Chilton's auto repair manual 1976

american cars
from 1969 to 1976

President	William A. Barbour
Executive Vice President	K. Robert Brink
Vice President and General Manager	William D. Byrne
Editor-In-Chief	John D. Kelly
Managing Editor	John H. Weise, S.A.E.
Assistant Managing Editor	Peter J. Meyer, S.A.E.
Technical Editors	Robert J. Brown
	Stephen J. Davis, S.A.E.
	Kerry A. Freeman
	Ronald L. Sessions
Production Manager	Warren Owens

CHILTON BOOK COMPANY Radnor, Pennsylvania

Published in Radnor by Chilton Book Company
Chilton Way, Radnor, Pa. 19089 215-687-8200
ISBN: 0-8019-6328-1 Library of Congress Catalog Card No. 76-648878

contents

Car Section

Unit Repair Section

INDEX

American Motors

YEAR IDENTIFICATION

SERIES 10, REBEL AND MATADOR

1969 Rebel

1970 Rebel

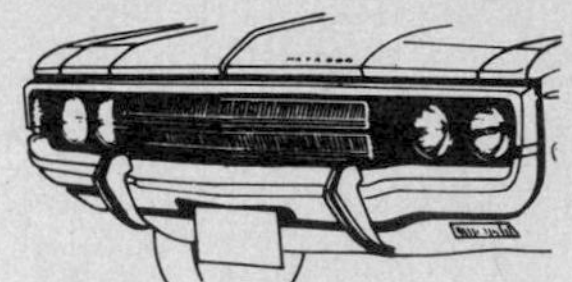
1971 Matador

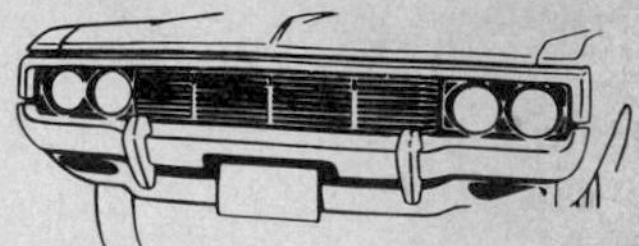
1972 Matador

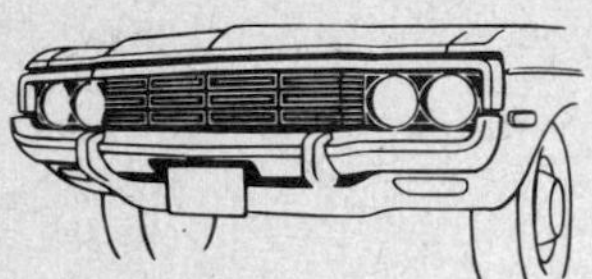
1973 Matador

1974-1975 Matador Coupe

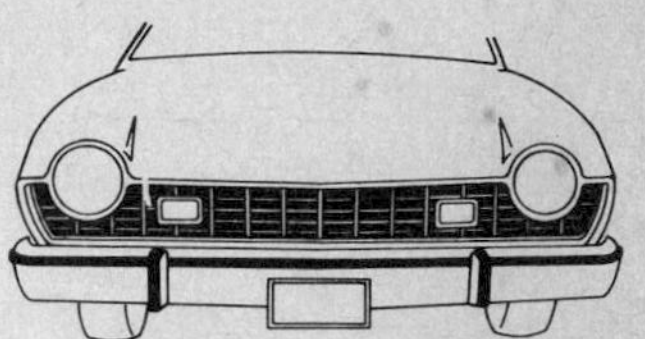
1976 Matador Coupe

SERIES 80, AMBASSADOR AND MATADOR

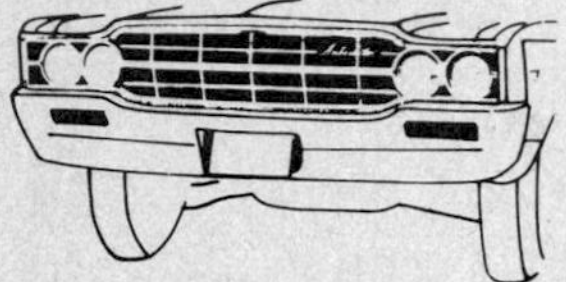
1969 Ambassador

1970 Ambassador

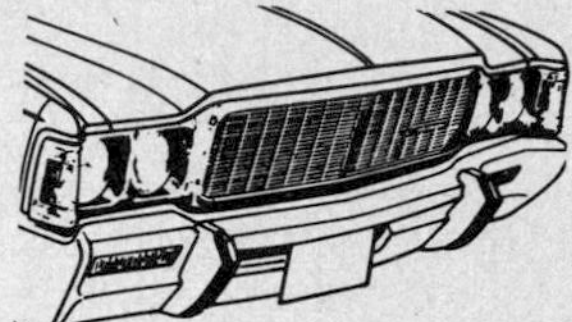
1971 Ambassador

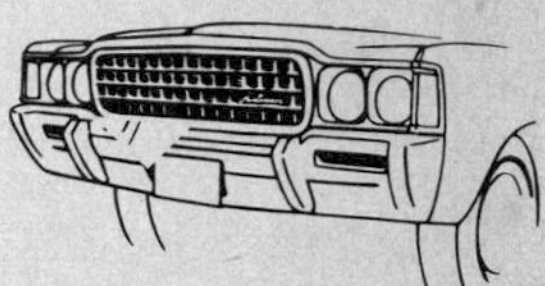
1972 Ambassador

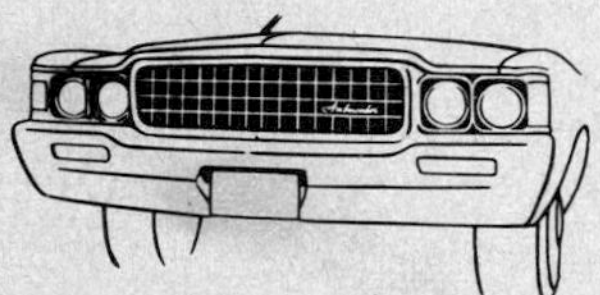
1973 Ambassador

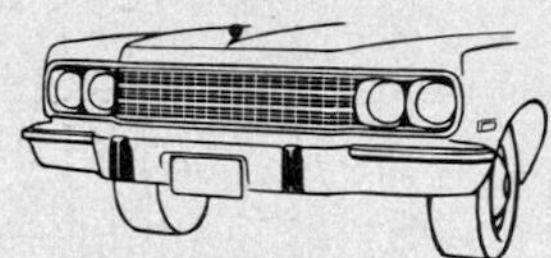
1974 Ambassador

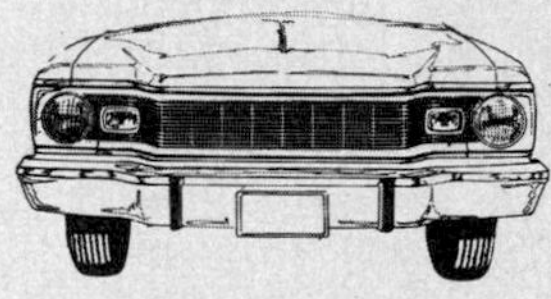
1975 Matador Sedan, Wagon

1976 Matador Sedan, Wagon

SERIES 01 AND 40, GREMLIN AND HORNET

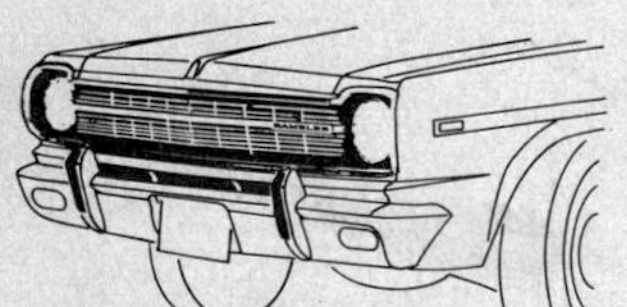
1969 American

1970-72 Hornet

1973 Hornet

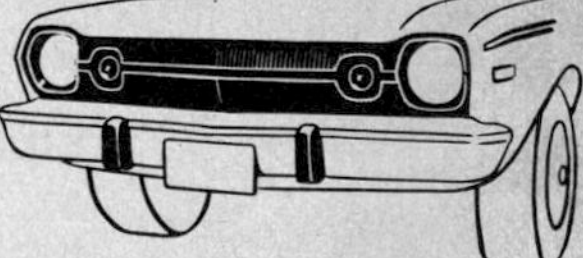
1974 Hornet

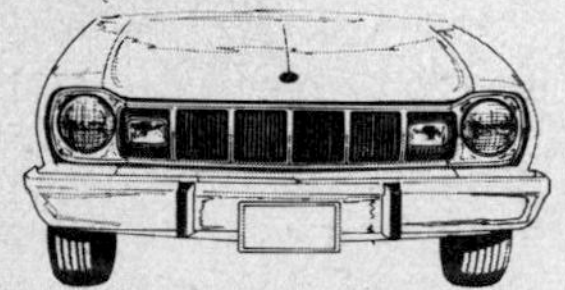
1975 Hornet

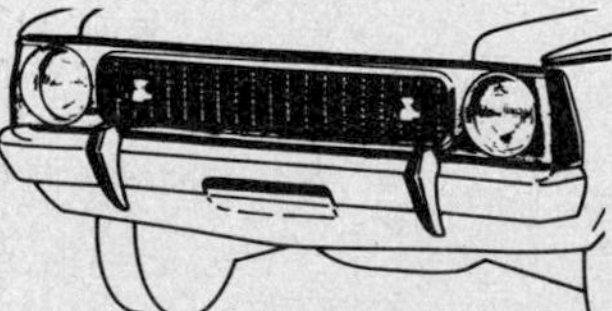
1970 Gremlin

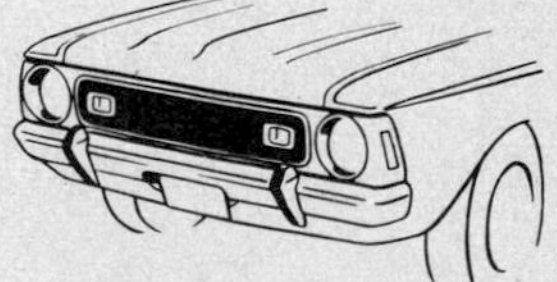
1971-72 Gremlin

1973 Gremlin

1974 Gremlin

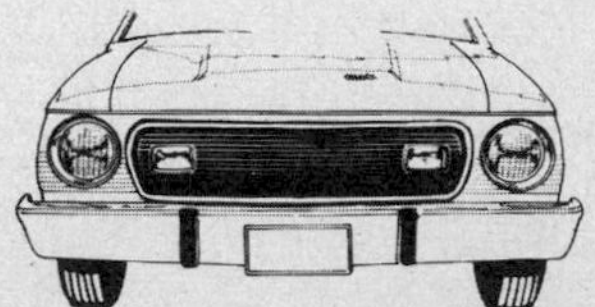
1975 Gremlin

1976 Gremlin

SERIES 70, JAVELIN

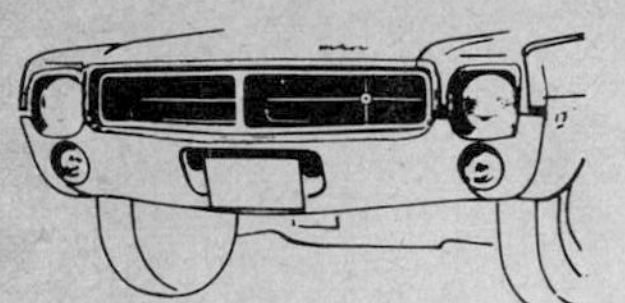
1969 Javelin

1970 Javelin

1971 Javelin SST

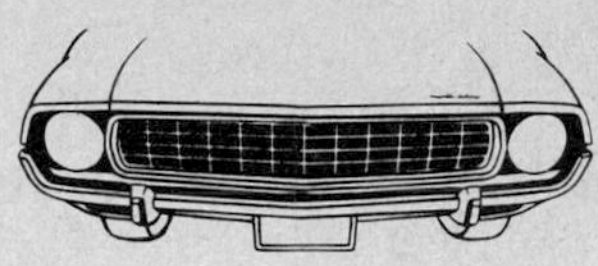
1972 Javelin SST

1973 Javelin

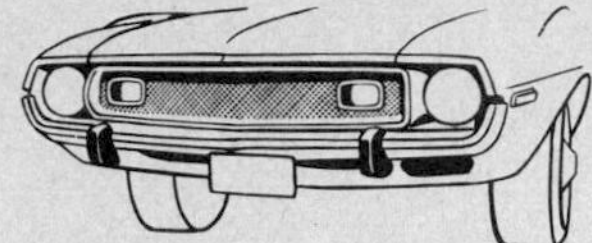
1974 Javelin

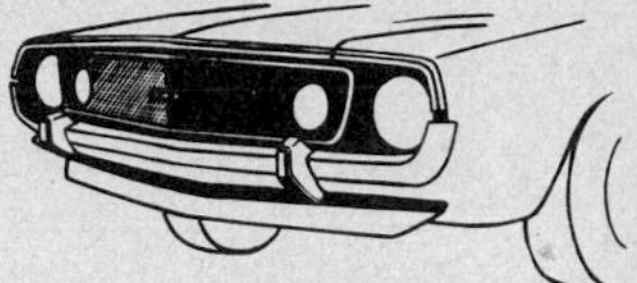
1971 Javelin AMX

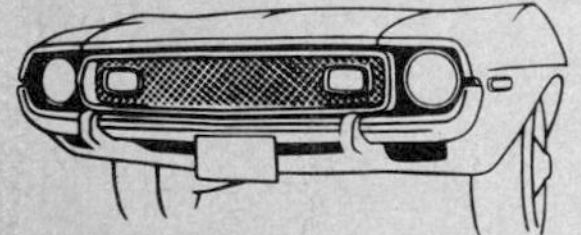
1972 Javelin AMX

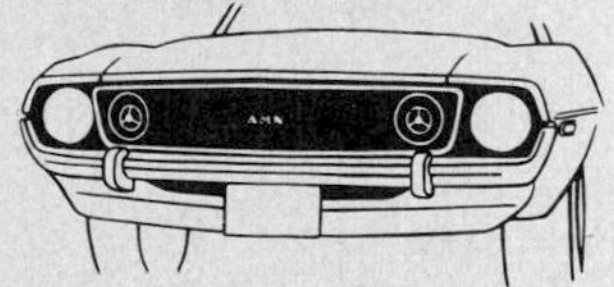
1973 Javelin AMX

1974 Javelin AMX

SERIES 30, AMX

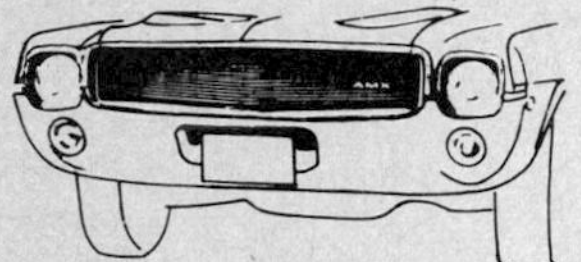
1969 AMX

1970 AMX

SERIES 60, PACER

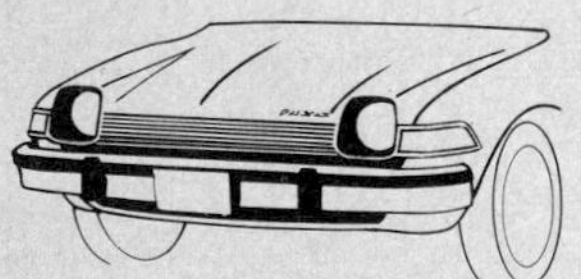
1975 Pacer

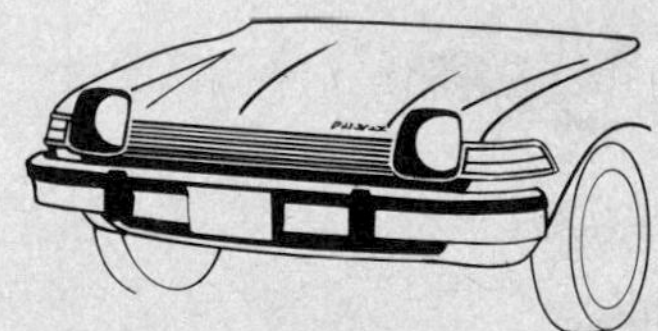
1976 Pacer

FIRING ORDER

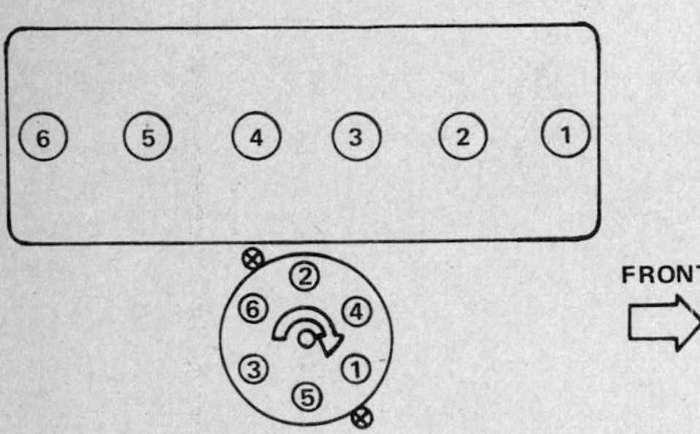

FRONT

CLOCKWISE ROTATION
1-5-3-6-2-4

6 cylinder OHV 199, 232 and 258
(© American Motors Corp)

CLOCKWISE ROTATION
1-8-4-3-6-5-7-2

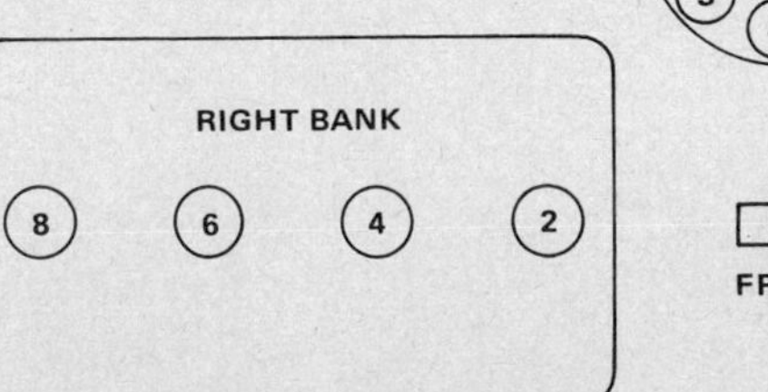

FRONT

290, 304, 343, 360, 390 and 401—V8
(© American Motors Corp)

CAR SERIAL NUMBER LOCATION

The thirteen digit car serial number is stamped on the left top of the dashboard, visible through the windshield. On 1970 and later vehicles, this number also can be found on a non-removable sticker on the front, left-side door pillar.

Engine Identification Code

Six—199, 232, 258—Stamped on right upper side of block.

V8—290, 304, 343, 360, 390, 401—Stamped on a tag attached to right-hand front of valve cover.

NOTE: All V8 engines have their cubic inch displacement cast into block, on both banks, between the first and second core plugs. This is the best way to tell engine displacement, because valve covers are interchangeable between engines.

6 cyl. engine code location

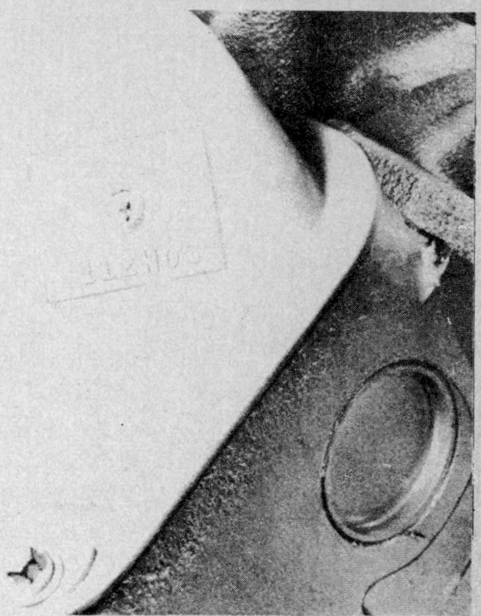

V8 engine code location
(© American Motors Corp)

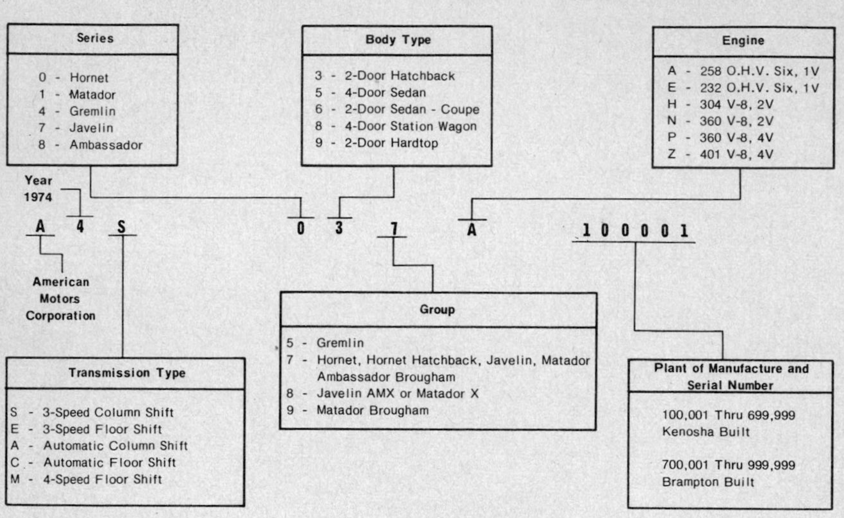

Vehicle Identification Number (VIN) decoding chart (© American Motors Corp)

ENGINE CODE

The engine code is the 4th digit of the engine build code stamped on a machined surface of the cylinder block between No. 2 and No. 3 cylinders on 6 cylinder engines and stamped on a tag attached to the right bank valve cover on V8 engines. In addition, the engine code is the 7th digit of the Vehicle Identification Number. (V.I.N.) The V.I.N. is stamped on a plate located at the left side of the instrument panel visible through the windshield on 1970 and later models.

Disp	Carb. No. Bbls.	Hp	'69	'70	'71	'72	'73	'74	'75	'76
6-Cylinder Models										
199	1	128	J	A						
232	1	90, 100 (net)				E	E	E	E	E
232	1	135			E					
232	1	145	L	E						
232	2	155	L	G						
258	1	95, 110 (net)				A	A	A	A	A
258	1	150			A					
258	2	120 (net)								A

Disp	Carb. No. Bbls.	Hp	'69	'70	'71	'72	'73	'74	'75	'76
8-Cylinder Models										
290	2	200	H							
290	4	225	N							
304	2	120, 150 (net)				H	H	H	H	H
304	2	210		H	H					
343	2	235	S							
343	4	280	Z							
360	2	140, 175 (net)				N	N	N	N	N
360	4	180, 195, 220# (net)				P	P	P	P	P
360	2	245		N	N					
360	4	290		P	P					
390	4	315	X							
390	4	325		X						
390	4	340		Y						
401	4	225 (net)				Z	Z	Z	Z	
401	4	330			Z					

With dual exhaust

GENERAL ENGINE SPECIFICATIONS

Year	Engine No. Cyl. Displacement Cu. In.	Carburetor Type	Horsepower @ rpm ■	Torque @ rpm (ft lbs) ■	Bore and Stroke (in.)	Compression Ratio	Oil Pressure @ 2050 rpm
'69	6-199	1 bbl	128 @ 4400	182 @ 1600	3.750 x 3.000	8.5:1	46
	6-232	1 bbl	145 @ 4300	215 @ 1600	3.750 x 3.500	8.5:1	46
	6-232	2 bbl	155 @ 4400	222 @ 1600	3.750 x 3.500	8.5:1	46
	8-290	2 bbl	200 @ 4600	285 @ 2800	3.750 x 3.280	9.0:1	46
	8-290	4 bbl	225 @ 4700	300 @ 3200	3.750 x 3.280	10.0:1	46
	8-343	2 bbl	235 @ 4400	345 @ 2600	4.080 x 3.280	9.0:1	46
	8-343	4 bbl	280 @ 4800	365 @ 3000	4.080 x 3.280	10.2:1	46
	8-390	4 bbl	315 @ 4600	425 @ 3200	4.165 x 3.754	10.2:1	46
'70	6-199	1 bbl	128 @ 4400	182 @ 1600	3.750 x 3.000	8.5:1	46
	6-232	1 bbl	145 @ 4300	215 @ 1600	3.750 x 3.500	8.5:1	46
	6-232	2 bbl	155 @ 4400	222 @ 1600	3.750 x 3.500	8.5:1	46
	8-304	2 bbl	210 @ 4400	305 @ 2800	3.750 x 3.440	9.0:1	46
	8-360	2 bbl	245 @ 4400	365 @ 2400	4.080 x 3.440	9.0:1	46
	8-360	4 bbl	290 @ 4800	395 @ 3200	4.080 x 3.440	10.0:1	46
	8-390	4 bbl	325 @ 5000	420 @ 3200	4.165 x 3.574	10.0:1	46
	8-390	4 bbl	340 @ 5100	430 @ 3600	4.165 x 3.574	10.0:1	46
'71	6-232	1 bbl	135 @ 4000	210 @ 1600	3.750 x 3.500	8.0:1	46
	6-258	1 bbl	150 @ 3800	240 @ 1800	3.750 x 3.900	8.0:1	46
	8-304	2 bbl	210 @ 4400	300 @ 2600	3.750 x 3.444	8.4:1	46
	8-360	2 bbl	245 @ 4400	365 @ 2600	4.080 x 3.444	8.5:1	46
	8-360	4 bbl	285 @ 4800	330 @ 5000	4.080 x 3.444	8.5:1	46
	8-401	4 bbl	330 @ 5000	430 @ 3400	4.650 x 3.680	9.5:1	46
'72	6-232	1 bbl	100 @ 3600	185 @ 1800	3.750 x 3.500	8.0:1	46
	6-258	1 bbl	110 @ 3500	195 @ 2000	3.750 x 3.900	8.0:1	46
	8-304	2 bbl	150 @ 4200	245 @ 2500	3.750 x 3.440	8.4:1	46
	8-360	2 bbl	175 @ 4000	285 @ 2400	4.080 x 3.440	8.5:1	46
	8-360	4 bbl	195 @ 4400	295 @ 2900	4.080 x 3.440	8.5:1	46
	8-401	4 bbl	255 @ 4600	345 @ 3300	4.165 x 3.680	8.5:1	46
'73	6-232	1 bbl	100 @ 3600	185 @ 1800	3.750 x 3.500	8.0:1	46
	6-258	1 bbl	110 @ 3500	195 @ 2000	3.750 x 3.900	8.0:1	46
	8-304	2 bbl	150 @ 4200	245 @ 2500	3.750 x 3.440	8.3:1	46
	8-360	2 bbl	175 @ 4000	285 @ 2400	4.080 x 3.440	8.3:1	46
	8-360	4 bbl	195 @ 4400	295 @ 2900	4.080 x 3.440	8.3:1	46
	8-360①	4 bbl	220 @ 4400	315 @ 3100	4.080 x 3.440	8.3:1	46
	8-401	4 bbl	255 @ 4600	345 @ 3300	4.165 x 3.680	8.5:1	46
'74	6-232	1 bbl	100 @ 3600	185 @ 1800	3.750 x 3.500	8.0:1	46
	6-258	1 bbl	110 @ 3500	195 @ 2000	3.750 x 3.900	8.0:1	46
	8-304	2 bbl	150 @ 4200	245 @ 2500	3.750 x 3.440	8.4:1	46
	8-360	2 bbl	175 @ 4000	285 @ 2400	4.080 x 3.440	8.25:1	46
	8-360	4 bbl	195 @ 4400	295 @ 2900	4.080 x 3.440	8.25:1	46
	8-360①	4 bbl	220 @ 4400	315 @ 3100	4.080 x 3.440	8.25:1	46
	8-401	4 bbl	255 @ 4600	345 @ 3300	4.165 x 3.680	8.25:1	46

GENERAL ENGINE SPECIFICATIONS (Cont'd)

Year	Engine No. Cyl. Displacement Cu. In.	Carburetor Type	Horsepower @ rpm ■	Torque @ rpm (ft lbs) ■	Bore and Stroke (in.)	Compression Ratio	Oil Pressure @ 2050 rpm
'75	6-232	1 bbl	100 @ 3600	185 @ 1800	3.750 x 3.500	8.0:1	37-75②
	6-258	1 bbl	110 @ 3500	195 @ 2000	3.750 x 3.900	8.0:1	37-75②
	8-304	2 bbl	150 @ 4200	245 @ 2500	3.750 x 3.440	8.4:1	37-75②
	8-360	2 bbl	175 @ 4000	285 @ 2400	4.080 x 3.440	8.25:1	37-75②
	8-360	4 bbl	195 @ 4400	295 @ 2900	4.080 x 3.440	8.25:1	37-75②
	8-360①	4 bbl	220 @ 4400	315 @ 3100	4.080 x 3.440	8.25:1	37-75②
	8-401	4 bbl	255 @ 4600	345 @ 3300	4.170 x 3.680	8.25:1	37-75②
'76	6-232	1 bbl	90 @ 3050	163 @ 2200	3.750 x 3.500	8.0:1	37-75②
	6-258	1 bbl	95 @ 3050	179 @ 2100	3.750 x 3.900	8.0:1	37-75②
	6-258	2 bbl	120 @ 3600	200 @ 2000	3.750 x 3.900	8.0:1	37-75②
	8-304	2 bbl	120 @ 3200	220 @ 2000	3.750 x 3.440	8.4:1	37-75②
	8-360	2 bbl	140 @ 3300	251 @ 1600	4.080 x 3.440	8.25:1	37-75②
	8-360①	4 bbl	180 @ 3600	280 @ 2800	4.080 x 3.440	8.25:1	37-75②

■ Beginning 1972, horsepower and torque are SAE net figures. They are measured at the rear of the transmission with all accessories installed and operating. Since the figures vary when a given engine is installed in different models, some are representative rather than exact.

① Dual exhaust

② At 1600 or more rpm

American, Hornet Gremlin, Rebel, Matador, Ambassador, Pacer

TUNE-UP SPECIFICATIONS

When analyzing compression test results, look for uniformity among cylinders rather than specific pressures.

Year	ENGINE No. Cyl Displacement (cu in.)	ENGINE hp	SPARK PLUGS Type	SPARK PLUGS Gap (in.)	DISTRIBUTOR Point Dwell (deg)	DISTRIBUTOR Point Gap (in.)	IGNITION TIMING (deg) ▲ Man Trans •	IGNITION TIMING (deg) ▲ Auto Trans	VALVES Intake Opens ■ (deg)	Fuel Pump Pressure (psi)	IDLE SPEED • (rpm) ▲ Man Trans	IDLE SPEED • (rpm) ▲ Auto Trans
'69	6-199	128	N-14Y	.035	33	.016	TDC	5B	12½	4-5½	600	525
	6-232	145	N-14Y	.035	33	.016	TDC	TDC①	12½	4-5½	600	525
	6-232	155	N-14Y	.035	33	.016	TDC	TDC①	12½	4-5½	600	525
	8-290	200	N-12Y	.035	30	.016	TDC	TDC	18½	4-5½	650	550
	8-290	225	N-12Y	.035	30	.016	TDC	TDC	18½	4-5½	650	550
	8-343	235	N-12Y	.035	30	.016	TDC	TDC	18½	4-5½	650	550
	8-343	280	N-12Y	.035	30	.016	TDC	TDC	18½	4-5½	650	550
	8-390	315	N-12Y	.035	30	.016	TDC	TDC	18½	4-5½	650	550
'70	6-199	128	N-14Y	.035	33	.016	3B	3B	12½	4-5½	600	550
	6-232	145	N-14Y	.035	33	.016	3B	3B	12½	4-5½	600	550
	6-232	155	N-14Y	.035	33	.016	3B	3B	12½	4-5½	600	550
	8-304	210	N-12Y	.035	30	.016	5B	5B	18½	4-5½	650	600
	8-360	245	N-12Y	.035	30	.016	5B	5B	18½	4-5½	650	600
	8-360	290	N-12Y	.035	30	.016	5B	5B	18½	4-5½	650	600
	8-390	325	N-12Y	.035	30	.016	5B	5B	18½	4-5½	650	600
	8-390	340	N-12Y	.035	30	.016	5B	5B	18½	4-5½	650	600
'71	6-232	135	N-12Y	.035	33	.016	3B	5B	12½	4-5½	700	600
	6-258	150	N-12Y	.035	33	.016	5B	5B	12½	4-5½	700	600
	8-304	210	N-12Y	.035	30	.016	2½B	2½B	14¾	4-5½	750	650
	8-360	245	N-12Y	.035	30	.016	2½B	2½B	14¾	4-5½	750	650
	8-360	285	N-12Y	.035	30	.016	2½B	2½B	14¾	4-5½	750	650
	8-401	330	N-12Y	.035	30	.016	2½B	2½B	25½	4-5½	750	650

TUNE-UP SPECIFICATIONS (Cont'd)

When analyzing compression test results, look for uniformity among cylinders rather than specific pressures.

ENGINE			SPARK PLUGS		DISTRIBUTOR		IGNITION TIMING (deg) ▲		VALVES	Fuel	IDLE SPEED ● (rpm) ▲	
Year	No. Cyl Displacement (cu in.)	hp	Type	Gap (in.)	Point Dwell (deg)	Point Gap (in.)	Man Trans ●	Auto Trans	Intake Opens ■ (deg)	Pump Pressure (psi)	Man Trans	Auto Trans
'72	6-232	100	N-12Y	.035	33	.016	5B(3B)	5B(3B)	12	4-5½	600(700)	550(600)
	6-258	110	N-12Y	.035	33	.016	5B(3B)	5B(3B)	12	4-5½	600(700)	550(600)
	8-304	150	N-12Y	.035	30	.016	5B	5B	14¾	4-5½	750	650(700)
	8-360	175	N-12Y	.035	30	.016	5B	5B	14¾	4-5½	750	700
	8-360	195	N-12Y	.035	30	.016	5B	5B	14¾	4-5½	750	700
	8-401	255	N-12Y	.035	30	.016	5B	5B	25½	4-5½	750	650(700)
'73	6-232	100	N-12Y	.035	33	.016	5B(3B)	5B(3B)	12	4-5½	700	600
	6-258	110	N-12Y	.035	33	.016	5B(3B)	5B(3B)	12	4-5½	700	600
	8-304	150	N-12Y	.035	30	.016	5B	5B	14¾	4-5½	750	700
	8-360	175	N-12Y	.035	30	.016	5B	5B	14¾	4-5½	750	700
	8-360	195	N-12Y	.035	30	.016	5B	5B	14¾	4-5½	750	700
	8-401	255	N-12Y	.035	30	.016	5B	5B	25½	4-5½	750	700
'74	6-232	100	N-12Y	.035	33	.016	5B(3B)	5B(3B)	12	4-5½	700	600
	6-258	110	N-12Y	.035	33	.016	5B(3B)	5B(3B)	12	4-5½	700	600
	8-304	150	N-12Y	.035	30	.016	5B	5B (2½ B)	14¾	5-6½	750	700
	8-360	175	N-12Y	.035	30	.016	5B	5B	14¾	5-6½	750	700
	8-360	195	N-12Y	.035	30	.016	5B	5B	14¾	5-6½	750	700
	8-401	255	N-12Y	.035	30	.016	5B	5B	25½	5-6½	750	700
'75	6-232	100	N-12Y	.035	electronic		5B	5B	12	4-5	600	550(700)
	6-258	110	N-12Y	.035	electronic		3B	3B	12	4-5	600	550(700)
	8-304	150	N-12Y	.035	electronic		5B	5B	14¾	5-6½	750	700
	8-360	175	N-12Y	.035	electronic		5B	5B	14¾	5-6½	750	700
	8-360	195	N-12Y	.035	electronic		5B	5B	14¾	5-6½	750	700
	8-401	255	N-12Y	.035	electronic		5B	5B	25½	5-6½	750	700
'76	All				See Underhood Specifications Sticker							

▲ See text for procedure
● Figure in parentheses indicates California engine
■ All figures Before Top Dead Center

B Before Top Dead Center
TDC Top Dead Center
— Not applicable

① For Rogue model, figure is 5 degrees Before Top Dead Center

AMX-Javelin TUNE-UP SPECIFICATIONS

When analyzing compression test results, look for uniformity among cylinders rather than specific pressures.

ENGINE			SPARK PLUGS		DISTRIBUTOR		IGNITION TIMING (deg) ▲		VALVES	Fuel	IDLE SPEED (rpm) ▲	
Year	No. Cyl Displacement (cu in.)	hp	Type	Gap (in.)	Point Dwell (deg)	Point Gap (in.)	Man Trans ●	Auto Trans	Intake Opens ■ (deg)	Pump Pressure (psi)	Man Trans ●	Auto Trans
'69	6-232	145	N-14Y	.035	31-34	.016	TDC	TDC	12½	4-5½	600	525
	8-290	200	N-12Y	.035	29-31	.016	TDC	TDC	18½	5-6½	650	550
	8-290	225	N-12Y	.035	29-31	.016	TDC	TDC	18½	5-6½	650	550
	8-343	280	N-12Y	.035	29-31	.016	TDC	TDC	18½	5-6½	650	550
	8-390	315	N-12Y	.035	29-31	.016	TDC	TDC	18½	5-6½	650	550
'70	6-232	145	N-14Y	.035	31-34	.016	3B	3B	12½	4-5½	600	550
	8-304	210	N-12Y	.035	29-31	.016	5B	5B	18½	5-6½	650	600
	8-360	245	N-12Y	.035	29-31	.016	5B	5B	18½	5-6½	650	600
	8-360	290	N-12Y	.035	29-31	.016	5B	5B	18½	5-6½	650	600
	8-390	325	N-12Y	.035	29-31	.016	TDC①	TDC①	18½	5-6½	650	600
'71	6-232	135	N-12Y	.035	31-34	.016	3B	5B	12½	4-5½	700	600
	6-258	150	N-12Y	.035	31-34	.016	—	5B	12½	4-5½	—	600

TUNE-UP SPECIFICATIONS (Cont'd)

When analyzing compression test results, look for uniformity among cylinders rather than specific pressures.

Year	ENGINE No. Cyl Displacement (cu in.)	ENGINE hp	SPARK PLUGS Type	SPARK PLUGS Gap (in.)	DISTRIBUTOR Point Dwell (deg)	DISTRIBUTOR Point Gap (in.)	IGNITION TIMING (deg) ▲ Man Trans •	IGNITION TIMING (deg) ▲ Auto Trans	VALVES Intake Opens ■ (deg)	Fuel Pump Pressure (psi)	IDLE SPEED (rpm) ▲ Man Trans •	IDLE SPEED (rpm) ▲ Auto Trans
	8-304	210	N-12Y	.035	29-31	.016	2½B	2½B	14¾	5-6½	750	650
	8-360	245	N-12Y	.035	29-31	.016	2½B	2½B	14¾	5-6½	750	650
	8-360	285	N-12Y	.035	29-31	.016	2½B	2½B	14¾	5-6½	750	650
	8-401	330	N-12Y	.035	29-31	.016	2½B	2½B	25½	5-6½	750	650
'72	6-232	100	N-12Y	.035	31-34	.016	5B	5B	12½	4-5½	600(700)	550(600)
	6-258	110	N-12Y	.035	31-34	.016	—	3B	12½	4-5½	—	550(600)
	8-304	150	N-12Y	.035	29-31	.016	5B	5B	14¾	5-6½	750	650(700)
	8-360	175	N-12Y	.035	29-31	.016	—	5B	14¾	5-6½	—	700
	8-360	195	N-12Y	.035	29-31	.016	5B	5B	14¾	5-6½	750	700
	8-401	255	N-12Y	.035	29-31	.016	5B	5B	25½	5-6½	750	650(700)
'73	6-232	100	N-12Y	.035	31-34	.016	5B	5B	12½	4-5½	700	600
	6-258	110	N-12Y	.035	31-34	.016	—	3B	12½	4-5½	—	600
	8-304	150	N-12Y	.035	29-31	.016	5B	5B	14¾	5-6½	750	700
	8-360	175	N-12Y	.035	29-31	.016	—	5B	14¾	5-6½	—	700
	8-360	190	N-12Y	.035	29-31	.016	5B	5B	14¾	5-6½	750	700
	8-401	255	N-12Y	.035	29-31	.016	5B	5B	25½	5-6½	750	700
'74	6-232	100	N-12Y	.035	31-34	.016	5B	5B	12½	4-5½	600(700)	550(600)
	6-258	110	N-12Y	.035	31-34	.016	—	3B	12½	4-5½	—	550(600)
	8-304	150	N-12Y	.035	29-31	.016	5B	5B (2½ B)	14¾	5-6½	750	650(700)
	8-360	175	N-12Y	.035	29-31	.016	—	5B	14¾	5-6½	—	700
	8-360	190	N-12Y	.035	29-31	.016	5B	5B	14¾	5-6½	750	700
	8-401	255	N-12Y	.035	29-31	.016	5B	5B	25½	5-6½	750	650(700)

▲ See text for procedure
■ All figures Before Top Dead Center
• Figure in parentheses indicates California engine
— Not applicable

① For vehicles prior to engine code No. 209X26, adjust ignition timing to 5 degrees before Top Dead Center
B Before Top Dead Center
TDC Top Dead Center

CAPACITIES

Year	ENGINE No. Cyl. Displacement (cu in.)	Engine Crankcase Add 1 Qt For New Filter	TRANSMISSION Pts To Refill After Draining Manual 3-Speed	Manual 4-Speed	Automatic	Drive Axle (pts)	Gasoline Tank (gals)	COOLING SYSTEM (qts) With Heater	With A/C
'69	6-199	4	1.5	—	18.5	3	See	10.5	10.5
	6-232	4	1.5①	—	18.5	3	chart	10.5	10.5
	8-290	4	3	2.5	18.5	4	below	14	14
	8-343	4	—	2.5	20	4		13	13
	8-390	4	—	2.5	20	4		13	13
'70	6-199	4	1.5	—	18.5	3		10.5	10.5
	6-232	4	1.5①	—	18.5	3		10.5	10.5
	8-304	4	3	2.5	18.5	4		14	14
	8-360	4	—	2.5	20	4		13	13
	8-390	4	—	2.5	20	4		13	13
'71	6-232	4	1.5①	—	18.5	3③		10.5	10.5
	6-258	4	2.5	—	18.5	3③		10.5	10.5
	8-304	4	2.5	2.5	18.5	4		14	14
	8-360	4	3	2.5	20	4		13	13
	8-401	4	—	2.5	20	4		13	13

CAPACITIES

Year	ENGINE No. Cyl. (cu in.) Displacement	Engine Crankcase Add 1 Qt For New Filter	TRANSMISSION Pts To Refill After Draining Manual 3-Speed	Manual 4-Speed	Automatic	Drive Axle (pts)	Gasoline Tank (gals)	COOLING SYSTEM (qts) With Heater	With A/C
'72	6-232	4	1.5①	—	17	3③		10.5	10.5
	6-258	4	2.5	—	17	3③		10.5	10.5
	8-304	4	2.5	2.5	17	4		14	14
	8-360	4	2.5	2.5	19	4		13	13
	8-401	4	2.5	2.5	19	4		13	13
'73	6-232	4	2.5	—	17	3③		10.5	10.5
	6-258	4	2.5	—	17	3③		10.5	10.5
	8-304	4	2.5	2.5	17	4		14	14
	8-360	4	2.5	2.5	19	4		13	14
	8-401	4	2.5	2.5	19	4		13	14
'74	6-232	4	2.5	—	17	3③		11	11.5
	6-258	4	2.5	—	17	3③		11	11.5
	8-304	4	2.5	2.5	17	4		16④	16④
	8-360	4	2.5	2.5	19	4		15.5⑤	15.5⑤
	8-401	4	2.5	2.5	19	4		15.5⑤	15.5⑤
'75-'76	6-232	4	3.5②	—	17	3③		11⑧	11.5⑥
	6-258	4	3.5②	—	17	3③		11⑧	11.5⑥
	8-304	4	3.5	—	17	4		16.5④	16④⑦
	8-360	4	—	—	19	4		15.5⑤	15.5⑤
	8-401	4	—	—	19	4		15.5⑤	15.5⑤

① Fully synchronized transmission 2.25 pts
② 4 pts with overdrive
③ 8.875 ring gear—4 pts
④ Matador Coupe—18.5 qts, with coolant recovery system—20.5 qts; Hornet and Gremlin—16 qts
⑤ Matador Coupe—17.5 qts, with coolant recovery system—19.5 qts
⑥ 13.5 qts in Matador Coupe, 15.5 qts in Matador Coupe with coolant recovery system, 14.5 qts in Pacer
⑦ 16.5 qts in Matador Sedan and Wagon
⑧ 14.5 qts in Pacer
— Not applicable

CAPACITIES

GASOLINE TANK CAPACITIES (gals)

Model	'69	'70	'71	'72	'73	'74	'75	'76
Ambassador	21.5	21.5	19.5	19.5	19.5	24.9		
American	16							
AMX	19	19						
Javelin	19	19	16	16	16	16		
Rebel	21.5	21.5						
Rambler	16	16						
Gremlin			21	21	21	21	21	21
Hornet			16	16	16	16	17	22
Matador			19.5	19.5	19.5	24.9	24.5	24.5
MatadorWagon	19	19	17	20	20	21	21	21
Pacer							22	22

VALVE SPECIFICATIONS

Year	Engine No. Cyl. Displacement (cu in.)	Seat Angle (deg) ■	Face Angle (deg) ●	Spring Test Pressure (lbs @ in.)	Spring Installed Height (in.)	Stem to Guide Clearance (in.) Intake	Stem to Guide Clearance (in.) Exhaust	Stem Diameter (in.) Intake	Stem Diameter (in.) Exhaust
'69	6-199	44	44	195 @ 1.44	1 13/16	.0010-.0030	.0010-.0030	.3720	.3720
	6-232	44	44	195 @ 1.44	1 13/16	.0010-.0030	.0010-.0030	.3720	.3720
	8-290	45	44.5	200 @ 1.39	1 13/16	.0010-.0030	.0010-.0030	.3720	.3720
	8-343	45	44.5	200 @ 1.39	1 13/16	.0010-.0030	.0010-.0030	.3720	.3720
	8-390	45	44.5	200 @ 1.39	1 13/16	.0010-.0030	.0010-.0030	.3720	.3720
	8-390①	45	44.5	250 @ 1.33	1 13/16	.0010-.0030	.0010-.0030	.3720	.3720
'70	6-199	44	44	195 @ 1.44	1 13/16	.0010-.0030	.0010-.0030	.3720	.3720
	6-232	44	44	195 @ 1.44	1 13/16	.0010-.0030	.0010-.0030	.3720	.3720
	8-304	45	44.5	200 @ 1.39	1 13/16	.0010-.0030	.0010-.0030	.3720	.3720
	8-360	45	44.5	200 @ 1.39	1 13/16	.0010-.0030	.0010-.0030	.3720	.3720
	8-390	45	44.5	200 @ 1.39	1 13/16	.0010-.0030	.0010-.0030	.3720	.3720
	8-390①	45	44.5	250 @ 1.33	1 13/16	.0010-.0030	.0010-.0030	.3720	.3720
'71	6-232	44.5	44	195 @ 1.44	1 13/16	.0010-.0030	.0010-.0030	.3720	.3720
	6-258	44.5	44	195 @ 1.44	1 13/16	.0010-.0030	.0010-.0030	.3720	.3720
	8-304	45	44.5	189 @ 1.39	1 13/16	.0010-.0030	.0010-.0030	.3720	.3720
	8-360	45	44.5	189 @ 1.39	1 13/16	.0010-.0030	.0010-.0030	.3720	.3720
	8-401	45	44.5	189 @ 1.39	1 13/16	.0010-.0030	.0010-.0030	.3720	.3720
	8, All①	45	44.5	250 @ 1.33	1 13/16	.0010-.0030	.0010-.0030	.3720	.3720
'72	6-232	44.5	44	195 @ 1.44	1 13/16	.0010-.0030	.0010-.0030	.3720	.3720
	6-258	44.5	44	195 @ 1.44	1 13/16	.0010-.0030	.0010-.0030	.3720	.3720
	8-304	45	44.5	218 @ 1.39	1 13/16	.0010-.0030	.0010-.0030	.3720	.3720
	8-360	45	44.5	218 @ 1.39	1 13/16	.0010-.0030	.0010-.0030	.3720	.3720
	8-401	45	44.5	218 @ 1.39	1 13/16	.0010-.0030	.0010-.0030	.3720	.3720
	8, All①	45	44.5	250 @ 1.33	1 13/16	.0010-.0030	.0010-.0030	.3720	.3720
'73	6-232	44.5	44	195 @ 1.44	1 13/16	.0010-.0030	.0010-.0030	.3720	.3720
	6-258	44.5	44	195 @ 1.44	1 13/16	.0010-.0030	.0010-.0030	.3720	.3720
	8-304	44.5	44	218 @ 1.39	1 13/16	.0010-.0030	.0010-.0030	.3720	.3720
	8-360	44.5	44	218 @ 1.39	1 13/16	.0010-.0030	.0010-.0030	.3720	.3720
	8-401	44.5	44	218 @ 1.39	1 13/16	.0010-.0030	.0010-.0030	.3720	.3720
'74	6-232	44.5	44	195 @ 1.44	1 13/16	.0010-.0030	.0010-.0030	.3720	.3720
	6-258	44.5	44	195 @ 1.44	1 13/16	.0010-.0030	.0010-.0030	.3720	.3720
	8-304	45	44	216 @ 1.39	1 13/16	.0010-.0030	.0010-.0030	.3720	.3720
	8-360	45	44	216 @ 1.39	1 13/16	.0010-.0030	.0010-.0030	.3720	.3720
	8-401	45	44	216 @ 1.39	1 13/16	.0010-.0030	.0010-.0030	.3720	.3720
'75-'76	6-232	44.5	44	195 @ 1.44	1 13/16	.0010-.0030	.0010-.0030	.3720	.3720
	6-258	44.5	44	195 @ 1.44	1 13/16	.0010-.0030	.0010-.0030	.3720	.3720
	8-304	44.5	44	213 @ 1.36	1 13/16	.0010-.0030	.0010-.0030	.3720	.3720
	8-360	44.5	44	213 @ 1.36	1 13/16	.0010-.0030	.0010-.0030	.3720	.3720
	8-401	44.5	44	213 @ 1.36	1 13/16	.0010-.0030	.0010-.0030	.3720	.3720

■ Exhaust valve face angles are shown
All intake valve seat angles are 30°

● Exhaust valve seat angles are shown
All intake valve face angles are 29°

① With high-performance camshaft; optional through 1970, or dealer-installed 1971-72

TORQUE SPECIFICATIONS

All readings in ft lbs

Year	Engine No. Cyl. Displacement (cu in.)	Cylinder Head Bolts	Rod Bearing Bolts	Main Bearing Bolts	Crankshaft Pulley Bolt	Flywheel to Crankshaft Bolts	MANIFOLD Intake	MANIFOLD Exhaust
'69-'76	6-All	80⑤	26-30	75-85	50-60⑥	95-120	18-28	18-28
	8-All	①	②	90-105	20-25③	95-120	37-47	20-30

① 1969—90-100; 1970-76—100-120
② 290, 304, 343, 360—26-30; 390, 401—35-40; 1975-76—26-30
③ Pulley-to-damper bolts; 1975-76—18-28 ft. lbs.
④ No. 5 (rear main 55 ft. lbs.)
⑤ 1973-76—95-115 ft. lbs.
⑥ Pulley-to-damper bolts; 1975-76—23 ft. lbs.

CRANKSHAFT AND CONNECTING ROD SPECIFICATIONS

All measurements are given in inches

Year	Engine No. Cyl. Displacement (cu in.)	CRANKSHAFT Main Brg. Journal Dia	CRANKSHAFT Main Brg. Oil Clearance	CRANKSHAFT Shaft End-Play	CRANKSHAFT Thrust on No.	CONNECTING ROD Journal Diameter	CONNECTING ROD Oil Clearance	CONNECTING ROD Side Clearance
'69	6, All	2.4986-2.5001	.001-.002	.0015-.007	3	2.0934-2.0955	.001-.002	.008-.010
	8, All	①	.001-.002②	.003-.008	3	③	.001-.002	.009-.015
'70-'76	6, All	2.4986-2.5001	.001-.002⑧	.0015-.007⑤	3	2.0934-2.0955	.001-.002⑧	.008-.010⑥
	8, All	①	.001-.002②	.003-.008	3	④	.001-.002⑧	.009-.015⑦

① Nos. 1-4—2.7474-2.7489; No. 5—2.7464-2.7479
② Rear main—.002-.003
③ 8-290, 343—2.0934-2.0955; 8-390—2.2471-2.2492
④ 1970-74 390, All 401—2.2471-2.2485; 304, 360—2.0934-2.0955, 1975-76 401—2.2464-2.2485
⑤ 1972-76—.0015-.0065
⑥ 1972-76—.005-.014
⑦ 1975-76—.006-.018
⑧ 1975-76—.001-.003

RING GAP

All measurements are given in inches

Year	Engine	Top Compression	Bottom Compression
'69-'76	All engines	.010-.020	.010-.020

Year	Engine	Oil Control
'69-'71	All engines	.015-.055
'72-'76	6-232, 258, 8-304	.010-.025
'72-'76	8-360	.015-.045
'72-'76	8-401	.015-.055

RING SIDE CLEARANCE

All measurements are given in inches

Year	Engine	Top Compression	Bottom Compression
'69-'71	6-199, 232, 258	.0015-.0035	.0015-.0035
'69-'71	8-290, 343, 390, 304, 360, 401	.002-.004	.002-.004
'72-'73	All engines	.0015-.0035	.0015-.0035
'74-'76	6-232, 258	.0015-.0030	.0015-.0030
'74-'76	8-304	.0015-.0035	.0015-.0030
'74-'76	8-360, 401	.0015-.0030	.0015-.0035

Year	Engine	Oil Control
'69-'71	All engines	.0000-.0050
'72-'76	6-232, 258, 8-304	.0011-.0080
'72-'76	8-360, 401	.0000-.0070

PISTON CLEARANCE

Year	Engine	Piston-to-Bore Clearance (in.)
'69	6-199, 232	.0005-.0013
	V8-290, 390	.0010-.0018
	V8-343	.0012-.0020
'70	6-199, 232	.0005-.0013
	V8-304, 390	.0010-.0018
	V8-360	.0012-.0020

Year	Engine	Piston-to-Bore Clearance (in.)
'71	6-232, 258	.0005-.0013
	V8-304, 401	.0010-.0018
	V8-360	.0012-.0020
'72-'76	6-232, 258	.0009-.0017
	V8-304, 401	.0010-.0018
	V8-360	.0012-.0020

ALTERNATOR AND REGULATOR SPECIFICATIONS

	ALTERNATOR			REGULATOR						
					Field Relay			Regulator		
Year	Part No. or Manufacturer	Field Current @ 12 V	Output (amps)	Part No. or Manufacturer	Air Gap (in.)	Point Gap (in.)	Volts to Close	Air Gap (in.)	Point Gap (in.)	Volts @ 75°F
'69-'70	3195534(5)	2.4-2.5	35	3195003	Not adjustable, sealed at factory					
	A12NAM456(7)	2.0-2.6	35	R2AM4	Not adjustable, sealed at factory					
	A12NAM606(2)	1.8-2.4	55	R2AM4	Not adjustable, sealed at factory					
'71	6-70D44186C01①	2.4-2.5	35	8RB2005	Not adjustable, sealed at factory					
	8-70D44187C01①	2.0-2.6	35	8RB2005	Not adjustable, sealed at factory					
	6-70D44188C01② } 8-70D44189C01 }	1.8-2.4	55	8RB2005	Not adjustable, sealed at factory					
'72-'73	8AL2025F	1.8-2.4	37	8RB2005	Not adjustable, sealed at factory					
	8AL2026F③	1.8-2.4	55	8RB2005	Not adjustable, sealed at factory					
'74	8AL2025F	1.8-2.5	37	8RH2005	Not adjustable, sealed at factory					
	8AL2015K, 16K②	1.8-2.5	51	8RH2005	Not adjustable, sealed at factory					
	8AL2044L, 45L③	1.8-2.5	62	8RH2005	Not adjustable, sealed at factory					
'75-'76	1100927	1.8-2.5	37	1116387	Not adjustable, sealed at factory					
	1102465	1.8-2.5	63	1116387	Not adjustable, sealed at factory					
	960928	1.8-2.5	55	1116387	Not adjustable, sealed at factory					
	8AL2044L	1.8-2.5	62	8RH2003	Not adjustable, sealed at factory					
	8AL2045L	1.8-2.5	62	8RH2003	Not adjustable, sealed at factory					
	8AL2033L	1.8-2.5	62	8RH2003	Not adjustable, sealed at factory					

① C02 for Matador
② Std. with A/C or rear defogger.
③ Std. All Ambassadors, A/C, rear defogger or "Command-Air"

BATTERY AND STARTER SPECIFICATIONS

		BATTERY			STARTER						
					Lock Test			No-Load Test			
Year	Engine No. Cyl. Displacement (cu in.)	Ampere Hour Capacity	Volts	Terminal Grounded	Amps	Volts	Torque (ft lbs)	Amps	Volts	RPM	Brush Spring Tension (oz)
'69	6 All	50	12	Neg.	290	4.3	6.5	63	10.6	7,850	35
	8 All	60	12	Neg.	500	4.5	9	70	12	9,500	40
	8 (opt.)	70	12	Neg.	500	4.5	10	70	12	9,500	40
'70-'76	6, 8-304	50	12	Neg.	600①	3.4	13	65	12	9,250	40
	8-360, 401	60	12	Neg.	600①	3.4	13	65	12	9,250	40
	All (opt.)	70②	12	Neg.	600①	3.4	13	65	12	9,250	40

① 1970—500 @ 4.5
② 80 amp-hour—fleet or dealer option

BRAKE SPECIFICATIONS

All measurements are given in inches

Year	Model	Master Cylinder Disc	Master Cylinder Drum	Wheel Cylinder Front Disc	Wheel Cylinder Front Drum	Wheel Cylinder Rear	Brake Disc or Drum Diameter Front Disc	Brake Disc or Drum Diameter Front Drum	Brake Disc or Drum Diameter Rear
'69	American, Rebel	1.0	1.0	2.00	1.12②	.94④	11.19	9.0①	9.0①③
	Rebel (Wag.)	1.0	1.0	2.00	1.09②	.94	11.19	10.0	10.0
	Ambassador	1.0	1.0	2.00	1.12②	.94⑥	11.19	10.0	10.0
	Javelin	1.0	1.0	2.00	1.19②	.94⑤	11.19	10.0	10.0
	AMX	1.0	—	2.00	—	.88	11.19	—	10.0
'70	Hornet	1.0	1.0	2.00	1.12②	.94	11.19	9.0①	9.0①
	Gremlin	—	1.0	—	1.12	.88	—	9.0	9.0
	Rebel	1.0	1.0	2.00	1.12②	.94⑤	11.19	10.0	10.0
	Rebel (Wag.)	1.0	1.0	2.00	1.09②	.94	11.19	10.0	10.0
	Ambassador	1.0	1.0	2.00	1.12②	.94⑥	11.19	10.0	10.0
	Ambassador (Wag.)	1.0	1.0	2.00	1.19	.94	11.19	10.0	10.0
	Javelin	1.0	1.0	2.00	1.19	.94⑤	11.19	10.0	10.0
	AMX	1.0	—	2.00	—	.88	11.19	—	10.0
'71-'73	Hornet, Gremlin-6	⑦	1.0	2.75	1.12	.88⑪	11.00	9.0	9.0③
	Hornet, Gremlin-8	⑦	1.0	2.75	1.19	.88	11.00	10.0	10.0
	Matador	⑦	1.0	2.75	1.09⑧	.94⑩	11.00	10.0	10.0
	Ambassador	⑦	1.0	2.75	1.19	.94⑩	11.00	10.0	10.0
	Javelin-6	⑦	1.0	2.75	1.12	.88⑨	11.00	9.0	9.0③
	Javelin, AMX-8	⑦	1.0	2.75	1.19	.88⑨	11.00	10.0	10.0
'74	Hornet, Gremlin-6	⑦	1.0	2.75	1.12	.88⑪	11.00	9.0	9.0
	Hornet, Gremlin-8	⑦	1.0	2.75	1.19	.88	11.00	10.0	10.0
	Matador	⑦	1.0	2.75	1.09⑧	.94	11.00	10.0	10.0
	Ambassador	⑦	—	2.75	—	.94	11.00	—	10.0
	Javelin, AMX	⑦	—	2.75	—	.88	11.00	—	10.0⑬
'75-'76	Hornet, Gremlin-6	1.0⑫	1.0	3.10	1.125	.875⑪	10.75	9.0	9.0
	Hornet, Gremlin-8	1.0⑫	1.0	3.10	1.187	.875	10.75	10.0	10.0
	Matador	1.13⑫	—	3.10	—	.875⑨	10.75	—	10.0
	Pacer	1.0⑫	1.0	3.10	1.094	.875	10.75	10.0	9.0

① 10 in. with V8
② 1.19 in. with V8
③ With disc brakes 10 in.—'71-'73
④ 0.91 in. with V8
⑤ 6 cyl disc brakes 1 in.
⑥ Disc brakes 1.12 in.
⑦ Optional disc brakes on Hornet, Gremlin, Javelin, Matador and Ambassador: Hornet, Gremlin, Javelin—1.063 in. man./1.000 in. power; Matador, Ambassador—1.125 in. power. Starting 1973, power disc brakes became standard on Ambassador and Javelin.
⑧ 6 cyl std. models; V8 models use 1.19 in. bores
⑨ 0.937 in. rear bores with front discs
⑩ 1.00 in rear bores on wagons with disc brakes
⑪ Gremlin-6—0.812 in.
⑫ Non-Power disc brakes—1.063 in.
⑬ Javelin-6—9 in. drums
Wag. Station wagon
Man. Manual
Std. Standard
— Not applicable

WHEEL ALIGNMENT SPECIFICATIONS

Year	Model	CASTER Range (deg)	CASTER Pref Setting (deg)	CAMBER Range (deg)	CAMBER Pref Setting (deg)	Toe-in (in.)	Steering Axis Inclin. (deg)	WHEEL PIVOT RATIO (deg) Inner Wheel	WHEEL PIVOT RATIO (deg) Outer Wheel
'69	Series 01, 30, 70	½N to ½P▲	0	⅜N to ⅜P	0	1/16 to 3/16	6½	25	22
	Series 10, 80	0 to 1N	½N	⅜N to ⅜P	0	1/16 to 3/16	6½	25	22
'70-'71	All Series	½P to 1½P	1P	⅜N to ⅜P	0	1/16 to 3/16	7¾	25	22
'72-'74	All Series	½P to 1½P	1P③	①	②	1/16 to 3/16	7¾	25	22
'75-'76	Series 01, 40	½P to 1½P	0	①	②	1/16 to 3/16	7¾	25	22
	Series 10, 80, 60	½P to 1½P	1P	①	②	1/16 to 3/16	7¾	25	22

▲ With power steering ½P to 1½P
① Left: ⅛P to ⅝P; Right: 0 to ½P
② Left ⅜P; Right: ⅛P
③ 1973 01-40 Series—0 deg.
N Negative P Positive
PS Power steering

Series 01 American/Hornet
10 Rebel/Matador through 1974/1975-76 Matador coupe
30 AMX
40 Gremlin
60 Pacer
70 Javelin
80 Ambassador/1975-76 Matador Sedan and Wagon

CHARGING SYSTEM

General information on generator and regulator repair and troubleshooting can be found in the Unit Repair Section.

Regulator Removal

Disconnect plug to the regulator. Remove the metal screws which hold the regulator to the sheet metal and lift off the regulator.

NOTE: Starting 1975, the Delco-Remy alternator has a solid state voltage regulator built into the end frame. The unit is integral with the alternator assembly and cannot be adjusted.

Alternator R & R

1. Disconnect battery cables.
2. Disconnect alternator wires or plug, then loosen adjusting bolt.
3. Remove V-belt, mounting bolts and alternator.
4. To install, reverse removal procedure. V8 brackets have a hole to use as a tensioner bar fulcrum.

Alternator Precautions

Caution Since the alternator and regulator are designed for use on only one polarity system, the following precautions must be observed:

1. The polarity of the battery, generator and regulator must be matched and considered before making any electrical connections in the system.
2. When connecting a booster battery, be sure to connect the negative battery terminals respectively and the positive battery terminals respectively.
3. When connecting a charger to the battery, connect the charger positive lead to the battery positive terminal. Connect the charger negative lead to the battery negative terminal.
4. Never operate the alternator on open circuit. Be sure that all connections in the circuit are clean and tight.
5. Do not short across or ground any of the terminals on the alternator regulator.
6. Do not attempt to polarize the alternator.
7. Do not use test lamps of more than 12 volts for checking diode continuity.
8. Avoid long soldering times when replacing diodes or transistors. Prolonged heat is damaging to these units.
9. Disconnect the battery ground terminal when servicing any AC system. This will prevent the possibility of accidental reversing of polarity.
10. If electronic welding equipment is used on the car, be sure to completely disconnect the alternator.

STARTING SYSTEM

American Motors cars are equipped with an integral positive engagement drive starter and a separate starter relay.

Starter repair procedures can be found in the Unit Repair Section.

Starter Removal

6 Cylinder

Disconnect the battery lead from the starter and the solenoid lead from the starter. From underneath the vehicle, remove the bolts which hold the starter to the bell housing and lift off the starter.

V8

Disconnect the battery wire and the solenoid wire at the starter. From underneath the vehicle, remove the bolts which hold the starter to the flywheel housing and lift off the starter.

IGNITION SYSTEM

On all cars with emission control systems, the distributor uses a cam lubricator. The lubricator should be rotated one-half turn every 12,000 miles and replaced at 24,000 mile intervals. Never oil the lubricator; always replace it at the proper interval. It is a good idea, however, to apply a small amount of high-melting-point lubricant to the breaker cam itself, when the points are replaced.

A transmission-controlled spark (TCS) is used on 1971–72 models equipped with 304 and 360 cu in. V8 engines, with automatic transmissions and on all cars sold in California. In 1973-75, it is used on all cars, except those with 401 cu in. engines (which are not sold in California). For details of this system, see the section on emission controls.

Starting 1975, all American Motors cars are equipped with the Breakerless Inductive Discharge (BID) ignition system. The system consists of an electronic ignition control unit, a standard type ignition coil, a distributor that contains an electronic sensor and trigger wheel instead of a cam, breaker points and condenser, and the usual high tension wires and spark plugs.

The electronic control unit is a solid-state, moisture proof component. The parts are permanently sealed in a resin potting material. This unit can not be repaired and must be serviced as a unit.

The sensor component of the distributor is a small coil of fine wire which receives an alternating current signal from the electronic control unit. The sensor develops an electromagnetic field used to detect the presence of metal. The sensor detects the metal edges of the spokes of the trigger wheel. When the leading edge of a trigger wheel spoke aligns with the center of the sensor coil, a signal is sent to the control unit to open the coil primary circuit and cause the secondary ignition spark.

There are no contacting (and thus wearing) surfaces between the trigger wheel and the sensor. The dwell angle remains the same and never requires adjustment. The dwell angle is determined by the control unit and the angle between the trigger wheel spokes.

For more information and repair procedures, see the "Electronic Ignition" Unit Repair Section.

Distributor Removal

6-Cylinder Models

The distributor is mounted on the side of the engine. Remove the distributor cap and mark the position of the rotor relative to the distributor body, then mark the distributor body relative to the block. Remove the distributor hold-down screw, disconnect the ignition primary wire and the vacuum advance tube. Lift the distributor out of the block.

V8 Models

1. Remove the distributor cap, mark the position of the rotor relative to the distributor body and mark the body relative to the block. Remove the carburetor air cleaner, the distributor primary wire and the distributor vacuum lines.
2. Remove the hold-down bolt and take the distributor up out of the block.

The rotor and body are marked so that they can be returned to the position from which they were removed. Do not turn the engine after the distributor has been taken off.

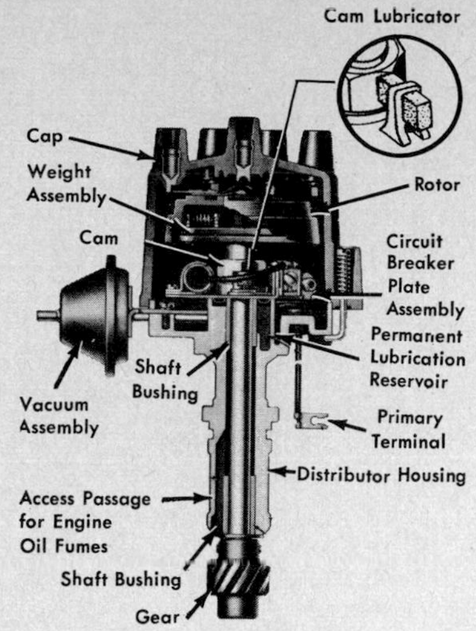

Distributor—all V8
(© American Motors Corp)

Distributor Installation

Engine Not Disturbed—Timing Retained

Install the distributor in the reverse order of removal. Be sure that the rotor and distributor are installed with the marks, which were made during removal, in alignment. Adjust the timing as required.

Engine Disturbed—Timing Lost

If the rotor position was not noted during removal, or if the engine was cranked with the distributor out, install it as follows:

1. Remove the spark plug from the no. one cylinder and position a compression gauge or a thumb over the spark plug hole.
2. Slowly crank the engine, until compression pressure starts to build up.
3. Continue cranking the engine so that the timing mark or pointer aligns with the TDC mark.
4. Install the distributor with its drive meshed, so that the rotor points to the no. one terminal on the distributor with engine at TDC.
5. Complete installation in the reverse order of removal and adjust the timing as required.

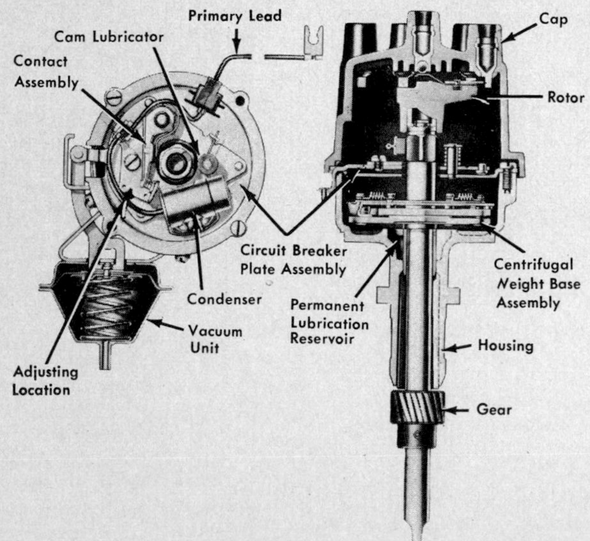

Distributor—199/232/258 6 cylinder
(© American Motors Corp)

Point Replacement

6-Cylinder Models

The condenser and primary leads are retained by spring tension. Remove the distributor rotor and cap, release the tension and remove the leads. Loosen contact base screw and remove contact point assembly. Install a new condenser, set approximate point gap of new contact set, lubricate cam lobes or reverse lubricator and install rotor and cap. Check dwell and adjust if necessary.

V8 Models

Remove the distributor cap, condenser and primary leads which are attached to the nylon terminal. Loosen the two base screws and remove points. When installing points, make sure pilot hole is properly positioned over hole in breaker plate. Install new condenser, then attach primary and condenser leads to nylon terminal. Reverse lubricator and check that terminal leads will not touch rotor. Install rotor, making sure round and square holes are lined up with their respective dowels. Adjust point dwell to specification by turning Allen screw on point set through window in side of cap.

Ignition Timing Adjustment

A scale located on the timing chain cover and a notch milled into the vibration damper are used as references to set ignition timing.

NOTE: Connect a tachometer to the BID ignition system in the conventional way; to the negative (distributor) side of the coil and to a ground. Some tachometers may not work with a BID ignition system and there is a possibility that some could be damaged. Check with the manufacturer of the tachometer to make sure it can be used.

1. On the 1970-76 models, disconnect the vacuum hose(s), at the distributor vacuum unit on six-cylinder engines, or at the carburetor on V8 engines. Plug the

vacuum return line to prevent leakage.
2. Connect a timing light and a tachometer in accordance with the manufacturer's instructions. If the timing light has an advance control, be sure that it is in the "off" position.
3. Start the engine. Adjust the carburetor curb idle screw so that the engine idles at 500 rpm.
4. Adjust the timing by loosening the distributor clamp and rotating the distributor. Set the timing to the proper specification.

NOTE: On some models, a white paint mark is applied to the scale for the specified, initial timing setting. Do not mistake this mark for TDC.

5. Check the timing again after tightening the distributor clamp.
6. Connect the vacuum hoses and set the idle speed to normal specifications.

FUEL SYSTEM

On cars equipped with vacuum-operated windshield wipers (through 1971) a double-action, vacuum booster fuel pump is used. If the car is equipped with an electric wiper motor, a conventional single-action fuel pump is fitted.

Emission controls are covered in the sections which deal with them, except when their service is part of the carburetor adjustment. In this case, their adjustment is covered in this section.

Fuel Pump R & R

Disconnect both gas lines from the fuel pump, disconnect the vacuum line, if it is a vacuum pump. Remove the two bolts which hold it to the block and lift off the pump.

Installation is the reverse of removal.

Fuel Filter R & R

For 1969, an inline fuel filter is located in the carburetor inlet. To change these filters (24,000 miles), unscrew the gas line at the carburetor, remove the element and install a new element. Do not try to clean these elements.

In 1970, the inline filter was changed to a 15 micron paper element unit. The filter assembly is located in the carburetor fuel intake line and secured to it by means of clamps and two short lengths of rubber hose. It should be replaced every 12,000 miles on 1970-72 models or every 15,000 miles, starting in 1973.

Carburetor Adjustments

1969-71

Adjust with air cleaner installed.

NOTE: Do not allow the engine to idle for more than three minutes at a time. If the idle mixture adjustment is not completed at the end of three minutes, run the engine at 2000 rpm for one minute. Continue the adjustments at the specified rpm.

1. Start engine and allow it to warm up to operating temperature. Connect a tachometer. *On engine with air pumps, disconnect air bypass hose at valve.*
2. Adjust carburetor idle speed screw to obtain 600 rpm for 6-cylinder manual, 525 rpm for 1969 6-cylinder automatic (in Drive), 550 rpm for 1970 6-cylinder automatic (in Drive), 650 rpm for V8 manual, 550 rpm for 1969 V8 automatic (in Drive), or 600 rpm for 1970 V8 automatic (in Drive), 700 rpm for six-cylinder manual, 600 rpm for 1971 six-cylinder automatic, 750 rpm for the 1971 V8 manual, and 650 rpm for the 1971 V8 automatic.
3. Starting from full rich stop/s (or two turns from seated on 4-BBL. manual V8) turn mixture screw/s clockwise until engine speed drops off.
4. Turn mixture screw/s counterclockwise until engine speed picks up to former level. The highest idle speed obtainable within the range of the limiter caps (or between the rich drop-off and lean drop-off points for 4-BBL. manual V8) is the "lean best idle setting." Both mixture screws should be turned equally unless the engine definitely demands otherwise.
5. If idle speed changes more than 30 rpm during mixture adjustment, reset carburetor idle speed screw and readjust mixture.

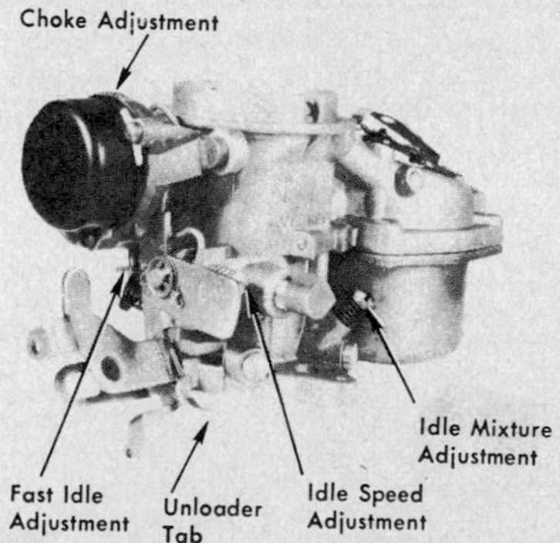

Carter RBS carburetor adjustments
(© American Motors Corp)

6. On cars with air pumps, reconnect air bypass valve hose.

NOTE: if idle quality is poor within the range of the limiter caps, the caps may be removed and the idle speed set using the corrective procedure. Keep in mind that a combustion gas analyzer is necessary to meet the critical federal exhaust emission standards. All cars should have a 14:1 air/fuel ratio except 4-BBL. manual transmission V8's, which should be set up at 13.5:1 (air bypass hose disconnected).

Idle Quality Corrective Procedure

1. Remove idle limiter caps by inserting a sheet metal screw into the center of the cap.
2. Adjust carburetor idle speed screw to obtain 50 rpm less than specified idle speed for all 6-cylinder, and all V8 automatic. Manual transmission V8's should be set to specified idle speed.
3. Turn in the mixture screw(s) until they are gently seated, then back out one turn. Connect a tachometer.

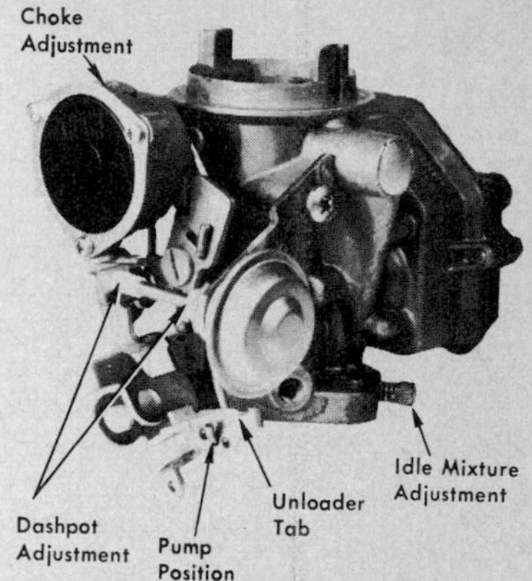

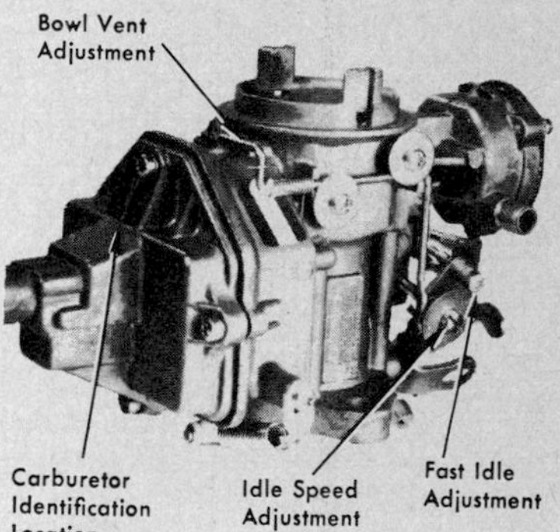

Holley 1931 carburetor adjustments
(© American Motors Corp)

4. Start the engine and turn the mixture screw(s) counterclockwise until the engine speed drops off slightly. On 2 bbl and 4 bbl carburetors, turn both mixture screws equally unless the engine definitely demands otherwise.
5. Turn the mixture screw(s) inward until the speed is regained, then continue inward until the speed begins to fall off again.
6. Turn the mixture screw(s) outward until the speed is regained. This is the "lean best idle" setting.
7. Readjust the idle speed screw to obtain the proper idle speed. Disconnect the tachometer.
8. Install new service idle limiter caps with ears against full rich stops.

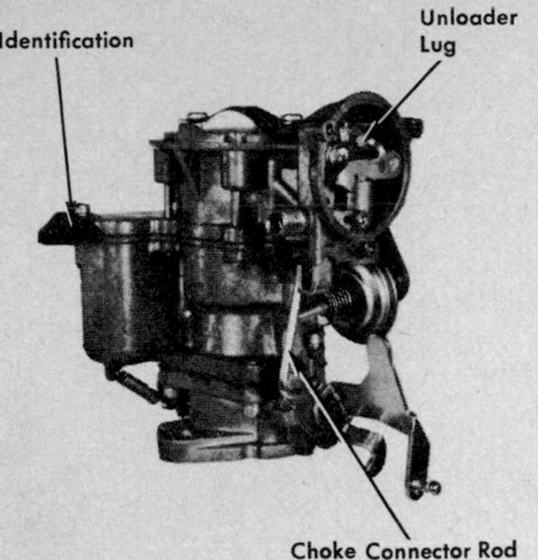

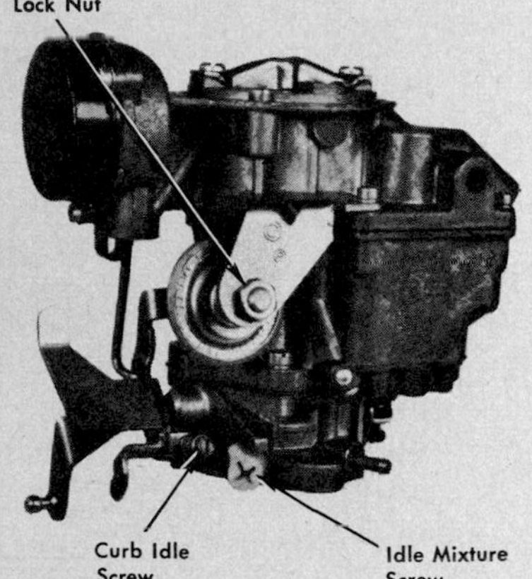

Carter YF carburetor adjustments
(© American Motors Corp)

1972

The basic procedure for adjusting the 1972 emission control carburetors is the same as that for 1969–71, above. There are, however, some variations.

1. Six-cylinder engines use the following rpm settings for idle speed:
   a. Manual transmissions — 600 rpm/National; 700 rpm/California.
   b. Automatic transmissions — 500 rpm (in Drive)/National; 600 rpm (in Drive)/California.
2. V8 engines use the following idle settings:
   a. Manual transmissions — 750 rpm/all engines.
   b. Automatic transmissions — set the 304 and 401 cu in. engines at 650 rpm (in Drive)/National; at 700 rpm (in Drive)/California. The 360 cu in. engine is set at 700 rpm/National and California.
3. On 360 and 401 cu in. V8 engines, with automatic transmissions, set the idle speed by adjusting the throttle stop solenoid, if so equipped, to the specified figure. Then adjust the engine idle to 500 rpm with the idle stop solenoid disconnected. Reconnect the solenoid.

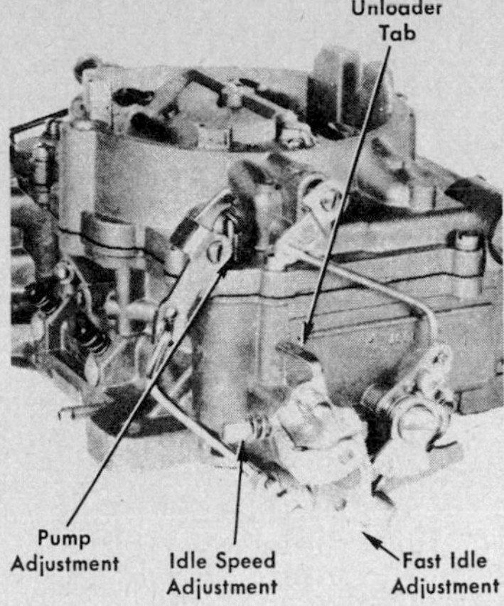

Carter AFB carburetor adjustments
(© American Motors Corp)

Caution When adjusting the idle speed on a car equipped with an automatic transmission, set in the Drive range, be sure that the parking brake is firmly on and that the front wheels are blocked.

1973-74

Adjust with air cleaner installed.

NOTE: Do not allow the engine to idle more than three minutes at a time. If the idle/mixture adjustment is not completed by the end of three minutes, run the engine for one minute at 2,000 rpm. Return to specified rpm and continue the adjustment.

1. Remove the idle limiter cap(s) by inserting a screw in its center. Turn the cap clockwise to remove it.
2. Discard the old cap(s).
3. Start the engine and allow it to reach normal operating temperature.
4. Install a tachometer of known accuracy, in accordance with its manufacturer's instructions.
5. Adjust the idle speed to 30 rpm above the speed specified in the "Tune-Up Specifications" chart.

NOTE: On 1973-74 V8, automatic transmission equipped cars and 1974

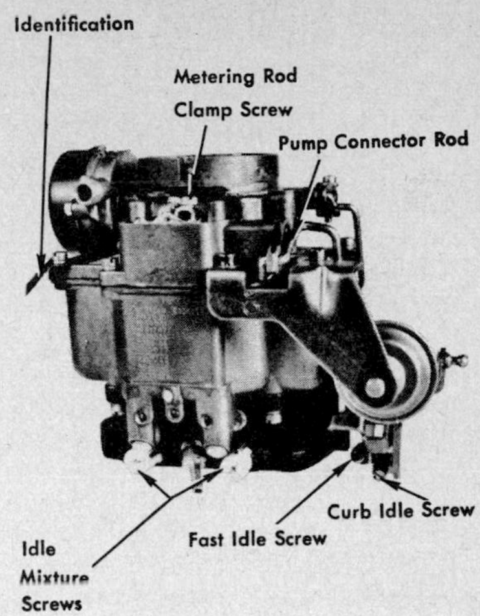

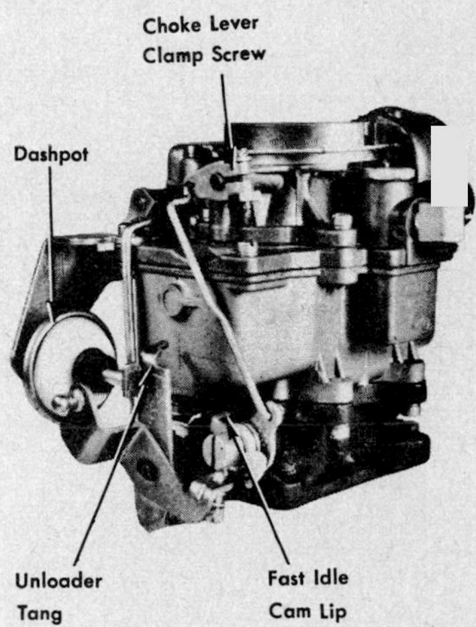

WCD carburetor adjustments
(© American Motors Corp)

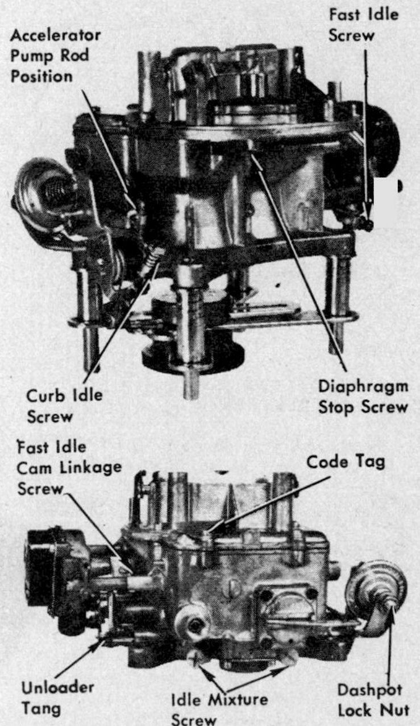

Autolite/Motorcraft 2100 carburetor adjustments (© American Motors Corp)

California sixes with automatic transmission, adjust the idle speed by turning the hex screw on the throttle stop solenoid.

6. Turn the mixture screws until they are seated against their full-rich stops.
7. Then turn the mixture screws clockwise (leaner) until a drop in engine idle speed is noted.
8. Turn the mixture screws counterclockwise from this position until the highest rpm is obtained.

NOTE: When adjusting the idle mixture on a carburetor which has two mixture screws, turn both screws equally unless satisfactory idle cannot be obtained in this manner.

9. If the idle speed changes more than 30 rpm during the mixture adjusting procedure, set the idle to 30 rpm above specification and repeat steps 6-8 again.
10. After completing steps 1-9 satisfactorily, turn the mixture screws clockwise until the engine idle speed drops the amount specfied below:

Engine/Transmission	*RPM*
6 cyl/manual	35
6 cyl/automatic	20
V8/All	40

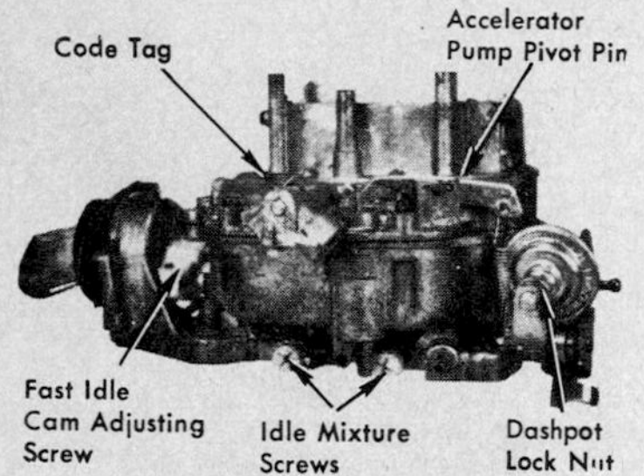

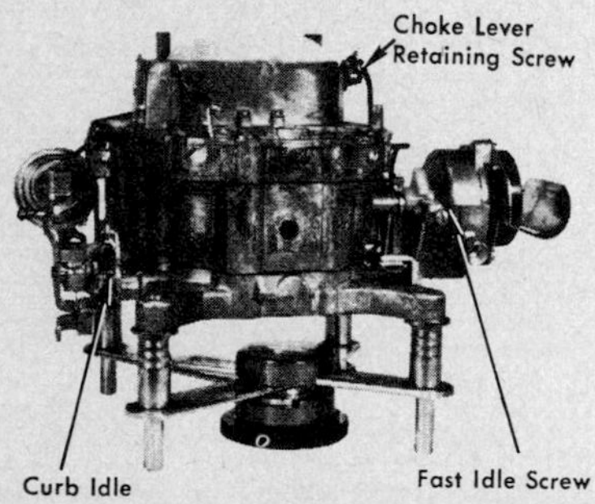

Autolite/Motorcraft 4300 carburetor adjustments (© American Motors Corp)

11. Install new service idle limiter caps.

Caution When adjusting the idle speed/mixture on a car with its automatic transmission set in Drive range, be sure that the parking brake is firmly on and that the front wheels are blocked.

1975-76

NOTE: This adjustment is performed with the air cleaner installed. Do not allow the engine to idle more than three minutes at a time. If the idle/mixture adjustment is not completed by the end of three minutes, run the engine for one minute at 2,000 rpm. Return to the specified rpm and continue the adjustment.

1. Adjust the idle screw(s) to the full rich stop(s). Note the position of the screw head slot inside the limiter cap slots.
2. Carefully remove the idle limiter cap(s) by installing a sheet metal screw in the center of the cap and turning clockwise. Discard the old caps.
3. Install a tachometer on the engine.
4. Start the engine and allow it to reach normal operating temperature.
5. Adjust the idle speed to 30 rpm above the specified idle speed. See the Tune-Up Specifications chart.

NOTE: On all V8 engines with automatic transmissions and California six cylinder engines with automatic transmissions the idle is adjusted with the throttle stop solenoid.

6. Starting from the full rich stop position, as noted in step 1, turn the mixture screw(s) clockwise (leaner) until the engine looses speed.
7. Turn the mixture screw(s) counterclockwise until the highest rpm reading is obtained at the lean best idle setting.

NOTE: On engines with two mixture screws, turn both of the screws an equal number of turns unless the engine demands otherwise.

8. If the idle speed has changed more than 30 rpm during the mixture adjustment, reset the idle to 30 rpm above the specified idle rpm as indicated in the "Tune-Up Specifications" chart.
9. Turn the mixture adjustment screw(s) clockwise until the rpm drops as follows:

Six cylinder	automatic	25 rpm
Six cylinder	manual	25 rpm
Six cylinder	manual with with EGR and catalytic converter	35 rpm
Six cylinder	manual with EGR	50 rpm
V8	automatic	20 rpm
V8	manual	40 rpm

10. Install new blue service idle limiter cap (s) over the idle mixture screw(s) with the limiter cap tang(s) positioned against the full rich stop(s). Be careful not to disturb the idle mixture setting while installing the cap(s). Press the cap(s) firmly into place.

Dashpot Adjustment

Some carburetors are equipped with a dashpot to prevent stalling. The dashpot adjustment procedure for these carburetors is as follows:

1. Be sure that the throttle valves are closed (curb idle position) and that the diaphragm stem is fully depressed.
2. Measure the clearance between the dashpot stem and the throttle lever with a feeler gauge. For the proper clearance specification see the chart below.
3. If the clearance is not correct, adjust it by loosening the locknut and rotating the dashpot until the proper clearance is obtained. Tighten the locknut.

Year	*Carburetor*		*Clearance (Gauge size in.)*
1969	RBS(1-V)	All	0.095
	6200(2-V)	All	0.140
	AFB(4-V)	All	0.160-0.170
1970	YF(1-V)	4768S	0.120
		4770S	0.095
	WCD(2-V)	All	0.095
	2100(2-V)	All	0.125
	4300(4-V)	All	0.125
1971	YF(1-V)	All	0.110
	2100(2-V)	All	0.125
	4300(4-V)	1TM4	0.065
		1TA4	0.125
1972-74	YF(1-V)	All	0.095
	2100(2-V)	2DM2	0.110
		2DA2, 3DM2, 4DM2	0.140
	4300(4-V)	All	0.140
1975	YF (1-V)	All	0.075
	2100 (2-V)	All	0.093

COOLING SYSTEM

American Motors cars are equipped with a conventional cooling system which utilizes a vertical flow radiator, a water pump, and a thermostat. The Pacer has a crossflow radiator. An internal by-pass port is used on the six-cylinder engine, which allows water to flow through the engine when the thermostat is closed. The V8 engine uses an external hose to perform the same function.

Information on the water temperature gauge can be found in the Unit Repair Section.

Radiator Removal

Raise the hood, drain the radiator, remove the upper and lower radiator hose. On models equipped with the optional coolant recovery system, disconnect its hose from the radiator. Remove the radiator shroud, if so equipped. Take out the bolts which hold the radiator to its cradle and, if the car is fitted with an oil cooler for the transmission, disconnect the oil cooler lines and lift the core up and out.

Water Pump Removal

The water pump is a centrifugal unit having a non-adjustable packless seal. It is non-serviceable and must be replaced if defective—no maintenance is required.

6 Cylinder

1. Drain the cooling system. Disconnect the negative (—) cable from the battery.
2. Unfasten the radiator and the heater hoses at the pump.
3. Loosen the adjustment bolts from the alternator and the power steering pump (if so equipped). Remove the V-belts.
4. Unfasten the fan ring securing bolts. Remove the fan and pump pulley assembly. Withdraw the fan ring (or shroud).
5. Remove the securing bolts from the water pump. Withdraw the pump along with its gasket.

Installation is the reverse order of removal. Always use a new pump gasket. Bleed the radiator by running the engine and opening the heater control valve. Run the engine long enough so that the thermostat opens. Check the coolant level.

The water pump securing bolts should be tightened to 10–15 ft lbs.

V8

1. Drain the cooling system at the radiator. Remove the upper hose from the radiator. Disconnect the negative (—) cable from the battery.

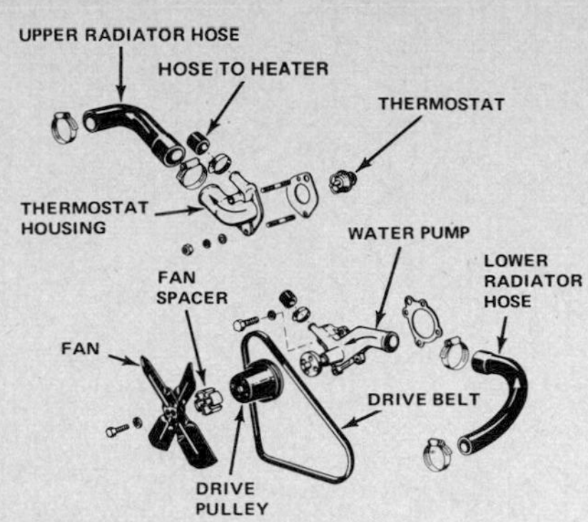

Cooling system components and coolant flow for 6 cylinder engines (© American Motors Corp)

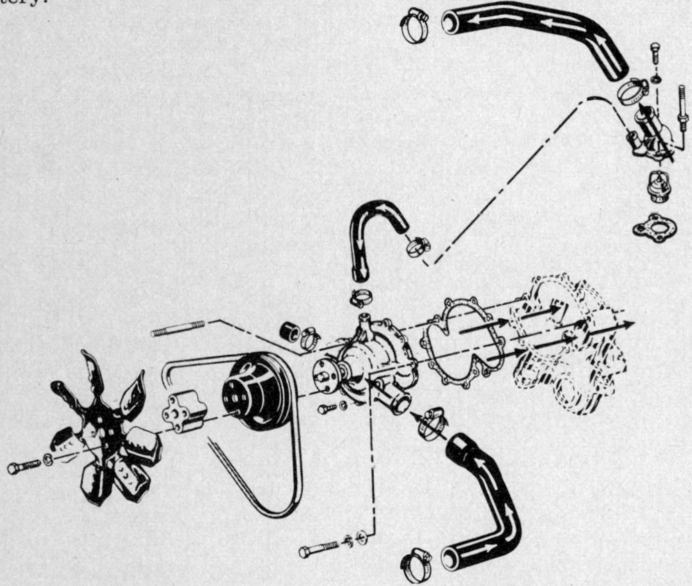

Water pump components and coolant flow 1969-76 V8 (© American Motors Corp)

2. Remove the air cleaner.
3. Remove the fan shroud. Remove the drive belts, the fan, and hub assembly by withdrawing the attaching bolts.
4. If the car is equipped with power steering, remove the pump assembly from its bracket.
5. If the car is equipped with an emission control air pump. Remove the three cap screws from the bracket at the cylinder head, and remove the pump, complete with bracket.
6. Loosen the bolts attaching the alternator bracket. Leave one bolt in position, so that the alternator may be swung to one side. Do not disconnect the wire from the alternator.
7. Disconnect the heater hose at the water pump.
8. On cars equipped with A/C, disconnect the compressor bracket and set it and the compressor out of the way. Remove the back idler. Do not discharge the air conditioning system.
9. Remove the by-pass and the lower radiator hoses from the pump.
10. Remove the pump and clean the gasket areas.

Installation is the reverse of removal. Always install a new pump gasket. Tighten the pump bolts to 40–50 in. lbs. Bleed the cooling system by starting the engine and opening the heater valve. Leave it open until the thermostat opens. Check the coolant level.

Chilton's TIME SAVER

On V8 engines, water pumps have two different shaft lengths depending on application. Long-shaft pumps can be used in short-shaft applications if the flange on the pump shaft is pressed further down towards the pump (using an axle press) and the fan spacer drilled to receive the longer shaft.

Thermostat Removal

The thermostat is located in the water outlet housing at the top of the cylinder head, or on V8 models in front of the manifold.

Disconnect the upper radiator hose and remove the bolts which hold the water outlet neck to the engine. Remove the thermostat.

When installing the thermostat, be sure that the wax pellet and coil spring are facing the engine. Thermostats are marked on the outer flange with the proper installing direction.

The bleed hole on the thermostats used on six-cylinder engines must be installed up (at 12 o'clock), to prevent "burping" caused by air trapped in the block.

Caution Tightening the housing bolts unevenly, or with the thermostat cocked in its recess, will cause the housing to crack.

EMISSION CONTROLS

See the "Unit Repair Section" for testing and repair of the various emission control system components.

1969 All Models

An air injection system (Air-Guard) was used to meet the emission requirements on all V8s with manual transmission.

This system consists of:

1. A belt-driven, vane-type pump which feeds air through a manifold and into each exhaust port via a stainless steel nozzle. The air mixes with the hot exhaust gases and aids in burning them completely in the exhaust manifold.
2. A carburetor with a different flow characteristic and a dashpot which is used to control throttle closing speed (except on six-cylinder models with automatic transmissions).
3. A distributor with a different advance curve and a special cam lubricator.
4. A positive crankcase ventilation system (PCV) retained from earlier models.

All other engines used a system of "engine modifications" to meet the new Federal emissions standards.

These engine modifications consist of:

1. A composition head gasket to replace the steel head gasket.

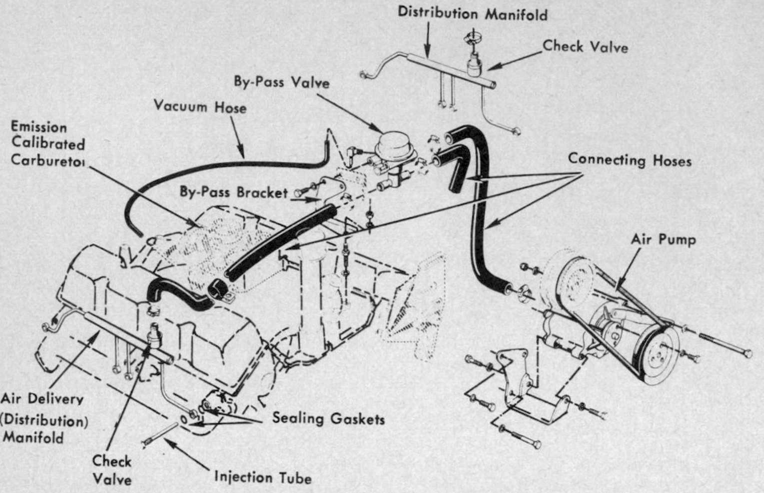

"Air-Guard" air injection system components
(© American Motors Corp)

2. An emission-calibrated carburetor, equipped with idle limiter caps to prevent the fuel/air mixture from being set over rich.
3. A distributor with a centrifugal advance curve designed to retard the timing only at idle speed, while still retaining normal performance characteristics.
4. A positive crankcase ventilation system (PCV) retained from earlier models.
5. A "low-quench" combustion chamber on six-cylinder engines.
6. A thermostatically controlled air cleaner (TAC) on all V8s, except those equipped with a 2V carburetor and manual transmission. The TAC allows only air heated by a stove on the exhaust manifold to enter the air cleaner when the under-hood temperature is less than 120° F. When the air is above this temperature, the valve opens, allowing under-hood air to be drawn through the air cleaner snorkle, in a conventional manner.

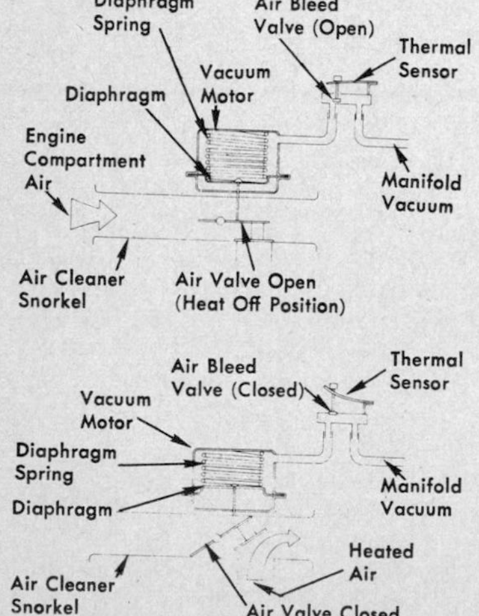

Thermostatically controlled air cleaner (TAC) —V8 engine application
(© American Motors Corp)

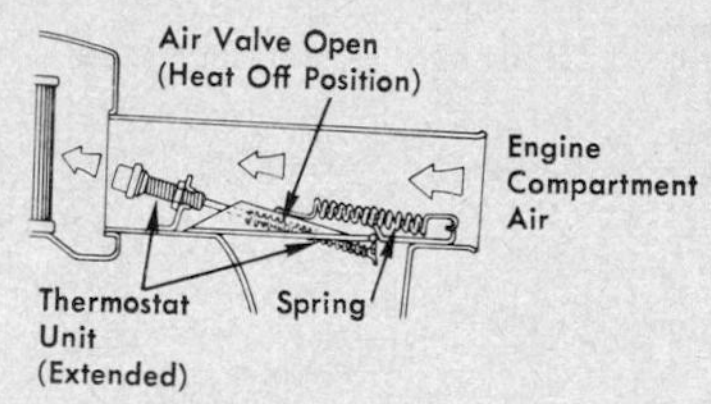

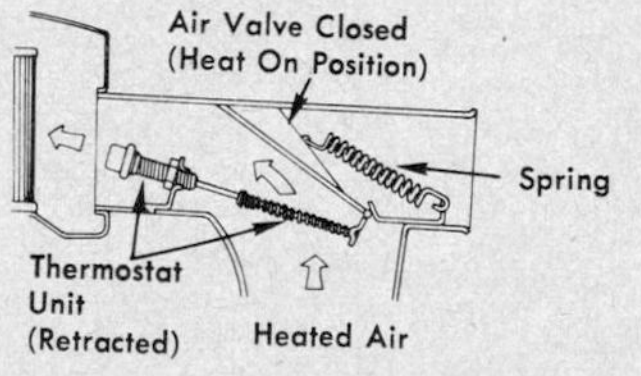

Thermostatically controlled air cleaner (TAC) —6 cylinder application
(© American Motors Corp)

1970 All Models

All of the 1969 emission controls have been carried over to 1970. In addition, the following controls are added:

1. A deceleration valve is added to the 199, 232, and 390 cu. in. engines when equipped with manual transmissions. When the car is decelerating and intake manifold pressure rises to a specific value, the valve closes off the vacuum spark port opening. Direct intake manifold vacuum is supplied to the advance diaphragm (dual-diaphragm distributor). This permits maximum ignition timing advance, to prevent afterburning in the engine exhaust system.
2. A dual-diaphragm distributor is used on all engines equipped with a deceleration valve and on the 304 and 360 cu in. V8 engines. It is not used on the 232 or 390 cu in. engines with automatic transmissions. It has a retard (secondary) diaphragm in addition to the advance (primary) diaphragm. The secondary diaphragm permits additional timing retardation during closed throttle deceleration and idle, thus reducing hydrocarbon emissions.

1970 California Models

In addition to the above modifications, all cars sold in California, starting with 1970 models, have to be equipped with an evaporative emission control system (EEC).

The American Motors EEC System consists of:

1. A fuel expansion tank that is integral with the fuel tank.
2. A closed vent system on the fuel tank.
3. A fuel check valve used to prevent the flow of *liquid* fuel through the closed vent system (not used on Gremlin models).
4. A special pressure and vacuum relief filler cap.

The EEC system routes raw fuel vapor into the PCV system, where it is burned along with regular crankcase emissions and the fuel-air mixture.

1971 All Models

The use of the evaporative emission control (EEC) system has been extended to the nationwide emission control package. All other systems have been retained, except for the dual-diaphragm distributor and the deceleration valve.

In addition, a charcoal canister has been added to the EEC system, on V8 engines equipped with automatic transmissions. The canister is used for fuel vapor storage.

1971 California

To meet oxides of nitrogen (NO_x) emission standards for California, a transmission-controlled spark (TCS) has been adapted, in addition to the other emission control systems. The TCS system is also used nationally on the 304 and 360 cu in. V8 engines, when equipped with an automatic transmission.

The TCS system functions to lower peak combustion temperature and pressures, thus reducing exhaust emissions of oxides of nitrogen.

The TCS system consists of:

1. A transmission control switch which opens or closes, depending upon car speed and the gear selected.
2. A solenoid vacuum valve that is activated by the transmission switch. It vents ported vacuum into the atmosphere, resulting in no distributor vacuum advance, when it is energized.
3. A temperature override switch, mounted on the front crossmember, is used to complete the circuit to the battery if the ambient temperature is more than 63° F.

If the temperature is lower than this, the TCS system does not function.

The TCS system prevents vacuum advance from occurring when the car is in a low or intermediate gear and the ambient temperature is above 63° F. When the car is in high gear (or above 34 mph—automatic transmission) or the temperature is higher than 63° F, full vacuum advance is supplied to the distributor.

1972 All Models

The 1972 emission controls have remained similar to those used in 1971. Several detail improvements have been incorporated. These consist of:

1. A charcoal canister is used on the EEC system of all V8 models with automatic transmissions, for fuel vapor storage. A "purge valve" is used to empty the canister into the PCV system at normal cruising speed.
2. The thermostatically controlled air cleaner (TAC) is extended in use to all engines in 1972. The TAC used on the V8 engines has a vacuum assist motor to operate the door in the air cleaner snorkle. The six-cylinder engine TAC works by spring tension against a thermostatically controlled door.

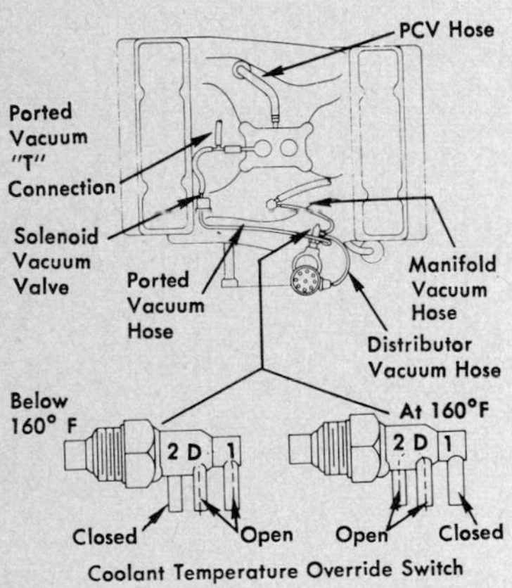

TCS hose routing, when equipped with a coolant temperature override switch (© American Motors Corp)

3. A coolant temperature operated vacuum valve is used on cars equipped with V8 engines and automatic transmissions. If the coolant temperature is above 160° F, intake manifold vacuum is blocked off and carburetor ported vacuum is sent through a hose to the distributor advance diaphragm, thus decreasing the amount of vacuum advance. On cars equipped with TCS, the distributor vacuum advance is controlled by the TCS system once 163° F is reached.

1973 All Models

All six cylinder models are equipped with TCS. A description of this system can be found above under "1972 California."

New in 1973 is an Exhaust Gas Recirculation (EGR) system which is used on all V8s and six cylinder Matadors. This system directs a portion of the exhaust gases back into the intake manifold where they combine with the incoming mixture. This diluting of the mixture lowers peak combustion temperatures and reduces NO_x. The EGR valve, which is controlled by carburetor vacuum, controls the amount of exhaust gas, if any, that is recycled into the engine. Two ambient temperature switches and one coolant temperature valve control the flow of vacuum to the valve. The low temperature ambient valve is mounted in the radiator support, near the grille, and opens at temperatures below 60°F to vent carburetor vacuum to the atmosphere. The high temperature ambient valve is mounted on the firewall and opens when ambient temperature rises above 115°F. When either of these valves is open the EGR valve will be closed, preventing exhaust gas from entering the engine. The coolant temperature valve is mounted in either the intake manifold or engine block and is closed to block vacuum when coolant temperature is below 115°F (160° on 304 V8 with manual transmssion).

Also new for 1973 is an electrically-assisted automatic choke used on V8 models equipped with 4-bbl carburetors.

Once under-hood temperatures reach 95°F (± 15°F), a bimetallic switch located in the choke cap closes, allowing a ceramic heating element to draw power from a special tap on the alternator.

This causes the choke valve to open faster than normal, thus reducing CO emission during engine warm-up.

After the engine is shut off, the bimetallic switch remains closed until under-hood temperature drops below 65°F. Thus, if the engine is turned off for only a short time or if the ambient temperature is above 65°F, the choke will function for only a limited period of time.

All Matador wagons and all V8s are equipped with an AIR pump which is described above under "1969 All Models."

1973½—74 All Models

Starting with vehicles made on or after 15 March 1973, the ambient temperature overrides were dropped from both the TCS and EGR systems.

Dropping these overrides on six-cylinder engines caused driveability problems, so a spark temperature override was added. This override provides normal vacuum advance below a coolant temperature of 160°F. Addition of the spark temperature override meant that the EGR coolant temperature override had to be dropped from the six-cylinder engines.

At the same time these changes were made, a new transmission controlled spark (TCS) was incorporated on all models equipped with automatic transmissions.

NOTE: The new TCS switch was used on Kenosha-built cars after VIN A3AXXXX229935 and on Brampton-built cars after VIN A3AXXXX723815 (6 cyl) or VIN A3AXXXX726274 (V8).

An adjustable TCS solenoid control switch, which is operated by transmission governor oil pressure, is mounted at the right rear of the block on sixes or at the rear of the right-hand valve cover on V8s. The switch is present at the factory and should not normally require adjustment. If adjustment becomes necessary, the procedure for it may be found in the emission control unit repair section.

For 1974, most of the changes made in March are retained, except that the EGR coolant temperature override has been returned to the six-cylinder engines.

In addition, 1974 cars also have the following:

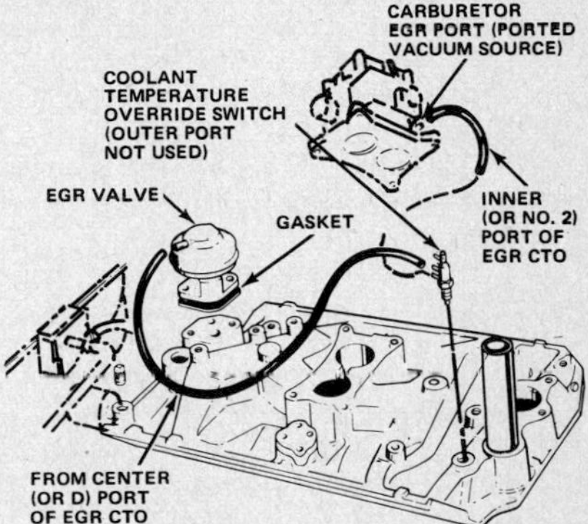

1974 V8 EGR system without backpressure sensor
(© American Motors Corp)

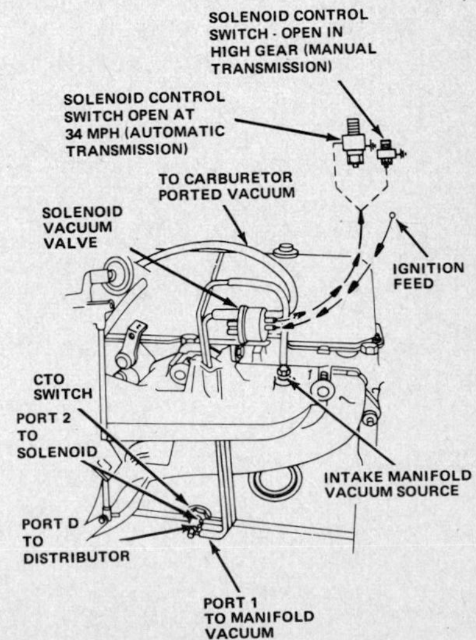

1974 TCS system—6 cylinder
(© American Motors Corp)

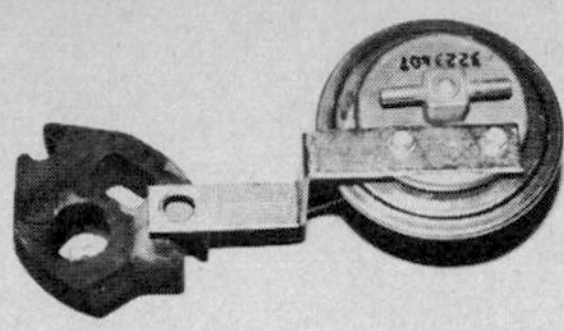

The backpressure sensing device used on some 1974 California engines when equipped with EGR

New diverter valves used with "Air Guard" on 1974-75 AMC cars

1. A back pressure sensing device to prevent EGR from occurring during idle, is used on all California six-cylinder engines when equipped with EGR valves, and V8s with automatic transmissions (except for the 401 cu in. V8).
2. Exhaust gas recirculation (EGR) has been extended to all six-cylinder engines, as well as V8s, except for the following:

   232 cu in. six—all Hornet sedans, Hornet hatchback, and Gremlin.

   258 cu in. six—Hornet 2-door sedan, Hornet hatchback, and Gremlin.
3. A new style diverter valve is used with air injection. The relief valve is now part of the diverter valve, rather than being mounted on the pump.
4. All engines for 1974 use a charcoal canister which is purged through the air cleaner snorkel. There is no purge valve on the canister.
5. The electrically assisted choke is retained on all 4-bbl V8 engines.

1975

All American Motors cars built for sale in California are equipped with the following emission control equipment:

a. Air guard air injection system
b. Catalytic converter (all V8s have two converters)
c. Exhaust gas recirculation (EGR)
d. Fuel tank vapor control system (FTVC)
e. Fuel vapor return system
f. Positive crankcase ventilation system (PCV)
g. Thermostatically controlled air cleaner (TAC)
h. Transmission controlled spark (TCS)
i. Exhaust back-pressure sensor (BPS)
j. EGR coolant temperature override switch
k. Vacuum advance (distributor) coolant tempertature override switch

American Motors cars built for sale in the remaining 49 states are equipped with all of the emission control devices California cars have with the following exceptions:

a. All six cylinder vehicles except manual transmission Matadors, do not have catalytic converters. All V8s and the 258 Matador Six with manual transmission have one catalytic converter; the 360 4 bbl V8 has two converters.
b. All Gremlin sixes and automatic transmission Hornet sixes and Pacers do not have the Air Guard air injection system.
c. All six cylinder vehicles except the Matador and Pacer automatic do not have the Fuel Vapor Return System.

See the "Emission Controls Unit Repair Section" for more information.

Air Pump R & R

Caution Never place the pump in a vise or attempt to dismantle it. The pump has no internal parts that are replaceable and it is serviced as a unit. Never pry or hammer on the pump housing.

1. Loosen the bolts on the pump pulley.
2. Loosen the air pump attachment bracket. On V8 models with air conditioning, loosen the power steering pump to aid in drive belt removal.
3. Disconnect the air supply hoses at the pump.
4. Remove the drivebelt and pulley from the hub.
5. Unscrew the bolts on the bracket and remove the pump.

Installation is as follows:

1. Place the pump on its mounting bracket and install, but do not tighten, the attaching bolts.
2. With the rotor shaft used as a center, fit the pulley into the hub and install the drive belt over the pulley.
3. Tighten the pulley attaching bolts, using care not to snap them off.
4. Adjust the pump until the belt is secure. Tighten the mounting bolts and the adjusting screw to 18-20 ft lbs.
5. Attach the hoses and clamps.

Air Pump Relief Valve R & R

NOTE: 1973-74 air pumps do not have a relief valve mounted on them. It is part of the diverter valve.

1. Use a gear puller and a steel bridge to remove the relief valve from the pump.
2. Remove the pressure plug from the new relief valve assembly (if so equipped).
3. Insert the relief valve into its housing mounting hole.
4. Place a block of wood over the valve. Use a hammer to tap the valve until it lightly registers against the housing. Use care not to distort the housing.
5. Press the pressure plug into the center of the relief valve.

Centrifugal Filter Fan R & R

NOTE: Never attempt to clean the filter fan. It is almost impossible to remove the fan without destroying it.

1. Remove the air pump from the car.
2. Gently pry the outer disc off and pull off the remaining portion. Be careful that no fragments from the fan enter the pump air intake.
3. Install a new filter fan pulling it into place with the pump pulley and attaching bolts.
4. Alternately torque the bolts so that the fan is drawn down *evenly*. Be sure that the outer edge of the fan fits into the pump housing.

Caution Never hammer or press the fan into place; damage to it and the pump will result.

5. Install the pump on the car.

NOTE: For the first 20-30 miles of operation, the fan may squeal until its lip has worn in. This is normal and does not indicate a damaged pump.

Exhaust Tube R & R

1. Remove the exhaust tube by grasping *it* (never the pump body) in a vise or a pair of pliers. Pull the tube out with a gentle twisting motion.
2. Install the new exhaust tube by tapping it into the hole with a hammer and a wooden block. Be careful not to damage its end.
3. Tap it until 7/8 in. of the tube remains above the pump cover.

NOTE: Do not clamp the pump in a vise while installing the exhaust tube.

By-Pass (Diverter) Valve R & R

1. Disconnect the hoses from the valve.
2. Remove the screws that attach the valve bracket to the engine, if so equipped. Remove the valve and bracket assembly.
3. Installation is the reverse of removal.

Air Injection Manifold and Check Valve Assembly R & R

6 Cylinder

1. Remove the intake/exhaust manifold assembly, after disconnecting the hoses from the air injection manifold.
2. Place the assembly in a vise and remove the retaining nuts on the air injection manifold at each cylinder exhaust port.
3. Lightly tap the injection tubes, then pull the injection manifold away from the exhaust manifold.
4. If the tubes have become fused to the injection manifold, remove them by applying heat while rotating them with pliers.

Installation of the injection manifold and tubes is performed as follows:

1. Insert new air injection tubes into the exhaust manifold. Tighten the injection tubes to 20 ft lbs.

NOTE: the shorter tubes go into the no. three and four cylinders.

2. Using a new gasket, assemble the exhaust/intake manifold to the engine.
3. Using new gaskets, install the air injection manifold on to the exhaust manifold in the reverse order of removal.

V8

1. Disconnect the air delivery hose at the check valve.
2. Loosen the air injection manifold attachment nuts from the cylinder head. Carefully, ease the air injection manifold away from the head.

NOTE: On some models it may be necessary to lower the bottom steering shaft clamp to gain access to the left rear mounting bolt; or to disconnect the right engine support and raise the engine to remove the right air injection manifold assembly. On Hornets and Gremlins, it may be easier to just remove the right-hand exhaust manifold completely.

3. On newer cars, loosen the air injection tubes and remove the manifold and tubes as an assembly.
4. On older models, or if the tubes are hard to remove, use an "easy-out" to twist the tube out gradually.

NOTE: Some interference may be encountered because of the normal carbon buildup on the tubes. Injection tubes which are removed with an "easy-out" must be replaced with new ones.

Installation is the reverse of removal.

PCV Valve R & R

The PCV valve must be replaced at periodic intervals or if it becomes inoperative. It cannot be cleaned or repaired.

1. Remove the PCV valve from the grommet on the intake manifold on V8 engines or the valve cover on the sixes.
2. Disconnect the hose from the valve.
3. Installation is the reverse of removal.

EGR Valve R & R

1. Remove the air cleaner assembly from the carburetor, on V8 engines.
2. Disconnect the vacuum line from the top of the EGR valve.
3. Loosen and remove the two screws which secure the valve to the manifold.
4. Remove the EGR valve and gaskets.

Installation of the EGR valve is the reverse of its removal. Always use a new gasket. Tighten the valve securing bolts to 13 ft lbs.

EGR Valve and Passage Cleaning

1. Remove the EGR valve.
the deposits from the stainless
2. Use a wire brush to clean all of
steel pintle.
3. Press down on the pintle to open the EGR valve and then release it to close the valve. Replace the valve assembly if it will not close fully.
4. Inspect the manifold passages. If necessary, clean them with a spiral wire brush.

NOTE: On six-cylinder engines, deposits will build up most rapidly in the upper passage. If the deposits cannot be removed with the wire brush, use a 9/16 in. drill bit. Rotate the drill by hand, after coating it with heavy grease.

5. Install the EGR valve with a new gasket.

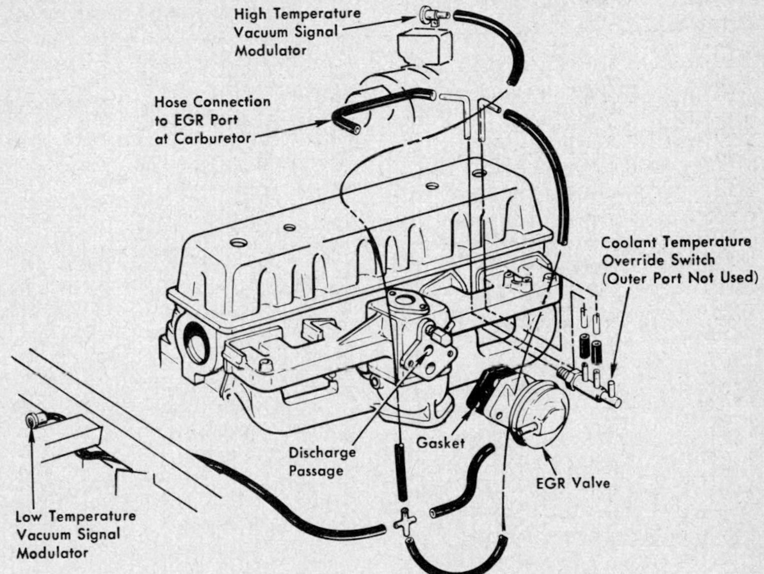

EGR valve installation and hose routing—6 cylinder
(© American Motors Corp)

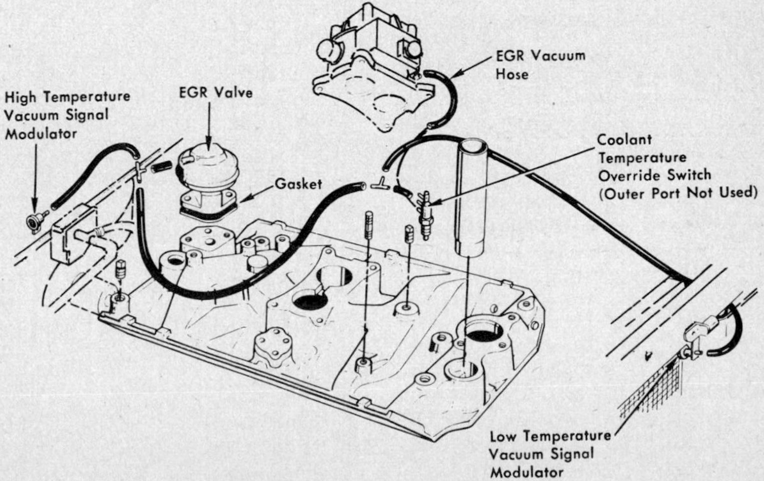

EGR valve installation and hose routing—V8
(© American Motors Corp)

EGR Coolant Temperature Override (CTO) Switch R & R

6 Cylinder

1. Drain the cooling system at the radiator.
2. Disconnect the vacuum hoses from the temperature override switch.
3. Place a drain pan underneath the switch.
4. Unscrew the switch from the block, using a 7/8-in. open-end wrench.

Installation is the reverse of removal.

V8

Use the same Steps as for six-cylinder engines. In addition, it will be necessary to remove the air cleaner and move the coil aside, in order to remove the CTO switch. To move the coil, unfasten its mounting bracket screw and tip the coil out of the way. Remember to secure the coil mounting bracket during installation.

EGR Valve w/Backpressure Sensor R & R

1. Remove the vacuum lines from both the EGR valve and the backpressure sensor.
2. Remove the screws which secure the valve section of the backpressure sensor.
3. Remove the two bolts which secure the EGR valve.
4. Take off the EGR valve/backpressure sensor assembly, the restrictor plate (if so equipped), and gasket(s).
5. Clean all joining surfaces, the EGR valve port, and the backpressure sensing valve port.

Installation is performed in the reverse order of removal. Use a new gasket(s). On sixes, the backpressure sensor should extend toward the *front* of the car; on V8s, it should extend towad the *left-side*. Tighten the EGR valve mounting bolts to 13 ft lbs.

ENGINE

In 1969, two 290 cu. in. V8s, one having 200 horsepower and the other 225 (depending on carburetion), were available. Two 343 cu. in. engines having 235 and 280 horsepower were also available. From 1969 to 1971, a 390 cu. in. V8, based on the 343, was available. This engine had a forged steel crankshaft and was rated at 315 horsepower.

In 1970, the 290 became a 304 and the 343 a 360. Horsepower figures increased by ten, except for the 300 horsepower, four-barrel 360. The 390 power rating was increased to 335 horsepower the same year. In 1971, the 390 engine was replaced by the similar 401 cu. in. unit.

From 1969-70, the seven-main-bearing six was offered in either a 199 or a 232 cu in. displacement version. The 232 cu in. engine was available with a 1V or a 2V carburetor. In 1970 a 258 cu in. engine was added to the six-cylinder line-up. The 199 cu in. engine was dropped in 1972, and the 232 became the base six-cylinder engine.

The 2V carburetor 258 six was not used from 1971 through 1975. In 1976, it was introduced for use in the Pacer only.

Engine R & R

All 1969-76 6-Cylinder

1. Remove hood; mark hinge position for easy assembly. Remove the fender braces, if so equipped.
2. Remove battery and air cleaner.
3. Drain engine oil and cooling system.
4. On automatic transmission equipped cars: drain transmission oil and remove cooler lines (if so equipped).
5. Remove power steering pump, smog pump and air conditioner compressor and condenser (if so equipped), and set them aside.

Caution Do *not* disconnect air conditioner or power steering lines.

6. Disconnect all hoses, tubes and wiring connecting engine and radiator to body and chassis. Remove radiator and starter motor for extra clearance in some models.
7. Disconnect exhaust pipe at manifold.
8. Disconnect speedometer cable and shift linkage. Disconnect the accelerator linkage at the carburetor.
9. Support engine and transmission and remove rear engine crossmember.
10. On Javelins with engine restraints, remove the restraint bracket from the transmission.
11. Disconnect front motor mounts at engine, then lift engine and transmission forward and out through hood opening, while allowing slip joint to pull out of extension housing.

Installation is the reverse of removal.

1969-76 V8—All Models

1. Follow Steps 1-6, inclusive, of six-cylinder procedure, then continue as follows:
2. Disconnect exhaust pipes from manifolds.
3. Support engine with chain hoist.
4. Remove engine rear crossmember.
5. Disconnect speedometer cable at transmission.
6. Disconnect automatic transmission shift linkage or standard transmission shift rods at transmission. If equipped with American Motors four-speed shifter, remove boot from floor pan and pull the two bolts that hold shift lever to shift mechanism; the mechanism can remain attached. If equipped with Hurst linkage, the shift lever should be removed from transmission for adequate clearance (see illustration).
7. Disconnect front motor mounts and pull engine forward and upward, while supporting driveshaft as slip joint is removed from extension housing. On Javelins with engine restraints, remove the restraint bracket from the transmission.

NOTE: if desirable, remove entire driveshaft beforehand by disassembling rear U-joint.

Installation procedure is the reverse of removal.

Engine Manifolds

Intake Manifold R & R

6 Cylinder

The intake manifold is mounted on the left-hand side of the engine and bolted to the cylinder head. A gasket is used between the intake manifold and the head, none is required for the exhaust manifold. The manifold on the 1969 Rogue 232 incorporates an internal water tube to supply carburetor heat; it is secured with a tapered fitting.

1. Remove the air cleaner and carburetor.
2. Disconnect the accelerator cable from the accelerator bellcrank.
3. Disconnect the PCV vacuum hose from the intake manifold and the TCS solenoid and bracket, if so equipped.
4. On 1969 Rogue 232 six cylinder engines, remove the coolant hoses from the intake manifold and plug the ends.
5. Remove the spark CTO switch and EGR valve (or exhaust back-pressure sensor) vacuum lines from each of these components.
6. Disconnect the hoses from the air pump and the injection manifold check valve. Disconnect the vacuum line from the diverter valve and remove the diverter valve with hoses, if so equipped.
7. Remove the air pump and power steering bracket (if so equipped) and remove the air pump. Move the power steering pump aside, out of the way, without disconnecting the hoses.
8. Remove the air conditioning drive belt idler assembly from the cylinder head, if so equipped. On some models it is necessary to remove the A/C compressor. Do not discharge the A/C system; just lie the compressor aside.

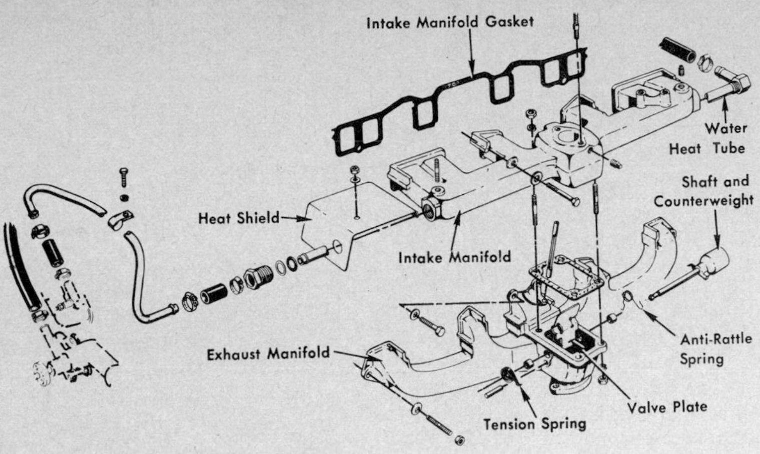

6 cylinder intake and exhaust manifold
(© American Motors Corp)

9. Remove the EGR valve (and exhaust back-pressure sensor) from the exhaust manifold.
10. Disconnect the exhaust pipe from the manifold.
11. Remove the manifold attaching bolts, nuts, and clamps and remove the intake and exhaust manifolds as an assembly. Discard the gasket. The two manifolds are separated at the heat riser.

To install the intake and exhaust manifolds:

1. Clean all of the mating surfaces on the cylinder head and the manifolds.
2. Assemble the two manifolds together and finger tighten the heat riser retaining nuts.
3. Position the manifold to the engine together with a new intake manifold gasket and tighten the manifold attaching bolts and nuts in the proper sequence to 23 ft lbs.

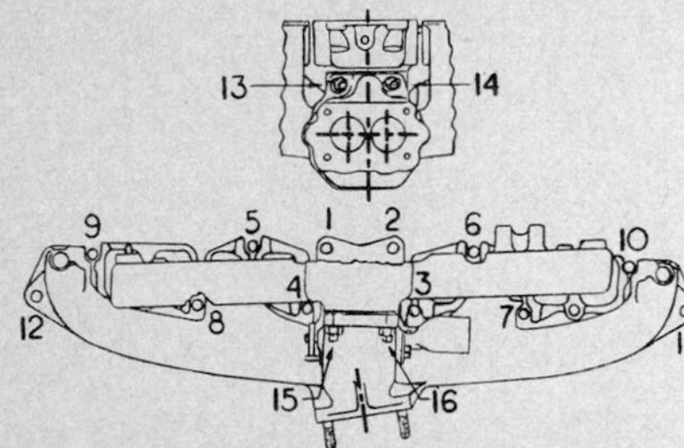

Intake manifold torque sequence—OHV 232 and 258 6 cylinder (© American Motors Corp)

4. Install the remaining components in the reverse order of removal. Adjust the automatic transmission throttle linkage, if so equipped. Adjust the drive belt(s) tension.

V8 Engines

The cast iron manifold completely encloses and seals the tappet valley between the cylinder heads. The manifold contains water passages, a crankcase vent passage, exhaust crossover and induction passages. A one-piece metal gasket seals the intake manifold to cylinder head joint and also serves as an oil baffle. The left-hand carburetor bores supply cylinders No. 1, 7, 4 and 6; the right-hand bores cylinders No. 3, 5, 2 and 8.

1. Drain the cooling system.
2. Remove the air cleaner assembly from the carburetor.
3. Mark and remove the spark plug wires.
4. Remove the spark plug wire guides from the cylinder head cover, ignition coil and by-pass valve brackets.
5. Disconnect the radiator upper hose and the by-pass hoses from their fittings on the intake manifold. Disconnect the temperature gauge sending unit electrical lead.
6. Remove the ignition coil and bracket. Set the coil/bracket assembly out of the way.
7. Remove the TCS solenoid, if so equipped, from the right-hand valve cover.
8. Disconnect any of the emission control wiring or hoses as necessary. Disconnect the heater hose from the rear of the intake manifold.
9. Disconnect the throttle linkage and fuel and vacuum lines from the carburetor.
10. On cars equipped with air injection, remove the by-pass (diverter) valve bracket. Set the valve assembly (with hoses) out of the way, forward of the engine.
11. If the car is equipped with "Cruise Command" (automatic speed control), remove the vacuum servo mounting bracket and set the servo assembly aside.
12. Remove the carburetor assembly from the manifold.
13. Remove the intake manifold assembly complete with gasket and end seals.

Always use a new gasket when installing the intake manifold. Use a good commercial sealer on both sides of the metal gasket and on the rubber end seals. Align the gasket at the rear first, then at the front.

The rest of the installation procedure is the reverse of removal. Torque the manifold bolts to 40-45 ft lbs, evenly.

Exhaust Manifold R & R

V8—Except Gremlin and Hornet w/Air Pump

NOTE: The mating surfaces of both

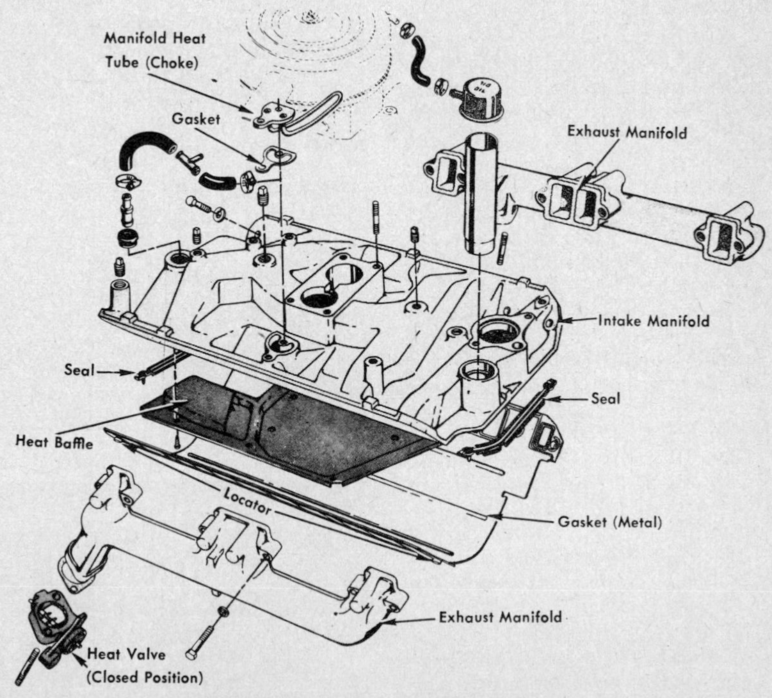

Two-barrel intake manifold—V8
(© American Motors Corp)

the exhaust manifold and the cylinder head are machined smooth, thus eliminating any need for a gasket between them.

1. Disconnect the wires from the spark plugs after marking them for firing order.
2. On models equipped with air injection, disconnect the air delivery hoses from the injection manifold. Remove the injection manifold and nozzles from the exhaust manifold.
3. Disconnect the exhaust from the exhaust manifold flange.
4. Remove the bolts and washers used to retain the manifold.
5. Remove the shields from the spark plugs.
6. Remove the exhaust manifold from the cylinder head.
7. Clean the machined surfaces of the manifold and head. Installation is the reverse of removal.

Gremlin and Hornet V8 with Air Pump

The exhaust manifold on the left-side may be removed in the same manner as detailed for other V8 engines, however, the right-side manifold on Gremlins and Hornets equipped with air pumps, must be removed in the following order:

1. Raise the car and securely support it with jackstands.
2. Disconnect the exhaust pipe from the manifold flange.
3. Support the engine at the vibration damper, by placing a jack with a block of wood on its lifting pad underneath it.
4. Remove the bolts which secure the engine mounting bracket on the right-side.
5. Remove the air cleaner assembly, including the tube which runs to the manifold heat stove.
6. Disconnect the battery cables. Remove the spark plug leads after marking them for installation.
7. Disconnect the air supply hose from the air injection manifold.
8. Remove the air injection tubes from the exhaust manifold.
9. On cars with automatic transmissions, remove the dipstick and the screw which secures the transmission dipstick tube.
10. Working from the rear, unscrew the exhaust manifold mounting bolts.
11. Raise the engine. Remove the exhaust manifold and the air injection manifold as an assembly.

Prior to installation, clean the joining surfaces of the manifold and cylinder head. Be careful not to nick or scratch either surface.

The rest of installation is the reverse of removal. Torque the manifold securing bolts to specification, starting from the rear and working forward.

6 Cylinder

Exhaust manifold is removed along with *intake* manifold; see previous instructions.

Valve System

American Motors cars use hydraulic tappets; thus, no mechanical valve adjustment is necessary. The valve guides are integral with the head on all engines.

The valve stem oil deflectors should be replaced whenever valve service is performed on the six-cylinder engines. The V8 engines use valve stem oil seals which must be replaced only if damaged, or worn.

Valve Guide Service

American Motors engines do not have replaceable valve guides.

Measure the stem to guide clearance in one of two ways. The valve stem can be measured with a micrometer and the guide measured using calibrated pilots, then the difference computed. The best way is to install the valve into the guide, without spring, and measure the lateral movement using a dial indicator. If stem to guide clearance is excessive, guides must be reamed to the proper oversize. Three oversize valves are available with stems 0.003, 0.015 and 0.030 in. larger than standard diameter.

NOTE: the exhaust valve stem is tapered 0.0005-0.001 in., smaller diameter toward valve head. Proper stem to guide clearance is 0.001-0.003 in. for both intake and exhaust valves.

No provision is made for adjustment of hydraulic tappet travel. Tappets having various thicknesses of push rod seats are available and can be installed to get a standard center travel position under normal operating conditions.

Rocker Assembly R & R

1969-72 All V8, and 1973 360, 401 V8

Individually mounted, pressed steel rocker arms operate the valves. These rockers are mounted on threaded studs and are held by a pivot ball and locknut. The hollow pushrods conduct oil from each hydraulic tappet to the rockers. There is a metering system in each tappet,

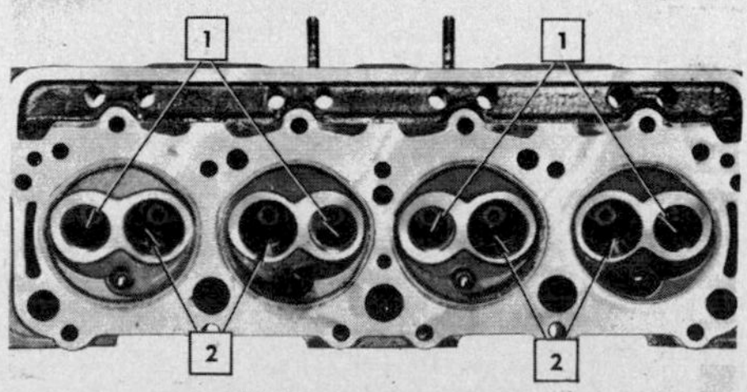

Valve sequence V8
(© American Motors Corp)
1 Exhaust valves
2 Intake valves

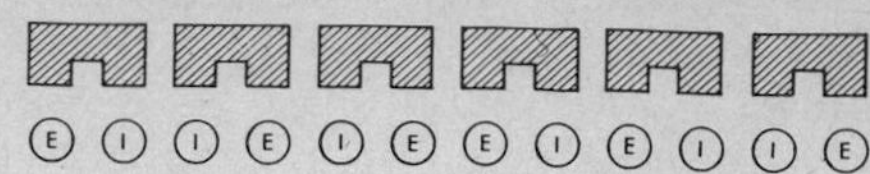

Valve sequence—OHV 6 199/232/258 —bottom view
(© American Motors Corp)

Correct Valve Facing

Incorrect Valve Facing

(© American Motors Corp)

Removing valve spring keepers
(© American Motors Corp)

consisting of a stepped lower pushrod cap surface and a flat plate. Any loss of lubrication to the rockers usually can be traced to failure of this part, or to a blocked pushrod oil passage. The pushrods rub against the cylinder head during operation and serve to maintain the correct rocker to valve stem angle.

1. Remove valve covers, after first removing any accessories and the air cleaner preheat tube.
2. Loosen and remove the retaining locknuts, ball pivots and rocker arms. It is a good idea to lay them out in order, along with their respective pushrods.
3. Installation is the reverse of removal.

NOTE: when installing new threaded studs, make sure hex nut is fully seated and tightened to 65-70 ft. lbs. Retaining locknuts are tightened to 20-25 ft. lbs.

1969-72 and 1974 6 Cylinder

The rocker shaft assembly is secured to the cylinder head with six cap bolts. Oil pressure for rocker lubrication is supplied via No. 3 camshaft bearing from the main oil gallery to No. 5 rocker support. Rocker shaft is 0.8575-0.8585 in. diameter; oil clearance is 0.003-0.005 in.

1. Remove valve cover.
2. Unbolt cap bolts and remove rockers and shaft.
3. Installation is the reverse of removal.

NOTE: hold rockers in place using large rubber bands.

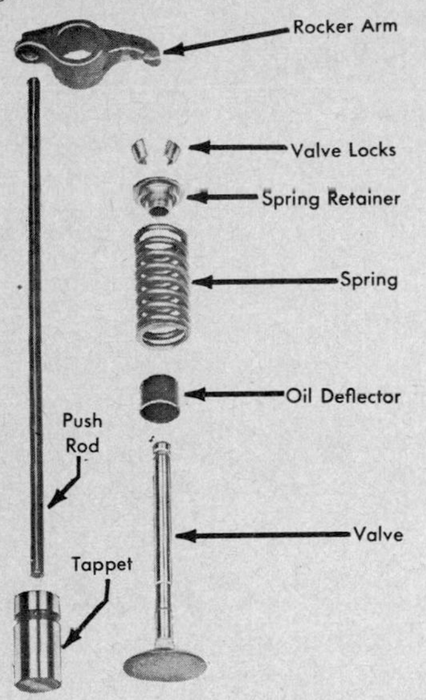

Valve assembly sequence—6 cylinder, 1969-72 and 1974 (© American Motors Corp)

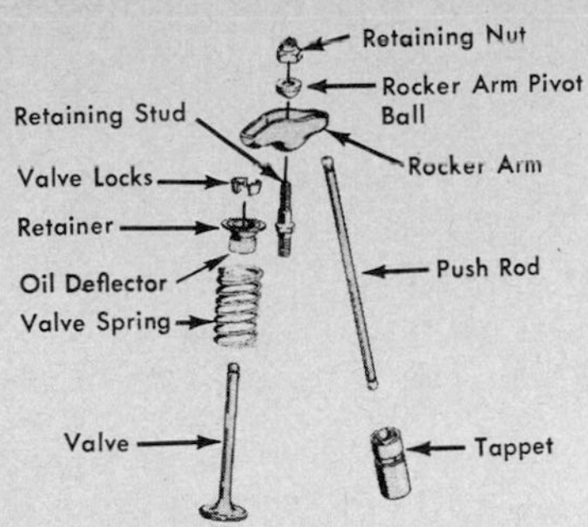

V8 rocker arm assembly (© American Motors Corp)

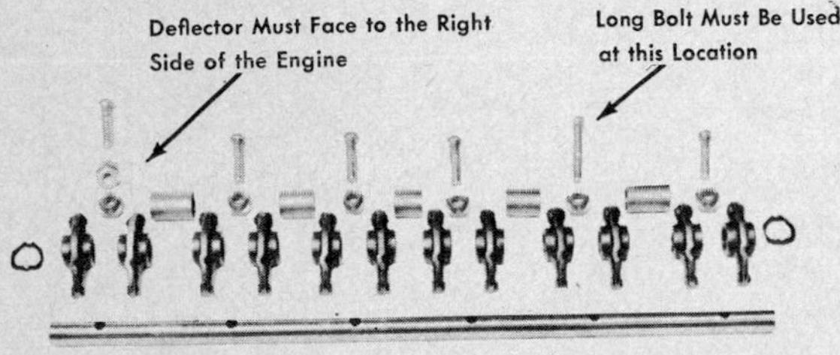

199/232/258 6 cylinder rocker arm assembly (1969-72 and 1974) (© American Motors Corp)

1973 and 1975-76 6 Cylinder, 304 V8 and All 1974-76 V8s

NOTE: *Be careful when ordering new valve train components, not to get parts for the wrong year. Some 1973 sixes may have come from the factory with the wrong tappets installed; check for this fault on any car which has noisy valves.*

1. Remove any accessories which are in the way and remove the valve cover, complete with gasket.
2. Unscrew the rocker arm capscrews.
3. Remove the pivot assemblies, rocker arms, and pushrods.

NOTE: *Be sure to keep all parts in the same order in which they were removed.*

4. Clean all parts in solvent. Blow all oil passages in the rocker arms and pushrods dry with compressed air.

Replace any deeply pitted rocker arms and scuffed or worn pushrods. If the pushrod is worn from lack of oil, replace it, its valve lifter and rocker arm, as well.

Installation is performed in the following order:

1. Insert the pushrods in their bores, be sure to center the bottom of each rod in the plunger cap of the hydraulic valve lifter.
2. Install the rocker arms, pivot assemblies and capscrews. Tighten the capscrews to the following specifications: 1973 and 1975-76 6 cylinder and 304 V8—21 ft lbs. 1974 All V8—19 ft lbs.

NOTE: *Be sure that the pushrods, pivot assemblies, and capscrews are returned to exactly the same places from which they were removed.*

3. Install the valve cover and gasket; secure them with retaining screws and washers.
4. Install anything which was removed to gain access to the valve covers.

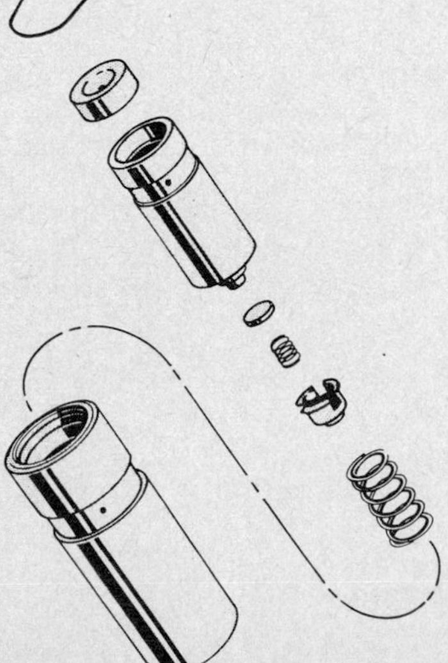

Exploded view of hydraulic tappet (metering disc not shown) (© American Motors Corp)

Cylinder Head R & R

All 6 Cylinder

1. Drain the cooling system. Disconnect throttle linkage, fuel lines, water hoses, spark plug wires and vacuum line. Remove the air cleaner, PCV hose, and the temperature sender.
2. Remove the valve cover and its gasket. Remove the rocker arm/shaft assembly and the pushrods. Keep the pushrods in order.
3. Remove the intake and exhaust manifold assembly from the head.
4. Disconnect the spark plug wires and remove the plugs.
5. Disconnect the battery ground cable, the coil, and the coil bracket from the head. Disconnect the temperature sending unit wire.
6. If the vehicle is equipped with air conditioning, remove the drive belt idler pulley bracket from the cylinder head. Loosen the alternator drive belt and remove the bolts from the compressor mounting bracket and set the compressor aside.
7. Remove the bolts and remove the cylinder head from the block.
8. Clean the gasket surfaces of both the head and the block. Remove the carbon deposits from the top of each piston and from the combustion chambers.
9. Check the head for straightness If the head (or the block) is 0.008 in. out of true over its entire length, 0.001 in. in 1 in., or 0.003 in. in 6 in., the head requires resurfacing.

Installation of the cylinder head is performed in the following order:

1. Use a new head gasket and coat both of its sides with sealer. The word "top," on the gasket, faces upward.
2. Tighten the head bolts in three stages and proper sequence, see the illustration, to the proper torque specification.

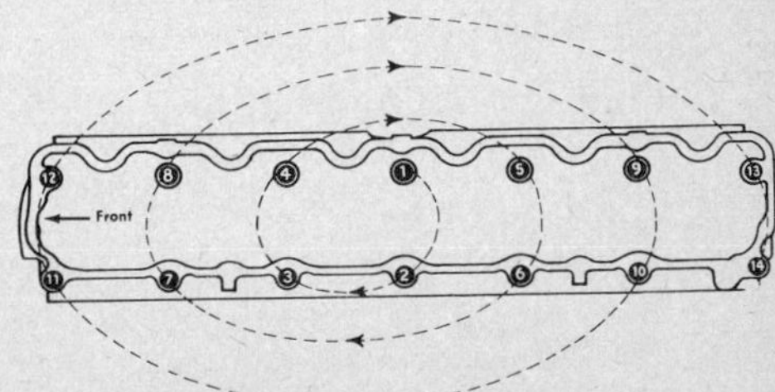

Cylinder head torque sequence for all 6 cylinder engines

3. The rest of installation is the reverse of the removal. Remember to refill the cooling system when completed.

V8

The cylinder heads have two holes to assist head location. Maximum out of true is 0.006 in. for the entire length of head; 0.001 in every 1 in. Make sure the rear rocker arm bolts are properly installed, otherwise no oil will get to the rockers.

1. Remove oil filler tube, rocker covers, power steering pump, alternator, exhaust manifolds and air conditioner. Move air conditioner compressor out of the way without disconnecting its hoses.
2. Drain the cooling system. Remove rockers and pushrods.
3. Disconnect water hoses, fuel lines, wiring, vacuum lines; remove distributor and intake manifold.
4. Remove cylinder head bolts and lift off heads carefully.

There are two locating dowels on the cylinder block to assist in gasket alignment during installation. Apply a commercial sealing compound to both sides of the head gasket. The word "top" and "A.M." should always face upward when installing the gasket. Tighten the head bolts to specifications in three steps in the sequence illustrated. The rest of removal is the reverse of installation.

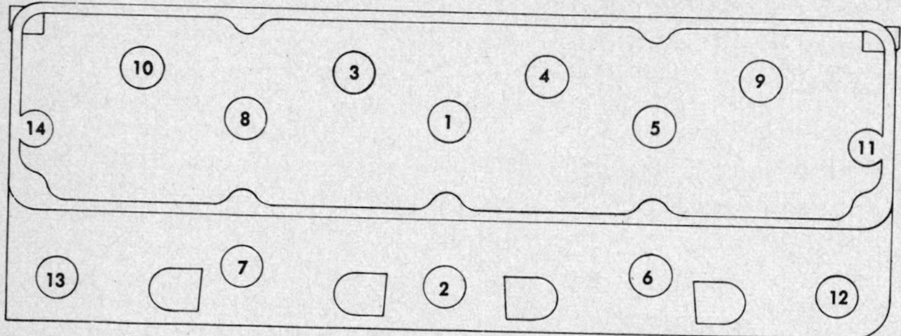

Cylinder head torque sequence for all V8 engines

Timing Cover, Chain, and Camshaft

Vibration Damper Removal

All Models

Remove the radiator core and the fan. Remove the nut from the center of the pulley and, using a puller, remove the pulley from the front of the crankshaft.

Timing Case Cover R&R

6 Cylinder

1. Remove all V-belts, fan blades and pulley.
2. Remove vibration damper.
3. Remove oil pan to cover bolts and cover to block bolts.
4. Raise cover and pull oil pan front seal up far enough to extract the tabs from the holes in cover.
5. Remove cover gasket from block; cut off seal tab flush with front face of block.
6. Clean all mating surfaces and remove oil seal.
7. Install new front oil seal, using proper size arbor.
8. Install new neoprene front oil pan seal, cutting off protruding tab to match original.
9. Position cover on block and install bolts. Tighten cover bolts to 4-6 ft. lbs.; four lower bolts to 10-12 ft. lbs.
10. Install vibration damper, tightening bolt to 50-60 ft. lbs.

NOTE: front oil seal can be installed with cover in place only if proper tool or duplicate is available.

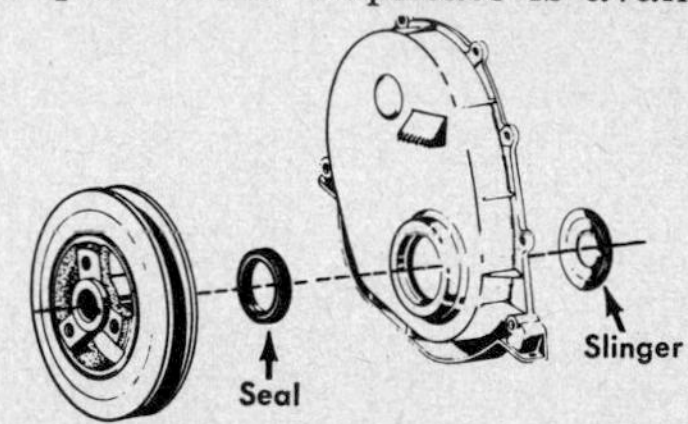

Timing chain cover assembly—199/232/258 6 cylinder
(© American Motors Corp)

V8

The die-cast timing cover incorporates an oil seal at the vibration damper hub. This seal must be installed from the rear; therefore the cover must be removed from engine in every case to replace front seal.

1. Drain coolant and remove hoses from water pump.
2. Remove distributor, fuel pump, alternator drive belt, accessory drive belts, fan and hub assembly.
3. Remove the vibration damper bolt, then pull off the damper.
4. Remove air conditioner compressor and power steering pump, if so equipped, and swing them out of the way *without* disconnecting hoses.
5. Remove the two front oil pan bolts from beneath the car, then remove the eight 9/16 in. hex head cover bolts.

NOTE: The timing case cover attaching bolts are of different lengths and must be replaced in their original locations.

6. Remove cover from block, then clean all parts and mating surfaces and remove oil seal.
7. Coat new seal lips with Petroleum jelly and seal surface with sealer, then drive seal into cover bore until it seats against the outer cover face. Use a proper size arbor for this job.
8. Remove lower dowel pin from cylinder block; this must be replaced when cover is in position but before bolts are installed.
9. Cut the oil pan gasket flush with the block on both sides of the oil pan.
10. Cut corresponding pieces of gasket from another oil pan gasket and cement them to cover. Install neoprene oil pan front seal into cover and align cork gasket tabs with pan seal.
11. Apply Permatex No. 2 to gaskets, then position cover. Install oil pan bolts and tighten evenly until cover lines up with upper dowel pin.
12. Install lower dowel pin, then cover to block bolts; tighten to 20-30 ft. lbs.
13. Install all removed pieces and adjust ignition timing.

Timing Chain Check—all 6 Cylinder

To check valve timing, remove valve cover and spark plugs, then rotate crankshaft until No. 6 piston is at TDC on compression stroke. Compression stroke can be determined by holding a finger in the No. 6 spark plug hole while turning the engine by hand—finger will be forced out by compression pressure. Set the valves of No. 1 cylinder to 0.003 in. clearance and rock the crankshaft

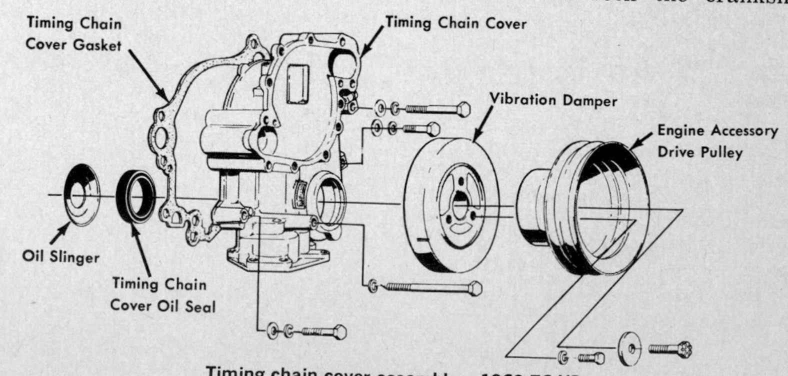

Timing chain cover assembly—1969-76 V8
(© American Motors Corp)

back and forth. The exhaust valve should open before the TDC mark on the pulley lines up with the pointer—measure the actual distance. The intake valve should open the same distance *past* the pointer—if it varies more than ½ in., remove the timing cover and inspect the chain.

Timing Chain Check—all V8

To check the valve timing, remove the rocker covers and spark plugs, then rotate the crankshaft until No. 6 piston is at TDC on compression stroke. This places No. 1 piston on TDC of the exhaust stroke in the valve overlap position. Rotate the crankshaft counterclockwise 90° (¼ turn) and install a dial indicator on No. 1 intake rocker pushrod end. Crank the engine in the normal direction of rotation (clockwise) until the pushrod moves 0.020 in. (304, 360 V8) or 0.025 in. (401 V8), as indicated on the dial. In this position, the timing pointer should align with TDC mark on the crankshaft vibration damper. If this varies more than ½ in. in either direction remove timing cover for chain inspection.

Timing Chain and Sprocket R&R

6 Cylinder - All

1. Remove the drive belt(s).
2. Remove the engine fan and hub assembly.
3. Remove the vibration damper pulley and remove the vibration damper.
4. Remove the timing case cover. Remove the seal from the timing case cover, because the seal should be replaced every time the cover is removed from the engine.
5. Remove the camshaft sprocket retaining bolt and washer.
6. Turn the crankshaft until the 0 timing mark on the crankshaft sprocket is closest to and in a centerline with the timing pointer of the camshaft sprocket.
7. Remove the crankshaft sprocket, camshaft sprocket and timing chain as an assembly. Disassemble the chain and sprockets.

To install the timing chain and sprockets:

8. Assemble the timing chain, crankshaft sprocket, and camshaft sprocket with the timing marks aligned as shown in the illustration.
9. Install the assembly to the crankshaft and camshaft.
10. Install the camshaft sprocket retaining bolt and washer and tighten the bolt to 50 ft lbs.
11. To ensure the correct installation of the timing chain, locate the timing mark of the camshaft sprocket at about the 1 o'clock position. This should place the

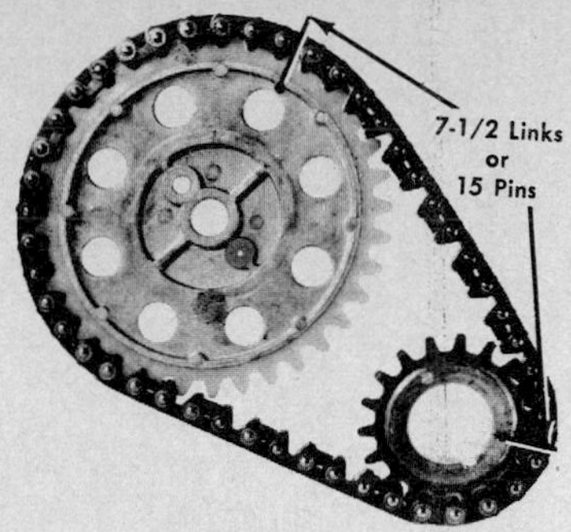

Correct timing chain installation—199/232/258 6 cylinder
(© American Motors Corp)

timing mark on the crankshaft sprocket where the sprocket teeth mesh with the chain. There should be 15 timing chain pins between the timing marks of both sprockets.

V8 - All

1. Remove the timing case cover and gasket.
2. Remove the crankshaft oil slinger.
3. Remove the camshaft sprocket retaining bolt and washer.
4. Remove the distributor drive gear and the fuel pump eccentric.
5. Turn the crankshaft until the 0 timing mark on the crankshaft sprocket is closest to and on a center line with the 0 timing mark on the camshaft sprocket.
6. Remove the crankshaft sprocket, camshaft sprocket and the timing chain as an assembly.

To install the timing chain and sprockets:

7. Assemble the timing chain, and the two sprockets with the timing marks aligned vertically, and install the assembly to the crankshaft and camshaft.
8. Install the fuel pump eccentric and the distributor drive gear. The fuel pump eccentric is installed with the word "REAR" toward the camshaft sprocket.
9. Install the camshaft sprocket, washer, and retaining bolt, tightening the bolt to 30 ft lbs.
9. To ensure the timing chain is installed correctly, turn the crankshaft until the timing mark on the camshaft sprocket is placed horizontally at the 3 o'clock position. Starting with the timing chain pin directly opposite the camshaft sprocket timing mark, count the number of pins down to the timing mark on the crankshaft sprocket. There should be 20 pins between the two timing marks. The crankshaft timing mark must be between the 20th and 21st pin.
10. Install the crankshaft oil slinger.
11. Install the timing case cover together with a new gasket.

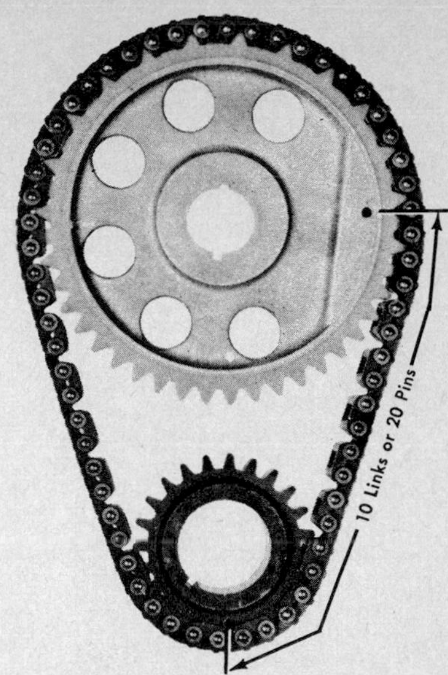

Correct timing chain installation—V8
(© American Motors Corp)

Camshaft R & R

6 Cylinder—All

1. Drain the cooling system and remove the radiator.
2. If the car is equipped with air conditioning, remove the condenser and the receiver unit as a *charged assembly*, only.

NOTE: Do not discharge the A/C system.

3. Remove the valve cover and gasket.
4. Remove the rocker arm/shaft assembly and withdraw the cylinder head complete with gaskets. Remove the tappets.

NOTE: Pushrods and tappets should be kept in the proper order. They must be returned to their original places during assembly.

5. Remove the drivebelt(s), fan assembly, accessory pulley(s), vibration damper, and the timing chain cover.
6. Remove the fuel pump. Take off the distributor assembly, including spark plug wires.
7. Turn the crankshaft until the "0" timing mark on the crankshaft sprocket is nearest to, on a centerline with, and aligns with the timing pointer on the camshaft sprocket.
8. Remove the sprockets and the timing chain as an assembly.
9. Remove the front bumper and/or grille as necessary. Withdraw the camshaft through the opening.
10. Inspect the bearing journals, distributor drive, cam lobes, and tappets for wear or damage. Replace parts, as required.

Camshaft installation is performed in the following order:

1. Use a generous amount of a suitable engine oil supplement on the camshaft. Install it in the block,

using care not to damage any surfaces.

2. Install the timing chain and sprocket assembly as outlined above.
3. Install the timing chain cover and a new oil seal, as outlined above.
4. Install the vibration damper and the accessory drive pulley (s).
5. Install the engine fan assembly and the drive belt(s). Tighten the belts to the proper tension.
6. Install the fuel pump.
7. With the number one piston at TDC of its compression stroke, fit the distributor so that the rotor is aligned with the no. one terminal on the cap (distributor fully seated on the block). Install the cap and the spark plug wires.
8. Install the tappets, cylinder head, its gasket, valve train (pushrods in the same order, as removed), valve cover and its gasket.

NOTE: All valve train components must be lubricated with engine oil supplement. The supplement must remain in the engine for at least the first 1000 miles. It does not require draining until the next regular oil change.

9. Install the air conditioner receiver and condenser, without discharging any coolant (if so equipped).
10. Install the radiator and top up the cooling system.
11. Install the front bumper and/or grille.

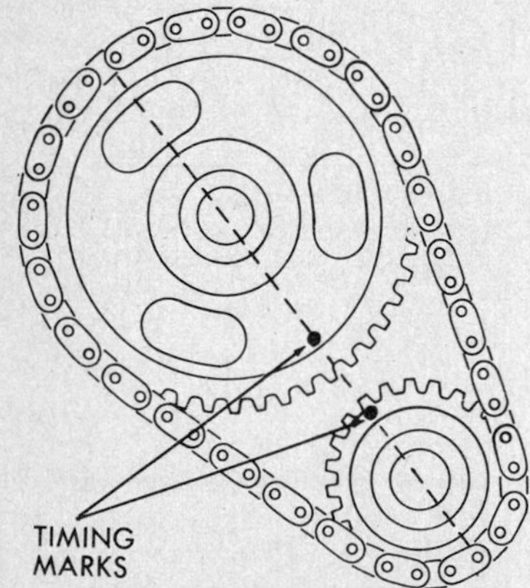

Six-cylinder timing chain and sprockets

V8 —All

1. Disconnect the battery cable.
2. Drain the radiator and both banks of the cylinder block. Remove the radiator, the hoses, and the thermostat housing. Remove the air conditioning condenser and receiver assembly as a charged unit, if so equipped.
3. Remove the distributor, complete with spark plug wires and the coil from the intake manifold.
4. Remove the intake manifold as a complete assembly.

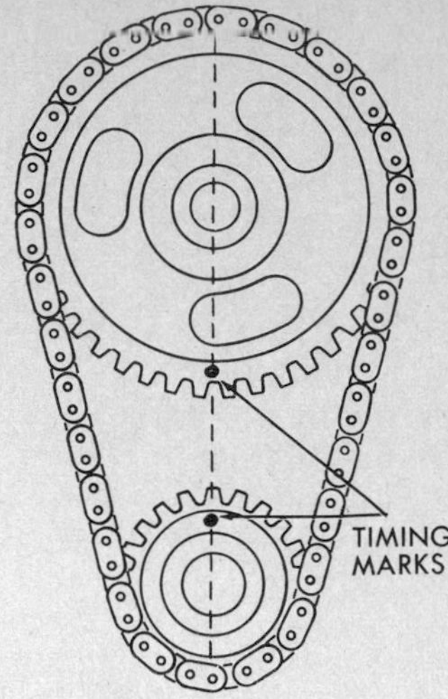

V8 timing chain and sprockets

5. Take off the valve cover and take out the valve train, including the hydraulic tappets.

NOTE: Keep the valve train components in proper order. They must be returned to their original place during assembly.

6. Remove the power steering pump from its bracket, without disconnecting the hoses. Set it out of the way.
7. Remove the fan assembly and then the fuel pump. Disconnect heater hose at the water pump.
8. Unbolt the alternator bracket and set it out of the way, complete with the alternator. Do not disconnect the alternator wiring.
9. Remove the crankshaft pulley and the vibration damper.
10. With the timing marks in vertical alignment, remove the front cover, distributor/oil pump drive gear, fuel pump eccentric, sprockets, and the timing chain.
11. Remove the hood latch upper support bracket attachment screws. Move the bracket, as necessary, to permit removal of the camshaft.
12. Use care during camshaft removal, so that the journal bearings are not damaged.
13. Inspect all parts for wear and damage. Replace them as required.

Installation of the cam is the reverse of removal. Install the timing chain and cover as outlined above. Adjust the belt tension and fill up the cooling system.

NOTE: Lubricate the camshaft, tappets, and the valve train with a suitable engine oil supplement. Add the remaining supplement to the crankcase, and leave it in the engine for at least the first 1000 miles. It does not require draining until the next regular oil change.

Piston Removal

All Engines

1. Drain the cooling system and remove the cylinder head assembly as outlined in the applicable section above.

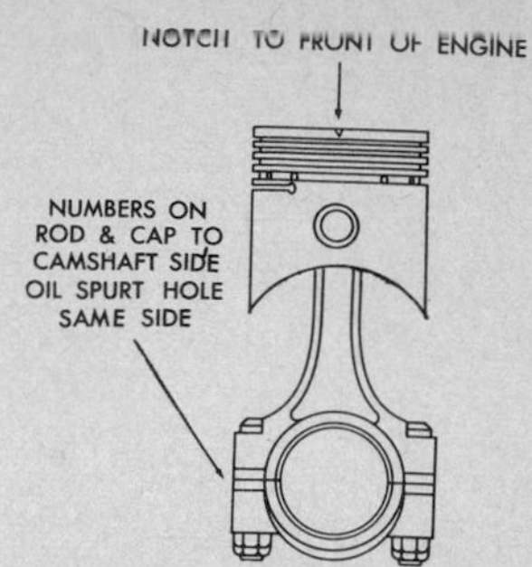

Piston and rod assembly 6 cylinder engine

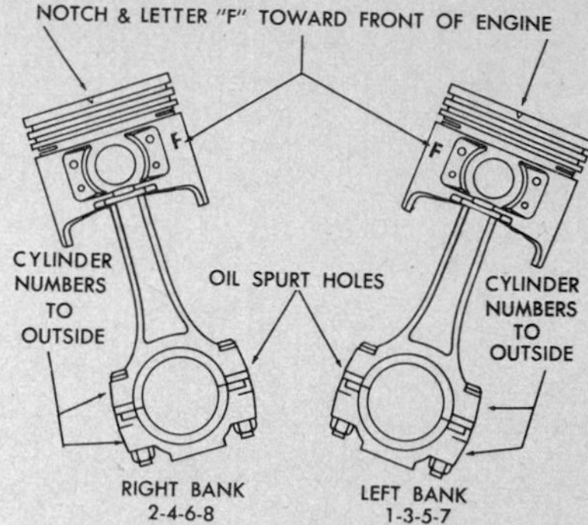

Piston and rod assembly—V8 engines

2. Use a ridge reamer to remove the ridge at the top of the cylinder wall. Each cylinder must be done separately with the piston at the bottom of its stroke.
3. Drain the oil and remove the oil pan.
4. Remove the connecting rod bearing caps and inserts from below.

NOTE: The rods and caps have the number of the cylinder, to which they were assembled, stamped on them. It is important that they be kept in the order in which they were removed.

5. Remove the piston and connecting rod assemblies through the *top* of the cylinder bore. Use care not to scratch the connecting rod journals or the cylinder walls with the rod bolts.

Ring Replacement

All Engines

1. Clean the carbon from the oil ring grooves, the oil drain openings and the pin boss. Use care not to remove any metal from the ring grooves or lands, as this will change clearance.
2. Measure the ring clearances and the cylinder bore taper as outlined in the "Engine Rebuilding" section.
3. Remove the glaze from the cylinder bore wall with an *expanding* hone. Ten strokes (down and return) are sufficient to clean the walls; more than ten will change clearances.

Caution Never use a rigid hone to remove cylinder glaze; it will destroy cylinder taper.

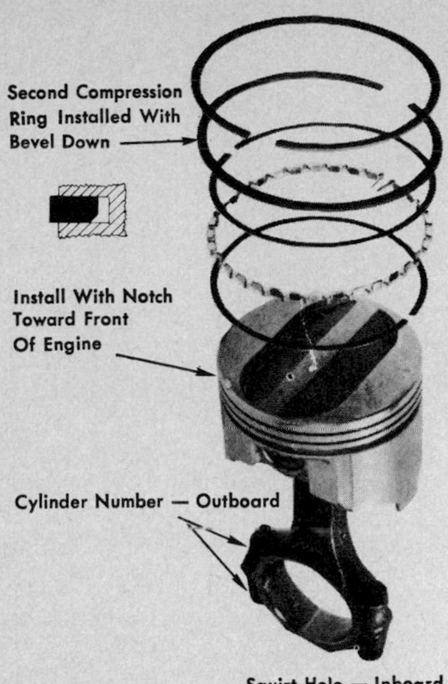

Piston ring assembly sequence
(© American Motors Corp)

4. Install the oil control rings on the pistons, first. Then install the compression rings with the top side (which is marked) up. Use a ring tool on the compression ring to prevent distortion and breakage.

Rod and Piston Installation

On engines using split-skirt pistons, the slit in the skirt must be installed opposite the oil squirt hole in the connecting rod. Solid skirt pistons are assembled so that the boss, or dimple, (and, in some instances, the letter F) at the top of the piston is on the same side of the connecting rod as the boss. This will be found on the connecting rod channel about halfway up the rod.

The piston and rod assemblies are united to the engine from the top and the dimple, or dot, on the top of the piston goes toward the front. On those engines having split-skirt pistons, the slit in the skirt of the piston goes to the left side of the engine.

Pistons of the 199 engine can be identified by their flat head and two notches; 232 and 258 pistons have a concave head with one notch.

Engine Lubrication

Full pressure lubrication is used throughout the engine, except for the piston pins. The piston pins receive lubrication by means of squirt holes in the connecting rods, as well as, oil splash.

A positive pressure, gear-type pump supplies oil pressure. The pump is mounted on a boss which is next to the number four main bearing behind the oil pan, on the six-cylinder engines.

The oil pump is incorporated in the timing case cover on the V8 engines. A cavity in the cover form the body of the pump while the drive and idler gear rotate in the cavity. The drive gear shaft is driven by the distributor.

Oil Pan R & R

NOTE: It is much easier to remove the engine in most cases.

6 Cylinder Engines (Except Pacer)

1. Disconnect front cushions from engine bracket and remove right bracket from engine.
2. Disconnect ground strap.
3. Remove valve cover and air cleaner.
4. If equipped, remove fan shroud.
5. Raise engine as far as possible.
6. Disconnect idler arm from side sill.
7. If equipped, disconnect stabilizer bar.
8. Loosen strut rod bolts at lower control arms.
9. Remove bolts retaining crossmember, and, with weight of car on wheels, pry down crossmember and insert wooden blocks to hold it down.
10. Drain oil and remove pan.
11. To install, reverse removal procedure.

Pacer

1. Drain the engine oil.
2. Install an engine lifting device and support the weight of the engine.
3. Disconnect the steering shaft flexible joint and hold it aside with a length of wire.
4. Raise and support the car.
5. Remove the front engine support through bolts.
6. Disconnect the front brake lines at the wheel cylinders.
7. Disconnect the upper ball joints from the spindles. Make sure the shock absorbers are attached securely.
8. Remove the upper control arm and move it aside.
9. Support the front crossmember with a jack.
10. Remove the nuts from the front crossmember rear mounts and swing the crossmember down and forward.
11. Remove the starter motor.
12. Remove the oil pan attaching screws and then the oil pan.
13. Remove the oil pan front and rear neoprene oil seals and thoroughly clean the gasket mating surfaces and inside of the oil pan.
14. Install a new oil pan front seal to the timing chain cover and apply a generous amount of silicone sealer to the end tabs.
15. Cement a new oil pan side gasket set into position on the engine block, applying a generous amount of silicone sealer to the gasket ends.
16. Coat the inside curved surface of the new oil pan rear seal with soap and apply silicone sealer to the side gasket contacting surface of the seal end tabs.
17. Install the seal in the recess of the rear main bearing cap, making sure it is fully seated.
18. Apply engine oil to the contacting surface of the front and rear oil pan seals and the oil pan.
19. Install and assemble the remaining components in the reverse order of removal, tightening the 1/4-20 oil pan screws to 7 ft lbs, 5/16-18 oil pan screws to 11 ft lbs, the crossmember attaching nuts to 50 ft lbs, the upper control arm cross shaft bolt and nut to 60 ft lbs, brake lines-to-wheel cylinders to 100 in. lbs, and the engine mount nuts to 25 ft lbs. Fill the crankcase with oil and bleed the brakes.

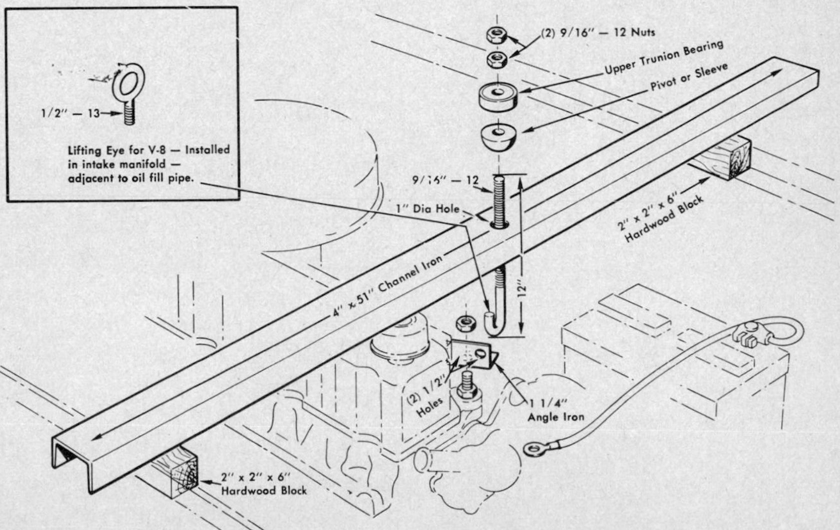

Lifting fixture can be fabricated as illustrated to facilitate oil pan and motor mount removal
(© American Motors Corp)

V8 Engines

1. Turn crankshaft until mark on damper is 180° from cover marks.
2. Disconnect engine cushion mounts from crossmember; remove fan shroud, if so equipped.
3. Disconnect battery ground strap; disconnect cushion mount brackets from block on American.
4. Remove starter motor.
5. Remove idler arm, except on 1969 Ambassador.
6. Ambassador sway bar: disconnect at side sills. American, Javelin, AMX, Rebel, Matador, Gremlin, Hornet sway bar: loosen links at lower control arms as far as possible.
7. Disconnect shock absorbers at lower control arms on all 1969 except Ambassador.
8. Attach chain hoist or lifting fixture and raise engine as far as possible.
9. Remove cushion mounts and brackets from American.
10. Loosen strut rod bolts at lower control arms; remove crossmember side sill bolts.
11. With car weight on front wheels, pry crossmember down far enough for clearance. Use wood blocks for support between crossmember and side sills.
12. Remove oil pan bolts and oil pan.

Reverse the removal procedure to install the oil pan. Use new oil pan-to-timing chain cover front seal. Coat the end tabs with sealer. Use new side and rear gaskets, coat them, as well.

Oil Pump Service

6 Cylinder

The oil pump is driven by the distributor drive shaft. Oil pump R&R does not, however, affect distributor timing because the drive gear remains in mesh with the camshaft gear.

1. Drain the oil and remove the oil pan.

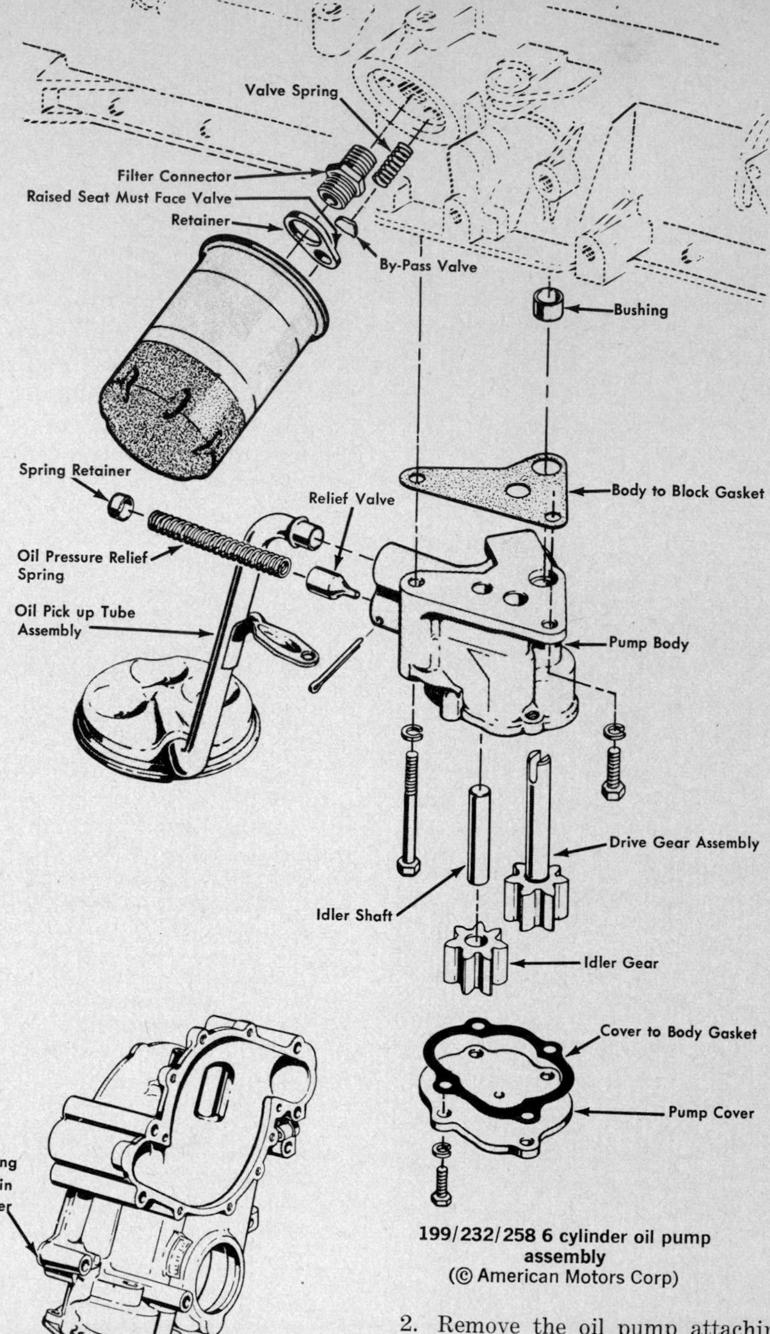

199/232/258 6 cylinder oil pump assembly
(© American Motors Corp)

2. Remove the oil pump attaching screws. Remove the pump and gasket from the engine block.
3. Remove the pump cover.

With a straightedge across the pump body and gears, clearance should be 0.001-0.003 in. (gears should project above body). Do not disturb location of tube in pump body if possible. Now, measure clearance between gears and wall of gear cavity opposite point of gear mesh; should be 0.0005-0.0025 in. for six. The oil pressure relief valve is set at the factory and is not adjustable.

Installation is the reverse of removal.

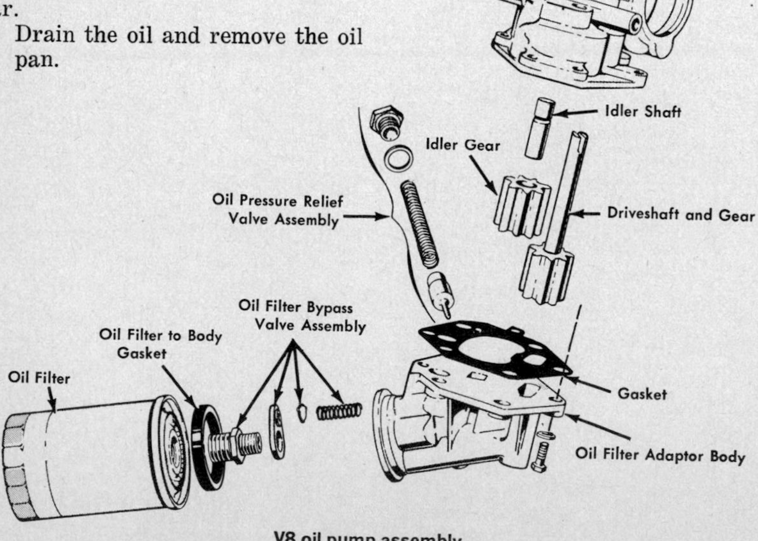

V8 oil pump assembly
(© American Motors Corp)

V8

The oil pump is located in, and as part of, the timing cover. The pump is driven by the distributor drive

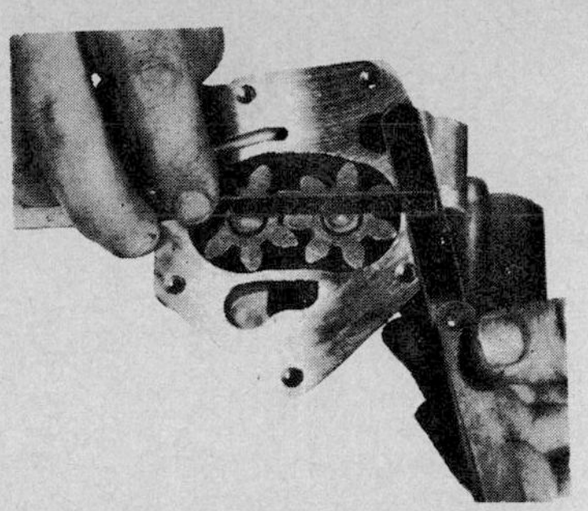

Checking oil pump gear end clearance
(© American Motors Corp)

Checking oil pump gear to body clearance
(© American Motors Corp)

shaft. Oil pump R&R does not, however, affect distributor timing.

Remove pump cover and place a straightedge across pump body and gears. Clearance should be 0.0025-0.0065 in. (gears projecting above body). Measure clearance between gears and wall of gear cavity opposite point of gear mesh; should be 0.002-0.004 in. The oil pressure relief valve is set to 75 psi up to 1969, 85 psi in 1970, and returned to 75 psi the following year. The valve is not adjustable.

Rear Main Bearing Oil Seal R & R

6 Cylinder Engines

1. Remove oil pan, as previously described.
2. Scrape clean all gasket surfaces, then remove rear main cap.
3. Discard lower portion of seal; drive out upper portion, using a brass drift, until it can be grasped with pliers.
4. Clean main cap, then *loosen* all remaining main cap bolts.
5. Lightly oil all surfaces, then coat the block-side surface of the new upper seal with soap and the seal lip with SAE 40 engine oil.
6. Install upper seal portion with the lip facing the front.
7. Coat the cap and block-side seal surface with Permatex No. 2.
8. Coat the back surface of new lower seal with soap, the lip with SAE 40 engine oil. Install lower seal firmly into main cap.
9. Coat both chamfered edges of rear main cap with Permatex No. 2, install bearing inserts (if removed) and tighten cap bolts to 75-80 ft. lbs, 100 ft. lbs for 1975.
10. Cement oil pan gasket to block; coat gasket tongues with Permatex No. 2 where they fit into rear main cap, as well as front neoprene seal.
11. Coat rear pan seal with soap and place into proper recess, then install oil pan bolts (¼ in.—5-8 ft. lbs.; 5/16 in.—10-12 ft. lbs).

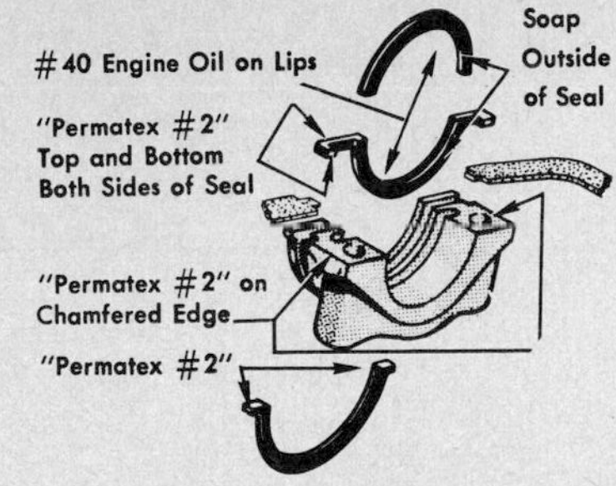

Rear main bearing oil seal 6 cylinder and V8
(© American Motors Corp)

V8 Engines

A neoprene seal, consisting of two pieces, is used. Procedure is identical to that used for the 6 cylinder, except that main cap bolts are tightened to 95-105 ft. lbs.

CLUTCH

The clutch is a single-plate, dry-disc, coil spring type. A semi-centrifugal clutch assembly is used with the 4-speed transmission V8, three rollers (six with 390) being equally spaced between the three clutch levers. These rollers are forced outward by centrifugal force and supply additional force to the pressure plate to prevent clutch slippage. The driven plate is spring-cushioned and has riveted linings. The throwout bearing is a ball bearing, pre-packed with grease at the factory.

No adjustment for wear is provided in the clutch itself, although an adjustment is built into the clutch cover to allow the release lever height to be varied. These adjusting nuts normally are not disturbed unless the clutch pressure plate is removed for overhaul.

Pedal travel decrease due to normal wear of the linings can be compensated for by adjusting the clutch pedal free-play.

Pedal Free Play Adjustment

Adjust the free-play of the clutch pedal to ⅞-1⅛ in. This is done by changing the length of the link between the throwout lever rod and the bellcrank assembly.

NOTE: On models equipped with guide pin holes for adjusting clutch pedal height, adjust clutch pedal height, by inserting a 5/16 in. x 4½ in. long pin into the alignment holes in the pedal bracket and pedal. Adjust pedal height so that pin slides freely.

Clutch Removal

Remove the transmission and starter motor, then disconnect the clutch linkage at the release lever and remove the capscrews that hold the bellhousing (clutch housing) to the engine. It may be necessary to move the rear of the engine up or down to gain wrench clearance.

Any shims between the housing and engine must be replaced in exactly the same place to prevent misalignment.

Matchmark the clutch cover, pressure plate and flywheel before removal to ensure proper balance. Loosen each clutch cover capscrew a few turns at a time until spring tension is released, then remove the cover, pressure plate, and disc.

Pilot Bushing

Check the pilot bushing in the end of the crankshaft for scoring or looseness. If it is necessary to replace the bushing, use either an expanding-end slidehammer or a suitable tap. Screwing the tap into the bore until it bottoms will force the bushing out.

Lubricate the bushing with wheel bearing grease or Molykote before installing the clutch.

Flywheel

Inspect the flywheel surface for heat cracks, scoring, or blue heat marks. Check the flywheel capscrews for proper torque (105 ft. lbs.). It will be necessary to lock-up the flywheel ring gear with a block or flywheel holding clamp tool before tightening these capscrews.

Throwout Bearing

The throwout (release) linkage consists of a forked, pivoted lever contacting the bearing at one end and the linkage pushrod on the other. A return spring keeps the lever in contact with the ball pivot.

The throwout bearing itself is pre-lubricated and cannot be repacked if dry. Failure is evidenced by uneven clutch pedal pressure and a grinding, rattling noise when the pedal is depressed. Replace any noisy throwout bearings as soon as is practicable to prevent disintegration and possible transmission or clutch damage.

Clutch Installation

Slide the new clutch disc onto the transmission input shaft to check for binding. Remove any burrs from either the splines or hub using emery paper, then clean with a safe solvent and lubricate the splines and hub with Molykote. Place the clutch disc against the flywheel and secure it by inserting a dummy pilot shaft (such shafts, made of wood, are available from automotive jobbers) or an old transmission input shaft.

Place the new pressure plate (it's always good policy to replace the pressure plate when installing a new disc) in position, after first making sure that the clutch disc is facing the proper direction (flywheel side is so marked), and that matchmarks are aligned if old pressure plate is used.

Install all the capscrews finger-tight. Tighten the screws a little at a time, working around the pressure plate to avoid distorting it, to 28 ft. lbs on 6 cylinder engines and 38 ft. lbs on V8s. Remove the pilot shaft.

Do not depress clutch pedal until transmission is installed or throwout bearing will fall out.

Install the clutch housing, throwout bearing and transmission. Hook up clutch linkage and check adjustment.

MANUAL TRANSMISSION

American Motors cars use Borg-Warner manual transmissions. For specific details of transmission overhaul, see the "Unit Repair Section."

An identification tag, containing Borg-Warner and American Motors part numbers, is located at the rear of the transmission. The model number is usually cast into the side of the case. Starting 1975 the identification code is stamped on the left front case flange. These numbers are important when ordering replacement parts, so always see that the tag is installed when the transmission is overhauled.

Starting 1970, cars built for Georgia and Tennessee have certain components identified by a nonrepeating number stamped on the left side of the transmission case.

Transmission R & R

All Models

NOTE: Open the hood to avoid damage to it, when the rear crossmember is removed.

1. Split the rear universal joint and slide the driveshaft off the back of the transmission. (See Universal Joints and Drive Lines.)
2. Remove shift mechanism linkage to the transmission, and disconnect the clutch linkage and speedometer cable; disconnect the back-up light switch wiring, and TCS switch wiring, also. Support the engine.
3. Disconnect the overdrive mechanism (if so equipped) and remove the rear mounts.
4. On Pacers with overdrive, remove the cotter pin from the parking brake equalizer and disconnect the front cable from the equalizer. Remove the cable adjuster and hooks from the floorpan bracket and lower equalizer and rear brake cables to provide clearance. Also, remove the ground strap from the floorpan.

NOTE: on V8 models with dual exhaust, exhaust pipes must be disconnected from manifolds and lowered so to gain working clearance. On Javelin and AMX models having Hurst shifter, entire shifter should be removed so that transmission can slide back far enough for removal.

5. Remove the transmission support crossmember, remove the two studs which hold the transmission to the bell housing and replace these two studs with two long pilot studs.
6. Remove the two bottom studs and slide the transmission assembly along the pilot studs and out of the car.

Installation of the manual transmission is performed in the following order:

1. Fit the throwout bearing and the sleeve assembly in the clutch fork. Center the bearing over the clutch lever.
2. Install two pilot studs in the clutch housing, instead of the lower clutch housing cap screws.
3. Carefully slide the transmission into place. Be careful not to damage the clutch driven plate splines.
4. Install the upper screws, which attach the case to the housing. Remove the pilot studs and install the lower cap screws.
5. If the car is equipped with a floor shift, install the shift mechanism.
6. Attach the speedometer cable, connect the back-up light switch wires and the transmission controlled spark (TCS) wire, if so equipped.
7. Raise the transmission. Attach the rear crossmember and support to the transmission. Fasten the crossmember to the side sills. Install the parking brake cables and ground strap on a Pacer with overdrive.
8. Attach the exhaust pipes to the exhaust manifolds, on V8 engines, if they were removed.
9. Install the front U-joint yoke on the transmission, as detailed elsewhere. Do the same for the rear U-joint at the differential.
10. Connect the shift rods on the column shift transmissions and the reverse lock-up rod (if so equipped) on the floor shift transmission. Check the transmission oil level and add lubricant, as needed.
11. Remove the supports and lower the car.
12. Install the shift lever, the boot, the bezel, and the retainer, if the car is equipped with a floor-shift transmission.
13. Adjust the shift linkage, as detailed below.

Shift Lever Adjustment

Column Shift—1969

Loosen the trunnion locknuts on the shift rods, then position the two operating levers in the center of the jacket tube cut-out. Insert a 3/16 in. drill through any existing aligning holes in the shift levers, shift gate and bracket. With the levers in neutral, adjust the trunnions for a free fit, without binding, in the levers. Lock the trunnions in this position, then check the shift lever positions for binding.

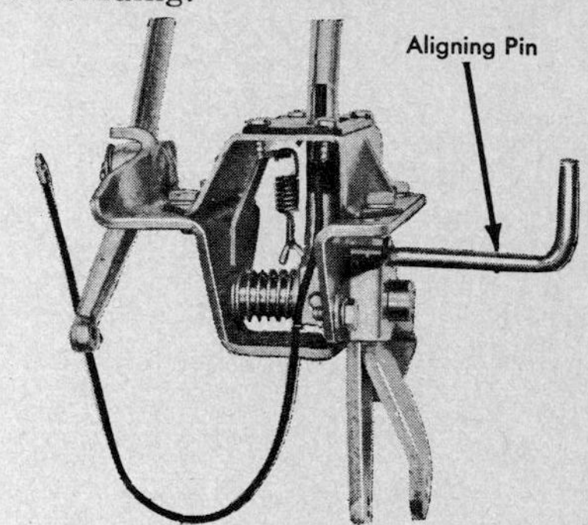

Aligning shift levers
(© American Motors Corp)

Column Shift—1970-76

1. Disconnect the shift rods from the shift levers. Insert a 3/16 in. drill through the column shift lever holes.
2. Shift into Reverse and lock the column with the ignition key. Position the First/Reverse shift lever in Reverse.
3. Adjust the shift rod trunnion to a free pin fit in the outer shift lever. Tighten the trunnion locknuts.
4. Unlock the column and move the gearshift to Neutral. Both of the transmission outer shift levers should be in the Neutral detent.
5. Repeat step three for the Second/Third shift rod trunnion.
6. Remove the drill from the column levers. Shift through all gears and check for a free crossover into Neutral.

Aligning shift levers column shift models with gauge hole
(© American Motors Corp)

7. Shift into Reverse and lock the column. The column should lock without any binding.

Three-Speed Floorshift—1969

Place the transmission shift levers in neutral. Loosen the 2-3 transmission lever attaching nut and adjustment bolt. With the 1-R shift rod in neutral position, align the 2-3 rod so the shift notch is exactly aligned with the 1-R shift rod notch. Tighten the adjustment bolt and attaching nut. Operate the shift lever to make sure there is no binding in the 1-2 shift.

To adjust the back-up light switch, loosen the two jam nuts and slide the switch forward or backward.

Three-Speed Floorshift—1970-71

Loosen the reverse lock rod trunnion locknuts about ½ in. Shift into reverse and lock the steering column. It may be necessary to move the lower column lever upward until it is in the locked position.

Tighten the lower trunnion locknut until it contacts the trunnion. Tighten the upper locknut while holding the trunnion centered in the column lever. Unlock the steering column, shift in neutral, and check that the transmission shift levers are in their neutral positions.

Loosen the 2-3 transmission lever attaching nut and adjustment bolt. With the 1-R shift rod in the neutral position, align the 1-R and 2-3 shift rod notches. Tighten the adjustment bolt and attaching nut.

Shift through the gears, checking for binding in the 1-2 shift in particular. Shift into reverse and lock the column—this operation should be smooth with no binding.

Three-Speed Floorshift—1972-76

For the correct standard steering column adjustment procedure, refer to "Three-Speed Floorshift—1969."

If the car is equipped with an adjustable steering column, refer to the 1970–71 floor-mounted shift linkage adjustment procedures.

Four-Speed AMC Floorshift—1969

Loosen the transmission shift lever nuts (two per lever) and loosen the locknuts on the reverse shift rod at the trunnion.

Install a ¼ in. drill through the selector lever retainer, through the levers, spacer plate and aligning hole in the mounting bracket (this is the neutral position).

Place all three transmission levers in neutral, then adjust the trunnion on the reverse shift rod so that it enters freely into the reverse lever without binding. Lock the nuts on the reverse rod and install washer and cotter pin.

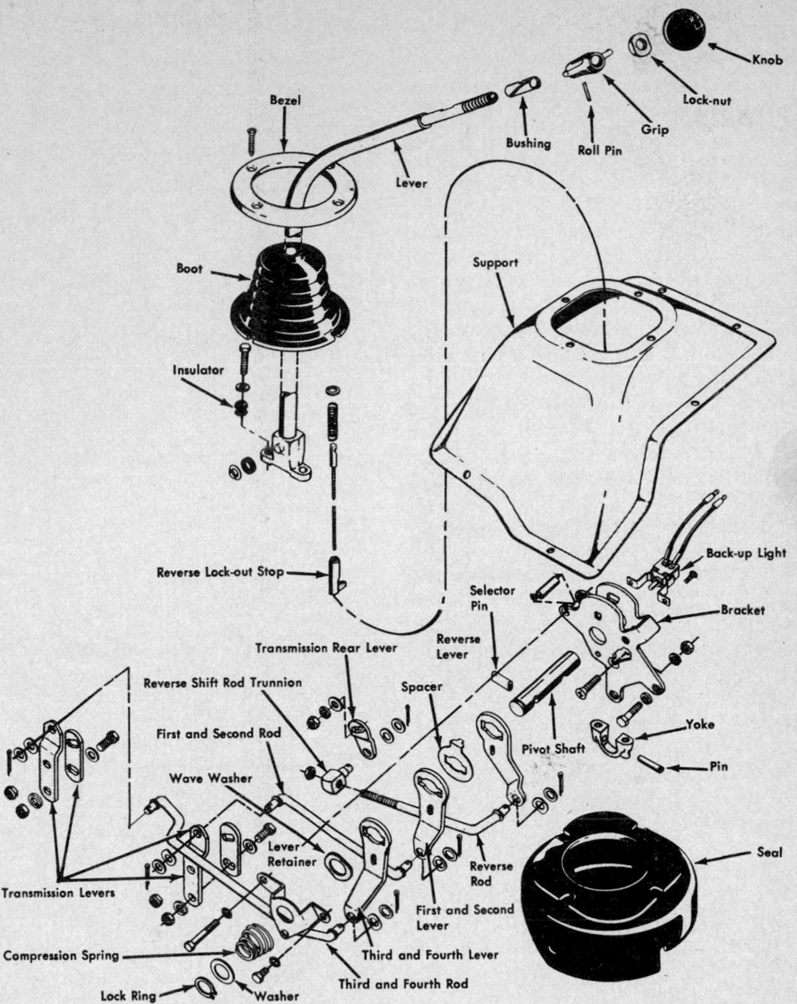

Four speed American Motors floorshift linkage (© American Motors Corp)

Tighten the lower nuts on the shift levers, making sure the outer levers stay in position, then tighten the upper nut to approximately 10 ft. lbs.

Caution Do not overtighten these nuts, otherwise the shift shafts might break.

Remove the ¼ in. drill rod, then lubricate the shift rod ends with chassis grease and check operation of shifter in all gears.

Four-Speed Hurst Floorshift—1969-74

NOTE: It may be necessary to lower the rear of the transmission to install the shift lever aligning pin. Before lowering the transmission, open the hood and remove the air cleaner. Then disconnect the exhaust system and the rear crossmember.

Remove the boot assembly or plug and loosen the lower nuts and bolts on the two transmission forward speed shift levers. Loosen the two self-locking nuts at the center of the shift levers. Loosen the two locknuts on the reverse shift rod trunnion.

With the shifter in neutral position, insert a ¼ in. diameter aligning pin into the shifter housing and through the center of the three shifter levers. Make sure that the pin enters the notch in the far side of the housing. Check that the transmission levers are in their neutral positions. Remove and reinsert the aligning pin. The pin should slide in freely. If it does not, the shifter is not correctly aligned in the neutral position.

Tighten the lower bolts and nuts at the transmission forward speed shift levers. Tighten the self-locking nuts to 10 ft. lbs. Make sure the transmis-

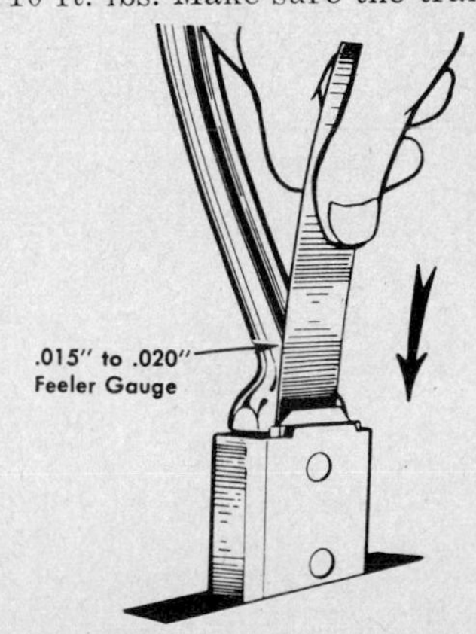

Removing lever from Hurst shifter (© American Motors Corp)

sion reverse lever is in the neutral position. Tighten the trunnion nuts, being careful not to bind the trunnion in the reverse lever, then remove the aligning pin.

NOTE: On 1970-74 models, loosen the steering column reverse lock-up rod trunnion locknuts about ½ in. each. Shift into reverse and lock the column. It may be necessary to move the lower column lever upward until it is in the locked position. Tighten the lower trunnion locknut until it contacts the trunnion. Tighten the upper locknut while holding the trunnion centered in the column lever. Unlock the column and check for proper shifting. The column should lock without binding.

AUTOMATIC TRANSMISSION

The Borg-Warner automatic transmission is used through model year 1971 and is called Shift Command. Shift-Command transmissions use a modified valve body to enable the driver to manually select a gear and hold the transmission in that gear.

In 1972, American Motors elected to use Chrysler Corporation Torqueflite automatic transmissions in all their cars. These transmissions are the same as the equivalent Chrysler units, the only differences being in case design required by the difference in American Motors' bell-housing configuration and driveshafts.

Identification

Shift Command

All Shift Command automatic transmissions are similar in appearance, construction, design, and operation. The only difference is in calibration for different engine application.

There is a transmission identification tag located on the left side of the transmission that will show the model number, serial number and the American Motors part number.

Cars built for sale in Georgia and Tennessee after 1970 have certain components identified by a non-repeating number. This special identification number is stamped on a machined pad on the left side of the transmission case.

Shift-Command automatic transmission identification tags
(© American Motors Corp)

SHIFT COMMAND TRANSMISSION IDENTIFICATION

Year	Transmission (Model)	Engine (cu. in.)
1969	36	199
	37	232
	11	290 2 bbl
	40	290 2 bbl
	11	290 4 bbl 343
	12	390
1970	42	199
	43	232
	43	232
	44	304
	11B	360
	12	390
1971	43	232
	44	258 304
	11B	360
	12	401

Torque Command

There are three models of Torque Command automatic transmissions; 904, 998, and 727. The 727 model is physically larger than the other two models, being designed for use with V8 engines and heavy duty applications. Physical identification of the 727 model transmission is assisted by the fact that the slope of the converter housing is much more gradual than the other two.

The 904 and 998 models are similar in size and are designed for lighter duty applications. The 998 model has reinforcing ribs on the top of the rear servo boss on the case which distinguish it from the 904 model.

A seven-digit part number is stamped on the case on the left side above the oil pan mating surface. Following the part number is a coded, four-digit number which indicates the date of manufacture. The last group of numbers stamped on the case is the serial number.

Cars built for sale in Georgia and Tennessee have certain components that differ and are identified by a non-repeating number. This special identification number is stamped on the right side of the converter housing on the starter housing boss.

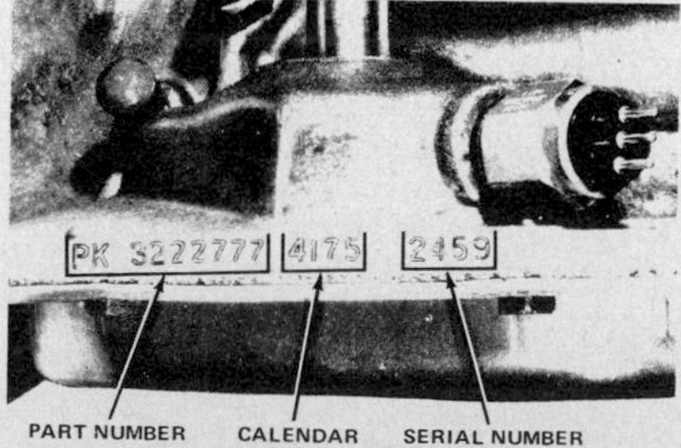

Torque-Command automatic transmission identi fication numbers
(© American Motors Corp)

TORQUE COMMAND TRANSMISSION IDENTIFICATION

Year	Transmission (Model)	Engine (cu. in.)
1972	904	232 258
	998	304
	727	360 401
1973-76	904	232[1] 258
	998	304[1]
	727	360[1]
		401

① Model 727 optional on 258 six and all V8s except Pacer

Neutral Safety Switch Replacement and Adjustment

Column Shift—1969-71

The neutral safety switch is combined with the back-up light switch, thus, adjustment of the neutral safety switch will automatically adjust the back-up light switch. The switch is mounted in the steering column jacket, below the instrument panel.

NOTE: Engage the parking brake fully before beginning adjustment procedures.

1. Loosen the two screws that attach the switch to the steering column jacket.
2. Select Neutral with the gear lever.
3. Insert a 3/32 in. punch in the hole on the switch face. Turn the switch until the pin freely enters the hole in the toggle.
4. Tighten the two mounting screws. Remove the punch. Be sure that the switch tang entered the channel on the operating shaft, *before* tightening the screws. Check the switch for proper operation.

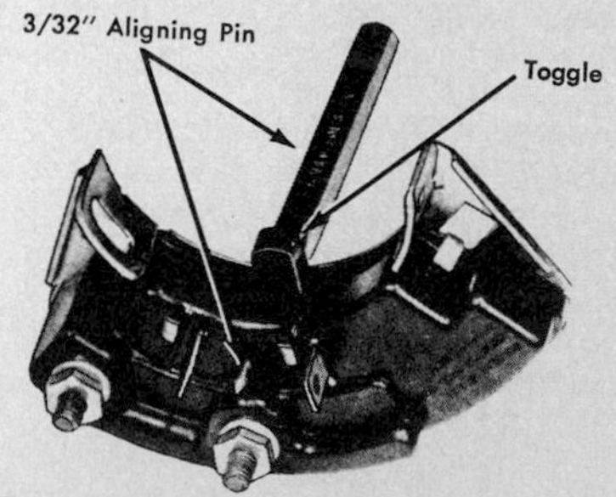

Steering column mounting neutral safety switch adjustment—1969-71
(© American Motors Corp)

5. Remove the mounting screws to remove the switch.

Console Shift—1969-71

The neutral safety switch is combined with the back-up light switch and is located in the center console. Before starting adjustment procedures be sure that the parking brake is firmly set.

1. Place the selector in Neutral.
2. Take the selector knob off the shift lever, except on 1971 Javelin models.
3. Remove the attachment screws from the console, raise it up and over the selector lever.
4. On the 1971 Javelin models, remove the console cover attaching screws and slide the cover up the selector lever.
5. Loosen the two switch attaching screws.

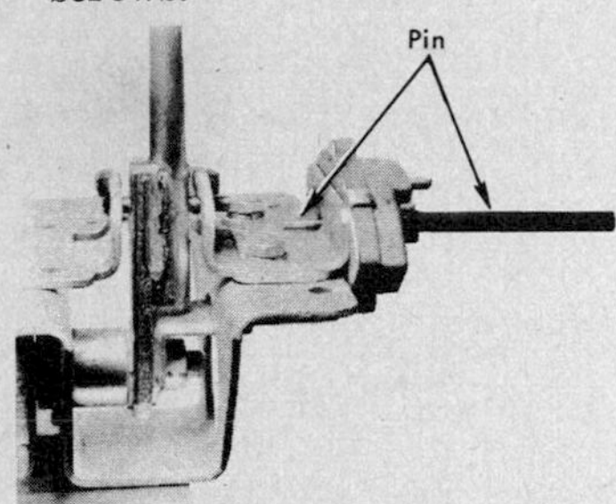

Console mounted neutral safety switch adjustment—1969-71
(© American Motors Corp)

6. Insert a 3/32 in. punch in the hole in the face of the switch. Move the switch as necessary to freely fit the punch through the hole in the toggle.
7. Tighten the two screws and remove the punch. Check for proper switch operation. The car should only start in Park or Neutral.
8. If the switch is to be completely removed, take out the screws and remove the switch.
9. When adjustments are completed, assemble the console and shift selector.

All Models—1972-76

On all 1972-76 American Motors cars, a combination back-up light/-neutral safety switch is mounted on the left side of the transmission case. This switch cannot be adjusted; failure requires replacement.

To test the switch, proceed in the following manner:

1. Disconnect the wiring connector from the switch.
2. Use a 12V test lamp to check for continuity between the center pin of the switch and the transmission case. The lamp should only light in Park or Neutral.
3. If the lamp lights up in other positions, check the transmission linkage adjustments before replacing the switch.
4. To test the back-up light function of the switch repeat step two, by bridging the outside pins to test continuity. The light should only light in Reverse. No continuity should be present from either of the pins to the case.

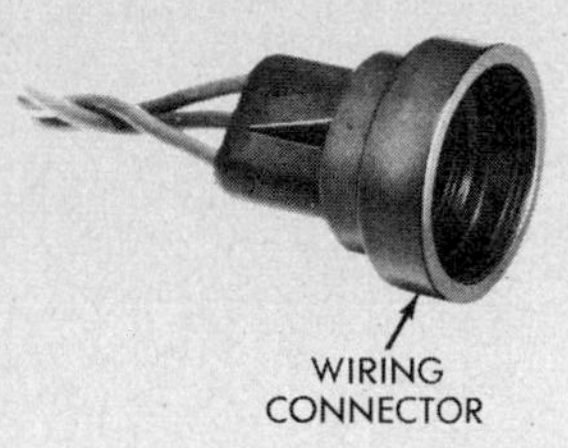
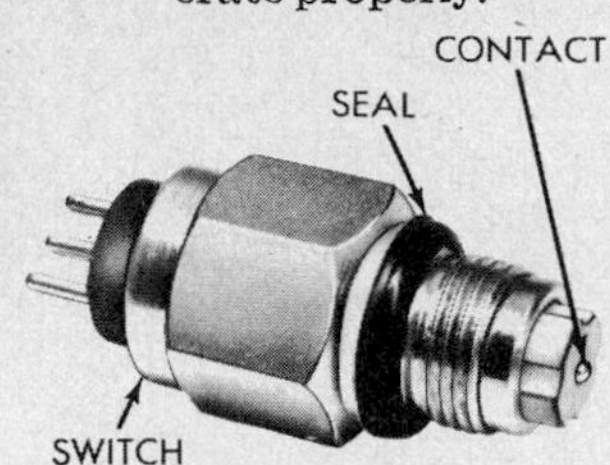
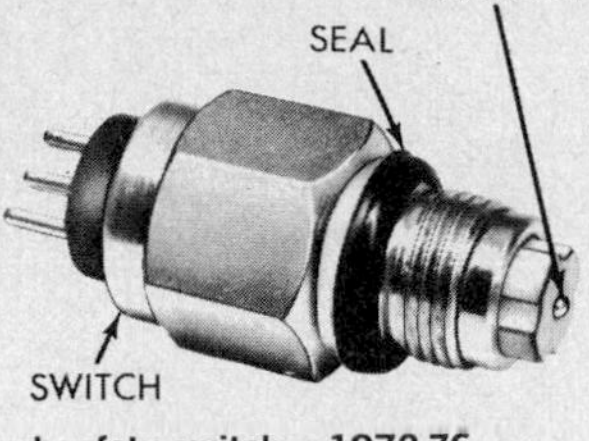

Torque-Command neutral safety switch—1972-76
(© Chrysler Corp)

To remove the switch, proceed as follows:

1. Place a container under the switch to catch transmission fluid. Unscrew the switch.
2. Select Park and then Neutral while checking to see that the operating fingers for the switch are centered in the case opening.
3. Screw a new switch and a *new* seal into the transmission. Tighten the switch to 24 ft. lbs.
4. Retest continuity. Replenish the transmission fluid, as required.

Manual Linkage Adjustment

1969-71

1. Place selector in Neutral.

NOTE: Low gear for American series.

2. Push shift rod against Neutral stop on shift gate.
3. Push selector lever forward to remove free play, then adjust clevis for free pin fit.
4. Connect linkage and check action, then test drive car.
5. On 1970 and 1971 models, place selector in Park and check column lock operation.

Console Shift—1970-71

1. Loosen park lockup rod trunnion locknuts.
2. Place console lever in Neutral.
3. Place transmission shift lever in neutral position.
4. Adjust shift rod for a free pin fit.
5. Place console lever in Park. Lock the steering column. It may be necessary to move the lower column lever upward until it is in the locked position.
6. Tighten the lower trunnion locknut until it contacts the trunnion. Tighten the upper locknut while holding the trunnion centered in the column lever.

Torque-Command—1972-76

1. With the engine off, place the selector in Park and the transmission shifting lever in the Park detent.
2. Adjust the shift rod, as necessary, for a free pin fit.
3. See that the steering column lock and the neutral safety switch operate properly.

Kick Down Band Adjustment

Torque-Command—1972-73

The adjustment screw for the kick-down band is located on the left side of the transmission, above the throttle and manual linkage levers.

1. Loosen the locknut. Back off the screw five turns.
2. Using a torque wrench tighten the screw to 72 in. lbs. (36 in. lbs on Pacer).
3. Back off two turns on the adjustment screw on the 904 and 998 series transmission.
4. Back off two and one-half turns with the 360 cu in. engines or two turns with the 401 cu in. engine when used with the 727 series transmission.
5. Hold the adjusting screw and tighten the locknut to 29 ft lbs.

Torque-Command—1974-76

The basic adjustment procedures are the same as for 1972-73 transmissions. However, the adjustment screw on all 998 and all 727 transmissions should be backed off two and one-half turns in Step 4. On all transmissions, hold the adjusting screw and tighten the lock-nut to 35 ft lbs, after completing the adjustment.

Downshift Solenoid R & R

Shift-Command—1969-71

1. Drain the fluid and remove pan, then disconnect solenoid wire from transmission case terminal.
2. Push in on the solenoid, while twisting, to disconnect it from the control valve. Take care not to lose the downshift valve spring.
3. To install, reverse the removal procedure, using a new O-ring.

Pan R & R

1969-71 All

1. Jack up the car and disconnect the filter tube at the transmission, then drain the transmission.

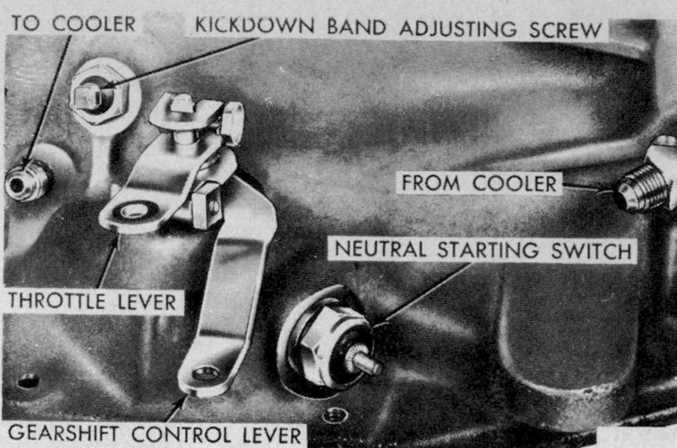

Torque-Command external adjustments
(© Chrysler Corp)

2. Remove pan screws and lock-washers, then remove pan and gasket.
3. Remove Alnico magnet from the head of the rear servo hold-down bolt, then remove inlet screen.

NOTE: Do not use air pressure, or any solvents other than ATF, to clean.

4. To install, reverse removal procedure, tightening pan screws to 15 ft. lbs.

Torque-Command—1972-76

1. Raise the car on a lift.
2. Place a container with a large mouth under the pan.
3. Remove the pan retaining bolts. Tap the pan at one corner in order to break it loose. Allow the fluid to drain from the transmission then remove the pan.
4. Clean the pan before installing it. Always use a *new* gasket. Tighten the pan bolts to 151 in. lbs.
5. Add DEXRON transmission fluid.

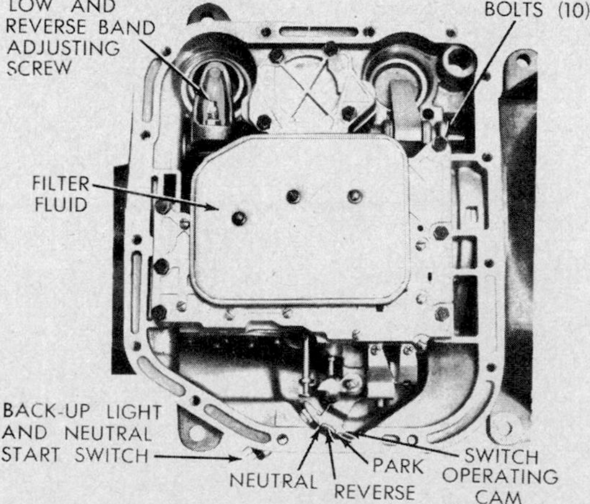

Torque-Command adjustments with the pan removed
(© Chrysler Corp)

Band Adjustments

Front Band—1969-71

1. Drain transmission fluid and remove pan.
2. Check for debris, "scorched" smelling fluid, and loose parts.
3. Check pick up screen for clogging, then check that all valve body cap screws and servo bolts are tight.
4. Check that delivery tubes are in place and snug.
5. To adjust, insert a ¼ in. gauge block between the front servo, adjusting screw and the piston rod, then tighten adjusting screw to 10 in. lbs.

NOTE: The adjusting screw on M11, M11B and M12 transmissions has a left-hand thread.

6. Inspect the adjuster wire for proper clearance—one screw thread must be exposed between the wire and the servo actuating lever.
7. Clean and install the pan, using a new gasket, then install proper quantity of approved fluid.

Rear Band—1969-71

1. Place a hydraulic jack under the transmission, then remove the four crossmember fasteners and the crossmember.

NOTE: Not necessary to remove crossmember on most Ambassador models. On AMX and Javelin equipped with power steering, lift the hood before lowering transmission to keep the power steering fluid reservoir wingnut from hitting the hood.

2. Lower the transmission, then loosen the rear band adjusting screw locknut and tighten the adjusting screw to 10 ft. lbs.
3. Back off adjusting screw ¾ turn for M36, M37, M40, M43, and M44 transmissions, 1¼ turns for M11, M11B, and M12 transmissions. Tighten locknut to 28 ft. lbs.
4. Raise transmission and replace crossmember.

Low and Reverse Band 904—1972-73; 998 and 727—1972-76

1. Remove the pan.
2. Loosen the locknut on the adjustment screw and back the screw off five turns.
3. Tighten the screw to 72 in. lbs.
4. Make the following adjustments:
   a. Series 904 transmission—back off three and one-quarter turns on the screw
   b. Series 998 transmission—back off four turns on the screw
   c. Series 727 transmission—back off two turns on the screw
5. Hold the adjusting screw while tightening the locknut to 35 ft. lbs.
6. Install the pan and a new gasket. Refill the transmission with DEXRON fluid.

Low and Reverse Band 904—1974-76

1. Drain the fluid and remove the pan as detailed above.
2. Check the fluid for particles or burning.
3. Remove the locknut from the adjusting screw.
4. With a torque wrench and a ¼ in. socket, tighten the adjusting screw to 41 in. lbs.
5. Back off 7 turns on the adjusting screw.
6. While holding the adjusting screw, install the locknut and tighten it to 35 ft lbs.
7. Install the pan and a new gasket. Refill with DEXRON transmission fluid.

Filter R & R

Torque-Command—1972-76

1. With the pan removed, remove the screws which secure the filter to the valve body and the filter.
2. Inspect the filter for metal particles and chips. If these are present, the transmission has worn or damaged parts.
3. Install a new filter. Tighten the filter securing screws to 28 in. lbs.
4. Clean the pan and install it. Always use a new gasket. Fill the transmission with DEXRON fluid.

REAR AXLE

Axle Shaft, Bearing and Seal

Removal and Installation

1. The hub and drum are separate units and are removed after the wheel is removed. The hub and axle shaft are serrated together on the taper. An axle shaft key assures propper alignment during assembly.
2. Attach a puller to the rear hub and remove the hub. The use of a "Knock-out" puller should be discouraged, since it may result in damage to the axle shaft or wheel bearings.
3. Disconnect the parking brake cable at the equalizer.
4. Disconnect the brake tube at the wheel cylinder and remove the brake support plate assembly, oil seal, and axle shims. Note that the axle shims are located on the left side only.
5. Using a screw type puller, remove the axle shaft and bearings from the axle housing.
6. Remove the axle shaft inner oil seal and install new seals at assembly.
7. The bearing is a press fit and should be removed with an arbor press.
8. The axle shaft bearings have no provision for lubrication after assembly. Before installing the bearings, they should be packed with a good quality wheel bearing lubricant.
9. Press the axle shaft bearings onto the axle shaft with the small diameter of the cone toward the outer (tapered) end of the shaft.
10. Soak the inner axle shaft seal in light lubricating oil. Coat the outer surface of the seal with sealant.
11. Install the inner oil seal with suitable installer.
12. Install the axle shafts, indexing the splined end with the differential side gears.
13. Install the outer bearing cup.
14. Install the brake support plate. Sealant should be applied to the axle housing flange and brake support mounting plate.
15. Install the original shims, oil seal and brake support plate. Torque the nuts to 30-35 ft lbs.
16. To adjust the axle shaft end-play, strike the axle shafts with a lead mallet to seat the bearings. Install a dial indicator on the brake support plate and check the play while pushing and pulling the axle shaft. End-play should be 0.004-0.008 in., with 0.006 in. desirable. Add shims to the left side only to decrease the play and remove shims to increase the play.
17. Slide the hub onto the axle shafts aligning the serrations and the keyway on the hub with the axle shaft key.
18. Tighten the axle shaft nut to 250 ft lbs. If the cotter pin hole is not aligned with a castellation on the nut, tighten the nut to the next castellation.

NOTE: a new hub must be installed whenever a new axle shaft is installed. Tighten the hub onto the shaft until the face of the hub is 3/16 in. from the edge of the outer taper of the shaft.

19. Install the rear drum and wheel.
20. Connect the parking brake cable at the equalizer.
21. Connect the brake tube at the wheel cylinder and bleed the brakes.

U-JOINTS

A one-piece, tubular driveshaft is used. Some rear yokes are held to the pinion shaft by a bolt, others by the pinion nut.

Removal and Installation

1. Disassemble rear U-joint by removing nuts.
2. Drop rear of driveshaft and slide front yoke out of transmission.
3. To install, reverse removal procedure, tightening U-joint nuts to 15 ft lbs.

Universal Joint Repairs

1. Remove the lock rings from the inner side of two opposite bearings and press on the outer side of one of the bearings, forcing the cross over. This will force the bearing on the opposite side out of its yoke.
2. Remove the bearing which was forced out of the yoke, then press the cross in the opposite direction to force the other bearing out.
3. Repeat this procedure on the third and fourth bearing.
4. When installing the new bearings in the universal joint yoke, it is possible to put them in with a driver of some type, but it is recommended that this work be done in an arbor press because a heavy jolt on the needle bearings can very easily misalign them, and greatly shorten their life.

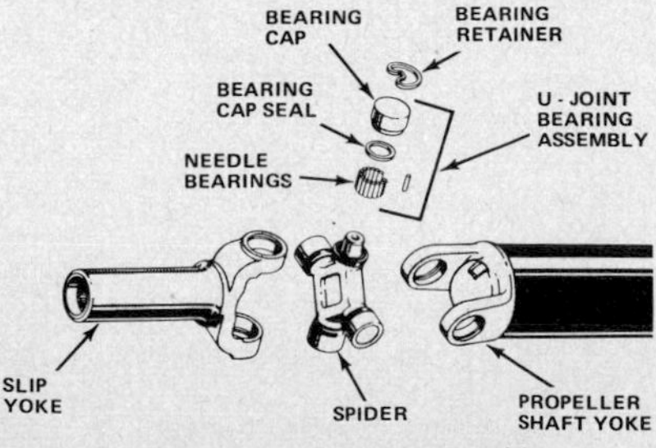

Front universal joint assembly
(© American Motors Corp)

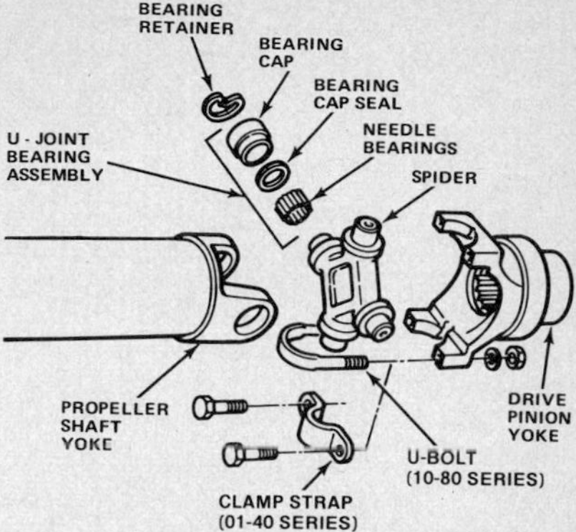

Rear universal joint assembly
(© American Motors Corp)

JACKING, HOISTING

1. Jack car, at front, under lower support arms and, at rear, under rear axle housing.
2. To lift, contact car at rear lift pads marked lift just forward of rear wheels (at the rear spring hangers on a Pacer). Front lift points are on underbody sill just to the rear of strut rod-to-sill mounting bracket. On a Pacer, the front lift points are located just to the rear of the dash panel on the front wheelwell sill.

FRONT SUSPENSION

The front suspension on all models is an independent linked type with the coil springs located between seats in the wheelwell panels and seats in the upper control arms. Rubber insulators between the springs and seats reduce noise transmission to the body.

Direct acting, telescopic shock absorbers are located inside the coil springs on 1970-76 models and the control arms are attached to the body via rubber bushings.

In 1969, the lower control arm contained a single ball joint which attached to the steering knuckle, while the upper portion of the knuckle was attached to a trunnion. In 1970, this system was replaced by a double ball joint design, both upper and lower control arms each having one joint.

On all models, strut rods serve to support the lower control arms. Stabilizer bars are used on some models.

The Pacer front suspension is different from all other AMC cars. The coil spring is mounted between the

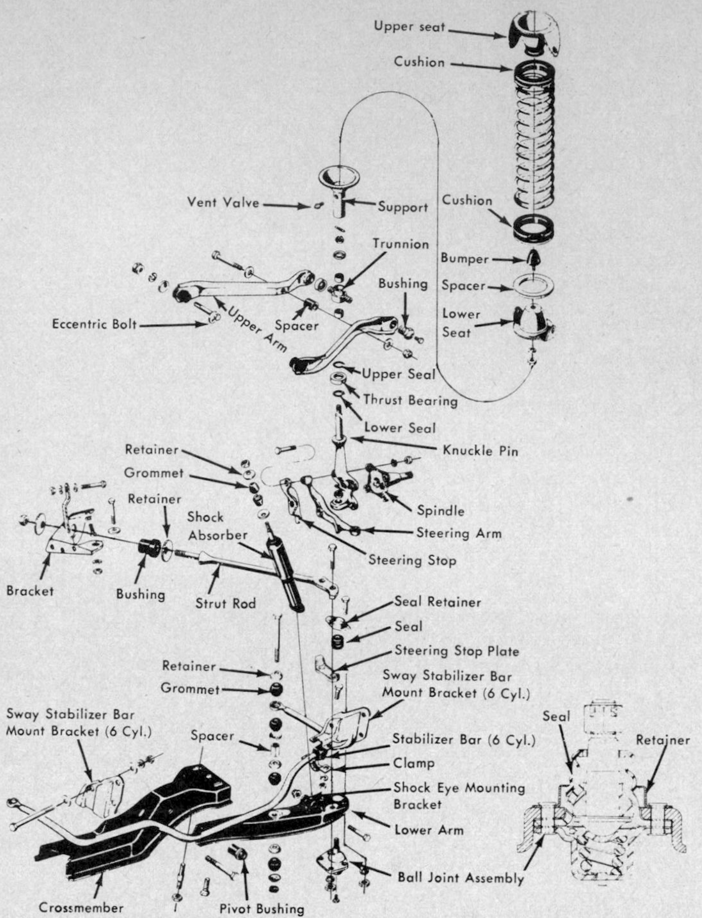

Typical front suspension—1969 Ambassador, and Rebel
(© American Motors Corp)

two control arms; seated at the bottom on the lower control arm and at the top in the suspension/engine mount crossmember. The crossmember is isolated from the rest of the body structure by rubber mounting points. The shock absorbers are mounted inside the coil spring. The steering knuckle is attached to the upper and lower control arms by upper and lower ball joints. A front stabilizer bar is optional.

Shock Absorber R & R

1969

The shock absorbers can be removed with the car resting on the ground or with it raised, but the weight of the car must be on the springs.

1. Remove the nut, washer, and grommet holding the bottom end to the lower control arm.
2. Remove the nut, washer, and grommet on the top stud of the shock.
3. Remove the shock absorber.

NOTE: *Steps 2 and 3 sound easy, but very often the retaining nuts are rusted in place. Penetrating oil helps, and very often you have to find a way to stop the shock absorber shaft from turning while you remove the top nut.*

4. On installation, make sure that you have all the washers and grommets in the right place. This is easy if you only remove one shock at a time. Fastener torques are 30 ft lbs at the top and 55 ft lbs at the bottom. You don't have to torque these.

1970-76
(Except Pacer)

1. Remove the two lower shock absorber attaching nuts. Remove the washers and the grommets.
2. Remove the upper mounting bracket nuts and bolts.
3. Remove the bracket, complete with shock.
4. Remove the upper attaching nut and separate the shock from the mounting bracket.

Install the shock as follows:

1. Fit the grommets, washers, upper mounting bracket and nut on the shock, in the reverse order of removal. Tighten the nut to 30 ft lbs (1970-72) or to 8 ft lbs (1973-76).
2. Fully extend the shock and install two grommets on the lower mounting studs.
3. Lower the shock through the hole in the wheel arch. Fit the lower attachment studs through the lower spring seat.
4. Install the grommets, washers, and nuts. Tighten the nuts to 8 ft

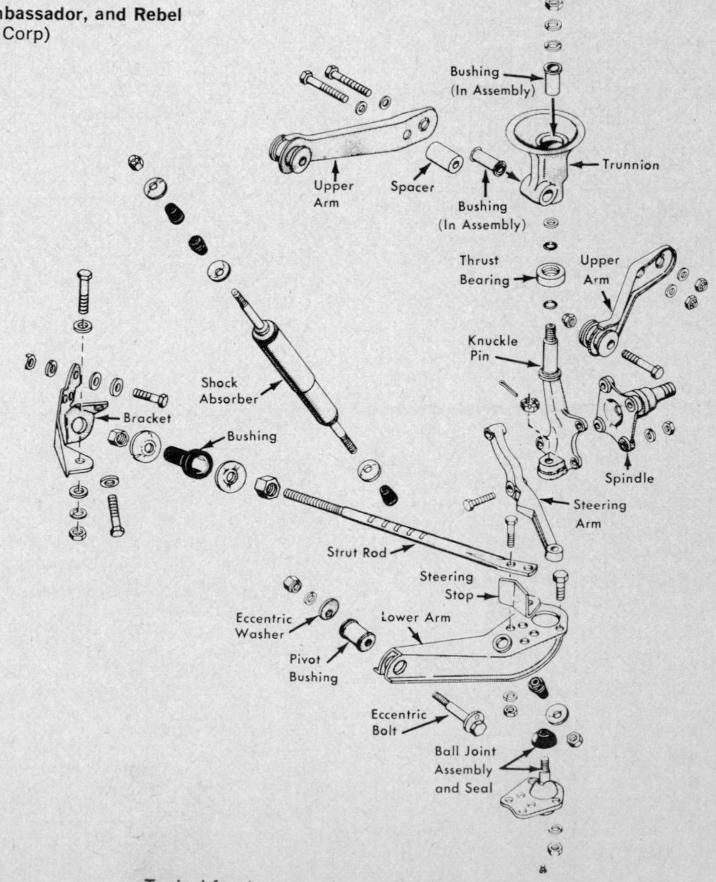

Typical front suspension—1969 American, Javelin and AMX
(© American Motors Corp)

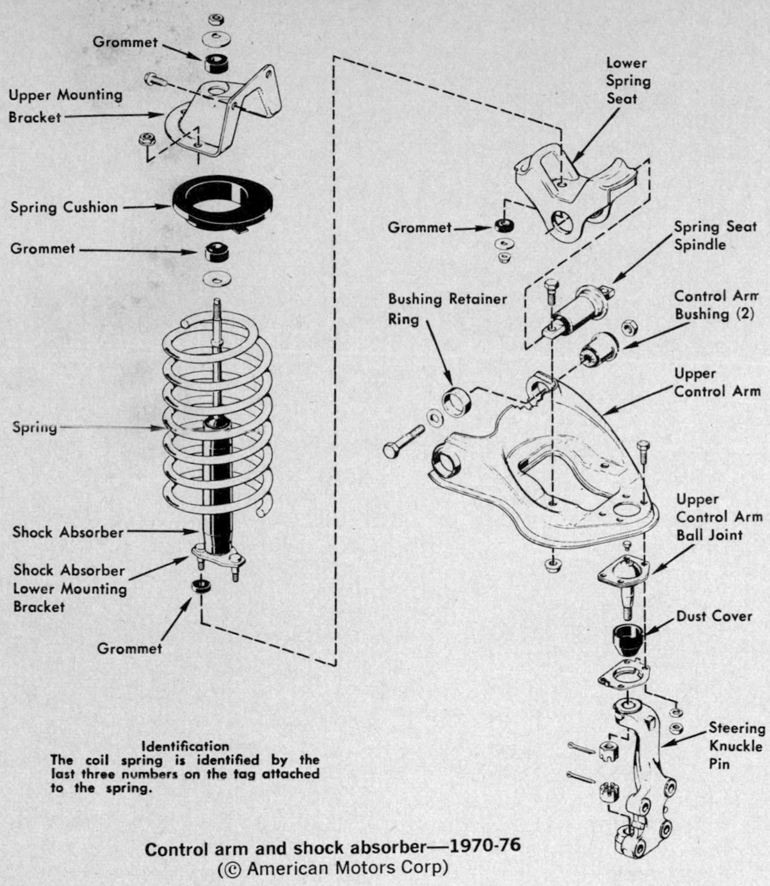

Control arm and shock absorber—1970-76
(© American Motors Corp)

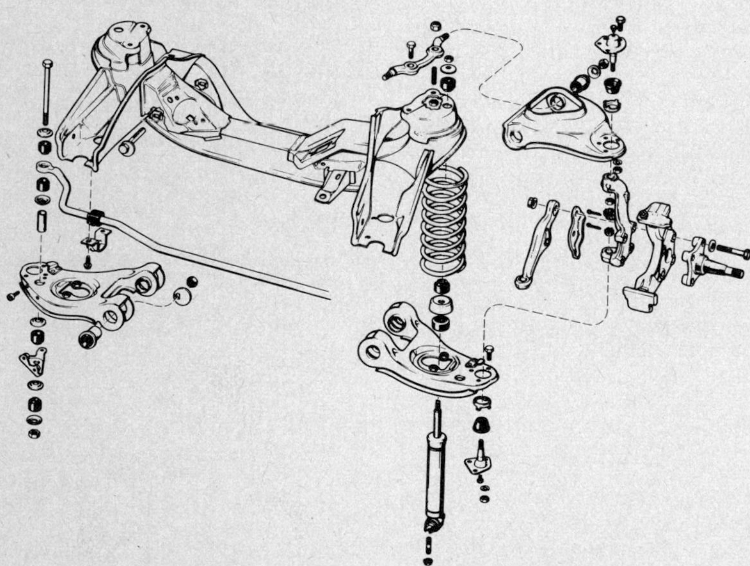

Exploded view of the Pacer front suspension, 1975-76
(© American Motors Corp)

lbs (1970-73) or 15 ft lbs (1974-76).

5. Secure the upper mounting bracket with its attachment nuts and bolts. Tighten them to 20 ft lbs.

1975-76 Pacer

1. Raise the front of the car and support it. Remove the wheels.
2. Remove the two lower shock absorber attaching bolts.
3. Remove the upper shock absorber attaching nut through the opening in the upper control arm.
4. Remove the shock absorber through the bottom of the lower control arm.

To install the front shock absorbers:

5. Install the rubber grommets and spacers to the shock absorber and install the shock up through the opening in the lower control arm. Place the rubber grommets and washers over the stud protruding through the mounting hole. Install the attaching nut and tighten the nut just enough to slightly compress the rubber grommets.
6. Position the lower shock mounting to the lower control arm and install the rubber grommets, washers and attaching nuts. Tighten the nuts until the grommets are slightly compressed.

Front Spring Removal and Installation

1969

Raise rear of car at diagonal corner from front spring to be removed. Install hooks in holes provided in spring seats while compressed. Release load and lower rear corner. This allows spring removal from car.

To install new spring, compress it by means of hydraulic press or jack with seats in place. Be sure holes in seats are aligned. Install hooks to hold spring in compression while placing in position. Reversing the above removal procedures will control position to release hooks when spring is in place.

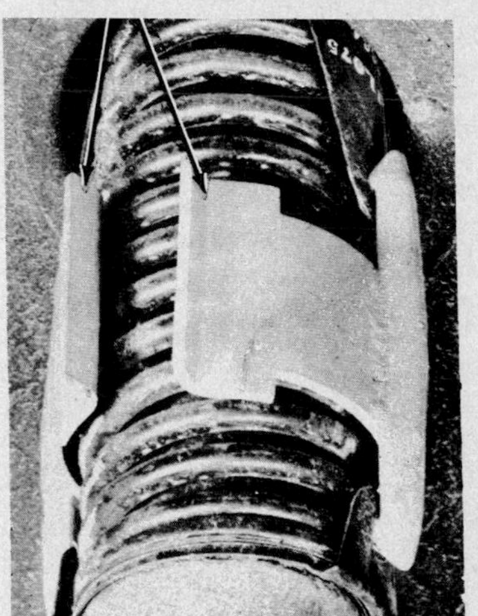

Front coil spring removal tools in place (arrows)
(© American Motors Corp)

1970-76 (Except Pacer)

Jack up the car far enough to reach the two lower shock absorber nuts. Remove the nuts, washers and grommets, then remove the upper mounting bracket screws and bolts from the wheelwell. Lift the bracket and shock absorber from the panel.

Lower the car to the floor, then install a spring compressor through the upper spring seat opening and bolt it to the lower spring seat using the lower shock absorber mounting holes. Remove the lower spring seat spindle retaining nuts, then tighten the compressor tool to compress the spring about 1 in.

Jack up the front of the car and support it on axle stands at the subframe (allowing the control arms to hang free). Remove the front wheel and pull the lower spring seat

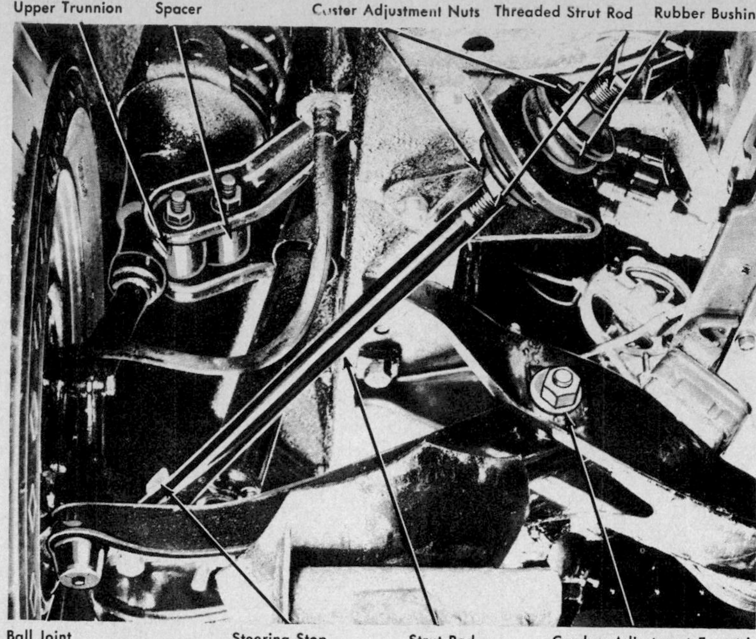

Rear view of front suspension—1969
(© American Motors Corp)

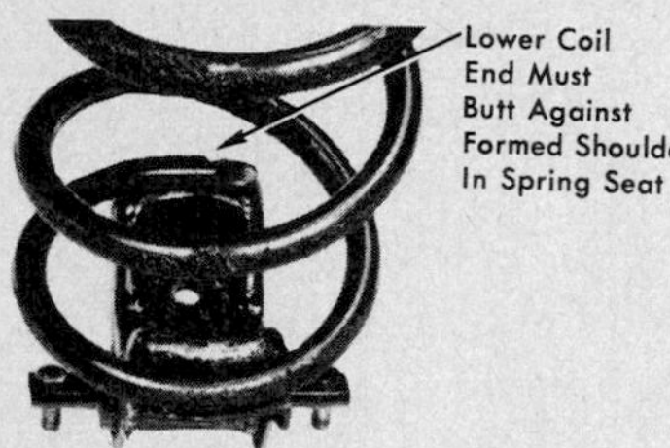

Lower spring seat installation—1970-76 front coil springs
(© American Motors Corp)

out away from the car, then slowly release the spring tension and remove the coil spring and lower spring seat.

To install, place the spring compressor through the coil spring and tape the rubber spring cushion to the small-diameter end of the spring (upper). Place the lower spring seat against the spring with the end of the coil against the formed shoulder in the seat. The shoulder and coil end face inwards, toward the engine, when the spring is installed.

Place the spring up against the upper seat, then align the lower spring seat pivot so that the retaining studs will enter the holes in the upper control arm. Compress the coil spring and install the spring, then install the wheel and tire and lower the car to the floor (to place weight on suspension). Install and tighten lower spring seat spindle retaining nuts and tighten them to 35 ft. lbs. Remove the spring compressor and install the shock absorber.

1975-76 Pacer

1. Disconnect the upper end of the shock absorber.
2. Raise the front end of the car and support it.
3. Disconnect the lower end of the shock absorber and remove it.
4. Disconnect the stabilizer bar at the lower control arm, if so equipped.
5. Remove the wheel, brake drum, or caliper and rotor. Do not allow the break hose to support the weight of the caliper; use a length of wire to suspend the caliper from the frame.
6. Remove the two bolts that attach the steering arm to the steering knuckle and move the steering arm aside.
7. Use a spring compressor to compress the coil spring.
8. Remove the cotter pin and nut from the lower ball joint stud and disengage the stud from the steering knuckle with a puller.
9. Move the steering knuckle, steering spindle, and support plate, or anchor plate assembly, aside to provide working clearance. Do not allow the brake hose to support the weight of these components. Use wire to hang the components from the upper control arm.
10. Move the lower control arm aside and remove the spring.

To install the front coil spring:

11. Position the upper end of the spring in the spring seat of the front crossmember. Align the cut-off end of the bottom coil with the formed shoulder in the spring seat. Use a floor jack or jack stand to support the spring until the spring compressor is installed. Install the spring compressor.
12. Assemble the remaining components of the front suspension in the reverse order of removal.

Tighten the ball joint stud nut to 75 ft lbs, the steering arm-to-knuckle attaching bolts to 80 ft lbs, the shock absorber mounting nuts to 20 ft lbs, and the stabilizer bar locknut to 8 ft lbs.

Control Arm R & R

Upper-Control Arm—1969

1. Remove front spring as described above.
2. Remove front or rear arm by disconnecting it at the trunnion, at wheelhouse panel mounting bolt, and the control arm spacer. Upon reassembly, torque spacer bolt nut to 80-90 ft. lbs.
3. Both front and rear arms may be removed as an assembly by disconnecting them from the mounting bracket. Remove lower spring seat support, lock pin and nut from the knuckle pin.

NOTE: to facilitate caster and camber adjustments upon reassembly, mark position of eccentric washers before disassembly.

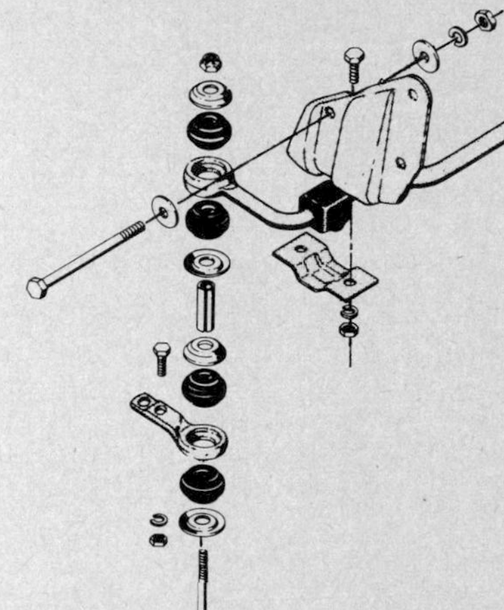

Front stabilizer bar assembly sequence—Rebel, and Ambassador, 1969
(© American Motors Corp)

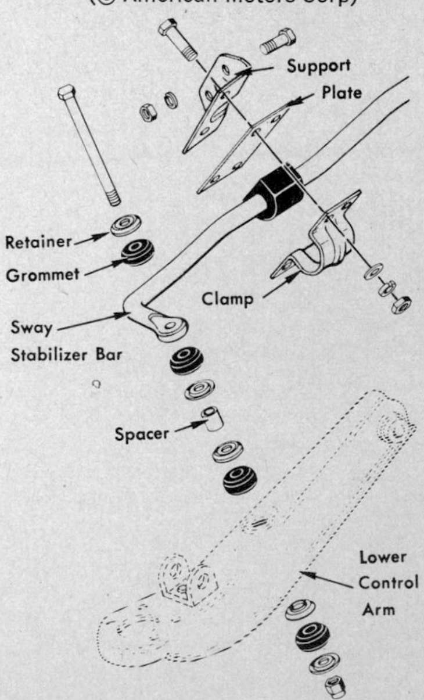

Front stabilizer bar assembly sequence—American, Javelin and AMX, 1969
(© American Motors Corp)

Upper Control Arm—1970-76 (Except Pacer)

Remove the shock absorber and compress the coil spring approximately 2 in., using the procedure outlined earlier under Front Spring Removal and Installation—1970-76.

Jack up the front of the car and support the body on jackstands placed under the subframes (allow the control arms to hang free). Remove the wheel and the upper ball joint cotter pin and retaining nut. Separate the ball joint stud from the steering knuckle using two hammers—one as a brace and the other to apply shock to the knuckle. Remove the inner pivot bolts from the panel, then remove the control arm.

To install, reverse the removal procedure. Do not tighten the pivot bolt nuts until the full weight of the car is on the wheels. The ball joint stud nut must be tightened to 45 ft. lbs., the lower spring seat pivot retaining nuts to 35 ft. lbs., and the control arm inner pivot bolts to 60 ft. lbs.

NOTE: it may be necessary to align the front end.

Upper Control Arm—1975-76 Pacer

1. Raise and support the front of the vehicle.
2. Remove the wheel and tire.
3. Remove the cotter pin and retaining nuts from the upper ball joint stud.
4. Install two service nuts onto the upper ball joint stud and strike the nuts with a hammer to loosen the stud from the steering knuckle.
5. Support the lower control arm with a floor jack.
6. Remove the two service nuts and disengage the stud from the steering knuckle.
7. Remove the retaining bolt and studlocknut that attach the cross-shaft to the front crossmember and remove the upper control arm assembly.
8. Install the upper control arm in the reverse order of removal, tightening the cross-shaft retaining nuts to 80 ft lbs, the upper ball joint stud nut to 75 ft lbs, and if new bushings were installed, tighten them last after the car is lowered to the floor with the wheel and tire installed to 60 ft lbs.

Lower Control Arm—1969-76 (Except Pacer)

The inner end of the lower control arm is attached to a removable crossmember. The outer end is attached to the steering knuckle pin and ball joint assembly.

NOTE: On 1969 models, it is recommended that the coil spring be removed.

To remove, jack up the car and support it on axle stands under the subframes. Remove the brake drum or caliper and rotor from the spindle, then disconnect the steering arm from the knuckle pin. Remove the lower ball joint stud cotter pin and nut. Separate the ball joint from the knuckle pin using two hammers—one as a brace and the other to apply shock to the knuckle.

Disconnect the sway bar from the control arm, then unbolt the strut rod. Remove the inner pivot bolt and the control arm.

To install, reverse the removal procedure; do not tighten inner pivot bolt until car weight is on wheels. Tighten ball joint retaining nut to 45 ft. lbs., strut rod bolts to 70 ft. lbs., sway bar bolts to 8 ft. lbs., steering arm bolts to 70 ft. lbs., and control arm inner pivot bolt to 95-100 ft. lbs.

Lower Control Arm—1975-76 Pacer

1. Disconnect the upper end of the shock absorber, raise the front end of the car and disconnect the lower end of the shock absorber and remove the shock absorber.
2. Disconnect the stabilizer bar at the lower control arm, if so equipped.
3. Remove the wheel, brake drum, or caliper and rotor. Do not allow the brake hose to support the weight of the caliper. Use wire to support it from the frame.
4. Remove the two bolts attaching the steering arm to the steering knuckle and move the steering arm aside.
5. Install a spring compressor and compress the spring.
6. Remove the cotter pin and nut from the lower ball joint stud. Thread two nuts onto the ball joint stud and strike the stud (nuts) with a hammer to loosen it from the steering knuckle. Remove the ball joint from the steering knuckle.
7. Move the steering knuckle assembly out of the way. Support the assembly with wire from the upper control arm.
8. Remove the two pivot bolts that attach the lower arm to the front crossmember and remove the lower control arm.
9. Install the lower control arm in the reverse order of removal, tightening the ball joint stud nut to 75 ft lbs, the steering arm attaching bolts to 80 ft lbs, the shock absorber attaching nuts to 20 ft lbs, the stabilizer bar locknut to 8 ft lbs, and lastly, after the car has been lowered to the ground with the wheel and tire installed, tighten the lower control arm pivot bolts to 95 ft lbs. Check the front end alignment.

Ball Joints

Inspection

NOTE: *Be sure that the front wheel bearings are adjusted to specification before checking the upper ball joint.*

1. Jack up the front of the car and place jackstands under the frame side sills.

NOTE: *The control arms must hang free if an accurate reading is to be obtained.*

2. Check the lower ball joints by grasping the lower portion of the wheel and pulling it in and out.
3. If there is noticeable vertical or lateral free play, the lower ball joint is worn and must be replaced.
4. To check the condition of the upper ball joint, place a dial indicator with its plunger against the tire scrub bead.
5. Move the upper portion of the wheel and tire toward the car's center, while watching the dial indicator.
6. Move the wheel and tire back out while watching the indicator.
7. The upper ball joint should be replaced if its *total* movement is greater than 0.160 in.

Removal and Installation

Lower Ball Joint

1. On all vehicles except Pacer, place a 2 x 4 x 5 in. block of wood on the side sill so that it supports the control arm.
2. Jack up the front end of the car and place jackstands underneath the frame side sills to support the body.

Place the wooden block, where illustrated, when removing either ball joint
(© American Motors Corp)

3. Remove the wheel and the brake drum. On cars equipped with disc brakes, remove the caliper and rotor.
4. Disconnect the lower control arm strut and take the steering stop off the control arm (except Pacer). Disconnect the stabilizer bar, if so equipped.
5. Separate the steering arm from the steering knuckle.
6. Remove the ball stud retaining nut, after removing its cotter pin.

7. Install a suitable ball joint puller; then loosen the ball stud in the knuckle pin. Leave the puller in place.
8. Place a jackstand under the lower control arm.
9. Chisel the heads off the rivets which secure the ball joint to the control arm. Use a punch to remove the rivets.
10. Remove the puller from the ball stud.
11. Remove the ball stud from the knuckle pin and remove the joint from the control arm.

Installation of a new lower ball joint is as follows:

1. Position the new ball joint so that its securing holes align with the rivet holes in the control arm.
2. Install the special 5/16 in. bolts, used to secure the ball joint, loosely.

Caution Use only the hardened 5/16 in. bolts supplied with the ball joint replacement kit; standard bolts are not strong enough.

3. Install the steering strut and stop on the lower control arm. Tighten their bolts to 75 ft lbs.
4. Tighten the 5/16 in. ball joint securing bolts to 25 ft lbs.
5. Fit the knuckle pin and retaining nut on the ball stud; tighten the nut to 45 ft lbs (75 ft lbs on Pacer) Install the cotter pin.
6. Complete the installation procedure in the reverse order of removal and then check front end alignment.

Upper Ball Joint—1970-76

1. Perform Steps 1-3 of the "Lower Ball Joint Removal" procedure.

NOTE: *It is not necessary to remove the brake drum in Step 3.*

2. Next, perform Steps 6-9 of the "Lower Ball Joint Removal" procedure to the upper ball joint.
3. Separate the upper ball joint from the control arm.
4. Remove the ball joint puller from the knuckle pin.

Installation of a new upper ball joint is as follows:

1. Perform Steps 1-2 of the "Lower Ball Joint Installation" procedure.
2. Skip Step 3 and go on to Steps 4-5 of the "Lower Ball Joint Installation" procedure.
3. Complete the installation in the reverse order of removal and check front end alignment.

Wheel Bearings

Inspection

Check to see that the inner cones of the bearings are free to "creep" on the spindle. Polish and lubricate the spindle to allow "creeping" movement and to keep rust from forming.

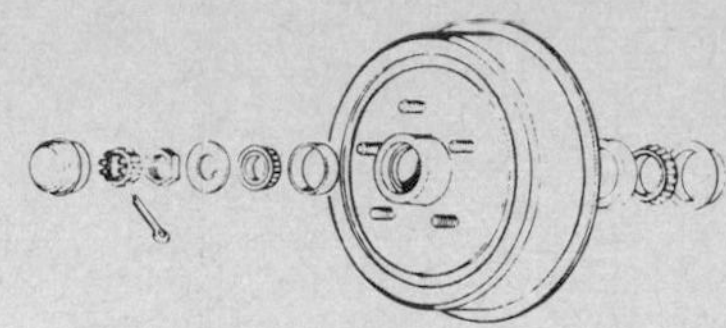

Front wheel bearing components
(© American Motors Corp)

Adjustment

1. With the tire and wheel removed and the car supported by a suitable and safe means, remove the dust cover from the spindle.
2. Remove the cotter pin and nut retainer.
3. Rotate the wheel while tightening the spindle nut to 20-25 ft lbs.
4. Loosen the spindle nut ⅓ of a turn.
5. Rotate the wheel while tightening the spindle nut to 6-10 in. lbs.
6. Fit the nut retainer over the spindle and align the slots in it with the cotter pin hole. Insert the cotter pin.
7. Install the dust cover.

REAR SUSPENSION

All 1969-76 American, Javelin, Hornet, Gremlin, Pacer, and AMX use a four or five-leaf semi-elliptic spring, and Hotchkiss drive rear suspension. Shock absorbers are mounted at their lower ends to studs and are bayonet type at their upper ends. Upper shock nuts are accessible by removing cover plates or by removing trunk floormat; except for AMX models. The upper ends of the shocks in the AMX are mounted to bolted-on brackets, which must be removed in order to remove the shocks.

The rear suspension on Rebel, Ambassador, and Matador models is a four-trailing arm, coil spring type. The two lower control arms are attached to the outer ends of the axle tubes and to the body side sills, while the two upper control arms are attached to the differential housing and to a rear crossmember. Rubber bushings are used on the lower arms and on the crossmember ends of the upper arms. The lower ends of the upper arms are attached to pressed in bushings in ears on the differential case. Shock absorbers are accessible at their upper ends by removing cover plates in the body or by removing brackets from underneath the car.

Shock Absorber R & R

1. Support the rear axle with jacks or a lift; this allows the weight of the car to compress the rear spring.
2. Remove the nut which secures the eye of the shock to the stud.
3. Remove the access plate on the rear underbody panel and remove the upper securing nut. It may be necessary to hold the top of the shock while unfastening the nut.

NOTE: Some models do not have an access plate. On these cars, remove the upper attachment plate complete as an assembly.

4. Remove the shock from under the car.
5. Installation is the reverse of removal.

Rear Spring R & R

1969-76 American, Javelin, Hornet, Pacer and Gremlin

1. Raise the car. Support the rear axle with jacks or a lift to take the load off the rear springs.
2. Disconnect the rear shock from the lower mounting stud. Lower the axle so that the rear springs hang free.
3. Disconnect the spring hangers.
4. Remove the nut from the bolt which attaches the eye of the spring to the front mount.
5. Remove the bolts from the rear shackle.
6. Installation is the reverse of removal.

1969-76 Ambassador and Matador

1. Raise the rear of the car and support the rear axle with jacks or a lift to take the load off the rear springs.
2. Disconnect the shock from the axle tube. Lower the axle to the fullest extent of its travel (limited by the control arms).
3. Pull down the axle tube to completely release the spring.
4. Reverse the above to install the spring.

BRAKES

All American Motors cars come equipped with dual tandem master cylinders. This allows one set of brakes to operate, should the other set fail. A switch in the system, connected to a warning light on the instrument panel, indicates a difference in pressure between the front and rear brake lines, thus indicating the failure of one brake system. Repair procedures for both the master cylinder and the switch are found in the "Unit Repair Section."

All drum brakes have automatic brake adjusters. These automatically compensate for lining wear, by operating when the brakes are applied while the car is backing up. The automatic mechanism is attached to the star wheel adjuster, which it works through.

Information on brake adjustments, lining replacement, bleeding procedure, master and wheel cylinder overhaul can be found in the Unit Repair Section.

Master Cylinder R & R

1. Disconnect the front and rear brake lines from the master cylinder. On cars equipped with drum brakes, the check valves will keep the fluid from draining out of the cylinder. If the car is equipped with disc brakes, one or both of the outlets must be plugged, to prevent fluid loss.
2. Remove the nuts which attach the master cylinder to the firewall or the power brake booster (if so equipped).
3. On cars that have manual brakes, disconnect the pedal push rod from the brake pedal.
4. Remove the master cylinder from the car.

Installation is the reverse of removal. Remember to bleed the brake system once the master cylinder has been installed. (See the "Unit Repair Section.")

Power Brake Unit R & R

Remove the clevis pin from the power-unit operating rod. Disconnect the vacuum line and the hydraulic lines from the power unit, remove the stop light wires, remove the mounting bolts and lift off the power cylinder.

Installation is the reverse order of the above.

Parking Brake Cable Replacement

All Models

1. Disconnect the lower end of the cable at the cross-shaft or equalizer, disconnect it at the handbrake end.
2. Remove the brackets which retain it to the body and firewall and thread it out of the vehicle.

When a new cable is to be installed, it is always a good idea to tie the new one to the end of the old one so that it will thread through in the same route as the old cable. This, sometimes, will require the service of a helper to guide it.

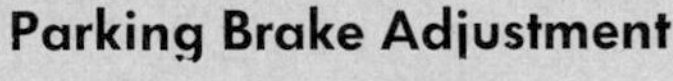

Parking Brake Adjustment

1969-76

NOTE: before adjusting the parking brake, adjust the service brakes, as outlined in the "Unit Repair Section."

1. On cars that have a foot-operated parking brake lever, set the lever on the first notch from the released position.
2. If the car has an "T" handle under the dashboard, set it on the fifth notch from the released position.
3. Tighten the cable at the equalizer so that the wheels cannot be turned forward.
4. Release the parking brake and check for rear brake drag. The wheels should rotate freely with the parking brake off.

STEERING

Power Steering Pump R & R

1. Remove the fan belt.
2. Place a container under the pump to catch fluid. On a Pacer, remove the fuel vapor storage canister.
3. Disconnect the hoses and cap the outlets, so that the power steering unit does not loose fluid.
4. On a Pacer with air conditioning, loosen the idler pulley adjusting bolt and idler pulley, air pump adjusting strap mounting bolt and remove the compressor drive belt from the idler pulley. Loosen the two nuts that attach the upper leg of the aluminum idler pulley mounting bracket to the cylinder head and remove the bolt that attaches the lower leg of the mounting bracket to the engine front cover.
5. Unbolt the pump bracket and remove the pump assembly.

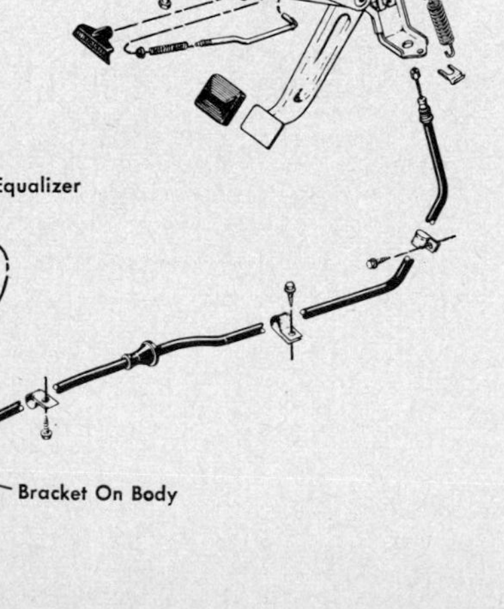

Typical foot pedal type parking brake linkage
(© American Motors Corp)

Installation is performed in the following manner:

1. Place the pump assembly on the engine and secure it with the attaching bolts.
2. Connect the hoses, being sure that the fittings are tightened evenly.
3. Position the filler neck of the reservoir upright, by loosening the attachment screw and rotating it to the correct position. Tighten the screw to 15–20 ft lbs.
4. Attach the A/C compressor on Pacers so equipped.
5. Fill the reservoir to the proper level with automatic transmission fluid and adjust the belt tension.

Steering Wheel R & R

1. Disconnect the battery and remove the horn button by one of the following methods:
   a. center button—lift upward.
   b. trim cover—remove the screws, which hold the cover on, from the rear. On "rimblow" wheels, remove the center contact.
2. Remove the steering wheel center nut. Before removing the wheel, note the position of the index marks on the wheel and the steering shaft.
3. Remove the wheel with a suitable puller.

Installation is the reverse of removal. Tighten the steering wheel nut to 20 ft lbs.

NOTE: Do not hammer on the end of the steering shaft; you could shear the plastic retainers which maintain the rigidity of the energy-absorbing steering column.

Turn Signal Switch R & R

1969

1. Disconnect the ground cable at the battery and remove the steering wheel as detailed above.
2. Remove the cancelling cam and the spring.
3. If the car is equipped with an adjustable steering wheel, remove the turn signal and the release levers.
4. Push the hazard warning knob in and remove it (if so equipped).
5. Remove the automatic shift quadrant (if so equipped).
6. Disconnect the turn signal switch wiring from the terminal block.
7. Remove the turn signal cover and the switch securing screws.
8. Remove the switch, however, first attach a string to the original switch wiring and pull the string through the steering column as the wiring is removed.

Leave the string in the column to aid in installing the wiring for the new switch.

Turn-signal switch installation is the reverse of removal. The new wiring must be inserted into the terminal block by color code, after switch installation.

1970-76

1. Disconnect the ground cable from the battery. Remove the steering wheel as outlined above.
2. Loosen the anti-theft cover attaching screws and remove the cover from the column. Do not remove the screws from the cover; they are attached to it with plastic retainers.
3. To remove the lockplate, a special compressor is required (see illustration). Depress the lockplate and pry the snap-ring from the groove in the steering shaft. Remove the tool, snap-ring, plate, turn signal cam, upper bearing preload spring, and the thrust washer from the shaft.

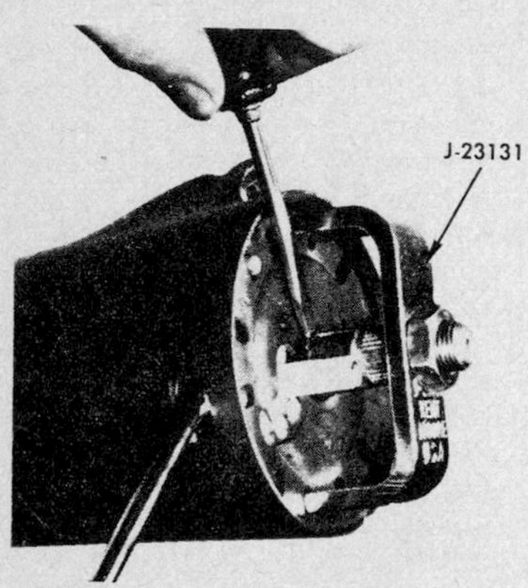

Using the special lockplate removal tool
(© American Motors Corp)

4. Place the turn signal lever in the right turn position and remove it.
5. Depress the hazard warning switch button and remove it, by rotating it counterclockwise.
6. Disconnect the wire harness connector block at its mounting bracket, which is located on the right side of the lower column.
7. If the car (Hornets only, after 1973) is equipped with a column-mounted automatic transmission selector, use a paper clip to depress the locktab that holds the shift quadrant light wire in the connector block (the grey wire at terminal "D").

NOTE: This is not necessary on 1974-76 Matador and Ambassador models.

8. Remove the switch attaching screws. Withdraw the switch and wire harness from the column.

Install the new switch in the reverse order of removal.

INSTRUMENT PANEL

Current is supplied to the instruments and the instrument panel lights through a printed circuit which is attached to the rear of the instrument cluster. The disconnect plug is part of the panel wiring harness and connects to pins attached to the printed circuit. A keyway located on the printed circuit board insures that the plug is always mounted correctly.

Caution Never pry under the plug to remove it, or damage to the printed circuit will result.

An instrument voltage regulator is wired in series with the gauges to supply a constant five volts to them. On the Hornet and Gremlin it is integral with the temperature gauge; on other models it is a separate unit.

Ignition Switch R & R

1969 Rebel and Ambassador

1. Disconnect battery.
2. Disconnect switch wires.
3. Remove escutcheon nut and remove switch toward rear of panel.

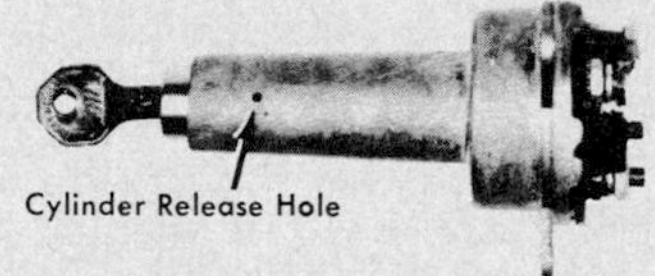

Ignition switch assembly—1969 Rebel and Ambassador
(© American Motors Corp)

4. With switch removed, turn key to Acc. position and insert wire (paper clip) in small hole in housing. Depress retainer while turning and pulling out cylinder.
5. Install in reverse of above.

All Other 1969 Models

1. Disconnect battery.

Ignition switch assembly—1969
(© American Motors Corp)

2. Depress switch and turn counterclockwise.
3. Remove switch through rear of panel and bevel from front.
4. Remove wires from switch.
5. Remove cylinder as in Step 4 of the above.
6. Install in reverse of above.

1970-71

The ignition switch on all models is mounted on the lower steering column tube and is connected to the lock cylinder via a lock rod.

1. Place key in "OFF-LOCK".
2. Remove switch mounting screws.
3. Disconnect lock rod, remove harness connector and switch.
4. To install, first place both key and switch slide in "OFF-LOCK" positions.
5. Insert a 3/32 in. drill bit into switch alignment hole.
6. With drill in place, hook up lock rod and remove all slack by sliding switch toward steering wheel.
7. Install mounting bolts and tighten securely. Remove drill and hook up wires.

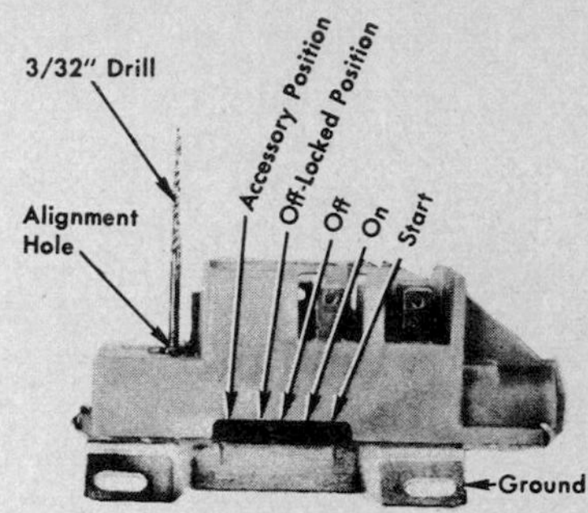

Ignition switch positions—1970-76
(© American Motors Corp)

1972-76

Removal of the column mounted ignition switch is the same as for the 1970-71 models. However, installation is slightly different:

1. On the standard column, move the switch slide to the left, as far as it will go. On the tilt-column, push the slide to the extreme right.
2. Position the lock rod into the hole on the switch slide.
3. Install the switch on the steering column. Be sure that the slide stays in its detent.

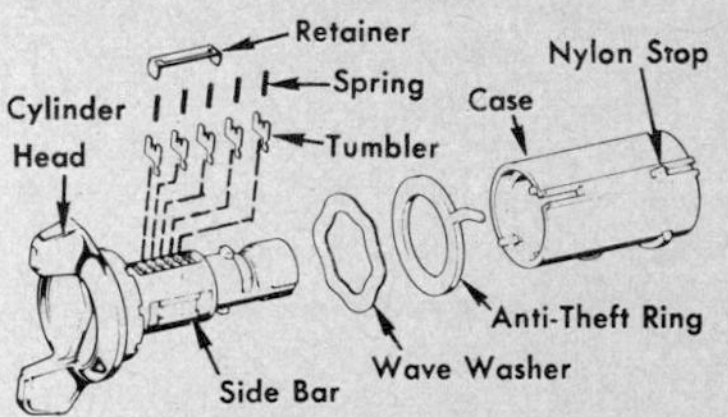

Ignition key lock—1970-76
(© American Motors Corp)

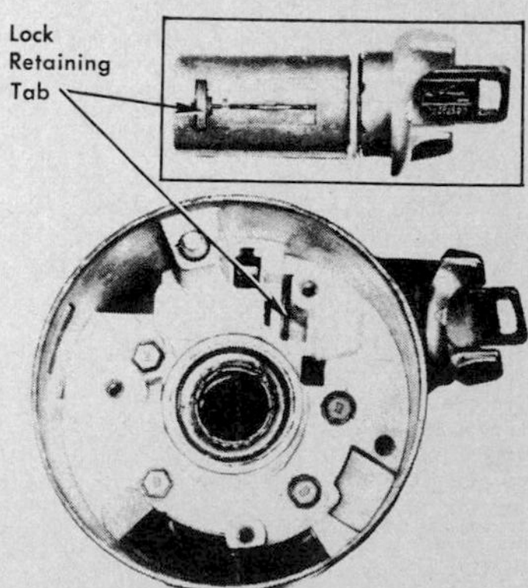

Lock cylinder removal—1970-76
(© American Motors Corp)

4. On the tilt-column, do not tighten the mounting screws. Instead, push the switch down the column, away from the steering wheel. This will remove any slack from the lock rod.
5. Tighten the switch mounting screws.

Lock Cylinder R & R—1970-76

Remove steering wheel.

1. Loosen anti-theft cover screws and remove cover from column.
2. Depress lock plate as far as possible, using a spacer and steering wheel nut.
3. Remove wire snap-ring from shaft groove, then remove compressor tool, snap-ring, lock plate, turn signal cam, upper bearing preload spring and thrust washer.
4. Place turn signal lever in "right turn" position and remove lever.
5. Depress hazard warning switch and remove button by turning counterclockwise.
6. Remove turn signal switch retaining screws and pull switch and wires out of column, as far as wiring will allow.
7. Place key in "LOCK" position, then depress lock cylinder retaining tab and remove cylinder.

To install the lock cylinder, proceed in the following manner:

1. Hold the lock cylinder sleeve and turn the lock cylinder clockwise until it contacts the stop.
2. Align the lock cylinder key with the keyway in the housing and slip the cylinder into the housing.
3. Lightly depress the cylinder against the sector, while turning it counterclockwise, until the cylinder and sector are engaged.
4. Depress the cylinder until the retaining tab engages, and the lock cylinder is secured.
5. Install the turn signal switch. Be sure that the actuating lever pivot is properly seated and aligned in the top of the housing boss, before installing it with its screws.
6. Install the turn signal stalk and check the operation of the switch.
7. Install the thrust washer, spring and turn signal cancelling cam on the steering shaft.
8. Align the lockplate and steering shaft splines, and position the lockplate so that the turn signal camshaft protrudes from the "dogleg" opening in the lockplate.
9. Use snap-ring pliers to install the snap-ring on the end of the steering shaft.
10. Secure the anti-theft cover with its screws.
11. Install the button on the hazard warning switch. Install the steering wheel, as detailed above.

Headlight Switch R & R

1969-76 (except Javelin)

Light switches are similar in all models. Some variation occurs in the shape and position of the nut mounting the switch to dash.

1. Disconnect battery and remove the switch overlay cover attaching screws so the cover can be pulled forward.
2. With switch in position press the release button and remove the knob and shaft.
3. Remove screws, attaching switch or bracket to panel.
4. Reverse for installation, positioning switch so that the shaft is lined up properly before tightening the bracket screws.

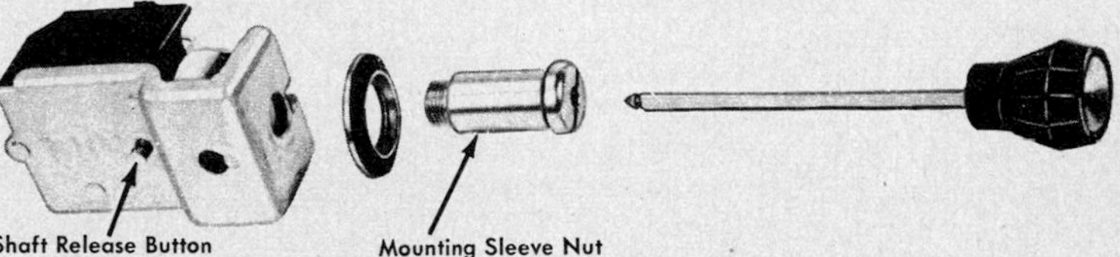

Light switch assembly (© American Motors Corp)

1971-74 Javelin

1. Remove the toggle switch knob by inserting a screwdriver in the groove on its left side. Pry upward, toward the knob, to release the spring clip that retains the knob.
2. Remove the screws that secure the lower cover to the steering column and withdraw the cover.
3. Disconnect the wire connectors and the retaining screws from the switch. Remove the switch.
4. Install the switch in the reverse order of removal.

WINDSHIELD WIPERS

Motor R & R

1969-74 American, Javelin, AMX, Hornet, and Gremlin 1973-74 Ambassador and Matador (except 1974 Matador Coupe)

The wiper motor is mounted on the engine side of the firewall and is easily accessible from under the hood.

1. Remove four screws that hold motor to firewall.
2. Remove hose and control cable, if equipped with vacuum wipers.
3. Unplug harness plug under dash, if equipped with electric wipers.
4. Disconnect motor link and remove motor.
5. To install, reverse removal procedure.

1975-76 Gremlin, Hornet, Matador Sedan and Wagon

1. Remove the wiper arms and blades.
2. Remove the screws holding the motor adpater plate to the dash panel.
3. Separate the wiper wiring harness connector at the motor.
4. Pull the motor and linkage out of the opening to expose the drive link-to-crank stud retaining clip. Raise up the lock tab of the clip with a screwdriver and slide the clip off the stud.
5. Install the windshield wiper motor in the reverse order of removal.

1969-72 Rebel, Matador, and Ambassador

1. Remove wiper arms and blades and the cowl air intake cover.
2. Slide the link-to-motor retainer clip off of the motor arm stud. Remove the link from the motor.
3. Disconnect control cable and vacuum hose or wiring harness from the motor.
4. Remove the motor and mounting plate-to-dash screws, and the motor assembly.
5. Install by reversing removal procedure.

1974-76 Matador Coupe

1. Remove the wiper arm/blade assemblies.
2. Open the hood and remove the cowl screen from the cowl opening.
3. Separate the linkage drive arm from the motor arm crankpin, by unfastening the retaining clip.
4. Disconnect the two multiconnectors from the motor.
5. Remove the wiper motor securing screws and withdraw the motor from the opening.

NOTE: *If the output arm hangs up on the dash panel during motor removal, rotate the arm clockwise by hand, so that it clears the panel opening.*

Installation is performed in the reverse order of removal. Prior to installation, make sure that the output arm is in the "park" position. Tighten the motor securing screws to 90-120 in lbs.

1975-76 Pacer

1. Remove the vacuum canister mounting bracket and canister.
2. Disconnect the linkage drive arm from the motor output arm crankpin by removing the retaining clip.
3. On vehicles equipped with air conditioning:

a. Remove the two nuts on the left side of the heater housing.
b. Remove the one nut on the right side of the heater housing.
c. Remove the screw from the heater housing support.

4. On vehicles not equipped with air conditioning:
   a. Remove the two nuts and one screw on the left side of the heater housing.
   b. Remove the one nut on the right side of the heater housing.
   c. Remove the screw from the heater housing support. Pull the heater housing forward.
5. Remove the wiper motor mounting plate attaching screws and remove the wiper motor assembly from the cowl.
6. Disconect the two wire connectors from the wiper motor.
7. Remove the wiper motor attaching screws and remove the wiper motor.
8. Install the wiper motor in the reverse order of removal.

Transmission R & R

1969-76 American, Javelin, AMX, Hornet, and Gremlin

To remove the pivot shaft body and link assembly after the link has been disconnected from the motor:

1. Remove pivot shaft spacer mounting nut, spacer and gaskets.
2. Disconnect washer hose.
3. Remove cowl ventilator air intake cover fastened to the cowl top by one screw at the front on each side and a retainer pin in the rear center of the cover.
4. The retainer pin is welded to the cover and inserted into a rubber grommet in the cowl top which serves as a retainer.
5. After the air intake cover is removed, the pivot shaft body retaining nuts are accessible for removal. The pivot shaft body and link assembly can then be removed from inside the body.

1969-76 Rebel, Matador (except 1974-76 Coupe), and Ambassador

1. Remove the wiper arm and blade assembly and pivot shaft to cowl top nut and spacer.
2. Disconnect the link end from the motor arm, after removing cowl air intake.
3. Close hood and remove two capscrews that hold each pivot shaft body. Remove assembly through cowl opening.
4. Install by reversing removal procedure.

1974-76 Matador Coupe

1. Remove the wiper arm/blade assemblies.
2. Open the hood and remove the cowl screen from the cowl opening.
3. Remove the screws which secure the left and right pivot shaft bodies to the cowl.
4. Separate the linkage drive arm from the motor arm crankpin, by removing the retaining clips.
5. Remove the pivot shaft body assembly through the cowl opening.

Installation is performed in the reverse order of removal. Tighten the pivot shaft body retaining screws to 90-120 in. lbs. Be sure that the retaining clips are securely fastened.

1975-76 Pacer

1. Remove the wiper arms and blades.
2. Remove the screws retaining the right and left pivot shaft bodies to the cowl.
3. Disconnect the linkage drive arm from the motor output arm crankpin by removing the retaining clip.
4. Remove the pivot shaft body assembly.
5. Position the pivot shaft body assembly on the car.
6. Install the retaining screws and tighten them to 50-70 in. lbs.
7. Connect the linkage drive arm to the motor output arm crankpin and install the retaining clip.

RADIO

The following precautions should be observed when working on a car radio:

1. Always observe the proper polarity of the power connections; i.e., positive (+) goes to the power source and negative (—) to ground (negative ground electrical system).
2. Never run the radio without a speaker; damage to the output transistors will result. If a replacement speaker is used, be sure that it is the correct impedance (ohms) for the radio. The proper impedance is stamped on the case of American Motors radios.
3. If a new antenna or antenna cable is used, adjust the antenna trimmer for the best reception of a weak AM station around 1400kc; the trimmer is located either behind the tuning knob or on the bottom of the radio case.

Removal and Installation

1969 American

1. Disconnect the battery ground lead.
2. Disconnect the antenna, power, and speaker wires from the radio.
3. Remove the radio bracket from the dash panel flange.
4. Pull the control knobs off and unfasten the control shaft bushing retainer nuts. Remove the ash tray assembly, if necessary.
5. Slide the radio back and down to remove it from underneath the instrument panel.

NOTE: if equipped with A/C, remove the glovebox and withdraw the radio through its opening.

Installation is the reverse of removal.

1969-73 Rebel, Matador, and Ambassador

1. Disconnect the battery ground cable.
2. Disconnect the antenna, power, ground, and speaker wires from the radio.
3. Remove the radio bracket from the dash panel flange.
4. Remove the cluster overlay.
5. Remove the radio mounting screws and withdraw the radio.

Installation is the reverse of removal.

1974-76 Matador and Ambassador

1. Remove the knobs from the radio and unfasten the control shafts retaining nuts.
2. Remove the bezel securing screws, and remove the bezel.
3. Loosen, but do not remove, the upper radio securing screw.
4. Raise the rear of the radio to separate its bracket from the upper securing screw.
5. Pull the radio forward slightly, and disconnect all of the leads from it. Remove the radio.

Radio installation is performed in the reverse order of removal. Adjust the antenna trimmer screw as detailed above.

1969-70 Javelin and AMX

1. Disconnect the battery ground cable.
2. Remove the ash tray. Remove the bolt from inside the ash tray which attaches to the radio (if so equipped).
3. Remove the radio knobs and remove the shaft retaining nuts. Remove the bezel retaining screws and the bezel on 1970 Javelin/AMX models.
4. Disconnect all of the leads from the radio.
5. Tip the back of the radio up, toward the toe board. Withdraw it from the rear edge of the center instrument panel pad.

NOTE: If equipped with A/C, remove the discharge duct to gain clearance for radio removal.

Installation is the reverse of removal.

1970-76 Hornet and Gremlin

1. Disconnect the battery ground cable.
2. Remove the ash tray and bracket.
3. Pull off the radio knobs and remove shaft retaining nuts.
4. Remove the bezel retaining screws and remove the bezel.
5. Disconnect the speaker, antenna, and power leads, and remove the radio.

Installation is the reverse of removal.

1971-74 Javelin

1. Disconnect the battery ground lead.
2. Remove the upper crash pad retaining screws, which are located next to the windshield.
3. Open the passenger-side door and remove the two panel securing screws from the door pillar area.
4. Remove the five securing screws from the upper flange of the instrument cluster bezel.
5. Remove the molding attaching screws and the passenger assist handle.
6. Remove the map light to gain access to the crash pad mounting stud which is located behind it. Remove the nut from the stud.

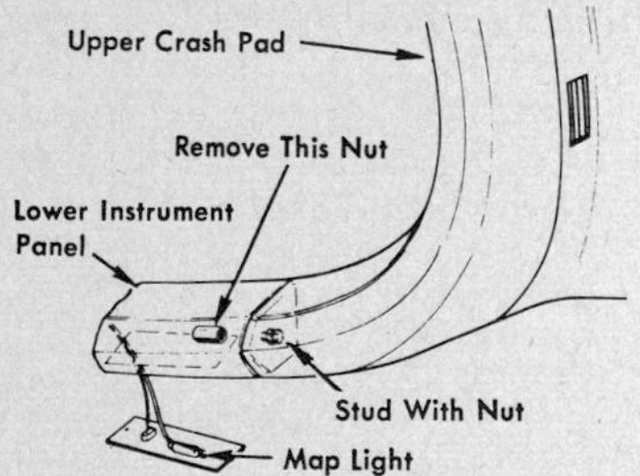

The lower retaining nut for the crash pad is hidden under the map light on the 1971-74 Javelin
(© American Motors Corp)

7. Remove the entire crash pad assembly.
8. Remove the three speaker mounting plate screws. Remove the speaker.
9. Slide the radio rearward and lift it up, in order to disconnect the speaker and light bulb leads.
10. Disconnect the radio power lead at the fuse block. Tie a string to the power lead, to aid in pulling it back through to the fuse block during assembly.
11. Remove the radio, complete with power lead.

Installation is the reverse of removal. Be sure to install the upper radio attaching screws and the speaker bracket mounting bolts, as these are part of the ground system.

1975-76 Pacer

1. Disconnect the negative battery cable.
2. Remove the radio overlay cover.
3. Loosen the radio-to-instrument panel attaching screw.
4. Disconnect the electrical connections and the antenna and remove the radio.
5. Install in the reverse order of removal.

HEATER

NOTE: It is recommended, unless you are trained in air conditioning servicing procedures, that you not disconnect any of the air conditioning refrigerant lines or vessels.

Heater Core R & R

Rebel, Matador and Ambassador —1969-73

1. Disconnect hoses from core and plug hoses and tubes. It will not be necessary to drain entire cooling system. On A/C equipped cars disconnect vacuum hoses at damper vacuum motor.
2. Remove lower blower housing attaching nuts and washers in engine compartment.
3. Remove glove compartment door and glove compartment.
4. Remove remaining heater housing screws in passenger compartment, and remove core and housing as an assembly.
5. Slide core from housing.
6. Install in reverse order of above.

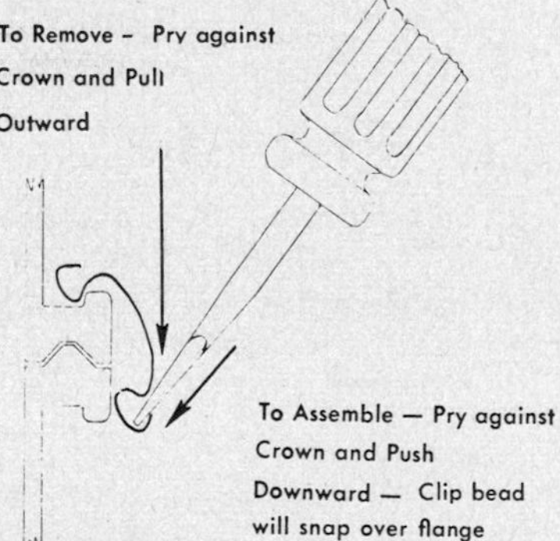

Removal and installation of evaporator housing cover retainer clip
(© American Motors Corp)

1974 Matador and Ambassador

1. Drain about two quarts of coolant from the cooling system.
2. Disconnect and plug the hoses which run to the heater core tubes in the engine compartment.
3. Disconnect the cable from the negative (—) battery terminal.
4. Remove the instrument panel lower finish panel and the glove compartment as follows:
   a. Remove the screws which secure the instrument cluster bezel and remove the bezel.
   b. Remove the screws from the lower glove compartment opening, which secure the crash padding.
   c. On cars without A/C, remove the mounting screws and remove the fresh air vent cable assemblies from the left and right-sides of the lower panel.
   d. On models with an optional inside hood release, remove the screws retaining its cable assembly to the lower panel and remove the assembly.
   e. Remove the lower finish panel-to-bracket retaining screws.
   f. Pull the panel down, disconnect any electrical connections, and remove the panel.
   g. Working from underneath the instrument panel, remove the nuts securing the glove compartment door hinge, and remove the door and hinge as assembly.
   h. Remove the fuse panel retaining screws, disconnect the electrical leads (mark them for installation first), and lift out the fuse panel.
   i. Remove the sheet metal screws which secure the glove compartment liner and remove the liner.
5. Disconnect the air blend door cable at the heater core housing.
6. On cars equipped with A/C, remove the hoses from the vacuum motors.
7. Remove the screws which secure the heater core housing. On models without A/C, unfasten the fresh air door cable.
8. Remove the housing and core as an assembly. Separate the core from the housing, as necessary.

Installation is the reverse of removal. Adjust the cable on the air blend door for proper operation. Refill the cooling system to capacity.

1975-76 Matador

1. Disconnect the negative battery cable.
2. Drain about 2 quarts of coolant from the cooling system.
3. Disconnect the heater hoses from the heater core in the engine compartment and plug the hoses.
4. On air conditioned cars, disconnect the blend-air damper cable at the heater core housing and remove the fuse panel. On non-A/C cars, disconnect the blend-air damper door and fresh air door cables.
5. Remove the lower instrument finish panel and remove the glove box door and liner.
6. Remove the right windshield pillar and corner finish mouldings for access to the upper right

heater core housing mounting screws.
7. On air conditioned cars, remove the vacuum motor hoses.
8. Remove the remaining heater core housing attaching screws.
9. On air conditioned cars, remove the capscrew retaining the instrument panel to the right body pillar. Pull the right side of the instrument panel slightly rearward.
10. Remove the heater core housing and heater core. Remove the heater core from the housing.
11. Install the heater core and housing in the reverse order of removal.

American—1969; Javelin and AMX—1969-74

1. Drain 1½ qts. (2 qts. beginning '70) of coolant from system.
2. Disconnect hoses from heater core tubes in engine compartment. Install corks in hoses and tubes.
3. Disconnect blower motor wires.
4. Remove housing attaching nuts at blower motor opening in dash.
5. Remove glove compartment door and glove compartment.

NOTE: on Javelin and AMX, remove glove box hinge bracket.

6. Disconnect air and defroster cables from damper levers.
7. Remove assembly.
8. Remove the core, defroster, and blower housing assembly from the car.
9. Remove the core from the housing assembly.

Installation is the reverse of removal.

Gremlin and Hornet—1970-76

1. Disconnect the negative battery cable and open heater valve and drain 2 qts. of coolant.
2. Disconnect heater hoses and plug hoses and core fittings.
3. Disconnect blower wires and remove motor and fan assembly.
4. On 1975-76 models, remove the housing attaching nut from the stud in the engine compartment.
5. Remove package shelf, if so equipped.
6. Disconnect wire at resistor, located below glove box.
7. Remove instrument panel center bezel, air outlet and duct, on A/C models.
8. Disconnect air and defroster cables from damper levers.
9. Remove right-side windshield pillar molding, the instrument panel upper sheet metal screws and the capscrew at the right door post.
10. Remove the right cowl trim panel after 1975.
11. Remove right kick panel and heater housing attaching screws.
12. Pull right side of instrument panel outward slightly and remove housing.
13. Remove core, defroster and blower housing.
14. Remove core from housing.

Installation is the reverse of removal.

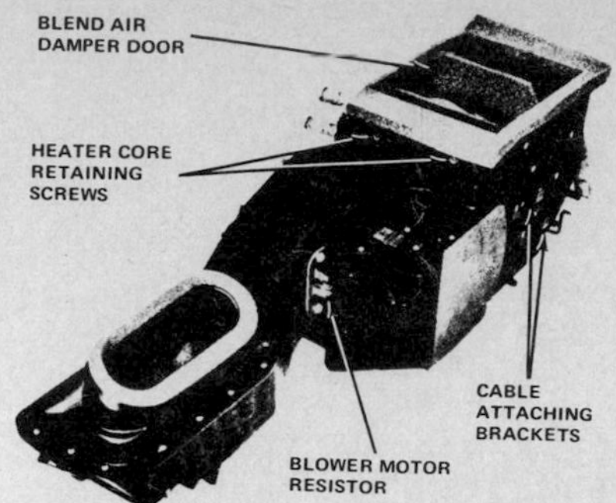

1973-76 Gremlin and Hornet heater assembly
(© American Motors Corp)

1975-76 Pacer

1. Drain about two quarts of coolant from the radiator.
2. Disconnect the heater hoses from the heater core tubes and install plugs in the heater hoses.
3. Remove the vacuum hoses from the heater core housing cover clip and move the lines aside.
4. Remove the heater core housing cover screws.
5. Disconnect the overcenter spring from the cover and remove the cover.
6. Remove the heater core-to-houing attaching screws and remove the heater core.
7. Install the heater core in the reverse order of removal.

Heater Blower R & R

Rebel, Matador, Ambassador —1969-73

1. Remove water valve from blower housing. It is not necessary to disconnect hoses and control cable.
2. Remove nuts, washers and screws attaching blower housing to dash panel in engine compartment.
3. Remove motor and fan, then separate fan from motor.
4. Install in reverse of above.

Blower housing attachment
(© American Motors Corp)

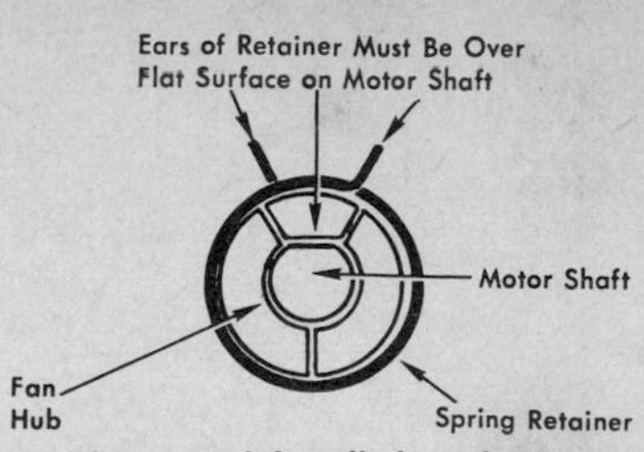

Blower retaining clip installation
(© American Motors Corp)

Javelin, AMX, American, Hornet and Gremlin—1969-76

1. Disconnect blower wires.
2. Remove three retaining nuts for scroll cover and remove motor and fan assembly.
3. To install, reverse removal procedure.

1974-76 Matador and Ambassador

1. Working from the engine compartment side of the firewall, disconnect the blower motor leads.
2. Remove the screws which secure the blower motor mounting plate to the blower motor housing.
3. Remove the motor, mounting plate, and fan as an assembly.

Installation is the reverse of removal.

1975-76 Pacer without A/C

1. Disconnect the negative battery cable.
2. Remove the right side windshield finish moulding.
3. Remove the instrument panel crash pad.
4. Remove the right scuff plate and cowl trim panel.
5. Remove the lower instrument panel-to-right A-pillar attaching screws.
6. Pull the instrument panel to the rear and replace the lower attaching screw in the right A-pillar. Allow the instrument panel to rest on the screw.
7. Remove the heater core housing attaching nuts and screw.
8. Remove the vacuum hoses from the heater core housing clip and set the lines aside.
9. Disconnect the blend-air door cable from the heater core housing.
10. Pull the heater core housing forward and set atop the upper control arm.
11. Remove the blower motor ground wire at the relay.
12. Disconnect the wires at the blower motor resistor.
13. Remove the blower motor housing brace.
14. Loosen the heater housing-to-dash panel attaching nuts.
15. Pull the blower housing to the rear and downward.
16. Disconnect the vacuum hoses from the vacuum motors.

17. Remove the blower housing.
18. Remove the blower housing cover.
19. Disconnect the white blower wire inside the housing.
20. Remove the blower motor mounting plate-to-housing screws and remove the blower motor assembly.
21. Remove the blower fan from the motor shaft and remove the mounting plate from the motor housing.
22. Install the blower motor in the reverse order of removal.

1975-76 Pacer With A/C

1. Disconnect the negative battery cable.
2. Remove the right scuff plate and cowl trim panel.
3. Remove the radio overlay cover.
4. Remove the instrument panel crash pad.
5. Remove the instrument panel-to-right A-pillar attaching screws.
6. Remove the two upper instrument panel-to-lower instrument panel attaching screws above the glove box.
7. Disconnect the blend-air door cable from the heater core housing.
8. Remove the housing brace-to-floorpan screw.
9. Disconnect the wire at the blower motor resistor.
10. Disconnect the vacuum hoses from the vacuum motors.
11. Remove the heater core housing attaching nuts and screw.
12. Remove the vacuum hoses from the housing clip and set the lines aside.
13. Pull the heater core housing forward and set it atop the upper control arm.
14. Remove the floor outlet duct.
15. Disconnect the wires from the blower motor relay.
16. Remove the blower housing attaching screw located in the engine compartment on the dash panel.
17. Loosen the evaporator housing-to-dash panel attaching nuts.
18. Remove the blower housing-to-dash panel attaching screw.
19. Pull the blower housing to the rear and downward.
20. Pull the right side of the instrument panel to the rear and remove the blower housing from under the panel.
21. Remove the floor door vacuum motor attaching screws and motor to gain access to the blower housing cover attaching screws.
22. Remove the blower housing cover attaching screws and remove the cover.
23. Remove the blower motor mounting plate and remove the blower motor assembly.
24. Remove the blower fan from the motor shaft and the mounting plate from the body of the motor.
25. Install the motor in the reverse order of removal.

SEAT BELTS

Warning System —1972-73

Operation

A red light flashes and a buzzer sounds to warn the driver and/or outboard front seat passenger to fasten his/their seat belt(s), under the following conditions:

1. When the ignition is on.
2. When the outboard front seat is occupied (pressure-sensitive switch closed).
3. When the seat belt(s) is/are not fastened.
4. When the automatic transmission selector is placed in any drive range (Forward or Reverse).
5. When the parking brake is released on manual transmission-equipped cars.

The light and buzzer will cease to function as soon as the seat belts are extended from the retractor and fastened over the laps of the driver and/or front seat passenger.

NOTE: If a package, handbag, etc., is placed on the right-hand front seat, the warning system might function even if there is no one sitting in the passenger's seat.

Warning Buzzer and Lamp R & R

To replace the buzzer, which is located under the instrument panel to the left of the instrument cluster, remove the sheetmetal screws (or tape), unfasten the multiconnector and withdraw the buzzer.

Installation is the reverse of removal.

On all series except the Javelin, pry the lamp assembly out of the instrument panel, working from the front, with a penknife or other suitable tool.

NOTE: Be careful not to scratch the painted surface of the instrument panel.

Disconnect the lamp connector and replace the lamp assembly as a complete unit.

On Javelin models, the two seat belt warning lamps are replaced like any other instrument panel warning lamp.

Seat Belt Retractor Switches

If the seat belt retractor switches fail, the entire seat belt assembly must be replaced, as these are not individually serviced components.

The switches are of the normally closed type.

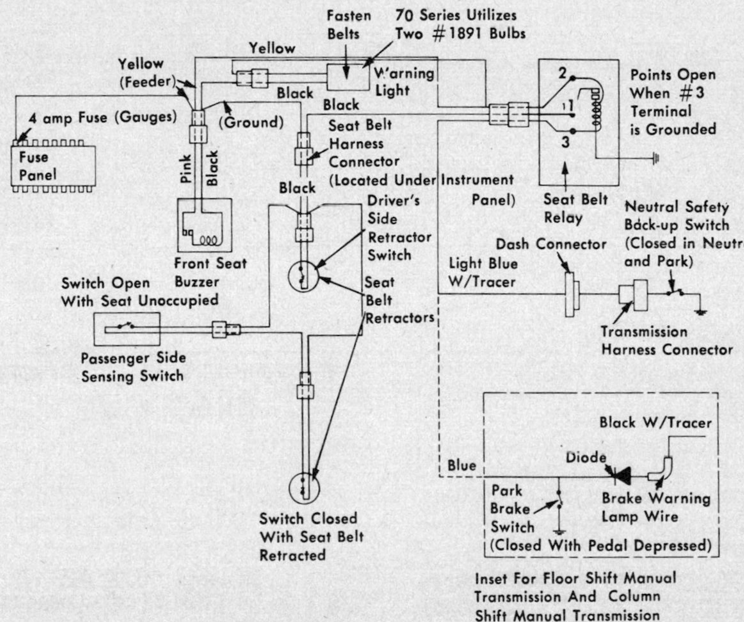

Schematic for seat belt warning system (© American Motors Corp)

Passenger Seat Sensing Switch

The pressure-sensitive switch used in the outboard front passenger seat is normally opened. It requires between 8-40 lbs pressure to close the warning circuit.

If the switch is overly sensitive, it can be adjusted in the following manner:

Depress the seat cushion above the switch location by applying your full weight on one knee.

This will cause seat cushion to bottom fully, thus bending the metal switch contract strips.

Repeat this procedure until proper sensitivity is attained.

NOTE: The switch used in bucket seats is not adjustable in this manner.

Relay

On some models, a relay is used to control the ground circuit of the warning buzzer and lamp. The relay is normally closed and it completes the ground circuit through its case. Grounding the number 3 terminal will cause the points to open, thus breaking the ground circuit for the warning system.

An improperly grounded relay case will cause the seat belt warning system not to function at all, while a burned-out relay could cause the warning system to function all of the time regardless of seat belt position. The relay is located below the lower left-hand instrument panel either next to the courtesy lamp or the brake pedal support bracket.

Diode

On manual transmission-equipped cars, a diode is used between the parking brake warning lamp and the pressure-sensitive switch to prevent feedback between the seat belt warning circuit and the parking brake warning circuit.

Failure of this diode will cause the parking brake warning light to remain lighted at all times.

Seat Belt/Starter Interlock System —1974-75

Operation

In addition to the light and buzzer used in 1972-73, a starter interlock has been incorporated into the seat belt warning system beginning 1974.

The car cannot be started unless the seat belts are fastened in a specific order. The driver (and front seat passenger) must get into the car, close the door(s), sit down, and then fasten the seat belts). If the seat belts are not fastened, or if they are fastened before the driver (and passenger) sit down, the car will not start. This prevents the belts from being permanently fastened and shoved behind the seats.

In case of a system failure and to make it easier for mechanics working on a car, a manual by-pass button is located under the hood. Pushing this button allows one "free start," i.e., without fastening the seat belt; each additional free start requires that the button be pushed again.

In addition to the components used for the 1972-73 warning system, a logic module (transistorized), a starter relay/by-pass button and two additional pressure-sensitive seat switches are used. The sensor switches that determine if the seat belt is fastened have been moved from the retractors to the seat belt buckles. This system is no longer required on new cars and may be disabled on those in service, provided that the warning light is left in operation.

Component Location

The logic module is located under the center of the instrument panel. The starter relay/by-pass switch is mounted under the hood, next to the starter solenoid on the right-hand inner fender panel.

Disabling the Interlock

The interlock may be disabled by unplugging the override relay and connecting the green with tracer, and the green wires together.

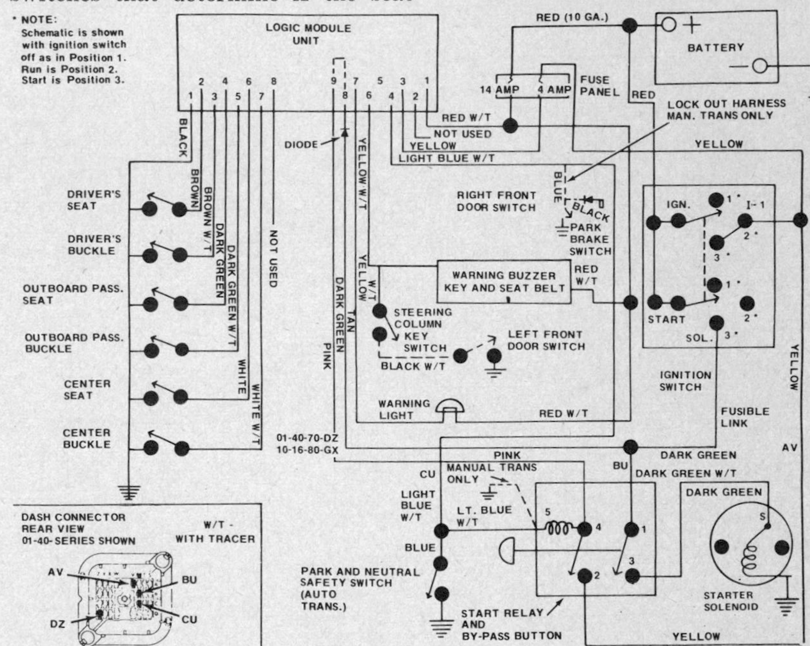

Schematic of the seat belt interlock system on 1974-75 American Motors cars (© American Motors Corp)

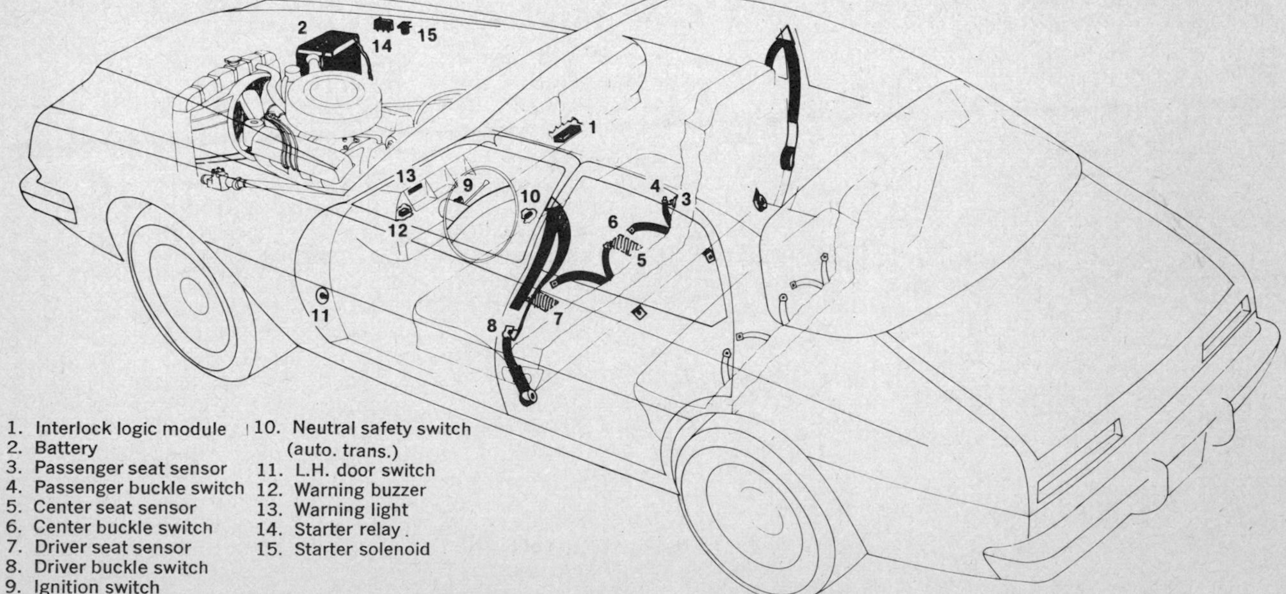

Component location for the seat belt/starter interlock system (© American Motors Corp)

Astre · Firebird · Grand Am · GTO · LeMans · Tempest · Ventura · Sunbird

YEAR IDENTIFICATION

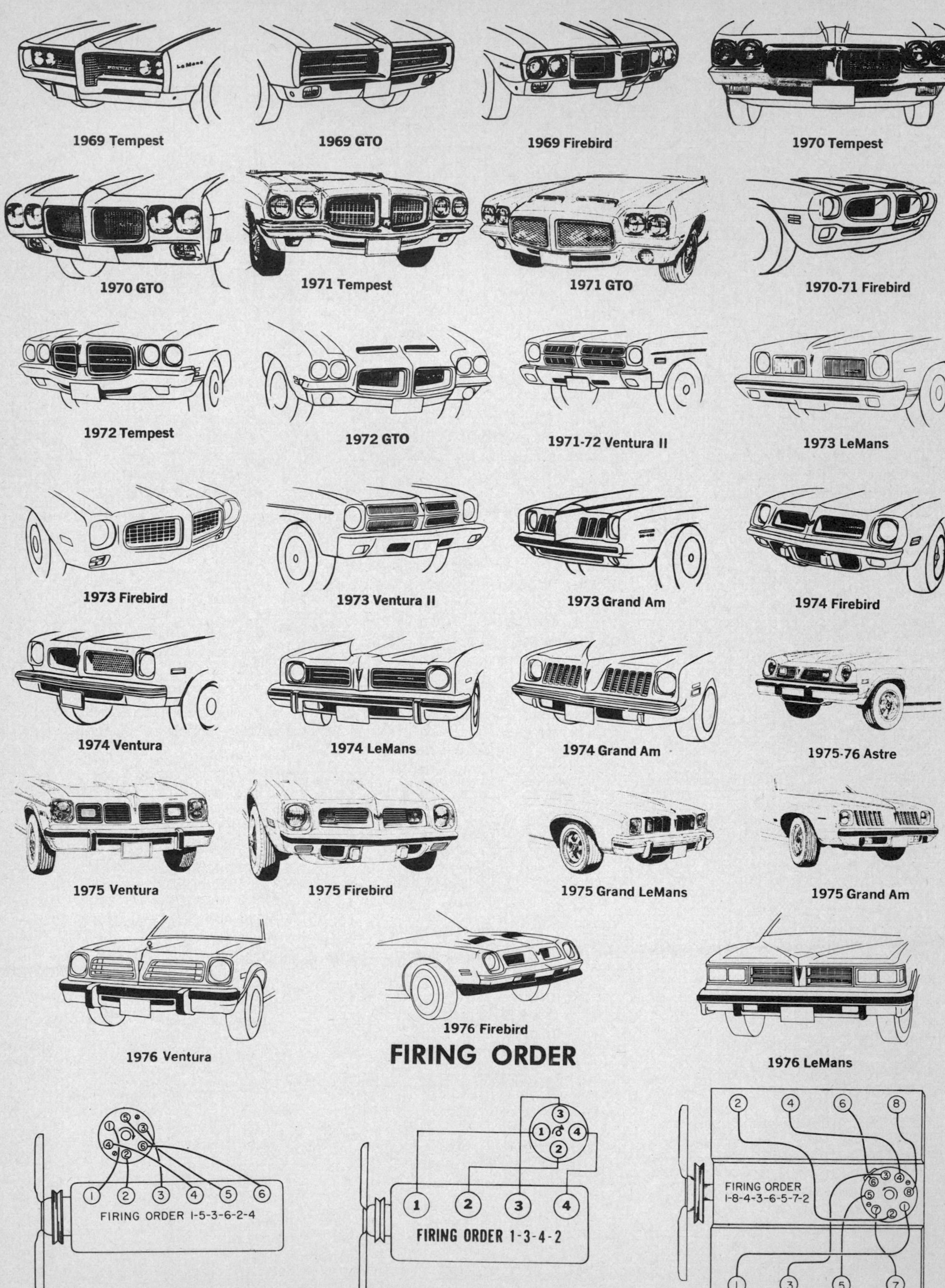

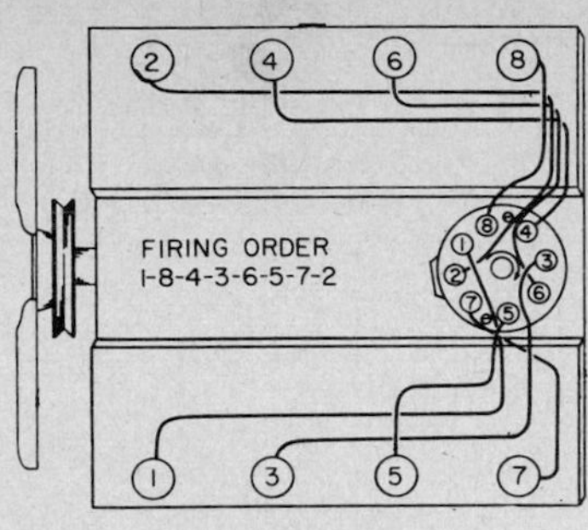

307 V8

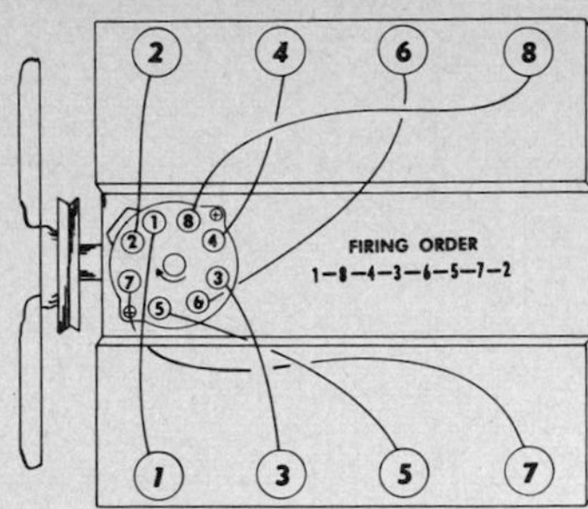

1975-76 Ventura 350

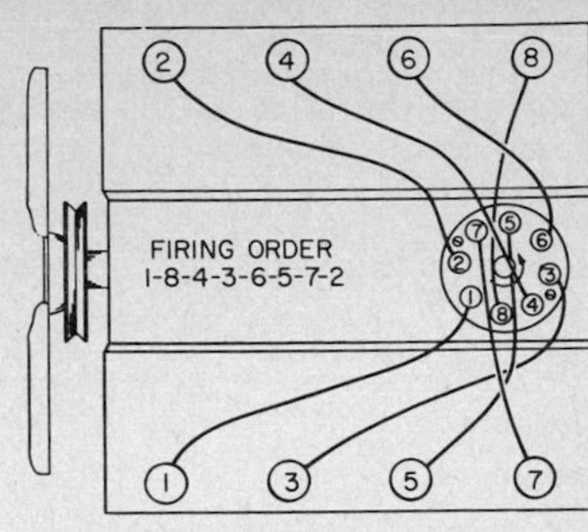

260 V8

CAR SERIAL NUMBER LOCATION

The car serial number is located on a plate attached to the top of the instrument panel, left-hand side, visible through the windshield. The number is interpreted as follows:

1969-71

First digit: Car division
Second and third digits: Series number
Fourth and fifth digits: Body style code
Sixth digit: Year manufactured
Seventh digit: Plant
Eighth digit: Engine used.
Ninth to thirteenth digits—sequential serial number

1972-74

First digit: Car division
Second digit: Series number
Third and fourth digits: Body style code

OHV 6-cyl engine number location
(© Pontiac Div., G.M. Corp)

Fifth digit: Engine used
Sixth digit: Year manufactured
Seventh digit: Plant
Eighth to thirteenth digits: Sequential serial number

1975-76

First digit: 2, for Pontiac division

Engine number and code location—1970 and later 350 (except 1975-76 Ventura), 400, 455 V8 engines
(© Pontiac Div., G.M. Corp)

Second, third, and fourth digits: Body style
Fifth digit: Engine used
Sixth digit: Year manufactured, 5 for 1975, 6 for 1976
Seventh digit: Assembly plant
Eighth to thirteenth digits: Sequential serial number

ENGINE IDENTIFICATION

Engine identification is made by means of a letter/number code stamped on the cylinder head contact surface of the block behind the oil filler pipe on 250 OHC six-cylinder engines; stamped on the distributor mounting pad at the right-side of the block or on the left rear side of the block on OHV six-cylinder engines; stamped on a machined pad, on the right side, above the starter motor on the OHC four-cylinder engine; and located on the machined face of the cylinder block, below and in front of the right cylinder head on all V8 engines.

Displacement (cu. in.)	Carburetor (no. Bbls.)	Hp.	'69	'70	'71	'72	'73	'74	'75	'76
4 Cylinder Models										
140 OHC	1	78 (net)							A②	
140 OHC	2	87 (net)							B②	
6 Cylinder Models										
250 OHC	1	175	ZK①							
			ZN①							
			ZC							
			ZF							
250 OHC	4	215	ZE①							
			ZL							
250 OHC	4	230	ZD①							
			ZH							
250 OHV	1	155		ZB						
				ZG						
250 OHV	1	145			CAA					
					CAB					
					ZB					
					ZG					

ENGINE IDENTIFICATION (con't.)

Engine identification is made by means of a letter/number code stamped on the cylinder head contact surface of the block behind the oil filler pipe on 250 OHC six-cylinder engines; stamped on the distributor mounting pad at the right-side of the block or on the left rear side of the block on OHV six-cylinder engines; stamped on a machined pad, on the right side, above the starter motor on the OHC four-cylinder engine; and located on the machined face of the cylinder block, below and in front of the right cylinder head on all V8 engines.

Displacement (cu. in.)	Carburetor (no. Bbls.)	Hp.	'69	'70	'71	'72	'73	'74	'75	'76
6 Cylinder Models										
250 OHV	1	110 (net)				CBA				
						CBC				
						CBG				
						CBJ				
						W6				
						Y6				
250 OHV	1	100 (net)					CCA	CCR	JU	
							CCB	CCW	JT	
							CCC	CCX	JL	
							CCD			
8 Cylinder Models										
260	2	110 (net)							QA	
									QD	
									QE	
									QJ	
									TE	
									TJ	
307	2	200			CCA					
					CCC					
307	2	130 (net)				CAY				
						CAZ				
						CKG				
						CKH				
350	2	265	WC①							
			WP①							
			XL①							
			XR①							
			YJ①							
			YN①							
			WM							
			WU							
			XB							
			XS							
			YE							
			YU							
350	2	255		WU						
				YU						
350	2	250			WR					
					WU					
					YU					
					XR					
350	2	160, 175# (net)				WR				
						YR				
						YV				
350	2	150, 175# (net)					XR			
							XV			
							Y2			
							YL			
							YR			
							YV			
							ZR			
							ZV			

ENGINE IDENTIFICATION (con't.)

Engine identification is made by means of a letter/number code stamped on the cylinder head contact surface of the block behind the oil filler pipe on 250 OHC six-cylinder engines; stamped on the distributor mounting pad at the right-side of the block or on the left rear side of the block on OHV six-cylinder engines; stamped on a machined pad, on the right side, above the starter motor on the OHC four-cylinder engine; and located on the machined face of the cylinder block, below and in front of the right cylinder head on all V8 engines.

Displacement (cu. in.)	Carburetor (no. Bbls.)	Hp.	'69	'70	'71	'72	'73	'74	'75	'76
8 Cylinder Models										
350	2	145 (net)							YA YB	
350	2	155, 170# (net)						AA WA WB YA YB YC ZA ZB	RS RI	
350	4	325	WN XC							
350	4	330	WV XU							
350	4	165 (net)							RW RX RN RO	
350	4	170, 200# (net)						WN WP YN YP YS ZP	WN YN ZP	
400	2	265	XM① XX	XX	WS XX					
400	2	175, 200# (net)				YX ZX				
400	2	170, 185# (net)					YP YX YZ ZK ZX			
400	2	175, 190# (net)						AH YH ZH ZJ	YH	
400	4	330	WZ YT	WT XV YS						
400	4	335	WQ YW							
400	4	350	WT YS	WT YS						
400	4	345	WH XN							
400	4	366	WS YZ	WS YZ						
400	4	370	WW XP	WW XP WH XN						
400	4	300			WK WT YS					
400	4	200, 250# (net)				WK WS YS				

ENGINE IDENTIFICATION (con't.)

Engine identification is made by means of a letter/number code stamped on the cylinder head contact surface of the block behind the oil filler pipe on 250 OHC six-cylinder engines; stamped on the distributor mounting pad at the right-side of the block or on the left rear side of the block on OHV six-cylinder engines; stamped on a machined pad, on the right side, above the starter motor on the OHC four-cylinder engine; and located on the machined face of the cylinder block, below and in front of the right cylinder head on all V8 engines.

Displacement (cu. in.)	Carburetor (no. Bbls.)	Hp.	'69	'70	'71	'72	'73	'74	'75	'76
8 Cylinder Models										
400	4	230 (net)					WK			
							WP			
							WS			
							Y3			
							YS			
							YT			
							YY			
							ZS			
400	4	225 (net)						AT		
								WT		
								YT		
								YZ		
								ZT		
400	4	210 (net)							YT	
									ZT	
									WT	
									YS	
455	4	370		WA						
				YC						
455	4	325			YC					
455	4	335			WC					
					WL					
					YE					
455	4	230, 250# (net)				YA				
						YC				
455HO	4	300 (net)				WM				
						YB				
455	4	250 (net)					WT	AU		
							WW	YY		
							YA	YW		
							YC	ZU		
							YD	ZW		
							YK			
							ZA			
							ZC			
455	4	215 (net)							YW	
									ZU	
455SD	4	310 (net)					W8			
							Y8			
455SD	4	290 (net)						W8		
								Y8		

① Early production small valve engine with 30° intake valve angle
② Fifth digit
With dual exhaust

GENERAL ENGINE SPECIFICATIONS

Year	Engine No. Cyl. Displacement Cu. In.	Carburetor Type	Horsepower @ rpm ■	Torque @ rpm (ft lbs) ■	Bore and Stroke (in.)	Compression Ratio	Oil Pressure @ 2050 rpm
'69	6-250 OHC	1 bbl	175 @ 4800	240 @ 2600	3.8762 x 3.530	9.0:1	31①
	6-250 OHC	4 bbl	215 @ 5200	255 @ 3500	3.8762 x 3.530	10.5:1	31①
	6-250 OHC	4 bbl	230 @ 5400	260 @ 3600	3.8762 x 3.530	10.5:1	31①
	8-350	2 bbl	265 @ 4600	325 @ 2800	3.8762 x 3.750	9.2:1	35
	8-350	4 bbl	325 @ 5100	380 @ 3200	3.8762 x 3.750	10.5:1	35
	8-350	4 bbl	330 @ 5100	380 @ 3200	3.8762 x 3.750	10.5:1	35
	8-400	2 bbl	265 @ 4600	397 @ 2400	4.1212 x 3.750	8.6:1	35
	8-400	4 bbl	330 @ 4800	430 @ 3300	4.1212 x 3.750	10.75:1	58
	8-400 HO	4 bbl	335 @ 5000	430 @ 3400	4.1212 x 3.750	10.75:1	58
	8-400 Ram Air	4 bbl	345 @ 5400	430 @ 3700	4.1212 x 3.750	10.75:1	58
	8-400 Ram Air	4 bbl	366 @ 5100	445 @ 3600	4.1212 x 3.750	10.75:1	58
	8-400 Ram Air IV	4 bbl	370 @ 5500	445 @ 3900	4.1212 x 3.750	10.75:1	58
'70	6-250	1 bbl	155 @ 4200	235 @ 1600	3.876 2x 3.530	8.5:1	53②
	8-350	2 bbl	255 @ 4600	355 @ 2800	3.8762 x 3.750	8.8:1	35
	8-400	2 bbl	265 @ 4600	397 @ 2400	4.1212 x 3.750	8.8:1	35
	8-400	4 bbl	330 @ 4800	430 @ 3000	4.1212 x 3.750	10.25:1③	35
	8-400 Ram Air	4 bbl	345 @ 5000	430 @ 3400	4.1212 x 3.750	10.5:1	35
	8-400	4 bbl	350 @ 4800	445 @ 2900	4.1212 x 3.750	10.0:1	35
	8-400	4 bbl	366 @ 5100	445 @ 3600	4.1212 x 3.750	10.5:1	35
	8-400	4 bbl	370 @ 5500	445 @ 3900	4.1212 x 3.750	10.5:1	35
	8-455	4 bbl	360 @ 4600	500 @ 3100	4.1522 x 4.210	10.25:1	35
'71	6-250	1 bbl	145 @ 4200	230 @ 1600	3.8750 x 3.530	8.5:1	38④
	8-307	2 bbl	200 @ 4600	300 @ 2400	3.8750 x 3.250	8.5:1	40②
	8-350	2 bbl	250 @ 4400	350 @ 2400	3.8762 x 3.750	8.0:1	35
	8-400	2 bbl	265 @ 4400	400 @ 2400	4.1212 x 3.750	8.2:1	58
	8-400	4 bbl	300 @ 4800	400 @ 3600	4.1212 x 3.750	8.2:1	58
	8-455	4 bbl	325 @ 4400	455 @ 3200	4.1522 x 4.210	8.2:1	35
	8-455 HO	4 bbl	335 @ 4800	480 @ 3600	4.1522 x 4.210	8.4:1	35
'72	6-250	1 bbl	110 @ 3800	185 @ 1600	3.8750 x 3.530	8.5:1	40②
	8-307	2 bbl	130 @ 4400	230 @ 2400	3.8750 x 3.250	8.5:1	40②
	8-350	2 bbl	160 @ 4400	270 @ 2000	3.8762 x 3.750	8.2:1	35
	8-400	2 bbl	175 @ 4000	310 @ 2400	4.1212 x 3.750	8.2:1	35
	8-400	4 bbl	200 @ 4000	295 @ 2800	4.1212 x 3.750	8.2:1	35
	8-400	4 bbl	250 @ 4400	325 @ 3200	4.1212 x 3.750	8.2:1	35
	8-455	4 bbl	250 @ 3600	375 @ 2400	4.1522 x 4.210	8.2:1	35
	8-455	4 bbl	300 @ 4000	415 @ 3200	4.1522 x 4.210	8.4:1	35
'73	6-250	1 bbl	100 @ 3600	175 @ 1600	3.8750 x 3.530	8.2:1	50-65②
	8-350 SE	2 bbl	150 @ 4000	270 @ 2000	3.8762 x 3.750	7.6:1	55-60⑤
	8-350 DE	2 bbl	175 @ 4400	280 @ 2400	3.8782 x 3.750	7.6:1	55-60⑤
	8-400 SE	2 bbl	170 @ 3600	320 @ 2000	4.1212 x 3.750	8.0:1	55-60⑤
	8-400 DE	2 bbl	185 @ 4000	320 @ 2400	4.1212 x 3.750	8.0:1	55-60⑤
	8-400 DE	4 bbl	230 @ 4400	325 @ 3200	4.1212 x 3.750	8.0:1	55-60⑤
	8-455 DE	4 bbl	250 @ 4000	370 @ 2800	4.1522 x 4.210	8.0:1	55-60⑤
	8-455S.D. DE	4 bbl	310 @ 4000	390 @ 3600	4.1522 x 4.210	8.4:1	75-80⑤

GENERAL ENGINE SPECIFICATIONS (con't.)

Year	Engine No. Cyl. Displacement Cu. In.	Carburetor Type	Horsepower @ rpm ■	Torque @ rpm (ft lbs) ■	Bore and Stroke (in.)	Compression Ratio	Oil Pressure @ 2050 rpm
'74	6-250	1 bbl	100 @ 3600	175 @ 1600	3.8750 x 3.530	8.2:1	36-41②
	8-350 SE	2 bbl	155 @ 4000	275 @ 2400	3.8762 x 3.750	7.6:1	55-60⑤
	8-350 DE	2 bbl	170 @ 4400	290 @ 2400	3.8782 x 3.750	7.6:1	55-60⑤
	8-350 SE	4 bbl	170 @ 4000	280 @ 2000	3.8762 x 3.750	7.6:1	55-60⑤
	8-350 DE	4 bbl	200 @ 4000	295 @ 2800	3.8762 x 3.750	7.6:1	55-60⑤
	8-400 SE	2 bbl	175 @ 3600	315 @ 2000	4.1212 x 3.750	8.0:1	55-60⑤
	8-400 DE	2 bbl	190 @ 4000	330 @ 2400	4.1212 x 3.750	8.0:1	55-60⑤
	8-400 DE	4 bbl	225 @ 4000	330 @ 2800	4.1212 x 3.750	8.0:1	55-60⑤
	8-455 SE	4 bbl	215 @ 3600	355 @ 2400	4.1522 x 4.210	8.0:1	55-60⑤
	8-455 DE	4 bbl	250 @ 4000	380 @ 2800	4.1522 x 4.210	8.0:1	55-60⑤
	8-455S.D. DE	4 bbl	290 @ 4000	395 @ 3200	4.1522 x 4.210	8.4:1	75-80⑤
'75-'76	4-140 OHC	1 bbl	78 @ 4200	120 @ 2000	3.501 x 3.625	8.0:1	40⑥
	4-140 OHC	2 bbl	87 @ 4400	122 @ 2800	3.501 x 3.625	8.0:1	40⑥
	V6-231	2 bbl	110 @ 4000	175 @ 2000	3.800 x 3.400	8.0:1	40⑧
	6-250	1 bbl	100 @ 3600	175 @ 1600	3.8750 x 3.530	8.2:1	36-41②
	8-260	2 bbl	110 @ 3400	205 @ 1600	3.500 x 3.385	7.4:1	30-45④
	8-350	2 bbl	155 @ 4000	275 @ 2400	3.8762 x 3.750	7.6:1	55-60⑤
	8-350	4 bbl	170 @ 4000	280 @ 2000	3.8762 x 3.750	7.6:1	55-60⑤
	8-350 Ventura	2 bbl	145 @ 3200	270 @ 2000	3.800 x 3.850	8.1:1	37⑦
	8-350 Ventura	4 bbl	165 @ 3800	260 @ 2200	3.800 x 3.850	8.1:1	37⑦
	8-400	2 bbl	175 @ 3600	315 @ 2000	4.1212 x 3.750	7.6:1	55-60⑤
	8-400	4 bbl	210 @ 4000	315 @ 2800	4.1212 x 3.750	7.6:1	55-60⑤
	8-455	4 bbl	215 @ 3600	355 @ 2400	4.1522 x 4.210	7.6:1	55-60⑤

■ Beginning 1972 horsepower and torque are SAE net figures. They are measured at the rear of the transmission with all accessories installed and operating. Since the figures vary when a given engine is installed in different models, some are representative, rather than exact.

① Oil pressure at 2800 rpm

② Oil pressure at 2000 rpm

③ For vehicles equipped with automatic transmissions, compression ratio is 10.0:1

④ Oil pressure at 1500 rpm

⑤ Oil Pressure above 2600 rpm

⑥ Pressure at 1000 rpm

⑦ Pressure at 2400 rpm

⑧ Oil pressure at 1000 rpm

HO High Output

OHC Overhead Cam

SE Single Exhaust

DE Dual Exhaust

TUNE-UP SPECIFICATIONS

Tempest, 1969-73 GTO, LeMans, Grand Am

When analyzing compression test results, look for uniformity among cylinders rather than specific pressures.

ENGINE			SPARK PLUGS		DISTRIBUTOR		IGNITION TIMING (deg) ▲		VALVES	Fuel	IDLE SPEED ● (rpm) ▲	
Year	No. Cyl Displacement	hp (cu in.)	Type	Gap (in.)	Point Dwell (deg)	Point Gap (in.)	Man Trans ●	Auto Trans	Intake Opens ■ (deg)	Pump Pressure (psi)	Man Trans	Auto Trans
'69	6-250 OHC	175	R-44NS	.035	32½	.019	TDC	TDC	14	4-5½	700①/500	600①/500
	6-250 OHC	215	R-44NS	.035	32½	.019	5B	5B	22/14	4-5½	850①/600	600①/500
	6-250 OHC	230	R-44NS	.035	32½	.019	5B	5B	22/14	4-5½	850①/600	600①/500
	8-350	265	R-46S	.035	30	.016	9B	9B	22	5-6½	850	650
	8-350	330	R-45S	.035	30	.016	9B	9B	38/23	5-6½	1000	650
	8-400	265	R-46S	.035	30	.016	9B	9B	22	5-6½	850	650
	8-400	330	R-45S	.035	30	.016	9B	9B	23	5-6½	1000	650
	8-400	350	R-45S	.035	30	.016	9B	9B	23	5-6½	1000	650
	8-400 Ram Air	366	R-45S	.035	30	.016	9B	9B	23	5-6½	1000①/650	650/500①
	8-400 Ram Air	370	R-44S	.035	30	.016	15B	15B	42	5-6½	1000①/650	650/500①

TUNE-UP SPECIFICATIONS (con't.)

Tempest, 1969-73 GTO, LeMans, Grand Am

When analyzing compression test results, look for uniformity among cylinders rather than specific pressures.

Year	ENGINE No. Cyl Displacement (cu in.)	hp	SPARK PLUGS Type	Gap (in.)	DISTRIBUTOR Point Dwell (deg)	Point Gap (in.)	IGNITION TIMING (deg) ▲ Man Trans ●	Auto Trans	VALVES Intake Opens ■ (deg)	Fuel Pump Pressure (psi)	IDLE SPEED ● (rpm) ▲ Man Trans	Auto Trans
'70	6-250	155	R-46T	.035	32½	.019	TDC	4B	16	4-5	830/750①	630/600①
	8-350	255	R-46S	.035	30	.016	9B	9B	22	5-6½	800	650
	8-400	265	R-46S	.035	30	.016	9B	9B	22	5-6½	800	650
	8-400	330	R-45S	.035	30	.016	9B	9B	30	5-6½	950	650
	8-400	350	R-46S	.035	30	.016	9B	9B	23	5-6½	950	650
	8-400 Ram Air	366	R-46S	.035	30	.016	9B	9B	31	5-6½	950	650
	8-400 Ram Air	370	R-46S	.035	30	.016	15B	15B	40	5 6½	1000①/650	750①/500
	8-455	360	R-46S	.035	30	.016	9B	9B	31/23	5-6½	950	650
'71	6-250	145	R-45T	.035	32½	.019	4B	4B	16	4-5	850/550①	650/500①
	8-350	250	R-47S	.035	30	.016	12B	12B	26/30	5-6½③	800	600
	8-400	265	R-47S	.035	30	.016	—	8B	26	5-6½③	—	600
	8-400	300	R-46S	.035	30	.016	12B	12B	23	5-6½③	1000/600①	700
	8-455	325	R-46S	.035	30	.016	—	12B	23	5-6½③	—	650
	8-455	335	R-46S	.035	30	.016	12B	12B	31	5-6½③	1000/600①	700
'72	6-250	110	R-45T	.035	32½	.019	4B	4B	16	4-5	700/450①	600/450①
	8-350	160	R-46TS	.035	30	.016	8B	10B	26/30④	5-6½	800	625
	8-400	175	R-46TS	.035	30	.016	—	10B	23/26④	5-6½	—	625
	8-400	200	R-46TS	.035	30	.016	8B	10B	23	5-6½	1000/600①	700/500①
	8-455	250	R-45TS	.035	30	.016	—	10B	23	5-6½	—	650/500①
	8-455	300	R-45TS	.035	—	—	8B	10B	31	5-6½	1000/600①	700/500①
'73	6-250	100	R-46T	.035	32½	.019	6B	6B	16	4-5	700/450①	600
	8-350 SE	150	R-46TS	.040	30	.016	10B	12B	26/30④	5-6½	900/600①	650
	8-350 DE	175	R-46TS	.040	30	.016	10B	12B	26/30④	5-6½	900/600①	650
	8-400 SE	170	R-46TS	.040	30	.016	10B	12B	26	5-6½	—	650
	8-400 DE	185	R-46TS	.040	30	.016	10B	12B	23/30④	5-6½	—	650
	8-400 DE	230	R-45TS	.040	30	.016	10B	12B	23/30④	5-6½	1000/600①	650
	8-455 DE	250	R-45TS	.040	30	.016	10B	12B	23	5-6½	—	650
	8-455 S.D. DE	310	R-44TS	.040	30	.016	10B	12B	42	5-6½	1000/600①	750/500①
'74	6-250	all	R-46T	.035	32½	.019	6B	6B	16	4-5	850/450①	600/450①
	8-350 2 bbl	all	R-46TS	.040	30	.016	10B	12B(10B)	26	5-6½	900/600①	650(625)
	8-350 4 bbl	all	R-46TS	.040	30	.016	10B	12B(10B)	26	5-6½	1000/600	650(625)
	8-400 2 bbl	all	R-46TS	.040	30	.016	10B	12B(10B)	26	5-6½	—	650(625)
	8-400 4 bbl	all	R-45TS	.040	30	.016	10B	12B(10B)	23/30④	5-6½	1000/600①	650(625)
	8-455	all	R-45TS	.040	30	.016	10B	12B(10B)	23	5-6½	—	650(625)
'75	6-250	100	R-46TX	.060	Electronic		10B	10B	16	4-5	850	550(600)
	8-350 2 bbl	155	R-46TSX	.060	Electronic		—	16B	26	5-6½	—	600
	8-350 4 bbl	170	R-46TSX	.060	Electronic		—	16B(12)	26	5-6½	—	650(625)
	8-400 2 bbl	175	R-46TSX	.060	Electronic		—	16B	26	5-6½	—	650
	8-400 4 bbl	210	R-45TSX	.060	Electronic		—	16B(12)	30	5-6½	—	650(600)
	8-455 4 bbl	215	R-45TSX	.060	Electronic		—	16B(10)	23	5-6½	—	650(675)
'76	6-250	100	R-46TX	.060	Electronic		—	10B	16	4½-5½	850	550(600)⑥
	8-260	110	R-46SX	.080	Electronic		16B(14)	18B(14)	14	7-8½	750	550(600)⑦
	8-350 2 bbl	155	R-46TSX	.060	Electronic		—	16B	22	7-8½	—	550⑦
	8-350 4 bbl	175	R-45TSX	.060	Electronic		—	16B	26	7-8½	—	600⑦
	8-400 2 bbl	170	R-46TSX	.060	Electronic		—	16B	26	7-8½	—	550⑦
	8-400 4 bbl	185	R-45TSX	.060	Electronic		—	16B	30	7-8½	—	575⑦
	8-455	200	R-45TSX	.060	Electronic		—	16B(12)	23	7-8½	—	550(600)⑦

SE Single Exhaust
DE Dual Exhaust
▲ See text for procedure
● Figure in parentheses indicates California engine
■ All figures are in degrees Before Top Dead Center. Where two figures appear, the first represents timing with manual transmission, the second with automatic transmission.
① Lower figure indicates idle speed with solenoid disconnected
② not used
③ 6½-8 with A/C
④ Lower figure represents manual transmission models; higher figure indicates automatic transmission.
⑥ 575 rpm for non-California models with air conditioning
⑦ 675 rpm with air conditioning on and compressor clutch wires disconnected
B Before Top Dead Center
TDC Top Dead Center

Firebird

TUNE-UP SPECIFICATIONS

When analyzing compression test results, look for uniformity among cylinders rather than specific pressures.

	ENGINE		SPARK PLUGS		DISTRIBUTOR		IGNITION TIMING (deg) ▲		VALVES	Fuel	IDLE SPEED ● (rpm) ▲	
Year	No. Cyl Displacement (cu in.)	hp	Type	Gap (in.)	Point Dwell (deg)	Point Gap (in.)	Man Trans	● Auto Trans	Intake Opens ■ (deg)	Pump Pressure (psi)	Man Trans	Auto Trans
'70	6-250	155	R-46T	.035	32½	.019	TDC	4B	16	4-5½	850/500①	650/500①
	8-350	255	R-46S	.035	30	.016	9B	9B	22	5-6½	800	650
	8-400	265	R-46S③	.035	30	.016	9B	9B	22	5-6½	800	650
	8-400	330	R-45S	.035	30	.016	9B	9B	30	5-6½	950	650
	8-400 Ram Air	345	R-44S	.035	30	.016	9B	9B	30	5-6½	950	650
	8-400 Ram Air	370	R-44S	.035	30	.016	15B	15B	30	5-6½	1000/650①	750/500①
'71	6-250	145	R-45T	.035	32½	.019	4B	4B	16	4-5	850/550①	650/500①
	8-350	250	R-47S	.035	30	.016	12B	12B	26/30⑤	④5-6½	800	600
	8-400	265	R-47S	.035	30	.016	—	8B	26	④5-6½	—	600
	8-400	300	R-46S	.035	30	.016	12B	12B	23	④5-6½	1000/600①	700
	8-455	325	R-46S	.035	30	.016	—	12B	23	④5-6½	—	650
	8-455	335	R-46S	.035	30	.016	12B	12B	31	④5-6½	1000/600①	700
'72	6-250	110	R-45T	.035	32½	.019	4B	4B	16	4-5	700①/450	600①/450
	8-350	160	R-46TS	.035	30	.016	8B	10B	26/30⑤	5-6½	800	625
	8-400	175	R-46TS	.035	30	.016	—	10B	23/26⑤	5-6½	—	625
	8-400	250	R-45TS	.035	30	.016	8B	10B	23	5-6½	1000/600①	700/500①
	8-455	300	R-45TS	.035	30	—	8B	10B	31	5-6½	1000/600①	700/500①
'73	6-250	100	R-46T	.035	32½	.019	6B	6B	16	4-5	700/450	600/450
	8-350 SE	150	R-46TS	.040	30	.016	10B	12B	26/30⑤	5-6½	900/600①	1500/650
	8-350 DE	175	R-46TS	.040	30	.016	10B	12B	26/30⑤	5-6½	900/600①	650
	8-400 SE	170	R-46TS	.040	30	.016	10B	12B	26	5-6½	—	650
	8-400 DE	230	R-45TS	.040	30	.016	10B	12B	23/30⑤	5-6½	1000/600①	650
	8-455 DE	250	R-45TS	.040	30	.016	10B	12B	23	5-6½	1000/600①	650
	8-455 S.D. DE	310	R-44TS	.040	30	.016	10B	12B	42	5-6½	1000/600①	750/500①
'74	6-250	all	R-46T	.035	32½	.019	6B	6B	16	4-5	850/450①	600/450①
	8-350 2 bbl	all	R-46TS	.040	30	.016	10B	12B(10B)	26	5-6½	900/600①	650(625)
	8-350 4 bbl	all	R-46TS	.040	30	.016	10B	12B(10B)	26	5-6½	1000/600	650(625)
	8-400 2 bbl	all	R-46TS	.040	30	.016	10B	12B(10B)	26	5-6½	—	650(625)
	8-400 4 bbl	all	R-45TS	.040	30	.016	10B	12B(10B)	23/30⑤	5-6½	1000/600①	650(625)
	8-455	all	R-45TS	.040	30	.016	10B	12B(10B)	23	5-6½	—	650(625)
	8-455 S.D.	290	R-45TS	.040	30	.016	10B	12B	38	5-6½	1000/600①	750/500①
'75	6-250	100	R-46TX	.060	Electronic		10B	10B	16	4-5	850	550(600)
	8-350 2 bbl	155	R-46TSX	.060	Electronic		—	16B	26	5-6½	—	600
	8-350 4 bbl	170	R-46TSX	.060	Electronic		12B	16B(12)	26	5-6½	775	650(625)
	8-400 4 bbl	210	R-45TSX	.060	Electronic		12B	16B(12)	30	5-6½	775	650(600)
'76	6-250	100	R-46TX	.060	Electronic		—	10B	16	4½-5½	850	550(600)⑥
	8-350 2 bbl	155	R-46TSX	.060	Electronic		—	16B	22	7-8½	—	550⑦
	8-350 4 bbl	175	R-45TSX	.060	Electronic		—	16B	26	7-8½	—	600⑦
	8-400	185	R-45TSX	.060	Electronic		12B	16B	30	7-8½	775	575⑦
	8-455	200	R-45TSX	.060	Electronic		12B	16B(12)	23	7-8½	—	550(600)⑦

SE Single Exhaust DE Dual Exhaust ▲ See text for procedure
● Figure in parentheses indicates California engine
■ All figures are in degrees Before Top Dead Center. Where two figures appear, the first represents timing with manual transmission, the second with automatic transmission.
① Lower figure indicates idle speed with solenoid disconnected

② Not used
③ AC-R-45S with automatic transmission.
④ 6½-8 with A/C
⑤ Lower figure represents manual transmission models; higher figure indicates automatic transmission.
⑥ 575 rpm for non-California models with air conditioning
⑦ 675 rpm with air conditioning on and compressor clutch wires disconnected

B Before Top Dead Center TDC Top Dead Center — Not applicable

Ventura, 1974 GTO, Astre, Sunbird

TUNE-UP SPECIFICATIONS

When analyzing compression test results, look for uniformity among cylinders rather than specific pressures.

ENGINE			SPARK PLUGS		DISTRIBUTOR		IGNITION TIMING (deg) ▲		VALVES	Fuel	IDLE SPEED ● (rpm) ▲	
Year	No. Cyl Displacement (cu in.)	hp	Type	Gap (in.)	Point Dwell (deg)	Point Gap (in.)	Man Trans ●	Auto Trans	Intake Opens ■ (deg)	Pump Pressure (psi)	Man Trans	Auto Trans
'71	6-250	145	R-45T	.035	31-34	.019	4B	4B	16	4-5	500	500
	8-307	200	R-45TS	.035	29-31	.019	4B	8B	28	5½-7½	600	550
'72	6-250	110	R-45T	.035	31-34	.019	4B	4B	16	4-5	700①/450	600①/450
	8-307	130	R-45TS	.035	29-31	.019	4B	8B	28	5½-7½	900①/450	600①/450
	8-350	160	R-46TS	.035	29-31	.019	10B	10B	16	5-6½	800	625
'73	6-250	110	R-46T	.035	31-34	.019	6B	6B	16	4-5	700/450①	600
	8-350 SE	150	R-46TS	.040	29-31	.019	10B	12B	16	5-6½	900/600①	650
	8-350 DE	175	R-46TS	.040	29-31	.019	10B	12B	16	5-6½	900/600①	650
'74	6-250	all	R-46T	.035	32½	.019	6B	6B	16	4-5	850/450①	600/450①
	8-350 2 bbl	all	R-46TS	.040	30	.019	10B	12B(10B)	26	5-6½	900/600①	650(625)
	8-350 4 bbl	all	R-46TS	.040	30	.019	10B	12B(10B)	26	5-6½	1000/600①	650(625)
'75	4-140 1 bbl	78	R-43TSX	.060	Electronic		8B	10B	22④	3-4½	1000	750
	4-140 2 bbl	87	R-43TSX	.060	Electronic		10B	12B	28④	3-4½	1000	750
	6-250	100	R-46TX	.060	Electronic		10B	10B	16	4-5	850	550(600)
	8-260	110	R-46SX	.080	Electronic		16B	18B(16)	14	5-6½	—	600
	8-350 2 bbl	145	R-45TSX	.060	Electronic		—	12B	19	5-6½	—	650(625)
	8-350 4 bbl	165	R-45TSX	.060	Electronic		—	12B	19	5-6½	—	650(625)
'76	4-140 1 bbl	69	R-43TSX	—	Electronic		8B	10B	22	3-4½	700	750
	4-140 2 bbl	87(80)	R-43TSX	—	Electronic		8B	10B	28	3-4½	700	750
	V6-231	110	R-44SX	.060	Electronic		12B	12B	17	3-4½	800	600
	6-250	100	R-46TX	.060	Electronic		—	10B	16	4½-5½	850	550(600)⑤
	8-260	110	R-46SX	.080	Electronic		16B(14)	18B(14)	14	7-8½	750	550(600)⑥
	8-350 2 bbl	135	R-45TSX	.060	Electronic		—	12B	22	7-8½	—	—
	8-350 4 bbl	155	R-45TSX	.060	Electronic		—	12B	26	7-8½	—	600

① Lower figure indicates idle speed with solenoid disconnected
④ See text for valve lash adjustment
⑤ 575 rpm for non-California models with air conditioning
⑥ 675 rpm with air conditioning on and compressor clutch wires disconnected

CAPACITIES

Year	ENGINE No. Cyl. Displacement (Cu. In.)	Engine Crankcase Add 1 Qt For New Filter	TRANSMISSION Pts To Refill After Draining Manual 3-Speed	4-Speed	Automatic ●	Drive Axle (pts)	Gasoline Tank (gals)	COOLING SYSTEM (qts) With Heater	With A/C
'70	6-250	4	3.5	——	6	3④	20②	13	——
	8-350	5	3.5③	2.5	6	3④	20②	19.9	19.9
	8-400	5	2.5	2.5	7.5	3④	20②	18.3	18.3
	8-455	5	2.5	2.5	7.5	3④	20②	17.5	17.5
'71	6-250	4	3.5	——	6	3④	19	13	12.4
	8-350	5	3.5③	2.5	6	3④	19	20	20.5
	8-400	5	2.8	2.5	7.5	3④	19	18.6	20.8
	8-455	5	2.8	2.5	7.5	3④	19	17.9	16.8
'72	6-250	4	3.5	——	6	3④	20②	13	12.4
	8-350	5	3.5	2.5	6	3④	20②	20	20.5
	8-400	5	2.8	2.5	7.5	3④	20②	18.6	20.8
	8-455	5	——	2.5	7.5	3④	20②	17.9	19

Tempest, 1969-73 GTO, LeMans, Grand Am — CAPACITIES (con't.)

Year	ENGINE No. Cyl. Displacement (Cu. In.)	Engine Crankcase Add 1 Qt For New Filter	TRANSMISSION Pts To Refill After Draining — Manual 3-Speed	Manual 4-Speed	Automatic ●	Drive Axle (pts)	Gasoline Tank (gals)	COOLING SYSTEM (qts) With Heater	With A/C
'73	6-250	4	3.5	—	7.5	4.25	21.8	13.3	—
	8-350	5	3.5	2.5	7.5	4.25⑦	21.8⑧	22.0	23.1
	8-400	5	2.8/3.5⑥	2.5	7.5	4.25⑦	21.8⑧⑨	22.0/23.0⑩	23.1/24.0⑩
	8-455	5	—	2.5	7.5	4.25⑦	21.8⑨	21.1	22.2
'74	6-250	4	3.5	—	7.5	4.25	21.8	13.3	—
	8-350	5	2.8/3.5⑥	2.5	7.5	4.25⑦	21.8⑧	22.0	23.2
	8-400	5	—	2.5	7.5	4.25⑦	21.8⑧⑨	22.0/23.0⑩	23.2/24.0⑩
	8-455	5	—	—	7.5	4.25⑦	21.5⑨	21.2	21.3
'75-'76	6-250	4	3.5	—	7.5	3	21.0	14.8	14.8
	8-350	5	—	—	7.5	3⑪	21.0⑧	21.8	21.8
	8-400	5	—	—	7.5	3⑪	21.0⑧⑨	23.8	21.8
	8-455	5	—	—	7.5	3⑪	21.0⑨	21.6	21.6

- ● '70 and later specifications do not include torque converter
- ① GTO close ratio 4-speed transmission—2.5 pts
- ② Station wagons: '69—20 gals, '70—22.5 gals, '72—23 gals less 1 gal for California cars—'70
- ③ 2.8 pts with heavy duty 3-speed transmission
- ④ 5 pts with 8.875 in. ring gear
- ⑤ 16 pts with 3-speed transmission
- ⑥ Lower figure represents 3-speed Muncie transmission; higher figure indicates 3-speed Saginaw transmission
- ⑦ 5.5 pts with 8.875 in. ring gear (station wagon)
- ⑧ 22 gals station wagon
- ⑨ 25 gals Grand Am
- ⑩ Lower figure indicates 2 bbl engine; higher figure indicates 4 bbl engine
- ⑪ 4.9 on wagon, optional on sedans
- OHC Overhead cam engine
- — Not applicable

Firebird — CAPACITIES

Year	ENGINE No. Cyl. Displacement (Cu. In.)	Engine Crankcase Add 1 Qt For New Filter	TRANSMISSION Pts To Refill After Draining — Manual 3-Speed	Manual 4-Speed	Automatic ●	Drive Axle (pts)	Gasoline Tank (gals)	COOLING SYSTEM (qts) With Heater	With A/C
'69	6-250 OHC	5	3.5	3.5	15④	3	21.5	11.9	12.3
	8-350	5	3.5①	2.5	15④	3	21.5	19.9	20.3
	8-400	5	2.8	2.5	19	3②	21.5	18.3	18.7
'70	6-250	4	3.5	—	6	3②	19.5③	13	—
	8-350	5	3.5①	2.5	6	3②	19.5③	19.9	19.9
	8-400	5	2.5	2.5	7.5	3②	19.5③	18.3	18.3
	8-455	5	2.5	2.5	7.5	3②	19.5③	17.5	17.5
'71	6-250	4	3.5	—	6	4.25	17	12	12.4
	8-350	5	3.5①	2.5	6	4.25	17	20	20.5
	8-400	5	2.8	2.5	7.5	4.25	17	18.6	18.7
	8-455	5	2.8	2.5	7.5	4.25	17	17.9	16.8
'72	6-250	4	3.5	—	6	4.25	17	12	12.4
	8-350	5	3.5	2.5	6	4.25	17	20	20.5
	8-400	5	2.8	2.5	7.5	4.25	17	18.6	18.7
	8-455	5	—	2.5	7.5	4.25	17	17.9	19
'73	6-250	4	3.5	—	7.5	4.25	18	12.5	—
	8-350	5	3.5	2.5	7.5	4.25	18	22.4	22.7
	8-400	5	—	2.5	7.5	4.25	18	22.4	22.7/23.5④
	8-455	5	—	2.5	7.5	4.25	18	20.9	21.8

Firebird CAPACITIES (con't.)

Year	ENGINE No. Cyl. Displacement (Cu. In.)	Engine Crankcase Add 1 Qt For New Filter	TRANSMISSION Pts To Refill After Draining Manual 3-Speed	Manual 4-Speed	Automatic ●	Drive Axle (pts)	Gasoline Tank (gals)	COOLING SYSTEM (qts) With Heater	With A/C
'74	6-250	4	3.5	—	7.5	4.25	20.2	12.5	—
	8-350	5	3.5	2.5	7.5	4.25	20.2	22.4	22.8
	8-400	5	—	2.5	7.5	4.25	20.2	22.4	22.7/23.6④
	8-455	5	—	2.5	7.5	4.25	20.2	20.9	21.9
'75-'76	6-250	4	3.5	—	8.0	4.25	21.5	13.5	13.5
	8-350	5	—	2.5	8.0	4.25	21.5	21.6	21.6
	8-400	5	—	2.5	8.0	4.25	21.5	23.5	23.5

● '70 and later specifications do not include torque converter
① 2.8 pts with heavy duty 3-speed transmission
② 4 pts with heavy duty axle
③ California cars—18.5 gals
④ Lower figure indicates 2 bbl model; higher figure indicates 4 bbl engine
OHC Overhead camshaft
— Not applicable

Ventura, 1974 GTO, Astre CAPACITIES

Year	ENGINE No. Cyl. Displacement (Cu. In.)	Engine Crankcase Add 1 Qt For New Filter	TRANSMISSION Pts To Refill After Draining Manual 3-Speed	Manual 4-Speed	Automatic ●	Drive Axle (pts)	Gasoline Tank (gals)	COOLING SYSTEM (qts) With Heater	With A/C
'71	6-250	4	3	—	6	3.75	16	12	—
	8-307	4	3	—	6①	3.75	16	15	16
'72	6-250	4	3	—	6	3.75	16	12	16
	8-307	4	3	—	6①	3.75	16	15	16
	8-350	5	—	—	5	3.75	16	19.4	20.3
'73	6-250	4	3.5	—	6	4.25	21.5	12.1	—
	8-350	5	3.5	2.5	5	4.25	21.5	12.1	12.1
'74	6-250	4	3.5	—	6	4.25	20.5	12.1	—
	8-350	5	3.5	2.5	7.5	4.25	20.5	19.2	19.3
'75-'76	4-140 OHC	3	3	3	8	2.8	16	7.6	8
	V6-231	4	—	3	6	2.8	18.5	13.4	14.2
	6-250	4	3.5	—	5.0	3.75	20.5	13.5	13.5
	8-260	4	3.5	—	5.0	3.75	20.5	18.5	19.5
	8-350	4	—	—	5.0	3.75	20.5	18.5	19.5

• Specifications do not include torque converter
① 5 pts with 3-speed transmission
— Not applicable

Tempest, 1969-73 GTO, Lemans, Grand Am VALVE SPECIFICATIONS

Year	Engine No. Cyl. Displacement (cu in.)	Seat Angle (deg) ■	Face Angle (deg) ●	Outer Spring Test Pressure▲ (lbs @ in.)	Spring Installed Height (in.)	STEM TO GUIDE Clearance (in.) Intake	Exhaust	STEM Diameter (in.) Intake	Exhaust
'69	6-250 1 bbl	45	44	98 @ 1.63	1 5/8	.0016-.0033	.0021-.0038	.3416	.3411
	6-250 4 bbl	45	44	65 @ 1.63	1 5/8	.0016-.0033	.0021-.0038	.3416	.3411
	8-350 2 bbl	45	44	63 @ 1.58	1 37/64	.0016-.0033	.0021-.0038	.3416	.3411
	8-350 4 bbl	45	44	83 @ 1.59	1 19/32	.0016-.0033	.0021-.0038	.3416	.3411
	8-400 2 bbl	30	29	63 @ 1.58	1 37/64	.0016-.0033	.0021-.0038	.3416	.3411
	8-400 4 bbl	30	29	66 @ 1.56	1 5/8	.0016-.0033	.0021-.0038	.3416	.3411
	8-400 R.A.	30	29	83 @ 1.59	1 19/32	.0016-.0032	.0021-.0038	.3416	.3411
	8-400 R.A. IV	30	29	75 @ 1.82	1 53/64	.0016-.0033	.0021-.0038	.3416	.3411

Tempest, Lemans, Grand Am 1969-73 GTO, VALVE SPECIFICATIONS (con't.)

Year	Engine No. Cyl. Displacement (cu in.)	Seat Angle (deg) ■	Face Angle (deg) ●	Outer Spring Test Pressure▲ (lbs @ in.)	Spring Installed Height (in.)	STEM TO GUIDE Clearance (in.) Intake	STEM TO GUIDE Clearance (in.) Exhaust	STEM Diameter (in.) Intake	STEM Diameter (in.) Exhaust
'70	6-250 1 bbl	46④	45⑤	60 @ 1.66	1 21/32	.0010-.0027	.0021-.0027	.3414	.3414
	8-350 2 bbl	45	44	63 @ 1.58	1 37/64	.0010-.0033	.0021-.0038	.3416	.3416
	8-400 2 bbl	45	44	63 @ 1.58	1 37/64	.0016-.0033	.0021-.0038	.3416	.3411
	8-400② 4 bbl	30	29	61 @ 1.59	1 19/32	.0016-.0033	.0021-.0038	.3416	.3411
	8-400③ 4 bbl	30	29	66 @ 1.56	1 9/16	.0016-.0033	.0021-.0038	.3416	.3416
	8-400 R.A. IV	30	29	76 @ 1.82	1 13/16	.0016-.0033	.0021-.0038	.3416	.3411
	8-455	30	29	66 @ 1.56	1 9/16	.0016-.0033	.0021-.0038	.3416	.3411
'71	6-250 1 bbl	46④	45⑤	61 @ 1.66	1 21/32	.0010-.0027	.0010-.0027	.3414	.3414
	8-350 2 bbl	45	44	61 @ 1.59	1 19/32	.0016-.0033	.0012-.0038	.3416	.3411
	8-400⑥	30	29	60 @ 1.60	1 19/32	.0016-.0033	.0021-.0038	.3416	.3411
	8-400 2 bbl	45	44	61 @ 1.59	1 19/32	.0016-.0033	.0021-.0038	.3416	.3411
	8-400 4 bbl	30	29	65 @ 1.57	1 9/16	.0016-.0033	.0021-.0038	.3416	.3411
	8-455	30	29	65 @ 1.57	1 9/16	.0016-.0033	.0021-.0038	.3416	.3416
	8-455 H.O.	30	29	66 @ 1.56	1 9/16	.0016-.0033	.0021-.0038	.3416	.3416
'72	6-250	46④	45⑤	60 @ 1.66	1 21/32	.0010-.0027	.0010-.0027	.3414	.3414
	8-350	45	44	61 @ 1.59	1 19/32	.0016-.0033	.0021-.0038	.3416	.3411
	8-400⑥	30	29	60 @ 1.60	1 19/32	.0016-.0033	.0021-.0038	.3416	.3411
	8-400 2 bbl	45	44	61 @ 1.59	1 19/32	.0016-.0033	.0021-.0038	.3416	.3411
	8-400 4 bbl	30	29	65 @ 1.57	1 9/16	.0016-.0033	.0021-.0038	.3416	.3411
	8-455	30	29	64 @ 1.57	1 9/16	.0016-.0033	.0021-.0038	.3416	.3416
	8-455 H.O.	30	29	66 @ 1.56	1 9/16	.0016-.0033	.0021-.0038	.3416	.3416
'73	6-250	46④	45⑤	60 @ 1.66	1 21/32	.0010-.0027	.0010-.0027	.3414	.3414
	8-350	45	44	61 @ 1.59	1 19/32	.0016-.0033	.0021-.0038	.3416	.3411
	8-400 4 bbl	30	29	60 @ 1.60	1 19/32	.0016-.0033	.0021-.0038	.3416	.3411
	8-400 2 bbl	45	44	61 @ 1.59	1 19/32	.0016-.0033	.0021-.0038	.3416	.3411
	8-400 4 bbl auto.	30	29	65 @ 1.57	1 9/16	.0016-.0033	.0021-.0038	.3416	.3411
	8-455	30	29	64 @ 1.57	1 9/16	.0016-.0033	.0021-.0038	.3416	.3411
	8-455 S.D.	45	44	70 @ 1.82	1 9/16	.0016-.0033	.0021-.0038	.3416	.3416
'74	6-250	46④	45⑤	60 @ 1.66	1 21/32	.0010-.0027	.0010-.0027	.3414	.3414
	8-350	45	44	61 @ 1.59	1 19/32	.0016-.0033	.0021-.0038	.3416	.3411
	8-400 4 bbl	30	29	60 @ 1.60	1 19/32	.0016-.0033	.0021-.0038	.3416	.3411
	8-400 2 bbl	45	44	61 @ 1.59	1 19/32	.0016-.0033	.0021-.0038	.3416	.3411
	8-400 4 bbl auto.	30	29	65 @ 1.57	1 9/16	.0016-.0033	.0021-.0038	.3416	.3411
	8-455	30	29	64 @ 1.57	1 9/16	.0016-.0033	.0021-.0038	.3416	.3411
'75-	6-250	46④	45⑤	57 @ 1.27	1 21/32	.0010-.0027	.0015-.0032	.3414	.3414
'76	8-350	45	44	61 @ 1.59	1 19/32	.0016-.0033	.0021-.0038	.3416	.3411
	8-400 2 bbl	45	44	61 @ 1.59	1 19/32	.0016-.0033	.0021-.0038	.3416	.3411
	8-400 4 bbl	30	29	60 @ 1.60	1 9/16	.0016-.0033	.0021-.0038	.3416	.3411
	8-455 4 bbl	30	29	65 @ 1.57	1 9/16	.0016-.0033	.0021-.0038	.3416	.3411

■ Intake valve seat angles are shown. All exhaust valve seat angles are 45° unless otherwise indicated.
● Intake valve face angles are shown. All exhaust valve face angles are 44° unless otherwise indicated.
① Not used
② Standard and Ram Air GTO with manual transmission
③ Standard GTO with automatic transmission
④ Exhaust valve seat angle 46°
⑤ Exhaust valve face angle 45°
⑥ All 400 cu in. engines with manual transmission
— Not specified

▲INNER SPRING TEST PRESSURE

Year	Engine	Pressure
'69	6-250 4 bbl	34 @ 1.59
	8-350 2 bbl	35 @ 1.54
	8-350 4 bbl	45 @ 1.64
	8-400 2 bbl	35 @ 1.54
	8-400 4 bbl	38 @ 1.52
	8-400 RA IV	45 @ 1.52⑩
'70	8-350 2 bbl	35 @ 1.54
	8-400 2 bbl	35 @ 1.54
	8-400⑪ 4 bbl	57 @ 1.52
	8-400⑫ 4 bbl	38 @ 1.52
	8-400 RA IV	40 @ 1.75
	8-455	38 @ 1.52
'71	8-350 2 bbl	33 @ 1.55
	8-400⑬	56 @ 1.53
	8-400 2 bbl	33 @ 1.55
	8-450 4 bbl	36 @ 1.53
	8-455	37 @ 1.53
	8-455 HO	38 @ 1.52
'72	8-350	33 @ 1.55
	8-400⑬	56 @ 1.53
	8-400 2 bbl	33 @ 1.55
	8-400 4 bbl	36 @ 1.53
	8-455	37 @ 1.53
	8-455 HO	38 @ 1.52
'73	8-350	33 @ 1.55
	8-400 4 bbl	56 @ 1.53
	8-400 2 bbl	33 @ 1.55
	8-400 4 bbl auto.	36 @ 1.53
	8-455	37 @ 1.53
	8-455 S.D.	40 @ 1.75
'74-'76	8-350	33 @ 1.55
	8-400 4 bbl	56 @ 1.53
	8-400 2 bbl	33 @ 1.55
	8-400 4 bbl auto.	36 @ 1.53
	8-455	37 @ 1.53

⑦ Not used
⑧ Not used
⑨ Not used
⑩ With manual trans.—38 @ 1.52
⑪ Standard GTO with manual transmission and all Ram Air
⑫ Standard GTO with automatic transmission
⑬ All 400 cu in. engines with manual transmission

Firebird, Ventura, 1974 GTO, Astre, Sunbird — VALVE SPECIFICATIONS

Year	Engine No. Cyl. Displacement (cu in.)	Seat Angle (deg) ■	Face Angle (deg) ●	Outer Spring Test Pressure▲ (lbs @ in.)	Spring Installed Height (in.)	STEM TO GUIDE Clearance (in.) Intake	Exhaust	STEM Diameter (in.) Intake	Exhaust
'69	6-250 1 bbl	45	44	97 @ 1.63	1 5/8	.0016-.0033	.0021-.0038	.3416	.3411
	6-250 4 bbl	45	44	65 @ 1.63	1 5/8	.0016-.0033	.0021-.0038	.3416	.3411
	8-350 2 bbl	45	44	63 @ 1.58	1 37/64	.0016-.0033	.0021-.0038	.3416	.3411
	8-350 4 bbl	45	44	83 @ 1.59	1 19/32	.0016-.0033	.0021-.0038	.3416	.3411
	8-400 4 bbl	30	29	66 @ 1.56	1 5/8	.0016-.0033	.0021-.0038	.3416	.3411
	8-400 Ram Air	30	29	83 @ 1.59	1 19/32	.0016-.0033	.0021-.0038	.3416	.3411
	8-400 Ram Air II	30	29	75 @ 1.82	1 53/64	.0016-.0033	.0021-.0038	.3416	.3411
'70	6-250 1 bbl	46④	45④	60 @ 1.66	1 21/32	.0010-.0027	.0010-.0027	.3414	.3414
	8-350 2 bbl	45	44	63 @ 1.58	1 37/64	.0016-.0033	.0021-.0038	.3416	.3416
	8-400 2 bbl	45	44	63 @ 1.58	1 37/64	.0016-.0033	.0021-.0038	.3416	.3411
	8-400② 4 bbl	30	29	61 @ 1.59	1 19/32	.0016-.0033	.0021-.0038	.3416	.3411
	8-400③ 4 bbl	30	29	66 @ 1.56	1 9/16	.0016-.0033	.0021-.0038	.3416	.3416
	8-400 Ram Air	30	29	61 @ 1.59	1 19/32	.0016-.0033	.0021-.0038	.3416	.3411
'71	6-250 1 bbl	46④	45④	61 @ 1.66	1 21/32	.0010-.0027	.0010-.0027	.3414	.3414
	8-307 2 bbl	46④	45④	80 @ 1.70	1 45/64	.0010-.0027	.0010-.0027	.3414	.3414
	8-350 2 bbl	45	44	61 @ 1.57	1 19/32	.0016-.0033	.0021-.0058	.3416	.3411
	8-400②	30	29	60 @ 1.60	1 19/32	.0016-.0033	.0021-.0038	.3416	.3411
	8-400 2 bbl	45	44	61 @ 1.59	1 19/32	.0016-.0033	.0021-.0038	.3416	.3411
	8-400 4 bbl	30	29	65 @ 1.57	1 9/16	.0016-.0033	.0021-.0038	.3416	.3411
	8-455	30	29	65 @ 1.57	1 9/16	.0016-.0033	.0021-.0038	.3416	.3416
	8-455 H.O.	30	29	66 @ 1.56	1 9/16	.0016-.0033	.0021-.0038	.3416	.3416

Firebird, Ventura, 1974 GTO, Astre, Sunbird

VALVE SPECIFICATIONS (con't.)

Year	Engine No. Cyl. Displacement (cu in.)	Seat Angle (deg) ■	Face Angle (deg) ●	Outer Spring Test Pressure▲ (lbs @ in.)	Spring Installed Height (in.)	STEM TO GUIDE Clearance (in.)		STEM Diameter (in.)	
						Intake	Exhaust	Intake	Exhaust
'72	6-250 1 bbl	46④	45④	60 @ 1.66	1 21/32	.0010-.0027	.0010-.0027	.3414	.3414
	8-307 2 bbl	46④	45④	81 @ 1.70	1 45/64	.0010-.0027	.0010-.0027	.3414	.3414
	8-350⑤ 2 bbl	46④	45④	60 @ 1.66	1 21/32	.0010-.0027	.0010-.0027	.3414	.3414
	8-350⑥ 2 bbl	45	44	61 @ 1.59	1 19/32	.0016-.0033	.0021-.0038	.3414	.3411
	8-400②	30	29	60 @ 1.60	1 19/32	.0016-.0033	.0021-.0038	.3416	.3411
	8-400 2 bbl	45	44	61 @ 1.59	1 19/32	.0016-.0033	.0021-.0038	.3416	.3411
	8-400 4 bbl	30	29	65 @ 1.57	1 9/16	.0016-.0033	.0021-.0038	.3416	.3411
	8-455 H.O.	30	29	66 @ 1.56	1 9/16	.0016-.0033	.0021-.0038	.3416	.3416
'73	6-250 1 bbl	46④	45④	60 @ 1.66	1 21/32	.0010-.0027	.0010-.0027	.3414	.3414
	8-350 2 bbl	45	44	61 @ 1.59	1 19/32	.0016-.0033	.0021-.0038	.3414	.3411
	8-400②	30	29	60 @ 1.60	1 19/32	.0016-.0033	.0021-.0038	.3416	.3411
	8-400 2 bbl	45	44	61 @ 1.59	1 19/32	.0016-.0033	.0021-.0038	.3416	.3411
	8-400 4 bbl	30	29	65 @ 1.57⑦	1 9/16	.0016-.0033	.0021-.0038	.3416	.3411
	8-455	30	29	66 @ 1.56⑨	1 9/16	.0016-.0033	.0021-.0038	.3416	.3411⑨
'74	6-250 1 bbl	46④	45④	60 @ 1.66	1 21/32	.0010-.0027	.0010-.0027	.3414	.3414
	8-350	45	44	61 @ 1.59	1 19/32	.0016-.0033	.0021-.0038	.3414	.3411
	8-400 2 bbl	45	44	61 @ 1.59	1 19/32	.0016-.0033	.0021-.0038	.3416	.3411
	8-400 4 bbl	30	29	65 @ 1.57⑩	1 9/16	.0016-.0033	.0021-.0038	.3416	.3411
	8-455	30	29	66 @ 1.56	1 9/16	.0016-.0033	.0021-.0038	.3416	.3411
	8-455 SD	45	44	70 @ 1.82	1 9/16	.0016-.0033	.0021-.0038	.3416	.3416
'75-	4-140 OHC	46④	45④	75 @ 1.75	1 3/4	.0010-.0027	.0010-.0027	.3414	.3414
'76	V6-231	45	45	64 @ 1.73	1 47/64	.0015-.0035	.0015-.0032	.3407	.3407
'76	6-250	46④	45④	57 @ 1.27	1 21/32	.0010-.0027	.0015-.0032	.3414	.3414
	8-260	45⑪	44⑫	81 @ 1.67	—	.0010-.0027	.0015-.0032	.3429	.3424
	8-350	45	44	61 @ 1.59	1 19/32	.0016-.0033	.0021-.0038	.3416	.3411
	8-350 Ventura	45	45	75 @ 1.73	1 23/32	.0015-.0035	.0015-.0032	.3725	.3727
	8-400	30	29	60 @ 1.60	1 9/16	.0016-.0033	.0021-.0038	.3416	.3411

■ Intake valve seat angles are shown. All exhaust valve seat angles are 45° unless otherwise indicated.
● Intake valve face angles are shown. All exhaust valve face angles are 44° unless otherwise indicated.
① Not used
② Manual transmission with 400 cu in. engine
③ Automatic transmission with 400 cu in. engine
④ Exhaust valve seat and face angles are the same as intake valve seat and face angles
⑤ Ventura II only
⑥ Firebird only
⑦ 59 @ 1.50 with manual transmission
⑧ 70 @ 1.82 for 455 S.D. engine
⑨ .3416 in. for 455 S.D. engine
⑩ 60 @ 1.60 with manual transmission
⑪ Exhaust—31
⑫ Exhaust—30
— Not specified

▲INNER SPRING TEST PRESSURE
(lbs @ in.)

Year	Engine No. Cyl Displacement (cu in.)	Test Pressure
'69	6-250 4 bbl	34 @ 1.59
	8-350 2 bbl	35 @ 1.54
	8-350 4 bbl	45 @ 1.52
	8-400 4 bbl	38 @ 1.32
	8-400 Ram Air II	45 @ 1.52③
'70	8-350 2 bbl	35 @ 1.54
	8-400 2 bbl	35 @ 1.54
	8-400 4 bbl	57 @ 1.52④
	8-400 4 bbl	45 @ 1.52⑤
	8-400 Ram Air	57 @ 1.52
'71	8-350 2 bbl	33 @ 1.55
	8-400	56 @ 1.53④
	8-400 2 bbl	33 @ 1.55
	8-400 4 bbl	36 @ 1.53
	8-455	37 @ 1.53
	8-455 H.O.	38 @ 1.52
'72	8-400	56 @ 1.53④
	8-400 2 bbl	33 @ 1.55
	8-400 4 bbl	36 @ 1.53
	8-455 H.O.	38 @ 1.52
'73	8-350	33 @ 1.55
	8-400	56 @ 1.53④
	8-400 2 bbl	33 @ 1.55
	8-400 4 bbl	36 @ 1.53
	8-455	36 @ 1.53⑥
'74-'76	8-350⑦	33 @ 1.55
	8-400	56 @ 1.53④
	8-400 2 bbl	33 @ 1.55
	8-400 4 bbl	36 @ 1.53
	8-455	36 @ 1.53⑥

① Not used
② Not used
③ With manual transmission: 38 @ 1.52
④ 400 cu in. engine with manual transmission
⑤ 400 cu in. engine with automatic transmission
⑥ 40 @ 1.75 for 455 S.D.
⑦ Except '75-'76 Ventura 350

TORQUE SPECIFICATIONS

All readings in ft lbs

Year	Engine No. Cyl. Displacement (cu in.)	Cylinder Head Bolts	Rod Bearing Bolts	Main Bearing Bolts	Crankshaft Damper or Pulley Bolt	Flywheel to Crankshaft Bolts	MANIFOLD Intake	MANIFOLD Exhaust
'69	6-250 OHC	85-100	30-35	60-70	Pressed on	60-70	25-40	15-25
	8-350, 400	85-100	40-46	90-110④	130-190	85-100	20-35	30-45
'70-'74	6-250	95	35	65	Pressed on	60	25-30①	25
	8-350, 400, 455	95	43②	90-110④	160	95	40	30
	8-307 ('71-'72)	65	45	75	60	60	30	25
'75-'76	4-140 OHC	60	35	65	80	60	30	30
	6-231	75	40	115	150③	55	45	25
	6-250	95	35	65	Pressed on	60	25-30①	25③
	8-260	85	42	120	310	90	40	25
	8-350, 400, 455	95	43	100④	160	95	40	30
	8-350 Ventura	80	40	115	140	60	45	28

① End bolts 15-20 ft. lbs.
② 63 ft lbs on 455 S.D. engine
③ With integral intake manifold cast into head—18-23 for four end bolts, 30-35 for all others
④ Rear cap—120

CRANKSHAFT AND CONNECTING ROD SPECIFICATIONS

All measurements are given in inches

Year	Engine No. Cyl. Displacement (cu in.)	CRANKSHAFT Main Brg. Journal Dia	CRANKSHAFT Main Brg. Oil Clearance	CRANKSHAFT Shaft End-Play	CRANKSHAFT Thrust on No.	CONNECTING ROD Journal Diameter	CONNECTING ROD Oil Clearance	CONNECTING ROD Side Clearance
'69	8-400	3.00	.0002-.0017	.0035-.0085	4	2.250	.0005-.0026	.006-.011①
	6-250 OHC	2.30	.0003-.0019	.002-.006	7	2.000	.0007-.0027③	.0085-.0135
	8-350	3.00	.0002-.0017④	.0035-.0085	4	2.250	.0005-.0025	.006-.011①
	8-400	3.00	.0002-.0017④	.0035-.0085	4	2.250	.0005-.0026⑤	.006-.011①
'70	6-250	2.30	.0003-.0029	.002-.006	7	2.000	.0007-.0027	.009-.013
	8-350	3.00	.0002-.0017	.0035-.0085	4	2.250	.0005-.0025	.012-.017①
	8-400	3.00	.0002-.0017⑥	.0035-.0085	4	2.250	.0005-.0026⑤	.012-.017①
	8-455	3.25	.0005-.0021	.0035-.0085	4	2.250	.0010-.0031	.012-.017①

CRANKSHAFT AND CONNECTING ROD SPECIFICATIONS (con't.)

All measurements are given in inches

Year	Engine No. Cyl. Displacement (cu in.)	CRANKSHAFT				CONNECTING ROD		
		Main Brg. Journal Dia	Main Brg. Oil Clearance	Shaft End-Play	Thrust on No.	Journal Diameter	Oil Clearance	Side Clearance
'71-'74	6-250	2.30	.0003-.0029	.002-.006	7	2.000	.0007-.0027	.009-.014⑩
	8-307 ('71-'72)	⑦	⑧	.002-.006	5	2.099-2.100	.0013-.0035	.002-.006①
	8-350	3.00	.0002-.0017	.003-.009	4	2.250	.0005-.0025	.012-.017①
	8-400	3.00	.0002-.0017	.003-.009	4	2.250	.0005-.0025	.012-.017①
	8-455	3.25	⑨⑪⑫	.003-.009	4	2.250	.0005-.0025⑬	.012-.017①
'75-'76	4-140 OHC	2.30	.0003-.0027⑮	.002-.007	4	2.000	.0007-.0038	.009-.014
	V6-231	2.4995	.0004-.0015	.004-.008	2	2.000	.0002-.0023	.006-.014
	6-250	2.30	.0003-.0029	.002-.006	7	2.000	.0007-.0027	.009-.014
	8-260	2.50	.0005-.0021⑯	.004-.008	3	2.124	.0005-.0026	.006-.020
	8-350, 400	3.00	.0002-.0017	.003-.009	4	2.250	.0005-.0025	.012-.017⑭
	8-350 Ventura	3.00	.0004-.0015	.003-.009	3	2.000	.0005-.0026	.006-.020
	8-455	3.25	.0005-.0021	.003-.009	4	2.250	.0005-.0025	.012-.017⑭

① Total for 2 connecting rods
② Not used
③ .0007-.0028 on 6 Cyl. 4-BBL. engine option
④ .0012-.0028 on Ram Air IV engine option
⑤ .0015-.0031 on Ram Air IV engine option
⑥ No.'s 1, 2, 3, 4 on Ram Air IV option—.0007-.0023
No.'s 1, 2, 3, 4 on Ram Air IV option—.0012-.0028
No. 5 on Ram Air IV option—.0007-.0022
⑦ No.'s 1, 2, 3, 4—2.4484-2.4493
No. 5—2.4479-2.4488
⑧ No. 1—.0008-.0020
No.'s 2, 3, 4—.0011-.0023
⑨ No. 1 bearing cap w/small valve—.0003-.0019
All others—.0005-.0021
⑩ .007-.016 in 1973
⑪ 1973-74—.0005-.0021 (455); .0010-.0026 (455 S.D.)
⑫ No. 1 on 1974 455—.0035-.0020
⑬ .0015-.0031 in 455 SD
⑭ Total for two
⑮ .0003-.0020 for no. 1
⑯ .0015-.0031 for no. 5

RING GAP

All measurements are given in inches

Year	Engine No. Cyl. Displacement (cu. in.)	Top Compression	Bottom Compression
'69	6-250	.005-.025	.005-.025
'69	8-350, 400	.010-.030	.010-.030
'71-'72	8-307	.010-.020	.010-.020
'70-'76	8-350, 400	.019	.015
'70-'76	8-455	.021	.015
'70-'76	6-250	.010-.020	.015-.055
'75-'76	4-140 OHC	.015-.025	.009-.019
'75-'76	8-350 Ventura	.010-.020	.010-.020
'75-'76	V6-231, 8-260	.010-.023	.010-.023

Year	Engine	Oil Control
'69-'74	All engines	.015-.055
'75-'76	4-140 OHC	.010-.030
'75-'76	6-250	.015-.055
'75-'76	8-350 Ventura	.015-.035
'75-'76	8-350, 400, 455	.035
'75-'76	V6-231, 8-260	.015-.055

RING SIDE CLEARANCE

All measurements are given in inches

Year	Engine No. Cyl. Displacement (cu. in.)	Top Compression	Bottom Compression
'69	6-250	.0015-.0050	.0015-.0050
'70-'76	6-250, 8-307 ('71-'72)	.0012-.0027	.0012-.0032
'69-'76	8-350, 400, 455	.0015-.0050	.0015-.0050
'75-'76	4-140 OHC	.0012-.0027	.0012-.0027
'75-'76	8-350 Ventura	.0030-.0050	.0030-.0050
'75-'76	8-260	.0020-.0040	.0020-.0040

Year	Engine	Oil Control
'69	6-250	.0015-.0050
'70-'76	6-250	.0001-.0050
'71-'72	8-307	.0020-.0070
'69-'76	8-350, 400, 455	.0015-.0050
'75-'76	4-140 OHC	.0000-.0050
'75-'76	8-350 Ventura	.0035-.0095
'75-'76	8-260	.0010-.0050

PISTON CLEARANCE

Year	Engine No. Cyl. Displacement (cu. in.)	Piston-to-Bore Clearance (in.)
'69	6-250 OHC	.0022-.0028
	8-350, 400	.0025-.0031
	8-400 Ram Air	.0055-.0061
'70	6-250	.0005-.0015
	8-350, 400	.0025-.0033
	8-400 Ram Air	.0055-.0061
'71	6-250	.0005-.0015
	8-350, 400	.0025-.0033
	8-307	.0005-.0011
'72	6-250	.0005-.0015
	8-350, 400, 455	.0025-.0033
	8-307	.0005-.0011
'73-'76	6-250	.0005-.0015
	8-350, 400	.0029-.0037
	8-455	.0021-.0029①
	8-455 S.D.	.0060-.0068②
'75-'76	4-140 OHC	.0018-.0028
	V6-231	.0008-.0014
	8-260	.0010-.0020
	8-350 Ventura	.0008-.0020

① .0025-.0033 for 1973
② .0064-.0072 for 1974

BATTERY AND STARTER SPECIFICATIONS

		BATTERY			STARTER						
					Lock Test			No-Load Test			
Year	Engine No. Cyl. Displacement (cu in.)	Ampere Hour ● Capacity	Volts	Terminal Grounded	Amps	Volts	Torque (ft lbs)	Amps	Volts	RPM	Brush Spring Tension (oz)
'69	6-250 OHC	44①	12	Neg.	Not Recommended			49-76	10.6	6,200-9,600	35
	8-350	53①	12	Neg.	Not Recommended			65-100	10.6	3,600-5,100	35
	8-400	61	12	Neg.	Not Recommended			Not Recommended			35
'70-'73	6-250	45①	12	Neg.	Not Recommended			Not Recommended			35
	6-Ventura II	45	12	Neg.	Not Recommended			50-80	9	5,500-10,500	35
	8-Ventura II (307—1971-72)	61	12	Neg.	Not Recommended			50-80	9	5,500-10,500	35
	8-350 P	53①	12	Neg.	Not Recommended			Not Recommended			35
	8-400, 455	61	12	Neg.	Not Recommended			Not Recommended			35
'74	6-250	2300, 4000	12	Neg.	Not Recommended			Not Recommended			35
	8-350, 400	2900, 3250	12	Neg.	Not Recommended			Not Recommended			35
	8-455	3250, 3750	12	Neg.	Not Recommended			Not Recommended			35
'75-'76	4-140 OHC	2300, 3200	12	Neg.	Not Recommended			Not Recommended			35
	6-250	2300, 3200, 4000	12	Neg.	Not Recommended			Not Recommended			35
	8-260, 350, 455	3200, 3500	12	Neg.	Not Recommended			Not Recommended			35
	Maintenance free option	3750	12	Neg.	Not Recommended			Not Recommended			35

① 61 amp battery used w/AC or H.D. battery option.
● Starting 1974, cranking power in watts is given

ALTERNATOR AND REGULATOR SPECIFICATIONS

	Alternator			Regulator						
					Field Relay			Regulator		
Year	Part No.	Field Current @ 12 V	Output (amps)	Part No.	Air Gap (in.)	Point Gap (in.)	Volts to Close	Air Gap (in.)	Point Gap (in.)	Volts @ 75°
'69	1100761	2.2-2.6	37	1119515②	.015	.030	1.5-3.2	.067	.014	13.5-16.0
	1100704	2.2-2.6	37	1119515	.015	.030	1.5-3.2	.067	.014	13.5-16.0
	1100832③	4.0-4.5	37	1119515	.015	.030	1.5-3.2	.067	.014	13.5-16.0
	1100830③	4.0-4.5	37	1119515	.015	.030	1.5-3.2	.067	.014	13.5-16.0
	1100700	2.2-2.6	55	1119515	.015	.030	1.5-3.2	.067	.014	13.5-16.0
	1100760	2.2-2.6	55	1119515	.015	.030	1.5-3.2	.067	.014	13.5-16.0
'70	1100704	2.2-2.6	37	1119515②	.015	.030	1.5-3.2	.067	.014	13.5-16.0
	1100888	2.2-2.6	55	1119515	.015	.030	1.5-3.2	.067	.014	13.5-16.0
	1100905	2.2-2.6	37	1119515	.015	.030	1.5-3.2	.067	.014	13.5-16.0
	1100700	2.2-2.6	55	1119515	.015	.030	1.5-3.2	.067	.014	13.5-16.0
	1100891	2.2-2.6	55	1119515	.015	.030	1.5-3.2	.067	.014	13.5-16.0
	1100892	2.2-2.6	55	1119515	.015	.030	1.5-3.2	.067	.014	13.5-16.0
	1100906	2.2-2.6	55	1119515	.015	.030	1.5-3.2	.067	.014	13.5-16.0
	1100895	2.2-2.6	61	1119515	.015	.030	1.5-3.2	.067	.014	13.5-16.0
'71-'74	1100550	4.0-4.5	37	1119515	.015	.030	1.5-3.2	.067	.014	13.8-14.8
	1100834	4.0-4.5	37	1119515	.015	.030	1.5-3.2	.067	.014	13.8-14.8
	1100927	4.0-4.5	37	Integral with Alternator						13.8-14.8
	1100566④	4.0-4.5	37	1119515	.015	.030	1.5-3.2	.067	.014	13.8-14.8
	1100836④	4.0-4.5	37	1119515	.015	.030	1.5-3.2	.067	.014	13.8-14.8
	1100920	4.0-4.5	55	Integral with Alternator						13.8-14.8
	1100928	4.0-4.5	55	Integral with Alternator						13.8-14.8
	1100843④	4.0-4.5	61	1119515	.015	.030	1.5-3.2	.067	.014	13.8-14.8
	11001015	4.0-4.5	80	Integral with Alternator						13.8-14.8
	1100497	4.0-4.9	37	Integral with Alternator						13.8-14.8
'75	1100545	4.0-4.5	32	Integral with Alternator						13.8-14.8
	1100560	4.0-4.5	55	Integral with Alternator						13.8-14.8
	1100497, 1102491	4.0-4.5	37	Integral with Alternator						13.8-14.8
	1102399, 1102388	4.0-4.5	37	Integral with Alternator						13.8-14.8
	1102457, 1102390	4.0-4.5	55	Integral with Alternator						13.8-14.8
	1102347, 1102486	4.0-4.5	61	Integral with Alternator						13.8-14.8
	1102481, 1102384	4.0-4.5	37	Integral with Alternator						13.8-14.8
	1102482 1102385	4.0-4.5	55	Integral with Alternator						13.8-14.8
	1101027, 1101016	4.0-4.5	80	Integral with Alternator						13.8-14.8
	1102483, 1102394	4.0-4.5	37	Integral with Alternator						13.8-14.8
	1102488, 1102840	4.0-4.5	55	Integral with Alternator						13.8-14.8

① Not used
② Transistor regulator 1116368 optional equipment until 1970
③ Integrated Circuit Generator (C.S.I.—no external regulator) optional on 1969 Firebird
④ Used only on Ventura

BRAKE SPECIFICATIONS

Year	Model	Master Cylinder Bore (in.) Disc	Master Cylinder Bore (in.) Drum	Wheel Cylinder Bore (in.) Front Disc	Wheel Cylinder Bore (in.) Front Drum	Wheel Cylinder Bore (in.) Rear	Brake Disc or Drum Diameter (in.) Front Disc	Brake Disc or Drum Diameter (in.) Front Drum	Brake Disc or Drum Diameter (in.) Rear
'69-'72	Tempest, Le Mans, GTO	1.125	1.0	2.938	1.125	.875	11.0	9.5	9.5
'73-'76	LeMans, Grand Am	1.0①	—	2.938	—	.875②	11.0	—	9.5③
'69	Firebird	1.125	1.0	2.938	1.125	.875	11.0	9.5	9.5
'70-'76	Firebird	1.0①	—	2.938	—	.875	11.0	—	9.5
'71-'76	Ventura	1.125	1.0	2.938	1.125	.875	11.0	9.5	9.5
'75-'76	Astre, Sunbird	1.159④	—	1.875	—	.750	9.88	—	9.0

① 1.125—with power brakes
② .9375 in. on station wagon
③ 11.0 in. on station wagon
④ 1.267—with power brakes
— Not applicable

WHEEL ALIGNMENT SPECIFICATIONS

Year	Model	Caster Range (deg)	Caster Pref Setting (deg)	Camber Range (deg)	Camber Pref Setting (deg)	Toe-in (in.)	Steering Axis Inclin. (deg)	Wheel Pivot Ratio (deg) Inner Wheel	Wheel Pivot Ratio (deg) Outer Wheel
'69	Exc. Firebird	2N to 1N	1½N	¼N to ¾P	¼P	0 to ⅛	9	20	18.25
'69	Firebird	0 to 1P	½P	¼N to ¾P	¼P	⅛ to ¼	8.25 to 9.25	20	—
'70-'71	Tempest, LeMans	1N to 2N	1½N	¼N to ¾P	¼P	0 to ⅛	9	20	22
	Station Wagon	1½N to 2½N	2N	¼N to ¾P	¼P	0 to ⅛	9	20	22
	Firebird	½N to 1½N	1N	¼P to 1¼P	¾P	⅛ to ¼	8.25 to 9.25	20	22
'71-'72	Tempest, LeMans	2N to 1N	1½N	½N to ½P	0	1/16 to 3/16	9	20	22
	Firebird	½N to ½P	0	½P to 1½P	1P	⅛ to ¼	8.25 to 9.25	20	22
	Ventura II	0 to 1P	½P	¼ to ¾P	¼P	⅛ to ¼	N.A.	20	22
'73	LeMans, Grand Am	③	④	①	②	0 to ⅛	10.35	20	22
	Firebird	½N to ½P	0	½P to 1½P	1P	⅛ to ¼	10.35	20	22
	Ventura II	0 to 1P	½P	¼N to ¾P	¼P	⅛ to ¼	8.5 to 9.5	20	22
'74	LeMans, Grand Am	③	④	①	②	0 to ⅛	10.35	20	22
	Firebird	1N to 1P	0	¾P to 1¾P	1P	1/16 to 5/16	10.35	20	22
	Ventura	½N to 1½P	½P	½N to 1P	¼P	1/16 to 5/16	9	20	22
'75-'76	Astre, Sunbird	¼N to 1¼N	¾N	¼N to ¾P	¼P	3/16 to 5/16	8.55	—	—
	Ventura	⑦	⑧	¼P to 1¼P	¾P	0 to ⅛	8.75	—	—
	Firebird	½N to ½P	0	½P to 1½P	1P	0 to ⅛	9.50	—	—
	LeMans, Grand Am	⑥	⑤	①	②	0 to ⅛	10.50	—	—

N Negative   P Positive
① LH: ½P to 1½P; RH: 0 to 1P
② LH: 1P; RH: ½P
③ Manual steering—1½N to ½N
Power steering—½N to ½P
④ Manual steering—1N
Power steering—0
⑤ Manual steering—1P
Power steering—2P
⑥ Manual steering—½P to 1½P
Power steering—1½P to 2½P
⑦ Manual steering—½N to 1½N
Power steering—½P to 1½P
⑧ Manual steering—1N
Power steering—1P
— Not specified

CHARGING SYSTEM

NOTE: For V6 and 260 V8 engine service procedures, refer to the Buick Apollo, Century, Gran Sport, Regal, Skyhawk, Skylark, Special Section.

Alternator R & R

1. Disconnect the battery cables.
2. Remove the alternator wires or connector.
3. Loosen the adjusting and pivot bolts.
4. Remove the V-belt.
5. Remove the alternator adjusting and pivot bolts.
6. Remove the alternator.
7. To install, reverse the removal procedure.

Adjust the belt tension so that the longest span of belt between pulleys can be depressed about ½ in. in the middle by moderate thumb pressure.

Caution Pull out on the alternator by hand to avoid damage to the housing and overtightening, which could damage the bearings.

Tighten first the adjuster bolt, then the pivot bolt.

Voltage Regulator R&R through 1970

1. Disconnect the battery cables.
2. Disconnect the wiring from the voltage regulator.
3. Remove the screws holding the regulator to the firewall or front bulkhead, depending on the car.
4. Reverse the removal procedure for installation.

Voltage Regulator R&R beginning 1971

The voltage regulator is inside the alternator. See "Charging and Starting Systems" in the "Unit Repair Section."

STARTING SYSTEM

Starter

The starter circuit consists of the battery, battery cables, starting motor, starter motor solenoid switch, ignition-starter switch and the neutral safety switch (automatic transmission) or clutch start switch (manual transmission).

The starting motor and solenoid assembly is mounted on the flywheel housing.

The solenoid switch closes the circuit between the battery and the starting motor. It also operates the shift lever that moves the drive pinion into mesh with the flywheel ring gear.

Repair procedures can be found in the "Charging and Starting Systems" section of the "Unit Repair Section." in the "Charging and Starting Systems" section of the "Unit Repair Section."

Starter Removal—OHC Four and Inline Six

1. Disconnect positive battery cable.
2. Disconnect solenoid wires.
3. Disconnect starter brace, if so equipped.
4. Remove starter-to-engine bolts and starter.

Starter Removal—V8

1. Jack up car and support on axle stands.
2. Follow Steps 1-4 of six-cylinder procedure, working from underneath car.

Starter Drive R & R

1. Disconnect the field straps from the solenoid and remove the starter through bolts.
2. Remove the commutator end frame, field frame, and armature from the drive housing.
3. To remove the overrunning clutch from the armature shaft:
   a. Slide the thrust collar from the end of the armature shaft.
   b. Slide a standard ½ in. pipe coupling (or an old pinion of suitable size) onto the armature shaft so that it butts against the snap-ring retainer. Tap the end of the pipe with a hammer, driving the retainer off of the snap-ring.
   c. Remove the snap-ring from the groove in the armature shaft.
   d. Slide the retainer and clutch from the armature shaft.
4. To reassemble, reverse the above procedure, being sure to:
   a. Slide the snap-ring, after it has been forced onto the armature shaft, past the grease groove to the snap-ring groove.
   b. Use two pairs of pliers at the same time, on opposite sides of the armature shaft, and grip the retainer and thrust collar and squeeze until the retainer is forced over the snap-ring.

IGNITION SYSTEM

Three types of distributors are used: a 12 volt aluminum internal point adjustment distributor used on six-cylinder engines, a 12 volt aluminum external point adjustment distributor used on eight-cylinder engines, and a 12 volt aluminum unitized transistor ignition distributor. During the 1974 model year, the unitized distributor was replaced by the similar HEI (High Energy Ignition) distributor used on other GM products. V8 HEI distributors have the coil mounted in the distributor cap. On the OHC four and inline six, the coil is mounted separately.

NOTE: There is a tachometer connecting terminal next to the ignition switch connector on the V8 HEI or unitized distributor cap. On the OHC four and the inline six, connect the tachometer to the terminal opposite the battery terminal on the remote-mounted coil. Most tachometers will work when connected to this terminal and to a ground. Some must connect from this terminal to the positive battery terminal. Some tachometers

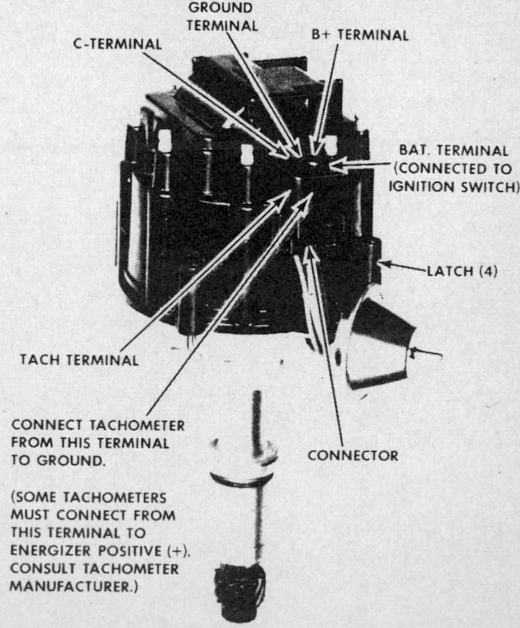

Tachometer hookup for V8 HEI system (© Pontiac Div., G.M. Corp)

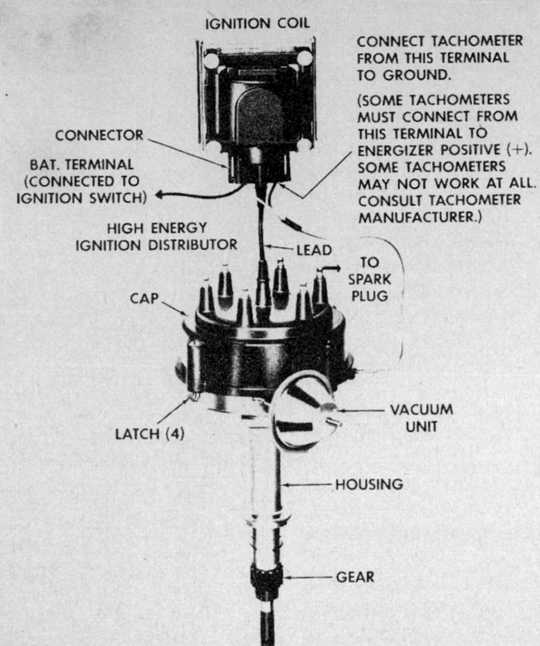

Tachometer hookup for OHC four and inline six HEI system (© Pontiac Div., G.M. Corp)

won't work at all with this system or may require a special hookup.

Never ground the tachometer terminal; the system will be damaged.

All the units perform the same function. They induce a high voltage surge into the coil and time these surges with regard to piston movements. They use centrifugal and vacuum ignition timing advance mechanisms to time the surges. They then direct these high-voltage surges through the distributor rotor, distributor cap, and high-tension wiring to the spark plugs.

Distributor Removal

1. Disconnect the distributor primary wire (the thin wire) from the coil on breaker point systems. On OHC four and inline six HEI systems, detach the wiring harness connector from the coil. On V8 HEI systems, disconnect the ignition switch battery feed wire from the distributor cap. Don't use a screwdriver or other tool to release the lock tab.
2. Remove the distributor cap. Unlatch the cap by using a screwdriver to disengage the spring-loaded latches. Sixes with breaker points have captive retaining screws.
3. Make reference marks on the block and the distributor housing that align with the tip of the rotor. Do not crank the engine after these marks have been made.
4. Disconnect the vacuum line at distributor.
5. Remove the distributor clamp screw and hold-down clamp.
6. Lift out the distributor. Notice the slight rotation of the rotor as the distributor is removed from the block.

Distributor Installation

Installation procedure is the reverse of the removal procedure. It should be noted, however, that while inserting a gear-driven distributor into the block, the rotor should be moved slightly to one side. This is necessary because of the helical cut of the distributor and camshaft gears. As the distributor seats in its bore, the rotor will turn slightly so the reference marks will once again be in line.

Installation—If Engine Has Been Disturbed

Inline Six and V8

1. With No. 1 piston coming up on compression stroke, continue cranking the engine until the pulley timing mark indexes with the zero (0) mark on the engine timing scale.
2. Replace the distributor.
3. Install the distributor in the block so that the vacuum diaphragm faces the left side of the engine on V8 engines, and to the front of the engine on six-cylinder engines. The rotor should point toward the contact in the cap for no. 1 cylinder. Move the rotor slightly to the side because, as the distributor is pressed into its bore, it will turn a small amount.
4. Reverse the removal procedure to complete installation.

OHC 4 Cylinder

1. Remove No. 1 spark plug and place a finger over the plug hole. Remove the center coil wire and crank the engine until compression is felt in No. 1 cylinder. Rotate the engine until the timing pulley pointer is aligned with the 0° TDC mark.
2. Install the distributor with the vacuum advance unit pointing toward the front of the engine and the punchmarks on the drive gear (if any) in line with the No. 1 cap tower. The rotor must point to the No. 1 distributor cap tower.
3. Install the hold-down clamp. Tighten the clamp bolt.
4. Install the rotor, cap and vacuum line.
5. Connect the wiring connector to the coil.
6. Check and adjust the ignition timing.

Contact Point and Condenser Replacement and Adjustment

1. Remove the distributor cap and the rotor.
2. Remove the V8 radio frequency interference (R.F.I.) shield, if so equipped.
3. Remove the screws holding the points in place.
4. Remove the condenser lead and ignition primary lead from the points. Loosen the clamp and slide the condenser out. Remove the point set.
5. Install a new set of points and tighten the attaching screws.
6. Slide the new condenser into the clamp. Connect the condenser and primary leads to the points.
7. Apply a very small amount of high temperature grease to the distributor breaker cam.
8. On sixes, adjust the point gap after turning the engine so that the fiber rubbing block of the point set is on the high point of the breaker cam. Set the dwell with the engine cranking. You don't have to adjust the gap on V8s at this point if you are installing preset points.
9. Install the V8 R.F.I. shield. (The half covering the points should be installed first.) You don't need the shield if the unitized point and condenser set is being used on V8s.
10. Install the rotor and distributor cap.
11. Set the V8 dwell using a dwell meter with the engine running. Using a 1/8 in. allen wrench, rotate the adjusting screw through the cap window until the dwell meets specifications.

Ignition Timing

Timing marks are located on the front engine cover and harmonic balancer or pulley.

1. Disconnect and plug the distributor vacuum advance hose.

2. Make sure that the dwell is adjusted to specifications on models with breaker points.

NOTE: it may be necessary to put a small amount of white paint or chalk on the timing marks to make them more visible.

3. Connect a timing light to no. 1 spark plug.
4. Loosen the distributor hold-down clamp.
5. Start the engine and rotate the distributor until the correct mark on the cover lines up with the pulley or harmonic balancer mark. Tighten the distributor clamp, and recheck the timing.

FUEL SYSTEM

Information on the fuel gauge and carburetors will be found in the Unit Repair Section.

The inline six and V8 fuel pump is of the single action diaphragm-type, equipped with a pulsation dampening chamber for stabilizing fuel flow.

A vapor diverter is incorporated into the fuel pumps used on air conditioned V8 and 4-BBL. models. The fuel pump is not repairable and must be replaced as a unit if defective.

The Astre uses an in-tank electric pump.

Fuel Pump R & R Inline Six and V8

1. Disconnect fuel inlet, outlet and vapor return lines at pump and plug pump inlet line.
2. Remove two pump mounting bolts and lockwashers; remove pump and gasket.
3. On Ventura II 307 V8 engines, if rocker arm pushrod is to be removed: take out the two adapter bolts and lockwashers and remove adapter and gasket.
4. Install pump with new gasket coated with sealer. Coat mounting bolt threads with sealer and tighten bolts.

NOTE: on Ventura II 307 V8 engines, mechanical fingers or heavy grease can be used to hold pump pushrod in place during installation. Coat pipe plug threads or adapter gasket with sealer if pushrod was removed.

5. Connect inlet and outlet lines, start engine and check for leaks.

Chilton's TIME SAVER

When replacing a fuel pump on a 307 cu. in. engine, considerable time can be saved as follows:

1. **Before removing the old pump, remove the upper bolt from the engine's right front mounting boss. This bolt hole is in direct alignment with the fuel pump pushrod. The threaded bolt hole continues into the pump pushrod bore. The bolt acts as an oil plug.**
2. **Temporarily insert a longer bolt, (about 3/8—16 x 2 in.) into the hole. Screw the bolt into the bore until it bottoms against the pump pushrod. (Don't tighten the bolt with a wrench or the rod can be damaged.)**
3. **The mechanic is now free to remove and install the fuel pump without worrying about fuel pump pushrod misalignment.**

CAUTION: don't forget to reinstall original motor bolt.

OHC 4 Cylinder

The electrical fuel pump is an integral part of the fuel tank unit assembly, which includes the fuel gauge metering unit. The fuel pump is energized by the ignition switch when the key is in the start position. After the engine starts, the pump receives current through the engine oil pressure safety switch as long as there is approximately 2 psi oil pressure.

1. Disconnect the battery ground cable and siphon the fuel from the tank.
2. Disconnect the gauge sending-unit and pump wires at the rear harness connector.
3. Raise the car. Disconnect the fuel line at the gauge unit pickup line.
4. Disconnect the tank vent line to the vapor separator, which is mounted in the tank.
5. Disconnect the gauge wire ground screw from the floorpan.
6. Remove the tank strap bolts and, very carefully, lower the tank.
7. Use a special wrench, or a suitable substitute, to unscrew the retaining cam ring. Do not strike any part of the tank with a metal tool, such as a hammer; there is a danger of explosion from sparks.
8. Remove the gauge sending-unit and fuel pump assembly.
9. Remove the flat wire conductor from the plastic clip on the fuel tube.
10. While squeezing the clamp, pull the pump straight back 1/2 in. for access to the terminals. Remove the two nuts, lockwashers, and wires from the pump.
11. Squeeze the clamp and pull the pump straight back to completely remove it from the sending unit.

Caution Be careful not to bend the circular support bracket.

12. Slide the replacement pump through the circular support bracket until it rests against the rubber coupling. Be sure that the rubber isolator and saran strainer, supplied in the service package, are attached to the pump.
13. Attach the two pump terminals, using lockwashers and nuts. Be sure that the flat conductor is attached to the terminal farthest away from the float arm.
14. Squeeze the clamp and push the pump into the rubber coupling.
15. Replace the flat wire conductor in the plastic clip on the fuel tube.
16. Install the pump and gauge unit into the tank opening. Tighten the cam ring.
17. Install the fuel tank using a reverse of the removal procedure.

Fuel Filter

Paper and Bronze Types

1. Disconnect fuel line connection at inlet of carburetor.
2. Remove inlet fuel filter nut from carburetor using a box wrench.
3. Remove filter element and spring.
4. If a bronze element, blow through cone end—element should allow air to pass freely.
5. Install element spring and new element into carburetor. Bronze elements are installed with small section of cone facing outward.
6. Install new gasket on fitting nut and install nut.
7. Install fuel line and tighten securely. Start engine and check for leaks.

Idle Stop Solenoid

The idle stop solenoid is used on some engines to prevent after-run when the ignition is turned off. After-run is caused largely by today's higher engine operating temperatures and wider throttle plate openings which are necessary for emission controls. Ordinarily, when the ignition is shut off the loss of spark is enough to stop the engine. However, if the engine has sufficiently high cylinder temperatures, enough air-fuel mixture can pass the wide throttle plate opening and be ignited without the spark plug and the engine will continue running even after the key is turned off. The idle solenoid is attached to the carburetor to solve this problem. The solenoid has an adjustable plunger and is electrically operated. When the ignition is turned on, the plunger is extended and contacts the carburetor throttle lever opening the throttle plate wide enough for the engine to idle properly. When the ignition is turned off, the plunger retracts and the throttle lever falls back on the lever stop. When the throttle lever is on its stop, the throttle plate opening is very small and will not allow enough air-fuel mixture to pass to run the engine with the ignition turned off.

Hot Idle Compensator

The hot idle compensator is used with automatic transmissions. Its purpose is to offset the enrichening effects caused by changes in air density and fuel vapors generated during hot engine operation. It is in a chamber on the float bowl casting. The compensator is a temperature-sensitive unit which opens and closes a passage leading from the atmosphere to an orifice below the throttle valve. At normal operating temperatures, the valve is closed, blocking the passage. During very hot engine operation, low air density and excessive fuel vapors in the carburetor enter the engine manifold causing a rich mixture, rough idling, and stalling. At a predetermined temperature, the compensator opens and allows enough air to offset the rich mixture and maintain a smooth idle. When the engine cools, the compensator closes and operation returns to normal.

Idle Speed and Mixture Adjustments

1969

Adjust with air cleaner installed.

V8 Engines

1. Turn in idle mixture screws until lightly seated, then back out 4 turns (2-BBL.) or 6 turns (4-BBL.).
2. Connect a tachometer, start engine and allow it to warm up to normal operating temperature. On automatic transmission, A/C cars, turn off A/C.
3. Place automatic in Drive, manual in Neutral. With idle stop solenoid energized, adjust mixture screws for best lean idle speed.
4. Adjust idle stop solenoid screw to obtain specified idle speed for 1969 Ram Air; use idle screw for all other 1969 cars.
5. Disconnect idle stop solenoid, then adjust idle speed screw on carburetor to obtain 650 rpm idle for manual transmission 4-BBL., 500 rpm for all others.

NOTE: do not re-adjust mixture screws.

6. Place fast idle lever on top step of cam and adjust fast idle speed.

Inline Six Engines

1. Turn in mixture screws until they lightly seat, then back out 5 turns.
2. Start engine, connect tachometer, and allow engine to warm up to normal operating temperature. On automatic transmission cars, place selector in Drive and turn off A/C, if so equipped.
3. Adjust idle stop solenoid screw to obtain 610 rpm for auto. transmission (1-BBL. and 4-BBL.), 730 rpm for manual transmission 1-BBL., and 880 rpm for manual transmission 4-BBL.
4. Turn mixture screws clockwise to obtain 600 rpm for auto. transmission (1-BBL. and 4-BBL.), 700 rpm for manual transmission 1-BBL., and 850 rpm for manual transmission 4-BBL.
5. Disconnect idle stop solenoid and adjust idle speed screw on carburetor to obtain 600 rpm for manual transmission 4-BBL., 500 rpm for all others.

NOTE: don't disturb idle mixture screws or stop solenoid after this point.

6. Reconnect solenoid and adjust fast idle speed.

1970

Adjust with air cleaner installed.

1. On California cars, remove fuel filler cap.
2. Disconnect and plug distributor vacuum advance hose.
3. Plug hot idle compensator on all automatic transmission V8's with Quadrajet (4 MV) carburetor *except* Ram Air III and IV. Also plug compensator on all L-6 and V8 2-BBL. with automatic and A/C.
4. With automatic in Drive, manual in Neutral, adjust curb idle speed as follows:

Inline six and Ram Air IV

a. With idle stop solenoid energized, adjust solenoid screw to obtain 830 rpm for L-6, 1,000 rpm for R.A. IV, 630 rpm for automatic L-6, and 750 rpm for automatic R.A. IV.

b. Adjust mixture screws equally to obtain lean best idle at 1,000 rpm for manual R.A. IV, 750 rpm for automatic R.A. IV, 750 rpm for manual L-6, and 600 rpm for automatic L-6.

c. Disconnect solenoid wire and adjust carburetor idle speed screw to obtain 400 rpm for L-6, 500 rpm for R.A. IV automatic, and 650 rpm for R.A. IV manual.

350, 400, 455 Engines

a. Back out mixture screws 3-5 turns from lightly seated positions.

b. Adjust carburetor idle speed screw to obtain 850 rpm for manual 350 and 400 2-BBL., 1,050 rpm for manual 400 and 455 4-BBL., or 675 rpm for all automatic 350, 400, 455 engines.

c. Lean mixture screws equally (turn in) to obtain 800 rpm for manual 350 and 400 2-BBL., 950 rpm for manual 400 and 455 4-BBL., or 650 rpm for all automatic 350, 400, 455 engines.

1971-72

Adjust with air cleaner installed.

On some models, the idle stop solenoid is no longer used, having been replaced by the combination emission control valve. This valve is energized through the transmission to increase idle speed under conditions of high gear deceleration and to provide full vacuum spark advance during high gear operation. The valve is de-energized at curb idle and in the lower gears to provide a retarded spark under these conditions, the result of which is lower hydrocarbon emission.

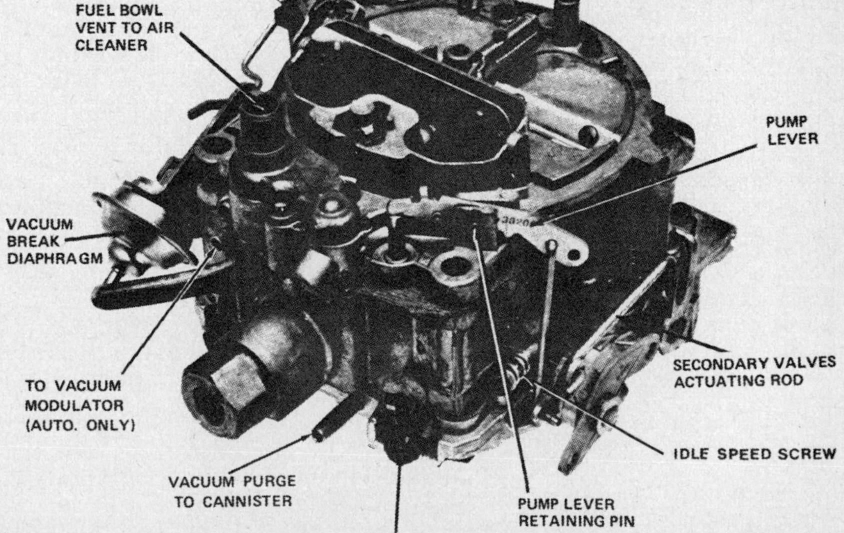

Rochester 4 bbl (© Pontiac Div., G.M. Corp)

The valve need not be adjusted unless the solenoid or throttle body is removed, or the carburetor overhauled.

V-8 Idle Speed

1. Disconnect carburetor "EVAP" hose from vapor storage canister.
2. Disconnect and plug carburetor-to-vacuum (distributor vacuum) solenoid hose at solenoid. Disconnect throttle solenoid wire on 4-BBL. manual transmission engines.
3. Set dwell and timing (in that order) at specified idle speed.
4. Adjust carburetor speed screw to obtain specified idle speed, automatic in Drive, manual in Neutral.
5. On 4-BBL. manual transmission models, reconnect throttle solenoid wire, manually extend solenoid screw and adjust to specified idle rpm.
6. Place automatic in Park, manual in Neutral and check fast idle speed with screw on top step of cam. Adjust fast idle screw to obtain 1,700 rpm.

NOTE: 2-BBL. carburetors are not adjustable for fast idle.

7. Reconnect distributor vacuum and vapor storage hoses.

6 Cyl. Idle Speed

1. Disconnect fuel tank "EVAP" hose from vapor storage canister.
2. Disconnect and plug distributor vacuum advance hose.
3. Set dwell and timing (in that order) at specified idle speed.
4. Adjust carburetor idle speed screw to obtain 550 rpm for manual, 500 rpm for automatic (in Drive). Do not adjust solenoid screw.
5. Place automatic in Park and manual in Neutral, then place fast idle tang on top step of fast idle cam and check fast idle speed. Adjust to obtain 2,400 rpm.

V-8 and 6 Cyl. Idle Mixture

If the carburetor has been overhauled, or the plastic locks removed from the mixture screws, the following procedure must be used to adjust idle speed and mixture. It must be emphasized that the manufacturer does not recommend this procedure as a substitute for the preceding methods, in that exhaust emission quality can be adversely affected unless the proper test equipment is available.

1. Turn in mixture screw/s until lightly seated, then back out 3½ turns.
2. Start engine and adjust carburetor idle speed screw to obtain a speed 25 rpm above specified idle (automatic), 75 rpm higher for L-6 and 2-BBL. V8 (manual), or 100 rpm higher for 4-BBL. V8 (manual).
3. Turn mixture screw/s in equally until specified idle speed is obtained. At this point, a CO meter should be employed to adjust mixture. A reading of 1.0% or less must be maintained.
4. Shut off engine and install new limiter caps
5. Adjust fast idle speed, as described previously.

1973-74

Six-Cylinder Idle Speed

1. Disconnect the fuel tank "evap" hose from the vapor canister in the engine compartment. Plug the line.
2. Disconnect and plug the distributor vacuum line.
3. Check that dwell and timing are correct.
4. Detach the idle stop solenoid wire (not the C.E.C. solenoid wire) and set the low idle speed to 450 rpm by using a ⅛ in. allen wrench inside the six-sided nut on the solenoid.

NOTE: The engine must be at normal operating temperature.

5. Reconnect the idle stop solenoid wire.
6. Set the normal idle speed to that specified in the Tune-Up Specifications chart. Adjust by turning the six-sided nut on the solenoid.

NOTE: The automatic transmission must be in Drive. Block the wheels.

7. On 1973 manual transmission models, pull the C.E.C. solenoid plunger out as far as it will go. The plunger should contact the throttle lever and produce an 850 rpm idle speed. Adjust by turning the plunger.
8. Set the automatic transmission in Park and the manual transmission in Neutral. Set the fast idle tang on the top step of the fast idle cam. The fast idle speed should be 2,400 rpm for 1973 and 1,800 rpm for 1974. Bend the tang to adjust.

V8 Idle Speed

1. Disconnect and plug the carburetor hose from the vapor canister.
2. Disconnect and plug the distributor and EGR valve vacuum hoses. Plug any open vacuum tubes on the carburetor.
3. Check the dwell and timing.
4. Disconnect the idle stop solenoid wire.
5. Adjust the carburetor idle speed screw to the low rpm specified in the Tune-Up Specifications chart.
6. Reconnect the solenoid wire and adjust the solenoid plunger screw to obtain the specified idle speed.

NOTE: You might have to work the throttle linkage by hand first, since the solenoid isn't always powerful enough to move it.

7. On four-barrel carburetors, check the fast idle speed with the fast idle speed screw on the top step of the fast idle cam. Adjust the speed by turning the fast idle screw. Fast idle speed is 1,500 rpm for all engines except the 1974 455 S.D., which is 2,000 rpm.

NOTE: The fast idle speed screw is NOT the same one used in Step 5. You can't make this adjustment on two-barrel carburetors.

Idle Mixture

1. Set the parking brake and block the wheels.
2. Disconnect and plug the carburetor hose from the vapor canister in the engine compartment. Disconnect and plug the distributor vacuum hose.
3. If the idle mixture limiter caps are intact and a CO meter is available, attempt to obtain an idle setting of 0.2% CO by adjusting the mixture screws. If this doesn't work, remove the caps and proceed to the next step.

NOTE: The engine must be at normal operating temperature.

Engine	*Year*	*Manual*	*Automatic*
6-250	1973	800	700
8-350, 2 bbl.	1973	1100	700
8-400, 2 bbl.	1973	—	700
8-400, 455, 4 bbl.	1973	1200	700
6-250	1974	950	650
6-250, Calif.	1974	950	630
8-350, 2 bbl.	1974	1150	750
8-350, 2 bbl., Calif.	1974	—	720
8-350, 4 bbl.	1974	1200	730
8-350, 4-bbl., Calif.	1974	—	720
8-400, 2 bbl.	1974	—	720
8-400, 2 bbl., Calif.	1974	—	690
8-400, 4 bbl.	1974	1310	720
8-400, 4 bbl., Calif.	1974	—	685
8-455, 4 bbl.	1974	—	680
8-455, 4 bbl., Calif.	1974	—	675
8-455, S.D.	1974	1420	825

4. Remove the idle mixture limiter caps. If you have a CO meter, adjust the mixture screws equally to get a reading of 0.2% CO.
5. Run the screws in until they are lightly seated, then back them out six turns for 1973 and seven for 1974.

NOTE: Sixes have only one screw.

6. Turn the air conditioner off, place the automatic transmission in Drive (block the wheels), place the manual transmission in Neutral, leave the air cleaner off and plug the air cleaner manifold vacuum fitting. Adjust the idle speed screw or the idle stop solenoid to obtain the following temporary idle speed:
7. Turn the mixture screws in equally to get the highest idle speed. Then set the speed back to that listed in Step 6.
8. Turn the mixture screws in equally until the engine speed drops to the normal idle speed given in the Tune-Up Specifications chart.
9. Install the air cleaner. If the idle speed changes, adjust the mixture screws slightly to compensate.

1975

OHC Four-Cylinder, 1-Bbl. Carburetor

1. The adjustment must be made with the engine at normal operating temperature, with the air conditioner off, and the air cleaner in place. Automatic transmissions must be in Drive and manual transmissions in neutral.
2. Set the parking brake and block the wheels.
3. Disconnect the fuel tank vent hose at the vapor canister. Detach and plug the distributor vacuum hose to prevent any vacuum advance.
4. Use pliers to break off the plastic mixture screw limiter cap.
5. Adjust the idle solenoid screw to get the specified idle speed. The tachometer hookup for the HEI ignition system is covered earlier under Ignition System.
6. Back out the mixture screw to get the fastest possible idle.
7. Use the solenoid screw to return to the specified idle speed.
8. Turn the mixture screw in until the idle speed drops 50 rpm for automatic, and 100 rpm for manual transmission.
9. Correct the idle speed using the solenoid screw.
10. Replace the distributor and canister hoses.

OHC Four-Cylinder, 2-Bbl. Carburetor

1. The adjustment must be made with the engine at normal operating temperature, with the air conditioner off, and the air cleaner removed. Automatic transmissions must be in Drive and manual transmissions in Neutral.
2. Set the parking brake and block the wheels.
3. Disconnect the fuel tank vent hose at the vapor canister. Detach and plug the distributor vacuum hose to prevent any vacuum advance.
4. Use pliers to break off the plastic mixture screw limiter cap.
5. Adjust the idle speed screw to get an idle speed of 830 rpm. On California manual transmission cars, adjust the solenoid screw to get an idle speed of 820 rpm. The tachometer hookup for the HEI ignition system is covered earlier under Ignition System.
6. Back out the mixture screw to get the fastest possible idle.
7. Correct the idle speed to that specified in Step 5.
8. Turn the mixture screw in until the idle speed drops to 750 rpm with automatic and 700 with manual transmission.
9. Correct the idle speed.
10. Replace the distributor and canister hoses, and the air cleaner.

Carter 2 bbl (© Pontiac Div., G.M. Corp)

Inline Six-Cylinder and V8

1. The adjustment must be made with the engine at normal operating temperature, with the air conditioner off, and the air cleaner removed. The air cleaner vacuum fitting in the manifold should be plugged. Automatic transmissions should be in Drive and manual transmissions in neutral.
2. Set the parking brake and block the wheels.
3. Disconnect and plug the carburetor hose from the vapor canister. Detach and plug the distributor vacuum hose to prevent any vacuum advance on the 350 2-bbl. engine, except in the Ventura.
4. Use pliers to break off the plastic idle mixture screw limiter caps. Sixes have only one screw. Turn in the mixture screws until they seat lightly, then back them out five turns.
5. Adjust the idle speed screw or idle solenoid screw to get the "before lean drop idle" speed listed on the underhood specifications sticker. The tachometer hookup for the HEI ignition system is covered earlier under Ignition System.
6. Adjust the mixture screws equally (quarter-turn increments are recommended) to obtain the highest possible idle speed. Check the adjustment by shifting into Neutral, running the engine at 2,000 rpm for 5-10 seconds, returning to idle, shifting back into Drive, and letting the speed stabilize for 10 seconds.
7. Return the idle speed to that set in Step 5.
8. Repeat Steps 6 and 7, until no further speed increase is possible.
9. Turn in the mixture screws equally until the normal idle speed is reached.
10. Replace and connect the air cleaner. Use the mixture screws

to make any slight idle speed correction necessary.
11. Replace the distributor and canister hoses.

COOLING SYSTEM

Radiator

A cross-flow radiator is used instead of a conventional down-flow and center type. With the cross-flow design, coolant flows horizontally through the core and the tanks are located on each side.

Advantages of the cross-flow radiator are improved cooling capability and a low silhouette.

Automatic transmission radiators have oil coolers built into the right-hand tank, air-conditioned and high-performance models have greater cooling capacity than standard. The drain cock is located at the inside, lower left-hand corner of the radiator.

To refill and bleed the cooling system after repair, first fill the radiator with coolant mixture. Leave the cap off and run the engine with the heater on until the thermostat opens. Then fill the radiator as necessary, with the engine running. Replace the radiator cap. If there is a coolant reservoir, add coolant mixture until the level is between the two marks.

Radiator R & R

All Except Astre

1. Drain coolant.
2. Remove fan shield assembly on the six. Remove the fan.
3. Disconnect upper and lower hoses.
4. Disconnect and plug oil cooler lines, if equipped with automatic transmission.

NOTE: on 1969 Tempest models remove fan blade, then remove entire radiator and shroud as an assembly.

5. Lift radiator and shroud straight up and out of car.
6. To install, reverse removal procedure, making sure lower cradles are properly located and automatic transmission is full.

Astre

There are two radiators: a standard type and a larger heavy duty radiator equipped with a fan shroud.

1. Drain the radiator.
2. On models with the heavy duty radiator, remove the fan shroud.
3. Disconnect the intake and outlet hoses and the coolant recovery hose. Disconnect the coolant level indicator lead.
4. Remove the upper mounting panel or bracket.
5. Lift the radiator up and out of the lower brackets.
6. To install, reverse the removal procedure.

Fan Shroud R & R—Astre

1. Remove the two screws which secure the shroud to the upper radiator brackets.
2. Remove the screw which holds the two halves of the shroud together at the lower left-hand corner.
3. Remove the left and right sections of the shroud from the clips at the bottom of the radiator.
4. To install, reverse the above procedure.

Water Pump R & R

Inline Six and V8

This is a centrifugal-type water-pump. It is die cast, with sealed bearings and is pressed together. Therefore, it is serviced as a unit.

1. Disconnect the battery and drain the radiator.
2. Loosen the alternator and remove the fan belt.
3. Remove the power steering and air conditioning belts, if so equipped.
4. Remove the fan and water pump pulley.
5. Remove the V8 front alternator bracket.
6. Remove the heater hose and radiator hose at the pump.

NOTE: remove the upper front timing cover and the two accessory drive housing bolts on OHC six engines.

7. Remove the water pump retaining bolts and the pump.
8. Install the pump by reversing the above steps. Make sure that all gasket surfaces are clean and smooth. Always use a gasket sealer on both sides of the gasket. Torque the retaining bolts to 20 ft lbs on six-cylinder engines, 30 ft lbs on the 307, and 15 ft lbs on all other V8 engines.

OHC 4 Cylinder

The water pump is located on the front of the engine block immediately above the crankshaft pulley. The pump bearings are permanently lubricated during manufacture and do not require periodic maintenance other than keeping the air vent (top of housing) and drain holes (bottom of housing) free of dirt and grease.

The pump components cannot be serviced separately and, in the event of pump failure, the complete assembly must be replaced as a unit, as follows:

1. Raise the hood and install a bolt through the hood hold-open link.
2. Disconnect the battery negative cable.

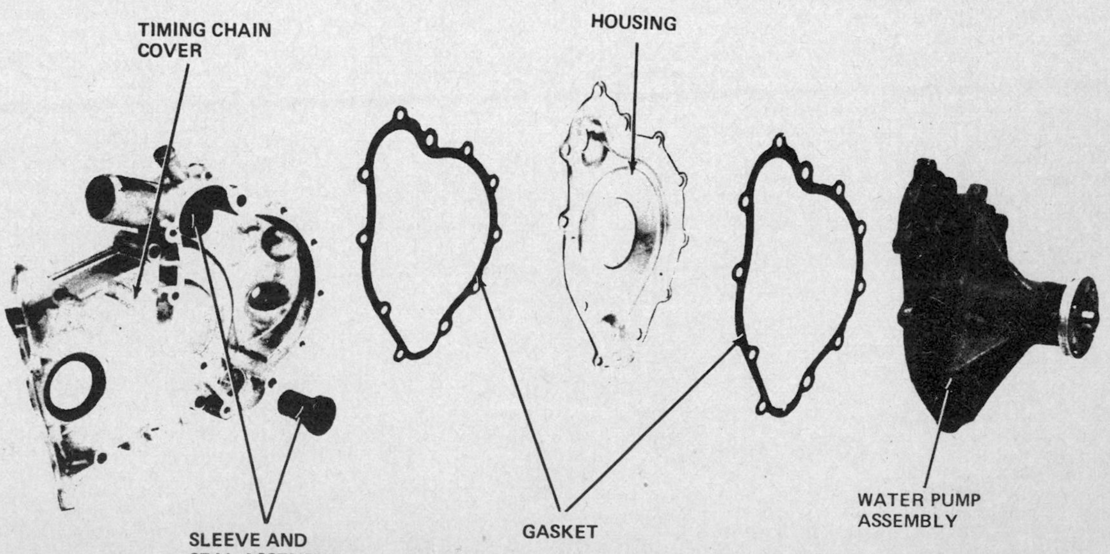

350 (except 1975-76 Ventura), 400, 455 V8 water pump assembly
(© Pontiac Div., G.M. Corp)

3. Remove the fan and spacer.

Caution No attempt should be made to repair a bent or damaged fan. The fan assembly must be in proper balance and an improperly balanced fan may cause extensive damage.

4. Loosen, but do not remove, the two lower timing belt cover retaining screws. The holes in the cover are slotted so that the cover is easily removed.
5. Remove the two upper timing belt cover retaining screws and remove the cover.
6. Drain the coolant.
7. Loosen the water pump bolts to relieve the tension on the timing belt.
8. Remove the hoses from the water pump.
9. Remove the water pump bolts, pump and gasket.
10. Thoroughly clean the old gasket material from the pump and block.
11. To install, position the water pump on the block using a new gasket and loosely install the water pump bolts. Make sure that the V grooves of the belt are aligned with the grooves in the water pump.

NOTE: use an anti-seize compound on the water pump bolt threads.

12. A special tool is available to adjust the timing belt. It fits into the round hole in the square lug to the upper right (facing) of the water pump and bears against the pump housing midway between the bolt holes. If this tool is available, apply 15 ft lbs of torque against the water pump (and belt). If the tool is not available, apply a force to the pump in a similar manner. Tighten the pump bolts to 15 ft lbs.
13. Install the radiator and heater hoses to the pump.
14. Install the timing belt cover, lowering the cover lower screw slots over the screws. Loosely tighten the screws against the cover.
15. Install the two upper timing cover screws, then tighten the upper and lower screws to 50 in. lbs.
16. Install the fan spacer and fan, tightening the bolts to 20 ft lbs.
17. Fill the cooling system, connect the battery negative cable, start the engine and check for leaks
18. Remove the bolt from the hood hold-open link and close the hood.

Thermostat R & R

Inline Six and V8

1. Drain coolant to below thermostat level.
2. Disconnect upper hose and remove water outlet assembly.
3. Replace by reversing the above steps. Clean the gasket surfaces and use a gasket sealer and a new gasket.
4. Refill and bleed cooling system.

OHC 4 Cylinder

The thermostat is located in a housing at the cylinder head water outlet adjacent to the intake manifold.

1. Drain the cooling system.
2. Disconnect the upper radiator hose at the engine.
3. If the alternator is attached to the water outlet, loosen the swivel bolt attachment and move it out of the way.
4. Unbolt the housing and remove the housing, gasket, and thermostat.
5. Replace the thermostat and housing, using a new gasket.
6. Install the alternator and adjust the drive belt.
7. Replace the radiator hose, fill the cooling system, start the engine, and check for leaks.

EMISSION CONTROLS

There are three types of emissions to be controlled: crankcase emissions, carburetor and gas tank gas vapor emissions, and exhaust emissions. See the "Unit Repair Section" for troubleshooting and repair information.

1969

A new concept, Combustion Control System (C.C.S.) utilizes engine modification. Essentially the C.C.S. increases combustion efficiency through carburetor and distributor calibrations and by increasing engine operating temperature.

Carburetors are calibrated leaner and initial ignition timing is retarded. Another carburetor feature is the idle fuel mixture limiting orifice. It is located at the base of the idle mixture screw and makes sure that, even if the idle mixture screw is turned too far, the fuel enrichment will not greatly affect exhaust emissions.

The C.C.S. also incorporates a higher engine operating temperature. A 195° thermostat is used. Engines that run hotter provide a more complete vaporation of the fuel and reduce quench area in the combustion chamber. Quench area is the relatively cool area near the cylinder wall and combustion chamber surfaces. Fuel in these areas does not burn properly because of the lower temperatures. This increases emissions.

The C.C.S. uses a thermostatically controlled air cleaner called the Auto-Therm air cleaner. It is designed to keep the temperature of the air entering the carburetor at approximately 100°. This allows the lean carburetor to work properly, minimizes carburetor icing, and improves engine warm-up characteristics. A sensor unit located on the clean air side of the air filter senses the temperature of the air passing over it and regulates the vacuum supplied to a vacuum diaphragm in the inlet tube of the air cleaner. The colder the air, the greater the amount of vacuum supplied to the vacuum diaphragm. The vacuum diaphragm, depending on the vacuum supplied to it, opens or closes a damper door in the inlet tube of the air cleaner. If the door is open, it allows air from the engine compartment to go to the carburetor. If the door is closed, air flows from the heat stove located on the exhaust manifold into the carburetor. In this way, heated air is supplied to the carburetor on cold days, and when first starting the engine and warming it up.

Since 1968, all car manufacturers have posted idle speeds and other pertinent data relative to the specific engine-car application in a conspicuous place in the engine compartment.

1970

The more stringent 1970 laws require tighter control of emissions. Crankcase emissions are controlled by the Positive Crankcase Ventilation System, and exhaust emissions by the engine Controlled Combustion System (C.C.S.), in conjunction with the new Transmission Controlled Spark System (T.C.S.)

In addition, cars sold in California are equipped with an Evaporation Control System that limits the amount of gasoline vapor discharged into the atmosphere (usually from the carburetor and fuel tank).

The T.C.S. system consists of a transmission switch, a solenoid valve, and a temperature switch. Under normal conditions, the system permits the vacuum distributor (spark) advance to operate only in high gear (both manual and automatic transmissions) and reverse.

The transmission switch is located on the transmission and senses when the transmission is in one of the lower gears. When it is in a lower gear, the switch activates the vacuum solenoid valve. This valve is located in the vacuum line that runs from the carburetor to the distributor and it shuts off vacuum to the distributor advance when it is activated. There is also an engine-temperature sensing switch which overrides the transmission switch. It will allow vacuum advance in the lower gears when engine temperature is below 85° or above 220°. There is always vacuum advance in high gear and reverse.

1971

In 1971, the Combination Emission Control System (C.E.C.), was introduced. It uses the C.C.S. of 1968–69 and incorporates several, but not all, of the features in the T.C.S. of 1970. Although distributor vacuum advance is eliminated in the lower gears, as in the T.C.S. system, it is eliminated in a different manner. A C.E.C. solenoid valve is used to regulate distributor vacuum advance.

The C.E.C. solenoid valve is mounted on the carburetor. Vacuum from the intake manifold passes through a port at the base of the solenoid before it reaches the distributor. When the solenoid receives an electrical signal, the plunger extends, opening the port, which allows vacuum to the distributor. At the same time, the plunger head contacts the carburetor throttle lever increasing the idle speed. When the solenoid is de-energized, the spring-loaded plunger returns to its unextended position closing the port and allowing the throttle lever to rest against the idle speed adjusting screw.

The switch is energized by two switches and one relay.

The time-delay relay is used to energize the C.E.C. solenoid and provide vacuum advance for the first 15 seconds after the ignition is turned on. This happens regardless of engine temperature. After the 15 seconds, the solenoid is again regulated by the temperature switch and the transmission switch.

One of the controlling switches is an engine temperature switch. It allows vacuum advance in all gears, by energizing the C.E.C. solenoid, when the engine temperature is below 82° or above 220°. In between 82° and 220°, this switch will allow no vacuum advance and the solenoid will be de-energized.

The other switch is the transmission switch. When the transmission is in the lower gears, this switch keeps the C.E.C. solenoid in the de-energized position eliminating vacuum advance. In high gear, the solenoid is energized by current from the battery and vacuum advance is supplied.

Engine dieseling is controlled by use of lower throttle plate openings (lower carburetor idle speeds).

On air-conditioned (A/C), automatic transmission cars, a solid-state time device engages the A/C compressor for about three seconds after the ignition is turned off. The load from the compressor effectively stalls the engine and prevents dieseling or overrun.

The evaporation control system was added to all cars in 1971. This system limits the amount of gasoline vapor discharged into the air from the gas tank and carburetor. The fuel tank has a non-vented cap. As vapors are generated in the fuel tank, they flow through a liquid vapor separator to a canister where they are stored. From the canister, the vapors are routed to the carburetor where they are burned when the engine is running.

1972

All six-cylinder models with manual transmissions, and all models with a 307 V8—regardless of type of transmission—use the C.E.C. system. All six-cylinder models with automatic transmissions use the A.I.R. system. All V8s equipped with a manual four-speed transmission use the T.C.S. system. All V8 models equipped with a three-speed manual transmission or an automatic transmission use the new Speed Control Spark System (S.C.S.)

Every engine/transmission combination uses the Auto-Therm air cleaner, P.C.V. system, and the evaporation control system.

The Speed Controlled Spark (S.C.S.), system uses a solenoid valve in the vacuum line running between the carburetor and the distributor. This valve is the same as the transmission-controlled spark valve. The difference in this system is that the valve is regulated by vehicle speed using a speed control spark switch. The S.C.S. solenoid valve is energized below 38 mph in any gear, under normal operating temperature, allowing no vacuum advance. Above 38 mph, in any gear, or any time engine temperature is higher or lower than normal operating temperature, the solenoid valve is de-energized allowing full vacuum advance to the distributor.

Normal S.C.S. engine operating temperatures range from 95° to 230°. An engine-temperature sensing switch is located in the head and de-energizes the solenoid until operating temperature is reached regardless of vehicle speed.

1973

The Controlled Combustion System (C.C.S.) is standard on all engines. The C.E.C./E.G.R. (Exhaust Gas Recirculation) system is used on all 6 cyl engines with manual transmission. The Air Injection Reactor (A.I.R.) is used on all 6 cyl, 350 with manual transmission, and 350/400 California engines. A combination of the Transmission Controlled Spark and Exhaust Gas Re-circulation (E.G.R.) is found on all V8 engines.

E.G.R. is a system used to reduce nitrous oxide (NO_x) emissions. It functions by allowing a small amount of exhaust gas into the air fuel mixture in the intake manifold, under certain conditions.

The EGR TCS system consists of a temperature switch which senses when the engine temperature is under 71° or over 230°, a second temperature switch sensing engine temperature between 140° and 230°, an EGR solenoid, a vacuum advance solenoid, a transmission switch, and a time delay relay.

The under 71° and over 230° switch is mounted on the left cyl head. The 140° to 230° switch is mounted in the right cyl head. The time delay relay is mounted on the vacuum advance solenoid.

The 71° to 230° switch grounds the circuit for the solenoids below 71° and above 230°. The 140° switch passes current to the transmission switch when engine temperature is between 140° and 230°. The transmission switch then grounds the circuit for the solenoids in first gear only. Between 71° and 140° the temperature switches are both open and the solenoids are in the normal positions.

The vacuum advance solenoid is normally closed, allowing no vacuum advance. The EGR solenoid is normally open, allowing exhaust gas recirculation.

Below 71° there is a complete circuit and both solenoids are energized, allowing vacuum advance and cutting off EGR.

From 71° to 140° there is an open circuit, the solenoids return to their normal positions, and vacuum advance is cut off and EGR is allowed.

From 140° to 230°, in first gear, there is an open circuit and the solenoids are in their normal positions. The time delay relay maintains the open circuit for 33 to 55 seconds after the transmission shifts into second gear. However, after the time delay in second and third gear, the solenoids are energized to allow vacuum advance and cut off EGR.

Over 235° the solenoids are energized and vacuum advance occurs and there is no EGR.

The C.E.C. system operates as previously, except that the time-delay relay now provides 20 seconds of vacuum advance before the solenoid is de-energized, and the engine temperature switch provides vacuum advance when engine coolant temperature is below 93°F.

1973½

A mid-year redesign of the emission control system was necessitated by newly-announced Federal standards. On cars equipped with A.I.R., air is not supplied to nos. 3 and 6 cylinders. This is done by internal changes in the cylinder heads. Mid-year A.I.R. cylinder heads can usually be identified by the absence of a drilled passage and metal sealing ball at the nos. 3 and 6 cylinder locations.

The new engines have a relocated vacuum source for the air cleaner. Vacuum is supplied through a tee in the hose feeding vacuum to the distributor vacuum spark thermal valve.

The mid-year EGR system operates basically on the same principle as the

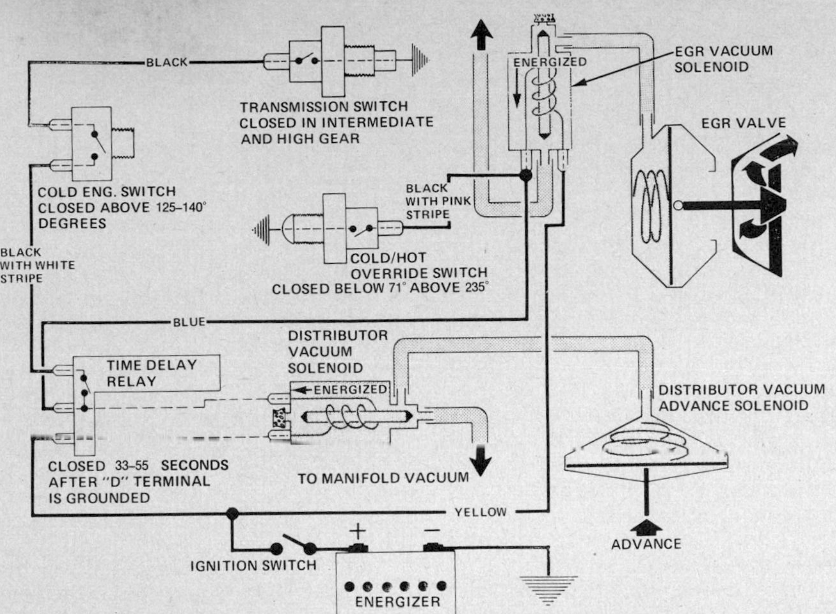

1973 combined TCS and EGR system (© Pontiac Div., G.M. Corp)

1973 system, except for two major differences:

1. The EGR and TCS systems now work completely independent of each other.
2. A new EGR thermal vacuum valve is used to sense the temperature of the intake manifold coolant. Below 95°F, no EGR; above 95°F, EGR.

In the TCS system, full vacuum advance is provided below 62°F. When the temperature rises above 62°F, the distributor vacuum spark thermal valve closes and from this point on the distributor solenoid must be energized to get vacuum advance. The upper temperature limit for vacuum advance cut-in is now 240°F.

The Start-Up Relay Switch gives full advance (ported for manual transmission) in any gear for 20 seconds after all engine starts. After the 20 seconds has elapsed, the switch breaks ground and the distributor solenoid is de-energized, shutting off the vacuum advance.

1974

The A.I.R. system is carried over from 1973 and is used on all manual transmission and California six-cylinder engines, 350 2 bbl manual transmission V8s, all 350 cu in. California engines and 400 cu in. 2 bbl California engines.

The EGR/TCS system is once again together, as in pre-1973½ systems, and consists of a thermal vacuum valve, vacuum advance solenoid, EGR valve, hot coolant switch, cold feed switch and a time-delay relay for engine starting. The system is found on all V8s. Pontiac six-cylinder engines use the Chevrolet system without any changes.

On the EGR/TCS system, the distributor spark-EGR thermal vacuum valve senses the temperature of the air/fuel mixture inside the intake manifold. Below 62°F, EGR is off and full vacuum advance is provided. When the temperature rises above 62°F, EGR is on (operated by a port above the throttle blade, so that it only comes on above idle). From this point on the distributor vacuum advance solenoid must be energized by the other components and switches to provide vacuum advance.

When the cylinder head metal temperature goes above 125°, 140°, 155°F (depending on use), the cold feed switch closes. This sends the 12V current to the TCS switch looking for a ground. The TCS switch provides a ground only when the transmission shifts into high gear. There is no time delay after shifting into high gear.

Any time the coolant temperature goes over 240°F, the hot coolant switch provides a ground for the distributor solenoid. Since the hot coolant switch will ground whether the TCS switch does or not, vacuum advance will be supplied to the distributor in any gear when the coolant temperature reaches 240°F or above.

There is a distributor vacuum spark delay valve on some models, between the distributor solenoid and the distributor acting as a restrictor on vacuum supplied to the distributor. This merely slows down the rate vacuum is initially supplied to the distributor. Full vacuum is eventually supplied.

EXHAUST GAS RECIRCULATION (EGR)

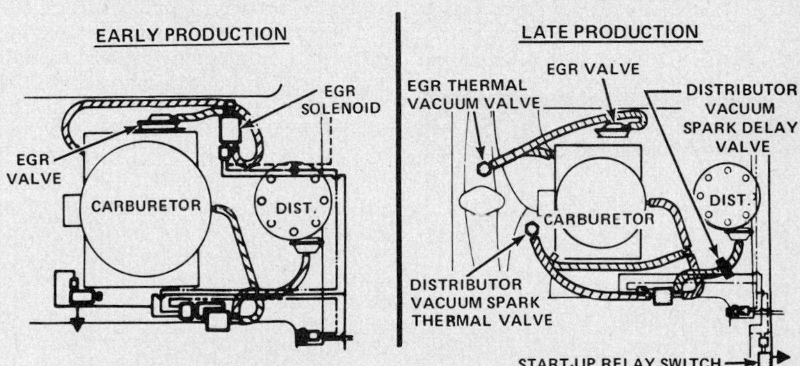

EGR system—1973 mid-year changes (© Pontiac Div, G.M. Corp)

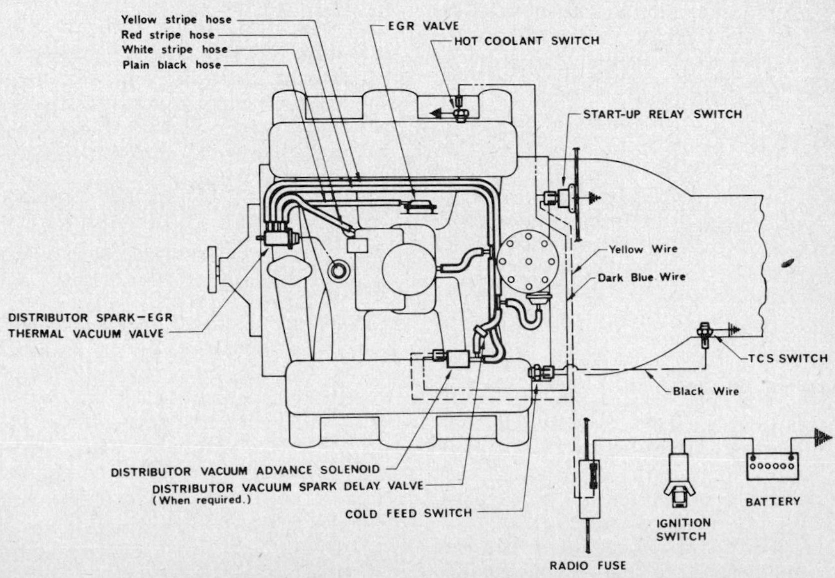

1974 Emissions Control System (© Pontiac Div., G.M. Corp)

The function of the start-up relay switch is identical to 1973½. See Pontiac section for further details.

1975-76

The Controlled Combustion System (C.C.S.) is continued on all non-California engines. It introduces preheated carburetor intake air during engine warmup.

The Air Injection Reactor (A.I.R.), or air pump system is continued in some applications.

E.G.R. (Exhaust Gas Recirculation) is used with the exhaust gas introduced into the intake mixture in the intake manifold and modulated by an exhaust backpressure modulating valve.

All models have high energy ignition (H.E.I.) to prevent any possible catalyst damage caused by ignition miss. Refer to the "Electronic Ignition" Unit Repair Section for details.

Oxidizing catalytic converters are used on all models to control hydrocarbons and carbon monoxide. Refer to the "Emission Control" Unit Repair Section for details on this system.

All engines have outside air intakes. The cooler outside air improves driveability.

A heat valve on the exhaust manifold diverts exhaust gases through the intake manifold for a faster warmup.

ENGINE

Inline Six-Cylinder Engine

1970-76

The overhead cam six-cylinder engine was replaced by an overhead valve, 250 cu. in., six-cylinder engine in 1970. It has a cast iron block and cylinder head, uses hydraulic valve lifters, and is similar in construction to the Chevrolet engine. Starting 1975, the intake manifold is integral with the cylinder head.

NOTE: For V6 engine servce procedures, refer to the Buick Apollo, Century, Gran Sport, Regal, Skyhawk, Skylark, Special Section.

V8 Engine

In 1968, an all-new 350 cu in. engine of Pontiac design was introduced. This engine is used as the standard base engine up to the present.

In 1970, the 400 cu. in. engine was available in two Ram Air versions for use in the GTO—the Ram Air III and IV. For the first time, a high output version of the 455 cu. in. engine, also with four-bolt main caps, was made available in the GTO. This engine was used in the Trans Am Firebird and GTO Judge in 1971, and in the LeMans and Grand Am in 1973.

The 1971-72 Ventura II has, as an option, a 307 cu. in. V8 similar to the Chevrolet design. This engine was supplemented in 1972 by the Pontiac 350 cu. in. V8. The 307 cu. in. V8 was dropped for 1973.

Two new engines were introduced in 1975 for use in the Ventura only. These are the 260 V8, which is similar to the Oldsmobile design, and the 350 V8, which is similar to the Buick design. The Pontiac design 350 continues in all other models.

OHC 4 Cylinder Engine

The Astre engine is a single overhead camshaft, four-cylinder design using a die cast aluminum cylinder block and a cast iron cylinder head. The iron-plated aluminum pistons ride directly on honed and electrochemically treated aluminum bores. The cylinder block is cast of an alloy containing silicon which, after suitable etching, provides a proper bore surface for the pistons and rings.

The valve train is completely contained in the head, with a straight-line vertical valve configuration. The camshaft is driven by a timing belt which in turn is driven from a front crankshaft pulley.

The 140 cu in. engine is available in the base single-barrel and an optional version with a two-barrel carburetor and high-performance camshaft.

Engine R & R

Inline Six and V8

1. Disconnect battery.
2. Drain cooling system.
3. Scribe alignment marks on hood and remove hood from hinges.
4. Disconnect the engine wiring harness and ground straps, alternator wires, and the engine-temperature and oil-pressure sending-unit wires.
5. Remove air cleaner and fan shield or shroud.
6. Disconnect radiator and heater hoses.
7. Remove radiator.

NOTE: On some models you can do the job by removing only the radiator or the fan, but it is generally easier to remove them both.

8. Remove fan and fan pulley.

NOTE: if equipped with power steering and/or air conditioning, disconnect and swing aside pump/compressor *without* disconnecting hoses.

9. Disconnect accelerator linkage.
10. Disconnect automatic transmission vacuum modulator line and power brake vacuum line at carburetor.

NOTE: on 1969 Firebird with air conditioning, remove wiper motor.

11. Raise the front of the car and drain the engine oil.
12. Disconnect fuel lines at pump.
13. Disconnect exhaust pipes.
14. Disconnect the starter wires and remove the starter on six-cylinder models.
15. If equipped with automatic transmission, remove converter cover and three converter retaining bolts, then slide converter to the rear.
16. If equipped with manual transmission, disconnect clutch linkage and remove clutch cross-shaft.

NOTE: remove starter and lower flywheel cover on 1970 and later V8s.

17. Remove four lower bellhousing bolts (two per side). Remove the three right side bolts on the 260 V8.
18. Disconnect transmission filler tube support (automatic) and starter wire shield from cylinder heads.
19. Remove two front motor mount-to-frame bracket bolts.
20. Lower car to floor then, using a jack and a wood block, support the transmission. Support the engine with a hoist.
21. Remove two remaining bellhousing bolts. Remove the three left side bolts on the 260 V8.
22. Raise transmission slightly, using the jack and wood block, then, using a chain hoist, remove the engine.
23. To install, reverse removal procedure. Install the two upper bellhousing bolts first (with jack still under transmission).

NOTE: do not lower engine completely until jack and wood block are removed.

OHC 4 Cylinder

1. Raise the hood and install a bolt in the hold-open link.
2. Disconnect the battery cables.
3. Drain the cooling system and disconnect the hoses at the radiator.
4. Disconnect the heater hoses at the water pump and at the heater inlet (bottom hose).
5. Disconnect the following emission hoses:
   a. PCV at the cam cover.
   b. The canister vacuum hose at the carburetor.
   c. PCV vacuum hose at the intake manifold.
   d. Bowl vent at the carburetor.
6. Remove the radiator, fan, fan spacer and air cleaner.
7. Disconnect the following electrical leads:
   a. Alternator.
   b. Ignition coil.
   c. Starter solenoid.
   d. Oil pressure sending unit.

e. Temperature sending unit.
f. Ground strap at the firewall.

8. Disconnect:
   a. Turbo Hydra-Matic detent cable.
   b. Fuel line at the rubber hose, rearward of the carburetor.
   c. Automatic transmission vacuum modulator and air conditioning vacuum line at the intake manifold.
   d. Throttle cable at the manifold bellcrank.
9. On cars with air conditioning, disconnect the compressor at the front support, rear support, rear lower bracket and remove the drive belt from the compressor.

NOTE: Do not disconnect any air conditioning lines or fittings.

10. Being careful not to crimp or bend the hoses, move the compressor slightly forward, allowing the front of the compressor to rest on the frame forward brace. Secure the rear of the compressor to the engine compartment so that it does not interfere with the engine removal.
11. If so equipped, disconnect the power steering pump and position it out of the way.
12. Raise the car on a hoist.
13. Disconnect the exhaust pipe at the exhaust manifold.
14. Remove the engine flywheel lower cover or the torque converter underpan.
15. On vehicles equipped with automatic transmission:
    a. Mark the converter-to-flywheel relationship for reassembly.
    b. Remove the converter to flywheel retaining bolts and install a converter safety strap, to keep the converter from falling out.
    c. Remove the converter housing to engine retaining bolts.
    d. Loosen the engine front mount retaining bolts at the frame attachment and lower the vehicle on the hoist.
    e. Install a floor jack under the transmission and an engine hoist to raise the engine slightly from its mounts.
    f. Remove the engine front mount retaining bolts.
    g. Remove the engine from the vehicle. Pull the engine forward enough to clear the transmission while slowly lifting the engine.
16. On vehicles with manual transmission:
    a. Remove the flywheel housing to engine retaining bolts.
    b. Proceed with Step 15, parts d, e, f, and g.

To install engine:

17. Install two guide pins into the upper bolt holes in the engine block. Guide pins can be fabricated by cutting the heads off two bolts and sawing screwdriver slots into them.
18. Lower the engine into place, aligning the engine with the transmission.
19. Install the front mount bolts hand-tight.
20. Install the converter or clutch housing-to-engine bolts, replacing the guide pins. Remove the torque converter retaining strap, if one was used.
21. Torque the clutch housing-to-engine bolts to 25 ft lbs and the converter housing-to-engine bolts to 35 ft lbs.
22. After checking to make sure that the front engine mounts are aligned and not making metal to-metal contact, tighten them to 20 ft lbs.
23. Align the previously made converter and flywheel marks, and torque the bolts to 35 ft lbs.
24. Install the flywheel dust cover or torque converter underpan.
25. Connect the exhaust pipe at the manifold.
26. If so equipped, install the air conditioning compressor and power steering pump. Adjust the alternator belt.
27. Reconnect:
    a. the accelerator cable,
    b. the automatic transmission vacuum modulator line and the air conditioning vacuum line,
    c. the fuel line, and
    d. the Turbo Hydra-Matic detent cable.
28. Attach the following electrical connections:
    a. alternator
    b. coil
    c. starter solenoid
    d. oil pressure switch
    e. temperature switch
    f. engine ground strap
29. Replace the air cleaner and install these hoses:
    a. vent tube at the air cleaner base
    b. carburetor bowl vent
    c. PCV vacuum line
    d. vacuum canister hose
30. Install the radiator, radiator panel or shroud, spacer, and fan.
31. Connect the heater and radiator hoses. Fill the cooling system.
32. Connect the battery cables. Start the engine and check for leaks. Remember to remove the bolt from the hood hold-open link.

Manifolds

Intake Manifold R & R

NOTE: Pontiac doesn't recommend a specific manifold bolt torque sequence, except for the 260, 307, and 1975-76 Ventura 350 V8s. However, one of the torque sequences shown should be adopted for other engines.

V8 Except Ventura II 307

1. Remove the EGR valve. Drain the radiator and block.

NOTE: You can drain most of the coolant through the radiator drain if you raise the rear of the car 15-18 in.

2. Remove air cleaner and upper radiator hose. On the 260 V8, remove the thermostat bypass hose and the heater hose.
3. Disconnect heater hose.
4. Disconnect temperature gauge wire, then remove two spark plug wire brackets from manifold. On the 260 V8, remove the coil mounting bolt.
5. Disconnect power brake vacuum and distributor vacuum lines. On the 1975-76 350 Ventura engine, remove the compressor bracket bolt, loosen the compressor bolt, and slide the bracket out.

NOTE: vacuum retard line is located at lower rear of vacuum unit on some exhaust emission distributors.

6. Disconnect fuel line at carburetor.
7. Disconnect crankcase vent hose and accelerator linkage.
8. Remove bolts that secure accelerator linkage bracket, then remove intake manifold bolts and nuts. If the intake manifold will not clear the distributor, remove the distributor after noting the position of the rotor and the distributor housing.
9. Remove manifold and gasket.

Caution make sure the O-ring between the intake manifold and timing chain cover is in place, where used.

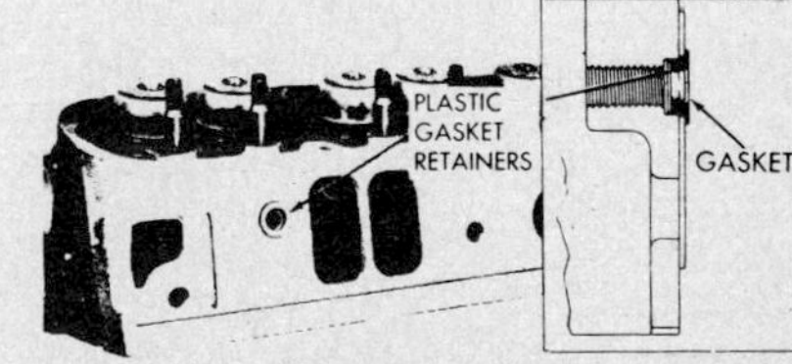

350 (except 1975-76 Ventura), 400, 455 V8 intake manifold gaskets can be held in place by using plastic retainers, available at Pontiac dealers

(© Pontiac Div., G.M. Corp)

10. To install, reverse removal procedure, tightening timing chain cover to manifold bolts to 10-20 ft. lbs., manifold hold-down bolts and nuts evenly to the specified torque.

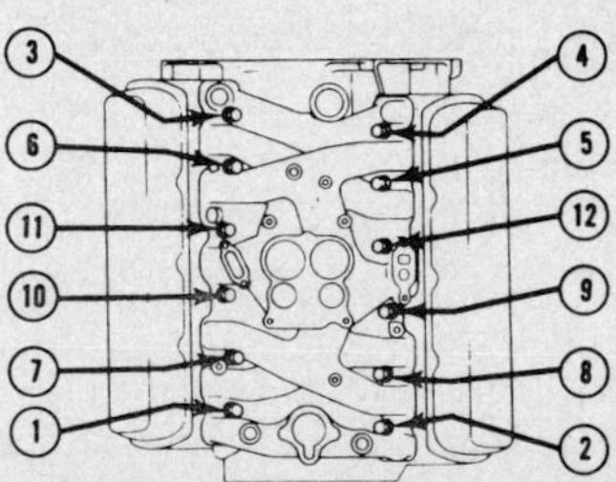

260 V8 intake manifold bolt torque sequence

(© G.M. Corp)

1975-76 Ventura 350 V8 intake manifold bolt torque sequence (© Pontiac Div., G.M. Corp)

1971-72 Ventura II 307 V8

1. Drain water from radiator and both sides of block.
2. Disconnect battery cables, upper radiator hose, accelerator linkage, carburetor fuel line, coil and temperature sender wires.
3. Disconnect power brake hose at carburetor base and spark advance hose at distributor.
4. Disconnect PCV hoses, then remove distributor cap and matchmark rotor and housing.
5. Remove distributor hold-down clamp and pull out distributor.
6. Remove upper alternator bracket and coil.
7. Remove manifold-to-head bolts, then remove manifold from engine.
8. To install, reverse removal procedure. Stick manifold end seals in position with sealer and tighten manifold bolts to 30 ft. lbs.

OHC 4 Cylinder

1. Raise the hood and install a bolt through the hold-open link.
2. Disconnect the negative battery cable.
3. Drain the cooling system.
4. Remove the EGR tube retaining clamps from both the intake and exhaust manifolds. Remove the EGR tube by carefully driving it off.
5. Disconnect the heater hose at the fitting on the intake manifold.
6. Disconnect the vent tube at the base of the air cleaner, then remove the air cleaner.
7. Remove the air cleaner silencer.
8. Disconnect:
   a. The choke rod at the carburetor.
   b. PCV valve at the cam cover.
   c. Fuel line at the carburetor.
   d. The carburetor bowl vent line at the carburetor.
   e. Throttle linkage and the transmission throttle valve linkage.
   f. Power steering pump brace at the manifold.
9. Remove the alternator to thermostat housing through-bolt and loosen the alternator swivel bolt. Move the alternator aside to gain access to the manifold bolt.
10. Remove the four intake manifold bolts and remove the manifold.
11. Remove from the manifold:
    a. The carburetor and carburetor linkage.
    b. Pipe plug.
    c. Vacuum fittings.
    d. Hot water nipple.
12. Install the items removed in Step 10 above to the new manifold.
13. Clean the gasket surfaces on the manifold and the cylinder head.
14. Position a new gasket over the dowels on the cylinder head, then carefully install the manifold. Make sure that the gasket remains in place.
15. Install the manifold bolts, tightening to 30 ft. lbs. The stud goes in the hole nearest No. 3 intake port.
16. Connect the power steering pump brace to the manifold.
17. Install the alternator to thermostat housing through bolt and adjust the belt tension.
18. Connect:
    a. The choke rod at the carburetor.
    b. The PCV valve at the cam cover.
    c. Fuel line at the carburetor.
    d. Carburetor bowl vent line at the carburetor.
    e. The throttle and transmission throttle valve linkage.
    f. Vacuum connections at the carburetor.
19. Install the air cleaner silencer and secure it to the heat stove tube.
20. Install the air cleaner. Connect the vent tube at the base of the air cleaner.
21. Connect the heater hose to the intake manifold fitting and fill the cooling system.
22. Raise the car. Install the EGR tube on the intake and exhaust manifolds.
23. Install the EGR tube retaining clamps. Lower the car.
24. Connect the negative battery cable and start the engine. Check for leaks and adjust the carburetor.

Inline Six Cylinder Intake and Exhaust Manifold R & R, through 1974

1. Remove air cleaner.
2. Disconnect accelerator linkage and return spring.
3. Disconnect fuel and vacuum lines at carburetor; disconnect choke rod.
4. Disconnect exhaust pipe at manifold flange.
5. Remove manifold bolts and clamps, then remove manifolds.

NOTE: intake manifold can be separated from exhaust manifold by removing one bolt and two nuts. These fasteners should be tightened to 25 ft. lbs. after the manifolds are bolted to the engine.

6. To install, reverse removal procedure, tightening center clamp bolts to 30 ft. lbs., end bolts to 15-20 ft. lbs. (for OHV engines), or all bolts to 30 ft. lbs. (for OHC engines).

Inline Six Cylinder Exhaust Manifold R & R, 1975-76

This procedure is for inline sixes with the intake manifold integral with the cylinder head.

1. Remove the air cleaner.
2. Remove the power steering and air pump brackets.
3. Remove the heat riser bracket.
4. Disconnect the throttle controls and the throttle return spring.
5. Detach the exhaust pipe at the manifold flange.
6. Unbolt and remove the manifold.
7. Replace the manifold with a new gasket. Torque the bolts to specifications in the illustrated sequence.
8. Replace the exhaust pipe.
9. Connect the throttle controls and return spring.
10. Replace the air cleaner and heat riser.

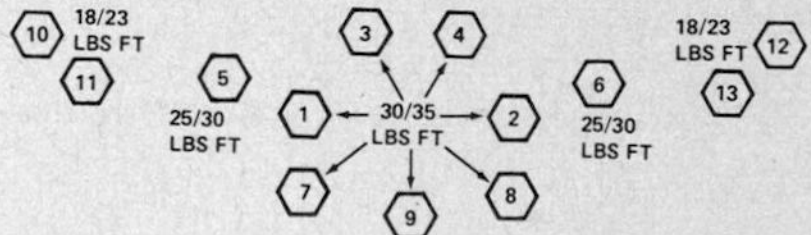

Torque sequence for exhaust manifold on inline six-cylinder with integral intake manifold (© G.M. Corp)

V8 Right-Side Exhaust Manifold R & R

1. On 307 engines, disconnect the battery ground cable.
2. On 307 engines, remove the air cleaner pre-heater stove.
3. Disconnect the exhaust pipes from the manifolds. On 1975-76 manual transmission 350 Ventura, remove the clutch equalizer shaft.
4. Straighten the tabs on the manifold bolts, if used, and remove the manifold bolts, manifold, and gasket.
5. Clean the gasket surfaces.
6. Replace the exhaust manifold, using a new gasket; the holes in the end of the gasket are slotted.

NOTE: the installation of the gasket may be simplified by first install-

ing the manifold using only the front and rear bolts to retain the manifold. Allow clearance of about 3/16 in. between the cylinder head and the exhaust manifold. After inserting the gasket between the head and the manifold, the remaining bolts may be installed.

7. On the 307 engine, torque the center bolts to 30 ft lbs, and the end bolts to 20 ft lbs. On all other engines, torque all bolts evenly to 30 ft lbs.
8. Bend the tabs against the sides of the bolt heads.
9. Attach the exhaust pipe, using a new gasket.
10. Connect the battery ground cable on the 307 (only).
11. Install air cleaner pre-heater stove on the 307 (only).

V8 Left-Side Exhaust Manifold R & R

1. Remove the alternator belt, alternator and mounting bracket as an assembly.
2. Remove the spark plugs from 307 engines. On the 1975-76 Ventura 350, remove the left front engine mount bolt and loosen the right one, in order to raise the engine.
3. Disconnect the exhaust pipes from the manifolds.
4. Remove the air pre-heater shroud from 260 and 307 engines.
5. Straighten the tabs, if used, on the manifold bolt locks and remove the bolts and manifold.
6. Clean the gasket surfaces.
7. Reverse the removal procedures for installation. The notes for the right-side apply here.

OHC 4 Cylinder Exhaust Manifold R & R

1. From under the car, disconnect the exhaust pipe from the manifold.
2. Remove the intake manifold.
3. Disconnect the oil dipstick bracket at the exhaust manifold.
4. Remove the exhaust manifold bolts, then remove the manifold and carburetor heater assembly.
5. Install the carburetor heater assembly on the new manifold.
6. Install the exhaust manifold and manifold bolts (loosely). The upper bolts are shorter.
7. Tighten the manifold bolts to 30 ft. lbs.
8. Connect the exhaust pipe to the manifold.

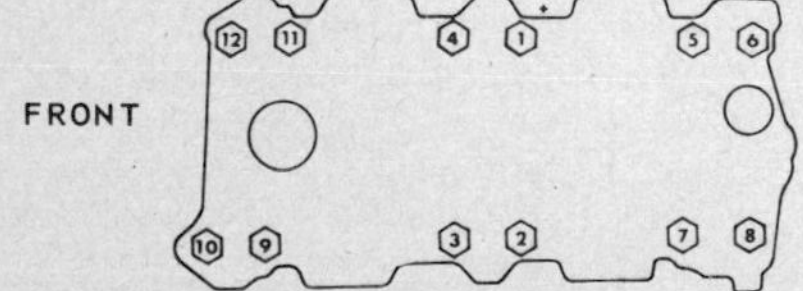

307 V8 intake manifold torque sequence
(© Pontiac Div., G.M. Corp)

9. Connect the oil dipstick bracket to the exhaust manifold.
10. Install the intake manifold as described above.

Valve System

Valve Guides

Pontiac engines have integral valve guides. Pontiac offers valves with oversize stems for worn guides (0.003 and 0.005 in. being available for most engines). To fit these, enlarge valve guide bores with valve guide reamers to an oversize that cleans up wear. If a large oversize is required, it is best to approach that size in stages by using a series of reamers of increasing diameter. This helps to maintain the concentricity of the guide bores with the valve seats. The correct valve stem to guide clearance is given in the Valve Specifications table at the beginning of this section.

As an alternate procedure, some local automotive machine shops fit replacement guides that use standard stem valves.

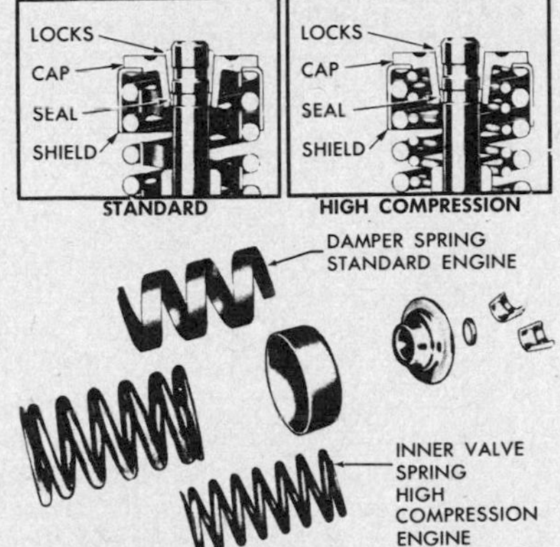

Typical 350 (except 1975-76 Ventura), 400, 455 V8 valve spring assemblies
(© Pontiac Div., G.M. Corp)

Rocker Arm R&R

OHV Six and 350 (except 1975-76 Ventura), 400, 455 V8

1. Remove the valve covers.
2. Remove the rocker arm nut and rocker arm ball.
3. Lift the rocker arm off the rocker arm stud. Always keep the rocker arm assemblies together and assemble them on the same stud.
4. Remove the pushrod from its bore. Make sure the rods are returned to their original bores, with the same end in the block.
5. Reverse the removal procedure to install the rocker arms. On V8s, tighten the rocker arm ball retaining nut to 20 ft lbs. On inline sixes, tighten the rocker arm nut with the lifter on the base circle of the camshaft lobe until valve train play is removed, then tighten a full turn further.

1975-76 Ventura 350 V8

1. Remove the rocker arm cover.
2. Remove the rocker arm shaft assembly bolts and the assembly.
3. Remove the nylon arm retainers by breaking them below their head with a chisel.
4. Remove the rocker arms.

NOTE: Each pair of rocker arms must be installed so that the external rib on each arm points away from the rocker arm shaft bolt that is located between each pair of rocker arms.

5. Install the rocker arms on the shaft and lubricate them with oil.
6. Center each arm on the ¼ in. hole in the shaft. Install new nylon rocker arm retainers in the holes using a ½ in. drift.
7. Locate the push rods in the rocker arms and insert the shaft-to-cylinder head bolts. Tighten the bolts a little at a time until they are tight.
8. Install the rocker cover and use a new gasket.

260 V8

Remove the valve covers. Remove the two bolts that attach the rocker arm pivot to the cylinder head. Remove the rocker arms in pairs. Install the pairs of rocker arms for each cylinder only when the lifters are off the cam lobe and the valves are closed. Lubricate all pivot and rocker arm wear points with white grease. Torque the hardened flanged retaining bolts to 25 ft. lbs.

Valve Adjustment

1969 6 Cylinder OHC

This engine is equipped with hydraulic valve lash adjusters. These adjusters are located in the cylinder head and serve as a fulcrum of the rocker arms, and locate the rocker arms accurately with the camshaft lobes. This lash adjuster is identical to that of a lifter used in a conventional pushrod engine. However, the lash adjuster remains stationary to maintain adjustment at all times.

These adjusters are to be serviced in the same manner as conventional hydraulic tappets.

Adjuster R & R

1. Remove rocker cover assembly.
2. Remove rocker arm and hydraulic lash adjuster assemblies, keeping them in proper order for correct installation in original positions.
3. If lash adjuster sticks in its bore, proceed as follows:
   a. Remove rocker arm.
   b. Fill vent hole adjacent to lifter with SAE 30 oil.
   c. Insert a 4 in. length of 3/16 in. diameter rod into the vent hole and strike the end of the rod sharply with a hammer.

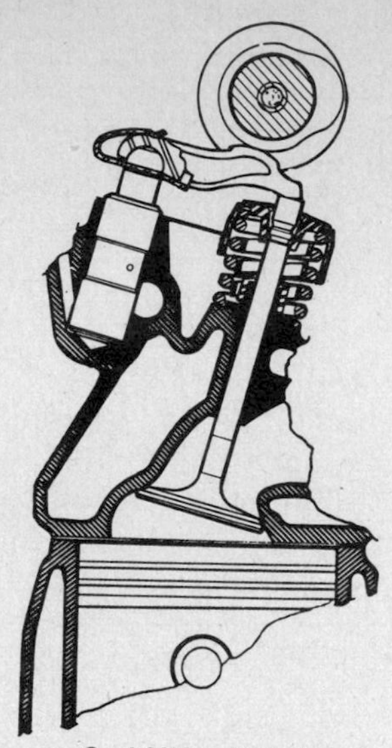
6 cyl OHC valve train
(© Pontiac Div., G.M. Corp)

NOTE: the hydraulic pressure generated in this operation should be sufficient to dislodge even the most stubborn adjuster.

4. To install, reverse removal procedure, with the exception of Step 3.

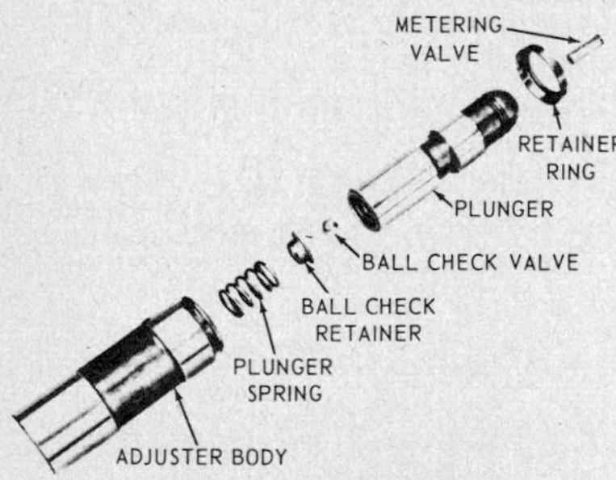

6 cyl OHC valve lash adjuster
(© Pontiac Div., G.M. Corp)

Compressing valve spring OHC 6 cyl
(© Pontiac Div., G.M. Corp)

OHC 4 Cylinder

1. Mark the locations of No. one and four spark plug wires on the side of the distributor with chalk. (Refer to the firing order illustration.)
2. Remove the distributor cap, air cleaner, and valve cover.
3. Turn the engine until the rotor points to the no. one position. The no. one intake and exhaust, no. two intake and no. three exhaust valves are adjusted at this position. The intake valve is the front valve for each cylinder, and the exhaust valve is the rear one.
4. Insert the correct size feeler gauge between the camshaft lobe and the valve tappet. If the clearance is between 0.014 and 0.017 in. for intakes or 0.029 and 0.032 in. for exhausts, no adjustment is necessary. This is due to the fact that the adjusting mechanism only allows adjustments in increments of 0.003 in.
5. If lash is 0.003 in. or more out of adjustment, insert a 1/8 in. allen wrench into the tappet adjusting screw and turn it one full turn. Turning clockwise tightens; turning counterclockwise loosens.
6. Check the lash again and adjust further if necessary. Always turn the adjuster screw one full turn. You can feel the flat spot by pressing down on the tappet while adjusting.
7. Turn the engine so that the rotor points to no. four. Adjust no. two exhaust, no. three intake, and no. four intake and exhaust valves in this position.
8. Replace the valve cover, air cleaner, and distributor cap.

Rocker Arm Stud R & R

OHV 6 Cylinder

1. Remove the rocker arm cover.
2. Remove the rocker arm.
3. If the original 3/8—24 N.F. stud threads are stripped, use a 3/8—16 N.C. tap to rethread it.
4. Put a stack of flat washers on the stud and tighten down the nut to pull the stud up. It may be necessary to remove the nut and add more washers to get the stud out.
5. If an oversize stud is to be installed (0.003 and 0.013 in. oversizes are available), ream the stud hole.
6. To install, coat the press fit area of the stud with axle lubricant, then press or hammer it into place. Make sure that the stud protrudes the same amount as the original ones.

NOTE: The factory recommends that a special tool, J-6880, be used. This is a sleeve that protects the threads from damage and ensures that the stud is driven in to the correct depth. A substitute can be fabricated. Do not hammer directly on the stud; it may fracture.

All V8 through 1973 Except GTO and Ventura II 307

Caution This procedure can be used **only** on engines with pressed-in rocker studs. GTO and some special high performance engines have screwed-in rocker studs which are easily identified by their hex head lower portion. All 1974 and later engines have screwed-in studs. Another common stud-securing repair procedure on standard engines is "pinning" pressed-in studs by drilling through the stud boss and stud and inserting an interference-fit roll pin. Make sure any such pins are removed before attempting the following procedure.

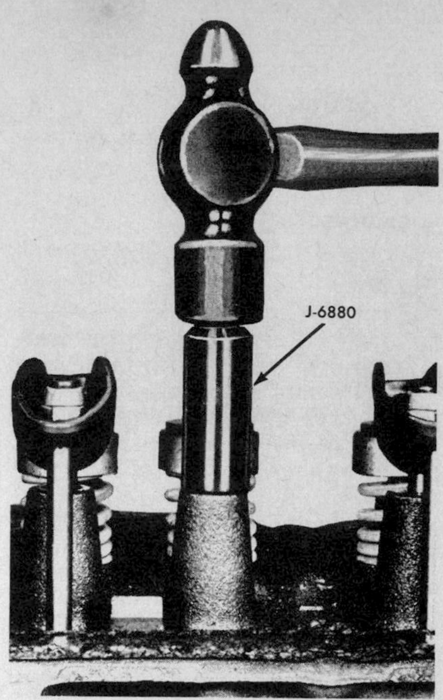

Installing rocker arm stud—OHV 6 cyl
(© Pontiac Div., G.M. Corp)

1. Disconnect battery and drain cooling system.
2. Remove rocker cover.
3. Pack oily rags around stud holes and engine openings.
4. Remove rocker arm and pushrod, then file two slots 3/32-1/8 in. deep on opposite sides of the stud. The top of the slots should be 1/4-3/8 in. below thread travel.
5. Place a spacer over the stud, then position stud remover on stud.
6. Place a spacer over the remover, then thread a 7/8 in. nut on stud remover and turn in until stud pulls from head.
7. If an oversize stud is to be used (0.003 in. oversize studs are available), ream stud hole to the proper size, then clean chips from area.
8. To install, refer to Step 6 of OHV 6 cylinder stud replacement procedure, substituting factory tool number J-23342 for J-6880.

GTO Screwed-In Rocker Studs

1. Remove rocker cover.
2. Remove rocker arm and nut.
3. Remove stud, using a deep socket.
4. Install new stud, tightening to 50 ft. lbs.

1971-72 Ventura II 307 V8

1. Remove rocker cover.

2. Place a stack of 3/8 in. washers over stud so that about 8-10 threads show.
3. Thread a 3/8—24 nut onto stud and turn it down with a wrench until stud begins to move. It will be necessary to remove nut and add more washers as the stud comes out.

NOTE: Stud can be rethreaded to 3/8—16 if it's stripped.

4. To install, coat the stud with hypoid lube, then press in using tool J-6880, as for OHV six.

The following is a method for replacing valve springs, oil seals or spring retainers without removing the cylinder head.

1. **Obtain a spark plug hole airchuck adapter from an auto parts store.**
2. **To this adapter add an airchuck so that the hose from an air compressor can be attached. This assembly will be used later to pressurize the cylinder.**
3. **Remove the valve rocker cover. Remove the rocker arm from the valve to be worked on.**
4. **Remove the spark plug from the cylinder to be worked on.**
5. **Turn the crankshaft to bring the piston of this cylinder down, away from possible contact with the valve head. Sharply tap the valve retainer to loosen the valve lock.**
6. **Then turn the crankshaft to bring the piston in this cylinder to the Exact Top of its Compression Stroke.**
7. **Screw in the chuck-equipped tool.**
8. **Hook up an air hose to the chuck and turn on the pressure (about 200 lbs.).**
9. **With a strong and constant supply of air holding the valve closed, compress the valve spring and remove the lock and retainer.**
10. **Make the necessary replacements and reassemble.**

NOTE: it is important that the operation be performed exactly as stated, in this order. The piston in the cylinder must be on exact top-center to prevent air pressure from turning the crankshaft.

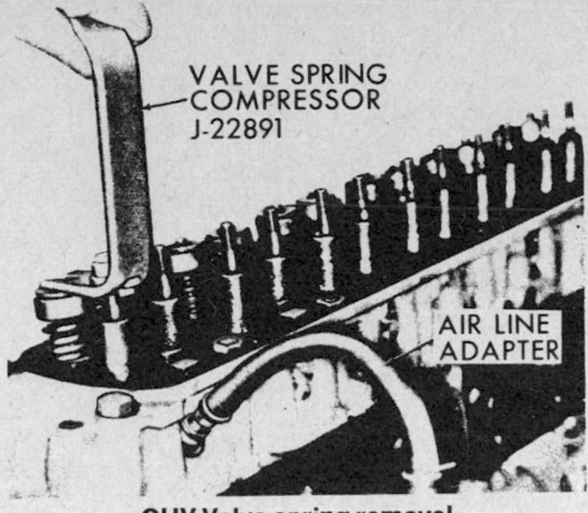

OHV Valve spring removal
(© Pontiac Div., G.M. Corp)

Cylinder Head

1969 OHC 6 Cylinder

Removal

1. Drain cooling system and remove air cleaner.
2. Disconnect accelerator pedal cable at bellcrank on manifold, and fuel and vacuum lines at carburetor.
3. Disconnect exhaust pipe at manifold flange, then remove manifold bolts and clamps and remove manifolds and carburetor as an assembly.
4. Remove timing belt top front cover.
5. Align timing marks, remove belt tension then remove belt from camshaft sprocket.
6. Remove rocker arm cover assembly.
7. Remove timing belt upper front cover mounting support bracket and rear lower cover.
8. Disconnect spark plug wires.
9. Remove rocker arms and hydraulic valve lash adjusters. Keep rocker arms and hydraulic lash adjusters in proper sequence for exact location for installation.
10. Remove cylinder head bolts and gasket.
11. Clean gasket surfaces and carbon from cylinder head and block.

Installation

When installing head, transfer all serviceable parts to new head using new seals on intake and exhaust valves and new intake and exhaust manifold gaskets.

1. Place new cylinder head gasket in position over dowels in cylinder block.
2. Guide cylinder head into place over dowels and gasket.
3. Start all cylinder head bolts in threads.

NOTE: bolts are of two different lengths. When inserted into proper holes, all bolts will project an equal distance from the head. Do not use sealer of any kind on threads.

4. Tighten cylinder head a little at a time with a torque wrench. Tighten center bolts and then the end bolts. Final torque should be 90-100 ft. lbs. Tighten the bolts to specifications in three stages.
5. Reverse Steps 1-9 of removal to complete installation procedure.

1970-76 OHV 6 Cylinder

Removal

1. Drain cooling system, remove air cleaner. Disconnect radiator hoses.
2. Disconnect accelerator pedal rod at bellcrank, fuel and vacuum lines at carburetor. Disconnect exhaust pipe at manifold flange.
3. Remove manifold-to-cylinder head attaching bolts and manifolds.
4. Remove rocker arm cover assembly, temperature sender and coil wires.
5. Loosen rocker arm nuts and rotate rocker arms so the pushrods can be removed.
6. Remove pushrods and store them so they can be installed in their original locations.
7. Disconnect spark plug wires. Remove the spark plugs.
8. Remove cylinder head bolts.
9. Lift off the head.
10. Remove cylinder head gasket.

Installation

1. Position new cylinder head gasket on block, on locating dowels.
2. Place cylinder head in position.
3. Install cylinder head attaching bolts. Tighten to specifications in three stages.
4. Install pushrods in original location and position.
5. Position rocker arm with lifter on base circle of camshaft and tighten rocker arm nuts until valve train play is removed. Tighten one more turn.
6. Install rocker arm cover.
7. Install manifold-to-cylinder head bolts and torque to specifications.

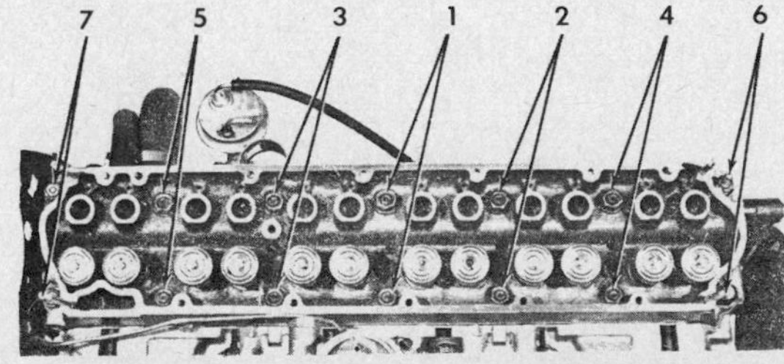

Cylinder head torque sequence—OHC 6 cyl
(© Pontiac Div., G.M. Corp)

Cylinder head torque sequence—OHV 6 cyl
(© Pontiac Div., G.M. Corp)

8. Install pushrod cover and crankcase breather outlet pipe.
9. Connect all wires, hoses and linkage; fill cooling system and check for leaks.
10. Replace the spark plugs and connect spark plug wires.

All V8

Removal

NOTE: drain the cooling system, including the block.

1. Remove intake manifold, valley cover, and rocker arm cover. Position the alternator and air conditioner compressor out of the way.
2. Loosen all rocker arm retaining nuts and pivot rockers off pushrods. Remove the rocker shaft on the 1975-76 Ventura 350. To remove the 1975-76 Ventura 350 left head, remove the dipstick and power steering pump.
3. Remove pushrods and place in order.
4. On the 260 and 1975-76 350 Ventura V8, remove the exhaust manifolds. On all others, remove the exhaust pipe-to-manifold attaching bolts. In order to remove the left head of the 455 S.D., it is necessary to remove the exhaust manifold attaching nuts and drop the manifold. Remove the inner panel of the carburetor heat stove from the two center cylinder head bolts.

NOTE: on 1968-70 air-conditioned Firebird models, remove compressor hold-down bolts and move compressor aside *without* disconnecting hoses.

5. Remove battery ground strap and engine ground strap on left head; engine ground strap and automatic transmission oil filler tube bracket on right head.
6. Remove cylinder head bolts and head, with exhaust manifold attached.

NOTE: left head must be maneuvered to clear power steering and power brake units except on Ventura II.

NOTE: on 1969-70 air-conditioned Firebird models, the right motor mount-to-frame bolt must be removed and the engine jacked up about 2 in. to gain access to the right rear rocker arm cover bolt and cylinder head bolt.

Installation

1. Check head surface for straightness, then place a new head gasket on block.

CAUTION: on 1969-70 air-conditioned Firebird models, install right rear head bolt into head *before* placing head on block.

NOTE: bolts are of three different lengths on 350 (except 1975-76 Ventura), 400, and 455 V8s. When bolts are properly installed, they will project an equal distance from head.

2. Install all bolts and tighten evenly to specified torque. Tighten the bolts to specifications in three stages.
3. Install pushrods in original positions.
4. Install the rocker assembly. Adjust as explained under Rocker Arm R & R.
5. Replace rocker arm cover.
6. Replace valley cover.
7. Replace ground straps, oil filler tube bracket, intake manifold, and right motor mount bolt (on A/C Firebird models).
8. Install exhaust pipe flange nuts. Install the exhaust manifolds, with new gaskets.

NOTE: 350 (except 1975-76 Ventura), 400, and 455 left and right cylinder heads are interchangeable within a single year; large- and small-valve heads should not be used on the same engine.

OHC 4 Cylinder R & R

NOTE: Cylinder head gasket R&R does not require separating the intake and exhaust manifolds from the cylinder head.

1. Remove the timing belt cover and camshaft cover. Drain the cooling system.
2. Remove the timing belt and camshaft sprocket.
3. Remove the intake and exhaust manifolds.
4. Disconnect the water hose at the thermostat housing (outlet).
5. Remove the cylinder head bolts, then the head and gasket.

NOTE: If the head sticks, bump the starter a few times to loosen it with compression. Do not insert any tools between the head and block to pry them apart.

6. Using a new gasket (smooth side up), carefully position the cylinder head on the block.
7. Install the cylinder head bolts finger-tight. Use an anti-seize compound on the threads. Install

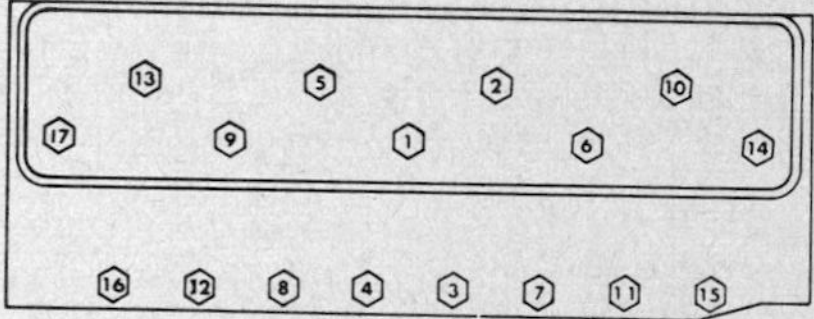

Cylinder head torque sequence—1971-72 307 V8 (© Pontiac Div., G.M. Corp)

1975-76 Ventura 350 head bolt torque sequence

260 V8 cylinder head bolt torque sequence
(© G.M. Corp)

Cylinder head torque sequence—350 (except 1975-76 Ventura), 400, 455 V8
(© Pontiac Div., G.M. Corp)

the lifting bracket under the second head bolt from the front on the spark plug side. The 6-3/8 in. bolts are installed on the manifold side and the 5-5/8 in. bolts are installed on the spark plug side.

8. Tighten the head bolts to 60 ft. lbs. (in steps), using the recommended sequence.
9. Connect the water hose to the thermostat housing.
10. Install the intake and exhaust manifolds.
11. Install the timing bolt and sprocket.
12. Install the front cover and camshaft cover.

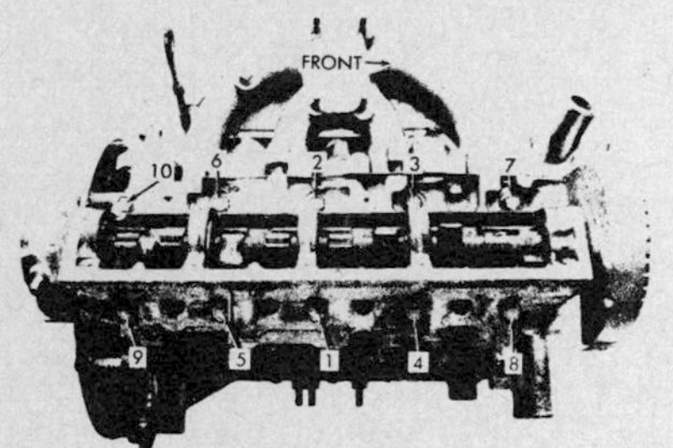

OHC four-cylinder head bolt torque sequence
(© Pontiac Div., G.M. Corp)

Timing Case

Timing Gear or Chain Cover and Oil Seal R & R

1970-76 OHV 6 Cylinder

1. Drain cooling system and disconnect radiator hoses at radiator.
2. Remove fan and water pump pulley.
3. Remove radiator and fan belt.
4. Remove harmonic balancer, using a puller.
5. Remove the two oil pan-to-front cover bolts. Remove or lower the oil pan on 1970-73 models.
6. Remove timing gear cover bolts, pull the cover forward and, on 1974 and later models, cut off the oil pan seal flush with the block, then remove cover and gasket.
7. Pry out oil seal using a screwdriver.

NOTE: seal can be replaced with cover installed.

8. Install new seal, with lip toward inside of cover. Drive it into place, using proper seal installer or an old wheel bearing outer race.
9. Inspect oil nozzle for damage and replace if necessary, then clean all gasket surfaces.
10. On 1974 and later models, cut the tabs from a new oil pan front seal and install the seal to the front cover, pressing the tips into the holes in the cover. Use sealer at the joints. Install cover and gasket (stick gasket to block with grease), making sure cover is centered properly on crankshaft end. Replace the two oil pan bolts, on 1974 and later models.
11. Tighten cover bolts, then install harmonic balancer. Replace the oil pan on 1970-73 models.

350 (except 1975-76 Ventura), 400, 455 V8

1. Drain radiator and cylinder block.
2. Loosen alternator adjusting bolts.
3. Remove fan, fan pulley, and accessory drive belts.
4. Disconnect radiator hoses. Remove the water pump.
5. Remove fuel pump.

NOTE: not necessary if only seal is being replaced.

6. Remove harmonic balancer bolt and washer.
7. Remove harmonic balancer.

NOTE: do not pry on rubber-mounted balancers. Seal can be removed, using a screwdriver, at this point. Install new seal with lip inward.

8. Remove front four oil pan to timing cover bolts.
9. Remove timing cover bolts and nuts and cover to intake manifold bolt.
10. Pull cover forward and remove.
11. Remove O-ring from recess in intake manifold, then clean all gasket surfaces.
12. To replace seal, pry it out of the cover using a screwdriver. Install the new seal with lip inwards.

NOTE: seal can be replaced with cover installed.

13. To install, reverse removal procedure, making sure all gaskets are replaced. Tighten four oil pan bolts to 12 ft. lbs., harmonic balancer bolt to 160 ft. lbs., and fan pulley bolts to 20 ft. lbs.

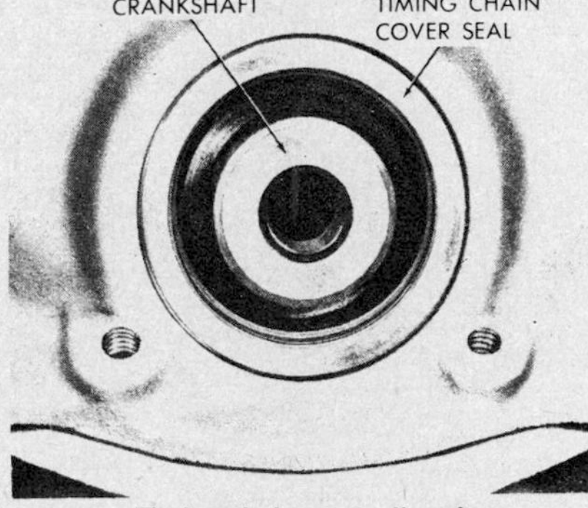

Timing chain cover oil seal
(© Pontiac Div., G.M. Corp)

1971-72 Ventura II 307 V8

NOTE: Removal is similar to 350, 400, and 455 V8 engines with the exceptions noted.

1. Remove oil pan, as outlined in the Lubrication Section.
2. Lower engine back onto motor mounts.
3. Remove harmonic balancer, using a puller.
4. Remove water pump, as outlined previously.
5. Remove timing cover bolts and cover.
6. Install by reversing removal procedure. Tighten cover bolts to 80 in. lbs.

260 V8

The timing case cover and the water pump housing are a one-piece casting.

1. Drain the cooling system and disconnect the radiator and heater hoses, remove the radiator core, the fan blades and pulley.
2. Remove the vibration damper and crankshaft pulley.
3. Drain the oil and remove the oil pan (see Engine Lubrication section).
4. Remove the front cover attaching bolts and remove the cover, timing indicator and water pump from the front of the engine.
5. Install in the reverse order of removal using a new gasket with sealing compound. Tighten self-tapping water pump attaching screws to 13 ft. lbs., 5/16 in. front cover attaching bolts to 22 ft. lbs. and the four bottom bolts (cover plate) to 35 ft. lbs. Torque the pulley hub bolt to 310 ft lbs, crankshaft pulley bolts to 10 ft lbs, and fan bolts to 20 ft lbs.

1975-76 Ventura 350

1. Drain cooling system and remove radiator, shroud, fan, pulleys, and belts.
2. Remove crankshaft pulley, fuel pump and distributor.
3. Remove alternator and power steering pump, if necessary.
4. Loosen and slide rearward front clamp on thermostat by-pass hose. Remove harmonic balancer.
5. Remove bolts attaching timing chain cover to cylinder block and oil pan to timing chain cover bolts. Remove timing chain cover assembly and gasket. Clean cover thoroughly, being careful not to damage the gasket surface.
6. Turn the crankshaft so that the timing marks on the sprockets are adjacent to each other on a line with the shaft centers.
7. Remove crankshaft oil slinger.
8. Remove bolt, special washer, distributor drive gear, and fuel pump eccentric from camshaft.
9. Pry camshaft and crankshaft sprockets forward until camshaft sprocket is free. Then remove both sprockets and chain.

If oil seal appears worn or has been leaking, replace as follows:

10. Use a punch to drive out the old seal and retainer. Drive from

front to rear of the timing chain cover.

11. Coil new packing around opening so that ends are at top. Drive in retainer. Stake the retainer in at least three places. Size the packing by rotating a hammer handle, etc. around the packing until the balancer hub fits through the packing.

If engine has been disturbed since chain and sprockets were removed:

12. Turn crankshaft until No. 1 piston is at top dead center.
13. Mount sprocket temporarily and turn camshaft so that timing mark is straight down.
14. Assemble chain and sprockets and mount on shafts with their timing marks closest to each other.
15. Mount slinger on sprocket with the concave side to the front.
16. Reinstall fuel pump eccentric with oil groove forward, distributor drive gear, special washer, and bolt on camshaft. Tighten the bolt to 50 ft lbs.
17. Remove oil pump cover and pack the space around the oil pump gears full of petroleum jelly, leaving no air spaces. Reinstall oil pump cover with new gasket. This step is very important. If it is not done the oil pump will not begin to pump oil as soon as the engine is started.
18. Reinstall timing chain cover with new gasket. Replace the harmonic balancer.

Keep engine speed low for a short time after installation of a new oil seal.

Timing Belt, Crankshaft Sprocket, or Lower Crankcase Cover Seal R & R—1969 OHC 6 Cylinder

Radiator removal is a distinct advantage for this operation.

1. Remove upper front timing cover.
2. Align timing marks.

NOTE: there are three sets of timing marks that must be aligned. One set is located on the harmonic balancer and the lower front belt cover. A second set is located on the accessory drive housing pulley and the lower front belt cover. The third set is the camshaft pulley set.

The mark on the harmonic balancer must be aligned with zero (0°) on the cover with the no. 1 cylinder on TDC of the compression stroke. The mark on the drive pulley should point toward the water pump and align with its mark on the belt cover. The camshaft pulley mark aligns with a mark on a bolt head located directly below the camshaft pulley.

All three sets of marks must be aligned at the same time when replacing the camshaft drive belt.

3. Remove fan and water pump pulley.
4. Remove harmonic balancer.
5. Remove timing belt lower front cover.
6. Loosen accessory drive mounting bolts to provide slack in timing belt.
7. Remove timing belt.
8. Remove crankshaft timing belt flange and sprocket.
9. Carefully remove seal from crankcase cover.
10. Install new seal, with lip of seal inward.
11. Replace crankshaft timing belt sprocket and flange.
12. Align timing marks and replace timing belt.
13. Replace timing belt lower cover and harmonic balancer.
14. Adjust timing belt tension.
15. Replace water pump pulley and fan.
16. Replace timing belt upper front cover.

Front Crankcase Cover and Gasket R & R—1969 OHC 6 Cylinder

1. Remove timing belt sprocket.
2. Remove four front oil pan-to-crankcase cover retaining bolts.
3. Loosen remaining oil pan bolts, as necessary, to provide clearance between crankcase cover and oil pan.
4. Remove five front crankcase cover attaching bolts.
5. Remove front crankcase cover and gasket, clean off the old gasket.
6. Inspect cover seal for wear or distortion.
7. Using new gasket installed over dowels and, if ncecessary, new seal, reverse removal procedures, torque oil pan and crankcase cover bolts to 10-15 ft. lbs.

Accessory Drive Housing Assembly, Oil Pump, Distributor and Fuel Pump—1969 OHC 6 Cylinder

The housing is unique, and consists of the oil pump, distributor and the fuel pump. The oil filter is also attached to this housing. The housing carries the drive sprocket for the above units and is used as a tensioner for the timing belt.

Oil Pressure Regulator R & R

1. Remove cap washer and spring from housing assembly.
2. Using magnet, remove valve from housing assembly.
3. Install valve on spring and install as an assembly.
4. Install cap washer.

Oil Pump R & R

1. Remove oil pump cover and gasket.
2. Remove drive gear and driven gear.
3. Install gears.
4. Replace cover using new gasket. Torque attaching bolts to 20 ft. lbs.

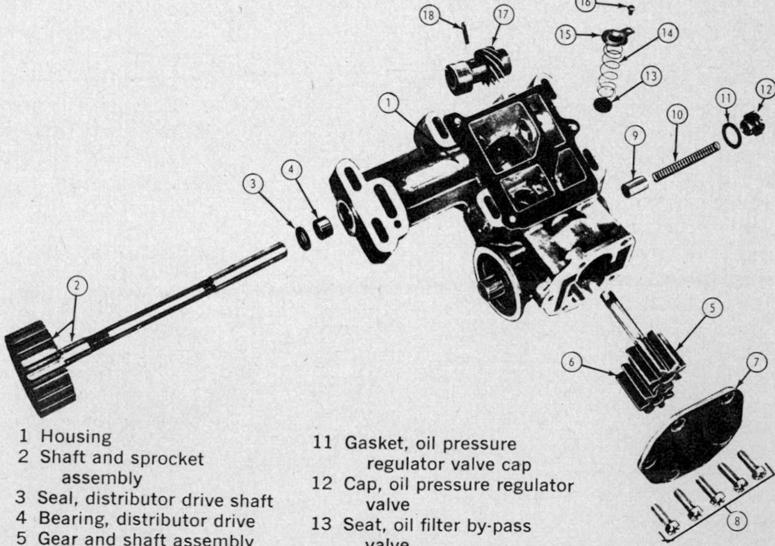

1 Housing
2 Shaft and sprocket assembly
3 Seal, distributor drive shaft
4 Bearing, distributor drive
5 Gear and shaft assembly oil pump drive
6 Gear, oil pump driven cover, oil pump
7 Cover, oil pump
8 Bolt, oil pump cover to housing
9 Valve, oil pressure regulator
10 Spring, oil pressure regulator
11 Gasket, oil pressure regulator valve cap
12 Cap, oil pressure regulator valve
13 Seat, oil filter by-pass valve
14 Spring, oil filter by-pass valve
15 Retainer, oil filter by-pass valve
16 Screw, oil filter by-pass valve retainer
17 Gear and eccentric
18 Pin, distributor oil and fuel pump gear and eccentric

OHC 6 cyl oil pump housing and distributor drive assembly
(© Pontiac Div., G.M. Corp)

Housing Assembly R & R

1. Remove timing belt top front cover.
2. Align timing marks.
3. Loosen six housing assembly retaining bolts from cylinder block.
4. Remove timing belt from camshaft sprocket and distributor drive.
5. Disconnect fuel lines from fuel pump.
6. Remove distributor cap, vacuum lines and wires from distributor.
7. Remove housing by removing six retaining bolts.
8. Install, using a new gasket, and loosely install housing assembly to cylinder block with six retaining bolts.
9. Align timing marks and install timing belt.
10. Connect fuel lines to fuel pump.
11. Replace distributor cap, vacuum lines and wires.
12. Adjust timing belt tension, see timing belt adjustment.
13. Replace timing belt top front cover.

1969 OHC Timing Belt Adjustment

1. Remove timing belt top front cover.
2. Using J-22232-2 calibration bar, set the pointer of timing belt tension fixture J-22232-1 to zero.

NOTE: this calibration must be performed before each use of J-22232 fixture to insure an accurate timing belt adjustment.

3. Remove camshaft sprocket to camshaft bolt and install J-22232-1 (tension fixture) on the belt with the rollers on the outside (smooth) surface of belt. Thread the fixture mounting bolt into camshaft sprocket bolt location, finger-tight.
4. Squeeze indicator end (upper) of fixture and quickly release so the fixture assumes released or relaxed position.
5. With J-22232-1 installed, as above, adjust accessory drive housing up or down, as required, to obtain a tension adjustment indicator reading centered in the green range, with drive housing mounting bolts torqued to 15 ± 3 ft. lbs.
6. Remove tension fixture and install sprocket retaining bolt, making sure bolt threads and washers are free of dirt.
7. Install upper front timing belt cover.

OHC 4 Cylinder Timing Cover, Belt and Camshaft

Front Cover R & R

1. Raise the hood and install a bolt in the hood hold-open link.
2. Disconnect the negative battery cable.
3. Remove the fan and spacer.
4. Loosen the two lower cover retaining screws.
5. Remove the top cover retaining screw and nut and remove the cover, lifting it until the slots clear the lower screws.
6. To install, position the cover, lowering it until the slots are over the lower screws. Loosely tighten the lower screws.
7. Install the upper screw and nut, then tighten all four screws to 50 in lbs.
8. Install the spacer and fan, tightening the bolts to 20 ft. lbs.
9. Connect the battery cable and remove the bolt from the hood hold-open link.

Timing Belt and Sprocket R & R

1. Raise the hood and install a bolt in the hood hold-open link.
2. Disconnect the negative battery cable.
3. Loosen the air conditioner and alternator as necessary and remove the drive belts.
4. Remove the crankshaft pulley and four pulley-to-sprocket bolts. Remove the pulley and damper or washer as applicable.

NOTE: it is not necessary to remove the pulley if only the camshaft sprocket is being removed.

5. Drain the engine coolant and loosen the water pump bolts to relieve the tension on the timing belt.
6. Remove the timing belt lower cover.
7. Remove the timing belt.
8. Align one of the holes in the camshaft timing sprocket with the bolt behind the sprocket. Using a socket on the bolt to keep the sprocket from rotating, remove the sprocket retaining bolt and washer.
9. Remove the camshaft sprocket.
10. The crankshaft sprocket may be removed with a puller.
11. Press the crankshaft sprocket back on. Make sure that the timing mark is facing out and that the key is installed.
12. To install the camshaft sprocket, align the dowel in the camshaft with the locating hole in the end of the camshaft.
13. Install the sprocket retaining bolt, tightening to 80 ft. lbs.
14. Align the timing mark on the camshaft sprocket with the notch on the timing belt upper cover and the crankshaft sprocket timing mark with the cast rib on the oil pump cover.
15. Install the timing belt on the crankshaft sprocket, then with the back of the belt positioned in the water pump track, install the belt on the camshaft sprocket. Make sure that both sprockets maintain their indexed positions.
16. Install the lower timing belt cover, using anti-seize compound on the threads of the bolts and tightening them to 50 in. lbs.
17. Adjust the timing belt tension as described under Water Pump R&R.
18. Fill the cooling system.
19. Install the accessory drive pulley to the crankshaft sprocket, aligning the tang on the pulley with the keyway on the crankshaft. Install the damper locating dowel in the locating hole of the sprocket.
20. Loosely install the four sprocket bolts, then install the crankshaft (center) bolt. Tighten the crankshaft bolt to 80 ft. lbs. and the four sprocket bolts to 15 ft. lbs.
21. Install the alternator and air conditioning compressor as applicable and adjust the belts.
22. Install the engine front cover, fan and fan spacer.
23. Connect the battery cable and remove the bolt from the hood hold-open link.

Camshaft R & R

1970-76 OHV 6 Cylinder

1. Drain cooling system.
2. Remove radiator, fan, and water pump pulley.
3. Remove grill.
4. Remove valve cover and gasket, then loosen rocker arm nuts and pivot rockers out of the way.
5. Remove pushrods. Keep them in order.
6. Remove distributor, fuel pump, and spark plugs.
7. Remove coil, pushrod (tappet gallery) covers and gasket; reach in and remove tappets, keeping them in order.
8. Pull off the harmonic balancer, then loosen the oil pan bolts and allow the pan to drop.
9. Remove timing gear cover.
10. Remove two camshaft thrust plate bolts by rotating cam gear holes to gain clearance.
11. Remove the camshaft by pulling it straight forward.

NOTE: support the camshaft; the cam bearings could be dislodged.

12. If cam gear is to be replaced, press it from the shaft using an arbor press.

CAUTION: thrust plate must be positioned so that Woodruff key does not damage it during removal.

13. New cam gear must be pressed onto the shaft, with the shaft supported in back of the front bearing journal.

NOTE: the thrust plate end-play should be 0.001-0.005 in. If less than 0.001 in., replace spacer ring; if greater than 0.005 in., replace thrust plate.

14. Carefully install the camshaft into the engine, then turn crankshaft and camshaft so that timing marks coincide; tighten thrust plate bolts to 5-8 ft. lbs.

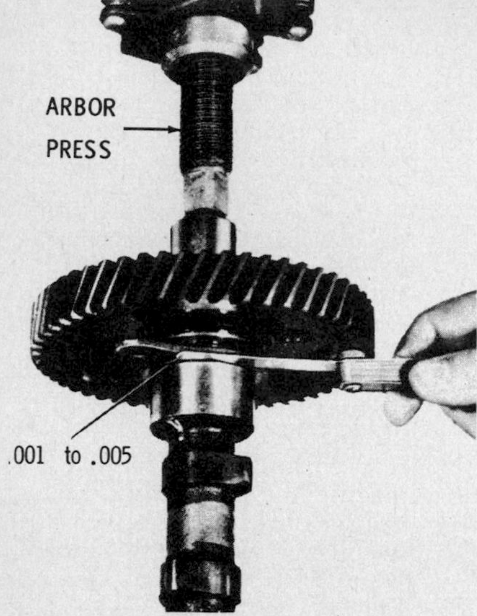

Installing OHV 6 camshaft gear and checking thrust plate end-play
(© Pontiac Div., G.M. Corp)

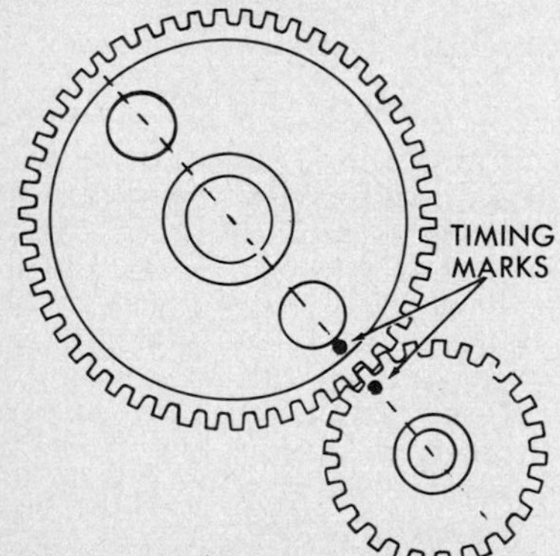

OHV 6 cyl timing mark alignment

Checking OHV 6 camshaft gear runout
(© Pontiac Div., G.M. Corp)

15. Check camshaft and crankshaft gear runout using a dial indicator. Cam gear runout should not exceed 0.004 in., crank gear should not exceed 0.003 in.

NOTE: if runout is excessive, remove gear and clean burrs from shaft.

16. Check gear backlash using a dial indicator; it should not exceed 0.006 in. and should not be less than 0.004 in.
17. To complete installation, reverse Steps 1-9.

NOTE: install distributor with No. 1 piston at TDC on compression stroke as indicated by the damper timing mark so that vacuum diaphragm faces forward and rotor points to No. 1 spark plug wire cap tower. Make sure oil pump drive shaft is properly indexed with distributor drive shaft.

350 (except 1975-76 Ventura), 400, 455 V8

1. Drain cooling system and remove air cleaner.
2. Disconnect all water hoses, vacuum lines and spark plug wires. Remove the radiator.
3. Disconnect accelerator linkage, temperature gauge wire, and fuel lines.
4. Remove hood latch brace.
5. Remove PCV hose, then remove rocker covers.

NOTE: on air-conditioned models, remove alternator and bracket.

6. Remove distributor, then remove intake manifold.
7. Remove valley cover.
8. Loosen rocker arm nuts and pivot rockers out of the way.
9. Remove pushrods and lifters (keep them in proper order).
10. Remove harmonic balancer, fuel pump, and four oil pan to timing cover bolts.
11. Remove timing cover and gasket, then remove fuel pump eccentric and bushing.
12. Align timing marks, then remove timing chain and sprockets.
13. Remove camshaft thrust plate.
14. Remove camshaft by pulling straight forward, being careful not to damage cam bearings in the process.

NOTE: it may be necessary to jack up the engine slightly to gain clearance, especially if motor mounts are worn.

15. Install new camshaft, with lobes and journals coated with heavy (SAE 50-60) oil, into the engine, being careful not to damage cam bearings.

NOTE: most specialty cams come with a special "break-in" lubricant for the lobes and journals; if such lubricant is available, use it instead of heavy oil.

16. Install camshaft thrust plate and tighten bolts to 20 ft. lbs.
17. To install, reverse Steps 1-12, tightening camshaft sprocket bolt to 40 ft lbs, timing cover bolts and nuts to 30 ft. lbs., oil pan bolts to 12 ft. lbs., and harmonic balancer bolt to 160 ft. lbs.

1971-72 Ventura II 307 V8

1. Remove intake manifold, valve lifters and timing chain cover (requires oil pan removal).

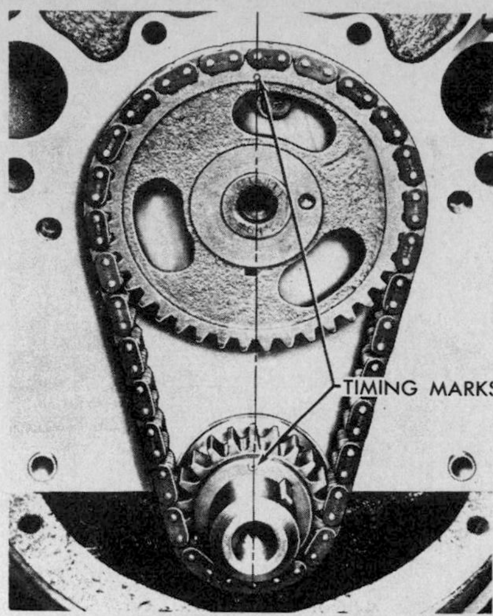

350 (except 1975-76 Ventura), 400, 455 V8 timing gear alignment marks
(© Pontiac Div., G.M. Corp)

2. Remove the two center bolts and the one lower bolt that secure the hood latch support. This will give adequate clearance for the cam. Remove radiator.
3. Remove fuel pump and pump pushrod.
4. Remove camshaft sprocket bolts, sprocket and timing chain. A light blow to the lower edge of a tight sprocket should free it (use a plastic mallet).
5. Install two 5/16—18 x 4 in. bolts in cam bolt holes and pull cam from block.
6. To install, reverse removal procedure, aligning timing marks as illustrated.

NOTE: cam lobes must be lubricated with Molykote® or equivalent before installation. All cam journals are the same diameter, so make sure cam bearings are not dislodged during installation.

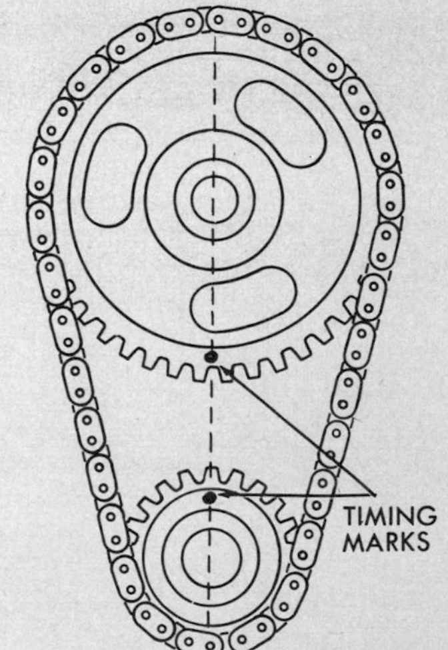

Typical Timing mark alignment—260, 307, 1975-76 Ventura 350 V8

260 V8

1. Disconnect the battery ground cable.
2. Drain the coolant. Remove the radiator.
3. Disconnect the fuel pump line.

4. Remove the air cleaner; discon nect the throttle cable.
5. Remove the alternator belt. Move the alternator and power steering pump aside. Move the air conditioning compressor to one side, but don't disconnect the refrigerant lines.
6. At the water pump, disconnect the thermostat bypass hose and heater hose.
7. Detach all engine electrical and vacuum connections.
8. Remove the distributor, exhaust crossover pipe, starter, and detach the exhaust pipe from the manifold.
9. Remove the crankshaft pulley and balancer bolt. Use a puller to remove the balancer.
10. Support the engine with a hoist. Remove the engine mount to bracket bolts, raise the engine as far as possible, and unbolt the mounts from the engine.
11. Remove the flywheel inspection cover and the oil pan.
12. Place wood blocks between the exhaust manifolds and the front crossmember to support the engine. Remove the hoist.
12. Remove the timing chain cover.
13. Remove the rocker covers. Remove the intake manifold.
14. Remove the oil filler pipe and the water temperature sender.
15. Remove the rocker arms, pushrods, and lifters. Keep all these parts in order so that they can be replaced in their original locations.
16. Remove the bolt, fuel pump eccentric, camshaft gear, oil slinger, and timing chain.
17. Carefully slide the camshaft out of the front of the engine.
18. On installation, coat the camshaft with special lubricant. Make sure to install the timing indicator before the power steering pump bracket. Install the flywheel inspection cover after the starter.

1975-76 Ventura 350 V8

1. Remove the intake manifold.
2. Remove the rocker covers. Remove the rocker shafts, pushrods, and lifters. Keep these components in order so they can be replaced in their original locations.
3. Remove the timing chain cover and the chain and sprockets.
4. Slide the camshaft out carefully.
5. Reverse the procedure for installation.

1969 OHC 6 Cylinder

1. Remove camshaft sprocket and seal.
2. Remove rocker cover assembly.
3. Using an adapter and a slide hammer, drive camshaft to the rear. Make sure bearing surfaces are not damaged during this operation.
4. Disconnect slide hammer and remove camshaft from rear of rocker cover.
5. Remove thrust washer, retaining washer, and bolt from rear of camshaft.
6. Clean and inspect all parts for wear or damage, then inspect bearing surfaces for wear or scoring.
7. Clean camshaft oil passages.
8. To install, reverse removal procedure making sure thrust washer is installed as illustrated. Tighten retaining bolt to 40 ft. lbs.
9. Check camshaft end-play, using a dial indicator on the front sprocket; end-play should be 0.003-0.009 in. and is controlled by the camshaft bore plug.

NOTE: lubricate camshaft lobes and rockers with special lubricant, available at Pontiac dealers. Tighten rocker cover bolts and nuts to 15 ft. lbs. from center outward.

Camshaft thrust washer position—OHC 6 (© Pontiac Div., G.M. Corp)

OHC 4 Cylinder

NOTE: A special valve tappet depressing tool is necessary for camshaft removal. The procedure given here uses the factory tool; it may vary slightly with those produced by tool companies.

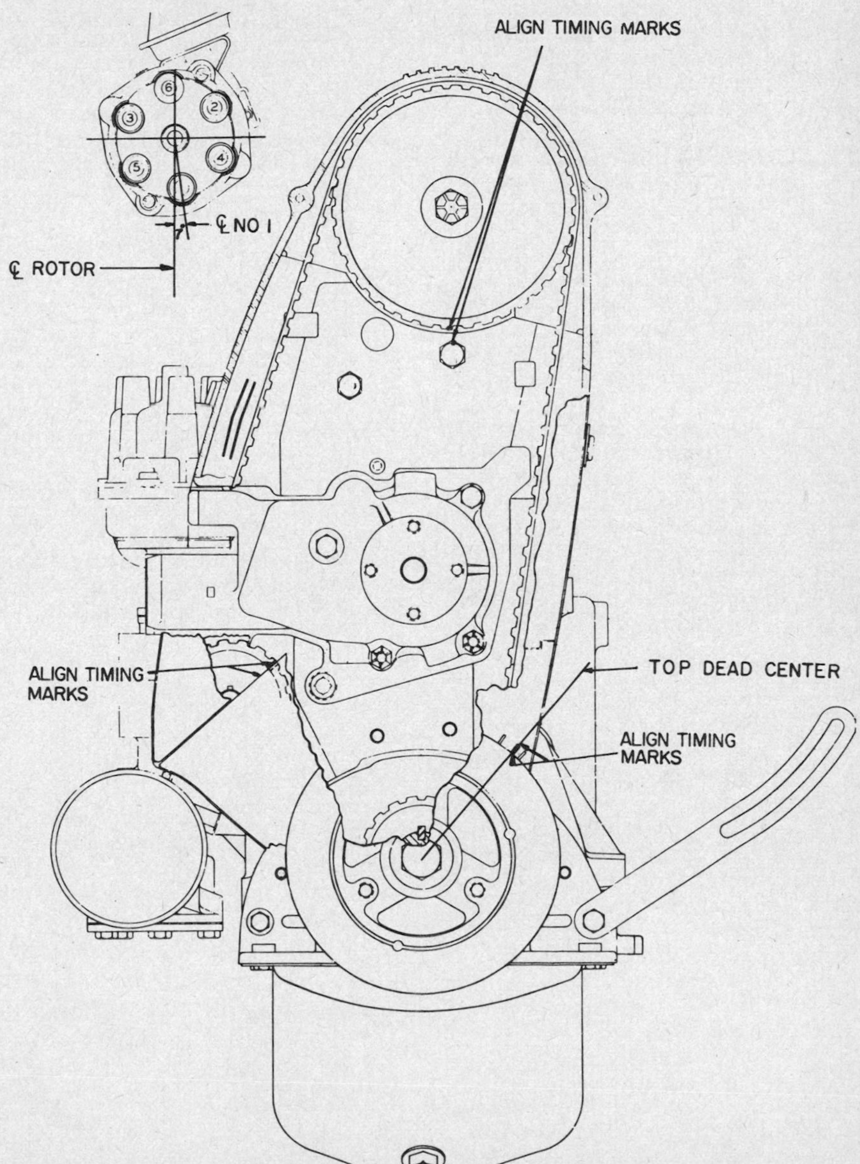

Timing marks OHC 6 cyl (© Pontiac Div., G.M. Corp)

1. Remove the hood.
2. Remove the camshaft timing sprocket.
3. Remove the three screws securing the camshaft seal and retainer assembly and timing cover to the cylinder head.
4. Inspect the seal, prying it out and replacing it if necessary.
5. Remove the camshaft cover.
6. Disconnect the fuel line at the carburetor.
7. Remove:
   a. Idle solenoid from its bracket.
   b. The choke coil, cover and rod assembly.
   c. Ignition distributor.
8. Raise the vehicle on a hoist, disconnect the front engine mounts at the body attachment, raise the front of the engine and install wood blocks, about 1-½ in. thick, between the engine mounts and the body.
9. Install camshaft removal tool on the cylinder head to hold down the lifters so that the camshaft may be removed.
   a. Position the tool so that the attaching holes are aligned with the lower cam cover bolt holes and the tappet levers of the tool are aligned to depress both valves of each cylinder.
   b. Back off the bolts in the bottom of the tool so that they are not contacting the bosses beneath the tool.
   c. Install the tool attaching bolts, tightening them securely.
   d. Tighten the bolts in the bottom of the tool until they just touch the bosses of the cylinder head. Before depressing the tappets, rotate the crankshaft pulley timing mark 90° clockwise from the timing mark on the tab. This assures that the pistons are not at TDC and will prevent valve-to-piston contact.
   e. Grease the ball end of the lever depressing bolts and tighten the bolts to depress the tappets.

NOTE: torque the lever bolts to 10 ft. lbs. If more tightening is required, check to see that the tool is properly installed, then proceed cautiously to prevent damaging the depressing lever.

10. Slide the camshaft forward until it clears the head.

NOTE: the camshaft bearings may be removed. It is not necessary to remove the camshaft end plug. Gently tap out the bearings, starting at the forward end. Tap out the rear bearing slowly into the distributor housing, being careful not to unseat the end plug. Crush the rear bearing to remove it from the distributor housing. Install, starting with the rear bearing. The oil holes in the three rear bearings must align with the oil holes in the case. On the first two bearings the oil holes are at 11 o'clock (as seen from the front of the engine) and the oil groove in the number one bearing toward the front of the engine.

11. Install the camshaft with the journals seated in the bores.
12. With the car up on a hoist, raise the front of the engine and remove the wood blocks from the engine mounts.
13. Install the front engine mounts, then lower the vehicle.
14. Using a new gasket, install the timing belt upper cover and retainer plate and seal assembly. Tighten the retaining bolts to 15 ft. lbs.
15. Using a dial indicator, measure the camshaft end-play. If it is not 0.004-0.012 in., select a camshaft retainer (according to cam locator thickness) which will provide more or less end-play as required.
16. Remove the tappet depressing tool by first releasing the tappet depressing lever bolts, and then removing the tool attaching bolts.
17. Install:
   a. Camshaft timing sprocket.
   b. The timing belt.
   c. Front engine cover.
   d. Distributor.
   e. Vehicle hood.
18. Adjust the valve tappets.
19. Install the camshaft cover.
20. Install and adjust the carburetor choke coil, cover and rod assembly.
21. Connect the carburetor fuel line.
22. Install the idle solenoid to the bracket.
23. Check and adjust the ignition timing and idle speed.

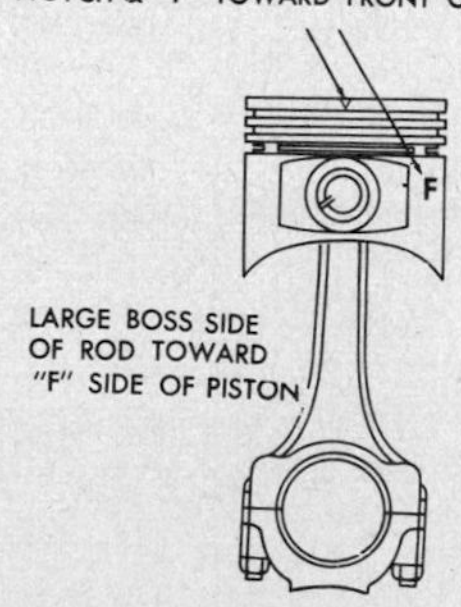

Piston and rod assembly—OHV 6 cyl

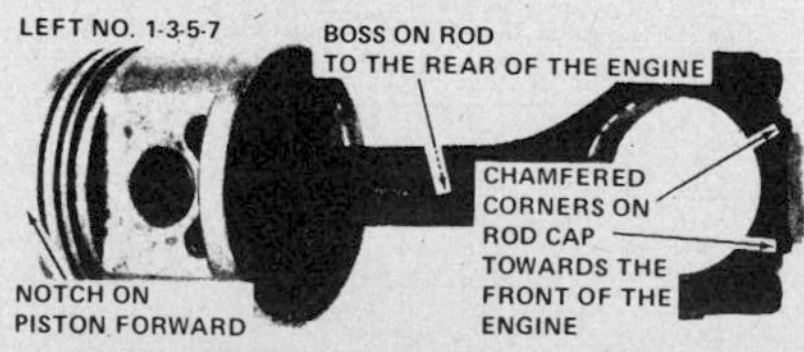

1975-76 Ventura 350 V8 piston and rod assembly, left bank
(© Pontiac Div., G.M. Corp)

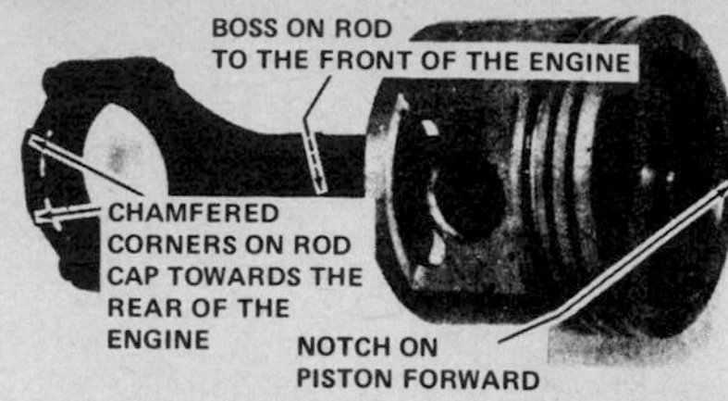

1975-76 Ventura 350 V8 piston rod assembly, right bank (© Pontiac Div., G.M. Corp)

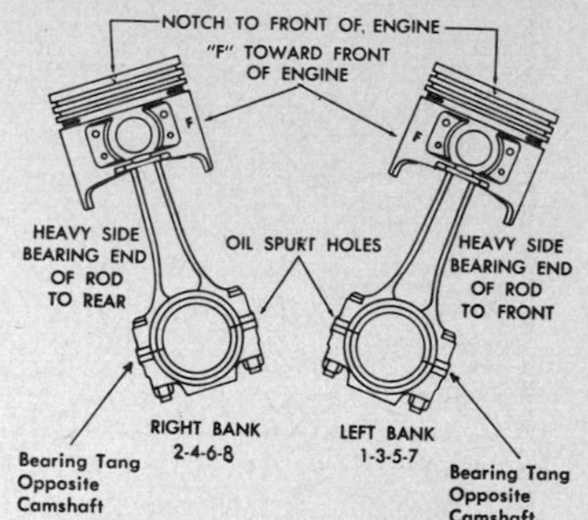

307 V8 piston and rod assembly

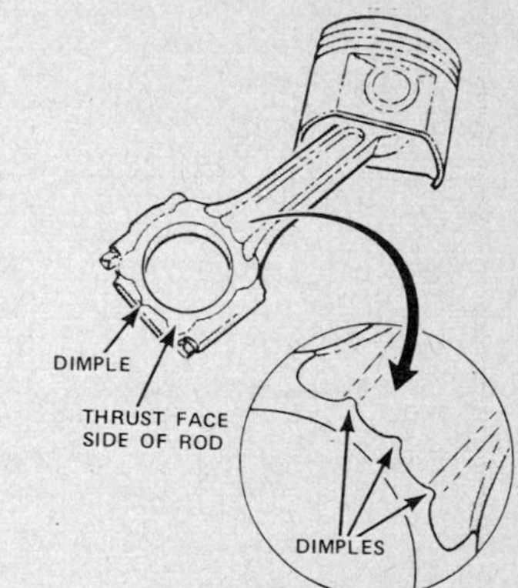

The dimples identify the connecting rod thrust faces on some V8 engines
(© Pontiac Div., G.M. Corp)

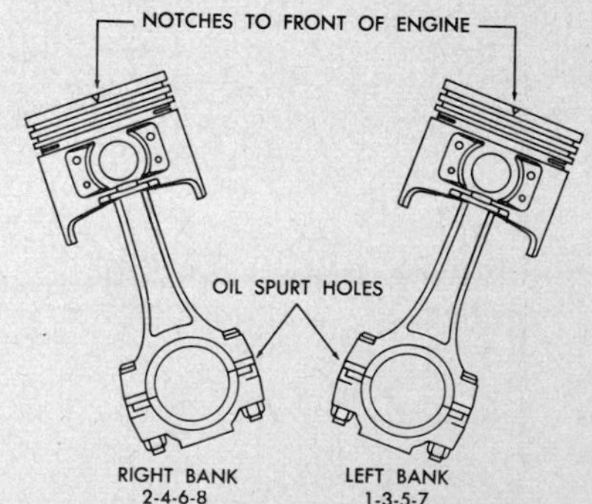

260, 350 (except 1975-76 Ventura), 400, 455 V8 piston and rod assembly
(© Pontiac Div., G.M. Corp)

Piston and Connecting Rod

The letter F, or the notch in the edge of the piston, goes to the front of the engine. The oil spurt holes on the connecting rod must face the camshaft. Some 1973, and all 1974 and later 350 (except 1975-76 Ventura) 400, and 455, V8 engines don't have these holes. These connecting rods have three dimples on one side of the

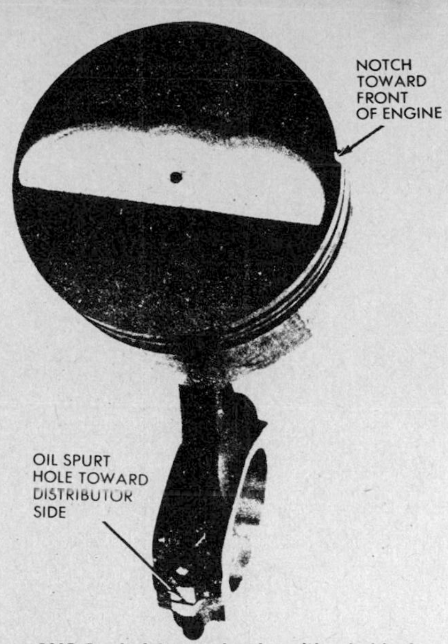

OHC 6 cyl piston and rod position in block
(© Pontiac Div., G.M. Corp)

rod and a single dimple on the connecting rod cap. The dimples must face forward on the left bank, and to the rear on the right.

Lubrication

Oil Pan R & R

1969-70 V8 and 1971 Tempest V8 with Manual Transmission

1. Remove engine from car.
2. Remove oil pan bolts.
3. Remove oil pan.

NOTE: 1970 Tempest V8 oil pan can be removed, in some cases, in a manner similar to 1969 Firebird V8.

1969 Firebird V8

1. Disconnect battery cable at battery.
2. Remove distributor cap and fan shield.
3. Remove fan and fan pulley on air-conditioned models.
4. Disconnect engine ground straps.
5. On air-conditioned models, remove compressor and swing it out of the way without disconnecting hoses.
6. Jack up front of car and drain engine oil.
7. Disconnect steering idler arm from frame.
8. Remove exhaust crossover pipe on single exhaust cars; disconnect exhaust pipes at manifold flanges on dual exhaust cars.
9. Remove starter motor, starter motor bracket, and flywheel cover.
10. Support engine with a chain hoist, then remove motor mounts and loosen rear transmission mount.

NOTE: it may be necessary, in individual cases, to remove the rear transmission mount.

11. Remove oil pan bolts, raise engine about 4½ in., and move engine forward about 1½ in.
12. Remove oil pan by rotating clockwise (to clear oil pump) and pulling down.
13. To install, reverse removal procedure.

1970½ Firebird and All 1971-76 V8 Models

1. On the 260 V8, remove the distributor cap and align the rotor with the no. 1 plug wire in the cap.
2. Disconnect battery cables.
3. Remove the fan and fan shroud. Tilt the power steering pump out of the way. Tilt the 1975-76 Ventura 350 air conditioning compressor in as far as possible. Remove the 260 V8 dipstick.
4. Move all water hoses and wiring out of the way.
5. Raise car and drain engine oil. Disconnect idler arm from frame and pitman arm from shaft on Firebird.
6. Disconnect exhaust pipe/s at manifold.
7. Remove starter and bracket, then remove flywheel inspection cover.
8. Support engine with a wood-padded jack.
9. Remove both frame-to-motor mount bolts.
10. Jack up engine for clearance, then remove oil pan bolts and pan.
11. To install, reverse the removal procedure. Silicone sealer is recommended at all gasket joints. Tighten pan bolts to 12 ft. lbs. Tighten the rear bolts, through the reinforcement straps, to 18 ft. lbs.

1970-76 OHV 6 Cylinder

1. Remove upper radiator shield assembly.
2. Disconnect battery ground cable.
3. Jack up front of car and drain engine oil.
4. Disconnect exhaust pipe at manifold flange.
5. Remove starter motor and flywheel cover.
6. Raise engine slightly, using a chain hoist, then remove both front motor mount to frame bolts and right motor mount.
7. Remove oil pan bolts, then raise engine and remove oil pan.
8. To install, reverse removal procedure.

NOTE: bolts into timing gear cover should be installed last. They are installed at an angle and holes line up after rest of oil pan bolts are tightened finger-tight.

1969 OHC 6 Cylinder

1. Disconnect battery.
2. Remove air cleaner assembly.
3. On air conditioned cars, remove compressor from mounting brackets and position to one side.
4. Inspect all water hoses and wiring harness for routing and possible interference. (Engine is raised at least 4½ in. on Tempest, 2 in. on Firebird.)

NOTE: Before raising the car, prop the hood open at least 6 in. to ensure enough clearance between timing belt cover and inner hood panel.

5. Raise car and drain crankcase.
6. Remove starter assembly and flywheel cover.
7. Reroute or disconnect any wiring between bellhousing and floor pan to insure against damage when bellhousing contacts pan.
8. Loosen transmission insulator to crossmember retaining bolts.
9. Remove right and left engine insulator to frame bracket through-bolts.
10. Rotate harmonic balancer until timing mark is at bottom. (This properly positions crankshaft counterweights.)
11. With suitable equipment, raise engine until insulators clear frame brackets.
12. Remove oil pan bolts.
13. Raise engine. Apply a rearward force on the engine-transmission assembly until oil pan clears the flywheel housing. Then, remove the oil pan.
14. Reverse the removal procedure to install the oil pan.

OHC 4 Cylinder

1. Raise the vehicle and drain the engine oil. Support the front of the engine, being careful not to distort the pan.
2. Remove the frame crossmember and both front crossmember braces.
3. Disconnect the steering idler arm at the frame side rail. On vehicles with air conditioning, disconnect the idler arm at the relay rod.
4. Mark the position of the steering linkage pitman arm to the steering gear pitman shaft and remove the pitman arm.

NOTE: do not rotate the steering gear pitman shaft while the linkage is disconnected, because the steering wheel alignment will be changed.

5. Remove the flywheel cover or converter underpan.
6. Remove the oil pan bolts, tap the oil pan to break the seal, then remove the pan.
7. Remove the pick-up screen-to-support retaining bolt and the pick-up screen-to-baffle support bolts, then remove the support from the baffle.
8. Remove the bolt which secures the oil drain back tube to the baffle, then rotate the baffle 90° toward the left side of the car

and remove the baffle from the pick-up screen.

9. The oil pump screen and pick up tube may be removed as follows:
   a. Remove the two self-locking mounting bolts (in block).
   b. Lightly tap on the U section of the pick-up tube to remove the tube from the casting.
   c. If damaged, the tube and screen assembly are replaced as a unit. It is recommended that once the assembly has been removed, it should not be reused.
   d. Apply sealing compound to the pick-up tube sealing surface.
   e. Install the tube into its bore, using an open end wrench on the tube boss, tapping the wrench with a mallet. Make sure that the retaining brackets are aligned with the bolt holes.
   f. Using anti-seize compound on the threads, install the retaining bolts. Tighten the bolts to 25 ft. lbs.
10. Install the oil pan and baffle in the reverse order of removal. Use sealing compound on the oil pump gasket surface. Tighten the oil pan bolts to 15 ft. lbs. Tighten frame crossmember and brace bolts to 35 ft. lbs.

Oil Pump R & R

V8 and OHV 6 Cylinder Engines

1. Remove engine oil pan. (See previous procedure.)
2. Remove pump attaching screws and carefully lower the pump.
3. Reinstall in reverse order.

NOTE: OHC 6 cylinder oil pump R & R is covered earlier in this section.

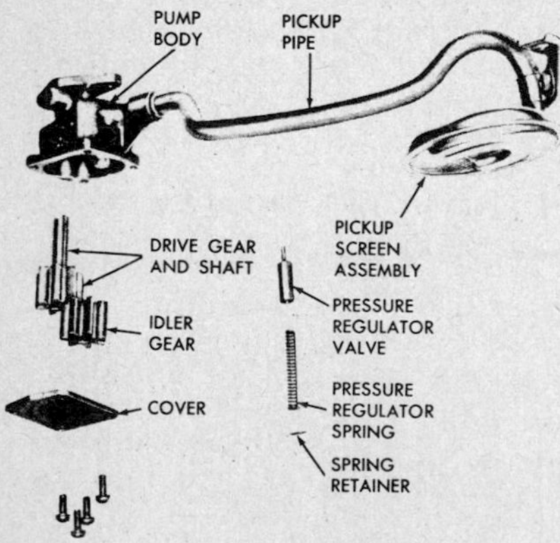

OHV 6 oil pump
(© Pontiac Div., G.M. Corp)

1975-76 Ventura 350

1. Remove the oil filter.
2. Remove the screws which attach the oil pump cover assembly to the timing chain cover. Remove the cover assembly and slide out the oil pump gears.
3. To install, reverse the removal procedure, being sure to check the clearance between the gear faces and the pump gasket surface. Clearance should be between 0.002 and 0.006 in.

NOTE: Pack the pump gears with petroleum jelly only. Unless the pump is packed with petroleum jelly, it may not prime itself when the engine is started.

OHC 4 Cylinder

1. Remove:
   a. Front engine cover.
   b. Accessory drive pulley.
   c. Timing belt.
   d. Timing belt lower cover.
   e. Crankshaft sprocket.
2. Raise the vehicle on a hoist and drain the engine oil.
3. Remove the oil pan and baffle.
4. Remove the oil pump bolts and the pump.
5. Inspect the oil pump for wear. The pump gears and body are not serviced separately. Replacement of the entire oil pump is required. Check the pressure regulator for free operation.
6. When installing, clean all gasket surfaces. Be sure that the pump drive key is installed properly. Use anti-seize compound on the threads of the pump mounting bolts, tightening them to 15 ft. lbs. The stud is installed in the upper right (facing pump) and tightened to 30 ft. lbs. Install the oil pan before tightening the timing cover bolts.

Oil Pump (Front Cover) Seal R & R

1. Remove the following:
   a. Engine front cover.
   b. Accessory drive pulley.
   c. Timing belt.
   d. Timing belt lower cover.
   e. Crankshaft timing sprocket.
2. Pry out the old seal, being careful not to damage the housing seal surfaces.
3. Coat the lips of the new seal with oil and apply sealing compound to the outside diameter of the seal.
4. Install the seal with the closed end outward.
5. Install all components removed in Step 1 above.

Rear Main Bearing Oil Seal

All 6 Cylinder Engines

Always replace both upper and lower seal halves. It is not necessary to remove the crankshaft to install the seal.

1. Remove the engine oil pan.
2. Remove the rear main bearing cap.
3. Remove the oil seal from the groove in the cap by prying from the bottom with a small screwdriver.
4. Insert a new seal, well lubricated with engine oil, into the bearing cap groove.
5. Remove the upper half of the seal. Use a small hammer and brass pin and tap one end of the oil seal until it protrudes far enough to be removed with pliers.
6. Install a new seal with the lip toward the front of the engine.
7. Install the bearing cap and torque it to specifications.

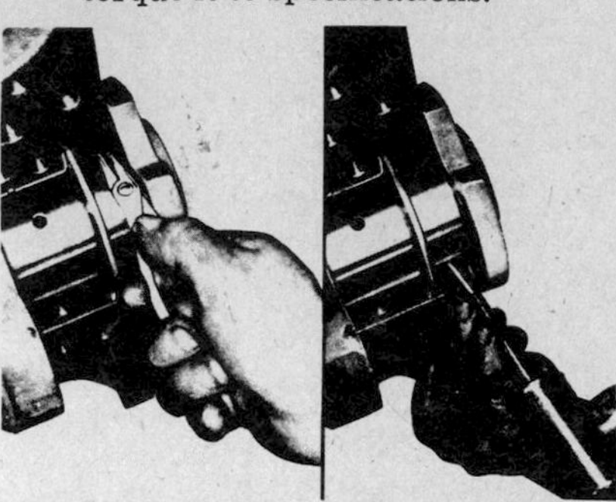

Rear main oil seal removal—upper half
(© Pontiac Div., G.M. Corp)

V8 Except 307

1. Remove the oil pan and baffle.
2. Remove the rear main bearing cap.

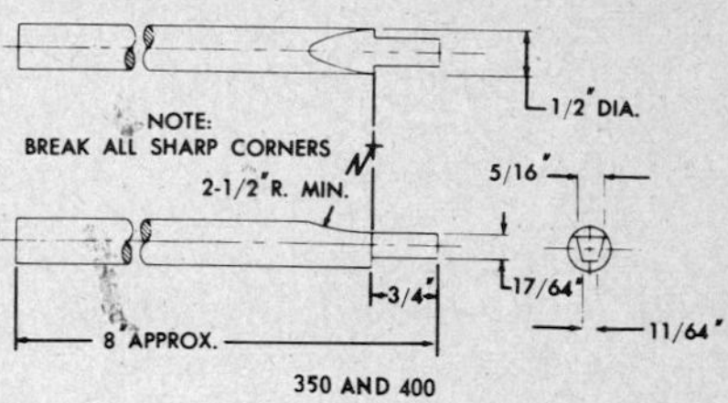

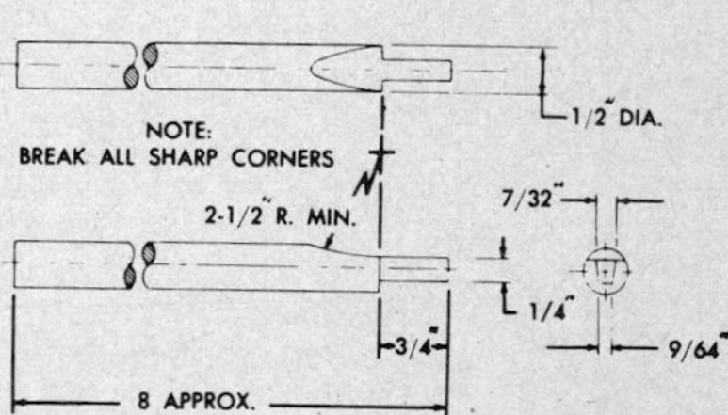

350 (except 1975-76 Ventura), 400, 455 V8
Rear main bearing upper seal tool. The bottom tool is for the 455
(© Pontiac Div., G.M. Corp)

3. Make a seal tool as illustrated.
4. Insert the tool against one end of the oil seal in the block and drive the seal gently into the groove until it bottoms. Repeat on the other end of the seal.
5. Form a new seal in the cap. Cut four 3/8 in. long pieces from this seal.
6. Work two of the pieces into each of the gaps which have been made at the end of the seal in the block. Do not cut off any material to make them fit.
7. Form a new seal in the bearing cap.
8. Apply a 1/16 in. bead of silicone sealer from the center of the seal across to the external gasket groove.
9. Reassemble the cap and torque to specifications.

307 V8 Engine

1. Remove the oil pan, baffle, oil pump, and rear main bearing cap.
2. Remove the upper half of the seal with a hammer and brass punch.
3. Install a new upper seal.
4. Remove the lower seal half from the bearing cap.
5. Install a new lower seal in the bearing cap.
6. Install the bearing cap and torque it to specifications.

OHC 4 Cylinder

NOTE: This repair can be made without removing the engine, but the transmission must be removed so that the crankshaft can be lowered.

1. Remove the oil pan and baffle.
2. Remove the rear main bearing cap and discard the lower seal.
3. Loosen the remaining bearing caps to allow the crankshaft to be lowered.
4. Push the upper seal on one end enough so that the other end can be grasped with pliers. It may help to turn the crankshaft. Pull out the upper seal.
5. Cut and form a new braided fabric upper seal in the bearing cap. Taper the end of the seal and insert a piece of soft wire through the seal about ¼ in. from the end. Wrap the wire around the seal to form a secure attachment.
6. Thread the wire through the upper seal groove, then start the seal and pull it into position.
7. Tighten all the bearing caps except the rear cap to 65 ft. lbs.
8. Cut the seal flush to 1/64 in. below the bearing edge, making a clean cut and leaving no raveled edges.
9. Install and cut a seal flush in the rear main bearing cap.
10. Install the rear main bearing cap and measure the clearance with Plastigage, tightening the cap bolts to 65 ft. lbs. If the bearing clearance is within specifications, the seal is properly seated.
11. Install the bearing cap, tightening to 65 ft. lbs.
12. Install rear main bearing cap side sealant. This is available in a kit, complete with plunger applicator. Force the compound firmly into place to ensure that there are no air bubbles.
13. Install the oil pan and baffle.

CLUTCH

A single-plate, dry-disc, diaphragm-spring clutch is used on all models. The clutch assembly consists of the driven plate, the pressure plate, and the release mechanism.

Two types of diaphragm type pressure plates are used—a bent finger type, for the high performance OHC six-cylinder and V8s of more than 350 cu. in. displacement, and a flat finger type, for low performance V8s and six-cylinder standard engines. The diaphragm spring design is such that no overcenter spring is required.

A clutch safety switch prevents engine cranking unless the clutch is disengaged. The only periodic clutch service required, other than adjustment for normal wear, is the periodic lubrication of all linkage pivot points.

Clutch R & R

All except Astre

1. Raise car and support on jackstands. Disconnect the battery.
2. Support rear of engine.
3. Remove driveshaft.
4. Remove rear crossmember bolts from frame and transmission mounts, and remove crossmember.
5. Disconnect transmission shift linkage, speedometer cable and clutch return spring. Clutch fork pushrod will now hang free.
6. Remove clutch housing cover plate screws and let plate hang from starter gear housing.
7. Lower engine enough to gain access to clutch housing bolts at engine block, then remove all but uppermost bolt.
8. Hold transmission and clutch housing assembly against block over dowel pins while removing last bolt. Remove transmission and clutch housing as an assembly.
9. Matchmark pressure plate and flywheel with paint to make sure correct balance is maintained.
10. Loosen the cover plate attaching screws, a little at a time, until clutch diaphragm spring tension is released. Remove bolts and clutch assembly.
11. The pilot bearing is an oil-impregnated type bearing press-into the crankshaft. Inspect and renew, if necessary.
12. Install clutch disc with long hub forward (toward flywheel).
13. Install pressure plate and cover assembly, then align clutch disc by inserting pilot tool, or old transmission mainshaft, into splines. Align mark on clutch cover with mark on flywheel, then align nearest bolt holes.
14. Install the bolts in the cover and tighten them alternately. Tighten them to 25 ft. lb. (35 for Ventura II through 1973).
15. Remove clutch pilot tool and check to see that it can be reinserted and moved freely.
16. Instal clutch fork and dust boot into clutch housing. Lubricate throwout bearing with high melting poit greast.
17. Complete the reassembly of clutch housing and transmission by reversing removal method. Tighten housing bolts to 40 ft. lbs. (30 for Ventura II through 1973). Begining 1974, tighten all models to 35 ft lbs.
18. Adjust shifter and clutch release linkage.

Astre

1. Raise vehicle on hoist.
2. Remove transmission.
3. Remove clutch fork cover then disconnect clutch return spring and control cable from clutch fork.
4. Remove main drive gear oil seal from clutch release bearing sleeve.
5. Remove flywheel housing lower cover.
6. Remove flywheel housing from engine.
7. To remove the release bearing from clutch fork and sleeve, slide lever off ball stud against spring action. If necessary to replace ball stud, remove cap, locknut and stud from housing.
8. If assembly marks on clutch assembly and flywheel are not distinguishable, remark with paint or center-punch.
9. Loosen clutch cover to flywheel attaching bolts one turn at a time until spring pressure is released, to avoid bending clutch cover flange.
10. Support the pressure plate and cover assembly then remove the bolts and clutch assembly.

Caution Do not disassemble the clutch cover, spring and pressure plate for repair. If defective replace complete assembly.

11. Index alignment marks on clutch assembly and flywheel. Place driven plate on pressure plate with long end of splined end facing forward, damper springs inside pressure plate, and insert a dummy clutch gear shaft through the cover and driven plate.
12. Position the complete assembly against the flywheel and insert the dummy shaft into the pilot bearing in the crankshaft.
13. Index the alignment marks and install clutch cover to flywheel bolts finger-tight.

Caution Tighten all bolts evenly and gradually until tight to avoid possible clutch distortion. Torque bolts 18 ft. lbs. and remove dummy shaft.

14. Lubricate the clutch fork ball socket and the fingers at the release bearing with high melting poit grease.
15. Lubricate the recess on the inside of the throwout bearing collar and the fork groove with high melting point grease. Install fork in housing but not on stud.

16. Install bearing on sleeve, then position clutch fork over bearing in housing and slide fork onto ball stud.
17. Install flywheel housing and lower cover. Tighten bolts to 25 ft. lbs.
18. Install transmission.
19. Adjust clutch.
20. Lower and remove vehicle from hoist.

Clutch Adjustment

Through 1971

1. Remove the return spring.
2. With the pedal against the stop, loosen the locknut on the clutch fork pushrod.
3. Turn the rod until the release bearing contacts the pressure plate fingers lightly.
4. Rotate the pushrod 3½ turns in.
5. Tighten the locknut.
6. Replace the spring.
7. There should be 1 in. free play at the pedal.

1972-76 Except Astre

1. Disconnect the clutch fork return spring.
2. Loosen the pushrod locknut.
3. Detach the swivel or pushrod from the countershaft lever.
4. Install the swivel or pushrod in the gauge hole on the countershaft lever.
5. Push on the countershaft lever so that the clutch pedal is up against the stop.
6. Hold the clutch fork to the rear so that the release bearing lightly contacts the release levers.
7. Adjust the pushrod length to remove all lash from the linkage.
8. Reinstall the swivel or pushrod in the original hole on the countershaft lever. Tighten the locknut.
9. Replace the spring. Pedal free travel should now be ¾-1¼ in.

Astre

Adjustment for normal clutch wear is accomplished by turning the clutch fork ball stud counterclockwise to give .90 ± .25 in. lash at clutch pedal.

1. Remove ball stud cap and loosen locknut on ball stud end located to the right of the transmission on the clutch housing.
2. Adjust ball stud to obtain .90 ± .25 in. free travel.
3. Tighten locknut to 25 ft lbs. being careful not to change adjustment and install ball stud cap.
4. Check operation of clutch.

MANUAL TRANSMISSION

Three-Speed

Three different three-speed manual transmissions have been used in these cars. All light and normal-duty models, and the Astre, use a Saginaw transmission, which can be identified by having only one bolt boss casting "ear" at the center top of the side cover. Heavy-duty 1969 models use a Dearborn (Ford) transmission. This is the only top cover transmission used in these cars. For 1970-74, the heavy-duty three-speed is a Muncie unit. This is similar in appearance to the Saginaw, but has two bolt boss casting "ears" at the top of the side cover.

Three-Speed Transmission R & R

All except Astre

1. Disconnect the battery and release the parking brake before raising the car.
2. Disconnect the speedometer cable.
3. Disconnect the transmission shifter levers from the transmission shifter shafts. On six-cylinder engines, disconnect the electrical lead from the T.C.S. switch. On floor-shift models, remove the two shifter assembly-to-shifter support bolts and remove the shifter from the transmission. If it is not necessary to remove the shifter from the car, it may be left hanging from its floor seal. Mark the differential flange and the driveshaft yoke to assure proper reassembly. Remove the driveshaft.
4. Support the rear of the engine and remove the transmission mount.
5. Remove the four crossmember bolts and slide the member rearward.
6. Remove the four transmission-to-bell housing bolts. It is a good idea to remove the upper bolts first and replace them with headless guide pins. This prevents any possible damage caused by the transmission hanging by its input shaft.
7. Slide the transmission rearward until it clears the clutch assembly and bell housing, then remove the transmission.
8. Reverse the removal procedure to install the transmission. Put the transmission in gear and turn the output shaft as necessary to start the splines into the clutch plate.

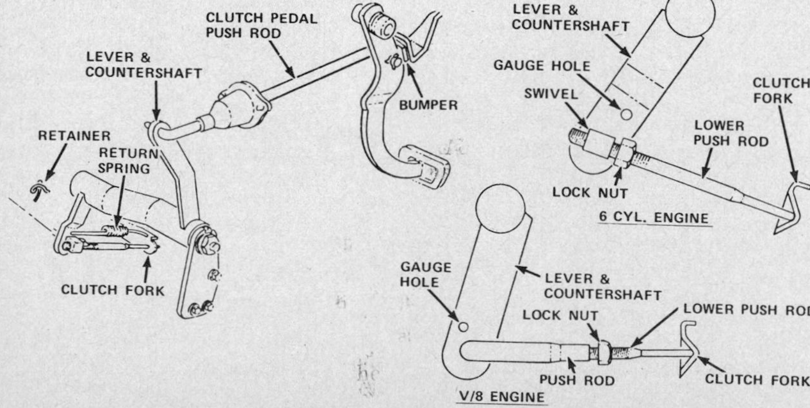

Typical clutch linkage and adjustment points, models through 1971 don't have the gauge hole
(© Pontiac Div., G.M. Corp)

Three-Speed Linkage Adjustment—Column Shift

1969-76 Saginaw Transmission except Ventura

1. Place gearshift lever in Reverse and lock ignition.
2. On the Tempest, loosen the swivel clamp bolt at the rear transmission shift lever (First and Reverse) and the bolt at the equalizer shaft and lever assembly.
3. On the Firebird, loosen the swivel clamp nut at the rear transmission shift lever (First and Reverse) then loosen the nut (D) at the idler lever.
4. Position the front transmission shift lever (Second and Third) in Neutral and the rear transmission shift lever (First and Reverse) in Reverse.
5. Tighten the First and Reverse swivel clamp bolt or nut, then unlock the steering column and shift into Neutral. On the Firebird, tighten both swivel clamp nuts, unlock the steering column, and check the complete shift pattern.
6. Unlock the column and align the lower gearshift levers (on column) in Neutral position, then insert a 0.185 in. diameter gauge pin through the hole in the lower control levers.
7. Tighten the swivel clamp bolt or nut, then remove the gauge pin and check the shift pattern.

1971-76 Ventura

1. Set the shift lever in Reverse and lock the column. Loosen the swivel clamp nuts at both shifter levers.
2. Pull down slightly on 1st-Rev rod to remove slack, then tighten swivel clamp nut at 1st-Rev lever.
3. Unlock steering column and shift into Neutral. Align column levers and insert a .185-.186 in. gauge pin through alignment holes.
4. Position 2nd-3rd transmission lever in Neutral, then tighten swivel clamp nut.
5. Remove gauge pin and check shift pattern and ignition lock. With lever in Reverse, key must move to LOCK freely. This should not be possible in any other gear.

Three-Speed Linkage Adjustment—Floor Shift

1969 Dearborn, 1970-74 Muncie, 1970-76 Saginaw

1. Place gearshift lever in Neutral.
2. Loosen swivel clamp on gearshift control rod.
3. Loosen trunnion locknuts on 1st-Reverse and 2nd-3rd transmission control rods.
4. Insert a 1/4 in. drill rod into shifter assembly.
5. If gearshift lever is not properly aligned with floor opening:
   a. *Console*—loosen two shifter to support bolts and align shifter. Tighten bolts.
   b. *Without console*—loosen two shifter to support bolts and center shifter in boot; tighten bolts.
6. Position both transmission shift levers in Neutral and tighten locknuts.
7. Remove gauge pin and check shift pattern.
8. Place gearshift lever in Reverse, then place steering column lower lever in Lock position and lock ignition.
9. Push up on gearshift control rod to take up lash in column lock mechanism, then tighten adjusting swivel clamp.

Four-Speed

The Saginaw is used as standard equipment on the Astre and all other four-speed models. The four-speed Muncie is used in heavy duty applications through 1974. Both transmissions are fully synchronized in all forward gears. They can easily be identified by their shift linkage. On the Muncie, two shift rods go to levers on the side cover and one rod (reverse) goes to a lever on the case extension housing. On the Saginaw, all three shift rods go to levers on the side cover. Starting 1975, the heavy duty transmission, used only in the Firebird, is the Warner Gear T-10, which can be identified by a 9 bolt curved bottom side cover. It also has a reverse shift lever on the extension housing.

Four-Speed Transmission R & R

All except Astre

The R&R procedures for these four-speed transmissions are the same as for three-speed units.

Astre Three and Four-Speed Transmission R & R

1. Raise the car and drain the transmission.
2. Remove the driveshaft.
3. Disconnect the speedometer cable, TCS switch, and the back-up light switch.
4. Detach the control rods and levers from the transmission, tie them together, and position them out of the way.
5. Remove the crossmember-to-transmission mounting bolts.
6. Support the engine and remove the crossmember-to-frame bolts. Remove the crossmember.
7. Remove the top transmission-to-clutch housing bolts and install guide pins in the holes.
8. Remove the lower bolts and pull the transmission back and out of the car.
9. On installation, guide the input shaft through the throwout bearing and into the pilot bearing.
10. Install the transmission retaining bolts and lockwashers. Tighten the bolts to 40 ft lbs.
11. Position the crossmember on the frame and install the retaining bolts hand-tight.
12. Install the crossmember-to-transmission bolts and then tighten all bolts to 28 ft lbs.
13. Remove the engine support.
14. Install the transmission control rods to the shifter. Adjust the linkage.
15. Connect the speedometer cable, TCS switch, and back-up light switch.
16. Install the driveshaft.
17. Fill the transmission to the level of the filler plug.
18. Lower the car and check transmission operation.

Four-Speed Linkage Adjustment

1969-76 All except Astre

1. Place gearshift lever in Neutral and ignition switch in "off".
2. Loosen adjusting swivel clamp on gearshift control rod.
3. For 1969 Saginaw, loosen trunnion locknuts on 1st-2nd and Reverse shift rods, then disconnect trunnion from lever. Loosen locknuts for all others.
4. Insert a 1/4 in. drill rod into gauge pin hole in shifter.
5. If Muncie or Warner gearshift lever is not properly aligned with floor opening:
   a. *Console*—loosen two shifter to support bolts and align shifter. Tighten bolts.
   b. *Without console*—loosen two shifter to support bolts and center shifter in boot; tighten bolts.
6. Place transmission shift levers in Neutral and tighten locknuts.
7. Align trunnion with hole in 3rd-4th shifter lever, insert trunnion and secure with washer and cotter pin for 1969 Saginaw.
8. Remove gauge pin and check shift pattern.
9. Place gearshift lever in Reverse, set steering column lower lever in Lock position and lock ignition.
10. Push up on gearshift control rod to take up lash in steering column lock mechanism, then tighten adjusting swivel clamp nut.

Astre Three and Four-Speed Linkage Adjustment

1. Turn the ignition switch to "Off" and place the shift lever in neutral.
2. Raise the car.
3. Loosen the lock nuts on the control rods. Position the transmission side cover levers in their neutral detents.
4. With the floor shift lever in neutral, align the shifter levers and insert a gauge pin into the levers and bracket.
5. Tighten the First/Reverse (First/Second on four-speed) control rod lock nut against its swivel.
6. Tighten the Second/Third (Third/Fourth on four-speed) control rod lock nut against its swivel.
7. On four-speeds, tighten the Reverse control rod lock nut against its swivel.

NOTE: All lock nuts are tightened to 120 in. lbs.

8. Remove the gauge pin and check shifter operation.

AUTOMATIC TRANSMISSION

The M-35 two-speed (G.M. Type 300) automatic was used in 1969 and was replaced by the M-35 two-speed Powerglide in 1970. The two-speed transmission was dropped for 1974. There are three three-speed automatic transmissions used. The Astre uses a Turbo Hydra-Matic 250, sixes and smaller V8s use a Turbo Hydro-Matic 350 (M-38), and the larger

V8s use a Turbo Hydra-Matic (M-40) 400. The 350 can readily be identified by its downshift cable between the accelerator linkage and the transmission. The 400 uses an electrical downshift switch at the accelerator pedal.

Pan R & R, Fluid and Filter Change

The fluid should be drained with the transmission warm.

1. Support the Astre transmission at the vibration damper. Remove the crossmember.
2. Prepare a large pan to catch the transmission fluid.
3. Loosen all the pan screws, then pull one corner down to drain most of the fluid.
4. Remove the pan screws and empty out the pan. The pan can be cleaned out with solvent but it must be dried thoroughly before replacement. Be very careful not to leave any lint or threads from rags in the pan.
5. Remove the filter or strainer retaining bolt (two on Turbo Hydra-Matic 250 and 350). A reuseable strainer is used on two-speed transmissions and the Turbo Hydra-Matic 250. The strainer may be cleaned in solvent and air-dried thoroughly. Filters are to be replaced.
6. Assemble a new O-ring and filter to the intake pipe on the Turbo Hydra-Matic 400. Use a new gasket on all other models.
7. Install the new filter or cleaned strainer.
8. Install the pan with a new gasket. Tighten the bolts evenly (12 ft lbs) in a criss-cross pattern.
9. Replace the Astre crossmember.
10. Add DEXRON or DEXRON II transmission fluid through the dipstick tube. Add 5 pts for Turbo Hydra-Matic 250, 3 for the 350, and 7 for the 400.
11. Start the engine and let it idle. Do not race the engine. Shift through all the indicator positions, holding the brakes. Check the fluid level with the engine idling in Park. The level should be between the two dimples on the dipstick, about 1/4 in. below the ADD mark. Add fluid as necessary.
12. Check the fluid level after the car has been driven enough to thoroughly warm up the transmission. The level should be at the FULL mark on the dipstick. If the transmission is overfilled, the excess must be drained off. Overfilling causes aerated fluid, resulting in transmission slippage and probable damage.

Vacuum Modulator R&R

1. Disconnect the vacuum hose from the modulator.
2. Remove the modulator bolt and retainer.
3. Slide the modulator out of the case.
4. Reverse the removal procedure to install. Use a new O-ring seal and check the fluid level.

Band Adjustments

Low Band—Two-Speed (M-35)

This adjustment is required at fluid change intervals, or whenever slippage is evident.

1. Place the shifter lever in Neutral and raise the vehicle.
2. Remove the adjusting screw protecting cap.
3. Loosen the adjusting screw locknut 1/4 turn.

Caution Be sure to hold the adjusting screw locknut at 1/4 turn loose during the adjusting procedure.

4. Tighten the adjusting screw to 70 in. lbs (40 for 1969) and then back off *exactly* four complete turns for a band with 6,000 miles or more of use, three turns for a band with less than 6,000 miles of use.
5. Tighten the locknut and install the protective cap.

Turbo Hydra-Matic 350, 400

Band adjustments are made during overhaul and cannot be accomplished without disassembly of the transmission.

Intermediate Band—Turbo Hydra-Matic 250

This adjustment is required at fluid change intervals, or whenever slippage is evident.

1. Position the shift lever in Neutral.
2. Loosen the locknut on the right side of the transmission and tighten the adjusting screw to 30 in lbs.
3. Back the screw out three turns and then tighten the locknut to 15 ft lbs.

Shift Linkage Adjustment

All Column Shift

1. Loosen screw (nut on Firebird) on adjusting swivel clamp.
2. Place gearshift lever in Park and lock ignition.
3. Place transmission shift lever in Park detent.
4. Push up on gearshift control rod until lash is taken up in steering column lock mechanism, then tighten screw or nut on swivel clamp.
5. Readjust the transmission neutral start switch if necessary.

Turbo Hydra-Matic Floorshift, except Astre and 1971-74 Ventura TH-M 350

1. Disconnect shift cable from transmission shift lever by removing nut from pin.
2. Adjust back drive linkage (as in Step 4, above).
3. Unlock ignition and rotate transmission shift lever counterclockwise two detents.
4. Place console lever in Neutral and move against forward Neutral stop.
5. Assemble shift cable and pin to transmission shift lever so that no binding exists, then tighten nut.
6. Readjust the transmission neutral start switch if necessary.

Two-Speed Floorshift

1. Place console lever in Park and lock ignition.
2. Disconnect shift cable from transmission shift lever pin. Loosen the screw on the adjusting swivel at the shaft lever.
3. Rotate transmission shift lever clockwise to Park position and push up on control rod to take up slack.
4. Tighten swivel.
5. Unlock ignition and rotate range lever on transmission counterclockwise two positions.
6. Place shift lever in Neutral and move forward against Neutral stop.
7. Assemble shift cable and pin to transmission lever (free fit) and tighten pin nut.
8. Readjust the transmission neutral start switch if necessary.

Ventura Turbo Hydra-Matic 350 Floorshift, through 1974

1. Loosen both swivel nuts on the shift control rod.
2. Place transmission lever in Drive position.
3. Set pawl rod into Drive notch.
4. Apply a forward load on actuating lever until pawl rod contacts detent.
5. Place a 0.094 in. spacer between front swivel nut and swivel. Run in front nut until it hits spacer, then release load and tighten rear nut to 40 in. lbs.
6. Place transmission shift lever in Park position and lock ignition.
7. Loosen not at the bottom of idler lever, then remove play by rotating shift lever downward. Tighten nut to 20 ft. lbs.

Astre Turbo Hydra-Matic 250 Floorshift

1. Loosen the nut and swivel at the transmission lever.
2. Set the transmission lever in Neutral by moving it counterclockwise to the L1 detent and then clockwise three detent positions to Neutral.
3. Position the shift lever in the Neutral notch of the detent plate.

4. Place the flat of the swivel into the slot of the control rod. Install the washer and cotter pin.
5. Tighten the locknut. Adjust the neutral safety switch, if necessary.

Neutral Safety/Backup Light Switch Adjustment

Through 1971

NOTE: The switch is on the steering column. This procedure applies to switches marked "ADJUST" and "RESET".

Caution After the switch has been adjusted, but before starting the engine to test the shifting pattern, make sure that the brakes are securely locked. This is necessary because a misadjusted switch will allow the engine to start in any of the forward or reverse gears.

1. Place the shifter lever in Park.
2. Loosen the switch retaining screws. Make sure that the switch drive tang is engaged in the shifter tube slot and that it stays engaged during adjustment.
3. Rotate the switch in its slot until it is in the Park position and then tighten the screws.
4. After observing the above caution, check the shifter pattern by placing the shifter lever in Neutral. If the transmission does not shift into Neutral, place the lever back in Park and rotate the switch slightly until the shift pattern is correct.
5. If it is possible to move the shift lever a large distance without having the transmission respond, check for a worn switch drive tang or bad electrical contacts inside the switch. In either case, replace the switch.

1972-76 Floorshift, 1971-76 Column Shift—except Astre

NOTE: This procedure applies to all switches with an adjusting pin hole in the back.

1. Place the shift lever in Neutral, except for 1971 models which must be placed in Drive. 1972 floorshift models must be in Park, except for Ventura, which must be in Drive.
2. Loosen the switch mounting screws.
3. Move the switch until you can insert a 0.092 (0.082 beginning 1975) in. diameter adjusting pin into the hole in the back of the switch about 3/8 in.
4. Tighten the screws and remove the pin.
5. Step on the brake pedal and check that the engine will start only in Neutral or Park.

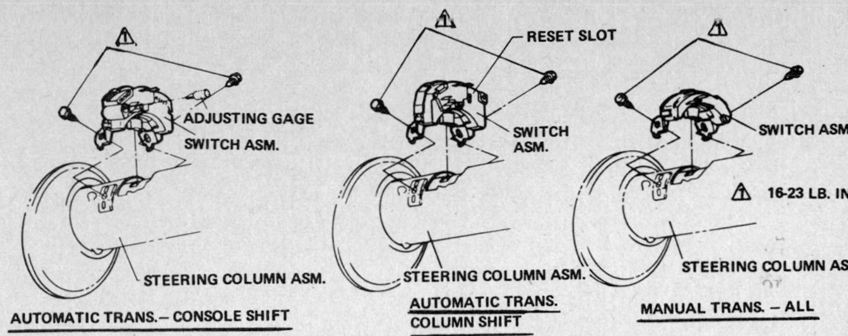

Neutral start switch (© Pontiac Div., G.M. Corp)

Astre

1. Remove screws securing floor console.
2. Disconnect the electrical plugs on the back-up, seat belt warning, neutral start, and seat belt buzzer contacts of the neutral safety switch.
3. Place shift lever in Neutral.
4. Remove two screws securing shift indicator plate.
5. Remove two screws securing shift lever curved cover.
6. Remove two screws securing neutral start switch to lever assembly.

NOTE: screws are hidden beneath lever cover.

7. Tilt switch assembly to right as you lift switch out of lever hole.
8. Make sure shift lever is in Neutral before installing switch assembly.
9. Assemble switch assembly to control lever bracket by inserting drive tang into hole in neutral start switch lever.

NOTE: When installing the same neutral switch, align the contact support slot with the service adjustment hole in the switch and insert a 3/32 in. drill to hold the switch in neutral. Remove the drill after the switch is fastened to the shift lever mounting bracket.

10. Tighten two mounting screws securing switch assembly to lever bracket.
11. Install curved shift lever cover and secure with two screws.
12. Install shift indicator plate and attach with two screws.
13. Moving control lever out of Neutral will shear the new switch plastic locating pin.
14. Plug electrical connectors into switch assembly; apply parking brake and start vehicle—check for starting in Neutral and Park only. Also check for back-up lamps on in Reverse.
15. Turn off ignition and install console cover securing with four screws.

Downshift Cable Adjustment —Turbo Hydra-Matic 250, 350

Tempest, LeMans

1. With engine off and throttle butterflies closed (off fast idle), position retainer against insert on cable (from inside car).
2. To adjust, grasp accelerator pedal lever adjacent to downshift cable and pull carburetor cable to wide open throttle position. Check for full cable travel.

Firebird

1. With engine off and throttle butterflies closed (off fast idle), position the retainer (under the hood) rearward against washer and insert (or Snap Lock up).
2. To adjust, push carburetor extension lever to wide open throttle position and push the Snap Lock down. Check for full cable travel.

Ventura

1. Disengage the Snap Lock on the detent cable.
2. Place carburetor lever at wide open position, against stop.
3. With detent cable through detent, push Snap Lock downward until its top is flush with the cable.

Astre

1. Remove the air cleaner.
2. Insert a screwdriver on each side of the snap-lock on the bracket at the front of the transmission and pry up to release the lock.
3. Compress the lock tabs and disconnect the snap-lock assembly from the bracket.
4. Position the carburetor lever in the wide open throttle position.
5. Hold the carburetor lever in position and push the Snap Lock on the cable down until the top is flush with the cable.

NOTE: The cable should not be lubricated.

6. Install the air cleaner.

Throttle Valve (TV) Linkage Adjustment—Two-Speed 1970-73

6 Cylinder Models

1. Remove air cleaner.
2. Disconnect TV control rod swivel and clip from carburetor lever, then disconnect TV return spring from bellhousing.

3. Push TV control rod rearward until transmission TV lever is against internal transmission stop.
4. Holding TV control rod in this position, hold carburetor lever in wide open throttle position and adjust TV control rod swivel so that pin freely enters hole in carburetor lever without binding.
5. Secure swivel, connect return spring and check linkage action for binding.
6. Install air cleaner.

V8 Models

1. Remove air cleaner.
2. Disconnect accelerator linkage at carburetor.
3. Disconnect throttle and TV rod return springs.
4. Pull TV rod forward until transmission is through detent, hold in this position and open carburetor butterflies to wide open position.
5. The butterflies must reach wide open position at the same time that the ball stud contacts end of slot in upper TV rod (± 1/32 in.).
6. If necessary, adjust swivel end of upper TV rod.
7. Connect linkage and springs, then check linkage for binding.
8. Install air cleaner.

U-JOINTS

A splined yoke and universal assembly and a rear universal joint are used to accommodate changes in length and orientation of the driveshaft as the car moves over bumps.

Driveshaft R&R

1. Mark the driveshaft rear yoke and the differential flange to assure correct alignment upon reassembly.
2. Remove the U-bolts and nuts from the differential flange.
3. Remove the driveshaft assembly by first sliding the driveshaft sufficiently forward to disengage the differential flange, then slide the shaft downward and rearward to disengage the front splined yoke from the transmission output shaft.
4. Installation is the reverse of removal. Be sure to align the match mark made before disassembly.

U-Joint R & R—All Front and Rear U-Joints

Removal

1. Remove the driveshaft.

NOTE: the universal may have snap-rings that are used to retain the bearing cups in the yokes. These snap-rings may be located at the outside of each yoke or in a groove at the base or open end of each bearing cap. In both cases, there are four snap-rings for each universal joint and they must be removed before proceeding further.

2. Support the splined yoke (front universal) or the journal (rear universal) in a manner that will allow the fixed yoke on the driveshaft to be moved. Support the opposite end so that the driveshaft will be in a horizontal position.
3. Using a piece of pipe, or a similar tool with a large enough diameter, apply force to the fixed yoke until the bearing is almost completely pushed out of the yoke and into the pipe. Remove the bearing completely by inserting a spacer between the seal and the bearing cup and finish pressing the bearing out of its yoke, or by tapping around the circumference of the exposed portion of the bearing with a punch and small hammer.

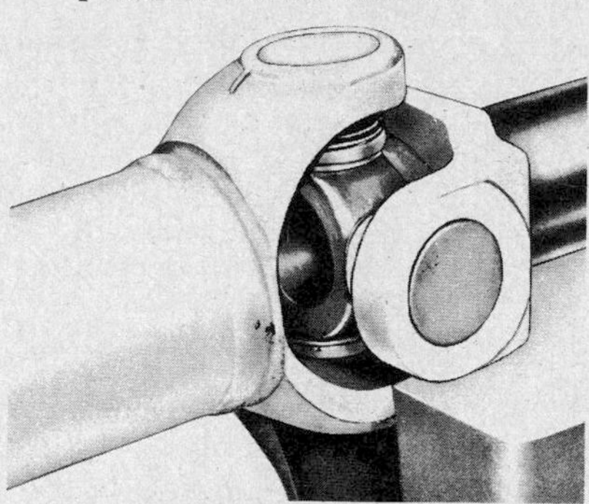

Supporting splined yoke
(© Pontiac Div., G.M. Corp)

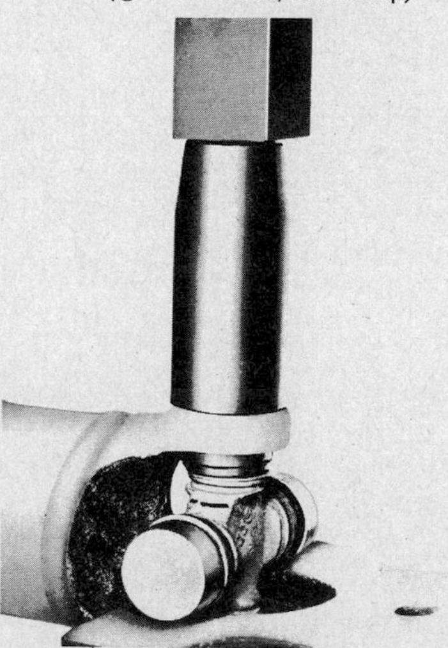

Bearing removal
(© Pontiac Div., G.M. Corp)

NOTE: The plastic which retains the bearing will be sheared when the bearing cup is pressed out. Be sure to remove the remains of the plastic retainer from the ears of the yoke. It is easier to remove the remains if a small pin or punch is first driven through the injection holes in the yoke. Failure to remove all of the plastic remains may prevent the bearing cups from being pressed into place and the bearing retainers from being properly seated.

4. Remove the rest of the bearings following the same procedure.

Installing journal
(© Pontiac Div., G.M. Corp)

Installation

1. Install a bearing one-quarter of the way into one side of the splined yoke (front universal) or fixed yoke (rear universal).
2. Insert the journal into the yoke so that an arm of the journal seats into the bearing.
3. Press in the bearing the remaining distance.
4. Install the opposite bearing. Do not allow the bearing rollers to jam. Continually check for free movement of the journal in the bearings as they are pressed into the yoke.
5. Install the rest of the bearings in the same manner.

REAR AXLE

Axle Shaft, Bearing, and Seal

Removal and Installation

These cars use two different types of drive axle, the C- and the non C-type. Axle shafts in the C-type are retained by C-shaped locks, which fit grooves at the inner end of the shaft. Axle shafts in the non C-type are retained by the brake backing plate, which is bolted to the axle housing. Bearings in the C-type axle consist of an outer race, bearing rollers and a roller cage, retained by snap-rings.

The non C-type axle uses a unit roller bearing (inner race, rollers and outer race), which is pressed onto the shaft, up to a shoulder. When servicing C- or non C-type axles, it is imperative to determine the axle service The Astre uses the C-type axle.

Non C—Type

Caution Before attempting any service to the drive axle or axle shafts, remove the axle carrier cover and visually determine if the axle shafts are retained by C-shaped locks at the inner end, or by the brake backing plate at the outer end. If the shafts are *not* retained by C-locks, proceed as follows.

Design allows for maximum axle shaft end-play of 0.022 in., which can be measured with a dial indicator. If end-play is found to be excessive, the bearing should be replaced. Shimming the bearing is not recommended as this ignores end-play of the bearing itself and could result in improper seating of the bearing.

1. Remove the wheel, tire and brake drum.
2. Remove the nuts holding the retainer plate to the backing plate. Disconnect the brake line.
3. Remove the retainer and install nuts, fingertight, to prevent the brake backing plate from being dislodged.
4. Pull out the axle shaft and bearing assembly, using a slide hammer.
5. Using a chisel, nick the bearing retainer in three or four places. The retainer does not have to be cut, merely collapsed sufficiently, to allow the bearing retainer to be slid from the shaft.
6. Press off the bearing and install the new one by pressing it into position.
7. Press on the new retainer.

NOTE: do not attempt to press the bearing and the retainer on at the same time.

8. Assemble the shaft and bearing in the housing, being sure that the bearing is seated properly in the housing.
9. Install the retainer, drum, wheel and tire. Bleed the brakes.

C—Type

Caution Before attempting any service to the drive axle or axle shafts, remove the carrier cover and visually determine if the axle shafts are retained by C-shaped locks at the inner ends or by a brake backing plate at the outer end. If they *are* retained by C-shaped locks, proceed as follows.

1. Raise the vehicle and remove the wheels.
2. The differential cover has already been removed (see Caution note above). Remove the differential pinion shaft lock-screw and the differential pinion shaft.
3. Push the flanged end of the axle shaft toward the center of the vehicle and remove the C-lock from the end of the shaft.
4. Remove the axle shaft from the housing, being careful not to damage the oil seal.
5. Remove the oil seal by inserting the button end of the axle shaft behind the steel case of the oil seal. Pry the seal loose from the bore.
6. Seat the legs of the bearing puller behind the bearing. Seat a washer against the bearing and hold it in place with a nut. Use a slide hammer to pull the bearing.
7. Pack the cavity between the seal lips with wheel bearing lubricant and lubricate a new wheel bearing with the same.
8. Use a suitable driver and install the bearing until it bottoms against the tube. Install the oil seal.
9. Slide the axle shaft into place. Be sure that the splines on the shaft do not damage the oil seal. Make sure that the splines engage the differential side gear.
10. Install the axle shaft C-lock on the inner end of the axle shaft and push the shaft outward so that the C-lock seats in the differential side gear counterbore.
11. Position the differential pinion shaft through the case and pinions, aligning the hole for the case with the hole for the lock-screw.
12. Install the pinion shaft lock-screw.
13. Use a new gasket and install the carrier cover. Be sure that the gasket surfaces are clean before installing the gasket and cover.
14. Fill the axle with lubricant to the bottom of the filler hole.
15. Install the brake drum and wheels and lower the car. Check for leaks and road test the car.

JACKING, HOISTING

Jack car at front spring seats of lower control arms. Jack car at rear under axle housing, or under a frame member.

FRONT SUSPENSION

Front Shock Absorber R&R

New shock absorbers must be purged of air before installation. This is done by repeatedly extending the shock in its normal mounted position, inverting, and compressing it.

Except Astre

1. Remove the nut, retainer, and grommet which are attached to the upper end of the shock absorber and seat against the frame bracket.

NOTE: it may be necessary to hold the shock absorber shaft to remove the nut. This may be done with a wrench on the end of the shaft.

2. Raise the car to allow the shock to be dropped from the lower control arm.
3. Remove the two shock absorber lower attaching screws and lower the shock from the control arm.
4. Install the shock absorber by reversing the removal steps.
5. Make sure all grommets are in the correct position. Tighten the upper nut to 10 ft. lbs.

Astre

1. Pry out the access plug in the engine compartment so that the upper mount is visible.
2. Raise the front of the car and safely support it.
3. Turn the wheels for clearance.
4. Hold the upper shock stud with a wrench. Loosen and remove the locknut.
5. Unbolt the lower end and pull the shock down and out.
6. Place the lower retainer and rubber grommet on the shock stud.
7. Put the shock in place and tighten the lower bolts. Torque to 20 ft lbs.
8. Place the upper grommet, retainer, and nut on the shock stud.
9. Hold the stud with a wrench and tighten the nut. Torque to 120 in. lbs.

Coil Spring R & R

Except Astre

1. Jack up car and support on jack stands at frame side rails.
2. Remove shock absorber.
3. Disconnect stabilizer bar at lower control arm.

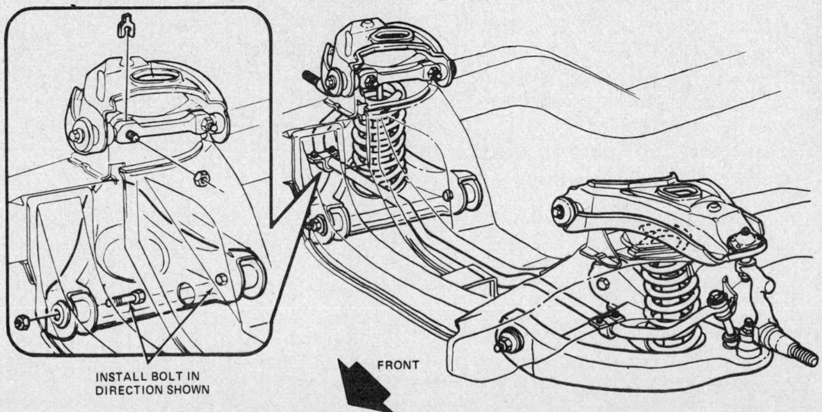

Front suspension—Ventura (© Pontiac Div., G.M. Corp)

4. Support lower control arm with a hydraulic floor jack, then remove the two inner control arm to front crossmember pivot bolts.
5. Carefully lower the control arm, allowing the spring to relax.

Caution Allow the spring to completely expand before attempting to remove it.

6. Reach in and remove spring.
7. **To install, reverse the removal procedure.** Tighten the lower control arm pivot bolts to 105 ft. lbs. or the nuts to 95 ft. lbs. with the weight of the car on the springs.

Astre

1. Raise the front of the car and support it with jackstands placed under the front crossmember braces.
2. Remove the wheel, shock absorbers, and stabilizer bar.
3. Support the lower control arm outer end with a hydraulic floor jack and a block of wood.
4. Securely fasten the spring to the lower control arm with a heavy chain.
5. To detach the tie rod, remove the cotter pin and nut, and tap on the steering arm (not the tie-rod end) with a hammer. Hold another hammer behind the steering arm to take the force of the tapping. The tie rod should then fall free.
6. Remove the lower ball joint stud from the steering knuckle.
7. Very cautiously lower the jack until the spring is fully expanded.
8. Place the spring in its pads on the lower control arm and shock tower. Secure it with a chain as in step four.
9. Carefully raise the jack.
10. Place the lower ball joint stud in the steering knuckle. Torque the stud nut to 60 ft lbs. If the cotter pin does not align, tighten it further 1 6 of a turn and insert a new cotter pin.
11. Install the tie-rod end to the steering arm. Torque the nut to 35 ft lbs. If the cotter pin hole does not align, tighten further up to a maximum of 50 ft lbs. Insert a new cotter pin.
12. Replace the shock absorber. Do not attach the top end of the shock at this point.
13. Install the stabilizer bar. Tighten the bracket bolts to 30 ft lbs and the control arm bolts to 10 ft lbs.
14. Replace the wheel and lower the car. Install the upper end of the shock absorber.

Upper Control Arm Removal

1. **Support car weight at outer end of lower control arm.**
2. **Remove wheel and tire.**
3. Remove cotter pin and loosen the nut on the upper control arm ball stud.
4. **Remove the stud from the knuckle** with a pry bar, while tapping with a hammer. The preferred method of doing this is to use a ball joint stud remover tool to push the stud out.
5. **Remove two nuts that hold the upper control arm cross-shaft to front crossmember. Count number of shims at each bolt.**

NOTE: on 1969 V8 Firebird models with air conditioning, swing compressor out of the way.

Upper Control Arm Installation

1. **Install bolts through holes and install upper control arm to crossmember.**
2. Secure two nuts and washers to the bolts holding the upper control arm shaft to front corssmember. Install same number of shims as removed at each bolt. Torque bolts to 50 ft. lbs. on all 1969-71 and 1975-76 models and 1972-76 Ventura. On 1972-74 Firebird, LeMans and Grand Am, tighten the bolts to 80 ft lbs. Torque the bolts to 60 ft lbs. on the Astre.
3. Lubricate ball joint with chassis lube.
4. **Install ball joint stud through knuckle. Install nut, and torque** to 50 ft. lbs. (40 ft. lbs.—1972-74, 30 ft. lbs.—Astre). Insert cotter pin.

Caution Care should be taken to insure that the steering knuckle hole, ball stud, and nut are free of dirt and grease before tightening the nut. Turn the nut only in the tightening direction to align the slot with the hole to insert the cotter pin. DO NOT BACK OFF THE NUT. Maximum torque to align the slot with the hole, except on Astre, should not exceed 70 ft. lbs. (100 for 1975 and later).

5. **Install wheel and tire assembly.**
6. **Lower car to floor.**
7. Be sure to recheck caster and camber.

Ball Joint Inspection

NOTE: before performing this inspection, make sure the wheel bearings are adjusted correctly and that the A arm bushings are in good condition.

1. Jack the car up under the front lower control arm at the spring seat.
2. Raise the car until there is 1–2 in. of clearance under the wheel.
3. Insert a bar under the wheel and pry upward. If the wheel raises more than 1/8 in., the ball joints are worn. Determine whether the upper or lower ball joint is worn by visual inspection while prying on the wheel.

NOTE: due to the distribution of forces in the suspension, the lower ball joint is usually the defective joint.

Alternate Ball Joint Inspection Method

Upper

1. Disengage the ball stud from the steering knuckle, the weight of the car being supported by a jack under the spring seat on the side being checked.
2. Install the stud nut onto the stud and check the torque required to rotate the ball stud.
3. If the torque is less than 1/2 ft lb, the joint must be replaced.

Lower

1. Place a jack under the lower control arm spring seat and jack up the car.
2. Remove the grease fitting from the lower ball joint.
3. Remove the hub and backing plate, or caliper assembly.
4. Separate the lower ball stud from the steering knuckle using a pry bar and hammer.

NOTE: Make sure that the seal is not damaged.

5. Place the probe of the dial indicator into the grease fitting hole until it touches the base of the ball joint.
6. Preload and zero the indicator, then pull up and down on the threaded portion of the stud and measure the play.
7. If the play exceeds 0.050 in., the ball joint must be replaced.

Lower Ball Joint Wear Indicators —1974 Firebird and LeMans, All Models beginning 1975

These cars have a visual wear indicator on the lower ball joint. Wear is indicated by the position of the 1/2 in. nipple into which the grease fitting is screwed. On a new joint, the nipple should project .050 in. beyond the ball joint cover surface. If the nipple is flush or inside the cover surface, replace the ball joint.

Upper Ball Joint Removal

1. Perform Steps 1-4 of Upper Control Arm Removal. Prickpunch the center of the four rivets.

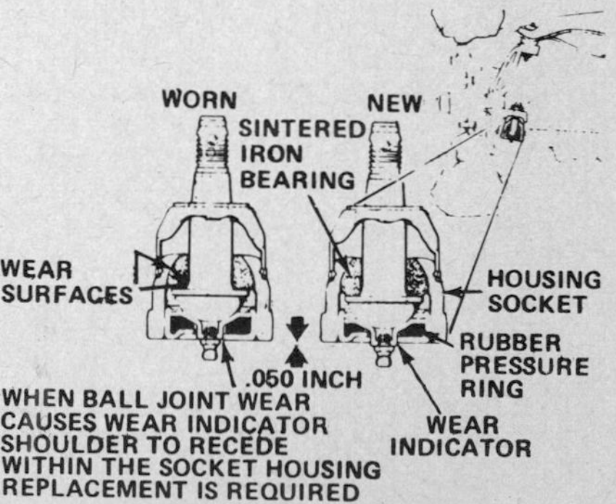

Lower ball joint wear indicator
(© Pontiac Div., G.M. Corp)

2. Drill through the heads of these rivets.
3. Chisel off rivet heads and tap out rivets with a punch.

Upper Ball Joint Installation

1. Install new ball joint against top side of upper control arm. Secure joint to control arm with the four special alloy bolts and nuts furnished with the replacement part.
2. Torque these bolts and nuts to 9 ft. lbs.

NOTE: use special bolts only.

Lower Control Arm and Ball Joint R & R

1. Remove coil spring and lower control arm inner bolts.
2. Separate lower ball joint from steering knuckle by prying, while hammering sharply on steering knuckle.
3. Press lower ball joint from lower control arm using suitable arbors and a large bench vise.
4. To install, reverse removal procedure, tightening lower ball joint stud nut to 85-90 ft. lbs. (70 ft. lbs—1972-76). Tighten the nut to 60 ft. lbs. on the Astre.

NOTE: if only ball joint is to be removed, remove brake caliper or hub and backing plate, with jack under lower arm. Begin with Step 2.

Wheel Bearing Inspection and Adjustment

Inspection

1. Raise the car and support it under the front lower control arm.
2. Spin the wheel to check for any unusual noise. Bad wheel bearings sometimes squeal or sound as though there is sand in the bearing.
3. If bearings are noisy or loose, they should be cleaned, inspected, and repacked before adjustment.
4. To check for loose bearings, grip the tire at top and bottom and move the wheel in and out. Movement less than 0.001 in. or greater than 0.005 in. indicates improper adjustment or excessive wear.

Adjustment

1. Lift the wheel off the ground by jacking under the lower control arm.
2. Remove the dust cap from the hub.
3. Remove the cotter pin and discard it.
4. Snug up the spindle nut while spinning the wheel to seat the bearings (12 ft. lbs). Then back off the nut ¼-½ turn.
5. Retighten the nut by hand until it is finger-tight.
6. Loosen the nut until the nearest hole in the spindle lines up with a slot in the spindle nut and then insert a new cotter pin. When the bearing is properly adjusted, there will be 0.001-0.005 in. endplay.

NOTE: under no circumstances is the final bearing nut adjustment to be even finger-tight.

7. Replace the dust cover and lower the car.

REAR SUSPENSION

Shock Absorber R&R

New shock absorbers must be purged of air before installation. This is done by repeatedly extending the shock in its normal mounted position, inverting, and compressing it.

Except Astre

1. Raise the car at the axle housing.
2. Remove the nut, retainer, and grommet, or nut, and lockwasher, which attach the lower end of the shock absorber to its mounting.
3. Remove the two shock absorber upper attaching screws and the shock absorber.
4. Reverse the removal procedures to install. Tighten the lower nut to 65 ft lbs. on LeMans and Grand Am, to 10 ft lbs. on Firebird and to 55 (45 beginning 1975) ft lbs. on Ventura.

Astre

1. Raise the vehicle and support the rear axle.
2. Remove upper attaching bolts and lower through-bolt.
3. Remove the shock absorber.
4. Install retainer and rubber grommet onto the new shock.
5. Place shock absorber into installed position and install upper retaining bolts. Torque to 18 ft. lbs.
6. Install the through bolt and a rubber grommet on each side of the shock eye. Torque the nut to 42 in. lbs.
7. Lower the car.

Rear Coil Spring R & R

Tempest, LeMans, Grand Am

1. Raise the rear of the car and support it solidly on the frame rails.
2. Remove the clip that attaches the brake hose to its bracket on the frame crossmember.
3. Support the rear axle with a jack.
4. Remove the nut and lockwasher from the shock absorber and disconnect the shock from the axle. It may be necessary to adjust the height of the jack to disconnect the shock. On models beginning 1973, disconnect the upper control arms from the axle housing.
5. Carefully lower the jack until the spring is free and remove the spring. Note the position of the spring and replace it with the lower coil pointing in the same direction.
6. Reverse the removal steps to install the spring.

Astre

1. Raise vehicle and support the rear axle, with a hydraulic jack.
2. Disconnect both shock absorbers from lower brackets.
3. Lower axle and remove springs and spring insulators.

NOTE: one or both springs may be removed at this point.

Caution When lowering axle do not stretch brake hose running from frame to axle.

4. Install insulators on top and bottom of springs and position on axle.
5. Raise axle and reconnect shock absorbers. Torque the bottom stud or bolt nuts to 42 in. lbs.
6. Lower the vehicle.

Rear Leaf Spring R & R

Firebird, Ventura

1. Jack up the car at the rear axle. Then support the major portion of the weight of the car on the frame rails, leaving the jack in place under the axle. At this point the jack should be supporting the axle only; there should be no tension on the spring.
2. Disconnect the shock at the axle and move it out of the way.
3. Remove the spring and shock absorber anchor plate nuts and remove the anchor plate and lower spring cushion pad.
4. Raise the axle with the jack and remove the upper spring cushion pad.
5 Loosen the upper and lower spring shackle pin nuts.
6. Loosen the front spring eye bolt.
7. Remove the screws securing the spring front mounting bracket to the floor pan and carefully let the spring swing down.

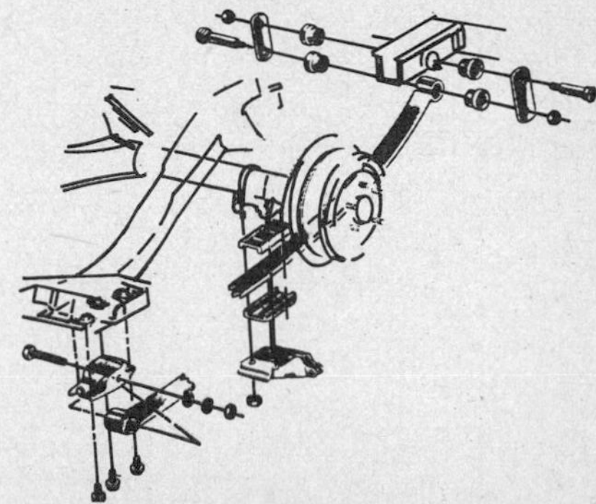

Rear spring installation—Ventura II with single leaf springs (© Pontiac Div., G.M. Corp)

8. Remove the lower shackle pin from the rear of the spring and remove the spring from the car.
9. Install the front spring mounting bracket on the front spring eye and loosely insert the bolt and nut. Do not tighten the spring eyebolt until the weight of the car is on the springs.
10. Place the spring into the shackles at the rear of the car and loosely install the lower shackle pin and nut. Do not tighten them.
11. Raise the front end of the spring and install the spring mounting bracket to the floor pan and torque the bolts to 30 ft lbs. Make sure the tab on the spring mounting bracket is indexed in the slot in the floor pan and that the parking brake cables are on the top side of the spring.
12. Place the upper spring cushion pan on the spring and lower the axle onto spring.
13. Install the lower spring cushion and shock absorber anchor plate and torque the anchor plate nuts to 40 ft lbs.
14. Install the shock absorber.
15. Put the weight of the car on the springs and torque the shackle pin nuts to 50 ft lbs. Tighten front eyebolt to 80 ft lbs.

BRAKES

Drum brakes are of the duo-servo, self-adjusting type. The self-adjusting feature operates only when the brakes are applied with car moving in reverse. On the Astre, the self-adjusters work when the handbrake is operated.

A dual-type master cylinder is used. For detailed information on this cylinder, see Unit Repair Section.

Information on brake service can be found in the Unit Repair Section.

Single-piston, sliding-caliper disc brakes have been available as optional equipment on most models (standard with high performance packages and Firebird starting 1970, on all models except Ventura since 1971, and on Ventura since 1975). These brakes have a vented, cast-iron rotor with two braking surfaces.

Disc brakes need no adjustment because, during operation, the application and release of hydraulic pressure causes the piston and caliper to move only slightly. In the released position, the pads do not move very far from the rotor thus, as pads wear down, the piston simply moves farther out of the caliper bore and the caliper repositions itself on its mounting bolts to maintain proper pad-to-rotor clearance.

A metering valve in the front brake circuit prevents the discs from operating until about 75 psi exists in the system. This enables the rear drum brakes to operate in synchronization with the front discs and reduces the possibility of unequal brake application and premature front brake lock-up. A proportioning valve in the rear brake circuit of some models limits the amount of hydraulic pressure that can be applied to the rear brakes, preventing the rear brakes from locking up. Starting 1971, a two- or three-function combination valve replaces the separate units used previously. The pressure required to operate front brakes is now 110-150 psi. Beginning 1974, all models have a lining wear indicator. As the lining material wears down, a steel sensor approaches the rotor. When enough lining material has worn away, the sensor makes contact with the rotor causing noise which is audible to the driver. See the Unit Repair Section of this manual for service procedures.

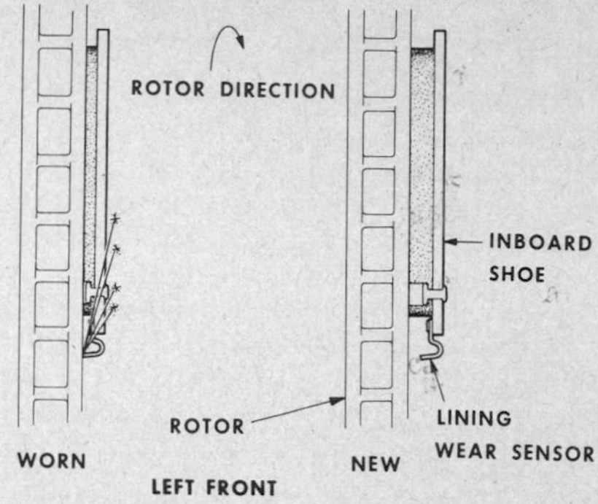

Disc brake lining wear indicator (© Pontiac Div, G.M. Corp)

Parking Brake Adjustment

Except Astre

The automatic self-adjusting feature incorporated in the rear brake mechanism normally maintains proper parking brake adjustment. For this reason, the rear brake adjustment must be checked before any adjustment of the parking brake cables is done. Check the parking brake

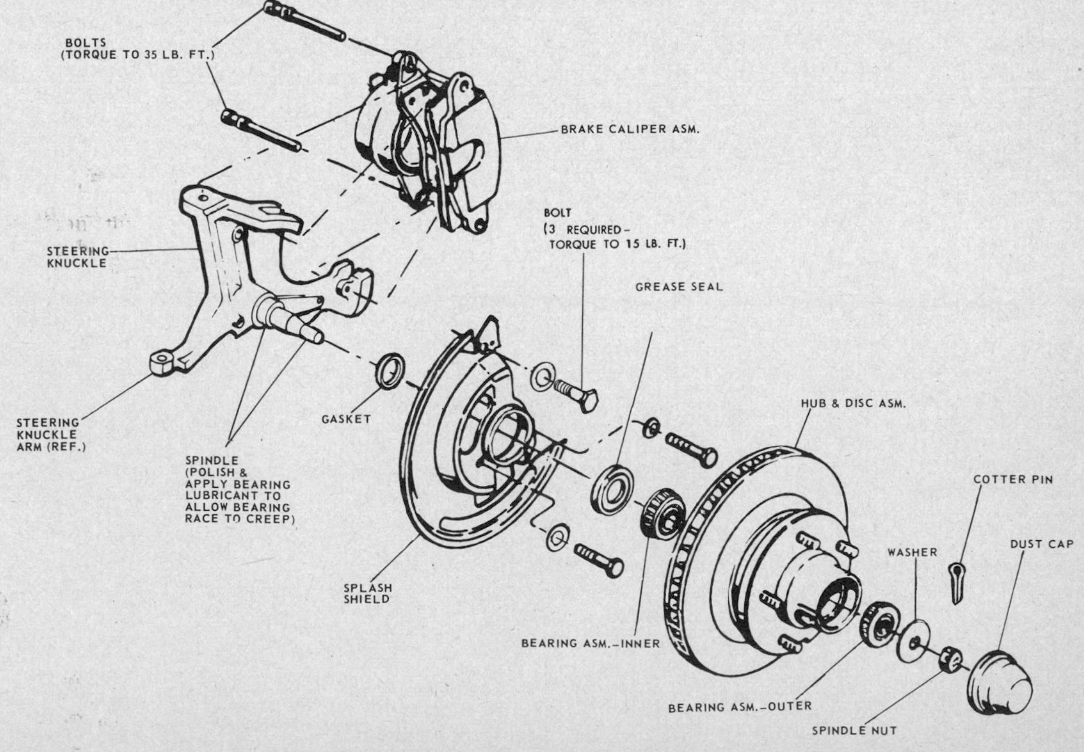

Steering knuckle, hub and disc assembly—1970-76 Firebird, 1973-76 LeMans and Grand Am (© Pontiac Div., G.M. Corp)

mechanism and cables for free movement and lubricate all working surfaces before proceeding.

Caution It is very important that the parking brake cables are not too tight. If the cables are too tight, they create a drag and position the secondary shoes so that the self-adjusters continue to operate in compensation for drag wear. The result is rapidly worn rear brake linings.

1. Jack up both rear wheels.
2. Push parking brake pedal 5-7 notches from full release position for Tempest and GTO up to 1970, 2 notches for Firebird up to 1970 and 1975-76 Firebird and Ventura, 3 notches for 1975-76 LeMans and Grand Am, 4-8 notches for all series 1971-72, 8 notches for all series 1973-74.
3. Loosen rear equalizer locknut and adjust forward nut until light rear brake drag is felt as wheels are rotated by hand. On 1975 and later models the wheels should be able to turn backward but not forward.
4. Tighten locknut and release parking brake pedal; no drag should be felt.

Astre

1. Raise and support the rear of the car.
2. Apply the parking brake one notch from the fully released position.
3. Loosen the adjusting locknut at the cable equalizer and tighten the adjusting nut until a slight drag is felt when the rear wheels are rotated.
4. Tighten the locknut securely.
5. The rear wheels should rotate freely when the parking brake is fully released.
6. Lower the vehicle.

Master Cylinder R & R

1. Disconnect hydraulic line/s at master cylinder; disconnect clevis at pedal (except on power brakes).
2. Remove the two retaining nuts and lockwashers that hold cylinder to the firewall or power booster.
3. Remove the master cylinder, gasket and rubber boot.
4. Position master cylinder on firewall; reconnect pushrod clevis to brake pedal.
5. Install nuts and lockwashers.
6. Install hydraulic line/s, then check brake pedal free play.
7. Bleed brakes, as described in Unit Repair Section.

NOTE: cars having disc brakes do not have a check valve in the front outlet port of the master cylinder. If one is installed, front discs will immediately wear out due to residual hydraulic pressure holding pads against rotor.

Power Brake Booster R & R

1. Remove the vacuum hose from the front housing and discard the grommet. Remove the master cylinder and position away from the booster. It is not necessary to disconnect the lines from the master cylinder if it is not to be repaired.
2. Remove the clevis pin retainer from the brake pedal inside the car.
3. Remove the nuts from the vacuum cylinder studs under the dash and remove the vacuum power section.
4. Reverse the removal procedure to install the booster.

STEERING

The manual steering gear is the recirculating-ball nut type. The steering shaft, worm shaft, and worm nut are all in line. The steering shaft and worm shaft are separated by a flexible coupling. This coupling permits the gear to be removed independently of the steering shaft and steering column.

All models use a variable-ratio power steering gear. The gear is the recirculating-ball type, incorporating a wormshaft and a rack-piston. A rotary valve is contained in the gear housing, eliminating the need for individually mounted valve and cylinder assemblies.

Hydraulic pressure for the power steering is provided by a constant displacement vane-type pump. It is located on the front of the engine and is belt-driven by the engine crankshaft pulley.

Tie Rod End R&R

1. Loosen the tie rod adjuster sleeve clamp nuts.
2. Remove the tie rod stud nut cotter pin and nut.

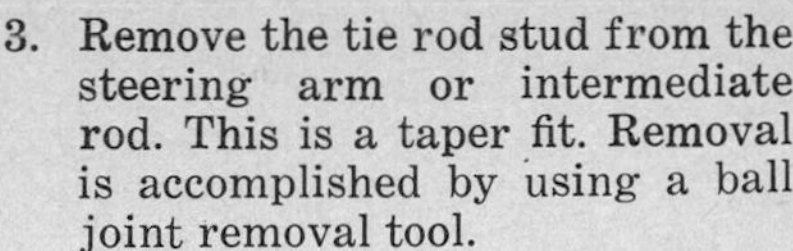

3. Remove the tie rod stud from the steering arm or intermediate rod. This is a taper fit. Removal is accomplished by using a ball joint removal tool.
4. Unthread the tie rod from the adjuster sleeve. Outer tie rods have right-hand threads and inner tie rods have left-hand threads. Count the number of turns the tie rod must be rotated to remove it from the adjusting sleeve. This will allow a reasonably accurate realignment upon reassembly.

Tie rod clamp installation (© Pontiac Div., G.M. Corp)

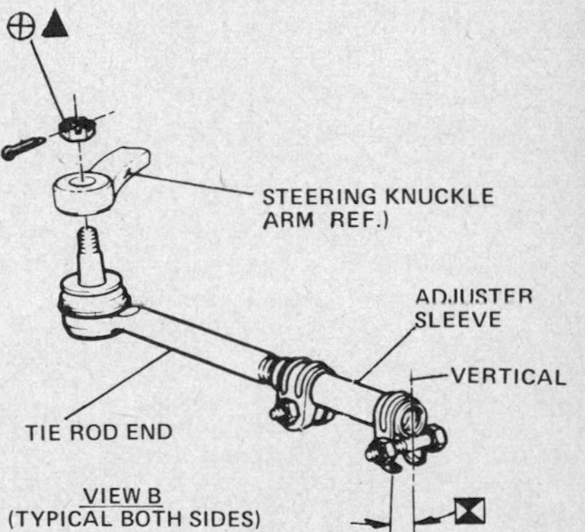

Tie rod assembly—typical (© Pontiac Div., G.M. Corp)

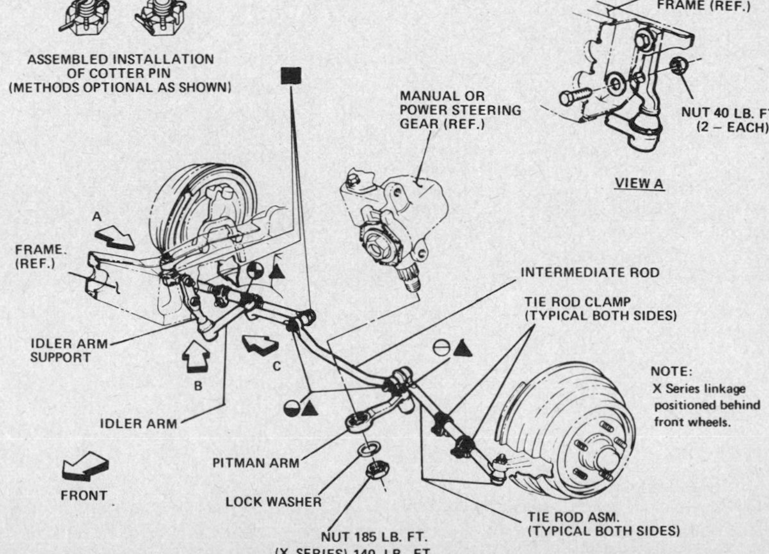

Steering linkage (© Pontiac Div., G.M. Corp)

5. Reverse the removal procedures for installation. Clean all rust and dirt from the threads. Check the alignment and adjust if necessary.

Power Steering Pump R&R

1. Disconnect the hoses at the pump.
2. Remove the drive pulley attaching nut.
3. Loosen the bracket-to-pump mounting bolts and remove the drive belt.
4. Slide the pulley from the shaft with a gear puller. Do not hammer on the pulley.
5. Remove the bracket-to-pump mounting bolts and remove the pump.
6. Reverse the removal steps for installation. Bleed the pump of air by turning the pulley counterclockwise until no bubbles appear in the reservoir.
7. Bleed the system.

Power Steering System Bleeding

The system must be bled of air whenever any parts of the pump circuit have been disconnected or replaced.

1. Fill the reservoir. Be careful not to overfill, because the level is normally checked at operating temperature after expansion has taken place. Allow the fluid to remain undisturbed for at least two minutes.
2. Start the engine and run it for only about two seconds.
3. Fill again as necessary.
4. Repeat Steps 1 to 3 until the level remains constant.
5. Raise the front wheels off the ground.
6. Run the engine at about 1,500 rpm and turn the wheels gently against the stops in either direction.
7. Fill again as necessary.
8. Lower the car to the ground. Turn the wheels gently against the stops in either direction with the engine running.
9. Fill again as necessary.

Steering Wheel R&R

Except Astre

1. On deluxe models, remove the screws holding the trim cover to the wheel, or if equipped with a horn button, lift the button off.
2. Remove the snap-ring and steering wheel nut from the steering shaft.
3. Position the wheels in the straight-ahead position and make match marks on the steering shaft and steering wheel.
4. Using a puller, remove the steering wheel.

Caution Don't pound on the steering wheel or the steering shaft. The collapsible column could be damaged enough to require replacement.

5. Disconnect the horn wire insulator by rotating the insulator counterclockwise to the unlock position and then pull up.
6. Reverse the removal procedures for installation. Make sure the match marks are lined up when installing the wheel.

Astre

1. Disconnect the battery ground cable.
2. Remove the two screws from the back of the wheel, allowing the shroud (horn actuator bar) to be removed. Lift the Formula wheel horn button off.
3. Set the wheel straight ahead. Mark the relationship of the wheel to the shaft and remove the snap-ring and nut.
4. Remove the steering wheel with a puller, using the two threaded holes in the wheel. Disconnect the horn wire insulator by rotating the insulator counterclockwise to the unlock position and then pulling up.
5. Install the wheel, aligning the previously made marks. Make sure that the turn signal switch is in the neutral position. Torque the nut to 30 ft lbs.
6. Make sure that the lower horn insulator, eyelet, and spring are in place.
7. Position the shroud, seating the pin on the right side of the wheel in the hole in the shroud. Replace the formula wheel horn button.
8. Replace the two screws in the rear of the wheel. Connect the battery cable.

Turn Signal Switch R & R

1. Remove the steering wheel.
2. Remove the three cover screws and lift the cover off the shaft.
3. Depress the lockplate and remove the snap-ring. Remove the retaining ring and lockplate.
4. Slide the upper bearing spring and turn signal cam off the shaft. Remove the thrust washer.
5. Remove the turn signal lever screw and lever.
6. Push the hazard warning switch in and remove the knob.
7. Pull the wiring connector out of the bracket and disconnect it. Wrap it with tape to prevent snagging.
8. Pull the switch straight up and remove it from the housing.
9. Reverse the removal procedures for installation.

INSTRUMENT PANEL

Ignition Switch R & R

The ignition and steering wheel locking switch is located just below the gear selector lever on the steering column.

1. Disconnect battery.
2. Loosen toe pan screws.
3. Remove column to panel nuts, lower steering column, and disconnect switch wire connectors.

Caution Be extremely careful with the steering column. Never let it hang unsupported.

4. Remove switch attaching screws and switch.
5. To install, move key lock to OFF-LOCK position.
6. Move actuator rod hole in switch to OFF-LOCK position.
7. Install switch, with rod in hole, then reverse removal procedure.

Switch Adjustment—Standard Column

1. Place switch in OFF position.
2. Position switch on column, then move slider to extreme left (toward wheel).
3. Move slider back two positions to the right of ACCESSORY position.
4. Place key in any run position and shift transmission into any position but Park for automatics or Reverse for manual.
5. Position lock toward ACCESSORY with a light finger pressure and secure switch.

Switch Adjustment—Tilt Column

1. Place key in ACCESSORY position; leave key in lock.
2. Loosen switch mounting screws.
3. Push switch upward toward wheel to make certain it is in ACCESSORY detent.
4. Hold key in full counter clockwise ACCESSORY position and tighten switch mounting screws.
5. Switch is properly adjusted if: it will go into ACCESSORY position, the key can be removed when in lock, and switch will go into START position.

Lock Cylinder Replacement

1. Remove steering wheel.
2. Pull turn signal switch up far enough to allow access to spring latch slot.
3. Place key in RUN position, insert a thin screwdriver into the slot next to the switch mounting screw boss and depress spring latch.

NOTE: there is a casting flash over this slot if the lock has never before been removed. It is necessary sometimes to use substantial force to

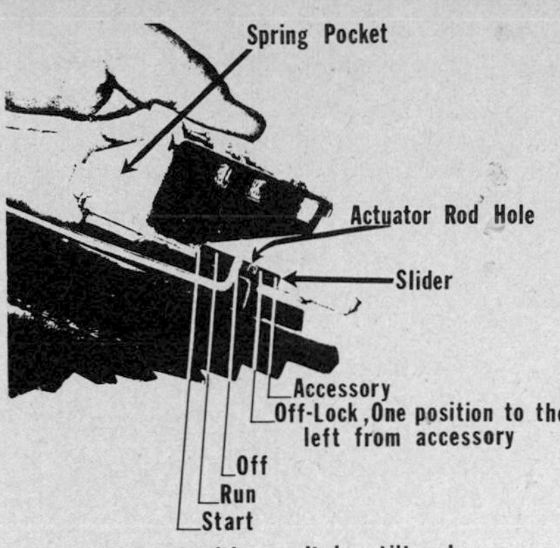

Adjusting ignition switch—tilt column
(© Pontiac Div., G.M. Corp)

break it. Be careful not to damage anything beneath the flashing when penetrating the slot.

4. Remove lock from housing.
5. To install, first hold lock cylinder sleeve and rotate knob clockwise against stop, looking at the key end.

Depressing lock cylinder spring latch
(© Pontiac Div., G.M. Corp)

6. Lay a 1/16 in. drill on housing surface next to housing bore. This isn't necessary on 1975 and later models, except Astre.

NOTE: the 1/16 in. drill prevents forcing the lock cylinder inward beyond its normal latched position. The buzzer switch and spring latch can hold the lock cylinder too far inward. Complete disassembly of the upper bearing housing is necessary to release an improperly installed lock cylinder.

7. Insert cylinder into housing bore, aligning keyway, and push in to abutment.
8. Rotate knob counterclockwise, pushing in slightly, until cylinder mates with sector.
9. Push in until spring latch pops into groove, then remove drill.

Light Switch Replacement

1. Disconnect battery.
2. Pull knob to on position.
3. Reach under instrument panel and depress the switch shaft retainer, then remove knob and shaft assembly.

NOTE: disconnect vacuum hose on vacuum-operated headlamp models.

4. Remove retaining ferrule nut.
5. Remove switch from instrument panel.
6. Disconnect multi-plug connector from switch.
7. Install in reverse of above. (In checking lights before installation, switch must be grounded to test dome lights on some models).

WINDSHIELD WIPERS

Motor R & R

1. Remove hoses and wire terminals that are connected to wiper unit.
2. Remove clip or nut that secures wiper crank to wiper linkage arm.

NOTE: this clip is under leaf screen on depressed-park (hidden wiper) motors, and accessible only after firewall bolts are removed on some standard motors. On some models, the wiper arm must be removed to facilitate motor removal.

3. Remove screws that secure wiper motor assembly to firewall.
4. Position wiper assembly on firewall and secure.
5. Connect wire terminals and hoses.
6. Connect wiper crank with wiper linkage arm.

Wiper Linkage R & R

1. Remove arm and blade assemblies.
2. Remove fresh air intake grille.
3. Remove wiper linkage retaining screws.
4. Loosen, but do not remove, wiper crank to linkage nuts.
5. Remove wiper linkage through cowl opening.
6. To install, reverse above procedure. Make sure wiper blades are in park position after they are installed.

RADIO

Radio R & R

1969-70, except 1970 Firebird

1. Disconnect antenna and power leads, remove tape deck and multiplex.
2. Loosen hex screws and remove knobs.
3. Remove escutcheon retaining nuts.
4. Remove screw that holds receiver to panel bracket, then remove ash tray.

NOTE: with air conditioner, outlet duct and bezel must be removed.

5. Remove speaker by disconnecting output connector and mounting bracket screws.
6. Reverse above procedure to reinstall.

NOTE: this procedure is very general, and some combinations of accessories may require slight modifications.

1970-76 Firebird

1. Disconnect battery.
2. Remove glove box, glove box door and lower right A/C duct.
3. Remove radio knobs, nuts and trim plate.
4. Disconnect antenna and power lines.
5. Disconnect speaker leads, then remove radio bracket and radio from passenger side of dashboard.
6. To install, reverse removal procedure.

1971-72 LeMans and GTO, 1971-76 Ventura

1. Disconnect battery. Remove lower A/C duct on Tempest.
2. Remove radio knobs, bezels and hex nuts.
3. Remove support bracket bolt. Remove the Ventura radio side-brace screw.
4. Disconnect electrical and antenna leads; remove radio from under dash.
5. To install, reverse removal procedure.

1973-76 LeMans

1. Disconnect the battery.
2. Remove the radio knobs and bezels.
3. Remove the upper and lower instrument panel trim plates.
4. Remove the two radio side (two front on 1974 and later) retaining screws.
5. Remove the radio from the panel opening, disconnecting the electrical connections and the antenna lead.
6. To install, reverse the removal procedure. If the radio is to be replaced, remove the bushing from the rear of the radio and install it on the replacement radio.

1973-76 Grand Am and Grand LeMans

1. Disconnect the battery.
2. Remove the radio knobs and bezels and the retaining hex nut from the right-hand radio tuning shaft.
3. Remove the four retaining screws and the trim plate.
4. Remove the two side (one front on 1974 and later) retaining screws and the mounting bracket screw.
5. Remove the radio and the mounting bracket from the dash, disconnecting the electrical connections and the antenna lead.
6. To install, reverse the removal procedure.

Astre

1. Remove battery ground cable.
2. Remove knobs, controls, washers and nuts from radio bushings.
3. Disconnect antenna lead, power connector, and speaker connectors from rear of receiver.
4. Remove two screws securing radio mounting bracket to instrument panel lower reinforcement and lift out radio receiver.
5. To install, reverse the removal procedure.

HEATER

Heater Blower R & R—Non Air-Conditioned Cars

1969 Tempest, GTO, and Firebird

1. Remove battery and battery tray.
2. Remove inner fender skirt.
3. Remove blower power wire.
4. Remove blower retaining screws and blower.
5. To install, reverse removal procedure.

NOTE: if duct was removed, make sure it is properly sealed during installation.

1970-72 Tempest and LeMans, 1970-76 Firebird

1. Jack up front of car and remove right front wheel.
2. Cut access hole along stamped outline on right fender skirt, using an air chisel.
3. Disconnect blower power wire.
4. Remove blower.
5. To install, reverse removal procedure, covering access hole with a metal plate secured with sealer and sheet metal screws.

1973-76 LeMans & Grand Am

1. Disconnect the blower motor feed wire and the ground wire.
2. Remove the blower motor retaining screws and remove the motor.
3. To replace, reverse the removal procedure.

1971-76 Ventura

1. Disconnect the battery.
2. Detach the heater hoses from the clips on the right front fender skirt.
3. Raise the car and remove all fender skirt attaching bolts except those which attach the skirt to the radiator support.
4. Pull down on the skirt and block the skirt to all clearance for removal of the blower motor.
5. Disconnect the electrical wiring from the motor.
6. Remove the attaching screws and remove the blower motor. Pry the motor flange gently if the sealer acts as an adhesive.
7. Remove the blower impeller retaining nut and separate the motor from the impeller.
8. To replace, reverse the removal procedure.

Astre

1. Disconnect the battery ground cable.
2. Disconnect the blower motor lead wire. Disconnect the motor cooling tube on air-conditioned models.
3. Scribe the blower motor flange to case position.
4. Remove the blower to case attaching screws and remove the blower wheel and motor assembly. Pry the flange gently if the sealer is retaining the assembly.
5. Remove the blower wheel retaining nut and separate the motor and wheel.
6. To install, reverse Steps 1-5, lining up the match-marks on the motor flange and case which were made at removal.

NOTE: assemble the blower wheel to the motor with the open end of the blower away from the motor. Reseal the motor flange, if necessary.

Heater Core R & R—Non Air-Conditioned Cars

1969-76 Tempest, GTO, LeMans, and Firebird

1. Drain radiator.
2. Disconnect heater hoses at air inlet assembly.
3. Remove nuts from core studs on firewall (under hood). Remove the glove box.

NOTE: on 1970-76 Firebird, remove glove box and door, then remove heater outlet from case. Remove defroster duct screw on all 1971-76 models.

4. From inside the car, pull the heater assembly from the firewall.
5. Disconnect control cables and wires, then remove heater assembly.
6. To remove core, unhook retaining springs or strips.
7. To install, reverse removal procedure, making sure core is properly sealed during installation.

1971-76 Ventura

1. Disconnect battery.
2. Drain radiator, disconnect heater hoses at core and plug core tubes.
3. Remove nuts from core case studs on firewall.
4. Remove glove box and glove box door.
5. From inside car, drill out lower right hand heater case stud with 1/4 in. drill.
6. Pull entire heater case, with core, from firewall.
7. Disconnect cables and blower resistor connector, then remove case from car.
8. Remove core from case.
9. To install, reverse removal procedure. Use sealer around core and replace drilled stud with new screw and stamped nut.

Astre

1. Disconnect the battery ground cable.
2. Disconnect the blower motor lead wire.
3. Place a pan under the vehicle. Disconnect the heater hoses at the core connections and secure the ends of the hoses in a raised position.
4. It may be necessary to remove the coil bracket to dash panel stud nut and move the coil out of the way.
5. Remove the blower intake to dash panel screws and nuts and remove the blower intake, blower motor and wheel as an assembly.
6. Remove the core retaining strap screws and remove the core from the vehicle.
7. To install, reverse Steps 1-6.

NOTE: be sure that the blower intake sealer is intact, replace if necessary.

Heater Blower R&R—Air-Conditioned Cars

1969 Firebird, Tempest, and GTO

1. Remove the fender brace, battery, and tray.
2. Scribe alignment marks and remove hood.
3. Remove the right front fender and skirt as an assembly.
4. Disconnect the motor wire and cooling tube from the motor.
5. Remove the motor attaching screws and the motor.
6. Reverse the above steps for installation.

1970-76 All Models

This procedure is the same as for non air-conditioned cars.

Heater Core and Case R&R—Air-Conditioned Cars

1969 Tempest, GTO, and Firebird

1. Remove the glove box.
2. Remove the lower instrument panel air-conditioning duct and outlet assembly by removing the five attaching screws and retainer.
3. Lower the duct and outlet assembly after disconnecting the right and left-side nozzle connections.
4. Disconnect the temperature control cable and vacuum hose.
5. Drain the cooling system and remove the two water hoses attached to the heater core.

6. Remove the six heater core-to-cowl attaching nuts. It is necessary to cut a 1 in. diameter hole in the right-hand fender skirt to remove the lower nut.
7. Remove two screws from the heater core and case evaporator housing seal and remove the seal and retainer.
8. Remove the core and case assembly.
9. Mark the heater cam and bracket assembly to ensure proper reinstallation and remove the heater cam and bracket.
10. Remove the front case-to-rear case attaching screws and separate the cases.
11. Remove the heater core retaining screws and core.
12. Reverse the above steps for installation.

1970-76 Tempest, GTO, LeMans, and Grand Am

1. Drain the coolant.
2. Disconnect the water hoses at the heater core tubes to prevent spilling coolant during removal.
3. Remove the glove compartment.
4. Remove the cold air duct and heater outlet.
5. Remove the defroster duct attaching screw.
6. Remove the screws and nuts which retain the case to the dash. Remove the blower motor resistor to gain access to the upper retaining nut inside the evaporator case.
7. Move the core and case assembly rearward to free the attaching studs from the cowl and remove the core and case assembly.
8. Disconnect the temperature cable and vacuum hoses from the core and case assembly.
9. Remove the core and case assembly from the car.
10. Remove the heater core retaining screws and core.
11. Reverse the above steps for installation.

1970-76 Firebird

1. Drain the coolant.
2. Remove the glove box and door.
3. Remove the cold air duct on the lower right-hand side.
4. Remove the left and center lower A/C ducts.
5. Raise the car and remove the rocker panel trim on the right side and remove the screws holding the forward trim brackets.
6. Remove the three lower fender bolts at rear of the fender.
7. Remove the four fender-to-skirt bolts at the rear of the wheel opening.
8. Remove the two fender skirt bolts near the blower motor area.
9. Pry the rear portion of the fender out at the bottom to gain access to the hose clamp on the water valve-to-core hose and disconnect the hose at the heater core.
10. Disconnect the water pump hose at the heater core.
11. Remove the two heater case retaining nuts under the hood at the dash.
12. Remove the two heater case retaining bolts inside the car.
13. Remove the console and tape player if equipped.
14. Disconnect the temperature cable at the heater case.
15. Remove the heater outlet duct.
16. Remove the lower defroster duct screw at the heater case.
17. Remove the right kick panel, and the heater core and case as an assembly.
18. Disconnect the vacuum hoses from the heater case and remove the core from the case.
19. Reverse the above steps for installation.

1971-76 Ventura

1. Disconnect the battery and drain the coolant.
2. Disconnect the upper heater hose at the core pipe and remove the accessible heater core and case assembly attaching nuts.
3. Remove the right front fender skirt bolts and lower the skirt to gain access to the lower heater hose clamp. Loosen the clamp and disconnect the hose.
4. Remove the lower right-hand heater core and case assembly attaching nut.
5. Remove the glove compartment and door.
6. Remove the recirculation vacuum diaphragm at the right-hand kick panel.
7. Remove the heater outlet and cold air distributor duct.
8. Remove the heater case extension screws and separate the extension from the heater case on models through 1974.
9. Disconnect the heater cables and electrical connectors, and remove the case and core as an assembly.
10. Separate the core from the case.
11. Reverse the above steps for installation.

Astre

1. Disconnect the battery ground cable.
2. Disconnect the heater hoses at the core and plug them.
3. Remove the firewall selector stud nuts, the glove box, and door.
4. Disconnect the left-side flexible dash outlet hose from the center distributor duct.
5. Remove the right-side dash outlet and hose assembly.
6. Remove the steering column lower plastic retainer, insulation, and screws. Remove the column instrument panel stud nuts and let the column rest on the seat.

Caution Be extremely careful with the steering column. Never let it hang unsupported.

7. Remove the instrument panel bezel, ash tray, and tray retainer.
8. Take out the air conditioning control panel screws.
9. Disconnect the radio and antenna leads.
10. Remove the instrument cluster to panel screws, cover the column to prevent scratches, and let the cluster rest on the column. Detach the speedometer cable.
11. Push the air conditioning controls forward and let them rest on the floor.
12. Remove the center distributor duct screws at the selector duct. Remove the duct instrument panel upper retainer and remove the duct by sliding it to the left to clear the lower instrument panel to cluster tab, and then to the right.
13. Remove the defroster duct-to-selector duct screw. Remove the remaining selector duct-to-dash screws and pull the duct back far enough to allow the electrical and vacuum lines to be disconnected.
14. Disconnect the lines and the control cable and remove the selector duct assembly.
15. Pry off the temperature door bellcrank, being careful not to bend the arm or damage the selector case.
16. Remove the temperature door. Remove the backing plate and temperature door cable retainer screws.
17. Remove the heater core and backing plate as an assembly. Remove the core retaining straps and withdraw the core.
18. Reverse the removal procedure to install the core.

SEAT BELTS

Buzzer System—1973

The front seat belt warning system consists of a switch in each belt retractor, a sensor switch in the seat cushion on the passenger side, a reminder light, and a warning buzzer. The circuit wiring is routed through the ignition switch and parking brake warning switch on manual transmission models or through the ignition switch and transmission switch on models equipped with automatic transmissions.

With the ignition switch on and the parking brake released on cars equipped with manual transmissions, or with the shift selector in a forward position on automatic transmission models, the warning circuit (light and buzzer) is closed (activated) until the driver's seat belt is extended to open (de-activate) the circuit. The seat sensor on the passenger side will react to weights on the seat cushion and close the warning circuit. Extending the passenger belt will open the circuit.

Seat Belt/Starter Interlock—1974-75

All Pontiacs are equipped with the sequential interlock seat belt system. The sequential interlock system requires the driver and right front seat occupant to first sit in their seats, then fasten their seat belts before the engine can be started. The middle seat position, on cars equipped with a front bench seat, is not included in the interlock system. The seat sensors are similar to those found in the 1973 buzzer systems.

Engine restarting is possible without interference from the interlock system if the driver has not left his seat. In the event of system malfunction, an emergency by-pass switch under the hood permits starting when the ignition key is in the ON position.

The buzzer/warning light system will be activated if a front seat belt is not fastened at an occupied front seat after the engine is started and the transmission is shifted from Park or Neutral to a forward gear.

Disabling the Interlock System

Since the requirement for the interlock system was dropped during the 1975 model year, those systems installed on cars built earlier may now be legally disabled. The seat belt warning light is still required.

1. Disconnect the negative battery cable.
2. Locate the interlock harness connector under the left side of the instrument panel on or near the fuse block.
3. Cut and tape the ends of the green wire on the body side of the connector.
4. Remove the buzzer from the fuse block or connector.

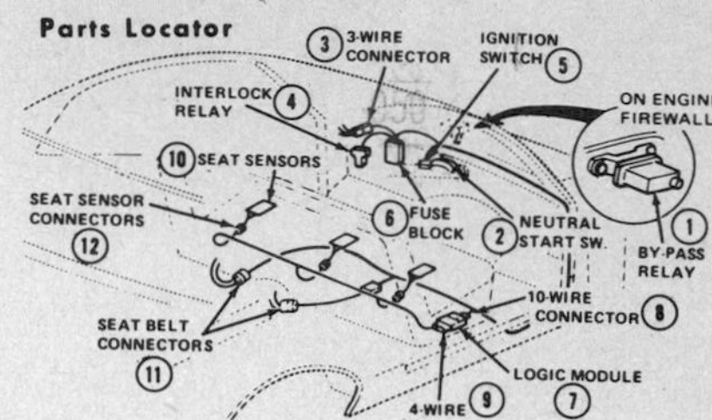

Seat belt/starter interlock component location (© Pontiac Div., G.M. Corp)

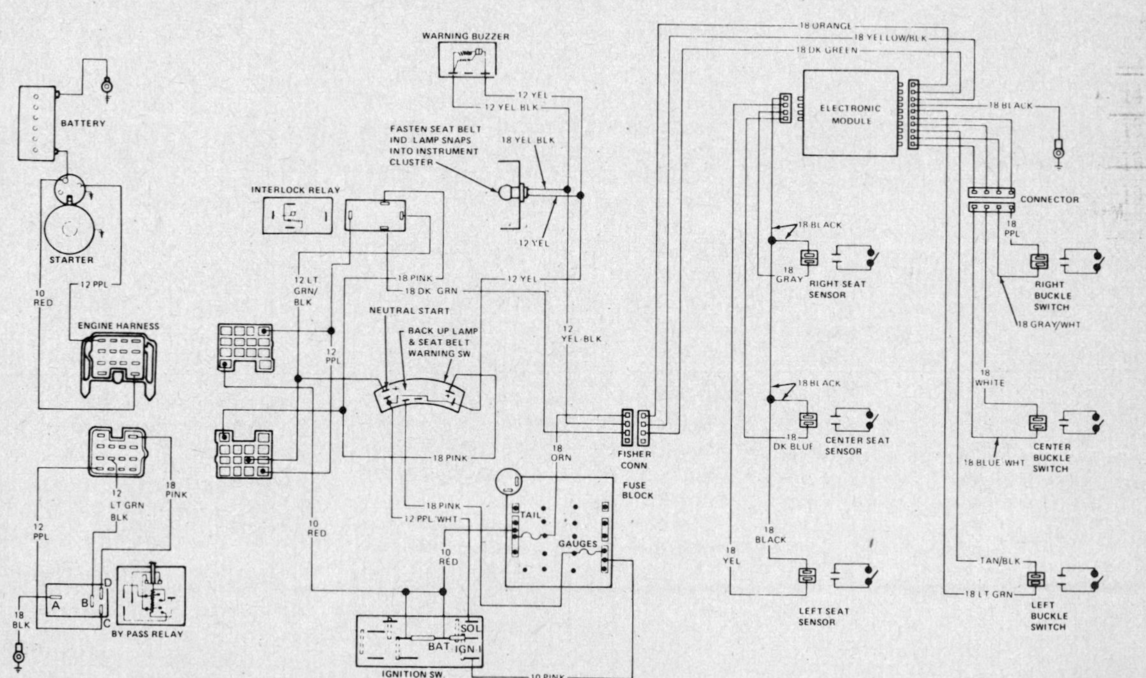

Ventura interlock system schematic, automatic transmission (© Pontiac Div., G.M. Corp)

INDEX

Barracuda · Challenger · Dart · Valiant · Aspen · Volare

YEAR IDENTIFICATION

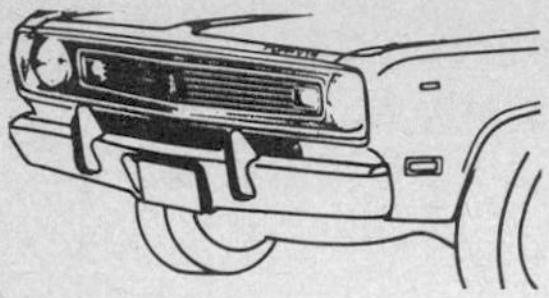

1969 Valiant

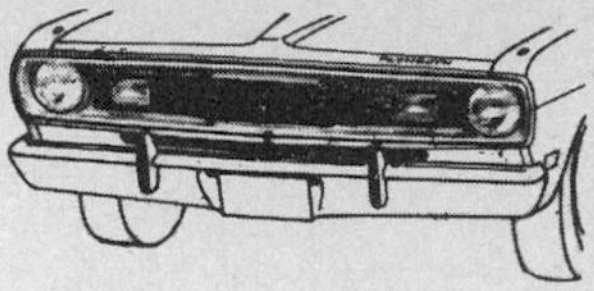

1970-72 Valiant and Duster

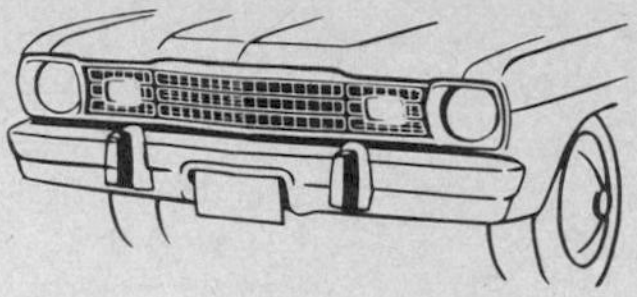

1973 Valiant and Duster

1974 Valiant and Duster

1970 Plymouth Cuda

1971 Cuda

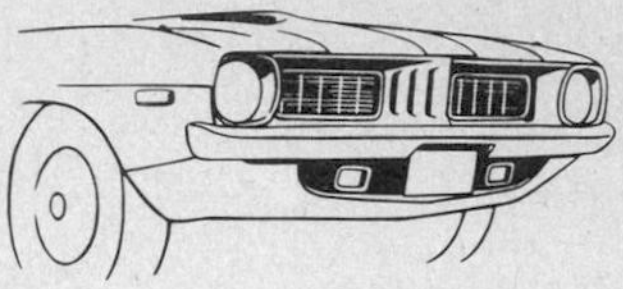

1972 Cuda

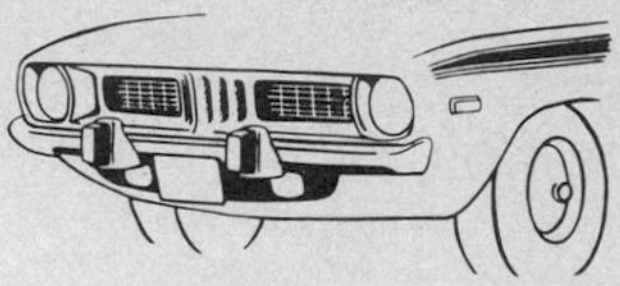

1973 Cuda

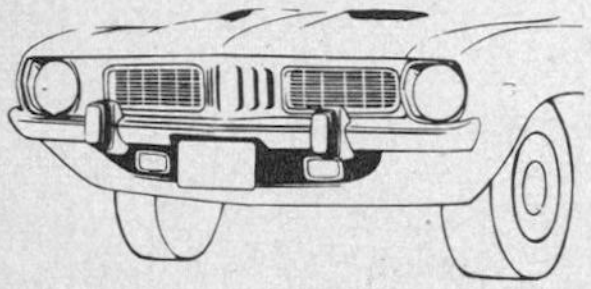

1974 Cuda

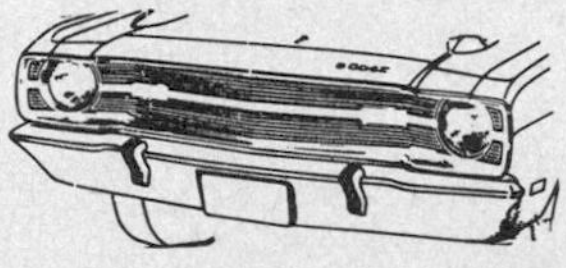

1969 Dart

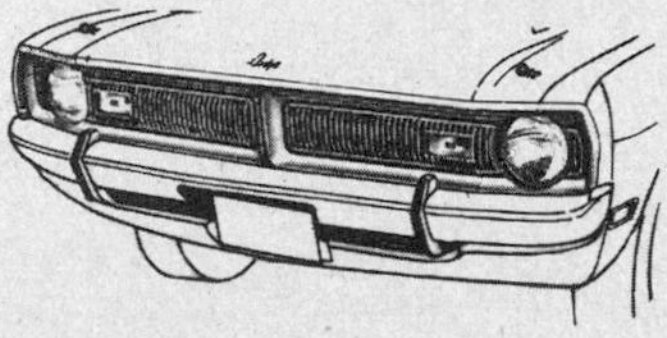

1970 Dart

1970-71 Challenger

1971 Demon

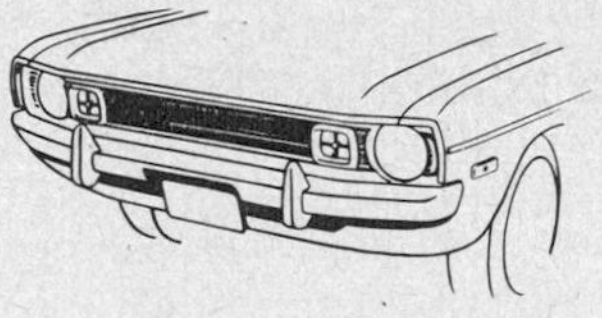

1972 Dart and Demon

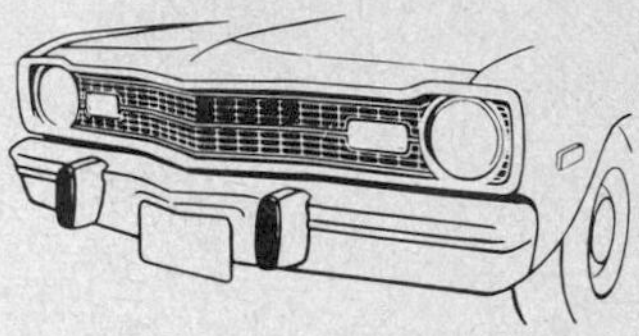

1973 Dart

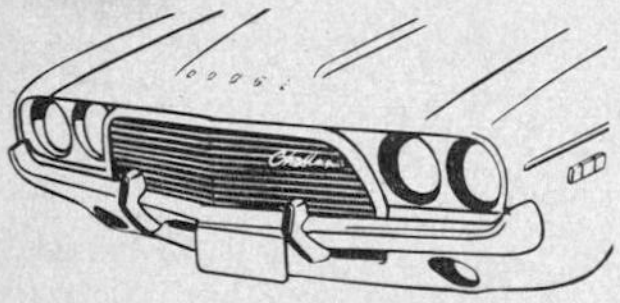

1972 Challenger

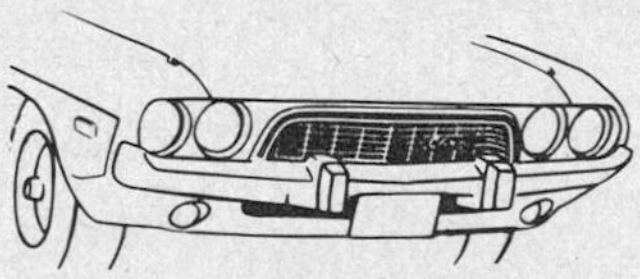

1973 Challenger

1974 Challenger

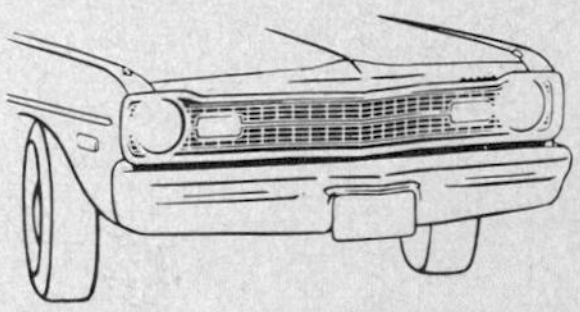

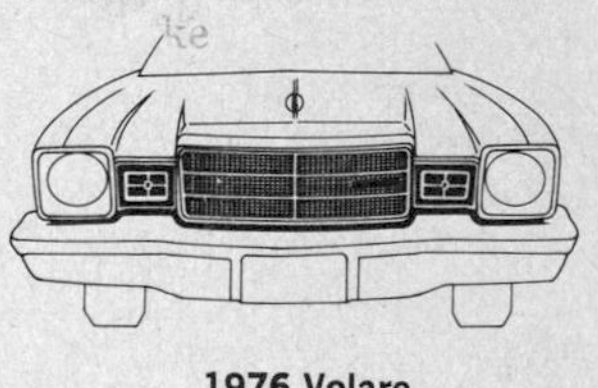

1974 Dart

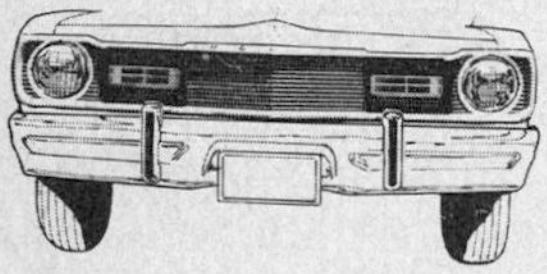

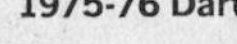

1975-76 Dart

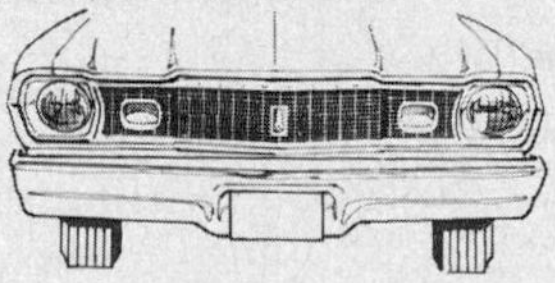

1975-76 Valiant

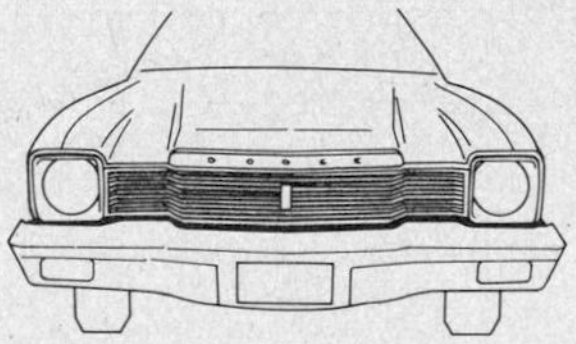

1976 Aspen

1976 Volare

FIRING ORDER

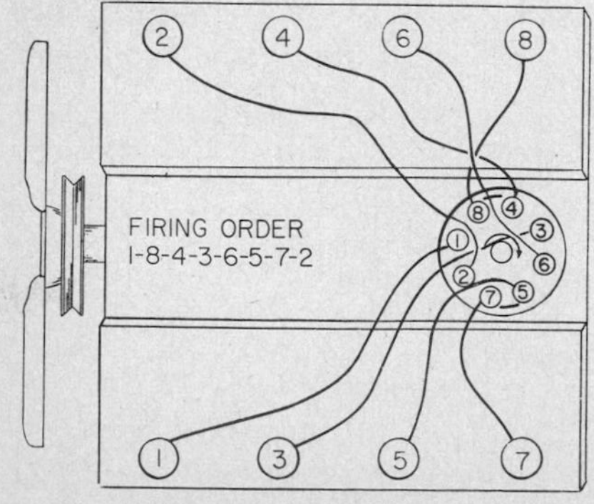

273, 318, 340, 360 cu. in.
(© Chrysler Corp)

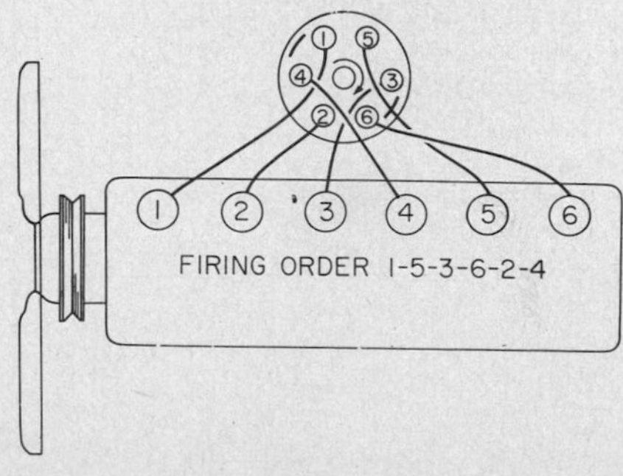

170, 198, 225 cu. in.
(© Chrysler Corp)

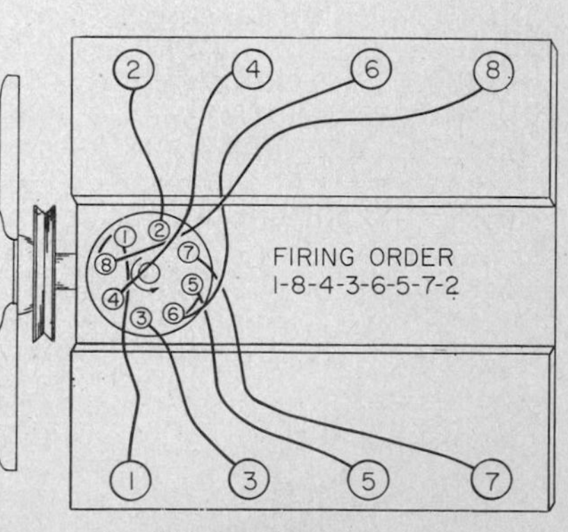

383, 426, 440 cu. in.
(© Chrysler Corp)

ENGINE IDENTIFICATION

Engine Number Location

170, 198 and 225 cu. in. six engines . . . stamped on joint face of block, next to No. 1 cylinder.

273, 318, 340, and 360 cu. in. V8 engines . . . stamped on front of block, just below left cylinder head.

383, 400, 426 and 440 cu. in. V8 engine . . . stamped on cylinder block pan rail, at left rear corner below starter opening.

Engine code location—273, 318, 340, 360
(© Chrysler Corp)

Engine code location—383, 440
(© Chrysler Corp)

ENGINE CODE

The engine code designation is the 5th digit of the vehicle identification number (V.I.N.). The V.I.N. is stamped on a plate located at the left side of the instrument panel visible through the windshield and located to the rear of the right engine mount on the oil pan rail on all models.

Disp	Bbl	Hp	'69	'70	'71	'72	'73	'74	'75	'76
6-Cylinder Models										
170	1	115	A							
198	1	95 (net)					B	B		
198	1	100 (net)				B				
198	1	125		B	B					
225	1	95							C	C
225	1	105 (net)					C	C		
225	1	110 (net)				C				
225	1	145	B	C	C					
8-Cylinder Models										
273	2	180	D							
318	2	145, 150 (net)				G	G	G	G	G
318	2	230	F	G	G					
340HP	4	240 (net)				H	H			
340HP	4	275			H					
360	4	190	P	H						J
360HP	4	230						J		
360HP	4	245 (net)							L	L
383	2	275			L					
383	2	290		L						
383	4	300			N					
383	4	330	H	L						
383	4	335		N						
426	8	425		R	R					
440	4	375		U						
440	6	385			V					
440	6	390		V						

GENERAL ENGINE SPECIFICATIONS

Year	Engine No. Cyl. Displacement (Cu. In.)	Carburetor Type	Horsepower @ rpm ■	Torque @ rpm (ft lbs) ■	Bore and Stroke (in.)	Compression Ratio	Oil Pressure @ 2050 rpm
'69	6-170	1 bbl	115 @ 4400	155 @ 2400	3.406 x 3.125	8.5:1	55
	6-225	1 bbl	145 @ 4000	215 @ 2400	3.406 x 4.125	8.4:1	55
	8-273	2 bbl	190 @ 4400	260 @ 2000	3.625 x 3.310	9.0:1	55
	8-318	2 bbl	230 @ 4400	340 @ 2400	3.910 x 3.310	9.2:1	55
	8-340	4 bbl	275 @ 5000	340 @ 3200	4.040 x 3.310	10.5:1	55
	8-383	4 bbl	330 @ 5200	410 @ 3600	4.250 x 3.375	10.0:1	55
'70	6-198	1 bbl	125 @ 4400	180 @ 2000	3.406 x 3.640	8.4:1	55
	6-225	1 bbl	145 @ 4000	215 @ 2400	3.406 x 4.125	8.4:1	55
	8-318	2 bbl	230 @ 4400	320 @ 2000	3.910 x 3.310	8.8:1	55
	8-340	4 bbl	275 @ 5000	340 @ 3200	4.040 x 3.310	10.5:1	55
	8-383	2 bbl	290 @ 4400	390 @ 2800	4.250 x 3.375	8.7:1	55
	8-383	4 bbl	330 @ 5000	425 @ 3200	4.250 x 3.375	9.5:1	55
	8-383 HP	4 bbl	335 @ 5200	425 @ 3400	4.250 x 3.375	10.5:1	55
	8-426 Hemi	2 x 4 bbl	425 @ 5000	490 @ 4000	4.250 x 3.750	10.2:1	55
	8-440 HP	4 bbl	375 @ 4600	480 @ 3200	4.320 x 3.750	9.7:1	55
	8-440 Six Pack	3 x 2 bbl	390 @ 4700	490 @ 3200	4.320 x 3.750	10.5:1	55

GENERAL ENGINE SPECIFICATIONS

Year	Engine No. Cyl. Displacement (Cu. In.)	Carburetor Type	Horsepower @ rpm ■	Torque @ rpm (ft lbs) ■	Bore and Stroke (in.)	Compression Ratio	Oil Pressure @ 2050 rpm
'71	6-198	1 bbl	125 @ 4400	180 @ 2000	3.406 x 3.640	8.4:1	55
	6-225	1 bbl	145 @ 4000	215 @ 2400	3.406 x 4.125	8.4:1	55
	8-318	2 bbl	230 @ 4400	320 @ 2000	3.910 x 3.310	8.6:1	55
	8-340	4 bbl	275 @ 5000	340 @ 3200	4.040 x 3.310	10.3:1	55
	8-340	3 x 2 bbl	290 @ 5000	340 @ 3200	4.040 x 3.310	10.3:1	55
	8-383	2 bbl	275 @ 4400	375 @ 2800	4.250 x 3.375	8.5:1	55
	8-383 HP	4 bbl	300 @ 4800	410 @ 3400	4.250 x 3.375	8.5:1	55
	8-426 Hemi	4 bbl	425 @ 5000	490 @.4000	4.250 x 3.750	10.2:1	55
	8-440 Six Pack	2 x 4 bbl	385 @ 4700	490 @ 3200	4.320 x 3.750	10.3:1	55
'72	6-198	1 bbl	100 @ 4400①	160 @ 2400②	3.406 x 3.640	8.4:1	55
	6-225	1 bbl	110 @ 4000③	185 @ 2000④	3.406 x 4.125	8.4:1	55
	8-318	2 bbl	150 @ 4000	260 @ 1600	3.910 x 3.310	8.6:1	55
	8-340	4 bbl	240 @ 4800	290 @ 3600	4.040 x 3.310	8.5:1	55
'73	6-198	1 bbl	95 @ 4000	155 @ 1600	3.406 x 3.640	8.4:1	55
	6-225	1 bbl	105 @ 4000	185 @ 1600	3.406 x 4.125	8.4:1	55
	8-318	2 bbl	150 @ 3600	265 @ 2000	3.910 x 3.310	8.6:1	55
	8-340HP	4 bbl	240 @ 4800	295 @ 3600	4.040 x 3.310	8.5:1	55
'74	6-198	1 bbl	95 @ 4000	145 @ 2000	3.406 x 3.640	8.4:1	55
	6-225	1 bbl	105 @ 3600	180 @ 1600	3.406 x 4.125	8.4:1	55
	8-318	2 bbl	150 @ 4000	255 @ 2200	3.910 x 3.310	8.6:1	55
	8-360HP	4 bbl	245 @ 4800	320 @ 3600	4.000 x 3.580	8.4:1	55
'75-'76	6-225	1 bbl	95 @ 3600	170 @ 1600	3.406 x 4.125	8.4:1	55
	8-318	2 bbl	145, 150 @ 4000	255 @ 2200	3.910 x 3.310	8.5:1	55
	8-360⑤	2 bbl	190 @ 4000	270 @ 3200	4.000 x 3.580	8.4:1	55
	8-360HP	4 bbl	230 @ 4800	300 @ 3600	4.000 x 3.580	8.4:1	55

■ Beginning 1972, horsepower and torque are SAE net figures. They are measured at the rear of the transmission with all accessories installed and operating. Since the figures vary when a given engine is installed in different models, some figures are representative rather than exact.

① For California vehicles, advertised horsepower is 94 @ 4400 rpm

② For California vehicles, advertised torque is 158 @ 2400 rpm

③ For California vehicles, advertised horsepower is 97 @ 4000 rpm

④ For California vehicles, advertised torque is 180 @ 2000 rpm

HP High Performance

⑤ 1976 only

Valiant, Dart, Aspen, Volare TUNE-UP SPECIFICATIONS

When analyzing compression test results, look for uniformity among cylinders rather than specific pressures.

ENGINE Year	ENGINE No. Cyl Displacement (cu in.)	ENGINE hp	SPARK PLUGS Type	SPARK PLUGS Gap (in.)	DISTRIBUTOR Point Dwell (deg)	DISTRIBUTOR Point Gap (in.)	IGNITION TIMING (deg) ▲ Man Trans ●	IGNITION TIMING (deg) ▲ Auto Trans	VALVES Intake Opens ■ (deg)	Fuel Pump Pressure (psi)	IDLE SPEED (rpm) ▲ Man Trans	IDLE SPEED (rpm) ▲ Auto Trans
'69	6-170	115	N-14Y	.035	42-47	.020	5A	2½A	10	3½-5	750	750
	6-225	145	N-14Y	.035	42-47	.020	TDC	TDC	10	3½-5	700	650
	8-273	190	N-14Y	.035	30-35	.017	2½A	2½A	10	5-7	700	650
	8-318	230	N-14Y	.035	30-35	.017	TDC	TDC	10	5-7	700	650
	8-340	275	N-9Y	.035	27-32③	.017	TDC	5B	22	5-7	750	700
	8-383	330②	J-11Y	.035	27-32③	.017	TDC	5B	21	3½-5	700	650
'70	6-198	125	N-14Y	.035	41-46	.020	2½B	TDC	10	3½-5	750	750①
	6-225	145	N-14Y	.035	41-56	.020	TDC	TDC	10	3½-5	700	650①
	8-318	230	N-14Y	.035	30-34	.017	TDC	TDC	10	5-7	750	700
	8-340	275	N-9Y	.035	27-32③	.017	5B	5B	22	5-7	900	900

Valiant, Dart, Aspen, Volare TUNE-UP SPECIFICATIONS

When analyzing compression test results, look for uniformity among cylinders rather than specific pressures.

ENGINE			SPARK PLUGS		DISTRIBUTOR		IGNITION TIMING (deg) ▲		VALVES	Fuel	IDLE SPEED (rpm) ▲	
Year	No. Cyl Displacement (cu in.)	hp	Type	Gap (in.)	Point Dwell (deg)	Point Gap (in.)	Man Trans ●	Auto Trans	Intake Opens ■ (deg)	Pump Pressure (psi)	Man Trans	Auto Trans
'71	6-198	125	N-14Y	.035	41-46	.020	2½B	2½B	16	3½-5	800	800
	6-225	145	N-14Y	.035	41-46	.020	TDC(2½B)	TDC(2½B)	16	3½-5	750	750
	8-318	230	N-14Y	.035	30-34	.017	TDC	TDC	10	5-7	750	700
	8-340 HP	275	N-9Y	.035	27-32③	.017	5B	5B	22	5-7	900	900
'72	6-198	100	N-14Y	.035	41-46	.020	2½B	2½B	16	2½-5	800(700)	800(700)
	6-225	110	N-14Y	.035	41-46	.020	TDC(2½B)	TDC(2½B)	16	2½-5	750(700)	750(700)
	8-318	150	N-13Y	.035	30-34	.017	TDC	TDC	10	5-7	750	750(700)
	8-340 HP	240	N-9Y	.035	30-34	.017	TDC(2½D)	2½B	22	5 7	900(850)	750
'73	6-198	95	N-14Y	.035	Electronic		2½B	2½B	16	4-5½	800	750
	6-225	105	N-14Y	.035	Electronic		TDC	TDC	16	4-5½	750	750
	8-318	150	N-13Y	.035	Electronic		2½B	TDC	10	6-7½	750	700
	8-360 HP	245	N-9Y	.035	Electronic		5B	2½B	22	6-7½	850	850
'74	6-198	95	N-14Y	.035	Electronic		2½B	2½B	16	3½-5	800	750
	6-225	105	N-14Y	.035	Electronic		TDC	TDC	16	5-7	800	750
	8-318	150	N-13Y	.035	Electronic		TDC	TDC	10	5-7	750	750
	8-360 HP	245	N-12Y	.035	Electronic		5B(2½B)	5B	22	5-7	850	850
'75	6-225	95	BL-13Y	.035	Electronic		TDC	TDC	16	3½-5	800	750
	8-318	145, 150	N-13Y	.035	Electronic		2B	2B	10	5-7	750	750
	8-360	H.P.	N-12Y	.035	Electronic		—	2B	22	5-7	—	750
'76	6-225	NA	RBL-13Y	.035	Electronic		6B⑤	2B	16	4-5½	750⑥	750
	8-318	NA	RN-12Y	.035	Electronic		2B	2B	10	6-7½	750	750
	8-360-2V	NA	RN-12Y	.035	Electronic		—	6B	18	6-7½	—	700
	8-360 H.P.	NA	RN-12Y	.035	Electronic		—	2B	22	6-7½	—	850

▲ See text for procedure
■ All figures Before Top Dead Center
● Figure in parentheses indicates California engine
H.P. High Performance
① A/C only
② Dart only
③ Adjust both sets of points to this figure. With both sets connected, total reading should be 37-42 degrees.
④ Figure is 22 degrees for automatic transmission
⑤ 2B in California
⑥ 800 rpm in California
A After Top Dead Center B Before Top Dead Center

Barracuda, Challenger TUNE-UP SPECIFICATIONS

When analyzing compression test results, look for uniformity among cylinders rather than specific pressures.

ENGINE			SPARK PLUGS		DISTRIBUTOR		IGNITION TIMING (deg) ▲		VALVES	Fuel	IDLE SPEED (rpm) ▲	
Year	No. Cyl Displacement (cu in.)	hp	Type	Gap (in.)	Point Dwell (deg)	Point Gap (in.)	Man Trans ●	Auto Trans	Intake Opens ■ (deg)	Pump Pressure (psi)	Man Trans	Auto Trans
'69	6-225	145	N-14Y	.035	45	.020	TDC	TDC	10	3½-5	700	650
	8-318	230	N-14Y	.035	33	.017	TDC	TDC	10	5-7	700	650
	8-340	275	N-9Y	.035	30②	.017	TDC	5B	22	5-7	750	700
	8-383	330	J-11Y	.035	30②	.017	TDC	5B	21	3½-5	700	650
'70	6-225	145	N-14Y	.035	44	.020	TDC	TDC	10	3½-5	700	650
	8-318	230	N-14Y	.035	32	.017	TDC	TDC	10	5-7	750	700
	8-340	275	N-9Y	.035	30②	.017	5B	5B	22	5-7	900	900
	8-383	290	J-14Y	.035	30½	.019	TDC	2½B	18	3½-5	750	650
	8-383	330	J-11Y	.035	30½	.019	TDC	2½B	18	3½-5	750	700
	8-383	335	J-11Y	.035	30½	.019	TDC	2½B	21	3½-5	750	750
	8-426	425	N-10Y	.035	30②	.017	TDC	2½B	36	7-8½	900	900
	8-440	375	J-11Y	.035	30½	.019	TDC	2½B	21	3½-5	900	800
	8-440	390	J-11Y	.035	30②	.017	5B	5B	21	6-7½	900	900

Barracuda, Challenger TUNE-UP SPECIFICATIONS

When analyzing compression test results, look for uniformity among cylinders rather than specific pressures.

Year	ENGINE No. Cyl Displacement (cu in.)	ENGINE hp	SPARK PLUGS Type	SPARK PLUGS Gap (in.)	DISTRIBUTOR Point Dwell (deg)	DISTRIBUTOR Point Gap (in.)	IGNITION TIMING (deg) ▲ Man Trans	IGNITION TIMING (deg) ▲ ● Auto Trans	VALVES Intake Opens ■ (deg)	Fuel Pump Pressure (psi)	IDLE SPEED (rpm) ▲ Man Trans	IDLE SPEED (rpm) ▲ Auto Trans
'71	6-198	125	N-14Y	.035	44	.020	2½B	2½B	16	3½-5	800	800
	6-225	145	N-14Y	.035	44	.020	TDC(2½B)	TDC(2½B)	16	3½-5	750	750
	8-318	230	N-14Y	.035	32	.017	TDC	TDC	10	5-7	750	700
	8-340	275	N-9Y	.035	32②	.017	5B	5B	22	5-7	900	900
	8-383	275	J-14Y	.035	30½	.019	TDC	2½B	18	3½-5	750	700
	8-383	300	J-11Y	.035	30½	.019	TDC	2½B	21	3½-5	900	800
	8-426	425	N-10Y	.035	30	.017	TDC	2½B	36	7-8½	900	900
	8-440	385	J-11Y	.035	30	.017	5B	5B	21	6-7½	950	950
'72	6-225	110	N-14Y	.035	44	.020	TDC(2½B)	TDC(2½B)	16	2½-5	750(700)	750(700)
	8-318	150	N-13Y	.035	32	.017	TDC	TDC	10	5-7	750	750(700)
	8-340	240	N-9Y	.035	Electronic		TDC(2½B)	2½B	22	5-7	900(850)	750
'73	8-318	150	N-13Y	.035	Electronic		2½B	TDC	10	6-7½	750	700
	8-340	240	N-9Y	.035	Electronic		5B	2½B	22	6-7½	850	850
'74	8-318	150	N-13Y	.035	Electronic		TDC	TDC	10	5-7	750	750
	8-360	245	N-12Y	.035	Electronic		5B(2½B)	5B	22	5-7	850	850

▲ See text for procedure
● Figure in parentheses indicates California engine
■ All figures Before Top Dead Center
① Not used
② Adjust both sets of points to this figure. With both sets connected, the total reading should be 40 degrees.
A After Top Dead Center
B Before Top Dead Center
TDC Top Dead Center
— Not applicable

MECHANICAL VALVE LIFTER CLEARANCE

Year	Engine	Intake (Hot) In.	Exhaust (Hot) In.
1969-72	All 6 cylinder	.010	.020

CAPACITIES

Year	Engine No. Cyl. Displacement (Cu. In.)	Engine Crankcase Add 1 Qt For New Filter	TRANSMISSION Pts To Refill After Draining Manual 3-Speed	Manual 4-Speed	Automatic	Drive Axle (pts)	Gasoline Tank (gals)	COOLING SYSTEM (qts) With Heater	With A/C
'69	6-170	4	6.5	—	16	2	18	12	14
	6-225	4	6.5	—	16	2	18	13	15
	8-273	4	6.5	7.5	16	2⑤	18	17	19
	8-318	4	6	7.5	16	2④	18	17	19
	8-340	4	—	7.5	16	4	18	16	16
	8-383	4	—	7.5	16	4	18	16	16
'70	6-198	4	6.5①	—	17	2	18	13	14
	6-225	4	6.5①	—	17	2	18	13	14
	8-318	4	4.75	7.5	16	4	18	16	17
	8-340	4	4.75	7	16	4	18	15.5	15.5
	8-383	4	4.75	7.5	19③	4	18	14.5	15
	8-426	6	—	7.5	17	5.5	18	17	—
	8-440	6	—	7.5	19	5.5	18	17	—
'71	6-198	4	6.5①	—	17	2⑥	17⑦	13	14
	6-225	4	6.5①	—	17	2⑥	17⑦	13	14
	8-318	4	4.75	—	17	4.5	17⑦	16	17.5
	8-340	4	4.75	7	16.3	4.5	17⑦	15.5	15.5
	8-383	4	4.75	7.5	19③	4.5	18	14.5	15
	8-426	6	—	7.5	16.3	5.5	18	17	—
	8-440	6	—	7.5	19	5.5	18	15.5	17

CAPACITIES

Year	Engine No. Cyl. Displacement (Cu. In.)	Engine Crankcase Add 1 Qt For New Filter	TRANSMISSION Pts To Refill After Draining — Manual 3-Speed	Manual 4-Speed	Automatic	Drive Axle (pts)	Gasoline Tank (gals)	COOLING SYSTEM (qts) With Heater	With A/C
'72	6-198	4	6.5	—	17	2	16	13	14
	6-225	4	6.5①	—	17	2	16⑧	13	14
	8-318	4	4.75	—	17	4.5	16⑧	16	17
	8-340	4	4.75	7②	16.3	4.5	16⑧	15	15
'73	6-198	4	6.5	—	17	2	16	13	13
	6-225	4	6.5	—	17	2	16	13	14
	8-318	4	4.75	—	17	4.5	16⑧	16	17.5
	8-340	4	4.75	7②	16.3	4.5	16⑧	15.5⑨	15.5
'74	6-198	4	6.5	—	13.5	2	16⑦	13	—
	6-225	4	4.75	—	13.5	2	16⑦	13	14.0
	8-318	4	4.75	7.0②	13.5	4.5	16⑦	16	17.5
	8-360	4	4.75	7.0②	14.0	4.5	16⑦	16	16.0
'75-'76	6-225	4	3.5	7.0	13.5	2	16⑩	13	14
	8-318	4	4.75	7.0	13.5	4.5	16⑩	16	17.5
	8-360	4	—	—	14.0	4.5	16⑩	16	16

① Barracuda, Challenger—4.75 pts
② Barracuda, Challenger—7.5 pts
③ Hi-performance—16 pts
④ Manual transmission—4 pts
⑤ 4-speed transmission—4 pts
⑥ Barracuda, Challenger—4.5 pts
⑦ Barracuda, Challenger—18 gals
⑧ Barracuda—16.5 gals, Challenger—18 gals
⑨ Barracuda, Challenger—15 qts
⑩ Aspen, Volare—18 gals
— Not applicable

VALVE SPECIFICATIONS

Year	Engine No. Cyl. Displacement (cu in.)	Seat Angle (deg)	Face Angle (deg)	Spring Test Pressure (lbs @ in.)	Spring Installed Height (in.)	STEM TO GUIDE Clearance (in.) Intake	Exhaust	STEM Diameter (in.) Intake	Exhaust
'69	6-170	45	①	144 @ 1.31	1 11/16	.0010-.0030	.0020-.0040	.3725	.3715
	6-225	45	①	144 @ 1.31	1 11/16	.0010-.0030	.0020-.0040	.3725	.3715
	8-273	45	①	177 @ 1.31	1 11/16	.0010-.0030	.0020-.0040	.3725	.3715
	8-318	45	①	177 @ 1.31	1 11/16	.0010-.0030	.0020-.0040	.3725	.3715
	8-340	45	①	242 @ 1.22	1 11/16	.0010-.0030	.0020-.0040	.3725	.3715
	8-383	45	45	246 @ 1.36	1 7/8	.0010-.0030	.0020-.0040	.3725	.3715
'70	6-198	45	①	144 @ 1.31	1 11/16	.0010-.0030	.0020-.0040	.3725	.3715
	6-225	45	①	144 @ 1.31	1 11/16	.0010-.0030	.0020-.0040	.3725	.3715
	8-318	45	①	177 @ 1.31	1 11/16	.0010-.0030	.0020-.0040	.3725	.3715
	8-340	45	①	242 @ 1.22	1 11/16	.0015-.0035	.0025-.0045	.3720	.3710
	8-383②	45	45	200 @ 1.44	1 7/8	.0010-.0030	.0020-.0040	.3727	.3717
	8-383③	45	45	246 @ 1.72	1 7/8	.0015-.0032	.0025-.0042	.3722	.3712
	8-426	45	45	310 @ 1.38	1 7/8	.0020-.0040	.0030-.0050	.3090	.3080
	8-440	45	45	310 @ 1.38	1 7/8	.0015-.0032	.0025-.0042	.3725	.3715
'71	6-198	45	①	144 @ 1.31	1 11/16	.0010-.0030	.0020-.0040	.3725	.3715
	6-225	45	①	144 @ 1.31	1 11/16	.0010-.0030	.0020-.0040	.3725	.3715
	8-318	45	①	177 @ 1.31	1 11/16	.0010-.0030	.0020-.0040	.3725	.3715
	8-340	45	①	238 @ 1.31	1 11/16	.0015-.0035	.0025-.0045	.3720	.3710
	8-383②	45	45	200 @ 1.44	1 7/8	.0010-.0030	.0020-.0040	.3727	.3717
	8-383③	45	45	246 @ 1.72	1 7/8	.0015-.0032	.0025-.0042	.3722	.3712
	8-426	45	45	310 @ 1.38	1 7/8	.0020-.0040	.0030-.0050	3090	.3080
	8-440	45	45	200 @ 1.44	1 7/8	.0010-.0030	.0020-.0040	.3727	.3717

VALVE SPECIFICATIONS

Year	Engine No. Cyl. Displacement (cu in.)	Seat Angle (deg)	Face Angle (deg)	Spring Test Pressure (lbs @ in.)	Spring Installed Height (in.)	Stem to Guide Clearance (in.) Intake	Exhaust	Stem Diameter (in.) Intake	Exhaust
'72	6-198	45	①	144 @ 1.31	1 11/16	.0010-.0030	.0020-.0040	.3725	.3715
	6-225	45	①	144 @ 1.31	1 11/16	.0010-.0030	.0020-.0040	.3725	.3715
	8-318	45	①	177 @ 1.31	1 11/16	.0010-.0030	.0020-.0040	.3725	.3715
	8-340	45	①	208 @ 1.31	1 11/16	.0015-.0035	.0025-.0045	.3720	.3710
'73	6-198	45	④	160 @ 1.24	1 21/32	.0010-.0030	.0020-.0040	.3725	.3715
	6-225	45	④	160 @ 1.24	1 21/32	.0010-.0030	.0020-.0040	.3725	.3715
	8-318	45	④	189 @ 1.28	1 21/32	.0010-.0030	.0020-.0040	.3725	.3715
	8-340	45	④	238 @ 1.22	1 21/32	.0015-.0035	.0025-.0045	.3720	.3710
'74	6-198	45	46	160 @ 1.24	1 21/32	.0010-.0030	.0020-.0040	.3725	.3715
	6-225	45	46	160 @ 1.24	1 21/32	.0010-.0030	.0020-.0040	.3725	.3715
	8-318	45	46	189 @ 1.28	1 21/32	.0010-.0030	.0020-.0040	.3725	.3715
	8-360	45	46	238 @ 1.22	1 21/32	.0010-.0030	.0025-.0045	.3725	.3715
'75-'76	6-225	45	46	162 @ 1.24	1 21/32	.0010-.0030	.0020-.0040	.3725	.3715
	8-318	45	46	185 @ 1.28	1 21/32	.0010-.0030	.0020-.0040	.3725	.3715
	8-360	45	46	195 @ 1.24⑤	1 21/32	.0010-.0030	.0020-.0040	.3725	.3715

① Intake 45°, Exhaust 43°
② 2 bbl carburetor
③ 4 bbl carburetor
④ Intake 45°, Exhaust 47°
⑤ 238 @ 1.22 for high performance model

TORQUE SPECIFICATIONS

All readings in ft lbs

Year	Engine No. Cyl. Displacement (cu in.)	Cylinder Head Bolts	Rod Bearing Bolts	Main Bearing Bolts	Crankshaft Pulley Bolt	Flywheel to Crankshaft Bolts	Manifold Intake	Manifold Exhaust
'69-'76	6-All	70	45	85	Press fit	55	10①	10
'69-'76	8-273, 318, 340, 360	95	45	85	②	65⑤	40⑥	30⑦
'69-'71	8-383, 440	70	45	85	②	55	40	30
'70-'71	8-426 Hemi	75	75	100③	135	70	④	35

① Intake to exhaust bolts—20 ft. lbs.
② Vibration damper bolts—15 ft. lbs. for 1969, 9 ft. lbs. for 1970-73. End of crankshaft bolt (except 1971 with 318 or 340 engine) 135 ft. lbs., 1971 with 318 or 340 engine—100 ft. lbs., 100 ft. lbs. with 318 and 360 engines in 1974-76.
③ Cross bolt mains—45 ft. lbs.
④ Torque the four center bolts on either side to 6 ft. lbs., all others to 4 ft. lbs.
⑤ 55 ft. lbs. on 318 and 360 in 1974-76
⑥ 35 ft. lbs. on 318 and 360 in 1974-76
⑦ 15 ft. lbs. on nuts and 20 ft. lbs. on screws on 318 and 360 in 1974-76

CRANKSHAFT AND CONNECTING ROD SPECIFICATIONS

All measurements are given in inches

Year	Engine No. Cyl. Displacement (cu in.)	Crankshaft Main Brg. Journal Dia	Main Brg. Oil Clearance	Shaft End-Play	Thrust on No.	Connecting Rod Journal Diameter	Oil Clearance	Side Clearance
'69-'76	6-170, 198, 225	2.7495-2.7505	.0005-.0015	.002-.007	3	2.1865-2.1875	.0005-.0015	.006-.012
'69-'74	8-273, 318, 340	2.4995-2.5005	.0005-.0015	.002-.007	3	2.124-2.125	.0005-.0025	.009-.017
'69-'71	8-383	2.6245-2.6255	.0005-.0015	.002-.007	3	2.3740-2.3750	.0005-.0015	.009-.017
'70-'71	8-440	2.7495-2.7505	.0005-.0015	.002-.007	3	2.3740-2.3750	.0010-.0020	.009-.017
'70	8-426 Hemi	2.7495-2.7505	.0015-.0025	.002-.007	3	2.374-2.375	.0015-.0025	.009-.017
'71	8-426 Hemi	2.7490-2.7500	.0015-.0030	.002-.007	3	2.3738-2.3745	.0015-.0025	.013-.017
'75-'76	8-318	2.4495-2.5005	.0005-.0015	.002-.007	3	2.124-2.125	.0005-.0025	.009-.017
'74-'76	8-360	2.8095-2.8105	.0005-.0020	.002-.007	3	2.124-2.125	.0005-.0020	.010-.015

RING GAP

All measurements are given in inches

Year	Engine No. Cyl. Displacement (cu. in.)	Top Compression	Bottom Compression
'69-'72	6-170, 198, 225 8-273, 318, 340	.010-.020	.010-.020
'69-'71	8-383, 440	.013-.023	.013-.023
'70	8-426	.013-.023	.013-.023
'71	8-426	.013-.025	.013-.025
'73	All engines except 8-340	.010-.020	.010-.020
'73	8-340	.013-.023	.013-.023
'74-'76	6-198, 225 8-318, 360	.010-.020	.010-.020

Year	Engine No. Cyl. Displacement (cu. in.)	Oil Control
'69-'73	All engines except 6-170	.015-.055①
'69	6-170	.010-.020

① Not applicable in 1974-76

MECHANICAL VALVE LIFTER CLEARANCE

Year	Engine	Intake (Hot) In.	Exhaust (Hot) In.
1969-76	All six cylinder	.010	.020

RING SIDE CLEARANCE

All measurements are given in inches

Year	Engine No. Cyl. Displacement (cu. in.)	Top Compression	Bottom Compression
'69-'76	All engines	.0015-.0030	.0015-.0030

Year	Engine No. Cyl. Displacement (cu. in.)	Oil Control
'69	6-170	.0015-.0030
'69-'76	6-198, 225, 8-273, 318, 340, 360, 426	.0002-.0050
'69-'71	8-383, 440	.0000-.0050

PISTON CLEARANCE

All measurements are given in inches

Year	Engine No. Cyl. Displacement (cu. in.)	Piston-to-Bore Clearance (in.)
'69	6-170	0.0005-0.0015
'70-'74	6-198	0.0005-0.0015
'69-'76	6-225	0.0005-0.0015
'69	8-273	0.0005-0.0015
'69-'76	8-318	0.0005-0.0015

Year	Engine No. Cyl. Displacement (cu. in.)	Piston-to-Bore Clearance (in.)
'73	8-340	0.0005-0.0015
'69-'71	8-383	0.0003-0.0013
'70-'71	8-426	0.0025-0.0035
'70-'71	8-440	0.0003-0.0013
'74-'76	8-360	0.0005-0.0015

ALTERNATOR AND REGULATOR SPECIFICATIONS

	ALTERNATOR			REGULATOR							
					Field Relay			Regulator			
Year	Part No. or Manufacturer	Field Current @ 12 V	Output (amps)	Part No. or Manufacturer	Air Gap (in.)	Point Gap (in.)	Volts to Close	Air Gap (in.)	Point Gap (in.)	Volts @ 75°
'69	6 Cyl Models	2.38-2.75	26	2098300①	.050①	.014	13.8	.050	.015	13.8-14.4
	8 Cyl Std.	2.38-2.75	35	2098300①	.050①	.014	13.8	.050	.015	13.8-14.4
	Heavy Duty, A/C	2.38-2.75	44	2098300①	.050①	.014	13.8	.050	.015	13.8-14.4
	Special Equip.	2.38-2.75	51	2098300①	.050①	.014	13.8	.050	.015	13.8-14.4
'70-'71	6 Cyl Models	2.38-2.75	26	3438150			Not Adjustable			13.8-14.4
	8 Cyl Std.	2.38-2.75	34②	3438150			Not Adjustable			13.8-14.4
	Heavy Duty, A/C	2.38-2.75	45	3438150			Not Adjustable			13.8-14.4
	Special Equip.	2.38-2.75	51	3438150			Not Adjustable			13.8-14.4

ALTERNATOR AND REGULATOR SPECIFICATIONS

Year	ALTERNATOR: Part No. or Manufacturer	Field Current @ 12 V	Output (amps)	REGULATOR: Part No. or Manufacturer	Field Relay: Air Gap (in.)	Field Relay: Point Gap (in.)	Field Relay: Volts to Close	Regulator: Air Gap (in.)	Regulator: Point Gap (in.)	Volts @ 75°
'72-'73	6 Cyl Models	2.5-3.1	39	3438150			Not Adjustable			13.8-14.4
	8 Cyl Std.	2.5-3.1	41	3438150			Not Adjustable			13.8-14.4
	Heavy Duty, A/C	2.5-3.1	50	3438150			Not Adjustable			13.8-14.4
	Special Equip.	2.5-3.1	60	3438150			Not Adjustable			13.8-14.4
'74	6 Cyl Models	2.5-3.1	34, 41	3438150			Not Adjustable			13.8-14.4
	8 Cyl Std.	2.5-3.1	50	3438150			Not Adjustable			13.8-14.4
	Special Equipment	2.5-3.1	60, 65	3438150			Not Adjustable			13.8-14.4
'75-'76	6 Cyl Models	2.5-3.1	41	3755960			Not Adjustable			14.0-14.6
	8 Cyl Std.	2.5-3.1	50	3755960			Not Adjustable			14.0-14.6
	Special Equipment	2.5-3.1	60, 65	3755960			Not Adjustable			14.0-14.6

① Essex wire regulator, #2444980, used interchangeably. Air gap setting is .032-.042 in., all other dimensions are identical with #2098300

② '71 models use a standard 44 amp alternator

BATTERY AND STARTER SPECIFICATIONS

Year	Engine No. Cyl. Displacement (cu in.)	BATTERY: Ampere Hour Capacity	Volts	Terminal Grounded	STARTER Lock Test: Amps	Volts	Torque (ft lbs)	No-Load Test: Amps	Volts	RPM	Brush Spring Tension (oz)
'69	6-170	38	12	Neg.	380	4	—	90	11	2,950	32-36
	6-225, 273, 318, 340	48	12	Neg.	425	4	—	90	11	2,300	32-36
	8-383	59	12	Neg.	425	4	—	90	11	2,300	32-36
'70	6 & 8-198, 225, 318, 340	46	12	Neg.	400-450	4	—	90	11	1,925-2,600	32-36
	8-383	59	12	Neg.	400-450	4	—	90	11	1,925-2,600	32-36
	8-426, 440	70	12	Neg.	400-450	4	—	90	11	1,925-2,600	32-36
'71	6 & 8-198, 225, 318	46	12	Neg.	400-450	4	—	90	11	1,925-2,600	32-36
	8-340, 383	59	12	Neg.	400-450	4	—	90	11	1,925-2,600	32-36
	8-426, 440	70	12	Neg.	400-450	4	—	90	11	1,925-2,600	32-36
'72-'73	6 & 8-198, 225, 318, 340	46	12	Neg.	400-450	4	—	90	11	1,925-2,600	32-36
	6 & 8-198, 225, 318, 340	59	12	Neg.	400-450	4	—	90	11	1,925-2,600	32-36
	6 & 8-198, 225, 318, 340	70	12	Neg.	400-450	4	—	90	11	1,925-2,600	32-36
'74	6 & 8-198, 225, 318, 360	48	12	Neg.	475-550	4	—	90	11	3,700-4,200	32-36
	6 & 8-198, 225, 318, 360	70	12	Neg.	475-550	4	—	90	11	3,700-4,200	32-36
'75-'76	6 & 8-225, 318, 360	48	12	Neg.	475-550	4	—	90	11	3,700-4,200	32-36
	6 & 8-225, 318, 360	70	12	Neg.	475-550	4	—	90	11	3,700-4,200	32-36

BRAKE SPECIFICATIONS

(All measurements are given in in.)

Year	Model	MASTER CYLINDER: Disc	MASTER CYLINDER: Drum	WHEEL CYLINDER Front: Disc	WHEEL CYLINDER Front: Drum	WHEEL CYLINDER: Rear	BRAKE DISC OR DRUM DIAMETER Front: Disc	Front: Drum	Rear
'69	All 6 cyl	—	1.00	—	1.00	13/16	—	9.0	9.0
	All V8	—	1.00	—	1 1/8	15/16	—	10.0	10.0
	All with disc brakes	④	—	⑤	—	15/16	⑥	—	10.0
'70	All Valiant	1.00	1.00	1.638	1.187	.9375	10.79	9.0	9.0
	6 cyl Barracuda and Challenger	1.125	1.00	2.750	1.187	.9375	10.72	10.0	10.0
	V8 Barracuda, Challenger	1.125	1.00	2.750	1.187	.9375	10.72	11.0⑦	11.0
	6 cyl Dart	1.00	1.00	1.638	1.187	.8125	10.79	10.0	9.0
	V8 Dart	1.00	1.00	1.638	1.187	.9375	10.79	10.0	10.0

BRAKE SPECIFICATIONS

(All measurements are given in in.)

Year	Model	Master Cylinder		Wheel Cylinder			Brake Disc or Drum Diameter		
				Front		Rear	Front		Rear
		Disc	Drum	Disc	Drum		Disc	Drum	
'71	6 cyl Dart and Valiant	1.03	1.03	1.625	1.00	.8125	11.04	9.0	9.0
	V8 Dart and Valiant, 6 cyl H.D., 6 cyl Barracuda, Challenger	1.03	1.03	1.625	1.187	.9375	11.04	10.0	10.0
	V8 Barracuda, Challenger	1.03⑧	1.03	2.750	1.187	.9375	10.72⑦	11.0	11.0⑦
'72	6 cyl Dart and Valiant	1.03	15/16	1.638	1.00	13/16	10.98	9.0	9.0
	6 cyl H.D., V8 Dart and Valiant, All Barracuda, Challenger	1.03	1.03	2.751	1 3/16	15/16	10.98	10.0	10.0⑨
'73	Valiant, Dart	1.03⑩	15/16	2.6	1 1/16	13/16⑪	10.82	9.0	9.0⑫
	Barracuda, Challenger	1.00⑬	—	2.75	—	15/16	10.84	—	10.0
'74	Valiant, Dart	1.03⑩	1.03	2.6	1 1/8	13/16⑭	10.98	10.0	9.0⑫
	Barracuda, Challenger	1.00⑬	—	2.75	—	15/16	10.98	—	10.0
'75-'76	Valiant, Dart	1.03⑩	1.03	2.60⑯	1 1/8	13/16⑪	10.82	10.0	9.0⑫
	Aspen, Volare	1.03⑮	—	2.75	—	15/16	10.84	—	10.0⑰

① Not used
② Not used
③ Not used
④ Kelsey Hayes 1 in.
Kelsey Hayes (floating caliper) 1 1/8 in.
Bendix 1 7/8 in.
⑤ Kelsey Hayes 1.636 in.
Kelsey Hayes (floating caliper) 2 3/4 in.
Bendix 2 in.
⑥ Kelsey Hayes 11.04 in.
Kelsey Hayes (floating caliper) 11.75 in.
Bendix 11.19 in.
⑦ 318, 340, 383 2 bbl engines—10 in.
⑧ 426 Hemi—1.125 in.
⑨ 11 in. optional on Barracuda and Challenger
⑩ 15/16 in. with power disc brakes
⑪ 15/16 in. rear drums with front disc brakes
⑫ 10 in. rear drums with front disc brakes
⑬ 1.03 in. with power brakes
⑭ 15/16 in. with 10 in. drums
⑮ 1.0 with non-power brakes
⑯ All 1975 models—2.75 in.
⑰ Wagons—11.0 in.
— Not applicable

WHEEL ALIGNMENT SPECIFICATIONS

Year	Model	Caster		Camber		Toe-in (in.)	Steering Axis Inclin. (deg.)	Wheel Pivot Ratio (deg)	
		Range (deg)	Pref Setting (deg)	Range (deg)	Pref Setting (deg)			Inner Wheel	Outer Wheel
'69	Manual	1N to 0⑥	1/2N	⑤	⑤	3/32 to 5/32	7 1/2	20	17.6
	Power	1/4P to 1 1/4P⑥	3/4P	⑤	⑤	3/32 to 5/32	7 1/2	20	17.6
'70	Valiant Manual	1/2N ± 1/2	1/2N	①	②	1/8 ± 1/32	7 1/2	20	17.5
	Valiant Power	3/4P ± 1/2	3/4P	①	②	1/8 ± 1/32	7 1/2	20	17.5
	Dart Manual	0 to 1N	1/2N	①	②	1/8 ± 1/32	7 1/2	20	17.6
	Dart Power	1/4P to 1 1/4P	3/4P	①	②	1/8 ± 1/32	7 1/2	20	17.6
	Barracuda Manual	1 5/16N to 15/16N	1N	①	②	3/32 to 5/32	7 1/2	20	17.5
	Barracuda Power	15/16P to 3/8N	1/16N	①	②	3/32 to 5/32	7 1/2	20	17.5
	Challenger Manual	1 5/16N to 15/16N	1N	①	②	3/32 to 5/32	7 1/2	20	17.8
	Challenger Power	15/16P to 3/8N	1/16N	①	②	3/32 to 5/32	7 1/2	20	17.8
'71-'72	Manual	1N to 0	1/2N	①	②	3/8 ± 5/32	7 1/2	20	17.5
	Power	1/4P to 1 1/4P	3/4P	①	②	3/8 ± 5/32	7 1/2	20	17.5
'73	Valiant, Dart, Barracuda, Challenger								
	Manual	0 to 1N	1/2N	③	④	3/32 to 5/32	7 1/2	20	17.5
	Power	1/4P to 1 1/4P	3/4P	③	④	3/32 to 5/32	7 1/2	20	17.5
'74	Valiant, Dart, Barracuda, Challenger								
	Manual	1 3/4N to 1/2P	1/2N	⑦	④	1/16 to 1/4	7 1/2	20	18.5
	Power	1/2N to 1 3/4P	3/4P	⑦	④	1/16 to 1/4	7 1/2	20	18.5

WHEEL ALIGNMENT SPECIFICATIONS

Year	Model	Caster Range (deg)	Caster Pref Setting (deg)	Camber Range (deg)	Camber Pref Setting (deg)	Toe-in (in.)	Steering Axis Inclin. (deg.)	Wheel Pivot Ratio (deg) Inner Wheel	Wheel Pivot Ratio (deg) Outer Wheel
'75-'76	Valiant, Dart, Aspen, Volare								
	Manual	1 5/16N to 1/16P	5/8N	⑧	④	1/16 to 1/4⑨	7 1/2⑩	20	18.5
	Power	1 5/16 to 1/16N	5/8P	⑧	④	1/16 to 1/4⑨	7 1/2⑩	20	18.5

① Left wheel—1/2P ± 1/4; Right wheel—1/4P ± 1/4
② Left wheel—1/2P; Right wheel—1/4P
③ Left wheel—1/4P to 3/4P; Right wheel—0 to 1/2P
④ Left wheel—1/2P; Right wheel—1/4P
⑤ Right side—0 to 1/2P, 1/4P preferred; left side—1/4P to 3/4P, 1/2P preferred
⑥ Dart: manual—1/16P to 1 1/16N; power—3/16P to 1 5/16P
⑦ Left wheel—0 to 1P; Right wheel—1/4N to 3/4P
⑧ Left wheel—1/8P to 7/8P; Right wheel—1/8N to 5/8P
⑨ Aspen, Volare—3/32 to 9/32 toe-in
⑩ Aspen, Volare—8.0
N Negative P Positive

FRONT END HEIGHT

Year	Model	Front End Height
'69	All M.S.	2 ± 1/8①
	All P.S.	2 ± 1/8①
'70	M.S.—Valiant, Dart	2 1/8 ± 1/8
	P.S.—Valiant, Dart	2 1/8 ± 1/8
	M.S.—Barracuda, Challenger	1 3/16 ± 1/8
	P.S.—Barracuda, Challenger	1 3/16 ± 1/8
'71-'72	All M.S.	②
	All P.S.	②

Year	Model	Front End Height
'73	All	③
'74	Dart, Valiant,	1 7/8 ± 1/8
	Barracuda, Challenger	1 1/8 ± 1/8
'75-'76	Valiant, Dart	10 15/16 ± 1/8

① Barracuda—1 3/8 ± 1/8
② Dart, Valiant 4DR—2 1/8 ± 1/8
Dart, Valiant 2DR—1 5/8 ± 1/8
Barracuda, Challenger—1 ± 1/8
③ Dart, Valiant 4DR—2 1/8 ± 1/8
Dart, Valiant 2DR—1 7/8 ± 1/8
Barracuda, Challenger—1 1/8 ± 1/8

CHARGING SYSTEM

Caution Because alternator design is unique, special care must be taken when servicing the charging system.

1. Battery polarity should be checked before any connections, such as jumper cables or battery charger leads, are made. Reversed battery connections will damage the diode rectifiers. It is recommended that the battery cables be disconnected before connecting a battery charger.
2. The battery must *never* be disconnected while the alternator is running because the regulator will be damaged.
3. Always disconnect the battery ground lead before replacing the alternator.
4. Do not attempt to polarize an alternator.
5. Do not short across or ground any alternator terminals.
6. Always disconnect the battery ground lead before removing the alternator output cable, whether the engine is running or not.
7. If electric arc welding has to be done on the car, first disconnect the battery and alternator cables. Never start the car with the welding unit attached.

NOTE: See Unit Repair Section for charging system troubleshooting and repairs.

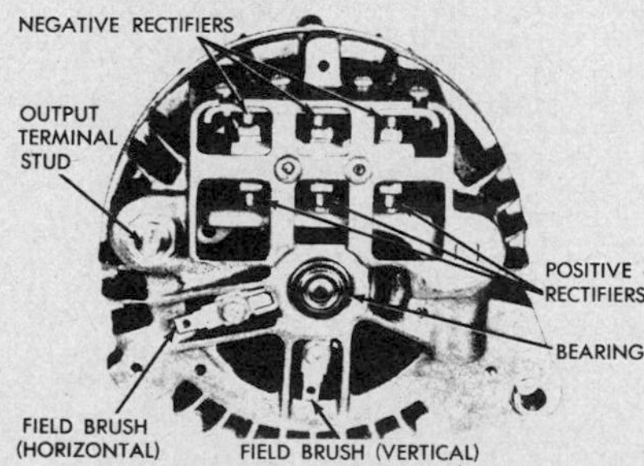

Rear view of the alternator
(© Chrysler Corp)

Alternator R & R

1. Disconnect battery ground cable.
2. Disconnect BAT and FLD leads from alternator. Disconnect the ground wire.
3. Remove alternator by removing two mounting bolts and belt tensioner bracket bolt.
4. To reinstall, reverse above.

NOTE: Never attempt to polarize an alternator, nor short the regulator.

Regulator R & R

1. Disconnect the cables from the battery posts.
2. Disconnect each electrical lead from the voltage regulator.
3. Remove the regulator by withdrawing its securing screws.
4. Installation is the reverse of the above. Be sure that the electrical leads are connected to the correct terminals and that all connections are clean and tight.

STARTING SYSTEM

All models are equipped with either a reduction-gear starter, with a 3.5:1 or 2:1 reduction gear set, or a direct-drive starter. Both types have solenoids which are mounted on the starter assembly.

See the Unit Repair Section for starting system troubleshooting and repair.

Starter R & R

1. Disconnect the ground cable at the battery.
2. Remove the cable from the starter.
3. Disconnect the solenoid leads at their solenoid terminals.
4. Remove the starter securing bolts and withdraw the starter from the engine flywheel housing. On some models with automatic transmissions, the oil cooler tube bracket will interfere with starter removal. In this case, remove the starter securing bolts, slide the cooler tube bracket off the stud, and then withdraw the starter.
5. Installation is the reverse of the above. Be sure that the starter and flywheel housing mating surfaces are free of dirt and oil.

IGNITION SYSTEM

The ignition system used on most models is of conventional design using primary and secondary ignition circuits. A separate ballast resistor unit is wired in the primary circuit between the battery and the coil. This resistor controls the current flow in the primary circuit, according to engine speed, reducing the current flow at low engine speeds and increasing the current flow at higher engine speeds. The ballast resistor is bypassed during starter operation to allow full battery voltage to flow to the ignition primary circuit.

Certain 1971 and 1972 models are equipped with the Chrysler Electronic Inition System. Beginning 1973, electronic ignition is standard on all models. For further details, refer to the section on electronic ignition systems in the "Unit Repair Section."

Distributor Removal

1. Disconnect the vacuum advance line at the distributor.
2. Disconnect the primary wire at the coil.
3. Unfasten the distributor cap retaining clips and lift off the cap.
4. Mark the distributor body and the engine block to indicate the position of the body in the block. Scribe a mark on the edge of the distributor housing to indicate the position of the rotor on the distributor. These marks can be used as guides when installing the distributor in a correctly timed engine.
5. Remove the distributor hold-down clamp screw and clamp.
6. Carefully lift the distributor out of the block.

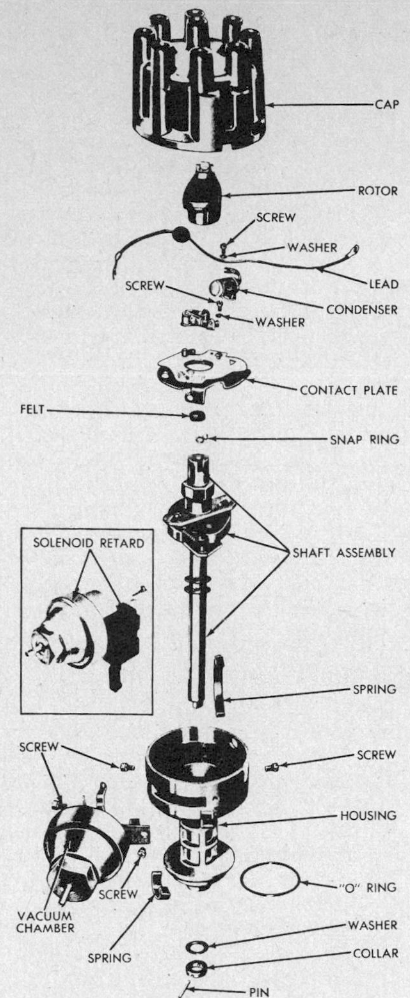

Chrysler distributor components—conventional ignition (© Chrysler Corp)

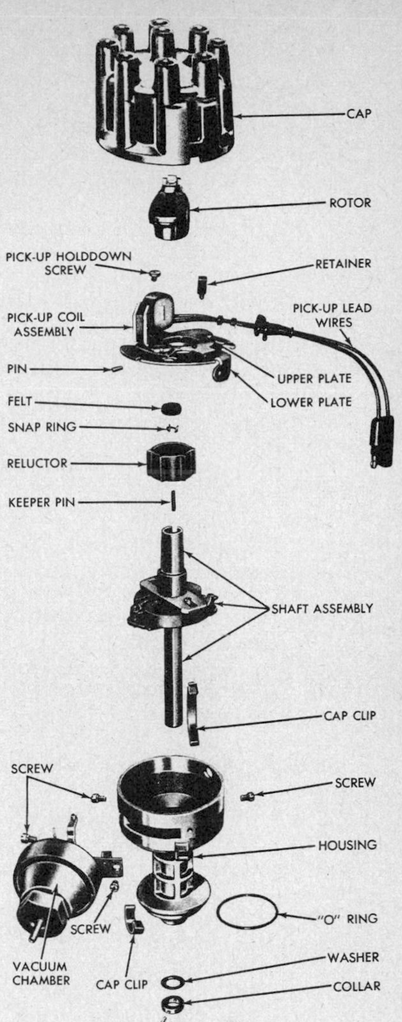

Exploded view of the electronic ignition distributor—V8. Six-cylinder distributor has a drive gear on the end of the shaft (© Chrysler Corp)

Distributor Installation

If the crankshaft has not been rotated while the distributor was removed from the engine, installation is the reverse of the removal procedure. (See step two or three of the procedure below.) Use the reference marks that were made before removal to correctly position the distributor in the block. Check the point gap and, before connecting the vacuum advance line, adjust the ignition timing.

If the crankshaft has been rotated or otherwise disturbed (as during engine rebuilding) after the distributor was removed, proceed as follows to install the distributor.

1. Bring the no. 1 piston to top dead center (TDC) by removing the no. 1 spark plug and inserting a finger into the hole, while rotating the crankshaft. Compression pressure can be felt as the no. 1 piston approaches TDC. The TDC timing mark on the crankshaft vibration damper should now be opposite the indicator on the timing chain case.
2. *For six-cylinder engines*: Note the position of the distributor cap (which should be connected to the engine by the spark plug cables). Hold the distributor so that the rotor will be in position *just ahead* of the distributor cap terminal for the no. 1 spark plug when the distributor is installed. Now lower the distributor into its engine block opening, engaging the distributor gear with the camshaft drive gear. Be sure that the rubber O-ring seal is in the groove in the distributor shank. When the distributor is properly seated, the rotor should be under the no. 1 distributor cap terminal with the contact points just opening. Proceed with step four.
3. *For eight-cylinder engines*: Clean the top of the engine block around the distributor opening to ensure a good seal between the distributor base and the block.

Note the position of the distributor cap (which should be connected to the engine by the spark plug cables). Hold the distributor so that the rotor will be in position *directly under* the distributor cap terminal for the no. 1 spark plug when the distributor is installed. Now lower the distributor into its engine block opening, engaging the tongue of the distributor shaft with the slot in the distributor and oil pump drive gear. Proceed with step four.

4. Install the distributor hold-down clamp and tighten its retaining screw finger-tight.
5. Check the point gap and refit the distributor cap. Connect the primary wire to the coil.
6. Check and adjust the point dwell and the ignition timing as described below.
7. Connect the vacuum advance line to the distributor.

Contact Point Replacement and Adjustment

Single Point Distributor

Use the procedure described below to remove, install, and adjust a single-contact point set.

1. Pull back the spring clips and lift off the distributor cap. Remove the rotor.
2. Loosen the terminal screw nut and remove the primary and condenser leads.
3. Remove the stationary contact lockscrew and remove the contact point set.
4. Remove the condenser and the retaining screw. Lift out the condenser.
5. Install the new condenser and tighten its retaining screw.
6. Install the point set but do not fully tighten its lockscrew.
7. Connect the condenser and primary leads.
8. If necessary, align the contacts by bending the stationary contact bracket only. *Never bend the movable contact arm to correct alignment.*
9. With the rubbing block of the movable contact arm resting on a peak of the cam lobe, adjust the point gap by inserting a screwdriver in the vee notch of the stationary contact base and using the screwdriver to move the stationary contact.
10. Tighten the lockscrew and recheck the gap setting. Reset if necessary.
11. Install the new rotor and refit the distributor cap.
12. Connect a dwell meter to the engine.
13. Start the engine and run it at idle speed. Note the dwell meter reading. If it is not within specifications, the point gap may be incorrect or the movable contact arm may be distorted. Readjust the contact points and recheck the dwell. Be sure that the correct point set has been installed.

Dual Point Distributor

Removal and installation of dual contact points is the same as for a single point set. However, adjustment of dual points using a dwell meter is slightly different because one set of contacts must be blocked open with a clean insulator while the opposite point set is adjusted to specifications, using the single point set adjustment procedure. When adjusted correctly, tighten the lockscrew. Then block open this contact set and adjust the other set in the same manner as the first. Check the total point dwell. If the contacts have been installed and adjusted correctly, the dwell angle should be as specified for both contact sets.

Ignition Timing

Ignition timing must be checked only when the engine is hot and running at its correct idle speed.

1. Disconnect the vacuum line at the distributor (on all models). On later models with either the ignition retard solenoid or the ignition advance solenoid, the timing must be set with the solenoids connected.
2. Connect a stroboscopic timing light, start the engine, and adjust the idle speed to specification (with the transmission in neutral).
3. Loosen the distributor hold-down screw so the housing can be rotated.
4. Check the ignition timing with the strobe light. If necessary, advance or retard the timing by rotating the distributor housing, until the correct timing is obtained.
5. Tighten the distributor hold-down screw and connect the vacuum line. Stop the engine and disconnect the timing light.

FUEL SYSTEM

Carburetors

Dodge and Plymouth compact and intermediate models have used many different types of carburetors. However, the adjustment procedure for all these carburetors, with a few exceptions, is the same. All 1968 and later carburetors incorporate modifications to reduce engine exhaust emissions. Carburetor modifications through 1969 are part of Chrysler's Cleaner Air Package, and 1970 and later models are part of the Cleaner Air System. The only carburetor changes used with the Cleaner Air Package are the installation of carburetor mixture limiter stops on the carburetor idle mixture adjustment screws, and leaner carburetor mixtures. With the Cleaner Air System, in addition to the above mentioned changes, faster acting chokes were added and, on some models, solenoid operated throttle stops and distributor retard mechanisms. The throttle stop raises the engine idle speed to reduce engine emissions, but de-energizes when the ignition is shut off to prevent the engine from dieseling. The distributor retard solenoid is activated when the idle speed adjustment screw returns to the curb idle position and contacts a sensor, mounted on the carburetor, which retards ignition timing while the engine is at idle. These carburetors also incorporate an internally mounted hot idle compensator which opens to induct additional air into the carburetor during low speed-high temperature operation.

The 426 Hemi and the 340 and 440 engines were available with multiple carburetor options. The 426 Hemi was equipped with two Carter AFB carburetors. Both carburetors had complete idle systems which must be adjusted and synchronized. The 340 and 440 Six-Pack engines were equipped with three Holley 2300 two-venturi carburetors. Only the center carburetor on these engines was equipped with an idle system and the inboard and outboard carburetors contained no idle adjustments.

Idle Speed and Mixture Adjustments (See Illustrations in Dodge Section)

1969-76 with CAP or CAS Except 426 Hemi

Adjust with air cleaner installed.

NOTE: this is the basic carburetor adjustment procedure, any specific exceptions are listed below.

1. Run engine at fast idle to stabilize engine temperature.
2. Make sure choke plate is fully released.
3. Attach a tachometer of known accuracy to the engine. With electronic ignition, connect one tachometer lead to the negative coil primary lead and the other to a good ground.
4. Connect an exhaust analyzer to the engine and insert the probe as far into the tailpipe as possible. On vehicles with dual exhaust, insert the probe into the left tailpipe as this is the side without the heat riser valve.
5. Check ignition timing and adjust it as required to conform to specification.
6. If equipped with air conditioning, turn the air conditioner OFF. On models with six-cylin-

der engines, turn the headlights on high beam.

7. Place the transmission in the Neutral position. Make sure the hot idle compensator valve is fully seated in the closed position.
8. Turn the engine idle speed adjustment screw in or out to adjust idle speed to specification. If equipped with an electric solenoid throttle positioner, turn the solenoid adjusting screw in or out to obtain specified rpm. Then, adjust the curb idle speed screw until it just touches the stop on the carburetor body. Now, back the curb idle speed adjusting screw out one full turn.
9. Turn each idle mixture adjustment screw 1/16 turn richer (counterclockwise). Wait 10 seconds and observe the reading on the exhaust gas analyzer. Continue this procedure until the meter indicates a definite increase in the richness of the mixture.

NOTE: this step is very important. A carburetor that is set too lean will cause the exhaust gas analyzer to give a false reading indicating a rich mixture. Because of this, the carburetor must first be known to have a rich mixture to verify the reading on the exhaust gas analyzer.

10. After verifying the reading obtained on the meter, adjust the mixture screws to get an air/fuel ratio of 14.2:1. Turn the mixture screws clockwise (leaner) to raise the meter reading or counterclockwise (richer) to lower the meter reading.

1969 383 and 440 V8

The carburetors used on these engines (Ball & Ball 2V, Carter 4V or Holley 4V) have lead or cup plugs installed over the idle mixture screws and an additional off idle mixture control screw added to the body of the carburetor. When adjusting the carburetor idle speed and mixture, use the off idle adjustment screw to alter the idle speed air /fuel mixture so it conforms to the 14.2:1 ratio specified. If unable to obtain an acceptable engine idle by adjusting this screw, refer to the procedure to correct rough idle and low speed surge.

Rough Idle and Low Speed Surge

Rough idle and low speed surge can be the result of improper balance of the idle mixture adjustment in the right and left carburetor bores. To correct this condition, perform the following operation.

1. On 1969 383 or 440 V8, remove the lead plugs from the two limited screws in the base of the carburetor (Ball & Ball or Carter) or the cup plugs from the sides of the primary metering body (Holley). The best way to remove the lead plugs is with a small drill and easy-out. Use a sharp punch to remove cup plugs from a Holley carburetor.
2. On all other models, remove the plastic limiter caps from the idle mixture adjustment screws.
3. Perform Steps 1-8 of the idle speed and mixture adjustment procedure.
4. On 1960 383 or 440 V8, turn the single off idle mixture adjustment screw counterclockwise (richer) until it is seated, then turn it clockwise (lean) 3/4 turn. Do not disturb this adjustment during the remainder of this procedure.
5. Turn both idle mixture adjustment screws clockwise until they are lightly seated. On some models, the idle mixture screws have a prevailing torque feature which causes the screws to become more difficult to turn as they approach the seated position.
6. On Ball & Ball carburetors, turn both idle mixture screws 1½ turns counterclockwise. On Carter and Holley carburetors, turn both idle mixture screws 2-3 turns clockwise.
7. Start the engine and perform Steps 9-11 of the idle speed and mixture adjustment procedure.

NOTE: in order to obtain a smooth idle, it is important that both mixture adjustment screws are adjusted an equal number of turns from the fully seated position.

8. Install lead plugs, cup plugs, or plastic caps on the idle mixture screws.

426 Hemi

See the Dodge/Plymouth Section.

Fuel Filter

Removal and Installation

Locate the filter in the fuel line between the fuel pump and the carburetor. Using hose-clamp pliers, remove the attaching clamps and pull the filter off. Reverse this procedure for installation. Be sure that the arrow on the filter is pointing toward the carburetor (direction of fuel flow).

Fuel Pump

The fuel pump used on the six-cylinder, 383 and 440 V8 engines are driven by a small cam eccentric cast into the main camshaft. On the 273, 318, 340, and 360 V8 engines, the pump is driven by a pressed steel eccentric secured on the gear end of the camshaft.

On the six-cylinder and 273, 318, 340, and 360 V8 engines, the pump is driven directly by the pump rocker arm pressing on the cam eccentric. On the 383, 426, and 440 big block V8s, there is a pushrod located between the pump rocker arm and the driving eccentric.

Removal and Installation

1. Wipe the pump exterior to remove all dirt and oil.
2. Taking note of positions, remove the pump fuel lines.
3. Remove the bolts securing the pump to the block and remove the pump.
4. Remove all gasket material from machined surfaces. Using a sealer of good quality, coat both sides of the pump gasket.
5. Install the pump to the block. If difficulty is encountered engaging the pump drive, rotate slightly.
6. Connect the fuel lines and tighten the pump bolts. Start the engine and check it for leaks.

COOLING SYSTEM

The cooling system is of conventional design consisting of a radiator, water pump, and thermostat. On those models that are equipped with automatic transmissions, there is a cooler located in the bottom of the radiator tank for the transmission fluid.

Some models are fitted with special cooling fan units which use a silicone fluid coupling device to engage the fan under certain conditions.

One of these fluid coupling units is called Torque Control Drive and it allows the fan to be driven in the normal manner at low engine speeds while limiting the top speed of the fan to a predetermined level at higher engine speeds. The other unit is only used on air-conditioned models and is called Thermal Control Drive. This device is essentially the same as the Torque Control Drive unit except for a thermostatic spring.

Radiator R & R

1. Drain the cooling system.
2. On cars with automatic transmissions, disconnect the fluid cooler lines at the radiator bottom tank. To avoid fluid loss or dirt contamination, plug the cooler lines.
3. Remove the upper and lower radiator hoses.
4. Remove the fan shroud securing screws and separate the shroud from the radiator. Move the shroud toward the engine as far as possible to obtain maximum clearance for removing the radiator.
5. Remove the radiator mounting screws.
6. Lift the radiator out of the engine compartment.

Caution Extreme care should be taken not to damage the radiator cooling fins or water tubes during removal.

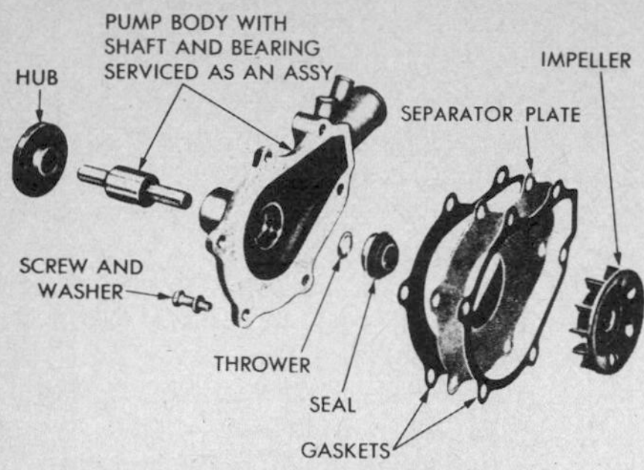

Water pump—6 cylinder
(© Chrysler Corp)

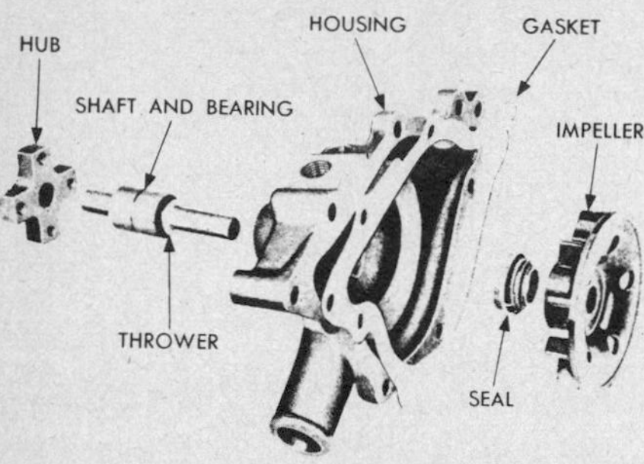

Water pump—273, 318, 340, and 360
(© Chrysler Corp)

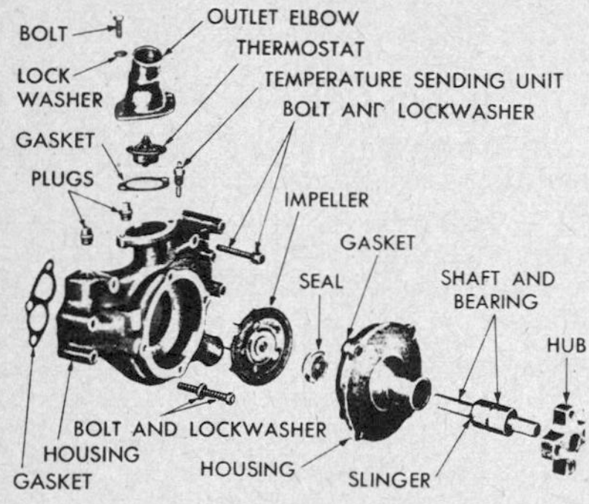

Water pump—383 and 440
(© Chrysler Corp)

7. Reverse the above to install the radiator. Fill the cooling system to 1 ¼ in. below the filler neck with the correct water and antifreeze mixture. Warm up the engine and check the coolant level. On cars with automatic transmissions, check the fluid level after warm-up and add fluid as required.

Water Pump R & R

NOTE: the water pump is serviced only as an assembly. When replacing the water pump, do not install a standard water pump on an air-conditioned car or vice versa.

1. Drain the cooling system.
2. Remove the fan shroud securing screws and move the shroud out of the way.
3. It may be necessary to remove the radiator on some models to obtain the working clearance necessary to remove the water pump.
4. Loosen the alternator mounting bolts. Loosen the mounting bolts for the power steering pump, idler pulley, air conditioning compressor, and air pump (if so equipped). Remove all the accessory belts.
5. Remove the fan, spacer or fluid drive, and the pulley.

Caution For fluid-coupled fan drives, do not position the drive unit with its shaft pointing downward. This will prevent the silicone fluid from draining into the fan-drive bearing and thereby contaminating the grease.

6. On some models, it may be necessary to remove the alternator or compressor mounting bracket bolts from the water pump to swing the alternator or compressor out of the way.
7. Withdraw the bolts which secure the water pump body to its engine block housing. Remove the water pump and discard the gasket.
8. Install the water pump with a new gasket on its housing. Torque its securing bolts to 30 ft lbs.
9. Rotate the pump shaft by hand to be sure that it rotates freely. Refit the alternator or compressor mounting bracket to the pump if either was removed. Install the pulley, spacer or fluid drive, and the fan. Torque their retaining nuts to 15 ft lbs.
10. Refit all the accessory drive belts.
11. Install the radiator if it was removed.
12. Install the fan shroud. Fill the cooling system to 1 ¼ in. below the filler neck with correct water and antifreeze mixture. Warm up the engine and inspect the water pump for any leaks. Check the coolant level and add as required.

Thermostat

Removal and Installation

1. Drain the cooling system to below the level of the thermostat.
2. Remove the upper radiator hose from the thermostat housing flange. Remove the housing bolts and take out the thermostat and housing.
3. To install the thermostat, use a new gasket. On V8s, be sure that the pellet end is facing toward engine. Six-cylinder models must have the vent hole facing up. From this point, reverse the removal procedure.

EMISSION CONTROLS

Positive Crankcase Ventilation

All models are equipped with a positive crankcase ventilation (PCV) system which draws air into the engine through the oil filler cap or the air cleaner and circulates it through the engine. The air combines with vapors in the crankcase and exits the engine through a metering valve mounted in the rocker arm cover. The air vapor mixture then re-enters the engine through the carburetor or intake manifold and passes into the combustion chambers where it is burned.

Cleaner Air Package (CAP)

All 1969 models use this package to reduce engine exhaust emissions. Changes include the addition of limiters to the carburetor idle mixture and vacuum controlled ignition timing retard mechanisms. In addition, the intake manifold and combustion chambers are reshaped to improve better mixture distribution, and a camshaft with increased overlap is used.

Cleaner Air System (CAS)

All 1970 and later models are

Cleaner Air System (© Chrysler Corp)

equipped with this type of exhaust emission control. This system consists of: heated carburetor air cleaner intake ducts, carburetor modifications, ignition timing controls, and reduced engine compression ratios.

Ignition Retard Solenoid—1971 and Earlier

The function of this unit is to retard the ignition timing at closed throttle. Located on the distributor side, this solenoid must be operating when the ignition tming is adjusted. To be sure that the solenoid is operating, disconnect the ground lead after the timing is set. If the engine idle speed increases noticeably, the solenoid is functioning properly.

Disconnect the solenoid when checking the dwell. If this is not done, the dwell meter will not read accurately.

Evaporative Control System

All 1970 vehicles sold in California and all 1971 and later vehicles have an Evaporation Control System to reduce evaporation losses from the fuel system. The system has an expansion tank in the main fuel tank. This prevents spillage due to expansion of warm fuel. A special filler cap with a two-way relief valve is used. An internal presure differential, caused by thermal expansion, opens the valve, as does an external pressure differential caused by fuel usage. Fuel vapors from the carburetor and fuel tank are routed to the crankcase ventilation system. A separator is installed to prevent liquid fuel from entering the crankcase ventilation system.

Evaporation control systems used on 1972 vehicles also include a charcoal canister and an overflow limiting valve.

The limiting valve prevents the fuel tank from being overfilled by trapping fuel in the filler when the tank is full. When pressure in the tank becomes greater than the valve operating pressure, the valve opens and allows the gasoline vapors to flow into the charcoal canister.

The charcoal canister is mounted in the engine compartment. It absorbs vapors and retains them until clean air is drawn through a line from it that runs to the PCV valve. Absorption occurs while the car is parked and cleaning occurs when the car engine is running.

Air Injection System (Air Pump)

In 1972-73 the air injection system was used on all six cylinder engines sold in California only. All 1975-76 California and most other 1975-76 engines use air pumps.

A belt-driven air pump, mounted on the front of the engine, is used to inject air into the exhaust ports. This causes oxidation of these gases and a considerable reduction in carbon monoxide and hydrocarbons. The system consists of the pump, a check valve to protect the hoses and pump from hot gases, and a diverter-pressure relief valve assembly.

Exhaust Gas Recirculation

1972—California

In order to reduce the emission of oxides and nitrogen (NOx), exhaust gases are ducted from the intake manifold crossover passage to dilute (with inert, oxygen-free gas) the fuel/air mixture. These gases are introduced to the intake manifold floor by small jets.

1973—All

Starting 1973, all Chrysler Corp. cars use exhaust gas recirculation (EGR). All engines have floor jets like those used on the 1972 models sold in California.

In addition to the floor jets, all 1973 engines except the 340 use an EGR control valve. This valve directs exhaust gas from the crossover passage into the intake manifold. By using either ported-vacuum or venturi-vacuum signals, the EGR valve is able to proportion the exhaust gas flow to the amount of vacuum present in the carburetor. Ported-vacuum is used on the 318 cu. in. (except California). Venturi-vacuum is used on all other engines except the 340.

A thermal switch is used to deenergize the EGR valve when the outside

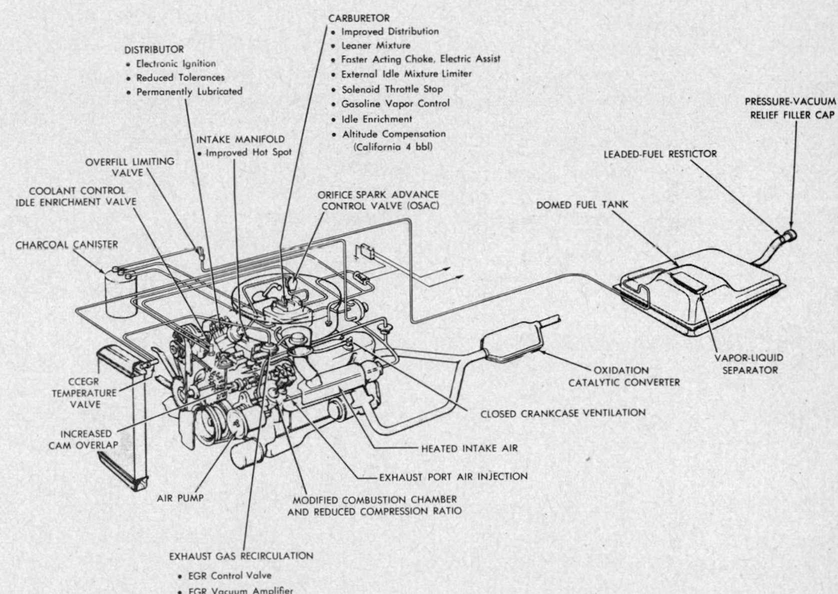

1975 Emission control systems (© Chrysler Corp)

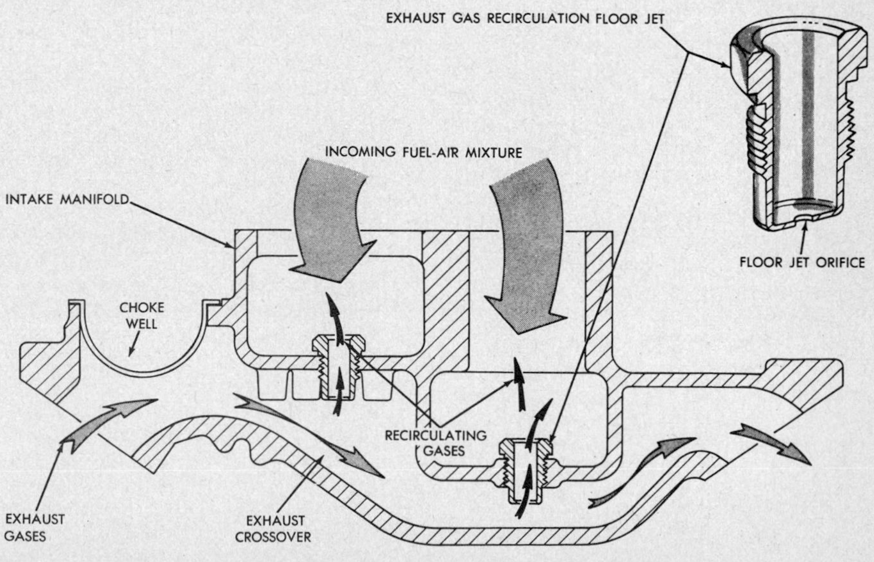

Exhaust Gas Recirculation—Floor Jet System
(© Chrysler Corp)

temperature is below 58° F, to provide better driveability.

Starting around 15 March 1973, the ambient temperature sensor was dropped. It was replaced by a thermostatic valve which is threaded into the top tank of the radiator. A hose runs from one valve nipple to the EGR vacuum amplifier. The other nipple has a filter fitted over it. When the coolant temperature is below 62° F, the valve is opened to the atmosphere, thus preventing the EGR valve diaphragm from getting vacuum. Above 62° F, the valve closes and the EGR valve is allowed to function.

1974-76—All

Floor jets have been dropped from all 1974 and later engines. The EGR temperature switch (mounted in the upper radiator tank , which was introduced in March 1973, has been retained.

NOTE: *The thermostatic switch for the EGR system is mounted on the thermostat housing on the 360–4 V engine.*

All 1974 engines, except for the following have a vacuum amplifier:

V8-318—All

V8-360—4-bbl High Performance

All 1975 engines use an EGR amplifier.

Electrically Assisted Choke

1973

During warm weather a heating element, located in the automatic choke well, comes on to shorten the period of choke operation and thus reduce hydrocarbon emissions. The heating element is operated by a time-delay control switch located next to the choke well. The assist choke draws about three amps of current during operation.

1974

A two-stage electric assist choke is used for 1974. The two-stage choke may be identified by its external resistor:

Blue resistor 5 ohm—V8-318

White resistor 10 ohm—All other V8s

Below 58° F, the heating element gets full, low amperage current from the choke control. Above 58° F, the resistor cuts the current in half. After several minutes of operation above 58° F, the control opens the circuit so that the heating element gets no current at all.

Most engines use a 20-watt heating element, except for the 360-V8—which uses a 40 watt element.

The 40-watt choke has a white paint spot on the choke cover.

1975-76

Most 1975 and later models have a single-stage electric choke which is similar to that used on all 1973 models. However, there are two exceptions to this; 318 cu in. with manual transmissions and 360 cu in. with 4-bbl carburetors have a two-stage electric assist choke which is similar to that used on 1974 models.

NO_x System

Many 1971 and 1972 vehicles sold in California have a NO_x system to control the emission of oxides of nitrogen. Engines with this system all have a special camshaft and a 185° F thermostat.

The manual transmission NO_x system uses a transmission switch, a thermal switch, and a solenoid vacuum valve. The transmission switch is screwed into the transmission housing and is closed, except in high gear. The thermal switch, mounted on the firewall, is open whenever the ambient temperature is above 70° F. With the transmission in any gear except high and the temperature above 70°, the solenoid vacuum valve is energized. This shuts off the distributor vacuum advance line preventing vacuum advance. Below 70°, the vacuum advance functions normally.

The NO_x system for automatic transmissions is more complex than the manual transmission system. It prevents vacuum advance when the ambient temperature is above 70° F, speed is below 30 mph, or the car is accelerating. The solenoid vacuum valve is interchangeable with that used in the manual transmission system. The speed switch senses vehicle speed and is driven by the speedometer cable. The control unit is mounted on the firewall. It contains a control module, thermal switch, and a vacuum switch. The control unit senses ambient temperature and manifold vacuum.

OSAC Valve

1973

Starting with the 1973 models, an orifice spark advance control (OSAC) valve is used to delay distributor vacuum advance for about 15 seconds during acceleration.

NOTE: *The amount of time-delay varies slightly from one engine size to another.*

To aid in cold weather engine operation, a temperature sensing switch is built in to the OSAC valve so that it will not function when the air temperature is below 68° F.

Some time after 1 March and before 15 March 1973, the temperature sensor was removed from the OSAC valve, but the general appearance and location of the valve were not changed. The valve can be recognized by a white gasket and a stick-on label with the new part number (3755499).

At the same time, the ignition timing was changed to TDC.

NOTE: *See the engine tune-up specifications decal for further timing information.*

1974-76

The OSAC valve has been moved from the firewall to the air cleaner for 1974-76 and the temperature control restored. There are six different time delay and operating temperature combinations for the valve. These combinations are identified by a color code tape on the top of the valve. These codes are as follows:

Color	*Time (sec)*	*Temperature (°F)*
Green	17	58
Red	17	50
Blue	17	①
White	27	58
Orange	27	①
Yellow	27	58

① No temperature control used

The OSAC valve is no longer used on 1976 225 and 318 engines.

Catalytic Converter

All 1975-76 Chrysler products sold in California except the 360 HP V8, and all sold nationwide except some 318-2V and all 360 HP V8 applications, are equipped with catalytic converters. These devices are used to oxidize excess carbon monoxide (CO) and hydrocarbons (HC) in the exhaust system before they can escape out the tailpipe and into the atmosphere. The converter is installed in front of the mufflers, underneath the car, and protected by a heat shield.

The expected catalyst life is 50,000 miles, provided that the engine is kept in tune and unleaded fuel is used.

To keep the catalyst from being overheated by an overly rich mixture during deceleration, a catalyst protection system (CPS) is used on 1975 models only. The system consists of a throttle positioner solenoid (not to be confused with the idle stop solenoid), a control box, and an engine rpm sensor.

Any time that the engine speed is more than 2,000 rpm while decelerating from highway speeds, the solenoid is energized and keeps the throttle butterfly from fully closing, thus preventing the mixture from becoming too rich. The CPS (throttle kicker) is not used on 1976 models.

Coolant Control Idle Enrichment (CCIE) System

The CCIE system is used on 1975 models with automatic transmissions. The system consists of a vacuum-operated valve built into the carburetor, which shuts off the idle circuit air bleeds when vacuum is supplied to its diaphragm.

Depending upon engine application, vacuum is either routed through a coolant controlled vacuum valve and an EGR vacuum control solenoid.

Vacuum is passed to the valve diaphragm below a predetermiend temperature, and on models with an EGR control solenoid for only 35 seconds after the engine is started. The CCIE valve action closes off the air bleed passages, which richens the mixture, and allows a smoother cold idle.

The CCIE system is not used on 1976 225 engines.

ENGINE

The standard equipment engine in most Chrysler Corperation compacts is the slant six. Although this engine has a very long stroke by modern standards (it is/was available in 170, 198, and 225 cu in. versions), it presents a low profile because the entire block is canted 30 degrees to the right.

The 273, 318, 340 and 360 cu in. engines are Chrysler's "A" block series of V8s. All of the V8s utilize hydraulic tappets. They are of the valve-in-head type, and they vary in compression ratio, piston displacement, camshafts, valve springs, carburetors, intake manifolds, and exhaust systems. Of some interest is the 340 Six Pack high-performance engine. With modified valve train, different heads, and three Holley 2-BBL 2300 carburetors, this engine was Chrysler's hottest small-block offering.

Chrysler's "B" block series consists of the 383 and 440 cu in. engines. Actually, these may be divided into two types: the 383 low-block engine and a 440 high-block entry. Basically, the difference is a larger, deeper block on the 440 to accommodate a longer stroke crank. In addition, main journal diameter, connecting rod length, pushrod length, and intake manifolds are different. Otherwise, these engines are similar and many parts will interchange.

In 1968, the 383 found its way into the Barracuda. In 1970, the 440 was added to the option list; it was available in both 4-BBL and 6-BBL versions.

In 1970, the 426 Hemi was added to the Barracuda/Challenger option list. It is basically a "B" series, raised-block engine, but with so many differences that it must be treated as a completely separate engine. It has hemispherical combustion chambers with 2.25 in. intake and 1.95 in. exhaust valves actuated by rocker arms mounted on separate intake and exhaust rocker shafts. The spark plugs are centrally located in the combustion chambers, and aluminum tubes protect the plugs and wires from oil where they pass through the rocker covers. Because of the huge intake ports, there is no room for head bolts on the intake side. Instead studs are mounted in the head which extend down into the valley between the cylinder heads. To reduce piston side thrust, Hemis use longer connecting rods than other raised-block "B" engines, and to strengthen the lower end, the main caps are crossbolted. The Hemi engine was discontinued in 1971 and is no longer available.

See the Dodge/Plymouth section for all repair procedures for the 426 Hemi engine.

Special Engine Markings

Over and undersize engine components are identified by various marks. These marks may be located on top right front engine pads or on the crankshaft counterweights. In addition, some big-block engines may have oversize valve stem markings stamped on cylinder head ends on the untapped boss. For explanation of the meanings of the various markings, consult your local Dodge/Plymouth dealership.

Engine R & R

6 Cylinder

1. Scribe the hood hinge outlines on the underside of the hood, then remove the hood.
2. Drain the cooling system, remove the battery and carburetor air cleaner.
3. Remove radiator and heater hoses, then the radiator. Remove PCV and evaporative control system (if so equipped).
4. Remove the outlet vent pipe from the cylinder head cover.
5. Disconnect fuel lines, linkage and wiring to the engine.
6. Disconnect exhaust pipe at exhaust manifold.
7. Raise car on hoist.
8. If equipped with automatic transmission, it must be drained. Remove the oil cooler lines, filler tube and shift cable.
9. Remove the clutch torque shaft, brake cables and rods.
10. Remove the speedometer cable and gear shift rods.
11. Disconnect driveshaft and tie out of the way.
12. Install an engine support fixture to the rear of the engine.
13. Remove the engine rear support crossmember.
14. Remove transmission mounting bolts from clutch housing.
15. Remove the transmission.
16. Lower the car.
17. Position engine lifting fixture onto the engine, and attach chain hoist to the fixture eyebolt.
18. Remove the engine support fixture.
19. Remove the engine front mounting bolts.

TIME SAVER

It is possible to remove the engine without removing the transmission. If the engine is to be removed from the vehicle without removing the transmission, care must be exercised not to allow the weight of the engine to rest on the torque converter hub (automatic transmission) or transmission input shaft (standard transmission).

To remove the engine without removing the transmission, perform Steps 1-7 and 10 of the engine removal operation. If the vehicle is equipped with an automatic transmission, attach a remote starter switch to the engine, remove the inspection plate from the bellhousing, crank the engine to gain access to the torque converter-to-driveplate attaching nuts and remove the nuts. If the vehicle is equipped with a manual transmission, disconnect the clutch torque shaft from the engine block and the clutch linkage from the adjustment rod. Remove the bolt that attaches the transmission filler tube to the engine (automatic transmission). Support the transmission and remove the bolts that attach the transmission to the engine or clutch bell housing. When removing the engine, place a block of wood on the lifting point of a floor jack and position the jack under the transmission. As the engine is removed from the vehicle, raise and lower the jack as required so the angle of the transmission duplicates as nearly as possible the angle of the engine.

When installing the engine into a vehicle with an automatic transmission, keep in mind that the crankshaft flange bolt circle, the inner and outer circle of holes in the driveplate, and the four tapped holes in the front face of the converter all have one hole offset. To insure proper engine-torque converter balance, the torque converter must be mounted to the driveplate in the same location it was originally installed.

When installing the engine into a vehicle with a manual transmission, it may be necessary to turn the crankshaft pulley, with the transmission in gear, to get the transmission input shaft spline to mesh with the inner hub on the clutch disc.

20. Lift the engine out of the engine compartment and lower it onto a substantial work stand.
21. To install the engine, reverse the above procedure.

V8

1. Scribe the outline of the hood hinge brackets on the bottom of the hood and remove the hood.
2. Drain the cooling system and remove the radiator.
3. Remove the battery.
4. Remove the fuel line from the fuel pump and plug the line.
5. Remove all wires and hoses that attach to the engine.
6. If equipped with air conditioning and/or power steering, remove the unit from the engine and position it out of the way *without disconnecting the lines.*
7. Attach lifting sling to the engine. On models equipped with a 426 Hemi engine, never attempt to remove the engine with the lifting sling attached to the intake manifold.
8. Raise the vehicle on a hoist and install an engine support fixture to support the rear of the engine.
9. On automatic transmission models, drain the transmission. On standard transmission models, disconnect the clutch torque shaft from the engine.
10. Disconnect the exhaust pipe/s from the exhaust manifold/s.
11. Remove the driveshaft.
12. Disconnect the transmission linkage and any wiring or cables that attach to the transmission.
13. Remove the engine rear support crossmember and remove the transmission.
14. Remove the bolts that attach the motor mounts to the chassis.
15. Lower the vehicle and attach a chain hoist or other lifting device to the engine.
16. Raise the engine and carefully remove it from the engine compartment.
17. Reverse the above procedure to install the engine.

Manifolds

6 Cylinder Combination Manifold

Removal

1. Remove air cleaner.
2. Remove vacuum control tube at carburetor and distributor. Remove the EGR line at the carburetor.
3. Remove fuel line and carburetor.
4. Remove three bolts that hold the flange.
5. Remove nuts and washers holding the intake and exhaust manifolds to the cylinder head.
6. Remove the assembly from the head.
7. Remove three bolts holding the intake and exhaust manifolds together.
8. Clean manifold mating and attaching surfaces with a straight edge and feeler gauge. All mating surfaces should be flat and plane within .008 in.

Installation

1. Place a new gasket between intake and exhaust manifolds and install three attaching bolts, loosely.
2. With a new gasket in place, position the complete manifold combination on the cylinder head.
3. Install conical washers (cupped side away from the nut) and nuts. Torque alternately to a final 10 ft. lbs.
4. Now, torque the three intake-to-exhaust manifold nuts to 15 ft. lbs.
5. Connect the exhaust pipe to the manifold flange and torque these two bolts to 30 ft. lbs.
6. Install carburetor and connect line, vacuum line and throttle linkage.
7. Install air cleaner. Start engine and check for intake and exhaust leaks.

V8 Intake Manifold R&R

All Engines Except 426 Hemi

1. Drain the cooling system. Disconnect the negative battery cable.
2. Remove the air cleaner and disconnect the fuel line from the carburetor.
3. Disconnect all vacuum lines that attach to the carburetor or intake manifold.
4. Disconnect the spark plug wires from the plugs and remove the distributor cap and wires as an assembly.
5. Disconnect the wires from the coil and the temperature sending unit.
6. Disconnect the heater hose and bypass hose from the intake manifold.
7. Remove the intake manifold attaching bolts and remove the manifold, carburetor and coil from the engine as an assembly.
8. Clean all gasket mounting surfaces and firmly cement new gaskets to the engine.
9. Reverse above precedure to install.

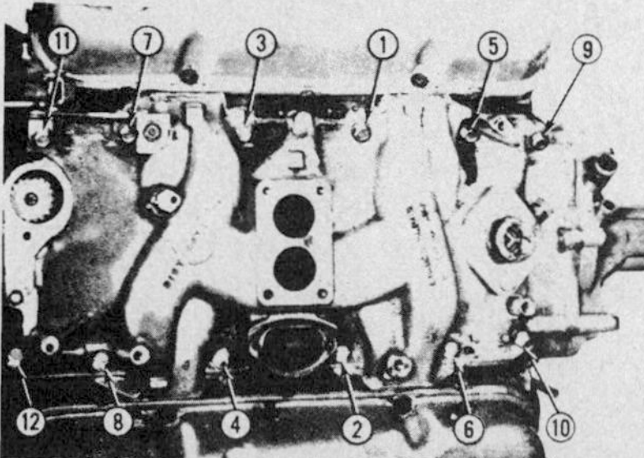

Intake manifold tightening sequence for V8 engines (except 426 Hemi)
(© Chrysler Corp)

426 Hemi

See Dodge-Plymouth section.

V8 Exhaust Manifold R&R

Disconnect the exhaust manifold at the pipe flange. Access to these bolts is underneath the vehicle. If so equipped, disconnect the Air Injection nozzles and carburetor heated air stove. Disconnect any components of the EGR system which are in the way. Remove the exhaust manifold by removing the securing bolts and washers. To reach these bolts, it may be necessary to jack the engine slightly off its front mounts. When the exhaust manifold is removed, sometimes the securing studs will come out with the nuts. If this occurs, studs must be replaced with the aid of sealing compound on the coarse thread ends. If this is not done, water leaks may develop at the studs. To install the exhaust manifold, reverse the removal procedure.

Valve System

All valves used in Chrysler engines (except 426 Hemi) are arranged in line in the cylinder head; they ride in guides that are integrally cast with the head. Service valves with oversize stems are available; therefore, valve guides may be reamed if required. Do not attempt to ream guides in one step to their maximum .030 in. oversize; work in .005, .015, and .030 in. steps. This allows the guide to be reamed true in relation to its seat.

All six-cylinder engines used in Chrysler vehicles are equipped with solid (mechanical) lifters. All V8s utilize hydraulic lifters. With the exception of the 340 Six Pack engine and the 426 Hemi, these hydraulic lifters are non adjustable.

Rocker Shaft Removal

All Engines except 426 Hemi

1. Remove closed ventilation system (PCV). On V8s, remove the spark plug wires.
2. Remove valve cover with gasket.

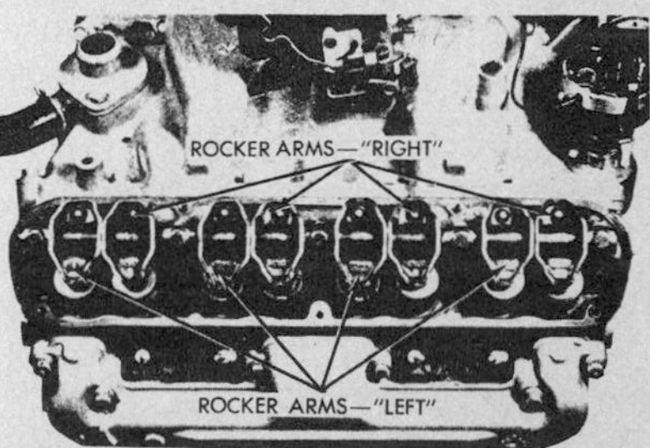

Identification of valve rocker arms for V8 engines (except 426 Hemi)
(© Chrysler Corp)

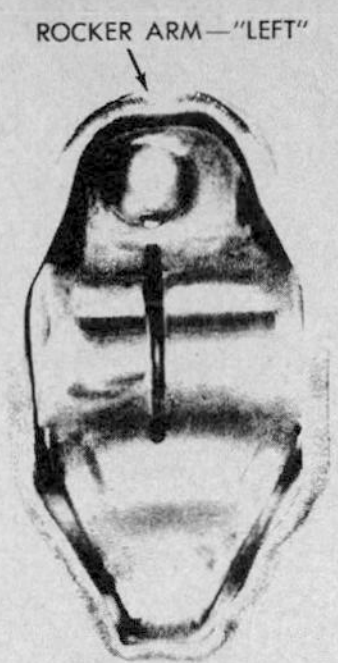

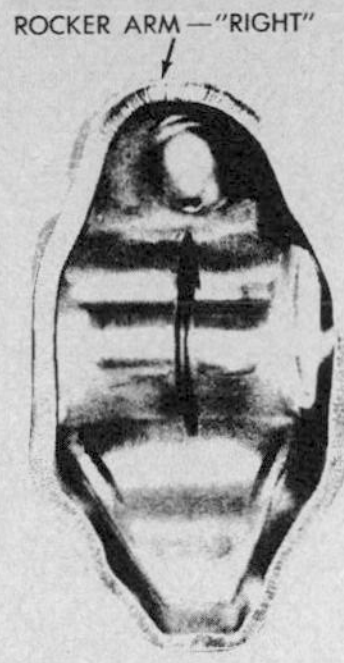

Proper location and installation of rocker arms on the shaft—V8 engines (except 426 Hemi) (© Chrysler Corp)

3. Remove rocker shaft bolts with retainers.
4. To replace the rocker arms, reverse the removal procedure. Be sure to torque rocker arm bolts to 25 ft lbs. On engines with adjustable lifters, set the valves. When replacing the valve cover, use a new gasket.

NOTE: when replacing rocker arms, be sure to align the oil holes.

426 Hemi

See the Dodge/Plymouth section.

Valve Adjustment

170, 198, 225, and 273 Cu. In. Engines

1. Warm up the engine until it reaches its normal operating temperature (water temperature of about 185°F).
2. Set the engine idle speed to 550 rpm and run the engine at this speed for five minutes.
3. Remove the valve cover by withdrawing its securing bolts. Be careful of the hot oil which will splash off the rocker assembly when the cover is removed.
4. Using the proper thickness feeler gauge, measure the clearance between the valve stem tip and the end of the rocker arm adjusting screw at each valve. If necessary, turn the adjusting screw to obtain the correct valve clearance.
5. After all of the valves have been checked and adjusted, stop the engine and replace the valve cover, using a new gasket between the cover and cylinder head. If much oil was lost during the valve adjustment procedure, check the oil level in the crankcase.

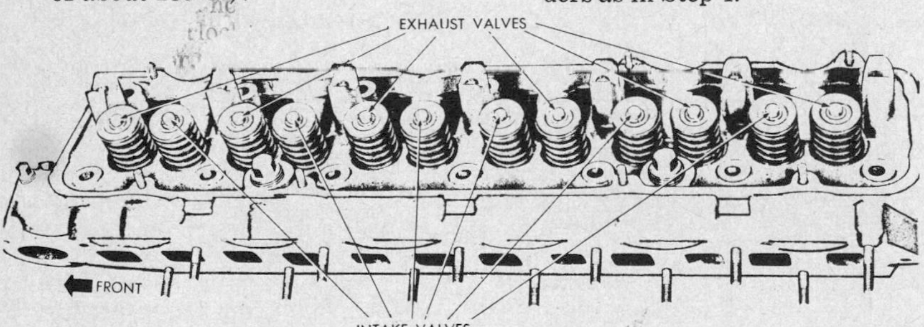

Cylinder head, showing valve sequence—170, 198 and 225 engines (© Chrysler Corp)

340 Six Pack and 426 Hemi

1. Adjust ignition timing to TDC.
2. Mark crankshaft damper with chalk at TDC and 180° opposite TDC.
3. Rotate crankshaft until No. 1 cylinder is at TDC and points are just opening.
4. Adjust intake tappets on No. 2 and No. 7 cylinders and exhaust tappets on No. 4 and No. 8 cylinders. On 1968-69 engines, adjust the intake valves to have a clearance of .028 in. and the exhaust valves .032 in. with the engine COLD. On 1970–71 engines, adjust the valves to have zero lash, then tighten the adjustment screw an additional 1½ turns. Tighten the locknuts to 25 ft lbs.
5. Rotate crankshaft 180° in normal direction of rotation until points open to fire No. 4 cylinder.
6. Adjust intake tappets on No. 1 and No. 8 cylinders and exhaust tappets on No. 3 and No. 6 cylinders as in Step 4.
7. Rotate crankshaft 180° in normal direction of rotation until points open to fire No. 6 cylinder.
8. Adjust intake tappets on No. 3 and No. 4 cylinders and exhaust tappets on No. 5 and No. 7 cylinders as in Step 4.
9. Rotate crankshaft 180° in normal direction of rotation until points open to fire No. 7 cylinder.
10. Adjust intake tappets on No. 5 and No. 6 cylinders and exhaust tappets on No. 1 and No. 2 cylinders as in Step 4.
11. Set ignition timing to operating specifications and install rocker covers.

Cylinder Head

6 Cylinder Removal

1. Drain the cooling system.
2. Remove carburetor air cleaner and fuel lines.
3. Disconnect accelerator linkage.
4. Remove all of the vacuum lines from the carburetor.
5. Carefully disconnect spark plug wires by pulling straight, in line with plug.
6. Disconnect heater hose and clamp holding the by-pass hose.
7. Disconnect the heat indicator-sending-unit wire.
8. Disconnect exhaust pipe at the exhaust manifold flange. If so equipped, disconnect the diverter valve vacuum line from the intake manifold; also remove the air injection assembly (if applicable).
9. Remove the intake and exhaust manifold and carburetor as an assembly.
10. Remove the outlet vent tube, evaporative control system, and cylinder head cover.
11. Remove the rocker arms and shaft.
12. Remove the pushrods and place them in order.
13. Remove the head bolts and lift off the cylinder head.
14. Place cylinder head on bench and remove the spark plugs and tubes.

6 Cylinder Installation

1. Clean carbon from the combustion area. Clean all gasket surfaces of both head and cylinder block. Install spark plugs (the aluminum plug shields act as satisfactory gasket material between spark plug body and cylinder head.)
2. If there is any cause to suspect leakage, check all surfaces with a straightedge. If out of flatness exceeds 0.00075 times the span length in any direction, replace head or machine head gasket surface. For example, on a 12 in. span the maximum allowable out of flat is 12 x 0.00075 or 0.009 in.
3. Apply a reliable sealer to the new gasket and install the gasket and cylinder head.
4. Install the 14 cylinder head bolts. Starting at the top center, tighten all cylinder head bolts to specification in three steps.
5. Inspect all push rods for bends or wear. Replace if necessary.
6. Insert the pushrods, small ends down into the tappets.
7. Install rocker arms and shaft assembly with flat on the end of the shaft on top and pointing toward the front of the engine. This is necessary to provide lubrication to the rocker assemblies. Torque the attaching bolts to 25 ft. lbs.
8. Loosen the three bolts that connect the intake and exhaust manifolds. (This is necessary to obtain proper alignment.)
9. Position intake and exhaust manifold and carburetor assembly onto the cylinder head. Put the cup side of the conical washers

against the manifolds, install the attaching nuts and torque to specifications.

10. Retighten the three intake-to-exhaust manifold bolts to specifications. Be sure to torque the inner bolt first.
11. Connect the heater hose and bypass hose clamp.
12. Connect the heat indicator sending-unit wire, the accelerator linkage and the spark plug wires. If applicable, install vacuum control tube at the carburetor, the air injection assembly, and the diverter valve.
13. Install carburetor vacuum line(s).
14. Connect exhaust pipe to the exhaust manifold.
15. Install the fuel line and carburetor air cleaner.
16. Refill the cooling system.
17. Start the engine and let run until operating temperatures have been reached.
18. Adjust valve tappet clearance to .010 in. (intake) and .020 in. (exhaust.) The adjusting screw in the pushrod end of the rocker arm should have a minimum of 3 ft. lbs. (36 in. lbs.) tension as it is turned. If less, replace the adjusting screw and the rocker arm.
19. Place the new cylinder head cover gasket in position and install cylinder head cover. Torque attaching nuts to 40 in. lbs. (3 1/3 ft. lbs.).
20. Install outlet vent tube, and evaporative control system (if applicable).

273, 318, 340, and 360 V8 Removal

1. Drain cooling system and disconnect battery.
2. Remove alternator, air cleaner and fuel line.
3. Disconnect accelerator linkage.
4. Remove vacuum hose(s) from the carburetor.
5. Remove distributor cap and wires. If removing heads in vehicle, remove plugs to prevent breaking them.
6. Disconnect coil wires, temperature sending wire, heater hoses, and bypass hose.
7. Remove closed ventilation system (PCV), evaporative control system if so equipped, and valve covers.
8. Remove intake manifold, ignition coil, and carburetor as an assembly.
9. Remove exhaust manifolds.
10. Remove rocker arm and shaft assemblies. Remove pushrods and identify to ensure installation in original location.
11. Remove 10 head bolts from each cylinder head and lift off heads.
12. Clean all surfaces.
13. Inspect all surfaces with straight edge if there is any reason to suspect leakage. If out of flatness exceeds 0.00075 times span length in any direction, replace head or machine mating surface. For example, if span length is 12 in., maximum out of flatness is 12 x 0.00075 or 0.009 in.
14. Reverse procedure to install. Be sure to torque the cylinder head to specifications in three stages.

Chilton's TIME SAVER

If only one head is to be removed, it is possible to leave the intake manifold on the engine while removing the head:

1. **Remove the head bolts from the intake manifold on the side from which the head is to be removed.**
2. **Loosen, but do not remove, the bolts on the opposite side of the manifold 1½-2 turns.**
3. **Perform steps 9-11 above.**
4. **Slip the head out from under the intake manifold.**
5. **Perform steps 12-14 above.**

383 and 440 Wedge V8s and 426 Hemi V8

See Dodge-Plymouth Section.

Chilton's TIME SAVER

Frequently valves become bent or warped or their seats become blocked with carbon or other material. Left unattended, this can cause burnt valves, damaged cylinder heads and other expensive troubles. To detect leaking valves early, perform this test whenever the cylinder head is removed.

1. **After removing head, replace sparkplugs. Removing sparkplugs before removing heads eliminates breakage.**
2. **Place head on bench with valves, springs, retainers and keys installed and combustion chambers up.**
3. **Pour enough gasoline in each combustion chamber to completely cover both valves. Watch combustion chambers for two minutes for any leakage.**

Cylinder Head Bolt Tightening Sequence

NOTE: torque to specifications in three steps.

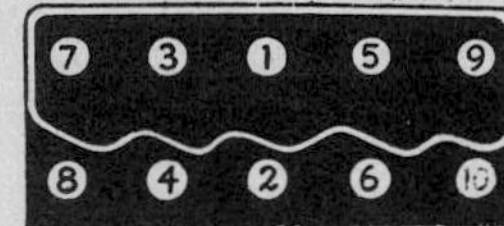

273, 318, 340, 360 cu. in. V8
(© Chrysler Corp)

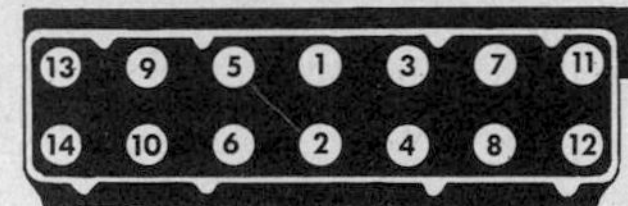

6 cylinder
(© Chrysler Corp)

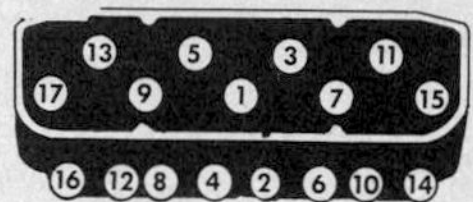

383, 440 cu. in. V8
(© Chrysler Corp)

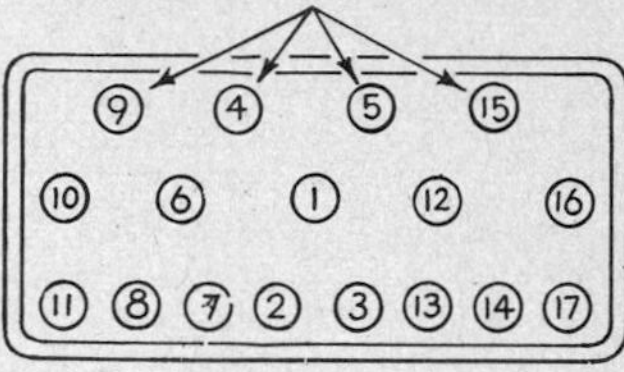

426 Hemi V8
(© Chrysler Corp)

Timing Cover, Chain, and Camshaft

Timing Chain and Cover Replacement

1. Drain the cooling system.
2. Disconnect the upper and lower radiator hoses from the engine. Disconnect the transmission cooler lines from the radiator.
3. If equipped with a fan shroud, remove it from the radiator and position it rearward over the fan.
4. Remove the radiator attaching screws and remove the radiator from the vehicle.

NOTE: it may not be necessary to remove the radiator and shroud if there is enough room to work the timing cover out.

5. Remove the bolts that attach the fan to the water pump and remove the fan, fan spacer (if so equipped) and pulley from the engine.
6. Disconnect the negative battery cable. Remove the bolts that attach the alternator mounting bracket to the engine and remove the alternator and bracket from the engine and position them out of the way with the wires attached.
7. If equipped with power steering, remove the bolts that attach the

power steering pump mounting bracket to the engine. Remove the pump and bracket from the engine and position them out of the way with the lines attached.

8. Remove the water pump from the engine.
9. Remove the bolt and washer that attach the vibration damper to the crankshaft.
10. Using a puller, remove the vibration damper.
11. Remove the bolts that attach the timing chain cover to the block and the front of the oil pan. Remove the cover from the engine.
12. To check timing chain slack, place a scale next to the timing chain to detect any movement in the chain. Place a torque wrench and socket on the camshaft sprocket attaching bolt. Apply either 30 ft lbs. (if cylinder heads are installed on the engine) or 15 ft lbs. (cylinder heads removed) of force to the bolt and rotate the bolt in the direction of crankshaft rotation to remove all slack from the chain. While applying torque to the camshaft sprocket bolt, the crankshaft should not be allowed to rotate. It may be necessary to block the crankshaft to prevent rotation. Position the scale over the edge of a timing chain link and apply an equal amount of torque in the opposite direction. If the movement of the chain exceeds 3/16 in., replace the chain.
13. To remove the timing chain, crank the engine until the timing marks on the sprockets are aligned, remove the bolt that attaches the cam sprocket to the camshaft, and slide the chain and both sprockets forward and remove them from the engine as an assembly.

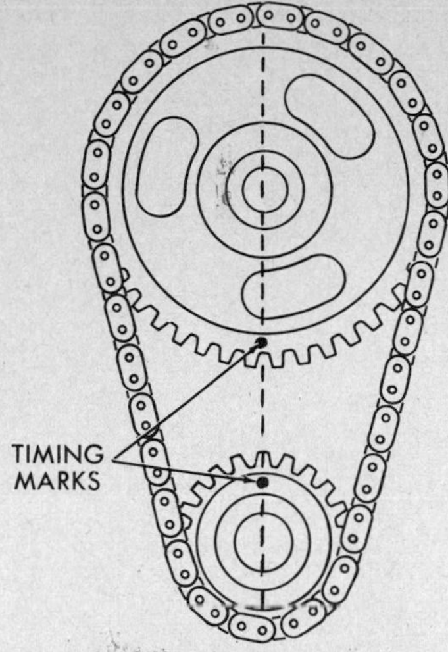

Alignment of timing marks—V8
(© Chrysler Corp)

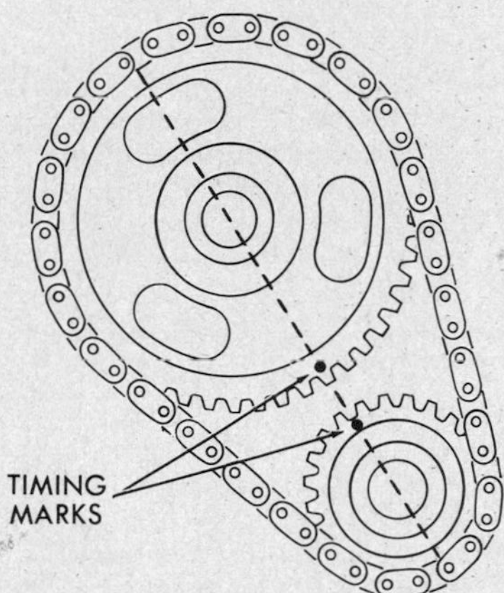

Alignment of timing marks—6 cylinder
(© Chrysler Corp)

14. Reverse above procedure to install, making sure the timing marks on the camshaft and crankshaft sprockets are aligned when they are installed on the engine.

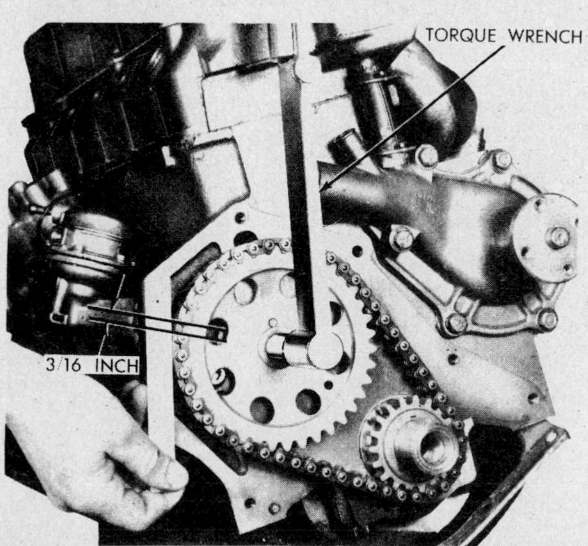

Measuring timing chain stretch
(© Chrysler Corp)

Timing Chain Cover Seal Replacement

All Engines

1. Using a puller, separate the seal from the retainer.
2. Using fingers and a screwdriver, pull the seal from the case.
3. To install the seal, place it in the case with the rubber side downward.
4. Seat the seal tightly against the cover face. There should be maximum clearance of 0.0014 in. between the seal and the cover. Be certain not to overcompress seal.

Camshaft Removal and Installation

NOTE: Whenever a new camshaft and/or new tappets are installed, the manufacturer recommends that one qt of their engine oil supplement, or equivalent, be added to the engine oil to aid break-in. This oil mixture should be left in the engine for a minimum of 500 miles.

The manufacturer recommends that the engine be removed from the vehicle before removing the camshaft. However, in some cases it may be possible to remove the camshaft from the engine with the engine still in the car by removing the radiator and grille and sliding the camshaft out through the front of the vehicle.

6 Cylinder Engines

1. Remove the timing gear cover, camshaft sprocket, and timing chain.
2. Remove the valve tappets, keeping them in order to ensure installation in their original location.
3. Remove the crankshaft sprocket.
4. Remove the distributor and the oil pump.
5. Remove the fuel pump.
6. Fit a long bolt into the front of the camshaft to facilitate camshaft removal.
7. Remove the camshaft, being careful not to damage the cam bearings with the cam lobes.
8. Lubricate the camshaft lobes and bearing journals with camshaft lubricant. Insert the camshaft into the engine block.
9. Install the fuel pump and oil pump.
10. Install the distributor. (Refer to the "Distributor Installation" procedure.)
11. Inspect the crowns of all the tappet faces with a straightedge. Replace any tappets that have dished or worn surfaces. Install the tappets.
12. Replace the timing gear and timing gear cover.

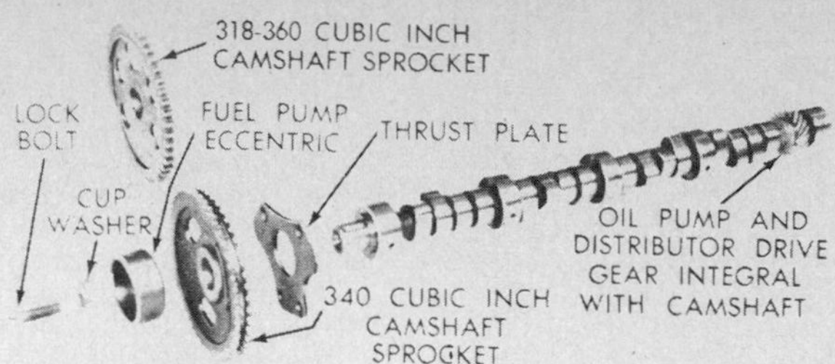

Camshaft and sprocket assembly—V8
(© Chrysler Corp)

V8 Engines

1. Remove the timing gear cover, camshaft and crankshaft sprocket, and the timing chain.
2. Remove the valve tappets, keeping them in order to ensure installation in their original location.
3. Remove the distributor and lift out the oil pump and distributor driveshaft.
4. Remove the camshaft thrust plate (is so equipped). Take note of the location of the oil tab.
5. Fit a long bolt into the front of the camshaft and remove the camshaft, being careful not to damage the cam bearings with the cam lobes.
6. Lubricate the camshaft lobes and bearing journals with camshaft lubricant. Insert the camshaft into the engine block within 2 in. of its final position in the block.
7. Have an assistant support the camshaft with a screwdriver to prevent the camshaft from contacting the freeze plug in the rear of the engine block. Position the screwdriver against the rear side of the cam gear and be careful not to damage the cam lobes.
8. Refit the camshaft thrust plate (if so equipped), and the chain oil tab. Be sure its tang enters the lower right hole in the thrust plate. Tab top edge must be flat against the thrust plate.
9. Install the oil pump and the distributor driveshaft. Install the distributor. (Refer to the "Distributor Installation" procedure.)
10. Inspect the crown of all the tappet faces with a straightedge. Replace any tappets that have dished or worn surfaces. Install the tappets.
11. Install the timing gear and gear cover.

Pistons and Connecting Rods

Piston Removal and Ring Replacement

1. Remove the cylinder heads.
2. Remove the oil pan.
3. Turn the crankshaft until the No. 1 piston is at the bottom of its stroke. Place a rag over the top of the piston, and using a ridge reamer, remove the ridge of carbon from the top of the cylinder wall. Repeat this operation on all cylinders.
4. Remove the connecting rod cap from the No. 1 piston connecting rod. Rotate the engine so the piston and connecting rod assembly are centered in the cylinder bore. Place a block of wood against the bottom of the piston and carefully drive the piston-connecting rod assembly from the cylinder block. Replace the connecting rod cap and bearing half on the connecting rod so they do not become mixed. Repeat this operation until all the pistons have been removed.

NOTE: Number the pistons, rods and caps to aid in identification during assembly.

5. Using a piston ring removal tool remove the piston rings.
6. If cylinder bore is in satisfactory condition, place each ring in bore in turn and square it in bore with head of piston. Measure ring gap. If ring gap is greater than limit, use new ring. If ring gap is less than limit, file end of ring to obtain correct gap.
7. Check ring side clearance by installing rings on piston, and inserting feeler gauge of correct dimension between ring and lower land. Gauge should slide freely around ring circumference without binding. Any wear will form a step on lower land. Replace any pistons having high steps. Before checking ring side clearance be sure ring grooves are clean and free of carbon, sludge, or grit.
8. Space ring gaps at equidistant intervals around piston circumference. Be sure that the compression ring gaps are staggered around the circumference of the piston so that neither is in line with the oil ring rail gap. Be sure to install piston in its original bore. Install short lengths of rubber tubing over connecting rod bolts to prevent damage to rod journal. Install ring compressor over rings on piston. Lower piston rod assembly into bore until ring compressor contacts block. Using wooden handle of hammer push piston into bore while guiding rod onto journal.

Engine Lubrication

Oil Pan Removal

Slant Six—1969-76 Dart and Valiant 1969 Barracuda

1. Disconnect the battery and drain the radiator. Disconnect the upper and lower radiator hoses, and remove the oil dipstick.
2. Remove the radiator shroud attaching screws and position it rearward on the engine (if so equipped).
3. Jack up the vehicle and drain the oil.
4. Remove the steering center link from the steering and idler arms.
5. Position a jack stand at the right front corner of the engine oil pan. Be sure not to support the engine at the crankshaft pulley or vibration damper.
6. Remove the front engine mount bolts. Raise the engine about 1½–2 in.
7. Remove the oil pan bolts, rotate the engine crankshaft to clear the counterweights, and remove the oil pan.
8. Using a new pan gasket set, install the oil pan and torque it to 200 in. lbs.
9. Lower the engine into its original position and install the front engine mount bolts. Torque to specifications.
10. Connect the steering and idler arms to the center link. Torque to specification; be sure to install the cotter pins.
11. If removed, install the radiator hoses and replace the fan shroud.
12. Fill the cooling system, install the dipstick, replace the oil, and check for leaks. Connect the battery and start the vehicle. Run for five minutes, then check again for leaks.

Slant Six—1970—72 Barracuda and Challenger

1. Disconnect the battery and remove the oil dipstick. Jack up the vehicle and drain the oil.
2. Remove the steering center link with the idler arm attached.
3. Disconnect the exhaust pipe from its manifold and secure it out of the way.
4. Remove the oil pan attaching bolts. Rotate the engine crankshaft in order to clear the counterweights. Remove the oil pan.
5. To install the oil pan, reverse the removal procedure. Torque the pan bolts to 200 in. lbs.

273, 318, 340, and 360 V8s —All Models

1. Disconnect the battery and remove the dipstick.
2. Jack up the vehicle and drain the oil. If so equipped, remove the torque converter-to-engine left housing strut.
3. Disconnect the steering center link from the steering and idler arms.
4. Disconnect the exhaust pipes from the manifolds and secure them out of the way.
5. Visually check to see if there is sufficient clearance to reach all of the oil pan bolts. If there is not, it will be necessary to raise the engine about 1½–2 in. Do this by loosening the motor mounts and jacking or hoisting the engine until the bolts in question become accessible. Be sure to raise the engine only the minimum amount necessary to reach these bolts. Remove the oil pan bolts, rotate the engine crankshaft to clear the counterweights, and remove the pan with a twisting motion.
6. When installing the oil pan, be sure that the oil strainer will be parallel with and will contact the pan bottom. Use a new gasket and torque the pan bolts to 200 in. lbs.
7. If it was necessary to jack the engine from its mounts, return it to its proper position at this time. Torque the engine mount bolts to specifications.
8. Install the engine-to-converter housing strut (if so equipped).
9. From this point, reverse the removal procedure.

383, 426, and 440 V8s —All Models

1. Disconnect the battery and remove the dipstick.
2. Jack up the vehicle and remove the center steering link from the steering and idler arms.
3. Disconnect the exhaust pipes from the manifolds and secure them out of the way.
4. If there is not sufficient clearance for the oil pan to clear the exhaust pipe, remove the clamp attaching the exhaust pipe to the extension and remove the exhaust pipe.
5. Drain the oil.
6. Remove the dust shield from the torque converter.
7. Extract the oil pan bolts. On some models, it may be necessary to jack the engine off its mounts (1½–2 in.) to reach the oil pan bolts. Do this by loosening the motor mounts and jacking or hoisting the engine. Raise the engine only the minimum amount required to reach the bolts in question. When removing the oil pan, be sure to rotate the crankshaft to clear the counterweights. Remove the pan with a twisting motion.
8. When installing the oil pan, be sure to use a new gasket. Torque the pan bolts to 200 in. lbs.
9. If it was necessary to jack the engine, lower it now and torque the engine mounts to specifications. To proceed, reverse the order of removal. After completion, be sure to start the vehicle and idle for at least five minutes. Check for leaks.

Oil Pump

Six Cylinder Removal

1. Drain radiator, disconnect upper and lower hoses, and remove fan shroud.
2. Raise vehicle on hoist, support front of engine with jack stand placed under right front corner of oil pan, and remove engine mount bolts. Do not support engine at crankshaft pulley or vibration damper.
3. Raise engine approximately 1½—2 in.
4. Remove oil filter, oil pump attaching bolts, and pump assembly.

273, 318, 340, and 360 Engines

1. Remove oil pan.
2. Remove oil pump from rear main bearing cap.

383, 426, and 440 V8s

1. The oil pump is located on the bottom side of the engine block at the filter.
2. Removal consists of taking out the attaching bolts and removing the pump and filter as an assembly.
3. To install the pump, reverse the removal procedure.

Rear Main Bearing Oil Seal

Service replacement seals are of split rubber type composition. This type of seal makes it possible to replace the upper half of the rear main oil seal without removing the engine from the car, or the crankshaft from the engine. When installing rubber seals, they must be replaced as a set and cannot be combined with the rope type rear main seal. The following procedure is for removing the rope type seal and replacing it with the rubber type seal.

NOTE: on vehicles with a 426 Hemi engine, remove the transmission and vibration damper in addition to the procedure listed below.

Replacement

1. Remove the oil pan.
2. Remove the rear seal retainer and the rear main bearing cap.
3. Remove the lower rope seal by prying from the side with a small screwdriver.
4. To remove the upper rope seal, drive up on either exposed end of the seal with a 6 in. piece of 3/16 in. brazing rod. When the opposite end of the seal starts to protrude from the block, have an assistant grasp it with pliers and gently pull it from the block while the opposite end is being driven.
5. Wipe crankshaft clean and lightly oil crankshaft and new seal before installing seal.
6. Loosen all main bearing caps slightly to lower the crankshaft which will ease installation.

Caution Do not allow the crankshaft to drop enough to permit the main bearings to become displaced on the crankshaft.

7. Hold the seal tightly against the crankshaft with the thumb (with paint stripe to the rear) and install the seal in the block groove. Rotate the crankshaft if necessary while installing the seal in the groove. *Make sure the sharp edges on the block groove do not cut or nick the rear of the seal.*
8. Install lower half of seal (with paint stripe to the rear) into the lower seal retainer.
9. Install rear main bearing cap.
10. Tighten all main bearing caps to specification.

NOTE: make sure all main bearings are located in their proper position before tightening the main bearing caps.

CLUTCH

All models utilize a single, dry plate clutch operated by a pedal suspended under the dash. All models are equipped with a return spring; some models have centrifugal rollers assembled between the pressure plate and cover. 1969-71 six-cylinder and light-duty V8 models utilize a non-centrifugal clutch while six-cylinder heavy-duty usage and most V8s use a semi-centrifugal type. All 1972 and later models use the semi-centrifugal type.

Clutch Removal

1. Remove the transmission.
2. Remove the clutch housing pan.
3. Disconnect the fork return spring from the clutch housing and release fork.
4. Remove the spring washer fastening the fork rod to the torque shaft lever pin. Remove the pin from the rod and release fork.
5. On models with three-speed transmissions (if this procedure is applicable to vehicle in question) remove the clip and plain washer securing the interlock

rod to the torque shaft lever and remove the washers and rod from the torque shaft.
6. Remove the sleeve assembly and clutch release bearing from the clutch release fork.
7. Punch-mark the clutch cover and flywheel so they may be installed in the same relative positions.
8. Loosen the clutch cover attaching screws in two stages to avoid bending the cover flange.
9. Remove the clutch assembly. Be careful not to contaminate the clutch with grease or oil.

Clutch Installation

1. Lightly lubricate the drive pinion bushing in the end of the crankshaft. Use about ½ teaspoonful of long-life chassis grease. Lubricant should be inserted in the radius in back of the bushing.
2. Thoroughly clean the surfaces of the flywheel and pressure plate with fine sandpaper. All oil or grease must be removed at this time.
3. Position the clutch disc, pressure plate, and cover in the mounting position. Springs on disc damper must be facing away from the flywheel. Do not touch the disc facing at any time. Insert a clutch disc aligning arbor or suitable substitute (such as a spare transmission drive pinion) through the disc hub and into the bushing.
4. Align the punch marks that were made at removal. Install the clutch cover bolts but do not tighten them.
5. Tighten all bolts a few turns at a time in an alternate sequence. Torque 5/16 in. bolts to 20 in. lbs. and 3/8 in. bolts to 30 ft lbs. Remove the alignment tool.
6. Pack the bearing sleeve cavity with an appropriate NLGI Grade 2 EP grease. Apply the same lubricant to the release fork pads of the sleeve.

Replacing clutch release bearing (© Chrysler Corp)

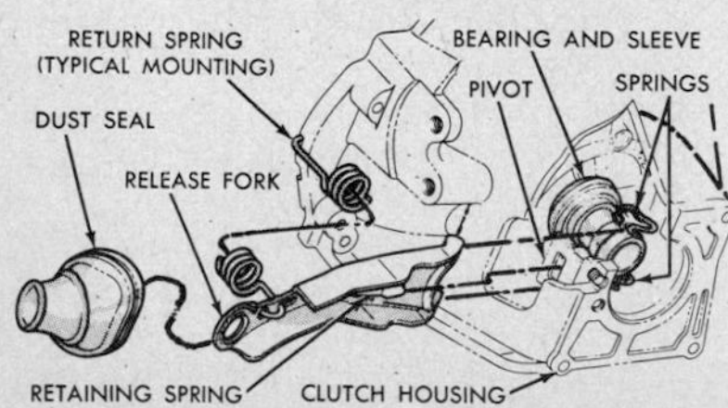

Clutch release fork, bearing and sleeve (© Chrysler Corp)

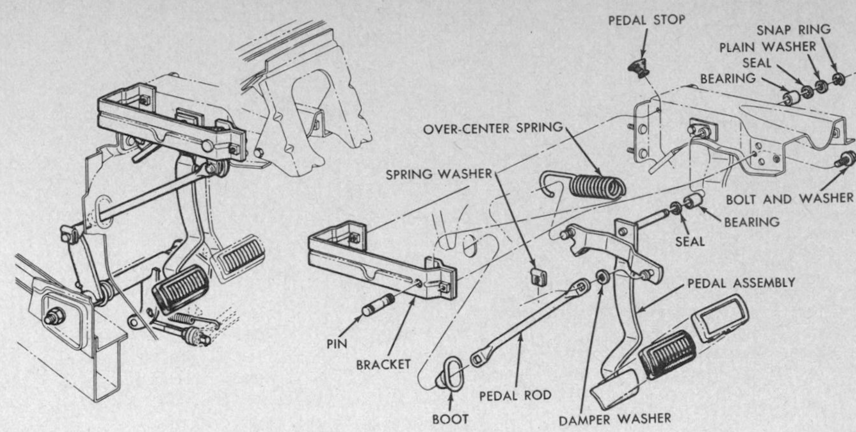

Typical clutch pedal and linkage (© Chrysler Corp)

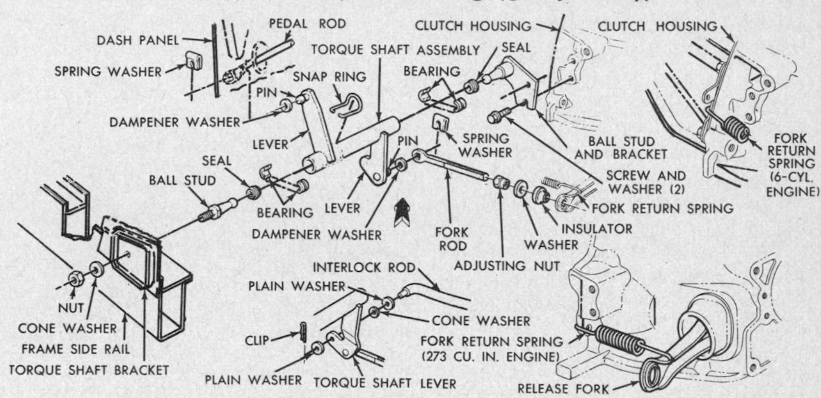

Typical clutch linkage (© Chrysler Corp)

Chrysler semi-centrifugal clutch (© Chrysler Corp)

7. Insert the release bearing and sleeve assembly into the clutch housing as far forward as possible. Lightly lubricate the fork fingers and retaining spring.
8. Insert the fork fingers under the clutch sleeve retaining springs. Retaining springs on the sleeve must have lateral freedom.
9. Make sure that the groove in the seal is properly seated in the seal opening flange in the clutch housing. Replace the pedal rod on the torque shaft lever pin and secure it with a spring washer.
10. Insert the threaded end of the fork rod assembly in the opening provided in the end of the release fork rod. Replace the eye end of the fork rod on the torque shaft lever pin and lock it with a spring washer.
11. If applicable, install the fork return spring between the release fork and the clutch housing.
12. If applicable, install the spring and plain washer with interlock rod in the torque shaft lever and lock it in position with a washer and clip.
13. When installing the transmission, be sure not to allow grease to settle on the splines or pilot end of the transmission drive pinion.
14. Install the transmission and adjust the clutch pedal free-play.

Clutch Linkage (Height and Free-Play) Adjustment

1. If the vehicle is equipped with a gearshift interlock rod, disconnect it by loosening the rod swivel clamp screw.
2. Adjust the fork rod by rotating the self-locking nut to provide

5/32 in. free-play at the fork end. This adjustment will result in the proper 1 in. free-play at the clutch pedal.

3. If the gearshift interlock was disconnected, refer to its adjustment below.

Gearshift Interlock Adjustment

1. Disconnect the interlock pawl from the clutch rod swivel.
2. Adjust the clutch pedal free-play.
3. With the first-reverse lever on the transmission in the neutral (middle detent) position, the interlock pawl should enter the slot in the first-reverse lever.
4. Loosen the swivel clamp bolt and move the swivel on the rod to enter the pawl. Install the washers with a clip. Hold the interlock pawl forward and torque the swivel clamp bolt to 100–125 in. lbs. The clutch pedal must be in the fully returned position during this adjustment.

NOTE: Under no circumstances should the clutch rod be pulled rearward to engage the pawl swivel.

5. Shift the clutch through all gear positions at least three times. Clutch action should be normal.
6. Disengage the clutch and shift halfway to first or reverse gear. The clutch should be held down by the interlock to within 1–2 in. of the floor.

MANUAL TRANSMISSION

Chrysler Corporation has used six different manual transmissions in its 1969-76 compact and sporty cars. Applications are as follows: a top cover three-speed A-745 with synchromesh on second and third only used on 1969 V8 and 6-cylinder fleet models; a top cover three-speed A-903 with synchromesh on second and third gears only used on 1969-72 6-cyliner models; a top cover three-speed A-250 with synchromesh on second and third gears only used on 1973-74 6-cylinder models; a side cover fully synchronized three-speed A-230 used on 1970-76 V8 and 6-cylinder fleet models; a top cover fully synchronized three-speed A-390 used on 1975-76 6-cylinder models; a side cover fully synchronized four-speed A-833 transmission available on all 1969-76 V8 models. The A-833 transmission was offered for both sixes and V8s with an overdrive fourth gear beginning 1975.

Removal

Top Cover Three Speed

1. Drain transmission.
2. Disconnect driveshaft at rear universal joint. Carefully pull shaft yoke out of transmission.
3. Disconnect speedometer cable, TCS switch and back up light switch.
4. Install engine support fixture or jack up engine about 1 in. and block in place.
5. Disconnect transmission extension housing from center crossmember.
6. Support transmission with jack and remove crossmember. Remove bolts that attach transmission to clutch housing.
7. Slide transmission rearward until pinion shaft clears clutch disc before lowering transmission.
8. Lower transmission and remove.

Fully Synchromesh, Side Cover Three Speed

1. Remove shift rods from transmission levers.
2. Drain transmission fluid.
3. Disconnect driveshaft at rear universal joint. Mark both parts for reassembly.
4. Carefully pull yoke out of transmission extension.
5. Disconnect speedometer cable, the TCS switch and back-up lights.
6. Remove part of exhaust if it blocks transmission.
7. Raise engine slightly and block in place.
8. Support transmission with jack, and remove crossmember.
9. Remove transmission to clutch housing bolts.
10. Slide transmission to rear until drive pinion shaft clears clutch disc, lower transmission, and remove from vehicle.

Four Speed

1. Raise vehicle on a hoist and drain transmission.
2. Disconnect all shift controls from transmission levers. Remove three bolts securing shift unit to extension housing.
3. Disconnect driveshaft at rear universal joint. Carefully pull yoke out of transmission extension.
4. Disconnect speedometer cable, TCS switch and back-up light switch leads.
5. Disconnect left exhaust pipe or dual exhausts. Disconnect parking brake cable.
6. Raise engine slightly and block in place.
7. Disconnect transmission extension from crossmember.
8. Remove crossmember.
9. Support transmission with jack. Remove clutch housing to transmission bolts.
10. Slide transmission to rear until drive pinion shaft clears clutch disc.
11. Lower transmission and remove from vehicle.

Manual Transmission Installation

Lightly grease the inner end of the pilot shaft bushing in the flywheel. In addition, grease the pinion bearing retainer pilot at the clutch release shaft.

Position the transmission so that the drive pinion is centered in the clutch housing bore. Push the transmission forward until the pinion shaft enters the clutch disc. Place the transmission in gear. Twist the output shaft until the splines are in alignment. Push the transmission forward until it is seated against the clutch housing.

Caution The transmission must not hang after the pinion is inside the clutch.

Replace the transmission coupling bolts. Torque them to 50 ft lbs. With a drift, align the crossmember bolt holes and install the bolts. Torque them to 40–50 ft lbs. Remove the engine support fixture and hooks. Install the extension housing and bolt in position. If so equipped, tighten the engine mount-to-crossmember bolt. Install and perform the gearshift linkage adjustment. Connect the driveshaft and universal joints. Connect the exhaust system and fill the transmission with an appropriate lubricant. Road-test the vehicle.

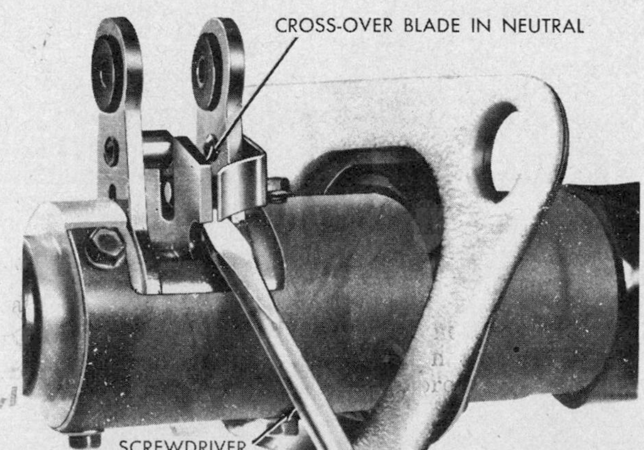

Holding cross-over blades in neutral (© Chrysler Corp)

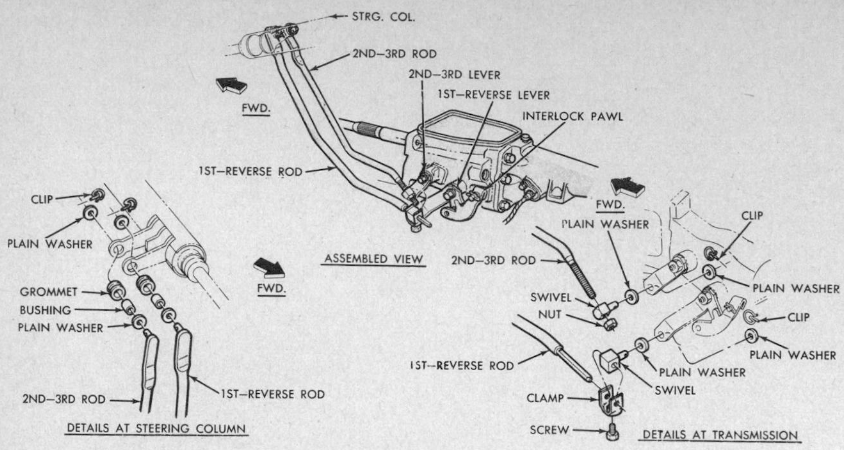

3-speed column shift linkage—1969-71 Models
(© Chrysler Corp)

Linkage Adjustment

Column Mounted 1969

1. Remove both shift rod lever swivels at the transmission levers.
2. Make sure both transmission levers are in the Neutral (middle) position.
3. Adjust the 2nd-3rd shift rod swivel so it will enter the 2nd-3rd (forward) lever at the transmission while the hand lever on the steering column is held 10° above the horizontal (neutral) position. Position the swivel in the lever and install the washer and clip and tighten the attaching nut to 70 in. lbs.
4. Place a screwdriver or other suitable tool between the cross-over blade and the 2nd-3rd lever at the base of the steering column, so that both lever pins are engaged by the cross-over blade.
5. Adjust the 1st-reverse shift rod swivel so it will freely enter the lever on the transmission. Position the swivel in the transmission lever and install the washer and clip and tighten the attaching nut to 100 in. lbs.
6. Remove the tool from the cross-over blade at the steering column and check linkage operation.

Column Mounted 1970-76

1. Remove both shift rod swivels from the transmission.
2. Make sure the transmission levers are in the Neutral (middle) position.
3. Move the shift lever on the steering column to line up the locating slots in the bottom of the steering column housing and bearing housing. Install a suitable tool in the slots and lock the ignition switch.
4. Place a screwdriver between the cross-over blade and the 2nd-3rd lever at the base of the steering column so that both lever pins are engaged by the cross-over blade.
5. Set the 1st-reverse (rear) lever on the transmission to the Reverse (forward) position.
6. Adjust the 1st-reverse rod swivel so it will freely enter the lever on the transmission. Insert the swivel into the lever on the transmission and install the washer and clip and tighten the attaching nut to 100 in. lbs.
7. Remove the tool from the slots in the steering column, unlock the ignition switch and place the shift lever on the column in the Neutral position.
8. Adjust the 2nd-3rd shift rod swivel so it will freely enter the lever on the transmission. Insert the swivel into the lever and install the washer and clip and tighten the attaching nut to 100 in. lbs.
9. Remove the tool from the cross-over blades on the steering column and check linkage operation.

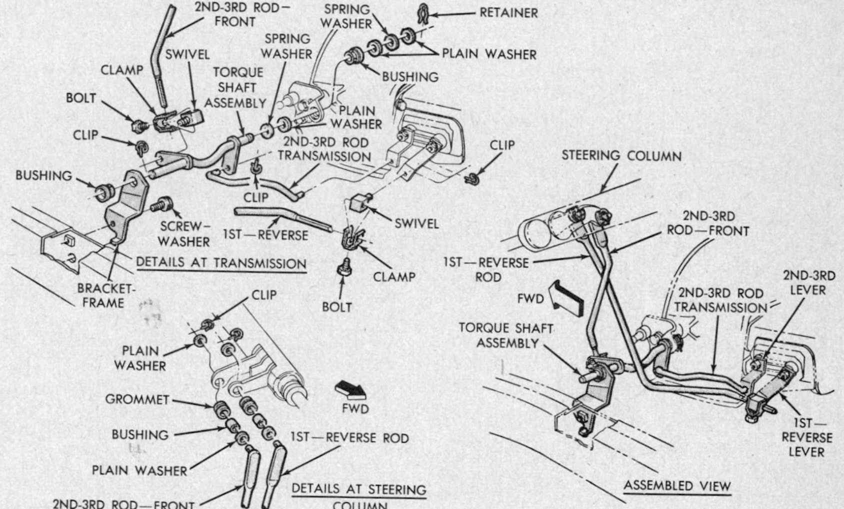

Manual three-speed linkage—1972-76 (© Chrysler Corp)

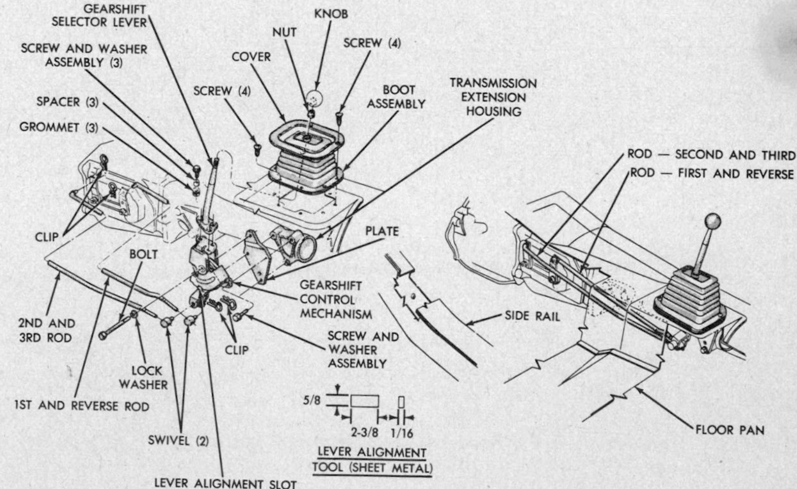

Three-speed floor shift linkage—Barracuda and Challenger; Valiant and Dart similar
(© Chrysler Corp)

Floor Mounted Three and Four Speed—1969-76

NOTE: This procedure is for Chrysler Corporation linkage only.

1. Make up a lever aligning tool from 1/16 in. thick metal or 1/4 in. diameter rod, as illustrated.
2. With transmission in neutral,

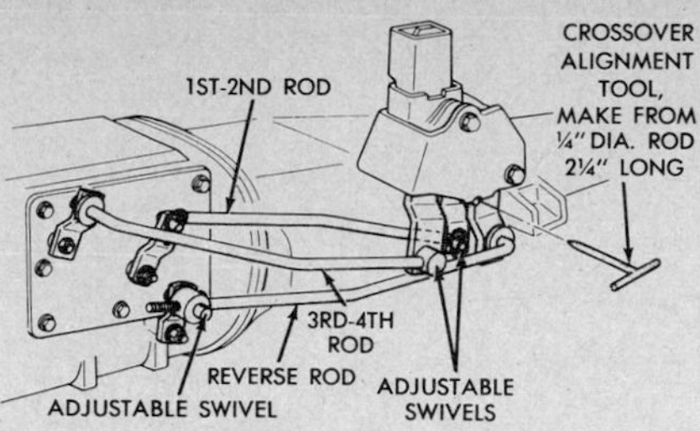

Four-speed floor shift linkage adjustment—1972-76 (© Chrysler Corp)

disconnect all control rods from the transmission levers.

3. Insert lever aligning tool through the slots in the levers, making sure it is through all the levers and against the back plate.
4. Now that all levers are locked in neutral, adjust length of control rods so they enter the transmission levers freely, without any forward or reverse movement.
5. Install control rod flat washers and retaining clips. Then, remove the aligning tool.
6. Check linkage for ease of shifting into all gears and for crossover smoothness.

AUTOMATIC TRANSMISSION

Two different transmission models are used in all models. On 1969-71 models, the model may be identified by the model number, which is embossed on the lower left side of the bell housing. On 1972 and later models, the model may be identified by the part number, which is stamped on a pad on the left side of the case oil pan flange. Generally speaking, all 6 cylinder, 273 and 318 V8 engines for normal use are equipped with a model A-904 Torqueflite, while all larger V8s use the model A-727. Fleet, police, and taxi service 6 cylinder, 273 and 318 V8 engines use the A-727 also.

The transmission combines a torque converter and a fully automatic three-speed gear system. The converter housing and transmission case are an integral aluminum casting. The transmission consists of two multiple disc clutches, an overrunning clutch, two servos and bands, and two planetary gear sets to provide three forward ratios and a reverse ratio. The common sun gear of the planetary gear sets is connected to the front clutch by a driving shell splined to the sun gear and to the front clutch retainer. The hydraulic system consists of the oil pump and a single valve body that contains all valves except the governor valve.

Cooling the converter is accomplished by circulating the transmission fluid through an oil-to-water type cooler located in the lower tank of the radiator. The torque converter assembly is a sealed unit that cannot be disassembled.

Draining, Refilling, Filter Service

For most models in normal service, the automatic transmission fluid need not be changed. However, for vehicles used in severe service, and for an extra measure of protection, fluid should be changed at 36,000 mile intervals. If the vehicle is used in competition, or for trailer towing, it is recommended that fluid be changed at 12,000 mile intervals.

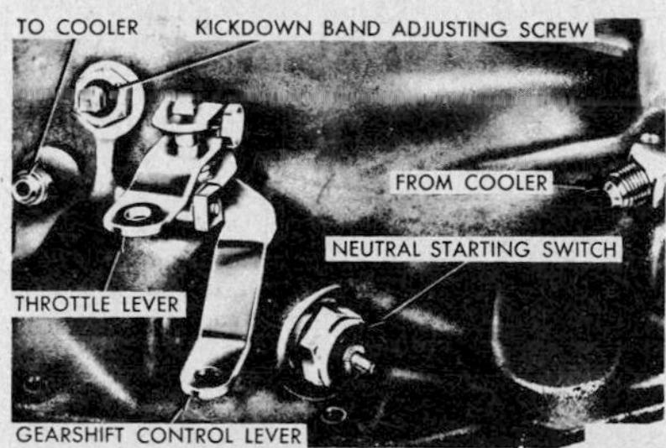

Torqueflite external controls
(© Chrysler Corp)

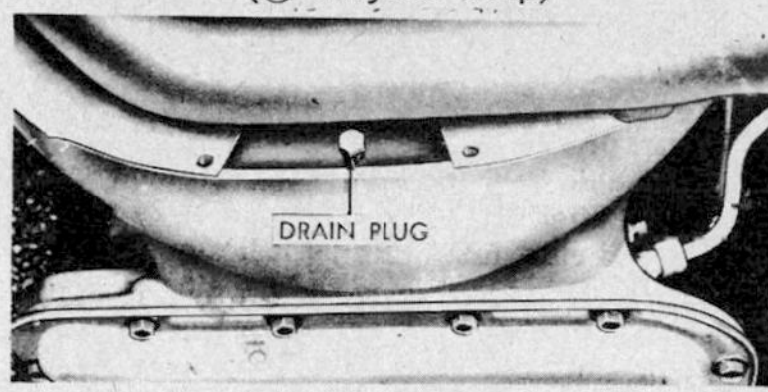

Converter drain plug
(© Chrysler Corp)

To drain the transmission fluid, raise the car on a hoist or jack up the front of the car and support it with suitable stands. Place a container, which has a large opening, under the transmission oil pan. Loosen the pan bolts at one corner, tap the pan to break the seal, and allow the fluid to drain. Remove the oil pan and filter. Remove the access plate from in front of the torque converter, with a socket wrench on the vibration damper bolt, rotate the engine clockwise to bring the converter drain to bottom. Position the container under the converter, withdraw the drainplug, and allow the fluid to drain.

Refit the converter drainplug and torque it to 110 in. lbs. Install the access plate. Place a new filter on the bottom of the valve body and tighten the retaining screws to 35 in. lbs. Clean the oil pan, fit a new gasket, and install the assembly. Torque the pan bolts to 150 in. lbs. Remove the container and lower the car.

Fill the transmission with six qt of Dexron automatic transmission fluid. Start the engine and allow it to idle for at least two minutes. With the parking brake engaged, move the selector lever momentarily to each position, ending in the neutral position. Add enough fluid to bring the level to the mark on the dipstick. Road-test the vehicle to thoroughly warm up the transmission and recheck the fluid level, with the engine idling and the parking brake engaged, after the transmission is at its normal operating temperature. The fluid level should then be between the "full" and "add one pint" marks.

Neutral Start Switch

The neutral switch is mounted in the transmission case on all models. When the transmission manual lever is placed in either the Park or Neutral position, a cam, which is attached to the transmission throttle lever inside the transmission, contacts the neutral start switch and provides a ground to complete the starter solenoid circuit. On late model compacts and intermediates, the back-up light switch has been incorporated into the neutral switch. The combination neutral and back-up light switch can be identified by the three electrical terminals on the rear of the switch. On this type of switch, the center terminal is for the neutral switch and the two outer terminals are for the back-up lights.

NOTE: in order for the neutral start switch to function properly, the transmission manual linkage must be properly adjusted and the actuator cam in the transmission must be centered in the neutral switch mounting hole in the transmission.

To remove switch, remove all wiring and, with the aid of a wrench, remove switch. Have a container of adequate size at hand to catch draining fluid. When replacing switch, be sure to use a new seal. Torque switch to 24 ft. lbs. Replace fluid.

Shift Linkage Adjustment

1969 Column Shift

1. Place the gear shift selector lever in the Park position.

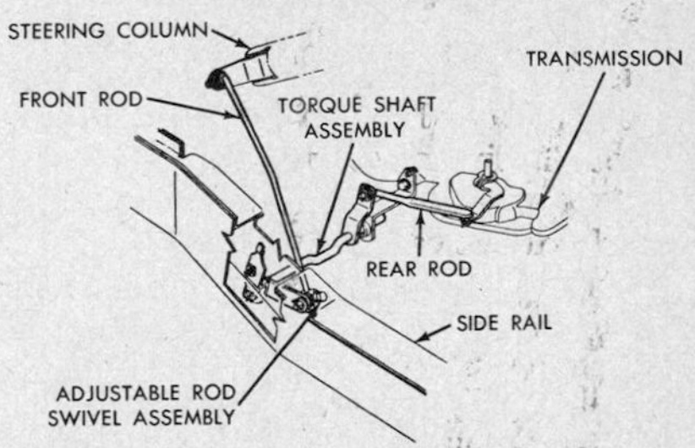

Column shift linkage—1970-74 Barracuda and Challenger (© Chrysler Corp)

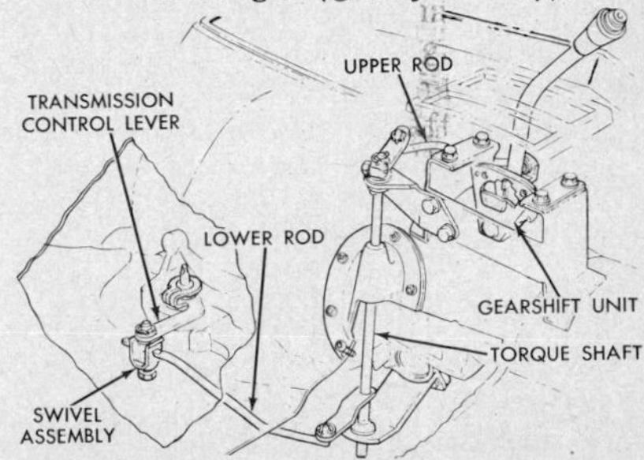

Automatic console shift linkage—1971-76 Valiant and Dart (© Chrysler Corp)

2. Loosen the transmission linkage control rod swivel clamp screw a few turns.
3. Manually move the transmission lever to the Park (rear) position.
4. With the control lever on the transmission in the Park detent and the selector lever in Park, tighten the swivel clamp screw to 100 in. lbs.

1969 Console Shift

1. With gearshift selector lever in park position, loosen bolt in lower rod adjusting lever.
2. Move transmission control lever all the way to the rear (park detent.)
3. With control lever in transmission in park position detent, and selector lever in park position, tighten the bolt in the lower rod adjusting lever securely.

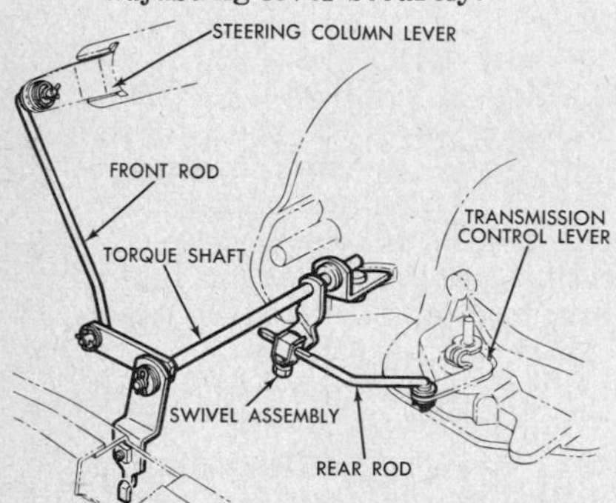

Automatic column shift linkage—1970-73 Valiant and Dart (© Chrysler Corp)

All 1970-76

1. On models equipped with a steering column lever, place the gearshift control lever in Park. Lock the steering column. On models equipped with a console-mounted shift lever, at the upper end of the steering column align the locating slots in the bottom of the shift housing and the bearing housing. Install an appropriate tool to hold this alignment and lock the steering column with the ignition key.
2. Move the gearshift control lever (located on the transmission, see neutral start switch illustration) fully rearward (in Park).
3. Position the adjustable rod to the proper length and install it with no load in any direction on the linkage. Tighten the locknut.
4. Check the adjustment by determining that the shift effort is free and the detents engage crisply. Gate stops must be positive. The position of the detents should be close enough to the gate stops in neutral and Drive so that the hand lever will slide into position when placed against the gate and then released. In addition, key starts must occur only when the transmission shift lever is in neutral or Park.

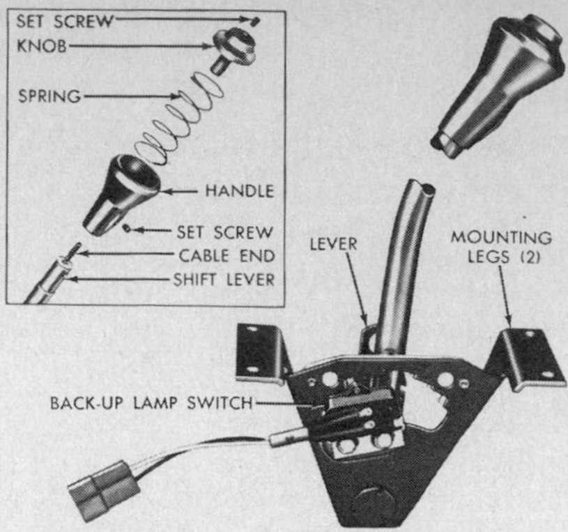

Automatic console shift unit disassembled—Valiant and Dart shown (© Chrysler Corp)

Band Adjustments

Kickdown Band

The kickdown band adjusting screw is located on the left-hand side of the transmission case near the throttle lever shaft.

1. Loosen the locknut and back off about five turns. Be sure the adjusting screw is free in the case.
2. Using an in. lbs torque wrench, torque the adjusting screw to 47–50 in. lbs. If adapter is not used, tighten adjusting screw to 72 in. lbs which is the true torque.
3. Back off the adjusting screw exactly to specification. Keep the screw from turning, and torque the locknut to specification.

Kickdown Band Adjustments

A-904	
1969-70 170 six	2⅝ turns
1969-76 198 and 225 six	2 turns
1969 273 V8	2 turns
1969-76 318 V8	2 turns
A-727	
1969-70 sixes and V8 except Hemi	2 turns
1970-71 Hemi V8 and 440-6	1½ turns
1971-76 225 six, 318, 340, 360, 383	2½ turns
1971 440 w/dual exhaust	2 turns
A-904 kickdown (1969-70) locknut torque	25 ft. lbs.
A-727 kickdown (1969-73) locknut torque	29 ft. lbs.①
A-904 (1971-73) kickdown locknut torque	29 ft. lbs.①

① 35 ft. lbs. in 1974-76

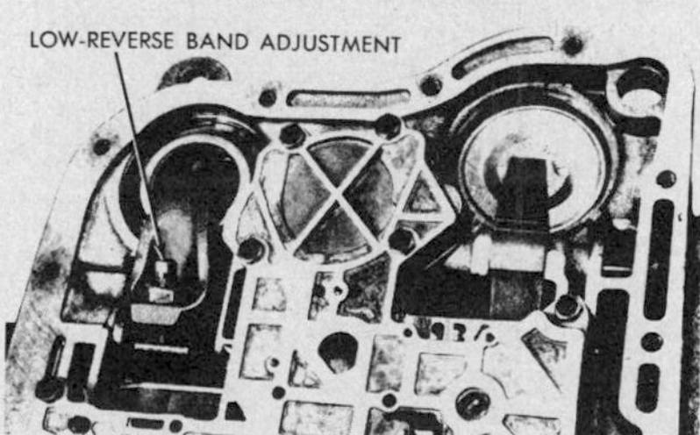

Low-Reverse band adjustment screw location (© Chrysler Corp)

Low and Reverse Band

Access to the low and reverse band requires pan removal.

1. Raise the car, drain transmission and remove the transmission oil pan.
2. Loosen the band adjusting screw locknut and back off the nut about five turns. Be sure the adjusting screw turns freely in the lever.
3. With the same tools as used on the kickdown band adjustment, tighten the adjusting screw to 47–50 in. lbs. If adapter is not used, torque to 72 in. lbs., the true torque.
4. Back off the adjusting screw exactly to specification. Keep the screw from turning and torque the locknut to specification.
5. Reinstall oil pan, using new gasket, and torque the pan bolts to 150 in. lbs.
6. Refill transmission to prescribed level.

Low and Reverse Band Screw Adjustment

A-904	
1969-73 except 318 V8	3¼ turns
1974-76 except 318 V8	7 turns
1969-76 318 V8	4 turns
Locknut torque (1969-70)	20 ft. lbs.
Locknut torque (1971-73)	35 ft. lbs.
(1974-75)	30 ft. lbs.
A-727	
1969-76	2 turns
Locknut torque	30 ft. lbs.
(1969-73)	35 ft. lbs.
(1974-76)	30 ft. lbs.

U-JOINTS

All Dodge and Plymouth vehicles use a cross and roller universal joint at both the front and rear. Two basic types of driveshafts are used: a solid tube type and a type that incorporates an internal vibration damper inside the tube itself. On certain applications, the driveshaft may be found to incorporate an inertia-type ring at the front universal joint. Servicing of all driveshafts is identical.

U-Joint Replacement

1. Raise the vehicle.
2. Mark the position of the rear driveshaft yoke in relation to the pinion flange so the driveshaft can be returned to its original location.
3. Disconnect the rear U-Joint from the pinion flange and remove the loose bearing caps. Pull the driveshaft rearward until it clears the transmission extension housing. Remove the driveshaft from the car.
4. Place the driveshaft in a vise and remove the snap-rings from the U-Joint to be removed.
5. Using a suitable tool, drive one of the bearing caps on the U-Joint to be removed toward the center of the driveshaft.

6. Remove the opposite bearing cap from the one being driven as it emerges from the driveshaft.
7. Repeat Step 6 until all bearing caps have been removed.
8. Remove the U-Joint spider from the driveshaft.
9. To install, position the spider in the driveshaft and drive the bearing caps onto the spider.
10. Install the snap-rings in the driveshaft.
11. Reinstall the driveshaft in its original location in the car.

REAR AXLE

Four different rear axle assemblies have been used. A 7¼ in. (ring gear diameter) unitized carrier axle is used with all six cylinder applications and on some late production 318 V8 models. An 8¼ in. unitized carrier axle is installed in most mid 1972 and later models with 318, 340, or 360 V8s. An 8¾ in. removable differential carrier axle is used on models through 1974 with 273, 318, 340, or 383 engines. A 9¾ in. unitized carrier axle is installed in 1970-71 Barracuda and Challenger models equipped with the high-performance 426 Hemi or 440 V8s.

These axles can be visually identified as follows:
The 7¼ in. axle has a 9 bolt rear cover with a filler plug. The 8¼ in. has a 10 bolt rear cover without a filler plug. The 8¾ in. has a welded rear cover. The 9¾ in. has a 10 bolt rear cover with a filler plug.

Axle Shaft, Bearing, and Seal

Removal and Installation

Because the axle shafts are slightly different from one rear axle assembly to another, individual service procedures are required for each axle shaft assembly. Two very important points to remember when servicing any rear axle assembly are:

1. Always elevate *both* rear wheels when performing any rear axle service, or when using the engine or other means to rotate the axle.

2. On those cars that are equipped with a Sure-Grip differential, you must never rotate one axle shaft without rotating the other. If it is necessary to rotate one of the axle shafts, *both* shafts must be in position and both must be rotated. Otherwise, alignment of the axle shafts will be very difficult.

7¼ In. Axle

NOTE: *Whenever this axle assembly is serviced, both the brake support plate gaskets and the inner axle shaft oil seal must be renewed.*

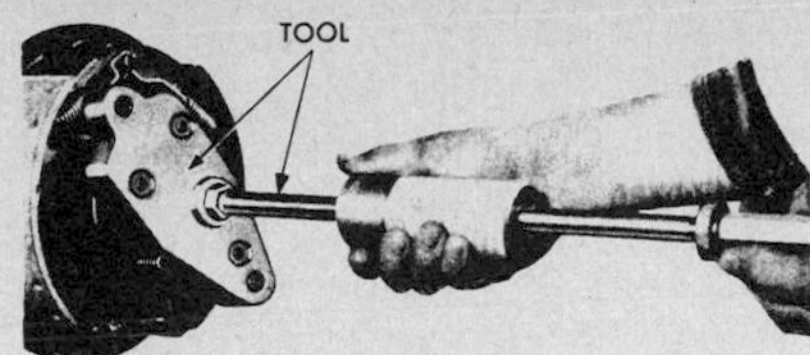

Removing axle shaft (© Chrysler Corp)

1. Support the rear of the car and remove the rear wheels.
2. Detach the clips which secure the brake drum to the axle shaft studs and remove the brake drum.
3. Disconnect the brake lines at the wheel cylinders and block off the lines.
4. Through the access hole in the axle shaft flange, remove the axle shaft retaining nuts.
5. Attach a suitable puller to the axle shaft flange and remove the axle shaft.
6. Remove the brake assembly from the axle housing.
7. Remove the axle shaft oil seal from the axle housing.

CAUTION: *Never use a torch or other heat source as an aid in removing any axle shaft components as this will result in serious damage to the axle assembly.*

8. Place the axle shaft housing retaining collar in a vise. With a chisel, cut deeply into the retaining collar at 90° intervals.
9. To assemble and install the axle shaft, replace the retainer plate bearing, and bearing retainer collar on the axle shaft, using a suitable press or puller.
10. Insert new axle shaft oil seals in the axle housing and lightly grease the outside diameter of the bearing.
11. Replace the foam gasket on the studs of the axle housing and install the brake support plate assembly on the axle housing studs. Refit the outer gasket.
12. Very carefully slide the axle shaft assembly through the oil seal and engage the splines of the differential slide gear. Using a non-metallic hammer, lightly tap the end of the axle shaft to position the axle shaft bearing in the recess of the axle housing. Install the retainer plate over the axle housing studs and torque the securing nuts to 35 ft lbs.
13. Reconnect the brake lines to the wheel cylinders and bleed the hydraulic system.
14. Install the brake drum and retaining clips.
15. Refit the rear wheels and lower the car.

8¼ In. Axle

1. Raise the vehicle and remove the wheels. Drain the oil from the rear axle.
2. Remove the differential cover, if not already removed.
3. Remove the differential pinion shaft lockscrew and the differential pinion shaft.
4. Push the flanged end of the axle shaft toward the center of the vehicle and remove the C-lock from the end of the shaft.
5. Remove the axle shaft from the housing being careful not to damage the oil seal. The axle shaft may not slide easily out of the housing. If so, obtain an axle puller.
6. The axle bearing will come out with the axle and will have to be replaced at an automotive repair shop.
7. Pry the axle seal loose from the bore and tap a new seal into place.
8. Installation is the reverse of removal. Use new gaskets for reassembly.

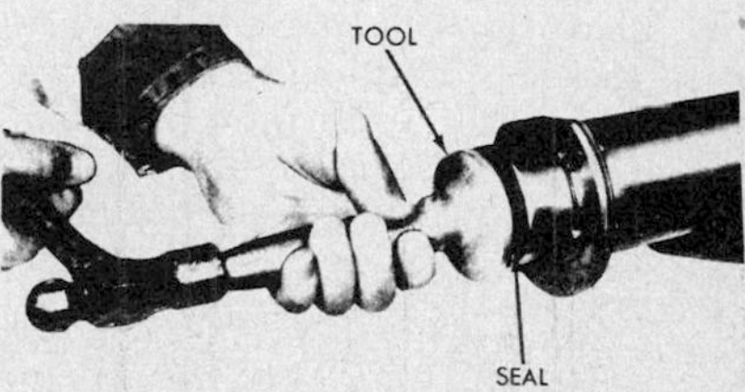

Installing axle shaft seal (© Chrysler Corp)

NOTE: *Mid 1972 and later models with an 8¼ in. axle no longer use a paper gasket under the rear axle cover. Instead of the paper gasket, a bead of gel type non sticking sealant is now used in production. The sealant should be applied as follows:*

1. Scrape away any remains of the paper gasket.
2. Clean the cover surface with mineral spirits. Any axle lubricant on the cover or axle housing will prevent the sealant from taking.
3. Apply a 1/16–3/32 in. bead of sealant to the clean, dry, cover flange. Apply the bead in a continuous bead along the bolt circle of the cover, looping inside the bolt holes.
4. Allow the sealant to air dry.
5. Clean the carrier gasket flange and air dry. Install the cover. If, for any reason, the cover is not installed within 20 minutes of applying the sealant, remove the sealant and start over.

8 ¾ and 9¾ In. Axles

NOTE: *Whenever this axle assembly is serviced, both the brake support plate gaskets and the inner axle shaft oil seal must be renewed.*

1. Jack up the rear of the car and remove the rear wheels.
2. Detach the clips which secure the brake drum to the axle shaft studs, and remove the brake drum.
3. Through the access hole in the axle shaft flange, remove the axle shaft retaining nuts. The right-side axle shaft has a threaded adjuster in the retain-

er plate and a lock under one of its studs which should be removed at this time.

4. Remove the parking brake strut.
5. Attach a suitable puller to the axle shaft.
6. Remove the brake assembly from the axle housing.
7. Remove the axle shaft oil seal from the axle housing.

CAUTION: *It is advisable to position some sort of a protective sleeve over the axle shaft seal surface next to the bearing collar to protect the seal surface. Never use a torch or other heat source as an aid in removing any axle shaft components as this will result in serious damage to the axle assembly.*

8. Wipe the axle housing seal bore clean. Install a new axle shaft oil seal.
9. Place the axle shaft housing retaining collar in a vise. With a chisel, cut deeply into the retaining collar at 90° intervals. Remove the bearing with a suitable puller.
10. Remove the bearing roller retainer flange by cutting off the lower edge with a chisel.
11. Grind or file a section off the flange of the inner bearing cone and remove the bearing rollers.
12. Pull the bearing roller retainer down as far as possible and cut it off with side cutters.
13. Remove the roller bearing cup with its protective sleeves.
14. To prevent damage to the seal journal when the bearing cone is removed, protect the journal with a single wrap of shim stock that is 0.002 in. thick and is held in place by a rubber band.
15. Using a suitable puller, remove the bearing cone. Remove the seal in the bearing retainer plate and replace it with a new seal.
16. To assemble the axle, first install the retainer plate and seal assembly on the axle shaft.
17. Grease the wheel bearing and install them.
18. Install a new axle shaft bearing cup, cone and collar on the shaft by using a suitable puller. Check the axle shaft seal journal for imperfections and if necessary, polish with no. 600 crocus cloth.
19. Thoroughly clean the axle housing flange face and brake support. Install a new rubber/asbestos gasket onto the axle housing studs. Next, install the brake support plate assembly on the left side of the axle housing.
20. Lightly grease the outside edge of the bearing cup. Install the bearing cup in the bearing bore.
21. Replace the foam gasket on the studs of the left-side axle housing and very carefully slide the axle shaft assembly through the oil seal and engage the splines of the differential side gear.
22. Using a non-metallic hammer, lightly tap the end of the axle shaft to position the axle shaft bearing in the recess of the axle housing. Install the retainer plate over the axle housing studs and, starting with the bottom securing nut, torque the nuts to 30–35 ft lbs.
23. Repeat step 19 for the right-side axle housing.
24. At the right side of the axle housing, back off the threaded adjuster until the inner face of the adjuster is flush with the inner face of the retainer plate. Very carefully slide the axle shaft assembly through the oil seal and engage the splines of the differential side gear. Repeat step 22.
25. Mount a dial indicator on the left brake support. Turn the adjuster clockwise until both wheel bearings are seated and there is zero end-play in the axle shafts. Back off the adjuster about four notches to establish an end-play of 0.008-0.018 in. on 8¾ in. axles and 0.008-0.012 for the 9¾.
26. Lightly tap the end of the left shaft with a non-metallic hammer. This will seat the right wheel bearing cup against the adjuster. Turn the axle shaft several times so that a true end-play reading is obtained.
27. Remove one retainer plate nut and install the adjuster lock. If the lock tab does not mate with the notch in the adjuster, turn the adjuster slightly until it does. Refit the nut and torque it to 30–35 ft lbs.
28. Recheck the axle shaft end-play. If it is not within 0.008–0.018 in., repeat the adjustment. When the adjustment is complete, remove the dial indicator.
29. Install the parking brake strut. Refit the brake drum and retaining clips.
30. Install the rear wheels and lower the car.

JACKING, HOISTING

Jack car at front control arms and at rear under axle housing.

To lift at frame use adapters, so that contact will be made at points shown. Lifting pads must extend beyond sides of supporting structure.

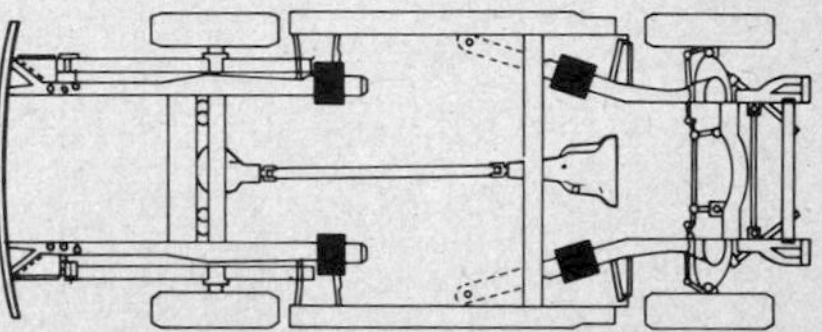

Positioning lift adapter (© Chrysler Corp)

FRONT SUSPENSION

All Chrysler vehicles utilize a torsion bar type front suspension. On Valiant, Dart, Barracuda and Challenger models, a pair of longitudinally mounted torsion bars are mounted between the lower control arms and the engine rear support crossmember.

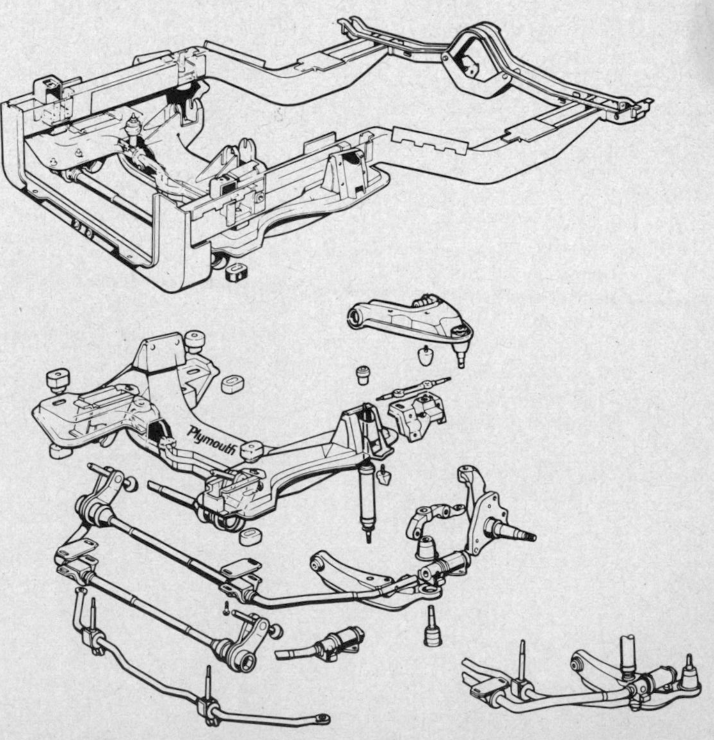

1976 Aspen, Volare isolated front suspension including transverse torsion bar (© Chrysler Corp)

On Volare and Aspen models, a pair of transverse mounted torsion bars are installed ahead of the front wheels, between the lower control arms and the opposite front subframe member. With the transverse setup, the lower control arm stabilizing struts are eliminated. On both types, conventional telescopic shock absorbers, upper and lower control arms, and compression type ball joints are used. A spring steel front stabilizer bar is standard equipment on all Volare and Aspen models, and optional on other models.

Lubrication

Balloon-type and semi-permanently lubricated steering linkage and front suspension ball joints are used. Relubrication at these points is required at about 36,000 miles, or three year periods (whichever comes first.) However, the balloon seals should be inspected for leaks, or other damage, two or three times a year.

When lubricating these points, use only multi-mileage long-life chassis grease. Remove the threaded plug from each joint to be lubricated, and temporarily install lube fittings. Inject lubricant, while feeling the seal with the fingers. Stop just before the seal starts to balloon. Remove lube fittings and reinstall plugs.

Shock Absorber Removal and Replacement

1. Remove the washer and nut from shock absorber upper end. Be sure to note the positions of all small parts.
2. Jack the vehicle until the wheels clear the floor. Remove the shock absorber lower attaching bolt. Allow the control arm mounting bracket to lower itself.
3. Fully compress the shock absorber by pushing upward. Pull the shock firmly and remove it from the vehicle.
4. Fully compress the new shock absorber. Insert the mount through the upper bushing and install the retainer and nut. Torque to specifications. Be sure that all the retainers are installed with the concave side in contact with rubber.
5. Position and align the lower mount of shock absorber. Install the bolt (on some models it must be installed from the rear) with nut and finger-tighten it. Lower the vehicle and torque to specifications with the full weight of the vehicle on the wheels.

Wheel Bearing Adjustment

1969-72

1. Raise the front of the car and remove the hub caps and grease caps from the front wheels. Remove the cotter pin from the spindle and remove the adjusting nut lock.
2. The wheel must be rotated while the bearing adjusting nut is tightened. For all Dart and Valiant models and 1969 Barracudas the adjusting nut should be tightened to 70 in. lbs.
3. Place the lock over the nut so that one pair of slots aligns with the cotter pin hole.
4. Back the nut and lock assembly off one slot. Install the cotter pin. This adjustment should yield 0.0–0.003 in. end-play.
5. Clean the grease cap. Coat, but do not fill, the cap with grease. Install it on the hub.
6. Lower the car and road-test it

1973-76

1. Jack up or hoist the car, so that the front wheels are off the floor.
2. Remove the hub caps, grease cup, cotter pin and nut lock.
3. Back off on the adjusting nut.
4. Check for free wheel rotation. If binding is present, repair the threads as required.
5. While rotating the wheel, tighten the wheel bearing adjustment nut to 240–300 in. lbs.
6. Release the torque. Retighten the nut so that it is finger tight.
7. Position the nut lock so that one pair of slots is in line with the cotter pin hole and install the cotter pin.
8. Install the rest of the items removed. Repeat the procedure for the other wheel and lower the car.

Front Height Adjustment

1969-74

1. Jounce the car and measure from the lowest point, at the centerline, of the lower ball joint to the floor (measurement B).

Measuring the front suspension height—1969-74 Valiant and Dart. Other cars are similar. (© Chrysler Corp)

2. Measure from the lowest area of the torsion bar adjusting blade to the floor (measurement A).
3. Subtract B from A. This is the front end height.
4. Measure the other side in the same way. Compare figures obtained with figure given in the wheel alignment specifications table in the front of this section.
5. Adjust, if necessary, by turning the torsion bar adjusting bolt, in to raise; out to lower.

1975-76

Except Volare and Aspen

1. Jounce the car several times, releasing it in the downward motion.
2. Measure the distance between the lowest point of the lower control arm torsion bar anchor (at a point one inch forward of the rear face of the anchor) and the ground. This is measurement "A".
3. Compare measurement "A" with the figure given under "Front End Height" in the "wheel Alignment Specifications" chart at the beginning of this car section.
4. Adjust, if necessary, by rotating clockwise to increase front end height, or rotating counterclockwise to decrease the height.
5. Check the adjustment on both sides. Maximum variation of front end height is ⅛ in.

Torsion Bars

Except Volare and Aspen

Contrary to appearance, the torsion bars are not interchangeable from right to left. They are marked with an R or an L, according to their location.

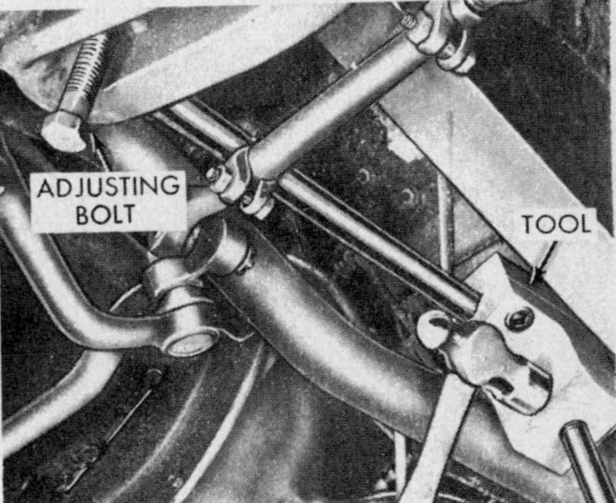

Removing torsion bar (© Chrysler Corp)

Removal

1. Remove the upper control arm rebound bumper before raising the car.
2. Lift the car, by the body, high enough to free the front suspension of all load. If the car is to be raised with jacks, place jack under center of K-member and raise until suspension is free of all load.
3. Release load from torsion bar by backing off anchor adjusting nuts. Remove the adjusting nut and swivel bolt.
4. Remove the lower control arm strut, if necessary.
5. Remove the lock spring from the rear of torsion bar rear anchor. Remove the automatic transmission torque shaft on 1974-75

models.

6. Install tool or clamp, and remove torsion bar rearward by striking the clamping tool with a hammer.

NOTE: do not apply heat to the front or rear anchors. Do not scratch or otherwise mar the skin of the torsion bar during removal or installation.

7. Remove the clamping tool and slide the rear anchor balloon seal off the front end of the bar.
8. Remove torsion bar by sliding the bar rearward and out through the rear anchor.

Installation

1. Clean the hex openings of both front and rear anchors, also clean the male ends of the torsion bar.
2. Feed the torsion bar through the rear anchor.
3. Slide the balloon-type seal over the torsion bar, with the large cupped side of the seal facing the rear.
4. Coat both ends of the torsion bar with multi-purpose grease.
5. When starting the bar into the anchor in the lower control arm, position the adjusting arm about 60° below the horizontal plane. This will permit windup for future adjustment.
6. Position the lock-ring into the rear anchor, then move torsion bar rearward until the bar contacts the lock-ring.
7. Pack the annular opening in the rear anchor with multi-purpose grease. Slide the rear anchor balloon type seal into position over the rear anchor until the lip of the seal fits in the groove.
8. Position swivel bolt on the control arm and hold in place while installing the adjusting nut and seat. Tighten the adjustment about ten turns before lowering car to the floor.
9. Install lower control arm strut.
10. Lower car to the floor and adjust front suspension height.

Upper and Lower Ball Joints

See Dodge-Plymouth section.

REAR SUSPENSION

All Dodge and Plymouth models utilize rear springs of the semi-elliptical leaf type. They are engineered to operate with little or no camber under conditions of small or no load. Heavy-duty springs are offered as an option on all models. They serve to increase the stability of the vehicle under conditions of heavy load. All vehicles with leaf springs are constructed with zinc interleaves between the normal leaves. They have the purpose of reducing spring corrosion and lengthening spring life.

Shock absorbers used on Chrysler vehicles are not utilized to support vehicle load. Their sole purpose is to control ride motion.

Chrysler shock absorbers have a built-in fluid weep. This is usually evident only during cold weather. Consequently, a slight fluid weep is not reason to replace a shock absorber.

Rear Shock Absorbers

Removal and Installation

1. Jack the vehicle under the axle assembly in such a manner as to relieve load from the shock absorbers.
2. Remove the nut attaching the shock to the spring mounting plate stud and withdraw the bolt.
3. At the upper mount, remove the shock attaching bolt and the shock.
4. To install the shock, position it so the upper bolt may be inserted. Hand-tighten only.
5. Align the shock with the spring mounting plate stud and install the bolt and nut. Hand-tighten only.
6. Lower the vehicle and tighten the shock absorber mounting bolts.

Rear Springs

Removal and Installation

1. Jack the vehicle and remove the wheels. Position jack stands under the axle in such a manner so as to relieve weight from the rear springs.
2. Disconnect the rear shock absorbers at the bottom attaching bolts. Lower the axle assembly to allow the rear springs to hang free. Disconnect the rear sway bar links, if so equipped.
3. Remove U-bolt nuts and withdraw bolts and spring plates. Remove the nuts securing the front spring hanger to the body mounting bracket.
4. Remove the rear spring hanger bolts and allow the spring to drop enough to allow the front spring hanger bolts to be removed. On the Barracuda and Challenger, loosen and remove the rear shackle nuts and plate and remove the shackle.
5. Remove the front pivot bolt from the front spring hanger.
6. Remove the shackle nuts and shackle from the rear spring.
7. To begin installation, assemble the shackle and bushings in the rear of the spring and hanger. Start the shackle bolt nut. Do not lubricate rubber bushings to ease installation. Do not tighten the bolt nut.
8. Install the front spring hanger to the front spring eye and insert the pivot bolt and nut. Do not tighten them.
9. Install the rear spring hanger-to-body bracket and torque the bolts to 35–40 ft lbs.
10. With the aid of a helper, raise the spring and insert the bolts in the spring hanger mounting bracket holes. Install the nuts and torque them to 30 ft lbs.
11. Position the axle assembly so it is correctly aligned with the spring center bolt.
12. Position the center bolt over the lower spring plate. Insert the U-bolt and nut. Connect the rear shock absorbers.
13. Lower the vehicle. Torque the pivot bolts to 85 ft lbs and tighten the shackle nuts.

BRAKES

A dual (tandem) master cylinder is used. In operation, this type master cylinder provides braking even if one section of the system should develop a leak.

Both drum and disc type brake systems are hydraulically operated. Power assist is offered as an option.

With the exception of heavy-duty fleet units, brakes are self-adjusting.

Beginning 1973, front disc brakes are standard on all models with the exception of six-cylinder Valiants and Darts.

Master Cylinder

Removal and Installation

1. Disconnect the brake lines from the master cylinder. If equipped

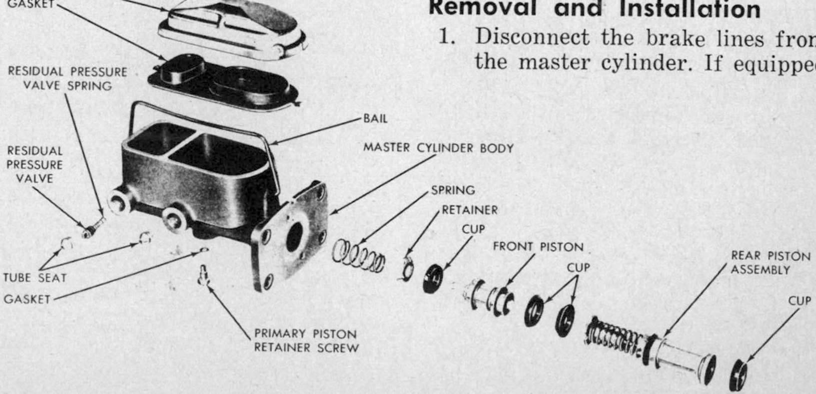

Dual type master cylinder (disc brakes) (© Chrysler Corp)

with disc brakes, plug the rear brake line outlet to prevent fluid loss.
2. Remove the nuts that attach the master clyinder to the cowl panel or brake booster.
3. On models with standard brakes, it is not necessary to disconnect the master cylinder pushrod from the brake pedal.
4. Slide the master cylinder straight out and off the cowl panel or brake booster.
5. Reverse above procedure to install and bleed brake system.

Power Brake Booster Removal and Installation

1. Remove the nuts that attach the master cylinder to the brake booster and position the master cylinder out of the way without disconnecting the lines. Use care not to kink the brake lines.
2. Disconnect the vacuum hose from the brake booster.
3. Working under the dash, remove the nut and bolt that attaches the brake booster pushrod to the brake pedal. On linkage type brake boosters, remove the lower pivot retaining bolt.
4. Remove the four brake booster attaching nuts and washers.
5. Remove booster assembly from the vehicle.
6. Reverse above procedure to install.

Parking Brake Adjustment

1. Release the parking brake lever and clean and lubricate the parking brake cable adjusting nut and threads. Loosen the cable adjusting nut.
2. Tighten the cable adjusting nut until a slight drag is felt in the rear wheels when the rear wheels are rotated. Loosen the cable adjusting nut until the rear wheels can be rotated freely. Back off the cable adjusting nut two additional turns.
3. Apply and release the parking brake several times and check to verify that the rear wheels rotate freely, without any brake drag.

STEERING

A worm and recirculating ball type steering gear is used with the manual steering system.

The worm shaft is supported at each end by ball-type thrust bearings.

The sector shaft includes an integral sector gear which meshes with helical grooves on the worm shaft ball nut.

The sector shaft is supported, and rotates, in two needle bearings in the housing and one in the housing cover.

Constant-Control power steering is an option on all models. Hydraulic power is provided by a vane type, belt-driven pump. A double-groove pump pulley is used.

Some power steering pumps were equipped from the factory with oil coolers. These were used on vehicles with high-performance engines and/or special axle ratios.

Power Steering Pump Removal and Installation

NOTE: Before beginning removal, take careful note of exact hose routine. Hoses must be routed and installed in the exact same manner as they were removed. Read the entire procedure before beginning pump service.

1. Back off the pump mounting and locking bolts, and remove the pump drive belt.
2. Disconnect all hoses at the pump.
3. Remove the pump bolts and pump with the bracket.
4. To install the pump, place the pump in position and install the mounting bolts.
5. Install the pump drive belt and adjust to specifications. Torque the mounting bolts to 25–30 ft lbs.
6. Connect the pressure and return hoses. On the 1.06 cu in. pump, install a new pressure hose O-ring.
7. Fill the pump with power steering fluid.
8. Turn the vehicle on and rotate the steering wheel from stop to stop at least 10 times. This will tend to bleed the system. Check the pump oil level and fill as required.
9. The pump end hose fitting torque is 24-30 ft lbs. The gear end fitting torque is 16 in. lbs. Be certain the hoses are at least 2 in. from the exhaust manifolds and are not kinked or twisted.

Steering Wheel Removal and Installation

1. Disconnect the negative battery cable.
2. Remove the horn ring ornament assembly.
3. Disconnect the wire from the horn switch. Remove the screws that attach the horn ring and switch to the steering wheel and remove the ring and switch.
4. Remove the steering wheel attaching nut(s) and washer(s) and, using a puller, remove the steering wheel from the steering shaft. On models equipped with a collapsible steering column cylinder, remove the cylinder attaching nut and remove the cylinder from the column.
5. To install the steering wheel, reverse the removal procedure.

Turn Signal Switch Removal and Installation

1. Disconnect the battery and remove the steering wheel.
2. Disconnect the horn and turn signal wires.
3. Tie a piece of string to the turn signal wires. Remove the turn signal switch screws while holding the other end of the string to prevent the wires from falling inside the steering column.
4. Remove the turn signal switch retainer ring and extract the switch.
5. To install the turn signal switch, reverse the removal procedure.

INSTRUMENT PANEL

Headlight Switch Removal and Installation

1969 All Models and 1970-76 Valiant and Dart

1. Remove the fuse box attaching screw and position the fuse box out of the way.
2. Press the release button on the body of the headlight switch and pull the control knob and shaft from the switch.
3. Disconnect the multiple connector from the rear of the headlight switch.
4. Remove the bezel nut that attaches the headlight switch to the dash and remove the switch.
5. Reverse above procedure to install.

1970-74 Barracuda and Challenger

1. Disconnect the negative battery cable.
2. Remove the six lamp panel mounting screws and carefully slide the lamp panel out of the dash and lay it on top of the instrument panel. It is not necessary to disconnect the wiring harness.
3. Remove the four switch bezel mounting screws. Carefully slide the switch bezel out and to the right, overlapping the center instrument cluster, then lower it until it is free of the instrument panel and disconnect the wiring harness.
4. Remove the two headlight switch mounting screws and remove the switch from the bezel assembly.
5. Install in reverse order.

Ignition Switch Removal and Installation

1969 All Models

1. Disconnect the multiple connector from the rear of the switch.

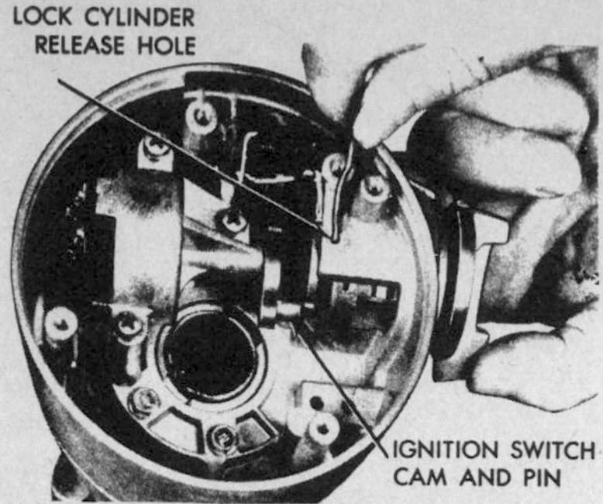

Lock cylinder removal
(© Chrysler Corp)

2. Remove the bezel nut that attaches the ignition switch to the dash and remove the switch.
3. Reverse procedure to install.

Ignition Lock Cylinder Removal and Installation

1969

1. Insert the ignition key into the lock cylinder.
2. Insert a piece of stiff wire into the small hole in the front face of the cylinder and apply pressure to the wire.
3. Turn the ignition key counterclockwise toward the "acc" position.
4. Pull the lock cylinder and key from the instrument panel.
5. Insert a new lock cylinder into the instrument panel and it will lock itself in place.

Ignition Switch and/or Ignition Lock Cylinder Removal and Installation

1970-76 Standard Steering Column

1. Disconnect the negative battery cable. Remove the steering wheel.
2. Remove the screw that attaches the turn signal lever to the steering column.
3. Remove the three screws that attach the upper bearing retainer to the turn signal switch.
4. Pull the turn signal switch as far upward as possible.
5. Using snap-ring pliers, remove the upper bearing housing snapring from the steering shaft.
6. Remove the screw that attaches the ignition key light assembly to the upper bearing housing.
7. Using care not to damage any components, pry the upper bearing housing off the steering shaft by lifting upward on alternate sides of the bearing housing with screwdrivers.
8. Lift upward as far as possible on the steering shaft lockplate and place a screwdriver or other object under it to hold it in the raised position. If this operation does not provide adequate working room under the lockplate, it will be necessary to press out the pin that attaches the lockplate to the steering shaft and remove the lockplate from the steering shaft. If the ignition switch is being replaced, the lockplate must be removed.
9. Using an offset screwdriver, remove the two screws that attach the lock lever guide plate to the steering column.
10. With the ignition lock cylinder in the "lock" position and the ignition key removed, insert a stiff wire into the lock cylinder release hole in the steering column. Push in on the wire to release the spring-loaded lock retainer and pull the lock cylinder out of the steering column.
11. If the ignition switch is being replaced, remove the two screws that attach the ignition key buzzer switch to the steering column and the three screws that attach the ignition switch to the steering column. Lift the ignition switch out of the housing.
12. Reverse the above procedure for installation.

1970-76 Tilt Steering Column

1. Disconnect the negative battery cable.
2. Remove the steering wheel.
3. Remove the three attaching screws and the shaft lock cover.
4. Remove the screws that attach the tilt control lever and the turn signal lever to the steering column and remove the levers.
5. Push the hazard warning knob in and unscrew the knob from the turn signal switch. Remove the ignition key lamp assembly.
6. Using a suitable tool, depress the lockplate to gain access to the lockplate retaining snap-ring. Remove the snap-ring from the steering shaft.
7. Remove the lockplate, cancelling cam, and spring.
8. Remove the three turn signal switch attaching screws, place the shift lever in the low (1) position, and pull the switch and wires as far upward as possible.
9. With the ignition lock cylinder in the "lock" position, insert a small screwdriver into the lock release slot in the housing cover.
10. Press down with the screwdriver to release the spring latch at bottom of the slot and pull the lock cylinder from the housing. The following steps are for ignition switch replacement only.
11. Remove the three screws that attach the upper steering column housing to the steering column and remove the housing.
12. Install the column tilt control lever and move the column to the full "up" position.
13. Insert a screwdriver into the slot in the spring retainer and press the retainer in approximately 3/16 in. Turn the retainer approximately 1/8 turn to the left until the ears align with the grooves in the housing. Remove the spring retainer, spring, and guide.
14. Push the steering shaft inward to enable removal of the inner race and seat. Remove the race and seat.
15. Make sure the ignition switch is in the "lock" position, then remove the wire connector from the ignition switch and remove the screws that attach the ignition switch to the outside of the steering column.
16. Lift the ignition switch from the column and twist it to disengage the switch actuating rod from the rack. Remove the switch.
17. To install the ignition lock cylinder, insert the cylinder into the housing with the cylinder in the lock position and the key removed.
18. Move the cylinder into the housing until it contacts the switch actuator. Move the switch actuator rod up and down to align the parts. When the parts are aligned the cylinder will move inward and lock into place. The following steps are for ignition switch installation only.
19. With the ignition switch in the "lock" position, insert the actuating rod into the steering column.
20. Twist the switch and rod assembly as required to engage the actuating rod with the rack. Make sure the ignition lock cylinder is in the "lock" position.
21. Install the ignition switch mounting screws but do not tighten them.
22. Move the ignition switch downward away from the steering wheel and tighten the switch mounting screws. Make sure the ignition switch has not moved out of the lock detent.
23. Attach the switch wiring connector.

WINDSHIELD WIPERS

Motor Removal

1969-76 Valiant and Dart and 1969 Barracuda

1. Disconnect battery.
2. Disconnect wiper motor wiring harness.
3. Remove three wiper motor mounting nuts. On vehicles without air conditioning it is easier to remove crank arm nut and crank arm from under instru-

ment panel first and omit steps 4 and 5. On 1968 models, disconnect the drive link from the left wiper pivot.

4. Work motor off mounting studs far enough to gain access to crank arm mounting nuts.

CAUTION: Do not force or pry motor from mounting studs as drive link can be easily distorted.

5. Using ½ in. open end wrench, remove motor crank arm nut. Carefully pry arm off shaft.
6. Remove wiper motor.

1970-74 Barracuda and Challenger

1. Disconnect battery.
2. Carefully remove wiper arm and blade assemblies.
3. Remove left cowl screen.
4. Remove drive crank arm retaining nut and drive crank. Disconnect wiring to motor.
5. Remove three wiper motor mounting nuts and remove motor.

Linkage Removal

1969-76 Valiant, Dart, and 1969 Barracuda

1. Disconnect battery.
2. If air conditioning equipped, remove duct supplying left spot cooler to provide easier access to left wiper pivot. Insert wide blade screwdriver between plastic link bushing and pivot crank arm. Gently twist screwdriver to force bushing and link from pivot pin. Remove three motor mounting nuts, pull motor away from bulkhead and remove motor crank arm retaining nut. Hold the motor crank when removing the nut to prevent stressing the gears. After crank arm is removed from motor shaft, remove drive link assembly from under left side of panel. Remove motor drive crank arm retaining nut and pry crank arm off motor shaft. Gently pry drive link and bushing from left pivot crank arm pin and withdraw assembly from under panel. Remove motor drive crank arm from drive link after removal of assembly from vehicle.
3. To remove connecting link from pivots, remove glove box. Reaching through glove box opening, gently pry bushing and link from right pivot pin. Lift link from pivot crank arm pin and repeat operation at left pivot. Withdraw from under left side of panel.

1970-74 Barracuda and Challenger

1. Remove wiper arm and blade assemblies.

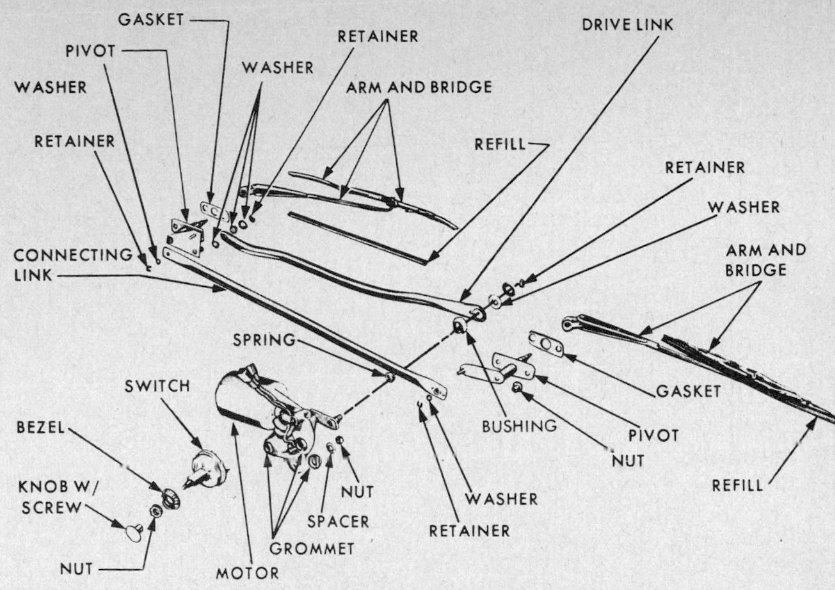

Single speed windshield wiper and linkage
(© Chrysler Corp)

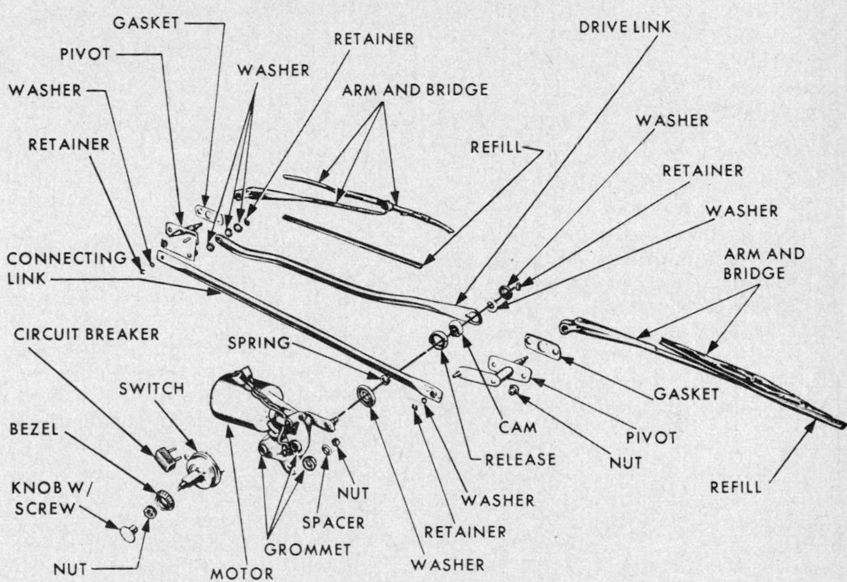

Variable speed windshield wiper and linkage
(© Chrysler Corp)

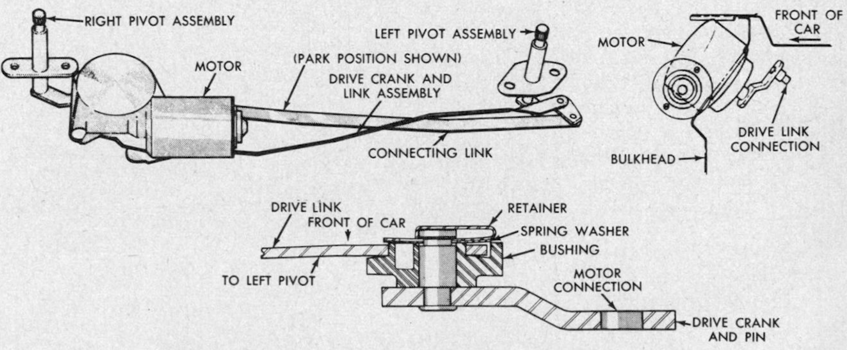

Valiant and Dart windshield wiper linkage (© Chrysler Corp)

2. Remove left cowl screen for access to linkage.
3. Disconnect battery.
4. Remove crank arm nut and crank from motor shaft.
5. Remove bolts mounting left and right pivots to body.
6. Remove links and pivots through cowl top opening.

RADIO

Removal

1969 Valiant, Dart, and Barracuda

1. Disconnect battery.
2. From under panel disconnect speaker and wiring leads at radio.
3. Remove two radio mounting nuts from radio mounting bracket.
4. Move radio down and out from under instrument panel.

1970-76 Valiant, Dart; 1970-74 Barracuda, and Challenger

1. Disconnect battery.
2. From under panel, disconnect speaker and wiring leads at radio.
3. Remove channel selector shaft and knobs if so equipped.
4. Remove two radio mounting screws from under panel and loosen radio to lower support bracket mounting nut. Hold radio in position and remove radio bracket.
5. Move radio toward the front of the car, down, and out from under instrument panel.

NOTE: If the car is equipped with air conditioning, it will be necessary to remove the two air outlet assembly-to-instrument panel mounting nuts from the underside of the panel and drop the assembly down and remove it from under the instrument panel. It will also be necessary to remove the ash tray and ash tray housing.

1970-71 Dart and Valiant with Rallye Dash

1. Disconnect the negative battery cable.
2. Remove the control knobs from the front of the radio.
3. On models equipped with air conditioning, remove the two air conditioner outlet duct retaining nuts and remove the duct. Disconnect the right-side defroster hose and hose bracket and position them out of the way of the radio.
4. Remove the bottom screw from the radio mounting bracket.
5. Remove the left-side defroster hose.
6. Loosen the top screw on the radio mounting bracket and remove the bracket.
7. Disconnect the speaker and antenna leads.
8. Remove the radio mounting nuts from the front of the radio.
9. Remove the radio bezel.
10. Lower the radio and disconnect the radio power lead.
11. Remove the radio from under the instrument panel.

HEATER

Heater Assembly Removal

1969-76 Valiant and Dart and 1969 Barracuda

1. Drain radiator and disconnect battery.
2. Disconnect heater hoses from heater and remove heater hoses to dash retainer plate. Disconnect heater motor wires.
3. Remove heater motor seal retainer plate from dash panel.
4. Disconnect heater-defroster and temperature control cables from heater assembly.
5. Remove heater motor resistor wire from resistor.
6. Remove defroster tubes from heater assembly.
7. Disconnect heater housing support rod from fresh air duct.
8. Remove heater assembly.

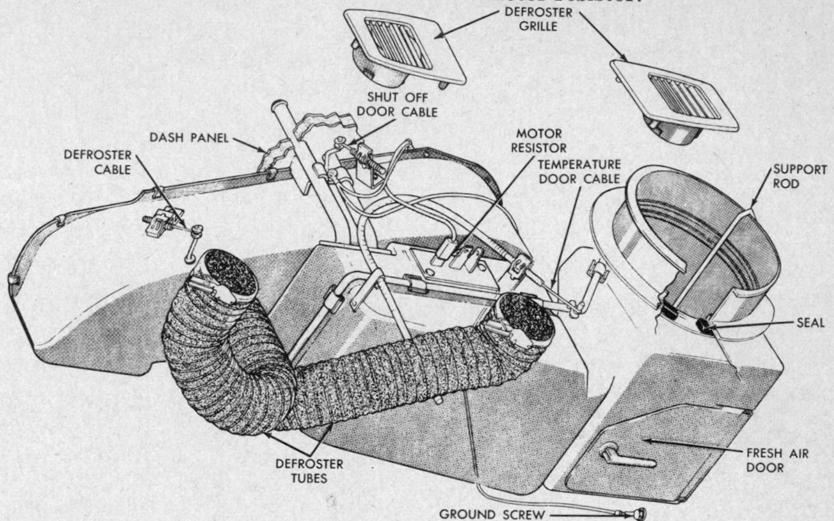

Heater assembly—Valiant and Dart 1969-76
(© Chrysler Corp)

1970-74 Barracuda and Challenger

1. Disconnect battery.
2. Drain coolant.
3. Disconnect heater hoses from core tubes at dash panel. Plug core tubes to prevent spilling coolant on interior of car.
4. Remove three mounting nuts from studs around blower motor and remove flange and air seal.
5. Unplug antenna from radio and place wire to one side.
6. Remove screw from housing to plenum support rod on right side of housing above fresh air opening.
7. Disconnect three air door cables.
8. Disconnect wires from blower motor resistor.
9. Tip unit down and out from under instrument panel.

Heater Blower Motor Removal —Non Air-Conditioned Cars

1969-76 Valiant and Dart and 1969 Barracuda

1. Remove the heater assembly.
2. Remove the seal from around the heater blower motor mounting studs.
3. Remove the spring clips that retain the spacers and the blower motor to the heater housing.
4. Remove the blower motor from the heater housing.

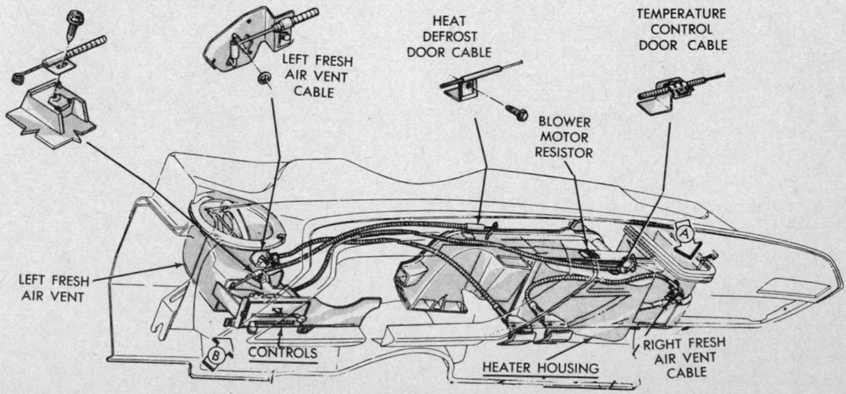

Barracuda and Challenger heater assembly
(© Chrysler Corp)

1970-74 Barracuda and Challenger

1. Remove heater assembly from car.
2. Disconnect blower motor lead from resistor block and ground wire from mounting plate.
3. Remove six sheet metal screws and six retaining clips holding blower motor assembly from housing.
4. Remove blower wheel from motor shaft.
5. Remove two retaining nuts and separate motor from mounting plate.

Heater Core Removal—Non Air-Conditioned Cars

1969-76 Valiant and Dart and 1969 Barracuda

1. Remove the heater assembly and the heater blower motor as outlined above.
2. Remove the fresh air door seal from either the inner or outer heating housing half only.
3. Remove the clips that retain the heater housing halves together.
4. Separate the heater housing halves.
5. Remove the screw that attaches the seal retainer and seal around the heater core tubes.
6. Remove the heater core tube support clamp.
7. Remove the screws that attach the heater core to the heater housing and remove the heater core.
8. Reverse above procedure to install.

1970-74 Barracuda and Challenger

1. Remove the heater assembly.
2. Remove the nine spring clips and four screws that hold the front cover to the heater housing.
3. Cut the sponge rubber plenum-to-heater housing air seal in two places where the front cover separates the cover from the housing.
4. Remove the core tube retaining screw from behind the housing, between the core tubes.
5. Remove the two sponge rubber gaskets from the heater core tubes and remove the core from the heater housing.

Heater Core Removal—Air-Conditioned Cars

1969-73 Dart and Valiant, 1969 Barracuda

1. The core and cover are serviced as an assembly. They are located just forward of the instrument panel.
2. Disconnect the battery and remove the air cleaner. Remove glove box, the air outlet assembly, and the right defroster tube.
3. Drain the cooling system and remove the heater hoses at the core.
4. Disconnect the vacuum hoses from the fresh air recirculating actuator, the electrical wires from the resistor block, the temperature control cable, the evaporator temperature control switch control cable, and the ground wire from the heater core.
5. Extract the screws holding the heater to the evaporator assemblies. Disconnect the heater housing support rod from its position at the fresh air duct.
6. Take out the entire heater assembly.
7. Remove the fresh air recirculating door actuator.
8. Remove the operating link between the recirculating door and the bellcrank.
9. Remove the fresh air intake seal from either the front or rear heater housing halves only.
10. Remove the clips holding the heater housing halves together. Pull the halves apart. Take out the screws which secure the heater core to the housing and remove the core.
11. To begin installation, place a small amount of sealer into the heater housing flange. Replace the heater core in the housing and install the attaching screws.
12. Place weatherseal on the inner lip of the heater core flange. Squeeze a small amount of sealer onto the heater housing cover.
13. Install the two housing halves together and install their retaining clips. Wipe off any excess sealer.
14. Install the link between the recirculating door and the bellcrank. It may require some adjustment; the fresh air door should be fully open when the recirculating door is closed. Replace the fresh air door recirculating actuator.
15. Place the heater assembly in the vehicle. Replace the temperature control cable on the outer operating arm; position it so that it is in the full heat position with the end of the cable housing ¼ in. beyond the edge of the retainer clip.
16. Replace the evaporator temperature control switch cable on the inner operating arm. In the full heat position, the end of the cable housing should be ¼ in. beyond the edge of the cable clip.
17. Install the heater assembly on the dash panel. Replace the heater support rod to the fresh air duct and install the evaporator assembly screw.
18. Replace the electrical connections to the resistor block. Install the vacuum hoses to the fresh air recirculating actuator. Be certain the red stripe is facing the rod side. Install the heater core ground wire.
19. Install the defroster tube, the glove box, and the air outlet assembly.
20. Replace the heater hoses, fill the cooling system, connect the battery and replace the air cleaner.
21. Start engine and bring to operating temperature. Test operation of the heater.

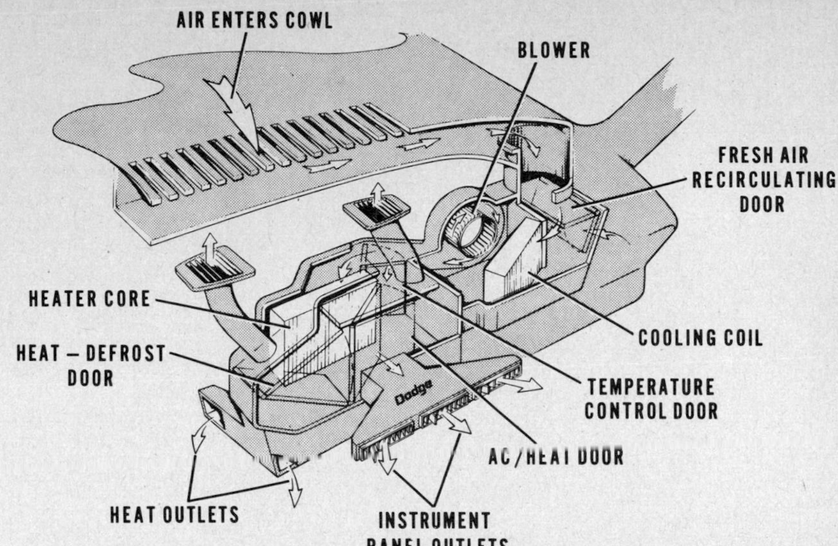

1969-73 Dart and Valiant heater and air conditioner assembly (© Chrysler Corp)

1974-76 Valiant and Dart

1. Disconnect the battery.
2. Drain the cooling system and disconnect the heater hose from the unit.
3. Remove the core tube seal nut, bracket and seal.
4. Remove the air conditioning duct.
5. Remove the ash tray and housing.

6. Remove the radio.
7. Remove the heat-defrost vacuum actuator pot and let it hang by its rod.
8. To remove the heat distribution duct, remove the three screws on the front cover, two on each end and work the housing out of the lip and remove it to the left-side.
9. Remove the left defroster duct. Remove the right defroster duct from the unit and let it hang from the top.
10. Remove the rear distribution housing. You may reach through the radio opening for some of the screws; three on top, three on the bottom, and one at the left end.
11. With the distribution housing off, the heater core will be loose. Separate it from the seal and lift it out.

1970-74 Barracuda and Challenger

NOTE: This procedure requires evacuation of the air conditioner refrigerant, use proper safety precautions.

1. Remove the air cleaner and disconnect the battery.
2. Drain the cooling system. Disconnect the heater hoses at the dash panel. Plug the core tubes to prevent spillage.
3. Discharge refrigerant from the system.
4. Disconnect the refrigerant lines at the dash panel (use two wrenches for this procedure). Leave the expansion valve attached to the line. Plug all refrigerant openings.
5. Disconnect the blower motor electrical connections. Remove the motor cooling tube and remove the blower motor.
6. Remove the glove box assembly.
7. Remove the appearance shield from the lower edge of the instrument panel.
8. Remove the left spot cooler duct and the air distribution housing.
9. Disconnect all wires from the blower motor resistor, and the antenna wire from the radio bottom.
10. Remove the radio.
11. Disconnect the vacuum harness from the control switch rear.
12. Remove the water valve cable from the bracket on the housing left end.
13. In the engine compartment, remove the nuts from the housing mounting studs.
14. Remove the rubber drain tube.
15. Take the support bracket from the plenum-to-housing panel.
16. Remove the unit from beneath the instrument panel.
17. With the unit removed from the vehicle, remove the plenum air seal.
18. Remove the vacuum hose from the fresh air door actuator and bypass door actuator. Remove the air seal from the evaporator core tubes and heater.
19. Remove the 18 screws securing the front and rear covers, extract one screw from between the evaporator core tubes. Pull the housings apart.
20. Extract the three screws from the evaporator core access plate and remove the plate. With access now clear to the 2 evaporator core mounting screws, remove them. In addition, remove the four screws securing the evaporator core to the front cover and remove the core.
21. Carefully lift the left housing half seal from the rear cover. Do not remove the entire seal; the lower portion acts as a water seal.
22. Remove the two core retaining screws from the mounting plate. From the back of the rear cover, remove one screw from between the core tubes. Lift the heater core from the housing.
23. To begin assembly and installation, place the heat door in the "up" position. Place the heater core into the rear cover. Install its retaining screws.
24. Apply rubber cement to the bottom of the raised portion of the housing seal; carefully replace it in its original position over the heater core.
25. Insert the evaporator core into the front cover and replace its four securing screws.
26. Place the front and rear covers together. Make sure the cover seal is seated properly. Replace the 18 securing screws (and the screw between the evaporator core tubes at the back of the rear cover).
27. Replace the air seal over the heater and evaporator core tubes.
28. Connect all vacuum hoses to their respective actuators. Connect the hose with the red tracer to the actuator rod side.
29. Install the evaporator core access cover plate to the housing front and replace its three sheet metal screws.
30. Apply rubber cement to the plenum air seal and install it in position.
31. Position the housing up under the instrument panel. Connect the housing-to-plenum support bracket.
32. In the engine compartment, install four retaining nuts on the housing mounting studs; torque them to 24 in. lbs.
33. Install the vacuum harness to the rear of the control switch. Install the water valve control cable in its retaining bracket.
34. Install the radio.
35. Install all blower motor resistor wiring. Plug the antenna lead into the radio bottom.
36. Replace the center outlet air distribution housing. Replace the left spot cooler duct.
37. Replace the appearance shield at the instrument panel bottom.
38. Replace the glove box.
39. Replace the blower motor and connect its wiring. Install the blower motor cooling tube and replace the evaporator drain tube.
40. Connect the refrigerant lines to the evaporator core tubes. Freely lubricate the fittings and O-rings with refrigerant oil. Use two wrenches to avoid twisting the tubes.
41. Connect the heater hoses to the core tubes. Fill the cooling system.
42. Sweep the system. Evacuate the system. Charge the system and check for leaks.

SEAT BELTS

Seat Belt/Starter Interlock System

All 1974 and some 1975 models are equipped with Chrysler Corporation's seat belt/starter interlock system, which prevents starting of the car engine until front seat belts are fastened. For full information on this system, refer to the Dodge/Plymouth and Chrysler Cordoba/Imperial car sections.

INDEX

Bobcat · Mustang II · Pinto

YEAR IDENTIFICATION

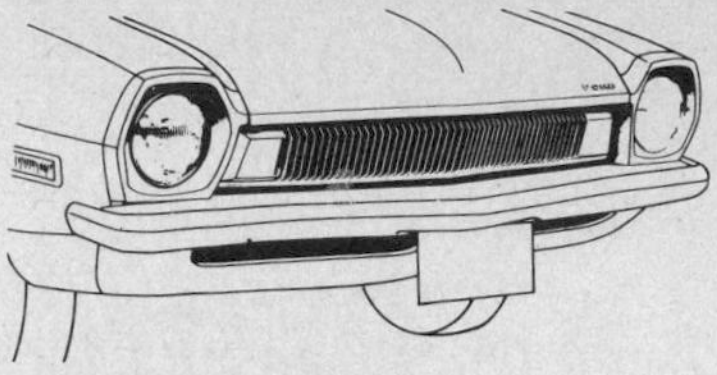

1971-72 Pinto

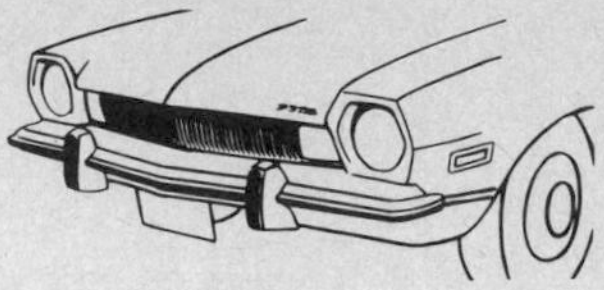

1973

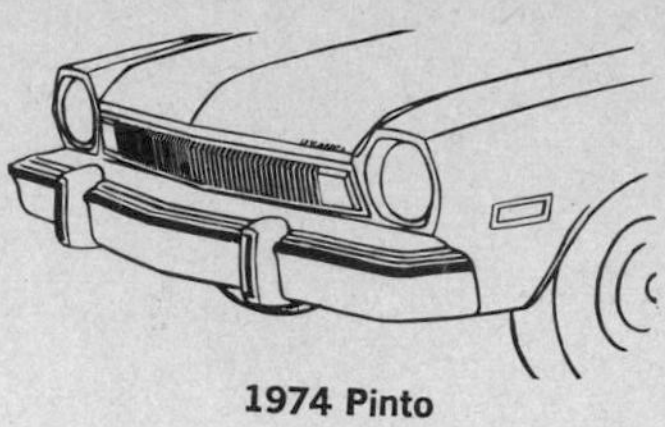

1974 Pinto

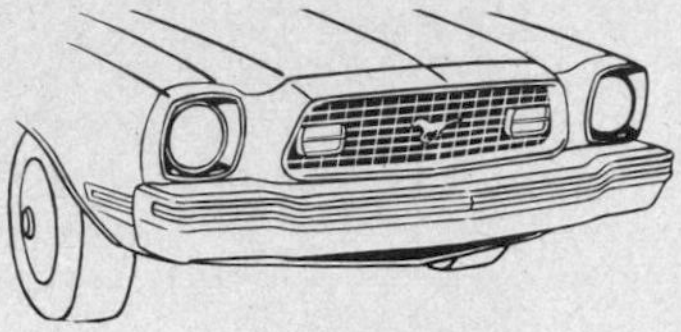

1974 Mustang II

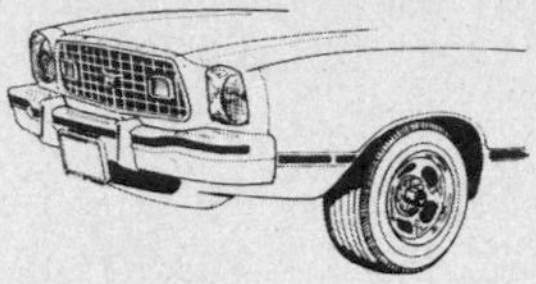

1975-76 Mustang II

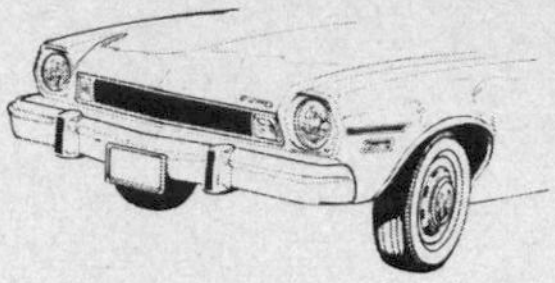

1975 Pinto

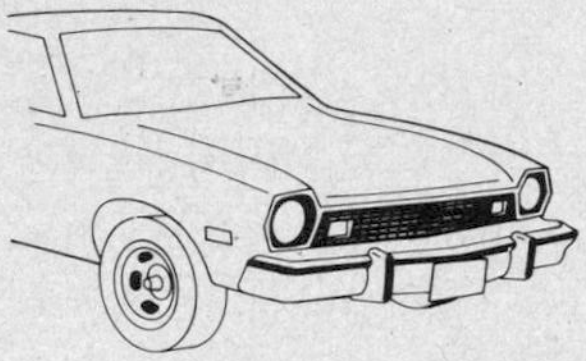

1976 Pinto

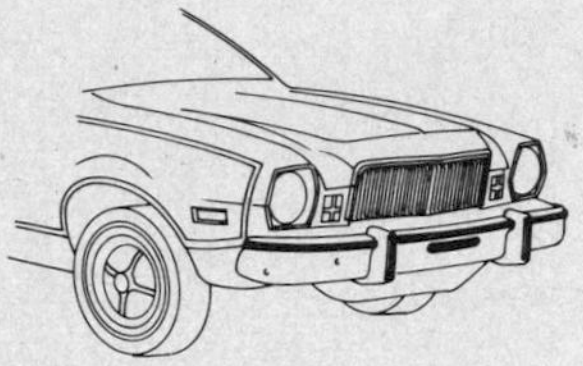

1976 Bobcat

FIRING ORDER

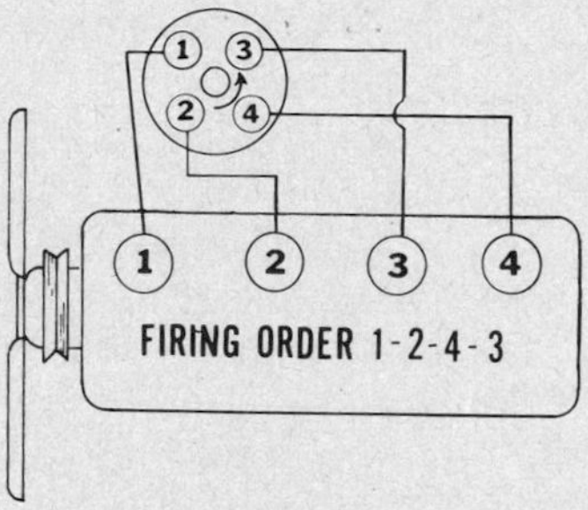

1
3
2
4
1
2
3
4
FIRING ORDER 1-2-4-3

1600 cc

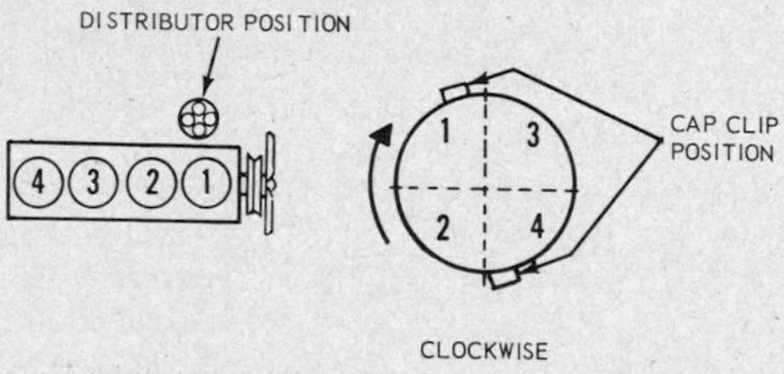

DISTRIBUTOR POSITION
4
3
2
1
1
3
2
4
CAP CLIP POSITION
CLOCKWISE

FIRING ORDER –1–3–4–2

2000 cc

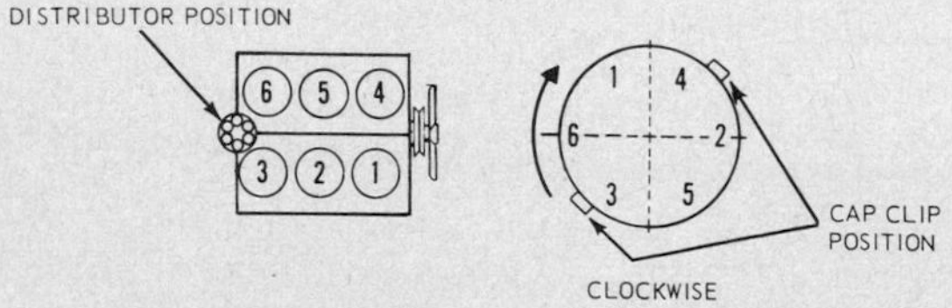

DISTRIBUTOR POSITION
6
5
4
3
2
1
1
4
6
2
3
5
CAP CLIP POSITION
CLOCKWISE

FIRING ORDER – 1–4–2–5–3–6

2800 cc V6 (© Ford Motor Co)

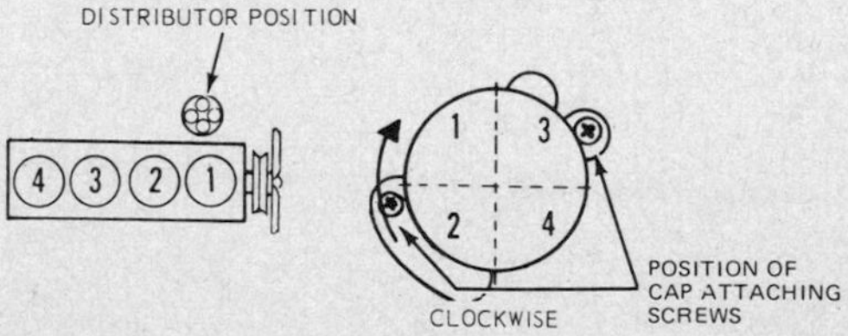

DISTRIBUTOR POSITION
4
3
2
1
1
3
2
4
CLOCKWISE
POSITION OF CAP ATTACHING SCREWS

FIRING ORDER –1–3–4–2

2300 cc (© Ford Motor Co)

1
2
3
4
FIRING ORDER
1-5-4-2-6-3-7-8
5
6
7
8

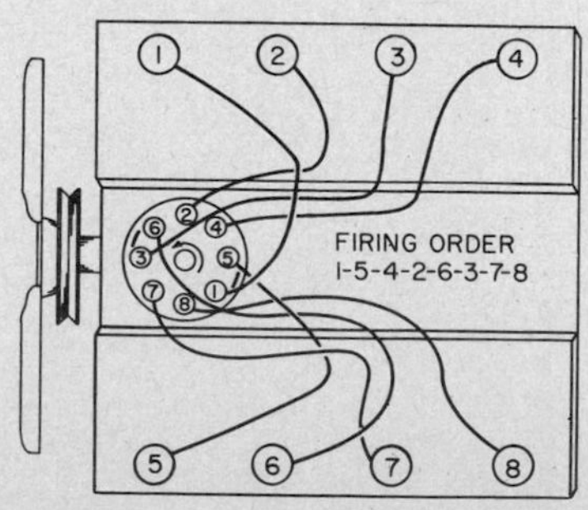

302 V8

CAR SERIAL NUMBER LOCATION

Vehicle Identification Number

The Vehicle Identification Number is located on a tab mounted on the upper left-hand corner of the dashboard, visible through the windshield. The VIN also appears on the Vehicle Certification Label, and is interpreted according to the illustration of this label.

Vehicle Certification Label

The Vehicle Certification Label is located on the rear edge or lock pillar of the driver's door. Alteration or removal of this label will result in its destruction, or the appearance of the word VOID.

Vehicle identification number plate

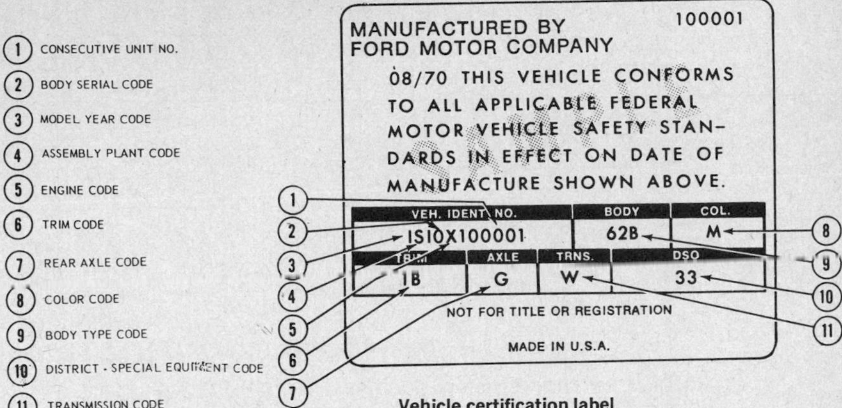

Vehicle certification label

ENGINE CODE

The engine code designation is the 5th digit of the vehicle identification number (V.I.N.). The V.I.N. is stamped on a plate located at the left side of the instrument panel visible through the windshield on all models.

Disp	Bbl	Hp	'71	'72	'73	'74	'75	'76
4-Cylinder Models								
98 (1600cc)	1	54 (net)		W	W			
98 (1600cc)	1	75	W					
122 (2000cc)	2	80 (net)				X		
122 (2000cc)	2	85, 86 (net)*		X	X			
122 (2000cc)	2	100	X					
140 (2300cc)	2	82, 88 (net)				Y		
140 (2300cc)	2	83 (net)					Y	Y
6-Cylinder Models								
171 (2800cc)	2	105 (net)				Z		
171 (2800cc)	2	97 (net)					Z	Z
8-Cylinder Models								
302 V8	2	129 (net)					F	F

* Net horsepower rating varies with model application

GENERAL ENGINE SPECIFICATIONS

Year	Engine No. Cyl. Displacement Cu. In.	Carburetor Type	Horsepower @ rpm ■	Torque @ rpm (ft lbs) ■	Bore and Stroke (in.)	Compression Ratio	Oil Pressure @ 2050 rpm
'71	4-97.6 (1600 cc)	1 bbl	75 @ 5000	96 @ 3000	3.188 x 3.056	8.0:1	38
	4-122 (2000 cc)	2 bbl	100 @ 5600	120 @ 3600	3.575 x 3.029	8.6:1	50①
'72	4-97.6 (1600 cc)	1 bbl	54 @ 4600	80 @ 2400	3.188 x 3.056	8.0:1	38
	4-122 (2000 cc)	2 bbl	86 @ 5400	103 @ 3200	3.575 x 3.029	8.2:1	50①
'73	4-97.6 (1600 cc)	1 bbl	54 @ 4600	80 @ 2400	3.188 x 3.056	8.0:1	38
	4-122 (2000 cc)	2 bbl	86 @ 5400	103 @ 3200	3.575 x 3.029	8.2:1	50①

GENERAL ENGINE SPECIFICATIONS (con't.)

Year	Engine No. Cyl. Displacement Cu. In.	Carburetor Type	Horsepower @ rpm ■	Torque @ rpm (ft lbs) ■	Bore and Stroke (in.)	Compression Ratio	Oil Pressure @ 2050 rpm
'74	4-122 (2000 cc)	2 bbl	80 @ 5400	98 @ 3000	3.575 x 3.029	8.2:1	50①
	4-140 (2300 cc)	2 bbl	88 @ 5000②	116 @ 2600	3.781 x 3.126	8.4:1	50
	6-170.8 (2800 cc)	2 bbl	105 @ 4600	140 @ 3200	3.660 x 2.700	8.2:1	40-55①
'75-'76	4-140 (2300 cc)	2 bbl	83 @ 4800	109 @ 2800	3.781 x 3.126	8.4:1③	50
	6-170.8 (2800 cc)	2 bbl	97 @ 4400	138 @ 3200	3.660 x 2.700	8.2:1④	40-55①
	8-302	2 bbl	129 @ 4000	213 @ 1800	4.000 x 3.000	8.0:1	50-70

■ Beginning 1972, horsepower and torque are SAE net figures. They are measured at the rear of the transmission with all accessories installed and operating. Since the figures vary when a given engine is installed in different models, some are representative rather than exact.

① Oil pressure at 1500 rpm.
② 88 hp in Mustang II; 82 hp in Pinto
③ 9.0:1 in 1976
④ 8.7:1 in 1976

TUNE-UP SPECIFICATIONS

When analyzing compression test results, look for uniformity among cylinders rather than specific pressures.

ENGINE		SPARK PLUGS		DISTRIBUTOR		IGNITION TIMING (deg) ▲		VALVES	Fuel	IDLE SPEED (rpm) ▲	
Year	No. Cyl. Displacement (cu in.)	Type	Gap (in.)	Point Dwell (deg)	Point Gap (in.)	Man Trans •	Auto Trans	Intake Opens ■ (deg)	Pump Pressure (psi)	Man Trans	Auto Trans
'71	4-97.6 (1600 cc)	AGR-22	.030	40	.025	12B	—	17	3½-5½	800/500③	—
'71	4-122 (2000 cc)	BRF-32①	②	40	.025	6B-10B	6B-10B	24	3½-5½	750/500③	650/500③
'72	4-97.6 (1600 cc)	AGR-22	.030	40	.025	12B	—	17	3½-5½	800/500③	—
'72	4-122 (2000 cc)	BRF-42	.034	40	.025	6B-10B	6B-10B	24	3½-5½	750/500③	650/500③
'73	4-97.6 (1600 cc)	AGR-32	.034	40	.025	12B	—	17	3½-5½	800/500③	—
	4-122 (2000 cc)	BRF-42	.034	40	.025	6B-10B	6B-10B	24	3½-5½	750/500③	650/500③
'74	4-122 (2000 cc)	BRF-42	.034	39	.025	6B④	6B④	24	3½-4½	750	750
	4-140 (2300 cc)	AGRF-52	.034	39	.025	6B	6B	22	3½-4½	750⑤	650⑤
	6-170.8 (2800 cc)	AGR-42	.044	38	.025	12B	12B	20	3½-4½	750	650
'75	4-140 (2300 cc)	AGRF-52	.034	Electronic		6B	6B(10B)	22	3½-4½	550⑦	550⑧
	6-170.8 (2800 cc)	AGR-42	.034	Electronic		6B	10B(8B)⑥	20	3½-4½	850	700
	8-302	ARF-42	.044	Electronic		—	6B	20	5½-6½	—	650
'76	4-140 (2300 cc)	AGRF-52	.034	Electronic		6B @ 550	20B @ 550	22	3½-4½	850	750
	6-170.8 (2800 cc)	AGR-42	.034	Electronic		10(8)B @ 700(650)	12(8)B⑩ @ 700	20	3½-4½	850	700
	8-302	ARF-42/52⑨	.044	Electronic		—	8/6B⑨ @ 500	20	5½-6½	—	700

▲ See text for procedure
■ All figures Before Top Dead Center
① BRF-42 recommended service plug
② For BRF-32, set gap to .025 inches and for BRF-42, set gap to .034 inches
③ First figure is for idle speed with solenoid energized and automatic transmission in Drive, while the second figure is for idle speed with solenoid disconnected and automatic transmission in Neutral. Cars without a solenoid use higher figure.
④ 3B at 650 for California Pinto
⑤ 850 man, 750 auto in Pinto
⑥ 8B(10B) for Bobcat
⑦ 850(900) for Bobcat
⑧ 750 for Bobcat
⑨ Depends on emission equipment, check underhood specifications sticker
⑩ In Drive

B Before Top Dead Center
— Not applicable
• Figure in parentheses is for California

CAPACITIES

Year	ENGINE No. Cyl. Displacement (Cu. In.)	Engine Crankcase Add 1 Qt For ■ New Filter	TRANSMISSION Pts To Refill After Draining: Manual 3-Speed	Manual 4-Speed	Automatic	Drive Axle (pts)	Gasoline Tank (gals)	COOLING SYSTEM (qts) With Heater	With A/C
'71-'72	4-97.6 (1600 cc)	3	—	2.5	—	2.2	11①	7.75	—
	4-122 (2000cc)	4	—	2.5	16	2.2	11①	8.50	8.50
'73	4-97.6 (1600 cc)	3	—	2.8	—	2.2	11①	7.80	—
	4-122 (2000cc)	4	—	2.8	16	2.2	11①	8.50	8.50

CAPACITIES

Year	Engine No. Cyl. Displacement (Cu. In.)	Engine ■ Crankcase Add 1 Qt For New Filter	Transmission Pts To Refill After Draining Manual 3-Speed	Manual 4-Speed	Automatic	Drive Axle (pts)	Gasoline Tank (gals)	Cooling System (qts) With Heater	With A/C
'74	4-122 (2000 cc)	4	—	2.8	16	3	13①	8.50	8.50
	4-140 (2300 cc)	4	—	4④	16	3	13①	8.80③	9.20③
	6-170.8 (2800 cc)	4②	—	4	16	3	13	12.5	12.8
'75-'76	4-140 (2300 cc)	4	—	3.5④	16	3⑧	13⑤⑥	8.7	9.0
	6-170.8 (2800 cc)	4.5②	—	3.5④	15⑦	4	13⑤⑥	12.5	13.2
	8-302	4	—	—	15	4	13⑥	16.3	16.3

■ ½ quart for 1600cc
— Not applicable
① Wagon—12 gals
② Add 0.5 qt for filter
③ 8.5 qt in Pinto
④ 2.8 qt in Pinto, Bobcat
⑤ 14 gals on station wagon
⑥ 16.5 gals with auxiliary tank in Mustang II
⑦ 14 pt in Pinto, Bobcat
⑧ 2.3 pt in Pinto, Bobcat

VALVE SPECIFICATIONS

Year	Engine No. Cyl. Displacement (cu in.)	Seat Angle (deg)	Face Angle (deg)	Spring Test Pressure (lbs @ in.)	Spring Installed Height (in.)	Stem to Guide Clearance (in.) Intake	Exhaust	Stem Diameter (in.) Intake	Exhaust
'71	4-97.6 (1600 cc)	45	45	47 @ 1.26	1 17/64	.0008-.0030	.0017-.0039	.3100	.3100
	4-122 (2000 cc)	45	45	67 @ 1.42	1 13/32	.0015-.0015	.0015-.0025	.3149	.3149
'72	4-97.6 (1600 cc)	45	45	50 @ 1.26	1 17/64	.0008-.0027	.0017-.0036	.3102	.3093
	4-122 (2000 cc)	45	46	69 @ 1.42	1 13/32	.0008-.0025	.0018-.0035	.3163	.3153
'73	4-97.6 (1600 cc)	45	44	47 @ 1.263	1 17/64	.0008-.0027	.0017-.0036	.3102	.3093
	4-122 (2000 cc)	45	44	69 @ 1.418	1 13/32	.0008-.0025	.0018-.0035	.3163	.3153
'74	4-122 (2000 cc)	45	46	69 @ 1.418	1 47/64	.0008-.0025	.0018-.0035	.3163	.3153
	4-140 (2300 cc)	45	46	75 @ 1.560	1 53/64	.0010-.0027	.0015-.0022	.3419	.3415
	6-170.8 (2800 cc)	45	44	64 @ 1.585	1 29/32	.0008-.0025	.0018-.0035	.3162	.3153
'75-'76	4-140 (2300 cc)	45	46	75 @ 1.56	1 9/16	.0006-.0023	.0015-.0032	.3424	.3415
	4-170.8 (2800 cc)	45	46	64 @ 1.59	1 19/32	.0008-.0025	.0018-.0035	.3162	.3153
	8-302	45	46	80 @ 1.60	1 11/16	.0007-.0027	.0015-.0032	.3420	.3415

TORQUE SPECIFICATIONS

All readings in ft lbs

Year	Engine No. Cyl. Displacement (cu in.)	Cylinder Head Bolts	Rod Bearing Bolts	Main Bearing Bolts	Crankshaft Pulley Bolt	Flywheel to Crankshaft Bolts	Manifold Intake	Manifold Exhaust
'71-'76	4-97.6 (1600 cc)	65-70	30-35	65-70	24-28	50-55	12-15	15-18
	4-122 (2000 cc)	65-80	29-34	65-75	39-43	47-51	12-15	12-15①
	4-140 (2300 cc)	80-90	30-36	80-90	80-114②	54-64	14-21	16-23
	6-170.8 (2800 cc)	65-80	21-25	65-75	92-103②	47-51	15-18	14-18
	8-302	65-72	19-24	60-70	70-90	75-85	23-25	12-16

① 15-18 in 1974
② Crankshaft damper bolt

CRANKSHAFT AND CONNECTING ROD SPECIFICATIONS

All measurements are given in inches

Year	Engine No. Cyl. Displacement (cu in.)	CRANKSHAFT Main Brg. Journal Dia	CRANKSHAFT Main Brg. Oil Clearance	CRANKSHAFT Shaft End-Play	CRANKSHAFT Thrust on No.	CONNECTING ROD Journal Diameter	CONNECTING ROD Oil Clearance	CONNECTING ROD Side Clearance
'71	4-97.6 (1600 cc)	2.1253-2.1261	.0004-.0018	.003-.011	3	1.9368-1.9376	.0004-.0024	.004-.010
	4-122 (2000 cc)	2.2432-2.2440	.0005-.0015	.004-.008	3	2.0464-2.0472	.0006-.0026	.004-.010
'72-'73	4-97.6 (1600 cc)	2.1253-2.1261	.0005-.0016	.003-.011	3	1.9368-1.9376	.0004-.0024	.004-.010
	4-122 (2000 cc)	2.2432-2.2440	.0006-.0016	.003-.011	3	2.0464-2.0472	.0006-.0026	.004-.010
'74	4-122 (2000 cc)	2.2432-2.2440	.0006-.0016	.003-.011	3	2.0464-2.0472	.0006-.0015	.004-.011
	4-140 (2300 cc)	2.3982-2.3990	.0008-.0015	.004-.012	3	2.0465-2.0472	.0006-.0027	.0008-.0026
	6-170.8 (2800 cc)	2.2433-2.2441	.0006-.0019	.003-.011	3	2.0464-2.0472	.0006-.0022	.004-.011
'75-'76	4-140 (2300 cc)	2.3982-2.3990	.0008-.0026	.004-.008	3	2.0465-2.0472	.0008-.0024	.0035-.0105
	6-170.8 (2800 cc)	2.2433-2.2437	.0006-.0019	.004-.008	3	2.0464-2.1256	.0006-.0026	.004-.011
	8-302	2.2482-2.2486	.0005-.0024	.004-.008	3	2.1228-2.1236	.0008-.0026	.010-.020

RING GAP

All measurements are given in inches

Year	Engine	Top Compression	Bottom Compression
'71-'73	4-97.6 (1600 cc)	.009-.014	.009-.014
'71-'72	4-122 (2000 cc)	.019-.021	.019-.021
'73-'74	4-122 (2000 cc)	.015-.023	.015-.023
'74	4-140 (2300 cc)	.010-.020	.010-.020
'74	6-170.8 (2800 cc)	.015-.023	.015-.023
'75-'76	4-140 (2300 cc)	.010-.035	.010-.020
'75-'76	6-170 (2800 cc)	.015-.022	.015-.022
'75-'76	8-302	.010-.020	.010-.020

Year	Engine	Oil Control
'71-'73	1600 cc	.009-.014
'71-'74	2000 cc	.016-.055
'74	2300 cc	.015-.055
'74	2800 cc	.015-.055
'75-'76	2300 cc	.010-.035
'75-'76	2800 cc	.016-.055
'75-'76	8-302	.015-.055

RING SIDE CLEARANCE

All measurements are given in inches

Year	Engine	Top Compression	Bottom Compression
'71-'73	4-97.6 (1600 cc)	.0016-.0036	.0016-.0036
'71-'74	4-122 (2000 cc)	.0019-.0038	.0019-.0038
'74-'76	4-140 (2300 cc)	.0020-.0040	.0020-.0040
'74-'76	6-170.8 (2800cc)	.0020-.0033	.0020-.0033
'75-'76	8-302	.002-.004	.002-.004

Year	Engine	Oil Control
'71-'73	1600 cc	.0018-.0038
'71-'74	2000 cc	Snug
'74-'76	2300 cc	Snug
'74-'76	2800 cc	Snug
'75-'76	8-302	Snug

PISTON CLEARANCE

Year	Engine	Piston-to-Bore Clearance (in.)
'71-'73	4-1600 cc	.0016-.0022* .0019-.0025**
'71-'74	4-2000 cc	.0010-.0020
'74-'76	4-2300 cc	.0013-.0021
'74-'76	6-2800 cc	.0010-.0021
'75-'76	8-302	.0018-.0026

* No. 1, 2, and 3
** No. 4

ALTERNATOR AND REGULATOR SPECIFICATIONS

	ALTERNATOR			REGULATOR						
					Field Relay			Regulator		
Year	Part No. or Manufacturer	Field Current @ 12 V	Output (amps)	Part No. or Manufacturer	Air Gap (in.)	Point Gap (in.)	Volts to Close	Air Gap (in.)	Point Gap (in.)	Volts @ 75°
'71	D0ZF-B	2.4	38	D0AF-A	Not Adjustable		2.5-4.0	Not Adjustable		13.5-15.3
	D0AF-G	2.9	42	D0AF-A	Not Adjustable		2.5-4.0	Not Adjustable		13.5-15.3
'72	D2ZF-AA	2.4	38	D2AF-AA	Not Adjustable		2.5-4.0	Not Adjustable		13.5-15.3
	D2AF-AA	2.9	42	D2AF-AA	Not Adjustable		2.5-4.0	Not Adjustable		13.5-15.3
	D2SF-AA	2.9	55	D2AF-AA	Not Adjustable		2.5-4.0	Not Adjustable		13.5-15.3
	D2AF-CA	2.9	61	D2AF-AA	Not Adjustable		2.5-4.0	Not Adjustable		13.5-15.3
	D2OF-AA	2.9	65	D2AF-AA	Not Adjustable		2.5-4.0	Not Adjustable		13.5-15.3
'73	D2ZF-AC	2.4	38	D3AF-AA	Not Adjustable		2.5-4.0	Not Adjustable		13.5-15.3
	D2OF-DB	2.9	42	D3AF-AA	Not Adjustable		2.5-4.0	Not Adjustable		13.5-15.3
	D2OF-CB	2.9	61	D3AF-AA	Not Adjustable		2.5-4.0	Not Adjustable		13.5-15.3
	D2ZF-BA	2.9	61	D3AF-AA	Not Adjustable		2.5-4.0	Not Adjustable		13.5-15.3
	D2ZF-AB	2.9	70	D3TF-AA	Not Adjustable		2.5-4.0	Not Adjustable		13.5-15.3
'74-'76	D3ZF-AA, D4ZF-EA, D42F-EA, D42F-AA, D4ZF-BA, D32F-AA	2.9	38	D4AF-AA	Not adjustable		2.5-4.0	Not Adjustable		13.5-15.3
	D30F-EA, D32F-BA D40F-DA, D34F-AA	2.9	61	D4AF-AA	Not adjustable		2.5-4.0	Not Adjustable		13.5-15.3
	D30F-AA, D42F-AA, D32F-AA, D40F-EA, D42F-CA, D4ZF-AA	—	70	D4TF-AA	Not adjustable		2.5-4.0	Not Adjustable		13.5-15.3
	D52-F-AA, D30F-FA, D3TF-CA	—	42	D4AF-AA	Not adjustable		2.5-4.0	Not adjustable		13.5-15.3

BATTERY AND STARTER SPECIFICATIONS

		BATTERY			STARTER						
					Lock Test			No-Load Test			
Year	Engine Displacement (cu in.)	Ampere Hour Capacity	Volts	Terminal Grounded	Amps	Volts	Torque (ft lbs)	Amps	Volts	RPM	Brush Spring Tension (oz)
'71-'76	All Models①	41, 45, 53	12	Neg.	460	5	9	70	12	9500	40
	All Models②	41, 45, 53	12	Neg.	670	5	15.5	80	12	9500	80

① With 4 in. diameter starter
② With 4.5 in. diameter starter

BRAKE SPECIFICATIONS

All measurements are given in inches

		MASTER CYLINDER		WHEEL CYLINDER			BRAKE DISC OR DRUM DIAMETER		
				Front			Front		
Year	Model	Disc	Drum	Disc	Drum	Rear	Disc	Drum	Rear
'71-'73	All Models	.9375	.9375	2.125	1.000	.7187①	9.3	9.0	9.0
'74-'76	All Models	.9375	—	2.600	—	.8750	9.3	—	9.0

① .8750 on station wagons

WHEEL ALIGNMENT SPECIFICATIONS

Year	Model	CASTER Range (deg)	CASTER Pref Setting (deg)	CAMBER Range (deg)	CAMBER Pref Setting (deg)	Toe-in (in.)	Steering Axis Inclin.	WHEEL PIVOT RATIO (deg) Inner Wheel	WHEEL PIVOT RATIO (deg) Outer Wheel
'71	All models	1P to 2P	1½P	0 to 1½P	¾P	0 to ¼	8.968	20	18.95
'72	All models	½N to 3½P	1½P	¼N to 1¾P	¾P	1/16 to 7/16	8.968	20	18.94
'73	All models	1N to 3P	1P	¼N to 1¾P	¾P	0 to ¼	8.968	20	18.94
'74	Mustang II	⅜N to 1⅞P	⅞P	½N to 1½P	½P	0 to ¼	9.763	20	18.84
'74-'76	Pinto, Bobcat	¾N to 3¼P	1¼P	¼N to 1¾P	¾P	⅛ to ⅜	10.018	20	18.84
'74-'76	Sta. Wag.	½N to 3½P	1½P	¼N to 1¾P	¾P	⅛ to ⅜	10.018	20	18.84
'75-'76	Mustang II	⅛N to 1⅞P	⅞P	½N to 1½P	½P	⅛	9.763	—	—

N Negative P Positive

NOTE: The Mustang II, beginning 1974, is in this section. Mustang models through 1973 are in the Comet car section. More extensive details on the 302 V8 may also be found in the Comet section.

CHARGING SYSTEM

The charging system consists of the battery, the alternator, the regulator and the wires and cables required to connect these units. Repair and testing of the alternator and regulator are covered in the "Unit Repair Section."

Caution Precautions that should be taken into consideration when working on this, or any other, AC charging system are as follows:

1. Never switch battery polarity.
2. When installing a battery, always connect the grounded terminal first.
3. Never disconnect the battery while the engine is running.
4. If the molded connector is disconnected from the alternator, do not ground the hot wire.
5. Never run the alternator with any charging system component disconnected.
6. Never electric weld around the car without disconnecting the alternator.
7. Never apply any voltage in excess of 12 volts during testing.
8. Never "jump" a battery for starting purposes with more than 12 volts.

Alternator Removal

1. Disconnect the battery negative cable.
2. Disconnect the electrical leads.
3. Loosen the three mounting bolts and tilt the alternator in towards the engine.
4. Remove the fanbelt, then remove the mounting bolts and the alternator.

Alternator Installation

1. Position the alternator and loosely install the mounting bolts.
2. Install fanbelt, pry on the front of the alternator so as to place tension on the belt (¼ in. deflection at belt midpoint), then tighten mounting bolts.
3. Connect alternator wires and the battery cable.

Regulator R & R

NOTE: The regulator is preset at the factory and is not adjustable.

1. Disconnect the battery ground cable.
2. Remove the wiring harness from the regulator.
3. Remove the regulator retaining screws and remove the regulator.
4. Position the regulator on the car and install the retaining screws.
5. Attach the wiring to the regulator and connect the ground cable.

STARTING SYSTEM

The engine is equipped with an Motorcraft positive engagement starter. Internal starter repair procedures can be found in the Unit Repair Section.

Starter Removal and Installation

2000 cc

1. Remove the ground cable from the battery.
2. Raise the car on a hoist and disconnect the starter cable.
3. Remove the 3 starter retaining bolts. Grasp the starter and rotate the solenoid housing outward and remove the starter forward between the engine mount and the crossmember.
4. Rotate the starter solenoid housing outward and position the starter motor to the engine.
5. Install the 3 retaining bolts and connect the starter cable.
6. Lower the car and install the battery ground cable.

2300 cc

1. Remove the ground cable from the battery.
2. Raise the car on the hoist and disconnect the starter cable at the starter.
3. Remove the 3 bolts retaining the steering gear to the crossmember and position the gear down out of the way.
4. On the Mustang II, remove the removable crossmember.
5. Remove the 3 starter retaining bolts and remove the starter out and between the crossmember (on the Pinto) and engine mount.
6. Position the starter motor to the engine and install it in the reverse order of removal.

2800 cc V6

1. Disconnect the battery ground cable.
2. Raise the car on a hoist and remove the four bolts retaining the crossmember under the bellhousing.
3. Remove the flex coupling clamping screw at the attachment point to the steering gear.
4. Remove the 3 nuts and bolts which attach the steering gear to the crossmember.
5. Disengage the steering gear from the flex coupling and pull

the steering gear down to provide access to the starter motor.
6. Disconnect the starter cable from the starter motor.
7. Remove the starter motor attaching bolts and remove the starter.
8. Install the starter motor in the reverse order of removal.

IGNITION SYSTEM

Distributor

The 1600 cc engine uses an Autolite distributor which is mounted on the right side of the engine and rotates counterclockwise. The 2000 cc and V6 engines are equipped with a Bosch distributor driven by an auxiliary shaft. The distributor is located on the left side of the engine and rotates in a clockwise direction. Both distributors are the dual advance type; that is, they have both centrifugal and vacuum advance. Some models are equipped with a vacuum retard mechanism which retards ignition timing during deceleration and idling.

Beginning 1975, all Ford engines have electronic ignition which does not use replaceable contacts. This system, while retaining most of the features of the conventional system, uses a unique armature and magnetic pickup coil assembly inside the distributor and a solid state amplifier module.

Tachometer Hookup for Solid State Ignition

The new solid state ignition coil connector allows a tachometer test lead with an alligator clip type tip to be connected to the distributor electronic control terminal without removing the connector.

Connect the clip to the Tach Test cavity. If the coil connector must be removed pull it out straight until it disconnects.

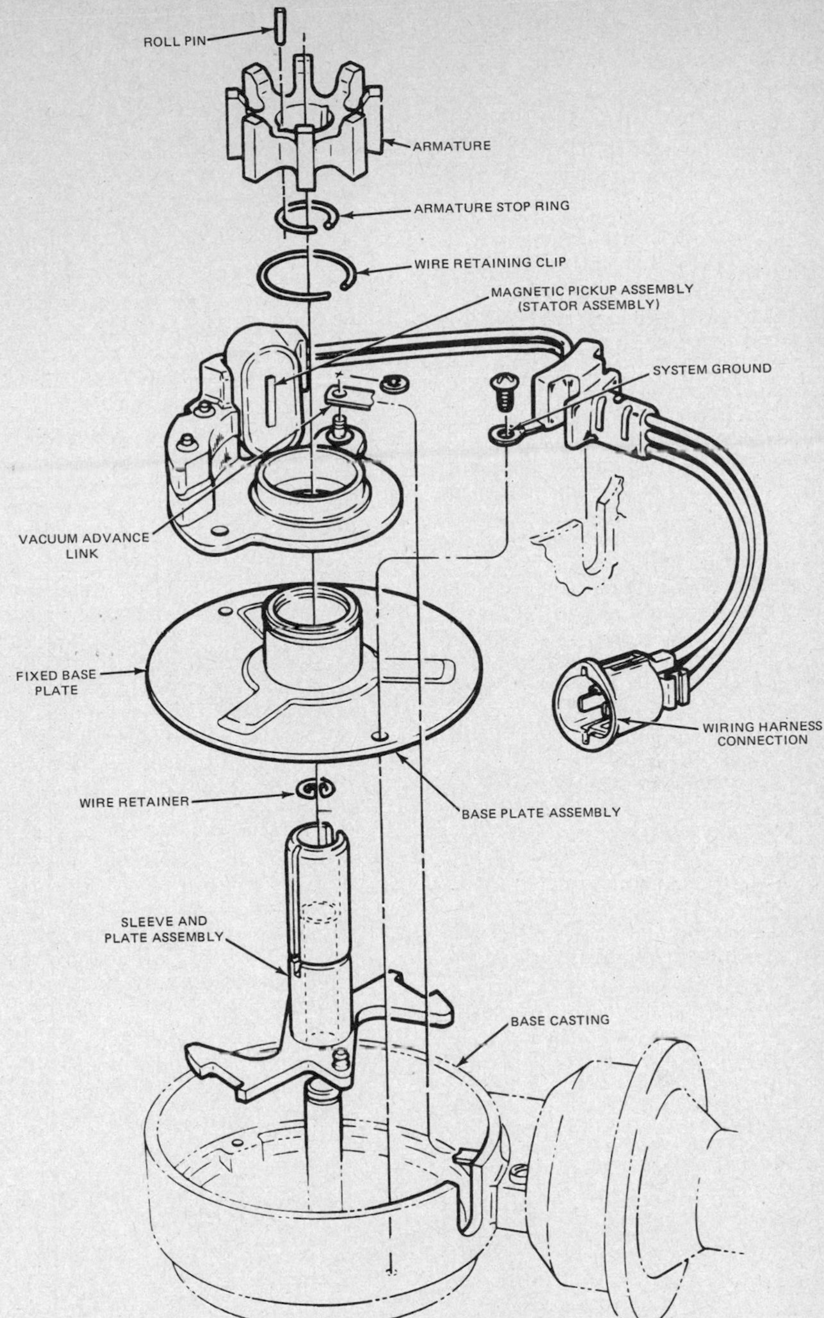

Exploded view of solid state ignition distributor (© Ford Motor Co.)

Removal

1. Remove the air cleaner on V6 engines. On the 4 cylinder engines equipped with an air pump, remove the one mounting bolt and the drive belt, then swing the pump to one side to gain access to the distributor. It may be necessary to disconnect the air pump system air filter and lines. Unsnap the two clips and remove the distributor cap.
2. Note their positioning, and then disconnect the vacuum lines from the distributor.
3. Matchmark the distributor housing and the engine block, then scribe another mark on the housing to indicate the rotor position.
4. Remove the bolt that holds the distributor, then carefully pull out the unit.

NOTE: The hex shaft which drives the oil pump may stick in the distributor shaft and be withdrawn from the pump. When installing the distributor coat one end of the hex shaft with heavy grease and insert that end into the hex hole in the distributor shaft.

Installation

1. Align matchmarks, if engine has not been disturbed, and install distributor.

NOTE: keep in mind that the helical gear will tend to rotate the distributor as it is pushed down.

2. If engine has been disturbed, turn crankshaft until No. 1 piston is at TDC on compression stroke and timing marks are aligned. Place the cap on the distributor and scribe the location of no. one spark plug tower. Install the distributor so that the rotor points toward no. one. Tighten the hold-down bolt.
3. Tighten the hold-down bolt and connect the primary and high-tension wires. Adjust contact breaker points and ignition timing. Connect the vacuum line(s).

Contact Point Replacement and Adjustment

1600 cc

1. Remove the distributor cap. Remove the screw that retains the primary and condenser wires to the point set.
2. Remove the two retaining screws and lift out the point set. It is best to replace the condenser and point set at the same time.
3. Lubricate the cam with silicone cam lube. Place the point set on the breaker plate, making sure the tab on the bottom engages the indentation in the plate. Tighten the retaining screw.
4. Install the primary and condenser wires to the point set, making sure that the connectors are parallel to each other and to the ground when tightened.
5. Turn the engine to bring the point set rubbing block onto one of the cam's high points. Insert a feeler gauge, thickness equal to the point gap specified in the "Tune-Up Specifications" chart, between the contacts.
6. Adjust the gap if the feeler gauge does not fit between the contacts with just a slight drag. Partially loosen the retaining screws and insert a screwdriver in the breaker plate notch at the top of the points. Twist the screwdriver until the correct gap is obtained, and then tighten the retaining screws.
7. Install the distributor cap, aligning the tab in the cap with the notch in the distributor. Check the dwell angle with a meter, if one is available.

2000 cc, 2300 cc, and 2800 cc V6

1. Remove the distributor cap. Pull the breaker point wire from the condenser connector near the outside edge of the distributor body.
2. Remove the retaining screws and lift out the point set.
3. To replace the condenser: remove the attaching screw, grasp the condenser and wire, and work the rubber grommet out of the distributor body. Disconnect the ignition wire connector from the coil and disconnect the coil wire from the condenser.

   The condenser is mounted inside the distributor on the 2300 cc engine. Remove it by disconnecting the condenser lead, removing the retaining screw, and lifting the condenser from the distributor.
4. To install the condenser: place the condenser and wire assembly on the side of the distributor and work the grommet into the distributor body. Install the retaining screw and position the end of the wire attached to the condenser on the "dist" coil post. Install the ignition wire on the coil post over the condenser wire.

   Install the condenser on the 2300 cc engine by placing the condenser in position in the distributor, installing the hold-down screw and connecting the condenser lead to the points terminal.
5. Position the point set on the breaker plate and tighten the retaining screw. Connect the breaker point wire to the condenser. Lubricate the cam with silicone cam lube.
6. Turn the engine to bring the point set rubbing block onto one of the cam's high points. Insert a feeler gauge, the thickness of which is equal to the point gap specified in the "Tune-Up Specifications" chart, between the contacts.

Caution When rotating the engine manually, never turn the pulley counterclockwise or the camshaft drive belt may slip and alter the timing.

7. Adjust the gap if the feeler gauge does not fit between the contacts with just a slight drag. Slightly loosen the retaining screw and insert a screwdriver between the boss on the breaker plate and the notch on the points. Twist the screwdriver until the correct gap is obtained, and then tighten the retaining screw.
8. Install the distributor cap, aligning the tab in the cap with the notch in the distributor. Check the dwell angle with a meter if one is available.

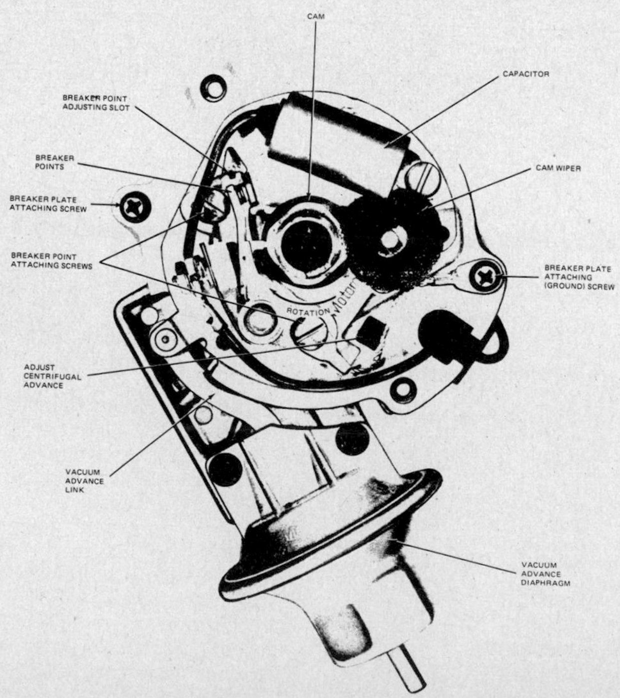

View of the inside of the 2300 cc distributor (© Ford Motor Co)

Ignition Timing

1. Locate the timing marks and pointer on the lower engine pulley and front cover. Clean the marks and pointer, and then scribe the mark and pointer with chalk. (See "Tune-Up Specifications" chart for the correct timing.)
2. Hook up a timing light to no. one spark plug according to the manufacturer's instructions. Disconnect the one or two vacuum lines and plug the open end(s).
3. Attach a tachometer and adjust the engine idle speed to 600 rpm. (See "Idle Speed Adjustment".)
4. Aim the timing light at the pulley marks. If the marks do not align, loosen the distributor hold-down screw or bolt and slowly rotate the distributor until the marks align. Tighten the hold-down screw or bolt.
5. Recheck the timing, and then adjust the engine to normal idle speed.

FUEL SYSTEM

Carburetor

The carburetor used on the 1600 cc engine is an Autolite single-barrel downdraft unit having idle, main, power valve, and accelerator pump systems. Cars equipped with exhaust emission controls have a tamper-proof slow-running volume screw that limits the rich mixture setting.

All other engines are equipped with an Autolite model 5200 carburetor. The 5200 model is a two stage, two venturi carburetor. The primary stage venturi bore is of smaller diameter than the secondary stage venturi bore. The secondary stage is actuated by mechanical linkage when the primary throttle plates reach an opening of approximately 45°. The primary stage includes a curb idle system, accelerator pump system, idle transfer system, main metering system and power enrichment system.

The secondary stage includes a transfer system, main metering system and power system. Both stages share a common fuel bowl.

On both carburetors, the automatic choke is mounted on the carburetor housing. It has a bimetallic thermostatic coil which winds up when cold and unwinds when hot. A vacuum diaphragm and spring controls the initial operation of the choke. Engine coolant flowing through a choke water cover heats the bimetal coil and controls the final choke opening.

Fuel Pump

All of the engines use a diaphragm-type mechanical fuel pump. All of the fuel pumps are mounted on the front, left-side of the engine, except on the 1600 cc engine where it is on the right-side.

The fuel pump is operated by a lever running on an eccentric on the camshaft on the 1600 cc, the 1974 and later 2000 and 2300 cc, and the 302 V8. All 1971-73 2000 cc, and the 2800 cc V6 engines have a pushrod operated fuel pump driven by an eccentric on the auxiliary shaft.

All of the fuel pumps are sealed and must be replaced when defective.

Removal and Installation

1. Disconnect the fuel lines from the fuel pump and plug the inlet line from the gas tank to prevent gas leakage.
2. Remove the fuel pump retaining screws and remove the pump.
3. Remove the fuel pump actuating rod, if so equipped.
4. Clean all gasket mounting surfaces.
5. Install the fuel pump actuating rod, if so equipped.
6. Apply oil-resistant sealer to the fuel pump, position the pump on the engine and install the retaining screws.

NOTE: Make sure the fuel pump rocker arm is riding on the camshaft eccentric.

7. Connect the fuel lines to the fuel pump, start the engine and check for leaks.

Fuel Filter Removal and Installation

1600 cc

The fuel filter is located in the fuel line beneath the battery; therefore, it is necessary to remove the battery to replace the filter.

1. Disconnect the battery cables. Remove the hold-down retaining nut and remove the battery.

Caution Be careful not to spill electrolyte from the battery as you are removing it.

2. Loosen the filter clamps, remove the lines from the old filter, and install the replacement filter.
3. Tighten the filter clamps and replace the battery.

2000 cc through 1973 and 2800 cc V6

The fuel filter is located in the fuel line between the fuel pump and the carburetor.

1. Squeeze the tabs on the fuel filter clamps together and remove the old filter.
2. Compress the clamp tabs and install the replacement filter, positioning the clamps near the ends of the filter.

1974 and later 2000 cc and 2300 cc, 302 V8

1. Remove the air cleaner.
2. Loosen the retaining clamp securing the fuel inlet hose to the fuel filter.
3. Unscrew the fuel filter from the carburetor. Disconnect the fuel filter from the hose.
4. Install the fuel filter in the reverse order of removal.

Idle Speed and Mixture Adjustment

The following prerequisites are necessary for adjustment on all models: bring the engine to normal operating temperature, switch on the high beams, remove the air cleaner, and attach a tachometer to the engine.

1600 cc

1. Check the idle speed. If it is necessary to make an adjustment, turn the nut on the bottom of the carburetor solenoid to correct the speed.

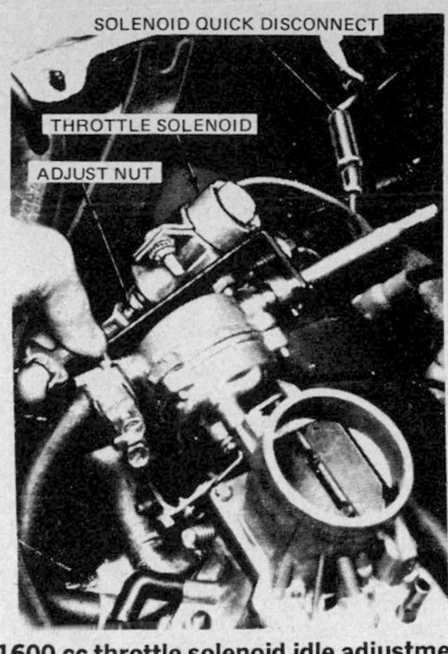

1600 cc throttle solenoid idle adjustment
(© Ford Motor Co)

2. When the idle speed is correct, disconnect the solenoid at the quick-disconnect.
3. Idle speed should equal the lower figure in the "Tune-Up Specifications" chart. Turn the carburetor idle screw if an adjustment is necessary.
4. Reconnect the solenoid. Open the throttle slightly and check to see that the solenoid plunger extends. Idle speed should be increased to the higher figure given in the "Tune-Up Specifications" chart.
5. Adjust the idle mixture screw until a smooth idle is obtained.
6. Turn the engine off and install the air cleaner. Recheck the idle speed and, if it is not correct, remove the air cleaner and readjust the idle speed. Repeat this operation until the idle speed is correct.

2000 cc, 2300 cc Without Air Conditioning, and all V6

1. Start the engine and check the idle speed. Make this check on automatic-equipped cars with the

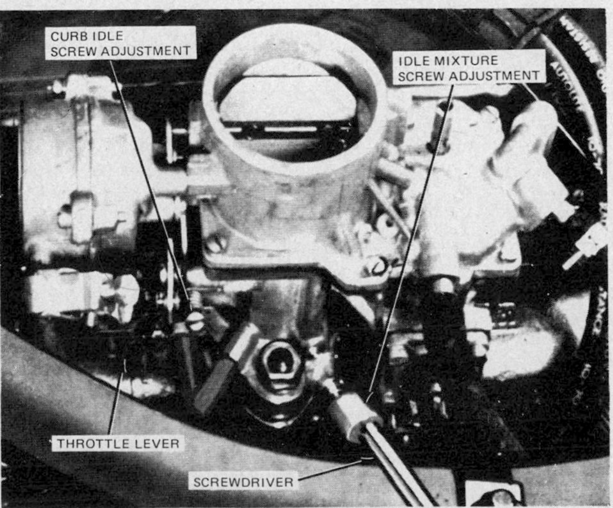

1600 cc idle speed and mixture adjustment screws
(© Ford Motor Co)

Throttle solenoid adjustment on the Autolite 5200 carburetor
(© Ford Motor Co)

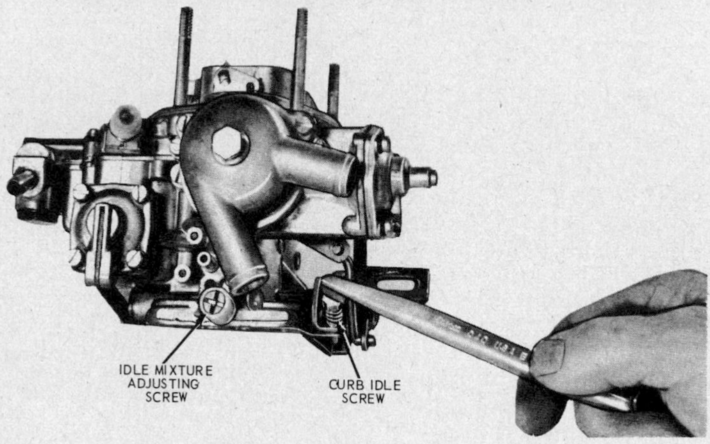

Autolite 5200 carburetor idle adjustments
(© Ford Motor Co)

selector in Drive and the wheels blocked.

2. Turn the carburetor curb idle screw in or out as necessary to correct the idle speed to the figure in the "Tune-Up Specifications" chart.
3. Adjust the carburetor idle mixture adjusting screw to obtain the smoothest idle.
4. Turn off the engine and install the air cleaner. Restart the engine and check the idle speed. If the idle speed has changed, remove the air cleaner and readjust the idle speed. Repeat this operation until the idle speed is correct.

2000 cc, 2300 cc With Air Conditioning

1. Turn the air conditioner on and, if equipped with automatic transmission, block the wheels and place the selector in Drive.
2. Check the idle speed and, if it isn't equal to the higher figure given in the "Tune-up Specifications" chart, turn the adjusting nut on the bottom of the carburetor solenoid to correct it.
3. Disconnect the solenoid at the quick-disconnect. Turn the air conditioner off and, on automatic-equipped cars, put the selector in neutral.
4. Check the idle speed. If it does not conform with the lower figure in the "Tune-Up Specifications" chart, adjust the carburetor curb idle screw to correct it.
5. Reconnect the solenoid. Open the throttle slightly and check to see that the solenoid plunger extends. The idle speed should be increased to the higher figure listed in the "Tune-Up Specifications" chart.
6. Turn the carburetor idle mixture screw until the smoothest idle is obtained.
7. Turn the engine off and install the air cleaner. Restart the engine and check the idle speed (A/C on, automatic transmission in Drive). If an adjustment is necessary, turn the engine off and remove the air cleaner. Start the engine and adjust the idle speed. Repeat this operation as many times as necessary.

302 V8

1. Warm up the engine to normal operating temperature.
2. Check timing and adjust if necessary.
3. If applicable, remove the spark delay valve and connect the part throttle vacuum line to the advance side of the distributor. Leave the manifold vacuum line connected to the retard side.
4. Disconnect the EGR valve and plug the line.
5. With the dashpot set at 0.080 in. (manual transmission models only), manual transmission in neutral; automatic in Drive, set the idle speed to that specified with the idle speed screw.
6. In neutral, raise the engine speed to 2200 RPM for about 5 seconds.
7. Let the engine return to normal idle and readjust if necessary, remembering to check the dashpot setting on manual transmission models.
8. Replace the spark delay valve and reconnect the vacuum line to the EGR valve.

COOLING SYSTEM

The cooling system consists of the water pump, fan, thermostat, radiator, and connecting lines. Coolant is circulated from the bottom of the radiator up through the water pump and into the cylinder block and cylinder head to the thermostat. If the engine is at operating temperature (or hotter), the coolant is returned to the radiator top tank, from where it flows down through the radiator tubes to be cooled by air. If the engine is cold, the coolant flows through a bypass hose to allow the coolant in the block and head to warm up quickly.

Radiator Removal and Installation

1. Remove the radiator cap and drain the coolant.
2. Disconnect the charcoal canister line from the clip on the radiator.
3. Disconnect the radiator hoses from the radiator.
4. Disconnect the transmission oil cooler lines from the bottom of the radiator, if so equipped.
5. Place a block of wood under the radiator for support and remove the mounting bolts. Position the fan shroud, if so equipped, rearward over the fan. Remove the radiator.
6. Reverse the removal procedure to install the radiator. Refill the cooling system.

Water Pump Removal and Installation

1. Drain the cooling system.

2. Disconnect the lower radiator hose and heater hose from the water pump.
3. Loosen the alternator retaining and adjusting bolt, and remove the drive belt.
4. Remove the fan and water pump pulley. On 2000 and 2300 cc engines, remove the camshaft drive belt cover.
5. Remove the water pump retaining bolts and remove the pump from the engine.
6. Clean all mating surfaces and install the pump with a new gasket coated with sealer. If a new pump is being installed, transfer the heater hose fitting from the old pump.
7. Reverse the removal steps to install the pump. Refill the cooling system.

Thermostat Removal and Installation

1. Drain the cooling system.
2. Remove the thermostat housing attaching bolts.

NOTE: On the 2800 cc V6, the thermostat is located on the bottom of the water pump housing. The thermostat housing connects to the radiator lower hose, instead of the upper hose.

3. On 1600 cc and 302 V8 engines, lift the thermostat housing from the engine and remove the thermostat and gasket.
4. On 2000 cc engines, remove the retaining clip, thermostat, thermostat seal, and gasket from the housing.
5. Clean the gasket mating surfaces and the thermostat housing.
6. Install the thermostat, gasket, seal, and retaining clip (2000 cc only) in the thermostat housing. Coat the gasket with sealer.
7. Install the attaching bolts and tighten them to 12–15 ft lbs.
8. Refill the cooling system.

EMISSION CONTROLS

Testing and diagnosis of emission control equipment that is not covered in this section is included in the "Emission Control" section of the "Unit Repair Section."

Distributor Controls

Dual-Diaphragm Distributor

Certain models use a dual-diaphragm distributor. This distributor has a normal set of centrifugal advance weights and vacuum diaphragm advance, with the addition of another diaphragm controlled by manifold vacuum. This second diaphragm acts to retard the spark under deceleration and idle, when manifold vacuum is greatest. While this decreases the power of the engine at these times, there is an increase in the braking effect of the engine and hydrocarbon emissions are reduced.

Coolant Temperature Control Valve

Certain models use a coolant temperature control valve which screws into the water jacket. Vacuum lines connect it to the carburetor, outer distributor vacuum chamber (advance), and the intake manifold. This valve helps prevent overheating by connecting intake manifold vacuum to the distributor and allowing vacuum advance during idling when the coolant temperature reaches a certain point.

Spark Delay Valve

Some models utilize a spark delay in the vacuum line to the vacuum advance chamber of the distributor. This valve cuts off vacuum advance during certain heavy throttle applications for a period of seconds.

Electronic Spark Control

This system blocks carburetor vacuum to the distributor vacuum advance mechanism under certain speed and temperature conditions. It consists of a temperature sensor, a speed sensor, an amplifier, and a distributor modulator vacuum valve. This system prevents ignition advance by blocking carburetor vacuum from the distributor advance mechanism until the car reaches 35 mph when the ambient temperature is over 65°F.

The temperature sensor monitors outside air temperature and relays this information to the amplifier. The amplifier controls the distributor modulator vacuum valve, which is connected into the carburetor-to-distributor vacuum line and is normally open. When the temperature is over 65°F, the sensor sends a signal to the amplifier which relays the signal to the distributor vacuum modulator. The modulator closes, cutting off ignition advance, until vehicle speed reaches 35 mph as signaled by the speed sensor in the speedometer cable. When the ambient temperature is below 49° the system does not function.

Exhaust Gas Recirculation

Some models utilize an Exhaust Gas Recirculation System (EGR) to control oxides of nitrogen. On V6 engines, exhaust gases travel through the exhaust gas crossover passage in the intake manifold. A portion of these gases are diverted into a spacer which is mounted under the carburetor. The EGR control valve, which is attached to the rear of the spacer, consists of a vacuum diaphragm with an attached plunger which normally block off exhaust gases from entering the intake manifold. On 4 cylinder engines, an external tube carries exhaust manifold gases to the carburetor spacer. The EGR valve is controlled by a vacuum line from the carburetor.

A new exhaust gas recirculation signal vacuum control system is used on the 302 V8. The new system uses an exhaust backpressure transducer to regulate the EGR valve spark port vacuum signal which modulates the flow of EGR. This matches the amount of EGR to the engine load more accurately; improving engine driveability and fuel economy.

Thermactor

From 1974 on, some models are equipped with an air injection system. The thermactor system consists of an air pump, check valves, anti-backfire valve, and air distribution and injection tubes. The belt driven air pump injects air into the exhaust manifold near the cylinder head. The air combines with the gases leaving the cylinders and burns off some of the harmful exhaust gases.

Catalytic Converter

Starting 1975, some Pintos, Bobcats, and Mustang IIs and all California cars, are equipped with catalytic converter units. While the unit does not require servicing until replacement, there are some precautions that must be observed.

1. Use unleaded fuel; the use of leaded fuel in a converter equipped car will invalidate the warranty.
2. Running out of gas may cause damage to the catalyst.
3. Proper engine maintenance is important. Misfires and other malfunctions can cause overheating and converter damage.
4. Do not run the engine for more than 30 seconds with a plug wire off or shorted.
5. Do not run an overly rich mixture for a long period of time.
6. Check ignition performance with an oscilloscope rather than by pulling a plug wire off.

Fuel System Controls

Carburetors

Carburetors are calibrated for leaner mixtures to decrease unburned hydrocarbon emissions. Idle mixture adjusting screws are equipped with limiter caps to prevent their being adjusted for excessively rich air-fuel mixtures at idle. The 1600 cc engine and 2000 cc engines equipped with air conditioning have a throttle positioning solenoid, which raises the idle speed when energized and retracts from the throttle lever when de-energized to prevent dieseling.

Deceleration Valve

1971-72 All Models; 1973 2000 cc With Manual Transmission; All Models 1974 and later

This valve is a vacuum-actuated valve which is attached to the intake manifold and connected to the carburetor with an air-fuel line. High vacuum during deceleration opens the valve and draws a metered air-fuel mixture through the hose from the carburetor. This enters the intake manifold and then the combustion chamber, where it is burned. This extra mixture slows the engine's deceleration rate and reduces the usually high exhaust emissions during slow-down. Tests and parts replacement procedures follow. A malfunctioning deceleration valve can be caused by one of three things: a leaking diaphragm, a defective poppet valve, or improper adjustment.

Decel Valve Replacement

1. Disconnect the air-fuel hose from the decel valve.
2. Loosen the union nut that attaches the decel valve to the intake manifold.
3. Reverse the removal steps to install the valve.

Poppet Valve Replacement

1. While holding the decel valve cover, loosen the four retaining screws.
2. Remove the screws and gradually release the spring pressure from the cover.
3. Remove the cover and invert the valve to remove the poppet valve and spring.
4. Install the new valve using a reverse of the removal procedure.

Diaphragm Replacement

1. Remove the bottom cover from the decel valve.
2. Remove the diaphragm and spring retainer.
3. Install the replacement diaphragm and spring retainer into the bottom of the housing.
4. Install the bottom cover on the decel valve.

Heated Air Intake Air Cleaner

The air cleaner is equipped with a thermostatically controlled door in the air cleaner snorkel. When the underhood temperature is under 90°F, the door is closed, blocking off cooler underhood air from the air cleaner and allowing heated air from a shroud over the exhaust manifold to enter. When the temperature is over 130°F, the door opens allowing the cooler underhood air to enter the air cleaner.

Evaporative Emission Control System

All models are equipped with a fuel vapor control system. The system has four major components—the fuel tank, the vapor separator, the three-way control valve, and the vapor absorbing charcoal canister. The fuel tank is equipped with a non-vented filler cap and has the vapor separator welded to its top side. The vapor separator cannot be serviced separately if defective—the entire fuel tank must be replaced.

The tank fuel filler neck is double-sealed and, in addition to fulfilling its primary function of receiving fuel, vents air through a secondary chamber and indicates fuel level.

The vapor separator (see illustration) serves to prevent the entry of liquid fuel into the three-way control valve supply line.

The three-way control valve has three internal valves—a check valve to regulate fuel control (0.3-0.65 psi), a safety pressure relief valve to permit vapor blow-off in case of a plugged vapor line, and a vacuum relief air valve to replace air in the tank as fuel is consumed (to prevent tank collapse).

Crankcase Emission Controls

Crankcase emission control equipment consists of an oil separator (mounted on the side of the engine block), a positive crankcase ventilation (PCV) valve (mounted on the top of the oil separator), a closed oil filler cap, and connecting hoses.

ENGINE

The standard engine used in the Pinto through 1973 is a 1600 cc, four-cylinder, inline overhead valve unit having a cross-flow cylinder head and piston-shaped combustion chambers. The cylinder bores are machined in the cast-iron block and cooled by full-length water jackets.

The crankshaft is made of cast iron and runs in five main bearings. End-play is controlled by half thrust washers on each side of the center main bearing.

The connecting rods are forged steel and pistons are solid skirt aluminum alloy with two compression rings and one oil ring. Piston pins are full-floating.

The camshaft is driven in a conventional manner, at one-half engine speed, by a single-row roller chain. A helical gear on the cam drives the distributor and oil pump, while an eccentric operates the fuel pump.

The cast-iron cylinder head has integral valve guides; although guide replacement is possible and sleeves are available. Intake valves are aluminum coated, and cannot be refaced.

The 2000 and 2300 cc, overhead camshaft, four-cylinder engine is of cast-iron construction. The crankshaft is supported by five main bearings and the camshaft by three bearings. The camshaft is belt driven by the crankshaft. Belt tension is adjusted by a spring loaded idler pulley.

The pistons are made from an aluminum alloy and forged steel connecting rods are used.

The 2800 cc engine is a V6 overhead valve design. The cylinder heads and engine block are made of cast iron. Four main bearings support the crankshaft. The distributor and the oil pump are driven by an eccentric at the front of the camshaft. The connecting rods are forged steel with replaceable copper-lead alloy insert bearings. The intake manifold is made from aluminum and has individual passages to the openings in the cylinder heads. The V6 has a full pressure lubrication system fed by a rotor type oil pump mounted at the rear of the crankcase.

Starting 1975, the Mustang II was offered with an optional 302 cubic inch V8. This is the same engine as used in other Ford cars, an overhead valve design with wedge shaped combustion chambers.

Caution Metric and standard thread bolts are mixed throughout all the four and six cylinder engines and transmissions. Only metric tools should be used to remove metric bolts.

If any repair operation requires the removal of a component of the air conditioning system (on vehicles so equipped), do not disconnect the refrigerant lines. If it is impossible to move the component out of the way with the lines attached, have the system evacuated. Air conditioning systems contain pressurized Freon, which is very dangerous to the untrained.

NOTE: For more extensive details on the 302 V8, see the Comet car section.

Engine Removal—1600 cc

1. Remove hood, after scribing matchmarks around hinges.
2. Disconnect battery cables.
3. Drain the cooling system.

NOTE: drain engine block as well as radiator.

4. Disconnect radiator hoses and remove radiator.
5. Remove air cleaner assembly.
6. Disconnect heater hoses from water pump and intake manifold.
7. Disconnect throttle linkage.
8. Disconnect oil pressure and temperature sender wires, then dis-

connect alternator wires. Disconnect the carburetor solenoid and coil battery wires.

NOTE: it is a good idea to tag these wires.

9. Disconnect exhaust pipe from manifold and remove hot air tubes.
10. Disconnect fuel inlet line at fuel pump.

NOTE: plug the line so that gas does not siphon from tank.

11. Disconnect coil wires, then remove spark plug wires and distributor cap.
12. Jack up the front of the car and support on axle stands.
13. Disconnect starter wires, remove starter and oil pan shield.
14. Remove clutch cover. Drain the oil.
15. Lower the car to the floor.
16. Remove clutch housing-to-engine bolts, then install lifting brackets and chain hoist.
17. Disconnect the front motor mounts, while supporting engine with chain hoist.
18. Place an axle stand or wooden block under the transmission.
19. Raise the engine slightly, while pulling forward to separate the transmission input shaft from the clutch; lift engine out of car.

Engine Installation—1600 cc

1. Position the engine assembly in the engine compartment and start the input shaft into the clutch disc. It may be necessary to adjust the position of the transmission if the input shaft doesn't enter the clutch disc properly. If the engine won't move after the shaft enters the clutch, turn the crankshaft pulley slowly with the transmission in gear until the splines on the input shaft align with those on the clutch disc.
2. Slide the engine rearward, making sure the flywheel upper cover plate engages the dowels on the clutch housing. Align the front motor mounts and the exhaust manifold with the exhaust pipe.
3. Install the front motor mount nuts and tighten them to 20–30 ft lbs.
4. Install and tighten the upper clutch housing-to-engine attaching bolts. Make sure that the engine ground strap is secured by the upper left bolt.
5. Install the distributor cap and wires. Connect the fuel line to the fuel pump.
6. Connect the oil pressure water temperature sending unit wires. Connect the carburetor solenoid and distributor battery wires.
7. Connect the alternator wires.
8. Connect the exhaust pipe to the exhaust manifold and install the heat duct on the manifold.
9. Connect the throttle linkage to the carburetor.
10. Connect the heater hoses to the engine.
11. Install the radiator and connect the hoses.
12. Install the air cleaner.
13. Jack the front of the car up and support it with stands.
14. Install the starter and connect the cable.
15. Install the lower clutch housing cover.
16. Install the oil pan drain plug and the cooling system drain plug in the block. Close the radiator petcock.
17. Remove the jack stands and lower the car.
18. Fill the engine with oil and the cooling system with coolant.
19. Connect the negative battery cable.
20. Start the engine and allow it to idle. Check for leaks and perform any necessary adjustments.
21. Install the hood.

Engine Removal—2000 cc

1. Drain the engine of coolant and oil. Remove the hood.
2. Remove the air cleaner and the exhaust manifold shroud.
3. Disconnect the battery ground cable.
4. Remove the upper and lower hoses from the radiator.
5. Remove the radiator and fan.
6. Disconnect the heater hose from the water pump and carburetor choke fitting.
7. Disconnect the wires from the alternator and starter. It is good practice to tag these wires to prevent confusion during installation.
8. Disconnect the carburetor accelerator cable. If the vehicle is equipped with air conditioning, remove the compressor from the mounting bracket and lay it aside.

NOTE: leave the refrigerant lines attached.

9. Disconnect the flexible fuel line from the fuel tank line and plug the fuel tank line.
10. Disconnect the coil primary wire and the water temperature and oil temperature sending units.
11. Jack up vehicle and remove the starter.
12. Remove the flywheel (or converter housing) upper mounting bolts.

NOTE: Two 10 mm × 3/8 in. studs are used to attach the upper housing to the engine. If the studs are removed, make sure they are reinstalled with the metric threads in the engine block.

13. Disconnect the exhaust pipe at the exhaust manifold. Unbolt the engine right and left mount at the underbody bracket. Remove the flywheel (or converter housing) cover.
14. On vehicles equipped with manual transmissions, remove the flywheel housing lower mounting bolts. On automatic transmission vehicles, disconnect the converter from the flywheel and remove the converter housing lower mounting bolts. It is necessary to turn the crankshaft pulley to gain access to the four converter - to - flywheel attaching nuts.
15. Lower the vehicle and support the transmission or converter housing with a hydraulic jack.
16. Attach the engine lifting apparatus and carefully pull the engine from the engine compartment.
17. On automatic transmission-equipped vehicles, match-mark the flywheel and the torque converter so they can be rejoined correctly.

Engine Installation—2000 cc

1. Place a new gasket over the exhaust pipe.
2. Carefully, lower the engine into the engine compartment. Be sure that the exhaust manifold studs are aligned with the holes in the exhaust pipe flange. On a vehicle with automatic transmission, start the converter pilot shaft into the crankshaft. On manual transmission cars, start the transmission drive gear into the clutch disc. It may be necessary to adjust the position of the transmission with relation to the engine if the input shaft fails to enter the clutch disc. If the engine hangs up after the shaft enters, turn the crankshaft slowly with the transmission in gear, until the input shaft splines mesh with the clutch disc splines.
3. Remove the lifting apparatus and install the flywheel (or converter housing) upper mounting bolts.
4. Remove the jack from the transmission and jack up vehicle.
5. Install the flywheel (or converter housing) lower mounting bolts. On an automatic transmission car, attach the converter to the flywheel and torque to 23-28 ft. lbs.
6. Install the flywheel (or converter housing) dust cover.
7. Install the engine left and right mounting brackets to the underbody.
8. Unplug the fuel tank line and connect it to the flexible line. Tighten the exhaust pipe and exhaust manifold.
9. Lower the vehicle and connect the water and oil temperature

sending units, coil primary wire and accelerator cable.

10. Install and connect the starter. Connect the alternator wires, and heater hose to the water pump and carburetor choke fitting.
11. Install the fan pulley, fan and drive belt. On vehicles equipped with air conditioning, install the compressor on the mounting bracket and adjust the belt tension. Drive belt should sag approximately ½ in. under thumb pressure at the middle of the longest side.
12. Install the radiator and connect the upper and lower hoses. Fill and bleed the cooling system. Fill the engine with the proper amount and grade of engine oil.
13. Connect the battery ground cable and operate the engine at fast idle, checking all gaskets and hoses for leaks.
14. On automatic transmission vehicles, adjust the transmission control linkage.
15. Install the air cleaner and connect the crankcase ventilation hose.
16. Install the hood.

Engine Removal—2300 cc

1. Raise the hood and fasten it up.
2. Drain the coolant from the radiator and the oil from the crankcase.
3. Remove the air cleaner and the exhaust manifold shroud.
4. Disconnect the ground cable from the battery.
5. Remove the radiator upper and lower hoses.
6. Remove the radiator and fan.
7. Disconnect the heater hose from the water pump and carburetor choke fitting.
8. Disconnect the alternator wires from the alternator, starter cable from the starter, and the accelerator cable from the carburetor. With air conditioning, remove the compressor from the mounting bracket, and position it out of the way, leaving the refrigerant lines attached.
9. Disconnect the flexible fuel line at the fuel pump line and plug the fuel line.
10. Disconnect the coil primary wire at the coil. Disconnect the oil pressure and the water temperature sending unit wires at the sending units.
11. Remove the starter.
12. Raise the vehicle. Remove the flywheel or converter housing upper attaching bolts.
13. Disconnect the headpipe at the exhaust manifold. Disconnect the engine right and left mounts at the underbody bracket. Remove the flywheel or converter housing cover.

    With automatic transmission, disconnect the converter from the flywheel. Remove the converter housing lower attaching bolts.

    With manual transmission, remove the flywheel housing lower attaching bolts.
14. Lower the vehicle. Support the transmission and the flywheel or converter housing with a jack.
15. Attach the engine lifting device to the existing lifting brackets.
16. Carefully lift the engine out of the engine compartment.

Engine Installation—2300 cc

1. Carefully lower the engine into the engine compartment.
2. Make sure that the studs on the exhaust manifold are aligned with the holes in the lead pipe.

   With automatic transmission, start the converter pilot into the crankshaft.

   With manual transmission, start the transmission main drive gear into the clutch disc. It may be necessary to adjust the position of the transmission in relation to the engine if the input shaft will not enter the clutch disc. If the engine hangs up after the shaft enters, turn the crankshaft slowly clockwise, with the transmission in gear, until the shaft splines mesh with the clutch disc splines.
3. Install the flywheel or converter housing upper attaching bolts. Remove the engine lifting sling hooks.
4. Remove the jack from the transmission. Raise the vehicle.
5. Install the flywheel or converter housing lower attaching bolts.

   With automatic transmission, attach the converter to the flywheel.
6. Install the flywheel or converter housing dust cover.
7. Install the engine left and right mount to the underbody bracket.
8. Remove the plug from the fuel line and connect the flexible fuel line to the fuel pump line. Install the exhaust manifold to headpipe nuts.
9. Lower the vehicle. Connect the oil pressure and engine temperature sending unit wires. Connect the coil primary wire. Connect the accelerator cable.
10. Install the starter motor. Connect the starter cable. Connect the alternator wires. Connect the heater hose at the water pump and carburetor for the choke fitting.
11. Install the pulley, fan, and drive belt. Adjust the drive belt tension. With air conditioning, install the compressor on the mounting bracket, and adjust the belt tension. Install the radiator. Connect the radiator upper and lower hoses. Fill and bleed the cooling system. Fill the crankcase with the proper type and quantity of motor oil.
12. Connect the battery ground cable.
13. Operate the engine at fast idle and check all gaskets and hose connections for leaks.

    With an automatic transmission, adjust the transmission control linkage, as necessary.
14. Install the air cleaner and connect the PCV hose.

Engine Removal—2800 cc V6

1. Disconnect the battery, drain the cooling system and remove the hood.
2. Remove the air cleaner and intake duct assembly.
3. Disconnect the upper and lower hoses at the radiator.
4. Remove the fan shroud attaching bolts and position the shroud over the fan. Remove the radiator and shroud.
5. Remove the alternator and bracket. Position the alternator out of the way. Disconnect the alternator ground wire from the cylinder block.
6. Disconnect the heater hoses at the block and water pump.
7. Remove the ground wires from the cylinder block.
8. Disconnect the fuel line at the fuel pump. Plug the fuel tank line.
9. Disconnect the accelerator cable or linkage at the carburetor and intake manifold. Disconnect the automatic transmission downshift linkage.
10. Disconnect the engine wire loom at the ignition coil. Disconnect the brake booster vacuum line
11. Raise the vehicle on a hoist.
12. Disconnect the headpipes at the exhaust manifolds.
13. Disconnect the starter cable and remove the starter.
14. Remove the engine front support through-bolts; remove engine insulator to block bolts.
15. With automatic transmission, remove the converter inspection cover and disconnect the flywheel from the converter.

    Remove the downshift rod.

    Remove the converter housing-to-engine block bolts and the adapter plate-to-converter housing bolt.

    With manual transmission, remove the clutch linkage and remove the bellhousing-to-engine block bolts.
16. Lower the vehicle.
17. Attach an engine lifting device to the lifting brackets at the exhaust manifolds.
18. Position a jack under the transmission.

19. Raise the engine slightly and carefully pull it from the transmission. Carefully lift the engine out of the engine compartment so that the rear cover plate is not bent or parts damaged.

Engine Installation—2800 cc V6

1. Lower the engine carefully into the engine compartment. Make sure that the exhaust manifolds are properly aligned with the headpipes.

   With manual transmission, start the transmission main driveshaft into the clutch disc. It may be necessary to adjust the position of the transmission in relation to the engine if the input shaft will not enter the clutch disc. If the engine hangs up after the shaft enters, turn the crankshaft slowly, with the transmission in gear, until the shaft splines mesh with the clutch disc splines.

   With automatic transmission, start the converter pilot into the crankshaft.
3. Install the bellhousing or converter housing upper bolts, making sure that the dowels in the cylinder block engage the flywheel housing. Remove the jack from under the transmission.
4. Remove the lifting device from the engine.
5. With automatic transmission, position the downshift rod on the transmission and engine.
6. Raise the vehicle on a hoist.
7. With automatic transmission, position the transmission linkage bracket and install the remaining converter housing bolts. Install the adapter plate-to-converter housing bolts. Install the converter-to-flywheel nuts and install the inspection cover. Connect the downshift rod on the transmission.

   On manual transmission cars, install the lower bellhousing bolts and connect the clutch linkage to the engine block.
8. Install the starter and connect the cable.
9. Connect the muffler inlet pipes at the exhaust manifolds.
10. Install the engine front support through-bolts.
11. Lower the vehicle.
12. Install the ground wire. Install the engine wire loom and connect it to the ignition coil, then install the water temperature sending unit and oil pressure sending unit. Connect the brake booster vacuum line.
13. Install the accelerator linkage and connect the automatic transmission downshift rod. Connect the vacuum lines. Connect the fuel tank line at the fuel pump.
14. Connect the ground wire at the cylinder block. Install the heater hoses at the water pump and cylinder block.
15. Install the alternator and bracket. Connect the alternator ground wire to the cylinder block. Install the drive belt and adjust the belt tension.
16. Position the fan shroud over the fan. Install the radiator and connect the upper and lower radiator hoses. Install the fan shroud attaching bolts.
17. Fill and bleed the cooling system. Fill the crankcase with oil. Adjust the automatic transmission downshift linkage. Connect the battery.
18. Operate the engine at fast idle until it reaches normal operating temperature and check all gaskets and hose connections for leaks. Adjust the ignition timing and idle speed.
19. Install the air cleaner and intake duct. Install and adjust the hood.

Engine Manifolds

Intake Manifold Removal

All 4 Cylinder Models

1. Drain the cooling system.
2. Remove the air cleaner and disconnect the throttle shaft at the carburetor throttle lever.
3. Disconnect the fuel line and vacuum line from the carburetor. Disconnect the carburetor solenoid wire at the quick-disconnect.
4. Remove the choke thermostatic spring and water housing.
5. Disconnect the water outlet hose and crankcase ventilation hose from the intake manifold.
6. Disconnect the decel valve-to-carburetor hose at the carubretor.
7. Remove the intake manifold attaching bolts and remove the manifold.
8. Remove all gasket material.
9. If the intake manifold is to be replaced, transfer all necessary components to the new manifold. Loosen the union fitting on the manifold and remove the decel valve from the intake manifold. Remove the decel valve adaptor from the manifold by inserting a large allen wrench into the adaptor and turning the adaptor out of the manifold.

Intake Manifold Installation

All 4 Cylinder Models

1. Clean the cylinder head and intake manifold mating surfaces thoroughly.
2. Carefully coat the mating surfaces with sealer and position a new gasket on the studs. Install the manifold and torque the nuts alternately and evenly.
3. Further installation is the reverse of removal.

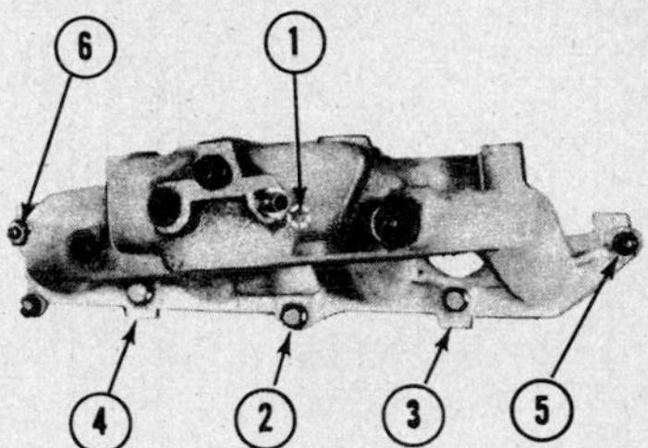

Intake manifold tightening sequence—2000 cc engine (© Ford Motor Co.)

Intake Manifold Removal and Installation

2800 cc V6

1. Remove the air cleaner assembly and disconnect the battery.
2. Disconnect the throttle cables.

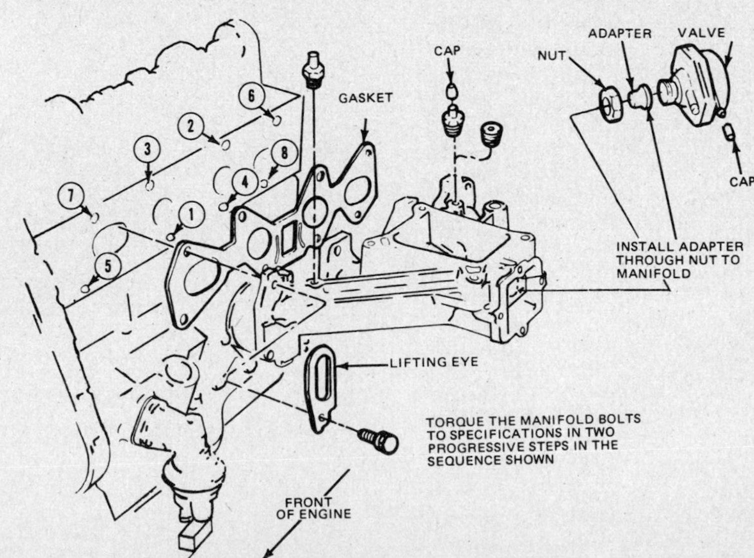

Intake manifold tightening sequence—2300 cc engine (© Ford Motor Co.)

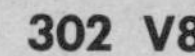

3. Drain the cooling system. Disconnect and remove the hose from the water outlet to the radiator and the hoses and line from the water outlet to the water pump.
4. Remove the distributor cap and spark plug wires as an assembly. Disconnect the distributor wire and the vacuum line.
5. Mark the position of the distributor and remove it.
6. Remove the fuel line and filter between the fuel pump and the carburetor and then remove the rocker arm covers.
7. Remove the intake manifold bolts and nuts. Tap the manifold lightly with a plastic hammer to break the gasket seal, and then lift off the manifold.
8. Remove all the gasket material and dirt from the manifold and cylinder heads.
9. Apply sealing compound to the joining surfaces. Place the manifold gasket in place. (Make sure that the tap on the right bank of the cylinder head gasket fits into the cutout of the manifold gasket.)

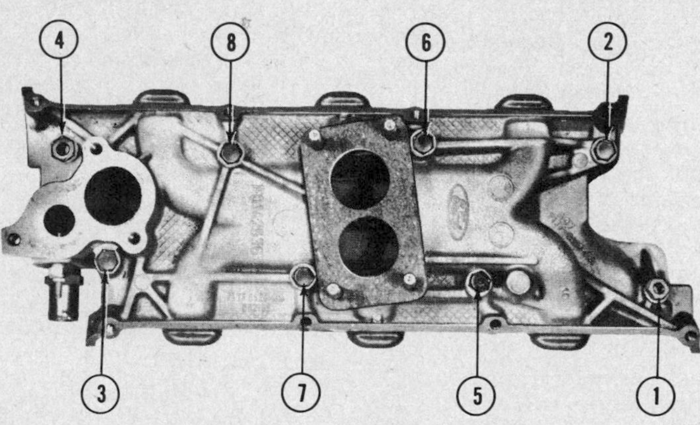

V6 intake manifold tightening sequence
(© Ford Motor Co)

10. Install the intake manifold. Tighten the attaching bolts until they are hand tight, and then tighten them, in sequence, to the proper torque.

NOTE: Tightening bolt no. 7 with a torque wrench will require an attachment called a "crow's foot."

11. Install the distributor so the rotor is pointing to the mark made previously.
12. Connect the distributor wire and vacuum line.
13. Install the carburetor, fuel line, fuel filter, and the rocker arm covers.
14. Install the distributor cap and wires.
15. Install and adjust the carburetor linkage.
16. Install the air cleaner assembly and air cleaner tube to the carburetor. Connect the battery.
17. Adjust the ignition timing.

302 V8

1. Drain the cooling system, remove the air cleaner assembly and disconnect the crankcase ventilation hose and choke heated air inlet hose.
2. Disconnect the throttle linkage from the carburetor; remove the automatic transmission and brake booster lines from the intake manifold.
3. Remove the air pump; remove the spark plug wires and distributor cap assembly with wires attached.
4. Remove the EGR vacuum amplifier, gas inlet line and automatic choke heat tube.
5. Remove the distributor and thermostat upper hose and sending unit assembly; remove the hose from the choke assembly to the intake manifold.
6. Remove the water pump bypass hose, and crankcase vent hose at the rocker arm cover.
7. Remove the air conditioner compressor-to-intake manifold brackets.
8. Remove the carburetor and intake manifold as an assembly.

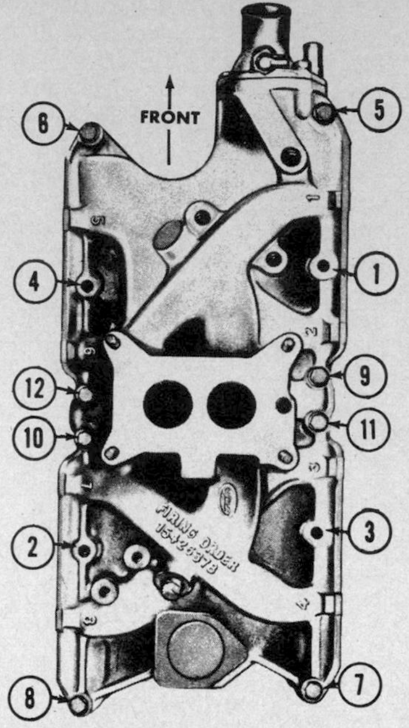

Intake manifold tightening sequence—302 V8 (© Ford Motor Co.)

NOTE: It may be necessary to pry the manifold away from the cylinder heads. Use caution to avoid damaging the sealing surfaces. Discard the intake manifold attaching bolt sealing washers.

9. If the manifold is to be disassembled, mark all vacuum hoses before disconnecting them.
10. For installation, clean the mating surfaces of the manifold and engine block.
11. Put new gaskets on the cylinder head and new seals on the engine block, checking to make sure they interlock. Apply sealer to the outside of each seal.

NOTE: Most sealers set up quickly so it is important that the rest of the operation be done as quickly as possible.

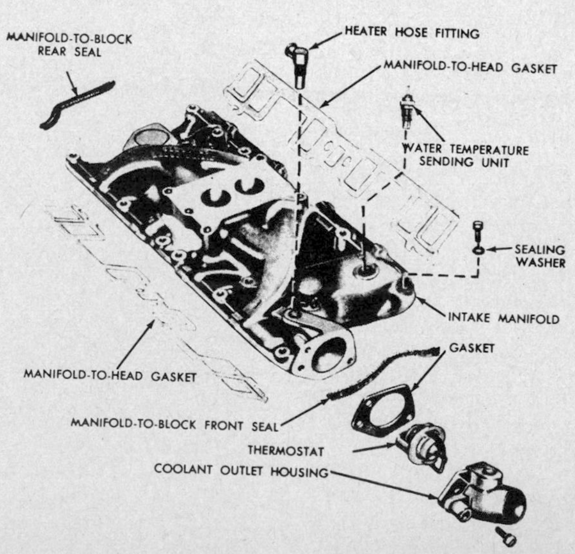

Intake manifold assembly with gaskets and seals—302 V8 (© Ford Motor Co.)

12. Lower the manifold to the block. When it is in place, run your finger around the seals to make sure they are in place.
13. Install the attaching nuts and bolts and torque to specifications in sequence.
14. Replace the distributor.
15. To complete the operation, reverse the procedure in the Steps 1-7.

Exhaust Manifold R & R

1600 cc

1. Remove the air cleaner.
2. Place a block of wood under the front of the exhaust pipe and disconnect the exhaust pipe from the manifold.
3. Remove the exhaust manifold attaching nuts and bolts, and remove the manifold.
4. If a new manifold is to be installed, remove the heat shroud from the old manifold and install it on the new manifold.
5. Clean the exhaust manifold and cylinder head mating surfaces.
6. Install a new gasket over the center studs on the cylinder head.
7. Position the exhaust manifold near the cylinder head and install the end exhaust manifold gaskets between the manifold and the head.
8. Install the attaching nuts and bolts and tighten them to the proper torque.
9. Connect the exhaust pipe to the manifold, remove the wood support, and install the air cleaner.

2000 and 2300 cc

1. Remove the air cleaner. Remove the heat shroud from the exhaust manifold.
2. Place a block of wood under the exhaust pipe, and then disconnect it from the manifold.

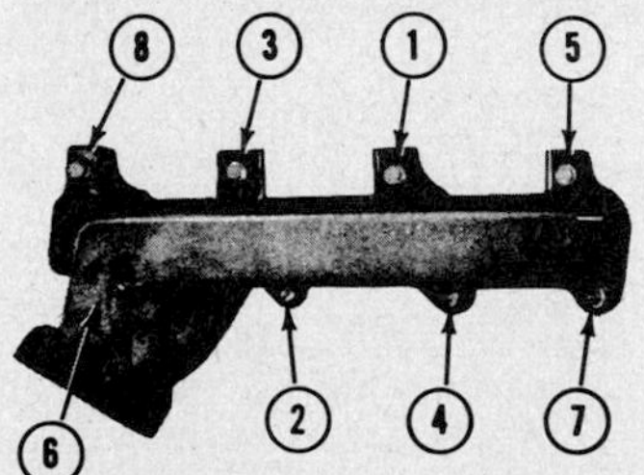

Exhaust manifold tightening sequence—2000 cc engine; 2300 cc is tightened in the same sequence
(© Ford Motor Co)

3. Remove the attaching nuts and remove the manifold from the head. Clean the mating surfaces.
4. Install a light coat of graphite grease on the exhaust manifold mating surface and position the manifold on the cylinder head.
5. Install the attaching nuts and tighten them to the proper torque.
6. Connect the exhaust pipe to the manifold and remove the wood support from under the pipe.
7. Install the air cleaner.

2800 cc

1. Remove the air cleaner.
2. Remove the four attaching nuts from the exhaust manifold shroud (right side only).
3. Disconnect the attaching nuts from the muffler inlet pipe.
4. Remove the exhaust manifold attaching nuts and remove the manifold.
5. These manifolds do not use gaskets. When installing the manifold, smear a light coat of graphite grease on the mating surfaces.
6. Position the manifold on the studs and install the bolts handtight then torque them evenly to the proper torque.
7. Install a new inlet pipe gasket and the attaching nuts.
8. Position the exhaust manifold shroud on the manifold and install the attaching nuts (right side).
9. Install the air cleaner.

302 V8

1. On the right exhaust manifold, remove the air cleaner, automatic choke heat tube and air cleaner heat ducts.
2. Disconnect the exhaust manifold(s) from the muffler inlet pipe(s).
3. Remove the manifold attaching bolts and remove the manifold(s).
4. Reverse the procedure to reinstall, using new inlet pipe gaskets.

Valve System

1600 cc

The valves are mounted vertically in the cylinder head, the intake valve heads being larger than the exhaust valve heads. The exhaust valves are stellite-coated for better heat and wear resistance, while the intake valves are coated with diffused aluminum for the same reason. *The factory does not recommend grinding the intake valves or lapping the intake valve seats, because the grinding operation removes the coating and shortens the life of the valve.* Exhaust valves, on the other hand, may be ground if necessary.

Valve stems are phosphate-coated for better wear resistance. Valve guides are cast integral with the head, although sleeves are available if guides become worn. In addition, valves are available with 0.003 and 0.015 in. oversize stem diameters.

The valve keepers do not grip the stem, allowing the valves to rotate freely during operation.

Valve Removal

1. Remove cylinder head, as previously described.
2. Compress valve springs, using valve spring compressor.
3. Remove valve locks or keys.
4. Release valve springs.

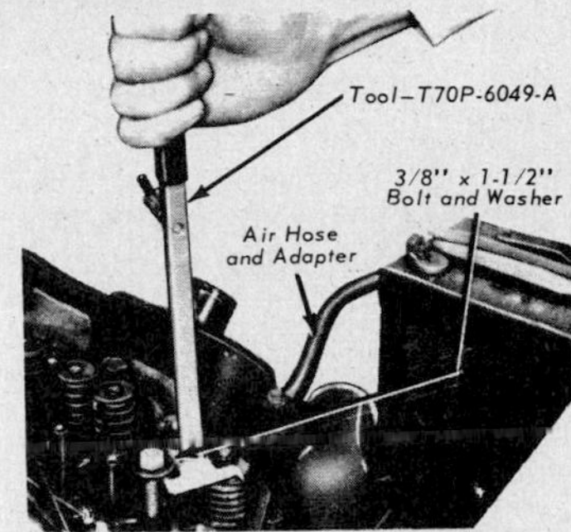

Removing valve spring with cylinder head installed—1600 cc
(© Ford Motor Co)

5. Remove valve springs, retainers, oil seals, and valves. Check valve spring squareness—5/64 in. is maximum permissible tolerance.

NOTE: if a valve does not slide out of the guide easily, check end of stem for mushrooming or heading over. If head is mushroomed, file off excess material, remove and discard valve. If valve is not mushroomed, lubricate stem, remove valve and check guide for galling. Valve seat width (minimum and desirable) is 1/16 in. for intakes, 5/64 in. for exhausts.

Valve Adjustment

1600 cc

Valves are set with the engine at normal operating temperature and turned off.

1. Remove the air cleaner. Disconnect the carburetor solenoid wire at the connector near the rear of the valve cover.
2. Remove the throttle cable retaining screw, pry the end of the throttle cable off the carburetor stud, and position the cable out of the way.
3. Remove the valve cover. Identify the spark plug wires and disconnect them.

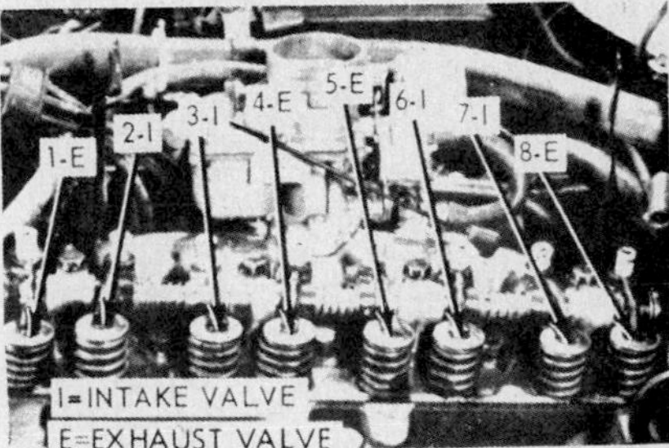

1600 cc engine valve identification
(© Ford Motor Co.)

4. Turn the engine to depress the proper valves by turning the crankshaft pulley.

Chilton's TIME SAVER

The following is a method for replacing valve springs, oil seals or spring retainers without removing the cylinder head.

1. **Obtain an air hose spark plug hole adaptor.**
2. **Remove the valve rocker cover.**
3. **Remove the rocker arm from the valve to be worked on.**
4. **Remove the spark plug from the cylinder to be worked on.**
5. **Turn the crankshaft to bring the piston of this cylinder down, away from possible contact with the valve head. Sharply tap the valve retainer to loosen the valve lock.**
6. **Then turn the crankshaft to bring the piston in this cylinder to the Exact Top of its Compression Stroke.**
7. **Screw in the spark plug hole adaptor.**
8. **Hook up an air hose to the chuck and turn on the pressure.**
9. **With a strong and constant supply of air holding the valve closed, compress the valve spring and remove the lock and retainer.**
10. **Make the necessary replacements and reassemble.**

NOTE: it is important that the operation be performed exactly as stated, in this order. The piston in the cylinder must be on exact top-center to prevent air pressure from turning the crankshaft.

Valve Clearance Adjustment

1600 cc Engine—Set Hot

Valve Depressed	*Valves to Adjust to .010*	*.017*
No. 1	No. 3	No. 8
No. 2	No. 7	No. 5
No. 3	No. 6	No. 1
No. 5	No. 2	No. 4

5. Insert a feeler gauge of the specified thickness between the tip of the rocker arm and the top of the valve. If an adjustment is necessary, turn the adjusting screw in or out as necessary.
6. Install the removed or disconnected components in a reverse order of removal. Tighten the valve cover retaining screws to 2.5–3.5 ft lbs.

2000 cc

Valves are set with engine cold.

1. Remove the air cleaner. Identify the spark plug wires and remove them, positioning them out of the way.

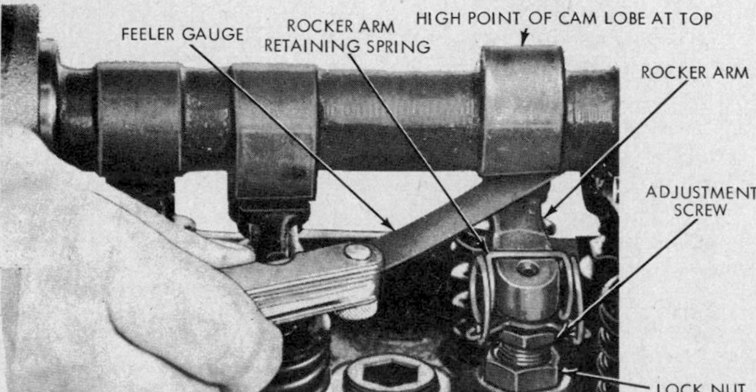

Checking valve clearance—2000 cc
(© Ford Motor Co)

2. On non-air-conditioned models, move the heater hose attached to the carburetor choke housing off the valve cover and out of the way. On air-conditioned models, disconnect the carburetor choke heater hose from the heater hot water valve and position it out of the way.

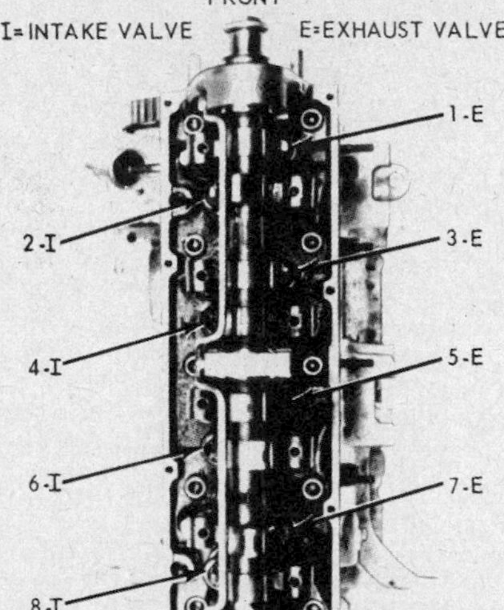

2000 cc engine valve identification
(© Ford Motor Co.)

3. Remove the valve cover retaining screw (note the position of the screws with rubber coated washers) and remove the valve cover.
4. Turn the crankshaft pulley to depress the valves specified in the chart.

Caution Never turn the pulley in a counterclockwise direction, as the camshaft drive belt may slip and alter the timing.

5. Check clearance according to the following chart:

Valve Clearance Adjustment

2000 cc Engine—Set Cold

Valve Depressed	*Valves to Adjust to .008*	*.010*
No. 1	No. 6	No. 7
No. 2	No. 8	No. 3
No. 3	No. 2	No. 5
No. 6	No. 4	No. 1

Clearance is checked between the rocker arm and the cam. Use a screwdriver to snap the retaining spring off the rocker arm until it hangs loose. Use a feeler gauge of the specified thickness to check the clearance.

6. If an adjustment is necessary, loosen the locknut and turn the adjusting screw in or out as necessary. When the adjustment is correct, tighten the locknut and snap the retaining spring back into place.
7. Replace the removed or disconnected components in a reverse order of removal. Tighten the rear valve cover cap screws to 4–6 ft lbs. from the back forward, the two vertical cap screws to 1–2 ft lbs, the two lateral cap screws to 4–6 ft lbs, and retighten the two vertical cap screws to 4–6 ft lbs.

2300 cc

This engine uses hydraulic lash adjusters. Thus, no routine valve adjustment is required.

2800 cc

Preliminary Adjustment (Cold)

1. Remove the rocker arm covers. Make sure that the rocker arm stand bolts are tight.
2. The valves are adjusted by positioning each piston in succession at TDC on the compression stroke in the firing order sequence, 1-4-2-5-3-6.
3. Rotate the crankshaft clockwise, as viewed from the front of the vehicle, until the No. 1 piston is on TDC at the end of the compression stroke.
4. With the crankshaft in the correct position, set the valve lash to 0.014 in. on the intake valve and 0.016 on the exhaust valve using a step-type feeler gauge (go and no go). Adjust the clearance by turning the adjusting

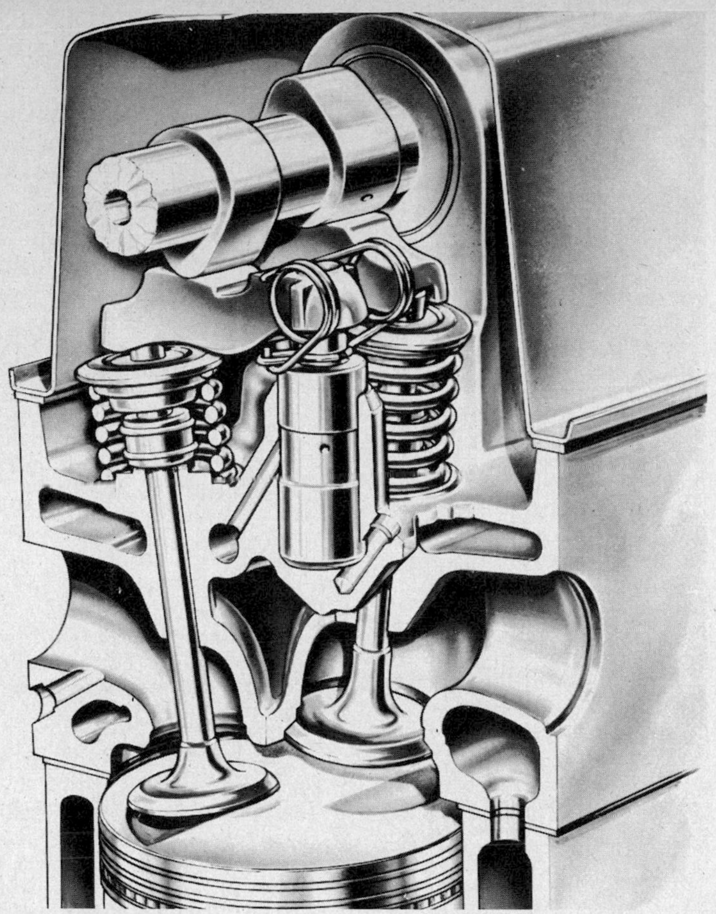

2300 cc engine valve train—not all engines will have the hairpin springs shown (© Ford Motor Co.)

nuts on the rockers. The adjusting nuts are self-locking.

The valve arrangement on the right bank, from front to rear, is: I-E-I-E-E-I; on the left bank, I-E-E-I-E-I.

5. Adjust the valves in the remaining cylinders following the firing order. This can be done by rotating the crankshaft in increments of 1/3 of a revolution (120 degrees) after adjusting the valves in each cylinder. This brings the next piston in the sequence to TDC.

Final Adjustment (Hot)

1. Start the engine and allow it to reach normal operating temperature.
2. With the engine idling, set the valve lash using a step-type feeler gauge (go and no go). Set the clearance to 0.014 in. on the intake valves and 0.016 in. on the exhaust valves.
3. Stop the engine and install the rocker covers.

302 V8

This hydraulic lifter adjustment is required whenever the valve train has been removed or disturbed, as in removing the cylinder heads.

1. Crank the engine until #1 cylinder is at TDC of the compression stroke and the timing pointer is aligned with the mark on the crankshaft damper.
2. Scribe a mark on the damper at this point.
3. Scribe three more marks on the damper, dividing the damper into quarters.
4. With the first mark aligned with the timing pointer, adjust the valves on #1 cylinder by backing off the adjusting nut until the pushrod has free play in it. Then, tighten the nut until it contacts the rocker shoulder, then torque to 18-20 ft lbs.
5. Repeat this procedure for each valve, turning the crankshaft ¼ turn to the next mark each time and following the engine firing order.

Rocker Arm or Shaft Replacement

1600 cc

1. Remove the valve cover as described under "Valve Adjustment." Disconnect the spark plug wires and move them out of the way.
2. Loosen each rocker shaft attaching bolt one turn at a time until all the bolts are loose.
3. Remove the rocker shaft.
4. To install, position the rocker shaft on the head and align the pushrods with the rocker arm adjusting screws.
5. Starting from the front of the engine and working back, tighten each bolt one turn at a time until the shaft is mounted on the head. Finally, tighten each bolt to 25-30 ft lbs.
6. Adjust the valves as previously described. Install the valve cover and spark plug wires.

2000 cc

1. Remove the valve cover as described under "Valve Adjustment."
2. Rotate the crankshaft in a clockwise direction until the cam lobe for the rocker arm that is to be removed is pointing straight up.
3. Remove the retaining spring from the rocker arm.
4. Depress the valve spring that corresponds to the rocker arm that is to be removed just enough to remove the rocker arm.
5. To install, position the rocker arm on the valve and adjusting screw and install the rocker arm retaining spring.
6. Adjust the valve clearance as previously described.
7. Install the valve cover, air cleaner, and any other components that were removed or disconnected in a reverse order of removal.

2300 cc

1. Remove the valve cover and associated parts as required.
2. Rotate the camshaft so that the base circle of the cam is against the cam follower you intend to remove.
3. Remove the retaining spring from the cam follower, if so equipped.
4. Using special tool T74P-6565-B or a valve spring compressor tool for a 2300 cc engine, collapse the lash adjuster and/or depress the valve spring, as necessary, and slide the cam follower over the

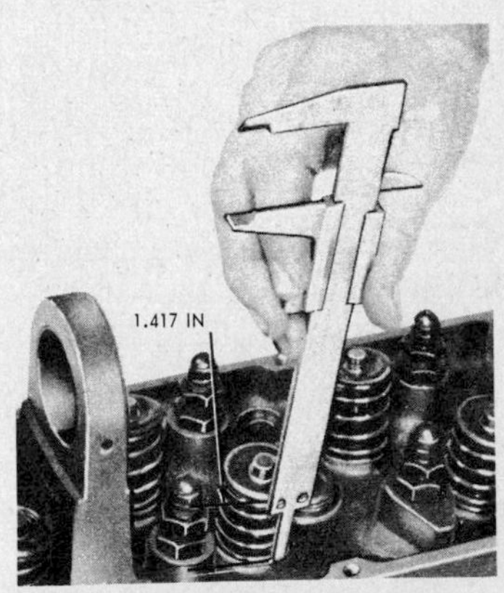

Checking Valve Spring Assembled Height (© Ford Motor Co.)

lash adjuster and out from under the camshaft.

5. Install the cam follower in the reverse order of removal. Make sure that the lash adjuster is collapsed and released before rotating the cam shaft.

2800 cc

1. Remove any emission control equipment as necessary to remove the rocker cover(s), remove the spark plug wires, remove the throttle linkage to the carburetor as necessary, and remove the valve rocker cover(s).
2. Remove the rocker arm shaft stand retaining bolts; loosen them each 2 turns at a time in sequence. Lift off the rocker arm and shaft assembly and the oil baffle.
3. Before installing the rocker shaft assemblies, back off the adjusting screws on the rockers a few turns. Install the rocker shafts in the reverse order of removal; tighten the rocker shaft stand retaining bolts 2 turns at a time in sequence until they are tight.

Cylinder Head

Removal—1600 cc

1. Remove the air cleaner, then disconnect the fuel line at the pump and the carburetor.
2. Drain the cooling system.
3. Disconnect spark plug wires, then disconnect heater and vacuum hoses from the intake manifold and choke housing.
4. Disconnect temperature sender wire, then disconnect exhaust pipe at manifold flange.
5. Disconnect throttle linkage and distributor vacuum line at carburetor. Disconnect the carburetor solenoid wire.
6. Remove thermostat housing and thermostat.
7. Remove rocker arm cover and gasket, then remove the rocker shaft bolts, evenly, and the rocker shaft assembly.
8. Remove pushrods and place them aside in proper order for correct installation.
9. Remove cylinder head bolts, head, and gasket.

Installation—1600 cc

1. Place a new head gasket on the block.
2. Position the cylinder head and install the bolts. Tighten evenly in sequence to proper torque.

NOTE: manifolds may be installed prior to placing head on block.

3. Install pushrods in correct order, then place rocker arms and shaft assembly on head and locate pushrods in rocker arm screws. Tighten rocker arm bolts to 25-30 ft. lbs.

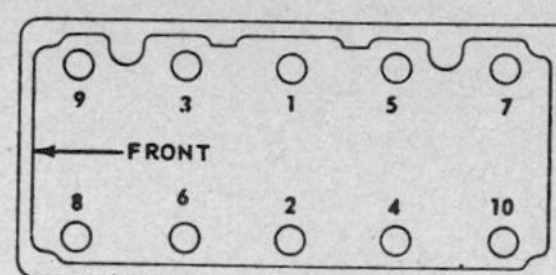

1600 cc cylinder head bolt tightening sequence

4. Adjust valve clearance, then install rocker arm cover and gasket.
5. Continue installation by reversing Steps 1-6 of removal procedure.

Removal—2000 cc and 2300 cc

1. Drain the cooling system.
2. Remove the air cleaner and the valve rocker cover.
3. Remove the intake and exhaust manifolds. The intake manifold, decel valve and carburetor can be removed as an assembly.
4. Remove the camshaft drive belt cover.
5. Loosen the drive belt tensioner and remove the drive belt.
6. Remove the water outlet from the cylinder head.
7. Remove the cylinder head bolts evenly, and remove the cylinder head.

NOTE: A special 12-point allen wrench is necessary to remove the head bolts on the 2000 cc engine. The cylinder head bolts on the 2300 cc engine have a 10-sided head, requiring a special tool.

Installation—2000 cc and 2300 cc

1. Position a new cylinder head gasket on the block.
2. Position the cylinder head and camshaft assembly on the block. Install the bolts finger tight, then torque according to specifications.

NOTE: If difficulty in positioning the head on the block is encountered, guide pins may be fabricated by cutting the heads off two extra cylinder head bolts.

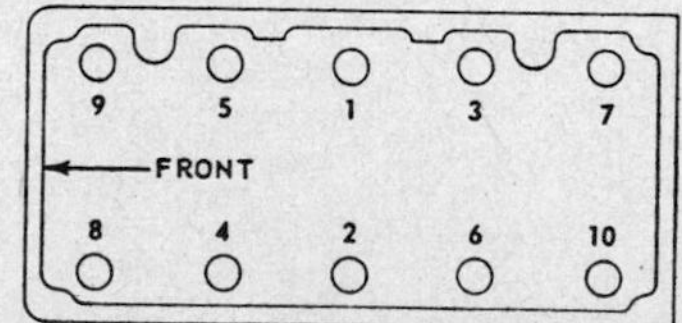

Cylinder head bolt tightening sequence 2000 cc and 2300 cc (© Ford Motor Co.)

3. Set the crankshaft at TDC and be sure that the camshaft drive gear and distributor are positioned correctly.
4. Install the camshaft drive belt and release the tensioner. Rotate the crankshaft two full turns to remove all slack from the belt. The timing marks should again be aligned. Tighten the tensioner lockbolt and pivot bolt.
5. Install the camshaft drive belt cover.
6. Apply sealer to the water outlet and new gasket, and install.
7. Install the intake and exhaust manifolds.
8. Adjust the valve clearance.
9. Install a new valve cover gasket and install the valve cover.
10. Install the air cleaner and crankcase ventilation hose.
11. Refill the cooling system.

Removal and Installation—2800 cc and 302 V8

1. Remove the air cleaner assembly and disconnect the battery and accelerator linkage. Drain the cooling system.
2. Remove the distributor cap with the spark plug wires attached. Remove the distributor vacuum line and distributor. Remove the hose from the water pump to the water outlet which is on the carburetor.
3. Remove the valve covers, fuel line and filter, carburetor, and the intake manifold.
4. Remove the rocker arm shaft and oil baffles. On the 302 V8, loosen the rocker arm stud nuts and rotate them to the side. Remove the pushrods, keeping them in the proper sequence for installation. Remove the exhaust valve stem caps on the 302 V8.
5. Remove the exhaust manifold, referring to the appropriate procedures.
6. Remove the cylinder head retaining bolts and remove the cylinder heads and gaskets.

Caution do not lay the cylinder head flat on its surface.

7. Remove all gasket material and carbon from the engine block and cylinder heads.
8. Place the head gaskets on the engine block.

NOTE: The left and right gaskets are not interchangeable.

9. Install guide studs in the engine block. Install the cylinder head assemblies on the engine block one at a time. Tighten the cylinder head bolts in sequence, and in steps, to 65-80 lbs.
10. Install the intake and exhaust manifolds.
11. Install the pushrods in the proper sequence. Install the oil baffles and the rocker arm shaft assemblies. Adjust the valve clearances.

Cylinder head bolt tightening sequence 302 V8 (© Ford Motor Co.)

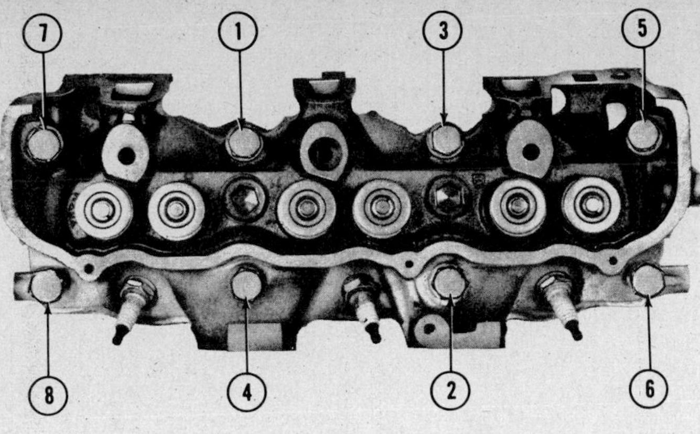

V6 cylinder head tightening sequence
(© Ford Motor Co)

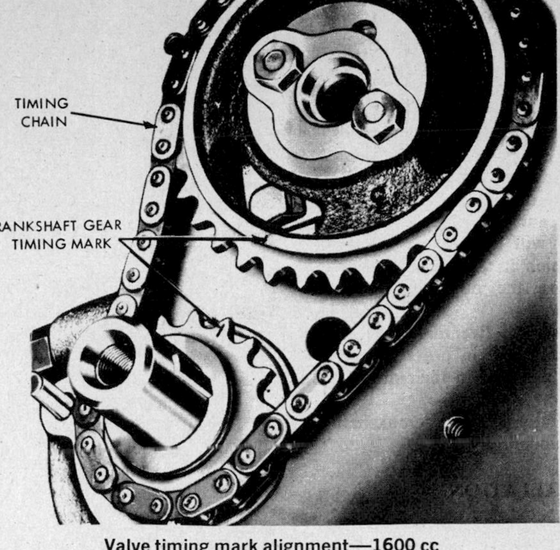

Valve timing mark alignment—1600 cc
(© Ford Motor Co)

12. Install the valve covers with new gaskets.
13. Install the distributor and set the ignition timing.
14. Install the carburetor and the distributor cap with the spark plug wires.
15. Connect the accelerator linkage, fuel line, with fuel filter installed, and distributor vacuum line to the carburetor. Fill the cooling system.

Timing Cover, Chain, and Camshaft—1600 cc

Timing Cover and Chain Replacement

1. Drain coolant.
2. Disconnect radiator hoses at the engine, then remove radiator.
3. Remove fanbelt, fan, and water pump pulley.
4. Remove the water pump.
5. Remove the crankshaft pulley, using a puller only.
6. Remove the front cover.

NOTE: cover is secured by four oil pan bolts as well.

Perform steps 7 through 13 to remove and install the timing chain.

7. With the transmission in Neutral, have an assistant tap the starter to align the cam and crankshaft sprockets.
8. Remove the timing chain tensioner.

Timing chain tensioner—1600 cc
(© Ford Motor Co)

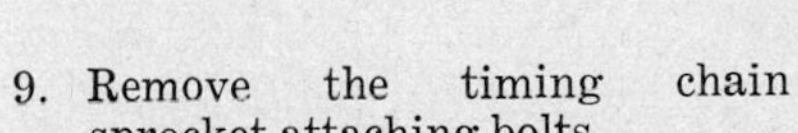

9. Remove the timing chain sprocket attaching bolts.
10. Slide the timing chain and the camshaft sprocket off the engine as an assembly.

NOTE: The timing chain tensioner pad is designed so that two grooves are gradually worn into it. Do not alter the grooves. Replace the chain and tensioner as a unit.

11. Install the replacement timing chain on the camshaft and crankshaft sprockets and align the timing marks.
12. Position the sprockets and timing chain on the engine. Be sure that the timing marks on the sprockets are aligned as shown in the figure.
13. Install the camshaft sprocket attaching bolts.
14. Coat the front cover gasket with sealer and position it and the cover on the engine.
15. Using a large socket wrench or other suitable tool to center the cover on the engine, install the cover attaching bolts.
16. Tighten the bolts to 5–7 ft lbs and remove the centering tool.
17. Install the four front oil pan bolts and tighten them to 7–9 ft lbs.
18. Install the lower engine pulley and the water pump. Adjust the engine drive belts.
19. Install the radiator and fill the cooling system.

Camshaft and Valve Lifter Replacement

The 1600 cc engine utilizes mushroom lifters, i.e., the bottom diameter is larger than the top diameter. For this reason, it is necessary to remove the engine, remove most of its external components, and invert it to remove the camshaft and/or lifters.

1. Remove the engine from the car and mount it securely on a stand.
2. Remove the fuel and oil pumps.
3. Remove the distributor.
4. Remove the valve cover, rocker shaft, and pushrods.
5. Remove the front cover and timing chain.
6. Place a pan under the engine and invert it on the stand.
7. Remove the oil pan.
8. Remove the camshaft thrust plate and remove the camshaft.
9. Remove the lifters.
10. Install the camshaft and/or lifters using a reverse of the removal procedure. Be sure to utilize the specific instructions on installing the timing chain and distributor. Adjust the valve clearance as previously described.

Camshaft, Auxiliary Shaft and Timing Belt —2000 cc and 2300 cc

Should the camshaft drive belt jump timing by a tooth or two, the engine could still run; but very poorly. To visually check for correct timing of the crankshaft, auxiliary shaft, and the camshaft on the 2000 cc and 2300 cc engines, follow this procedure:

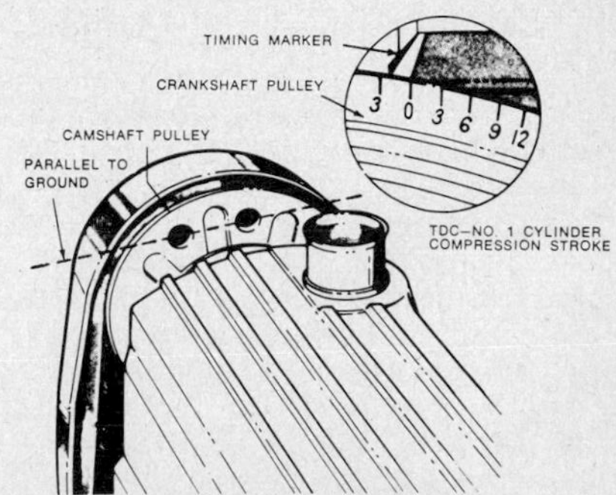

Checking camshaft timing
(© Ford Motor Co)

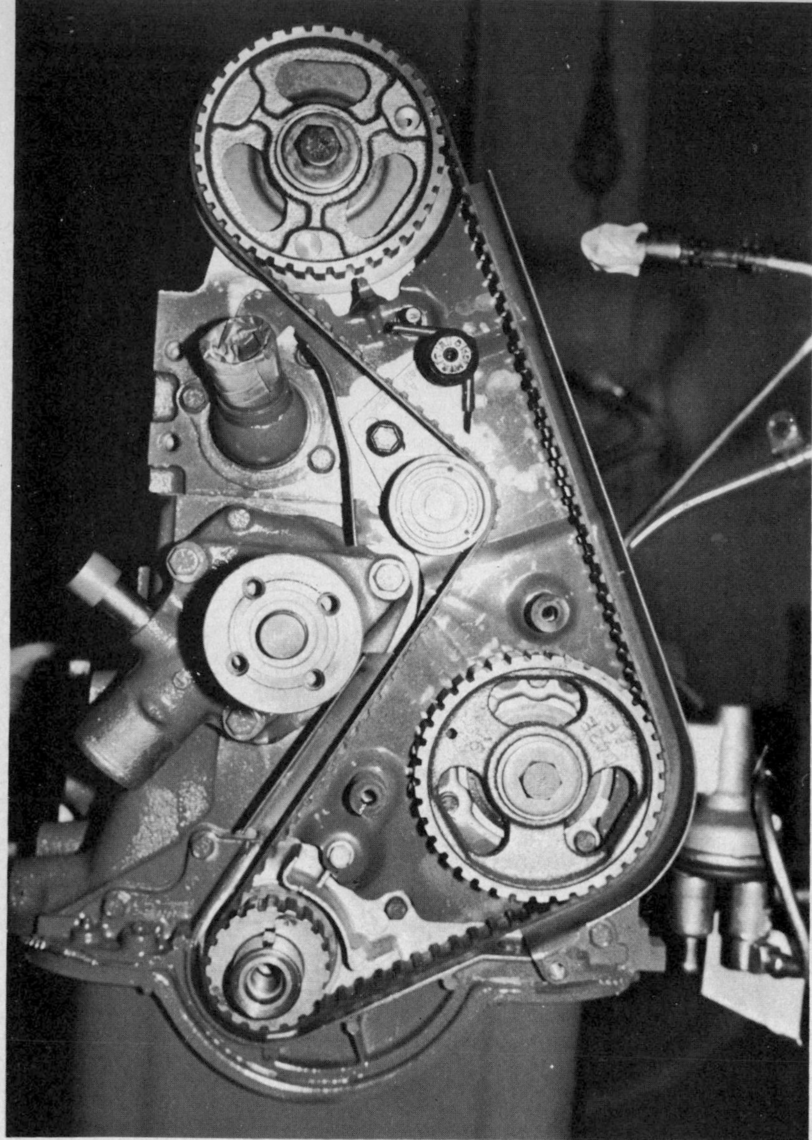

2300 cc engine camshaft drive—note the alignment tab for the camshaft sprocket and the alignment slot for the crankshaft sprocket

On 2000 cc engines, turn the crankshaft over until the two round locating holes in the camshaft pulley are visible from the rear side of the pulley, looking forward from the left-side of the car. When these two holes are parallel to the ground, the timing pointer on the crankshaft pulley should point to TDC. If the drive belt is dislocated, the crankshaft damper will be retarded or advanced 19° per cog on the belt.

If the engine you are working on does not have the two locating holes on the rear side of the camshaft pulley, then you will have to remove the drive belt cover and observe that when the crankshaft timing marks are aligned to TDC of the compression stroke of the No. 1 cylinder, the distributor rotor is pointing to the index mark on the upper lip of the distributor housing which coincides with No. 1 spark plug tower, and the pointer on the camshaft pulley is aligned with the index mark on the cylinder head.

On 2300 cc engines, there is an access plug provided in the cam drive belt cover so that the camshaft timing can be checked without removing the drive belt cover. Remove the access plug, turn the crankshaft until the timing marks on the crankshaft indicates TDC, and observe that the timing mark on the camshaft drive sprocket is aligned with the pointer on the inner belt cover. Also, the rotor of the distributor must align with the No. 1 cylinder firing position.

NOTE: Never turn the crankshaft of any of the overhead cam engines in the opposite direction of normal rotation. Backward rotation of the crankshaft may cause the timing belt to slip and alter the timing.

Timing Belt Replacement

1. Remove the camshaft drive belt cover.
2. Remove the distributor cap from the distributor and position it out of the way.
3. Turn the engine clockwise until:
   a. The timing pointer is aligned with the "0" mark on the crankshaft pulley.
   b. The pointer on the camshaft sprocket is aligned with the ball in the belt guide plate.
   c. The distributor rotor is aligned with the timing mark on the upper lip of the distributor housing.
4. Loosen the drive belt tensioner bolt and move the tensioner as far left as possible. Tighten the tensioner adjustment bolt.
5. Remove the belt from the pulleys.
6. Preconditions should be as in step three. Install the belt on the three sprockets, making sure that the cogs in the belt engage the slots in the sprockets.
7. Loosen the tensioner adjustment bolt and allow the full spring pressure of the tensioner to force the tensioner against the belt.
8. Turn the crankshaft pulley clockwise two complete turns to remove all slack from the belt.
9. Continue to turn the pulley until the marks described in step three are aligned. If the belt has slipped, remove the belt and repeat the installation procedure.
10. Position the drive belt tensioner so there is no free-play in the drive belt and tighten the tensioner adjustment bolt. Be careful not to overtighten the belt.

Camshaft Replacement

1. Remove the cylinder head as previously described.
2. Remove the rocker arms.
3. Remove the camshaft drive gear attaching bolt and washer, and remove the gear and belt guide plate.
4. Carefully slide the camshaft out of the rear of the cylinder head on the 2000 cc engine.

   On the 2300 cc engine, the camshaft is removed through the front of the cylinder head.
5. Reverse the removal procedure to install the camshaft and cylinder head.

NOTE: Coat the camshaft with oil before sliding it into the cylinder head.

Auxiliary Shaft Replacement

1. Remove the camshaft drive belt cover.
2. Remove the drive belt. Remove the auxiliary shaft sprocket. A puller may be necessary to remove the sprocket.
3. Remove the distributor and fuel pump.

Crankshaft, camshaft, and distributor timing marks—2000 cc engine
(© Ford Motor Co)

4. Remove the auxiliary shaft cover and thrust plate.
5. Withdraw the auxiliary shaft from the block.

NOTE: The distributor drive gear and the fuel pump eccentric on the auxiliary shaft must not be allowed to touch the auxiliary shaft bearings during removal and installation. Completely coat the shaft with oil before sliding it into place.

6. Slide the auxiliary shaft into the housing and insert the thrust plate to hold the shaft.
7. Install a new gasket and auxiliary shaft cover.
8. Fit a new gasket into the fuel pump and install the pump.
9. Insert the distributor and install the auxiliary shaft sprocket.
10. Align the timing marks and install the drive belt.
11. Install the drive belt cover.
12. Check the ignition timing.

Timing Case and Camshaft—V6 and V8

Front Cover Removal and Installation

1. Remove the oil pan as described in the following section.
2. Remove the radiator and any other necessary parts such as the water pump, to allow clearance.
3. Remove the alternator and drive belts. Remove the water pump and water lines.
4. Remove the fan.
5. Remove the crankshaft pulley with a puller and, if necessary, remove the guide sleeves from the cylinder block. On the V8 remove the fuel pump.
6. Remove the front cover retaining bolts and remove the front cover. If the front cover plate gasket needs replacement, remove the two screws and the plate to replace the gasket.
7. To install, reverse the procedures, cleaning all surfaces of gasket material and installing new gaskets and sealing compound.

NOTE: If the guide sleeves were removed, install them with new seal rings but do not use sealing compound.

V8 Front Oil Seal Removal and Installation

1. Remove the timing cover.
2. Drive out the old seal with a punch and make sure that the inside rim is clean.
3. Coat a new seal with grease and place it into position on the case.
4. Drive the seal in until fully seated; check to make sure that the spring is properly positioned in the seal.
5. Reinstall the timing cover.

Camshaft Removal and Installation

1. Drain the cooling system.
2. Remove the radiator.
3. Remove the distributor cap with the spark plug wires attached. Remove the distributor vacuum line, distributor, alternator, rocker arm covers, fuel line and filter, carburetor, and intake manifold; on the V8 remove the accelerator rod and spring.
4. Remove the rocker arm and shaft assemblies. (On the V8, rotate them to the side.) Lift out the pushrods and mark them so they can be replaced in the same location.
5. Remove the oil pan. (See the following sections.)
6. Remove the timing chain cover. On the V8 remove the front oil seal.
7. Remove the camshaft gear retaining bolt and slide the gear off the camshaft. Remove the camshaft thrust plate.
8. Remove the valve lifters from the engine block with a magnet. Lifters should be identified to permit installation in the same location.
9. Carefully pull the camshaft from the engine block, avoiding damage to the camshaft bearings. Remove the key and spacer ring.
10. Coat the camshaft with a moly cam lubricant or SAE 90 gear oil.
11. Install the camshaft, carefully avoiding damage to the bearings.

NOTE: When installing the camshaft, do not push it hard into the engine. There is an oil plug at the rear of the engine block called the "bore plug." If the camshaft is installed too far into the engine or forced into the engine, it could push this plug out, resulting in oil leaking on the clutch and pressure plate and causing serious damage.

12. Install the spacer ring with the worn side toward the engine. Insert the camshaft key. Install the thrust plate.

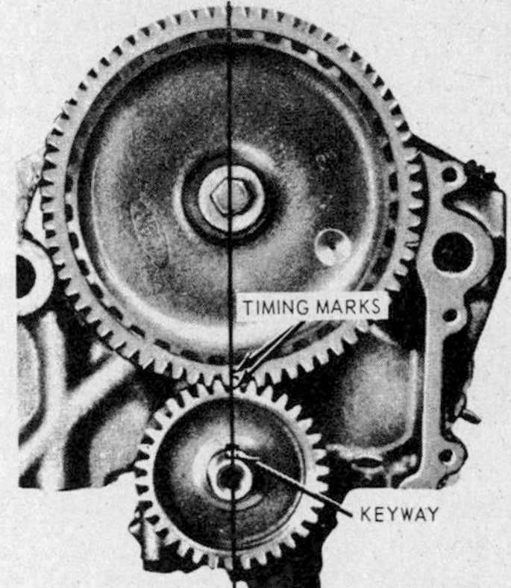

V6 timing gear installation
(© Ford Motor Co)

13. Install the camshaft timing gear and align the timing marks. Install the retaining washer and bolt. On the V8, install the front oil seal.
14. Install the valve lifters.
15. Install the timing cover.

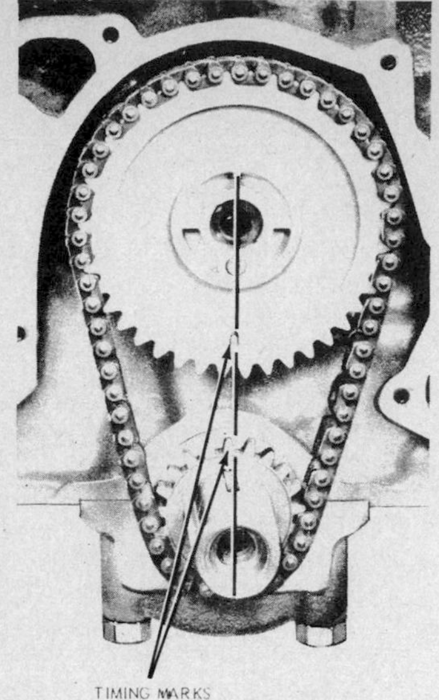

Aligning the camshaft timing marks, 302 V8
(© Ford Motor Co.)

16. Install the belt drive pulley and secure it with the washer and retaining bolt.
17. Install the oil pan.
18. Install the pushrods in the same locations from which they were removed. Install the intake manifold.
19. Install the oil baffles and rocker arm shaft assemblies. Adjust the valves to the cold setting.
20. Install the carburetor, fuel line and filter, alternator, distributor cap, and wires.
21. Fill the cooling system.

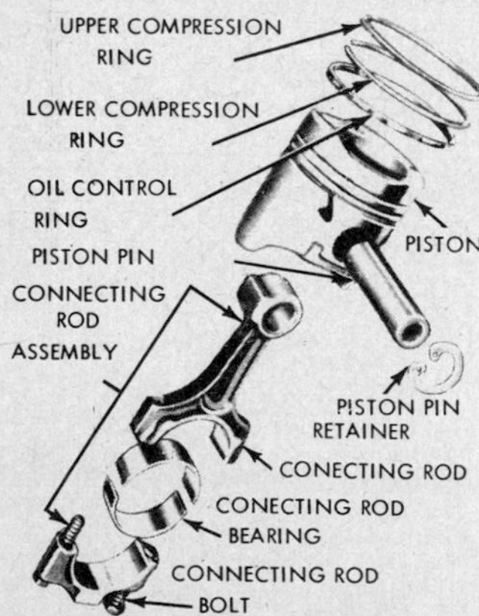

Connecting rod and piston assembly for the 1600 cc engine (© Ford Motor Co)

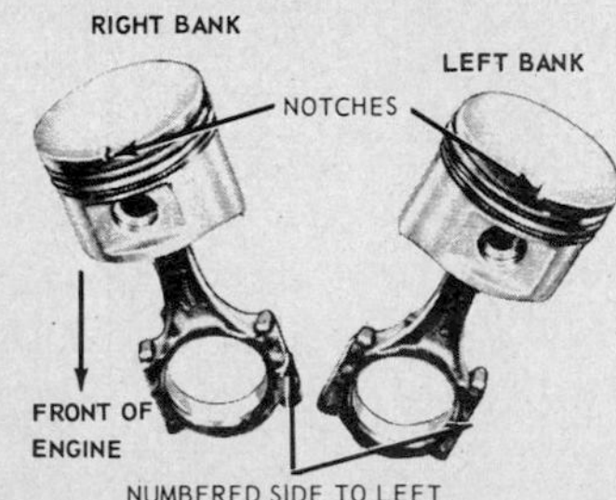

Piston and rod positioning for installation—2800 cc V6
(© Ford Motor Co)

Piston and rod positioning for installation in 2000 cc and 2300 cc engines
(© Ford Motor Co)

22. Install the rocker arm covers but not permanently. Run the engine, check for leaks, and set the ignition timing.
23. Set the valves at their hot setting. Install the valve covers permanently.

Engine Lubrication

Oil Pan Replacement

1600, 2000, and 2300 cc

1. Drain the crankcase.
2. Remove the oil dipstick.
3. On 1600 cc engines, disconnect the negative battery cable, remove the starter motor retaining bolts and remove the starter from the engine.
4. Disconnect the steering shaft connection from the rack and pinion.
5. Disconnect the rack and pinion from the crossmember and move it forward to provide clearance.
6. Remove the flywheel housing inspection cover.
7. Remove the oil pan attaching bolts and remove the pan.
8. Clean the gasket mounting surface of the block and the pan.
9. Coat the block surface and the oil pan gasket with oil resistant sealer and position the gasket on the block.
10. Coat the oil pan front oil seal and the cylinder front cover with oil resistant sealer and position the seal on the front cover, making sure the ends of the seal contact the oil pan gasket.
11. Coat the rear oil pan seal with oil resistant sealer and install it in the rear main bearing cap.
12. Position the pan on the block and tighten the bolts to specification. On 1600 cc engines tighten the bolts to a torque of 6-8 ft lbs, and on 2000 and 2300 cc engines to 4-6 ft lbs.
13. Reverse steps 1-6 to complete installation.

2800 cc V6

1. Remove the dipstick. Remove the bolts attaching the fan shroud to the radiator. Position the shroud over the fan. Disconnect the battery ground cable at the battery. Loosen the alternator bracket and adjusting bolts.
2. Raise the vehicle on a hoist.
3. Drain the crankcase.
4. Remove the splash shield. Remove the starter.
5. Remove the engine front support nuts.
6. Raise the engine and place wood blocks between the engine front supports and the chassis brackets.
7. Remove the oil pan attaching bolts and remove the oil pan.
8. Clean the gasket surfaces of the block and the oil pan. The oil pan has a two-piece gasket.
9. Coat the block surface and the oil pan gasket with sealer. Position the oil pan gaskets on the cylinder block.
10. Position the oil pan front seal on the cylinder front cover. Be sure that the tabs on the seal are over the oil pan gasket.
11. Place the end seals in position flush with the cylinder block oil pan rail, if previously removed.

    Position the oil pan rear seal on the rear main bearing cap. Be sure that the tabs on the seal are over the oil pan gasket.
12. Position the oil pan centered on the cylinder block. Install two bolts at both ends (front and rear) of the oil pan, then install the remaining bolts and tighten them to 5-7 ft lbs, starting with the bolt at the left front corner (looking from the rear) on the leading edge of the oil pan and working around the circumference of the pan.
13. Replace the converter housing or clutch cover.
14. Raise the engine and remove the wood blocks from between the engine supports and chassis brackets. Lower the engine and install the engine support nuts.
15. Replace the starter and splash shield.
16. Lower the vehicle.
17. Install the alternator.
18. Connect the battery ground wire.
19. Install the fan shroud.
20. Install the dipstick. Fill the crankcase with oil. Start the engine and check for leaks.

Oil Pump R & R—1600

The oil pump and filter assembly is bolted to the left side of the block and can be serviced with the engine installed in the car.

Two types of oil pump have been installed during production—an eccentric bi-rotor type and a sliding vane type. These pumps are readily identified by their end covers—the eccentric bi-rotor type has four recesses cast into its cover while the sliding vane type has a flat cover. These two pumps are interchangeable, although their internal parts are not.

1. Lift the hood and place a drain pan under the oil pump.
2. Remove the three bolts which hold the pump and filter assembly.

NOTE: Tighten these bolts to 13-15 ft. lbs. when installing pump.

3. Remove filter from pump.
4. To install, reverse removal procedure.

Oil Pump R & R—All except 1600

The oil pump, of bi-rotor design, is mounted to the bottom of the cylinder block, inside the oil pan. To remove the pump, remove the oil pan and remove the two bolts that mount the oil pump to the block.

NOTE: Under no circumstances should the oil pump on a 2300 cc engine be disassembled. If the pump is found to be defective, it should be replaced as a unit.

Crankshaft Rear Main Oil Seal Replacement

1600 cc

1. Remove transmission and unbolt the right and left engine mounts from the cylinder block.
2. Raise and support the engine above the engine mounts.
3. Remove the pressure plate bolts in sequence, a few turns at a time, and remove the pressure plate and clutch disc.
4. Remove the flywheel.
5. Remove the oil pan and gaskets.
6. Remove the rear oil seal carrier.
7. Remove the seal from the carrier and install a new one.
8. Locate a new gasket on the rear oil seal carrier. Fit the carrier to the block rear face. Tighten the bolts evenly to 12-15 ft lbs.
9. Position new gaskets on the block flange. Position the cork packing strips with the chamfered ends into the grooves. Install the oil pan.
10. Assemble the clutch, transmission, and motor mounts in the reverse order of removal.

2000 cc and 2800 cc V6

1. Remove the transmission. Remove the clutch pressure plate and clutch disc, if so equipped.
2. Remove the flywheel, flywheel housing and rear plate.
3. Punch two holes in the crankshaft rear oil seal on opposite sides of the crankshaft just above the bearing cap-to-cylinder block split line. Install a sheet metal screw in each of the holes and pry the crankshaft rear main oil seal from the block.

NOTE: Use extreme caution not to scratch the crankshaft oil seal surface.

Clean the oil seal recess in the cylinder block and main bearing cap.

4. Coat the seal and all of the seal mounting surfaces with oil and install the seal in the recess, driving it in place with an oil seal installation tool.
5. Install the clutch and/or transmission in the reverse order of removal.

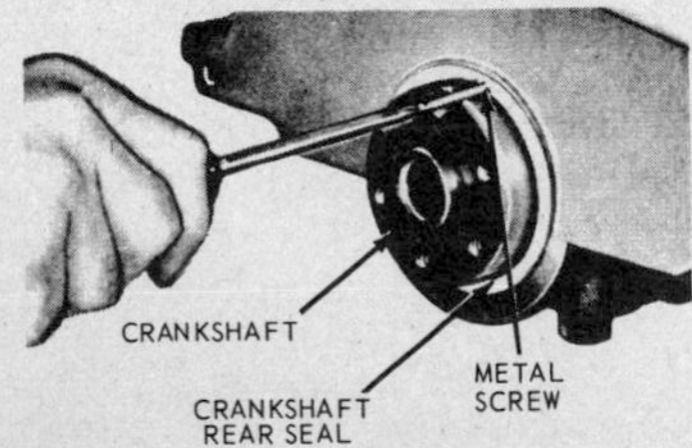

Removing the crankshaft rear main oil seal—2000 cc and 2800 cc V6
(© Ford Motor Co)

2300 cc and 302 V8

1. Remove the oil pan and oil pump, if required.
2. Loosen all the main bearing cap bolts, thereby lowering the crankshaft slightly but not more than 1/32 in.
3. Remove the rear main bearing cap, and remove the oil seal from the bearing cap and the cylinder block. Install a small sheet metal screw in one end of the cylinder block half of the seal, and pull on the screw to remove the seal. Remove the oil seal retaining pin from the bearing cap if so equipped.
4. Clean the seal grooves in the cap and block with a brush and solvent. Dry the area thoroughly. No solvent should come in contact with the seal.
5. Dip the seal halves in clean engine oil.
6. Carefully install the upper seal (block half) into its groove with the undercut side of the seal toward the front of the engine, by rotating it on the seal journal of the crankshaft until about 3/8 in. protrudes below the parting surface. Be sure that no rubber has been shaved off. Wipe all oil from the mating surface of the bearing cap and cylinder block.
7. Tighten the bearing cap bolts to specifications.
8. Install the lower seal in the rear main bearing cap with the undercut side of the seal toward the front of the engine. Allow the seal to protrude about 3/8 in. above the parting surface to mate with the upper seal when the cap is installed.

NOTE: Install the seals so that the locating tab faces the rear of the engine. (2300 cc only).

9. Apply a *small* amount of sealer to the mating surface of the bearing cap. No sealer compound should come in contact with the rubber seals when the bearing cap is installed and tightened.
10. Install the oil pump (if removed) and oil pan. Fill the crankcase with oil, and operate the engine, checking for leaks.

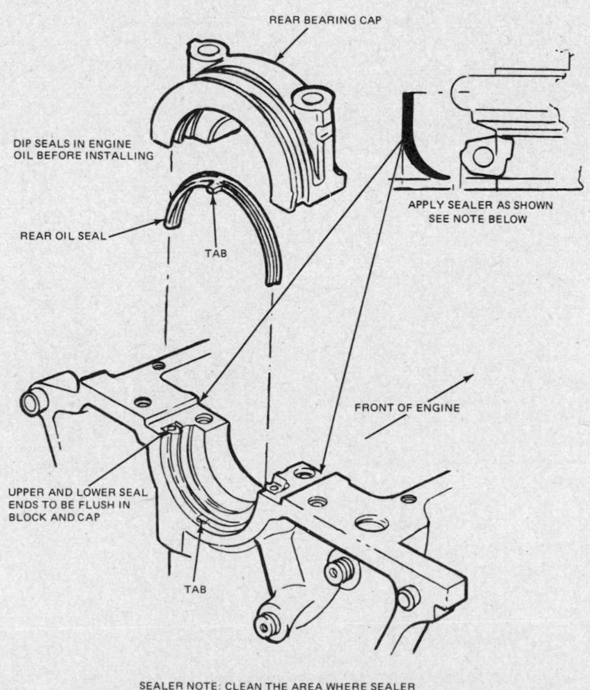

Replacement of the crankshaft rear main oil seal—2300 cc engine (© Ford Motor Co)

CLUTCH

Adjustment

Pinto Built Before 10/1/70

1. From under the car, pull the clutch cable toward the front of the vehicle until the C-clip can be removed from the cable. Remove the clip.
2. Continue to pull the cable toward the front of the vehicle until all free movement has been eliminated from the clutch release bearing.
3. While holding the cable in the zero free play position, insert a 0.135 in. spacer against the flywheel boss on the engine side and install the C-clip in the closest possible groove next to the spacer.
4. Remove the spacer and release the cable.

Pinto and Bobcat Built After 10/1/70

1. Working under the car, loosen the clutch adjusting nut, the front locknut and the rear locknut (if so equipped).
2. Pull the clutch cable toward the front of the car until all freeplay is removed from the clutch release lever.
3. Holding the cable in this position, place a 1/4 in. spacer against the engine side of the flywheel housing and tighten the adjusting nut finger-tight against the spacer.
4. Hold the adjusting nut so that it maintains its position and tighten the front locknut against the adjusting nut.
5. Remove the spacer and tighten the rear locknut (if so equipped) against the transmission side of the flywheel housing.

Mustang II

1. Remove the cable retaining clip at the dash panel.
2. Remove the screw holding the cable attaching bracket on the fender apron.
3. Pull the cable toward the front of the vehicle until the adjusting nut can be turned. Rotate the nut away from the adjustment sleeve about 1/4 in.
4. Release the cable, and then pull the cable again until free movement of the release lever is eliminated.
5. Rotate the adjusting nut toward the adjustment sleeve until contact is made, then index it into the next notch.
6. Reinstall the cable retaining clip and cable attaching bracket, and screw on the fender apron.

Clutch, Clutch Housing, and Transmission

Removal

1. Place the gearshift lever in the neutral position. Raise the car and remove the back-up light switch from the transmission extension housing.
2. Loosen the shift lever locknut. Remove the knob and the locknut from the shift lever. Remove the four rubber boot attaching screws and remove the boot.
3. Compress the corrugated rubber spring, then remove the retaining snap-ring and slide the spring upward on the lever.
4. Bend the shift lever locktabs up, then thread the plastic dome nut from the extension housing.
5. Lift the shift lever from the extension housing.
6. Working from under the hood, remove the upper flywheel housing-to-engine attaching bolts.
7. Raise the vehicle and matchmark the driveshaft and the rear axle pinion.
8. Disconnect and remove the driveshaft. Place rags in the extension housing to prevent loss of lubricant.
9. Remove the clutch release lever dust cover.
10. Disconnect the clutch cable from the clutch release lever.
11. Remove the starter motor attaching bolts and position the motor out of the way.
12. Remove the speedometer cable-to-transmission attaching screw and remove the cable and gear from the transmission. Plug the opening in the transmission to prevent lubricant spillage.
13. Support the rear of the engine with a jack and remove the crossmember-to-body attaching bolts.
14. Remove the bolts that attach the crossmember to the transmission extension housing and remove the crossmember from the car.
15. Lower the engine to gain working room, and remove the remaining flywheel housing-to-engine attaching bolts.
16. Slide the transmission rearward and remove it from the car.
17. If the clutch is to be removed loosen the six pressure plate attaching bolts evenly to release spring pressure gradually. If the

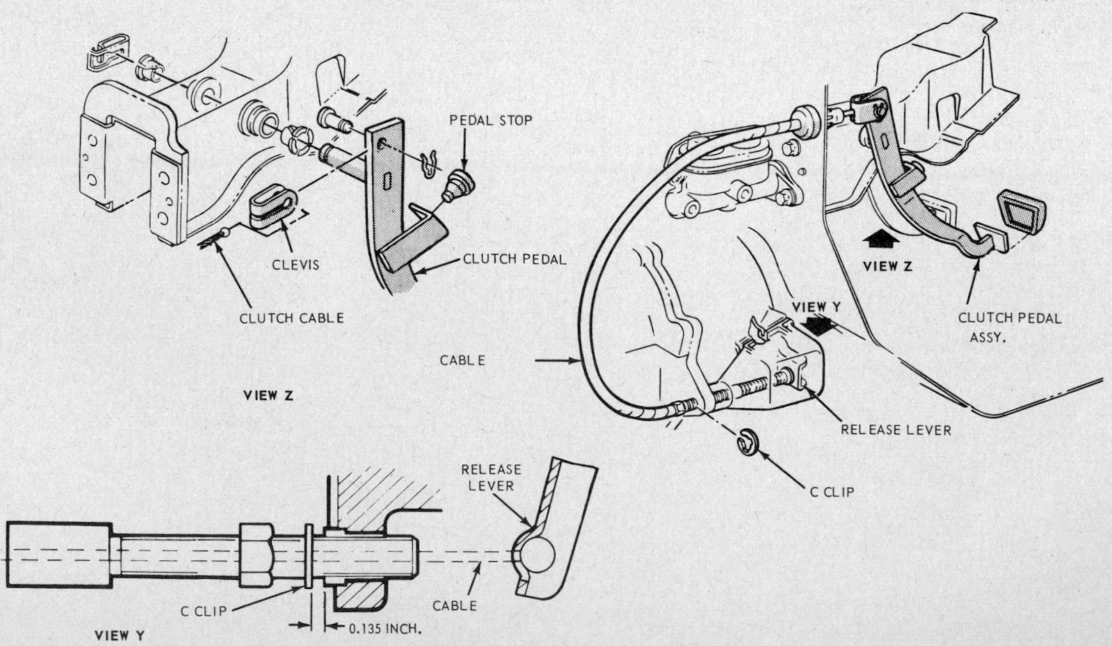

Clutch linkage for a Pinto (© Ford Motor Co)

same pressure plate and cover are to be reused, mark the position of the pressure plate and flywheel so they can be returned to their original location.

18. Remove the pressure plate attaching bolts and remove the pressure plate and clutch from the car.

Installation

1. Position the clutch and pressure plate on the flywheel and install the attaching bolts loosely.

NOTE: the three dowel pins on the flywheel must be aligned with the pressure plate.

2. Align the clutch assembly, using a pilot shaft or other suitable tool, and alternately tighten the bolts.
3. Position the transmission and flywheel assembly on the studs on the cylinder block and install the retaining bolts.
4. Reverse removal procedure to install remaining equipment. The shift lever must be installed before the back-up light switch.

MANUAL TRANSMISSION

A four-speed manual transmission is standard equipment on all models. Some 1600 cc Pintos have an English built transmission. The majority of 1600 cc Pintos and all other Pintos and Bobcats use a German built transmission. These transmissions can be identified from the transmission ID code on the identification tag at the left front of the extension housing. The Mustang II uses an American built transmission. See the Manual Transmissions Unit Repair section for further details.

Transmission R&R

See *Clutch, Clutch Housing, and Transmission Removal and Installation* in this car section.

AUTOMATIC TRANSMISSION

All models use a C4 automatic transmission, except for those with the 2300 cc engine. 2300 models use a C3 transmission. The Vehicle Certification Label gives the transmission code letter, V for C3, and W for C4.

In Car Service

Downshift Linkage Adjustment

1. Disconnect the downshift lever return spring.
2. Hold the throttle shaft lever in the wide open position. Hold the downshift rod against the through detent stop. Adjust the downshift screw to obtain 0.050-0.070 in. clearance between the screw tip and the throttle shaft lever tab.
3. Connect the downshift lever return spring.

Shift Linkage Adjustment

1. Place the transmission selector lever in the Drive position.
2. Raise the vehicle and loosen the manual linkage shift rod at the selector lever.
3. Move the transmission manual lever to the Drive position (fourth detent position from the rear of the transmission).
4. Tighten the nut on the manual linkage shift rod to 10-20 ft. lbs.
5. Lower the car and check transmission operation.

Neutral Start Switch Adjustment

1. Place the transmission selector lever in the Neutral position.

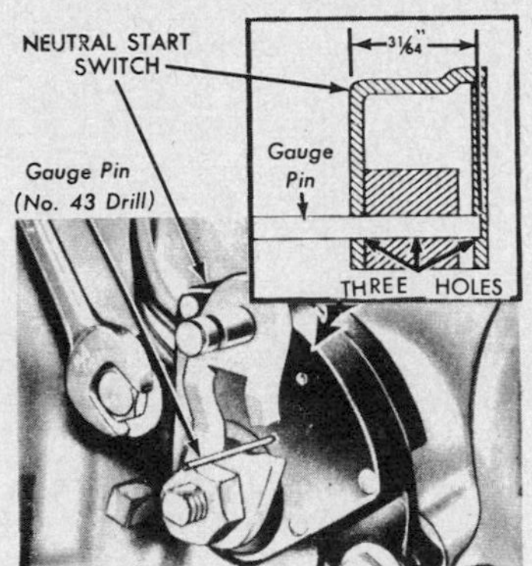

Neutral start switch adjustment
(© Ford Motor Co)

2. Raise the vehicle on a hoist and loosen the two bolts that attach the neutral switch to the transmission.
3. Rotate the switch until a gauge pin (shank end of a #43 drill bit) can be inserted through the gauge pin holes in the switch. The gauge pin must be inserted a full 31/64 in. into the switch, through all three holes in the switch.
4. Tighten the switch retaining bolts to 50-75 in. lbs. and remove the pin.

Neutral Start Switch Replacement

1. Raise the car, with the transmission in neutral, and disconnect the downshift linkage.
2. Remove the neutral switch attaching bolts and remove the switch and disconnect the wires.
3. Install the replacement switch and adjust it as described above.
4. Install the downshift outer lever.
5. Connect the downshift linkage rod to the downshift lever.

Band Adjustments

Caution The torque figures and numbers of turns given in these procedures must be exactly correct to prevent transmission damage.

NOTE: Perform the adjustments in the order listed here. The only band adjustment required on the C3 transmission is on the front band.

Intermediate (Front) Band

1. Wipe clean the area around the adjusting screw on the side of the transmission, near the left-front corner of the transmission.

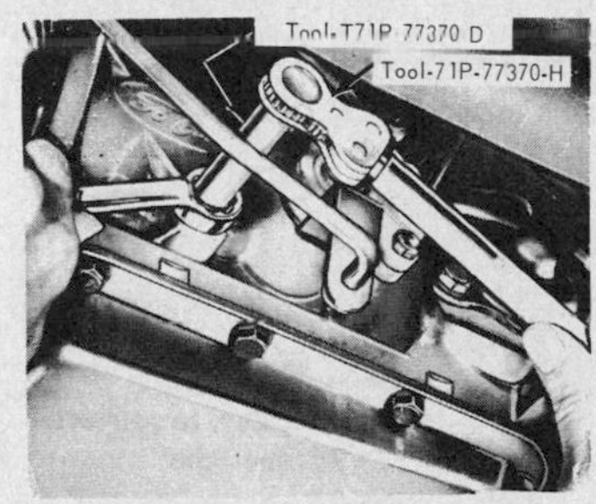

Intermediate band adjustment
(© Ford Motor Co)

2. Remove the adjusting screw locknut and discard it.
3. Install a new locknut on the adjusting screw but do not tighten it.
4. Tighten the adjusting screw to *exactly 10 ft lbs.*
5. Back off the adjusting screw *exactly 1¾ turns; 1½ turns on the C3.*
6. Hold the adjusting screw so that it *does not turn* and tighten the adjusting screw locknut to 35–45 ft lbs.

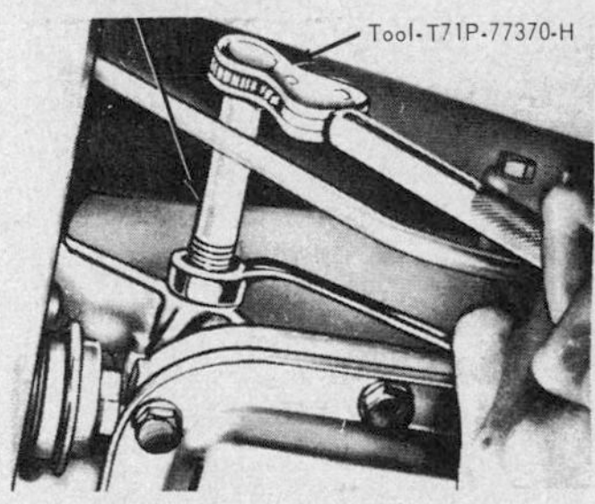

Low-reverse band adjustment
(© Ford Motor Co)

Low-Reverse Band

1. Wipe clean the area around the adjusting screw on the side of the transmission, near the right-rear corner.
2. Remove the adjusting screw locknut and discard it.
3. Install a new locknut on the adjusting screw but do not tighten it.
4. Tighten the adjusting screw to *exactly 10 ft lbs.*
5. Back off the adjusting screw *exactly 3 full turns.*
6. Hold the adjusting screw so that it *does not turn* and tighten the adjusting screw to 35–45 ft lbs.

Pan R & R, Fluid and Filter Change

1. Raise the car up on a lift.
2. Some C4 models require that the transmission fluid filler tube be disconnected to drain the pan; all others can be drained by loosening the pan bolts and letting the fluid drain out when the pan is lowered.
3. After the fluid has drained out, remove the rest of the attaching bolts, the pan and the gasket.
4. Remove the bolts holding the filter in place, remove the filter and replace it. The filter may be reused after cleaning in a non-detergent solution, such as new transmission fluid.
5. Replace the filter and gasket and attach the mounting bolts. Clean the edge of the transmission pan before installing the new gasket; bolt the pan to the transmission, and reattach the fluid filler tube if applicable.
6. Refill the transmission with the proper amount of Type F fluid (See Capacities Chart in the front of this section), and check for leaks around the pan.

Caution Add a little less than the specified amount of fluid at first, run the engine, shift through all positions, and check the level. It should be between ADD and FULL. The level should be at FULL after the transmission is fully warmed up. Be very cautious not to overfill.

U-JOINTS

U-Joint Removal and Installation

1. Raise the vehicle.
2. Mark the position of the rear driveshaft yoke in relation to the pinion flange so the driveshaft can be returned to its original location.
3. Disconnect the rear U-Joint from the pinion flange and remove the loose bearing caps. Pull the driveshaft rearward until it clears the transmission extension housing. Remove the driveshaft from the car.
4. Place the driveshaft in a vise and remove the snap-rings from the U-Joint to be removed.
5. Using a suitable tool, drive one of the bearing caps on the U-Joint to be removed toward the center of the driveshaft.
6. Remove the opposite bearing cap from the one being driven as it emerges from the driveshaft.
7. Repeat Step 6 until all bearing caps have been removed.
8. Remove the U-Joint spider from the driveshaft.
9. To install, position the spider in the driveshaft and drive the bearing caps onto the spider.
10. Install the snap-rings in the driveshaft.
11. Reinstall the driveshaft using a reverse of the removal procedure. Make sure that the yoke and pinion flange marks are aligned.

REAR AXLE

Axle Shaft, Bearing and Seal

Removal and Installation

NOTE: Bearings must be pressed on and off the shaft with an arbor press.

1. Remove the wheel, tire, and the brake drum.
2. Remove the nuts holding the axle retainer plate to the backing plate.
3. Remove the retainer and install the nuts fingertight to prevent the backing plate from being dislodged.
4. Using a slide hammer, remove the axle shaft and bearing assembly. If the end play is excessive, replace the bearing.
5. Using a chisel, nick the bearing retainer in three or four places.
6. Press off the old bearing and install the new one by pressing it into position.
7. Press on the new retainer.
8. With a slide hammer, remove the seal from the axle housing; when removed, clean the seal recess in the axle housing.
9. Place a new seal in position and drive it into place with a seal installation tool. The right and left seals are not interchangeable so make sure that the seal is on the proper axle.
10. Assemble the shaft and bearing in the housing and make sure that the bearing is seated properly.

Removing the rear wheel bearing retainer ring (© Ford Motor Co.)

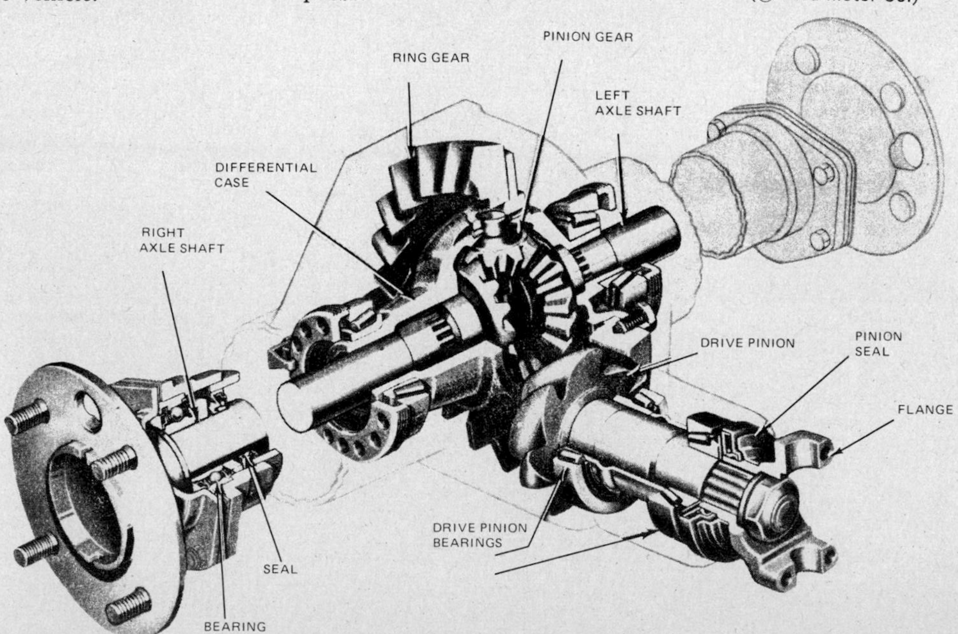

Cutaway view of rear axle (© Ford Motor Co.)

11. Install the retainer, the drum, the wheel, and the tire.

JACKING, HOISTING

Lift and jacking points are shown in the figure.

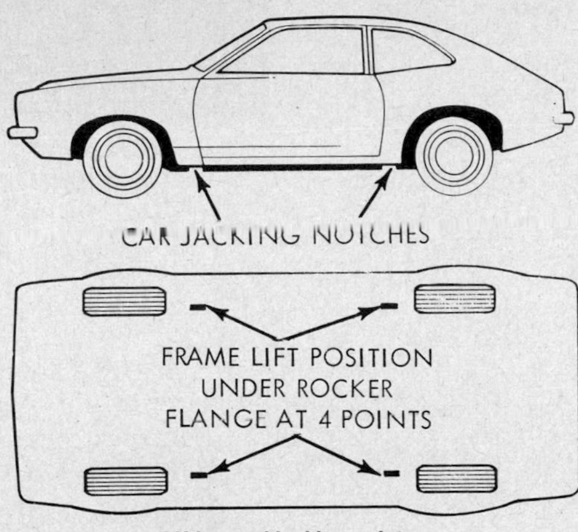

Lifting and jacking points
(© Ford Motor Co)

FRONT SUSPENSION

Upper Ball Joint

Inspection

1. Raise the vehicle by placing a floor jack under the lower arm. Do not allow the lower arm to hang freely with the vehicle on a hoist or bumper jack.
2. Have an assistant grasp the bottom of the tire and move the wheel in and out.
3. As the wheel is being moved, observe the upper control arm where the spindle attaches to it. Any movement between the upper part of the spindle and the upper ball joint indicates a bad ball joint which must be replaced.

NOTE: during this check the lower ball joint will be unloaded and may move; this is normal and not an indication of a bad ball joint. Also, do not mistake a loose wheel bearing for a defective ball joint.

Replacement

1. Raise the vehicle and allow the front wheels to fall into their full down position.
2. Drill a 1/8 in. hole completely through each ball joint attaching rivet.
3. Using a large chisel, cut off the head of each rivet and drive them from the upper arm.
4. Place a jack under the lower arm and lower the vehicle about 6 in.
5. Remove the cotter pin and attaching nut from the ball joint stud.
6. Using a suitable tool, loosen the ball joint stud from the spindle and remove the ball joint from the upper arm.
7. Clean all metal burrs from the upper arm and install the new ball joint, using the service part nuts and bolts to attach the ball joint to the upper arm. Do not attempt to re-rivet the ball joint once it has been removed.
8. Check front end alignment.

Lower Ball Joint

Inspection

1. Raise the vehicle by placing a floor jack under the lower arm; or, raise the vehicle on a hoist and place a jack stand under the lower arm and lower the vehicle onto it to remove the preload from the lower ball joint.
2. Have an assistant grasp the wheel top and bottom and apply alternate in and out pressure to the top and bottom of the wheel.
3. Radial play of ¼ in. is acceptable measured at the inside of the wheel adjacent to the lower arm.

NOTE: this radial play is multiplied at the outer circumference of the tire and should be measured only at the inside of the wheel.

Replacement

1. Raise the vehicle and allow the front wheels to fall to their full down position.
2. Drill a ⅛ in. hole completely through each ball joint attaching rivet.
3. Use a ⅜ in. drill in the pilot hole to drill off the head of the rivet.
4. Drive the rivets from the lower arm.
5. Place a jack under the lower arm and lower the vehicle about 6 in.
6. Remove the lower ball joint stud cotter pin and attaching nut.
7. Using a suitable tool, loosen the ball joint from the spindle and remove the ball joint from the lower arm.
8. Clean all metal burrs from the lower arm and install the new ball joint, using the service part nuts and bolts to attach the ball joint to the lower arm. Do not attempt to re-rivet the ball joint once it has been removed.
9. Check front end alignment.

Upper Control Arm

Replacement

1. Raise the vehicle on a hoist.
2. If equipped with drum brakes, remove the tire, wheel and brake drum as an assembly. If equipped with disc brakes, remove the tire and wheel, remove the caliper attaching bolts and position the caliper out of the way with the brake hose attached. Remove the rotor and hub from the spindle.
3. Disconnect the lower control arm and remove the coil spring.
4. Remove the cotter pin and attaching nut from the ball joint stud.
5. Using a suitable tool, loosen the upper ball joint from the spindle.
6. Remove the upper arm inner shaft attaching bolts and remove the arm and shaft from the chassis as an assembly.
7. Reverse above procedure to install.
8. Adjust front end alignment.

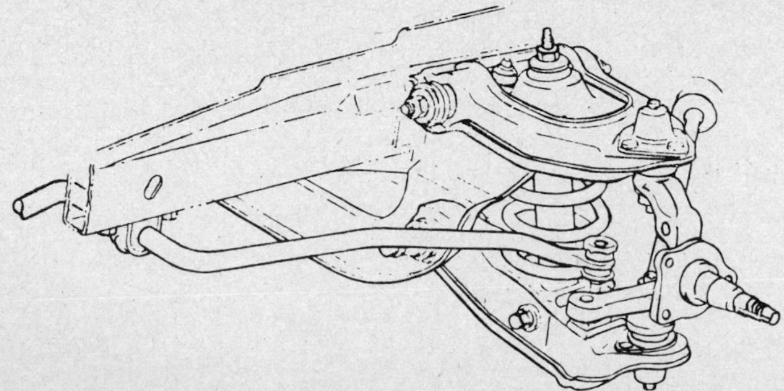

Left front suspension, Mustang II—Pinto is similar (© Ford Motor Co.)

Lower Control Arm

Replacement

1. Raise the car and support it with stands placed back of the lower arms.
2. If equipped with drum type brakes, remove the wheel and brake drums as an assembly. Remove the brake backing plate attaching bolts and remove the backing plate from the spindle. Wire the assembly back out of the way.
3. If equipped with disc brakes, remove the wheel from the hub. Remove the caliper from the rotor and wire it back out of the way. Remove the hub and rotor from the spindle.
4. Disconnect the shock absorber and remove it.
5. Remove the cotter pins from the upper and lower ball joint stud nuts.
6. Remove the two bolts and nuts holding the strut to the lower arm.
7. Loosen the lower ball joint stud nut two turns. Do not remove this nut.
8. Install a spreader tool between the upper and lower ball joint studs.
9. Expand the tool until the tool exerts considerable pressure on the studs. Tap the spindle near the lower stud with a hammer to loosen the stud in the spindle. Do not loosen the stud with tool pressure only.
10. Position a floor jack under the lower arm and remove the lower ball joint and nut.
11. Lower the floor jack and remove the spring and insulator.
12. Remove the A arm-to-crossmember attaching parts, and remove the arm from the car.
13. Reverse the above procedure to install. If the lower control arm was replaced because of damage, have front-end alignment checked.

Spring Replacement

1. Jack up the front of the car and support it with jackstands.
2. Remove the shock absorber.
3. Disconnect the strut bar from the lower control arm.
4. Place a floor jack under the lower control arm.
5. Remove the nut and bolt that attach the lower control arm to the front crossmember.
6. Carefully lower the jack, slowly, to relieve the spring pressure from the lower arm.
7. Remove the spring and upper insulator.
8. Place the upper insulator on the spring and secure it in place with tape.
9. Position the spring on the lower control arm. Make sure that the bottom of the spring properly engages the seat on the lower control arm.
10. Raise the lower control arm with the floor jack and guide the lower control arm and the top of the spring into place. Install the lower control arm attaching bolt and nut. Tighten the lower control arm attaching bolt to 75–110 ft lbs.
11. Install the shock absorber after removing the jack.
12. Remove the jack stands and lower the car.

Shock Absorber Replacement

1. Remove the nut, washer, and bushing from the upper end of the shock. If the shaft of the shock absorber turns while you are attempting to remove the nut, hold the shaft in place with an adjustable wrench while removing the nut.
2. Raise the front end of the car and install jackstands.
3. Disconnect the bottom of the shock absorber from the lower control arm. It may be necessary to raise the lower arm to remove the bottom bolt.
4. Remove the shock absorber from under the car.
5. Position the replacement shock absorber on the lower control arm and install the attaching bolts.
6. Remove the jackstands and lower the car.
7. Connect the top of the shock absorber to the upper spring pad.

Wheel Bearing Adustment

1. Jack the front of the car up and support it with jackstands.
2. Remove the dust cap and spindle nut cotter pin. Slide the nut lock off. Discard the pin.
3. Tighten the adjusting nut to 17–25 ft lbs while turning the wheel. Back the nut off one-half turn.
4. Tighten the nut to 10–15 in. lbs.
5. Install the nut lock on the adjusting nut so that two of the slots align with the hole in the spindle.
6. Install a new cotter pin and bend back its ends.
7. Install the dust cap and lower the car.

REAR SUSPENSION

The rear suspension consists of conventional three-leaf, longitudinal, semi-elliptic springs, located asymmetrically to the rear axle carrier and fastened by U-bolt clamps. Standard telescopic shock absorbers control vertical rebound.

Rear Shock Absorber Replacement

1. Disconnect the lower end of the shock absorber from the spring plate.
2. Remove the three bolts retaining the shock absorber mounting bracket at the upper end of the shock.
3. Compress and remove shock from car.
4. Transfer mounting bracket to new shock.
5. Position shock absorber on car and install attaching parts.

Rear Spring Replacement

1. Disconnect the lower end of the shock absorber from the spring plate and position the shock out of the way.
2. Raise the vehicle on a hoist and place supports under the axle and the underbody.
3. Remove the spring plate attaching nuts from the U-bolts. Remove the spring plate.
4. Disconnect and remove the rear shackle from the spring.
5. Remove the front hanger bolt and nut from the eye of the

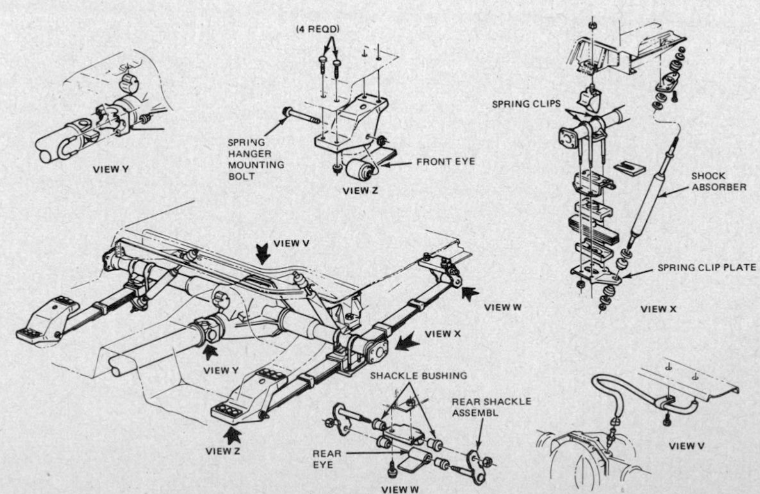

Mustang II rear suspension (© Ford Motor Co)

spring. Remove the spring from the car.

6. Reverse above procedure to install.

NOTE: all used attaching parts must be discarded and replaced with new parts.

BRAKES

The drum brake system incorporates single anchor, internal expanding and self adjusting brake assemblies. The brake hydraulic system employs a dual reservoir master cylinder, a pressure differential valve and a single cylinder, dual piston wheel cylinder mounted on each backing plate. Front disc brakes are available as an option.

The parking brake is operated through a floor-mounted lever located between the front seats. Pulling the lever transmits force through a two cable linkage to operate the rear drum brakes. A self-adjusting feature operates when there is excessive clearance between the brake shoes and drums.

Replacement and overhaul procedures are included in the "Unit Repair Section."

Master Cylinder

Removal and Installation

1. Working under the dash, disconnect the stop light switch wires from the stop light switch and remove the switch and master cylinder pushrod from the brake pedal. Use care not to damage the stop light switch during removal.
2. Raise the hood and remove the brake lines from the master cylinder.
3. Remove the capscrews and lockwashers that attach the master cylinder to the firewall and remove the master cylinder.
4. Reverse above procedure to install, but, leave the brake lines loose on the master cylinder.
5. Fill the master cylinder with Extra Heavy Duty Brake Fluid.
6. Bleed the master cylinder by slowly depressing the foot pedal.
7. Refill master cylinder and bleed the front, then the rear, brakes.

Vacuum Brake Booster

Removal and Installation

1. From inside the car, remove the stoplight switch connector from the switch; remove the pin retainer and washer from the pedal pin and slide the stoplight switch far enough to clear the pin and remove the switch. Slide the booster push rod, bushing and washer off the brake pin.
2. On four and six cylinder models, remove: air cleaner, accelerator cable (at carburetor), accelerator cable bracket, choke water inlet hose (at thermostat), and vacuum hose from EGR valve.
3. Disconnect the manifold vacuum hose from the booster.
4. Remove the primary and secondary brake lines from the outlet ports on the master cylinder. Cap the lines and the master cylinder ports.
5. Remove the master cylinder retaining nuts and remove the master cylinder.
6. From inside the car, remove the booster to dash retaining nuts. From the engine side, pull the booster until the pushrod clears the dash panel, rotate the booster ninety degrees, and pull up until it comes clear.
7. To install, put the booster in position with the check valve on the upper right side. Replace the booster pushrod assembly on the brake pedal pin; secure the booster to the dash panel and tighten the bolts.
8. Place the stoplight switch on the booster push rod with the slot toward the pedal and the hole just clearing the pin. Be careful not to damage the switch. Install the retaining washer and pin and connect the wiring connector.
9. Reconnect the manifold vacuum hose to the booster unit.
10. Reattach the master cylinder assembly, reconnect the items removed in Step 2 and bleed the brakes.

Parking Brake Adjustment

Through 1974

1. Fully release the parking brake.
2. Place the transmission in Neutral and raise the rear of the vehicle until the rear wheels clear the floor. Jack under the axle.
3. Tighten the adjusting nut against the cable equalizer or cable adjusting rod, until the rear brakes drag when the rear wheels are turned.
4. Loosen the adjusting nut until the rear wheels can be turned without the rear brakes dragging.
5. Lower the rear of the vehicle and check the operation of the parking brake.

1975 and later

1. Pry the cover of the parking brake handle assembly up by inserting a screwdriver under the rear edge and forcing up.
2. With the handle raised eight notches, loosen the lock nut, and tighten the adjusting nut. You shouldn't be able to turn the wheels.
3. Tighten the locknut.
4. Reinstall handle cover.

NOTE: This procedure is to be done with the weight of the car on the axles.

STEERING

The steering gear is of the rack and pinion type. The gear input shaft is connected to the steering shaft by means of a flexible cable. A pinion gear, machined on the input shaft, engages the rack and rotation of the input shaft pinion causes the rack to move laterally.

The tie-rod is attached at each end of the rack joint. This allows the tie-rods to move with the front suspension. The gear is sealed at each

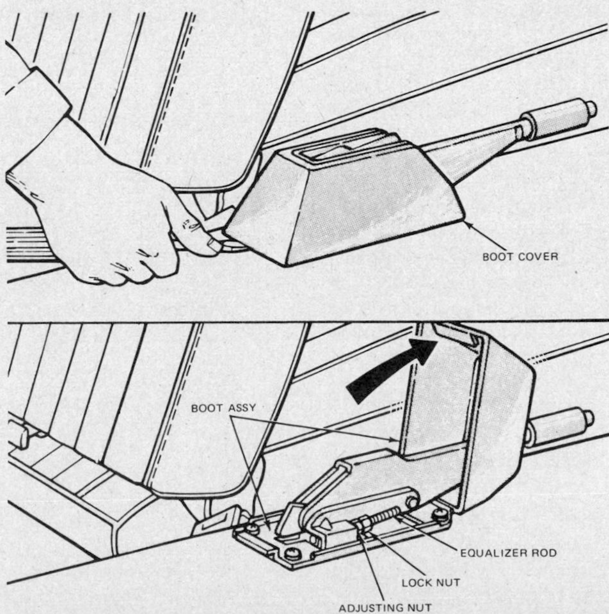

Parking brake adjustment (© Ford Motor Co)

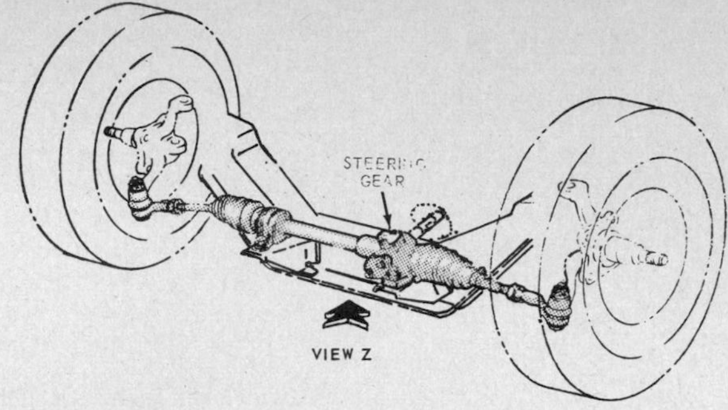

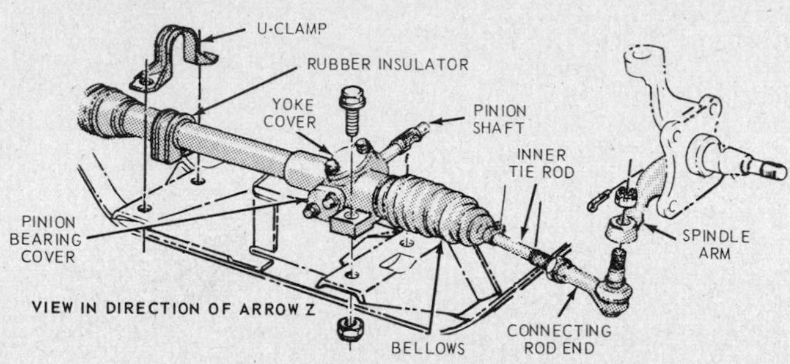

Rack and pinion steering
(© Ford Motor Co)

end with rubber bellows. The steering gear is filled with approximately 5 oz. of SAE-90 E.P. type oil at initial assembly and checking or refilling is not required unless fluid leakage is evident or repairs become necessary.

Couplings attaching the tie-rods are retained on the rack, are pinned and cannot be disassembled in service. Replacement of inner tie-rods, rack, housing, or upper pinion bearing requires installation of a new steering gear assembly.

Integral power rack and pinion steering is a hydraulic-mechanical unit, which uses an integral piston and rack design. Internal valving directs the flow of fluid from the pump and controls the pressure, as required. The unit contains a rotary hydraulic fluid control valve integrated to the input shaft of the steering gear and a boost cylinder integrated with the rack. See the Power Steering Unit Repair Section for details.

Caution When the front wheels of the vehicle are suspended completely off the ground, do not turn the wheels quickly or forcefully from lock to lock. This could cause a build-up of hydraulic pressure within the steering gear which could damage or blow out the bellows.

Power Steering Pump

Removal and Installation

1. Disconnect the fluid return hose at the reservoir, and drain the fluid from the pump.
2. Disconnect the pressure hose from the pump.
3. Remove the bolts from the front of the pump attaching it to the mounting bracket. Disconnect the belt from the pulley and remove the pump.
4. Install the pump in the reverse order of removal.
5. Fill the reservoir with fluid.
6. Turn the steering wheel from stop-to-stop several times. Do not hold the steering wheel in the far left or right position.
7. Recheck the fluid level and add fluid as necessary.
8. Start the engine and allow it to run for several minutes.
9. Stop the engine and recheck the fluid level in the reservoir; add fluid, as necessary.

Steering Wheel Removal and Installation

1. Disconnect the battery ground cable.
2. On models with a small horn button, remove the horn button by pushing down and turning it counterclockwise.
3. On deluxe steering wheels, remove the pad by removing the two screws from behind the steering wheel. Disconnect the horn wires from the pad.
4. Remove the steering wheel attaching nut and, using a puller, remove the steering wheel.
5. Align the mark on the hub with the mark on the shaft and install the wheel on the shaft.
6. Install the attaching nut and tighten it to 30–40 ft lbs.
7. Install the horn button or pad.

Turn Signal and Flasher Switch Removal and Installation

1. Remove the steering wheel as previously outlined.
2. Remove the turn signal lever by unscrewing it from the steering column.
3. Snap off the lower steering column shroud.
4. Disconnect the steering column wiring connectors from the steering column by lifting up on the tabs and removing the connectors from the brackets.
6. Remove the three screws that attach the head of the switch to the top of the steering column.
7. Pull the switch and wire assembly up and out of the steering column. A thin wire attached to the connector will make it easy to pull it down through the column on installation.
8. To install the switch, position it and the wires in the steering column and work the wires down the steering column.
9. Secure the wires and connectors to the base of the steering column.
10. Connect the wire connectors at the base of the column.
11. Install the switch head attaching screws.
12. Install the turn signal lever and steering wheel.

INSTRUMENT PANEL

Headlight Switch Removal and Installation

Pinto

1. Disconnect the battery ground cable.
2. Remove the instrument cluster.
3. Remove the headlight switch control knob, shaft and retaining nut.
4. Disconnect the multiple connector from the switch and remove the switch from instrument cluster opening.
5. Reverse above procedure to install.

Mustang II

1. Disconnect the battery ground cable.
2. Through the hole in the underside of the instrument panel, press the release button with a screwdriver, and remove the knob and shaft assembly.
3. Remove the bezel nut, lower the switch and disconnect the multiple connector.
4. Remove the switch.
5. Install the headlight switch in the reverse order of removal.

Ignition Switch

Removal

1. To gain access to the switch, remove the steering column shroud and disconnect and lower the steering column from the brake support bracket.
2. Disconnect the negative battery cable.
3. Disconnect the switch wiring at the multiple connector.
4. Remove the two nuts that retain the ignition switch to the steering column.
5. Remove the pin that connects the switch plunger to the actuating rod and remove the switch.

Installation

1. When installing the ignition switch, both the switch and the ignition lock must be in the LOCK position. The manual parts can be held in place by turning the ignition lock cylinder to the LOCK position with the transmission in PARK (automatic transmission) or REVERSE (standard transmission). To hold the switch in the LOCK position, insert a pin in the hole on the top of the switch, after manually moving the switch to the lock position.
2. Position the hole in the end of the switch plunger to the hole in the actuator and install the connecting pin.
3. Position the ignition switch on the steering column, and install, but do not tighten the retaining nuts.
4. Move the switch up and down on the steering column to find the mid-point of the actuating rod lash, then tighten the switch retaining nuts.
5. Remove the locking pin from the switch and install the steering column and shroud.

Ignition Lock Cylinder Removal and Installation

1. Disconnect the negative battery cable.
2. Remove the steering wheel as described under "Steering." Insert a stiff wire into the hole located in the lock cylinder housing.
3. Place the gearshift lever in Reverse on standard shift cars and in Park on cars with an automatic transmission, and turn the ignition key to the On position.
4. Depress the wire and remove the lock cylinder and wire.
5. Insert the new cylinder into housing and turn it to the Off position. This will lock the cylinder into position.
6. Reinstall the steering wheel and pad.
7. Connect the negative battery cable.

WINDSHIELD WIPERS

Motor Removal and Installation

1. Loosen the two nuts and disconnect the wiper pivot shaft and link assembly from the motor drive arm ball. A link retaining clip is used on the Mustang II.
2. Remove the three motor attaching screws and lower the motor away from the left side of the dash.
3. Disconnect the wiper motor wires and remove the motor.
4. To install, position the motor under the dash and install the wires. Operate the motor to ensure it is in Park position.
5. Position the motor to the dash and install the retaining screws.
6. Position the wiper pivot shaft and link assembly to the motor drive arm ball and tighten the two nuts. On the Mustang II, install the retaining clip.

Wiper Blade Pivot Removal and Installation

1. Remove the windshield wiper arms and blades from the pivot shafts.
2. Loosen the two nuts retaining the wiper pivot shaft and link assembly to the motor drive arm ball.
3. Remove the screws attaching each pivot shaft.
4. Remove the pivot shaft and link assembly from under the left side of the dash.
5. Reverse above procedure to install. Operate the wiper motor before installing the wiper blades to ensure the pivots are in Park.

NOTE: On a Pinto with air conditioning, the blower motor and housing must be removed to gain access to the wiper pivot and link assembly. After removing the blower motor and housing, follow the previous procedure.

RADIO

Removal and Installation

1. Disconnect the negative battery cable from the battery.
2. Remove the control knobs, discs, control shaft nuts and washers on the Mustang II.
3. On the Mustang II with a Motorola radio, pull the ash tray out to expose the lower mounting bolt. Remove the bolt.
4. Remove the radio rear support attaching nut or bolt.
5. On a Pinto, remove the four screws attaching the bezel to the instrument panel opening.
6. Remove the radio from the instrument panel; out through the front on a Pinto, or down from behind the instrument panel on a Mustang II.
7. Disconnect the electrical lead, antenna lead, and speaker leads from the radio and remove the radio from the vehicle.
8. Install the radio in the reverse order of removal.

HEATER

Heater Assembly Removal and Installation, Non-Air Conditioned Cars

1. Drain the cooling system and disconnect the negative battery cable.
2. Disconnect the blower motor ground wire (black) at the engine side of the dash panel.
3. Disconnect the heater hoses at the engine block.
4. Remove the four nuts that attach the heater assembly to the dash, from the engine side of the dash.
5. Working inside the car, remove the glove box.
6. Disconnect the control cables from the heater. Disconnect the motor lead. Remove the radio.
7. Remove the snap-rivet that at-

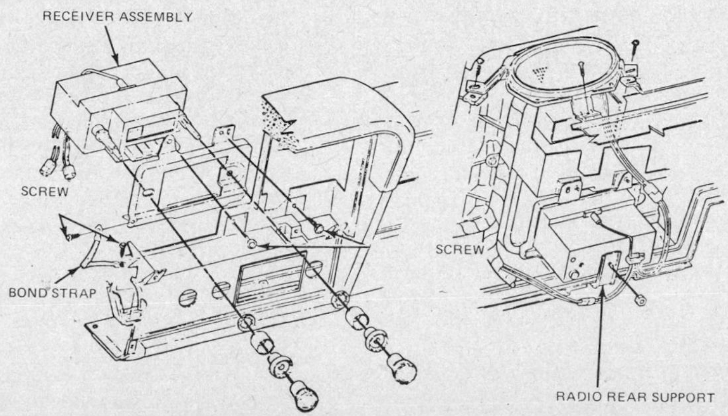

Radio installation Mustang II (© Ford Motor Co.)

taches the forward side of the defroster air duct to the heater assembly. Move the air duct back into the defroster nozzle and disengage it from the tabs on the heater box. Tilt the forward edge of the duct up and forward to disengage it from the nozzle, and remove it from the left side of the heater assembly.

8. Remove the heater assembly to dash panel support bracket mounting screw and remove the heater assembly. At the same time, pull the heater hoses through the dash panel. Then, disconnect the hoses from the heater core in the case.
9. Install in the reverse order of removal.

Blower Motor Removal and Installation, Non-Air Conditioned Cars

1. Remove the heater assembly.
2. Disconnect the blower motor lead wire from the resistor.
3. Remove the four blower motor mounting plate attaching nuts and remove the motor and wheel.
4. Install in the reverse order.

Heater Core Removal and Installation, Non-Air Conditioned Cars

1. Remove the heater assembly.
2. Remove the compression gasket from the cowl air inlet and remove the eleven clips from the case. Separate the case and remove the heater core.
3. Install in the reverse order.

Heater Assembly Removal and Installation, Air Conditioned Cars

1971-72 Models

NOTE: This procedure requires evacuation of the air conditioning refrigerant. Failure to exercise proper safety precautions could cause personal injury.

1. Disconnect the negative battery cable and drain the cooling system.
2. Evacuate the air conditioning system.
3. Disconnect the heater hose from the heater housing.
4. Remove the expansion valve from the evaporator core and tape the openings on the core closed.
5. Disconnect the green and brown vacuum hoses from the hot water valve and remove the two screws that attach the hot water valve and vacuum motor to the firewall.
6. Remove the three heater housing attaching nuts from the engine side of the firewall.
7. Remove the glove box door and the glove box. On models equipped with a console, remove the console.
8. Remove the radio and the kick panel from under the right side of the instrument panel.
9. Remove the three bolts that attach the right pillar brace to the lower edge of the instrument panel.
10. Disconnect the temperature control cable from the heater housing, and the purple and green vacuum hoses from the water valve vacuum switch on the heater housing.
11. Disconnect the white hose from the vacuum motor and the electrical leads from the blower motor resistor.
12. Disconnect the blower motor ground wire from the cowl and the red and yellow vacuum hoses from the vacuum motor above the heater blower motor.
13. Remove the cover plate from the bottom of the defroster duct that runs out of the blower motor.
14. Remove the two screws that attach the air distribution duct to the blower motor and remove the duct.
15. Reach through the opening left by the removal of the air distribution duct and remove the nut and lock plate that attaches the blower housing to the heater housing.
16. Turn the blower housing counterclockwise to disconnect it from the heater housing. Position the blower housing out of the way on the transmission tunnel.
17. Remove the drain hose from the heater housing and remove the screw that attaches the right side of the heater housing to the cowl upper support.
18. Remove the heater housing from under the instrument panel.
19. Reverse the above procedure to install the heater housing. After installation, charge the refrigerant system.

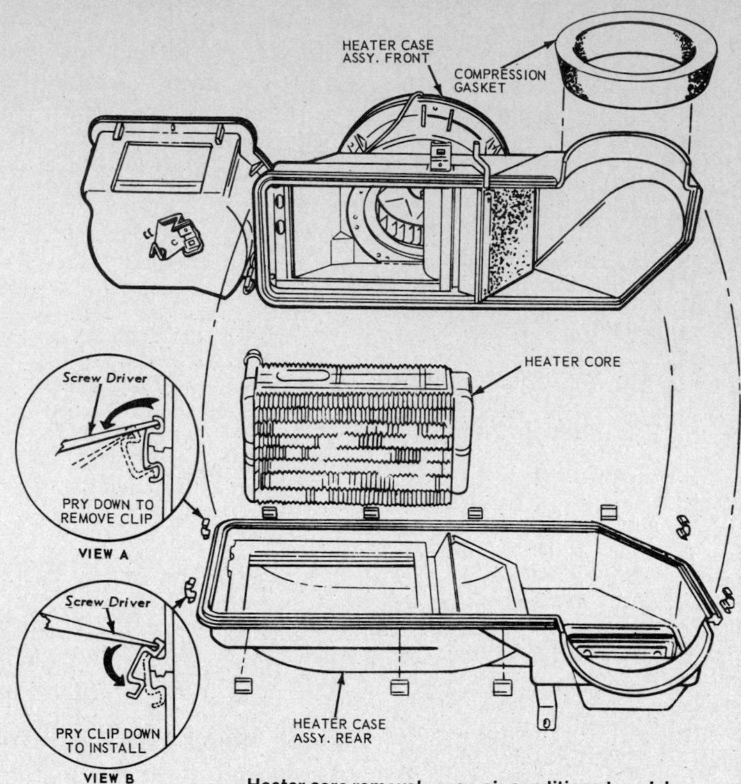

Heater core removal—non-air conditioned models
(© Ford Motor Co)

1973 Models

NOTE: This procedure requires evacuation of the air conditioning refrigerant. Failure to exercise proper safety precautions could cause personal injury.

1. Disconnect the negative battery cable and drain the cooling system.
2. Evacuate the air conditioning system.
3. Disconnect the heater hoses from the heater core tubes.
4. Disconnect the expansion valve from the evaporator core tubes and plug the openings in the core tubes.
5. Remove the three nuts that attach the heater assembly to the firewall.
6. Remove the glove box and disconnect the right and left air ducts from the heater housing.
7. Disconnect the blue vacuum hose from the A/C-defroster distribution housing. Open the access door in the bottom of the housing and remove the two screws that

attach the housing to the instrument panel defroster ducts. Remove the housing from the top of the blower motor housing.

8. Disconnect the red and the yellow vacuum hoses from the A/C-heat door vacuum motor (upper left side of housing).
9. Disconnect the white vacuum hose from outside recirculation door vacuum motor (upper right side of housing).
10. Disconnect the multiple vacuum connector from the rear of the A/C-heater control on the instrument panel.
11. Disconnect the control cable from the temperature control door crank arm.
12. Disconnect the purple and the green vacuum hoses from the water valve switch. The water valve switch is located on the heater housing just above the temperature door crank arm.
13. Remove the bracket that attaches the heater housing to the underside of the instrument panel.
14. Move the heater assembly rearward until it clears its mounting studs, then detach the vacuum hoses that are taped or clipped to the top of the housing.
15. Tag and disconnect the wiring that attaches to the heater housing.
16. Remove the heater housing from the car.
17. Reverse the above procedure to install the heater housing. Charge the refrigerant system.

1974-76 Models

NOTE: This procedure requires evacuation of the air conditioning refrigerant. Failure to exercise proper safety precautions could cause personal injury.

1. Drain the engine coolant, discharge the air conditioning system and disconnect the battery.
2. Remove the A/C refrigerant lines and the front half of the refrigerant manifold.
3. Remove the manifold mounting stud with vice-grips to provide clearance when removing the evaporator case assembly.
4. Disconnect the two heater hoses from the core tubes in the engine compartment.
5. Remove the A/C condensate drain hose in the engine compartment.
6. Remove the glove box.
7. Disconnect the vacuum hoses from the evaporator case.
8. Disconnect the temperature control cable from the blend door crank arm.
9. Remove the heat distribution duct. On the Mustang II, remove the mode door vacuum motor which is retained to the evaporator case assembly by two nuts and a spring nut.
10. On the Pinto, to remove the A/C defrost plenum:
    a. Cut and remove the two staples which retain the fold down door in the closed position on the plenum.
    b. Bend the fold down door away from the locating tabs on each side of the plenum to allow removal of the adaptor duct.
    c. Remove the adapter duct.

On the Mustang II, remove the lower section of the A/C defrost plenum which is retained by 3 screws and two retaining tabs.

11. Remove the blower motor and wheel from the blower scroll.
12. Install one ¼-20 hex-washer head screw to the mounting tab on the inlet duct to upper cowl bracket to hold the duct in place. Leave this screw in place when installing the case assembly.
13. Remove the three inlet duct-to-evaporator case attaching screws through the blower scroll opening.
14. Remove the one upper case-to-inlet duct attaching screw located under the outside-recirculating motor mounting bracket.
15. Remove the two evaporator-to-upper cowl bracket attaching screws.
16. Remove the four evaporator-to-dash panel attaching nuts in the engine compartment.
17. Rotate the evaporator assembly down and away from the dash panel and out from under the instrument panel.
18. Install the heater/evaporator case in the reverse order of removal. During installation, position the fold down door of the defrost plenum between the locating tabs on each side of the plenum and tape it in position with two pieces of black tape 1 in. wide by 4 in. long.

Blower Motor Removal and Installation, Air Conditioned Cars

1971-72 Models

1. Disconnect the negative battery cable. If equipped with a console, remove the console from the car.
2. Remove the radio.
3. Remove the fuse panel attaching screw, disconnect the multiple connector from the fuse panel and remove the fuse panel from the fuse panel support bracket which is attached to the brake pedal support bracket.
4. Remove the fuse panel support bracket from the brake pedal support bracket and position it out of the way.
5. Remove the instrument panel-to-cowl brace and position the fuse panel on the lower edge of the instrument panel.
6. Disconnect the lead wires from the blower motor resistor and the blower motor ground wire from the cowl.
7. Remove the red and yellow vacuum hoses from the vacuum motor over the blower motor.
8. Remove the cover plate from the bottom of the defroster outlet duct of the blower motor.
9. Remove the two screws that attach the air distribution duct to the blower motor housing.
10. Reach through the opening left by the removal of the air distribution duct and remove the nut and lock plate that attaches the blower motor housing to the heater housing.
11. Turn the blower motor counterclockwise to disconnect it from the heater housing and position the blower motor on the transmission tunnel.
12. Remove the steering column-to-instrument panel brace. It may be necessary to move the blower housing slightly rearward to gain access to the upper brace attaching bolt.
13. Cut the blower housing-to-heater housing gasket at the break in the two blower housing pieces.
14. Disconnect the A/C-heat door rod from the A/C-heat door.
15. Remove the seven clips and separate the two halves of the blower housing.
16. Remove the left half of the blower housing with the blower motor attached.
17. Remove the three blower motor mounting nuts and remove the blower motor and wheel.
18. Reverse the above procedure to install the blower motor.

1973 Models

1. Disconnect the negative battery cable.
2. Remove the two screws that attach the hot air distribution duct to the bottom of the blower housing and remove the duct.
3. Open the access door in the bottom of the A/C-defroster distribution housing and remove the two screws that attach the distribution housing to the instrument panel defroster ducts.
4. Working through the opening left by removal of the bottom heat distribution duct, remove the nut and lock plate that attaches the blower housing to the heater housing.
5. Turn the blower motor housing clockwise to disengage the two locking tabs on the blower housing from the pin on the heater housing.
6. Remove the blower housing from the car.

7. Cut the blower outlet gasket at the blower housing seams.
8. Remove the clips that secure the two halves of the blower housing, and separate the housing.
9. Remove the three blower motor attaching nuts and the motor.

1974-76 Models

The blower motor and wheel is integrally located within the scroll portion of the evaporator assembly on the right-side of the evaporator case. To remove the blower motor and wheel, remove the glove box and remove the four screws retaining the blower motor and wheel in the blower scroll. Install the blower motor and wheel in the reverse order of removal.

Heater Core Removal and Installation, Air Conditioned Cars

1971-73 Models

1. Remove the heater housing and remove the rubber seal from the housing.
2. Remove the eleven clips that hold the two halves of the heater housing together and separate the housing.
3. Remove the A/C thermostatic de-icing switch from the top of the housing.
4. Remove four screws and remove the evaporator core from the upper housing.
5. Remove four screws and the temperature blend door upper frame.
6. Remove the spring clip and crank arm and remove the temperature blend door from the housing.
7. Remove four screws and the temperature blend door lower frame.
8. Remove the heater core and gasket from the lower housing.

1974-76 Models

1. Remove the evaporator case assembly from the vehicle.
2. Remove the eight upper-to-lower case attaching screws.
3. Remove the rubber seal from the heater core tubes.
4. Remove the upper half of the evaporator case.
5. Move the rubber seal on the evaporator core forward to clear the case mounting stud and pull the core out of the lower case.
6. Remove the two heater core upper straps.
7. Remove the air deflector mounting screw on the lower case to the left of the heater core, remove the deflector and remove the heater core.
8. Install in the reverse order of removal. Be sure to install new rope sealer around the flange of the lower case before installing the upper half of the case. Install new O-rings on the manifold plate. Dip the new O-rings in refrigerant oil before installing them.

SEAT BELTS

Seat Belt/Starter Interlock System, 1974-75

All Ford vehicles are equipped with the Federally-required starter interlock system. The purpose of this system is to force the wearing of seat belts.

The system includes a warning light and buzzer (as in late 1972 and 1973), weight sensors in the front seats, switches in the outboard front seat belt retractors, and an electronic control module.

The electronic control module requires that the driver and right front passenger first sit down, then pull out their seat belts. If this is not done, the starter will not operate, but the light and buzzer will. The sequence must be followed each time the engine is started unless the driver and passenger have remained seated and buckled. If the seat belts have been pulled out and left buckled, the engine will not start. The switches in the retractors must be cycled for each start. If the belts are released after the start, the light and buzzer will operate.

If the system should fail, preventing starting, the interlock by-pass switch under the hood can be used. This switch permits one start without interference from the interlock system. This by-pass switch can also be used for servicing purposes.

Troubleshooting

If the starter will not crank or the warning buzzer will not shut off, perform the following checks:

Problem: Front seat occupant sits on a prebuckled seat belt.

Solution: Unbuckle the prebuckled belt, fully retract, extract, and then rebuckle the belt.

Problem: The front seat occupants are buckled, but the starter will not crank.

Solution: The unoccupied seat sensor switch stuck closed before the seat was occupied. Reset the unoccupied seat sensor switches by applying and then releasing 50 lbs or more of weight to the seat directly over the seat sensor switches.

Problem: Starter will not crank with a heavy parcel on the front seat.

Solution: Buckle the seat belt around the parcel, or place the parcel somewhere else in the car. Unbuckle the seat belt when the parcel is removed from the front seat.

Problem: Starter will not crank due to starter interlock system component failure.

Solution: An emergency starter interlock override switch is located under the hood on the fender apron. Depress the red push button on the switch and release it. This will allow one complete cycle of the ignition key from Off to Start and back to Off. Do not tape the button down as this will result in deactivation of the override feature.

Disabling the Interlock System

New automobiles are no longer required to have the interlock system. The system may legally be disabled on cars that do have it, but the following procedure must be used. The warning light is still required.

1. Locate the override switch and terminal connector attached to it.
2. Remove the no. 32 (red with a light blue stripe) wire(s) and no. 33 (white with pink dots), wire(s) and splice them together.
3. To remove the buzzer, remove the terminal connector from the buzzer, and tape it to the wiring harness to prevent rattling; then remove the buzzer unit.

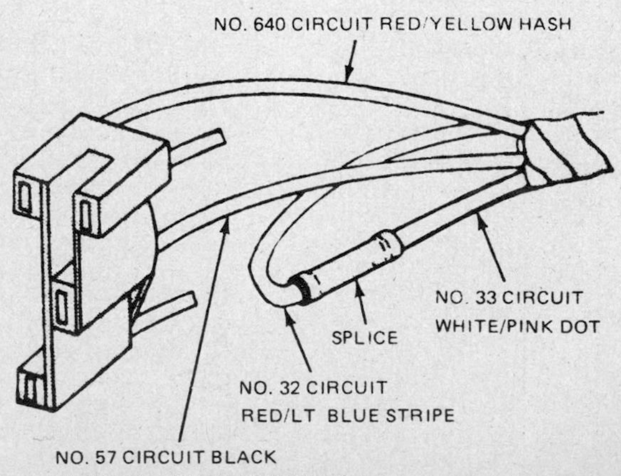

Seatbelt interlock override switch terminal connector and wires (© Ford Motor Co.)

INDEX

Buick

YEAR IDENTIFICATION

1969 Riviera

1969 Wildcat

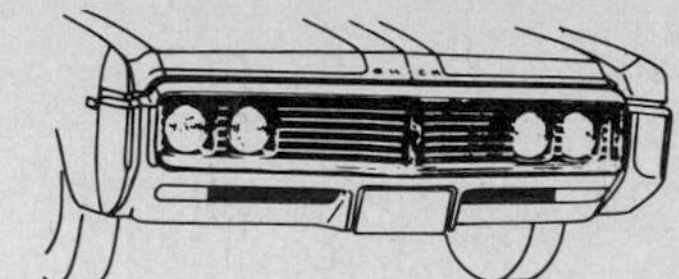
1969 Le Sabre

1969 Electra

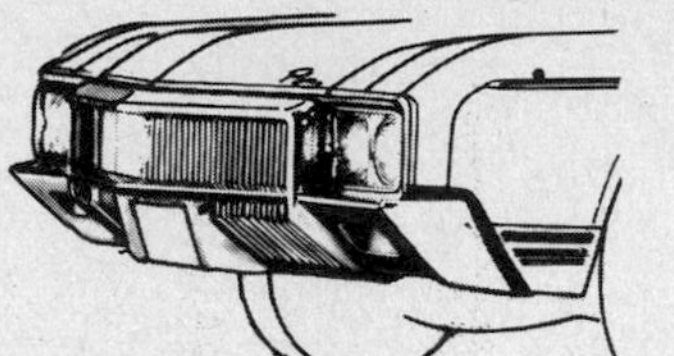
1970 Riviera

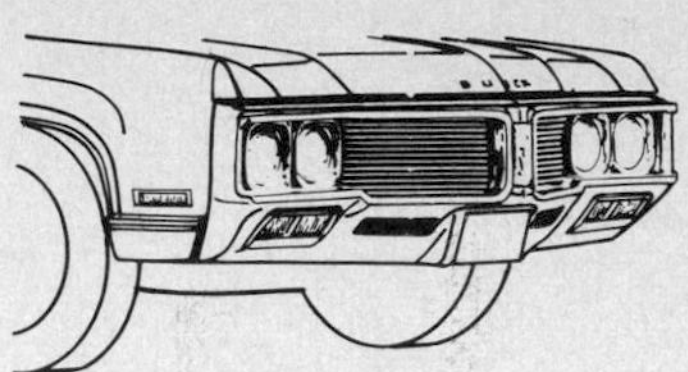
1970 Le Sabre

1971 Riviera

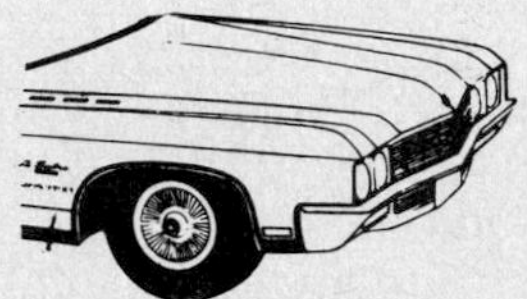
1971 Le Sabre

1971 Electra

1971 Centurion

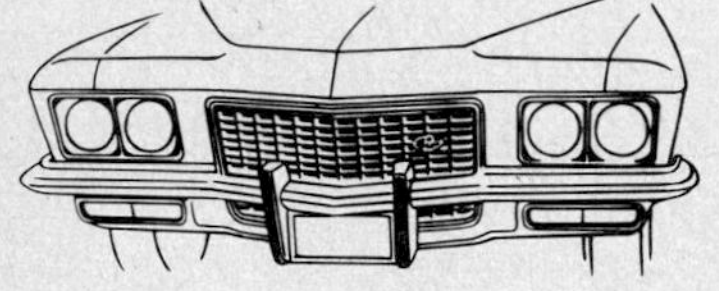
1972 Riviera

1972 Electra

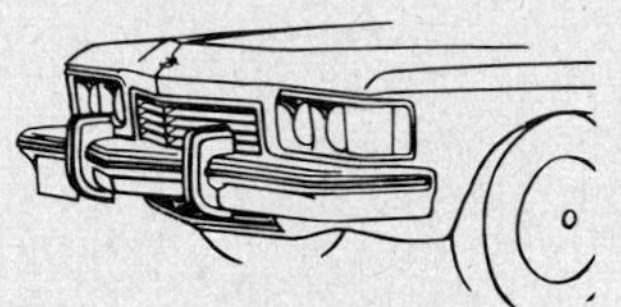
1973 Riviera

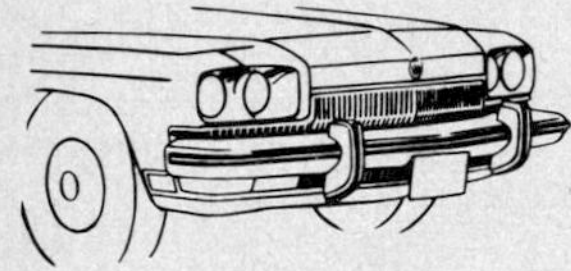
1973 Buick

1974 Riviera

1974 Electra

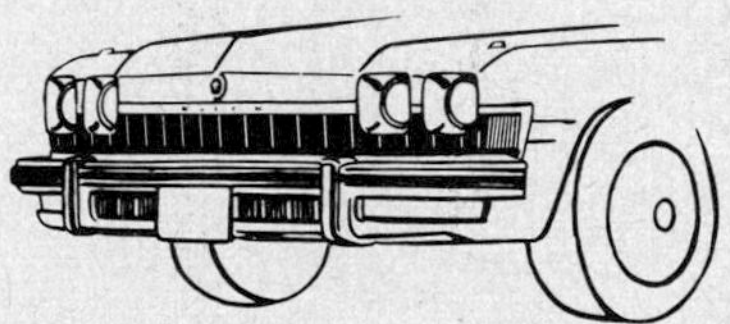
1974 Le Sabre

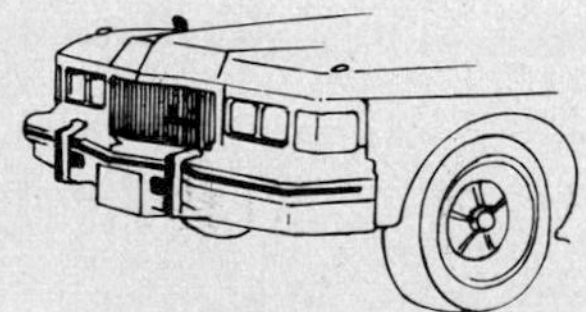
1975 Riviera

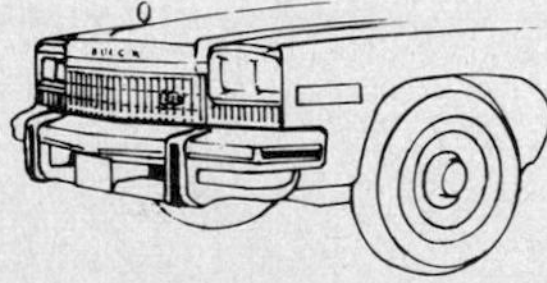
1975 Electra

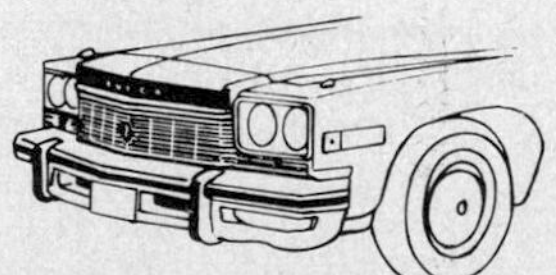
1975 LeSabre

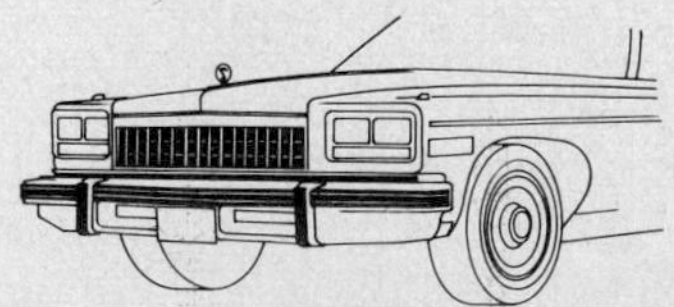
1976 Electra

1976 Electra Limited

FIRING ORDER

FIRING ORDER
1–8–4–3–6–5–7–2

350, 430, 455 cu in.

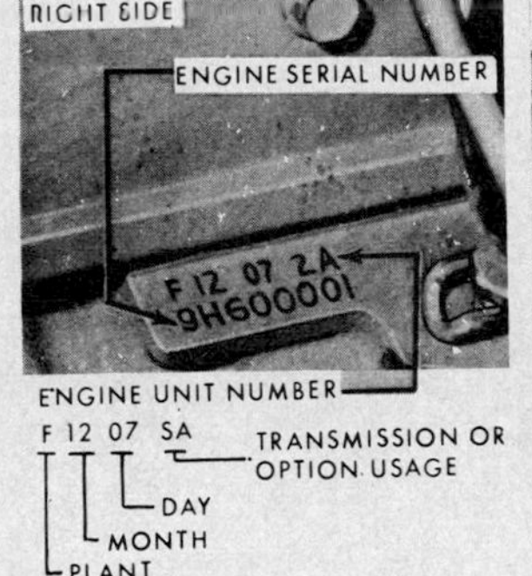

Typical production code number
(© Buick Div., G.M. Corp)

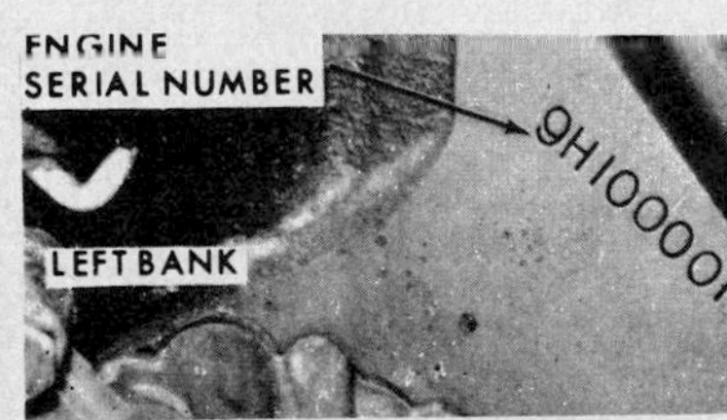

Engine numbers, 350 cu in. through 1971
(© Buick Div., G.M. Corp)

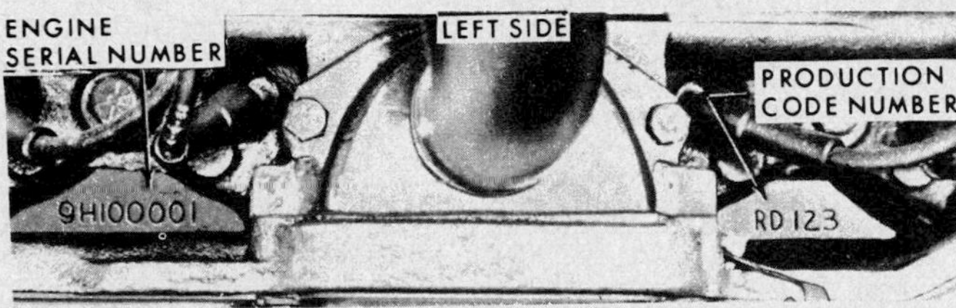

Engine numbers, 430, and 455 cu in. through 1971
(© Buick Div., G.M. Corp)

ENGINE PRODUCTION CODE

Disp	Bbl	Hp	'69	'70	'71	'72	'73	'74	'75	'76
8-Cylinder Models										
350	2	150, 165# (net)					XC	XC	AB	
350	2	155 (net)				WC				
350	4	160, 165 (net)							AM	
350	4	175, 195# (net)					XB	XB		
350	4	180 (net)				WB				
350	2	230	RO		TC TO					
350	2	260		SO						
350	4	260			TB TD					
350	4	280	RP							
350	4	285		SB						
350	4	315		SP						
455	4	205 (net)							AF	
455	4	225, (net)	PD	RD		WF	XF			
455	4	210, 230# (net)						XF		
455	4	260 (net)				WA	XA			
Stage 1										
455	4	245 (net)						XA		
455	4	315			TR					
455	4	330			TA					
455	4	350		SR						
455	4	370		SF						

\# Dual exhaust

CAR SERIAL NUMBER LOCATION AND ENGINE IDENTIFICATION

The car serial number is used for registration and other legal records. This number is unique to the individual car. The production code number identifies the type of engine and its production date. The Engine Production Code chart can be used to determine the type of engine in the particular vehicle. The engine number also appears on the vehicle identification plate following model and series identification.

1969

The serial number identification plate is attached to the top of the instrument panel on the left side.

On the 350 cu. in. engine, the serial number is on the front of the left cylinder bank just below the cylinder head. The production code number is between the left exhaust manifold and the two front spark plugs on the left bank.

On the 430 cu. in. engine, the serial number is between the two front spark plugs and the exhaust manifold on the left side. The production code number is between the two rear spark plugs and the exhaust manifold, also on the left side.

1970-71

The serial number identification plate is attached to the top of the instrument panel on the left side.

On the 350 cu. in. engine, the serial number is on the front of the left cylinder bank just below the cylinder head. The production code number is between the left exhaust manifold and the two front spark plugs on the left bank.

On the 455 cu. in. engine, the serial number is between the two front spark plugs and the exhaust manifold on the left side. The production code number is between the two rear spark plugs and the exhaust manifold, also on the left side.

1972-76

The car serial number identification plate is attached to the top of the instrument panel on the left-side.

On the 350 cu. in. engine, the engine serial number is on the front of the right cylinder bank. The production code number is between the left exhaust manifold and the two front spark plugs.

On the 455 cu. in. engine, the engine serial number is on the front of the right cylinder bank. The production code number is between the left exhaust manifold and the two rear spark plugs.

GENERAL ENGINE SPECIFICATIONS

Year	Engine No. Cyl. Displacement (cu. in.)	Carburetor Type	Horsepower @ rpm ■	Torque @ rpm (ft lbs) ■	Bore and Stroke (in.)	Compression Ratio	Oil Pressure @ 2400 rpm (psi)
'69	8-350	2 bbl	230 @ 4400	350 @ 2400	3.800 x 3.500	9.0:1	37
	8-350	4 bbl	280 @ 4600	375 @ 3200	3.800 x 3.850	10.25:1	37
	8-430	4 bbl	360 @ 5000	475 @ 3200	4.1875 x 3.900	10.25:1	40
'70	8-350	2 bbl	260 @ 4600	360 @ 2600	3.800 x 3.850	9.0:1	37
	8-350	4 bbl	285 @ 4600	375 @ 3200	3.800 x 3.850	10.25:1	37
	8-350	4 bbl	315 @ 4800	410 @ 3200	3.800 x 3.850	10.25:1	37
	8-455	4 bbl	370 @ 4600	510 @ 2800	4.3125 x 3.900	10.0:1	40
'71	8-350	2 bbl	230 @ 4400	350 @ 2400	3.800 x 3.850	8.5:1	37
	8-350	4 bbl	260 @ 4600	360 @ 3000	3.800 x 3.850	8.5:1	37
	8-455	4 bbl	315 @ 4400	450 @ 2800	4.3125 x 3.900	8.5:1	40
	8-455	4 bbl	330 @ 4600	455 @ 2800	4.3125 x 3.900	8.5:1	40
'72	8-350	2 bbl	155 @ 3800①	270 @ 2400②	3.800 x 3.850	8.5:1	37③
	8-350	4 bbl	180 @ 3800④	275 @ 2400⑤	3.800 x 3.850	8.5:1	37③
	8-455	4 bbl	225 @ 4000	360 @ 2600	4.3125 x 3.900	8.5:1	40
	8-455 DE	4 bbl	250 @ 4000	375 @ 2800	4.3125 x 3.900	8.5:1	40
	8-455	4 bbl	260 @ 4400	380 @ 2800	4.3125 x 3.900	8.5:1	40
'73	8-350	2 bbl	150 @ 3800	265 @ 2400	3.800 x 3.850	8.5:1	37
	8-350	4 bbl	175 @ 3800	270 @ 2400	3.800 x 3.850	8.5:1	37
	8-455	4 bbl	225 @ 4000	360 @ 2600	4.3125 x 3.900	8.5:1	37
	8-455 DE	4 bbl	250 @ 4000	375 @ 2800	4.3125 x 3.900	8.5:1	37
	8-455	4 bbl	260 @ 4400	380 @ 2800	4.3125 x 3.900	8.5:1	37
'74	8-350 SE	2 bbl	150 @ 3600	270 @ 2000	3.800 x 3.850	8.5:1	37
	8-350 DE	2 bbl	165 @ 3800	285 @ 2000	3.800 x 3.850	8.5:1	37
	8-350 SE	4 bbl	175 @ 3800	260 @ 2000	3.800 x 3.850	8.5:1	37
	8-350 DE	4 bbl	195 @ 4000	280 @ 2000	3.800 x 3.850	8.5:1	37
	8-455 SE	2 bbl	175 @ 3400	355 @ 2000	4.3125 x 3.900	8.5:1	37
	8-455 DE	2 bbl	190 @ 3600	370 @ 2000	4.3125 x 3.900	8.5:1	37
	8-455 SE	4 bbl	210 @ 3600	335 @ 2200	4.3125 x 3.900	8.5:1	37
	8-455 DE	4 bbl	230 @ 3800	355 @ 2200	4.3125 x 3.900	8.5:1	37
	8-455 DE⑥	4 bbl	245 @ 4000	360 @ 2400	4.3125 x 3.900	8.5:1	37
'75-'76	8-350	4 bbl	165 @ 3800⑦	260 @ 2200	3.800 x 3.850	8.0:1	37
	8-455	4 bbl	205 @ 3800	345 @ 2000	4.3125 x 3.900	7.9:1	40

■ Beginning 1972, horsepower and torque are SAE net figures. They are measured at the rear of the transmission with all accessories installed and operating. Since the figures vary when a given engine is installed in different models, some are representative rather than exact.

SE Single Exhaust
DE Dual Exhaust

① For California vehicles, advertised horsepower is 150 @ 3800 rpm
② For California vehicles, advertised torque is 265 @ 2400 rpm
③ Adjust oil pressure at 2600 rpm
④ For California vehicles, advertised horsepower is 175 @ 3800 rpm
⑤ For California vehicles, advertised torque is 270 @ 2400 rpm
⑥ Stage I
⑦ 160 @ 3800 for California vehicles

TUNE-UP SPECIFICATIONS

Year	ENGINE No. Cyl Displacement (cu in.)	hp	SPARK PLUGS Type	Gap (in.)	DISTRIBUTOR Point Dwell (deg)	Point Gap (in.)	IGNITION TIMING (deg) ▲ Man Trans	Auto Trans	VALVES Intake Opens ■ (deg)	Fuel Pump Pressure (psi)	IDLE SPEED (rpm) ▲ Man Trans	Auto Trans
'69	8-350	230	R-45TS	.030	30	.016	TDC	TDC	24	4¼-5¾	700	600
	8-350	280	R-45TS	.030	30	.016	TDC	TDC	24	4¼-5¾	700	600
	8-430	360	R-44TS	.030	30	.016	—	TDC	14	5½-7	—	550
'70	8-350	260	R-45TS	.030	30	.016	6B	6B	24	4¼-5¾	700	600
	8-350	285	R-45TS	.030	30	.016	6B	6B	24	4¼-5¾	700	600
	8-350	315	R-45TS	.030	30	.016	6B	6B	24	4¼-5¾	700	600
	8-455	350	R-44TS	.030	30	.016	6B	6B	18	4¼-5¾	700	600
	8-455	370	R-44TS	.030	30	.016	6B	6B	18	4¼-5¾	700	600
'71	8-350	230	R-45TS	.030	30	.016	6D	10B②	24	4¼-5¾	1100/800③	600
	8-350	260	R-45TS	.030	30	.016	6B	4B	28	4¼-5¾	1100/800③	600
	8-455	315	R-45TS	.030	30	.016	6B	4B	12	4¼-5¾	1100/700③	600
	8-455	330	R-44TS	.030	30	.016	10B	10B	12	4¼-5¾	1100/700③	600
'72	8-350	155	R-45TS	.040	30	.016	4B	4B	24	4¼-5¾	800③/600	650③/500
	8-350	180	R-45TS	.040	30	.016	4B	4B	24	4¼-5¾	800③/600	650③/500
	8-455	225	R-45TS	.040	30	.016	4B	4B	12(14)④	4¼-5¾	900③/600	650③/500
	8-455	250	R-45TS	.040	30	.016	4B	4B	12(14)④	4¼-5¾	900③/600	650③/500
	8-455	260	R-45TS	.040	30	.016	4B	4B	12(14)④	4¼-5¾	900③/600	650③/500
'73	8-350	150	R-45TS	.040	30	.016	—	4B	24	4¼-5¾	—	600/500③
	8-350	175	R-45TS	.040	30	.016	—	4B	24	4¼-5¾	—	600/500③
	8-455	225	R-45TS	.040	30	.016	—	4B	14	4¼-5¾	—	650/500③
	8-455	250	R-45TS	.040	30	.016	—	4B	14	4¼-5¾	—	650/500③
	8-455	260	R-45TS	.040	30	.016	—	4B	14	4¼-5¾	—	650/500③
'74	8-350	All⑥	R-45TS	.040	30	.016	—	4B	19⑤⑦	4¼-5¾	—	650/500③
	8-455	All⑥	R-45TS	.040	30	.016	—	4B	10⑤	4¼-5¾	—	650/500③
'75	8-350	165	R-45TSX	.060	Electronic		—	12B	19⑤	4¼-5¾	—	600
	8-455	205	R-45TSX	.060	Electronic		—	12B	10⑤	4¼-5¾	—	600
'76	8-350	All	R-45TSX	.060	Electronic		—	12B	19	5-6½	—	600
	8-455	205	R-45TSX	.060	Electronic		—	12B	10	7½-9	—	600

▲ See text for procedure
■ All figures Before Top Dead Center
① Not used
② 4B for LeSabre
③ Lower figure indicates idle speed with solenoid disconnected
④ Figure in parentheses indicates California vehicle.
⑤ These figures do not represent a change from 1973; however, the reference point is changed to be consistent with information required for government certification.
⑥ See engine compartment tune-up sticker on engines with H.E.I. electronic ignition system.
⑦ 25 on California cars
B Before Top Dead Center
N.A. Not available
TDC Top Dead Center
— Not applicable

CAPACITIES

Year	ENGINE No. Cyl. Displacement (cu. in.)	Engine Crankcase Add 1 Qt For New Filter	TRANSMISSION Pts To Refill After Draining Manual 3-Speed	4-Speed	Automatic •	Drive Axle (pts)	Gasoline Tank (gals)	COOLING SYSTEM (qts) With Heater	With A/C
'69	8-350	4	3.5	—	5	3	25	13.2	13.6
	8-430	4	3.5	—	7	4.25	25	16.7	17
	Riviera	4	—	—	7	4.25	21	16.7	17
'70	8-350	4	3.5	—	6	3	25	16.2	16.6
	8-455	4	3.5	—	7	4.25	25①	19.7	20
	Riviera	4	—	—	7	4.25	21	19.7	20

CAPACITIES

Year	ENGINE No. Cyl. Displacement (cu. in.)	Engine Crankcase Add 1 Qt For New Filter	TRANSMISSION Pts To Refill After Draining Manual 3-Speed	Manual 4-Speed	Automatic •	Drive Axle (pts)	Gasoline Tank (gals)	COOLING SYSTEM (qts) With Heater	With A/C
'71	8-350	4	3.5	—	6	4.25	25	16.2	16.6
	8-455	4	3.5	—	7	5.5	25②	18.7	19
	Riviera	4	—	—	7	5.5	24	19.7	20
'72	8-350	4	—	—	6	4.25	25	19	19.3
	8-455	4	—	—	7	5.5	25②	18.7	19
	Riviera	4	—	—	7	5.5	24	18.7	19
'73	8-350	4	—	—	6	4.25	26	18.9	19.3
	8-455	4	—	—	7	5.4	26③	18.7	19④
	Riviera	4	—	—	7	5.4	26	18.7	19④
'74	8-350	4	—	—	6	4.25	26	18.9	19.3
	8-455	4	—	—	7⑤	5.4	26③	18.7	19④
	Riviera	4	—	—	7	5.4	26	18.7	19④
'75-'76	8-350	4	—	—	6	4.25	26	16.9	17.2
	8-455	4	—	—	7⑤	5.4	26③	19.6	21.4
	Riviera	4	—	—	7	5.4	26	19.6	21.4

• Specifications do not include torque converter
① Estate wagon—24 gals
② Estate wagon—23 gals
③ Estate wagon—22 gals
④ 20.2 with H.D. cooling
— Not applicable
⑤ LeSabre 455—6 pts

VALVE SPECIFICATIONS

Year	Engine No. Cyl. Displacement (cu in.)	Seat Angle (deg)	Face Angle (deg)	Spring Test Pressure (lbs @ in.)	Spring Installed Height (in.)	STEM TO GUIDE Clearance (in.) Intake	Exhaust	STEM Diameter (in.) Intake	Exhaust
'69	8-350	45	45	180 @ 1.34	1 23/32	.0015-.0025	.0015-.0032	.3725	.3727
	8-430	45	45	177 @ 1.45	1 29/32	.0015-.0035	.0015-.0032	.3725	.3727
'70	8-350	45	45	180 @ 1.34	1 23/32	.0015-.0025	.0015-.0032	.3725	.3725
	8-455	45	45	177 @ 1.45	1 29/32	.0015-.0035	.0015-.0032	.3725	.3725
'71	8-350	45	45	180 @ 1.34	1 23/32	.0015-.0035	.0015-.0032	.3725	.3725
	8-455	45	45	177 @ 1.45	1 29/32	.0015-.0035	.0015-.0032	.3725	.3727
'72	8-350	45	45	180 @ 1.34	1 23/32	.0015-.0035	.0015-.0032	.3725	.3727
	8-455	45	45	177 @ 1.45	1 29/32	.0015-.0035	.0015-.0032	.3725	.3727
'73	8-350	45	45	180 @ 1.34	1 23/32	.0015-.0035	.0015-.0032	.3725	.3730
	8-455	45	45	177 @ 1.45	1 29/32	.0015-.0035	.0015-.0032	.3725	.3730
'74	8-350	45	45	180 @ 1.34	1 23/32	.0015-.0035	.0015-.0032	.3725	.3730
	8-455	45	45	177 @ 1.45	1 29/32	.0015-.0035	.0015-.0032	.3725	.3730
'75-'76	8-350	45	45	180 @ 1.34①	1 47/64	.0015-.0035	.0015-.0032	.3725	.3727
	8-455	45	45	177 @ 1.45	1 57/64	.0015-.0035	.0015-.0032	.3725	.3727

① Exhaust—175 @ 1.34

TORQUE SPECIFICATIONS

All readings in ft lbs

Year	Engine Displacement (cu in.)	Cylinder Head Bolts	Rod Bearing Bolts	Main Bearing Bolts	Crankshaft Pulley or Balancer Bolt	Flywheel to Crankshaft Bolts	MANIFOLD Intake	MANIFOLD Exhaust
'69-'72	350	75	35	95	120	60	55	18
	430, 455	100	35①	110	200	60	55②	18
'73	350	80	35③	115	140	60	55	18
	455	100	45	115	200	60	65	18
'74-'76	350	80	40	115	140	60	45	28
	455	100	45	115	200	60	45	28

① 1970 455 cu in.—45 ft. lbs.
② 1970-72 455 cu in.—65 ft. lbs.
③ 40 with cap screws

CRANKSHAFT AND CONNECTING ROD SPECIFICATIONS

All measurements are given in in.

Year	Engine Displacement (cu in.)	CRANKSHAFT Main Brg. Journal Dia	CRANKSHAFT Main Brg. Oil Clearance	CRANKSHAFT Shaft End-Play	CRANKSHAFT Thrust on No.	CONNECTING ROD Journal Diameter	CONNECTING ROD Oil Clearance	CONNECTING ROD Side Clearance
'69	350	2.9995	.0004-.0015	.003-.009	3	2.0000	.0002-.0023	.006-.014
	430	3.2500	.0007-.0018	.003-.009	3	2.2495	.0002-.0023	.005-.012
'70-'72	350	2.9995	.0004-.0015	.003-.009	3	2.0000	.0002-.0023	.006-.014
	455	3.2500	.0007-.0018	.003-.009	3	2.2495	.0002-.0023	.005-.012
'73	350	2.9995	.0004-.0015	.003-.009	3	2.0000	.0002-.0023	.006-.020
	455	3.2500	.0007-.0018	.003-.009	3	2.2495	.0002-.0023	.005-.012
'74	350	3.0000	.0004-.0015	.003-.009	3	2.0000	.0002-.0023	.006-.020
	455	3.2500	.0007-.0018	.003-.009	3	2.2495	.0002-.0023	.005-.012
'75-'76	350	2.9995	.0004-.0015	.003-.009	3	1.9995	.0005-.0026	.006-.026
	455	3.2500	.0007-.0018	.003-.009	3	2.2491	.0005-.0026	.005-.025

RING GAP

All measurements are given in inches

Year	Engine No. Cyl Displacement (cu in.)	Top Compression	Bottom Compression	Oil Control
'69-'70	8-350	.010-.020	.010-.020	.015-.035
	8-430, 455	.013-.023	.013-.023	.015-.055
'71-'72	8-350	.013-.023	.013-.023	.015-.035
	8-455	.013-.023	.013-.023	.015-.055
'73-'74	8-350	.010-.020	.010-.020	.015-.035
	8-455	.013-.023	.013-.023	.015-.055
'75-'76	8-350	.013-.023	.013-.023	.015-.035
	8-455	.013-.023	.013-.023	.015-.035

PISTON CLEARANCE

Year	Engine No. Cyl. Displacement (cu. in.)	Piston to Bore Clearance (in.)
'69	8-350	.0008-.0014
	8-430	.0007-.0013
'70-'74	8-350	.0008-.0020
	8-455	.0010-.0016
'75-'76	8-350	.0008-.0014
	8-455	.0010-.0016

RING SIDE CLEARANCE

All measurements are given in inches

Year	Engine	Top Compression	Bottom Compression	Oil Control
'69-'76	All	.003-.005	.003-.005	.0035-.0095①

① .0035 Maximum—'73 and later

ALTERNATOR AND REGULATOR SPECIFICATIONS

	ALTERNATOR			REGULATOR						
					Field Relay			Regulator		
Year	Part No.	Field Current @ 12 V	Output (amps)	Part No.	Air Gap (in.)	Point Gap (in.)	Volts to Close	Air Gap (in.)	Point Gap (in.)	Volts @ 75°
'69-'70	1100691	2.2-2.6	42	1119515	.015	.030	1.5-3.2	.067	.014	13.6-14.4
	1100774	2.2-2.6	55	1119507	.015	.030	3.8-7.2	.067	.014	13.6-14.4
	1100774	2.2-2.6	55	1119515	.015	.030	1.5-3.2	.067	.014	13.6-14.4
	1100860	2.2-2.6	61	1119515	.015	.030	1.5-3.2	.067	.014	13.6-14.4
'71	1100943	2.2-2.6	42	1119515	.015	.030	1.5-3.2	.067	.014	13.5-14.5
	1100926	4.0-4.5	42	1116384		Transistor type—no adjustment				13.6-14.3
	1100931	2.2-2.6	55	1119515	.015	.030	1.5-3.2	.067	.014	13.5-14.5
	1100932	2.2-2.6	61	1119515	.015	.030	1.5-3.2	.067	.014	13.5-14.5
	1100933	2.8-3.2	63	1119519	.015	.030	1.5-3.2	.067	.014	13.5-14.5
	1100924	4.0-4.5	55	1116384		Transistor type—no adjustment				13.6-14.3
'72	1102448	2.2-2.6	55	1119515	.015	.030	1.5-3.2	.067	.014	13.5-14.5
	1102442	2.2-2.6	55	1119515	.015	.030	1.5-3.2	.067	.014	13.5-14.5
	1102450	2.2-2.6	61	1119515	.015	.030	1.5-3.2	.067	.014	13.5-14.5
	1102447	2.8-3.2	63	1119519	.015	.030	1.5-3.2	.067	.014	13.5-14.5
	1100926	4.0-4.5	42			Transistor type—no adjustment				13.5-14.5
	1100924	4.0-4.5	55			Transistor type—no adjustment				13.5-14.5
'73-'74	1100946	4.0-4.5	50			Transistor type—no adjustment				13.5-14.5
	1100948	4.0-4.5	55			Transistor type—no adjustment				13.5-14.5
	1100925	4.0-4.5	58			Transistor type—no adjustment				13.5-14.5
'75	1102389	4.0-4.5	42			Transistor type—no adjustment				13.6-14.2
	1102391	4.0-4.5	61			Transistor type—no adjustment				13.6-14.2
	1102939	4.0-4.5	63			Transistor type—no adjustment				13.6-14.2

BATTERY AND STARTER SPECIFICATIONS

		BATTERY			STARTER						
					Lock Test			No-Load Test			
Year	Engine Displacement (cu in.)	Ampere Hour Capacity	Volts	Terminal Grounded	Amps	Volts	Torque (ft lbs)	Amps	Volts	RPM	Brush Spring Tension (oz)
'69-'70	350	61	12	Neg.	Not Recommended			55-85	9	3,100-4,900	35
	430, 455	70	12	Neg.	Not Recommended			48-74	9	4,100-6,300	35
'71-'72	350	61	12	Neg.	Not Recommended			80	9	3,500-6,000	35
	455	70	12	Neg.	Not Recommended			45-80	9	4,000-6,500	35
'73-'74	350	①	12	Neg.	Not Recommended			55-80	9	3,500-6,000	35
	455	②	12	Neg.	Not Recommended			45-80	9	4,000-6,500	35
'75-'76	350	③	12	Neg.	Not Recommended			—	—	—	35
	455	④	12	Neg.	Not Recommended			—	—	—	35

① Side Terminal—Cranking power 2,900 watts @ 0°F
② Side Terminal—Cranking power 3,000 watts @ 0°F
③ Cranking power—3,200 watts @ 0°F
④ Cranking power—3,500 watts @ 0°F

BRAKE SPECIFICATIONS

All measurements given in in.

Year	Model	Master Cylinder Disc	Master Cylinder Drum	Wheel Cylinder Front Disc	Wheel Cylinder Front Drum	Wheel Cylinder Rear	Brake Disc or Drum Diameter Front Disc	Brake Disc or Drum Diameter Front Drum	Brake Disc or Drum Diameter Rear
'69	All	1.125	1.00	2.125	1.188	1.00①	11.920	12.002	12.002
'70	All	1.125	1.00	2.938	1.188	1.00①	11.00	12.002	12.002
'71-'76	All	1.125	—	2.938	—	.938②	11.86	—	11.002③

① Riviera—.9375
② Estate Wagon—1.000
③ Estate Wagon—12.002
— Not applicable

WHEEL ALIGNMENT SPECIFICATIONS

Year	Model	Caster Range (deg)	Caster Pref Setting (deg)	Camber Range (deg)	Camber Pref Setting (deg)	Toe-in (in.)	Steering Axis Inclin.	Wheel Pivot Ratio (deg) Inner Wheel	Wheel Pivot Ratio (deg) Outer Wheel
'69	All exc. Riviera	1/4P to 1 1/4P	3/4P	1/2N to 1/2P	0	3/16 to 5/16	10.75	20	19 1/2
	Riviera	1/2P to 1 1/2P	1P	1/4N to 3/4P	1/4P	5/32 to 9/32	10.75	20	16 3/4
'70	All exc. Riviera	1/4P to 1 1/4P	3/4P	1/2N to 1/2P	0	3/16 to 5/16	10.5	20	19 1/2
	Riviera	1/2P to 1 1/2P	1P	1/4N to 3/4P	1/4P	1/8 to 1/4	10.5	20	16 3/4
'71	All	1/2P to 1 1/2P	1P	1/4N to 3/4P	1/4P	1/8 to 1/4	10.5	20	18 1/2
'72	All	1/2P to 1 1/2P	1P	0 to 1P	1/2P	1/8 to 1/4	9.0	20	18 1/2
'73	All	1/2P to 1 1/2P	1P	1/4N to 3/4P	1/4P	1/8 to 1/4	9.6①	20	18 1/2
'74	All	1/2P to 1 1/2P	1P	1/2P to 1 1/2P LH 0 to 1P RH	1P LH 1/2P RH	0 to 1/8	9.6①	20	18 1/2
'75-'76	All	1P to 2P	1 1/2P	1/2P to 1 1/2P LH 0 to 1 1/2P RH	1P LH 1/2 RH	0 to 1/8	9.6①	20	18 1/2

① Estate Wagon 10.7
N Negative P Positive
LH Left-hand side
RH Right-hand side

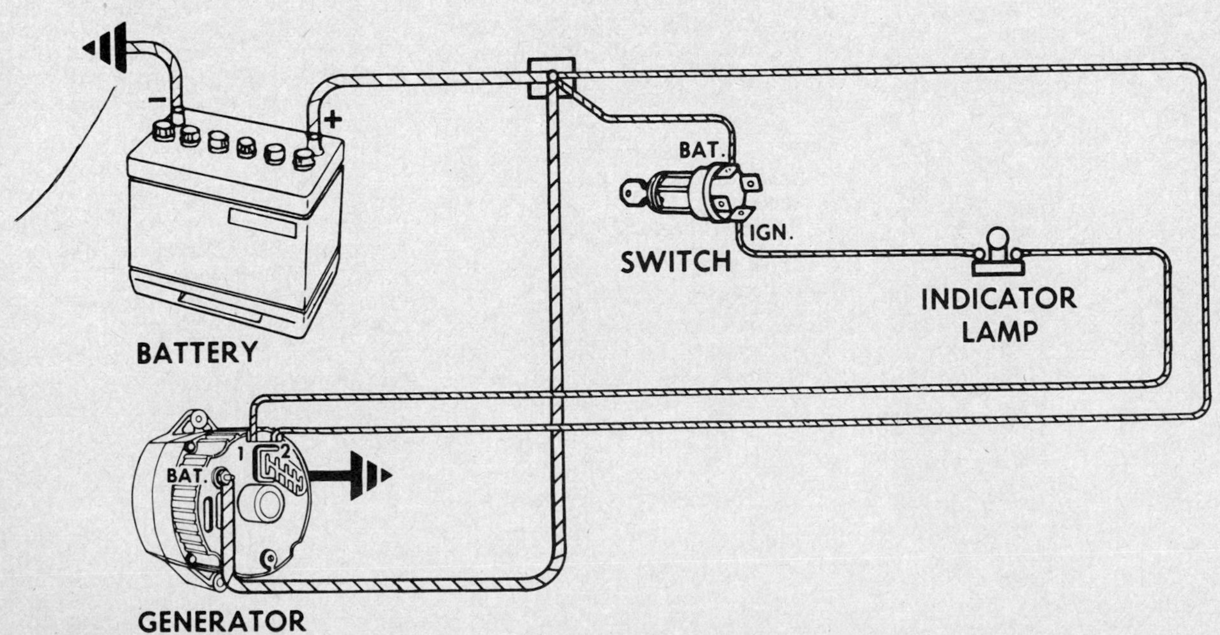

Charging system schematic
(© Buick Div., G.M. Corp.)

CHARGING SYSTEM

See the "Unit Repair Section" for rebuilding procedures and trouble-shooting.

Caution Since the Delcotron and regulator are designed for use on only one polarity system, the following precautions must be observed:

1. The polarity of the battery, generator and regulator must be matched and considered before making any electrical connections in the system.
2. When connecting a booster battery, be sure to connect the negative battery terminals together and the positive battery terminals together.
3. When connecting a charger to the battery, connect the charger positive lead to the battery positive terminal. Connect the charger negative lead to the battery negative terminal.
4. Never operate the Delcotron on open circuit. Be sure that all connections in the circuit are clean and tight.
5. Do not short across or ground any of the terminals on the Delcotron regulator.
6. Do not attempt to polarize the Delcotron.
7. Do not use test lamps of more than 12 volts for checking diode continuity.
8. Avoid long soldering times when replacing diodes or transistors. Prolonged heat is damaging to these units.
9. Disconnect the battery ground terminal when servicing any component of the charging system.

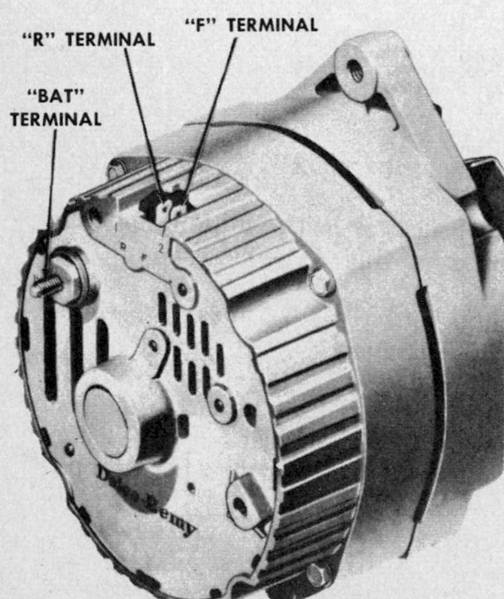

Delcotron wire connections
(© Buick Div., G.M. Corp)

Voltage Regulator R & R through 1970

1. Disconnect the battery cables.
2. Disconnect the wiring from the voltage regulator.
3. Remove the screws holding the regulator to the firewall or front bulkhead depending on the car.
4. Reverse the removal procedures to install.

Voltage Regulator R & R 1971 and later

The voltage regulator is inside the alternator. For R&R procedures see the Charging and Starting Systems Unit Repair Section.

Alternator R & R

Remove the bolt holding the tension bar to the alternator. On some models, it may be necessary to loosen and rotate the fan shroud to get at the pivot bolt. Push the alternator in toward the engine to release the drive belt. Remove the alternator mounting bolt to release the alternator from the engine.

When reinstalling, adjust the alternator drive belt to allow ½ in. play on the longest run between pulleys.

NOTE: on A/C models, remove the compressor brace.

STARTING SYSTEM

See the "Unit Repair Section" for rebuilding procedures and trouble-shooting.

Starter R & R

1. Disconnect battery.
2. Jack up car and remove the four flywheel inspection cover screws.
3. Disconnect wires from solenoid.
4. Remove the starter bolts.
5. Remove starter.

NOTE: On some models, it may be necessary to move exhaust pipe to gain clearance.

6. Reverse the above steps to install.

Starter Drive R & R

1. Remove the bolt which holds the field leads to the solenoid motor terminal and disconnect the leads. Remove the two solenoid attaching bolts, rotate and remove the solenoid.
2. Remove the two through bolts, end frame, and field frame assembly.
3. Pull both brush holder pivot pins and lift out each pair of brush holder assemblies. Disconnect the leads and brushes.
4. Remove the shift lever pivot bolt, plunger, shift lever, and armature from the drive housing.
5. Remove the drive assembly from the armature by first using a suitable tool (such as a ½ in. pipe coupling) to disengage the snap-ring retainer from the snap-ring. After removing the snap ring and retainer, slide the drive assembly off the armature shaft.
6. Inspect all parts for wear or damage and replace where necessary. When cleaning all parts, be sure not to use any degreasing or high temperature method on the armature, field coils, and drive assembly.

To assemble:

7. Lubricate the armature shaft and install the drive assembly with the pinion out.
8. Slide the snap-ring retainer onto the shaft with the recessed side out.
9. Use a block of wood and a hammer to get the new snap-ring started on the shaft. Install the snap-ring in the shaft groove.
10. Slide the thrust collar onto the shaft, move the snap-ring retainer up to the snap-ring, and squeeze the retainer and thrust collar together with two pairs of pliers. The retainer should be forced over the snap-ring.
11. Lubricate the drive frame bushing and shift lever linkage and install the shift lever in the drive end frame.
12. Install the armature and spacers into the drive end frame, making sure that the shift lever is in place.
13. Assemble the brushes and leads to the brush holders. Place the brush holders and springs in the field frame and install the pivot pins.
14. Install the field frame over the armature, spreading the brush holders to prevent damage.
15. Lubricate the commutator end frame bushing and install the frame.
16. Install the through-bolts.
17. Move the armature toward the commutator end frame. Measure the clearance between the snap-ring retainer and drive end housing with feeler gauges. It should be 0.005-0.050 in. Use spacers to adjust the clearance.

IGNITION SYSTEM

Distributor Removal

Disconnect the distributor primary wire from the coil and the hose from the vacuum unit. Remove distributor cap by inserting a screwdriver into upper slotted end of cap latches, pressing down and turning 90° counter-clockwise.

Make a mark on the distributor body in line with the rotor. Matchmark position of vacuum unit to the engine.

Remove clamp to release distributor and remove from crankcase.

NOTE: 1970-73 distributors have a radio interference shield over the contact points. Only snap-lock point sets can be used because screw-type connectors will hit this shield and short ignition. The shield isn't necessary if a unitized point and condenser set is installed. The unitized set is standard equipment beginning 1974.

Distributor Installation

If engine was inadvertently turned over while distributor was out, proceed as follows:

Remove right rocker arm cover. Using a wrench on the crankshaft pulley bolt, turn the engine over until both valves for No. 1 cylinder are closed. The timing mark on the harmonic balancer behind the crankshaft pulley should be aligned with the zero degree mark. No. 1 cylinder is now at firing point.

Install distributor in engine with rotor in position to fire No. 1 cylinder. The vacuum unit should align with the match-mark made when distributor was removed. Press down lightly on distributor if it does not seat correctly. Use starter to turn engine until the tang on the distributor shaft slips into the slot in the oil pump shaft. This will not disturb the relationship between the distributor and the camshaft because the drive gear engages before the tang. However, it will be necessary to return the engine to the No. 1 firing point and check that rotor is also at No. 1 firing point. Reconnect vacuum tube and primary wire. Rotate the distributor body slightly until contacts just start to open. Install and tighten distributor clamp. Install distributor cap. Start engine and adjust point dwell.

If the engine has not been disturbed since the distributor was removed proceed as follows:

Insert distributor into the block so that the rotor is pointing to the mark made on distributor housing and the vacuum advance unit is aligned with the match-mark made on the engine. Connect the vacuum tube, primary wire, and install the distributor cap. Install distributor clamp. Check that spark plug wires are correctly routed. Start engine and adjust point dwell and then adjust ignition timing. Rotate distributor body counterclockwise to advance the timing.

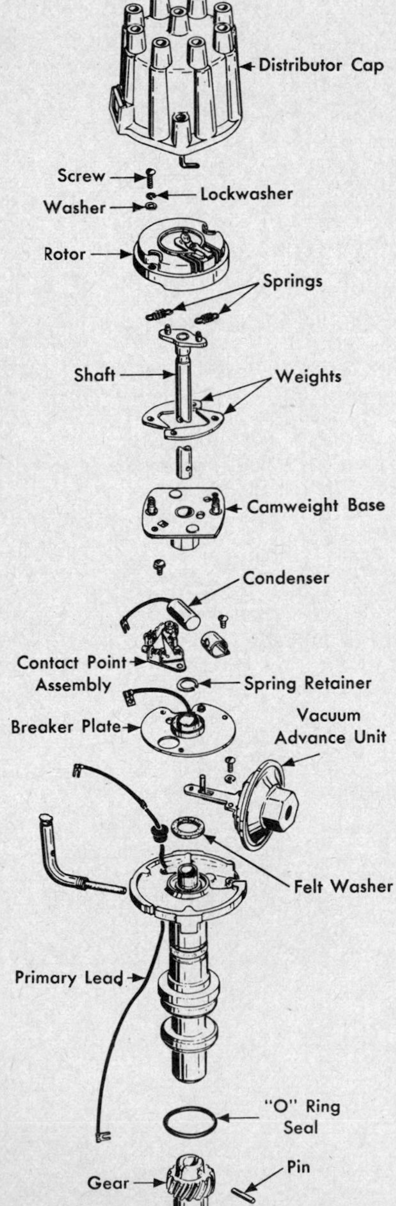

Distributor—exploded view
(© Buick Div., G.M. Corp)

Contact Point Replacement and Adjustment

NOTE: the condenser should be replaced when the points are replaced.

1. Remove the distributor cap and rotor. If equipped with an interference shield, remove the shield.
2. Loosen the two screws holding the contact point set in place and remove the point set.
3. Disconnect the condenser and primary leads from their terminals on the points.

Installing RFI shield 1970-73
(© Buick Div., G.M. Corp)

4. Connect the wires to a new set of points and install them into the distributor.
5. Put a small amount of grease on the breaker cam or turn the lubricator.
6. Reinstall the shield, rotor, and cap. Install the shield half that covers the points first.
7. Adjust the dwell to specification.
8. Check the timing.

Ignition Timing

Timing marks are located on the front engine cover and on the harmonic balancer.

1. Disconnect the distributor vacuum advance hose from the distributor and plug the hose.
2. Make sure the dwell is correct.

NOTE: it may be necessary to put a small amount of white paint or chalk on the timing marks to make them more visible.

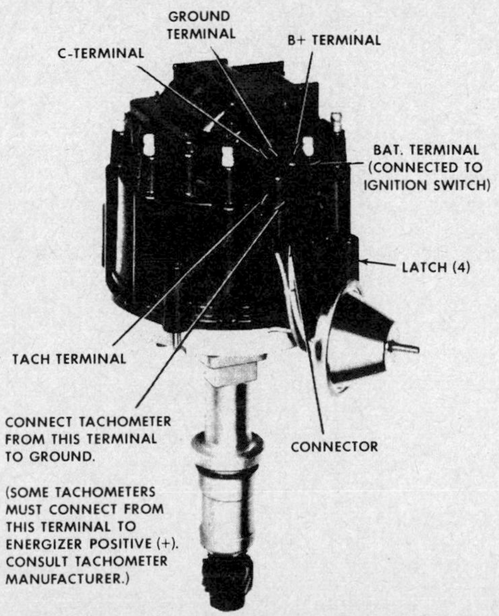

Tachometer connection for the HEI system (© Buick Div., G.M. Corp)

3. Connect a timing light to No. 1 cylinder.
4. Loosen the distributor clamp.
5. Start the engine and rotate the distributor until the correct marks line up. Tighten the distributor clamp and recheck the timing.
6. Reconnect the vacuum hose.

Solid State Ignition

Beginning 1974, a solid state, high energy ignition (HEI) system is offered as an option on all Buick engines. Beginning 1975, the HEI system is standard equipment on all models. There are no points or condenser to replace, nor any cam or rubbing block to wear out. Precision timing and proper tuning are maintained over a greater interval than conventional point - and - condenser systems, and the high energy coil delivers 50 to 75% more voltage than a conventional electronic system. In addition, the high energy system is completely unitized.

There is a convenient tachometer terminal at the top of the distributor cap on HEI systems. The terminal is marked "TACH". Connect the positive tachometer lead to the distributor terminal and the negative tachometer lead to a ground. Some tachometers must connect from the distributor terminal to the positive terminal of the battery. Follow the tachometer manufacturer's instructions.

Note: Never ground the HEI tachometer terminal.

The procedure for checking the timing on this system is the same as for conventional ignition systems.

FUEL SYSTEM

Fuel Pump

These models use a single action fuel pump mounted on the lower side of the engine front cover. Flexible gas lines are used.

The fuel pump is not rebuildable.

1969-70 Riviera Only

These models have a turbine type electric fuel pump mounted at the bottom of the fuel tank. This pump maintains a steady pressure whenever the engine is running. The electrical circuit to the pump is completed by an oil pressure switch which is bypassed for starting. If oil pressure fails, the fuel pump will not operate.

All Engines with Air Conditioners, All 430, 455 Cu. In.

All air-conditioner equipped cars have a special fuel pump with a metering outlet for a vapor return system. Hot fuel and fuel vapor is returned to the fuel tank. The fuel pump is continuously cooled by circulating fuel from the tank, thus greatly reducing the possibility of vapor lock.

Fuel Pump R & R

1. Disconnect the fuel inlet, outlet, and vapor return hoses.
2. Remove the two bolts holding the pump to the engine.
3. Remove the old fuel pump.

To install:

1. Install a new pump and gasket.
2. Install the two bolts.
3. Reconnect the hoses to the pump. Do not force the threaded fittings, use very light pressure until it is obvious that the threads are started properly.
4. Start the engine and check for leaks.

Fuel Filter Replacement

The filter is located in the carburetor inlet behind the large hex nut. This is a small pleated paper or sintered bronze filter.

1. Remove the fuel inlet line from the carburetor.
2. Remove the large nut from the carburetor body.
3. Remove the old filter.
4. Install a new filter with the spring inserted before the filter.
5. Install the large hex nut and fuel line.
6. Start the engine and check for leaks.

Idle Speed and Mixture Adjustments

Through 1970

NOTE: The air cleaner must be in place for idle mixture adjustment.

1. Check PCV system for proper operation.
2. Connect tachometer; warm engine to normal operating temperature.
3. Place manual transmission in N, automatic in D (wheels blocked).
4. To make sure the Thermo Vacuum switch does not switch distributor vacuum over to full manifold vacuum due to overheated coolant, remove the hose from the distributor and plug.

NOTE: check that the compressor for the Automatic Level Control. if so equipped, is not running. The compressor now has a regulating valve to shut off vacuum at idle speed. If the compressor is running, this valve is faulty and must be replaced before a good idle can be obtained.

5. Adjust throttle stop screw to obtain an idle speed 20 rpm faster than specified.
6. Turn in each mixture needle, alternately, to obtain an idle speed 10 rpm less *per needle* than the basic idle setting of Step 5 (for a total of 20 rpm less).
7. Press down on the hot idle compensator, if so equipped. If idle

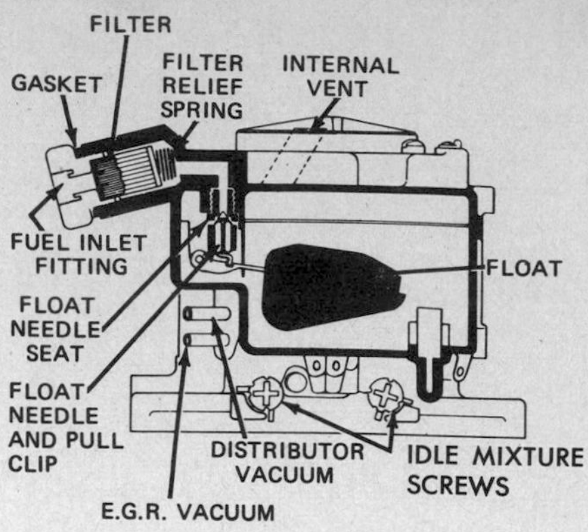

2 bbl carburetor
(© Buick Div., G.M. Corp)

drops, valve is open and should be unstuck and idle reset.

1971

NOTE: The air cleaner must be in place to get the proper idle mixture.

1. Check PCV system for proper operation.
2. Connect tachometer; warm engine to normal operating temperature.
3. Place manual transmission in N, automatic in D (wheels blocked).
4. Remove distributor hose and plug.

NOTE: check that the compressor for the Automatic Level Control, if so equipped, is not running. The compressor has a regulating valve to shut off vacuum at idle speed. If the compressor is running, this valve is faulty and must be replaced before a good idle can be obtained.

5. Adjust throttle stop screw to obtain specified idle speed.
6. Adjust idle mixture needles, alternately, to obtain highest tachometer reading.
7. Readjust throttle stop and mixture screws as required to obtain an idle speed 50 rpm faster than specified, then turn in each screw (leaner) to reduce idle speed 25 rpm *per needle* (for a total reduction of 50 rpm).
8. Adjust fast idle speed.

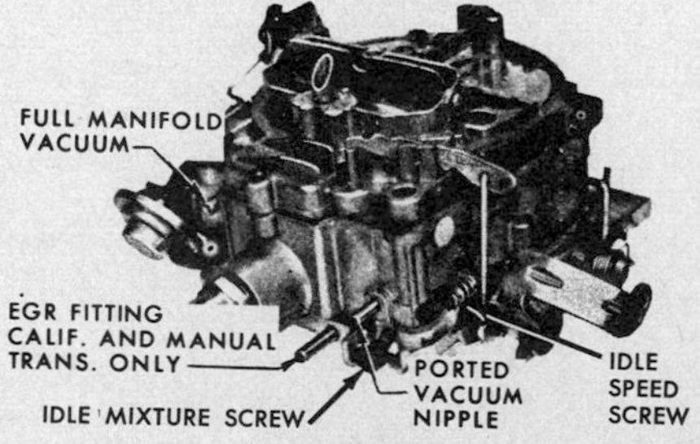

4 bbl carburetor
(© Buick Div., G.M. Corp)

1972-73

1. Connect a tachometer to the engine.
2. Start the engine and run it until it is warmed up.
3. Remove and plug the vacuum hose to the distributor.

4. Place manual transmissions in neutral and automatic transmissions in D.
5. Open the throttle sufficiently to allow the solenoid to extend and contact the throttle lever pad in the idle position.
6. Adjust the solenoid set screw to obtain the specified rpm. This is the higher figure in the specification chart.
7. Disconnect the solenoid wire to disengage solenoid.
8. Adjust the carburetor idle screw to obtain specified idle speed, which is the lower figure in the specification chart.
9. Reconnect the solenoid wire.
10. Adjust the idle mixture needles, one at a time, to obtain the highest tachometer reading. After the highest reading is reached, readjust the solenoid plunger to obtain 50 rpm over the specified idle speed. Turn each mixture needle in to reduce the idle speed 25 rpm for each needle. This reduces the idle speed to the recommended rpm.
11. Adjust the fast idle speed on all four-barrel carburetors. Fast idle must be adjusted after slow idle speed and mixture have been adjusted. Automatic transmission cars are adjusted on the low step of the fast idle cam in Drive to 700 RPM. Manual transmission cars are adjusted on the low cam step to 820 RPM for 350 engines, and 920 RPM for 455 engines.
12. Connect the distributor vacuum hose.
13. Install the "red" service idle needle limiter caps on the mixture screws.

1974-75

NOTE: Idle speed and mixture must be set with the engine at normal operating temperature, the air conditioner off, the air cleaner on, and the transmission in drive. If a CO meter is available, set the idle mixture to that specified on the underhood specifications sticker.

1. Set the parking brake and block the wheels.
2. Disconnect the evaporative emission hose at the air cleaner. Disconnect and plug the distributor vacuum line at the distributor. Disconnect and plug the EGR vacuum line at the EGR valve.
3. Adjust the idle speed to that specified in the "Tune-Up Specifications" chart. First adjust the idle speed screw with the solenoid disconnected to get the lower speed, then adjust the solenoid screw with the solenoid connected to get the higher speed.
4. Cut the tabs off the mixture screw caps, then equally richen (turn out) the mixture screws until the maximum idle speed is achieved.
5. Using the solenoid screw, adjust, if necessary, the idle speed to 70 rpm above the specified speed for 455 engines, and 60 rpm above for the 350 (1974). On 1975 vehicles, adjust the idle speed to 80 rpm above specification.
6. Turn in (lean) the mixture screws equally until the engine returns to the specified idle speed.
7. Reconnect all the hoses removed in Step 2.

COOLING SYSTEM

Radiator Core R & R

On models equipped with a fan shroud, remove the shroud from the radiator and position it rearward over the fan.

Remove the capscrews that hold the fan blades to the fan hub and take off the blades, spacer and pump pulley. Drain the cooling system and remove the top and bottom radiator hoses and the two automatic transmission oil coder lines from the radiator. Remove the bolts that hold the radiator core to the cradle and lift the core straight up. Reverse the above steps to install.

Water Pump R & R

It is possible to remove and replace the water pump on all Buicks without disturbing the radiator core. This is accomplished by removing the fan belt, fan blades, and pulley, disconnecting the hoses and removing the water pump attaching bolts. Reverse the removal procedure to install. Use a new gasket and make sure all gasket surfaces are clean.

Thermostat R & R

The thermostat is contained in the water outlet elbow mounted on the front of the intake manifold.

To replace the thermostat, disconnect the upper radiator hose, remove the water outlet attaching bolts, lift off the outlet and take out the thermostat.

Caution When installing a thermostat always place the end of the thermostat with the spring inside the engine.

EMISSION CONTROLS

There are three types of emissions to be controlled: crankcase emissions, carburetor and gas tank fuel vapor emissions, and exhaust emissions. See the "Unit Repair Section" for troubleshooting and repair information.

1969

A new concept, Combustion Control System, (CCS), uses engine modifications. Essentially, the CCS increases combustion efficiency through carburetor and distributor calibrations and by increasing engine operating temperature.

Carburetors are calibrated leaner and initial ignition timing is retarded. Another carburetor feature is the idle fuel mixture limiting orifice. It is located at the base of the idle mixture screw and makes sure that even if the idle mixture screw is turned out too far, the fuel enrichment will not greatly affect exhaust emissions.

The CCS incorporates a higher engine operation temperature with a 195°F thermostat. Engines that run hotter provide more complete vaporazation of the fuel and reduce quench area in the combustion chamber. Quench area is the relatively cool area near the cylinder wall and combustion chamber surfaces. Fuel in these areas does not burn properly because of the lower temperatures. This incomplete burning increases emissions.

The CCS uses a thermostatically controlled air cleaner called the Auto-Therm air cleaner. It is designed to keep the temperature of the air entering the carburetor at approximately 100°F. This allows the lean carburetor to work properly, minimizes carburetor icing, and improves engine warm-up characteristics. A sensor unit, located on the clean air side of the air filter, senses the temperature of the air passing over it and regulates the vacuum supplied to a vacuum diaphragm in the inlet tube of the air cleaner. The colder the air, the greater the amount of vacuum supplied to the vacuum diaphragm. The vacuum diaphragm, depending on the vacuum supplied to it, opens or closes a damper door in the inlet tube of the air cleaner. If the door is open, it allows air from the engine compartment to go to the carburetor. If the door is closed, air flows from the heat stove that is located on the exhaust manifold into the carburetor. It is in this way that heated air is supplied to the carburetor during cold days and when first starting the engine and warming it up.

1970-71

The more stringent 1970 laws require tighter control of emissions. Crankcase emissions are controlled by the Closed Positive Crankcase Ventilation System, and exhaust emissions by the engine Controlled Combustion System (CCS), in conjunction with the new Transmission Controlled Spark System (TCS).

In addition, cars sold in California are equipped with an Evaporation Control System that limits the amount of gasoline vapor discharged into the atmosphere (usually from the carburetor and fuel tank).

The TCS system consists of a transmission switch, a solenoid valve, and a temperature switch. Under normal conditions, the system permits the vacuum distributor (spark) advance to operate only in high gear (both manual and automatic transmissions) and reverse.

The transmission switch is located on the transmission and senses when the transmission is in one of the lower gears. When in a lower gear, the switch activates the vacuum solenoid valve. This valve is located in the vacuum line that runs from the carburetor to the distributor and shuts off vacuum to the distributor advance when it is activated. There is also an engine-temperature sensing switch which overrides the transmission switch. It will allow vacuum advance in the lower gears when engine temperature is below 85°F or above 220°F. There is always vacuum advance in high gear and reverse.

The Evaporative Emission Control System was introduced in 1970. Vapors generated in the gas tank while the car is at rest are transferred to an activated charcoal canister located in the engine compartment. When the car is running the vapors are removed from the canister and burned by the engine.

1972

In 1972, all engines are equipped with positive crankcase ventilation, transmission controlled vacuum spark advance (TCS) and the controlled combustion system (CCS). The air injection reactor system is standard on all engines except the non-California 350 cu in. with automatic transmissions. All California cars and all cars with manual transmissions have Exhaust Gas Recirculation (EGR).

CCS is explained in the 1969 section, and TCS in the 1970-71 section.

The EGR system is used to reduce oxides of nitrogen emissions. To lower the formation of nitrogen oxides, it is necessary to reduce combustion temperatures. This is done by introducing exhaust gases into the intake manifold to be burned.

An EGR valve is mounted on the right rear of the intake manifold and is used to regulate the amount of exhaust gases and the time the exhaust gases enter the intake manifold. As the engine speeds up, carburetor vacuum is applied to the valve which opens a port connecting the intake manifold to the exhaust gas passage that is cast in the intake manifold. This allows exhaust gases to pass into the intake manifold. The EGR system is not in operation during engine idle.

1973

All engines are equipped with Positive Crankcase Ventilation, Controlled Combustion, Air Injection Reactor System, Exhaust Gas Recirculation, Transmission Controlled Vacuum Spark Advance System and Evaporative Emission Control. With the exception of a low temperature cut-out valve that was added to the EGR system, the emission control systems remain unchanged from previous years.

The EGR system is the same one that was used on 1972 California cars with a new temperature valve. This black and white plastic valve is located in the vacuum line to the EGR valve and it senses ambient temperature above the engine intake manifold. At temperatures below 55°F, the temperature valve closes to prevent carburetor vacuum from opening the EGR valve. When the temperature above the manifold rises above 60°F, the valve opens and allows carburetor vacuum to control the operation of the EGR valve. Whenever installing a new valve, always make sure the side of the valve marked EGR faces toward the EGR valve.

1974

The 1974 Buick emission control system is unchanged from 1973, except for a required change in the EGR temperature sensor. An Environmental Protection Agency order necessitated that the EGR ambient temperature sensor either be removed or changed to record coolant temperature on engines produced after March 15, 1973. Although the system design remains unchanged, there has been an extensive refinement and recalibration of components to insure greater efficiency.

1975

All 1975 models have a catalytic converter which helps control emissions by burning them away. Details on this system can be found in the "Emission Control" Unit Repair Section. A new fast engine warm-up system routes exhaust gases through the intake manifold for a faster warm-up. Exhaust gases also operate the fast acting choke, so that lean mixtures can be used as soon as possible. High Energy Ignition is standard on all models to prevent catalyst damage caused by engine missing.

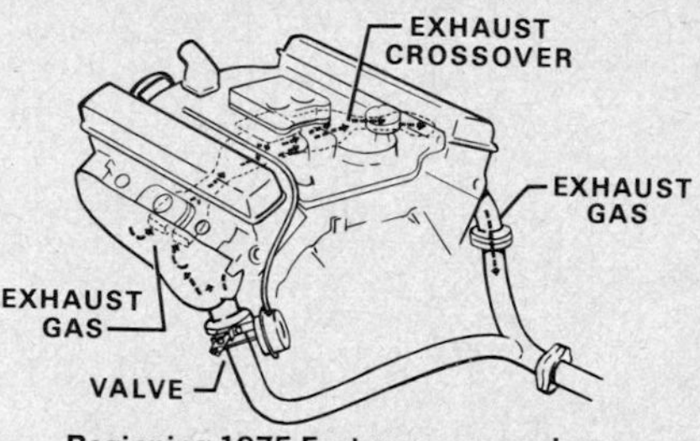

Beginning 1975 Fast warm-up system
(© Buick Div., G.M. Corp)

ENGINE

Engine R & R

1. Drain cooling system.
2. Scribe hinge outline on underside of hood. Remove hood attaching bolts and remove hood.

VACUUM TO BE CONNECTED TO TIMED PORT IN CARBURETOR
DIAPHRAGM COVER
SPRING
VALVE SHAFT
SEAL
ACTUATING DIAPHRAGM
VALVE CHAMBER
VALVE OPEN
VALVE CLOSED
VALVE SEAT
TO INTAKE MANIFOLD
EXHAUST GAS PORT INLET

EGR valve
(© Buick Div., G.M. Corp)

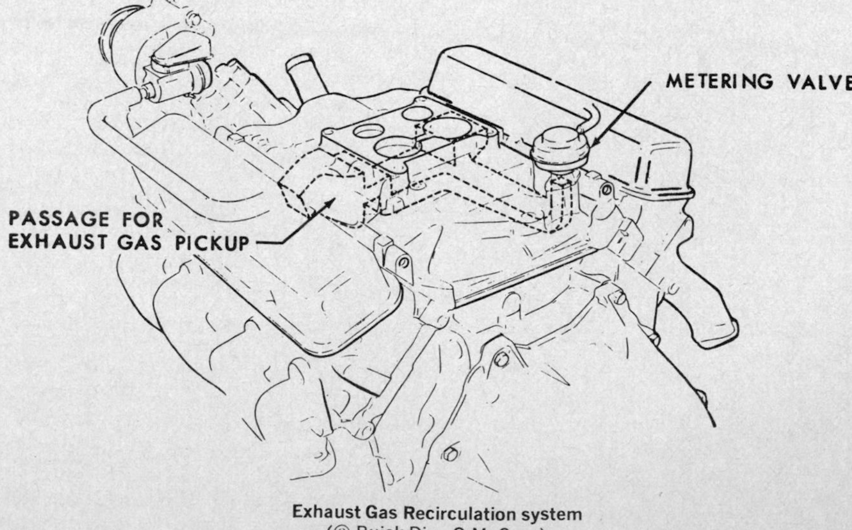

Exhaust Gas Recirculation system
(© Buick Div., G.M. Corp)

3. Disconnect battery cables.
4. Remove radiator and heater hoses and remove the air cleaner.
5. Disconnect transmission oil cooler lines. Remove fan shroud, fan belts, and pulleys.
6. Remove attaching bolts and lift out radiator.
7. Disconnect exhaust pipe or pipes at the exhaust manifold/s.
8. Disconnect vacuum line to power brake unit.
9. Disconnect accelerator to carburetor linkage.
10. Disconnect all engine component wiring that would interfere with engine removal, such as generator wires, gauge sending unit wires, primary ignition wires, engine-to-body ground strap, etc.
11. Disconnect gas line at fuel pump.
12. Detach power steering pump and position to the left. Do not disconnect the hoses.
13. Detach air conditioner compressor at bracket and position to the right. Do not disconnect hoses.

Caution If the compressor refrigerant lines do not have enough slack to position the compressor out of the way without disconnecting the refrigerant lines, the air conditioning system will have to be removed by a trained air conditioning specialist. Under no conditions should an untrained person attempt to disconnect the air conditioning refrigerant lines. These lines contain pressurized freon which can be extremely dangerous to the untrained.

14. Disconnect transmission control linkage.
15. Disconnect vapor emission lines on 1970 and later models.
16. Attach lifting device to the engine and raise enough to support the engine weight.
17. Remove flywheel cover pan. On cars equipped with an automatic transmission, remove the flywheel to-torque converter bolts. Match-mark the flywheel and torque converter for reassembly.
18. Separate engine from transmission at bell housing on cars equipped with automatic transmission. On cars equipped with a manual transmission, separate the transmission from the bellhousing.
19. Remove engine attachment thru-bolts at the engine mounts.
20. Lift engine forward and upward to clear engine compartment.
21. Install by reversing above procedure. When installing an engine, the front mounting pad to frame bolts should be the last mounting bolts to be tightened. Note that there are dowel pins in the block that have matching holes in the bellhousing. These pins must be in almost perfect alignment before the engine will go together with the transmission.

Manifolds

Intake Manifold R & R

1. Drain the cooling system and disconnect the battery.
2. Remove carburetor air cleaner. Disconnect all tubes and hoses from the carburetor. Disconnect and remove the coil.
3. Disconnect temperature indicator wire from sending unit.
4. Disconnect accelerator and transmission linkage at carburetor. Disconnect throttle return spring.
5. Slide front thermostat by-pass hose clamp back on the hose. Disconnect upper radiator hose at outlet.
6. Disconnect heater hose at the temperature control valve inlet.

Intake manifold tightening sequence—350 and 455 V8 beginning 1971 (© Buick Div., G.M. Corp)

Force the end of the hose down to permit coolant to drain from intake manifold.

7. Loosen the air conditioning compressor bracket bolt and swing the bracket out of the way.
8. Remove manifold attaching bolts.
9. Remove intake manifold and carburetor as an assembly by sliding rearward to disengage the thermostat by-pass hose from the water pump. Remove intake manifold gasket.
10. Reverse the above steps to install. Torque the bolts in the sequence shown.

NOTE: New intake manifold gasket and seals must be used whenever a manifold is removed.

Exhaust Manifolds R & R

1. Jack up car and support on jack stands.
2. Disconnect exhaust pipe from manifolds on both sides of engine and lower. If equipped with dual exhaust, disconnect and lower only on the side being worked on.
3. If equipped with manual transmission, remove equalizer shaft.

Note: On right side, it may be necessary to remove A/C, power steering, or alternator. On 1971-1972 left-side exhaust manifolds on models other than LeSabre, the pitman arm must be removed and the steering linkage pushed out of the way.

4. Remove exhaust manifold-to-cylinder head bolts.
5. Remove manifold from beneath car.
6. Reverse the above steps to install.

Valve System

Rocker Arm R & R

1969 V8

Removal

1. Remove the rocker arm cover and four rocker arm and shaft assembly bolts. Remove the assembly.
2. Remove the shaft end-cap by splitting the side of the cap with a chisel.
3. Remove the rocker arms and springs. Keep the parts in order.

Installation

1. Install the rocker arms and springs on the shaft and lubricate the shaft with oil as the rocker arms are installed.
2. Install a new end-cap on the rocker arm shaft.

NOTE: when installing the rocker arm shaft assembly, be sure that the drill mark is facing up and toward the rear on the left cylinder head and toward the front of the right cylinder head.

3. After locating the top of each push rod in its rocker arm seat, draw the rocker arm and shaft assembly down by tightening the bracket bolts a little at a time until they are tight.
4. Install the rocker arm cover with a new gasket.

1970 and later V8

Removal

1. Remove the rocker arm cover.
2. Remove the rocker arm shaft assembly bolts and then the assembly.
3. Remove the nylon arm retainers by prying them out with pliers or breaking them with a chisel.
4. Remove the rocker arms. Remove any retainer pieces from the inside of the shaft.

Installation

1. Install the rocker arms on the shaft and lubricate them with oil.
2. Center each arm on the 1/4 in. hole in the shaft. Install new nylon rocker arm retainers in the holes using a drift 1/2 in. in diameter.

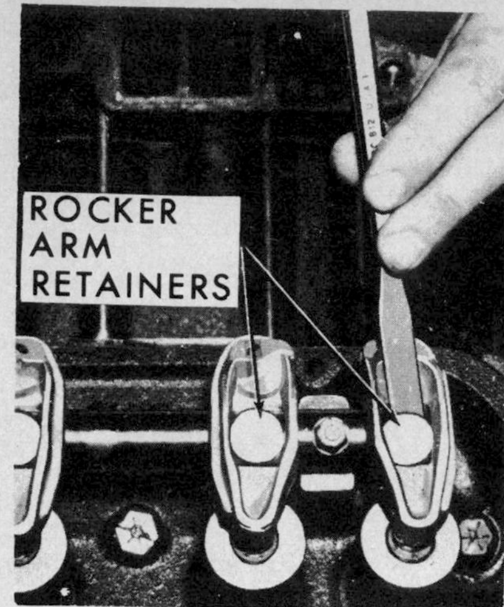

Removing nylon rocker arm retainers —350 and 455 beginning 1971 (© Buick Div., G.M. Corp)

NOTE: On engines through 1972, each pair of rocker arms must be installed so that the external rib on each arm points away from the rocker arm shaft bolt that is located between each pair of rocker arms. On 1973 and later engines, replacement rocker arms are marked R and L. From the front of the engine on the left bank, the sequence should be L-R, L-R, L-R, L-R. On the right bank, it should be R-L, R-L, R-L, R-L.

3. Locate the push rods in the rocker arms and insert the shaft-to-cylinder head bolts. Tighten the bolts a little at a time to 25-30 ft lbs.
4. Install the rocker cover and use a new gasket.

Valve Adjustment

After the shaft assembly-to-cylinder head bolts are torqued to specification, the valves are automatically-properly adjusted.

Valve Guide Replacement

Valve guides are cast into the cylinder heads of all engines. The valve guides must be reamed and fitted with valves with oversize stems to be repaired.

Valve Springs

To check the condition of the valve springs, line up the intake valve springs on a flat surface and, using a straightedge, compare the height of the springs. If all of the springs are the same height, as determined by the straightedge, it may be assumed that the springs are in good condition, since it is very unlikely that all of the springs would collapse the same amount.

If one or more of the springs are lower than the rest it is advisable to procure at least one new spring and then compare the other springs with the new one for free length.

Chilton's TIME SAVER

The following is a method for replacing valve springs, oil seals or spring retainers without removing the cylinder head.

1. **Obtain a spark plug hole air chuck adaptor from an auto parts store.**
2. **Add an air chuck to this adaptor so the hose from an air compressor can be attached. This assembly will be used later to pressurize the cylinder.**
3. **Remove the valve rocker cover. Remove the rocker arm from the valve to be worked on.**
4. **Remove the spark plug from the cylinder to be worked on.**
5. **Turn the crankshaft to bring the piston of this cylinder down, away from possible contact with the valve head. Sharply tap the valve retainer to loosen the valve lock.**
6. **Then turn the crankshaft to bring the piston in this cylinder to the Exact Top of its Compression Stroke.**
7. **Screw in the chuck-equipped tool.**
8. **Hook up an air hose to the chuck and turn on the pressure (about 200 lbs.).**
9. **With a strong and constant supply of air holding the valve closed, compress the valve spring and remove the lock and retainer.**
10. **Make the necessary replacements and reassemble.**

NOTE: it is important that the operation be performed exactly as stated, in this order. The piston in the cylinder must be on exact top-center to prevent air pressure from turning the crankshaft.

Replace all springs that do not come up to the standard established by the new one.

Repeat the operation on the exhaust valve springs.

Valve Removal

Unbolt and remove the cylinder heads. Take the heads to a bench and, using a C-type or lever type valve spring compressor, compress the valve springs, remove the keepers, release the valve springs, and push the valves to the combustion chamber side of the head.

NOTE: All 350 and some 455 engines use progressively wound valve springs. The coils are closer together at one end than at the other. The close wound end must go against the cylinder head.

Hydraulic Lifters, Removal

To remove the lifters, remove the rocker cover and take off the rocker shaft assemblies and lift out the pushrods. Then remove the intake manifold.

The lifters are barrel type which come right up out of their bores requiring no other tools than the fingers. Store the lifters in such a way that they can be reinstalled in their original positions.

If more effort is required than can be given by the fingers, it indicates gum or sticky substances present in the oil which probably caused the failure.

NOTE: 0.010 in. oversize lifters are sometimes installed at the factory. These are identified by an O on the lifter bore and two grooves on the lifter body.

Cylinder Head

Cylinder Head R & R

1. Disconnect the battery.
2. Drain the coolant.
3. Remove the air cleaner.
4. Remove the air conditioning from the engine, but do not disconnect any lines.
5. Remove the intake manifold.
6. When removing the right cylinder head, loosen the alternator belt and remove the alternator; if equipped with an air conditioning compressor, remove the compressor from the mounting bracket and position it out of the way WITH THE HOSES CONNECTED, then remove the alternator with the mounting bracket; finally, disconnect the metal temperature indicator wire (1973 and later models only).
7. When removing the left cylinder head, remove the dipstick and the power steering pump without disconnecting any hoses.

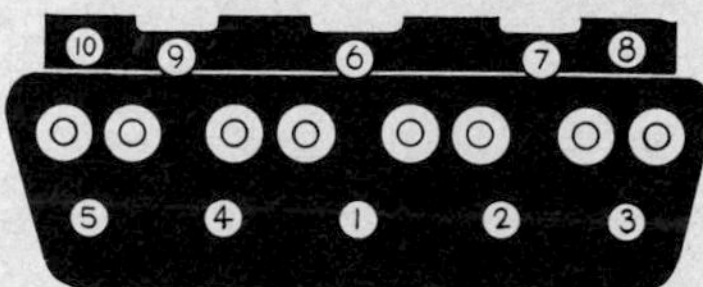

1969 350, 430 cu in. cylinder head torque sequence

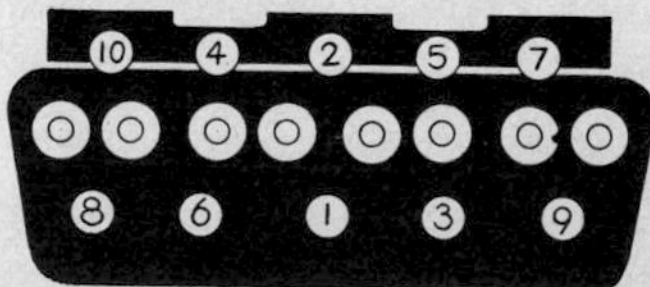

Cylinder head torque sequence for 350, 455 cu in. beginning 1970

8. Disconnect the plug wires.
9. Disconnect the exhaust manifold from the head being removed.
10. Remove the rocker arm cover and rocker shaft assembly. Lift out the push rods. Disconnect the AIR hoses from the cylinder head.
11. Remove the cylinder head bolts.
12. Remove the cylinder head and gasket.
13. Reverse the above steps to install. Torque the head bolts to specifications in three steps.

Timing Case Cover, Timing Chain and Camshaft

Vibration Damper Removal

Remove the radiator core and take out the cap screws that hold the fan pulley to the vibration damper. Remove the large bolt from the center of the crankshaft and insert a bolt type puller into the holes which held the fan pulley. Pull off the vibration damper.

Timing Chain and Front Oil Seal Replacement

350 Cu. In.

1. Drain cooling system and remove radiator, shroud, fan, pulleys, and belts.
2. Remove crankshaft pulley, fuel pump and distributor.
3. Remove Delcotron and power steering pump, if necessary.
4. Loosen and slide rearward front clamp on thermostat by-pass hose. Remove harmonic balancer.
5. Remove bolts attaching timing chain cover to cylinder block and oil pan to timing chain cover bolts. Remove timing chain cover assembly and gasket. Clean cover thoroughly, being careful not to damage the gasket surface.
6. Turn the crankshaft so that the timing marks on the sprockets are adjacent to each other on a line with the shaft centers.
7. Remove crankshaft oil slinger.
8. Remove bolt, special washer, distributor drive gear, and fuel pump eccentric from camshaft.
9. Alternately pry camshaft and crankshaft sprockets forward until camshaft sprocket and chain are free. Then remove the crankshaft sprocket.
   If oil seal appears worn or has been leaking, replace as follows:
10. Use a punch to drive out the old seal and retainer. Drive from front to rear of the timing chain cover.
11. Coil new packing around opening so that ends are at top. Drive in retainer. Stake the retainer in at least three places. Size the packing by rotating a hammer handle, etc. around the packing until the balancer hub fits through the packing.
    If engine has been disturbed since chain and sprockets were removed:
12. Turn crankshaft until No. 1 piston is at top dead center of the compression stroke.
13. Mount sprocket temporarily and turn camshaft so that timing mark is straight down.
14. Assemble chain and sprockets and mount on shafts with their timing marks closest to each other and aligned vertically.
15. Mount slinger on sprocket with the concave side to the front.
16. Reinstall fuel pump eccentric, distributor drive gear, special washer, and bolt on camshaft. Reinstall Woodruff key with oil groove forward.
17. Remove oil pump cover and pack the space around the oil pump gears full of petroleum jelly, leaving no air spaces. Reinstall oil pump cover with new gasket. This step is very important. If it is not done the oil pump will not begin to pump oil as soon as the engine is started.
18. Reinstall timing chain cover with new gasket.

Keep engine speed low for a short time after installation of a new oil seal.

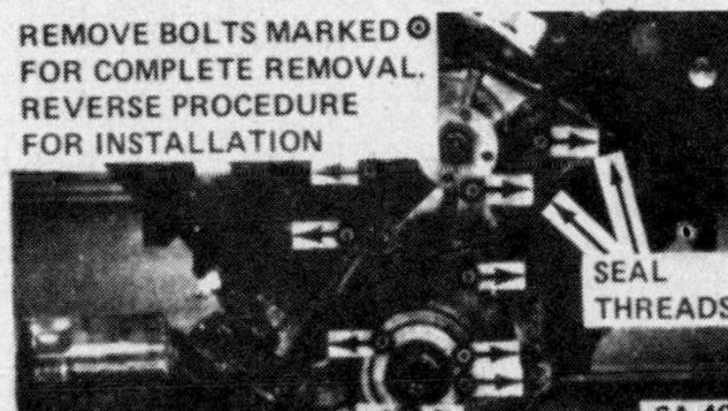

350 timing cover bolts (© Buick Div., G.M. Corp)

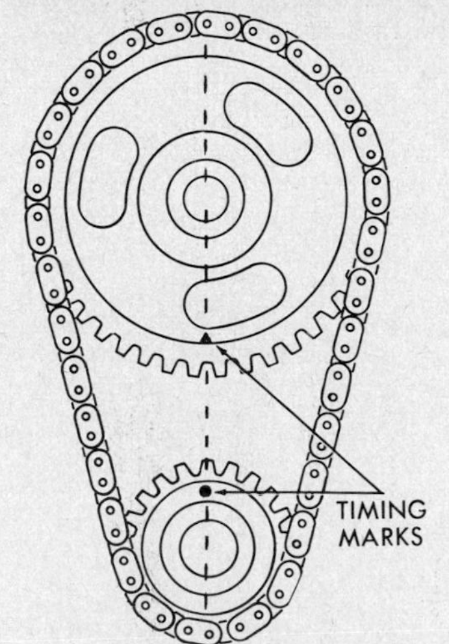

Timing chain and sprocket marks

430, 455 Cu. In.

This procedure is identical to that outlined for 350 cu. in. engines with

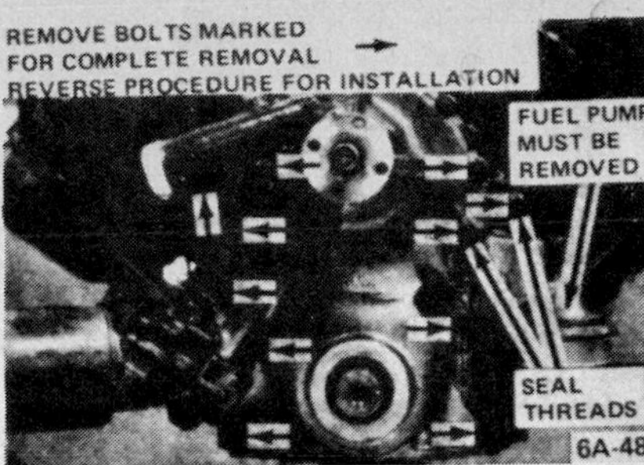

455 timing cover bolts (© Buick Div., G.M. Corp)

the substitution of the following steps:

8. Remove oil pan. Remove camshaft sprocket bolts.
16. Reinstall oil pan. Reinstall camshaft sprocket bolts.

Camshaft R & R

1. Remove the intake manifold, distributor, radiator, air conditioning condenser and grille.
2. Remove the rocker arm covers.
3. Remove the rocker arm and shaft assemblies, push rods, and valve lifters.
4. Remove the timing chain cover, timing chain, and camshaft sprocket.
5. Slide the camshaft forward, through the grille opening, and out from the bearing bores. Carefully avoid marring the bearing surfaces.
6. Reverse the above steps to install.

Connecting Rods, Rings And Pistons

When new rings are installed without reboring the cylinders, cylinder wall glaze should be broken. This can be done by using the finest grade stones in a cylinder hone. Check the piston - to - cylinder wall clearance after honing.

New piston rings must be checked for clearance and gap in the cylinder bores and for side-clearance while installed on the piston.

If piston pin bosses are worn out of round or oversize, the piston and pin should be replaced. Oversize pins are not practical because the pin is

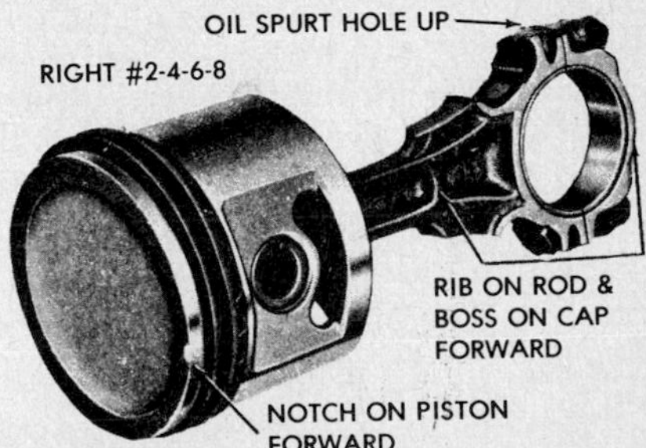

350 piston and connecting rod assembly —right bank
(© Buick Div., G.M. Corp)

a press fit in the connecting rod. Piston pins must fit the piston with an easy finger push at 70°F.

When the rod assemblies are replaced in the engine, the connecting rod bearing oil spurt hole must point up toward the camshaft.

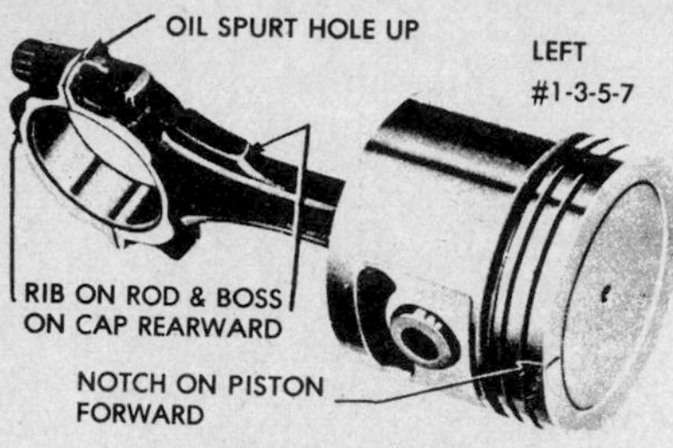

350 piston and connecting rod assembly —left bank
(© Buick Div., G.M. Corp)

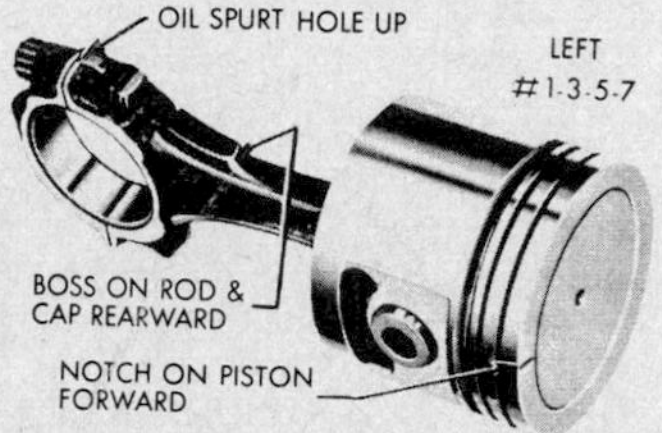

430, 455 piston and connecting rod assembly—left bank
(© Buick Div., G.M. Corp)

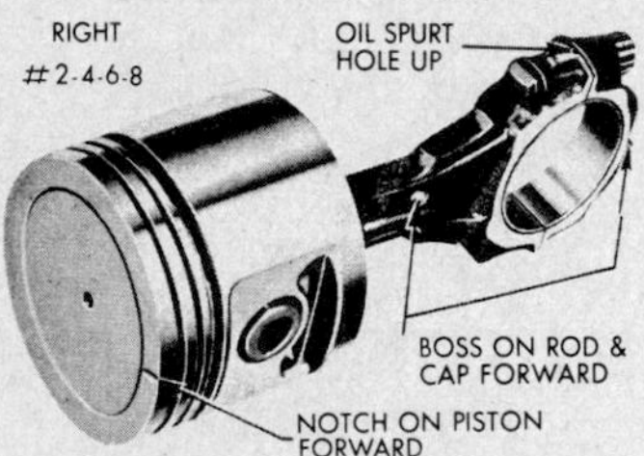

430, 455 piston and connecting rod assembly—right bank
(© Buick Div., G.M. Corp)

Engine Lubrication

Oil Pan R & R

1. Disconnect the battery.
2. Remove the fan shroud-to-radiator tie bar screws.
3. Remove the air cleaner and disconnect the throttle linkage.
4. Raise the car and support it on jackstands.
5. Drain the oil.
6. On cars equipped with manual transmission, loosen the clutch equalizer bracket-to-frame attaching bolts and remove the exhaust crossover pipe.
7. On cars equipped with automatic transmissions, remove the lower flywheel housing, remove the shift linkage attaching bolt and swing it out of the way, and disconnect the exhaust crossover pipe at the engine.
8. On 1970-72 models, disconnect the idler arm at the frame and push the steering linkage forward to the crossmember.
9. Remove the front engine mounting bolts.
10. Raise the engine by placing a jack under the crankshaft pulley mounting.

Caution On air conditioned cars, place a support under the right-side of the transmission before raising the engine. If you don't do this, the engine and transmission will cock to the right due to the weight of the air conditioning equipment.

11. Remove the oil pan bolts and remove the pan. It may be necessary to rotate the crankshaft to get enough clearance to remove the pan.
12. Reverse the above steps to install. Use gasket sealer and new gaskets. Tighten the bolts evenly to 14 ft lbs.

Oil Pump Removal

The oil pump is located in the timing chain cover on the right-hand side. It is connected by a drilled passage in the crankcase to an oil screen housing and pipe assembly. The screen is submerged in the oil supply in the oil pan.

The pump can be disassembled as follows:

1. Remove the oil filter.
2. Unbolt the pump cover assembly from the timing chain cover.
3. Remove the cover assembly and slide out the pump gears.
4. Remove the oil pressure relief valve cap, spring, and valve. Do not remove the oil filter by-pass valve and spring.
5. Check that the relief valve spring isn't worn on its side or collapsed. Check that the relief valve is no more than an easy slip fit in its bore in the cover. If there is any perceptible side-play, replace the valve. If there is still side-play, replace the cover.
6. Check the filter by-pass valve for good condition.

To assemble the pump:

7. Lubricate and install the pressure relief valve and spring in the cover bore. Install the gasket and cap, torquing the cap to 35 ft. lbs.
8. Install the gears and check that gear-to-cover end clearance is between 0.002-0.006 in. If the clearance is less, check the timing cover gear pocket for wear.
9. Remove the gears and pack the gear pocket full of petroleum jelly. Don't use grease.

Caution Unless the pump is primed this way, it won't produce any oil pressure when the engine is started.

10. Install the gears. Install a new gasket and the cover. Torque the bolts evenly to 10 ft lbs. Replace the filter.

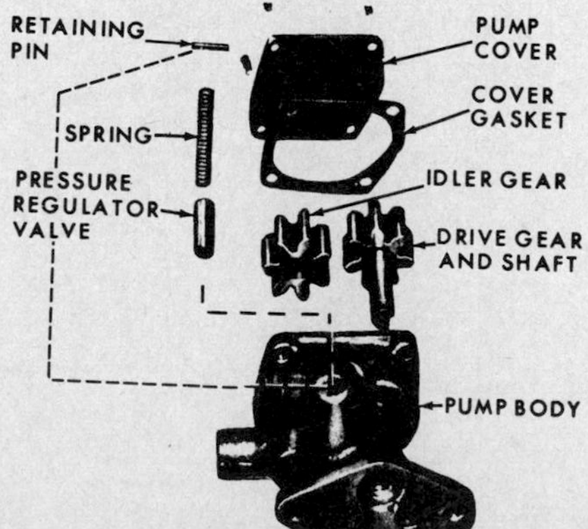

Typical oil pump assembly
(© Buick Div., G.M. Corp)

Rear Main Bearing Oil Seal Replacement

Buick uses an oil slinger and groove, a braided fabric seal and two neoprene strips to seal the rear main bearing. The braided fabric seal can be installed in the crankcase half (upper) only when crankshaft is removed. However, the seal can be replaced in the lower half whenever the lower half (cap) has been removed. To renew the seals in the cap proceed as follows:

Remove the oil pan. Remove the old seals and clean the cap. Place new braided seal in groove with both ends projecting above parting surface of cap. Force seal into groove by rubbing down with a hammer handle or other smooth tool until seal is seated in groove and ends project above the parting face of the cap not more than 1/16 in. Using a razor blade, cut off ends flush with parting surface.

On 350 cu in. engines only, just before installing the bearing cap, lightly lubricate the neoprene side seals and install in bearing cap with the upper ends protruding about 1/16 in. The seals must not be cut to length.

NOTE: The neoprene side seals may fit loosely in the side grooves of the rear main bearing cap when first installed, and may even leak for a short time. However, the seals swell considerably when they come in contact with oil and heat and will soon seal properly if installed correctly.

After installing the cap, force the seals up into the cap with a blunt instrument to insure a seal at the line between the cap and the case.

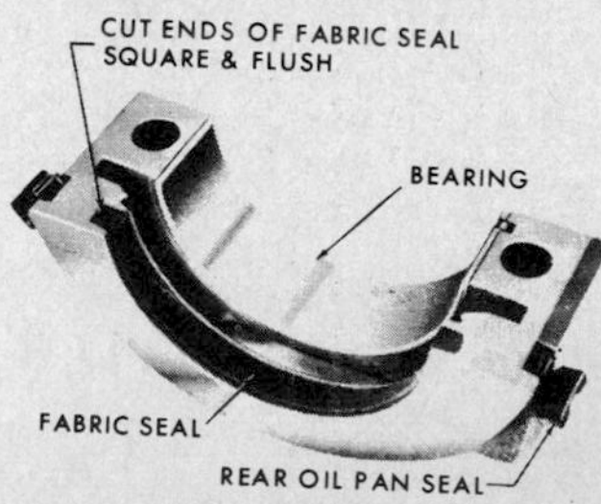

Rear main bearing cap—455 cu in.
(© Buick Div., G.M. Corp)

NOTE: the 430 and 455 cu. in. engines use a rear bearing cap which does not have the neoprene side seals. These engines are sealed at this point by a rear oil pan seal.

Caution The engine must be operated at slow speed when first started after installation of new braided seals.

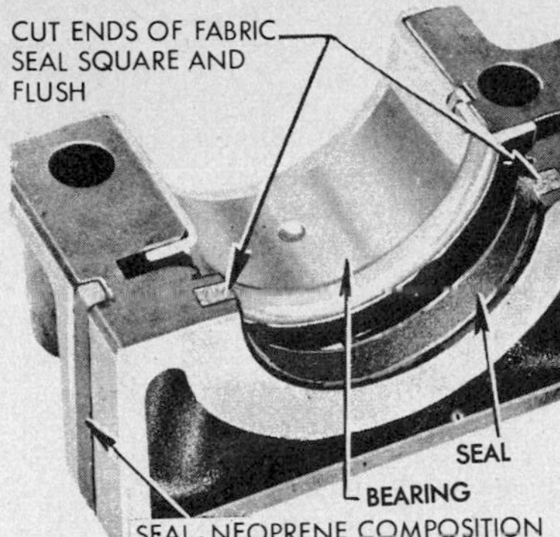

Rear main bearing cap—except 455 cu in.
(© Buick Div., G.M. Corp)

Chilton's TIME SAVER

Top Half, Rear Main Bearing Oil Seal Replacement

1. Drain engine oil and remove oil pan.
2. Remove rear main bearing cap.
3. With a 6 in. length of 3/16 in. brazing rod, drive up on either exposed end of the top half oil seal. When the opposite end of the seal starts to protrude, have a helper grasp it with pliers and pull gently while the driven end is being tapped. It is surprising how easily most of these seals can be removed by this method.

To replace the woven fabric-type seal:

1. Obtain a 12 in. piece of copper wire (about the same gauge as that used in the strands of an insulated battery cable).
2. Thread one strand of this wire through the new seal, about ½ in. from the end, bend back and make secure.
3. Thoroughly saturate the new seal with engine oil.
4. Push the copper wire up through the oil seal groove until it comes down on the opposite side of the bearing.
5. Pull (with pliers) on the protruding copper wire while the crankshaft is being turned and the new seal is slowly fed into place.

CAUTION: this snaking operation slightly reduces the diameter of the new seal and care will have to be used to keep the seal from slipping too far through the top half of the bearing.

6. When an equal amount of seal is extending from each side, cut off the copper wire close to the seal and tamp both ends of the seal up into the groove (this will tend to expand the seal again).

NOTE: don't worry about the copper wire left in the groove, it is too soft to cause damage.

7. Replace the seal in the cap in the usual way and replace the oil pan.

CLUTCH

The only service adjustment that can be made on a Buick clutch is that of pedal clearance. If difficulty is experienced with the clutch and adjusting the clearance does not correct it, it will be necessary to remove the clutch from the car, since no practical in-car service is possible.

On models through 1971, there is a safety switch attached to the clutch pedal arm inside the car to prevent the engine from being started unless the clutch pedal is depressed.

Clutch Removal and Installation

Through 1971

1. Remove transmission.
2. Remove pedal return spring from clutch fork. Disconnect rod assembly from clutch fork.
3. Remove flywheel housing.
4. Remove throwout bearing from clutch fork.
5. Disconnect clutch fork from ball stud by moving toward center of flywheel housing.
6. Mark clutch cover and flywheel so that cover can be reinstalled in the same position. This is important to proper balance.
7. Loosen clutch cover to flywheel attaching bolts one turn at a time to maintain even spring pressure.
8. Support pressure plate and cover assembly while removing bolts. Remove pressure plate and driven plate. Caution should be used to keep the driven plate clean.
9. Reinstall by receiving the removal procedure. Use a dummy shaft to align the clutch plate. Tighten pressure plate to 30-40 ft lbs.

Clutch Pedal Adjustment

Through 1971

Clutch pedal clearance is adjusted under the car at the link between the clutch throwout fork and the equalizer. There should be ⅝-⅞ in. free-play of the clutch pedal before the throwout bearing strikes the fingers (or diaphragm).

MANUAL TRANSMISSION

See the "Unit Repair Section" for overhaul procedures.

The backup light switch is mounted on the steering column under the instrument panel in the same location as the neutral start and backup light switch on automatic transmission models. The switch is operated by the movement of the column shift tube. The mounting bracket has slotted holes for adjustment.

Transmission Removal

Through 1971

1. Mark universal joint and transmission shaft companion flange for proper indexing at time of installation. Remove two U-bolts and disconnect driveshaft at the front joint. Slide the driveshaft rearward as far as possible and remove.
2. Disconnect shift linkage from transmission.
3. Disconnect speedometer cable at transmission. Remove driven gear and sleeve.
4. Loosen all three exhaust pipe ball joints to permit transmission and rear of engine to be lowered.
5. Remove two bolts holding transmission mounting pad to transmission support. Leave mounting pad bolted to transmission.
6. With a padded jack under the engine, raise the unit until the transmission mounting pad clears the transmission support.
7. Remove four bolts holding transmission support to body members. Remove support, then lower the jack to allow transmission to clear the underbody.
8. Remove the two top transmission-to-flywheel housing bolts and insert guide pins.

NOTE: If guide pins are not used, damage to the clutch driven plate can result.

9. Remove the two lower transmission attaching bolts. Slide the transmission back until the drive gear shaft disengages the clutch disc and clears the flywheel housing. Lower the transmission.

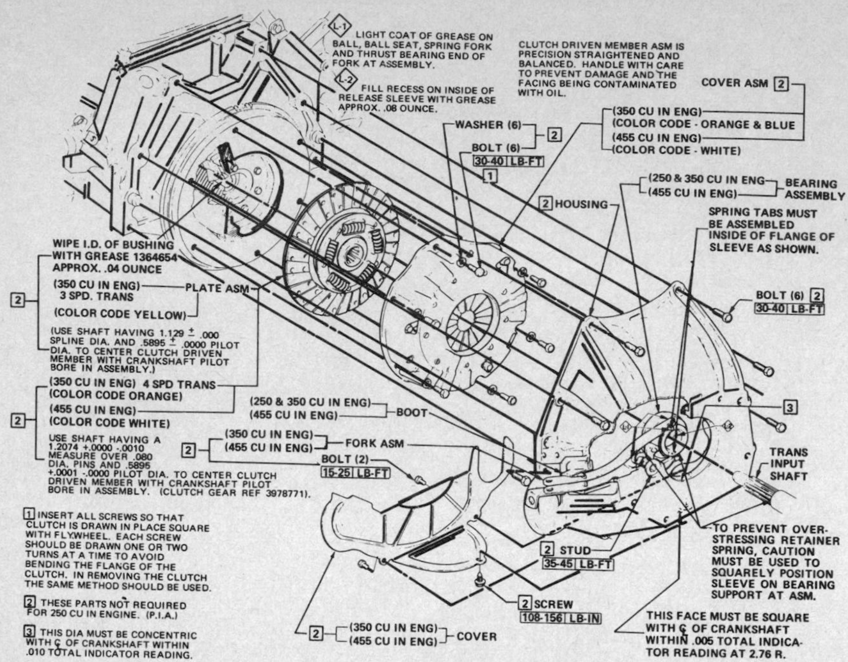

Typical clutch assembly sequence—1971 illustrated (© Buick Div., G.M. Corp)

10. Install transmission by reversing the above procedure.

Shift Linkage Adjustment—Three-Speed Column Shift

Through 1971

1. Place column selector lever in reverse position. Loosen first-reverse adjusting clamp bolts.
2. Shift first-reverse transmission lever into reverse. Tighten first-reverse adjusting clamp bolt to 17-23 ft. lbs.
3. Shift transmission levers into neutral positions. Loosen second-third adjusting clamp.
4. Install 3/16 in. rod into alignment holes. Tighten second-third adjusting clamp bolt to 17-23 ft. lbs.

AUTOMATIC TRANSMISSION

The Super Turbine 300 transmission is standard equipment on Le Sabre models with the smallest engine in 1969. In 1969, the Turbo Hydra-Matic 400 is optional on small engine Le Sabres and standard on all other models. In 1970, the Super Turbine 300 is eliminated; the Turbo Hydra-Matic 350, 375B, and 400 are the only automatic transmissions used on 1970 to present Buicks.

Identification

Super Turbine 300—1969

The production day and shift built number, transmission model and model year numbers are stamped on the low servo cover located on the middle right side of the transmission case. Also, the car serial number is stamped on the lower left side of the transmission case, next to the detent solenoid case connector.

SUPER TURBINE 300 MODEL CODE AND USAGE

MODEL	USAGE
MH	All Sport Wagons
ME	All 350 V8 Except Sport Wagons
LC	All 250 Six

Turbo Hydra-Matic 350 and 375

The production day and shift built number, transmission model and model year are stamped on the transmission in the following locations:

through 1972, the intermediate clutch accumulator cover located on the middle right side of the transmission.

Location of the 350 and 375 automatic transmission model identification, through 1972 (© Buick Div., G.M. Corp)

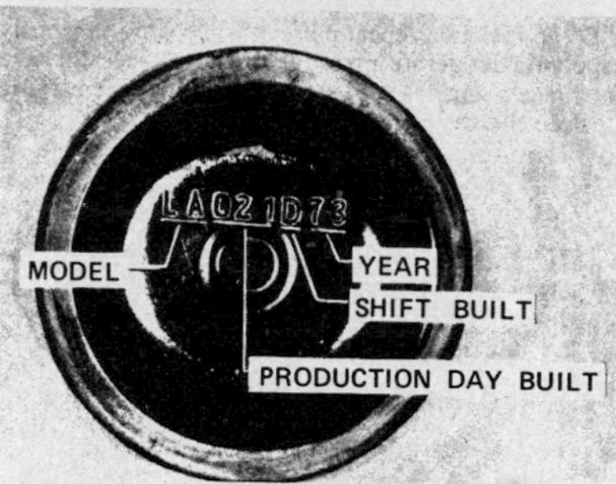

Location of the 350 and 375 automatic transmission model identification, 1973 and later (© Buick Div., G.M. Corp)

1973 and later, the inside of the governor cover located at the left rear of the transmission. The

TURBO HYDRA-MATIC 400 MODEL CODE AND USAGE

Year	Model	Usage
1969	BT	430 V8 Riviera
	BU	350 V8 LeSabre 400
	BC	430 V8 Wildcat, Electra
1970	BT	455 V8 Riviera
	BC	455 V8 Wildcat, Electra, LeSabre 455, Estate Wagon
1971	BT	455 V8 Riviera
	BC	455 V8 LeSabre, Centurion, Electra, Estate Wagon
1972-76	BC	455 V8 LeSabre, Centurion, Electra, Estate Wagon, Riviera with standard axle
	BT	Same as above but with high performance axle.

NOTE: The most notable characteristic distinguishing between the 350, 375 and 400 transmissions is the kick-down arrangement. The 350 and 375 kick-down linkage is by a cable attached to the accelerator linkage. The 400 kick-down is performed electrically by a switch at the accelerator pedal.

cover is held to the transmission by a retaining wire.

The vehicle serial number is located on the lower left side of the transmission case, next to the manual shifting shaft.

TURBO HYDRA-MATIC 350-375 MODEL CODE AND USAGE

YEAR	MODEL	USAGE
1969	Full size Buicks did not use the 350 transmission in 1969.	
1970	JS	LeSabre
1971-76	KL	LeSabre

NOTE: The only difference between the 350 and 375 transmissions is that the 375 has 5 direct clutch plates instead of 4. This increases torque capacity. There is no way to tell the difference between the two from the outside.

Turbo Hydra-Matic 400

The production identification number is stamped on a metal tag located in the lower right side of the transmission case. The vehicle serial number is stamped on a pad located just above the bottom pan face on the left side of the transmission.

Neutral Start Switch Adjustment

This safety switch prevents starting except in Neutral or Park positions. The switch combines function with the back-up light switch and is actuated by the transmission linkage. On column shift cars, the switch is on the steering column under the instrument panel. On console shift cars, the switch is inside the console up to 1970, on the column thereafter. To check switch adjustment:

1. Turn on ignition switch.
2. Place shift control lever in Reverse, and make sure back-up lights are on.
3. Set parking brake. Hold foot brake. Place shift control in Neutral and make sure engine will start. Repeat in Park, Drive, and Reverse. Engine must start only in Neutral or Park.
4. To adjust the switch, place the shift lever in the Neutral position and insert a 3/32 in. (No. 41) drill bit through the hole in the back of the switch. Move the switch until the bit goes in about ⅜ in. Tighten the mounting screws.
5. Check the adjustment as in Step 3.

Shift Linkage Adjustment

Column Shift through 1970

1. Place the manual control lever against the Drive stop.
2. Loosen the adjusting clamp bolt at the transmission.
3. Place the transmission lever in the Drive position (the third detent from the back).
4. Tighten the adjusting clamp bolt to 17-23 ft lbs. Overtightening will cause hard shifting.

1971 and later Column Shift

1. Loosen adjusting clamp bolt.
2. Place selector lever in Neutral.
3. Place transmission lever, at transmission, in Neutral.
4. Tighten adjusting clamp bolt to 17-23 ft. lbs.
5. Start engine. Check for proper shifting into all ranges.

Floorshift

These units are operated by a cable linkage. Adjust as follows:

1. Loosen the trunnion bolt at the transmission end of the cable on models through 1971. On 1972 and later models, pull the clip from the cable housing at the side of the transmission.
2. Set the console shift lever against the Drive stop on models through 1971. On 1972 and later

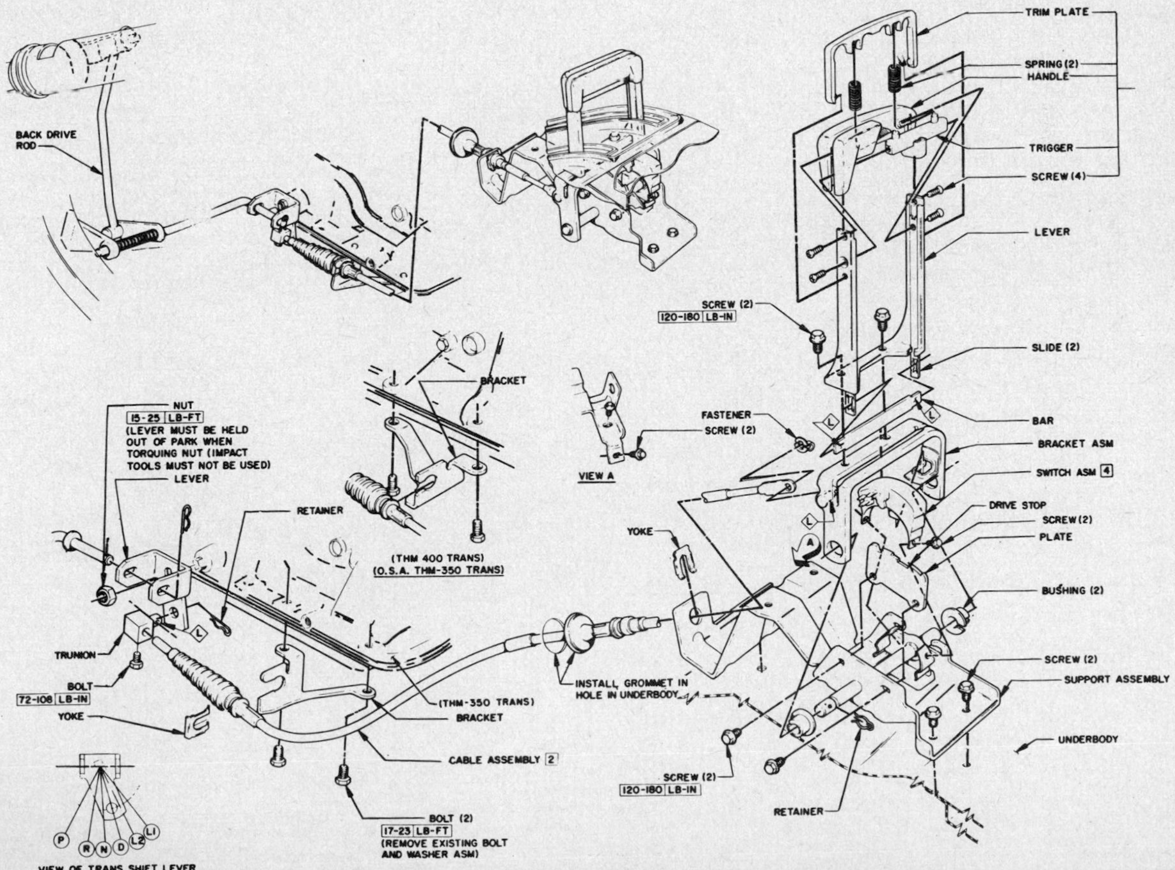

Cable type console shift linkage—Turbo-Hydramatic 400, 1969-71
(© Buick Div., G.M. Corp)

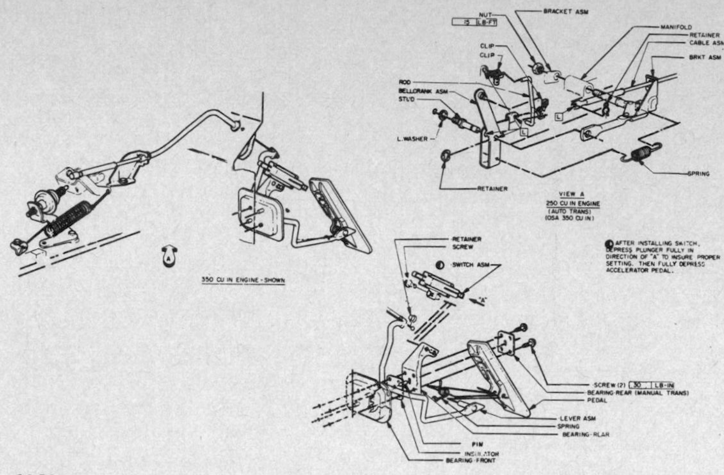
1969 Super Turbine 300 detent switch adjustment (© Buick Div., G.M. Corp)

models, set it in the Park detent.

3. Set the transmission shift lever in the Drive position on models through 1971. This is the third position from the back. On 1972 and later models, set it in the Park, or most forward, position.
4. On models through 1971, tighten the trunnion bolt against the cable end to 6-9 ft lbs. On 1972 and later models, replace the clip to hold the cable housing in position.
5. Place the console shift lever in the Park position on models through 1971.
6. Loosen back drive rod clamp screw or nut.
7. Push back drive rod (from linkage to steering column) up and hold lightly against stop.
8. Tighten screw in clamp at end of back drive rod to 17-23 ft. lbs.
9. Start engine. Check for proper shifting into all ranges.

Detent Switch Adjustment

1969 Super Turbine 300
1969-76 Super Turbine 400, Turbo Hydra-Matic 400

Refer to the accompanying illustrations for these adjustment procedures.

On 1972 and later models, the initial adjustment on installation is made by pushing the switch lever all the way toward the firewall. The final adjustment is made automatically the first time the accelerator pedal is fully depressed.

Pan R & R, Fluid and Filter Change

Turbo Hydra-Matic 350 and 375, Super Turbine 300

1. Raise the car and support it with jack stands.
2. Place a container under one of the pan corners and loosen the pan attaching screws. Pull the corner down to drain some of the fluid.
3. After the fluid has drained, remove the pan, clean and dry it

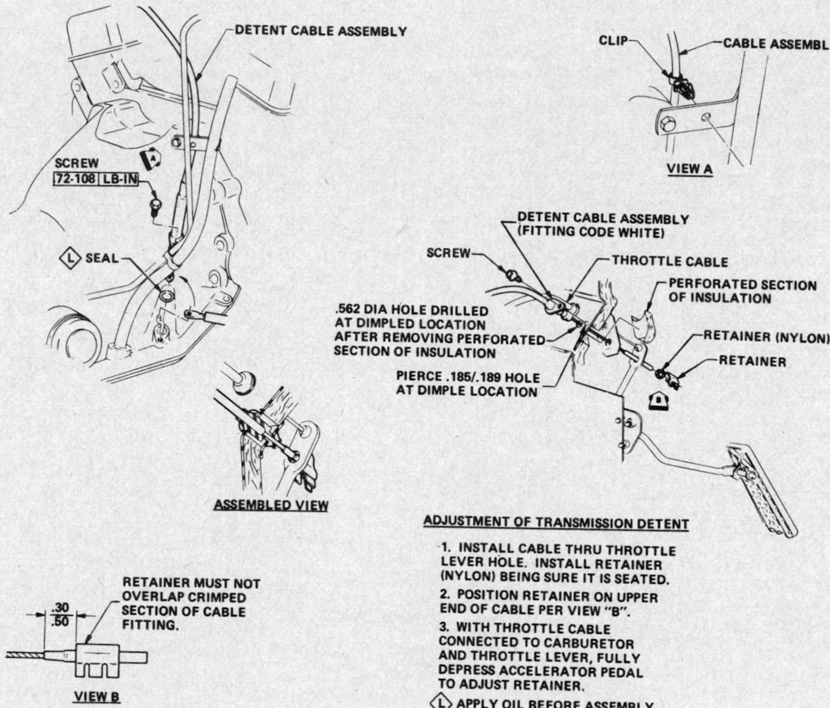

Detent switch adjustment—1971 (© Buick Div., G.M. Corp)

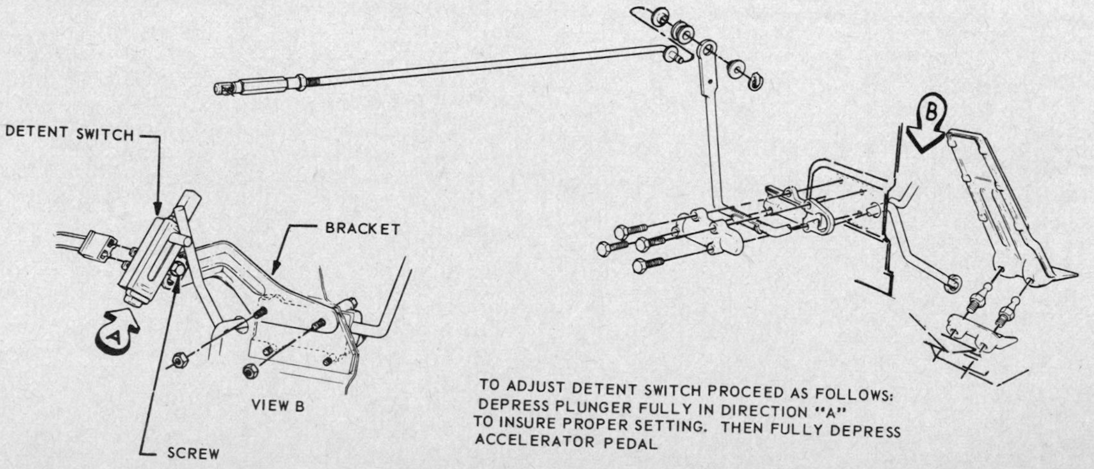

1969-70 Super Turbine 400 and Turbo-Hydramatic 400 detent switch adjustment (© Buick Div., G.M. Corp)

thoroughly. Be very careful not to leave any lint from cleaning rags in the pan.

4. Remove the filter assembly and gasket (O-ring on 300) by removing the two retaining screws.
5. Install a new filter-to-valve body gasket (O-ring on 300) on the filter and install the filter. Tighten the retaining screws.
6. Install the pan with a new gasket. Tighten the retaining screws to 13 ft lbs.

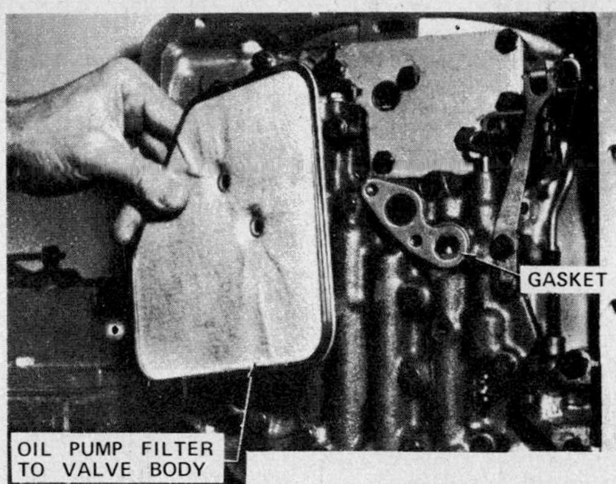

Removing/installing the filter and gasket on a 350 or 375 automatic transmission
(© Buick Div., G.M. Corp)

7. Lower the car and add 3 pints of transmission fluid through the filler neck.
8. With the shift lever in Park, start the engine, but do not race it. Move the shift lever through each range.
9. Immediately check the fluid level with the selector lever in Park and the engine running. Make sure the vehicle is resting on a level surface.
10. Add additional fluid as necessary to bring the level to 1/4 in. below the "ADD" mark on the dipstick. Do not overfill.

Turbo Hydra-Matic 400

The procedure for removing the pan and changing the fluid and filter are the same as for the 350 and 375. The filter of the 400 is attached by one bolt and has an O-ring seal on the end of the intake pipe. Make sure that the O-ring is removed from its seat if it does not come out with the filter and intake pipe. Install a new O-ring. Tighten the filter retaining bolt to 12 ft lbs. Add 5 pints of fluid through the filler tube.

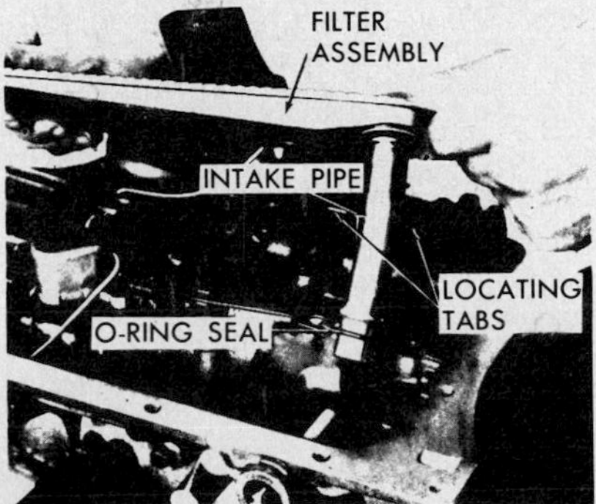

Removing/installing the filter and O-ring seal on a 400 automatic transmission
(© Buick Div., G.M. Corp)

U-JOINTS

Driveshaft Removal

1969-70 Riviera

1. Mark pinion flange and rear joint for reassembly. At rear pinion flange, remove U-bolt clamps from rear universal; on Riviera, remove four rear CV joint to pinion flange bolts. Use tape to secure bearings on the spider.
2. Remove four center bearing attaching bolts; two bolts on Riviera.
3. Support rear end of shaft. Slide assembly rearward until front yoke is free of transmission shaft splines. On Riviera, slide complete shaft assembly rearward through frame tunnel.
4. Protect the oil seal surface on the front yoke from dirt or marring.

NOTE: do not bend CV joint to its extreme angle at any time.

1969-70, Except Riviera, All 1971 and later

1. Mark shaft and pinion flange for reassembly.
2. Remove U-bolts from rear pinion flange. Use tape to secure bearings on the spider.
3. Remove shaft assembly by sliding rearward to disengage splines on transmission shaft.

Driveshaft Disassembly

Single Universal Joint

Nylon-injected composite universal joints are used.

1. Remove the driveshaft.
2. By using a piece of pipe or similar tool, slightly larger than 1⅛ in. to encircle the bearing shell, apply force on the yoke until downward movement of the yoke and stationary position of journal force the bearing assembly almost out of the top of the yoke (the force applied on the yoke will shear nylon retainers which lock bearings in place).
3. Rotate propeller shaft 180° and repeat preceding step to partially remove the opposite bearing.
4. Complete removal of these bearings by tapping around the circumference of exposed portion of bearing.
5. Remove journal from driveshaft rear yoke.
6. Remove bearings and journal from splined yoke in the same way.

NOTE: New bearings and journal assembly kits must be used upon reassembly. The kit includes snaprings and Delrin washers.

7. Install by inserting one bearing one-quarter way in one side of splined yoke, using brass hammer.
8. Insert journal into splined yoke (with dust shields installed).

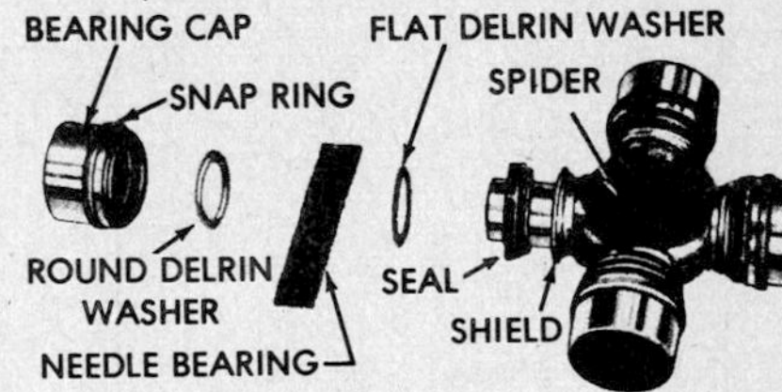

Typical U-joint
(© Buick Div., G.M. Corp)

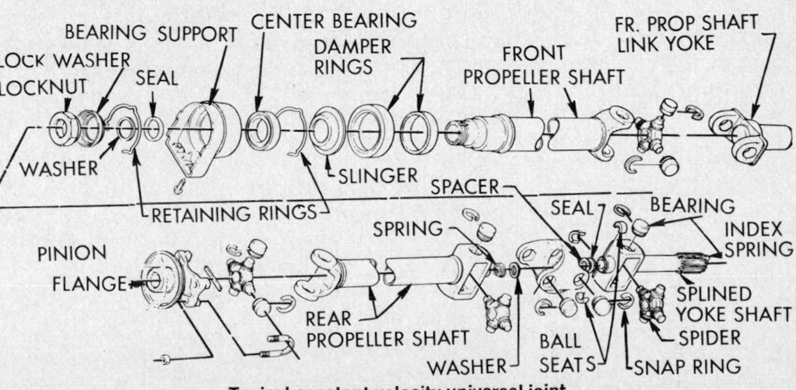

Typical constant velocity universal joint
(© Buick Div., G.M. Corp)

9. Install opposite bearing, ensuring that the bearing rollers do not jam on journal. Check free rotary movement of journal in bearing.
10. Now, press both bearings into place (just far enough to install snap rings).
11. Assemble opposite end universal in the same way.

Double Cardan Constant-Velocity Rear U-Joint

Removal

1. Mark the link yoke and the adjoining yokes, with a punch, before disassembly to ensure proper reassembly and driveshaft balance.

NOTE: It is easier to remove the flange yoke first. The first pair of flange yoke universal joint bearings to be removed is the pair in the link yoke.

2. With the driveshaft in a horizontal position, solidly support the link yoke. (A 1⅞ in. pipe will do.)
3. Apply force to the bearing cup on the opposite side with a 1⅛ in. pipe or a socket the size of the bearing cup. Use a hammer, vise, or press to apply force. Force the cup inward as far as possible.

NOTE: In the absence of a press, a heavy vise may be used, but make sure that the universal to be removed is at a right angle to the jaws of the vise. Do not cock the bearing cups in their bores.

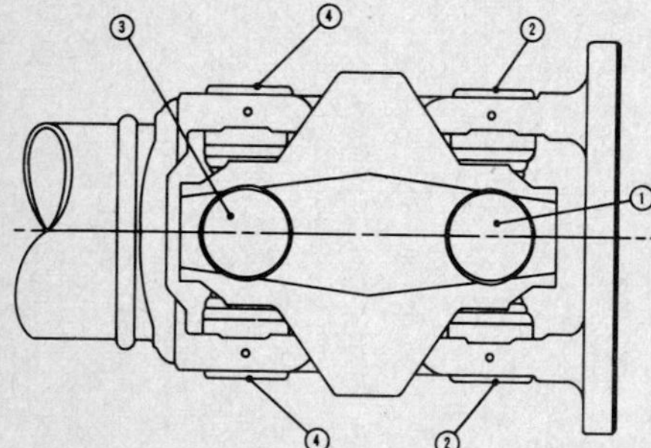

Bearing cap removal sequence—double Cardan joint starting 1971
(© Buick Div., G.M. Corp)

4. Remove the pieces of pipe and complete the removal of the protruding bearing cup by tapping around the circumference of the exposed portion of the bearing with a small hammer.
5. Reverse the positions of the pieces of pipe and apply force to the exposed journal end. This will force the other bearing cup out of its bore and allow removal of the flange.

NOTE: There is a ball joint located between the two universals. The ball portion of this joint is on the inner end of the flange yoke. Care must be taken not to damage the ball. On 1973 and later models the centering ball is a press-fit and is replaceable. On previous models the ball can not be removed. The ball seat is in the end of the driveshaft. To remove the seat, pry the seal out with a screwdriver.

6. To remove the journal from the flange, use steps two through five.
7. Remove the universal joint bearings from the driveshaft using the steps from two through five. The first pair of bearing caps that should be removed is the pair in the link yoke.

Installation

1. Examine the ball stud seat and ball stud for scores or wear. Worn seats can be replaced with a kit. A worn ball, however, requires the replacement of the entire propeller shaft yoke and flange assembly on all except 1973 and later models. Clean the ball seat cavity and fill it with grease. Install the spring, washer, ball seats, and spacer, if removed.
2. Install the universal joints in the opposite order from which they were disassembled.
3. Install a bearing ¼ of the way into one side of the yoke.
4. Insert the journal into the yoke so that an arm of the journal seats into the bearing.
5. Press the bearing in the remaining distance and install its snapring.
6. Install the opposite bearing. Do not allow the bearing rollers to jam. Continually check for free movement of the journal in the bearings as they are pressed into the yoke.
7. Install the rest of the bearings in the same manner.

REAR AXLE

Axle Shaft, Bearing and Seal

Removal and Installation

1. Jack up the vehicle and remove the wheel and brake drum on the side to be serviced.

NOTE: There are two types of axles installed in Buicks; one with the axle shafts attached to the differential side gears with C-clips and the other with the axle shafts held in by retainer plates attached to the brake backing plate. The only way to be sure of which type you are working on is to remove the differential cover and look for the C-clips.

2. On models with the C-clips:
   a. Remove the bolts and differential carrier cover and allow the lubricant to drain out.

Axle shaft C-clips inside the differential
(© Buick Div., G.M. Corp)

   b. Remove the pinion shaft lock bolt and pinion shaft from the differential.
   c. Push the axle shafts inward to permit the removal of the C-clips and remove the axle shafts.
3. On models with retainer plates:
   a. Remove the nuts holding the retainer plates to the brake backing plates.
   b. Pull the retainers clear of the bolts and reinstall two opposite nuts finger tight to hold the brake backing plate in position.
   c. Pull the axle shaft out using an axle puller (slide hammer).
4. On axles with C-clips, the bearing and seal are removed and installed from the axle housing with special bearing and seal tools.
5. On axles with the retainer plates, and axle bearing retainer ring must be cracked with a chisel, and the bearing pressed off and on with an arbor press. Press on a new retainer ring.

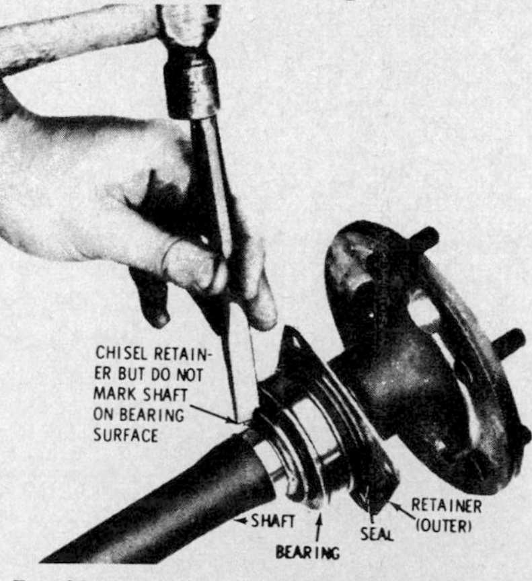

Breaking the bearing retainer with a chisel
(© Buick Div., G.M. Corp)

6. Install the axle shafts in the reverse order of removal. Apply a small amount of lubricant to the splines of the axle shaft to facilitate installation. If the differential is a limited slip type, use a limited slip differential type lubricant.

JACKING, HOISTING

Jack car at front spring seat of lower control arm or center of cross-member.

Jack car at rear, at axle housing.

To lift at frame, use side rails in front of body floor pan and at rear side rail at lower control arm front pivot.

FRONT SUSPENSION

Figures covering the caster, camber, toe-in, king pin inclination, and turning radius can be found in the Wheel Alignment table.

Shock Absorber R & R

1. Remove the upper shock absorber attaching nut, grommet retainer, and grommet.
2. Remove the lower retaining screws. Lower the shock through the hole in the lower control arm.
3. Reverse the above steps to install.

COIL SPRING
UPPER CONTROL ARM
RUBBER BUMPER
UPPER BALL JOINT
STEERING KNUCKLE
STABILIZER
SHIM AS REQUIRED
STABILIZER LINK
RUBBER BUMPER
BRAKE REACTION ROD
BOLT "A" FRONT
BOLT "B" REAR
LOWER CONTROL ARM

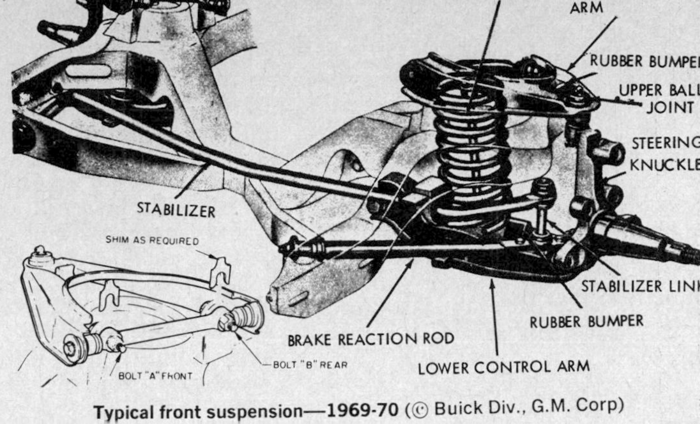

Typical front suspension—1969-70 (© Buick Div., G.M. Corp)

Ball Joints

Inspection

Through 1972

NOTE: before performing this inspection, make sure that the wheel bearings are adjusted correctly and that the A-arm bushings are in good condition.

1. Jack the car up under the front lower control arm at the spring seat.
2. Raise the car until there is 1–2 in. of clearance under the wheel.
3. Insert a bar under the wheel and pry upward. If the wheel raises more than 1/8 in., the ball joints are worn. Determine whether the upper or lower ball joint is worn by visual inspection while prying on the wheel.

NOTE: due to the distribution of forces in the suspension, the lower ball joint is usually the defective joint.

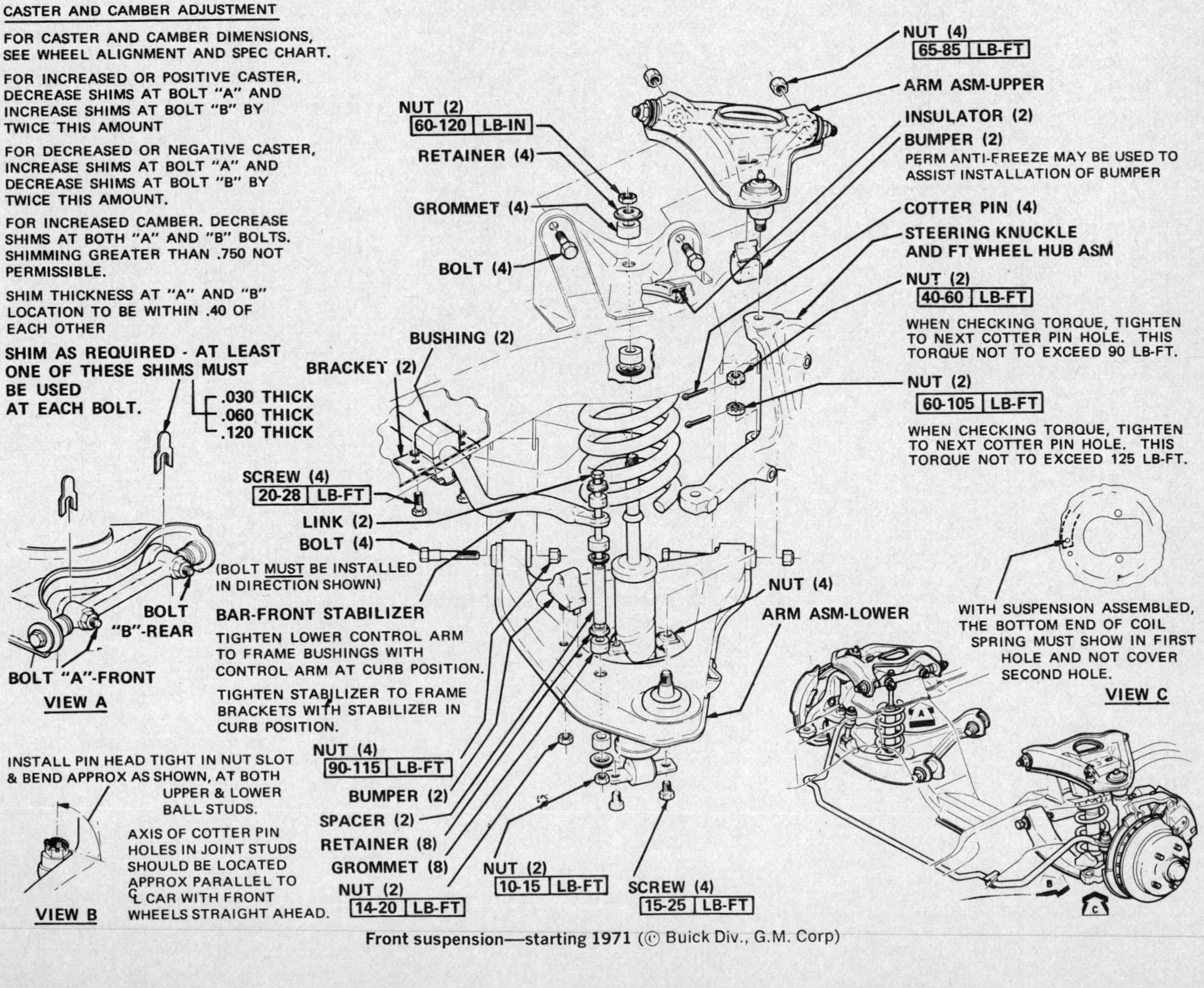

CASTER AND CAMBER ADJUSTMENT
FOR CASTER AND CAMBER DIMENSIONS, SEE WHEEL ALIGNMENT AND SPEC CHART.
FOR INCREASED OR POSITIVE CASTER, DECREASE SHIMS AT BOLT "A" AND INCREASE SHIMS AT BOLT "B" BY TWICE THIS AMOUNT
FOR DECREASED OR NEGATIVE CASTER, INCREASE SHIMS AT BOLT "A" AND DECREASE SHIMS AT BOLT "B" BY TWICE THIS AMOUNT.
FOR INCREASED CAMBER. DECREASE SHIMS AT BOTH "A" AND "B" BOLTS. SHIMMING GREATER THAN .750 NOT PERMISSIBLE.
SHIM THICKNESS AT "A" AND "B" LOCATION TO BE WITHIN .40 OF EACH OTHER
SHIM AS REQUIRED - AT LEAST ONE OF THESE SHIMS MUST BE USED AT EACH BOLT.
.030 THICK
.060 THICK
.120 THICK
BOLT "B"-REAR
BOLT "A"-FRONT
VIEW A
INSTALL PIN HEAD TIGHT IN NUT SLOT & BEND APPROX AS SHOWN, AT BOTH UPPER & LOWER BALL STUDS.
AXIS OF COTTER PIN HOLES IN JOINT STUDS SHOULD BE LOCATED APPROX PARALLEL TO ℄ CAR WITH FRONT WHEELS STRAIGHT AHEAD.
VIEW B
NUT (2) 60-120 LB-IN
RETAINER (4)
GROMMET (4)
BOLT (4)
BUSHING (2)
BRACKET (2)
SCREW (4) 20-28 LB-FT
LINK (2)
BOLT (4)
(BOLT MUST BE INSTALLED IN DIRECTION SHOWN)
BAR-FRONT STABILIZER
TIGHTEN LOWER CONTROL ARM TO FRAME BUSHINGS WITH CONTROL ARM AT CURB POSITION.
TIGHTEN STABILIZER TO FRAME BRACKETS WITH STABILIZER IN CURB POSITION.
NUT (4) 90-115 LB-FT
BUMPER (2)
SPACER (2)
RETAINER (8)
GROMMET (8)
NUT (2) 14-20 LB-FT
NUT (2) 10-15 LB-FT
SCREW (4) 15-25 LB-FT
NUT (4) 65-85 LB-FT
ARM ASM-UPPER
INSULATOR (2)
BUMPER (2)
PERM ANTI-FREEZE MAY BE USED TO ASSIST INSTALLATION OF BUMPER
COTTER PIN (4)
STEERING KNUCKLE AND FT WHEEL HUB ASM
NUT (2) 40-60 LB-FT
WHEN CHECKING TORQUE, TIGHTEN TO NEXT COTTER PIN HOLE. THIS TORQUE NOT TO EXCEED 90 LB-FT.
NUT (2) 60-105 LB-FT
WHEN CHECKING TORQUE, TIGHTEN TO NEXT COTTER PIN HOLE. THIS TORQUE NOT TO EXCEED 125 LB-FT.
NUT (4)
ARM ASM-LOWER
WITH SUSPENSION ASSEMBLED, THE BOTTOM END OF COIL SPRING MUST SHOW IN FIRST HOLE AND NOT COVER SECOND HOLE.
VIEW C

Front suspension—starting 1971 (© Buick Div., G.M. Corp)

Beginning 1973

The lower ball joints contain a visual wear indicator. The lower ball joint grease plug screws into the wear indicator which protrudes from the bottom of the ball joint housing. As long as the wear indicator extends out of the ball joint housing, the ball joint is not worn. If the tip of the wear indicator is parallel with, or recessed into the ball joint housing, the ball joint is defective.

Control Arms, and/or Ball Joint, Spring—R & R

Upper Control Arm

1. Raise car with jack under the frame. Remove wheel and tire.
2. Remove cotter pin from upper ball joint stud.
3. Loosen, but do not remove nut.

Caution If the nut is removed, the full force of the coil spring could be released.

Rap the knuckle sharply in the area of the tapered stud to free the stud from the knuckle.

4. With another jack, support the car weight under the outer edge of the lower control arm. Raise jack enough to free upper control arm from upper ball stud.
5. Wire brake and knuckle in place to prevent brake hose damage, then, lift upper arm from knuckle.

NOTE: If only ball joints are to be replaced, stop at this point. Center punch and drill out the four rivets, then chisel off their heads. Remove old ball joint—the new joint comes with four specially hardened bolts, which must be torqued to 8 ft. lbs. The nut goes on top.

6. Remove the upper control arm shaft-to-bracket nuts and lock washers. Carefully note the number, thickness, and location of the adjusting shims. Remove control arm assembly.
7. Reverse the above steps to install.

Caution When installing the cotter pin, never loosen the nut to align the cotter pin holes. Always tighten the nut to the next slot that lines up with the hole.

Lower Control Arm, or Spring

1. Raise the front of the car and remove the tires, wheels, hub and drum or rotor.
2. Disconnect and remove shock absorber.
3. Remove front stabilizer rod link from lower control arm.
4. Disconnect brake reaction rod from lower control arm but leave it attached to the front frame crossmember up to 1970 models.
5. Remove control arm bumper up to 1970 models.
6. As a safety precaution and to gain maximum leverage, place a jack about ½ in. below the lower ball joint stud. Now, remove the ball stud cotter pin and loosen the nut about ⅛ in. Do not remove the nut.
7. Rap the steering knuckle in the area of the stud to separate the stud from the knuckle.
8. After the stud has broken loose from the knuckle, raise the jack against the control arm. Remove nut and separate the steering knuckle from the tapered stud.
9. Carefully lower jack under the control arm and release the spring. With the jack entirely lowered, it may be necessary to pry the spring off its seat on the lower control arm with a pry bar.
10. After the spring is removed, the lower control arm may be removed by removing the lock nut attaching the control arm to the frame.
11. Install by reversing removal procedure. Tighten castellated nut to 85 ft. lbs.

Lower Ball Joint R & R

1. Perform steps two through eight, inclusive, in the "Lower Control Arm R&R" procedure.
2. Remove the ball joint by pressing the joint from the lower control arm. It may be necessary to remove the ball joint and lower control arm as an assembly and have the ball joint removed in a press if suitable tools are not available.
3. Install a new ball joint and reverse the removal procedure.

Front Wheel Bearing Adjustment

Through 1970

Adjustment of freshly cleaned and repacked roller bearings is as follows:

1. Torque spindle nut to 19 ft. lbs. while rotating the wheel.
2. Back off the nut until bearings are loose.
3. Retorque spindle nut to 11 ft. lbs. while rotating the wheel.
4. If either cotter pin hole in spindle lines up with nut castellations, back off the nut one-twelfth turn and install cotter pin. Otherwise, back off the nut to the first position that will accept a horizontal or vertical cotter pin.
5. Install cotter pin and lock spindle nut into position.

NOTE: .002-.006 in. end-play is normal.

1971-76

1. Lift the wheel off the ground by jacking under the lower control arm.
2. Remove the dust cap from the hub.
3. Remove the cotter pin and discard.
4. Snug up the spindle nut to seat the bearings. Then back off the nut 1/4–1/2 turn.
5. Retighten the nut by hand until it is finger-tight.
6. Loosen the nut 1/12 of a turn (no more than 1/6) and line up the hole in the spindle with the nearest slot in the spindle nut, and insert a new cotter pin. There should be 0.001-0.005 in. end-play.

NOTE: Under no circumstances is the final bearing nut adjustment to be even finger-tight.

7. Replace the dust cover and lower the car.

REAR SUSPENSION

Shock Absorber R & R

1. Raise the car at the axle housing.
2. Remove the nut, retainer, and grommet or nut, and lockwasher, as equipped, which attach the lower end of the shock absorber to its mounting.
3. Remove the two shock absorber upper attaching screws and remove the shock absorber.
4. Reverse the removal procedures to install. On 1973-75 models the upper attaching nut should be tightened to 10-15 ft lbs.

Rear Leaf Spring Replacement —1971-76 Station Wagon

1. Jack up car at axle housing. Make sure you don't crush exhaust pipe.
2. Support car at both frame side rails in front of and behind the springs, using axle stands.
3. Remove nut and lockwasher from lower shock stud.
4. Move shock out of the way.
5. Disconnect the right side exhaust system by removing the screw that attaches the exhaust pipe hanger to the rear frame crossmember. Support the exhaust system to prevent damage from bending.
6. Remove spring anchor plate nuts, then remove anchor plate and cushion.
7. Jack axle housing up and remove upper cushion.
8. Loosen upper and lower spring shackle nuts.
9. Loosen spring eye bolt.
10. Remove eye bolt and carefully lower spring.
11. Support spring and remove lower shackle pin.
12. Remove spring.

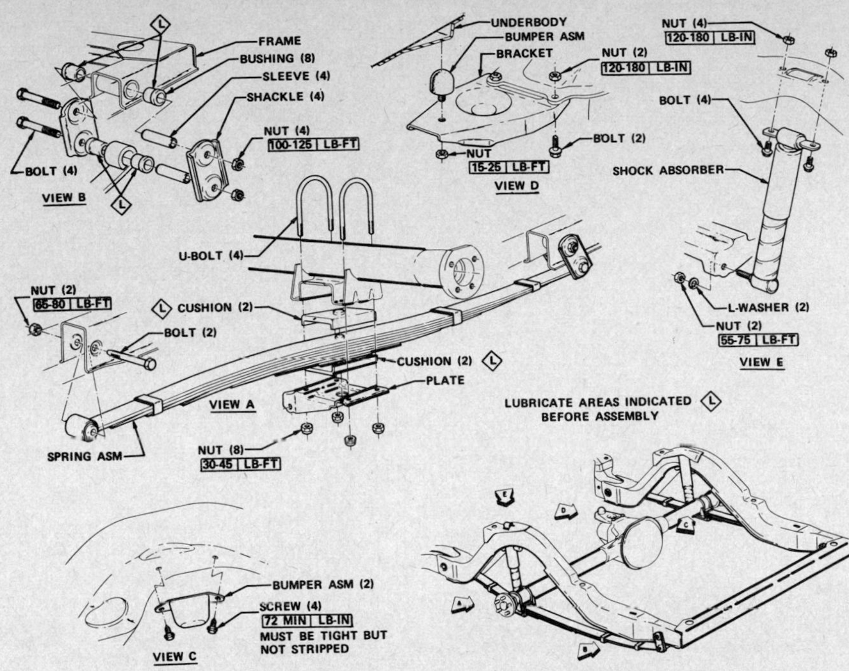

Rear suspension details—Estate Wagon with leaf springs, 1971 and later
(© Buick Div., G.M. Corp)

13. To install, reverse removal procedure. Tighten front eye bolt to 80-100 ft lbs., shackle nuts to 75-95 ft lbs., anchor plate nuts to 35-50 ft lbs, and lower shock nut to 55-75 ft lbs.

Rear Coil Spring Replacement

1. Jack up the back of the car and support both sides on stand jacks on the frame, in front of the rear axle. Disconnect shock absorbers.

NOTE: It may be necessary to disconnect the rear brake line in order to obtain sufficient axle drop to remove the spring. If this is done, first depress and secure the brake pedal at least 1 in. from the relaxed position to prevent the master cylinder from draining when the rear brake line is disconnected.

2. Place a jack under the lower control arms and remove the bolts which hold the upper control arms to the rear axle housing.

NOTE: Spring can often be removed without disconnecting lower control arm.

3. Slowly, and very carefully, let the trailing arms come down until the tension is released from the rear coil springs. Then, take off the coil spring. Note the direction the end of the last coil is pointing. Reinstall the spring in the same position.
4. When starting a new coil spring, make certain that the bottom of the coil is properly inserted into the socket in the frame and into the form plate on the trailing arm.
5. Jack the trailing arms into place and reinstall the trailing arm rear bolts.

NOTE: Don't tighten the bolts yet.

6. Lower the car to rest on its wheels.
7. Tighten the bolts to 65-85 ft lbs.

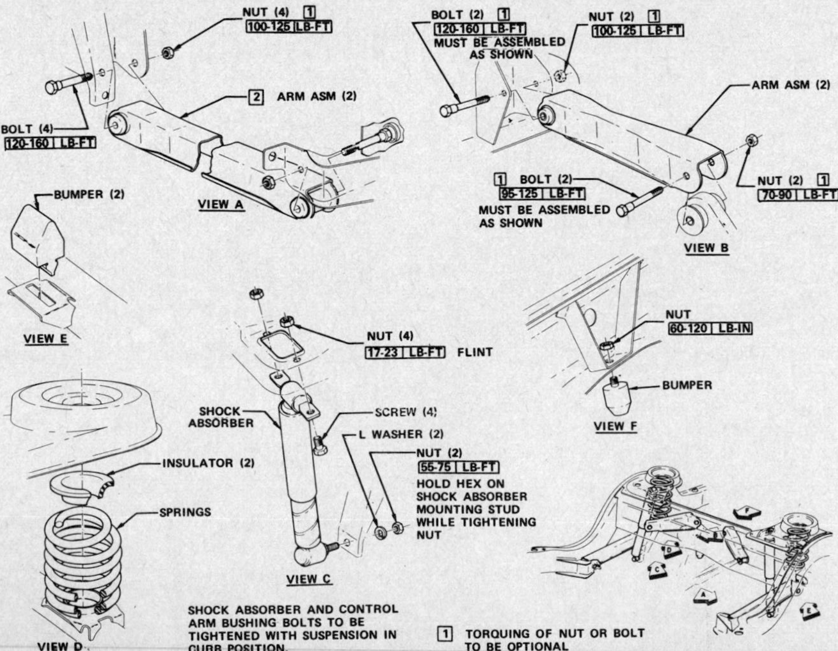

BRAKES

A dual master cylinder is used on all models. Information on the system and brake adjustments, lining replacement, bleeding procedure, master and wheel cylinder overhaul can be found in the Unit Repair Section.

Some models are equipped with front wheel disc brakes. Beginning 1969 these disc brakes operate with single cylinder per wheel design. However, some 1969 models have the earlier four piston disc brakes. For details, consult the Unit Repair Section.

Master Cylinder R & R

1. Disconnect brake pipe or pipes from master cylinder and tape end of pipe or pipes to prevent entrance of dirt.
2. Disconnect brake pedal from master cylinder at the pushrod.

NOTE: Step 2 is not necessary with power brakes.

3. Remove master cylinder-to-dash or booster retaining bolts. Remove the master cylinder.
4. Reverse the above steps to install. Bleed the brakes and check for leaks after installation.

Power Brake Unit R & R

1. Unbolt the master cylinder from the power unit. Being careful not to kink or bend the brake lines, pull the master cylinder away from the power unit without disconnecting the brake lines.
2. Disconnect and plug the vacuum hose.
3. Disconnect the power brake pushrod from the brake pedal.
4. Unbolt the power brake unit from the firewall.
5. Remove the unit.
6. Mount the unit to the firewall.
7. Install the master cylinder to the power unit and torque the nuts to 25 ft lbs.
8. Connect the vacuum hose.
9. Connect the power brake pushrod to the brake pedal.

Parking Brake Lever R & R

The parking brake lever on all models is a foot-operated treadle.

To remove the treadle first disconnect the cable and then unbolt the treadle frame from its mounting under the dash.

Parking Brake Cable Replacement

Front Cable

1. Raise car.
2. Remove jam nut and adjusting nut from equalizer. Remove retainer clip from rear portion of front cable at frame on models through 1971 and at the lever arm on 1972 and later cars. The retainer clip is not used on the 1969-70 Riviera.
3. At front of cable, bend snap-in retainer fingers in, so that retainer can be removed.
4. Disconnect cable from pedal assembly and remove cable.

NOTE: installation of a new cable can be eased by tying a cord to either end of the cable being removed and then pulling the new cable through the proper routing by use of the same cord. This is necessary since the cable is not long enough to follow a new path.

5. Install cable by reversing removal procedure.
6. Adjust the parking brake.

Center Cable

1. Raise car.
2. Remove jam nut and adjusting nut from equalizer.
3. Unhook connector at each end and disengage hooks and guides.
4. Install new cable by reversing removal procedure.
5. Adjust the parking brake.
6. Apply the parking brake firmly three times and repeat adjustment.

Rear Cable

1. Raise car.
2. Remove rear wheel and brake drum.
3. Loosen jam nut and adjusting nut at equalizer.
4. Disengage rear cable at connector.
5. Remove two bolts attaching cable assembly to backing plate on the Estate Wagon and bend the retainers on all other models. Disengage cable at brake shoe operating lever.
6. Install new cable by reversing removal procedure.
7. Adjust the parking brake.

Parking Brake Adjustment

Adjustment of the parking brake is necessary whenever the rear brake cables have been disconnected or the parking brake pedal can be depressed more than sixteen rachet clicks (13 on 1974-76 models) under foot pressure. The car should first be raised on a lift.

1. Make sure that service brakes are properly adjusted.
2. Depress parking brake pedal three ratchet clicks (six on 1974-76 Estate wagons).
3. Loosen jam nut on equalizer adjusting nut. Tighten adjusting nut until rear wheels can just be turned rearward by hand but not forward.
4. Release rachet one click; the rear wheels should rotate rearward freely and forward with a slight drag.
5. Release rachet fully; the rear wheels should turn freely in either direction.

NOTE: be sure that the parking brake does not drag. An overtightened, dragging parking brake on a car with automatic brake adjusters will result in an extremely short life for rear brake linings.

STEERING

Instructions covering the overhaul of the steering gear will be found in the Unit Repair Section. No manual steering is available on full-size Buicks starting in 1971. Troubleshooting and overhaul procedures are given in the "Unit Repair Section."

Power Steering Pump Removal and Installation

Disconnect the drive belt and remove the pump pulley with a suitable puller. On some models, the pulley has bolt access holes which make pulley removal unnecessary. Disconnect the hoses from the pump and unbolt the pump from the bracket. Use caps or tape to cover the hose connectors, unions, and hose ends to keep out dirt.

Reinstall by reversing procedure. The drive belt should be adjusted to have about ½ in. play on the longest run between pulleys. After replacing pump, fill reservoir and bleed pump by idling engine for three minutes before moving the steering wheel. Then rotate steering wheel slowly throughout its entire range. Recheck level.

Tie Rod End Inspection

1. Raise the car under the lower control arm.
2. Make sure control arm ball joints are good and that the wheel bearings are adjusted. Grasp the tire on either side and move the tire from side to side. If excessive play is present (more than 1/16 in.), visually inspect the linkage as the tire is moved.

Tie Rod End R & R

1. Loosen the tie-rod adjuster sleeve clamp nuts.
2. Remove the tie-rod stud nut cotter pin and nut.
3. Remove the tie-rod stud from the steering arm or intermediate rod. This is a taper fit. Removal is accomplished using a ball joint removal tool or by hitting the tie rod stud sharply with a hammer. If the ball joint is to be reused, the removal tool must be used.

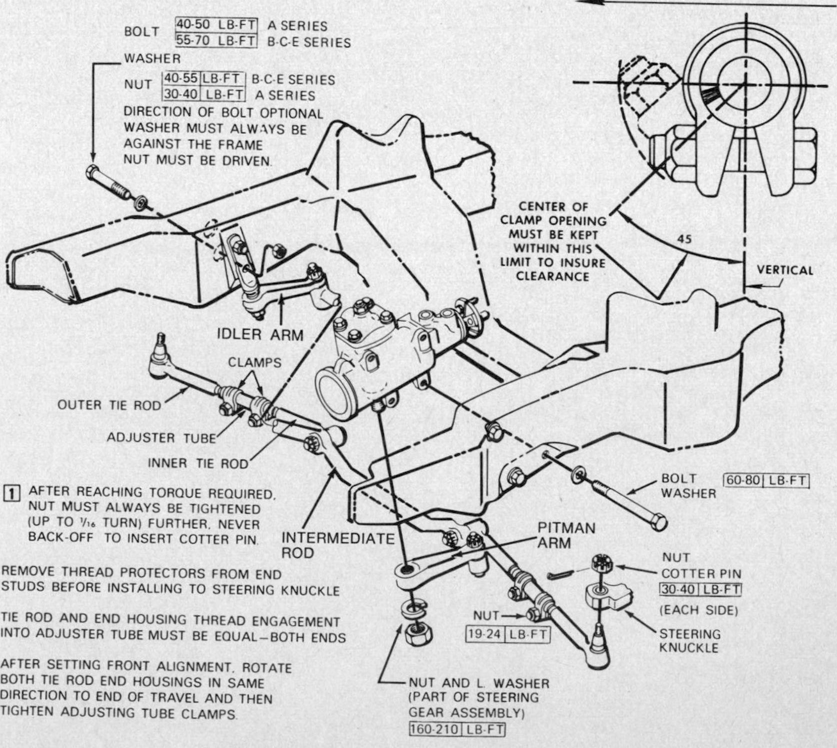

Steering linkage (© Buick Div., G.M. Corp)

4. Unthread the tie rod from the adjuster sleeve. Outer tie rods have right-hand threads and inner tie rods have left-hand threads. Count the number of turns the tie rod must be rotated to remove it from the adjusting sleeve. This will allow a reasonably accurate realignment upon reassembly.
5. Reverse the removal procedures to install. Clean rust and dirt from the threads. Check the front end alignment and adjust if necessary.

Intermediate Rod R & R

1. Remove the left and right-side inner tie-rod ends from the intermediate rod. These are taper fits; remove them as described in the tie rod section.
2. Remove the intermediate rod studs from the idler and pitman arms. These are taper fits.
3. Remove the intermediate rod.
4. Reverse the above steps to install.

Pitman Arm R & R

1. Remove the intermediate rod stud from the pitman arm. This is a taper fit, remove it as described in the tie rod section.
2. Remove the pitman arm nut and lockwasher from the pitman shaft.
3. Remove the pitman arm from the pitman shaft using a puller. Do not hammer on the end of the puller or serious internal damage will be done to the steering gear box.
4. Reverse the above steps to install.

Idler Arm R & R

1. Remove the intermediate arm stud. This is a taper fit; see the tie rod section for removal.
2. Remove the two bolts attaching the idler arm to the frame.
3. Remove the idler arm from the intermediate rod by tapping the intermediate rod with a hammer, using a heavy hammer as a backing.
4. Reverse the above steps to install.

Steering Wheel R & R

1. Unplug the horn wire connector from the steering column.
2. On cars with standard wheel or optional wood-rim wheel, pull off cap, remove three screws and bushing spacer, receiver cup, and Belleville spring. On cars with bar-type horn actuator remove screws securing actuator from underside of steering wheel, pull out lead connector plug, and remove actuator assembly.
3. Loosen steering wheel nut.
4. Apply steering wheel puller and pull wheel up to the nut. Now remove puller, nut and steering wheel.

Caution Don't pound on the steering wheel in either direction or the collapsible steering column will collapse, requiring replacement.

5. Install wheel with the location mark aligned with that of the shaft.

NOTE: Location marks are provided on the steering wheel and shaft to simplify proper indexing at the time of installation.

6. Install the wheel nut and torque to 30 ft lbs.
7. Reinstall horn button or actuator assembly.

Special Procedure for Cars with A.C.R.S. (Air Bags)

Some 1974 and later models have an air cushion, or air bag, restraint system. One of the elements of this complex system is an air cushion module in the top of the steering wheel. The steering wheel can be removed in the manner described in this section after the module has been removed.

To remove the module:

1. Turn the ignition lock to the LOCK position.
2. Disconnect the battery ground cable and tape the end to prevent any possibility of a complete circuit.
3. Remove the 4 module-to-steering wheel screws. A special tool is available to do this.
4. Lift up the module and disconnect the horn wire.
5. Disconnect the module wire connector. A special tool is available to do this, too.

WARNING: The driver air cushion module should always be carried with the vinyl cover away from all parts of one's body and should always be laid on a flat surface with the vinyl side up. This is necessary so that a free space is provided to allow the air cushion to expand in case of accidental deployment.

Do not attempt to repair any portion of the module. The module must be serviced as a unit. Attempting repairs such as soldering wires, changing covers, etc. may cause accidental inflation or impair operation of the driver module and cause serious injury.

Do not dispose of a module in any way. The highly inflammable material in the module can cause serious burns if ignited. Modules must be exchanged at an authorized dealer's parts department.

To install the module:

6. Hold the module with the emblem in the lower right corner.
7. Loop the air cushion harness clockwise from the 11 O'clock position to the 6 O'clock position.
8. Install the module connector by pushing it onto the column circuit firmly. Check that it is fully seated.
9. Install the horn wire.
10. Position the module, making sure that the wiring is still in place, and install the 4 screws. Torque them to 40 in. lbs.
11. Reconnect the battery ground cable.
12. Turn the ignition lock to any position other than LOCK and check that the restraint indicator light operates correctly.

Turn Signal Switch R & R

Tilt and Non-Tilt Column

NOTE: The steering wheel must always be supported. Use extreme care not to bend steering column.

1. Remove the steering wheel.
2. Remove the three cover screws and remove the cover.
3. Depress the lockplate and remove the snap-ring. Remove the lockplate.
4. Remove the spring and horn contact signal cancelling cam. Remove the thrust washer from the upper steering shaft.
5. Remove the turn signal lever, depress and remove the hazard warning knob, and tilt column lever, if equipped.

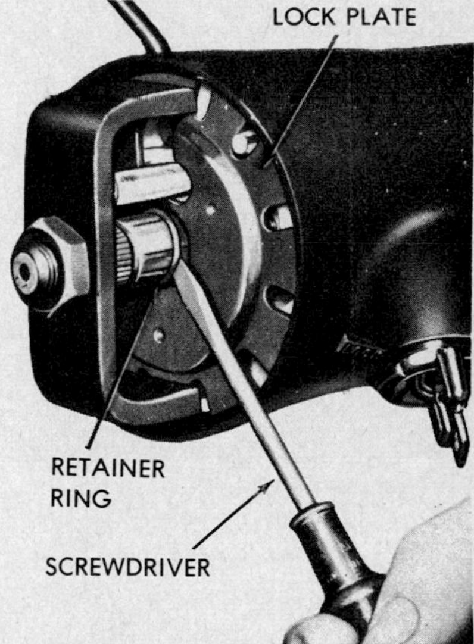

Depress the lock plate to remove the retaining ring (© Buick Div., G.M. Corp)

6. Tape the wiring harness connector to the wires so it will slip easily up the steering column.
7. Remove the three turn signal switch mounting screws. Pull the connector out from the bracket on the column.
8. Pull the switch straight up with the wire protector and wire harness.
9. Reverse the above steps to install.

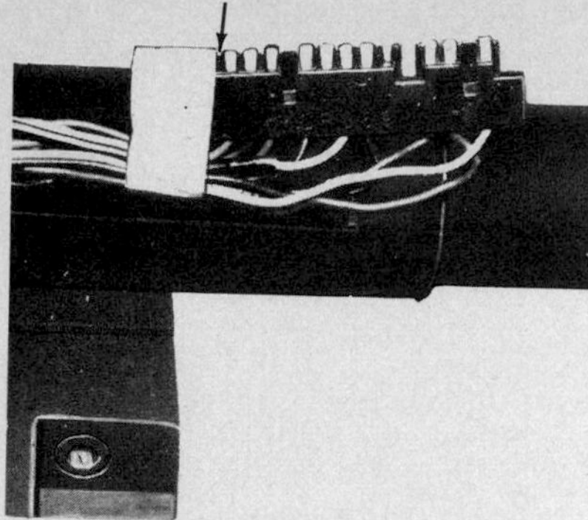

Tape the connector to the wires so that it will slip easily up the steering column (© Buick Div., G.M. Corp)

1974 and later with A.C.R.S. (Air Bags)

Follow the procedure for removing the steering wheel and air cushion module which appears previously under "Steering Wheel R&R, Special Procedure for Cars with A.C.R.S."

1. Remove the 3 screws from the retainer and cover. Carefully lift the cover and retainer from the column.
2. Carefully insert a screwdriver blade into the locking tab at the side and lift the slip ring from the column.
3. Now proceed with Steps 3-8 of the "Tilt and Non-Tilt Column Turn Signal Switch R & R" procedure.
4. To replace the slip ring, align the slip ring locating tab with the slot in the bowl and push the slip ring into position. Make sure that all 3 locking tabs are securely positioned.
5. Install the cover and retainer, aligning the cover over the locating tab. Torque the screws to 15 in. lbs.

INSTRUMENT PANEL

Ignition Switch

Lock Cylinder and/or Switch Replacement

The ignition switch occupies a position on the steering column, just above the gear selector lever. This lock prevents shifting the transmission and locks the steering. The ignition lock cylinder cannot be removed until the steering column is partially disassembled to gain access to the internal lock cylinder retainer. The steering wheel, lock plate, and turn signal switch assembly must be removed first.

Standard Column

1. Remove steering wheel using proper puller.
2. Remove three cover screws and cover; remove retainers.
3. Depress lock plate, then remove wire snap-ring and lock plate.
4. Slide upper bearing preload spring and cancelling cam off shaft.
5. Slide thrust washer off shaft, then remove turn signal lever screw and lever.
6. Push in four-way flasher switch; remove knob.
7. Remove three turn signal switch mounting screws, pull connector out of its bracket on the column and tape the upper part of connector and wires together.
8. Pull turn signal switch out of column jacket.
9. Insert a small screwdriver into the slot next to the turn signal switch mounting screw boss (right-hand slot), depress spring latch and remove key lock.

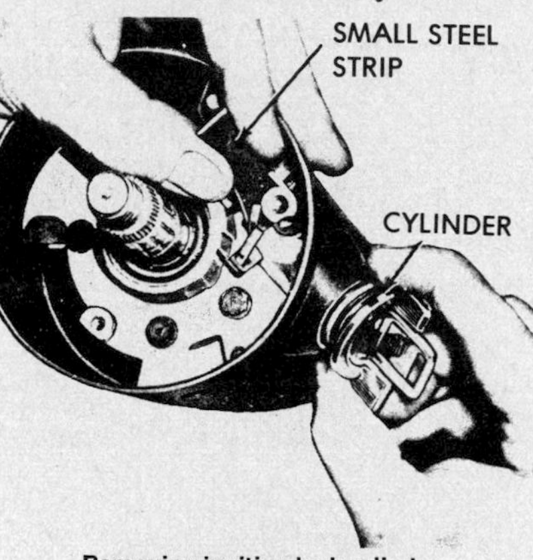

Removing ignition lock cylinder (© Buick Div., G.M. Corp)

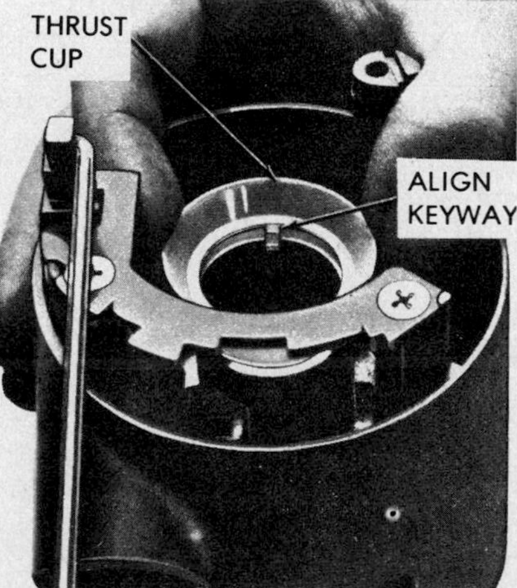

Removing the buzzer switch on a standard steering column (© (© Buick Div., G.M. Corp)

10. Pull buzzer switch straight out, depressing switch clip with pliers. If the ignition switch is to be removed, disconnect the steering column mounting bracket from the lower edge of the instrument panel and lower the steering column. Support the column so that it does not flex.
11. Place ignition switch in accessory position by pulling up on connecting rod until there is a definite stop or detent felt.
12. Remove two attaching screws and ignition switch.
13. Assembly is the reverse of the above. However, note the following steps before proceeding with the reassembly.
14. To install the steering lock, hold the lock cylinder sleeve and rotate the knob clockwise against the stop. Insert the cylinder into the cover bore with the key on the cylinder sleeve aligned with the keyway in the housing. Then push the cylinder in until it bottoms. Maintaining a light inward pressure, rotate the knob counterclockwise until the drive section of the cylinder mates with the drive shaft. Push in until the snap ring pops into the groove and the lock cylinder is secured in the cover. Check for free rotation.
15. When installing the ignition switch, be sure the lock cylinder is in the lock position. Put the shift bowl or shroud in the park position. Make sure the ignition switch is in the lock position. Then insert the actuator rod into the switch and assemble the switch to the column.
16. The neutral start switch is adjusted with the shift lever in the drive position.

Tilt Column

1. Remove column mounting bracket from column.

NOTE: be careful not to damage the "breakaway" capsules.

2. Remove steering wheel using proper puller.
3. Remove turn signal wire protector (lower column).
4. Remove three column cover screws and cover.
5. Remove tilt release lever, turn signal switch lever, push four-way flasher knob in and remove knob, and remove upper shift lever.
6. Depress lock plate and remove the snap-ring; remove lock plate.
7. Remove cancelling cam and spring.
8. Remove three turn signal switch screws, tape wires to wire connector at upper end and place shift bowl in Low. Pull switch straight up and out.
9. Insert a small screwdriver into the slot next to the turn signal switch mounting screw boss (right-hand slot), depress spring latch and remove key lock.
10. If ignition switch is to be replaced, remove buzzer switch straight out, depressing switch clip with pliers.
11. Remove three housing cover screws and cover.

Removing the buzzer switch on a tilt steering column (© Buick Div., G.M. Corp)

12. Install tilt release lever and place column in full UP position.
13. Place screwdriver in slot of tilt spring retainer, press in about 3/16 in. and turn counterclockwise. Remove spring and guide.

NOTE: spring is very strong—be careful.

14. Place column in neutral position, push in on upper steering shaft, remove inner race seat and race.
15. Remove upper flange pinch bolt, place ignition switch in accessory position, remove two switch mounting screws and switch.

NOTE: neutral start switch can be removed at this time, if necessary.

16. Assembly is the reverse of the above. However, note the following steps before proceeding with the reassembly.
17. To install the steering lock, hold the lock cylinder sleeve and rotate the knob clockwise against the stop. Insert the cylinder into the cover bore with the key on the cylinder sleeve aligned with the keyway in the housing. Then push the cylinder in until it bottoms. Maintaining a light inward pressure, rotate the knob counterclockwise until the drive section of the cylinder mates with the drive shaft. Push in until the snap ring pops into the groove and the lock cylinder is secured in the cover. Check for free rotation.
18. When installing the ignition switch, be sure the lock cylinder is in the lock position. Put the shift bowl or shroud in the park position. Make sure the ignition switch is in the lock position. Then insert the actuator rod into the switch and assemble the switch to the column.
19. The neutral start switch is adjusted with the shift lever in the drive position.

Light Switch

Replacement

1. Disconnect battery.
2. Pull switch knob to last notch and depress spring loaded latch button on top of switch, while pulling knob and rod out of switch.
3. Remove escutcheon and retaining nut. Remove switch from cluster.

NOTE: remove left trim plate on 1971 and later models.

4. Disconnect multiple connector.
5. Install in reverse of above.

WINDSHIELD WIPERS

Motor R & R

Through 1970

1. Disconnect wire connectors from motor and pump.
2. Remove washer hoses from the pump.
3. Remove left side air intake grille.
4. Remove spring retainer clip from wiper motor shaft lever.
5. Lift transmission drive links off motor shaft lever.
6. Remove motor attaching bolts, then lift out motor.
7. Install by reversing the above procedure.

1971-76

1. Raise the hood and remove the cowl screen.
2. Loosen the transmission drive link-to-crankarm attaching nuts through the cowl screen opening.
3. Remove the transmission drive link(s) from the motor crank arm.
4. Disconnect the wiring and washer hoses.
5. Remove the motor attaching screws.
6. Remove the motor while guiding the crank arm through the hole.

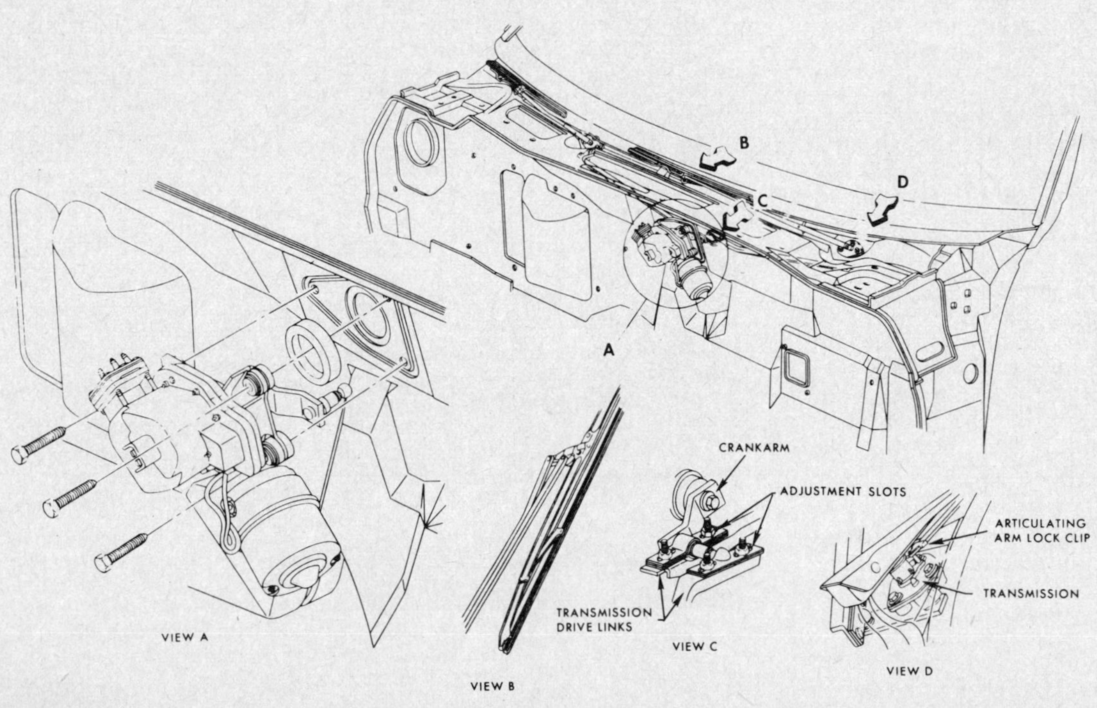

Windshield wiper system—1971 and later (© Buick Div., G.M. Corp)

7. Install the wiper motor in the reverse order of removal. The motor must be in the Park position when assembling the crank arm to the transmission drive link(s).

Wiper Transmission (Linkage) R & R

1. Remove the wiper blade and arm, shaft and escutcheon retaining nuts and the escutcheon from the transmission shaft.
2. Remove air intake grille.
3. Remove spring retainer clip from wiper motor shaft. Lift drive links off motor shaft.

NOTE: on 1971 and later models, loosen attaching nuts and slip drive link off crank arm.

4. Remove the transmission retaining screws.
5. Slide transmission and drive link toward opposite side of car. Lift transmission up at opening and remove.
6. Install by reversing the above procedure.

RADIO

Always disconnect the battery ground cable before working on any part of the instrument panel.

Removal and Installation

1969-70 Riviera

1. Remove ash tray assembly.
2. Remove knobs, escutcheons, and hex nuts.
3. Unplug antenna and wiring leads.
4. Remove radio downward.
5. Install by reversing procedure.

1969-70 Except Riviera

1. Remove center air-conditioning duct.
2. Remove right instrument trim panel and screw in bottom of radio.
3. Remove radio knobs, escutcheons, and two hex nuts.
4. Unplug antenna and wiring leads.
5. Remove radio downward.
6. Install by reversing procedure.

1971-76 All Models

1. Remove knobs and escutcheons from radio. If equipped with Trip-Set and/or Speed-Alert, remove cone-shaped knobs.
2. Remove face plate by pulling outward. *Disconnect Seelight before completely removing face plate, if equipped with Trip-Set/Speed-Alert.*
3. Remove the two hex nuts from the control shafts.
4. Remove ash tray and frame.
5. Disconnect the two connectors behind dash and unplug antenna.
6. Unscrew the support bracket nuts and remove radio to the rear and downwards.
7. Install by reversing removal procedure.

1974 and later with A.C.R.S. (Air Bags)

1. Turn the ignition lock to the LOCK position.
2. Disconnect the battery ground cable and tape its end thoroughly to prevent any possibility of a circuit.
3. Remove both lower instrument panel cover trim plates after prying them out.
4. Disconnect the parking brake release cable and remove the lower left instrument panel cover assembly by removing the 8 retaining screws.
5. Remove:
   a. 2 horizontal screws below the instrument panel
   b. 4 vertical screws on the upper horizontal instrument panel surface.
   c. 2 screws from the outside of the glove box door hinge
   d. 1 screw from the right-side of the instrument panel cover.
6. Disconnect the radio, speakers, convector (remote unit) connectors, and antenna lead cable from the radio.
7. Release the 4 clips behind the instrument panel by grasping the tongue of the far right-side clip, squeezing, and pulling forward.
8. Remove the radio knobs and escutcheons from the shafts.
9. Carefully pull the trim plate off the instrument panel housing.
10. Remove the retaining nuts from the shafts.
11. Unscrew and remove the power antenna relay.
12. Loosen the nut on the left radio support. Remove the right support nut.
13. Lower the radio from beneath the instrument panel.
14. If the car has a radio/tape unit, remove the two convector (remote unit) mounting screws and remove the convector from the right-side of the instrument panel housing support.
15. Reverse all these steps on installation.

HEATER

NOTE: On procedures which call for removal of fender in order to gain access to the blower motor, it is possible to cut a trap door in the inner fender panel to gain access to the blower motor. Using a torch or sheet metal cutter, cut the door on three sides and bend it out of the way. Remove and install the motor. Bend the trap door back and weld it in place. Then, spray the welds and door with undercoating.

Blower and Heater Core Assembly R & R w/o A/C

1969-70 Riviera

1. Remove the right front fender.
2. Disconnect the vacuum hoses.
3. Disconnect the wire that is attached to the motor and remove the connector from the blower resistor. If just the blower motor is to be replaced, remove the blower motor attaching screws and the blower.
4. Disconnect the control wire attached to the temperature door lever.
5. Drain the coolant and remove the heater hoses at the firewall.
6. Remove the 12 screws securing the blower and heater assembly to the firewall and remove the assembly.
7. Reverse the above steps to install.

Blower Only R & R w/o A/C

All Models Except Riviera through 1970

1. Remove the right front fender.
2. Disconnect the blower motor wire.
3. Remove the blower motor attaching screws and remove the motor.
4. Reverse the above steps to install.

1971-76 All Models

1. Support the hood and loosen the hood hinge from the extension and plate assembly.
2. Remove the extension and plate assembly.

NOTE: Steps 1 and 2 are not necessary on the 1974-76 Riviera.

3. Disconnect the blower motor wire.
4. Remove the blower motor attaching screws and the motor.

Heater Core R & R w/o A/C

1969-76 All Models Except 1969-70 Riviera

1. Drain the radiator and disconnect the heater inlet and outlet hoses at the dash.
2. Disconnect the control wires from the defroster door and vacuum hose diverter door actuator diaphragm and control cable from the temperature door lever.
3. Remove the nuts securing the heater assembly to the dash.
4. Remove the screw securing the defroster outlet tab to the heater assembly.

5. Remove the heater from the car.
6. Reverse the above steps to install.

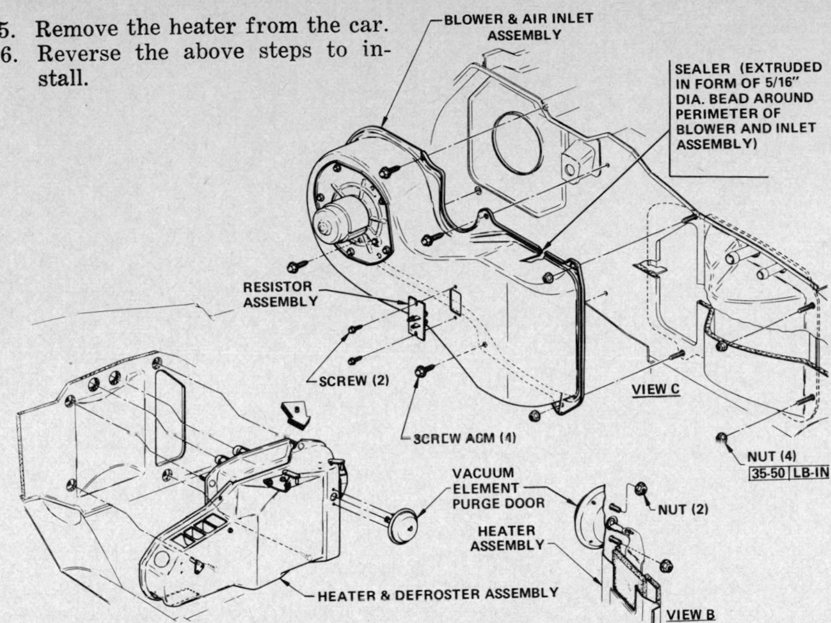

Heater blower removal—beginning 1971 (© Buick Div., G.M. Corp)

Blower Motor R & R with A/C

1969-70 Riviera

1. Remove the right front fender inner panel.
2. Remove the motor wires.
3. Remove the five blower motor securing screws and remove the motor.
4. Reverse the above steps to install.

1969-70 All Models Except Riviera

1. Remove the blower motor wires.
2. Remove the five blower motor securing screws and remove the motor.
3. Reverse the above steps to install.

1971-76 All Models Including Riviera

1. Support the hood and loosen the hood hinge from the extension and plate assembly.
2. Remove the extension and plate assembly.

NOTE: Steps 1 and 2 are not necessary on the 1974-76 models.

3. Disconnect the blower motor wires.
4. Remove the blower motor securing screws and remove the motor.

Heater Core R & R with A/C

1969-70 Riviera

1. Drain the radiator and disconnect the heater hoses from the heater core.
2. Disconnect the temperature door control cable and blower wires.
3. Remove the six screws securing the air conditioner assembly to the firewall and remove the assembly.
4. Reverse the above steps to install.

1969-70 All Models except Riviera

1. Drain the radiator and disconnect the hoses from the heater core.
2. Remove the instrument panel cover with the center A/C outlet and right A/C outlet with hose attached.
3. Remove the center A/C duct, A/C distributor duct and defroster outlet manifold assembly.
4. Disconnect the defroster and temperature control wires and the pink hose from the mode door diaphragm.
5. Remove the seven screws from the inside and the two screws from the engine compartment and remove the core assembly.

1971-76 All Models Including Riviera

1. Drain the radiator and disconnect the hoses from the core.
2. Disconnect the wires from the defroster door, diverter door and temperature door.
3. Remove the four nuts securing the core assembly to the dash.
4. Remove the screw securing the defroster outlet tab to the heater assembly.
5. Remove the core assembly.
6. Reverse the above steps to install.

SEAT BELTS

Buzzer System—1973

The front seat belt warning system consists of a switch in each belt retractor, a sensor switch in the seat cushion on the passenger side, a reminder light, and a warning buzzer. The circuit wiring is routed through the ignition switch and the parking brake warning switch on manual transmission models, or through the ignition switch and the transmission switch on models equipped with automatic transmissions.

With the ignition switch on and the parking brake released (manual transmission), or with the selector in a forward position on automatic transmission models, the warning circuit (light and buzzer) is closed (activated) until the driver's seat belt is extended to open (deactivate) the circuit. The seat sensor on the passenger side will react to weights in excess of 0-47 lbs on the seat cushion and close the warning circuit. Extending the passenger belt will open the circuit.

Seat Belt/Starter Interlock System—1974-75

The seat belt/starter interlock system makes it necessary for outboard front seat occupants to fasten their seat belts before the engine can be started. Employing seat weight sensors similar to 1973 models, the new system does not require a passenger occupying the middle portion of the front seat to buckle up, but failure to do so will cause the seat belt alarm buzzer to sound.

When an outboard front seat is occupied, a sensor under the seat signals an electronic relay module which then requires verification from a switch in the buckle, indicating the belt has been fastened, before completing the starting circuit. An override by-pass switch under the hood, which is activated with the ignition key in the ON position, permits starting in the event of system malfunction.

Disabling the Seat Belt/Starter Interlock and Buzzer System

It is legal to disconnect the seat belt interlock and buzzer system, but not the seat belt warning light. Disconnect the system as follows:

NOTE: If the vehicle is not equipped with a starter interlock, proceed to Step 4 to disconnect the buzzer only.

1. Disconnect the negative battery cable.
2. Locate the interlock wiring harness under the left side of the instrument panel on or near the fuse block. The connector has orange, yellow and green wires.
3. Cut and tape the ends of the green wire on the body side of the harness.
4. Disconnect the seat belt warning

buzzer from the installed position under the left side of the instrument panel by removing the buzzer from the fuse block or connector and removing the two yellow wires with black tracers from the multiple connector into which the buzzer is plugged. Tape the terminal and reinstall the buzzer.

5. Connect the battery ground cable.

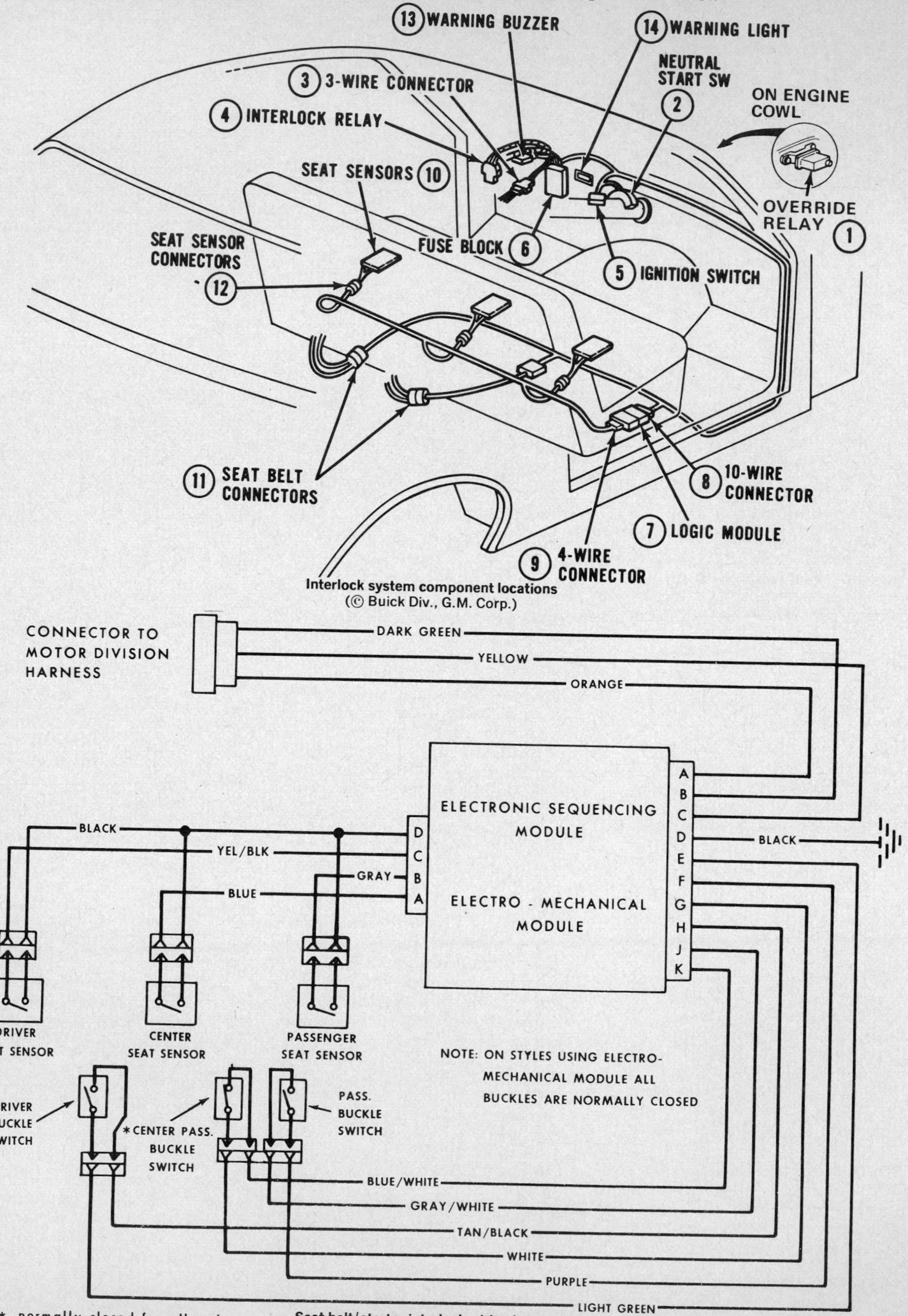

Interlock system component locations (© Buick Div., G.M. Corp.)

Seat belt/starter interlock wiring harness schematic for all GM cars (© G.M. Corp)

INDEX

Buick Apollo · Century · Gran Sport · Regal · Skyhawk · Skylark · Special

YEAR IDENTIFICATION

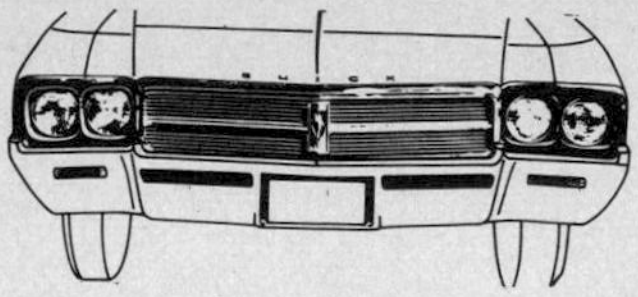

1969 Special

1969 G.S. 400

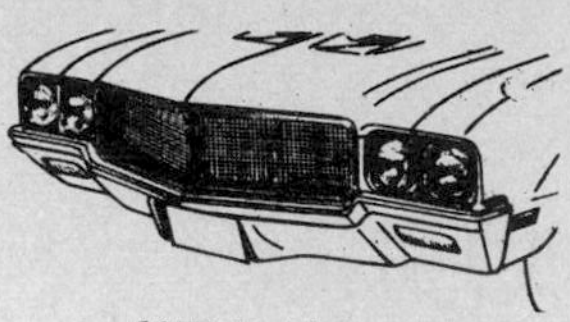

1970 Buick Special

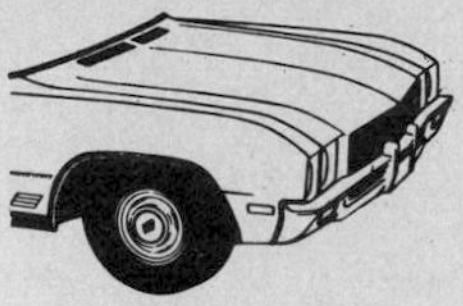

1971 Skylark

1971 G.S.

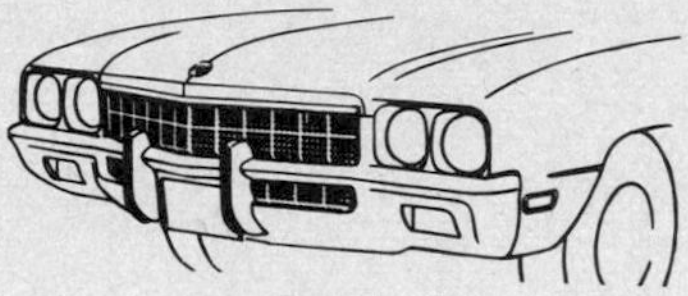

1972 Skylark

1972 Buick Gran Sport

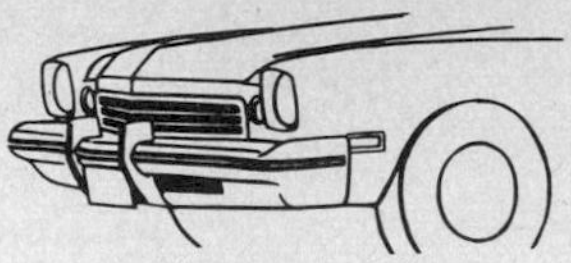

1973 Buick Century

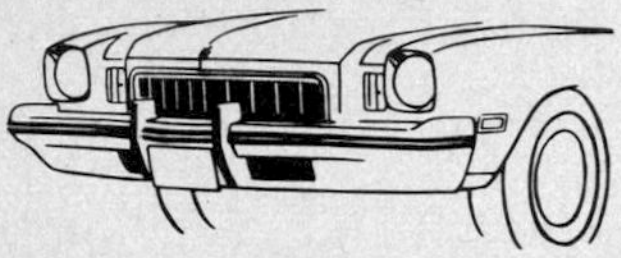

1973 Buick Regal

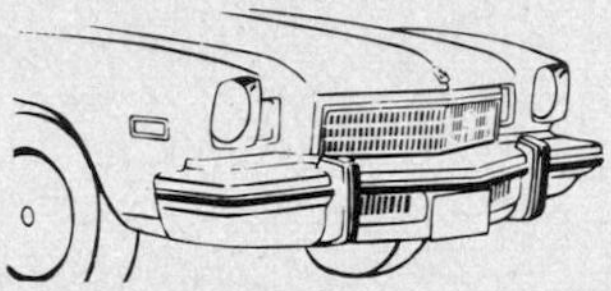

1974 Buick Regal

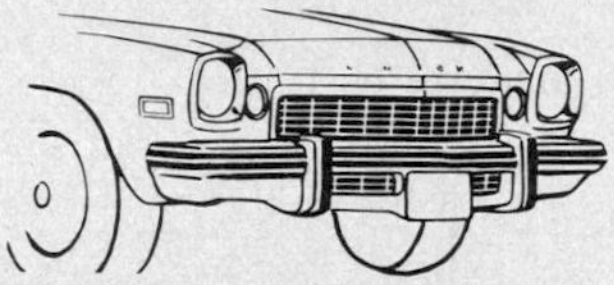

1974 Buick Century

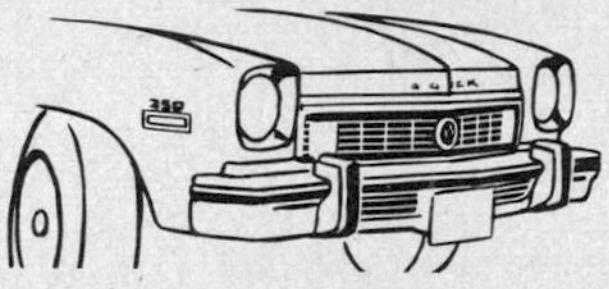

1974 Apollo

1975 Century

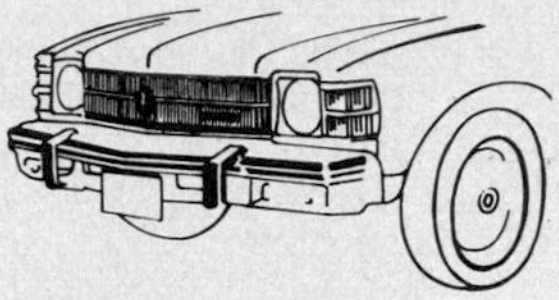

1975 Skylark, Apollo

1975 Skyhawk

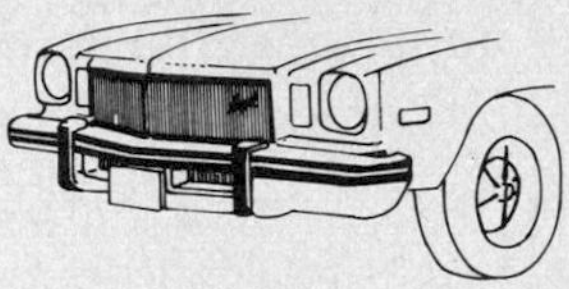

1975 Regal

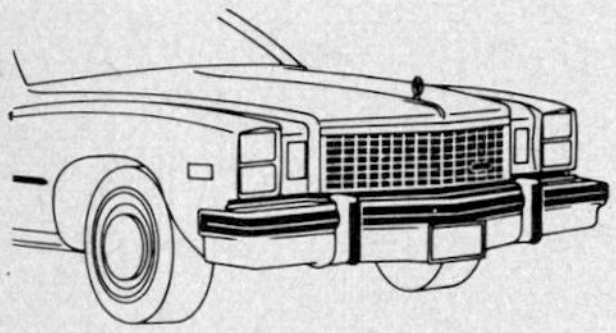

1976 Century

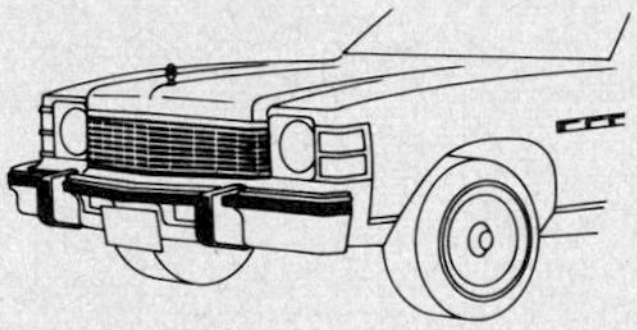

1976 Skylark, Apollo

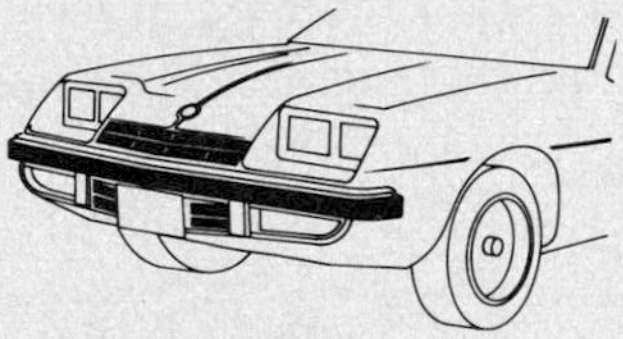

1976 Skyhawk

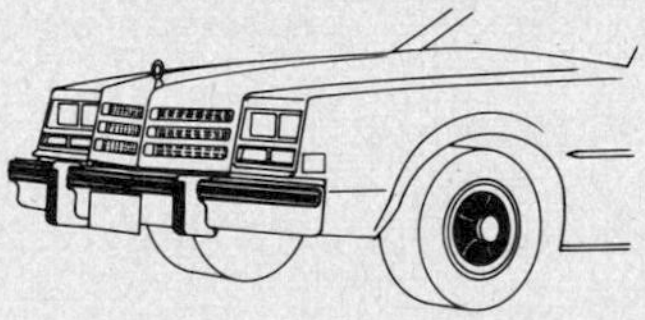

1976 Century Special

FIRING ORDER

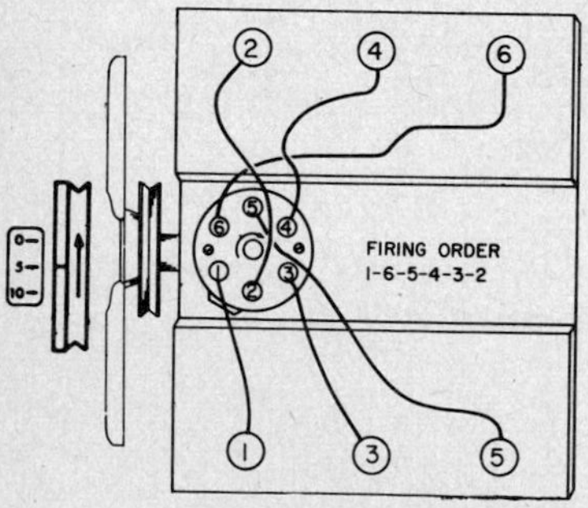

FIRING ORDER
1-6-5-4-3-2

V6 engine

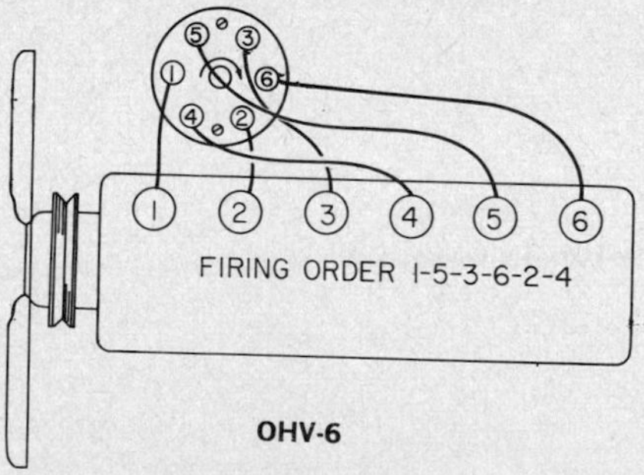

FIRING ORDER 1-5-3-6-2-4

OHV-6

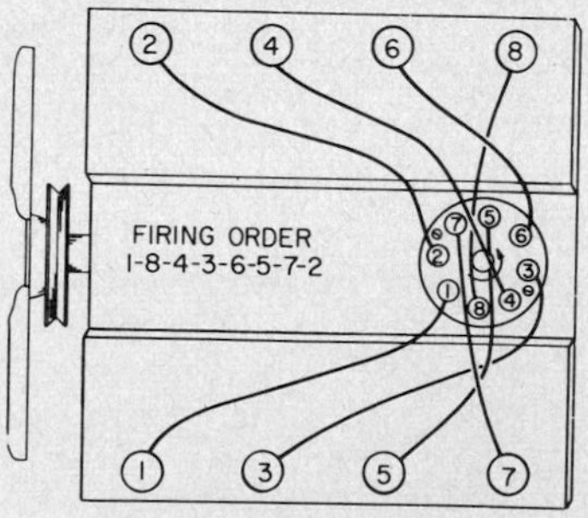

FIRING ORDER
1-8-4-3-6-5-7-2

260 V8

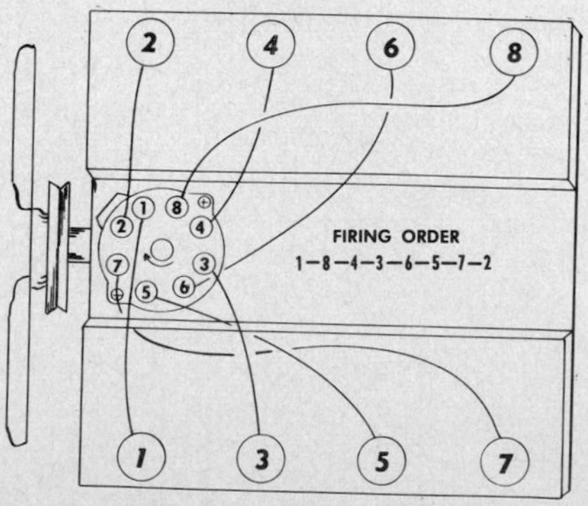

FIRING ORDER
1—8—4—3—6—5—7—2

350, 400, 455 cu in.

CAR SERIAL NUMBER LOCATION AND ENGINE IDENTIFICATION

The car serial number is used for registrations and other legal records. This number is unique to the individual car. The production code number identifies the type of engine and its production date. The Engine Identification Code chart can be used to determine the type of engine installed in the vehicle. The engine serial number also appears on the vehicle identification plate following model and series identification. The engine serial and car serial numbers are the same.

1969

The serial number identification plate is attached to the top of the instrument panel on the left side and can be seen through the windshield.

On the 250 cu. in. OHV6 engine, the engine number and the production code number are on the right side, rearward of the distributor.

On the 350 cu. in. V8 engine, the engine number is on the front of the left bank of cylinders. The production code number is between the left exhaust manifold and the two front spark plugs.

On the 400 cu. in. engine, the production code number is between the two rear spark plugs and the left exhaust manifold. The engine number is between the two front plugs and the left exhaust manifold.

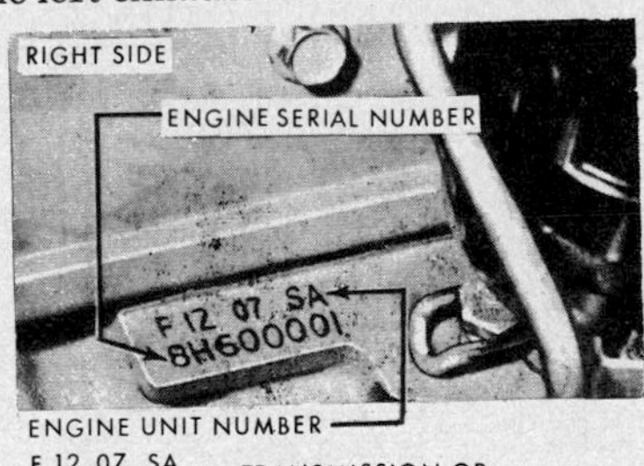

Serial number and production code location (OHV 6)
(© Buick Div., G.M. Corp)

1970-71

The serial number identification plate is attached to the top left of the instrument panel. It can be seen through the windshield.

On the 250 cu. in. OHV6 engine, the engine number and production code number are on the right side, to the rear of the distributor.

On the 350 cu. in. V8 engine, the engine number is on the front of the left bank of cylinders. The production code number is between the left exhaust manifold and the two front spark plugs.

ENGINE PRODUCTION CODE

Disp	Bbl	Hp	'69	'70	'71	'72	'73	'74	'75	'76
6-Cylinder Models										
231	2	110							AD	
250	1	145			ZB ZG					
250	1	155	LA LE MA ME	SA SB						
250	1	100 (net)						CCR, CCW, CCK, CCX		
8-Cylinder Models										
350	2	145							AB	
350	4	165							AM	
350	2	150, 165# (net)					XC	XC		
350	2	155 (net)				WC				
350	4	175, 190# (net)					XB	XB		
350	4	180, 195# (net)				WB				
350	2	230	RO		TC TO					
350	2	260		SO						
350	4	260			TB TD					
350	4	280	RP							
350	4	285		SB						
350	4	315		SP						
400	4	340	RR							
455	2	190 (net)						—		
455	4	225 (net)				WF WA	XF	XF		
Stage 1										
455	4	255 (net)						XS		
455	4	270 (net)				WS	XS			
Stage 1										
455	4	315			TR					
455	4	345			TS					
Stage 1										
455	4	450		SR						
455	4	360		SS						
Stage 1										

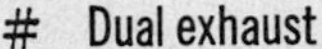

Dual exhaust

Serial number and production code location (400 and 455 cu in. through 1971)

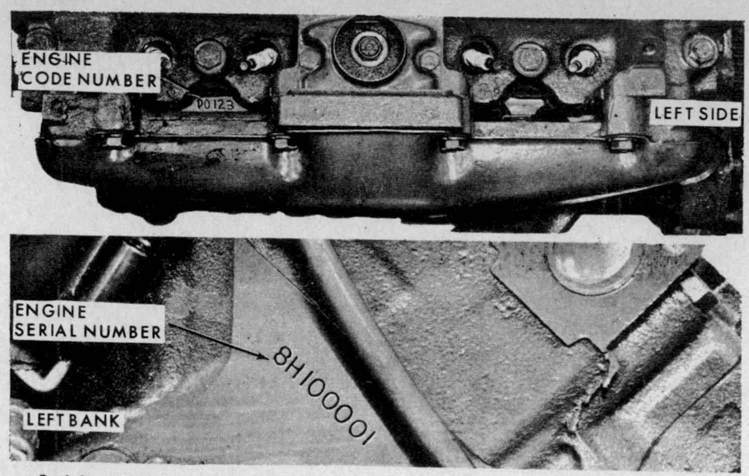

Serial number and production code number location (350 cu in. through 1971)
(© Buick Div., G.M. Corp)

On the 455 cu. in. engine, the production code number is between the two rear spark plugs and the left exhaust manifold. The engine number is between the two front spark plugs and the exhaust manifold.

1972-76

The car serial number identification plate is attached to the top of the instrument panel on the left-side.

On the 250 cu in. six-cylinder engine, the engine number and production code number are on the right-side, to the rear of the distributor.

On the V6 engine, the production code number is between the front and middle branches of the right exhaust manifold. The engine serial number is just below the front of the left cylinder head.

On the 260 cu in. engine, the engine serial and production code is on the oil filler tube on the front of the engine.

On the 350 cu in. engine, the engine serial number is on the front of the right cylinder bank. The production code number is between the left exhaust manifold and the two front spark plugs.

On the 455 cu in. engine, the engine serial number is on the front of the right cylinder bank. The production code number is between the left exhaust manifold and the two rear spark plugs.

On most 1975 and later engines, the production code can be found with the serial number.

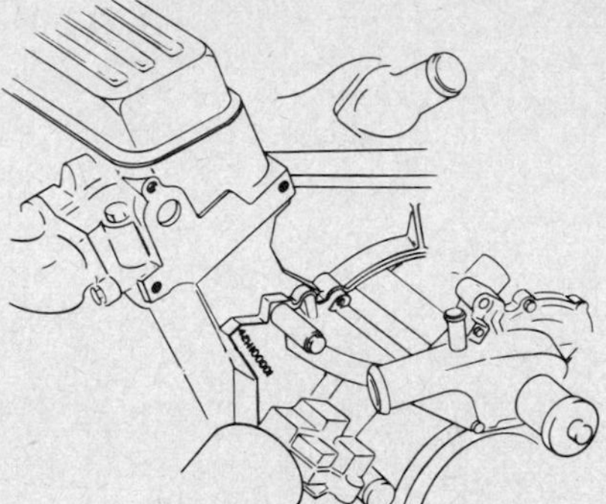

Engine serial number location for all V8s except 260 beginning 1972
(© Buick Div., G.M. Corp)

GENERAL ENGINE SPECIFICATIONS

Year	Engine Displacement (Cu. In.)	Carburetor Type	Horsepower @ rpm ■	Torque @ rpm (ft lbs) ■	Bore and Stroke (in.)	Compression Ratio	Oil Pressure @ 2400 rpm
'69	6-250	1 bbl	155 @ 4200	235 @ 1600	3.875 x 3.530	8.5:1	37①
	8-350	2 bbl	230 @ 4400	350 @ 2400	3.800 x 3.500	9.0:1	37
	8-350	4 bbl	280 @ 4600	375 @ 3200	3.800 x 3.850	10.25:1	37
	8-400	4 bbl	340 @ 5000	440 @ 3200	4.040 x 3.900	10.25:1	40
'70	6-250	1 bbl	155 @ 4200	235 @ 1600	3.875 x 3.530	8.5:1	37①
	8-350	2 bbl	260 @ 4600	360 @ 2600	3.800 x 3.850	9.0:1	37
	8-350	4 bbl	285 @ 4600	375 @ 3000	3.800 x 3.850	9.0:1	37
	8-350	4 bbl	315 @ 4800	410 @ 3200	3.800 x 3.850	10.25:1	37
	8-455	4 bbl	350 @ 4600	510 @ 2600	4.3125 x 3.900	10.0:1	40
	8-455 Stage 1	4 bbl	360 @ 4600	510 @ 2600	4.3125 x 3.900	10.5:1	40
'71	6-250	1 bbl	145 @ 4000	235 @ 2400	3.875 x 3.530	8.5:1	37①
	8-350	2 bbl	230 @ 4400	350 @ 2400	3.800 x 3.850	8.5:1	37
	8-350	4 bbl	260 @ 4600	360 @ 3000	3.800 x 3.850	8.5:1	37
	8-455	4 bbl	315 @ 4400	450 @ 2800	4.3125 x 3.900	8.5:1	40
	8-455 Stage 1	4 bbl	345 @ 5000	460 @ 3000	4.3125 x 3.900	8.5:1	40
'72	8-350	2 bbl	155 @ 3800②	270 @ 2400③	3.800 x 3.850	8.5:1	37④
	8-350	4 bbl	180 @ 3800⑤	275 @ 2400	3.800 x 3.850	8.5:1	37④
	8-350⑥	4 bbl	195 @ 4000⑦	290 @ 2800⑧	3.800 x 3.850	8.5:1	37④
	8-455	4 bbl	225 @ 4000	360 @ 2600	4.3125 x 3.900	8.5:1	40
	8-455 Stage 1	4 bbl	270 @ 4400	390 @ 3000	4.3125 x 3.900	8.5:1	40

GENERAL ENGINE SPECIFICATIONS

Year	Engine Displacement (Cu. In.)	Carburetor Type	Horsepower @ rpm ■	Torque @ rpm (ft lbs) ■	Bore and Stroke (in.)	Compression Ratio	Oil Pressure @ 2400 rpm
'73	8-350	2 bbl	150 @ 3800	265 @ 2400	3.800 x 3.850	8.5:1	37
	8-350	4 bbl	175 @ 3800	270 @ 2400	3.800 x 3.850	8.5:1	37
	8-350	4 bbl	190 @ 4000	285 @ 2800	3.800 x 3.850	8.5:1	37
	8-455	4 bbl	225 @ 4000	360 @ 2600	4.3125 x 3.900	8.5:1	37
	8-455	4 bbl	270 @ 4400	390 @ 3000	4.3125 x 3.900	8.5:1	37
'74	6-250	1 bbl	100 @ 3600	175 @ 1600	3.875 x 3.530	8.3:1	40⑨
	8-350	2 bbl	150 @ 3600	270 @ 2000	3.800 x 3.850	8.5:1	37
	8-350	4 bbl	175 @ 3800	260 @ 2000	3.800 x 3.850	8.5:1	37
	8-455 DE	2 bbl	190 @ 3600	370 @ 2000	4.3125 x 3.900	8.5:1	40
	8-455 DE	4 bbl	230 @ 3300	355 @ 2200	4.3125 x 3.900	8.5:1	40
	8-455 DE⑧	4 bbl	255 @ 4400	370 @ 2800	4.3125 x 3.900	8.5:1	40
'75-'76	V6-231	2 bbl	110 @ 4000	175 @ 2000	3.800 x 3.400	8.0:1	37
	6-250	1 bbl	105 @ 3800	185 @ 1200	3.875 x 3.530	8.25:1	36-41⑨
	8-260	2 bbl	110 @ 3400	210 @ 1600	3.550 x 3.385	8.5:1	30-45
	8-350	2 bbl	145 @ 3200	270 @ 2000	3.800 x 3.850	8.1:1	37
	8-350	4 bbl	165 @ 3800	260 @ 2200	3.800 x 3.850	8.0:1	37

■ Beginning 1972, horsepower and torque are SAE net figures. They are measured at the rear of the transmission with all accessories installed and operating. Since the figures vary when a given engine is installed in different models, some are representative rather than exact.

① Oil pressure at 1500 rpm

② For California vehicles, advertised horsepower is 150 @ 3800 rpm

③ For California vehicles, advertised torque is 265 @ 2400 rpm

④ Oil pressure at 2600 rpm

⑤ For California vehicles, advertised torque is 285 @ 2800 rpm

⑥ Dual exhaust

⑦ For California vehicles, advertised horsepower is 190 @ 4000 rpm

⑧ Stage I Gran Sport

⑨ Oil pressure at 2000 rpm

DE Dual exhaust

TUNE-UP SPECIFICATIONS

When analyzing compression test results, look for uniformity among cylinders rather than specific pressures.

	ENGINE		SPARK PLUGS		DISTRIBUTOR		IGNITION TIMING (deg) ▲		VALVES	Fuel	IDLE SPEED (rpm) ▲	
Year	No. Cyl Displacement (cu in.)	hp	Type	Gap (in.)	Point Dwell (deg)	Point Gap (in.)	Man Trans •	Auto Trans	Intake Opens ■ (deg) •	Pump Pressure (psi)	Man Trans	Auto Trans
'69	6-250	155	R-46N	.035	32½	.019	TDC	4B	62	4-5	700/400	500/400
	8-350	230	R-45TS	.030	30	.016	TDC	TDC	24	4¼-5¾	700	600
	8-350	280	R-45TS	.030	30	.016	TDC	TDC	24	4¼-5¾	700	600
	8-400	340	R-44TS	.030	30	.016	TDC	2½B	14	4¼-5¾	700	600
'70	6-250	155	R-46T	.035	32½	.019	TDC	4B	16	4-5	750/400	600/400
	8-350	260	R-45TS	.030	30	.016	6B	6B	24	4¼-5¾	700	600
	8-350	285	R-45TS	.030	30	.016	6B	6B	24	4¼-5¾	700	600
	8-350	315	R-45TS	.030	30	.016	6B	6B	24	4¼-5¾	700	600
	8-455	350	R-44TS	.030	30	.016	6B	6B	18	4¼-5¾	700	600
	8-455 Stage 1	360	R-44TS	.030	30	.016	10B	10B	18	4¼-5¾	700	600
'71	6-250	145	R-46T	.035	32½	.019	4B	4B	16	4-5	550	600
	8-350	230	R-45TS	.030	30	.016	6B	10B	24	4¼-5¾	800	600
	8-350	260	R-45TS	.030	30	.016	6B	6B	28	4¼-5¾	800	600
	8-455	315	R-45TS	.030	30	.016	6B	6B	12	4¼-5¾	700	600
	8-455 Stage 1	270	R-45TS	.030	30	.016	10B	10B	28	4¼-5¾	700	600
'72	8-350	155	R-45TS	.040	30	.016	4B	4B	24	4¼-5¾	800/600	650/500
	8-350	180	R-45TS	.040	30	.016	4B	4B	24	4¼-5¾	800/600	650/500
	8-350	195	R-45TS	.040	30	.016	4B	4B	24	4¼-5¾	800/600	650/500
	8-455	225	R-45TS	.040	30	.016	4B	4B	24(14)	4¼-5¾	900/600	650/500
	8-455 Stage 1	360	R-45TS	.040	30	.016	8B	10B	24(14)	4¼-5¾	900/600	650/500

TUNE-UP SPECIFICATIONS

When analyzing compression test results, look for uniformity among cylinders rather than specific pressures.

Year	ENGINE No. Cyl Displacement (cu in.)	ENGINE hp	SPARK PLUGS Type	SPARK PLUGS Gap (in.)	DISTRIBUTOR Point Dwell (deg)	DISTRIBUTOR Point Gap (in.)	IGNITION TIMING (deg) ▲ Man Trans	IGNITION TIMING (deg) ▲ Auto Trans	VALVES Intake Opens ■ (deg) ●	Fuel Pump Pressure (psi)	IDLE SPEED③ (rpm) ▲ Man Trans	IDLE SPEED③ (rpm) ▲ Auto Trans
'73	8-350	150	R-45TS	.040	30	.016	4B	4B	24	4¼-5¾	800/600	650/500
	8-350	175	R-45TS	.040	30	.016	4B	4B	24	4¼-5¾	800/600	650/500
	8-350	190	R-45TS	.040	30	.016	4B	4B	24	4¼-5¾	800/600	650/500
	8-455	225	R-45TS	.040	30	.016	4B	4B	24	4¼-5¾	900/600	650/500
	8-455 Stage 1	270	R-45TS	.040	30	.016	8B	10B	24	4¼-5¾	900/600	650/500
'74	6-250	All	R-46T	.035	32½	.019	8B	6B	16④	4-5	950/450	600/450
	8-350	All	R-45TS	.040	30	.016	—	4B	19(25)④	4¼-5¾	—	650/500
	8-455	All	R-45TS	.040	30	.016	—	4B	10④	4¼-5¾	—	650/500
	8-455 Stage 1	255	R-45TS	.040	30	.016	—	10B	10④	4¼-5¾	—	650/500
'75	V6-231	175	R-44SX	.060	Electronic		12B	12B	17	3-4½⑤	800/600③	700
	6-250	100	R-46TX	.060	Electronic		10B	10B	14	4-5	850	550
	8-260	110	R-465X	.060	Electronic		—	18B(14B)	22	4¼-5¾	—	650
	8-350	All	R-45TSX	.060	Electronic		12B	12B	19	4¼-5¾	—	600
'76	V6-231	110	R-44SX	.060	Electronic		12B	12B	17	3-4½⑤	600/800	600
	8-260	110	R-46SX	.080	Electronic		—	18B(14) @ 1100	22	4¼-5¾	—	550/650 (600/650⑥)
	8-350	All	R-45TSX	.060	Electronic		—	12B	19	4¼-5¾	—	600

▲ See text for procedure
● Figure in parentheses indicates California engine
■ All figures Before Top Dead Center
① Not used
② A/C on
③ Lower figure indicates idle speed with solenoid disconnected
④ These figures do not represent a change from 1973; however, the reference point is changed (from .004 inch valve lift to .004 inch cam lift) to be consistent with information required for Government certification.
⑤ 4¼-5¾ on mechanical pumps
⑥ Air conditioning on, compressor clutch wires disconnected

CAPACITIES

Year	ENGINE No. Cyl. Displacement (cu. in.)	Engine Crankcase Add 1 Qt For New Filter	TRANSMISSION Pts To Refill After Draining Manual 3-Speed	TRANSMISSION Manual 4-Speed	TRANSMISSION Automatic ●	Drive Axle (pts)	Gasoline Tank (gals)	COOLING SYSTEM (qts) With Heater	COOLING SYSTEM (qts) With A/C
'69	6-250	4	3.4	—	5	3	20	11.3	13
	8-350	4	3.4	—	5	3	20	13.5	13.5
	8-350GS	4	3.4	3	6	3	20	13.5	13.5
	8-400GS	4	3.5	3	7	3	20	16.2	16.7
'70	6-250	4	3.4	—	6	3	20	16	16
	8-350	4	3.4	—	6	3	20①	16.5	16.5
	8-350GS	4	3.5	3	7	3	20	16.5	16.5
	8-455	4	3.5	3	7	4.25	20	19.2	19.7
'71	6-250	4	3.4	—	6	4.25	20	16	16
	8-350	4	3.4	—	6	4.25	20①	16.5	16.5
	8-350GS	4	3.4	3	6	4.25	20	16.5	16.5
	8-455	4	—	3	7	5.5	20	19.2	19.7
'72	8-350	4	3.4	—	6	4.25	20①	16.5	16.9
	8-350GS	4	3.4	3	6	4.25	20	16.2	16.6
	8-455	4	—	3	7	5.5	20	19.2	19.7
'73	8-350	4	3.4	—	6	4.25	22	16.5	16.9
	8-350GS	4	3.4	3.4	6	4.25	22	16.5	16.9
	8-455	4	—	3.4	6	4.25	22	16.2	16.6
'74	6-250	4	3.5	—	6	4.25	21	14.0	②
	8-350 Apollo	4	—	—	6	4.25	21	18.9	19.3
	8-350	4	—	—	6	4.25	22	16.5	16.9
	8-455	4	—	—	6	4.25	22	16.2	16.6

CAPACITIES

Year	ENGINE No. Cyl. Displacement (cu. in.)	Engine Crankcase Add 1 Qt For New Filter	TRANSMISSION Pts To Refill After Draining Manual 3-Speed	4-Speed	Automatic •	Drive Axle (pts)	Gasoline Tank (gals)	COOLING SYSTEM (qts) With Heater	With A/C
'75-'76	V6-231, Skyhawk	4	—	3.5	6	2.8	18.5	13.35	14.19
	V6-231, Skylark	4	3.5	—	6	4.25	21	17.09	17.0
	V6-231, Other	4	3.5	—	6	4.25	22	15.35	15.32
	6-250	4	3.5	—	6	4.25	21	16.92	17.0
	8-260	4	—	—	6	4.25	21	18.9	19.3
	8-350, Apollo/Skylark	4	—	—	6	4.25	21	18.9	19.3
	8-350, Other	4	—	—	6	4.25	22	16.88	17.16

• Specifications do not include torque converter
① Sportwagon—23 gals
② Optional—16 qts

GS Gran Sport
— Not applicable

TORQUE SPECIFICATIONS

All readings in ft lbs

Year	Engine No. Cyl. Displacement (cu in.)	Cylinder Head Bolts	Rod Bearing Bolts	Main Bearing Bolts	Crankshaft Pulley or Balancer Bolts	Flywheel to Crankshaft Bolts	MANIFOLD Intake	Exhaust
'69	6-250	90-95	35-45	60-70	60	55-65	25-35	②
	8-350	65-70	30-35	50-55①	140-160	50-60	25-30	10-15
	8-400	100	45	110	200	50-60	55	18
'70-'76	6-250	95	35	60-70	60	55-65	35	②
	6-231	75	40	115	150③	55	45	25
	8-260	85	42	120	200③	60	40	25
	8-350	80	35④	115	140③	60	45	28
	8-455	100	45	115	200③	60	45	28

① Rear Main Bearing—65-75
② Center Bolts 25-30; End Bolts 15-20
③ Minimum
④ 40 with capscrews

CRANKSHAFT AND CONNECTING ROD SPECIFICATIONS

All measurements are given in inches

Year	Engine No. Cyl. Displacement (cu in.)	CRANKSHAFT Main Brg. Journal Dia	Main Brg. Oil Clearance	Shaft End-Play	Thrust on No.	CONNECTING ROD Journal Diameter	Oil Clearance	Side Clearance
'69	6-250	2.3004	.0003-.0029	.004	7	2.0000	.0007-.0027	.009-.013
	8-350	2.9995	.0004-.0015	.006	3	2.0000	.0002-.0023	.006-.014
	8-400	3.2500	.0007-.0018	.006	3	2.2500	.0002-.0023	.005-.012
'70-'74	6-250①	2.3004	.0003-.0029	.002-.006	7	2.0000	.0007-.0027	.009-.014
	8-350	2.9995③	.0004-.0015	.002-.006②	3	2.0000	.0002-.0023	.006-.020
	8-455	3.2500	.0007-.0018	.003-.009	3	2.2500	.0002-.0023	.005-.019
'75-'76	V6-231	2.4995	.0004-.0015	.004-.008	2	2.0000	.0002-.0023	.006-.014
	6-250	2.2999	.0003-.0029	.002-.006	7	2.0000	.0007-.0027	.007-.016
	8-260	2.4995	.0005-.0021	.004-.008	3	2.1240	.0005-.0026	.006-.020
	8-350	2.9995	.0004-.0015	.002-.006	3	2.0000	.0005-.0026	.006-.026

① 1970-71, '74
② 1972 and later, V8—350; .003-.009 in.
③ 3.0000 for 1974 and later

VALVE SPECIFICATIONS

Year	Engine No. Cyl. Displacement (cu in.)	Seat Angle (deg)	Face Angle (deg)	Spring Test Pressure (lbs @ in.)	Spring Installed Height (in.)	STEM TO GUIDE Clearance (in.) Intake	STEM TO GUIDE Clearance (in.) Exhaust	STEM Diameter (in.) Intake	STEM Diameter (in.) Exhaust
'69	6-250	46	45	186 @ 1.27	1 21/32	.0010-.0027	.0010-.0027	.3414	.3414
	8-350	45	45	180 @ 1.34	1 23/32	.0015-.0025	.0015-.0032	.3725	.372
	8-400	45	45	177 @ 1.45	1 29/32	.0015-.0035	.0015-.0032	.3725	.3727
'70	6-250	46	45	186 @ 1.27	1 21/32	.0010-.0027	.0010-.0027	.3414	.3414
	8-350	45	45	180 @ 1.34	1 23/32	.0015-.0025	.0015-.0032	.3725	.3727
	8-455	45	45	177 @ 1.45	1 29/32	.0015-.0035	.0015-.0032	.3725	.3727
'71	6-250	46	45	186 @ 1.27	1 21/32	.0010-.0027	.0010-.0027	.3414	.3414
	8-350	45	45	180 @ 1.34	1 23/32	.0015-.0035	.0015-.0032	.3725	.3727
	8-455	45	45	177 @ 1.45	1 29/32	.0015-.0035	.0015-.0032	.3725	.3727
'72	8-350	45	45	180 @ 1.34	1 23/32	.0015-.0035	.0015-.0032	.3725	.3727
	8-455	45	45	198 @ 1.45	1 29/32	.0015-.0035	.0015-.0032	.3725	.3727
'73	8-350	45	45	180 @ 1.34	1 23/32	.0015-.0035	.0015-.0032	.3720	.3730
	8-455	45	45	198 @ 1.45	1 29/32	.0015-.0035	.0015-.0032	.3725	.3727
'74	6-250	46	45	186 @ 1.27	1 21/32	.0010-.0027	.0010-.0027	.3413	.3413
	8-350	45	45	180 @ 1.34	1 29/32	00015-.0035	.0015-.0032	.3725	.3727
	8-455	45	45	178 @ 1.45	1 29/32	.0015-.0035	.0015-.0032	.3725	.3727
'75-'76	V6-231	45	45	164 @ 1.34②	1 47/64	.0015-.0035	.0015-.0032	.3407	.3407
	6-250	46	45	186 @ 1.27	1 21/32	.0010-.0027	.0010-.0020	.3413	.3413
	8-260	45④	46④	187 @ 1.27	—	.0010-.0027	.0015-.0032	.3428	.3424
	8-350	45	45	180 @ 1.34③	1 47/64	.0015-.0035	.0015-.0032	.3725	.3727

① Inner spring test pressure—76 @ 1.25
② Exhaust—182 @ 1.34
③ Exhaust—175 @ 1.34
④ Exhaust—59 seat, 60 face

RING GAP

All measurements are given in inches

Year	Engine No. Cyl. Displacement (cu. in.)	Top Compression	Bottom Compression
'69	6-250 8-350	.010-.020	.010-.020
'69	8-400	.013-.023	.013-.023
'70-'74	8-455	.013-.023	.013-.023
'71-'76	6-250	.010-.020	.010-.020
'71-'72	8-350	.013-.023	.013-.023
'73-'76	8-350	.010-.020	.010-.020
'75-'76	V6-231	.013-.023	.013-.023
'75-'76	8-260	.010-.023	.010-.023

Year	Engine No. Cyl. Displacement (cu. in.)	Oil Control
'69-'76	8-350	.015-.035
'69-'72	8-400, 455	.015-.055
'73-'74	8-455	.015-.035
'69-'71	6-250	.015-.025
'75-'76	6-250	.015-.055
'75-'76	V6-231	.015-.035
'75-'76	8-260	.015-.055

RING SIDE CLEARANCE

All measurements are given in inches

Year	Engine No. Cyl. Displacement (cu. in.)	Top Compression	Bottom Compression	Oil Control
'69-'72	8-350, 400, 455	.003-.005	.003-.005	.0035-.0095
'73-'76	8-350, 455	.003-.005	.003-.005	.0035 Max.
'69-'76	6-250	.0012-.0027	.0012-.0032	.0000-.0050
'75-'76	8-260	.002-.004	.002-.004	.001-.005

PISTON CLEARANCE

Year	Engine No. Cyl. Displacement (cu. in.)	Piston to Bore Clearance (in.)
'69	6-250	.0005-.0011
	8-350	.0008-.0014
	8-400	.0007-.0013
'70-'71	6-250	.0005-.0011
	8-350	.0008-.0020
	8-455	.0010-.0016
'72-'73	8-350	.0008-.0020
	8-455	.0010-.0016

Year	Engine No. Cyl. Displacement (cu. in.)	Piston to Bore Clearance (in.)
'74	6-250	.0005-.0015
	8-350	.0008-.0020
	8-455	.0010-.0016
'75-'76	V6-231	.0008-.0014
	6-250	.0005-.0015
	8-350	.0008-.0014
	8-260	.002-.004

ALTERNATOR AND REGULATOR SPECIFICATIONS

	ALTERNATOR			REGULATOR						
					Field Relay			Regulator		
Year	Part No.	Field Current @ 12 V	Output (amps)	Part No.	Air Gap (in.)	Point Gap (in.)	Volts to Close	Air Gap (in.)	Point Gap (in.)	Volts @ 75°
'69	1100761	2.2-2.6	37	1119515	.015	.030	2.3-3.7	.060	.014	13.6-14.4
	1100691	2.2-2.6	42	1119515	.015	.030	2.3-3.7	.060	.014	13.6-14.4
'70	1100761	2.2-2.6	37	1119515	.015	.030	2.3-3.7	.060	.014	13.6-14.4
	1100691	2.2-2.6	42	1119515	.015	.030	2.3-3.7	.060	.014	13.6-14.4
'71	1100905	2.2-2.6	37	1119515	.015	.030	1.5-3.2	.067	.014	13.5-14.4
	1100931	2.2-2.6	55	1119515	.015	.030	1.5-3.2	.067	.014	13.5-14.4
'72	1102449	2.2-2.6	37	1119515	.015	.030	1.5-3.2	.067	.014	13.5-14.5
	1102448	2.2-2.6	55	1119515	.015	.030	1.5-3.2	.067	.014	13.5-14.5
'73	1100947	4.0-4.5	37	Transistor type, integral with alternator, no adjustment						13.5-14.5
	1100926	4.0-4.5	42	Transistor type, integral with alternator, no adjustment						13.5-14.5
'74	1100947	4.0-4.5	37	Transistor type, integral with alternator, no adjustment						13.5-14.5
	1100926	4.0-4.5	42	Transistor type, integral with alternator, no adjustment						13.5-14.5
	1101018	4.0-4.5	80	Transistor type, integral with alternator, no adjustment						13.5-14.5
	1100497	4.0-4.5	37	Transistor type, integral with alternator, no adjustment						13.5-14.5
	1100947	4.0-4.5	37	Transistor type, integral with alternator, no adjustment						13.5-14.5
	1100946	4.0-4.5	55	Transistor type, integral with alternator, no adjustment						13.5-14.5
'75	1102394	4.0-4.5	37	Transistor type, integral with alternator, no adjustment						13.6-14.2
	1102495	4.0-4.5	55	Transistor type, integral with alternator, no adjustment						13.6-14.2
	1102388	4.0-4.5	37	Transistor type, integral with alternator, no adjustment						13.6-14.2
	1102390	4.0-4.5	55	Transistor type, integral with alternator, no adjustment						13.6-14.2

BATTERY AND STARTER SPECIFICATIONS

		BATTERY			STARTER						
					Lock Test			No-Load Test			
Year	Engine No. Cyl. Displacement (cu in.)	Ampere Hour Capacity	Volts	Terminal Grounded	Amps	Volts	Torque (ft lbs)	Amps	Volts	RPM	Brush Spring Tension (oz)
'69	L6-250	44	12	Neg.	Not Recommended			68	10.6	6,700	35
	8-350	61	12	Neg.	Not Recommended			70	9	4,000	35
	8-350 G.S.	61	12	Neg.	Not Recommended			70	9	4,000	35
	8-400 G.S.	70	12	Neg.	Not Recommended			61	9	5,200	35
'70-'72	L6-250	44	12	Neg.	Not Recommended			49-87	9	6,200-10,700	35
	8-350	61	12	Neg.	Not Recommended			55-85	9	3,100-6,000①	35
	8-455	70	12	Neg.	Not Recommended			48-80	9	4,100-6,500②	35
'73	8-350	③	12	Neg.	Not Recommended			55-85	9	3,500-6,000	35
	8-455	④	12	Neg.	Not Recommended			48-80	9	4,000-6,500	35

BATTERY AND STARTER SPECIFICATIONS

Year	Engine No. Cyl. Displacement (cu in.)	BATTERY Ampere Hour Capacity	BATTERY Volts	BATTERY Terminal Grounded	STARTER Lock Test Amps	STARTER Lock Test Volts	STARTER Lock Test Torque (ft lbs)	STARTER No-Load Test Amps	STARTER No-Load Test Volts	STARTER No-Load Test RPM	Brush Spring Tension (oz)
'74	6-250	⑤	12	Neg.	Not Recommended			50-80	9	5,500-10,500	35
	8-350	③	12	Neg.	Not Recommended			55-80	9	3,500-6,000	35
	8-455	④	12	Neg.	Not Recommended			45-80	9	4,000-6,500	35
'75-'76	V6-231	⑥	12	Neg.	Not Recommended			55-80	9	3,500-6,000	35
	6-250	⑦	12	Neg.	Not Recommended			50-80	9	5,500-10,500	35
	8-260	⑧	12	Neg.	Not Recommended			55-80	9	3,500-6,000	35
	8-350	⑧	12	Neg.	Not Recommended			55-80	9	3,500-6,000	35

① 1972—3,500-6,000 rpm
② 1972—4,000-6,500 rpm
③ Side Terminal—Cranking power 2,900 or 3,250 watts @ 0°F
④ Side Terminal—Cranking power 3,250 watts @ 0°F
⑤ Side Terminal—Cranking power 2,300 or 3,750 watts @ 0°F
⑥ Cranking power 2,300 or 2,500 watts @ 0°F
⑦ Cranking power 2,300 watts @ 0°F
⑧ Cranking power 3,200 watts @ 0°F

BRAKE SPECIFICATIONS

Year	Model	MASTER CYLINDER Disc	MASTER CYLINDER Drum	WHEEL CYLINDER Front Disc	WHEEL CYLINDER Front Drum	WHEEL CYLINDER Rear	BRAKE DISC OR DRUM DIAMETER Front Disc	BRAKE DISC OR DRUM DIAMETER Front Drum	BRAKE DISC OR DRUM DIAMETER Rear
'69	Special, Skylark, GS	1.125	1.0	2.937	1.125	.875	11.0	9.5	9.5
	Sportwagon	1.125	1.0	2.937	1.125	1.0	11.0	9.5	9.5
'70-'72	All	1.125	1.0	2.937	1.125	.875	11.0	9.495-9.505	9.495-9.505
'73	All	1.001①	1.0	2.937	1.125	.875	11.0	9.5	9.5
'74	All	1.125	1.0	2.937	1.125	.875	11.0	9.5	9.5
'75	Skyhawk	0.75	—	1.875	—	.75	9.88	—	9.0
	All other models	1.125②	—	2.937	—	.875	11.0	—	9.5③
'76	Skyhawk	0.88	—	1.875	—	.812	9.88	—	9.5
	Skylark	1.125	—	2.94	—	.875	11.0	—	9.5
	All other models	1.125④	—	2.938	—	.937	11.0	—	11.0

① Power disc—1.125
② Non power—1.000
③ 11.0 on wagons
④ Non power—0.938

WHEEL ALIGNMENT SPECIFICATIONS

Year	Model	CASTER Range (deg)	CASTER Pref Setting (deg)	CAMBER Range (deg)	CAMBER Pref Setting (deg)	Toe-in (in.)	Steering Axis Inclin. (deg)	WHEEL PIVOT RATIO (deg) Inner Wheel	WHEEL PIVOT RATIO (deg) Outer Wheel
'69	All	1N to 0	½N	0 to 1P	½P	⅛ to ¼	8	20	18½
'70-'72	All	1N to 0	½N	0 to 1P	½P	⅛ to ¼	8	20	18½
'73	All	0 to 1P	½P	0 to 1P①	½P	1/16 to ⅛	8	—	—
'74	Apollo	½N to 1½P	½P	½N to 1P	¾P	1/16 to 5/16	9	—	—
	Century, Regal, Luxus	1N to 1P	0	¼N to 1¼P RH ¼P to 1¾P LH	½P RH 1P LH	0 to 3/16	8	—	—
'75-'76	Skyhawk	1¼N to ¼N	¾N	½N to ¾P	¼P	0 to ⅛	8.55	—	—
	Apollo/Skylark, manual steer.	½N to 1½N	1N	¼P to 1¼P	¾P	0 to ⅛	10	—	—
	Apollo/Skylark, power steer.	½P to 1½P	1P	¼P to 1¼P	¾P	0 to ⅛	10	—	—
	Century, Regal	1½P to 2½P	2P	½P RH ½P to 1½P LH	½P RH 1P LH	0 to ⅛	8	—	—

① Right wheel given, left wheel is 0 to 2P, preferred 1P
N Negative P Positive
RH Right hand side
LH Left hand side
—Not specified

CHARGING SYSTEM

Complete information on charging system troubleshooting and repairs can be found in the "Unit Repair Section."

Alternator R & R

Remove bolt holding tension bar to unit. Release drive belt. Unfasten mounting bolt to release Delcotron from engine. When reinstalling, adjust drive belt to allow ½ in. play on the longest run between pulleys.

NOTE: on some models, it may be necessary to loosen and rotate fan shroud. On all A/C models, remove compressor bracket.

Voltage Regulator R & R through 1970

1. Disconnect the battery cables.
2. Disconnect the wiring from the voltage regulator.
3. Remove the screws holding the regulator to the firewall or front bulkhead, depending on the car.
4. Reverse the removal procedures to install.

Voltage Regulator R & R beginning 1971

The voltage regulator is inside the alternator. For R&R procedures see "Charging and Starting Systems" in the "Unit Repair Section."

STARTING SYSTEM

The starter circuit consists of the battery, battery cables, starting motor, starter motor solenoid switch, ignition-starter switch and the neutral safety switch (used on cars with automatic transmission). Manual transmission models have a clutch safety switch instead of the neutral safety switch.

The starting motor and solenoid assembly is mounted on the right side of the engine. The solenoid switch closes the circuit between the battery and the starting motor. It also operates the shift lever that moves the drive pinion into mesh with the flywheel ring gear.

Starter R & R

Inline 6 Cylinder

1. Disconnect battery and solenoid wires.
2. Remove the flywheel inspection cover.
3. On 1974 and later models, disconnect the starter support bracket.
4. Remove attaching bolts and lift out starter.

V6

Disconnect the negative battery cable from the battery. Note the locations of the wiring connections and disconnect the electrical leads from the starter. Remove the capscrew which secures the starter motor to the angle bracket on the side of the engine. Remove the two capscrews which secure the drive end of the starter motor to the cylinder block and remove the starter. Install the starter in the reverse order of removal.

V8

1. Disconnect battery.
2. Jack up car.
3. Remove four screws (⅜ in.) that hold flywheel inspection cover.
4. Disconnect wires from solenoid.
5. Remove one bolt from starter bracket to engine block, then remove two rear starter bolts using a 9/16 in. socket.

NOTE: the bracket bolt is hidden and must be removed using a short ½ in. open-end wrench. This bolt must be started by hand when installing. The bracket was used only through 1972.

6. Remove starter motor.

Skyhawk, Automatic Transmission

1. Disconnect the battery and raise the car.
2. Remove the exhaust crossover pipe and flywheel cover.
3. Remove the two transmission mount to transmission bolts and support the transmission extension housing.
4. Remove the right transmission support bolt and loosen the left bolt enough to let the transmission support pivot down.
5. Lower the transmission and disconnect the oil cooler lines at the transmission.
6. Remove the starter mounting bolts; remove the starter wires, and lower the starter from the engine.
7. Installation is the reverse of removal.

Starter Drive Removal and Installation

1. Remove the bolt which holds the field leads to the solenoid motor terminal and disconnect the leads. Remove the two solenoid attaching bolts, rotate, and remove the solenoid.
2. Remove the two through-bolts, end frame, and field frame assembly.
3. Pull both brush holder pivot pins and lift out each pair of brush holder assemblies. Disconnect the leads and brushes.
4. Remove the shift lever pivot bolt, plunger, shift lever, and armature from the drive housing.
5. Remove the drive assembly from the armature by first using a suitable tool (such as a ½ in. pipe coupling) to disengage the snap-ring retainer from the snap-ring. After removing the snap-ring and retainer, slide the drive assembly off of the armature shaft.
6. Inspect all parts for wear or damage and replace where necessary. When cleaning all parts, be sure not to use any degreasing or high temperature method on the armature, field coils, and drive assembly.

To assemble:

7. Lubricate the armature shaft and install the drive assembly with the pinion out.
8. Slide the snap-ring retainer onto the shaft with the recessed side out.
9. Use a block of wood and a hammer to get the new snap-ring started on the shaft. Install the snap-ring in the shaft groove.
10. Slide the thrust collar onto the shaft, move the snap-ring retainer up to the snap-ring, and squeeze the retainer and thrust collar together with two pair of pliers. The retainer should be forced over the snap-ring.
11. Lubricate the drive frame bushing and shift lever linkage and install the shift lever in the drive end frame.
12. Install the armature and spacers into the drive end frame, making sure that the shift lever is in place.
13. Assemble the brushes and leads to the brush holders. Place the brush holders and springs in the field frame and install the pivot pins.
14. Install the field frame over the armature, spreading the brush holders to prevent damage.
15. Lubricate the commutator end frame bushing and install the frame.
16. Install the through-bolts.
17. Move the armature toward the commutator end frame. Measure the clearance between the snap-ring retainer and drive end housing with feeler gauges. It should be 0.005-0.050 in. Use spacers to adjust the clearance.

IGNITION SYSTEM

Distributor Removal

1. Remove distributor cap, primary wire and vacuum line at the distributor. On inline sixes with HEI, remove No. 1 and 2 spark plug wires and the coil connectors. Unplug the V6 and V8 distributor cap HEI connectors.
2. Scribe a mark on the distributor

body, locating the position of the rotor and scribe another mark on the engine block, showing the position of the body in the block.
3. Remove the hold-down clamp and lift the distributor out of the block.

Distributor Installation

For firing order and cylinder numbering, see specifications.

1. If engine has been disturbed, rotate the crankshaft to bring the piston of No. 1 cylinder to the top of its compression stroke. If the engine has not been disturbed, insert the distributor into the engine, making sure the tip of the rotor is aligned with the marks that were scribed on the distributor housing and the engine block.
2. Position the distributor in the block with the rotor at No. 1 firing position. Make sure the oil pump intermediate drive shaft is properly seated in the oil pump.
3. Install the distributor lock but do not tighten.
4. Rotate the distributor body clockwise until the breaker points are just starting to open. Tighten the retaining screw.
5. Connect the primary wire and the vacuum line to the distributor, then install distributor cap.

NOTE: Design of the V6 engine requires a special form of distributor cam. The distributor may be serviced in the regular way and should cause no more problems than any other distributor, if the firing plan is thoroughly understood. The distributor cam is not ground to standard six cylinder indexing intervals. This particular form requires that the original pattern of spark plug wiring be used. The engine will not run in balance if number one spark plug wire is inserted into number six distributor cap tower, even though each wire in the firing sequence is advanced to the next distributor tower. There is a difference between the firing intervals of each succeeding cylinder through the 720° engine cycle.

6. Start the engine and check the timing with a timing light.

Contact Point Replacement and Adjustment

Inline Six-Cylinder through 1974

1. Loosen the captive distributor cap retaining screws and remove the cap.
2. Pull off the rotor.
3. Disconnect the primary and condenser leads from the point set.
4. Remove the retaining screw and the point set.
5. Remove the condenser and clamp.
6. Rotate the sponge cam lubricator or apply a trace of petroleum jelly or distributor lubricant to the cam.
7. Insert the new point set and the attaching screw.
8. Install the new condenser and clamp.
9. Connect the leads to the point set.
10. Turn the engine so that the points are open their maximum.
11. Adjust the gap with a feeler gauge. Use the screwdriver slot to lever the points open or closed.
12. Check the dwell with the engine either cranking or running. Set the dwell by adjusting the point gap.
13. Check the timing.

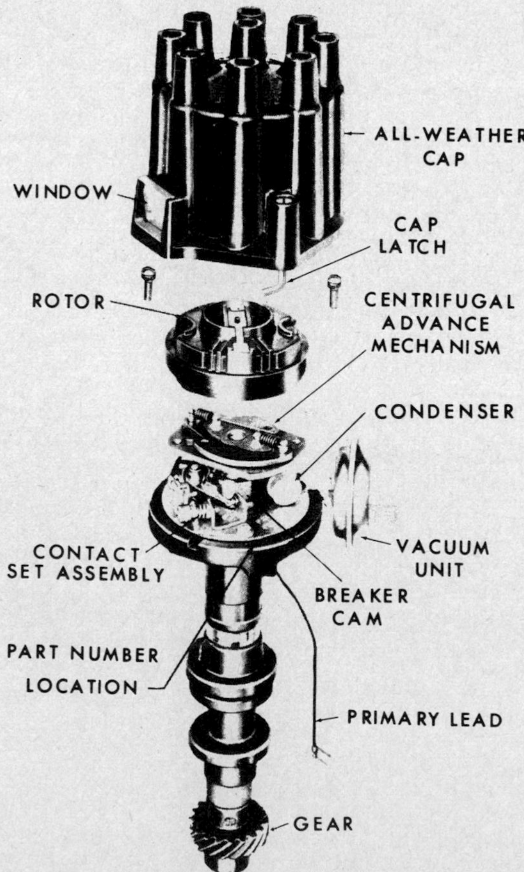

Distributor assembly, R.F.I. shield was used 1970-73
(© Buick Div., G.M. Corp)

V6 and V8 through 1974

NOTE: the condenser should be replaced when the points are replaced.

1. Remove the distributor cap and rotor. If equipped with an interference shield, remove the shield.
2. Disconnect the condenser and primary leads from their terminal on the points.
3. Loosen the two screws holding the contact point set in place and remove point set.
4. Connect the wires to a new set of points and install them into the distributor.

NOTE: 1970-73 distributors have a radio interference shield over the contact points. Only snap-lock point sets can be used because screw-type connectors will hit this shield and short the ignition. The shield isn't needed if the later type unitized point condenser set is installed.

Installing R.F.I. shield
(© Buick Div., G.M. Corp)

5. Put a small amount of grease on the breaker cam or rotate the lubricator.
6. Reinstall the shield, rotor, and cap. Install the shield half that covers the points first. The shield isn't necessary if a unitized point and condenser set is installed.

The unitized set is standard equipment beginning 1974. It can be installed in all General Motors V8 distributors.

7. Adjust the dwell to specifications using a 1/8 in. allen wrench through the cap window.
8. Check the timing.

Ignition Timing

Timing marks are located on the front engine cover and on the harmonic balancer.

1. Disconnect the distributor vacuum advance hose from the distributor and plug the hose.
2. Make sure the dwell is adjusted.

NOTE: it may be necessary to put a small amount of white paint or chalk on the timing marks to make them more visible.

3. Connect a timing light to no. 1 cylinder.
4. Loosen the distributor clamp.
5. Start the engine and rotate the distributor until the correct marks line up. Tighten the distributor clamp and recheck the timing.
6. Reconnect the vacuum hose.

High Energy Ignition System

Beginning 1974, a solid state, high energy ignition system is offered as an option on all Buick V8 engines. On 1975 and later Buicks, it is standard equipment. There are no points or condenser to replace, nor any cam or rubbing block to wear out. Precision timing and proper tuning are maintained over a greater interval than conventional point-and-condenser systems, and the high energy coil delivers 50 to 75% more voltage than a conventional electronic system. In addition, the high energy system is completely unitized.

The procedure for checking the timing on this system is the same as for conventional ignition systems.

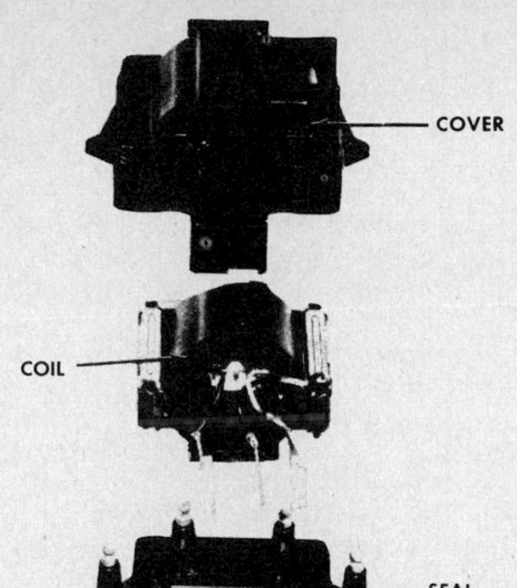

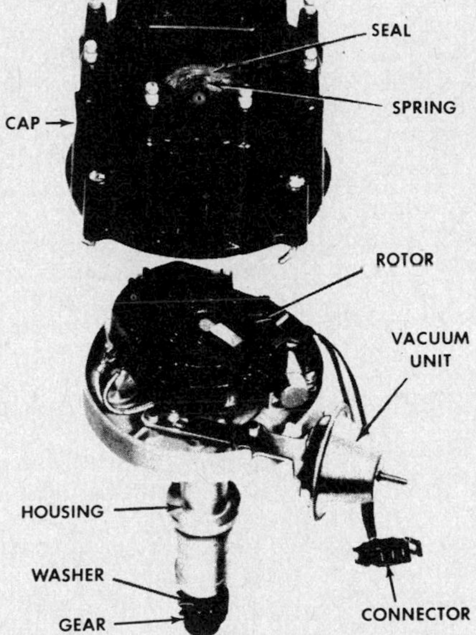

Exploded view of V8 or V6 HEI distributor
(© Buick Div., G.M. Corp)

High Energy Ignition System Tachometer Hookup

Some 1974, and all 1975 and later Buicks are equipped with the High Energy Ignition System which uses a different tachometer hookup than was used in previous years.

1. On the V6 and V8 engines, connect the tachometer to the TACH terminal on the distributor and to a suitable ground.

NOTE: Some tachometers must connect to the TACH terminal on the distributor and to the positive terminal on the battery. If there is any doubt check the tachometer manufacturer's instructions.

2. On the inline six cylinder, connect the tachometer to the TACH terminal on the coil, opposite the BAT terminal, and to a ground.

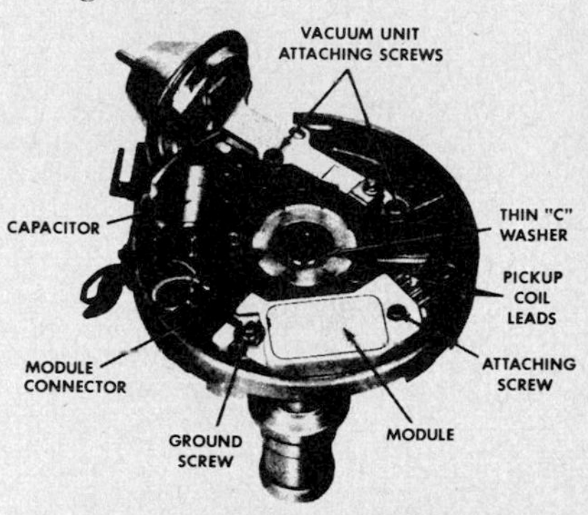

Internal components of HEI distributor
(© Buick Div., G.M. Corp)

FUEL SYSTEM

Idle Speed and Mixture Adjustment

1969-70 V8

1. Connect a tachometer to the engine.

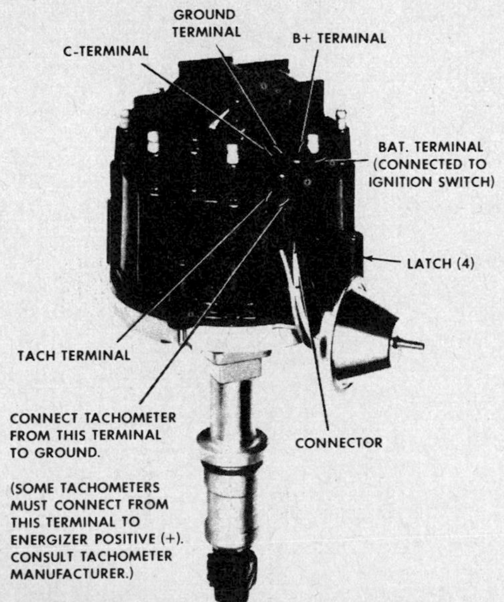

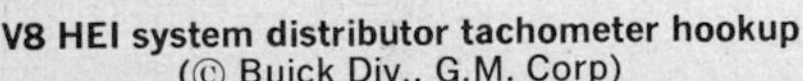

V8 HEI system distributor tachometer hookup
(© Buick Div., G.M. Corp)

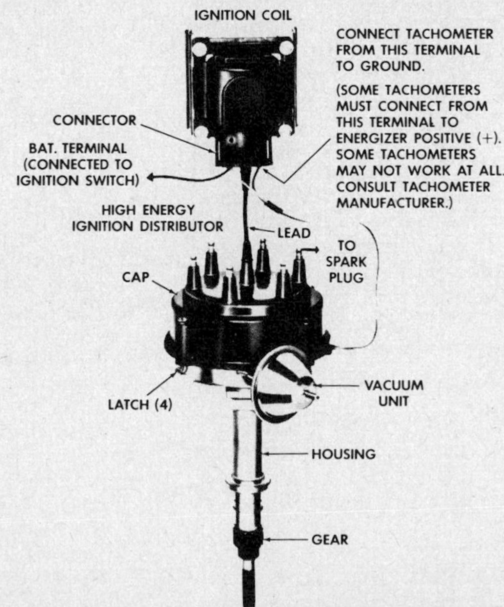

Tachometer connection, inline six cylinder engine with HEI system
(© Buick Div., G.M. Corp)

2. Run the engine until it is warmed up.
3. Remove and plug the vacuum hose to the distributor.
4. Place a manual transmission in neutral, and an automatic transmission in Drive.

NOTE: check to see that the compressor for the Automatic Level Control, if equipped, is not running. The compressor now has a regulating valve to turn off vacuum at idle speed. If the compressor is running, this valve is faulty and must be adjusted or replaced before a good idle can be obtained.

5. Adjust the throttle stopscrew to set the idle speed according to specifications.
6. Adjust the idle mixture needles, one at a time, to obtain the highest tachometer reading. Readjust the throttle stopscrew to obtain 20 revolutions per minute (rpm) faster than specified idle speed. Turn each mixture needle to reduce engine speed 10 rpm. This reduces idle speed to specifications.

1969 6 Cyl

See Note in previous procedure about Automatic Level Control.

1. Connect a tachometer to the engine.
2. Start the engine and warm it up.
3. Remove and plug the vacuum hose to the distributor.
4. Place manual transmissions in neutral and automatics in Drive. Make sure the wheels are blocked and the brakes are securely set.
5. Adjust the solenoid plunger screw to set the specified idle speed. This is the higher figure in the specification table.
6. Adjust the idle mixture needles, one at a time, to obtain the highest tachometer reading. Readjust the solenoid plunger to obtain 20 rpm higher than the specified idle.
7. Turn in the mixture needle to drop engine speed 20 rpm. This will achieve the specified idle.
8. Disconnect the wire from the idle stop solenoid to de-energize the solenoid. Adjust the carburetor throttle stopscrew to obtain the specified slow-idle speed.
9. Reconnect the solenoid wire and check the fast-idle speed.

1970 6 Cyl.

See the note in the 1969-70 V8 section on Automatic Level Control.

1. Connect a tachometer to the engine.
2. Start the engine and warm it up.
3. Remove and plug the vacuum hose to the distributor.
4. Place manual transmissions in Neutral and automatics in Drive. Make sure the wheels are blocked and the brakes are securely set.
5. Adjust the solenoid plunger screw to set the specified idle speed. This is the higher figure in the specification table.
6. Stop the engine and turn the mixture screw in until it contacts the seat lightly, then turn it out four turns. Restart the engine.
7. Readjust the solenoid screw to get 830 rpm for manual transmissions and 630 rpm for automatics.
8. Adjust the mixture screw in to achieve the specified idle speed.
9. Disconnect the wire from the idle stop solenoid to de-energize the solenoid.
10. Adjust the carburetor throttle stopscrew to obtain specified slow-idle speed. This is the lower figure in the specification table. Reconnect the solenoid wire and check the fast-idle speed.

1971 All

NOTE: On models with a V8 engine and manual transmission, the relay and solenoid located near the carburetor are emission control devices and should not be adjusted. See the note in the 1969–70 V8 procedure on automatic level control.

1. Connect a tachometer to the engine.
2. Start the engine and warm it up.
3. Remove the hose to the distributor and plug it up.
4. Adjust the throttle stopscrew to set the specified idle speed.
5. Adjust the idle mixture screws (one screw on 6 cyl) to obtain the highest idle within the limited travel of the screws.
6. Readjust the throttle stopscrew to obtain the specified idle speed.

1972-73 All

See the note in the 1969–70 V8 procedure on automatic level control.

1. Connect a tachometer to the engine.
2. Start the engine and run it until it is warmed up.
3. Remove and plug the vacuum hose to the distributor.
4. Place manual transmissions in Neutral and automatic transmissions in Drive.
5. Open the throttle sufficiently to allow the solenoid to extend and contact the throttle lever pad in the idle position.
6. Adjust the solenoid plunger to obtain the specified rpm. This is the higher figure in the specification chart.
7. Disconnect the solenoid wire to disengage solenoid.
8. Adjust the carburetor idle screw to obtain specified idle speed, this is the lower figure in the specification chart.
9. Reconnect the solenoid wire.
10. Adjust the idle mixture needles, one at a time, to obtain the highest tachometer reading. After the highest reading is reached, readjust the solenoid plunger to obtain 50 rpm over the specified idle speed. Turn each mixture needle in to reduce the idle speed 25 rpm for each needle. This reduces the idle speed to the recommended rpm.
11. Adjust the fast idle speed on all four-barrel carburetors. Fast idle must be adjusted after the slow idle speed and mixture have been adjusted. Automatic transmission cars are adjusted on the low step of the fast idle cam, in Drive, to 700 rpm. Manual transmission cars are adjusted on the low cam step to 820 rpm for 350 engines, and 920 rpm for 455 engines.
12. Connect the distributor vacuum hose.
13. Install the red service idle needle limiter caps on the mixture screws.

1974-75 Six-Cylinder

NOTE: Idle speed and mixture must be set with the engine at normal operating temperature, the air conditioner off, the air cleaner on, and the automatic transmission in Drive.

1. Set the parking brake and block the wheels.
2. Disconnect the fuel tank vent hose at the vapor canister. Dis-

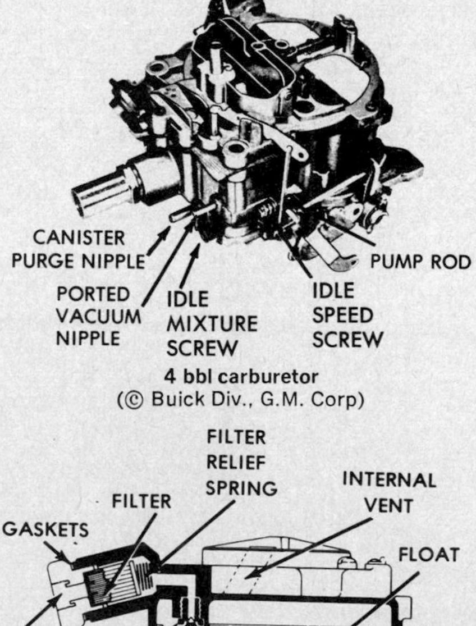

4 bbl carburetor
(© Buick Div., G.M. Corp)

2 bbl carburetor
(© Buick Div., G.M. Corp)

connect and plug the distributor vacuum line at the distributor.

3. Adjust the idle speed to the higher figure specified in the "Tune-Up Specifications" chart. Adjust the solenoid screw with the solenoid connected.
4. Cut the tab off the idle mixture screw cap.
5. Using the solenoid screw, set the idle speed to the higher speed specified on the underhood sticker. This is usually 30-350 rpm above normal idle speed.
6. Adjust the mixture screw (usually out) until the maximum engine idle speed is reached.
7. Lean the mixture by turning the mixture screw in until the engine slows to the idle speed you started with in Step 3. Adjust the idle speed to the lower figure from the "Tune-Up Specifications" chart with the solenoid disconnected.
8. Reconnect all the hoses removed in Step 2.

1974-75 V6 and V8

NOTE: Idle speed and mixture must be set with the engine at normal operating temperature, the air conditioner off, the air cleaner on, and the transmission in Drive. If a CO meter is available, set the idle mixture to obtain .3% or less at idle.

1. Set the parking brake and block the wheels.
2. Disconnect the evaporative emission hose at the air cleaner. Disconnect and plug the distributor vacuum line at the distributor. Disconnect and plug the EGR vacuum line at the EGR valve.
3. Adjust the idle speed to that specified in the "Tune-Up Specifications" chart. First adjust the idle speed screw with the solenoid disconnected to get the lower speed, then adjust the solenoid screw with the solenoid connected to get the higher speed.
4. Cut the tabs off the mixture screw caps.
5. On all V8s except 260 using the solenoid screw, adjust the idle speed to the higher speed specified on the underhood sticker. This is usually 60-100 rpm above normal idle speed.
6. Turn in the mixture screws equally until the engine returns to the normal idle speed.
7. Reconnect all the hoses removed in Step 2.

Fuel Pump

An AC fuel pump is used. The pump lever works from the underside of a camshaft eccentric. It is of the single-action diaphragm type. Fuel pumps are sealed units. They are not to be repaired.

All air conditioned cars with V8 engines and all cars with 400 and 455 cu. in. engines have a special fuel pump. This pump has a vapor return line which returns hot fuel and fuel vapor to the fuel tank. The possibility of vapor lock is thus greatly reduced by keeping cool fuel circulating through the pump.

Fuel Pump R & R

All except Skyhawk

1. Disconnect the fuel inlet hose from the pump. Disconnect the vapor return hose, if equipped. Disconnect the outlet hose.
2. Remove the two ½ inch (in.) bolts.
3. Remove the fuel pump.
4. Install a new gasket.
5. Install a new pump and bolts.
6. Tighten the bolts alternately and evenly.
7. Reconnect the hoses, start the engine, and check for leaks.

Skyhawk

The fuel pump used in the Skyhawk is an electric pump, mounted in the gas tank.

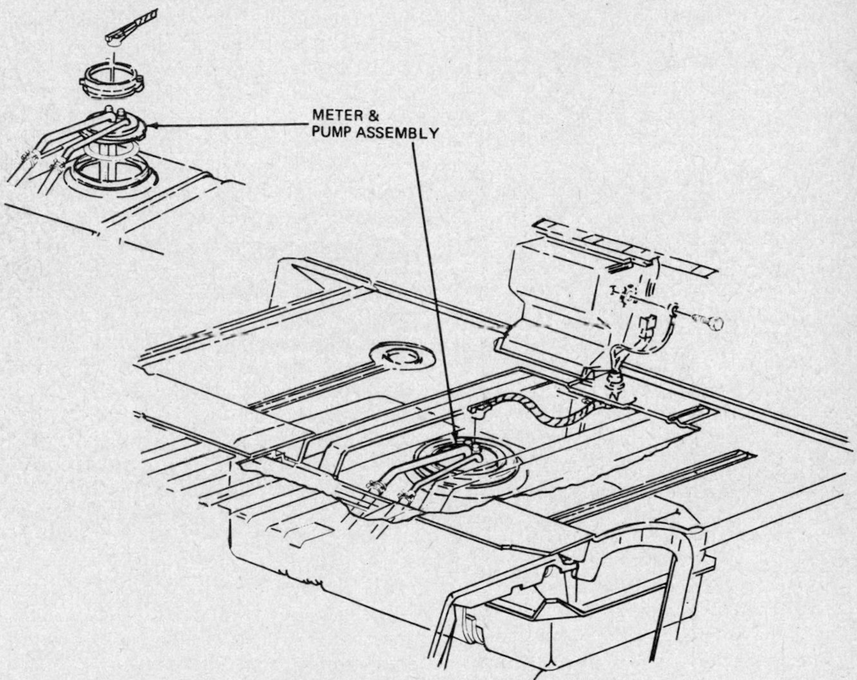

Skyhawk fuel pump location
(© Buick Div., G.M. Corp)

1. Disconect the fuel pump wires at the rear wiring harness connector.
2. Raise the car on a hoist and drain the gas tank.
3. Disconnect the gas line hose at the tank, and the vent hose.
4. Remove the gas gauge ground wire from the bottom of the tank.
5. Remove the tank retaining straps, and lower the tank carefully.
6. A special spanner wrench is needed to unscrew the pump retaining ring.
7. Installation is the reverse of removal.

Fuel Filter

These engines have a pleated paper or a bronze fuel filter located in the carburetor inlet.

Fuel Filter Replacement

1. Disconnect the fuel line connection at the inlet of the carburetor.
2. Remove the inlet fuel filter nut from the carburetor with a box wrench.

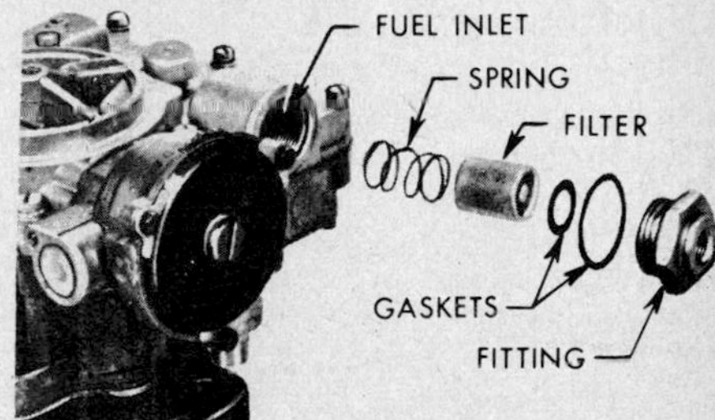

Fuel filter
(© Buick Div., G.M. Corp)

3. Remove the filter element and spring.
4. If a bronze element, blow through the cone end—the element should allow air to pass freely.
5. Install the element spring and a new element into the carburetor. Bronze elements are installed with the small section of the cone facing outward.
6. Install a new gasket on the fitting nut and install the nut.
7. Install the fuel line and tighten it securely. Start the engine and check for leaks.

COOLING SYSTEM

The cooling system is pressurized to about 15 psi. Coolant temperature is controlled by a thermostat housed in the forward (outlet) end of the intake manifold. This thermostat controls circulation and temperature in the intake manifold as well as in the engine. In the OHV 6 engine, the thermostat is in the top front of the cylinder head.

Thermostat R & R

To replace the thermostat, remove the two bolts holding the water neck in place. Remove the water neck and the thermostat will lift out. Use a new gasket when reinstalling a new thermostat.

Caution Be sure the thermostat is not reversed in its installed position. The temperature-sensitive side should extend toward the rear or down.

Water Pump R & R

Inline Six-Cylinder

1. Drain the radiator.
2. Disconnect the heater hose and the lower radiator hose from the pump.
3. Loosen the alternator bolt and remove the belt.
4. Remove the fan blades and pulley.
5. Unbolt the power steering pump from the water pump. Unbolt the water pump from the engine.
6. Remove the pump. Be careful to pull it straight out, to avoid impeller damage.
7. On installation, use a new, sealer coated gasket.
8. Reverse the procedure for installation.

V6

1. Drain the cooling system; remove the fan shroud.
2. Remove the fan belt and the fan and pulley from the hub on the water pump.
3. Disconnect the hoses from the water pump.
4. Remove the capscrews which secure the water pump to the engine and remove the pump from the vehicle.
5. Clean all of the mating surfaces, install new gaskets with sealer applied and install the water pump in the reverse order of removal.

V8 Removal

1. Drain the cooling system; on all 1975-76 models, the fan shroud must be removed. On the Skyhawk, the fan shroud and fan must be removed together.
2. Loosen belt or belts, then remove fan blades and pulley or pulleys from hub on water pump shaft. Remove belt or belts.
3. Disconnect hose from water pump inlet and heater hose from nipple. Remove bolts, then remove pump and gasket from the timing case cover.

V8 Installation

1. Install pump assembly with new gasket. Bolts and lock washers must be torqued evenly.
2. Connect radiator hose to pump inlet and heater hose to nipple. Fill cooling system and check all points of possible coolant leaks.
3. Install fan pulley or pulleys and fan blade. Install belt or belts and adjust for correct tension.

Radiator R & R

The radiator mounting is a four-point system using rubber inserts on U-shaped brackets for the lower mounting. The radiator upper mounting points are part of the upper radiator panel. The radiator is removed by removing the upper radiator panel, disconnecting the hoses and automatic transmission lines if equipped, and lifting the radiator out of the car. On models equipped with a fan shroud, remove the shroud from the radiator and position it rearward over the fan. Installation is the reverse of removal.

EMISSION CONTROLS

There are three types of emissions to be controlled: crankcase emissions, carburetor and gas tank gas vapor emissions, and exhaust emissions. See the "Unit Repair Section" for troubleshooting and repair information.

1969

A new concept, Combustion Control System (CCS) utilizes engine modifications. Essentially the CCS increases combustion efficiency through carburetor and distributor calibrations and by increasing engine operating temperature.

Carburetors are calibrated leaner and initial ignition timing is retarded. Another carburetor feature is the idle fuel mixture limiting orifice. It is located at the base of the idle mixture screw and makes sure that fuel enrichment will not greatly affect exhaust emissions even if the idle mixture screw is turned out too far.

The CCS also incorporates a higher engine operation temperature. A 195° thermostat is used. Engines running hotter provide more complete vaporation of the fuel and reduce quench area in the combustion chamber. Quench area is the relatively cool area near the cylinder wall and combustion chamber surfaces. Fuel in these areas does not burn properly because of the lower temperatures.

This incomplete burning increases emissions.

The CCS uses a thermostatically controlled air cleaner called the Auto-Therm air cleaner. It is designed to keep the temperature of the air entering the carburetor at approximately 100°. This allows the lean carburetor to work properly, minimizes carburetor icing, and improves engine warm-up characteristics. A sensor unit located on the clean air side of the air filter senses the temperature of the air passing over it and regulates the vacuum supplied to a vacuum diaphragm in the inlet tube of the air cleaner. The colder the air the greater the amount of vacuum supplied to the vacuum diaphragm. The vacuum diaphragm, depending on the vacuum supplied to it, opens or closes a damper door in the inlet tube of the air cleaner. If the door is open, it allows air from the engine compartment to go to the carburetor. If the door is closed, air flows from the heat stove located on the exhaust manifold into the carburetor. In this way heated air is supplied to the carburetor during cold days and when first starting the engine and warming it up.

1970-71

The more stringent 1970 laws require tighter control of emissions. Crankcase emissions are controlled by the Closed Positive Crankcase Ventilation System; exhaust emissions are controlled by the engine Controlled Combustion System (CCS), in conjunction with the new Transmission Controlled Spark System (TCS).

In addition, cars sold in California in 1970 and all 1971 models are equipped with an Evaporation Control System that limits the amount of gasoline vapor discharged into the atmosphere (usually from the carburetor and fuel tank).

The TCS system consists of a transmission switch, a solenoid valve, and a temperature switch. Under normal conditions, the system permits the vacuum distributor (spark) advance to operate only in high gear (both manual and automatic transmissions) and reverse.

The transmission switch is located on the transmission and senses when the transmission is in one of the lower gears. When in a lower gear, the switch activates the vacuum solenoid valve. This valve is located in the vacuum line that runs from the carburetor to the distributor and shuts off vacuum to the distributor advance when it is activated. There is also an engine-temperature sensing switch which overrides the transmission switch. It will allow vacuum advance in the lower gears when the engine temperature is below 85° or above 220°. There is always vacuum advance in high gear and reverse.

The Evaporative Emission Control System was introduced in 1970. Vapors generated in the gas tank while the car is at rest are transferred to an activated charcoal canister located in the engine compartment. When the car is running the vapors are removed from the canister and burned by the engine.

1972

In 1972, all engines are equipped with Positive Crankcase Ventilation, Transmission Controlled Vacuum Spark Advance, and the Controlled Combustion System. See the 1970-71 section for an explanation of TCS. The Air Injection Reactor System is standard on all engines except non-California 350 cu in. engines with automatic transmissions. All California cars and all cars with manual transmissions have Exhaust Gas Recirculation (EGR).

The EGR System is used to reduce oxides of nitrogen emissions. To lower the formation of nitrogen oxides, it is necessary to reduce combustion temperatures. This is done by introducing exhaust gases into the intake manifold to be burned.

An EGR valve is mounted on the right rear of the intake manifold and is used to regulate the amount of exhaust gases and the time the exhaust gases enter the intake manifold. As the engine speeds up, carburetor vacuum is applied to the valve which opens a port connecting the intake manifold to the exhaust gas passage that is cast in the intake manifold. This allows exhaust gases to pass into the intake manifold. The EGR system is not in operation during engine idle.

1973

All engines are equipped with Positive Crankcase Ventilation, Controlled Combustion, Air Injection Reactor System, Exhaust Gas Recirculation, Transmission Controlled Vacuum Spark Advance System, and Evaporative Emission Control. With the exception of a low temperature cut-out valve that added to the EGR system, the emission control systems remain unchanged from previous years.

The EGR system is the same one that was used on 1972 California cars with a new temperature valve. This black and white plastic valve is located in the vacuum line to the EGR valve and it senses ambient temperature above the engine intake manifold. At temperatures below 0-0°F, the temperature valve closes to prevent carburetor vacuum from opening the EGR valve. When the temperature above the manifold rises above 60°F, the valve opens and allows carburetor vacuum to control the operation of the EGR valve. Whenever installing a new valve, always make sure the side of the valve marked EGR faces toward the EGR valve.

1974

The 1974 Buick emission control system is unchanged from 1973, except for a required change in the EGR temperature sensor. An Environmental Protection Agency order necessitated that the EGR ambient temperature sensor either be removed or changed to record coolant temperature on engines produced after March 15, 1973. Although the system design remains unchanged, there has been an extensive refinement and recalibration of components to insure greater efficiency.

1975

The 1975 Buick emission control system has three additions to the 1974 system, while dropping the Transmission Controlled Spark system used since 1970. The additions are: a catalytic converter, a choke air modulator, and an early fuel evaporation system (EFE).

The catalytic converter is a device used to reduce hydrocarbons and carbon monoxide in the exhaust system. See the Unit Repair Section for more details.

The choke air modulator, located in the bottom of the air cleaner, provides heated air to the choke thermostatic coil housing to improve drivability and performance.

The EFE valve promotes quick heating of the incoming fuel to the carburetor by directing the flow of exhaust gas through the intake manifold crossover passage underneath the carburetor.

ENGINE

Engine Removal

1. Scribe marks at the hood hinges and the hinge brackets. Remove the hood.
2. Disconnect the battery and drain the coolant.
3. Remove the air cleaner.
4. On cars with air conditioning (A/C), disconnect the compressor ground wire from the bracket. Remove the electrical connector from the compressor. Remove the compressor and position the compressor out of the way. Do not disconnect any hoses.

Caution If the compressor refrigerant lines do not have enough slack to position the compressor out of the way without disconnecting the refrigerant lines, the air conditioning system will have to be removed by a trained air conditioning specialist. Under no conditions should an untrained person attempt to disconnect the air conditioning refrigerant lines. These lines contain pressurized freon, which can be extremely dangerous to the untrained.

5. Remove the fan blade, pulley, and belts.
6. Disconnect the radiator and heater hoses. Remove the radiator and shroud assembly.
7. Remove the power steering pump and move it out of the way. Do not disconnect any hoses.
8. Remove the fuel pump hoses and plug them.
9. Disconnect the vapor emission lines, on 1970 and later models, from the carburetor, the vacuum supply hose from the carburetor to the vacuum manifold, and the power brake vacuum hoses, if equipped.
10. Disconnect the throttle linkage at the carburetor.
11. Disconnect the oil and coolant switch.
12. Disconnect the engine-to-body ground strap.
13. Raise the car and disconnect the starter wires.
14. Disconnect the pipe from the exhaust manifold and support the exhaust system.
15. Remove the flywheel and converter cover.
16. On cars equipped with automatic transmissions, remove the flywheel-to-converter attaching bolts. Match-mark the converter to the flywheel. On standard transmission models, disconnect the clutch linkage.
17. Remove the transmission-to-engine attaching bolts.

NOTE: On inline sixes, leave the engine and transmission bolted together. They are removed as a unit. Unbolt the transmission rear mount from the crossmember and remove the driveshaft.

18. Support the transmission.
19. Remove the thru-bolts from the motor mounts.
20. Lower the car, making sure the transmission is adequately supported.
21. Disengage the engine from the transmission and remove the engine from the car.

Engine Installation

Install the engine in the reverse order of removal.

Note that there are dowel pins in the block that have matching holes in the bellhousing. These dowel pins must be in almost perfect alignment before the engine will go together with the transmission.

Manifolds

Inline Six-Cylinder

This engine uses a combined intake and exhaust manifold, equipped with thermostatic heat-riser valve.

To remove the manifold assembly, disconnect the exhaust pipe flange and remove all connections to the carburetor. Take off the vacuum lines at the manifold and also at the carburetor. Remove power steering pump and bracket. Remove the EFE valve bracket.

Remove the carburetor. Unbolt the manifold from the side of the cylinder head. The intake manifold can be separated from the exhaust manifold by removing one bolt and two nuts. These fasteners should be tightened to 15-30 ft lbs after the manifolds are bolted to the engine.

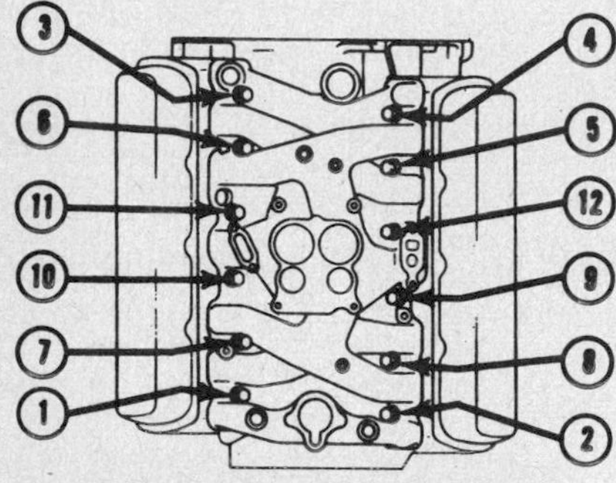

260 V8 intake manifold torque sequence (© Buick Div., G.M. Corp)

V8 (except 260) intake manifold torque sequence (© Buick Div., G.M. Corp)

Intake manifold bolt tightening sequence, V8 except 260 (© Buick Div., G.M. Corp)

Intake Manifold R & R

V8 Engines

The manifold incorporates an exhaust heat passage to warm the carburetor throttle body. Engine coolant flows out of the engine through the water passages in the manifold and through the thermostat and water outlet elbow located at the front of the manifold.

1. Drain cooling system and disconnect the battery.
2. Remove carburetor air cleaner. Disconnect all tubes and hoses from the carburetor. Disconnect and remove the coil.
3. Disconnect temperature indicator wire from sending unit. Loosen the air conditioning compressor bracket bolt and alternator bracket and swing the bracket out of the way.
4. Disconnect accelerator and transmission linkage at carburetor. Disconnect throttle return spring.
5. Slide front thermostat by-pass hose clamp back on the hose. Disconnect upper radiator hose at outlet.
6. Disconnect heater hose at the temperature control valve inlet. Force the end of the hose down to permit coolant to drain from intake manifold.
7. Remove manifold-to-head attaching bolts.
8. Remove intake manifold and carburetor as an assembly by sliding rearward to disengage the thermostat by-pass hose from the water pump. Remove intake manifold gasket. Reverse the above steps to install, torquing the bolts in the sequence illustrated.

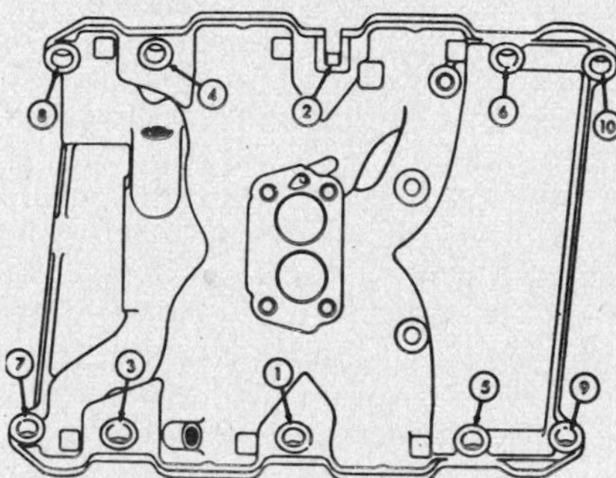

V6 intake manifold torque sequence (© Buick Div., G.M. Corp)

V6

1. Disconnect the crankcase vent hose, exhaust manifold line, choke heat tube, distributor vacuum hose, and the fuel line at the carburetor.
2. Disconnect the two distributor leads from the ignition coil.
3. Disconnect the wiring harness from the coolant temperature sending unit.
4. Remove the ten cap bolts which attach the intake manifold to the cylinder heads.
5. Remove the intake manifold and carburetor as an assembly.
6. Clean all of the mating surfaces of the intake manifold and cylinder heads, removing all traces of gasket material.
7. Install a new rubber intake manifold seal at the front and rear rails of the cylinder block. Be sure the pointed ends of the seals fit snugly against the block and cylinder heads.
8. Set the intake manifold in place on the cylinder block between the cylinder heads. Thread two cap bolts through the manifold into each cylinder head as guide bolts. Lift the manifold slightly and insert each of the two gaskets into position between the manifold and corresponding cylinder head. Be certain that the gasket is installed with its three apertures aligned with the ports of the head and manifold. One gasket should be installed in position on the right side and the other gasket reversed and installed on the left side.
9. Install the manifold attaching bolt in the open bolt hole at the right center side of the intake manifold. During manufacture, this open bolt hole is held to close tolerances so that the bolt in this location serves to locate the manifold front and rear.
10. Install the remaining intake manifold attaching bolts. The longer bolts are installed in the two forward holes on either side.
11. Tighten the intake manifold bolts to the proper torque in the proper sequence.
12. Assemble the remaining components to the engine in the reverse order of removal.

Exhaust Manifold

V8 Engines

Some engines have a heat control valve in one of the exhaust manifolds. This valve has a thermostat spring which tends to hold the valve closed under cold operating conditions.

This tension causes pressure build-up in the exhaust manifold, which forces exhaust through the crossover passage under the carburetor in the intake manifold to the opposite exhaust manifold and out the pipe and muffler.

Heat Riser Operation Check

1. Locate the heat riser counterweight.
2. If the weight is operating correctly it will rotate freely on its axis.
3. If the weight is stuck, tap the axle on which the weight rotates after soaking it with penetrating oil. Do not attempt to force the weight as this will only shear the axle.

Heat Riser R & R

1. Remove the exhaust pipe flange bolts.

2. Move the exhaust pipe out of the way and remove the heat riser.
3. Replace the heat riser, exhaust pipe, and bolts after cleaning the gasket surfaces.

Exhaust Manifold R & R

All V8 except Apollo Left-Side

1. Jack up car and support on axle stands.
2. Disconnect exhaust pipe from manifolds on both sides of engine and lower. If equipped with dual exhaust, disconnect and lower only on the side being worked on.
3. If equipped with manual transmission, remove equalizer shaft.

NOTE: on right side, it may be necessary to remove A/C, power steering, or alternator.

4. Remove exhaust manifold-to-cylinder head bolts.
5. Remove manifold from beneath car.

NOTE: On GS 400 models, it may be necessary to pull pitman arm from pitman shaft and to swing steering linkage forward to gain clearance.

6. Reverse the above to install. Always use the bolt locks.

Apollo V8, Left-Side Only

1. Raise and support the front end.
2. Disconnect the crossover pipe.
3. Remove the left engine mount through-bolt and loosen the right one.
4. Raise the engine.
5. Unbolt and remove the manifold.
6. Reverse the procedure to replace the manifold.

V6

1. Raise the vehicle on a hoist, and remove the crossover pipe.
2. On the right side, disconnect the choke pipe; on the left side, disconnect the EFE line.
3. Remove the exhaust manifold to cylinder head bolts, and lower the exhaust manifold.

Valve System

All V8 and V6 engines, except the 260, use rocker arm shafts while the inline six and the 260 V8 use rocker arm studs. All lifters are the hydraulic type.

NOTE: All 250, 350, and some 455 engines use progressively wound valve springs. The coils are closer together at one end than at the other. The close wound end must go against the cylinder head.

Rocker Arm R & R

Inline Six-Cylinder

NOTE: these rocker arms are of the individual pedestal design and need not be removed to remove head.

1. Remove rocker arm cover.
2. Remove rocker arm nuts, rocker arm balls, rocker arms, and push rods. These should be reinstalled in their original locations.

1969 V8

1. Remove the rocker arm cover and four rocker arm and shaft assembly bolts. Remove the assembly.
2. Remove the shaft end cap by splitting the side of the cap with a chisel.
3. Remove the rocker arms and springs. Keep the parts in order.
4. Install the rocker arms and springs on the shaft and lubricate the shaft with oil as the rocker arms are installed.
5. Install a new end cap on the rocker arm shaft.

NOTE: When installing the rocker arm shaft assembly, be sure that the drill mark is facing up and toward the rear on the left cylinder head and toward the front on the right cylinder head.

6. After locating the top of each push rod in its rocker arm seat, draw the rocker arm and shaft assembly down by tightening the bracket bolts a little at a time until tight.
7. Install the rocker arm cover with a new gasket.

1970 and later V8 and V6

1. Remove the rocker arm cover.
2. Remove the rocker arm shaft assembly bolts and the assembly.
3. Remove the nylon arm retainers by breaking them below their head with a chisel.

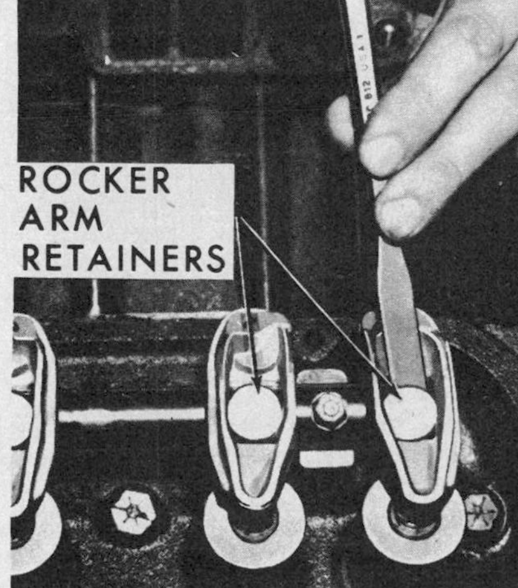

Removing nylon rocker arm retainer
(© Buick Div., G.M. Corp)

4. Remove the rocker arms.

NOTE: On 1970-72 engines, each pair of rocker arms must be installed so that the external rib on each arm points away from the rocker arm shaft bolt that is located between each pair of rocker arms. On 1973 and later engines, the rocker arms are marked R and L. From the front of the engine on the left bank, the sequence should be L-R, L-R, L-R, L-R. On the right bank, it should be R-L, R-L, R-L, R-L.

5. Install the rocker arms on the shaft and lubricate them with oil.
6. Center each arm on the 1/4 in. hole in the shaft. Install new nylon rocker arm retainers in the holes using a 1/2 in. drift.
7. Locate the push rods in the rocker arms and insert the shaft-to-cylinder head bolts. Tighten the bolts a little at a time until they are tightened to 30 ft lbs.
8. Install the rocker cover and use a new gasket.

260 V8

1. Remove the valve cover.
2. Remove the rocker arm bolts, and the rocker arm pivot.
3. Remove the rocker arm assembly. Remove each rocker arm assembly as a unit before proceeding to the next one.
4. Place a rocker arm assembly in the proper position, and lubricate the rocker arms and pivot assembly.
5. Install the rocker arm bolts, alternately tightening them to 25 ft lbs.
6. Proceed to the next rocker arm assembly until installation is complete; install the rocker arm cover.

Rocker Arm Stud Removal and Installation

Inline Six-Cylinder

1. Remove the rocker cover and rocker arms.
2. File two slots 3/32-1/8 in. deep on opposite sides of the stud. The bottom of the slots should be 1/2 in. from the top of the stud hole.
3. Place a spacer washer over the stud, then position a stud remover on the stud and tighten it securely.
4. Place a spacer (socket) over the stud remover, then thread a 7/8 in. nut on the stud remover and turn in until the stud pulls from the head.
5. If an oversize stud is to be used (0.003 and 0.013 in. oversize studs are available), ream the stud hole to the proper size.
6. To install, coat the press-fit area of the stud with axle lube, then press or hammer it into place.

NOTE: The factory recommends that tool J-6880 be used for this job. This tool is simply a sleeve that is held in place with an allen screw and protects the threads from damage. Any homemade tool will work if care is exercised. Do not hammer directly on the stud because it is hardened; it will fracture if subjected to shock.

Rocker arms and shaft, 455 cu in. through 1972
(© Buick Div., G.M. Corp)

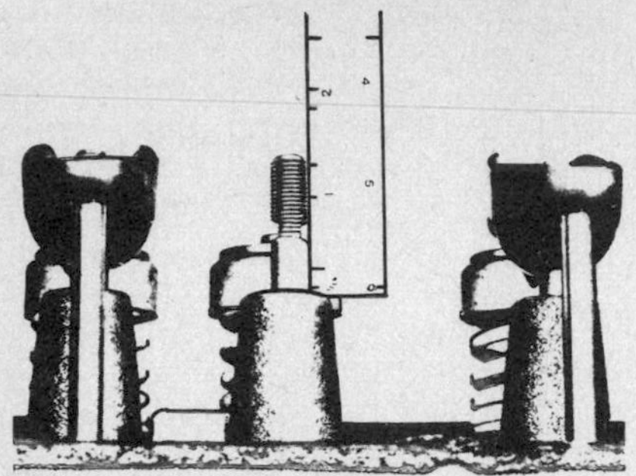

Slots for removing six-cylinder rocker arm stud
(© Buick Div., G.M. Corp)

Installing new six-cylinder rocker arm stud
(© Buick Div., G.M. Corp)

Inline Six Cylinder Hydraulic Valve Lifter Adjustment

When the rocker arms have been removed and replaced, it will be necessary to adjust the valves as follows:

1. Adjust each rocker arm nut to eliminate any valve lash. This must be done when the lifter is on the base of the circle of the cam.
2. Remove the distributor cap and crank the engine until the distributor points to No. 1 cylinder position, with the points (if any) open.

The following valves can be adjusted with the engine in No. 1 firing position:

Intake: No. 1, 2, 4; Exhaust: 1, 3, and 5.

The valve positions on the inline six cylinder engine are:

Front to Back: E I I E E I I E E I I E

3. Turn each adjusting nut until all lash is removed. This can be determined by checking pushrod side play while tightening the adjusting nut. When all play has been removed, turn the adjusting nut one more turn. This will place the lifter plunger in the center of its travel.
4. Follow steps 2 and 3 to adjust the remaining valves.

The following valves can be adjusted with the engine in the No. 6 firing position.

Intake: No. 3, 5, and 6; Exhaust: No. 2, 4, and 6.

The following is a method for replacing valve springs, oil seals, or spring retainers without removing the cylinder head.

1. **Obtain a spark plug hole air chuck adapter from an auto parts store.**
2. **Add an air chuck to this adaptor so the hose from an air compressor can be attached. This assembly will be used later to pressurize the cylinder.**
3. **Remove the valve rocker cover. Remove the rocker arm from the valve to be worked on.**
4. **Remove the spark plug from the cylinder to be worked on.**
5. **Turn the crankshaft to bring the piston of this cylinder down, away from possible contact with the valve head. Sharply tap the valve retainer to loosen the valve lock.**
6. **Turn the crankshaft to bring the piston in this cylinder to the exact top of its compression stroke.**
7. **Screw in the chuck-equipped tool.**
8. **Hook up an air hose to the chuck and turn on the pressure (about 200 lbs).**
9. **With a strong and constant supply of air holding the valve closed, compress the valve spring and remove the lock and retainer.**
10. **Make the necessary replacements and reassemble.**

NOTE: it is important that the operation be performed exactly as stated, in this order. The piston in the cylinder must be on exact top-center to prevent air pressure from turning the crankshaft.

Cylinder Head R & R

Removal Inline Six

1. Drain coolant.
2. Disconnect the exhaust pipe at the manifold flange, then remove the manifold bolts and clamps and remove the manifolds and carburetor as an assembly.
3. Remove the air conditioning compressor, if equipped, *but do not disconnect any lines.* Disconnect the air pump hose at the check valve.
4. Disconnect the spark plug wires from the plugs.
5. Disconnect the fuel and vacuum lines from the retaining clip at the water outlet. Disconnect the wires from the temperature sending unit, and accelerator pedal at bellcrank.
6. Remove the upper radiator hose.
7. Remove the coil and rocker arm cover.
8. Loosen the rocker arm nuts and rotate the rocker arms so the pushrods can be removed, then remove the pushrods and store them so they can be installed in their original locations.
9. Remove the cylinder head bolts, cylinder head, and gasket.

Installation Inline Six

1. Clean all gasket surfaces, install a new gasket, and place the head on the block.
2. Install the head bolts. Torque the head bolts to specifications in three stages.
3. Reverse steps one through eight to finish installation.

Inline six-cylinder engine head torque sequence (© Buick Div., G.M. Corp)

V6

1. Remove the intake manifold.
2. Remove the rocker cover.

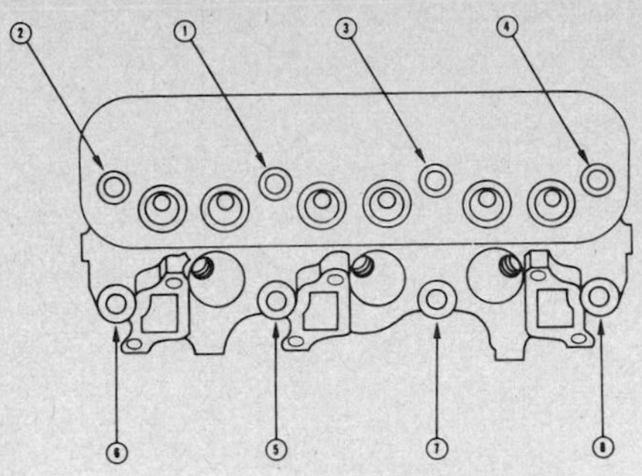

V6 cylinder head bolt torque sequence
(© Buick Div., G.M. Corp)

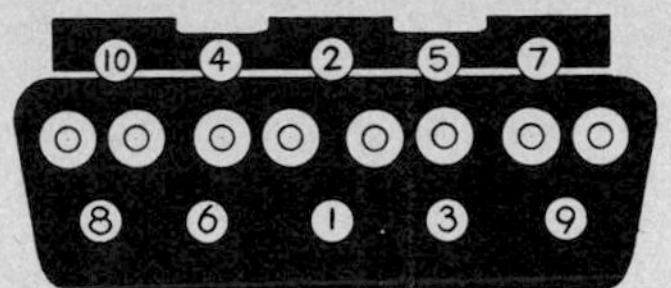

1970 and later 350, 455 cu in. cylinder head torque sequence

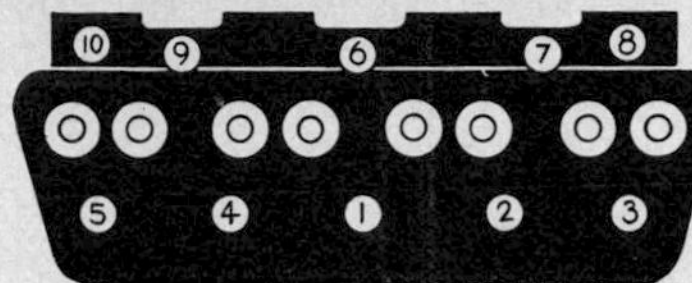

1969 400 cu in., 1969 350 cu in. cylinder head torque sequence

260 V8 cylinder head bolt torque sequence
(© Buick Div., G.M. Corp)

455 timing chain cover
(© Buick Div., G.M. Corp)

3. Remove the exhaust pipes at the flanges.
4. Remove the alternator in order to remove the right head.
5. Remove the dipstick and power steering pump, if so equipped, in order to remove the left head.
6. Remove the valve cover and the rocker assemblies. Mark these parts so that they can be reinstalled in exactly the same positions.
7. Unbolt the head bolts and lift off the cylinder head(s). It is very important that the inside of the engine be protected from dirt. The hydraulic lifters are particularly susceptible to being damaged by dirt.
8. To install, use the reverse procedure.

V8

1. Disconnect the battery.
2. Drain the coolant.
3. Remove the air cleaner.
4. Remove the air conditioning compressor, *but do not disconnect any lines.*
5. Remove the intake manifold.
6. When removing the right cylinder head, loosen the alternator belt and remove the alternator.
7. When removing the left cylinder head, remove the dipstick, power steering pump and AIR pump if so equipped.
8. Disconnect the plug wires.
9. Disconnect exhaust manifold from the head being removed.
10. Remove the rocker arm cover and rocker shaft assembly. Lift out the push rods.
11. Remove the cylinder head bolts.
12. Remove the cylinder head and gasket.
13. Reverse the above steps to install. Torque the head bolts to specifications in three steps.

Timing Cover, Chain, and Camshaft

Timing Chain, Cover Oil Seal, & Cover R & R

Inline Six Removal and Installation

This engine uses timing gears instead of sprockets and chain. The factory recommends that the engine be removed for this operation, but the following procedure should allow you to save a lot of time by leaving it in place.

1. Drain the cooling system and disconnect the radiator hoses at the radiator.
2. Remove the fan and water pump pulley.
3. Remove the radiator and fan belt.
4. Remove the harmonic balancer, using a puller.
5. Loosen the oil pan bolts and allow the pan to rest against the front crossmember.
6. Remove the timing gear cover bolts, then remove the cover and gasket.
7. Pry out the oil seal using a screwdriver.

NOTE: The seal can be replaced with the cover installed.

8. Install a new seal with the lip toward the inside of the cover. Drive it into place, using the proper seal installer or an old wheel bearing outer race.
9. Inspect the oil nozzle for damage and replace it if necessary, then clean all gasket surfaces.
10. Install the cover and gasket (stick the gasket to the block with Petroleum jelly or wheel bearing grease), making sure the cover is centered properly on the crankshaft end.
11. Tighten the cover bolts to 7 ft lbs, then install the oil pan and harmonic balancer.

Removal 455 Cu. In.

1. Drain cooling system.
2. Remove radiator, fan, fan pulley and belt, and crankshaft pulley and pulley reinforcement.
2. Remove fuel pump and Delcotron alternator.
4. Remove distributor.
5. Loosen clamp on thermostat bypass hose.
6. Remove harmonic balancer.
7. Remove timing chain cover to crankcase bolts. Remove oil pan to timing chain cover bolts. Thoroughly clean cover and crankcase surface. Pry the seal out with a screwdriver. Do not distort the cover.
8. Align timing marks on sprockets.
9. Remove oil pan.
10. Remove crankshaft oil slinger. Remove camshaft sprocket bolts.
11. Use two large screwdrivers to alternately pry the camshaft sprocket, then the crankshaft sprocket, forward and off their respective shafts.

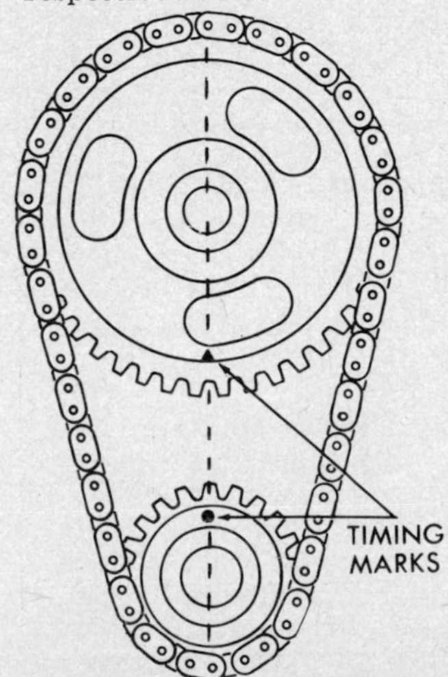

Valve timing marks—V8 and V6

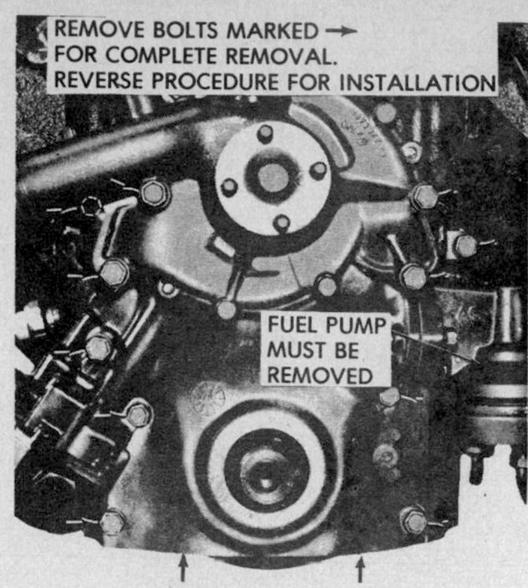

350 timing chain cover
(© Buick Div., G.M. Corp)

Removal 350, 400 Cu. In.

This procedure is the same as that detaiied above for the 455 cu. in. engine with the substitution of the following steps:

9. Delete Step 9.
10. Remove bolt, special washer, camshaft distributor drive gear, and fuel pump eccentric from camshaft. Remove crankshaft oil slinger.

Installation 350, 400 Cu. In.

1. Make sure, with sprockets temporarily installed, that No. 1 piston is at top dead center and the camshaft sprocket O-mark is straight down and on the centerline of both shafts.
2. Remove the camshaft sprocket and assemble the timing chain on both sprockets. Then slide the sprockets-and-chain assembly on the shafts with the O-marks in their closest together position and on a centerline with the sprocket hubs.
3. Assemble slinger on crankshaft with I.D. against the sprocket, (concave side toward front of engine).
4. Slide fuel pump eccentric on camshaft and Woodruff key with oil groove forward.
5. Install distributor drive gear.
6. Install drive gear and eccentric bolt and retaining washer. Torque to 40-55 ft. lbs.
7. Reinstall timing case cover. Install a new seal by lightly tapping it in place. The lip of the seal faces inward. By reversing removal procedure, paying particular attention to the following points.
   A. Remove oil pump cover and pack space around the oil pump gears completely full of petroleum jelly. There must be no air space left inside the pump. Reinstall the pump cover using new gasket.
   B. The gasket surface of the block and timing chain cover must be clean and smooth. Use a new gasket correctly positioned.
   C. Install chain cover being certain the dowel pins engage the dowel pin holes before starting the attaching bolts.
   D. Lube the bolt threads before installation and install them.
   E. If the car has power steering, the front pump bracket should be installed at this time.
   F. Lube the O.D. of the harmonic balancer hub before installation to prevent damage to the seal when starting the engine.

Installation 455 Cu. In.

This procedure is similar to that above for 350, 400 cu in. V8, with the substitution of the following steps:

4. Delete Step 4.
5. Reinstall oil pan.
6. Install camshaft sprocket bolts. Torque to 22 ft. lbs.

260 V8

1. Drain the cooling system, remove the radiator hoses, the fan shroud, and the radiator.
2. Remove all engine belts, the fan and fan pulley, the crankshaft pulley, and the harmonic balancer.
3. Drain the oil and remove the oil pan.
4. Remove the mounting bolts, and pry off the cover, the timing indicator, and the water pump assembly.
5. Remove the fuel pump eccentric from the camshaft.
6. Remove the oil slinger, the cam shaft sprocket and timing chain.
7. Remove the key from the crankshaft sprocket then remove the sprocket. Because of the close fit of the crankshaft sprocket, it may be necessary to use a gear puller to remove it.
8. Install the camshaft and crankshaft sprockets, and the timing chain together, and align their timing marks. When the two marks are in alignment. No. 6 cylinder is at TDC. To obtain TDC for No. 1 cylinder, rotate the camshaft one revolution. This will bring No. 1 to TDC.
9. Install the fuel pump eccentric on the camshaft gear.
10. Install the key into the crankshaft sprocket.
11. Reinstall the oil slinger.
12. Install a new cover gasket, and install the front cover assembly. Tighten the bolts evenly in a criss-cross pattern.
13. Install the oil pan; lubricate the pulley hub seal surface and install the pulley hub and bolt, torquing the bolt to 255 ft lbs.
14. From this point on, reverse the removal procedure to finish installing the components.

V6

1. Remove the water pump and crankshaft pulley.
2. Remove the two bolts that attach the oil pan to the timing chain cover.
3. Remove the five bolts that attach the timing chain cover to the engine block.
4. Remove the cover and gasket.
5. Remove the crankshaft front oil seal.
6. From the rear of the timing chain cover, coil new packing around the crankshaft hole in the cover so that the ends of the packing are at the top. Drive in the new packing with a punch. It will be necessary to ream out the hole to obtain clearance for the crankshaft vibration damper hub.
7. Make sure that the timing marks on the crankshaft and the camshaft sprockets are aligned. This will make installing the parts easier.

   NOTE: It is not necessary to remove the timing chain dampers (tensioners) unless they are worn or damaged and require replacement.
8. Remove the front crankshaft oil slinger.
9. Remove the bolt and the special washer that hold the camshaft distributor drive gear and fuel pump eccentric at the forward end of the camshaft. Remove the eccentric and the gear from the camshaft.
10. Alternately pry forward the camshaft sprocket and then the crankshaft sprocket until the camshaft sprocket is pried from the camshaft.
11. Remove the camshaft sprocket, sprocket key, and timing chain from the engine.
12. Pry the crankshaft sprocket from the crankshaft.

Install as follows:

1. If the engine has not been disturbed proceed to Step 4 for installation procedures.
2. If the engine has been disturbed turn the crankshaft so that number one piston is at top dead center.
3. Temporarily install the sprocket key and the camshaft sprocket on the camshaft. Turn the camshaft so that the index mark of the sprocket is downward. Remove the key and sprocket from the camshaft.
4. Assemble the timing chain and sprockets. Install the keys, sprockets, and chain assembly on the camshaft and crankshaft so that the index marks of both the sprockets are aligned.

   NOTE: It will be necessary to

hold the spring loaded timing chain damper out of the way while installing the timing chain and sprocket assembly.

5. Install the front oil slinger on the crankshaft with the inside diameter against the sprocket (concave side toward the front of the engine).
6. Install the fuel pump eccentric on the camshaft and the key, with the oil groove of the eccentric forward.
7. Install the distributor drive gear on the camshaft. Secure the gear and eccentric to the camshaft with the retaining washer and bolt.
8. Torque the bolt to 40-55 ft lbs.
9. Replace the cover.

Camshaft R & R

Inline Six-Cylinder

1. Drain cooling system.
2. Remove radiator, fan, and water pump pulley.
3. Remove grille.
4. Remove valve cover and gasket, then loosen rocker arm nuts and pivot rockers out of the way.
5. Remove pushrods.
6. Remove distributor, fuel pump, and spark plugs.
7. Remove coil, pushrod (tappet gallery) covers and gasket; reach in and remove tappets, keeping them in order.
8. Remove harmonic balancer, then loosen oil pan bolts and allow pan to drop.
9. Remove timing gear cover.
10. Align the timing marks. Remove two camshaft thrust plate bolts by rotating cam gear holes to gain clearance.
11. Remove the camshaft by pulling it straight forward.

NOTE: do not wiggle the camshaft; cam bearings could be dislodged.

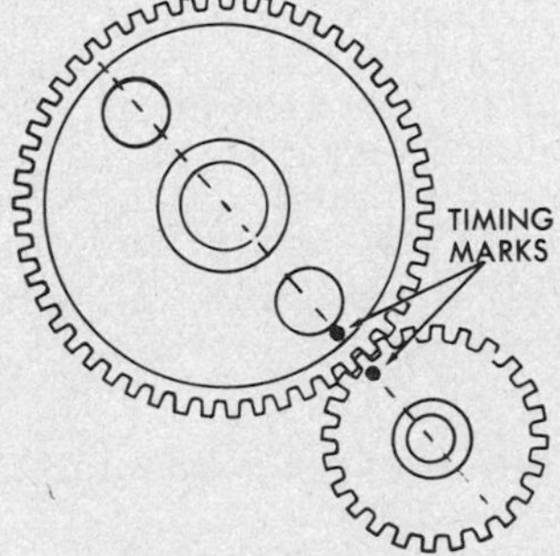

Valve timing marks—inline 6

12. If cam gear is to be replaced, press it from the shaft using an arbor press.

NOTE: thrust plate must be positioned so that Woodruff key does not damage it during removal.

13. New cam gear must be pressed onto the shaft, with the shaft supported in back of the front bearing journal.

NOTE: the thrust plate end-play should be 0.001-0.005 in. If less than 0.001 in., replace spacer ring; if greater than 0.005 in., replace thrust plate.

14. Carefully install the camshaft into the engine, then turn crankshaft and camshaft so that timing marks coincide; tighten thrust plate bolts to 5–8 ft. lbs. Lubricate the camshaft lobes and bearings with heavy oil.
15. Check camshaft and crankshaft gear runout using a dial indicator. Cam gear runout should not exceed 0.004 in., crank gear runout should not exceed 0.003 in.

NOTE: if runout is excessive, remove gear and clean burrs from shaft.

16. Check gear backlash using a dial indicator; it should not exceed 0.006 in. and should not be less than 0.004 in.
17. To complete installation, reverse Steps 1-9.

NOTE: install distributor with No. 1 piston at TDC on compression stroke so that vacuum diaphragm faces forward and rotor points to No. 1 spark plug wire cap tower. Make sure oil pump drive shaft is properly indexed with distributor drive shaft.

V6

1. Remove the engine.
2. Remove the intake manifold and carburetor assembly.
3. Remove the distributor.
4. Remove the fuel pump.
5. Remove the alternator, drive belts, cooling fan, fan pulley, and water pump.
6. Remove the crankshaft pulley and the vibration damper.
7. Remove the oil pump.
8. Remove the timing chain cover.
9. Remove the timing chain and the camshaft sprocket, along with the distributor drive gear and the fuel pump eccentric.
10. Remove the rocker arm assemblies.

NOTE: The push rods need not be removed. But if they are, be sure that they are replaced in their original positions.

11. Lift the tappets up so that they are not in contact with the camshaft. Use wire clips or clip-type clothes pins to hold the tappets up.
12. Carefully guide the camshaft forward out of the engine. Avoid marring the bearing surfaces.
13. Install in reverse order of the above procedure.

V8

1. Drain the cooling system.
2. Remove the radiator, fan, and water pump pulley.
3. Remove the grille.
4. Remove the valve cover, rocker shaft assemblies, and push rods. Keep these parts in order. They must be reassembled in the same order.
5. Remove the distributor and fuel pump.
6. Remove the harmonic balancer, water pump timing chain cover assembly, timing chain, and sprocket.
7. Remove the intake manifold and the valley cover.
8. Remove the hydraulic lifters and keep them in order.

NOTE: 0.010 in. oversize lifters are sometimes installed. These are identified by an O on the lifter bore and two grooves on the lifter body.

9. Slide the camshaft forward out of the bearing bores. Do this very carefully to avoid marring the bearing surfaces.
10. Reverse the above steps to install. Clean all gasket surfaces and use new gaskets. Make sure the camshaft timing marks are aligned. Lubricate the camshaft lobes and bearings with heavy oil.

260 V8

1. Disconnect the battery.
2. Drain the radiator, remove all radiator hoses, disconnect the transmission cooler lines, remove the fan shroud, and remove the radiator.
3. Disconnect the fuel line at the pump, remove the air cleaner and disconnect the throttle cable.
4. Remove the alternator belt and move the alternator to one side; remove the power steering pump and belt and set it aside out of the way.
5. Remove the air conditioner compressor mounting bracket and move the assembly out of the way. *Do not disconnect the lines.*
6. Remove the thermostat bypass hose and all heater hoses; disconnect any electrical and vacuum connections that are in the way; disconnect the sparkplug wires.
7. Remove the distributor, engine oil pan, starter and exhaust crossover pipe.
8. Remove the harmonic balancer and pulley; remove the flywheel inspection cover, the engine front cover, both valve covers and the intake manifold.
9. Remove the rocker arm assembly.
10. If the car is equipped with air conditioning move the condensor to the side.
11. Remove the fuel pump eccentric, the camshaft sprocket, the oil slinger and the timing chain.
12. Remove the camshaft by carefully sliding it out of the front of the engine.

Installation is the reverse of removal but note the following points:

1. Make sure that the camshaft and bearings are liberally coated with heavy oil.
2. Make sure that the camshaft and crankshaft sprockets are properly aligned.
3. Before installing the power steering pump make sure that the timing indicator attaching stud is installed and properly torqued (35 ft lbs.).
4. Install the flywheel inspection cover after installing the starter.
5. The left side rear oil gallery plug, just behind the distributor, is used for distributor lubrication. There is a cup plug on top of the threaded plug which has to be removed before lubricant can be added. The front oil gallery plug is on the right side and provides lubrication for the timing chain and gears.

Piston Assembly

All V8 engines are numbered 1-3-5-7, left bank; and 2-4-6-8, right bank. The inline 6 engine is numbered 1-2-3-4-5-6, front to rear.

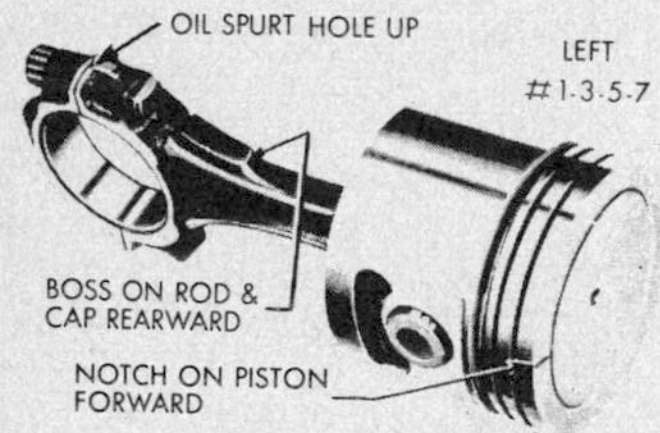

Piston and rod assembly, left bank—350, 400, 455
(© Buick Div., G.M. Corp)

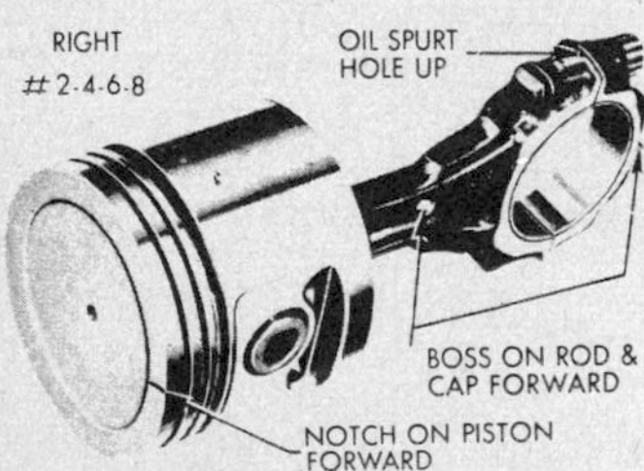

Piston and rod assembly, right bank—350, 400, 455
(© Buick Div., G.M. Corp)

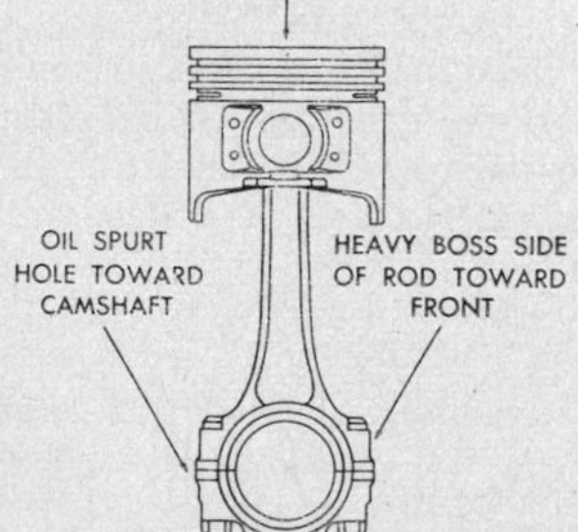

Piston and rod assembly—inline 6

V6

Starting at the front end of the crankcase, the cylinders in the right bank are numbered 2-4-6 and in the left bank are numbered 1-3-5.

All compression rings are marked with a dimple, a letter "T", a letter "O", or the word "TOP" to identify the side of the ring which must face toward the top of the piston.

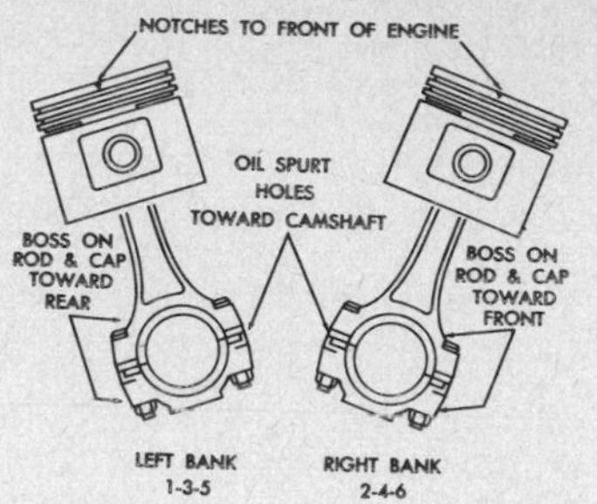

Piston and rod assembly—V6

When the piston and connecting rod assembly is properly installed, the oil spurt hole in the connecting rod will face the camshaft. The rib on the edge of the bearing cap will be on the same side as the conical boss on the connecting rod web. These marks on the rib and the boss will be toward the other connecting rod on the same crankpin. The notch on the piston will face the front of the engine.

Lubrication

The engine lubrication system is the force feed type, in which oil is supplied under pressure to the crankshaft, connecting rods, camshaft bearings and valve lifters. Oil is supplied under controlled volume to the rocker arm bearings and pushrods.

Oil Pump Removal and Installation

On the inline 6, the oil pump is located in the oil pan and mounted to the front section of the cylinder block where it is connected to an oil screen housing and pipe assembly. On the V8s, the oil pump is located in the left side of the timing chain cover, where it is connected by a drilled passage in the cylinder crankcase to an oil screen housing and standpipe assembly.

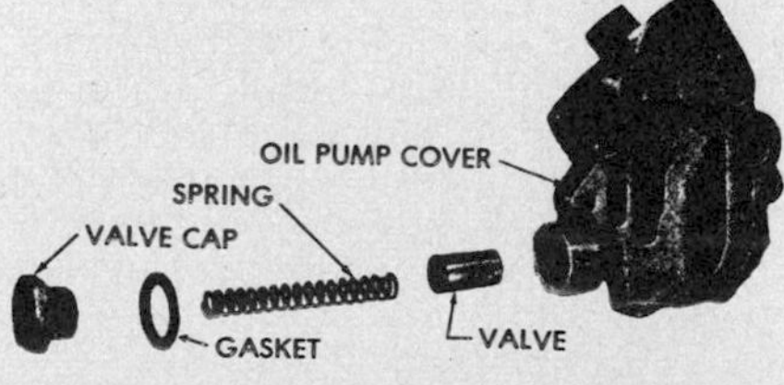

Oil pump cover and pressure relief valve—V8
(© Buick Div., G.M. Corp)

Inline Six-Cylinder

1. Drain the oil and remove the oil pan.
2. Remove the two flange mounting bolts and the pickup pipe bolt and remove the pump and screen as an assembly.
3. To install, reverse the above procedure, being sure to tighten the mounting bolts to 9 ft lbs.

NOTE: The oil pump should slide easily into place. If not, remove it and relocate the slot.

V6

1. Remove the oil filter.
2. Disconnect the lead from the oil pressure indicator switch in the filter by-pass valve cap.
3. Remove the screws that attach the oil pump cover assembly to the timing chain cover.
4. Remove the cover assembly and slide out the oil pump.
5. Install the oil pump in the reverse order of removal. Replenish the crankcase oil supply to the proper level.

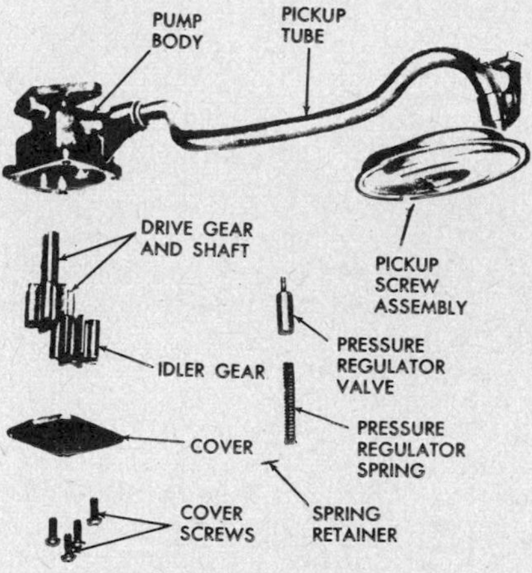

Inline 6 oil pump—exploded view
(© Buick Div., G.M. Corp)

V8 except 260

The pump can be disassembled as follows:

1. Remove the oil filter.
2. Unbolt the pump cover assembly from the timing chain cover.
3. Remove the cover assembly and slide out the pump gears.
4. Remove the oil pressure relief valve cap, spring, and valve. Do not remove the oil filter by-pass valve and spring.
5. Check that the relief valve spring isn't worn on its side or collapsed. Check that the relief valve is no more than an easy slip fit in its bore in the cover. If there is any perceptible side-play, replace the valve. If there is still side-play, replace the cover.
6. Check the filter by-pass valve for good condition.

To assemble the pump:

7. Lubricate and install the pressure relief valve and spring in the cover bore. Install the gasket and cap, torquing the cap to 35 ft lbs.
8. Install the gears and check that gear-to-cover end clearance is between 0.002-0.006 in. If the clearance is less, check the timing cover gear pocket for wear.

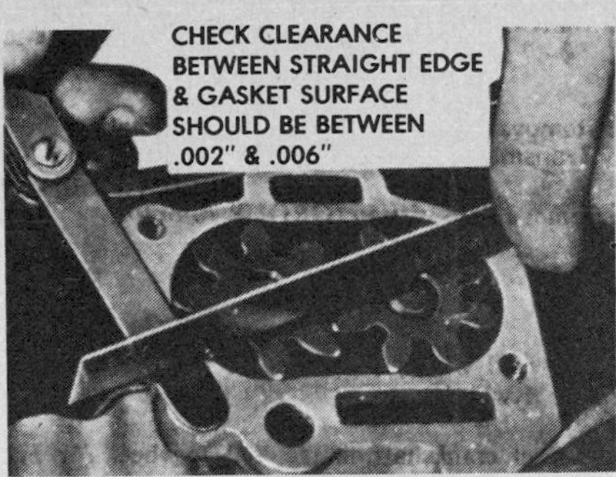

Checking oil pump end clearance—V6 and V8
(© Buick Div., G.M. Corp)

9. Remove the gears and pack the gear pocket full of petroleum jelly. Don't use grease.

Caution Unless the pump is primed this way, it won't produce any oil pressure when the engine is started.

10. Install the gears. Install a new gasket and the cover. Torque the bolts evenly to 10 ft lbs. Replace the filter.

260 V8

1. Remove the oil pan.
2. Remove the oil pump to rear main bearing cap mounting bolts.
3. Remove the pump and drive shaft extension.
4. Installation is the reverse of removal.

Oil Pan Removal and Installation

V8 Engines except 260

1. Disconnect the battery ground cable.
2. Remove the fan shroud-to-radiator tie bar screws.
3. Remove the air cleaner and disconnect the throttle linkage.
4. Raise the front end and support it on jackstands.
5. Drain the oil.
6. Disconnect the exhaust crossover pipe at the engine. The clutch equalizer bracket will have to be unbolted from the frame on some earlier models.
7. Remove the lower flywheel housing cover.
8. Remove the shift linkage bolt and swing it out of the way.
9. Remove the front engine mount bolts.
10. Raise the front of the engine, either by placing a block of wood and a jack under the crankshaft pulley mounting or lifting it with a hoist.

Caution On air conditioned cars, place a support under the right-side of the transmission before raising the engine. If you don't do this, the engine and transmission will flop to the right due to the weight of the air conditioning equipment.

11. On Apollo, disconnect the idler arm at the frame and swing the assembly down.
12. Unbolt and remove the pan. It may be necessary to turn the crankshaft so that it doesn't interfere with the front of the pan.
13. Reverse the procedure for installation.

260 V8

1. Remove distributor cap and place rotor at TDC for No. 1 cylinder by turning crankshaft pulley.
2. Disconnect the battery cable; remove the dipstick.
3. Put the car on a lift and drain the oil.
4. Remove the flywheel cover and starter assembly.
5. Disconnect the exhaust and exhaust crossover pipes.
6. Jack up the engine to disconnect the engine mounts then raise the front of the engine as far as possible.
7. Remove the oil pan mounting bolts and remove the pan.
8. Install the front and rear seals, the pan gasket, and replace the pan.
9. Reverse the removal steps to install.

1969 Inline Six-Cylinder

To remove the oil pan, it is necessary to remove the engine from the car. See Engine Removal.

Inline Six-Cylinder beginning 1970

1. Disconnect battery, remove air cleaner and disconnect throttle linkage.
2. Remove fan shroud-to-radiator tie bar screws.
3. Jack up car and support on axle stands under lower A-frames.
4. Drain engine oil.
5. If equipped with automatic transmission:
   a. Remove flywheel housing inspection cover.
   b. Remove shift linkage bolt and swing linkage out of way.
   c. Disconnect exhaust pipe at manifold.
6. Remove front motor mount bolts.
7. Jack up engine as far as it will go, with padded jack under crank pulley mounting.
8. Remove front motor mounts completely to gain clearance. Remove the left mount and frame bracket, on Apollo.
9. On Apollo, disconnect the steering rod at the idler lever, then move the linkage to one side.
10. On Apollo, unbolt and move the brake line away from the front crossmember.
11. Turn the crankshaft until the timing mark on the damper is at the bottom.
12. Unbolt the pan. On Apollo, lower it slightly and roll it into the area from which you removed the left engine mount, tilt the front of the pan up and pull it down and out to the rear.
13. Reverse the procedure on installation. Tighten the bolts to 7-10 ft lbs, except for those that go into the front cover. These must be installed last and tightened to 5 ft lbs.

Rear Main Bearing Oil Seal Replacement

Inline Six-Cylinder

1. The rear main bearing oil seal can be replaced without removing the crankshaft. Remove the oil pan and rear main bearing cap.
2. Remove the seal from the bearing cap and clean the groove.
3. Remove the upper seal half by tapping the seal out with a brass punch until it can be grasped with pliers.
4. To replace the bearing cap seal, lubricate the groove in the cap and lightly press the seal in place. Do not cut the end of the seal. Do not get any oil on the parting line surface.
5. To replace the upper seal, lubricate the new seal with oil. Gradually push the seal in the groove in the block, while turning the crankshaft, until the seal is rolled into place.
6. Install the rear main bearing cap and torque it to specifications. Be sure the cross seal tabs are in place and properly seated. Make sure there is no oil on the parting line between the bearing cap and the block. Run the engine slowly for the first few minutes.

V6

1. Remove the oil pan and the crankshaft. When the rear main bearing cap is removed, remove the fabric packing type seal from the radius portion of the cap and the neoprene seals from the grooves on the side of the cap.
2. With an ice pick or similar tool pry the upper half of the seal from the block.
3. Place the new seal in the groove in the rear main bearing cap with both ends protruding above the parting surface of the cap. Force the seal into the groove by rubbing down with a hammer handle or similar tool until the seal projects above the groove no more than 1 16 in. Cut the ends off flush with the mating surface of the cap with a razor blade. Lubricate the seal with engine oil just before installing it in the engine.

4. Lubricate all of the main bearings and install the crankshaft. Install all the main bearing caps and tighten them to the correct torque.
5. Dip the neoprene main bearing cap side seals in kerosene (any light oil will do) for 1-½ minutes. This will cause the seals to swell; so you will have to work quickly. Install the seals into the bearing cap grooves. The protruding ends of the seals should then be squirted with kerosene (or oil), wiped off, and peaned over with a hammer to be sure of a seal at the upper mating surface of the cap and cylinder block.

NOTE: Do not cut the seals to length before installing them.

6. Attach the connecting rods to the crankshaft and install the oil pan in the reverse order of removal.

V8

1. Braided fabric seals are used. The upper seal half cannot be replaced without removing the crankshaft, unless you use the Time Saver in this section.
2. Remove the oil pan and rear main bearing cap.
3. Remove the old seal from the bearing cap and place a new seal in the groove with both ends projecting above the parting surface of the cap.
4. Force the seal into the groove by rubbing down with a hammer handle or smooth tool, until the seal projects above the groove not more than 1/16 in. Cut the ends off flush with the surface of the cap. Use a razor blade.
5. Use the same procedure to install a new upper seal half after removing the engine from the car and the crankshaft from the engine.

Chilton's TIME SAVER

Top Half, Rear Main Bearing Oil Seal Replacement

Although the factory recommends removing the crankshaft to replace the top half of the oil seal, the following procedure can be used without removing the crankshaft.

1. **Remove the oil pan and rear main bearing cap.**
2. **Loosen the rest of the crankshaft main bearings and allow the crankshaft to drop about 1/16 in.**
3. **Remove the old upper half of the oil seal.**
4. **Wrap some soft copper wire around the end of the new seal and leave about 12 in. on the end. Generously lubricate the new seal with oil.**
5. **Slip the free end of the copper wire into the oil seal groove and around the crankshaft. Pull the wire until the seal protrudes an equal amount on each side. Rotate the crankshaft as the seal is pulled into place.**
6. **Remove the wire. Push any excess seal that may be protruding back into the groove.**
7. **Before tightening the crankshaft bearing caps, visually check the bearings to make sure they are in place. Torque the bearing cap bolts to specifications. Make sure there is no oil on the parting surfaces.**
8. **Replace the oil pan. Run the engine slowly for the first few minutes of operation.**

CLUTCH

A single plate, dry disc clutch is used in cars with manual transmissions. The unit is conventional in design with a diaphragm spring assembly. The clutch is not adjustable except for pedal clearance.

Clutch Removal

1. Remove pedal return spring from clutch fork. Remove the transmission.
2. Remove flywheel housing.
3. Remove throw-out bearing from clutch fork.
4. Disconnect clutch fork from ball stud.
5. Mark clutch cover and flywheel to assure proper balance on reassembly.
6. Loosen clutch cover to flywheel bolts one turn at a time until spring pressure is released.
7. Support pressure plate and cover assembly while removing last bolts, then remove cover assembly and driven plate.

Clutch Installation

Install clutch by reversing removal procedure. Use a clutch aligning pilot or a spare main drive gear through the hub of driven plate and into the pilot bushing. Be sure to align the clutch cover-to-flywheel index marks.

Clutch Linkage Adjustment

All except Skyhawk

Check pedal lash (free-play) by pushing down on the pedal by hand. Lash should be approximately ¾ in. measured at the pedal pad.

1. Make sure the pedal is at full release position, contacting the rubber bumper stop. Remove return spring.
2. Adjust clutch release rod underneath car to give zero lash at the clutch pedal.
3. Back off release rod adjustment 2-3 turns to give ¾ in. lash at pedal pad. (Equals 1/16-⅛ in. at pushrod.)
4. Tighten locknut on clutch release rod.

Skyhawk

1. Make sure that the pedal is at full release position, contacting the rubber bumper stop. Remove the return spring.
2. Push the clutch fork forward until the throwout bearing just touches the clutch spring (about 1¾ in.).
3. Tighten the screw pin on the cable to obtain about ¼ in. fork free play; this will produce ¾-1 in. free play at the clutch pedal.
4. Attach the return spring

MANUAL TRANSMISSION

Three different, fully-synchronized three-speed transmissions have been available in these cars. A Ford-built, top cover transmission was used through 1969 in high-performance applications. It is the only top cover transmission found in these cars. A Muncie transmission was used in 1970-71 GS models. It can be identified by the two casting "ears" or bolt bosses on the case at the top of the side cover. A Saginaw transmission is used in all years. It is the only 3-speed manual transmission used on the Apollo and Century. It can be identified by the single casting "ear" or bolt boss on the case at the top of the side cover. The production code and transmission serial number are on the right side of the transmission case.

The Muncie 4-speed is the only 4-speed transmission used in cars made before 1975.

In the Skyhawk, a fully synchronized, four speed Saginaw transmission is used. The production code and transmission serial number are stamped on the right side of the transmission case.

For repair procedures, see the Unit Repair Section.

Removal and Installation

1. Mark the universal joint and transmission shaft companion flange for proper indexing at the time of installation. Remove the two U-bolts and disconnect the driveshaft at the rear joint. Slide the driveshaft rearward as far as possible and remove it.
2. Disconnect the shift linkage from the transmission.

3. Disconnect the speedometer cable at the transmission.
4. Loosen all exhaust pipe joints to permit the transmission and the rear of the engine to be lowered if necessary.
5. Remove the two bolts holding the transmission mounting pad to the transmission support. Leave the mounting pad bolted to the transmission.
6. With a padded jack under the engine, raise the unit until the transmission mounting pad just clears the transmission support.
7. Remove the four bolts holding the transmission support to the body members. Remove the support, then lower the jack to allow the transmission to clear the underbody.
8. Remove the two top transmission-to-flywheel housing bolts and install guide pins.

NOTE: If guide pins are not used, damage to the clutch driven plate can result.

9. Remove the other transmission attaching bolts. Slide the transmission back until the drive gear shaft disengages the clutch disc and clears the flywheel housing. Lower the transmission.
10. On installation, install the guide pins in the upper and lower right-side bolt holes for alignment. If the guide pins aren't used, the clutch plate might be damaged.

Linkage Adjustment

Three-Speed Column Shift

1969 and later

1. Place the column shift lever in Reverse. Turn the ignition lock to the LOCK position.
2. Loosen first-reverse clamp bolt.
3. Place the transmission first-reverse lever (the rear one) into the reverse (forward) position. Pull down on the shift rod and tighten the clamp bolt to 17-23 ft. lbs.
4. Unlock the ignition lock and shift the transmission levers into their neutral (center) positions.
5. Loosen second-third clamp bolt.
6. Install a 3/16 in. dia. rod through second-third lever, selector plate, first-reverse lever, and alignment plate at the bottom of the column.
7. Tighten second-third clamp bolt to 17-23 ft. lbs.
8. With the shift lever in Reverse, the key must move freely to the LOCK position. You should not be able to get into the LOCK position in any gear position other than Reverse.

Three-Speed Floorshift

1. Place transmission levers into neutral.
2. Loosen shift rod adjusting clamp bolts.
3. Place a 5/16 in. dia. rod in notch in rear portion of shift bracket assembly.
4. Move both shift levers back against rod.
5. Tighten shift rod adjusting bolts to 17-23 ft. lbs.

Four-Speed Floorshift

All except Skyhawk

1. Place transmission levers in neutral positions.
2. Place a 5/16 in. dia. rod in rear lower portion of shift bracket assembly.

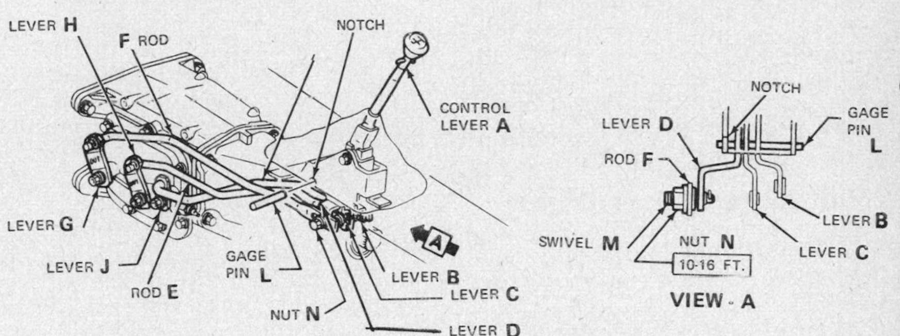

Skyhawk 4 speed transmission linkage (© Buick Div., G.M. Corp)

3. Adjust all three shift levers back against rod.
4. Tighten adjusting clamp bolts to 17-23 ft. lbs.

Skyhawk

1. Loosen the rod retaining nuts at the base of the shift lever; set the third and fourth, first and second, and reverse gear levers into neutral. This can be done by moving the levers counterclockwise one detent and then clockwise one detent.
2. Move the shift lever into neutral and then align the holes of the reverse, first and second, and third and fourth gear levers with the notch on the shifter assembly. When they are aligned, insert a pin to hold them in place.
3. Attach the third and fourth gear rod to the third and fourth gear lever.
4. Attach the third and fourth gear rod and retaining nut loosely to the swivel on the third and fourth gear lever. When installed, tighten the retaining nut.
5. Repeat steps 3 and 4 for the first and second, and for the reverse gear adjustment.
6. When the adjustments have been completed, remove the pin.

Hurst Shift Linkage Adjustment

1. Shift transmission into Reverse.
2. Push "back drive" (steering lock) rod up into reverse detent in steering column (if applicable).
3. Tighten clamp screw to 17-23 ft. lbs.
4. Place all transmission and control levers in Neutral.
5. Insert a ¼ in. drill rod through adjustment hole in shifter and make sure all shift rods fit into their respective levers without tension. Adjust length of rods as necessary, then tighten swivel nuts.

Clutch Start Switch

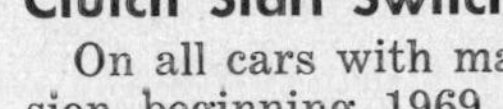

On all cars with manual transmission beginning 1969, a clutch start switch on the clutch pedal bracket prevents starting unless the clutch pedal is fully depressed. This switch is connected in series with the circuit from the ignition switch to the starter solenoid; therefore a no-start condition could be caused by its failure.

Backup Light Switch

The backup light switch is mounted on the steering column under the instrument panel in the same location as the neutral start and backup light switch on automatic transmission models. The switch is operated by the movement of the column shift tube. The mounting bracket has slotted holes for adjustment.

AUTOMATIC TRANSMISSION

All the Buick models covered in this section except the 1969-71 Gran Sport, use the 350-375B Turbo Hydra-Matic transmission. The identification number for this transmission is located on the lower left side. The 1969-71 Gran Sport uses a Turbo Hydra-Matic 400 transmission with its identification number in the same place as the 350-375B transmission. The 1969 Buick Special Deluxe uses a Super Turbine 300 transmission; its identification number is also on the lower left side, next to the detent solenoid case connector.

One way to tell the difference between the 350-375B transmission and the 400 transmission is the detent switch. On the 350-375B series, the detent cable runs from the throttle linkage down to the right side of the transmission. On the 400 series, there is an electrically operated detent switch in the engine compartment, on the firewall, next to the throttle lever.

Detent Cable Adjustment—Turbo Hydra-Matic 350 and 375B

Refer to the accompanying illustration for this procedure.

Detent Switch Adjustment—Turbo Hydra-Matic 400

The switch is on the firewall, inside the car, near the accelerator pedal. The initial adjustment on installation is made by pushing the switch lever all the way toward the firewall. The final adjustment is made automatically the first time the accelerator pedal is floorboarded.

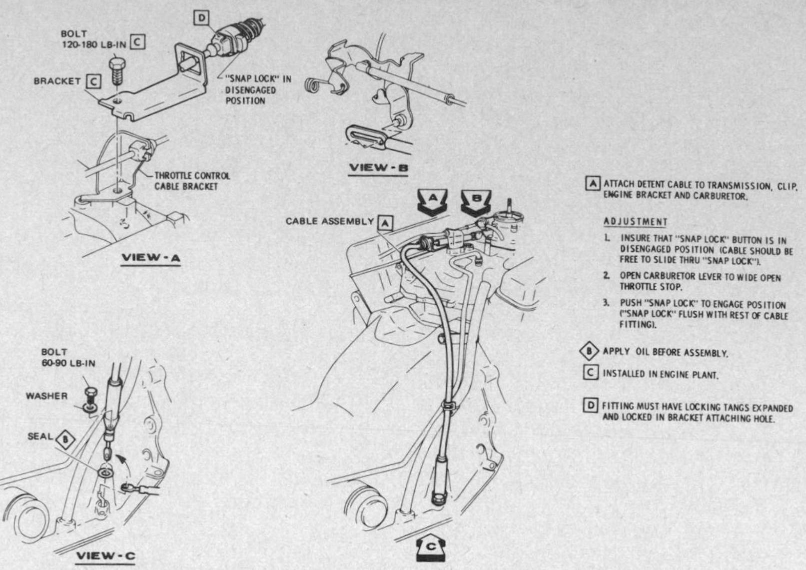

Apollo Turbo Hydra-Matic 350 detent switch installation and adjustment
(© Buick Div., G.M. Corp)

Shift Linkage Adjustment

Column Shift

1. Place selector lever in Drive (Neutral for 1971 up).
2. Loosen adjusting clamp bolt.
3. Place lever at transmission in drive (Neutral for 1971 up) position.
4. Tighten clamp bolt to 17-23 ft. lbs.

Console Shift

There are two procedures that can be used, depending on the shape of the transmission end of the shifter cable. On early models, the cable ends in a straight rod with a clamp (trunnion) bolt. On later models, the cable ends in a flattened eye with a fixed bolt through it.

1. Loosen the trunnion bolt at the transmission end of the cable on early models. On later models, pull the clip from the cable housing at the side of the transmission.
2. Set the console shift lever against the Drive stop on early models. On later models, set it in the Park detent.
3. Set the transmission shift lever in the Drive position on early

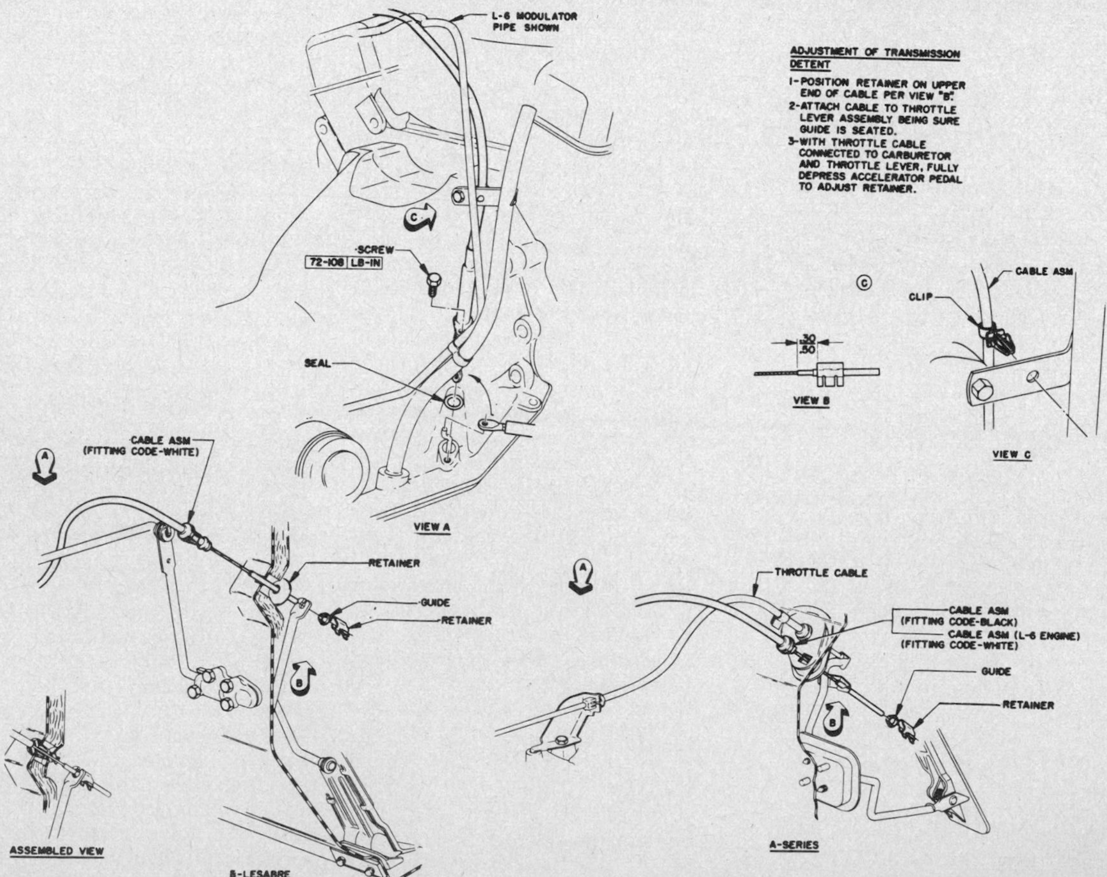

Transmission detent cable adjustment—Turbo Hydra-Matic 350 (© Buick Div., G.M. Corp)

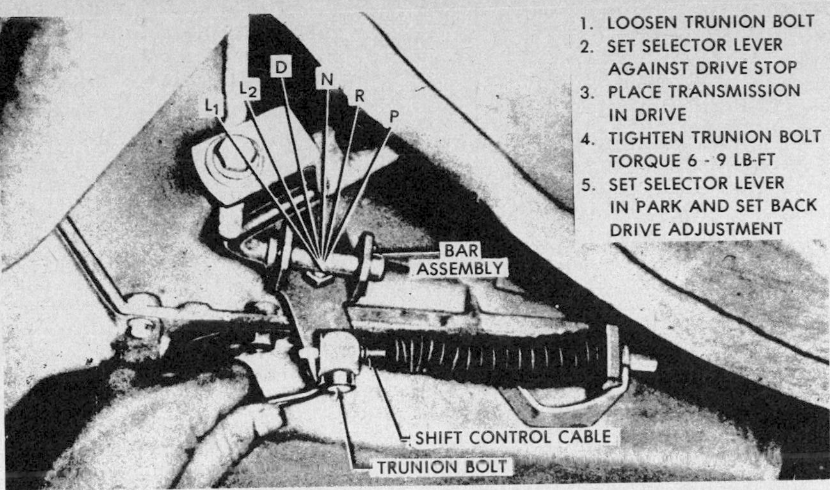

Turbo Hydra-Matic 350 and 400 linkage adjustment console shifter (early models) (© Buick Div., G.M. Corp)

models. This is the third position from the back. On later models, set it in the Park, or most forward, position.

4. On early models, tighten the trunnion bolt against the cable end to 6-9 ft lbs. On later models, replace the clip to hold the cable housing in position.
5. Place the console shift lever in the Park position.
6. Set the console shift lever in Park. Loosen the clamp at the bottom of the back drive rod (the one that goes to the steering column). Push the back drive rod up against the stop and tighten the clamp screw.

Neutral Safety Switch

This switch prevents the engine from being started in any transmission position except Neutral or Park. The back-up light switch is combined with the neutral safety switch. On column shift cars and 1971 and later models with console shift, the switch is located on the steering column under the instrument panel. On earlier console shift cars, the switch is located inside the console. When the neutral start portion of the switch is correctly adjusted, the back-up portion is adjusted automatically. Slotted mounting screw holes permit switch movement for adjustment. To adjust the switch, place the shift lever in the Neutral position and insert a 3/32 in. drill bit through the hole in the back of the switch. Move the switch until the bit goes in about 3/8 in. Tighten the mounting screws and check the adjustment.

Caution when checking to see if engine will start in transmission positions other than Neutral or Park, always hold the service brake firmly.

Pan Removal and Installation Fluid and Filter Change

Turbo Hydra-Matic 350, 375 B

1. Raise the car on a lift, remove the pan bolts and washers. Loosen the bolts gradually so that the fluid can drain out of one corner of the pan without spilling.
2. Remove the old gasket and clean the pan.
3. Remove the two screws holding the filter in place and remove it, remove the filter to valve body gasket.
4. Install the new filter to valve body gasket on the filter and install the assembly. Replace the pan, torquing the bolts to 13 ft lbs.
5. Lower the car and add three pints of Dexron automatic transmission fluid; then start the car and shift it through each gear.
6. Check the transmission fluid level and add if necessary.

Turbo Hydra-Matic transmission filter and gasket (© Buick Div., G.M. Corp)

Turbo Hydra-Matic 400

The procedure is the same, but when the filter is removed, the intake pipe O-ring seal must be replaced. The pan bolts are torqued to 10 ft lbs.

U-JOINTS

The driveshaft is a one piece unit with a splined slip yoke and a universal joint at the transmission end, and a second universal joint at the differential end. The shaft, depending on application, can be a one-piece solid steel unit, or can be composed of two concentric tubes damped with rubber.

Driveshaft R & R

1. Mark the driveshaft rear yoke and the differential flange to assure correct alignment upon reassembly.
2. Remove the bolts and straps from the differential flange.
3. Remove the driveshaft assembly by first sliding the driveshaft sufficiently forward to disengage the differential flange and then slide the shaft downward and rearward to disengage the front splined yoke from the transmission output shaft.
4. Installation is the reverse of removal. Be sure to align the match marks made before disassembly.

Universal Joint R & R

Nylon-injected composite universal joints are used. To replace universal joints:

1. Remove the driveshaft.
2. By using a piece of pipe or similar tool, slightly larger than 1⅛ in. to encircle the bearing shell, apply force on the yoke until downward movement of the yoke and stationary position of journal force the bearing assembly almost out of the top of the yoke (the force applied on the yoke will shear nylon retainers which lock bearings in place).
3. Rotate the shaft 180° and repeat preceding step to partially remove the opposite bearing.
4. Complete removal of these bearings by tapping around the circumference of exposed portion of bearing.
5. Remove journal from driveshaft rear yoke.
6. Remove bearings and journal from splined yoke in the same way.

NOTE: new bearings and journal assembly kits must be used upon reassembly. The kit includes snap-rings and Delrin washers.

7. Install by inserting one bearing one-quarter way in one side of splined yoke, using brass hammer.
8. Insert journal into splined yoke (with dust shields installed).
9. Install opposite bearing, ensuring that the bearing rollers do not jam on journal. Check free rotary movement of journal in bearing.
10. Now, press both bearings into place (just far enough to install snap rings).
11. Assemble opposite end universal in the same way.

REAR AXLE

Axle, Shaft, Bearing, and Seal

Removal and Installation

These cars use two different types of drive axle, the C- and the non C-type. Axle shafts in the C-type are retained by C-shaped locks, which fit grooves at the inner end of the shaft. Axle shafts in the non C-type are retained by the brake backing plate, which is bolted to the axle housing. Bearings in the C-type axle consist of an outer race, bearing rollers and a roller cage, retained by snap-rings. The non C-type axle uses a unit roller bearing (inner race, rollers and outer race), which is pressed onto the shaft up to a shoulder. When servicing C or non C type axles, it is imperative to determine the axle type before attempting any service.

Non C-Type

Caution Before attempting any service to the drive axle or axle shafts, remove the axle carrier cover and visually determine if the axle shafts are retained by C-shaped locks at the inner end, or by the brake backing plate at the outer end. If the shafts are *not* retained by C-locks, proceed as follows.

Design allows for maximum axle shaft end-play of 0.022 in., which can be measured with a dial indicator. If end-play is found to be excessive, the bearing should be replaced. Shimming the bearing is not recommended as this ignores end-play of the bearing itself and could result in improper seating of the bearing.

1. Remove the wheel, tire and brake drum.
2. Remove the nuts holding the retainer plate to the backing plate. Disconnect the brake line.
3. Remove the retainer and install nuts, fingertight, to prevent the brake backing plate from being dislodged.
4. Pull out the axle shaft and bearing assembly, using a slide hammer.
5. Using a chisel, nick the bearing retainer in three or four places. The retainer does not have to be cut, merely collapsed sufficiently. to allow the bearing retainer to be slid from the shaft.
6. Press off the bearing and install the new one by pressing it into position.
7. Press on the new retainer.

NOTE: do not attempt to press the bearing and the retainer on at the same time.

8. Assemble the shaft and bearing in the housing, being sure that the bearing is seated properly in the housing.
9. Install the retainer, drum, wheel and tire. Bleed the brakes.

C-Type

Caution Before attempting any service to the drive axle or axle shafts, remove the carrier cover and visually determine if the axle shaft(s) are retained by C-shaped locks at the inner ends or by a brake backing plate at the outer end. If they *are* retained by C-shaped locks, proceed as follows.

1. Raise the vehicle and remove the wheels.
2. The differential cover has already been removed (see Caution note above). Remove the differential pinion shaft lock-screw and the differential pinion shaft.

Removing pinion shaft lock bolt from differential
(© Buick Div., G.M. Corp)

3. Push the flanged end of the axle shaft toward the center of the vehicle and remove the C-lock from the end of the shaft.

Removing the axle shaft C lock
(© Buick Div., G.M. Corp)

4. Remove the axle shaft from the housing, being careful not to damage the oil seal.
5. Remove the oil seal by inserting the button end of the axle shaft behind the steel case of the oil seal. Pry the seal loose from the bore.
6. Seat the legs of the bearing puller behind the bearing. Seat a washer against the bearing and hold it in place with a nut. Use a slide hammer to pull the bearing.
7. Pack the cavity between the seal lips with wheel bearing lubricant and lubricate a new wheel bearing with same.
8. Use a suitable driver and install the bearing until it bottoms against the tube. Install the oil seal.
9. Slide the axle shaft into place. Be sure that the splines on the shaft do not damage the oil seal. Make sure that the splines engage the differential side gear.
10. Install the axle shaft C-lock on the inner end of the axle shaft and push the shaft outward so that the C-lock seats in the differential side gear counterbore.
11. Position the differential pinion shaft through the case and pinions, aligning the hole in the case with the hole for the lock-screw.
12. Install the pinion shaft lock-screw.
13. Use a new gasket and install the carrier cover. Be sure that the gasket surfaces are clean before installing the gasket and cover.
14. Fill the axle with lubricant to the bottom of the filler hole.
15. Install the brake drum and wheels and lower the car. Check for leaks and road test the car.

JACKING, HOISTING

Jack car at front spring seat of lower control arm or center of cross member.

Jack car at rear at axle housing.

To lift at frame, use side rails in front of body floor pan and at rear side rail at lower control arm front pivot.

FRONT SUSPENSION

Ball joints, located at the outer ends of the upper and lower control arms, act as pivot points for both the vertical movement of the wheel and rotation of the steering knuckle. The spherical joints have a fixed boot grease seal to protect against dirt and water. Steering knuckles and spindles are one-piece forgings.

Rubber bushings at the upper inner control arm ends pivot on shafts attached to the frame. By varying shim thickness at this point, caster and camber are adjusted. The inner ends of the lower control arms are also rubber mounted and are attached to the front crossmember by brackets.

The upper ends of the coil springs are seated in the frame, while the lower ends rest on the lower control arms. Double-action shock absorbers are located inside the coil springs, the rubber insulated upper end of each

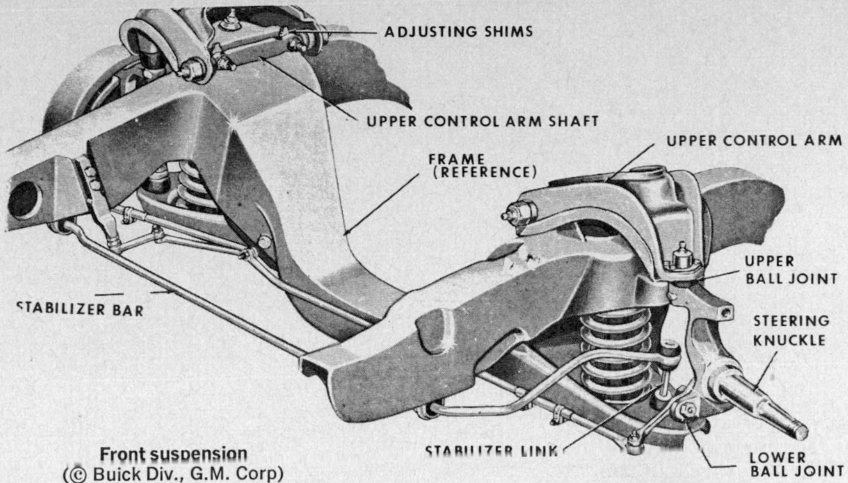

Front suspension
(© Buick Div., G.M. Corp)

unit being fastened to the frame, the similarly insulated lower end to the lower control arm.

For increased roll stability, a stabilizer bar is rubber mounted to the frame and is connected to the lower control arms via links at each end.

Ball Joint Inspection

Through 1972

NOTE: before performing this inspection, make sure the wheel bearings are adjusted correctly and that the A arm bushings are in good condition.

1. Jack up the car under the front lower control arm at the spring seat.
2. Raise the car until there is 1–2 in. of clearance under the wheel.
3. Insert a bar under the wheel and pry upward. If the wheel raises more than 1/8 in. the ball joints are worn. Determine if the upper or lower ball joint is worn by visual inspection while prying on the wheel.

NOTE: due to the distribution of forces in the suspension, the lower ball joint is usually the defective joint.

1973 and later

Beginning 1973, on all cars except the 73-74 Apollo, lower ball joints have a visual wear indicator. The lower ball joint grease plug screws into the wear indicator which protrudes from the bottom of the ball joint housing. As long as the wear indicator extends out of the ball joint housing, the ball joint is not worn. If the tip of the wear indicator is parallel with, or recessed into the ball joint housing, the ball joint is defective.

Through 1972, 1973-74 Apollo

1. Place a jack under the lower control arm spring seat. Raise the wheel off the floor.
2. Measure the distance from the tip of the grease fitting to the end of the ball joint stud with calipers. What you are measuring here is the total length of the ball joint.
3. Insert a bar under the tire and pry up. Measure the length of the ball joint, with the wheel raised.
4. If there is a difference in the two measurements of more than 1/16 in., the joint is worn.

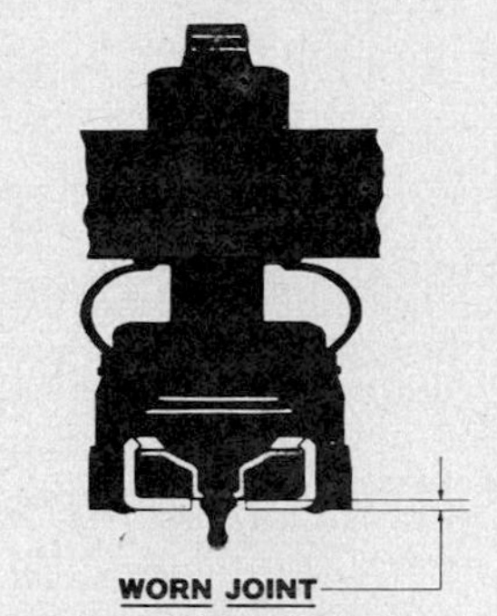

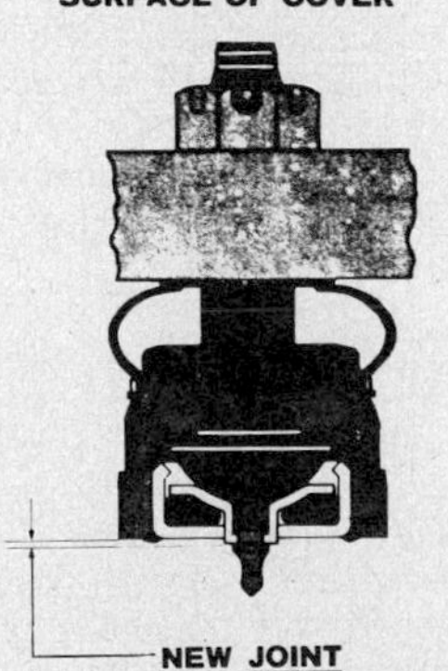

The wear indicating lower ball joint is used beginning 1973 on all models except Apollo, and beginning 1975 on Apollo
(© Buick Div., G.M. Corp)

Control Arm, and/or Ball Joint, Spring—Removal and Installation

Upper Control Arm

1. Raise the car and place a jack under the frame. Remove the wheel and tire.
2. Remove the cotter pin from the upper ball joint stud.
3. Loosen, but do not remove, the nut.

Caution If the nut is removed, the full force of the coil spring could be released.

Rap the knuckle sharply in the area of the tapered stud or use a ball joint removal tool to free the stud from the knuckle.

4. With another jack, support the car weight under the outer edge of the lower control arm. Raise the jack enough to free the upper control arm from the upper ball stud.
5. Wire the brake and knuckle in place to prevent brake hose damage, then lift the upper arm from the knuckle.

NOTE: If only the ball joints are to be replaced, stop at this point. Center punch and drill out the four rivets, then chisel off their heads. Remove the old ball joint. The new joint comes with four specially hardened bolts which must be torqued to 8 ft lbs. The nut goes on top.

6. Remove the upper control arm shaft-to-bracket nuts and lock washers. Carefully note the number, thickness, and location of the adjusting shims. Remove the control arm assembly.
7. Reverse the above steps to install.

Caution When installing the cotter pin, never loosen the nut to align the cotter pin holes. Always tighten the nut to the next slot that lines up with the hole.

Lower Control Arm or Spring

1. Raise the front of the car and remove the tires, wheels, hub, and drum or rotor.
2. Disconnect and remove the shock absorber.
3. Remove the front stabilizer rod link from the lower control arm.
4. Disconnect the brake reaction rod from the lower control arm but leave it attached to the front frame crossmember up to 1970 models. On the Skyhawk, mark the position of the front alignment cam bolts to aid in reassembly.
5. Remove the control arm bumper up to 1970 models.
6. As a safety precaution and to gain maximum leverage, place a jack about 1/2 in. below the lower ball joint stud. Now, remove the ball stud cotter pin and loosen the nut about 1/8 in. Do not remove the nut.

Caution If the nut is removed, the full force of the coil spring could be released.

7. Rap the steering knuckle in the area of the stud or use a ball joint removal tool to separate the stud from the knuckle.
8. After the stud has broken loose from the knuckle, raise the jack

against the control arm. Remove the nut and separate the steering knuckle from the tapered stud.

9. Carefully lower the jack under the control arm and release the spring. With the jack entirely lowered, it may be necessary to pry the spring off its seat on the lower control arm with a pry bar.
10. After the spring is removed, the lower control arm may be removed by removing the lock nut which attaches the control arm to the frame.
11. Install by reversing the removal procedure. Tighten the castellated nut to 85 ft lbs.

Lower Ball Joint Removal and Installation

1. Perform Steps 2-8, inclusive, in the "Lower Control Arm" procedure.
2. Remove the ball joint by pressing the joint from the lower control arm. It may be necessary to remove the ball joint and lower control arm as an assembly and have the ball joint removed in a press if suitable tools are not available.
3. Install a new ball joint and reverse the removal procedure.

Front Wheel Bearing Adjustment

Through 1970

Adjustment of freshly cleaned and repacked roller bearings is as follows:

1. Torque the spindle nut to 19 ft lbs while rotating the wheel.
2. Back off the nut until the bearings are loose.
3. Retorque the spindle nut to 11 ft lbs while rotating the wheel.
4. If either cotter pin hole in the spindle lines up with the nut castellations, back off the nut ½ turn and install the cotter pin. Otherwise, back off the nut to the first position that will accept a horizontal or vertical cotter pin.
5. Install the cotter pin and lock spindle nut into position.

NOTE: 0.002-0.006 in. end-play is normal.

1971 and later

1. Lift the wheel off the ground by jacking under the lower control arm.
2. Remove the dust cap from the hub.
3. Remove the cotter pin and discard it.
4. Snug up the spindle nut to seat the bearings while turning the wheel. Then back off the nut ¼-½ turn.

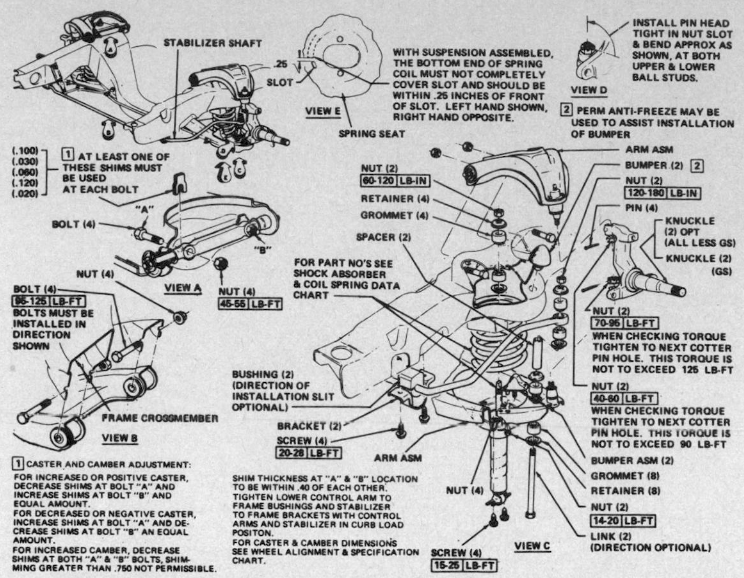

Typical front suspension and wheel alignment details
(© Buick Div., G.M. Corp)

5. Retighten the nut by hand until it is finger-tight.
6. Loosen the nut until the nearest hole in the spindle lines up with a slot in the spindle nut, and insert a new cotter pin.

NOTE: Under no circumstance is the final bearing nut adjustment to be even finger-tight.

7. Feel the looseness in the hub assembly. There will be 0.001-0.005 in. end-play.
8. Replace the dust cover and lower the car.

Shock Absorber R & R

1. Remove the upper shock absorber attaching nut, grommet retainer, and grommet.
2. Remove the lower retaining screws. Lower the shock through the hole in the lower control arm.
3. Reverse the above steps to install.

REAR SUSPENSION

The rear suspension on the Skyhawk is not independent, consisting of a rigid axle, a torque arm and two trailing links, Panhard rod, coil springs and an antisway bar. Other models are similar but do not have the torque arm or Panhard rod. The Apollo uses leaf springs instead of trailing arms.

Shock Absorber R & R

1. Raise car at the axle housing.
2. Remove the nut, retainer, and grommet or nut and lockwasher, as equipped, which attach the lower end of the shock absorber to its mounting.
3. Remove the two shock absorber upper attaching screws and remove the shock absorber.
4. Reverse the removal procedures to install.

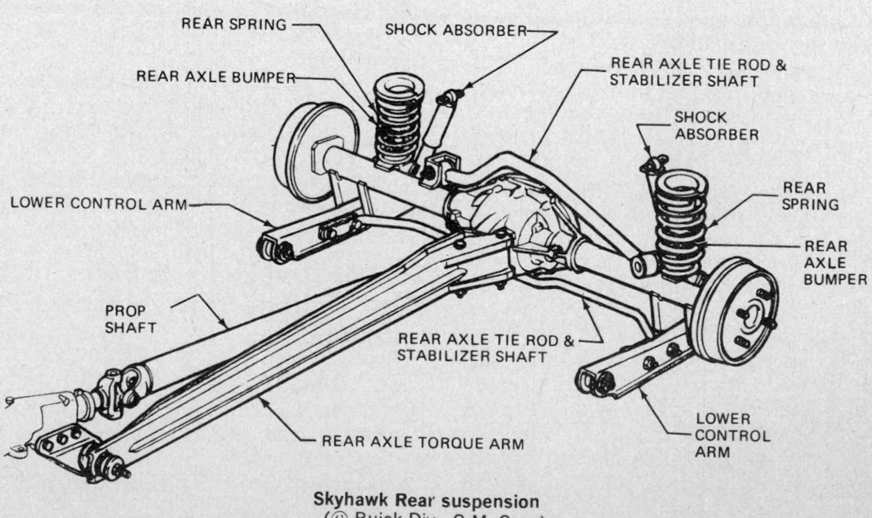

Skyhawk Rear suspension
(© Buick Div., G.M. Corp)

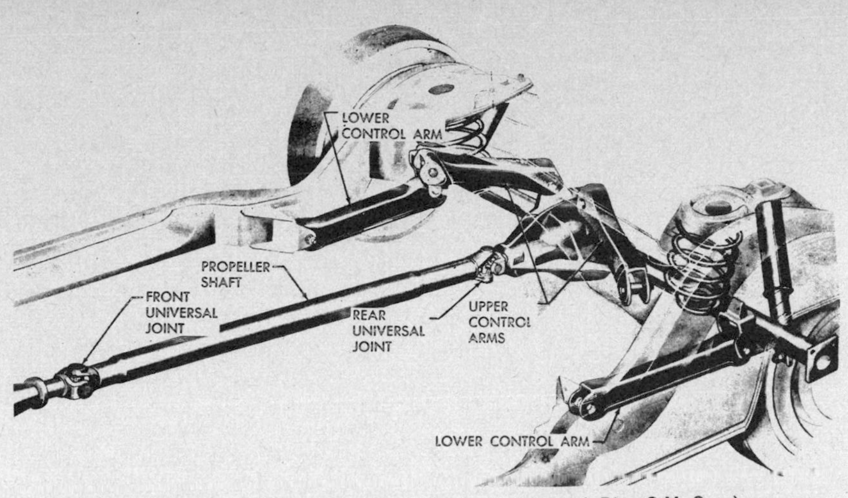

Rear suspension except Apollo and Skyhawk (© Buick Div., G.M. Corp)

Rear Leaf Spring Replacement

1. Raise the rear of the car on stands.
2. Support the rear axle to take its weight off the springs.
3. Disconnect the bottom of the shock absorber.
4. Loosen the front spring eye bolt.
5. Unbolt the spring front bracket from the underbody.
6. Lower the axle slightly and remove the front bracket from the spring.
7. Pry the parking brake cable out of its retainer bracket on the axle spring mounting plate.
8. Unbolt the spring from the axle.
9. Remove the spring plate and cushion from the bottom of the spring. There should also be a cushion between the axle and the spring.
10. Remove the upper bolt from the rear spring shackle. Lower the spring and remove the bottom bolt.
11. On installation, attach the front bracket to the spring eye. The head of the bolt should be toward the center of the car.
12. Assemble the shackle loosely to the rear spring eye.
13. Raise the rear end of spring and install the upper shackle bolt loosely, making sure that the parking brake cable goes under the spring.
14. Raise the front end of the spring and loosely attach the front bracket to the underbody. Make sure that the bracket tab goes into its slot.
15. Make sure that the upper and lower spring cushions are aligned properly. The upper one has locating ribs and the lower one, a locating dowel.
16. Install the spring lower mounting plate over the locating dowel and loosely install the nuts. Don't forget the parking brake cable bracket.
17. Attach the bottom of the shock absorber.
18. Attach the parking brake cable to the bracket on the lower spring plate.
19. Let the vehicle weight down on the springs. Tighten all the bolts. Torques are: rear shackle bolts —40-60 ft lbs, front bracket screws—25-35 ft lbs, front eye bolt—65-80 ft lbs, and axle bolts —35-50 ft lbs.

Rear Coil Spring Replacement

1. Jack up the back of the car and support both sides on stand jacks on the frame, in front of the rear axle. Disconnect the shock absorber.

NOTE: *It may be necessary to disconnect the rear brake line in order to obtain sufficient axle drop to remove the spring. If this is done, first depress and secure the brake pedal at least 1 in. from the relaxed position to prevent the master cylinder from draining when the rear brake line is disconnected.*

2. On 1973 and later models, detach the upper control arms at the differential. This may be necessary on some earlier models also.
3. Slowly, and very carefully, let the axle come down until the tension is released from the rear coil spring. Then, take off the coil spring. Note the direction in which the end of the last coil is pointing. Reinstall the spring in the same position.
4. When starting a new coil spring, make certain that the bottom of the coil is properly inserted into the socket in the frame and into the form plate on the trailing arm.
5. Jack the axle into place and reinstall the control arm bolt. Tighten the bolts to 75-95 ft lbs with the car's weight on the springs.

BRAKES

Drum Brakes

The service brakes are of the conventional type, hydraulically operated.

The brakes are self-adjusting. The system is designed to react and progressively tighten the star wheel adjuster, a notch at a time, as required. The self-adjusters only operate when the brakes are applied while the car is moving rearward.

For detailed service brake information, see Unit Repair Section.

Master Cylinder

A tandem master cylinder is standard equipment on all models. This type system is covered in the Unit Repair Section.

Disc Brakes

Disc brakes were optional on the front wheels of some models until the 1973 model year when they became standard equipment. Information on disc brakes is in the Unit Repair Section.

Master Cylinder Removal

1. Disconnect brake pipe or pipes from master cylinder and tape end of pipe or pipes to prevent entrance of dirt.
2. Disconnect brake pedal from master cylinder at the pushrod.

NOTE: *This step isn't required with power brakes.*

3. Remove master cylinder-to-dash retaining bolts. Remove the master cylinder. Reverse the above steps to install. Bleed the master cylinder after it is reinstalled.

Power Brake Unit R & R

1. Unbolt the master cylinder from the power unit. Being careful not to kink or bend the brake lines, pull the master cylinder away from the power unit without disconnecting the brake lines.
2. Disconnect and plug the vacuum hose.
3. Disconnect the power brake pushrod from the brake pedal.
4. Unbolt the power brake unit from the firewall.
5. Remove the unit.
6. Mount the unit to the firewall.
7. Install the master cylinder to the power unit and torque the nuts to 25 ft lbs.
8. Connect the vacuum hose.
9. Connect the power brake pushrod to the brake pedal.

Parking Brake Adjustment

Adjustment of the parking brake is necessary whenever the rear brake cables have been disconnected or the parking brake pedal can be depressed more than eight rachet clicks under heavy foot pressure. The car should first be raised on a lift.

1. Make sure that service brakes are properly adjusted.

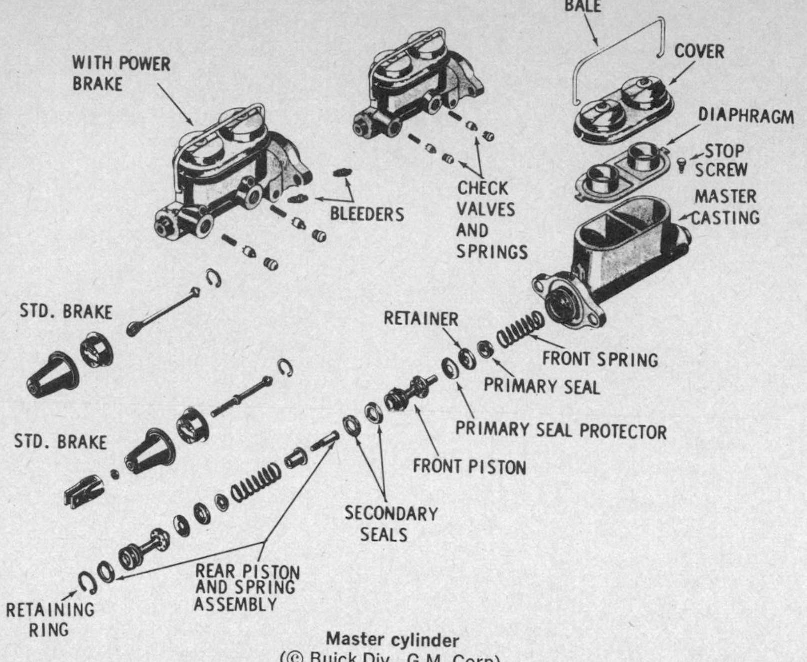

Master cylinder
(© Buick Div., G.M. Corp)

2. Depress parking brake pedal three rachet clicks, two on Apollo.
3. Loosen jam nut on equalizer adjusting nut. Tighten adjusting nut until rear wheels can just be turned rearward by hand but not forward.
4. Release rachet one click; the rear wheels should rotate rearward freely and forward with a slight drag.
5. Release rachet one more click; rear wheels should turn freely in either direction.

NOTE: be sure that the parking brake does not drag. An overtightened, dragging parking brake on a car with automatic brake adjusters will result in an extremely short life for rear brake linings.

STEERING

The manual steering gear is the recirculating ball nut type. The steering shaft, worm shaft, and worm nut are all in line. This coupling permits the gear to be removed independently of the steering shaft and steering column.

All Buicks use a variable-ratio power steering gear. The gear is the recirculating ball type incorporating a wormshaft and a rack-piston.

Hydraulic pressure for the power steering is provided by a constant displacement vane type pump. It is located on the left front of the engine and is belt driven off the engine crankshaft pulley.

See the "Unit Repair Section" for rebuilding procedures.

Refer to the Unit Repair Section for adjustments and repairs to steering gear, both manual and power-assisted.

Steering Wheel

Removal

1. Unplug the horn wire connector from the steering column.
2. On cars with standard wheel or optional wood-rim wheel, pull off cap, remove three screws and contact, insulator, and spring. On cars with bar-type horn actuator, remove screws securing actuator from underside of steering wheel, pull out lead connector plug, and remove actuator assembly.
3. Loosen steering wheel nut.
4. Apply steering wheel puller and pull wheel up to the nut. Now remove puller, nut and steering wheel.

Caution Don't pound on the steering wheel in either direction or the collapsible steering column will collapse, requiring replacement.

Installation

NOTE: location marks are provided on the steering wheel and shaft to simplify proper indexing at the time of installation.

1. Install wheel with the location mark aligned with that of the shaft.
2. Install the wheel nut and torque to 30 ft. lbs.
3. Reinstall horn button or actuator assembly.

Tie-Rod End R & R

1. Loosen the tie-rod adjuster sleeve clamp nuts.
2. Remove the tie-rod stud nut cotter pin and nut.
3. Remove the tie-rod stud from the steering arm or intermediate rod. This is a taper fit. Removal is accomplished using a ball joint removal tool or by hitting the steering arm sharply with a hammer, while using a heavy hammer as a backup. If the joint is to be reused the removal tool must be used.
4. Unthread the tie rod from the adjuster sleeve. Outer tie rods have right-hand threads and inner tie rods have left-hand threads. Count the number of turns the tie rod must be rotated to remove it from the adjusting sleeve. This will allow a reasonably accurate realignment upon reassembly.
5. Reverse the removal procedures to install. Clean rust and dirt from the threads. Check the alignment and adjust if necessary.

Turn Signal Switch R & R

NOTE: the steering wheel must always be supported. Use extreme care not to bend the steering column.

1. Remove the steering wheel.
2. Remove the three cover screws and the cover.
3. Depress the lockplate and remove the snap-ring. Remove the lockplate.

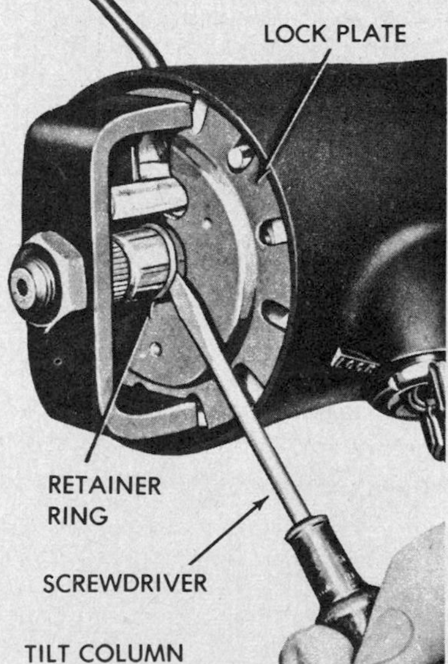

Removing lock plate
(© Buick Div., G.M. Corp)

4. Remove the spring and horn contact signal cancelling cam. Remove the thrust washer.
5. Remove the turn signal lever, depress the hazard warning knob, and remove the knob and tilt column lever—if equipped.
6. Remove the three turn signal switch mounting screws. Pull the connector out of the bracket on the column.

7. Pull the switch straight up with the wire protector and wire harness.
8. Reverse the above steps to install.

INSTRUMENT PANEL

Ignition Switch and Lock Cylinder R & R

The ignition switch and lock is located in the steering column. The ignition lock also locks the steering and the transmission.

Standard Column

1. Remove steering wheel using proper puller.
2. Remove three cover screws and cover; remove retainers.
3. Depress lock plate, then remove wire snap-ring and lock plate.
4. Slide upper bearing preload spring and cancelling cam off shaft. Remove the steering column-to-instrument panel attaching bolts (2), and carefully lower the column.

NOTE: steering shaft is now unsupported and could slide out the bottom of the column.

5. Slide thrust washer off shaft, then remove turn signal lever screw and lever.
6. Push in four-way flasher switch; remove knob.
7. Remove three turn signal switch mounting screws, pull connector out of its bracket on the column and tape the upper part of connector and wires together.
8. Pull turn signal switch out of column jacket.
9. Insert a small screwdriver into the slot next to the turn signal switch mounting screw boss (right-hand slot), depress spring latch and remove key lock.
10. Pull buzzer switch straight out, depressing switch clip with pliers.
11. Place ignition switch in accessory position by pulling up on connecting rod until there is a definite stop or detent felt.
12. Remove two attaching screws and ignition switch.
13. Assembly is the reverse of the above. However, note the following steps before proceeding with the reassembly.
14. To install the steering lock, hold the lock cylinder sleeve and rotate the knob clockwise against the stop. Insert the cylinder into the cover bore with the key on the cylinder sleeve aligned with the keyway in the housing. Then push the cylinder in until it bottoms. Maintaining a light inward pressure, rotate the knob counterclockwise until the drive section of the cylinder mates with the drive shaft. Push in until the snap-ring pops into the groove and the lock cylinder is secured in the cover. Check for free rotation.
15. When installing the ignition switch, be sure the lock cylinder is in the LOCK position. Put the shift bowl or shroud in the PARK position. Make sure the ignition switch is in the LOCK position. Then insert the actuator rod into the switch and assemble the switch to the column.
16. The neutral start switch is adjusted with the shift lever in the Drive position.

Tilt Column

1. Remove column mounting bracket from column.

NOTE: be careful not to damage the "breakaway" capsules.

2. Remove steering wheel using proper puller.
3. Remove turn signal wire protector (lower column).
4. Remove three column cover screws and cover.
5. Remove tilt release lever, turn signal switch lever, push four-way flasher knob in and remove knob, and remove upper shift lever.
6. Depress lock plate and remove the snap-ring; remove lock plate.
7. Remove cancelling cam and spring.
8. Remove three turn signal switch screws, tape wires to wire connector at upper end and place shift bowl in Low. Pull switch straight up and out.
9. Insert a small screwdriver into the slot next to the turn signal switch mounting screw boss (right-hand slot), depress spring latch and remove key lock.
10. Remove buzzer switch straight out, depressing switch clip with pliers.
11. Remove three housing cover screws and cover.
12. Install tilt release lever and place column in full UP position.
13. Place screwdriver in slot of tilt spring retainer, press in about 3/16 in. and turn counterclockwise. Remove spring and guide.

NOTE: spring is very strong—be careful.

14. Place column in neutral position, push in on upper steering shaft, remove inner race seat and race.
15. Remove upper flange pinch bolt, place ignition switch in accessory position, remove two switch mounting screws and switch.

NOTE: neutral start switch can be removed at this time, if necessary.

16. Assembly is the reverse of the above. However, note the following steps before proceeding with the reassembly.
17. To install the steering lock, hold the lock cylinder sleeve and rotate the knob clockwise against the stop. Insert the cylinder into the cover bore with the key on the cylinder sleeve aligned with the keyway in the housing. Then push the cylinder in until it bottoms. Maintaining a light inward pressure, rotate the knob counterclockwise until the drive section of the cylinder mates with the drive shaft. Push in until the snap-ring pops into the groove and the lock cylinder is secured in the cover. Check for free rotation.
18. When installing the ignition switch, be sure the lock cylinder is in the LOCK position. Put the shift bowl or shroud in the PARK position. Make sure the ignition switch is in the LOCK position. Then insert the actuator rod into the switch and assemble the switch to the column.
19. The neutral start switch is adjusted with the shift lever in the Drive position.

Light Switch Replacement

1. Disconnect battery.
2. Disconnect multiple connector from switch.
3. Pull switch knob to last notch and depress spring loaded latch button on top of switch while pulling knob and rod out of switch.

NOTE: on A/C cars, remove left duct if so equipped.

4. Remove escutcheon and switch.
5. Install in reverse of above.

WINDSHIELD WIPERS

All wiper motors are located on the engine side of the firewall. The transmission and linkage are located on the passenger compartment side of the firewall directly forward of the instrument panel. The cowl screen must be removed to allow the drive link to be disconnected from the crank arm.

The wiper-washer switch is included in the instrument cluster.

Windshield Wiper Motor R & R

Non-Depressed Park

1. Disconnect the battery.
2. Remove the cowl screen. Beginning 1974, this is necessary only on Apollo.
3. Loosen the two nuts on the adjustable motor drive link at the crank arm and slip the drive link off.

4. Remove the electrical connectors from the washer motor and pump.
5. Disconnect the washer pump hoses.
6. Remove the three bolts securing the motor to the cowl and carefully lift the motor away from the cowl.
7. Reverse the above steps for installation.

Depressed Park

1. Disconnect the battery.
2. Remove the hoses from the washer nozzles.
3. Remove the rubber weatherstrip and cowl screen.
4. Loosen the two nuts on the adjustable motor drive link at the crank arm and slip the drive link off.
5. Disconnect the washer hoses and electrical connectors.
6. Remove the three wiper motor-to-cowl retaining screws and the motor.
7. Reverse the above steps to install.

Windshield Wiper Linkage R & R

1. Disconnect the washer hose from the washer nozzles.
2. Remove the rubber weatherstrip from the front of the cowl screen and the five snap-clips from the rear of the screen then remove the screen.
3. Loosen the two nuts on the drive link at the crank arm and slip the link off the crank arm.
4. Remove both wiper arm and blade assemblies.
5. Remove the right and left linkage-to-body attaching screws. On the Skyhawk, remove the linkage snap ring, hex nut, and washer.
6. With the assembly loose, remove it through the cowl plenum chamber.
7. Reverse the above steps to install.

RADIO

Radio Removal and Installation

1969-72

NOTE: if equipped with stereo tape, remove tape player before starting Step 2.

1. Disconnect battery ground lead.
2. Remove radio knobs, escutcheons, and hex nuts.
3. Remove two screws from radio filler plate and remove plate.
4. Remove ashtray assembly.
5. Remove center air conditioning duct, if so equipped.
6. Remove radio bracket.
7. Remove two instrument panel attaching nuts at radio face.
8. Disconnect wiring and remove radio downward.
9. Install in reverse order of removal.

1973 and later, except Skyhawk

NOTE: *Use Steps 1, 2, 5, and 6 for the Apollo.*

1. Disconnect the battery ground cable.
2. Remove the radio knobs and escutcheons.
3. Remove the two screws and remove the center air conditioning duct assembly control. Disconnect the left air conditioning hose.
4. Disconnect the antenna, power, and speaker leads.
5. Loosen the support nut or screw at the side of the radio.
6. Remove the radio shaft nuts and slide the radio back and down.
7. Reverse the procedure on installation, adjusting the trimmer screw before replacing the right knob.

Caution Don't turn on the radio without the speaker connected. Failure will result.

Skyhawk

1. Disconnect the battery; remove the clock knob and trim panel.
2. Remove the instrument panel cover, glove compartment, and four attaching nuts from above the glove compartment door.
3. Lower the steering column by removing the nuts holding the column to the upper bracket guide.

Caution Be extremely careful not to let the column drop or hang unsupported.

4. Disconnect the speedometer cable from the speedometer; remove the instrument cluster assembly.
5. Remove all the knobs and escutcheons from the radio; remove the radio support bracket retaining screw from the lower dash.
6. Disconnect the electrical connections and antenna lead wire, remove the radio.
7. Installation is the reverse of removal.

HEATER

Heater Core R & R without A/C

1969-72

1. Remove right front inner fender panel.
2. Drain radiator.
3. Disconnect control cables from defroster door and outside air inlet door. Disconnect temperature control cable from temperature door.
4. Remove nuts from heater assembly studs.
5. Disconnect inlet and outlet hoses.
6. Remove connector from blower motor resistor.
7. Remove screws securing defroster outlet assembly to top of heater assembly.
8. Work heater assembly rearward until studs clear dash. Remove heater assembly.
9. Install in reverse of above.

1973 and later, except Apollo

1. Drain the radiator and disconnect the heater inlet and outlet hoses at the dash. On the Skyhawk, remove the blower inlet to dash screws, remove the blower inlet, motor and wheel as an assembly.
2. Disconnect the control wires from the defroster door and vacuum hose diverter door actuator diaphragm and control cable from the temperature door lever, except on the Skyhawk.
3. Remove the four nuts securing the heater assembly to the dash. On the Skyhawk, remove the core retaining strap screws and remove the core.
4. Remove the screw securing the defroster outlet tab to the heater assembly, except on the Skyhawk.
5. Remove the heater from the car.
6. Reverse the above steps to install.

Apollo

1. Disconnect the battery ground cable.
2. Drain the radiator.
3. Disconnect the heater hoses and plug the tubes to prevent spillage, when you remove the assembly from inside the car.
4. Remove the retaining nuts from the studs on the engine side of the firewall.
5. Remove the glove compartment and door.
6. Drill out the lower right heater case stud from inside the car.
7. Pull the core and case assembly from below the instrument panel.
8. Detach the cables and wiring from the case and remove the case from the car.
9. Remove the core from the case.
10. Reverse the procedure on installation, replacing the drilled out stud with a new screw and stamped nut.

Heater Blower R & R without A/C

1969-72

1. Remove right front inner fender panel.

2. Remove nuts and screws securing blower and air inlet assembly to cowl.
3. Disconnect blower motor wire and remove assembly.
4. Install in reverse of above.

1973 and later, except Apollo and Skyhawk

1. Disconnect the blower motor wire.
2. Remove the blower motor attaching screws and the motor.

Apollo

1. Disconnect the battery ground cable.
2. Raise the car. Remove all the fender skirt bolts except those holding the skirt to the radiator support.
3. Pull out and down on the fender skirt. Put a wood block between the skirt and fender to allow clearance for removing the motor.
4. Disconnect the motor wiring.
5. Remove the screws and the motor.
6. Reverse the procedure on installation.

Skyhawk

See Heater Core R & R without A/C, 1973 and later, except Apollo.

Blower Motor R & R with A/C

1969-70

1. On 1970 cars, remove the right front inner fender panel. On 1969 models, remove the fender.
2. Disconnect the motor wiring.
3. Remove the five securing screws and remove the motor.
4. Reverse the above steps to install.

1971-72

1. Support the hood and remove the extension and plate assembly from the hood hinge.
2. Disconnect the motor wiring.
3. Remove the screws securing the motor to the firewall and remove the motor.
4. Reverse the above steps to install.

1973 and later

1. Follow the same procedures as described in the Blower R&R without A/C.

Heater Core R & R with A/C

1969-70

1. Drain the radiator and disconnect the heater hoses from the heater core.
2. Remove the instrument panel cover with the right-side A/C outlet and hose still attached.
3. Remove the center A/C duct, left A/C outlet duct, A/C distributor duct, and the defroster assembly.
4. Disconnect the defroster and temperature control wires.
5. Remove the four nuts and two screws securing the air conditioner heater assembly to the dash and remove the assembly.
6. Reverse the above steps to install.

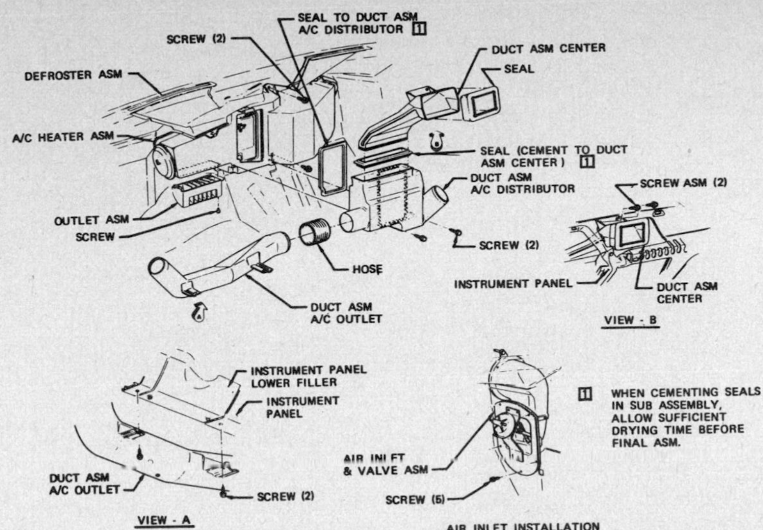

1972 air conditioning ducts (© Buick Div., G.M. Corp)

1971-72

1. Drain the radiator and disconnect the heater inlet and outlet hoses from the dash.
2. Disconnect the control wires from the defroster door and vacuum hose diverter door actuator diaphragm and control cable from the temperature door lever.
3. Remove the four nuts securing the heater assembly to the dash.
4. Remove the screw securing the defroster outlet tab to the heater assembly.
5. Move the heater assembly rearward until the studs clear the dash and then remove the heater assembly.
6. Reverse the above steps to install.

1973 and later, except Apollo and Skyhawk

1. Drain the radiator and disconnect the heater hoses.
2. Disconnect the temperature control cable and the vacuum hoses.
3. Remove the resistor assembly. Reach through the opening and remove the attaching nut. Remove the attaching nut directly over the transmission and the two attaching nuts to the upper and lower inboard evaporator case half.
4. From inside the car, remove the screw in the lower right corner on the passenger side.
5. Remove the lower attaching outlets. Work the assembly to the rear until the studs clear. Remove the heater assembly.
6. On installation, adjust the control cable to get about 1/8 in. springback in the hot position.

Apollo

1. Disconnect the battery ground cable.
2. Drain the coolant.
3. Disconnect the upper heater hose and remove all the heater case assembly nuts you can reach.
4. Remove the right front fender skirt bolts and lower the skirt to remove the lower heater hose clamp. Remove the lower right case nut while you're in there.
5. Plug the heater core tubes to prevent spillage inside the car.
6. Remove the glove compartment and door.
7. Remove the diaphragm at the right kick panel.
8. Remove the heater outlet at the bottom of the heater case.
9. Remove the cold air duct from the heater case.
10. Remove the heater case extension screws and separate the extension from the case.
11. Disconnect the heater cables and wiring.
12. Remove the core and case assembly.
13. Reverse the whole procedure on installation.

Skyhawk

Caution This procedure requires purging the air conditioning system of refrigerant. Do not attempt this unless you are a qualified air conditioning technician.

1. Disconnect the battery and purge the refrigerant from the air conditioning system.
2. Remove the glove compartment, the right side air outlet duct, the

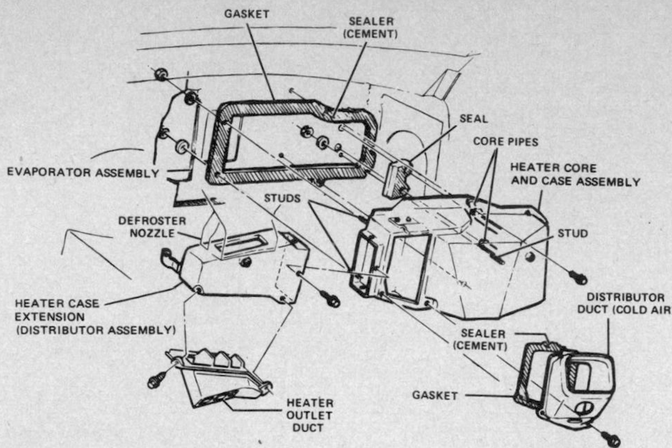

Heater case assembly for Apollo with factory installed air conditioning
(© Buick Div., G.M. Corp)

instrument bezel and pad, and air outlet duct on the left side.

3. Lower the steering column.

NOTE: Make sure that the steering column is adequately supported when lowered to avoid major damage.

4. Remove the instrument panel assembly and heater-air conditioner control assembly from the instrument panel.
5. Remove the radio and the defroster duct.
6. Remove the large center distributor duct, and the heater hoses at the core pipes.
7. Clean the VIR (receiver vessel) of any dirt which may have accumulated on it. Disconnect the compressor inlet line, oil bleed line and condenser outlet line; cap all these lines.
8. Loosen the evaporator inlet and outlet lines; remove the VIR mounting clamp and slide the VIR off the evaporator, outlet line first.
9. Remove and discard all the old O ring gaskets and plug all open lines to prevent contamination.
10. Remove the heater to cowl attaching nuts and remove the heater-distributor assembly, disconnect all electrical and vacuum connections.
11. Separate the heater case from the distributor assembly; separate the heater core from the heater case.
12. Installation is the reverse of removal, but when raising the steering column to its proper position, be careful not to damage any if its components. If the mounting bracket for the steering column is damaged, replace it.

SEAT BELTS

Buzzer System—1973

The front seat belt warning system consists of a switch in each belt retractor, a sensor switch in the seat cushion on the passenger side, a reminder light and a warning buzzer. The circuit wiring is routed through the ignition switch and parking brake warning switch on manual transmission models, or through the ignition switch and transmission switch on models equipped with automatic transmissions.

With the ignition swicch on and the parking brake released with manual transmission, or with the selector in a forward position on automatic transmission models, the warning circuit (light and buzzer) is closed (activated) until the driver's seat belt is extended to open (deactivate) the circuit. The seat sensor on the passenger side will react to weights in excess of 0-47 lbs on the seat cushion and close the warning circuit. Extending the passenger belt will open the circuit.

Seat Belt/Starter Interlock System 1974-75

The seat belt/starter interlock system makes it necessary for outboard front seat occupants to fasten their seat belts before the engine can be started. Employing seat weight sensors similar to 1973 models, the new system does not require a passenger occupying the middle portion of the front seat to buckle up, but failure to do so will cause the seat belt alarm buzzer to sound.

When an outboard front seat is occupied, a sensor under the seat signals an electronic relay module which then requires vertification from a switch in the buckle, indicating the belt has been fastened, before completing the starting circuit. An override by-pass switch under the hood, which is activated with the ignition key in the ON position, permits starting in the event of system malfunction.

Disabling the Interlock System

The seat belt interlock and warning buzzer are no longer mandatory. These may now be disabled, but the seat belt warning light must remain in operation.

1. Disconnect the battery, and locate the interlock terminal connector. This is a connector with orange, yellow and green wires, located under the left side of the instrument panel, near the fuse box.
2. Cut and tape the green wire on the body harness side of the connector.
3. Remove the warning buzzer from the fuse block or terminal connector on all Skyhawk, Skylark, and Apollo models.
4. On all other models, remove and tape the terminal with two yellow wires with black stripes. This terminal is located near the fuse block.

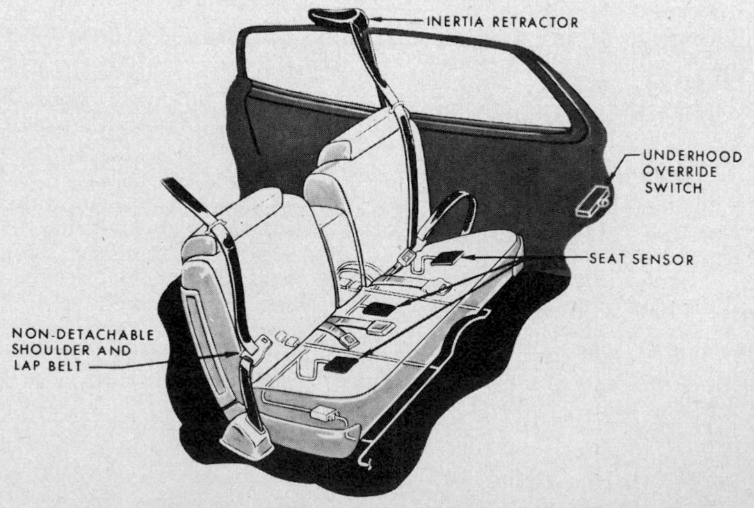

Seat belt/starter interlock system (© Buick Div., G.M. Corp)

Cadillac · Seville

YEAR IDENTIFICATION

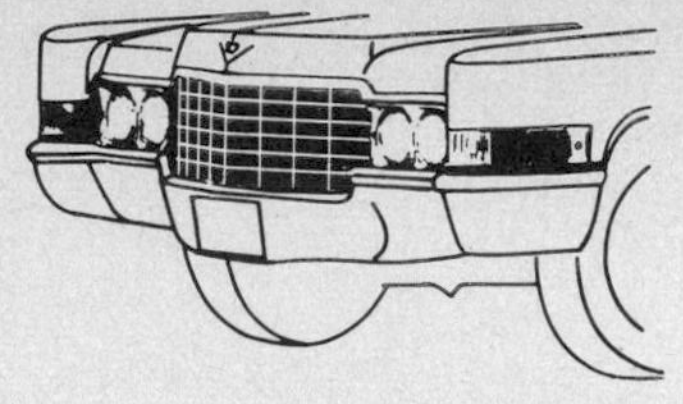

1969-70

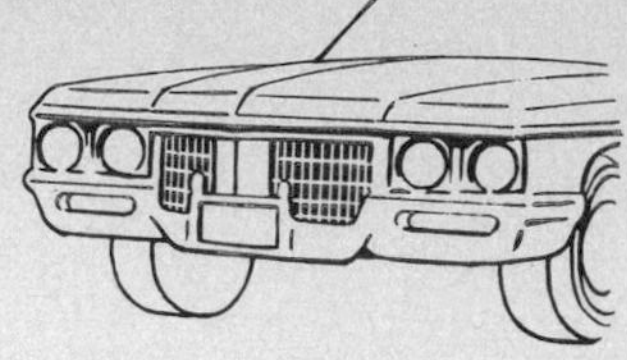

1971

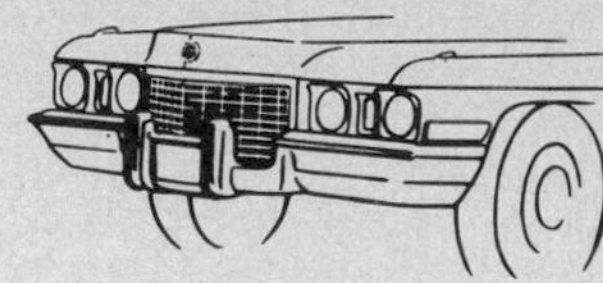

1972

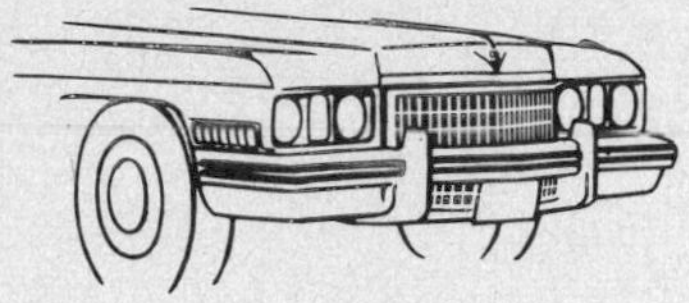

1973

1974

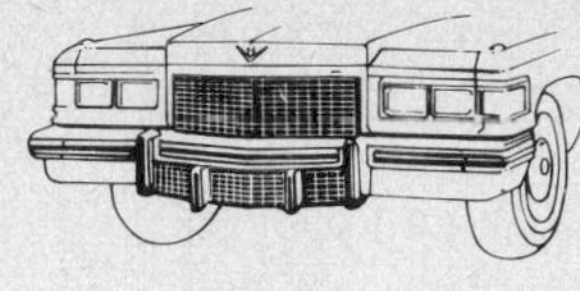

1975

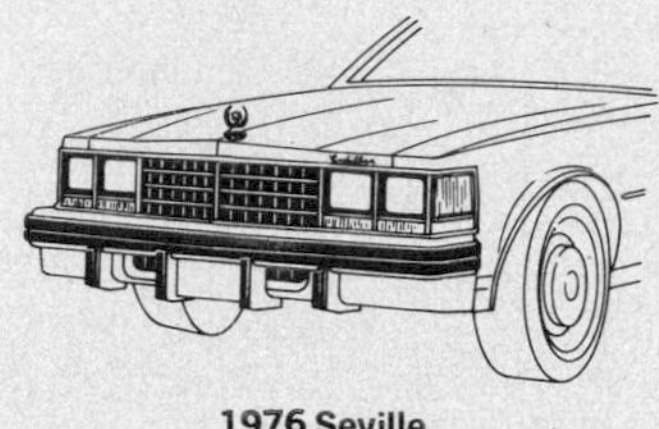

1976 Seville
(© Cadillac Div., G.M. Corp.)

FIRING ORDER

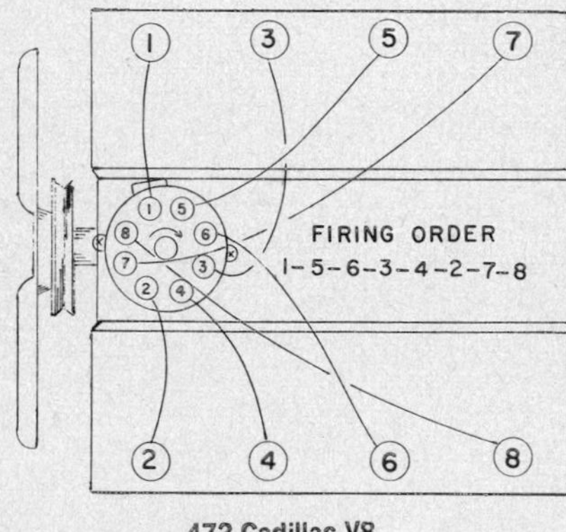

472 Cadillac V8

FIRING ORDER
1-8-4-3-6-5-7-2

350 Seville V8
(© Cadillac Div., G.M. Corp.)

CAR SERIAL NUMBER LOCATION AND ENGINE IDENTIFICATION

1969-70

The vehicle identification plate is located on the top left side of the dashboard, and is visible through the windshield. The eight digit serial number consists of a sales code letter, the last digit of the model year (8, 9, or 0), and a six digit sequential serial number.

All models utilize a 472 cu. in. V8 engine. The vehicle identification number, less sales code, is stamped on the top rear of the engine block, adjacent to the transmission.

1971-76

The vehicle identification plate is located on the top left side of the dashboard, and is visible through the windshield. The thirteen digit serial number consists of the G.M. Division Code (6), a four digit series and model number, the last digit of the model year, plant designation, and a six digit sequential serial number.

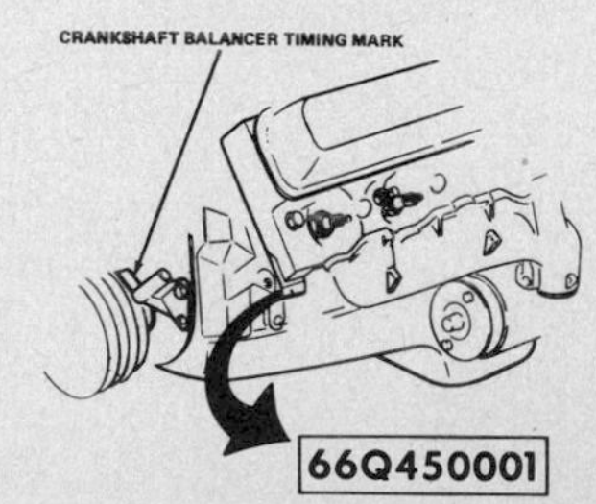

Engine identification number location on the Seville 350 V8 (© G.M. Corp.)

All models except the Seville utilize a 472 cu. in. V8 engine. A derivative of the vehicle identification number is stamped on the top rear of the engine block behind the intake manifold.

1972-76 models have the engine code located on the left rear of the engine block behind the left cylinder head.

The engine number on the 350 cu in. Seville V8 is on a boss at the left front side of the cylinder block directly below the front spark plug.

GENERAL ENGINE SPECIFICATIONS

Year	Engine Displacement Cu. In.	Carburetor Type	Horsepower @ rpm ■	Torque @ rpm (ft lbs) ■	Bore and Stroke (in.)	Compression Ratio	Oil Pressure @ 2050 rpm
'69	8-472	4 bbl	375 @ 4400	525 @ 3000	4.300 x 4.060	10.5:1	38
'70	8-472	4 bbl	375 @ 4400	525 @ 3000	4.300 x 4.060	10.0:1	38
'71	8-472	4 bbl	345 @ 4400	500 @ 2800	4.300 x 4.060	8.5:1	38
'72	8-472	4 bbl	220 @ 4000	365 @ 2400	4.300 x 4.060	8.5:1	35
'73	8-472	4 bbl	220 @ 4000	365 @ 2400	4.300 x 4.060	8.5:1	35
'74	8-472	4 bbl	220 @ 4000	365 @ 2400	4.300 x 4.060	8.25:1	35
'75-'76	8-500	4 bbl	235 @ 3800	386 @ 2400	4.300 x 4.304	8.5:1	35
	8-350	EFI	180 @ 4400	275 @ 2000	4.057 x 3.385	8.0:1	35

■ Beginning 1972 horscpower and torque are SAE net figures. They are measured at the rear of the transmission with all accessories installed and operating. Since the figures vary when a given engine is installed in different models, some are representative rather than exact.

TUNE-UP SPECIFICATIONS

When analyzing compression test results, look for uniformity among cylinders rather than specific pressures.

ENGINE			SPARK PLUGS		DISTRIBUTOR		IGNITION TIMING (deg) ▲		VALVES	Fuel	IDLE SPEED (rpm) ▲	
Year	No. Cyl Displacement (cu in.)	hp	Type	Gap (in.)	Point Dwell (deg)	Point Gap (in.)	Man Trans	Auto Trans	Intake Opens ■ (deg)	Pump Pressure (psi)	Man Trans	Auto Trans
'69	8-472	375	R-44-N	.035	30	.016	—	5B	18	5¼-6½	—	550①
'70	8-472	375	R-46-N	.035	30	.016	—	7½B	18	5¼-6½	—	600①
'71	8-472	345	R-46-N	.035	30	.016	—	8B	38	5¼-6½	—	600②/400
'72	8-472	220	R-46-N	.035	30	.016	—	8B	34	5¼-6½	—	600②/400
'73	8-472	220	R-46-N	.035	30	.016	—	8B	34	5¼-5¾	—	600②/400
'74*	8-472	220	R-45-NS	.035	30	.016	—	10B	21	5¼-6½	—	600②/400
'75	8-500	235	R-45NSX	.060	Electronic		—	6B③	34	5¼-6¼	—	600②/400
	8-350	180	R-46SX	0.80	Electronic		—	10B	22	39	—	600
'76	8-500	190	R-45NSX	.060	Electronic		—	6B	34	5¼-6¼	—	600
	8-500 EFI	215	R-45NSX	.060	Electronic		—	12B	34	39 min.	—	600
	8-350	180	See Underhood Specifications Sticker									

▲ See text for procedure
■ All figures Before Top Dead Center
* No point gap or dwell with electronic ignition
① Adjust idle to 900-950 rpm with idle speed-up on. See text for special procedure.
② Lower figure indicates idle speed with solenoid disconnected
B Before Top Dead Center
EFI Electronic fuel injection
③ 12B for fuel injected engines

CAPACITIES

Year	ENGINE No. Cyl. Displacement (Cu. In.)	Engine Crankcase Add 1 Qt For New Filter	TRANSMISSION Pts To Refill After Draining Manual 3-Speed	4-Speed	Automatic ●	Drive Axle (pts)	Gasoline Tank (gals)	COOLING SYSTEM (qts) With Heater	With A/C
'69	All	4	—	—	8	5	26①	21.3	21.8②
'70	All	4	—	—	8	5	26①	21.3	21.8②
'71	All	4	—	—	8	5	27.5	21.3	21.8②
'72	All	4	—	—	8	5	27.5	21.3	21.8②
'73	All	4	—	—	8	5	27.5	21.3	21.8②③
'74	All	4	—	—	8	5	27.5	21.3	21.8②③
'75-'76	8-500	4	—	—	8	5	27.5	21.3	23.8④
	8-350	4	—	—	8	5	27.5	21.3	23.8②
		4	—	—	8	5	21	18.9	18.9

● Specifications do not include torque converter
① Fleetwood—20 gals
② Fleetwood—24.8 qts
③ Trailer package—2 qts additional
④ Fleetwood—26.8 qts

VALVE SPECIFICATIONS

Year	Engine No. Cyl. Displacement (cu in.)	Seat Angle (deg)	Face Angle (deg)	Spring Test Pressure (lbs @ in.)	Spring Installed Height (in.)	STEM TO GUIDE Clearance (in.) Intake	Exhaust	STEM Diameter (in.) Intake	Exhaust
'69	8-472	45	44	160 @ 1.50	1 15/16	.0005-.0025	.0010-.0025	.3420	.3418
'70	8-472	45	44	160 @ 1.50	1 15/16	.0005-.0025	.0010-.0025	.3420	.3418
'71	8-472	45	44	160 @ 1.50	1 15/16	.0010-.0027	.0010-.0025	.3420	.3418
'72	8-472	45	44	168 @ 1.50	1 15/16	.0010-.0027	.0012-.0027	.3420	.3418
'73	8-472	45	44	168 @ 1.50	1 15/16	.0010-.0027	.0012-.0027	.3420	.3418
'74	8-472	45	44	165 @ 1.50	1 15/16	.0010-.0027	.0016-.0027	.3420	.3418
'75-'76	8-500	45	44	168 @ 1.50	1 15/16	.0010-.0027	.0012-.0027	.3418	.3416
	8-350	①	②	187 @ 1.27	1 43/64	.0010-.0027	.0015-.0032	.3429	.3424

① Intake 45°; exhaust 30°
② Intake 40°; exhaust 31°

TORQUE SPECIFICATIONS

All readings in ft lbs

Year	Engine Displacement (cu in.)	Cylinder Head Bolts	Rod Bearing Bolts	Main Bearing Bolts	Crankshaft Pulley Bolt	Flywheel to Crankshaft Bolts	MANIFOLD Intake	Exhaust
'69-'76	472,500	115	40	90	Press fit①	75	30	35
'75-'76	350	85	42	120②	310③	60	40	25

NOTE—Some bolts and nuts are marked on the heads to indicate the grade of steel used. Do not use bolts of a lower grade than those originally installed. The marks consist of lines: SAE5—3 lines; SAE7—5 lines; SAE8—6 lines

① Pulley-to-harmonic damper screw—17 ft lbs
② 80 ft lbs. on No. 5
③ Balancer-to-crankshaft

CRANKSHAFT AND CONNECTING ROD SPECIFICATIONS

All measurements are given in inches

Year	Engine Displacement (cu in.)	Crankshaft: Main Brg. Journal Dia	Crankshaft: Main Brg. Oil Clearance	Crankshaft: Shaft End-Play	Crankshaft: Thrust on No.	Connecting Rod: Journal Diameter	Connecting Rod: Oil Clearance	Connecting Rod: Side Clearance
'69-'73	472	3.250	.0003-.0026	.002-.012	3	2.5000	.0005-.0035	.008-.016
'74	472	3.250	.0013-.0026	.002-.012	3	2.0250	.0005-.0028	.011-.021
'75-'76	500	3.250	.0013-.0026	.002-.012	3	2.5000	.0005-.0028	.008-.016
'75-'76	350	2.4995-2.4985①	.0005-.0021②	.004-.008	3	2.1238-2.1248	.0004-.0033	.006-.020

① No. 1—2.4988-2.4998 in.
② No. 5—.0015-.0031 in.

RING GAP

Year	Engine	Top Compression	Bottom Compression
'69-76	472, 500	.013-.025	.013-.025
'75-'76	350	.010-.023	.010-.023

Year	Engine	Oil Control
'69-'76	All engines	.015-.055

RING SIDE CLEARANCE

Year	Engine	Top Compression	Bottom Compression
'69-'74	8-472	.0017-.0040	.0017-.0040
'75-'76	8-500	.0017-.0040	.0017-.0040
'75-'76	8-350	.0020-.0040	.0020-.0040

Year	Engine	Oil Control
'69-'76	472, 500	None (side sealing)
'75-'76	350	.0006-.0096

PISTON CLEARANCE

Year	Engine	Piston to Bore Clearance
'69	472	.0006-.0010
'70	472	.0006-.0010
'71	472	.0006-.0010
'72	472	.0006-.0010
'73	472	.0006-.0010
'74	472	.0006-.0010
'75-'76	500	.0006-.0010
'75-'76	350	.0010-.0020

BATTERY AND STARTER SPECIFICATIONS

Year	Engine Displacement (cu in.)	Battery: Ampere Hour Capacity	Battery: Volts	Battery: Terminal Grounded	Starter Lock Test: Amps	Starter Lock Test: Volts	Starter Lock Test: Torque (ft lbs)	Starter No-Load Test: Amps	Starter No-Load Test: Volts	Starter No-Load Test: RPM	Brush Spring Tension (oz)
'69-'70	472	74	12	Neg.	510	Not Recommended		70-99	10.6	7,800	35
'71-'76	472, 500	74	12	Neg.	510	Not Recommended		65-90	9	7,000	35

ALTERNATOR AND REGULATOR SPECIFICATIONS

	ALTERNATOR			REGULATOR						
					Field Relay			Regulator		
Year	Part No. or Manufacturer	Field Current @ 12 V	Output (amps)	Part No. or Manufacturer	Air Gap (in.)	Point Gap (in.)	Volts to Close	Air Gap (in.)	Point Gap (in.)	Volts @ 75
'69	1100696	2.2-2.6	42	1119515	—	—	—	—	—	13.5-14.4
	1100694	2.2-2.6	55	1119515	—	—	—	—	—	13.5-14.4
	1100742	2.2-2.6	63	1119519	—	—	—	—	—	13.5-14.4
'70	1100908	2.2-2.6	42	1119515	—	—	—	—	—	13.5-14.4
	1100694	2.2-2.6	55	1119515	—	—	—	—	—	13.5-14.4
	1100910	2.8-3.2	63	1119519	—	—	—	—	—	13.5-14.4
'71-'75	1100842, 1100543, 1102459	2.2-2.6	42	1119515, 1116387	—	—	—	—	—	13.5-14.4
	1100742, 1102849, 1100554, 1102451	4.0-4.5	63	1119519	—	—	—	—	—	13.5-14.4
	1101019, 1101030	4.0-4.5	80	1116387	—	—	—	—	—	—

BRAKE SPECIFICATIONS

All measurements are given in inches

		MASTER CYLINDER		WHEEL CYLINDER			BRAKE DISC OR DRUM DIAMETER		
				Front			Front		
Year	Model	Disc	Drum	Disc	Drum	Rear	Disc	Drum	Rear
'69	All Series	1.00	—	2¾	—	13/16①	12.0	—	12.0
'70	All Series	1.00	—	2¾	—	13/16①	11.9	—	12.0
'71-'76	All Cadillac Series	1.12	—	2 15/16	—	15/16	11.9	—	12.0
	Seville	1.12	—	2 15/16	—	15/16	11.0	—	11.0

① 7/8 for the Fleetwood '75 Sedan and Limousine

WHEEL ALIGNMENT SPECIFICATIONS

		CASTER		CAMBER				WHEEL PIVOT RATIO (deg)	
Year	Model	Range (deg)	Pref Setting (deg)	Range (deg)	Pref Setting (deg)	Toe-in (in.)	Steering Axis Inclin. (deg)	Inner Wheel	Outer Wheel
'69-'70	All Series	1½N to ½N	1N	3/8N to 3/8P	0	1/8 to 1/4	6	20	18
'71-'73	All Series	1½N to ½N	1N	①	①	1/8 to 1/4	6	20	18
'74-'76	All Cadillac Series	½N to ½P	0	②	①	1/16 to 3/16	6	20	18
	Seville	1½P to 2½P	2P	②	②	0 to 1/8	—	—	—

① Left 3/8P to 3/8N; zero preferred
Right 1/8P to 5/8N; 1/4N preferred

② Left 0 to 1P; ½P preferred
Right 1/4N to 3/4P; 1/4P preferred

N Negative P Positive

CHARGING SYSTEM

Two types of alternators are used on the various Cadillac models, both of which have an integrated circuit regulator mounted inside the alternator. For charging system trouble shooting and repair information, consult the "Unit Repair Section."

Alternator Removal

1969-72

Disconnect the battery. Disconnect the wire leads at the alternator. Remove alternator adjusting strap drive belt. Remove alternator.

NOTE: heavy duty alternator used on commercial chassis is slid backwards off its lower mounting bolts, after first loosening belt tensioner and removing fan belt and upper bolt.

1973-76

1. Disconnect the negative battery cable.
2. Disconnect the electrical leads from the alternator.
3. Remove the screw from the alternator adjusting link.
4. Remove the screw from the rear of the alternator, retaining the shims for reinstallation.
5. Loosen the alternator pivot bolt and remove the drive belt.
6. Remove the AIR pump pulley for access to the AIR pump bolt behind the pulley.
7. Loosen the two screws securing the front bracket to the engine.
8. Remove the alternator, spacer and lower through bolt by twisting the alternator toward the fender for clearance.
9. Install the alternator in the reverse order of removal.

Caution Since the Delcotron and regulator are designed for use on only one polarity system, the following precautions must be observed:

1. The polarity of the battery, generator, and regulator must be matched and considered before making any electrical connections in the system.
2. When connecting a booster battery, be sure to connect the negative battery terminals together and the positive battery terminals together.
3. When connecting a charger to the battery, connect the charger positive lead to the battery positive terminal. Connect the charger negative lead to the battery negative terminal.
4. Never operate the Delcotron on open circuit. Be sure that all connections in the circuit are clean and tight.
5. Do not short across or ground any of the terminals on the Delcotron regulator.
6. Do not attempt to polarize the Delcotron.
7. Do not use test lamps of more than 12 volts for checking diode continuity.
8. Avoid long soldering times when replacing diodes or transistors. Prolonged heat is damaging to these units.
9. Disconnect the battery ground terminal when servicing any A.C. system. This will prevent the possibility of accidental reversing of polarity.

STARTING SYSTEM

Cadillac starter motors are located on the right hand side of the engine, except on the Seville 350 V8 where it is on the left side.

Information on starter overhaul can be found in the Unit Repair Section.

Starter R & R

1. Disconnect battery cable and jack up car.
2. Disconnect battery lead and two wires from solenoid.
3. Remove bolt that holds support bracket to starter.
4. Remove two starter-to-engine bolts.
5. Remove motor by pulling it forward and down, or toward right front wheel and over the steering linkage.
6. To install, reverse removal procedure, tightening starter-to-engine bolts to 46 ft. lbs., bracket bolt to 12 ft lbs. and nut to 6 ft lbs.

Starter Drive Removal and Installation

Caution When the starter is disassembled, do not clean the starter drive, armature, or the field in solvent as this will dissolve the lubricant in the drive mechanism and damage the insulation on the armature.

1. Remove the field coil connector from the solenoid motor terminal.
2. Remove the two screws and lockwashers which secure the solenoid switch assembly to the starter drive housing. Pull off the solenoid and its return spring by turning the solenoid assembly counterclockwise to disengage the flange from the center frame.
3. Remove the housing through-bolts and the commutator end frame with the leather brake washer.
4. Remove the center frame assembly and the snap-ring which holds the shift lever pivot pin. Remove the pin.
5. Pull the plunger, shift lever, armature, and the starter drive from the drive housing.
6. Use the following procedure to remove the starter drive from the armature shaft.
   a. Remove the thrust collar from the armature shaft.
   b. Using a 5/8 in. deep socket, slide it over the end of the shaft so that the end of the socket butts against the edge of the retainer. With a hammer, tap the end of the socket to drive the retainer toward the armature and off of the snap-ring.
   c. Remove the snap-ring. Examine its condition and replace if necessary.
   d. The drive can now be removed from the armature shaft.
7. To install the unit, reverse the removal procedure.

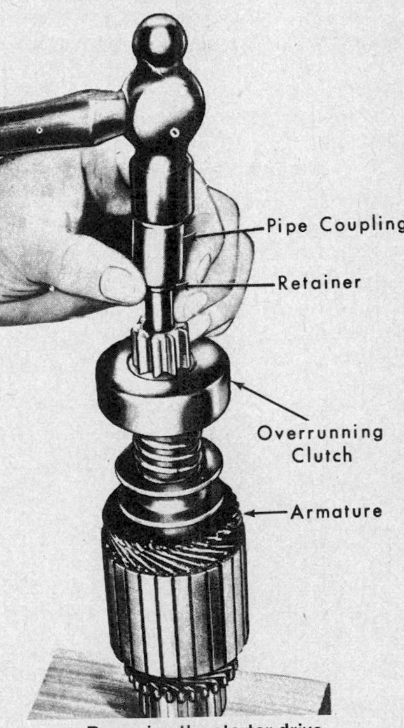

Removing the starter drive
(© Cadillac Div., G.M. Corp.)

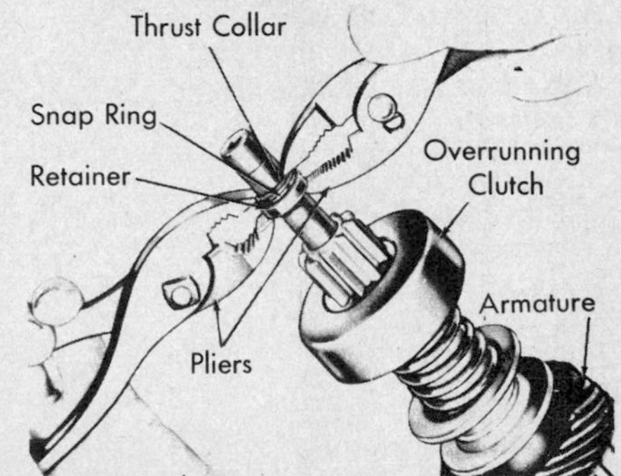

Installing the snap ring retainer
(© Cadillac Div., G.M. Corp.)

IGNITION SYSTEM

The distributor used in Cadillacs is a single-point type using clockwise rotation. It is constructed of aluminum alloy and is located at the top left front of the engine.

The High Energy Ignition system was optional in 1974 and became standard equipment in 1975. The HEI system consists of an ignition coil, electronic module and a magnetic pick-up assembly all within the distributor.

The ignition coil performs in the same manner as a coil in a breaker point type ignition; boosting primary voltage to the proper secondary voltage. The magnetic pick-up assembly is an electronic signaling device that tells the electronic module when to break the primary ignition circuit and cause the secondary spark. The electronic module mounted in the distributor housing, is a solid state unit containing five complete circuits which control secondary spark triggering, switching, current limiting, dwell control and distributor pick-up. The dwell angle is controllled by a transistor circuit within the module and is varied in direct relation to engine speed.

Centrifugal and vacuum advance mechanisms are basically the same as for breaker-type ignitions.

A terminal in the top of the distributor cap is provided for the connection of a tachometer. The terminal is marked "TACH".

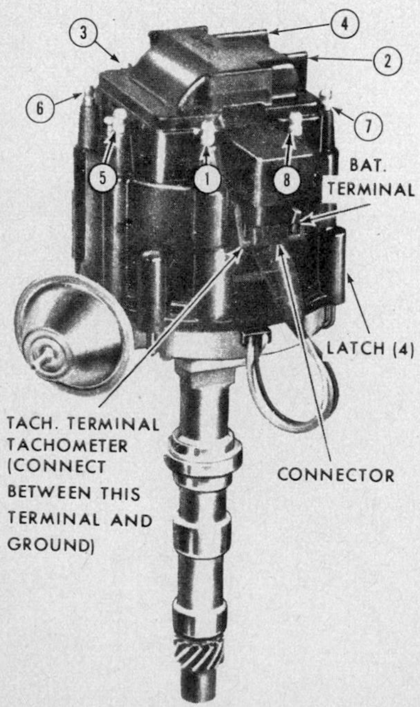

Tachometer connection on HEI system
(© Cadillac Div., G.M. Corp.)

Distributor Point Replacement

1. Remove distributor cap by depressing and turning the retaining screws.
2. Remove two screws securing rotor cap and remove cap.
3. Remove condenser and primary leads from nylon insulated connection.
4. Loosen two screws holding base of contact assembly in place and remove points.
5. Inspect weight assembly, replace or lubricate as required.
6. Place new points under the two screws and tighten screws.
7. Connect the condenser and primary leads at the nylon insulated connection.

NOTE: be sure leads do not interfere with cap, weight base, or breaker advance.

8. Install rotor cap. Square and round lugs must be properly aligned.
9. With 1/8 in. Allen wrench inserted, turn until points close while rubbing block is on high point of lobe. Then turn screw counterclockwise one-half turn.

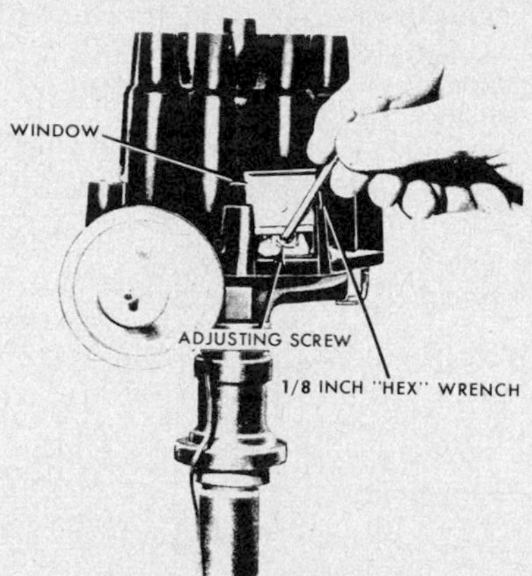

Distributor point adjustment
(© Cadillac Div., G.M. Corp)

10. Replace distributor cap.
11. With engine warmed up and off fast idle, set points to get proper dwell angle.

Distributor Removal

Unplug (HEI) and remove distributor cap. Disconnect vacuum line. Disconnect primary lead at distributor.

Turn the engine to top dead center for No. 1 cylinder so that the rotor points to the No. 1 cylinder tower in the distributor cap and the pointer on the timing case cover points to the O-mark on the crankshaft pulley.

Using a scribe mark, index the vacuum advance unit to the cylinder block, and the tip of the rotor to the distributor housing so that the distributor body will be correctly replaced at reassembly. Remove clamp bolt and distributor.

Distributor Installation

Install the distributor so that the vacuum advance unit aligns with the match-mark made at removal. Turn the rotor slightly left of center so that as the gear engages the camshaft it will revolve into the proper position, pointing to the No. 1 contact in the cap.

NOTE: if the engine has been cranked, remove the No. 1 spark plug. Crank the engine until the No. 1 piston is in firing position with the pointer and the O-mark on the crank-shaft pulley aligned. Then proceed as above.

Install the hold-down clamp. Connect the primary lead and install the cap.

Fill the distributor oiler tube with 10W oil or rotate lubricator.

Plug the distributor vacuum line to the carburetor.

Insert an adapter pin alongside the No. 1 wire in the distributor cap and connect a timing light.

Clean the crankshaft pulley markings and the pointer.

Set the timing to specifications.

Tighten clamp bolt to 18 ft. lbs.

Remove plug and adapter pin and reconnect the vacuum line to the advance unit.

Distributor Installation (If Engine Has Been Disturbed)

If the engine has been disturbed (cranked) after removing the distributor, perform the following procedure for installation:

1. Crank the engine until no. 1 piston is at the top of its compression stroke. The compression stroke can be determined by removing the spark plug from no. 1 cylinder and placing your thumb over the hole while an assistant slowly cranks the engine. Crank until compression is felt at the hole and then continue cranking slowly until the timing mark on the crankshaft pulley lines up with the zero degrees (0°) timing mark located on the timing chain cover.
2. Position the distributor in the block but do not, at this time, allow it to engage with its drive gear at the base of the mounting hole. Observe the position of the vacuum control unit on the distributor. If the distributor is located correctly, the vacuum unit will be positioned normally so that the vacuum hose can easily connect to it.
3. Rotate the distributor shaft so that the rotor points to the front of the engine, turn the rotor counterclockwise about 1/8 turn toward the left (driver's side), and push the distributor down to engage the camshaft. It may be

necessary to turn the rotor a small amount in either direction in order to achieve this engagement. If installed correctly, the rotor should point toward the no. 1 spark plug terminal in the distributor cap.

4. Press firmly downward on the distributor housing. This will ensure that the distributor shaft engages the oil pump shaft, thereby allowing the distributor to fully contact the engine block.
5. Install the hold-down clamp and tighten the bolt until it is snug.
6. Turn the distributor slightly until the points just open and then tighten down on the bolt.
7. Install the distributor cap, making sure that the rotor points to no. 1 terminal in the cap.
8. Attach all wires and the vacuum advance hose.
9. Start the engine. If it fails to start, or runs roughly, the distributor is 180° out of time. Lift up on the distributor, turn the rotor one-half revolution, and install the distributor. Repeat steps 1–9 if the engine continues to run poorly.
10. Check the timing and change it as necessary.

Thermal Vacuum Switch

The thermal vacuum switch was added to the distributor vacuum circuit to prevent engine overheating in heavy traffic. This switch is so designed to provide full vacuum advance in prolonged idling, or high temperature, situations. Under these conditions, the switch sends full manifold vacuum, instead of the normal carburetor vacuum, to the advance unit. Vacuum switch units having four ports, instead of the normal three, allow manifold vacuum to operate an idle speed-up devise (the adjustment of which is found under *Fuel System*). The cut-off temperature of the switch is 220°F. An overheating condition may be due to a faulty switch.

To check the switch, proceed as follows:

1. Idle engine at 600 rpm and at normal operating temperature.
2. With an assistant in the car with his foot on the brake, and transmission in Reverse, disconnect the line from the distributor advance unit and check that vacuum is available (from port D). If vacuum is not available, the separate vacuum solenoid may be at fault.
3. Remove the line between the switch and the vacuum break T at carb. Vacuum still should be available at distributor line (from port D) and should not be available at the line just removed from port MT.
4. Block radiator with a piece of cardboard until "Engine Temp" light comes on.
5. Reconnect line removed in Step 3 and disconnect line between carburetor and switch port C. Vacuum now should be available at distributor line (from port D) and should not be available at line disconnected from port C.
6. If the previous checks indicate a faulty switch, replace the unit.

Ignition Timing

1. Loosen the distributor hold-down bolt so that the distributor can be turned without it being too loose.
2. Remove the hose from the vacuum advance and tape the free end closed. The end must be taped as a manifold leak will affect the timing.
3. Remove the vacuum hose from the parking brake and tape the end.
4. Connect the timing light. With HEI, connect it at the No. 1 distributor terminal. Make certain that the timing marks are visible.
5. Connect a tachometer to the engine and, after securing the parking brake, start the engine and place the selector lever in Drive.
6. Adjust the idle speed to 600 rpm.
7. Point the timing light at the pulley and observe the notch in the pulley in relation to the notches on the front cover. Check the specification chart for the correct timing setting.
8. If the setting is not correct, rotate the distributor until the correct timing is obtained then tighten the distributor clamp nut to 18 ft lbs and recheck the timing.
9. Untape and reconnect the vacuum hoses on the parking brake and the vacuum advance.

FUEL SYSTEM

Carbureted Engines

The standard Cadillac fuel system (except Seville) includes the fuel pump, fuel filter line, carburetor and intake manifold.

Fuel Injected Engines

Electronic Fuel Injection (EFI) is optional on all models except the Fleetwood, Limousine, and Commercial Chassis vehicles.

EFI provides a means of precisely controlling the air/fuel mixture for combustion by monitoring selected engine operating conditions and electronically metering the fuel requirements to meet those conditions.

The EFI system consists of four basic subsystems; the fuel delivery system, air induction system, the network of sensors, and the electronic control unit (ECU).

Fuel Delivery System

The fuel delivery subsystem is made up of an in-tank fuel pump and a chassis mounted fuel pump, fuel filter, a fuel pressure regulator, fuel rails, an injector for each cylinder, and supply and return lines.

Fuel Pumps

The electric fuel pumps are connected in parallel to the ECU and are

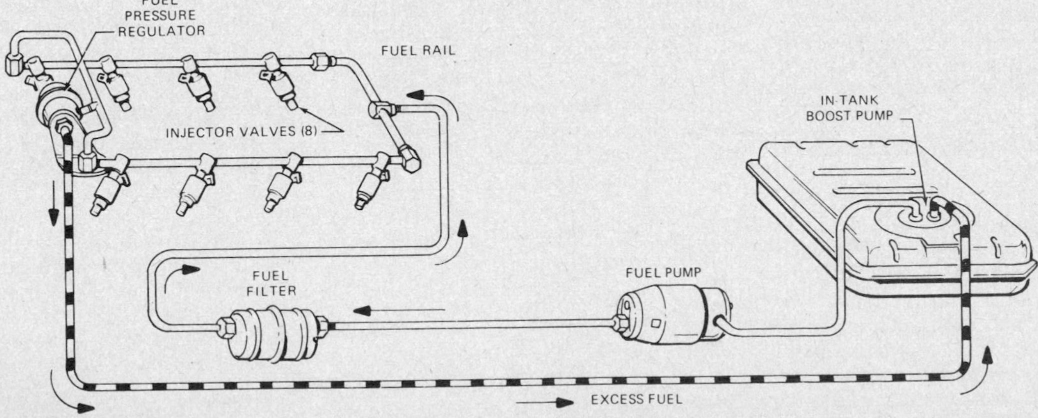

Fuel delivery system—EFI
(© Cadillac Div., G.M. Corp.)

activated by the ECU when the ignition is turned on and the engine is cranking or operating. If the engine stalls or if the starter is not engaged, the fuel pumps will stop in about one second. The fuel is pumped from the fuel tank, through the supply line and filter, through the pressure regulator, fuel rails and to the injectors, with excess fuel being returned to the fuel tank.

The in-tank boost pump is located in the fuel tank and is an integral part of the fuel gauge tank unit. This pump supplies fuel to the chassis mounted fuel pump and helps prevent vapor lock on the suction side of the system.

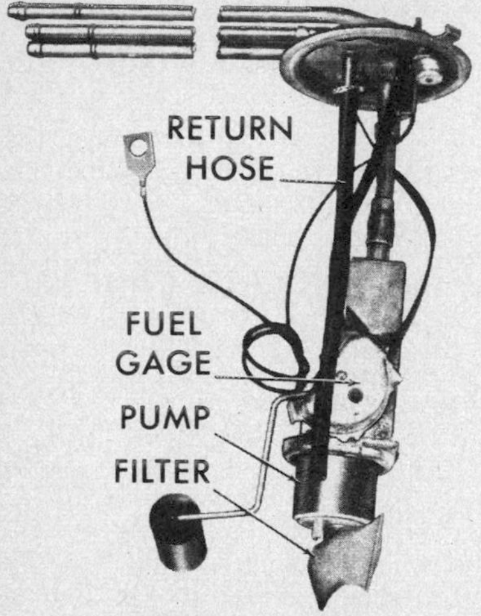

In-tank fuel pump—EFI
(© Cadillac Div., G.M. Corp.)

The chassis mounted fuel pump is a constant-displacement, roller-vane pump with a check valve to prevent fuel from flowing back into the tank. This pump has a flow rate of 33 gallons per hour and maintains a minimum presure of 39 psi. An internal relief valve opens at 55-95 psi to protect the system from excessive pressure. The pump is mounted under the vehicle, forward of the left rear wheel on all vehicles except the Eldorado, where it is mounted in front of the right rear wheel.

Fuel Filter

The fuel filter is located on a bracket on the lower left front of the engine. The filter consists of a casing with an internal throwaway type paper filter element. The filter element should be replaced every 22,500 miles.

Fuel Pressure Regulator

The fuel pressure regulator, located on the fuel rail at the front of the engine, maintains a constant 39 psi pressure across the fuel injectors. The regulator contains an air chamber and fuel chamber separated by a spring-loaded diaphragm. The air chamber is connected by a hose to the throttle body assembly. The pressure in the air chamber of the regulator is identical to the pressure in the intake manifold. The changing manifold pressure and the spring control the action of the diaphragm valve, opening or closing an orifice in the fuel chamber of the regulator. At this point excess fuel is routed out of the regulator and back to the fuel tank.

Fuel Injector

The fuel injector is a solenoid operated pintle valve that meters fuel to each cylinder. The injectors are controlled by an electronic pulse signal from the ECU. When energized, the valve opens for precisely the proper amount of time to spray the exact amount of fuel droplets required by the engine. When the injector is deenergized, it prevents any futher fuel flow to the engine.

The eight injectors are divided into two groups of four each. Cylinders 1, 2, 7, and 8 form group 1 and the remaining injectors form group 2. All four injectors in each group are opened and closed simultaneously; while the two groups operate alternately.

The injectors are located on the intake manifold above the intake valve of each cylinder.

Air Induction System

The air induction system is made up of the throttle body assembly, fast idle valve assembly, and the intake manifold.

Throttle Body

Air for combustion enters the throttle body and is controlled by the throttle valves which are connected to the accelerator pedal linkage, much like a conventional carburetor. The throttle body consists of a housing with two bores and two shaft mounted throttle valves. The throttle valves are pre-set slightly open when the throttle lever is resting against the idle stop position. *The adjustment is not to be tampered with.* An adjustable set screw on the front of the throttle body adjusts an idle by-pass air passage incorporated within the throttle body and allows a regulated amount of air to by-pass the throttle valves, adjusting warm engine idle speed.

A large port on top of the throttle body contains the fast idle valve.

Fast Idle Valve

The fast idle valve, installed on the top of the throttle body, consists of a plastic body that houses an electric heater, a spring and plunger, and a temperature sensitive unit.

The fast idle valve is connected electrically to the fuel pump circuit through the ECU. When the engine is started cold, the open valve allows extra air to bypass the throttle valves. The heater warms the thermal element which expands and forces the spring and plunger toward the air orifice, restricting the flow of extra air and gradually reducing the engine speed to the normal idle rpm. The fast idle valve has no affect after the thermal element reaches about 140°F. The rate at which the valve closes is a function of time and temperature. The warmer the air, the faster the valve closes. At 68°F the valve will close in about 90 seconds and at −20°F the valve will require about 5 minutes to close.

Intake Manifold

The intake manifold is basically the same as those installed on carbureted engines. There are, however, a few minor differences: Only air travels through the intake manifold. There is a hole above each cylinder for injector installation. A port is made available for the installation of the air temperature sensor. There is no exhaust heat cross-over passage. The exhaust passage from the right cylinder head is for EGR only.

Engine Sensors

All of the engines sensors are electrically connected to the Electronic Control Unit (ECU). Each of the sensors operates independently, monitors a specific engine operating condition, and transmits this information via electronic signal to the ECU. The sensors continuously send information signals to the ECU while the ignition switch is in the On or Start position.

Manifold Absolute Pressure Sensor

The manifold absolute pressure (MAP) sensor monitors pressure changes within the intake manifold which are the direct result of engine load, speed, and barometric pressure. As pressure in the intake manifold increases, additional fuel is required. The MAP sensor sends this information to the ECU so that the length of time the injectors are energized is increased or decreased accordingly.

The sensor is mounted within the electronic control unit. A manifold pressure line is routed with the engine harness and is connected to the front of the throttle body at one end to the MAP sensor at the other end.

Throttle Position Switch

The throttle position switch is mounted to the throttle body, connected to the throttle valve shaft, and monitors the opening or closing of the throttle valves. The switch senses the shaft movement and position and transmits electrical signals to the ECU. The ECU processes these signals to determine the fuel requirement for the engine.

Temperature Sensors

The two air and coolant temperature sensors vary electrical current resistance as a function of temperature. Low temperatures provide low resistance and vice versa. Voltage changes across each sensor is monitored by the ECU.

The air temperature sensor is located on the rear of the intake manifold and is connected to the engine harness. The coolant temperature sensor is located on the heater hose fitting at the rear of the right cylinder head.

The sensors are identical and completely interchangeable.

Speed Sensor

The speed sensor is incorporated within the ignition distributor, and consists of two components. The first is a plastic housing containing two reed switches. The second is a rotor with two magnets attached to it and rotating with the distributor shaft.

The rotation of the magnets past the reed switches causes them to open and close, providing two bits of information: one for synchronization of the ECU and the proper injector group with the intake valve timing; and the engine rpm for fuel scheduling.

Electronic Control Unit

The electronic control unit (ECU), installed above the glove box in the passenger compartment on big Cadillacs and below the radio in the Seville, is a preprogrammed analog computer. The ECU is electrically connected to the vehicle's power supply, all of the EFI system electrical components, plus the EGR activation solenoid by a harness routed through the firewall.

When the ECU is energized by the ignition switch being turned to the On or Crank position, it continuously receives information from all of the engine sensors, and activates the fuel pumps, fast idle valve, fuel injectors, and the EGR solenoid.

The commands for proper air/fuel ratios for various driving and atmospheric conditions are designed into the ECU. As the elctronic signals are received from the sensors, the ECU analyzes the signals and computes the exact fuel requirement for the engine. The ECU then causes the fuel injectors to open for a specific amount of time. The duration of time the injectors are open varies as the engine operating conditions change.

The electronic control units are calibrated differently depending on where the car is sold (California or 49 states) and in which vehicle the unit is installed. Each ECU is labeled for its intended use. The proper unit must be used for each application.

Troubleshooting

NOTE: Because a special electronic tester is necessary to diagnose problems in the ECU, this section will deal with troubleshooting only mechanical and basic electrical problems of the EFI system. If the ECU is diagnosed as being the possible cause of a problem, the car should be taken to a Cadillac dealer where the special electronic tester and trained personel are available.

NOTE: Before disconnecting any part of the fuel delivery system on EFI equipped vehicles, the pressure within the fuel lines must be bled off. On early model cars without a pressure fiitting in the rear fuel rail, cover the fitting to be removed with a shop towel while loosening. Dispose of the gasoline soaked cloth safely.

On models with the "Schrader" pressure relief valve in the rear fuel rail, arrange a shop towl or suitable container at the valve so the fuel will be contained. Remove the protective cap, depress the valve, and bleed the pressure out of the system. Dispose of the fuel or fuel soaked cloth safely. Replace the protective cap on the valve and proceed with the service.

ELECTRONIC FUEL INJECTION TROUBLE-SHOOTING CHART

PROBLEM: Engine cranks but will not start
POSSIBLE CAUSE:
NOTE: The following possible causes assume that the rest of the vehicle electrical system is functioning properly.

1. Blown 10 amp in-line fuel pump fuse (located under the instrument panel near the ECU wiring harness connectors). To check, listen for the whine of the chassis-mounted fuel pump when the ignition key is turned to the On position. The fuel pump should only operate for one second before shutting off. Do not turn the ignition key to the Start position.
2. Poor connection of the green wire at the fuel pump wiring harness near the ECU harness below the instrument panel. Check the operation of the fuel pump in the same manner as in POSSIBLE CAUSE 1 above.
3. Malfunction in the chassis-mounted pump.
4. Open circuit in the purple wire between the starter solenoid and the ECU.
4. Open circuit in the green wire between the alternator BAT terminal and the ECU.
6. Poor connection at the engine coolant sensor or an open circuit in the wiring or the sensor, with the engine cold only. To check, connect an ohmmeter to the temperature sensor connector terminals. If the resistance in the sensor is greater than 1600 ohms, replace the sensor.
7. Poor connection of the ECU wiring harness.
8. Poor connection at the speed sensor on the distributor.
9. The speed sensor trigger is stuck closed.
10. The wide-open-throttle section of the throttle position switch is shorted. To check, disconnect the switch; the engine should start.
11. A restriction in the fuel delivery system.

PROBLEM: Hard starting
POSSIBLE CAUSE:

1. Open circuit in the engine coolant temperature sensor. This should occur only when the engine is cold or partially warm. The engine should start satisfactorily when hot.
2. The wide-open-throttle section of the throttle position switch is shorted. To check, disconnect the switch; the engine should start.
3. The fuel pressure regulator is malfunctioning.
4. The chassis-mounted fuel pump is malfunctioning.

PROBLEM: Poor fuel economy
POSSIBLE CAUSE:

1. The manifold absolute air pressure sensor is disconnected or leaking.
2. The vacuum hose at the fuel pressure regulator or throttle body is disconnected.
3. The air temperature or coolant temperature sensors are malfunctioning. Check the coolant temperature sensor as outlined under "Engine cranks but will not start", number 6. Check the air temperature sensor by connecting an ohmmeter to the sensor connector terminals; if the sensor resistance is less than 700 ohms, replace the sensor.

PROBLEM: Engine stalls after being started
POSSIBLE CAUSE:

1. A poor connection or open circuits in the black and yellow ignition signal wire between the fuse block and the ECU.
2. A poor connection or open circuit in the wiring or body of the engine coolant temperature sensor; cold or warm engine only. Check as outlined under "Engine cranks but will not start", number 6.

PROBLEM: Rough idle
POSSIBLE CAUSE:

1. Disconnected, leaking, or pinched manifold absolute air pressure sensor vacuum hose.
2. Poor connection or an open circuit in the air temperature sensor or wiring; cold engine only. See "Poor fuel economy", number 3.

3. Poor connection or short in the sensor or wiring of the engine coolant temperature sensor. See "Engine cranks but will not start", number 6.
4. Poor connection at the injectors.

PROBLEM: Fast idle condition is prolonged

POSSIBLE CAUSE:

1. Throttle position switch needs adjusting.
2. Poor connection at the fast idle valve or an open circuit in the heating element.
3. A vacuum leak in or around the throttle body.

PROBLEM: Hesitation of the engine under acceleration

POSSIBLE CAUSE:

1. Leaking, restricted, or disconnected manifold absolute air pressure sensor vacuum hose.
2. Throttle position switch needs adjusting or is malfunctioning.
3. Poor connecton of the ECU wiring harness at the ECU.
4. Poor connection at the EGR valve solenoid or the solenoid is stuck open; cold engine only.
5. Intermittent malfunction of the speed sensor trigger at the distributor.

PROBLEM: High speed performance is poor

POSSIBLE CAUSE:

1. The wide-open-throttle section of the throttle position switch needs adjusting or the switch is malfunctioning.
2. The fuel filter is blocked or restricted.
3. The chassis-mounted fuel pump is malfunctioning.
4. Intermittent malfunction of the speed sensor trigger.
5. An open circuit in the purple wire between the starter solenoid and the ECU.

Fuel Pump and Filter

The fuel pump on carbureted engines is mounted on the left-hand side of the engine. The pump is driven by an eccentric machined as an integral part of the camshaft. There is a fuel filter between the fuel pump and the carburetor. The fuel filter is an integral part of the fuel pump. The filter should be replaced every 12,000 miles. On air conditioned cars, the fuel filter has a passage and a connecting line to the fuel tank to return fuel vapors to the tank under high temperature conditions.

Vehicles with EFI have two electric fuel pumps; one is mounted in the fuel tank and is integral with the fuel level sending unit and the other, a chassis-mounted pump located in front of the rear axle either on the right or left side. A fuel filter is mounted on a bracket at the lower left front of the engine.

Pump R & R
Carbureted Engines

NOTE: on air conditioned cars, be sure to disconnect the flexible line connecting the fuel filter to the vapor return line from the tank.

1. If equipped with A.I.R. system, it may be necessary to remove air pump and bracket for clearance.
2. Remove center coil wire. Jack up front of car and support on axle stands so that pump can be removed from underneath.
3. Loosen one bolt and one stud nut.
4. Turn over engine so that tension on mounting bolts is relieved.
5. Disconnect pump inlet line and pump outlet line. Plug inlet line. Disconnect the vapor return line.
6. Remove two mounting bolts and pump.
7. To install, reverse removal procedure. Make sure pump arm is properly positioned on cam eccentric; tighten bolts to 15 ft. lbs.

Fuel Injected Engines

Chassis-Mounted Pump

1. Relieve the pressure in the fuel lines and remove the fuel inlet and outlet hoses from nipples on the pump.
2. Peel back the rubber boot and remove the two nuts, one from each electrical terminal. Remove the electrical leads.

NOTE: These nuts have metric threads.

3. Remove the two screws and flat washers holding the fuel pump to the bracket and remove the pump assembly.
4. Install the fuel pump in the reverse order of removal. Connect the green wire to the positive terminal on the pump and the black wire to the negative terminal. Check to make sure the fuel pump is resting evenly on its two mounts and not grounding against the bracket or frame.

In-Tank Pump

1. Disconnect the battery, open the fuel tank filler door and disconnect the tan sending unit feed wire.
2. Siphon the fuel from the fuel tank. If the rear of the car is raised one foot higher than the front, more fuel can be taken out.
3. Raise the rear of the car and remove the screw securing the ground wire to the cross member.
4. Disconnect the fuel line, evaporative emission lines and the fuel return lines at the front of the tank.
5. Support the tank with a jack and wooden block and remove one screw on each side securing the fuel tank support straps to the body at the front of the tank.
6. Lower the jack and tank enough so that the fuel pump electrical lead can be disconnected. Disconnect the wire.
7. Remove the fuel tank from the car.
8. Remove the locknuts securing the fuel gauge tank unit and fuel pump feed wires to the tank unit.
9. Turn the cam locking ring counterclockwise with a soft non-ferrous punch and hammer. When the lock ring is disengaged, remove it and lift the gauge/pump unit from the tank.
10. Install in the reverse order of removal. Tighten the fuel tank retaining strap screws to 25 ft lbs.

Filter R & R
Carbureted Engines

1. Jack up car and support on stands.
2. Clamp or plug rubber section of inlet hose.
3. Disconnect fuel pump outlet line at fuel pump.
4. Remove fuel outlet nut and remove filter.

NOTE: use two wrenches to prevent loosening of nut welded to pump cover.

5. Install in reverse of above.

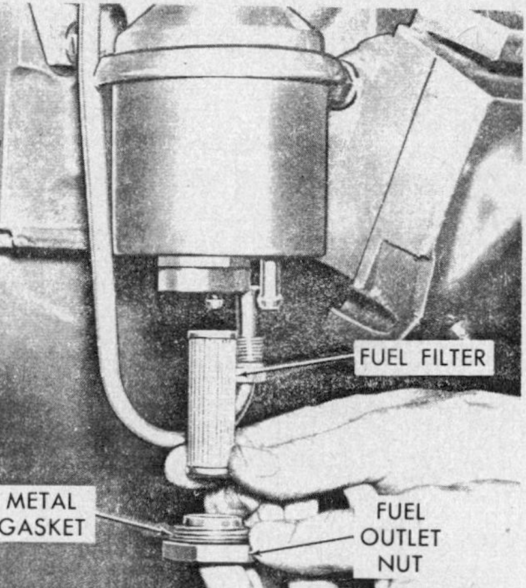

Fuel filter (© Cadillac Div., G.M. Corp)

Fuel Injected Engines

NOTE: The fuel filter element can be replaced by unscrewing the bottom cover and removing it.

1. Bleed the pressure from the fuel delivery system and remove the fuel inlet and outlet hoses from the fuel filter.
2. Remove the two screws retaining the fuel filter to the bracket and remove the filter from the engine.
3. Remove the inlet and outlet fittings from the filter assembly if they are needed for the new filter.
4. Install the fittings to the new filter, using a sealer on the threads.

5. Attach the filter to the bracket and tighten the retaining screws to 12 ft lbs.
6. Connect the inlet and outlet line, using new clamps.

NOTE: It may require considerable cranking before the engine starts due to the drained fuel lines.

Throttle Body Assembly R & R

Fuel Injected Engines

1. Remove the air cleaner.
2. Disconnect the two throttle return springs from the throttle lever.
3. Remove the cruise control chain retainer and chain, if so equipped.
4. Remove the clip and disconnect the throttle cable from the throttle lever.
5. Remove the left rear throttle body mounting screw and remove the one screw holding the throttle bracket to the intake manifold.
6. Remove the downshift switch from the throttle lever and position bracket. Move the switch and linkage aside.
7. Disconnect the throttle position and fast idle valve electrical connectors. Slide the fast idle valve wiring out of the notch in the throttle body.
8. Disconnect the vacuum lines from the throttle body.
9. Remove the remaining throttle body retaining screws and remove the throttle body.
10. Remove all gasket material from the intake manifold and the throttle body.
11. Install the throttle body in the reverse order of removel. Install the throttle return springs between the throttle lever and pressure regulator bracket with the open end of the spring on the outside of the throttle lever.

Throttle Position Switch R & R

Fuel Injected Engines

1. Remove the throttle body from the engine.
2. Remove the two mounting screws and remove the switch from the throttle body.
3. Install the switch on the right side of the throttle body so that the tab on the switch engages the flat on the throttle shaft.
4. Install the two mounting screws and tighten the screws so that the switch will move but is still firmly attached.
5. Adjust the throttle position switch as outlined under "Adjustments".
6. Reinstall the throttle body.

Fast Idle Valve R & R

Fuel Injected Engines

1. Remove the air cleaner and disconnect the fast idle valve heater electrical connection.
2. Remove the air cleaner mounting stud.
3. Push down and twist the fast idle valve heater counterclockwise 90° to remove it.
4. Remove the fast idle valve, spring and seat from the throttle body.

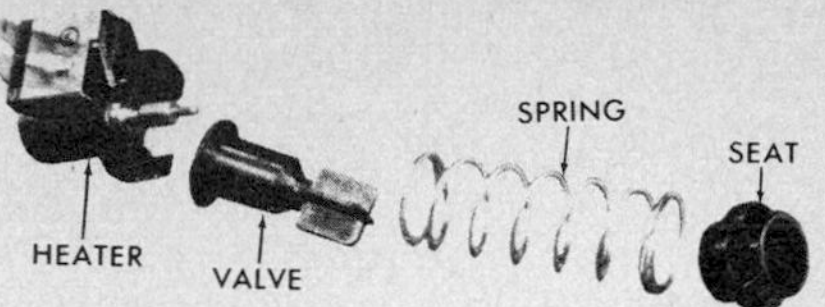

Fast idle valve assembly—exploded view—EFI
(© Cadillac Div., G.M. Corp.)

5. Install the fast idle valve seat, spring and valve in the throttle body.
6. Position the heater on top of the fast idle valve and push it down to compress the spring. Be careful to avoid damaging the microswitch contact arm on the bottom of the heater housing.
7. Align the tabs on the fast idle valve heater with the cut-out portion of the throttle body and compress the spring further.
8. Rotate the heater clockwise 90° to secure it in position.
9. Connect the electrical lead and install the air cleaner stud and air cleaner.

Fuel Injector R & R

Fuel Injected Engines

1. Remove the front and rear fuel rails.
2. Remove the electrical conduit from the injector brackets.
3. Remove the two screws holding each injector bracket to the intake manifold and remove the brackets and grommets.
4. Disconnect the electrical lead from all of the injectors on the fuel rail being removed.

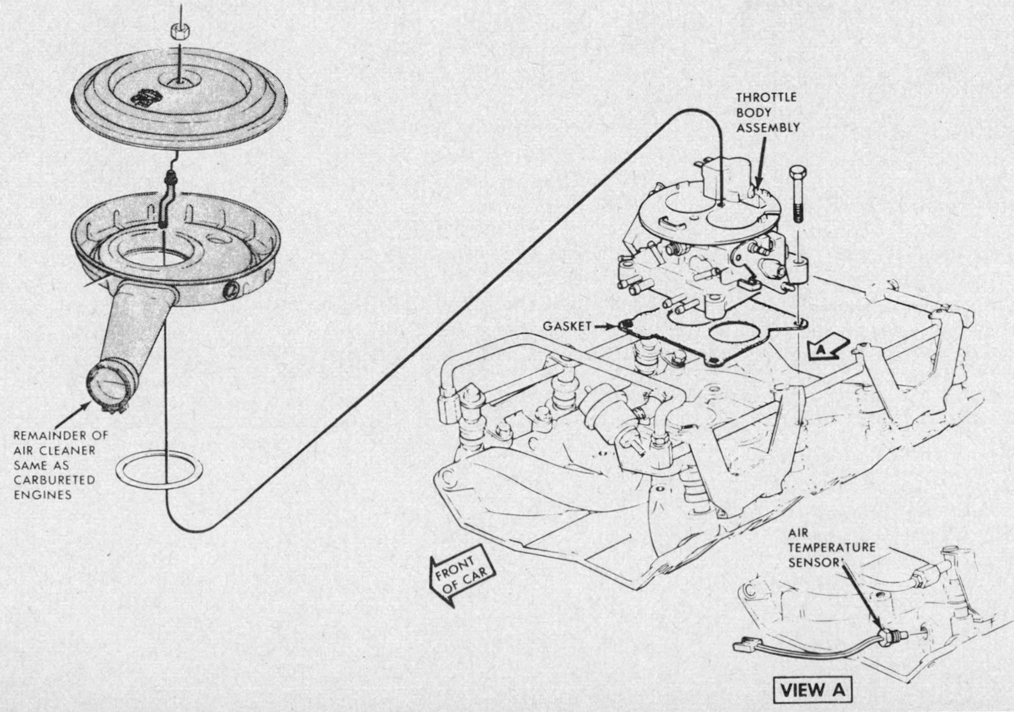

Mounting of the throttle body assembly and air temperature sensor—EFI
(© Cadillac Div., G.M. Corp.)

5. Remove the fuel rail and injectors from the engine as an assembly. Some injectors may stick to the intake manifold and others will come off with the fuel rail. Remove the injectors from the fuel rail and manifold as required.
6. Remove and discard all of the used O-rings used to seal the injectors at the fuel rail and intake manifold.
7. Before installing the new O-ring seals, lubricate them with a suitable lubricant and install the O-rings on the fuel rail end of each injector.
8. Install the injectors into the fuel rail with the electrical connector facing inward.
9. Install new O-rings into each injector port in the intake manifold.
10. Install the fuel rail/injector assembly to the intake manifold. Make certain that each injector is properly positioned in the manifold O-ring.
11. Install the rubber grommets, flanges down, on the fuel rail and install the injector brackets in position.
12. Install and tighten the bracket retaining screws to 5 ft lbs.
13. Route and secure the electrical harness along the bracket. Connect the injectors as follows: The front injectors are connected to the red/black wires and the two center injectors are connected to the black/white wires.
14. Install the front and rear fuel rails.
15. Turn the ignition On and Off a few times to build up fuel pressure in the system and check for leaks.
16. Start the engine and check for leaks. It may require considerable cranking to start the engine due to the drained condition of the fuel lines.

Fuel Pressure Regulator R & R

Fuel Injected Engines

1. Remove the vacuum hose from the top of the pressure regulator.
2. Bleed off the pressure in the fuel delivery system and disconnect the flexible fuel hose between the fuel rail and the regulator. Disconnect the fuel return line.
3. Remove the one nut securing the pressure regulator to the bracket. This nut has metric threads.
4. Remove the regulator.
5. Install the regulator in the reverse order of removal.

Air Valve (Dashpot)

A vacuum-operated throttle check is used on some models. It operates by a combination of spring pressure and engine vacuum. Adjust length of plunger for correct operation.

Adjustment is made by seating the vacuum diaphragm. With the diaphragm in this position there must be 0.030 in. clearance between the dashpot rod and the end of the slot in the air valve lever. When making this measurement, make certain that the diaphragm plunger is totally compressed inward. Bend the rod at the air valve end to make adjustments.

Speed-Up Control Adjustment

Cars equipped with air conditioning have a vacuum-powered, solenoid-operated speed-up control attached to the carburetor.

This device increases the engine idle speed to 900 rpm when the transmission is in neutral and the air conditioner switch is on.

1969

On these models, the speed-up control is actuated by water temperature, working only when radiator reaches 220°F. Air conditioner does not have to be on to have idle speed up. Curb and fast idle adjustments should be made before attempting the speed-up idle adjustment.

1. Warm up engine.
2. With engine off, remove air cleaner.
3. Disconnect vacuum hose leading from thermo vacuum switch to reducing nipple near dash, at reducing nipple.
4. Disconnect vacuum hose at diverter valve and connect to reducing nipple.
5. Disconnect and plug distributor vacuum hose at vacuum unit.
6. Disconnect manifold vacuum hose from thermo vacuum switch nipple at "MT" and connect to distributor vacuum unit. This is the nipple closest to the block.
7. Turn air conditioner to HIGH and turn temperature dial to 65.
8. With transmission in Neutral or Park, start engine and make adjustment at screw on idle speed-up control arm (900-950 rpm).
9. Turn engine off, reconnect hoses and install air cleaner.

1970 Fleetwood 75 and Commercial

Operation is similar to 1969. Different vacuum routing requires a slightly different procedure.

1. Set curb and fast idle.
2. Stop engine and remove air cleaner and heat duct.
3. Disconnect and plug distributor advance hose.
4. Disconnect vacuum hose at vacuum break tank and connect it to distributor advance unit.
5. Disconnect vacuum hose that goes from Thermo Vacuum switch to reducing nipple, at the reducing nipple.
6. Disconnect vacuum hose connector at carburetor vacuum break T.
7. Connect a 25 in. section of 3/16 in. vacuum hose between T and reducing nipple.
8. Turn A/C to HIGH and set dial to 65°F.
9. Start and warm up engine, then adjust idle speed-up in Neutral. Turn adjusting screw, as illustrated, to maintain 900-950 rpm.

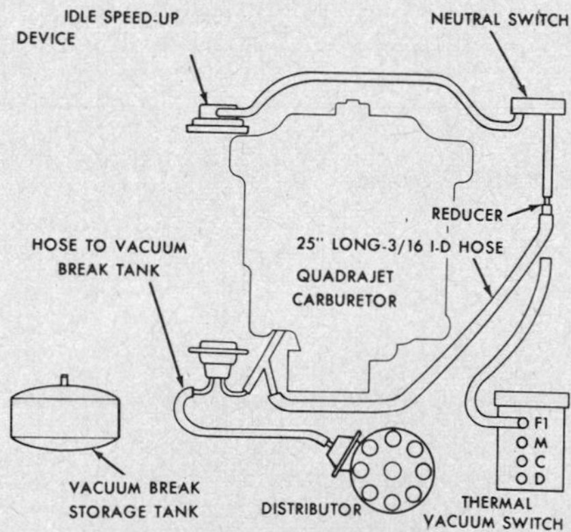

Idle speed-up adjustment—1970 (© Cadillac Div., G.M. Corp)

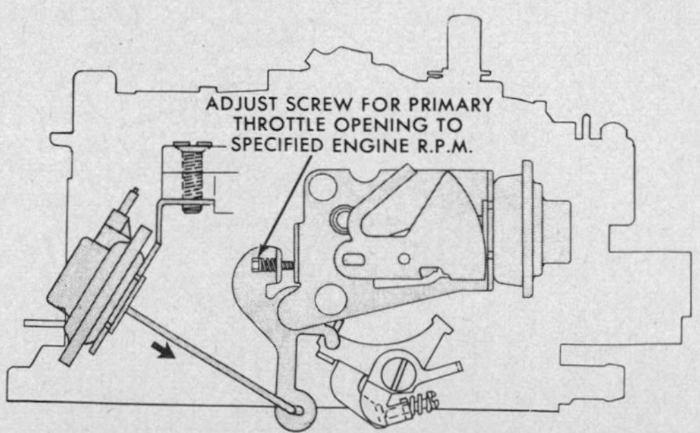

Speed-up control adjustment. The adjustment is on the rod on earlier models (© Cadillac Div., G.M. Corp)

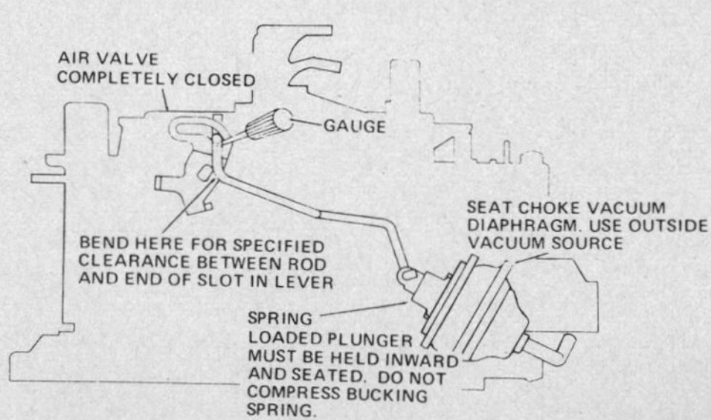

Air valve adjustment (© Cadillac Div., G.M. Corp)

NOTE: pull rod on idle speed-up unit should move when selector lever is moved to Park or Neutral. If it does not, check neutral switch or for vacuum leaks.

10. Turn off engine, reconnect hoses and install air cleaner.

Carbureted Engine Idle Speed and Mixture Adjustments

1969

Make all adjustments with the air cleaner removed.

1. Make sure the PCV valve is clean and working properly.
2. Disconnect the parking brake vacuum hose at the vacuum cylinder and connect a vacuum gauge to the hose.
3. Connect a tachometer to the engine and set the parking brake. Allow the engine to reach normal operating temperature.
4. Remove the air cleaner and make certain that the dashpot is disengaged.
5. With the parking brake on, place the transmission in Drive. Make sure that the parking brake holds securely.
6. Disconnect and plug distributor vacuum advance hose.

NOTE: plug parking brake vacuum hose instead of using a gauge.

7. Adjust air adjusting screw to obtain an idle speed of 480-500 rpm for cars without Air Injection Reactor system, 550 rpm for A.I.R. equipped cars. (A/C should be *off* for A.I.R. cars, *on* for all others.)

NOTE: press down on brass hot idle compensator pin while making adjustments. Be careful of the bimetallic strip, as it is easily damaged.

8. Set idle speed screw 1½ turns in after contacting primary lever, both mixture screws out 4 turns from seated position.
9. Turn one idle mixture screw clockwise to obtain highest tach reading. Continue to turn screw until speed falls off 20 rpm—this is the lean idle fall-off point. Back off screw 1 turn for 1969 A.I.R. cars.
10. Repeat Step 9, turning other mixture screw.
11. Reset idle speed as in Step 7, then repeat Steps 9 and 10 if speed exceeds 500 rpm for non-A.I.R. cars or 550 rpm for A.I.R. cars.
12. Install air cleaner and recheck idle speed.
13. Shut off engine, disconnect tach, connect parking brake vacuum line and reconnect distributor vacuum advance.

1970

Adjust with air cleaner removed.

1. Disconnect and plug distributor vacuum advance line.
2. Disconnect and plug parking brake vacuum line at vacuum release cylinder.
3. Connect a tachometer, set parking brake and remove air cleaner.
4. Make sure dashpot is not touching linkage, then turn slow idle speed screw in approximately 1½ turns after it contacts primary throttle lever. Turn in both mixture screws until they seat gently, then unscrew them approximately 6 turns.
5. Place car in Drive after warming up engine. Turn off Air Conditioning.

NOTE: press down on hot idle compensator pin while making adjustments.

6. Adjust slow idle screw to obtain 620 rpm.
7. Turn one mixture screw clockwise until speed falls off 10 rpm, then repeat Steps 6 and 7 for other mixture screw. Idle speed now should be 600 rpm, indicating a 10 rpm drop per mixture needle.
8. Install air cleaner, shut off engine and disconnect tach.
9. Connect parking brake vacuum line and distributor vacuum line.

1971-76

Adjust with air cleaner removed.

Idle speed is adjusted at a new anti-dieseling solenoid located where the dashpot was located in previous years. The throttle must be opened slightly to allow the plunger to move out all the way, then it must be closed against the now-extended solenoid plunger before making the idle speed adjustment. The solenoid plunger will retract when the ignition is shut off.

1. Disconnect and plug distributor vacuum advance hose and parking brake vacuum hose (at the release cylinder). If equipped with "self-leveling", remove and plug the air leveling compressor hose at the air cleaner. Remove the air cleaner but keep the vacuum hoses connected.
2. Connect a tachometer and set the parking brake with transmission in Neutral.
3. Turn in mixture screws until they seat gently, then turn the screws out approximately 6 turns 1971-73 or 4 turns—1974-76.
4. Start engine and allow it to warm up. Make sure choke is off.
5. Place car in Drive (DR) with A/C off.

NOTE: press down on hot idle comments. This applies to Fleetwood 75 and Commercial models only.

6. Set idle speed to 620 rpm—1971-73 or 640 rpm—1974-76 by adjusting anti-dieseling solenoid. Tighten jam nut.
7. Turn each mixture screw clockwise ¼ turn at a time alternately until idle speed of 600 rpm is obtained.
8. Install limiter caps, then disconnect wire that energizes solenoid. The plunger should retract to allow a slower idle speed of 350-400 rpm.
9. Shut off engine, disconnect tach, connect vacuum lines and solenoid wire and install air cleaner.

Idle Speed Adjustment

Fuel Injected Engines

1. Adjust the ignition timing to the correct specifications.
2. Disconnect and plug the distributor vacuum line, the parking brake release cylinder vacuum line, and the air leveling compressor hose at the air cleaner.
3. Connect a tachometer to the engine, start it, allow the engine to reach normal operating temperature.
4. Place the transmission selector in Drive, and turn the air conditioning Off.
5. Loosen the lock nut on the idle by-pass adjusting screw on the front of the throttle body.
6. Adjust the idle by-pass adjusting screw to obtain an idle speed of 600 rpm.
7. Tighten the lock nut on the adjusting screw, stop the engine, remove the tachometer, and install the air cleaner and vacuum hoses.

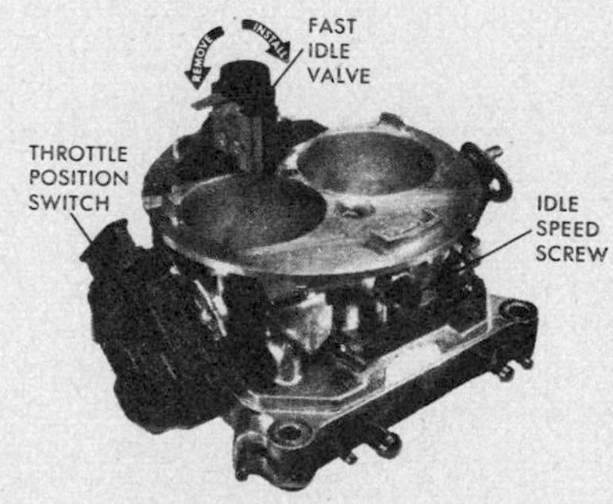

Throttle body adjustments—EFI
(© Cadillac Div., G.M. Corp.)

Throttle Position Switch

Fuel Injected Engines

1. Loosen the two throttle position switch mounting screws.
2. While holding the throttle valves in the idle position, turn the throttle position switch counterclockwise carefully until the endstop is reached.
3. Tighten the mounting screws.
4. Check and make sure that the throttle valves close to the throttle stop. Readjust, if necessary.

Adjusting the idle speed—EFI
(© Cadillac Div., G.M. Corp.)

COOLING SYSTEM

Cadillac uses a sealed cooling system. The sealed system is designed to remain sealed at all times. A coolant reservior allows the pressurized system to be kept sealed even when fresh coolant is added. There is no need to open the radiator cap.

Information on the water temperature gauge can be found in the Unit Repair Section.

Radiator R & R

1. Disconnect battery cable.
2. Drain cooling system.
3. Disconnect air conditioning compressor, if so equipped, and position out of the way without disconnecting hoses.
4. Remove clamp that holds A/C high pressure vapor line to cradle.
5. Loosen hose clamps and disconnect upper and lower radiator hoses.
6. Disconnect two transmission oil cooler lines and plug them.

NOTE: disconnect heater return hose, if so equipped.

7. Remove two top radiator cradle clamps or straps and fan shroud. Disconnect reservoir hose from 1969.
8. Remove vacuum hoses, if so equipped. Mark for proper installation.
9. Pull radiator straight up and out of car.

Water Pump R & R

1. Disconnect negative battery cable.
2. Drain radiator and remove fan shroud.
3. Remove fan assembly. The screws cannot be removed entirely due to lack of clearance between fan and radiator. Slide loosened assembly near power steering pump to remove bolts and spacer.
4. Loosen alternator mounting screws and remove generator belt.
5. Loosen power steering pump mounting screws and remove belts.
6. On applicable models, remove A.I.R. pump and belt.
7. Remove water pump pulley, disconnect water inlet and remove 11 screws and pump.

Thermostat R & R

Removal

1. Drain the cooling system until the coolant level is below the level of the thermostat.
2. Remove the upper radiator hose at the thermostat housing.
3. Remove the thermostat housing.
4. Pull the thermostat from the engine block.

Installation

1. Position the thermostat in the block with the valve up.
2. Install a new gasket coated with sealer onto the engine block.
3. Position and secure the thermostat housing; tighten screws to 10 ft lbs.
4. Connect the radiator hose and refill the system to the proper level.

EMISSION CONTROLS

Positive Crankcase Ventilation (PCV) Systems

A simple valve, operated by intake manifold vacuum, is used to meter the flow of air and vapors through the crankcase. Air is drawn in through the breather assembly, located between the left rocker cover and the carburetor air cleaner (closed system). When the car is decelerating or the engine is idling, high manifold vacuum opens the valve; this allows full flow of the crankcase vapor into the intake manifold. During acceleration or at a constant speed, the intake manifold vacuum drops. the valve spring forces the valve closed and restricts the flow of vapors into the intake manifold from the crankcase. If a backfire occurs the valve closes, preventing the vapor in the crankcase from being ignited.

Air Injection

The 1969 cars were the first to be equipped with an Air Injection Reactor (AIR) in addition to the PCV system. This AIR system consists of an engine-driven pump which forces air into the exhaust port of each cylinder to promote further oxidation and reduce the concentration of hydrocarbons.

The 1970 models did not use the AIR system but substituted the Controlled Combustion System (CCS). The PCV system was retained on all 1970 models. The CCS system is composed of a thermac air cleaner and a transmission-controlled spark advance.

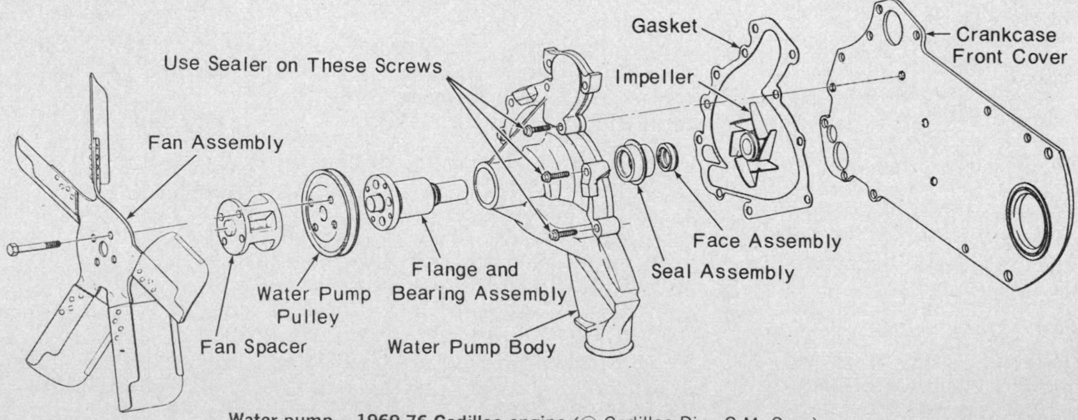

Water pump—1969-76 Cadillac engine (© Cadillac Div., G.M. Corp)

Thermostatically Controlled Air Cleaner

The thermatic air cleaner regulates the air temperature at the air cleaner inlet so that it maintains a constant temperature of 105°F. A damper in the air cleaner, when the engine is cold (85°F or below) allows the intake air to be heated by the exhaust manifold before it enters the carburetor. As the engine reaches operating temperature, the damper opens and allows a mixture of outside cool air and heated air to mix to obtain the 105° F intake air.

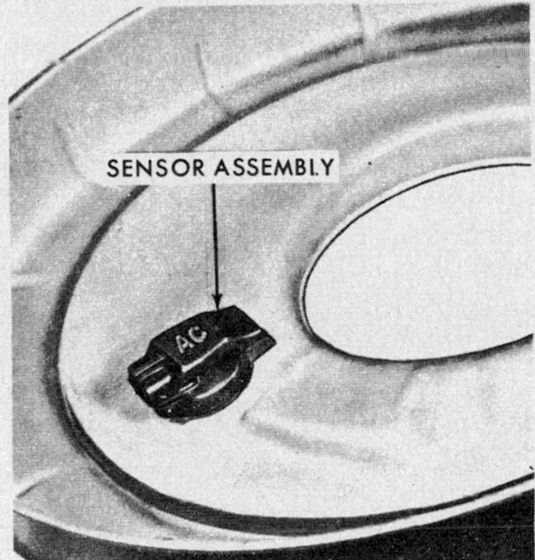

Location of the Thermac air cleaner sensor (© Cadillac Div., G.M. Corp)

Transmission Controlled Spark (TCS)

The transmission-controlled spark system is composed of a transmission switch, a thermal vacuum switch, and a vacuum solenoid. The switch is positioned in the block with vacuum lines from the intake manifold, the distributor and the carburetor running to it. The line between the carburetor and the thermal vacuum switch has the solenoid attached to it. The solenoid has a wire which connects it with the transmission. Inside the thermal vacuum switch there is a ball check valve system which opens and closes the ports in the switch.

The vacuum switch has two vacuum sources attached to it: intake manifold vacuum and carburetor vacuum. In the normal running position, the ball check blocks the passage of vacuum from the intake manifold to the distributor and allows vacuum to pass from the carburetor to the distributor. This vacuum is regulated by the transmission solenoid. If the engine should overheat at idle speed, the ball check valve blocks the carburetor-to-distributor vacuum and allows the intake manifold-to-distributor vacuum port to be uncovered allowing the stronger intake manifold vacuum to advance the ignition timing and cool the engine.

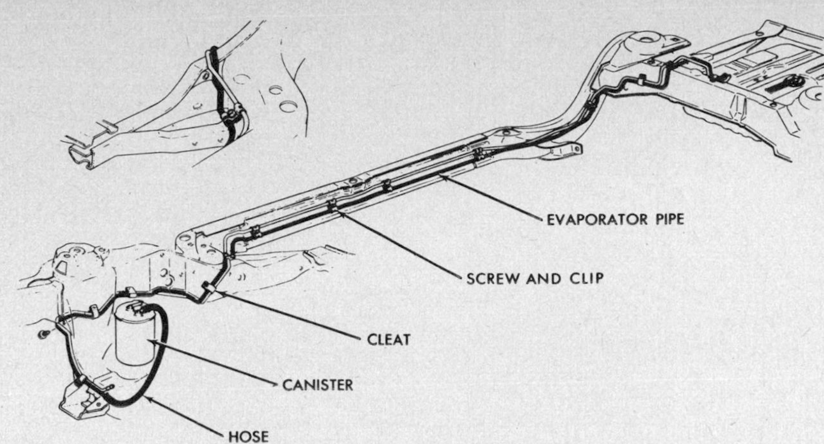

Evaporative control system (© Cadillac Div., G.M. Corp)

The vacuum solenoid is a type of regulator between the carburetor vacuum line, the thermal vacuum switch, the distributor, and the transmission. When the transmission is in neutral, first, or second gear, the solenoid is energized which eliminates vacuum advance to the distributor. When the transmission shifts into third gear the solenoid is de-energized allowing the vacuum advance to pass to the distributor.

Evaporative Loss Control (ELC)

Evaporative Loss Control (ELC), also known as evaporative control system (E.C.S.), was used in California cars in 1970 and nationally starting in 1971. The concept of this system is, the venting of the fuel tank through a canister containing charcoal. Both liquid fuel and fuel vapors from the tank are fed into the liquid vapor separator which is located ahead of the fuel tank. The vapors are collected in the charcoal canister which is mounted on the front of the radiator. The vapors are drawn from the canister by a vacuum line which is connected to the air cleaner. The liquid fuel which is ducted to the separator is returned to the fuel tank.

Exhaust Gas Recirculation (EGR)

The Exhaust Gas Recirculation System (EGR), used from 1973 on, is a control system used to reduce nitrous oxides released into the air. The basic function of the system is to reduce the temperature in the combustion chambers. This will lessen nitrogen oxidation and reduce pollution. It is accomplished by recirculating a small amount of engine exhaust through ports in the intake manifold and into the carburetor for reburning.

This channeling of exhaust is governed by the EGR valve which is mounted at the rear of the intake

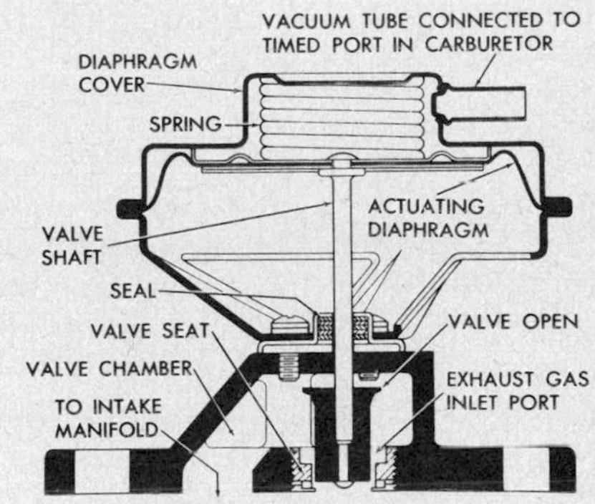

E.G.R. valve in the open position (© Cadillac Div., G.M. Corp)

manifold. As the engine speed increases, vacuum is applied to the vacuum diaphragm in the valve and this opens the exhaust port allowing exhaust gases to enter. As vacuum decreases at idle speed and wide open throttle, the valve closes and the gases are cut off.

Temperature overrides are used to prevent exhaust gas recirculation from occurring when the engine is cold. Prior to March 15, 1973, these overrides depended upon ambient temperature; overrides used after this date were enclosed in shrouds, making them dependent upon engine temperature. The temperature override switch blocks vacuum to the EGR valve at temperature below 60°F.

All 1974 models sold in California use an exhaust backpressure transducer which is connected to the EGR valve to prevent exhaust gases from being recirculated at idle, and wide open throttle because the higher volume of gas recirculated on these models would cause poor performance.

The EGR system is slightly different on EFI engines. The EGR vacuum solenoid valve is controlled by the ECU and installed in the signal line to the EGR valve. The ECU keeps the solenoid valve closed when coolant temperatures are below about 130°F, blocking the signal to the EGR valve. This is to improve cold starting and engine warm up. When the coolant

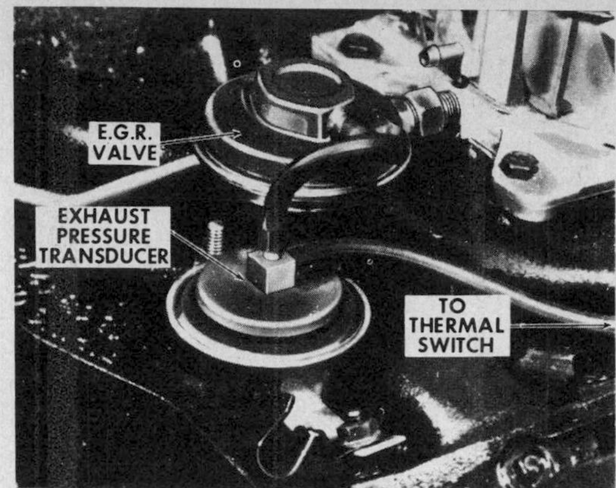

Exhaust pressure transducer and EGR valve—1974 and later
(© Cadillac Div., G.M. Corp.)

temperature goes above 130°F, ported vacuum is directed to the EGR valve and exhaust pressure transducer. A thermal delay valve is not used.

Catalytic Converter

Catalytic converters are used on 1975 Cadillacs to meet the tougher 1975 Federal emission standards. The converter is located in the exhaust pipe, under the floor on the passenger's side.

For more information on how the converter works, as well as service procedures for it, see the "Emission Controls" Unit Repair Section.

Model Usage

Models made in 1969 use PCV and air injection (AIR). 1970 models sold in California, use an evaporative loss control (ELC) system.

In 1971 transmission controlled spark (TCS) and the thermostatically controlled air cleaner were used for the first time. The ELC system was expanded to include cars sold nationally and PCV was continued.

In the 1971 model year all cars were equipped with the PCV, AIR, and ELC systems.

The 1972 cars use the PCV, AIR, ELC, and a Speed Control Spark (SCS) which controls the spark advance to the distributor at low speeds. The switch is mounted within the transmission and connected to the speedometer gear. The switch is closed prior to 33 mph, allowing no vacuum advance to the distributor during speeds from 0 to 33 mph. When the vehicle reaches 33 mph, the contacts in the switch separate, allowing the vacuum port to be uncovered. Once the port is uncovered the vacuum causes the distributor to advance.

1973-74 models use EGR, PCV, AIR, and ELC.

1975 models use catalytic converters, AIR, PCV, ECS, and EGR.

Component Removal and Installation

PCV Valve

1. Disconnect the valve from its connection in the valve cover.
2. Remove the hose clamp and the hose from the ventilator valve grommet.
3. To install, place a small amount of silicone sealer on both ends of the new valve and install the small end of the valve into the hose. Secure with the clamp.
4. Place the large end of the valve into the grommet in the valve cover.

AIR Pump

NOTE: Pump service should be limited to replacement of the entire unit. At no time should the pump be opened.

1. Raise and support the vehicle.
2. Remove the air hose from the diverter valve and disconnect the vacuum line from the other side of the valve.
3. Remove the three screws which hold the pulley to the pump and remove the pulley and belt.
4. Remove the mounting bolt from the top of the air pump and the adjusting bolt from the bottom rear.
5. Remove the pump and the diverter valve as an assembly.
6. To install, lift the pump through the space between the lower radiator hose and the oil filter. Turn the pump so that the diverter valve passes over the oil filter.
7. Place the pump against the mounting bracket and loosely install the upper screw and adjusting bolt.
8. Install the pulley and drive belt and adjust the belt.
9. The adjusting and mounting bolts should be torqued to 25 ft lbs.
10. Connect the air hose to the larger fitting of the diverter valve and tighten the clamp. The vacuum hose is installed on the small fitting of the valve.

Centrifugal Filter Fan R & R

NOTE: Never attempt to clean the filter fan. It is impossible to remove the fan without destroying it.

1. Remove the air pump from the car, as detailed above.
2. Gently pry the outer disc off and pull off the remaining portion. Be careful that no fragments from the fan enter the pump air intake.
3. Install a new filter fan pulling it into place with the pump pulley and attaching belts.
4. Alternately torque the bolts so that the fan is drawn down *evenly*. Be sure that the outer edge of the fan fits into the pump housing.

Caution Never hammer or press the fan into place; damage to it and the pump will result.

5. Install the pump on the car.

NOTE: For the first 20-30 miles of operation, the fan may squeal until its lip has worn in. This is normal and does not indicate a damaged pump.

Thermac Temperature Sensor

1. Remove the hose from between the sensor and the manifold fitting.
2. Remove the air cleaner.
3. Remove the hose between the sensor and the vacuum motor.
4. Pull the retainer from the sensor vacuum fittings and remove the retainer.
5. Pull the sensor from the air cleaner.
6. To install, place the gasket on the sensor and install the sensor into the air cleaner.
7. Press the retainer on the vacuum connections.
8. Connect the vacuum hose between the sensor and the vacuum motor. Place the vacuum hose on the remaining fitting.
9. Position the air cleaner making certain that the heat tube engages the heat shroud on the exhaust manifold.
10. Connect the vacuum hose between the sensor and the manifold.

Exhaust Gas Recirculation Valve

1. Remove the air cleaner and the vacuum hoses from the air cleaner and the front of the carburetor.
2. Remove the valve attaching nuts and the vacuum signal line and remove the valve.
3. To install, place the valve on the manifold studs and install the attaching nuts.
4. Connect the vacuum signal line to the E.G.R. valve and the two

vacuum hoses to the air cleaner.
5. Install the air cleaner.

Evaporative Control System Canister

1. Remove the hoses from the top of the canister.
2. Remove the canister strap bracket from the radiator cradle.
3. Remove both the strap and the canister from the cradle.
4. To install, position the canister onto the radiator cradle bracket with the fittings on the top facing toward the engine.
5. Tighten the hold-down strap and connect the two hoses to the top of the canister. The smaller diameter hose is connected to the carburetor while the larger diameter hose goes to the tank.

Evaporative Control System Canister Filter

1. Remove the canister from its cradle.
2. Pull out the element by squeezing it under the retainer bar.
3. To install, push the element under the bar and locate it evenly around the entire bottom of the canister.
4. Install the canister.

For troubleshooting and adjustment of the Cadillac emission control systems consult the "Unit Repair Section."

ENGINE

Engine Removal and Installation

Except Seville

1. Disconnect negative battery cable.
2. Remove hood, after scribing hood hinge outline for proper alignment.
3. Remove air cleaner and heat shroud.
4. Drain cooling system. Unfasten the fender struts from the radiator shroud.
5. Remove radiator hose bracket, radiator cover and fan.
6. Remove upper radiator hose.
7. Disconnect throttle and Cruise Control linkage at carburetor.
8. Remove Cruise Control power unit on cars so equipped.
9. Disconnect power steering pump bracket and swing pump out of way with hoses still connected. Position power steering fluid cooler out of the way.
10. Remove A/C compressor bracket bolts and swing compressor out of way with hoses still connected.
11. Disconnect temperature sender wire, idle speed-up wire (if so equipped), ignition primary wire, downshift switch wire, S.C.S. or T.C.S. solenoid (if so equipped) and anti-dieseling solenoid wires, electronic ignition connector, block temperature sender lead, and all ground straps.
12. Bend back clips and position wiring harness out of the way.
13. Disconnect all vacuum hoses, and purge hose from E.L.C. canister. Disconnect the automatic level control line, on models, so equipped.
14. Disconnect alternator, heater switch and oil pressure sender wires.
15. Remove wiring harness from clips.
16. Remove water hose from fitting at rear of right-hand cylinder head.

NOTE: on A/C cars up to 1969, remove blower relay, power servo, and master switch from heater air selector.

17. Loosen and remove alternator and A.I.R. pumps and remove belts.
18. Disconnect tie struts and swing out of the way.
19. Remove upper two transmission-to-engine bolts. Remove two screws that secure right air deflector to lower radiator cradle.
20. Jack up car and support on axle stands.
21. Remove starter motor, then disconnect exhaust pipes from manifolds.
22. Remove front engine mount bolts, then disconnect and plug vapor return line at fuel pump (A/C cars only) and fuel inlet line. Remove oil filter, after draining engine oil.
23. Disconnect lower radiator hose and remove flywheel housing cover.
24. Remove the three screws that secure flex plate to converter. Engine must be rotated for access.
25. Remove four transmission-to-engine bolts.
26. Lower the car to the ground.
27. Connect a lifting bracket to the engine.
28. Support transmission with a wood-padded floor jack.
29. Raise engine slightly and pull forward to disengage from transmission, then pull engine up and out.
30. Reverse the above procedure to install the engine.

Seville

1. Disconnect the negative battery cable.
2. Drain the cooling system.
3. Remove the hood. Scribe marks on the hinges and their mounting points for installation.
4. Remove the air cleaner assembly.
5. Remove the struts from both right and left wheelhousings.
6. Remove the radiator cover.
7. Disconnect the power brake hose at the point where it joins the steel tube to the rear of the left cylinder head.
8. Disconnect the left and right side section of the wiring harness and position them out of the way.
9. Disconnect the heater hose from the rear of the intake manifold.
10. Disconnect the upper and lower radiator hoses from the engine and remove the fan assembly from the water pump.
11. Remove the distributor cap and spark plug wires.
12. Disconnect the two ground wires from the compressor bracket and position the harness out of the way.
13. Disconnect the accelerator linkage and vapor canister hose from the throttle body.
14. Disconnect the fuel inlet line from the fuel rail and plug the line.
15. Remove the power steering gear from the engine and move it out of the way.
16. Disconnect the fuel return line from the pressure regulator outlet fitting.
17. Remove the air conditioner compressor from the engine without disconnecting the refrigerant lines and move it out of the way.
18. Raise the car on a hoist.
19. Disconnect the exhaust pipe and exhaust crossover pipe from the exhaust manifolds.
20. Remove the torque converter cover.
21. Remove the starter motor.
22. Remove the screw and clip securing the transmission oil cooler lines to the engine oil pan.
23. Remove the three screws securing the flexplate to the convertor.
24. Remove the through-bolt from each engine mount.
25. Remove the screws holding the engine and transmission together.
26. Lower the car.
27. Remove the screws securing the heater water valve to the evaporator and move the valve out of the way.
28. Support the transmission with a jack and a block of wood placed between the jack and the transmission case.
29. Install a suitable lifting device on the engine and raise the engine off of the motor mounts. Reposition the transmission support.
30. Raise the engine carefully, pull it forward and lift it from the car.
31. Install the engine in the reverse order of removal.

Manifolds

Exhaust Manifold Removal

1. In order to remove the left exhaust manifold remove the air cleaner assembly, then remove the air cleaner bracket and heat stove from the manifold, by unfastening the manifold nuts from the studs on the Nos. 2 and 8 cylinders.
2. Unfasten the nuts which secure the downpipes to either manifold.
3. Remove the bolts which secure the manifold to the cylinder heads.

NOTE: It may not be possible to remove the fifth bolt from the front of the cylinder head completely. Back the bolt all the way out and remove it with the manifolds.

4. Lift the manifold out of the engine compartment.

Installation is performed in the reverse order of removal. Lubricate the cylinder head installation surface with moly grease. Install the fifth screw from the front prior to installing the manifold. Tighten the bolts to specifications.

Intake Manifold Removal

Carbureted Engines

1. Remove the negative battery cable, air cleaner, heat tube, and crankcase vent.
2. Disconnect the throttle linkage and the Cruise Control.
3. Remove the coil leads and the connector from the SCS solenoid.
4. Disconnect the downshift switch and the temperature sender. On some models it is necessary to remove the anti-dieseling solenoid and the SCS solenoid.
5. Disconnect all vacuum lines. Remove the carburetor fuel line.
6. On cars with air conditioning, it is necessary to partially remove the compressor.
7. Remove the manifold hold-down bolts and lift the manifold from the engine.
8. To install the intake manifold, reverse the above procedure. The intake manifold bolts are torqued to 30 ft lbs, using a diagonal torque pattern beginning from the center of the manifold and working toward the ends.

Fuel Injected Engines

1. Disconnect the negative battery cable and remove the air cleaner and crankcase filter.
2. Disconnect the throttle cable and cruise control linkage at the throttle body. Remove the cable from the bracket and move it aside.
3. Disconnect the coolant temperature switch wire, the HEI wire, speed sensor wire, downshift switch wire, and the injector wiring harness from the fuel rail brackets and move the harness out of the way.
4. Disconnect the two vacuum hoses from the throttle body to the thermal vacuum switch (TVS).
5. Disconect the vacuum hoses and power brake pipe from the rear of the throttle body.
6. Bleed the pressure from the fuel delivery system and disconnect the fuel line from the fuel rail.
7. Disconnect the EGR solenoid wires, air temperature sensor wire and the MAP sensor vacuum hose.
8. Remove the PCV valve from the rocker cover and move it out of the way.
9. Remove the spark plug wires and the distributor cap.
10. Remove the front fuel rail.
11. Remove the air conditioner compressor from the engine. Do not disconnect the refrigerant lines.
12. Remove the fuel return line hose from the fuel pressure regulator.
13. Remove the 12 intake manifold retaining screws and remove the manifold. Do not pry or lift the manifold by the fuel rails or their mounting brackets.
14. Clean all gasket material from the mating surfaces of the manifold, cylinder heads and block.
15. Place new rubber intake manifold seals over the rails at the front and rear of the cylinder block. The tabs on the gasket should be positioned in the holes in the rails and the beveled ends of the gasket tucked into the slot at the mating of the head and rail.
16. Apply gasket sealer to the sheet metal gasket-shield on the engine. The holes in the gasket should engage the dowel pins on the cylinder heads. Be careful not to use too much sealer near the injector tips.
17. Carefully position the manifold on the top of the engine. Install and tighten the intake manifold retaining screws to 30 ft lbs.
18. Assemble and install the remaining components in the reverse order of removal.

Valve System

All Cadillacs use hydraulic lifters. Valve systems with hydraulic lifters operate with zero clearance in the valve train. The rocker arms are non-adjustable. The lifter itself will compensate if there is slack in the system but if there is excessive play, the entire system should be examined.

Rocker Arm Removal and Installation

The rocker arms are mounted in pairs (four pairs to each cylinder head). They are of the modified pedestal-mounted type.

Rocker arms may be removed in pairs and do not require cylinder-head removal.

Torque rocker arm mounting screws to 60 ft lbs—1969-73; or 70 ft lbs—1974 and later.

Checking the Valve Guides

Check the valve stem to guide clearance using a 1/16 in. (wide) strip of 0.005 in shim stock. With the valve removed, bend the shim and hang it in the valve guide on the push-rod side. The shim should not extend more than ¼ in. into the guide. With the shim in the guide, place the valve stem into the guide. If it does not slide into the guide, it is within the allowable limits.

If the valve guides are found to be worn past allowable limits, the valve guides will have to be rebored and valves with oversize stems installed. Three oversize valves of different stem diameters are available for each engine.

Sometimes a valve guide bore is made oversize at the factory. Oversize valve guide bores from the factory are marked on the inboard side of the cylinder heads on a machined surface just above the intake manifold surface on the 350 V8 in the Seville and on the cylinder head gasket surface in line with the oversize valve on the 472 V8 in the full-size Cadillacs.

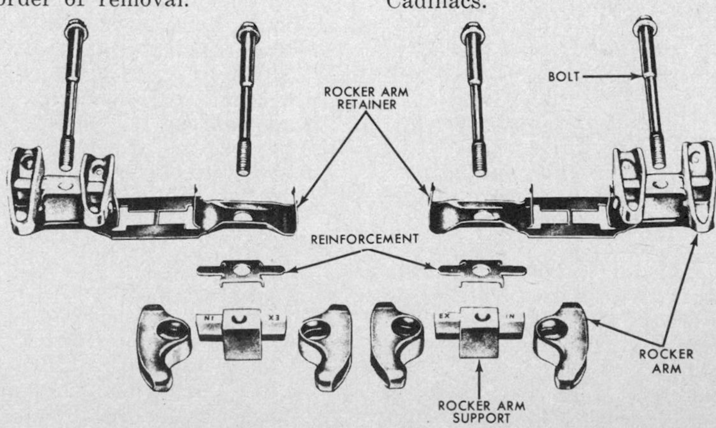

Cadillac engine rocker arm assembly (© Cadillac Div., G.M. Corp)

Valve Lifter Removal

Lifters may be removed without taking off the cylinder head.

1. Remove throttle and gas lines from the carburetor, disconnect hoses, vacuum lines and wires that pass over the rocker covers.
2. Remove the distributor cap and disconnect the wires at the spark plugs.
3. Remove the bolts that hold the rocker covers to the cylinder head and lift off the rocker covers to the cylinder head and lift off the rocker covers leaving the spark plug wires attached to them.
4. Remove the bolts that hold the intake manifold to the cylinder block and lift off the intake manifold. If desired, the carburetor can be detached from the manifold first, but this is not necessary.
5. Remove the valve chamber cover plate.
6. Remove the bolts that hold the rocker shafts to the cylinder head and lift off the rocker shafts holes in the cylinder heads. Pull the pushrods up through the
7. Pull the lifters up out of their bores.

Sometimes gum residue forms on the bottom of the lifter, making it very difficult to pull the lifter up out of its bore.

However, even when gum is present on the bottom of the lifter body, the lifter can be pulled up out of its bore using special pliers. These pliers are designed to grip the lifter firmly, without scoring or scratching it.

If a special tool isn't available, a good substitute can be made by grinding the teeth out of an ordinary pair of pliers and grinding a circle almost the size of the valve lifter body. When the pliers are squeezed down on the lifter body, it will contact a large surface, thus preventing scoring.

NOTE: Some 350 V8 Seville engines have both standard and .010 in. oversize valve lifters. The oversize lifters have "O" etched on the side of the lifter and the same marking on the lifter housing boss on the cylinder block.

Cylinder Heads

Cylinder Head Removal and Installation

Service Note

Care must be used when replacing Cadillac engine cylinder-head bolts. They are different lengths.

1. Remove intake manifold.
2. Drain engine coolant.
3. Disconnect ground strap at rear of cylinder heads from cowl. Disconnect wiring connector for high engine temperature warning system from sending unit at rear of left cylinder head.
4. Remove alternator, if working on the right cylinder head, or partially remove the steering pump if working on the left head. Remove the heater hose from the rear of the right cylinder head.
5. Disconnect A.I.R. injection pump tubes from cylinder heads.
6. Remove clamps holding the wire harness to the cylinder heads and tie harness back out of the way.
7. Remove screws holding exhaust manifolds to cylinder heads.
8. Remove screws holding the rocker arm cover to the heads.
9. Remove the rocker cover.
10. Remove screws holding each rocker arm support to cylinder head, then remove rocker arm assemblies. Store these assemblies so that they may be reinstalled in their correct locations.
11. Remove pushrods and store them with their respective rocker arm assemblies.
12. Install two 7/16 x 6 in. screws to be used as lifting handles in two of the rocker arm support screw holes.
13. Remove ten cylinder-head bolts.
14. Lift cylinder head off the block.
15. Remove all gasket material from the cylinder head and block mating surfaces.
16. Install by reversing removal procedures.

When torquing the head bolts, use the three-step method. Starting from the middle of the center row of bolts and working outward (toward each end), torque the bolts to 1/3 of the total torque listed. Once this is done, repeat the same procedure, this time torquing all the bolts to 2/3 of the total listed torque. Finally torque the bolts to the recommended torque.

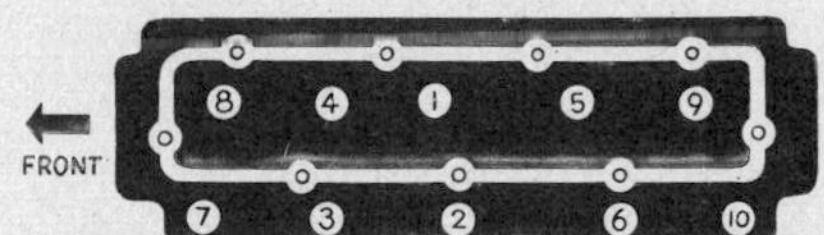

Cylinder head bolt tightening sequence —Cadillac engine

Cylinder head bolt tightening sequence —Seville 350 V8 (© G.M. Corp.)

Cylinder head bolt location and length—1970-76 Cadillac engine

FRONT OF ENGINE

Bolt Location	Length
A (Bolt)	4.36"
B (Bolt)	4.77"
C (Bolt)	3.02"
D (Bolt/Stud)	3.02"
E (Bolt/Stud)	4.77"

Cylinder head bolt location and length—1969 (© Cadillac Div., G.M. Corp.)

Timing Case Cover— Chains and Camshaft

Timing Chain Cover, Chain, and Sprocket Removal

1. Disconnect negative battery cable and drain cooling system.
2. Detach upper radiator hose retainer from cradle and position hose out of the way.
3. Remove fan, generator belt and power steering belts.
4. Remove four capscrews that secure crank pulley to harmonic balancer, then remove both pulley and balancer.
5. Remove plug from end of crankshaft, and install balancer puller pilot in one bore in the end of the crankshaft and remove balancer hub from the end of the crankshaft.
6. Drain engine oil and remove oil pan.
7. Disconnect lower radiator hose from water pump, then remove the ten screws that hold front cover to engine. Remove cover with water pump attached.
8. Remove distributor and fuel pump.
9. Remove oil slinger and fuel pump eccentric.
10. Remove two capscrews that secure camshaft sprocket.
11. Remove camshaft sprocket along with timing chain.
12. To install, reverse removal procedure.

Mount the timing chain over the camshaft and the crankshaft sprocket and start the camshaft sprocket over the shaft, being certain the aligning dowel is in a position where it will enter the hole in the camshaft freely. Make certain that the timing marks on the sprockets are in line between shaft centers.

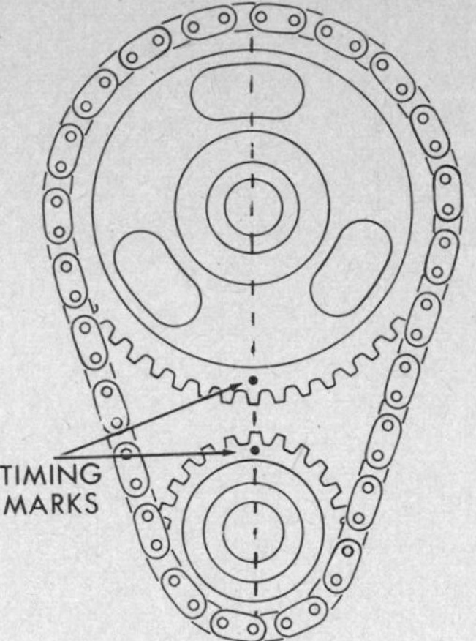

Timing mark alignment

Camshaft sprockets sometimes install a little stiffly. However, a comparatively easy way to install a tight-fitting sprocket is to draw it on carefully with two bolts somewhat longer than the regular mounting bolts. By drawing alternately against each bolt, and tapping gently with a plastic hammer, even a very tight camshaft gear sprocket can be installed.

When the camshaft is secured, turn the engine two full revolutions until the timing marks again assume the original position. Check to make certain that the punch marks, which are stamped into the front face of the sprockets, are in line between the shaft centers.

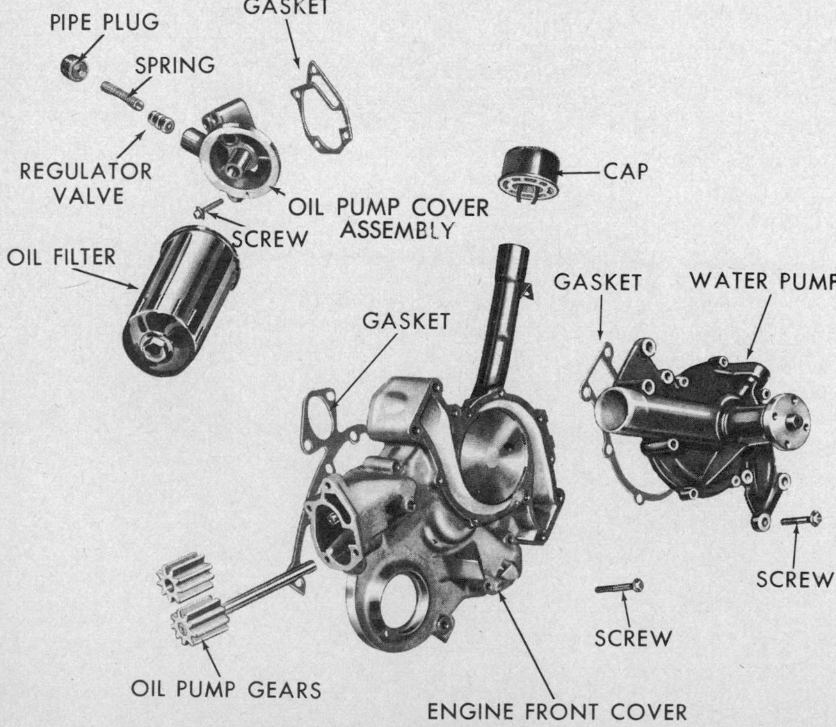

Engine front cover disassembled—Cadillac engine
(© Cadillac Div., G.M. Corp)

Timing Cover Oil Seal R & R

All models are equipped with a molded-type front cover crankshaft oil seal. The seal may be replaced without removing the engine front cover.

1. Disconnect the battery and remove carburetor air cleaner.
2. Remove power steering pump drive belt.
3. Remove generator drive belt.
4. On air conditioned cars, and cars equipped with the A.I.R. system. remove the pump drive belts.
5. Raise and support the front of the car on stands. Remove the fan.
6. Remove pulley and harmonic balancer, as outlined in Timing Chain and Sprocket Removal.
7. With a thin blade screwdriver, pry out front cover oil seal.
8. Lubricate new dual-lip oil seal with wheel bearing grease. Position seal on end of crankshaft with garter spring side toward engine.
9. Using a seal installer drive the front seal into the front cover until it bottoms.
10. Assemble and install the remaining parts in reverse order of disassembly.

Camshaft Removal and Replacement

1. Remove the radiator.
2. Remove the engine front cover and the distributor.
3. Remove the oil pump and the oil slinger from the crankshaft.
4. Remove the fuel pump and the fuel pump eccentric from the camshaft.
5. Remove the camshaft sprocket and the timing chain.

NOTE: Make certain that the aligning marks on the two sprockets are correctly aligned before removing the timing chain.

6. Remove the lifters and slide the camshaft carefully out of the engine block.

NOTE: Do not allow the camshaft lobes to scratch the camshaft bearings.

7. To install the camshaft, reverse the above procedure. Before installation, the camshaft should be lubricated with a thin coat of rear axle lubricant and then carefully inserted to avoid bearing damage.
8. The camshaft sprocket screws should be torqued to 18 ft lbs while the fuel pump eccentric screw is tightened to 35 ft lbs.

Piston and Rod Installation

The numbers on the connecting rods face away from the camshaft; that is, the numbers on the left bank, (even) face to the left; the numbers on the right bank, (odd) face to the right. As a double check, the word *rear*, (or "R"), stamped on the piston, faces the rear of the engine on both banks and an arrow on the piston top points to the front of the engine. The rod nuts are torqued to 40 ft lbs.

On the 350 Seville V8, the piston is placed in the cylinder with the notch in the top of the piston and the "F" on the side of the piston facing toward the front of the engine. The oil spurt hole in the connecting rod faces toward the camshaft.

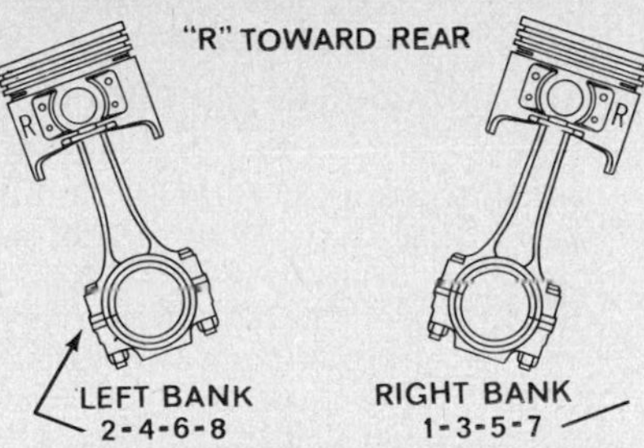

Piston to connecting rod relationship —Cadillac engine

Lubrication

Oil Pump Removal and Installation

472 V8

1. Jack up car and remove oil filter.
2. Remove five capscrews that secure oil pump to engine.

NOTE: Remove screw nearest pressure regulator last.

3. Slide drive shaft, drive gear and driven gear out of housing.
4. Remove plug from housing cover, using 5/16 in. wrench. Remove pressure regulator valve and spring.
5. Check free length of regulator spring—it should be 2.57-2.69 in. from 1969 through 1975 models.
6. Inspect gears and housing for burrs or scoring.
7. Check pump clearance limits.
8. Assembly, and installation is the reverse of disassembly and removal.

472 V8 OIL PUMP SPECIFICATIONS

Backlash between drive gears, 0.008-0.012 in.

Clearance between body and shaft not to exceed 0.005 in.

Clearance between body and gears not to exceed 0.005 in.

Gear end-play not to exceed 0.006 in.

350 V8

1. Remove the oil pan.
2. Remove the oil pump-to-rear main bearing cap attaching bolts and remove the oil pump and drive shaft extension.
3. Remove the drive shaft extension. Do not attempt to remove the washers from the shaft. The shaft extension and washers must be serviced as an assembly if the washers are not 1-11/32 in. from the end of the shaft.
4. Remove the cotter pin, spring and the pressure regulator valve. Place your thumb over the pressure regulator bore before removing the cotter pin to contain the spring.
5. Remove the oil pump cover attaching screws and remove the cover and gasket.
6. Remove the idler gear and drive gear from the pump body.
7. Check the gears for scoring and any other damage. Install new gears, if necessary. Check the end clearance of the pump gears and the pressure regulator valve -to-bore clearance.
8. Assemble and install the oil pump in reverse order of removal. The end of the drive shaft extension nearest the washers is inserted into the drive shaft.

Piston and connecting rod positioning —Seville 350 V8

350 V8 OIL PUMP SPECIFICATIONS

Gear end clearance, 0.0025-0.0065 in. Pressure regulator valve-to-bore clearance, 0.0025-0.0050 in.

Oil Pan Removal and Installation

472 V8

1. Drain engine oil and disconnect positive battery cable.
2. Disconnect exhaust crossover pipe at exhaust manifold.
3. Disconnect exhaust support bracket at transmission extension housing, and position exhaust system to one side.
4. Remove starter motor.
5. Remove two idler arm support mounting screws from frame side member, and lower support.
6. Disconnect pitman arm at drag link, and lower steering linkage.
7. Remove transmission lower cover.
8. Remove engine oil pan.
9. When reinstalling, reverse above procedure and torque oil pan screws and nuts to 10 ft lbs. The transmission cover screws should be torqued to 20 ft lbs.

350 V8

1. Remove the wheelhousing struts from the fenders.
2. Remove the radiator cover.
3. Raise the car.
4. Remove the through-bolt from each motor mount
5. Remove the exhaust crossover pipe.
6. Remove the starter motor.
7. Remove the torque converter cover.
8. Drain the crankcase and remove the oil pan attaching screws.
9. Raise the engine as far as necessary with a jack placed under the crankshaft pulley and remove the oil pan.
10. Clean all of the gasket material from the oil pan and engine block mating surfaces and install the oil pan in the reverse order of removal, using a new gasket kit and sealer. The rubber front and rear seals cover the tabs on the oil pan gaskets at the front cover.

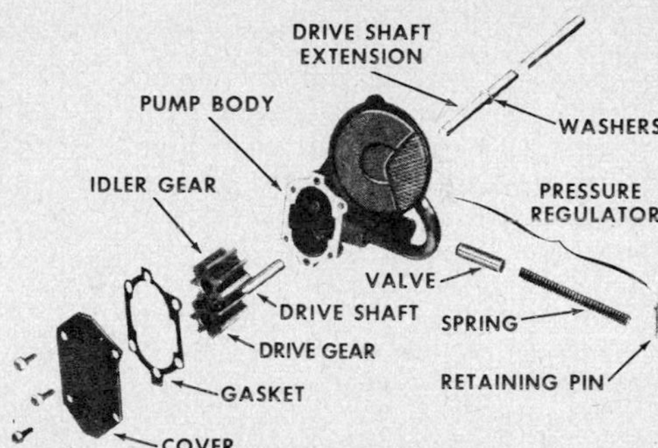

Exploded view of 350 Seville V8 oil pump (© Cadillac Div., G.M. Corp.)

Rear Main Seal R & R

472 V8

1. Remove the oil pan, after removing spark plug wires and plugs.
2. Remove the rear main bearing cap and loosen the bolts holding the other four bearings about three turns each. Remove the old rear main bearing seals.
3. Clean the groove in the cap and in the block. Lubricate seals with engine oil.
4. Make an installation tool, as illustrated.
5. Start the upper half into the groove in the block with the lip facing forward and rotate it into position, using the tool as a guide. Press firmly on both ends to be sure it is protruding uniformly on each side.
6. Install the lower half of the seal into the bearing cap with the lip facing forward and one end of the seal over the ridge and flush with the split line. Hold one finger over this end to prevent it from slipping, and push the seal into seated position by applying

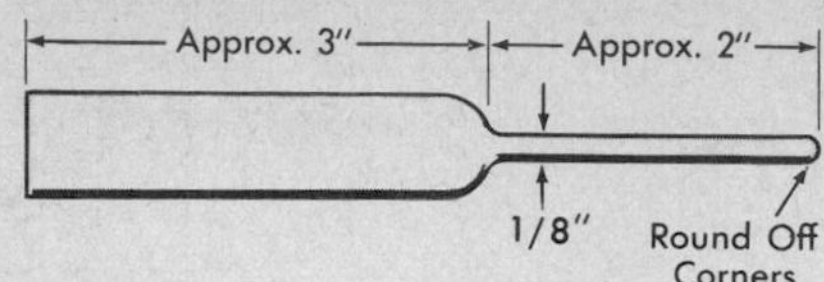

Rear main bearing oil seal installation tool
(© Cadillac Div., G.M. Corp)

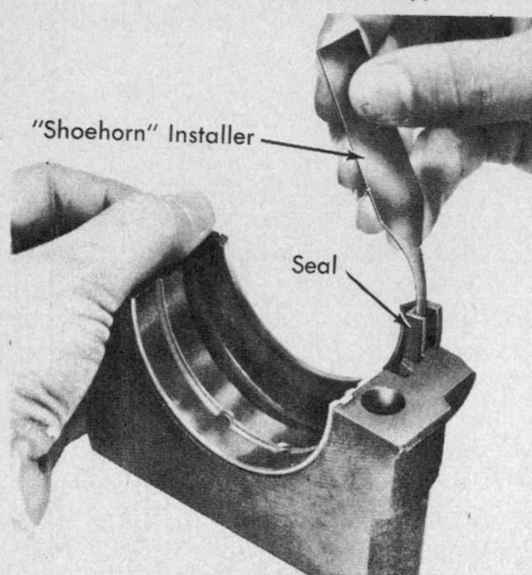

Installing rear main bearing oil seal
(© Cadillac Div., G.M. Corp)

pressure to the other end. Be sure the seal is firmly seated and protrudes evenly on each side. Do not apply pressure to the lip. This may damage the effectiveness of the seal.

7. Apply rubber cement to the mating surfaces of the block and cap being careful not to get any cement on the bearing, the crankshaft or the seal. The cement coating should be about .010 in. thick.
8. Install the bearing cap, tightening the bolts with the fingers only.
9. Move the crankshaft forward and rearward by pounding on the counterweight with a plastic hammer to assure alignment of the rear main bearing thrust surfaces.
10. Tighten the bearing bolts to 90-100 ft. lbs. Be sure to tighten the bolts of the other four bearings also.
11. Reinstall the oil pan.

350 V8

The crankshaft need not be removed to replace the rear main bearing upper oil seal.

1. Drain the crankcase and remove the oil pan and rear main bearing cap.
2. Using a blunt-ended tool, drive the upper seal into its groove on each side until it is tightly packed. This is usually ¼-¾ in.
3. Cut pieces of new seal 1/16 in. longer than required to fill the grooves and install, packing into place.
4. Carefully trim any protruding seal, being sure not to scratch or damage the bearing surface.
5. Install a new seal in the bearing cap and install cap, tightening bolts to the proper torque. Install the oil pan.

AUTOMATIC TRANSMISSION

All Cadillac cars use a Turbo Hydra-matic 400 automatic transmission.

Neutral Safety Switch through 1973

NOTE: switch is on steering column under dash.

Removal

1. Position the gear selector in the Neutral position.
2. Release the clamp and remove the switch without moving the contact carrier. The position of the carrier should be marked.
3. Remove the vacuum hoses after they have been marked and disconnect the wires from the switch.
4. Installation is accomplished by reversing the above procedure.

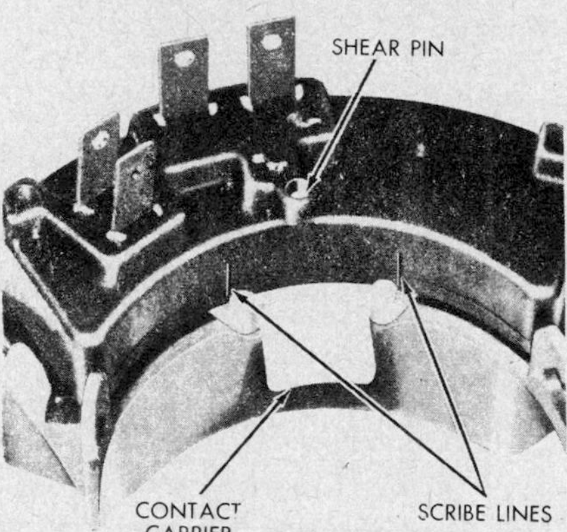

Neutral safety switch
(© Cadillac Div., G.M. Corp)

Adjustment

1. Check that the gear lever is correctly adjusted and that the neutral safety switch is properly positioned by this check.
2. Set the handbrake. Put the hand lever on the steering column in drive. Hold the ignition key on and slowly move the hand lever toward Neutral or Park until the starter cranks and the engine runs.
3. Without moving the lever farther, press the accelerator to determine whether the transmission is really in Neutral or Park.
4. If all is correct, the engine will have started when the hand lever got to the neutral position and the transmission will not be in gear. Also, back-up lights will go on with transmission in Reverse.

NOTE: a vacuum leak that can be corrected by moving shift lever is an indication that the switch only needs adjustment and is not defective.

5. Adjust the neutral safety switch by turning it and its mounting bracket until the above conditions are met.

Neutral Safety Switch—1974 and later

On all models 1974 and later, the neutral safety switch works mechanically, rather than electrically. When the transmission selector is any position other than Park or Neutral, the key cannot be turned to "Start."

Shift Linkage Adjustment

1. Loosen nut on steering column manual lever on full-size Cadillacs and the adjustment screw on the relay lever on Seville.
2. From under the car, pull relay rod up, positioning transmission shift valve in Park, then push rod down to the Neutral third step.
3. Position selector lever in Neutral.
4. Tighten nut on steering column manual lever on full-size Cadillacs and the adjustment screw on the relay lever on Seville.
5. Check that positions selected on selector lever correspond with appropriate detents on transmission.

Kickdown Adjustment

1. Remove the air cleaner.
2. Make certain that the idle speed is set correctly and that the carburetor is operating on the low-speed circuit.
3. Loosen the switch mounting screws and insert 0.094 in. wire gauge into the hole in the lower wire terminal.
4. With the gauge in place, adjust the position of the switch so that the lever just touches the carburetor adaptor plate arm. The switch should make contact above 60° of throttle opening.
5. After adjusting, tighten the mounting screws and remove the gauge.
6. Reinstall the air cleaner.

Pan Removal and Installation, Fluid and Filter Change

1. Either use a suction gun to remove two quarts of fluid through the oil filler tube, or raise the vehicle and loosen on corner of the transmisson pan and allow the fluid to drain into an appropriate container.
2. Remove the remaining pan attaching screws and remove the pan and gasket. Discard the gasket.
3. Clean the pan with solvent and dry it throughly.
4. Remove the filter retaining bolt.
5. Remove the intake pipe and filter assembly. Remove the intake pipe O-ring and discard the filter and O-ring.

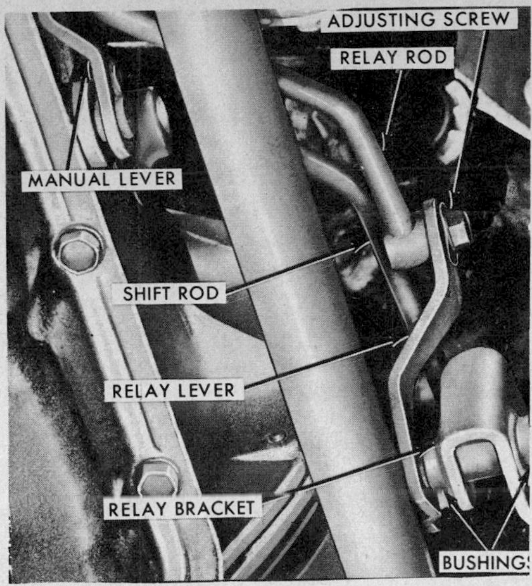

Manual linkage adjustment—1969 (© Cadillac Div., G.M. Corp)

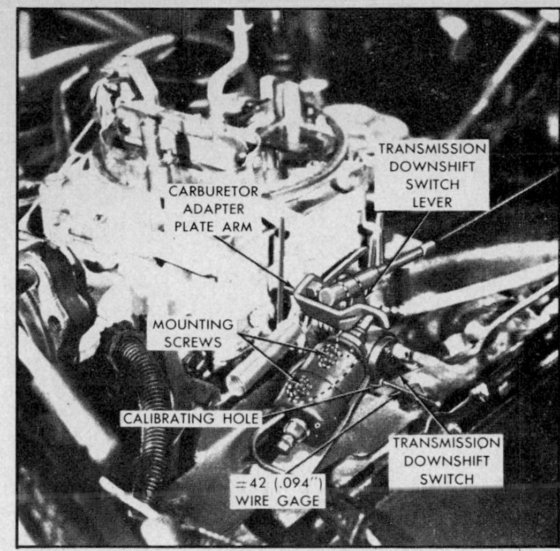

Downshift switch adjustment
(© Cadillac Div., G.M. Corp.)

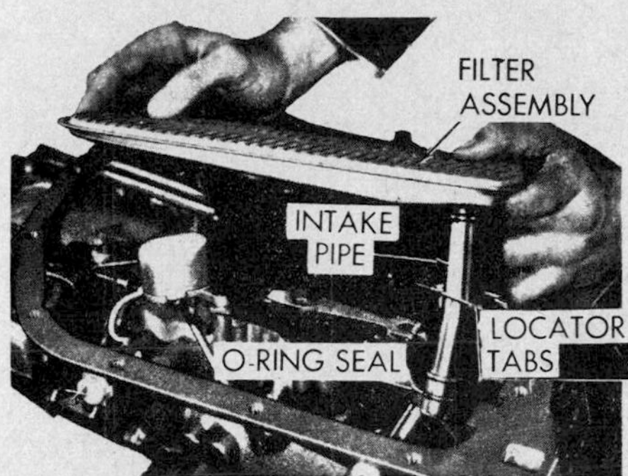

Removing the transmission filter assembly
(© Cadillac Div., G.M. Corp.)

6. Install the new intake pipe O-ring on the pipe and install the intake pipe into the new filter assembly.
7. Install the intake pipe and filter assembly into the case bore. Install the filter retaining bolt.
8. Install a new gasket on the pan and install the pan, tightening the retaining screws to 12 ft lbs.
9. Lower the car and add 4 quarts of Dexron automatic transmission fluid through the filter tube. If the filter was not replaced, only add 2 quarts.
10. Start the engine and allow it to run at normal idle speed for 1½ minutes with the gear selector in Park.
11. Check the fluid level. With the fluid below normal operating temperature the level should be ¼ in. below the ADD mark on the dip stick. Add fluid as necessary.

U-JOINTS

Universal joints and drive lines can be divided into three groups: single-shaft models, two-piece shaft models (except Commercial after 1969), and two-piece shaft models (Commercial up to 1969).

Single-Piece Type

Two double Cardan constant velocity universal joints are used on full-size Cadillacs with the single-shaft type: one at the front, and one at the rear. This type propeller shaft is serviced as a complete assembly.

The Seville uses a one piece drive shaft assembly with a single Cardan universal joint at the front end and a double Cardan constant velocity joint at the rear end. The double Cardan constant velocity joint consists of two single joints connected by a link yoke. A ball and socket device located between the crosses of the two single joints is used to center them and maintain their relative positions. This causes each cross to operate through ½ of the total angle across the joint.

Two-Piece-Shaft Type—Except 1969 Commercial Models

The two-piece propeller shaft uses three constant velocity universal joints, located at each end and at the approximate center of the shaft assembly. This shaft is used on 1970 up commercial models.

At the front end of the rear section of the propeller shaft is a splined male slip yoke that fits into a splined coupling in the rear end of the front section of the front shaft. This slip spline satisfies the normal lengthening and shortening of the propeller shaft due to road conditions and rear axle movement.

The propeller shaft assembly is attached to the transmission by means of a slip yoke, and to the differential drive pinion by a double flange connection. The propeller shaft assembly is supported midway by a bracket and bearing combination attached to a frame crossmember.

With the exception of the center bearing and support combination, the propeller shaft is serviced as an assembly.

Two-Piece-Shaft Type—1969 Commercial Models

A two-piece propeller shaft assembly, using three standard universal joints, is used on commercial vehicles.

Standard joints are used at each end of the shaft assembly and at the center support.

The universal joints are replaceable, but cannot be repacked. On original universal joints, the injected nylon ring that locks the bearing cup in the slip yoke will shear off when the bearing is removed. There are no provisions for replacing this nylon ring.

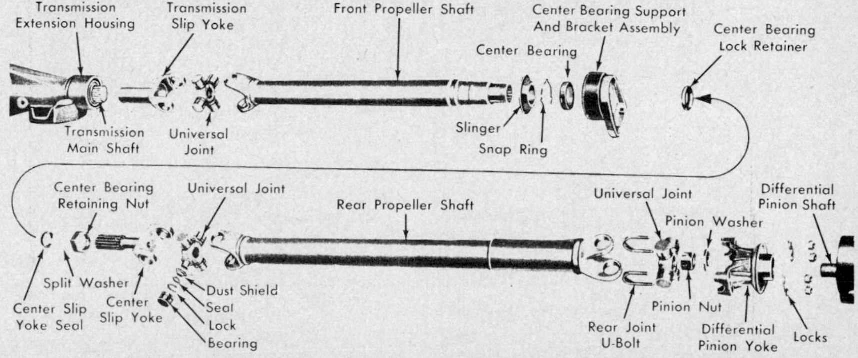

Driveshaft 1969 Commercial (© Cadillac Div., G.M. Corp)

When the joint becomes noisy or otherwise needs attention, renew the joint.

Front and rear sections of this shaft are splined together the same as in two-piece passenger car models.

The commercial vehicle two-piece-shaft type unit is attached to the transmission by means of a front slip yoke. The assembly is attached to the differential carrier by two U-bolts that hold the rear joint cross bearings to the differential carrier pinion yoke. The propeller shaft assembly is supported at the center by an adjustable center bearing support and bracket attached to a frame crossmember. The center bearing support is adjustable to compensate for various load influences.

Single-Piece Shaft R & R

Full-Size Cadillac

1. Place transmission in Neutral and jack up car; support on axle stands.
2. Remove the two accessible rear U-joint flange capscrews.
3. Rotate driveshaft and remove other two capscrews, after supporting rear of shaft on a chain. Never let the full weight of the driveshaft be supported only by the front constant velocity joint.
4. Push shaft forward to clear pinion flange, then pull rearward to disengage slip yoke from transmission. Plug transmission to prevent oil leak.
5. Lubricate slip yoke inside diameter with gear lube, outside of splines with A.T.F.
6. To install, reverse removal procedure, tightening rear U-joint fasteners to 70 ft. lbs. Place transmission in Park to hold shaft while tightening capscrews.

Seville

1. Raise the vehicle with the transmission in Park and the front of the car slightly lower than the rear, if possible.
2. Mark the position of the ball support yoke in relation to the axle pinion flange.
3. Remove the ball support yoke attaching screws. Support the drive shaft as the last screw is being removed.
4. Remove the drive shaft by pushing it forward into the rear of the transmision until the ball support yoke clears the differential pinion flange, and then pulling it rearward out of the transmission. Fluid could leak out of the rear of the transmission if the front isn't lowered enough. Plug the opening with a clean lint free cloth, if necessary.
5. Install the drive shaft in the reverse order of removal.

Two-Piece Shaft R & R

1. Follow Steps 1-6 of *Single-Piece Shaft R & R*, with the addition of the following step:

1A. Remove center bearing support after matchmarking it and crossmember. When installing, tighten the bolts to 16 ft. lbs.

U-Joint Removal and Installation

1. Remove the drive shaft.
2. Remove the lockrings from the bearings. If the original universal joints are being replaced, the nylon ring will sear off when the bearing is removed.
3. Match-mark the yoke and the shaft so that the shaft parts can be reassembled easily.
4. Position the yoke or bearing trunnion on vise jaws. Using a bearing remover, or a similar tool, and a hammer tap the remover until the bearing is driven out of the yoke about ½ in.
5. Place the tool in the vise and then drive the yoke away from the tool until the bearing is removed. (See illustration.)
6. Use the no. 4 and 5 procedures for all other bearings.
7. To install the bearings lubricate the cross arm ends with universal joint grease and install the joint cross into position.

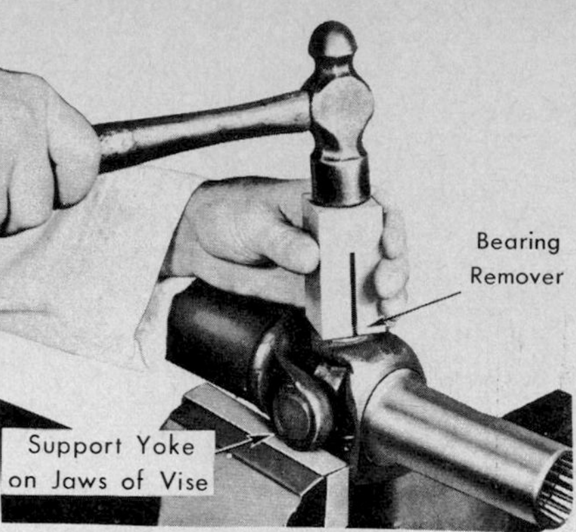

Using the bearing removal tool (© Cadillac Div., G.M. Corp)

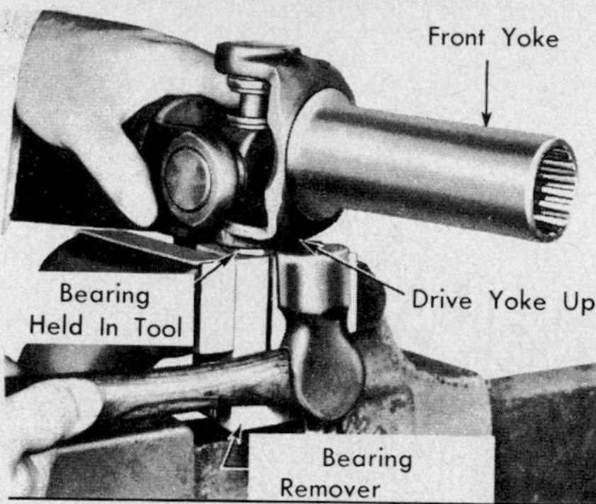

Removing the universal joint bearing (© Cadillac Div., G.M. Corp)

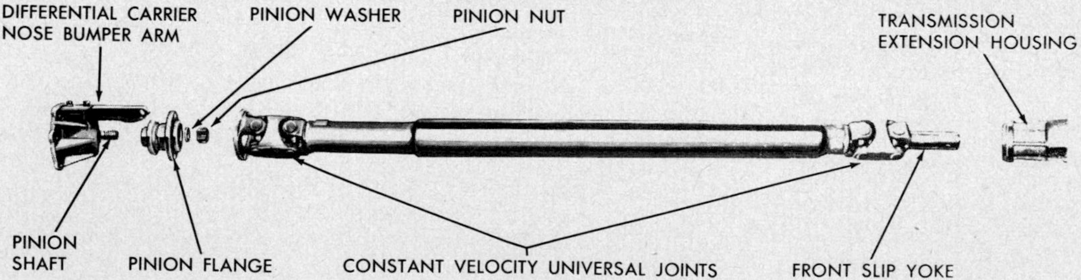

Single-piece driveshaft (© Cadillac Div., G.M. Corp)

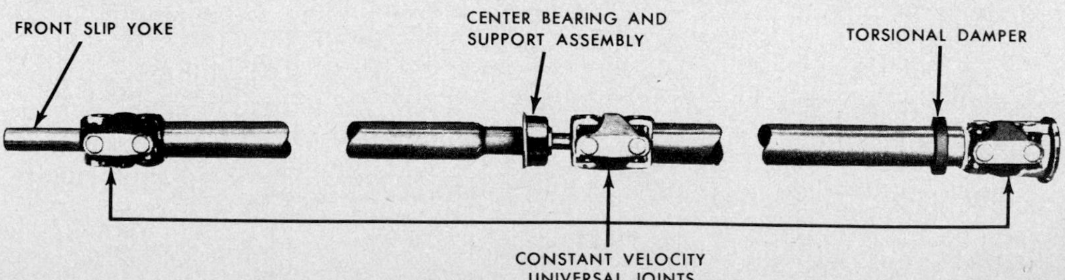

Two-piece driveshaft with C.V. joints (© Cadillac Div., G.M. Corp)

8. Start the bearings into the driveshaft yoke and press them into position using a vise.

NOTE: If the bearings are not positioned with normal vise pressure, there is a possibility that one of the needle bearings has fallen out of place.

9. Use the same installation procedure for the other bearings.
10. Install the lock rings.

REAR AXLE

Removal and Installation

Full-Size Cadillac

1. Raise the rear of the car and support it. Remove the wheel and brake drum.
2. Remove the four nuts that secure the retainer and backing plate to the axle housing.
3. Remove the axle shaft with a slide hammer.

NOTE: When the axle shaft is removed the outer bearing race may remain in the axle housing. This does not indicate bearing failure. If the bearing is to be replaced, make sure the old outer bearing race is removed from the axle housing.

4. Using a chisel and hammer, split the bearing retainer next to the bearing. Be careful not to damage the bearing of the axle shaft. Remove and discard the retainer.
5. Stand the axle shaft upright on the flanged end and use two screwdrivers to pry the oil seal away from the bearing.
6. Remove axle bearing from the axle shaft with a press.
7. Make sure that the axle shaft and bearing are clean and install the bearing seal onto the axle shaft. The oil seal is properly installed when it can't be pushed on any further.
8. Apply a light coat of wheel bearing grease to the bearing.
9. If a tapered roller bearing is used, position the bearing on the axle shaft with the narrow ring of the bearing facing the flanged end of the axle shaft. If a straight roller bearing is installed, the loose ring at one end of the inner race must be installed toward the flange.
10. Press the bearing onto the axle shaft until the bearing bottoms against the shoulder on the shaft.
11. Press the retainer on the axle shaft until the retainer bottoms against the bearing.
12. If the axle bearing has been replaced because of bearing failure, inspect the axle housing and differential carrier for metal chips and clean thoroughly.
13. Apply a thin film of wheel bearing grease to the wheelbearing bore in the axle housing. Also, lubricate the oil seal and the outer race of the bearing with wheel bearing grease.
14. Install a new gasket on the brake backing plate.
15. Install the axle shaft onto the axle housing, using extreme care to align the oil seal cover with the axle housing mounting bolts. Rotate the axle shaft so the axle shaft splines engage the differential side gear splines.
16. Install the four nuts on the axle housing flange bolts to hold the gasket, brake backing plate, and oil seal cover in place. Tighten the nuts to 50 ft lbs. Install the brake drum and one nut to push it on. Remove the nut to install the wheel. Lower the car.

Seville

1. Raise the car on a hoist and remove the wheel and brake drum.
2. Clean any dirt from the differential cover and loosen the cover attaching screw, allowing the lubricant to drain out into a suitable container.
3. Remove the pinion shaft lockscrew and remove the pinion shaft.
4. Push in on the flanged end of the axle shaft and remove the "C" lock from the splined end of the axle shaft.
5. Remove the axle shaft from the housing, being cautious not to damage the oil seal.
6. Use a screwdriver to pry the oil seal out of the bore. Use an axle shaft bearing puller on a slide hammer to remove the axle bearing from the bearing bore.
7. Install the new bearing in the bearing bore until it is 0.550 in. from the end of the axle tube. Use a block of wood and a hammer to tap the bearing in place. Install the axle shaft bearing seal until it is flush with the end of the axle tube.
8. Slide the axle shaft into the housing until the splines on the end of the shaft engage the splines of the differential side gear. Handle the shaft gently when trying to engage the splines.
9. Install the axle shaft "C" lock on the splined end of the axle shaft in the differential. Push the shaft outward so that the shaft lock seats in the counterbore of the differential side gear.
10. Install the pinion cross shaft through the differential case and pinion gears. Aligne the lock screw hole and install the lock screw, tightening it to 25 ft lbs.
11. Clean the differential housing and cover mating surfaces and install the cover with a new gasket.
12. Fill the differential with lubricant, install the brake drum and wheel, and lower the car.

JACKING, HOISTING

All Except Seville

When jacking under front suspension arms, make sure lift is made from the flattened portion on the flange of the lower arms.

When lifting on frame area, make sure of solid contact at the corners of the perimeter of the frame with the lift points close to the bend at front and rear of the frame.

Seville

To raise the car on a twin-post suspension hoist, place the lift adapters under the lower control arms at the front and under the axle tube near the spring mounting pads at the rear.

When using a framehoist, place the lift adapters under the front subframe members just in front of the rear cross member and under the rear sub-frame members opposite the front rear spring shackles.

FRONT SUSPENSION

All Cadillacs use the same front suspension system (except Eldorado). The system is a coil spring suspension which consists of two upper and two lower control arm assemblies, shock absorbers, front struts, a stabilizer bar and two steering knuckles, and a pair of steel coiled springs.

For further information on front suspension alignment consult the "Unit Repair Section."

Shock Absorber R & R

1. Open the hood. Remove the retaining nut from the frame spring tower. Use a box wrench to prevent the shock stem from turning while the nut is being unfastened.
2. Take off the bolt, nut, and lockwasher which secure the lower end of the shock to the suspension arm.
3. Remove the shock through the bottom of the lower arm.

Installation is performed in the following order:

If you are replacing the grommet, dip it in soapy water and twist it through the frame hole.

NOTE: Don't use silicone lubricant.

4. Install the retainer in the upper stem.
5. Extend the shock rod as far as it will go.
6. Install the shock up through the coil spring and guide the stem into the grommet.

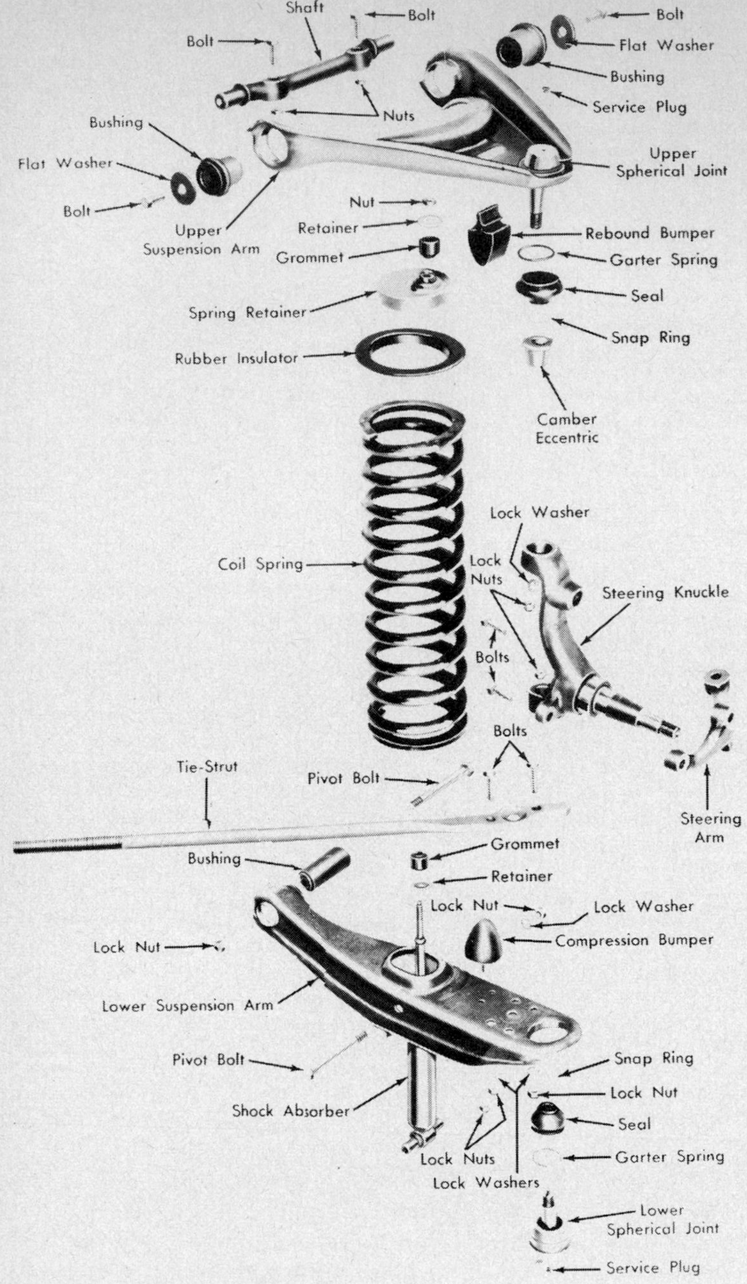

Typical front suspension—1969-70 (© Cadillac Div., G.M. Corp)

7. Position the lower end of the shock on the lower control arm. Install the bolt lockwasher and nut. Tighten the bolt to 40 ft lbs —1969; or to 55 ft lbs—1970-76. (19 ft lbs on Seville)
8. Tighten the retaining nut on the upper stem to 180 in lbs, while holding the stem with a box wrench to keep it from turning. On Seville, tighten the nut to the end of the threads about 1⅛ in. of stud is above the nut.

Lower Control Arm and Coil Spring R & R

1. Disconnect front shock at its upper mount.
2. Raise car and support under front frame side rails.
3. Remove wheel and tire assembly.
4. Disconnect stabilizer link from lower arm or spring to be removed.
5. Disconnect tie-strut at lower arm.
6. Remove bolt holding shock to lower arm, and remove shock from car.
7. Remove nut from pivot bolt in lower arm at frame mount.
8. Position jack under outboard end of lower suspension arm so that jack is supporting the arm.
9. Remove locknut from lower ball joint stud. Install standard nut on joint stud and run nut to within two threads of knuckle.
10. Strike knuckle with a hammer in area of ball joint stud to loosen the joint. Raising the opposite rear corner of the car will help compress the spring and assist in removing the joint stud from the knuckle.
11. Use jack to lift spring load from nut and remove nut from joint stud. Wrap a chain around the spring and through the lower control arm as a safety measure.
12. Slowly lower jack and remove spring.
13. Remove pivot bolt from lower arm at frame mount and remove the arm.
14. Install by reversing the removal procedure.

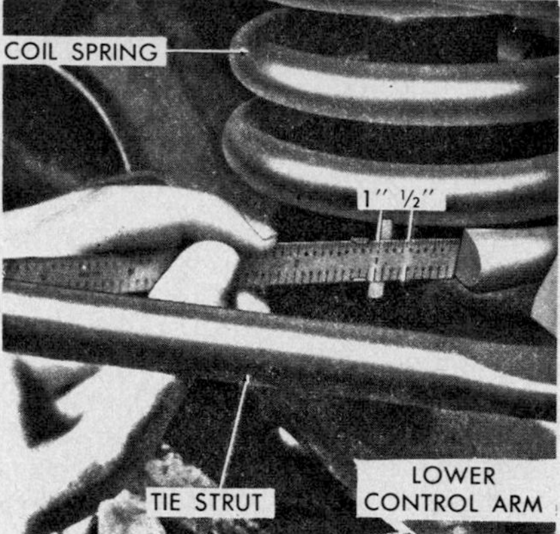

Install the front coil spring on a full size Cadillac so that the end of the coil is ½ to 1 in. from the edge of the lower control arm

(© Cadillac Div., G.M. Corp.)

Ball Joint Inspection

NOTE: Before performing this inspection, make sure the wheel bearings are adjusted correctly and that the A-arm bushings are in good condition.

1. Jack the car up under the front lower control arm at the spring seat.
2. Raise the car until there is 1–2 in. of clearance under the wheel.
3. Insert a bar under the wheel and pry upward. If the wheel raises more than ⅛ in. the ball joints are worn. Determine if the upper or lower ball joint is worn by visual inspection while prying on the wheel.

NOTE: Due to the distribution of forces in the suspension, the lower ball joint is usually the defective joint. Also, 1973 and later Cadillacs are equipped with wear indicators on the lower ball joint. As long as the wear indicator neck extends below the ball stud seat, replacement is unnecessary.

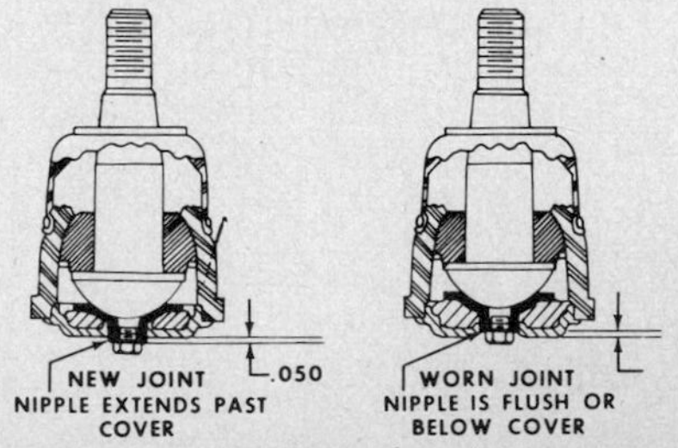

Lower ball joint wear indicator—1973 and later
(© Cadillac Div., G.M. Corp.)

SHIM
SHAFT
SPHERICAL JOINT
UPPER SUSPENSION ARM
BUSHING
WASHER
NUT
BUMPER
COIL SPRING
BUSHING
FRAME
SPLASH SHIELD
BRAKE CALIPER
STEERING KNUCKLE
STABILIZER BAR
SPHERICAL JOINT
NUT
HUB AND ROTOR ASSEMBLY
CAP
LINK BOLT
BEARING CUP
SHOCK ABSORBER
BEARING
WASHER

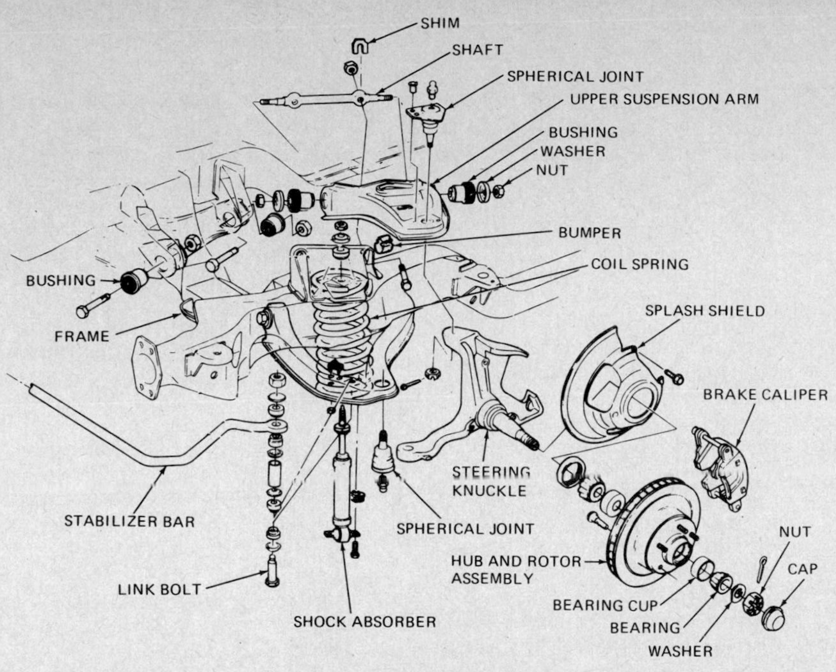

Exploded view of Seville front suspension
(© Cadillac Div., G.M. Corp.)

Lower Ball Joint R & R

1. Follow Steps 1-12 of *Lower Control Arm and Coil Spring R & R.*
2. Remove band and seal from ball joint.
3. If ball joint vertical movement exceeds 1/16 in. (.062 in.), press old ball joint out of lower control arm, using press tool.
4. Press new joint into arm until it bottoms on flange, using standard nut and flat washer to pull joint into position.
5. Reverse Steps 1-12 of *Lower Control Arm and Coil Spring R & R,* tightening stud nut to 85 ft lbs.

Upper Ball Joint R & R

Full-Size Cadillac

1. Jack up front of car and support on jack stands under coil springs.
2. Remove wheel and tire assembly.
3. Loosen upper ball joint locknut.
4. Matchmark camber eccentric and steering knuckle for proper alignment.
5. Strike steering knuckle near upper joint until joint taper is free.

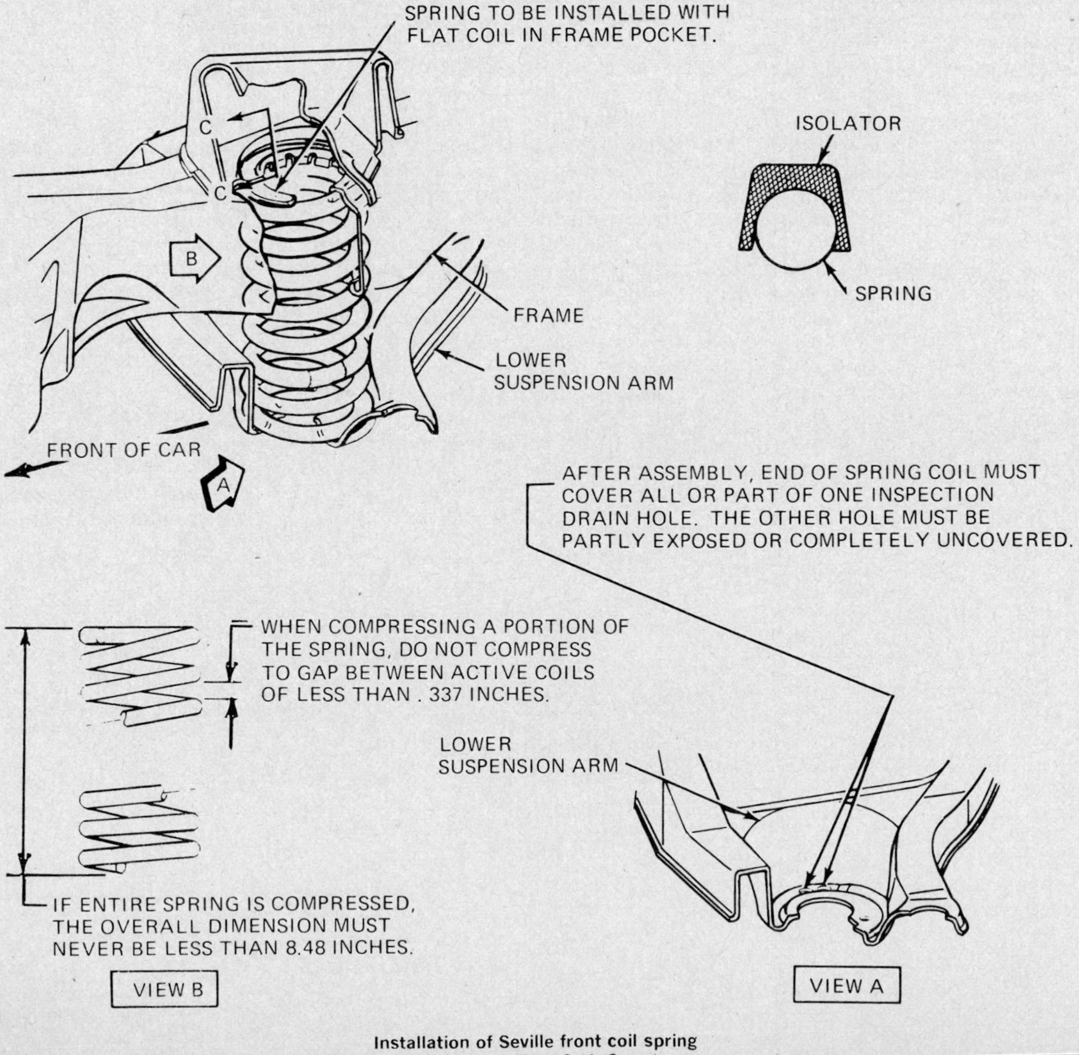

SPRING TO BE INSTALLED WITH FLAT COIL IN FRAME POCKET.
C
C
B
FRAME
LOWER SUSPENSION ARM
FRONT OF CAR
A
ISOLATOR
SPRING
AFTER ASSEMBLY, END OF SPRING COIL MUST COVER ALL OR PART OF ONE INSPECTION DRAIN HOLE. THE OTHER HOLE MUST BE PARTLY EXPOSED OR COMPLETELY UNCOVERED.
WHEN COMPRESSING A PORTION OF THE SPRING, DO NOT COMPRESS TO GAP BETWEEN ACTIVE COILS OF LESS THAN . 337 INCHES.
LOWER SUSPENSION ARM
IF ENTIRE SPRING IS COMPRESSED, THE OVERALL DIMENSION MUST NEVER BE LESS THAN 8.48 INCHES.
VIEW B
VIEW A

Installation of Seville front coil spring
(© Cadillac Div., G.M. Corp.)

6. Remove locknut, then remove camber eccentric using a puller.
7. Clean ball joint and install another nut on top of the reinstalled locknut. Turn the joint using a torque wrench. If torquc exceeds or is less than 2-4 ft. lbs., the entire upper control arm with integral ball joint must replace as an assembly.
8. To install, reverse removal procedure. Tighten locknut on stud of ball joint to 60 ft. lbs.

NOTE: Use a standard ½-20 nut and washer to pull camber eccentric into position.

Seville

1. Raise the car on a hoist.
2. Remove the wheel and tire.
3. Remove the upper ball joint stud cotter pin.
4. Remove the brake caliper assembly and support it from the frame with a length of wire.
5. Loosen the stud nut, but not more than one turn.
6. Strike the top of the steering knuckle until the ball joint is free of the steering knuckle.
7. Support the lower control arm with a jack so that the steering knuckle can be disconnected from the ball joint.
8. Remove upper ball joint stud nut and remove the joint from the steering knuckle and allow the knuckle to swing out of the way.
9. Lift the upper control arm and place a block of wood between it and the frame as a support.
10. If the ball joint has any perceptible side-to-side shake or can be turned in its socket with your fingers, then it should be replaced.
11. Remove the rivets from the upper control arm with either a chisel or a grinding wheel. Drive them out with a punch after removing the heads. Do not damage the ball joint seat.
12. Install the new ball joint in the upper control arm and attach it with the nuts and bolts provided. Insert the bolts from the bottom and tighten them to 25 ft lbs.
13. Turn the ball joint stud so the cotter pin hole runs front-to-rear.
14. Remove the block of wood from between the frame and the upper control arm.
15. Before installing the ball joint stud in the steering knuckle, check the tapered hole and remove any dirt or debris. If the hole is distorted or damaged, the steering knuckle must be replaced.
16. Install the ball joint stud in the hole in the top of the steering knuckle. Install the castellated nut and tighten it to 60 ft lbs. Tighen the nut to a maximum of 100 ft lbs to install the cotter pin. Do not back the nut off in order to install the cotter pin.
17. Install the brake caliper assembly.
18. Grease the ball joint.
19. Install the wheel and tire and lower the car.

Wheel Bearing

Removal and Installation

1. Raise the vehicle and position it securely.
2. Remove the wheel and tire.
3. On drum brake models, remove the dust cap, cotter pin, spindle nut, washer, and the outer bearing assembly. Remove the brake drum from the steering knuckle spindle.
4. On disc brake models, remove the two bolts which hold the caliper to the knuckle and slide the caliper off the disc and secure it to the upper control arm.

NOTE: Never allow the caliper to hang from the brake hose.

Remove the dust cap, cotter pin, spindle nut, washer, and the outer bearing assembly. Pull off the hub and disc assembly from the steering knuckle spindle.
5. Remove the inner bearing grease seal and the inner bearing.
6. Before installation, lubricate the hub bore with a thin film of grease. (On disc brake units use #2 grade lithium type.) Also, pack the bearing cone and the bearings themselves. The bearings should be packed with a commercial packer or with your hands by forcing grease through the larger end of the bearing until it protrudes through the smaller end.
7. Install the inner bearing and seal and install the drum or disc assembly onto the spindle.
8. Install the outer bearings, washer, and spindle nut. Tighten the nut hand tight.
9. On disc brake models, install the caliper.
10. Replace the wheel and tire.
11. Adjust the wheel bearings. (See "Wheel Bearing Adjustment.")
12. Tighten the wheel lugs and lower the vehicle.

Inspection

1. Clean the bearing assemblies with clean solvent and, if there is damage, replace the complete assembly.
2. Check the bearing races and the hub surface for nicks or other defects. Replace if necessary.
3. Make certain that the inner race is not turning inside the hub. Replace the hub and race if necessary.
4. Examine the spindle bearing seats for wear. Replace if necessary.

Adjustment

Drum Brakes

1. Tighten the adjusting nut to 30 ft lbs while rotating the wheel.

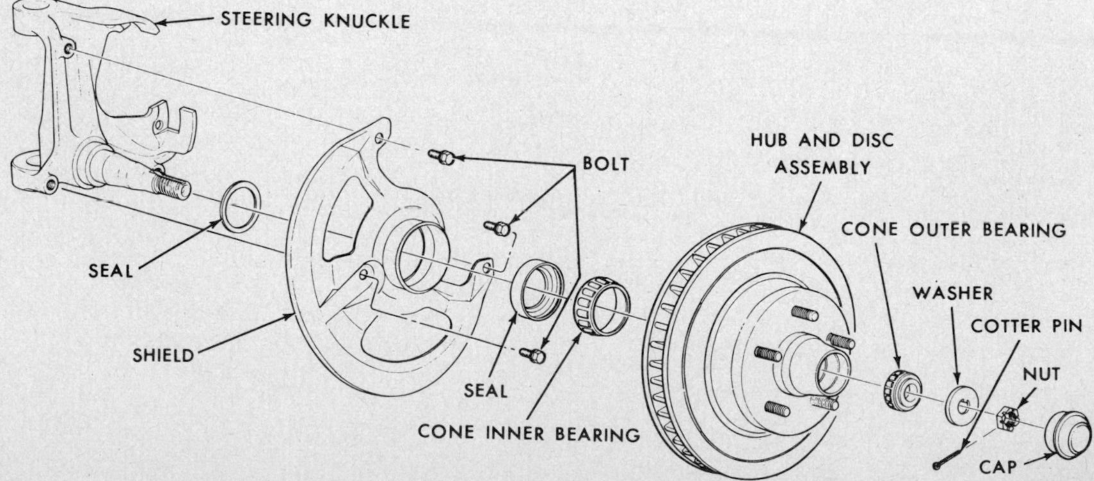

Front disc brake hub assembly (© Cadillac Div., G.M. Corp)

2. Back off ¼ turn (90°) and insert the cotter pin. If the pin cannot be inserted, loosen the adjusting nut until it can be installed.
3. Peen the cotter pin over so that it cannot be moved within its hole.

Disc Brakes

1. Rotate the wheel and tighten the adjusting nut to 15 ft lbs.
2. Back off the nut until it is free and then tighten it finger tight.
3. Insert the cotter pin. If the pin cannot be installed in this position, back off the nut until the holes align. Make certain that the pin fits tight. If it can be moved with your fingers, it should be replaced.

REAR SUSPENSION

All Except Commercial and Seville

A four-link rear suspension system, consisting of upper and lower control arms, coil springs and shock absorbers is used. The coil springs are placed on brackets on the rear axle housing at their lower ends, the upper ends being seated in the frame crossmember. The upper and lower control arms are so placed to give the car good lateral stability. Cars can be equipped with Automatic Level Control, described later.

Commercial Chassis and Seville

The Commerical chassis and Seville uses semi-elliptic leaf springs. They are approximately 2½ in. wide in a conventional Hotchkiss drive layout. The springs have zinc, full length polyethylene, or teflon inner liners between leaves to provide correct interleaf friction and to prevent corrosion. Direct acting shock absorbers are provided, connected between the U-bolt spring plates and brackets welded to the frame cross-member. Automatic Level Control, with individual valving is optional.

Shock Absorber Removal and Installation

1. Raise the rear of the vehicle and support both the frame and the axle with separate jacks.
2. If the vehicle is equipped with Automatic Level Control, remove the air lines at the shocks.

Caution The shocks act as rebound stops for the rear suspension and under no circumstances should the rear end be raised excessively high while disconnecting the shocks, unless both the rear axle and the frame are supported.

3. Remove the upper retaining bolts and nuts. To perform this, bend a ½ in. box end wrench to form a 45° angle at a point one inch from the center of the box diameter. This is used to hold the upper mounting nut.

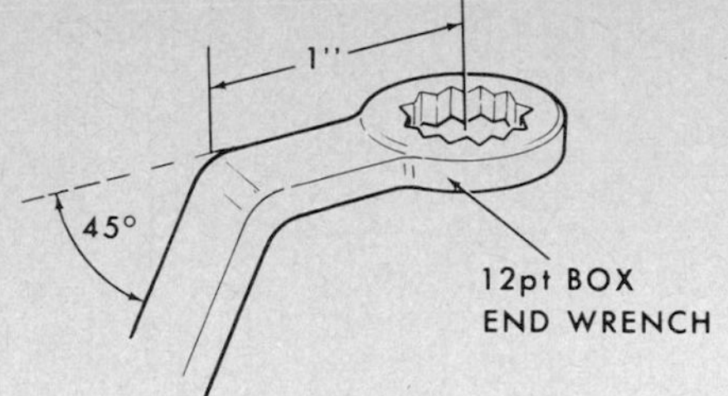

Rear shock absorber wrench
(© Cadillac Div., G.M. Corp)

4. Remove the lower retaining nut while holding the stem by the grommet to keep the stem from turning. Pull the shock off.
5. Installation is the reverse of removal.

Coil Spring R & R

1969-70

1. Jack up rear of car and place axle stands under frame side rails.
2. Place a jack under the differential housing.
3. Remove tire and wheel assemblies.
4. If car has A.L.C., disconnect link at overtravel lever and position it in center position.

Caution The shock absorbers act as stops for the suspension. Make certain that both the axle and frame are supported before proceeding further.

5. Remove shock absorber lower retaining nuts and washers.
6. Remove rear bolts from upper control arms, then free links from mountings.

NOTE: it may be necessary to place another jack under differential pinion housing to facilitate bolt removal.

7. If removing right spring, disconnect brake hose at crossmember bracket and disconnect parking brake cable strap. Lower jacks under differential.

Caution Do not allow the differential to wind up as it is lowered as the spring may fly out.

8. Place floor jack under control arm opposite of spring being removed. (If removing right spring, place jack under left control arm and vice-versa.)
9. Jack up on lower control arm until spring can be removed.
10. To install, reverse removal procedure. Tighten upper and lower control arm bolts to 75 ft. lbs.

1971-76

1. Follow Steps 1-5 of previous procedure.
2. Position container to catch brake fluid, then disconnect brake hose from steel line at frame.
3. Remove brake hose and clip from frame.
4. Disconnect rear U-joint and support driveshaft on a chain.
5. Remove nuts and bolts that secure both upper control arms to axle brackets.
6. Lower rear axle assembly slowly until springs are free.

Caution Do not allow the differential to wind up as it is lowered as the spring may fly out.

7. To install, reverse removal procedure. Tighten upper and lower control arm bolts to 75 ft. lbs.

Leaf Spring R & R

Commercial Chassis

1. Jack up car and support on axle stands at frame side rails.
2. Place axle stands under axle housing, after jacking up housing.
3. Remove front eye bolt nut and drive out bolt.
4. Disconnect shock absorber from U-bolt plate.
5. Remove rear shackle nuts.
6. Remove U-bolt plate nuts, plate and insulators.
7. Disconnect rear shackle links and lower spring.
8. To install, reverse removal procedure. Tighten shackle nuts to 70 ft. lbs., U-bolt nuts to 45 ft. lbs., and lower shock nuts to 50 ft. lbs.

Seville

1. Raise the rear of the car and support it so the axle can be raised or lowered. Raise the axle so that all tension is relieved from the spring.
2. Disconnect the rear automatic leveling valve overtravel lever from its link and hold the lever in the exhaust position (down) to deflate the shock absorbers.
3. Disconnect the lower half of the shock absorbers and move them out of the way.
4. Loosen the parking brake adjustment at the equalizer and remove the parking brake cable clip from the front retaining bracket on the spring. Remove the cable clamps from the under side of the springs.
5. Loosen the spring front eye bushing-to-retaining bracket bolt.
6. Remove the bolts retaining the front spring bracket to the underbody.
7. Lower the axle enough to permit access to the front eye bolt and remove the bracket from the spring.

NOTE: The front eye bushing can be replaced at this time.

8. Remove the U-bolt and T-bolt nuts retaining the lower spring plate to the axle and stabilizer bar brackets.
9. Remove the upper and lower spring pads and spring plate.
10. Support the spring with a jack stand and remove the two nuts from the rear shackle.
11. Separate the shackle and remove the spring from the vehicle.
12. If the spring is being replaced, remove the spring damper for installation on the new spring by removing the clamp bolt and bending the bottom half of the clamp down about 2 in. Slide the clamp rearward over the damper and remove the damper from the spring.
13. Position the spring damper on the new spring and position it 1/8 in. from the front spring eye. Slide the clamp forward over the damper and position the clamp at the second leaf of the spring.

NOTE: The clamp must face upward and the nut must be on the outside of the spring.

Install the clamp bolt pointing up and tighten to 20 ft lbs.

NOTE: Do not tighten any of the attaching hardware to specifications until step 25. Allow the retaining nuts and bolts to remain only finger tight until the entire spring is assembled; before lowering the car.

14. Position the front eye of the spring to the front mounting bracket and install the attaching bolt with the head on the inside. Tighten the bolt to 105 ft lbs.
15. Install the upper shackle bushings in the frame. Position the shackles to the bushings and install the bolt and nut, tightening to 50 ft lbs.
16. Install the bushing halves in the rear spring eye and install the spring to the shackle, tightening the lower shackle bolt and nut to 50 ft lbs.
17. Raise the front end of the spring and position the bracket to the underbody. Make sure the tab on the bracket is aligned in the slot in the underbody.
18. Install the screws retaining the front spring bracket to the underbody and tighten to 30 ft lbs.
19. Position the spring upper cushion between the spring and the axle bracket so the cushion ribs align with the bracket locating ribs.
20. Position the lower mounting plate over the locating dowel on the lower spring pad and install the retaining nuts, tightening them to 45 ft lbs.
21. Position the stabilizer brackets to the lower spring plate and tighten the retaining bolts and nuts to 30 ft lbs.
22. Connect the lower shock absorber mount to the lower spring bracket and tighten to 45 ft lbs.
23. Install the parking brake cable under the leaf spring and secure it at the front of the spring with the wire clip and clamp. Adjust the parking brake cable.
24. Connect the rear leveling valve overtravel lever to its link.
25. Tighten all of the attaching hardware to the specifications given in the preceding text.
26. Lower the vehicle.

Automatic Level Control

The system consists of a vacuum-operated air compressor and a control valve mounted at rear suspension crossmember. The valve is then connected to Superlift rear shock absorbers.

The Superlift shock absorber is essentially a conventional shock absorber enclosed in an air chamber. A pliable nylon-reinforced neoprene boot seals the air dome to air piston. It will extend or retract under the pressure controlled by the valve.

As load is added to the vehicle, the control valve admits air under pressure to these shock absorbers, lifting vehicle to normal position. As load is reduced, the valve releases air and lowers vehicle to the previous normal level.

The valve is connected by a link to the right rear upper control link. A deflection of at least 1/2 in. is required to make it operative.

A delay mechanism is built into the valve housing. This requires that an attitude be assumed for four to 15 seconds in order for the valve to operate. It prevents operation during normal road motions.

Pressure at the shock absorber units is kept equal by means of the line connecting the two units, with only one unit connected directly to the control valve. This keeps approximately 8-15 psi. on shock absorber units at all times. The pressure is released at the control valve and the equalizing pressure is maintained through a check valve at the release fitting.

The compressor is located in the engine compartment. It is operated by vacuum surge through a line connected just forward of the carburetor insulator connection on all full size Cadillacs. On a Seville, vacuum is supplied to the compressor by a line connected to the PCV vacuum line. Air, at atmospheric pressure, is taken into the compressor through a line connected to the air cleaner. The compressed air from the compressor is supplied to a reservoir and then to the control valve.

Any service work on this system, or other parts of the vehicle, that may cause deflation wll require system reinflation to approximately 140 psi.

All lines are 1/8 in. diameter flexible black tubing. In working on this system, use care not to kink this tubing. Keep tubing away from the exhaust system.

BRAKES

All Cadillacs have power-assisted, hydraulic front and rear brakes. They also use a vacuum-release operated parking brake. All cars are equipped with single-piston, sliding-caliper front disc brakes and the rear drum system.

For information relating to brake shoe replacement and adjustment, wheel cylinder and caliper overhaul, and brake bleeding refer to the brake "Unit Repair Section."

A dual master cylinder is used. This system enables one pair of brakes to function even if the other pair fails.

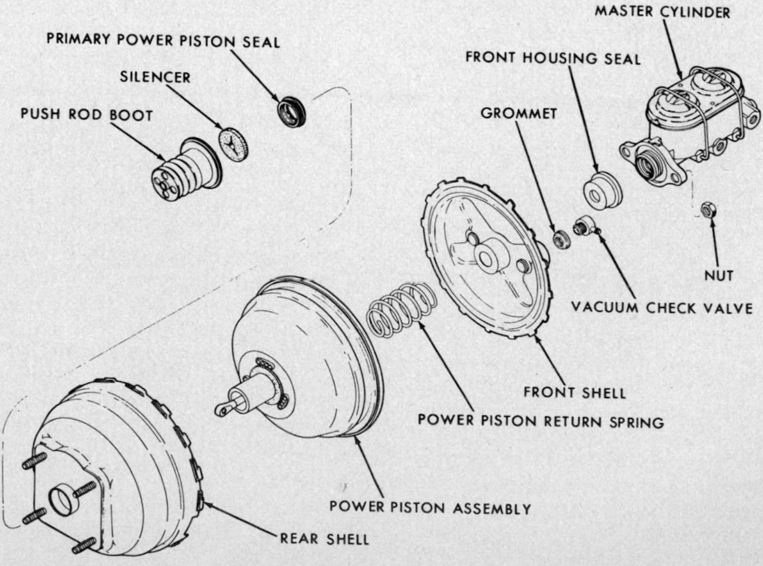

Brake master cylinder and power head (© Cadillac Div., G.M. Corp)

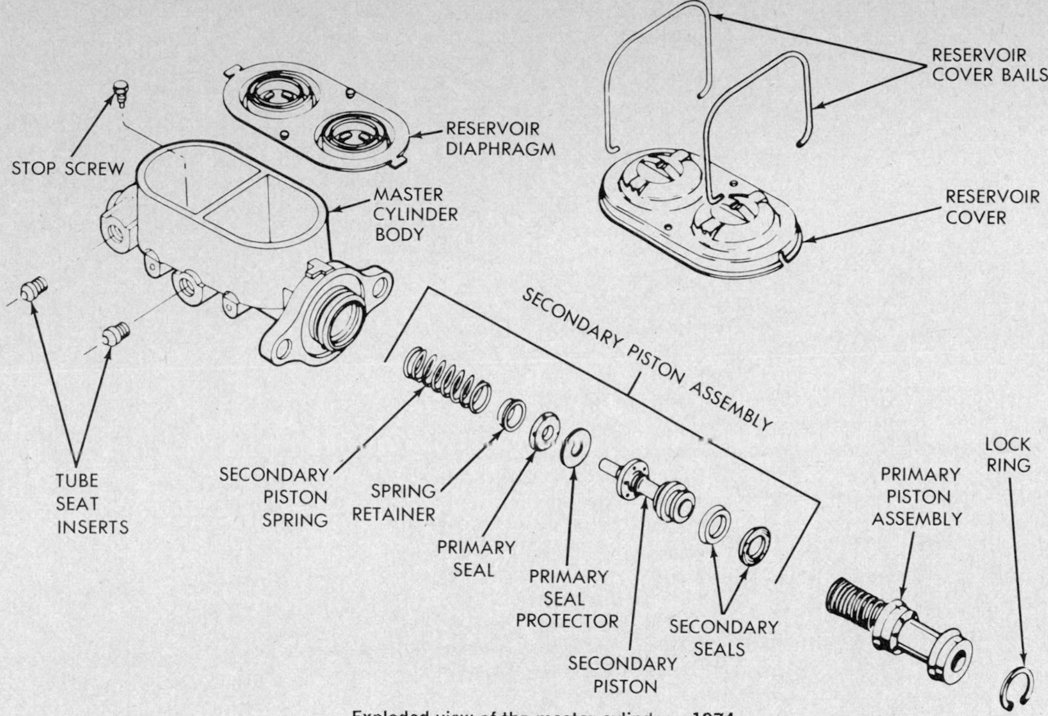

Exploded view of the master cylinder—1974
(© Cadillac Div., G.M. Corp.)

Power Brake Unit R & R

Full Size Cadillac

1. Disconnect and cap hydraulic lines from master cylinder.
2. Disconnect vacuum line from vacuum check valve on unit.
3. Remove steering column lower cover, as described under *Panel and Cluster R & R.*
4. Remove cotter pin, washer and spring spacer that secure power unit pushrod to brake pedal arm.
5. Remove the four nuts that secure power unit to firewall, then remove power unit.
6. To install, reverse removal procedure. The torque on the brake lines should be no greater than 20 ft lbs. Bleed the hydraulic system.

Seville

1. Remove any vacuum from the booster by depressing the brake pedal several times.
2. Disconnect the two front and one rear brake outlet lines and electrical connector from the combination valve. Plug the lines and outlets to prevent entry of dirt.
3. Remove the two attaching nuts securing the master cylinder to the booster, and discard the nuts. Remove the master cylinder and combination valve assembly from the car.
4. Disconnect the booster vacuum hose from the check valve.
5. From under the instrument panel, remove the clip and washer from the brake pedal push rod pin. Do not remove the push rod from the brake pedal assembly yet.
6. Remove the two screws retaining the twilight sentinel amplifier, if so equipped, to the brake pedal bracket. Lower the amplifier and discard the connectors.
7. Remove the four booster-to-cowl retaining nuts and discard the nuts. Slide the studs through the cowl. Move the booster toward the engine and keep the mounting surface parallel to the cowl. Slide the push rod from the brake pedal pin and remove the booster from the car.
8. Install the booster in the reverse order of removal, using new attaching nuts. Tighten the booster-to-cowl nuts to 15 ft lbs, and the master cylinder-to-booster nuts to 20 ft lbs.
9. Bleed the brake hydraulic system. Start the engine and check the brake vacuum system for leaks and operation.

Rear Drum Brakes

The rear braking system of all models consists of power-assisted, hydraulic service brakes.

The service brake has a self-adjusting brake shoe mechanism consisting of a link, actuator, pawl, and pawl return spring. The actuator is held against the secondary shoe by means of a hold-down cup and spring. The pawl is connected to the actuator and held in position by the pawl return spring.

The automatic adjustment takes place only when the brakes are applied when the car is moving rearward.

Over-adjustment is prevented by the shoe-to-drum clearance limiting secondary shoe travel to less than that required for the pawl to engage the next tooth of the star wheel.

Care must be used that the correct star wheel assembly is installed at the proper wheel, to insure that the self-adjusters work correctly.

Vacuum Release Parking Brake

A vacuum release assists the foot-operated parking brake. With the engine running, the brake automatically releases when the car is put into gear. This device eliminates the possibility of driving the car with the parking brake engaged.

Parking Brake Adjustment

NOTE: make certain that the rear brakes are properly adjusted before adjusting the parking brake.

1. Make a check of the parking brake linkage for the free movement of all the cables. Lubricate, if necessary.
2. Making a correct measurement with a ruler, depress the parking brake pedal exactly 1¾ in.—1969-72; 1.0 in.—1973-76.
3. Raise the rear wheels off the ground.
4. While holding the cable stud to keep it from turning, tighten the equalizer nut until a light drag is felt on either wheel when they are spun in the forward direction.

5. When the parking brake is released there should be no brake shoe drag.
6. When the brake is adjusted properly there should be 1⅛–2⅛ in. of pedal travel when a 50 lbs force is applied to the pedal —1969-72; or 2-3 in. when 125 lbs force is applied to the pedal 1973—76 full size Cadillacs and 5-6 in. with 125 lbs of force on the Seville.

Master Cylinder Removal and Installation

NOTE: It is possible to remove the master cylinder unit without removing the power booster from the vehicle.

1. Disconnect from the master cylinder and cover the front and rear brake lines.
2. Remove the two securing nuts which hold the master cylinder to the power booster.
3. Remove the master cylinder.
4. To install, reverse the removal procedure. Bleed the hydraulic system.

STEERING

Steering Wheel Removal

NOTE: For models equipped with air bags, perform the special procedure detailed below, prior to removing steering wheel.

1. Remove the screws on the underside of the steering wheel spokes near the center and remove the pad assembly.
2. Remove the horn contact wire from the plastic tower by pushing in on the wire and turning it counterclockwise.
3. Remove the nut holding the steering wheel to the steering shaft.
4. On tilt wheels, remove locking lever and flange and screw assembly.
5. Note the match-marking of the shaft and wheel and use a puller to remove the steering wheel.
6. When reinstalling, tighten nut to 30-35 ft lbs. for 1969-70 models. 20 ft lbs for 1971 and 30 ft lbs for the 1972-76 models.

Special Procedure for Cars with A.C.R.S. (Air Bags)

Some 1974 and later models have an air cushion, or air bag, restraint system. One of the elements of this complex system is an air cushion module in the top of the steering wheel. The steering wheel can be removed in the manner described in this section after the module has been removed.

To remove the module:

1. Turn the ignition lock to the LOCK position.
2. Disconnect the battery ground cable and tape the end to prevent any possibility of a complete circuit.
3. Remove the 4 module-to-steering wheel screws. A special tool is available to do this.
4. Lift up the module and disconnect the horn wire.
5. Disconnect the module wire connector. A special tool is available to do this, too.

WARNING: The driver air cushion module should always be carried with the vinyl cover away from all parts of one's body and should always be laid on a flat surface with the vinyl side up. This is necessary so that a free space is provided to allow the air cushion to expand in case of accidental deployment.

Do not attempt to repair any portion of the module. The module must be serviced as a unit. Attempting repairs such as soldering wires, changing covers, etc. may cause accidental inflation or impair operation of the driver module and cause serious injury.

Do not dispose of a module in any way. The highly inflammable material in the module can cause serious burns if ignited. Modules must be exchanged at an authorized dealer's parts department.

To install the module:

6. Hold the module with the emblem in the lower right corner.
7. Loop the air cushion harness clockwise from the 11 o'clock position to the 6 o'clock position.
8. Install the module connector by pushing it onto the column circuit firmly. Check that it is fully seated.
9. Install the horn wire.
10. Position the module, making sure that the wiring is still in place, and install the 4 screws. Torque them to 40 in. lbs.
11. Reconnect the battery ground cable.
12. Turn the ignition lock to any position other than LOCK and check that the restraint indicator light operates correctly.

Turn Signal Switch Removal and Replacement

Full Size Cadillac Models w/o A.C.R.S. (Air Bags)

1. Remove the steering wheel.
2. Remove the lockplate cover assembly.
3. After compressing the lockplate spring, remove the snap-ring from the groove in the shaft.

Caution When the snap-ring is removed do not allow the shaft to slide out the bottom of the column.

4. Remove the lockplate and slide the turn signal cam and the upper bearing preload spring off the upper steering shaft. Remove horn contact carrier.
5. Remove the thrust washer from the shaft.

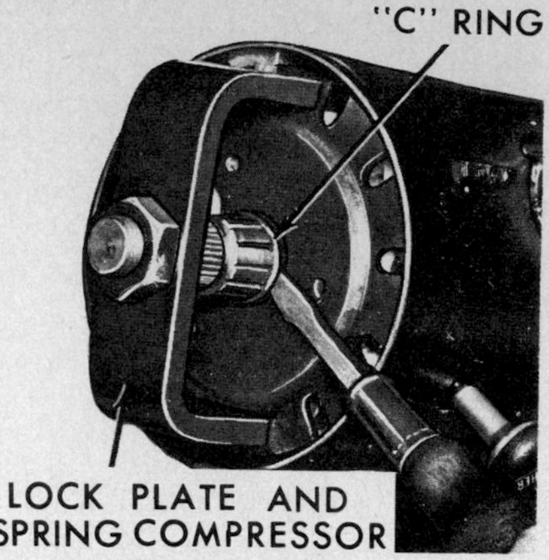

Removing the C-ring (© Cadillac Div., G.M. Corp)

6. Remove the hazard warning switch from the column along with the turn signal lever.
7. Use the following procedure if the car is equipped with Cruise Control.
   a. Attach a length of wire to the connector on the Cruise Control switch harness.
   b. Gently pull the harness up and out of the column.
8. Remove the two vertical bolts at the steering column upper support. Remove the shim packs. Keep the shims in order for reinstallation.
9. Remove the four screws securing the column upper mounting bracket to the column and remove the bracket.
10. Remove the turn signal switch mounting screws.
11. Slide the switch connector out of the bracket on the steering column.
12. If the switch is known to be bad, cut the wires and discard the switch. Tape the connector of the new switch to the old wires, and pull the new harness down through the steering column while removing the old wires.

If the original switch is to be reused, wrap tape around the wire and connector and pull the harness up through the column. It may be helpful to attach a length of wire or string to the harness connector before pulling it up through the column to facilitate installation.

13. After freeing the switch wiring protector from its mounting, pull the turn signal switch straight up and remove the switch, switch harness, and the connector from the column.
14. To reassemble reverse the removal procedure.

1974 and Later Full Size Cadillac Models with A.C.R.S. (Air Bags)

Follow the procedure for removing

Turn signal switch
(© Cadillac Div., G.M. Corp.)

the steering wheel and air cushion module which appears previously under "Steering Wheel Removal, Special Procedure for Cars with A.C.R.S."

1. Remove the 3 screws from the retainer and cover. Carefully lift the cover and retainer from the column.
2. Carefully insert a screwdriver blade into the locking tab at the side and lift the slip-ring from the column.
3. Now proceed with Steps 3-10 of the "Turn Signal Switch Removal and Replacement" procedure.
4. To replace the slip-ring, align the slip-ring locating tab with the slot in the bowl and push the slip-ring into position. Make sure that all 3 locking tabs are securely positioned.
5. Install the cover and retainer, aligning the cover over the locating tab. Torque the screws to 15 in. lbs.

Seville

1. Disconnect the battery and remove the steering wheel.
2. Remove the rubber sleeve bumper from the steering shaft.
3. Remove the plastic retainer with a screwdriver, disengaging the tabs on the retainer from the C-ring.
4. Compress the upper steering shaft preload spring with a compressor and remove the C-ring.
5. Remove the spring compressor and remove the upper steering shaft lock plate, horn contact carrier and the preload spring.
6. Remove the steering column lower cover.
7. Unscrew and remove the turn signal lever. If equipped with cruise control:
   a. Disconnect the cruise control wire from the harness near the bottom of the steering column.
   b. Slide the protector off the cruise control wire and wind the wire around the turn signal lever until the lever is disconnected. Do not remove the wire from the column.
8. Remove the two nuts and shim packs from the upper column support. Keep the shims together as a unit for reinstallation.
9. Remove the bracket from the steering column.
10. Disconnect the turn signal wiring harness from the car harness and remove the wires from the plastic protector.
11. Remove the turn signal switch retaining screws and pull the switch up out of the steering column.
12. If the switch is to be replaced, cut the wires from the switch and tape the new switch connector to the old wires. Carefully pull the new harness down through the column as the old wires are removed.
13. If the old switch is to be reused, tape the connector to the wires and carefully pull the harness up out of the column.
14. Feed the wiring harness down through the steering column to replace the old switch.
15. Secure the switch in the steering column.
16. Install the upper shaft preload spring.
17. Install the lock plate and carrier assembly. Make sure that the flat on the lower end of the steering shaft is pointing up and that the small plastic tab on the carrier is up or nearest the top of the column. The flat surface of the lock plate must be installed facing down against the turn signal switch.
18. Install the spring compressor, compress the preload spring and lock plate and install the C-ring with the wide side toward the keyway.
19. Remove the spring compressor and install the plastic retainer on the C-ring.
20. Install the rubber sleeve bumper over the steering shaft and install the steering wheel.
21. Install the turn signal lever. If the vehicle is equipped with cruise control:
   a. Turn the turn signal lever clockwise exactly 6 turns to wind the harness tightly around the lever.
   b. Position the lever to the switch and screw it in, unwinding the harness as the lever is installed.
22. Remove the tape from the end of the harness and connect the switch and cruise control, if so equipped, to the car harness.
23. Cover both harnesses with the plastic protector and position it to the column. The turn signal connector slides on the tabs of the column.
24. Position the steering column upper bracket over the turn signal switch harness plastic protector.
25. Install the mounting bracket nuts and shims in their original positions.
26. Install the steering column lower cover.

Steering Linkage Removal and Replacement

1. Remove cotter pins and nuts from outer tie-rod pivots.
2. Remove outer tie rod pivots from steering knuckles using tie-rod end puller.
3. Remove idler arm screws and lockwashers from side member.
4. Remove pitman arm cotter pin. nut and washer at steering linkage.
5. Remove steering linkage from pitman arm.
6. Remove drag link with tie-rods and idler arm attached.
7. Remove cotter pins and nuts from idler arm pivot and inner tie-rod pivots.
8. Remove tie-rod.
9. Remove idler arm from drag link.
10. Remove dust seals from pitman arm and idler arm pivot studs.
11. Remove outer tie-rod pivots by loosening nuts on outer clamp bolts and unscrewing the pivot-from adjuster tubes.
12. To install, reverse removal procedure. Tighten the idler arm nuts to 40 ft lbs and install the cotter pin. Do not tighten above 50 ft lbs.

Power Steering Pump Removal and Installation

1. On a Seville, remove the alternator and bracket.
2. Disconnect the pump lines and seal them to prevent fluid loss.
3. Remove the pump mounting from the engine block. Remove the drive belt.
4. By releasing the bottom pivot screw the pump can be removed with the mounting bracket attached.
5. The installation procedure is the reverse of the removal. Remember to adjust the pump belt tension and bleed the hydraulic line system.

NOTE: To adjust power steering pump belt, loosen pump to mounting bracket screws, move pump upward until belt is tight. Tighten mounting bracket screws. Run the engine faster than idle speed, turn steering wheel

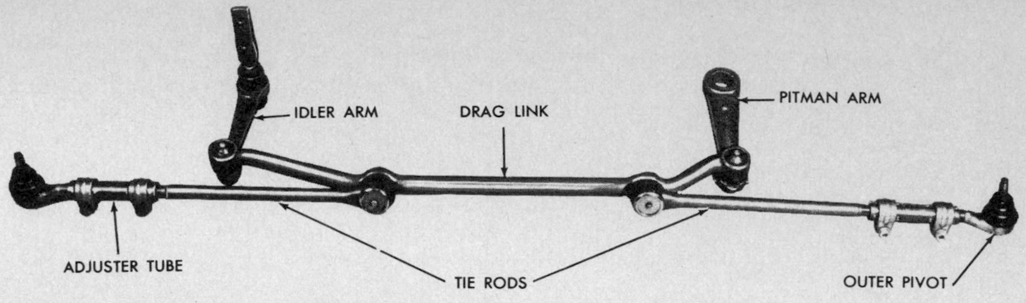

Cadillac Steering linkage (© Cadillac Div., G.M. Corp)

full right or left. If belt squeals, it is too loose and should be tightened more.

INSTRUMENT PANEL

Ignition Switch Replacement

1. Disconnect battery.
2. Position lock cylinder in "lock" position.
3. Remove steering column lower cover.
4. Loosen two nuts on upper steering column, allowing column to drop.

Caution Do not remove nuts, as column may bend under its own weight.

5. Disconnect ignition switch connector at switch.
6. Remove two screws securing ignition switch to steering column. Remove switch.
7. To install, first assemble ignition switch on actuator rod and adjust to "lock" position, as follows:
   a. *Standard Column*—Hold switch actuating rod stationary with one hand while moving switch toward bottom of column until switch reaches end of travel (Acc. position). Back off one detent, then, with key also in "lock" position, tighten two switch mounting screws to 35 in. lbs.
   b. *Tilt column*—Hold switch actuating rod stationary with one hand while moving switch toward upper end of column until switch reaches end of travel (Acc. position). Back off one detent, then, with key also in "lock" position, tighten two switch mounting screws to 35 in. lbs.
8. Connect wires, tighten two steering column nuts, install lower cover and reconnect battery.

Ignition Switch Adjustment

1974-76

From 1974, Cadillac models use a mechanical neutral safety switch, which is part of the ignition switch linkage. Because of this, the following adjustments should be made whenever the ignition switch is removed or serviced:

1. Disconnect the battery negative (—) cable.
2. Set the ignition switch to "OFF-UNLOCKED."
3. Place the gear selector lever in Neutral (N).
4. Turn the key toward "LOCK" and hold it there while installing the ignition switch.
5. Make sure that the gear selector moves through all ranges.
6. Connect the battery cable.
7. Apply the service brake; confirm that the engine starts only in Park (P) or Neutral (N), but not in any other range.

Lock Cylinder Replacement

NOTE: On 1974 and later models, equipped with air bags (A.C.R.S.), perform the special procedure for removing the air bag module from the steering wheel, prior to removing the lock cylinder.

Standard Steering Column

1. Remove the steering wheel.
2. Remove the lockplate cover assembly.
3. After compressing the lockplate spring, remove the snap-ring from the groove in the shaft.

Caution When the snap-ring is removed do not allow the shaft to slide out the bottom of the column.

4. Remove the lockplate and slide the turn signal cam and the upper bearing preload spring off the upper steering shaft.
5. Remove the thrust washer from the shaft.
6. Remove the hazard warning switch from the column along with the turn signal lever.
7. Use the following procedure if the car is equipped with Cruise Control.
   a. Attach a piece of stiff wire to the connector on the Cruise Control switch harness.
   b. Gently pull the harness up and out of the column.
8. Remove the turn signal switch mounting screws.
9. Slide the switch connector out of the bracket on the steering column.
10. After freeing the switch wiring protector from its mounting, pull the turn signal switch straight up and remove the switch, switch harness and the connector from the column.
11. Turn the ignition switch to "on" or "run" and then insert a small screwdriver into the slot next to the switch mounting screw boss. Push the lock cylinder tab and remove the lock cylinder.

Tilt Column

1. Remove the steering wheel.

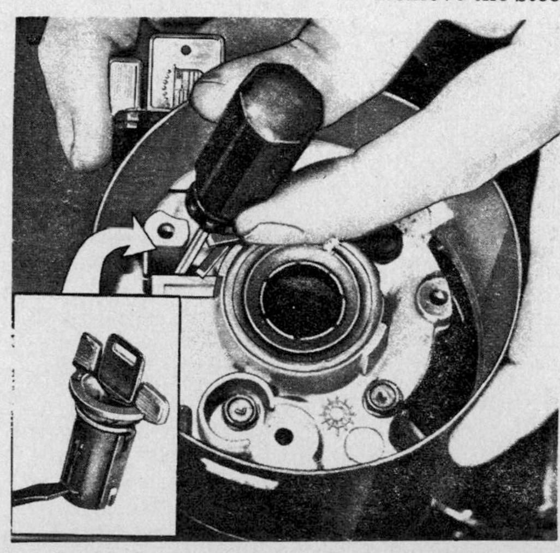

Removing the lock cylinder (© Cadillac Div., G.M. Corp)

2. Remove the rubber sleeve bumper from the steering shaft.
3. Using a small screwdriver remove the plastic retainer.
4. Using a spring compressor, compress the upper steering shaft spring and remove the C-ring. Release the steering shaft lockplate, the horn contact carrier, and the upper steering shaft preload spring.
5. Remove the four screws which hold the upper mounting bracket and then remove the bracket.
6. Slide the harness connector out of the bracket on the steering column. Tape the upper part of the harness and connector.
7. Disconnect the hazard button and position the shift bowl in Park. Remove the turn signal lever from the column.
8. Use the following procedure for cars with Cruise Control.
   a. Remove the harness protector from the harness.
   b. Attach a piece of piano wire to the switch harness connector.
   c. Before removing the turn signal lever, loop a piece of piano wire and insert it into the turn signal lever opening. Using the wire, pull the Cruise Control harness out through the opening.
   d. Pull the rest of the harness up through and out of the column.
   e. Remove the guide wire from the connector and secure the wire to the column.
   f. Remove the turn signal lever.
9. Pull the turn signal switch up until the end connector is within the shift bowl. Remove the hazard flasher level. Allow the switch to hang.
10. Place the ignition key in the "run" position.
11. Depress the center of the lock cylinder retaining tab with a screwdriver and then remove the lock cylinder.
12. To install reverse the above procedure.

Headlight Switch R & R

Full Size Cadillac

1. Disconnect the negative battery cable and remove the lower cover of the steering column.
2. Release the wiring harness retainer which runs below the headlight switch.
3. Depress the knob release button which is located on the top of the headlight switch. While the button is depressed, remove the rod and knob.
4. Remove the two mounting screws and the ground wire which is located at the bottom of the switch housing.
5. Pull the headlight switch assembly down and rearward, disconnect the wiring harness connectors, and the two bulbs, and then remove the assembly.
6. Unfasten the hex-head sleeve which holds the headlight switch to the housing case, then remove the switch from the case.
7. On units with Guide-Matic or Twilight Sentinel, use the following additional procedure.
   a. Remove the two screws securing the backplate and the lens to the bezel. Then remove the backplate and the lens.
   b. Remove the control ring and the washer on units equipped with one of the systems only. On cars with both systems, a dual control with an inner and outer shaft is used.
   c. Remove the hex nut securing the control switch and then remove the switch from the backplate.
8. To reassemble reverse the removal procedure.

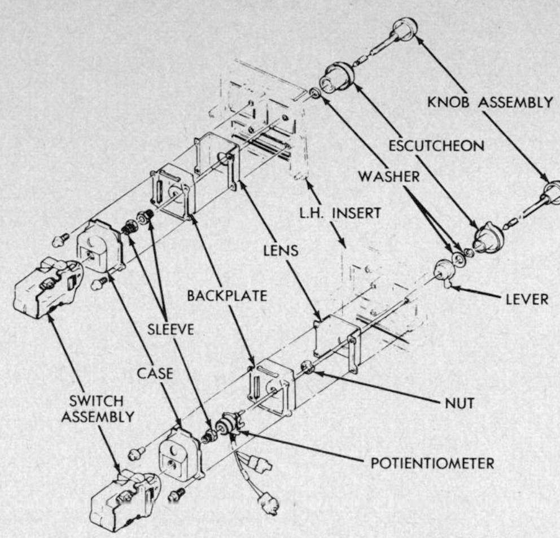

Seville headlight switch components
(© Cadillac Div., G.M. Corp.)

Seville

1. Disconnect the negative battery cable.
2. Remove the lower steering column cover and instrument cluster bezel.
3. Remove the trim screw from the left side of the lower panel.
4. Remove the 2 screws securing the left lower instrument panel to the top cover.
5. Loosen the screw securing the lower panel to the reinforcement.
6. Pull the left lower instrument panel out to gain access to the connectors. Disconnect the climate control electrical and vacuum connectors, cruise control and headlight connectors, illumination bulbs and sockets, and ground wires.
7. Pull the knob on the headlight switch On and depress the spring loaded button on the bottom of the switch. Remove the headlight switch knob and rod.
8. Remove the headlight switch case-to-instrument panel insert screws and separate the headlight switch assembly from the left lower instrument panel assembly.
9. Remove the sleeve that secures the switch to the case.
10. Without Guide-Matic and/or Twilight Sentinel, remove the sleeve that secures the escutcheon, washer and lens to the backplate.
    If the vehicle is equipped with Guide-Matic and/or Twilight Sentinel, remove the Guide-Matic knob, wave washer and Twilight Sentinel lever by carefully pulling straight out. The lens may be removed without any further disassembly. Remove the spanner nut to remove the potentiometer(s) from the backplate.
11. Install the headlight switch in the reverse order.

WINDSHIELD WIPERS

Wiper and Washer Motor R & R

1969-70

1. Disconnect negative battery cable.
2. Disconnect three washer hoses from control valve. Matchmark hoses and valve nipples for proper assembly sequence.
3. Disconnect two-way connector at washer unit and three-way connector at wiper unit.
4. Remove rubber grommet or cover plate above wiper motor on firewall.
5. Loosen two locknuts that secure crank arm to ball socket. Disen-

gage arm from socket, without removing the locknuts.
6. Remove three screws that secure wiper/washer to firewall and remove assembly.
7. To install, reverse removal procedure, making sure wiper crank is in Park position.

1971-76

1. Disconnect negative battery cable, after raising hood.
2. Remove cowl screen.
3. Reach through opening and disengage transmission drive link from wiper crank arm by loosening two nuts.
4. Disconnect wiring and washer hoses.
5. Remove three screws that secure wiper/washer unit to firewall.
6. Remove entire assembly.
7. To install, reverse removal procedure, making sure wiper crank arm is in Park position.

Wiper Linkage R & R

1. Remove both wiper arms.
2. Remove six clips that secure rubber hood seal to cowl. Position seal out of the way.
3. Remove screws that secure cowl vent screen; remove screen.
4. Remove the three screws on each side that hold the linkage to the cowl.
5. Remove cover plate on firewall above wiper motor.
6. Loosen the two retaining locknuts and disengage motor crank arm.

Caution Do not remove lock nuts from the ball socket studs.

7. Remove the linkage through the right-hand cowl opening.
8. To install, reverse removal procedure, after lubricating ball sockets.

RADIO

Removal

1969-70 Full Size Cadillac

1. Remove steering column lower cover.
2. Remove defroster hose behind radio.
3. Remove radio knobs, washers and rings by pulling straight out.
4. Using spanner nut wrench, remove spanner nuts securing control shafts to instrument panel.
5. Disconnect wire connectors and antenna lead-in cable. On cars with stereos, disconnect the single lead to the rear speaker and the four-way connector to the front speaker. Disconnect the two-way speaker connector on AM/FM units.
6. Remove screws securing support bracket to radio and panel center support and remove bracket.
7. Pull radio rearward and down.
8. Disconnect dial bulb socket and remove radio.

1971-73 Full Size Cadillac

This procedure is the same as 1969-70 procedure, except that Step 2 can be eliminated.

Seville

1. Remove the electronic fuel injection electronic control unit.
2. Remove the screw holding the climate control outlet extension to the heater case.
3. Disconnect the antenna.
4. Remove the nut retaining the rear radio support rod to the radio and move it out of the way.
5. Remove the control knobs, springs, control rings and both hex nuts from the control shafts at the front of the radio. The control knobs on radios with 8-track tape players are secured by set screws with 5/64 in. allen heads.
6. Slide the radio forward and pivot the rear downward to disconnect the electrical connectors.
7. Remove the radio from the vehicle.
8. Install in the reverse order.

1974-76 Full Size Cadillacs w/o Air Bags (A.C.R.S.)

1. Remove the 4 screws each which secure the lower steering column cover to its reinforcement and the instrument panel support.
2. Take the lower cover off.
3. Unfasten the screws which secure the lower ash tray bracket, and then remove the two screws from the left-hand ash tray bracket.
4. Unfasten the right-hand ash tray securing screw. Remove the ash tray assembly from the dash panel.
5. Remove the knobs, washers, outer rings, and shaft retaining nuts.
6. Remove the radio-to-dash panel lower support brace nut from the back of the radio.
7. Loosen, but don't remove, the screw which secures the brace to the support, and turn the brace clockwise.
8. Slide the radio back from the instrument panel. Detach the speaker connector, power connector, and antenna lead from it.
9. Turn the dial side of the radio (front) so that it is facing down, and lower the left-side of the receiver. Withdraw it through the ash tray opening.

Installation is performed in the reverse order of removal.

1974-76 Full Size Cadillacs with Air Bags (A.C.R.S.)

1. Turn the ignition switch to "Lock."
2. Remove the negative (—) battery cable and tape its terminal end.

Caution If the battery cable is not disconnected and taped, there is a chance that the air bag could accidently deploy.

3. Remove the 3 screws which retain the glovebox in the dash, but don't remove the two striker screws.
4. Remove the glovebox partition screws, and set the glovebox aside, without disconnecting the wiring.
5. Remove the tape storage compartment retaining screws and remove the compartment.
6. Remove the ash tray assembly retaining screws, pull the assembly out partway, unfasten the electrical leads, and remove the assembly.
7. Remove the knee restraint left trim screw.
8. Remove the screws, and loosen, but don't remove, the fifth screw (under the steering column) from the bottom of the knee restraint.
9. Remove the 4 knee restraint securing screws working from the tape storage compartment and ash tray openings.
10. Perform Steps 5-7 of the radio removal procedure for 1974-76 Cadillacs without air bags.
11. Through the knee restraint opening, disconnect the antenna lead, depress the locktabs and push the electrical connections upwards to disengage them.
12. Clear the instrument panel support by turning the radio to the left. Slide the radio away from you, lower the front of the radio (dial), and withdraw it, front first, through the knee restraint opening.

Installation is the reverse of removal.

HEATER

Heater Blower—Non-Air-Conditioned Cars

1969-70

1. Disconnect negative battery cable.
2. Drain cooling system.
3. Remove one screw that secures antenna bracket to wheelhousing.
4. Disconnect blower electrical connector.
5. Remove five screws that secure blower to case and remove blower motor by rotating it 180° while pulling out.

6. Remove heater hoses.
7. Disconnect green vacuum hose at vacuum power unit.
8. Disconnect temperature valve cable and remove cable clamp.
9. Remove screw that secures check valve and position valve out of the way.
10. Position power brake vacuum line out of the way.
11. Disconnect three-way connector at blower resistor.
12. Remove seat warmer relay, if so equipped.
13. Remove wiring harness from clip.
14. Remove seven screws that secure the bottom of the blower assembly to cowl.
15. Remove five screws and one nut that secure top of blower assembly to cowl.
16. Remove blower case assembly.
17. To install, reverse removal procedure.

1971-76

1. Disconnect negative battery cable.
2. Disconnect electrical connector.
3. Remove five blower-to-case screws and blower motor.

Heater Blower— Air-Conditioned Cars

1. Disconnect negative battery cable.
2. On 1969-70 models only, remove screw that secures antenna bracket to wheelhousing.
3. Remove rubber cooling hose from nipple and blower motor.
4. Disconnect electrical connector.
5. Remove screws that secure motor to case, then twist motor 180° and pull out.

Heater Core— Non-Air-Conditioned Cars

1969-70

1. Disconnect the negative battery cable.
2. Drain the cooling system.
3. Disconnect the electrical connector lead to the heater blower motor.
4. Remove the attaching screws of the blower motor and remove the motor.
5. Remove screws from each side of heater core, securing wire retaining clamps to blower case, then remove clamps.
6. Pull core out of case and remove grommets from inlet and outlet fittings.
7. Install in reverse of above.

1971-76

1. Drain cooling system.
2. Remove heater hoses from core nipples. Plug the nipples.
3. Remove instrument panel top cover.
4. Remove screws and position center ventilator duct and sleeve out of the way.
5. Remove vacuum hoses from diverter door and defroster door vacuum actuators.
6. Unfasten the bowden cable from temperature door and case and move out of way.
7. Take out the screws, securing heater case to cowl.
8. Work heater case from position under instrument panel.
9. Remove the screws and clips securing the core to heater case, and lift out core.
10. To install, reverse removal procedure.

Heater Core— Air-Conditioned Cars

1969-70

1. Disconnect negative battery cable.
2. Remove air cleaner.
3. Drain coolant.
4. Disconnect two heater hoses at heater air selector.
5. Remove blower relay connector.
6. Remove connector from power servo.
7. Remove neutral switch, vacuum storage tank, and Automatic Level Control hoses from vacuum check valve.
8. Remove right and left tie struts.

NOTE: if equipped with Automatic Level Control, position left tie strut out of the way in the engine compartment.

9. Disconnect Thermal Vacuum Switch hose.
10. Disengage wiring harness from clips, then remove white vacuum hose at water valve.
11. Remove vacuum harness connector from cowl, then remove six air selector to cowl screws.
12. Remove one nut and blower relay ground wire from air selector stud.
13. Remove fuse block and position it out of the way.
14. Remove four mode selector screws.
15. Pull vacuum harness connector into passenger compartment and disconnect.
16. Guide heater and air modulator assembly from engine compartment.
17. Remove four screws that secure heater core frame to case.
18. Remove gasket, then pull heater

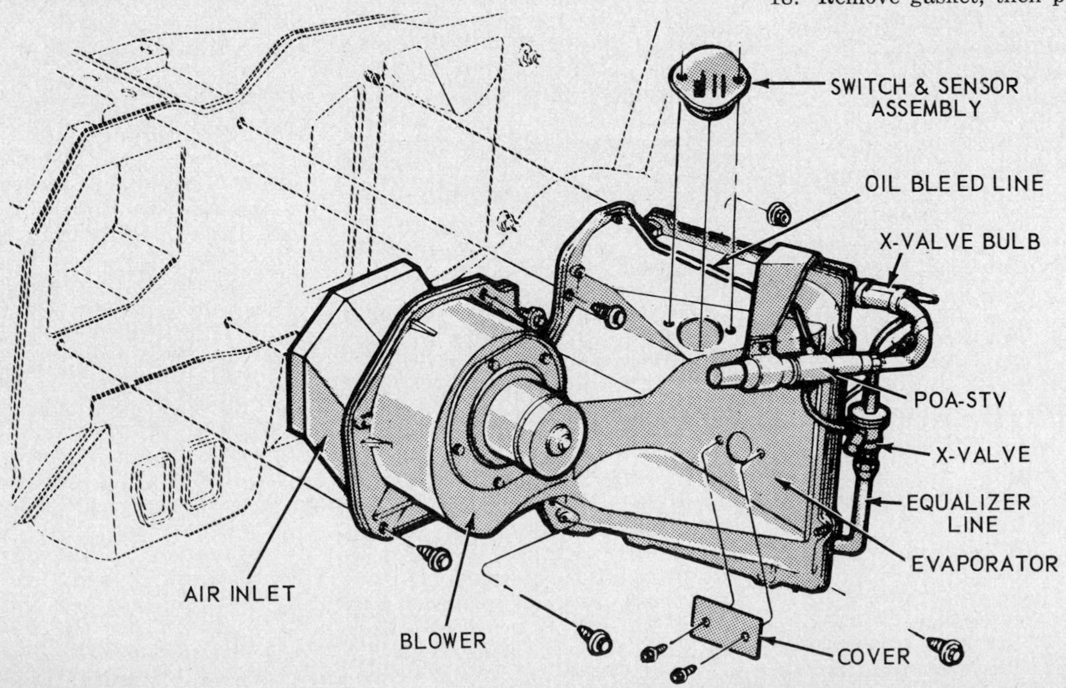

1971-73 blower, air inlet, and evaporator (© Cadillac Div., G.M. Corp)

core and frame away from case.
19. Remove rubber grommets from air inlet and outlet fittings.
20. Remove four screws, retaining clamps and heater core.
21. To install, reverse removal procedure.

1971-76 Full Size Cadillac

NOTE: On 1974 and later models equipped with air bags (A.C.R.S.), the passenger air bag restraint assembly must be removed first. This dangerous procedure is best left to a dealer shop.

1. Drain cooling system.
2. Remove hoses from heater core nipples. Plug the nipples.
3. Remove instrument panel top cover.
4. Remove right and left A/C outlet hoses and center outlet connector.
5. Remove screws securing A/C distributor to heater case and lift off distributor.
6. Remove defroster nozzle.
7. Remove glove box.
8. Disconnect vacuum hoses at recirculator door, water valve, control head supply hose, and programmer (if equipped).
9. Disconnect aspirator hose from in-car sensor.
10. Take off instrument panel braces.
11. On engine side of cowl remove the nuts securing heater case to cowl.
12. Work the heater case out from under dash.
13. Remove rubber seals from around core nipples.
14. Remove the screw and clip from beneath the seal.
15. Take out screws and clip from opposite end of core and remove core.
16. Reverse the above procedure for installation.

Seville

NOTE: In order to remove the heater core, the air conditioning system must be discharged and the evaporator case assembly removed from the car. If you are not knowledgeable about or properly equipped to service automotive air conditioning systems, do not attempt to discharge the system.

1. Discharge the air conditioning system.
2. Drain the cooling system and remove the right side wheelhousing strut.
3. Support the front of the hood and tape a pad to the right rear corner of the hood. Remove the right hood hinge.
4. Remove the electrical connections from the components mounted on the evaporator assembly and move the wiring harness out of the way.
5. Remove the heater hose at the heater core side of the hot water valve. Remove the two screws securing the valve to the evaporator case and move the valve out of the way.
6. Jack up the front of the car and support it with jackstands. Remove the right front wheel.
7. Remove the five screws securing the wheelhousing to the fender at the wheel opening.
8. Remove the two screws attaching the wheelhousing at the front.
9. Remove the three plastic retainers securing the wheel housing seal at the rear of the wheelwell, front of the wheelwell, and at the fender, forward of the wheel opening.
10. Remove the two screws behind the wheelwell securing the wheelhousing to the cowl brace.
11. Remove the battery and battery tray.
12. Remove the three screws and retainer securing the wheelhousing to the radiator support under the horns.
13. Remove the wheelhousing damper upper mounting bolt and move the damper out of the way.
14. Remove the wheelhousing from the car. Some prying and bending may be necessary.
15. Remove the heater hoses from the heater core nipples.
16. Disconnect and plug the refrigeration lines at the receiver.
17. Remove the screws and nuts retaining the evaporator case and remove the case from the vehicle.
18. Separate the case and remove the heater core.
19. Install in the reverse order. Use new O-rings at the connection of the refrigeration lines to the receiver. Fill the cooling system and evacuate and recharge the refrigeration system of the air conditioning.

SEAT BELTS

Warning System

1972-73

The seat belt warning system consists of lap belt retractor switches, a pressure-sensitive switch underneath the right-hand front passenger's seat, a warning lamp and a buzzer.

On cars having automatic transmissions, the seat belt warning circuit is wired through the ignition switch and the combination back-up lamp/neutral safety switch.

With the ignition key in the "RUN" position, a weight of 40-50 lbs on the seat (pressure-sensitive switch), energizes the circuit when the gear selector is placed in a forward drive range.

A warning light will glow and a buzzer will sound with the circuit energized, until the seat belts are withdrawn from the retractors and fastened over the laps of the two outboard front seat occupants.

Seat Belt/Starter Interlock System

1974-75

As required by law, all 1974-75 Cadillac passenger cars could not be started until the front seat occupants sit down and then fasten their seat belts. If the proper sequence is not followed, e.g., the occupants fasten the seat belts and then sit on them, the car cannot be started.

If, after the car is started, the seat belts are unfastened, a warning buzzer and light will be activated in a similar manner to that described above for 1972-73 models.

The shoulder harness and lap belt are permanently fastened together, so that they both must be worn. The shoulder harness uses an inertia-lock reel to allow freedom of movement under normal driving conditions.

NOTE: This type of reel locks up when the car decelerates rapidly, as during a crash.

The lap belts use the same ratchet-type retractors that the 1972-73 models use.

The switches for the interlock system have been removed from the lap belt retractors and placed in the belt buckles. The seat sensors remain the same as those used in 1972-73, except that two more have been added.

For ease of service, the car may be started from outside, by reaching in and turning the key but without depressing the seat sensors.

In case of system failure, an override switch is located under the hood. This is a "one start" switch and it must be reset each time it is used.

Disabling the Seat Belt Interlock and Buzzer

It is now legal to disconnect the seat belt interlock and buzzer system, but not the seat belt warning light.

1. Disconnect the negative battery cable.
2. Locate the interlock harness connector under the left side of the instrument panel on or near the fuse block with orange, yellow and green wires.
3. Cut and tape the green wire on the body harness side of the interlock connector.
4. Disconect the seat belt warning buzzer from its position under the left side of the instrument panel by removing the lower steering column cover. Remove the connector and seat belt buzzer from the left body bracket and disconnect the buzzer from the harness and reinstall the connector to the bracket. Install the lower steering column cover.

INDEX

Cadillac Eldorado

YEAR IDENTIFICATION

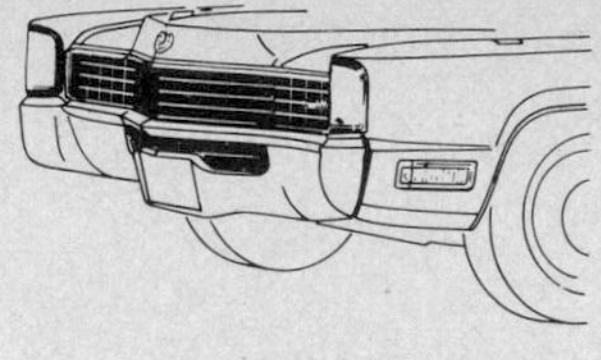

1969

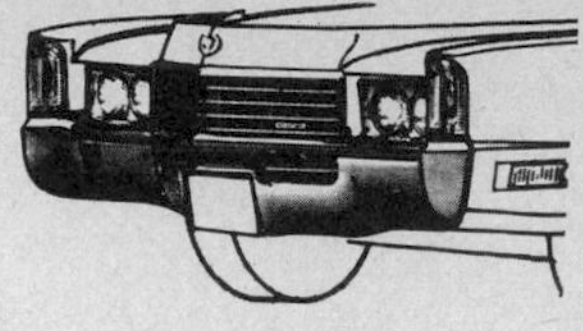

1970

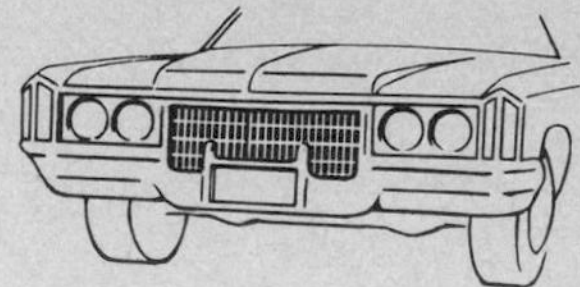

1971

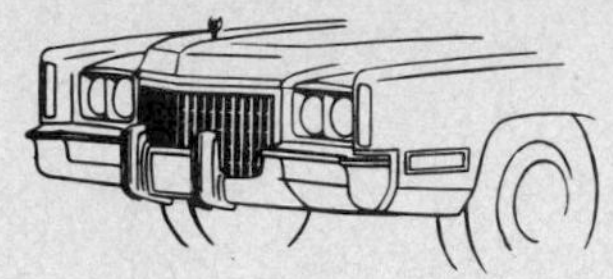

1972

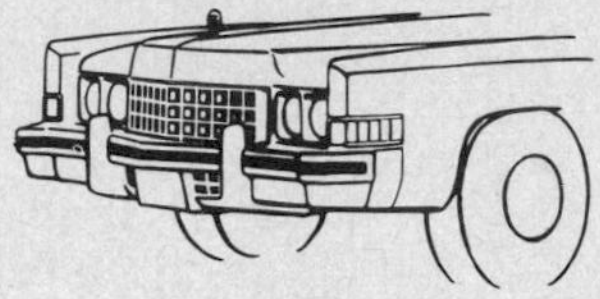

1973

1974

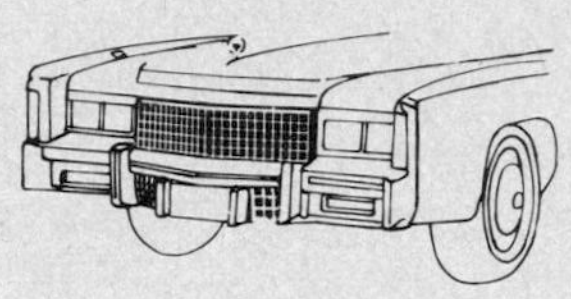

1975

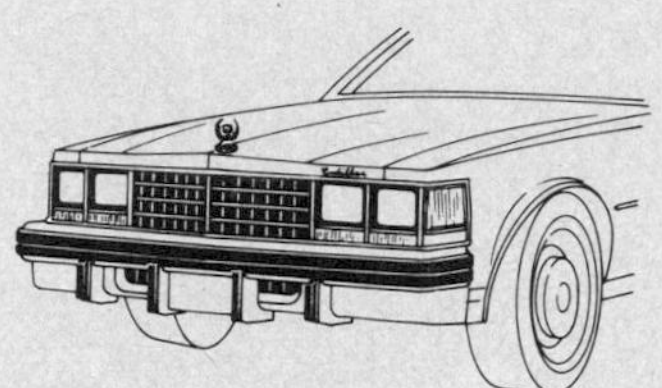

1976 Cadillac Seville

FIRING ORDER

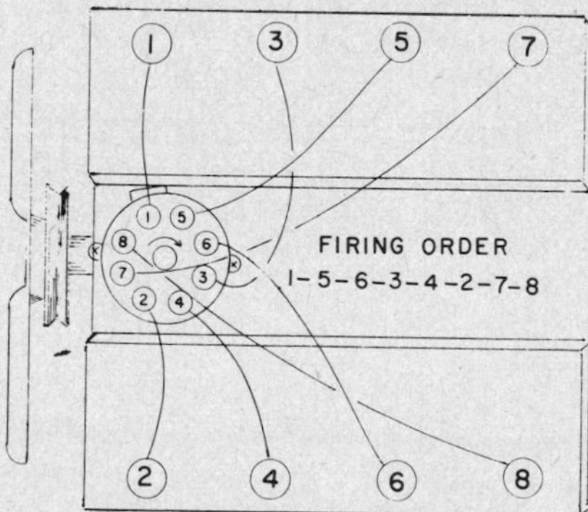

CAR SERIAL NUMBER LOCATION AND ENGINE IDENTIFICATION

1969-70

The vehicle identification plate is located on the top left side of the dashboard, and is visible through the windshield. The eight digit serial number consists of a sales code letter. The last digit of the model year (8, 9, or 0), and a six digit sequential number.

1969 models use a 472 cu. in. engine. A 500 cu. in. engine is used in 1970. The vehicle identification number, less sales code, is stamped on the top rear of the engine block, adjacent to the transmission.

1971-76

The vehicle identification plate is located on the top left side of the dashboard, and is visible through the windshield. The thirteen digit serial number consists of the G.M. Division Code (6), a four digit series and model number, the last digit of the model year, plant designation, and a six digit sequential serial number.

All models utilize a 500 cu. in. V8 engine. A derivative of the vehicle identification number is stamped on the top rear of the engine block, adjacent to the transmission.

1972-76 models have the engine code located on the left rear of the engine block, behind the intake manifold.

GENERAL ENGINE SPECIFICATIONS

Year	Engine Cu. In. Displacement	Carburetor Type	Horsepower @ rpm ■	Torque @ rpm (ft lbs) ■	Bore and Stroke (in.)	Compression Ratio	Oil Pressure @ 2050 rpm
'69	8-472	4 bbl	375 @ 4400	525 @ 3000	4.300 x 4.060	10.5:1	38
'70	8-500	4 bbl	400 @ 4400	550 @ 3000	4.300 x 4.304	10.0:1	38
'71	8-500	4 bbl	365 @ 4400	535 @ 2800	4.300 x 4.304	8.5:1	38
'72	8-500	4 bbl	235 @ 3800	385 @ 2400	4.300 x 4.304	8.5:1	35
'73	8-500	4 bbl	235 @ 3800	385 @ 2400	4.300 x 4.304	8.5:1	35
'74	8-500	4 bbl	210 @ 3600	380 @ 2000	4.300 x 4.304	8.25:1	35
'75-'76	8-500	4 bbl	210 @ 3600	380 @ 2000	4.300 x 4.304	8.25:1	35
'75-'76	8-500	EFI	210 @ 3600	380 @ 2000	4.300 x 4.304	8.25:1	35

■ Beginning 1972 horsepower and torque are SAE net figures. They are measured at the rear of the transmission with all accessories installed and operating. Since the figures may vary when a given engine is installed in different models, some are representative rather than exact.

EFI—Electronic Fuel Injection

TUNE-UP SPECIFICATIONS

When analyzing compression test results, look for uniformity among cylinders rather than specific pressures.

Year	ENGINE No. Cyl Displacement (cu in.)	ENGINE hp	SPARK PLUGS Type	SPARK PLUGS Gap (in.)	DISTRIBUTOR Point Dwell (deg)	DISTRIBUTOR Point Gap (in.)	IGNITION TIMING (deg) ▲ Man Trans	IGNITION TIMING (deg) ▲ Auto Trans	VALVES Intake Opens ■ (deg) ●	Fuel Pump Pressure (psi)	IDLE SPEED (rpm) ▲ Man Trans	IDLE SPEED (rpm) ▲ Auto Trans
'69	8-472	375	R-44-N	.035	30	.016	—	5B	18	5¼-6½	—	550②
'70	8-500	400	R-46-N	.035	30	.016	—	7½B	18	5¼-6½	—	600③/400
'71	8-500	365	R-46-N	.035	30	.016	—	8B	38	5¼-6½	—	600③/400
'72	8-500	235	R-46-N	.035	30	.016	—	8B	34	5¼-6½	—	600③/400
'73	8-500	235	R-46-N	.035	30	.016	—	8B	34	5¼-6½	—	600③/400
'74	8-500	210	R-45NS	.035	30	.016	—	10B	21	5¼-6½	—	600③/400
	8-500 (H.E.I.)	210	R-45NS	.035	Electronic		—	10B	21	5¼-6½	—	600③/400
'75	8-500	210	R-45NSX	.060	Electronic		—	6B	21	5¼-6½	—	600③/400
	8-500 (EFI)	210	R-45NSX	.060	Electronic		—	2B	21	39 min.	—	600
'76	8-500	190	R-45NSX	.060	Electronic		—	6B	21	5¼-6¼	—	600
	8-500 (EFI)	215	R-45NSX	.060	Electronic		—	12B	21	39 min.	—	600

▲ See text for procedure
■ All figures Before Top Dead Center
● Figures in parentheses are for California only
① For A/C equipped vehicles, adjust idle to 900-950 rpm in neutral with A/C and idle speed-up on
② Adjust idle to 900-950 rpm with idle speed-up on. See text for special procedure.
③ Lower figure indicates idle speed with solenoid disconnected
④ See engine compartment decal
B Before Top Dead Center
— Not applicable
H.E.I.—High Energy Ignition
EFI—Electronic Fuel Injection

CAPACITIES

Year	ENGINE No. Cyl. Displacement (cu. in.)	Engine Crankcase Add 1 Qt For New Filter	TRANSMISSION Pts To Refill After Draining Manual 3-Speed	Manual 4-Speed	Automatic ●	Drive Axle (pts)	Gasoline Tank (gals)	COOLING SYSTEM (qts) With Heater	COOLING SYSTEM (qts) With A/C
'69	All	5	——	——	11.9	4.5	24	21.3	21.8
'70	All	5	——	——	11.9	4.5	24①	21.3	21.8
'71	All	5	——	——	11.9	4.0	27.5	21.3	21.8
'72	All	5	——	——	11.9	4.0	27.5	21.3	21.8②
'73	All	5	——	——	11.9	4.0	27.5	21.3	21.8②
'74	All	5	——	——	11.9	4.0	27.5	21.3	21.8②
'75	All	5	——	——	10.0	4.0	27.5	25.8	25.8
'76	All	5	——	——	10.0	4.0	27.5	25.8	25.8

● Specifications do not include torque convertor
① California cars—22 gals
② Trailer package—2 qts additional
—— Not applicable

VALVE SPECIFICATIONS

Year	Engine No. Cyl. Displacement (cu in.)	Seat Angle (deg)	Face Angle (deg)	Spring Test Pressure (lbs @ in.)	Spring Installed Height (in.)	STEM TO GUIDE Clearance (in.)		STEM Diameter (in.)	
						Intake	Exhaust	Intake	Exhaust
'69	8-472	45	44	160 @ 1.50	1 15/16	.0005-.0025	.0010-.0025	.3420	.3418
'70	8-500	45	44	160 @ 1.50	1 15/16	.0005-.0025	.0010-.0025	.3420	.3418
'71	8-500	45	44	160 @ 1.50	1 15/16	.0010-.0027	.0010-.0025	.3420	.3418
'72	8-500	45	44	168 @ 1.50	1 15/16	.0010-.0027	.0012-.0027	.3418	.3416
'73	8-500	45	44	168 @ 1.50	1 15/16	.0010-.0027	.0012-.0027	.3418	.3416
'74	8-500	45	44	168 @ 1.50	1 15/16	.0010-.0027	.0012-.0029	.3418	.3416
'75-'76	8-500	45	44	160 @ 1.50	1 15/16	.0010-.0027	.0010-.0027	.3416	.3416

TORQUE SPECIFICATIONS

All readings in ft lbs

Year	Engine Displacement (cu in.)	Cylinder Head Bolts	Rod Bearing Bolts	Main Bearing Bolts	Crankshaft Pulley Bolt	Flywheel to Crankshaft Bolts	MANIFOLD	
							Intake	Exhaust
'69-'76	472, 500	115	40	90	Press fit	75	30	35

NOTE—Some bolts and nuts are marked on the heads to indicate the grade of steel used. Do not use bolts of a lower grade than those originally installed. The marks consist of lines: SAE 5—3 lines; SAE 7—5 lines; SAE 8—6 lines

CRANKSHAFT AND CONNECTING ROD SPECIFICATIONS

All measurements are given in inches

Year	Engine Displacement (cu in.)	CRANKSHAFT				CONNECTING ROD		
		Main Brg. Journal Dia	Main Brg. Oil Clearance	Shaft End-Play	Thrust on No.	Journal Diameter	Oil Clearance	Side Clearance
'69-'73	472, 500	3.250	.0003-.0026	.002-.012	3	2.5000	.0005-.0035	.008-.016
'74	500	3.250	.0003-.0026	.002-.012	3	2.5000	.0005-.0028	.011-.021①
'75-'76	500	3.250	.0001-.0026	.002-.012	3	2.6426	.0005-.0028	.008-.020

① Total 2 Rods

RING GAP

All measurements are given in inches

Year	Engine No. Cyl. Displacement (cu in.)	Top Compression	Bottom Compression
'69-'76	8-472, 500	.013-.025	.013-.025

Year	Engine	Oil Control
69-'76	All engines	.015-.055

RING SIDE CLEARANCE

All measurements are given in inches

Year	Engine	Top Compression	Bottom Compression
'69-'76	8-472, 500	.0017-.0040	.0017-.0040

Year	Engine	Oil Control
'69-76	All engines	None (side sealing)

PISTON CLEARANCE

Year	Engine	Piston to Bore Clearance
'69	472	.0006-.0010
'70	500	.0006-.0010
'71	500	.0006-.0010
'72	500	.0006-.0010
'73	500	.0006-.0010
'74	500	.0006-.0010
'75-'76	500	.0006-.0010

ALTERNATOR AND REGULATOR SPECIFICATIONS

	ALTERNATOR			REGULATOR						
					Field Relay			Regulator		
Year	Part No. or Manufacturer	Field Current @ 12 V	Output (amps)	Part No. or Manufacturer	Air Gap (in.)	Point Gap (in.)	Volts to Close	Air Gap (in.)	Point Gap (in.)	Volts @ 75°
'69	1100734	2.2-2.6	42	1119515	.015	.030	2.3-3.7	.060	.014	13.5-14.4
	1100803	2.2-2.6	55	1119515	.015	.030	2.3-3.7	.060	.014	13.5-14.4
'70	1100908	2.2-2.6	42	1119515	—	—	—	—	—	13.5-14.4
	1100910	2.8-3.2	63	1119515	—	—	—	—	—	13.5-14.4
'71-'74	1100940 w/o A.C.	4.0-4.5	42	—	Transistor type—no adjustment					
	1100937 w/A.C.	4.0-4.5	63	—	Transistor type—no adjustment					
	1101015 w/TP	4.0-4.5	80	—	Transistor type—no adjustment					
'75-'76	1100554, 1102840	4.0-4.5	63	—	Transistor type—no adjustment					
	1101019, 1101030	4.0-4.5	80	—	Transistor type—no adjustment					

w/o A.C.—Without Air Conditioning
w/A.C.—With Air Conditioning
w/TP—With Trailer Package

BATTERY AND STARTER SPECIFICATIONS

		BATTERY			STARTER						
					Lock Test			No-Load Test			
Year	Engine Displacement (cu in.)	Ampere Hour Capacity	Volts	Terminal Grounded	Amps	Volts	Torque (ft lbs)	Amps	Volts	RPM	Brush Spring Tension (oz)
'69-'70	472, 500	74	12	Neg.	Not Recommended			70-99	10.6	7,800	35
'71-'76	500	74	12	Neg.	Not Recommended			65-95	9.0	7,000-10,500	35

BRAKE SPECIFICATIONS

All measurements are given in inches

Year	Model	Master Cylinder Disc	Master Cylinder Drum	Wheel Cylinder Front Disc	Wheel Cylinder Front Drum	Wheel Cylinder Rear	Brake Disc or Drum Diameter Front Disc	Brake Disc or Drum Diameter Front Drum	Brake Disc or Drum Diameter Rear
'69-'70	Eldorado	1.125	—	2 15/16	—	7/8	11.0	—	11.0
'71-'76	Eldorado	1.125	—	2 15/16	—	15/16	11.0	—	11.0

WHEEL ALIGNMENT SPECIFICATIONS

Year	Model	Caster Range (deg)	Caster Pref Setting (deg)	Camber Range (deg)	Camber Pref Setting (deg)	Toe-in (in.)	Steering Axis Inclin.	Wheel Pivot Ratio (deg) Inner Wheel	Wheel Pivot Ratio (deg) Outer Wheel
'69-'70	Eldorado	1½N to 2½N	2N	3/8N to 3/8P	0	0 to 1/8	11	20	18 1/6
'71-'73	Eldorado	½N to 1½N	1N	3/8N to 3/8P	0	1/16N to 1/16P	11	20	18 1/6
'74-'76	Eldorado	½N to ½P	0	LH—3/8N to 3/8P RH—1/8N to 5/8P	0 ¼	1/16N to 1/16P	11	20	18 1/6

N Negative P Positive
LH—Left-hand
RH—Right-hand

CHARGING SYSTEM

Caution The following are a few precautions to observe in servicing the Delcotron (AC) generator and the regulator.

1. When installing a battery, be certain that the ground polarity of the battery and the ground polarity of the generator and regulator are the same.
2. When connecting a booster battery, be sure to connect the correct battery terminals together.
3. When hooking up a charger, connect the correct charged leads to the battery terminals.
4. Never operate the generator on an open circuit. Be sure all connections in the charging circuit are tight.
5. Do not short across or ground any of the terminals on the generator or regulator.
6. Never polarize an AC system.

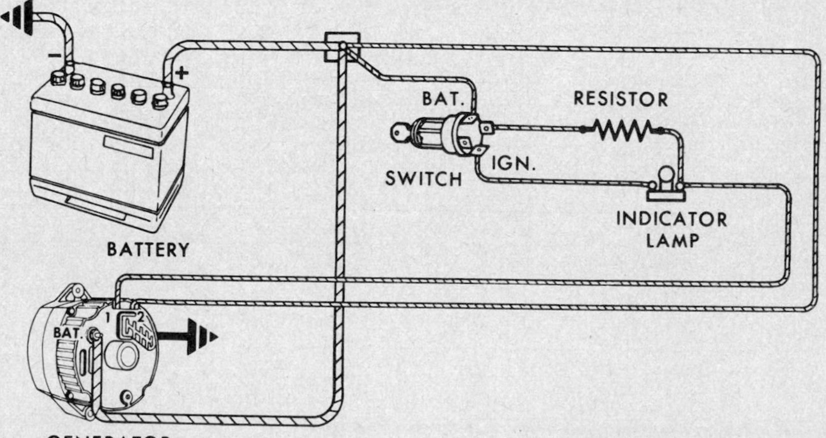

Charging system diagram (© Cadillac Div., G.M. Corp)

Alternator Removal and Installation

Except 80 Amp Alternator

1. Disconnect negative battery cable.
2. Disconnect A.I.R. hose at check valve and remove heater hose clip from adjusting link (if so equipped).
3. For 1969 models, remove strut rod between adjusting link and cylinder head.
4. Remove cap, if installed, from "+" terminal.
5. Disconnect wires from "+" terminal.
6. Unplug multiple connector.
7. Disconnect black wire from ground terminal (if used).
8. Remove link adjusting screw and raise link, then loosen lower alternator mounting screw and remove V-belt.
9. Remove lower mounting screw, spacer and washer.

NOTE: it may be necessary to twist alternator towards fender to do this.

10. Remove alternator.
11. To install, reverse removal screws to 17-20 ft. lbs.

80 Amp H. D. Alternator

1. Disconnect the negative battery cable.
2. Disconnect all wiring connections from the alternator.
3. Loosen the belt tension adjusting bolts and remove the belt.

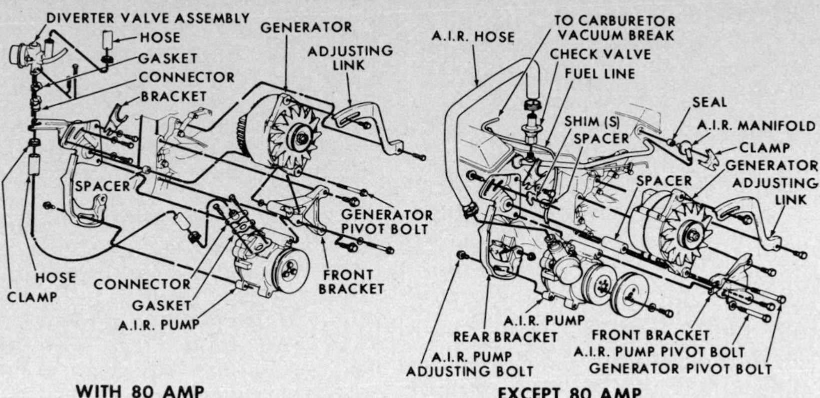

Alternator mounting positions (© Cadillac Div., G.M. Corp)

4. Remove the 2 nuts and lockwashers from the lower mounting bolts, leaving the bolts in place.
5. Remove the upper mounting bolt and remove the alternator by sliding it rearward off the lower mounting bolts.
6. Installation is the reverse of removal. Adjust the belt tension.

STARTING SYSTEM

For detailed testing and repair procedures consult the "Unit Repair Section."

Starter R & R

1. Disconnect the negative battery cable.
2. Disconnect the starter harness which is located at the right rear of the engine.
3. Raise the front of the car.
4. Remove the spring clip securing wire which is attached to the solenoid housing.
5. Remove the support bracket which holds the starter to the crankcase.
6. Remove the two screws which attach the starter to the crankcase.
7. Remove the starter from the car by first pulling it forward and then toward the right front wheel and then up over the steering linkage.
8. To install the unit, position it properly onto the engine crankcase and then tighten the attaching screws to 46 ft lbs.
9. Install the support bracket. Tighten the screws to 12 ft lbs and the nut to 6 ft lbs.
10. Install the spring clip and lower the car. Connect the starter harness and the negative battery cable.

IGNITION SYSTEM

The Eldorado distributor is constructed of aluminum alloy and positioned at the top left, front part of the engine. It is of a single point type with an internal vacuum advance. It is driven by a gear located on the camshaft; driving the distributor cam in a clockwise direction as viewed from the front of the engine compartment.

In 1974, GM "High Energy Ignition" (HEI) was offered as an option; it became standard equipment starting in 1975.

HEI is a breakerless system which has the coil and the control module integral with the distributor. For futher description as well as repair procedures, see "Electronic Ignition" in the unit repair section.

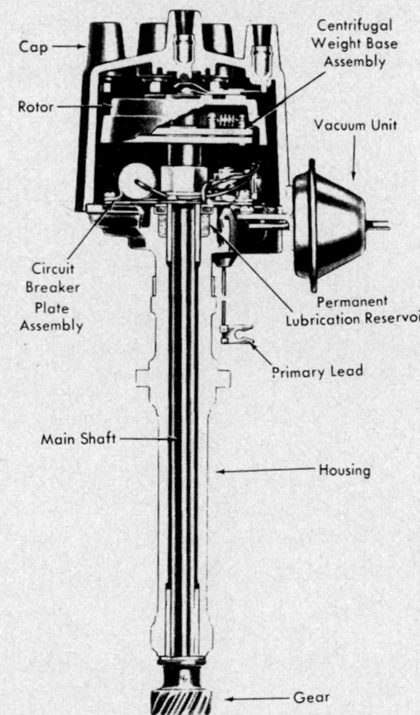

Conventional distributor showing major components (© Cadillac Div., G.M. Corp)

Contact Point Replacement and Adjustment—1969-74

1. Remove distributor cap by depressing and turning the retaining screws.
2. Remove the two rotor screws.
3. Remove condenser and primary leads from nylon insulated connection.
4. Loosen two screws holding base of contact assembly in place and remove points.
5. Inspect weight assembly, replace or lubricate as required.
6. Place new points under the two screws and tighten screws.
7. Connect the condenser and primary leads at the nylon insulated connection.

NOTE: be sure leads do not interfere with cap, weight base, or breaker advance.

8. Install rotor. Square and round lugs must be properly aligned.
9. With 1/8 in. Allen wrench, turn until points close while rubbing block is on high point of lobe. Then turn screw counterclockwise one-half turn.
10. Replace distributor cap.
11. With engine warmed up and at idle, set points to proper dwell angle.

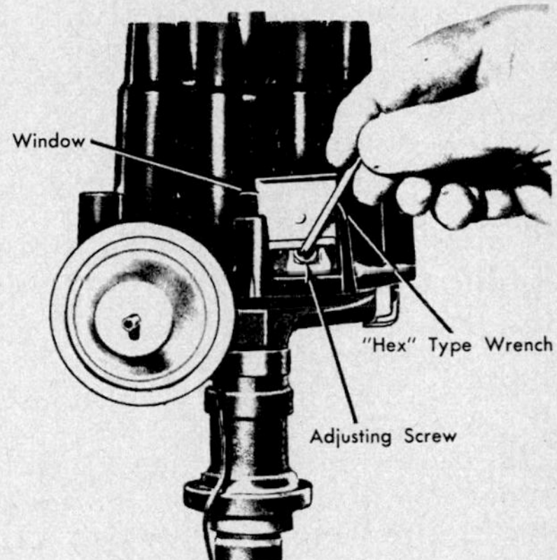

Adjusting distributor points (© Cadillac Div., G.M. Corp)

Distributor Removal

1. Remove distributor cap. Disconnect vacuum hose. Disconnect primary lead at the coil.
2. Crank the engine to top dead center for No. 1 cylinder. The pointer on the timing case cover will point to the O-mark on the crankshaft pulley and the rotor will face No. 1 plug wire on the cap.
3. Match-mark the vacuum advance unit to the cylinder block so that the distributor body will be correctly replaced at reassembly.
4. Remove hold-down clamp and lift the distributor straight up.

Distributor Installation

1. Install rubber seal-ring below distributor housing mounting flange.
2. Install the distributor so that the vacuum advance unit aligns with the match-mark made at removal. Turn the rotor slightly left of center so that as the gear engages the camshaft it will revolve into the proper position, pointing to No. 1 contact in the cap.

3. Install the distributor hold-down and connect the distributor lead to the coil.
4. Check the condition of the contact points and the breaker gap.
5. Install the cap and set the timing. (See "Ignition Timing.")
6. Reconnect the vacuum hose to the vacuum advance unit.

NOTE: if the engine has been cranked, remove No. 1 spark plug. Crank the engine until No. 1 piston is in firing position with the pointer and the O-mark on the crankshaft pulley aligned. Lower the distributor into position with the rotor pointing to No. 1 contact on the distributor cap.

Tachometer Hook-up to HEI Ignition

In the distributor cap, there is a "tach" terminal. Connect the tachometer to this terminal and to ground. Some tachometers must connect from the "tach" terminal to the battery positive (+) terminal; follow the manufacturer's instructions.

Caution Grounding the "tach" terminal could damage the HEI electronic module.

Ignition Timing

1. Loosen the distributor clamp enough to allow the distributor to be turned by hand without excessive looseness.
2. Disconnect the vacuum advance at the distributor and tape the end of the hose to prevent any air leaks.
3. Disconnect the parking brake vacuum hose at the diaphragm and tape the end.
4. Connect a timing light to the engine.
5. Connect a tachometer to the engine.

NOTE: Make sure that the timing mark on the pulley and the aligning plate on the front cover are clean.

6. Disconnect the automatic level control hose on cars so equipped.
7. Allow the engine to reach operating temperature.
8. Set the idle speed with the selector lever in Drive.
9. Set the timing to specifications. At the correct setting tighten the hold-down bolt of the distributor to 18 ft lbs. and recheck the timing.
10. Connect the 3 vacuum hoses and remove both the timing light and the tachometer from the engine.

FUEL SYSTEM

Mechanical Fuel Pump

The fuel pump is mounted on the left-front of the engine and is driven by an eccentric on the camshaft. The fuel filter is an integral part of the fuel pump on 1969-74 models. A strainer is also located behind the fuel inlet nut on the carburetor (this is the filter on 1975-76 models).

See the Cadillac section for filter replacement.

All air conditioned cars have a provision to return excess fuel vapor to the gasoline tank to prevent vapor lock under high temperature conditions. The line runs directly from the fuel pump.

Fuel Pump R & R

1. If equipped with A.I.R. system, it may be necessary to remove air pump and bracket for clearance.
2. Remove center coil wire.
3. Jack up the front of the car and support on axle stands so that pump can be removed from underneath.
4. Loosen two mounting bolts, or one bolt and one nut.
5. Turn over engine to relieve tension on pump arm.
6. Disconnect pump inlet and outlet lines. Plug inlet line.
7. Disconnect vapor return line on 1969 and later models.
8. Remove mounting bolts and fuel pump.
9. To install, reverse removal procedure.

Fuel Filter

See Cadillac section.

Thermal Vacuum Switch and Idle Speed-up Device

See Cadillac section.

Electric Fuel Pump

Models equipped with electronic fuel injection (EFI) have two electric fuel pumps. For fuel pump service on cars so equipped, see the Cadillac section.

Carburetor

Idle Speed and Mixture Adjustments

1969

Adjust with air cleaner removed.

1. Make sure PCV valve is free and working properly.
2. Disconnect parking brake vacuum hose at vacuum release cylinder and plug.
3. Connect a tachometer, set parking brake and allow engine to come up to normal operating temperature in Neutral.
4. Remove air cleaner and make sure dashpot is disengaged.
5. With wheels chocked, place transmission in Drive.
6. On 1968-69 cars, disconnect and plug distributor vacuum line.
7. Adjust air adjusting screw to obtain an idle speed of 550 rpm with A/C *off* for A.I.R. cars, 480-500 rpm with A/C *on* for non-A.I.R. cars.
8. NOTE: press down on brass hot idle compensator pin while making adjustments.
9. Set idle speed screw 1½ turns in after contacting primary lever, both mixture screws out 4 turns from seated position.
10. Turn one mixture screw clockwise to obtain highest tach reading. Continue to turn screw until speed falls off 20 rpm—this is the lean idle fall off point. Back off 1 turn.
11. Repeat Step 10, turning other mixture screw.
12. Reset idle speed as in Step 7, then repeat Steps 10 and 11 if speed exceeds 500 rpm for non-A.I.R. cars or 550 rpm for A.I.R. cars.
13. Install air cleaner and recheck idle speed.
14. Shut off engine, disconnect tach, reconnect parking brake vacuum line and distributor vacuum line on 1968-69 models.

1970

Adjust with air cleaner removed.

1. Disconnect and plug distributor vacuum advance line.
2. Disconnect and plug parking brake vacuum line at vacuum release cylinder.
3. Connect a tachometer, set parking brake and remove air cleaner.
4. Make sure dashpot is not touching linkage, then turn slow idle speed screw in approximately 1½ turns after it contacts primary throttle lever. Turn in both mixture screws until they seat gently, then unscrew them approximately 6 turns.
5. Place car in Drive after warming up engine. Turn off A/C.

NOTE: press down on hot idle compensator pin while making adjustments.

6. Adjust slow idle screw to obtain 620 rpm.
7. Turn one mixture screw clockwise until speed falls off 10 rpm, then repeat Steps 6 and 7 for other mixture screw. Idle speed now should be 600 rpm, indicating a 10 rpm drop per mixture needle.
8. Install air cleaner, shut off engine and disconnect tach.
9. Connect parking brake vacuum line and distributor vacuum line.

1971-1974

Adjust with air cleaner removed.

Idle speed is adjusted at a new anti-dieseling solenoid located where the dashpot was located in previous years. The throttle must be opened slightly to allow the plunger to move out all the way, then it must be closed against the now-extended solenoid plunger before making the idle speed adjustment. The solenoid plunger will retract when the ignition is shut off.

1. Disconnect and plug distributor vacuum advance hose and parking brake vacuum hose (at the release cylinder).
2. Connect a tachometer and set the parking brake with transmission in Neutral.
3. Remove the air cleaner and turn in mixture screws until they seat gently, then turn the screws out approximately 6 turns (4 turns, 1974).
4. Start engine and allow it to warm up.
5. Place car in Drive with A/C off.
6. Set idle speed to 620 rpm (640 rpm, 1974 by adjusting anti-dieseling solenoid. Tighten jam nut.
7. Alternately, turn each mixture screw clockwise ¼ turn at a time until idle speed reaches 600 rpm.
8. Disconnect wire that energizes solenoid. The plunger should retract to allow a slower idle speed of 350-400 rpm.
9. Shut off engine, disconnect tach, connect vacuum lines and solenoid wire and install air cleaner.

1975

1. Disconnect the hose from the parking brake vacuum release cylinder. Plug the hose.
2. Apply the parking brake. Block the wheels. Remove and plug the air leveling compressor hose at the air cleaner.
3. Connect a tachometer. Allow the engine to reach normal operating temperature. The choke should fully open and the cam follower should be off the fast idle cam completely.

Caution Do not allow the engine to idle or fast idle for excessive periods of time; catalyst damage could result.

4. Place the transmission in Drive and shut-off the air conditioner.
5. Adjust the idle speed screw to obtain 600 rpm (unless the mixture is to be adjusted).
6. Remove the air cleaner but leave its vacuum hoses connected.
7. Remove the limiter caps and screw both mixture screws out 5 turns from fully seated.
8. Set the idle speed to 650 rpm on 49-state cars or 620 rpm on California cars with the idle speed screw.
8. Use a hex-driver with an extension to turn in each mixture screw ¼-turn at a time until the normal idle speed of 600 rpm is obtained.
9. Shut off the engine. Install service replacement limiter caps on the idle mixture screws and install the air cleaner.
10. Remove the tachometer. Connect all the vacuum hoses.

Electronic Fuel Injection (EFI)

Starting 1975, electronic fuel injection (EFI) was offered as an option on all Cadillacs, including Eldorado models.

For a description of the EFI system, as well as adjustment and service procedures, see the Cadillac section.

COOLING SYSTEM

Eldorados use a sealed cooling system which maintains 15 lbs maximum pressure. The radiator is constructed with two vertical tanks that connect to the enclosed cross-flow tubing. The coolant enters the upper left-hand inlet tank and circulates through the cross-flow tubes and enters the right return tank.

Further information on the cooling system may be found in the Cadillac section under the same year model. Also, system capacities can be found in the "Capacities Table."

Radiator R & R

1. Remove the negative battery cable.
2. Open the drain plug on the radiator and drain the coolant. Remove the radiator cap so that the liquid flows more quickly.
3. Remove the hose clamps and remove the upper hose.
4. Remove the heater return hose which is located at the right radiator tank.
5. Disconnect the two transmission cooler lines from the bottom of the radiator. Plug the ends of the lines to prevent loss of fluid.
6. On the 1969-70 cars, remove the two top cradle clamps and then the three screws which fasten the finger guard to the cradle.
7. On 1971 through 1975 cars it is necessary to remove the screw which holds the upper radiator hose to the cover panel and then remove the cover panel by removing the six panel screws.
8. On 1971 through 1976 cars, remove the reservoir hose from the filler neck and the two straps from the top of the radiator.
9. Remove the radiator, being careful not to damage the radiator or the fan. Pull the unit straight up.
10. Installation is the reverse of removal.

Water Pump and Thermostat R & R

See the Cadillac section under the specific year.

EMISSION CONTROLS

The Cadillac Eldorado uses the same emission control systems as the rest of the Cadillac line.

For a description of these controls, as well as their removal and installation (where applicable), see Emission Controls in the Cadillac car section.

For emission control tests and adjustments, see Emission Control Systems in the Unit Repair Section.

ENGINE

1969 Eldorados use a 472 cu in. V8, while 1970-75 models use a longer stroke version displacing 500 cu in. All V8s in Cadillacs are overhead valve, 90° models. The five main bearing crankshaft uses shell type bearing inserts and end thrust is taken on the center main bearing. Cast aluminum pistons are used with 2 compression rings and 1 oil ring. To provide a non-scuffing surface during break-in, the pistons are tin plated. The camshaft is supported by five bearings and is driven through a timing chain from the crankshaft. Hydraulic valve lifters are used on all engines and the lifter plunger and body are selectively fitted in matched pairs.

On the Eldorado, special mounting brackets welded to the frame provide the front attaching points and a special crossmember is used for the rear mount.

Engine R & R

Caution If it is necessary to reposition the air conditioner compressor or the lines, do not disconnect the lines.

1. Follow Steps 1-16 of procedure in Cadillac Section.
2. Disconnect left exhaust pipe at manifold flange.
3. Remove screw that holds transmission cooler lines to motor mount.
4. Remove nut that secures dipstick tube to manifold. Remove the upper screw holding the steering gear flex coupling shroud to the frame.
5. Jack up car and remove the steering gear flex coupling shroud.
6. Remove starter motor.
7. Disconnect right exhaust pipe at manifold flange.
8. Remove transmission inspection cover.

9. Disconnect and plug vapor return line and fuel inlet at fuel pump.
10. Remove lower radiator hose at water pump.
11. Remove three screws that secure flex plate to converter.
12. Remove four screws that secure engine to transmission.
13. Remove front motor mount bolts and bolt that secures final drive to mount.
14. Remove right drive axle spindle nut and cotter pin.
15. Remove drive axle-to-output shaft screws and lockwashers.

NOTE: discard screws and washers. Have an assistant hold brake pedal to prevent shaft from turning.

16. Remove shaft support-to-engine bolts, and one support-to-brace screw.
17. Rotate inboard end of drive axle rearward toward starter motor.
18. Pull output shaft straight out, then lower and remove from underside of car. Proceed with engine removal procedure.
19. Lower car, install lifting bracket and chain hoist and place a wood-padded jack under the transmission pan.
20. Raise engine and pull forward to disengage transmission. Lift engine out of car.
21. To install, reverse removal procedure. See Cadillac Section for flex-plate alignment.

Manifolds

Intake Manifold R & R

With Carburetor

1. Remove the negative battery cable.
2. Remove the air cleaner, heat tube, crankcase breather, carburetor linkage, and the Cruise Control linkage.
3. Remove the coil wires or HEI connector and disconnect the SCS solenoid.
4. Remove the primary coil wire (if so equipped) and then remove the distributor cap.
5. Disconnect the single connector near the ignition coil and the green wire to the temperature sender.
6. Remove the two orange wires from the downshift switch and disconnect the antidieseling solenoid.
7. Remove the ignition coil (if so equipped) antidieseling solenoid, and the SCS solenoid.
8. Remove the power brake vacuum hose and the vacuum modulator hose which is located at the rear of the carburetor.
9. On air-conditioned cars, disconnect the compressor clutch electrical connection. Remove the vacuum hose for the air conditioner from the rear of the carburetor.
10. Remove the fuel line from the carburetor and remove the distributor vacuum advance at the carburetor.
11. Disconnect the PCV valve and remove the 12 manifold retaining bolts.
12. Remove the manifold. Also remove the inner manifold shield and gasket and the front and rear gaskets.
13. To reassemble reverse the above procedure.

With Electronic Fuel Injection (EFI)

For intake manifold removal and installation on 1975-76 models with electronic fuel injection, see the Cadillac section.

Cylinder Head Removal

NOTE: Care must be used when replacing cylinder-head bolts. They are of different lengths.

1. Remove intake manifold.
2. Drain engine coolant.
3. Disconnect ground strap at rear of cylinder heads from cowl. Disconnect wiring connector for high engine temperature warning system from sending unit at rear of left cylinder head.
4. Remove alternator and heater hose, if working on the right cylinder head, or partially remove the steering pump if working on the left head.
5. Disconnect AIR injection pump tubes from cylinder heads.
6. Remove clamps holding the wire harness to the cylinder heads and tie harness back out of the way.
7. Remove screws holding exhaust manifolds to cylinder heads.
8. Remove screws holding the rocker arm cover to the heads.
9. Remove the cover.
10. Remove the screws holding each rocker arm support to cylinder head, then remove rocker arm assemblies. Store these assemblies so that they may be reinstalled in their correct locations.
11. Remove pushrods and store them with their respective rocker arm assemblies.
12. Install two 7/16 x 6 in. screws to be used as lifting handles in two of the rocker arm support screw holes.
13. Remove ten cylinder-head bolts.
14. Lift cylinder head off the block.
15. Remove all gasket material from the cylinder head and block mating surfaces.

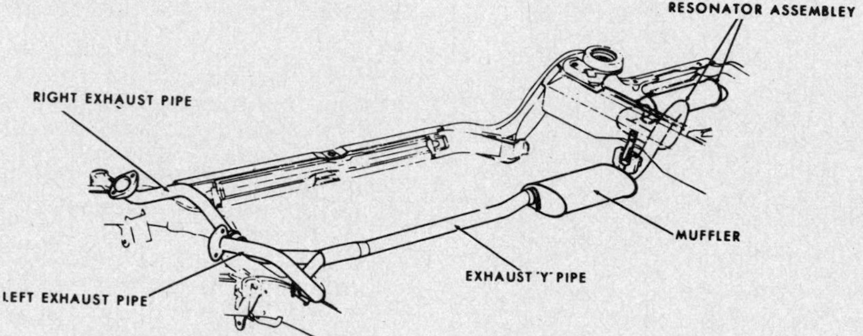

Typical Cadillac Eldorado exhaust system (1972 shown) (© Cadillac Div., G.M. Corp)

Exhaust Manifold R & R

1. If the work is to be done on the left-side manifold, remove the carburetor air cleaner and the heat duct. Remove the nuts from no. 2 and no. 6 cylinders and the heat shroud from around the manifold.
2. Remove the dipstick tube.
3. Release the eight securing screws, disconnect the manifold from the exhaust pipe, and remove the manifold. The 5th screw from the front may not be removable due to frame interference. Back it out and remove it with the manifold.
4. Use the same procedure for removing the other side.
5. Reassembly is the reverse of the above procedure.

Valve System

Rocker Arm R & R and Valve Adjustment

Valve rocker arms are mounted in pairs (four pairs to each cylinder head). They are of the modified pedestal-mounted type.

Rocker arms may be removed in pairs and do not require cylinder-head removal.

Torque rocker arm mounting screws to 60 ft lbs.

Cylinder Head Installation

When torquing the head bolts, use the three-step method. Starting from the middle of the center row of bolts and working outward (toward each end), torque the bolts to 1/3 of the total torque listed. Once this is done, repeat the same procedure, this time torquing all the bolts to 2/3 of the total listed torque. Finally torque the bolts to the recommended torque.

By using this procedure, head warping is eliminated. It ensures equal pressure on the head gasket over its entire surface.

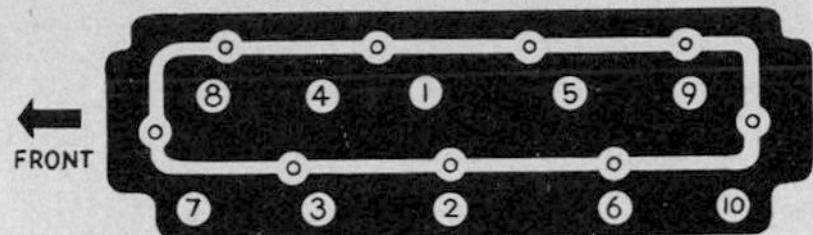

Cylinder head bolt tightening sequence
See text in "Cadillac" section for bolt location and length

Assembling Rod and Piston Assemblies to the Block

The numbers on the connecting rods face away from the camshaft; that is, the numbers on the left bank face to the left; the numbers on the right bank face to the right. As a double check, the word *rear*, (or "R"), stamped on the piston, faces the rear of the engine on both banks and an arrow on the piston top points to the front of the engine.

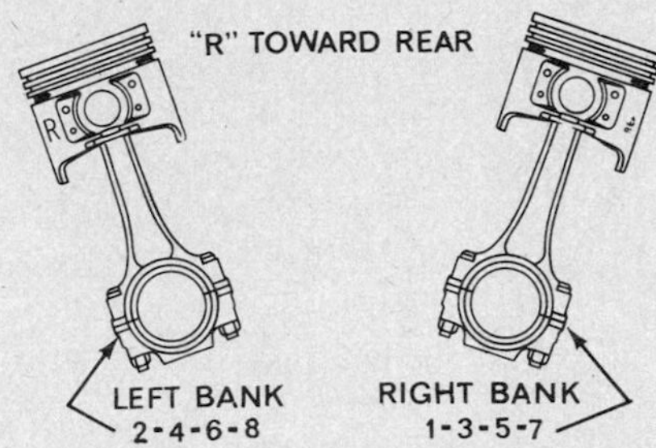

Piston-to-connecting rod relationship

Rear Main Bearing Oil Seal Replacement

1. Remove the oil pan, after removing spark plug, wires and plugs.
2. Remove the rear main bearing cap and loosen the bolts holding the other four bearings about three turns each. Remove the old rear main bearing seals.
3. Clean the groove in the cap and in the block. Lubricate seals with engine oil.
4. Make an installation tool, as illustrated.
5. Start the upper half into the groove in the block with the lip facing forward and rotate it into position, using the tool as a guide. Press firmly on both ends to be sure it is protruding uniformly on each side.
6. Install the lower half of the seal into the bearing cap with the lip facing forward and one end of the seal over the ridge and flush with the split line. Hold one finger over this end to prevent it from slipping, and push the seal into seated position by applying pressure to the other end. Be sure the seal is firmly seated and protrudes evenly on each side. Do not apply pressure to the lip. This may damage the effectiveness of the seal.
7. Apply rubber cement to the mating surfaces of the block and cap being careful not to get any cement on the bearing, the crankshaft or the seal. The cement coating should be about .010 in. thick.
8. Install the bearing cap, tightening the bolts with the fingers only.
9. Tighten the bearing bolts to 90-100 ft lbs. Be sure to tighten the bolts of the other four bearings also.
10. Reinstall the oil pan.

Timing Cover, Chain and Camshaft

Timing Cover, Chain and Sprockets R & R

The engine must be removed from the car before the front cover can be removed. The procedure is otherwise identical to that for the same year Cadillac as found in the Cadillac Section.

Camshaft R & R

See Cadillac section.

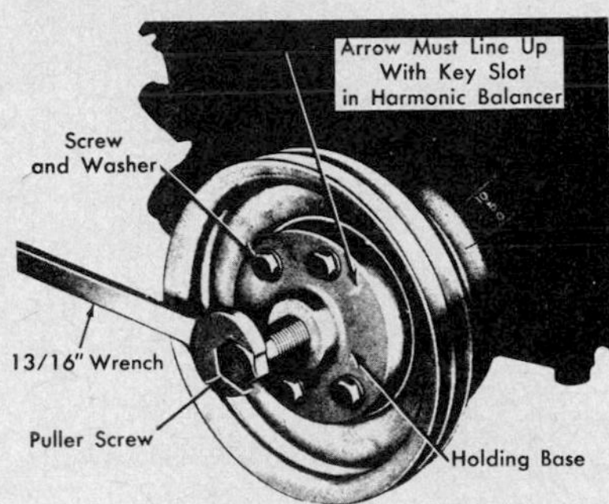

Balancer assembly removal
(© Cadillac Div., G.M. Corp)

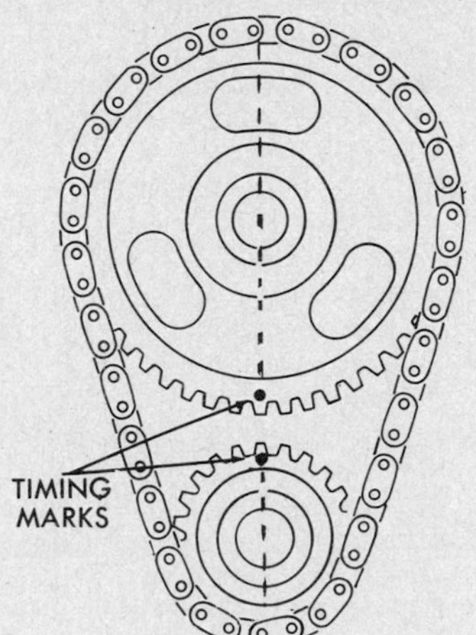

Timing sprocket location marks

Lubrication

Oil Pan Removal

1. Remove engine as previously described in Engine R & R.
2. Drain engine oil.
3. Remove the transmission lower cover.
4. Remove two brackets-to-block bolts on each side of engine front mounting support.
5. Remove nuts and cap screws that hold oil pan to cylinder block and engine front cover, then remove the oil pan.
6. Remove side gaskets and rubber front and rear seals from oil pan. Discard the gaskets and seals.
7. Install by reversing the removal procedure. Torque to 10 ft lbs.

Oil Pump Service

Removal, Inspection, Installation

1. Jack up car and remove oil filter.
2. Remove five capscrews that secure oil pump to engine.

NOTE: remove screw nearest pressure regulator last.

3. Slide drive shaft, drive gear and driven gear out of housing.
4. Remove plug from housing cover, using 5/16 in. wrench. Remove pressure regulator valve and spring.
5. Check free length of regulator spring—it should be 2.57-2.69 in.
6. Inspect gears and housing for burrs or scoring.
7. Check pump clearance limits.
8. Assembly, and installation is the reverse of disassembly and removal.

Oil Pump Specifications

Backlash between drive gears, 0.008-0.012 in. (through 1974) or 0.001-0.13 in. (1975 and later).
Clearance between body and shaft not to exceed 0.005 in.
Clearance between body and gears not to exceed 0.005 in.
Gear end-play not to exceed 0.006 in.

AUTOMATIC TRANSMISSION

The Turbo Hydra Matic transmission used on the Eldorado is a fully automatic transmission used for front wheel drive applications. It consists primarily of a three-element hydraulic torque converter, dual sprocket and link assembly, compound planetary gear set, three multiple-disc clutches, a sprag clutch, a roller clutch, two band assemblies, and an hydraulic control system.

Automatic Transmission R & R

Removal

1. Disconnect the battery.
2. Remove the hood.
3. Remove the transmission dipstick, then remove the bolt holding the filler tube bracket to exhaust manifold and remove the

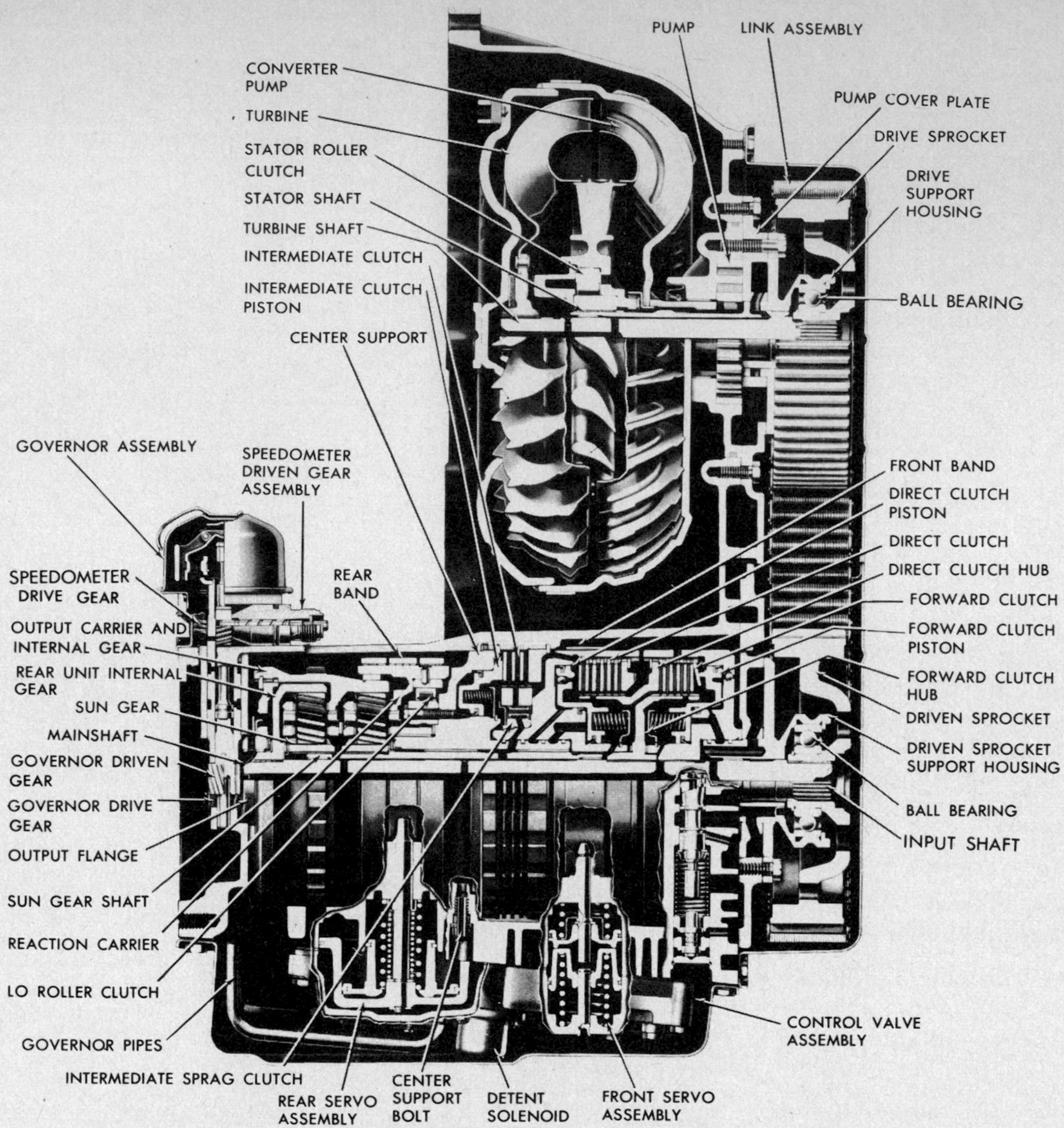

Turbo Hydra-Matic transmission components (© Cadillac Div., G.M. Corp)

filler tube. Discard the O-ring seal.

4. Remove bolts at locations A, B and C, holding the final drive case to the transmission. (See illustration).
5. Disconnect speedometer cable from the governor assembly, unplug T.C.S. wiring if so equipped and disconnect the detent solenoid.
6. Disconnect oil cooler pipes at the transmission and at the radiator. Cap the pipes and plug connector holes in transmission and radiator.
7. Remove bolt holding the cooler pipe bracket to final drive bracket and position pipes outboard of governor assembly.
8. Remove nut at location H, holding final drive to the transmission.
9. Remove bolts at locations I, J, K and L, holding transmission to engine and adapter plate.
10. Remove upper left bolt holding rear motor mount bracket to the transmission.
11. Remove bolt holding the ground strap to left side of cowl. Remove ground strap.
12. Remove upper left bolt holding converter cover plate to transmission, (use 7/16 in. socket with universal and extension to reach underneath the left exhaust manifold).

NOTE: loosen two screws holding A.L.C. compressor and position compressor out of the way.

13. Position cable with looped ends under engine intake manifold and hook looped ends to chain fall and cable, putting engine mounts under tension.
14. Position safety chain over top of transmission.
15. Raise car and place on jack stands, adjusting chain fall as necessary.
16. Disconnect leads from starter.
17. Remove bolt at location O holding starter motor to transmission case and remove the ground strap.
18. While holding the starter, remove bolt at location P and remove starter.
19. Remove three remaining screws holding the converter cover plate to the transmission and remove the cover plate.
20. Position transmission jack, equipped with front end drive transmission adapter plate to transmission and install nut and bolt holding adapter brace to transmission at starter motor lower mounting bolt hole.
21. Disconnect electrical connector from transmission.
22. Remove vacuum line from vacuum modulator.
23. Secure transmission to transmission jack with safety chain.
24. Remove three flexplate-to-converter attaching bolts.

Transmission attaching bolt location (© Cadillac Div., G.M. Corp)

25. Remove bolts at locations M and N holding transmission to engine and adapter plate.
26. Remove cotter pin securing relay rod to manual yoke on left side of transmission and separate rod from yoke.
27. Remove bolts at locations D, E and F and nut at location G holding final drive to transmission.

NOTE: position a clean drain pan under a point where transmission and final drive meet to avoid leakage onto floor when the two units are separated.

28. Remove five bolts and washers holding the rear of acromat to front crossbar and frame horns and allow acromat to hang free.
29. Through access holes in bottom of front crossmember, remove two nuts and studs. Turn steering wheel to left lock.
30. Have a helper, using a large pry bar, shift engine forward, while mechanic uses small pry bar to help separate transmission from engine and final drive.
31. Following initial separation, allow transmission to drain at the separation.
32. Remove two bolts on right side, holding the rear motor mount to the transmission.
33. Through access holes in the bottom of transmission support bar, remove two bolts, one on each side, holding the rear motor mounts to transmission support bar, and position motor mounts and bracket rearward to underbody.
34. While a helper pries and holds engine forward, move transmission rearward to disengage transmission case from dowels on engine adapter and to disengage final drive from studs on transmission case. Top of transmission should be tilted slightly rearward.
35. Slowly lower transmission, until converter is about half-way exposed from flexplate.
36. Install converter holding clamp, J-21366, using a 5/16 in.—18 nut to hold clamp screw to transmission case at location N.

Caution Converter holding clamp, J-21366, must be used to prevent the converter becoming disengaged when the transmission is removed.

37. Lower transmission from car.

Caution Rear motor mount bracket will follow transmission from car. To avoid damage or injury, remove bracket as soon as there is sufficient clearance.

38. Remove and discard final drive gasket and clean mounting surface of final drive.

Installation

1. Position transmission on jack, equipped with adapter plate, under the car.
2. Saturate new gasket with transmission fluid, then place gasket on final drive.
3. Position rear motor mount bracket on top of transmission support bar against underbody.
4. Raise transmission in place until converter is about half-way covered by flexplate, then remove converter holding clamp from transmission.
5. While helper pries engine forward with a pry bar, continue raising transmission, making sure the top of the transmission case clears splined input shaft of final drive, and position to engine.
6. Align the engine to the final drive, with the assistance of a helper by watching the following items:
   A. Studs on transmission case to mounting holes in final drive.
   B. Guide holes in transmission case to dowels on adapter.
   C. Internal flange on final drive to transmission.

Caution Since engagement of splined final drive input shaft to transmission is hidden, care must be taken to avoid damaging transmission or final drive assembly.

   D. To help engagement of final drive splines, rotate one front wheel while helper holds the other.

NOTE: when alignment is complete and correct, the gap between the final drive and transmission should not exceed ¼ in.

7. Loosely install bolts at locations D and F attaching transmission to final drive and bolt at location N attaching transmission to engine through adapter, alternately tightening bolts to avoid cocking the transmission. Do not torque bolts.
8. Working in the engine compartment, loosely install bolt at location J attaching transmission to adapter. Do not torque at this time.
9. Install bolt at location M holding transmission to adapter plate. Do not torque.
10. Position rear motor mount bracket to transmission and loosely install three bolts holding bracket to transmission.

NOTE: upper left bolt is installed from engine compartment.

11. Position rear engine mounts and bracket to transmission support bar, and loosely install bolts through access holes in bottom of bar, attaching mounts to bar.
12. Reposition engine assembly, as necessary, and install left bolt securing front motor mount to front cross bar. Torque front motor mount bolts to 30 ft. lbs.
13. Separate safety chain, remove nut and bolt securing jack adapter plate to transmission case and remove jack.
14. Torque the following bolts as specified:
    A. Rear engine mounts to transmission support bar, 55 ft. lbs.
    B. Rear engine mounts to transmission (two on right side), 55 ft. lbs.
    C. Transmission to adapter to engine, 30 ft. lbs.
    D. Transmission to adapter (location M), 30 ft. lbs.

Caution The following procedure for attaching the converter to the flexplate must be strictly followed to prevent improper installation and damage to flexplate and transmission.

15. Rotate converter until two of the three weld nuts on the converter line up with two of the three bolt holes in the flexplate. Position converter so that weld nuts are flush with flexplate. Be sure converter is not cocked and that pilot in center of converter is properly seated in crankshaft.
16. Install two flexplate to converter attaching bolts through access holes in flexplate and torque to 28 ft. lbs.

NOTE: bolts must be tightened at this time to assure proper alignment of converter.

17. Rotate flexplate and converter until third bolt hole is accessible. Install third bolt and torque to 28 ft. lbs.
18. Install vacuum hose on vacuum modulator assembly.
19. Install electrical connector to transmission connector.
20. Position converter cover plate to transmission case and install two lower and one upper right bolts holding the cover plate to the transmission. Torque to 5 ft. lbs.
21. Position the starter to the transmission case and install bolt at P position.
22. Position ground strap to transmission and install bolt holding the ground strap and starter to the transmission at location O. Torque bolts at locations O and P to 25 ft. lbs.
23. Install leads to starter motor.
24. Install bolts at locations C and E and a nut at G holding transmission to final drive.
25. Torque bolts at locations C through F to 25 ft. lbs.
26. Position acromat to front cross bar and frame horns and install five retaining bolts and washers.
27. Position relay rod to manual yoke and secure with a cotter pin.
28. Check operation of manual linkage and adjust, if necessary.
29. Disconnect chain fall and lower the car.
30. Remove cable from intake manifold and safety chain from transmission.
31. Install bolts at locations A and B and nut at location H holding transmission to final drive. Torque bolts to 25 ft. lbs.
32. Install upper left bolt holding converter cover plate to transmission in the manner described for removing it, the reversal of Step 12.
33. Install bolts at locations I, K and L, holding transmission to engine and adapter.
34. Torque bolts at locations I, J, K and L to 25 ft. lbs.
35. Tighten brass cooler pipe connectors at case to 28 ft. lbs. Clean connections and connect cooler pipes at transmission, using cooler pipe wrench J-21477. Torque to 28 ft. lbs.
36. Connect oil cooler pipes to radiator with the same wrench. Torque to 40 ft. lbs.
37. Install cooler pipe clamp.
38. Install speedometer cable to governor.
39. Install new O-ring on transmission filler tube and install filler tube through hole in final drive case.
40. Position transmission filler tube bracket to exhaust manifold and install retaining bolt.
41. Install body ground strap to firewall and secure it with a nut.
42. Connect battery.
43. Bring transmission to fluid level. Bring engine to operating temperature, then recheck fluid level.
44. Thoroughly check entire power train for oil and coolant leaks.
45. Install and align hood assembly.

Neutral Safety Switch, All Models

NOTE: switch is on steering column under dash.

Removal

1. Position the gear selector in the Neutral positon.
2. Release the clamp and remove the switch without moving the contact carrier. The position of the carrier should be marked.
3. Remove the vacuum hoses after they have been marked and disconnect the two wires from the switch.
4. Installation is accomplished by reversing the above procedure.

Adjustment

1. Check that the gear lever is correctly adjusted and that the neutral safety switch is properly positioned by this check.
2. Set the handbrake. Put the hand lever on the steering column in drive. Hold the ignition key on and slowly move the hand lever toward Neutral or Park until the starter cranks and the engine runs.
3. Without moving the lever farther, press the accelerator to determine whether the transmission is really in Neutral or Park.
4. If all is correct, the engine will start wih the lever in Park. The transmission will not be in gear. Also, back-up lights will go on with transmission in Reverse.

NOTE: a vacuum leak that can be corrected by moving shift lever is an indication that the switch only needs adjustment and is not defective.

5. Adjust the neutral safety switch by turning it and its mounting bracket until the above conditions are met.

Shift Linkage Adjustment

1. Place the transmission shift valve into the Park position and then move the relay rod to the Neutral step which is the third one in the downward position.
2. Loosen the adjusting screw on the relay lever and place the selector lever in the Neutral detent position.
3. Tighten the relay rod adjusting screw with the shift lever held against the neutral stop.
4. Check the adjustment by:
   a. Moving the selector lever to the Neutral detent making sure that the lever fits securely into the notch on the steering column.
   b. Move the lever to Drive. Make sure that the lever is secure in this gear. Move the lever to Reverse and check for gear security.

Caution When the linkage is adjusted check the operation of the Neutral Safety Switch, parking brake release and the back-up lights.

Kickdown Adjustment

1. Remove the air cleaner.
2. Make certain that the idle speed is set correctly and that the carburetor is operating on the low-speed circuit.
3. Loosen the switch mounting screws and insert a 0.094 in. wire gauge into the hole in the lower wire terminal.
4. With the gauge in place, adjust the position of the switch so that the lever just touches the carburetor adaptor plate arm. The switch should make contact above 60° of throttle opening.
5. After adjusting, tighten the mounting screws and remove the gauge.
6. Reinstall the air cleaner.

Pan Removal and Installation, Fluid Change

1. Remove the transmission dipstick.
2. Insert a rubber hose attached to a suction gun into the filler tube. Remove enough fluid to prevent the pan from overflowing when it is removed.
3. Raise the car and support it securely. Place a container under the transmission pan to catch fluid.
4. Remove the pan and gasket. Throw the old gasket away. Drain and clean the pan.

Installation is as follows:

1. Place a new gasket on the pan and install the pan. Tighten the attaching screws to 12 ft lbs.

2. Lower the car.
3. Add 4 qts of DEXRON® transmission fluid through the filler tube.
4. Start the engine and run it at 800 rpm for 1½ minutes with the gear selector in Park (P).
5. Return the engine speed to idle. Check the level and add fluid as necessary. The level should be between *add* and *full*.

Filter Replacement

1. Remove the transmission pan.
2. Remove the intake pipe/filter assembly.
3. Remove the intake pipe O-ring and discard it.
4. Insert a new O-ring in the pipe bore.
5. Install a new intake pipe/filter assembly in the pipe bore.
6. Install the pan and add fluid.

Drive Sprocket

If it should be necessary to replace either the drive sprocket, chain, or driven sprocket, the three unit combination must be replaced as a set. They are matched and are not to be serviced separately.

Removal

1. Remove 18 cover housing attaching bolts.
2. Remove cover housing and gasket. Discard the gasket.
3. Install J-4646 snap-ring pliers into sprocket bearing retaining snap-rings located under the drive and driven sprockets and remove snap-rings from retaining grooves in support housings.

Removing sprocket snap-ring
(© Cadillac Div., G.M. Corp)

NOTE: do not remove snap-rings from beneath the sprockets. Leave them in a loose position between the sprockets and the bearing assemblies.

4. Remove drive and driven sprockets, link assemblies, bearings and shaft simultaneously by alternately pulling upward on the drive and driven sprockets until the bearings are out of the drive and driven support housings.

NOTE: it may be necessary to pry up on the sprockets. Use care.

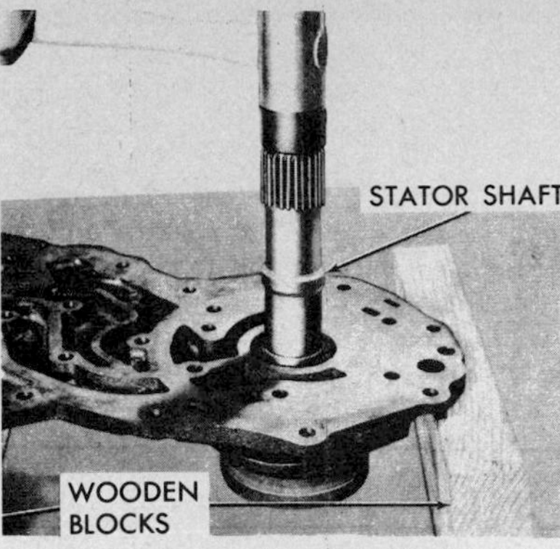

Removing the drive sprocket support
(© Cadillac Div., G.M. Corp)

Removing tight sprockets
(© Cadillac Div., G.M. Corp)

Caution Do not pry on the guide links or the aluminum case. Pry only on the sprockets.

5. Remove link assembly from drive and driven sprockets.

Removing sprockets and link assembly
(© Cadillac Div., G.M. Corp)

6. Remove two hook type oil seal rings from turbine shaft.
7. Inspect drive and driven sprocket bearing assemblies for rough or defective bearings.

NOTE: do not remove bearing assemblies from drive or driven sprockets unless they need replacement.

8. If removal of bearing assembly from drive and/or driven sprockets is necessary, proceed as follows:
   A. Remove sprocket to bearing assembly retaining snap-ring using tool J-5589, snap-ring pliers.

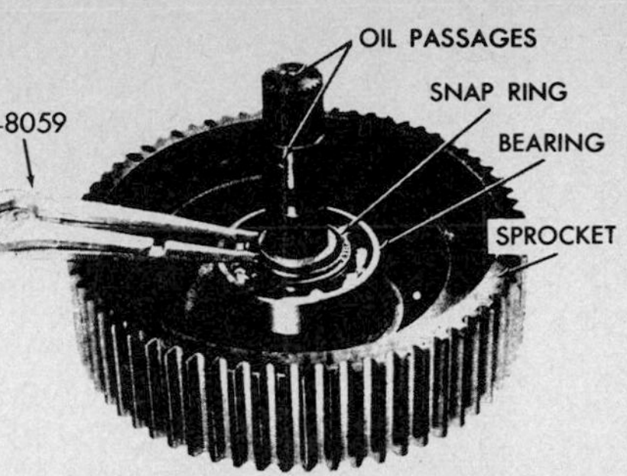

Removing sprocket bearing snap-ring
(© Cadillac Div., G.M. Corp)

   B. Mount sprocket with turbine or input shaft placed in hole in work bench on two 2 x 4 x 10 in. pieces of wood.
   C. With a hammer and brass rod, drive the inner race alternately through each of the access openings until the bearing assembly is removed from the sprocket hub. Drive the sprocket, and turbine shaft and link assembly.

Inspection

1. Inspect drive sprocket teeth for nicks, burrs, scoring, gauling and excessive wear.
2. Inspect drive sprocket to ball bearing retaining snap-ring for damage.
3. Inspect drive sprocket ball bearing inner race mounting surface for damage.
4. Inspect turbine shaft for open lubrication passages. Run a tag wire through the passages to be sure they are open.
5. Inspect spline for damage.
6. Inspect the ground bushing journals for damage.
7. Inspect the two hook-type oil seal grooves for damage or excessive wear.
8. Inspect the turbine shaft for cracks or distortion.
9. Inspect the link assembly for damage or loose links.

NOTE: take particular notice of the guide links. They are the wide outside links on each side of the link assembly.

Driven Sprocket at Input Shaft

Inspection

1. Inspect driven sprocket teeth for nicks, burrs, scoring, gauling and excessive wear.
2. Inspect sprocket to ball bearing retaining snap-ring for damage.
3. Inspect ball bearing inner race mounting surface for damage.
4. Inspect input shaft for open lubrication holes. Run a tag wire through the holes to be sure they are open.
5. Inspect spline for damage.
6. Inspect ground bushing journals for damage.

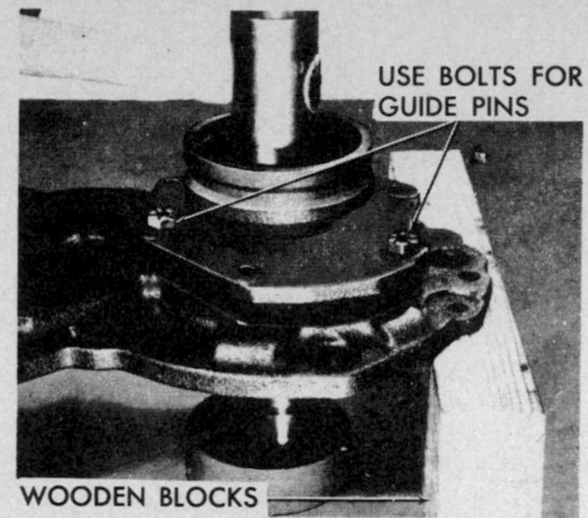

Installing driven sprocket support
(© Cadillac Div., G.M. Corp)

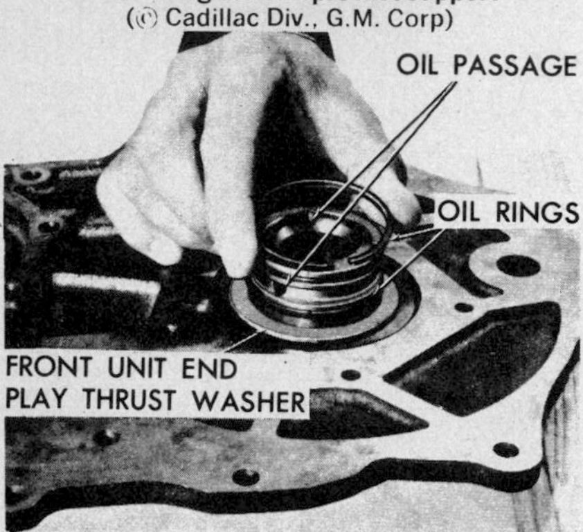

Installing oil rings on driven sprocket support
(© Cadillac Div., G.M. Corp)

Sprocket Bearings

Installation

1. Turn sprocket so that turbine or input shaft is pointing upward.
2. Install new sprocket bearing as follows:
   A. Install snap-ring, letter side down on shaft.
   B. Assemble bearing assembly on turbine or input shaft.
   C. Using a piece of pipe, drive the bearing assembly onto the hub of the sprocket until it is resting on the bearing seat of the sprocket.
   D. Install sprocket to bearing assembly retaining snap-ring into groove sprocket hub.
3. Install two hook-type oil seal rings on turbine shaft.

Front Unit End-Play Check

Make front unit end-play check as follows:

A. Install front unit end-play checking tool J-22241 into driven sprocket housing so that the urethane on the tool can engage the splines and the forward clutch housing. Let the tool bottom on the main shaft and then withdraw it approximately 1/16-⅛ in.

B. Remove two of the 5/16—18 bolts from the driven support housing.

C. Install 5/16—18 threaded hammer bolt with jam nut into one bolt hole in driven support housing.

NOTE: do not thread slide hammer bolt deep enough to interfere with forward clutch travel.

D. Mount dial indicator on rod and index indicator to register with the forward clutch drum that can be reached through second bolt removed from driven support housing.

E. Push end-play tool down to remove slack.

F. Push and hold output flange outward. Place a screwdriver in case opening at parking area and push upward on output carrier.

G. Place another screwdriver between the metal lip of the end-play tool and the drive sprocket housing. Now push upward on the metal lip of the end-play tool and read the resulting end-play. This should be between .003-.024 in. The selective washer controlling this end play is the phenolic thrust washer located between the driven support housing and the forward clutch housing. If more or less washer thickness is required to bring the end-play within specifications, select the proper washer from the chart.

U-JOINTS

See Drive Axle.

DRIVE AXLES

Drive axles are a complete flexible assembly and consist of an axle shaft and an inner tri-pot joint and outer constant velocity joint. The inner tri-pot joint has complete flexibility, plus inward and outward movement. The outer constant velocity joint has complete flexibility at the angle of operation.

Drive Axle—Right Side

Removal—1969-71

1. Hoist car under lower control arms.

NOTE: battery should be disconnected.

2. Remove drive axle, cotter pin, nut and washer.
3. Using a wood-padded hammer, tap on end of drive axle to unseat axle at hub assembly.

NOTE: install a piece of rubber hose over torsion bar connector at lower control arm to prevent *seal* damage.

4. Remove inner constant velocity joint attaching bolts.

NOTE: Disconnect tie-rod end at steering knuckle and disconnect upper ball joint before proceeding to Step 5.

5. Remove two output shaft support-to-engine bolts and one support-to-brace screw.
6. Rotate inboard end of axle rearward toward starter motor.
7. Slide output shaft straight out and remove.
8. Rotate drive axle inboard and toward front of car, guiding over front crossmember.

Removal 1972-1976

1. Remove the negative battery cable and the wheel disc.
2. If the drive axle is to be removed, release the cotter pin and loosen but do not remove the spindle nut.
3. Raise the car at the lower control arms.
4. Loosen but do not remove the right front shock absorber lower mounting nut. Then pry the shock absorber along the lower mounting stud until it reaches the nut. Do not remove the shock absorber from the lower mount.
5. To keep the torsion bar connectors from being damaged, cover them with a short length of rubber hose.

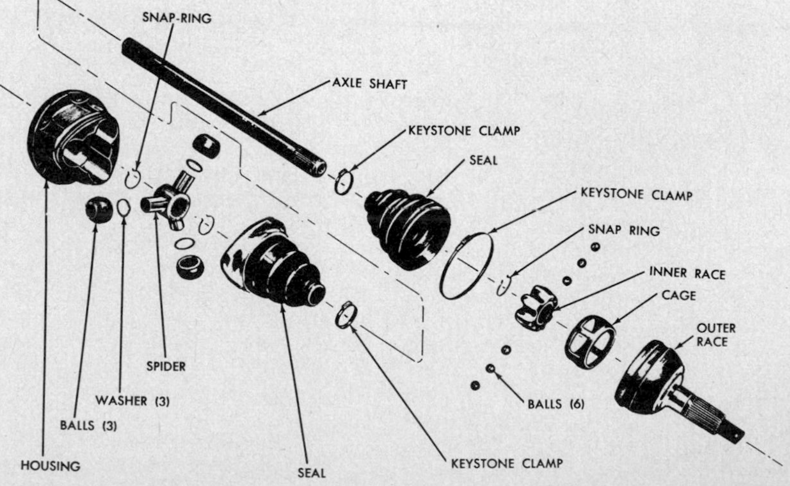

Drive axle—exploded view (© Cadillac Div., G.M. Corp)

6. Remove the screws securing the drive axle to the output shaft.
7. Position the inside end of the drive axle toward the starter motor to gain access to the output shaft. Then remove the screw which supports the output shaft to the final drive housing.
8. Remove the two screws which support the right output shaft support to the engine.
9. Remove the output shaft, support, and strut as an assembly in the following manner.
   a. Slide the output shaft outward to disengage the splines.
   b. Move the inside end of the assembly forward and downward until it is clear of the car.
10. If the drive axle is to be removed, use the following procedure.
   a. Using a hammer and a wooden block tap the end of the drive axle to unseat the axle at the hub.

NOTE: The spindle nut should be loosened but not removed.

   b. Rotate the axle inward and toward the front of the car positioning the axle over the front crossmember and out from under the car.

Caution Care must be exercised so that constant velocity joints do not turn to full extremes, and that seals are not damaged against shock absorber or stabilizer bar.

Installation—1969-76

1. Carefully place right-hand drive axle assembly into lower control arm and enter outer race splines into knuckle.
2. Lubricate final drive output shaft seal, with wheel bearing grease.
3. Install right-hand output shaft into final drive and attach the support bolts to engine and brakes. Torque the bolts to 50 ft. lbs.
4. Install brace.
5. Move right-hand drive axle assembly toward front of car and align with right-hand output shaft. Install attaching bolts and torque to 65 ft. lbs.
6. Install washer and nut on drive axle.
7. Remove floor stands and lower hoist.
8. Tighten wheel lugs to 105 ft. lbs. and drive axle nut to 105–110 ft, lbs., (1972-76 to 150 ft lbs.) Install cotter pin.

Drive Axle—Left Side

Removal and Installation

1. Hoist car under lower control arms.
2. Remove wheel and tire.
3. Remove drive axle cotter pin, nut and washer.
4. Install a piece of rubber hose over lower control arm torsion bar connector.
5. Remove six drive axle-to-output shaft screws and washers.
6. Loosen upper shock mounting bolt. Disconnect stabilizer bar link up to 1970.
7. Remove upper control arm ball joint cotter pin and nut.
8. Using hammer and brass drift, drive on knuckle until upper ball joint stud is free.
9. Remove brake hose bracket.
10. Tip upper part of knuckle and support outward so that brake hose is not damaged.
11. Carefully guide drive axle assembly outboard.

NOTE: care must be exercised so that constant velocity joints do not turn to full extremes and that seals are not damaged against shock absorber or stabilizer bar.

12. To install, reverse removal procedure. Tighten upper shock bolt to 75 ft. lbs., drive axle and wheel lug nuts to 105-110 ft. lbs., and output shaft-to-axle screws to 65 ft. lbs.

Constant Velocity Joint (Out of Car)

The constant velocity joints are to be replaced as a unit and are only disassembled for repacking and replacement of seals.

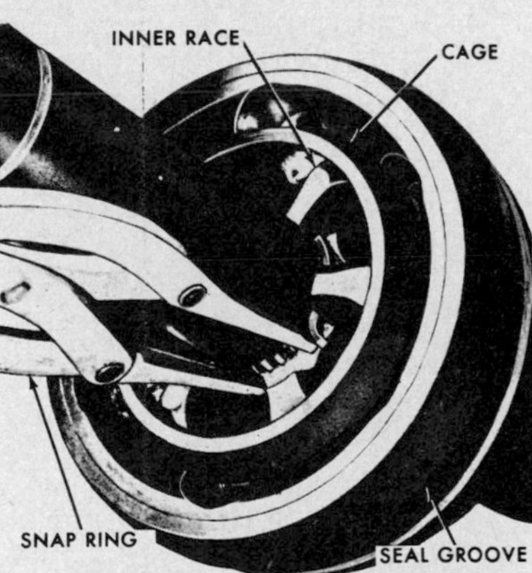

Removing outer axle joint
(© Cadillac Div., G.M. Corp)

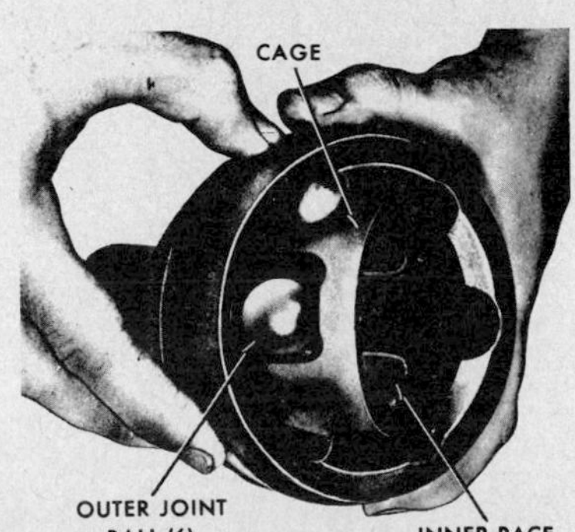

Removing balls from outer joint
(© Cadillac Div., G.M. Corp)

Outer C.V. Joint Disassembly

1. Insert axle assembly in vise. Hold by the mid-portion of the axle shaft.
2. Remove inner and outer seal clamps.
3. Slide seal down axle shaft to gain access to C. V. joint.
4. Using snap-ring pliers, spread retaining ring until C. V. joint can be removed from axle spline.
5. Remove retaining ring.
6. Slide seal from axle shaft.
7. Remove grease from constant velocity joint.
8. Holding constant velocity joint with one hand, tilt cage and inner race so that one ball can be removed. Continue until all six balls are removed.
9. Turn cage 90° and with large slot in cage aligned with land in outer race, lift out.

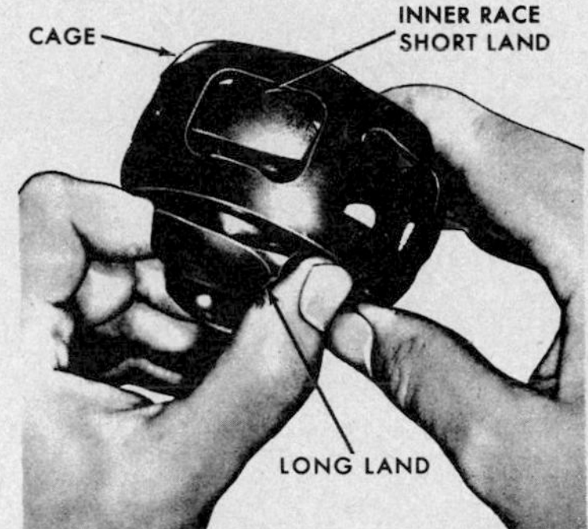

Removing inner race from cage
(© Cadillac Div., G.M. Corp)

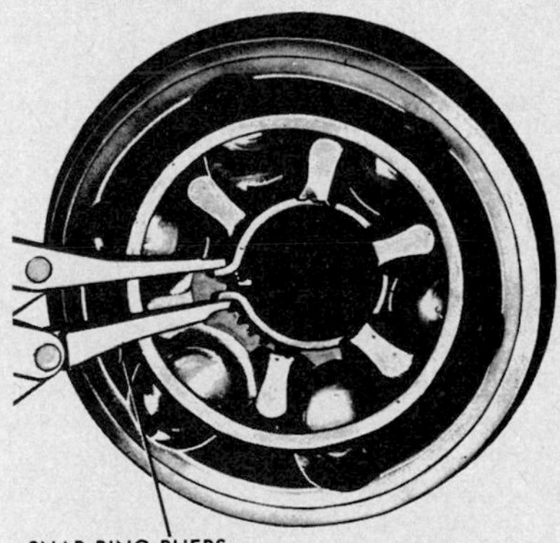

Removing inner race snap-ring
(© Cadillac Div., G.M. Corp)

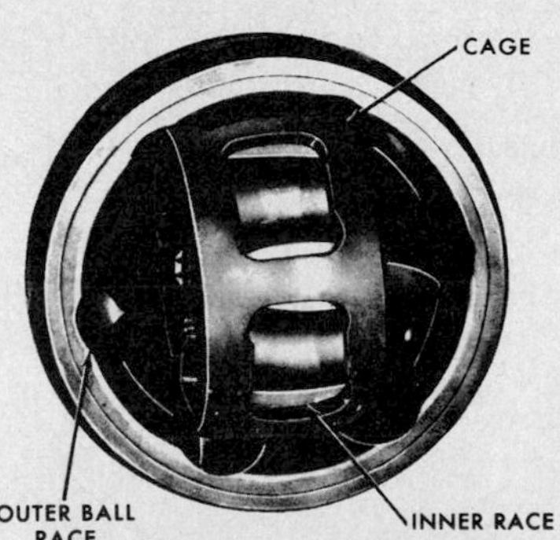

Removing cage and inner race
(© Cadillac Div., G.M. Corp)

10. With cage and inner race assembly, turn inner race 90° to align with large hole in cage. Lift land on inner race up through large hole in cage and turn up and out to separate parts.

Assembly

1. Insert land of inner race into large hole in cage and pivot to install in cage.
2. Align inner race and pivot inner race 90° to align in outer race.
3. Insert balls into outer race one at a time until all six balls are installed. Inner race and cage will have to be tilted so that each ball can be inserted.
4. Pack constant velocity joint full of lubricant (Part No. 1050530).
5. Pack inside of seal with the same lubricant, until folds of seal are full.
6. Place small keystone clamp on axle shaft.
7. Install seal onto axle shaft.
8. Install retaining ring into inner race.
9. Insert axle shaft into splines of outer constant velocity joint until retaining ring secures shaft.
10. Position seal in slot of outer race.
11. Install large keystone clamp over seal and secure.

Inner Tri-pot Joint Disassembly

1. Insert axle assembly in vise. Clamp on mid-portion of axle shaft.
2. Remove small seal clamp.
3. Remove large end of seal from C. V. joint by prying out peened spots and driving off C. V. joint with hammer and chisel.
4. Slide the seal and adapter down the axle shaft until the tri-pot joint is exposed.

NOTE: the tri-pot housing is now free to slide off the joint. Use care to prevent the spider leg balls from sliding off the spider legs. Each leg ball contains multiple bearing rollers.

5. Cup one hand under the tri-pot joint to prevent dropping spider leg balls and rollers while sliding housing off of joint.
6. Remove spider leg ball.
7. Remove O-ring seal from outer housing.
8. Wipe excess grease from outer housing to gain access to snap ring and remove spider outer snap-ring.
9. With a plastic hammer, tap alternately on spider legs to drive spider off shaft.
10. Remove spider inner snap-ring.
11. Slide seal off axle shaft.
12. Remove rollers from spider leg balls.

Caution Do not lose any of the needle bearings in the spider leg balls.

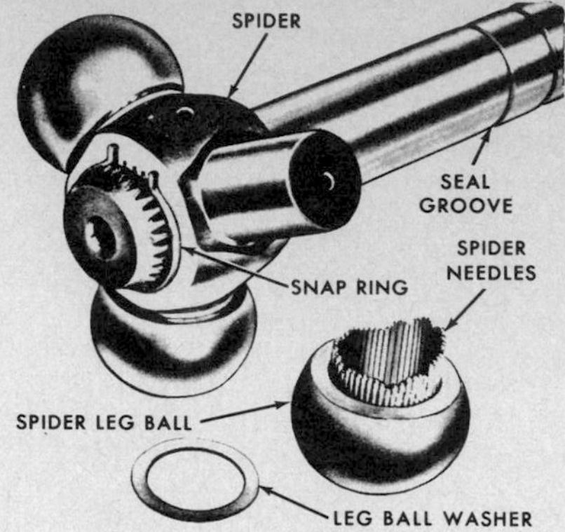

Assembly

1. Insert axle assembly in a vise. Hold by mid-portion of axle shaft.
2. Place small keystone clamp on axle shaft.
3. Position seal on shaft.
4. Place spider inner snap-ring in position on shaft.
5. Apply lubricant to axle and the spider splines.
6. Align spider on axle shaft.
7. With a plastic hammer, tap alternately on spider legs to drive spider into position on axle shaft.
8. Install spider outer snap-ring on axle shaft.
9. Place O-ring on tri-pot joint housing.
10. Apply a thin coat of lubricant to inner race of leg balls, and install leg ball rollers.
11. Apply lubricant to spider leg balls and legs.
12. Remove axle from vise then install washers and three spider leg balls, one at a time as a unit on the spider.

NOTE: when installing leg balls, use the leg ball washers as retainers for the spider rollers.

13. Pack inside of seal with special drive axle joint lubricant until the folds of the seal are full.
14. Pack housing with special drive axle joint lubricant and install by sliding housing over spider leg balls.
15. Position seal adapter over lip on joint housing and stake with blunt chisel.
16. Seat seal in groove on axle shaft, and secure keystone clamps.

JACKING, HOISTING

When jacking the front of the vehicle, make certain that the jack is placed so that it contacts the lower suspension arm just inside the stabilizer bar. If the vehicle is lifted from the rear, place the jack as far in to the middle of the frame as possible so that the Automatic Level Control and the fuel and brake lines are not damaged.

Ideally, the best lift is one which contacts both the front and rear suspension at the same time.

Caution The rear lower control arm should never be used as a lift point for the vehicle.

When working on the vehicle in the

Front jacking position
(© Cadillac Div., G.M. Corp)

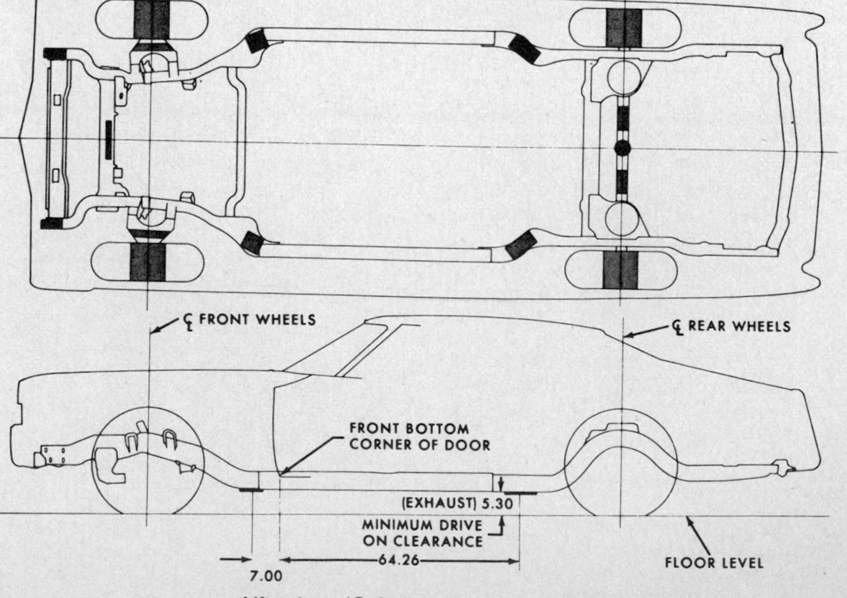

Lift points (© Cadillac Div., G.M. Corp)

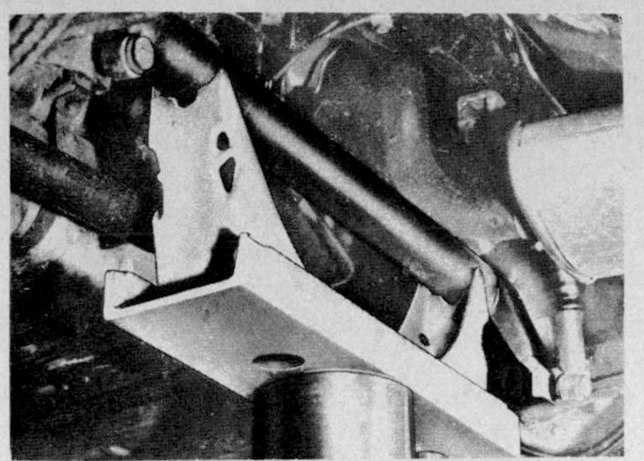

Rear jacking position
(© Cadillac Div., G.M. Corp)

raised position, it is recommended that two jackstands be placed under the front frame crossmember. Also, the vehicle should never be supported at the very ends of the frame with anything other than the jack provided with the car.

DIFFERENTIAL

A bevel gear-type differential is used on all front wheel drive models. This design supersedes the original planetary-type final drive. While unit removal and installation procedures are typical, the assembly, or its components are not interchangeable with the earlier design.

Overheauling the differential assembly is not recommended. Cadillac recommends that the unit be serviced by replacement only.

Output Shafts, Bearings and Seals

Right Side Shaft Removal

1. Disconnect battery.
2. Hoist car and remove the wheel.
3. Place a short length of rubber hose over control arm torsion bar connector.
4. Disconnect right-hand drive axle from the output shaft.
5. Disconnect support from engine and brace. Loosen lower shock bolt.
6. Rotate the inside end of the drive axle toward the starter motor and slide the output shaft straight out toward the side of the car.
7. When the splined end has cleared the drive unit, tilt and remove it from the underside of the car. Be careful not to damage the drive oil seal.
8. If seal is to be removed, pry it out with a large screwdriver.
9. If output shaft bearing is to be removed, it can be removed as follows:
   a. Remove three self-tapping screws that secure bearing retainer.
   b. Clamp output shaft in a vise.
   c. Make two steel plates ¼x3x8 in. and install as illustrated.
   d. Install four ⅜—24 bolts about 5 in. long through output shaft flange.
   e. Tighten bolts alternately and bearing will be forced from its seat.

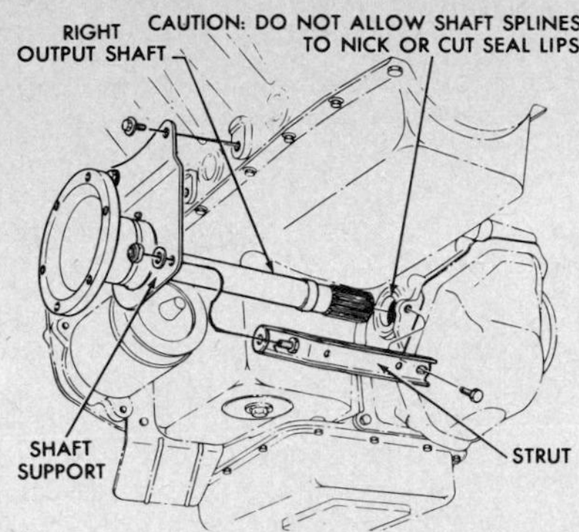

Output shaft, right-side
(© Cadillac Div., G.M. Corp)

Installation

1. If output bearing was removed, assemble parts as illustrated.
2. Position assembly in a press and install bearing until seated.
3. Pack area between bearing and retainer with wheel bearing grease, then install slinger.
4. If seal was removed, it can now be installed.
5. Apply special seal lubricant to output shaft seal, then install output shaft into final drive, indexing the splines of both units.
6. Install support to engine and brace bolts.

NOTE: seat washers in old grooves in output shaft support to ensure output shaft alignment. If new support is installed, carefully center output shaft in support with bolts loosely installed, then tighten bolts to 50 ft. lbs. Do not allow shaft to hang unsupported in final drive.

7. Connect drive axle to output shaft. Tighten screws to 65 ft. lbs.
8. Remove protective rubber hose.
9. Connect battery, check engine oil level and check for oil leaks.

Left Side Shaft Removal

1. Remove the cotter pin from the drive spindle and loosen the spindle nut.
2. Raise the car. Remove the wheel and the drive spindle nut.
3. Remove the left drive axle. (See "Left Drive Axle Removal.")
4. Remove the bolt which holds the left-hand output shaft.
5. Remove the output shaft by pulling it out in the same manner as was used in the right side removal procedure.

Installation

1. If seal was removed, install new seal.
2. Apply special seal lubricant to seal, then insert output shaft into final drive assembly, indexing splines of output shaft with splines of final drive.
3. Install left-hand output shaft retaining bolt and torque to 45 ft. lbs.
4. Install left drive axle.

Final Drive

Cadillac recommends that the final drive unit not be serviced. It should be serviced by replacement only.

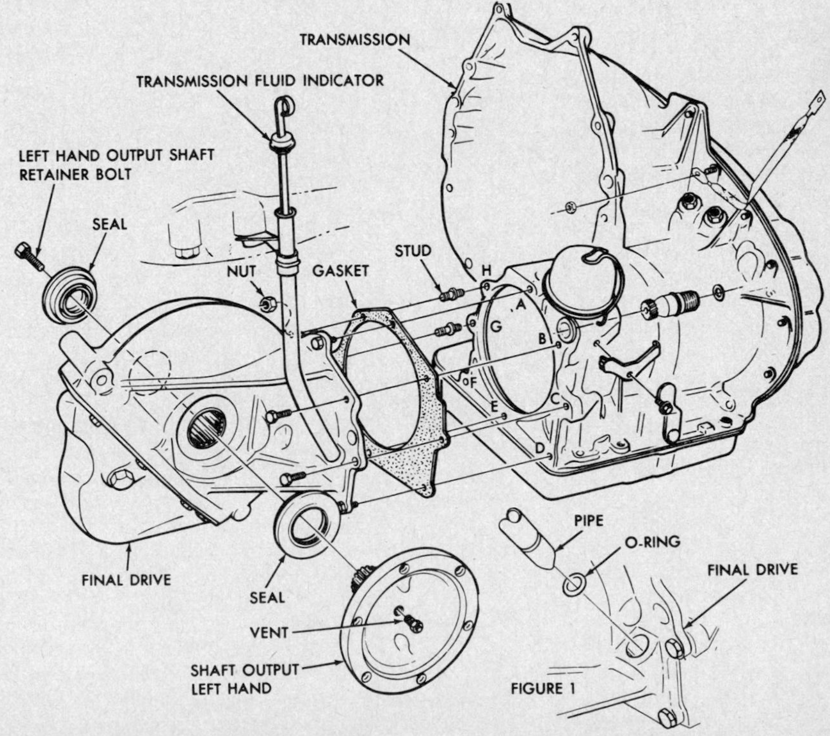

Final drive-to-transmission assembly (© Cadillac Div., G.M. Corp)

Removal—1969-71

1. Disconnect battery.
2. Pump about one gallon of transmission fluid out of filler tube. Remove bolt on the bracket that secures filler tube and remove filler tube, plugging the filler tube hole.
3. Remove bolts A and B and nut H. (See illustration.)
4. Remove the bolt holding the transmission cooler line to the final drive support bracket.
5. Remove the nut from the large through-bolt and remove the final drive support bracket from the final drive unit.
6. Remove the nut and bolt securing the left front engine mount support bracket to the engine.
7. Remove the bolt securing the final drive support bracket to the left front engine mount support.
8. Raise car and remove wheels and tires.
9. Install lengths of rubber hose on both lower torsion bar connectors.
10. Loosen twelve screws and washers that secure drive axles to output shafts.
11. Loosen, BUT DO NOT REMOVE, lower shock nut on right side.
12. Remove the brace from the final drive case and right-hand output shaft support.
13. Remove the battery clip attached to the frame above the right-hand drive axle.
14. Remove the 2 bolts securing the right-hand output shaft support to the engine.
15. Rotate the drive axle rearward toward the starter to gain access to the output shaft.
16. Remove right output shaft.
17. Remove six screws and lock-washers that secure left output shaft to axle.
18. Raise and block the steering gear out of the way.
19. Loosen screws that secure final drive cover to final drive. Allow lubricant to drain then remove screws and cover.
20. Compress left drive axle inner constant velocity joint and secure drive axle to frame.
21. Remove final drive support bracket.
22. Remove bolts C, D, E, and F and nut G.
23. Disengage final drive splines from transmission.
24. Remove final drive unit, permitting ring gear to rotate up over steering gear.
25. Remove transmission to final drive gasket and discard.

Installation—1969-71

1. Positioning new gasket on transmission, install final drive unit, permitting ring gear to rotate up over steering linkage.
2. Align final drive splines with splines in transmission.
3. Align bolt studs G and H on transmission with holes in final drive.
4. Install bolts C, D, E and F and nut G finger tight.
5. Install support bracket on final drive unit.
6. Install other support brackets.
7. Install bolt in oil cooler lines clamp and tighten to 8 ft. lbs.
8. Tighten bolts C, D, E and F and nut G to 25 ft. lbs.
9. Reposition left drive axle and install screws to 65 ft. lbs.
10. Install right output shaft and axle.
11. Position final drive cover to final drive and install screws to 30 ft. lbs.
12. Fill final drive unit. Tighten lower shock nut to 75 lbs.
13. Install wheels and tires, tightening nuts finger tight.
14. Lower car and tighten wheel nuts to 105 ft. lbs.
15. Install bolts A and B and nut H, tightening to 25 ft. lbs.
16. Install new O-ring on transmission filler tube, remove plug in filler tube hole and install filler tube.
17. Position the transmission cooler line clips and secure the support bracket with the screw torqued to 8 ft lbs.
18. Connect battery.
19. Check engine oil and transmission fluid. Start engine and add fluid as needed.
20. After running check the seals for leaks.

Removal—1972-76

1. Disconnect the negative battery cable.
2. Unbolt the transmission filler tube bracket and remove the filler tube.
3. Remove screws A, B and the nut H.
4. Disconnect the transmission cooler lines from the final drive support bracket and slide the clip out of the way.
5. Remove the locknut, washer and long through-bolt holding the final drive support brace to the engine mount bracket.
6. Remove the right-hand output shaft.

Caution The shock absorbers act as rebound stops. Before performing the following Step, be sure that the right-hand shock absorber lower sleeve cannot be dislodged from the stud.

7. Place jackstands under the front frame side rails and lower the hoist that was used when removing the right-hand output shaft.
8. Remove the final drive cover and allow the lubricant to drain into a drain pan.
9. Remove the 6 screws holding the left-hand drive axle to the output shaft. Compress the drive axle inner C.V. joint and hold it in this position to remove the final drive unit with the left-hand output shaft installed.
10. Remove the bolt, washer, and nut holding the left tie strut to the frame crossmember. Loosen the bolt holding the strut to the side rail and rotate the strut outboard until the strut is clear of the final drive area.
11. Remove the large through-bolt nut and washers, securing the final drive support bracket to the final drive.
12. Remove the final drive support bracket.
13. Remove the final drive cover and gasket(s).
14. Remove the final drive with a transmission lift and adapter. The adapter should have a rotating feature to ease removal and installation.
15. Place a drain pan under the transmission and remove screws C, D, E, F and nut G.
16. Disengage the final drive splines from the transmission and let the unit drain.
17. Rotate the final drive unit from under the car by sliding the unit toward the front of the car and permitting the ring gear to rotate over the steering linkage. Lower the housing from the car.
18. Remove and discard the final drive-to-transmission gasket.

Installation—1972-76

See "Installation—1969-71."

FRONT SUSPENSION

The front suspension consists of control arms, stabilizer bar, shock absorbers and a right and left torsion bar. Torsion bars are used in place of conventional coil springs. The front end of the torsion bar is attached to the lower control arm. The rear of torsion bar is mounted into an adjustable arm at the torsion bar crossmember. The carrying height of the car is controlled by this adjustment.

Wheel Hub (Front) R & R

1. Remove hub cap, loosen wheel nuts, remove drive axle cotter pin and loosen drive axle nut.
2. Jack up car and place axle stands under lower control arms.
3. Remove axle nut and wheel and tire assembly.
4. Remove brake drum, or with disc brakes remove brake hose and caliper.

NOTE: Match-mark disc and hub, then remove disc.

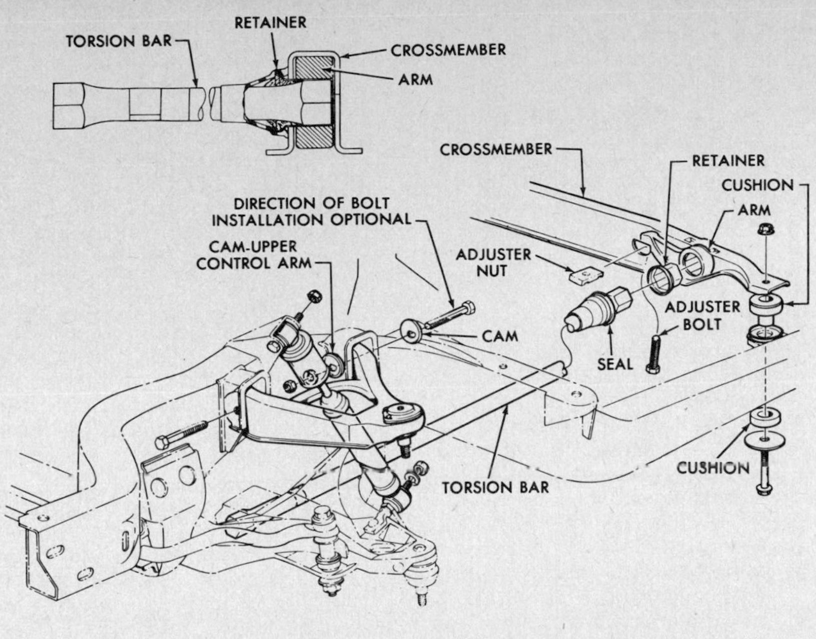

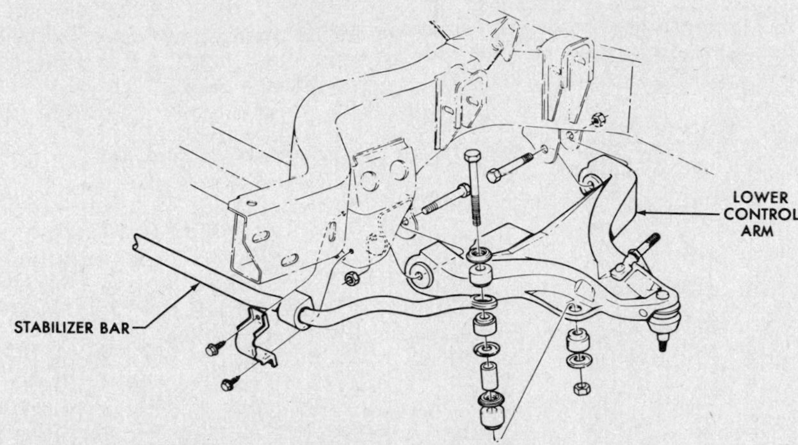

Front suspension disassembled. No retainer is used after 1969; crossmember mounts are slightly different starting 1971
(© Cadillac Div., G.M. Corp)

5. Disconnect brake hose from steel line if equipped with drum brakes.
6. Remove upper ball joint cotter pin and loosen stud nut.
7. Strike steering knuckle near upper joint to separate it from taper.
8. Remove tie-rod end cotter pin and nut.
9. Separate tie-rod end from steering knuckle using a tie-rod splitter.
10. Remove lower ball joint cotter pin and stud nut.
11. Disconnect lower ball joint.
12. Remove hub, backing plate and steering knuckle as an assembly.
13. To install, reverse removal procedure. Tighten both ball joint stud nuts to 40 ft. lbs. up to 1969, 85 ft. lbs. starting 1970 and tie-rod nut to 30 ft. lbs. Drive axle nut must be tightened to 105–110 ft lbs. except 1972 which has a torque of 150 ft lbs. to prevent loosening in service.

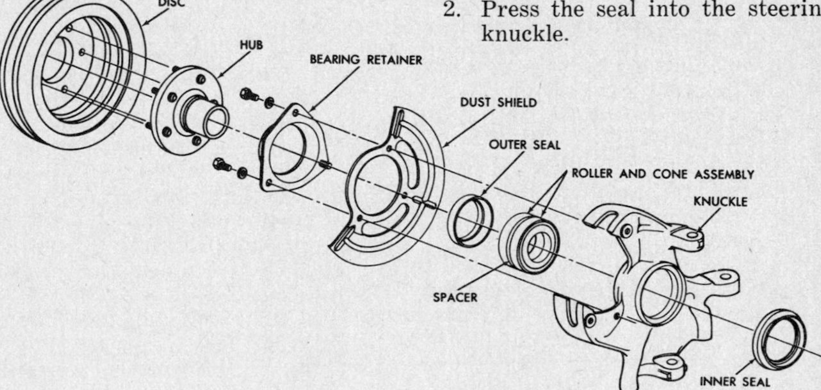

Front hub, bearing, and retainer (© Cadillac Div., G.M. Corp)

Steering Knuckle and Seal Replacement

Removal

1. Remove the wheel disc.
2. Remove the drive axle cotter pin and loosen the nut.
3. Loosen the wheel mounting nuts.
4. Support the car under the lower control arms.
5. Remove the hub nut, washer and lug nuts.
6. Remove the wheel.
7. Remove the upper ball joint cotter pin and nut.
8. Remove the brake line hose clip from the upper ball joint stud, but do not loosen the ball joint stud.
9. Install one or two lug nuts to prevent the disc from falling off the hub when removing the caliper.
10. Remove the 2 bolts securing the caliper and remove the caliper.
11. Suspend the caliper with wire attached to the frame.
12. Matchmark the hub and disc and remove the disc.
13. Place a short length of rubber hose over the lower control arm torsion bar connector to prevent damaging the tri-pot joint.
14. Position the brake hose out of the way. Strike the steering knuckle in the area of the upper ball joint and loosen the upper ball joint stud.
15. Remove the cotter pin and nut from the tie-rod end.
16. Remove the tie-rod from the steering knuckle.
17. Remove the cotter pin and nut from the lower ball joint stud.
18. Disconnect the lower ball joint at the steering knuckle.
19. Remove the hub and knuckle by guiding it over the drive axle.
20. Use a screwdriver to remove the inner seal.

Installation

1. Apply a moderate amount of high melting point lithium base grease into the lips of the steering knuckle inner seal.
2. Press the seal into the steering knuckle.
3. Align the splines in the hub with the splines on the drive axle and install the hub and knuckle on the drive axle.
4. Further installation is the reverse of removal. The cotter pin on the upper ball joint stud must be crimped flat against the nut to avoid damaging the drive axle

C.V. joint or seal. Tighten the upper ball joint nut to 60 ft lbs. Tighten the tie-rod end to 40 ft lbs. Tighten the lower ball joint nut to 80 ft lbs. If the cotter pin cannot be installed, tighten the nut until it can be installed. Tighten the drive axle to hub nut to a minimum of 110 ft lbs and tighten it further until the cotter pin can be installed.

Check the standing height and front end alignment. Be sure that the front brake hose is not twisted.

Torsion Bar

Removal—1969-70

1. Raise car and place jack under rear axle. Raise front of car and place jacks under front lower control arms.
2. Install torsion bar remover and installer on torsion bar crossmember. Tighten center bolt on this tool until torsion bar adjusting arm is raised enough to permit removal of adjusting bolt and lock nut. Remove adjusting bolt and lock nut.
3. Remove torsion bar installer and remover and install on other end of torsion bar crossmember and repeat Step 2. Remove tool.
4. Remove torsion bar crossmember mounting bolts, bushings, retainers and parking brake cable clip.
5. Drive crossmember down, then rearward until both torsion bars are free. Adjusting arms will fall out.
6. Lift up on crossmember. Remove torsion bars by sliding them out of lower control arm connectors.

Installation—1969-70

1. Lubricate both ends of torsion bar for approximately 3 in. with extreme pressure chassis lubricant.
2. Place torsion bar in retainer at chassis crossmember.
3. Lubricate lower control arm torsion bar connector and slide torsion bar into connector.

NOTE: The torsion bars are stamped "L" and "R" for left and right. The end which is stamped is inserted in the lower control arm torsion bar connector.

4. Repeat procedure for other torsion bar.
5. Place torsion bar adjusting arm in crossmember, then slide torsion bar toward rear of car until seated in adjusting arm.
6. Repeat for other torsion bar.
7. Install bushings and retainers between crossmember and frame on both sides.
8. Raise front of car, positioning jacks under lower control arms.
9. Install crossmember mounting bolts and tighten to 40 ft. lbs.
10. Install torsion bar remover and installer on crossmember and tighten center bolt until torsion bar adjusting arm is high enough to permit installation of adjusting bolt and locknut. Install locknut and adjusting bolt.
11. Remove torsion bar remover and installer and install on other end of crossmember and repeat Step 10 for other torsion bar.
12. Remove torsion bar remover and installer.
13. Check the standing height and the front wheel alignment.
14. Raise car, removing jacks, and lower car.

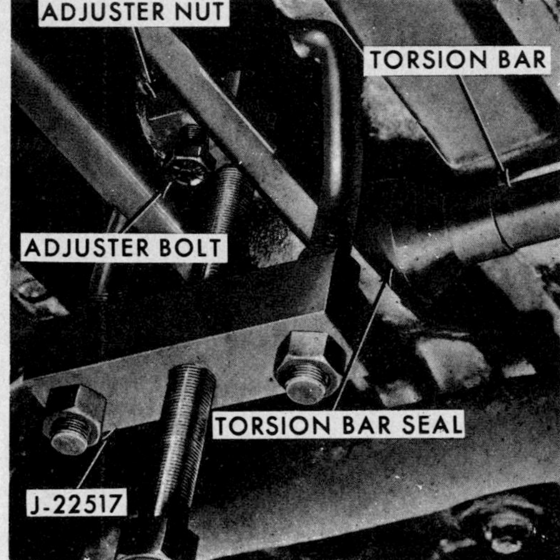

Torsion bar remover and installer (© Cadillac Div., G.M. Corp)

Removal—1971-76

1. Jack up car and support so that front suspension hangs at full rebound.
2. Remove adjusting bolt from both torsion bar locknuts.
3. Install torsion bar remover and installer tool on torsion bar crossmember.
4. Tighten center bolt of tool until adjusting arm is raised high enough to permit removal of locknut. Remove locknut.
5. Repeat Steps 3 and 4 on other side of crossmember.
6. Remove parking brake cable guide at right side of underbody.
7. Remove torsion bar crossmember bolts and retainers from both sides. On 1974-76 models with air bags (ACRS), remove the lock pins and retainers from either end of the crossmember.
8. Move crossmember toward side opposite the torsion bar being removed. One side of crossmember should clear frame at this point.
9. Lower the free end on the crossmember and drive it rearward until torsion bar is free. It may be necessary to loosen parking brake adjuster nut to gain slack in cable.

NOTE: although both torsion bars can be removed at this point, it has been found much easier to do only one side at a time.

10. Remove torsion bar from lower control arm.

NOTE: nicks or scratches in torsion bar can cause its failure.

Installation—1971-76

1. Lubricate 3 in. of each end of torsion bar. Bars are marked L or R for left and right sides—do not interchange.
2. Slide torsion bar into lower control arm as far as it will go after installing the torsion bar seal.
3. Position adjusting arm in crossmember. Holding arm in place, slide torsion bar rearward until it is seated in adjusting arm. The torsion bars are stamped "L" for left and "R" for right. The stamped end is installed in the lower control arm.
4. Position crossmember to frame and reverse Steps 1-7 of *Removal* procedure.

Upper Control Arm

Removal

NOTE: the upper control arm can be serviced as an assembly, although bushings and upper ball joint kits are available.

1. Hoist car and remove wheel. Support the car on jackstands as close to the ball joints as possible.
2. Remove upper shock absorber attaching bolt.
3. Remove cotter pin and nut on upper ball joint.
4. Disconnect brake hose clamp from ball joint stud. Remove caliper.
5. Using hammer and a drift, drive on spindle until upper ball joint stud is disengaged.

6. Remove upper control arm cam assemblies and remove control arm from car.

Installation

1. Guide upper control arm over shock absorber and install bushing ends into frame horns.
2. Install cam assemblies.

NOTE: front cam is mounted up, rear cam is mounted down.

3. Install ball joint stud into knuckle. Install caliper.
4. Install brake hose clip on ball joint stud.
5. Install ball joint nut. Torque to 40 ft. lbs. for 1969, 85 ft. lbs. from 1970-1971 and 60 ft. lbs. in 1972 and later, and insert cotter pin, crimp.

NOTE: cotter pin must be crimped toward upper control arm to prevent interference with outer C. V. joint seal.

6. Install upper shock attaching bolt and nut. Torque to 75 ft. lbs.
7. Install wheel.
8. Lower hoist.
9. Check camber, caster and toe-in, and adjust if necessary.

Upper Control Arm Bushing on the Car

The upper control arm bushings can be removed and installed without removing the control arm.

Removal

1. Hoist car and remove wheel.
2. Disconnect upper shock absorber attaching bolt.
3. Remove cam assemblies from control arms.
4. Move control arms out of frame horns and attach bushing removal tools. The bushings can be sprayed with silicone lubricant to ease removal.

Installation

1. Install tools and press bushings into control arm.
2. Move control arm into frame horns and install cam assemblies. Front cam is mounted up, rear cam is mounted down.
3. Connect upper shock absorber attaching bolt. Torque to 75 ft. lbs.
4. Replace wheel and lower car.
5. Align front wheels.

Lower Control Arm

Removal

1. Remove wheel disc and loosen wheel mounting nuts.
2. Remove hub cotter pin. Loosen nut.
3. Raise car and remove wheel and tire.
4. Remove torsion bar, as described previously.
5. Remove hub nut and washer, and brake line clips attached to frame.
6. Remove cotter pin, nut and brake line clip from upper ball joint and remove joint from steering knuckle with a hammer and drift.
7. Disconnect shock absorber and remove.
8. Disconnect tie-rod end at steering knuckle with tie-rod end puller.
9. Disconnect stablizer bar and nut and link bolt.
10. Disconnect lower ball joint with ball joint puller and adapter.
11. Disengage hub, knuckle and disc as an assembly and secure to upper control arm with wire.
12. Remove lower control arm to frame nuts and bolts and disengage arm from frame mounts.

Installation

1. Install hub, disc and knuckle assembly on drive axle.
2. Install lower control arms into mounts at chassis.

NOTE: do not tighten nuts now.

3. Install lower control arm ball joint into steering knuckle. Tighten nut to 40 ft. lbs. for 1969, 85 ft. lbs. from 1970 to 1971 and 80 ft. lbs. in 1972 and later. Install the cotter pin.
4. Tighten lower control arm bolts to 75 ft lbs (80 ft lbs 1974 and later).
5. Install shock absorber and tighten nut to 75 ft. lbs.
6. Install upper control arm ball joint into steering knuckle and install brake line clip. Tighten nut to 40 ft. lbs. for 1969, 85 ft. lbs. from 1970 to 1971 and 60 ft. lbs from 1972 and later. Install cotter pin.
7. Install brake line clip to chassis.
8. Install tie-rod end in steering knuckle, tightening nut to 30 ft. lbs. (40 ft lbs 1974 and later).
9. Install stabilizer bar.
10. Install hub to drive axle washer and nut.
11. Install torsion bar.
12. Install wheel and tire.
13. Lower car.
14. Tighten hub to drive axle nut to 110 ft. lbs. and install cotter pin. Tighten wheel nuts to 105 ft. lbs. (130 ft lbs 1974 and later).
15. Install wheel disc.

Lower Control Arm Bushings

Removal

Remove lower control arm and press bushings out of arm. To install, press bushings into arm and install arm. Check standing height and front wheel alignment if necessary.

Ball Joint Checks

Vertical Check

1. Raise the car and position floor stands under the left and right lower control arm, as near as possible to each lower ball joint. Car must be stable and should not rock on floor stands.
2. Position dial indicator to register vertical movement at wheel hub.
3. Place a pry bar between the lower control arm and the outer race, and pry down on the bar. Very little pressure is necessary. Often the weight of the bar is sufficient. Care must be used so that the drive axle seal is not damaged. The vertical reading must not exceed 0.125 in.

Horizontal Check

1. Place car on floor stands as outlined in Step 1 in the Vertical Check.
2. Position dial indicator at the rim of the wheel, to indicate side play.
3. Grasp wheel, top and bottom, and push in on the bottom of the tire while pulling out at the top. Read gauge, then reverse the push-pull procedure. Horizontal deflection on the gauge should not exceed 0.125 in. at the wheel rim.

Lower Control Arm Ball Joint

Removal

1. Remove the lower control arm.
2. Using chisel, cut the three rivet heads off.
3. By using a 7/32 in. drill bit, drill side rivets 3/16 in. deep.
4. Using hammer and punch, drive center rivet of joint, until joint is out of the control arm.

Installation

1. Install service ball joint into control arm and torque bolts and nut.
2. Reverse lower control arm removal.

Lower Control Arm Ball Joint Seal

The lower ball joint seal can be installed with lower control arm either in or out of the car.

Removal

1. Remove steering knuckle.
2. Using hammer and chisel, tap lightly on the seal retainer.
3. Work the retainer off the joint with a small screwdriver.
4. Wipe grease from ball joint and stud.

Installation

1. Position new seal over ball joint stud.
2. Lubricate jaws of camber adjusting wrench and carefully slide jaw between seal and retainer.
3. Tap lightly with hammer on cen-

ter bolt of the wrench until retainer is fully seated.

4. Install knuckle.
5. Lubricate the ball joint fitting until grease is apparent in seal.

Stabilizer Bar

Removal

1. Raise the car and support it on jack stands.
2. Remove link bolts, nuts, grommets, spacers and retainers from lower control arm. Discard bolts.
3. Remove two bolts attaching dust shield to frame, both sides.
4. Remove bracket to frame attaching bolts and remove stabilizer bar from front of car.

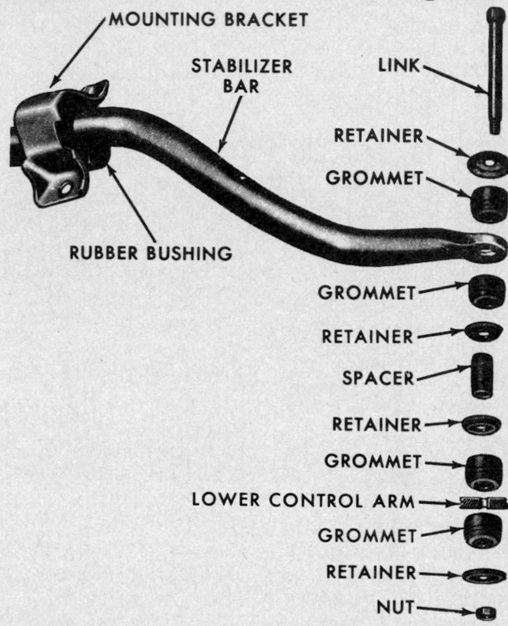

Eldorado front stabilizer linkage (© Cadillac Div., G.M. Corp)

Installation

Reverse removal procedure.

NOTE: new link bolts are torqued to 13 ft lbs., then cut off to leave 1/4 in. of bolt remaining.

Front Shock Absorber

Replacement

The front shock absorbers should be removed with the car on a platform type hoist, so that the vehicle weight is supported on the front suspension. If a platform hoist is available, ignore Steps 1-3. If no platform hoist is available, support the car as indicated in Steps 1-3.

1. Remove wheel disc and loosen wheel mounting nuts.
2. Raise car, place on jacks, and remove wheel and tire.
3. Place a hydraulic jack under lower control arm and raise so that load is taken off shock absorber.
4. Disconnect shock absorber at upper and lower mount.
5. Compress shock absorber, working lower mount free from mount bolt.
6. Remove shock absorber.
7. Install by reversing procedure above, tightening shock absorber nuts to 75 ft. lbs. and wheel mounting nuts to 105 ft lbs. (130 ft lbs 1974 and later).

Standing Height—1969-70

The standing height is controlled by the adjustment setting of the torsion bar adjusting bolts. Clockwise rotation of the bolts increases the front height. It is very important that this height be considered and made correct before steering geometry is established.

For quick checks only, the locations at frame-to-ground points A and B, as illustrated, can be used up to 1970. However, locations C and D, are preferred and should always be used for proper measurements of standing heights up to 1970.

Measuring Height—All Years

Before measuring standing height, check and correct the following items:

1. Car must be on a level surface.
2. Gas tank should be full or a compensating weight added. Estimate the amount of gasoline in the tank and add weights in the trunk in the space immediately above the float access hole area.
3. Front seat should be adjusted all the way to its rearmost position.
4. Front and rear tires should be inflated to proper pressure.
5. Both doors closed.
6. No passengers or additional weight should be in the car or trunk (except as indicated above).

Checking Rear Height with Automatic Level Control Disconnected

Though rear height readings can be taken without disconnecting the ALC, it is preferred that measurements be taken with the leveling system disconnected—to eliminate the possibility of the ALC system affecting the reading.

The ALC can be disconnected at the black line connection at the leveling valve.

After the measurement is taken and the black line is reconnected, the ALC system should be refilled by use of an air pressure hose to insure pressure reserve in the tank.

If rear of car raises when the automatic leveling system is reconnected, the leveling system should be checked and adjusted.

Quick Reference Locations —to 1970

Location A is at a point 2 in. behind the front edge of the door. This is

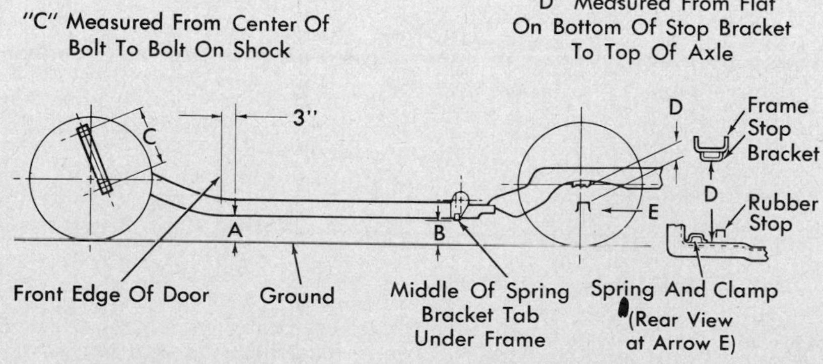

Reference Locations Frame To Ground		Preferred Locations	
"A" Front	"B" Rear	"C" Front True Shock Length	"D" Rear Standing Height
6¼" TO 6⁷⁄₁₆"	5¹⁵⁄₁₆" TO 6½"	14⅝" TO 14⅞"	4-23/32" To 5-15/32"

1969-70 Eldorado standing height chart (© Cadillac Div., G.M. Corp)

39½ in. from the centerline of the front wheel.

Location B is at the middle of the spring bracket tab under the frame. This is 32¼ in. forward of the rear axle centerline.

Preferred Locations—to 1970

Location C is from center to center of the shock absorber upper and lower mounting bolts.

Location D is from the flat on the bottom of the stop bracket to the top of the axle. The rear view of D, as illustrated, shows this location more clearly.

Standing Height—1971-76

The procedure for checking standing height has been modified slightly starting with 1971 production. A quick check of height on these models can be made by measuring the distance between the lower edge of the front shock absorber dust cover and the lower shock bolt centerline (front) and the distance between the lower edge of the frame "kickover" and the top of the axle tube (rear). If equipped with Automatic Level Control, loosen the air lines at the rear shocks to bleed all air from the system.

Standing Height—1971-74

Model	Front	Rear
Coupe	8.0-8.25"	3.88-4.64"
Convertible	8.0-8.25"	3.88-4.64"

Standing Height—1975-76

Model	Front	Rear
Coupe	8.25-8.50"	5.06-5.31"
Convertible	8.25-8.50"	5.06-5.31"

Caution Do not accidentally slip the measuring rule or device into the slot for the rubber bumper in the rear axle, because doing so would give a false reading. Also remove all air from Automatic Level Control before the measurement.

Acceptable specifications are also given in illustration. Frame to ground dimensions must be within 1 in. from front to rear and within ⅝ in. from side to side.

If dimensions are not within tolerance, torsion bars wheel alignment must be adjusted.

Alignment Procedures Setting Camber & Caster

1. Check camber. The preferred setting for camber is in the specifications. To adjust proceed as follows:
   - A. Loosen nut on upper control arm front and rear cam bolts.
   - B. Note camber reading and rotate front bolt to correct for one-half of the incorrect reading or as near to that amount as possible. Tighten front nut.
   - C. Loosen nut on upper control arm rear cam bolt and rotate rear cam bolt to bring camber reading to 0°. Tighten rear nut.
   - D. Check caster. Preferred reading is in the specifications.

NOTE: if caster requires adjustment, proceed with Step E; if not, move to Step I.

   - E. Loosen front cam bolt nut.
   - F. Using camber scale on alignment equipment, rotate front bolt so that the camber changes an amount equal to one-quarter of the desired castor change.

NOTE: if adjusting to correct for excessive negative caster, rotate front bolt to increase positive camber. If adjusting to correct for excessive positive caster, rotate front bolt to increase negative camber.

   - G. Tighten front nut.
   - H. Loosen nut on rear cam bolt and rotate the rear bolt until camber setting returns to 0°. This results in the correct caster setting.
   - I. Tighten upper control arm cam nuts to 75 ft. lbs. up to 1969, 95 ft. lbs. starting 1970. Hold head of bolt securely; any movement of the cam will affect final setting and will require a recheck of the camber and caster adjustments.

Caster, camber cam locations
(© Cadillac Div., G.M. Corp)

Relationship of Front and Rear Cams

When setting camber and caster, remember this relationship:

Front cams. If turned for more positive camber, then caster also becomes more positive.

In other words, when turning the front cams to obtain a more positive setting for camber, caster will follow to a more positive setting.

The same is true when turning for more positive caster: more positive camber will follow.

Rear cams. If turned for more positive camber, then caster becomes more negative.

When turning the rear cams to obtain a more positive setting for camber, caster will advance in the opposite direction toward a more negative setting.

Toe-in Adjustment

- A. Center steering wheel, raise car and check wheel runout.
- B. Loosen tie-rod adjuster nuts, and adjust to proper setting.
- C. Tighten tie-rod adjuster nuts. Torque nuts 22 ft. lbs. Position tie-rod clamps so operning of clamps are facing UP. This is a very necessary setting. Interference and a possible tie up of front end linkage could occur, if clamps hit anything while turning.

Front Wheel Bearing Adjustment

1. Raise the front of the car and remove the wheel covers from the wheels and the dust covers, nut locks and cotter pins from the spindles.
2. On 1969 to 1971 models tighten the adjusting nut to 30 ft lbs. while on 1972 to 1976 models torque the nut to 15 ft lbs.
3. Once the correct torque is obtained, on 1969 to 1971 models back the nut off to 0 pounds of torque. 1972 to 1976 models require that the nut be backed off until it is just loose (1 flat).
4. Tighten the nut on 1969 to 1971 models to 6 ft lbs of torque. 1972-76 models are tightened finger tight only.
5. Install cotter pin.

NOTE: If the cotter pin cannot be installed, back the adjusting nut off to the next hole. DO NOT tighten the nut over 6 lbs on 1969 to 1971 models.

REAR SUSPENSION

1969-70

The rear suspension on the Cadillac Eldorado consists of two single leaf, semi-elliptical springs, two vertical and two horizontal shock absorbers.

1971-76

A new rear suspension system, introduced in 1971, has replaced the old leaf spring type used previously. This new system is a four-link, coil spring suspension having no components interchangeable with other Cadillac models. Instead of two vertical and two horizontal shock absorbers, as used on earlier models, Automatic Level Control Superlift shock absorbers are used exclusively.

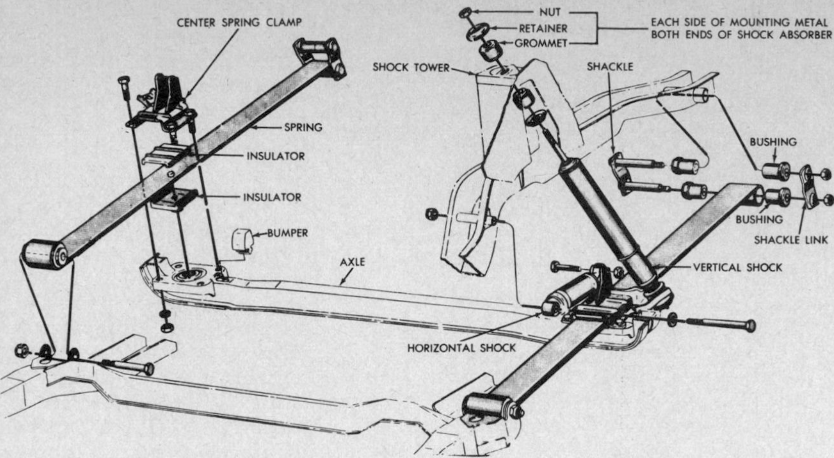

Rear suspension—1969-70 (© Cadillac Div., G.M. Corp)

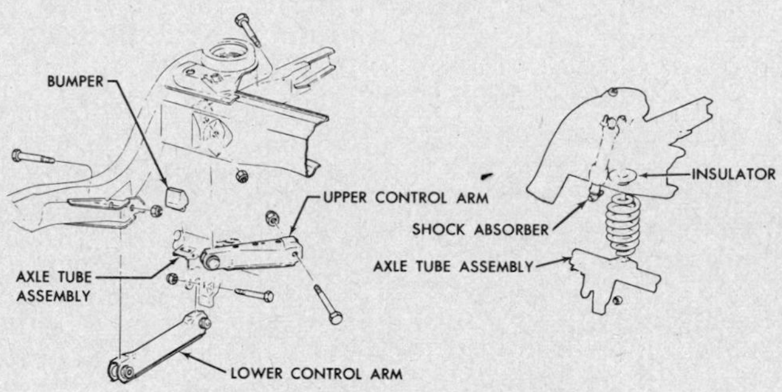

Rear suspension—1971-76 Eldorado (© Cadillac Div., G.M. Corp)

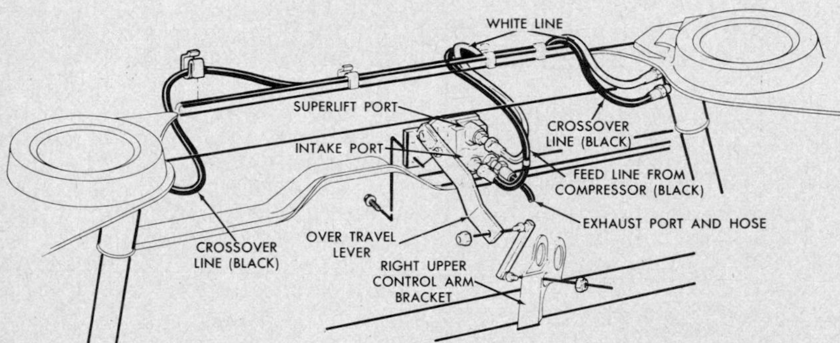

Location of the automatic level control components (© Cadillac Div., G.M. Corp)

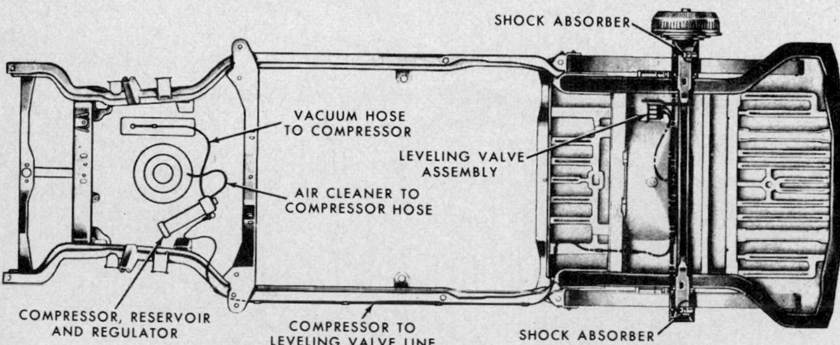

Automatic leveling system (© Cadillac Div., G.M. Corp)

Automatic Level Control

This system is basically the same as that used on other Cadillac models and functions identically. However, the on-car location of major components is different. Procedures will be found in the Cadillac section.

Rear Leaf Spring Removal —1969-70

1. Raise car.
2. Support rear axle at center with hydraulic jack.
3. Remove rear wheel from side being worked on.
4. Remove nut that secures Automatic Level Control link to axle bracket and remove link.
5. Remove nut that secures front of spring to frame bracket.

NOTE: do not remove bolt now.

6. Remove two nuts at rear shackle outer link and remove link.
7. Remove four nuts and lockwashers that secure center spring clamp to rear axle and position out of the way.
8. Lower hydraulic jack until axle is free from spring.
9. Remove rear shackle assembly from spring and body.
10. Remove bolt from front of spring and remove spring.

Upper Control Arm R & R—1971-76

1. Jack up car and support rear on axle stands under frame side members.
2. Disconnect Automatic Level Control system over-travel link at right upper control arm axle bracket, then position lever in "center" position.
3. Disconnect lower shock bolt and position shock out of the way.
4. Jack up under rear axle to unload upper control arm.
5. Remove bolt and nut that secures upper arm to axle bracket.
6. Remove bolt and nut that secures upper arm to crossmember; remove arm.

NOTE: bushings can be replaced at this point.

7. Install upper arm to brackets and install bolts and nuts. Do not tighten nuts at this time.
8. Install lower shock bolt and shock.
9. Jack up on rear axle and remove axle stands under frame side members.
10. With weight of car on axle only, tighten upper arm-to-crossmember nuts to 100 ft lbs (145 ft lbs 1974-76) and lower axle bracket nuts to 75 ft lbs (110 ft lbs 1974-76).
11. Install A.L.C. overtravel lever, lower car and inflate system to 140 psi.

NOTE: control arm pivot bolts must be tightened at standing height or ride rate will be affected.

12. Inspect brake lines for damage.

Lower Control Arm R & R—1971-76

1. Jack up car.
2. Remove bolts and nuts that secure lower arm to axle and frame.
3. Remove lower control arm.
4. Install lower arm and tighten bolts to 100 ft lbs (145 ft lbs 1974-76).

Rear Coil Spring R & R—1971-76

1. Remove both upper control arms from their axle mountings.
2. Disconnect both rear shocks at lower ends.
3. Disconnect brake hose and cap brake line.
4. Lower axle carefully, using a floor jack, until springs can be removed.

Caution If axle is lowered beyond full rebound, springs can jump from their seats with considerable force. For this reason, lower axle only far enough to allow springs to be lightly compressed by hand and removed.

5. Inspect rubber insulators for damage.
6. Insert springs and jack up axle until springs are compressed.
7. Reconnect shocks and upper control arms.
8. Connect brake hose and bleed rear brake circuit.

Rear Axle Assembly

1969-70

The rear axle consists of a welded beam-type, drop center axle having spindles pressed into and bolted to the axle flanges. The rear wheels run on tapered roller bearings very similar to those used on the front wheels of Cadillac models other than the Eldorado.

1971-76

The rear axle was changed in 1971 to a straight, hollow tube design. The spindles still are pressed and bolted to the axle flanges and tapered roller bearings are used. The Track Master system, optional on 1971 and later Eldorado models, uses a hollow spindle through which the drive cables for the speed sensors run.

Removal—1969-70

1. Raise car, and remove rear wheels.
2. Remove rear brake drum, then hub assembly.
3. Disconnect brake lines and hose and parking brake cable.
4. Disconnect overtravel lever link from bracket on rear axle.
5. Remove spring guides that hold parking brake cable to center spring clamp.
6. Remove brake backing plates.
7. Supporting rear axle at center with hydraulic jack, remove four nuts on each side of spring clamp assemblies.
8. Lower jack and remove rear axle.
9. To install, reverse removal.

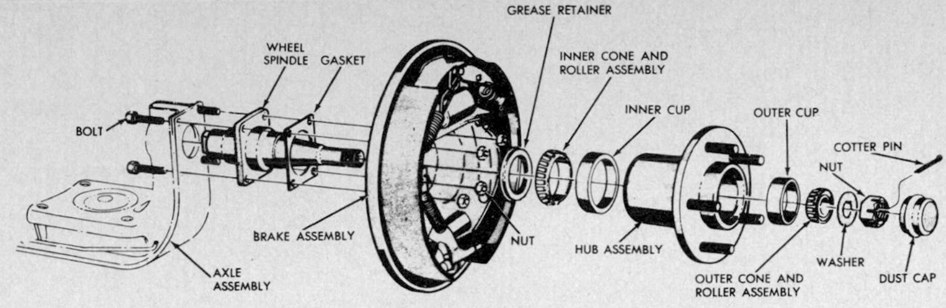

Rear axle disassembled—1969-70 (© Cadillac Div., G.M. Corp)

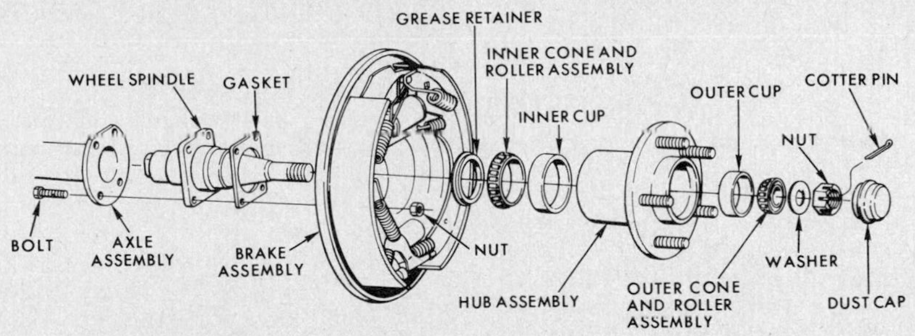

Rear axle disassembled—1971-76 (© Cadillac Div., G.M. Corp)

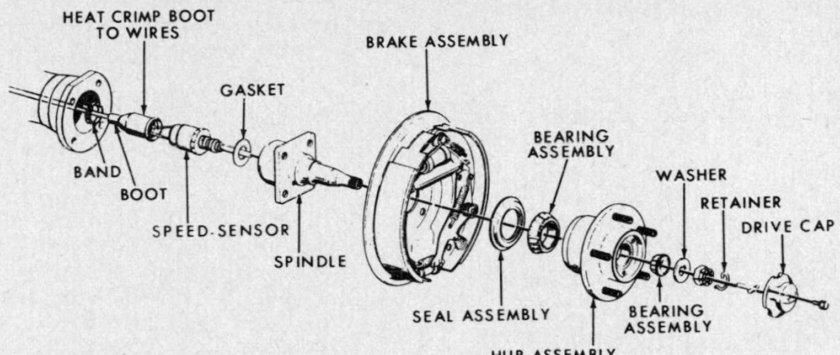

Rear axle disassembled—1971-72 with Track Master (© Cadillac Div., G.M. Corp)

Removal—1971-76

1. Jack up rear of car and support on stands under frame rails. Raise hoist far enough to support weight of rear axle.
2. Remove both tire and wheel assemblies. Remove the stabilizer bar (1971-74).
3. Remove hubs as follows:
   a. Remove brake drums.
   b. If equipped with Track Master (T.M.), remove three screws that secure drive cap, remove cap, retainer rings, spindle nut, washer and bearings.
   c. If equipped with standard axle, remove dust cap, cotter pin, spindle nut, washer and bearings.
   d. Pull hub off spindle.
4. Disconnect brake lines at wheel cylinders.
5. Disconnect rubber hose and cap to prevent brake fluid loss.
6. Disconnect overtravel link at axle bracket, then deflate shocks.
7. Remove brake backing plates and pull spindle using a slide hammer.

NOTE: make sure the sensor wiring is not damaged if equipped with T.M.

8. Disconnect brake lines from clips on axle.
9. If car is equipped with T.M., remove screw and clip that secures sensor cable to axle. Pull cable through ⅝ in. hole in axle and disconnect.
10. Disconnect lower shock bolts and position shocks out of the way.
11. Jack up on axle to relieve tension on upper control arm.
12. Remove bolts and nuts that secure upper control arms to axle.
13. Lower axle and remove coil springs.

Caution Stand clear of the axle assembly as the springs may snap from their seats.

14. Remove bolts and nuts that secure lower control arms to axle.
15. Remove brake junction from axle and rubber stop bumpers.
16. Remove axle from car.
17. To install, reverse removal procedure.

Rear Wheel Bearing Adjustment

Regularly scheduled wheel bearing repacking is not required. When major brake service is required, it is recommended that the rear wheel bearings be cleaned and repacked with a high melting point grade 2 lithium grease.

1971-72

1. Adjustment should be made

while revolving the wheel at least 3 times the speed of nut rotation through at least 3 revolutions.

2. Check to be sure that the hub is completely seated on the spindle.
3. While rotating the wheel assembly, tighten the spindle nut to 30 ft lbs (1971) or 15 ft lbs (1972).
4. On 1971 models, back off the spindle nut 90°. On 1972 models, back the nut off until it is free.
5. On 1971 models, insert the cotter pin after backing the nut off 90°. On 1972 models, tighten the nut finger-tight and insert the cotter pin.
6. If the cotter pin cannot be inserted in either of the 2 holes, back the nut off until it can be inserted.
7. Peen the end of the pin securely.
8. If equipped with Track Master, insert the pin into the end of the sensor assembly using pliers, and install insulators on each end of the pin. The pin should protrude equally from each end of the sensor.
9. Install the dust cap, or if equipped with Track Master, install the drive cap.

1973-76

1. Adjustment should be made while rotating the wheel at least 3 times the speed of the nut rotation through at least 3 revolutions.
2. While rotating the hub, tighten the spindle nut to 25-30 ft lbs.
3. Back the nut off ½ turn and tighten it to 24 in. lbs. Install the cotter pin.
4. If the cotter pin cannot be installed, back the nut off until it can be installed.
5. The final adjustment should be 24 in. lbs nut torque to 0.004 in. bearing play.
6. Peen the end of the cotter pin and install the dust cap.

BRAKES

Single-piston, sliding caliper Delco-Moraine disc brakes are standard equipment on the front wheels of all Eldorado models. The master cylinders used with these brakes are the same as for the same year Cadillac, even though the Eldorado uses tandem power booster units.

A foot-operated, vacuum parking brake working on the rear drums via mechanical linkage is used. This is virtually identical to the parking brake used on other Cadillac models.

For brake service, see the Unit Repair Section of this manual.

Master Cylinder R & R

See Cadillac section.

Power Brake Booster R & R

1. Disconnect hydraulic lines from master cylinder.
2. Disconnect vacuum line from vacuum check valve on unit.
3. Remove steering column lower cover.
4. Remove cotter pin, washer and spring spacer that secure power unit pushrod to brake pedal arm.
5. Remove the four nuts that secure power unit to firewall, then remove power unit.
6. To install, reverse removal procedure.

Brake System Check

1. Start engine and allow it to idle in Neutral. Depress brake pedal and hold—if pedal gradually falls away, a hydraulic system leak is indicated.
2. Check pedal travel from rest to full on position. Pedal travel should not exceed 2 in. for 1969-70 and 2 1/16 in. for 1971-76.
3. If pedal travel exceeds specifications, the system is probably contaminated by air bubbles and should be bled.

NOTE: disc brakes—tap calipers around piston area with plastic hammer to dislodge all air bubbles. Less common causes of excessive pedal travel include malfunctioning rear brake self-adjusters, tapered rear linings, worn out rear linings or complete loss of fluid from one brake circuit.

Parking Brake

Preliminary Check

1. Check vacuum cylinder piston travel (on brake pedal support) by running engine at idle and shifting from Drive to Neutral. The manual release lever should move up and down as vacuum is applied and released.
2. If no movement is observed, check for kinked or loose vacuum line connections all the way out to the intake manifold. Check neutral switch adjustment and vacuum release valve.
3. If movement is slow (greater than 2 seconds), vacuum diaphragm may be leaking or lines kinked partially closed.
4. If vacuum piston completes full stroke, but does not release brake, parking brake assembly is faulty and must be replaced as a unit.
5. If parking brake does not remain fully engaged in all gears with engine off, the assembly must be replaced.

Parking Brake Cable Adjustment

See Cadillac section.

STEERING

The steering linkage on the Eldorado is composed of a pitman arm, idler arm, a pair of tie rod assemblies, a drag link, and a shock absorber. The pitman arm connects the left side of the drag link to the steering gear while the idler arm connects the right side of the drag link to the frame. The small shock absorber connects the drag link to the frame and serves to dampen the vibrations in the linkage. The tie rods connect the drag link with the steering knuckles.

For steering gear overhaul see the "Unit Repair Section."

Steering Gear R & R

1. Remove the pressure lines from the gear and tape or plug the lines.
2. Raise the car.
3. Remove the cotter pin and nut from the pitman arm and then, using a puller, disconnect the pitman arm from the drag link.
4. Separate the flexible coupling.
5. Release the three screws which hold the gear to the side frame rail. The gear is removed by pulling it forward and downward and out of the car.
6. Installation is the reverse of removal. If the pitman arm is removed from the shaft the nut should be torqued to 185 ft lbs upon assembly. The side rail mounting screws should be torqued to 70 ft lbs while the flexible coupling torque should be 20 ft lbs and the pitman arm nut which secures it to the drag link should be tightened to 60 ft lbs. The return line hoses should be tightened to 30 ft lbs.

Steering Linkage R & R

1. Remove the front wheels.
2. Remove the steering damper from the frame (1969-74).
3. Remove all the cotter pins and nuts from the pitman arm and the idler arm pivots on the drag link.
4. Using a puller, remove both the idler and pitman arm pivots from the drag link.

NOTE: It may be necessary to loosen the steering gear from the frame to remove the drag link from the pitman arm.

5. The cotter pins and nuts from the outer tie rod pivots should be removed at the steering knuckles. Then separate the tie rod pivots from the steering knuckles.
6. The linkage can be removed from the frame.
7. If the idler arm is to be removed, loosen the locknut and bolt which fastens it to the frame.
8. Installation is accomplished by reversing the removal procedure.

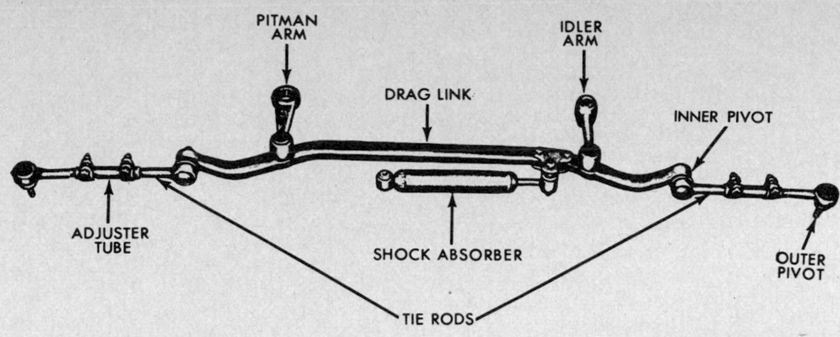

Steering linkage (shock absorber not used—1975-76) (© Cadillac Div., G.M. Corp)

The torque on the damper should be 40 ft lbs while the tie rod torque is 60 ft lbs. When installing the idler arm on the frame tighten the bolt to 95 ft lbs.

Power Steering Pump R & R, Steering Wheel R & R, and Turn Signal Switch R & R

See the Cadillac section.

INSTRUMENT PANEL

Headlight Switch R & R

1969

1. Remove instrument panel upper cover.
2. Remove steering column lower cover.
3. Remove two screws that secure air conditioning duct to bezel assembly and remove duct.
4. Disconnect wiring harness that is below headlight switch assembly.
5. Depress spring loaded release button on top of headlight switch and remove switch, knob and rod assembly.
6. Remove screws that secure switch assembly to bezel.
7. Pull assembly rearward, disconnect wiring connectors, two bulbs and remove assembly.
8. Install in reverse of above.

1970-76

1. Disconnect negative battery cable. Remove steering column lower cover.
2. Disconnect wiring harness retainer below headlight switch assembly.
3. Depress spring loaded release button on top of headlight switch and remove switch, knob and rod assembly (switch "on").
4. Remove screw with ground wire at bottom of switch housing.
5. Pull assembly down and rearward, disconnect wiring harness connectors, two bulbs and remove assembly.
6. Install in reverse of above.

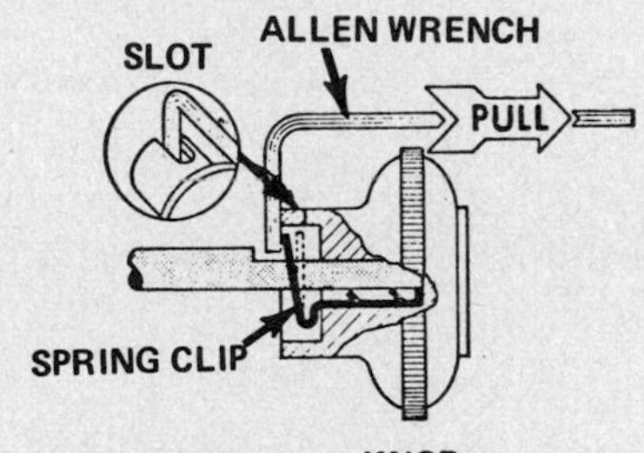

1971-76 radio knob removal
(© Cadillac Div., G.M. Corp)

Ignition Switch R & R

See *Cadillac Section.*

Ignition Lock Cylinder R & R

See *Cadillac Section.*

WINDSHIELD WIPERS

The windshield wiper system consists of the wiper motor and transmission assembly. It is similar to that used on other Cadillac models.

Linkage R & R

1969-70

1. Remove wiper arm and blade assemblies.
2. Remove screws that secure air inlet screen to cowl; remove screen.
3. Remove two screws and cover plate on firewall.
4. Remove locknut which secures wiper crank to ball socket.
5. Remove 3 linkage mounting screws (each side) and both transmissions, after disengaging ball socket.
6. To install, reverse removal procedure, making sure that the ball socket is fully seated.

NOTE: driver side linkage arm must point *down*, passenger side *up*.

1971-76

1. Raise hood and remove cowl vent screen.
2. Remove wiper arm and blade assembly from side being serviced.
3. Loosen, but do not remove, attaching nuts securing drive linkage to motor crank arm. If only left linkage is being removed, it is not necessary to loosen right attaching nuts.
4. Disconnect drive linkage from motor crank arm.
5. Remove the attaching screws of the linkage being serviced, then remove through plenum chamber opening.
6. To install, reverse removal procedure. Motor must be in "Park" position.

Motor R & R

See Cadillac section.

RADIO

See Cadillac section.

HEATER

Blower Assembly and Motor R & R

1969-70

1. Drain cooling system.
2. Remove rubber cooling hose from nipple and blower motor.
3. Disconnect blower motor electrical connector.
4. Remove five attaching screws and blower motor.
5. Remove left cowl-to-fender strut rod.
6. Remove heater hoses from blower case.
7. Disconnect Bowden cable from temperature door.
8. Disconnect connector from motor resistor.
9. Disconnect vacuum hoses, then remove twelve screws from blower case.
10. Pull blower assembly away from cowl and remove from car.
11. To install, reverse removal procedure, using a new gasket.

1971-76

See Cadillac section.

Heater Core R & R

1969-70

1. Remove heater blower motor and assembly.
2. Remove four screws, two on each side, that secure retaining clamps.
3. Remove retaining clamps and heater core.

1971-76

See Cadillac section.

SEAT BELTS

Seat Belt/Starter Interlock System —1974-75

The seat belt starter interlock system consists of an electronic module, seat sensor switches, seat buckle switches, interlock relay and an override relay.

The electronic module receives signals from the seat sensor switches and the buckle switches to monitor the proper belt buckling sequence. If the proper sequence is followed, the module opens the interlock relay and allows the engine to be started. It is located underneath the right-hand front seat cushion.

The seat sensor switches are normally open and are located in the seat cushion.

The seat belt buckle switches on the outboard buckles are normally open, while the center buckle switch is normally closed.

The interlock relay is located near the fuse block and the points are open when the coil is energized.

For emergencies, an override relay is provided. Two fuses protect the interlock system, the "Clk-Ltr-Ctsy-Lt" and "Gauges-Trans" fuses.

Disabling the Seat Belt/ Starter Interlock and Buzzer

The seat belt/starter interlock was used only on early production 1975s. A special act of Congress repealed its mandatory installation.

It is now legal to disable the seat belt/starter interlock, but *not* the warning light. To do this, proceed as follows:

1. Disconnect the negative (—) battery cable.
2. Locate the interlock harness connector, which is on or near the fuse block. The connector has orange, yellow, and green leads running to it.
3. Cut and tape the green lead on the body harness side of the interlock connector.
4. Remove the steering column lower cover.
5. Remove the buzzer connector from its mounting bracket and separate the buzzer from it. Install the connector back on the bracket.
6. Replace the steering column lower cover.
7. Connect the negative battery cable.
8. Check system operation by starting the car with the seat belt unfastened.

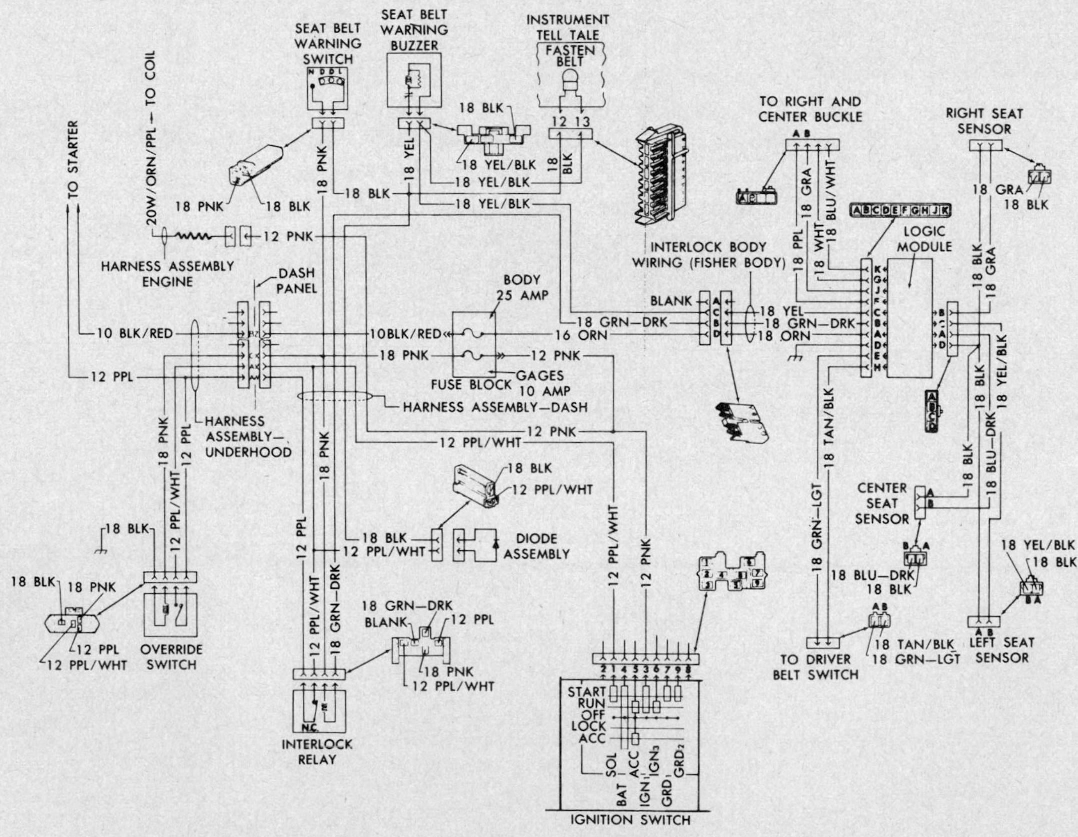

Seat belt interlock/starter wiring diagram (© Cadillac Div., G.M. Corp)

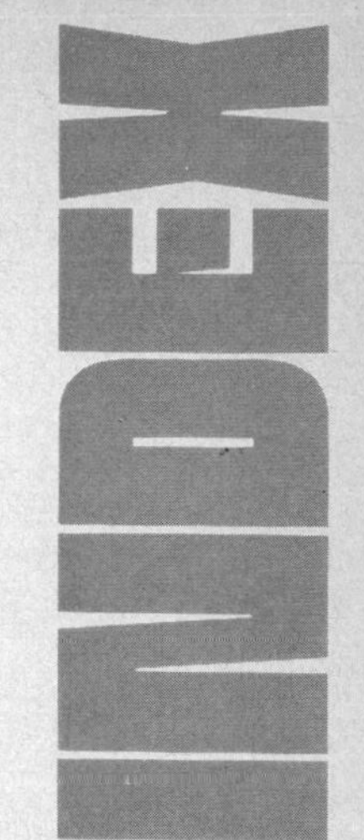

Camaro · Chevelle · Monte Carlo · Nova

YEAR IDENTIFICATION

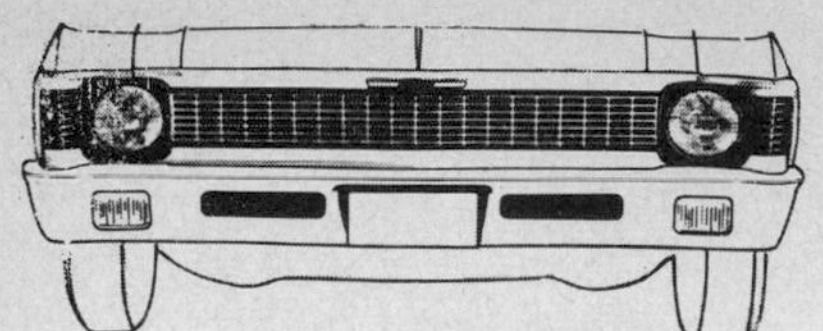

1969-72 Nova

1973 Nova

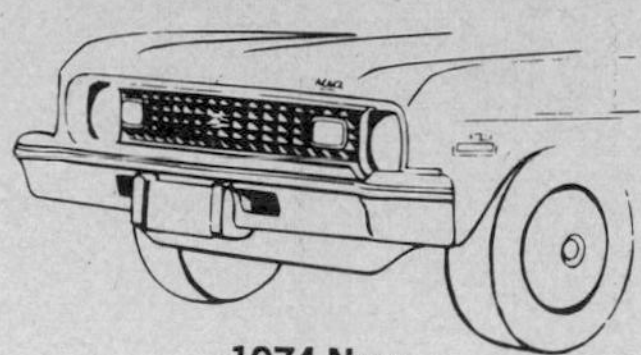

1974 Nova

1975 Nova LN

1976 Nova LN

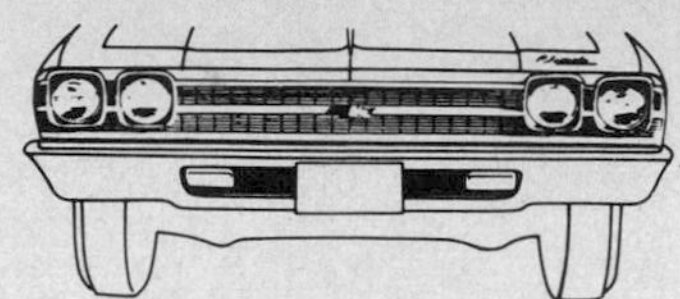

1969 Chevelle

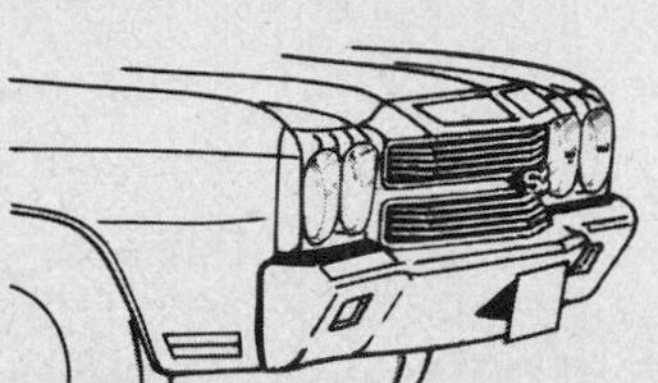

1970 Chevelle

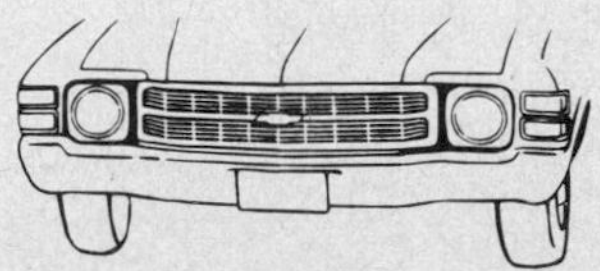

1971 Chevelle

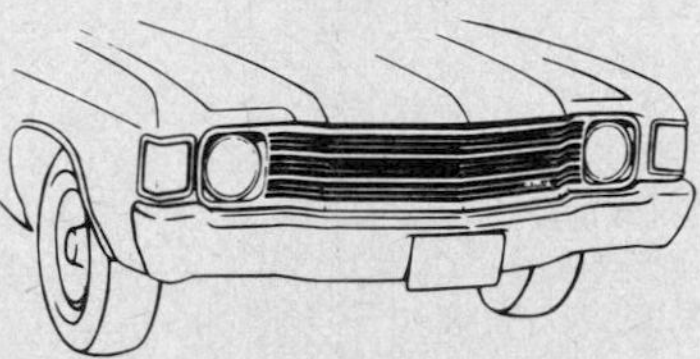

1972 Chevelle

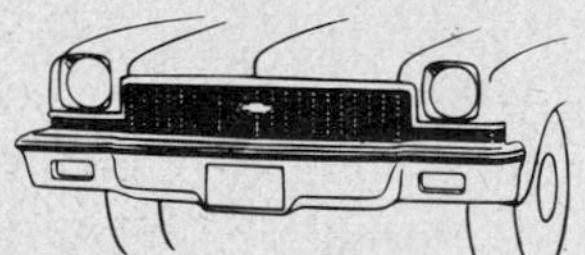

1973 Chevelle

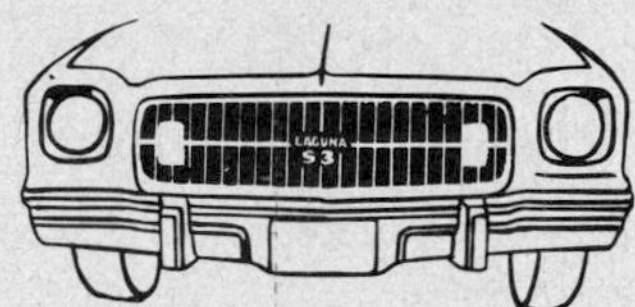

1974 Chevelle Laguna

1975 Malibu Classic

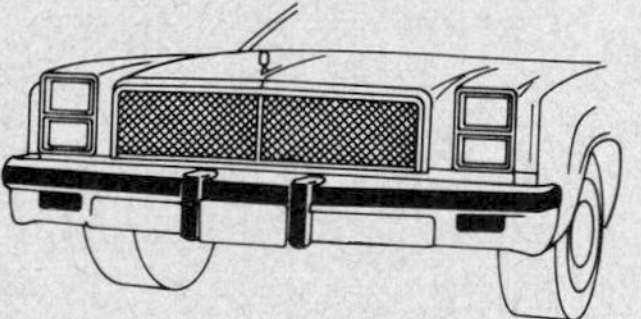

1976 Malibu Classic

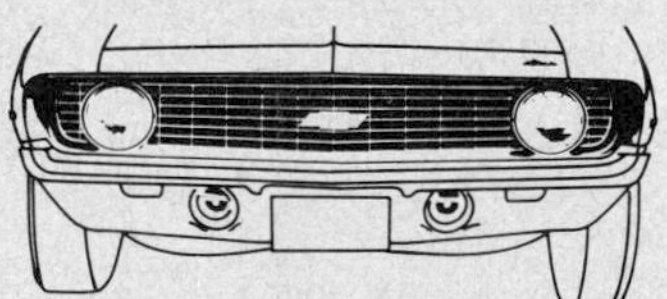

1969 Camaro

1969 Camaro SS

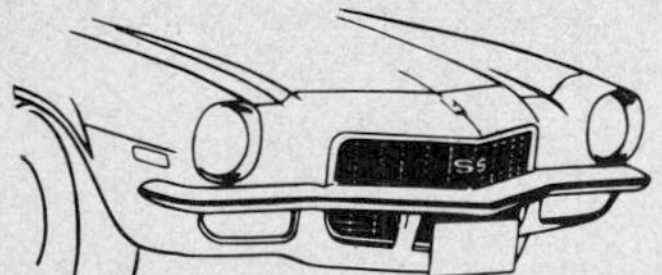

1970-71 Camaro

1972 Camaro

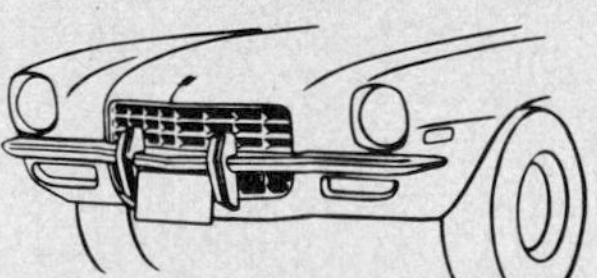

1973 Camaro

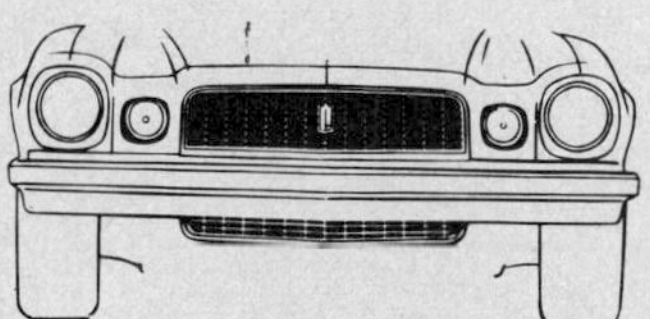

1974 Camaro

1975 Camaro

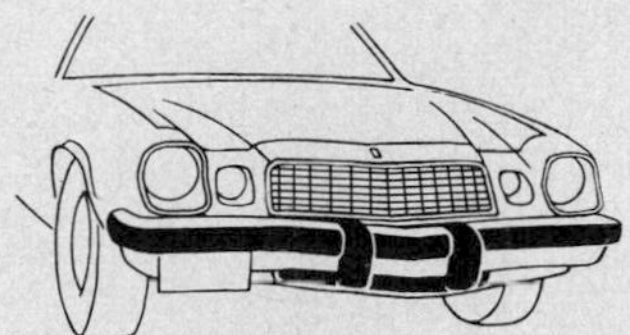

1976 Camaro

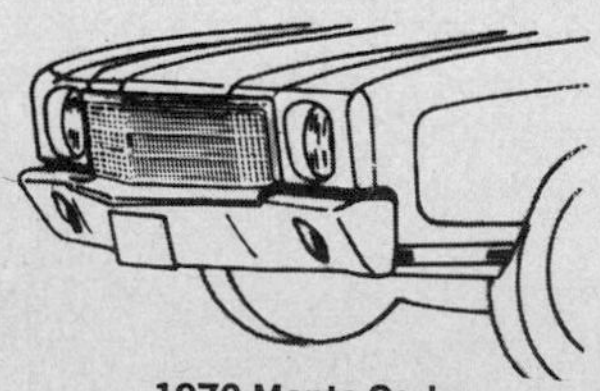

1970 Monte Carlo

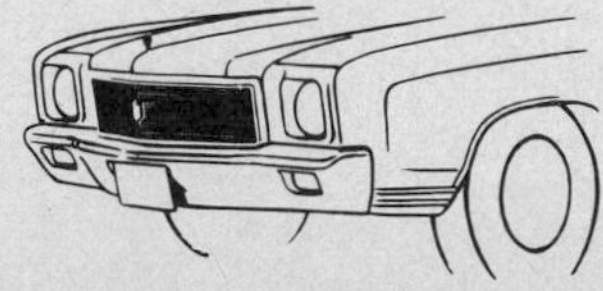

1971 Monte Carlo

1972 Monte Carlo

YEAR IDENTIFICATION

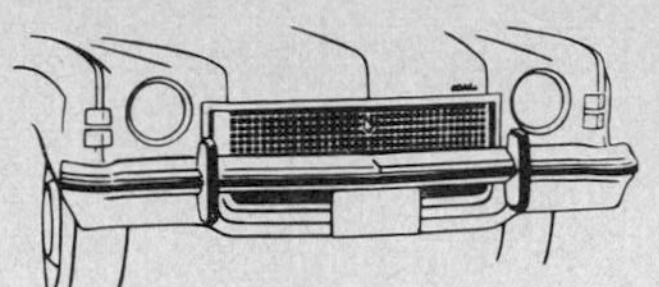

1973 Monte Carlo

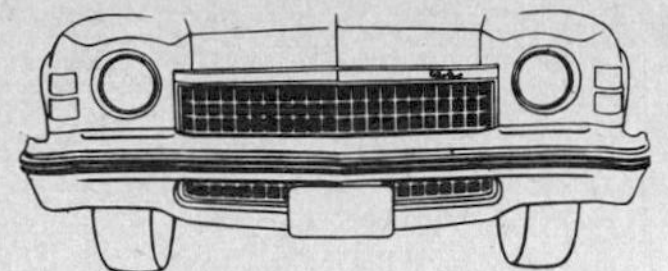

1974 Monte Carlo

1975 Monte Carlo

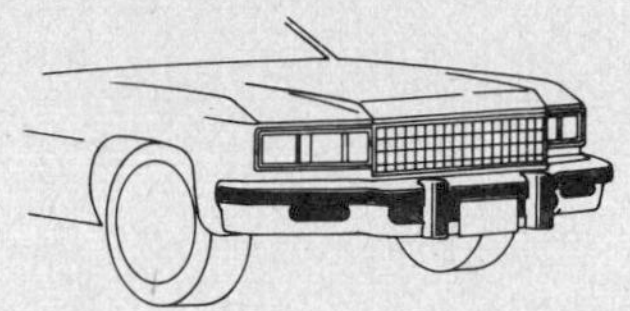

1976 Monte Carlo

FIRING ORDER

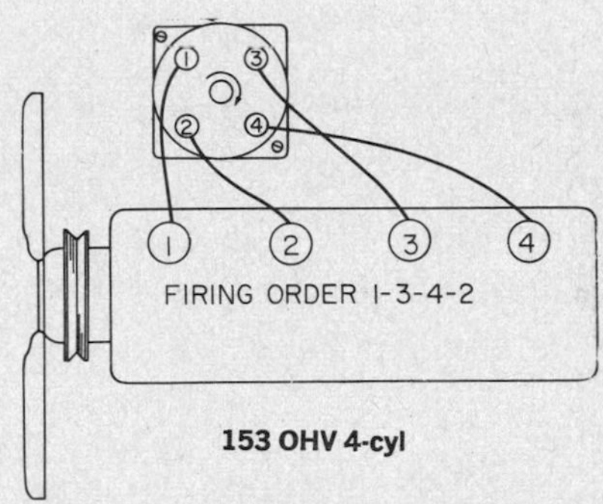

153 OHV 4-cyl

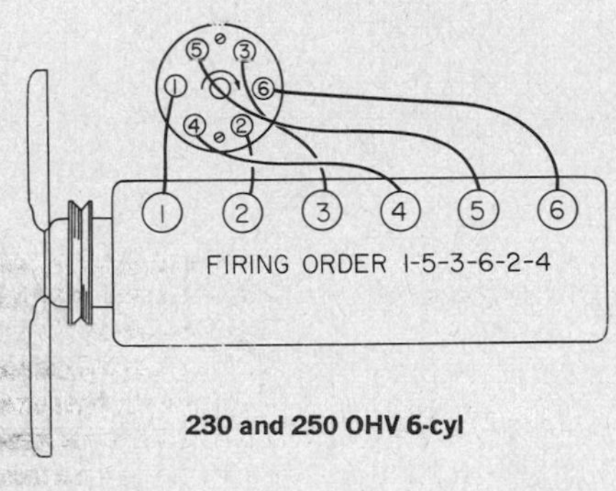

230 and 250 OHV 6-cyl

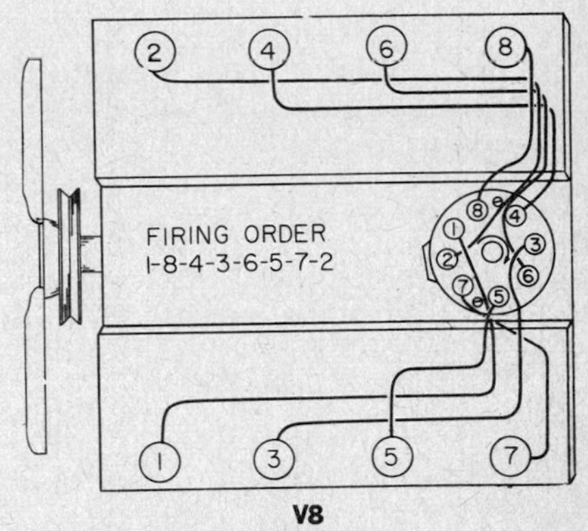

V8

CAR SERIAL NUMBER LOCATION

Car serial number is located on the top left-hand side of the instrument panel, visible through the windshield.

Car Serial Number Interpretation

A typical vehicle serial number tag yields manufacturer's identity, vehicle type, model year, assembly plant and production unit number when broken down as shown in the following charts.

through 1971

Mfr. Identity[1]	*Body Style*[2]	*Model Year*[3]	*Assy. Plant*[4]	*Unit No.*[5]
1	5645	8	F	100025

1. Manufacturer's identity number assigned to all Chevrolet built vehicles.
2. Model Identification
3. Last number of model year (1968).
4. F-Flint
5. Unit numbering will start at 100,001 at all plants.

1972 and later

Mfr. Identity[1]	*Series Code Letter*[2]	*Body Style*[3]	*Engine Model*[4]	*Model Year*[5]	*Assy. Plant*[6]	*Unit No.*[7]
1	N	47	R	4	F	100025

1. Manufacturer's identity number assigned to all Chevrolet built vehicles.
2. Series
3. Body Style
4. Engine code
5. Last number of model year (1974)
6. Assembly Plant (F-Flint)
7. Unit numbering will start at 000001 or 100001 depending on the model.

ENGINE IDENTIFICATION

Nova 4-6 Cyl.—Pad at front right-hand side of cylinder block at rear of distributor.
V8—Pad at front right-hand side of cylinder block.

No. Cyls.	Cu. In. Displ.	Type	YEAR AND CODE 1969	1970	1971	1972	1973	1974	1975
4	153	M.T.	AA	CCA					
4	153	PG, Torque Dr.	AB	CCB					
6	230	PG, w/ex. EM	AN						
6	230	PG, AC	AQ						
6	230	T.H. 350	AO						
6	230	AC	AP						
6	230	T.H. 350, AC	AR						
6	230	M.T.	AM						
6	230	Torque Dr.	AN	CCD					
6	250	M.T.	BE	CCG, CRF	CCI, CCL	CBG, CDM	CCC	CCR	

ENGINE IDENTIFICATION (Continued)

Nova 4-6 Cyl.—Pad at front right-hand side of cylinder block at rear of distributor.
V8—Pad at front right-hand side of cylinder block.

No. Cyls.	Cu. In. Displ.	Type	YEAR AND CODE 1969	1970	1971	1972	1973	1974	1975
6	250	PG, w/ex. EM	BB	CCM		CSD	CCA		
6	250	PG, AC	BC						
6	250	T.H. 350	BD	CCK				CCK	
6	250	AC	BF						
6	250	T.H. 350, AC	BH						
6	250	Torque Dr.	BB, BC						
6	250	M.T.		CAA					
6	250	PG, TD		CAB					
6	250	M.T., w/NB2					CCD		
6	250	PG, w/NB2					CCB		
6	250	T.H. California						CCW	
6	250								CJL, CJM,
									CJT, CJU
									KJR, CJS,
8	262								CZF, CZH,
									CZJ, CZK,
									CZL, CZM
8	307	M.T.				CKG	CHB		
8	307	PG				CKH			
8	307	T.H.				CTK	CHH		
8	307	M.T., w/ex. EM				CAR			
8	307	PG, w/ex. EM				CAZ			
8	307	T.H., w/ex. EM				CMA			
8	307	M.T., w/NB2					CHD		
8	307	T.H., w/NB2					CHC		
8	307	M.T.	DA	CNC					
8	307	PG	DC	CNE					
8	307	T.H. 350	DD	CNF					
8	307	4-spd.	DE	CND					
8	307	M.T.		CCA	CCA				
8	307	PG		CCC	CCC				
8	350	M.T.	HB, HD	CNI(250),		CKA	CKA, CKB		
				CNJ(300)		CKK			
8	350	T.H.	HA, HQ	CNN(250),		CTL	CKW		
				CRE(300)		CKD	CKW		
8	350	2-BBL.	HC						
8	350	PG	HE, HR	CNK, CNM					
8	350	PG, 2-BBL.	HF						
8	350	T.H.	HS						
8	350	PG		CGB(250)	CGB				
8	350	M.T.		CGK(300)	CGK				
8	350	T.H. 350		CGL(300)	CGL	CDD			
				CJD(300)		CMD			
8	350	M.T.		CJG(300)		CDG			
8	350	M.T., w/NB2					CKC, CKH	CKH	
8	350	A.T., w/NB2					CKK, CKD	CKD	
8	350	3-spd., 2-BBL.						CMC	
8	350	4-spd., 4-BBL.						CKB	
8	350	T.H., 2-BBL.						CMA	
8	350	T.H., 4-BBL.						CKD	
8	350								CMU, CMY,
									CRC, CRD,
									CRT, CRU,
									CRX, CUH,
									CUJ, CRZ,
									CUM, CUS
8	396	HP	JF						
8	396	SHP	JH, KA, KC						
8	396	HP, T.H. 400	JI						
8	396	SHP, T.H. 400	JL						

ENGINE IDENTIFICATION (Continued)

Nova 4-6 Cyl.—Pad at front right-hand side of cylinder block at rear of distributor.
V8—Pad at front right-hand side of cylinder block.

No. Cyls.	Cu. In. Displ.	Type	YEAR AND CODE 1969	1970	1971	1972	1973	1974	1975
8	396	T.H. 400	JM	CTW(350), CTY(375), CKN(325)					
8	396	PG	JU						
8	396	M.T.	KE	CTX(350), CKO(375)					
8	396	T.H. 400#		CKP(375)					
8	396	M.T., HDC		CTZ(350), CKQ(375)					
8	396	B.T., HDC#		CKU(375)					
8	396	M.T.#		CKT(375)					
8	402	M.T.		CKR(330)					
8	402	M.T., HDC		CKS(300)					

AC—air conditioned
HDC—heavy duty clutch
HP—high performance engine
SHP—special high performance engine
PCV—positive crankcase ventilation
OD—overdrive
w/ex. EM, or EM—with exhaust emission
M.T.—manual transmission
PG—Powerglide transmission.
3-spd.—three speed transmission
4-spd.—four speed transmission
T.H.—Turbo Hydra-Matic
#—Aluminum heads
TD—Torque Drive
NB2—Calif. only

Chevelle and Monte Carlo

Engine identification code letter follows immediately after engine serial number.
6 Cyl.—Pad at front right-hand side of cylinder block at rear of distributor.
V8—Pad at front right-hand side of cylinder block.

No. Cyls.	Cu. In. Displ.	Type	YEAR AND CODE 1969	1970	1971	1972	1973	1974	1975
6	230	HDC	BC						
6	230	HDC, AC	BB						
6	230	PG	BF						
6	230	PG, w/ex. EM	AN						
6	230	T.H., AC	AR						
6	230	T.H.	AD						
6	230	M.T.	AM						
6	230	3-spd. AC	AP						
6	230	PG, AC	AQ						
6	250	3-spd. or OD	BE	CCL					
6	250	3-spd. AC	BF						
6	250	PG	BB	CCM		CBJ			
6	250	PG, AC	BC						
6	250	T.H.	BD	CCK			CCA	CCX	
6	250	T.H., AC	BH						
6	250	M.T.			CAA	CBG	CCC	CCR	
6	250	M.T., w/NB2					CCD		
6	250	T.H., w/NB2					CCB	CCW	
6	250								CJL, CJR, CJT, CJU, CJS
8	307	T.H.	DD	CNF		CTK	CMA		
8	307	M.T.	DA	CNC			CHB		
8	307	4-spd.	DE	CND					
8	307	PG	DC	CNE		CKH			
8	307	M.T.			CCA	CKG			
8	300	T.H., w/NB2					CHC		
8	350	M.T.	HA			CKK, CKA	CKA, CKB		
8	350	T.H.	HB						
8	350	2-BBL., M.T.	HC					CMC	
8	350	2-BBL., T.H.	HD					CMA	
8	350	PG	HE	CNM(250)					
8	350	PG, 2-BBL.	HF						
8	350	M.T.	HP	CNI(250)					

ENGINE IDENTIFICATION (Continued)

Chevelle and Monte Carlo

Engine identification code letter follows immediately after engine serial number.
6 Cyl.—Pad at front right-hand side of cylinder block at rear of distributor.
V8—Pad at front right-hand side of cylinder block.

No. Cyls.	Cu. In. Displ.	Type	YEAR AND CODE 1969	1970	1971	1972	1973	1974	1975
8	350	M.T.	HR	CNJ(300)					
8	350	PG	HR	CNK(300)		CKB, CDB			
8	350	T.H.	HS	CRE(300)		CT, CKD	CKL, CKJ		
8	350	M.T.			CGA(245)				
8	350	PG			CGB(245)				
8	350	M.T.			CGK(270)				
8	350	T.H. 350			CGL(270)				
					CJD(270)				
8	350	M.T.			CJJ(270)				
8	350	M.T., w/NB2				CKC, CKH			
8	350	T.H., w/NB2				CKD, CKK		CKD	
8	350	3-spd., 4-BBL.						CKH	
8	350								CMY, CRU, CMJ, CMH, CRX, CR2, CUS, CMM
8	396	HDC	ED						
8	396	HP	JC						
8	396	SHP	JD						
8	396	PG	EK						
8	396	PG, HP	EL						
8	396	T.H. (325 hp)	ET						
8	396	T.H. (350 hp)	EU						
8	396	M.T.	JA	CTX(350)					
				CKT(375)					
				CKO(375)					
8	396	HP, 3-spd. T.H. 400	JE						
8	396	T.H. 400	JK	CTW(350)					
8	396	SHP, T.H. 400 (#—CKP only)	KF	CTY(375),					
				CKP(375)					
				CKU(375)					
8	396	M.T.	KG						
8	396	T.H. 400	KH	CKN(325)					
8	396	M.T., HP	KB						
8	396	M.T.	JV						
8	396	SHP, M.T.	KD						
8	396	M.T.	KI						
8	396	M.T., HDC		CTZ(350),					
				CKQ(375)					
8	400	T.H., 4-BBL.						CTC	
8	400	T.H., 4-BBL., California						CTA	
8	400								CTU, CTX, CTB
8	402	M.T.		CKR					
8	402	M.T., HDC (330 hp)		CKS		CLA, CLS			
8	402	T.H. 350 (Mk. IV)							
8	402	T.H. 400 (Mk. IV)			CLB	CLB			
8	402	M.T. (Mk. IV)							
8	402	4-spd. (Mk. IV)			CLL				
8	402	M.T. Police (Mk. IV)			CLR				
8	402	M.T. (Mk. IV)			CLS				
8	402	M.T. (Mk. IV)			CPR				
8	400	M.T. (Mk. IV)			CPA	CPA			
					CPG				
					CPD				
					CPP				

ENGINE IDENTIFICATION (Continued)

Chevelle and Monte Carlo

Engine identification code letter follows immediately after engine serial number.
6 Cyl.—Pad at front right-hand side of cylinder block at rear of distributor.
V8—Pad at front right-hand side of cylinder block.

No. Cyls.	Cu. In. Displ.	Type	YEAR AND CODE						
			1969	1970	1971	1972	1973	1974	1975
8	454	M.T. (390 hp)		CRN, CRT					
8	454	T.H. 400		CRQ					
8	454	T.H. 400 (450 hp)		CRR		CPD			
8	454	T.H. 400# (450 hp)		CRS					
8	454	M.T.		CRV			CWA	CWA	
8	454	T.H.					CWB	CWX	
8	454	M.T., w/NB2					CWC		
8	454	T.H. w/NB2					CWD	CWD	
8	454								CXW

AC—air conditioned
HDC—heavy duty clutch
HP—high performance
M.T.—manual transmission
OD—overdrive
PG—powerglide transmission
PCV—positive crankcase ventilation
w/ex. EM—with exhaust emission
w/T. Ign.—with transistor ignition
4-BBL.—four-barrel carburetor
T.H.—Turbo Hydra-Matic
#—Aluminum heads
NB2—Calif. only

Camaro

Engine identification code letter follows immediately after engine serial number.
6 Cyl.—Pad at front right-hand side of cylinder block at rear of distributor.
V8—Pad at front right-hand side of cylinder block.

No. Cyls.	Cu. In. Displ.	Type	YEAR AND CODE						
			1969	1970	1971	1972	1973	1974	1975
6	230	3 or 4-spd.	AM	CCC					
6	230	PG, Torque Dr.	AN	CCD					
6	230	PG, AC	AQ						
6	230	T.H. 350	AO						
6	230	AC	AP						
6	230	T.H. 350, AC	AR						
6	250	3 or 4-spd.	BE						
6	250	AC	BF						
6	250	PG, Torque Dr.	BB						
6	250	PG, AC	BC						
6	250	PG, AC, w/ex. EM	BC						
6	250	T.H. 350	BD						
6	250	T.H. 350, AC	BH						
6	250	M.T.			CAA	CBG	CCC	CCR	
6	250	PG			CCA	CBJ			
6	250	T.H.					CCA	CCX	
6	250	M.T., w/NB2					CCP		
6	250	T.H., w/NB2					CCB	CCW	
6	250								CJL, CJT, CJU
8	302	Z28	DZ*						
8	307	M.T.	DA	CNC					
8	307	P.G.	DC	CNE					
8	307	T.H. 350	DD	CNF		CTK	CHH		
8	307	4-spd.	DE	CND					
8	307	M.T.			CCA	CKG	CHB		
8	307	PG			CCA	CKH			
8	307	M.T., w/NB2					CHJ		
8	307	T.H., w/NB2					CHK		

ENGINE IDENTIFICATION (Continued)

Camaro

Engine identification code letter follows immediately after engine serial number.
6 Cyl.—Pad at front right-hand side of cylinder block at rear of distributor.
V8—Pad at front right-hand side of cylinder block.

No. Cyls.	Cu. In. Displ.	Type	YEAR AND CODE 1969	1970	1971	1972	1973	1974	1975*
8	350	3 or 4-spd.	HA, HQ	CNJ(300)					
8	350	PG	HE, HR	CNK(300)					
8	350	T.H.	HB, HS	CRE(300)		CKD			
8	350	2-BBL.	HC	CNJ(250)					
8	350	T.H., 2-BBL.	HD	CNM(250)				CMA	
8	350	PG, 2-BBL.	HF	CNN(250)					
8	350	PG			CGB(245)				
8	350	T.H. 400			CGR(330)		CLK	CLK	
8	350	M.T.			CGK(270)	CKA	CKB		
					CJG(270)	CRG			
8	350	T.H. 350			CGL(270)	CTL	CKU	CKU	
					CJD(270)	CRD	CKW		
8	350	M.T.			CJG(330)	CKK			
8	350	M.T., 4-spd., Z28					CLJ	CLJ	
							CKA		
8	350	M.T., w/NB2					CLM	CKH	
							CKY		
8	350	T.H., w/NB2					CKH	CKD	
							CLL		
							CKX		
							CKD		
8	350	M.T., 2-BBL.						CMC	
8	350	M.T., 4-BBL.						CKB	
8	350								CMU, CMB, CRX, CHW, CML
8	396	T.H. 400	JG	CJI(350)					
8	396	SHP	JH						
8	396	HP, T.H.	JI						
8	396	HP	JF						
8	396	PG	JB						
8	396	M.T.#	JJ, KE						
8	396	SHP, T.H. 400	JL	CJL(375)					
8	396	T.H. 400#	JM						
8	396	M.T.	JU	CJF(350)					
8	396	M.T., SHP	KA, KC	CJH(375)					
8	402	T.H.		CTW(350), CKN(325), CTY(375)		CTB			
8	402	M.T.		CTX(350),		CLA			
				CKO(375)		CTA			
8	402	T.H.			CLD(300)	CLB			
8	402	M.T.			CLC(300)				

AC—air conditioned
HDC—heavy duty clutch
HP—high performance
SHP—special high performance
M.T.—manual transmission
PG—Powerglide transmission
w/ex. EM—with exhaust emission
4-BBL.—four-barrel carburetor
2-BBL.—two-barrel carburetor
T.H.—Turbo Hydra-Matic
*—CNA = late production
#—Aluminum heads
NB2—Calif. only

GENERAL ENGINE SPECIFICATIONS

Year	Engine No. Cyl. Displacement (cu in.)	Carburetor Type	Horsepower @ rpm ■	Torque @ rpm (ft lbs) ■	Bore and Stroke (in.)	Compression Ratio	Oil Pressure @ 2000 rpm
'69	4-153	1 bbl	90 @ 4000	152 @ 2400	3.875 x 3.250	8.5:1	58
	6-230	1 bbl	140 @ 4400	220 @ 1600	3.875 x 3.250	8.5:1	58
	6-250	1 bbl	155 @ 4200	235 @ 1600	3.875 x 3.530	8.5:1	58
	8-302	4 bbl	290 @ 5800	290 @ 4200	4.000 x 3.000	11.0:1	45
	8-307	2 bbl	200 @ 4600	300 @ 2400	3.875 x 3.250	9.0:1	58
	8-350	2 bbl	250 @ 4800	345 @ 2800	4.000 x 3.480	9.0:1	62
	8-350	4 bbl	300 @ 4800	380 @ 3200	4.000 x 3.480	10.25:1	62
	8-396	4 bbl	325 @ 4800	410 @ 3200	4.094 x 3.760	10.25:1	62
	8-396	4 bbl	350 @ 5200	415 @ 3400	4.094 x 3.760	10.25:1	62
	8-396	4 bbl	375 @ 5600	415 @ 3600	4.094 x 3.760	11.0:1	62
'70	4-153	1 bbl	90 @ 4000	152 @ 2400	3.875 x 3.250	8.5:1	40
	6-230	1 bbl	140 @ 4400	220 @ 1600	3.875 x 3.250	8.5:1	40
	6-250	1 bbl	155 @ 4200	235 @ 1600	3.875 x 3.530	8.5:1	40
	8-307	2 bbl	200 @ 4600	300 @ 2400	3.875 x 3.250	9.0:1	40
	8-350	2 bbl	250 @ 4800	345 @ 2800	4.000 x 3.480	9.0:1	40
	8-350	4 bbl	300 @ 4800	380 @ 3200	4.000 x 3.480	10.25:1	40
	8-400	2 bbl	265 @ 4400	400 @ 2400	4.125 x 3.760	9.0:1	40
	8-402	4 bbl	330 @ 4800	410 @ 3200	4.126 x 3.760	10.25:1	40
	8-402	4 bbl	350 @ 5200	415 @ 3400	4.126 x 3.760	10.25:1	40
	8-454	4 bbl	360 @ 4400	500 @ 3200	4.251 x 4.000	10.25:1	40
'71	6-250	1 bbl	145 @ 4200	230 @ 1600	3.875 x 3.530	8.5:1	40
	8-307	2 bbl	200 @ 4600	300 @ 2400	3.875 x 3.250	8.5:1	40
	8-350	2 bbl	245 @ 4800	350 @ 2800	4.000 x 3.480	8.5:1	40
	8-350	4 bbl	270 @ 4800	360 @ 3200	4.000 x 3.480	8.5:1	40
	8-350	4 bbl	330 @ 5000	275 @ 5600	4.000 x 3.480	9.0:1	40
	8-402	4 bbl	300 @ 4800	400 @ 3200	4.126 x 3.760	8.5:1	40
	8-454	4 bbl	365 @ 4800	465 @ 3200	4.251 x 4.000	8.5:1	40
	8-454	4 bbl	425 @ 5600	475 @ 4000	4.251 x 4.000	9.0:1	40
'72	6-250	1 bbl	110 @ 3800	185 @ 1600	3.875 x 3.530	8.5:1	40
	8-307	2 bbl	130 @ 4000	230 @ 2400	3.875 x 3.250	8.5:1	40
	8-350	2 bbl	165 @ 4000	280 @ 2400	4.000 x 3.480	8.5:1	40
	8-350	4 bbl	200 @ 4400	300 @ 2800	4.000 x 3.480	8.5:1	40
	8-350	4 bbl	255 @ 5600	280 @ 4000	4.000 x 3.480	9.0:1	40
	8-402	4 bbl	240 @ 4400	345 @ 3200	4.126 x 3.760	8.5:1	40
	8-454	4 bbl	220 @ 4000	390 @ 3200	4.251 x 4.000	8.5:1	40
'73	6-250	1 bbl	100 @ 3800	175 @ 1600	3.875 x 3.530	8.25:1	40
	8-307	2 bbl	115 @ 4000	205 @ 2000	3.875 x 3.250	8.5:1	40
	8-350	2 bbl	145 @ 4000	255 @ 2400	4.000 x 3.480	8.5:1	40
	8-350	4 bbl	175 @ 4400	270 @ 2400	4.000 x 3.480	8.5:1	40
	8-350	4 bbl	245 @ 5200	280 @ 4000	4.000 x 3.480	9.0:1	40
	8-454	4 bbl	245 @ 4000	375 @ 2800	4.251 x 4.000	8.5:1	40
'74	6-250	1 bbl	100 @ 3600	175 @ 1800	3.875 x 3.530	8.25:1	40
	8-350②	2 bbl	145 @ 3600	250 @ 2200	4.000 x 3.480	8.5:1	40
	8-350③	4 bbl	160 @ 3800	245 @ 2400	4.000 x 3.480	8.5:1	40
	8-350	4 bbl	185 @ 4000	270 @ 2600	4.000 x 3.480	8.5:1	40
	8-350/Z28	4 bbl	245 @ 5200	280 @ 4000	4.000 x 3.480	9.0:1	40
	8-400②	2 bbl	150 @ 3200	295 @ 2600	4.126 x 3.750	8.5:1	40
	8-400③	4 bbl	180 @ 3800	290 @ 2400	4.126 x 3.750	8.5:1	40
	8-454	4 bbl	235 @ 4000	360 @ 2800	4.251 x 4.000	8.25:1	44

GENERAL ENGINE SPECIFICATIONS (con't.)

Year	Engine No. Cyl. Displacement (cu in.)	Carburetor Type	Horsepower @ rpm ■	Torque @ rpm (ft lbs) ■	Bore and Stroke (in.)	Compression Ratio	Oil Pressure @ 2000 rpm
'75-'76	6-250	1 bbl	105 @ 3800	185 @ 1200	3.875 x 3.530	8.25:1	40
	8-262	2 bbl	110 @ 3600	200 @ 2000	3.671 x 3.10	8.5:1	40
	8-305	2 bbl	N.A.	N.A.	3.736 x 3.480	N.A.	40
	8-350②	2 bbl	145 @ 3800	250 @ 2200	4.000 x 3.480	8.5:1	40
	8-350	4 bbl	155 @ 3800	245 @ 2400④	4.000 x 3.480	8.5:1	40
	8-400	4 bbl	175 @ 3600	305 @ 2000	4.126 x 4.000	8.5:1	40
	8-454②	4 bbl	215 @ 4000	350 @ 2400	4.251 x 4.000	8.15:1	44

■ Starting 1972, horsepower and torque are SAE net figures. They are measured at the rear of the transmission with all accessories installed and operating. Since the figures vary when a given engine is installed in different models, some are representative rather than exact.

② Not available—Calif.

③ Calif. only

④ 250 @ 2400 in wagon

Camaro

TUNE-UP SPECIFICATIONS

Year	ENGINE No. Cyl. Displacement (cu in.)	hp	SPARK PLUGS Type	SPARK PLUGS Gap (in.)	DISTRIBUTOR Point Dwell (deg)	DISTRIBUTOR Point Gap (in.)	IGNITION TIMING (deg) ▲ ● Man Trans	IGNITION TIMING (deg) ▲ ● Auto Trans	VALVES Intake Opens ■ (deg) ●	Fuel Pump Pressure (psi)	IDLE SPEED (rpm) ▲ Man Trans	●	IDLE SPEED (rpm) ▲ Auto Trans.
'69	6-230	140	R-46N	.035	31-34	.019	TDC	4B	16	4-5	700		500/400③
	6-250	155	R-46N	.035	31-34	.019	TDC	4B	16	4-5	700		500/400③
	8-302	290	R-43	.035	28-32	.019	4B	—	N.A.	5-6½	900		—
	8-307	200	R-45S	.035	28-32	.019	2B	2B	28	5-7½	700		600
	8-327	210	R-45S	.035	28-32	.019	2A	2B	28	5-6½	700		600
	8-350	255	R-44	.035	28-32	.019	TDC	4B	28	5-6½	700		600
	8-350	300	R-44	.035	28-32	.019	TDC	4B	28	5-6½	700		600
	8-396	325	R-44N	.035	28-32	.019	4B	4B	28	5-8½	800		600
	8-396	350	R-43N	.035	28-32	.019	TDC	4B	56	5-8½	800		600
	8-396	375	R-43N	.035	28-32	.019	4B	4B	N.A.	5-8½	750		750/400
'70	6-250	155	R-43	.035	29-31	.019	TDC	4B	16	3½-4½	750		650/400③
	8-307	200	R-46T	.035	31-34	.019	2B	8B	28	5-6½	700		600/450③
	8-350	250	R-44	.035	29-31	.019	TDC	4B	28	7-8½	750		600/450③
	8-350	300	R-44	.035	29-31	.019	TDC	4B	28	7-8½	700		600
	8-350	360	R-43	.035	29-31	.019	8B	8B	42½	7-8½	800		750/500③
	8-396	350	R-44T	.035	29-31	.019	TDC	4B	56	5-8½	700		600
	8-396	375	R-43T	.035	29-31	.019	4B	4B	N.A.	5-8½	750		700
'71	6-250	145	R-46TS	.035	31-34	.019	4B	4B	16	3½-4½	550		550②
	8-307	200	R-45TS	.035	29-31	.019	4B	8B	28	5-6½	600		550②
	8-350	245	R-45TS	.035	29-31	.019	2B	6B	28	7-8½	600		550②
	8-350	270	R-44TS	.035	29-31	.019	4B	8B	28	7-8½	600		550②
	8-350	300	R-43TS	.035	29-31	.019	8B	12B	42⅔	7-8½	700		700
	8-402	300	R-44TS	.035	28-30	.019	8B	8B	28	7-8½	600		600
'72	6-250	110	R-46T	.035	31-34	.019	4B	4B	16	3½-4½	700		600
	8-307	130	R-44T	.035	29-31	.019	4B	8B	28	5-6½	900		600
	8-350	165	R-44T	.035	29-31	.019	6B	6B	28(44)	7-8½	900		600
	8-350	200	R-44T	.035	29-31	.019	4B	8B	28(44)	7-8½	800		600
	8-350	255	R-44T	.035	29-31	.019	8B	12B	42⅔	7-8½	900		700
	8-402	240	R-44TS	.035	28-30	.019	8B	8B	28	7-8½	800		600
'73	6-250	100	R-46T	.035	31-34	.019	6B	6B	16	3½-4½	700/450③		600/450
	8-307	115	R-44T	.035	29-31	.019	4B	4B	28	5-6½	900/450③		600/450
	8-350	145	R-44T	.035	29-31	.019	8B	8B	28	7½-8½	900/450③		600/450
	8-350	175	R-44T	.035	29-31	.019	8B	12B	28	7½-8½	900/450③		600/450
	8-350	245	R-44T	.035	29-31	.019	8B	12B	52	7½-8½	900/450③		700/450

Camaro TUNE-UP SPECIFICATIONS

When analyzing compression test results, look for uniformity among cylinders rather than specific pressures.

Year	ENGINE No. Cyl. Displacement (cu in.)	hp	SPARK PLUGS Type	Gap (in.)	DISTRIBUTOR Point Dwell (deg)	Point Gap (in.)	IGNITION TIMING (deg) ▲ • Man Trans	Auto Trans	VALVES Intake Opens ■ (deg) •	Fuel Pump Pressure (psi)	IDLE SPEED (rpm) ▲ Man Trans •	Auto Trans.
'74	6-250	100	R-46T	.035	31-34	.019	6B	6B	16	4-5	800/450③	600/450
	8-350	145	R-44T	.035	29-31	.019	4B	8B	28	7½-9	900/450③	600/450
	8-350	160	R-44T	.035	29-31	.019	4B	8B	44	7½-9	900/450③	600/450
	8-350	185	R-44T	.035	29-31	.019	4B	8B	28	7½-9	900/450③	600/450
	8-350	245	R-44T	.035	29-31	.019	8B	8B	52	7½-9	900/450③	700/450
'75	6-250	105	R-46TX	.060	Electronic		10B	10B	16	4-5	800/425③	550/425③④ (600/425)
	8-350	145	R-44TX	.060	Electronic		6B	6B	28	7½-9	800	600
	8-350	155	R-44TX	.060	Electronic		6B	8B(6B)	28	7½-9	800	600
'76	6-250	105	R-46TS	.035	Electronic		6B	6B	16	4-5	850	550⑤(600)
	8-305	All	R-45TS	.045	Electronic		6B	8B(0)	28	7½-9	800	600
	8-350	155	R-45TS	.045	Electronic		8(6)B	8(6)B	28	7½-9	800	600

▲ See text for procedure. For those cars equipped with an idle solenoid, disconnect solenoid and adjust idle to 450 rpm
● Figure in parentheses indicates California engine
■ All figures Before Top Dead Center
① Not used
② A/C on
③ Lower figure with Idle Solenoid disconnected
④ Without intake manifold integral with head—600/450
A After Top Dead Center
B Before Top Dead Center
⑤ Air conditioning on
TDC Top Dead Center
— Not applicable

MECHANICAL VALVE LIFTER CLEARANCE

Year	Engine		Intake (Hot) In.	Exhaust (Hot) In.
1969	V8-302	290 hp	.030	.030
1970	V8-350	360 hp	.024	.030
1971	V8-350	300 hp	.024	.030
1972	V8-350	255 hp	.024	.030

Nova TUNE-UP SPECIFICATIONS

When analyzing compression test results, look for uniformity among cylinders rather than specific pressures.

Year	ENGINE No. Cyl. Displacement (cu in.)	hp	SPARK PLUGS Type	Gap (in.)	DISTRIBUTOR Point Dwell (deg)	Point Gap (in.)	IGNITION TIMING (deg) ▲ • Man Trans	Auto Trans	VALVES Intake Opens ■ (deg) •	Fuel Pump Pressure (psi)	IDLE SPEED (rpm) ▲ Man Trans •	Auto Trans.
'69	4-153	90	D-46N	.035	31-34	.019	TDC	4B	28	4-5	750	600
	6-230	140	R-46N	.035	31-34	.019	TDC	4B	16	4-5	700	550/400③
	6-250	155	R-46N	.035	31-34	.019	TDC	4B	16	4-5	700	550/400③
	8-307	200	R-45S	.035	31-34	.019	2B	2B	28	5½-7½	700	600
	8-350	250	R-45S	.035	29-31	.019	TDC	4B	28	5½-7½	700	600
	8-350	300	R-44S	.035	29-31	.019	TDC	4B	28	7½-9	700	600
	8-396	350	R-43N	.035	28-32	.019	TDC	4B	56	5-8½	800	600
	8-396④	375	R-43N	.035	28-32	.019	4B	4B	44	5-8½	750	750/400
'70	4-153	90	R-46N	.035	31-34	.019	TDC	4B	17½	4-5	750	650
	6-230	140	R-46N	.035	31-34	.019	TDC	4B	16	4-5	700	550/400③
	6-250	155	R-46N	.035	31-34	.019	TDC	4B	16	4-5	700	550/400③
	8-307	200	R-45	.035	29-31	.019	2B	8B	28	5½-7½	700	600/450③
	8-350	250	R-44	.035	29-31	.019	TDC	4B	28	5½-7½	750	600/450③
	8-350	300	R-44	.035	29-31	.019	TDC	4B	28	7½-9	700	600
'71	6-250	145	R-46TS	.035	31-34	.019	4B	4B	16	4-5	550	500
	8-307	200	R-45TS	.035	29-31	.019	4B	8B	28	5½-7½	600	550②
	8-350	245	R-45TS	.035	29-31	.019	2B	6B	28	7½-9	600	550②
	8-350	270	R-44TS	.035	29-31	.019	4B	8B	28	7½-9	600	550②

TUNE-UP SPECIFICATIONS

When analyzing compression test results, look for uniformity among cylinders rather than specific pressures.

Year	ENGINE No. Cyl. Displacement (cu in.)	hp	SPARK PLUGS Type	Gap (in.)	DISTRIBUTOR Point Dwell (deg)	Point Gap (in.)	IGNITION TIMING (deg) ▲ ● Man Trans	Auto Trans	VALVES Intake Opens ■ (deg) ●	Fuel Pump Pressure (psi)	IDLE SPEED (rpm) ▲ ● Man Trans	Auto Trans.
'72	6-250	110	R-46T	.035	31-34	.019	4B	4B	16	4-5	700	600
	8-307	130	R-44T	.035	29-31	.019	4B	8B	28	5½-7½	900	600
	8-350	165	R-44T	.035	29-31	.019	6B	6B	28(44)	7½-9	900	600
	8-350	200	R-44T	.035	29-31	.019	4B	8B	28(44)	7½-9	800	600
'73	6-250	100	R-46T	.035	31-34	.019	6B	6B	16	3½-4½	700/450③	600/450
	8-307	115	R-44T	.035	29-31	.019	4B	8B	28	5-6½	900/450③	600/450
	8-350	145	R-44T	.035	29-31	.019	8B	8B	28	7-8½	900/450③	600/450
	8-350	175	R-44T	.035	29-31	.019	8B	12B	28	7-8½	900/450③	600/450
'74	6-250	100	R-46T	.035	31-34	.019	6B	6B	16	4-5	800/450③	600/450
	8-350	145	R-44T	.035	29-31	.019	4B	8B	28	7½-9	900/450③	600/450
	8-350	160	R-44T	.035	29-31	.019	4B	8B	44	7½-9	900/450③	600/450
	8-350	185	R-44T	.035	29-31	.019	4B	8B	28	7½-9	900/450③	600/450
'75	6-250	105	R-46TX	.060	Electronic		10B	10B	16	4-5	800/425③	550/425③④ (600/425)
	8-262	110	R-44TX	.060	Electronic		8B	8B	26	7½-9	800	600
	8-350	145	R-44TX	.060	Electronic		6B	6B	28	7½-9	800	600
	8-350	155	R-44TX	.060	Electronic		6B	8B(6B)	28	7½-9	800	600
'76	6-250	105	R-46TS	.035	Electronic		8B	6B	16	4-5	850	550⑤(600)
	8-350	All	R-45TS	.045	Electronic		6B	8B(0)	28	7½-9	800	600
	8-350	145	R-45TS	.045	Electronic		8(6)B	8(6)B	28	7½-9	800	600

▲ See text for procedure
● Figure in parentheses indicates California engine
■ All figures Before Top Dead Center
① Not used
② A/C on
③ Lower figure with Idle Solenoid disconnected
④ Adjust mechanical valve lifter clearance to .024 in. for intake with engine hot, and to .028 in. for exhaust with engine hot
⑤ Air conditioning on

A After Top Dead Center
B Before Top Dead Center
TDC Top Dead Center
— Not applicable

Chevelle, Monte Carlo

TUNE-UP SPECIFICATIONS

When analyzing compression test results, look for uniformity among cylinders rather than specific pressures.

Year	ENGINE No. Cyl. Displacement (cu in.)	hp	SPARK PLUGS Type	Gap (in.)	DISTRIBUTOR Point Dwell (deg)	Point Gap (in.)	IGNITION TIMING (deg) ▲ ● Man Trans	Auto Trans	VALVES Intake Opens ■ (deg) ●	Fuel Pump Pressure (psi)	IDLE SPEED (rpm) ▲ ● Man Trans	Auto Trans.
'69	6-230	140	R-46N	.035	31-34	.019	TDC	4B	16	3-4½	700	550/400③
	6-250	155	R-46N	.035	31-34	.019	TDC	4B	16	3-4½	700	550/400③
	8-307	200	R-45S	.035	28-32	.019	2B	2B	28	5-6½	700	600
	8-350	250	R-44	.035	28-32	.019	TDC	4B	28	5-6½	700	600
	8-350	300	R-44	.035	28-32	.019	TDC	4B	28	5-6½	700	600
	8-396	325	R-44N	.035	28-32	.019	4B	4B	28	5-8½	800	600
	8-396	350	R-43N	.035	28-32	.019	TDC	4B	56	5-8½	800	600
	8-396	375	R-43N	.035	28-32	.019	4B	4B	44	5-8½	750	750/400
'70	6-250	155	R-46T	.035	31-34	.019	TDC	4B	16	3-4½	750	600/400③
	8-307	200	R-43	.035	28-32	.019	2B	8B	28	5-6½	700	600/450③
	8-350	250	R-44	.035	28-32	.019	TDC	4B	28	5-6½	750	600/450③
	8-350	300	R-44	.035	28-32	.019	TDC	4B	28	5-6½	700	600
	8-396	350	R-44T	.035	28-32	.019	TDC	4B	56	5-8½	700	600
	8-396	375	R-43T	.035	28-32	.019	4B	4B	N.A.	5-8½	750	700
	8-400	265	R-44	.035	28-32	.019	4B	8B	28	5-8½	700	600/450③
	8-400	330	R-44T	.035	28-32	.019	4B	4B	28	5-8½	700	600
	8-454	360	R-43T	.035	28-32	.019	6B	6B	56	5-8½	700	600

TUNE-UP SPECIFICATIONS

Chevelle, Monte Carlo

When analyzing compression test results, look for uniformity among cylinders rather than specific pressures.

	ENGINE		SPARK PLUGS		DISTRIBUTOR		IGNITION TIMING (deg) ▲ ●		VALVES	Fuel	IDLE SPEED (rpm) ▲	
Year	No. Cyl. Displacement (cu in.)	hp	Type	Gap (in.)	Point Dwell (deg)	Point Gap (in.)	Man Trans	Auto Trans	Intake Opens ■ (deg) ●	Pump Pressure (psi)	Man Trans ●	Auto Trans.
'71	6-250	145	R-46TS	.035	31-34	.019	4B	4B	16	3½-4½	550	500
	8-307	200	R-45TS	.035	29-31	.019	4B	8B	28	5-6½	600	550
	8-350	245	R-45TS	.035	29-31	.019	2B	6B	28	7-8½	600	550
	8-350	270	R-44TS	.035	29-31	.019	4B	8B	28	7-8½	600	550
	8-400	255	R-44TS	.035	29-31	.019	4B	8B	28	7-8½	600	550
	8-402	300	R-44TS	.035	29-31	.019	8B	8B	28	7-8½	600	600
	8-454	365	R-42TS	.035	29-31	.019	8B	8B	56	7-8½	600	600
	8-454	425	R-42TS	.035	29-31	.019	8B	12B	44	7-8½	700	700
'72	6-250	110	R-46TS	.035	31-34	.019	4B	4B	16	3½-4½	700	600
	8-307	130	R-44T	.035	29-31	.019	4B	8B	28	5-6½	900	600
	8-350	165	R-44T	.035	29-31	.019	6B	6B	28	7-8½	900	600
	8-350	175	R-44T	.035	29-31	.019	4B	8B	28	7-8½	800	600
	8-402	240	R-44T	.035	29-31	.019	8B	8B	30	7-8½	750	600
	8-454	270	R-44T	.035	29-31	.019	8B	8B	56	7-8½	750	600
'73	6-250	100	R-46T	.035	31-34	.019	6B	6B	16	3½-4½	700/450③	600/450
	8-307	115	R-44T	.035	29-31	.019	4B	8B	28	5-6½	900/450③	600/450
	8-350	145	R-44T	.035	29-31	.019	8B	8B	28	7-8½	900/450③	600/450
	8-350	175	R-44T	.035	29-31	.019	8B	12B	28	7-8½	900/450③	600/450
	8-454	245	R-44T	.035	29-31	.019	10B	10B	55	7-8½	900/450③	600/450
'74	6-250	100	R-46T	.035	31-34	.019	6B	6B	16	4-5	800/450③	600/450
	8-350	145	R-44T	.035	29-31	.019	4B	8B	28	7½-9	900/450③	600/450
	8-350	160	R-44T	.035	29-31	.019	4B	8B	44	7½-9	900/450③	600/450
	8-400	150	R-44T	.035	29-31	.019	—	8B	28	7½-9	—	600/450
	8-400	180	R-44T	.035	29-31	.019	—	8B	44	7½-9	—	600/450
	8-454	235	R-44T	.035	29-31	.019	10B	10B	55	7½-9	800/450③	600/450
'75	6-250	105	R-46TX	.060	Electronic		10B	10B	16	4-5	850/425③	550/425 ③④ (600/425)
	8-350	145	R-44TX	.060	Electronic		6B	6B	28	7½-9	800	600
	8-350	155	R-44TX	.060	Electronic		—	6B	28	7½-9	—	600
	8-400	175	R-44TX	.060	Electronic		—	8B	28	7½-9	—	600
	8-454	215	R-44TX	.060	Electronic		—	16B	55	7½-9	—	600/500③
'76	6-250	105	R-46TS	.035	Electronic		6B	6B	16	4-5	850	550⑤(600)
	8-305	All	R-45TS	.045	Electronic		—	8B(0)	28	7½-9	—	600
	8-350	145	R-45TS	.045	Electronic		—	6B	28	7½-9	—	600
	8-350	155	R-45TS	.045	Electronic		—	8(6)B	28	7½-9	—	600
	8-400	175	R-45TS	.045	Electronic		—	8B	28	7½-9	—	600

▲ See text for procedure
● Figure in parentheses indicates California engine
■ All figures Before Top Dead Center
①② Not used
③ Lower figure with idle solenoid disconnected
④ Without intake manifold integral with head—600/450
A After Top Dead Center
B Before Top Dead Center
⑤ Air conditioning on

TDC Top Dead Center
— Not applicable

MECHANICAL VALVE LIFTER CLEARANCE

Year	Engine	Intake (Hot) in.	Exhaust (Hot) in.
1969-1971	V8-396 375 hp	.024	.028
1971	V8-454 425 hp	.024	.028

CAPACITIES

Year	ENGINE No. Cyl. Displacement (Cu. In.)	Engine Crankcase Add 1 Qt For * New Filter	TRANSMISSION Pts To Refill After Draining Manual 3-Speed	4-Speed	Automatic ●	Drive Axle (pts)	Gasoline Tank (gals)	COOLING SYSTEM (qts) With Heater	With A/C
'69	4-153	3.5	3	—	6	3.5	shown in the	9	9
	6-230	4	3③	—	6⑬	3.5④	following	13	13
	6-250	4	3③	—	6⑬	3.5④	chart.	13	13
	8-302	4	3③	3	6⑬	3.5④		17	—
	8-307	4	3③	3	6⑬	3.5④		17	18⑦
	8-350	4	3③	3	6⑬	3.5④		16	17⑦
	8-396	4	3③	3	8	3.5④		23	24
'70	4-153	3.5	3	—	6	3.75⑧		9	9
	6-230	4	3	—	6⑬	3.75⑧		12	13
	6-250	4	3	—	6⑬	3.75⑧		12	13
	8-307	4	3	—	6⑬	3.75⑧		15	16
	8-350	4	3	3	6.5⑨⑬	3.75⑧		16	16
	8-400	4	3	3	8	3.75⑧		16	16
	8-396	4	3	3	8	3.75⑧		23	24
	8-400	4	3	3	8	3.75⑧		23	24
	8-454	4	3	3	8	3.75⑧		22	23
'71	6-250	4	3	—	6	3.75		12	—
	8-307	4	3	—	6⑬	3.75		15	16
	8-350	4	3	3	6.5⑬	3.75		16	16
	8-400	4	3	3	8	3.75		23	23
	8-454	4	—	3	8	3.75		22	23
'72	6-250	4	3	—	6⑬	4.25		12	—
	8-307	4	3	—	6⑬	4.25		15	16
	8-350	4	3	3	6.5⑩⑬	4.25		16	16
	8-402	4	—	3	8	4.25⑪		24	24
	8-454	4	—	3	8	4.25⑪		23	24
'73	6-250	4	3	—	6⑬	4.25		12.5	—
	8-307	4	3	—	5	4.25		16⑭	17⑮
	8-350	4	3	3	5⑩	4.25		16⑭	17⑮
	8-454	4	—	3	8	4.25⑪		23	24
'74	6-250	4	3	—	8	4.25		12.5	—
	8-350	4	3	3	8	4.25		16⑭	17⑮
	8-400	4	—	—	8	4.25⑪		16	17
	8-454	4	—	3	9	4.9		23	24
'75-'76	6-250	4	3	—	8	4.25		14⑰	15⑯
	8-262	4	3	—	8	4.25		17	18
	8-305	4	3	3	8	4.25		17	18
	8-350	4	3	3	8	4.25		17	18⑱
	8-400	4	—	—	8	4.25⑪		17⑲	18
	8-454	4	—	3	9	4.9		23	23

* Add ½ qt with filter change on 4 cyl engine
● Specifications do not include torque converter
①② Not used
③ 3.5 pts with heavy duty transmission
④ 4 pts with 8.875 in. ring gear
⑥ 14 qts on Camaro
⑦ Less one qt on Nova
⑧ 4:25 pts with 8⅞ in. ring gear
⑨ 8 pts with 360 hp engine
⑩ 8 pts with Z-28 350
⑪ 4.9 pts in Monte Carlo, El Camino, or Chevelle with 8⅞ in. ring gear
⑫ Not used
⑬ 5 pts with Turbo Hydramatic 350
⑭ 15.5 Nova
⑮ 16.5 Nova
⑯ 16 Chevelle
⑰ 15 Nova
⑱ 17 Nova
⑲ 18 Monte Carlo
— Not applicable

GAS TANK CAPACITIES (Gals)

Year	Nova	Chevelle, Monte Carlo	Camaro
'69	18	20①	18
'70	18	20②	19
'71	16	19②	17
'72	16	19②	18
'73	21	22③	18
'74	21	22③	21
'75-'76	21	22③	21

① 22 gals in station wagon
② 18 gals in station wagon
③ 26 gals in El Camino

VALVE SPECIFICATIONS

Year	Engine No. Cyl. Displacement (cu in.)	Seat Angle (deg)	Face Angle (deg)	Spring Test Pressure (lbs @ in.)	Spring Installed Height (in.)	STEM TO GUIDE Clearance (in.)		STEM Diameter (in.)	
						Intake	Exhaust	Intake	Exhaust
'69	4-153	46③	45	81 @ 1.66	1 21/32	.0010-.0037	.0015-.0052	.3414	.3414
	6-230	46③	45	59 @ 1.66	1 21/32	.0010-.0037	.0015-.0052	.3414	.3414
	6-250	46③	45	59 @ 1.66	1 21/37	.0010-.0037	.0015-.0052	.3414	.3414
	8-302	46③	45	80 @ 1.70	1 5/32	.0010-.0037	.0010-.0047	.3414	.3414
	8-307	46③	45	80 @ 1.70	1 5/32	.0010-.0037	.0010-.0047	.3414	.3414
	8-350	46③	45	80 @ 1.70	1 5/32	.0010-.0037	.0010-.0047	.3414	.3414
	8-396①	46③	45	90 @ 1.88	1 7/8	.0010-.0035	.0012-.0047	.3719	.3719
	8-396④	46③	45	100 @ 1.88	1 7/8	.0010-.0035	.0012-.0047	.3719	.3719
'70	4-153	46③	45	81 @ 1.66	1 21/32	.0010-.0037	.0015-.0052	.3414	.3414
	6-230	46③	45	59 @ 1.66	1 21/32	.0010-.0037	.0015-.0052	.3414	.3414
	6-250	46③	45	59 @ 1.66	1 21/32	.0010-.0037	.0015-.0052	.3414	.3414
	8-307	46③	45	80 @ 1.70	1 23/32	.0010-.0037	.0012-.0049	.3414	.3414
	8-350	46③	45	80 @ 1.70	1 23/32	.0010-.0037	.0012-.0049	.3414	.3414
	8-400	46③	45	80 @ 1.70	1 7/8	.0010-.0037	.0012-.0047	.3414	.3414
	8-402	46③	45	75 @ 1.88⑤	1 7/8	.0010-.0037	.0012-.0047	.3719	.3717
	8-454	46③	45	75 @ 1.88⑤	1 7/8	.0010-.0037	.0012-.0047	.3717	.3719
'71	6-250	46	45	60 @ 1.66	1 21/32	.0010-.0037	.0015-.0052	.3414	.3414
	8-307	46	45	80 @ 1.70	1 23/32	.0010-.0037	.0012-.0049	.3414	.3414
	8-350	46	45	80 @ 1.70	1 23/32	.0010-.0037	.0012-.0049	.3414	.3414
	8-402	46	45	75 @ 1.88⑤	1 7/8	.0010-.0037	.0012-.0047	.3719	.3717
	8-454	46	45	75 @ 1.88⑤	1 7/8	.0010-.0037	.0012-.0047	.3719	.3717
'72	6-250	46	45	60 @ 1.66	1 21/32	.0010-.0037	.0015-.0052	.3414	.3414
	8-307	46	45	80 @ 1.70	1 23/32	.0010-.0037	.0012-.0049	.3414	.3414
	8-350	46	45	80 @ 1.70	1 23/32	.0010-.0037	.0012-.0049	.3414	.3414
	8-402	46	45	75 @ 1.88⑤	1 7/8	.0010-.0037	.0012-.0047	.3719	.3717
	8-454	46	45	75 @ 1.88⑤	1 7/8	.0010-.0037	.0012-.0047	.3719	.3717
'73	6-250	46	45	60 @ 1.66	1 21/32	.0010-.0027	.0015-.0032	.3414	.3414
	8-307	46	45	80 @ 1.61⑥	1 5/8⑦	.0010-.0027	.0012-.0029	.3414	.3414
	8-350	46	45	80 @ 1.70⑥	1 23/32⑦	.0010-.0027	.0012-.0027	.3414	.3414
	8-454	46	45	80 @ 1.88	1 7/8	.0010-.0027	.0012-.0027	.3719	.3417
'74	6-250	46	45	60 @ 1.66	1 21/32	.0010-.0027	.0010-.0027	.3414	.3414
	8-350	46	45	80 @ 1.70⑥	1 23/32⑦	.0010-.0027	.0010-.0027	.3414	.3414
	8-400	46	45	80 @ 1.70⑥	1 23/32⑦	.0010-.0027	.0010-.0027	.3414	.3414
	8-454	46	45	80 @ 1.88	1 7/8	.0010-.0027	.0010-.0027	.3719	.3719

VALVE SPECIFICATIONS

Year	Engine No. Cyl. Displacement (cu in.)	Seat Angle (deg)	Face Angle (deg)	Spring Test Pressure (lbs @ in.)	Spring Installed Height (in.)	STEM TO GUIDE Clearance (in.) Intake	Exhaust	STEM Diameter (in.) Intake	Exhaust
'75-'76	6-250	46	45	60 @ 1.66	1 21/32	.0010-.0027	.0010-.0027	.3414	.3414
	8-305, 8-262	46	45	80 @ 1.70⑥	1 23/32⑦	.0010-.0027	.0010-.0027	.3414	.3414
	8-350	46	45	80 @ 1.70⑥	1 23/32⑦	.0010-.0027	.0010-.0027	.3414	.3414
	8-400	46	45	80 @ 1.70⑥	1 23/32⑦	.0010-.0027	.0010-.0027	.3414	.3414
	8-454	46	45	90 @ 1.80	1 5/64	.0010-.0027	.0010-.0027	.3719	.3719

① 325 hp
② Not used
③ 45° on aluminum heads
④ 350 hp
⑤ Inner spring—30 @ 1.78
⑥ 80 @ 1.61 for exhaust
⑦ 1 39/64 for exhaust

TORQUE SPECIFICATIONS

All readings in ft lbs

Year	Engine No. Cyl. Displacement (cu in.)	Cylinder Head Bolts	Rod Bearing Bolts	Main Bearing Bolts	Crankshaft Pulley or Damper Bolt	Flywheel to Crankshaft Bolts	MANIFOLD Intake	Exhaust
'69-'76	6-230, 250	95	35	65	—	60	35⑧	30⑦⑩
'69-'76	8-305, 8-262, 302, 307, 350, 400	70	45	75②	60⑥	60	30	⑤
'69-'76	8-396, 402 (Big Block)	80①	50	110	85⑥	65	30	30
	8-454	80①	50④	110	85⑨	65	30	20

① Aluminum Heads—Short bolts 65, Long bolts 75
② Engines with 4-bolt mains—Outer bolts 65
③ Not used
④ 7/16 Rod bolts—70
⑤ Center bolts—30, end bolts 20
⑥ Where applicable
⑦ Exhaust-to-intake
⑧ Manifold-to-head
⑨ 65 starting 1975
⑩ With intake manifold integral with head—30 center, 20 on four end bolts

CRANKSHAFT AND CONNECTING ROD SPECIFICATIONS

All measurements are given in inches

Year	Engine No. Cyl. Displacement (cu in.)	CRANKSHAFT Main Brg. Journal Dia	Main Brg. Oil Clearance	Shaft End-Play	Thrust on No.	CONNECTING ROD Journal Diameter	Oil Clearance	Side Clearance
'69	4-153	2.2983-2.2993	.0003-.0029	.002-.006	5	1.999-2.000	.0007-.0027	.009-.013
	6-230	2.2983-2.2993	.0003-.0029	.002-.006	7	1.999-2.000	.0007-.0027	.009-.013
	6-250	2.2983-2.2993	.0003-.0029	.002-.006	7	1.999-2.000	.0007-.0027	.009-.013
	8-302 (Z28)	2.4479-2.4488	.0008-.003	.003-.011	5	2.099-2.100	.0007-.0028	.009-.013
	8-307	2.4479-2.4488	.0008-.002②	.003-.011	5	2.099-2.100	.0007-.0027	.009-.013
	8-327	2.4479-2.4488	.0008-.002②	.003-.011	5	2.099-2.100	.0007-.0028	.009-.013
	8-350	2.4479-2.4488	.0008-.002②	.003-.011	5	2.099-2.100	.0007-.0028	.009-.013
	8-396	③	⑤	.006-.010	5	2.199-2.200	.0009-.0025	.015-.021
	8-396 (375 H.P.)	④	.0013-.0025⑥	.006-.010	5	2.1985-2.1995	.0014-.0030	.019-.025
'70	4-153	2.2983-2.2993	.0003-.0029	.002-.006	5	1.999-2.000	.0007-.0027	.009-.013
	6-230	2.2983-2.2993	.0003-.0029	.002-.006	7	1.999-2.000	.0007-.0027	.009-.013
	6-250	2.2983-2.2993	.0003-.0029	.002-.006	7	1.999-2.000	.0007-.0027	.009-.013
	8-307, 350	2.4484-2.4493①	.0003-.0015⑦	.002-.006	5	2.099-2.100	.0007-.0028	.008-.014
	8-350 (Z28)	2.4484-2.4493①	.0013-.0025⑧	.002-.006	5	2.099-2.100	.0013-.0035	.008-.014
	8-400 (Monte Carlo)	2.6584-2.6493⑫	.0008-.0020⑮	.002-.006	5	2.099-2.100	.0009-.0025	.008-.014
	8-402	2.7487-2.7496⑨	.0007-.0019⑩	.006-.010	5	2.199-2.200	.0009-.0025	.013-.023
	8-454	2.7485-2.7494④	.0013-.0025⑪	.006-.010	5	2.199-2.200	.0009-.0025	.015-.021

CRANKSHAFT AND CONNECTING ROD SPECIFICATIONS (Continued)

All measurements are given in inches

Year	Engine No. Cyl. Displacement (cu in.)	CRANKSHAFT Main Brg. Journal Dia	Main Brg. Oil Clearance	Shaft End-Play	Thrust on No.	CONNECTING ROD Journal Diameter	Oil Clearance	Side Clearance
'71	6-250	2.2983-2.2993	.0003-.0029	.002-.006	7	1.999-2.000	.0007-.0027	.009-.014
	8-307, 350	2.4484-2.4493⑭	.0008-.0020⑮	.002-.006	5	2.099-2.100	.0013-.0035	.008-.014
	8-350 (Z28)	2.4484-2.4493⑭	.0013-.0025⑧	.002-.006	5	2.099-2.100	.0013-.0035	.008-.014
	8-402	2.7487-2.7496⑨	.0007-.0019⑩	.006-.010	5	2.199-2.200	.0009-.0025	.013-.023
	8-454 (365 H.P.)	2.7485-2.7494④	.0013-.0025⑪	.006-.010	5	2.199-2.200	.0009-.0025	.015-.021
	8-454 (425 H.P.)	2.7481-2.7490①	.0013-.0025⑬	.006-.010	5	2.1985-2.1995	.0009-.0025	.019-.025
'72	6-250	2.2983-2.2993	.0003-.0029	.002-.006	7	1.999-2.000	.0007-.0027	.009-.014
	8-307, 350	2.4484-2.4493⑭	.0008-.0020⑮	.002-.006	5	2.099-2.100	.0013-.0035	.008-.014
	8-350 (Z28)	2.4484-2.4493⑭	.0013-.0025⑧	.002-.006	5	2.099-2.100	.0013-.0035	.008-.014
	8-402	2.7487-2.7496⑨	.0007-.0019⑩	.006-.010	5	2.199-2.200	.0009-.0025	.013-.023
	8-454	2.7485-2.7494④	.0013-.0025⑪	.006-.010	5	2.199-2.200	.0009-.0025	.015-.021
'73	6-250	2.3004	.0003-.0029	.002-.006	7	1.999-2.000	.0007-.0027	.009-.014
	8-307, 350	2.4502⑯	.0008-.0020⑮	.002-.007	5	2.099-2.100	.0013-.0035	.008-.014
	8-454	2.7492⑰	.0007-.0019⑱	.006-.010	5	2.199-2.200	.0009-.0025	.015-.023
'74	6-250	2.3004	.0003-.0029	.002-.006	7	1.999-2.000	.0007-.0027	.007-.016
	8-350	2.4502⑯	.0008-.0020⑮	.002-.007	5	2.099-2.100	.0013-.0025	.008-.014
	8-400	2.6503⑲	.0008-.0020⑮	.002-.007	5	2.099-2.100	.0013-.0025	.008-.014
	8-454	2.7499⑳	.0007-.0019⑱	.006-.010	5	2.199-2.200	.0013-.0035	.015-.023
'75-'76	6-250	2.2999	.0003-.0029	.002-.006	7	1.999-2.000	.0007-.0027	.007-.016
	8-262	2.4502⑯	.0008-.0020⑮	.002-.007	5	2.098-2.099	.0013-.0035	.008-.014
	8-305, 8-350	2.4502⑯	.0008-.0020⑮	.002-.007	5	2.099-2.100	.0013-.0035	.006-.016
	8-400	2.6503⑲	.0008-.0020⑮	.002-.007	5	2.099-2.100	.0013-.0025	.008-.014
	8-454	2.7499⑳	.0007-.0019⑩	.006-.010	5	2.199-2.200	.0009-.0025	.015-.023

① No. 5—2.4478-2.4488
② No. 5—.0018-.0034
③ Nos. 1-2—2.7484-2.7493
Nos. 3-4—2.7481-2.7490
No. 5—2.7478-2.7488
④ No. 1—2.7484-2.7493
Nos. 2-4—2.7481-2.7490
No. 5—2.7478-2.7488
⑤ Nos. 1-2—.0010-.0022
Nos. 3-4—.0013-.0025
No. 5—.0015-.0031
⑥ No. 5—.0015-.0031
⑦ Nos. 2-4—.0006-.0018
No. 5—.0008-.0023
⑧ w/Man. trans.—No. 5—.0023-.0033
w/Auto. trans.—No. 1—.0019-.0031
Nos. 2-4—.0013-.0025
No. 5—.0023-.0033
⑨ Nos. 3-4—2.7481-2.7490
No. 5—2.7473-2.7483
⑩ Nos. 2-4—.0013-.0025
No. 5—.0019-.0035
⑪ No. 5—.0024-.0040
⑫ No. 5—2.6479-2.6488
⑬ No. 5—.0029-.0045
⑭ Nos. 2-4—2.4481-2.4490
No. 5—2.4479-2.4488
⑮ Nos. 2-4—.0011-.0023
No. 5—.0017-.0033
⑯ No. 5—2.4508
⑰ Nos. 2-4—2.7504
No. 5—2.7499
⑱ Nos. 2-4—.0013-.0028
No. 5—.0019-.0035
⑲ No. 5—2.6509
⑳ Nos. 2-4—2.7504
No. 5—2.7505

RING GAP

All measurements are given in inches

Year	Engine	Top Compression	Bottom Compression
'69-'76	4-153, 6-230, 250, 8-262, 307, 396, 400, 402, 454	.010-.020	.010-.020
'69	8-302	.013-.023	.013-.025
'76	8-305	.010-.020	.010-.025
'69	8-350	.013-.023	.013-.025
'70-'72	8-350①	.010-.020	.013-.025
'73-'76	8-350	.010-.020	.013-.025

Year	Engine	Oil Control
'69-'76	4-153, 6-230, 250, 8-307, 350, 396, 400, 402, 454	.015-.055
'69	8-396	.010-.030
'75-'76	8-262	.010-.025
'76	8-305	.010-.035

① 255, 330 hp Top .010-.020
2nd .013-.023

RING SIDE CLEARANCE

All measurements are given in inches

Year	Engine	Top Compression	Bottom Compression
'69-'76	4-153, 6-230, 8-302, 307, 400	.0012-.0027 ③	.0012-.0032 ③
'69	8-396	.0017-.0032	.0017-.0032
'69-'76	6-250	.0012-.0027	.0012-.0032
'69-'76	8-262, 350	.0012-.0032①	.0012-.0027②
'70-'76	8-402, 454	.0017-.0032	.0017-.0032

① .0012-.0027 on 1975-76 2 bbl. 350
② 145, 155, 165, 245, 250 hp 350 cu in. engine .0012-.0032
③ 330 hp 400 cu in. engine
Top .0017-.0032
2nd .0017-.0032
④ .002-.007 for 1970-74 350 2 bbl and 1974-76 350 4 bbl, except 1974 Z28

Year	Engine	Oil Control
'69-'76	4-153, 6-230, 250, 8-262, 302, 307, 350, 400	.0000-.0050④
'69-'76	8-396, 402, 454	.0005-.0065

PISTON CLEARANCE

① 1971 Only

Year	Engine	Horsepower	Piston to Bore Maximum Service Clearance (in.)
'70	4-153, 6-230, 250, 8-307	All	.0025
	8-302	All	.0061
	8-350	250, 300	.0027
	8-400	265	.0034
	8-402	All	.0038
	8-454	360	.0049
'71-'72	6-250, 8-307	All	.0025
	8-350	245, 270	.0027
	8-350	330	.0061
	8-402	All	.0035
	8-454	365	.0049
	8-454①	425	.0065
'73	6-250, 8-307	All	.0025
	8-350	145, 175	.0027
	8-350	245	.0061
	8-454	All	.0035
'74	6-250	100	.0025
	8-350	145, 160, 185	.0027
	8-350	245	.0051
	8-400	150, 180	.0034
	8-454	235	.0035
'75-'76	6-250	105	.0025
	8-262	110	.0025
	8-350	145	.0025
	8-350	155	.0027
	8-400	175	.0034
	8-454	215	.0035

ALTERNATOR AND REGULATOR SPECIFICATIONS

	ALTERNATOR			REGULATOR						
					Field Relay			Regulator		
Year	Part No.	Field @ 12 V Current	Output (amps)	Part No.	Air Gap (in.)	Point Gap (in.)	Volts to Close	Air Gap (in.)	Point Gap (in.)	Volts @ 85°
'69	1100834	2.2-2.6	37	1119515	.015	.030	2.3-3.7	.067	.014	13.5-14.4
	1100836	2.2-2.6	37	1119515	.015	.030	2.3-3.7	.067	.014	13.5-14.4
'70	1100834	2.2-2.6	37	1119515	.015	.030	2.3-3.7	.067	.014	13.5-14.4
	1100837	2.2-2.6	37	1119515	.015	.030	2.3-3.7	.067	.014	13.5-14.4
'71	1100838	2.2-2.6	37	1119515	.015	.030	2.3-3.7	.067	.014	13.5-14.4
	1100839	2.2-2.6	37	1119515	.015	.030	2.3-3.7	.067	.014	13.5-14.4
'72	1100566	2.2-2.6	35	1119515	.015	.030	1.5-3.2	.067	.014	13.8-14.8
	1100917	2.8-3.2	59	1119519	.030	.030	1.5-3.2	.067	.014	13.8-14.8
	1100843	2.8-3.2	58	Integrated with alternator						13.8-14.8
'73	1100497	2.8-3.2	36	Integrated with alternator						13.8-14.8
	1100934	2.8-3.2	37	Integrated with alternator						13.8-14.8
'74	1100934	4-4.5	37	Integrated with alternator						13.8-14.8
	1102347	4-4.5	61	Integrated with alternator						13.8-14.8
	1100497	4-4.5	37	Integrated with alternator						13.8-14.8
	1100573	4-4.5	42	Integrated with alternator						13.8-14.8
	1100597	4-4.5	61	Integrated with alternator						13.8-14.8
	1100560, 1100575	4-4.5	55	Integrated with alternator						13.8-14.8

ALTERNATOR AND REGULATOR SPECIFICATIONS

Year	Alternator Part No.	Alternator Field @ 12 V Current	Alternator Output (amps)	Regulator Part No.	Field Relay Air Gap (in.)	Field Relay Point Gap (in.)	Field Relay Volts to Close	Regulator Air Gap (in.)	Regulator Point Gap (in.)	Regulator Volts @ 85°
'75	1100497, 1102397	4-4.5	37	Integrated with alternator						13.8-14.8
	1102483	4-4.5	37	Integrated with alternator						13.8-14.8
	1100560, 1100575	4-4.5	55	Integrated with alternator						13.8-14.8
	1100597, 1102347	4-4.5	61	Integrated with alternator						13.8-14.8

BATTERY AND STARTER SPECIFICATIONS

Year	Engine No. Cyl. Displacement (cu in.)	Battery Ampere Hour Capacity •	Battery Volts	Battery Terminal Grounded	Starter Lock Test Amps	Starter Lock Test Volts	Starter Lock Test Torque (ft lbs)	Starter No-Load Test Amps	Starter No-Load Test Volts	Starter No-Load Test RPM	Brush Spring Tension (oz)
'69	4 & 6, 8-307	45	12	Neg.	Not Recommended			—	10.6	—	35
	8-302, 350, 396	61	12	Neg.	Not Recommended			—	9	—	35
'70-'71	4 & 6, 8-307	45	12	Neg.	Not Recommended			50-80	9	5,500-10,500	35
	8-350	61	12	Neg.	Not Recommended			55-80	9	3,500-6,000	35
	8-402 (396)	61	12	Neg.	Not Recommended			65-95	9	7,500-10,500	35
	8-454	62	12	Neg.	Not Recommended			65-95	9	7,500-10,500	35
'72	6-250	45	12	Neg.	Not Recommended			50-80	9	5,500-10,500	35
	8-307, 350, 402	61	12	Neg.	Not Recommended			50-80①	9	5,500-10,500	35
	8-454	76	12	Neg.	Not Recommended			65-95	9	7,500-10,500	35
'73	6-250	45	12	Neg.	Not Recommended			50-80	9	5,500-10,500	35
	8-307	61	12	Neg.	Not Recommended			50-80	9	5,500-10,500	35
	8-350, 454	76	12	Neg.	Not Recommended			65-95	9	7,500-10,500	35
'74	6-250	2300	12	Neg.	Not Recommended			50-80	9	5,500-10,500	35
	8-350, 400	2900	12	Neg.	Not Recommended			65-95	9	7,500-10,500	35
	8-454	3750	12	Neg.	Not Recommended			65-95	9	7,500-10,500	35
'75-'76	6-250	2500	12	Neg.	Not Recommended			50-80	9	5,500-10,500	35
	8-262	2500	12	Neg.	Not Recommended			55-80	9	3,500-6,000	35
	8-350, 400	3200	12	Neg.	Not Recommended			65-95	9	7,500-10,000	35
	8-454	4000	12	Neg.	Not Recommended			65-95	9	7,500-10,000	35

① 350 & 402 use 454 starter below
• Cranking Power in watts @ 0°F is given, starting 1974

BRAKE SPECIFICATIONS

All measurements are given in inches

Year	Model	Master Cylinder Disc	Master Cylinder Drum	Wheel Cylinder Front Disc	Wheel Cylinder Front Drum	Wheel Cylinder Rear	Brake Disc or Drum Diameter Front Disc	Brake Disc or Drum Diameter Front Drum	Brake Disc or Drum Diameter Rear
'69	Chevelle	1.00	1.00	2.063	1.125	.938①	11.0	9.5	9.5
	Nova, Camaro	1.125	1.00	2.938	1.125	.875	11.0	9.5	9.5
'70-'72	Nova, Chevelle	1.125	1.000	2.938	1.125	.875	11.00	9.5	9.5
	Camaro, Monte Carlo	1.125	—	2.938	—	.875	11.00	—	9.5
'73	Nova	1.125	1.000	2.938	1.125	.875	11.00	9.5	9.5
	Chevelle, Camaro	1.000②	—	2.938	—	.875	11.00	—	9.5
	Chevelle wagon	1.000②	—	2.938	—	.939	11.00	—	11.0
	Monte Carlo	1.125	—	2.938	—	.875	11.00	—	9.5

BRAKE SPECIFICATIONS

All measurements are given in inches

Year	Model	Master Cylinder Disc	Master Cylinder Drum	Wheel Cylinder Front Disc	Wheel Cylinder Front Drum	Wheel Cylinder Rear	Brake Disc or Drum Diameter Front Disc	Brake Disc or Drum Diameter Front Drum	Brake Disc or Drum Diameter Rear
'74	Nova	1.000	1.000	2.938	1.125	.875	11.00	9.5	9.5
	Chevelle, Camaro, Monte Carlo S	1.000	—	2.938	—	.875	11.00	—	9.5
	Chevelle wagon	1.000	—	2.938	—	.938	11.00	—	11.0
'75	Nova, Chevelle, Camaro	1.000②	—	2.938	—	.875	11.00	—	9.5
	Chevelle wagon	1.000②	—	2.938	—	.938	11.00	—	11.0
	Monte Carlo S	1.000	—	2.938	—	.875	11.00	—	9.5
'76	Nova, Camaro	1.000②	—	2.938	—	.938	11.00	—	9.5
	Chevelle	0.938②	—	2.938	—	1.000③	11.00	—	11.0
	Monte Carlo	1.125	—	2.938	—	.938	11.00	—	11.0

① .875 with disc brakes
② 1.125 with Power assist
③ .938 with power brakes
— Not applicable

— Not applicable

WHEEL ALIGNMENT SPECIFICATIONS

Year	Model	Caster Range (deg)	Caster Pref Setting (deg)	Camber Range (deg)	Camber Pref Setting (deg)	Toe-in (in.)	Steering Axis Inclination (deg)	Wheel Pivot Ratio (deg) Inner Wheel	Wheel Pivot Ratio (deg) Outer Wheel
'69	Nova	0 to 1P	½P	¼N to ¾P	½P	⅛ to ¼	8¾	20	N.A.
	Chevelle	1½N to ½N①	1N	0 to 1P	½P	⅛ to ¼	8¼	20	18½
	Camaro	0 to 1P	½P	¼N to ¾P	½P	⅛ to ¼	8¾	20	N.A.
'70-'71	Nova	0 to 1P	½P	¼N to ¾P	½P	⅛ to ¼	8¼ to 9¼	20	N.A.
	Chevelle, Monte Carlo	1½N to ½N①	1N	0 to 1P	½P	⅛ to ¼	7¾ to 8¾	20	N.A.
	Camaro	0 to 2P	1P	¼N to 1¾P	¾P	⅛ to ¼	10 to 11	20	N.A.
'72	Nova	0 to 1P	½P	¼N to ¾P	¼P	⅛ to ¼	8¾ to 9¼	—	—
	Chevelle	1½N to ½N	1N	¼P to 1¼P	¾P	⅛ to ¼	7¾ to 8¾	—	—
	Monte Carlo	½N to ½P	0	¼P to 1¼P	¾P	⅛ to ¼	7¾ to 8¾	—	—
	Camaro	½N to ½P	0	½P to 1½P	1P	⅛ to ¼	9 to 10	—	—
	Camaro Z28	1½N to ½N	1N	¼P to 1¼P	¾P	⅛ to ¼	9¼ to 10¼	—	—
'73	Nova	½N to 1½P	½P	½N to 1P	¾P	1/16 to 5/16	9	—	—
	Chevelle	1¾N to ¾N	1¼N	½P to 1½P	1P②	⅛ to ¼	9½	—	—
	Monte Carlo	4¼P to 5¼P	4¾P	½P to 1½P	1P②	0 to ⅛	9½	—	—
	Camaro	1N to 1P	0	¼P to 1¾P	1P	1/16 to 5/16	10½	—	—
	Camaro Z28	2N to 0	1N	1½N to 0	¾N	1/16 to 5/16	10½	—	—
'74	Nova	0 to 1P	½P	¼P to ¾P	¼P	⅛ to ¼	8¾	—	—
	Chevelle③	1½ to ½N	1N	½P to 1½P	1P	0 to ⅛	10½	—	—
	Chevelle④	½N to ½P	0	½P to 1½P	1P	0 to ⅛	10½	—	—
	Monte Carlo S	4½ to 5½P	5	½P to 1½P	1P	0 to ⅛	10½	—	—
	Camaro	½N to ½P	0	½P to 1½P	1P	⅛ to ¼	9½	—	—
	Camaro Z28	1½N to ½N	1N	¼P to 1¼P	¾P	⅛ to ¼	9¾	—	—
'75-'76	Nova③	1¾N to ¼N	1N	¼N to 1¾P	¾P	0 to ⅛	10	—	—
	Nova④	¾N to ¾P	0	0 to 1½P	¾P	0 to ⅛	10	—	—
	Chevelle	1½P to 2½P	2P	½P to 1½P②	1P	0 to ⅛	9 19/32	—	—
	Monte Carlo S	4¼P to 5¼P	4¾P	½P to 1½P②	1P	0 to ⅛	9 19/32	—	—
	Camaro	1N to 1P	0	¼P to 1¾P	1P	0 to ⅛	10 11/32	—	—

N Negative P Positive
① SS 396, El Camino—0 to 1P
② Left wheel given, right wheel is ½P ± ½
③ Manual steering
④ Power steering
N.A. Not available

CHARGING SYSTEM

Alternator and regulator troubleshooting and repair are covered in the Unit Repair Section.

Alternator Precautions

The following are a few precautions to observe in servicing the Delcotron (AC) generator and the regulator.

1. When installing a battery, be certain that the ground polarity of the battery and the ground polarity of the generator and regulator are the same.
2. When connecting a booster battery, be sure to connect the correct battery terminals together.
3. When hooking up a charger, connect the correct leads to the battery terminals.
4. Never operate the generator on an open circuit. Be sure all connections in the charging circuit are tight.
5. Do not short across or ground any of the terminals on the generator or regulator.
6. Never polarize an AC system.
7. Do not use test lamps of more than 12 volts for checking diode continuity.
8. Avoid long soldering times when replacing diodes or transistors, as prolonged heat will damage them. Always use a heat sink.
9. Always disconnect the battery ground terminal when servicing any AC system. This will prevent accidentally reversing polarity.
10. Always disconnect the battery and AC generator if electric arc welding equipment is being used on the car.

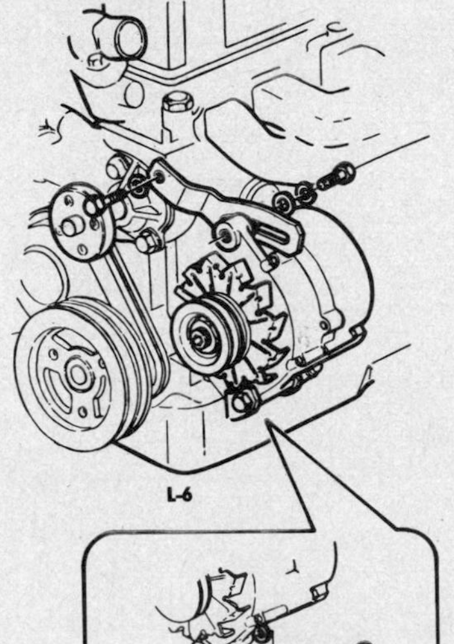

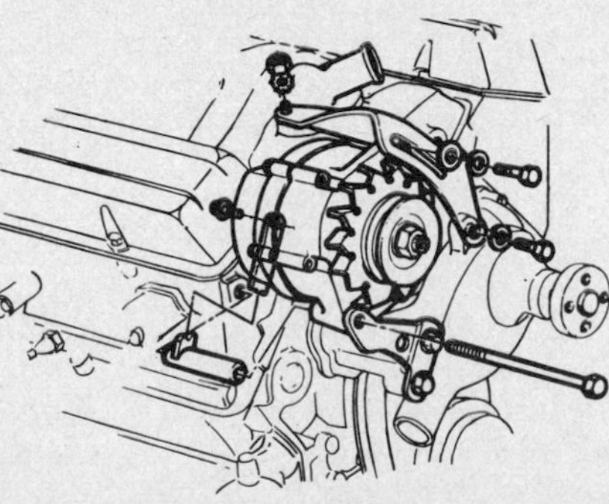

Delcotron installation (© Chevrolet Div., G.M. Corp)

Alternator Removal and Installation

1. Disconnect battery ground cable to prevent diode damage.
2. Disconnect the alternator wiring.
3. Remove brace bolt. If power steering equipped, loosen pump brace and mount nuts. Detach drive belt (s).
4. Support the alternator and remove mount bolt(s). Remove unit from vehicle.
5. Reverse procedure to install. Adjust drive belt to have ¼-½ in. play on longest run of belt.

Regulator R & R, through 1972

1. Disconnect the ground cable at the battery.
2. Disconnect the wiring harness from the regulator.
3. Remove the mounting screws and remove the regulator.
4. Make sure that the regulator base gasket is in place before installation.
5. Clean the attaching area for proper grounding.
6. Install the regulator. Do not overtighten the mounting screws, as this will cancel the cushioning effect of the rubber grommets.

NOTE: An integral alternator/regulator has been optional since 1969 and standard equipment since 1973. Separate removal or adjustment of the regulator is not possible with this unit. Complete disassembly of this unit is described in the "Unit Repair Section."

STARTING SYSTEM

Starter motor troubleshooting and repairs are covered in the Unit Repair Section.

Starter Removal and Installation

1. Disconnect battery ground cable.
2. Raise and support vehicle.
3. Disconnect all wires at solenoid terminals. Note color coding of wires for reinstallation.
4. Remove starter front bracket and two mount bolts. On engines with solenoid heat shield, remove front bracket upper bolt and detach bracket from starter motor.
5. Remove front bracket bolt or nut. Rotate bracket clear. Lower starter front end first. Remove starter.
6. Reverse procedure to install. Torque mount bolts to 25-35 ft. lbs.

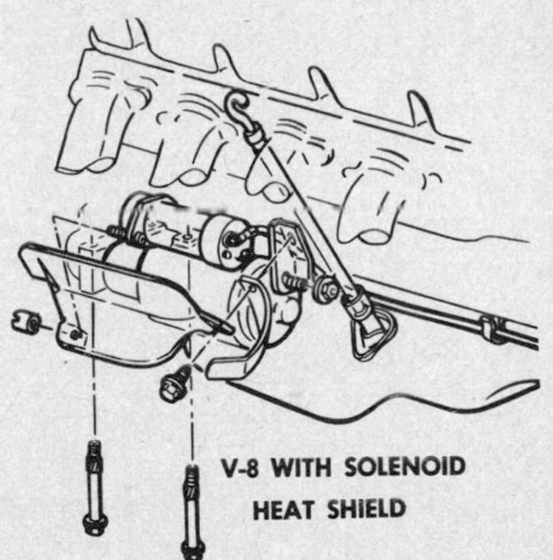

Starter motor installation
(© Chevrolet Div., G.M. Corp)

IGNITION SYSTEM

All models are equipped with the HEI distributor and ignition system starting 1975. This system uses no points and is, therefore, maintenance free. See the Electronic Ignition section for unit description.

Caution When using an auxiliary starter switch the primary distributor lead on point-type systems must be disconnected from the negative post of the ignition coil and the ignition switch must be on. On HEI systems, the distributor BATT lead must be disconnected. Failure to do this may cause damage to the grounding circuit in the ignition switch.

Inline 4 and 6 Cylinder Models

The four and six cylinder distributors are similar. Mounting is on the forward right side of the engine. Both units use centrifugal and vacuum controlled advance mechanism. Direction of rotation (as viewed from the top) is clockwise for both models.

V8 Models

The distributor is located between the two banks of cylinders at the back of the block.

HEI System Tachometer Hookup

There is a terminal marked TACH on the side of the V8 HEI distributor. Connect one tachometer lead to this terminal and the other to ground. On some tachometers, the leads must be connected to the TACH terminal and to the battery positive terminal. The

1 Condenser
2 Contact point assembly
3 Retaining ring

4 Breaker plate
5 Felt washer
5a Plastic seal
6 Vacuum advance unit

7 Housing
7a Tanged washer
8 Shim washer
9 Drive gear pin
10 Drive gear

11 Cap
12 Rotor
13 Radio frequency interference shield
14 Weight springs

15 Mainshaft
16 Advance weights
17 Cam weight base assembly

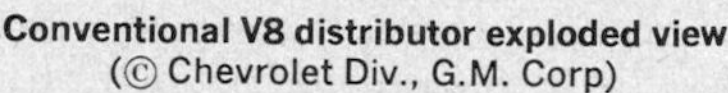

Conventional V8 distributor exploded view
(© Chevrolet Div., G.M. Corp)

hookup is the same for the six-cylinder HEI system, except that the TACH terminal is opposite the BAT terminal on the connector plug on the remote-mounted coil.

Caution Never ground the TACH terminal; serious system damage will result. If there is any doubt as to the correct tachometer hookup, check with the tachometer manufacturer.

Distributor Removal and Installation

The drive gear is attached to the distributor shaft. If it becomes necessary to remove the distributor, carefully mark the position of the rotor in relation to the engine block and the distributor housing so that, if the engine is not turned after the distributor is taken out, the rotor can be returned to the position from which it was removed without difficulty.

To remove the distributor, take off the V8 carburetor air cleaner, disconnect the coil primary wire and the vacuum line, remove the distributor cap, take out the distributor body. With a pencil, mark the position of the body relative to the block, and then work the distributor up out of the block.

When installing the distributor, turn the rotor about 1/8 turn counter clockwise past the alignment mark before pushing the distributor into place. The marks should align when the distributor seats. Check the timing.

Distributor Installation (Engine Disturbed)

1. Turn the crankshaft until the No. 1 cylinder is at the top of its compression stroke. Remove the No. 1 spark plug to feel the compression.
2. Align the timing mark on the vibration damper with the TDC indicator or 0 mark on the timing scale.
3. With distributor body oriented in its normal position, hold the rotor pointing toward the No. 1 plug wire location, then turn the rotor approximately 1/8 turn counterclockwise and push the distributor down until it engages the camshaft, rotating the shaft slightly if necessary.

NOTE: on Mark IV (big block) V8 engines there is a punch mark on the distributor drive gear which indicates the rotor position. Thus, the distributor may be installed with the cap in place. Align the punch mark 2° clockwise from the No. 1 cap terminal, then rotate the distributor body 1/8 turn counterclockwise and push the distributor down into the block.

4. Press down on the distributor and crank the engine to make sure the oil pump shaft is engaged.
5. Return the crankshaft to No. 1 cylinder compression stroke with the timing marks aligned.
6. Turn the distributor body counterclockwise until the points are just beginning to open, then tighten the distributor clamp bolt.
7. Install the distributor cap, checking that the rotor points to the No. 1 terminal. Make sure that the spark plug wires are in their supports and are securely connected.
8. Connect distributor vacuum line and primary wire.
9. Start engine and set the timing.

Breaker Point Adjustment

NOTE: 1970-73 distributors are equipped with a radio static-shield which must be removed for access to the points. If a unitized point and condenser set is used, the shield isn't needed.

Breaker point gap (dwell) adjustment is accomplished for four and six cylinder engines by loosening the point assembly attaching screw and adjusting the points with a screwdriver until the correct gap clearance is obtained (use a feeler gauge). Tighten the point assembly attaching screw and install the distributor cap. Use a dwell meter to check the dwell angle, readjusting if necessary. Dwell can be checked with the engine cranking or running.

On V8 models there is a window in the distributor cap so that the dwell angle may be set while the engine is running. Use an allen (hex) wrench to make the adjustment.

See Tune-Up Specifications at the beginning of this section for correct breaker point gap and dwell angle.

The distributor cam lubricator should be rotated 180° or switched end-for-end every 12,000 miles, and replaced every 24,000 miles. Do not oil these lubricator wicks.

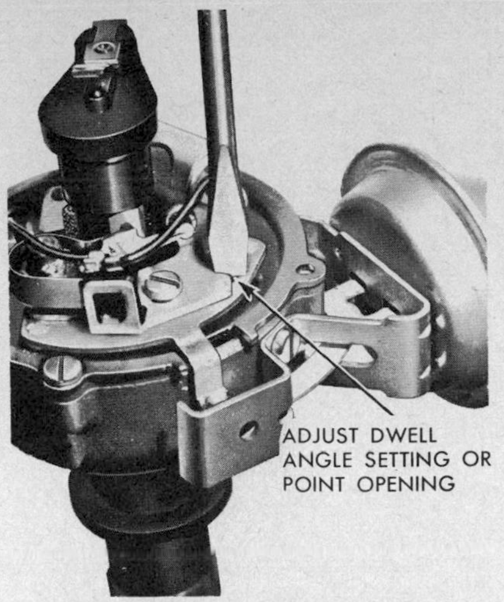

Inline six-cylinder point adjustment
(© Chevrolet Div., G.M. Corp)

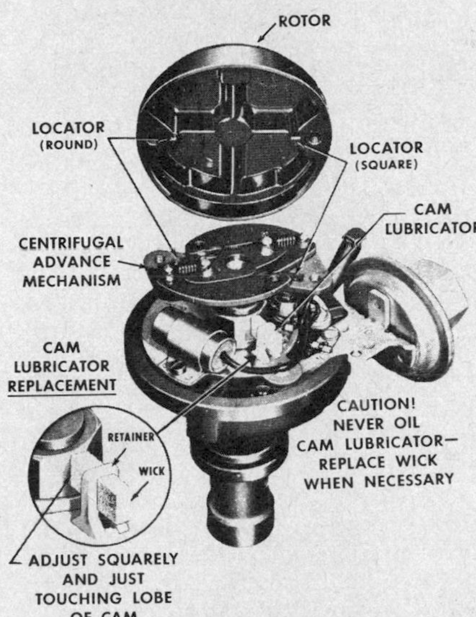

V8 distributor cam lubricator
(© Chevrolet Div., G.M. Corp)

Caution On V8 models the distributor body is involved in the engine lubricating system. The lubricating circuit to the right-bank valve train can be interrupted by mis-alignment of the distributor body. This can cause serious trouble and may be hard to diagnose. See Firing Order and Timing illustrations for correct distributor positioning.

Ignition Timing

Remove the spark plug wire from No. 1 plug and attach a timing light between the wire and the plug. With HEI, use an adapter at the no. 1 distributor terminal. Disconnect the distributor spark advance hose and plug the vacuum opening. Start the engine and run it at idle speed. Aim the timing light at the degree scale just over the harmonic balancer. Adjust the timing by loosening the securing clamp and rotating the distributor until the desired ignition advance is achieved, then tighten the clamp. To advance the timing, rotate the distributor opposite to the normal direction of rotor rotation. Retard the timing by rotating the distributor in the normal direction of rotor rotation.

FUEL SYSTEM

Fuel Pump

The fuel pump is the single action AC diaphragm type.

The pump is actuated by an eccentric located on the engine camshaft. On inline engines, the eccentric actuates the pump rocker arm. On V8 engines, a pushrod between the camshaft eccentric and the fuel pump actuates the pump rocker arm.

Fuel Pump R & R

1. Disconnect fuel inlet and outlet lines at pump and plug pump inlet line.
2. Remove two pump mounting bolts and lockwashers; remove pump and gasket.
3. On all small-block engines, if rocker arm pushrod is to be removed: take out the two adapter bolts and lockwashers and remove adapter and gasket.
4. On big-block V8 engines, if rocker arm pushrod is to be removed: take out pipe plug.
5. Install pump with new gasket coated with sealer. Coat mounting bolt threads with sealer and tighten bolts.

NOTE: on V8 engines, mechanical fingers or heavy grease can be used to hold pump pushrod in place during installation. Coat pipe plug threads or adapter gasket with sealer if pushrod was removed.

6. Connect inlet and outlet lines, start engine and check for leaks.

Chilton's TIME SAVER

When replacing a fuel pump on small block V8 engines, considerable time can be saved as follows:

1. **Before removing the old pump, remove the upper bolt from the engine's right front mounting boss. This bolt hole is in direct alignment with the fuel pump pushrod. The threaded bolt hole continues into the pump pushrod bore. The bolt acts as an oil plug.**
2. **Temporarily insert a longer bolt, (about ⅜—16 x 2 in.) into the hole. Screw the bolt into the bore until it bottoms against the pump pushrod. (Don't tighten the bolt with a wrench or the rod can be damaged.)**
3. **The mechanic is now free to remove and install the fuel pump without worrying about fuel pump pushrod misalignment.**

CAUTION: don't forget to reinstall original motor bolt.

Fuel Filter R & R

Paper and Bronze Types

1. Disconnect fuel line connection at inlet of carburetor.
2. Remove inlet fuel filter nut from carburetor using a box wrench.
3. Remove filter element and spring.
4. If a bronze element, blow through cone end—element should allow air to pass freely.
5. Install element spring and new element into carburetor. Bronze elements are installed with small section of cone facing outward.
6. Install new gasket on fitting nut and install nut.
7. Install fuel line and tighten securely. Start engine and check for leaks.

Paper fuel filter
(© Chevrolet Div., G.M. Corp)

Idle Speed and Mixture Adjustments

NOTE: *the Carburetor Usage Chart will help in identifying the type of carburetor installed on a particular car. Idle speed figures listed in this section are approximate. Consult the tune-up chart in the front of this section for exact figures.*

1969

Adjust with air cleaner installed.

1. Turn in idle mixture screw/s until they seat gently, then back out three turns.
2. Start engine and allow it to come up to operating temperature. Make sure choke is fully open and preheater valve is open, then adjust idle speed screw to obtain specified idle speed (automatic in Drive, manual in Neutral).

NOTE: on A/C cars, turn off A/C *except* on 4 and 6 cylinder engines with auto transmission. On these engines, idle is set with A/C on.

Carburetor Usage Chart

Year	Engine	Carburetor	Models
1969	4 153	Rochester M	Nova
	6 230, 250	Rochester MV	Chevelle, Nova, Camaro
	V8 302 (290 Z28)	Holley 4150	Camaro
	V8 307 (200)	Rochester 2GV (1¼)	Chevelle, Nova
	V8 327 (210)	Rochester 2GV (1¼)	Camaro
	V8 350 (300)	Rochester 4MV	Chevelle, Nova, Camaro
	V8 396 (325)	Rochester 4MV	Chevelle, Camaro
	V8 396 (350) (375)	Holley 4150	Chevelle, Nova, Camaro
1970 exc. below	4-153	Rochester M	Nova
	6-230	Rochester MV	Nova
	6-250	Rochester MV	Nova, Chevelle
	V8 307 (200)	Rochester 2GV (1¼)	Nova, Chevelle
	V8 350 (250)	Rochester 2GV (1½)	Chevelle, Monte Carlo, Chevelle
	V8 350 (300)	Rochester 4MV	Nova, Monte Carlo, Chevelle
	V8 400 (265)	Rochester 2GV (1½)	Monte Carlo
	V8 402 (330)	Rochester 4MV	Monte Carlo, Chevelle (396)
	V8 454 (360)	Rochester 4MV	Monte Carlo, Chevelle
	V8 400 (350)	Rochester 4MV	Chevelle
1970½ and 1971	6-250	Rochester MV	Chevelle, Nova, Camaro
	V8 307 (200)	Rochester 2GV (1¼)	Chevelle, Nova, Camaro
	V8 350 (245)	Rochester 2GV	Nova, Monte Carlo, Chevelle, Camaro
	V8 350 (270)	Rochester 4MV	Nova, Monte Carlo, Chevelle, Camaro
	V8 350 (330 Z28)	Holley 4150	Camaro
	V8 402 (300)	Rochester 4MV	Chevelle, Monte Carlo, Camaro
	V8 454 (365)	Rochester 4MV	Monte Carlo, Chevelle
	V8 454 (425)	Holley 4150	Monte Carlo, Chevelle
1972	6-250	Rochester MV	Chevelle, Camaro, Nova
	V8-307	Rochester 2GV (1¼)	Chevelle, Camaro, Nova
	V8-350	Rochester 2GV (1½)	Chevelle, Monte Carlo, Camaro, Nova
	V8-350 Z28	Holley 4150	Camaro
	V8-350	Rochester 4MV	Chevelle, Monte Carlo, Camaro, Nova
	V8-402	Rochester 4MV	Chevelle, Camaro
	V8-454	Rochester 4MV	Chevelle, Monte Carlo
1973	6-250	Rochester MV	Chevelle, Camaro, Nova
	V8-307	Rochester 2GV (1¼)	Chevelle, Camaro, Nova
	V8-350	Rochester 2GV (1½)	Nova, Chevelle, Monte Carlo, Camaro
	V8-350	Rochester 4MV	Chevelle, Monte Carlo, Nova, Camaro (incl. Z28)
	V8-454	Rochester 4MV	Chevelle, Monte Carlo
1974	6-250	Rochester MV	Chevelle, Camaro, Nova
	V8-350	Rochester 2GV	Chevelle, Nova, Camaro, Monte Carlo
	V8-350	Rochester 4MV	Chevelle, Nova, Camaro, Monte Carlo
	V8-400	Rochester 2GV	Monte Carlo, Chevelle
	V8-400	Rochester 4MV	Monte Carlo, Chevelle
	V8-454	Rochester 4MV	Monte Carlo, Chevelle
1975	6-250	Rochester MV	Chevelle, Camaro, Nova
	V8-262	Rochester 2GC	Nova
	V8-350	Rochester 2GC	Chevelle, Camaro, Monte Carlo, Nova
	V8-350	Rochester 4MCA	Chevelle, Monte Carlo, Camaro
	V8-400	Rochester 4MC	Chevelle, Monte Carlo
	V8-454	Rochester 4MC	Chevelle, Monte Carlo

3. Adjust idle mixture screw/s to obtain highest steady idle speed, then readjust idle speed screw to obtain specified speed. On cars having idle stop solenoid, adjust as follows:
   a. Adjust idle speed to specified rpm by turning hex on solenoid plunger.
   b. Disconnect wire at solenoid. This allows throttle lever to seat against idle screw.
   c. Adjust idle screw to obtain specified solenoid-off rpm, then reconnect wire.
4. Adjust one mixture screw to obtain a 20 rpm drop in idle speed, then back out screw ¼ turn from this point.
5. Repeat Steps 3 and 4 for second mixture screw, if so equipped.
6. Readjust idle speed to obtain specified idle speed.

1970

Adjust with air cleaner installed.

1. Disconnect "FUEL TANK" line from vapor canister (E.E.C.).
2. Connect a tachometer to engine, start engine and allow it to come up to operating temperature. Make sure choke and preheater valves are fully open.
3. Turn off A/C and set parking brake. Disconnect and plug distributor vacuum line.
4. Make the following adjustments:

4 cylinder 153

a. Set mixture screw to obtain maximum idle rpm.
b. Adjust idle speed screw to obtain 750 rpm for manual transmission (in Neutral), 650 rpm for automatic (in Drive).
c. Adjust mixture screw to obtain a 20 rpm drop in idle speed, then back out ¼ turn from this point.
d. Readjust idle speed to obtain specified rpm, then reconnect vacuum line.

6 cylinder 230/250

a. Turn in mixture screw until it gently seats, then back out screw four turns.
b. Adjust solenoid screw to obtain 830 rpm for manual transmission (in Neutral) or 630 rpm for automatic (in Drive).
c. Adjust mixture screw to obtain 750 rpm for manual transmission (in Neutral) or 600 rpm for automatic (in Drive).
d. Disconnect solenoid wire and set idle speed to 400 rpm, then reconnect.
e. Reconnect distributor vacuum line.

V8 307 and 400 (265 H.P.)

a. Turn in mixture screws until they seat gently, then back out four turns.
b. Adjust carburetor idle speed screw to obtain 800 rpm for manual transmission (in Neutral), or adjust solenoid screw to obtain 630 rpm

for automatic transmission (in Drive).

c. Adjust both mixture screws equally inward to obtain 700 rpm for manual transmission, 600 rpm for automatic (in Drive).

d. On cars with automatic, disconnect solenoid wire, set carburetor idle screw to obtain 450 rpm and reconnect solenoid.

e. Reconnect distributor vacuum line.

V8 350 (250 H.P.)

a. Turn in mixture screws until they gently seat, then back out four turns.

b. Adjust solenoid screw to obtain 830 rpm for manual transmission (in Neutral), 630 rpm for automatic (in Drive).

c. Adjust both mixture screws equally inward to obtain 750 rpm for manual transmission or 600 rpm for automatic (in Drive).

d. Disconnect solenoid wire, set carburetor idle screw to obtain 450 rpm and reconnect solenoid.

e. Reconnect distributor vacuum line.

V8 350 (300 H.P.) and 400 (330 H.P.)

a. Turn in both mixture screws until they gently seat, then back out four turns.

b. Adjust carburetor idle screw to obtain 775 rpm for manual transmission, 630 rpm for automatic (in Drive).

c. Adjust mixture screws equally to obtain 700 rpm for manual transmission, 600 rpm for automatic (in Drive).

d. Reconnect distributor vacuum line.

V8 396 (350 H.P.) and 454 (360 H.P.)

a. Turn in both mixture screws until they gently seat, then back out four turns.

b. Adjust carburetor idle screw to obtain 700 rpm for manual transmission or 630 rpm for automatic (in Drive).

c. For cars with automatic transmission: adjust mixture screws equally to obtain 600 rpm with transmission in Drive.

d. For cars with manual transmission: turn in *one* mixture screw until speed drops to 400 rpm, then adjust carburetor idle screw to obtain 700 rpm. Turn in the *other* mixture screw until speed drops 40 rpm, then regain 700 rpm by adjusting carburetor idle screw.

e. Reconnect distributor vacuum line.

5. Disconnect tachometer and reconnect fuel vapor line.

1971

Adjust with air cleaner installed.

The idle stop solenoid is no longer used, having been replaced by the combination emission control valve. This valve is energized through the transmission to increase idle speed under conditions of high gear deceleration and to provide full vacuum spark advance during high gear operation. The valve is de-energized at curb idle and in the lower gears to provide a retarded spark under these conditions, the result of which is lower hydrocarbon emission. *The valve need not be adjusted unless the solenoid or throttle body is removed, or the carburetor overhauled.*

On all 1971 vehicles except those with solid lifter cams, i.e., 350/330 (Z28) and 454/425 (LS-6), idle limiter caps are installed on the mixture screws of the carburetors. Chevrolet does not recommend removing these caps, and does not recommend adjusting the mixture. Adjusting the mixture without the proper test gear will result in hydrocarbon emission levels in excess of the specified minimum.

1. Follow Steps 1-3 of 1970 procedure.
2. Make the following adjustments:

6 cylinder 250

a. Adjust carburetor idle speed screw to obtain 550 rpm for manual transmission (in Neutral) or 500 rpm for automatic (in Drive). *Do not adjust solenoid screw.*

b. Reconnect vapor line and distributor vacuum advance line.

V8 307 (200 H.P.) and 350 (245 H.P.)

a. Adjust carburetor idle speed screw to obtain 600 rpm for manual transmission (in Neutral) with A/C off, or 550 rpm for automatic (in Drive) with A/C on. *Do not adjust solenoid screw.*

b. Reconnect vapor line and distributor vacuum advance line.

V8 350 (270 H.P.)

a. Adjust carburetor idle speed screw to obtain 600 rpm for manual transmission (in Neutral) with A/C off, or 550 rpm for automatic (in Drive) with A/C on. *Do not adjust solenoid screw.*

b. Place fast idle cam follower on second step of fast idle cam, turn A/C off and adjust fast idle to 1,350 rpm for manual transmission (in Neutral) or 1,500 rpm for automatic (in Park).

c. Reconnect vapor line and distributor vacuum advance line.

V8 350 (330 H.P. Z28) and 454 (425 H.P.)

a. Adjust mixture screws to obtain maximum speed (rpm at idle), then adjust carburetor idle speed screw to obtain 700 rpm (manual in Neutral and automatic in Drive).

b. Turn in one mixture screw to obtain a 20 rpm drop in speed, then back out 1/4 turn.

c. Repeat Step "b" for other mixture screw, then reset idle to 700 rpm. *Do not adjust solenoid screw.*

d. Reconnect vapor line and distributor vacuum line.

V8 396 (300 H.P.) and 454 (365 H.P.)

a. Turn off A/C and adjust carburetor idle speed screw to obtain 600 rpm with manual transmission in Neutral and automatic in Drive. *Do not adjust solenoid screw.*

b. Place fast idle cam follower on second step of fast idle cam, turn off A/C and adjust fast idle to 1,350 rpm for manual transmission (in Neutral) or 1,500 rpm for automatic (in Park).

c. Reconnect vapor line and distributor vacuum line.

1972

Disconnect the fuel tank line from the vapor canister. Disconnect the distributor vacuum hose and plug the opening. All carburetors are equipped with idle mixture limiter caps. Do not try to adjust the mixture or remove the caps. Adjust the idle speed with the engine running at its normal temperature, choke open, and parking brake set. Turn the air conditioner off, if so equipped. Chock the wheels on automatic transmission cars. Manual transmissions should be in Neutral, and automatic transmissions in Drive.

250 cu in. 6 cylinder

Adjust the idle stop solenoid (not the C.E.C. solenoid, which is the larger of the two carburetor-mounted solenoids) for a speed of 700 rpm (M.T.) or 600 rpm (A.T.).

307, 350 and 400 cu in. V8s (two-barrel carburetor)

Adjust the idle stop solenoid screw for 900 rpm (M.T.) or 600 rpm (A.T.). Set the carburetor fast idle cam screw for 1850 rpm on 307 engines and 2200 rpm on 350 and 400 engines.

350 cu in. V8 (Quadrajet four-barrel carburetor)

Adjust the idle stop solenoid screw to obtain 800 rpm (M.T.) or 600 rpm (A.T.). Position the fast idle follower on the second step of the fast idle cam and set the fast idle to 1350 rpm (M.T.) or 1500 rpm (A.T.).

350 cu in. V8 (Holley four-barrel carburetor)

Adjust the idle stop solenoid screw for 900 rpm.

402 and 454 cu in. V8s (Quadrajet four-barrel carburetor)

Adjust the idle stop solenoid screw for 800 rpm (M.T.) or 600 rpm (A.T.). Position the fast idle follower on the second step of the fast idle cam and set the fast idle at 1350 rpm (M.T.) or 1500 rpm (A.T.).

1973

All models are equipped with idle limiter caps and idle solenoids. Disconnect the fuel-tank line from the evaporative canister. The engine must be running at operating temperature, choke off, parking brake on, and rear wheels blocked. Disconnect the distributor vacuum hose and plug it. After adjustment, reconnect the vacuum and evaporative hoses.

250 cu. in. 6 cylinder

Adjust the idle stop solenoid for 700 rpm on manual transmission models or 600 rpm on automatics. On manual models, make no attempt to adjust the CEC solenoid (the larger of the two carburetor solenoids) or a decrease in engine braking could result.

Two-barrel 307, 350, and 400 cu. in. V8's

1. With air conditioning switched off, if so equipped, adjust the idle stop solenoid screw for a speed of 900 rpm on manual models; 600 rpm on automatics.
2. De-energize the idle stop solenoid and adjust the idle speed screw (screw resting on lower step of the cam) for 450 rpm on 307, 400 rpm on 350 and 400 engines with automatic transmission, or 500 rpm on 350 engines with a manual transmission.

Four-barrel 350 and 454 cu. in V8's

1. Adjust the idle stop solenoid screw for 900 rpm on manual transmission models; 600 rpm on automatics.
2. Connect the distributor vacuum hose and position the fast idle cam follower on the top step of the fast idle cam (turn air conditioning off if so equipped) and adjust the fast idle to 1300 rpm on manual transmission 350 engines; 1600 on manual 454 engines and all automatics (in Park).

Z28

1. Adjust the idle stop solenoid screw (air conditioning off if so equipped) for a speed of 900 rpm on manual transmission; 700 rpm on automatic (in Drive).
2. Connect the distributor vacuum hose and position the fast idle cam follower on the top step of the cam (turn air conditioning off if so equipped) and adjust the fast idle to 1300 rpm on manual models; 1600 rpm on automatics.

1974

The same preconditions as 1973 apply.

250 cu. in. 6 cylinder

Adjust the idle stop solenoid hex nut for 850 rpm on manual transmission; 600 rpm on automatics (in Drive).

Two-barrel 350 and 400 cu. in. V8s

1. Turn the air conditioning off, if so equipped. Adjust the idle stop solenoid screw for 900 rpm on manual transmission models; 600 rpm on automatics (in Drive).
2. De-energize the solenoid and adjust the carburetor idle cam screw (on low step of cam) for 400 rpm on automatic models (in Drive); 500 rpm on 350 engines with manual transmission.

Four-barrel 350 and 400 cu. in. V8s

1. Turn the air conditioning off, if so equipped. Adjust the idle stop solenoid screw for 900 rpm on manual transmission models; 600 rpm on automatics (in Drive).
2. Connect the distributor vacuum hose. Position the fast idle cam follower on the top step of the fast idle cam and adjust the fast idle speed to 1300 rpm on manual transmission models; 1600 on automatics (in Park).

Z28

1. Turn the air conditioning off, if so equipped. Adjust the idle stop solenoid for 900 rpm on manual transmission models; 700 rpm on automatics (in Drive).
2. Connect the distributor vacuum hose. Position the fast idle cam follower on the top step of the cam and adjust the fast idle to 1300 rpm on manual transmission cars; 1500 rpm on automatics (in Park).

454 cu. in. V8

1. Shut off the air conditioning, if so equipped. Adjust the idle stop solenoid screw for 800 rpm on manual transmission models; 600 rpm on automatics (in Drive).
2. Connect the distributor vacuum hose and position the fast idle cam follower on the top step of the cam and adjust the fast idle to 1600 rpm on manual transmission cams; 1500 rpm on automatics (in Park).

1975

The engine must be at normal operating temperature with the air cleaner on, the choke open, the air conditioner off, and the timing correctly set.

1. Set the brake and block the wheels.
2. Set the automatic transmission in Drive and the manual in neutral. Disconnect the fuel tank hose from the vapor canister in the engine compartment.
3. Use needle nose pliers to break off the mixture screw cap or caps.
4. Adjust the idle speed to the higher of the two speeds specified on the underhood emission specifications sticker. If the information isn't available, set the idle speed 50 rpm above that specified.
5. Turn out the mixture screws equally until the highest possible idle speed is reached. If the speed becomes excessive,reset the idle speed to that in Step 4 and continue.
6. Turn in the mixture screws equally until the normal idle speed is reached.
7. Replace the vapor canister hose.

COOLING SYSTEM

A standard pressure cooling system is used on all models. The radiator cap is designed to maintain a cooling system pressure of about 13 or 15 psi above atmospheric. The water pump requires no attention except to make certain the air vent at the top of the housing and the drain holes in the bottom do not become clogged.

Radiator R & R

1. Drain radiator.
2. Disconnect hoses and oil cooler lines.
3. Remove radiator upper panel and shroud (if so equipped).
4. Remove radiator attaching bolts and lift radiator out of car.
5. Slide radiator into position.
6. Install attaching bolts, shroud, and upper panel.
7. Install hoses and close drain.
8. Fill cooling system, run engine with radiator cap off until operating temperature has been

reached. Again fill cooling system and check for leaks.

Water Pump R & R

1. Drain the radiator and loosen the fan pulley bolts.
2. Disconnect the heater hose, lower radiator hose and, if applicable, the bypass hose at the water pump.
3. On V8 engines, remove the alternator upper brace. Loosen the swivel bolt and remove the fan belt.
4. On Mark IV (big block) engines, disconnect the power steering and air conditioning belts and swivel the power steering pump to one side.
5. Remove the fan blade and pulley.

NOTE: thermostatic fan clutches must be kept in an "in-car" position. When removed from the car the assembly should be supported so that the clutch disc remains in a vertical plane to prevent silicone fluid leakage.

6. Remove the water pump attaching bolts and, if applicable, the power steering-to-pump bolts and remove the pump and gasket.

NOTE: on four and six-cylinder engines, pull the pump straight out of the block first to avoid damage to the impeller.

7. Install the pump assembly using a new gasket. Coat the gasket on both sides with sealer. Tighten the 5/16 in. bolts to 15 ft lbs. (four and six-cylinder) and the 3/8 in. bolts (V8) to 30 ft lbs.
8. Install the pulley and fan.
9. On Mark IV engines, install the power steering and air conditioning bolts.
10. Connect the hoses and fill the cooling system.
11. On V8 engines, install the alternator upper brace and fan belt. Install the power steering pump bolt.
12. Adjust the belts, then start the engine and check for leaks.

Thermostat R & R

The thermostat is located inside a housing on the front of the cylinder head on four and six-cylinder engines and inside the front of the intake manifold casting on V8 engines. It is not necessary to remove the radiator hose from the thermostat housing when removing the thermostat.

1. Remove the two retaining bolts from the thermostat housing and lift up the housing with the hose attached. Remove the thermostat.
2. Insert the new thermostat, spring end down, and install the housing with a new gasket. Tighten the housing retaining bolts to 30 ft lbs.

EMISSION CONTROLS

NOTE: see the Unit Repair Section for emission control systems troubleshooting.

Positive Crankcase Ventilation

In this system, crankcase vapors are drawn into the intake manifold and burned as part of engine combustion. The system draws clean air from the carburetor air cleaner. The ventilation flow is regulated by the PCV valve.

Air Injection Reactor

The AIR system injects air into the exhaust system, near enough to the exhaust valves to continue the burning of the normally unburned segment of the exhaust gases. To do this it employs an air injection pump and a system of hoses, valves, tubes, etc., necessary to carry the compressed air from the pump to the exhaust manifolds. Carburetors and distributors for AIR engines have specific modifications to adapt them to the air injection system; those components should not be interchanged with those intended for use on engines that do not have the system.

A diverter valve is used to prevent backfiring. The valve senses sudden increases in manifold vacuum and ceases the injection of air during fuel-rich periods. During coasting, this valve diverts the entire air flow through the pump muffler and during high engine speeds, expels it through a relief valve. Check valves in the system prevent exhaust gases from entering the pump.

Air Pump R & R

Caution Do not pry on the pump housing or clamp the pump in a vise: the housing is soft and may become distorted.

1. Disconnect the air hoses at the pump.
2. Hold the pump pulley from turning and loosen the pulley bolts. Remove the pulley.
3. Loosen the pump mounting bolts. Remove the drive belt.
4. Remove the mounting bolts, and then remove the pump.
5. Install the pump using a reverse of the removal procedure.

Diverter (Anti-afterburn) Valve R & R

1. Detach the vacuum sensing line from the valve.
2. Remove the other hose(s) from the valve.
3. Unfasten the diverter valve from the elbow or the pump body.

Installation is the reverse of removal. Always use a new gasket. Tighten the valve securing bolts to 85 in. lbs.

Controlled Combustion System

C.C.S. increases combustion efficiency through leaner carburetor adjustments and revised distributor calibration. Thermostatically controlled air intakes are also used on most models. A higher temperature thermostat is used on C.C.S. cars.

Evaporative Emission Control

Introduced on California cars in 1970, and nationwide in 1971, this system reduces the amount of escaping gasoline vapors. Float bowl emissions are controlled by internal carburetor modifications. Redesigned bowl vents, reduced bowl capacity, heat shields, and improved intake manifold-to-carburetor insulation serve to reduce vapor loss into the atmosphere. The venting of fuel tank vapors into the air has been stopped. Fuel vapors are now directed through lines to a canister containing an activated charcoal filter. Unburned vapors are trapped here until the engine is started. When the engine is running, the canister is purged by air drawn in by manifold vacuum. The air and fuel vapors are then directed into the engine to be burned. All 1973 into the engine to be burned. Most 1973 and later models have integral vapor separators within the fuel tank.

Charcoal Canister R & R

NOTE: The filter can usually be replaced without removing the canister.

1. Raise the vehicle and securely support it on jackstands.
2. Note the proper installation positions of the hose connections on the canister and then remove the hoses.
3. Loosen the screws which secure the canister mounting clamps and remove the canister assembly.
4. If the filter requires replacement, pull it from the bottom of the canister with your fingers.

Check the condition of the hoses and hose fittings. Replace as required.

NOTE: If new hoses are being used, use only those which are fuel resistant and are marked "EVAP".

Check the purge valve which is located on the top of the canister, by applying vacuum to it. A good valve should retain the vacuum. If the valve is defective, slowly unsnap its top (the diaphragm is held in place by spring tension). Withdraw the diaphragm, spring, and spring retainer. Assemble the valve in the reverse order of disassembly.

Replace the filter in the bottom of the canister if necessary. Install the canister assembly in the vehicle in the reverse order of removal.

Transmission Controlled Spark

Introduced in 1970, this system controls exhaust emissions by eliminating vacuum advance in the lower forward gears.

The 1970 system consists of a transmission switch, solenoid vacuum switch, time delay relay, and a thermostatic water temperature switch. The solenoid vacuum switch is energized in the lower gears via the transmission switch and closes off distributor vacuum. The two-way transmission switch is activated by the shifter shaft on manual transmissions, and fluid pressure on automatic transmissions. The switch de-energizes the solenoid in high gear, the plunger extends and uncovers the vacuum port, and the distributor receives full vacuum. The temperature switch overrides the system when engine temperature is below 63° or above 232°. This allows vacuum advance in all gears. A time delay relay opens 15 seconds after the ignition is switched on. Full vacuum advance during this delay eliminates the possibility of stalling.

The 1971 system is similar, except that the vacuum solenoid (now called a Combination Emissions Control or CEC solenoid) serves two functions. One function is to control distributor vacuum; the added function is to act as a deceleration throttle stop in high gear. This cuts down on emissions when the vehicle is coming to a stop in high gear. The CEC solenoid is controlled by a temperature switch, a transmission switch, and a 20 second time delay relay. This system also contains a reversing relay, which energizes the solenoid when the transmission switch, temperature switch or time delay completes the CEC circuit to ground. This system is directly opposite the 1970 system in operation. The 1970 vacuum solenoid was normally open to allow vacuum advance and when energized, closed to block vacuum. The 1971 system is normally closed blocking vacuum advance and when energized, opens to allow vacuum advance. The temperature switch completes the CEC circuit to ground when engine temperature is below 82°. Some Camaros also have a high temperature terminal on the switch to complete the CEC circuit when coolant temperature reaches 232°. The time delay relay allows vacuum advance (and raised idle speed) for 20 seconds after the ignition key is turned to the "on" position. Models with an automatic transmission and air conditioning also have a solid state timing device which engages the air conditioning compressor for three seconds after the ignition key is turned to the "off" position to prevent the engine from running-on.

The 1972 6 cylinder system is similar to that used in 1971, except that an idle stop solenoid has been added to the system. In the energized position, the solenoid maintains engine speed at a predetermined fast idle. When the solenoid is de-energized by turning off the ignition, the solenoid allows the throttle plates to close beyond the normal idle position; thus cuting off the air supply and preventing engine run-on. The 6 cylinder is the only 1972 engine with a C.E.C. valve, which serves the same deceleration function as in 1971. The 1972 time delay relay delays full vacuum 20 seconds after the transmission is shifted into high gear. V8 engines use a vacuum advance solenoid similar to that used in 1970. This relay is normally closed to block vacuum and opens when energized to allow vacuum advance. The solenoid controls distributor vacuum advance and performs no throttle positioning function. The idle stop solenoid used operates in the same manner as the one on 6 cylinder engines. All air-conditioned cars have an additional anti-diesel (run-on) solenoid which engages the compressor clutch for three seconds after the ignition is switched off. The 1973 TCS system differs from the 1972 system in three ways. The 32 second upshift delay has been replaced by a 20 second starting relay. This relay closes to complete the TCS circuit and open the TCS solenoid, allowing vacuum advance, for 20 seconds after the key is turned to the "on" position. The operating temperature of the temperature overide switch has been raised to 93°, and the switch that was used to engage the A/C compressor when the key was turned "off" has been eliminated. All models are equipped with an electric throttle control solenoid to prevent run-on. The 1973 TCS system is used on all models equipped with a 307 engine, all V8 models equipped with a manual transmission, and all full-size station wagons equipped with a 165 hp 350 or a 170 hp 400.

The 1974 TCS system is used only on manual transmission models. System components remain unchanged from 1973. The vacuum advance solenoid is located on the coil bracket.

For 1975, the system is used in conjunction with the catalytic converter. Air is injected into the exhaust manifold ahead of the converter.

For diagnosis procedures, see the Unit Repair Section. Any of the methods of exhaust emission control requires close and frequent attention to tune-up factors of engine maintenance.

Early Fuel Evaporation System

1975 models are equipped with this system to reduce engine warm-up time, improve driveability, and reduce emissions. On start-up, a vacuum motor acts to close a heat valve in the exhaust manifold which causes exhaust gases to enter the intake manifold heat riser passages. Incoming fuel mixture is then heated and more complete fuel evaporation is provided during warm-up.

Catalytic Converter

All models are equipped with a catalytic converter. The converter is located midway in the exhaust system. Stainless steel exhaust pipes are used ahead of the converter. The converter is stainless steel with an aluminized steel cover and a ceramic felt blanket to insulate the converter from the floorpan. The catalyst pellet bed inside the converter consists of noble metals which cause a reaction that converts hydro-carbons and carbon monoxide into water and carbon monoxide into water and carbon dioxide. See the "Unit Repair" section for a complete description.

Exhaust Gas Recirculation

All 1973-75 engines are equipped with exhaust gas recirculation (EGR). This system consists of a metering valve, a vacuum line to the carburetor, and cast-in exhaust gas passages in the intake manifold. The EGR valve is controlled by carburetor vacuum, and accordingly opens and closes to admit exhaust gases into the fuel/air mixture. The exhaust gases lower the combustion temperature, and reduce the amount of oxides of nitrogen (NO_x) produced. The valve is closed at idle and wide open throttle, but is open between the two extreme throttle positions.

Some California engines are equipped with a dual diaphragm EGR valve. This valve further limits the exhaust gas opening (compared to the single diaphragm EGR valve) during high intake manifold vacuum periods, such as high-speed cruising, and provides more exhaust gas recirculation during acceleration when manifold vacuum is low. In addition to the hose running to the thermal vacuum switch, a second hose is connected directly to the intake manifold.

EGR Valve R & R

1. Pull the vacuum sensing line

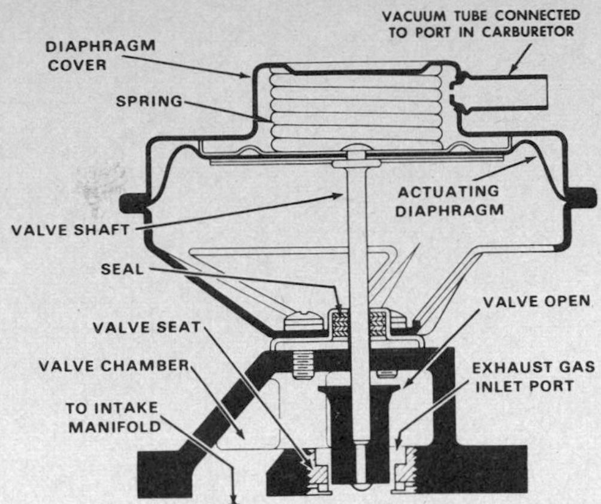

Cutaway view of an EGR valve
(© Chevrolet Div., G.M. Corp)

from the fitting on top of the EGR valve.

2. Unfasten the bolt which secures the valve clamp to the manifold.
3. Withdraw the clamp and the EGR valve from the manifold.

Install the EGR valve in the reverse order of removal. Use a new valve gasket. Tighten the clamp bolt to 20 ft lbs and lock it with its tab.

ENGINE

Four, six, and eight cylinder engines are used. The four cylinder engine is a 153 cu. in. inline design with five main bearings. The six cylinder engines are also of the inline type, with seven main bearings. They have been built in 230 and 250 cu. in. displacements. V8 engines are of two basic types. All engines of each type are generally similar in design and have some interchangeability of parts. The first type is the small block V8 series. This includes the 262, 302, 307, 350, and 400 cu. in. engines. The second type is the big block or Mark IV, V8 series. This includes engines of 396, 402, and 454 cu. in. displacement.

The big block 402 was last offered in 1972. The small block 400 was offered starting 1974.

Engine R & R

NOTE: unless otherwise stated, the following operations cover the 4 cylinder, 6 cylinder and V8 engines.

Caution Do not discharge the compressor or disconnect the A/C lines. Damage to the A/C system or personal injury could result.

Removal

1. Raise car and place on jackstands.
2. Drain cooling system, transmission, and crankcase.
3. Scribe alignment marks on underside of hood and around hood hinges, and remove hood from hinges.
4. Disconnect coolant and heater hoses at engine attachment.
5. Disconnect battery cables at battery.
6. Remove radiator and shroud assembly. Remove fan and pulley.
7. Remove air cleaner.
8. Disconnect coil, starter and alternator wires, engine-to-body ground strap, oil pressure and engine temperature sender wires, C.E.C. wire, and any other wires.
9. Disconnect gas line at fuel pump.
10. Disconnect accelerator control linkage at firewall.
11. Disconnect hand choke linkage (4 cylinder), and power brake vacuum line.
12. Disconnect exhaust pipe from manifold. Disconnect the crossover pipe on V8 models, if so equipped.
13. Disconnect clutch shaft bracket at frame and disconnect clutch linkage. On automatic transmission models, remove transmission oil filler tube and plug the opening.
14. Attach engine lifting apparatus. Attach to hoist and secure the engine.
15. Remove driveshaft.
16. Remove and set aside power steering pump and air conditioning compressor. Do not disconnect hoses.
17. Remove engine rear mounting bolts.
18. Disconnect speedometer cable, transmission control rod linkage lower ends, T.C.S. switch, and transmission oil cooler lines.
19. Loosen front engine mounting bolts.
20. Raise engine slightly and remove bolts.
21. Remove transmission crossmember and free the transmission rear mounting.
22. Remove engine and transmission as a unit from the car.

Installation

1. Bolt engine lifting tool to engine and lower engine and transmission into chassis as a unit. Guide engine to align front engine mounts with mounts on frame.
2. Install one rear transmission crossmember side bolt, swing crossmember up under transmission mount and install bolt in opposite side rail.
3. Align and install rear mount bolts.
4. Install engine front mount bolts and remove lifting tool from engine.
5. Install and connect all items in reverse order of engine removal procedure.

Separating Transmission and Clutch from Engine

Manual Transmission

1. Remove clutch housing cover plate screws.
2. Remove bolts holding clutch housing to engine block. Remove clutch housing and transmission assembly.
3. Remove starter and clutch housing cover plate.
4. Loosen clutch-to-flywheel bolts, alternately, until spring pressure is released. Remove all bolts, clutch disc and pressure plate assembly.
5. Re-attach transmission by reversing above process.

Automatic Transmission

1. Lower the engine and support it on suitable blocks.
2. Remove starter and converter housing underpan.
3. Remove flywheel-to-converter assembly attaching bolts.
4. Support transmission on blocks.
5. Remove transmission-to-engine mounting bolts.
6. With engine hoist attached, remove blocks from engine only and slowly guide the engine from the transmission.
7. Re-attach automatic transmission by reversing above process.

Manifolds

Refer to the Chevrolet section for intake and exhaust manifold removal and installation procedures for both inline and V8 engines. Use the following procedure for exhaust manifold removal and installation on sixes with the intake manifold integral with the cylinder head.

Exhaust Manifold R & R—1975 and Later Six Cylinder Engine with Integral Intake Manifold

1. Remove the air cleaner.
2. Remove the power steering and air pump brackets.

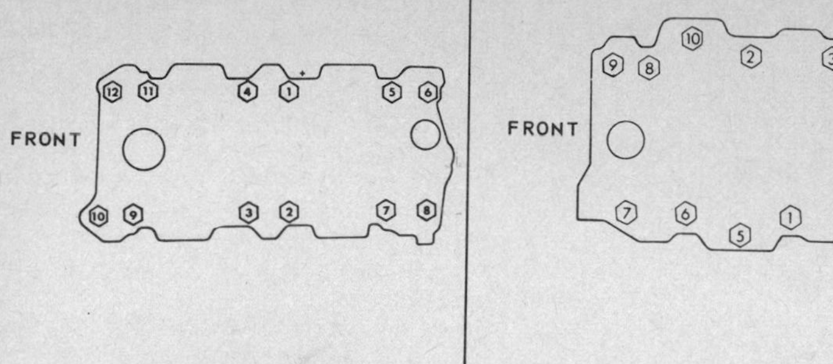

"SMALL V8" "MARK IV V8"

Intake manifold torque sequence—V8 engines (©Chevrolet Div., G.M. Corp)

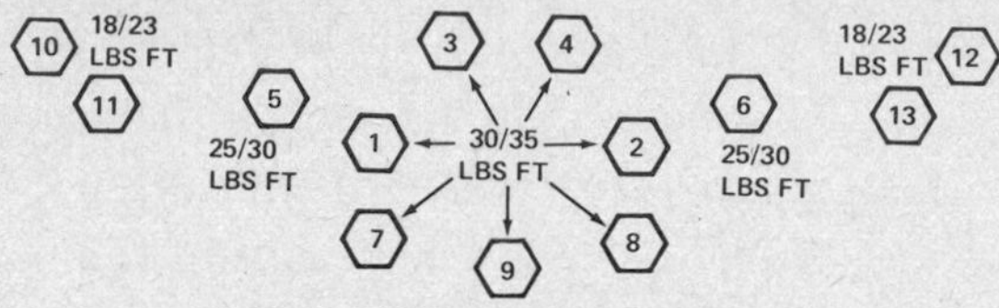

Exhaust manifold torque sequence—
inline six cylinder with integral intake manifold
(© Chevrolet Div., G.M. Corp.)

3. Remove the EFE valve bracket.
4. Disconnect the throttle linkage and return spring.
5. Unbolt the exhaust pipe from the flange.
6. Unbolt and remove the manifold.
7. Reverse the procedure for installation. Tighten the four end bolts to specifications last.

Valve System

Chevrolet uses a hydraulic tappet system with adjustable rocker mounting nuts to obtain zero lash.

A few high-performance V8s through 1972 use mechanical tappets (valve lifters) which require periodic adjustment.

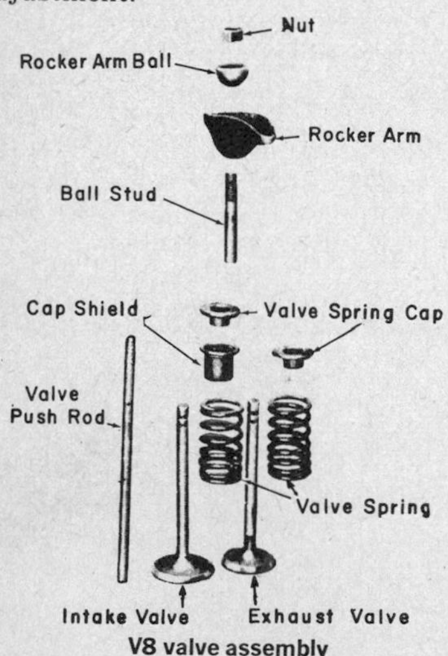

V8 valve assembly
(© Chevrolet Div., G.M. Corp)

Hydraulic Valve Lifter Adjustment

Preliminary Adjustment

In the case of disassembly, or any other cause for valve tappet adjustment, proceed as follows:

1. Remove the rocker arm covers.

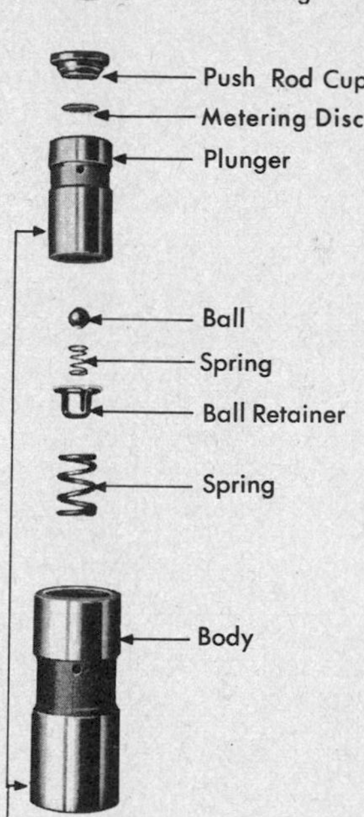

Hydraulic lifter plunger and body are fitted pairs and must not be mismated
(© Chevrolet Div., G.M. Corp)

2. Remove distributor cap and crank engine until distributor rotor points to No. 1 cylinder terminal, with points open. The crankshaft damper timing marks should be aligned.

The following valves can be adjusted with the engine in No. 1 firing position:

OHV 4—Intake No. 1, 2, Exhaust No. 1, 3
OHV 6—Intake No. 1, 2, 4, Exhaust No. 1, 3, 5
V8—Intake No. 1, 2, 5, 7, Exhaust No. 1, 3, 4, 8

3. Turn the rocker arm mounting nut until all lash is removed from each valve train. This can be determined by rotating the

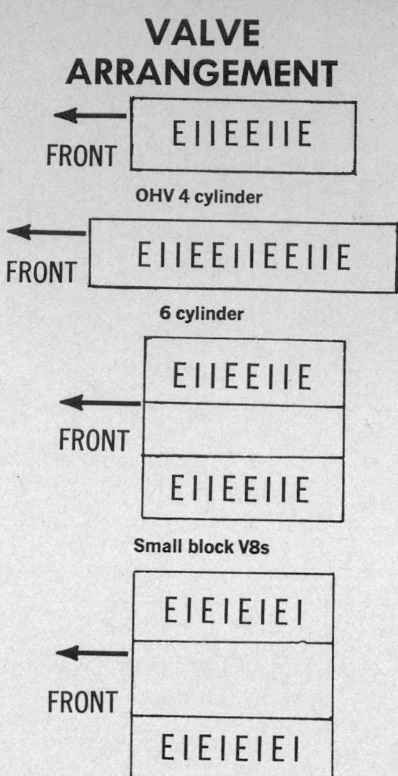

pushrod while turning the adjustment. When all play has been removed, turn adjusting nut one more turn. This will place the lifter plunger in the center of its travel.

4. Turn the engine 360° clockwise.

The following valves can be adjusted with the engine in the No. 6 firing position (No. 4 on OHV 4):

OHV 4—Intake No. 3, 4, Exhaust No. 2, 4
OHV 6—Intake No. 3, 5, 6, Exhaust No. 2, 4, 6
V8—Intake No. 3, 4, 6, 8, Exhaust No. 2, 5, 6, 7

Running Adjustment

Adjust the lifters as follows with the engine hot and running.

1. Remove rocker arm covers and gaskets.

Adjusting valve clearance—6 cyl hydraulic lifters
(© Chevrolet Div., G.M. Corp)

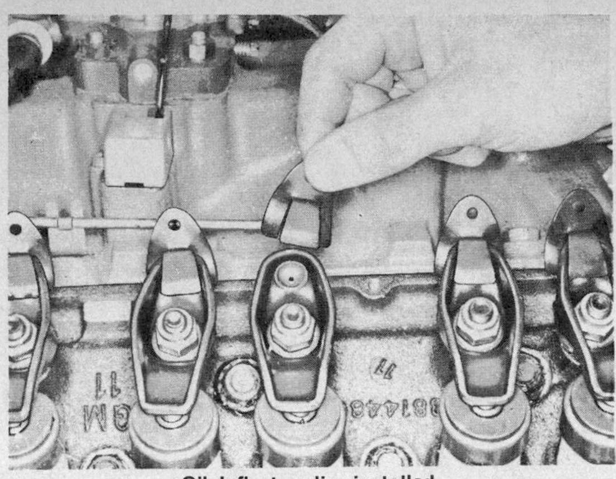

Oil deflector clips installed
(© Chevrolet Div., G.M. Corp)

2. Place oil deflector clips on rocker arms.
3. With engine running at idle, back off rocker arm nut until it starts to clatter.
4. Turn nut down until clatter stops. This is the zero lash position.
5. Tighten nut down one-quarter turn. Pause ten seconds. Repeat additional quarter turns and ten second pauses until nut has been tightened down one full turn from the zero lash position.
6. Repeat steps 3, 4, and 5 for all rocker arms.
7. Remove oil deflector clips and replace rocker arm covers.

Mechanical Valve Lifter Adjustment

1. Set engine in No. 1 firing position.
2. Adjust the clearance between the valve stems and the rocker arms using a feeler gauge. Adjust the rocker arm mounting nut. Check the Tune-Up Specifications table for the proper clearance. Adjust the following Valves in No. 1 firing position: Intake No. 2, 7, Exhaust No. 4, 8.
3. Turn crankshaft one-half revolution (180°) clockwise. Adjust the following valves: Intake No. 1, 8, Exhaust No. 3, 6.

Adjusting valve clearance—V8 w/mechanical lifters
(© Chevrolet Div., G.M. Corp)

4. Turn crankshaft one-half revolution clockwise to No. 6 firing position. Adjust the following valves in No. 6 firing position: Intake No. 3, 4, Exhaust No. 5, 7.
5. Turn crankshaft one-half revolution clockwise. Adjust the following valves: Intake No. 5, 6, Exhaust No. 1, 2.
6. Run engine until normal operating temperature is reached. Reset all clearances, hot and running, using oil deflectors.

Cylinder Head

R & R

Caution Do not discharge the compressor or disconnect the A/C lines. Damage to the A/C system or personal injury could result.

4 and 6 Cylinder Engines

1. Drain cooling system and remove air cleaner. Disconnect P.C.V. hose.
2. Disconnect choke cable (4 cylinder), accelerator pedal rod at bell crank on manifold, and fuel and vacuum lines at carburetor.
3. Disconnect exhaust pipe at manifold flange, then remove manifold bolts and clamps and remove manifolds and carburetor as an assembly.
4. Remove fuel and vacuum line retaining clip from water outlet. Then disconnect wire harness from heat sending unit and coil, leaving harness clear of clips on rocker arm cover.
5. Disconnect radiator hose at water outlet housing and battery ground strap at cylinder head.
6. Disconnect wires and remove spark plugs. On the 6 cylinder engine disconnect coil to distributor primary wire lead at coil and remove the coil.
7. Remove rocker arm cover. Back off rocker arm nuts, pivot rocker arms to clear push rods and remove push rods.
8. Remove cylinder-head bolts, cylinder head and gasket.
9. Place a new cylinder-head gasket over dowel pins in cylinder block.
10. Guide and lower cylinder head into place over dowels and gasket.
11. Oil cylinder-head bolts, install and run them down snug.
12. Tighten the cylinder-head bolts a little at a time with a torque wrench in the correct sequence. Final torque should be as specified.

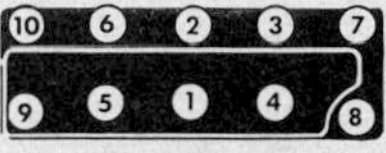

OHV 4 cylinder engine cylinder head torque sequence

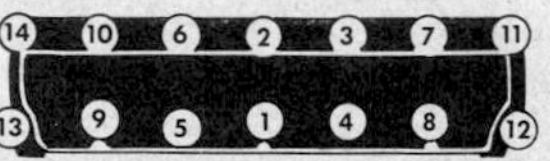

6 cylinder engine cylinder head torque sequence

13. Install valve pushrods down through the cylinder-head openings and seat them in their lifter sockets.
14. Install rocker arms, balls and nuts and tighten rocker arm nuts until all pushrod play is taken up.
15. Install thermostat, thermostat housing and water outlet using new gaskets. Then connect radiator hose.
16. Install heat sending switch and torque to 15–20 ft. lbs.
17. Clean spark plugs or install new ones.
18. Torque 13/16 in. hex plugs to 20 ft lbs and 5/8 in. hex plugs to 15 ft lbs. Tapered seat plugs are used on some engines starting in 1970 and all engines beginning in 1971.
19. Install coil (on six cylinder engine) then connect heat sending unit and coil primary wires, and connect battery ground cable at the cylinder head.
20. Clean surfaces and install new gasket over manifold studs. Install manifold. Install bolts and clamps and torque as specified.
21. Connect throttle linkage, and choke wire (on four cylinder engine).
22. Connect P.C.V., fuel and vacuum lines and secure lines in clip at water outlet.
23. Fill cooling system and check for leaks.
24. Adjust valve lash.
25. Install rocker arm cover and position wiring harness in clips.
26. Clean and install air cleaner.

V8 Engines

Removal and Installation

1. Drain coolant. Remove air cleaner.

2. Disconnect:
   a. battery
   b. radiator and heater hose from manifold
   c. throttle linkage
   d. fuel line
   e. coil wires
   f. temperature sending unit
   g. power brake hose, distributor vacuum hose, and crankcase vent hoses.
3. Remove:
   a. distributor, marking position
   b. alternator upper bracket
   c. coil and bracket
   d. manifold attaching bolts
   e. intake manifold and carburetor.
4. Remove:
   a. rocker arm covers
   b. rocker arm nuts, balls, rocker arms, and push rods. These items must be replaced in their original locations.
5. Remove cylinder head bolts, cylinder head, and gasket.
6. Reverse procedure to install. Tighten head bolts evenly to the specified torque. On engines having steel gasket, use sealer on both sides. No sealer should be used on steel-asbestos gaskets. Adjust the valve lash.

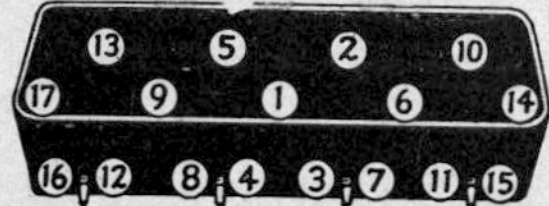

Small block V8 cylinder head torque sequence

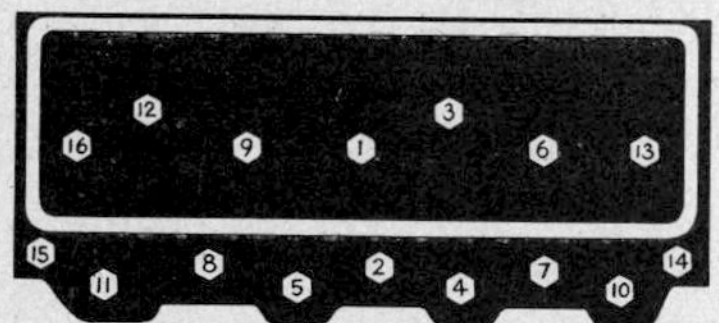

Big block V8 cylinder head torque sequence

Timing Cover, Chain, and Camshaft

All 4 and 6 cylinder engines have gear driven camshafts, while all V8 camshafts are driven by a timing chain. 4 or 6 cylinder timing gear replacement requires camshaft removal.

NOTE: the 6 cylinder engine uses a harmonic balancer that closely resembles the Chevrolet V8-type. The removal procedure for this damper will be the same as that for the Chevrolet V8. Driving the damper back onto the crankshaft without supporting the pulley can cause damage. A replacement tool must be used during the reassembly operation.

Cover Removal and Installation

1. Drain and remove radiator.
2. Remove harmonic balancer, (6 and 8 cylinder) or a crankshaft pulley, (4 cylinder) using a puller.
3. Drain the engine oil and remove

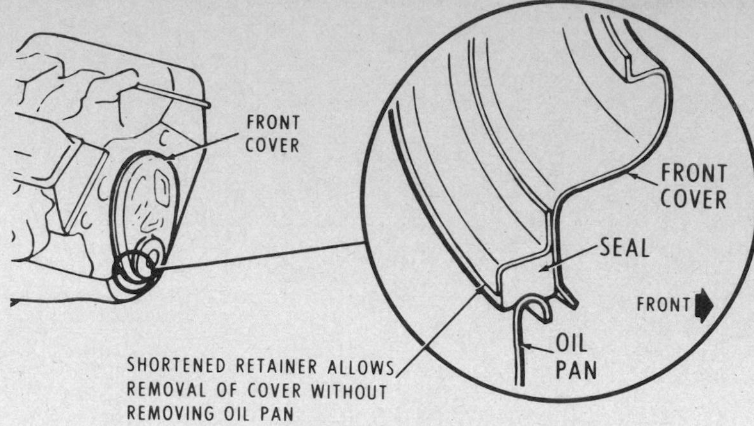

On 1975 and later small block V8s, it is no longer necessary to remove or lower the oil pan to remove the timing cover. The seal retainer is shortened enough to clear the pan
(© Chevrolet Div., G.M. Corp)

the oil pan on all engines through 1972, and on small block V8s through 1974. Remove the V8 water pump. If the oil pan isn't to removed, cut the pan seal off flush with the block.

4. Remove timing gear cover attaching screws, and cover and gasket.
5. Reverse procedure to install. Use silicone sealer at the oil pan to cylinder block joint.

Caution The 6 and 8 cylinder engines use a harmonic balancer. Breakage may occur if the balancer is hammered back onto the crankshaft.

This balancer must be drawn back into place.

When replacing the crankshaft damper, it has been found that lightly polishing the inside diameter with crocus cloth will greatly ease replacement. This procedure will also assist in any future removals, as it is sometimes difficult to pull a damper even with a puller. Be sure that the polishing is not overdone, or the damper will wobble on the crankshaft.

Oil Seal R & R

1. After removing gear cover, pry oil seal out of front of cover with large screwdriver.
2. Install new lip seal with lip (open side of seal) inside and drive or press seal carefully into place.

Timing Chain Replacement

V8 Models

V8 models are equipped with a timing chain. To replace the chain, remove the radiator, water pump harmonic balancer, and the crankcase front cover. This will allow access to the timing chain. Crank the engine until the marks punched on both sprockets are closest to one another and in line between the shaft centers. Take out the three bolts that hold the camshaft gear to the camshaft. This gear is a light press fit on the camshaft and will come off readily. It is located by a dowel. The chain comes off with the camshaft gear. A gear puller will be required to remove the crankshaft gear.

Without disturbing the position of the engine, mount the new crank gear on the shaft, then mount the chain over the camshaft gear. Arrange the camshaft gear in such a way that the timing marks will line up between the shaft centers and the camshaft locating dowel will enter the dowel hole in the cam sprocket.

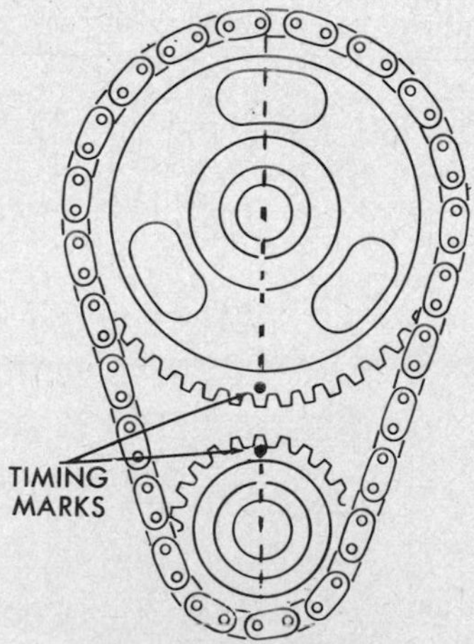

V8 engine timing marks

Place the cam sprocket, with its chain mounted over it, in position on the front of the camshaft and pull up with the three bolts that hold it to the camshaft.

After the gears are in place, turn the engine two full revolutions to make certain that the timing marks are in correct alignment between the shaft centers.

Camshaft R & R

4 and 6 Cylinder engines

The manufacturer recommends that the engine be removed from the car to remove the camshaft. However, in most cases the following procedure can be used. You may also have to raise the front of the engine for clearance.

1. In addition to removing the timing gear cover, remove the grille assembly.
2. Remove valve cover and gasket, loosen all the valve rocker arm nuts and pivot the arms clear of the pushrods.
3. Remove distributor and fuel pump.
4. Remove coil, side cover and gasket. Remove pushrods and valve lifters.
5. Remove the two camshaft thrust plate retaining screws by working through holes in the camshaft gear.
6. Remove camshaft and gear assembly by pulling it out through the front of the block.

NOTE: if renewing either camshaft or camshaft gear, the gear must be pressed off the camshaft. The replacement parts must be assembled in the same manner (under pressure). In placing the gear on the camshaft, press the gear onto the shaft until it bottoms against the gear spacer ring. The end clearance of the thrust plate should be .001 to .005 in.

7. Install camshaft assembly in the engine.
8. Turn crankshaft and camshaft to align and bring the timing marks together. Push the camshaft into this aligned position. Install camshaft thrust plate-to-block screws and torque them to 6-7½ ft. lbs.
9. Runout on either crankshaft or camshaft gear should not exceed .003 in.

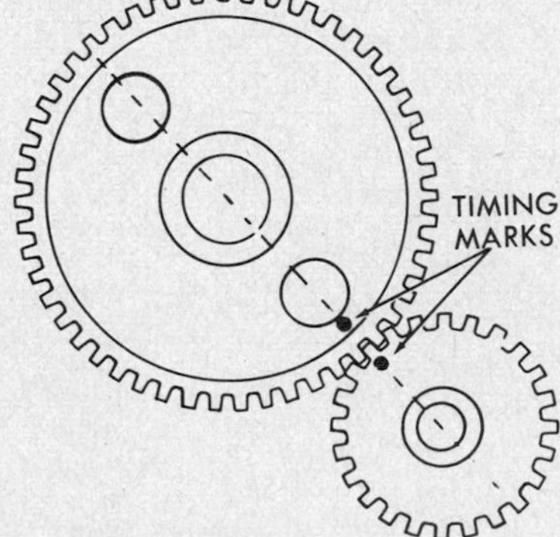

OHV 4 and 6 cylinder timing marks

10. Backlash between the two gears should be between .004 and .006 in.
11. Install timing gear cover and gasket.
12. Install oil pan and gaskets.
13. Install harmonic balancer.
14. Line up keyway in balancer with key on crankshaft and drive balancer onto shaft until it bottoms against crankshaft gear.
15. Install valve lifters and pushrods. Install side cover with new gasket. Attach coil wires; install fuel pump.
16. Install distributor and set timing as described under distributor at the beginning of the section.
17. Pivot rocker arms over pushrods and adjust the valves.
18. Add oil to the engine. Install and adjust fan belt.
19. Install radiator or shroud.
20. Install grille assembly.
21. Fill cooling system, start engine and check for leaks.
22. Check and adjust timing.

V8 Engines

1. Remove intake manifold, valve lifters and timing chain cover as described in this section.
2. Remove grille, except on Nova and 1969 Camaro. On these models, remove both front motor mount bolts and right motor mount, then lower engine until it rests on frame.
3. On Nova and 1969 Camaro, remove the two center bolts and the one lower bolt that secure the hood latch support. This will give adequate clearance for the cam.
4. Remove fuel pump and pump pushrod.
5. Remove camshaft sprocket bolts, sprocket and timing chain. A light blow to the lower edge of a tight sprocket should free it (use a plastic mallet).
6. Install two 5/16—18 x 4 in. bolts in cam bolt holes and pull cam from block.
7. To install, reverse removal procedure aligning the sprocket timing marks.

NOTE: cam lobes must be lubricated with Molykote® or SAE 90 gear oil before installation. All cam journals are the same diameter, so be careful that the cam bearings are not dislodged during installation.

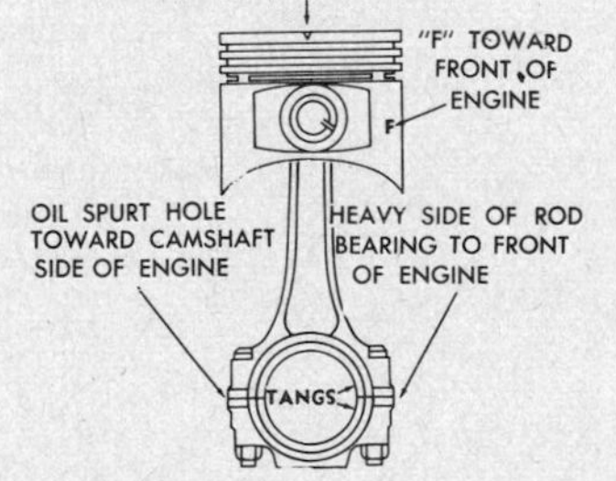

Piston and rod assembly—OHV 4 and 6 cylinder

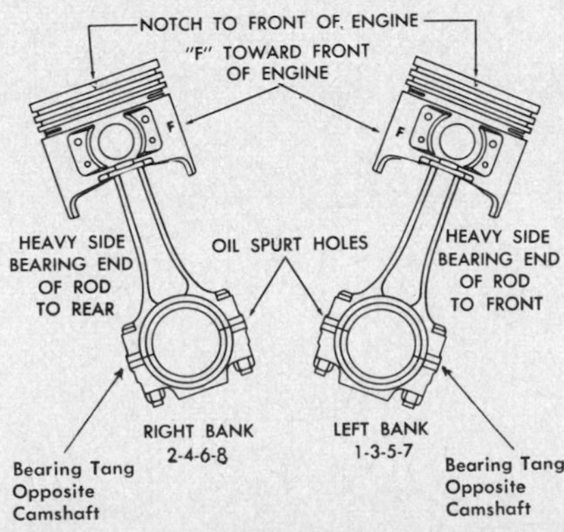

Piston-to-rod relationship—small block V8

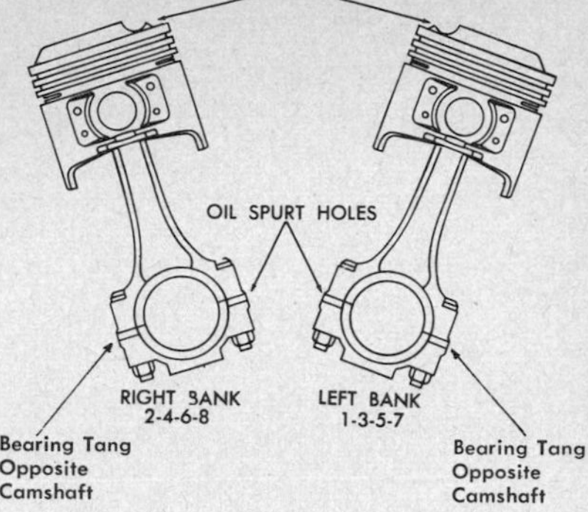

Piston-to-rod relationship—Mk IV (big block) V8

Lubrication

Oil Pan R & R

1969-76 Nova, Camaro—4 and 6 Cylinder

1. Disconnect battery ground cable.
2. Remove front engine mount bolts.

NOTE: 1970 up, remove upper radiator panel or side mount bolts.

3. Drain coolant. Remove radiator hoses.
4. Remove fan.
5. Drain engine oil.
6. Disconnect and remove starter.
7. Disconnect oil cooler lines and remove converter or flywheel housing underpan.
8. On Nova through 1974 and Camaro through 1972, disconnect steering rod at idler lever. Swing linkage to one side for pan clearance.
9. Rotate crankshaft until timing mark on torsional damper is at 6:00 o'clock position.
10. On Camaro, raise engine enough to insert 2 X 4 in. blocks under engine mounts.
11. Unbolt oil pan. On some models it may be necessary to remove the oil pump and intake pipe for clearance. On Nova, remove the left engine mount and frame bracket. Lower the pan slightly and roll it into the area where the mount was. Then tilt the front of the pan up and pull it down and to the rear. Lower pan.

1969 Chevelle with Standard Transmission—6 Cylinder

1. Remove engine from car.
2. Place engine on stands, supported at each front mount and at transmission extension.

Caution As a safety precaution, leave engine lift attached and most of the weight supported from above.

3. Remove starter, then the oil pan.

1969 Chevelle with Automatic Transmission, 1970-72 Chevelle —6 Cylinder

1. Disconnect battery ground cable.
2. Remove radiator upper mounting panel. Place a piece of heavy cardboard between fan and radiator.
3. Remove starter. Disconnect fuel line.
4. Drain engine oil; disconnect brake line from front crossmember.
5. Remove converter housing underpan and splash shield.
6. Rotate crankshaft until timing mark on torsional damper is at 6:00 o'clock position.
7. Remove front engine mount through bolts.
8. Raise engine approximately three inches, remove engine mounts, and lower oil pan.

1969-76 Camaro, Nova, Chevelle, Monte Carlo—V8

See the next procedure for Chevelle and Monte Carlo through 1972 with big block V8.

1. Disconnect battery ground cable.
2. Remove distributor cap.
3. Remove radiator upper mounting panel.
4. Remove fan. On big block (Mark IV) engine models, place a piece of heavy cardboard between the radiator and fan.
5. Drain engine oil.
6. Disconnect exhaust or crossover pipes.
7. Remove converter housing underpan and splash shield.
8. On Nova through 1974 and Camaro through 1972, disconnect steering idler lever at the frame. Swing linkage down.
9. Rotate crankshaft until timing mark on torsional damper is at 6:00 o'clock position.
10. Remove starter.
11. On small V8 through 1970, remove fuel pump.
12. Remove front engine mount through bolts.
13. Raise engine and insert blocks under engine mounts. Block thickness should be 2 in. for Nova and Camaro, and 3 in. for Chevelle.
14. Remove oil pan.

Installing blocks for oil pan removal—V8
(© Chevrolet Div., G.M. Corp)

1969-72 Chevelle and Monte Carlo —396, 402, 454 V8

1. Disconnect battery ground cable.
2. Remove:
   a. air cleaner
   b. dipstick
   c. distributor cap
   d. radiator shroud and upper mounting panel.
3. On 396 models, place a piece of heavy cardboard between radiator and fan.
4. Disconnect engine ground straps.
5. Disconnect accelerator control cable.
6. Drain oil.
7. Remove driveshaft and plug rear of transmission.
8. Remove starter.
9. Disconnect transmission linkage at transmission or remove floorshift lever.
10. Disconnect speedometer cable and back-up switch connector.
11. On manual transmission vehicles disconnect clutch chaft at frame. On automatic transmission vehicles, disconnect cooler lines, detent cable, rod or switch wire, and modulator pipe.
12. Remove crossmember bolts. Jack up engine. Move crossmember rearward.
13. Remove crossover or disconnect dual exhaust pipes.
14. Remove:
   a. flywheel housing cover
   b. transmission
   c. flywheel housing and throwout bearing (manual transmission)
   d. front engine mount through bolts.
15. Raise rear of engine approximately 4 inches. Support engine by hoist.
16. Raise front of engine approximately 4 inches and insert 2 in. blocks under front engine mounts.
17. Rotate crankshaft until timing mark on torsional damper is at 6:00 o'clock position.
18. Unbolt and remove oil pan.

Oil Pump R & R

1. Remove oil pan.
2. Remove pump and pickup tube and screen assembly on inline engine and pump to rear main bearing cap bolt on V8. Remove the pump and extension shaft on the V8.
3. To install, reverse removal procedure.

Rear Main Seal R & R

The rear main bearing seal may be replaced without removing the crankshaft. Seals should only be replaced as a pair. Fabrication of a seal installation tool as shown in the figure will prevent damaging the bead on the cylinder block. The seal lips should face the front of the engine when properly installed.

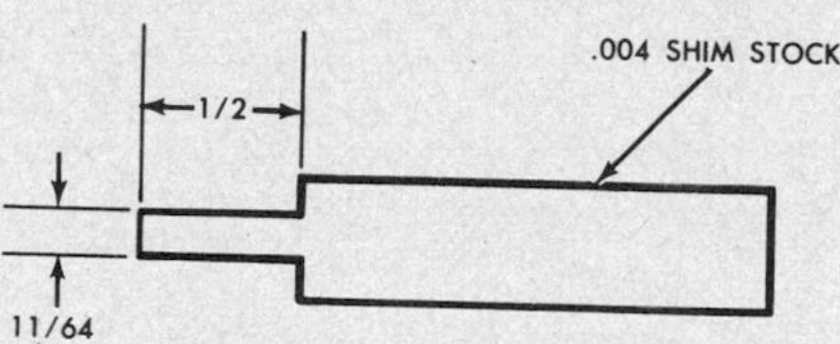

Rear main bearing seal installation tool
(© Chevrolet Div., G.M. Corp)

1. Remove the oil pan and pump as previously outlined, and remove the rear main bearing cap.
2. Pry the lower seal out of the bearing cap with a screwdriver, being careful not to gouge the cap surface.
3. Remove the upper seal by lightly tapping on one end with a brass pin punch until the other end can be grasped and pulled out with pliers.
4. Clean the bearing cap, cylinder block, and crankshaft mating surfaces with solvent. Inspect all these surfaces for gouges, nicks, and burrs.
5. Apply light engine oil on the seal lips and bead, but keep the seal ends clean.
6. Insert the tip of the installation tool between the crankshaft and the seal seat of the cylinder block. Place the seal between the tip of the tool and the crankshaft, so that the bead contacts the tip of the tool.
7. Be sure that the seal lip is facing the front of the engine, and work the seal around the crankshaft, using the installation tool to protect the seal from the corner of the cylinder block.

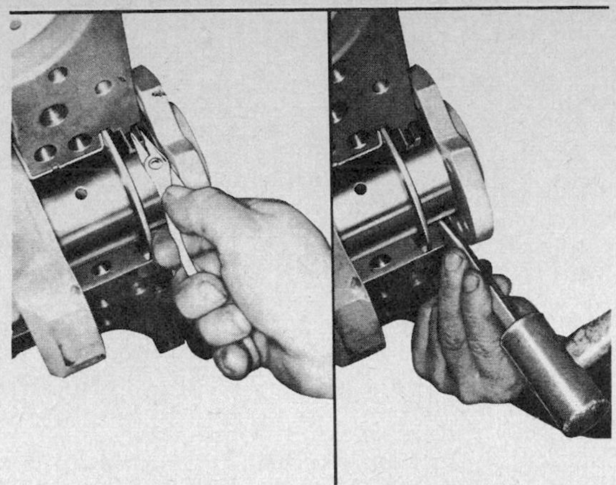

Rear main seal installation
(© Chevrolet Div., G.M. Corp)

NOTE: do not remove the tool until the opposite end of the seal is flush with the cylinder block surface.

8. Remove the installation tool, being careful not to pull the seal out at the same time.
9. Using the same procedure, install the lower seal into the bearing cap. Use your finger and thumb to lever the seal into the cap.
10. Apply sealer to the cylinder block only where the cap mates to the surface. Do not apply sealer to the seal ends.
11. Install the rear cap and torque the bolts to specifications. Install the oil pan and pump as previously described.

CLUTCH

A diaphragm type clutch assembly is used with all manual transmissions. A flat finger diaphragm clutch is used for normal service. V8 engines with four speed transmissions have a bent finger, centrifugal diaphragm clutch assembly. In this design the release fingers are bent back to gain a centrifugal boost and to insure quick re-engagement at high engine speeds. The centrifugal type clutch has the advantage of low pedal effort with high plate load.

The clutch release bearings used with the flat and bent finger diaphragms are not interchangeable. Using the flat finger release bearing with the bent finger clutch assembly will result in slippage and rapid wear.

The only service adjustment necessary on the clutch is to maintain the correct pedal free play. Clutch pedal free play, or throwout bearing lash, decreases with driven disc wear.

Further information on clutches may be found in the Unit Repair Section.

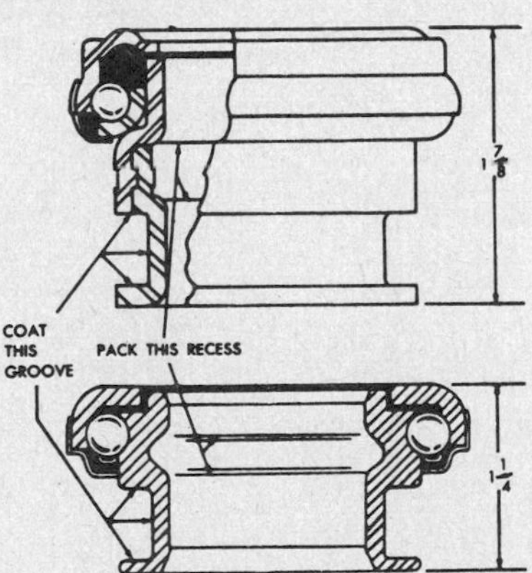

Clutch release bearing lubrication, flat finger type at top, bent finger type at bottom
(© Chevrolet Div., G.M. Corp)

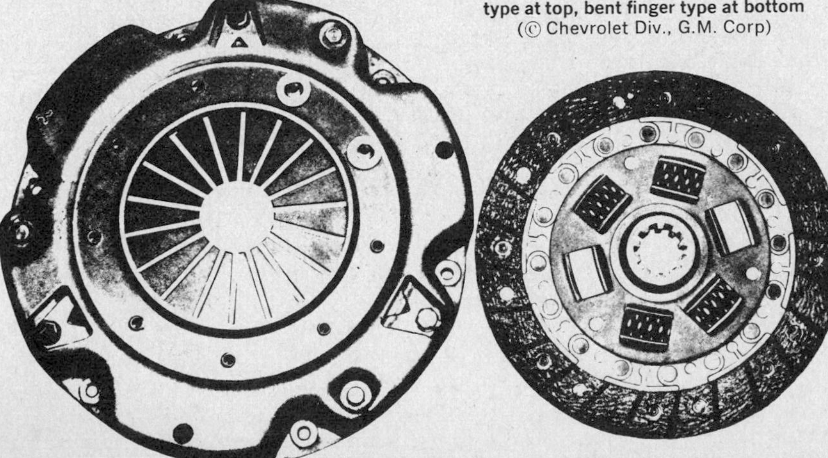

Single disc diaphragm clutch assembly (© Chevrolet Div., G.M. Corp)

Removal

1. Support engine and remove transmission.
2. Disconnect clutch fork push rod and spring.
3. Remove flywheel housing.
4. Slide clutch fork from ball stud and remove fork from dust boot. Ball stud is threaded into clutch housing and may be replaced, if necessary.
5. Install an alignment tool (dummy shaft) to support the clutch assembly during removal. Mark flywheel and clutch cover for reinstallation, if they do not already have X marks.
6. Loosen clutch to flywheel attaching bolts evenly, one turn at a time, until spring pressure is released. Remove bolts and clutch assembly.

Installation

1. Clean pressure plate and flywheel face.
2. Support clutch disc and pressure plate with alignment tool. The driven disc is installed with the damper springs on the transmission side. The grease slinger is always on the transmission side.
3. Turn clutch assembly until mark on cover lines up with mark on flywheel, then install bolts. Tighten down evenly and gradually to avoid distortion.
4. Remove alignment tool.
5. Lubricate ball socket and fork fingers at release bearing end with high melting point grease. Lubricate recess on inside of throwout bearing and throwout fork groove with a light coat of graphite or other high melting point grease.
6. Install clutch fork and dust boot into housing. Install throwout bearing to throwout fork. Install flywheel housing. Install transmission.
7. Connect fork push rod and spring. Lubricate spring and pushrod ends.
8. Adjust shift linkage and clutch pedal free play.

Free Play Adjustment

This adjustment must be made under the vehicle on the clutch operating linkage. Free play is measured at the clutch pedal.

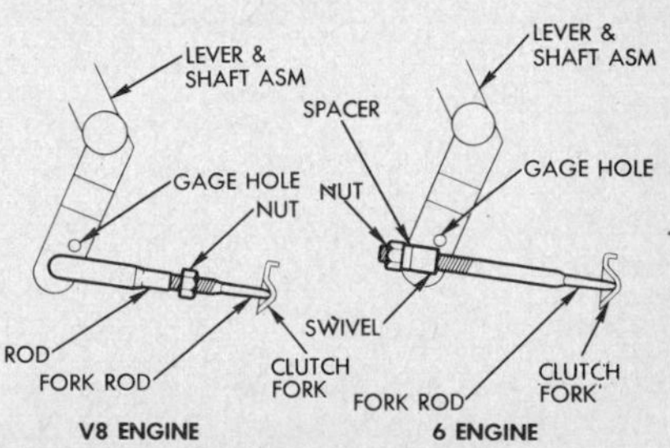

Clutch pedal free-play adjustment
(© Chevrolet Div., G.M. Corp)

Chevelle, Monte Carlo, and Camaro through 1970, Nova through 1971

1. Disconnect the return spring at the clutch operating fork.
2. Use the linkage to push the clutch pedal up against its rubber bumper stop.
3. Loosen the operating rod locknut and lengthen the adjustable rod until it pushes the fork back enough that the release bearing can just be felt to contact the pressure plate fingers.
4. Shorten the rod three turns and tighten the locknut.
5. Replace the spring and check the free play at the pedal pad.

1971 Chevelle, Monte Carlo, and Camaro, All Models starting 1972

You can also use this procedure on any earlier models that have a gauge hole in the clutch pivot shaft arm.

1. Disconnect the return spring at the clutch operating fork.
2. Use the linkage to push the clutch pedal up against its rubber bumper stop.
3. Push the end of the clutch operating fork to the rear until the release bearing can just be felt to contact the pressure plate fingers.
4. Detach the front end of the operating rod from the clutch pivot shaft arm and place it in the gauge hole on the arm.
5. Loosen the locknut and lengthen the rod just enough to take all the play out of the linkage. Tighten the locknut.
6. Replace the operating rod in its original location.
7. Replace the return spring and check the free play at the pedal pad.

Clutch Pedal Free Play

Vehicle	Free Play at Pedal Pad (in.)
1971-72 Nova	1-1½
1968-69 Camaro 1969-70 Nova	1-1⅛
1969-72 Chevelle, 1970-72 Camaro	1⅛-1¾
1973-76 Nova, Camaro 1973-76 Chevelle	¾-1⅜ ¾-1 5/16

Clutch Start Switch

This switch, used on standard shift models, is operated by linkage from the clutch pedal arm, inside the vehicle. The function of the switch is to prevent the engine from being started unless the clutch pedal is fully depressed. There is no adjustment necessary for this switch.

MANUAL TRANSMISSION

The normal-duty three-speed transmission is the Saginaw unit, while the heavy-duty three-speed used through 1974 is the Muncie. The Saginaw has one bolt boss casting "ear" at the center top of the side cover, while the Muncie has two such "ears".

The normal-duty four-speed is the Saginaw, while the heavy-duty unit used through 1974 is the Muncie. During 1974, the Muncie four-speed was phased out and the Warner T-10 heavy-duty four-speed introduced in the Camaro only. On the Saginaw, all three shift linkage rods go to the levers on the side cover. On the Muncie, two shift rods go to levers on the side cover and one rod (reverse) goes to a lever on the case extension housing. The Warner T-10 linkage is similar to that on the Muncie, but the transmission has a 9 bolt curved bottom side cover.

Transmission R & R

1. On floorshift models, remove the shift knob, and the spring and T-handle on four-speeds. Remove the boot.
2. Raise the car.
3. Disconnect the speedometer cable and TCS switch wiring at the transmission.
4. Remove the driveshaft.
5. On models through 1972, remove the crossmember to shifter brace.
6. Support the rear of the engine and remove the crossmember. On models through 1972, the crossmember may be slid rearward.
7. Detach the shift rods from the transmission levers.
8. On floorshift models, remove the shifter from the transmission.
9. Remove the upper transmission to clutch housing bolts and replace them with headless guide pins. Remove the lower bolts.
10. Slide the transmission back along the guide pins until the input shaft clears the clutch. Remove the transmission.
11. Reverse the procedure for installation. If the input shaft won't engage the clutch splines, put the transmission in gear and turn the output shaft slightly. Torque the transmission to clutch housing bolts to 55 ft lbs through 1972, and to 75 ft lbs beginning 1973.

Shift Linkage Adjustment

Column Shift

1. With transmission in Reverse, place ignition switch in Off position up to 1970, Lock for 1971 and later.
2. Loosen shift rod lock nuts.
3. Set transmission first-reverse lever in reverse position. Push up on first-reverse control rod to 1970, pull down for 1971 and later until column lever is in reverse detent position. Tighten first-reverse lock nut.
4. Unlock the switch and shift the column and transmission levers to neutral position. Insert a 3/16 in. dia. rod into alignment holes in levers.
5. Tighten second-third locknut.
6. Remove alignment rod. Shift column lever to reverse. Turn key to Lock. Ignition switch must move freely to Lock position and it must not be possible to turn key to Lock when in any transmission position other than reverse. If this interlock binds, leave switch in Lock position and readjust first-reverse rod.
7. Check shifting.

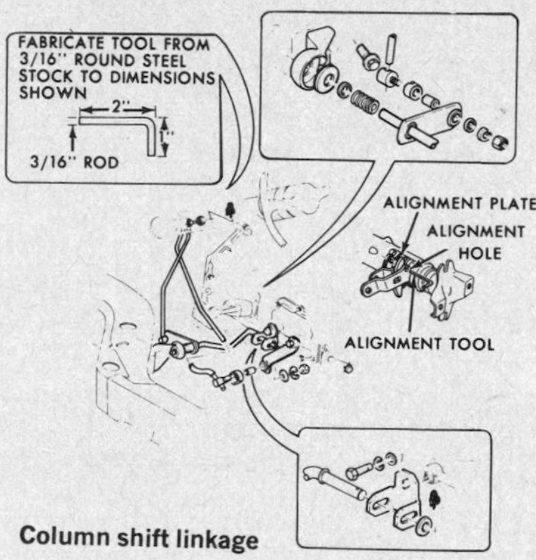

Column shift linkage
(© Chevrolet Div., G.M. Corp)

Floorshift

1. Turn ignition switch to Lock position up to 1970, Off starting 1971.
2. Loosen locknuts on shift rods and back drive rod.
3. Set transmission levers in neutral positions.
4. Set floorshift lever in neutral. Install locating gauge, ⅛ thick X 41/64 wide X 3 in. long, into control lever bracket assembly alignment slot. Some later models may take a locating pin.
5. Adjust length of shift rods. Tighten locknuts.
6. Remove locating gauge. Shift into reverse and lock the switch.
7. Pull down slightly on back drive rod to remove any slack and tighten locknut. Ignition switch must move freely to Lock position and it must not be possible to turn key to Lock when in any transmission position other than reverse. If this interlock binds, leave the switch in Lock position and readjust back drive rod.
8. Check shifting operation.

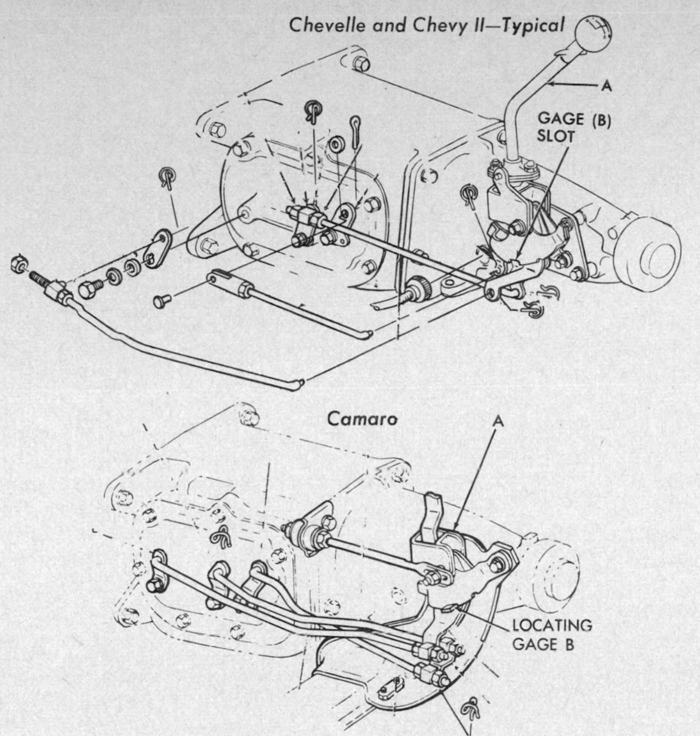

Typical four speed floorshift linkage (© Chevrolet Div., G.M. Corp)

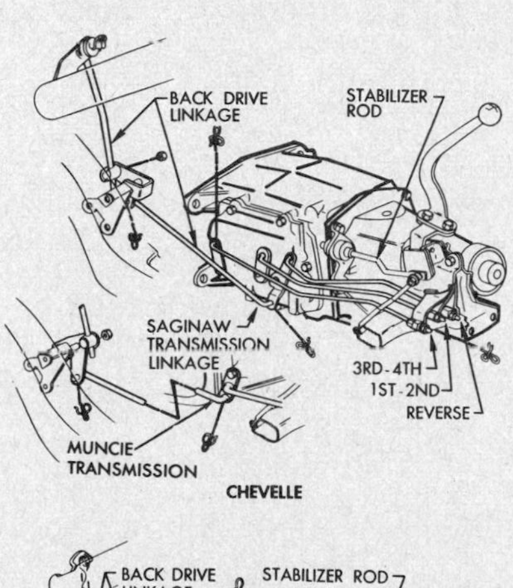

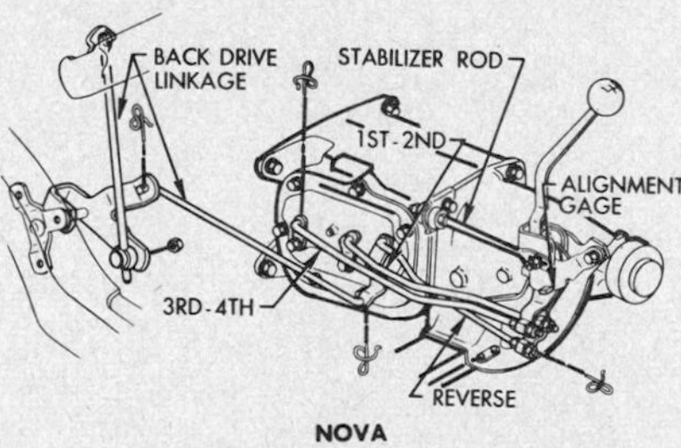

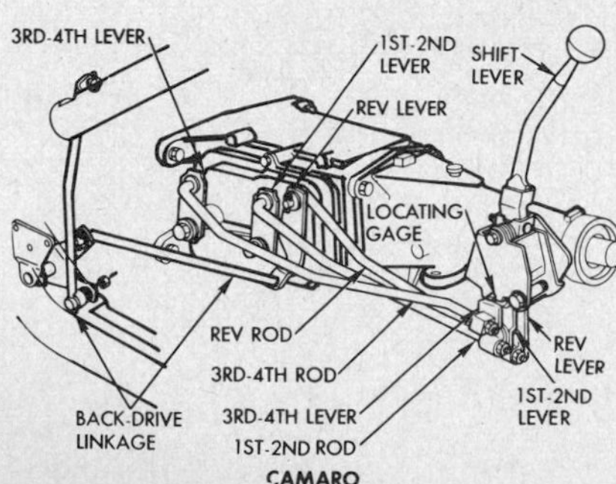

Saginaw four speed linkages (© Chevrolet Div., G.M. Corp)

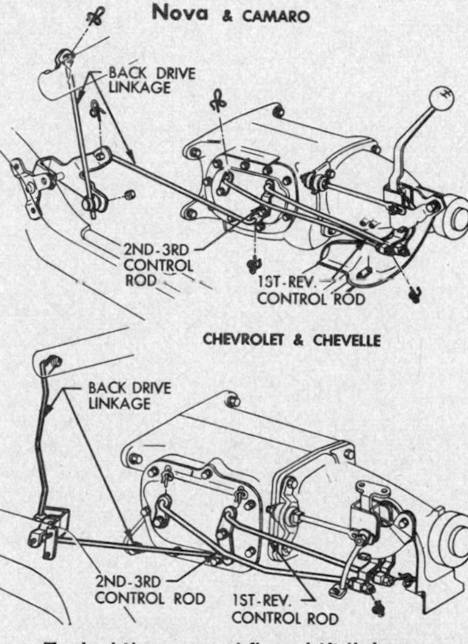

Typical three speed floorshift linkage (© Chevrolet Div., G.M. Corp)

AUTOMATIC TRANSMISSION

There are two basic automatic transmissions. The first is the two speed Powerglide. A variation on the Powerglide, dropped in 1971, is the Torque Drive transmission. The Torque Drive unit is a Powerglide with the automatic shifting provisions removed. Torque Drive is shifted manually, but has no clutch. The Powerglide transmission was dropped in mid-1973. The second type is the three speed Turbo Hydra-Matic.

This transmission is available in several load capacities, the Turbo Hydra-Matic 250, 350, 375, and 400.

The Turbo Hydra-Matic 250 is used only in 1974 and later six-cylinder models. The 250 may be identified by the intermediate band adjusting screw on the right side of the case. The intermediate band replaces the intermediate clutch on the larger capacity models. The 250 and 350 have a cable operated downshift linkage running from the accelerator linkage to the right side of the transmission, while the 375 and 400 have a downshift solenoid activated by a switch on the accelerator linkage. There is no external difference between the 375 and 400; they differ internally in numbers of clutch plates and other items related to torque capacity.

Powerglide Shift Linkage Adjustment

Column Shift through 1972

1. Loosen adjustment clamp at cross-shaft. Set transmission lever in drive by rotating lever counterclockwise to low detent, then clockwise one detent to drive.
2. Set selector lever in Drive. Remove any free play by holding cross-shaft upward and pulling shift rod downward.
3. Tighten the clamp and check the adjustment.
4. Place shift lever in Park and ignition switch in Lock. Loosen back drive rod clamp nut. Remove column lash and tighten clamp nut.
5. With selector lever in Park, the ignition key should move freely to Lock position. Lock position should be obtainable only when transmission is in Park.

Torque Drive through 1971

1. Loosen swivel at idler lever.
2. Place transmission lever in Hi position.
3. Set shift lever at lower end of column up against first position stop.
4. Adjust rod in swivel and tighten retaining nut.
5. Place shift lever in Park and ignition switch in Lock. Loosen back drive rod clamp nut. Remove column lash and tighten clamp nut.
6. With selector lever in Park, the ignition key should move freely to Lock position. Lock position should be obtainable only when transmission is in Park.

Nova Floorshift through 1970

This is a rod operated linkage.

1. Loosen adjustment nuts at swivel. Set transmission lever in drive position by moving counterclockwise to low detent, then clockwise one detent to drive.
2. Set floorshift lever in Drive.

Hold floorshift unit lower operating lever forward against shift lever detent.

3. Place a 3/32 (.0094 in.) spacer between rear nut and swivel. Tighten rear nut against spacer.
4. Remove spacer and tighten front nut against swivel, locking swivel between nuts.
5. Place shift lever in Park position. Adjust column (back drive) rod. With shift lever in Park, the ignition key must move freely to Lock, and Lock position must not be obtainable in any transmission position other than Park.

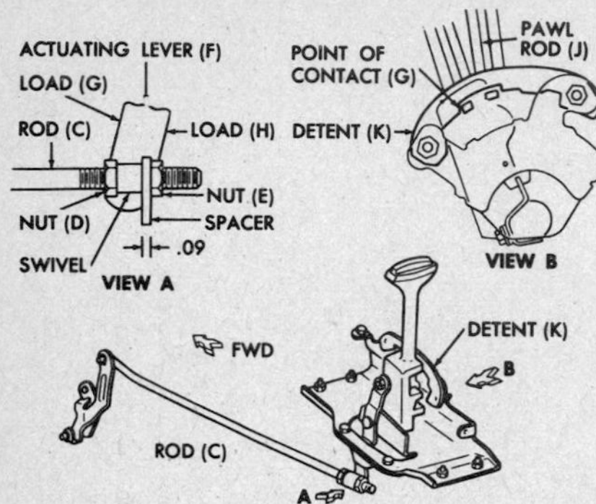

Automatic transmission rod operated floorshift linkage, Nova (© Chevrolet Div., G.M. Corp)

Camaro, Chevelle, Monte Carlo Floorshift through 1972

These models use a cable operated linkage.

1. Place shift lever in Drive position.
2. Disconnect cable from transmission lever. Place transmission lever in drive by rotating lever counterclockwise to low detent, then clockwise one detent to drive.
3. Measure distance from rearward face of attachment bracket to center of cable attachment pin. Adjust this dimension to 5.5 in. by loosening and moving cable end stud nut.
4. Place shift lever in Park and ignition switch in Lock position.
5. Loosen and adjust column (back drive) rod.
6. With selector lever in Park position, the ignition key should move freely to Lock position. Lock position should not be obtainable in any transmission position other than Park.

Turbo Hydra-Matic Shift Linkage Adjustment

Column Shift

1. Loosen the swivel at the lower end of the rod that comes from the column.
2. On 1973 and later models, set the transmission lever in the Neutral detent by turning the lever counterclockwise to the L1 detent, then clockwise three positions. On models through 1972, set the lever in the Drive detent by turning the lever counterclockwise to the L1 detent, then clockwise two positions.

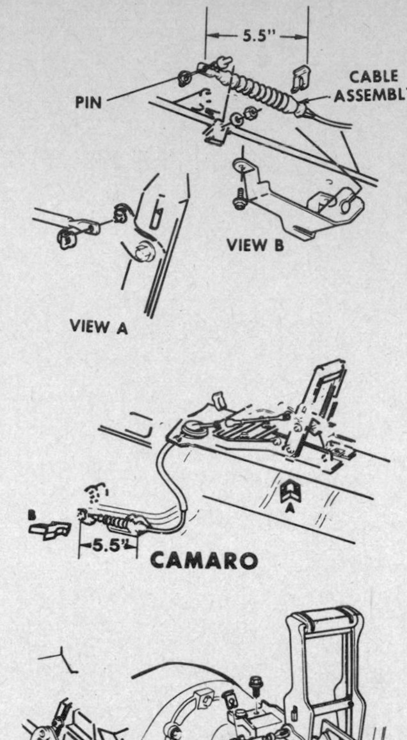

Automatic transmission cable operated floorshift linkage, Camaro and Chevelle (© Chevrolet Div., G.M. Corp)

3. Put the column lever in Neutral for 1973 and later models, and in Drive for models through 1972. The important thing here is not where the indicator points but that the lever be in the correct position.
4. Tighten the swivel.
5. Check that the key cannot be removed and that the wheel is not locked with the key in RUN. Check that the key can be removed in LOCK with the lever in Park, and that the steering wheel is locked.

Nova Floorshift through 1974

This is a rod operated linkage, very similar to the rod operated linkage used on the Nova Powerglide floorshift through 1970. The adjustment procedure is the same, except that 1972 and later models are adjusted in Neutral, rather than Drive. The Turbo Hydra-Matic Drive position is obtained by turning the transmission lever counterclockwise to the L1 detent, then clockwise two positions. The Neutral position is obtained by turning the lever clockwise three positions from the L1 detent.

Camaro, Chevelle, Monte Carlo Floorshift through 1972

This is a cable operated linkage, very similar to the cable linkage used on the Camaro, Chevelle, and Monte Carlo Powerglide floorshift through 1972. The adjustment procedure is the same, except that the Turbo Hydra-Matic Drive position is obtained by turning the transmission lever counterclockwise to the L1 detent, then clockwise two positions.

Camaro, Chevelle, Monte Carlo Floorshift 1973 and later; Nova Floorshift 1975 and later

This is a cable operated linkage.

1. Loosen the swivel at the lower end of the rod that comes from the steering column.
2. Loosen the pin at the transmission end of the cable.
3. Set the floorshift lever in the Drive detent.
4. Set the transmission lever in the Drive detent by moving it counterclockwise to the L1 detent, then clockwise three detent positions.
5. Tighten the nut on the pin at the transmission end of the cable.
6. Put the floorshift lever in Park and the ignition switch in LOCK.
7. Pull down lightly on the rod from the column and tighten its clamp nut.

Powerglide Throttle Valve Linkage Adjustment

Inline Engines through 1973

1. Fully depress the accelerator pedal.
2. Bellcrank must be at wide open throttle position.
3. On models through 1971, the dash lever at the firewall must be 1/64-1/16 in. off the lever stop.
4. Transmission lever must be against transmission internal stop.

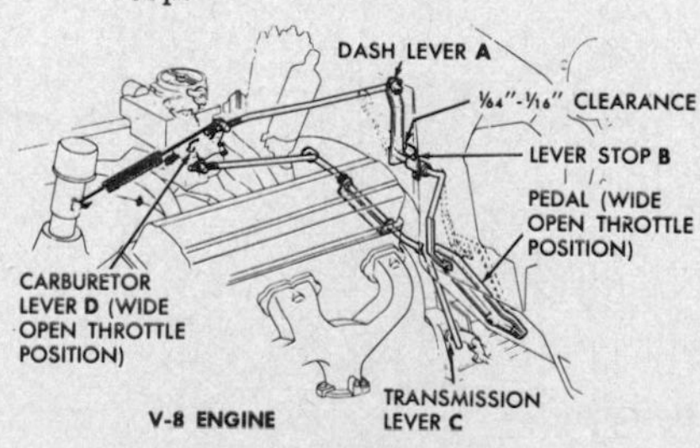

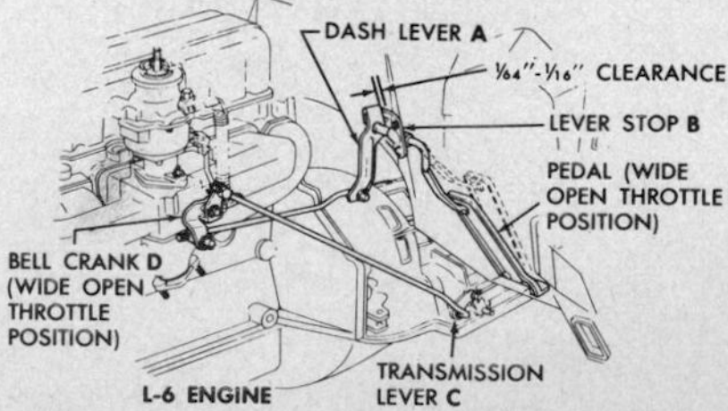

Powerglide throttle valve linkage adjustment V8, 1969-73 inline engines (© Chevrolet Div., G.M. Corp)

5. Adjust linkage to simultaneously obtain conditions in Steps 1-4, above.

V8 Engines through 1972

1. Remove air cleaner.
2. Disconnect accelerator linkage at carburetor.
3. Disconnect both return springs.
4. Pull throttle valve upper rod forward until transmission is through detent.
5. Open carburetor to wide open throttle position. Adjust swivel on end of upper throttle valve rod so carburetor reaches wide open throttle position at the same time that the ball stud contacts the end of the slot in the upper throttle valve rod. A tolerance of 1/32 in. is allowable.

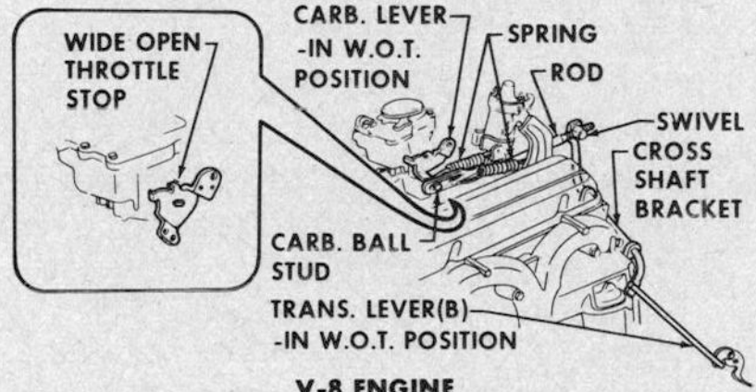

Powerglide throttle valve linkage—1969-73 V8 (© Chevrolet Div., G.M. Corp)

Turbo Hydra-Matic 250 and 350 Detent Cable Adjustment

The Turbo Hydra-Matic 250 and 350 have a detent, or downshift, cable between the carburetor linkage and the transmission.

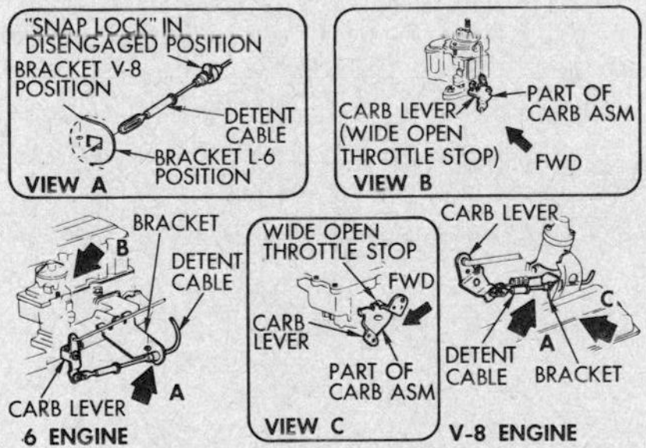

Turbo Hydra-Matic 350 detent cable adjustment (© Chevrolet Div., G.M. Corp)

1969-76 Nova and Camaro, Chevelle and Monte Carlo through 1972

1. Remove air cleaner.
2. Loosen detent cable screw or disengage snap lock.
3. Place carburetor lever in wide open throttle position. Make sure lever is against stop. On vehicles with Quadrajet carburetors, disengage the secondary lock out before placing lever in wide open throttle position.

NOTE: detent cable must be pulled through detent position.

4. Engage snap lock or tighten detent screw.

1973 and Later Chevelle and Monte Carlo

On these models, the cable adjusts itself the first time the accelerator pedal is floorboarded.

Turbo Hydra-Matic 375 and 400 Detent Switch Adjustment

The Turbo Hydra-Matic 375 and 400 transmission has an electrical detent, or downshift, switch operated by the throttle linkage.

Nova and Camaro through 1972

1. Loosen the switch mounting bolts. Place the carburetor lever in the wide open throttle position.
2. Make sure the choke is off.
3. Depress the switch plunger all the way.
4. Adjust switch mounting to obtain distance between depressed switch plunger and throttle lever paddle of .22-.24 in.
5. Tighten the switch mounting bolts.

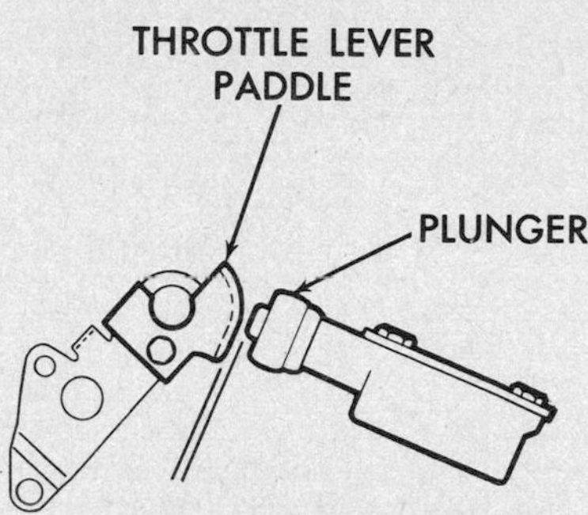

Turbo Hydra-Matic 400 detent switch adjustment—Nova and Camaro (© Chevrolet Div., G.M. Corp)

Chevelle and Monte Carlo through 1972

1. Pull detent switch driver rearward until hole in switch body aligns with hold in driver. Insert a .092 in. dia. pin through the aligned holes to hold the driver in position.
2. Loosen mounting bolt.
3. Depress accelerator to wide open throttle position. Move switch forward until driver contacts accelerator lever.
4. Tighten mounting bolt. Remove pin.

1973 and Later

After installation, the switch adjusts itself the first time the accelerator is floorboarded.

Neutral Safety Switch

The neutral safety switch prevents the engine from being started in any transmission position except Neutral or Park. On all column shift models and floorshift models from late 1972, the switch is located on the upper side of the steering column under the instrument panel. On floorshift models thru early 1972, the switch is located inside the shift console.

Switch Replacement

1. Remove console for access on early floorshift models.
2. Disconnect wiring connectors.
3. Remove switch.
4. Position the shift lever in Neutral on column shift models from late 1972. Put it in Drive on earlier column shift models, and in Park on floorshift models with the column mounted switch. On column shift models, locate lever tang against transmission selector plate.
5. Align slot in contact support with hole in switch. Insert 3/32 in. dia. pin to hold support in place. Switch is now aligned.

NOTE: 1973 and later neutral safety switches have a shear-pin installed to aid in proper new switch alignment so that insertion of a pin is unnecessary. Moving the shift lever shears the pin.

6. Place contact support drive slot over drive tang. Install screws.
7. Remove pin. Connect wiring. Replace console.

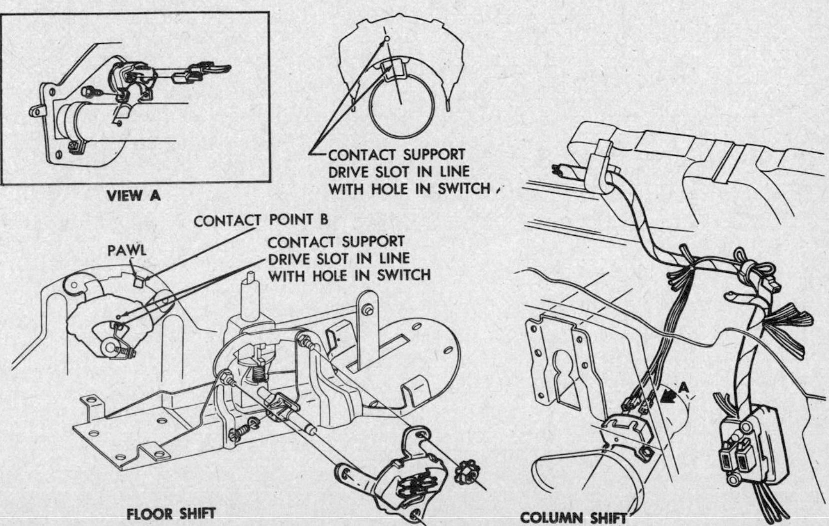

Typical neutral safety switch installation (© Chevrolet Div., G.M. Corp)

8. Set parking brake and footbrake. Check to see that engine will start only in Park or Neutral.

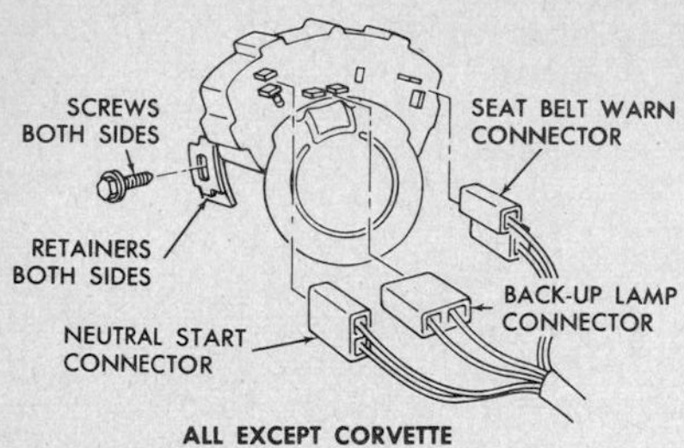

1973 combination neutral start switch connections
(© Chevrolet Div., G.M. Corp)

Band Adjustments

There are no band adjustments possible or required for the Turbo Hydra-Matic 350, 375, or 400.

Low Band—Powerglide and Torque Drive

The low band must be adjusted at the first required fluid change or whenever there is slippage.

1. Position the shift lever in Neutral.
2. Remove the protective cap from the adjusting screw on the left side of the transmission.
3. Loosen the locknut 1/4 turn and hold it with a wrench during the entire adjusting procedure.
4. Tighten the adjusting nut to 70 in. lbs, using a 7/32 allen wrench.
5. Back off the adjusting nut exactly three turns for a band used less than 6,000 miles. Back off exactly four turns for a band used 6,000 miles or more.
6. Torque the locknut to 15 ft lbs. and replace the cap.

Intermediate Band—Turbo Hydra-Matic 250

The intermediate band must be adjusted with every required fluid change or whenever there is slippage.

1. Position the shift lever in Neutral.
2. Loosen the locknut on the right side of the transmission and tighten the adjusting screw to 30 in lbs.
3. Back the screw out three turns and then tighten the locknut to 15 ft lbs.

Pan Removal and Installation, Fluid and Filter Change

The fluid should be changed with the transmission warm.

1. Raise and support the vehicle, preferably in a level attitude.
2. On Nova with Turbo Hydra-Matic 250 or 350, support the transmission and remove the support crossmember.
3. Place a large pan under the transmission pan. Remove all the front and side pan bolts. Loosen the rear bolts about four turns.
4. Pry the pan loose and let it drain.
5. Remove the pan and gasket. Clean the pan thoroughly with solvent and air dry it. Be very careful not to get any lint from rags in the pan.
6. Remove the strainer to valve body screws, the strainer, and the gasket. Most 350 transmissions will have a throw-away filter instead of a strainer. On the 400 transmission, remove the filter retaining bolt, filter, and intake pipe O-ring.
7. If there is a strainer, clean it in solvent and air dry.
8. Install the new filter or cleaned strainer with a new gasket. Tighten the screws to 12 ft lbs. On the 400, install a new intake pipe O-ring and a new filter, tightening the retaining bolt to 10 ft lbs.
9. Install the pan with a new gasket. Tighten the bolts evenly to 12 ft lbs (8 for Powerglide and Torque Drive).
10. Lower the car and add 5 pts (3 on Powerglide and Torque Drive) of DEXRON® or DEXRON II® automatic transmission fluid through the dipstick tube.
11. Start the engine in Park and let it idle. Do not race the engine. Shift into each shift lever position, shift back into Park, and check the fluid level on the dipstick. The level should be 1/4 in. below ADD. Be very careful not to overfill. Recheck the level after the car has been driven long enough to thoroughly warm up the transmission. Add fluid as necessary. The level should then be at FULL.

U-JOINTS

Driveshafts are of a one-piece design, using Cardan type universal joints. The universal joints are lubricated and sealed at the factory and require no periodic maintenance. The front yoke is splined, providing a slip joint for length variations in the drive line. There is a damper on some models: this damper is not serviced separately.

Two basic universal joints are used. The Dana or Cleveland type uses snap-ring bearing cap retainers. The Saginaw uses injection molded plastic to retain the bearing caps. On the Saginaw type there is a snap-ring groove in the bearing housing inboard of the yoke to facilitate installation of a repair kit.

Driveshaft R & R

Disconnect the rear universal joint flange. On some models, the bearing caps are bolted directly to the differential flange with clamps or U-bolts. Pull the front yoke from the transmission. Watch for oil leaks from the transmission output housing. Install in the reverse order of removal.

Universal Joint R & R

Dana and Cleveland Type

1. Remove the driveshaft.
2. Remove the snap-rings from the trunnion yoke.
3. Using a vise and suitably sized sockets, press on the trunnion until the bearing cap is almost out. Grasp the cap in the vise and work it out of the yoke. Repeat the above procedure for the rest of the bearing caps.
4. Pack the rollers in grease and fill the grease reservoir.
5. To install, position the trunnion in the yoke and partially install one bearing cap. Start the trunnion in the bearing cap and partially install the other cap. Align the trunnion with the caps and press into place.
6. If necessary, repeat Step 5 above for the other yoke.
7. Install the snap-rings.
8. Install the driveshaft in the vehicle.

Saginaw Type

Remove and install the bearing caps and trunnion as described for the Dana and Cleveland type universal joints. On an original universal joint, however, the bearing caps will be secured in the yokes with injected plastic. The plastic will shear when the bearing caps are pressed. Service snap-rings are installed in the groove on the inside (of yoke) of the installed caps.

REAR AXLE

Axle Shaft, Bearing and Seal

Removal and Installation

These cars use, basically, two different types of drive axle, the C- and the non C-type. Axle shafts in the C-type are retained by C-shaped locks, which fit grooves at the inner end of the shaft. Axle shafts in the non C-type are retained by the brake backing plate, which is bolted to the axle housing. Bearings in the C-type axle consist of an outer race, bearing rollers and a roller cage, retained by snap-rings. The non C-type axle uses a unit roller bearing (inner race, rollers and outer race), which is pressed onto the shaft, up to a shoulder. When servicing C or non C-type axles, it is imperative to determine the axle type before attempting any service.

Non C Type

Caution Before attempting any service to the drive axle or axle shafts, remove the axle carrier cover and visually determine if the axle shafts are retained by C-shaped locks at the inner end, or by the brake backing plate at the outer end. If the shafts are *not* retained by C-locks, proceed as follows.

Design allows for maximum axle shaft end-play of 0.022 in., which can be measured with a dial indicator. If end-play is found to be excessive, the bearing should be replaced. Shimming the bearing is not recommended as this ignores end-play of the bearing itself and could result in improper seating of the bearing.

1. Remove the wheel, tire and brake drum.
2. Remove the nuts holding the retainer plate to the backing plate. Disconnect the brake line.
3. Remove the retainer and install nuts, fingertight, to prevent the brake backing plate from being dislodged.
4. Pull out the axle shaft and bearing assembly, using a slide hammer.
5. Using a chisel, nick the bearing retainer in three or four places. The retainer does not have to be cut, merely collapsed sufficiently, to allow the bearing retainer to be slid from the shaft.
6. Press off the bearing and install the new one by pressing it into postion.
7. Press on the new retainer.

NOTE: do not attempt to press the bearing and the retainer on at the same time.

8. Assemble the shaft and bearing in the housing, being sure that the bearing is seated properly in the housing.
9. Install the retainer, drum, wheel and tire. Bleed the brakes.

C—Type

Caution Before attempting any service to the drive axle or axle shafts, remove the carrier cover and visually determine if the axle shaft(s) are retained by C-shaped locks at the inner ends or by a brake backing plate at the outer end. If they *are* retained by C-shaped locks, proceed as follows.

1. Raise the vehicle and remove the wheels.
2. The differential cover has already been removed (see Caution note). Remove the differential pinion shaft lock-screw and the differential pinion shaft.
3. Push the flanged end of the axle shaft toward the center of the vehicle and remove the "C" lock from the end of the shaft.
4. Remove the axle shaft from the housing, being careful not to damage the oil seal.
5. Remove the oil seal by inserting the button end of the axle shaft behind the steel case of the oil seal. Pry the seal loose from the bore.
6. Seat the legs of the bearing puller behind the bearing. Seat a washer against the bearing and hold it in place with a nut. Use a slide hammer to pull the bearing.
7. Pack the cavity between the seal lips with wheel bearing lubricant and lubricate a new wheel bearing with same.
8. Use a suitable driver and install the bearing until it bottoms against the tube. Install the oil seal.
9. Slide the axle shaft into place. Be sure that the splines on the shaft do not damage the oil seal. Make sure that the splines engage the differential side gear.
10. Install the axle shaft, C-lock on the inner end of the axle shaft and push the shaft outward so that the C-lock seats in the differential side gear counterbore.
11. Position the differential pinion shaft through the case and pinions, aligning the hole in the case with the hole for the lock-screw.
13. Use a new gasket and install the carrier cover. Be sure that the gasket surfaces are clean before installing the gasket and cover.
14. Fill the axle with lubricant to the bottom of the filler hole.
15. Install the brake drum and wheels and lower the car. Check for leaks and road test the car.

JACKING, HOISTING

1. Jack car at front spring seat of lower control arm. Jack car at rear axle housing except when equipped with rear stabilizer bar. On these models, jack at frame rails.
2. To lift at frame, use side rails in front of body floor pan and at rear corner at squared off corner of box ahead of rear wheel.

FRONT SUSPENSION

Coil Spring R & R

1. Remove the shock absorber. Disconnect the stabilizer bar.
2. Suport the car at the frame so the control arms hang free.
3. Support the inner end of the control arm with a floor jack. (dealers have a device that cradles the inner bushings).
4. Raise the jack enough to take the tension off the lower control arm pivot bolts.
5. Chain the spring to the lower control arm, for safety's sake.
6. Remove first the rear, then the front pivot bolt.
7. Cautiously lower the jack until all spring tension is released.
8. Note the way in which the spring is installed to the control arm and remove it.
9. On installation, position the spring to the control arm and raise it into place.
10. Install the pivot bolts and torque the nuts to 100 ft lbs for all 1974 and later models except for 1974 Nova. Torque the 1974 Nova and all models through 1973 to 85 ft lbs.
11. Replace the shock absorber and stabilizer bar.

Shock Absorber R & R

1. Remove the upper stem nut while holding the stem to keep it from turning.
2. Remove the two bolts holding the shock absorber to the lower control arm, and pull the shock through the arm.
3. Extend the new shock absorber and insert it up through the lower control arm. Make sure that the upper stem goes through the hole in the upper control arm frame bracket.

NOTE: Purge new shocks of air by repeatedly compressing them while inverted and extending them in their normal installed position.

4. Install the grommet, retainer cup, and nut to the shock absorber upper stem.
5. Hold the shock absorber stem and tighten the upper nut to 8 ft lbs.
6. Install the lower control arm retaining bolts and tighten to 20 ft lbs.

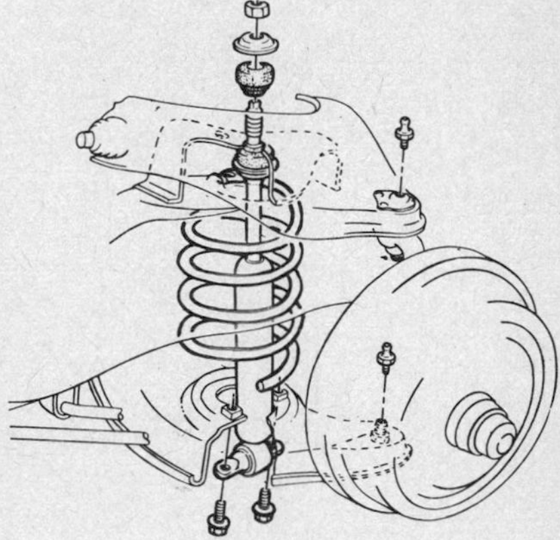

Chevelle, Camaro, 1969 Nova shock absorber installation
(© Chevrolet Div., G.M. Corp)

Front Wheel Bearing Adjustment

1. Jack the car up and support it at the lower arm.
2. Remove the hub dust cover and spindle cotter pin. Loosen the nut.

3. While spinning the wheel, snug the nut down to seat the bearings. Do not exert over 12 ft lbs of force on the nut.
4. Back the nut off 1/4–1/2 a turn or until it is just loose. Line up the cotter pin hole in the spindle with the hole in the nut.
5. Insert a new cotter pin. Endplay should be between 0.001 and 0.005 in. If play exceeds this tolerance, the wheel bearings should be replaced.

Ball Joints

Ball Joint Inspection

NOTE: before performing this inspection, make sure the wheel bearings are adjusted correctly and that the A-arm bushings are in good condition.

1. Jack the car up under the front lower control arm at the spring seat.
2. Raise the car until there is 1–2 in. of clearance under the wheel.
3. Insert a bar under the wheel and pry upward. If the wheel raises more than 1/8 in., the ball joints are worn. Determine if the upper or lower ball joint is worn by visual inspection while prying on the wheel.
4. The upper ball joint can be further inspected after partial suspension disassembly. If the stud has any detectable side-to-side movement or if it can be twisted with your fingers it should be replaced.

NOTE: due to the distribution of forces in the suspension, the lower ball joint is usually the defective joint. Because of this, 1974 and later Chevelle, Camaro, and Monte Carlo and 1975 and later Nova models are equipped with wear indicators on the lower ball joint. As long as the indicator extends below the ball stud seat, replacement is unnecessary.

Upper Ball Joint R & R

1. Raise the car on a hoist.
2. Remove the tire and wheel assembly.
3. Support the lower control arm with a jack.
4. Remove the upper ball stud nut.
5. Remove the ball stud from the knuckle.
6. Chisel or grind off the ball joint mounting rivets.
7. Drill out the ball stud attaching holes to accept the service ball joint attaching bolts.
8. Install the ball joint with the nuts and bolts supplied with the new joint, nuts on top.
9. Install the lube fitting in the new joint.
10. Mate the upper control arm to the steering knuckle and install the ball stud through the knuckle boss.
11. Tighten the ball stud nut to 55 ft lbs. plus whatever is necessary to align the cotter pin holes. Install the cotter pin.

NOTE: Do not back off on the nut to align the cotter pin.

12. Install the wheel and lower the vehicle.

Lower Ball Joint R & R

1. Raise the vehicle on a hoist and remove the wheel.
2. Support the lower control arm with a jack.
3. Loosen the lower ball stud nut. Break the ball stud loose. Remove the ball stud nut.
4. Remove the ball stud from the steering knuckle.
5. The ball joint in 1969-70 models is attached with rivets which must be chiseled or ground off. Beginning with 1971 models, the ball joint is pressed in and must be pressed out.
6. Install the new ball joint, using the bolts supplied with the service ball joint (drill out the rivet holes to accommodate the mounting bolts) on 1969-70 models. The thick-headed bolt is installed on the forward side of the control arm. Press in the ball joint on 1971 and later models.
7. Install the ball stud in the steering knuckle boss. This may be done by raising the lower control arm with the jack.
8. Install the nut on the ball stud, tightening to 50 ft lbs on all models through 1973 and 1974 Nova; 60 ft lbs on 1974 Chevelle, Monte Carlo, and Camaro, and 83 ft lbs on all 1975 and later models.
9. Install the lube fitting.

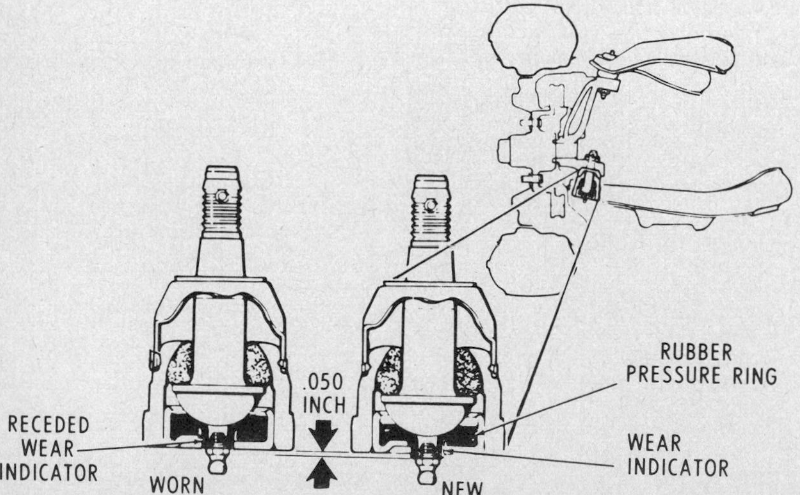

1974 and later Chevelle, Monte Carlo, and Camaro and 1975 and later Nova models are equipped with wear indicators on the lower ball joint
(©Chevrolet Div., G.M. Corp)

Lower Control Arm R & R

1. Remove the spring as described earlier.
2. Remove the ball stud from the steering knuckle.
3. Remove the control arm.
4. To install, reverse the above procedure.

Upper Control Arm R & R

1. Raise the vehicle on a hoist.
2. Support the outer end of the lower control arm with a jack.
3. Remove the wheel.
4. Separate the upper ball joint from the steering knuckle as described above under "Upper Ball Joint R&R"
5. Remove the control arm shaft to frame nuts.

NOTE: tape the shims together and identify them so that they can be installed in the positions from which they were removed.

6. Remove the bolts which attach the control arm shaft to the frame and remove the control arm. Note the positions of the bolts.
7. Install in the reverse order of removal. Make sure the shaft to frame bolts are installed in the same position they were in before removal and that the shims are in their original positions. Tighten the shaft to frame bolts to 55 ft lbs on Nova through 1974 and Chevelle and Monte Carlo through 1972; 75 ft lbs on all 1975 and later models; 80 ft lbs on Camaro through 1973; and 90 ft lbs on 1973-74 Chevelle and Monte Carlo, and 1974 Camaro. The control arm shaft nuts are torqued to 40 ft lbs on Chevelle and Monte Carlo through 1973 and Nova through 1974; 65 ft lbs on Camaro through 1974 and 1974 Chevelle and Monte Carlo; and 75 ft lbs on all 1975 and later models.

REAR SUSPENSION

The Chevelle and Monte Carlo have a coil spring rear suspension located by two lower control arms and two diagonally mounted upper control arms. Fore and aft axle movement is prevented by the lower control arms. Lateral movement is prevented by the upper control arms and the axle-to-frame tie-rod.

The Camaro and Nova have a leaf spring rear suspension.

All models use staggered shock absorbers to prevent axle hop on hard acceleration. The right shock absorber is mounted forward of the axle and the left shock absorber is mounted behind the axle.

Shock Absorber R & R

1. Jack the car to a convenient working height.
2. If the car is equipped with superlift shock absorbers, disconnect the air line.
3. On Chevelle and Monte Carlo: remove the two retaining bolts from the upper mounting bracket. Hold the hex on the bottom stud and disconnect the lower mounting. Remove the shock absorber.
4. On Camaro: with the rear axle supported, remove the lower shock absorber nut, retainer, and grommet. Remove the upper bolts, and remove the shock.
5. On Nova: remove the lower shock absorber eye bolt. Remove the upper bolts, and remove the shock absorber.
6. Install the shock absorbers in a reverse of the removal procedure. Torque the upper fasteners: 12 ft lbs on Chevelle and Monte Carlo and 18 ft lbs on Nova and Camaro. Torque the bottom fasteners: 65 ft lbs on Chevelle and Monte Carlo, 45 ft lbs on Nova (60 ft lbs with performance suspension) and 8 ft lbs on Camaro.

Chevelle rear shock absorber mounting
(© Chevrolet Div., G.M. Corp)

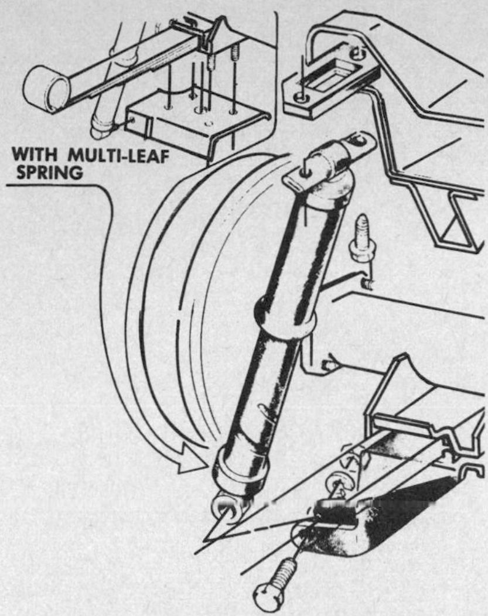

Nova rear shock absorber mounting
(© Chevrolet Div., G.M. Corp)

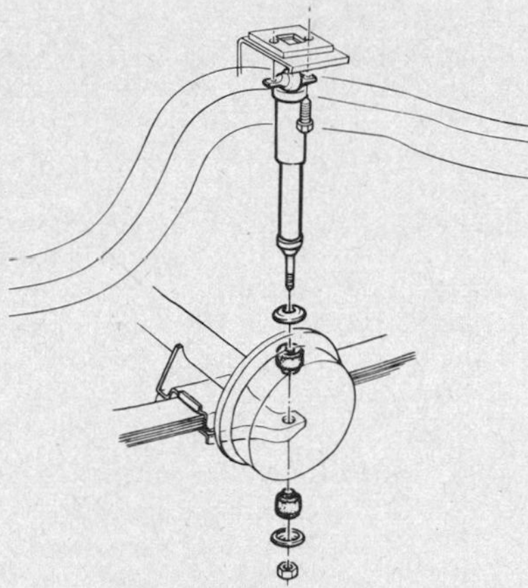

Camaro rear shock absorber mounting
(© Chevrolet Div., G.M. Corp)

Spring R & R

Chevelle and Monte Carlo

If the springs have been in use for any length of time, it will probably be necessary to replace both to maintain an even ride height.

1. Raise the car by the frame so that the rear axle can be independently raised and lowered.
2. Support the rear axle with a floor jack.
3. Disconnect the shock absorber from the axle. You don't have to disconnect both shocks unless you are removing both springs.
4. On 1973 and later models, disconnect the brake line at the axle housing junction block. Disconnect the upper control arm at the axle. You don't have to disconnect both unless you are removing both springs.

   NOTE: This step makes the job easier on earlier models, too.
5. Lower the axle to the limits of its travel, being careful of the brake lines.
6. Pry the lower end of the spring over the axle bracket vertical retainer. Remove the spring and insulator. Reverse the procedure for installation. Torque the upper control arm to axle mount to 80 ft lbs.

Nova and Camaro

1. Raise the car by the frame so that the rear axle can be independently raised and lowered.
2. Support the rear axle with a floor jack.
3. Disconnect the shock absorber lower mount.
4. Loosen the retaining bolt through the front spring eye. Unbolt the front bracket from the body.
5. Lower the axle enough to remove the bracket and retaining bolt from the front spring eye.
6. Pry the parking brake cable from the spring mounting plate retainer.
7. Remove the U-bolt nuts, the spring plate, and the upper and lower spring pads.
8. Remove the lower rear shackle bolt. Remove the spring.

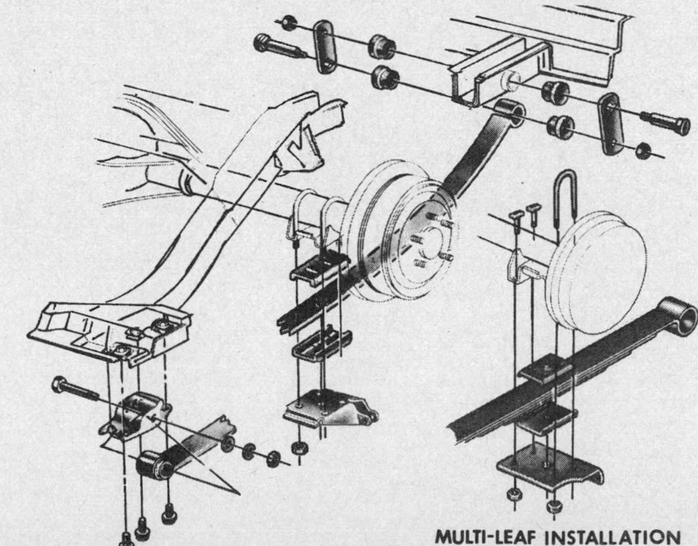

Rear spring mounting—Nova and Camaro
(© Chevrolet Div., G.M. Corp)

9. On installation, install the front bracket to the spring eye, install the rear shackle, bolt the front bracket in place, install the U-bolts, and replace the shock absorber. Tighten the bolts with the weight of the car on the springs. Torque the front bracket mounting bolts to 25-30 ft lbs, the front eye bolt to 75 ft lbs, the U-bolts to 40 ft lbs, and the rear shackle bolts to 50 ft lbs.

BRAKES

A dual type master cylinder is used on all models. The front portion of the master cylinder supplies hydraulic pressure for the front wheels. Pressure for rear wheel brake application is supplied from the rear portion of the master cylinder.

Brake lining replacement and adjustment, wheel and master cylinder overhaul and brake bleeding procedures can be found in the Unit Repair Section.

As an option, power brakes are available. Data on these power brakes can be found in the Unit Repair Section.

Front wheel disc brakes are standard on late models and optional on earlier models.

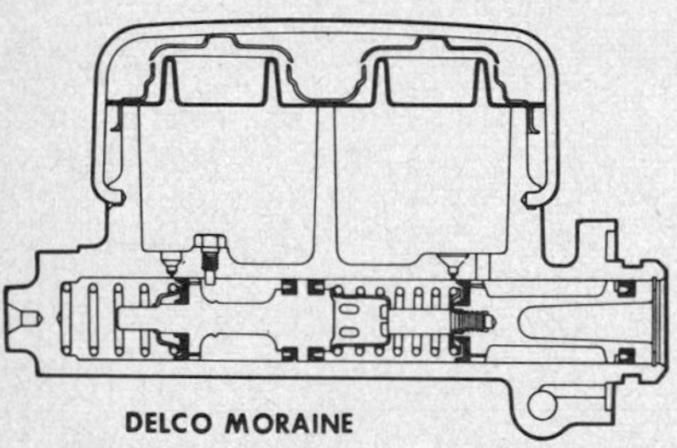

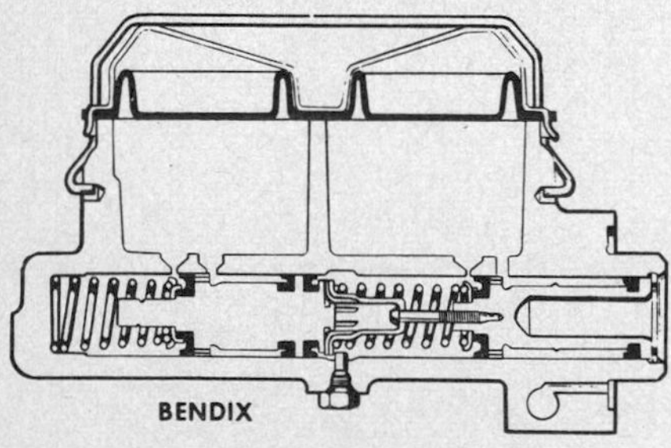

Dual type master cylinders—typical
(© Chevrolet Div., G.M. Corp)

Master Cylinder R & R

1. Disconnect hydraulic line/s at master cylinder.
2. Remove the retaining nuts and lockwashers that hold cylinder to firewall. Disconnect pushrod at brake pedal.
3. Remove the master cylinder, gasket and rubber boot.
4. Position master cylinder on firewall, making sure pushrod goes through the rubber boot into the piston. Reconnect pushrod clevis to brake pedal.
5. Install nuts and lockwashers.
6. Install hydraulic line/s, then check brake pedal free play.
7. Bleed brakes, as described in Unit Repair Section.

NOTE: cars having disc brakes do not have a check valve in the front outlet port of the master cylinder. If one is installed, front discs will immediately wear out due to residual hydraulic pressure holding pads against rotor.

Power Brake Booster R & R

1969-76 Except the Following Chevelle and Monte Carlo Models

1. Disconnect vacuum hose from vacuum check valve.
2. Disconnect hydraulic lines at master cylinder.
3. Disconnect pushrod at brake pedal assembly.
4. Remove nuts and lockwashers that secure booster to firewall and remove booster from engine compartment.
5. Install by reversing removal procedure. Make sure to check operation of stop lights and bleed brakes. Allow engine vacuum to build before applying brakes.

1969 Chevelle with Manual Transmission, 1970 Chevelle Station Wagon, 1971-76 Chevelle and Monte Carlo—All

1. Remove master cylinder from vacuum booster.
2. Remove vacuum line from vacuum check valve.
3. On 1971 and later models, remove brake line clip from booster.
4. From inside vehicle, remove nuts and lockwashers that secure booster to firewall.
5. Push brake pedal to the floor. This will disengage booster from firewall and adequate clearance for removal of the pushrod pivot pin will be gained.
6. Remove clip from pivot pin, then remove power unit from car.
7. Install by reversing removal procedure. Make sure to check operation of stop lights and bleed brakes. Allow engine vacuum to build before applying brakes.

Parking Brake

The parking brake is pedal operated on all models. It functions through an equalizer and cables to the rear brake shoes.

Parking Brake Adjustment

1. Jack up rear of car and support with both rear wheels off floor.
2. Apply parking brake two notches from fully released position.
3. Loosen the equalizer locknut, then tighten the adjusting nut until a light to moderate drag is felt when the rear wheels are rotated.
4. Tighten the locknut.
5. Fully release parking brake and rotate rear wheels—no drag should be felt.

STEERING

Tie-Rod R & R

1. Remove the cotter pins and nuts from the tie-rod end studs.
2. Tap on the steering arm near the tie-rod end (use another hammer as backing) and pull down on the tie-rod, if necessary, to free it.
3. Remove the inner stud in the same manner as the outer.
4. Loosen the clamp bolts and unscrew the ends if they are being replaced.

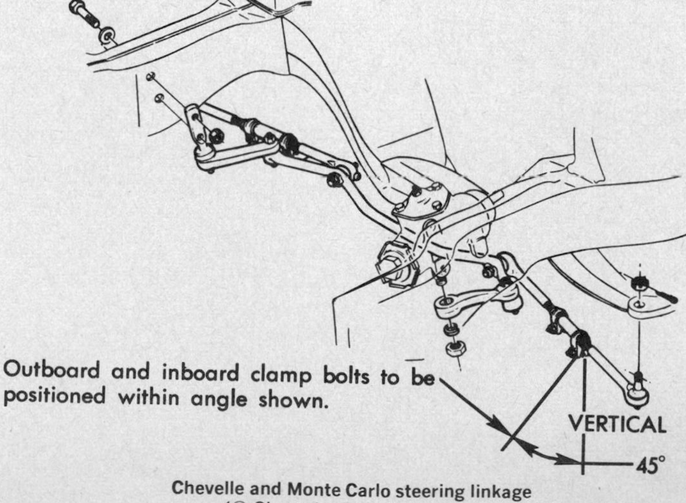

Chevelle and Monte Carlo steering linkage
(© Chevrolet Div., G.M. Corp)

5. Lubricate the tie-rod end threads with chassis grease if they were removed. Install each end assembly an equal distance from the sleeve.
6. Ensure that the tie-rod end stud threads and nut are clean. Install new seals and install the studs into the steering arms and relay rod.
7. Install the stud nuts. Tighten to 35 ft lbs. If necessary, you can tighten the nuts to as much as 50 ft lbs to install the cotter pins.
8. Adjust the toe-in.

NOTE: before tightening the sleeve clamps, ensure that the clamps are positioned so that adjusting sleeve slot is covered by the clamp.

Relay Rod R & R

1. Remove the inner tie-rod ends from the relay rod as outlined under tie-rod R&R. Remove the steering damper, if so equipped.
2. Remove the relay rod stud nut and cotter pin from the pitman arm. Free the relay rod from the pitman arm, moving the steering linkage if necessary. Repeat this operation to remove the relay rod from the idler arm and remove the relay rod from the car.
3. Install the relay rod on the idler arm. Tighten the nut to 35 ft lbs.
4. Raise the relay and install it on the pitman arm. Tighten the nut to 45 ft lbs.
5. Adjust the toe-in.

Pitman Arm R & R

1. Remove the pitman arm stud nut and cotter pin.
2. Tap the relay rod off the pitman arm, using another hammer as backing. Pull the relay rod off the pitman arm stud.
3. Remove the pitman arm nut and mark the arm-to-shaft relationship.
4. Remove the pitman arm using a puller.
5. Install the pitman arm on the shaft, aligning the previously made marks. Install the pitman shaft nut and tighten it to 180 ft lbs (140 on 1973-74 Nova).
6. Install the relay rod on the pitman arm. Tighten the nut to 45 ft lbs. and install a cotter pin.

Idler Arm R & R

The idler arm assembly requires replacement if a vertical force of 25 pounds at the relay rod end applied with the arm in the straight ahead position produces more than 1/8 in. up and down play.

1. Remove the idler arm-to-frame nut, washer, and bolt.
2. Remove the cotter pin and nut from the idler arm-to-relay rod ball end stud.
3. Tap the relay rod with a hammer, using another hammer as backing, to remove the relay rod from the idler arm.
4. Remove the idler arm.
5. Place the idler arm on the frame and install the bolts, washers, and nuts. Tighten to 35 ft lbs on all models through 1972, Chevelle and Monte Carlo through 1973, and Nova through 1974; 50 ft lbs for all others.
6. Install the relay rod to the idler arm, making sure that the stud seal is in place. Tighten the nut to 50 ft lbs for models through 1971, and 35 ft lbs for all 1972 and later models. Insert a cotter pin.

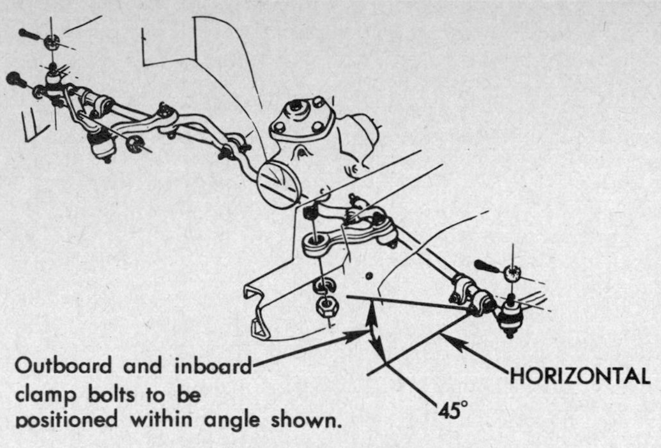

Camaro steering linkage
(© Chevrolet Div., G.M. Corp)

HORIZONTAL
30°
30°
Outboard and inboard clamps bolts to be positioned within angle shown.

Nova steering linkage
(© Chevrolet Div., G.M. Corp)

Power Steering Pump R & R

All models use an integral type of power steering gear. A pump delivers hydraulic pressure through two hoses to the steering gear itself.

Detailed service coverage is found in the Unit Repair Section.

1. Remove the hoses at the pump and tape the openings shut to prevent contamination. Position the disconnected lines in a raised position to prevent leakage.
2. Remove the pump belt.
3. Loosen the retaining bolts and any braces, and remove the pump.
4. Install the pump on the engine with the retaining bolts hand-tight.
5. Connect and tighten the hose fittings.
6. Refill the pump with fluid and bleed by turning the pulley counterclockwise (viewed from the front). Stop the bleeding when air bubbles no longer appear.
7. Install the pump belt on the pulley and adjust the tension.

Bleeding Power Steering System

1. Fill the fluid reservoir.
2. Let the fluid stand undisturbed for two minutes, then crank the engine for about two seconds. Refill reservoir if necessary.
3. Repeat Steps 1 and 2 above until the fluid level remains constant after cranking the engine.
4. Raise the front of the car until the wheels are off the ground, then start the engine. Increase the engine speed to about 1,500 rpm.
5. Turn the wheels lightly against the stops to the left and right, checking the fluid level and refilling if necessary.

Steering Wheel R & R

Caution Disconnect the battery ground cable before removing the steering wheel. When installing a steering wheel, always make sure that the turn signal lever is in the neutral position.

1969 Standard Wheel and 1970-76 Padded Rim Wheel

1. Pry out the center cap and retainer. Remove the shaft snap-ring on 1975 and later models.
2. Remove the steering wheel nut and washer.
3. Remove the three receiving cup screws and remove the cup, belleville spring, bushing, and pivot ring.
4. Mark the wheel-to-shaft relationship, and then remove the wheel with a puller.
5. Install the wheel on the shaft, aligning the previously made marks. Tighten the nut to 30 ft lbs.
6. Install the belleville spring (dished side up), pivot ring, bushing, and receiving cup. Install the center cap and reconnect the battery.

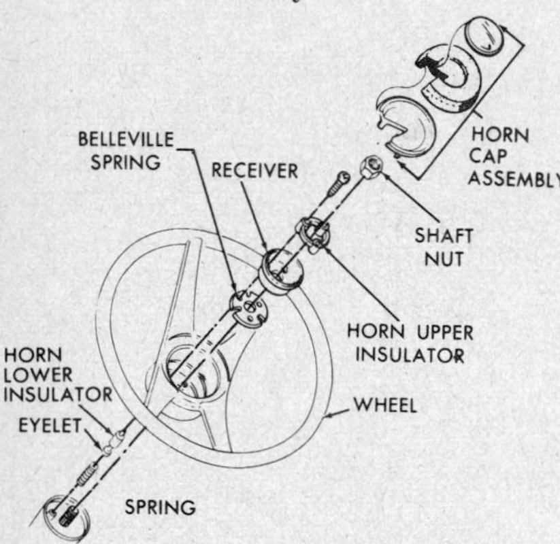

Cushioned rim steering wheel assembly
(© Chevrolet Div., G.M. Corp)

1969 Deluxe Wheel and 1970-76 Standard Wheel

1. Remove the trim retaining screws from behind the wheel.
2. Lift the trim off and pull the horn wires from the turn signal cancelling cam.
3. Remove the steering wheel nut.
4. Mark the wheel-to-shaft relationship, and then remove the wheel with a puller.
5. Install the wheel on the shaft, aligning the previously made marks. Tighten the nut to 30 ft lbs.
6. Insert the horn wires into the cancelling cam.

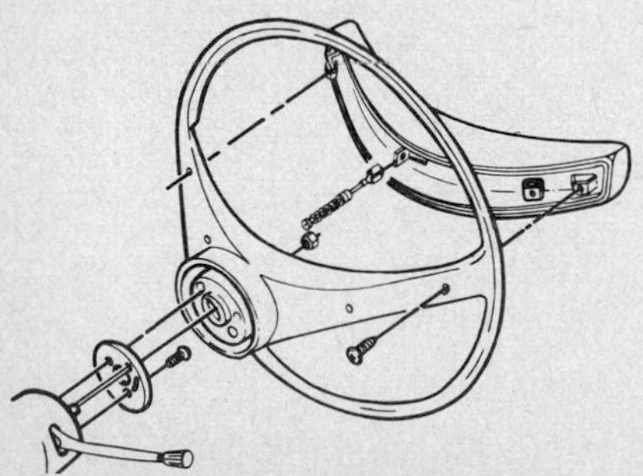

1969 Deluxe and 1970-76 standard steering wheel
(©Chevrolet Div., G.M. Corp)

7. Install the center trim and reconnect the battery cable.

NOTE: The 1969 simulated wood wheel does not require pulling for removal. Remove the center cap and horn contact assembly. Reverse the disassembly procedure to install the wheel.

Turn Signal Switch R & R

1. Remove the steering wheel as previously outlined. Remove the trim cover.
2. Loosen the cover screws and lift the cover off the shaft.
3. Position the U-shaped lockplate compressing tool on the end of the steering shaft and compress the lock plate by turning the shaft nut clockwise. Pry the wire snap-ring out of the shaft groove.

Depressing the lock plate and removing the snap-ring
(© Chevrolet Div., G.M. Corp)

4. Remove the tool and lift the lock-plate off the shaft.
5. Slip the cancelling cam, upper bearing preload spring, and thrust washer off the shaft.
6. Remove the turn signal lever. Push the flasher knob in and unscrew it.
7. Pull the switch connector out of the mast jacket and tape the upper part to facilitate switch removal. Attach a long piece of wire to the turn signal switch connector. When installing the turn signal switch, feed this wire through the column first, and then use this wire to pull the switch connector into position. On tilt wheels, place the turn signal and shifter housing in Low position and remove the harness cover.
8. Remove the three switch mounting screws. Remove the switch by pulling it straight up while guiding the wiring harness cover through the column.
9. Install the replacement switch by working the connector and cover down through the housing and under the bracket. On tilt models, the connector is worked down through the housing, under the bracket, and then the cover is installed on the harness.
10. Install the switch mounting screws and the connector on the mast jacket bracket. Install the column-to-dash trim plate.
11. Install the flasher knob and the turn signal lever.
12. With the turn signal lever in neutral and the flasher knob out, slide the thrust washer, upper bearing preload spring, and cancelling cam onto the shaft.
13. Position the lock plate on the shaft and press it down until a new snap-ring can be inserted in the shaft groove.
14. Install the cover and the steering wheel.

INSTRUMENT PANEL

Ignition Switch Replacement

All models have the ignition lock cylinder located on the upper right side of the steering column. The ignition switch is inside the channel section of the brake pedal support. The switch is inaccessible unless the steering column is lowered.

1. Lower steering column. The column must be carefully supported to prevent damage.
2. Remove lock cylinder.

NOTE: pull actuating rod for switch up until a definite stop is felt, then push it down one detent to Lock position.

3. Remove two switch screws and switch assembly.
4. When replacing switch, make sure switch and lock are in Lock position. Do not use switch screws longer than the originals, or the compressibility feature of the column may be lost.

Lock Cylinder Replacement

1. Remove steering wheel and directional signal switch as previously outlined in "Steering."
2. Place lock cylinder in Lock position up to 1970, Run position starting 1971.

Caution Do not remove the ignition key buzzer.

3. Insert a small screwdriver into the turn signal housing slot. Keeping the screwdriver to the right side of the slot, break the housing flash loose and depress the spring latch at the lower end of the lock cylinder. Remove the lock cylinder.

NOTE: considerable force may be necessary to break this casting flash, but be careful not to damage any other parts. When ordering a new lock cylinder, specify a cylinder assembly. This will save assembling the cylinder, washer, sleeve, and adaptor.

4. To install, hold the lock cylinder sleeve and rotate the knob clockwise against the stop. Insert the

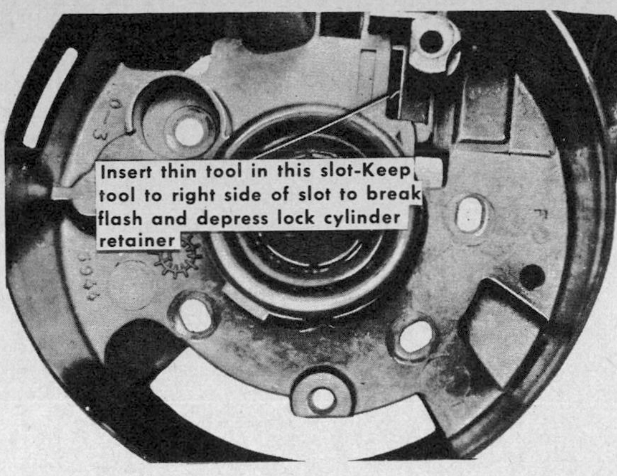

Removing the lock cylinder
(© Chevrolet Div., G.M. Corp)

cylinder into the housing, aligning the key and keyway. Hold a .070 in. drill between the lock bezel and housing. Rotate the cylinder counterclockwise, maintaining a light pressure until the drive section of the cylinder mates with the sector. Push in until the snap ring pops into the grooves. Remove drill. Check cylinder operation.

Caution The drill prevents forcing the lock cylinder inward beyond its normal position. The buzzer switch and spring latch can hold the lock cylinder in too far. Complete disassembly of the upper bearing housing is necessary to release an improperly installed lock cylinder.

Light Switch Replacement

1969-76 Nova, 1969 Camaro and Chevelle

1. Disconnect battery.
2. Pull knob out to on position.
3. Reach under instrument panel and depress the switch shaft retainer, and remove knob and shaft assembly.
4. Remove the retaining ferrule nut.
5. Remove switch from instrument panel.
6. Disconnect the multi-plug connector from the switch.
7. Reverse the procedure to install.

1970-76 Chevelle, Monte Carlo

1. Disconnect battery ground cable.
2. Remove six screws and instrument panel pad.
3. Remove left radio speaker.
4. Pull knob to on position.
5. Reach behind instrument panel and depress switch shaft retainer. Remove knob and shaft assembly.
6. Remove ferrule nut and switch assembly from instrument panel.
7. Reverse procedure to install.

1970-76 Camaro

1. Disconnect battery negative cable.

Light switch
(© Chevrolet Div., G.M. Corp)

2. Remove steering column lower cover (six screws).
3. Reach up under cluster on the left side and depress light switch shaft retainer, while pulling gently on shaft.
4. Remove nut that secures switch to cluster carrier.
5. Remove four cluster carrier screws in front and two from rear, then tilt right side of cluster out. Cigarette lighter grounding ring may have to be freed.
6. Unplug harness connector from switch.
7. Remove switch.
8. To install, reverse removal procedure. Make sure all ground connections are refastened.

WINDSHIELD WIPERS

Motor R & R

1. Make sure wiper motor is in park position.
2. Disconnect washer hoses and electrical connectors.
3. Remove the plenum chamber grille or access cover. Disconnect the drive link from the motor crank arm.
4. Remove the retaining screws or nuts and remove motor.
5. Reverse procedure to install, checking sealing gaskets at motor.

Linkage R & R

1. Make sure wiper motor is in park position.
2. Disconnect battery ground cable.
3. Remove wiper arm and blade assemblies from linkage. On articulated left arm assemblies, remove carburetor type clip retaining pinned arm to blade arm.

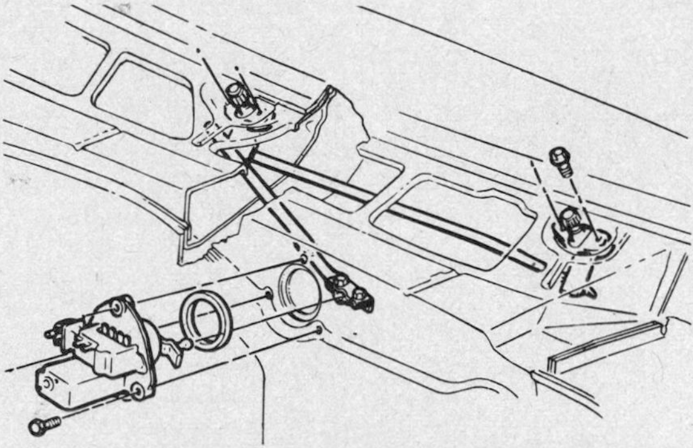

Wiper motor and linkage—Camaro
(© Chevrolet Div., G.M. Corp)

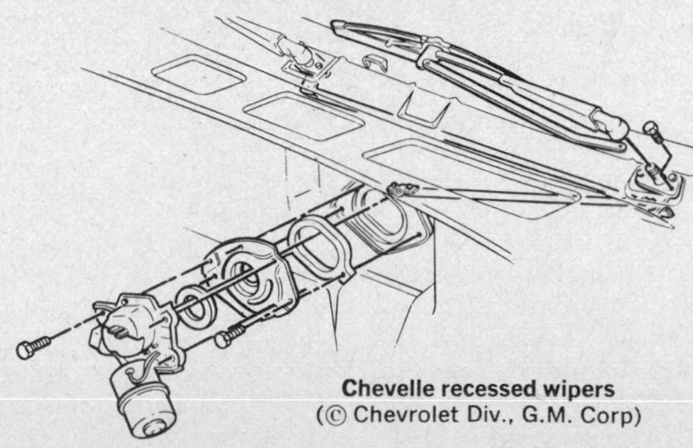

Chevelle recessed wipers
(© Chevrolet Div., G.M. Corp)

4. Remove plenum chamber air intake grille or screen.
5. Loosen nuts retaining drive rod ball stud to crank arm and detach drive rod from crank arm.
6. Remove linkage retaining screws. Lower linkage and drive rod assemblies into plenum chamber.
7. Remove linkage from plenum chamber through cowl opening.
8. Reverse procedure to install, making sure wiper blade assemblies are installed in park position.

RADIO

Radio R & R

through 1972

1. Disconnect battery ground cable.
2. Remove ash tray and ash tray housing as necessary.
3. Remove knobs, controls, washers, trim plate, and nuts from radio.
4. Remove hoses from center air conditioning duct as necessary.
5. Disconnect all wiring leads.
6. Remove screw from radio rear mounting bracket and lower radio.
7. To install, reverse above procedure.

1973 and Later Chevelle and Monte Carlo

1. Disconnect the battery ground cable.
2. Remove the left air conditioner lap cooler duct.
3. Pull off the knobs and bezels.
4. Remove the control shaft nuts and washers. You will probably need a deep well socket.
5. Remove the support bracket stud nut. Disconnect the antenna, speaker, and power wires.
6. Move the radio back until the shafts clear the instrument panel. Lower it from behind the panel.
7. Reverse the procedure for installation. Make sure to hook up the speaker leads before turning the radio on; operating without a speaker will damage the transistors.

1973 and Later Nova and Camaro

1. Disconnect the battery ground cable.
2. Pull off the knobs and bezels.
3. Remove the control shaft nuts and washers. A deep well socket will be needed on the Camaro.
4. Remove the mounting bracket screws or nuts.
5. Move the radio back until the shafts clear the instrument panel. Lower it and disconnect the antenna, speaker, and power wires.
6. Remove the radio. Reverse the procedure for installation. Make sure to hook up the speaker leads before turning the radio on; operating without a speaker will damage the transistors.

HEATER

Heater Blower R & R

1969 Camaro

1. Disconnect battery ground cable.
2. Disconnect hoses and wiring from fender skirt.
3. Remove wheel opening trim.
4. Remove rocker panel molding.
5. Loosen rear lower fender to body bolt.
6. Remove nine rearmost fender skirt attaching screws.
7. Pull lower rear edge of fender out. Pull skirt down. Place a block of wood between fender and skirt.
8. Remove blower to case attaching screws. Remove the air-cooling hose from the motor on air-conditioned cars. Remove blower assembly.
9. Remove blower wheel retaining nut. Separate blower and motor.
10. Reverse procedure to install. Open end of blower should be away from motor.

1969-72 Chevelle and Monte Carlo, 1969-76 Nova, 1970-76 Camaro

1. Disconnect battery ground cable.
2. Disconnect hoses and wiring from right side inner fender panel.
3. Remove all right side inner fender panel attaching bolts except those attaching panel to radiator support. On 1974 and later Nova, remove the eight rear fender skirt screws instead.
4. Pull out, then down, on panel. Place a block between panel and fender.
5. Remove blower to case attaching screws. Remove the air-cooling hose from the motor on air-conditioned cars. Remove blower assembly. On 1974 and later Nova, separate the blower wheel and motor first.
6. Remove blower wheel retaining nut and separate the motor and wheel.
7. Reverse procedure to install. Open end of blower should be away from motor.

1973 and Later Chevelle and Monte Carlo

1. Disconnect the battery ground cable.
2. Disconnect the motor lead wire.
3. Remove the blower to case screws and the blower.
4. Remove the retaining nut to separate the motor and wheel.
5. Reverse the procedure for installation. The open end of the blower wheel should be away from the motor.

Heater Core R & R

All Non Air-Conditioned Models

1. Disconnect battery ground cable.
2. Drain radiator.
3. Disconnect heater hoses. Plug core inlet and outlet. *Note: The larger hose goes to the water pump.*
4. Remove nuts from air distributor duct studs on firewall.
5. On Nova, remove glove compartment and door assembly.
6. From under Nova dash, drill out lower right hand distributor duct stud with a 1/4 in. drill.
7. On 1970 and later Camaro: remove glove box and radio, then defroster duct to distributor duct screw.
8. Pull distributor duct from firewall mounting. Remove resistor wires.
9. Remove core assembly from distributor duct.
10. Reverse procedure to install.

Chevelle and Monte Carlo with Air Conditioning through 1972

1. Drain the cooling system and disconnect the battery ground cable. It is not necessary to purge the A/C refrigerant.
2. Remove the heater hoses at the firewall and plug the openings.
3. Remove the case stud nuts from the firewall.
4. Remove the glove compartment on 1969 models.
5. Remove the right kick pad cover and the recirculating air valve.
6. Remove the center duct from the distributor, and remove the floor distributor duct.
7. From inside the passenger compartment, drill the lower right distributor duct stud out.
8. Remove the remaining air distributor-to-firewall screws, electrical connectors, and control cables.
9. Scribe the temperature door camming plate - to - distributor duct relationship and remove the plate.
10. Remove the heater core housing and core.
11. Reverse the removal procedure to install the core. Replace the drilled-out stud with a screw and speed nut.

1973 and Later Chevelle and Monte Carlo with Air Conditioning

1. Disconnect the battery ground cable and drain the radiator. Don't purge the air conditioning system.
2. Detach the heater hoses and plug the core tubes.
3. Remove the nuts from the firewall distributor case studs inside the car.
4. Remove the resistor assembly, reach through the opening, and remove the last distributor stud nut.

5. Remove the screws holding the right lap cooler duct to the instrument panel. Remove the duct.
6. Remove the center duct.
7. Remove the glove box strap screw, strap, and glove box.
8. Remove the floor outlet.
9. Remove the defroster to distributor duct screw at the lower distributor duct screw at the lower right of the duct.
10. Pull the distributor assembly back far enough that the studs and core tubes clear. Lower it and detach the electrical and vacuum connections.
11. Disconnect the temperature door cable.
12. Remove the distributor assembly.
13. Remove the screws holding the core clamps to the distributor assembly and remove the core.
14. Reverse the procedure for installation.

Nova with Air Conditioning

1. Disconnect the battery ground cable and drain the cooling system. It is not necessary to purge the refrigerant from the A/C system.
2. Disconnect the heater hose from the upper pipe at the firewall.
3. Remove the nuts from the heater studs in the firewall.
4. Remove the right front inner fender panel screws and lower the panel onto the tire.
5. Remove the remaining stud nut and the lower heater hose.
6. Remove the glove compartment.
7. Remove the right kick pad recirculating air valve.
8. Detach the center duct from the selector duct.
9. Remove the floor duct and separate the two selector halves.
10. Remove the selector duct from the firewall.
11. Disconnect the control cables and electrical wires.
12. Scribe the temperature door camming plate-to-selector duct relationship and remove the plate.
13. Place the selector duct on the floor and remove the heater core housing and core.
14. Reverse the removal steps to install the core.

1969 Camaro with Air Conditioning

1. Drain the cooling system and disconnect the battery ground cable. It is not necessary to purge the refrigerant from the A.C. system.
2. Disconnect the upper heater hose at the firewall.
3. Remove all accessible heater stud nuts from the firewall.
4. Remove the lower right side rocker molding.
5. Remove the bottom fender retaining bolts, inner panel-to-fender, and inner panel-to-reinforcement screws.
6. Pull the lower part of the fender out and pry the skirt away from the fender flange and firewall. Insert a 2 x 4 in. block of wood to hold the skirt out.
7. Disconnect the bottom heater hose and remove the lower right hand stud nut.
8. Remove the glove compartment and right kick pad recirculating valve.
9. Disconnect both side and center dash outlet hoses from the center duct. Remove the center duct from the distributor assembly.
10. Remove the floor outlet duct and separate the two distributor halves.
11. Detach the distributor from the firewall and carefully lower it. Remove the control cables and electrical connections.
12. Remove the distributor. Scribe the temperature door camming plate-to-distributor relationship and remove the plate.
13. Remove the heater core housing and core from the distributor.
14. Reverse the removal procedure to install the heater core.

1970-76 Camaro with Air Conditioning

1. Disconnect the battery ground cable and drain the cooling system. It is not necessary to purge the refrigerant from the A.C. system. On 1974 and later models, remove the 8 to 10 rearmost inner fender skirt screws and block the skirt out with a 4 in. wood block for access.
2. Disconnect the heater hoses at the firewall and plug the openings.
3. Remove the nuts from the heater studs protruding through the firewall.
4. Remove the glove compartment and radio.
5. Remove the defroster duct-to-distributor duct screw and pull the defroster duct rearward.
6. Pull the distributor duct from its dash mounting. Disconnect the control cables and electrical wires when there is sufficient clearance.
7. Remove the distributor duct and core from the car.
8. Remove the retainers and remove the heater core.
9. Reverse the removal procedure to install the heater core.

SEAT BELTS

Warning Buzzer and Light

1972-73

Beginning 1 January 1972, all cars are required to have a warning system which operates a buzzer and a warning light if either the driver's or the right-hand front passenger's seat belts are not fastened when the seats are occupied and the car is in forward motion.

On Chevrolet products, this system consists of seat belt retractor switches, pressure sensitive front seat switches, a parking brake switch, (M.T.), or a transmission switch (A.T.), a warning light, and a buzzer.

The seat belt warning system is wired through the 20 amp "Gauges" fuse.

The warning light is located in the instrument cluster; and the buzzer, which is shared with the ignition key warning system, is taped to the instrument cluster wiring harness.

The warning system is activated when the ignition switch is ON, the front seats are occupied, and the seat belts are left in their retractors. Only when the front seat belts are extended and properly fastened, will the warning light and buzzer stop.

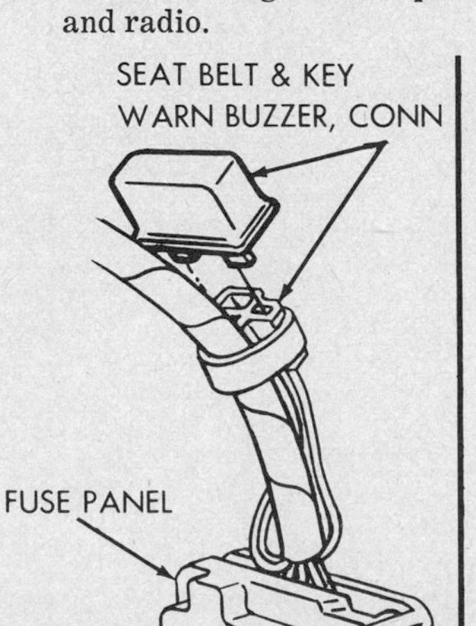

Seat belt/ignition switch warning buzzer location (© Chevrolet Div., G.M. Corp)

Two different types of switches are used to control the operation of the system, depending upon the type of transmission used:

On manual transmission cars, the parking brake warning light switch is used to activate the seat belt warning circuit through a relay as soon as the parking brake is released. A diode is used in the circuit to prevent feedback to the brake warning system.

On automatic transmission models, the seat belt warning system is activated by the neutral safety/back-up lamp switch, when the car is placed into any forward gear and the seat belts are not used.

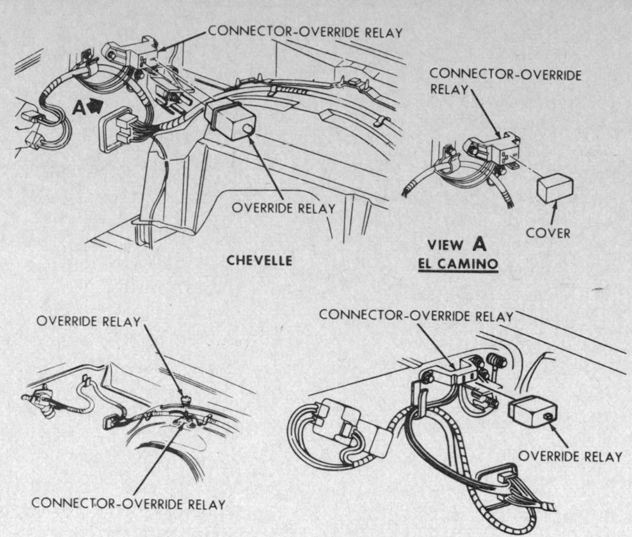

Starter interlock override relay locations
(© Chevrolet Div., G.M. Corp)

Seat Belt/Starter Interlock System

1974-75

As required by law, all 1974 and some 1975 Chevrolet passenger cars cannot be started until the front seat occupants are seated and have fastened their seat belts. If the proper sequence is not followed, the engine cannot be started.

If, after the car is started, the seat belts are unfastened, a warning buzzer and light will be activated in a similar manner to that described above for 1972-73 models.

The shoulder harness and lap belt are permanently fastened together, so that they both must be worn. The shoulder harness uses an inertia-lock reel to allow freedom of movement under normal driving conditions.

NOTE: This type of reel locks up when the car decelerates rapidly, as during a crash.

The lap belts use the same ratchet-type retractors that the 1972-73 models use.

The switches for the interlock system have been removed from the lap belt retractors and placed in the belt buckles. The seat sensors remain the same as those used in 1972-73.

For ease of service, the car may be started from outside, by reaching in and turning the key, but without depressing the seat sensors.

In case of system failure, an override switch is located under the hood. This is a "one start" switch and it must be reset each time it is used.

Disabling the Interlock System

Since the requirement for the interlock system was dropped during the 1975 model year, those systems installed on cars built earlier may now be legally disabled. The seat belt warning light is still required.

1. Disconnect the negative battery cable.
2. Locate the interlock harness connector under the left side of the instrument panel on or near the fuse block. It has orange, yellow, and green leads.
3. Cut and tape the ends of the green wire on the body side of the connector.
4. Remove the buzzer from the fuse block or connector.

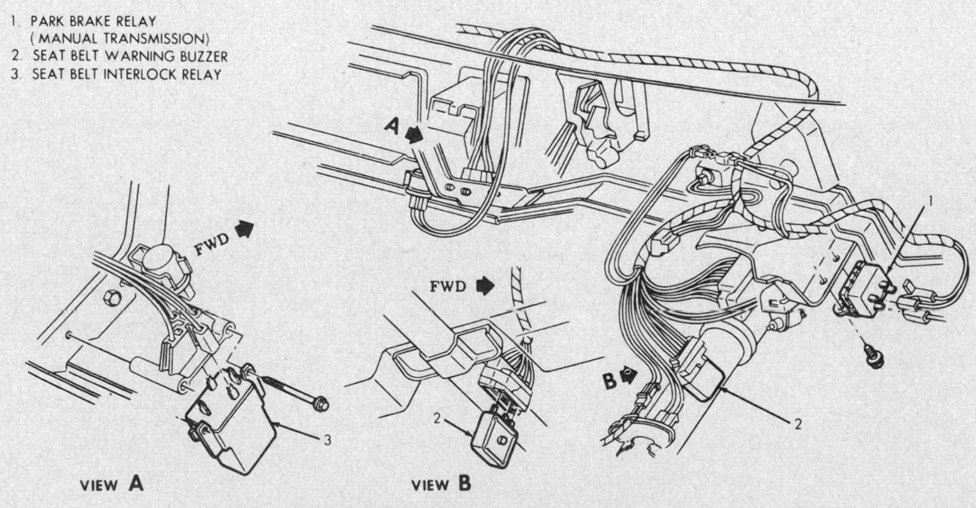

Nova seat belt warning and starter interlock system
(© Chevrolet Div., G.M. Corp)

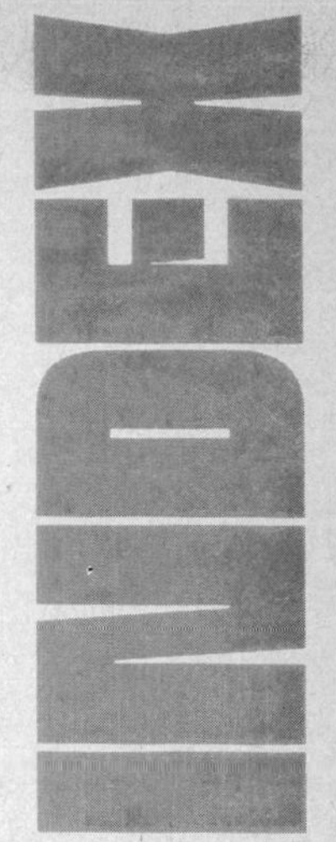

Chevrolet · Corvette

YEAR IDENTIFICATION

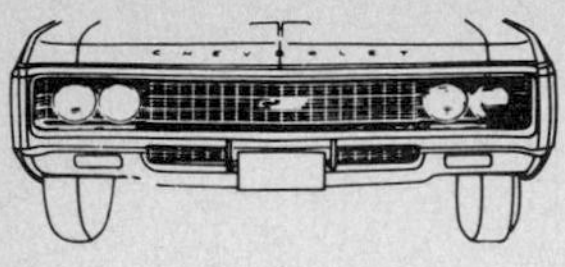

1969

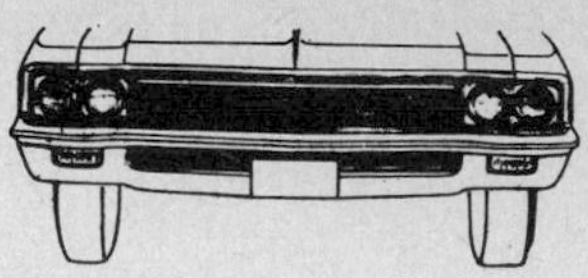

1970

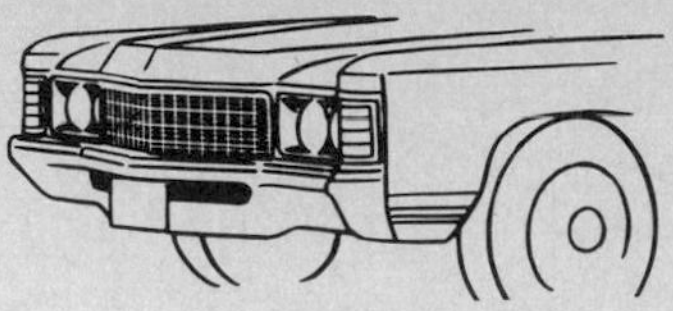

1971

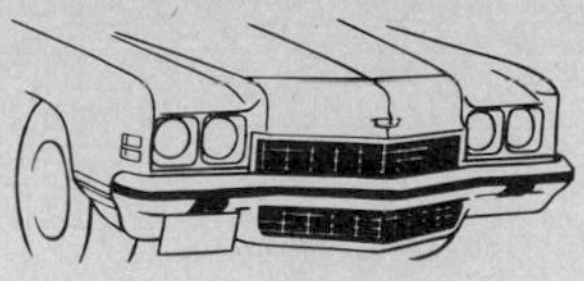

1972 Caprice

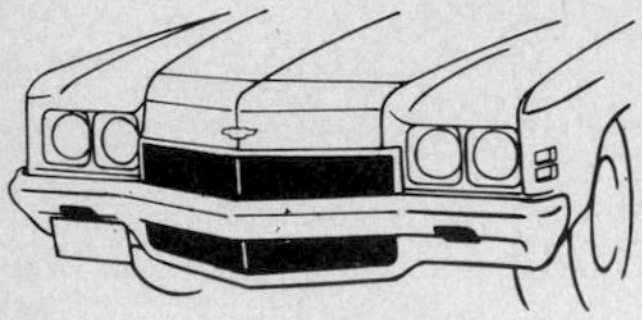

1972 Impala

1973 Impala

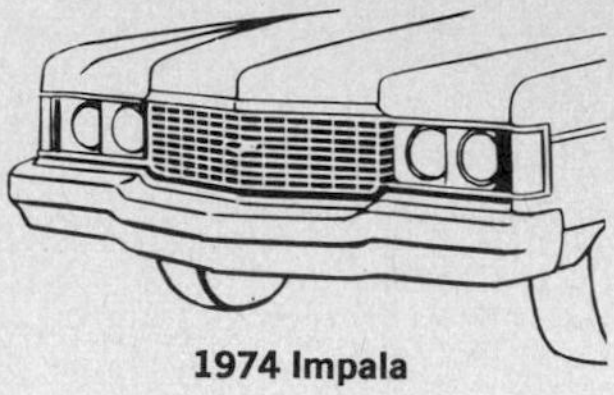

1974 Impala

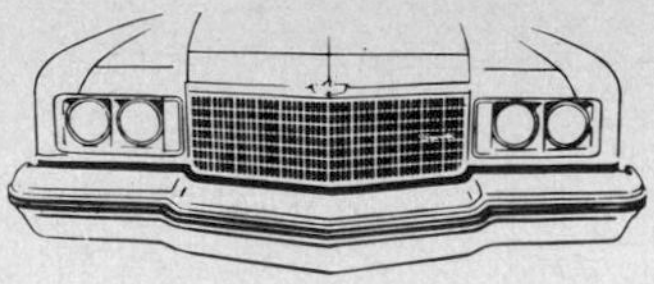

1974 Caprice

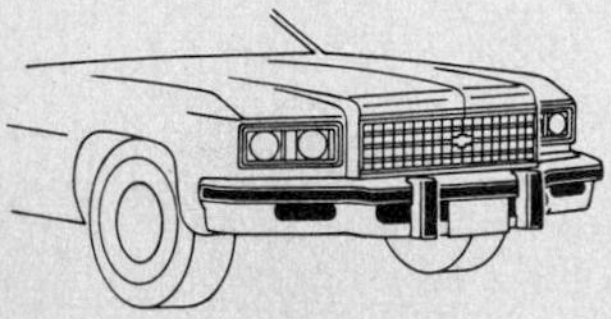

1975 Caprice

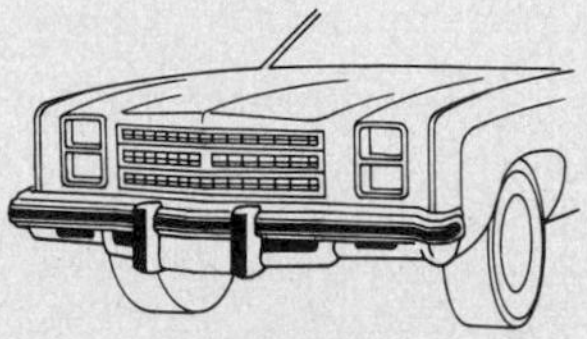

1976 Caprice

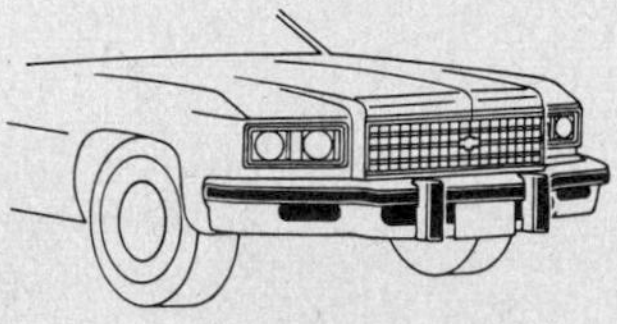

1976 Impala

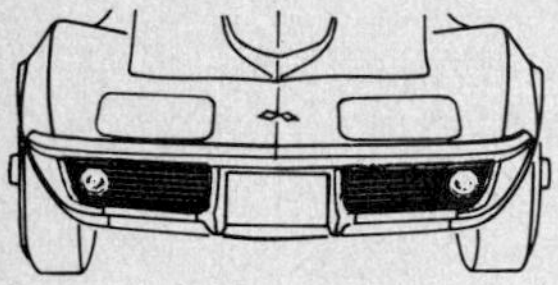

1968-69

1972

1973

1974

1975 Corvette

1976 Corvette

FIRING ORDER

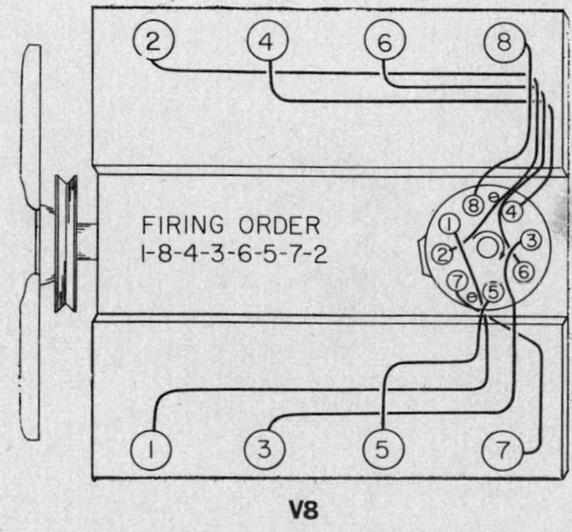

V8

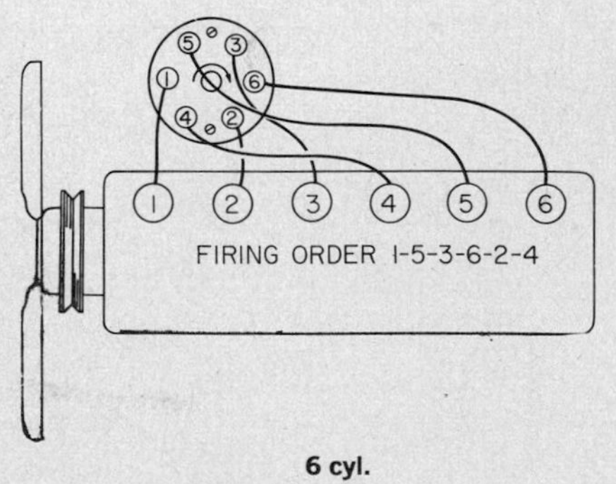

6 cyl.

CAR SERIAL NUMBER LOCATION

Vehicle serial number is found on a plate on the top left side of the instrument panel, visible through the windshield.

Car Serial Number Interpretation

A typical vehicle serial number tag yields manufacturer's identity, vehicle type, model year, assembly plant and production unit number when broken down as shown in the following charts.

Through 1971

Mfr. Identity[1]	*Body Style*[2]	*Model Year*[3]	*Assy. Plant*[4]	*Unit No.*[5]
1	5645	8	F	100025

1. Manufacturer's identity number assigned to all Chevrolet built vehicles.
2. Model identification.
3. Last number of model year (1968).
4. F-Flint.
5. Unit numbering will start at 100,001 at all plants.

1972 and Later

Mfr. Identity[1]	*Series Code Letter*[2]	*Body Style*[3]	*Engine Model*[4]	*Model Year*[5]	*Assembly Plant*[6]	*Unit Number*[7]
1	N	47	R	4	F	100025

1. Manufacturer's identity number assigned to all Chevrolet built vehicles.
2. Model Series
3. Body Style
4. Engine code
5. Last number of model year (1974)
6. Assembly Plant
7. Unit numbering will start at 000001 or 100,001 depending on the model.

Engine Identification

Six Cylinder Engines

The production code letters immediately follow the engine serial number. The number is found on a pad at the front right-hand side of the cylinder block, just to the rear of the distributor.

V8 Engines

The production code letters immediately follow the engine serial number. The number is found on a pad at the front right-hand side of the cylinder block.

Chevrolet ENGINE IDENTIFICATION

No. Cyls.	Cu. in. Displ.	Type	YEAR AND CODE 1969	1970	1971	1972	1973	1974	1975
6	250	PG, AC, w/ex. EM	BO						
6	250	M.T.	BA	CCG, CCH, CCZ, CRF, CRG	CAA	CNJ CDL	CCL		
6	250	M.T. California					CCM		
6	250	M.T., AC	BG			CBH			
6	250	Taxi, Police, M.T.	BP	CCL	CAC	CBJ			
6	250	PG			CAB	CBK			
6	250	PG, Taxi, Police	BJ, BL	CCM	CAD				
6	250	PG, AC	BO						
6	250	AC	BQ						
6	250	T.H. 350, Police			CCK				
8	327	M.T.	FA, FJ						
8	327	PG	FB, FK						
8	327	T.H. 350	FC, FL						
8	327	T.H. 400	FH						
8	327	Police	FG						
8	327	M.T., Taxi	FY						
8	327	PG, Taxi	FZ						
8	327	T.H. 350, Taxi	GA						
8	327	T.H. 400, Taxi	GB						
8	350	PG	GE, HK						
8	350	T.H. 350, 2-BBL.	HD, HM						
8	350	PG, 2-BBL.	HF, HL						
8	350	M.T.	HG, HD	CND (250),	CGA (245) CNQ (300)				
8	350	T.H. 400	HH, IA			CKB			

ENGINE IDENTIFICATION

No. Cyls.	Cu. in. Displ.	Type	1969	1970	1971	1972	1973	1974	1975
			YEAR AND CODE						
8	350	2-BBL.	HI						
8	350	T.H. 400, 2-BBL.	HJ						
8	350	T.H. 350	HN, HY	CNR (300) CNV (250)					
8	350	M.T.	HP, HT			CSJ			
8	350	PG	HU	CNS (300), CNU (250)	CGB				
8	350	M.T., Taxi, 2-BBL.	IL						
8	350	PG, Taxi, 2-BBL.	IM						
8	350	T.H. 350, Taxi, 2-BBL.	IN		CGJ			CMD	
8	350	T.H., 2-BBL.					CKL	CMA	
8	350	T.H., 2-BBL., California					CKK		
8	350	T.H., 2-BBL., Wagon					CLU		
8	350	T.H., 2-BBL., Wagon, Calif.					CLT		
8	350	T.H., 4-BBL., California Police and Taxi						CMK	
8	350	T.H., 4-BBL., Police						CMJ	
8	350								CRS
8	350								CRZ, CRF
8	350								CRX, CRY
8	350								CRU, CRW
8	350	T.H. 400, Taxi, 2-BBL.	IP						
8	350	M.T., Taxi, Police	IQ, IR	CNP (250)	CJB, CJH				
8	350	PG, Taxi, Police	IS, IX	CNW (250)		CAR, CSH			
8	350	T.H. 350, Taxi	IT, IY	CNT (300), CNX (250)	CGJ				
8	350	T.H. 400, Taxi	IV, IZ						
8	350	M.T., Taxi	IW						
8	350	T.H., 4-BBL.					CKJ	CMH	
8	350	T.H., 4-BBL., California					CKD	CKD	
8	350								CMX, CMY
8	396	M.T.	JT						
8	396	M.T., 2-BBL.	JN						
8	396	T.H. 400, Police, 2-BBL.	JO						
8	396	2-BBL., Police	JP						
8	396	T.H. 400, 2-BBL.	JQ						
8	396	M.T., Police	JR						
8	400	M.T. (265 hp)		CGR					
8	400	T.H. 350		CLK (265)		CDL, CDM			
8	400	T.H.					CSA		
8	400	T.H., California					CSD		
8	400	T.H., Wagon					CSK		
8	400	T.H., Wagon, California					CSM		
8	400	T.H., 2-BBL.						CTA	
8	400	T.H., 2-BBL., Police						CTB	
8	400	T.H., 4-BBL.						CTD, CTJ	
8	400	T.H., 4-BBL., California						CTC	
8	400	T.H., 4-BBL., California Police						CTK	
8	400								CSH, CSR
8	400								CSS, CST
8	400								CTL, CTM
8	400								CTR, CTS

Chevrolet

ENGINE IDENTIFICATION

No. Cyls.	Cu. in. Displ.	Type	YEAR AND CODE 1969	1970	1971	1972	1973	1974	1975
8	402	T.H. 350 (Mk. IV)	CKR	CLP (300)					
8	402	M.T., Police (Mk. IV)	CKN	CLR (330)		CLR, CTB			
8	402	M.T.				CLB			
8	402	M.T., w/AIR, Police				CTJ			
8	427	M.T., HDC							
8	427	SHP							
8	427	T.H., w/ex. EM							
8	427	M.T.	MA						
8	427	HP	LA						
8	427	4-BBL.	LB						
8	427	T.H. 400, HP	LC						
8	427	M.T., SHP	LD						
8	427	T.H. 400, 4-BBL.	LE						
8	427	T.H., Police, HP	LF						
8	427	M.T., Police, HP	LG, LZ, MB						
8	427	M.T., HP	LH, MC						
8	427	T.H. 400	LI						
8	427	T.H. 400, Police, 4-BBL.	LJ						
8	427	M.T., Police, 4-BBL.	LK						
8	427	T.H. 400, SHP	LS						
8	427	M.T., Police	LY						
8	427	M.T., SHP	MD						
8	454	M.T.		CGV (345), CGU (390)	CPD (365)				
8	454	M.T., Police		CGS (345), CGT (390)	CPG (365)				
8	454	T.H.				CPD			
8	454	T.H., Police				CPG			
8	454	T.H., w/AIR				CRW			
8	454	T.H., Police, w/AIR				CRY			
8	454	T.H.					CWL		
8	454	T.H., California					CWD		
8	454	T.H., 4-BBL.						CXA, CWY	
8	454	T.H., 4-BBL., Police						CWU	
8	454	T.H., 4-BBL., California Police						CWW	
8	454								CXK, CXL
8	454								CXX, CXY

AC—Air conditioned
HDC—Heavy duty clutch
HP—High performance
SHP—Special high performance
M.T.—Manual transmission
PG—Powerglide transmission

T.H.—Turbo-Hydramatic transmission
w/ex. EM—With exhaust emission controls
Trans. Ign.—Transistorized ignition
TD—Torque Drive
MT—Manual Transmission

ENGINE IDENTIFICATION

No. Cyls.	Cu. in. Displ.	Type	YEAR AND CODE 1969	1970	1971	1972	1973	1974	1975
8	350	HP	HW	CTN					
8	350	HP, AC	HX	CTO					
8	350	M.T.	HY	CTL					
8	350	T.H. 400	HZ	CTM					
8	350	HP, T. Ign.		CTP					
8	350	HP, T. Ign., AC		CTQ					
8	350	SHP		CTR					
8	350	SHP, T. Ign.		CTU					
8	350	SHP, T. Ign., M.T.		CTV					
8	350	M.T. (270 hp)			CGS				
8	350	M.T. (330 hp)			CGZ				
8	350	M.T. (200 hp)				CKW			
8	350	M.T., w/ex. EM (200 hp)				CDH			
8	350	T.H. (200 hp)				CKX			
8	350	T.H., w/ex. EM (200 hp)				CDJ			
8	350	M.T. (255 hp)				CKY			
8	350	HDMT (255 hp)				CKZ			
8	350	M.T., w/AIR (255 hp)				CRT			
8	350	T.H., w/AIR (255 hp)				CRS			
8	350	Hyd. 400 (270 hp)			CGT				
8	350	4-Spd. (330 hp)			CGY				
8	350	M.T. (190 hp)					CKZ	CKZ	
8	350	M.T., California (190 hp)					CLB	CLB	
8	350	T.H. (190 hp)					CLA	CLA	
8	350	T.H., California (190 hp)					CLC	CLC	
8	350	M.T. (250 hp)					CLR	CLR	
8	350	M.T., California (250 hp)					CLS	CLS	
8	350	T.H. (250 hp)					CLD	CLD	
8	350	T.H., California (250 hp)					CLH	CLH	
8	350	4-Spd.							CRJ, CUA
8	350	T.H. 400							CRK
8	350	4-Spd. HP							CRL, CUT
8	350	T.H. 400 HP							CRM
8	350	4-Spd. HP							CUD
8	350	4-Spd.							CUB
8	427	HP (390 hp), T.H.	LL, LM						
8	427	SHP	LO						
8	427	SHP (435 hp)	LR						
8	427	Aluminum Heads (435 hp)	LP						
8	427	HP, T.H. 400, 3-2-BBL.	LN						
8	427	HP, 3-2-BBL.	LQ						
8	427	SHP, HDC, 3-2-BBL.	LT						
8	427	Aluminum Heads, HDC	LU						
8	427	Aluminum Heads, T.H. 400	LW						
8	427	T.H. 400 (heavy duty)	LV						
8	427	SHP, T.H .400	LX						
8	454	HP, 4-BBL., T.H. 400		CGW					
8	454	HP, 4-BBL.		CZU					
8	454	Heavy duty, 4-BBL.		CZL					
8	454	T.H. 400, 4-BBL.		CZN					
8	454	HP, 4-BBL., T. Ign.		CRI					

Corvette

ENGINE IDENTIFICATION

No. Cyls.	Cu. in. Displ.	Type	YEAR AND CODE 1969	1970	1971	1972	1973	1974	1975
8	454	T.H. 400 (365 hp)			CPJ				
8	454	M.T. (365 hp)			CPH				
8	454	M.T. (425 hp)			CPW				
8	454	T.H. 400 (425 hp)			CPX				
8	454	M.T. (270 hp)				CPH			
8	454	T.H. (270 hp)				CPJ			
8	454	w/AIR (270 hp)				CSR			
8	454	w/AIR (270 hp)				CSS			
8	454	M.T.					CWM	CWM	
8	454	M.T., California					CWT	CWT	
8	454	T.H.					CWR	CWR	
8	454	T.H., California					CWS	CWS	

AC—Air conditioned
HP—High performance
SHP—Special high performance
M.T.—Manual transmission
PG—Powerglide Transmission
HDC—Heavy duty clutch
PS—Power steering
w/ex. EM—With exhaust emission
T. Ign.—With transistor ignition
4-BBL.—Four barrel carburetor
T.H.—With Turbo-Hydramatic
HDMT—Heavy duty 4-speed
w/AIR—With Air Injection Reactor

GENERAL ENGINE SPECIFICATIONS

Year	Engine No. Cyl. Displacement Cu. In.	Carburetor Type	Horsepower @ rpm ■	Torque @ rpm (ft lbs) ■	Bore and Stroke (in.)	Compression Ratio	Oil Pressure @ 2000 rpm
'69	6 250	1 bbl	155 @ 4200	235 @ 1600	3.875 x 3.530	8.5:1	58 @ 2000
	8-327	2 bbl	235 @ 4800	325 @ 2800	3.875 x 3.530	9.0:1	58 @ 2000
	8-350	4 bbl	255 @ 4800	365 @ 3200	4.000 x 3.480	9.0:1	58 @ 2000
	8-350	4 bbl	300 @ 4800	380 @ 3200	4.000 x 3.480	10.25:1	58 @ 2000
	8-350	4 bbl	350 @ 5600	380 @ 3600	4.000 x 3.480	11.0:1	58 @ 2000
	8-396	2 bbl	265 @ 4800	400 @ 2800	4.094 x 3.760	9.0:1	62 @ 2000
	8-427	4 bbl	335 @ 4800	460 @ 3200	4.251 x 3.760	10.25:1	62 @ 2000
	8-427	4 bbl	390 @ 4800	460 @ 3600	4.251 x 3.760	10.25:1	62 @ 2000
	8-427	3 x 2 bbl	400 @ 5400	460 @ 3600	4.251 x 3.760	10.25:1	62 @ 2000
	8-427	3 x 2 bbl	435 @ 5800	460 @ 4000	4.251 x 3.760	11.0:1	62 @ 2000
'70	6-250	1 bbl	155 @ 4200	235 @ 1600	3.875 x 3.530	8.5:1	58 @ 2000
	8-350	2 bbl	250 @ 4800	345 @ 2800	4.000 x 3.480	9.0:1	58 @ 2000
	8-350	4 bbl	300 @ 4800	380 @ 3200	4.000 x 3.480	10.25:1	58 @ 2000①
	8-350	4 bbl	350 @ 5600	380 @ 3600	4.000 x 3.480	11.0:1	40 @ 2000
	8-350	4 bbl	370 @ 6000	380 @ 4000	4.000 x 3.480	11.0:1	40 @ 2000
	8-400	2 bbl	265 @ 4400	400 @ 2400	4.125 x 3.750	9.0:1	58 @ 2000
	8-454	4 bbl	345 @ 4400	500 @ 3000	4.251 x 4.000	10.25:1	62 @ 2000
	8-454	4 bbl	390 @ 4800	500 @ 3400	4.251 x 4.000	10.25:1	62 @ 2000①
	8-454	4 bbl	460 @ 5600	490 @ 3600	4.251 x 4.000	11.25:1	62 @ 2000①

GENERAL ENGINE SPECIFICATIONS

Year	Engine No. Cyl. Displacement Cu. In.	Carburetor Type	Horsepower @ rpm ■	Torque @ rpm (ft lbs) ■	Bore and Stroke (in.)	Compression Ratio	Oil Pressure @ 2000 rpm
'71	6-250	1 bbl	145 @ 4200	230 @ 1600	3.875 x 3.530	8.5:1	40 @ 2000
	8-350	2 bbl	245 @ 4800	350 @ 2800	4.000 x 3.480	8.5:1	40 @ 2000
	8-350	4 bbl	270 @ 4800	360 @ 3200	4.000 x 3.480	8.5:1	40 @ 2000
	8-350	4 bbl	330 @ 5600	360 @ 4000	4.000 x 3.480	9.0:1	40 @ 2000
	8-400	2 bbl	255 @ 4400	390 @ 2400	4.125 x 3.750	8.5:1	40 @ 2000
	8-400 (402 Cu. In.)	4 bbl	300 @ 4800	400 @ 3200	4.126 x 3.760	8.5:1	40 @ 2000
	8-454	4 bbl	365 @ 4800	465 @ 4000	4.251 x 4.000	8.5:1	40 @ 2000
	8-454	4 bbl	425 @ 5600	475 @ 4000	4.251 x 4.000	9.0:1	40 @ 2000
'72	6-250	1 bbl	110 @ 3800	185 @ 1600	3.875 x 3.530	8.5:1	40 @ 2000
	8-350	2 bbl	165 @ 4000	280 @ 2400	4.000 x 3.480	8.5:1	40 @ 2000
	8-350	4 bbl	200 @ 4400	300 @ 2800	4.000 x 3.480	8.5:1	40 @ 2000
	8-350	4 bbl	255 @ 5600	280 @ 4000	4.000 x 3.480	9.0:1	40 @ 2000
	8-400	2 bbl	170 @ 3400	325 @ 2000	4.126 x 3.750	8.5:1	40 @2000
	8-402	4 bbl	210 @ 4400	320 @ 2400	4.126 x 3.760	8.5:1	40 @ 2000
	8-454	4 bbl	270 @ 4000	390 @ 3200	4.251 x 4.000	8.5:1	40 @ 2000
'73	6-250	1 bbl	100 @ 3600	175 @ 1600	3.875 x 3.530	8.25:1	40 @ 2000
	8-350	2 bbl	145 @ 4000	255 @ 2400	4.000 x 3.480	8.5:1	40 @ 2000
	8-350	4 bbl	175 @ 4000	260 @ 2800	4.000 x 3.480	8.5:1	40 @ 2000
	8-350	4 bbl	190 @ 4400	270 @ 2800	4.000 x 3.480	8.5:1	40 @ 2000
	8-350	4 bbl	250 @ 5200	285 @ 4000	4.000 x 3.480	9.0:1	40 @ 2000
	8-400	2 bbl	150 @ 3200	295 @ 2000	4.126 x 3.750	8.5:1	40 @ 2000
	8-454	4 bbl	245 @ 4000②	375 @ 2800③	4.251 x 4.000	8.25:1	40 @ 2000
	8-454	4 bbl	275 @ 4400	395 @ 2800	4.251 x 4.000	8.25:1	40 @ 2000
'74	8-350	2 bbl	145 @ 3600	250 @ 2200	4.000 x 3.480	8.5:1	40 @ 2000
	8-350	4 bbl	160 @ 3800	245 @ 2400	4.000 x 3.480	8.5:1	40 @ 2000
	8-350	4 bbl	195 @ 4400	275 @ 2800	4.000 x 3.480	8.5:1	40 @ 2000
	8-350	4 bbl	250 @ 5200	285 @ 4000	4.000 x 3.480	9.0:1	40 @ 2000
	8-400	2 bbl	150 @ 3200	295 @ 2000	4.126 x 3.750	8.5:1	40 @ 2000
	8-400	4 bbl	180 @ 3800	290 @ 2400	4.126 x 3.750	8.5:1	40 @ 2000
	8-454	4 bbl	235 @ 4000	360 @ 2800	4.251 x 4.000	8.25:1	40 @ 2000
	8-454	4 bbl	270 @ 4400	380 @ 2800	4.251 x 4.000	8.25:1	40 @ 2000
'75-'76	8-350④	2 bbl	145 @ 3800	250 @ 2200	4.000 x 3.480	8.5:1	40 @ 2000
	8-350	4 bbl	155 @ 3800	250 @ 2400	4.000 x 3.480	8.5:1	40 @ 2000
	8-350	4 bbl	165 @ 3800	255 @ 2400	4.000 x 3.480	8.5:1	40 @ 2000
	8-350	4 bbl	205 @ 4800	255 @ 3600	4.000 x 3.480	9.0:1	40 @ 2000
	8-400	4 bbl	175 @ 3600	305 @ 2000	4.126 x 3.750	8.5:1	40 @ 2000
	8-454④	4 bbl	215 @ 4000	350 @ 2400	4.251 x 4.000	8.15:1⑤	40 @ 2000

■ Beginning 1972, horsepower and torque are SAE net figures. They are measured at the rear of the transmission with all accessories installed and operating. Since the figures vary when a given engine is installed in different models, some are representative rather than exact.

① For Corvettes, oil pressure is 40 psi at 2000 rpm
② 215 in wagon
③ 345 in wagon
④ Not available in California
⑤ 8.25:1 for 1976

Chevrolet

TUNE-UP SPECIFICATIONS

When analyzing compression test results, look for uniformity among cylinders rather than specific pressures.

ENGINE			SPARK PLUGS		DISTRIBUTOR		IGNITION TIMING (deg) ▲		VALVES	Fuel	IDLE SPEED (rpm) ▲	
Year	No. Cyl Displacement	hp (cu in.)	Type	Gap (in.)	Point Dwell (deg)	Point Gap (in.)	Man Trans	● Auto Trans	Intake Opens ■ (deg) ●	Pump Pressure (psi)	Man Trans	Auto Trans
'69	6-250	155	R46N	.035	31-34	.019	TDC	4B	16	4-5	700	550/400③
	8-327	235	R45S	.035	29-31	.019	2A	2B	28	7½-9	700	600
	8-350	255	R44S	.035	29-31	.019	TDC	4B	28	7½-9	700	600
	8-350	300	R44S	.035	29-31	.019	TDC	4B	28	7½-9	700	600
	8-396	265	R44N	.035	29-31	.019	TDC	4B	28	7½-9	700	600
	8-427	335	R44N	.035	29-31	.019	4B	4B	28	7½-9	700	600
	8-427	390	R43N	.035	29-31	.019	4B	4B	56	7½-9	800②	600②
'70	6-250	155	R46T	.035	31-34	.019	TDC	4B	16	4-5	750/400③	600/400②
	8-350	250	R44	.035	29-31	.019	TDC	4B	28	7½-9	700/450③	600/450③
	8-350	300	R44	.035	29-31	.019	TDC	4B	28	7½-9	700	600
	8-400	265	R44	.035	29-31	.019	4B	8B	28	7½-9	700	600/450②
	8-454	345	R44T	.035	28-30	.019	6B	6B	30	7½-9	700	600
	8-454	390	R43T	.035	28-30	.019	6B	6B	56	7½-9	700	600
'71	6-250	145	R46TS	.035	31-34	.019	4B	4B	16	4-5	550	500②
	8-350	245	R44TS	.035	29-31	.019	2B	6B	28	7½-9	600	550②
	8-350	270	R44TS	.035	29-31	.019	4B	8B	28	7½-9	600	550②
	8-400	255	R44TS	.035	29-31	.019	4B	8B	28	7½-9	600	550②
	8-402	300	R44TS	.035	29-31	.019	8B	8B	28	7½-9	600	600②
	8-454	365	R43TS	.035	28-30	.019	8B	8B	56	7½-9	600	600
'72	6-250	110	R46T	.035	31-34	.019	4B	4B	16	4-5	700	600
	8-350	165	R44T	.035	29-31	.019	6B	6B	28(44)	7½-9	900	600
	8-400	170	R44T	.035	29-31	.019	2B	6B	28(44)	7½-9	900	600
	8-402	210	R44T	.035	29-31	.019	8B	8B	30(44)	7½-9	750	600
	8-454	270	R44T	.035	29-31	.019	8B	8B	56	7½-9	750	600
'73	6-250	100	R46T	.035	31-34	.019	6B	—	16	3½-4½	700/450③	—
	8-350	145	R44T	.035	29-31	.019	—	8B	28	7½-9	—	600/450③
	8-350	175	R44T	.035	29-31	.019	—	12B	28	7½-9	—	600/450③
	8-400	140	R44T	.035	29-31	.019	—	8B	28	7½-9	—	600/450③
	8-454	245⑤	R44T	.035	29-31	.019	—	10B	55	7½-9	—	600/450③
'74	8-350	145	R44T	.035	29-31	.019	—	8B	28(44)	7½-9	—	600
	8-350	160	R44T	.035	29-31	.019	—	12B(8B)	28(44)	7½-9	—	600
	8-400	150	R44T	.035	29-31	.019	—	8B	28(44)	7½-9	—	600
	8-400	180	R44T	.035	29-31	.019	—	8B	28(44)	7½-9	—	600
	8-454	235	R44T	.035	29-31	.019	—	10B	55	7½-9	—	600
'75	8-350	145	R-44TX	.060	Electronic		—	6B	28	7½-9	—	600
	8-350	155	R-44TX	.060	Electronic		—	6B	28	7½-9	—	600
	8-400	175	R-44TX	.060	Electronic		—	8B	28	7½-9	—	600
	8-454	215	R-44TX	.060	Electronic		—	16B	55	7½-9	—	650
'76	8-350	145	R-45TS	.045	Electronic		—	6B	28	7½-9	—	600
	8-350	155	R-45TS	.045	Electronic		—	6B	28	7½-9	—	600
	8-400	175	R-45TS	.045	Electronic		—	8B	28	7½-9	—	600
	8-454	215	R-45TSX	.060	Electronic		—	—	55	7½-9	—	550

▲ See text for procedure
● Figure in parentheses indicates California engine
■ All figures Before Top Dead Center
① Equipped with Air Injection Reactor System
② A/C on
③ Lower figure with Idle Solenoid disconnected
— Not applicable
④ Adjust mechanical valve lifter clearance to .020 inches for intake with engine hot and to .024 inches for exhaust with engine hot.
⑤ 215 in wagons
A After Top Dead Center
B Before Top Dead Center
TDC Top Dead Center

Corvette

TUNE-UP SPECIFICATIONS

When analyzing compression test results, look for uniformity among cylinders rather than specific pressures.

Year	ENGINE No. Cyl Displacement	hp (cu in.)	SPARK PLUGS Type	Gap (in.)	DISTRIBUTOR Point Dwell (deg)	Point Gap (in.)	IGNITION TIMING (deg) ▲ Man Trans	● Auto Trans	VALVES Intake Opens ■ (deg) ●	Fuel Pump Pressure (psi)	IDLE SPEED (rpm) ▲ Man Trans	Auto Trans
'69	8-350	300	R44S	.035	28-32	.019	TDC	4B	28	7½-9	700	600
	8-350	350	R44	.035	28-32	.019	4B	—	52	7½-9	750	—
	8-427	390	43N	.035	28-32	.019	4B	4B	56	7½-9	800②	600②
	8-427	400	43N	.035	28-32	.019	4B	4B	56	7½-9	800②	600②
	8-427	435	43N	.035	28-32	.019	4B	4B	44	7½-9	750	750/400
'70	8-350	300	R44	.035	29-31	.019	4B	4B	28	7½-9	700	600
	8-350	350	R44	.035	29-31	.019	4B	—	52	7½-9	750	—
	8-350	370	R43T	.035	—	—	8B	12B	42½	7½-9	700	—
	8-454	390	R43T	.035	28-30	.019	6B	6B	56	7½-9	800	600
	8-454	460	R43XL	.035	—	—	4B	4B	62	7½-9	750	600
'71	8-350	270	R44TS	.035	29-31	.019	8B	8B	28	7½-9	600	550
	8-350	330	R43TS	.035	—	—	8B	12B	42½	7½-9	700	700
	8-454	365	R43TS	.035	28-30	.019	8B	8B	56	7½-9	600	600
	8-454	425	R44TS	.035	—	—	8B	12B	44	7½-9	700	700
'72	8-350	200	R44T	.035	29-31	.019	8B	8B	28(44)	7½-9	800	600
	8-350	255	R44T	.035	29-31	.019	4B	8B	42½	7½-9	900	700
	8-454	270	R44T	.035	29-31	.019	8B	8B	56	7½-9	800	600
'73	8-350	190	R44T	.035	29-31	.019	12B	12B	28	7½-9	900/450③	600/450
	8-350	250	R44T	.035	29-31	.019	8B	8B	52	7½-9	900/450③	700/450
	8-454	275	R44T	.035	29-31	.019	10B	10B	55	7½-9	900/450③	600/450
'74	8-350	195	R44T	.035	29-31	.019	8B(4B)	8B	28(44)	7½-9	900	600
	8-350	250	R44T	.035	29-31	.019	8B	8B	52	7½-9	900	700
	8-454	270	R44T	.035	29-31	.019	10B	10B	55	7½-9	800	600
'75	8-350	165	R-44TX	.060	Electronic		6B	6B	28	7½-9	800	600
	8-350	205	R-44TX	.060	Electronic		12B	12B	52	7½-9	900	700
'76	8-350	165	R-45TS	.045	Electronic		—	—	28	7½-9	900	700①
	8-350	205	R-45TS	.045	Electronic		12B	12B	52	7½-9	900	700①

▲ See text for procedure
● Figure in parentheses iindicates California engine
■ All figures Before Top Dead Center
① Air conditioning on
② A/C on
③ Lower figure with Idle Solenoid disconnected
④ With A/C
⑤ Adjust solenoid screw with A/C on. Adjust idle screw with A/C off
A After Top Dead Center
B Before Top Dead Center
TDC Top Dead Center
— Not applicable

MECHANICAL VALVE LIFTER CLEARANCE

Year	Engine		Intake (Hot) In.	Exhaust (Hot) In.
1969	V8-427	435 hp	.024	.028
1970	V8-350	370 hp	.024	.030
1970	V8-454	460 hp	.024	.028
1971	V8-350	330 hp	.024	.030
1971	V8-454	425 hp	.024	.028
1972	V8-350	255 hp	.024	.030

Chevrolet — CAPACITIES

Year	ENGINE No. Cyl. (Cu. In.) Displacement	Engine Crankcase Add 1 Qt For New Filter	TRANSMISSION Pts To Refill After Draining — Manual 3-Speed	Manual 4-Speed	Automatic ●	Drive Axle (pts)	Gasoline Tank (gals) ■	COOLING SYSTEM (qts) With Heater	With A/C
'69	6-250	4	3	3	6⑦	3.5①	24	12	12
	8-327	4	3	3	6.5⑥	3.5①	24	17	17
	8-350	4	3.5	3	6.5⑥	3.5①	24	15	16
	8-396	4	3.5	3	6.5⑥	3.5①	24	23	24
	8-427	4	3.5	3	8	3.5①	24	22②	23
'70	6-250	4	3	—	6	3.5①	25	12	12
	8-350	4	3	—	6.5⑦	3.5①	25	16	16④
	8-400	4	—	—	5⑥	3.5①	25	16	17
	8-454	4	—	—	8	3.5①	25	22	22
'71	6-250	4	3	—	6	3.5①	24	12	—
	8-350	4	3	—	6.5⑦	3.5①	24	16	17
	8-400	4	3	—	5⑥	3.5①	24	16	17
	8-402	4	—	—	8	3.5①	24	23	24
	8-454	4	—	—	8	3.5①	24	22	23
'72	6-250	4	3	—	6	4.25⑤	23	12	—
	8-350	4	—	—	5	4.25⑤	23	16	17
	8-400	4	—	—	5	4.25⑤	23	16	17
	8-402	4	—	—	8	4.25⑤	23	23	24
	8-454	4	—	—	8	4.25⑤	23	22	23
'73	6-250	4	3	—	5	4.25⑤	26	12	12
	8-350	4	—	—	5	4.25⑤	26	16	17
	8-400	4	—	—	5	4.25⑤	26	16.5	17.5
	8-454	4	—	—	8	4.25⑤	26	23	24
'74	8-350	4	—	—	8	4.25⑤	26	16	16
	8-400	4	—	—	8⑧	4.25⑤	26	16	16
	8-454	4	—	—	9	4.25⑤	26	22	23
'75-'76	8-350	4	—	—	8	4.25⑤	26	16	16
	8-400	4	—	—	9	4.25⑤	26	16	16
	8-454	4	—	—	9	4.25⑤	26	22	23

● Specifications do not include torque converter
■ Station wagons: '68-'69—24 gals, '70—22 gals, '71—23 gals, '72-'75—22 gals
① 4 pts with 8.875 diameter ring gear
② 425 hp 427—23 qts
③ 3.5 pts with heavy duty 3-speed
④ 17 qts with 300 hp engine
⑤ 4.9 pts with 8.875 ring gear
⑥ 8 pts with 3-speed Turbo Hydramatic 400
⑦ 5 pts with 3-speed Turbo Hydramatic 350
⑧ 9 with 400 4 bbl
— Not applicable

Corvette — CAPACITIES

Year	ENGINE No. Cyl. (Cu. In.) Displacement	Engine Crankcase Add 1 Qt For New Filter	TRANSMISSION Pts To Refill After Draining — Manual 3-Speed	Manual 4-Speed	Automatic ●	Drive Axle (pts)	Gasoline Tank (gals)	COOLING SYSTEM (qts) With Heater	With A/C
'69	8-350	4	3	3	8	4	20	15	15
	8-427	5	—	3	8	4	20	22	22
'70	8-350	4	—	3	8	4	20	15①	18
	8-454	5	—	3	8	4	20	22	22
'71	8-350	4	—	3	8	4	18	15②	18
	8-454	5	—	3	8	4	18	22	22

CAPACITIES

Year	ENGINE No. Cyl. (Cu. In.) Displacement	Engine Crankcase Add 1 Qt For New Filter	TRANSMISSION Pts To Refill After Draining — Manual 3-Speed	Manual 4-Speed	Automatic ●	Drive Axle (pts)	Gasoline Tank (gals)	COOLING SYSTEM (qts) With Heater	With A/C
'72	8-350	4	—	3	8	4	18	15②	18
	8-454	5	—	3	8	4	18	22	24
'73	8-350	4	—	3	8	4	18	18	18
	8-454	5	—	3	8	4	18	24	24
'74	8-350	4	—	3	8	4	18	17	17
	8-454	5	—	3	8	4	18	22	23
'75-'76	8-350	4	—	3	8	4	18	17	17

● Specifications do not include torque converter
① 18 qts with 370 hp
② 18 qts with 330 hp
— Not applicable

VALVE SPECIFICATIONS

Year	Engine No. Cyl. Displacement (cu in.)	Seat Angle (deg)	Face Angle (deg)	Spring Test Pressure (lbs @ in.)	Spring Installed Height (in.)	STEM TO GUIDE Clearance (in.) Intake	Exhaust	STEM Diameter (in.) Intake	Exhaust
'69	6-250	46②	45	60 @ 1.66	1 21/32	.0010-.0037	.0010-.0047	.3414	.3414
	8-327	46②	45	80 @ 1.70	1 5/32	.0010-.0037	.0010-.0047	.3414	.3414
	8-350	46②	45	80 @ 1.70	1 5/32	.0010-.0037	.0010-.0047	.3414	.3414
	8-396	46②	45	90 @ 1.88	1 7/8	.0010-.0037	.0010-.0037	.3719	.3719
	8-427	46②	45	90 @ 1.88	1 7/8	.0010-.0037	.0010-.0037	.3719	.3719
	8-427③	46②	45	75 @ 1.88④	1 7/8	.0010-.0037	.0010-.0037	.3719	.3719
'70	6-250	46	45	60 @ 1.66	1 21/32	.0010-.0037	.0010-.0047	.3414	.3414
	8-350	46	45	80 @ 1.70	1 23/32	.0010-.0037	.0010-.0047	.3414	.3414
	8-400	46	45	80 @ 1.70	1 7/8	.0010-.0037	.0010-.0047	.3414	.3414
	8-454	46	45	75 @ 1.88⑥	1 7/8	.0010-.0037	.0010-.0047	.3718	.3718
	8-454⑦	46	45	75 @ 1.88⑧	1 7/8	.0010-.0037	.0010-.0047	.3718	.3718
'71	6-250	46	45	60 @ 1.66	1 21/32	.0010-.0037	.0010-.0047	.3414	.3714
	8-350	46	45	80 @ 1.70	1 23/32	.0010-.0037	.0010-.0047	.3414	.3714
	8-400	46	45	80 @ 1.70	1 23/32	.0010-.0037	.0010-.0047	.3414	.3714
	8-400⑨	46	45	75 @ 1.88⑥	1 7/8	.0010-.0037	.0010-.0047	.3719	.3717
	8-454	46	45	75 @ 1.88⑥	1 7/8	.0010-.0037	.0010-.0047	.3719	.3717
'72	6-250	46	45	60 @ 1.66	1 21/32	.0010-.0037	.0010-.0047	.3414	.3414
	8-350	46	45	80 @ 1.70	1 23/32	.0010-.0037	.0010-.0047	.3414	.3414
	8-400	46	45	80 @ 1.70	1 23/32	.0010-.0037	.0010-.0047	.3414	.3414
	8-402	46	45	90 @ 1.88	1 7/8	.0010-.0037	.0010-.0047	.3719	.3717
	8-454	46	45	75 @ 1.88⑥	1 7/8	.0010-.0037	.0010-.0047	.3719	.3717
'73	6-250	46	45	60 @ 1.66	1 21/32	.0010-.0027	.0010-.0027	.3414	.3414
	8-350	46	45	80 @ 1.70⑩	1 23/32	.0010-.0027	.0010-.0027	.3414	.3414
	8-400	46	45	80 @ 1.70⑩	1 23/32	.0010-.0027	.0010-.0027	.3414	.3414
	8-454	46	45	80 @ 1.88	1 7/8	.0010-.0027	.0010-.0027	.3719	.3717
'74	8-350	46	45	80 @ 1.70⑩	1 23/32	.0010-.0027	.0010-.0027	.3414	.3414
	8-400	46	45	80 @ 1.70⑩	1 23/32	.0010-.0027	.0010-.0027	.3414	.3414
	8-454	46	45	80 @ 1.88	1 7/8	.0010-.0027	.0010-.0027	.3719	.3717

VALVE SPECIFICATIONS

Year	Engine No. Cyl. Displacement (cu in.)	Seat Angle (deg)	Face Angle (deg)	Spring Test Pressure (lbs @ in.)	Spring Installed Height (in.)	STEM TO GUIDE Clearance (in.) Intake	STEM TO GUIDE Clearance (in.) Exhaust	STEM Diameter (in.) Intake	STEM Diameter (in.) Exhaust
'75-'76	8-350	46	45	80 @ 1.70⑩	1 23/32	.0010-.0027	.0010-.0027	.3414	.3414
	8-400	46	45	80 @ 1.70⑩	1 23/32	.0010-.0027	.0010-.0027	.3414	.3414
	8-454	46	45	90 @ 1.80	1 7/8	.0010-.0027	.0010-.0027	.3719	.3717

② 45° on engines with aluminum heads
③ 430 hp
④ Inner spring 41 @ 1.78
⑤ 350 hp
⑥ Inner spring 30 @ 1.78
⑦ 460 hp
⑧ Inner spring 41 @ 1.78
⑨ 300 hp
⑩ Intake, 80 @ 1.61 for exhaust spring

TORQUE SPECIFICATIONS

All readings in ft lbs

Year	Engine No. Cyl. Displacement (cu in.)	Cylinder Head Bolts	Rod Bearing Bolts	Main Bearing Bolts	Crankshaft Pulley Bolt	Flywheel to Crankshaft Bolts	MANIFOLD Intake	MANIFOLD Exhaust
'69-'73	6	95	35	65	—	60	30⑧	25⑦
'69-'76	8-392, 350, 400	60-70	45	75②	60⑥	60	30	⑤
'69-'76	8-396, 402 (Big Block)	80①	50	105	85⑥	65	30	30
	8-427, 454	80①	50④	105	85	65	30	30

① Aluminum Heads—Short bolts 65, Long bolts 75
② Engines with 4-bolt mains—Outer bolts 65
③ Not used
④ 7/16 Rod bolts—70
⑤ Center bolts—25-30, end bolts 15-20
⑥ Where applicable
⑦ Exhaust-to-intake
⑧ Manifold-to-head

CRANKSHAFT AND CONNECTING ROD SPECIFICATIONS

All measurements are given in in.

Year	Engine No. Cyl. Displace. (cu in.)	CRANKSHAFT Main Brg. Journal Dia	CRANKSHAFT Main Brg. Oil Clearance	CRANKSHAFT Shaft End-Play	CRANKSHAFT Thrust on No.	CONNECTING ROD Journal Diameter	CONNECTING ROD Oil Clearance	CONNECTING ROD Side Clearance
'69	6-250	2.2983-2.2993	.0003-.0029	.002-.006	7	1.9990-2.0000	.0007-.0027	.009-.013
	8-327	2.4484-2.4493①	.0008-.0020②	.003-.011	5	2.0990-2.1000	.0007-.0028	.009-.013
	8-350	2.4484-2.4493①	.0008-.0020②	.003-.011	5	2.0990-2.1000	.0007-.0028	.009-.013
	8-396	2.7484-2.7493③	.0010-.0022④	.006-.010	5	2.1990-2.2000	.0009-.0025	.015-.021
	8-427	2.7481-2.7490⑤	.0013-.0025⑥	.006-.010	5	2.1990-2.2000	.0009-.0025	.015-.021
	8-427 (435 H.P.)	2.7481-2.7490⑤	.0013-.0025⑥	.006-.010	5	2.1985-2.1995	.0014-.0030	.019-.025
'70	6-250	2.2983-2.2993	.0003-.0029	.002-.006	7	1.9990-2.0000	.0007-.0027	.009-.014
	8-350	2.4484-2.4493⑦	.0003-.0015⑧	.002-.006	5	2.0990-2.1000	.0007-.0028	.008-.014
	8-400 (265 H.P.)	2.6509	.0008-.0020⑨	.002-.006	5	2.0990-2.1000	.0009-.0030	.008-.014
	8-454	2.7485-2.7494③	.0013-.0025⑩	.006-.010	5	2.1990-2.2000	.0009-.0025	.015-.021
	8-454 (460 H.P.)	2.7481-2.7490⑤	.0013-.0025⑪	.006-.010	5	2.1985-2.1995	.0014-.0030	.019-.025
'71	6-250	2.2983-2.2993	.0003-.0029	.002-.006	7	1.9990-2.0000	.0007-.0027	.009-.014
	8-350	2.4484-2.4493⑦	.0008-.0020⑨	.002-.006	5	2.0990-2.1000	.0013-.0035	.008-.014
	8-350 (330 H.P.)	2.4484-2.4493⑦	.0013-.0025⑬	.002-.006	5	2.0990-2.1000	.0013-.0035	.008-.014
	8-400 (255 H.P.)	2.6484-2.6493⑭	.0008-.0020⑨	.002-.006	5	2.0990-2.1000	.0013-.0035	.008-.014
	8-402 (300 H.P.) (Mk. IV)	2.7487-2.7496⑮	.0007-.0019⑯	.006-.010	5	2.1990-2.2000	.0009-.0025	.013-.023
	8-454 (365 H.P.)	2.7485-2.7494⑰	.0013-.0025⑩	.006-.010	5	2.1990-2.2000	.0009-.0025	.015-.021
	8-454 (425 H.P.)	2.7481-2.7490⑤	.0013-.0025⑪	.006-.010	5	2.1985-2.1995	.0009-.0025	.019-.025

CRANKSHAFT AND CONNECTING ROD SPECIFICATIONS

All measurements are given in in.

Year	Engine No. Cyl. Displace. (cu in.)	CRANKSHAFT				CONNECTING ROD		
		Main Brg. Journal Dia	Main Brg. Oil Clearance	Shaft End-Play	Thrust on No.	Journal Diameter	Oil Clearance	Side Clearance
'72	6-250	2.2983-2.2993	.0003-.0029	.002-.006	7	1.9990-2.0000	.0007-.0027	.009-.014
	8-350	2.4484-2.4493⑫	.0008-.0020⑨	.002-.006	5	2.0990-2.1000	.0013-.0035	.008-.014
	8-350 (255 H.P.)	2.4484-2.4493⑫	.0013-.0025⑬	.002-.006	5	2.0990-2.1000	.0013-.0035	.008-.014
	8-400 (170 H.P.)	2.6484-2.6493⑭	.0008-.0020⑨	.002-.006	5	2.0990-2.1000	.0013-.0035	.008-.014
	8-402 (210 H.P.)	2.7487-2.7496⑮	.0007-.0019⑯	.006-.010	5	2.1990-2.2000	.0009-.0025	.013-.023
	8-454 (270 H.P.)	2.7485-2.7494⑰	.0013-.0025⑩	.006-.010	5	2.1990-2.2000	.0009-.0025	.015-.021
'73-'74	6-250	2.3004	.0003-.0029	.002-.006	7	1.9990-2.0000	.0007-.0027	.007-.016
	8-350	2.4502⑱	.0008-.0020⑨	.002-.006	5	2.0990-2.1000	.0013-.0035	.008-.014
	8-350	2.4502⑱	.0013-.0025⑬	.002-.006	5	2.0990-2.1000	.0013-.0035	.008-.014
	8-400	2.6503⑲	.0008-.0020⑨	.002-.007	5	2.0990-2.1000	.0013-.0035	.008-.014
	8-454	2.7504⑳	.0007-.0019⑯	.006-.010	5	2.1990-2.2000	.0009-.0025	.015-.021
'75-'76	8-350	2.4502⑱	.0008-.0020⑨	.002-.007	5	2.099-2.100	.0013-.0035	.008-.014
	8-350	2.4502⑱	.0013-.0025⑬	.002-.007	5	2.099-2.100	.0013-.0035	.008-.014
	8-400	2.6503⑲	.0008-.0020⑨	.002-.007	5	2.099-2.100	.0013-.0035	.008-.014
	8-454	2.7504㉑	.0007-.0019⑯	.006-.010	5	2.199-2.200	.0009-.0025	.015-.021

① No. 5—2.4470-2.4488
② No. 5—.0018-.0034
③ No.'s 3, 4—2.7481-2.7490; No. 5—2.7478-2.7488
④ No.'s 3, 4—.0013-.0025; No. 5—.0015-.0031
⑤ No. 5—2.7478-2.7488
⑥ No. 5—.0015-.0031
⑦ No. 5—2.4479-2.4488
⑧ No.'s 2, 3, 4—.0006-.0018; No. 5—.0008-.0023
⑨ No.'s 2, 3, 4—.011-.0023; No. 5—.0017-.0033
⑩ No. 5—.0024-.0040
⑪ No. 5—.0029-.0045
⑫ No.'s 2, 3, 4—2.4481-2.4490; No. 5—2.4479-2.4488
⑬ No. 5—.0023-.0033; with auto. trans. No. 1—.0019-.0031
⑭ No. 5—2.6479-2.6488
⑮ No.'s 3, 4—2.7481-2.7490; No. 5—2.7473-2.7483
⑯ No.'s 2, 3, 4—.0013-.0025; No. 5—.0019-.0035
⑰ No.'s 2, 3, 4—2.7481-2.7490; No. 5—2.7478-2.7488
⑱ No. 5—2.4508
⑲ No. 5—2.6509
⑳ No.'s 1, 5—2.7499
㉑ No. 1—2.7499; No. 5—2.7505

RING GAP

All measurements are given in inches

Year	Engine No. Cyl.	Top Compression	Bottom Compression
'69-'74	6-250	.010-.020	.010-.020
'69	8-327	.013-.023	.013-.025
'69-'71	8-350	.010-.020①	.013-.025①
'69-'76	8-396, 400, 402 427, 454	.010-.020	.010-.020
	All except 8-350	.010-.020	.010-.020
'73-'76	8-350	.010-.020	.013-.025②

① 250, 300 hp 350 cu in. Top .013-.023
2nd .013-.025
② 250, 255 hp 350 cu in. .013-.023

Year	Engine No. Cyl.	Oil Control
'69-'74	All engines except 8-396, 427	.015-.055
'69	8-396, 427	.010-.030
'75-'76	8-350	.015-.055
	8-400	.010-.035
	8-454	.010-.025

RING SIDE CLEARANCE

All measurements are given in inches

Year	Engine No. Cyl.	Top Compression	Bottom Compression
'69-'73	6-250	.0012-.0027	.0012-.0032
'69	8-327	.0012-.0032①	.0012-.0027①
'69	8-350	.0012-.0032	.0012-.0027
'70-'76	8-350 2 bbl	.0012-.0032	.0012-.0032
'70-'76	8-350 4 bbl	.0012-.0032	.0012-.0027
'69	8-396	.0017-.0032	.0017-.0032
'70-'76	8-400	.0012-.0027②	.0012-.0032②
'69	8-427	.0017-.0032	.0017-.0032
'71-'72	8-402	.0017-.0032	.0017-.0032
'71-'76	8-454	.0017-.0032	.0017-.0032

① 250, 275 hp 327 cu in.
Top .0012-.0027
2nd .0012-.0032
② 330 hp 400 cu in.
Top .0017-.0032
2nd .0012-.0032
③ 330 hp 400 cu in.
.0005-.0065

Year	Engine No. Cyl.	Oil Control
'69-'76	6-250, 327, 400	.000-.005③
'69-'76	8-350 2 bbl	.002-.007
'69-'76	8-350 4 bbl	.000-.005
'69	8-396	.0005-.0065
'71-'72	8-402	.0005-.0065
'69	8-427	.0005-.0065
'70-'76	8-454	.0005-.0065

PISTON CLEARANCE

Year	Engine		Piston to Bore Clearance (in.) ●
	Displacement cu in.	Advertised H.P.	
'69-'76	250		.0005-.0025
	327, 350	All 145	.0005-.0025
	350	145, 155, 165, 190, 250	.0007-.0027 .0007-.0027
		300	.0007-.0027
		350	.0020-.0036
		205, 245, 370	.0036-.0061
	396	350	.0018-.0038
		375	.0036-.0065
	400	150, 175, 180, 265	.0014-.0034
		330	.0018-.0038
	427	390	.0024-.0045
		400	.0024-.0045
		430	.0058-.0080
		435	.0040-.0065
	454	215, 235, 245, 275	.0018-.0035
		345	.0024-.0049
		360	.0024-.0049
		390	.0024-.0049
		450	.0040-.0065

● Service range—minimum to maximum

ALTERNATOR AND REGULATOR SPECIFICATIONS

	ALTERNATOR			REGULATOR						
					Field Relay			Regulator		
Year	Part No. or Manufacturer	Field Current @ 12 V	Output (amps)	Part No. or Manufacturer	Air Gap (in.)	Point Gap (in.)	Volts to Close	Air Gap (in.)	Point Gap (in.)	Volts @ 75°
'69	1100834	2.2-2.6	37	1119515	.015	.030	2.3-3.7	.067	.014	13.5-14.4
	1100836	2.2-2.6	37	1119515	.015	.030	2.3-3.7	.067	.014	13.5-14.4
	1100696	2.2-2.6	37	1119515	.015	.030	2.3-3.7	.067	.014	13.5-14.4
'70	1100834	2.2-2.6	37	1119515	.015	.030	2.3-3.7	.067	.014	13.5-14.4
	1100900	2.2-2.6	37	1119515	.015	.030	2.3-3.7	.067	.014	13.5-14.4
	1100901	2.2-2.6	37	1119515	.015	.030	2.3-3.7	.067	.014	13.5-14.4

ALTERNATOR AND REGULATOR SPECIFICATIONS

Year	Alternator Part No. or Manufacturer	Alternator Field Current @ 12 V	Alternator Output (amps)	Regulator Part No. or Manufacturer	Field Relay Air Gap (in.)	Field Relay Point Gap (in.)	Field Relay Volts to Close	Regulator Air Gap (in.)	Regulator Point Gap (in.)	Volts @ 75°
'71-'72	1100544	4.0-4.5	55	1119515	.015	.030	1.5-3.2	.067	.014	13.8-14.8
	1100543, 1100950	4.0-4.5	37	1119515	.015	.030	1.5-3.2	.067	.014	13.8-14.8
	1100566, 1100836, 1100837	2.2-2.6	35	1119515	.015	.030	1.5-3.2	.067	.014	13.8-14.8
	1100843	2.2-2.6	58	1119515	.015	.030	1.5-3.2	.067	.014	13.8-14.8
	1100917	2.8-3.2	59	1119519	.030	.030	1.5-3.2	.067	.014	13.8-14.8
	1100567	2.2-2.6	40	1119515	.015	.030	1.5-3.2	.067	.014	13.8-14.8
	1100497	2.8-3.2	37	Integrated with alternator						13.8-14.8
	1100934	2.8-3.2	37	Integrated with alternator						13.8-14.8
'73-'74	1100544	4.0-4.5	61	Integrated with alternator						13.8-14.8
	1102353, 1100573, 1102346, 1100950	4.0-4.5	42	Integrated with alternator						13.8-14.8
	1100934, 1100497	4.0-4.5	37	Integrated with alternator						13.8-14.8
	1102354, 1100542	4.0-4.5	63	Integrated with alternator						13.8-14.8
'75-'76	1102483	4.0-4.5	37	Integrated with alternator						13.8-14.8
	1100950	4.0-4.5	42	Integrated with alternator						13.8-14.8

BATTERY AND STARTER SPECIFICATIONS

Year	Engine No. Cyl. Displacement (cu in.)	Battery Ampere Hour Capacity	Battery Volts	Battery Terminal Grounded	Lock Test Amps	Lock Test Volts	Lock Test Torque (ft lbs)	No-Load Test Amps	No-Load Test Volts	No-Load Test RPM	Brush Spring Tension (oz)
'69	6 & 8-327, 396	45	12	Neg.	Not Recommended			73	9	4,500	35
	8-350, 427	61	12	Neg.	Not Recommended			85	9	10,000	35
	All Corvette Engines	62	12	Neg.	Not Recommended			85	9	10,000	35
'70	6	45	12	Neg.	Not Recommended			50-80	9	5,500-10,500	35
	8-350	61	12	Neg.	Not Recommended			55-80	9	3,500-6,000	35
	All Corvette Engines	62	12	Neg.	Not Recommended			55-80	9	3,500-6,000	35
	8-400	62	12	Neg.	Not Recommended			55-80	9	3,500-6,000	35
	8-454	62	12	Neg.	Not Recommended			65-95	9	7,500-10,500	35
'71-'72	6	45	12	Neg.	Not Recommended			50-80	9	5,500-10,500	35
	8-350	61	12	Neg.	Not Recommended			65-95	9	7,500-10,500	35
	8-400	61	12	Neg.	Not Recommended			65-95	9	7,500-10,500	35
	8-402	61	12	Neg.	Not Recommended			65-95	9	7,500-10,500	35
	8-454	76	12	Neg.	Not Recommended			65-95	9	7,500-10,500	35
	Corvette 350	62	12	Neg.	Not Recommended			65-95	9	7,500-10,500	35
	Corvette 454	76	12	Neg.	Not Recommended			65-95	9	7,500-10,500	35
'73-'74	6	①	12	Neg.	Not Recommended			50-80	9	5,500-10,500	35
	8-350, 400	②	12	Neg.	Not Recommended			65-95	9	7,500-10,500	35
	8-454	④	12	Neg.	Not Recommended			65-95	9	7,500-10,500	35
	Corvette 350	③	12	Neg.	Not Recommended			65-95	9	7,500-10,500	35
	Corvette 454	④	12	Neg.	Not Recommended			65-95	9	7,500-10,500	35
'75-'76	8-350, 400	②	12	Neg.	Not Recommended			65-95	9	7,500-10,500	35
	8-454	⑤	12	Neg.	Not Recommended			65-95	9	7,500-10,500	35
	Corvette 350	③	12	Neg.	Not Recommended			65-95	9	7,500-10,500	35

① Side Terminal—Cranking power 2,300 watts @ 0°F
② Side Terminal—Cranking power 2,900 watts @ 0°F
③ Side Terminal—Cranking power 3,250 watts @ 0°F
④ Side Terminal—Cranking power 3,750 watts @ 0°F
⑤ Side Terminal—Cranking power 4,000 watts @ 0°F

BRAKE SPECIFICATIONS

Year	Model	Master Cylinder Disc	Master Cylinder Drum	Wheel Cylinder Front Disc	Wheel Cylinder Front Drum	Wheel Cylinder Rear	Brake Disc or Drum Diameter Front Disc	Brake Disc or Drum Diameter Front Drum	Brake Disc or Drum Diameter Rear
CHEVROLET									
'69-'70	All	1 1/8	1.0	2 15/16	1 3/16	1.00	11.75	11.0	11.0
'71-'76	Exc. Sta. Wag.	1 1/8	—	2 15/16	—	15/16	11.86	—	11.0
	Sta. Wag.	1 1/8	—	2 15/16	—	1.00	11.86	—	12.0
CORVETTE									
'69-'71	All	1.0	—	1 7/8	—	1 3/8	11.75	—	11.75③
'72-'76	All	1.0②	—	1 7/8	—	1 3/8	11.75	—	11.75③

① Metallic linings—7/0 in.
② Power brakes—1 1/8 except 1974
③ Disc
— Not applicable

WHEEL ALIGNMENT SPECIFICATIONS

Year	Model	Caster Range (deg)	Caster Pref Setting (deg)	Camber Range (deg)	Camber Pref Setting (deg)	Toe-in (in.)	Steering Axis Inclin. (deg)	Wheel Pivot Ratio (deg) Inner Wheel	Wheel Pivot Ratio (deg) Outer Wheel
'69	Chevrolet	1/4P to 1 1/4P	1/4P	1/4N to 3/4P	1/4P	1/8 to 1/4	7 to 8	20	18
	Corvette	1/2P to 1 1/2P①	1P	1/2P to 1 1/4P②	3/4P	3/16 to 5/16②	6 1/2 to 7 1/2	20	18 1/2
'70	Chevrolet	1/4P to 1 1/4P	1/4P	1/4N to 3/4P	1/4P	1/8 to 1/4	7 to 8	20	18
	Corvette	1/2P to 1 1/2P①	1P	1/2P to 1 1/4P②	3/4P	3/16 to 5/16②	6 1/2 to 7 1/2	20	18 1/2
'71	Chevrolet	1 1/2N to 1/2N	1N	0 to 1P	1/2P	1/8 to 1/4	9 1/2 to 10 1/2	N.A.	N.A.
'71-'72	Corvette	1/2P to 1 1/2P①	1P	1/4P to 1 1/4P	3/4P	3/16 to 5/16	6 1/2 to 7 1/2	N.A.	N.A.
'72	Chevrolet	1/2P to 1 1/2P	1P	0 to 1P	1/2P	3/16 to 5/16	9 1/2 to 10 1/2	N.A.	N.A.
'73	Chevrolet	0 to 2P	1P	1/4P to 1 3/4P⑤	1P	1/16N to 3/16P	10 1/2	N.A.	N.A.
	Corvette	0 to 2P③	1P	0 to 1 1/2P④	3/4P	1/8 to 3/8④	6 7/8	N.A.	N.A.
'74	Chevrolet	1/2-1 1/2P	1P	1/2-1 1/2P⑤	1P⑥	1/16 to 3/16	9 1/2	N.A.	N.A.
	Corvette	1/2P-1 1/2P①	1P	1/4P-1 1/4P④	3/4P	3/32 to 5/32④	7 3/4	N.A.	N.A.
'75-'76	Chevrolet	1/2P-2 1/2P	1 1/2P	1/2-1 1/2P⑤	1P⑥	1/16 to 3/16	9 7/64	N.A.	N.A.
	Corvette	1/2P-1 1/2P①	1P	1/4P-1 1/4P⑦	3/4P	1/32 to 3/32⑦	7 3/4	N.A.	N.A.

① W/power steering—1 3/4P to 2 3/4P
② Rear wheel alignment: camber 1 1/8N to 5/8N to toe-in 1/32 to 3/32
③ W/power steering—1 1/4P to 3 1/4P, 2 1/4 preferred
④ Rear wheel alignment: camber 7/8N ± 1/4. toe-in 2/32 ± 1/32
⑤ Left wheel given, right wheel is 1/4N to 1 1/4P, preferred 1/2P
⑥ Left wheel given, right wheel is 1/2P
⑦ Rear wheel alignment: Camber—11/16N ± 1/4; Toe-in—0 ± 1/32
N Negative P Positive

CHARGING SYSTEM

Repair and test details on the Delcotron and its regulators can be found in the Unit Repair Section.

A resistance wire is used between the "ACC" connector of the ignition switch and the regulator.

Caution Since the Delcotron and regulator are designed for use on a single polarity system, the following precautions must be observed:

1. The polarity of the battery, generator, and regulator must be matched and considered before making any electrical connections in the system.
2. When connecting a booster battery, be sure to connect the negative battery terminals with one another, and the positive battery terminals with one another.
3. When connecting a charger to the battery, connect the charger positive lead to the battery positive terminal. Connect the charger negative lead to the battery negative terminal.
4. Never operate the Delcotron on open circuit. Be sure that all connections in the circuit are clean and tight.
5. Do not short across or ground any of the terminals on the Delcotron regulator.
6. Do not attempt to polarize the Delcotron.
7. Do not use test lamps of more than 12 volts or high amperage for checking diode continuity.
8. Avoid long soldering times when replacing diodes or transistors. Prolonged heat is damaging to these units. Always use a heat-sink when soldering these solid state devices.
9. Disconnect the battery ground terminal when servicing any AC system. This will prevent the possibility of accidentally reversing polarity.

Alternator R & R

1. Disconnect the battery cables from the battery terminals.
2. Disconnect and identify the wire leads from the alternator.
3. Remove the alternator brace bolt, then remove belt (s).
4. Remove the alternator pivot attaching bolt and remove alternator from vehicle.
5. To install, reverse the above procedure and adjust belt tension.

Regulator R & R

1. Disconnect the ground cable at the battery.
2. Disconnect the wiring harness from the regulator.
3. Remove the mounting screws and remove the regulator.
4. Make sure that the regulator base gasket is in place before installation.
5. Clean the attaching area for proper grounding.
6. Install the regulator. Do not overtighten the mounting screws, as this will cancel the cushioning effect of the rubber grommets.

NOTE: An integral alternator/regulator has been optionally available since 1969. Separate removal or adjustment of the regulator is not possible with this unit. Complete disassembly of this unit is described in the "Unit Repair Section."

STARTING SYSTEM

Detailed information on the starter can be found in the Starter Specifications table of this section. More information on starters can be found in the Unit Repair Section under Charging and Starting Systems.

Starter R & R

1. Disconnect the battery and the wires from the solenoid.

NOTE: 1975 models do not have a solenoid-to-ignition coil wire, thus eliminating the R terminal on the solenoid.

2. Remove the starter mounting bolt and lock washers. On V8s, a stud nut and lock washer are at the front of the starter.
3. Pull starter forward and out of car.
4. To install, reverse the above procedure.

IGNITION SYSTEM

Three types of ignition systems have been available: a conventional breaker type, an optional Corvette magnetic pulse system, and a High Energy Ignition (HEI) system. The magnetic pulse distributor, which was discontinued in 1972, requires no maintenance.

A resistance wire connects the ignition switch and the coil on the breaker type system. The magnetic pulse system utilizes two; one between the negative coil terminal and ground, the other resistance wire provides a voltage drop for the engine run circuit. The HEI system doesn't use a resistance wire.

The HEI system was used starting in 1974 on 454 cu. in. Chevrolets. All 1975-76 models are equipped with HEI. Description and troubleshooting for both the magnetic pulse and HEI systems are found in the electronic ignition "Unit Repair Section."

Distributor Removal

6 Cylinder Models

The distributor assembly is mounted on the right side of the block and is driven directly from the camshaft.

To remove the distributor, first detach the vacuum lines from the vacuum advance unit and lift off the distributor cap.

The distributor body is fastened to the block by a single cap screw which holds the octane selector plate down against the block. Scribe marks so that the distributor body and rotor can be installed in their original locations. Do not turn engine while the distributor is removed. Remove the retaining screw and lift the distributor out of the block.

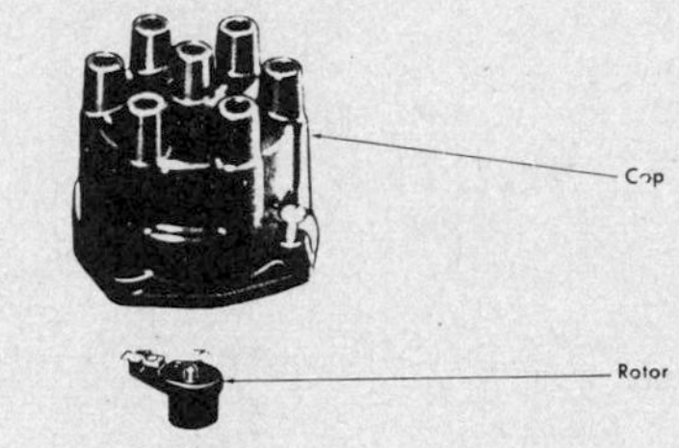

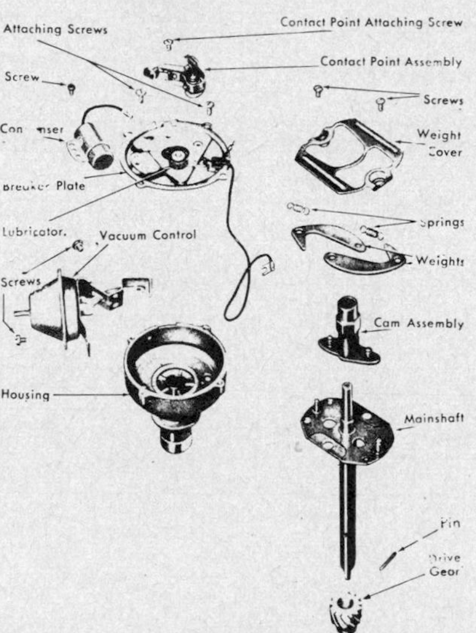

6-cylinder distributor, typical
(© Chevrolet Div., G.M. Corp)

V8 Models—Standard Distributor

The distributor is located between the two banks of cylinders at the back of the block.

The drive gear is attached to the distributor shaft; therefore, if it becomes necessary to remove the distributor, carefully mark the position of the rotor. Then, if the engine is not turned after the distributor is taken out, it can be installed in the same position from which is was removed.

To remove the distributor, disconnect the carburetor air cleaner, disconnect the coil primary wire and the vacuum line, remove the distributor

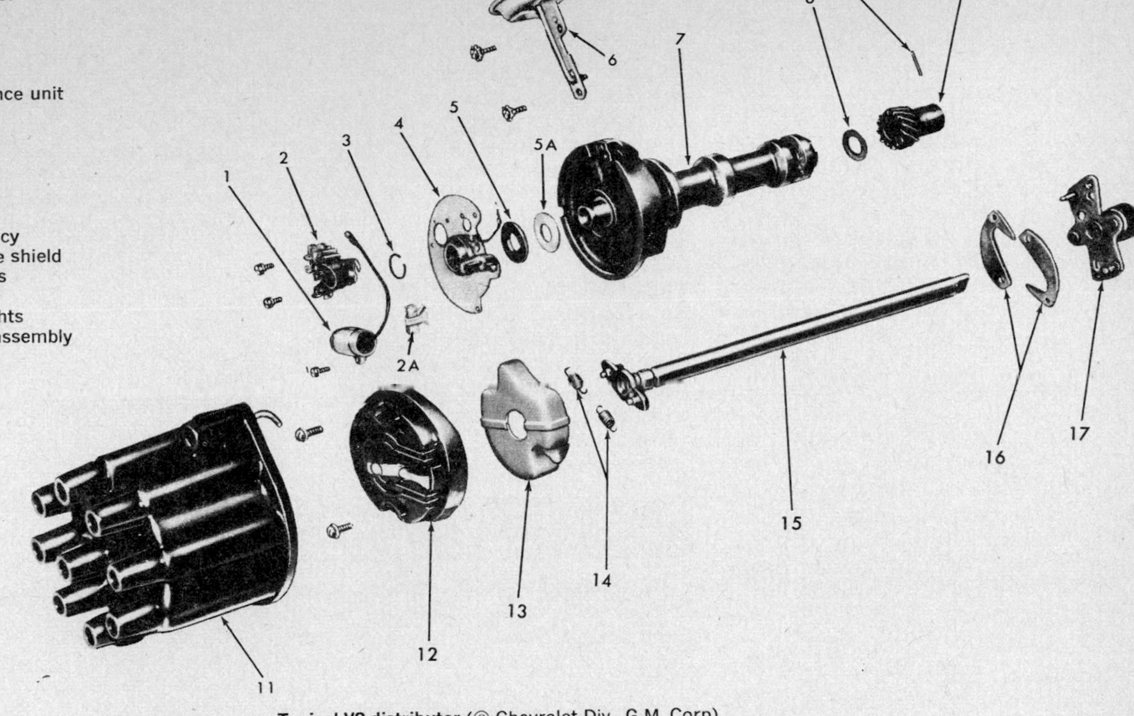

Typical V8 distributor (© Chevrolet Div., G.M. Corp)

cap, take out the single hold-down bolt located under the distributor body, mark the position of the body relative to the block and then work the distributor up out of the block.

Magnetic Pulse and HEI Distributor

1. Disconnect pick-up coil connector.
2. Remove distributor cap.
3. Crank engine so that rotor points to No. 1 cylinder plug tower and timing mark on crankshaft pulley is indexed with pointer. Mark the position of the tip of the rotor on the engine block.
4. Remove distributor vacuum line.
5. Remove distributor hold-down bolt and clamp, then remove distributor.
6. When installing the distributor, align the tip of the rotor with the mark that was made on the block.

Distributor Installation (Engine Disturbed)

1. Turn crank until the No. 1 cylinder is at the top of its compression stroke. Remove the No. 1 spark plug to feel the compression.
2. Align the timing mark on the flywheel or vibration damper with the indicator.
3. With distributor body oriented in its normal position, hold the rotor pointing toward the front of the engine, then turn the rotor approximately 1/8 turn counterclockwise and push the distributor down until it engages the camshaft, rotating the shaft slightly if necessary.

NOTE: on Mark IV engines there is a punch mark on the distributor drive gear which indicates the rotor position. Thus, the distributor may be installed with the cap in place. Align the punch mark 2° clockwise from the No. 1 cap terminal, then rotate the distributor body clockwise 1/8 turn counterclockwise and push the distributor down into the block.

4. Press down on the distributor and crank the engine to make sure the oil pump shaft is engaged.
5. Return the crankshaft to No. 1 cylinder compression stroke with the timing marks aligned.
6. Turn the distributor body counterclockwise until the points are just beginning to open, then tighten the distributor clamp bolt.
7. Install the distributor cap, checking that the rotor points to the No. 1 terminal. Make sure that the spark plug wires are in their supports and are securely connected.
8. Connect distributor vacuum line and primary wire.
9. Start engine and set the timing.

Caution When using an auxiliary starter switch for bumping the engine into position for timing, the primary distributor lead must be disconnected from the negative post of the ignition coil and the switch must be in the on position. Failure to do this may cause damage to the grounding circuit in the ignition switch.

Breaker Point Adjustment

NOTE: 1970-72 distributors are equipped with a radio static shield, which must be removed for access to the points.

Breaker point gap (dwell) adjustment is accomplished for 6-cylinder engines by loosening the point assembly attaching screw and adjusting it with a screwdriver until correct gap clearance is obtained (use a feeler gauge). Tighten the point assembly attaching screws and install the distributor cap. Use a dwell meter, if available, to check the dwell angle, readjusting if necessary.

On V8 models there is a window in the distributor cap so that the dwell

6-cylinder point adjustment
(© Chevrolet Div., G.M. Corp)

angle may be set while the engine is running. Use a ⅛ in. Allen (hex) wrench to make the adjustment.

See Tune-Up Specifications at the beginning of this section for correct breaker point gap and dwell angle.

Caution On V8 models the distributor body is involved in the engine lubricating system. The lubricating circuit to the right-bank valve train can be interrupted by mis-alignment of the distributor body. This can cause serious trouble and may be hard to diagnose. See Firing Order and Timing illustrations for correct distributor positioning.

HEI System Dwell/Tachometer Hookup

Connect one dwell/tach lead to the TACH terminal on the side of the distributor and the other to ground. Some tachometers must be connected to the TACH terminal and the battery positive terminal. Not all tachometers will operate correctly with the HEI system. Check with the manufacturer if there is any doubt.

Caution *The TACH terminal should never be connected to ground.*

When hooking up a remote starter switch, disconnect the BATT terminal.

Distributor Cam Lubricator Wick

The distributor cam lubricator should be rotated 180° (L6 engines) or switched end for end (V8 engines) every 12,000 miles, and replaced every 24,000 miles.

Caution Do not oil these lubricator wicks or directly lubricate the cam.

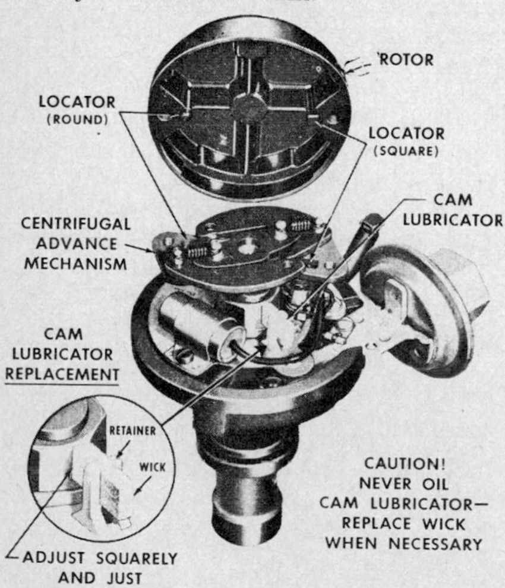

V8 distributor showing details of cam lubricator
(© Chevrolet Div., G.M. Corp)

Ignition Timing

Remove the spark plug wire from no. one plug and attach a timing light between the wire and the plug. Disconnect the distributor spark advance hose and plug the vacuum opening. Start the engine and run it at idle speed. Aim the timing light at the degree scale just over the harmonic balancer. The markings on the scale are in 2° increments with the greatest number of markings on the *before* side of the 0. Adjust the timing by loosening the securing clamp and rotating the distributor until the desired ignition advance is achieved, then tighten the clamp. To advance the timing, rotate the distributor opposite to the normal direction of rotor rotation. Retard the timing by rotating the distributor in the normal direction of rotor rotation. When timing an engine equipped with HEI, use an adapter at the No. 1 distributor terminal.

FUEL SYSTEM

Data on capacity of the gas tank can be found in the Capacities table. Data on correct engine idle speed and fuel pump pressure can be found in the Tune-up Specifications table.

Information covering operation and troubles of the fuel gauge is in the Unit Repair Section.

Fuel Pump R & R

To remove the fuel pump, disconnect the input line and the output line to the carburetor. The fuel pump then can be unbolted from the side of the block and lifted off. On V8 models, the pump is actuated by a pushrod in the block.

Caution A fuel pump may fail to function at the time of replacement as a result of error in positioning or damage to the fuel pump pushrod of the V8 engine. This pushrod can slip out of place during the process of pump replacement and result in no pump action from the newly replaced unit. Before tightening the fuel pump to the engine, have someone spin the engine with the starter while feeling the fuel pump body for movement. If the pump and pushrod are in correct position, movement will be felt in the pump as the pushrod pressure is applied and released from the pump arm.

Fuel Filter R&R

Fuel filters are integral with the carburetor body. The filter element can be replaced as follows:

1. Disconnect the fuel line.
2. Remove the fuel filter nut from the carburetor.
3. Remove the filter element and spring. Blow through the filter end. If the air does not flow freely, replace the element. Do not attempt to clean the filter element.
4. Install the spring, then the element. Bronze filters in Holley carburetors must have the small section of the cone facing out.
5. Install the inlet fitting using a new gasket.
6. Install the fuel line.

Carburetor Adjustments

NOTE: refer to the illustrations in the Camaro Section for idle speed and mixture screw locations.

Chilton's TIME SAVER

327, 350, 400 cu. in.

When replacing a fuel pump on a 327, 350, or 400 cu. in. engine, considerable time can be be saved as follows:

1. **Before removing the old pump, remove the upper bolt from the engine's right front mounting boss. This bolt hole is in direct alignment with the fuel pump pushrod. The threaded bolt hole continues into the pump pushrod bore. The bolt acts as an oil plug.**
2. **Temporarily insert a longer bolt, (about ⅜—16 x 2 in.) into the hole. Screw the bolt into the bore until it bottoms against the pump pushrod. (Don't tighten the bolt with a wrench or the rod can be damaged.)**
3. **The mechanic is now free to remove and install the fuel pump without worrying about fuel pump pushrod misalignment.**

CAUTION: don't forget to reinstall original motor bolt.

396, 427 and 454 cu. in.

The design of these engines prevents the use of the method of simplifying fuel pump pushrod positioning while installing a fuel pump. However, to hold the pump pushrod in position while installing the fuel pump, the following works satisfactorily;

1. **Clean oil from pushrod.**
2. **Pack a small quantity of non-fibrous grease in the area around the fuel pump pushrod to hold it in suspension long enough to position the fuel pump.**
3. **Install and check pump action, then torque attaching bolts.**

Idle mixture and speed adjustments are critical aspects of exhaust emission control. For a discussion of the various emission control systems see Exhaust Emission Control Systems later in this section. It is important that all tune-up instructions be carefully followed to ensure satisfactory engine performance and minimum exhaust pollution. The different combinations of emission systems application on the different engine models have resulted in a great variety of tune-up specifications. See the Tune-Up Specifications at the beginning of this section. All models have a decal conspicuously placed somewhere in the engine compartment giving tune-up specifications.

When adjusting a carburetor with two idle mixture screws, adjust them alternately and evenly, unless otherwise stated.

See the Unit Repair Section for illustrations and adjustment specifications of Carter, Holley and Rochester carburetors. In the following adjustment procedures the term "lean roll" means turning the mixture adjusting screws in (clockwise) from optimum setting to obtain an obvious drop in engine speed (usually 20 rpm).

All 1969

Adjust with air cleaner installed.

1. Turn the idle mixture screw/s in until lightly seated, then back out 3 turns.
2. With engine at operating temperature, adjust idle speed screw to obtain specified rpm, manual transmission in Neutral and automatic in Drive.

NOTE: On 1969 models, turn the air conditioner either on or off according to the instructions on the tune-up decal.

3. Adjust one idle mixture screw to obtain the highest steady idle speed.
4. Adjust the idle speed screw to the speed specified on the tune-up decal.

NOTE: on models equipped with an idle solenoid, adjust the solenoid plunger hex to obtain 500 rpm on the L6 engine and 600 rpm on V8 engines. Disconnect the wire at the solenoid to de-energize it, allowing the throttle lever to contact the carburetor idle speed screw. Adjust the carburetor idle screw to obtain 400 rpm.

5. Adjust the mixture screw in to "lean roll" position, then back out (rich) 1/4 turn.
6. Repeat Steps 3, 4 and 5 for the other idle mixture screw for 2-BBL. and 4-BBL. engines.
7. Readjust the idle speed screw to obtain final specified rpm, if necessary.

1970 Chevrolet

Adjust with air cleaner installed.

If the vehicle is equipped with Evaporative Emission, disconnect the fuel tank line from the vapor canister while making the idle speed and mixture adjustments. Warm up the engine and leave it running with the choke and, if applicable, air cleaner damper door fully open and the air conditioning off.

250 Engine

1. Disconnect and plug the distributor vacuum hose at the distributor end.
2. Turn the idle mixture screw in until it lightly contacts the seat, back it out 4 turns.
3. Adjust the solenoid plunger to obtain 830 rpm (manual transmission in Neutral) or 630 rpm (automatic transmission in Drive).
4. Adjust mixture screw in to obtain 750 rpm (manual transmission in Neutral) or 600 rpm (automatic transmission in Drive).
5. Disconnect the solenoid wire and, with the solenoid plunger depressed, adjust the carburetor idle speed screw to obtain 400 rpm.
6. Reconnect the solenoid wire and distributor vacuum hose.

400 (265 H.P.) Engine

1. Disconnect and plug the distributor vacuum hose at the distributor end.
2. Turn the idle mixture screws in until they lightly contact the seats, then back them out 4 turns.
3. With manual transmission in Neutral, adjust the carburetor idle speed screw to obtain 800 rpm. With automatic transmission in Drive, adjust the solenoid plunger to obtain 630 rpm.
4. Adjust the idle mixture screws in equally to obtain 700 rpm (manual transmission in Neutral) or 600 rpm (automatic transmission in Drive).
5. If equipped with automatic transmission, disconnect the solenoid wire and, with solenoid plunger depressed, set the carburetor idle speed screw to obtain 450 rpm.
6. Reconnect the solenoid wire and the distributor vacuum hose.

350 (250 H.P.) Engine

1. Disconnect and plug the distributor vacuum hose at the distributor end.
2. Turn the idle mixture screws in until they lightly contact the seats, then back them out 4 turns.
3. With manual transmission in Neutral, adjust the solenoid plunger to obtain 830 rpm. With automatic transmission in Drive, adjust the solenoid plunger to obtain 630 rpm.
4. Adjust the idle mixture screws in equally to obtain 750 rpm (manual transmission in Neutral) or 600 rpm (automatic transmission in Drive).
5. Disconnect the solenoid wire and, with the solenoid plunger fully depressed, set the carburetor idle speed screw to obtain 450 rpm.
6. Reconnect the solenoid wire and distributor vacuum hose.

350 (300 H.P.) Engine

1. Disconnect the vacuum hose at the distributor and plug the hose.
2. Turn the idle mixture screws in until they lightly contact the seats, then back them out 4 turns.
3. With manual transmission in Neutral, adjust the carburetor idle speed screw to obtain 775 rpm. With automatic transmission in Drive, adjust the carburetor idle speed screw to obtain 630 rpm.
4. Adjust the mixture screws in equally to obtain 700 rpm (manual transmission in Neutral) or 600 rpm (automatic transmission in Drive).
5. Reconnect the distributor vacuum hose.

1970 Corvette

Adjust with air cleaner installed.

If the vehicle is equipped with Evaporative Emission, disconnect the fuel tank line from the vapor canister while making the idle speed and mixture adjustments. Warm up the engine and leave it running while adjusting. The choke valve and, if applicable, air cleaner damper door should remain open. Leave the air conditioning off.

350 (300, 350 and 370 H.P.) Engines

1. Adjust the idle mixture screws equally to obtain maximum idle speed.
2. On the 300 H.P. engine with manual transmission in Neutral adjust the idle speed screw to obtain 700 rpm. On the 300 H.P. engine with automatic transmission in Drive, adjust the idle speed screw to obtain 600 rpm.
3. On the 350 and 370 H.P. engines, adjust the idle speed screw to obtain 750 rpm with the manual transmission in Neutral.

454 (450 H.P.) Engine

1. *Remove the air cleaner.*
2. Disconnect the distributor vacuum hose at the distributor and plug the hose.

3. Adjust the mixture screws for maximum idle speed.
4. With manual transmission in Neutral, adjust the carburetor idle speed screw to obtain 750 rpm. With automatic transmission in Drive, adjust the carburetor idle speed screw to obtain 700 rpm.
5. Turn one idle mixture screw to obtain a 20 rpm drop in idle speed, then back the screw out ¼ turn. Repeat for the second idle mixture screw.
6. Repeat Step 4 above.
7. Reconnect the distributor vacuum hose and install the air cleaner.

454 (345 H.P.) and 454 (390 H.P.) Engines

1. Disconnect the distributor vacuum hose at the distributor and plug the hose.
2. Turn the idle mixture screws in they are lightly seated, then back them out 4 turns.
3. With automatic transmission in Drive, adjust the carburetor idle speed screw to obtain 630 rpm. Adjust the idle mixture screws in equally to obtain 600 rpm.
4. With manual transmission in Neutral, adjust the carburetor idle speed screw to obtain 700 rpm. Turn one of the mixture screws in until the engine speed drops to 400 rpm. Readjust the idle speed screw to obtain 700 rpm. Turn in the other mixture screw until the engine speed drops 40 rpm. Readjust the idle speed screw to obtain 700 rpm.
5. Reconnect the distributor vacuum hose.

All 1971—Initial Adjustments

Adjust with air cleaner installed.

The following initial idle adjustments are part of the normal engine tune-up. There is a tune-up decal placed conspicuously in the engine compartment outlining the specific procedure and settings for each engine application. Follow all of the instructions when adjusting the idle. These tuning procedures are necessary to obtain the delicate balance of variables for the maintenance of both reliable engine performance and efficient exhaust emission control.

NOTE: all engines except the 350 (330 H.P.) and 454 (425 H.P.) have limiter caps on the mixture adjusting screws. The idle mixture is preset and the limiter caps installed at the factory in order to meet emission control standards. Do not remove these limiter caps unless all other possible causes of poor idle condition have been thoroughly checked out. Procedures for setting the idle mixture with the limiter caps removed are described under the heading "Complete Adjustment" later on.

The solenoid used on 1971 carburetors is different from the one used on earlier models. Combination Emission Control System (C.E.C. solenoid) valve regulates distributor vacuum as a function of transmission gear position.

Caution The C.E.C. solenoid is adjusted only after: 1) replacement of the solenoid, 2) major carburetor overhaul, or 3) after the throttle body is removed or replaced.

Instructions for C.E.C. solenoid plunger adjustment are contained in the Unit Repair Section.

All initial adjustments described below are made:

1. With the engine warmed up and running.
2. With the choke fully open.
3. With the fuel tank line disconnected from the Evaporative Emission canister on all models except the Corvette.
4. With the fuel tank gas cap removed on the Corvette.
5. With the vacuum hose disconnected at the distributor and plugged.

Be sure to reconnect the distributor vacuum hose and to connect the fuel tank to evaporative emission canister line or install the gas cap when idle adjustments are complete.

250 6-Cylinder Engine

Adjust the carburetor idle speed screw (NOT the solenoid plunger) to obtain 550 rpm (manual transmission in Neutral) or 500 rpm (automatic transmission in Drive).

350 and 400 (2-BBL) and 350 (4-BBL Quadrajet) Engines

Adjust the carburetor idle speed screw (NOT the solenoid plunger) to obtain 600 rpm (manual transmission in Neutral with the air conditioner off) or 550 rpm (automatic transmission in Drive with the air conditioner on).

350 and 454 (4-BBL Holley) Engines —Corvette

1. Adjust the carburetor idle speed screw (NOT the solenoid plunger) to obtain 700 rpm (manual transmission in Neutral or automatic transmission in Drive).
2. Adjust the idle mixture screws alternately to obtain the maximum smooth idle speed.

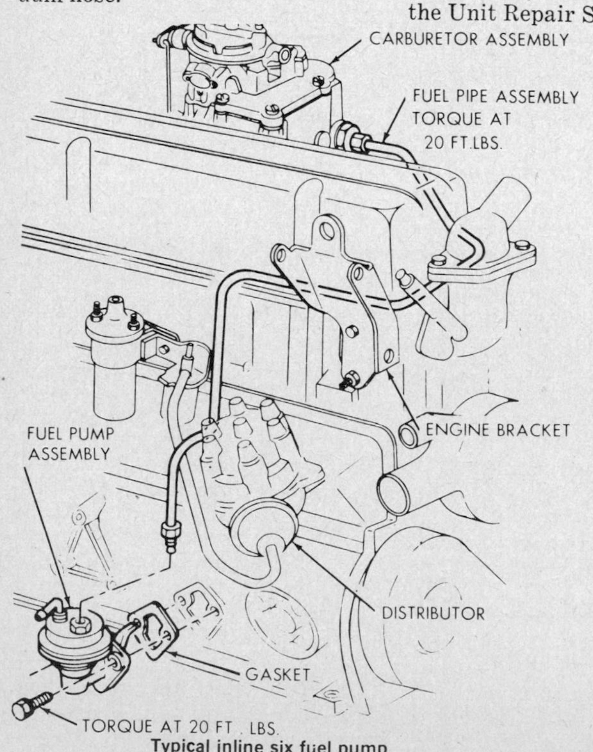

Typical inline six fuel pump
(© Chevrolet Div., G.M. Corp.)

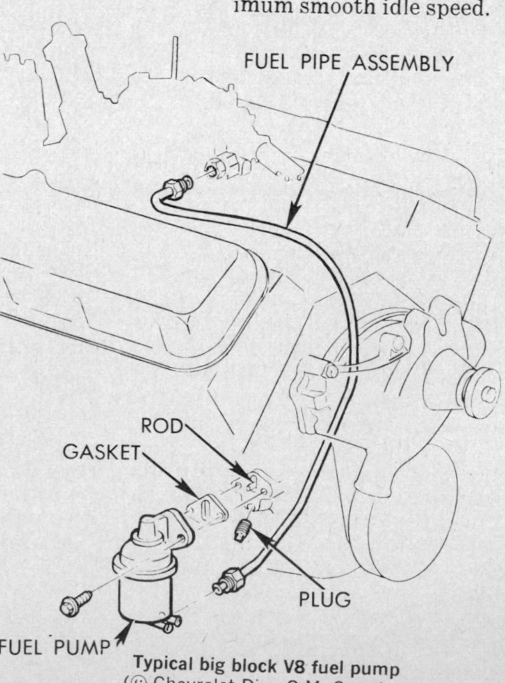

Typical big block V8 fuel pump
(© Chevrolet Div., G.M. Corp.)

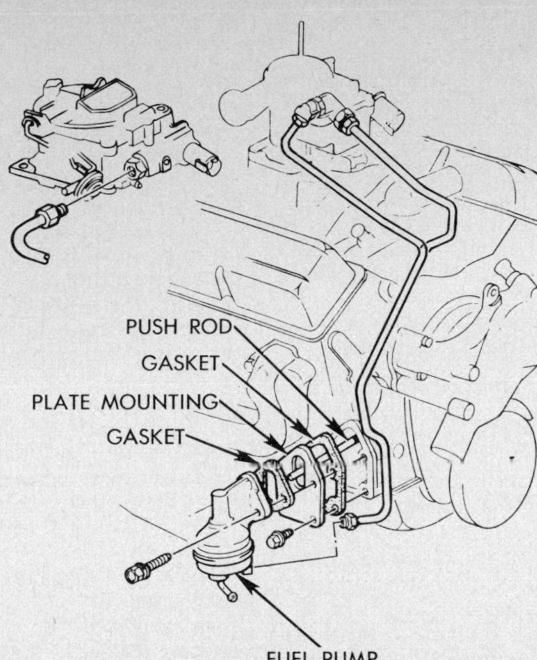

Typical small block V8 fuel pump installation
(© Chevrolet Div., G.M. Corp.)

3. Adjust one of the idle mixture screws to obtain a 20 rpm drop ("lean roll"), then back it out 1/4 turn.
4. Repeat Step 4 above for the other idle mixture screw.
5. Readjust the carburetor idle speed screw to obtain 700 rpm if necessary.

402 and 454 (4-BBL Quadrajet) Engines

Turn the air conditioner off. Adjust the carburetor idle speed screw (NOT the solenoid plunger) to obtain 600 rpm (manual transmission in Neutral or automatic transmission in Drive).

1972

NOTE: all carburetors are equipped with idle limiter caps and idle mixture is preset at the factory and should not require adjustment.

1. On Chevrolet models, disconnect the fuel tank line from the vapor storage canister. On Corvettes, remove the fuel filler cap but do not remove the vapor line.
2. Detach the distributor vacuum hose and plug the hose.
3. Set the parking brake and turn the air conditioner (if so equipped) off. On cars equipped with an automatic transmission, chock the wheels.
4. Allow the engine to reach normal operating temperature. Be sure that the choke is open.
5. If the car has an automatic transmission, set the selector in Drive. If the car has a manual transmission keep the transmission in Neutral.
6. Adjust the anti-dieseling solenoid to the *higher* of the two rpm figures given in the specifications.

Caution Do not turn the solenoid more than one complete turn unless the electrical lead is disconnected (solenoid de-energized).

7. Disconnect the solenoid lead and set the idle speed to the *lower* of the two figures given in the specifications. Use an allen wrench in the end of the solenoid for this adjustment, on six cylinder engines. On V8's use the normal idle speed adjusting screw.

NOTE: if no lower figure is given, adjust the idle to 450 rpm.

8. Reconnect all of the wires and hoses which were disconnected in order to perform these adjustments.

1973

All models are equipped with idle limiter caps and idle solenoids. Disconnect the fuel tank line from the evaporative canister. The engine must be running at operating temperature, choke off, parking brake on, and rear wheels blocked. Disconnect the distributor vacuum hose and plug it. After adjustment, reconnect the vacuum and evaporative hoses.

250 cu in. Six-Cylinder

Adjust the idle stop solenoid for 700 rpm on manual transmission models or 600 rpm on automatics. On manual models, make no attempt to adjust the CEC solenoid (the larger of the two carburetor solenoids) or a decrease in engine braking could result.

Two-barrel 350 and 400 cu in. V8s

1. With air conditioning switched off, adjust the idle stop solenoid screw for a speed of 900 rpm on manual models; 600 rpm on automatics.
2. De-energize the idle stop solenoid and adjust the idle speed screw (screw resting on lower step of the cam) for 400 rpm on 350 and 400 engines with automatic transmission, or 500 rpm on 350 engines with manual transmission.

Four-barrel 350 and 454 cu in. V8s

1. Adjust the idle stop solenoid screw for 900 rpm on manual, 600 rpm on automatic.
2. Connect the distributor vacuum hose and position the fast idle cam follower on the top step of the fast idle cam (turn air conditioning off) and adjust the fast idle to 1300 rpm on manual transmission 350 engines; 1600 on manual 454 engines and all automatics (in Park).

Optional Corvette 350 cu in. (L82) V8

1. Adjust the idle stop solenoid screw (air conditioning off) for a speed of 900 rpm on manual transmission; 700 rpm on automatic (in Drive).
2. Connect the distributor vacuum hose and position the fast idle cam follower on the top step of the cam (turn air conditioning off) and adjust the fast idle to 1300 rpm on manual; 1600 rpm on automatic.

1974

The same preconditions as for 1973 apply.

Two-barrel 350 and 400 cu in. V8s

1. Turn the air conditioning off. Adjust the idle stop solenoid screw for 900 rpm on manual; 600 rpm on automatic (in Drive).
2. De-energize the solenoid and adjust the carburetor idle cam screw (on low step of cam) for 400 rpm on automatic models (in Drive); 500 rpm on 350 engines with manual transmission.

Four-barrel 350 and 400 cu in. V8s

1. Turn the air conditioning off. Adjust the idle stop solenoid screw for 900 rpm on manual transmission models; 600 rpm on automatic (in Drive).
2. Connect the distributor vacuum hose. Position the fast idle cam follower on the top step of the fast idle cam and adjust the fast idle speed to 1300 rpm on manual; 1600 on automatic (in Park).

Optional Corvette 350 cu in. (L82) V8

1. Turn the air conditioning off. Adjust the idle stop solenoid for

900 rpm on manual; 700 rpm on automatic (in Drive).
2. Connect the distributor vacuum hose. Position the fast idle cam follower on the top step of the cam and adjust the fast idle to 1300 rpm on manual; 1600 rpm on automatic (in Park).

454 cu in. V8

1. Shut off the air conditioning. Adjust the idle stop solenoid screw for 800 rpm on manual; 600 rpm on automatic (in Drive).
2. Connect the distributor vacuum hose and position the fast idle cam follower on the top step of the cam and adjust the fast idle to 1600 rpm on manual; 1500 rpm on automatic (in Park).

1975

The same preconditions as 1974 apply.

Two-barrel

1. Turn the air conditioner off.
2. Adjust the idle speed to 600 rpm (check the idle speed given on the underhood tune-up decal and use that one if it differs) with the idle speed screw. No idle speed solenoid is used on the 1975 two-barrel carburetor.

Four-barrel

1. Turn the air conditioning off.
2. Disconnect the idle speed solenoid. Turn the idle speed screw to adjust for the lower of the two idle speeds specified on the underhood tune-up decal. Adjust automatic transmission cars in Drive with wheels blocked; manual transmission cars in neutral.
3. Connect the idle speed solenoid. Open the throttle to extend the solenoid plunger.
4. Use the soleoid plunger to adjust the idle speed to the higher of the two speeds on the underhood tune-up decal.

COOLING SYSTEM

Chevrolet engine cooling systems function at high pressure for increased cooling efficiency. The radiator cap has a pressure and vacuum relief valve.

Cooling system capacities for the various models can be found in the Capacities table at the beginning of this section. Information on the water temperature gauge can be found in the Unit Repair Section.

Radiator R & R

Chevrolet

1. Drain the cooling system.
2. Disconnect the radiator upper and lower hoses and, if applicable, transmission coolant lines. Remove the coolant recovery system line, if so equipped.
3. Remove the radiator upper panel if so equipped.
4. If there is a radiator shroud in front of the radiator, the radiator and shrould are removed as an assembly.
5. If there is a fan shroud, remove the shroud attaching screws let the shroud hang on the fan.
6. Remove the radiator attaching bolts and remove the radiator.
7. Installation is the reverse of the removal procedure.

1969-74 Corvette

1. Drain the radiator.
2. Raise the hood and insert a bolt in the hole of the hood support. Remove the hood.
3. Remove the radiator inlet and outlet hoses and, if applicable, the transmission coolant hoses.
4. If applicable, remove the supply tank hose at the radiator connection.
5. Remove the shroud to radiator support bracket screws (the L88 engine does not have a fan shroud).
6. Remove the shroud to radiator baffle bracket screws and let the shroud rest on the fan.
7. Remove the radiator upper support bracket screws and carefully lift the radiator from the car.
8. Install in the reverse order of removal.

1975-76 Corvette

1. Drain the radiator and disconnect the battery ground cable. Disconnect cooler lines on automatic transmission models.
2. Remove the hood. This is a two man job.
3. Remove the radiator support brackets attached to the fan shroud.
4. Remove the two front hood hinge bolts.
5. From inside the wheel well, remove the six radiator side support bolts.
6. Remove the two bottom radiator support bolts and the center brace.
7. Pull the radiator support forward and use a clamp to retain it to the right hood hinge.
8. Disconnect the two radiator hoses and the overflow hose.
9. Carefully lift the radiator out of the car.
10. If replacing the radiator, remove the shrouds and mount them on the new unit.
11. Installation is the reverse of removal.

Water Pump R & R

1. Drain the radiator and loosen the fan pulley bolts.
2. Disconnect the heater hose, lower radiator hose and, if applicable, the bypass hose at the water pump.
3. On V8 engines, remove the Delcotron upper brace. Loosen the swivel bolt and remove the fan belt.
4. On Mark IV engines, disconnect the power steering and air conditioning belts and swivel the power steering pump to one side.
5. Remove the fan blade and pulley. Replace a bent or damaged fan.

NOTE: thermostatic fan clutches must be kept in an "in-car" position. When removed from the car the assembly should be supported so that the clutch disc remains in a vertical plane to prevent silicone fluid leakage.

6. Remove the water pump attaching bolts and, if applicable, the power steering-to-pump bolts and remove the pump and gasket.

NOTE: on six-cylinder engines, pull the pump straight out of the block first to avoid damage to the impeller.

7. Install the pump assembly using a new gasket. Coat the gasket on both sides with sealer. Tighten the 5/16 in. bolts to 15 ft. lbs. (six-cylinder) and the ⅜ in. bolts (V8) to 30 ft. lbs.
8. Install the pulley and fan.
9. On Mark IV engines, install the power steering and air conditioning bolts.
10. Connect the hoses and fill the cooling system.
11. On V8 engines, install the Delcotron upper brace and fan belt. Install the power steering pump bolt.
12. Adjust the belts, then start the engine and check for leaks.

Thermostat R & R

The thermostat is located inside a housing on the front of the cylinder head on six-cylinder engines and between the intake manifold and the cylinder head (forward) on V8 engines. It is not necessary to remove the radiator hose from the thermostat housing.

1. Remove the two retaining bolts from the thermostat housing and lift up the housing with the hose attached. Remove the thermostat.
2. Insert the new thermostat, spring end down, and install the housing with a new gasket.

EMISSION CONTROLS

Positive Crankcase Ventilation

In this system, crankcase vapors are drawn into the intake manifold and burned as part of the engine combustion. The "closed positive" system draws clean air from the carburetor air cleaner. The ventilation flow is regulated by a PCV valve located in the valve cover.

Air Injection Reactor

The A.I.R. system injects compressed air into the exhaust system, close enough to the exhaust valves to continue the burning of the normally unburned segment of the exhaust gases. To do this it employs an air injection pump and a system of hoses, valves, tubes, etc., necessary to carry the compressed air from the pump to the exhaust manifolds. Carburetors and distributors for A.I.R. engines have specific modifications to adapt them to the air injection system; these components should not be interchanged with those intended for use on engines that do not have the system.

A diverter valve is used to prevent backfiring. The valve senses sudden increases in manifold vacuum and ceases the injection of air during fuel-rich periods. During coasting, this valve diverts the entire air flow through the muffler and during high engines speeds, expels it through a relief valve. Check valves in the system prevent exhaust gases from entering the pump.

On models with catalytic converters, it is not necessary to inject the air close to the exhaust valves. For this reason, not all models are equipped with manifolds on the exhaust manifolds for air injection as in previous years. Instead, one large pipe is used to inject air into the exhaust pipe ahead of the converter. Some models use part of the old system, but utilize only two or three of the injection nozzles on the exhaust manifold.

Air Pump R & R

1. Disconnect the air hoses at the pump.
2. Hold the pump pulley from turning and loosen the pulley bolts.
3. Loosen the pump mounting bolt and adjustment bracket bolt. Remove the drive belt.
4. Remove the mounting bolts and then remove the pump.
5. Install the pump using a reverse of the removal procedure.

Controlled Combustion System

This system increases combustion efficiency by means of leaner carburetor mixtures and revised distributor calibration. On most installations, thermostatically controlled air cleaner intakes draw warm air from an exhaust manifold shroud. This allows leaner carburetor settings and improves engine warm-up. A higher temperature thermostat is employed on C.C.S. cars.

Particular attention must be paid to the tuning of C.C.S. equipped engines to maintain performance and efficient exhaust emission control.

Evaporative Emission Control

Introduced on California cars in 1970, and nationwide in 1971, this system reduces the amount of escaping gasoline vapors. Float bowl emissions are controlled by internal carburetor modifications. Redesigned bowl vents, reduced bowl capacity, heat shields, and improved intake manifold - to - carburetor insulation serve to reduce vapor loss into the atmosphere. The venting of fuel tank vapors into the air has been stopped. Fuel vapors are now directed through lines to a canister containing an activated charcoal filter. Unburned vapors are trapped here until the engine is started. When the engine is running, the canister is purged by air drawn in by manifold vacuum. The air and fuel vapors are then directed into the engine to be burned. This system is designed to reduce fuel vapor emission. The canister filter should be replaced every 12 months or 12,000 miles. To replace the filter, proceed as follows:

The filter is located in the bottom of the canister. Pull out the old filter and work the new filter into place. It may be necessary, on earlier models, to remove the bottom of the canister for access.

Anti-Dieseling Solenoid

Some models may have an idle speed solenoid on the carburetor. All 1972-74 models have idle solenoids. Due to the leaner carburetor settings required for emission control, the engine may have a tendency to "diesel" or "run-on" after the ignition is turned off. The carburetor solenoid, energized when the ignition is on, maintains the normal idle speed. When the ignition is turned off, the solenoid is de-energized and permits the throttle valves to fully close, thus preventing run-on. For adjustment of carburetors with idle solenoids see Carburetor Adjustments.

Transmission Controlled Spark

Introduced in 1970, this system controls exhaust emissions by eliminating vacuum advance in the lower forward gears.

1970

The 1970 system consists of a transmission switch, solenoid vacuum switch, time delay relay, and a thermostatic water temperature switch. The solenoid vacuum switch is energized in the lower gears via the transmission switch and closes off distributor vacuum. The two-way transmission switch is activated by the shifter shaft on manual transmissions, and by oil pressure on automatic transmissions. The switch de-energizes the solenoid in high gear, the plunger extends and uncovers the vacuum port, and the distributor receives full vacuum. The temperature switch overrides the system when engine temperature is below 63° or above 232°. This allows vacuum advance in all gears. A time delay relay opens 15 seconds after the ignition is switched on. Full vacuum advance during this delay eliminates the possibility of stalling.

1971

The 1971 system is similar, except that the vacuum solenoid (now called a Combination Emissions Control solenoid) serves two functions. One function is to control distributor vacuum; the added function is to act as a deceleration throttle stop in high gear. This cuts down on emissions when the vehicle is coming to a stop in high gear. The CEC solenoid is controlled by a temperature switch, a transmission switch, and a 20 second time delay relay. This system also contains a reversing relay, which energizes the solenoid when the transmission switch, temperature switch or time delay completes the CEC circuit to ground. This system is directly opposite the 1970 system in operation. The 1970 vacuum solenoid was normally open to allow vacuum advance and when energized, closed to block vacuum. The 1971 system is normally closed blocking vacuum advance and when energized, opens to allow vacuum advance. The temperature switch completes the CEC circuit to ground when engine temperature is below 82°. Some Camaros and Corvettes also have a high temperature terminal on the switch to complete the CEC circuit when coolant temperature reaches 232°. The time delay relay allows vacuum advance (and raised idle speed) for 20 seconds after the ignition key is turned to the "on" position. Models with an automatic transmission and air conditioning also have a solid state timing device which engages the air conditioning compressor for three seconds after the ignition key is turned to the "off" position to prevent the engine from running-on. Two throttle settings are necessary; one for curb idle and one for emission control on coast. Both settings are described in the tune-up section.

1972-74

The 1972-73 L6 system is similar to that used in 1971, except that an idle stop solenoid has been added to the system. In the energized position, the solenoid maintains engine speed at a predetermined fast idle. When de-energized the solenoid allows the throttle plates to close beyond the normal idle position; thus cutting off the air supply and preventing engine run-on. The L6 is the only 1972-74 engine with a CEC valve, which serves the same deceleration function as in 1971. The 1972 time delay relay delays full vacuum 20 seconds after the transmission is shifted into high gear. On 1973-74 models, the delay relay is replaced by a time relay which energizes the CEC valve for 20 seconds after the key is turned to the On position. This relay is not used on 1973 V8 engines with small blocks. V8 engines use a vacuum advance solenoid similar to that used in 1970. This relay is normally closed to block vacuum and opens when energized to allow vacuum advance. The solenoid controls distributor vacuum advance and performs no throttle positioning function. The idle stop solenoid used operates in the same manner as the one on L6 engines. All air-conditioned cars have an additional anti-diesel (run-on) solenoid which engages the compressor clutch for three seconds after the ignition is switched off. The 1973-74 Chevrolet TCS system differs from the 1972 system in three ways.

The 23 second upshift delay has been replaced by a 20 second starting relay. This relay closes to complete the TCS circuit and open the TCS solenoid, allowing vacuum advance, for 20 seconds after the key is turned to the "on" position. The operating temperature of the temperature override switch has been raised to 93°, and the switch that was used to engage the A/C compressor when the key was turned "off" has been eliminated. All models are equipped with an electric throttle control solenoid to prevent run-on. The 1973 TCS system is used on all full-size station wagons equipped with a 165 hp 350 or a 170 hp 400. The 1974 TCS system is used only on manual transmission models. System components remain unchanged from 1973. The vacuum advance solenoid is located on the coil bracket.

1973-74 Corvette models are equipped with a Thermo-Override system instead of the normal TCS system. This system consists of a three-position temperature switch, which is mounted in the right cylinder head and a two-position vacuum advance solenoid. Three vacuum lines are connected to the solenoid, a ported vacuum line from the carburetor, a vacuum line from the intake manifold, and a vacuum line that runs to the distributor vacuum advance unit. When the engine temperature is between 93°F and 232°F, the temperature switch contacts are open and the vacuum solenoid is de-energized. This causes carburetor-ported vacuum to control the operation of the distributor vacuum advance unit. When the engine temperature is below 93°F or above 232°F, the temperature switch contacts are closed and the vacuum solenoid is energized. This moves the plunger in the solenoid to block the ported vacuum opening and connect manifold vacuum to the distributor. When the engine reaches normal temperature, the temperature switch contacts open and ported vacuum is restored to the distributor.

For diagnosis procedures, see the Unit Repair Section. Any of the methods of exhaust emission control requires close and frequent attention to tune-up factors of engine maintenance. TCS is not used on 1975 models.

Exhaust Gas Recirculation

All 1973-75 engines are equipped with exhaust gas recirculation (EGR). This system consists of a metering valve, a vacuum line to the carburetor, and cast-in exhaust gas passages in the intake manifold. The EGR valve is controlled by carburetor vacuum, and accordingly opens and closes to admit exhaust gases into the fuel/air mixture. The exhaust gases lower the combustion temperature, and reduce the amount of oxides of nitrogen (NO_x) produced. The valve is closed at idle and wide open throttle, but is open between the two extreme throttle positions.

As the car accelerates, the carburetor throttle plate uncovers the vacuum port for the EGR valve. At 3–5 in. Hg, the EGR valve opens and then some of the exhaust gases are allowed to flow into the air/fuel mixture to lower the combustion temperature. At full-throttle the valve closes again.

400 cu. in. California engines are equipped with a dual diaphragm EGR valve. This valve further limits the exhaust gas opening (compared to the single diaphragm EGR valve) during high intake manifold vacuum periods, such as high-speed cruising, and provides more exhaust gas recirculation during acceleration when manifold vacuum is low. In addition to the hose running to the thermal vacuum switch, a second hose is connected directly to the intake manifold.

EGR Valve R & R

1. Detach the vacuum line from the EGR valve.
2. Unfasten the two bolts which attach the valve to the manifold. Withdraw the valve.

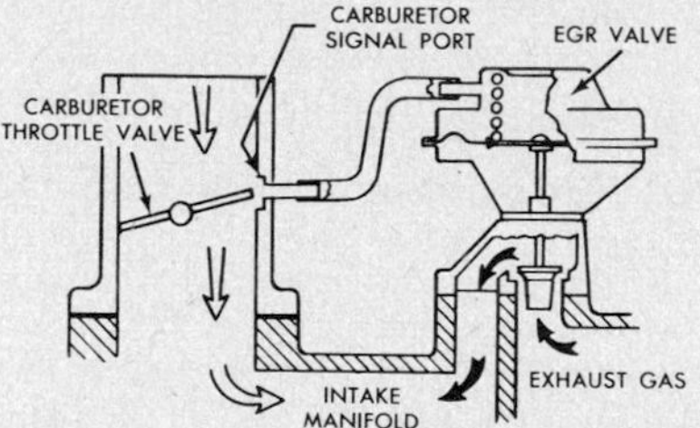

EGR system schematic
(© Chevrolet Div., G.M. Corp)

3. Installation is the reverse of removal. Always use a new gasket between the valve and the manifold.

Early Fuel Evaporation System

1975 models are equipped with this system to reduce engine warm-up time, improve driveability, and reduce emissions. On start-up, a vacuum motor acts to close a heat valve in the exhaust manifold which causes exhaust gases to enter the intake mani-

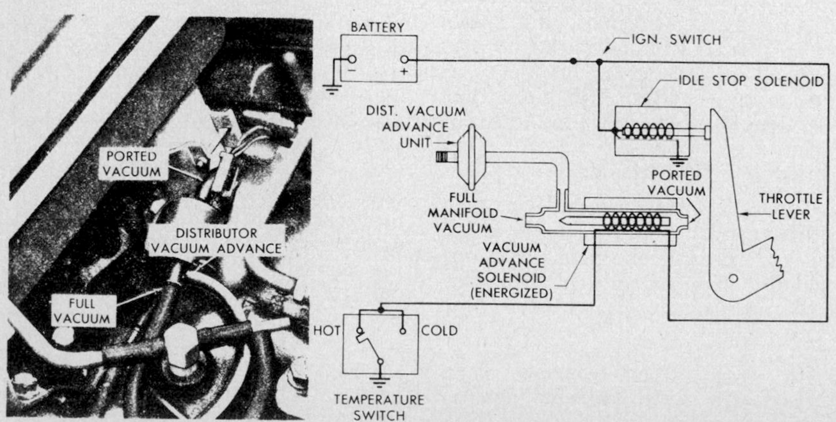

1973-74 Corvette Thermo-Override System (© Chevrolet Div., G.M. Corp)

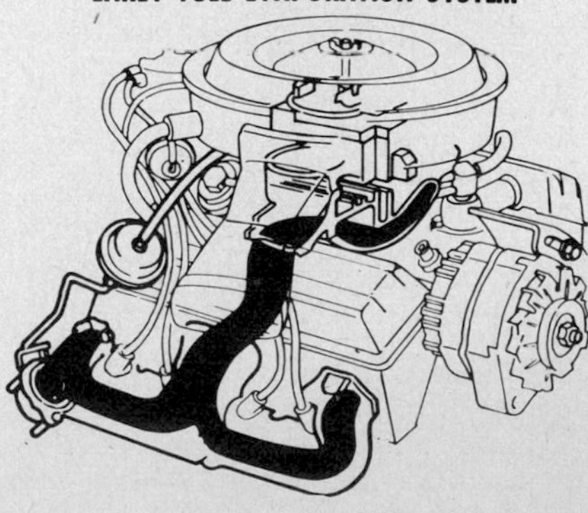

fold heat riser passages. Incoming fuel mixture is then heated and more complete fuel evaporation is provided during warm-up.

Catalytic Converter

Some Federal and all California models are equipped with a catalytic converter. The converter is located midway in the exhaust system. Stainless steel exhaust pipes are used ahead of the converter. The converter is stainless steel with an aluminized steel cover and a ceramic felt blanket to insulate the converter from the floorpan. The catalyst pellet bed inside the converter consists of noble metals which cause a reaction that converts hydrocarbons and carbon monoxide into water and carbon dioxide.

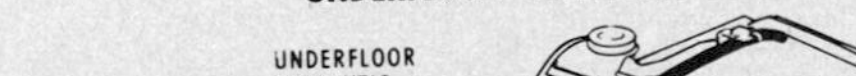
UNDERFLOOR CATALYTIC CONVERTER

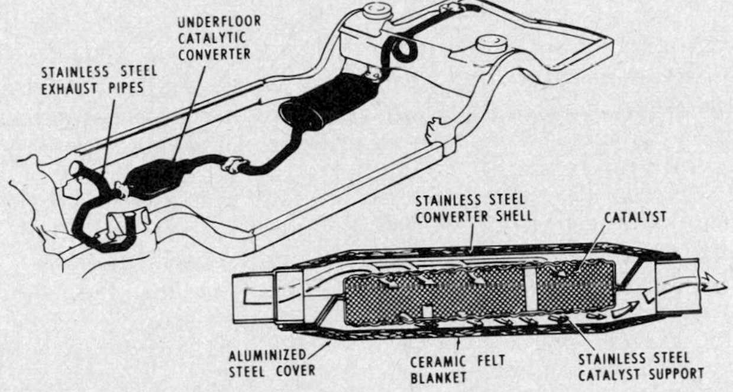

ENGINE

Engine application and specification tables may be found at the beginning of this section.

The following service procedures apply to all engines, except where differences are specified. The 396, 402, 427 and 454 V8 (Mark IV large blocks) are essentially the same engine. Similarly, the 327, 350, and 400 small block series engines all utilize the same design. The big block 402 was last offered in 1972. The small block 400 was offered in 1974 in both two and four-barrel form.

Engine R & R

Chevrolet

1. Remove the hood. Scribe lines around the hinges so that the hood can be installed in its original location.
2. Remove the air cleaner.
3. Disconnect the battery cables at the battery.
4. Remove the radiator and shroud.
5. Remove the fan blade and pulley.
6. Disconnect wires at:
    a. C.E.C. solenoid.
    b. Coil.
    c. Temperature switch.
    d. Delcotron.
    e. Starter solenoid.
    f. Oil pressure sending unit.
7. Disconnect:
    a. Accelerator linkage at the pedal.
    b. Oil pressure gauge line, if so equipped.
    c. Exhaust pipes at the manifold flanges.
    d. Engine cooler lines, if so equipped.
    e. Vacuum line to the power brake unit, if so equipped.
    f. Fuel line (front tank) at the fuel pump.
8. Remove the power steering pump, leaving the hoses attached to the pump.
9. Raise the car on a hoist.
10. Drain the cooling system and the crankcase.
11. Remove the driveshaft.

NOTE: if a plug for the driveshaft opening in the transmission is not available, drain the transmission.

12. Disconnect:
    a. Shift linkage at the transmission.
    b. Speedometer cable at the transmission.
    c. Transmission cooler lines, if so equipped.
    d. TCS switch at the transmission.
13. On vehicles with synchromesh transmissions, disconnect the clutch linkage at the cross-shaft then remove the cross-shaft at the frame bracket.
14. Lower the vehicle and remove the rocker arm covers and install engine lifting adapter on the cylinder heads.
15. Raise the engine enough to take the weight off the front mounts, then remove the front mount through bolts.
16. Remove the rear mount to crossmember bolts.
17. Raise the engine enough to take the weight off the rear mount, then remove the crossmember.

NOTE: on Chevrolets it is necessary to remove the mount from the transmission before the crossmember can be removed.

18. Remove the engine/transmission assembly as a unit.
19. To remove the clutch and transmission from the engine:
    a. Remove the clutch housing cover plate screws.
    b. Remove the clutch housing to engine attaching bolts, then, remove the transmission and clutch housing as a unit.

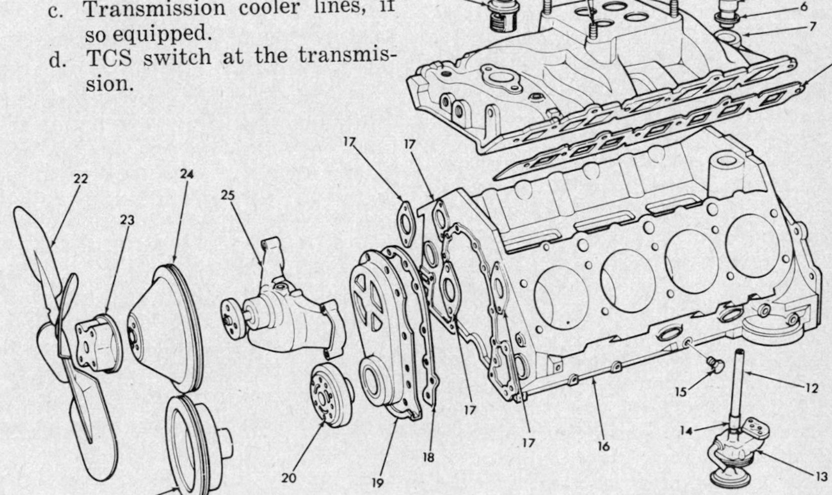

Mark IV (big block) exploded view (© Chevrolet Div., G.M. Corp)

1 Cap nipple
2 Rotor
3 Spring clip
4 Distributor
5 Distributor gear
6 Gasket
7 Intake manifold
8 Gasket
12 Oil pump shaft
13 Oil pump
14 Sleeve
15 Drain plug
16 Cylinder block
17 Gasket
18 Gasket
19 Timing cover
20 Damper
21 Pulley
22 Fan
23 Spacer
24 Pulley
25 Water pump
26 Thermostat
27 Water neck
28 Carburetor stud
29 Gasket
30 Shaft
31 Vacuum unit
32 Distributor cap

Caution Do not let the weight of the transmission hang on the spline because the clutch disc may be easily damaged.

c. Remove the starter and clutch housing rear cover plate.
d. Loosen the clutch mounting bolts one turn at a time (to prevent distortion of the clutch cover) until the spring pressure is released. Remove all the bolts, clutch disc and pressure plate assembly.

20. To remove the automatic transmission:
    a. Remove the starter and the converter housing underpan.
    b. Remove the flywheel to converter attaching bolts.
    c. Supporting both the engine and transmission, remove the transmission to engine mounting bolts.
    d. Slowly guide the engine from the transmission.

Corvette

This procedure is basically the same for all engines regardless of size and model year. Certain pieces of optional equipment require minor specific changes but the overall operation remains the same.

1. The engine may be removed separately from the transmission, through the top of the engine compartment. Begin by draining the cooling system and the engine crankcase.
2. Disconnect the battery cables from the battery terminals and remove the air cleaner and ignition shields. Cover the carburetor.
3. Disconnect wiring at the alternator, temperature sending unit, oil pressure switch, primary coil lead, and CEC solenoid when applicable. Also disconnect the engine ground wires and the accelerator rod at the bellcrank.
4. Disconnect the power brake hose at the manifold end when applicable. Disconnect the tachometer drive cable at the distributor and the throttle valve if so equipped. Scribe the hood hinge locations on the support brackets and remove the hood.
5. Remove the radiator shroud and radiator, then the fan and fan assembly. If the car is equipped with power steering, remove the pump mounting bolts and push the pump into the vacant radiator opening. An alternate method is to disconnect the pump lines and plug both ends.
6. Remove the heater hose from the clip at the alternator bracket, then disconnect the hose from the engine connections and move back for extra clearance. Remove the rocker arm covers and place the vehicle on jack stands.
7. Remove the center head bolt on each head, and install the lift tool to the engine. Unhook the distributor cap and move it forward. Cover the distributor with a clean cloth.
8. Disconnect the exhaust pipes at the manifold flanges. On cars equipped with large block engines, the front stud on each manifold must be removed before the exhaust pipes can be removed.
9. Disconnect the wire leads at the starter solenoid. Remove the gas tank line at the fuel pump and plug the line to prevent fuel siphoning.
10. Block the clutch pedal in the return position and remove the clutch cross-shaft. Remove the oil filter and oil cooler lines if so equipped. Remove the starting motor. If the Corvette is equipped with a manual transmission, remove the flywheel cover plate. If equiped with an automatic transmission, remove the converter underpan.
11. Remove the front engine mount thru-bolts. Support the transmission with a floor jack and remove the transmission-to-engine bolts. If the car has an automatic transmission, remove the converter-to-flywheel bolts and install the converter holding bracket to the transmission.
12. Move the engine forward and upward as needed to clear the engine compartment.
13. Replacement is the reversal of this procedure.

Manifolds

Combination Manifold Used on 6 Cylinder Engines

All Chevrolet six cylinder engines are equipped with a combination intake and exhaust manifold. The exhaust manifold is equipped with a heat riser valve which, when the engine is cold, deflects the hot exhaust gases against the intake manifold to assist in rapid warm up.

If the engine doesn't seem to warm up properly or, when operated at a high speed, acts lean, it is a good idea to check this heat riser valve to be certain that it is functioning freely. Failure of the heat riser valve to open will increase the time required to warm the engine. Failure of the heat riser valve to close after the manifold is hot will cause the engine to run lean.

To remove the manifold assembly, disconnect the exhaust pipe flange and remove all connections to the carburetor. Take off the vacuum lines at the manifold and at the carburetor.

Remove the carburetor, and the manifold may be unbolted from the side of the cylinder head using socket wrenches and box wrenches. If necessary to remove either exhaust or intake manifolds they may be separated by removing one bolt and two nuts at center of assembly.

Before reinstalling the manifold, thoroughly clean all mating surfaces.

Intake Manifold R & R—V8

1. Remove the air cleaner.
2. Drain the radiator.
3. Disconnect:
    a. Battery cables at the battery.
    b. Upper radiator and heater hoses at the manifold.
    c. Crankcase ventilation hoses as required.
    d. Fuel line at the carburetor.
    e. Accelerator linkage at the pedal lever.
    f. Vacuum hose at the distributor.
    g. Power brake hose at the carburetor base or manifold, if applicable.
    h. Ignition coil and temperature sending switch wires.
4. Remove the distributor cap and scribe the rotor position relative to distributor body.
5. Remove the distributor.
6. If applicable, remove the Delcotron upper bracket.
7. Remove the manifold to head attaching bolts, then remove the manifold and carburetor as an assembly.
8. If the manifold is to be replaced, transfer the carburetor (and mounting studs), water outlet and thermostat (use a new gasket), heater hose adapter and, if applicable, the choke coil and EGR valve with its vacuum line.
9. Before installing the manifold, thoroughly clean the gasket and seal surfaces of the cylinder heads and manifold.
10. Install the manifold end seals, folding the tabs if applicable, and the manifold/head gaskets, using a sealing compound around

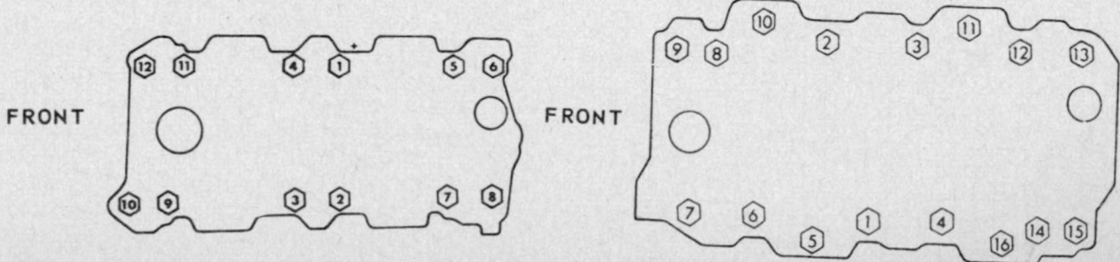

Intake manifold tightening sequence (left—small block V8; right—Mk. IV (big block) V8)
(© Chevrolet Div., G.M. Corp)

the water passages. Make sure the gaskets are firmly cemented in place before installing the manifold.

11. When installing the manifold, care should be taken not to dislocate the end seals. It is helpful to use a pilot in the distributor opening. Tighten the manifold bolts to 30 ft. lbs. in the sequence illustrated.
12. Install the ignition coil.
13. Install the distributor with the rotor in its original location as indicated by the scribe line. If the engine has been disturbed, refer to "Distributor R&R" above.
14. If applicable, install the Delcotron upper bracket and adjust the belt tension.
15. Connect all components disconnected in Step 3 above.
16. Fill the cooling system, start the engine, check for leaks and adjust the ignition timing and carburetor idle speed and mixture.

Exhaust Manifold R & R—V8

1. If equipped with A.I.R., remove the air injector manifold assembly. The ¼ in. pipe threads in the manifold are straight threads. Do not use a ¼ in. tapered pipe tap.
2. Disconnect the battery.
3. If applicable, remove the air cleaner pre-heater shroud.
4. Remove the exhaust pipe flange nuts, then hang the pipe with wire.
5. Remove the manifold mounting bolts (end bolts first), then remove the manifold.
6. To install, clean the mating surfaces, then install the manifold with the center bolts first. Install the end bolts, then tighten all bolts to 20 ft. lbs.
7. To complete installation, reverse Steps 1 through 3.

Valve System

Valve tappet clearances are listed in the Tune-Up Specifications table. Complete valve specifications are found in the Valve Specifications table.

Valve Guides

Valve guides are integral with the cylinder head. Valve guide bores may be reamed to accommodate oversize valve stems or the guides may be knurled (if wear permits) to allow the retention of standard size valves. Maximum allowable valve stem to guide bore clearance is .0027 in.

Valve Replacement

With cylinder head on bench and the rockers removed, compress the valve spring and remove the valve lock, seal, spring cap and spring.

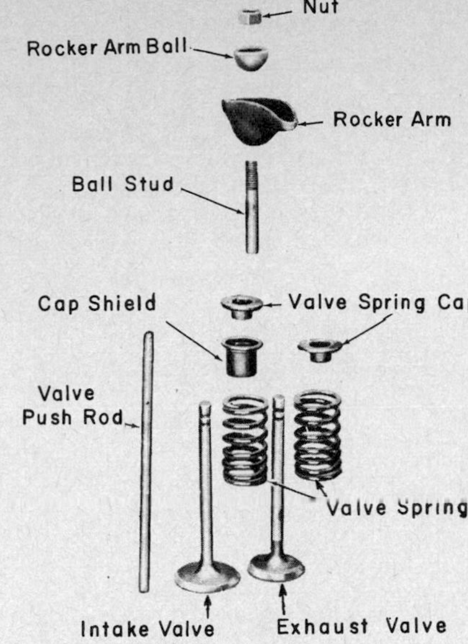

V8 engine valve system
(© Chevrolet Div., G.M. Corp)

Line the valve springs up on a flat surface. All should be the same height. Replace those that do not match with new.

Rocker Arm R & R

Rocker arms are removed by removing the adjusting nut. Be sure to adjust valve lash after replacing rocker arms.

NOTE: when replacing an exhaust rocker, move an old intake rocker to the exhaust rocker arm stud and install the new rocker arm on the intake stud.

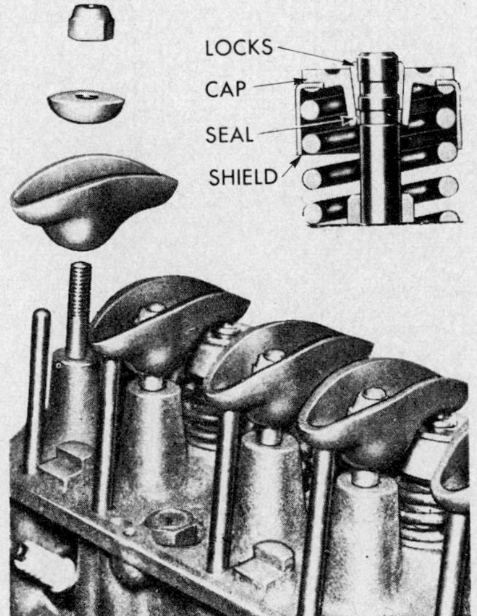

6-cylinder head and rocker arm assembly, 250 cu. in. engine
(© Chevrolet Div., G.M. Corp)

Rocker arm studs that have damaged threads or are loose in the cylinder heads may be replaced with new studs available in 0.003 in. and 0.013 in. oversize or the bores may be tapped and screw-in replacement studs used. Do not attempt to install an oversize stud without reaming the stud bore. Studs are press-fit. Mark IV and late high-performance small-block engines use screw-in studs and pushrod guide plates.

NOTE: if engine is equipped with the A.I.R. exhaust emission control system, the interfering components of the system must be removed. Disconnect the lines at the air injection nozzles in the exhaust manifolds.

Valve Tappet Adjustment

Hydraulic Lifters

On six-cylinder engines, crank the engine until the distributor rotor points to the No. 1 firing position and the breaker points are just opening. The following valves may be adjusted:

No. 1	exhaust	intake
No. 2		intake
No. 3	exhaust	
No. 4		intake
No. 5	exhaust	

To adjust the rest of the valves, crank the engine until the distributor rotor points to the No. 6 firing position and the breaker points are just opening. The following valves may be adjusted:

No. 2	exhaust	
No. 3		intake
No. 4	exhaust	
No. 5		intake
No. 6	exhaust	intake

On V8 engines, crank the engine until the No. 1 piston is at TDC of its compression stroke (the compression can be felt by placing a finger over the spark plug hole or by feeling the valves as the timing mark passes "0"—if the valves don't move, the No. 1 piston is at the top of its compression stroke). With the crankshaft in this position the following valves may be adjusted:

Exhaust—1, 3, 4, 8
Intake—1, 2, 5, 7

Rotate the crankshaft one full revolution until the timing pointer is again aligned with the "0". With the crankshaft thus in No. 6 cylinder firing position, the following valves may be adjusted:

Exhaust—2, 5, 6, 7
Intake—3, 4, 6, 8

Adjustment is made by backing off

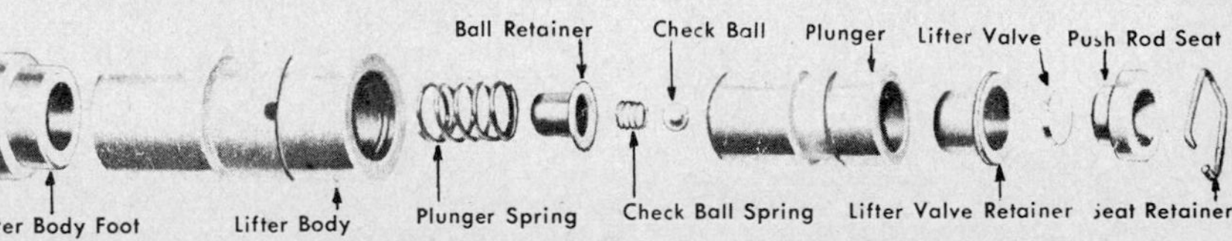

Typical hydraulic lifter exploded (© Chevrolet Div., G.M. Corp)

the rocker arm adjusting nut until there is play in the pushrod. Tighten the nut to remove the pushrod clearance (this can be felt by rotating the pushrod with the fingers while tightening the adjusting nut). When the pushrod cannot be freely turned, tighten the nut one additional turn to place the hydraulic lifter in the center of its travel. No further adjustment is required.

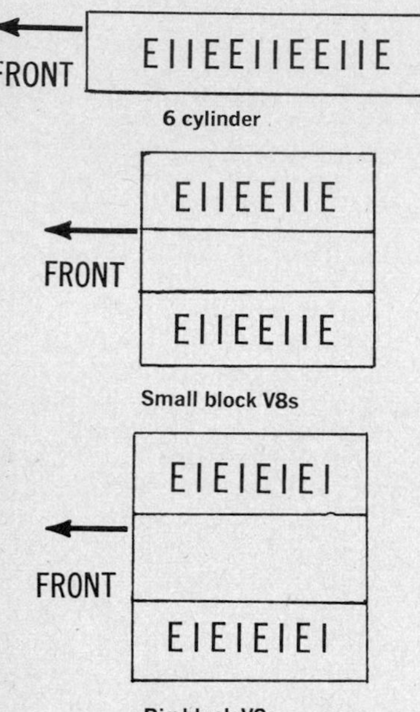

6 cylinder

Small block V8s

Big block V8s

Mechanical Lifters

Position the crankshaft for No. 1, then No. 6 cylinder firing positions as described for adjusting hydraulic lifters above. In the case of mechanical lifters, however, use a feeler gauge between the rocker arm and the valve stem to obtain the correct clearance. The final valve lash setting is made with the engine running at normal operating temperature. Specified valve lash (hot) can be found in the Tune-Up Specifications at the beginning of this section.

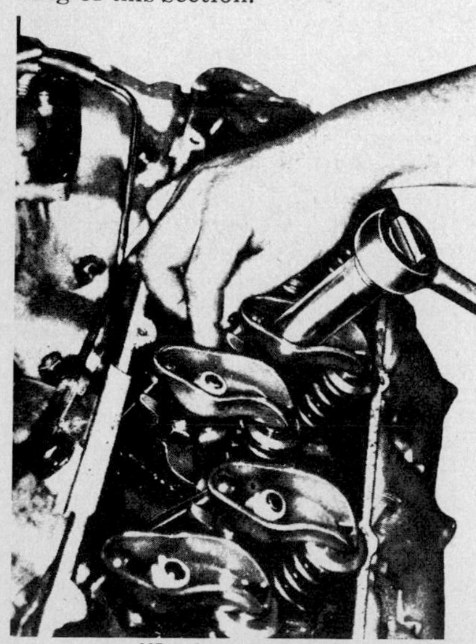

V8 valve adjustment
(© Chevrolet Div., G.M. Corp)

Cylinder Head

R & R

6 Cylinder Models

To remove the cylinder head, detach the air cleaner and all rods, lines and vacuum tubes at the carburetor and manifold.

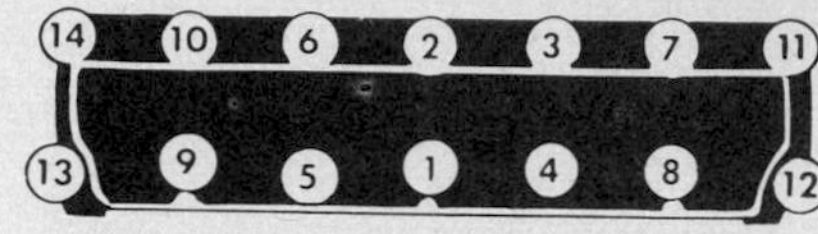

OHV 6 cylinder

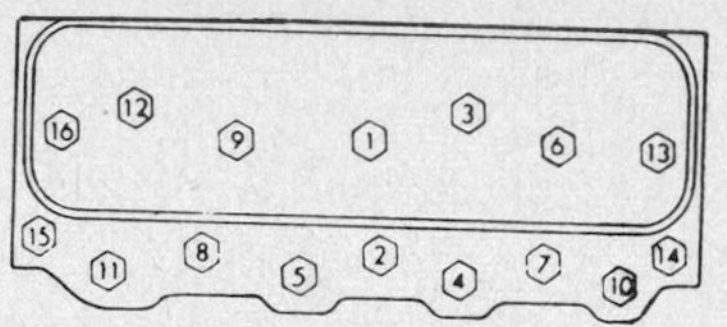

V8—327, 350, and 400

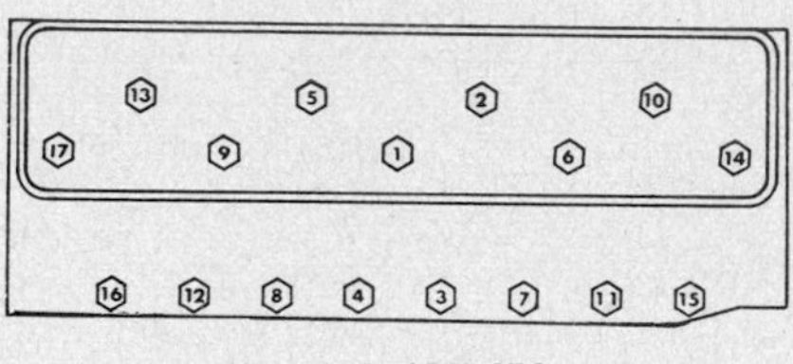

V8—402, 427, 454

NOTE: if the engine is equipped with an exhaust emission control system, the injector connections must be disconnected at the cylinder head. Disconnect any interfering components and tie back out of the way.

When installing, do not use sealer on the composition steel asbestos gasket. Coat the threads of the head bolts with sealing compound before installation. Tighten the head bolts in sequence (see the illustration at the beginning of this section) a little at a time until each is torqued to 95 ft. lbs. Install all components which were removed. Adjust the valve mechanism as described later.

Caution The 1/4 in. pipe threads at the cylinder head air injection nozzles are a straight pipe thread. Do not use a 1/4 in. tapered pipe tap. Hoses used in this air injection system are of special material. Do not substitute.

1. Unbolt the manifold from the cylinder head, but not from the exhaust pipe flange. The manifold is simply pulled away from the head.
2. Remove the engine side plate covers and the gas lines at the fuel pump. Unbolt and lift off the rocker cover, disconnect the oil line leads to the rockers.
3. The rocker levers are supported separately and may be left intact until the head is removed.
4. Unbolt and lift off the cylinder head.

V8 Models

1. Remove the intake manifold as described above.
2. Remove the exhaust manifolds as described above.
3. Back off the rocker arm nuts and pivot the rocker arms out of the way so that the pushrods can be removed. Identify the pushrods so that they can be reinstalled in their original locations.
4. Remove the cylinder head bolts and cylinder heads.
5. Install using new gaskets. The head gasket is installed with the bead up.

NOTE: coat a STEEL gasket on both sides with sealer. If a STEEL ASBESTOS gasket is used, do not apply sealer. Clean the bolt threads, apply sealing compound and install the bolts finger tight.

6. Tighten the head bolts a little at a time in the sequence illustrated in the Specifications at the beginning of this section. Tighten to a final torque of 65 ft. lbs. (small V8) or 85 ft. lbs. (Mark IV).
7. Install the exhaust and intake manifolds as described previously.
8. Adjust the valves as described later.

Timing Case

Crankshaft Pulley Replacement

NOTE: to prevent vibration damper damage, it is important that a puller be used to draw the pulley on the crankshaft.

6 Cylinder Models

1. Remove the radiator core and the fan belt. Remove accessory drive pulley and belt, if so equipped.
2. Use a screw-type puller to remove the balancer-pulley assembly.

V8 Models

1. Drain radiator and disconnect the hoses. Take off the fan belt, and the fan pulley assembly. Remove the battery.
2. Remove the fan shroud. Remove the radiator core. Unbolt the pulley portion of the balancer-pulley assembly.
3. Install screw-type puller and remove the balancer portion from the crankshaft.

Timing Case Cover and Front Oil Seal Replacement

NOTE: the timing case cover oil seal may be replaced without removing the case cover on all Corvettes and Chevrolets.

After gaining access to the oil seal, pry the old seal out of the cover with a screwdriver. Then, lubricate the new seal and drive it into place with tool J-8340, or equivalent.

Chilton's TIME SAVER

When replacing the crankshaft damper, it has been found that lightly polishing the crankshaft damper with crocus cloth will greatly ease replacement. This procedure will also assist in any future removals, as it is sometimes difficult to pull a damper even with a puller. Be sure that the polishing is not overdone, or the damper will wobble on the crankshaft.

6 Cylinder and 396, 402, 427, 454 V8

1. Remove the radiator, fan belts and, using a puller, remove the crankshaft pulley. On V8 engines, remove the water pump.
2. Remove the timing case-to-engine attaching bolts and remove the two oil pan-to-timing case bolts. The front cover is changed, beginning 1974.
3. Slide the front cover forward until a knife can be positioned behind the cover, then cut the ends of the oil pan front seal off flush with the cylinder block on the two ends of the front cover.
4. Remove the front cover and clean all gasket mounting surfaces on the front cover, the block and the exposed portion of the oil pan.
5. Temporarily position a new oil pan front seal on the front of the oil pan and trim off the edges of the new seal so that it will fit flush with the engine block.
6. Remove the new front seal, coat it with sealer and install it on the front cover. Apply a bead of silicone rubber sealer to the place on the front of the oil pan where the cut off portion of the old seal will mate with the new oil pan front seal.
7. Install a centering tool in the crankshaft snout hole in the front cover and install the front cover on the engine.
8. Install the front cover bolts finger tight, remove the centering tool and tighten the cover bolts. Install the pulley, fan belts and radiator.

Cutting oil pan front seal
(© Chevrolet Div., G.M. Corp)

327, 350, and 400 V8

1. Remove the crankshaft pulley. Remove the oil pan. The pan need not be removed on 1975 and later engines. Remove the water pump. Remove the screws holding the timing case cover to the block and remove the cover and gaskets.
2. Use a large screwdriver to pry the old seal out of the front face of the cover.
3. Install the new seal so that open end is toward the inside of the cover.
4. Check that the timing chain oil slinger is in place against the crankshaft sprocket.
5. Install the cover carefully onto the locating dowels.
6. Tighten the attaching screws to 6-8 ft. lbs.

Timing Chain Replacement

6 Cylinder Engines

Chevrolet timing gears are arranged so that (unless deliberately disturbed) the valve timing will remain as set at the factory. Unless the gears are badly worn or seriously damaged, the valve timing will remain constant within reasonable limits.

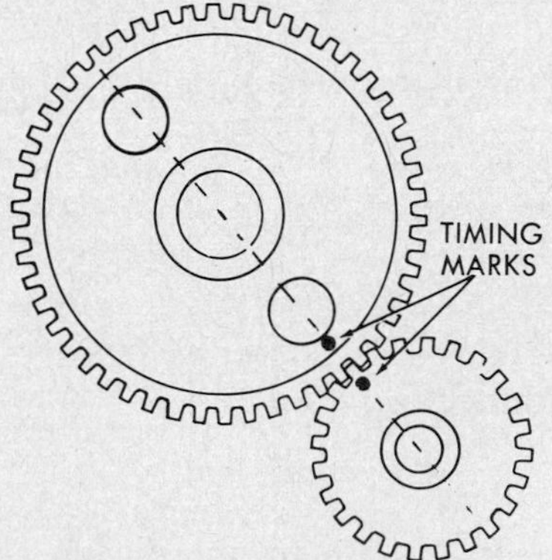

Timing mark alignment, 6 cylinder

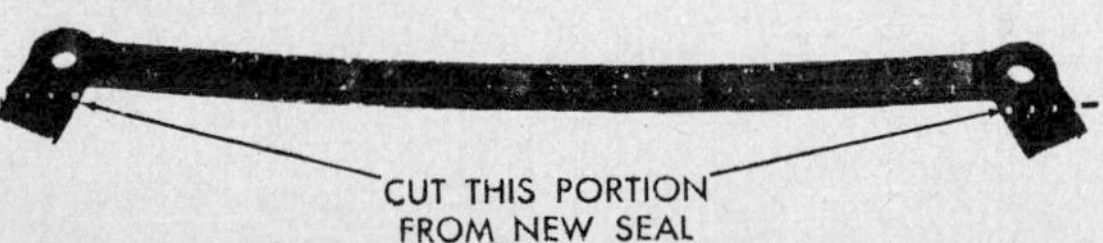

Fitting new oil pan front seal
(© Chevrolet Div., G.M. Corp)

If it becomes necessary to replace the timing gears due to wear or damage, remove the radiator core, disconnect the front motor mounts and jack up the front of the engine. Remove the fan belt, fan pulley, oil pan and timing case cover.

NOTE: the manufacturer recommends that the camshaft be removed from the car in order to remove and replace the gear in an arbor press.

Sometimes when the gear is being pressed on in place on the car, damage results to the thrust washer in back of the cam gear. Unfortunately, this damage is not noticed until the engine is started.

To replace the gear by removing the camshaft, remove the rocker arm assemblies and the distributor, take out all of the pushrods and all of the lifters. The camshaft may then be pulled out toward the front of the engine. It will be necessary to retime the ignition.

Runout of the timing gear should not exceed .004 in. Backlash between the two gears should not be less than .004 in. nor more than .006 in. End clearance of the thrust plate should be .001 to .005 in.

Caution The use of a dial indicator will reduce the possibility of driving the gear too far onto the camshaft. This would alter the desired camshaft thrust clearance of .001 to .005 in. Use care when approaching the final position of the gear on the shaft, because it is impossible to increase the thrust clearance without pulling the new gear. In the absence of a dial indicator, this end thrust can be measured with a feeler gauge. In this case, the thrust clearance is to be measured between the camshaft gear hub and the thrust plate. A feeler gauge strip, inserted in either of the two large gear holes, will reach this point.

V8 Models

To replace the chain, remove the radiator core, water pump, the harmonic balancer and the crankcase front cover. This will allow access to the timing chain. Crank the engine until the timing marks on both sprockets are nearest each other and in line between the shaft centers. Then take out the three bolts that hold the camshaft gear to the camshaft. This gear is a light press fit on the camshaft and will come off easily. It is located by a dowel.

The chain comes off with the camshaft gear.

A gear puller will be required to remove the crankshaft gear.

Without disturbing the position of the engine, mount the new crankshaft gear on the shaft, and mount the chain over the camshaft gear. Ar-

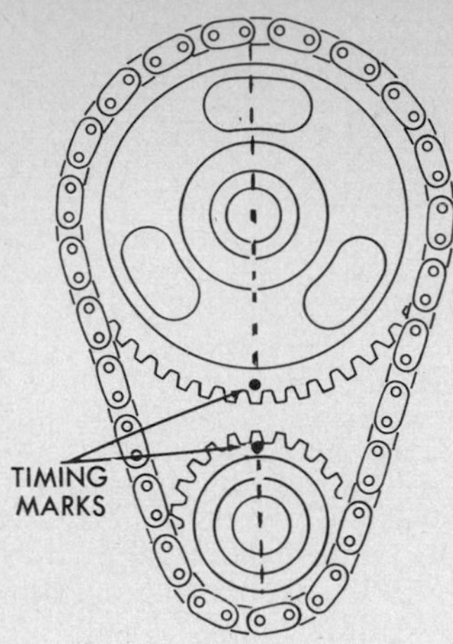

Timing mark alignment, V8

range the camshaft gear in such a way that the timing marks will line up between the shaft centers and the camshaft locating dowel will enter the dowel hole in the cam sprocket.

Place the cam sprocket, with its chain mounted over it, in position on the front of the car and pull up with the three bolts that hold it to the camshaft.

After the gears are in place, turn the engine two full revolutions to make certain that the timing marks are in correct alignment between the shaft centers.

End-play of the V8 camshaft is zero.

Camshaft Replacement

6 Cylinder Engines

Due to the length of the six cylinder camshaft, a large amount of working room will be required in front of the engine to remove the camshaft. There are two ways to go about this task: either remove the engine assembly from the car, or remove the radiator, grille and supports that are mounted directly in front of the engine, disconnect the motor mounts and raise the front of the engine as required to gain enough clearance to remove the cam from the engine. In either case the following equipment will have to be removed from the engine:

1. Remove the valve cover. Loosen each rocker arm mounting stud enough to turn it sideways and remove the pushrods. Keep the pushrods in their proper order.
2. Remove the fuel pump.
3. Remove the inspection plates from the side of the engine and remove the valve lifters. Keep the lifters in order when they are removed.
5. Remove the timing case cover.
6. Turn the crankshaft until the timing marks on the camshaft and crankshaft gears are aligned.
7. Remove the distributor cap and mark the position of the distributor rotor relative to the distributor body and the position of the distributor body relative to the engine block. Remove the distributor.
8. Remove the camshaft from the engine.

V8

1. Drain the cooling system and remove the radiator. On Corvettes, remove the hood.
2. Remove the water pump and the timing case cover.
3. Turn the crankshaft until the timing marks on the camshaft and crankshaft gears are aligned.
4. Remove the valve covers and loosen each rocker arm nut enough to turn the rocker to the side and remove the pushrods. Keep the pushrods in order when they are removed from the engine.
5. Remove the distributor cap and mark the position of the rotor relative to the distributor body and the position of the distributor body relative to the engine. Remove the distributor.
6. Remove the intake manifold, then remove the valve lifters from the engine. Keep the lifters in order when they are removed from the engine.
7. Remove the fuel pump.
8. Remove the timing chain and sprockets from the engine.
9. Install two 5/16 in. 18x4 bolts in the holes in the front of the cam and carefully slide it out of the engine.

NOTE: On some engine and model combinations it will be necessary to disconnect the motor mounts and jack up the front of the engine or remove the grille from the car in order to gain adequate clearance in front of the engine to get the camshaft out of the engine.

Pistons and Connecting Rods

NOTE: complete engine rebuilding procedures are contained in the "Engine Rebuilding Section."

Assembling Piston to Connecting Rod

6 Cylinder Engines

Where split skirt-type pistons are being installed, the split in the skirt of the piston should be placed opposite the clamp screw of the wristpin. This is also opposite the number on the bottom of the connecting rod.

Where solid skirt slipper-type pistons are being replaced, it is unimportant which way the piston is mounted onto the connecting rod. However, if the old pistons are being reinstalled, the piston should be carefully marked before it is detached from the connecting rod in order that it may be replaced on the same side from which it was removed.

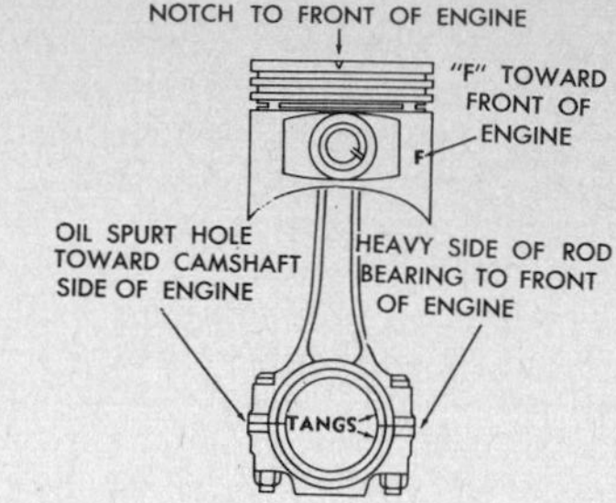

Correct relation of piston to rod, 6-cylinder 250 cu. in. engine

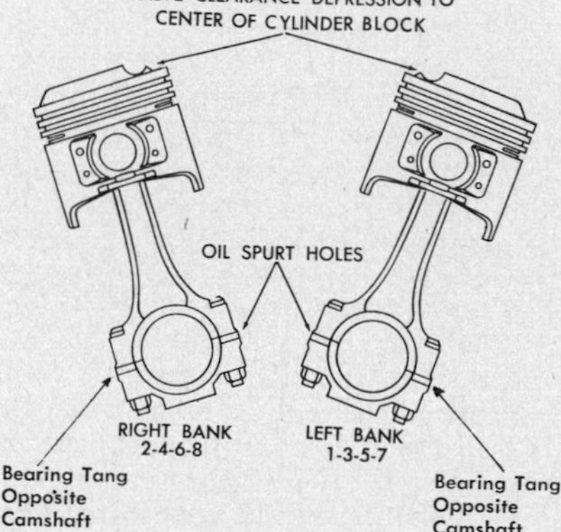

Piston-to-rod relationship—Mk. IV (big block) V8

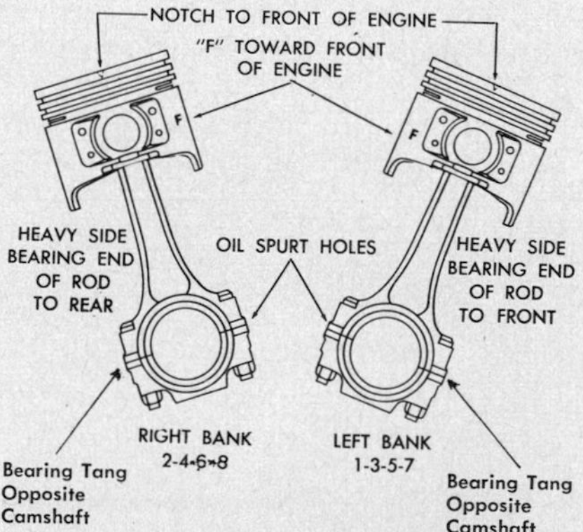

Piston-to-rod relationship—small block V8

V8 Engines

Pistons are marked with a cast depression at the top of the piston and also the letter F on the piston strut. This depression and F always go toward the front.

For the left bank, pistons Nos. 1, 3, 5, and 7, the heavy flange at the bottom of the connecting rod goes on the side of the piston having the depression and F mark. For the right bank, cylinders Nos. 2, 4, 6, and 8, the heavy flange on the connecting rod goes to the side opposite the stamped letter F and the cast depression in the top of the piston.

Assembling Piston and Rod Assembly to the Engine

6 Cylinder Models

When assembling the rods to the pistons and installing the pistons in their respective bores, be sure that the flange, or heavy side of the rod at the bearing end, is toward the front of the piston (cast depression in top of piston head). The oil hole in the connecting rod goes toward the camshaft side of the engine.

V8 Models

Place the piston and rod assemblies into the cylinder so that the depression cast into the top of the piston (and the letter F stamped on the boss of the piston) face front. Double check that the pistons are in the correct bank by noting that on the left bank, pistons Nos. 1, 3, 5 and 7, the heavy flange on the connecting rod will also face forward, but on the right bank, cylinders Nos. 2, 4, 6 and 8, the heavy flange on the connecting rod will face toward the rear.

Lubrication

Oil Pan Removal

Chevrolet 6 Cylinder Manual Transmission

The oil pan can be removed, either after removing engine, or as follows:

1. Drain radiator and oil pan.
2. Disconnect gas tank line at fuel pump and upper and lower radiator hoses.
3. Remove clutch housing-to-engine block bolt above dowel on right side.
4. Raise vehicle on hoist or place on jack stands.
5. Rotate engine to align distributor rotor No. 3. and No. 5 plug wire. (This locates No. 6 crank throw part way up.)
6. Remove starter and flywheel front cover plate.
7. Remove front mount through bolts.
8. Jack up front of engine. Raise as far as possible always using care by checking various dash and body tunnel clearances.
9. Remove front engine mount frame bracket on right side and remove oil filter where necessary.
10. Remove oil pan screws and lower pan to frame.
11. Remove oil pump to gain clearance, then remove oil pan by sliding and rotating front to right and then to rear, and down at an angle. (On certain earlier models, these procedures may be varied in some self-evident areas.)
12. Install in reverse of above.

NOTE: gasket can be replaced by completely removing pan from vehicle.

Chevrolet 6 Cylinder Automatic Transmission

1. Drain radiator and crankcase.
2. Disconnect gas tank line at fuel pump, and radiator hoses at radiator.
3. Remove clutch housing-to-engine block bolt above dowel pin on each side.
4. Rotate engine to align distributor between No. 3 and No. 5 plug wires. (This locates No. 6 crank throw part way up.)
5. Raise vehicle on hoist or on jack stands.
6. Remove converter cover pan, and starter assembly.
7. Follow Steps 7 through 12, listed above.

Chevrolet—V8

1. Disconnect battery negative cable.
2. Remove distributor cap from distributor to prevent breakage against firewall.
3. Drain cooling system. Remove radiator hoses, and remove oil dipstick and tube, where necessary.
4. Remove fan blade assembly.
5. Raise car, and drain engine oil.
6. Remove bolts from engine front mounts. Disconnect and remove starter.
7. On cars with automatic transmissions, remove converter housing underpan.
8. Disconnect the exhaust Y pipe from the manifolds.
9. Rotate crankshaft until timing mark on the damper is at six o'clock position.
10. Using a block of wood and a suitable jack, raise engine enough to insert 2 x 4 in. wood blocks under engine mounts then lower engine onto blocks.
11. Remove engine oil pan.
12. Install by reversing removal procedures.

NOTE: the 396, 402, 427, and 454 cu. in. engines use three 1/4 in. attaching bolts at crankcase front cover; one at each corner, and one at the lower center.

Corvette

1. Disconnect battery, and remove dipstick and tube.
2. Raise car and support on stands. Drain engine oil.
3. Remove starter and flywheel underpan.
4. Disconnect steering idler arm and lower steering linkage.
5. Remove oil pan and discard gaskets and seals.
6. On high performance engines, the oil baffle must be removed before additional operations can be performed.

NOTE: on the 427 and 454 cu. in. engine, the oil pan has three 1/4 in. attaching bolts at crankcase front cover; one at each front corner, and one at lower center.

7. Install by reversing removal procedure.

Oil Pump Replacement

On all Chevrolet engines, the oil pump is located in the oil pan, and it is driven by a tang from the distributor shaft.

On six-cylinder engines, the pump is flange-mounted to the under side of the crankcase with two cap screws.

On V8 models, the oil pump is bolted to the rear, main bearing cap. Oil is fed from the pump up through the rear, main bearing cap.

Rear Main Bearing Oil Seal R & R

1. Remove rear main bearing cap and pry old seal from groove. Insert new seal with lubricant only on the lip. Do not get oil on the glue-treated parting line surfaces. Lip faces front of engine.

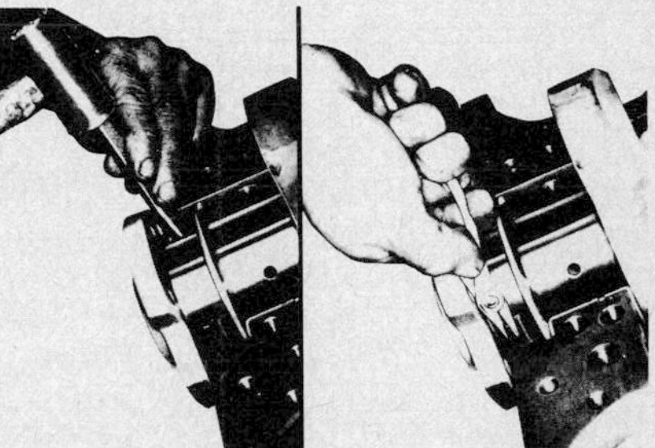

Rear main seal removal
(© Chevrolet Div., G.M. Corp)

2. Using a hammer and small punch, revolve the upper half of the seal until it protrudes far enough to remove with pliers.
3. Oil the seal except at the glue-treated ends and, using a hammer handle, roll the seal into place in the block.
4. These seals are made to size and require no trimming. Install the lower half over the crankshaft and in place onto the block.

CLUTCH

Clutches are of the diaphragm spring type. The throwout bearing is a ball bearing with no provision for lubrication. The throwout fork pivots on a ball stud which is mounted in the rear face of the bellhousing.

Clutch R & R

All Models

1. Support the engine and remove the transmission as described in "Manual Transmission R&R."

2. Disconnect the clutch fork push-rod and spring.
3. Remove the flywheel housing.
4. Slide the clutch fork from the ball stud and remove the fork from the dust boot. The ball stud is threaded into the clutch housing and is easily replaced, if necessary.
5. Install a clutch pilot tool.

NOTE: look for the assembly markings "X" on the flywheel and the clutch cover (pressure plate assembly). If there are none, scribe marks to identify the position of the clutch cover relative to the flywheel.

6. Loosen the clutch cover bolts evenly until the spring pressure is relieved, then remove the bolts and clutch assembly.
7. Before installing, clean the pressure plate and the flywheel face.
8. Position the disc and pressure plate assembly on the flywheel and install a pilot tool.

NOTE: the disc on six-cylinder engines is installed with the springs facing the flywheel. On V8 engines, the grease slinger must face the transmission.

9. Install the pressure plate assembly bolts. Make sure the mark on the cover is aligned with the mark on the flywheel. Tighten the bolts alternately and evenly to 35 ft. lbs.
10. Remove the pilot tool.
11. Remove the release fork and lubricate the ball socket and the fork fingers at the throwout bearing with graphite or Moly Grease. Reinstall the release fork.
12. Lubricate the inside recess and the fork groove of the throwout bearing with a light coat of graphite or Moly Grease.
13. Install the clutch release fork and dust boot in the clutch housing and the throwout bearing on the fork, then install the flywheel housing. Tighten flywheel housing bolts to 30 ft. lbs.
14. Connect the fork pushrod and spring.
15. Adjust the shift linkage as described later.
16. Adjust the clutch pedal free play as described previously.

Clutch Adjustment

1969-70 Chevrolet and 1969-74 Corvette

1. Disconnect the spring between the clutch push rod and cross shaft lever.
2. While holding the clutch pedal against the stop, loosen the two locknuts enough to allow the adjusting rod to move against the clutch fork until the throwout bearing lightly touches the pressure plate springs.

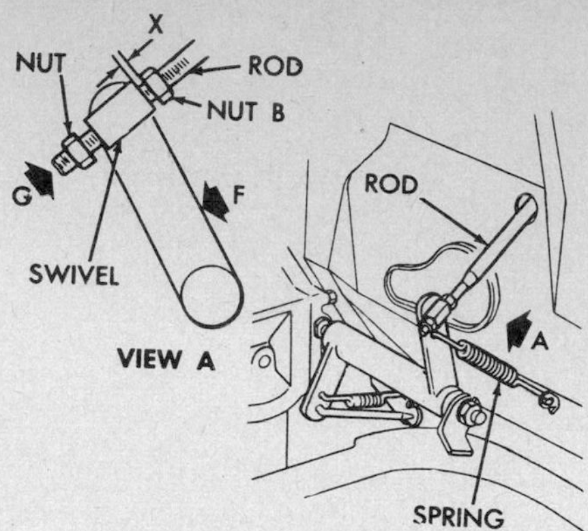

1969-70 Chevrolet clutch linkage
(© Chevrolet Div., G.M. Corp)

3. Turn the upper nut against the swivel and then back it off 4½ turns. Tighten the bottom locknut to look the swivel against the top nut.

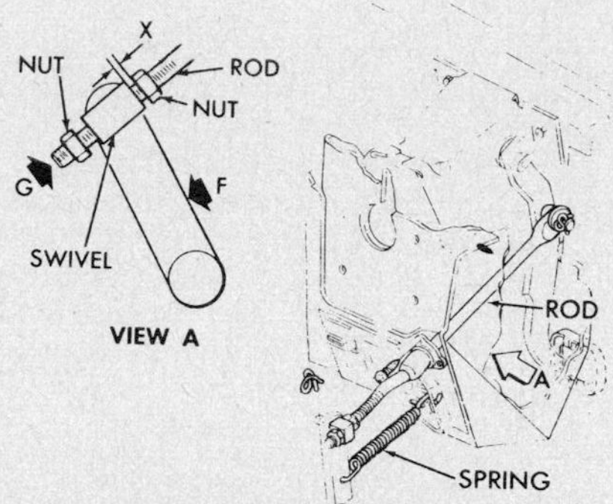

1969-74 Corvette clutch linkage
(© Chevrolet Div., G.M. Corp)

4. Reinstall the return spring. Pedal free travel, the distance the pedal can be moved before the throwout bearing contacts the pressure plate spring, should be:
1969-70 Chevrolet 1-1½ in.
1969-71 Corvette 1¼-2 in.
1969-70 Corvette with HD clutch 2-2½ in.
1972 Corvette 1¼-1¾ in.
1973 Corvette 1¼-1½ in.
1974 Corvette 1-1½ in.

1971-73 Chevrolet

1. Disconnect the return spring at the clutch fork.
2. Push the clutch lever and shaft assembly until the clutch pedal is tight against the rubber stop under the dash.
3. Push the outer end of the clutch fork backward until the throwout bearing just touches the pressure plate spring.
4. Install the pushrod into the upper hole on the lever and increase its length until all play is removed.
5. Remove the rod from the upper hole and reinsert it into the lower hole.
6. Tighten the locknut, being careful not to change the length of the push rod.
7. Install the return spring.
8. Check the pedal free travel. It should be 1¼-1¾ in.

1975-76 Corvette

1. Disconnect the return spring between the floor and the cross shaft.
2. Push the clutch lever and shaft assembly until the clutch pedal is tightly against the rubber stop under the dash.
3. Loosen the two locknuts on the shaft.
4. Push the shaft until the throwout bearing just touches the pressure plate spring.
5. Tighten the top locknut towards the swivel until the distance between it and the swivel is 0.4 in.
6. Tighten the bottom locknut against the swivel.
7. Check pedal free travel. It should be 1-1½ in.

MANUAL TRANSMISSION

Transmission refill capacities are in the Capacities table of this section.

Manual transmissions used in these models are the Muncie 3-speed, Saginaw 3-speed, Saginaw 4-speed, Muncie 4-speed, and Warner 4-speed. The Warner was installed in Corvettes beginning in mid-year 1974. All 1975-76 4-speed Corvettes are equipped with the Warner unit. Identification

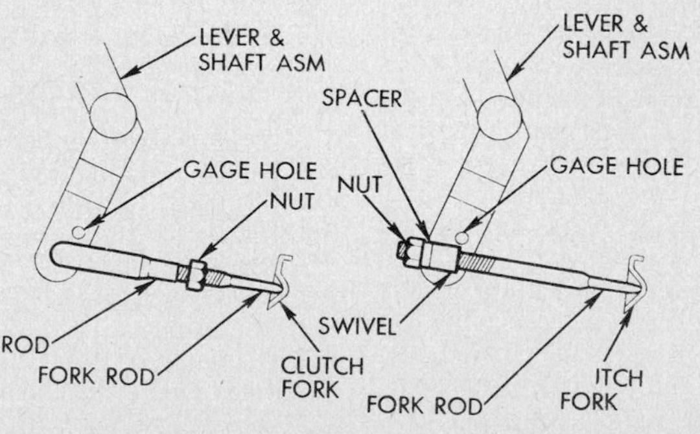

1971-73 Chevrolet clutch linkage
(© Chevrolet Div., G.M. Corp)

is determined by side cover design and linkage. The 3-speed Muncie side cover has two ears on the case at the top and the Saginaw 3-speed one. The Saginaw 4-speed linkage arms are all mounted through the side cover. The Muncie and Warner 4-speeds have the reverse fork mounted in the tailshaft. These two may be differentiated by the shape of the side cover; the Warner has a nine bolt curved bottom and the Muncie a seven bolt straight bottom.

Troubleshooting and repair of manual transmissions is covered in the Unit Repair Section.

Shift Linkage Adjustment

1969-73 Three-Speed Column Shift

1. With transmission in Reverse, place ignition switch in Off position up to 1970, Lock for 1971-73.
2. Loosen shift rod lock nuts.
3. Set transmission first-reverse lever in reverse position. Push up on first-reverse control rod to 1970, pull down for 1971-73 until column lever is in reverse detent position. Tighten first-reverse lock nut.
4. Shift column and transmission levers to neutral position. Insert a 3/16 in. dia. rod into alignment holes in levers and alignment plate.
5. Tighten second-third locknut.
6. Remove alignment rod. Shift column lever to reverse. Turn key to Lock. Ignition switch must move freely to Lock position and it must not be possible to turn key to Lock when in any transmission position other than reverse. If this interlock binds, leave switch in Lock position and readjust first-reverse rod.
7. Check shifting.

1969 Corvette Three-Speed Floorshift

1. Put the ignition switch in "off" and loosen the shift rod swivel locknuts. Set the transmission levers in to the neutral detent position.
2. Install a 1/8 thick X 41/64 wide X 3 in. long gauge in the bracket assembly.
3. Adjust the length of the shift rods for easy entry into the levers.
4. Remove the gauge and check the shift operation.
5. Shift the transmission into reverse.
6. Loosen the interlock bracket assembly bolts at the bottom of the steering column. Make sure that the bracket is not stuck to the dash and then tighten the bracket again.
7. Move the ignition key through "off" and "lock." If there is any binding, readjust the interlock linkage.

Four-Speed

Two makes of four-speed transmission have been used, Muncie and Saginaw. Linkage adjustments, however, are typical. Four-speeds were not available in the Chevrolet after 1969. A gauge 1/8 in. thick by 41/64 in. wide and 3 in. long should be used to locate and maintain neutral detent position of the shift lever while making linkage adjustments.

1969 Chevrolet Four Speed Floorshift

1. Place ignition switch in Lock position.
2. Loosen locknuts at swivels on shift rods and back drive control rod.
3. Set transmission shift levers in neutral positions.
4. Shift lever into neutral. Insert locating gauge, 1/8 thick X 41/64 wide X 3 in. long, into control lever bracket assembly.
5. Hold each lever against the gauge and adjust in turn. Tighten shift rod locknuts and remove gauge.
6. Shift lever into reverse, then pull down slightly on back drive rod to remove slack. Tighten back drive rod locknut.
7. Ignition switch must move freely to Lock position and it must not be possible to turn key to Lock when in any transmission position other than reverse. Readjust back drive rod, if necessary.
8. Check for proper shifting operation.

Corvette Four-Speed

1. Place the ignition switch in "off" (1969) or "lock" (1970-75).
2. Perform steps two through five

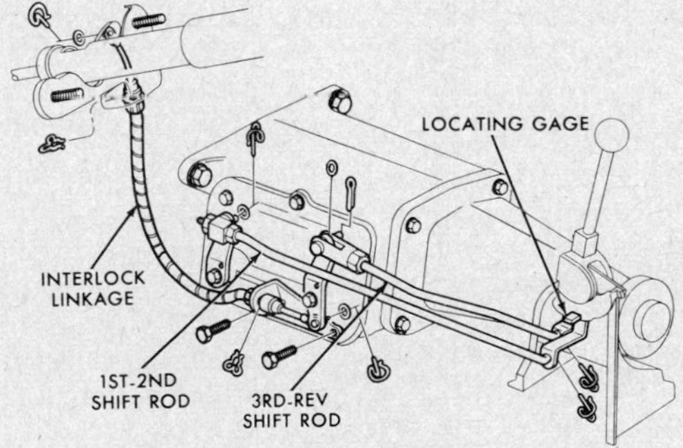

1969 Corvette 3-speed linkage adjustment
(© Chevrolet Div., G.M. Corp)

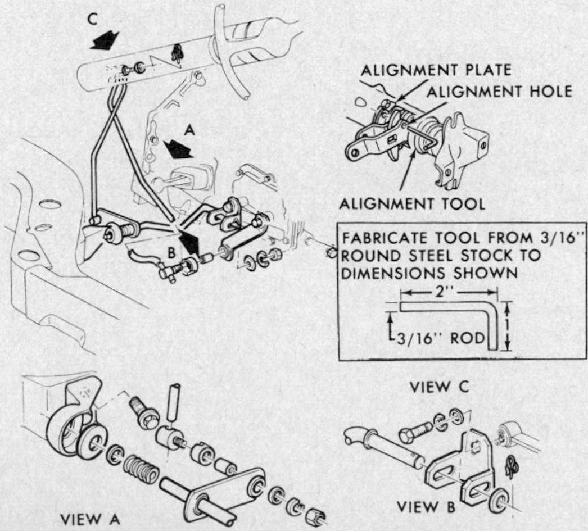

1969-73 3-speed column shift linkage adjustment
(© Chevrolet Div., G.M. Corp)

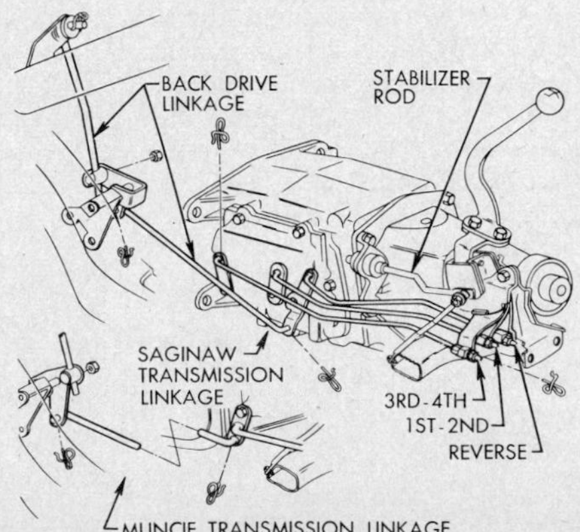

1969 Chevrolet 4-speed linkage adjustment
(© Chevrolet Div., G.M. Corp)

above, and then check the shifting operation.
3. Loosen the interlock bracket assembly bolts at the bottom of the steering column. Make sure that the bracket is not stuck to the dash and then tighten the bracket again.
4. Move the ignition key through "off" and "lock" positions. If there is any binding, readjust the interlock linkage.

4. Raise the vehicle on a hoist.
5. Remove the right and left exhaust pipes.
6. Disconnect the driveshaft at the transmission, lower the driveshaft and remove the slip yoke from the transmission.
7. Remove the rear mount to bracket bolts, then jack the engine enough to raise the transmission from the mount.
8. Remove the transmission linkage mounting bracket to frame bolts.
9. Disconnect the shift levers at the transmission.
10. Remove the bolts attaching gearshift assembly to mounting bracket and remove the mounting bracket. Remove the shifter mechanism with the rods attached.
11. Disconnect the speedometer cable and the TCS switch wiring.
12. Remove the transmission mount bracket.
13. Remove the transmission to clutch housing retaining bolts and the lower left extension bolt.
14. Pull the transmission rearward until it is clear of the clutch housing, then rotate it clockwise while pulling to the rear. Carefully lower the rear of the engine until the tachometer drive cable at the distributor just clears the firewall.

Caution The tachometer cable is easily damaged if it hits the firewall. Slide the transmission rearward until it clears the clutch, then tilt the front of it down and lower it from the car.

15. Installation is the reverse of removal. Adjust the shift linkage.

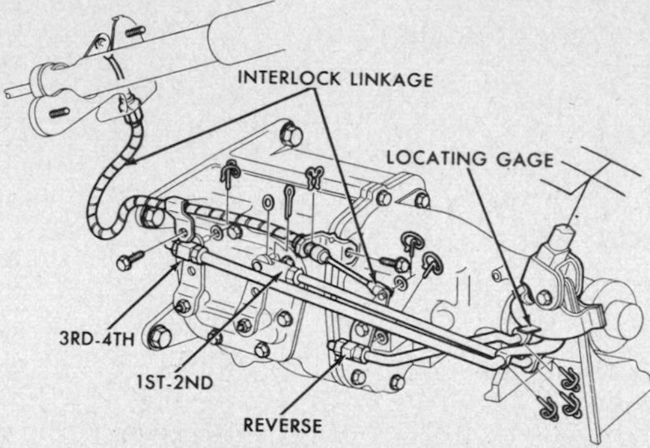

Corvette 4-speed linkage adjustment
(© Chevrolet Div., G.M. Corp)

Transmission Removal (Except Corvette)

1. Raise the car on a hoist and drain the transmission. Disconnect the speedometer cable and the control levers. Disconnect the propeller shaft. Remove two bolts attaching the center bearing to the frame. Remove nuts and U-bolts retaining the rear universal joint bearing to the differential pinion drive flange. Move the propeller shaft rearward to the left and under the rear axle housing to withdraw the front universal joint from the transmission output shaft. Remove the transmission rear mounting pad bolts and unbolt the support member from the frame.
2. On all models, remove the two top transmission-to-clutch housing cap screws, and insert guide pins to keep the weight of the transmission from falling on the clutch assembly.
3. Remove the lower transmission-to-clutch housing cap screws. Slide the transmission straight back on the guide pins until the input shaft of the transmission is free of the clutch.
4. Remove the transmission from under the car.
5. Install in reverse order of removal.

Transmission Removal (Corvette)

1. Disconnect the battery ground cable.
2. Remove the shifter ball and "T" handle.
3. Remove the console trim plate.

AUTOMATIC TRANSMISSION

Four automatic transmissions have been used. Powerglide was available only in Chevrolets. This 2-speed transmission was used for the last time in 1972. Three Turbo Hydra-Matics have been available, the 350, 375, and the 400. All are 3-speed transmissions. Identification can be made by the shape of the pan.

Powerglide pan

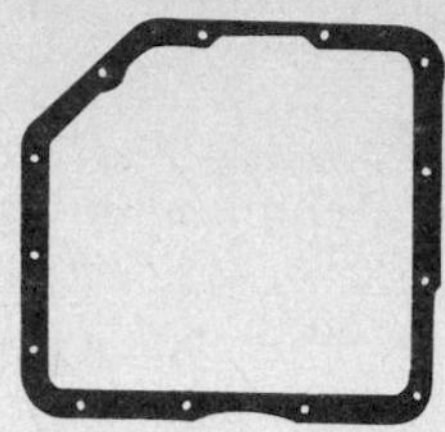
Turbo Hydra-Matic 350 pan

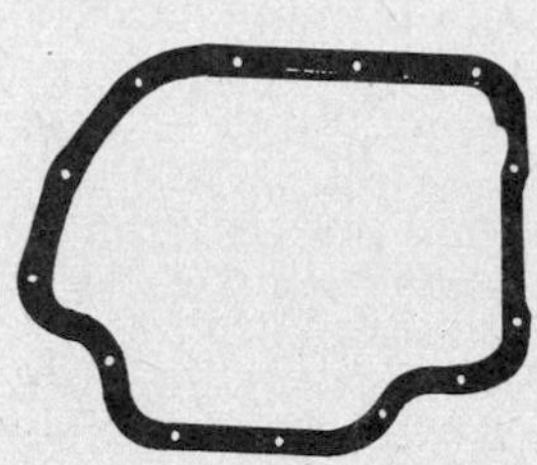
Turbo Hydra-Matic 375 and 400 pan

Neutral Safety Switch Adjustment

1969-71

In all models the adjustment is made with the shift lever in Drive position. Loosen the switch mounting screws. Align the slot in the contact support with the hole in the switch and insert a 3/32 in. pin to hold the support in place.

On column shift models, place the contact support drive slot over the shifter tube drive tang and tighten the screws.

On Corvettes, the shift control lever must be disconnected from the control rod and the shift control knob removed. Then remove the trim plate to get at the switch. Proceed as described in the first paragraph above, then place the contact support drive slot over the drive tang. Tighten the switch mounting screws, then remove the pin. Reinstall the shift control lever and trim plate.

On Chevrolet models with floor shift, the ash tray, trim plate assembly and indicator lens and housing must be removed from the console before proceding as described in the first paragraph above. Clamp the control lever pawl against the contact point of the detent. Tighten the switch mounting screws, then remove the pin and reinstall all the console components which were removed.

1972

Column Shift

1. Disconnect the wiring at the switch.
2. Remove the retaining screws and remove the switch from the steering column.
3. Put the shift level in neutral when installing the switch
4. Align the slot in the contact support with the hole in the switch and insert a 3/32 in. pin to hold the support in position. The switch is now in the Drive position.
5. Put the contact support drive slot over the shifter tube drive tang and tighten the screws. Remove the clamp and the pin.
6. Connect the wiring and check the switch for proper operation.

Floorshift

1. Disconnect the shift control lever arm from the control rod.
2. Remove the shift knob.
3. Remove the trim plate.
4. Remove the control assembly retaining screws and lift the assembly away from the seal.
5. Remove the neutral switch from the control assembly.

To install:

6. On early 1972 models put the shifter into Drive. Park on later Chevrolets (with neutral switch on column), or Neutral on later Corvettes.
7. Align the hole in the contact support with the hole in the switch and insert a 3/32 in. pin to hold the support in place.
8. Place the contact support drive slot over the drive tang and tighten the switch mounting screws. Remove the pin.
9. Install the control assembly mounting screws. Connect the switch wiring and check the switch operation.
10. Install the trim plate and shift knob.
11. Connect the shift lever arm to the transmission control rod.

1973-76

Use the procedure outlined previously except that during installation, the shift lever is positioned in Neutral on column shift or Drive on floor shift models. It is only necessary to use the 3/32 in. pin for alignment when the original switch pin has been sheared off.

Shift Linkage Adjustment

1969-72 Column Shift

1. Make sure that the shift lever works freely in the mast jacket.
2. Check for proper linkage adjustment:
   a. Pull the selector lever back and allow the lever to be positioned in Drive by the transmission detent.

   NOTE: do not use the indicator pointer as a reference. The indicator pointer will be adjusted after the linkage.

   b. Release the lever. The lever should not go into Low range unless it is lifted.
   c. Lift the shift lever and allow the lever to be positioned in Neutral by the transmission detent.
   d. Release the lever. The lever should not go into Reverse unless it is lifted.
   e. If the selector lever can move beyond the Neutral and Drive detents without being lifted, then the mechanical stops in the steering column are not coordinated with the transmission detents and adjustment is required.
3. To adjust, place the selector lever in Drive as determined by the transmission detent.
4. Loosen the adjustment clamp or swivel at the cross-shaft and position the selector lever in Drive.
5. With the selector lever in Drive and the transmission lever in Drive detent position, tighten the clamp or swivel bolt.
6. Repeat Step 2 above to check for proper adjustment.
7. If necessary, readjust the selector pointer to agree with the transmission detents.
8. Readjust the neutral safety switch if necessary.
9. When properly adjusted:
   a. From Reverse to Drive position travel, the transmission detent must be noted and related to the indicated position on the dial.
   b. In Drive and Reverse positions, the selector lever must drop back into position freely when lifted.

1973-76 Column Shift

1. Follow steps 1 and 2 of the preceding procedure.
2. Remove the retaining screw and spring washer from the linkage swivel.
3. Set the lever on the transmission in neutral by moving it counterclockwise to the L1 detent and then clockwise three detent positions to neutral.
4. Place the transmission selector lever in Neutral as determined by the stop in the steering column. Don't use the indicator pointer for reference. The pointer will be adjusted last.
5. Assemble the swivel, spring washer, and screw to the lever and tighten to 20 ft lbs.
6. Readjust the indicator needle, if necessary, to match the transmission detent positions. Readjust the neutral switch.
7. Make sure that the key cannot be removed with the key in the run position and the transmission in reverse. When the key is in the Lock position and shift lever in Park, be sure that the key can be removed, the steering is locked, and that the transmission remains in Park when the steering column is locked.

1969 Chevrolet Floorshift

NOTE: this procedure covers both Powerglide and Turbo Hydra-Matic transmissions.

1. Shift the lever into Drive.
2. Remove the cable clip and disconnect the cable from the lever. Position the transmission lever in Drive.
3. Measure the distance from the rear face of the attaching

NUT (D)
ROD
LEVER
BRACKET
CROSS SHAFT

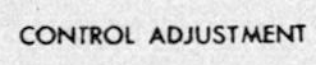

1. Set transmission lever in "Drive" position.
2. Set shift tube & lever assby. in "Drive" position.
3. Tighten nut (D) to 10 ft. lbs.
4. Check shift pattern in all ranges. Readjust if necessary.

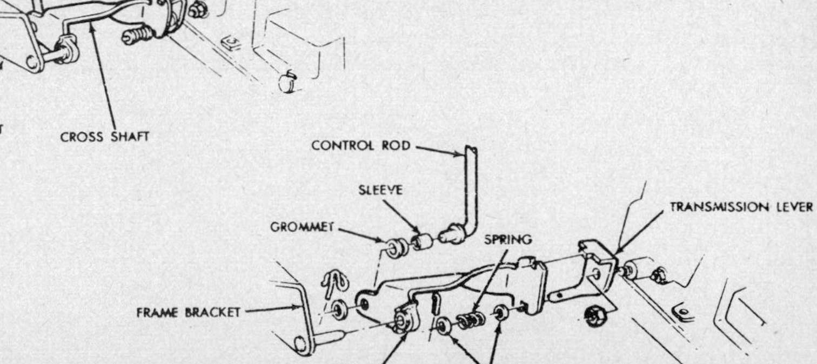

Turbo Hydra-Matic column linkage adjustment (© Chevrolet Div., G.M. Corp)

bracket to the stud on the transmission bracket. If this distance is not 5.5 in., loosen the stud and adjust it.

4. Adjust the end of the cable and reinstall it on the stud.
5. Remove the console quadrant cover and disconnect the cable from the shift lever.
6. A 0.07 in. feeler gauge should fit between the pawl and the Drive detent of the detent plate. Adjust the detent plate, if necessary.
7. Measure the distance from the front of the shifter bracket to the center of the cable pivot pin. If this distance is not 6.25 in., loosen the bolt and move the lever as necessary.
8. Reinstall the quadrant cover.

1969-72 Corvette (Turbo Hydra-Matic)

1. Disconnect the pushrod at the transmission lever.
2. With the transmission lever in Drive detent and the selector lever in Drive, rotate the pushrod until the hole lines up with the lever pin.
3. Install the pushrod on the pin and install the retainer clip.
4. Check operation of the linkage in all positions.

1973-76 Corvette

1. Loosen the nut on the transmission lever so that the pin can move in the slot. Remove the console cover.
2. Move the transmission lever counter-clockwise to the L1 position and then clockwise five detents to Park.
3. Place the shift lever in Park and insert a 0.40 in. spacer in front of the pawl.
4. Tighten the nut on the transmission lever to 20 ft. lbs.
5. Turn the ignition switch to Lock with the shift lever in Park.
6. Remove the cotter pin and washer from the backdrive cable at the column lever. Disconnect the cable.
7. Working under the dash, remove the two nuts at the steering column-to-dash bracket.
8. Turn the lock tube lever counterclockwise (when viewed from the front of the column) to remove any free-play from the column.
9. Move the bracket until the cable eye passes freely over the retaining pin on the bracket.
10. While holding the bracket in place, have an assistant tighten the bracket retaining nuts.
11. Install the cotter pin and washer to retain the cable to the lever retaining pin.

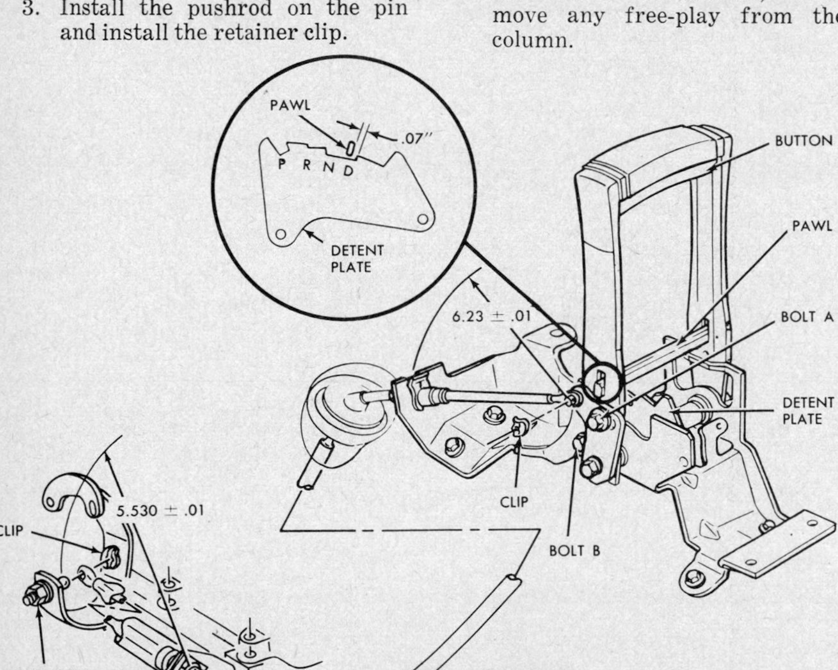

1969 Chevrolet automatic floorshift adjustment (© Chevrolet Div., G.M. Corp)

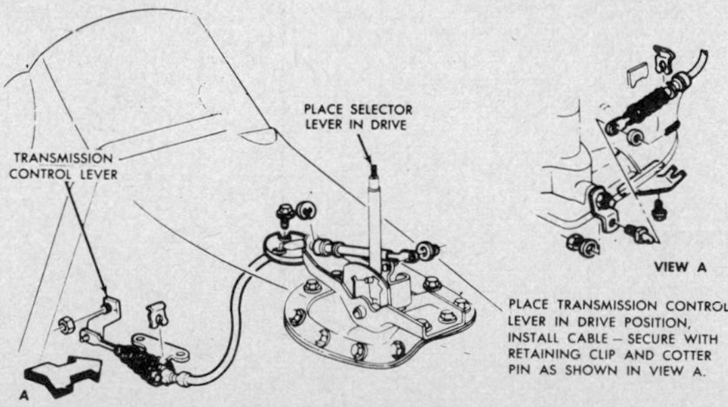

Corvette Turbo Hydra-Matic linkage adjustment (© Chevrolet Div., G.M. Corp)

Throttle Valve Adjustment

1969-73 6-Cylinder

Adjustment is made with the throttle pedal completely depressed and the bellcrank in wide open position.

Adjust the length of the linkage to obtain a 1/64 in. to 1/16 in. clearance between the lever on the firewall and its stop when the transmission lever is against its stop.

1969-72 V8 Powerglide

1. Remove the air cleaner and disconnect:
   a. Accelerator linkage at the carburetor.
   b. Accelerator return spring.
   c. Throttle valve rod return spring.
2. Pull the throttle valve upper rod forward until the transmission is through detent and place the carburetor in wide open position. The carburetor must reach wide open position at the same time that the ball stud contacts the end of the slot in the upper throttle valve rod.
3. Adjust the swivel on the end of the upper throttle valve rod to obtain the setting described in Step 2 above. Allowable tolerance is approximately 1/32 in.
4. Connect and adjust the carburetor linkage.

Detent Cable Adjustment

1969-72 Turbo Hydra-Matic 350 (Chevrolet)

1. Disengage the snap lock on the detent cable.
2. Place the carburetor in wide open position (lever against the stop). On Quadrajet carburetors, disengage the secondary locknut before placing the lever in wide open position.

NOTE: detent cable must be through detent.

3. Holding the carburetor in wide open position, push the snap lock on the detent cable downward until the top is flush with the cable.

1973-76 Turbo Hydra-Matic 350 (Chevrolet)

The cable adjusts itself the first time the accelerator pedal is depressed to the floor.

Detent Switch Adjustment

1969-72 Turbo Hydra-Matic 400 (Corvette)

The detent switch is located on the carburetor.

1. Pull the detent switch driver rearward until the hole in the switch body aligns with the hole in the driver.
2. Insert a 0.092 in. pin through the aligned holes to a depth of 0.10 in. to hold the driver in position.
3. Loosen the switch mounting bolt.
4. With the throttle held in wide open position, move the switch forward until the driver contacts the accelerator lever.
5. Tighten the mounting bolt and remove the pin.

1969-72 Turbo Hydra-Matic 400 (Chevrolet)

The detent switch is located on the carburetor.

1. Loosen the switch mounting bolt.
2. Holding the throttle in wide open position (choke fully open), depress the detent switch plunger until it bottoms in the switch. Move the switch toward the throttle lever paddle until there is a clearance of 0.23 ± 0.01 in. between the face of the lever paddle and the depressed detent switch plunger.
3. Tighten the switch mounting bolts.

1973-76 Turbo Hydra-Matic 375 and 400 (Chevrolet and Corvette)

The switch is located over the accelerator pedal. After installing a new switch, adjustment is made by pressing the plunger in. This presets the switch and it will self-adjust the first time the pedal is fully depressed.

Band Adjustment, Pan Removal and Installation, Fluid and Filter Change

Follow the procedures given in the Camaro section.

U-JOINTS

Driveshafts are of a one-piece design, using Cardan type universal joints. The universal joints are lube-sealed at the factory and require no periodic maintenance. The front yoke is splined, providing a slip joint for slight length variations in the drive line. There is a damper on some models: this damper is not serviced separately.

Two basic universal joints are used. The Dana or Cleveland type uses snap-ring bearing cap retainers. The Saginaw uses injection molded plastic to retain the bearing caps. On the Saginaw type there is a snap-ring groove in the bearing housing inboard of the yoke to hold the bearings in place.

Driveshaft R & R

Disconnect the rear universal joint flange. On some models, the bearing caps are bolted directly to the differential flange with clamps or U-bolts. Pull the front yoke from the transmission. Watch for oil leaks from the transmission output housing. Install in the reverse order of removal.

Universal Joint R & R

Dana and Cleveland Type

1. Remove the driveshaft.
2. Remove the snap-rings from the trunnion yoke.
3. Using a vise and suitably sized sockets, press on the trunnion until the bearing cap is almost out. Grasp the cap in the vise and work it out of the yoke. Repeat the above procedure for the rest of the bearing caps.
4. Pack the rollers in grease and fill the grease reservoir.
5. To install, position the trunnion in the yoke and partially install one bearing cap. Start the trunnion in the bearing cap and partially install the other cap. Align the trunnion with the caps and press into place.

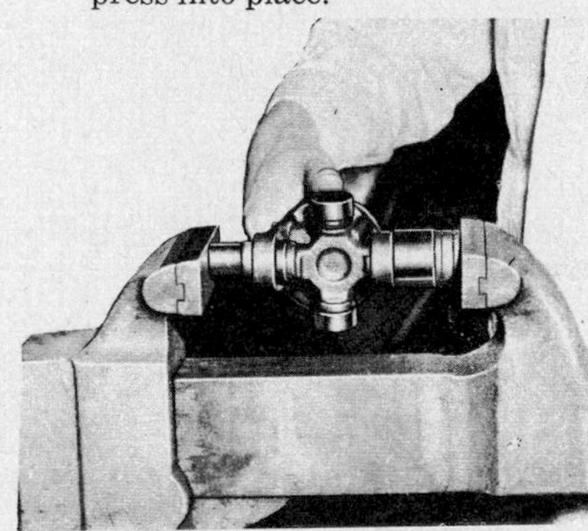

Assembling universal joint
(© Chevrolet Div., G.M. Corp)

6. If necessary, repeat Step 5 above for the other yoke.
7. Install the snap-rings.
8. Install the driveshaft in the vehicle.

Saginaw Type

Remove and install the bearing caps and trunnion as described for the Dana and Cleveland type universal joints. On an original universal joint, however, the bearing caps will be secured in the yokes with injected plastic. The plastic will shear when the bearing caps are pressed. Service snap-rings are installed in the groove on the inside (of yoke) of the installed caps.

Constant Velocity Type

Some models are equipped with driveshafts which incorporate constant velocity U-joints. The driveshaft yokes on each end of the driveshaft contain two U-joints which are connected within the yoke by a centering ball. Factory installed U-joints do not have grooves for snap-rings and are retained in the yokes by injected plastic. This makes the joints non-repairable by conventional methods. Some aftermarket kits are available with screw-in bearing caps to repair this type of joint.

DRIVE AXLES

Corvette

Corvette is equipped with an independent rear suspension. The differential is solidly attached to the car frame, the rear wheels being driven through tubular rear axles, each fitted with two universal joints. A transverse, multiple leaf rear spring provides rear suspension. Brake torque and driving forces are transmitted through radius arms to the frame. The spring supports vertical loads, while lateral forces, on turns etc., are taken by the axles and control rods to the fixed differential and to the frame.

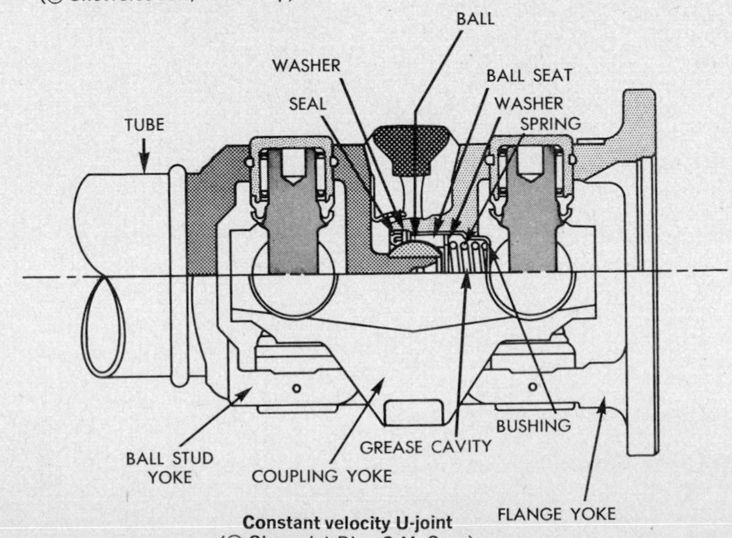

Constant velocity U-joint
(© Chevrolet Div., G.M. Corp)

1. Raise the vehicle on a hoist.
2. Disconnect the spring and link bolts.
3. Disconnect the axle shafts at the carrier by removing the U-bolts on the universal joint trunnions.
4. Disconnect the carrier front support bracket at the frame crossmember.
5. Disconnect the driveshaft at the companion flange.
6. Scribe marks indicating the cam and bolt relative location on the strut rod bracket and loosen the cam bolts.
7. Remove the four bolts which secure the bracket to the carrier lower surface and drop the bracket. Remove the camber cam bolts and swing the strut rods up and out of the way.
8. Remove the eight carrier to cover bolts, loosening the bolts gradually to permit the lubricant to drain out.
9. Pull the carrier partially out of the cover, drop the nose to clear the crossmember, then gradually work the carrier down and out.
10. To install, clean the carrier cover and grease the gasket surface.
11. Using a new gasket and two ½-13 x 1-¼ in. studs as aligning studs, raise the carrier into position.
12. Install the carrier to cover bolts, tightening securely.
13. Install the driveshaft to the companion flange, tightening the clamp bolts securely.
14. Install the rubber cushion on the bracket and position to the frame crossmember. Install the nut, tightening to 50 ft. lbs.
15. Install the axle trunnions to the yokes with the U-bolts.
16. Assemble the strut rods to the bracket and raise the bracket into position under the carrier. Install the four bolts, tightening to 35 ft. lbs.
17. Move the camber cams to the marked locations and tighten the cam nuts.
18. Connect the spring end link bolts.
19. Fill the housing with lubricant to the level of the filler hole.

Positraction Differential

No special attention is required in this area, except with the lubricant used.

Under no circumstances use anything but special Positraction lubricant.

Failure to follow these instructions may result in permanent damage to the unit.

REAR AXLE

For Chevrolet axle shaft, bearing, and seal service, refer to the Camaro section.

JACKING, HOISTING

When jacking the car, place the jack at the spring seat of the lower control arm in the front and at the axle housing in the rear. A bumper jack may be used on Chevrolet models, but not Corvettes.

To hoist the car, position the hoist arms at the frame side rails immediately in front of the rear wheels and immediately behind the front wheels.

FRONT SUSPENSION

Both Chevrolet and Corvette utilize conventional short-long arm suspension, with coil springs and tube shocks. A stabilizer bar is used between the lower arms to reduce roll.

Shock Absorber R & R

1. Remove the upper stem nut while holding the stem to keep it from turning.
2. Remove the two bolts holding the shock absorber to the lower control arm and pull the shock through the arm.
3. Extend the shock absorber and insert it up through the lower control arm. Make sure that the upper stem goes through the hole in the upper control arm frame bracket.
4. Install the grommet, retainer cup, and nut to the shock absorber upper stem.
5. Hold the shock absorber stem and tighten the upper nut to 8 ft lbs.
6. Install the lower control arm retaining bolts and tighten to 20 ft lbs. (Chevrolet) or 13 ft lbs. (Corvette).

Front Wheel Bearing Adjustment

1. Jack the car up and support it at the lower arm.
2. Remove the hub dust cover and spindle cotter pin.
3. While spinning the wheel, snug the nut down to seat the bearings. Do not exert over 12 ft lbs of force on the nut.
4. Back the nut off ¼–½ a turn. Tighten the nut *finger-tight* (if the roller bearings are preloaded with the wheel off the ground, the inner edges of the bearings will be forced against the bearing cage), then *loosen* the nut as required to line up the cotter pin hole in the spindle with the hole in the nut.
5. Insert the cotter pin. End-play should be between 0.001 and 0.008 in. If play exceeds this tolerance, the wheel bearings should be replaced.

Front Spring R & R

Chevrolet 1969-70

1. Remove shock absorber upper stem retaining nut and grommet.
2. Support the car by the frame so that the control arms hang free. Remove the wheel assembly, shock absorber, stabilizer to lower control arm link, strut rod to lower control arm attaching nuts, bolts and lockwashers, and the tie-rod end.
3. Scribe the position of the inner pivot camber adjusting cam bolt and then remove the nut, lock washer and outer cam.
4. Install a steel bar through the shock absorber mounting hole in the lower control arm so that the notch in the bar seats over the bottom spring coil and the bar extends inboard and under the inner bushing. Fit a 5 in. wood block between the bar and the lower arm inner support bushing.

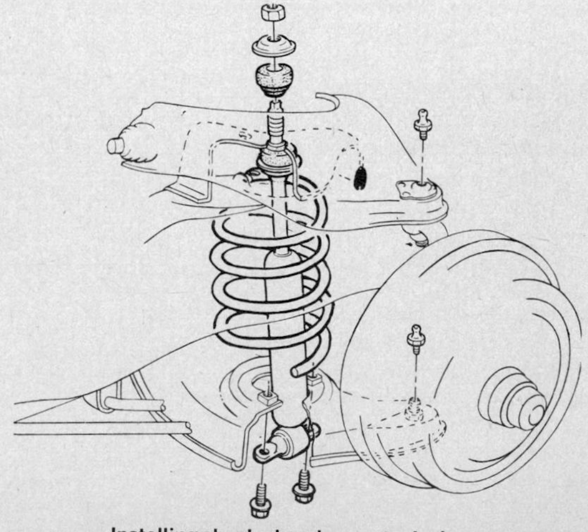

Installing shock absorbers—typical
(© Chevrolet Div., G.M. Corp)

5. With a floor jack, raise the end of the steel bar enough to remove tension from the inner pivot cam bolt. The bolt can then be removed.
6. Carefully lower the inner end of the control arm. Tension on the spring must be removed before the spring can be taken out of the car.
7. Remove the spring.
8. Install by reversing removal procedure.

NOTE: This tool is a cradle which, when fastened to a hydraulic jack, allows the lowering of the control arm and slow decompression of the spring. A similar tool can be fabricated in the shop. Always safety-chain the spring and control arm when using this method.

4. Remove cross shaft rear retaining nut and the two front retaining bolts.
5. Slowly release jack, swing control arm forward, then remove spring.

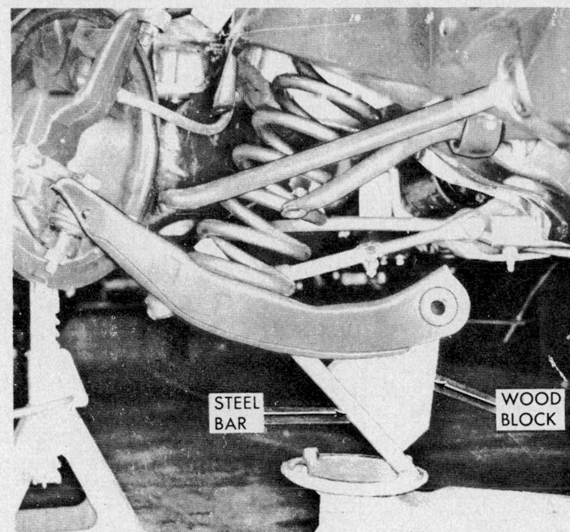

Chevrolet front spring removal
(© Chevrolet Div., G.M. Corp)

Chevrolet 1971-76
Corvette 1969-76

1. Raise car on hoist and remove nut, retainer and grommet from top of shock absorber. Support car so that control arms swing free.
2. Disconnect stabilizer bar from lower control arm and remove shock absorber.
3. Bolt spring remover tool (J-22944) to a suitable jack and place it under the lower control arm bushings so that the bushings seat in the grooves of the tool.

Corvette front spring removal
(© Chevrolet Div., G.M. Corp)

6. Install by reversing procedure above.

NOTE: Chevrolet recommends this cradle spring removal tool for all models, beginning in 1971. Either of the other two methods may be used, depending on the availability of tools.

Ball Joint Inspection

NOTE: before performing this inspection, make sure the wheel bearings are adjusted correctly and that the A arm bushings are in good condition.

1. Jack the car up under the front lower control arm at the spring seat.
2. Raise the car until there is 1-2 in. of clearance under the wheel.
3. Insert a bar under the wheel and pry upward. If the wheel raises more than 1/8 in. the ball joints are worn. Determine if the upper or lower ball joint is worn by visual inspection while prying on the wheel.

NOTE: due to the distribution of forces is the suspension, the lower ball joint is usually the defective joint. Also, 1973 and later Chevrolets are equipped with wear indicators on the lower ball joint. As long as the wear indicator neck extends below the ball stud seat, replacement is unnecessary.

Upper Ball Joint R & R

1. Raise the car on a hoist.
2. Remove the tire and wheel assembly.
3. Support the lower control arm with a jack.
4. Loosen the upper ball stud nut.
5. Install a ball joint remover tool and unseat the upper joint from the steering knuckle. Remove the upper stud nut and install a block of wood under the upper A-arm.
6. Chisel or grind off the ball joint mounting rivets.
7. Drill out the ball stud attaching holes to accept the service ball joint attaching bolts.
8. Install the ball joint with the nuts and bolts supplied with the new joint.
9. Install the lube fitting in the new joint.
10. Mate the upper control arm to the steering knuckle and install the ball stud through the knuckle boss.
11. Tighten the ball stud nut to 50 ft. lbs. plus whatever is necessary to align the cotter pin holes. Install the cotter pin.
12. Install the wheel and lower the vehicle.

Lower Ball Joint R & R

NOTE: On the 1971-76 Corvette, the lower ball joint removal and installation is the same as that described for the upper ball joint above. For all others:

1. On models through 1970, raise the vehicle on a hoist and remove the wheel. On vehicles equipped with disc brakes, remove the caliper assembly.
2. Support the lower control arm with a jack.
3. Loosen the lower ball stud nut. Break the ball stud loose. Remove the ball stud nut.
4. Remove the ball stud from the steering knuckle.
5. The ball joint in 1969-70 models is attached with rivets which must be chiseled or ground off. Beginning with 1971 models, the ball joint is pressed in and must be pressed out.
6. Install the new ball joint, using the bolts supplied with the service ball joint (drill out the rivet holes to accommodate the mounting bolts) on 1969-70 models. The thick-headed bolt is installed on the forward side of the control arm. Press in the ball joint on 1971 and later models.
7. Install the ball stud in the steering knuckle boss. This may be done by raising the lower control arm with the jack.
8. Install the nut on the ball stud, tightening to 80-90 ft. lbs.
9. Install the lube fitting.

Lower Control Arm R & R

1. Remove the spring as described above.

2. Remove the ball stud from the steering knuckle as described above.
3. Remove the control arm pivot bolts and remove the control arm. On some Corvettes, the pivot bolt is secured to the frame with two bolts.
4. To install, reverse the above procedure.

Upper Control Arm R & R

1. Raise the vehicle on a hoist.
2. Support the outer end of the lower control arm, with a jack.
3. Remove the wheel.
4. Separate the upper ball joint from the steering knuckle as described above under "Upper Ball Joint R&R"
5. Remove the control arm shaft to frame nuts.

NOTE: tape the shims together and identify them so that they can be installed in the positions from which they were removed.

6. Remove the bolts which attach the control arm shaft to the frame and remove the control arm. Note the positions of the bolts.
7. Install in the reverse order of removal. Make sure the shaft to frame bolts are installed in the same position they were in before removal and that the shims are in their original positions. Tighten the shaft to frame bolts to 85 ft. lbs. on the Chevrolet and to 55 ft. lbs. on the Corvette. The control arm shaft nuts are torqued to 60 ft. lbs.

REAR SUSPENSION

The Chevrolet uses a coil sprung Salisbury axle located by two trailing arms on each side, except the 1971–76 station wagon which has semi-elliptical leaf springs. The Corvette uses a three-link, independent suspension with a nine-leaf, transverse spring.

Rear Shock Absorber R & R

Chevrolet

1. Jack the car to a convenient working height.
2. If the car is equipped with superlift shock absorbers, disconnect the air line.
3. Remove the two retaining bolts from the upper mounting bracket.
4. Hold the hex on the bottom stud and disconnect the lower mounting. Remove the shock absorber.
5. Install the top two bolts hand-tight.
6. Install the lower stud into the axle bracket and install the lockwasher and nut hand-tight.
7. Torque the upper bolts to 12 ft lbs.
8. While holding the hex stud, torque the nut to 65 ft lbs.
9. Attach the air line, if so equipped, and lower the car.

Corvette

1. Jack the car to a convenient working height.
2. Remove the upper bolt and nut.
3. Remove the lower mounting nut and washers.
4. Pivot the top of the shock absorber out the frame bracket and pull the bottom off the strut shaft.
5. Slide the upper shock absorber eye into the frame bracket and install the bolt, lockwasher, and nut.
6. Install the rubber grommets on the lower shock eye and place the shock over the strut shaft. Install the washers and nut.
7. Torque the upper bolt to 50 ft lbs and the lower nut to 35 ft lbs. Lower the car.

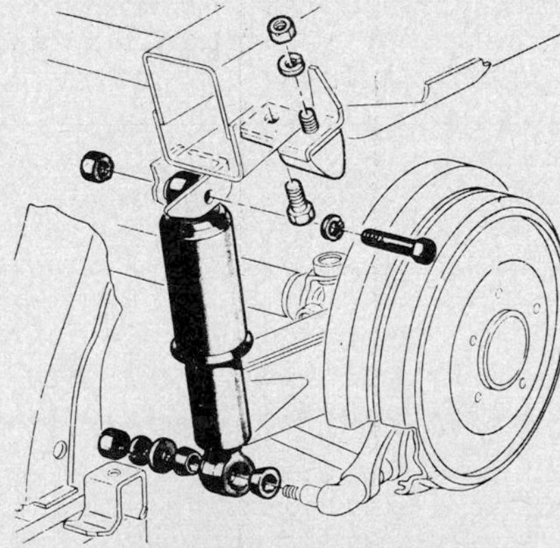

Shock absorber installation, Corvette
(© Chevrolet Div., G.M. Corp)

Coil Type Rear Springs (Chevrolet)

R & R

1. Raise rear of vehicle and place jack stands under frame. Support weight of vehicle at rear axle housing separately from above frame position.
2. Remove both rear wheels.
3. With car supported as in Step 1, and springs compressed by weight of vehicle:
   a. Disconnect both rear shocks from anchor pin lower connection.
   b. Loosen the upper control arm(s) rear pivot bolt (do not remove the nut).
   c. Loosen both left and right lower control arm rear attachment (do not disconnect from axle brackets).
   d. Remove rear suspension tie rod from stud on axle tube.
4. Slightly loosen the nut on the bolt that retains the spring and seat to control arm at lower seat of both rear springs. When bolt has been backed off the maximum distance, all threads of the nut should still be engaged on the bolt.

Caution Under no condition should the nut, at this time, be removed from the bolt in the seat of either spring.

5. Slowly lower the rear axle assembly, allowing the axle to swing down, carrying the springs out of the upper seat. This provides access for spring removal.
6. Remove the lower seat attaching parts from each spring, then remove springs from vehicle.
7. Position springs in upper seat and install lower seat parts on control arm. Install nut of spring retaining bolt finger-tight.

NOTE: Omit lockwasher under the special high carbon bolt, so that sufficient threads will be available to start the nut. Lockwashers will be installed later.

8. Alternately raise the axle slightly and retighten the nut on each spring lower seat bolt. Continue in until the weight is fully supported on the jack or lift. With spring now completely compressed to approximate curb

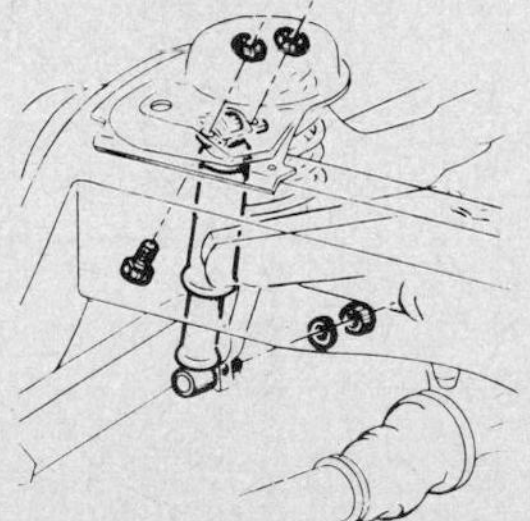

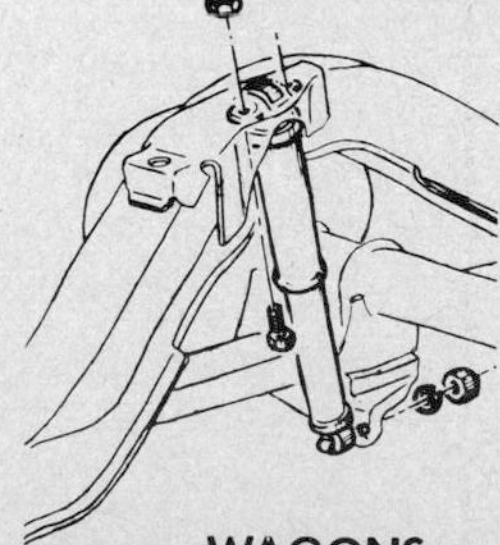

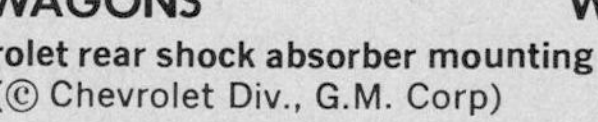

Chevrolet rear shock absorber mounting
(© Chevrolet Div., G.M. Corp)

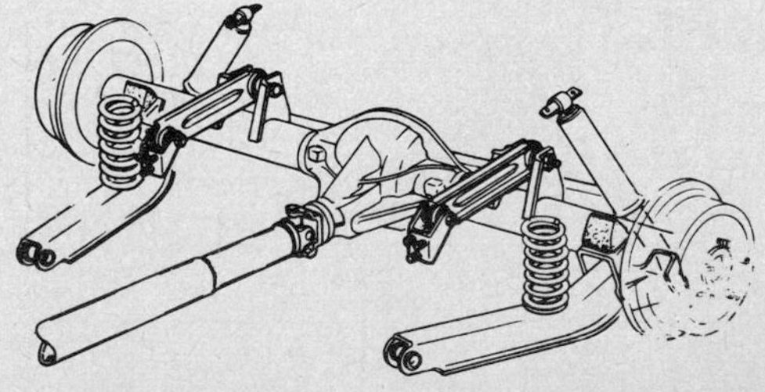

Chevrolet rear suspension except 1971-76 station wagon
(© Chevrolet Div., G.M. Corp)

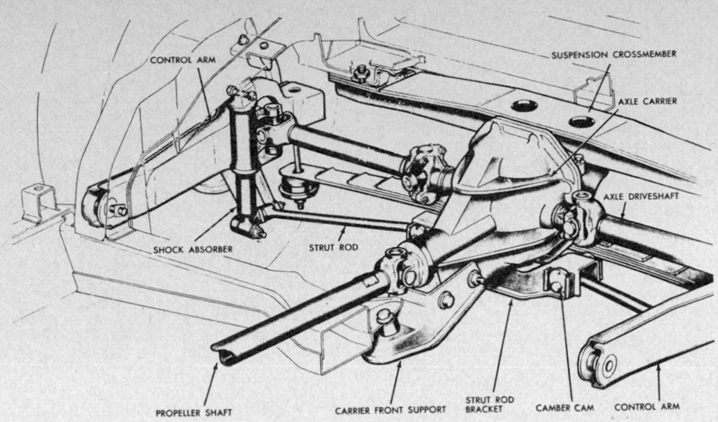

Corvette rear suspension
(© Chevrolet Div., G.M. Corp)

position, completely position the springs in the lower seats by torquing the nut on the lower seat bolt.

9. Reconnect shock absorbers, torque rear attachment of upper and lower control arms, and reconnect the axle tie-rod.
10. While still jacked under axle, remove the nut from the lower seat bolt of one rear spring and install lockwasher and replace nut and tighten. Similarly install lockwasher at other spring.
11. Install rear wheels and lower car to floor.

Transverse Leaf Spring (Corvette)

R & R

1. Raise car and support it by the frame, slightly forward of torque control pivot points. Remove wheel assemblies.
2. Place floor jack under spring near link bolt, and raise spring until nearly flat.
3. Tie the end of the spring to the suspension crossmember to hold this flat attitude, with a 1/4 in. or 5/16 in. chain and grab hook wrapped around the spring and crossmember. To prevent chain slipping, use a C-clamp on the spring adjacent to the chain.
4. Remove link bolt and rubber bushings.
5. Support and raise spring end, as before, and remove chain.
6. Carefully lower jack to completely relax spring.
7. Repeat foregoing procedure on the other side of car.
8. Remove four bolts and washers attaching the spring at the center.
9. Remove the spring by sliding it over the exhaust pipes and out one side of the car.
10. Install by reversing removal procedure.

Leaf Spring R & R Chevrolet 126 In. W.B. Station Wagon

1971-76

1. Raise the vehicle on a hoist and place an adjustable jack under the axle.
2. Raise the axle until all tension is relieved from the spring.
3. Disconnect the shock absorber from the spring retainer plate.
4. Remove the upper shackle retaining bolt, then the front spring eye bolt.
5. Remove the spring/axle U-bolts, lower plate, spring pads, and spring.
6. Remove the shackle from the spring.
7. Before installing the spring, install the shackle on the rearward end.
8. Place the upper cushion on the spring, then insert the front of the spring into the frame and attach the rear shackle, leaving the bolt loose.
9. Install the lower spring pad and retainer plate, tightening the U-bolt nuts to 40 ft. lbs.
10. Tighten the rear shackle bolts to 80 ft. lbs.
11. Tighten the front eye bolt to 115 ft. lbs.
12. Attach the shock absorber to spring retainer plate, tightening to 65 ft. lbs.
13. Remove the jack and lower the vehicle.

Strut Rod and Bracket (Corvette)

Rear Wheel Camber Adjustment

Due to the design of this rear suspension, it is important that the strut rod and rear wheel camber adjusting specifications and procedures be included.

Rod and Bracket—Removal

1. Raise car on a hoist.
2. Disconnect shock absorber lower eye from strut rod shaft.
3. Remove strut rod shaft cotter pin and nut. Withdraw shaft by pulling toward the front of the car.
4. Mark related position of camber adjustment, so that adjustment is maintained upon reassembly.
5. Loosen camber bolt and nut. Remove four bolts holding strut rod bracket to carrier and lower the bracket.
6. Remove cam bolt and cam bolt assembly. Pull strut down out of bracket and remove bushing caps.
7. Inspect strut rod bushings for wear and replace where necessary. Replace strut rod if it is bent or damaged in any way.
8. Install by reversing removal procedure.
9. Check rear wheel camber and adjust to specifications.

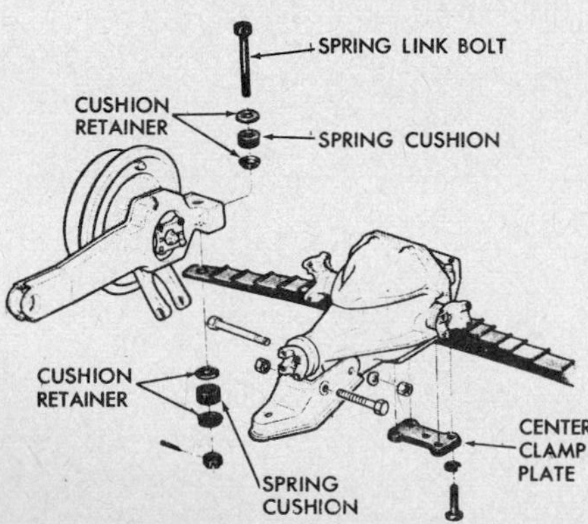

Spring mounting, Corvette
(© Chevrolet Div., G.M. Corp)

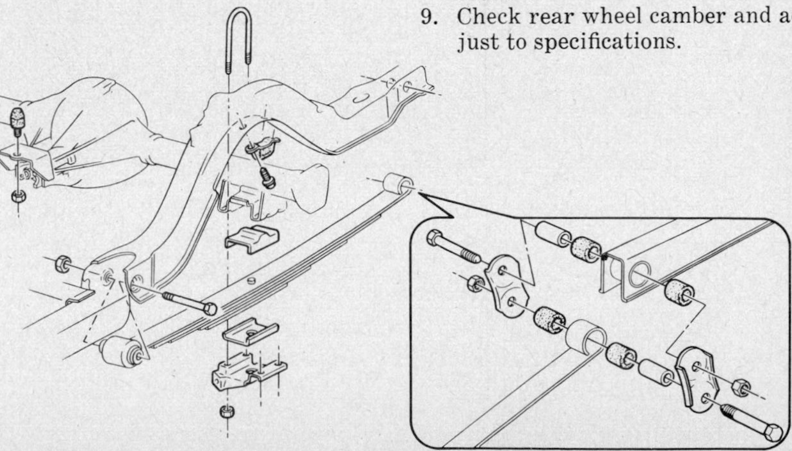

1971-76 126 in. W.B. station wagon rear suspension (© Chevrolet Div., G.M. Corp)

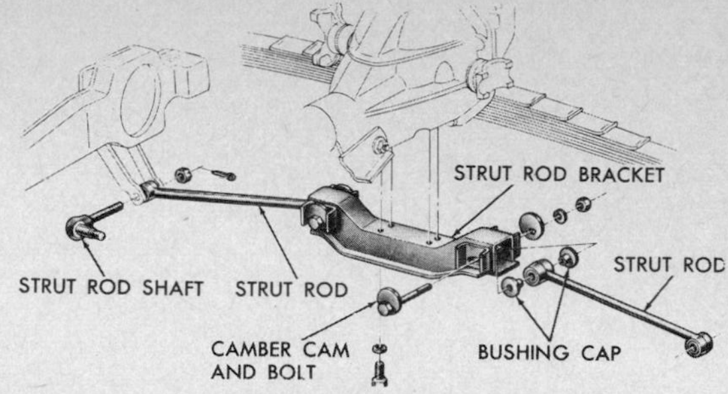

Strut rods, Corvette
(© Chevrolet Div., G.M. Corp)

Torque Control Arm R & R (Corvette)

1. Disconnect spring on the side from which the torque arm is to be removed. Follow procedure for Springs R & R.

NOTE: if so equipped, disconnect stabilizer rod from torque arm.

2. Remove shock absorber lower eye from strut rod shaft.
3. Disconnect and remove strut rod shaft and swing strut rod down.
4. Remove four bolts holding the axle driveshaft to spindle flange and disconnect drive shaft.
5. Disconnect brake line at wheel cylinder inlet or caliper and from torque arm. Disconnect parking brake cable.
6. Remove torque arm pivot bolt and toe-in shims, then pull torque arm out of frame. Tape shims together to assure relationship for reassembly.
7. To install, place torque arm in frame opening.
8. Position toe-in shims in original location on both sides of torque arm. Install pivot bolt and lightly tighten at this time.
9. Raise axle driveshaft into position and install to drive flange. Torque bolts to 75 ft. lbs.
10. Raise strut into position and insert strut rod shaft so that flat lines up with flat in spindle support fork. Install nut and torque to 80 ft. lbs.
11. Install shock absorber lower eye and tighten nut to 35 ft. lbs.
12. Connect spring end as outlined under Leaf Type Rear Springs R & R.

NOTE: if car is so equipped, connect stabilizer shaft.

13. Install brake drum or disc and caliper, and wheel. Then lower the car. Tighten torque pivot bolt to 50 ft. lbs.
14. Bleed brakes and check camber and toe-in.

BRAKES

Specific information on brake cylinder sizes can be found in the Brake Specifications table.

Brake adjustments, lining replacement, bleeding procedure, master and wheel cylinder overhaul can be found in the Unit Repair Section.

A dual hydraulic brake system is employed. The front and rear brakes are each separate systems with a common tandem master cylinder. In the event of a failure in either of the systems, the other will remain operable.

Corvette Parking Brake Adjustment

1. Jack the rear wheels off the ground and remove the wheels.
2. Rotate the disc until the adjusting screw can be seen through the hole in the disc.
3. Insert a screwdriver and adjust with an up-and-down motion.
4. Tighten the adjuster until the disc cannot move, then back off 6 to 8 notches.
5. Apply the parking brake to the fourth notch. Tighten the cables at the equalizer to give a light drag with the wheel mounted.
6. Release the parking brake and check for a no drag condition.

Power Brake Unit Removal

1. Remove vacuum hose from vacuum check valve.
2. Disconnect hydraulic lines at unit.
3. Disconnect push rod at brake pedal assembly.
4. Remove nuts and lockwashers that secure unit to firewall and remove unit.

Master Cylinder Removal

The pedals are pivoted from underneath the dash panel. The master cylinder is located on the engine side of the firewall.

1. To remove the master cylinder, disconnect the hydraulic lines, remove the clevis that connects

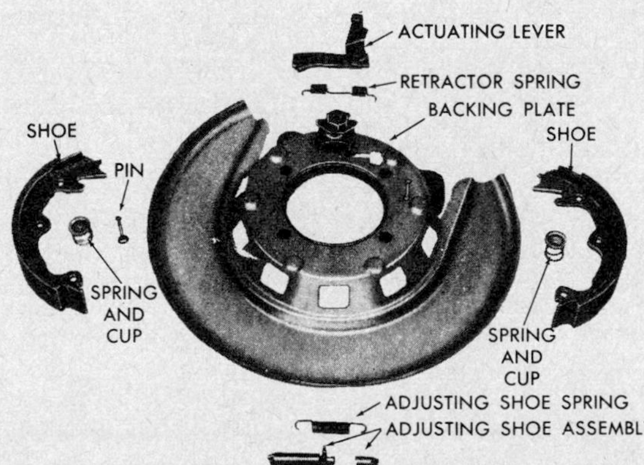

Corvette parking brake components
(© Chevrolet Div., G.M. Corp)

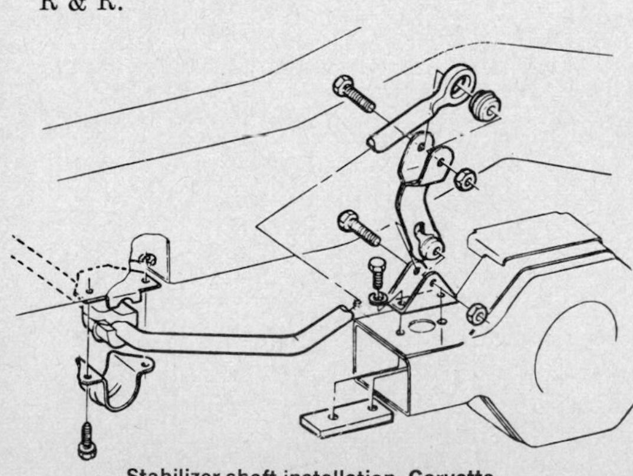
Stabilizer shaft installation, Corvette
(© Chevrolet Div., G.M. Corp)

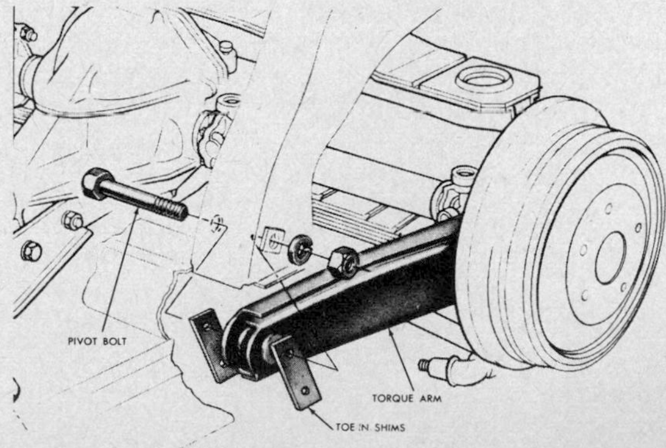

Torque control arm, Corvette
(© Chevrolet Div., G.M. Corp)

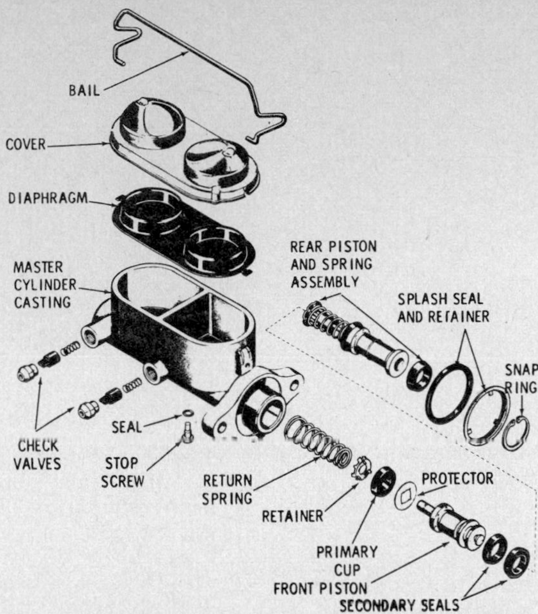

Master cylinder (Moraine) No front check valve with front disc brake
(© Chevrolet Div., G.M. Corp)

the brake pushrod to the brake pedal from under the dash.

2. Remove the mounting bolts that hold the master cylinder to the firewall and lift off the master cylinder.
3. To install, reverse the above procedure, and bleed the brake system when installation is complete.

Brake Pedal Free Travel Adjustment—Except Disc Brakes

The brake pedal stop is not adjustable, but brake pedal free travel is adjustable by setting the clearance between the pedal pushrod and the master cylinder.

1. Loosen the locknut on the pushrod.
2. Turn the pushrod until there is 1/16 to 1/4 in. pedal free travel (movement before the pushrod contacts the master cylinder pistons).
3. Tighten the locknut against the clevis and recheck the free travel.

Parking Brake Cable R & R

Before working under the dash to remove the front parking brake cable, disconnect the battery to avoid the possibility of shorting out any of the circuits.

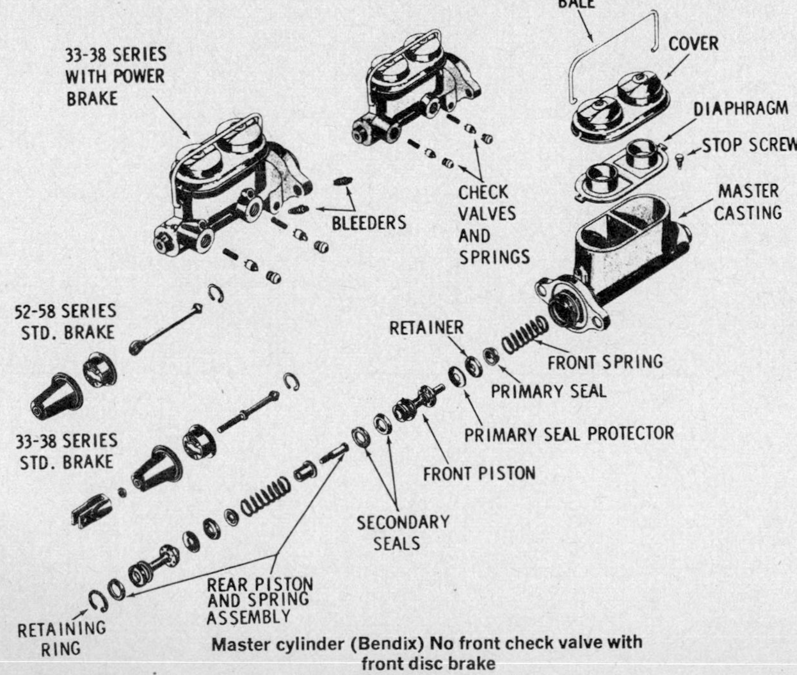

Master cylinder (Bendix) No front check valve with front disc brake
(© Chevrolet Div., G.M. Corp)

1969-70 Chevrolet

There are three parking brake cables: the front cable runs between the pedal assembly and the looped center cable; the center cable is a large loop, each end connected to the short rear cables and the center (forward) attached to the front cable with the equalizer; the rear cables are attached to brake shoe actuating levers.

To remove any of the cables, first release the brake pedal and loosen the equalizer adjusting nuts. The front cable slips into a clevis at the pedal lever and is connected to the equalizer by means of a threaded rod. The outer cable has locking fingers which secure it in a hole in the firewall.

The center cable is removed by disconnecting the equalizer, disconnecting each end from the rear cables and by removing it from the frame guides and hook. The rear cables are removed by disconnecting the forward end from the center cable, removing the retainers at the frame and by removing the rear end from the brake actuating levers. The brake drum and shoes must be removed to disconnect the rear cable from the actuating lever.

Adjust the parking brake after replacing any of the cables. Adjustment is made at the equalizer while the parking brake pedal is applied two notches from the full release position. Loosen the forward equalizer adjusting nut, tighten the rear nut until slight brake drag is obtained, then tighten the forward adjusting nut. Check operation after adjustment.

1971-76 Chevrolet

The parking brake cable design is essentially the same as that used in 1969-70 models with a forward, center and two rear cables. The front outer cable, however, is clipped to the pedal bracket. When replacing the front cable, tie a rope onto the top of the old cable and pull it through the cable route so that it may be used to pull the new cable into place. Remove the rear screws holding the inner fender panel to the fender to get at the cable grommet in the firewall. Adjustment is the same as that described for the 1968-1970 models above.

Corvette

To remove the front cable, remove the parking brake lever and the pulley. Remove the cable ball end from the hand lever. Remove the seal grommet from the underbody cable hole and pull the cable out of the vehicle. Installation is the reverse of the removal procedure.

To remove the rear cables, remove the retainer clips at the frame and disconnect the cables at the rear

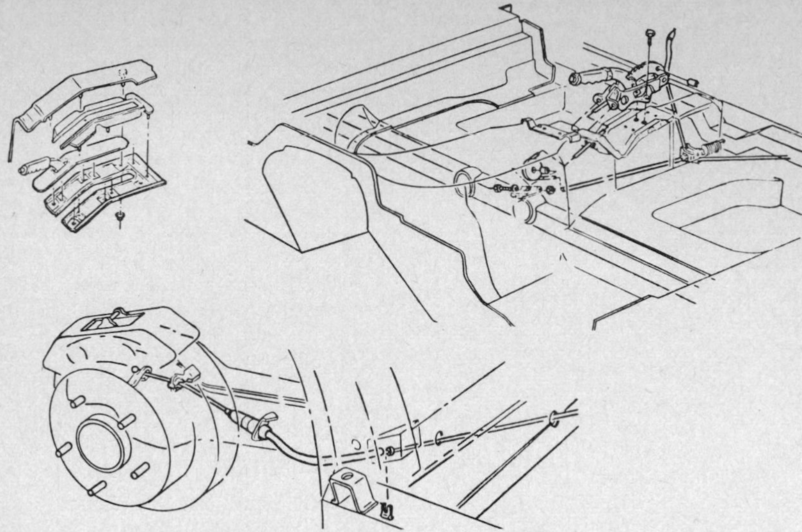

Corvette parking brake cables (© Chevrolet Div., G.M. Corp)

flange plate. Remove the ball from the recess of the brake lever clevis and disconnect the cables from the equalizer. Install in the reverse order of removal.

Adjustment of the parking brake is made with the lever set at two notches from the fully released position. Tighten the equalizer adjusting nuts until slight drag is felt at the rear wheels.

STEERING

Manual steering gear on both the Chevrolet and Corvette is of the recirculating ball type. Relay-type steering linkage is used on all models, with a pitman arm connected to one end of a relay rod and a frame-mounted idler arm at the other end. Two tie-rods assemblies connect the relay rod to the steering arms. The tie-rod ends are threaded into sleeves to provide adjustment.

Chevrolet power steering is the integral-gear type. The only external hydraulic lines on this system are the pressure and return hoses to the pump. The Corvette uses a linkage assist system. A valve attached to the linkage modulates pressure according to power requirements. A power cylinder supplies the actual assist.

Tie-Rod R & R

1. Remove the cotter pins and nuts from the tie-rod end studs.
2. Tap on the steering arm near the tie-rod end (use another hammer as backing) and pull down on the tie rod, if necessary, to free it.
3. Remove the inner stud in the same manner as the outer.
4. Loosen the clamp bolts and unscrew the ends if they are being replaced.
5. Lubricate the tie-rod end threads with chassis grease if they were removed. Install each end assembly an equal distance from the sleeve.
6. Ensure that the tie-rod end stud threads and nut are clean. Install new seals and install the studs into the steering arms and relay rod.
7. Install the stud nuts. Tighten the outer end nut to 35 ft lbs and the inner nut to 60 ft lbs (35 ft lbs on Corvette)
8. Adjust the toe-in as described in the "Front End Alignment" section.

NOTE: before tightening the sleeve clamps, ensure that the clamps are positioned so that the adjusting sleeve slot is covered by the clamp.

Idler Arm R & R

1. Remove the idler arm-to-frame nut, washer, and bolt (no washer is used on Corvette).
2. Remove the cotter pin and nut from the idler arm-to-relay rod ball end stud.
3. Tap the relay rod firmly with a hammer, using another heavy hammer as backing on the opposite side of the relay rod to remove the relay rod from the idler arm.
4. Remove the idler arm.
5. To install the idler arm on a Chevrolet, install the seal on the idler arm stud; position the stud up through the frame, and install the lockwasher and nut. Tighten the nut to 45 ft lbs.
6. To install the idler arm on a Corvette, place the idler arm on the frame and install the retaining bolts and nuts. Tighten the nuts to 35 ft lbs.
7. Position the relay rod on the idler arm. Ensure that the seal is on the stud. Install the nut and tighten to 40 ft lbs (Chevrolet) or 35 ft lbs (Corvette). Install a cotter pin.

Relay Rod R & R

Chevrolet

1. Remove the inner tie-rod ends from the relay rod as outlined under "Tie-Rod R&R."
2. Remove the relay rod stud nut and cotter pin from the pitman arm. Free the relay rod from the pitman arm, moving the steering linkage if necessary. Repeat this operation to remove the relay rod from the idler arm and remove the relay rod from the car.
3. Install the relay rod on the idler arm. Tighten the nut to 40 ft lbs.
4. Raise the relay and install it on the pitman arm. Tighten the nut to 45 ft lbs.

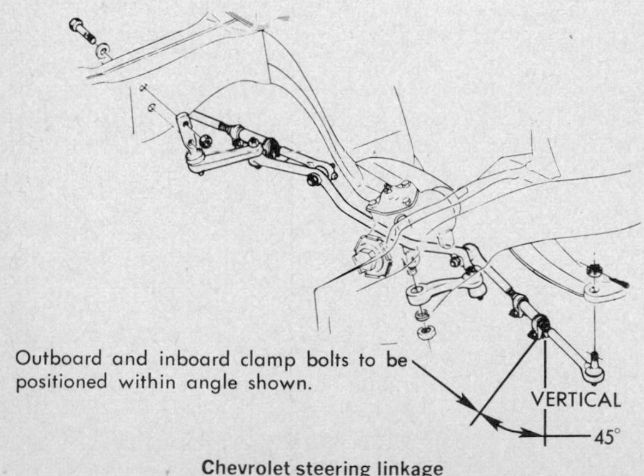

Chevrolet steering linkage
(© Chevrolet Div., G.M. Corp)

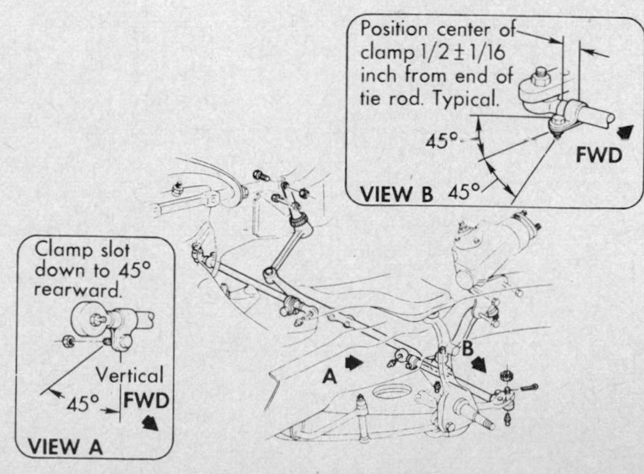

Corvette steering linkage
(© Chevrolet Div., G.M. Corp)

5. Adjust the toe-in as described in the "Front End Alignment" section.

Corvette

1. Remove the inner tie-rod ends from the relay rod as outlined in "Tie-Rod R&R."
2. Disconnect the relay rod at the pitman arm. Tap the stud out of the pitman arm and lower the relay rod.
3. Disconnect the relay rod from the idler arm and remove the rod. Remove the idler arm washer and seal.
4. Position the relay rod on the idler arm stud, ensuring that the seal and washer are in place, and then install the nut. Tighten the nut to 35 ft lbs and install a cotter pin.
5. Install a new pitman arm seal and clamp.
6. Install the inner spring seat and spring on the relay rod.
7. Raise the relay rod and install it on the pitman arm. Install the spring seat, spring, and end-plug.
8. Tighten the end-plug until the springs are compressed and the plug abuts, and then back it off ¾ of a turn. Insert a cotter pin to hold the adjustment.
9. Install the tie-rod ends as outlined under "Tie-Rod R&R."
10. Apply grease to the tie-rod ends and pitman arm-to-relay rod ball joint.
11. Adjust the toe-in as outlined in "Front End Alignment."

Pitman Arm R & R

1. Remove the pitman arm stud nut and cotter pin.
2. Tap the relay rod off the pitman arm, using another hammer as backing. Pull the relay rod off the pitman arm stud.
3. Remove the pitman arm nut and mark the arm-to-shaft relationship.
4. Remove the pitman arm using a puller.
5. Install the pitman arm on the shaft, aligning the previously made marks. Install the pitman shaft nut and tighten it to 180 ft lbs (Chevrolet) or 140 ft lbs (Corvette).

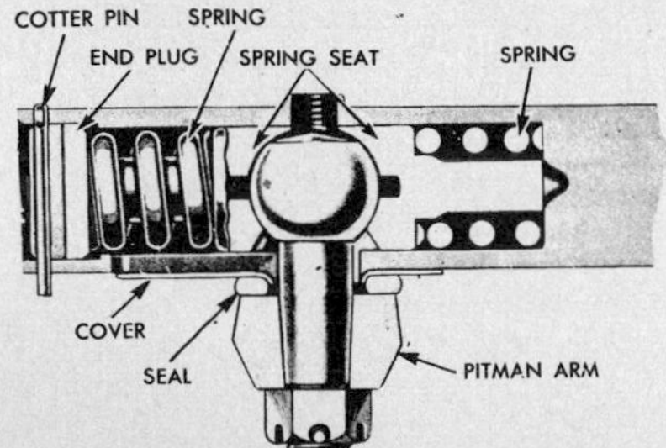

Corvette pitman arm attachment to relay rod (© Chevrolet Div., G.M. Corp)

6. Install the relay rod on the pitman arm. Tighten the nut to 45 ft lbs and install a cotter pin.

Power Steering Pump R & R

1. Remove the hoses at the pump and tape the openings shut to prevent contamination. Position the disconnected lines in a raised position to prevent leakage.
2. Remove the pump belt. On 427 and 454 Corvettes, loosen the alternator and remove the pump-to-alternator belt.
3. Loosen the retaining bolts and any braces, and remove the pump.
4. Install the pump on the engine with the retaining bolts hand-tight.
5. Connect and tighten the hose fittings.
6. Refill the pump and bleed by turning the pulley counterclockwise (viewed from the front). Stop the bleeding when air bubbles no longer appear.
7. Install the pump belt on the pulley and adjust the tension.

Bleeding Power Steering System

1. Fill the fluid reservoir.
2. Let the fluid stand undisturbed for two minutes, then crank the engine for about two seconds. Refill reservoir if necessary.
3. Repeat Steps 1 and 2 above until the fluid level remains constant after cranking the engine.
4. Raise the front of the car until the wheels are off the ground, then start the engine. Increase the engine speed to about 1,500 rpm.
5. Turn the wheels to the left and right, checking the fluid level and refilling if necessary.

Steering Wheel R & R

Caution Disconnect the battery ground cable before removing the steering wheel. When installing a steering wheel, always make sure that the turn signal lever is in the neutral position.

1975 and later models have a snap ring on the steering column which must be removed for steering wheel service.

Chevrolet 1969 Deluxe Wheel and Standard Wheel 1970-76

1. Remove the four trim retaining screws from behind the wheel.
2. Lift the trim off and pull the horn wires from the turn signal cancelling cam.
3. Remove the steering wheel nut.
4. Mark the wheel-to-shaft relationship, and then remove the wheel with a puller.
5. Install the wheel on the shaft, aligning the previously made marks. Tighten the nut to 30 ft lbs.
6. Insert the horn wires into the cancelling cam.
7. Install the center trim and reconnect the battery cable.

NOTE: The 1969 Chevrolet simulated wood wheel, the 1973 Chevrolet cushioned rim wheel, and the Corvette wheel do not require pulling for removal. Pry off the center cap and horn contact assembly. On the tilt/telescope Corvette wheel, remove the shim, center lock-screw, lock lever or knob, and the spacer. The wheel is held to the hub by phillips screws. Reverse the disassembly procedure to install the wheel.

Caution *On 1973 Chevrolets equipped with the air bag restraint system, refer to the Oldsmobile section for steering wheel and turn signal switch service.*

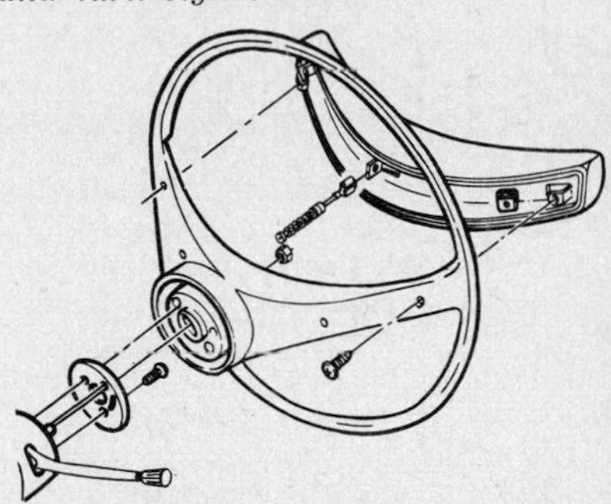

1969 Chevrolet Deluxe and 1970-76 standard steering wheel (© Chevrolet Div., G.M. Corp)

Turn Signal Switch R & R

Chevrolet and Corvette

1. Remove the steering wheel as previously outlined.
2. Loosen the three cover screws and lift the cover off the shaft.
3. Position the special lockplate compressing tool (J-23131 1969-70 or J-23653 1971-76) on the end of the steering shaft and compress the lockplate by turning the shaft nut clockwise. Pry the wire snap-ring out of the shaft groove.
4. Remove the tool and lift the lockplate off the shaft.
5. Slip the cancelling cam, upper bearing pre-load spring, and thrust washer off the shaft.
6. Remove the turn signal lever. Push the flasher knob in and unscrew it.
7. Pull the switch connector out of the mast jacket and tape the upper part to facilitate switch removal. On tilt wheels, place the turn signal and shifter housing in Low position and remove the harness cover.
8. Remove the three switch mounting screws. Remove the switch by pulling it straight up while guiding the wiring harness cover through the column.
9. Install the replacement switch by

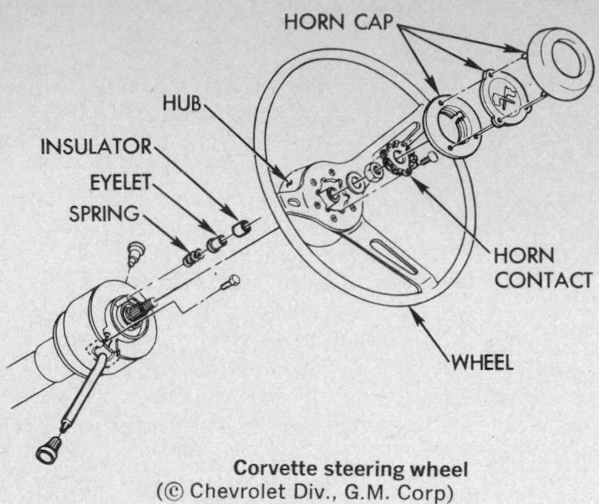

Corvette steering wheel
(© Chevrolet Div., G.M. Corp)

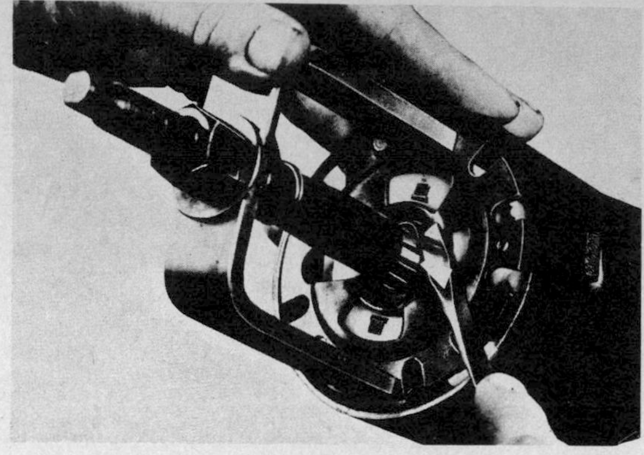

Compressing steering wheel lockplate and removing snap-ring
(© Chevrolet Div., G.M. Corp)

working the connector and cover down through the housing and under the bracket. On tilt models, the connector is worked down through the housing, under the bracket, and then the cover is installed on the harness.

10. Install the switch mounting screws and the connector on the mast jacket bracket. Install the column-to-dash trim plate.
11. Install the flasher knob and the turn signal lever.
12. With the turn signal lever in neutral and the flasher knob out, slide the thrust washer, upper bearing pre-load spring, and cancelling cam onto the shaft.
13. Position the lockplate on the shaft and press it down until a new snap-ring can be inserted in the shaft groove.
14. Install the cover and the steering wheel.

Corvette Tilt-Telescope

1. Remove the steering wheel as previously outlined and press off the hub with a puller.
2. Remove the steering column/dash trim cover.
3. Remove the C-ring plastic retainer, if so equipped.
4. Install the special lockplate compressing tool (J-23131 1969–70 or J-23653 1971-76) over the steering shaft. Position a 5/16 in. nut under each tool leg and reinstall the star screw to prevent the shaft from moving.
5. Compress the lockplate by turning the shaft nut clockwise until the C-ring can be removed.
6. Remove the tool and lift out the lock plate, horn contact carrier, and the upper bearing preload spring.

NOTE: 1969 Corvette assembly order is: horn control carrier, lockplate, and upper bearing preload spring.

7. Pull the switch connector out of the mast jacket and tape the upper part to facilitate switch removal.
8. Remove the turn signal lever. Push the flasher in and unscrew it.
9. Position the turn signal and shifter housing in Low position. Remove the switch by pulling it straight up while guiding the wiring harness out of the housing.
10. Install the replacement switch by working the harness connector down through the housing and under the mounting bracket.
11. Install the harness cover and clip the connector to the mast jacket.
12. Install the switch mounting screws, signal lever, and the flasher knob.
13. With the turn signal lever in neutral and the flasher knob out, install the upper bearing pre-load spring, horn contact carrier, and lockplate onto the shaft. Horn contact carrier is last on 1969 models.
14. Position the tool as in step four and compress the plate far enough to allow the C-ring to be installed.
15. Remove the tool. Install the plastic C-ring retainer.
16. Install the column/dash trim cover. Install the steering wheel.

INSTRUMENT PANEL

Caution Disconnect battery while working on the speedometer or gauges.

Ignition Switch Replacement

Chevrolet & Corvette

The switch is located inside the channel section of the brake pedal support and is completely inaccessible without first lowering the steering column. The switch is actuated by a rod and rack assembly. A gear on the end of the lock cylinder engages the toothed upper end of the rod.

1. Remove or lower the steering column as described under *Steering.* If steering column is lowered, be sure to properly support it.
2. Put the switch in "Lock" position. With the cylinder removed, the rod is in "Lock" position when it is in the next to the uppermost detent.
3. Remove the two switch screws and remove the switch assembly.
4. Before installing, place the new switch in "Lock" position and make sure the lock cylinder and actuating rod are in "Lock" position (second detent from the top).
5. Install the activating rod into the switch and assemble the switch on the column. Tighten the mounting screws. Use only the specified screws since over-length screws could impair the collapsibility of the column.
6. Reinstall the steering column.

Lock Cylinder R & R

1. Remove steering wheel and directional signal switch.

NOTE: see *Steering.*

2. Place lock cylinder in Lock position up to 1970, Run position starting 1971.

Caution Do not remove the ignition key buzzer.

3. Insert a small screwdriver into the turn signal housing slot. Keeping the screwdriver to the right side of the slot, break the housing flash loose and depress the spring latch at the lower end of the lock cylinder. Remove the lock cylinder.

NOTE: Considerable force may be necessary to break this casting flash, but be careful not to damage any other parts. When ordering a new lock cylinder, specify a cylinder assembly. This will save assembling the cylinder, washer, sleeve and adaptor.

4. To install, hold the lock cylinder sleeve and rotate the knob clockwise against the stop. Insert the cylinder into the housing, aligning the key and keyway. Hold a .070 in. drill between the lock bezel and housing. Rotate the cylinder counterclockwise, maintaining a light pressure until the

drive section of the cylinder mates with the sector. Push in until the snap ring pops into the grooves. Remove drill. Check cylinder operation.

Caution The drill prevents forcing the lock cylinder inward beyond its normal position. The buzzer switch and spring latch can hold the lock cylinder in too far. Complete disassembly of the upper bearing housing is necessary to release an improperly installed lock cylinder.

Headlight Switch Replacement

Chevrolet

1. Disconnect battery.
2. Pull knob out to on position.
3. Reach under instrument panel and depress the switch shaft retainer. Remove knob and shaft assembly.
4. Remove the retaining ferrule nut. (Tool J-4880 will assist.)
5. Remove switch from instrument panel.
6. Disconnect the multi-plug connector from the switch.
7. Replace in reverse of above. (In checking lights before installation, switch must be grounded to test dome light.)

Corvette

1. Disconnect the battery.
2. Remove mast jacket trim covers.
3. Unclip and remove the left forward console side trim panel.
4. Lower the steering column as described under *Steering*.
5. Remove the screws and washers which secure the left instrument panel to the door opening, the top of the dash and the left side of the center instrument cluster.
6. Pull the cluster assembly down and tilt it forward.
7. Depress the switch shaft retainer and remove the knob and shaft assembly.
8. Remove the switch retaining bezel.
9. Disconnect the vacuum lines, identifying them for correct reconnection.
10. Pry the connector from the switch.
11. Install in the reverse order of removal.

WINDSHIELD WIPERS

Motor R & R

Corvette and Chevrolet

1. With wiper motor in park position and hood open, disconnect the washer hoses and all wiring from the motor assembly.
2. Remove the plenum chamber grill on Corvettes or the access cover on Chevrolet models.
3. Loosen the nuts which retain the drive link to the crank arm ball stud on Chevrolet models. Remove the nut which retains the crank arm to the motor assembly on Corvette models.
4. On Corvettes, remove the ignition shield and distributor cap. Remove and identify the left bank spark plug leads.
5. Remove the motor mounting screws or nuts and remove the motor.
6. To install, reverse the above procedure.

Transmission R & R

Chevrolet and Corvette

1. Open the hood and disconnect the battery.
2. Make sure that the wiper motor is in park position.
3. On 1969-72 Corvette models, remove the rubber plug from the front of the wiper door actuator, then insert a screwdriver, pushing the internal piston rearward to open the door.
4. Remove the wiper arm and blade. On the articulated left hand arm assembly, remove the retaining clip from the pin on the drive arm.
5. Remove the plenum chamber air intake grill or screen.
6. Loosen the nuts which retain the drive rod ball stud to the crank arm and detach the drive rod from the crank arm.
7. Remove the transmission retaining screws or nuts, then lower the drive rod assemblies into the plenum chamber.
8. Remove the transmission and linkage from the plenum chamber through the cowl opening.
9. To install, reverse the above procedure.

RADIO

R & R

1969-72 Chevrolet

1. Disconnect battery.
2. Remove ash tray, retainer attaching screws and retainer.
3. Remove heater control panel retaining screws and push panel assembly from console.

NOTE: if interference between control panel and radio is met, loosen radio retaining nuts.

4. Remove radio control knobs, bezels and retaining nuts.
5. Disconnect radio wiring harness, and antenna lead-in.
6. Remove radio rear brace attaching screw, and remove radio from the car.
7. Remove speaker retaining bolt and remove speaker.
8. To install, reverse removal procedure.

1973-76 Chevrolet

1. Disconnect the negative battery cable.
2. On cars with A/C, remove the lap cooler duct.
3. Turn the radio control knobs until the slots in the bottom of the knobs are visible. Depress the metal retainers with a screwdriver and remove the knobs and bezels.
4. Remove the control shaft nuts and washers.
5. Remove the right side bracket-to-instrument panel bolt and the stud nut on the left side of the radio.
6. Pull the radio forward and disconnect the wiring from the radio and remove the radio from the car.

1969-71 Corvette Coupe

1. Disconnect battery.
2. Remove right and left door sill plates and kick pads.
3. Disconnect right and left side radio-to-speaker connectors.
4. Remove right side dash pad.
5. Remove right and left console forward trim pads.
6. Remove bolt and remove the heater floor outlet duct by pulling it through left hand opening.
7. From front of console, tape radio push buttons in depressed position. From rear of console, disconnect electrical connector, brace and antenna lead-in.
8. Remove radio knobs and bezel retaining nuts. Push radio assembly forward and remove from rear through right side opening.
9. Install by reversing procedure above.

1969-71 Corvette Convertible

1. Disconnect battery.
2. Remove right instrument panel pad.
3. Disconnect speaker connectors.
4. Remove wiper switch trim plate screws to gain access to switch connector and remove connector and trim plate from cluster assembly.
5. Unclip and remove right and left console forward trim pads and remove forwardmost screw on right and left side of console.
6. Inserting a flexible drive socket between the console and metal horseshoe brace, remove the nuts from the two studs on the lower edge of the console cluster. Remove the remaining screws that retain the cluster assembly to the instrument panel.
7. From rear of console, disconnect electric connector, brace and antenna lead-in.
8. Remove radio knobs and bezel retaining nuts.
9. Pull radio assembly forward and

remove through right side opening.
10. Install by reversing procedure above.

1972-76 Corvette

1. Disconnect the negative battery cable and remove the right instrument panel pad.
2. Disconnect the radio speaker connectors.
3. Remove the wiper switch trim plate screws and tip the plate forward to gain access to the switch connector. Remove the switch connector and trim plate from the dash.
4. Unclip and remove the right and left forward console trim pads. Remove the forwardmost screw on the left and right sides of the console.
5. Working with a flexible drive socket between the console and the metal horseshoe brace, remove the nuts from the studs on the lower edge of the console cluster.
6. Remove the remaining console attaching screws and disconnect the radio electrical connectors, antenna wire and radio brace from the rear of the console. Remove the radio knobs and nuts.
7. Pull the top of the console rearward and separate the radio from the console and remove it from the right side opening.

NOTE: The center instrument cluster trim panel is designed to collapse under impact. Do not deflect the panel to gain access to the radio. Also, the remotely located radio heat sink should be removed with the radio when servicing is required.

HEATER

Heater Blower R & R

Chevrolet

1. Disconnect battery.
2. Unclip hoses from fender skirt.
3. Disconnect electrical feed from motor. Disconnect the motor air-cooling hose on air-conditioned cars.
4. Turn vehicle front wheels to extreme right.
5. Remove right front fender skirt bolts and allow skirt to drop, resting it on top of tire. It may be wedged away from fender lower flange with block of wood to provide better access to bolts.
6. Remove screws attaching motor mounting plate to air inlet housing.
7. Remove screws attaching motor to mounting plate.
8. Remove clip attaching cage to shaft and remove blower motor.
9. Install in reverse of above.

Corvette (Non-Air Conditioned)

1. Remove the radiator supply tank from its retaining straps. Move it out of the way. Disconnect the battery.
2. Remove blower motor electrical connectors.
3. Scribe a reference mark on the blower motor mounting plate and the blower motor.
4. Remove the five screws that mount the blower mounting plate to the blower inlet assembly.
5. Withdraw the blower assembly from the inlet assembly.
6. Install in reverse of removal procedure.

Corvette with Air Conditioning

1. Remove the battery ground cable.
2. Disconnect the air cooling tube and electrical wire from the blower motor.
3. Remove the first three sill molding screws and pry the molding out to allow access to the right splash shield bolts.
4. Remove the splash shield.
5. Remove the motor retaining screws and drop the motor out through the splash shield opening. Pry on the mounting flange gently, if necessary to break the motor loose.
6. Reverse the removal steps to install the motor.

Heater Core R & R

All Except Air Conditioned Cars

1. Drain radiator.
2. Remove heater hoses at connections beside air inlet assembly.
3. Remove cable and electrical connectors from heater and defroster assembly.
4. On engine side of dash, remove screws and nuts holding air inlet to dash panel.
5. Inside vehicle, pull entire assembly from firewall and remove assembly from vehicle.
6. Remove core assembly retaining springs and remove core.
7. Install in reverse of above.

NOTE: This procedure is not applicable to air-conditioned cars, except pre-1970 models with the dealer-installed, under dash unit.

1969-71 Chevrolet with Air Conditioning

1. Remove the battery ground cable.
2. Drain the cooling system. It is not necessary to evacuate the A.C. refrigerant.
3. Remove the heater hoses at the firewall.
4. Remove the nuts from the heater distributor studs protruding through the firewall.
5. Remove the glove compartment.
6. Remove the five center distributor duct hoses, duct cables, center duct-to-selector duct screws, and the center duct.
7. From inside the car, drill out the lower case stud using a 1/4 in. drill.
8. Remove the floor distributor duct.
9. Remove the firewall screws and pull the selector from the firewall.
10. Remove all wires, vacuum lines, and cables attached to the assembly, and remove it from the car.
11. Scribe the temperature door camming plate-to-selector duct relationship and remove the plate.
12. Remove the heater core and core housing from the selector duct.
13. Reverse the removal steps to install.

1972-76 Chevrolet with Air Conditioning

1. Drain the cooling system. It is not necessary to evacuate the A.C. refrigerant.
2. Disconnect the battery ground cable and compressor clutch connector.
3. Disconnect the vacuum line from the vacuum check valve and push the grommet through the firewall into the passenger compartment.
4. Disconnect the heater hoses at the firewall.
5. Remove the three screws and nuts retaining the heater and selector duct. The inner fender must be pried out from the firewall to gain access to one screw.
6. Remove the lap cooler assembly.
7. Remove the glove compartment.
8. Remove the floor outlet duct and dash panel pad.
9. Disconnect the distributor duct hoses and connector.
10. Remove the duct from the selector.
11. Loosen the defroster duct and move it to provide access to the selector and core assembly.
12. Disconnect the temperature door cable.
13. Separate the inline vacuum connector and the outside air diaphragm line.
14. Lift the heater and air selector duct out as an assembly.
15. Remove the retaining screws and remove the heater core from the selector.

Corvette with Air Conditioning

1. Disconnect the battery ground cable.
2. Drain the cooling system. It is not necessary to evacuate the A.C. refrigerant.
3. Disconnect the heater hoses at the firewall and plug the pipes.
4. Remove the nuts from the distributor studs protruding through the firewall.
5. Remove the right side dash pad and center dash cluster (described under "Instruments").

HEATER CIRCUIT DIAGNOSIS

BLOWER MOTOR INOPERATIVE (ANY SPEED)

Check fuse (25 amp Heater A/C)

- **FUSE BLOWN**
  - With Ignition switch in "RUN" position and blower speed switch "ON" use meter to locate short in one of the following wires:
    1. From fuse panel to blower speed switch.
    2. From blower speed switch to heater resistor.
    3. From heater resistor to blower.

    Note: Short circuit may be intermittent. If meter does not indicate a short circuit, move harness around as much as possible to re-create short circuit. Watch and listen for arcing.
- **FUSE OK**
  - The following tests should be made with the ignition switch in "RUN" position the blower speed switch "ON" and the lever on heat position.
  - Check blower motor ground
    - **POOR OR NO GROUND** → Repair ground
    - **GROUND OK** → Check motor connector with 12 volt test light.
      - **LAMP LIGHTS** → Replace Motor
      - **LAMP DOES NOT LIGHT** → Check orange wire connector on resistor with 12 volt test light.
        - **LAMP DOES NOT LIGHT** → Use 12 volt test light and check feed terminal (brown) on blower speed switch.
          - **LAMP DOES NOT LIGHT** → Repair open in brown wire from blower speed switch to fuse panel.
          - **LAMP LIGHTS** → Replace switch
        - **LAMP LIGHTS** → Repair open in orange wire from resistor to blower motor.

BLOWER MOTOR INOPERATIVE (CERTAIN SPEEDS)**

Disconnect resistor connector, connect one lead of a self powered test light to any one terminal and use the other lead to probe each of the other two terminals.

- **TEST LIGHT DOES NOT LIGHT ON ALL TERMINALS** → Replace resistor
- **TEST LIGHT LIGHTS ON ALL TERMINALS** → With ignition "OFF", disconnect 3 wire connector from resistor. Connect a jumper lead from battery positive terminal to the yellow wire terminal in connector. Use 12 volt test light to check for voltage at yellow wire on blower speed switch. Repeat same test on other wires.
  - **LAMP LIGHTS ON ALL THREE WIRES** → Replace blower speed switch
  - **LAMP DOES NOT LIGHT ON ALL THREE WIRES** → Repair open in affected wire

** Vehicles with Engine Thermal Switch. Set blower switch on "LO". If engine temperature at switch is above 95° F, blower should operate. If blower is inoperative, remove switch connector and jump connector terminals. If blower now operates, replace switch. If blower is inoperative, proceed with resistor and blower switch checks.

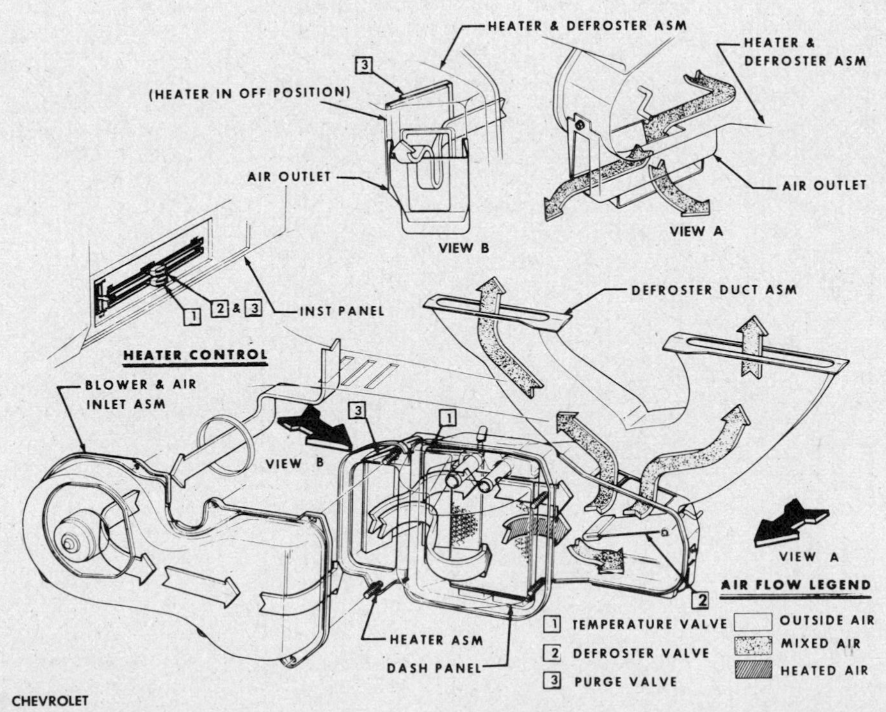

Heater Air-Flow
(© Chevrolet Div., G.M. Corp.)

6. Disconnect the right dash outlet from the center duct.
7. Remove the center duct from the selector duct.
8. Remove the selector duct to the dash panel and pull it to the right and to the rear.
9. Remove the cables and wiring connectors from the selector and remove it from the car.
10. Remove the temperature door cam plate from the selector duct.
11. Remove the heater core and housing from the selector.
12. Reverse the removal procedure to install.

SEAT BELTS

Warning System

1972-73

The seat belt warning system consists of lap belt retractor switches, a pressure-sensitive switch underneath the right-hand front passenger's seat, a warning lamp and a buzzer.

On manual transmission-equipped cars, the circuit is wired through the ignition switch, the parking brake warning light switch, and a relay, which is located between the instrument cluster wiring and the switch on the parking brake. A diode is used to prevent feedback into the parking brake warning circuit.

On cars having automatic transmissions, the seat belt warning circuit is wired through the ignition switch and the combination back-up lamp/neutral safety switch.

With the ignition key in the "RUN" position, a weight of 40-50 lbs on the driver's or passenger's seat pressure-sensitive switch) energizes the circuit when the parking brake is released (M/T) or the gear selector placed in a forward drive range (A/T).

A warning light will glow and a buzzer will sound with the circuit energized, unless the seat belts are withdrawn from the retractors and fastened over the laps of the two outboard front seat occupants.

Seat Belt/Starter Interlock System

As required by law, all 1974 and later Chevrolet passenger cars cannot be started until the front seat occupants are seated and have fastened their seat belts. If the proper sequence is not followed, e.g., the occupants fasten their seat belts and then sit on them, the engine cannot be started.

If, after the car is started, the seat belts are unfastened, a warning buzzer and light will be activated in a similar manner to that described for 1972-73 models.

The shoulder harness and lap belt are permanently fastened together, so that they both must be worn. The shoulder harness uses an inertia-lock reel to allow freedom of movement under normal driving conditions.

NOTE: This type of reel locks up when the car decelerates rapidly, as during a crash.

The lap belts use the same ratchet-type retractors that the 1972-73 models use.

The switches for the interlock system have been removed from the lap belt retractors and placed in the belt buckles. The seat sensors remain the same as those used in 1972-73.

For ease of service, the car may be started from outside, by reaching in and turning the key, but without depressing the seat sensors.

In case of system failure or for service, an override switch is located under the hood. This is a "one start"

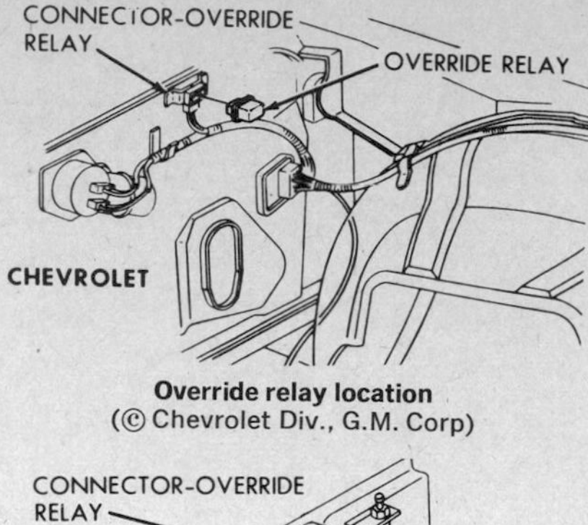

Override relay location
(© Chevrolet Div., G.M. Corp)

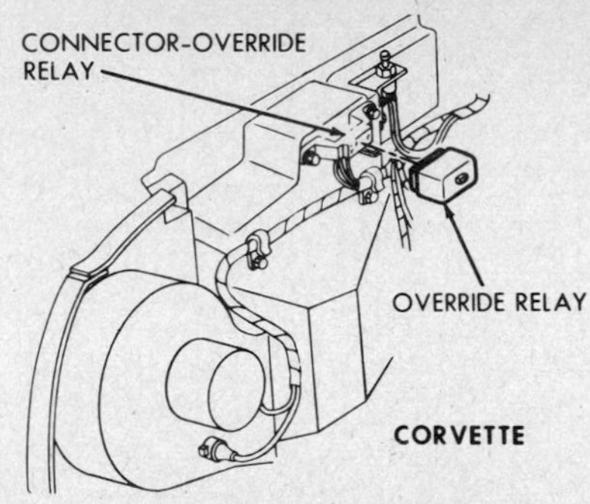

Override relay location
(© Chevrolet Div., G.M. Corp)

switch and it must be reset each time it is used.

Disabling the Interlock System

Since the requirement for the interlock system was dropped during the 1975 model year, these systems may now be legally disabled. The seat belt warning light is still required.

1. Disconnect the battery ground cable.
2. Locate the interlock harness connector under the left side of the instrument panel on or near the fuse block. It has orange, yellow, and green leads.
3. Cut and tape the ends of the green wire on the body side of the connector.
4. Remove the buzzer from the fuse block or connector.

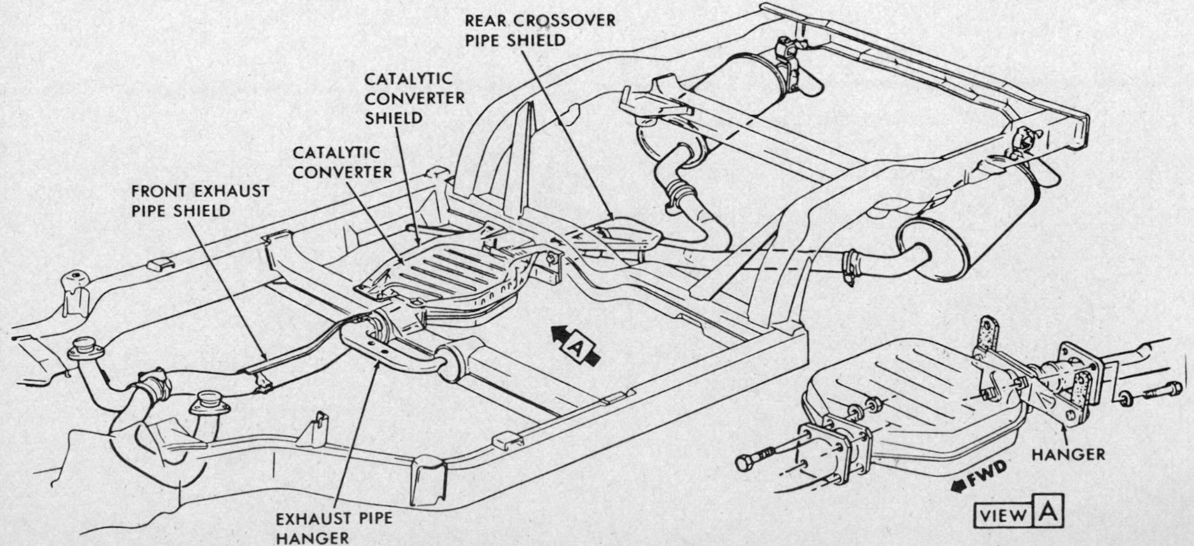

1975 Corvette exhaust system and catalytic converter
(© Chevrolet Div., G.M. Corp)

Chevette

YEAR IDENTIFICATION

1976

FIRING ORDER

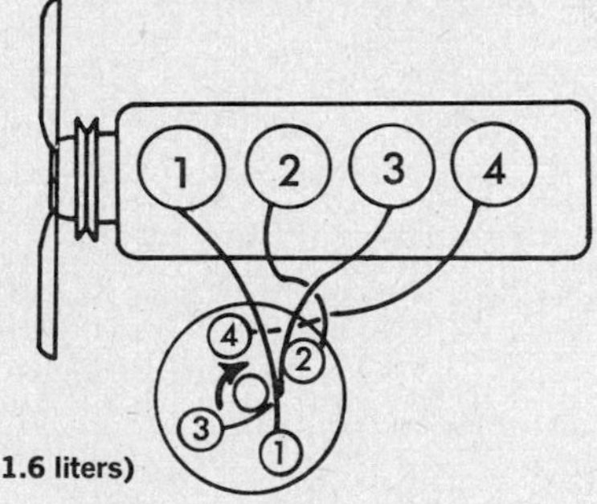

CHEVROLET Chevette 4-cyl. engine (1.4 & 1.6 liters)

Engine firing order: 1-3-4-2

Distributor rotation: clockwise

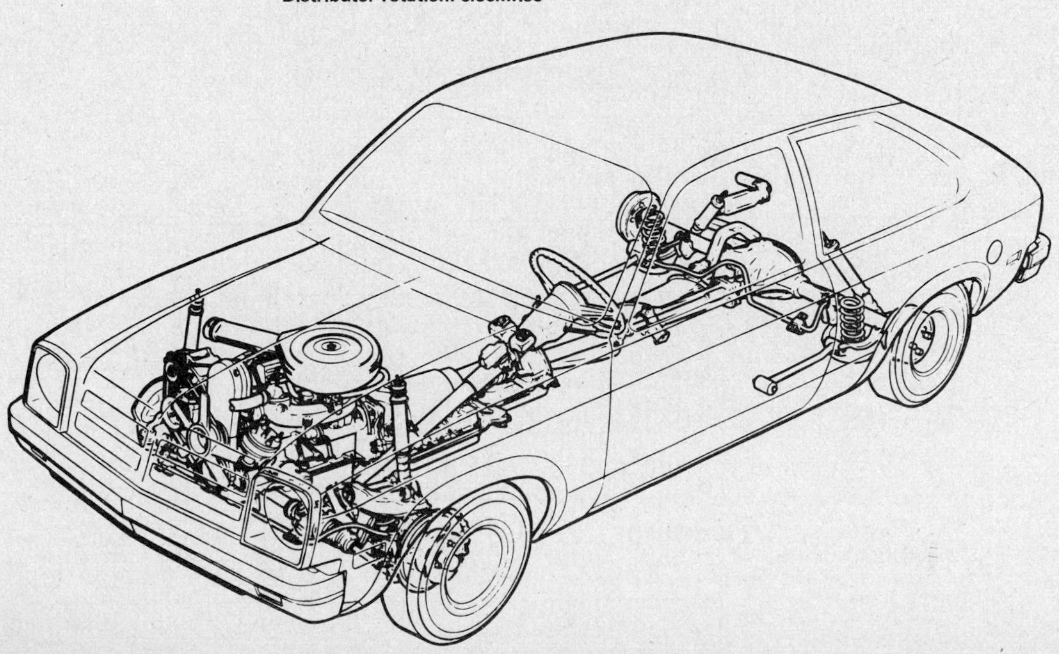

Chevette chassis layout cutaway

GENERAL ENGINE SPECIFICATIONS

Year	Engine No. Cyl. Displacement (Liters—Cu. In.)	Carburetor Type	Horsepower ■	Torque (ft lbs) ■	Bore x Stroke (in.)	Compression Ratio	Oil Pressure @ 6000 rpm
'76	4-1.4 (85)	1 bbl	52	67	3.228 x 2.606	8.5:1	55
	4-1.6 (97.6)	1 bbl	60	77	3.228 x 2.900	8.5:1	55

■ Estimated

TUNE-UP SPECIFICATIONS

When analyzing compression test results, look for uniformity among cylinders rather than specific pressures

Year	ENGINE No. Cyl. Displacement (liters)	SPARK PLUG Type	SPARK PLUG Gap (in.)	DISTRIBUTOR Point Dwell (deg)	DISTRIBUTOR Point Gap (in.)	IGNITION TIMING (deg) Man Trans	IGNITION TIMING (deg) Auto Trans	VALVES Intake Opens ■ (deg)	Fuel Pump Pressure (psi)	IDLE SPEED (rpm) Man Trans	IDLE SPEED (rpm) Auto Trans
'76	4-1.4	R43TS	.035	Electronic		①		43⅓	5-6.5	①	
	4-1.6	R43TS	.035	Electronic		①		43⅓	5-6.5	①	

① See Underhood Specifications Sticker
■ All figures before top dead center

CAPACITIES

Year	ENGINE No. Cyl. Displacement (liters)	Engine Crankcase Add 1 Qt For New Filter	TRANSMISSION Pts To Refill After Draining Manual 4-Speed	TRANSMISSION Pts To Refill After Draining Automatic	Drive Axle (pts)	Gasoline Tank (gals)	COOLING SYSTEM (qts)
'76	4-1.4	4	3	7	2.8	12	8.5
	4-1.6	4	3	7	2.8	12	9.0

VALVE SPECIFICATIONS

Year	Engine No. Cyl. Displacement (liters)	Seat Angle (deg)	Face Angle (deg)	Spring Test Pressure (lbs @ in.)	Spring Installed Height (in.)	Stem to Guide Clearance (in.) Intake	Stem to Guide Clearance (in.) Exhaust	Stem Diameter (in.) Intake	Stem Diameter (in.) Exhaust
'76	4-1.4	46	45	173 @ .89	1.26	.0018-.0021	.0026-.0029	.3141	.3133
	4-1.6	46	45	173 @ .89	1.26	.0018-.0021	.0026-.0029	.3141	.3133

CRANKSHAFT AND CONNECTING ROD SPECIFICATIONS

All measurements are given in inches

Year	Engine No. Cyl. Displacement (liters)	CRANKSHAFT Main Brg. Journal Dia	CRANKSHAFT Main Brg. Oil Clearance	CRANKSHAFT Shaft End-Play	CRANKSHAFT Thrust on No.	CONNECTING ROD Journal Diameter	CONNECTING ROD Oil Clearance	CONNECTING ROD Side Clearance
'76	4-1.4	2.0226	.0003-.0029	.004-.008	4	2.0078-2.0083	.0013-.0060	.004-.012
	4-1.6	2.0226	.0003-.0029	.004-.008	4	2.0078-2.0083	.0013-.0060	.004-.012

RING GAP

All measurements are given in inches

Year	Engine No. Cyl. Displacement (liters)	Top Compression	Bottom Compression
'76	4-1.4	.009-.018	.009-.018
	4-1.6	.009-.018	.009-.018

Year	Engine No. Cyl. Displacement (liters)	Oil Control
'76	4-1.4	.015-.055
	4-1.6	.015-.055

PISTON CLEARANCE

Year	Engine No. Cyl. Displacement (liters)	Piston to Bore Clearance (in.)*
'76	4-1.4	.0008-.0016
	4-1.6	.0008-.0016

*At top of skirt

ALTERNATOR AND REGULATOR SPECIFICATIONS

	ALTERNATOR			REGULATOR						
						Field Relay				
Year	Part No. or Manufacturer	Field Current @ 12 V	Output (amps)	Part No. or Manufacturer	Air Gap (in.)	Point Gap (in.)	Volts to Close	Air Gap (in.)	Regulator Point Gap (in.)	Volts @ 85°
'76	Delco Remy	—	32	—		Integral Regulator				13.8-14.8

BATTERY SPECIFICATIONS

		BATTERY		
Year	Engine No. Cyl. Displacement (liters)	Capacity (watts)	Volts	Terminal Grounded
'76	4-1.4	2500	12	N
	4-1.6	2500	12	N

BRAKE SPECIFICATIONS

All measurements are given in inches

		MASTER CYLINDER		WHEEL CYLINDER			BRAKE DISC OR DRUM DIAMETER		
				Front		Rear	Front		Rear
Year	Model	Disc	Drum	Disc	Drum		Disc	Drum	
'76	All	.750	—	1.875	—	.750	9.68	—	7.88

WHEEL ALIGNMENT SPECIFICATIONS

		CASTER		CAMBER				WHEEL PIVOT RATIO (deg)	
Year	Model	Range (deg)	Pref Setting (deg)	Range (deg)	Pref Setting (deg)	Toe-in (in.)	Steering Axis Inclin. (deg)	Inner Wheel	Outer Wheel
'76	All	—	5½P	—	½P	0	7.55	—	—

Chevette HEI distributor with remote-mounted coil

Chevrolet's Chevette is a new US-made economy car. Chassis layout follows the familiar American pattern of front engine-rear drive. The only body style produced is a two-door hatchback with a folding rear seat. The rear seat may be deleted on a special lightweight economy version.

Chevette offers a number of firsts. These are:

- The lightest US-made car—1,998 lbs.
- The first US-made all Metric car
- The most extensive anti-corrosion protection of any US-made car
- The smallest turning circle of any US-made car—30.2 ft.
- The first GM use of an on-vehicle diagnostic system
- The first Chevrolet to use a steering column lever for turn signal, headlight flasher, windshield wipers, and washers
- The first rack and pinion steering on a US-made GM car.

Chevette one-barrel carburetor

Steering

The Chevette uses rack and pinion steering gear, which is noted for its accuracy and durability. Though the steering is quick, the light weight of the car makes a power assist unnecessary. An energy absorbing column, the same design as in the Vega, is used. A sport steering wheel is available with the Rally 1.6 option group.

Brakes

The Chevette has floating caliper front disc brakes and drum rear brakes, with a hand-operated floor-mounted parking brake working on the rear brakes. An integral-type power booster is optional. The front brakes have wear sensors.

Body and Trim

The body and undercarriage have been treated to extensive rust-proofing. Some of the methods used are galvanized rocker panels, an enameled crossmember, plastic inner fender liners, a wax base spray on the lower surfaces of the doors, epoxy paint on the springs, zinc primer on inner panel sufaces, and an oil base coating on rear spring seats.

Chevette has a full range of optional equipment including an integrated air-conditioning system. There is a floor console with a package tray, AM and AM/FM radios with a fender-mounted antenna, swing-out rear quarter windows, tinted glass, vinyl top, body side protective molding, and radial tires. The one body is enhanced by six available option package variations:

- A two-passenger with floor mats, painted exterior trim, embossed fiberboard sidewalls, no rear seat, and other cost-cutters
- A well-equipped base model with carpeted floor, rear seat, chrome-plated trim, and added sound-deadening
- A custom exterior option consisting of various bright trim items, blackout headlight bezels, and body color door handle inserts and grille.
- A sport decor option with black molding and paint treatments
- A Rally 1.6 option with 1.6 engine, special suspension with rear stabilizer bar, gauges and tachometer, sport steering wheel, sport shifter, and a passenger grab handle.
- A Woody option, giving the appearance of a mini estate wagon.

Chevette prototype engine compartment layout

Chevette overhead camshaft four-cylinder engine and four-speed transmission

Engine

The Chevette engine is a water-cooled inline four, available in 1.4 liter (85 cu in.) and 1.6 liter (97.6 cu in.) displacements. The block and cylinder head are of cast iron for durability, while bolt-on parts such as the intake manifold and camshaft cover are of aluminum for light weight. The cylinder head is the cross-flow type with an overhead camshaft and wedge-shaped combustion chambers. The cross-flow design mounts the intake system at one side of the head and the free-flowing exhaust manifold at the other. The camshaft is driven by a toothed rubber timing belt, as proven in the Vega, and uses rocker arms with hydraulic lash adjusters. The HEI distributor, with remote-mounted coil, is driven off the crankshaft, as are the oil and fuel pumps. A lip-type rear crankshaft seal is used to keep engine length to a minimum. The air cleaner is the 50,000 mile type as on the Vega. A catalytic converter in the exhaust system is required. The optional 1.6 liter engine differs from the base 1.4 liter engine by increased stroke, a larger one-barrel carburetor, and a low restriction muffler and exhaust system with a resonator at the rear. The fuel filter is a paper element type in the carburetor inlet.

Chevette timing mark location

Rear Axle

Available axle ratios are 4.11:1 and 3.70:1. The axle itself is a non-independent live type with a unique modified torque-tube design. The torque-tube extends forward along the driveline to approximately the pivot point of the rear axle locating links. A short driveshaft is used between the rear of the transmission and the front of the torque-tube.

Chevette engine compartment, showing 50,000 mile air cleaner, free-flowing exhaust system, freedom battery, and shock absorber mount tower

Transmission

The Chevette four-speed manual transmission is an aluminum case unit with a single-rail internal shifter. It weighs 35 lbs. less than the current Chevrolet four-speed. A unique feature is helical gears for reverse to eliminate gear whine while backing up.

The optional three-speed automatic transmission is a new design—the Turbo Hydra-Matic 200. It weighs 35 lbs. less than the Turbo Hydra-Matic 250 used in the Vega. The weight reduction is achieved by replacing iron castings with welded steel stampings and scaling down components. The transmission is water-cooled by a fluid cooler in the radiator.

FRONT SUSPENSION

Suspension

The high-caster front suspension is mounted to a crossmember. The design mounts the coil springs between A-arms, and the shock absorbers between the body shell and the top of the upper A-arms. The high-caster setting assists in vehicle stability. Radial tires are optional. Wheel size is 13 x 5 in. Rear suspension is by coil springs and axle locating links. A rear axle track bar is standard equipment.

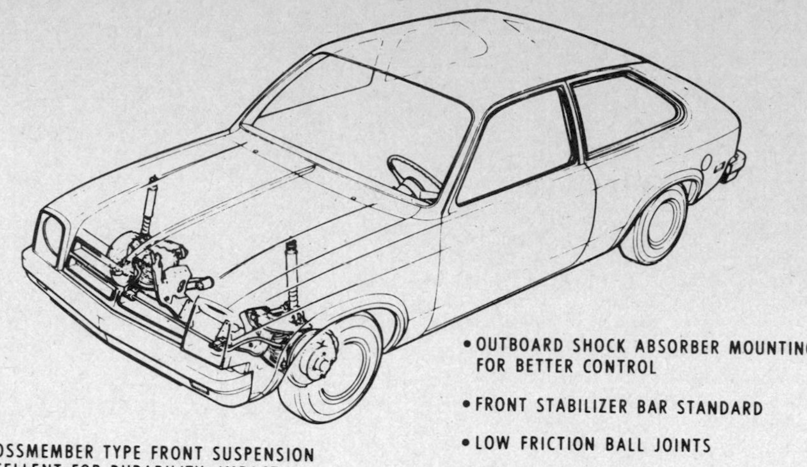

BASE EQUIPMENT DIAGNOSTIC SYSTEM

ADDITIONAL CIRCUITS MONITOR MAJOR OPTIONAL EQUIPMENT

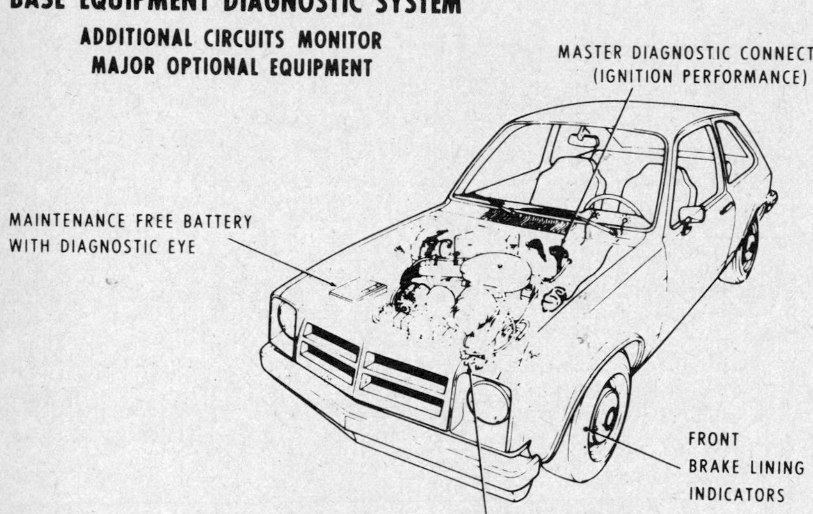

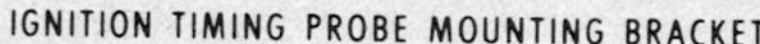

Diagnostic System

The Chevette maintenance-free battery and front brake lining wear indicators give direct indications if service is required. An underhood master electronic diagnostic connector and ignition probe bracket are used to speed diagnosis of malfunctions.

A special do-it-yourself owner maintenance booklet is included with each Chevette.

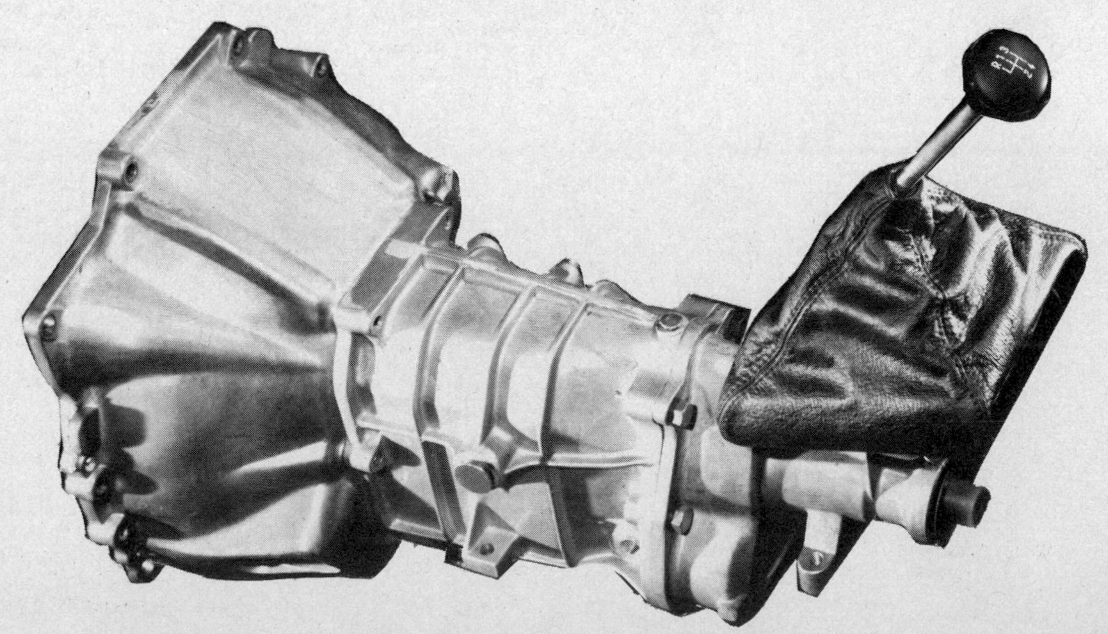

Chevette aluminum case four-speed transmission

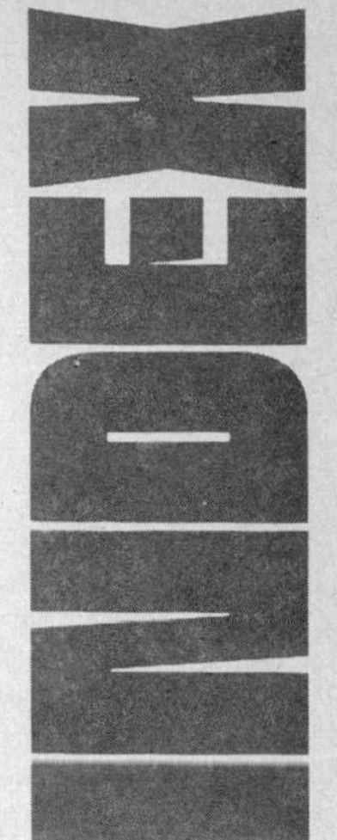

Chrysler · Cordoba · Imperial

YEAR IDENTIFICATION

Chrysler

1969 Newport

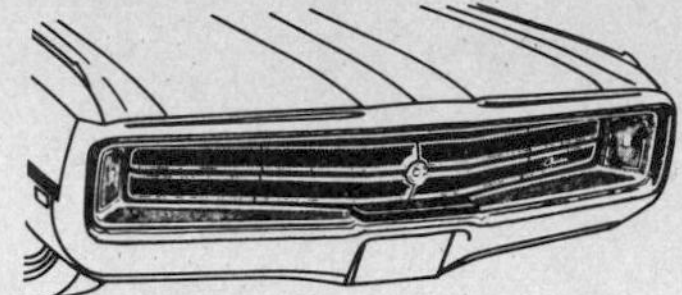

1969 "300"

1969 New Yorker

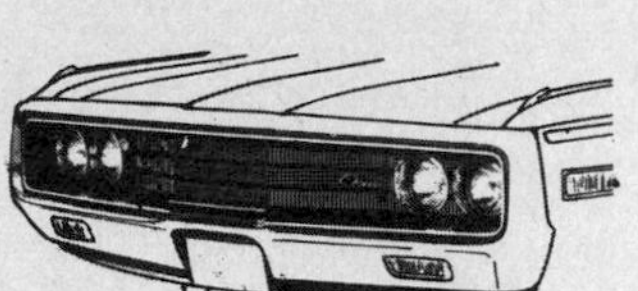

1970 Newport Custom

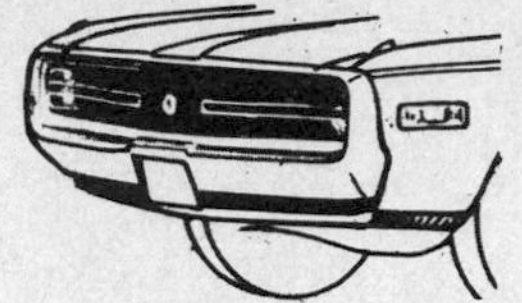

1970 "300"

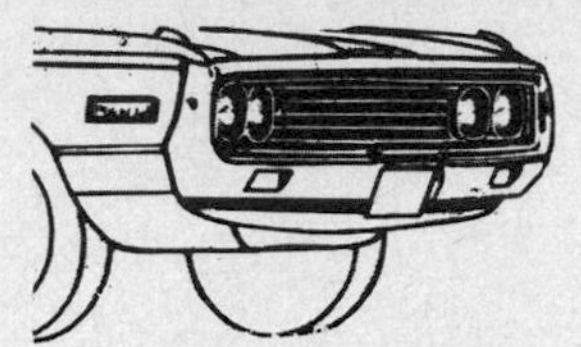

1970 New Yorker

1971 Newport

1972 Newport

1972 New Yorker

1973 Newport

1973 New Yorker

1974 New Yorker

1975 Newport

1975 Cordoba

1975 New Yorker Brougham

1976 Newport

1976 Cordoba

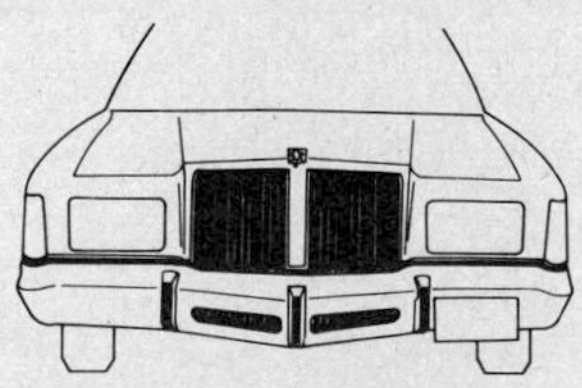

1976 New Yorker Brougham

Chrysler Imperial

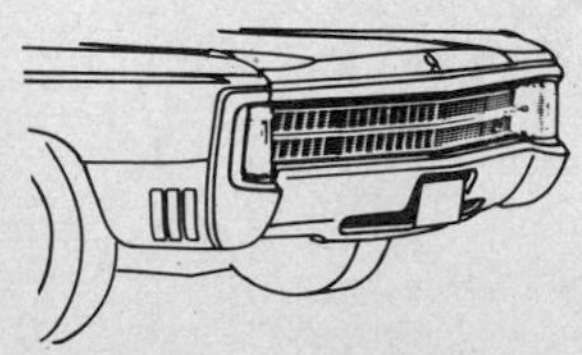

1969

1970 LeBaron

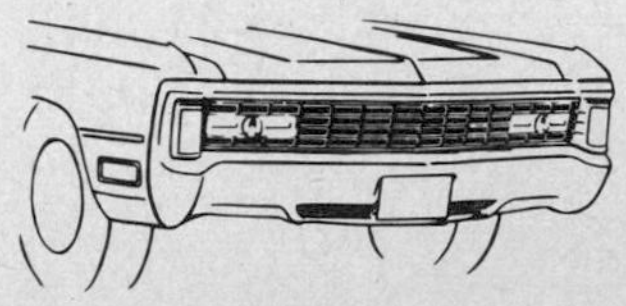

1971 LeBaron

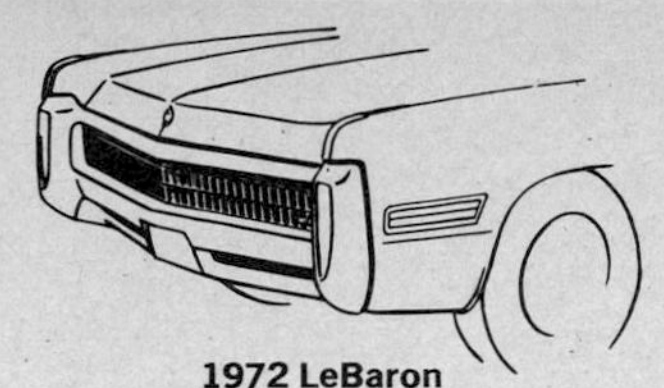
1972 LeBaron

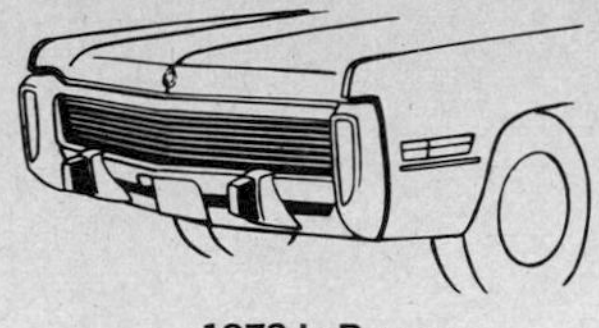
1973 LeBaron

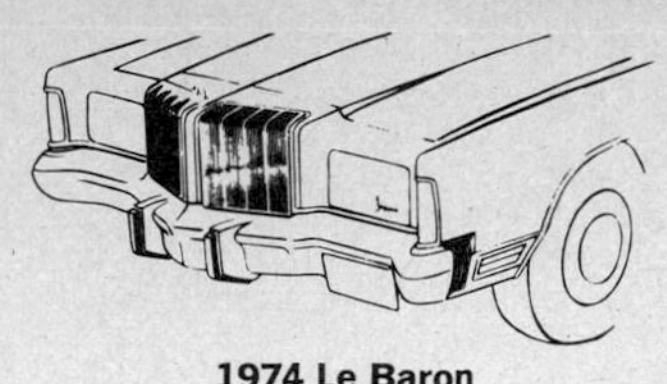
1974 Le Baron

1975 Imperial LeBaron

FIRING ORDER

2 4 6 8 SPARK PLUGS RIGHT BANK

1 3 5 7 SPARK PLUGS LEFT BANK

360 cu in engines—distributor rotates clockwise

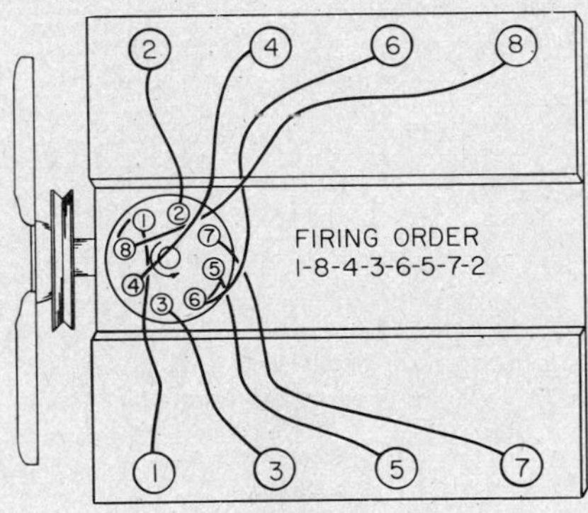

383, 400 and 440 cu in engines—distributor rotates counterclockwise

CAR SERIAL NUMBER LOCATION

Top of instrument panel, visible through windshield.

ENGINE CODE

The engine code designation is the 5th digit of the vehicle identification number (V.I.N.). The V.I.N. is stamped on a plate located at the left side of the instrument panel visible through the windshield, and located to the rear of the right engine mount on all engines.

Disp	Bbl	Hp	'69	'70	'71	'72	'73	'74	'75	'76
8-Cylinder Models										
318	2	150 (net)							G	G
360	2	180, 175 (net)			K				K	K
360	2	255			K					
360	4	200						J		
383	2	275			L					
383	2	290	G	L						
383	4	300			N					
383	2	330	H	N						
400	2	165							M	M
400	2	185 (net)					M	M		
400	4	190, 200, 205 (net)*						N	N	N
400	4	255 (net)				P				
440	4	235, 215, 230 (net)①					T	T	T	T
440	4	280 (net)				U				
440	4	335			T					
440	4	350	K	T						
440	4	370			U					
440	4	375	L	U						

① 1974 California cars—hp. 220 net
* 200 net hp. California; 205 net hp. 49 states

GENERAL ENGINE SPECIFICATIONS

Year	Engine No. Cyl. Displacement (Cu. In.)	Carburetor Type	Horsepower @ rpm ■	Torque @ rpm (ft lbs) ■	Bore and Stroke (in.)	Compression Ratio	Oil Pressure @ 2050 rpm
'69	8-383	2 bbl	290 @ 4400	390 @ 2800	4.250 x 3.375	9.2:1	45-65
	8-383	4 bbl	330 @ 5000	425 @ 3200	4.250 x 3.375	10.0:1	45-65
	8-440	4 bbl	350 @ 4400	480 @ 2800	4.320 x 3.750	10.1:1	45-65
	8-440	4 bbl	375 @ 4600	480 @ 3200	4.320 x 3.750	10.1:1	45-65
'70	8-383	2 bbl	290 @ 4400	390 @ 2800	4.250 x 3.375	8.7:1	45-65
	8-383	4 bbl	330 @ 5000	425 @ 3200	4.250 x 3.375	9.5:1	45-65
	8-440	4 bbl	350 @ 4400	480 @ 2800	4.320 x 3.750	9.7:1	45-65
	8-440	4 bbl	375 @ 4600	480 @ 3200	4.320 x 3.750	9.7:1	45-65
'71	8-360	2 bbl	255 @ 4000	360 @ 2400	4.000 x 3.580	8.7:1	45-65
	8-383	2 bbl	275 @ 4400	375 @ 2800	4.250 x 3.375	8.5:1	45-65
	8-383	4 bbl	300 @ 4800	410 @ 3400	4.250 x 3.375	8.5:1	45-65
	8-440	4 bbl	335 @ 4400	460 @ 3200	4.320 x 3.750	8.5:1	45-65
	8-440	4 bbl	370 @ 4600	480 @ 3200	4.320 x 3.750	9.5:1	45-65
'72	8-360	2 bbl	175 @ 4000	285 @ 2400	4.000 x 3.580	8.8:1	45-65
	8-400	2 bbl	190 @ 4400	310 @ 2400	4.342 x 3.375	8.2:1	45-65
	8-440	4 bbl	225 @ 4400	345 @ 3200	4.320 x 3.750	8.2:1	45-65
'73	8-400	2 bbl	185 @ 3600	310 @ 2400	4.340 x 3.380	8.2:1	45-65
	8-440	4 bbl	215 @ 3600①	345 @ 2000①	4.320 x 3.750	8.2:1	45-65
'74	8-360	4 bbl	200 @ 4000	290 @ 3200	4.000 x 3.580	8.4:1	45-65
	8-400	2 bbl	185 @ 4000	315 @ 2400	4.340 x 3.380	8.2:1	45-65
	8-400	4 bbl	205 @ 4400	310 @ 2400	4.340 x 3.380	8.2:1	45-65
	8-440	4 bbl	230 @ 4000	350 @ 3200②	4.320 x 3.750	8.2:1	45-65
'75-'76	8-318	2 bbl	150 @ 4000③	255 @ 1600③	3.910 x 3.310	8.5:1	45-65
	8-360	2 bbl	180 @ 4000	290 @ 2400	4.000 x 3.580	8.4:1	45-65
	8-360	4 bbl	190 @ 4000	270 @ 3200	4.000 x 3.580	8.4:1	45-65
	8-400	2 bbl	175 @ 4000④	300 @ 2400④	4.340 x 3.380	8.2:1	50-75
	8-400	4 bbl	195 @ 4000⑤	285 @ 3200⑤	4.340 x 3.380	8.2:1	50-75
	8-440	4 bbl	215 @ 4000⑥	330 @ 3200⑥	4.320 x 3.750	8.2:1	50-75
	8-400 HP	4 bbl	235 @ 4200	320 @ 3200	4.340 x 3.380	8.2:1	50-75
	8-440 HP	4 bbl	260 @ 4400⑦	355 @ 3200⑦	4.320 x 3.750	8.2:1	50-75

① California cars hp 208 @ 3600, torque 340 @ 2000
② California cars—hp. 220 @ 4000, torque 345 @ 3200
③ California—hp. 135 @ 3600, torque 245 @ 1600
④ Cordoba—hp. 165 @ 4000, torque 295 @ 3200; all 1976 models same
⑤ Cordoba—hp. 190 @ 4000, torque 290 @ 3200; Cordoba (California)—hp. 185 @ 4000, torque 285 @ 3200
⑥ California—hp. 210 @ 4000, torque 320 @ 3200
⑦ California—hp. 250 @ 4000, torque 350 @ 3200; 1975 only
HP High Performance
■ Starting 1972, horsepower and torque are SAE net figures. They are measured at the rear of the transmission with all accessories installed and operating. Since the figures vary when a given engine is installed in different models, some are representative rather than exact.

TUNE-UP SPECIFICATIONS

When analyzing compression test results, look for uniformity among cylinders rather than specific pressures.

	ENGINE		SPARK PLUGS		DISTRIBUTOR		IGNITION TIMING (deg) ▲ ●		VALVES	Fuel	IDLE SPEED (rpm) ▲	
Year	No. Cyl Displacement (cu in.)	hp	Type	Gap (in.)	Point Dwell (deg)	Point Gap (in.)	Man Trans	Auto Trans	Intake Opens ■ (deg)	Pump Pressure (psi)	Man Trans	Auto Trans
'69	8-383	290	J-14Y	.035	30-35	.017	TDC	7½B	18	3½-5	700	600
	8-383	330	J-11Y	.035	30-35	.017	—	5B	18	3½-5	700	650
	8-440	350	J-13Y	.035	30-35	.017	—	7½B	18	3½-5	700	600N
	8-440	375	J-11Y	.035	30-35	.017	TDC	5B	21	3½-5	700	650N
'70	8-383	290	J-14Y	.035	28½-32½	.018	TDC	2½B	18	3½-5	750	650
	8-383	330	J-11Y	.035	28½-32½	.018	TDC	2½B	18	3½-5	—	700
	8-440	350	J-13Y	.035	28½-32½	.018	—	5B	18	3½-5	—	650
	8-440	375	J-11Y	.035	28½-32½	.018	TDC	2½B	21	3½-5	900	800
'71	8-360	255	J-13Y	.035	30-34	.017	2½B	2½B	16	3½-5	750	700
	8-383	275	J-14Y	.035	30-34	.017	TDC	2½B	18	3½-5	750	700
	8-383	300	J-14Y	.035	28½-32½	.017	TDC	2½B	21	3½-5	900	800
	8-440	335	J-13Y	.035	28½-32½	.017	—	5B	18	3½-5	—	750
	8-440	370	J-11Y	.035	28½-32½	.017	TDC	2½B	21	3½-5	900	900
'72	8-360	175	N-13Y	.035	28½-32½	.017	—	TDC	16	5-7	—	700
	8-400	255	J-13Y	.035	28½-32½	.018	—	5B(2½B)⑦	18	3½-5	—	700
	8-440	280	J-11Y	.035	28½-32½	.018	—	10B(5B)	18	3½-5	—	900
'73	8-400	185	J-13Y	.035	Electronic		—	10B	18	4 5½	—	700
	8-440	215	J-11Y	.035	Electronic		—	10B	18	4-5½	—	700
'74	8-360	200	N-12Y	.035	Electronic		—	5B	22	5.9-7.4	—	750
	8-400	185	J-13Y	.035	Electronic		—	10B(5B)	18	4-5½	—	750
	8-400	205	J-11Y	.035	Electronic		—	10B(2½B)	21	4-5½	—	900
	8-440	230	J-11Y	.035	Electronic		—	10B	21	4-5½	—	750
'75	8-318	150	N-13Y	.035	Electronic		—	2B	10	5-7	—	750
	8-360	180	N-12Y	.035	Electronic		—	6B	18	5-7	—	750
	8-360	190	N-12Y	.035	Electronic		—	6B	18	5-7	—	750
	8-400	175	J-13Y	.035	Electronic		—	10B	18	4-5½	—	750
	8-400	195, 235	J-13Y	.035	Electronic		—	8B	18	4-5½	—	750
	8-440	215, 260	RY-87P	.040	Electronic		—	8B	18	4-5½	—	750
'76	8-318	NA	RN-12Y	.035	Electronic		—	2B	10	6-7½	—	750
	8-360-2V	NA	RN-12Y	.035	Electronic		—	6B	18	6-7½	—	700
	8-360-4V②	NA	RN-12Y	.035	Electronic		—	6B	18	6-7½	—	750
	8-400-2V	NA	RJ-13Y	.035	Electronic		—	10B	18	6-7½	—	700③
	8-400-4V	NA	RJ-13Y	.035	Electronic		—	6B①	18	6-7½	—	750④
	8-440-4V	NA	RJ-87P⑤	.035⑥	Electronic		—	8B	18	6-7½	—	750

▲ See text for procedure
● Figure in parentheses indicates California engine
■ All figures Before Top Dead Center
① 8B in California
② California only
③ 750 rpm in California
④ 850 rpm on 400-4V HP
⑤ Champion RJ-86P, Bosch WA95, WA96 on lean burn engines
⑥ Bosch plugs—.033 in.
⑦ Non-California cars built after Feb. 2, 7½B
A After Top Dead Center
B Before Top Dead Center
TDC Top Dead Center
— Not applicable

CAPACITIES

Year	ENGINE No. Cyl. Displacement (Cu. In.)	Engine Crankcase Add 1 Qt For New Filter	TRANSMISSION Pts To Refill After Draining Manual 3-Speed	Manual 4-Speed	Automatic	Drive Axle (pts)	Gasoline Tank (gals)	COOLING SYSTEM (qts) With Heater ▲	With A/C
'69	8-383	4	6	—	18.5①	4	24	17	17
	8-440	4	—	—	18.5	4	24	17	18
	Town & Country	4	—	—	18.5①	4	23	16	17
	Imperial	4	—	—	18.5	4	24	19	19
'70	8-383	4	4.75	—	19.0①	4	24	14.5②	16②
	8-440	4	—	—	19.0	4	24	15.5	17
	Town & Country	4	—	—	19.0①	4	23	16	17
	Imperial	4	—	—	19.0	4.4	24	18	18
'71	8-360	4	4.75	—	16.3	4.5	23	15.5	16
	8-383	4	4.75③	—	19.0①	4.5	23	14.5	15
	8-440	4	—	—	19.0	4.5	23	15.5	17
	Town & Country	4	—	—	19.0①	4.5	23	16	17
	Imperial	4	—	—	19.0	4.5	23	17.5	17.5
'72	8-360	4	—	—	16.3	4.4	23	15.5	16.5
	8-400	4	—	—	19.0	4.4	23	14.5	15.5
	8-440	4	—	—	19.0	4.4	23	17.5	17.5
	Town & Country	4	—	—	19.0	4.4	23	16	17
	Imperial	4	—	—	19.0	4.4	23	17.5	17.5
'73	8-400	4	—	—	19.0	4.5	23	16	16
	8-440	4	—	—	19.0	4.5	23	15.5	15.5
	Imperial	4	—	—	19.0	4.5	23	18	18
'74	8-360	4	—	—	16.1	4.5	26.5⑤	16	16
	8-400	4	—	—	18.9④	4.5	26.5⑤	16.5	16.5
	8-440	4	—	—	18.9	4.5	26.5⑤	16	16
	Imperial	4	—	—	16.5	4.5	26.5	17	17
'75-'76	8-318 Cordoba	4	—	—	16.5	4.5	25.5	16.5	18
	8-360	4	—	—	16.5	4.5	⑥	16.0	16.0
	8-400	4	—	—	16.5	4.5	⑥	16.5	16.5
	8-440	4	—	—	16.5	4.5	⑥	16.0	16.0
	Imperial	4	—	—	16.5	4.5	26.5	17.0	17.0

▲ Add 1.5 qts if equipped with rear seat heater
① 4 bbl carb—16 pts
② 4 bbl carb—15.5-17 pts
③ 2 bbl only
④ 16.1 with HP400 engine

⑤ Wagons—24 gals, Cordoba—25.5 gals, Cordoba with dual exhaust—20.5 gals
⑥ Cordoba—25.5
Chrysler full size except wagon—26.5
Chrysler full size wagon—24.0
— Not applicable

VALVE SPECIFICATIONS

Engine No. Cyl. Displacement	Seat Angle (deg)	Face Angle (deg)	Spring Test Pressure (lbs @ in.)	Spring Installed Height (in.)	Stem to Guide Clearance (in.) Intake	Stem to Guide Clearance (in.) Exhaust	Stem Diameter (in.) Intake	Stem Diameter (in.) Exhaust
'69 8-383①	45	45	200 @ 1.44	1 7/8	.0010-.0030	.0020-.0040	.3725	.3715
8-383②	45	45	246 @ 1.36	1 7/8	.0010-.0030	.0020-.0040	.3725	.3715
8-440	45	45	200 @ 1.44	1 7/8	.0010-.0030	.0020-.0040	.3725	.3715
8-440③	45	45	246 @ 1.36	1 7/8	.0010-.0030	.0020-.0040	.3725	.3715
'70 8-383	45	45	200 @ 1.44	1 7/8	.0010-.0030	.0020-.0040	.3725	.3715
8-440	45	45	200 @ 1.44	1 7/8	.0010-.0030	.0020-.0040	.3725	.3715
8-440③	45	45	246 @ 1.36	1 7/8	.0010-.0030	.0020-.0040	.3725	.3715
'71 8-360	45	④	177 @ 1.31	1 11/16	.0010-.0030	.0020-.0040	.3725	.3715
8-383①	45	45	200 @ 1.44	1 7/8	.0010-.0030	.0020-.0040	.3727	.3715
8-383②	45	45	246 @ 1.36	1 7/8	.0015-.0032	.0025-.0042	.3722	.3712
8-440	45	45	200 @ 1.44	1 7/8	.0010-.0030	.0020-.0040	.3727	.3717
8-440③	45	45	246 @ 1.36	1 7/8	.0015-.0032	.0025-.0042	.3722	.3712
'72 8-360	45	④	177 @ 1.31	1 11/16	.0010-.0030	.0020-.0040	.3725	.3715
8-400	45	45	200 @ 1.44	1 7/8	.0010-.0030	.0020-.0040	.3725	.3715
8-440	45	45	200 @ 1.44	1 7/8	.0010-.0030	.0020-.0040	.3725	.3715
'73 8-400	45	45	200 @ 1.42	1 55/64	.0015-.0032	⑤	.3722	⑥
8-440	45	45	200 @ 1.42	1 55/64	.0015-.0032	⑤	.3722	⑥
'74 8-360	45	④	208 @ 1.31	1 43/64	.0010-.0030	.0020-.0040	.3725	.3720
8-400	45	45	200 @ 1.43	1 55/64	.0010-.0027	⑤	.3727	⑥
8-400③	45	45	234 @ 1.40	1 55/64	.0015-.0032	⑥	.3722	⑥
8-440	45	45	234 @ 1.40	1 55/64	.0015-.0032	⑥	.3722	⑥
'75-'76 8-318	45	④	177 @ 1.31	1 21/32	.0010-.0030	.0020-.0040	.3725	.3715
8-360	45	④	⑦	1 21/32	.0010-.0030	.0020-.0040	.3725	.3715
8-400①	45	45	200 @ 1.43	1 55/64	.0010-.0027	⑤	.3726	⑥
8-400②	45	45	200 @ 1.43	1 55/64	.0015-.0032	⑧	.3726	⑥
8-440	45	45	246 @ 1.36	1 55/64	.0015-.0032	⑧	.3726	⑥

① 2 bbl
② 4 bbl
③ Hi-Performance
④ Intake valve face angle 45°
Exhaust valve face angle 43°
⑤ Hot end—.0020-.0037, cold end—.0010-.0027
⑥ Hot end—.3716, cold end—.3726
⑦ 2 bbl engine—177 @ 1.31
4 bbl engine—208 @ 1.31
⑧ Hot end—.0025-.0042, cold end—.0015-.0040

TORQUE SPECIFICATIONS

All readings in ft lbs

Year	Engine No. Cyl. Displacement (cu in.)	Cylinder Head Bolts	Rod Bearing Bolts	Main Bearing Bolts	Crankshaft Pulley Bolt	Flywheel to Crankshaft Bolts	Manifold Intake	Manifold Exhaust
'71-'72, '74-'76	8-360, 318	95	45	85	100	55	35	15
'69-'76	8-383, 400, 440	70	45	85	135	55	40	30

CRANKSHAFT AND CONNECTING ROD SPECIFICATIONS

All measurements are given in inches

Year	Engine No. Cyl. Displacement (cu in.)	CRANKSHAFT Main Brg. Journal Dia	CRANKSHAFT Main Brg. Oil Clearance	CRANKSHAFT Shaft End-Play	CRANKSHAFT Thrust on No.	CONNECTING ROD Journal Diameter	CONNECTING ROD Oil Clearance	CONNECTING ROD Side Clearance
'74-'76	8-318	2.4995-2.5005	.0005-.0025	.002-.007	3	2.124-2.125	.0005-.0020	.006-.014
'71-'72	8-360	2.8095-2.8105	.0005-.0025	.002-.007	3	2.124-2.125	.0005-.0020	.009-.017
'69-'76	8-383, 400	2.6245-2.6255	.0005-.0015	.002-.007	3	2.3740-2.3750	.0005-.0015	.009-.017
'69-'76	8-440	2.7495-2.7505	.0005-.0015	.002-.007	3	2.3750-2.3750	.0007-.0032	.009-.017

RING SIDE CLEARANCE

All measurements are given in inches

Year	Engine No. Cyl. Displacement (cu. in.)	Top Compression	Bottom Compression
'69-'76	All engines	.0015-.0030	.0015-.0030

Year	Engine No. Cyl. Displacement (cu. in.)	Oil Control
'69-'76	8-383, 400, 440	.0000-.005
'71-'72, '74-'76	8-360, 318	.0002-.005

RING GAP

All measurements are given in inches

Year	Engine No. Cyl. Displacement (cu. in.)	Top Compression	Bottom Compression
'69-'76	8-383, 440	.013-.025	.013-.025
'71-'72, '74-'76	8-360, 318	.010-.020	.010-.020

Year	Engine No. Cyl. Displacement (cu. in.)	Oil Control
'69-'76	All engines	.015-.055

PISTON CLEARANCE

Year	Engine	Piston to bore clearance (in.)
1969	383, 440	.0003-.0015
1970	383, 440	.0003-.0013
1971	360	.0005-.0015

Year	Engine	Piston to bore clearance (in.)
1971	383, 440	.0003-.0013
1972-76	318, 360	.0005-.0015
	400, 440	.0003-.0013

ALTERNATOR AND REGULATOR SPECIFICATIONS

		ALTERNATOR		REGULATOR						
					Field Relay			Regulator		
Year	Application	Field Current @ 12 V	Output (amps)	Part No. or Manufacturer	Air Gap (in.)	Point Gap (in.)	Volts to Close	Air Gap (in.)	Point Gap (in.)	Volts @ 75°
'69	Chrysler	2.38-2.75	35	2098300	.050②	.014	13.8	.015	.050	13.8-14.4
	Imperial	2.38-2.75	35	2875400	.050②	.014	13.8	.015	.050	13.8-14.4
'70-'71	Standard	2.38-2.75	34.5 ± 3	3438150	—	—	—	Not Adjustable		13.8-14.4
	Hvy. Duty and/or A/C	2.38-2.75	44.5 ± 3	3438150	—	—	—	Not Adjustable		13.8-14.4
'72-'74	Chrysler	2.5-3.1	41④	3438150	—	—	—	Not Adjustable		13.8-14.4
	Imperial	2.5-3.1	50⑤	3438150	—	—	—	Not Adjustable		13.8-14.4
	Special Equip. and A/C	2.5-3.1	60 ± 3⑤	3438150	—	—	—	Not Adjustable		13.8-14.4
'75-'76	Cordoba	2.5-3.1	50⑥⑦	3755960	—	—	—	Not Adjustable		14.0-14.6
	Chrysler	2.5-3.1	50⑦	3755960	—	—	—	Not Adjustable		14.0-14.6
	Imperial	2.5-3.1	65⑦	3755960	—	—	—	Not Adjustable		14.0-14.6

① not used
② Essex wire regulator, #2444980, used interchangeably. Air gap setting is .032-.042 in. All other dimensions are identical to #2098300
③ 41 amp model used with A/C, 51 amp model available as special equipment
④ Beginning 1974, 50 amp
⑤ Beginning 1974, 65 amp
⑥ 41 amp alternator on 1975-76 Cordoba with 400 cu. in. V8
⑦ 100 amp alternator available on all 1975-76 Cordoba, Chrysler and Imperial models equiped with rear window defroster, and alll fleet models

BATTERY AND STARTER SPECIFICATIONS

		BATTERY			STARTER						
					Lock Test			No-Load Test			
Year	Engine No. Cyl. Displacement (cu in.)	Ampere Hour Capacity	Volts	Terminal Grounded	Amps	Volts	Torque (ft lbs)	Amps	Volts	RPM	Brush Spring Tension (oz)
'69	8-383, 440, wo/AC	59①	12	Neg.	400-450	4	—	90	11	1,925-2,600	32-36
	All others	70	12	Neg.	400-450	4	—	90	11	1,925-2,600	32-36
'70-'71	8-360, 383, 400	59①	12	Neg.	400-450	4	—	90	11	1,925-2,600	32-36
	8-440	70	12	Neg.	400-450	4	—	90	11	1,925-2,600	32-36
'72	8-360	55①	12	Neg.	400-450	4	—	90	11	1,925-2,600	32-36
	8-400	59①	12	Neg.	400-450	4	—	90	11	1,925-2,600	32-36
	8-440	70	12	Neg.	400-450	4	—	90	11	1,925-2,600	32-36
'73-'74	8-400, 360	59①	12	Neg.	475-550	4	—	90	11	3,700-4,200	32-36
	8-440	70	12	Neg.	475-550	4	—	90	11	3,700-4,200	32-36
'75-'76	8-318 Coroba	48①	12	Neg.	475-550	4	—	90	11	3,700-4,200	32-36
	8-360, 400	70②	12	Neg.	475-550	4	—	90	11	5,700	32-36
	8-440	85	12	Neg.	475-550	4	—	90	11	5,700	32-36

① 70 amp model available as special equipment
② 85 amp model available as special equipment

BRAKE SPECIFICATIONS

All measurements are given in inches

Year	Model	Master Cylinder Disc	Master Cylinder Drum	Wheel Cylinder Front Disc	Wheel Cylinder Front Drum	Wheel Cylinder Rear	Brake Disc or Drum Diameter Front Disc	Brake Disc or Drum Diameter Front Drum	Brake Disc or Drum Diameter Rear
'69-'72	All with 4 wheel drums	—	1.0①	—	1.187	0.9375	—	11.0	11.0
	All with Budd disc brakes	1.125①	—	2.375	—	0.9375	11.87	—	11.0
	All with Kelsey Hayes disc	1.125①	—	2.75	—	0.9375	11.75	—	11.0
'73	Chrysler	1.03	—	2.75	—	0.9375	11.56	—	11.0
	Imperial	1.03	—	2.75	—	0.9375	11.56	—	11.0
'74-'76	Chrysler	1.031	—	3.10	—	0.9375	11.75	—	11.00
	Imperial (4-wheel discs)	1.063	—	3.10	—	2.6000	11.75	—	11.63
	Cordoba	1.03	—	2.75	—	0.9375	10.84	—	10.0

① 1971-72 models—1.03 in.
— Not applicable

WHEEL ALIGNMENT SPECIFICATIONS

Year	Model	Caster Range (deg)	Caster Pref Setting (deg)	Camber Range (deg)	Camber Pref Setting (deg)	Toe-in (in.)	Steering Axis Inclin. (deg.)	Wheel Pivot Ratio (deg) Inner Wheel	Wheel Pivot Ratio (deg) Outer Wheel
'69	Man, Pow. exc. Imp.	1N to 0	1/2N	①	①	3/32 to 5/32	7 1/2②	20	18.8
	Power Steering Imp.	1/4P to 1 1/4P	3/4P	①	①	3/32 to 5/32	9	20	17.9
'70-'72	Manual Steering	1/2N ± 9/16	1/2N	④	⑤	3/32 to 5/32	7 1/2	20	18.8
	Power Steering Chry.	1/2N ± 9/16⑥	1/2N	④	⑤	3/32 to 5/32	7 1/2	20	18.8
	Power Steering Imp.	3/4P ± 9/16⑥	3/4P	④	⑤	3/32 to 5/32	9	20	17.9
'73	Chrysler	1/16N to 1 5/16P	5/8P	⑦	⑤	1/8 ± 3/32	7 1/2	20	18.8
	Imperial	1/16N to 1 5/16P	5/8P	⑦	⑤	1/8 ± 3/32	9	20	17.9
'74	Chrysler, Imperial	1/2N to 1 3/4P	3/4P	⑧	⑤	1/16 to 1/4	9	20	18.3
'75-'76	Cordoba	1/16N to 1 5/16P	3/4P	⑦	⑤	3/32 to 3/16	8	20	18.0
	Chrysler, Imperial	1/16N to 1 5/16P	3/4P	⑦	⑤	3/16 ± 3/32	9	20	18.3

① Left side—P1/4 to P3/4. Preferred P1/2.
Right side—0 to P1/2. Preferred P1/4.
② Imperial 9 degrees.
③ not used
④ Left side—1/2P ± 1/4; Right side—1/4P ± 1/4
⑤ Left side—1/2P; Right side—1/4P
⑥ 1971-72—3/4P ± 1/2
⑦ Left side—1/8P to 7/8P
Right side—1/8N to 5/8P
⑧ Left side—0 to 1P
Right side—1/4N to 3/4P
N Negative P Positive

FRONT END HEIGHT▲

Year	Model	Front End Height
'69-'73	Chrysler	1 1/8 ± 1/8
	Imperial	1 3/4 ± 1/8
'74	Chrysler	1 ± 1/8
	Imperial	1 ± 1/8
'75-'76	Chrysler	10 1/8 ± 1/8
	Imperial	10 1/8 ± 1/8
	Cordoba	10 3/4 ± 1/8

▲ See text for procedure

NOTE: Service procedures for the Charging System, Starting System, Ignition System, Fuel System, Cooling System, Emission Control System, Engine, and Clutch on Chrysler, Cordoba, and Imperial cars can be found in the Dodge-Plymouth section.

MANUAL TRANSMISSION

Linkage Adjustment

1969

1. Remove the first and reverse rod swivel from the steering column; remove the second and third rod swivel from the torque shaft lever.
2. Be sure the transmission levers are in the neutral (middle detent) position. Adjust the second and third rod swivel by loosening the clamp bolt and positioning the swivel on the rod so it will enter the torque shaft lever while the gear selector on the steering column is held approximately 12° above the horizontal. Secure it in position with its washers and clip, and torque the swivel clamp bolt to 100 in. lbs.
3. Insert a screwdriver between the crossover blade and the second and third lever at the steering column. Be sure that both lever pins are engaged by the crossover blade.
4. Adjust the first and reverse rod swivel by loosening its locknut and rotating the swivel so it will enter the first and reverse lever at the steering column. Install the washers and clip, and torque the swivel locknut to 70 in. lbs.
5. Remove the screwdriver from the crossover blade at the steering column. Shift through all the gears to check the adjustment and crossover smoothness.
6. Disconnect the clutch rod swivel from the interlock pawl. Check the clutch pedal free-play; if it requires adjustment, refer to the proper procedure and perform this operation now.
7. Adjust the first and reverse lever on the transmission so that when it is in the neutral (middle detent) position, the interlock pawl will enter the slot in the first and reverse lever.
8. Loosen the swivel clamp bolt and position the swivel on the rod so it will enter the pawl; install its clip and washers. With the interlock lever held forward, torque the swivel clamp bolt to 100 in. lbs. While this adjustment is being performed, the clutch pedal must be in the fully returned position. *NOTE: do not pull the interlock rod rearward to engage the swivel with the pawl.*
9. Disengage the clutch, and shift in the normal manner from neutral to first, and then from neutral to reverse. Be sure to perform the above as you normally would while driving.
10. The action of the clutch should be normal. Disengage the clutch and shift halfway to first or reverse. If everything is properly operating, the clutch should be held down to between 1 to 2 in. off the floor by the interlock.

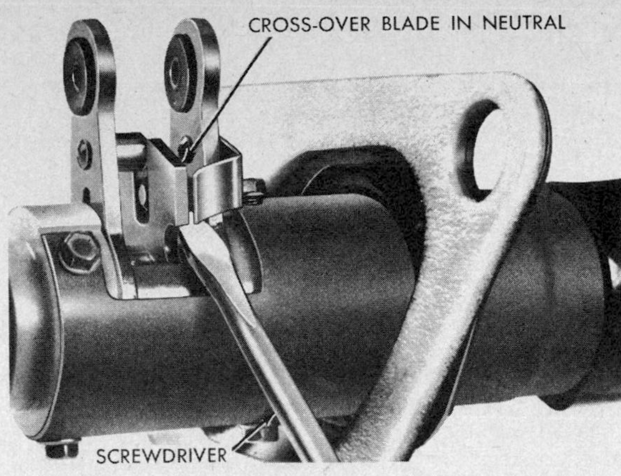

Holding the crossover blades in neutral—1969-71

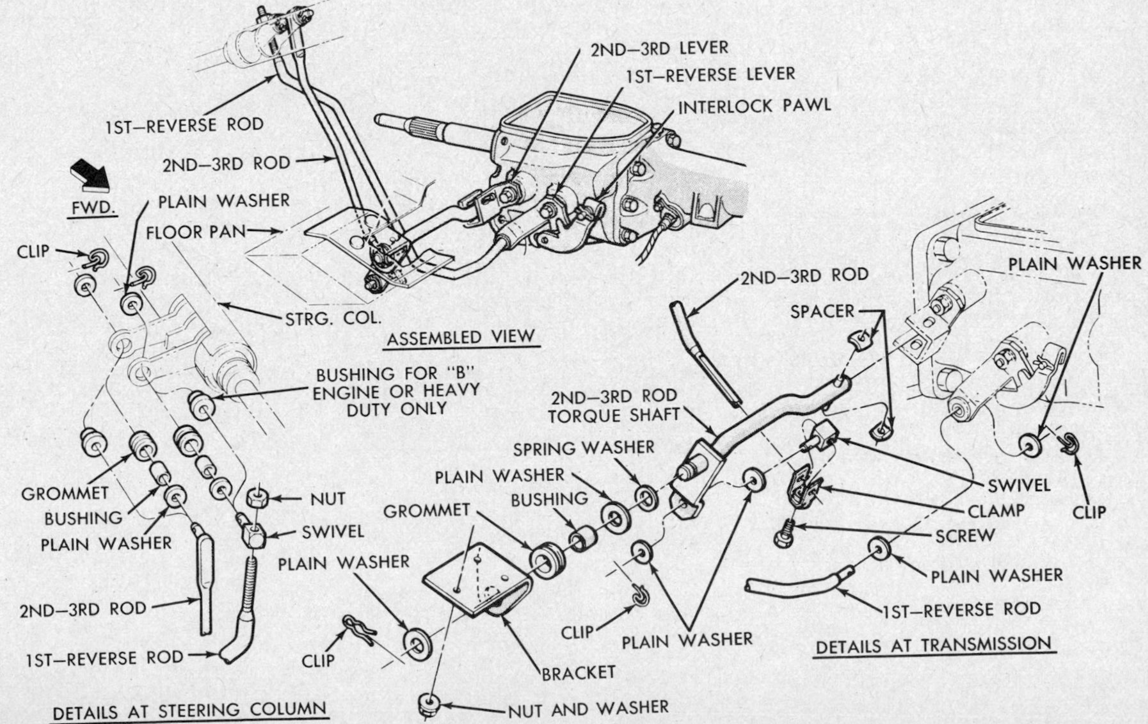

Typical linkage—1969—71 (© Chrysler Corp)

1970-71

1. Remove the shift rod swivels from the transmission shift levers. Be sure the transmission shift levers are in the neutral (middle detent) position.
2. Position the shift levers to align the locating slots in the bottom of the steering column shift and bearing housing. Install a suitable holding tool in the slot and lock the ignition switch.
3. Insert a screwdriver between the crossover blade and the second and third lever at the steering column. Both lever pins must be engaged by the crossover blade.
4. Rotate (clockwise) the first and reverse lever on the transmission to obtain the reverse position.
5. Adjust the first and reverse rod swivel by loosening the clamp bolt and positioning the swivel on the rod so it will enter the first and reverse lever at the transmission. Install its washers and clip; torque the swivel bolt to 100 in. lbs.
6. Remove the gearshift housing locating tool, unlock the ignition switch, and shift the steering column lever to the neutral position.
7. Adjust the second and third rod swivel by loosening the clamp bolt and positioning the swivel on the rod so it will enter the second and third lever at the transmission. Install its washers and clip; torque the swivel bolt to 100 in. lbs.
8. Remove the tool from the crossover blade at the steering column. Shift through all the gears to check the adjustment.
9. Check the operation of the steering lock in the reverse (1970–71) and second gear (1970 only) positions. With the linkage properly adjusted (for all years) the column should lock in the reverse position only.

AUTOMATIC TRANSMISSION

On 1969-71 models, model identification appears in large letters embossed on the lower side of the bell housing. While designs and servicing procedures are similar for all vehicles, internal parts are necessarily different. Therefore, when replacing parts refer to the 7-digit part number stamped on the left side of the transmission oil flange.

The transmission combines a torque converter and fully automatic 3-speed gear system. Converter housing and transmission case are an integral aluminum casting. The transmission consists of two multiple disc clutches, an overrunning clutch, two servos and bands, and two planetary gear sets to provide three forward ratios and a reverse ratio. The common sun gear of the planetary gear sets is connected to the front clutch by a driving shell splined to the sun gear and to the front clutch retainer. The hydraulic system consists of the oil pump and a single valve body that contains all valves except the governor valve.

Cooling the converter is accomplished by circulating the transmission fluid through an oil-to-water type cooler located in the radiator lower tank. The torque converter assembly is a sealed unit that cannot be disassembled.

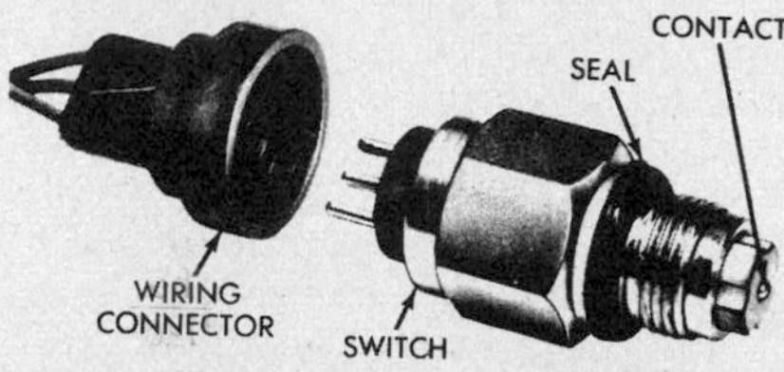

Combination neutral start and back-up light switch (© Chrysler Corp)

Neutral Start Switch

The neutral switch is mounted in the transmission case on all models. When the transmission manual lever is placed in either the Park or Neutral position, a cam, which is attached to the transmission throttle lever inside the transmission, contacts the neutral start switch and provides a ground to complete the starter solenoid circuit. On late model Chryslers and Imperials, the back-up light switch has been incorporated into the neutral switch. The combination neutral and back-up light switch can be identified by the three electrical terminals on the rear of the switch. On this type of switch, the center terminal is for the neutral switch and the two outer terminals are for the back-up lights.

NOTE: in order for the neutral start switch to function properly, the transmission manual linkage must be properly adjusted and the actuator cam in the transmission must be centered in the neutral switch mounting hole in the transmission.

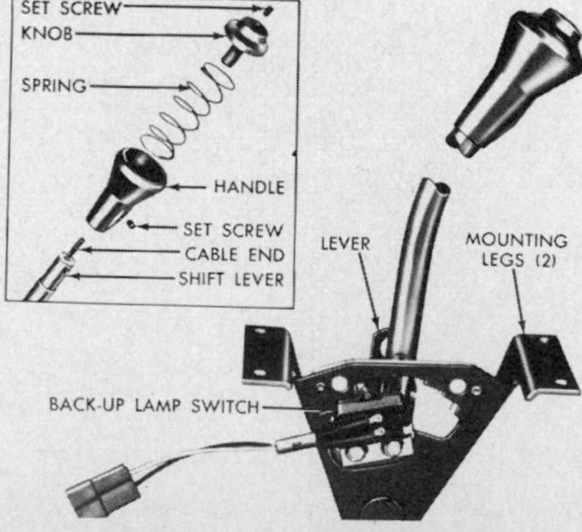

Automatic transmission console shifter (© Chrysler Corp)

To remove the switch, remove all the electrical leads while taking note of their position. Remove the switch with a wrench. Have a container of adequate size at hand to catch the draining fluid. When replacing the switch, be sure to use a new seal. Torque the switch to 24 ft lbs and replace the fluid.

Shift Linkage Adjustment

1969 Console Selector, 1969 Column Selector

1. Place selector lever in Park. Loosen control rod swivel clamp.
2. Move the transmission control lever fully to the rear (park detent).
3. Tighten the control rod swivel clamp to 100 in-lbs.

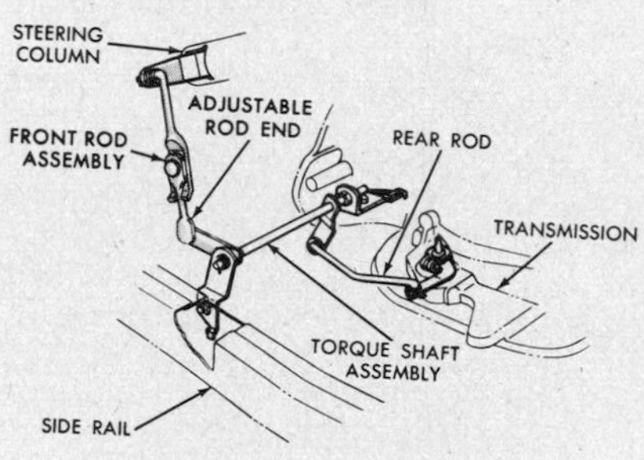

TorqueFlite column shift linkage—1970-72 Chrysler and Imperial (© Chrysler Corp)

1970-76 Console Selector 1970-76 Column Selector

1. Free adjustable rod ends.
2. Place selector lever in Park. Lock steering column. On console selector, line up locating slots in bottom of shift housing and bearing housing. Hold in place with a suitable tool.
3. Move selector to rear of Park detent.
4. Set adjustable rods to proper length.
5. Check adjustment:
   a. Detents and gate stops should be positive.
   b. Selector lever must not remain out of detent position when placed against gate and then released.

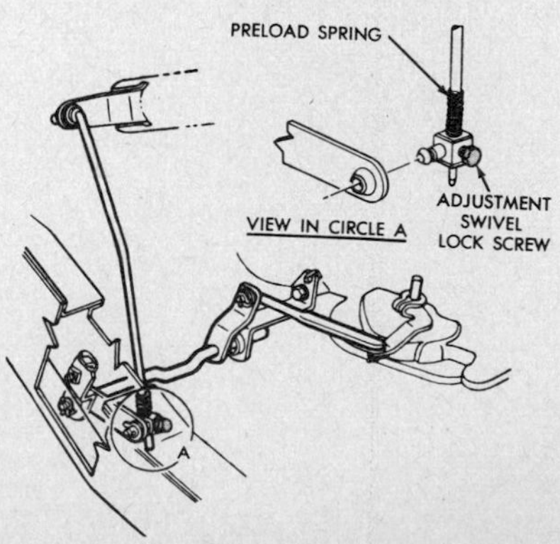

TorqueFlite column shift linkage—1974-76 Chrysler and Imperial (© Chrysler Corp)

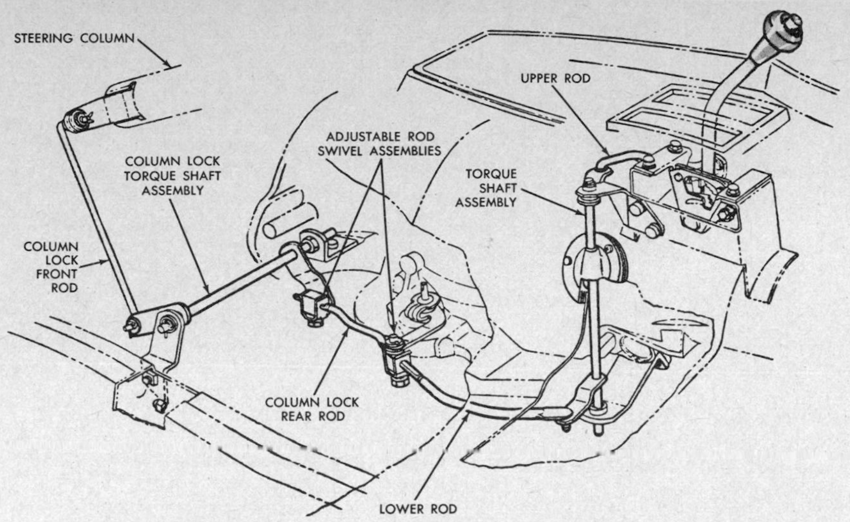

TorqueFlite console shift linkage—1970-71 Chrysler
(© Chrysler Corp)

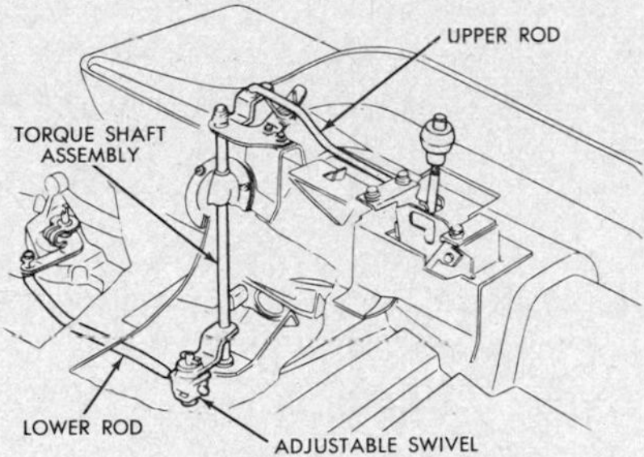

TorqueFlite console shift linkage —1975-76 Cordoba
(© Chrysler Corp)

c. Key start must occur with selector lever held against Park gate.

Band Adjustments

Kick-down Band

The kick-down band adjusting screw is located on the left-hand side of the transmission case near the throttle lever shaft.

1. Loosen the locknut and back it off about five turns. Be sure that the adjusting screw is free in the case.
2. Using an inch pounds torque wrench torque the adjusting screw to 72 in. lbs.
3. Back off the adjusting screw the exact number of turns specified below. Keep the screw from turning and torque the locknut to the value specified below.

1969-70 . . . . .2 turns
1971-76 . . . . .2½ turns
Kick-down band adjusting screw locknut torque (1969-71) . .29 ft lbs
(1972-76) . .35 ft lbs

Low and Reverse Band

The oil pan must be removed from the transmission to gain access to the low and reverse band adjusting screw.

1. Drain the transmission and remove the oil pan.
2. Loosen the band adjusting screw locknut and back it off about five turns. Be sure that the adjusting screw turns freely in the lever.
3. Using an inch pounds torque wrench, tighten the adjusting screw to 72 in. lbs if an adaptor is not used.
4. Back off the adjusting screw the exact number of turns specified below. Keep the screw from turning and torque the locknut to the value specified below.

1969-76 . . . . .2 turns
Low and reverse band adjusting screw locknut torque (1969-71) . .35 ft lbs
(1972-76) . .30 ft lbs

5. Using a new gasket, install the oil pan and tighten the attaching bolts to 150 in. lbs.
6. Fill the transmission.

U-JOINTS

All models use one-piece driveshafts with two U-joints. All full size Chrysler, Cordoba, and 1974-75 Imperial models have two cross-and-roller joints with a slip spline at the front U-joint. There are two constant-velocity U-joints with a sliding yoke at the front of 1969-73 Imperials.

Two basic types of driveshafts are utilized; a solid tube type, and one that incorporates an internal vibration damper inside the tube itself. On certain applications, the driveshaft may be found to incorporate an inertia type ring at the front U-joint. Servicing of all driveshafts is identical.

Driveshaft Removal

1969-76

1. Scribe alignment marks on the driveshaft, rear U-joint, and the drive pinion flange. This is necessary to ensure proper drive train balance upon installation of the various parts.
2. Remove both of the U-joint roller and bushing assembly clamps from the rear axle drive pinion flange. Be sure not to disturb the retaining strap (if so equipped) which holds the bushing assemblies on the U-joint cross. Do not allow the driveshaft to hang loose while removing either U-joint.

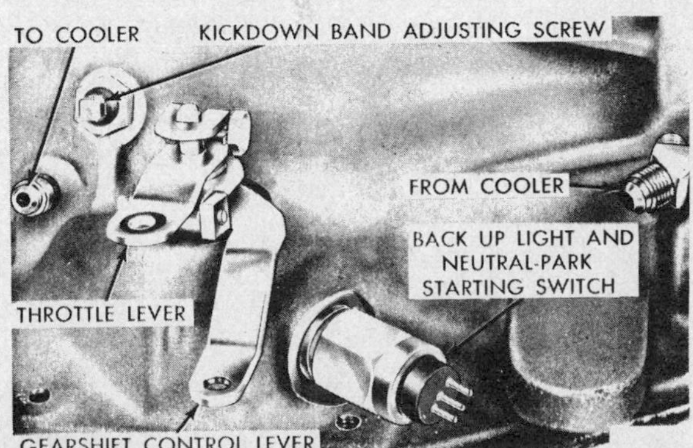

TorqueFlite transmission external controls, showing the location of the kick-down band adjustment
(© Chrysler Corp)

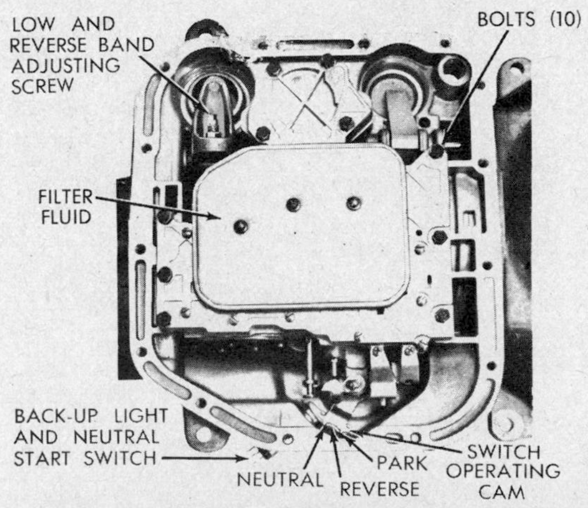

TorqueFlite transmission with the pan removed. Note the low and reverse band adjusting screw location
(© Chrysler Corp)

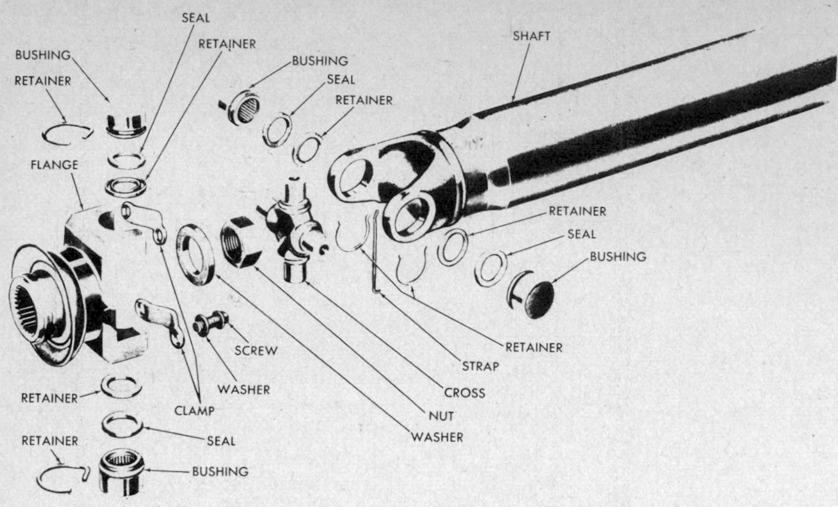

Rear cross and roller U-joint—All Chrysler, Cordoba, and 1974-75 Imperial

3. Slide the driveshaft with the front yoke from the transmission output shaft. Be careful not to damage the splines on the output shaft and the yoke. Do not disturb the yoke seal unless it is damaged or leaking. Remove the driveshaft and protect the sliding yoke from damage.
4. To install the driveshaft, clean the sliding yoke and inspect its machined surface. File off burrs if necessary. Carefully engage the yoke splines with the splines on the end of the transmission output shaft.
5. At the rear, align the scribe marks and install the U-joint cross and roller bushings into the drive pinion flange. Fit the bushing clamps and securing screws and torque to specifications.

Constant Velocity Universal Joint—1969-73 Imperial Only

Disassembly

Remove the driveshaft and, before disassembling any parts, mark the joints for proper indexing at the time of assembly.

1. Remove four screws and lockwashers. Remove spline yoke.
2. Remove two loose bearings from centering socket yoke.
3. Remove snap-rings holding the bearing assemblies in the center socket yoke shaft, and center yoke bores.
4. Press bearing assemblies from the yokes by using a ¾ in. socket as a remover and a pipe or socket with an inside diameter of not less than 1 1/16 in. as a receiver on the opposite bearing. With the aid of a press or vise, press one of the rear yoke bearings about ⅜ in. out of the yoke.
5. Clamp the exposed bearing in the vise and drive the yoke from the bearing with a brass drift.
6. Using the same procedure, press the exposed end of the cross to force the bearing on the opposite end about ⅜ in. out of the yoke. Remove the bearing from the yoke as previously described in Step 5.
7. Remove the remaining set of bearings from the propeller shaft yoke in the same way.
8. With the shaft held in the vise, press in on the yoke shaft and work the center joint off the cross.
9. Remove the cross from the propeller shaft yoke. Remove centering stud spring from the propeller shaft.
10. Remove the four roller bearing assemblies to separate the yoke shaft from the center yoke, as previously described.

If it is necessary to remove the centering ball and socket assembly, proceed as follows:

11. Carefully pry the centering ball seal assembly from the yoke shaft.
12. Remove seal from the centering stud seal retainer and the bearing rollers from the centering ball.
13. Fill the cavity behind the centering ball and inside the ball with lithium base grease.
14. Insert a rod, slightly smaller than the inside diameter of the centering ball, into the ball, then strike it sharply with a hammer. The force applied should force the ball and retainer from the yoke.

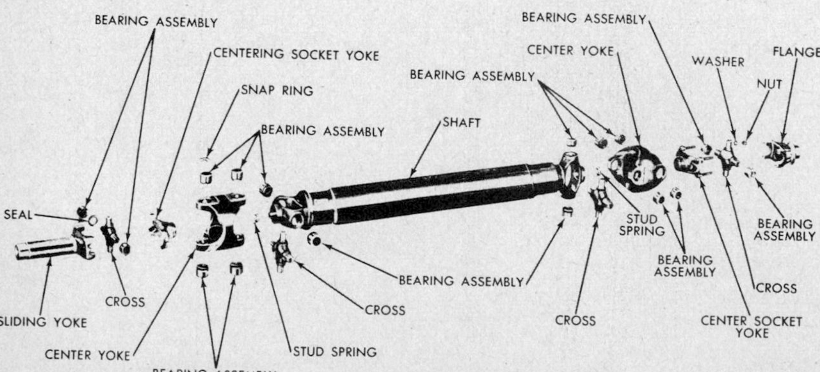

Constant Velocity U-joints and drive shaft—1969-73 Imperial
(© Chrysler Corp)

Assembly

1. Position the centering assembly in the yoke with the large diameter hole up, and press it firmly into its seat.
2. Apply grease on the inside surface of the centering ball. Install the 34 rollers. Install the centering stud seal in the ball.
3. Install centering ball seal assembly on the yoke and press firmly into place.
4. Coat the inside surfaces of the bearing races with the same grease, and install the 32 rollers. Also, pack the reservoirs in the ends of the cross with the same grease.
5. Place the cross in the shaft yoke. Insert one bearing assembly in the bearing bore of the shaft yoke. With the bar stock or socket used as a remover when disassembling, press the bearing into the bore. At the same time, guide the cross into the bearing. Press the bearing into the yoke far enough to install the snap-ring. Install the snap-ring. Reverse the position of the yoke and install the opposite bearing and snap-ring in th same manner.
6. Place the center yoke on the cross installed in the shaft yoke. Install the two bearings and snap-rings in the yoke, as previously described.
7. Install the cross and two bearings in the shaft yoke, in the same manner as previously described. Install snap-rings.
8. Install centering stud spring on the centering stud, (large end first). Apply grease to the stud.
9. Position the cross in the center universal joint of the propeller

shaft while guiding the centering ball on the centering stud, applying pressure at the same time. Work the center yoke over the cross. Don't damage the cross seals.
10. Install the two bearing assemblies in the rear bores of the center yoke as previously described. Install snap-rings.
11. Coat the splines of the center socket yoke with grease.
12. Install slip spline yoke on the constant velocity joints with screws and lockwashers. Torque to specifications.

Cross and Roller Bearing U-Joints—All Chrysler, Cordoba, and 1974-75 Imperial

Disassembly and Assembly

1. To disassemble the joint, remove the four bolts that hold the two bearing assemblies to the companion flange and knock the bearings off the flange.
2. To remove the bearings from the yoke, first remove the bearing retainer lock washers or C-washers, then pressing on one of the bearings, drive the bearing in toward the center of the joint. This will force the cross to push the opposite bearing out of the universal joint yoke. After it has been pushed all the way out of the yoke, pull up the cross slightly and pack some washers under it. Then press on the end of the cross from which the bearing was just removed to force the first bearing out of the yoke.
3. Perhaps the easiest way to reassemble is to start both bearing retainers into the yoke at the same time, hold the cross carefully in the fingers and squeeze both bearings in a vise or heavy C-clamp. Driving the bearings into place usually cocks the little rollers, greatly reducing the life of the bearings.
4. Install the locking devices.

REAR AXLE

Three different rear axle assemblies have been used on Chrysler, Imperial and Cordoba models. A removable carrier axle with an 8¾ in. ring gear diameter differential was installed on all 1969-72 models. Beginning 1973, two integral carrier axles are used; an 8¼ in. ring gear diameter unit with 318, 360 and 400 V8 engines, and a 9¼ in. ring gear diameter unit with the 440 V8. Both the 8¼ and 9¼ in. axles use C-clips to retain the axle shafts.

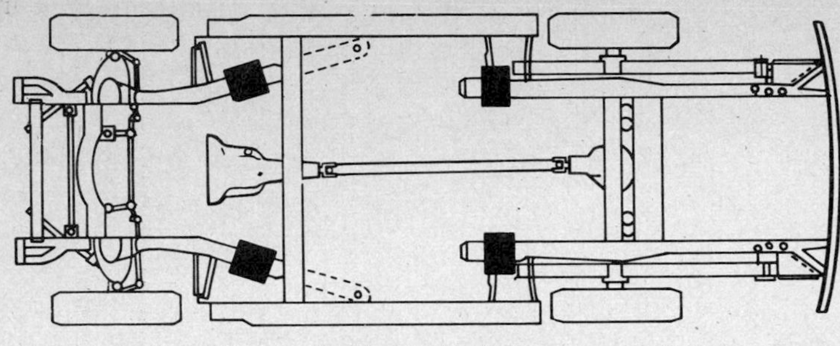

Positioning lift adapter
(© Chrysler Corp)

Axle Shaft, Bearing and Seal

Removal and Installation

See the Dodge/Plymouth section.

JACKING, HOISTING

Jack car at front under lower control arm and at rear under axle housing.

To lift at frame, use adapters so that contact will be made at points shown. Lifting pad must extend beyond sides of supporting structure.

FRONT SUSPENSION

All models utilize torsion bar front suspension. The rear anchors of the torsion bars are integral with the engine rear support crossmember; the front anchor points are part of the lower control arms, and are the means used to adjust the height of the vehicle. Compression type lower ball joints are used on all 1969-73 Chryslers. The lower ball joints are preloaded on all Imperials, Cordobas, and 1974-76 Chryslers. The ball joints and torsion bars at the front of the rear anchors use balloon type flexible seals; this serves to protect the components from road splash and dirt. When it is necessary to lubricate these balloon seals, avoid pressure type lubrcation guns; these seals burst easily, and should be filled slowly and manually only.

1969-73 Imperials use a rubber isolated front crossmember. It is effectively isolated from the stub frame by four large rubber bushing insulators. The crossmember that supports the torsion bar rear anchor is further isolated from the stub frame's crossmember by sandwich type insulators. The upper control arm is mounted on a pivot bar and the front wheel alignment is adjusted by two vertically mounted cam bolts. A link type sway bar is fitted; it mounts to the lower control arm and front crossmember.

When servicing, it is important to remember that all front suspension parts containing rubber should be tightened only when the suspension is at the proper height, and that the full weight of the vehicle must be on the wheels. Moreover, do not lubricate the ruber bushings wth oil at any time.

Front Shock Absorber Removal and Installation

1. Remove the nut and retainer from the shock absorber top.
2. Jack the front of the vehicle. It is sometimes necessary to remove the tire and wheel assembly and perform the removal operation from beneath the fender.
3. Remove the shock absorber lower attaching bolt nut. Remove the bolt from the shock absorber eye or shaft and lower the control arm mounting bracket.
4. Push upward on the shock absorber and fully compress it; pull the shock downward and out of its upper mounting bushings and remove from the vehicle. On 1969-73 Imperial models, the dust shield is removed with the shock absorber. It may be necessary to remove the upper control

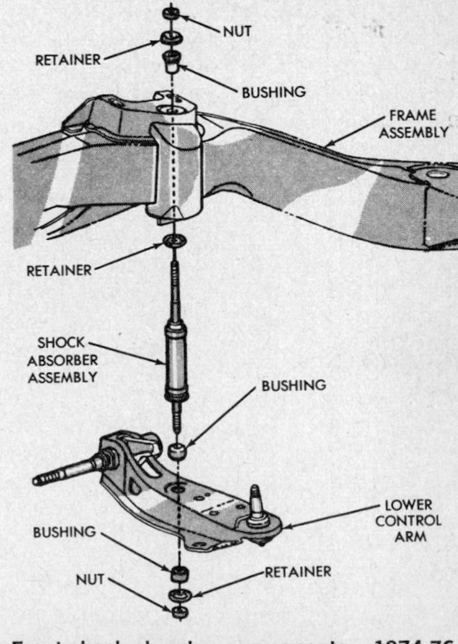

Front shock absorber components—1974-76 Chrysler and Imperial
(© Chrysler Corp)

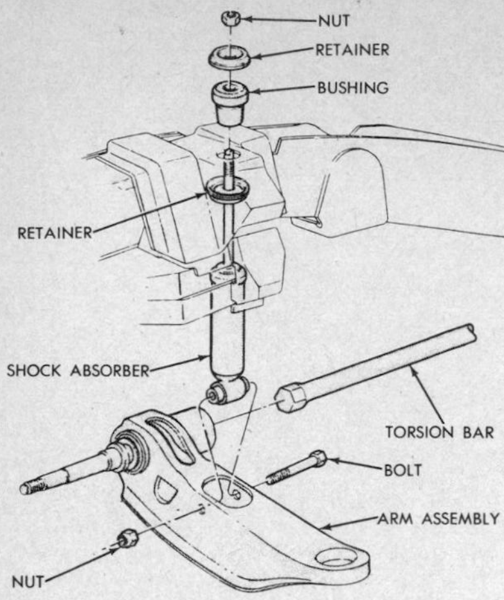

Front shock absorber and lower control arm assembly—Cordoba
(© Chrysler Corp)

arm bumper, on some models, to obtain enough clearance to remove the shock absorber assembly.

5. To begin the installation procedure fully compress the shock. Insert the rod through the upper bushing, install the retainer and nut, and tighten the nut. On 1969-73 Imperial models, place the retainer on the shock absorber upper rod; then install the dust shield. Install the rod to the upper bushing with its nut and retainer and tighten the nut. *NOTE: All retainers must be installed with the concave (sunken) side in contact with the rubber.* Align the shock lower eye or shaft with its lower control arm mountings. Install its retaining nut and bolt finger tight. Lower the vehicle and tighten the nut with the full weight of the vehicle on the wheels.

Front Height Adjustment

1969-74

1. Jounce vehicle several times, releasing it on downward motion.
2. Measure distance A. For 1969-73 Chrysler models, the measurement is taken from the lowest point of the adjusting blade. For all Imperial models and 1974 Chrysler models measure from the lowest point of the front torsion bar anchor at the rear of the lower control arm flange.
3. Measure distance B. This is the distance between the lowest point of the lower ball joint housing and the floor.
4. Subtract distance A from distance B to obtain front suspension height. Check this figure against the figure listed in the front end alignment table in the front of this section.
5. Measure the other side. There should be no more than 1/8 in.

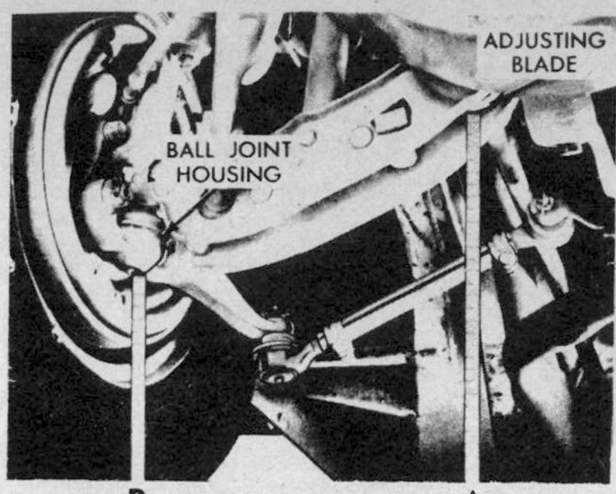

Measuring front suspension height—1969-73 Chrysler (© Chrysler Corp)

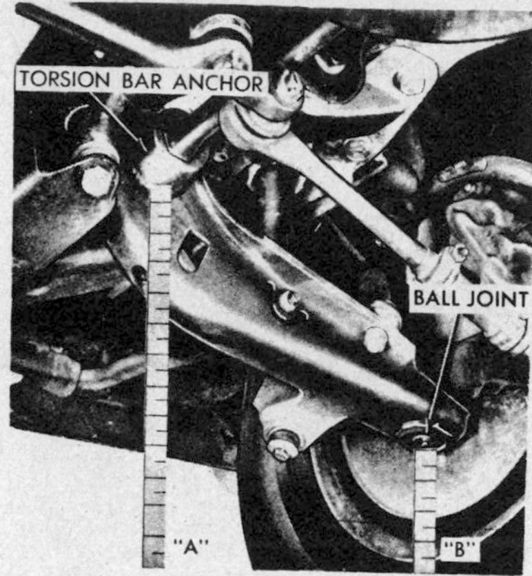

Measuring front suspension height—1969-74 Imperial and 1974 Chrysler
(© Chrysler Corp)

difference in height from one side to the other.

6. Adjust height, as necessary, by turning torsion bar adjusting bolt clockwise to increase height and counterclockwise to decrease height.

1975-76

1. Jounce the vehicle several times, releasing it in the downward position.
2. Measure distance "A". The measurement is taken from the lowest point of the lower control arm torsion bar anchor at a point 1 inch forward of the rear face of the anchor, to the ground. Check this figure against that listed in the "Front End Height" table in the front of this section.
3. Measure the other side. Maximum allowable variation in height from one side to another is 1/8 in.
4. Adjust height, as necessary, by rotating the torsion bar adjusting bolt clockwise to increase height and counterclockwise to decrease height.

Wheel Bearing Adjustment

1969-72

1. Jack the vehicle and remove the hub cap and grease cup. Take out the cotter pin, remove the nut lock and loosen the adjusting nut.
2. While rotating the wheel, tighten the wheel bearing adjusting nut to 90 in. lbs.
3. Align the nut lock on the nut so that one pair of slots is in line with the cotter pin hole.
4. Back off the adjusting nut lock assembly one slot and install a new cotter pin. This should yield an adjustment between zero (no preload) and 0.003 in. end-play.
5. Clean the grease cup. Coat, but do not fill, the inside of the cup with wheel bearing lubricant and install it on the vehicle. Install the hub caps and lower the vehicle.

1973-76

1. Raise the front of the car to allow the wheels to spin freely.
2. Remove the wheel cover, grease cup, cotterpin, and lock nut.
3. Tighten the wheel bearing adjusting nut to 240-300 in. lbs while spinning the wheel.
4. Back the nut off and retighten to finger tight.
5. Reinstall the lock nut, cotter pin, grease cup, and wheel cover.
6. Lower the car.

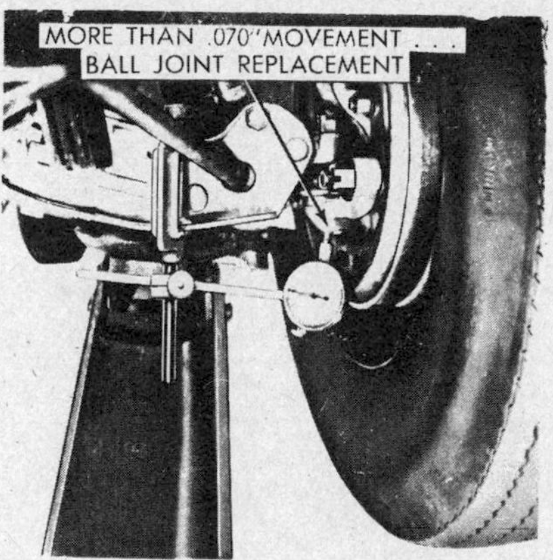

Measuring lower ball joint axial travel
(© Chrysler Corp)

Lower Ball Joint

Inspection

1. Raise the front of the vehicle by placing a floor jack under the lower control arm. Position the lifting point of the jack as close to the wheel as possible.
2. Have an assistant raise and lower the tire and wheel assembly and observe any movement at the lower ball joint.
3. On 1969-73 Chryslers, replace the ball joint of the axial play exceeds 0.070 in. On all Cordobas, 1969-76 Imperials, and 1974-76 full size Chryslers, the lower ball joints are preloaded and, if any free-play exists in excess of 0.020 in., the lower ball joint control arm assembly must be removed for service.

Removal—1969-73 Chrysler

The compression-type lower ball joint is integral with the steering arm and is not serviced separately.

1. Remove the upper control arm rebound bumper. Raise the vehicle on a hoist so the front suspension will drop to the downward limit of its travel.
2. Place a jack stand under the lower control arm, near the ball joint.
3. Lower the vehicle onto the jack stand. Off-load the torsion bars by rotating the adjusting bolts counterclockwise.
4. Remove the tire, wheel, and brake drum from the vehicle as an assembly. If equipped with disc brakes, remove the tire and wheel. Remove the brake pads, and remove the caliper from the steering knuckle and position it out of the way with the brake line attached. Remove the rotor from the spindle.
5. Remove the two lower bolts that attach the steering arm-ball joint assembly to the brake assembly mounting plate.
6. Using a suitable tool, disconnect the tie rod end from the steering arm, taking care not to damage the seal.
7. Remove the ball joint stud retaining nut and cotter pin.
8. Using a suitable tool, separate and remove the ball joint from the lower contol arm.

Installation

1. Position ball joint-steering arm assembly on the steering knuckle and install the two retaining bolts.
2. Insert the ball joint stud in the lower control arm and install the retaining nut and cotter pin.
3. Position the tie rod end in the steering knuckle and install the retaining nut and cotter pin.
4. Place a load on the torsion bar by turning the adjusting bolt in a clockwise direction.
5. Install the tire, wheel and brake drum assembly. If equipped with disc brakes, install the rotor, caliper, brake pads and tire and wheel assembly.
6. Lower vehicle and install upper control arm rebound bumper if so equipped.
7. Check and adjust front suspension height as required.

Removal—1969-73 Imperial

Lower ball joints on Imperial models are serviced only as ball joint-control arm assemblies.

1. Raise the vehicle on a hoist so the front suspension drops to the downward limit of its travel.
2. Remove the wheel and tire as an assembly.
3. Remove the load from *both* torsion bars by turning the adjusting bolts in a counterclockwise direction.
4. Disconnect the shock absorber from the lower control arm and position the shock out of the way. Disconnect the strut bar from the lower control arm.
5. Disconnect the brake hose from the caliper.
6. Remove the lower ball joint retaining nut and cotter pin.
7. Using a suitable tool, separate the ball joint stud from the steering knuckle.
8. Remove the nut and washer that attaches the lower control arm pivot shaft to the frame.
9. Using a brass drift and hammer, tap the end of the pivot shaft to loosen it (the shaft is a tapered fit in the front crossmember).
10. Remove the lower control arm and shaft from the vehicle as an assembly.
11. Position the control arm assembly in a press with the hex opening for the torsion bar in the up position and place a support under the outer edge of the control arm.
12. Insert a brass drift in the hex opening and press the shaft out of the control arm. The bushing inner arm will remain on the shaft.
13. Remove the torsion bar adjusting bolt and swivel from the control arm.

Installation

1. Position a new bushing on the pivot shaft (flange end of the bushing first) and seat the bushing on the shoulder of the pivot shaft.
2. Press the shaft and bushing assembly into the new control arm.
3. Install the torsion bar adjusting bolt and swivel on the new control arm.
4. Position a new seal on the ball joint and install the seal. To ease installation of the seal, the ball joint stud should be perpendicular to the body of the ball joint.
5. Position the control arm assembly on the crossmember in approximate operating position and install the nut and washer. *Do not tighten the nut until the full weight of the vehicle is on the wheels.*
6. Insert the lower ball joint stud in the steering knuckle and install the retaining nut and cotter pin.
7. Install the strut bar rear bushing and retainer on the strut bar and insert the strut bar through the crossmember.
8. Install the front strut bar bushing and retainer on the strut bar and install the retaining nut finger tight only.
9. Position the rear of the strut bar over the lower control arm and install the bumper and plate.
10. Connect the shock absorber to the lower control arm and install the retaining nut finger tight. Place a load on each torsion bar by turning the adjusting bolt clockwise.
11. Connect the brake line to the disc brake caliper and bleed the brakes.
12. Install the tire and wheel assembly.
13. Lower the vehicle to the floor. Tighten the strut bar, shock absorber and lower control arm attaching nuts.
14. Check and adjust front end height as required.

Removal—1974-76 Chrysler, Cordoba, and Imperial

Lower ball joints on these models may be serviced separately. The ball joints are a press-fit necessitating a special tool (see illustration) for removal.

1. Place the ignition switch in the "off" or "unlocked" position.
2. Remove the rebound bumper.
3. Raise the vehicle on a hoist so that the front suspension drops to the downward limit of its travel. Position jackstands beneath the front frame for extra support.

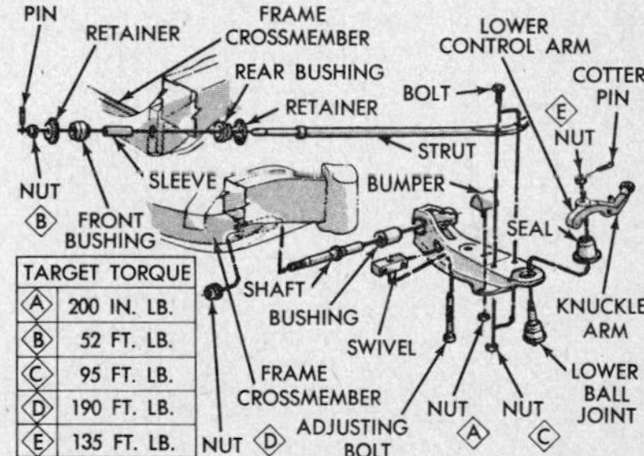

Lower control arm assembly exploded view—1974-76 Chrysler and Imperial
(© Chrysler Corp)

4. Remove the wheel and tire assembly.
5. Remove the caliper from its mounts and tie it up out of the way so that there is no strain on the flexible brake hose.
6. Remove the hub and rotor assembly, splash shield, lower shock absorber mounting nut, retainer and insulator.
7. Off-load the torsion bars by rotating the adjusting bolts counterclockwise.
8. Remove the upper and lower ball joint stud cotter pins and nuts. Using a ball joint press tool (such as C-3564A), slide the tool over the upper stud until the tool rests on the steering knuckle.
9. Then, turn the threaded portion of the tool so that it locks snugly against the lower stud. Tighten the tool enough to load the lower

ball joint stud, and then strike the steering knuckle arm with a hammer to loosen the stud. Under no circumstances should you attempt to force the stud from the knuckle using the tool alone.

10. Using a press (such as C-4212), press the ball joint out of the lower control arm.

Removing ball joint stud
(© Chrysler Corp)

Installation

1. Using the ball joint press (such as C-4212) press the new ball joint into the lower control arm.
2. Place a new seal over the ball joint (as necessary). Using an adapter tool (such as C-4034), press the retainer portion of the seal down over the ball joint housing until it locks into position.
3. Insert the ball joint stud through the opening in the knuckle arm and install the stud retaining nuts. Tighten to 85 ft lbs. Install the cotter pins and lubricate the ball joint.
4. Load the torsion bar by rotating the adjusting bolt clockwise.
5. Install the shock absorber retaining nut, retainer and insulator, the splash shield, hub and rotor assembly, and brake caliper. Install the wheel and tire assembly.
6. Adjust the front wheel bearings.
7. Remove the jackstands and lower the car. Install the rebound bumper. Adjust the front suspension height.

Upper Ball Joint

Replacement

1. Place the ignition in the "off" or "unlocked" position. Raise the vehicle by placing a floor jack under the lower control arm. Place the lifting point of the jack as close as possible to the wheel.
2. Remove the wheel, tire and drum as an assembly. On models

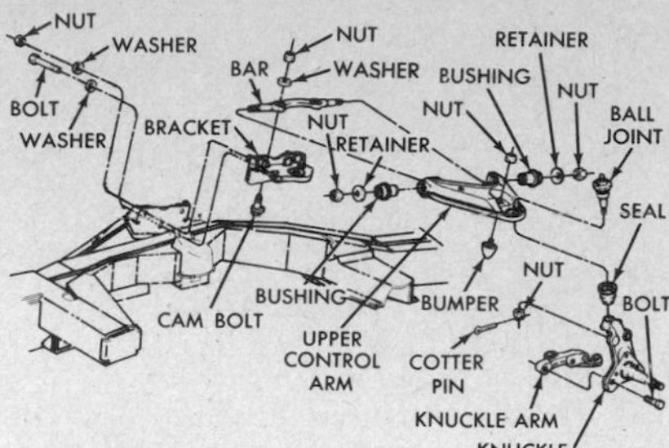

Imperial upper control arm—1969-73
(© Chrysler Corp)

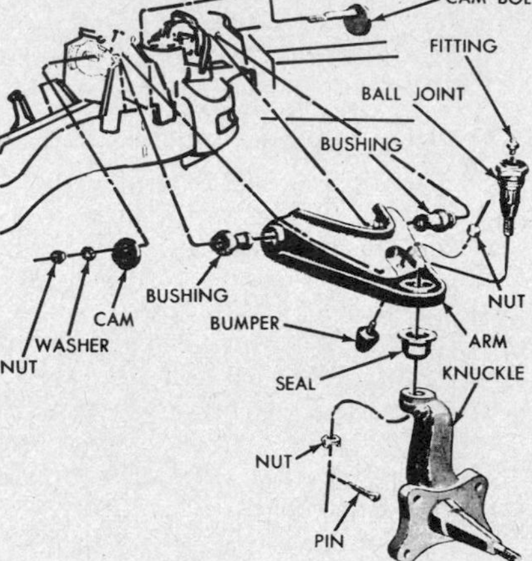

Chrysler upper control arm—1969-73
(© Chrysler Corp)

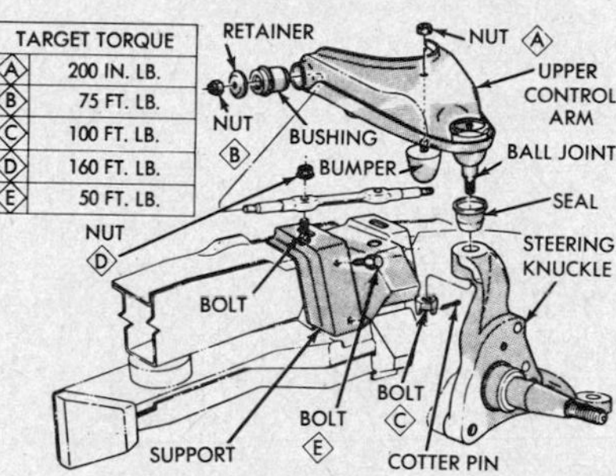

TARGET TORQUE	
A	200 IN. LB.
B	75 FT. LB.
C	100 FT. LB.
D	160 FT. LB.
E	50 FT. LB.

Upper control arm assembly—Cordoba
(© Chrysler Corp)

with disc brakes, remove the tire and wheel, remove the disc brake pads, remove the disc brake caliper from the steering knuckle and position the caliper out of the way with the brake line attached. Remove the brake rotor from the steering knuckle.

3. Remove the nut that attaches the upper ball joint to the steering knuckle and, using a suitable tool, loosen the ball joint stud from the steering knuckle.
4. Unscrew the upper ball joint from the upper control arm and remove it from the vehicle.
5. Position new ball joint on the upper control arm, screw the ball joint into the control arm until it bottoms and tighten the ball joint to a minimum of 125 ft. lbs. for Chrysler and Cordoba models, 150 ft. lbs. for Imperial models.

NOTE: when installing a ball joint, make certain the ball joint threads engage those of the upper control arm squarely if the original control arm is being used.

6. Position a new seal on the ball joint stud and install the seal in the ball joint making sure the seal is fully seated on the ball joint housing.
7. Position ball joint stud in the steering knuckle and install the retaining nut.
8. Lubricate ball joint and, if replacement ball joint is equipped with knock-off type grease fitting, break off that portion of the fitting over which the lubrication gun was installed.
9. If equipped with disc brakes, install the rotor, caliper and brake pads. Install the tire and wheel.
10. Lower the vehicle and adjust front suspension height as required.

Torsion Bar

The torsion bars are not interchangeable from right to left. They are marked with an R or an L, according to their location.

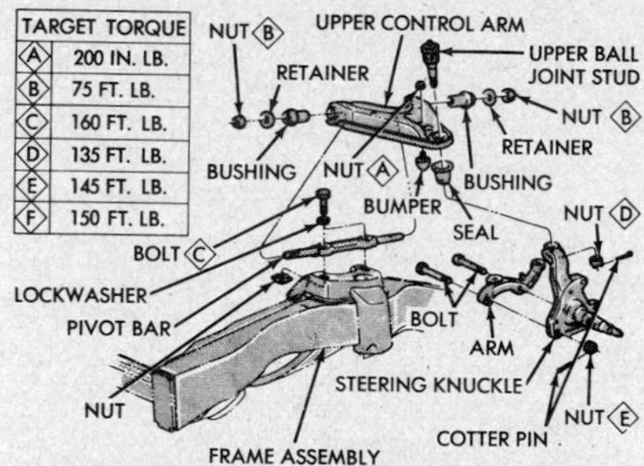

TARGET TORQUE	
A	200 IN. LB.
B	75 FT. LB.
C	160 FT. LB.
D	135 FT. LB.
E	145 FT. LB.
F	150 FT. LB.

Upper control arm assembly exploded view—1974-76 Chrysler and Imperial
(© Chrysler Corp)

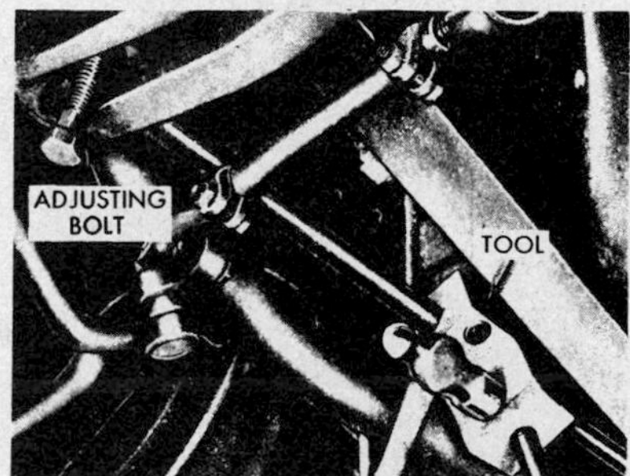

Removing the torsion bar
(© Chrysler Corp)

Torsion Bar Removal and Replacement

Removal

1. Raise the vehicle so the front suspension drops to the limit of its downward travel.
2. Remove the upper control arm rebound bumper if so equipped.
3. On all models except 1969-73 Imperials, remove the tension from the torsion bar to be replaced by turning the anchor adjusting bolt in a counterclockwise direction and removing the adjusting bolt and swivel. On

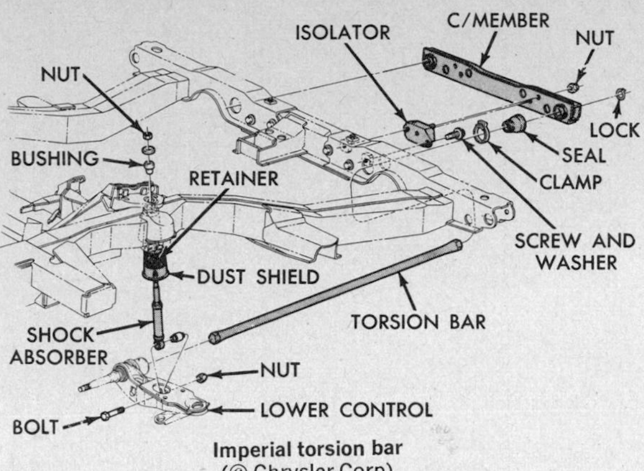

Imperial torsion bar
(© Chrysler Corp)

1969-73 Imperials, release the load on both torsion bars by turning each anchor adjusting bolt in a counterclockwise direction. This is necessary because the rubber insulator rear crossmember would be under load and could possibly cause severe damage or personal injury.

4. Slide rear anchor balloon seal off of the rear anchor and remove the lockring from the anchor. On Imperial models remove the balloon seal clamp.
5. On all models, remove the torsion bar from the vehicle by sliding it rearward and out of the torsion bar rear anchor.

Installation

1. Position the torsion bar in the chassis and apply a coating of chassis lubricant to both ends.
2. Install the lockring in the anchor, making sure it is seated in the groove.
3. Pack the annular opening in the rear anchor completely full of chassis lubricant and position the lip of the balloon seal in the groove of the anchor. On Imperial models, install the balloon seal clamp.
4. On all Chrysler, Cordoba, and 1974-75 Imperial models, turn the adjusting bolt in a clockwise direction to place a load on the torsion bar. On 1969-73 Imperial models, turn both adjusting bolts to load both torsion bars.
5. Lower the vehicle to the floor and adjust front end height as required.

REAR SUSPENSION

All models use a leaf-spring rear suspension and double-acting shock absorbers. The springs are of the semi-elliptical type, with zinc interleaves between the normal leaves to increase spring life and reduce corrosion. On most models, rubber insulators are used where the springs attach to the body to reduce road noise and vibration.

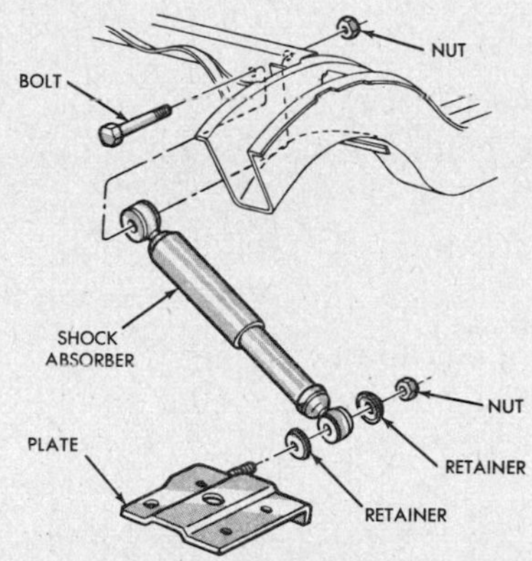

Rear shock absorber components—1974-76 Chrysler and Imperial shown; others similar
(© Chrysler Corp)

Rear Shock Absorber Removal and Installation

1. Jack the vehicle under the rear axle. Position the jackstands in such a manner that the shock absorbers are under no load.
2. At the bottom mount, remove the nut and retainer securing the shock to the spring seat isolator retainer plate; remove the shock from the stud.
3. At the top mount, remove the retaining nut and washer and then remove the shock. To replace the shock absorber, reverse the removal procedure. Remember that the shock absorber mounting bolts must not be fully tightened until the full vehicle weight is resting on the wheels.

Rear Spring R & R

1. Raise the vehicle on a hoist.
2. Place jack stands under the differential and lower the vehicle until the weight is removed from the rear springs.
3. Disconnect the rear shock absorber. If so equipped, remove the sway bar.
4. Loosen and remove the U-bolt nuts and U-bolts. Remove the spring plate.
5. Loosen and remove the nuts holding the front spring hanger to the front body mounting bracket.

Caution 1974 and later full-size models have preloaded rear springs. A special spring stretcher (tool no. C-4211) must be installed before releasing either end of the spring. Do not try to remove the spring without the stretcher; its sudden release could cause serious injury.

6. Remove the rear spring hanger bolts and let the spring drop far enough to pull the front spring hanger bolts out of the body mounting bracket.
7. Remove the front pivot bolt from the front spring hanger.
8. Loosen and remove rear shackle nuts and remove the rear shackle from the spring.
9. Remove rear spring from the vehicle.
10. Reverse above procedure to install. When installing the front and rear pivot nuts and bolts, do not tighten the bolts until the vehicle has been lowered to the floor and weight is on the wheels.

BRAKES

Front wheel disc brakes were optional equipment until 1973 when they became standard equipment. Information on this type of brake is in the Unit Repair Section. A compound brake system is used on all models. This system is, in effect, two independent hydraulic systems, one for the front brakes and another for the rear brakes. The master cylinder has two pistons in tandem and two fluid outlets. The front outlet tube is connected to the hydraulic system safety switch and to the rear brakes. The rear outlet tube is also connected to the safety switch and the front brakes. In the event of a pressure loss in either branch of the system, the safety switch causes a warning light to be illuminated on the instrument panel. Power brakes are available on all models. The power brake unit features a direct pedal connection to a vacuum unit mounted on the firewall with a master cylinder directly mounted to a vacuum booster.

This vacuum-suspended system utilizes engine intake manifold vacuum and atmospheric pressure for its power boost to the master cylinder.

The 1974-75 Imperial uses rear disc brakes. The system is similar to that employed on domestic sportscars, with internal drum brake shoes for the parking brake.

NOTE: Procedures for brake shoe or pad replacement and adjustment, wheel and master cylinder overhaul, and brake bleeding can be found in the "Unit Repair Section."

Master Cylinder Removal

1. Disconnect fluid lines. On disc brake cylinders, plug brake outlets to prevent leakage.
2. Remove nuts attaching master cylinder to cowl panel or to power brake unit.

NOTE: it is not necessary to disconnect the pedal push rod as it is possible to separate the master cylinder from the rod by pulling them apart after the master cylinder attaching nuts have been removed.

3. Disconnect pedal push rod (non-power brakes) from brake pedal.
4. Remove master cylinder from vehicle.
5. Reverse procedure to install.
6. Bleed brake system.

Power Brake Booster R & R

1. Remove the nuts attaching the master cylinder to the brake booster and position the master cylinder out of the way. If the brake lines do not have enough slack to allow the master cylinder to be moved without kinking the brake lines, it will be necessary to disconnect the brake lines.
2. Disconnect the vacuum hose from the brake booster.
3. Working under the dash, remove the attaching nut and bolt from the brake booster pushrod and disconnect the pushrod from the brake pedal. On linkage type power brake boosters, remove the lower pivot mounting bolt.
4. Remove the four nuts and washers that attach the brake booster to the interior side of the firewall.
5. Remove the booster from under the hood.
6. Reverse above procedure to install.
7. If the brake lines were disconnected, bleed the brake system.

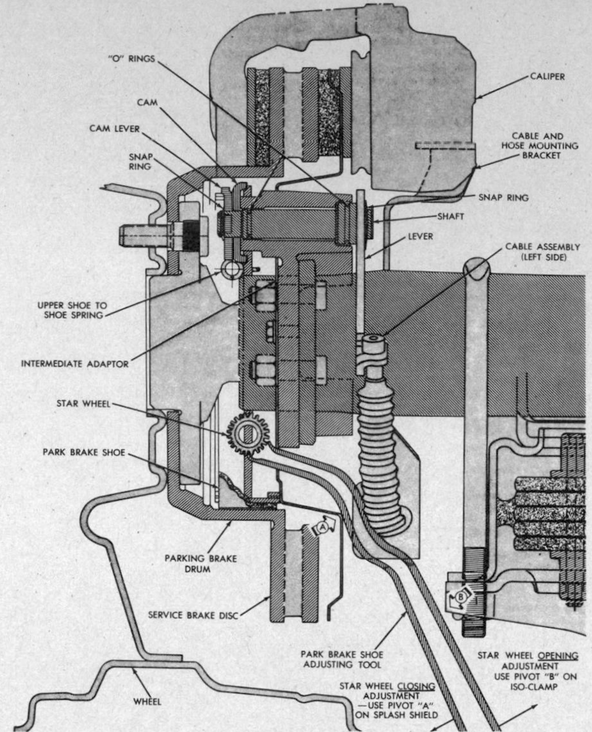

Parking brake shoe adjustment—1974-75 Imperial
(© Chrysler Corp)

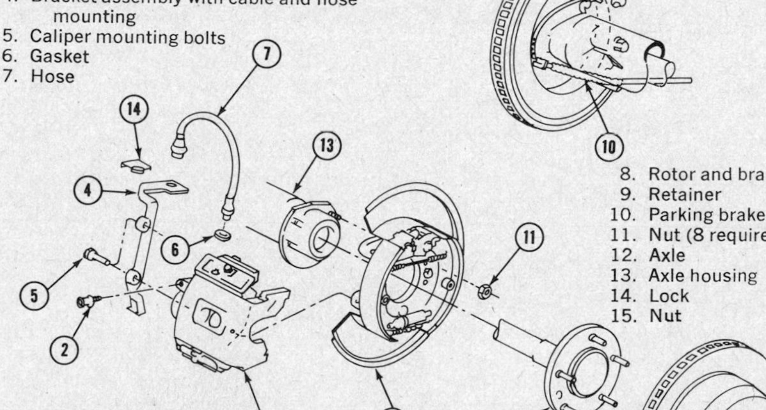

1. Housing assembly
2. Bleeder valve
3. Parking brake assembly with backing plate
4. Bracket assembly with cable and hose mounting
5. Caliper mounting bolts
6. Gasket
7. Hose
8. Rotor and brake disc
9. Retainer
10. Parking brake cable
11. Nut (8 required)
12. Axle
13. Axle housing
14. Lock
15. Nut

Details of the 1974-75 Imperial rear disc brake system. The internal expanding shoes are the parking brake
(© Chrysler Corp)

In a compound system one end of the car can develop a leak but the other half of the system will still operate. Two output lines identify this system.

FRONT AXLE
MASTER CYLINDER
REAR AXLE

Dual master cylinder circuit, typical
(© Chrysler Corp)

Parking Brake Adjustment

NOTE: On cars equipped with drum rear brakes, the rear brakes must first be properly adjusted before attempting a cable adjustment. On 1974-75 Imperials, the internal drum parking brake is first adjusted by inserting an adjusting spoon through an opening in the intermediate adapter (from the inboard side) and turning the starwheel until the parking brake shoes seat against the drum/disc surface. Then, back off the starwheel exactly 12 clicks so that the disc turns freely. Finally, adjust the cable as described below.

1. Raise and support vehicle. Release parking brake lever. Loosen cable adjusting nut.
2. Tighten cable adjusting nut until a slight drag is felt while rotating wheel.
3. Loosen cable adjusting nut until both rear wheels can be rotated freely. Back off cable adjusting nut two full turns.
4. Apply parking brake several times. Check to see that rear wheels rotate freely without dragging.

STEERING

A worm and recirculating ball type steering gear is used with the manual steering system. The worm shaft is supported at each end by ball type thrust bearings. The sector shaft includes an integral sector gear which meshes with helical grooves on the worm shaft ball nut. The sector shaft is supported, and rotates, in two needle bearings in the housing and one in the housing cover.

Constant-Control power steering is an option on all models. Hydraulic power is provided by a vane-type, belt-driven pump. A double-groove type pump pulley is used.

Some power steering pumps were equipped from the factory with oil coolers. These were used on vehicles with air conditioning, high-performance engines, and/or vehicles equipped with special axle ratios.

Most power steering pumps used an oil filter screen that was located in the oil return tube inside the reservoir. These only require service when they are completely clogged or when the pump is disassembled. Servicing is by replacement only.

Power Steering Pump Removal and Installation

1. Before beginning the removal procedure, carefully take note of the exact hose routing. The hoses must be installed in the exact same position as before removal. Read the entire removal procedure before beginning.
2. Back off the pump mounting and locking bolts and remove the pump drive belt.
3. Disconnect all hoses at the pump.
4. Remove the pump bolts and remove the pump with its bracket.
5. To install the pump, place it in position and install the mounting bolts.
6. Install the pump drive belt and adjust it to specifications. Torque the pump mounting bolts to 25–30 ft lbs.
7. Connect the pressure and return hoses. On the 1.06 cu in. pump, install a new pressure-hose O-ring.
8. Fill the pump with power steering fluid.
9. Start the engine and rotate the steering wheel from stop to stop at least 10 times. This will help to bleed the system. Check the pump oil level and fill as required.
10. Torque the pump end hose fitting to 24 ft lbs, and the gear end fitting to 160 in. lbs. Be certain the hoses are at least 2 in. from the exhaust manifolds and are not kinked or twisted.

Steering Wheel R & R

NOTE: Be careful when removing the steering wheel from vehicles that are equipped with a collapsible steering column. A sharp blow or excessive pressure on the column could cause it to collapse.

1. Disconnect the battery.
2. Depress the steering wheel center assembly and rotate it counterclockwise about ¼ turn. With the aid of a screwdriver, pry off the center assembly. On rim blow horn equipped models, the center assembly is secured by screws in the rear of the steering wheel spokes. Remove the screws and disconnect the wires to the rim blow horn.
3. Remove the large center nut. Remove the steering wheel from the column with a puller.
4. Reverse the procedure to install.

Turn Signal Switch R & R

1969

1. Disconnect the battery and remove the steering wheel.
2. Disconnect the horn and turn signal wires. Remove the snap-ring from the top of the steering shaft, if so equipped. Unscrew and remove the turn signal lever.
3. Tie a piece of string to the turn signal wires. Remove the turn signal switch screws.
4. Remove the turn signal switch retainer ring and extract the switch.
5. To install the switch, reverse the removal procedure. Transfer the string that was attached to the old switch to the new switch, and pull on the opposite end of the string to guide the wires through the column.

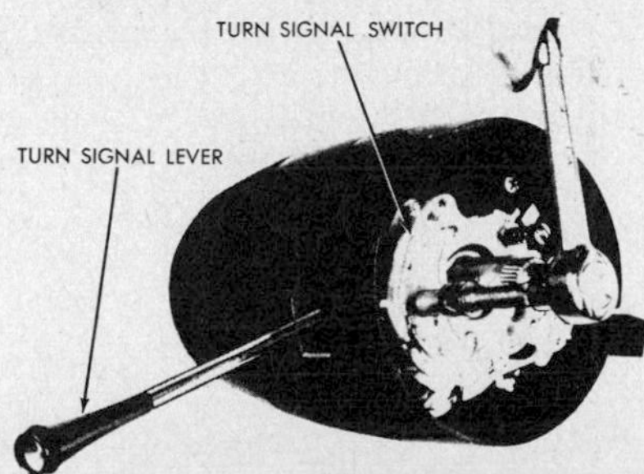

Removing the turn signal switch
(© Chrysler Corp)

1970-76

1. Remove the steering wheel.
2. Remove the three screws which fasten the turn signal switch to the steering column.
3. Remove the turn signal lever.
4. Unfasten the moulded wiring connector from the turn signal switch and withdraw the switch.
5. Installation is the reverse of the removal procedure.

INSTRUMENT PANEL

Ignition Switch Replacement —1969

1. Remove switch bezel nut.
2. Push switch through panel.
3. Disconnect wiring connector.
4. Remove switch.
5. To install, reverse procedure. Align key on switch with slot in panel.

Ignition Lock Cylinder Replacement—1969

1. Insert the ignition key into the lock cylinder.
2. Insert a piece of stiff wire into the small hole in the front face of the cylinder, and apply pressure to the wire.
3. Turn the ignition key counterclockwise toward the "acc" position.
4. Pull the lock cylinder and key from the instrument panel.
5. Insert a new lock cylinder into the instrument panel and it will lock itself in place.

Ignition Lock Cylinder and/or Ignition Switch Replacement —1970-76

1970-76 Standard Steering Column

1. Disconnect the negative battery cable. Remove the steering wheel.
2. Remove the screw that attaches the turn signal lever to the steering column.
3. Remove the three screws that attach the upper bearing retainer to the turn signal switch.
4. Pull the turn signal switch as far upward as possible.
5. Remove the upper bearing housing snap-ring from the steering shaft with snap-ring pliers.
6. Remove the screw that attaches the ignition key light assembly to the upper bearing housing.
7. Being careful not to damage any

components, pry the upper bearing housing off the steering shaft by lifting upward on alternate sides of the bearing housing with screwdrivers.

8. Lift upward on the steering shaft lockplate and place a screwdriver, or a substitute under it to hold it in the raised position. If this operation does not provide adequate working room beneath the lockplate, it will be necessary to press out the pin that attaches the lockplate to the steering shaft and remove the lockplate from the steering shaft. If the ignition switch is being replaced the lockplate must be removed.
9. Using an offset screwdriver, remove the two screws that attach the lock lever guide plate to the steering column.
10. With the ignition lock cylinder in the "lock" position and the ignition key removed, insert a stiff wire into the lock cylinder release hole in the steering column. Push in on the wire to release the spring-loaded lock retainer and pull the lock cylinder out from the steering column.
11. If the ignition switch is being replaced, remove the two screws that attach the ignition key buzzer switch to the steering column and the three screws that attach the ignition switch to the steering column. Lift the ignition switch out of the housing.
12. Reverse the above procedure for installation.

1970-76 Tilt Steering Column

1. Disconnect the negative battery cable.
2. Remove the steering wheel.
3. Remove the three attaching screws and remove the shaft lock cover.
4. Remove the screws that attach the tilt control lever and the turn signal lever to the steering column and remove the levers.
5. Push the hazard warning knob in and unscrew the knob from the turn signal switch. Remove the ignition key lamp assembly.
6. Using a suitable tool, repress the lockplate to gain access to the lockplate retaining snap-ring. Remove the snap-ring from the steering shaft.
7. Remove the lockplate, cancelling cam, and spring.
8. Remove the three turn signal switch attaching screws, place the shift lever in the low (1) position, and pull the switch and wires as far upward as possible.
9. With the ignition lock cylinder in the "lock" position, insert a small screwdriver into the lock release slot in the housing cover.
10. Press down with the screwdriver to release the spring latch at the bottom of the slot and pull the lock cylinder from the housing. The following steps are for ignition switch replacement only.
11. Remove the three screws that attach the upper steering column housing to the steering column and remove the housing.
12. Install the column tilt control lever and move the column to the full "up" position.
13. Insert a screwdriver into the slot in the spring retainer and press the retainer in approximately 3/16 in. Turn the retainer approximately 1/8 turn to the left until the ears align with the grooves in the housing. Remove the spring retainer, spring, and guide.
14. Push the steering shaft inward to enable removal of the inner race and seat. Remove the race and seat.
15. Make sure the ignition switch is in the "lock" position, then remove the wire connector from the ignition switch and remove the screws that attach the ignition switch to the outside of the steering column.
16. Lift the ignition switch from the column and twist it to disengage the switch actuating rod from the rack. Remove the switch.
17. To install the ignition lock cylinder, insert the cylinder into the housing with the cylinder in the lock position and the key *removed.*
18. Move the cylinder into the housing until it contacts the switch actuator. Move the switch actuator rod up and down to align the parts. When the parts are aligned the cylinder will move inward, where it will snap and lock into position.
19. With the ignition switch in the "lock" position insert the actuating rod into the steering column.
20. Twist the switch and rod assembly as required to engage the actuating rod with the rack. Make sure the ignition lock cylinder is in the lock position.
21. Install the ignition switch mounting screws but do not tighten them.
22. Move the ignition switch downward, away from the steering wheel, and tighten the switch mounting screws. Make sure the ignition switch has not moved out of the "lock" detent.
23. Attach the switch wiring connector.

Headlight Switch Replacement

1969-70 All Models

1. Disconnect the battery. Remove instrument cluster.
2. Remove headlamp switch from rear of cluster.
3. Install in reverse of above.

> **Chilton's TIME SAVER**
>
> **Although the Chrysler service literature calls for the removal of the instrument cluster to remove the headlight switch, the switch may be removed with the cluster in place. Working from under the instrument panel, remove the wires from the switch. Remove the switch retaining screws using a stubby screwdriver. Remove the switch from the panel.**

1971-76 All Models

1. Disconnect the battery. If equipped with air conditioning, remove the left air conditioning duct.
2. Remove the headlight switch shaft and knob by pulling the switch to the On position, reaching under the dash, and depressing the button on the bottom of the headlight switch case. Pull the knob and shaft from the switch.
3. Remove the sentinel and automatic dimmer control knobs if equipped with automatic headlight dimmer.
4. Remove the headlight switch attaching nut.
5. Remove the headlight switch from under the dash and disconnect the wires.
6. Reverse above procedure to install.

WINDSHIELD WIPERS

Wiper Motor Removal and Installation

1969-70 All Models

1. Disconnect battery ground cable.
2. Lift the wiper arm and insert a .090 pin or drill. Pull wiper arm from shaft with a rocking motion.
3. Remove windshield lower moulding.
4. Remove cowl screen.
5. Remove drive crank arm retaining nut and drive crank. To prevent damage to the gears, hold the crank arm nut with a wrench when removing the crank arm from the motor. Disconnect motor wiring.
6. Remove three mounting nuts. Remove motor.
7. Reverse procedure to install.

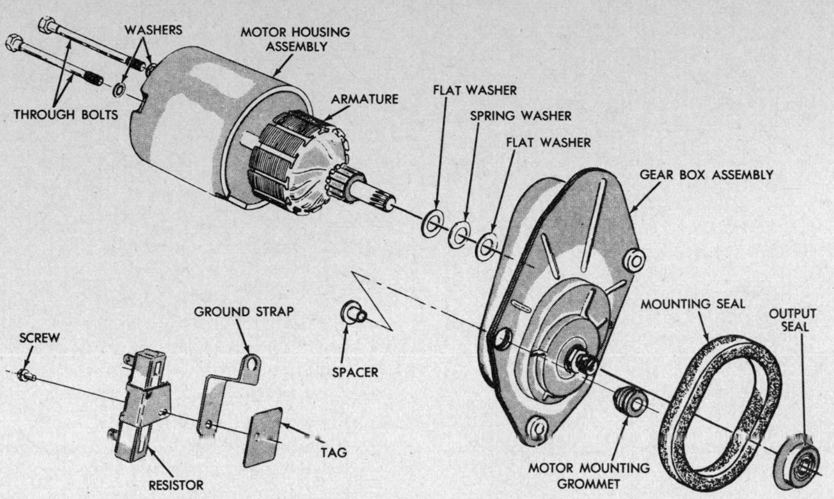

Two-speed wiper motor—exploded view (©Chrysler Corp)

1971-76 All Models

1. Disconnect the negative battery cable.
2. Lift the latch on each wiper arm and remove the arms and blades as an assembly.
3. Remove the cowl screen.
4. Remove the drive crank retaining nut and drive crank. To prevent damage to the gears, hold the crank arm nut with a wrench when removing the crank arm from the motor. Disconnect motor wiring.
5. Disconnect the lead wires from the wiper motor.
6. Remove the three wiper motor mounting bolts and remove the motor from the vehicle.
7. Reverse above procedure to install. When installing the wiper arms and blades, make sure the wiper motor is in the Park position.

Wiper Linkage

1969-76 All Models

1. Disconnect the battery. Insert a 0.090 in. pin in the base of each wiper arm and remove the arm and blade assemblies from the wiper pivots.
2. On 1969 models, remove the windshield lower moulding.
3. Remove the cowl screen.
4. Remove the crank arm retaining nut and crank arm from the wiper motor. To prevent stressing the gears, hold the motor crank with a wrench while removing the crank arm nut.
5. Remove the bolts that attach the right and left pivots to the body of the vehicle.
6. Remove the links and pivots as an assembly through the cowl opening.
7. Reverse above procedure to install.

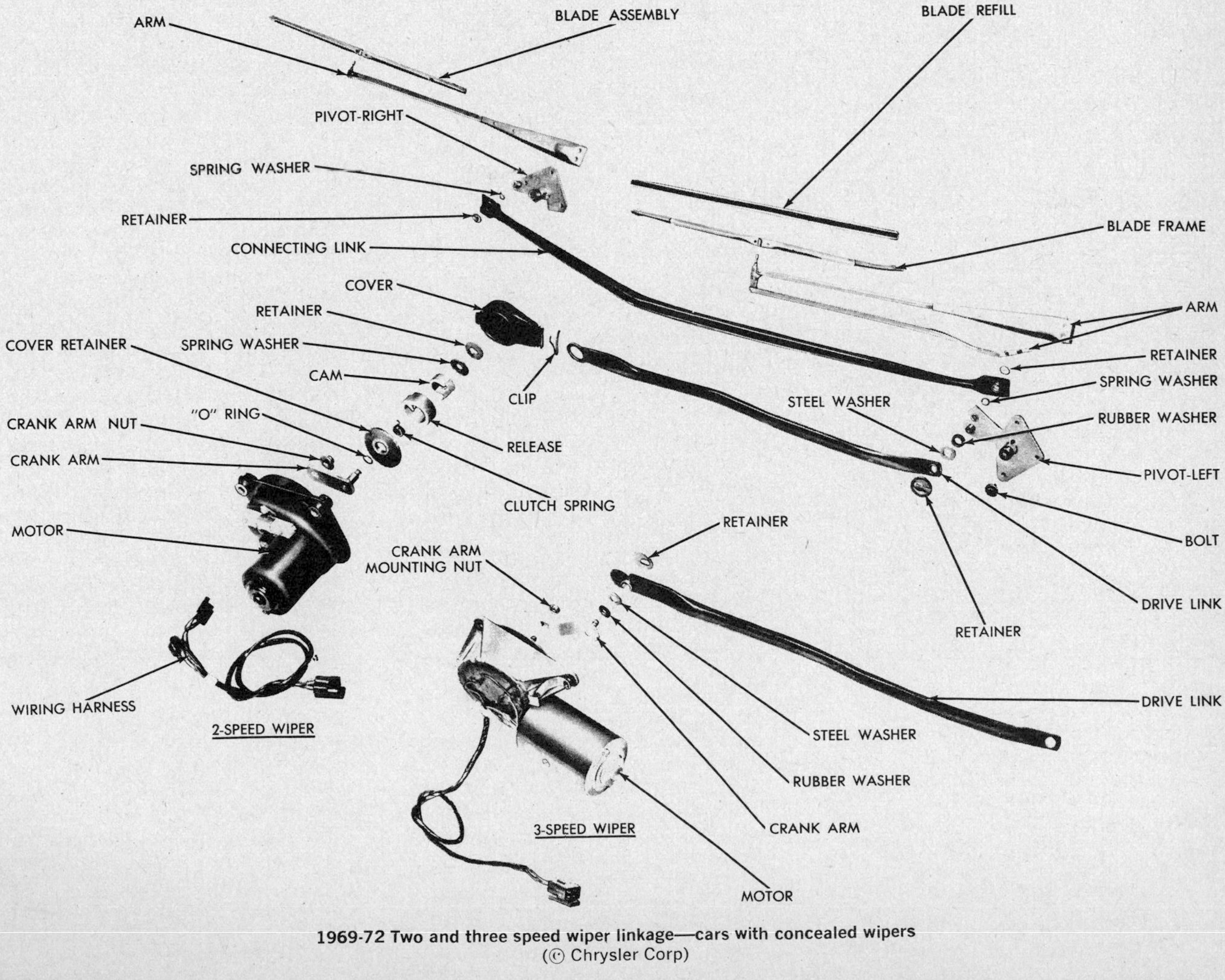

1969-72 Two and three speed wiper linkage—cars with concealed wipers
(© Chrysler Corp)

RADIO

Removal and Installation

1969-76 All Models

1. Disconnect battery ground cable.
2. Remove left ash tray.
3. On 1969-71 models, remove the steering column cover.
4. Unscrew stereo tape reset knob, if so equipped.
5. Disconnect radio wiring.
6. Move defroster vacuum actuator to facilitate radio removal.
7. Remove two radio mounting screws through access openings in lower instrument panel. On search-tune and AM radios, remove knobs, bezels, and nuts.
8. Remove radio support bracket (if so equipped) mounting screw from lower reinforcement. Support radio.
9. Remove radio support bracket or mounting screws through the access openings in the lower instrument panel. Remove radio from under instrument panel.
10. Reverse procedure to install.

HEATER

Heater Blower R & R—Non-Air Conditioned Models

1969-76 Chrysler and Imperial

The blower motor is mounted to the engine side housing under the right front fender between the inner fender shield and the fender. The inner fender shield must be removed to service the blower motor.

1975-76 Cordoba

1. Disconnect the negative battery cable.
2. Remove the entire heater assembly from the car, as outlined under "Heater Core Removal and Installation, Non-Air Conditioned Models."
3. Disconnect the blower motor lead from the resistor block, and the ground wire from the mounting plate.
4. Remove the 6 sheet metal screws and clips retaining the blower mount to the housing. Separate the mount and blower from the housing.
5. Remove the blower wheel from the motor shaft.
6. Remove the two retaining nuts and separate the motor from its mount.
7. Reverse the procedure to install.

Heater Core R & R—Non-Air Conditioned Models

1969-76 All Models

1. Disconnect battery ground cable. Drain coolant.
2. Disconnect heater hoses and plug fittings.
3. Slide front seat back. Unplug antenna from radio.
4. Remove vacuum hoses from trunk lock, if so equipped.
5. Disconnect blower motor resistor block.
6. Remove vacuum hoses from defroster actuator and heater shut off door actuator.

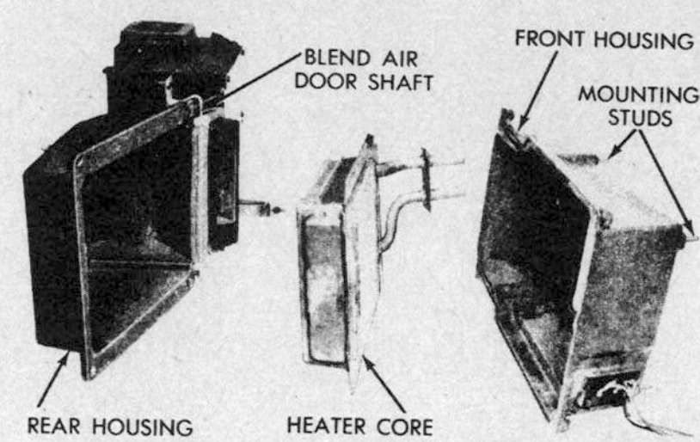

Removing heater core—non-air conditioned Chrysler (full-sized) models
(© Chrysler Corp)

7. Swing support bracket up out of the way.
8. Remove four retaining nuts from studs on engine side housing.
9. Remove locating bolt from bottom center of passenger side housing.
10. Roll or tip housing out from under instrument panel.
11. Remove temperature control cable retaining clip and cable from heat shut off door crank.
12. From inside housing, remove two retaining nuts from right side of heater core and four screws from outside of housing.
13. Remove core tube locating metal screw from top of housing.
14. Carefully pull heater core out of housing.
15. Reverse procedure to install.

Blower Motor Removal—Air Conditioned Models

1969-76 Chrysler and Imperial

1. The blower motor is mounted on the engine side housing, under the right front fender, between the inner fender shield and the fender. To service the motor, it is necessary to remove the inner fender panel by extracting its securing bolts. If the vehicle is equipped with a power antenna, it is necessary to disconnect it before the inner fender panel is removed.
2. For all models, disconnect the battery and feed wires and remove the air tube (if so equipped). Remove its mounting bolts and remove the blower assembly.
3. Installation is the reverse of the above.

1975-76 Cordoba

1. Disconnect the feed wire at its connector. Remove the air tube.
2. Remove the three nuts retaining the blower mount to the firewall (from the engine side.)
3. Lift out the blower motor and fan assembly.
4. Reverse the procedure to install.

Heater Core Removal—Air Conditioned Models

1969-73 Chrysler and Imperial

1. The heater core is located in the front cover of the passenger side housing. The air conditioning system need not be discharged to remove the heater core.
2. Disconnect the battery and drain the cooling system. Remove the air cleaner and disconnect the heater hoses. Plug the heater core tubes to prevent fluid loss.
3. Remove the left spot cooler duct and the steering column cover. On 1972 models, remove the linkage shield.
4. Disconnect the two actuator rods at the linkage on the left side of the housing. Remove the two cover retaining screws.
5. Remove the heat distribution duct securing screws, the duct, and the now-exposed screws in the bottom lip of the front cover.
6. Remove the glove box and the center spot cooler duct; also the right spot cooler duct and the air distribution housing.
7. Working in the glove box opening, remove the top and right side retaining screws from the housing. On vehicles with Auto-Temp, remove the aspirator tube from its clip before performing the above.
8. Disconnect all electrical leads at the resistor block. Remove the vacuum hoses from the recirculating housing actuator. On cars with Auto-Temp, remove the wires from the plastic strips and metal clip; remove the amplifier, master, and compressor switches.
9. Remove the nut from the housing end of the support bracket. Swing the bracket upward and out of the way, and carefully roll the heater core and front cover out from beneath the instrument panel. On 1972-73 models, remove the core from the housing by cutting the adhesive away, grasping it at the top, and pulling it from the housing.
10. (This step applies to 1969-71 models only.) To begin the installation procedure, install the heater core in the front cover and place the core and cover on the evaporator housing. Hold the front cover in position and swing the support bracket down over the stud on the front cover face. Install its retaining nut.

11. (This step applies to 1972-73 models only). To begin the installation procedure, remove the condensate seal from the heater core flange and cement a new seal in position. Install the heater core in the rear housing and secure with a screw at either end. Install the core and rear housing to the front housing. Hold the rear housing in position and swing the support bracket down and over the stud on the rear housing face; install its retaining nut.
12. Working through the glove box opening, install the housing top retaining screws and the screws at the right side of the front cover (1969–71) or the screws at the right side of the rear housing (1972-73).
13. Working beneath the instrument panel, replace all the screws securing the housings together. On 1972-73 models, install the two screws on the left side of the rear housing. (On these models, it is not necessary to reinstall the linkage shield.)
14. Install the heat distribution duct to the bottom of the housing.
15. Connect the actuator rods.
16. Connect all of the vacuum hoses to the actuators; install all electrical connections to the resistor block. On cars with Auto-Temp, secure the wires with the plastic straps and metal clip. Install the aspirator tube in the clip.
17. Working through the glove box opening, replace the air distribution housing, the center spot cooler duct, and the right spot cooler duct.
18. Install the steering column cover and the left spot cooler duct. Replace the glove box assembly. On Auto-Temp equipped vehicles, install the amplifier, master, and compressor switches.
19. From this point, reverse the removal procedure.

1974-76 Chrysler and Imperial

NOTE: *This procedure requires evacuation of the refrigerant in the air conditioning system. Therefore, it should not be attempted by persons not having the special tools and training required to perform the job safely.*

1. Purge the system of refrigerant
2. Disconnect the battery ground cable.
3. Remove the air cleaner and disconnect the heater hoses. Plug the core tubes.
4. Remove the 5/16" bolt in the center of the plumbing sealing plate.
5. Pull the refrigerant line assembly toward the front of the car.
6. Remove the two ¼-20 Allen screws and remove the "H" valve.
7. Slide the front seat back, out of the way. Remove the lap cooler and lower instrument panel cover.
8. Remove the A/C distribution duct.
9. Unplug the antenna lead from the radio.
10. Disconnect the wires and vacuum lines from unit.
11. Remove the drain tube. With automatic temperature control (ATC), remove the electrical connections and vacuum connector from the servo. Disconnect the amplifier wires. Disconnect the wires and vacuum hoses from the master and compressor switches. Disconnect the aspirator tube.
12. Remove the temperature control cable from the clip on the unit.
13. Remove the retaining nut from the support bracket.
14. Remove the six retaining nuts from the studs in the engine compartment.
15. Remove the housing from under the instrument panel, and place it on a work table.
16. Remove the mode door and the blend air door levers from the shaft. Remove the screws and lift off the top cover.
17. Remove the 4 retaining screws and the 3 screws for the core tube seal. Lift out the core.
18. Reverse the procedure to install.

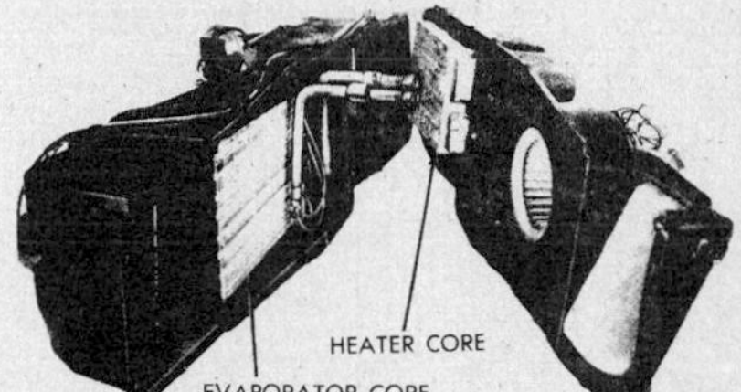

Heater and Evaporator core location—Cordoba
(© Chrysler Corp)

1975-76 Cordoba

See the "Heater Core Removal" procedure (for air-conditioned models) for the "1971-76 Satellite, Coronet, Charger and 1975-76 Fury" in the Dodge-Plymouth section.

SEAT BELTS

For all information concerning seat belt warning systems and the seat belt/starter interlock system used on Chrysler Corporation cars, see the Dodge-Plymouth section.

Seat belt interlock override switch—1974-75 models; pushing the switch button will permit the car to be started once for servicing purposes, without an occupant using the seat restraint system
(© Chrysler Corp)

Air conditioning-heater housing assembly—1974-76 Chrysler and Imperial
(© Chrysler Corp)

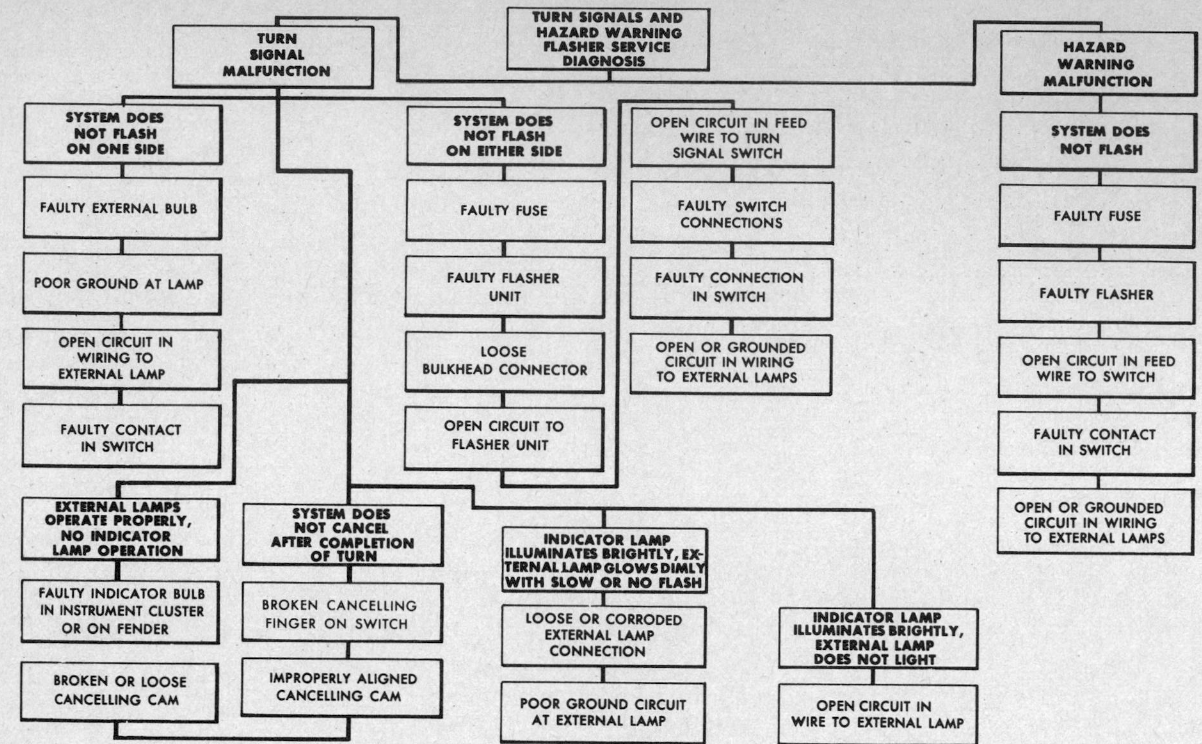

TURN SIGNALS AND HAZARD WARNING FLASHER SERVICE DIAGNOSIS
TURN SIGNAL MALFUNCTION
HAZARD WARNING MALFUNCTION
SYSTEM DOES NOT FLASH ON ONE SIDE
FAULTY EXTERNAL BULB
POOR GROUND AT LAMP
OPEN CIRCUIT IN WIRING TO EXTERNAL LAMP
FAULTY CONTACT IN SWITCH
SYSTEM DOES NOT FLASH ON EITHER SIDE
FAULTY FUSE
FAULTY FLASHER UNIT
LOOSE BULKHEAD CONNECTOR
OPEN CIRCUIT TO FLASHER UNIT
OPEN CIRCUIT IN FEED WIRE TO TURN SIGNAL SWITCH
FAULTY SWITCH CONNECTIONS
FAULTY CONNECTION IN SWITCH
OPEN OR GROUNDED CIRCUIT IN WIRING TO EXTERNAL LAMPS
SYSTEM DOES NOT FLASH
FAULTY FUSE
FAULTY FLASHER
OPEN CIRCUIT IN FEED WIRE TO SWITCH
FAULTY CONTACT IN SWITCH
OPEN OR GROUNDED CIRCUIT IN WIRING TO EXTERNAL LAMPS
EXTERNAL LAMPS OPERATE PROPERLY, NO INDICATOR LAMP OPERATION
FAULTY INDICATOR BULB IN INSTRUMENT CLUSTER OR ON FENDER
BROKEN OR LOOSE CANCELLING CAM
SYSTEM DOES NOT CANCEL AFTER COMPLETION OF TURN
BROKEN CANCELLING FINGER ON SWITCH
IMPROPERLY ALIGNED CANCELLING CAM
INDICATOR LAMP ILLUMINATES BRIGHTLY, EXTERNAL LAMP GLOWS DIMLY WITH SLOW OR NO FLASH
LOOSE OR CORRODED EXTERNAL LAMP CONNECTION
POOR GROUND CIRCUIT AT EXTERNAL LAMP
INDICATOR LAMP ILLUMINATES BRIGHTLY, EXTERNAL LAMP DOES NOT LIGHT
OPEN CIRCUIT IN WIRE TO EXTERNAL LAMP

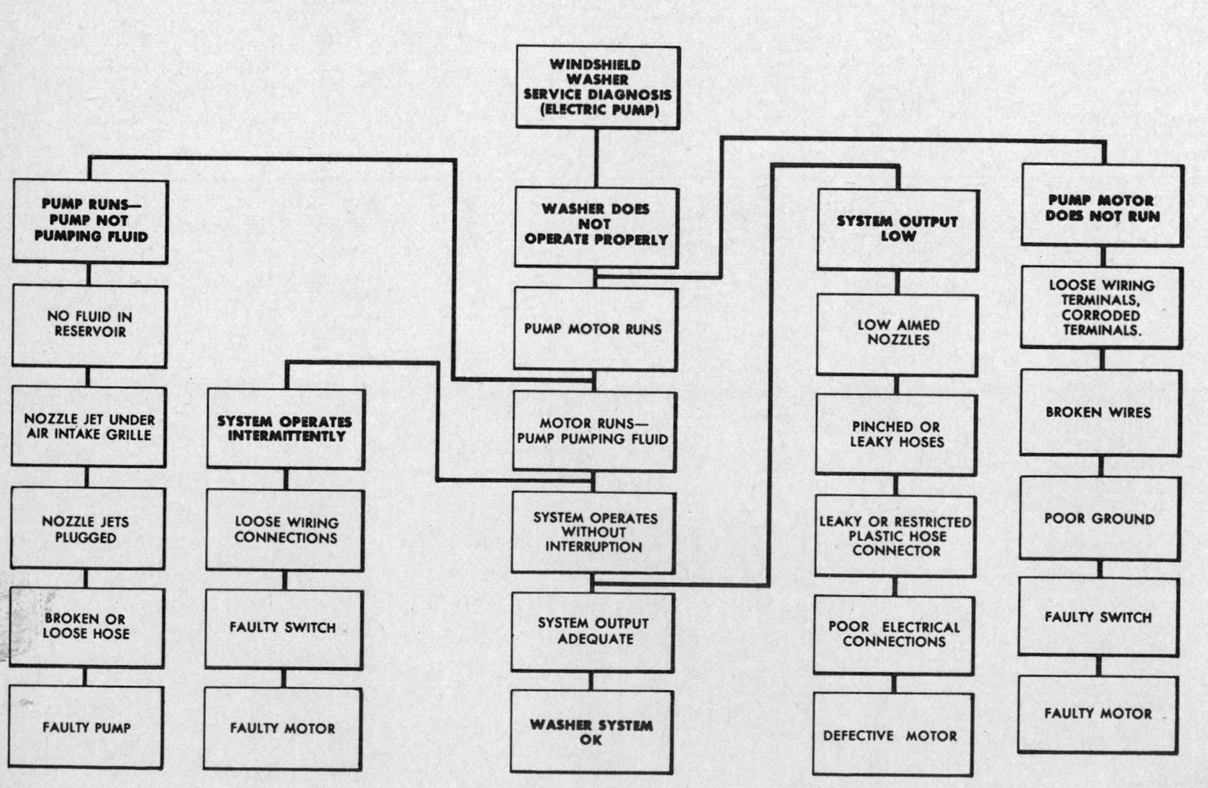

WINDSHIELD WASHER SERVICE DIAGNOSIS (ELECTRIC PUMP)
WASHER DOES NOT OPERATE PROPERLY
PUMP MOTOR RUNS
MOTOR RUNS—PUMP PUMPING FLUID
SYSTEM OPERATES WITHOUT INTERRUPTION
SYSTEM OUTPUT ADEQUATE
WASHER SYSTEM OK
PUMP RUNS—PUMP NOT PUMPING FLUID
NO FLUID IN RESERVOIR
NOZZLE JET UNDER AIR INTAKE GRILLE
NOZZLE JETS PLUGGED
BROKEN OR LOOSE HOSE
FAULTY PUMP
SYSTEM OPERATES INTERMITTENTLY
LOOSE WIRING CONNECTIONS
FAULTY SWITCH
FAULTY MOTOR
SYSTEM OUTPUT LOW
LOW AIMED NOZZLES
PINCHED OR LEAKY HOSES
LEAKY OR RESTRICTED PLASTIC HOSE CONNECTOR
POOR ELECTRICAL CONNECTIONS
DEFECTIVE MOTOR
PUMP MOTOR DOES NOT RUN
LOOSE WIRING TERMINALS, CORRODED TERMINALS.
BROKEN WIRES
POOR GROUND
FAULTY SWITCH
FAULTY MOTOR

Comet · Cougar · Elite · Fairlane · Falcon · Granada · Maverick · Monarch · Montego · Mustang · Torino

YEAR IDENTIFICATION

FAIRLANE AND TORINO

1969

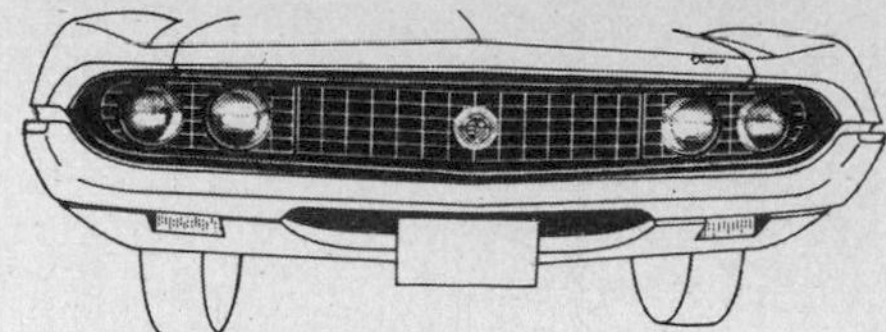

1970

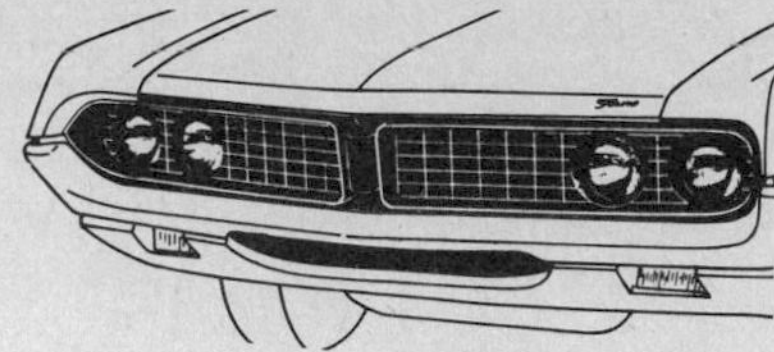

1971

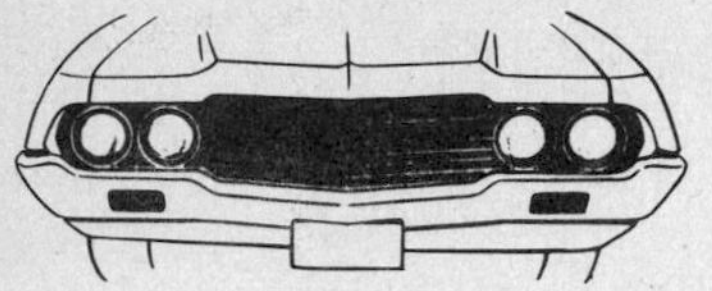

1972 Torino

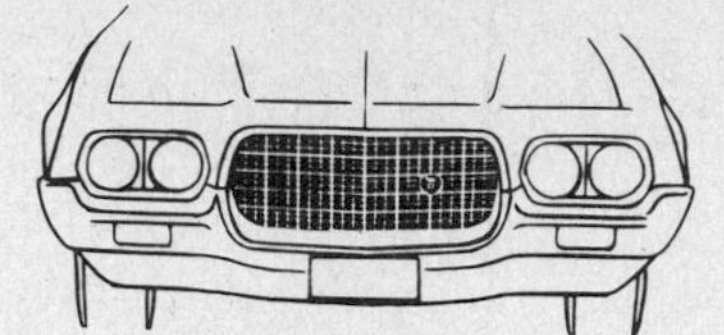

1972 Gran Torino

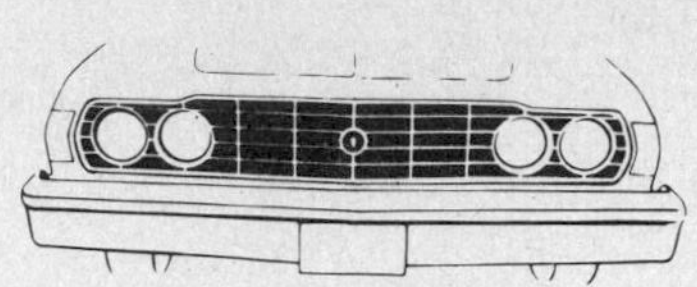

1973 Torino

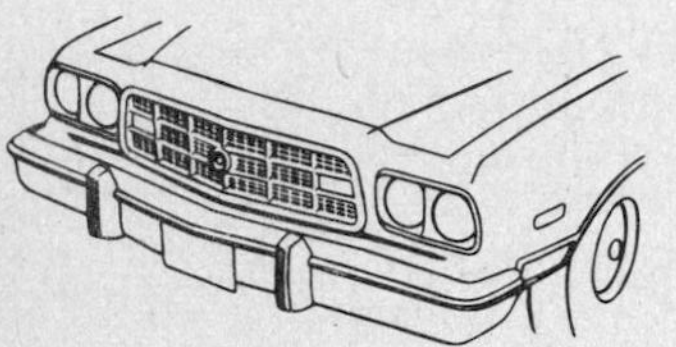

1973 Gran Torino

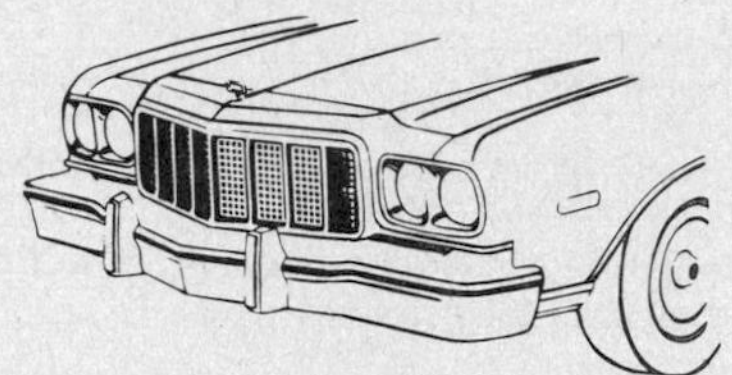

1974 Gran Torino

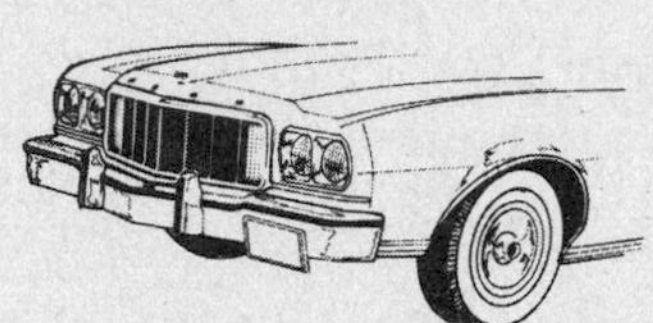

1975 Gran Torino Brougham

1974-75 Ford Elite

1976 Gran Torino Brougham

1976 Ford Elite

FALCON

1969

GRANADA

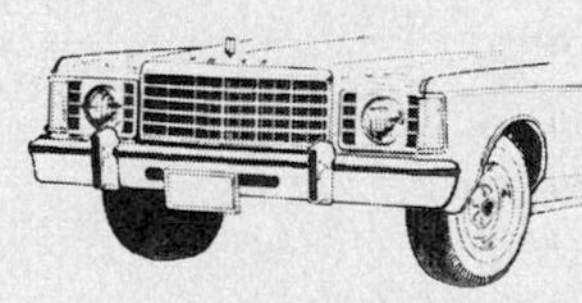

1975

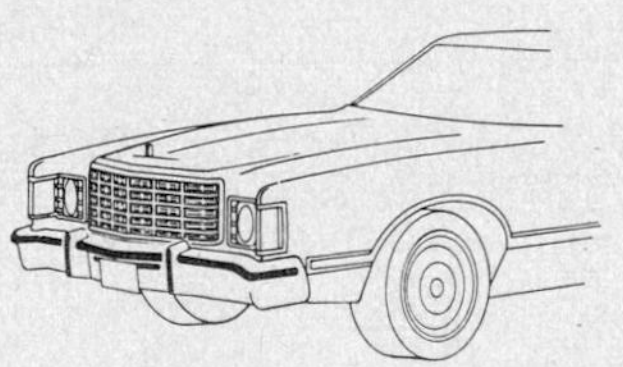

1976

COUGAR

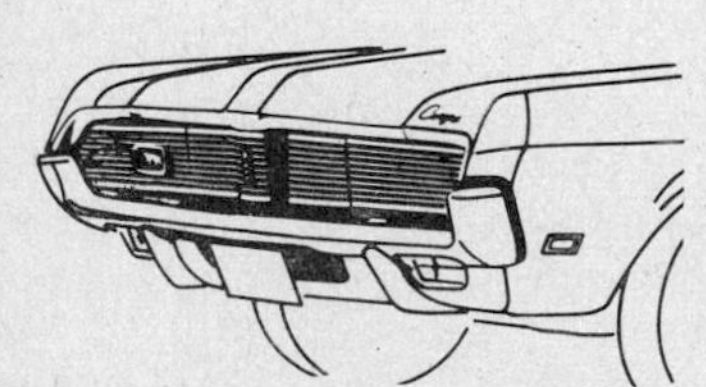

1969

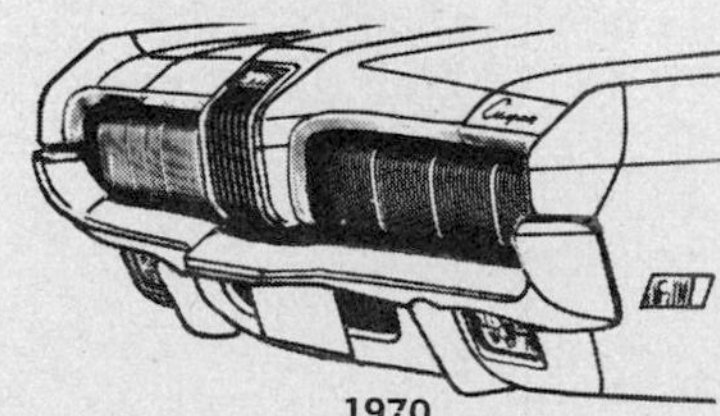

1970

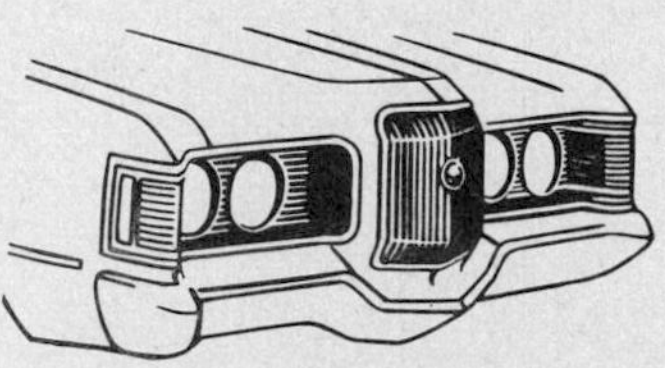

1971

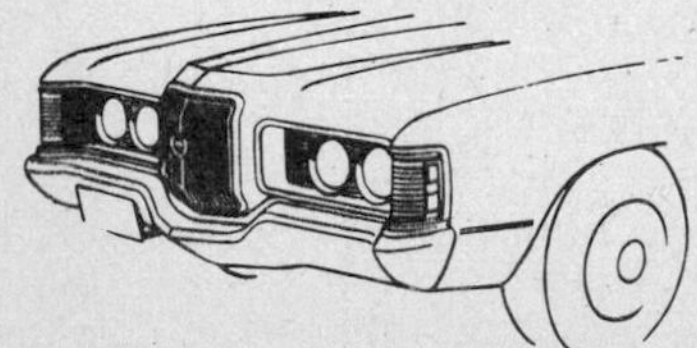

1972 XR-7

1973

1974-75

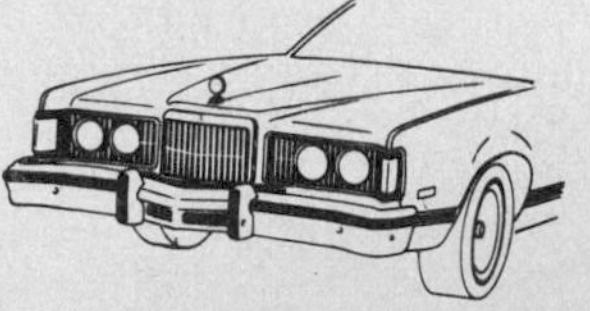

1976

MONARCH

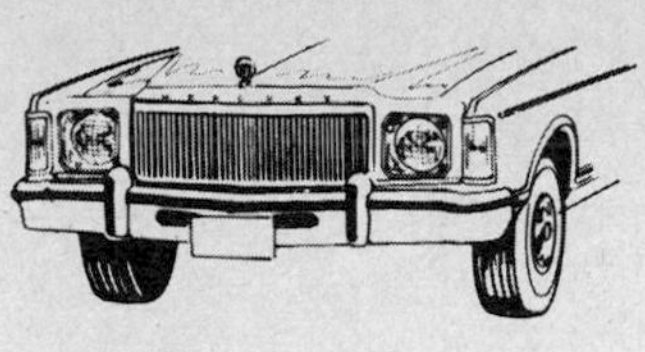

1975

1976

MUSTANG

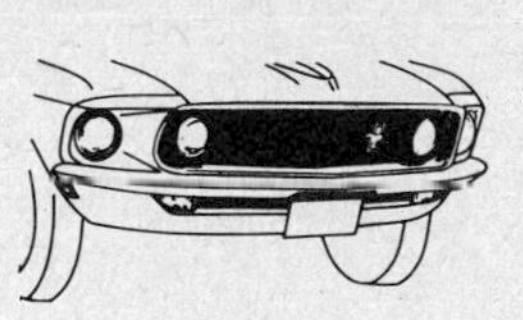

1969

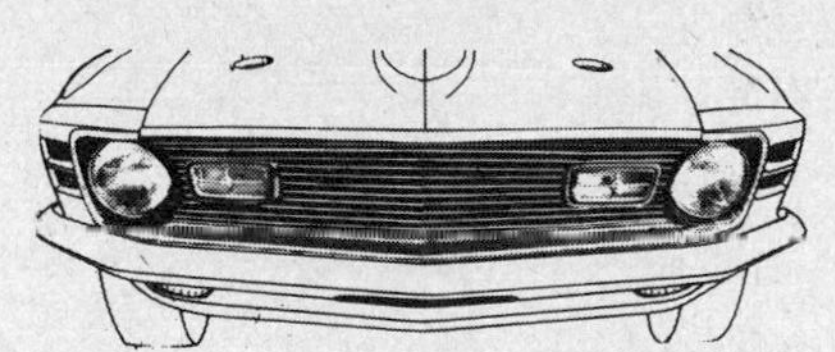

1970

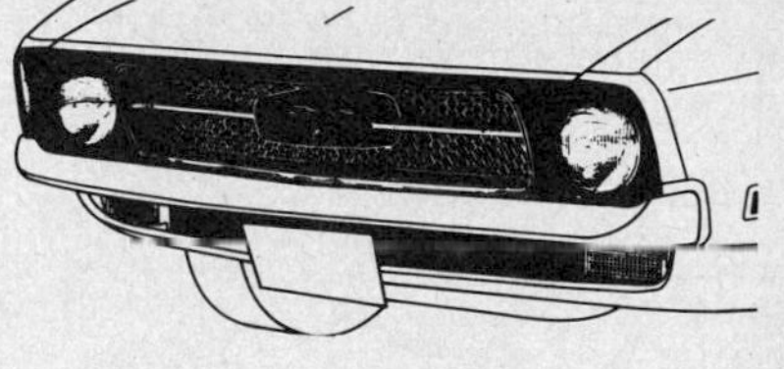

1971

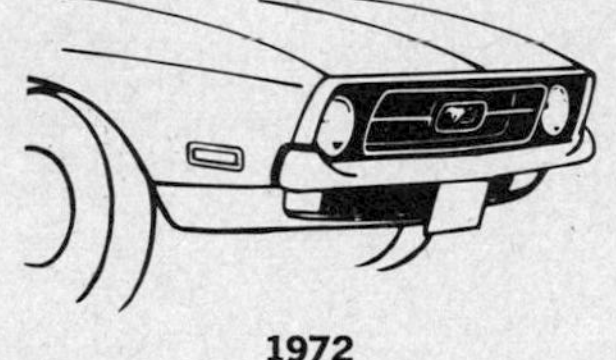

1972

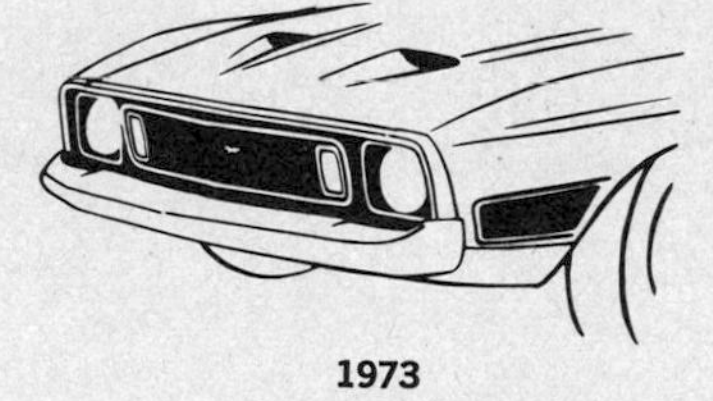

1973

COMET

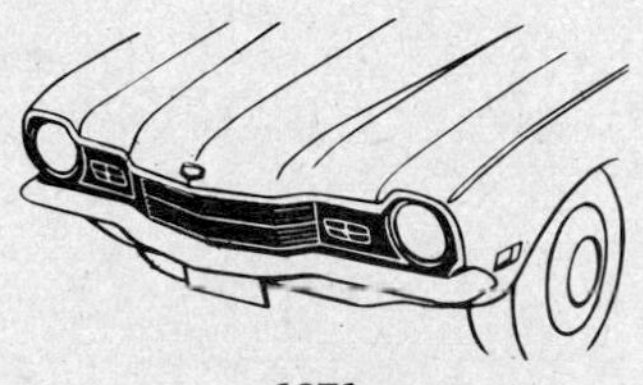

1971

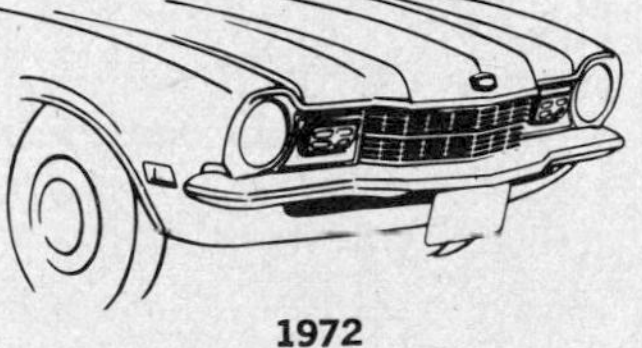

1972

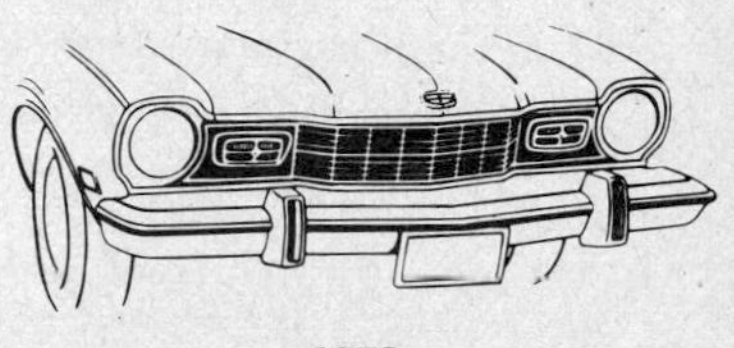

1973

1974

1975

1976

MONTEGO

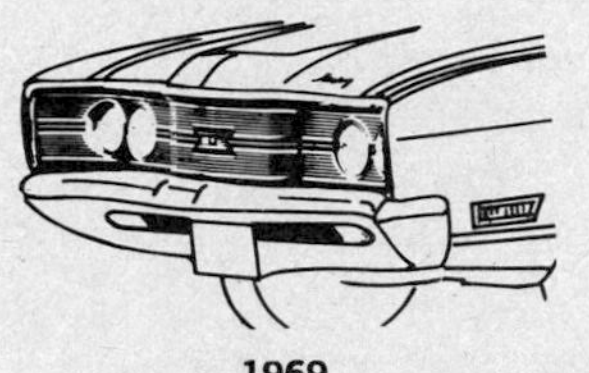

1969

1970

1971

1972

1973

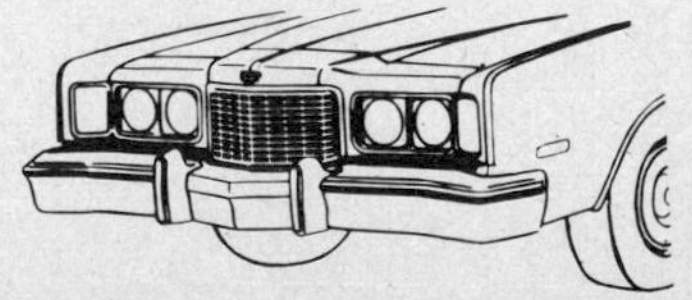

1974

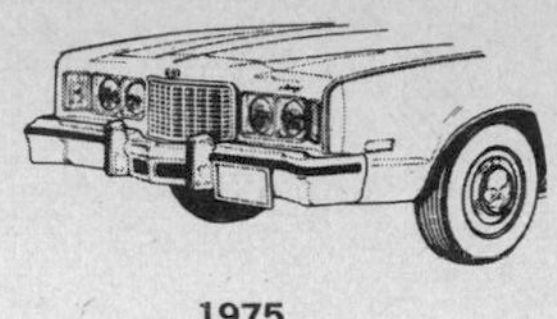

1975

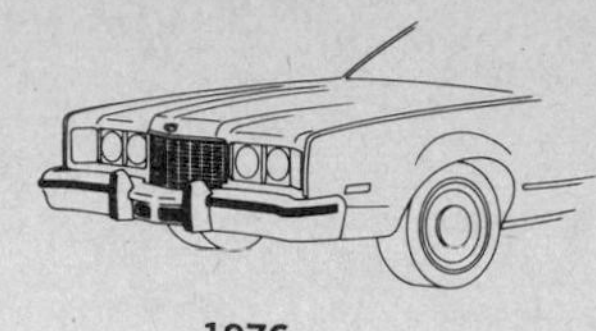

1976

MAVERICK

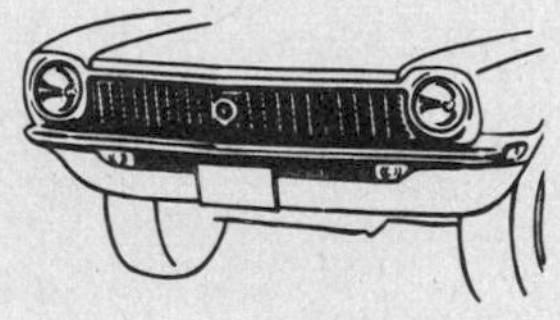

1970-72

1971-72 Grabber

1973

1974

1975

1976

FIRING ORDER

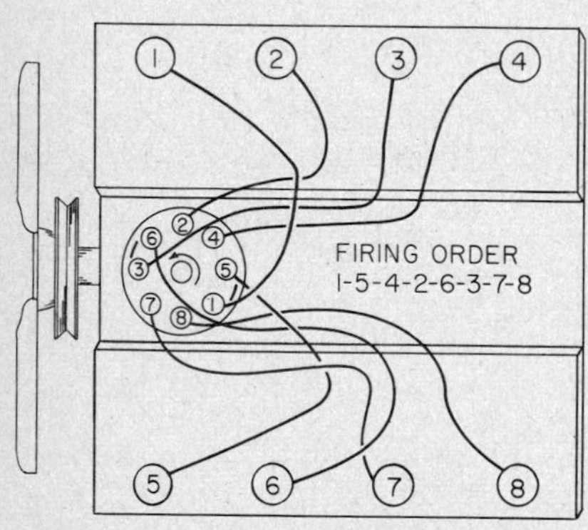

All V8 except 351, 400 V8

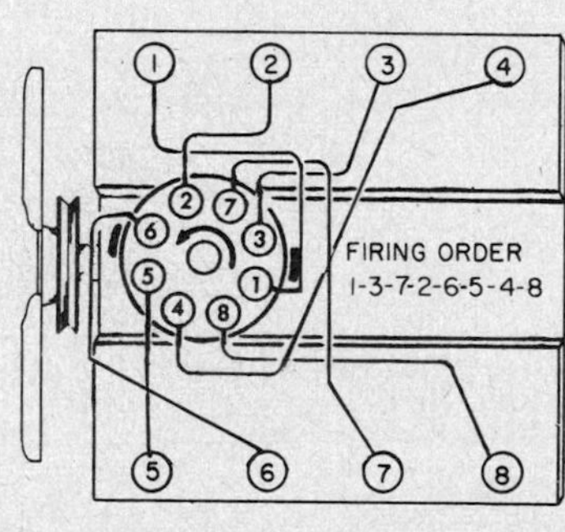

351 and 400 V8

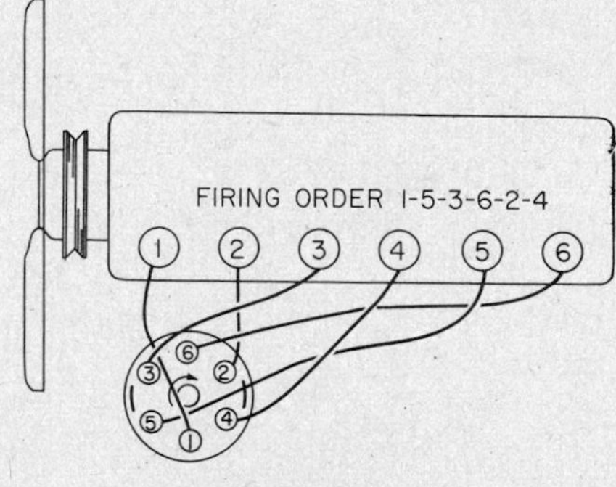

All 6 cylinder

CAR SERIAL NUMBER LOCATION AND ENGINE IDENTIFICATION

Vehicle Identification Number

The serial number is on a plate attached to the top of the instrument panel, visible through the windshield. The plate is interpreted as per the illustrations.

1. CONSECUTIVE UNIT NO
2. BODY SERIAL CODE
3. MODEL YEAR CODE
4. ASSEMBLY PLANT CODE
5. ENGINE CODE
6. TRIM CODE
7. REAR AXLE CODE
8. COLOR CODE
9. BODY TYPE CODE
10. DISTRICT SPEC EQUIP CODE
11. TRANSMISSION CODE

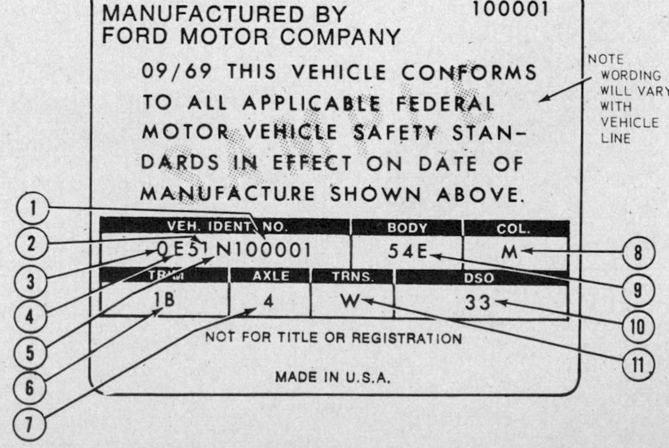

Vehicle certification label—1970-76

Vehicle Certification Label 1970-76

The vehicle certification label is located on the rear of the driver's door. The upper half of the label contains the name of the manufacturer, the month and year of manufacture, and the certification statement. For interpretation of the lower half of the label, see the illustration.

9Y83N100001

Typical vehicle identification number (VIN) tab

ENGINE CODE

The engine code designation is the 5th digit of the vehicle identification number (V.I.N.). The V.I.N. is stamped on a plate located at the left side of the instrument panel, visible through the windshield.

Disp	Bbl	HP	'69	'70	'71	'72	'73	'74	'75	'76
6-Cylinder Models										
170	1	82 (net)				U				
170	1	100			U					
170	1	105	U	U						
200	1	74, 75 (net)							T	T
200	1	84 (net)					T	T		
200	1	91 (net)				T				
200	1	115	T		T					
200	1	120		T						
250	1	70+, 79±, 72, 85 (net)							L	L
250	1	88, 91, 92, 99 (net)					L	L		
250	1	95, 98 (net)				L				
250	1	145			L					
250	1	155	L	L						
8-Cylinder Models										
302	2	135, 137, 138, 141 (net)					F			
302	2	115±, 122, 129 (net)							F	F
302	2	138, 140, 143 (net)				F		F		
302	2	210		F	F					
302	2	220	F	F						
302 (Boss)	4	290	G	G						
351W	2	153±, 143, 154 (net)							H	H
351W	2	156, 162 (net)					H	H		
351C	2	154, 159, 163, 177 (net)					H	H		
351①	2	161, 164, 177 (net)				H	H			
351M	2	150±, 148 (net)							Q	Q
351CJ	4	246, 255, 266 (net)				Q	Q	Q		
351HO	4	266 (net)				R				
351①	2	240			H					
351W	2	250	H	H						
351C	4	280			Q					
351C	4	285			M					
351W	4	290	M							
351C	4	300		M						
351 (Boss)	4	330			R					

TRANSMISSION CODES

1969

Code	Transmission	Code	Transmission
1	Three speed manual	Y	Automatic MX
5	Four speed manual-wide ratio	X	Automatic FMX
6	Four speed manual-close ratio	Z	Automatic C6 Special for Police and trailer towing
W	Automatic C4		
U	Automatic C6		

1970-71

Code	Transmission	Code	Transmission
1	Three speed manual	W	Automatic C4
5	Four speed manual-wide ratio	U	Automatic C6
6	Four speed manual-close ratio	X	Automatic FMX
V	Semi-Automatic stick shift	Z	Automatic C6 Special for Police and trailer towing

1972-76

Code	Transmission	Code	Transmission
1	Three speed manual	W	Automatic C4
5	Four speed manual	X	Automatic FMX
U	Automatic C6	Z	Automatic (C6 Special) for Police and trailer towing

ENGINE CODE

The engine code designation is the 5th digit of the vehicle identification number (V.I.N.). The V.I.N. is stamped on a plate located at the left side of the instrument panel, visible through the windshield.

Disp	Bbl	HP	'69	'70	'71	'72	'73	'74	'75	'76
390	4	320	S							
400	2	144±, 158 (net)							S	S
400	2	163, 168, 170 (net)					S	S		
400	2	168, 172 (net)				S				
428	4	335	Q	Q						
429	4	197, 201 (net)					N			
429	4	205, 208, 212 (net)				N				
429	4	360		N	N					
429CJ	4	370		C	C					
429SCJ	4	375		J	J					
429 (Boss)	4	375		Z						
460	4	217±, 216 (net)							A	A
460	4	202, 208, 195, 220 (net)						A		
460PI	4	226 (net)							C	C

① Both Windsor and Cleveland versions of the 351 2V engine have been available. The quickest method of identification is to disconnect a spark plug wire and examine the size of the plug. 1969-74 Windsor engines are equipped with standard 18mm spark plugs. Cleveland engines and Modified Cleveland engines (1975-76) are equipped with smaller 14mm spark plugs (as are 1975-76 Windsor engines).

± California horsepower rating

CJ Cobra Jet — C Cleveland
HO High output — SCJ Super Cobra Jet
W Windsor — PI Police Interceptor

GENERAL ENGINE SPECIFICATIONS

Year	Engine No. Cyl. Displacement Cu. In.	Carburetor Type	Horsepower @ rpm ■	Torque @ rpm (ft lbs) ■	Bore and Stroke (in.)	Compression Ratio	Oil Pressure @ 2000 rpm
'69	6-170	1 bbl	105 @ 4400	158 @ 2400	3.500 x 2.940	9.1:1	35-60
	6-200	1 bbl	120 @ 4400	190 @ 2400	3.680 x 3.130	8.1:1	35-60
	6-250	1 bbl	155 @ 4000	240 @ 1600	3.682 x 3.910	9.0:1	35-60
	8-302	2 bbl	210 @ 4400	295 @ 2400	4.000 x 3.000	9.5:1	35-60
	8-302 BOSS	4 bbl	290 @ 5800	290 @ 4300	4.000 x 3.000	10.5:1	35-60
	8-351 W	2 bbl	250 @ 4600	355 @ 2600	4.000 x 3.000	9.5:1	35-60
	8-351 W	4 bbl	290 @ 4800	385 @ 3200	4.000 x 3.000	10.7:1	35-60
	8-390	4 bbl	320 @ 4600	427 @ 3200	4.050 x 3.784	10.5:1	35-60
	8-428 CJ	4 bbl	335 @ 5200	440 @ 3400	4.130 x 3.984	10.6:1	35-60
	8-429 BOSS	4 bbl	375 @ 5200	450 @ 3400	4.360 x 3.590	10.5:1	45-60
'70	6-170	1 bbl	105 @ 4400	158 @ 2400	3.500 x 2.940	8.7:1	35-60
	6-200	1 bbl	120 @ 4400	190 @ 2400	3.680 x 3.130	8.7:1	35-60
	6-250	1 bbl	155 @ 4400	240 @ 1600	3.682 x 3.910	9.0:1	35-60
	8-302	2 bbl	210 @ 4400	295 @ 2400	4.000 x 3.000	9.5:1	35-60
	8-302 BOSS	4 bbl	290 @ 5800	290 @ 4300	4.000 x 3.000	10.5:1	35-60
	8-351 C or W	2 bbl	250 @ 4600	355 @ 2600	4.000 x 3.500	9.5:1	35-60
	8-351 C	4 bbl	300 @ 5400	380 @ 3400	4.000 x 3.500	11.4:1	35-60
	8-428 CJ	4 bbl	335 @ 5200	440 @ 3400	4.130 x 3.984	10.6:1	35-60
	8-429	4 bbl	360 @ 4600	480 @ 2800	4.362 x 3.590	10.5:1	35-60
	8-429 CJ	4 bbl	370 @ 5400	450 @ 3400	4.362 x 3.590	11.3:1	35-60
	8-429 SCJ	4 bbl	375 @ 5600	450 @ 3400	4.362 x 3.590	10.5:1	35-60
	8-429 BOSS	4 bbl	375 @ 5200	450 @ 3400	4.362 x 3.590	10.5:1	45-60
'71	6-170	1 bbl	100 @ 4200	148 @ 2600	3.500 x 2.940	8.7:1	35-60
	6-200	1 bbl	115 @ 4000	180 @ 2200	3.680 x 3.130	8.7:1	35-60
	6-250	1 bbl	145 @ 4000	232 @ 1600	3.682 x 3.910	9.0:1	35-60
	8-302	2 bbl	210 @ 4600	296 @ 2600	4.000 x 3.000	9.0:1	35-60
	8-351 C or W	2 bbl	240 @ 4600	355 @ 2600	4.000 x 3.500	9.5:1	35-60
	8-351 BOSS	4 bbl	330 @ 5800	380 @ 3400	4.000 x 3.500	11.0:1	35-60
	8-351 CJ	4 bbl	280 @ 5800	345 @ 3800	4.000 x 3.500	9.0:1	35-60
	8-351 C	4 bbl	285 @ 5400	370 @ 3400	4.000 x 3.500	10.7:1	35-60
	8-429	4 bbl	360 @ 4600	480 @ 2800	4.362 x 3.590	10.5:1	35-75
	8-429 CJ	4 bbl	370 @ 5400	450 @ 3400	4.362 x 3.590	11.3:1	35-75
	8-429 SCJ	4 bbl	375 @ 5600	450 @ 3400	4.362 x 3.590	11.3:1	35-75
'72	6-170	1 bbl	82 @ 4400	129 @ 1800	3.500 x 2.940	8.3:1	35-60
	6-200	1 bbl	91 @ 4000	154 @ 2200	3.680 x 3.130	8.3:1	35-60
	6-250	1 bbl	99 @ 3600	184 @ 1600	3.680 x 3.910	8.0:1	35-60
	8-302	2 bbl	141 @ 4000	242 @ 2000	4.000 x 3.000	8.5:1	35-60
	8-351 C or W	2 bbl	164 @ 4000	276 @ 2000	4.000 x 3.500	8.6:1	35-85
	8-351 CJ	4 bbl	248 @ 5400	290 @ 3800	4.000 x 3.500	8.6:1	35-85
	8-351 HO	4 bbl	266 @ 5400	301 @ 3600	4.000 x 3.500	8.6:1	35-85
	8-400	2 bbl	168 @ 4200	297 @ 2200	4.000 x 4.000	8.4:1	35-85
	8-429	4 bbl	205 @ 4400	322 @ 2600	4.362 x 3.590	8.5:1	35-75
'73	6-200	1 bbl	91 @ 4000	154 @ 2200	3.680 x 3.130	8.3:1	35-60
	6-250	1 bbl	99 @ 3600	184 @ 1600	3.680 x 3.910	8.0:1	35-60
	8-302	2 bbl	141 @ 4000	242 @ 2000	4.000 x 3.000	8.5:1	35-60
	8-351	2 bbl	164 @ 4000	276 @ 2000	4.000 x 3.500	8.6:1	35-85
	8-351	4 bbl	248 @ 5400	290 @ 3800	4.000 x 3.500	8.0:1	35-85
	8-400	2 bbl	168 @ 4200	297 @ 2200	4.000 x 4.000	8.0:1	35-85
	8-429	4 bbl	205 @ 4400	322 @ 2600	4.362 x 3.590	8.5:1	35-75

GENERAL ENGINE SPECIFICATIONS (con't.)

Year	Engine No. Cyl. Displacement (Cu. In.)	Carburetor Type	Horsepower @ rpm ■	Torque @ rpm (ft lbs) ■	Bore and Stroke (in.)	Compression Ratio	Oil Pressure @ 2000 rpm
'74	6-200	1 bbl	84 @ 3800	150 @ 1800	3.680 x 3.130	8.3:1	35-55
	6-250	1 bbl	91 @ 3200	190 @ 1600	3.680 x 3.910	8.0:1	35-55
	8-302	2 bbl	140 @ 3800	230 @ 2600	4.000 x 3.000	8.0:1	35-55
	8-351 W	2 bbl	162 @ 4000	275 @ 2200	4.000 x 3.500	8.0:1	50-70
	8-351 C	2 bbl	163 @ 4200	278 @ 2000	4.000 x 3.500	8.0:1	50-70
	8-351	4 bbl	255 @ 5600	290 @ 3400	4.000 x 3.500	7.9:1	50-70
	8-400	2 bbl	170 @ 3400	330 @ 2000	4.000 x 4.000	8.0:1	50-70
	8-460	4 bbl	195 @ 3800	355 @ 2600	4.362 x 3.850	8.0:1	35-75
	8-460	4 bbl	220 @ 4000	355 @ 2600	4.362 x 3.850	8.0:1	35-75
	8-460 PI	4 bbl	260 @ 4400	380 @ 2700	4.362 x 3.850	8.8:1	50-75
'75-	6-200 MT	1 bbl	75 @ 3200	145 @ 2000	3.680 x 3.130	8.3:1	30-50
'76	6-200 AT	1 bbl	74 @ 3400	132 @ 2400	3.680 x 3.130	8.3:1	30-50
	6-250 MT	1 bbl	85 @ 2900	180 @ 2000	3.680 x 3.910	8.0:1	40-60
	6-250 AT	1 bbl	72 @ 2900	180 @ 1400	3.680 x 3.910	8.0:1	40-60
	6-250 MT Cal.	1 bbl	79 @ 2800	177 @ 1600	3.680 x 3.910	8.0:1	40-60
	6-250 AT Cal.	1 bbl	70 @ 2800	175 @ 1400	3.680 x 3.910	8.0:1	40-60
	8-302 Granada, Monarch	2 bbl	129 @ 3800	220 @ 1800	4.000 x 3.000	8.0:1	40-60
	8-302 Maverick, Comet	2 bbl	122 @ 3800	208 @ 1800	4.000 x 3.000	8.0:1	40-60
	8-302 Cal.	2 bbl	115 @ 3600	203 @ 1800	4.000 x 3.000	8.0:1	40-60
	8-351 W Compact	2 bbl	143 @ 3600	255 @ 2200	4.000 x 3.500	8.2:1	40-65
	8-351-W Intermediate	2 bbl	154 @ 3800	268 @ 2200	4.000 x 3.500	8.2:1	40-65
	8-351 W Cal.	2 bbl	153 @ 3400	270 @ 2400	4.000 x 3.500	8.2:1	40-65
	8-351 M 49	2 bbl	148 @ 3800	243 @ 2400	4.000 x 3.500	8.0:1	50-75
	8-351 M Cal.	2 bbl	150 @ 3800	244 @ 2800	4.000 x 3.500	8.0:1	50-75
	8-400 49	2 bbl	158 @ 3800	276 @ 2000	4.000 x 4.000	8.0:1	50-75
	8-400 Cal.	2 bbl	144 @ 3600	255 @ 2200	4.000 x 4.000	8.0:1	50-75
	8-460 49	4 bbl	216 @ 4000	366 @ 2600	4.362 x 3.850	8.0:1	40-65
	8-460 Cal.	4 bbl	217 @ 4000	365 @ 2600	4.362 x 3.850	8.0:1	40-65
	8-460 PI	4 bbl	226 @ 4000	374 @ 2600	4.362 x 3.850	8.0:1	40-65

■ Beginning 1972 horsepower and torque are SAE net figures. They are measured at the rear of the transmission with all accessories installed and operating. Since the figures vary when a given engine is installed in different models, some are representative rather than exact.

W Windsor
C Cleveland
M Modified Cleveland
PI Police Interceptor

MT Manual Transmission
AT Automatic Transmission
49 49 states only
Cal California only

Maverick, Granada, Comet, Monarch

TUNE-UP SPECIFICATIONS

When analyzing compression test results, look for uniformity among cylinders rather than specific pressures.

Year	ENGINE No. Cyl Displacement (cu in.)	hp	SPARK PLUGS Type	SPARK PLUGS Gap (in.)	DISTRIBUTOR Point Dwell (deg) *	DISTRIBUTOR Point Gap (in.)	IGNITION TIMING (deg) ▲ Man Trans	IGNITION TIMING (deg) ▲ Auto Trans	VALVES Intake Opens ■ (deg)	Fuel Pump Pressure (psi)	IDLE SPEED (rpm) ▲ Man Trans ●	IDLE SPEED (rpm) ▲ Auto Trans
'70	6-170	105	BF-82	.034	37/39	.027/ .025	6B	6B	9	4½	750	550
	6-200	120	BF-82	.034	37/39	.027/ .025	6B	6B	9	4½	800/500	600/500
	6-250	155	BF-82	.034	37/39	.027/ .025	—	6B	10	4-6	—	550

Maverick, Granada, Comet, Monarch

TUNE-UP SPECIFICATIONS (con't.)

When analyzing compression test results, look for uniformity among cylinders rather than specific pressures.

Year	ENGINE No. Cyl Displacement (cu in.)	hp	SPARK PLUGS Type	SPARK PLUGS Gap (in.)	DISTRIBUTOR Point Dwell (deg)	DISTRIBUTOR * Point Gap (in.)	IGNITION TIMING (deg) ▲ Man Trans	IGNITION TIMING (deg) ▲ Auto Trans	VALVES Intake Opens ■ (deg)	Fuel Pump Pressure (psi)	IDLE SPEED (rpm) ▲ ● Man Trans	IDLE SPEED (rpm) ▲ ● Auto Trans
'71	6-170	100	BRF-82	.034	35/36	.027/ .025	6B	—	9	4-6	750	—
	6-200	115	BRF-82	.034	35/36	.027/ .025	6B	6B	9	4-6	800/500	600/500
	6-250	145	BRF-82	.034	35/36	.027/ .025	6B	6B	10	4-6	750/500	600/500
	8-302	210	BRF-42	.034	26/28	.021/ .017	6B	6B	16	4-6	800/500	600/500
'72	6-170	82	BRF-82	.034	37	.027/	6B	—	9	4-6	750	—
	6-200	91	BRF-82	.034	37	.027	6B	6B	9	4-6	800/500	600/500
	6-250	98	BRF-82	.034	37	.027	6B	6B	10	4-6	750/500	600/500
	8-302	143	BRF-42	.034	28	.017	6B	6B	16	4-6	800/500	600/500
'73	6-200	91	BRF-82	.034	37	.027/ .025	6B	6B	9	4-6	800/500	600/500
	6-250	98	BRF-82	.034	37	.027/ .025	—	6B	10	4-6	—	600/500
	8-302	143	BRF-42	.034	28	.017	6B	6B	16	4-6	800/500	600/500
'74	6-200	84	BRF-82	.034	37	.024/ .030	6B	6B	28	4½-5½	750/500	550/500
	6-250	91	BRF-82	.044	37	.024/ .030	6B	6B	26	4½-5½	750/500	600/500
	8-302	140	BRF-42	.044	27	.014/ .020	6B	6B	②	5½-6½	800/500	650/500①
'75	6-200	74, 75	BRF-82	.044	Electronic		6B	6B	20	4½-5½	750/500	600/500
	6-250	70, 72, 79, 85	BRF-82	.044	Electronic		6B	6B	26	4½-5½	850/500	600/500
	8-302	122, 129	ARF-42	.044	Electronic		6B	6B	20	5½-6½	900/500	650/500
	8-302	115	ARF-42	.044	Electronic		6B	8B	20	5½-6½	900/500	650/500
	8-351 W	143	ARF-42	.044	Electronic		—	4B	15	5½-6½	—	700/500
	8-351 W	153	ARF-42	.044	Electronic		—	6B	15	5½-6½	—	650/500
'76	6-200	All	BRF-82	.044	Electronic		③	③	20	4½-5½	800	650
	6-250	All	BRF-82	.044	Electronic		③	③	26	4½-5½	850	600
	8-302	All	ARF- 42/52③	.044	Electronic		③	③	20	5½-6½	750	650(700)
	8-351W	All	ARF-52	.044	Electronic		—	8(10)B④ @ 625(650)	15	5½-6½	—	625(650)

* Where two dwell or point gap figures are separated by a slash, the first figure is for engines equipped with dual diaphragm distributors and the second figure is for engines equipped with single diaphragm distributors

▲ See text for procedure

■ All figures Before Top Dead Center

● Where two idle speed figures are separated by a slash, the first figure is for idle speed with solenoid energized and automatic transmission in Drive, while the second is for idle speed with solenoid disconnected and automatic transmission in Neutral

B Before Top Dead Center

— Not applicable

① 600/500 with air conditioning

② 16° B—manual transmission
20° B—automatic transmission

③ Depends on emission equipment, check underhood specifications sticker

④ In Drive

Fairlane, Torino, Montego, Mustang, Cougar, Elite

TUNE-UP SPECIFICATIONS

When analyzing compression test results, look for uniformity among cylinders rather than specific pressures.

Year	ENGINE No. Cyl Displacement (cu in.)	ENGINE hp	SPARK PLUGS Type	SPARK PLUGS Gap (in.)	DISTRIBUTOR Point Dwell * (deg)	DISTRIBUTOR Point Gap (in.)	IGNITION TIMING (deg) ▲ Man Trans	IGNITION TIMING (deg) ▲ Auto Trans	VALVES Intake Opens ■ (deg)	Fuel Pump Pressure (psi)	IDLE SPEED (rpm) ▲ Man Trans ●	IDLE SPEED (rpm) ▲ Auto Trans
'69	6-200	115	BF-82	.034	38	.027	6B	6B	9	4½-5½	750	550②
	6-250	155	BF-82	.034	38	.025	6B	6B	10	4½-5½	700 700/500	550 550/450
	8-302	220	BF-42	.034	29③	.021④	6B	6B	16	4½-5½	650	550②
	8-302	290	BF-32	.035	32	.020	16B	—	40	4½-5½	800/500	—
	8-351	250	BF-42	.034	29	.017	6B	6B	11	4½-5½	650	550
	8-351	290	BF-32	.034	29	.017	6B	6B	11	4½-5½	675	575
	8-390	320	BF-42	.034	29③	.017⑤	6B	6B	16	4½-5½	700	550
	8-428	335	BF-32	.034	27⑥	.021④	6B	6B	18	4½-5½	700	650
'70	6-200	120	BF-82	.035	38	.027	6B	6B	9	4-6	750⑦	550①
	6-250	155	BF-82	.035	38	.025	6B	6B	10	4-6	750/500	600/500
	8-302	210	BF-42	.035	27	.021	6B	6B	16	4-6	800/500	600/500
	8-302	290	AF-32	.035	32	.020	16B	—	40	4½-6½	800/500	—
	8-351C	250	AF-42	.035	27	.021	6B	6B	12	5-7	700/500	600
	8-351W	250	BF-42	.035	27	.021	10B	10B	11	5-7	700/500	575 600/500
	8-351C	300	BF-32	.035	27/29	.021/ .017	6B	6B	16	5-6	800/500	600 600/500
	8-428	335	BF-32	.035	32	.020	6B	6B	18	4½-6½	725	675 675/500
	8-429	360	BF-42	.035	27/29	.021/ .017	6B	6B	16	5-7	700	600
	8-429CJ	370	AF-32	.035	27/29	.021/ .017	10B	10B	16	6½-8½	700 700/500	650
	8-429	BOSS	AF-32	.035	27/29	.021/ .017	10B	10B	16	6½-8½	650/500	700/500
'71	6-250	145	BRF-82	.034	36	.027/ .025	6B	6B	10	4-6	750	600
	8-302	210	BRF-42	.034	27	.021	6B	6B	16	4-6	800/500	575 600/500
	8-351C	240	ARF-42	.034	27	.021	6B	6B	12	5-7	700/500	600
	8-351W	240	BRF-42	.034	27	.021	6B	6B	12	5-7	700/500	575 600/500
	8-351CJ	280	ARF-42	.034	27	.021	6B	6B	18	5-7	800/500	600
	8-351C	285	ARF-32	.034	27/29	.021/ .017	6B	6B	18	5-7	800/500	600
	8-351	BOSS	ARF-32	.034	27/29	.021/ .017	6B	6B	18	4½-5½	800	590
	8-429	360	BRF-42	.034	27/29	.021/ .017	4B	4B	16	5-7	700	600 600/500
	8-429CJ	370	ARF-42	.034	25	.020	10B	10B	32	4½-6½	700	650 650/500
	8-429	SCJ	ARF-42	.034	28	.020	10B	10B	40½	4½-6½	650/500	700/500
'72	6-250	95	BRF-82	.034	37	.027	6B	6B	10(16)	4½-6½	750/500	600/500
	8-302	140	BRF-42	.034	28	.017	6B	6B	16	5½-6½	800/500	575 600/500
	8-351C	165	ARF-42	.034	28	.017	6B	6B	12	5½-6½		575/500 (625/500)

Fairlane, Torino, Montego, Mustang, Cougar, Elite

TUNE-UP SPECIFICATIONS (con't.)

When analyzing compression test results, look for uniformity among cylinders rather than specific pressures.

Year	ENGINE No. Cyl Displacement (cu in.)	ENGINE hp	SPARK PLUGS Type	SPARK PLUGS Gap (in.)	DISTRIBUTOR Point Dwell (deg) *	DISTRIBUTOR Point Gap (in.)	IGNITION TIMING (deg) ▲ Man Trans	IGNITION TIMING (deg) ▲ Auto Trans	VALVES Intake Opens ■ (deg)	Fuel Pump Pressure (psi)	IDLE SPEED (rpm) ▲ Man Trans ●	IDLE SPEED (rpm) ▲ Auto Trans
	8-351W	165	BRF-42	.034	28	.017	—	6B	12	5½-6½	—	575 600/500
	8-351CJ	266	ARF-42	.034	28	.017/.020	16B	16B⑪	14	5½-6½		700/500⑪ (800/500)
	8-351HO	N.A.	ARF-42	.034	28	.020	10B	—	17½	5½-6½	1000/500	—
	8-400	168	ARF-42	.034	28	.017	—	6B	17	4½-5½	—	625/500
	8-429	205	ARF-42	.034	28	.017	—	10B	8	5½-6½	—	600/500
'73	6-250	95	BRF-82	.034	37	.027/ .025	6B	6B	16	4½-6½	750/500	600/500
	8-302	140	BRF-42	.034	28	.017	6B	6B	16	5½-6½	800/500	575 600/500
	8-351C	165	ARF-42	.034	28	.017	—	6B	12	5½-6½	—	625/500
	8-351W	165	BRF-42	.034	28	.017	—	6B	12	5½-6½	—	575 600/500
	8-351CJ	266	ARF-42	.034	28⑬	.017⑩	16B	16B⑪	14	5½-6½	1000/500	800/500⑪
	8-400	168	ARF-42	.034	28	.017	—	6B	17	5½-6½	—	625/500
	8-429	205	ARF-42	.034	28	.017	—	10B	8	5½-6½	—	600/500
'74	6-250	91	BRF-82	.044	37	.027	6B	6B	26	5½-6½	800/500	625/500
	8-302	140	BRF-42	.044	28	.017	10B	6B	16⑮	5½-6½	800/500	625/500
	8-351W	162	BRF-42	.044	28	.017	—	6B	15	5½-6½	—	600/500
	8-351C	163	ARF-42	.044	28	.017	—	14B	11.5	5½-6½	—	600/500
	8-351CJ	255	ARF-42	.044	28	.017	—	20B⑭	14	5½-6½	—	800/500
	8-400	170	ARF-42	.044	Electronic		—	12B⑭	17	5½-6½	—	625/500
	8-460	195, 220, 260	ARF-42	.054	Electronic		—	14B	8	5½-6½	—	650/500
'75	8-351W	153, 154	ARF-42	.044	Electronic		—	6B	15	5½-6½	—	600/500
	8-351M	148, 150	ARF-42	.044	Electronic		—	6B	19½	5½-6½	—	700/500
	8-400	144, 158	ARF-42	.044	Electronic		—	6B	17	5½-6½	—	625/500
	8-460	216, 217	ARF-52	.044	Electronic		—	14B	8	5½-6½	—	650/500
	8-460PI	226	ARF-52	.044	Electronic		—	14B	18	5½-7	—	700/500
'76	8-351W	All	ARF-42/52⑧	.054	Electronic		—	⑧	15	5½-6½	—	650
	8-351M	All	ARF-42/52⑧	.044	Electronic		—	⑧	19½	5½-6½	—	650 (650/675⑧)
	8-400	All	ARF-42/52⑧	.044	Electronic		—	⑧	17	5½-6½	—	650(625)
	8-460	All	ARF-52	.044	Electronic		—	8/14B⑧⑨ @ 650	8	5½-6½	—	650
	8-460PI	226	ARF-52	.044	Electronic		—	14B⑨ @ 650	18	5½-7	—	650

* Where two dwell or point gap figures are separated by a slash, the first figure is for engines equipped with dual diaphragm distributors and the second figure is for engines equipped with single diaphragm distributors

▲ See text for procedure

● In all cases where two idle speed figures are separated by a slash, the first is for idle speed with solenoid energized and automatic transmission in Drive, while the second is for idle speed with solenoid disconnected and automatic transmission in Neutral. Figures in parentheses are for California

■ All figures are in degrees Before Top Dead Center

① For air conditioned vehicles, adjust idle speed to 600 rpm with A/C on

② A/C off

③ Figure is 27 degrees for automatic transmission

④ Figure is .017 for automatic transmission

⑤ Figure is .021 for automatic transmission

⑥ Figure is 29 degrees for automatic transmission

⑦ For air conditioned vehicles, adjust idle speed to 800 rpm with A/C on

⑧ Depends on emission equipment, check underhood specifications sticker
⑨ In Drive
⑩ Not Used
⑪ On Cougars with automatic transmission, set ignition timing to 6B and set idle speed to 650 rpm
⑫ Not used
⑬ Figure is 32°-35° on manual transmission model with dual point distributor with both point sets combined
⑭ At 500 rpm
⑮ 20° BTC for 302 automatic
B Before Top Dead Center
C Cleveland
M Modified Cleveland

CJ Cobra Jet
HO High Output
N.A. Not available

SCJ Super Cobra Jet
W Windsor
— Not applicable

MECHANICAL VALVE LIFTER CLEARANCE

Year	Engine	Intake (Hot) In.	Exhaust (Hot) In.
1969-1970	302 BOSS	.025	.025
1969-1970	429 BOSS	.013 (Cold)	.013 (Cold)
1970-1971	429 SCJ	.019	.019
1971	351 BOSS	.025	.025
1972	351 HO	.025	.025

Falcon

TUNE-UP SPECIFICATIONS

When analyzing compression test results, look for uniformity among cylinders rather than specific pressures.

Year	ENGINE No. Cyl Displacement (cu in.)	ENGINE hp	SPARK PLUGS Type	SPARK PLUGS Gap (in.)	DISTRIBUTOR Point Dwell (deg)	DISTRIBUTOR Point Gap (in.)	IGNITION TIMING (deg) ▲ Man Trans	IGNITION TIMING (deg) ▲ Auto Trans	VALVES Intake Opens ■ (deg)	Fuel Pump Pressure (psi)	IDLE SPEED (rpm) ▲ ● Man Trans	IDLE SPEED (rpm) ▲ ● Auto Trans
'69	6-170	100	BF-82	.034	37	.027	6B	6B	9	4½-5½	750	550
	6-200	115	BF-82	.034	37	.027	6B	6B	9	4½-5½	750	550①
	8-302	220	BF-42	.034	27/29	.021/.017	6B	6B	16	4½-5½	650	550①
'70	6-200	120	BF-82	.035	37	.027	6B	6B	9	4½-5½	750②	550③
	8-302	220	BF-42	.035	27/29	.021/.017	6B	6B	16	4½-5½	800/500	600/500

* Where two dwell or point gap figures are separated by a splash, the first figure is for engines equipped with dual diaphragm distributors, while the second is for engines equipped with single diaphragm distributors.
▲ See text for procedure
■ All figures Before Top Dead Center
● Where two idle speed figures are separated by a slash, the first is for idle speed with solenoid energized and automatic transmission in Drive; the second is for idle speed with solenoid disconnected and automatic transmission in Neutral
① A/C off
② For air conditioned vehicles, adjust idle speed to 800 rpm with A/C off
③ For air conditioned vehicles, adjust idle speed to 600 rpm with A/C off

CAPACITIES

Year	ENGINE No. Cyl. Displacement (Cu. In.)	Engine Crankcase Add 1 Qt For New Filter	TRANSMISSION Pts To Refill After Draining Manual 3-Speed	Manual 4-Speed	Automatic	Drive Axle (pts)	Gasoline Tank (gals)	COOLING SYSTEM (qts) With Heater	With A/C
'69	FALCON								
	6-170, 200	3.5	3.5	—	16	2.5	16①	9.5	9.5
	8-302	4	3.5	—	18	4	16①	13.5	13.5
	FAIRLANE, TORINO								
	6-250	3.5	3.5	—	18	4	20	10	10
	8-302	4	3.5	—	—	—	20	—	—
	8-351	4	3.5	4	22	5	20	14.5	16.5
	8-390, 428	4	3.5	4	26	5	20	20	20
	MUSTANG								
	6-200	3.5	3.5	—	16	4	20	9	9
	6-250	3.5	3.5	—	18	4	20	10	10
	8-302, 351	4	3.5	4	18⑥	4⑦	20	13.5	15
	8-390, 428	4	—	4	26	5	20	14.5	16
	MONTEGO								
	6-250	3.5	3.5	—	18	4	20	10	10
	8-302	4	3.5	4	18	4	20	13.5	13.5
	COUGAR, MONTEGO								
	8-351	4	3.5	4	22	5	20⑧	14.5	16
	8-390, 428	4	—	4	26	5	20⑧	20	20

CAPACITIES (con't.)

Year	ENGINE No. Cyl. Displacement (Cu. In.)	Engine Crankcase Add 1 Qt For New Filter	TRANSMISSION Pts To Refill After Draining — Manual 3-Speed	Manual 4-Speed	Automatic	Drive Axle (pts)	Gasoline Tank (gals)	COOLING SYSTEM (qts) With Heater	With A/C
'70	FALCON, MAVERICK								
	6-170, 200	3.5	3.5	—	16	2.5	16	9	9
	MAVERICK								
	6-250	3.5	—	—	18	2.5	16	10	10
	FAIRLANE, TORINO								
	6-250	3.5	3.5	—	18	4	22	11.5	11.5
	FALCON, FAIRLANE, TORINO								
	8-302	4	3.5	4	18	5	22	15.5	16.5
	FAIRLANE, TORINO								
	8-351	4	3.5	4	22	5	22	15.5	16.5
	8-429	6⑨	—	4	26	5	22	19.5	19.5
	MUSTANG								
	6-200	3.5	3.5	—	16	2.25	22	9	9
	6-250	3.5	3.5	—	18	4	22	10	10
	8-302	4	3.5	4	18	4	22	13.5	15
	8-351	4	3.5	4	22	5	22	14.5	16
	8-428	4	—	4	26	5	22	19.5	19.5
	MONTEGO								
	6-250	3.5	3.5	—	18	4	22	11.5	11.5
	8-302	3.5	3.5	—	18	4	22	15	15
	MONTEGO, COUGAR								
	8-351	4	3.5	4	22	4	22	15.5	16
	8-429, 428	4⑨	—	4	26	5	22	19.5	19.5
'71	MAVERICK, COMET								
	6-170, 200	3.5	3.5	—	16	2.5	15	9	9
	6-250	3.5	3.5	—	18	2.5	15	9.5	9.5
	8-302	4	3.5	—	18	4	15	13.5	14
	TORINO, MONTEGO								
	6-250	3.5	3.5	—	18	4	20⑩	11	11
	8-302	4	3.5	—	18	4	20⑩	15	15.5
	8-351	4	3.5	4	22	5	20⑩	15.5	16.5
	8-429	6⑨	—	4	26	5	20⑩	19.5	19.5
	MUSTANG								
	6-250	3.5	3.5	—	18	4	20	11	11
	8-302	4	3.5	—	18	4	20	15	15.5
	MUSTANG, COUGAR								
	8-351	4	3.5	4	22	5	20	15.5	16
	8-429	6⑨	—	4	26	5	20	19.5	19.5
'72	MAVERICK, COMET								
	6-170, 200	3.5	3.5	—	16	4	15	9	9
	6-250	3.5	3.5	—	18	4	15	9.5	10.5
	8-302	4	3.5	—	18	4	15	13.5	14.5
	TORINO, MONTEGO								
	6-250	3.5	3.5	—	18	4	22.5⑩	11.5	11.5
	8-302	4	3.5	—	18	4	22.5⑩	15	15
	8-351	4	—	4	20.5⑪	4	22.5⑩	15.5	16
	8-400	4	—	—	26	4	22.5⑩	17.5	17.5
	8-429	4	—	—	26	5	22.5	19	19

CAPACITIES (con't.)

Year	ENGINE No. Cyl. Displacement (Cu. In.)	Engine Crankcase Add 1 Qt For New Filter	TRANSMISSION Pts To Refill After Draining: Manual 3-Speed	Manual 4-Speed	Automatic	Drive Axle (pts)	Gasoline Tank (gals)	COOLING SYSTEM (qts) With Heater	With A/C
'72	MUSTANG								
	6-250	3.5	3.5	—	18	4	19.5	11	11
	8-302	4	3.5	—	18	4	19.5	15	15.5
	MUSTANG, COUGAR								
	8-351	4	3.5	4	22⑫	5	19.5	16	16
'73	MAVERICK, COMET								
	6-200	3.5	3.5	—	16	4	15	9	9
	6-250	3.5	3.5	—	18	4	15	9.5	10.5
	8-302	4	3.5	—	18	4	15	13.5	14.5
	TORINO, MONTEGO								
	6-250	3.5	3.5	—	18	4	22.5⑩	11.5	11.5
	8-302	4	3.5	—	18	4	22.5⑩	15	15
	8-351	4	—	4	20.5⑪	4	22.5⑩	15.5	16
	8-400	4	—	—	26	4	22.5⑩	17.5	17.5
	8-429	4	—	—	26	5	22.5	19	19
	MUSTANG								
	6-250	3.5	3.5	—	18	4	19.5	11	11
	8-302	4	3.5	—	18	4	19.5	15	15.5
	MUSTANG, COUGAR								
	8-351	4	—	4	22⑫	5	19.5	16	16
'74	MAVERICK, COMET								
	6-200	4	3.5	—	16	4	15	9.0	9.0
	6-250	4	3.5	—	18	4	15	9.7	9.7
	8-302	4	3.5	—	18	4	15	13.4	14.2
	TORINO, MONTEGO								
	6-250	4	—	—	⑬	4	26.5⑰	11.5	—
	8-302	4	3.5	—	⑬	4	26.5⑰	15.7	15.7
	TORINO, MONTEGO, COUGAR, ELITE								
	8-351	4	—	—	⑭	4⑯	26.5⑰	⑱	⑲
	8-400	4	—	—	25⑮	5	26.5⑰	17.7	18.3
	8-460	6	—	—	25⑮	5	26.5⑰	18.9	19.5
'75-'76	MAVERICK, COMET								
	6-200	4	3.5	—	16	4	16㉓	9.0	9.0
	6-250	4	3.5	—	18	4	16㉓	9.7	9.7
	8-302	4	3.5	—	18	4	16㉓	13.4	14.2
	TORINO, MONTEGO								
	8-351	4	—	—	⑳	4	26.5⑰	15.9㉑	16.2㉑
	8-400	4	—	—	⑳	5	26.5⑰	17.1	17.5
	8-460	4	—	—	⑳	5	26.5⑰	19.2	19.2
	COUGAR, ELITE								
	8-351	4	—	—	㉒	5	26.5	16.3	16.8
	8-400	4	—	—	㉒	5	26.5	17.7	18.3
	8-460	4	—	—	㉒	5	26.5	18.9	20.5
	GRANADA, MONARCH								
	6-200	4	3.5	—	—	4	19.2	9.9	9.9
	6-250	4	3.5	—	17.0	4	19.2	10.5	10.7
	8-302	4	3.5	—	17.0	4	19.2	14.6	14.6
	8-351	4	—	—	20.0	4	19.2	15.7	16.7

CAPACITIES

① 20 gals on station wagon
②③④⑤ Not used
⑥ 22 pts with 351 engine
⑦ 5 pts with 351 engine
⑧ 17 gals on Cougar
⑨ 429 4 bbl—4 qts
428, 429 CJ, SCJ—6 qts
add 1 qt if equipped with oil cooler
⑩ Less 2 gals—station wagon, Ranchero
⑪ 26 pts for 351 CJ
⑫ Less 1 pt with 4 bbl
⑬ C4—18 or 20 pts; FMX—22 pts
⑭ 351 2V with C-4—20 pts; 351-2V with FMX—22pts; 351 2V with C-6—25 pts; 351-4V (C6)—21 pts
⑮ Cougar—21 pts
⑯ Cougar—5 pts
⑰ Station wagon—21.2 gallons
⑱ 351 W 2V—16.4 qts
351 C 2V—15.9 qts
351 C 4V—15.9 qts
⑲ 351 W 2V—16.8 qts
351 C 2V—16.5 qts
351 C 4V—16.9 qts
⑳ C4—20 pts; C6—25 pts; FMX—22 pts
㉑ 17.1 qts with heater, 17.5 qts with AC on 351 C 2 bbl
㉒ C4—21 pts; C6—24.5 pts; FMX—22 pts
㉓ 19.2 gals in 1976
—— Not applicable

VALVE SPECIFICATIONS

Year	Engine No. Cyl. Displacement (cu in.)	Seat Angle (deg)	Face Angle (deg)	Spring Test Pressure (lbs @ in.)	Spring Installed Height (in.)	Stem to Guide Clearance (in.)		Stem Diameter (in.)	
						Intake	Exhaust	Intake	Exhaust
'69	6-170, 200	45	44	150 @ 1.22	1 19/32	.0008-.0025	.0010-.0027	.3104	.3102
	6-250	45	44	150 @ 1.22	1 19/32	.0008-.0025	.0010-.0027	.3104	.3102
	8-302	45	44	180 @ 1.23	1 21/32	.0010-.0027	.0015-.0032	.3420	.3415
	8-351	45	44	215 @ 1.34	1 25/32	.0010-.0027	.0015-.0032	.3420	.3415
	8-390	45	44	220 @ 1.38	1 13/16	.0010-.0027	.0015-.0032	.3715	.3710
	8-428	②	③	268 @ 1.31	1 13/16	.0010-.0027	.0015-.0032	.3715	.3710
'70	6-170, 200	45	44	150 @ 1.22	1 19/32	.0008-.0025	.0010-.0027	.3104	.3102
	6-250	45	44	150 @ 1.22	1 19/32	.0008-.0025	.0010-.0027	.3104	.3102
	8-302	45	44	180 @ 1.23	1 21/32	.0010-.0027	.0010-.0027	.3420	.3415
	8-302④	45	44	315 @ 1.31	1 13/16	.0010-.0027	.0015-.0032	.3420	.3415
	8-351⑤	45	44	215 @ 1.34	1 25/32	.0010-.0027	.0010-.0027	.3420	.3415
	8-351⑥	45	44	209 @ 1.42	1 13/16	.0010-.0027	.0015-.0032	.3420	.3415
	8-351⑦	45	44	285 @ 1.31	1 13/16	.0010-.0027	.0015-.0032	.3420	.3415
	8-428	②	③	265 @ 1.31	1 13/16	.0015-.0032	.0015-.0032	.3715	.3710
	8-429	45	44	253 @ 1.33	1 13/16	.0010-.0027	.0010-.0027	.3420	.3420
	8-429④	②	③	315 @ 1.31	1 13/16	.0010-.0024	.0020-.0034	.3715	.3705
	8-429⑧	②	③	306 @ 1.36	1 13/16	.0010-.0024	.0020-.0034	.3420	.3417
'71	6-170, 200	45	44	150 @ 1.22	1 19/32	.0008-.0025	.0010-.0027	.3104	.3102
	6-250	45	44	150 @ 1.22	1 19/32	.0008-.0025	.0010-.0027	.3104	.3102
	8-302	45	44	180 @ 1.23	1 21/32	.0010-.0027	.0015-.0032	.3420	.3415
	8-302④	45	44	315 @ 1.31	1 13/16	.0010-.0027	.0015-.0032	.3420	.3415
	8-351⑤	45	44	215 @ 1.34	1 25/32	.0010-.0027	.0015-.0032	.3420	.3415
	8-351⑥	45	44	210 @ 1.42	1 13/16	.0010-.0027	.0015-.0032	.3420	.3415
	8-351⑦	45	44	285 @ 1.31	1 13/16	.0010-.0027	.0015-.0032	.3420	.3415
	8-429	45	45	229 @ 1.33	1 13/16	.0010-.0027	.0010-.0027	.3420	.3420
'72	6-170, 200	45	44	150 @ 1.22	1 19/32	.0008-.0025	.0010-.0027	.3104	.3102
	6-250	45	44	150 @ 1.22	1 19/32	.0008-.0025	.0010-.0027	.3104	.3102
	8-302	45	44	200 @ 1.23	1 11/16	.0010-.0027	.0015-.0032	.3420	.3415
	8-351⑤	45	44	200 @ 1.34	1 25/32	.0010-.0027	.0015-.0032	.3420	.3415
	8-351⑥	45	44	210 @ 1.42	1 13/16	.0010-.0027	.0015-.0032	.3420	.3415

VALVE SPECIFICATIONS (con't.)

Year	Engine No. Cyl. Displacement (cu in.)	Seat Angle (deg)	Face Angle (deg)	Spring Test Pressure (lbs @ in.)	Spring Installed Height (in.)	STEM TO GUIDE Clearance (in.) Intake	Exhaust	STEM Diameter (in.) Intake	Exhaust
'72	8-351⑦	45	44	285 @ 1.23	1 13/16	.0010-.0027	.0015-.0032	.3420	.3415
	8-351④	45	44	315 @ 1.23	1 13/16	.0010-.0027	.0015-.0032	.3420	.3415
	8-400	45	44	226 @ 1.39	1 13/16	.0010-.0027	.0015-.0032	.3420	.3415
	8-429	45	45	229 @ 1.33	1 13/16	.0010-.0027	.0010-.0027	.3420	.3420
'73-	6-200	45	46	150 @ 1.22	1 19/32	.0008-.0025	.0010-.0027	.3104	.3102
'76	6-250	45	46	150 @ 1.22	1 19/32	.0008-.0025	.0010-.0027	.3104	.3102
	8-302	45	46	200 @ 1.22	1 9/16	.0010-.0027	.0015-.0032	.3420	.3415
	8-351⑤	45	46	200 @ 1.34	1 25/32	.0010-.0027	.0015-.0032	.3420	.3415
	8-351⑥	45	46	282 @ 1.32	1 13/16	.0010-.0027	.0015-.0032	.3420	.3415
	8-351⑦	45	46	285 @ 1.32	1 13/16	.0010-.0027	.0015-.0032	.3420	.3415
	8-400	45	46	226 @ 1.39	1 13/16	.0010-.0027	.0015-.0032	.3420	.3415
	8-460	45	46	253 @ 1.33	1 13/16	.0010-.0027	.0010-.0027	.3420	.3420

① Not used
② Intake valve seat angle 30°
Exhaust valve seat angle 45°
③ Intake valve face angle 29°
Exhaust valve face angle 44°
④ Boss
⑤ Windsor heads
⑥ Cleveland or modified Cleveland 2 bbl
⑦ Cleveland or modified Cleveland 4 bbl
⑧ Cobra Jet

TORQUE SPECIFICATIONS

All readings in ft lbs

Year	Engine No. Cyl. Displacement (cu in.)	Cylinder Head Bolts*	Rod Bearing Bolts	Main Bearing Bolts	Crankshaft Pulley Bolt	Flywheel to Crankshaft Bolts	MANIFOLD Intake	Exhaust
'69	6-170, 200, 250	70-75	19-24	60-70	85-100	75-85	—	13-18
	8-302	65-72	19-24	60-70	70-90	75-85	23-25	12-16
	8-351W	95-100	40-45	95-105	70-90	75-85	23-25	18-24
	8-390	80-90	40-45	95-105	70-90	75-85	32-35	18-24
	8-428	80-90	53-58	95-105	70-90	75-85	32-35	18-24
'70-'73	6-170, 200, 250	70-75	19-24②	60-70	85-100	75-85	—	13-18
	8-302	65-72	19-24③	60-70④	70-90	75-85	23-25	12-16
	8-351	95-100①	40-45⑥	95-105⑦	70-90	75-85	23-25 (5/16) 28-32 (3/8) 6-9 (1/4)	12-22
	8-400	95-105⑨	40-45	⑩	70-90	75-85	21-25 (5/16) 27-33 (3/8) 6-9 (1/4)	12-16
	8-428	80-90	53-58	95-105	70-90	75-85	32-35	18-24
	8-429, 460	130-140	40-45	95-105⑤	70-90	75-85	25-30	28-33
	8-429 Boss	90-95	85-90	70-80	70-90	75-85	25-30	28-33
'74-'76	6-200	70-75	19-24	60-70	85-100	75-85	—	13-18
	6-250	70-75	21-26	60-70	85-100	75-85	—	13-18
	8-302	65-72	19-24	60-70	35-50	75-85	19-27	12-16
	8-351W	105-112	40-45	95-105	35-50	75-85	19-27	18-24
	8-351C, 351M	95-105⑧	40-45	⑨	70-90	75-85	⑩	12-22
	8-400	95-105⑧	40-45	⑨	70-90	75-85	⑩	12-16
	8-460	130-140	40-45	95-105	35-50	75-85	22-32	28-33

① 351 Boss and HO three steps—40, 80, 120 ft. lbs.
② 250—21-26
③ 302 Boss—40-45
④ 302 Boss—outer bolts 35-40
⑤ 7/16 in. bolts—70-80
⑥ 351 Boss and HO—43-48 ft. lbs.
⑦ 3/8 in. bolts—34-45 ft. lbs.
⑧ Three steps—55, 75, then maximum figure
⑨ 1/2 in—13 bolts, 95-105, 3/8 in—16 bolts, 35-45
⑩ 5/16 in. bolt, 21-25; 3/8 in. bolt, 22-32; 1/4 in. bolt, 6-9
* Tighten cylinder head bolts in three steps

CRANKSHAFT AND CONNECTING ROD SPECIFICATIONS

All measurements are given in inches

Year	Engine No. Cyl. Displacement (cu in.)	CRANKSHAFT Main Brg. Journal Dia	Main Brg. Oil Clearance	Shaft End-Play	Thrust on No.	CONNECTING ROD Journal Diameter	Oil Clearance	Side Clearance
'69-'76	6-170	2.2482-2.2490	.0005-.0022	.004-.008	3	2.1232-2.1240	.0008-.0024	.003-.010
	6-200	2.2482-2.2490	.0005-.0022	.004-.008	5	2.1232-2.1240	.0008-.0024	.003-.010
	6-250	2.3982-2.3990	.0005-.0022	.004-.008	5	2.1232-2.1240	.0008-.0024	.003-.010
	8-302	2.2482-2.2490	.0005-.0024⑤⑪	.004-.008	3	2.1228-2.1236①	.0008-.0026②	.010-.020
	8-351W	2.2994-3.0002	.0013-.0030⑩	.004-.008	3	2.3103-2.3111	.0008-.0026	.010-.020
	8-351C or M	2.7484-2.7492	.0009-.0026⑦	.004-.008	3	2.3103-2.3111	.0008-.0026⑦⑨	.010-.020
	8-390	2.7484-2.7492	.0008-.0020	.004-.010	3	2.4380-2.4388	.0008-.0030	.010-.020
	8-400	2.9994-3.0002	.0011-.0028	.004-.008	3	2.3103-2.3111	.0011-.0026⑨	.010-.020
	8-428	2.7484-2.7492	.0010-.0020	.004-.010	3	2.4380-2.4388	.0010-.0030	.010-.020
	8-429, 460	2.9994-3.0002	.0010-.0020③⑧	.004-.008	3	2.4992-2.5000	.0008-.0028④	.010-.020

① Boss 302—2.1222-2.1230
② Boss 302—.0015-.0025
③ Boss 429—.0010-.0025
④ Boss 429—.0015-.0025
⑤ 302—.0001-.0005 No. 1 bearing only
⑥ Not used
⑦ Boss 351, 351 HO and 351 C or M 4-bbl—.0011-.0015
⑧ No. 1—.0010-.0015
⑨ .0008-.0015 in. in 1974-76
⑩ .0008-.0026 in. in 1974-76
⑩ .0005-.0015 in. in 1974-76

RING GAP

All measurements are given in inches

Year	Engine	Top Compression	Bottom Compression
'69-'73	6-170, 200, 250 8-302, 351, 400, 428, 429, 460	.010-.020	.010-.020
'74-'76	6-200, 250	.008-.016	.008-.016
	8-302, 351, 400, 460	.010-.020	.010-.020

Year	Engine	Oil Control
'69-'76	6-170, 200, 250	.015-.055
'69-'71	8-302, 351	.015-.069
'69	8-390	.015-.055
'69-'71	8-428, 429	.010-.035
'72-'76	8-302, 351	.015-.055①
'72-'76	8-400	.015-.069
'72-'76	8-429, 460	.015-.055

① .015-.069 in Cleveland built engine through 1973

RING SIDE CLEARANCE

All measurements are given in inches

Year	Engine	Top Compression	Bottom Compression
'69--'76	All engines	.002-.004	.002-.004

Year	Engine	Oil Control
'69-'76	All engines	Snug①

① 1974-'76 8-460—.002-.006 in.

PISTON CLEARANCE

Year	Engine	Piston-to-Bore Minimum	Clearance (in.) Maximum
'69	170, 200, 250	0.0014	0.0020
'69-'76	302, 351W	0.0018	0.0026
'69	390, 428	0.0015	0.0023
'70-'76	170, 200, 250	0.0013	0.0021
'70-'76	351C, 351M, 400, 429, 460	0.0014①	0.0022①
'70	429CJ, 429SCJ	0.0030	0.0038
'71	429CJ, 429SCJ	0.0042	0.0050
'72	351HO (CJ)	0.0034	0.0042

① 1974-'76 8-460—.0022-.0030 in.

ALTERNATOR AND REGULATOR SPECIFICATIONS

Year	ALTERNATOR Manufacturer	Field Current @ 12 V	Output (amps)	REGULATOR Manufacturer	Field Relay Air Gap (in.)	Field Relay Point Gap (in.)	Volts to Close	Regulator Air Gap (in.)	Regulator Point Gap (in.)	Volts @ 75°
'69	Autolite	2.8-3.3	38	Autolite	—	—	2.5	.049-.056	.017-.022	13.8-14.4
	Autolite	2.9-3.1	42	Autolite	.012-.022	.015-.022	2.5	.049-.056	.017-.022	13.8-14.4
	Autolite	2.9	45	Autolite	.015	—	2.5-4	.052	.019	13.8-14.6
	Autolite	2.9	55	Autolite	.015	—	2.5-4	.052	.019	13.8-14.6
	Leece-Neville	2.9	53	Leece-Neville	.012	.025	7	.047	.019	14.1-14.9
'70	Autolite Purple	2.4	38	Autolite	—	—	2-4.2	—	—	13.5-15.3
	Autolite Orange	2.9	42	Autolite	—	—	2-4.2	—	—	13.5-15.3
	Autolite Red	2.9	55	Autolite	—	—	2-4.2	—	—	13.5-15.3
	Autolite Green	2.9	61	Autolite	—	—	2-4.2	—	—	13.5-15.3
	Autolite Black	2.9	65	Autolite	—	—	2-4.2	—	—	13.5-15.3
'71	Autolite Purple	2.4	38	Autolite	—	—	2.5-4	—	—	13.5-15.3
	Autolite Orange	2.9	42	Autolite	—	—	2.5-4	—	—	13.5-15.3
	Autolite Red	2.9	55	Autolite	—	—	2.5-4	—	—	13.5-15.3
	Autolite Green	2.9	61	Autolite	—	—	2.5-4	—	—	13.5-15.3
	Autolite Black	2.9	65	Autolite	—	—	2.5-4	—	—	13.5-15.3
'72-'75	Motorcraft Purple	2.4	38	Motorcraft	—	—	2.5-4	—	—	13.5-15.4
	Motorcraft Orange	2.9	42	Motorcraft	—	—	2.5-4	—	—	13.5-15.4
	Motorcraft Red	2.9	55	Motorcraft	—	—	2.5-4	—	—	13.5-15.4
	Motorcraft Green	2.9	61	Motorcraft	—	—	2.5-4	—	—	13.5-15.4
	Motorcraft Black	2.9	65	Motorcraft	—	—	2.5-4	—	—	13.5-15.4
	Motorcraft Side Terminal	2.9	70	Motorcraft	—	—	2.5-4	—	—	13.5-15.4
	Motorcraft Side Terminal	2.9	90	Motorcraft	—	—	2.5-4	—	—	13.5-15.4

— Not Applicable (Non-Adjustable)

BATTERY AND STARTER SPECIFICATIONS

Year	Engine No. Cyl. Displacement (cu in.)	BATTERY Ampere Hour Capacity	Volts	Terminal Grounded	STARTER Lock Test Amps	Lock Test Volts	Lock Test Torque (ft lbs)	No-Load Test Amps	No-Load Test Volts	No-Load Test RPM	Brush Spring Tension (oz)
'69-'76	6-170	41, 45④	12	Neg.	460	5	9	50	12	9,500	40
	6-200, 250	41, 45④	12	Neg.	670	5	15.5	70	12	9,500	40
	8-exc. below	41, 53, 55③	12	Neg.	①	5	②	70	12	9,500	40
	8-351 4-BBL.	55③	12	Neg.	①	5	②	70	12	9,500	40
	8-400, 428, 429, 460	68, 73, 77	12	Neg.	670	5	15.5	70⑤	12	9,500	40⑥

① 4½ in. diameter starter—670; 4 in. diameter starter—460
② 4½ in. diameter starter—15.5; 4 in. diameter starter—9.0
③ 68AH battery optional; 73AH battery optional
④ 53AH battery optional
⑤ 90 amp 1974-76
⑥ 80 oz. 1974-76

BRAKE SPECIFICATIONS

All measurements are given in inches

Year	Model	MASTER CYLINDER		WHEEL CYLINDER				BRAKE DISC OR DRUM DIAMETER			
				Front		Rear		Front		Rear	
		Disc	Drum	Disc	Drum	Drum	Disc	Disc	Drum	Drum	Disc
'69	6 Falcon (200 cu in.)	.9375①	1.0	2.38	1 1/16	27/32	—	11.3	9.0	9.0	—
	6 Mustang	—	1.0	—	1 1/16	27/32	—	—	9.0	9.0	—
	Falcon & Fairlane Sta. Wag.	.9375①	1.0	2.38	1 3/32	15/16	—	11.3	10.0	10.0	—
	Falcon exc. 6 cyl. 200 and Sta. Wag., Fairlane 250 and 302 exc. Sta. Wag., Mustang V8 302	.9375①	1.0	2.38	1 1/8	7/8	—	11.3	10.0	10.0	—
	Fairlane and Montego conv. and pass. with 351, 390, and All Cougar, and all 8 Mustang exc. 302	.9375①	1.0	2.38	1 3/32	7/8	—	11.3	10.0	10.0	—
'70	6 Falcon, Maverick, Mustang	—	1.0	—	1 1/16	27/32	—	—	9.0	9.0	—
	All Cougar	1.0	1.0	2.38	1 1/8	29/32	—	11.3	10.0	10.0	—
	Falcon, Montego, Torino Sta. Wag.	.9375①③	1.0	2.38	1 1/8	31/32	—	11.3	10.0	10.0	—
	All Cougar, 8 Falcon Sed., Torino and Montego Sed.	.9375①③	1.0	2.38	1 1/8	29/32	—	11.3	10.0	10.0	—
	Mustang 8	1.0	1.0	2.38	1 1/8	7/8④	—	11.3	10.0	10.0	—
'71	Cougar	1.0	1.0	2.38	1 1/8	29/32	—	11.3	10.0	10.0	—
	6 Mustang	—	1.0	—	1 1/8	29/32	—	—	9.0	10.0	—
	8 Mustang	1.0	1.0	2.38	1 1/8	7/8	—	11.3	10.0	10.0	—
	6 Maverick	—	1.0	—	1 1/16	27/32	—	—	9.0	9.0	—
	8 Maverick	—	1.0	—	1 1/8	7/8	—	—	10.0	10.0	—
	6 Comet	—	1.0	—	1 1/16	27/32	—	—	10.0	10.0	—
	8 Comet	—	1.0	—	1 1/8	7/8	—	—	10.0	10.0	—
	Montego and Torino Sed.	.9375①	1.0	2.38	1 1/8	29/32	—	11.3	10.0	10.0	—
	Montego & Torino Sta. Wag.	.9375①	1.0	2.38	1 1/8	31/32	—	11.3	10.0	10.0	—
'72-'73	Cougar	1.0⑨	1.0	2.38	1 1/8	29/32⑧	—	11.3	10.0	10.0	—
	6 Comet⑥	—	1.0	—	1 1/8	27/32	—	—	9.0④	9.0④	—
	8 Comet⑥ (10 in.)	—	1.0	—	1 1/8	27/32	—	—	10.0	10.0	—
	Montego, Torino	1.0	1.0	3.10	—	1.0	—	10.72	—	10.0⑦	—
	Mustang	1.0⑨	1.0	2.38	1 1/8	7/8⑤	—	11.3	10.0	10.0	—
	Maverick⑥	—	1.0	—	1 1/8	27/32	—	—	9.0④	9.0④	—
'74	Maverick, Comet	.9380	.9380	2.60	1.125	0.843	—	11.03	10.0	10.0	—
	Torino, Montego, Cougar, Elite	1.0	—	3.10	—	1.0	—	10.72	—	10.0⑦	—
'75-'76	Maverick, Comet	.9380	.9375	2.60	1.125	0.875	—	11.03	10.0	10.0	—
	Torino, Montego, Cougar, Elite	1.0	—	3.10	—	1.0	—	10.72	—	10.0⑦	—
	Granada, Monarch	.9380⑩	—	2.60	—	0.875	2.10	11.03	—	10.0	10.66

① Also applies to all power brakes
② Not used
③ Torino and Montego only
④ 10″ brakes required for 1972 250 1-V cars equipped with optional D70-14 or DR78-14 tires, and all 1973 models
⑤ 29/32″ on all 1972 V8 equipped cars, and 27/32″ on all 1973 models
⑥ 10″ on 1972 302 V8 equipped cars, and on all 1973 models
⑦ 11″ on Station Wagons with 351, 400, 429 or 460 V8; All Station Wagons in 1974-76
⑧ 27/32″ all 1973
⑨ .9375 in 1973
— Not applicable
⑩ 4-wheel disc brake option uses 1.0 in. master cylinder

WHEEL ALIGNMENT SPECIFICATIONS

		CASTER		CAMBER				WHEEL PIVOT RATIO (deg)	
Year	Model	Range (deg)	Pref Setting (deg)	Range (deg)	Pref Setting (deg)	Toe-in (in.)	Steering Axis Inclin. (deg)	Inner Wheel	Outer Wheel
'69	Falcon, Torino, Montego	1¾N to ¼P	¾N	½N to 1P	¼P	⅛ to ¼	7	20	18⅛
	Cougar & Mustang	¾N to 1¼P	¼P	¼P to 1¾P	¾P	⅛ to ¼	6¾	20	18¾
'70-'71	Montego, Falcon, Torino	1¼N to ¼N	¾N	½N to 1P	¼P	⅛ to ⅜	7⅔	20	③
	Cougar & Mustang	1N to 1P	0	0 to 1½P⑤	1P	1/16 to 5/16	6¾	20	18⅔
	Maverick, Comet	1½N to ½P	½N	½N to ¼P	¼P	1/16 to 5/16	6¾	20	18¾④
'72	Torino, Montego	1¼N to 2¾P	¾P	¼N to 1¾P	¾P	1/16 to 7/16	7⅔	20	17¾
	Mustang, Cougar	2N to 2P	0	½N to 1½P	½P	1/16 to ⅜	6¾	20	17¾
	Maverick, Comet	2½N to 1½P	½N	¾N to 1¼P	¼P	1/16 to ⅜	6¾	20	18½④
'73	Torino, Montego	¾N to 2¼P	¾P	¼N to 1¾P	¾P	3/16 to 9/16	7⅔	20	17.73
	Mustang, Cougar	2N to 2P	0	½N to 1½P	½P	1/16 to ⅜	6¾	20	17.72
	Maverick, Comet	2½N to 1½P	½N	¾N to 1¼P	¼P	1/16 to ⅜	6¾	20	18.44④
'74-'76	Torino, Montego, Cougar, Elite	½P to 3½P	2P	⑥	⑦	0 to ⅜	9	20	18.11
	Maverick, Comet, Monarch, Granada	2½N to 1½P	½N	¾N to 1¼P	¼P	1/16 to ⅜	6¾	20	18.39④

①② Not used
② Falcon—6⅔
③ Falcon—18°6′; others with manual steering—17°19′; power steering—17°49′
④ 18.16° for power steering.
⑤ 1970 models—¼P to 1¾P
⑥ Left—⅜N to 1⅝P
Right—⅞N to 1⅛P
⑦ Left—⅝P
Right—⅛P
N Negative P Positive

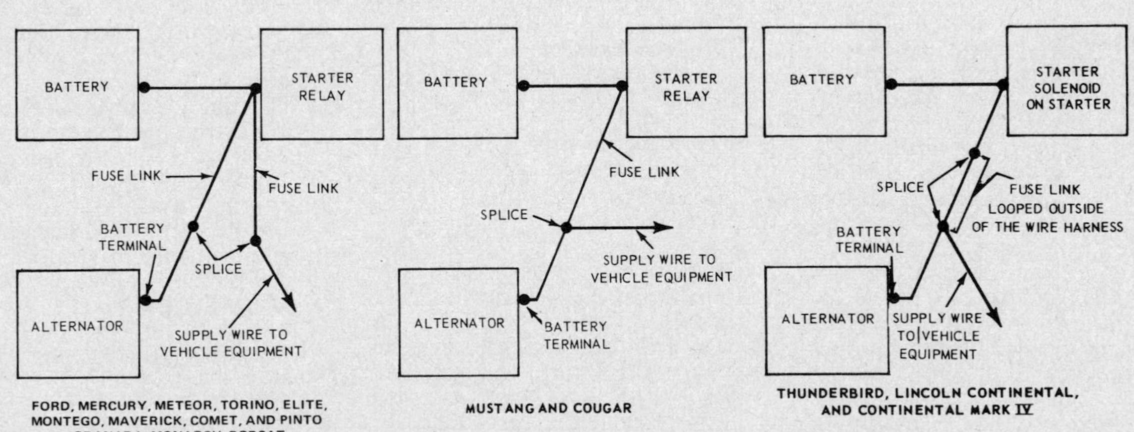

Fuse link locations
(© Ford Motor Co.)

NOTE: Mustang models through 1973 are covered in this section. Refer to the Bobcat, Mustang II, Pinto car section for coverage of 1974 and later Mustang II models.

CHARGING SYSTEM

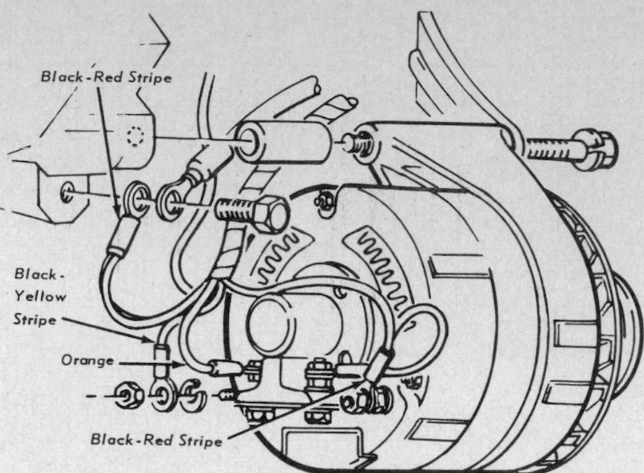

Typical alternator mounting (© Ford Motor Co)

All Ford cars from 1969 to the present have used alternating current (AC) charging systems.

Charging system troubleshooting and repair procedures can be found in the Unit Repair Section under Charging and Starting Systems.

Fuse Link

Since 1970, all Ford products have incorporated a fuse link in the charging system. The fuse link is a short length of insulated wire, several gauge sizes smaller than the system it protects. The fuse link blows out if a booster battery is hooked into the system incorrectly, or if a component of the electrical system is shorted to ground. When the fuse link blows, it leaves an open circuit in the charging system and the alternator will not charge the battery. A blown fuse link can be identified by bare wire ends or bubbled insulation. It is located in the engine wire harness on or near the starter relay and is marked FUSE LINK.

Alternator

The alternator is covered in the Charging and Starting Systems Unit Repair Section.

Caution Since the alternator and regulator are designed for use on only one polarity system, the following precautions must be observed:

1. The polarity of the battery, generator and regulator must be matched and considered before making any electrical connections in the system.
2. When connecting a booster battery, be sure to join the negative battery terminals together and the positive battery terminals together.
3. When connecting a charger to the battery, connect the charger positive lead to the battery positive terminal. Connect the charger negative lead to the battery negative terminal.
4. Never operate the alternator on open circuit. Be sure that all connections in the circuit are clean and tight.
5. Do not short across or ground any of the terminals on the alternator.
6. Do not attempt to polarize the alternator.
7. Do not use test lamps of more than 12 volts for checking diode continuity.
8. Avoid long soldering times when replacing diodes or transistors. Prolonged heat is damaging to these units.
9. Disconnect the battery ground terminal when servicing any AC system. This will prevent the possibility of accidental reversing of polarity.

Alternator R & R

1. Disconnect the battery ground cable.
2. Loosen the alternator mounting bolts and remove the adjustment arm to alternator attaching bolt. Disengage the alternator belt.
3. Remove the electrical connectors from the alternator and remove the alternator. On some models it is necessary to remove the alternator mounting bolts and the alternator wiring ground bolt from engine to gain access to the electrical connectors.
4. Reverse above procedure to reinstall.

Voltage Regulator R & R

1. Disconnect the negative battery cable.
2. Remove the regulator mounting screws.
3. Remove the cable quick-disconnect from the old regulator and attach to the new regulator.
4. Place the mounting bracket for the radio suppression capacitor over the hole for the lower regulator's mounting screw and install the screws.
5. Connect the negative battery cable.
6. Test the system for proper voltage regulation.

STARTING SYSTEM

The starter is a four-brush, series-parallel wound unit. The circuit is completed by means of a relay controlled switch which is part of the ignition switch.

Starting system troubleshooting and repair procedures can be found in the Charging and Starting Systems Unit Repair Section.

All models, except 1970-76 Torinos, Elites, Montegos, Mustangs, and Cougars with the 429 or 460 V8 have a positive engagement starter with a self-contained engagement mechanism. The 429 and 460 V8 engined models use a solenoid activated starter to which is mounted an outboard solenoid. Thede is no difference in procedures for removing or installing these two types of starters.

Starter R & R

Due to interference of the exhaust inlet pipe on some models, the steering idler arm must be lowered to provide clearance for starter removal.

1. Disconnect the starter cable at the starter terminal, remove the flywheel housing to starter retaining screws. Remove the starter assembly and the rubber dust ring.
2. Position the rubber dust ring on the flywheel housing.
3. Position the starter assembly to the flywheel housing, and begin on the starter retaining screws. On a car with an automatic transmission, the transmission dipstick tube bracket is mounted under the starter side mounting bolt. Snug all bolts, then tighten to 15 ft. lbs., tightening the middle bolt first.

NOTE: Intermittent starter operation on solenoid starter motor equipped 429 and 460 V8s may be due to the loosening of screws and terminals on the solenoid switch assembly. To remedy this, apply a small amount of Loctite® TL-290 or, its equivalent.

Starter Drive R & R

Positive Engagement Starters

1. After removing the starter from the engine, loosen and remove the brush cover band and the

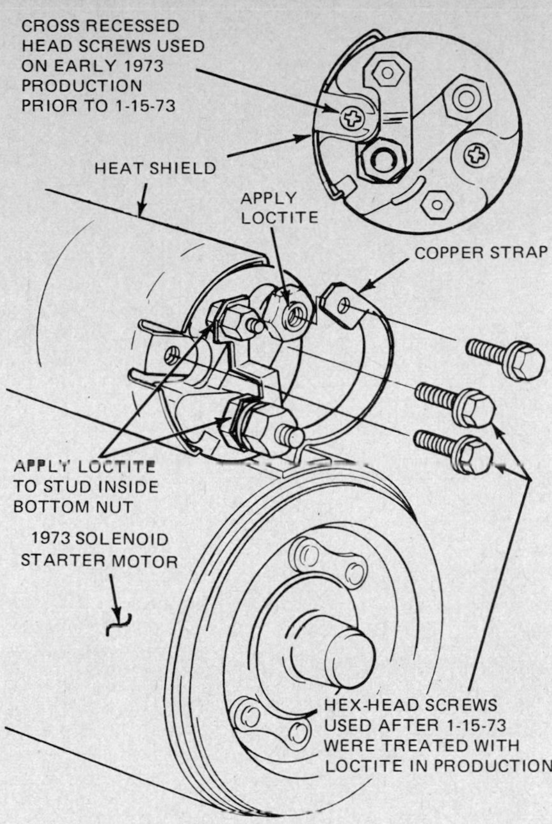

Solenoid-actuated starter motor (© Ford Motor Co)

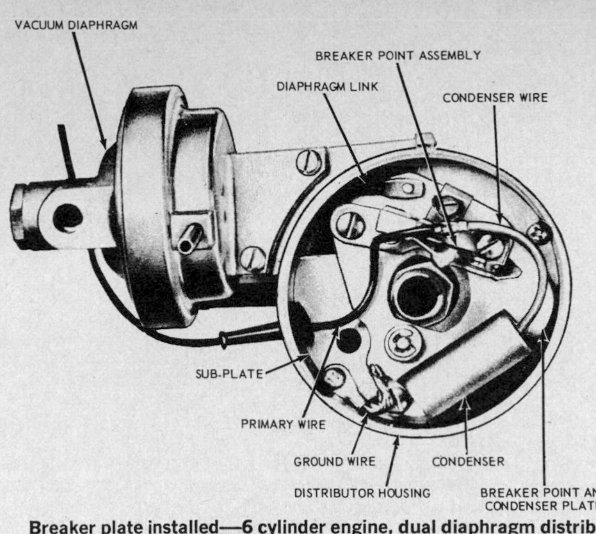

Breaker plate installed—6 cylinder engine, dual diaphragm distributor (© Ford Motor Co)

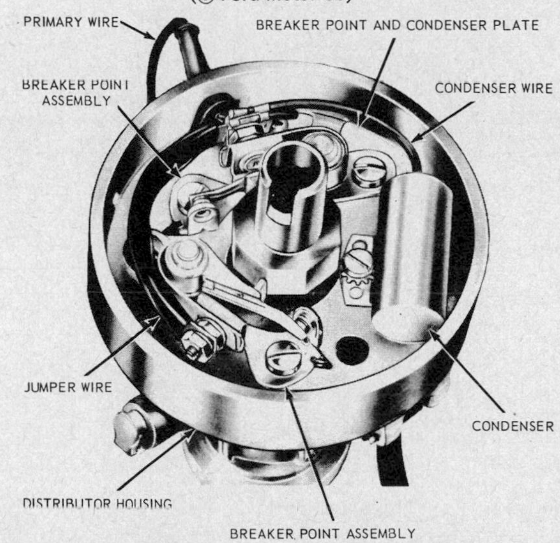

Dual point distributor breaker plate (© Ford Motor Co)

cover of the starter drive plunger lever.

2. Loosen the thru-bolts enough to facilitate the removal of the drive end housing and plunger lever return spring.
3. Some drive end housings are equipped with needle bearings. If the starter is so equipped, and you are not replacing the bearings, insert a dummy shaft through the housing to prevent the loss of any of the bearing needles.
4. Remove the retaining pivot pin and starter drive plunger lever.
5. Remove the stop-ring and retainer from the end of the armature shaft. Remove the drive gear assembly.
6. Apply a thin coat of white grease to the splines of the armature shaft. Install the drive gear assembly on the armature shaft and also install a new stop-ring.
7. Position the starter gear plunger lever on the starter frame and install the pivot pin. Check to see that the plunger lever properly engages the starter drive assembly.
8. Install a new stop-ring retainer. Remove the dummy shaft from the drive end housing and lightly grease the needle bearings, if so equipped. Position the starter drive plunger lever's return spring and the drive end housing to the starter frame.
9. Tighten the thru-bolts to 55–75 inch pounds (in. lbs).
10. Position the plunger lever cover and brush cover band, with its gasket, on the starter. Tighten the brush cover band retaining screw.

Solenoid-Actuated Starters

See the Charging and Starting Systems Unit Repair Section.

IGNITION SYSTEM

All pre-1974 compact and intermediate Ford cars use a conventional contact breaker ignition system, consisting of a distributor containing the points and condenser, a coil, and the high voltage wiring to the spark plugs.

Since 1968 all models use a dual advance distributor to provide more accurately timed ignition and cleaner, smog-free exhaust. Some of these distributors have dual diaphragm vacuum advance mechanisms. These have two vacuum lines to the distributor bellows, one to advance the timing during high speed road use, and one to retard the timing at idle.

Beginning 1974, Ford uses a solid state or "breakerless" ignition system on all 200 cu in and larger engines in the state of California, and on all 400 and 460 cu in V8s nationwide.

Starting 1975, breakerless ignition is standard on all Ford engines. This system is unique in that it eliminates the contact breaker points, replacing them with a permanent magnet low voltage generator.

Briefly, the system works as follows: When the ignition is on and the distributor is rotating, the low voltage generator in the distributor produces alternating current which is then sent to the electronic control module. The module senses the signal from the low voltage generator as the alternating current wave swings from positive to negative each time one of the gear teeth on the armature passes the magnetic field in the coil of the generator. When a gear tooth is directly opposite the magnetic field,

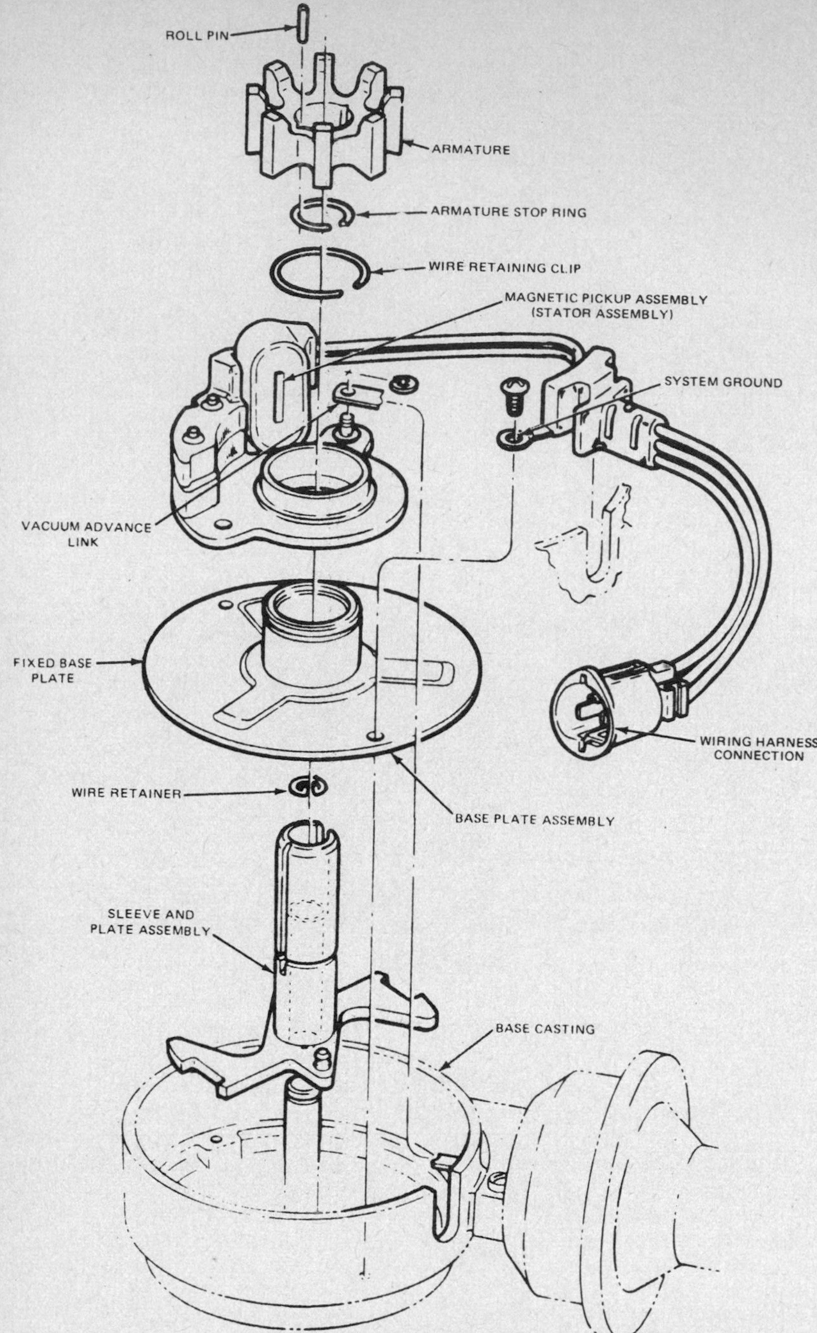

Breakerless V8 distributor diassembled
(© Ford Motor Co)

the alternating current wave is at crossover (neither negative nor positive). The control module senses this and cuts off electricity (low voltage) to the coil, causing it to fire (high voltage). After the coil fires, the timing circuitry in the module redirects the low tension voltage to the coil.

Other than the low voltage generator and the control module, the rest of the system is conventional in appearance, with a conventional distributor cap and rotor. Spark advance or retard is accomplished by moving the plate for the low voltage generator in the distributor.

NOTE: On 1975 and later models there is a terminal on the coil provided for connecting a tachometer. The terminal is labeled "Tach Test" and has a small arrowhead pointing to the proper terminal.

Dual Advance

The dual advance distributor has two independently operated spark-timing control systems. A centrifugal type and a vacuum-type control are used on each distributor of standard production engines. Centrifugal weights cause the cam to advance or rotate ahead, relative to the distributor shaft.

The vacuum control mechanism operates through a spring loaded diaphragm and movable breaker plate, about the same as the vacuum advance distributor.

Distributor Removal

1. Remove distributor cap. Disconnect the primary wire at the coil and the vacuum control line at the distributor.
2. Scribe a mark on the distributor body, showing position of the rotor. Then, scribe another mark on the distributor body and engine block, showing the position of the body in the block. These marks can be used to advantage when reassembling the distributor in an undisturbed engine.
3. Remove the screw, lockwasher and hold-down clamp. Pull the distributor out of the block. Do not rotate crankshaft while distributor is out of block because it will then be necessary to retime ignition.

Distributor Installation

1. If the engine was not cranked while the distributor was removed, install the distributor in the engine, aligning the tip of the rotor with the marks that were made on the distributor body and the engine. Proceed to Step 3. If the engine was cranked while the distributor was removed, rotate the crankshaft to bring No. 1 piston to T.D.C. of its compression stroke.
2. Position distributor in the block with the rotor at No. 1 firing position. Be sure that the oil pump intermediate driveshaft is properly seated in the oil pump.
3. Install, but do not tighten, the distributor retaining clamp and screw.

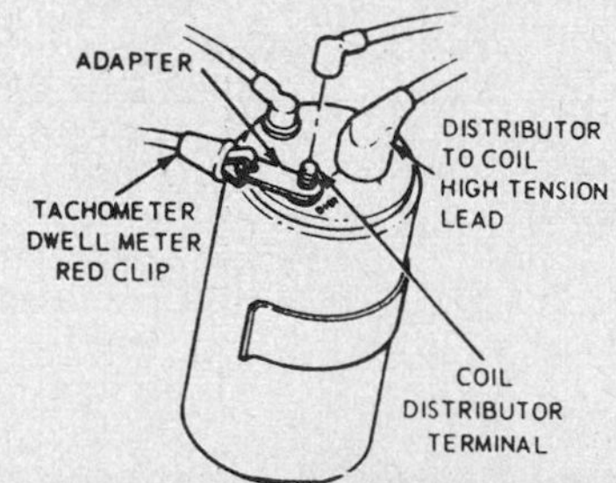

Installing dwell/tachometer adaptor on coil—1974 and earlier models equipped with conventional ignition
(© Ford Motor Co)

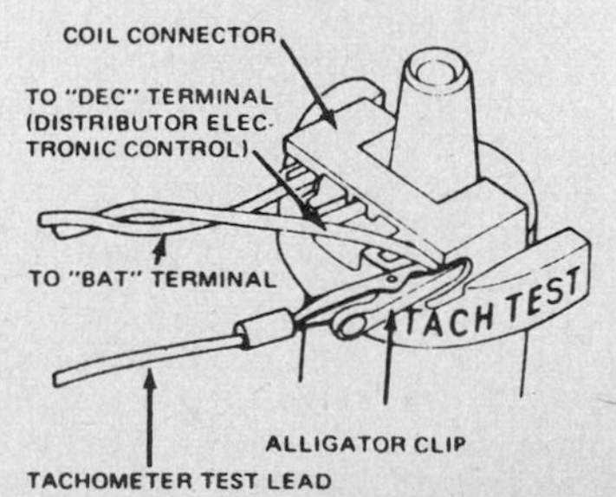

Attaching dwell/tachometer lead to coil connector—1975 and later models equipped with breakerless ignition
(© Ford Motor Co)

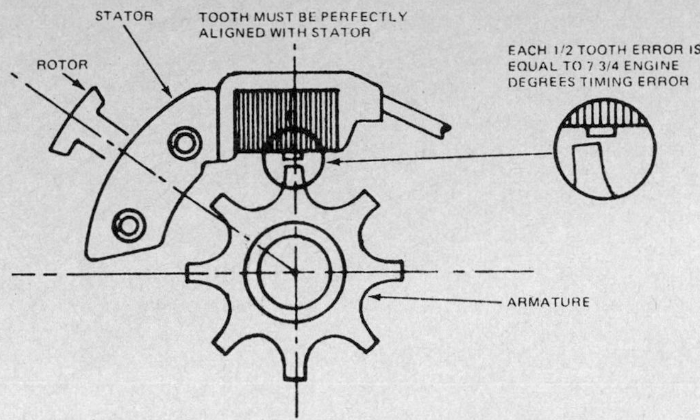

Breakerless ignition distributor static timing position
(© Ford Motor Co)

4. Rotate the distributor body clockwise until the breaker points start to open.
5. Tighten the retaining clamp screw.
6. Install distributor cap.
7. Connect distributor primary wire.
8. Start engine and run long enough to obtain engine operating temperature.
9. Idle engine to 500 rpm. Then, with a timing light, check the timing marks at the front pulley and make necessary corrections.
10. Connect the vacuum control line to the distributor and check advance characteristics with the timing light when the engine is accelerated.

Contact Point Replacement and Adjustment 1974 and earlier models

1. Unsnap the distributor cap retaining clips and position the cap clear of the breaker plate. Remove the rotor by pulling it straight up.
2. Remove the metal point shield, if so equipped.
3. Disconnect the primary lead and condenser wires from the contact point assembly. On dual-point distributors, remove the jumper strap also.
4. Remove the contact point and condenser retaining screws. Lift the contact point assembly and condenser from the distributor.
5. Lightly lubricate the distributor cam with heat-resistant lubricant.
6. Place the new contact point assembly and condenser in the distributor. Install, but do not tighten, the retaining screws.
7. On all V8 engines, except those equipped with a centrifugal advance distributor, place the ground wire under the contact point assembly screw farthest from the contacts. This ground wire is positioned under the condenser retaining screw on all six-cylinder engines.
8. Turn the engine until the rubbing block on the point assembly is resting on the high point of the distributor cam lobe. Insert a feeler gauge of specified thickness between the contact points and adjust the gap. Tighten the retaining screw and remove the feeler gauge.
9. Connect the primary and condenser wires to the contact point assembly in the same order as they were removed. On those distributors with a metal point shield, the wires should be positioned 180 degrees (180°) from each other. Install the shield.
10. Install the rotor and distributor cap.
11. If a dwell meter is available, check to see that the distributor dwell is within specifications.

Ignition Timing

1. Locate the timing marks and pointer on the lower engine pulley and engine's front cover.
2. Clean the marks and apply chalk or bright-colored paint to the pointer.
3. Attach a timing light according to the manufacturer's specifications.
4. Disconnect and plug all vacuum lines leading to the distributor.
5. If the recommended engine idle speed is in excess of 500 rpm, set the idle at 500 rpm for setting the timing. If the recommended idle speed is below 500 rpm, do not alter it.
6. Aim the timing light at the timing mark and pointer on the front of the engine. If the marks align when the timing light flashes, remove the timing light, set the idle to its proper specification, and connect the vacuum lines at the distributor. If the marks do not align when the light flashes, turn the engine off and loosen the distributor hold-down clamp slightly.
7. Start the engine again, and observe the alignment of the timing marks. To advance the timing, turn the distributor counter-clockwise, on six-cylinder engines, or clockwise, for V8 engines. When altering the timing, it is wise to tap the distributor lightly with a wooden hammer handle to move it in the desired direction. Grasping the distributor with your hand may result in a painful electric shock. When the timing marks are aligned, turn the engine off and tighten the distributor hold-down clamp.

FUEL SYSTEM

Fuel Pump

A single-action, permanently sealed Carter fuel pump is used on all models. On 6-cylinder engines the fuel pump is located on the lower, left center of the engine block. The V8 fuel pump is mounted on the left side of the cylinder front cover.

1975-76 Police Interceptor 460 V8s use a tank-mounted electric fuel pump.

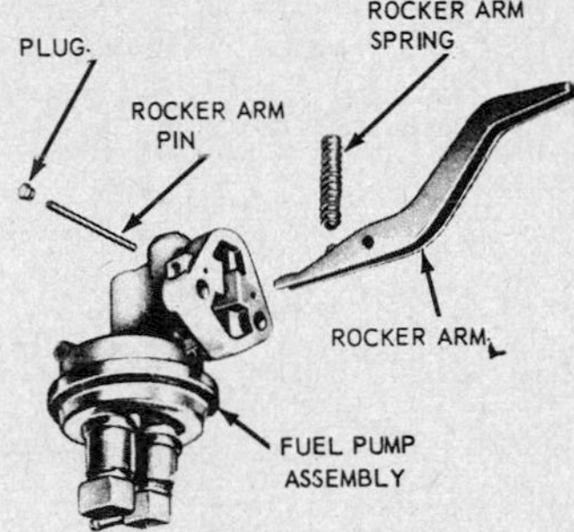

Typical fuel pump—V8 shown
(© Ford Motor Co)

R & R—All Models except 460 PI V8

1. Remove the inlet and outlet lines from the pump.
2. Remove the fuel pump retaining screws and remove the pump and gasket.
3. Clean all gasket material from the pump mounting surface on the engine, and apply a coat of oil-resistant sealer to the new gasket.
4. Position pump on engine and install retaining screws.
5. Reinstall lines, start engine and check for leaks.

NOTE: if resistance is felt while positioning the fuel pump on the block, the camshaft eccentric is in the high position. To ease installation, connect a remote engine starter switch to the engine and "tap" remote switch until resistance fades.

Fuel Filter

All models use a non-serviceable in-line fuel filter which is located at the carburetor fuel inlet.

Fuel Filter R & R

The filter is removed by removing the air cleaner, loosening the hose clamp on the inlet line, and unscrewing the filter. When installing, use a new hose clamp to prevent leakage.

Carburetor

Ford uses eleven types of carburetors: Autolite 1100, Carter YF and RBS (1-barrel), Autolite 2100 and 2150 (2-barrel), Autolite 4100, Autolite 4300, and 4350. Holley 4150 C, Carter Thermo-Quad® and Rochester Quadrajet 4MV (4-barrel).

Idle Speed and Mixture Adjustments

NOTE: Adjust with air cleaner installed.

Idle Speed Adjustment

This is the procedure for adjusting all carburetors; any exceptions are listed below.

NOTE: If the following adjustment fails to produce a satisfactory idle, the following items should be checked: vacuum leaks, ignition wiring continuity, spark plug condition, dwell angle, breaker point condition, ignition timing, carburetor float level, PCV valve condition, valve clearance, cylinder compression, and, failing all else, check for an overly lean air fuel mixture with a CO meter of known accuracy.

1. Run engine at fast idle to equalize operating temperature.
2. Make sure the choke plate is fully released.
3. Turn headlights on high beam. On models equipped with an automatic transmission, apply the parking brake and put the transmission selector lever in Drive.
4. If engine is equipped with hot idle compensator valve, make sure it is fully seated in the closed position.
5. Attach tachometer of known accuracy to the engine.
6. On cars equipped with air conditioning, 1969 models (except 200 6-cylinder and 302 V8 engines with automatic transmission) set idle speer with air conditioner turned ON. On all 1970 and later models the idle speed is set with the air conditioner turned OFF.
7. On 1969 and later models equipped with a temperature sensing valve in the distributor vacuum line, remove and plug the vacuum hoses from the intake manifold to the valve, at the valve located in the intake manifold. Also plug the intake manifold hose fitting on the valve.
8. Make sure the dashpot is working freely and not binding.
9. If it is not possible to adjust the idle speed with the air cleaner installed, the engine idle speed must be rechecked after installing the air cleaner. On cars with vacuum controlled heat ducts in the air cleaner, the vacuum line must be plugged if the carburetor is to be adjusted with the air cleaner removed.
10. On carburetors which do not have an electric throttle solenoid, turn the idle speed adjusting screw inward or outward to obtain the specified idle speed. On 1969–71 models which have a throttle solenoid, turn the solenoid plunger in or out to obtain the higher of the two idle speeds listed in the "Tune-up Specifications" table. On 1972-76 models which are equipped with a throttle solenoid, turn the throttle solenoid adjustment screw inward or outward to obtain the higher of the two idle speeds listed in the "Tune-up Specifications" table.
11. If equipped with a throttle solenoid, disconnect the lead wire from the solenoid and turn the curb idle adjusting screw on the carburetor to obtain the lower of the two idle speeds listed in the "Tune-up Specifications" table. On models equipped with an automatic transmission, place the transmission selector lever in Park or neutral before adjusting the lower idle speed.

NOTE: with the electric solenoid disengaged, the carburetor adjusting screw must make contact with the throttle shaft to prevent the throttle plates from jamming in the throttle bore when the engine is shut off.

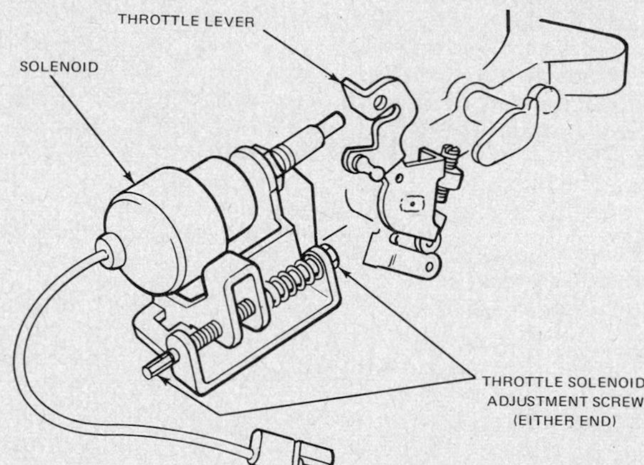

1972-74 throttle solenoid adjustment—Motorcraft 2100-D and 4300 installation shown (© Ford Motor Co)

Carburetor adjustments—solenoid equipped Carter RBS IV (© Ford Motor Co)

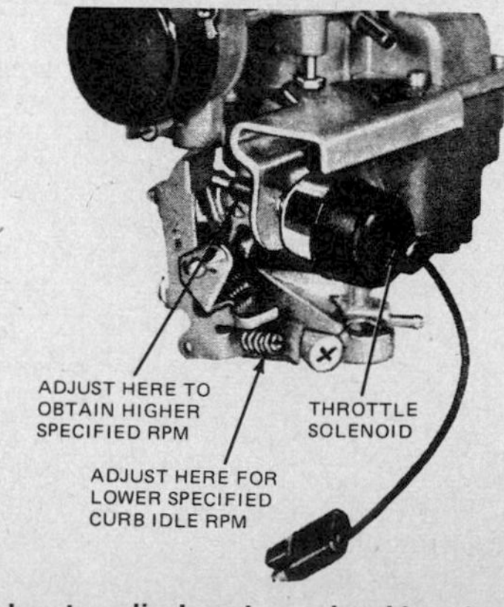

Carburetor adjustments—solenoid equipped Carter YF IV (© Ford Motor Co)

Fuel Mixture Adjustment

On 1968 and later models with idle mixture limiters, adjust by turning the idle mixture adjusting screw(s) inward to obtain the smoothest idle possible *within the range of the idle limiters. Limiter caps should not be removed,* unless a CO meter is available to bring the emissions within the legal limits.

Dashpot Adjustment

Type A Dashpots

1. Adjust throttle to fast idle position and turn dashpot adjusting screw out until it is clear of dashpot plunger assembly.
2. Turn screw in until it contacts plunger. Then turn dashpot adjusting screw in specified number of turns against plunger.

NOTE: Not all engines are equipped with dashpots, and not all are adjusted in this manner. This chart applies only to models mentioned.

Year, Engines and Models	*No. of Turns*
1969 Falcon and Mustang 200 six cylinder with automatic	2¼
1969 Falcon and Mustang 200 six cylinder with manual transmission	3¼

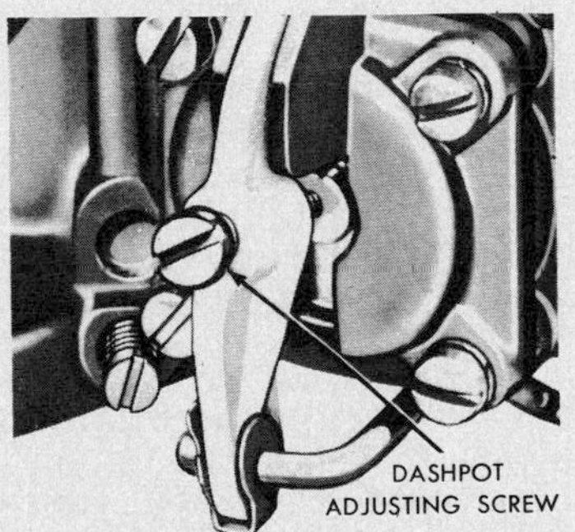

Type A dashpot adjustment (© Ford Motor Co)

Type B Dashpots

1. With engine idle speed and mixture properly adjusted and with engine at operating temperature, loosen dashpot lock nut.
2. Hold throttle in closed position and depress dashpot plunger. Measure clearance between plunger and cam. Adjust dashpot nut to give proper clearance.

Type B Anti-stall dashpot adjustment
(© Ford Motor Co)

NOTE: Not all engines have dashpots and not all are adjusted in this manner. This chart applies only to models mentioned.

Year, Model and Engine	*Clearance Manual (in.)*	*Clearance Automatic (in.)*
1969 Montego, Fairlane and Mustang 250 six except when solenoid equipped	0.080	
1969 302 2V	⅛	⅛
1969 351 Windsor 2V	7/64	
1969 351 Windsor 4V	3/32	
1969 390 4V	⅛	
1969 428 CJ	0.100	0.100
1969 Falcon 170 six	0.100	0.100
1970-71 170 and 200 six cylinder if so equipped	7/64	7/64
1970-71 Montego, Fairlane, and Mustang 250 six		7/32
1970 302 2V without air conditioning		⅛
1970-71 351 Windsor 2V without air conditioning		⅛
1970-71 351 Cleveland 2V without air conditioning		⅛
1970-71 351 Cleveland 4V without air conditioning		0.080
1970 429 4V Montego and Fairlane	0.070	0.070
1970 428 CJ without air conditioning	0.140	0.200

Throttle Linkage Adjustments

Linkage adjustment procedures are found in the Automatic Transmission Section.

COOLING SYSTEM

In the 6-cylinder engine, coolant flows from the cylinder head, past the thermostat (if it is open) and into the radiator upper tank. In the V8 engine, coolant from each cylinder head flows through water passages in the intake manifold, then past the thermostat (if it is open) and into the radiator upper tank.

A single water pump assembly is used. The pump has a sealed bearing integral with the water pump shaft. The bearing requires no lubrication. There is a bleed hole in the water pump housing. This is not a lubrication hole.

Some models are equipped with a coolant recovery or "constant full" system. These systems have a non-vented radiator cap that forces coolant expansion into an expansion reservoir. When adding coolant to these systems, add coolant to the reservoir only, not the radiator.

Radiator

Removal

1. Drain cooling system.
2. Disconnect upper and lower hoses at the radiator.
3. On automatic transmission-equipped cars, disconnect oil cooler lines at radiator.
4. On vehicles equipped with a fan shroud, remove the shroud retaining screws and position the shroud out of the way.
5. Remove radiator attaching bolts and lift out the radiator.

Installation

1. If a new radiator is to be installed, transfer the petcock from the old radiator to the new one. On cars equipped with automatic transmissions, transfer the oil cooler line fittings from the old radiator to the new one.
2. Position the radiator and install, but do not tighten, the radiator support bolts. On cars equipped with automatic transmissions, connect the oil cooler lines. Then tighten the radiator support bolts.
3. On vehicles equipped with a fan shroud, reinstall the shroud.
4. Connect the radiator hoses. Close the radiator petcock. Then fill and bleed the cooling system.
5. Start the engine and bring to operating temperature. Check for leaks.
6. On cars equipped with automatic transmissions, check the cooler lines for leaks and interference. Check transmission fluid level.

Water Pump R & R

1. Drain cooling system.
2. On 351C, 351M, and 400 V8, disconnect the negative battery cable.
3. On cars with power steering, remove the drive belt. On models with 390 or 428 engines, remove the power steering mounting retaining screws and remove the pump and bracket as an asembly and position it out of the way.
4. If the vehicle is equipped with air conditioning, remove the idler pulley bracket and air conditioner drive belt.
5. On engines with Thermactor, remove the belt.
6. Disconnect the lower radiator hose and heater hose from the water pump.
7. On cars equipped with a fan shroud, remove the retaining screws and position the shroud rearward.
8. Remove the fan and spacer from the engine, and if the car is equipped with a fan shroud, remove the fan and shroud from the engine as an assembly.
9. Loosen alternator mounting bolts, remove the alternator belt and remove the alternator adjusting arm bracket from the water pump.

10. Loosen bypass hose at water pump.
11. Remove water pump retaining screws and remove pump from engine.
12. Clean any gasket material from the pump mounting surface, and on 429 V8 remove the water pump backing plate and replace the gasket.

NOTE: The 250 6-cylinder engine originally uses a one-piece gasket for the cylinder front cover and water pump. Trim away the old gasket at the edge of the cylinder cover and replace with service gasket.

13. Remove the heater hose fitting from the old pump and install it on the new pump.
14. Coat both sides of the new gasket with a water-resistant sealer, then re-install pump reversing the above procedure.

Thermostat R & R

1. Open the drain cock and drain the radiator so the coolant level is below the coolant outlet elbow which houses the thermostat.
2. Remove the outlet elbow retaining bolts and position the elbow sufficiently clear of the intake manifold or cylinder head to provide access to the thermostat.
3. Remove the thermostat by rotating it in a counterclockwise direction and lifting it from the housing.
4. Clean the mating surfaces of the outlet elbow and the engine to remove all old gasket material and sealer. Coat the new gasket with water-resistant sealer and install it on the engine. Install the thermostat in the outlet elbow. On the above-mention engines (step three), the thermostat must be rotated clockwise to lock it in position.
5. Install the outlet elbow and retaining bolts on the engine. Torque the bolts to 12–15 ft lbs.
6. Refill the radiator. Run the engine at operating temperature and check for leaks. Recheck the coolant level.

EMISSION CONTROLS

All Models

All Ford cars covered in this text use positive crankcase ventilation (PCV) systems. The PCV system routes a harmful mixture of blow-by gases and condensation vapors, which were formerly dispelled into the atmosphere, through a modulating valve (PCV valve) and into the intake manifold where they combine with the carburetor air fuel mixture and are burned in the combustion chamber.

1969

On 1969 cars with manual transmissions, and 1969-71 high-performance V8 models, the Thermacter (air injection) system was used. This system, which injects fresh air into the exhaust ports to achieve afterburning of raw exhaust fumes, consists of an air pump, a bypass and a check valve, and external air manifolds (not an integral part of the engine exhaust manifolds), and air injector tubes in the exhaust ports.

In order to comply with federal antipollution laws, Ford Motor Company adopted the IMCO (IMproved COmbustion) emission control system in 1968. Rather than burning the exhaust gases in the exhaust manifolds, as in the Thermactor system, the IMCO system reduces carbon monoxide and hydrocarbons through more complete combustion in the combustion chambers. This is accomplished through the use of a heated air intake system which thermostatically supplies air, which has been warmed by the exhaust manifold, as needed, to the air cleaner, as well as idle mixture limiter caps which prevent the air fuel mixture from being adjusted to an overly rich condition at idle, and control of ignition timing by a dual diaphragm vacuum advance mechanism on the distributor and a ported vacuum or temperature override switch (PVS). The outer chamber of the dual vacuum advance is controlled by carburetor vacuum and the inner chamber by intake manifold vacuum. During normal engine operation the outer diaphragm advances ignition timing, while the inner diaphragm retards timing at idle. Three vacuum hoses are attached to the PVS switch; the top hose is connected to the carburetor, the second to the distributor, and the third to the intake manifold. When the engine is operating under normal temperature conditions, vacuum is supplied to the distributor vacuum advance by the carburetor. If the engine should overheat, the PVS switch connects intake manifold vacuum to the distributor which advances ignition timing while the engine is idling, thus speeding up the engine and lowering engine temperature.

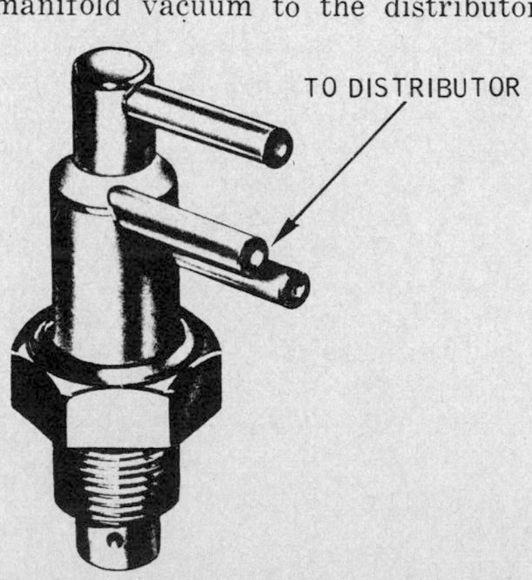

Distributor vacuum control valve (ported vacuum switch)
(© Ford Motor Co)

In 1969, to further aid in reducing emissions, a distributor vacuum advance (deceleration) control valve and a throttle solenoid were used on some models. The deceleration valve provides maximum intake manifold vacuum to the distributor and subsequent timing advance to prevent backfiring in the exhaust system when the vehicle is slowing down.

The throttle solenoid is located on the side of the carburetor. When the ignition key is turned On, the throttle solenoid plunger extends and contacts the carburetor throttle lever, raising the idle speed of the engine. When the ignition key is turned off, the solenoid lever retracts, allowing the carburetor throttle lever to fall back on the carburetor idle speed adjusting screw. This prevents the engine from running-on when the key is turned off.

1970-71

The fuel evaporative emission control system was used on California models in 1970, and nationwide in 1971. This system eliminates pollution due to evaporating fuel by channeling the breathing of the fuel tank and by the venting of the carburetor float bowl through a canister filled with activated charcoal, condensing the fuel vapors and returning them to the fuel system.

The IMCO system of emission control was further extended in 1970 to become the Distributor Modulator (Dist-O-Vac) System. The Dist-O-Vac system incorporated all of the IMCO features but included three units of equipment which control spark advance in a more sophisticated manner. A speed sensor is located between two sections of the speedometer cable and generates a small current which increases in direct proportion to speed. A thermal switch is located in the right door pillar and activates at outside temperatures of 58° or higher. The impulses of both are fed into the electonic control amplifier. The distributor vacuum advance hose is connected from the carburetor, through the electronic control amplifier, to the distributor. When ambient temperature is above 58°, the contacts in the temperature switch open, and a plunger in the amplifier prevents vacuum from being supplied to the distributor. When vehicle speed reaches approximately 30 mph, the signal from the speed sensor causes the control amplifier to open the vacuum line to the distributor and ignition timing is allowed to advance in the normal manner. When the ambient temperature is below 58°, the temperature switch closes, and normal vacuum is supplied to the distributor regardless of vehicle

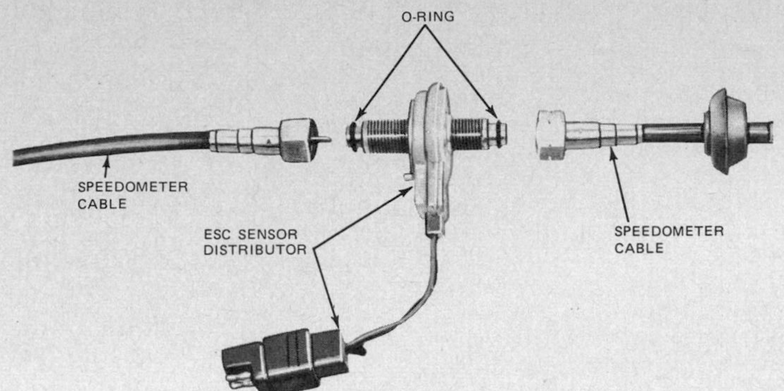

Speed sensor location (© Ford Motor Co)

speed. In the event of engine overheating, the ported vacuum switch (PVS), a carryover from the IMCO system, overrides the electronic control modulator by connecting intake manifold vacuum to the distributor.

1972

For 1972, the Dist-O-Vac system was replaced by two different spark control systems. The Electronic Spark Control (ESC) system is the same as the old Dist-O-Vac system except that the electronic control modulator was separated into two pieces, an amplifier and a distributor modulator valve. The amplifier judges the signals sent to it by the speed and temperature switches and tells the distributor modulator valve when to open and close and thus allow or prevent vacuum to reach the distributor. The Transmission Regulated Spark (TRS) is similar to the ESC system except that the speed sensor is replaced by a transmission switch. The switch is mounted on the side of the transmission and is hydraulically actuated on cars equipped with an automatic transmission and manually actuated on models equipped with a manual transmission. When the ambient temperature is above 55°, the transmission switch is closed whenever the transmission is in any gear other than high gear (manual transmission), or high gear or reverse (automatic transmission). When the transmission switch closes, it signals the distributor modulator valve to close and thus prevents carburetor vacuum from reaching the distributor. As in past systems, neither of these systems is functional below 55–58°, and both are bypassed by the PVS if the engine should overheat.

On most 1972 and later models, a spark delay valve was inserted into the vacuum advance line to the distributor. The valve closes under hard acceleration, blocking carburetor vacuum to the distributor for a predetermined period of seconds. The valves are color coded for identification purposes.

1973

1973 and later models utilize an Exhaust Gas Recirculation System (EGR) to control oxides of nitrogen. On V8 engines, exhaust gases travel through the exhaust gas crossover passage in the intake manifold. A portion of these gases is diverted into a spacer which is mounted under the carburetor The EGR control valve, which is attached to the rear of the spacer, consists of a vacuum diaphragm with an attached plunger which normally blocks off exhaust gases from entering the intake manifold. On 6 cylinder engines, an external tube carries exhaust manifold gases to the carburetor spacer. On all models except those equipped with a 250 six-cylinder and manual transmission, the EGR valve is controlled by a vacuum line from the carburetor which passes through a ported vacuum switch. The EGR ported vacuum switch provides vacuum to the EGR valve at coolant temperature above 125°F. The vacuum diaphragm then opens the EGR valve permitting exhaust gases to flow through the carburetor spacer and enter the intake manifold where they combine with the fuel mixture and enter the combustion chambers. The exhaust gases are relatively oxygen-free, and tend to dilute the combustion charge. This lowers peak combustion temperature thereby reducing oxides of nitrogen.

1973-74 Torinos and Montegos equipped with a 250 six-cylinder engine and manual transmission have a combined spark control and EGR system called "TRS+1." The spark control portion of this system is identical to the TRS system described under "1972." Operation of the EGR control valve is governed by vacuum from either the distributor vacuum port on the carburetor or the EGR vacuum port. When the TRS system is not in operation. EGR valve vacuum comes from the EGR port on the carburetor. The vacuum passes through a coolant temperature vacuum valve and a three-way solenoid valve. The coolant valve blocks vacuum from the EGR valve until the engine coolant temperature has reached 60° F. The vacuum lines from both the EGR and distributor vacuum ports on the carburetor connect to the three-way solenoid valve. The third line is an outlet line to the EGR valve. When the TRS system is not in operation, the three-way solenoid valve is deenergized. When the TRS system is in operation, the solenoid is energized, blocking the EGR port on the three-way solenoid, and opening the distributor port to the EGR valve. When the transmission is shifted into high gear, the TRS and three-way solenoids are de-energized. This restores normal vacuum to the distributor and the EGR valve.

All models equipped with a 250 six-cylinder engine and automatic transmission and built prior to March 15, 1973, use another system to control distributor spark advance. The system, known as the Temperature Activated Vacuum (TAV) system, contains a three-way solenoid valve, an ambient temperature switch, and a vacuum bleed line to the air cleaner. The operation of the three way solenoid valve is identical to the valve described above for 250 manual transmission engines. The only difference is that the output line of the three-way valve is connected to the distributor. When the ambient temperature is above 60°, the contacts in the temperature sensor close and complete the circuit to the three-way solenoid. This energizes the solenoid and connects the EGR vacuum port on the carburetor to the distributor vaccum advance. When the ambient temperature is below 49°, the solenoid is de-energized and the distributor

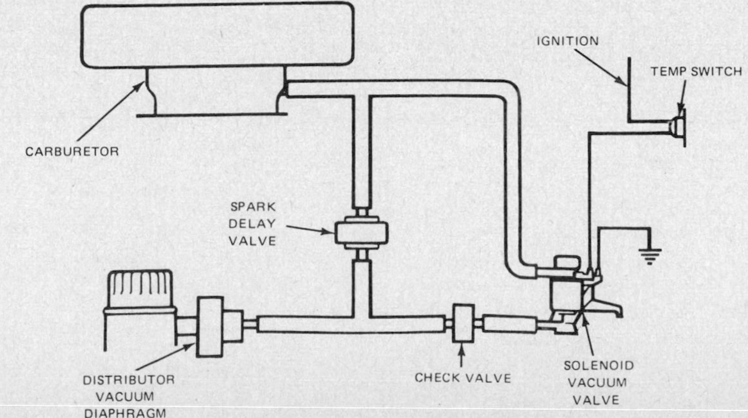

Delay vacuum by-pass system—DVB (© Ford Motor Co)

vacuum advance operates in the normal manner.

1973 Torino and Montego station wagons equipped with a 302 or 351W V8 and manual transmission and all 1973 models that are equipped with a 351C, 400, or 429 V8 built prior to March 15, 1973, use a Delay Vacuum By-Pass (DVB) spark control system. This system provides two paths by which carburetor vacuum can reach the distributor vacuum advance. The system consists of a spark delay valve, a check valve, a solenoid vacuum valve, and an ambient temperature switch. When the ambient temperature is below 49°F. the temperature switch contacts and the vacuum solenoid are open (de-energized). Under these conditions, vacuum will flow from the carburetor, through the open solenoid, and to the distributor. Since the spark delay valve resists the flow of carburetor vacuum, the vacuum will always flow through the vacuum solenoid when it is open, since this is the path of least resistance. When the ambient temperature rises above 60°F. the contacts in the temperature switch (which is located in the door post) close. This passes ignition switch current to the solenoid, energizing the solenoid. This blocks one of the vacuum paths. All distributor vacuum must now flow through the spark delay valve. When carburetor vacuum rises above a certain level on acceleration, a rubber valve in the spark delay valve blocks vacuum from passing through the valve for 5-30 seconds. After this delay, normal vacuum is supplied to the distributor. When the vacuum solenoid is closed (temperature above 60°), the vacuum line from the solenoid to the distributor is vented to atmosphere. To prevent the vacuum that is passing through the spark delay valve from escaping through the solenoid into the atmosphere, a one-way check valve is installed in the vacuum line from the solenoid to the distributor.

All 1973 and later models use an electric choke heating element. When ambient temperature is above 63°, and the ignition switch is turned on, a heating element in the choke housing raises the temperature of the choke bimetallic spring, thus preventing the choke from engaging.

1974

1974 models sold in California and all 1975 models are equipped with a Thermactor (air injection) system to reduce hydrocarbons and carbon monoxide. This system is used in addition to the previously mentioned EGR and IMCO systems, which are used to reduce oxides of nitrogen.

A Cold Temperature Actuated Vacuum (CTAV) System is installed on some 1973 models manfactured after March 15, 1973 and many 1974 models to control distributor spark advance. It is basically a refinement of the DVB or TAV spark control systems with the temperature switch relocated in the air cleaner and a latching relay added to maintain a strong vacuum signal at the distributor, whether it be EGR port or spark port carburetor vacuum, and to keep the system from intermittently switching vacuum signals when the intake air is between 49 and 60° F. When the temperature switch closes at 60° F, the latching relay (normally off) is energized and stays on until the ignition switch is turned off. The latching relay then overrides the temperature switch and forces the solenoid valve to keep the spark port vacuum system closed and open the EGR port vacuum system. This prevents full vacuum advance, once the engine is warmed-up, thereby lowering emissions.

The EGR/CSC system is used on most 1974 and later models. It regulates both distributor spark advance and EGR valve operation, according to coolant temperature, by sequentially switching vacuum sources. The major components are:

a. 95°F EGR-PVS valve,
b. spark delay valve (SDV), and
c. a vacuum check valve.

When coolant temperature is below 85°F, the EGR-PVS valve admits carburetor EGR port vacuum (at about 2500 rpm) directly to the distributor advance diaphragm through a one-way check valve. At the same time, EGR-PVS valve shuts off carburetor EGR vacuum to the EGR valve and transmission diaphragm.

When coolant temperature is above 95° F, the EGR-PVS valve is actuated and admits carburetor EGR vacuum to the EGR valve and transmission instead of the distributor. At temperatures between 82° and 95°F, the EGR-PVS valve may be open, closed, or in midposition.

1975-76

Catalytic converters are installed in all 1975 and later cars sold in California, and on most 1975 models sold in the 49 states with the following exceptions; 250 six-cylinder and 302 V8 Mavericks and Comets, 250 six-cylinder 2-door Granadas and Monarchs. Torino, Elite, Montego and Cougar models sold in California use dual converters.

All 1976 models use a catalytic converter system.

The catalyst units convert emissions of hydrocarbons and carbon monoxide into harmless carbon dioxide and water, and in some cases, small amounts of possibly harmful sulfur dioxide (rotten egg odor) or (when mixed with water) sulphuric acid. The reaction takes place inside the converters at great heat (1300-1500°F) using platinum and

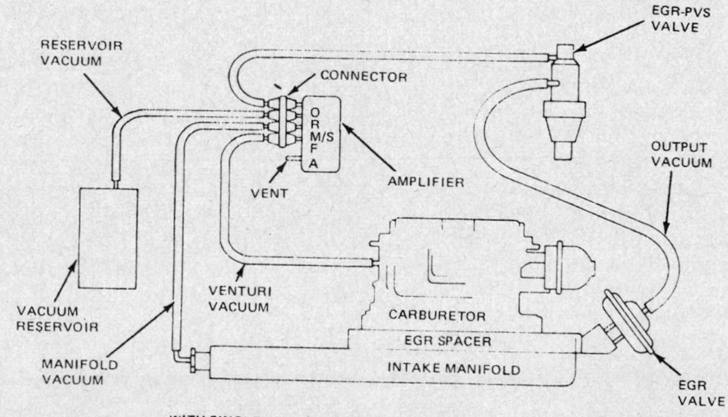

WITH SINGLE CONNECTOR VVA (1974 TYPE)

RESERVOIR VACUUM
VENT
EGR-PVS VALVE
AMPLIFIER
A
S R
V O
CHECK VALVE
VENTURI VACUUM
OUTPUT VACUUM
CONNECTOR
SPARK OR EGR PORT VACUUM
VACUUM RESERVOIR
CARBURETOR
EGR SPACER
INTAKE MANIFOLD
EGR VALVE
MANIFOLD VACUUM

Typical 1974-76 EGR system components
(© Ford Motor Co)

THERMACTOR NON-CATALYST SYSTEM
- Used on vehicles without catalytic converter.
- Same as 1974 except as shown.

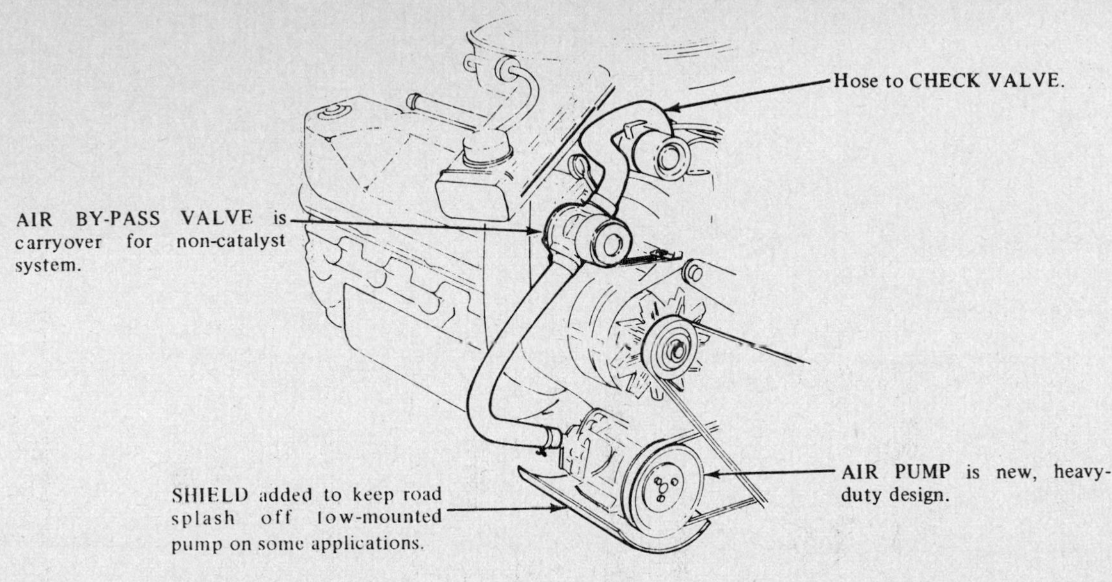

THERMACTOR CATALYST SYSTEM
- Used on vehicles with catalytic converter.

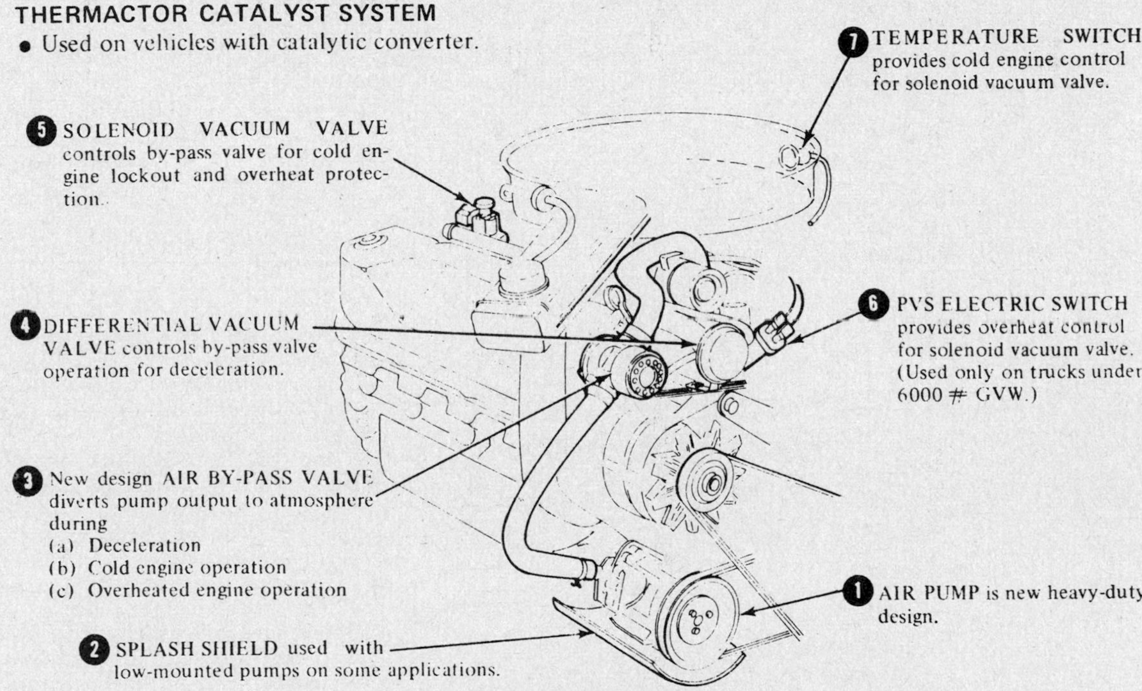

1975-76 Thermactor systems
(© Ford Motor Co)

palladium metals as the catalyst. The units are installed in the exhaust system, upstream from the mufflers. They are designed, if the engine is kept in proper tune and *only* unleaded fuel is used, to last 50,000 miles before replacement.

On models using the 460 V8 engine, a Cold Start Spark Advance (CSSA) System is used to improve cold engine operation. When the coolant temperature is below 125° F, carburetor ported vacuum is routed to the distributor through a spark delay valve and coolant temperature operated vacuum valve (PVS).

Another aid to cold engine operation is a "cold weather modulator," which is added to the heated air intake system. When the ambient temperature is below 55° F and the engine is cold, the cold weather modulator prevents the door in the air cleaner snorkel from opening to the fresh air position under hard acceleration. Above 55° F, the door works the same as in other years; i.e., opening under hard acceleration or when the engine has reached normal operating temperatures.

All 1975 engines have a spacer entry EGR valve mounted on a spacer beneath the carburetor. This replaces the "floor entry" system used on some 1974 engines.

Positive crankcase ventilation (PCV) and evaporative emission control systems are carryovers from previous years.

To futher aid cold start driveability during engine warmup, most 1975 engines use a vacuum Operated Heat Valve (VOHV) located between the exhaust manifold and the exhaust inlet (header) pipe.

When the engine is first started, the valve is closed, blocking exhaust gases from exiting from one bank of cylin-

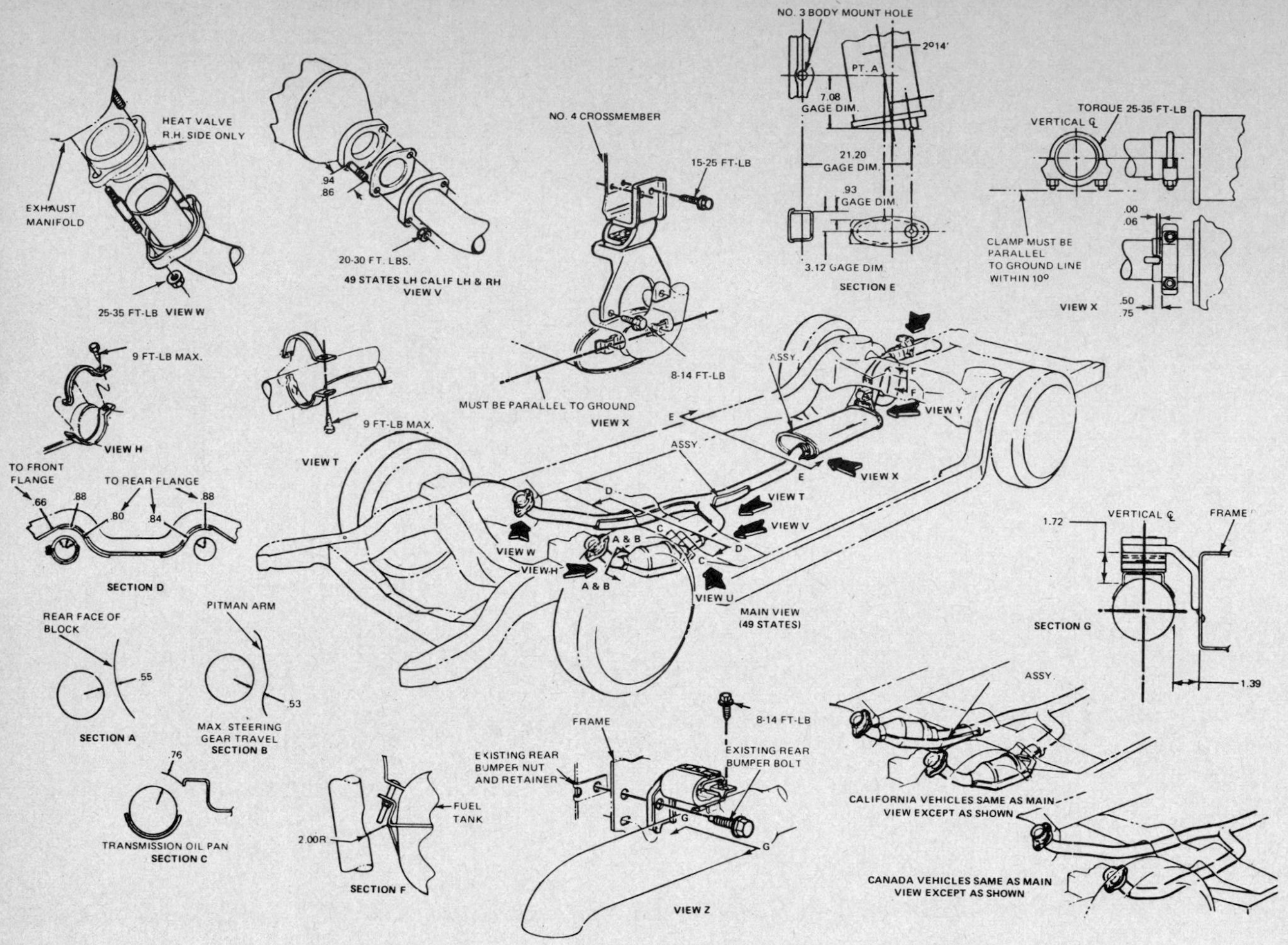

Typical catalytic converter installation—1975-76 Torino, Elite, Montego and Cougar (body/frame cars) shown
(© Ford Motor Co)

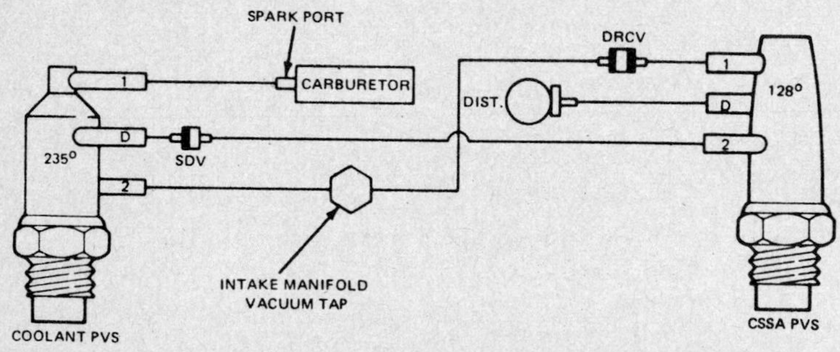

CSSA System schematic
(© Ford Motor Co)

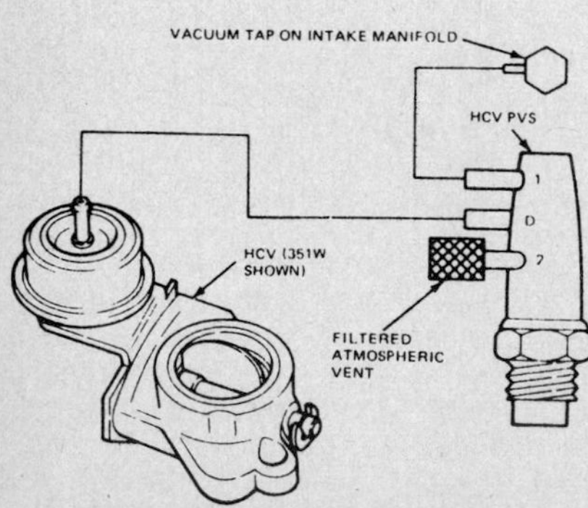

VOHV System schematic
(© Ford Motor Co)

ders. These gases are then diverted back through the intake manifold crossover passage under the carburetor and choke. The VOHV is controlled by a ported vacuum switch which uses manifold vacuum to keep the vacuum motor on the valve closed until the coolant reaches a predetermined "warm-up" value. When the engine is warmed-up, the PVS shuts off vacuum to the VOHV, and a strong return spring opens the VOHV butterfly.

The complexity of the emission control equipment on all Ford vehicles has been substantially reduced in 1976 due to the more extensive use of catalyst and catalytic converters. All 1976 model passenger cars have catalytic converters. The average number of emission control components has been reduced from 25 to 11 on most cars.

In addition, a new exhaust gas recirculation signal vacuum control system is used on all 1976 V8 engines. The new system uses an exhaust backpressure transducer to regulate the EGR valve spark port vacuum signal which modulates the flow of EGR. This more accurately matches the amount of EGR to the engine load; improving engine driveability and fuel economy.

For system checks and adjustments, see "Emission Control Systems" in the Unit Repair Section.

ENGINE

There were three different six-cylinder engines available in compact and intermediate size Ford products from 1968-72: the 170, the 200 and the 250 cu. in. engines. The 170 engine was dropped from production in 1973. These engines are all of the same family, and the only great difference among them is their bore and stroke. One distinguishing characteristic that makes these engines easily identifiable is the fact that the intake manifold is cast as an integral part of the cylinder head.

Optional V8 engines for these models are very numerous, and like the family of six-cylinder engines, there is a great amount of similarity among them.

Th most widely used are the 302 V8s. These are remarkably compact engines with stud-mounted rockers and wedge-shaped combustion chambers.

In 1969, Ford Motor Company introduced a longer stroke, higher block version of the 302 engine. This engine is the 351 Windsor engine and features the wedge-shaped combustion chambers and stud-mounted rockers of the small block engine in a new intermediate sized block.

A high-performance version of the 302 engine was also introduced in 1969. Called the Boss 302, this engine featured mechanical valve lifters and large valve—small spark plug cylinder heads similar to the ones that were used on the 1970 and later 351 Cleveland engines.

In 1970, Ford Motor Company added the 351 Cleveland engine. The 351 Cleveland engine has the same bore and stroke as the Windsor engine, and there most of the resemblance ends. It has different main bearing size, larger valves, smaller plugs, and semi-hemispherical combustion chambers. It is used concurrently with the Windsor engine and is found in many of the same models. A longer stroke, 400 cu in. version of the 351 Cleveland V8 was introduced in 1972. In 1975, all 351C engines are designated 351M, for modified Cleveland.

The Boss 302 V8 was eliminated from production in 1971, and it was replaced by a high-performance version of the 351 Cleveland engine. It is designated as the 351 HO (High Output) engine, available on 1971-72 models.

Starting in 1970, some Montegos, Cyclones and Torinos used the big block 429 V8. This V8 came in three forms. The first was the 429 engine, which is the same as was used in full sized Mercury and Ford cars. The second was the 429CJ engine which used stronger rods, big valve heads, smaller 14 mm. plugs, and an ignition governor set at 5,800 rpm. The third was the 429 Super CJ, which was similar to the 429 CJ except for forged pistons, four bolt main caps, solid lifters, and a 6,000 rpm governor. The 429 CJ and SCJ were discontinued after the 1971 model year run. The standard performance 429-4V V8 was available through 1973. Beginning 1974, a similar 460 4V V8 is used in some heavy-duty applications.

Engine Removal

1. Scribe the hood hinge outline on the under-hood, disconnect the hood and remove.
2. Drain the entire cooling system and crankcase.
3. Remove the air cleaner, disconnect the battery at the cylinder head. On automatic transmission equipped cars, disconnect oil cooler lines at the radiator.
4. Remove upper and lower radiator hoses and remove radiator. If equipped with air conditioning, unbolt compressor and position compressor out of way with refrigerant lines intact. Unbolt and lay refrigerant radiator forward without disconnecting refrigerant lines.

NOTE: If there is not enough slack in the refrigerant lines to position the compressor out of the way, the refrigerant in the system must be evacuated (using proper safety precautions) before the lines can be disconnected from the compressor.

On some 428 CJ engines and all 429 Super CJ, Boss 302, and Boss 429 engines disconnect inlet and outlet lines from engine oil cooler, remove hold-down bracket and remove cooler.

5. Remove fan, fan belt and upper pully.
6. Disconnect the heater hoses from the engine.
7. Disconnect the alternator wires at the alternator, the starter cable at the starter, the accelerator rod at the carburetor.
8. Disconnect fuel tank line at the fuel pump and plug the line.
9. Disconnect the coil primary wire at the coil. Disconnect wires at the oil pressure and water temperature sending units.
10. Remove the starter and dust seal.
11. On a car equipped with a manual-shift transmission, remove the clutch retracting spring. Disconnect the clutch equalizer shaft and arm bracket at the underbody rail and remove the arm bracket and equalizer shaft.
12. Raise the car. Remove the flywheel or converter housing upper retaining bolts.
13. Disconnect the exhaust pipe or pipes at the exhaust manifold. Disconnect the right and left motor mount at the underbody bracket. Remove the flywheel or converter housing cover.
14. On a car with manual shift, remove the flywheel housing lower retaining bolts.
15. On a car equipped with automatic transmission, disconnect throttle valve vacuum line at the intake manifold (2 lines on 1973 models) disconnect the converter from the flywheel. Remove the converter housing lower retaining bolts. On a car with power steering, disconnect power steering pump from cylinder head. Put drive belt and wire steering pump out of the way.
16. Lower the car. Support the transmission and flywheel or converter housing with a jack.
17. Attach an engine lifting hook. Lift the engine up and out of the compartment and onto an adequate workstand.

Engine Installation

1. Place a new gasket over the studs of the exhaust manifold/s.
2. Attach engine sling and lifting device. Lift engine from workstand.
3. Lower the engine into the engine compartment. Be sure the exhaust manifold/s is in proper alignment with the muffler inlet pipe/s, and the dowels in the block engage the holes in the flywheel housing.
   On a car with automatic transmission, start the converter pilot into the crankshaft.
   On a car with manual-shift transmission, start the transmission main drive gear into the clutch disc. If the engine hangs up after the shaft enters, rotate the crankshaft slowly (with transmission in gear) until the shaft and clutch disc splines mesh.
4. Install the flywheel or converter housing upper bolts.
5. Install engine support insulator to bracket retaining nuts. Disconnect engine lifting sling and remove lifting brackets.
6. Raise front of car. Connect exhaust line/s and tighten attachments.
7. Position dust seal and install starter.
8. On cars with manual-shift transmissions, install remaining flywheel housing-to-engine bolts. Connect clutch release rod. Position the clutch equalizer bar and bracket, and install retaining bolts. Install clutch pedal retracting spring.
9. On cars with automatic transmissions, remove the retainer holding the converter in the housing. Attach the converter to the flywheel. Install the converter housing inspection cover and the remaining converter housing retaining bolts.
10. Remove the support from the transmission and lower the car.
11. Connect engine ground strap and coil primary wire.
12. Connect water temperature gauge wire and the heater hose at coolant outlet housing. Connect accelerator rod at the bellcrank.
13. On cars with automatic transmission, connect the transmission filler tube bracket. Connect the throttle valve vacuum line.
14. On cars with power steering, install the drive belt and power

steering pump bracket. Install the bracket retaining bolts. Adjust drive belt to proper tension.
15. Remove plug from the fuel tank line. Connect the flexible fuel line and the oil pressure sending unit wire.
16. Install the pulley, belt, spacer, and fan. Adjust belt tension.
17. Tighten alternator adjusting bolts. Connect generator wires and the battery ground cable.
18. Install radiator. Connect radiator hoses. On air conditioned cars, install compressor and refrigerant radiator. On some 428 CJ engines, and all 429 Super CJ, Boss 302, and Boss 429 engines, install engine oil cooler and hold-down bracket and connect inlet and outlet lines.
19. On cars with automatic transmission, connect oil cooler lines.
20. Install oil filter. Connect heater hose at water pump, after bleeding the system.
21. Bring crankcase to level with correct grade of oil. Run engine at fast idle and check for leaks. Install air cleaner and make final engine adjustments.
22. Install and adjust hood.
23. Road-test car.

Intake Manifold R & R

6 Cylinder

170, 200 and 250 cu. in. sixes have intake manifolds that are integral with the cylinder head and cannot be removed.

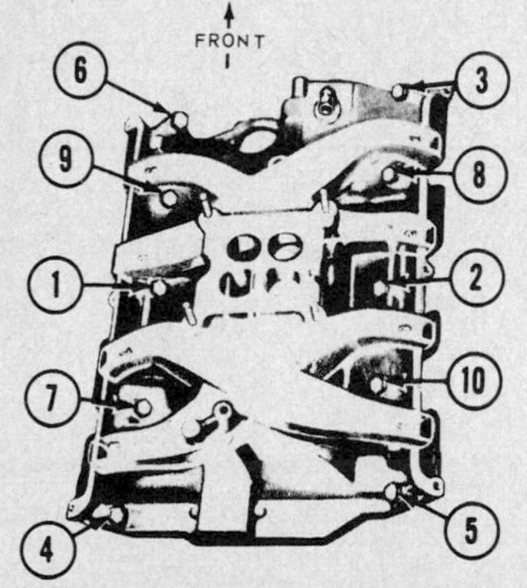

Intake manifold torque sequence— 390 and 428 V8
(© Ford Motor Co)

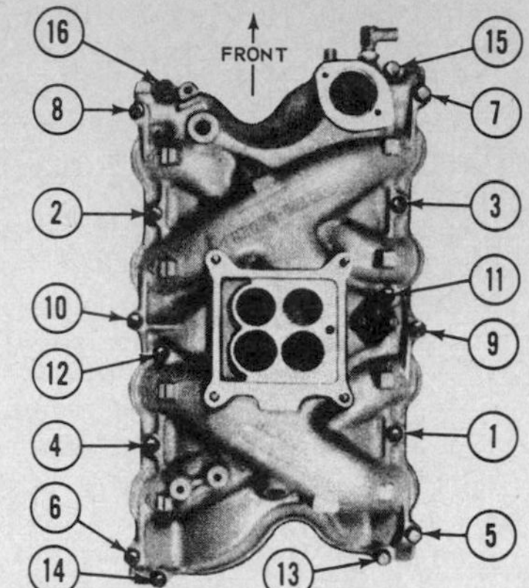

Intake manifold torque sequence—1970-73 429, 1974-76 460 V8
(© Ford Motor Co)

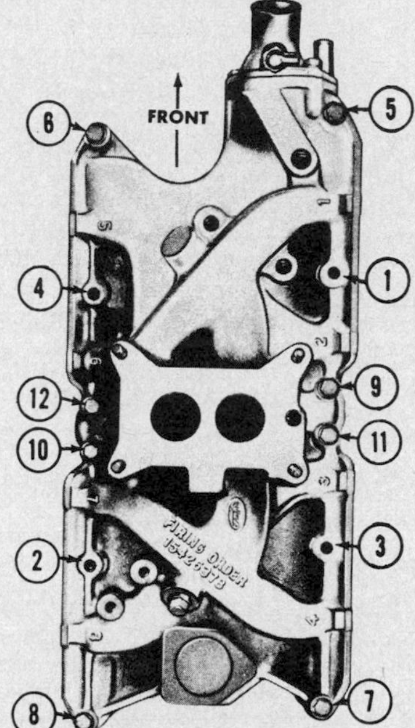

Intake manifold torque sequence—302 V8
(© Ford Motor Co)

302, 351W, 390, 428, 429, 429CJ, 429SCJ, and 460

1. Drain the cooling system.
2. Disconnect the upper radiator hose from the thermostat housing and the bypass hose from the manifold.
3. Remove the air cleaner and ducts.
4. Remove the distributor cap and wires from the engine. Mark the position of the distributor rotor in relationship to the intake manifold, remove the primary wire from the coil, then remove the distributor hold-down bolt and the distributor.
5. Remove all vacuum lines from the intake manifold and remove the temperature sending unit wire.
6. Disconnect the fuel line and any vacuum lines from the carburetor.
7. Remove all carburetor linkage and kickdown linkage that attaches to the intake manifold.
8. On 390, 427 and 428 engines, remove the valve covers, the rocker arm assemblies and the pushrods. The rocker arms should be removed by backing off each of the four bolts two turns in sequence from front to back. Keep pushrods in order so that they can be installed in their original position.
9. Remove the manifold attaching bolts and remove the manifold. If it is necessary to pry the manifold to loosen it from the engine, use care not to damage any gasket sealing surfaces.
10. Clean all gasket surfaces and firmly cement new gaskets in place. The gaskets should be securely locked in place before attempting to install the manifold.
11. Reverse above procedure to reinstall.

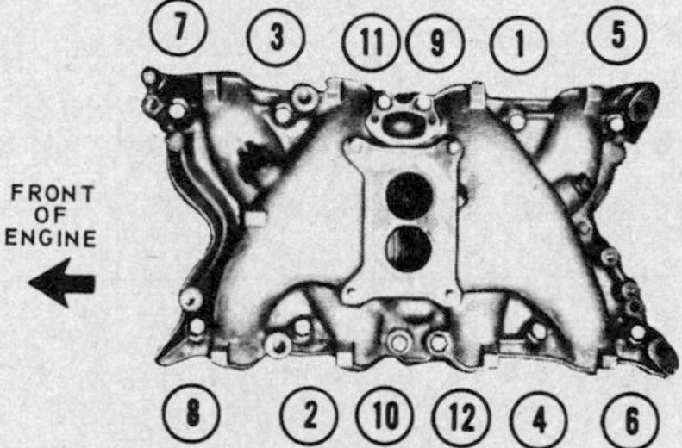

Intake manifold torque sequence—351C, 351M and 400 V8
(© Ford Motor Co)

302 Boss, 351C, 351M, 351HO and 400 V8

1. Drain cooling system and remove air cleaner. On Boss 302 engine, disconnect Thermactor air hose from check valve at rear of intake manifold and loosen hose clamp at hose bracket. Remove air hose and Thermactor air by-pass valve from bracket and position out of way.
2. Disconnect accelerator linkage and accelerator downshift linkage, if so equipped, and position out of way. On Boss 302, disconnect choke cable from carburetor.
3. Disconnect high tension lead and wires from coil. Disconnect engine wire loom and position out of way.
4. Disconnect spark plug wires from spark plugs by grasping,

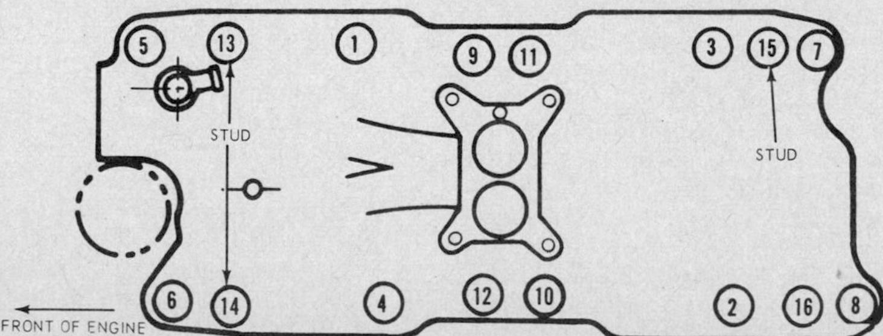

Intake manifold torque sequence—351W V8
(© Ford Motor Co)

twisting, and pulling molded cap only. Remove distributor cap and wire assembly.

5. Remove carburetor fuel inlet line.
6. Disconnect distributor vacuum hoses from distributor. Remove hold-down bolt and remove distributor.
7. Disconnect radiator upper hose from coolant outlet housing and disconnect temperature sender wire.
8. Loosen clamp on water pump by-pass hose at coolant outlet housing and slide hose off outlet housing.
9. Disconnect crankcase vent hose (PCV) at rocker cover.
10. If vehicle is air conditioned, remove compressor to intake manifold brackets.
11. Remove intake manifold and carburetor as an assembly. Discard all used gaskets and clean all mating surfaces.
12. Reverse procedure to install.

Exhaust Manifold Removal R & R

6 Cylinder Engines

1. Remove the air cleaner and heat duct body.
2. Disconnect the muffler inlet pipe and remove the choke hot air tube from the manifold.
3. Bend the exhaust manifold attaching bolt lock tabs back, remove the bolts and the manifold.
4. Clean all manifold mating surfaces and place a new gasket on the muffler inlet pipe.
5. Reinstall manifold by reversing above procedure, torque attaching bolts in sequence from the centermost bolt outward.

V8 Engines—Except 428 CJ and 429 Boss

1. On right exhaust manifold, remove the air cleaner, automatic choke heat tube and air cleaner heat ducts.
2. Disconnect the exhaust manifold(s) from the muffler inlet pipe(s).
3. Remove the manifold attaching bolts and remove the manifold(s).
4. Reverse above procedure to reinstall, using new inlet pipe gaskets.

NOTE: To remove the left side exhaust manifold from a car equipped with a 351C, 351M, or 400 engine, it is necessary to remove the oil filter and the transmission selector cross-shaft or clutch linkage and equalizer shaft bracket, depending on transmission type.

428 CJ Engine

This procedure is for removing both manifolds. If only one manifold is to be removed, do not remove any equipment located on or near the opposite side of the engine.

1. Remove the air cleaner, heat tubes, choke and vacuum lines from the manifold.
2. Remove the air cleaner heat tube mounting studs and the three forward attaching bolts from the right-side manifold.
3. Raise the car on a hoist, and remove the idler arm bracket from the frame.
4. Disconnect the starter cable and remove the starter motor.
5. Remove the remaining right-side manifold attaching bolts.
6. Disconnect all exhaust system hangers and lower the exhaust system.
7. Remove the inlet pipes from the manifolds.
8. On vehicles with manual transmission, remove the clutch linkage and equalizer bracket from the engine.
9. Disconnect the Pitman arm from the steering sector shaft and, on vehicles with power steering, remove the steering control valve bracket from the frame.
10. Lower the car, disconnect the steering shaft flex joint, unbolt and remove the steering gear box assembly from the frame.
11. Raise the car again and disconnect and remove both motor mounts and the rear crossmember support attaching bolts.
12. Position a jack under the engine and, using a piece of wood under the oil pan, raise the engine slightly.
13. Remove remaining manifold attaching bolts and remove the manifolds.
14. Clean all gasket surfaces and, using new inlet pipe gaskets, reverse above procedure to reinstall manifolds.

Valve System

The 6-cylinder engines are equipped with tubular pushrods and barrel type tappets. Valve lash is controlled by self locking adjusting screws.

V8 engines, except the 429 SCJ, and Boss 302, 351, and 429, use hydraulic tappets. The pushrods in the V8s also transfer oil under pressure to the friction areas of the rocker arms.

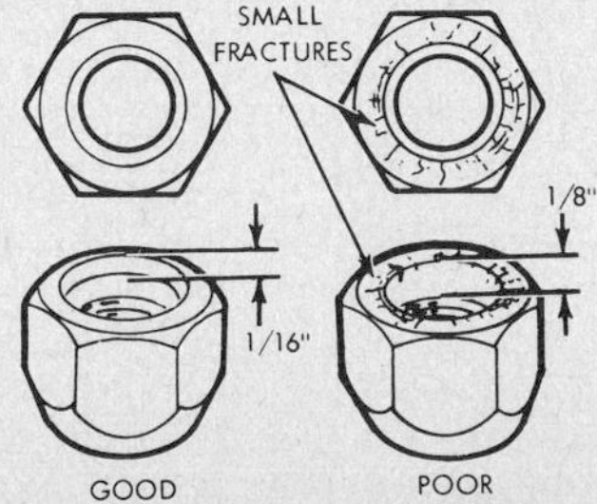

Rocker arm stud nut inspection
(© Ford Motor Co)

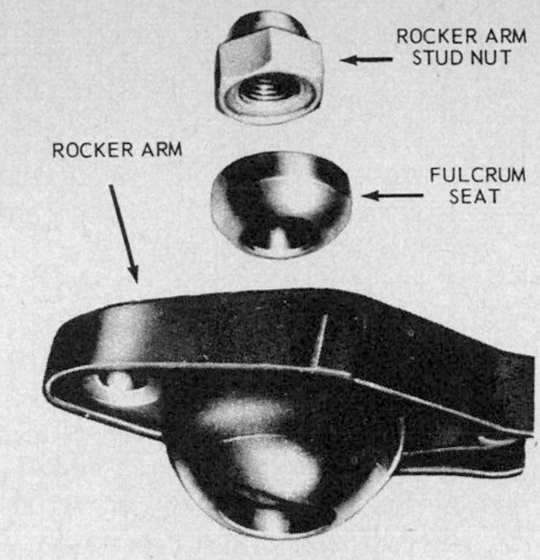

302, and 351 Windsor rocker arm assembly
(© Ford Motor Co)

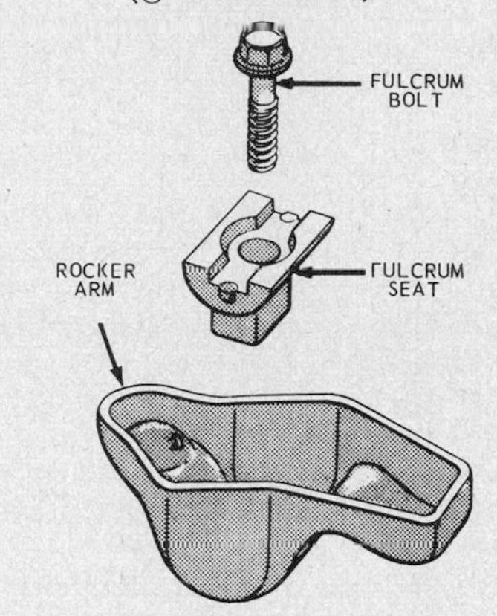

351 Cleveland V8 rocker arm assembly; 351M, 400 V8 similar (with oil deflector)
(© Ford Motor Co)

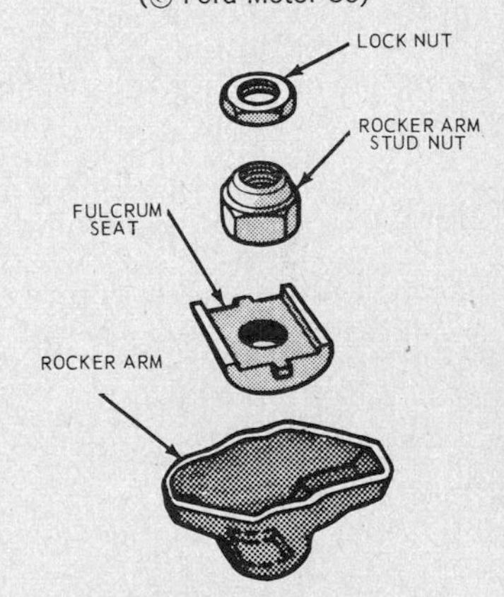

Boss 302 rocker arm assembly
(© Ford Motor Co)

Preliminary Valve Adjustment

V8

NOTE: The early 302 V8 engine has rocker arm mounting studs which do *not* incorporate a positive stop shoulder on the mounting stud. These engines were originally equipped with this kind of stud. However, due to production differences, it is possible some early 302 engines may be encountered that *are* equipped with positive stop rocker arm mounting studs. Before adjusting the valves, verify that the rocker arm mounting studs do not incorporate a positive stop shoulder. On studs without a positive stop, the shank portion of the stud that is exposed just above the cylinder head is the same diameter as the threaded portion, at the top of the stud, to which the rocker arm retaining nut attaches. If the shank portion of the stud is of greater diameter than the threaded portion, this identifies it as a positive stop rocker arm stud and the adjustment specifications for the 351 engine with adjusting nuts should be used. Only the 302, 351W and 1969-71 429 engines require a preliminary valve adjustment. All other V-8s use either a bolt and fulcrum (351C, 351M, 400, 460, and 1972-73 429) or rocker shafts (390 and 428). High performance versions of any of these V8s probably will be equipped with rocker arm adjusting nuts.

302, 351W and 1969-71 429
With Rocker Arm Adjusting Nuts

1. Crank the engine until #1 cylinder is at TDC of the compression stroke and the timing pointer is aligned with the marks on the crankshaft damper.
2. Scribe a mark on the damper at this point.
3. Scribe three more marks on the damper, dividing the damper into quarters.
4. With the first mark aligned with the timing pointer, adjust the valves on #1 cylinder by backing off the adjusting nut until the pushrod has free play in it. Then, tighten the nut until there is no free play in the rocker arm. This can be determined by turning the pushrod while tightening the nut; when the pushrod can no longer be turned, all clearance has been removed. After the clearance has been removed, tighten the nut an additional ¾ of a turn (302 V8 w/o positive stop rocker arm studs).

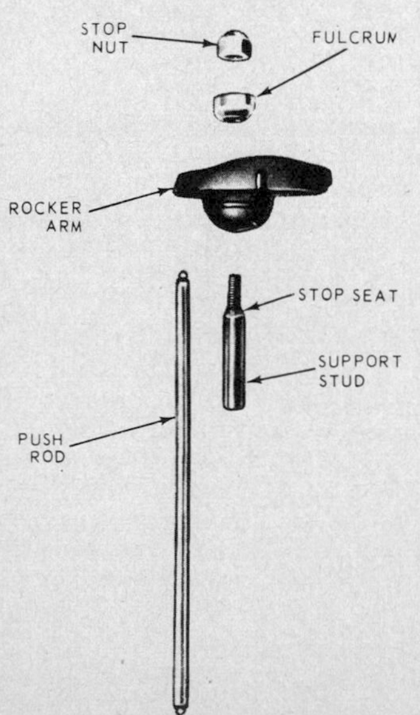

Positive Stop Rocker Arm Stud and Nut
(© Ford Motor Co)

5. Repeat this procedure for each valve, turning the crankshaft ¼ turn to the next mark each time and following the engine firing order.
6. Rocker arm adjusting nut tightening specifications are: 302 (with positive stop rocker arm studs) and 351W—tighten the nut until it contacts the rocker shoulder, then torque it to 18-20 ft lbs; 429—tighten the nut until it contacts the rocker shoulder then tighten the nut to 18-22 ft lbs.

6-Cylinder

All 6 Cylinder and 390 and 428 V8s

These engines are equipped with shaft-mounted rocker arms which do not require a preliminary valve adjustment. In the event of cylinder head or rocker arm removal, the rocker arm shaft bolts are tightened, front to rear, to 30-35 ft-lbs (6 cylinder) or 40-45 ft-lbs (390 an 428 V8).

351C, 351M, 400, 460, and
1972-73 429

These engines use a bolt and fulcrum rocker arm and require no preliminary valve adjustment. In the event that the valve train is disturbed, install the fulcrum, oil deflector, and tighten the bolt to 18-25 ft. lbs.

Boss 302, Boss 351 and Boss 429,
429 SCJ

1. Make primary valve adjustment in the following manner, and continue to install rocker covers and fill cooling system.

NOTE: Tappets must be adjusted while on the low radius of the cam.

2. If the distributor has not been disturbed and ignition timing is reasonably correct, proceed as follows: rotate crankshaft until the distributor rotor points to No. 1 plug wire tower of the distributor cap. Adjust valves in cylinder firing order according to rotor position.
3. If the distributor is out of time or has been removed from the engine: turn the crankshaft until No. 1 piston is at the top of its compression stroke. (intake valve of No. 6 cylinder just beginning to open), and the crankshaft damper is on T.D.C. Make three chalk marks on the crankshaft damper, 120° apart, starting with T.D.C. These marks will divide crankshaft travel into three parts, or six segments, of each engine cycle. Valve adjustment can then be made in firing sequence, beginning with No. 1 on TDC and progressing through the regular order of firing by advancing one chalk mark (120 crankshaft degrees) at a time.

V8 Mechanical Valve Lifter Final Adjustment

1. Run engine to bring to operating temperature.
2. Remove rocker covers.
3. Insert a feeler gauge of specified thickness between the rocker arm and valve, and with engine running, adjust rocker arm to obtain desired clearance.
4. Reinstall rocker cover.

Disassembly of Cylinder Heads

1. Remove cylinder heads.
2. Compress valve springs using valve spring compressor.
3. Remove valve locks or keys.
4. Release valve springs.
5. Remove valve springs, retainers, oil seals, and valves. On Boss 302 and Boss 429 engines, remove valve spring seals also.

NOTE: if a valve does not slide out of the guide easily check end of stem for mushrooming or heading over. If the stem is mushroomed, file off excess, remove and discard valve. If valve is not mushroomed, lubricate system of valve, remove, and check for stem wear or damage.

Valve Guides

Ford Motor Company engines use integral valve guides. Mercury and Ford dealers offer valves with oversize stems for worn guides. To fit these, enlarge valve guide bores with valve guide reamers to an oversize that cleans up wear. If a large oversize is required it is best to approach that size in stages by using a series of reamers of increasing diameter. This helps to maintain the concentricity of the guide bore with the valve seat. The correct valve guide to stem clearance is at front of this section. As an alternative, some local automotive machine shops will fit replacement guides that use standard stem valves.

Cylinder Head

6 Cylinder Removal

1. Drain cooling system, remove the air cleaner and disconnect the battery cable at the cylinder head.
2. Disconnect exhaust pipe at the manifold end, spring the exhaust pipe down and remove the flange gasket.
3. Disconnect the fuel and vacuum lines from the carburetor. Disconnect the intake manifold line at the intake manifold.

4. Disconnect the accelerator and retracting spring at the carburetor.
5. Disconnect the carburetor spacer outlet line at the spacer. Disconnect the radiator upper hose and the heater hose at the water outlet elbow. Disconnect the radiator lower hose and the heater hose at the water pump.
6. Disconnect the distributor vacuum control line at the distributor. Disconnect the gas filter line on the inlet side of the filter.
7. Disconnect the spark plug wires and remove the plugs.
8. Remove the rocker arm cover.
9. Back off all of the tappet adjusting screws to relieve tension on the rocker shaft. Loosen the rocker arm shaft attaching bolts and remove the rocker arm and shaft assembly. Remove the valve pushrods, in order, and keep them that way.
10. Remove one cylinder-head bolt from each end of the head (at opposite corners) and install cylinder head guide studs. Remove the remaining cylinder head bolts and lift off the cylinder head.

To help in removal and installation of cylinder head, two 6 in. x 7/16—14 bolts with heads cut off and the head end slightly tapered and slotted for installation and removal, with a screwdriver, will reduce the possibility of damage during head replacement. These guide studs make a handy tool during head removal and gasket and head replacement.

6 Cylinder Installation

1. Clean the cylinder head and block surfaces. Be sure of flatness and no surface damage.
2. Apply cylinder head gasket sealer to both sides of the new gasket and slide the gasket down over the two guide studs in the cylinder block.

NOTE: apply gasket sealer only to steel shim head gaskets. Steel-asbestos composite head gaskets are to be installed without any sealer.

Cylinder head bolt tightening sequence—170, 200, 250 cu. in. 6 cyl

3. Carefully lower the cylinder head over the guide studs. Place the exhaust pipe flange on the manifold studs (new gasket).
4. Coat the threads of the end bolts for the right side of the cylinder head with a small amount of water-resistant sealer. Install, but do not tighten, two head bolts at opposite ends to hold the head gasket in place. Remove the guide studs and install the remaining bolts.
5. Cylinder head torquing should proceed in three steps and in prescribed order. Tighten to 55 ft. lbs., then give them a second tightening to 65 ft. lbs. The final step is to 75 ft. lbs., at which they should remain undisturbed.
6. Lubricate both ends of the pushrods and install them in their original locations.
7. Apply a petroleum jelly-type lubricant to the rocker arm pads and the valve stem tips and position the rocker arm shaft assembly on the head. Be sure the oil holes in the shaft are in a down position.
8. Tighten all the rocker shaft retaining bolts to 30-35 ft. lbs. and do a preliminary valve adjustment (make sure there are no tight valve adjustments).
9. Hook up the exhaust pipe.
10. Reconnect the heater and radiator hoses.
11. Reposition the distributor vacuum line, the carburetor gas line and the intake manifold vacuum line on the engine. Hook them up to their respective connections and reconnect the battery cable to the cylinder head.
12. Connect the accelerator rod and retracting spring. Connect the choke control cable and adjust the choke.
13. Reconnect the vacuum line at the distributor. Connect the fuel inlet line at the fuel filter and the intake manifold vacuum line at the vacuum pump. Connect the windshield wiper vacuum line to the other side of the vacuum pump.
14. Lightly lubricate the spark plug threads, install them and torque to 25 ft. lbs. Connect spark plug wires and be sure the wires are all the way down in their sockets.
15. Fill the cooling system and bleed. Run the engine to stabilize all engine parts temperatures.
16. Adjust engine idle speed and idle fuel-air adjustment.
17. Coat one side of a new rocker cover gasket with oil-resistant sealer. Lay the treated side of the gasket on the cover and install the cover. Be sure the gasket seals evenly all around the cylinder head.

Cylinder head bolt tightening sequence—302, 302 Boss, 351W, 351C, 400 V8 shown; 390, 428, 429 Boss V8 have similar bolt pattern

All V8 Except 390, 428 and Boss 429

1. Remove the valve covers and disconnect the negative battery cable.
2. Remove the intake manifold and carburetor assembly.
3. On cars equipped with air conditioning, remove the compressor from the engine and position it to one side, *without disconnecting the refrigerant lines.*
4. If removing the left cylinder head, on cars equipped with power steering, remove the pump, bracket, and drive belt and position to one side *without disconnecting the lines.* On cars with Thermactor emission control system, disconnect the hose from the air manifold on the left cylinder head.
5. If removing the right cylinder head, remove the alternator mounting bracket bolt and spacer, ignition coil, and air cleaner inlet duct. On cars equipped with Thermactor emission control, remove the air pump and bracket. Disconnect the hose from the right cylinder head.
6. Disconnect the exhaust manifold/s from the exhaust pipe/s.
7. Loosen the rocker arm stud nuts so that the arms can rotate to the side to clear the pushrods. Remove the pushrods.
8. Remove the cylinder head bolts and lift off the cylinder head. On some 351 engines, it may be necessary to remove the exhaust manifold to gain access to the lower cylinder head bolts.
9. Reverse the above procedures for installation taking care to follow the specified torque sequence as per the diagrams. Perform a preliminary valve adjustment before starting the engine.

390 and 428 V8

1. Remove the intake manifold assembly as previously described.
2. Remove any remaining accessories that may obstruct removal.
3. Disconnect the exhaust manifold/s from the exhaust pipe/s.
4. Unbolt and remove heads.
5. Reverse above procedure for installation taking care to follow the specified torque sequence as per the diagrams.

Timing Cover, Chain, and Camshaft

6-Cylinder Cover and Chain

Removal

1. Drain the cooling system and crankcase.
2. Disconnect the upper radiator hose from the intake manifold and the lower hose from the

Frequently valves become bent or warped or their seats become blocked with carbon or other material. Left unattended, this can cause burnt valves, damaged cylinder heads and other expensive troubles. To detect leaking valves early, perform this test whenever the cylinder head is removed.

1. **After removing head, replace spark plugs. Removing spark plugs before removing heads eliminates breakage.**
2. **Place head on bench with valves, springs, retainers and keys installed and combustion chambers up.**
3. **Pour enough gasoline in each combustion chamber to completely cover both valves. Watch combustion chambers for two minutes for any leakage.**

water pump. On cars with automatic transmission, disconnect the cooler lines from the radiator.

3. Remove the radiator, fan and pulley, and engine drive belts. On models with air conditioning, remove the condenser retaining bolts and position the condenser forward. *Do not disconnect the refrigerant lines.*
4. On 170 and 200 cu. in. engines remove the cylinder front cover retaining bolts and front oil pan bolts and gently pry the cover away from the block. On 250 engines, it is necessary to remove the oil pan before removing the front cover.
5. Remove the crankshaft pulley bolt and use a puller to remove the vibration damper.
6. With a socket wrench of the proper size on the crankshaft pulley bolt, gently rotate the crankshaft in a clockwise direction until all slack is removed from the left side of the timing chain. Scribe a mark on the engine block parallel to the present position of the left side of the chain. Next, turn the crankshaft in a counterclockwise direction to remove all the slack from the right side of the chain. Force the left side of the chain outward with the fingers and measure the distance between the reference point and the present position of the chain. If the distance exceeds ½ inch, replace the chain and sprockets.
7. Crank the engine until the timing marks are aligned as shown in the illustration. Remove the bolt, slide sprocket and chain forward and remove as an assembly.

Installation

1. Position the sprockets and chain on the engine, making sure that the timing marks are aligned, dot to dot.
2. Reinstall the front cover, applying oil resistant sealer to the new gasket.

NOTE: on 170 and 200 engines, trim away the exposed portion of the old oil pan gasket flush with front of the engine block. Cut and position the required portion of a new gasket to the oil pan, applying sealer to both sides of it.

3. On 250 engines, reinstall the oil pan.
4. Install the fan, pulley and belts. Adjust belt tension.
5. Install the radiator, connect the radiator hoses and transmission cooling lines. If equipped with air conditioning, install the condenser.
6. Fill the crankcase and cooling system. Start the engine and check for leaks.

V8 Cover and Chain

Removal

1. Drain cooling system, remove air cleaner and disconnect the battery.
2. Disconnect radiator hoses and remove the radiator.
3. Disconnect heater hose at water pump. Slide water pump by-pass hose clamp toward the pump.
4. Loosen alternator mounting bolts at the alternator. Remove the alternator support bolt at the water pump. Remove Thermactor pump on all engines so equipped.
5. Remove the fan, spacer, pulley, and drive belt.
6. Remove pulley from crankshaft pulley adapter. Remove cap screw and washer from front end of crankshaft. Remove crankshaft pulley adapter with a puller.
7. Disconnect fuel pump outlet line at the pump. Remove fuel pump retaining bolts and lay the pump to the side.
8. Remove the front cover attaching bolts. On the 351C, 351M, and 400 engines, it is necessary to remove the oil pan before the front cover can be removed.
9. Remove the crankshaft oil slinger if so equipped.
10. Check timing chain deflection, using the procedure outlined in Step 6 of the six cylinder cover and chain removal.
11. Crank engine until sprocket timing marks are aligned as shown in valve timing illustration.
12. Remove crankshaft sprocket cap screw, washers, and fuel pump eccentric. Slide both sprockets and chain forward and off as an assembly.

Installation

1. Position sprockets and chain on the camshaft and crankshaft with both timing marks dot to dot on a centerline. Install fuel pump eccentric, washers and sprocket attaching bolt. Torque the sprocket attaching bolt to 30–35 ft lbs.
2. Install crankshaft front oil slinger.
3. Clean front cover and mating surfaces of old gasket material.
4. Coat a new cover gasket with sealer and position it on the block.

NOTE: On all except 351C, 351M, and 400 engines, trim away the exposed portion of the oil pan gasket flush with the cylinder block. Cut and position the required portion of a new gasket to the oil pan, applying sealer to both sides of it. On 351C, 351M, and 400 engines, after installing the cylinder front cover, install the oil pan using a new gasket.

5. Install front cover, using a crankshaft-to-cover alignment tool. Torque attaching bolts to 12-15 ft. lbs.
6. Install fuel pump, torque attaching bolts to 23-28 ft. lbs., connect fuel pump outlet tube.
7. Install crankshaft pulley adapter and torque attaching bolt to 70-90 ft. lbs. Install crankshaft pulley.

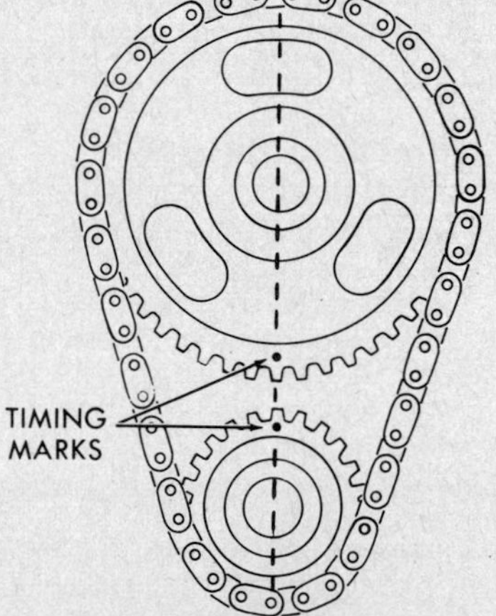

Timing mark alignment

8. Install water pump pulley, drive belt, spacer and fan.
9. Install alternator support bolt at the water pump. Tighten alternator mounting bolts. Adjust drive belt tension. Install Thermactor pump if so equipped.
10. Install radiator and connect all coolant and heater hoses. Connect battery cables.
11. Refill and bleed cooling system.
12. Start engine and operate at fast idle to operating temperature.
13. Check for leaks, install air cleaner. Adjust ignition timing and make all final adjustments.

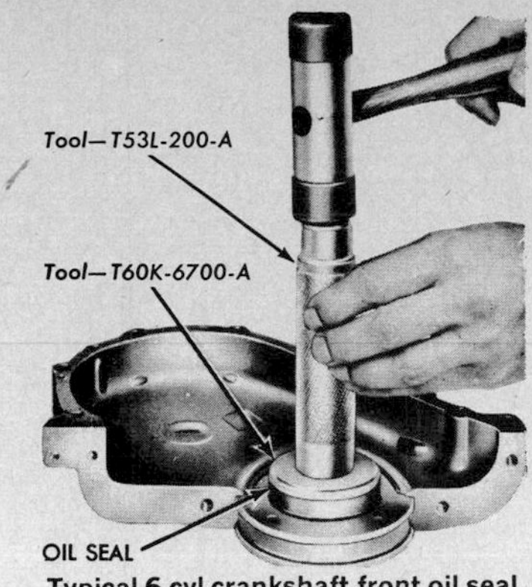

Typical 6 cyl crankshaft front oil seal replacement (© Ford Motor Co)

Cover Seal R & R

It is a recommended practice to replace the cover seal any time the front cover is removed.

1. With the cover removed from the car, drive the old seal from the rear of cover with a pin-punch. Clean out the recess in the cover.
2. Coat the new seal with grease and drive it into the cover until it is fully seated. Check the seal after installation to be sure the spring is properly positioned in the seal.

Camshaft R & R

6 Cylinder Engines

1. Remove the cylinder head as directed in that section.
2. Remove the cylinder front cover, timing chain and sprockets as outlined in the preceding section.
3. Disconnect and remove the grille. On Mustang models, remove the gravel deflector.
4. Using a magnet, remove the valve lifters and keep them in order so that they can be installed in their original positions.
5. Remove the camshaft thrust plate and remove the camshaft by pulling it from the front of the engine. Use care not to damage the camshaft lobes or journals while removing the cam from the engine.
6. Before installing the camshaft, coat the lobes with Lubriplate and the journals and all valve parts with heavy oil.
7. Reverse above procedure to install, following recommended torque settings and tightening sequences. Perform a preliminary valve adjustment before starting the engine.

V8 Engines

1. Remove the intake manifold as outlined previously.
2. Remove the cylinder front cover, timing chain and sprockets as directed previously.
3. Remove the grille, and, on models with air conditioning, remove the condenser retaining bolts and position it out of the way. *Do not disconnect refrigerant lines.*
4. Remove the rocker arm covers.
5. On 390 and 428 engines it is necessary to remove the rocker arm shafts to remove the intake manifold. On all other engines with individually mounted rocker arms, loosen the rocker arm fulcrum bolts and rotate the rocker arms to the side.
6. Remove the pushrods and lifters and keep them in order so that they can be installed in their original positions.
7. Remove the camshaft thrust plate and washer if so equipped. Remove the camshaft from the front of the engine. Use care not to damage camshaft lobes or journals while removing the cam from the engine.
8. Before installing the camshaft, coat the lobes with Lubriplate and the journals and valve parts with heavy oil.
9. Reverse above procedure to install.

NOTE: on engines with individually mounted rocker arms, it is necessary to perform a preliminary valve adjustment before starting the engine.

Lubrication

All engines are equipped with full-flow-type oil filters to condition the oil before it reaches the main bearings. The filter is equipped with an internal, relief, by-pass valve as a safety precaution.

Oil Pan R & R

NOTE: on certain engine-chassis combinations, interference will be encountered between the oil pan and oil pump while attempting to remove the oil pan. If this occurs, lower the oil pan and reach inside it and remove the two bolts retaining the oil pump and pickup tube to the engine block. Lower the pump and pickup tube assembly into the pan and remove it with the pan. To ensure proper gasket sealing, the oil pan retaining bolts should be tightened from the center outward.

1969-70 170, 200, and 250 6 Cylinder—All Models

1. Drain the crankcase. Remove the dipstick and the flywheel inspection plate.
2. In Mustangs and Cougars, disconnect the stabilizer bar and pull downward, out of the way.
3. Remove one bolt, loosen the other and swing no. 2 crossmember out of the way.
4. Remove the retaining bolts and oil pan. Reverse the above procedure to install.

1971-76 Maverick and Comet with 170 and 200 6 Cylinder

1. Drain the crankcase. Remove the dipstick and the flywheel inspection plate.
2. Remove the retaining bolts and oil pan. Reverse the above procedures to install, taking care to place the tabs of the front and rear oil seals over the pan gasket.

1971-76 Torino, Montego, Maverick, Monarch, Granada and Comet with 250 6 Cylinder, 1971-73 Mustang 6 Cylinder

1. Drain the crankcase and cooling system. Remove the dipstick and the flywheel inspection plate.
2. Remove the radiator. On cars with automatic transmissions, the oil cooler lines must be disconnected and plugged.
3. Raise the vehicle. Remove the stabilizer bar.
4. Remove the engine support thru-bolts and nuts.
5. Raise the engine with a jack and place two 2 in. wooden blocks between the engine supports and the chassis brackets.

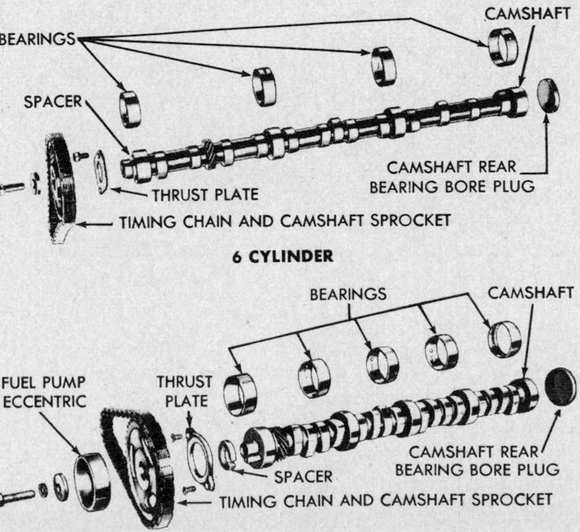

Camshaft and related parts (© Ford Motor Co)

6. Remove the retaining bolts and the starter motor.
7. Remove the retaining bolts and oil pan. Reverse the above procedures for installation.

1969 302, and 351 V8—All Models

1. Drain the crankcase. Remove the dipstick.
2. Disconnect the stabilizer bar from the lower control arms and pull the ends down.
3. Remove the oil pan retaining bolts and position the pan on the front crossmember.
4. Remove one oil inlet tube bolt, loosen the other and position the tube out of the way.
5. Turn the chankshaft as required for clearance to remove the pan.
6. Install in the reverse order from above.

1970 Mustang and Cougar 302, Boss 302, 351W, and 351C V8

1. Drain the crankcase. Remove the dipstick. Raise the vehicle.
2. Remove the stabilizer-to-frame retaining bolts.
3. Remove the two bolts retaining the crossmember to the chassis.
4. Remove the starter from cars with 351 Cleveland engines.
5. Remove the retaining bolts and the oil pan.
6. Turn the crankshaft as required for clearance to remove the pan.
7. Install in the reverse order from above.

1969 All models with 390 or 428 V8; 1970 Falcon, Fairlane, Torino, and Montego with 302 or 351 V8; 1970-76 All Models with 429 or 460 V8; 1971-76 All models with 302, 351 or 400 V8

1. Remove the dipstick.
2. Remove the fan shroud retaining bolts, on models so equipped, and position the shroud over the fan.
3. Raise the vehicle and drain the crankcase.
4. On vehicles with 351C, 351M, 400, and 429 engines, disconnect the negative battery cable and remove the starter.
5. Disconnect the stabilizer bar links and pull the ends down.
6. Remove the engine front support thru-bolts.
7. Install a wooden block on a jack and position the jack beneath the leading edge of the pan.
8. Raise the engine and place 1–1 ½ in. wood blocks between the engine supports and the chassis. Remove the jack from beneath the engine.
9. Remove the oil pan retaining bolts and lower the pan to the crossmember.
10. If the car is equipped with an automatic transmission, position the oil cooler lines out of the way.
11. Turn the crankshaft as required to obtain clearance to remove the pan.
12. Install in reverse of above.

NOTE: Oil leakage from the rear section of the oil pan gasket (not the rear main seal) has been a problem on some 429 and 460 Police Interceptor V8's. Ford has remedied the situation with a new style seal. However, if the neoprene seal is of the old type, the seal may be prevented from leaking by the application of silicone rubber sealer to the corners of the rear main bearing cap saddle, as shown, prior to installation. Once the silicone sealer is applied, install the oil pan immediately, as the sealer will begin to harden.

Oil Pump

Removal—All Engines

1. Remove oil pan.
2. Remove oil pump inlet tube and screen assembly.
3. Remove oil pump attaching bolts and remove oil pump gasket and intermediate shaft.

Installation—All Engines

1. Prime oil pump by filling inlet and outlet port with engine oil and rotating shaft of pump to distribute it.
2. Position intermediate drive shaft into distributor socket.
3. Position new gasket on pump body and insert intermediate drive shaft into pump body.

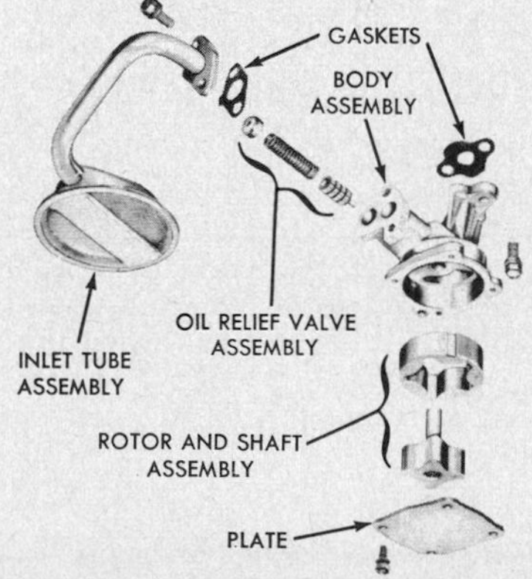

302, Boss 302, and 351 Windsor V8 oil pump (© Ford Motor Co)

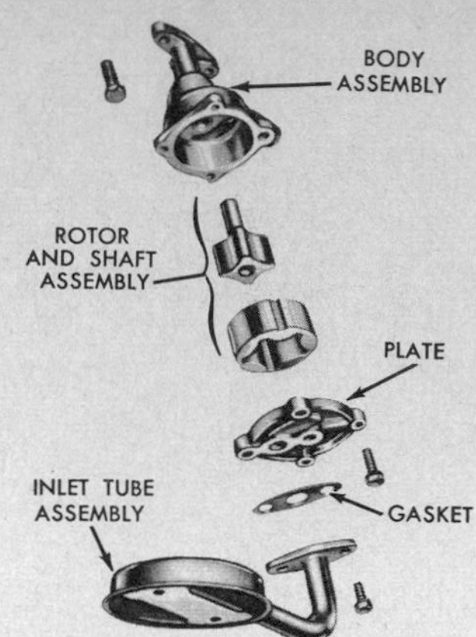

6 cyl oil pump (© Ford Motor Co)

4. Install pump and intermediate shaft as an assembly.

NOTE: do not force pump if it does not seat readily. The drive shaft may be misaligned with the distributor shaft. To align rotate intermediate drive shaft into a new position.

5. Install and torque oil pump attaching screws to 12-15 ft. lbs. on six cylinder, 20-25 ft. lbs. on V8s.
6. Install oil pan.

Rear Crankshaft Oil Seal R & R

1969 390 and 428, All 1970-76 Engines

NOTE: the rear oil seal installed in these engines is a rubber type seal.

1. Remove the oil pan, and, if required, the oil pump.
2. Loosen all main bearing caps allowing the crankshaft to lower slightly.

NOTE: the crankshaft should not be allowed to drop more than 1/32 in.

3. Remove the rear main bearing cap and remove the seal from the cap and block.
4. Carefully clean the seal grooves in the cap and block with solvent.
5. Soak the new seal halves in clean engine oil.

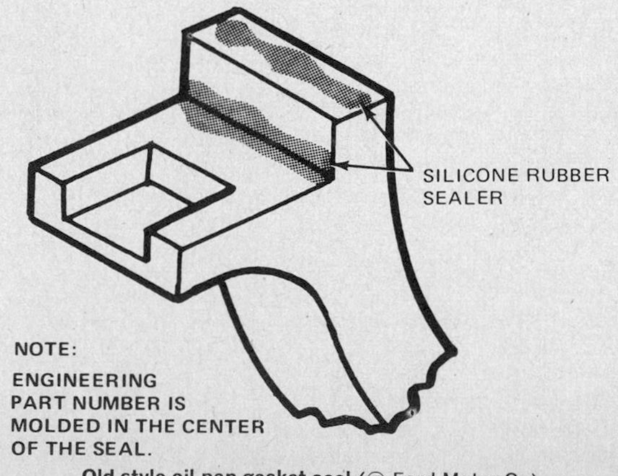

Old style oil pan gasket seal (© Ford Motor Co)

6. Install the upper half of the seal in the block with the undercut side of the seal toward the front of the engine. Slide the seal around the crankshaft journal until 3/8 in. protrudes beyond the base of the block.
7. Repeat above procedure on lower seal, allowing an equal length of the seal to protrude beyond the opposite end of the bearing cap.
8. Install rear bearing cap and torque all main bearings to specifications. Apply sealer only to the rear of the seals.
9. Dip the bearing cap side seals in oil, then immediately install them. Do not use any sealer on the side seals. Tap the seals into place and do not clip the protruding ends.
10. Install the oil pump and pan. Fill the crankcase with oil, start engine check for leaks.

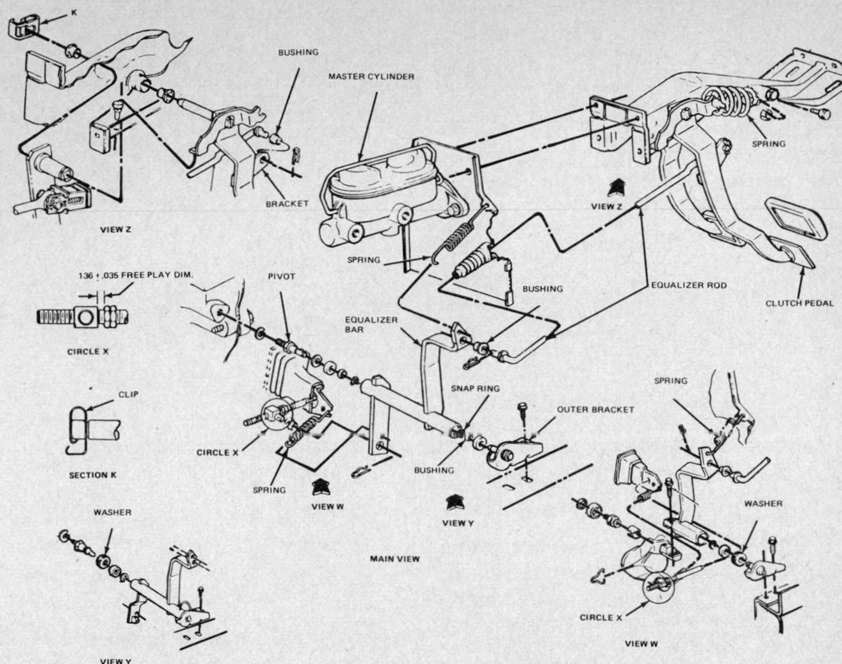

Clutch pedal and linkage adjustment—1970-74 Maverick and Comet
(© Ford Motor Co)

All Other Engines

NOTE: The rear oil seal originally installed in these engines is a rope (fabric) type seal. However, all service replacements are of the rubber type. To remove the rope type seal and install the rubber type, the following procedure is used.

1. Drain the crankcase and remove the oil pan.
2. Remove the lower half of the rear main bearing cap and, after removing the old seal from the cap, drive out the pin in the bottom of the seal groove with a punch.
3. Loosen all main bearing caps and allow the crankshaft to lower slightly.

NOTE: The crankshaft should not be allowed to drop more than 1/32 in.

4. With a 6 in. length of 3/16 in. brazing rod, drive up on either exposed end of the top half of the oil seal. When the opposite end of the seal starts to protrude, have a helper grasp it with pliers and gently pull, while the driven end is being tapped.
5. After removing both halves of the rope seal and the retaining pin from the lower half of the bearing cap, follow steps 4–10 of the above procedure for 1970-76 engines to install the rubber seal.

CLUTCH

The clutch is a single dry disc type and is mechanically engaged. Centrifugal weights are used to increase pressure plate grip at high rpm.

Pedal Adjustment

1. Disconnect clutch return spring from release lever.
2. Loosen release lever rod locknut and adjusting nut.
3. Move clutch release lever rear-

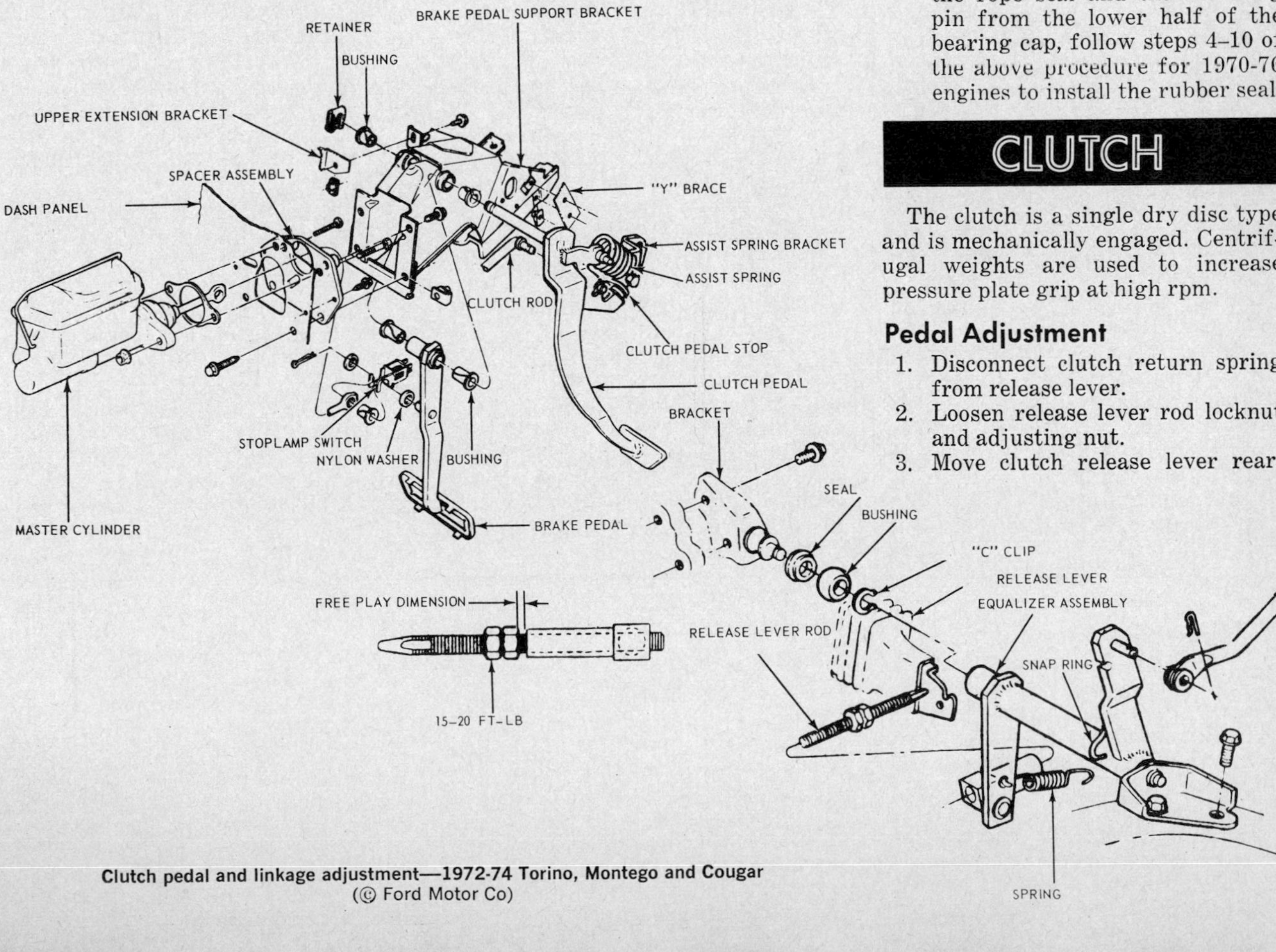

Clutch pedal and linkage adjustment—1972-74 Torino, Montego and Cougar
(© Ford Motor Co)

ward until release bearing lightly contacts clutch pressure plate release fingers.
4. Adjust rod length until rod seats in release lever pocket.
5. Insert specified feeler gauge between adjusting nut and swivel sleeve. Tighten adjusting nut against gauge.
6. Tighten lock nut against adjusting nut, taking care not to disturb adjustment. Torque locknut to 15-20 ft. lbs. and remove feeler gauge.
7. Install clutch return spring.
8. Check free travel at pedal. Readjust if necessary to obtain specified travel. Moving adjusting nut away from swivel sleeve increases travel. Moving adjusting nut toward swivel sleeve decreases travel.
9. As final check, measure pedal free travel with transmission in neutral and engine running at 3,000 rpm. If pedal travel is not minimum of ½ in., readjust free travel.

TIME SAVER

If a problem is encountered with clutch adjustment rods bending, check the clutch equalizer shaft. A bent or distorted equalizer shaft will allow the clutch pedal to travel too far, which will bend the adjustment rod.

Clutch Pedal Adjustment

Year and Engine	*Clearance* (in.)*	*Free Travel (in.)*
1969-71 except 390, 428 and 429	0.136	⅞-1⅛
1969-71 390, 428 and 429	0.178	⅞-1⅛
1972-74 Torino, Montego, Cougar and 1972-73 Mustang	0.194	⅞-1⅛
1972-76 Comet, Maverick, Monarch and Granada	0.136	⅞-1⅛

* Between adjusting nut and swivel sleeve

Clutch and/or Manual Transmission Removal

1. Disconnect and remove starter and dust ring, if the clutch is to be removed. On floor-shift models, remove the boot retainer and shifter lever.
2. Raise the car.
3. Disconnect the driveshaft at the rear universal joint and remove the driveshaft.

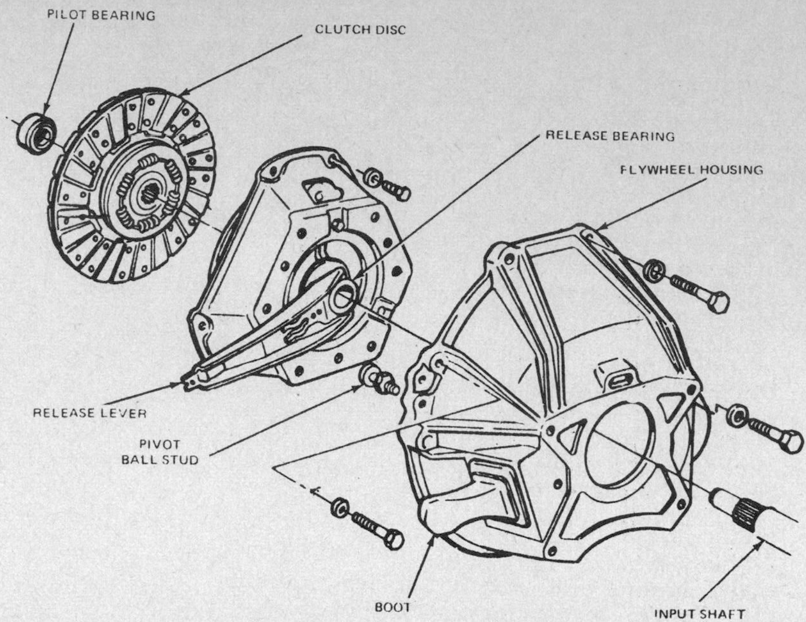

Exploded view of clutch and related parts
(© Ford Motor Co)

4. Disconnect the speedometer cable at the transmission extension. On cars with transmission regulated spark, disconnect the lead wire at the connector. Disconnect the seat belt sensor wires.
5. Disconnect the gear shift rods from the transmission shift levers. If car is equipped with four speed, remove bolts that secure shift control bracket to extension housing.
6. Remove the bolt holding the extension housing to the rear support, and remove the muffler inlet pipe bracket to housing bolt.
7. Remove the two rear support bracket insulator nuts from the underside of the crossmember. Remove crossmember.
8. Place a jack (equipped with a protective piece of wood) under the rear of the engine oil pan. Raise the engine, slightly.
9. Remove transmission - to - flywheel-housing bolts.

NOTE: on 429 and 460 cu in. engines the upper left-hand transmission attaching bolt is a seal bolt. Carefully note its position so that it may be reinstalled in its original position.

10. Slide the transmission back and out of the car.
11. To remove the clutch, remove release lever retracting spring and disconnect pedal at the equalizer bar.
12. Remove bolts that secure engine rear plate to front lower part of bellhousing.
13. Remove bolts that attach bell housing to cylinder block and remove housing and release lever as a unit.
14. Loosen six pressure plate cover attaching bolts evenly to release spring pressure. Mark cover and flywheel to facilitate reassembly in same position.
15. Remove six attaching bolts while holding pressure plate cover. Remove pressure plate and clutch disc.

Caution Do not depress the clutch pedal while the transmission is removed.

Clutch and/or Manual Transmission Installation

1. To install the clutch, first wash flywheel surface with alcohol.
2. Attach the clutch disc and pressure plate assembly to the flywheel with the bolts finger tight.
3. Align the clutch disc with the pilot bushing. Torque cover bolts to 12-20 ft. lbs.
4. Lightly lubricate the release lever fulcrum ends. Install the release lever in the flywheel housing and install the dust shield.
5. Apply very little lubricant on the release bearing retainer journal. Attach the release bearing and hub on the release lever.
6. Install the flywheel housing and torque the attaching bolts to 40-50 ft. lbs. on all V8s. Torque sixes to 23-33 ft. lbs. Install the dust cover and torque the bolts to 17-20 ft. lbs.
7. Connect the release rod and the retracting spring. Connect the pedal - to - equalizer - rod at the equalizer bar.
8. Install starter and dust ring.
9. Start the transmission extension housing up and over the rear support. After moving the transmission back just far enough for the pilot shaft to clear the clutch housing, move it upward and

into position on the flywheel housing.

10. Move the transmission forward and into place against the flywheel housing, and install the transmission attaching bolts finger-tight.
11. Tighten the transmission bolts to 37-42 ft. lbs. on all cars.
12. Slowly lower the engine onto the crossmember.
13. Install and torque the insulator-to-crossmember nuts to 25-35 ft. lbs. on all 1969 vehicles except 390 and 428 CJ Cougars and Mustangs. Torque 390 and 428 CJ Cougars and Mustangs to 30-42 ft. lbs. Torque 1970-76 Torinos, Montegos, Mavericks, Comets, Monarchs and Granadas to 30-50 ft. lbs. and 1970-74 Cougars and 1970-73 Mustangs to 25-35 ft. lbs.
14. Connect gear shift rods and the speedometer cable. On transmission regulated spark equipped cars, connect the lead wire at the connector.
15. Hook up the drive shaft.
16. Refill transmission to proper level. On floor-shift models, install the boot retainer and shift lever.

MANUAL TRANSMISSION

There are two manual transmissions used: (1) a heavy-duty, top cover, fully synchromesh three-speed used on all three-speed applications, and (2) a heavy-duty, top cover, fully synchromesh, Ford-built four-speed used on V8 engines through 1974. The four-speed manual transmission is not available on 1975 and later models.

Linkage Adjustment

Three-Speed Column Shift

With the transmission in neutral, the shift lever should be in a horizontal plane and parallel to the instrument panel line. Corrective adjustments should be made at the gear shift rods.

1. Place lever in neutral.
2. Loosen two gear shift rod adjustment nuts.
3. Insert 3/16 in. diameter alignment pin through first and reverse gear shift lever and second and third gear shift lever. Align levers to insert pin.
4. Tighten gear shift rod adjustment nuts, and remove pin.
5. Check gear lever for smooth crossover.

Three-Speed Floor and Console Shift

1. Loosen three shift linkage adjustment nuts.
2. Install a 1/4 in. diameter alignment pin through control bracket and levers.
3. Tighten three shift linkage adjustment nuts and remove alignment pin.
4. Check gear lever for smooth crossover.

Four-Speed

1. Place shifter lever in neutral position, then raise car on a hoist.
2. Insert a 1/4 in. rod into the alignment holes of the shift levers.
3. If the holes are not in exact alignment, check for bent connecting rods or loose lever lock nuts at the rod ends. Make replacements or repairs, then adjust as follows.
4. Loosen the three rod-to-lever retaining lock nuts and move the levers until the 1/4 in. gauge rod will enter the alignment holes. Be sure that the transmission shift

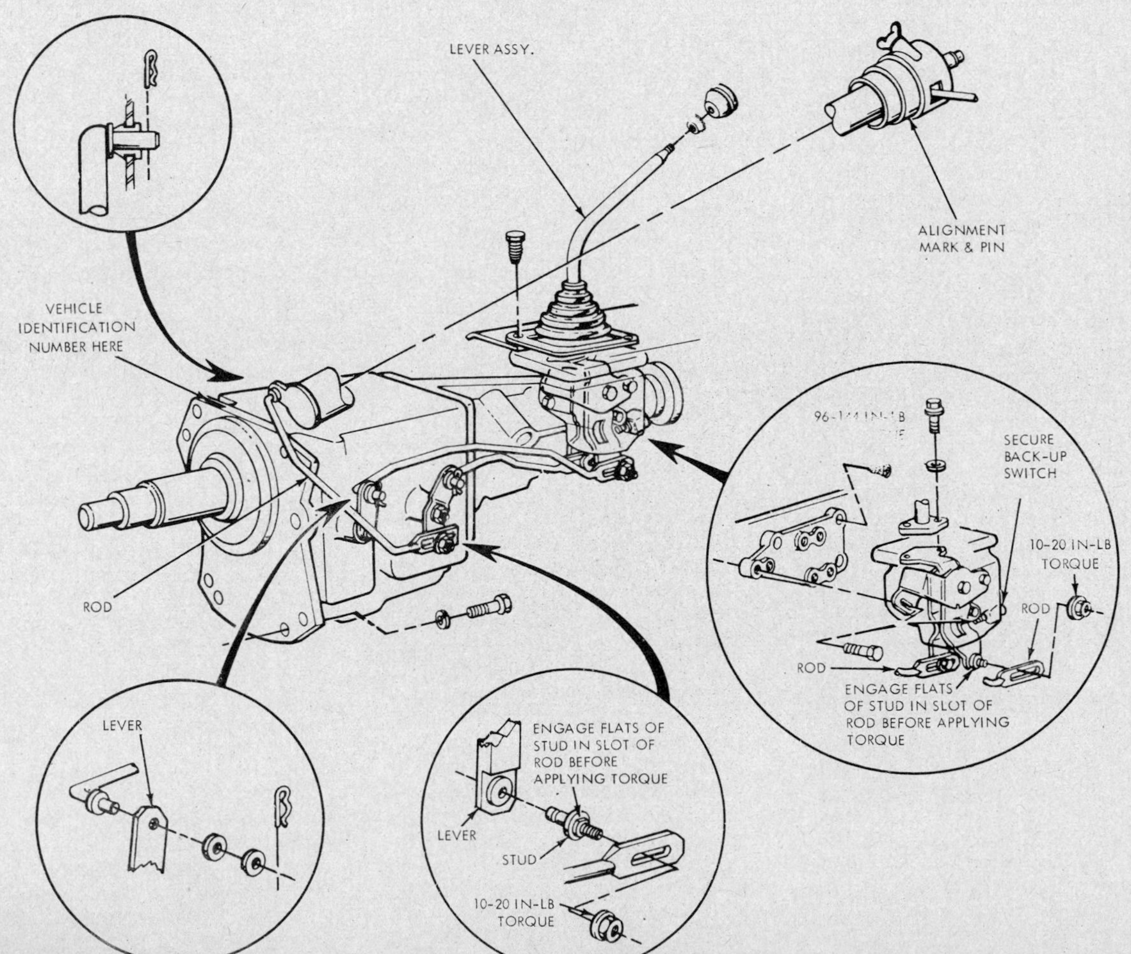

Three-speed floor shift linkage and lock rod
(© Ford Motor Co)

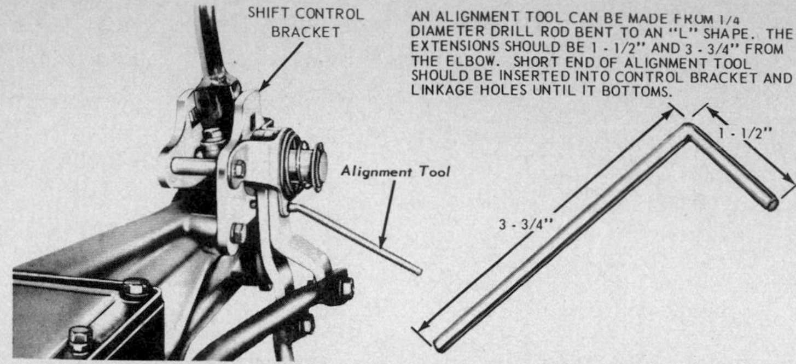

Manual transmission floor or console shift adjustment (© Ford Motor Co)

levers are in neutral and the reverse shifter lever is in the neutral detent.

5. Install the shift rods and torque the lock nuts to 18-23 ft. lbs.
6. Remove the ¼ in. gauge rod.
7. Operate the shift levers to assure correct shifting.
8. Lower the car and road test.

Transmission Lock Rod Adjustment

1970 and later models with floor or console mounted shifters and manual transmissions incorporate a transmission lock rod which prevents the shifter from being moved from the reverse position when the ignition lock is in the OFF position. The lock rod connects the shift tube in the steering column to the transmission reverse lever. The lock rod cannot be properly adjusted until the manual linkage adjustment is correct.

1. With the transmission selector lever in the neutral position, loosen the lock rod adjustment nut on the transmission reverse lever.
2. Insert a .180 in. diameter rod (No. 15 drill bit) in the gauge pin hole located at the 6 o'clock position on the steering column socket casting, directly below the ignition lock.
3. Manipulate the pin until the casting will not move with the pin inserted.
4. Torque the lock rod adjustment rod to 10-20 ft. lbs.
5. Remove the pin and check the linkage operation.

Transmission Removal

See Clutch and/or Transmission Removal.

AUTOMATIC TRANSMISSION

Three different automatic transmissions are used in Ford compact and intermediate cars: a C4, a C6, and a FMX. The C4 is a light duty transmission used on six cylinder and small block V8 engines. The FMX is an intermediate duty transmission used on medium duty V8s. The C6 is a heavy duty transmission used on high-performance and large displacement V8 engines.

Pan R & R, Fluid Change

Normal maintenance and lubrication requirements do not include periodic changes of transmission fluid. A change is required only when it is necessary to replace the transmission fluid. At this time the converter, oil cooler core, and cooler lines should be thoroughly flushed out to remove any dirt or deposits that might clog these units later.

When filling a completely dry (no fluid) transmission and converter, install five quarts of transmission fluid and then start the engine. Shift the selector lever through all gear positions briefly and set at Park position. Check the fluid level and add enough fluid to raise the level to between the marks on the dipstick. Do not overfill the transmission.

The procedure for a partial drain and refill of the transmission fluid is as follows:

1. Raise the car on a hoist or jack stands.
2. Place a drain pan under the transmission pan.

NOTE: On some models of the C4 transmission, the fluid is drained by disconnecting the filler tube from the transmission fluid pan.

3. Loosen the pan attaching bolts to allow the fluid to drain.
4. When the fluid has stopped draining to level of the pan flange, remove the pan bolts starting at the rear and along both sides of the pan, allowing the pan to drop and drain gradually.
5. When all the transmission fluid has drained, remove the pan and the fluid filter and clean them.
6. After completing the transmission repairs or adjustments, install the fluid filter screen, a new pan gasket, and the pan on the transmission. Tighten the pan attaching bolts on C4 and C6 transmissions to 12–16 ft lbs. On FMX and CW transmissions, tighten the pan attaching bolts to 10–13 ft lbs.

NOTE: Be sure to use Type "F" transmission fluid. The use of any other type of fluid such as Type "A" suffix "A," or DEXRON will materially affect the service life of the transmission.

7. Install three quarts of transmission fluid through the filter tube. If the filler tube was removed to drain the transmission, install the filler tube using a new 0-ring.
8. Start and run the engine for a few minutes at low idle speed and then at the fast idle speed (about 1,200 rpm) until the normal operating temperature is reached. Do not race the engine.
9. Move the selector lever through all gear positions and place it at the Park position. Check the fluid level, and add fluid until the level is between the "add" and "full" marks on the dipstick. Do not overfill.

C4

Throttle Linkage Adjustment

Initial Adjustments—All Models

1. Apply parking brake and place selector lever at N.
2. Run engine at normal idle speed. If engine is cold, run engine at fast idle speed (about 1200 rpm) until it reaches normal operating temperature. When engine is warm, slow it down to normal idle speed.
3. Connect tachometer to engine.
4. Adjust engine idle speed to specified rpm with transmission selector lever at D or D_1 or D_2.
5. The carburetor throttle lever must be against hot idle speed adjusting screw at specified idle speed in D or D_1 or D_2.

1969 Mustang, Falcon, and Cougar —Final Adjustments

1. With engine off, check accelerator pedal for height of 4½ in. measured from top of pedal at pivot point to floor pan. To obtain correct pedal height, adjust accelerator connecting link at point A in figure.
2. With engine off disconnect downshift control cable at point B from accelerator shaft lever.
3. With carburetor choke in off position, depress accelerator to floor. Block pedal to hold it in wide open position.
4. Rotate downshift lever C counter clockwise to place it against internal stop.
5. With lever held in this position, and all slack removed from cable, adjusting trunnion so that it will slide into accelerator shaft lever. Turn one additional turn clockwise, then secure it to lever with retaining clip.
6. Remove block to release carburetor linkage.

1969 Montego, Torino and Fairlane —Final Adjustment

1. Disconnect bellcrank to carburetor rod at point C and accelerator connecting link from throttle shaft at point B.
2. Disconnect stabilizer rod from stabilizer at point B.
3. Insert ¼ inch diameter pin through stabilizer and bracket.
4. Adjust length of stabilizer rod so that trunnion enters stabilizer freely. Secure stabilizer rod with retaining clip.
5. Secure carburetor to bellcrank rod to bell crank with attaching clip at point C.
6. Adjust length of accelerator rod connecting link to obtain accelerator pedal height of 4-4½ in. measured from top of pedal at pivot point. Connect accelerator connecting link to accelerator shaft with retaining clip after proper accelerator pedal height is obtained.
7. With engine off, disconnect downshift control cable at point D from accelerator shaft lever.
8. Rotate downshift lever E counter clockwise to place it against internal stop.
9. With lever held in this position, and all slack removed from cable, adjust trunnion so that it will slide into downshift lever. Turn it one additional turn clockwise, then secure it to accelerator shaft lever with retaining clip.
10. Remove block to release accelerator linkage.

1969-70 Mustang Six Cylinder, and 1970 Montego, Fairlane, Torino and Maverick Six Cylinder— Final Adjustments

1. Disconnect throttle return spring and remove trunnion and cable at bellcrank.
2. Hold transmission in full downshift against stop.
3. Hold carburetor throttle lever wide open against stop.
4. Adjust trunnion at bellcrank until ball stud on shaft and ball stud receiver on cable align. Then turn trunnion one full additional turn to increase length.
5. Release transmission and carburetor to normal free position.
6. Install throttle return spring.

1969-76 Cougar and 1969-73 Mustang V8s, and 1970-76 All Models—Final Adjustments

1. Disconnect throttle and downshift return springs.
2. Hold carburetor throttle lever in wide open position against stop.
3. Hold transmission in full downshift position against internal stop.
4. Turn adjustment screw on carburetor downshift lever to within 0.040-0.080 in. on 1971 and earlier models, 0.050–0.070 in. on 1972 models, and 0.010–0.080 on 1973 and later models, of contacting pickup surface of carburetor throttle lever.
5. Release transmission and carburetor to normal free positions.
6. Install throttle and downshift return springs.

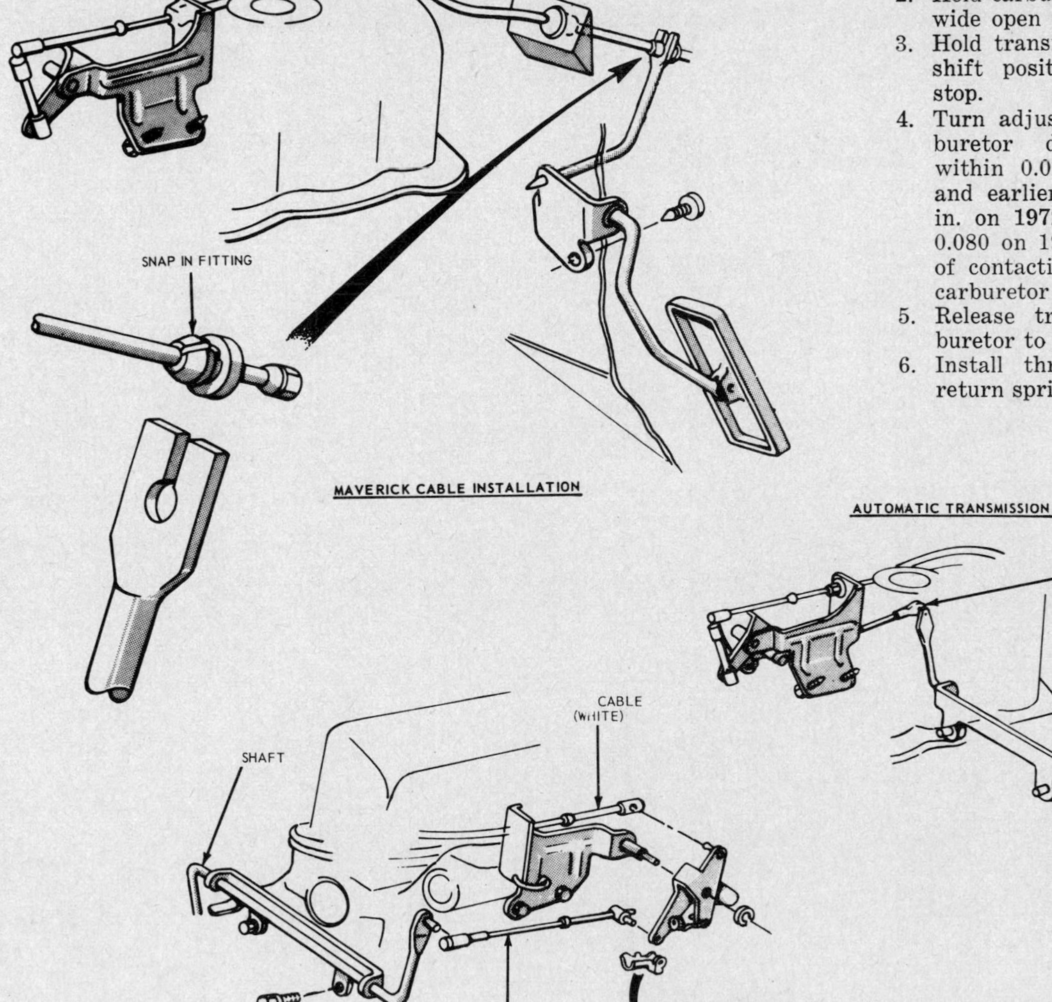

Throttle linkage adjustment—1970 Maverick (© Ford Motor Co)

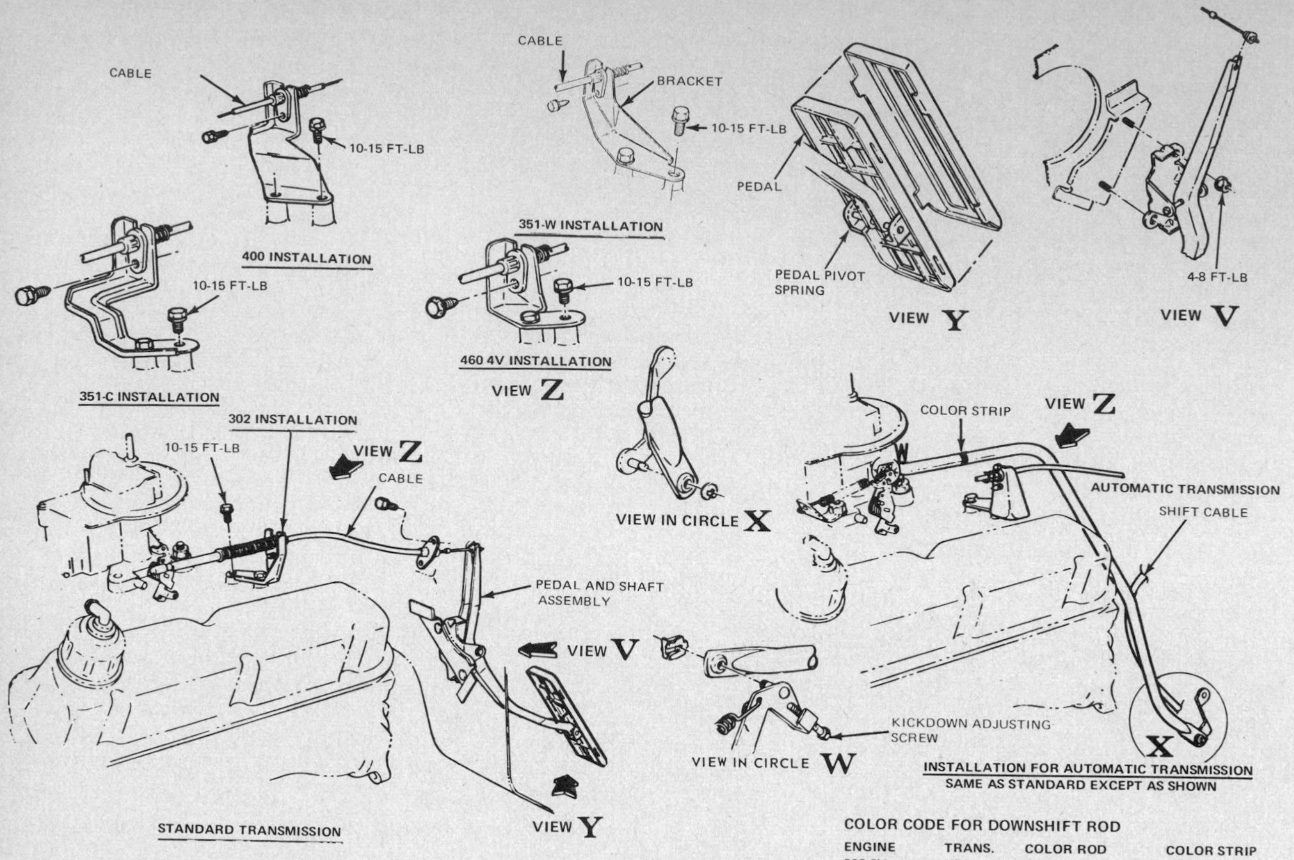

CABLE
10-15 FT-LB
400 INSTALLATION
CABLE
BRACKET
10-15 FT-LB
351-W INSTALLATION
10-15 FT-LB
460 4V INSTALLATION
VIEW Z
10-15 FT-LB
351-C INSTALLATION
PEDAL
PEDAL PIVOT SPRING
VIEW Y
4-8 FT-LB
VIEW V
302 INSTALLATION
10-15 FT-LB
VIEW Z
CABLE
PEDAL AND SHAFT ASSEMBLY
VIEW V
VIEW Y
STANDARD TRANSMISSION
VIEW IN CIRCLE X
COLOR STRIP
VIEW Z
AUTOMATIC TRANSMISSION
SHIFT CABLE
KICKDOWN ADJUSTING SCREW
VIEW IN CIRCLE W
INSTALLATION FOR AUTOMATIC TRANSMISSION SAME AS STANDARD EXCEPT AS SHOWN

KICK-DOWN CONTROL ADJUSTMENT

A. WITH CARBURETOR HELD AT W.O.T. POSITION AND THE KICKDOWN ROD HELD DOWNWARD AGAINST THE "THROUGH DETENT" STOP, ADJUST THE KICKDOWN ADJUSTING SCREW TO OBTAIN 0.010-0.080 INCH CLEARANCE BETWEEN THE SCREW AND THROTTLE ARM.

B. RELEASE CARBURETOR AND TRANSMISSION LEVERS TO FREE POSITIONS.

COLOR CODE FOR ACCELERATOR CABLE

ENGINE	COLOR
302-2V	YELLOW
351-2V	YELLOW
351-4V	BLUE
400-2V	YELLOW
460-4V P.I.	BLACK

COLOR CODE FOR DOWNSHIFT ROD

ENGINE	TRANS.	COLOR ROD	COLOR STRIP
302-2V	XP3	GOLD	YELLOW
351C-2V	XP3	GOLD	WHITE
351C-2V	XPL	GOLD	VIOLET-WHITE
351C-2V	FMX	GOLD	WHITE-BLUE
351W-2V	XP3	GOLD	RED-YELLOW
351W-2V	XPL	GOLD	BLACK-BLUE
351W-2V	FMX	GOLD	BROWN-SILVER
351-4V	XPL	GOLD	VIOLET
400-2V	XPL	GOLD	VIOLET
460-4V P.I.	XPL	GOLD	SILVER

Throttle and downshift linkage—1972-76 Torino, Elite, Montego and Cougar V8
(© Ford Motor Co)

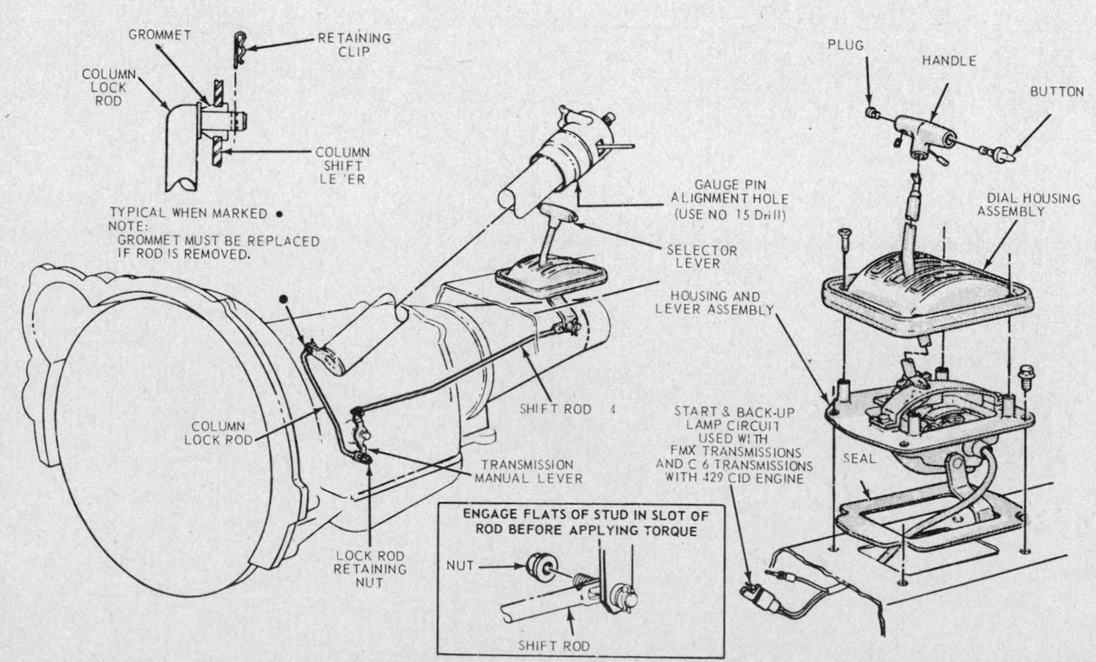

Automatic transmission floor mounted shift linkage and lock rod—1969-73 Mustang and Cougar
(© Ford Motor Co)

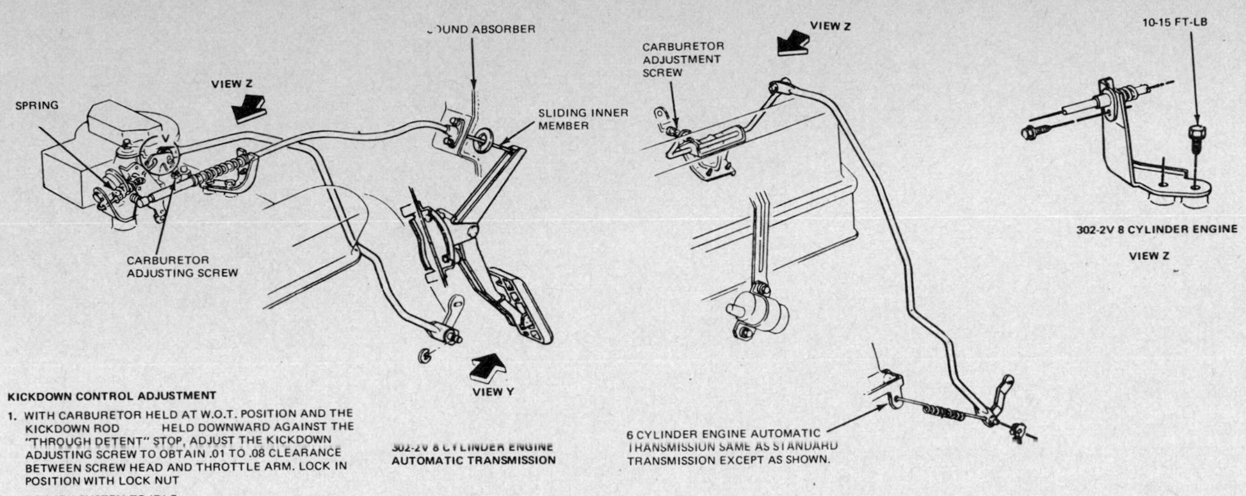

KICKDOWN CONTROL ADJUSTMENT

1. WITH CARBURETOR HELD AT W.O.T. POSITION AND THE KICKDOWN ROD HELD DOWNWARD AGAINST THE "THROUGH DETENT" STOP, ADJUST THE KICKDOWN ADJUSTING SCREW TO OBTAIN .01 TO .08 CLEARANCE BETWEEN SCREW HEAD AND THROTTLE ARM. LOCK IN POSITION WITH LOCK NUT
2. RETURN SYSTEM TO IDLE.

Throttle and downshift linkage—1971-76 Maverick and Comet
(© Ford Motor Co)

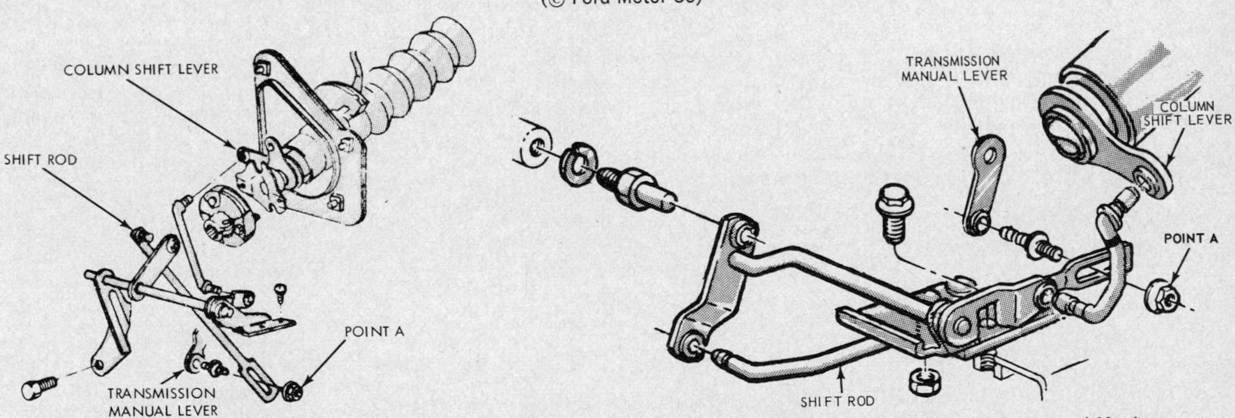

Column shift—1970-76 Maverick and 1971-76 Comet
(© Ford Motor Co)

Column shift—1969-70 Fairlane, Falcon, Torino and Montego
(© Ford Motor Co)

Shift Linkage Adjustment

Column Shift

1. With engine stopped, loosen clamp at shift lever at point A so that shift rod is free to slide in clamp. On vehicles equipped with a shift cable, remove the nut at point A and at manual lever stud.
2. Place transmission shift lever into D or D_1 (large dot) position. On Maverick with semi-automatic transmission, place lever in Hi.
3. Shift manual lever at transmission into D, D_1, or Hi. On transmission through 1971, D or Hi is the third detent from the rear. On 1972 and later transmissions, D is the second detent from the rear.
4. Tighten clamp on shift rod at point A to 10-20 ft. lbs. On vehicles equipped with a shift cable, position the cable end on the transmission manual lever stud, aligning the flats. Start the adjusting nut.
5. Check pointer alignment and transmission operation for all selector lever positions.

Floor or Console Shift

1. Place transmission shift lever in D.
2. Raise vehicle and loosen manual lever shift rod retaining nut. Move transmission lever to D_1 or D position. On all cars through 1970, D is fourth detent from rear. On 1971 cars, D is the third detent from the rear. On 1972 and later cars, D is second from rear.
3. With transmission shift lever and transmission manual lever in position, tighten nut at point A to 10-20 ft. lbs.
4. Check transmission operation for all selector lever detent positions.

NOTE: since 1970, all models with

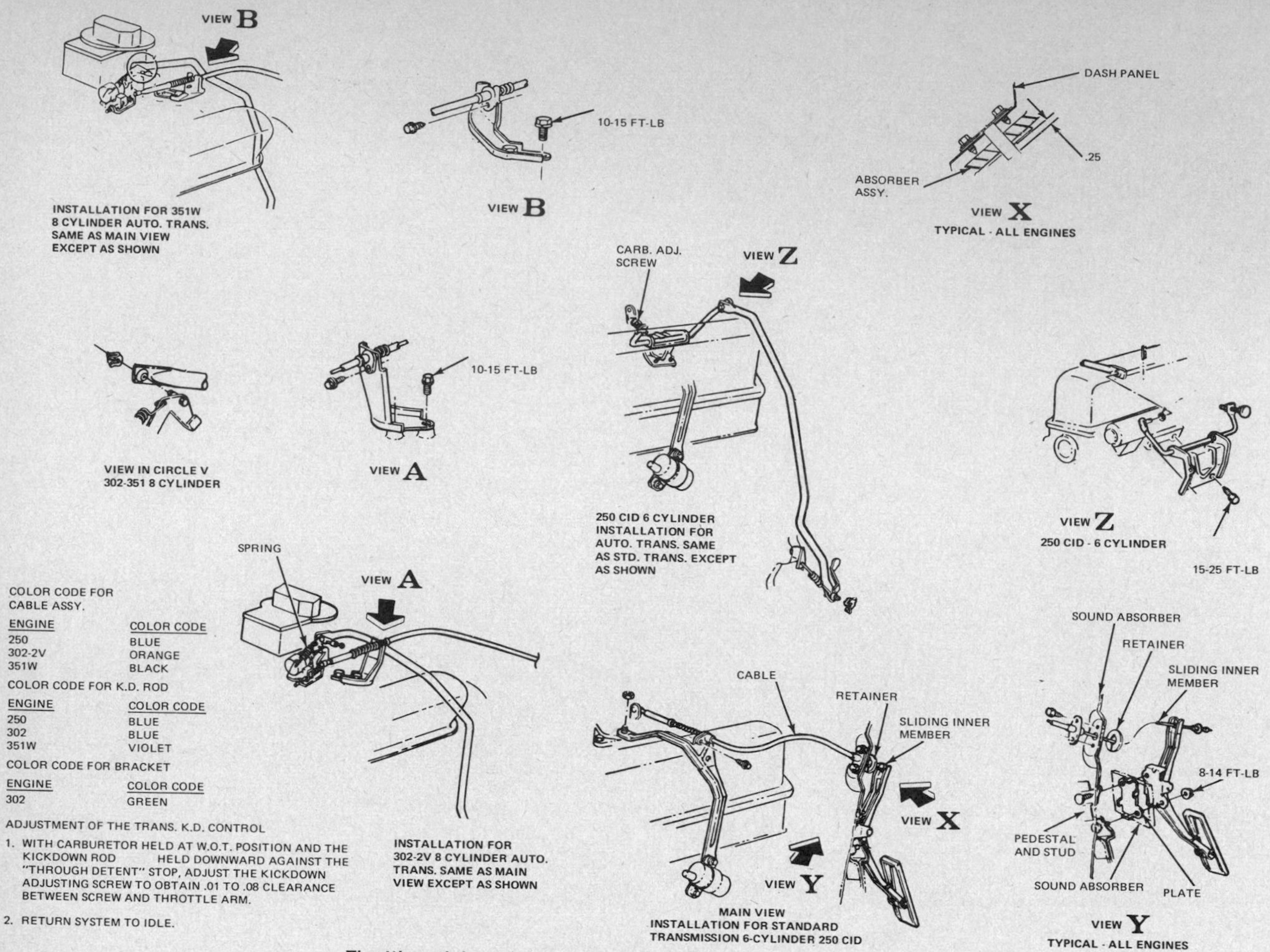

COLOR CODE FOR CABLE ASSY.

ENGINE	COLOR CODE
250	BLUE
302-2V	ORANGE
351W	BLACK

COLOR CODE FOR K.D. ROD

ENGINE	COLOR CODE
250	BLUE
302	BLUE
351W	VIOLET

COLOR CODE FOR BRACKET

ENGINE	COLOR CODE
302	GREEN

ADJUSTMENT OF THE TRANS. K.D. CONTROL

1. WITH CARBURETOR HELD AT W.O.T. POSITION AND THE KICKDOWN ROD HELD DOWNWARD AGAINST THE "THROUGH DETENT" STOP, ADJUST THE KICKDOWN ADJUSTING SCREW TO OBTAIN .01 TO .08 CLEARANCE BETWEEN SCREW AND THROTTLE ARM.
2. RETURN SYSTEM TO IDLE.

Throttle and downshift linkage—1975-76 Granada and Monarch
(© Ford Motor Co)

a floor or console mounted selector lever have incorporated a transmission lock out rod to prevent the transmission selector from being moved out of the PARK position when the ignition lock is in the OFF position. The lock rod connects the shift tube in the steering column to the transmission manual lever. The lock rod cannot be properly adjusted until the manual linkage adjustment is correct.

Lock Rod Adjustment

1. With the transmission selector lever in the DRIVE position, loosen the lock rod adjustment nut on the transmission manual lever.

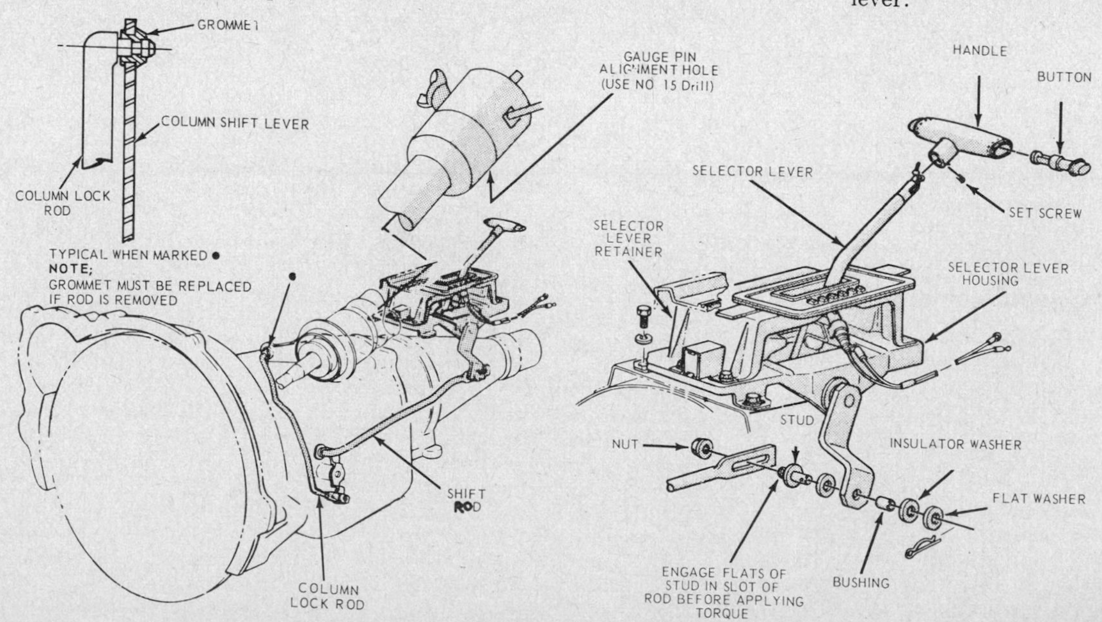

Automatic transmission floor mounted shift linkage and lock rod—1970-71 Fairlane, Torino and Montego
(© Ford Motor Co)

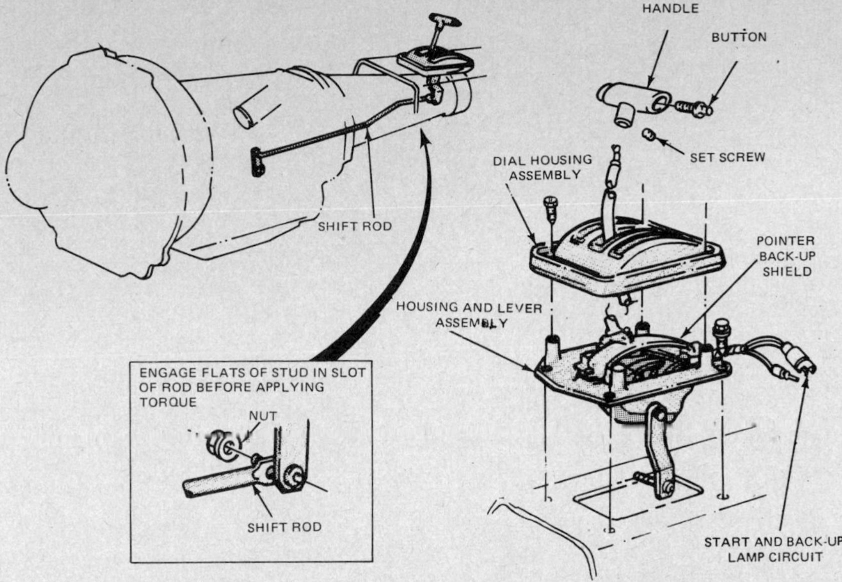

Automatic transmission floor mounted linkage—1972-76 Torino, Elite, Montego and Cougar
(© Ford Motor Co)

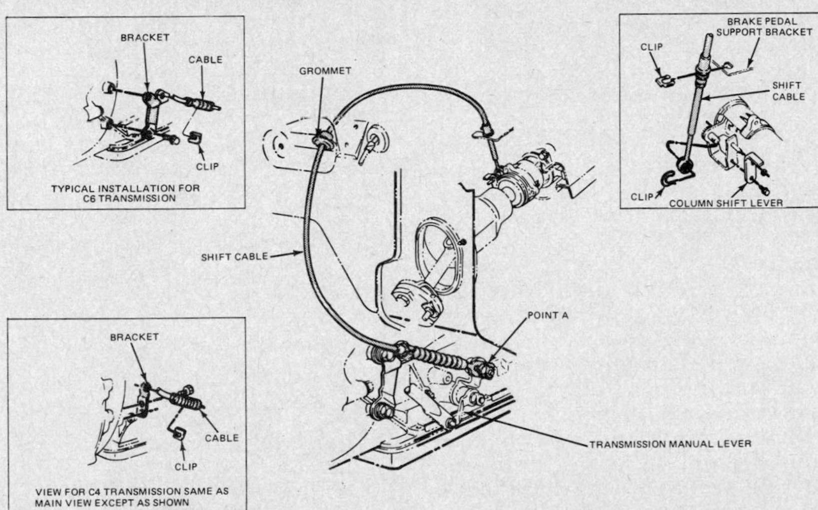

Automatic transmission column mounted linkage—1972-76 Torino, Elite, Montego, Cougar, Granada and Monarch

2. Insert a .180 in. diameter rod (No. 15 drill bit) in the gauge pin hole in the steering column socket casting, it is located at the 6 o'clock position directly below the ignition lock.
3. Manipulate the pin so that the casting will not move when the pin is fully inserted.
4. Torque the lock rod adjustment nut to 10-20 ft. lbs.
5. Remove the pin and check the linkage operation.

Band Adjustment

Intermediate Band

1. Clean all the dirt from the adjusting screw and remove and discard the locknut.
2. Install a new locknut on the adjusting screw. Using a torque wrench, tighten the adjusting screw to 10 ft lbs.

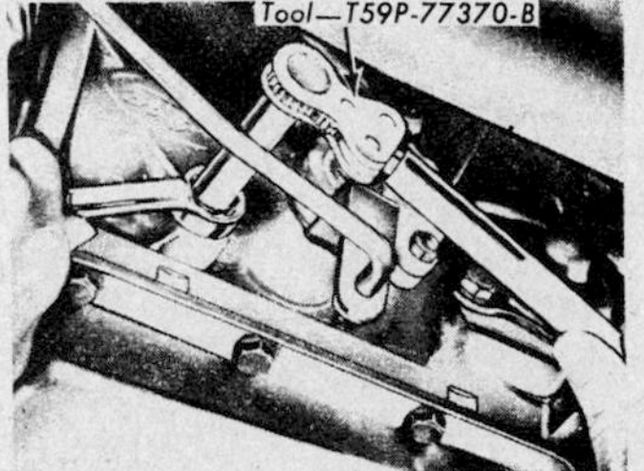

C4 Intermediate band adjustment
(© Ford Motor Co)

3. Back off the adjusting screw *exactly 1¾ turns.*
4. Hold the adjusting screw steady and tighten the locknut to the proper torque.

Low-Reverse Band

1. Clean all dirt from around the band adjusting screw, and remove and discard the locknut.
2. Install a new locknut on the adjusting screw. Using a torque wrench, tighten the adjusting screw to 10 ft lbs.

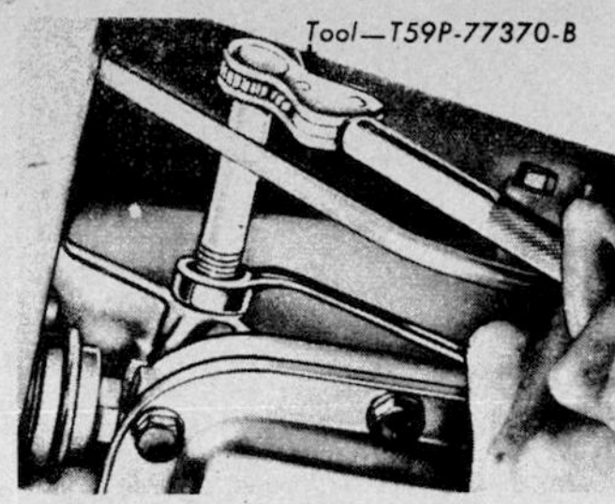

C4 Low-Reverse band adjustment
(© Ford Motor Co)

3. Back off the adjusting screw *exactly 3 full turns.*
4. Hold the adjusting screw steady and tighten the locknut to the proper torque.

C6

Throttle and Downshift Linkage

Initial Adjustments

See C4 section.

Montego, Torino and Fairlane with 390 Engine—Final Adjustments

1. Disconnect bellcrank to carburetor rod at point C and accelerator rod from throttle shaft at point B.
2. Disconnect stabilizer rod from stabilizer at point A.
3. Insert ¼ in. diameter pin through stabilizer and bracket.
4. Adjust length of stabilizer rod so that trunnion enters stabilizer freely. Secure stabilizer rod with retaining clip.
5. Secure carburetor to bellcrank rod to bellcrank with attaching clip at point C.
6. Adjust length of accelerator rod to obtain accelerator pedal height of 4-4½ in. measured at pedal.
7. Connect accelerator rod to accelerator shaft with retaining clip after proper accelerator pedal height has been established.
8. With engine off, disconnect downshift rod from lever at point D.
9. With carburetor choke in off position, depress accelerator pedal to floor; block pedal to hold it in open position.
10. Rotate downshift lever on transmission in counter clockwise direction to place it against internal stop.
11. Adjust trunnion at point D so that it enters downshift lever freely.
12. Turn it one additional turn counter clockwise to lengthen rod. Secure it to lever with retaining clip.
13. Remove block from accelerator pedal.

1969-76 All Models—Final Adjustments

See C4 section under 1969-76 Cougar V8.

Shift Linkage Adjustment, Transmission Lock Rod Adjustment

See C4 section.

Band Adjustment

Intermediate Band Adjustment

1. Raise the car on a hoist or place it on jackstands.
2. Clean the threads of the intermediate band adjusting screw.
3. Loosen the adjustment screw lock nut.
4. Tighten the adjusting screw to 10 ft lbs and back the screw off *exactly 1½ turns.* Tighten the adjusting screw locknut.

FMX

Since 1969, the FMX transmission has been used in some intermediate size Fords. It is usually used in conjunction with the 351 V8 engine. The throttle and downshift linkage adjustments are the same as used with the C4 transmission.

FMX Band Adjustment

See Ford section.

U-JOINTS

Rear Universal Joint Removal

The rear universal joint has two pillow blocks which are bolted to the pinion shaft flange.

Take out the four bolts that hold the bearing blocks to the pinion shaft and gently tap off the bearing blocks.

Lower the back end of the drive shaft and the front end can be slid out of the back of the transmission together with the transmission yoke portion of the front universal joint.

Carry the assembly—the front universal joint complete, the driveshaft and the rear universal joint—to the bench and remove the cross from the rear universal joint by taking out the lock rings from the inner side of the bearings. Using a large punch or an arbor press, drive one of the bearings in toward the center, which will force out the opposite bearing.

When it is pressed out far enough to grip it with a pair of pliers, grip it and pull it out of the driveshaft yoke.

Now drive the cross in the opposite direction until the opposite bearing has been driven far enough out for gripping with a pair of pliers.

When both bearings have been taken out, the cross can be lifted from between the two yokes.

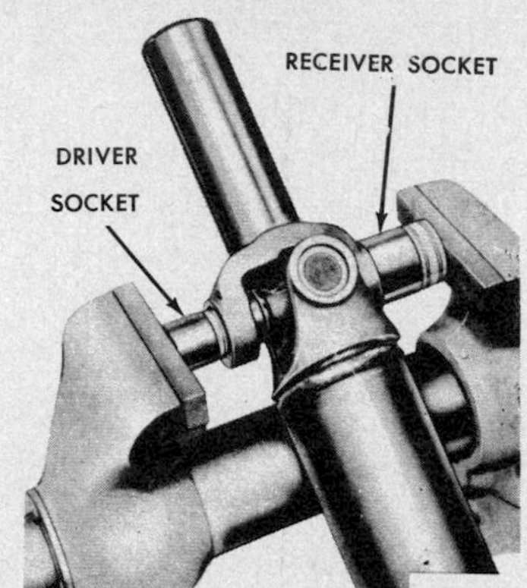

U-joint removal (© Ford Motor Co)

Front Universal Joint Removal

Follow the procedure given above for the rear universal joint but leave the rear universal joint cross in place on the driveshaft if it is not to be removed.

Remove the lock rings from the inner side of two opposite bearings and press on the outer side of one of the bearings, forcing the cross over, which will force the bearing on the opposite side out of its yoke.

Remove the bearing which was forced out of the yoke and then press the cross in the opposite direction to press the other bearing out.

Repeat this procedure on the third and fourth bearings.

When installing the new bearings in the universal joint yoke, it is possible to put them in with a driver of some type, but it is recommended that this work be done in an arbor press since a heavy jolt on the needle bearings can very easily misalign them, which will greatly shorten their life.

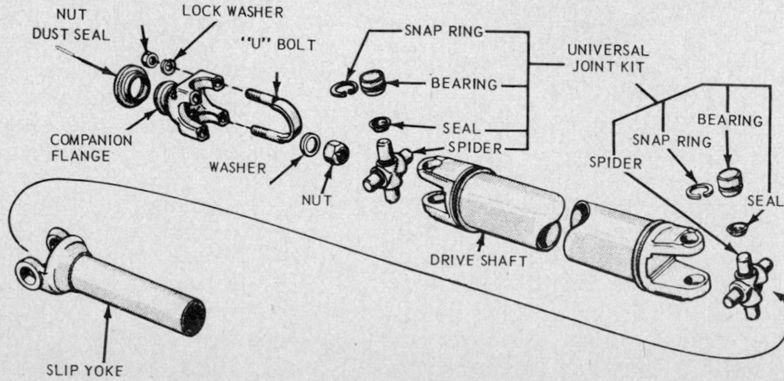

Driveshaft and universal joint assembly (© Ford Motor Co)

REAR AXLE

Axle Shaft

Shaft Removal and Installation, Bearing Replacement

NOTE: Bearings must be pressed on and off the shaft with an arbor press. Unless you have access to one, it is inadvisable to attempt any repair work on the axle shaft and bearing assemblies.

1. Remove the wheel, tire, and brake drum.
2. Remove the nuts holding the retainer plate to the backing plate. Disconnect the brake line.
3. Remove the retainer and install nuts, finger-tight, to prevent the brake backing plate from being dislodged.

NOTE: Some late-model cars using the integral carrier or WER axles have C-clips retaining the axle shafts. Prior to removing the shaft, remove the inspection plate and check for C-clips. The clips must be removed prior to shaft removal.

4. Pull out the axle shaft and bearing assembly, using a slide hammer.

NOTE: If end-play is found to be excessive, the bearing should be replaced. Shimming the bearing is not recommended as this ignores end-play of the bearing itself and could result in improper seating of the bearing.

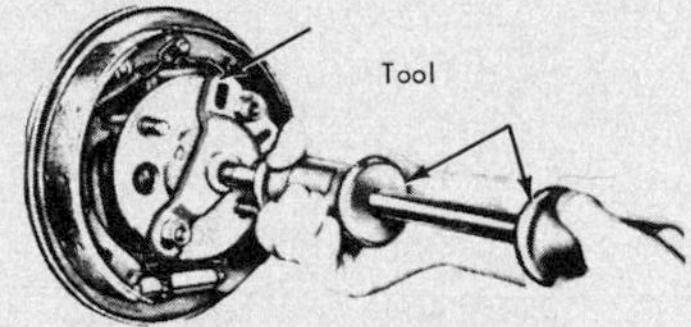

Removing axle shaft (© Ford Motor Co)

5. Using a chisel, nick the bearing retainer in 3 or 4 places. The retainer does not have to be cut, but merely collapsed sufficiently to allow the bearing retainer to be slid from the shaft.
6. Press off the bearing and install the new one by pressing it into position.
7. Press on the new retainer.

NOTE: Do not attempt to press the bearing and retainer on at the same time.

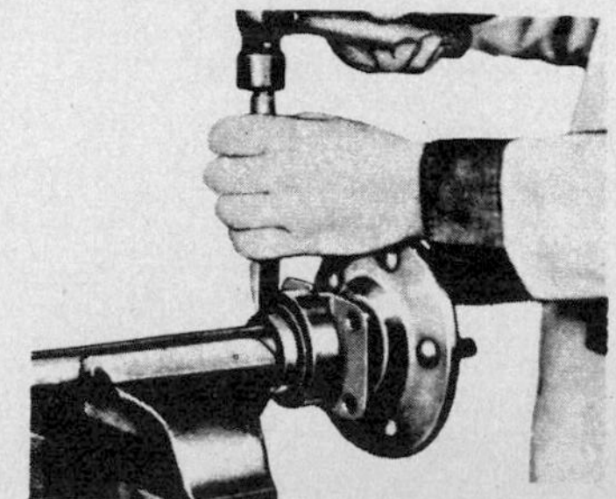

Removing rear wheel bearing retainer ring (© Ford Motor Co)

8. Assemble the shaft and bearing in the housing, being sure that the bearing is seated properly in the housing.
9. Install the retainer, drum, wheel, and tire. Bleed the brakes.

Axle Shaft Replacement

1. Remove the axle shaft from the rear axle assembly, following the procedures previously discussed.
2. Using a two-fingered seal puller (slide hammer), remove the seal from the axle housing.
3. Thoroughly clean the recess in the rear axle housing from which the seal was removed.
4. Position a new seal on the housing and drive it into place with a seal installation tool. If this tool is not available, a wood block may be substituted.

NOTE: Although the right and left-hand seals are identical, there are many different types of seals which have been used. It is advisable to have one of the old seals with you when you are purchasing new ones.

5. When the seal is properly installed, install the axle shaft.

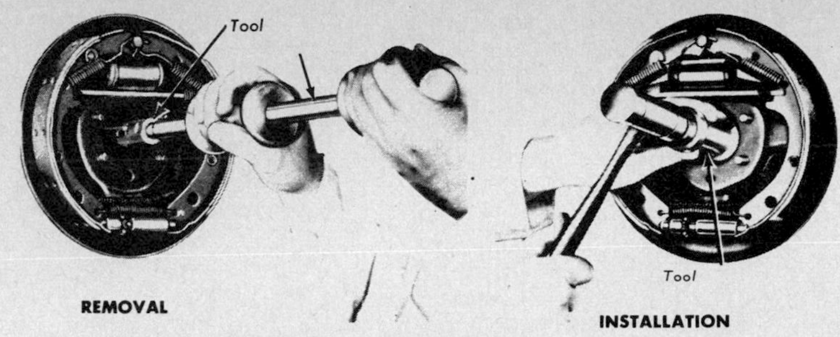

Removing and installing axle shaft seal (© Ford Motor Co)

JACKING, HOISTING

Jack car at front under spring seat of lower control arm. Jack car at rear axle housing close to differential case.

Twin post lifts—front adapters must be carefully placed, large enough to cover entire spring seat area. On models with leaf spring rear suspension, rear adapters or forks must be placed under axle not more than one in. outboard from welds near differential housing. Do not allow the lifts to contact the steering linkage.

Rear hoist contact area—cars with unitized construction (© Ford Motor Co)

On 1972 and later Torinos and Montegos, as well as 1974 and later Cougars and Elites, *do not* position the fork lifts outboard of the rear suspension lower arms. Place the forklifts under the axle housing inboard of the suspension arm brackets.

Frame contact lifts—on all except 1972 Torino and Montego and 1974 and later Cougar and Elite, place adapters as shown in diagram. Be sure that pads cover at least 12 sq. in. in area.

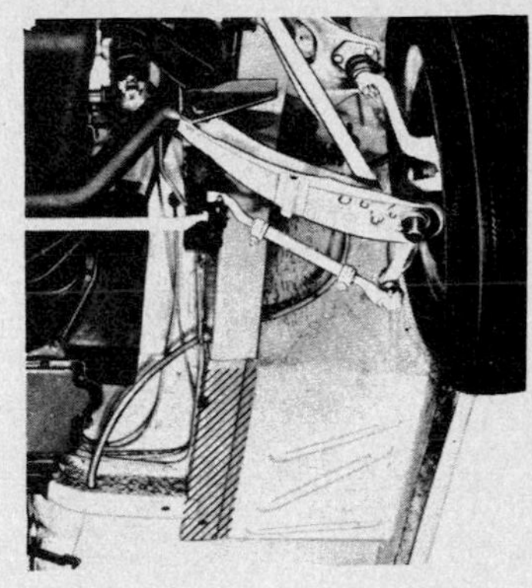

Front hoist contact area—cars with unitized construction (© Ford Motor Co)

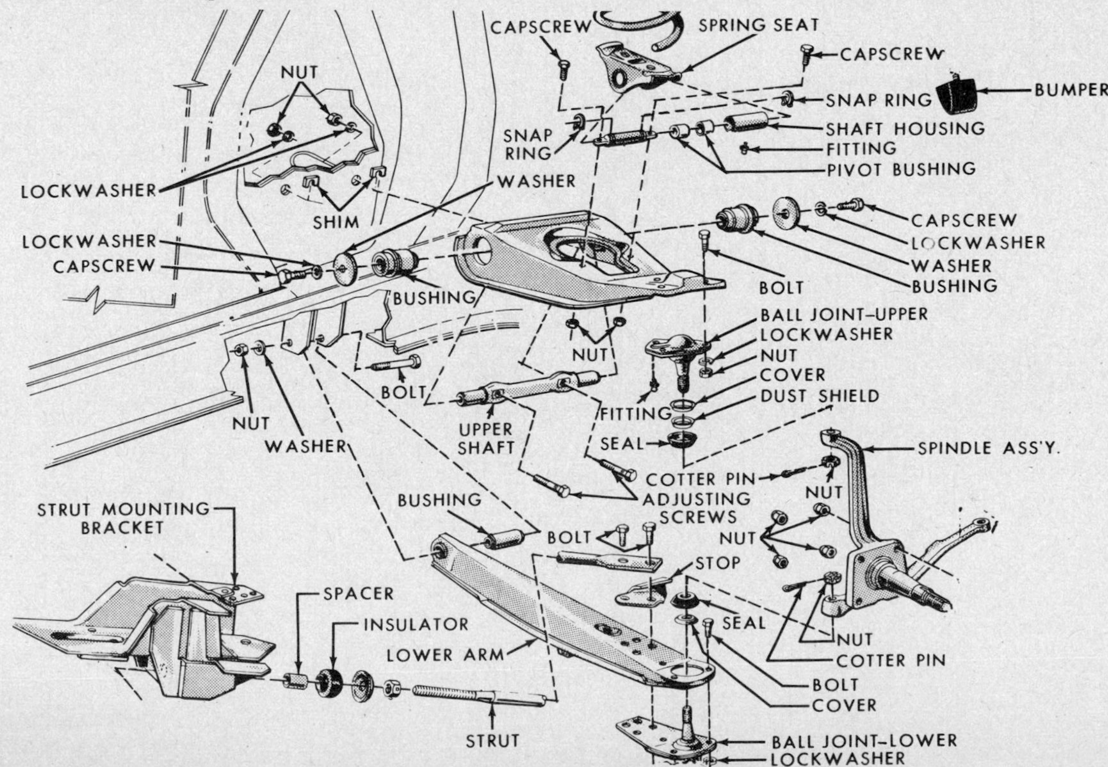

Front suspension—spring on upper arm (© Ford Motor Co)

FRONT SUSPENSION

On all compact and intermediate Ford Products, except the 1972 and later Torino and Montego and 1974 and later Cougar and Elite, the front coil springs are mounted on top of the upper control arm to a tower in the sheet metal of the body. This type of mounting provides good stability. The lower arm and stablizing strut substitute for the conventional a frame and serve to guide the lower part of the spindle through its cycle of up-and-down movement. The rod-type stabilizing strut is mounted between two rubber buffer pads at the front end to cushion fore and aft thrust of suspension. The effective length of this rod is variable and must be considered in maintenance. Ball joints are of the usual steel construction.

On 1972 and later Torinos and Montegos and 1974 and later Cougars and Elites, the front coil springs are mounted between the upper and lower control arm. This type of mounting, used on standard-sized Fords for many years, aids cornering ability by lowering the roll center.

Front end alignment procedures are given in the Unit Repair Section.

Figures covering the caster, camber, toe-in, kingpin inclination, and turning radius can be found in the Front Wheel Alignment table of this section.

Coil Spring on Upper Arm

Shock Absorber

Removal

1. Raise the hood and remove the three shock absorber-to-spring tower attaching bolts.
2. Raise the front of the vehicle and place jackstands under the lower control arms.
3. Remove the shock absorber lower attaching nuts, washers, and insulators.
4. Lift the shock absorber and upper bracket from the spring tower and remove the bracket from the shock absorber. Remove the insulators from the lower attaching studs.

Installation

1. Install the upper mounting bracket on the shock absorber. Install the insulators on the lower attaching studs.
2. Place the shock absorber and upper bracket assembly in the spring tower, making sure that the shock absorber lower studs are in the pivot plate holes.
3. Install the two washers and attaching nuts on the lower studs of the shock absorbers.
4. Install the three shock absorber upper mounting bracket attaching nuts.
5. Remove the jackstands and lower the vehicle.

Spring

Removal

1. Raise hood and remove shock absorber upper mounting bracket bolts.

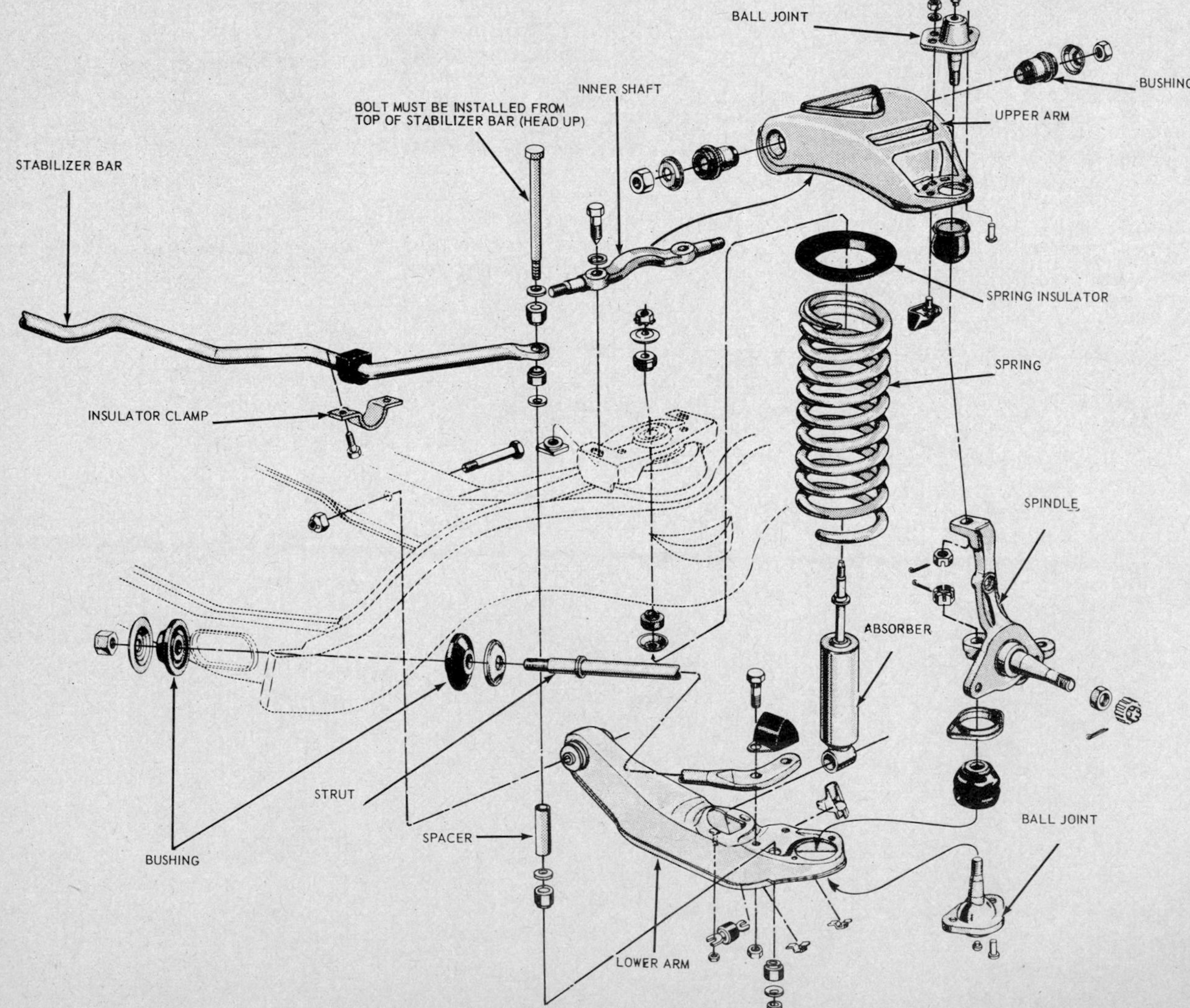

Front suspension—spring on lower arm (© Ford Motor Co)

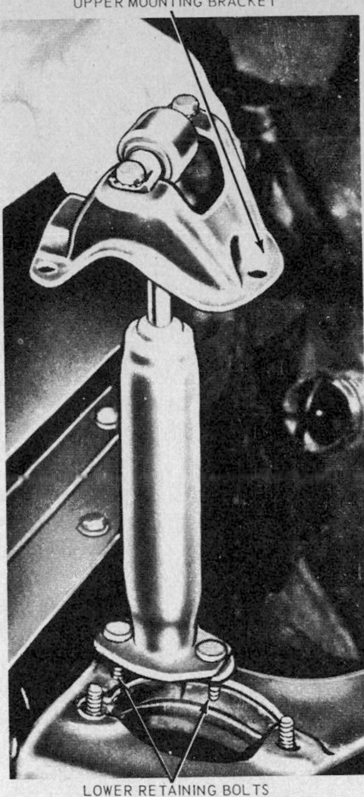

Removing shock absorber and bracket assembly—spring on upper arm
(© Ford Motor Co)

2. Raise front of vehicle, and place safety stands under inboard ends of lower control arms.
3. Remove shock absorber lower attaching nuts, washers and insulators.
4. Lift shock absorber and upper bracket from spring tower.
5. Remove wheel cover on hub cap.
6. Remove grease cap, cotter pin, nut lock, adjusting nut, and outer bearing.
7. Pull wheel, tire and hub and drum off spindle as an assembly. Remove the disc brake assembly, if so equipped.
8. Install spring compressor as shown in figures.
9. Compress spring until all tension is removed from control arms.
10. Remove two upper control arm attaching nuts and swing control arm out board.
11. Release spring compressor and remove.
12. Remove spring.

Installation

1. Place upper spring insulator on spring and secure in place with tape.
2. Position spring in spring tower and compress with spring compressor.
3. Swing upper control arm in board and install attaching nuts.
4. Release spring pressure and guide spring into upper arm spring seat. The end of the spring must be not more than ½ in. from tab on spring seat.
5. Remove spring compressor and position wheel, tire, and hub and drum on spindle. Install disc brake assembly, if so equipped.
6. Install bearing, washer and adjusting nut.
7. On disc brake cars, loosen adjusting nut three turns, and rock wheel hub and rotor assembly in and out to push disc brake pads away from rotor.
8. While rotating wheel, hub and drum assembly, torque adjusting nut to 17-25 ft. lbs. to seat bearing.

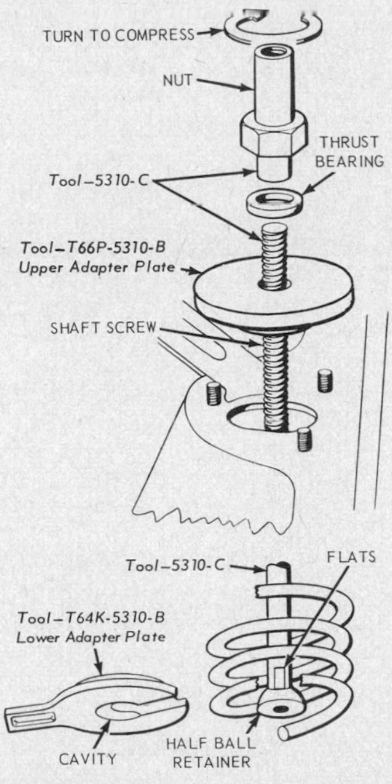

Spring compressor—spring on upper arm
(© Ford Motor Co)

9. With 1⅛ in. box wrench back off adjusting nut ½ turn, and tighten nut to 10-15 in. lbs. or finger tight.
10. Position lock on adjusting nut and install new cotter pin. Bend ends of pin around castellated flange of nut lock.
11. Check front wheel rotation and install grease cap and hub cap.
12. Install shock absorber and upper bracket assembly, making sure shock absorber lower studs have insulators and are in pivot plate holes.
13. Install nuts and washers on lower studs and torque to 8-12 ft. lbs. on 1970 and later models and 12-17 ft. lbs. on 1969 models.
14. Install nuts on shock absorber upper bracket.
15. Lower car.

Lower Ball Joint

On all intermediate size Ford cars which have the coil springs mounted on the upper control arm, the lower ball joint is an integral part of the lower control arm. If the lower ball joint is defective the entire lower control arm must be replaced.

Inspection

1. Raise the vehicle on a hoist or floor jack so that the front wheel falls to the full down position.
2. Have an assistant grasp the bottom of the tire and move the wheel in and out.
3. As the wheel is being moved, observe the lower control arm where the spindle attaches to it.
4. Any movement between the lower part of the spindle and the lower control arm indicates a bad control arm which must be replaced.

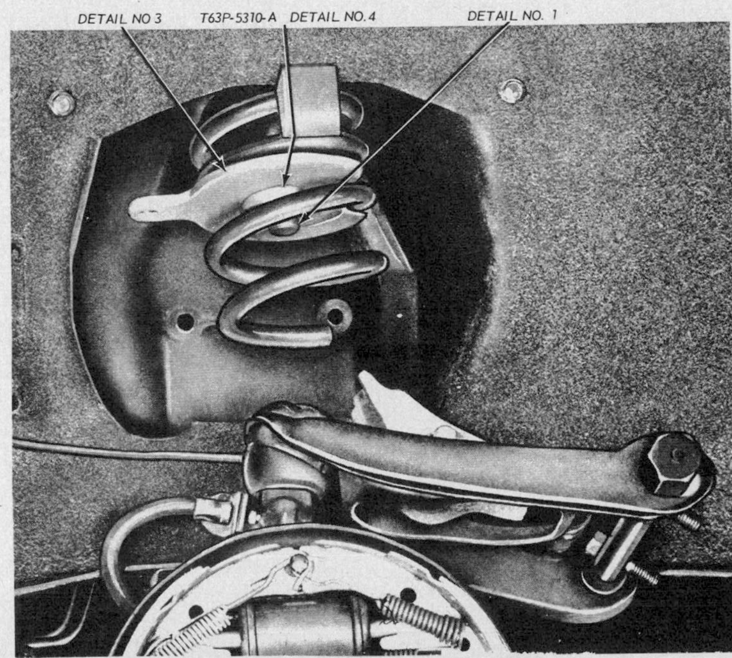

Compressing spring—spring on upper arm (© Ford Motor Co)

NOTE: during this check, the upper ball joint will be unloaded and may move; this is normal and not an indication of a bad ball joint. Also, do not mistake a loose wheel bearing for a worn ball joint.

Replacement

1. Position an upper control arm support between the upper arm and side rail as shown in the illustration.
2. Raise the vehicle, position jack stands and remove the wheel and tire.
3. Remove the stabilizer bar to link attaching nut and disconnect the bar from the link.
4. Remove the link bolt from the lower arm.
5. Remove the strut bar to lower attaching nuts and bolts.
6. Remove the lower ball joint cotter pin and back off the nut. Using a suitable tool, loosen the ball joint stud in the spindle.
7. Remove the nut from the arm and lower the arm.
8. Remove the lower arm to underbody cam attaching parts and remove the arm.
9. To install, position the lower arm in the underbody and install the ball joint and cam attaching parts loosely.
10. Install the stabilizer and strut and torque the attaching parts to specifications.
11. Torque the lower arm pivot and ball joint stud to specifications.
12. Lower the car and remove the upper arm support.
13. Front end alignment must be rechecked.

Upper Ball Joint

Inspection

1. Raise the vehicle on a hoist or floor jack so that the front wheels hang in full down position.
2. Have an assistant grasp the wheel top and bottom and apply alternate in and out pressure to the top and bottom of the wheel.
3. Radial play of $\frac{1}{4}$ in. is acceptable measured at the inside of the wheel adjacent to the upper arm.

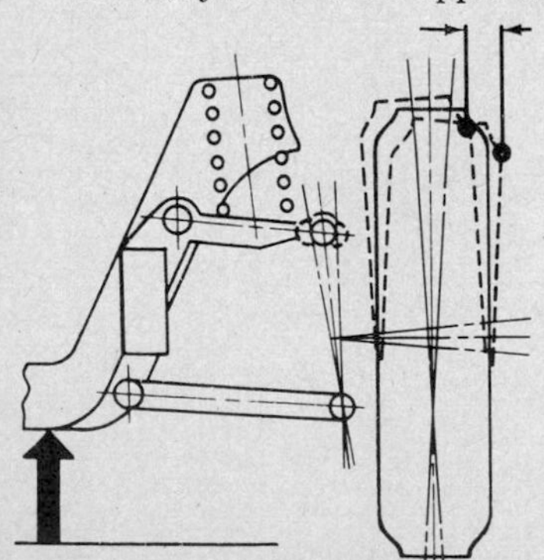

Measuring upper ball joint radial play —spring on upper arm (© Ford Motor Co)

NOTE: this radial play measurement is multiplied at the outer circumference of the tire and should not be measured here. Measure only at the inside of the wheel.

Replacement

1. Position support between the upper arm and frame rail as shown in illustration.
2. Raise the vehicle and remove the tire and wheel.
3. Remove the upper ball joint cotter pin and loosen the nut.
4. Using a suitable tool, loosen the ball joint in the spindle.
5. Remove the three ball joint retaining rivets using a large chisel.
6. Remove the nut from the ball joint stud and remove the ball joint.
7. Clean and remove all burrs from the ball joint mounting area of the control arm before installing new ball joint.
8. Install the ball joint in the upper arm using the service part nuts and bolts. Do not attempt to rivet a new ball joint to the arm.
9. Install and torque the ball joint stud nut and install the cotter pin.
10. Lubricate the new joint with a hand type grease gun only, using an air pressure gun may loosen the ball joint seal.
11. Install wheel, lower vehicle and remove upper arm support.
12. Check front end alignment.

Upper Control Arm

Replacement

1. Remove the shock absorber and upper mounting bracket from the car as an assembly.
2. Raise the vehicle and remove the wheel and tire as an assembly.
3. Install spring compressor tool.
4. Place a safety stand under the lower arm.
5. Remove the cotter pin from the upper ball joint stud and loosen the nut.
6. Using a suitable tool, loosen the ball joint in the spindle, then, remove the nut and lift the stud from the spindle.
7. Remove the upper arm attaching nuts from the engine compartment, and remove the upper arm.
8. To install the arm, position it on the mounting bracket and install the attaching nuts on the inner shaft attaching bolts.

NOTE: the original equipment keystone-type lockwashers must be used with the inner shaft attaching nuts and bolts.

9. Install the upper ball joint stud in the spindle and tighten the nut to specifications. Install a new cotter pin.
10. Remove spring compressor and position spring on upper arm. Install wheel and check front end alignment.

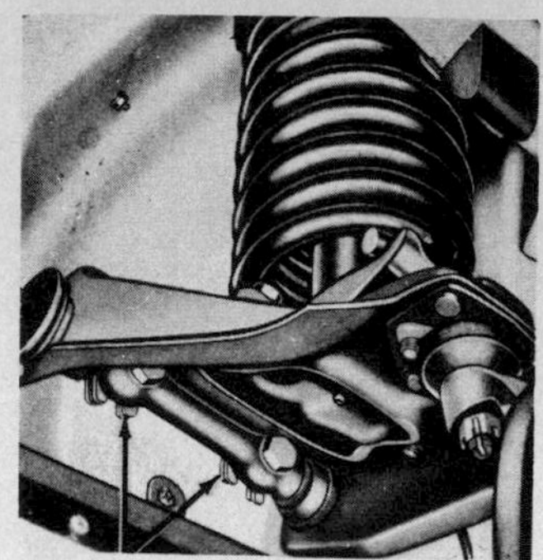

Upper control arm assembly—spring on upper arm (© Ford Motor Co)

Upper control arm lubricating tool (© Ford Motor Co)

When upper control arm bushings become low on lubrication, they become very noisy. This can often be corrected by lubrication and it is not necessary to replace the bushings. On early models that do not contain grease plugs it is necessary to drill and tap the bushing to accept a grease fitting.

On later models with grease plugs it is difficult to remove the plug and grease the bushing with conventional tools. Ford Motor Co. has available through its dealers an upper A-arm lubrication kit which greatly eases the performance of this operation.

Coil Spring on Lower Arm

Shock Absorber

Removal and Replacement

1. Remove the nut, washer, and bushing from the upper end of the shock absorber.
2. Raise the vehicle and install jackstands under the frame rails.

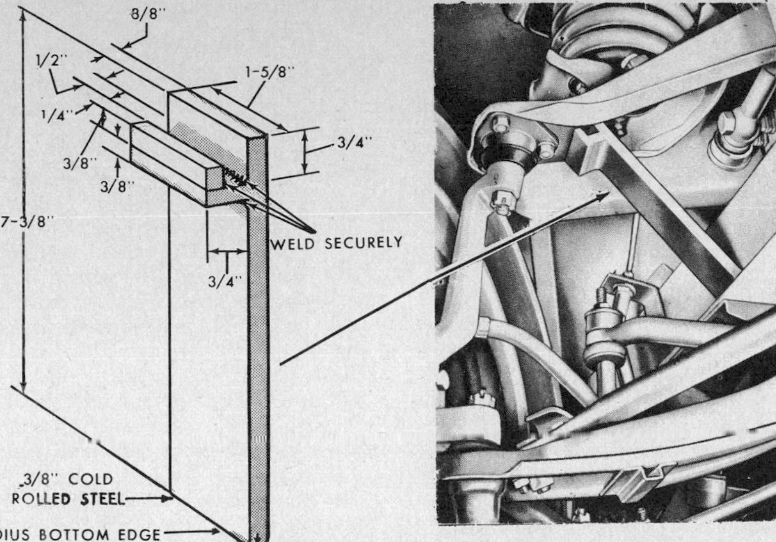

Upper control arm support—spring on upper arm (© Ford Motor Co)

3. Remove the two bolts securing the shock absorber to the lower control arm and remove the shock absorber.
4. Install a new bushing and washer on the top of the shock absorber and position the unit inside the front spring. Install the two lower attaching bolts and torque them to 8–15 ft lbs.
5. Remove the jackstands and lower the vehicle.
6. Place a new bushing and washer on the shock absorber top stud and install the attaching nut. Torque to 22–30 ft lbs.

Coil Spring and Lower Control Arm R & R

1. Raise car and support it with stands placed in back of lower arms.
2. If equipped with drum type brakes, remove the wheel and brake drum as an assembly. Remove the brake backing plate attaching bolts and remove the backing plate from the spindle. Wire the assembly back out of the way.
3. If equipped with disc brakes, remove the wheel from the hub. Remove the bolts and washers that hold the caliper and brake hose bracket to the spindle. Remove the caliper from the rotor and wire it back out of the way. Then, remove the hub and rotor from the spindle.
4. Disconnect lower end of the shock absorber and push it up to the retracted position.
5. Disconnect stabilizer bar link from the lower arm.
6. Remove cotter pins from the upper and lower ball joint stud nuts.
7. Remove two bolts and nuts holding the strut to the lower arm.
8. Loosen the lower ball joint stud nut two turns. Do not remove this nut.
9. Install a spreader tool between the upper and lower ball joint studs.
10. Expand the tool until the tool exerts considerable pressure on the studs. Tap the spindle near the lower stud with a hammer to loosen the stud in the spindle. Do not loosen the stud with tool pressure only.
11. Position floor jack under the lower arm and remove the lower ball joint stud nut.
12. Lower floor jack and remove the spring and insulator.
13. Remove the A-arm to crossmember attaching parts, and remove the arm from the car.
14. Reverse above procedure to install. If lower control arm was replaced because of damage, check front end alignment.

Coil spring and lower arm replacement —spring on lower arm (© Ford Motor Co)

Lower Ball Joint

Inspection

1. Raise the vehicle by placing a floor jack under the lower arm; or, raise the vehicle on a hoist and place a jack stand under the lower arm and lower the vehicle onto it to remove the preload from the lower ball joint.
2. Have an assistant grasp the wheel top and bottom and apply alternate in and out pressure to the top and bottom of the wheel.
3. Radial play of ¼ in. is acceptable measured at the inside of the wheel adjacent to the lower arm.

NOTE: this radial play is multiplied at the outer circumference of the tire and should be measured only at the inside of the wheel.

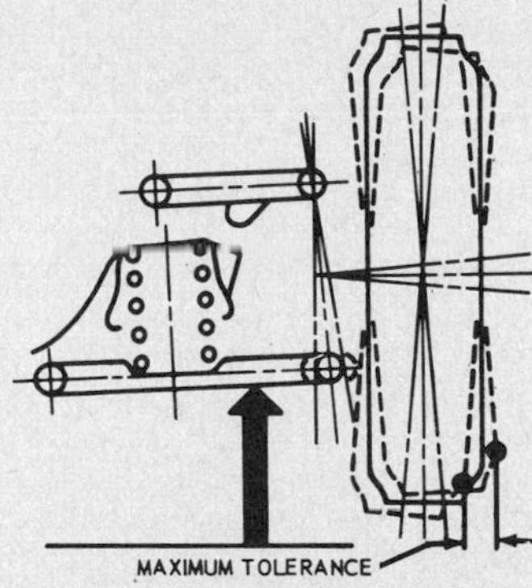

Measuring lower ball joint radial play —spring on lower arm (© Ford Motor Co)

Replacement

1. Raise the vehicle on a hoist and allow the front wheels to fall to their full down position.
2. Drill a 1/8 in. hole completely through each ball joint attaching rivet.
3. Use a ⅜ in. drill in the pilot hole to drill off the head of the rivet.
4. Drive the rivets from the lower arm.
5. Place a jack under the lower arm and lower the vehicle about 6 in.
6. Remove the lower ball joint stud cotter pin and attaching nut.
7. Using a suitable tool, loosen the ball joint from the spindle and remove the ball joint from the lower arm.
8. Clean all metal burrs from the lower arm and install the new ball joint, using the service part nuts and bolts to attach the ball joint to the lower arm. Do not attempt to rerivet the ball joint once it has been removed.
9. Check front end alignment.

Upper Ball Joint

Inspection

1. Raise the vehicle by placing a floor jack under the lower arm. Do not allow the lower arm to hang freely with the vehicle on a hoist or bumper jack.
2. Have an assistant grasp the bottom of the tire and move the wheel in and out.
3. As the wheel is being moved, observe the upper control arm where the spindle attaches to it. Any movement between the upper part of the spindle and the upper ball joint indicates a bad

ball joint which must be replaced.

NOTE: During this check the lower ball joint will be unloaded and may move; this is normal and not an indication of a bad ball joint. Also, do not mistake a loose wheel bearing for a defective ball joint.

Replacement

1. Raise the vehicle on a hoist and allow the front wheels to fall to their full down position.
2. Drill a 1/8 in. hole completely through each ball joint attaching rivet.
3. Using a large chisel, cut off the head of each rivet and drive them from the upper arm.
4. Place a jack under the lower arm and lower the vehicle about 6 in.
5. Remove the cotter pin and attaching nut from the ball joint stud.
6. Using a suitable tool, loosen the ball joint stud from the spindle and remove the ball joint from the upper arm.
7. Clean all metal burrs from the upper arm and install the new ball point, using the service part nuts and bolts to attach the ball joint to the upper arm. Do not attempt to rerivet the ball joint once it has been removed.
8. Check front end alignment.

Upper Control Arm

Replacement

1. Raise the vehicle on a hoist.
2. If equipped with drum brakes remove the tire, wheel and brake drum as an assembly. If equipped with disc brakes, remove the tire and wheel.
3. Remove the cotter pin and attaching nut from the ball joint stud.
4. Using a suitable tool, loosen the upper ball joint from the spindle.
5. Place a jack under the lower arm and lower the vehicle about 6 in.
6. Remove the upper arm inner shaft attaching bolts and remove the arm and shaft from the chassis as an assembly.
7. Reverse above procedure to install.
8. Adjust front end alignment.

REAR SUSPENSION

All intermediate and compact-sized Ford products, except the 1972 and later Torino and Montego, and 1974 and later Cougar and Elite, use a leaf-spring rear suspension. A pair of leaf springs support the axle housing, which is secured to the springs by two U-bolts and retaining plates. Each spring is suspended from the underbody side rails by a hanger at the front and a shackle at the rear. The shock absorbers are mounted between the leaf spring retaining plates and brackets bolted to the crossmember. Some 1969-71 high-performance models are equipped with staggered rear shock absorbers.

1972 and later Torinos and Montegos and 1974 and later Cougars and Elites, utilize a coil spring, rear suspension. The axle housing is suspended from the frame by an upper and lower trailing arm, and a shock absorber at each side of the vehicle. These arms pivot in the frame members and the rear axle housing brackets. Each coil spring is mounted between a lower seat which is welded to the axle housing and an upper seat integral with the frame. The shock absorbers are bolted to the spring upper seats at the top and brackets mounted on the axle housing at the bottom. A rear stabilizer, bar attached to the frame side rail brackets and the two axle housing brackets, is available as optional equipment.

Leaf Spring Suspension

Spring R & R

1. Raise the vehicle and place supports beneath the underbody and axle.
2. Disconnect the lower end of the shock absorber from the spring

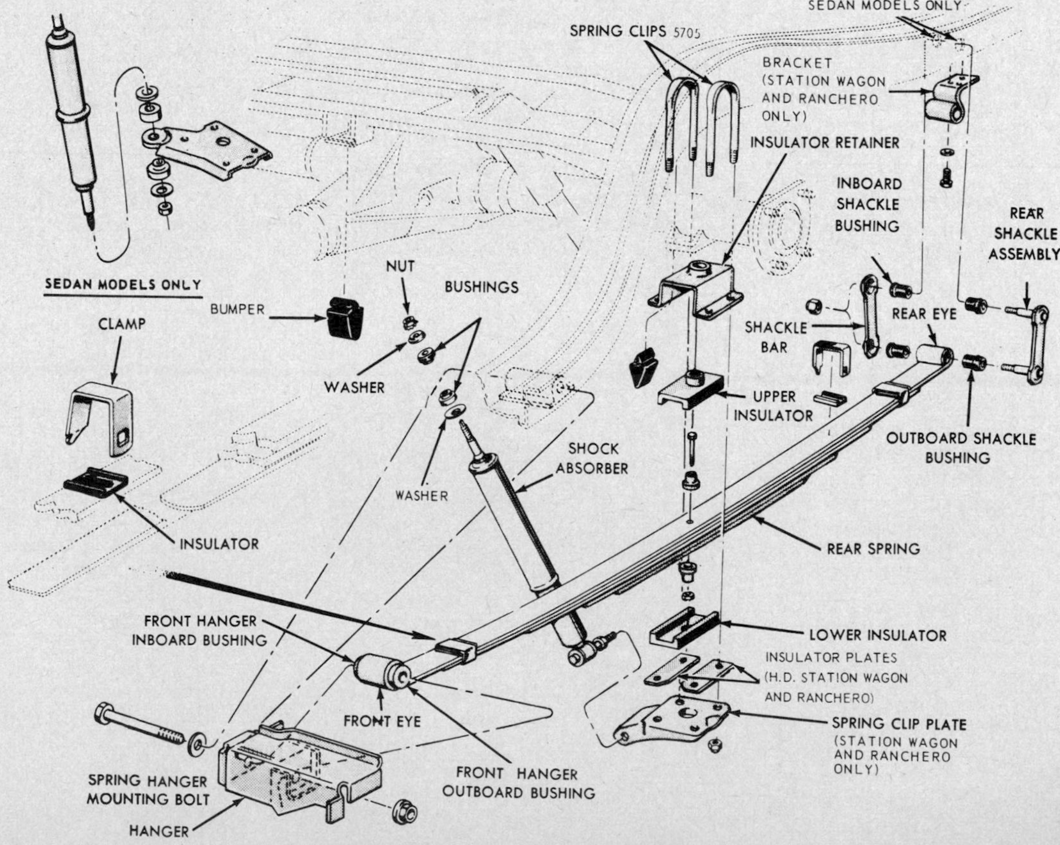

Exploded view of leaf spring rear suspension
(© Ford Motor Co)

clip plate and position it out of the way. Remove the supports from under the axle.

3. Remove the spring plate nuts from the U-bolt and remove the spring plate. With a jack, raise the rear axle just enough to remove the weight of the housing from the spring.
4. Remove the two rear shackle attaching nuts, the shackle bar, and the two inner bushings.
5. Remove the rear shackle assembly and the two outer bushings.
6. Remove the nut from the spring mounting bolt and tap the bolt out of the bushing at the front hanger. Lift out the spring assembly.

NOTE: all used attaching components (nuts, bolts, etc.) must be discarded and replaced with new ones prior to assembly.

7. Position the leaf spring under the axle housing and insert the shackle assembly into the rear hanger bracket and the rear eye of the spring.
8. Install the shackle inner bushings, the shackle plate, and the locknuts. Hand-tighten the locknuts.
9. Position the spring eye in the front hanger, slip the washer on the front hanger bolt, and, from the inboard side, insert the bolt through the hanger and eye. Install the locknut on the hanger bolt finger-tight.
10. Lower the rear axle housing so that it rests on the spring. Place the spring plate on the U-bolt and tighten the nuts.
11. Attach the lower end of the shock absorber to the spring plate using a new nut.
12. Place jackstands under the rear axle. Lower the vehicle until the spring is in the approximate curb load position, and tighten the front hanger locknut.
13. Tighten the rear shackle locknuts. Close the hole in the inner rail with a body plug.
14. Remove the jackstands and lower the vehicle.

Shock Absorber R & R

1969-73 Mustang and Cougar

1. Disconnect the shock absorber at the spring plate.
2. Remove the shock absorber access cover from the trunk. Remove the rear seat from convertibles to reach the access cover.
3. Remove the shock absorber upper retaining nut.
4. Compress and remove the shock absorber. Remove all bushings and washers from the unit.
5. Place new inner bushings and washers on the shock absorber studs.
6. Connect the upper stud to the mounting. Install a new outer bushing, washer, and nut on the stud. Install the access cover.
7. Connect the lower stud to the spring plate. Install a new outer bushing, washer, and nut on the stud. Be sure that the spring plate is free of burrs.

1969-70 Falcon and Fairlane, 1969-71 Torino and Montego All Models Except Convertible

1. Remove the spare from the trunk. On station wagons, remove the access cover from the opening in the seat riser over the shock absorber. On Rancheros, remove the attaching screws and remove the forward half of the floor panel, then remove the access cover from the opening in the floor pan. On all other models, fold back the trunk floor mat and remove the access cover.
2. Remove the nut, outer washer, and rubber bushing from the top of the shock absorber.
3. Raise the vehicle and remove the attaching nut, outer washer, and bushing from the shock absorber at the spring plate. Compress and remove the shock absorber. Remove all bushings and washers from the unit.
4. Position a new inner washer and bushing on each shock absorber stud.
5. Place the shock absorber between the spring plate and the mounting in the floor pan. Install a new outer bushing, washer, and nut on the lower stud. Make sure that the spring plate is free of burrs. Lower the vehicle.
6. Install the new outer bushing, washer, and nut on the upper stud.
7. On station wagon models, replace the retaining screws and floor bed panel. On Rancheros, install the access cover and the forward half of the bed. On all other models, install the access cover and secure the spare in the trunk.

1969-70 Fairlane, and 1969-71 Torino and Montego Convertibles

1. Remove the rear seat.
2. Raise the vehicle and install jackstands. Have an assistant hold the shock absorber from underneath the car and remove the nut, washer, and bushing from the top of the shock absorber.
3. Remove the lower shock absorber nut, washer, and bushing. Compress and remove the shock absorber. Remove the inner bushings and washers from the unit.
4. Place the new inner washers and bushings on the shock absorber. Secure the shock absorber at its lower attachment by installing the new outer bushing, washer, and nut on the lower mounting stud.
5. Lower the vehicle and install the new outer bushing, washer, and nut on the top of the shock absorber.
6. Install the rear seat.

1970-76 Maverick and 1971-76 Comet, 1975-76 Granada and Monarch

1. Remove the lower end of the shock absorber from the spring plate.
2. Remove the nut retaining the upper end of the shock absorber to the mounting bracket underneath the car.
3. Compress and remove the shock absorber.
4. Transfer the washers and bushings to the new shock absorber. Insert the upper stud through the mounting bracket, and install the attaching nut finger-tight.
5. Compress and install the shock absorber to the spring plate. Install the washers, bushings, and attaching nuts.
6. Tighten the upper and lower attaching nuts.

Coil Spring Suspension

Spring R & R

1. Place a jack under the rear axle housing. Raise the vehicle and place jackstands under the frame side rails.
2. Disconnect the lower studs of the shock absorbers from the mounting brackets on the axle housing.
3. Lower the axle housing until the springs are fully released.
4. Remove the springs and insulators from the vehicle.
5. Place the insulators in each upper seat and position the springs between the upper and lower seats.
6. With the springs in position, raise the axle housing until the lower studs of the rear shock absorbers reach the mounting brackets on the axle housing. Connect the lower studs and install the attaching nuts.
7. Remove the jackstands and lower the vehicle.

Shock Absorber R & R

1. Raise the vehicle and install jackstands.
2. Remove the shock absorber outer attaching nut, washer and insulator from the stud at the top side of the spring upper seat. Compress the shock sufficiently to clear the spring seat hole, and remove the inner insulator and washer from the upper attaching stud.
3. Remove the locknut and disconnect the shock absorber lower stud at the mounting bracket on

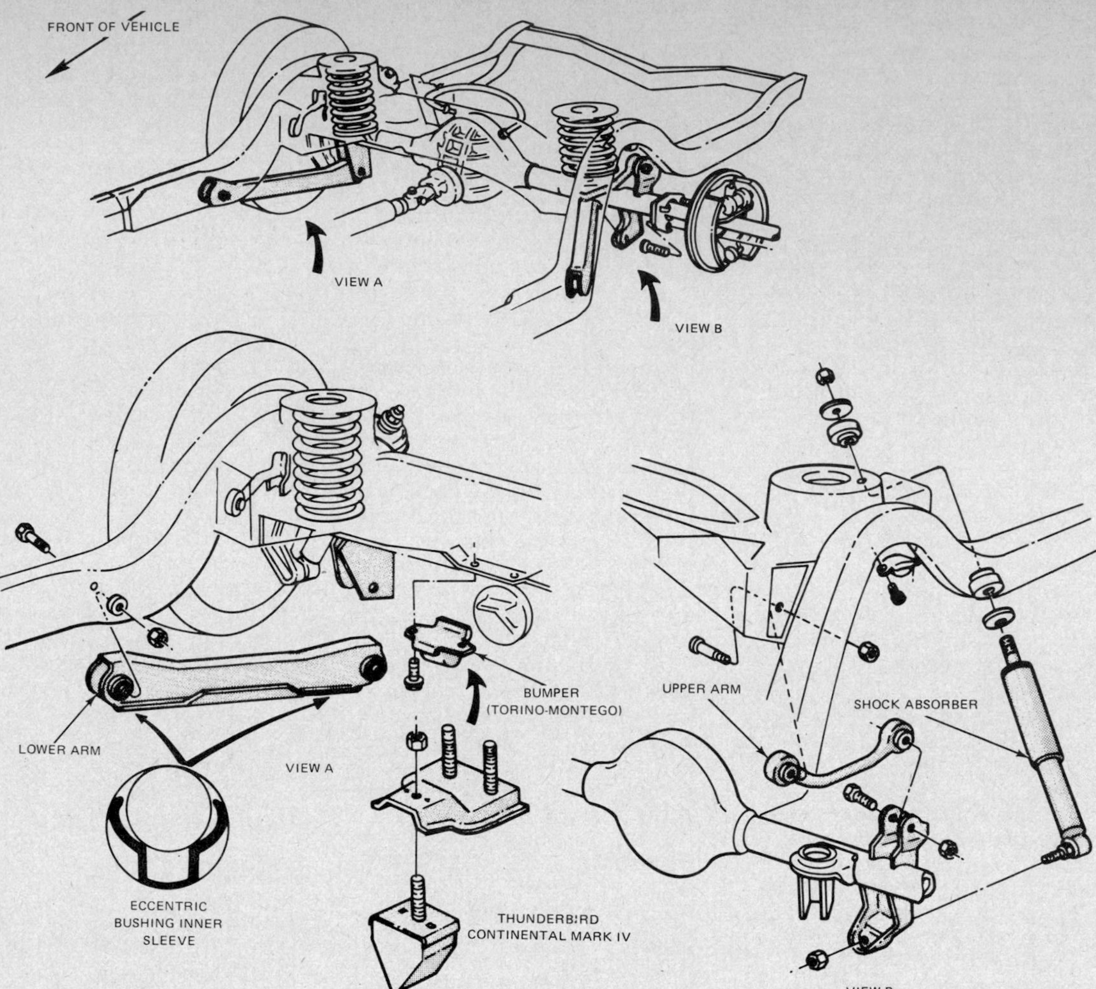

Coil spring rear suspension (© Ford Motor Co)

the axle housing. Remove the shock absorber.

4. Position a new inner washer and insulator on the upper attaching stud. Place the upper stud in the hole in the upper spring seat. While maintaining the shock in this position, install a new outer insulator, washer, and nut on the stud from the top side of the spring upper seat.
5. Extend the shock absorber. Locate the lower stud in the mounting bracket hole on the axle housing and install the locknut.

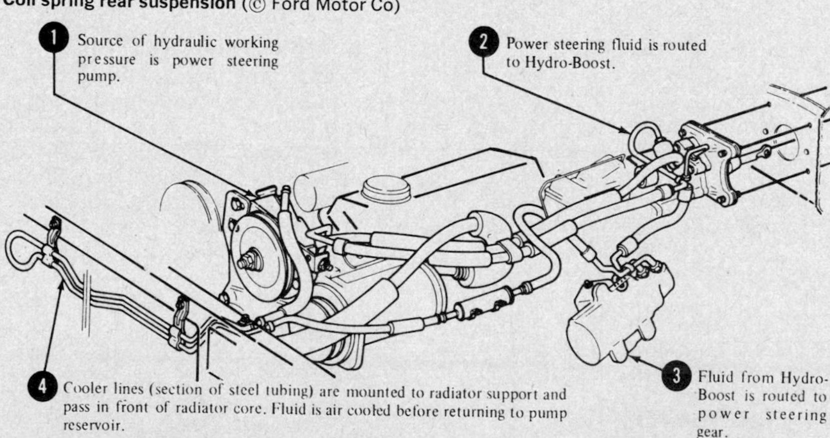

Hydro-Boost installation
(© Ford Motor Co)

BRAKES

An independent parking brake operates the rear wheel brake shoes or pads through a mechanical cable linkage. Brake shoe or pad replacement and adjustment procedures as well as wheel cylinder and master cylinder overhaul and brake bleeding procedures can be found in the Unit Repair Section.

Self-Adjusting Drum Brakes

The self-adjusting brake mechanism consists of a cable, cable guide, adjuster lever, and adjuster spring. The cable is hooked over the anchor pin at the top and is connected to the lever at the bottom. The cable is connected to the secondary brake shoe by means of the cable guide. The adjuster spring is hooked to the primary brake shoe and to the lever.

The automatic adjuster operates only when the brakes are applied while the car is moving rearward.

With the car moving rearward and the brakes applied, the wrapping action of the shoes following the drum forces the upper end of the primary shoe against the anchor pin. Action of the wheel cylinder moves the upper end of the secondary shoe away from the anchor pin. Movement of the secondary shoe causes the cable to pull the adjusting lever upward and against the end of a tooth on the adjusting screw star wheel. Upward travel of the lever increases as lining wear increases. When the lever can move far enough upward to pass over the end of the tooth, the adjuster spring pulls the lever downward causing the star wheel to turn and expand the shoes. The star wheel is turned one tooth at a time as the linings progressively wear.

Disc Brakes

Front disc brakes have been available on front wheels of most models. Rear disc brakes are available on Granada and Monarch when equipped with the hydraulically assisted Hydro-Boost System. Complete Service Procedures are covered in the Unit Repair Section.

Dual Master Cylinder R & R

Standard Brakes

1. Working under the dash, disconnect the master cylinder pushrod from the brake pedal. The pushrod cannot be removed from the master cylinder.
2. Disconnect the stoplight switch wires and remove the switch from the brake pedal, using care not to damage the switch.
3. Disconnect the brake lines from the master cylinder.
4. Remove the attaching screws from the firewall and remove the master cylinder from the car.
5. Reinstall in reverse of above order, leaving the brake line fittings loose at the master cylinder.
6. Fill the master cylinder, and with the brake lines loose, slowly bleed the air from the master cylinder using the foot pedal.

Power Brakes

1. Disconnect the brake line from the master cylinder.
2. Remove the two nuts and lockwashers that attach the master cylinder to the brake booster.
3. Remove the master cylinder from the booster.
4. Reverse above procedure to reinstall.
5. Fill master cylinder and bleed entire brake system.
6. Refill master cylinder.

Power Brakes

Vacuum Power Unit Removal

1. Working inside the car below the instrument panel, disconnect booster valve operating rod from the brake pedal assembly.
2. Open the hood, and disconnect the wires from the stop light switch at the brake master cylinder.
3. Disconnect the brake line at the master cylinder outlet fitting.
4. Disconnect manifold vacuum hose from the booster unit.
5. Remove the four bracket-to-dash panel attaching bolts.
6. Remove the booster and bracket assembly from the dash panel, sliding the valve operating rod out from the engine side of the dash panel.

Vacuum Power Unit Installation

1. Mount the booster and bracket assembly to the dash panel by sliding the valve operating rod in through the hole in the dash panel, and installing the attaching bolts.
2. Connect manifold vacuum hose to the booster.
3. Connect the brake line to the master cylinder outlet fitting.
4. Connect stop light switch wires.
5. Working inside the car below the instrument panel, install the rubber boot on the valve operating rod at the passenger side of the dash panel.
6. Connect the valve operating rod to the brake pedal with the bushings, eccentric shoulder bolt, and nut.

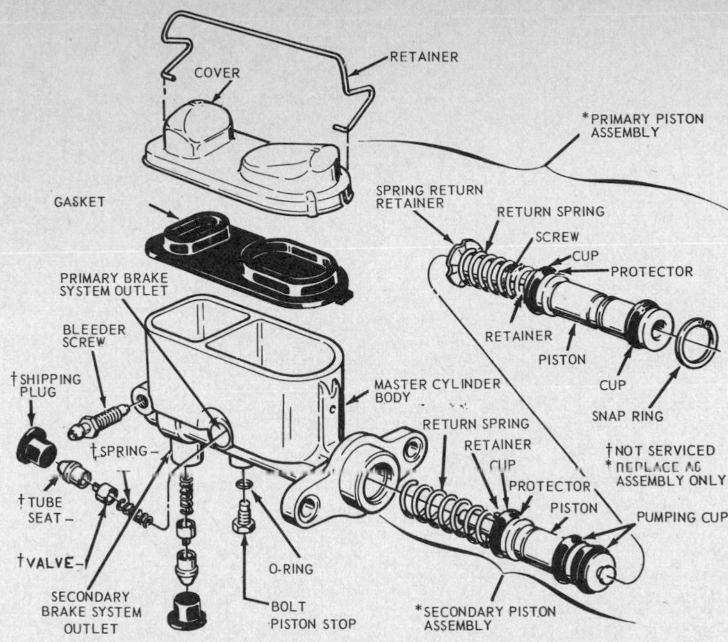

Dual master cylinder—disc brakes (© Ford Motor Co)

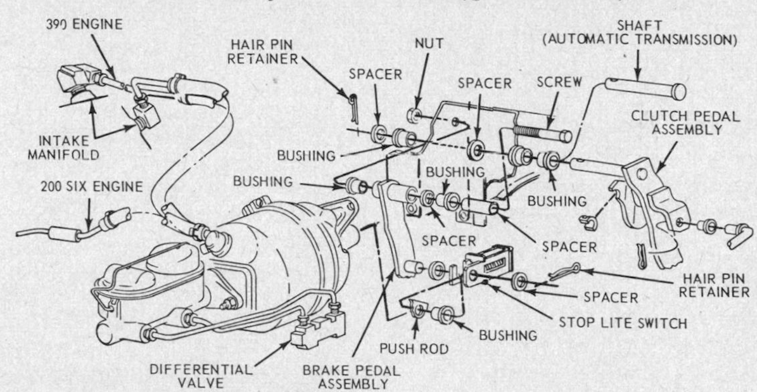

Vacuum brake booster installation (© Ford Motor Co)

Hydro-Boost Power Unit R & R

See the "Lincoln" section.

Parking Brake Adjustment

In most cases, a rear brake shoe adjustment will provide satisfactory parking brake action. However, if parking brake cables are excessively loose after releasing the handbrake, proceed as follows:

1. On handle-actuated systems pull up the handle to the third notch. On pedal-actuated systems, depress the parking brake pedal one notch from its normal released position.
2. Loosen locknut on equalizer rod under the car. Then loosen the nut in front of the equalizer, several turns.

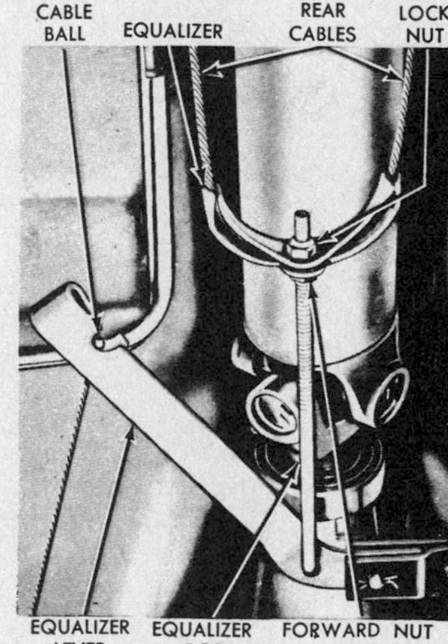

Parking brake linkage (© Ford Motor Co)

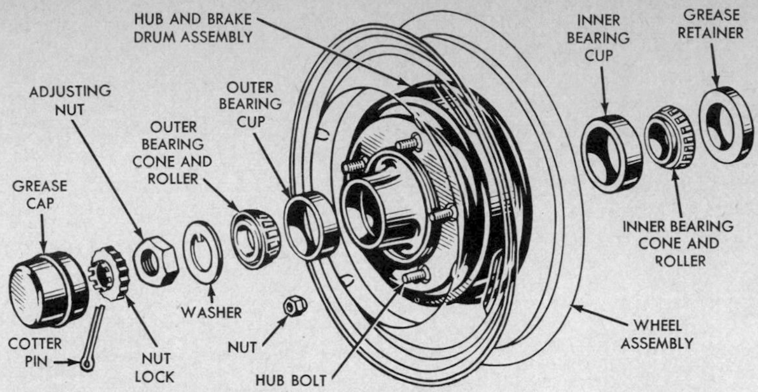

Front hub, bearings, and grease retainers—drum brakes shown, disc brakes similar (© Ford Motor Co)

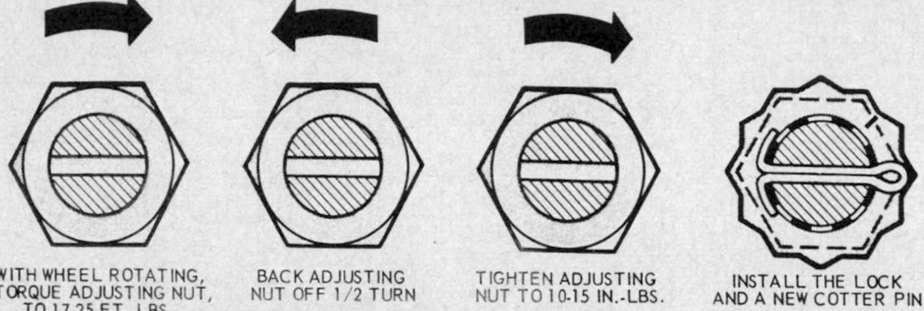

Adjusting wheel bearings (© Ford Motor Co)

3. Turn the locknut forward against the equalizer until the cables are tight enough so that the rear wheels cannot be turned by hand. Then, back off the adjustment until the rear wheels turn freely.
4. When cables are properly adjusted, tighten both nuts against the equalizer.
5. Release the brake and feel for freeness of rear wheels.

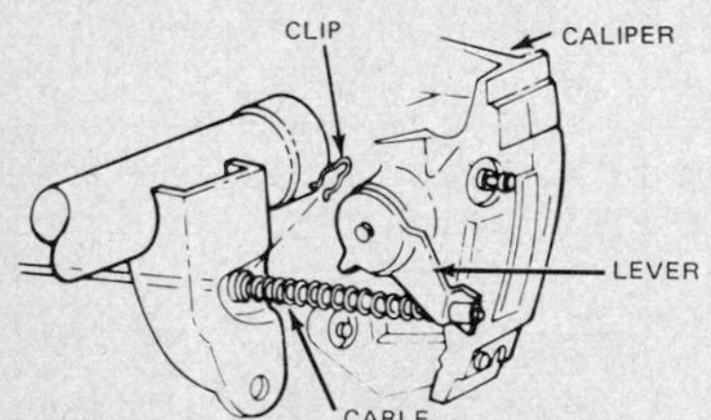

Parking brake cable and lever—Granada and Monarch with rear disc brakes
(© Ford Motor Co)

Granada and Monarch with Rear Disc Brakes

1. Fully release the parking brake.
2. Place the transmission in Neutral. If it is necessary to raise the car to reach the adjusting nut and observe the parking brake levers, use an axle hoist or a floor jack positioned beneath the differential. This is necessary so that the rear axle remains at the curb attitude, not stretching the parking brake cables.

Caution *If you are raising the rear of the car only, block the front wheels.*

3. Locate the adjusting nut beneath the car on the driver's side. While observing the parking brake actuating levers on the rear calipers, tighten the adjusting nut until the levers just begin to move. Then, loosen the nut sufficiently for the levers to fully return to the stop position.
4. Check the operation of the parking brake. Make sure the actuating levers return to the stop position by attempting to pull them rearward. If the lever moves rearward, the cable adjustment is too tight, which will cause a dragging rear brake and consequent brake overheating and fade.

STEERING

The manual steering gear is of the worm and recirculating ball type. The sector shaft is straddle-mounted in the cover above the gear and a housing-mounted roller bearing below the gear. The steering linkage consists of a Pitman arm, a steering (Pitman) arm to idler arm rod, an idler arm and tie-rods.

Power steering is available as an option. On all compact and intermediate Ford products, except the 1971–73 Mustang, 1972 and later Torino and Montego, the 1974 and later Cougar and the Elite, the power steering system is the Bendix non-integral type. The Bendix system utilizes the manual worm and recirculating ball steering gear. Hydraulic assist is provided externally to the steering linkage via a power steering pump, power cylinder, and control valve. The 1971-73 Mustangs and Cougars use the Saginaw integral system, while the Elites, 1972 and later Torinos and Montegos and 1974 and later Cougars use the Ford integral system. On both types, hydraulic assist is directly applied to the steering gear, eliminating all hoses and hardware which were previously mounted under the chassis on the Bendix system.

Wheel Bearing Adjustment

1. Raise the front of the vehicle.
2. Remove the wheel cover and grease cap.
3. Remove the cotter pin and nut lock.
4. Back off the adjusting nut and retighten the nut to 17–25 ft. lbs. Back off the adjusting nut again ½ turn. Retighten the nut to 10–15 in. lbs. Install the nut lock so that the castellations are aligned with the cotter pin hole. Install the cotter pin and bend the ends around the castellations of the nut lock to prevent interference with the radio static collector in the grease cap.
5. Install the grease cap and wheel cover.
6. Lower the vehicle.

Power Steering Pump R & R

1. Drain the fluid from the pump reservoir by disconnecting the fluid return hose at the pump. Then, disconnect the pressure hose from the pump.
2. Remove the mounting bolts from the front of the pump. On eight cylinder engines, there is a nut on the rear of the pump that must be removed. After removal, move the pump inward to loosen the belt tension and remove the belt from the pulley. Then, remove the pump from the car.
3. To reinstall the pump, position on mounting bracket and loosely install the mounting bolts and nuts. Put the drive belt over the pulley and move the pump outward against the belt until the proper belt tension is obtained. Measure the belt tension with a belt tension gauge for the proper adjustment. Only in cases where a belt tension gauge is not available should the belt deflection method be used.
4. Tighten the mounting bolts and nuts.

Steering Wheel R & R

1. Open the hood and disconnect the negative cable from the battery.
2. On models with safety crash pads, remove the crash pad attaching screws from the underside of the steering wheel spoke and remove the pad. On all models equipped with a horn button, remove the horn button or ring by pressing down evenly and turning it counterclockwise approximately 20° and then lifting it from the steering wheel. Disconnect the horn wires from the crash pad on models so equipped.
3. Remove the nut from the end of the shaft. Install a steering

wheel puller on the end of the shaft and remove the wheel.

Caution The use of knock-off type steering wheel puller or the use of a hammer on the steering shaft will damage the column bearing, on collapsible columns, the column itself may be damaged.

4. Lubricate the upper surface of the steering shaft upper bushing with white grease. Transfer all serviceable parts to the new steering wheel.
5. Position the steering wheel on the shaft so that the alignment marks line up. Install a locknut and torque it to 20–30 ft lbs. Connect the horn wires.
6. Install the horn button or ring by turning it clockwise or install the crash pad.

Turn Signal Switch R & R

1. Open the hood and disconnect the negative battery cable.
2. Remove the steering wheel.
3. Unscrew the turn signal handle from the side of the column. Remove the emergency flasher retainer and knob, if so equipped.
4. Remove the wire assembly cover and disconnect the wire connector plugs. Record the location and color code of each wire and tape the wires together. Make sure that the horn wires are disconnected. Remove the plastic cover from the wiring harness. Attach a piece of heavy cord to the switch wires to pull them through the column during installation.
5. Remove the retaining clips and attaching screws from the turn signal switch and pull the switch and wire assembly from the top of the column.
6. Tape the ends of the new switch wires together and transfer the pull cord to these wires.
7. Pull the wires down through the column with the cord and attach the new switch to the column hub.
8. Connect the wiring plugs to their mating plugs at the lower end of the column and install the plastic cover at the harness.
9. Install all retaining clips and wire assembly covers that were removed and install the turn signal handle. Install the emergency flasher retainer and knob, if so equipped.
10. Install the steering wheel and retaining nut.
11. Connect the negative battery cable.

INSTRUMENT PANEL

Ignition Lock Cylinder Replacement

1969

1. Insert key and turn to Acc. position.
2. With stiff wire in hole, depress lock pin and rotate cylinder counterclockwise, then pull out cylinder.

1970-76

1. Disconnect the negative battery cable.
2. On cars with a fixed steering column, remove the steering wheel trim pad and the steering wheel. Insert a stiff wire into the hole located in the lock cylinder housing. On cars with a tilt steering wheel, this hole is located on the outside of the steering column near the emergency flasher button and it is not necessary to remove the steering wheel.
3. Place the gear shift lever in Reverse on standard shift cars and in Park on cars with automatic transmission, and turn the ignition key to the ON or RUN position.
4. Depress wire and remove lock cylinder and wire.
5. Insert new cylinder into housing and turn to the OFF position. This will lock the cylinder into position.
6. Reinstall steering wheel and pad.
7. Connect negative battery cable.

Ignition Switch Replacement

1969

1. Remove cylinder as above.
2. Press in on rear of switch and rotate the switch one-eighth turn counterclockwise. Remove the bezel, switch and spacer.
3. Remove nut from back of switch. Remove the accessory and gauge feed wires from accessory terminal. Pull insulated plug from rear of switch.
4. Install in reverse of above.

1970-76

1. Disconnect the negative battery cable.
2. Remove shrouding from the steering column, and detach and lower the steering column from the brake support bracket.
3. Disconnect the switch wiring at the multiple plug.
4. Remove the two nuts that retain the switch to steering column.
5. On models with a steering column-mounted gearshift lever, disconnect the ignition switch plunger from the ignition switch actuator rod and remove the ignition switch. On models with a floor mounted gearshift lever, remove the pin that connects the switch plunger to the switch actuator and remove the switch.
6. To re-install the switch, place both locking mechanism at top of column and switch itself in lock

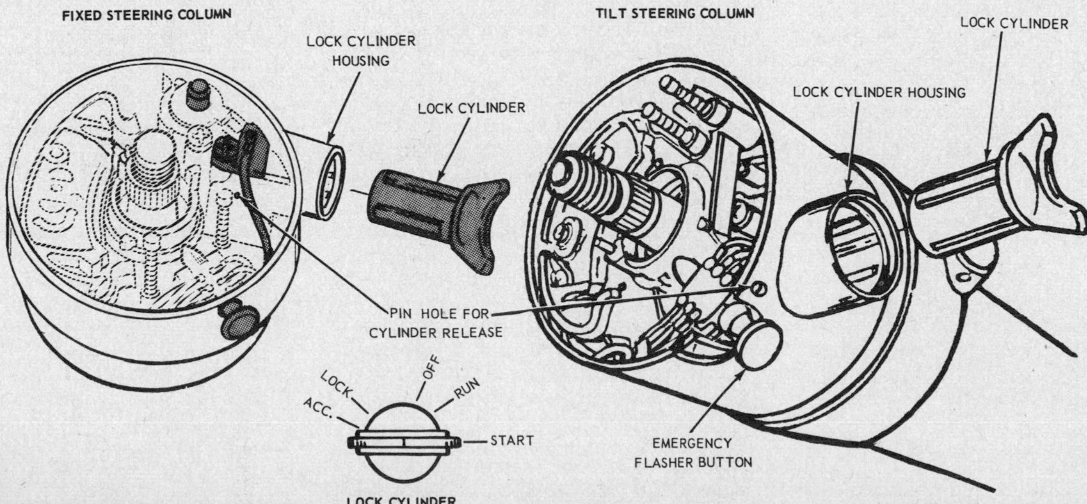

Lock cylinder replacement with locking column (© Ford Motor Co)

position for correct adjustment. To hold column in lock position, place automatic shift lever in PARK or manual shift lever in reverse, and turn to LOCK and remove the key. New switches are held in lock by plastic shipping pins. To pin existing switches, pull the switch plunger out as far as it will go and push back in to first detent. Insert 3/32 in. diameter wire into locking hole in the top of the switch.
7. Connect the switch plunger to the switch actuator rod.
8. Position the switch on the column and install the attaching nuts. Do not tighten them.
9. Move the switch up and down to locate the mid-position of rod lash, and then tighten the nuts.
10. Remove the locking pin or wire.
11. Attach the steering column to the brake support bracket and install the shrouding.

Headlight Switch Replacement

1. Disconnect the negative battery cable.
2. Remove the headlight switch control knob and shaft after depressing the release button on the rear of the switch. Some models require special procedures to gain access to the release button. They are:
   a. On Mustangs and Cougars through 1971, remove the two screws that attach the parking brake mechanism to the dash panel and lower the brake control with the vent cable attached to it.
   b. On 1970 and later Mavericks, Comets, Monarchs, and Granadas equipped with air conditioning, disconnect the left A/C duct from the duct-to-register connector, loosen the two nuts that retain the left register to the utility shelf and remove the connector from the register.
   c. On 1972–73 Mustangs and Cougars, insert a screwdriver through the hole in the bottom of the instrument panel beneath the headlight switch and depress the headlight switch release button with the screwdriver.

Headlight switch (© Ford Motor Co)

3. After pulling the switch shaft and knob from the switch, remove the bezel nut that attaches the switch to the instrument panel.
4. Lower the switch and disconnect the lead wires from the switch.
5. On models equipped with headlight doors, disconnect the vacuum hoses from the headlight switch.
6. Reverse the above procedure to install the new switch. When installing the new switch, insert the control knob and shaft into the switch until a distinct click is heard, signifying that the shaft is locked in place.

Neutral Safety and Back-Up Light Switch Assembly—Automatic Transmission

Ford small cars have used the same neutral switches and back up switches as full size Fords.

See the Ford section for a complete breakdown of years, transmissions, and adjustments.

Back-Up Light Switch—Manual Transmission

The back-up light switch may be located in either one of two places. The back-up light switch location, on cars with column shift selector and linkage controls, is at the bottom of the column.

The back-up light switch location, on cars with consoles and floor shift selector, is on the left side of the transmission back at the shift control bracket.

WINDSHIELD WIPERS

Motor R & R

1969 Montego, Falcon, Fairlane and Torino

1. Disconnect wiper motor wire connector.
2. Remove wiper arm and blade assemblies.
3. Remove cowl top grille panel retaining screws and remove cowl top grille.
4. Remove wiper link retaining clip from wiper motor arm.
5. Remove four wiper motor retaining bolts and remove wiper motor and mounting bracket.
6. To install position wiper motor and mounting bracket against dash panel and install four retaining bolts.
7. Place wiper link on motor drive arm and install retaining clip.
8. Install cowl top grille panel.
9. Connect wiper motor wiring connectors.
10. Check motor operation.

1969-70 Cougar and Mustang

1. Remove wiper arm and blade assemblies from pivot shafts and disconnect left side washer hose at T fitting on cowl grille.
2. Remove eight screws and remove cowl top grille.
3. Motor is located inside left fresh air plenum chamber. Disconnect motor ground wire by removing one screw at forward edge of plenum chamber.
4. Disconnect motor wire at plug and push it back into plenum chamber.
5. Disconnect linkage drive arm from motor output arm crank pin by removing retaining clip.
6. Remove three bolts that retain motor to mounting bracket, rotate motor output arm 180 degrees, and remove motor.
7. Before installing motor, rotate output arm 180 degrees. Before connecting linkage drive arm to motor, turn ignition to ACC position to allow motor to go to park position.

1970-71 Montego, Falcon, Fairlane, and Torino; 1972-76 Torino and Montego with Non-Depressed Wipers; 1971-73 Mustang and Cougar

1. Disconnect battery and wiper motor connector.
2. Remove cowl top left vent screen by removing four retaining drive pins.
3. Remove wiper link retaining clip from wiper motor arm.
4. Remove three wiper motor retaining bolts, and remove wiper motor and mounting bracket.
5. To install motor, place wiper motor and mounting bracket against dash panel and install three retaining bolts.
6. Position wiper link on motor drive arm, and install connecting clip. Be sure to force clip locking flange into locked position as shown in figure.
7. Install cowl top vent screen and secure with four drive pins.
8. Check motor operation and connect wiring plugs.

1970-76 Maverick, Comet, Monarch, and Granada

1. Remove instrument cluster.
2. If air conditioned, remove center connector and duct assembly. Remove mounting bracket screw behind center duct, disconnect assembly from plenum chamber and left duct, and pull center connector and duct assembly out through cluster opening.
3. Working through cluster opening, disconnect two pivot shaft links from motor drive arm by removing retaining clip.
4. Disconnect wiring plug at motor, remove three retaining bolts, and remove motor through cluster opening.

5. To install motor, bolt motor to mounting plate with three retaining bolts.
6. Connect right pivot shaft link to motor and then connect left pivot shaft link. Lock clip as shown.
7. On air conditioned vehicles, insert end of center connector and duct assembly near mounting bracket into left duct and opposite end into plenum chamber.
8. Secure assembly with mounting bracket screw.
9. Install instrument cluster, and check operation of wiper motor.

1972-73 Torino and Montego (Depressed Park)

1. Disconnect the negative battery cable.
2. Remove the wiper arms from the pivot shafts.
3. Disconnect the linkage drive arm from the motor output arm crankpin by removing the retaining clip.
4. From the engine side of the dash, disconnect the two wire connectors from the motor.
5. Remove the three retaining bolts and the motor from the dash.
6. If the output arm catches on the dash during removal, hand-turn the arm clockwise so it will clear the opening in the dash.
7. Reverse the above procedure for installation, making sure that the output arm is in the "park" position prior to installation.

1974-76 Torino, Elite, Montego and Cougar (Depressed Park)

1. Disconnect the battery ground cable.
2. Remove the wiper arm and blade assemblies from the pivot shafts.
3. Remove the left cowl screen for access through the cowl opening. Disconnect the linkage drive arm from the motor output arm crankpin by removing the retaining clip. From the engine side of the dash, disconnect the two push-on wire connectors from the motor.
4. Remove the three bolts which retain the motor to the dash and remove the motor. If the output arm catches on the dash during removal, hand turn the arm clockwise, so that it will clear the opening in the dash.
5. Before installing the motor, be sure that the output arm is in the Park position.

Pivot Shaft and Linkage R & R

1969 Montego, Falcon, Fairlane, and Torino

1. Remove wiper arms and blades.
2. Remove cowl top grille retaining screws and remove cowl top grille.
3. Remove clip retaining drive arm to pivot.
4. Remove three retaining screws from each pivot and remove pivot shaft and link assembly.
5. To install, position pivot shaft and link assembly in the cowl and install pivot shaft retaining screws.
6. Place left link on motor drive arm and install retaining clip.
7. Install wiper arms and blades, and check wiper operation.
8. Install cowl top grille panel.

1969-70 Cougar and Mustang

1. Disconnect battery.
2. Remove wiper arm and blade assemblies from pivot shafts.
3. Disconnect washer hose at T fitting on cowl grille.
4. Remove eight screws and remove cowl top grille.
5. Disconnect linkage drive arm from motor output arm crank pin by removing retaining clip.
6. Remove clip and disconnect right link from right arm and pivot shaft assembly.
7. Remove three retaining screws and remove right arm and pivot shaft assembly.
8. Remove three screws retaining left arm and pivot shaft.
9. Lift out pivot shaft and arm, left link, and linkage drive arm as one assembly. Assembly comes out to right.
10. When installing pivot shaft assemblies, tighten retaining bolts to 3-7 ft. lbs. Install left pivot shaft and linkage first. Be sure linkage connecting clips are forced into locked position as shown in figure.

1970-76 Maverick, 1971-76 Comet, 1975-76 Monarch and Granada—Left Side

1. Remove instrument cluster.
2. Remove wiper arm and blade assembly from pivot shaft.
3. Working through cluster opening, disconnect both pivot shaft links from motor drive arm by removing retaining clip.
4. Remove three bolts that retain left pivot shaft assembly to cowl and take left pivot shaft assembly out through cluster opening.

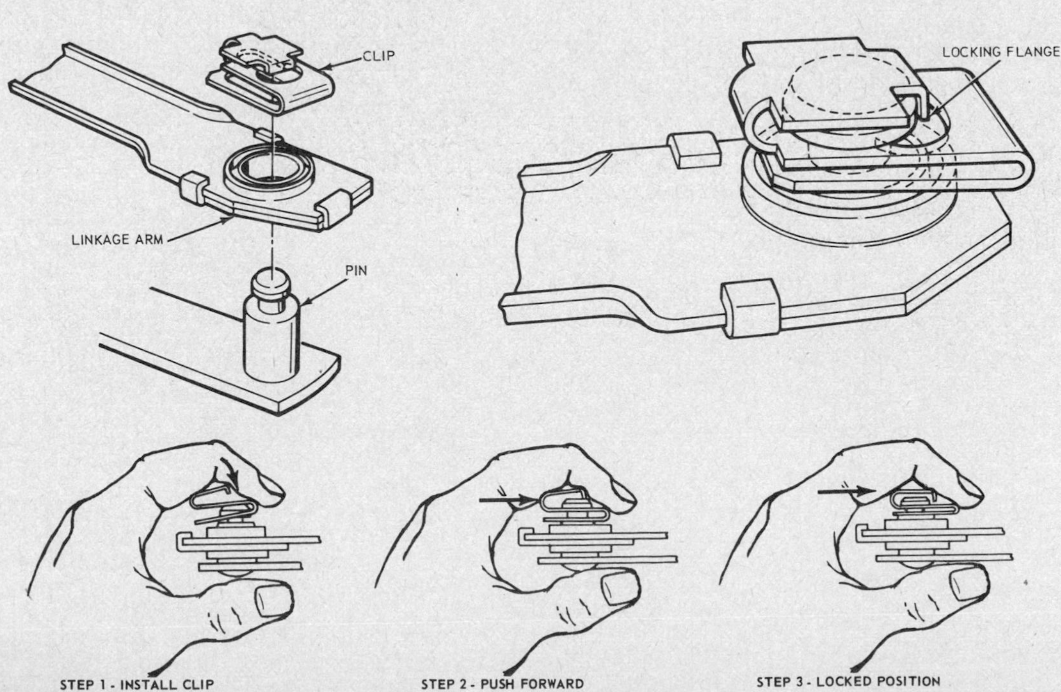

Installation of windshield wiper connecting clips (© Ford Motor Co)

5. Before installing, cement new gasket on pivot shaft mounting flange. Tighten retaining bolts to 3-7 ft. lbs. After installing pivot shaft and link assembly to cowl connect right pivot shaft link to motor drive arm first, and then connect left link. Be sure connecting clip is locked as shown in figure.

1970-76 Maverick, 1971-76 Comet 1975-76 Monarch and Granada —Right Side

1. Disconnect battery.
2. Remove wiper arm and blade assembly from pivot shaft.
3. If car is air conditioned, remove right duct assembly. Unclip duct from right connector, slide left end out of plenum chamber, and lower duct assembly out from under instrument panel.
4. From under instrument panel, disconnect first left and then right pivot shaft link from motor drive arm by removing remaining clip.
5. Reaching between utility shelf and instrument panel, remove three bolts that retain right pivot shaft and link assembly to cowl. Lower assembly out from under instrument panel.
6. Before installing, cement new gasket to pivot shaft mounting flange. After installing pivot shaft and link assembly to cowl, be sure right pivot shaft link is connected to motor drive arm before left pivot shaft link. Be sure connecting clip is in locked position as shown in figure.

1971-76 Torino, Elite, Montego, and Cougar, and 1971-73 Mustang

1. Disconnect the negative battery cable.
2. Remove the wiper arms from the pivot shafts.
3. Remove the four retaining drive pins and the cowl top vent screen.
4. Remove the drive arm-to-pivot retaining clip.
5. Remove the three retaining screws from each pivot and remove the pivot shaft and link assembly.
6. Transfer the right pivot, if necessary, by removing the connecting clip.
7. Position the pivot shaft and link assembly in the cowl, and install the pivot shaft retaining screws.
8. Position the left link on the motor drive arm and install the connecting clip.
9. Install the wiper arms.
10. Connect the negative cable and test wiper operation.
11. Install the cowl top vent screen.

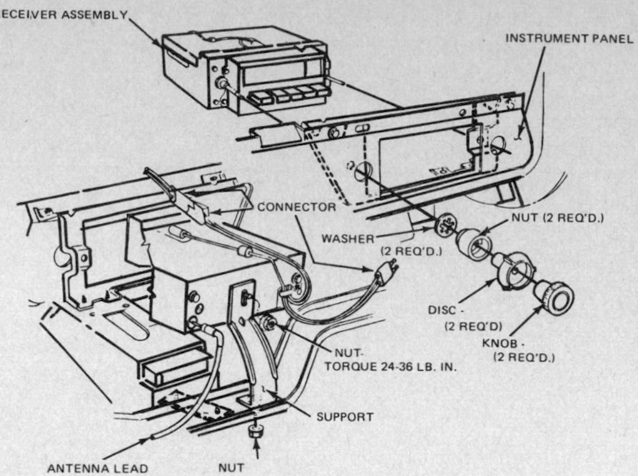

Radio removal—1974-76 Torino, Montego, Cougar and Elite (© Ford Motor Co)

RADIO

Removal and Replacement

1969-76 Montego, Fairlane, Torino Falcon, and 1974-76 Cougar

1. Disconnect battery.
2. Pull radio control knobs off shafts.
3. Remove radio support to instrument panel attaching screw.
4. Remove two bezel nuts from radio control shafts.
5. Lower radio and disconnect antenna, speaker, and power leads. Remove radio.
6. To install, connect antenna, speaker and power leads to radio.
7. Position radio in instrument panel and install two bezel nuts. Torque bezel nuts to 30-35 in. lbs.
8. Install radio support bracket to instrument panel attaching screw and torque to 30-35 in. lbs.
9. Connect battery.
10. Adjust antenna trimmer, if necessary.
11. Install radio control knobs and set push buttons for desired stations.

1969-70 Cougar and Mustang

1. Disconnect battery.
2. Pull control knobs, discs, and sleeve from radio control shafts.
3. Remove radio applique from instrument panel.
4. Remove right and left finish panels.
5. Remove two mounting plate attaching screws.
6. Pull radio out of instrument panel and disconnect wires from radio.
7. Remove mounting plate and rear support from radio.
8. Remove radio.
9. To replace, install mounting plate and rear support on radio.
10. Position radio near opening and connect wires to radio.
11. Install jumper wire to ground radio to instrument panel.
12. Connect battery and check operation of radio.
13. Adjust antenna trimmer.
14. Disconnect battery and remove jumper cable.
15. Insert radio and wires into panel opening. Be sure radio rear support slips over instrument panel reinforcement.
16. Install mounting plate attaching screws.
17. Install left and right finish panels.
18. Install radio applique, sleeve, discs, and control knobs.
19. Connect radio ground cable and set push buttons.

1971-73 Mustang and Cougar

1. Disconnect the negative battery cable.
2. Disconnect the radio antenna wire from the radio.
3. Pull off the radio control knobs and remove the two radio bezel nuts from the radio.
4. Remove the four radio bezel attaching screws.
5. Pull the radio away from the instrument panel and disconnect the lead wires from the radio as they become accessible.
6. To install the radio, position it on the instrument panel and connect the lead wires to it.
7. To complete installation, reverse the removal procedure. When positioning the radio in the instrument panel, make sure the radio support bracket on the rear of the radio engages the tab on the instrument panel.

1970-76 Maverick, Comet, Monarch and Granada

1. Disconnect battery.
2. Remove radio rear support nut and lock washer.
3. Remove four radio to instrument panel retaining screws.
4. Pull radio from instrument panel and disconnect antenna, speaker, and power leads.

5. Remove radio.
6. Remove knob and disc assemblies from radio shafts.
7. Remove two bezel retaining nuts and remove bezel.
8. To install radio, position bezel on radio and install two bezel retaining nuts.
9. Install disc and knob assemblies on radio shafts.
10. Connect antenna, speaker, and power connectors.
11. Position radio so that rear support mounting bolt enters hole in rear support mounting bracket.
12. Install four radio to instrument panel retaining screws.
13. Install radio rear support nut and lock washer.
14. Place speaker and power wire harnesses in clip on bezel.
15. Connect battery and check operation of radio.
16. Adjust selector buttons for desired stations.

HEATER

Vehicles without Air Conditioning

Heater R & R

1969-73 Cougar and Mustang

1. Disconnect battery and drain coolant.
2. Remove instrument panel pad.
3. Remove glove compartment liner and door.
4. Remove air distribution duct from heater.
5. Disconnect control cables from heater assembly.
6. Disconnect wires from blower motor resistor.
7. Remove right courtesy light located on underside of instrument panel, if so equipped.
8. Remove heater support to dash panel retaining screw.
9. Disconnect vacuum hoses and remove power air vent duct, if so equipped.
10. Remove blower motor ground wire grounding screw.
11. Disconnect heater hoses from heater at dash panel.
12. Working in engine compartment, remove five heater assembly retaining nuts.
13. Remove instrument panel to cowl attaching screws.
14. Remove instrument panel right side brace.
15. Pull heater assembly and right side of instrument panel rearward, and remove heater assembly. Reverse procedure to install.

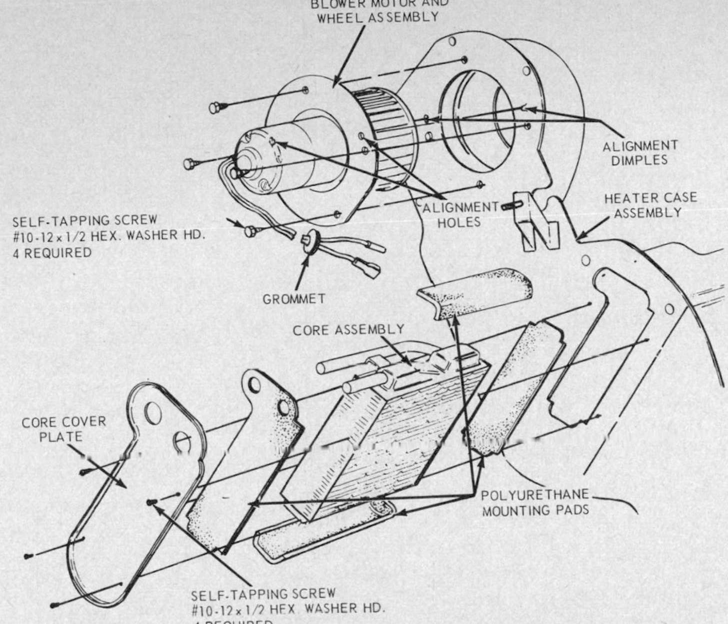

Heater, blower motor and core assemblies—1969-70 Fairlane and Falcon, 1969-76 Montego and Torino, 1974-76 Cougar and Elite; Granada and Monarch similar (© Ford Motor Co)

1969-70 Falcon and Fairlane, 1975-76 Granada and Monarch, 1969-76 Torino and Montego, 1974-76 Cougar and Elite

1. Drain coolant.
2. Disconnect both heater hoses at dash.
3. Remove nuts retaining heater assembly to dash.
4. Disconnect temperature and defroster cables at heater.
5. Disconnect wires from resistor, and disconnect blower motor wires and clip retaining heater assembly to defroster nozzle.
6. Remove glove box.
7. Remove bolt and nut right air duct control to instrument panel. Remove nuts retaining right air duct and remove duct assembly.
8. Remove heater assembly to bench.

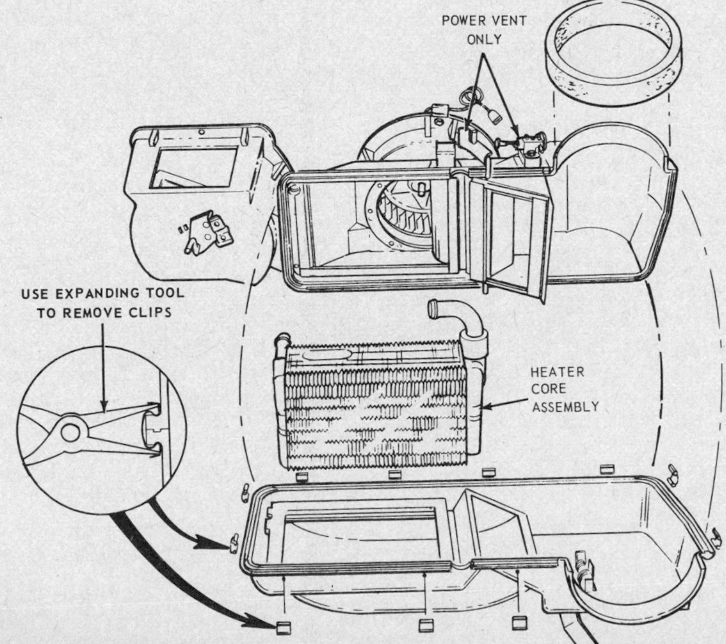

Heater core removal—1969-73 Cougar and Mustang; Maverick and Comet similar (© Ford Motor Co)

1970-76 Maverick, 1971-76 Comet

1. Drain the cooling system and disconnect the negative battery cable.
2. Disconnect the blower ground wire (black) from the fender apron.
3. Disconnect the heater hoses from the engine block.
4. Remove the five heater assembly to firewall attaching bolts from the firewall.
5. Working inside the car, remove the ignition switch and plate

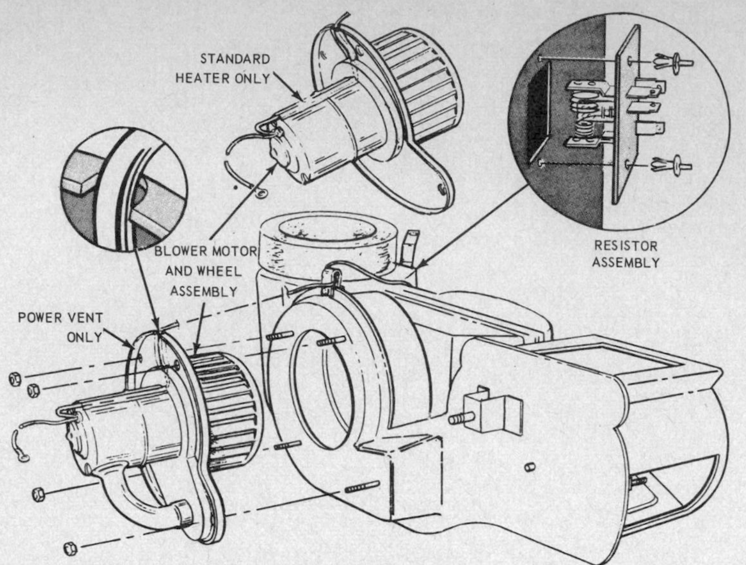

Heater blower and motor installation—1969-73 Mustang and Cougar, 1970-76 Maverick, 1971-76 Comet
(© Ford Motor Co)

from the package tray and remove the tray from the dash.

6. Remove the right kick panel and remove the package tray bracket.
7. Disconnect the heater control cables from the heater.
8. Disconnect the defroster air duct from the top of the heater.
9. Disconnect the heater blower motor lead wires from the resistor at the bottom of the heater.
10. Remove the one screw from the bracket that mounts the heater to the dash.
11. Remove the heater from the car by pulling the heater hoses through the firewall, then disconnecting them from the heater.

Heater Core R & R

1969-70 Cougar and Mustang, 1970-76 Maverick and Comet

1. Remove heater assembly.
2. Remove air inlet seal from heater assembly.
3. Remove eleven clips from heater assembly flange and separate heater assembly housing.
4. Remove heater core from heater assembly housing. Reverse procedure to install.

1969-76 Montego, Fairlane, Torino, Elite, Falcon, 1971-73 Mustang, 1971-76 Cougar, Monarch and Granada

The heater core is located in the heater case in a diagonal position. It is serviced through an opening in the back plate. With the heater assembly removed from the vehicle, remove heater core cover and pad and remove core. Reverse procedure to install.

Blower Motor R & R

The blower motor on all models is located inside the heater assembly. To replace the blower motor, remove the heater assembly from the car following the steps in the above procedures. Once the heater assembly is removed, it is a simple operation to remove the motor attaching bolts and remove the motor. On all models, the motor and cage are removed as an assembly.

Vehicles with Integral Heater-Air Conditioning

NOTE: removal of the heater-air conditioner housing requires evacuation of the air conditioner refrigerant. This operation requires special tools and training. Failure to follow proper safety precautions may cause personal injury.

Heater-Air Conditioner Housing R & R

1969-70 Falcon and Fairlane, 1969-71 Torino and Montego

Removal

NOTE: to remove the core, it is necessary to remove the entire evaporator assembly.

1. Remove the carburetor air cleaner.
2. Disconnect the battery ground cable.
3. Drain the cooling system.
4. Purge the system of refrigerant.
5. Disconnect the high and low pressure lines at the expansion valve.
6. Remove the two piece seal retainer from the dash panel and the refrigerant hose seal.
7. Disconnect the three heater hoses at the dash panel.
8. Disconnect the two clutch wires from the vacuum switch at the water valve mounting plate.
9. Disconnect the vacuum hoses at the water valves, clutch switch and vacuum supply tank. Push the hose-wire harness into the passenger compartment.
10. Remove the drain tube hose and seal from the evaporator housing.
11. Disengage the defroster nozzle from the plenum.
12. Disconnect the red-stripe hose from the vacuum motor.
13. Remove the plenum chamber.
14. Remove the glove compartment liner.
15. Disconnect the vacuum hose from the right vent motor.
16. Remove the right vent assembly.
17. Disconnect the four vacuum hoses and the temperature control cable from the control assembly.
18. Disconnect the wires from the blower resistor and icing switch.
19. Disconnect the flexible hoses from the center air duct.
20. Remove the center air duct.
21. Remove the defroster nozzle.
22. Remove the evaporator retaining nuts and remove the assembly.

Installation

To install, reverse the removal procedure. Evacuate, leak test, and charge the system with refrigerant.

1969-70 Mustang and Cougar

Removal

NOTE: to remove the core, it is necessary to remove the entire evaporator assembly.

1. Remove the carburetor air cleaner.
2. Disconnect the battery ground cable.
3. Drain the cooling system.
4. Purge the system of refrigerant.
5. Remove the heat shield from the expansion valve.
6. Disconnect the low pressure hose and service valve from the compressor.
7. Disconnect the high pressure hose at the quick disconnect.
8. Remove the straps retaining the refrigerant hoses to the dash-to-fender apron supports.
9. Disconnect the heater hoses from the heater core. Remove the upper and lower seal retainers and remove the hose seal.
10. Remove the evaporator housing and blower housing nuts from the engine side of dash panel.
11. Remove the instrument panel pad.
12. Remove the glove box assembly and support.
13. Remove the instrument cluster assembly.
14. Disconnect all vacuum hoses.

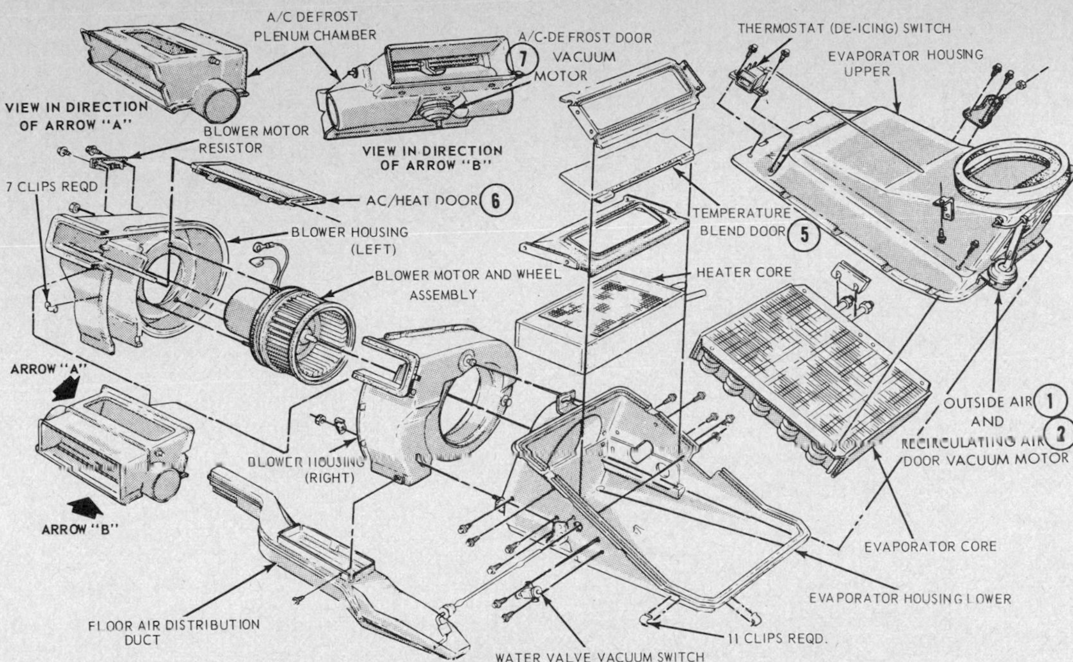

Heater-air conditioner assembly—1970-74 Maverick, 1971-74 Comet, 1975-76 Maverick and Comet similar
(© Ford Motor Co)

15. Disconnect the control cable from the temperature blend door, wires from the A/C thermostat switch.
16. Disconnect air ducts from the plenum chamber, remove the air ducts.
17. Remove the A/C defrost plenum chamber.
18. Remove the instrument right side brace, evaporator housing upper rear support.
19. Move the blower housing to the left away from the evaporator housing.
20. Cover carpet and pull drain tube from hole in floor pan.
21. Remove the instrument panel lower finish cover from around the steering column.
22. Remove nuts and bolts retaining the instrument panel to steering column support.
23. Position the instrument panel back and remove the evaporator housing from the vehicle.

Installation

To install, reverse the removal procedure, Evacuate. Leak test. Charge the system.

1970-76 Maverick, 1971-76 Comet

Removal

NOTE: to facilitate installation, tag vacuum lines and electrical wires, as to their proper location, before disassembling unit. To remove the core, it is necessary to remove the entire evaporator assembly.

1. Disconnect the battery and remove the air cleaner.
2. Drain the cooling system.
3. Connect a manifold gauge set to the compressor, and discharge the system.
4. Remove the expansion valve and disconnect the heater hoses from the heater core. Tape over openings to avoid entry of dirt.
5. Remove the three A/C assembly-to-dash panel mounting stud nuts. Remove the utility shelf and bracket from the lower edge of the instrument panel, and remove the right cowl trim panel and radio. Remove the glove compartment.
6. Disconnect the right and left A/C register air ducts from the plenum chamber.
7. Remove the floor distribution duct from the blower housing.
8. Remove the center register from the instrument panel. Then pull the plenum chamber part way through the register opening to disengage it from the blower housing. Disconnect the (blue) hose from the (7) door motor on the plenum chamber.
9. Disconnect the vacuum hoses from the doormotors.
10. Disconnect the vacuum harness multiple connector from the control assembly.
11. Disconnect the temperature control cable from the evaporator housing, and disconnect the vacuum hoses from the adjacent water valve vacuum switch.
12. Remove the screw which retains the evaporator housing to the cowl upper support and move A/C assembly rearward and away from the dash panel.
13. Remove any remaining hoses and disconnect wires from the blower resistor, the de-icing switch and the blower motor ground wire.
14. Remove the evaporator and blower housing assembly from the vehicle.

Installation

1. Install assembly into the vehicle by reversing the removal procedures, being careful to correctly connect the vacuum holes. When making connections to the water valve vacuum switch, connect the purple hose to the nipple closest to the switch plunger and attach the green hose to the water valve motor.
2. After installation, adjust the temperature control cable and, if neccessary, the water valve vacuum switch.
3. Evacuate, leak test and charge the system.

1971-73 Mustang and Cougar

Removal

NOTE: to remove the core, it is necessary to remove the entire evaporator assembly.

1. Remove the carburetor air cleaner.
2. Disconnect the battery.
3. Drain the cooling system.
4. Purge the system of refrigerant.
5. Disconnect the evaporator tubes from the expansion valve, disconnect the heater hoses.
6. Remove the housing-to-dash panel mounting stud nuts.
7. Remove the glove box and map light from the lower edge, right side of instrument panel.
8. Disconnect the vacuum hoses at the motor.

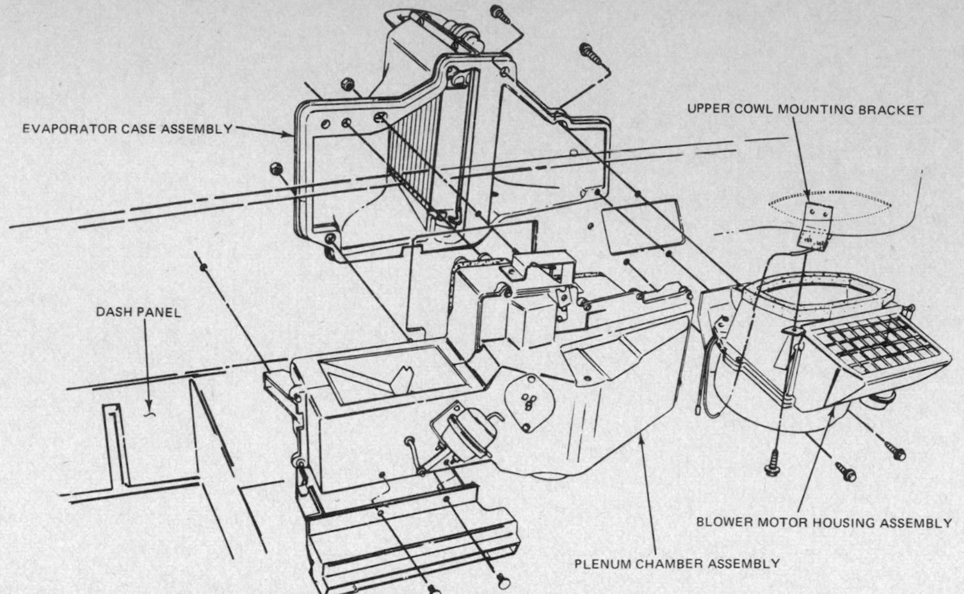

Heater-air conditioner assembly—1972-76 Torino, Montego, Cougar and Elite
(© Ford Motor Co)

9. Disconnect the two hoses from the water valve vacuum switch, and disengage the hoses from the slip at the top of the housing.
10. Disconnect the wires from the thermostatic (de-icing) switch.
11. Disconnect the cable from the door crank arm.
12. Remove the motor from the housing to allow clearance at the lower edge of the instrument panel, and remove the motor bracket.
13. Remove the motor to allow clearance at the right side of the housing during removal.
14. Remove the housing-to-cowl bracket.
15. Pull the drain hose from the hole in the floor pan.
16. Remove the two blower housing-to-cowl attaching screws, lower the blower housing slightly. Pull the housing away from the dash panel, move it to the right to separate it from the blower housing and remove it from the vehicle.

Installation

To install, reverse the removal procedure. Evacuate, Leak test, and Charge the refrigerant system.

1972-76 Torino, Montego 1974-76 Cougar and Elite

Removal

NOTE: to remove the core, it is necessary to remove the entire assembly.

1. Discharge system as outlined under instructions referring to units with six cylinder compressor.
2. Disconnect the heater hoses, and position them so coolant will not escape.
3. Disconnect liquid line to expansion valve, low pressure line to STV valve, and STV valve equalizer line.
4. Remove insulation around capillary tube, and remove tube from suction line. Remove expansion valve from evaporator.
5. Remove STV valve by disconnecting it from the evaporator.
6. Remove the two mounting flange nuts and three mounting flange screws that can be reached from the engine compartment. Remove the sheet metal mounting screws, plenum right lower mounting screws, and blower housing-to-evaporator housing screw from under the instrument panel. Remove the plenum mounting screws and move the plenum to the rear.
7. Remove the evaporator case from the engine compartment.

Installation

1. Reverse the removal procedures, observing the following precautions:
   a. After installing heater hoses, replace any coolant that may have been lost.
   b. Evacuate, leak test, and charge the system.

Heater Core R & R

1969-70 Falcon and Fairlane 1969-71 Torino and Montego

1. Remove the heater-air conditioner assembly.
2. Separate the heater housing from the plenum.
3. Slip the heater core out of the plenum.
4. Transfer the old heater core seal to the new core.
5. Slip the new core with seal into the plenum.
6. Install the heater housing to the plenum. Connect the wires at the resistor block, and install the seal and retainer at the evaporator tubes.
7. Install the heater-air conditoner assembly.

1969-73 Mustang and Cougar, 1970-76 Maverick, 1971-76 Comet

1. Remove the heater-air conditioner assembly.
2. Remove the flange clips and upper half of the housing assembly.
3. Remove the water valve vacuum switch from the lower half of the housing.
4. Remove the screw, retaining clip and temperature blend door shaft, the four screws and door upper frame, the door, and the four screws and door lower frame from the lower half of the housing.
5. Lift the heater core from the lower housing.
6. Transfer the pads from the old core to the new core.
7. Reverse the above procedures to install. Leak-test, evacuate and charge the refrigeration system.

1972-76 Torino and Montego 1974-76 Cougar

1. Drain the cooling system and disconnect the heater hoses at the core.
2. Remove the glove box.
3. Remove the two snap clips and the heater air outlet register from the plenum.
4. Remove the temperature control cable assembly mounting screw, and disconnect the end of the cable from the blend door crank arm.
5. Remove the blue and red vacuum hoses from the high-low door vacuum motor; the yellow hose

from the panel-defrost door motor, and the brown hose from the inline tee connector.

6. Disconnect the wires at the resistor block.
7. Remove the ten screws and the rear half of the plenum.
8. Remove the mounting nut from the heater core tube support bracket.
9. Reverse the above procedures to install, taking care to apply body sealer around the case flanges to insure a positive seal.

1975-76 Granada and Monarch

NOTE: The refrigerant system components and charge do not have to be disturbed when removing and installing the heater core.

1. Drain the coolant and disconnect the battery.
2. Disconnect 2 heater hose clamps at the dash panel in the engine compartment. Plug the core tubes to prevent coolant leakage during removal.
3. Remove the heat distribution duct from the instrument panel.
4. Remove the seat belt interlock module and bracket.
5. Remove the glovebox liner.
6. Loosen the right door sill scuff plate, right "A" pillar trim cover and remove the right cowl side trim panel.
7. Loosen instrument panel-to-right cowl side bolt and remove the instrument panel brace bolt at the lower rail, below the glove box.
8. Remove the instrument panel crash pad.
9. Remove the radio speaker or panel cowl brace.
10. Remove the 4 nozzle-to-cowl bracket mounting screws.
11. Lift the defroster nozzle upward through the crash pad opening.
12. Disconnect the vacuum hoses from the A/C-Defrost and Heat/Defrost door motors. Remove the screw from the clip holding the vacuum harness to the plenum.
13. Remove 2 Heat/Defrost door mounting nuts and swing the motor rearward on the door crankarm.
14. Remove 2 screws attaching the plenum to the left mounting bracket. Then remove the 2 screws and 3 clips securing the plenum to the evaporator case.
15. Swing the bottom of the plenum away from the evaporator case to disengage the S-clip on the forward flange of the plenum. Raise the plenum to clear the tabs on the top of the evaporator case.
16. Move the plenum to the left as far as possible, (about 4 inches) pulling rearward on the instrument panel to gain clearance. Take care when pulling back on the instrument panel to avoid cracking the plastic panel.

NOTE: There is very little clearance between the plenum and the wiper motor assembly.

17. Pull the heater core to the left using the tab molded into the rear heater core seal. As the rear surface of the heater core clears the evaporator case, pull the core rearward and downward to clear the instrument panel.
18. Reverse the above procedure to install.

NOTE: Before installing the core, make sure that the heater core tube to dash panel seal is in place between the evaporator case and the dash panel.

Blower Motor R & R

1969-70 Falcon and Fairlane
1969-76 Torino and Montego, 1974-76 Cougar

Removal

1. Disconnect the battery and take out the glove box.

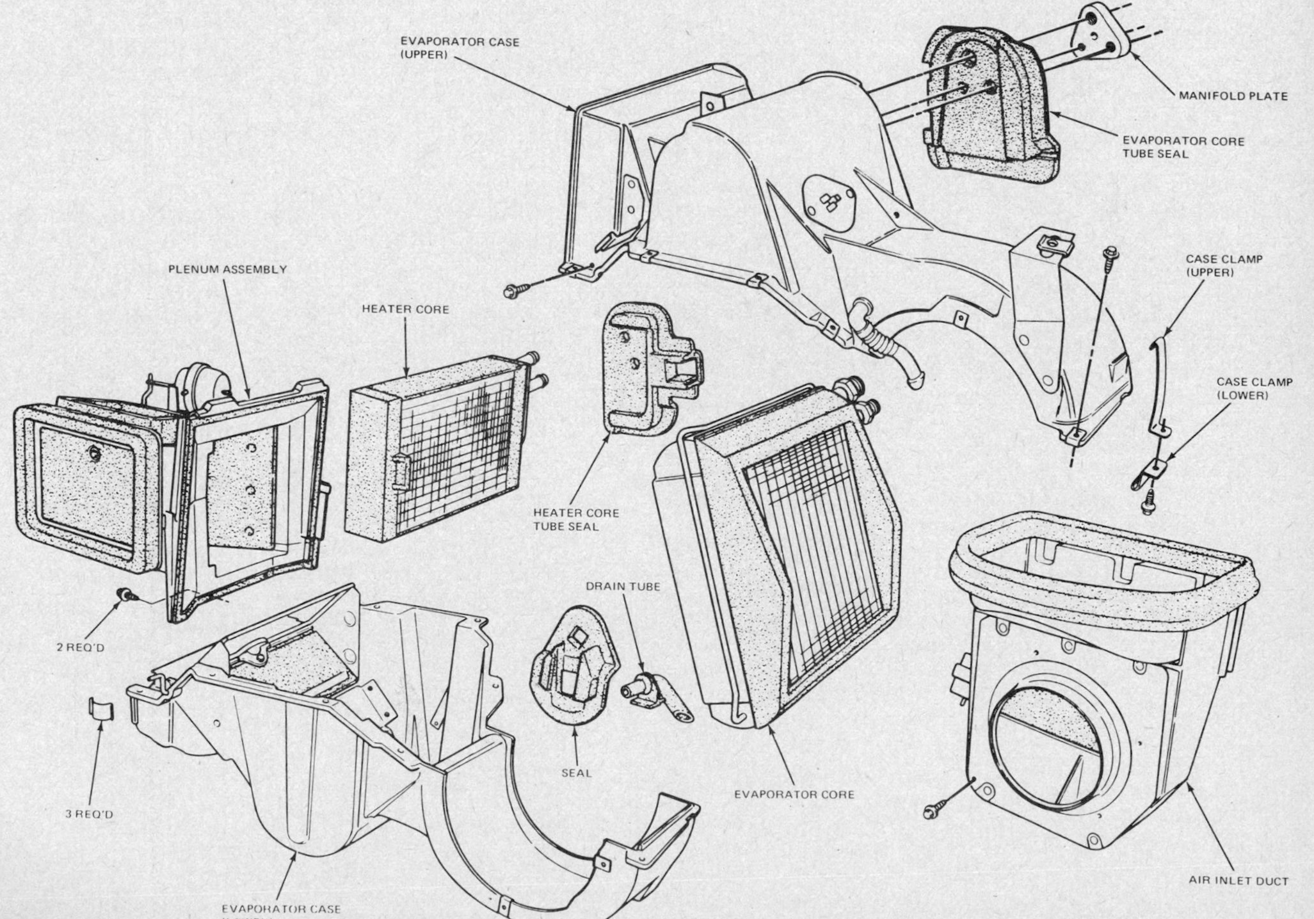

Heater core removal—Granada and Monarch with heater/air conditioner system
(© Ford Motor Co)

2. On 1971 and earlier models, take out the right hand fresh air duct. On 1972 and later models, remove recirculating air duct.
3. Remove the two screws which attach the blower lower housing to the dash panel.
4. Disconnect the vacuum line from the actuator and move it out of the way.
5. Disconnect the plug from the resistor block and lift out the resistor block.
6. On 1971 and earlier models, take off the blower motor cover and lift out the motor and the blower wheel. On 1972 and later models, remove all blower housing flange screws, separate blower housing halves, and unscrew and remove blower assembly.
7. Remove the blower wheel.

Installation

1. Install the blower wheel on the motor.
2. Install the motor and shell and ground wire in the case.
3. On 1971 and earlier models, install the blower cover. On 1972 and later models, install blower assembly into lower housing, and reassemble housing.
4. Connect the wires.
5. Fasten the resistor block to the plenum.
6. Install the fresh air duct on earlier models, recirculating air duct on 1972 and later models.
7. Install the two screws which attach the blower lower housing to the dash.
8. Install the glove box and connect the battery.

1969-70 Mustang and Cougar

Removal

1. Disconnect battery ground cable, and drain cooling system.
2. Remove instrument panel pad, glove compartment liner, and glove compartment door.
3. Remove the heater air distribution duct.
4. Disconnect the control cables, and the wires from the blower motor resistor.
5. Remove the right side courtesy light, if applicable.
6. Remove the heater support mounting screw from the dash.
7. Disconnect the vacuum hoses. If the vehicle is equipped with a power ventilation system, remove the power vent air duct.
8. Disconnect the heater hoses at the dash panel.
9. From the engine compartment, remove the blower motor ground screw, and the five heater assembly retaining nuts.
10. Remove the screws which hold the instrument panel to the cowl, and the instrument panel right side brace. Pull the right side of the instrument panel rearward, and remove the heater assembly.
11. Disconnect blower motor wires where they connect at the resistor.
12. Remove the four mounting plate nuts, and remove the blower and motor assembly.

Installation

1. To install, reverse the procedures, being careful to properly adjust the control cables.

1970-73 Maverick, 1971-73 Comet

Removal

1. Disconnect the battery and remove the radio asembly.
2. Remove the utility shelf, and air ducts from the plenum chamber.
3. Remove the air duct from the bottom of the blower housing.
4. Remove the blower housing mounting stud nut and lock plate.
5. Rotate the blower housing from the evaporator housing.
6. Disconnect the vacuum hoses, resistor and ground wires, and remove the housing.
7. Separate the left and right halves.

Installation

1. Set the motor in place.
2. Install the motor attaching nuts.
3. Set the blower fan on the motor shaft.
4. Install the blower motor and fan assembly.
5. Set the blower housing in place.
6. Install the blower housing attaching nuts, washers, and screws.
7. Install the water valve.
8. Reverse steps 1-3 to complete asembly.

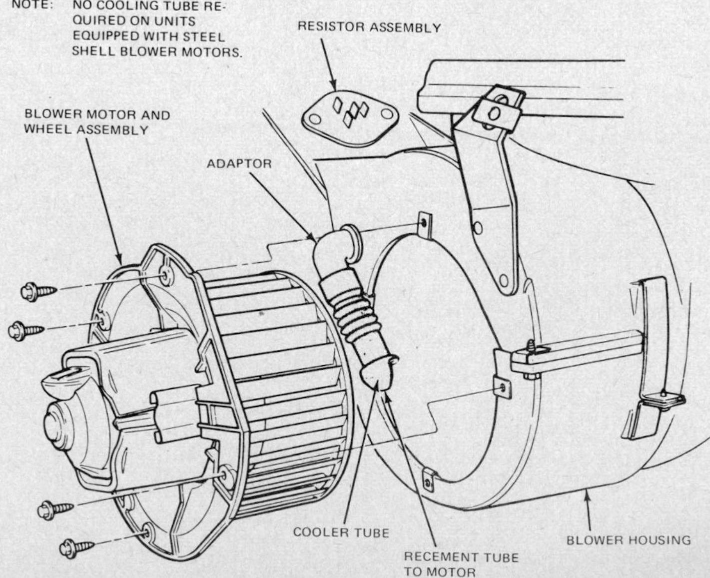

Blower motor removal—Granada and Monarch with heater/air conditioner system
(© Ford Motor Co)

1974-76 Maverick and Comet

1. Disconnect the battery and remove the radio.
2. Remove the floor air distribution duct retaining bolts, and disconnect the right and left A/C register air duct assemblies from the plenum chamber.
3 Remove the floor air distribution duct from the bottom of the blower housing.
4. Remove the blower housing mounting stud nut and lockplate.
5. Rotate the blower housing to unlock the slotted tabs on the blower housing from their lock pins on the evaporator housing. There are two tabs and pins. Disconnect the red and yellow hoses at the vacuum motor on the blower housing. Disconnect the resistor and ground wires, and remove the blower housing.
6. Cut the gaskets around the A/C outlets at the break line.
7. Remove the seven clips, and separate the left and right halves of the blower housing.
8. Remove the three blower motor mounting plate retaining nuts, and remove the motor and wheel assembly from the housing.
9. Assemble and install in the reverse order of removal, making sure that the A/C-Heat door is positioned properly before clipping the right and left housing halves together. Connect the battery.

1971-73 Mustang and Cougar

Removal

1. Disconnect the battery. Remove the blower housing mounting bracket stud nut (engine side of the dash panel.)
2. Remove the two blower housing-to-instrument panel support mounting screws.

3. Disconnect the blower motor ground wire (black) from the resistor.
4. Disconnect the blower motor lead wire (orange-black) from the resistor.
5. Rotate the blower housing to a diagonal position. Remove the blower motor mounting screws, and remove the blower motor and wheel as an assembly.

Installation

1. Position the assembly and secure the mounting screws.
2. Connect the blower motor lead and ground wires.
3. Position the blower motor on the blower housing and install the mounting bracket.
4. Install the battery.

1975-76 Granada and Monarch

1. Disconnect the negative battery cable.
2. Loosen the passenger side door sill scuff plate and the right "A" pillar trim cover. Remove the right cowl side trim panel.
3. Remove the bolt retaining the lower side of the instrument panel to the cowl. Remove the right cowl side brace bolt.
4. Disconnect the wiring harness connectors at the blower motor.
5. If so equipped, remove the cooling tube from the blower motor.
6. Remove the 4 screws retaining the blower motor and wheel assembly to the scroll. To remove the motor, pull rearward on the lower edge of the instrument panel to provide clearance.
7. Installation is the reverse of removal. If necesary, cement the cooling tube to the blower motor.

SEAT BELTS

Seat Belt/Starter Interlock System

On 1974-75 models, a starter interlock system is employed consisting of a warning light, buzzer, seat sensors, switches in the outboard belt retractors, and an electronic logic module. Basically, the starter will not engage unless the driver and other front seat passenger sit in the seat and pull out the seat belt. Unles the driver or passenger has remained seated and buckled, the sequence must be repeated every time the engine is started. Leaving the belts pulled all the way out also will prevent the engine from being started, as the belts must be retracted and buckled each time the engine is started. In the event of a starter interlock system failure, or to permit the use of a remote starter switch when working under the hood, a starter interlock by-pass switch is located in the engine compartment, thereby eliminating the need to perform the buckling sequence.

NOTE: Each time the by-pass switch is operated, the buckling sequence may be eliminated once and once only. The system may not be permanently by-passed.

Disconnecting Seat Belt/Starter Interlock

As of October 29, 1974, it is legal to disconnect the seat belt/starter interlock system. However the warning light portion of the system must be left operational.

1. Apply the parking brake and remove the ignition key.
2. Open the hood and locate the system emergency override switch and connector. Remove the connector.
3. Cut the white wire(s) with the pink dots (# 33 circuit) and the red wire(s) with the light blue stripe (#32 circuit).
4. Splice the two (four) wires together and tape the splice. Use a "butt" connector if available.

NOTE: Do not cut and splice the other connector wires. If the red/yellow hash wire is spliced to any of the other wires the car will start in gear.

6. Install the connector back on the override switch. Close the hood.
7. Apply the parking brakes, buckle the seat belt, and turn the key to the "ON" position. If the starter cranks in "ON" or any gear selected, the wrong wires have been cut and spliced. Repeat steps 3-6.
8. Unbuckle the belt and try to start the car. If the car doesn't start, repeat steps 3-6. If the car starts, everything is OK.
9. To stop the warning buzzer from operating, remove it from its connector and throw it away. Tape the connector to the wiring harness so that it can't rattle.

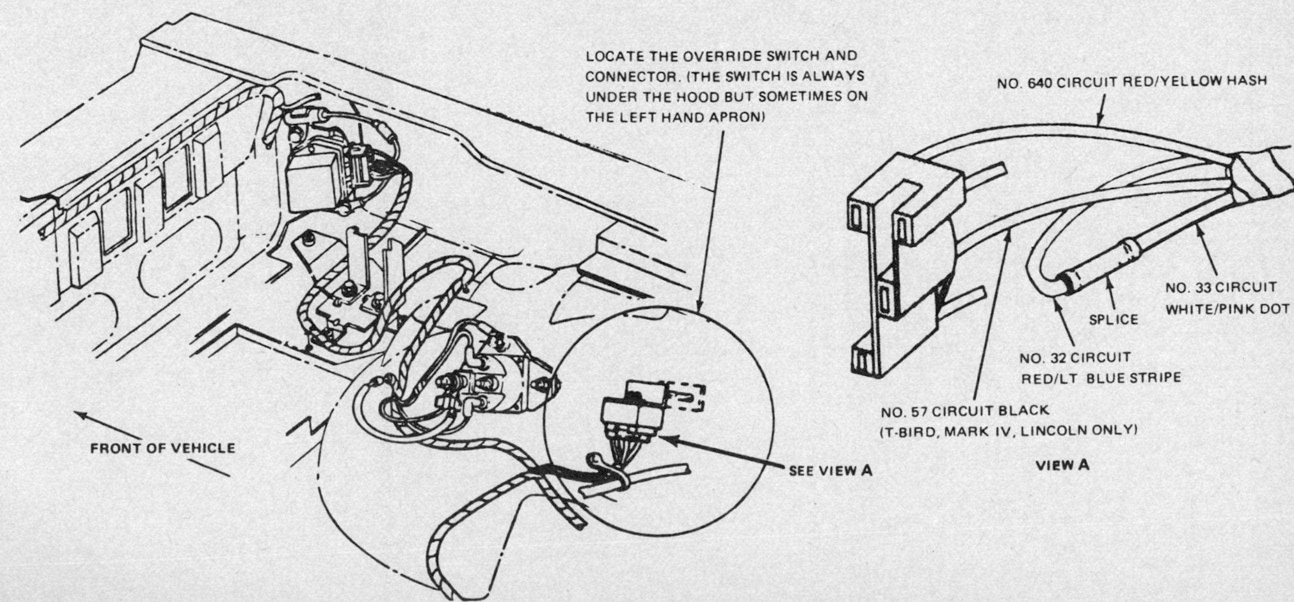

Disconnecting seat belt/starter interlock system
(© Ford Motor Co)

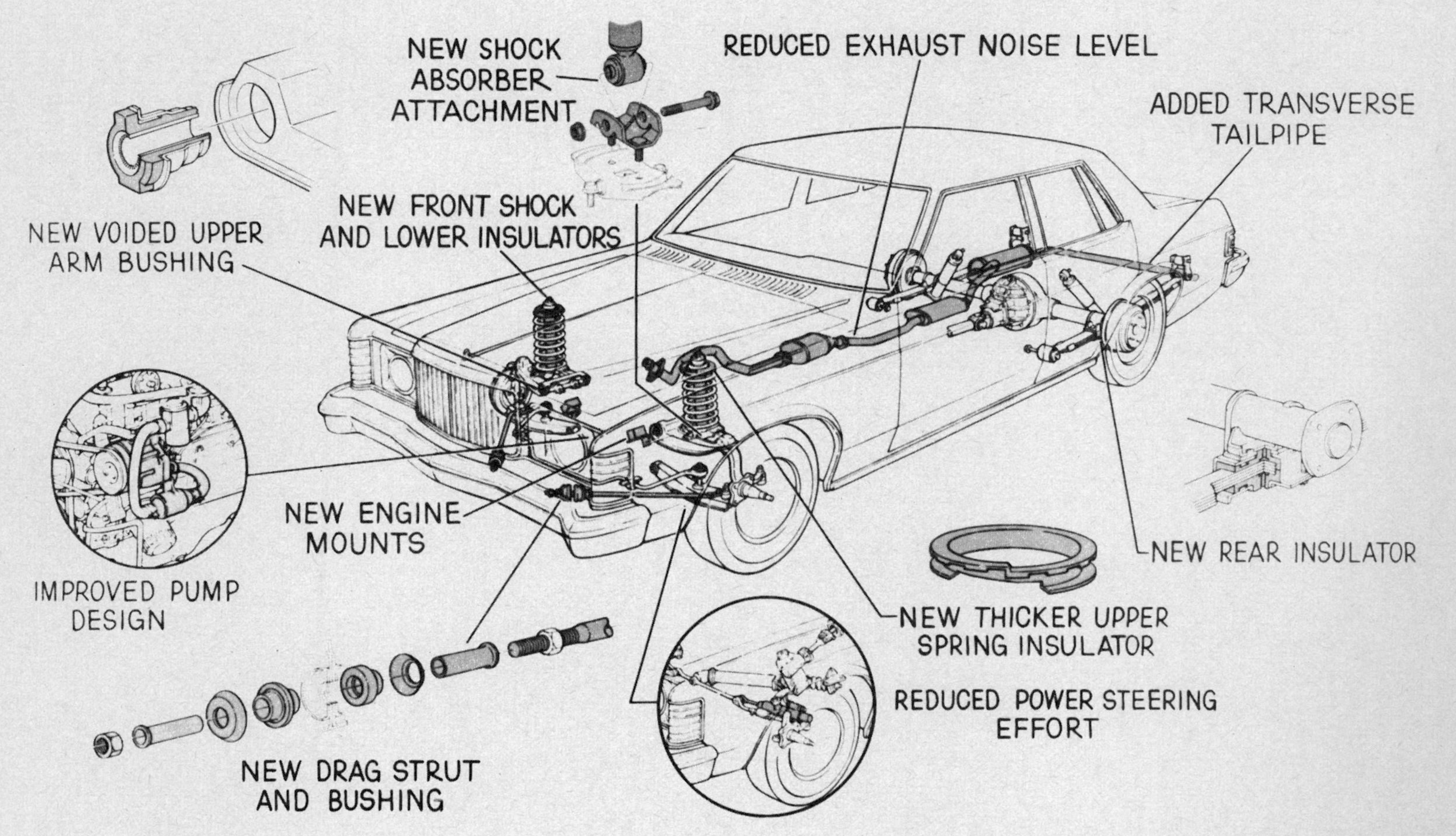

1976 Monarch/Granada ride improvement and noise reduction changes
(© Ford Motor Co.)

INDEX

Dodge · Plymouth

MODEL IDENTIFICATION

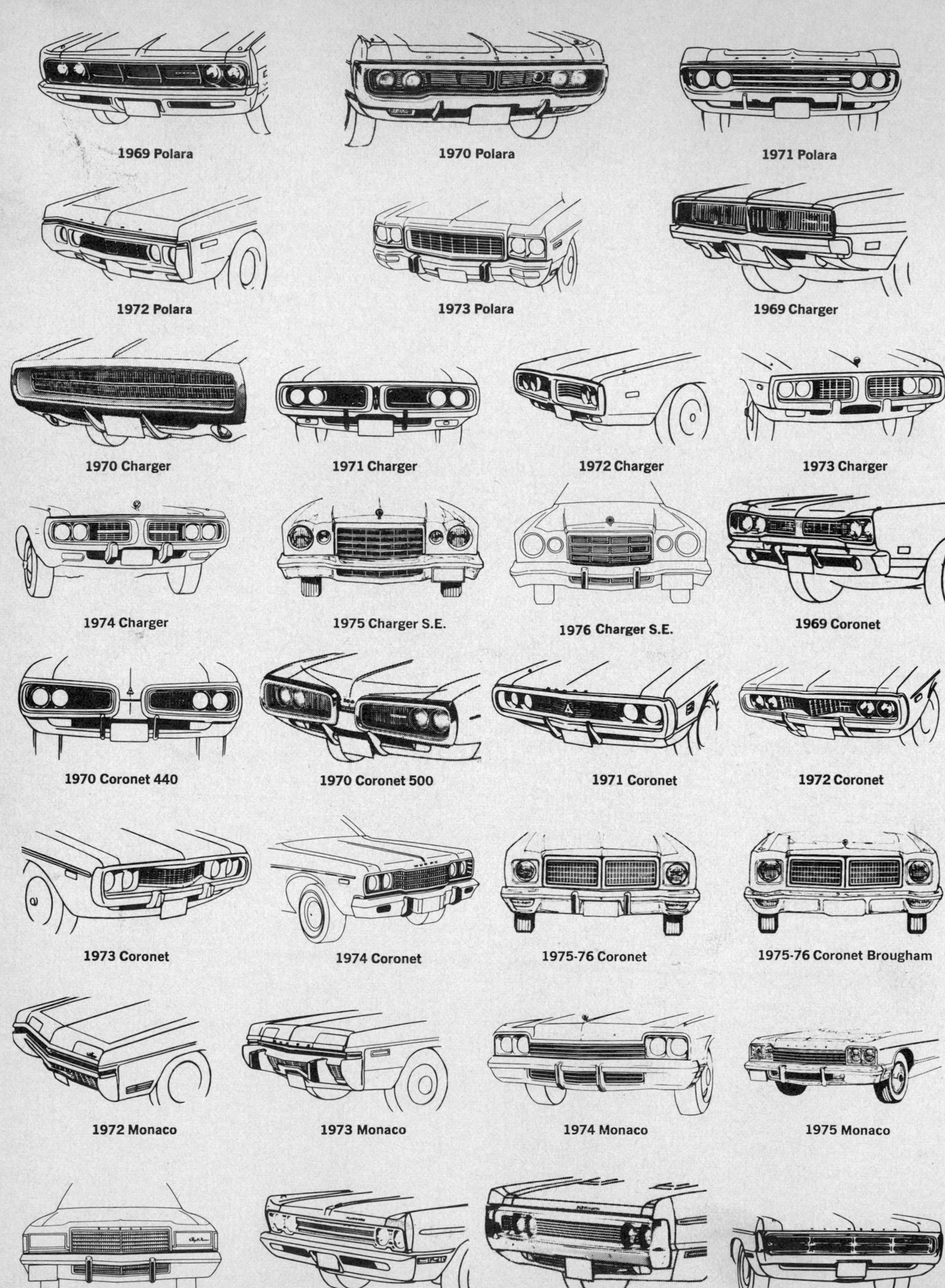

1969 Polara
1970 Polara
1971 Polara
1972 Polara
1973 Polara
1969 Charger
1970 Charger
1971 Charger
1972 Charger
1973 Charger
1974 Charger
1975 Charger S.E.
1976 Charger S.E.
1969 Coronet
1970 Coronet 440
1970 Coronet 500
1971 Coronet
1972 Coronet
1973 Coronet
1974 Coronet
1975-76 Coronet
1975-76 Coronet Brougham
1972 Monaco
1973 Monaco
1974 Monaco
1975 Monaco
1976 Monaco
1969 Fury
1970 Fury
1971 Fury

MODEL IDENTIFICATION (con't.)

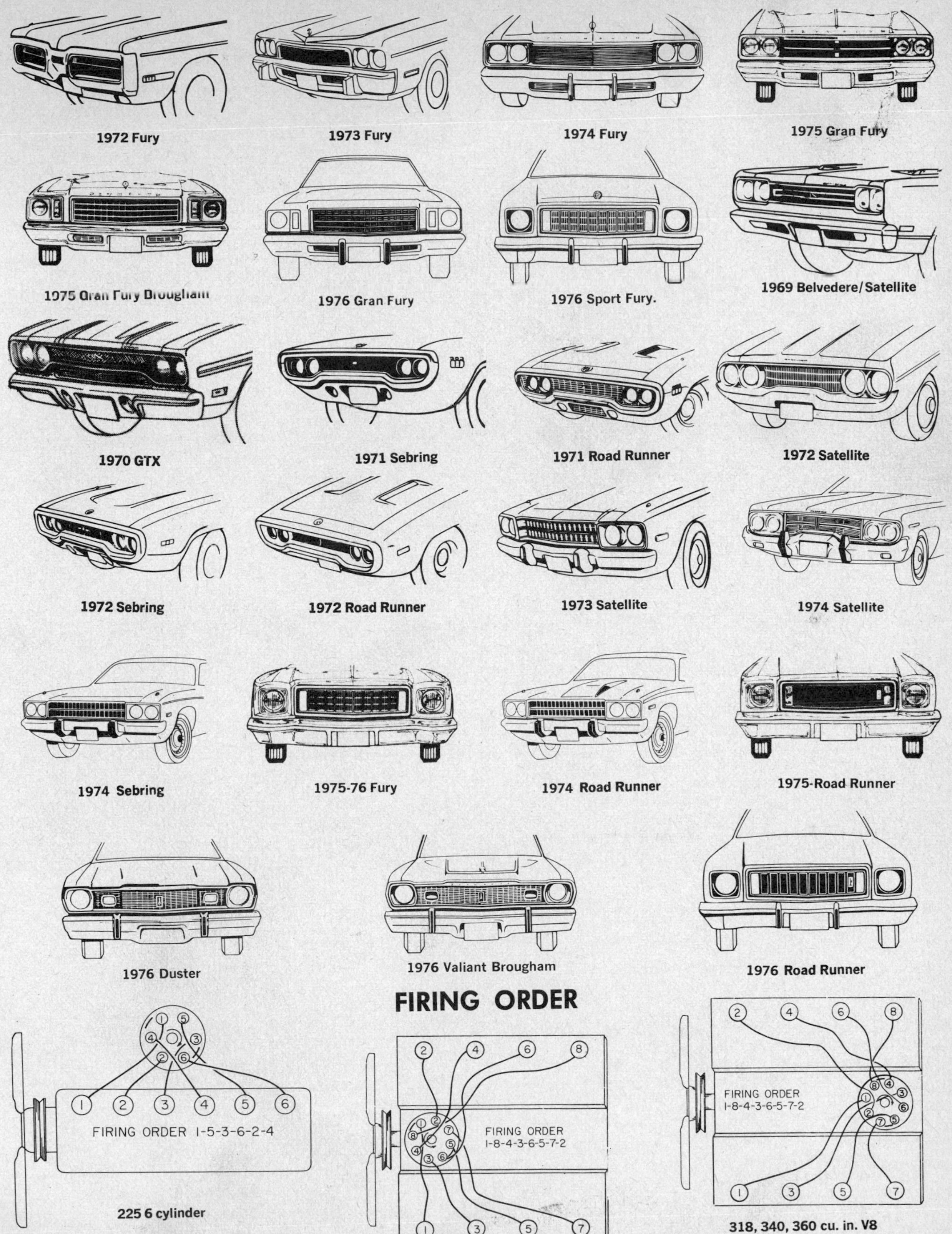

1972 Fury
1973 Fury
1974 Fury
1975 Gran Fury
1975 Gran Fury Brougham
1976 Gran Fury
1976 Sport Fury.
1969 Belvedere/Satellite
1970 GTX
1971 Sebring
1971 Road Runner
1972 Satellite
1972 Sebring
1972 Road Runner
1973 Satellite
1974 Satellite
1974 Sebring
1975-76 Fury
1974 Road Runner
1975-Road Runner
1976 Duster
1976 Valiant Brougham
1976 Road Runner

FIRING ORDER

225 6 cylinder

383, 426 Hemi, 400, 440 cu. in. with Chrysler distributor (No. 1 one space CW for Autolite and Prestolite distributors)

318, 340, 360 cu. in. V8

Car Serial Number Location

Top of instrument panel, visible through windshield.

ENGINE CODE

The engine code designation is the 5th digit of the vehicle identification number (V.I.N.). The V.I.N. is stamped on a plate located at the left side of the instrument panel visible through the windshield and located to the rear of the right engine mount on the oil pan rail.

Disp	Bbl	Hp*	'69	'70	'71	'72	'73	'74	'75	'76
6-Cylinder Models										
225	1	95 (net)							C	C
225	1	105 (net)					C	C		
225	1	110 (net)				C				
225	1	145	B	C	C					
8-Cylinder Models										
318	2	150, 170 (net)					G	G	G	G
318	2	230	F	G	G					
340HP	4	240 (net)				H	H			
340HP	4	275			H					
360	2	170 (net)				K	K			
360	2	180 (net)						K	K	K
360	4	190 (net)							J	J
360	4	200 (net)						J		
360HP	4	245 (net)						L	L	L
383	2	275			L					
383	2	290	G	L						
383	4	300			N					
383	4	330	H	L						
383	4	335	H	N						

Disp	Bbl	Hp*	'69	'70	'71	'72	'73	'74	'75	'76
8-Cylinder Models										
400	2	190 (net)				M				
400	2	175, 185 (net)					M	M	M	M
400	4	190 (net)							N	N
400	4	200, 205 (net)						N		
400HP	4	235 (net)							P	P
400HP	4	230, 240 (net)						P		
400HP	4	255 (net)④				P				
400HP	4	260 (net)					P			
426 Hemi	8	425	J	R	R					
440	4	215 (net)							T	T
440	4	220, 230 (net)					T	T		
440HP	4	275, 280 (net)					U	U		
440HP	4	290 (net)				U				
440	4	370				U				
440	4	375	L	U						
440	6	385			V					
440	6	390		V						

* Net horsepower rating varies with model application
④ Non-California cars with Fresh Air Pack—265 (net)

GENERAL ENGINE SPECIFICATIONS

Year	Engine No. Cyl. Displacement Cu. In.	Carburetor Type	Horsepower @ rpm ■	Torque @ rpm (ft lbs) ■	Bore and Stroke (in.)	Compression Ratio	Oil Pressure @ 2050 rpm
'69	6-225	1 bbl	145 @ 4000	215 @ 2400	3.400 x 4.125	8.40:1	55
	8-318	2 bbl	230 @ 4400	340 @ 2400	3.910 x 3.310	9.20:1	55
	8-383	2 bbl	290 @ 4400	390 @ 2800	4.250 x 3.375	9.20:1	55
	8-383	4 bbl	330 @ 5000	425 @ 3200	4.250 x 3.375	10.00:1	55
	8-383	4 bbl	335 @ 5200	425 @ 3400	4.250 x 3.375	10.00:1	55
	8-426 Hemi	2 x 4 bbl	425 @ 5000	490 @ 4000	4.250 x 3.750	10.25:1	55
	8-440	4 bbl	350 @ 4400	480 @ 2800	4.320 x 3.750	10.01:1	55
	8-440 HP	4 bbl	375 @ 4600	480 @ 3200	4.320 x 3.750	10.01:1	55
'70	6-225	1 bbl	145 @ 4000	215 @ 2400	3.400 x 4.125	8.40:1	55
	8-318	2 bbl	230 @ 4400	320 @ 2000	3.910 x 3.310	8.80:1	55
	8-383	2 bbl	290 @ 4400	390 @ 2800	4.250 x 3.375	8.70:1	55
	8-383	4 bbl	330 @ 5000	425 @ 3200	4.250 x 3.375	9.50:1	55
	8-383 HP	4 bbl	335 @ 5200	425 @ 3400	4.250 x 3.375	9.50:1	55
	8-426 Hemi	2 x 4 bbl	425 @ 5000	490 @ 4000	4.250 x 3.750	10.20:1	55
	8-440	4 bbl	350 @ 4400	480 @ 2800	4.320 x 3.750	9.70:1	55
	8-440 HP	4 bbl	375 @ 4600	480 @ 3200	4.320 x 3.750	9.70:1	55
	8-440	3 x 2 bbl	390 @ 4700	490 @ 3200	4.320 x 3.750	10.50:1	55

GENERAL ENGINE SPECIFICATIONS (con't.)

Year	Engine No. Cyl. Displacement Cu. In.	Carburetor Type	Horsepower @ rpm ■	Torque @ rpm (ft lbs) ■	Bore and Stroke (in.)	Compression Ratio	Oil Pressure @ 2050 rpm
'71	6-225	1 bbl	145 @ 4000	215 @ 2400	3.400 x 4.125	8.40:1	55
	8-318	2 bbl	230 @ 4400	320 @ 2000	3.910 x 3.310	8.60:1	55
	8-340	4 bbl	275 @ 5000	340 @ 3200	4.040 x 3.310	10.30:1	55
	8-360	2 bbl	255 @ 4400	360 @ 2400	4.000 x 3.580	8.70:1	55
	8-383	2 bbl	275 @ 4400	375 @ 2800	4.250 x 3.375	8.50:1	55
	8-383 HP	4 bbl	300 @ 4800	410 @ 3400	4.250 x 3.375	8.50:1	55
	8-426 Hemi	2 x 4 bbl	425 @ 5000	490 @ 4000	4.250 x 3.750	10.20:1	55
	8-440	4 bbl	335 @ 4400	460 @ 3200	4.320 x 3.750	8.50:1	55
	8-440 HP	4 bbl	370 @ 4600	480 @ 3200	4.320 x 3.750	9.50:1	55
	8-440	3 x 2 bbl	385 @ 4700	490 @ 3200	4.320 x 3.750	10.30:1	55
'72	6-225	1 bbl	110 @ 4000①	185 @ 2000②	3.400 x 4.125	8.40:1	55
	8-318	2 bbl	150 @ 4000	260 @ 1600	3.910 x 3.310	8.60:1	55
	8-340 HP	4 bbl	240 @ 4800	290 @ 3600	4.040 x 3.310	8.50:1	55
	8-360	2 bbl	175 @ 4000	285 @ 2400	4.000 x 3.580	8.80:1	55
	8-400	2 bbl	190 @ 4400③	310 @ 2400④	4.340 x 3.380	8.20:1	55
	8-400	4 bbl	255 @ 4800⑤	340 @ 3200⑥	4.340 x 3.380	8.20:1	55
	8-400⑪	4 bbl	265 @ 4800	345 @ 3200	4.340 x 3.380	8.20:1	55
	8-440	4 bbl	225 @ 4400⑦	345 @ 3200⑧	4.320 x 3.750	8.20:1	55
	8-440	4 bbl	280 @ 4800⑨	375 @ 3200⑩	4.320 x 3.750	8.20:1	55
	8-440⑪	4 bbl	290 @ 4800	380 @ 3200	4.320 x 3750	8.20:1	55
'73	6-225	1 bbl	105 @ 4000	185 @ 1600	3.400 x 4.125	8.4:1	55
	8-318	2 bbl	150 @ 3600	265 @ 2000	3.910 x 3.310	8.6:1	55
	8-340 HP	4 bbl	240 @ 4800	295 @ 3600	4.040 x 3.310	8.5:1	55
	8-360	2 bbl	170 @ 4000	285 @ 2400	4.000 x 3.580	8.4:1	55
	8-400	2 bbl	185 @ 3600	310 @ 2400	4.340 x 3.380	8.2:1	55
	8-400	4 bbl	260 @ 4800	335 @ 3600	4.340 x 3.380	8.2:1	55
	8-440	4 bbl	220 @ 3600	350 @ 2400	4.320 x 3.750	8.2:1	55
	8-440 HP	4 bbl	275 @ 4800	380 @ 3200	4.320 x 3.750	8.2:1	55
'74	6-225	1 bbl	105 @ 3600	180 @ 1600	3.400 x 4.125	8.4:1	55
	8-318	2 bbl	150 @ 4000	255 @ 2200	3.910 x 3.310	8.6:1	55
	8-318 HP	2 bbl	170 @ 4000	265 @ 2600	3.910 x 3.310	8.6:1	55
	8-360	2 bbl	180 @ 4000	290 @ 2400	4.000 x 3.580	8.4:1	55
	8-360	4 bbl	200 @ 4000	290 @ 3200	4.000 x 3.580	8.4:1	55
	8-360 HP	4 bbl	245 @ 4800	320 @ 3600	4.000 x 3.580	8.4:1	55
	8-400	2 bbl	185 @ 4000	315 @ 2400	4.340 x 3.380	8.2:1	55
	8-400	4 bbl	205 @ 4400	310 @ 2400	4.340 x 3.380	8.2:1	55
	8-400 HP	4 bbl	250 @ 4800	330 @ 3400	4.340 x 3.380	8.2:1	55
	8-440	4 bbl	230 @ 3600⑫	350 @ 3200⑫	4.320 x 3.750	8.2:1	55
	8-440 HP	4 bbl	275 @ 4400	375 @ 3200	4.320 x 3.750	8.2:1	55

GENERAL ENGINE SPECIFICATIONS (con't.)

Year	Engine No. Cyl. Cu. In. Displacement	Carburetor Type	Horsepower @ rpm ■	Torque @ rpm (ft lbs) ■	Bore and Stroke (in.)	Compression Ratio	Oil Pressure @ 2050 rpm
'75-'76	6-225	1 bbl	95 @ 3600	170 @ 1600	3.400 x 4.125	8.4:1	55
	6-225 Calif.	1 bbl	90 @ 3600	165 @ 1600	3.400 x 4.125	8.4:1	55
	8-318	2 bbl	150 @ 4000	255 @ 1600⑭	3.910 x 3.310	8.5:1	55
	8-318 Calif.	2 bbl	135 @ 3600⑬	245 @ 1600⑮	3.910 x 3.310	8.5:1	55
	8-360	2 bbl	180 @ 4000	290 @ 2400	4.000 x 3.580	8.4:1	55
	8-360	4 bbl	190 @ 4000	270 @ 3200	4.000 x 3.580	8.4:1	55
	8-400	2 bbl	165 @ 4000⑯	295 @ 3200⑰	4.340 x 3.380	8.2:1	55
	8-400	4 bbl	190 @ 4000⑱	290 @ 3200⑲	4.340 x 3.380	8.2:1	55
	8-400 Calif.	4 bbl	185 @ 4000	285 @ 3200	4.340 x 3.380	8.2:1	55
	8-400 HP	4 bbl	235 @ 4200⑳	320 @ 3200㉑	4.340 x 3.380	8.2:1	55
	8-440	4 bbl	215 @ 4000	330 @ 3200	4.320 x 3.750	8.2:1	55
	8-440 Calif.	4 bbl	210 @ 4000	320 @ 3200	4.320 x 3.750	8.2:1	55
	8-440 HP	4 bbl	260 @ 4000	355 @ 3200	4.320 x 3.750	8.2:1	55
	8-440 Calif.	4 bbl	250 @ 4000	350 @ 3200	4.320 x 3.750	8.2:1	55

■ Beginning 1972, horsepower and torque are SAE net figures. They are measured at the rear of the transmission with all accessories installed and operating. Since the figures vary when a given engine is installed in different models, some are representative rather than exact.

① For California vehicles, advertised horsepower is 97 @ 4000 rpm
② For California vehicles, advertised torque is 180 @ 2000 rpm
③ For California vehicles, advertised horsepower is 181 @ 4400 rpm
④ For California vehicles, advertised torque is 305 @ 2400 rpm
⑤ For California vehicles, advertised horsepower is 246 @ 4800 rpm
⑥ For California vehicles, advertised torque is 335 @ 3200 rpm
⑦ For California vehicles, advertised horsepower is 216 @ 4400 rpm
⑧ For California vehicles, advertised torque is 340 @ 3200 rpm
⑨ For California vehicles, advertised horsepower is 271 @ 4800 rpm
⑩ For California vehicles, advertised torque is 370 @ 3200 rpm
⑪ Not available in California
⑫ For California vehicles, h.p. 220, torque 345
⑬ Gran Fury, Monaco—145
⑭ Gran Fury, Monaco—260
⑮ Gran Fury, Monaco—250
⑯ Gran Fury, Monaco—175
⑰ Gran Fury, Monaco—300, Charger SE—295
⑱ Gran Fury, Monaco—195
⑲ Gran Fury, Monaco—285
⑳ Gran Fury, Monaco—240
㉑ Gran Fury, Monaco—325
HP High Performance

Belvedere, Satellite, 1975-76 Fury, Coronet, Charger (intermediate size)

TUNE-UP SPECIFICATIONS

When analyzing compression test results, look for uniformity among cylinders rather than specific pressures.

ENGINE		SPARK PLUGS		DISTRIBUTOR		IGNITION TIMING (deg) ▲		VALVES	Fuel	IDLE SPEED (rpm) ▲	
Year No. Cyl Displacement (cu in.)	hp	Type	(in.)	Point Dwell (deg)	Point Gap (in.)	Man Trans	● Auto Trans	Intake Opens ■ (deg)	Pump Pressure (psi)	Man Trans	● Auto Trans
'69 6-225	145	N-14Y	.035	45	.020	TDC	TDC	10	3½-5	700	650
8-318	230	N-14Y	.035	33	.017	TDC	TDC	10	5-7	700	650
8-383	290	J-14Y	.035	33	.017	TDC	7½B	18	3½-5	700	600
8-383	330	J-11Y	.035	33	.017	TDC	5B	18	3½-5	700	650
8-383	335	J-11Y	.035	30①	.017	TDC	5B	21	3½-5	700	650
8-426	425	N-10Y	.035	30①	.017	TDC	TDC	36	7-8½	800	800
8-440	375	J-11Y	.035	33②	.017	TDC	5B	21	6-7½	700	650

Belvedere, Satellite, 1975-76 Fury, Coronet, Charger (intermediate size)

TUNE-UP SPECIFICATIONS (con't.)

When analyzing compression test results, look for uniformity among cylinders rather than specific pressures.

ENGINE			SPARK PLUGS		DISTRIBUTOR		IGNITION TIMING (deg) ▲		VALVES	Fuel	IDLE SPEED (rpm) ▲	
Year	No. Cyl Displacement (cu in.)	hp	Type	(in.)	Point Dwell (deg)	Point Gap (in.)	Man Trans ●	Auto Trans	Intake Opens ■ (deg)	Pump Pressure (psi)	Man Trans ●	Auto Trans
'70	6-225	145	N-14Y	.035	44	.020	TDC	TDC	10	3½-5	700	650
	8-318	230	N-14Y	.035	32	.017	TDC	TDC	10	5-7	750	700
	8-383	290	J-14Y	.035	30	.018	TDC	2½B	18	3½-5	750	650
	8-383	330	J-11Y	.035	30	.018	TDC	2½B	18	3½-5	750	750
	8-383	335	J-11Y	.035	30	.018	TDC	2½B	21	3½-5	750	750
	8-426	425	N-10Y	.035	30①	.017	TDC	5B	36	7-8½	900	900
	8-440	375	J-11Y	.035	30	.018	TDC	2½B	18	3½-5	900	800
	8-440	390	J-11Y	.035	30①	.017	5B	5B	21	6-7½	900	900
'71	6-225	145	N-14Y	.035	44	.020	TDC(2½B)	TDC(2½B)	16	3½-5	750	750
	8-318	230	N-14Y	.035	32	.017	TDC	TDC	10	5-7	750	700
	8-340	275	N-9Y	.035	33②	.017	5B	5B	22	5-7	900	900
	8-383	275	J-14Y	.035	30	.018	TDC	2½B	18	3½-5	750	700
	8-383	300	N-11Y	.035	30	.018	TDC	2½B	21	3½-5	900	800
	8-426	425	N-10Y	.035	30①	.017	TDC	2½B	36	7-8½	950	950
	8-440	370	J-11Y	.035	30	.018	TDC	2½B	18	3½-5	900	800
	8-440	385	J-11Y	.035	30①	.017	12½B	12½B	21	6-7½	900	900
'72	6-225	110	N-14Y	.035	44	.020	TDC	TDC	16	3½-5	750(700)	750(700)
	8-318	150	N-13Y	.035	32	.017	TDC	TDC	10	5-7	750	750(700)
	8-340	240	N-9Y	.035	Electronic		2½B	2½B	22	5-7	900(850	750
	8-400	190	J-13Y	.035	30	.018	—	5B③	18	3½-5	—	700
	8-400	255④	J-11Y	.035	Electronic		TDC(2½B)	10B(5B)	21	3½-5	900(800)	750
	8-440	290	J-11Y	.035	Electronic		2½B	10B(5B)	21	3½-5	900(800)	900
'73	6-225	105	N-14Y	.035	Electronic		TDC	TDC	16	4-5½	750	750
	8-318	150	N-13Y	.035	Electronic		2½B	TDC	10	6-7½	750	700
	8-340	240	N-9Y	.035	Electronic		5B	2½B	22	6-7½	850	850
	8-400	175	J-13Y	.035	Electronic		—	10B	18	4-5½	—	700
	8-400	260	J-11Y	.035	Electronic		2½B	10B	21	4-5½	900	850
	8-440	275	J-11Y	.035	Electronic		—	10B	21	4-5½	—	800
'74	6-225	105	N-14Y	.035	Electronic		TDC	TDC	16	3½-5	800	750
	8-318	150	N-13Y	.035	Electronic		TDC	TDC	10	5-7½	750	750
	8-318	170	N-13Y	.035	Electronic		TDC	TDC	22	5-7½	750	750
	8-360	180	N-12Y	.035	Electronic		—	5B	16	5-7½	—	750
	8-360	200	N-12Y	.035	Electronic		—	5B	16	6-7½	—	750
	8-360	245	N-12Y	.035	Electronic		5B(2½B)	5B	22	6-7½	850	850
	8-400	205	J-13Y	.035	Electronic		—	5B	18	4-5½	—	900
	8-400	250	J-11Y	.035	Electronic		5B	5B(2½B)	21	4-5½	900	900
	8-440	275	J-11Y	.035	Electronic		—	10B(5B)	21	7-8.2	—	800
'75	6-225	95	BL-13Y	.035	Electronic		TDC	TDC	16	3½-5	800	750
	8-318	150	N-13Y	.035	Electronic		2B	2B	10	5-7	750	750
	8-360	180, 190, 200	N-12Y	.035	Electronic		—	6B	18	5-7	—	750
	8-360	H.P.	N-12Y	.035	Electronic		—	2B	22	5-7	—	750
	8-400	All	J-13Y	.035	Electronic		—	8B	18	4-5½	—	750

Belvedere, Satellite, 1975-76 Fury, Coronet, Charger (intermediate size)

TUNE-UP SPECIFICATIONS (con't.)

When analyzing compression test results, look for uniformity among cylinders rather than specific pressures.

Year	Engine No. Cyl Displacement (cu in.)	hp	Spark Plugs Type	Spark Plugs (in.)	Distributor Point Dwell (deg)	Distributor Point Gap (in.)	Ignition Timing (deg) ▲ Man Trans ●	Ignition Timing (deg) ▲ Auto Trans	Valves Intake Opens ■ (deg)	Fuel Pump Pressure (psi)	Idle Speed (rpm) ▲ Man Trans ●	Idle Speed (rpm) ▲ Auto Trans
'76	6-225	N.A.	RBL-13Y	.035	Electronic		6B⑦	2B	16	4-5½	750⑨	750
	8-318	N.A.	RN-12Y	.035	Electronic		2B	2B	10	6-7½	750	750
	8-360-2V	N.A.	RN-12Y	.035	Electronic		—	6B	18	6-7½	—	700⑩
	8-360-4V⑤	N.A.	RN-12Y	.035	Electronic		—	6B	18	6-7½	—	750
	8-400-2V	N.A.	RJ-13Y⑥	.035	Electronic		—	10B	18	6-7½	—	700⑩
	8-400-4V	N.A.	RJ-13Y⑥	.035	Electronic		—	6B⑧	18	6-7½	—	750
	8-400-4V	H.P.	RJ-13Y⑥	.035	Electronic		—	6B⑧	18	6-7½	—	850

▲ See text for procedure
● Figure in parentheses indicates California engine
■ All figures Before Top Dead Center
① Adjust each set of points to this figure. With both sets connected, the total reading should be 40 degrees.
② For vehicles with manual transmission, adjust each set of points to 30 degrees. With both sets connected, the total reading should be 40 degrees.
③ For non-California vehicles built after February 2, 1972, adjust ignition timing to 7½ degrees Before Top Dead Center
④ For Non-California vehicles equipped with Fresh Air Pack, figure is 265 hp
H.P.—High performance

A After Top Dead Center
B Before Top Dead Center
TDC Top Dead Center
— Not applicable
N.A.—Not Available

⑤ California only
⑥ Or RJ-87P
⑦ 2B in California
⑧ 8B in California
⑨ 800 rpm in California
⑩ 750 rpm in California

MECHANICAL VALVE LIFTER CLEARANCE

Year	Engine	Intake In.	Exhaust In.
1969-1976	All 6 cylinder	.010 (Hot)	.020 (Hot)
1969	426 Hemi	.028 (Cold)	.032 (Cold)

TUNE-UP SPECIFICATIONS

1969-74 Fury, 1975-76 Gran Fury, Polara, Monaco (full size)

When analyzing compression test results, look for uniformity among cylinders rather than specific pressures.

Year	Engine No. Cyl Displacement (cu in.)	hp	Spark Plugs Type	Spark Plugs Gap (in.)	Distributor Point Dwell (deg)	Distributor Point Gap (in.)	Ignition Timing (deg) ▲ Man Trans ●	Ignition Timing (deg) ▲ Auto Trans	Valves Intake Opens ■ (deg)	Fuel Pump Pressure (psi)	Idle Speed (rpm) ▲ Man Trans ●	Idle Speed (rpm) ▲ Auto Trans
'69	6-225	145	N-11Y	.035	42-47	.020	TDC	TDC	10	3½-5	700	650
	8-318	230	N-14Y	.035	30-35	.017	TDC	TDC	10	5-7	700	650
	8-383	290	J-14Y	.035	30-35	.017	TDC	7½B	18	3½-5	700	600
	8-383	330	J-11Y	.035	30-35	.017	TDC	5B	18	3½-5	700	650
	8-440	350	J-13Y	.035	28-33	.017	—	7½B	18	3½-5	—	600
	8-440	375	J-11Y	.035	②	.017	TDC	5B	21	6-7½	700	650
'70	6-225	145	N-14Y	.035	41-46	.020	TDC	TDC	10	3½-5	700	650
	8-318	230	N-14Y	.035	30-34	.017	TDC	TDC	10	5-7	750	700
	8-383	290	J-14Y	.035	28-32	.018	TDC	2½B	18	3½-5	750	650
	8-383	330	J-11Y	.035	28-32	.018	TDC	2½B	18	3½-5	750	750
	8-440	350	J-13Y	.035	28-33	.018	—	12½B	18	3½-5	—	650
	8-440	390	J-11Y	.035	27-32①	.017	5B	5B	21	6-7½	900	900
'71	6-225	145	N-14Y	.035	41-46	.020	TDC(2½B)	TDC(2½B)	16	3½-5	750	750
	8-318	230	N-14Y	.035	30-34	.017	TDC	TDC	10	5-7	750	700
	8-360	255	N-13Y	.035	30-34	.017	2½B	2½B	16	3½-5	750	700
	8-383	275	J-14Y	.035	28-32	.018	TDC	2½B	18	3½-5	750	700
	8-383	300	J-11Y	.035	28-32	.018	TDC	2½B	21	3½-5	900	800
	8-440	335	N-13Y	.035	30.34	.017	—	5B	18	3½-5	—	750
	8-440	370	J-11Y	.035	28-32	.018	TDC	2½B	21	3½-5	.900	800

TUNE-UP SPECIFICATIONS (con't.)

1969-74 Fury, 1975-76 Gran Fury, Polara, Monaco (full size)

When analyzing compression test results, look for uniformity among cylinders rather than specific pressures.

Year	ENGINE No. Cyl Displacement (cu in.)	hp	SPARK PLUGS Type	SPARK PLUGS Gap (in.)	DISTRIBUTOR Point Dwell (deg)	DISTRIBUTOR Point Gap (in.)	IGNITION TIMING (deg) ▲ Man Trans	IGNITION TIMING (deg) ▲ ● Auto Trans	VALVES Intake Opens ■ (deg)	Fuel Pump Pressure (psi)	IDLE SPEED (rpm) ▲ Man Trans	IDLE SPEED (rpm) ▲ ● Auto Trans
'72	8-318	150	J-11Y	.035	28-32	.018	—	TDC	10	5-7	—	750(700)
	8-360	175	N-13Y	.035	30-34	.017	—	TDC	16	5-7	—	750
	8-400	190	J-13Y	.035	28-32	.018	—	5B③	18	3½-5	—	700
	8-440	225	J-11Y	.035	28-32	.018	—	10B	18	3½-5	—	750(700)
'73	8-318	150	N-13Y	.035	Electronic		—	TDC	10	6-7½	—	700
	8-360	170	N-13Y	.035	Electronic		—	TDC	16	6-7½	—	750
	8-400	185	J-13Y	.035	Electronic		—	10B	18	4-5½	—	700
	8-440	220	J-11Y	.035	Electronic		—	10B	18	4-5½	—	700
'74	8-360	180	N-12Y	.035	Electronic		—	5B	16	5-7½	—	750
	8-400	185	J-13Y	.035	Electronic		—	5B	18	4-5½	—	750
	8-400	260	J-13Y	.035	Electronic		—	5B	18	4-5½	—	900 (750)
	8-440	275	J-11Y	.035	Electronic		—	10B	18	7-8.2	—	750
'75	8-318	150	N-13Y	.035	Electronic		—	2B	10	5-7	—	750
	8-360	All	N-12Y	.035	Electronic		—	6B	18	5-7	—	750
	8-400	175	J-13Y	.035	Electronic		—	10B	18	4-5½	—	750
	8-400	190	J-13Y	.035	Electronic		—	8B	18	4-5½	—	750
	8-440	215	RY-87P	.040	Electronic		—	8B	18	4-5½	—	750
'76	8-360-2V	N.A.	RN-12Y	.035	Electronic		—	6B	18	6-7½	—	700⑧
	8-360-4V⑤	N.A.	RN-12Y	.035	Electronic		—	6B	18	6-7½	—	750
	8-400-2V	N.A.	RJ-13Y	.035	Electronic		—	10B	18	6-7½	—	700⑧
	8-400-4V	N.A.	RJ-13Y	.035	Electronic		—	6B⑦	18	6-7½	—	700⑧
	8-440-4V	N.A.	RJ-87P④	.035⑥	Electronic		—	8B	18	6-7½	—	750

▲ See text for procedure
■ Before Top Dead Center
● Figure in parentheses indicates California engine
① Both sets 37°-40°
② Automatic transmission 30°-50°
Manual 27°-32°, both sets 37°-40°
③ Non-California cars built after Feb. 2, 7½B

A After Top Dead Center
B Before Top Dead Center
TDC Top Dead Center

N.A. Not Available
④ Or RJ-86P, WA95, WA96 with Lean Burn engines
⑤ California only
⑥ WA95 or WA96 plug—.033
⑦ 8B in California
⑧ 750 rpm in California

CAPACITIES

Year	ENGINE No. Cyl. Displacement (Cu. In.)	Engine Crankcase Add 1 Qt For New Filter	TRANSMISSION Pts To Refill After Draining Manual 3-Speed	Manual 4-Speed	Automatic	Drive Axle (pts)	Gasoline Tank (gals)	COOLING SYSTEM (qts) With Heater	With A/C
'69	6-225	4	6.5	—	15.5	2④	19⑩	13	15
	8-318	4	6	—	15.5	4	19⑩	16	19
	8-383⑭	4	6	7	18.5	4	19⑩	16	17
	8-383⑮	4	—	7.5	15.5	4	19⑩	16	17
	8-426	6	—	7.5	16	4⑤	19	18	—
	8-440	4	—	7.5	18.5	4⑤	19⑩	17	18
'70	6-225	4	4.75	—	17	2④	19⑩	13	15
	8-318	4	4.75	—	16	4	19⑩	16	19
	8-383⑭	4	4.75	—	19	4	19⑩	16	17
	8-383⑮	4	4.75	7.5	16	4	19⑩	16	17
	8-426	6	—	7.5	17	5.5	19	18	—
	8-440	4①	—	7.5	19	5.5⑥	19⑩	17	18

CAPACITIES (con't.)

Year	ENGINE No. Cyl. Displacement (Cu. In.)	Engine Crankcase Add 1 Qt For New Filter	TRANSMISSION Pts To Refill After Draining — Manual 3-Speed	Manual 4-Speed	Automatic	Drive Axle (pts)	Gasoline Tank (gals)	COOLING SYSTEM (qts) With Heater	With A/C
'71	6-225	4	6.5②	—	17	4⑦	21⑪	13	13
	8-318	4	4.75	—	17	4⑦	21⑪	16	16.5
	8-340	4	4.75	7.5	16.3	4	21	15	15
	8-360	4	4.75	—	16	4.5	23	15.5	15
	8-383	4	4.75	7.5	16③	4⑦	21⑪	14.5	15
	8-426	6	—	7.5	17	5.5	21	15.5	—
	8-440	4①	—	7.5	19	5.5⑦	21⑪	15.5	17
'72	6-225	4	6.5	—	17	4.5	21	13	14
	8-318	4	4.75	—	17	4.5	21⑪	16	17.5
	8-340	4	—	7.5	16.3	4.5	21	15	15.5
	8-360	4	—	—	16.3	4.5	23	16	16
	8-400⑭	4	—	—	19	4.5	21⑪	14.5	15
	8-440⑮	4	4.75	7.5	16.3	4.5	21⑪	14.5	14.5
'73	6-225	4	4.75	—	17	4.5	19.5	13	13
	8-318	4	4.75	7.5	17	4.5	19.5⑪⑱	16	17.5
	8-340	4	—	7.5	16.3	4.5	19.5	15	15.5
	8-360	4	—	—	16.3	4.5	19.5⑪	15.5	16
	8-400	4	—	7.5	19⑯	4.5	19.5⑪⑱	16	17⑲
	8-440	4	—	—	16.3⑰	4.5	19.5⑪	16.5⑳	16.5⑳
'74	6-225	4	4.75	—	17	4.4	19.5	13	—
	8-318	4	4.75	7.5	17 (17.5)	4.4	19.5⑱	16	18
	8-360 Satellite, Charger, Coronet	4	—	7.5	16.5 (17)	4.4	19.5⑱	16.5	16.5
	8-360 Fury, Polara, Monaco	4	—	—	16.5 (17.5)	4.4⑫	25.0⑧	16	16
	8-400 Satellite, Charger, Coronet	4	—	—	19 (20)	4.4⑫	19.5⑱	16.5	16.5
	8-400 HP Satellite, Charger, Coronet	4	—	7.5	16.5 (17)	4.4⑫	19.5⑱	16.5	17.5
	8-400 Fury, Polara, Monaco	4	—	—	19 (20.5)	4.4⑫	25.0⑧	16.5	16.5
	8-440 HP Satellite, Charger, Coronet	4	—	—	16.5	4.4	19.5	16	16
	8-440 Fury, Polara, Monaco	4	—	—	19 (20.5)	4.5	25.0⑧	16	16
'75-'76	6-225 Intermediate	4	4.75	—	16.5	4.5	25.5	13.0	—
	8-318 Intermediate	4	4.75	—	16.5	4.5	25.5⑱	16.5	18.0
	8-318 Full size	4	—	—	16.5	4.5	26.5	17.5	17.5
	8-360 Intermediate	4	—	—	16.5	4.5	25.5⑱	16.0	16.0
	8-360 Full size	4	—	—	16.5	4.5	26.5⑧	16.0	16.0
	8-400 Intermediate	4	—	—	16.5	4.5	25.5⑱㉑	16.5	16.5
	8-400 Full size	4	—	—	16.5	4.5	26.5⑧	16.5	16.5
	8-440 Full size	4	—	—	16.5	4.5	26.5⑧	16.0	16.0

① 3-2 bbl—6 qts
② Fury, Polara, Monaco—4.75 pts
③ 2 bbl—19 pts
④ Fury, station wagon—4 pts
⑤ Manual transmissions—5.5 pts
⑥ Fury, Polara, Monaco—4 pts
⑦ Fury, Polara, Monaco—4.5 pts
⑧ Station wagons—24 gals
⑨ Station wagon—22 gals
⑩ Fury, Polara, Monaco—24 gals, station wagon—23 gals
⑪ Fury, Polara, Monaco—23 gals
⑫ Station wagons—4.5 pts
⑬ Not used
⑭ With 2 bbl carburetor
⑮ With 4 bbl carburetor
⑯ Charger, Coronet, Satellite with 4 bbl—16.3 pts
⑰ Fury, Polara, Monaco—19 pts
⑱ Station wagons—21 gals
⑲ Fury, Polara, Monaco—16 qts
⑳ Fury, Polara, Monaco—15.5 qts
㉑ 400 4 bbl w/dual exhaust—20.5 gals.
— Not applicable

VALVE SPECIFICATIONS

Year	Engine No. Cyl. Displacement (cu in.)	Seat Angle (deg)	Face Angle (deg)	Spring Test Pressure (lbs @ in.)	Spring Installed Height (in.)	STEM TO GUIDE Clearance (in.) Intake	Exhaust	STEM Diameter (in.) Intake	Exhaust
'69	6-225	45	45①	144 @ 1.31	1 11/16	.0010-.0030	.0020-.0040	.3725	.3715
	8-318	45	45①	177 @ 1.31	1 11/16	.0010-.0030	.0020-.0040	.3725	.3715
	8-383③	45	45	200 @ 1.44	1 7/8	.0010-.0030	.0020-.0040	.3725	.3715
	8-383④	45	45	246 @ 1.36	1 7/8	.0010-.0030	.0020-.0040	.3725	.3715
	8-426	45	45	280 @ 1.38	1 7/8	.0020-.0040	.0030-.0050	.3090	.3080
	8-440	45	45	200 @ 1.44	1 7/8	.0010-.0030	.0020-.0040	.3725	.3715
	8-440⑥	45	45	246 @ 1.36	1 7/8	.0010-.0030	.0020-.0040	.3725	.3715
'70	6-225	45	45①	144 @ 1.31	1 11/16	.0010-.0030	.0020-.0040	.3725	.3715
	8-318	45	45①	177 @ 1.31	1 11/16	.0010-.0030	.0020-.0040	.3725	.3715
	8-383③	45	45	200 @ 1.44	1 7/8	.0010-.0030	.0020-.0040	.3727	.3717
	8-383④	45	45	246 @ 1.72	1 7/8	.0015-.0032	.0025-.0042	.3722	.3712
	8-426	45	45	200 @ 1.44	1 7/8	.0020-.0040	.0030-.0050	.3090	.3080
	8-440	45	45	246 @ 1.72	1 7/8	.0010-.0030	.0020-.0040	.3727	.3717
	8-440⑥	45	45	310 @ 1.38	1 7/8	.0015-.0032	.0025-.0042	.3722	.3712
'71	6-225	45	45①	144 @ 1.31	1 11/16	.0010-.0030	.0020-.0040	.3725	.3715
	8-318	45	45①	177 @ 1.31	1 11/16	.0010-.0030	.0020-.0040	.3725	.3715
	8-340	45	45①	238 @ 1.31	1 11/16	.0015-.0035	.0025-.0045	.3720	.3710
	8-360	45	45①	177 @ 1.31	1 11/16	.0010-.0030	.0020-.0040	.3725	.3715
	8-383③	45	45	200 @ 1.44	1 7/8	.0010-.0030	.0020-.0040	.3727	.3717
	8-383④	45	45	246 @ 1.72	1 7/8	.0015-.0032	.0025-.0042	.3722	.3712
	8-426	45	45	310 @ 1.28	1 7/8	.0020-.0040	.0030-.0050	.3090	.3080
	8-440	45	45	200 @ 1.44	1 7/8	.0010-.0030	.0020-.0040	.3722	.3717
	8-440⑥	45	45	246 @ 1.72	1 7/8	.0015-.0032	.0025-.0042	.3722	.3712
'72	6-225	45	45①	144 @ 1.31	1 11/16	.0010-.0030	.0020-.0040	.3725	.3715
	8-318	45	45①	177 @ 1.31	1 11/16	.0010-.0030	.0020-.0040	.3725	.3715
	8-340	45	45①	208 @ 1.31	1 11/16	.0015-.0035	.0025-.0045	.3720	.3710
	8-360	45	45①	177 @ 1.31	1 11/16	.0010-.0030	.0020-.0040	.3725	.3715
	8-400③	45	45	200 @ 1.44	1 7/8	.0010-.0030	.0020-.0040	.3727	.3717
	8-400④	45	45	246 @ 1.72	1 7/8	.0015-.0032	.0025-.0042	.3722	.3712
	8-440	45	45	200 @ 1.44	1 7/8	.0010-.0030	.0020-.0040	.3727	.3717
	8-440⑥	45	45	246 @ 1.72	1 7/8	.0015-.0032	.0025-.0042	.3722	.3712
'73	6-225	45	45②	160 @ 1.24	1 21/32	.0010-.0030	.0020-.0040	.3725	.3715
	8-318	45	45②	189 @ 1.28	1 21/32	.0010-.0030	.0020-.0040	.3725	.3715
	8-340	45	45②	238 @ 1.22	1 21/32	.0015-.0035	.0025-.0045	.3720	.3710
	8-360	45	45②	195 @ 1.24	1 21/32	.0010-.0030	.0020-.0040	.3725	.3715
	8-400③	45	45	200 @ 1.42	1 55/64	.0010-.0027	⑦	.3727	⑨
	8-400④	45	45	234 @ 1.40	1 55/64	.0015-.0032	⑧	.3722	⑩
	8-440	45	45	200 @ 1.42	1 55/64	.0010-.0027	⑦	.3727	⑨
	8-440⑥	45	45	234 @ 1.40	1 55/64	.0015-.0032	⑧	.3722	⑩
'74-	6-225	45	45①	143 @ 1.31	1 21/32	.0010-.0030	.0020-.0040	.3725	.3715
'76	8-318	45	45①	177 @ 1.31	1 21/32	.0010-.0030	.0020-.0040	.3725	.3715
	8-360	45	45①	208 @ 1.31⑪	1 21/32	.0010-.0030	.0025-.0040	3725	.3715
	8-400, 440 std.	45	45	200 @ 1.43	1 55/64	.0010-.0027	⑦	.3727	⑨
	8-400⑥	45	45	246 @ 1.36	1 55/64	.0015-.0032	⑩	3722	⑩
	8-440⑥	45	45	246 @ 1.36	1 55/64	.0015-.0032	⑩	.3722	⑩

① Exhaust 43°
② Exhaust 47°
③ 2 bbl carburetor
④ 4 bbl carburetor
⑤ Hemi
⑥ Hi-Performance
⑦ Hot end—.0020-.0037, cold end—.0010-.0027
⑧ Hot end—.0025-.0042, cold end—.0015-.0032
⑨ Hot end—.3716, cold end—.3726
⑩ Hot end—.3711, cold end—.3721
⑪ 177 @ 1.31 on 2 bbl engine

TORQUE SPECIFICATIONS

All readings in ft lbs

Year	Engine Displacement (cu in.)	Cylinder Head Bolts	Rod Bearing Bolts	Main Bearing Bolts	Crankshaft Pulley Bolt	Flywheel to Crankshaft Bolts	MANIFOLD Intake	MANIFOLD Exhaust
'69-'76	6-All	70	45	85	Press fit	55	10①	10
'69-'76	8-318, 340, 360	95	45	85	135②	55	35	15-20
	8-383, 400, 440	70	45	85	135	55	40	30
'69-'71	8-426 Hemi	75	75	100③	135	70	④	35

① Intake to exhaust bolts—20 ft. lbs.
② '71-'76 318, 340, 360 cu. in. engines—100 ft. lbs.
③ Cross bolt mains—45 ft. lbs.
④ 4 center bolts on either side—6 ft. lbs., others 4 ft. lbs.

CRANKSHAFT AND CONNECTING ROD SPECIFICATIONS

All measurements are given in inches

Year	Engine Displacement (cu in.)	CRANKSHAFT Main Brg. Journal Dia	Main Brg. Oil Clearance	Shaft End-Play	Thrust on No.	CONNECTING ROD Journal Diameter	Oil Clearance	Side Clearance
'69-'76	6-225	2.7495-2.7505	.0005-.0020	.002-.007	3	2.1865-2.1875	.0005-.0020	.006-.012
'69-'76	8-318, 340	2.4495-2.5005	.0005-.0020	.002-.007	3	2.124-2.125	.0005-.0025	.006-.014
'71-'76	8-360	2.8095-2.8105	.0005-.0025	.002-.007	3	2.124-2.125	.0005-.0020	.006-.014
'69-'76	8-383, 400	2.6245-2.6255	.0005-.0020	.002-.007	3	2.3740-2.3750	.0005-.0020	.009-.017
'69-'76	8-440	2.7495-2.7505	.0005-.0020	.002-.007	3	2.3740-2.3750	.001-.0020	.009-.017
'69-'70	426 Hemi	2.7495-2.7505	.0015-.0025	.002-.007	3	2.374-2.375	.0015-.0025	.009-.017
'71	426 Hemi	2.7490-2.7500	.0015-.0030	.002-.007	3	2.3738-2.3745	.0015-.0025	.013-.017

RING GAP

All measurements are given in inches

Year	Engine No. Cyl. Displacement (cu. in.)	Top Compression	Bottom Compression
'69-'72	6-225	.010-.020	.010-.020
	8-318, 340, 360, 8-383, 400, 426, 440	.013-.023	.013-.023
'73-'76	6-225, 8-318, 360	.010-.020	.010-.020
'73-'76	8-340, 400, 440	.013-.023	.013-.023

Year	Engine	Oil Control
'69-'76	All engines	.015-.055

RING SIDE CLEARANCE

All measurements are given in inches

Year	Engine No. Cyl. Displacement (cu. in.)	Top Compression	Bottom Compression
'69-'76	All engines	.0015-.0030	.0015-.0030

Year	Engine No. Cyl. Displacement (cu. in.)	Oil Control
'69-'76	6-225, 8-318, 426, 340, 360	.002-.005
	8-383, 440, 400	.0000-.005

PISTON CLEARANCE

Year	Engine No. Cyl. Displacement (cu. in.)	Piston to Bore Clearance (in.)
'69-'76	6-225	
	8-318, 340, 360	.0005-.0015
	8-383, 400, 440	.0003-.0013
'69-'71	8-426 Hemi	.0025-.0035

ALTERNATOR AND REGULATOR SPECIFICATIONS

Year	Model	Alternator: Field Current @ 12 V	Alternator: Output (amps)	Regulator: Part No.	Field Relay: Air Gap (in.)	Field Relay: Point Gap (in.)	Field Relay: Volts to Close	Regulator: Air Gap (in.)	Regulator: Point Gap (in.)	Volts @ 75°
'69	6 Cyl Models	2.38-2.75	26 ± 3	2098300①	.050①	.014	13.8	.015	.050	13.8-14.4
	V8 Std.—All	2.38-2.75	34.5 ± 3	2098300①	.050①	.014	13.8	.015	.050	13.8-14.4
	Heavy Duty, A/C	2.38-2.75	44 ± 3②	2098300①	.050①	.014	13.8	.015	.050	13.8-14.4
'70-'71	6 Cyl Models	2.38-2.75	26 ± 3	3438150			Not Adjustable			13.8-14.4
	V8 Std.—All	2.38-2.75	34.5 ± 3	3438150			Not Adjustable			13.8-14.4
	Heavy Duty, A/C	2.38-2.75	44.5 ± 3	3438150			Not Adjustable			13.8-14.4
	Special Equip.	2.38-2.75	51 ± 3	3438150			Not Adjustable			13.8-14.4
'72-'73	6 Cyl Models	2.5-3.1	26	3438150			Not Adjustable			13.8-14.4
	V8 Std.	2.5-3.1	39	3438150			Not Adjustable			13.8-14.4
	Heavy Duty, A/C	2.5-3.1	50	3438150			Not Adjustable			13.8-14.4
	Special Equip.	2.5-3.1	60	3438150			Not Adjustable			13.8-14.4
'74-'76	6 Cyl Models	2.5-3.7	41	3438150			Not Adjustable			13.8-14.4
	V8 Std.	2.5-3.7	50	3438150			Not Adjustable			13.8-14.4
	Special Equip.	2.5-3.7	60	3438150			Not Adjustable			13.8-14.4

① Chrysler built-used interchangeably with #2444900, which is Essex wire built. Air gap setting is .032-.042 in., all other dimensions are identical with #2098300

② 51 amp special equipment model available

BATTERY AND STARTER SPECIFICATIONS

Year	Engine No. Cyl. Displacement (cu. in.)	Battery: Ampere Hour Capacity	Battery: Volts	Battery: Terminal Grounded	Lock Test: Amps	Lock Test: Volts	Lock Test: Torque (ft lbs)	No-Load Test: Amps	No-Load Test: Volts	No-Load Test: RPM	Brush Spring Tension (oz)
'69	6-225, 8-318	48	12	Neg.	400-450	4	—	90	11	1,925-2,600	32-36
	8-383, 426, 440	70	12	Neg.	400-450	4	—	90	11	1,925-2,600	32-36
	8-426, Opt. all others	70	12	Neg.	310-445	4	—	78	11	3,800	32-36
'70-'72	6-225, 8-318, 340	48	12	Neg.	400-450	4	—	90	11	1,925-2,600	32-36
	8-360, 383, 400	59①	12	Neg.	400-450	4	—	90	11	1,925-2,600	32-36
	8-426, 440, Opt. all others	70	12	Neg.	400-450	4	—	90	11	1,925-2,600	32-36
'73	6-225, 8-318, 340	48	12	Neg.	400-450	4	—	90	11	1,925-2,600	32-36
	8-360, 400	59①	12	Neg.	475-550	4	—	90	11	4,300	32-36
	8-440	70	12	Neg.	475-550	4	—	90	11	4,300	32-36
'74-'76	6-225, 8-318	48	12	Neg.	475-550	4	—	90	11	3,700-4,200	32-36
	8-360, 400	59①	12	Neg.	475-550	4	—	90	11	3,700-4,200	32-36
	8-440	70	12	Neg.	475-550	4	—	90	11	3,700-4,200	32-36

① 55 amps for '72 8-400, '72-'76 8-360 installed in Fury, Polara, Monaco

BRAKE SPECIFICATIONS

All measurements in inches

Year	Model	Master Cylinder Disc	Master Cylinder Drum	Wheel Cylinder Front Disc	Wheel Cylinder Front Drum	Wheel Cylinder Rear	Brake Disc or Drum Diameter Front Disc	Brake Disc or Drum Diameter Front Drum	Brake Disc or Drum Diameter Rear
'69	Coronet, Charger, Belvedere, Satellite	—	1.0	—	1.125	.9375	—	10.0①	10.0①
	Polara, Monaco, Fury, VIP	—	1.0	—	1.125	.9375	—	11.0	11.0
	Coronet, Charger, Belvedere, Satellite	1.125	—	2.00	—	.9375	11.75	—	10.0
	Fury, Polara, Monaco, VIP	1.125	—	2.75	—	.9375	11.75	—	11.0
'70	Coronet, Charger, Belvedere, Satellite	—	1.0	—	1.125	.9375	—	10.0③	10.0③
	Polara, Monaco	—	1.0	—	1.125	.9375	—	11.0	11.0
	Coronet, Charger, Belvedere, Satellite models with disc brakes	1.125	—	2.750	—	.9375	10.72	—	11.0
	Fury, Polara, Monaco	1.125	—	2.750	—	.9375	11.75	—	11.0
'71-'72	Coronet, Charger, Satellite	—	1.0	—	1.187	.9375	—	10.0①	10.0①
	Polara, Monaco	—	1.0	—	1.187	.9375	—	11.0①	11.0①
	All with disc brakes	1.00④	—	2.750	—	.9375	11.75	—	11.0
'73-'76	Coronet, Charger, Satellite	1.00⑤	—	2.750	—	.9375	10.98	—	10.0⑥
	Polara, Monaco, 1973-74 Fury, 1975-76 Gran Fury	1.03	—	2.750⑦	—	.9375	11.75	—	11.0

① 11 in. standard on some models, optional on all others
② Not used
③ 11 in. brakes optional
④ 1⅛ in. with Hemi engine
⑤ 1.03 with power brakes
⑥ 11 in. on station wagons
⑦ 3.100 beginning 1974
— Not applicable

WHEEL ALIGNMENT SPECIFICATIONS

Year	Model	Caster Range (deg)	Caster Pref Setting (deg)	Camber Range (deg)	Camber Pref Setting (deg)	Toe-in (in.)	Steering Axis Inclin.	Wheel Pivot Ratio (deg) Inner Wheel	Wheel Pivot Ratio (deg) Outer Wheel
'69	M.S.—Coronet, Charger, Belvedere, Satellite	0 to 1N	½N	①	①	3/32 to 5/32	7½	20	17.8
	P.S.—Coronet, Charger, Belvedere, Satellite	¼P to 1¼P	¾P	①	①	3/32 to 5/32	7½	20	17.8
	M.S.—Fury, Monaco, Polara	0 to 1N	½N	①	①	3/32 to 5/32	7½	20	18.8
	P.S.—Fury, Monaco, Polara	¼P to 1¼P	¾P	①	①	3/32 to 5/32	7½	20	18.8
'70-'72	M.S.—Coronet, Charger, Belvedere, Satellite	½N ± ½	½N	①	①	3/32 to 5/32	7½	20	17.8
	P.S.—Coronet, Charger, Belvedere, Satellite	¾P ± ½	¾P	①	①	3/32 to 5/32	7½	20	17.8
	M.S.—Fury, Monaco, Polara	½N ± ½	½N	①	①	3/32 to 5/32	7½	20	18.8
	P.S.—Fury, Monaco, Polara	¼ to 1¼P⑤	¾P⑤	①	①	3/32 to 5/32	7½	20	18.8

WHEEL ALIGNMENT SPECIFICATIONS (con't.)

Year	Model	Caster Range (deg)	Caster Pref Setting (deg)	Camber Range (deg)	Camber Pref Setting (deg)	Toe-in (in.)	Steering Axis Inclin.	Wheel Pivot Ratio (deg) Inner Wheel	Wheel Pivot Ratio (deg) Outer Wheel
'73	M.S.—Coronet, Charger, Satellite	1 5/16N to 1/16P	5/8N	⑥	⑥	1/8 ± 3/32	7 1/2	20	17.8
	P.S.—Coronet Charger, Satellite	1/16N to 1 5/16P	5/8P	⑥	⑥	1/8 ± 3/32	7 1/2	20	17.8
	P.S.—Fury, Monaco, Polara	1/16N to 1 5/16P	5/8P	⑥	⑥	1/8 ± 3/32	7 1/2	20	18.8
'74	M.S.—Coronct, Charger, Satellite	1 3/4N to 1/2P	5/8N	⑦	⑦	1/16 to 1/4	8	20	18.0
	P.S.—Coronet, Charger, Satellite	1/2N to 1 3/4P	5/8P	⑦	⑦	1/16 to 1/4	8	20	18.0
	P.S.—Fury, Monaco, Polara	1/2N to 1 3/4P	5/8P	⑦	⑦	1/16 to 1/4	9	20	18.3
'75-'76	M.S.—Coronet, Charger, Fury	1 5/16N to 1/16P	1/2N	⑥	⑥	3/32 to 9/32	8	20	18.0
	Charger, P.S.—Coronet, Fury	1/16N to 1 5/16P	3/4P	⑥	⑥	3/32 to 9/32	8	20	18.0
	P.S.—Gran Fury, Monaco	1/16N to 1 5/16P	3/4P	⑥	⑥	3/32 to 9/32	8	20	18.3

M.S. Manual steering
P.S. Power steering
P Positive
N Negative

① Left—1/4P to 3/4P; 1/2P preferred
Right 0 to 1/2 P; 1/4P preferred
② Heavy duty—2 1/8 ± 1/8
③ Fury sta. wag., Monaco, Polara, Custom 880—1 1/8 ± 1/8
④ Sta. wag.—1 3/4 ± 1/8
⑤ 1970—0 to 1N (1/2N preferred)
⑥ Left—1/8P to 7/8P; 1/2P preferred
Right—1/8N to 5/8P; 1/4P preferred
⑦ Left—0 to 1P; 1/2P preferred
Right—1/4N to 3/4P; 1/4P preferred

FRONT END HEIGHT ▲

Year	Model	Front End Height
'69-'74	Coronet, Charger, Belvedere, Satellite	1 7/8 ± 1/8②
	Fury, Monaco, Polara	1 3/8 ± 1/8①③
'75-'76	Coronet, Satellite, Charger, Fury	10 3/4 ± 1/8
	Wagon	11 1/4 ± 1/8
	Gran Fury Monaco	10 1/8 ± 1/8

① Monaco, Polara—1 1/8 ± 1/8
② '71-'73—1 5/8 ± 1/8
③ 1974—1 in.
▲ See text for procedure

NOTE: Service procedures for the Charging System, Starting System, Ignition System, Cooling System, Fuel System, Emission Control Systems, Engine and Clutch apply to Chrysler and Imperial models, as well.

CHARGING SYSTEM

The alternator is basically an alternating current generator with solid-state rectifiers to convert AC current to DC current for charging the battery. The solid-state rectifiers are located between the battery alternator coils; since they are one-way current flow devices, they eliminate any need in the charging circuit for a cutout relay. A solid-state voltage regulator, used since 1970, maintains correct charging voltage by varying the duty cycle of a series of pulses to the alternator field. Pulse rate is controlled by the ignition frequency of the engine.

Before undertaking any electrical system service, the battery must be disconnected. Never attempt to polarize or short any component of the system.

Charging System troubleshooting and repairs can be found in the Unit Repair Section.

Alternator R&R

To remove alternator:

1. Disconnect battery.
2. Disconnect Bat. and Fld. leads from alternator.
3. Remove alternator by removing two mounting bolts and belt tensioner bracket bolt.
4. To reinstall: reverse the above.

Never attempt to polarize an alternator, and never short the regulator.

Regulator

Removal and Installation

1. Disconnect the battery.
2. Remove all electrical leads.
3. Remove all attaching bolts and lift off regulator.
4. To install reverse the removal procedure.

Caution Never attempt to short the regulator.

STARTING SYSTEM

All Chrysler models are equipped with one of two types of starter: a direct-drive type used on 1971-72 6 cylinder (225) fleet models equipped with an 11 in. clutch, or a 3.5:1 or 2.0:1 reduction gear type. The reduction gear type of starter may be identified by the battery treminal on the starter being installed at an angle; the direct-drive type starter battery terminal is parallel to the starter case.

Both types of starters have solenoids which are mounted directly on the starter assembly. Therefore, the starter must be removed from the car to service the solenoid and motor brushes.

Starter

Removal and Installation

1. Disconnect the ground cable at the battery.
2. Remove the cable from the starter.
3. Disconnect the solenoid leads at their solenoid terminals.
4. Remove the starter securing bolts and withdraw the starter from the engine flywheel housing. On some models with automatic transmissions, the oil cooler tube bracket will interfere with starter removal. In this case, remove the starter securing bolts, slide the cooler tube bracket off the stud and then withdraw the starter.
5. Installation is the reverse of the above. Be sure that the starter and flywheel housing mating surfaces are free of dirt and oil.

IGNITION SYSTEM

Chrysler used conventional ignition systems on all models to 1971 and most 1972 models. Conventional ignition systems may be divided into two circuits: a low-voltage primary section, consisting of the ammeter, battery, ignition switch, ballast resistor, ignition coil primary winding, vehicle frame, contact points, and condenser; and a secondary high-voltage section, consisting of the coil secondary winding, distributor cap and rotor, spark plugs, and vehicle frame.

Any ignition systems trouble should include a check of the ballast resistor. Its function is to reduce current flow during low-speed operation and allow high-current flow during high-speed operation. This tends to increase contact point life. While the starter is operating, the ballast resistor is bypassed, allowing full battery voltage to flow into the ignition primary system.

Ignition Retard Solenoid

1971 and Earlier Models

This unit's function is to retard ignition timing at closed throttle. *Located on the distributor side, this solenoid must be operating when ignition timing is checked.* To check whether the solenoid is operating, disconnect the ground lead after timing is set. If engine idle speed increases noticeably, the solenoid is functioning properly.

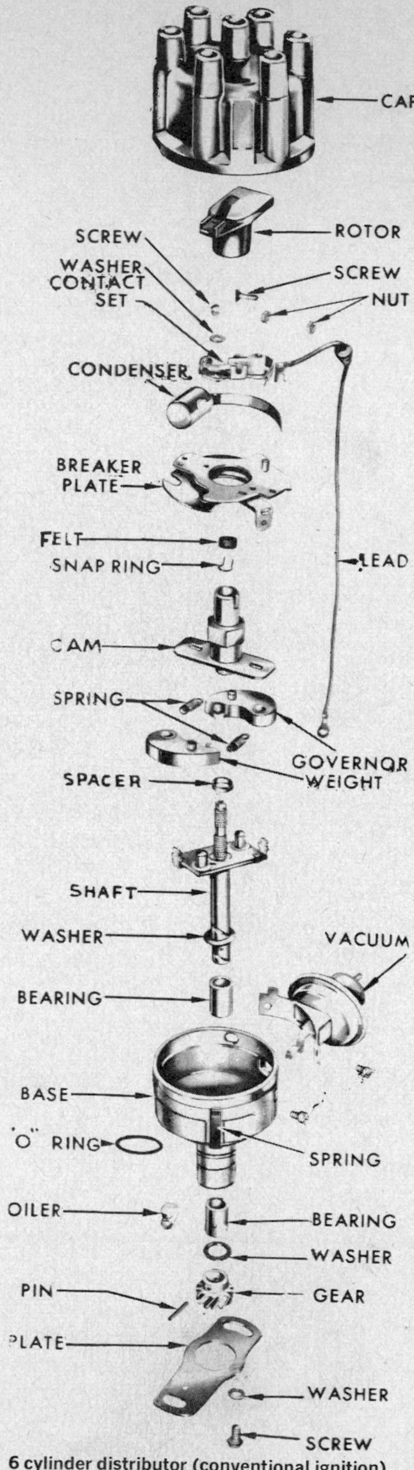

6 cylinder distributor (conventional ignition) (© Chrysler Corp)

Ignition Advance Solenoid

1972-74 Models Equipped with 400 or 440 4-V V-8

This solenoid, located on the distributor side, is connected to the starter relay so that it operates only during engine cranking to improve starting.

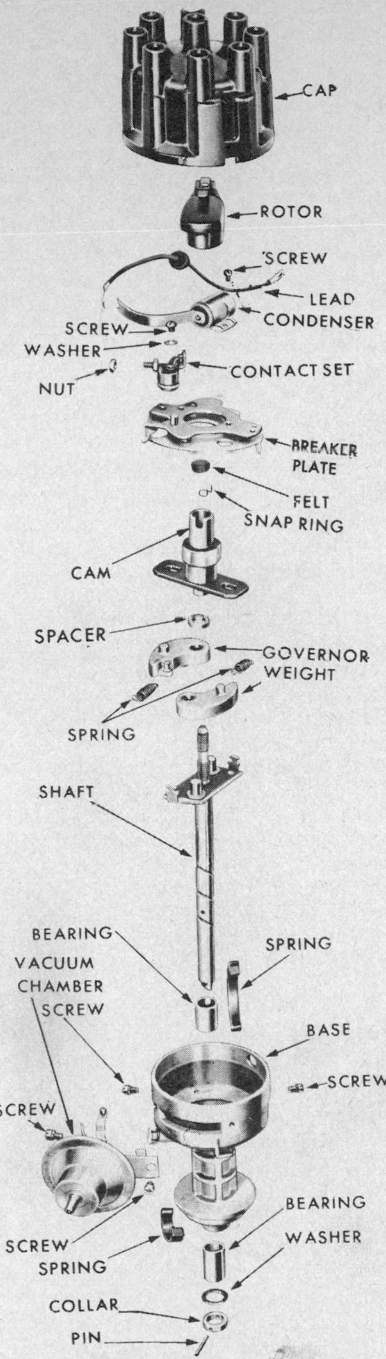

V8 distributor (conventional ignition)
(© Chrysler Corp)

When the engine fires, this solenoid ceases to operate. If the solenoid is not operating, it will affect starting, but not drivability. A possible sign of non-operation is popping through the carburetor during engine cranking.

To check operation, idle engine and connect a jumper wire from the battery to the solenoid lead. If the solenoid is operating properly, the engine speed will increase noticeably.

Caution Disconnect jumper wire as soon as possible after checking solenoid operation.

Electronic Ignition

An electronic ignition system is standard on all 1973 and later Chrysler Corporation vehicles. This type of ignition system has no contact points; consequently, there is no dwell adjustment. The only regular ignition system maintenance required is inspection of the wiring and spark plug replacement (check timing on occasion only).

To determine whether a car is equipped with electronic ignition, check for a double primary lead from the distributor, a dual ballast resistor located on the firewall, and a control unit located either on the left wheel housing or the firewall.

If the electronic ignition is not functioning properly but the wiring is in good condition, refer to the Unit Repair section for proper service.

Detailed information on distributor drive, direction of distributor rotation, cylinder numbering, firing order, point gap, point dwell, timing mark location, spark plugs, and spark advance will be found in the Specification Tables.

Distributor Assembly Removal

1. Take off the cap and wire assembly.
2. Disconnect the primary coil wire and vacuum control tube.
3. Mark the relative positions of the distributor and rotor on the engine block.
4. Loosen the distributor mounting and lift out the distributor.

NOTE: to simplify reinstallation, do not disturb the engine while the distributor is out.

5. Reinstall by reversing the above procedure, aligning the distributor rotor and the mark on the block when installing the distributor.

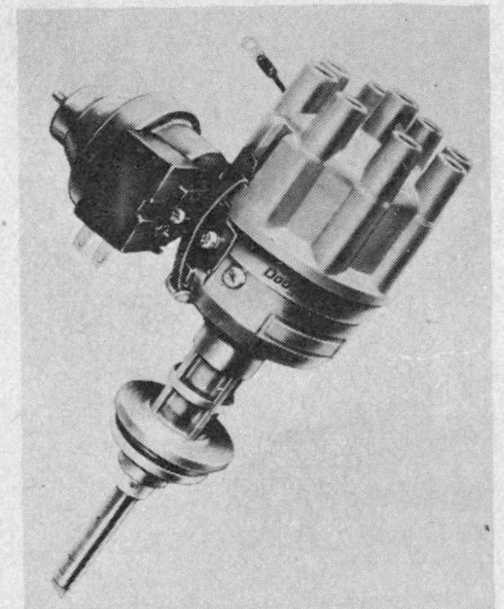

High performance distributor with solenoid retard
(©Chrysler Corp)

Distributor Replacement (When Engine has been Disturbed)

Slant 6 Engine

1. Remove No. 1 spark plug and, with the thumb closing the hole, rotate the engine until No. 1 piston is up on compression at top dead center. This is determined by the pressure on the thumb and the 0 mark on the crankshaft pulley hub being aligned with the timing pointer.
2. Rotate the rotor to a position just ahead of the No. 1 distributor cap terminal.
3. Lower the distributor into the opening, engaging distributor gear with drive gear on camshaft. With distributor fully seated on engine, rotor should be under the cap No. 1 tower with distributor contact points just opening.
4. Install cap, tighten hold-down arm screw and check timing with a timing light.

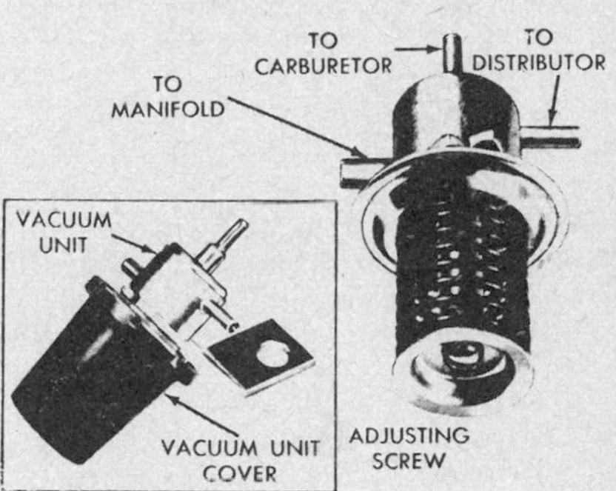

Distributor vacuum unit
(© Chrysler Corp)

V8 Engine

Rotate the crankshaft until No. 1 cylinder is at top dead center. The pointer on the chain case cover should be over the 0 mark on the crankshaft pulley. The slot in the intermediate shaft which carries the gear that drives the oil pump and the distributor, should be parallel with the crankshaft.

Hold the distributor over the mounting pad on the cylinder block so that the distributor body flange coincides with the mounting pad and the rotor points to the No. 1 cylinder firing position.

Install the distributor while holding the rotor in position, allowing it to move only enough to engage the slot in the drive gear.

Breaker Points and Condenser Replacement

Single Point Distributor

1. Remove the distributor cap. Do not pull the wires from the cap. Pull the rotor from the shaft.
2. Carefully note the position of all leads and remove the securing nut. Loosen the point plate lockscrew and remove the points and condenser from the vehicle.
3. With a clean, lint-free rag, wipe any of the old cam grease from the distributor cam. Apply fresh cam lubricant sparingly.

4. Insert a new point set with the contact heel resting on the highest point of the cam lobe. Set point gap to specifications with a feeler gauge. The setting is correct when the feeler gauge is removed with a light drag. Install the condenser and secure the leads. Lock the point securing screws.
5. Replace the distributor cap and rotor. Check the dwell with a dwell meter. Adjust the point gap as necessary.
6. Road-test vehicle.

Dual Point Distributor

The removal and installation of dual contact points is the same as for a single point set. The point adjustment is also the same, except that each set must be set while its rubbing block is on the high point of the cam lobe. The dwell adjustment of dual points is slightly different because one set of contacts must be blocked open with a clean insulator while the opposite point set is adjusted to specifications. When correctly adjusted, tighten the lockscrew. Block open this contact set and adjust this contact set in the same manner as the first. Check the point dwell. If the contacts have been installed and adjusted correctly, the dwell angle should be as specified for both contact sets.

Distributor (Point) Dwell Checking

Correct distributor dwell angle is essential to good ignition performance and contact life. To test:

1. Disconnect the vacuum line. If the vehicle is equipped with an ignition retard solenoid (some 1971 and earlier models only), disconnect it.
2. Connect the red lead of the dwell meter to distributor terminal of the coil and the black lead to ground. Set the selector switch to proper number of engine cylinders.
3. Start the engine and allow it to operate at idle speed.
4. Observe the dwell meter reading. If it is not within specifications, the contact gap may be incorrect, the cam may be worn, or the movable contact arm may be distorted. Connect the ignition retard solenoid (if so equipped) and the vacuum line.

Ignition Timing

NOTE: Before timing engine, check information on ignition retard/advance solenoids.

The ignition timing test indicates correct timing of the engine only at idle and with the engine hot. Check timing as follows:

1. Disconnect the vacuum hose at the distributor and plug the line.
2. Connect a strobe light to No. 1 spark plug and to the battery terminals.
3. Start the engine and set it to the specified idle speed with the transmission in Neutral.
4. Loosen the distributor locking screw so that the housing can be rotated.
5. Check the timing by aiming the strobe light at the vibration damper. If timing is ahead of the mark, turn the distributor housing in the direction of rotor-rotation. This will retard timing. If it is past the mark, rotate the distributor against its direction of rotation to advance the timing. When timing is adjusted to specifications, tighten the distributor lockscrew and reconnect the vacuum hose to the distributor.

FUEL SYSTEM

The fuel system consists of three basic parts: the fuel pump; filter, and carburetor(s). The fuel pumps used on the six-cylinder and all big blocks (383-440 cu in.) are driven by a small cam eccentric cast into the main camshaft. On the 318, 340, and 360 engines, the pump is driven by a pressed steel eccentric secured on the gear end of the camshaft. On the six-cylinder and 318, 340, and 360 engines, the pump is driven directly by the pump rocker arm pressing on the cam eccentric. On the big block engines, there is a push rod located between the pump rocker arm and the driving eccentric.

All Dodge and Plymouth vehicles are equipped with a fuel filter located in the fuel line between the fuel pump and carburetor. Servicing is by replacement only.

Dodge and Plymouth vehicles have utilized many different types of carburetors. All carburetors incorporate modifications to reduce engine exhaust emissions. Carburetor modifications for 1969 are part of Chrysler's Cleaner Air Package and 1970 and later models are part of the Cleaner Air System. The only carburetor changes used with the Cleaner Air Package are the installation of carburetor mixture limiter stops on the carburetor idle mixture adjustent screws, and leaner air/fuel mixture. With the Cleaner Air System, in addition to the above mentioned changes, faster-acting chokes were added, and as of 1972 the choke is not adjustable.

On some models, solenoid-operated throttle stops and distributor retard (until 1971) mechanisms were installed. On 1972-74 models, the distributor retard was exchanged for a distributor advance solenoid. The throttle stop raises the engine idle speed to reduce engine emissions, but de-energizes when the ignition is shut off to prevent the engine from dieseling. The distributor retard solenoid is activated when the idle speed adjustment screw returns to the curb idle position and contacts a sensor. This sensor, mounted on the carburetor, retards ignition timing when the engine idles. The distributor advance solenoid is connected to the starter relay so that it is activated only during engine cranking. It does not operate when the engine is running.

Some carburetors incorporate an internally mounted hot idle compensator. This compensator is designed to induct additional air to the carburetor during low-speed, high-temperature operation.

Until 1971, both the 426 Hemi and

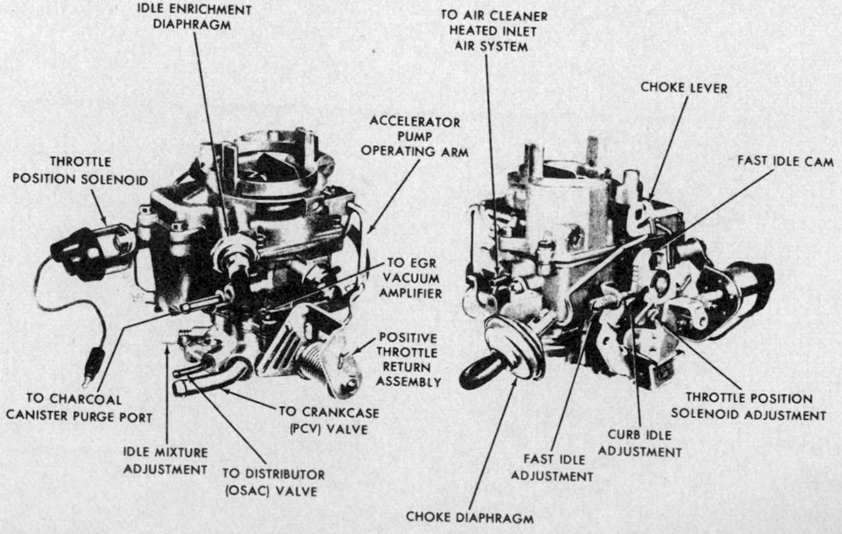

Holley 1945-1V Carburetor Adjustments
(© Chrysler Corp.)

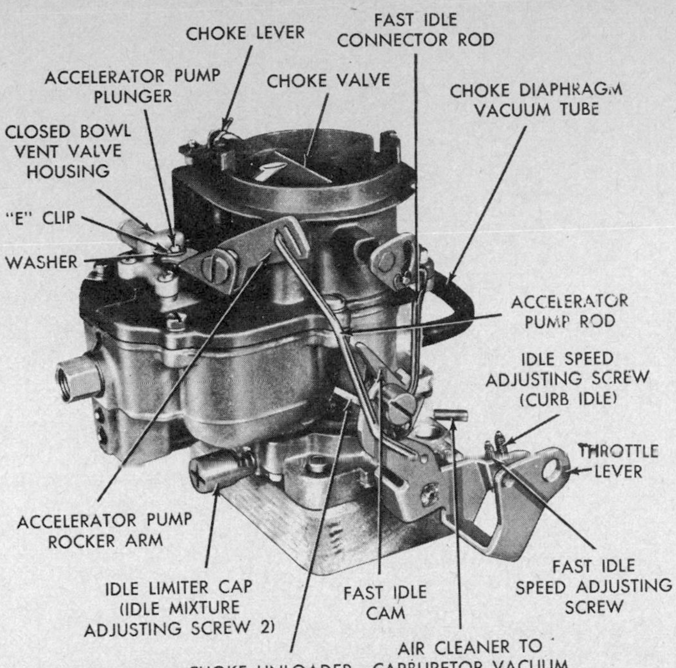

Carter carburetor adjustments
(© Chrysler Corp)

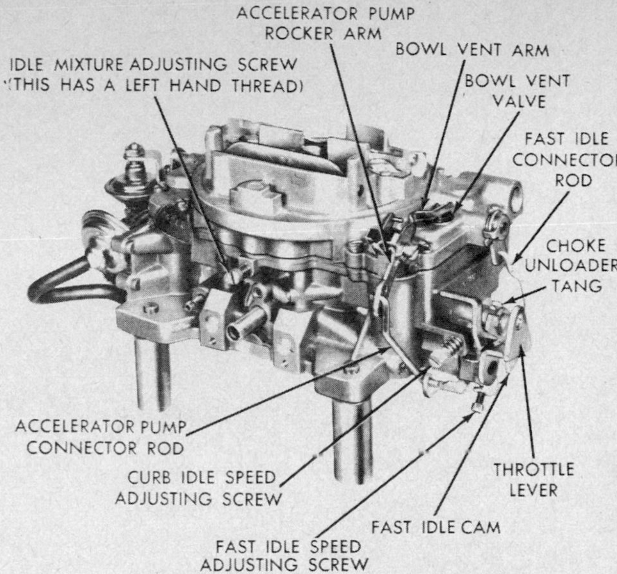

1969 Carter AVS carburetor adjustments
(© Chrysler Corp)

the 440 Six Pack engines were equipped with multiple carburetors. The Hemi used two Carter AFBs. Both carburetors were equipped with complete idle systems; they must be adjusted and synchronized to obtain a satisfactory engine idle. The 440 Six Pack was equipped with three Holley 2300 two-barrel carburetors. Only the center carburetor was equipped with an idle system; the inboard and outboard carburetors contained no idle adjustments.

Fuel Pump Removal

All Models

Remove all lines at the fuel pump, and the pump-to-block mounting screws. Remove the pump.

Fuel Filter

Removal and Installation

Locate the filter in the fuel line between the fuel pump and the carburetor. Using hose-clamp pliers, remove the attaching clamps and pull off the filter. Reverse the procedure to install. Be sure that the arrow on the filter is pointing toward the carburetor (direction of fuel flow).

Idle Speed and Mixture Adjustments

1969-76 with CAP or CAS Except 426 Hemi

Adjust with air cleaner installed.

NOTE: this is the basic carburetor adjustment procedure, any specific exceptions are listed below.

1. Run engine at fast idle to stabilize engine temperature.

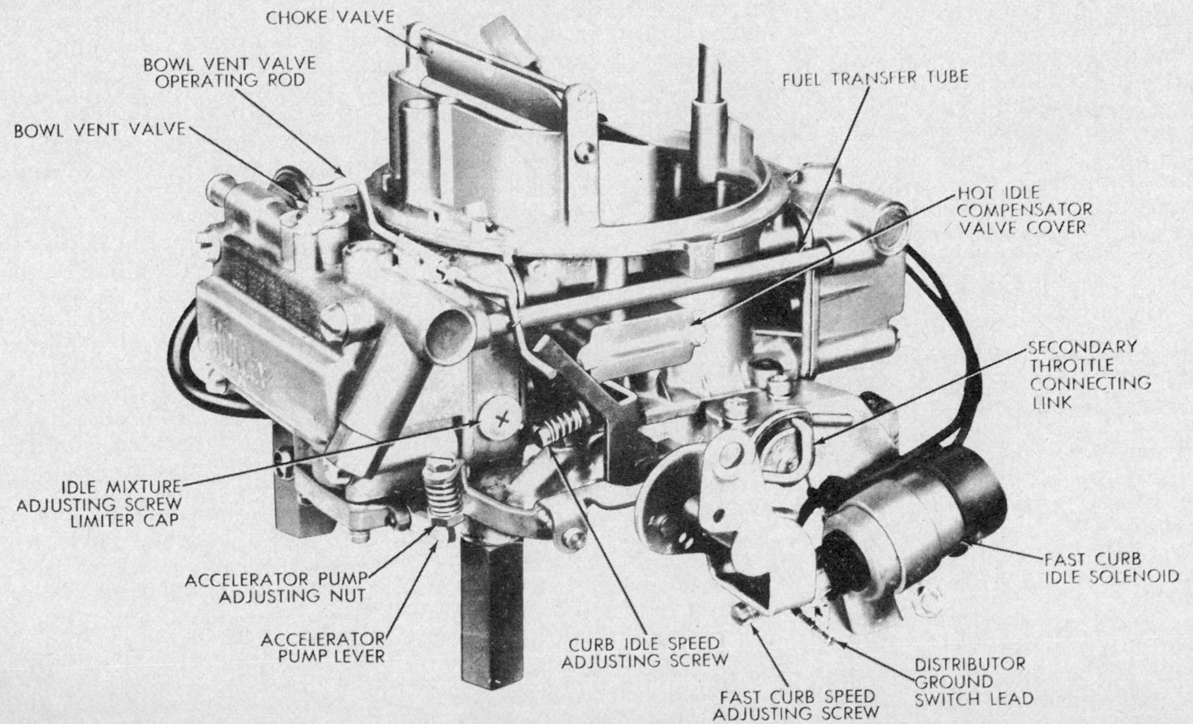

1970-71 Holley carburetor adjustments (© Chrysler Corp)

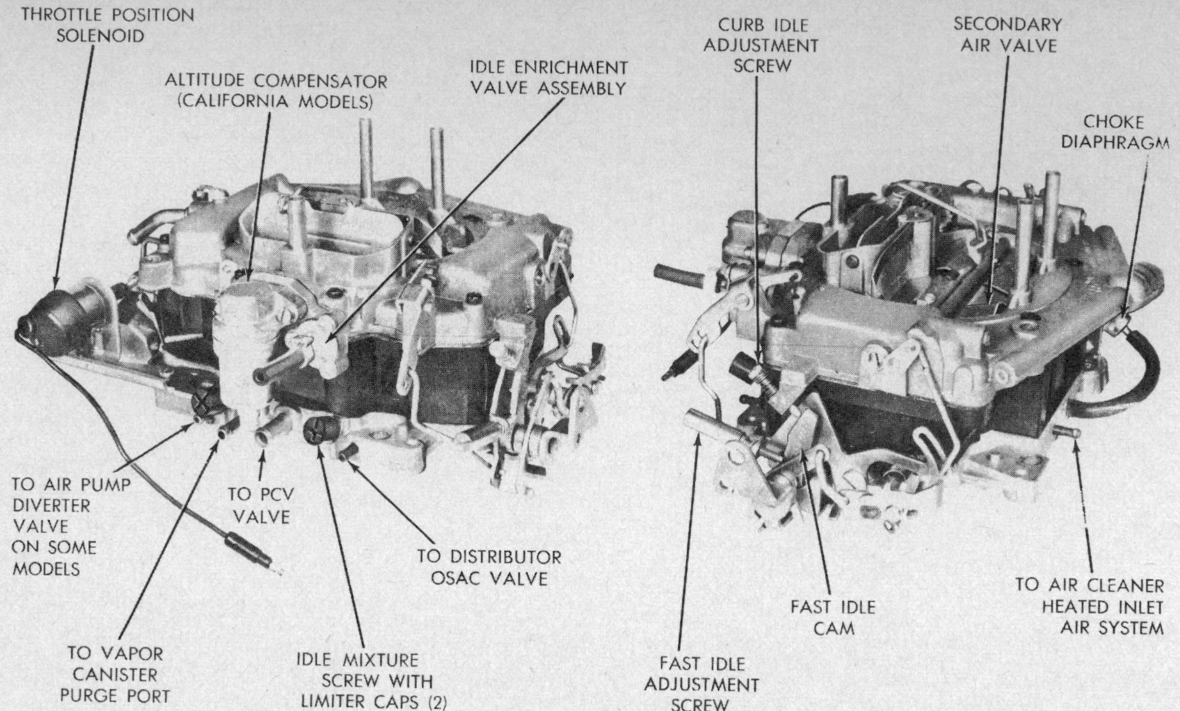

Carter Thermo-Quad® Carburetor Adjustments
(© Chrysler Corp.)

2. Make sure choke plate is fully released.
3. Attach a tachometer of known accuracy to the engine.
4. Connect an exhaust analyzer to the engine and insert the probe as far into the tailpipe as possible. On vehicles with dual exhaust, insert the probe into the left tailpipe as this is the side without the heat riser valve.
5. Check ignition timing and adjust it as required to conform to specification.
6. If equipped with air conditioning, turn the air conditioner off. On models with six-cylinder engines, turn the headlights on high beam.
7. Place the transmission in the Neutral position. Make sure the hot idle compensator valve is fully seated in the closed position.
8. Turn the engine idle speed adjustment screw in or out to adjust idle speed to specification. If equipped with an electric solenoid throttle positioner, turn the solenoid adjusting screw in or out to obtain specified rpm. Then, adjust the curb idle speed screw until it just touches the stop on the carburetor body. Now, back the curb idle speed adjusting screw out one full turn.
9. Turn each idle mixture adjustment screw 1/16 turn richer (counterclockwise). Wait 30 seconds and observe the reading on the exhaust gas analyzer. Continue this procedure until the meter indicates a definite increase in the richness of the mixture.

NOTE: this step is very important. A carburetor that is set too lean will cause the exhaust gas analyzer to give a false reading indicating a rich mixture. Because of this, the carburetor must first be known to have a rich mixture to verify the reading on the exhaust gas analyzer.

10. After verifying the reading obtained on the meter, adjust the mixture screws to get an air/fuel ratio of 14.2:1. Turn the mixture screws clockwise (leaner) to raise the meter reading or counterclockwise (richer) to lower the meter reading.

NOTE: Do not remove the plastic cap in order to obtain an over-rich mixture.

1969 383 and 440 V8

The carburetors used on these engines (Ball & Ball 2V, Carter 4V or Holley 4V) have lead or cup plugs installed over the idle mixture screws and an additional off idle mixture control screw added to the body of the carburetor. When adjusting the carburetor idle speed and mixture, use the off idle adjustment screw to alter the idle speed air/fuel mixture so it conforms to the 14.2:1 ratio specified. If unable to obtain an acceptable engine idle by adjusting this screw, refer to the procedure to correct rough idle and low speed surge.

Rough Idle and Low Speed Surge—All 1969-76 Except Hemi

Rough idle and low speed surge can be the result of improper balance of the idle mixture adjustment in the right and left carburetor bores. To correct this condition, perform the following operation.

1. On 1969 383 or 440 V8, remove the lead plugs from the base of the carburetor (Ball & Ball or Carter) or the cup plugs from the sides of the primary metering body (Holley). The best way to remove the lead plugs is with a small drill and easy-out. Use a sharp punch to remove cup plugs from a Holley carburetor.
2. On all other models, remove the plastic limiter caps from the idle mixture adjustment screws.
3. Perform Steps 1-8 of the idle speed and mixture adjustment procedure.
4. On 1969 383 or 440 V8, turn the single off idle mixture adjustment screw counterclockwise (richer) until it is seated, then turn it clockwise (lean) 3/4 turn. Do not disturb this adjustment during the remainer of this procedure.
5. Turn both idle mixture adjustment screws clockwise until they are lightly seated. On some models, the idle mixture screws have a prevailing torque feature which causes the screws to become more difficult to turn as they approach the seated position.
6. On Ball & Ball carburetors, turn both idle mixture screws 1½ turns counterclockwise. On Carter and Holley carburetors, turn both idle mixture screws 2-3 turns counterclockwise.

7. Start the engine and perform Steps 9-11 of the idle speed and mixture adjustment procedure.

NOTE: in order to obtain a smooth idle, it is important that both mixture adjustment screws are adjusted an equal number of turns from the fully seated position.

8. Install lead plugs, cup plugs, or plastic caps on the idle mixture screws.

426 Hemi

Because each carburetor is equipped with a complete idle system, accurate carburetor synchronization is very important. After adjusting the idle speed and mixture, it should be rechecked and rebalanced as required in the outside ambient temperature after a road test.

Adjust with air cleaner removed.

1. Run engine at fast idle to stabilize engine temperature.
2. Make sure the choke plate is fully released.
3. Attach a tachometer of known accuracy to the engine.
4. If equipped with a hot idle compensator valve, make sure it is fully seated in the closed position.
5. Place the transmission in the Neutral position.
6. Turn the idle speed adjustment screws in or out to adjust the engine idle speed to specification. If equipped with an electric solenoid throttle positioner, turn the solenoid adjusting screw in or out to obtain specified engine idle speed. Then, turn the curb idle speed adjusting screw clockwise until it just touches the stop on the carburetor throttle body. Next, back the curb idle speed adjusting screw out one full turn.
7. Adjust each idle mixture screw to obtain the highest rpm possible. Repeat this operation until all four mixture adjustment screws have been properly adjusted and balanced.
8. If the idle mixture adjustment procedure has changed the engine idle speed, adjust the idle speed.

Balancing Multiple-Carburetor Installations

426 Hemi

There is no actual adjustment of the external carburetor linkage to synchronize the twin carburetors. Proper balancing of the carburetor idle speeds as described in the idle speed for the 426 Hemi will ensure correct and mixture adjustment procedure carburetor synchronization.

440 Six Pack

Because only the center carburetor has provisions for adjusting the engine idle speed and fuel mixture, these adjustments are performed using the procedure for single-carburetor installations. The throttle rods which connect each outboard carburetor to the center carburetor can be adjusted for correct throttle synchronization using the procedure below.

1. Remove the air cleaner.
2. Remove the outboard throttle rod securing clips and disengage the front and rear rods from the throttle levers.
3. Be sure that the ignition switch is turned off. (This de-energizes the fast curb idle solenoid so that clearance can be obtained between the plunger and the fast curb idle adjusting screw.)
4. Close the throttle valves of all three carburetors and hold them in the closed position.
5. Shorten or lengthen the front and rear connector rods by turning each rod into or out of the threaded sleeve until the rod end can be inserted into the hole in the throttle lever smoothly.
6. Fit each throttle connector rod into its corresponding throttle lever and secure each rod with a clip.

Fast Curb Idle Speed Solenoid Adjustment

1970-76 Models (If So Equipped)

1. Bring the engine to operating temperature and attach a tachometer.
2. With the engine running, adjust the fast curb idle screw to the proper rpm for the vehicle in question.
3. Adjust the slow curb idle screw until the screw end just contacts the stop. Back the screw off one full turn; this should return the vehicle to the slow curb idle setting.

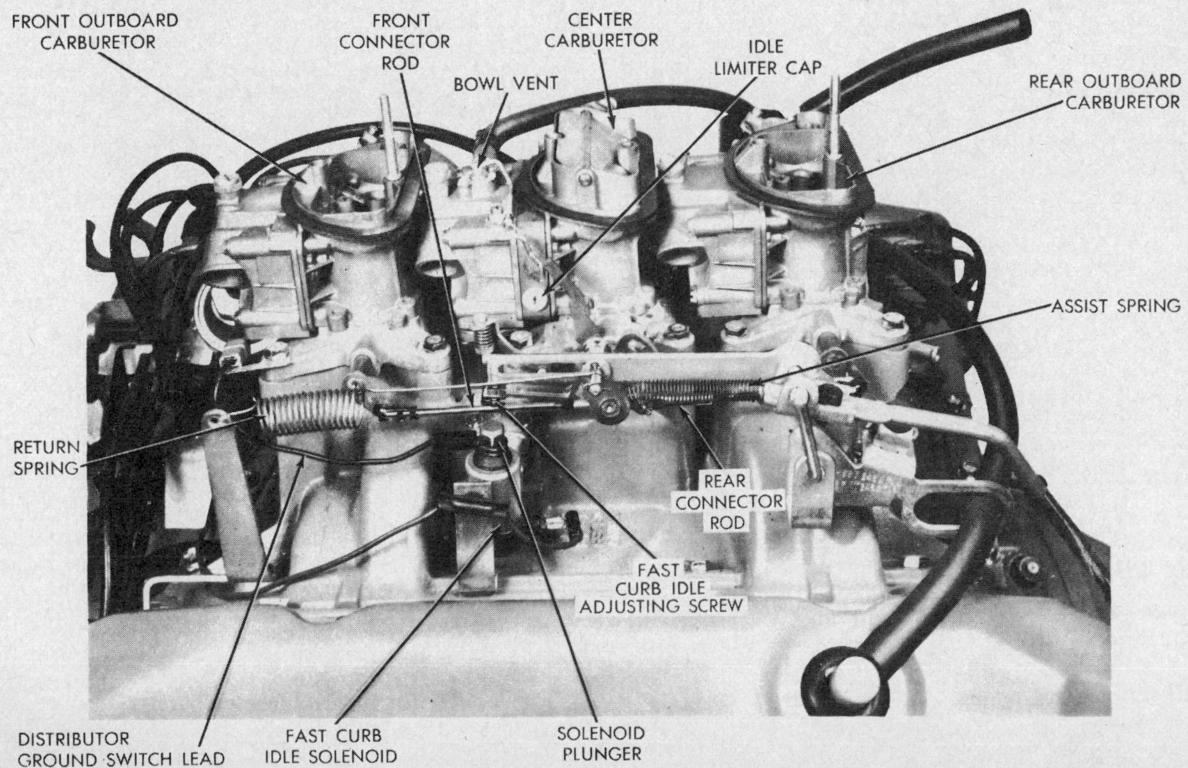

Holley Six Pack carburetor adjustments (© Chrysler Corp)

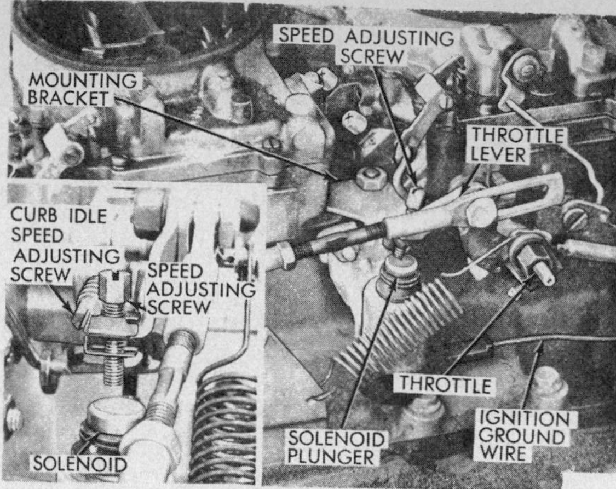

Solenoid throttle positioner adjustment
(© Chrysler Corp)

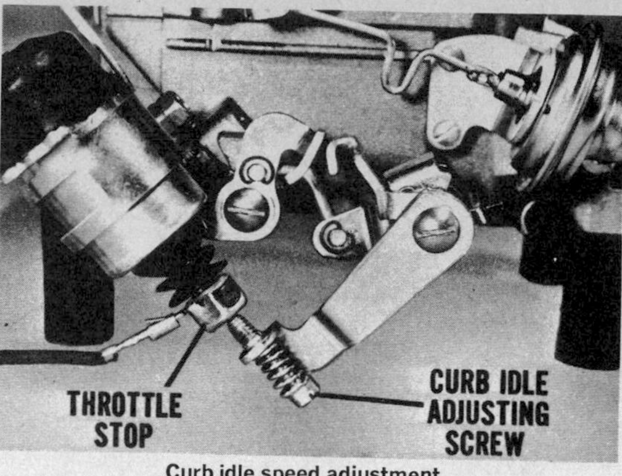

Curb idle speed adjustment
(© Chrysler Corp)

4. Test the above procedure by disconnecting the solenoid wire at the connector. Be sure not to let the lead short to the engine. Now reconnect the wire. The fast curb idle speed solenoid should not advance the throttle.

COOLING SYSTEM

The main cooling system components are a tube and spacer-type radiator, a thermostat (temperature specifications vary with year and model), a fan which may have a varying number of blades (and may be a viscous-drive type), and a water pump. The type of fan and radiator size/equipment (such as a radiator shroud) vary with engine, accessories, and intended usage.

Radiator Removal and Installation

1. Allow the cooling system to drain. On those vehicles with automatic transmissions, disconnect the oil cooler lines from the radiator bottom.
2. Remove both upper and lower radiator hoses. Remove the hose which runs to the coolant reserves system (if so equipped).
3. Remove the radiator shroud attaching bolts and tilt the shroud out of the way.
4. Remove the radiator attaching bolts. Remove radiator.

NOTE: When lifting the radiator, be sure not to damage the cooling fins.

5. To install the radiator, reverse the removal procedure. After finishing the installation, be sure to check the level of the coolant and the transmission oil.

Water Pump Removal

1969-71

1. Drain cooling system. Remove upper half of fan shroud if so equipped or set one piece shroud back on engine.

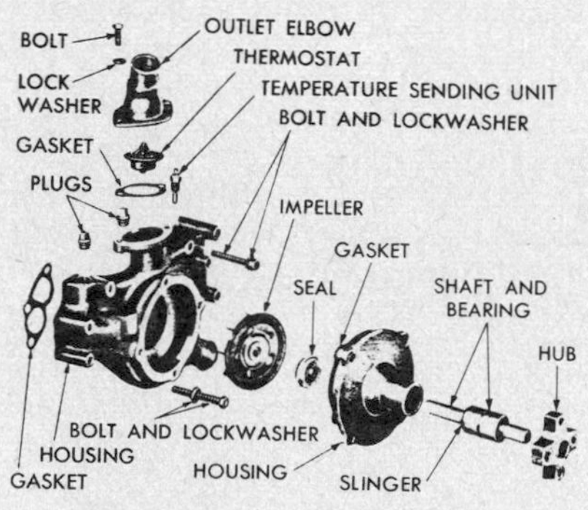

Typical water pump—B block engines
(© Chrysler Corp)

2. Loosen power steering pump, idler pulley and alternator. Remove all belts.
3. Remove fan, spacer or fluid drive, and pulley.

Caution Do not place a fluid drive unit with the shaft pointing downwards. Silicon fluid will drain into fan drive bearing and ruin grease.

4. Remove bolts attaching water pump to housing. Remove water pump and discard gasket.

1972-76

6 Cylinder Models without Air Conditioning and/or Air Pump

1. Drain the cooling system. Remove the battery. If the engine is equipped with a fan shroud, remove and swing it back over the engine.
2. Remove the power steering and alternator belts.
3. Take off the fan, spacer, pulley, and bolts as a unit.
4. Move the lower hose clamp to bypass the center of the hose. Disconnect the heater hose and the lower hose of the water pump.
5. Remove the water pump bolts and the pump.

6 Cylinder Models with Air Conditioning and/or Air Pump

1. Remove the battery and drain the cooling system. Remove the fan shroud and swing it back over the engine.
2. Disconnect the transmission oil cooler lines (if automatic transmission) and remove the lower radiator hoses. Cap the openings to prevent the entry of dirt and excessive fluid loss.
3. Remove the radiator.
4. Loosen the alternator, power steering pump, idler pulley, and air pump.
5. Take off the fan, spacer, pulley, and bolts as an assembly. Remove all belts.
6. Remove the compressor and/or air pump bracket and secure it out of way.
7. Move the lower hose clamp to bypass the center of the hose. Disconnect the heater hose.
8. Remove the water pump bolts and the pump.

V8 Removal

1. Drain the cooling system and move the fan shroud out of the way.
2. Disconnect the transmission oil cooler lines (automatic) and all radiator hoses. Cap the openings to prevent the entry of dirt or excessive fluid loss.
3. Remove the radiator, if necessary.
4. Loosen the alternator adjusting strap bolts. Remove the belts.
5. On 318-360 engines with no air conditioning, remove the alternator bracket bolts from the water pump. Swing the alternator out of the way and tighten the pivot bolt. On 318–360 engines with air conditioning, remove the idler pulley assembly and alternator with adjusting bracket.
6. Remove the fan, spacer/fluid drive, pulley, and bolts as an assembly.

Caution Do not let fluid drain into the fan-drive bearing.

7. Disconnect the heater and all by-pass hoses.
8. Remove the compressor-to-front mounting bracket bolts.

9. Remove the water pump attaching bolts and the water pump.
10. Carefully lift the compressor out of the way.

V8 Installation

1. Install the by-pass hose and position the clamp in the center of the hose.
2. Install the pump with a new gasket and torque it to 30 ft. lbs. Be sure that the pump turns freely.
3. Install the heater hose and route it near the by-pass hose clamps.
4. On V8s with air conditioning, install the front bracket on the compressor. Torque to 50 ft lbs. Torque the pump bolts to 30 ft lbs.
5. Replace the alternator, bracket, and idler pulley assembly. Torque to 30 ft lbs.
6. Install the compressor clutch assembly (if applicable).
7. Install the fan assembly. Check and adjust all belts.
8. Install the radiator, hoses, and transmission cooling lines.
9. Install fan shroud and fill the cooling system. Check the oil level in the transmission.

Thermostat

Removal and Installation

1. Drain the cooling system to below the level of the thermostat.
2. Remove the upper radiator hose from the thermostat housing flange. Remove the housing bolts, thermostat, and housing.
3. To install a thermostat, use a new gasket. On V8s, be sure that the pellet end is facing toward engine. Six-cylinder models must have the vent hole facing up. From this point, reverse the removal procedure. Tighten to 30 ft lbs.

EMISSION CONTROLS

NOTE: Additional information on the Emission Control System may be found in the emission systems unit repair section.

Positive Crankcase Ventilation

All models are equipped with a positive crankcase ventilation system which draws air into the engine through the oil filler cap or the air cleaner and circulates it through the engine. The air combines with vapors in the crankcase and exits the engine through a metering valve mounted in the rocker arm cover. The air-vapor mixture then re-enters the engine through the carburetor or intake manifold and passes into the combustion chamber where it is burned.

Cleaner Air Package (CAP)

All 1969 models use this package to reduce engine exhaust emissions. Changes include the addition of limiters to the carburetor idle mixture screws, leaner carburetor mixtures and vacuum controlled ignition timing retard mechanisms.

Cleaner Air System (CAS)

All 1970 and later models are equipped with this type of exhaust emission control. This system consists of: heated carburetor air cleaner intake ducts, carburetor modifications, ignition timing controls, and reduced engine compression ratios.

In addition to the aforementioned controls, many new ones were added or modified since.

Intake Manifold/Cylinder Head Design Change

A change has been incorporated in intake manifold design to place all manifold branch runners on one level. This is in contrast to the previous, two-level design. This change was made to improve fuel vaporization during warm-up, and hence, to allow the use of leaner fuel/air mixtures.

Cylinder head design has also been modified. By redesigning the intake ports to give more fuel turbulence and increasing the volume of the combustion chambers to increase quench area, the fuel/air mixture burns more uniformly and this results in a lower production of HC and CO.

Ignition Retard Solenoid 1971 and Earlier Models

The function of this unit is to retard the ignition timing at closed throttle. Located on the distributor side, this solenoid must be operating when the ignition timing is adjusted. To be sure that the solenoid is operating, disconnect the ground lead after the timing is set. If the engine idle speed increases noticeably, the solenoid is functioning properly.

In contrast to the above, disconnect the solenoid when checking the dwell. If this is not done, the dwell meter will not read accurately.

Ignition Advance Solenoid—1972-74

This solenoid, located on the distributor side, is connected to the starter relay so that it operates only during engine cranking, to improve starting. It is used on some 400 and 440 engines.

When the engine fires, this solenoid ceases to operate. It is designed to advance the timing only during cranking. If the solenoid is not operating, it will affect starting, but not drivability. A possible sign of failure is popping through the carburetor during engine cranking.

To check operation, idle the engine and connect a jumper wire from the battery to the solenoid lead. If the solenoid is operating properly, engine speed will increase noticeably.

Caution Disconnect the jumper wire as soon as possible when checking the operation of the solenoid.

Vapor Saver System (Evaporative Control System)

This system is used to prevent the loss of fuel vapor from the fuel tank and carburetor. It is required by law on all 1970 California vehicles, and on all (50 states) 1971 and later models.

By venting carburetor and fuel tank vapors to a charcoal canister for temporary storage fuel vapors are prevented from entering the atmosphere. The system is purged of vapors when the engine is running by means of air drawn through the canister by intake manifold vacuum.

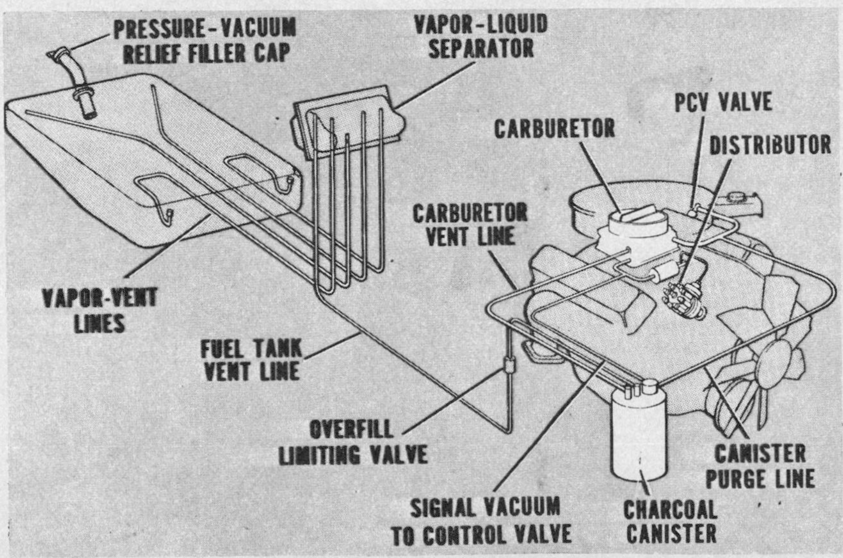

Vapor saver system (© Chrysler Corp)

In addition, a limiting valve is used to prevent fuel tank overfilling. Located in the fuel vapor vent line in the engine compartment, this valve prevents overfilling by closing when the filler tube is closed by incoming fuel.

Air Injection System (Air Pump)—1972-76

In 1972 the air injection system was used on the 225, 400 and 440 cu in. engines sold in California only. In 1973, the 225, 360 and 440 cu in. engines sold in California used air injection. In 1974, some of the 400 and 440 cu in. engines sold in California use air pumps, depending upon model usage. In 1975-76 most engines, California and 49 states, use the air pumps in conjunction with catalytic converters, except those using the "lean-burn" system.

A belt-driven air pump, mounted on the front of the engine, is used to inject air into the exhaust ports. This causes oxidation of these gases and a considerable reduction in carbon monoxide and hydrocarbons. The system consists of the pump, a check valve to protect the hoses and pump from hot gases, and a diverter-/pressure relief valve assembly.

Service to the air injection system is limited to belt tension adjustment every 12,000 miles. In addition, if any part fails in service, repair is effected by removal and replacement only.

Exhaust Gas Recirculation

In order to reduce the emission of oxides and nitrogen (NO_X), exhaust gases are ducted from the intake manifold crossover passage to contaminate the fuel/air mixture. (Do not confuse this system with other changes in the intake manifold.) These gases are introduced to the intake manifold floor by small jets. Every 12,000 miles, inspect these jets by looking through the carburetor. If the jet is plugged, remove, clean, and reinstall it.

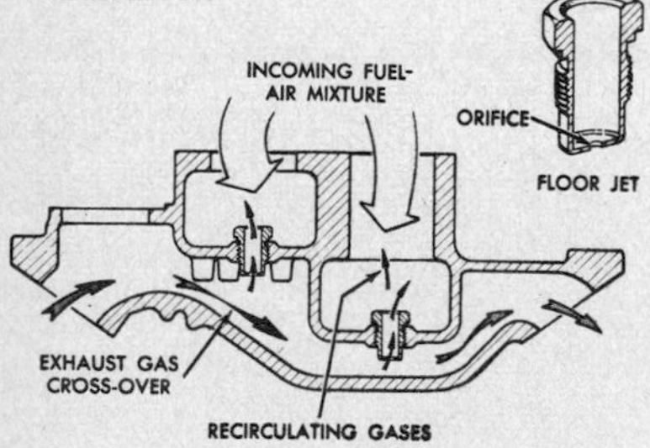

Exhaust gas recirculation—1973 floor jet type
(© Chrysler Corp)

1973—All

Starting with 1973, all Chrysler Corp. cars use exhaust gas recirculation (EGR). All engines have floor jets like those used on the 1972 models sold in California. The 340 and 400 cu in. engines equipped with 4-bbl carburetor use only floor jets for 1973.

In addition to the floor jets, all other 1973 engines use an EGR control valve. This valve directs exhaust gas from the crossover passage into the intake manifold. By using either ported-vacuum or venturi-vacuum signals, the EGR valve is able to proportion the exhaust gas flow to the amount of vacuum present in the carburetor. Ported-vacuum is used on the 318 cu in. (except California) and the 400 cu in. 2-bbl engines, as well as, the 440 cu in. 4-bbl high-performance engine. Venturi-vacuum is used on the six-cylinder engines, the 440 standard engines, and on the 318 2-bbl sold in California.

A thermal switch is used to de-energize the EGR valve when the outside temperature is below 58°F, to provide better driveability.

Starting around 15 March 1973, the ambient temperature sensor was dropped. It has been replaced by a thermostatic valve which is threaded into the top tank of the radiator. A hose runs from one valve nipple to the EGR vacuum amplifier. The other nipple has a filter fitted over it. When the coolant temperature is below 62°F, the valve is opened to the atmosphere, thus preventing the EGR valve diaphragm from getting vacuum. Above 62°F, the valve closes and the EGR valve is allowed to function.

1974-76—All

Floor jets have been dropped from all 1974 and later engines. The EGR temperature switch (mounted in the upper radiator tank), which was introduced in March 1973, has been retained.

NOTE: The thermostatic switch for the EGR system is mounted on the thermostat housing on the 360-4V engine.

All 1974 engines, except for the following, have a vacuum amplifier:

V8-318—All
V8-360—4-bbl High Performance
V8-400—4-bbl High Performance
V8-440—4-bbl High Performance

All 1975 engines use an EGR amplifier.

NOTE: *1976 engines equipped with the "lean-burn" system do not use EGR.*

1975 (CCIE System)

All 1975 engines have a Venturi type PEGR system with a 35 second time delay after starting. The system is coolant temperature controlled and provides for idle enrichment.

Electric Assist Choke

1973

During warm weather a heating element, located in the automatic choke well, comes on to shorten the period of choke operation and thus reduce hydro-carbon emissions. The heating element is operated by a time-delay control switch located next to the choke well. The assist choke draws about three amps of current during operation.

1974-76

A two-stage electric assist choke is used for 1974. The two-stage choke may be identified by its external resistor:

Blue resistor 5 ohm—all sixes/V8-318

White resistor 10 ohm—All other V8s

Below 58°F, the heating element gets full, low amperage current from the choke control. Above 58°F, the resistor cuts the current in half. After several minutes of operation above 58°F, the control opens the circuit so that the heating element gets no current at all.

Most engines use a 20-watt heating element, except for the following which have 4-bbl carburetors and use a 40-watt choke:

V8-440 (Thermo-Quad)—All states
V8-400 H.P. (Thermo-Quad)—All (except Calif.)
V8-440 H.P. (Thermo-Quad)—

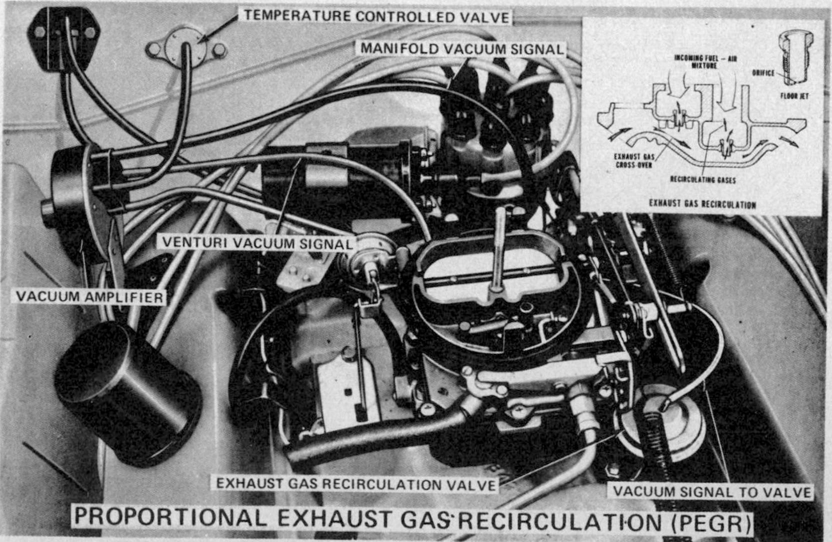

1973 Exhaust Gas recirculation system with venturi-vacuum amplifier
(© Chrysler Corp.)

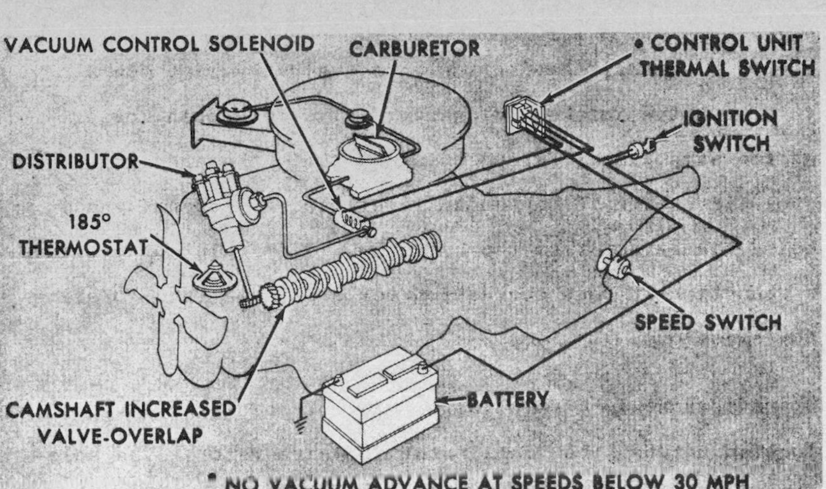

NO_X control system—automatic transmission (© Chrysler Corp)

Calif. only
V8-360—All states
V8-360 H.P.—All states

The 40-watt choke has a white paint spot on the choke cover.

For 1975, all engines except the 360 4-bbl and 318 V8s use the single-stage electric choke similar to 1973. The above mentioned V8s use the two-stage choke from 1974.

NOx System

Many 1971-72 cars have a NO_X system to control the emission of oxides of nitrogen. Engines with this system all have a special camshaft and a 185° F thermostat.

Manual Transmission

The manual transmission NO_X system uses a transmission switch, a thermal switch, and a solenoid vacuum valve. The transmission switch is screwed into the transmission housing and is closed, except in high gear. The thermal switch, mounted on the firewall, is open whenever the ambient temperature is above 70°F. With the transmission in any gear except high and the temperature above 70°, the solenoid vacuum valve is energized. This shuts off the distributor vacuum advance line preventing vacuum advance. Below 70°, the vacuum advance functions normally.

Automatic Transmission

The NO_X system for automatic transmissions is more complex than the manual transmission system. It prevents vacuum advance when the ambient temperature is above 70°F, speed is below 30 mph, or the car is accelerating. The solenoid vacuum valve is interchangeable with that used in the manual transmission system. The speed switch senses vehicle speed and is driven by the speedometer cable. The control unit is mounted on the firewall. It contains a control module, thermal switch, and a vacuum switch. The control unit senses ambient temperature and manifold vacuum.

OSAC Valve

1973

Starting with the 1973 models, an orifice spark advance control (OSAC) valve is used to delay distributor vacuum advance for about 15 seconds during acceleration.

NOTE: The amount of time-delay varies slightly from one engine size to another.

To aid in cold weather engine operation, a temperature sensing switch is built in to the OSAC valve so that it will not function when the air temperature is below 68°F.

Some time after 1 March and before 15 March 1973, the temperature sensor was removed from the OSAC valve, but the general appearance and location of the valve were not changed. The valve can be recognized by a white gasket and a stick-on label with the new part number (3755499).

At the same time, the ignition timing was changed to TDC.

NOTE: See the engine tune-up Specifications decal for further timing information.

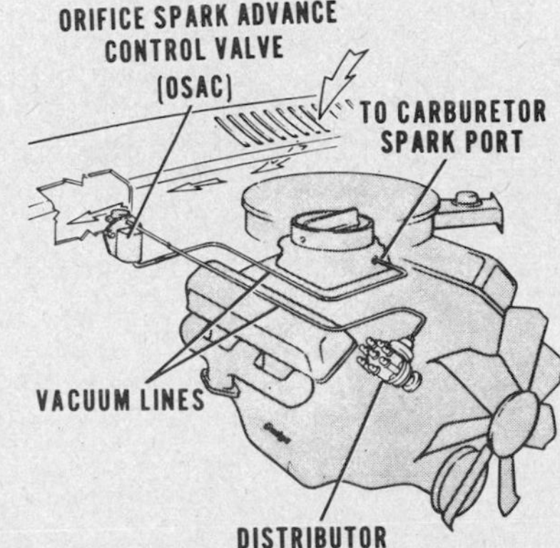

Orifice spark advance control (OSAC) valve—1973
(© Chrysler Corp.)

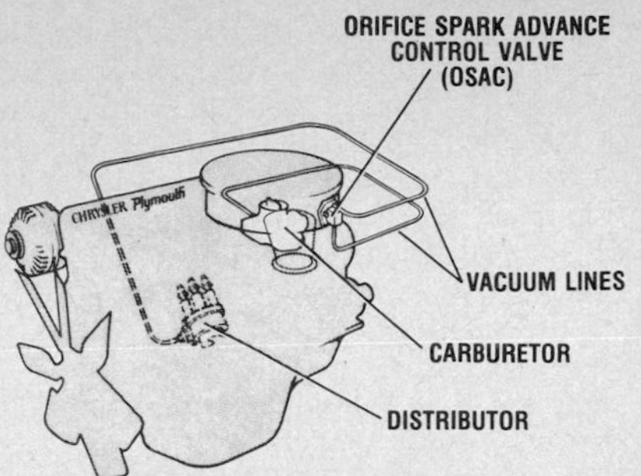

Typical OSAC valve vacuum hose routing and component layout—1974-75
(© Chrysler Corp.)

1974-76

The OSAC valve has been moved from the firewall to the air cleaner beginning 1974 and the temperature control restored. The OSAC valve is not used on 1976 models equipped with the 225 6 cylinder, 318 V8, 360-4V California V8, or on the 440-4V Federal V8. There are six different time delay and operating temperature combinations for the valve. These combinations are identified by a color code tape on the top of the valve. These codes are as follows:

Color	*Time (sec)*	*Temperature (°F)*
Green	17	58
Red	17	50
Blue	17	①
White	27	58
Orange	27	①
Yellow	27	58

①—No temperature control used

Caution Always replace the valve with one having the same color code. Failure to do so could result in poor vehicle performance or lack of compliance with the emission laws.

Catalytic Converter

All 1975-76 Chrysler products, except some 318 or 400HP V8 models and those 1976 full-sized models equipped with the "Lean-Burn" system, are equipped with catalytic converters. These devices are used to burn excess carbon monoxide and hydrocarbons in the exhaust system, that would otherwise escape out the exhaust pipe. The converters are installed in front of the front mufflers and are replaced at 50,000 miles intervals, providing that the engine is kept in tune.

To protect the catalyst from being confronted with an overly rich mixture during deceleration, a catalyst protection system is used on 1975 models. This consists of a throttle solenoid (not to be confused with the idle solenoid) which keeps the idle above 2,000 rpm during deceleration, and an electronic speed switch. 1976 models drop the system.

Available on 1976 full-sized Chrysler Corporation cars with the 400-4V or 440-4V engines is the electronic spark advance control or "lean-burn" system. This system (not to be confused with electronic "breakerless" ignition), through its precise regulation of spark timing, allows the engine to burn a leaner air/fuel mixture than was ever before possible on a modern, mass-produced vehicle. Most contemporary powerplants are tuned to an air/fuel mixture of approximately 14-½ parts air to one part fuel. The lean-burn engine, on the other hand, is most efficient at about 18 parts air to one part fuel. Six engine compartment-mounted sensors monitor all critical and fast changing factors that affect engine performance, and feed this data to the spark control computer which instantly calculates the precise moment to fire the mixture for the best combination of fuel economy, performance, and low emissions levels.

These sensors monitor engine (coolant) temperature, ambient (outside air temperature, intake manifold vacuum (engine load), engine speed (rpm) and position relative to Top Dead Center (TDC), throttle position, and rate of change in throttle position. With the lean-burn system, the following items of emission control may be dropped; catalytic converter (except California), air injection (air pump) system, exhaust gas recirculation system, OSAC valve, and distributor vacuum controls. The key is to clean up pollutants in the engine; not with power robbing hang-on devices.

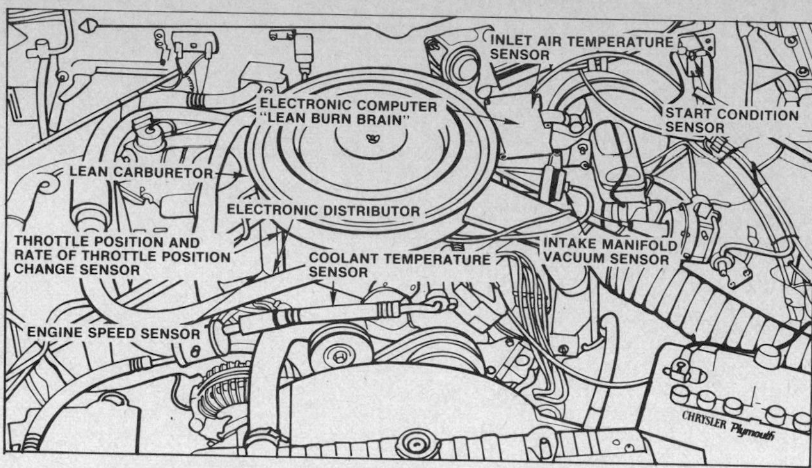

Electronic Spark Advance Control (Lean-Burn) System Components
(© Chrysler Corp.)

The OSAC valve is located in the air cleaner

IDLE STOP SOLENOID WITH CARBURETOR SWITCH
ELECTRONIC SPARK ADVANCE MODULE
●Vacuum Transducer
●Ambient Temperature Sensor
THROTTLE POSITION TRANSDUCER
WATER TEMPERATURE SENSOR
FRESH AIR INTAKE
TO IGNITION
BALLAST RESISTOR
CHRYSLER Plymouth
INLET AIR TEMPERATURE SENSOR
DUAL PICK-UP DISTRIBUTOR
IGNITION COIL
MAGNETIC TIMING

Lean-burn System Schematic
(© Chrysler Corp.)

ENGINE

The standard equipment engine in most Dodge and Plymouth car models is the 225 cu. in. slant six. Although this engine has a very long stroke by modern standards, it presents a low profile because the entire block is canted 30 degrees to the right.

The 318 cu. in. engines is a member of Chrysler Corporation's "A" block series of V8s. In 1971, a low compression 360 cu. in. V8 was added to the list of "A" block engines available.

Chrysler Corporation's "B" block series is really two series of engines, the low-block series and the raised-block series. These series differ in block deck height, main journal diameter, connecting rod length, and pushrod length. Otherwise these engines are similar and many parts interchange. The 383 and 400 cu. in. engines are low-block engines, and the 440 cu. in. V8 is a raised-block engine. All these engines are conventional V8s with wedge shaped combustion chambers and deep blocks that extend well below crankshaft centerline.

The 426 Hemi is Dodge and Plym-

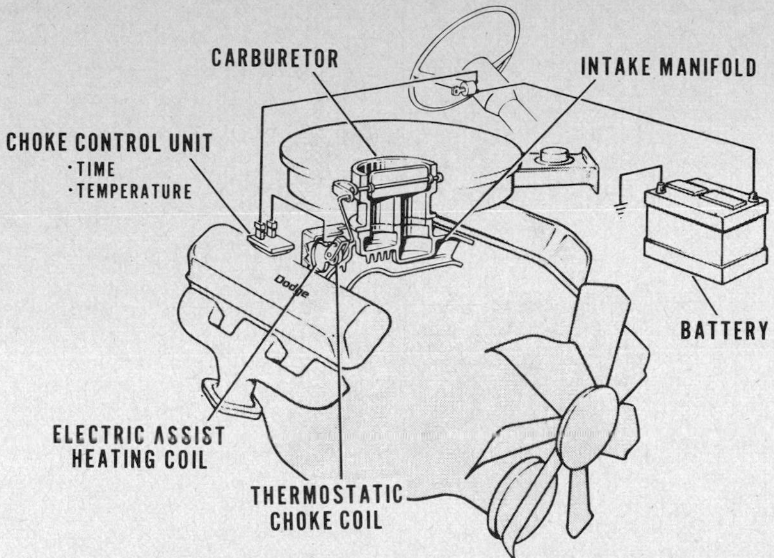

1973-76 electric assist choke system (© Chrysler Corp)

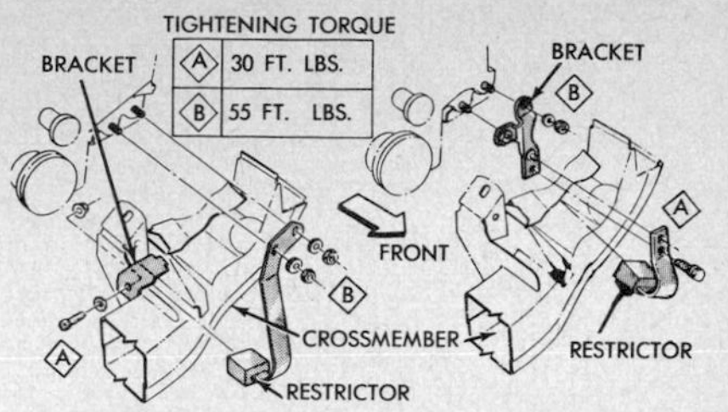

Spool-type engine mount tightening for 1973 and later Chrysler Corp. cars
(© Chrysler Corp)

outh's largest, heaviest, most complicated, and most powerful engine. It is basically a "B" series, raised-block engine, but with so many differences that it must be treated as a completely separate engine. It has hemispherical combustion chambers with 2.25 in. intake and 1.95 in. exhaust valves actuated by rocker arms mounted on separate intake and exhaust rocker shafts. The spark plugs are centrally located in the combustion chambers, and aluminum tubes protect the plugs and wires from oil where they pass through the rocker covers. Because of the huge intake ports, there is no room for head bolts on the intake side. Instead studs are mounted in the head which extend down into the valley between the cylinder heads. To reduce piston side thrust, Hemis use longer connecting rods than other raised-block "B" engines, and to strengthen the lower end, the main caps are crossbolted. The Hemi engine was discontinued in 1971 and is no longer available for street use.

Special Engine Markings

Over and undersize engine components are identified by various marks. These marks may be located on top, right-front engine pads or on the crankshaft counterweights. In addition, some big-block engines may have oversize valve stem markings stamped on the ends of the cylinder head on the untapped boss.

Engine R & R

1. Scribe the outline of the hood hinge brackets on the bottom of the hood and remove the hood.
2. Drain the cooling system and remove the radiator.
3. Remove the battery.
4. Remove the fuel line from the fuel pump and plug the line.
5. Remove all wires and hoses that attach to the engine. Remove all emission control equipment that may be damaged by the engine removal procedure.
6. If equipped with air conditioning and/or power steering, remove the unit from the engine and position it out of the way *without disconnecting the lines.*
7. Attach lifting sling to the engine. On V8 models (except the Hemi) remove the carburetor and attach the engine lifting fixture to the carburetor flange studs on the intake manifold. On models equipped with a 426 Hemi engine, never attempt to remove the engine with the lifting sling attached to the intake manifold. Attach lifting straps to the front of the left cylinder head, and the rear strap to the rear of the right cylinder head.
8. Raise the vehicle on a hoist and install an engine support fixture to support the rear of the engine.
9. On automatic transmission models, drain the transmission and torque converter. On standard transmission models, disconnect the clutch torque shaft from the engine.
10. Disconnect the exhaust pipe/s from the exhaust manifold/s.
11. Remove the driveshaft.
12. Disconnect the transmission linkage and any wiring or cables that attach to the transmission.
13. Remove the engine rear support crossmember and remove the transmission.
14. Remove the bolts that attach the motor mounts to the chassis.
15. Lower the vehicle and attach a chain hoist or other lifting device to the engine.
16. Raise the engine and carefully remove it from the vehicle.
17. Reverse above procedure to install.

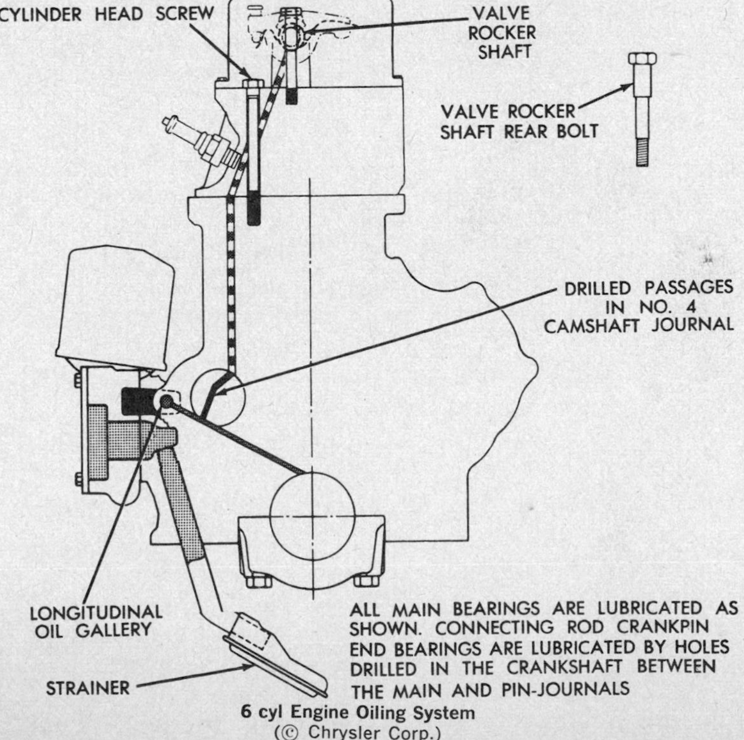

6 cyl Engine Oiling System
(© Chrysler Corp.)

Chilton's TIME SAVER

To remove the engine without removing the transmission, use the following operation. Perform Steps 1-7 and 10 of the "Engine R&R" operation. If the vehicle is equipped with an automatic transmission, attach a remote starter switch to the engine, remove the inspection plate from the bellhousing, crank the engine to gain access to the torque converter-to-driveplate attaching nuts and remove the nuts. If the vehicle is equipped with a manual transmission, disconnect the clutch torque shaft from the engine block and the clutch linkage from the adjustment rod. Remove the bolt that attaches the transmission filler tube to the engine (automatic transmission). Support the transmission and remove the bolts that attach the transmission to the engine or clutch bellhousing. When removing the engine, place a block of wood on the lifting point of a floor jack and position the jack under the transmission. As the engine is removed from the vehicle, raise and lower the jack as required so the angle of the transmission duplicates as nearly as possible the angle of the engine.

When installing the engine into a vehicle with an automatic transmission, keep in mind that the crankshaft flange bolt circle, the inner and outer circle of holes in the driveplate, and the four tapped holes in the front face of the converter all have one hole offset. To ensure proper engine-torque converter balance, the torque converter must be mounted to the driveplate in the same location it was originally installed.

When installing the engine into a vehicle with a manual transmission, it may be necessary to disconnect the driveshaft and turn the transmission output shaft, with the transmission in gear, to get the transmission input shaft splines to mesh with the inner hub on the clutch disc.

Manifolds

6 Cylinder Combination Manifold R&R

1. Remove the air cleaner and the fuel line from the carburetor.
2. Disconnect the accelerator linkage.
3. Disconnect the vacuum advance line at the carburetor.
4. Disconnect the exhaust pipe at the exhaust manifold flange.
5. Withdraw the manifold assemby-to-cylinder head bolts and remove the intake and exhaust manifolds, and the carburetor, as a single unit. The manifolds may be separated by removing the three bolts which hold them together.
6. Installation of the combination manifold and carburetor assembly is the reverse of the above. When installing the manifold assembly, use new gaskets and loosen the three bolts which secure the intake manifold to the exhaust manifold to maintain proper alignment. Torque these three bolts to 15 ft lbs in the sequence: inner bolt first, then the outer two bolts. Torque the manifold assembly-to-cylinder head bolts to 10 ft lbs.

Intake Manifold Removal

All V8 Engines Except 426 Hemi

1. Drain cooling system and disconnect battery.
2. Remove the air cleaner and fuel line from the carburetor.
3. Disconnect accelerator linkage.
4. Remove vacuum control between carburetor and distributor.
5. Remove distributor cap and wires.
6. Disconnect coil wires, temperature sending unit wire, heater hoses, and bypass hose.
7. Remove intake manifold, ignition coil, and carburetor as an assembly.

426 Hemi

1. Drain cooling system and disconnect battery.
2. Remove the air cleaner and fuel lines from the carburetors.
3. Disconnect accelerator linkage.
4. Remove vacuum control between carburetor and distributor. Remove distributor cap and wires.
5. Disconnect coil wires, heater hoses and bypass hose.
6. Remove two stud nuts and washers which retain intake manifold inlet heat tube to right hand exhaust header.

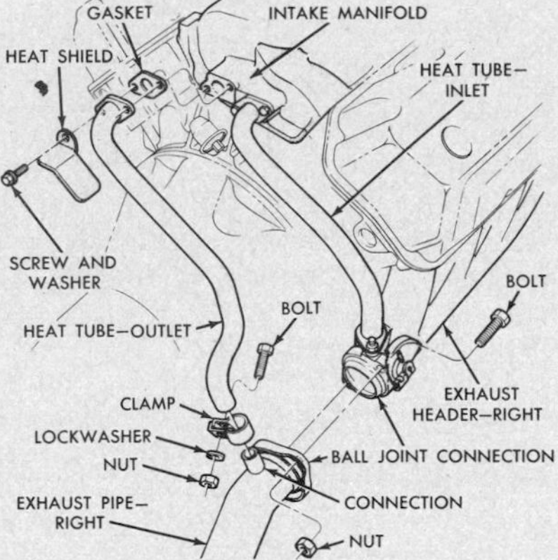

Manifold heat tubes—426 Hemi
(© Chrysler Corp)

Typical intake manifold tightening sequence (except Hemi and six-cylinder). Torque to specifications in two steps
(© Chrysler Corp)

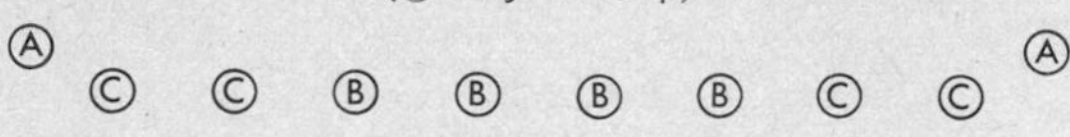

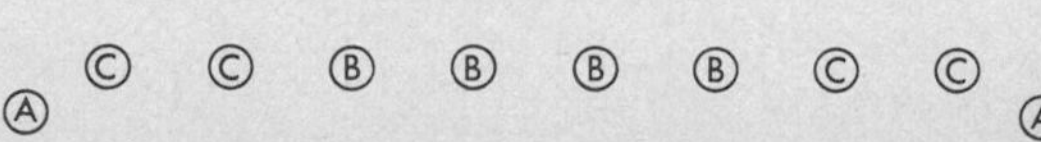

426 Hemi intake manifold tightening sequence in three steps
(© Chrysler Corp)

7. Remove screws attaching upper end of inlet tube to rear face of intake manifold.
8. Remove inlet tube and discard gaskets. Install new gaskets at assembly.
9. Remove nut, washer, and bolt from tube clamp at exhaust pipe. Remove clamp from outlet tube.
10. Remove screws attaching heat shield and outlet tube to rear face of intake manifold and remove tube and shield.
11. Remove intake manifold, coil and carburetors as an assembly.

Exhaust Manifold

Removal—All V8 Models

Disconnect the exhaust manifold at the pipe flange. Access to these bolts is underneath the vehicle. Disconnect the air injection nozzles and carburetor heated air stove (if so equipped). Remove the exhaust manifold by removing the securing bolts and washers. To reach these bolts, it may be necessary to jack the engine slightly off its front mounts. When the exhaust manifold is removed, sometimes the securing studs will come out with the nuts. If this occurs, the studs must be replaced with the aid of sealing compound on the coarse thread ends. If this is not done, water leaks may develop at the studs. To install the exhaust manifold, reverse the removal procedure.

Valve System

All valves used in Chrysler engines (except the 426 Hemi) are arranged in line in the cylinder head and ride in guides that are cast integrally. Service valves with overside stems are available; therefore, the valve guides may be reamed if that is required. Do not attempt to ream the guides in one step to their maximum .030 in. oversize; work in .005, .015, and .030 in. steps. This allows the guides to be reamed true in relation to valve seats.

All six-cylinder engines used in Chrysler vehicles are equipped with solid (mechanical) lifters. The 426 Hemi engine used solid lifters in 1969; beginning 1970, adjustable-type hydraulic lifters were used. All other V8 engines used in Dodge and Plymouth vehicles have used non-adjustable hydraulic lifters throughout their production.

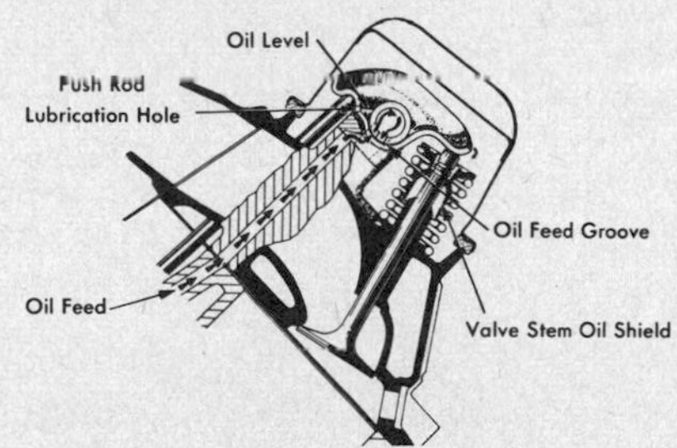

Rocker and shaft oil supply—B block engines
(© Chrysler Corp)

Rocker Shaft Removal

All Engines except 426 Hemi

1. Remove the closed ventilation system (PCV). On V8s, remove the spark plug wires.
2. Remove the valve cover with its gasket.
3. Remove the rocker shaft bolts with their retainers.
4. To replace the rocker arms, reverse the removal procedure. Be sure to torque the rocker arm bolts to 25 ft lbs. On those engines with mechanical lifters, adjust the valves. When replacing the valve cover, use a new gasket.

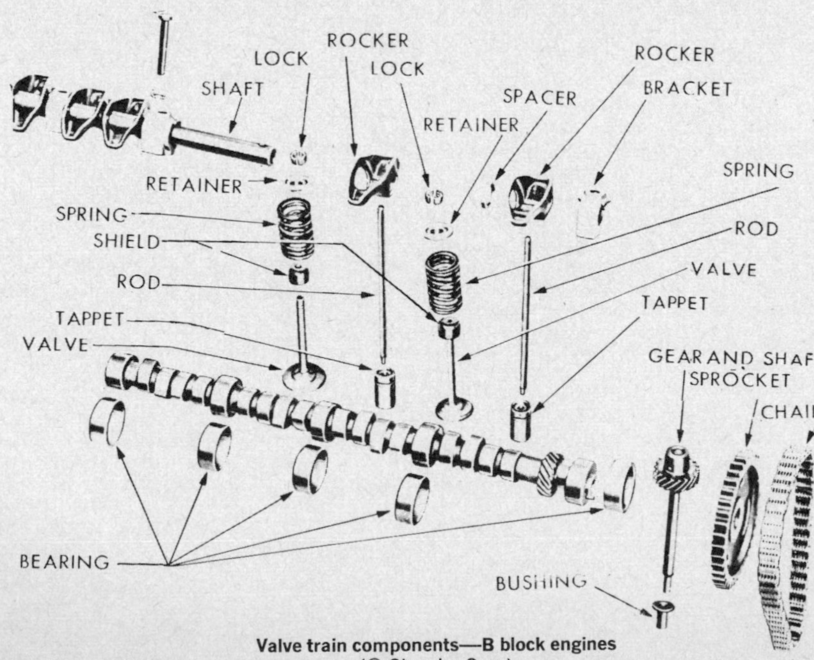

Valve train components—B block engines
(© Chrysler Corp)

NOTE: When replacing rocker arms, be sure to align the oil holes.

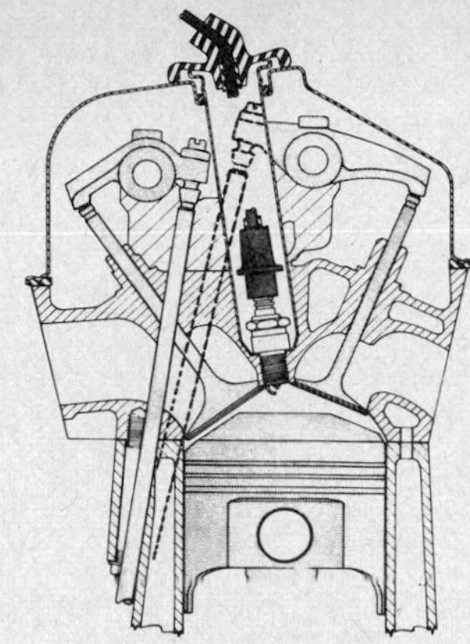

426 Hemi valve gear
(© Chrysler Corp)

426 Hemi

1. Remove air cleaner, and distributor cap with spark plug cables and secondry coil cable as an assembly.
2. Grasp secondary cables at plastic spark covers and pull covers straight out.
3. Remove spark plugs.
4. On left bank, disconnect brake lines at master cylinder, and remove cotter pin and clevis pin from linkage in back of power brake.
5. Remove four nuts attaching booster to mounting bracket and remove power brake and master cylinder assembly.
6. Remove rocker covers and gaskets.
7. Remove five bolts that attach rocker shafts assembly on each head.

NOTE: these rocker shaft assembly bolts pass through the head and into the block. Anytime rocker shaft assembly is removed, remove that head, fit a new gasket, reassemble and torque.

8. Lift off rocker shafts assembly.

Tappet Adjustment

6 Cylinder Engine

1. Start the engine and allow it to idle for 5 minutes.
2. Remove the rocker arm cover.
3. Start the engine and adjust the intake valves to have a clearance of 0.010 in. and the exhaust 0.020 in. with the engine HOT.

426 Hemi

1. Adjust ignition timing to TDC.
2. Mark crankshaft damper with chalk at TDC and 180° opposite TDC.
3. Rotate crankshaft until No. 1 cylinder is at TDC and points are just opening.
4. Adjust intake tappets on No. 2 and No. 7 cylinders and exhaust tappets on No. 4 and No. 8 cylinders. On 1968-69 engines, adjust

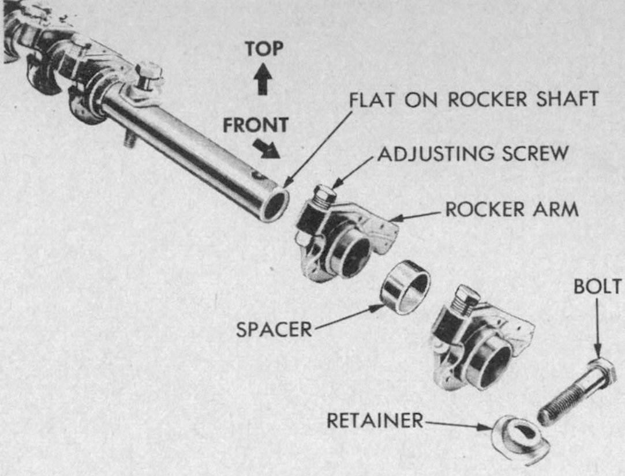

Slant six shaft and rockers
(© Chrysler Corp)

the intake valves to have a clearance of .028 in. and the exhaust valves .032 in. with the engine COLD. On 1970-71 engines, adjust the valves to have zero lash, then tighten the adjustment screw an additional 1½ turns. Tighten the locknuts to 25 ft. lbs.

5. Rotate crankshaft 180° in normal direction of rotation until points open to fire No. 4 cylinder.
10. Adjust intake tappets on No. 5 and No. 6 cylinders and exhaust tappets on No. 1 and No. 2 cylinders as in Step 4.
11. Set ignition timing to operating specifications and install rocker covers.

Valve Guides

Dodge and Plymouth engines do not have separate valve guides. They do have, however, 0.005, 0.015, and 0.030 in. oversize valves (stem diameter). To use these, ream the worn guides to the smallest oversize that will clean up wear. Always start with the smallest reamer and proceed in steps to the largest, as this maintains the concentricity of the guide with the valve seat.

As an alternate procedure, some local automotive machine shops bore out the stock guides and replace them with bronze or cast iron guides which are of stock internal dimensions.

> **Chilton's TIME SAVER**
>
> **The following is a method for replacing valve springs, oil seals or spring retainers without removing the cylinder head.**
>
> 1. **Entirely dismantle a spark plug and save the threaded shell.**
> 2. **To this shell, braze or weld an air chuck.**
> 3. **Remove the valve rocker cover. Remove the rocker arm from the affected valve.**
> 4. **Remove the spark plug from the affected cylinder.**
> 5. **Turn the crankshaft to bring the piston of this cylinder down, away from possible contact with the valve head. Sharply tap the valve retainer to loosen the valve lock.**
> 6. **Turn the crankshaft to bring the piston in this cylinder to the exact top of its compression stroke.**
> 7. **Screw in the chuck-equipped spark plug shell.**
> 8. **Hook up an air hose to the chuck and turn on the pressure (about 200 lbs.).**
> 9. **With a strong and constant supply of air holding the valve closed, compress the valve spring and remove the lock and retainer.**
> 10. **Make the necessary replacements and reassemble.**
>
> **NOTE: it is important that the operation be performed exactly as stated, in this order. The piston in the affected cylinder must be on exact top center to prevent air pressure from turning the crankshaft.**

6. Adjust intake tappets on No. 1 and No. 8 cylinders and exhaust tappets on No. 3 and No. 6 cylinders as in Step 4.
7. Rotate crankshaft 180° in normal direction of rotation until points open to fire No. 6 cylinder.
8. Adjust intake tappets on No. 3 and No. 4 cylinders and exhaust tappets on No. 5 and No. 7 cylinders as in Step 4.
9. Rotate crankshaft 180° in normal direction of rotation until points open to fire No. 7 cylinder.

Cylinder Head

Removal

Six Cylinder

1. Drain cooling system.
2. Remove air cleaner and fuel line.
3. Remove vacuum line at carburetor and distributor.
4. Disconnect accelerator linkage.
5. Disconnect spark plug wires by pulling straight out in line with plugs.
6. Disconnect heater hose and bypass hose clamp.
7. Disconnect temperature sending wire.
8. Disconnect exhaust pipe at exhaust manifold flange.
9. Remove intake and exhaust manifold as an assembly.
10. Remove closed vent system (PCV) and rocker cover.
11. Remove rocker shaft assembly.
12. Remove pushrods in sequence and save them to re-install in original bores.
13. Remove 14 head bolts.
14. Remove head.
15. Remove spark plugs and tubes.

318, 340, 360 Engines

1. Drain cooling system and disconnect battery.
2. Remove intake manifold.

NOTE: Removing the intake manifold is only necessary if both heads are to be removed. Otherwise remove the bolts from the head and loosen the bolts on the other side. Slip the head from under the manifold.

3. Remove exhaust manifolds.
4. Remove rocker shaft assemblies.
5. Remove pushrods in sequence and save them to install in their original bores.
6. Remove ten head bolts from each cylinder head.

383, 400, and 440 Engines

1. Drain cooling system and disconnect battery.
2. Remove alternator, air cleaner, and fuel line.
3. Remove intake manifold.
4. Remove tappet chamber cover.
5. Remove rocker covers and gaskets.
6. Remove exhaust manifolds.
7. Remove rocker shaft assemblies.
8. Remove pushrods in sequence and save them to install in their original bore.
9. Remove 17 head bolts from each cylinder head and remove heads.

426 Hemi—Removal and Installation

1. Remove rocker covers.
2. Remove rocker shaft assemblies.
3. Remove intake manifold.
4. Disconnect exhaust headers, and tie out of way.
5. Remove eight lower head bolts. Remove the nuts from the four

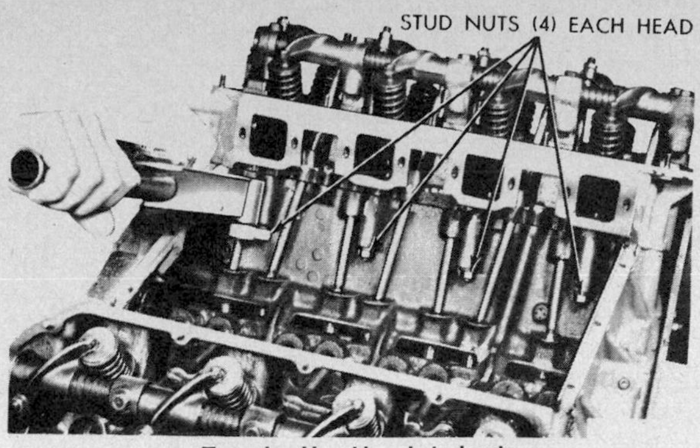

Torquing Hemi head stud nuts
(© Chrysler Corp)

cylinder studs inside of the tappet chamber.

6. Remove heads. Do not set heads on studs at any time. Because of the unusual use of rocker shaft bolts as head bolts follow installation procedure carefully.
7. Coat new head gasket with sealer and install with raised bead towards block.
8. Install cylinder heads taking care not to damage studs.
9. Install nuts on cylinder head studs and short cylinder head bolts in outer bolt holes, but do not tighten either.
10. Install pushrods in their original bores. The short rods go in the upper holes and the long rods go in the lower holes.
11. Position rocker shafts assemblies on heads and install five long head bolts in each after lining up pushrods with rockers.
12. Torque bolts and stud nuts in sequence given at front of section.
13. Adjust valve lash.
14. Install headers with new gaskets and torque to 35 ft. lbs.
15. Install new rocker cover gaskets and install rocker covers. Tighten nuts to 10 ft. lbs.
16. Gap plugs to 0.035 in. Slide spark plug tube shields over tubes. With six in. extension install spark plugs and tubes. Torque to 30 ft. lbs. Do not drop or bang spark plugs for this may change gap.
17. Install manifold.

Cylinder Head Bolt Tightening Sequence

NOTE: Torque to specifications in three stages.

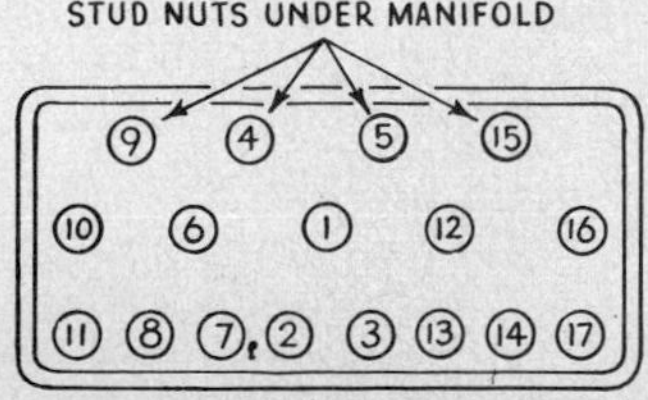

426 Hemi V8

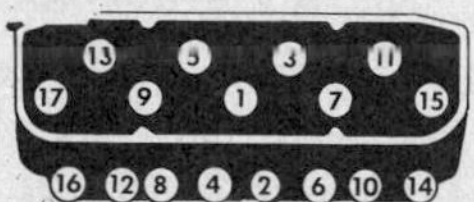

383, 400, 440 V8

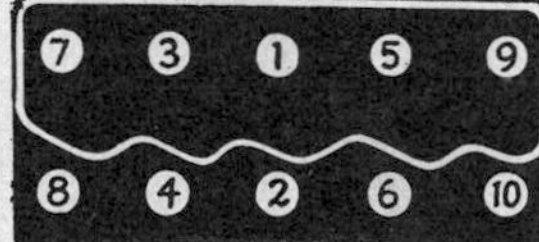

273, 318, 340 and 360 V8

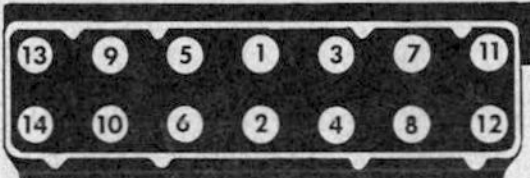

225 6-cylinder

Timing Cover, Chain, and Camshaft

Removal and Installation

NOTE: On both 6 and V8 models, it is normal to find particles of rubber collected between the seal retainer and the crankshaft oil slinger after the seal has been in service. Check the slack in the chain after completion of chain installation (procedure will be found below):

Six Cylinder Models—Removal

1. Drain the cooling system and disconnect the battery.
2. Remove radiator and fan.
3. With puller, remove vibration damper.
4. Loosen engine oil pan bolts to allow clearance, and remove timing case cover and gasket.
5. Slide crankshaft oil slinger off the front of crankshaft.
6. Remove the camshaft sprocket bolt.
7. Remove the timing chain with camshaft sprocket.

Six Cylinder Models—Installation

1. Turn crankshaft to line up the timing mark on the crankshaft sprocket with the centerline of canshaft (without the chain.)
2. Remove the camshaft sprocket and reinstall with chain.
3. Torque camshaft sprocket to 35 ft. lbs.

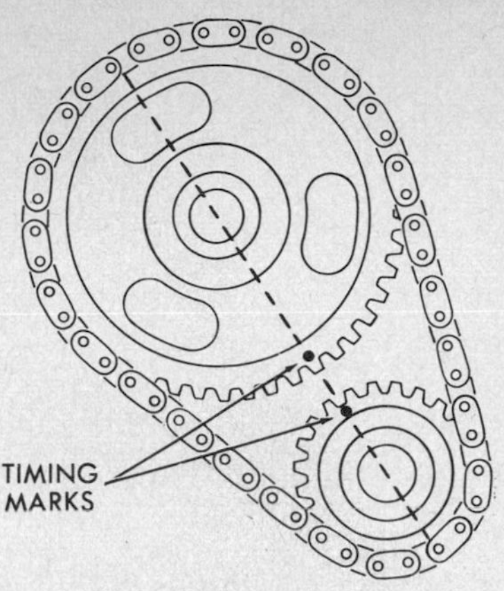

6 cylinder timing mark alignment

4. Replace oil slinger.
5. Reinstall timing case cover with new gasket and torque to 15 ft. lbs. Retighten engine oil pan to 17 ft. lbs.
6. Replace vibration damper.
7. Replace radiator and hoses.
8. Refill and bleed cooling system.

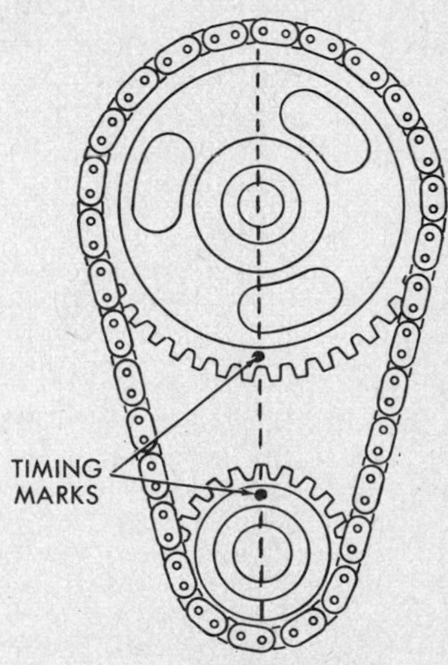

V8 timing mark alignment

V8 Models

Caution When installing a timing chain on a V-8 engine, have an assistant support the camshaft with a screwdriver to prevent the camshaft from contacting the freeze plug in the rear of the engine block. Remove the distributor and the oil pump/distributor drive gear. Position the screwdriver against the rear side of the cam gear and be careful not to damage the cam lobes.

1. Remove the timing gear cover and the crankshaft oil slinger.
2. On 318, 340, and 360 cu in. engines, remove the camshaft sprocket lockbolt, securing cup washer, and fuel pump eccentric. Remove the timing chain with the camshaft and crankshaft sprockets. On 383, 400, 440, and 426 cu in. engines, remove the camshaft sprocket lockbolt and remove the timing chain with the

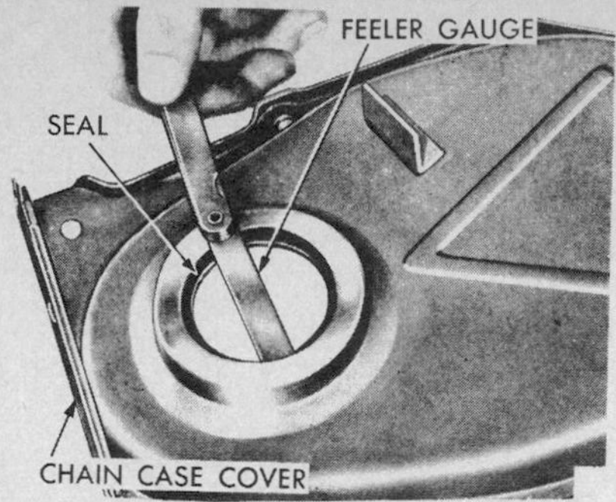

Checking seal for proper clearance (© Chrysler Corp)

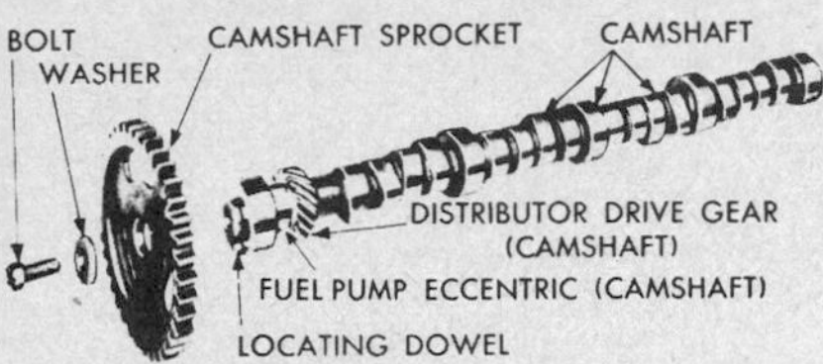

Camshaft and sprocket—318 V8 (© Chrysler Corp)

camshaft and crankshaft sprockets.

3. Place the camshaft and crankshaft sprockets on a flat surface with their timing marker on an imaginary centerline through both sprocket borers.
4. Position the timing chain around both sprockets.
5. Turn the crankshaft and camshafts to line up with the keyway location in the crankshaft sprocket and the dowel hole in the camshaft sprocket.
6. Lift the sprockets and timing chains while keeping the sprockets tight against the chain in the correct position, and slide both sprockets evenly onto their respective shafts.
7. Use a straightedge to measure the alignment of the sprocket timing marks.
8. On 318, 340, and 360 cu in. engines, install the fuel pump eccentric, cup washer, and camshaft sprocket lockbolt. Torque the lockbolt to 35 ft lbs. On 383 and 440 cu in. engines, install the washer and camshaft sprocket lockbolt. Torque the lockbolt to 35 ft lbs. Check that the rear face of the camshaft sprocket is flush with the camshaft end. On the 426 Hemi, install the washers and camshaft lockbolt. Torque the lockbolt to 40 ft lbs.

Checking Timing Chain Slack

To check timing chain slack, place a scale next to the timing chain to detect any movement in the chain. Place a torque wrench and socket on the camshaft sprocket attaching bolt. Apply either 30 ft lbs (if cylinder heads are installed on the engine) or 15 ft lbs (cylinder heads removed) of force to the bolt and rotate the bolt in the direction of crankshaft rotation to remove all slack from the chain. While applying torque to the camshaft sprocket bolt, the crankshaft should not be allowed to rotate. It may be necessary to block the crankshaft to prevent rotation. Position the scale over the edge of a timing chain link and apply an equal amount of torque in the opposite direction. If the movement of the chain exceeds 3/16 in., replace the chain.

Timing Chain Cover Seal Replacement

All Engines

1. Using a puller, separate the seal from the retainer.
2. Using fingers and a screwdriver, pull the seal from the case.
3. To install the seal place it in the case with the rubber side downward.
4. Seat the seal tightly against the cover face. There should be a maximum clearance of .0014 in. between the seal and the cover. Be careful not to over-compress the seal.

Camshaft R&R

1. Remove the timing chain and cover.
2. Remove the intake manifold.
3. Remove the rocker arm covers and rocker arm assemblies.
4. Remove the pushrods and valve lifters and keep them in order sc they can be returned to their original location in the engine.
5. Remove the distributor and distributor-oil pump driveshaft.
6. Remove the fuel pump from the engine and position it out of the way without disconnecting the fuel lines.
7. Remove the camshaft from the engine. Use care not to damage the lobes during removal.
8. Reverse above procedure to install, lubricating the cam before installation.

NOTE: when installing the camshaft and timing chain, do not allow the camshaft to contact the welch plug in the rear of the engine block as this could loosen the plug.

Pistons and Connecting Rods

When assembling pistons to connecting rods, and the assemblies to the engine, on the slant 6, be sure to locate the squirt hole to the proper side. The 1969-76 engine has the piston head notch at the front, with the oil squirt hole to the right side of the engine.

NOTE: Late in 1971, a new piston and crankshaft assembly was incorporated into the assembly of some 440 cu. in. non-high-performance engines. Because these pistons are lighter than the old style, they cannot be used as alternative replacements for the older engines. Engines equipped with this new style piston and crank assembly may be identified by the letter "C" on the information pad on the top, next to the left bank and tappet rail.

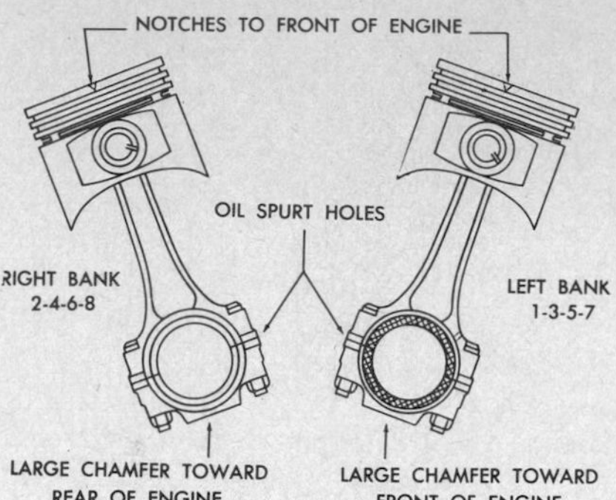

Relation of piston and rod—all V8s (© Chrysler Corp)

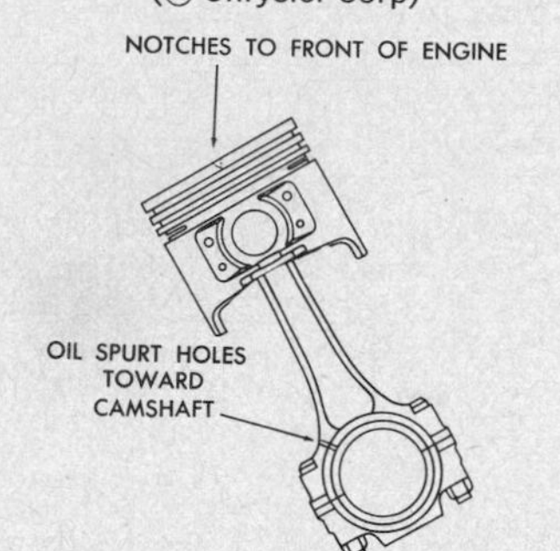

Relation of piston and rod—slant six (© Chrysler Corp)

Engine Lubrication

All Chrysler engines utilize a full-flow, replaceable-type oil filter. Six-cylinder engines utilize an externally mounted rotor-type oil pump located on the lower right side of the cylinder block. The 318, 340, and 360 V8s utilize an internally mounted oil pump. On the big-block engines, the pump is mounted externally, and is also of the rotor type.

Oil Pan Removal

Slant 6

1. Drain the radiator, disconnect the radiator hoses, disconnect the battery and remove the oil dipstick. On 1973-76 models, remove the fan shroud attaching screws, and loop the shroud rearward over the engine. Jack up the vehicle and drain the oil.
2. Remove the steering arm center link. Disconnect the idler arm ball joints.
3. Disconnect the exhaust pipe from its manifold and secure it out of the way.
4. On 1973-76 models, support the block with a jack and wooden block. Remove the front engine mounts and raise the engine 1½ to 2 inches. Take out the oil pan

attaching bolts. Rotate the engine crankshaft in order to clear the counterweights. Remove the oil pan.

5. To install the pan, reverse the removal procedure. Torque the pan bolts to 200 in. lbs.

318, 340, and 360 V8s

1. Disconnect the battery and remove the dipstick.
2. Jack up the vehicle and drain the oil. Remove the torque converter-to-engine left housing strut.
3. Remove the idler arm and steering linkage ball joints from the center link.
4. Disconnect the exhaust pipe(s) from the manifold and move it out of the way.

NOTE: On 360 HP 4 bbl engines installed in Satellites, Coronets and Chargers, raise the engine 1½ to 2 inches to clear the pan.

5. Remove the oil pan bolts and the oil pan.
6. To install the pan, be sure that the oil strainer will touch the bottom of the pan.
7. Using a new gasket, install the oil pan. Torque the bolts to 200 in. lbs. On 360 cu in. engines, be certain that the notches on the side gaskets overlap the rear seal.
8. Install the engine-to-converter housing strut.
9. From this point, reverse the removal procedure.

383, 400, 426, and 440 V8s

1. Disconnect the battery and remove the dipstick.
2. Jack up the vehicle and remove the steering linkage from the steering and idler arms.
3. Disconnect the exhaust pipes from the manifolds and move them out of the way.
4. Remove the clamp attaching the exhaust pipe to the extension and remove the exhaust pipe.
5. Drain the oil.
6. Remove the dust shield from the torque converter.
7. On 1973-76 Satellite, Coronet and Charger models, loosen the front engine mounts and raise the engine 1½ to 2 inches. Extract the oil pan bolts. Rotate the flywheel until the counterweight and connecting rods at the front of the crank are at their highest position. This will provide sufficient clearance for the pan to be lowered. Rotate the pan counterclockwise to clear the oil screen and suction pipe; lower the pan.
8. To install the pan, reverse the removal procedure. Torque to 200 in. lbs.

On 360 engines, be sure that the pan gasket is positioned as shown
(© Chrysler Corp)

Oil Pump Removal

Six Cylinder

1. Drain radiator, disconnect upper and lower hoses, and remove fan shroud.
2. Raise vehicle on hoist, support front of engine with jackstand placed under right front corner of oil pan, and remove engine mount bolts. Do not support engine at crankshaft pulley or vibration damper.
3. Raise engine approximately 1½ to 2 in.
4. Remove oil filter, oil pump attaching bolts, and pump assembly.

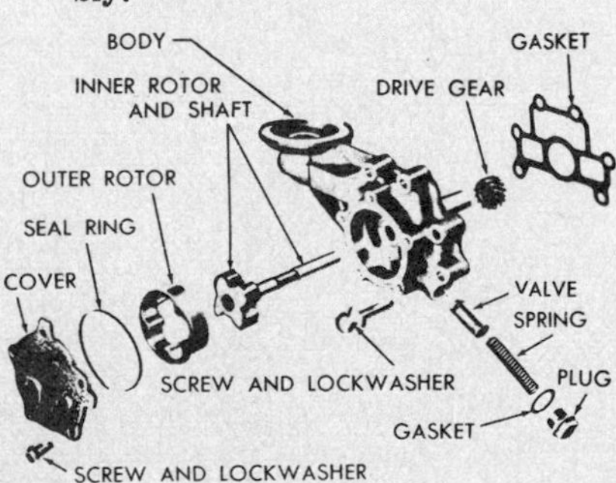

6 cylinder oil pump
(© Chrysler Corp)

318, 340 and 360 Engines

1. Remove oil pan.
2. Remove oil pump from rear main bearing cap.

383, 400, 440, and 426 Hemi Engines

1. Because the oil pump is externally mounted, it is unnecessary to remove the oil pan.
2. Remove oil pump from bottom side of engine.

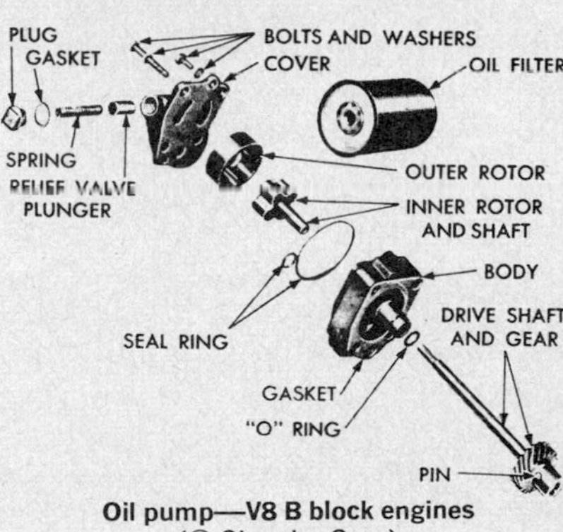

Oil pump—V8 B block engines
(© Chrysler Corp)

Rear Main Bearing Oil Seal

Service replacement seals are of split rubber type composition. This type of seal makes it possible to replace the upper half of the rear main oil seal without removing the engine from the car. When installing rubber seals, they must be replaced as a set and cannot be combined with the rope type rear main seal. The following procedure is for removing the rope type seal and replacing it with the rubber type seal.

Replacement

NOTE: on vehicles with a 426 Hemi engine, remove the transmission and vibration damper in addition to the procedure listed below.

1. Remove the oil pan.
2. Remove the rear seal retainer and the rear main bearing cap.
3. Remove the lower rope seal by prying from the side with a small screwdriver.
4. To remove the upper rope seal, drive up on either exposed end of the seal with a 6 in. piece of 3/16 in. brazing rod. When the opposite end of the seal starts to protrude from the block, have an assistant grasp it with pliers and gently pull it from the block while the opposite end is being driven.
5. Wipe crankshaft clean and lightly oil crankshaft and new seal before installing seal.
6. Loosen all main bearing caps slightly to lower the crankshaft which will ease installation.

Do not allow the crankshaft to drop enough to permit the main bearings to become displaced on the crankshaft.

7. Hold the seal tightly against the crankshaft with the thumb (with paint stripe to the rear) and install the seal in the block groove. Rotate the crankshaft if necessary while installing the seal in the groove. *Make sure the sharp edges on the block groove do not cut or nick the rear of the seal.*
8. Install lower half of seal (with paint stripe to the rear) into the lower seal retainer.
9. Install rear main bearing cap.
10. Tighten all main bearing caps to specification.

Note: make sure all main bearings are located in their proper position before tightening the main bearing caps.

CLUTCH

All models utilize a single, dry-plate type of clutch which is operated by a pedal suspended under the dash. All models are equipped with a return spring; some models have center the pressure plate and cover. On 1969-71 models, six-cylinder and light-duty V8 models utilize a non-centrifugal type of clutch while six-cylinder heavy-duty usage and most V8s use a semi-centrifugal type. All 1972 and later models use the semi-centrifugal type.

Clutch Removal

1. Remove the transmission.
2. Remove the clutch housing pan.
3. Disconnect the fork return spring from the clutch housing and release the fork.
4. Take off the spring washer fastening fork rod-to-torque shaft lever pin. Remove the pin from the rod and release the fork.
5. On those models with three-speed transmissions (if this procedure is applicable to the vehicle in question) remove the clip and the plain washer which secures the interlock rod-to-torque shaft lever and remove the washers and rod from the torque shaft.
6. Remove the sleeve assembly and the clutch release bearing from the clutch release fork.
7. Punch-mark the clutch cover and flywheel so they may be installed in their same relative positions.
8. Loosen the clutch cover attaching screws in two stages to avoid bending the cover flange.
9. Remove the clutch assembly. Be careful not to contaminate the clutch with grease or oil.

Clutch Installation

1. Lightly lubricate the drive pinion bushing in the end of the crankshaft with ½ teaspoon of long-life chassis grease. The lubricant should be inserted in the radius in back of the bushing.
2. Thoroughly clean the surfaces of the flywheel and pressure plate with fine sandpaper. All oil or grease must be removed at this time.
3. Position the clutch disc, pressure plate, and cover in the mounting position. The springs on the disc damper must be facing away from the flywheel. Do not touch the disc facing at any time. Insert a clutch disc aligning arbor or suitable substitute (such as a spare transmission drive pinion) through the disc hub and into the bushing.
4. Align the punch marks that were made at removal. Install the clutch cover bolt but do not tighten it.
5. Tighten all bolts a few turns at a time in an alternate sequence. Torque 5/16 in. bolts to 200 in. lbs and 3/8 in. bolts to 30 ft lbs. Remove the alignment tool.
6. Pack the bearing sleeve cavity with an appropriate NLGI Grade 2 EP grease. Apply the same lubricant to the release fork pads of the sleeve.
7. Insert the release bearing and sleeve assembly into the clutch housing as far forward as possible. Lightly lubricate the fork fingers and retaining spring.
8. Insert the fork fingers under the clutch sleeve retaining springs. The retaining springs on the sleeve must have lateral freedom.
9. Make sure that the groove in the seal is properly seated in the seal-opening flange in the clutch housing. Replace the pedal rod on the torque shaft lever pin and secure it with spring washer.
10. Insert the threaded end of the fork rod assembly into the opening provided in the end of the release fork rod. Replace the eye end of the fork rod on the torque shaft lever pin and lock it in place with a spring washer.
11. If applicable, install the fork return spring between the release fork and the clutch housing.
12. If applicable, install the spring and plain washer with the interlock rod in the torque shaft lever and lock it in position with a washer and clip.
13. When installing the transmission, be careful that no grease settles on the splines or pilot end of the transmission drive pinion.
14. Install the transmission and adjust clutch pedal free-play.

Clutch Linkage (Height and Free-Play) Adjustment

1. If the vehicle is equipped with a gearshift interlock rod (six-cylinder models and some light-duty V8s with three-speeds), disconnect it by loosening the rod swivel clamp screw.
2. Adjust the fork rod by rotating the self-locking nut to provide 5/32 in. free-play at the end of the fork. This adjustment will result in the proper one-inch free-play at the clutch pedal.
3. If the gearshift interlock was disconnected, refer to its adjustment procedure below.

Gearshift Interlock Adjustment

1. Disconnect the interlock pawl from the clutch rod swivel.
2. Adjust clutch pedal free-play.
3. With the first-reverse lever of the transmission in the neutral (middle detent) position, the interlock pawl should enter the slot in the first-reverse lever.
4. Loosen the swivel clamp bolt and move the swivel on the rod to enter the pawl. Install the washers with a clip. Hold the interlock pawl forward and torque the swivel clamp bolt to 100–125 in. lbs. The clutch pedal must be in the fully returned position during this adjustment. Under no circumstance should the clutch rod be pulled rearward to engage the pawl swivel.
5. Shift the clutch through all of the gear positions at least three times, clutch action should be normal.
6. Disengage the clutch and shift halfway to first or reverse gear. The clutch should be held down by the interlock within 1–2 in. of floor.

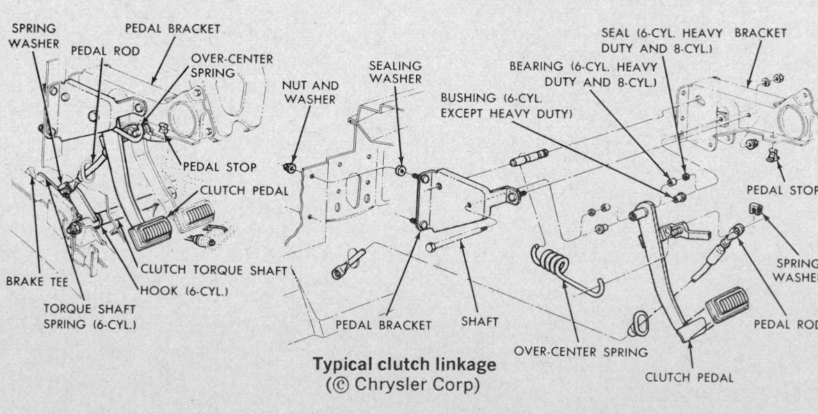

Typical clutch linkage
(© Chrysler Corp)

MANUAL TRANSMISSION

Dodge and Plymouth have used six different manual transmissions from 1969 to 1976. Six cylinder models are equipped with an A-903 three-speed from 1969 to 1972, and a similar A-250 three-speed in 1973-74. Both these units are provided with synchromesh engagement on second and third gears only. Starting 1975, all six cylinder cars use a fully synchronized A-390 three-speed as standard equipment. V8 models, as well as heavy-duty taxi and fleet usage models, are equipped with an A-745 three-speed in 1969 (sychromesh on second and third gears only), and a fully sychronized A-230 three-speed unit on all 1970 and later cars. A fully synchronized A-833 four-speed is available on all V8 models.

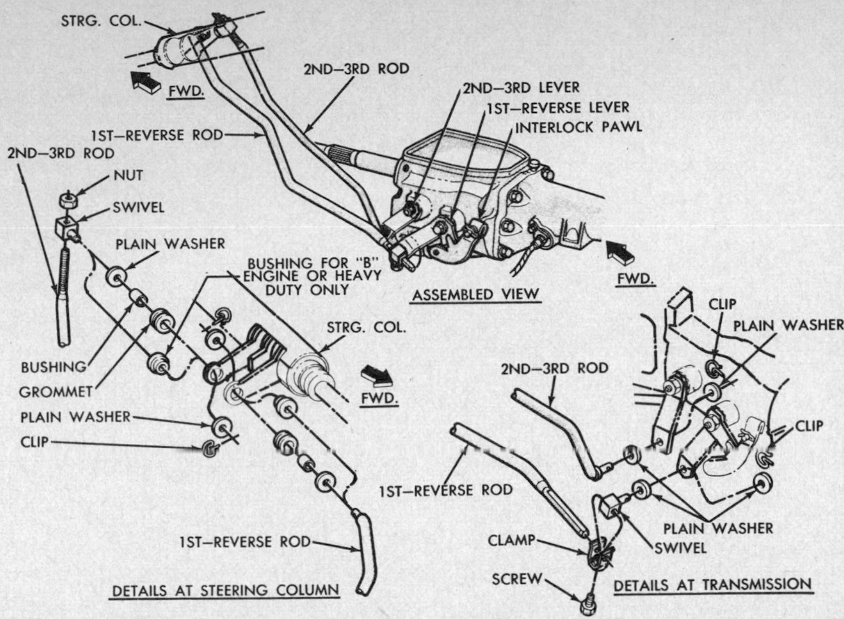

1969 Coronet, Charger, and Belvedere gearshift linkage (© Chrysler Corp)

Transmission Removal

All Top Cover 3 Speed Transmissions

1. Drain the transmission.
2. Disconnect the driveshaft at the rear universal joint. Carefully pull the shaft yoke out of the transmission.
3. Disconnect the speedometer cable and the back-up light switch.
4. Install the engine support fixture or jack up the engine about 1 in. and block it in place.
5. Disconnect the transmission extension housing from the center crossmember.
6. Support the transmission with a jack and remove the crossmember. Remove the bolts that attach the transmission to the clutch housing.
7. Slide the transmission rearward until the pinion shaft clears the clutch disc before lowering the transmission.
8. Lower the transmission and remove it.

Fully Synchromesh, Side Cover Three Speed

1. Remove shift rods from transmission levers.
2. Drain transmission fluid.
3. Disconnect drive shaft at rear universal joint. Mark both parts for reassembly.
4. Carefully pull yoke out of transmission extension.
5. Disconnect speedometer and backup lights.
6. Remove part of exhaust if it blocks transmission.
7. Raise engine slightly and block in place.
8. Support transmission with jack, and remove crossmember.
9. Remove transmission to clutch housing bolts.
10. Slide transmission to rear until drive pinion shaft clears. Clear clutch disc, lower transmission, and remove from vehicle.

Four Speed

1. Raise vehicle on a hoist and drain transmission.
2. Disconnect all shift controls from transmission levers. Remove three bolts securing shift unit to extension housing.
3. Disconnect driveshaft at rear universal joint. Carefully pull yoke out of transmission extension.
4. Disconnect speedometer cable and backup light switch leads.
5. Disconnect left exhaust pipe or dual exhausts. Disconnect parking brake cable.
6. Raise engine slightly and block in place.
7. Disconnect transmission extension from crossmember.
8. Remove crossmember.
9. Support transmission with jack. Remove clutch housing to transmission bolts.
10. Slide transmission to rear until drive pinion shaft clears clutch disc.
11. Lower transmission and remove from vehicle.

Manual Transmission Installation

Lightly grease the inner end of the pilot shaft bushing in the flywheel. In addition, grease the pinion bearing retainer pilot at the clutch release shaft.

Position the transmission so that the drive pinion is centered in the clutch housing bore. Push the transmission forward until the pinion shaft enters the clutch disc. Place the transmission in gear. Twist the output shaft until the splines align. Push the transmission forward until it is seated against the clutch housing.

Caution The transmission must not hang after the pinion is inside the clutch.

Replace the transmission coupling bolts. Torque them to 50 ft lbs. With the aid of a drift, align the crossmember bolt holes and install and torque the bolts to 40–50 ft lbs. Remove the engine support fixture and hooks. Install the extension housing and bolt in position. If so equipped, tighten the engine mount-to-crossmember bolt. Install and perform the gearshift linkage adjustment. Connect the driveshaft and universal joints. Connect the exhaust system and fill the transmission with the appropriate lubricant. Road-test vehicle.

Manual Shift Adjustments

Column Mounted Shifter

Three Speed 1969 Coronet, Charger and Belvedere

1. Remove second-third swivel from steering column lever and first-reverse swivel from transmission lever.
2. Make sure transmission shift levers are in neutral (middle detent) position.
3. Loosen lock nut and adjust second-third swivel so it will enter second-third lever at steering column while hand lever on steering column is held 12 degrees above horizontal position. Install washers and clip. Tighten swivel nut to 70 in. lbs.
4. Place screwdriver or suitable tool

between cross-over blade and second-third lever at steering column so that both lever pins are engaged by cross-over blade.

5. Adjust first reverse rod swivel by loosening clamp bolt and sliding swivel along rod so it will enter first-reverse lever at transmission. Install washers and slip. Tighten swivel bolt to 100 in. lbs.
6. Remove tool from cross-over blade at steering column and shift through all gears to check adjustment and cross over smoothness.

Three Speed 1969 Polara, Monaco, and Fury

1. Remove first-reverse rod swivel from steering column and second-third rod swivel from torque shaft lever.
2. Make sure transmission shift levers are in neutral (middle detent) position.
3. Adjust second-third rod swivel by loosening clamp bolt and sliding swivel along rod so it will enter torque shaft lever while hand lever on steering column is held 12 degrees above horizontal position. Install washers and clip. Tighten swivel clamp bolt to 100 in. lbs.
4. Place screwdriver or suitable tool between cross-over blade and second-third lever at steering column so that both lever pins are engaged by cross-over blade.
5. Adjust first-reverse rod swivel by loosening lock nut and turning swivel so it will enter first-reverse lever at steering column. Install washers and clip. Tighten swivel lock nut to 70 in. lbs.
6. Remove tool from cross-over blade at steering column and shift through all gears to check adjustment and cross-over smoothness.

Three Speed 1970-76

1. Remove both shift rod swivels from the transmission shift levers. Be sure that the transmission shift levers are in neutral (middle) position.
2. Move shift lever to line up locating slots in bottom of steering column shift housing and bearing housing. Place a suitable tool in the slot and lock the ignition switch.
3. Place a screwdriver or suitable tool between crossover blade and second-third lever at steering column so that both lever pins are engaged by cross-over blade.
4. Set first-reverse lever on transmission to reverse position (rotate clockwise).
5. Adjust first-reverse rod swivel by loosening clamp bolt and sliding swivel along rod. It should enter first-reverse lever at transmission. Install washers and clip. Tighten swivel bolt to 100 in. lbs.
6. Remove gearshift housing locating tool, unlock ignition switch, and shift column lever into neutral position.

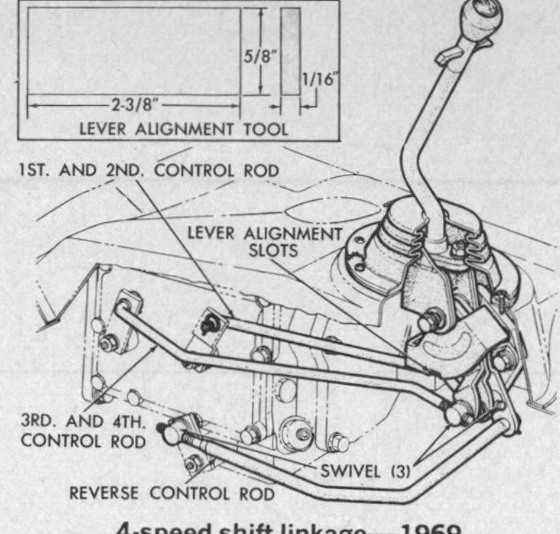

4-speed shift linkage—1969
(© Chrysler Corp)

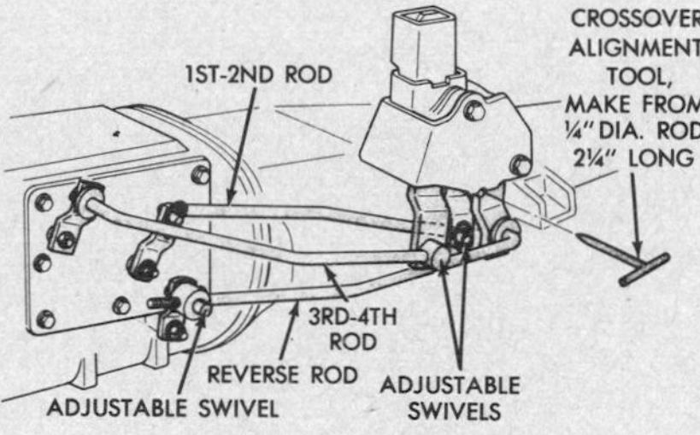

1972-76 four-speed gearshift linkage adjustment
(© Chrysler Corp)

7. Adjust second-third rod swivel by loosening clamp bolt and sliding swivel along rod so it will enter second-third lever at transmission. Install washers and clip. Tighten swivel bolt to 100 in. lbs.
8. Remove tool from crossover blade at steering column, and shift through all gears to check adjustment and cross-over smoothness.

Floor Mounted Shifter

1969-76 Three and Four Speed

1. Make up a lever aligning tool from 1/16 in. thick metal as in illustration.
2. With transmission in neutral, disconnect all control rods from the transmission levers.
3. Insert lever aligning tool through the slots in the levers and against the back plate. This locks the levers in neutral.
4. With all transmission levers in neutral, adjust the length of the control rods so they enter the transmission levers freely without rearward or forward movement.
5. Install control rod flat washers and retainers. Remove the aligning tool.
6. Check linkage for ease of shifting into all gears and for ease of crossover.

AUTOMATIC TRANSMISSION

On 1969-71 models, model indentification appears in large letters embossed on the lower side of the bell housing. While designs and servicing procedures are similar for all vehicles, internal parts are necessarily different. Therefore, when replacing parts refer to the 7-digit part number stamped on the left side of the transmission oil flange.

As a general rule, the A-904 Torqueflite is used on all 6 cylinder and light duty (318) V8 applications. The A-727 Torqueflite is used on all medium and heavy duty V8 applications.

Neutral Start Switch

The neutral switch is mounted in the transmission case on all models. When the transmission manual lever is placed in either the Park or Neutral position, a cam, which is attached to the transmission throttle lever inside the transmission, con-

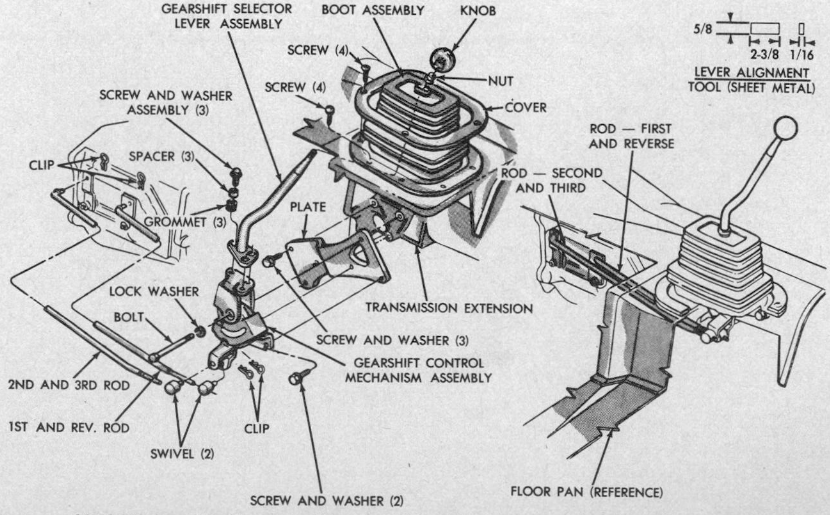

1971-75 Satellite, Coronet, Charger, 1975-76 Fury three-speed floor shift linkage
(© Chrysler Corp)

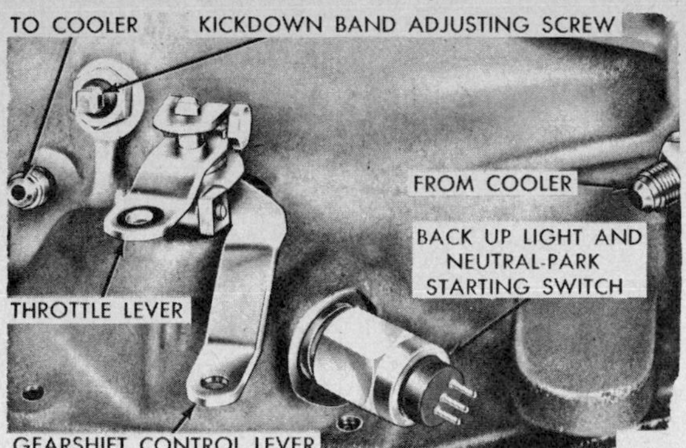

External adjustments and controls—1971-76
(© Chrysler Corp)

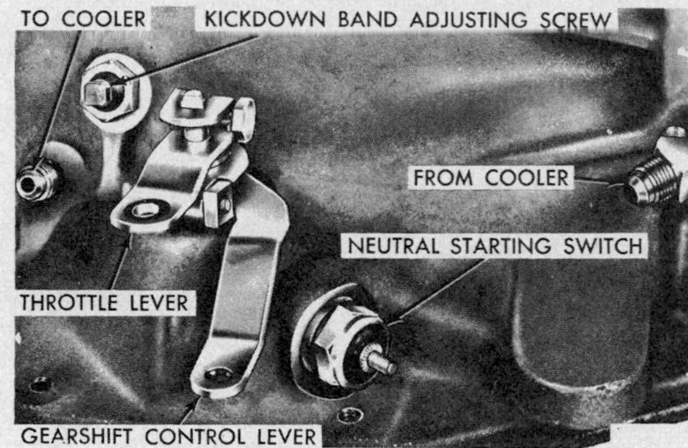

External adjustments and controls—1969-70
(© Chrysler Corp)

tacts the neutral start switch and provides a ground to complete the starter solenoid circuit. On late model Dodges and Plymouths, the back-up light switch has been incorporated into the neutral switch. The combination neutral and back-up light switch can be identified by the three electrical terminals on the rear of the switch. On this type of switch, the center terminal is for the neutral switch and the two outer terminals are for the back-up lights.

NOTE: in order for the neutral start switch to function properly, the transmission manual linkage must be properly adjusted and the actuator cam in the transmission must be centered in the neutral switch mounting hole in the transmission.

To remove the switch, remove all wiring and, with the aid of a wrench, remove the switch. Have a container of adequate size at hand to catch draining fluid. When replacing the switch, be sure to use a new seal. Torque the switch to 24 ft lbs. Replace the fluid.

Gearshift Linkage Adjustment

Column Shift 1969

1. Place gearshift selector lever in PARK position and loosen control rod swivel clamp screw a few turns.
2. Move transmission lever all the way to rear (in PARK detent).
3. With control lever on transmission in PARK position detent and selector lever in PARK position, tighten swivel clamp screw.

Console Shift 1969

1. Place gearshift selector lever in PARK position and loosen lower rod swivel clamp screw a few turns.
2. Move transmission lever all the way to rear (in PARK detent).
3. With control lever on transmission in PARK position detent, and selector lever in PARK position, tighten swivel clamp screw or adjusting lever bolt securely.

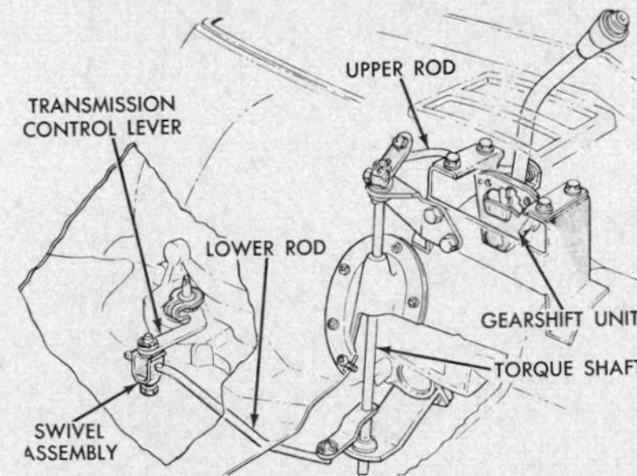

1969 Console shift linkage—intermediate and full size models (© Chrysler Corp)

Console Shift 1970-76

1. Place the gearshift control lever in the park position. Lock steering column with the ignition key.
2. Move the gearshift control lever (located on transmission, see neutral start switch illustration) fully rearward (in Park position).
3. Position the adjustable rod to the proper length and install it

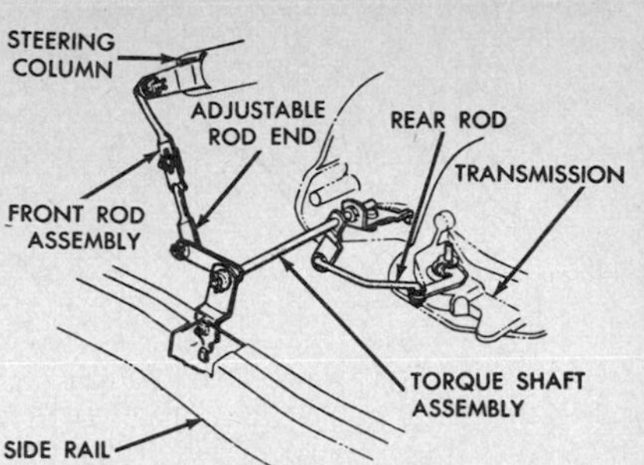

1970-72 column gearshift linkage—Fury, Polara, Monaco (© Chrysler Corp)

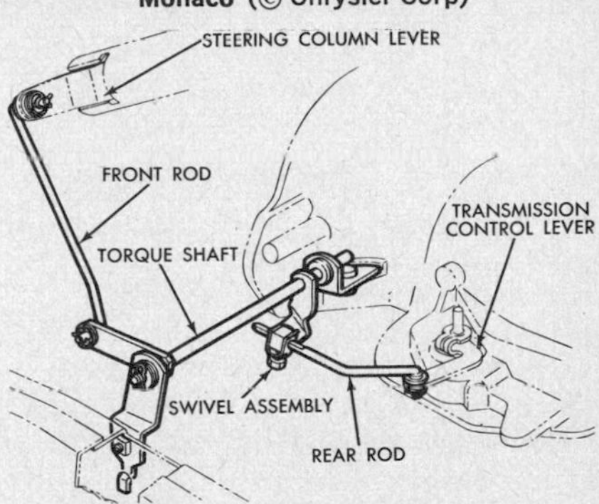

Automatic transmission column shift linkage —1969-70 Belvedere, Charger, Coronet
(© Chrysler Corp)

with no load in any direction on the linkage. Tighten the locknut.

4. Check the adjustment by determining that the shift effort is free and that the detents engage crisply. The gate stops must be positive. The position of the detents should be close enough to the gate stops in Neutral and Drive that the handlever will slide into position when placed against the gate and then released. Key starts must occur only when the transmission shift lever is in the Neutral or Park positions.

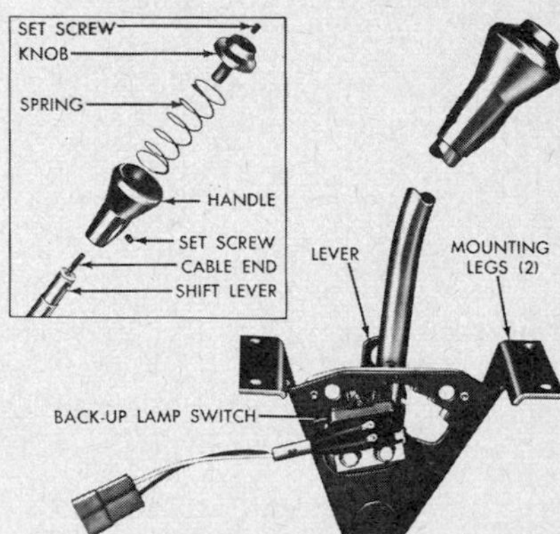

Automatic transmission console shifter
(© Chrysler Corp)

Console Shift 1970-76

1. Align the locating slots in the bottom of the shift housing and the bearing housing at the upper end of the steering column. Install the appropriate tool to hold this alignment; lock the steering column with the ignition key.
2. Move the console lever to the Park position; move the gear-

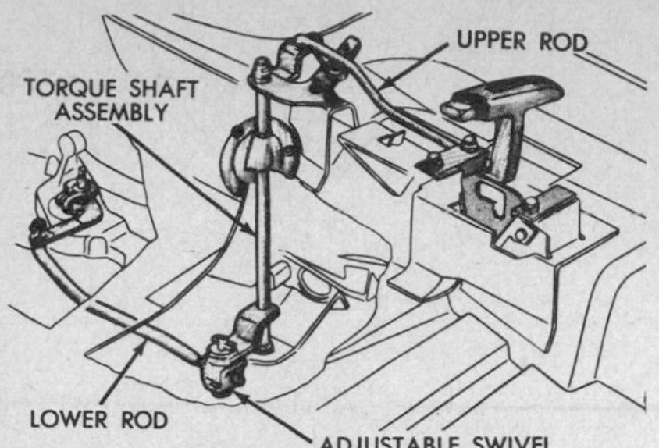

1971-76 console gearshift linkage—Satellite, Charger, Coronet (© Chrysler Corp)

shift control lever (located on the transmission, see neutral start switch illustration) fully rearward to the Park detent.

3. Position the adjustable rods to the correct length with no load, in any direction, on the rods or linkage. Tighten the locknut.
4. Check the adjustment by determining that the shift effort is free and that the detents engage crisply. The gate stops must be positive. The position of the detents should be close enough to the gate stops in Neutral and Drive so that the handlever will slide into position when it is placed against the gate and then released. In addition, key starts must occur only when the transmission shift lever is in the Neutral or Park positions.

Band Adjustments

Kick-down Band

The kick-down band adjusting screw is located on the left-hand side of the transmission case near the throttle lever shaft.

1. Loosen the locknut and back it off about five turns. Be sure that the adjusting screw is free in the case.
2. Using a torque wrench and, if necessary, suitable adaptors, torque the adjusting screw to 50 in. lbs, if an adaptor is used, or to 72 in. lbs if an adaptor is not used.
3. Back off the adjusting screw the exact number of turns specified below. Keep the screw from turning and torque the locknut to the value specified below.

Kick-down Band Adjustment Specifications

A—904	
1969-76 225 cu. in.	2 turns
1969-76 318 cu. in.	2 turns
A—727	
1969-70 six and eight-cylinder engines except Hemi	2 turns
1969-71 Hemi and 440 Six Pack	1½ turns
1971-76 225, 318, 340, 360, 383, 400, and 440 cu in.	2½ turns

Kick-down Band Adjusting Screw Locknut Torque

A-904 (1969-70)	25 ft. lbs.
A-904 (1971-72)	29 ft. lbs.
A-904 (1973-76)	35 ft. lbs
A-727 (1969-72)	29 ft. lbs.
A-727 (1973-76)	35 ft. lbs

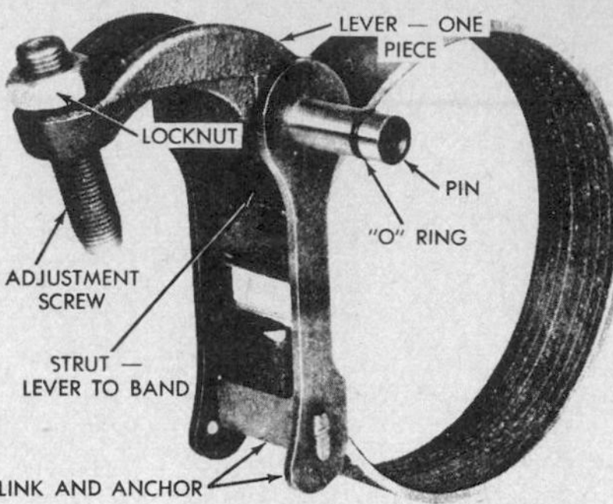

1974-76 A-904 six-cylinder low-reverse band adjustment (© Chrysler Corp)

Low and Reverse Band

The oil pan must be removed from the transmission to gain access to the First and Reverse band adjusting screw.

1. Drain the transmission and remove the oil pan.
2. Loosen the band adjusting screw locknut and back it off about five turns. Be sure that the adjusting screw turns freely in the lever.
3. Using a torque wrench and, if necessary, suitable adaptors, torque the adjusting screw to 47–50 in. lbs, if an adaptor is used, or to 72 in. lbs if an adaptor is not used. (1974-76 A-904 six cylinder applications—41 in. lbs)
4. Back off the adjusting screw the exact number of turns specified below. Keep the screw from turning and torque the locknut to the value specified below.
5. Using a new gasket, refit the oil pan and torque the pan bolts to 150 in. lbs. Refill the transmission to the proper fluid level.

First and Reverse Band Adjustment Specifications

A—904	
1969-73 6 cyl.	3¼ turns
1974-76 6 Cyl	7 turns
1969-76 318 cu in.	4 turns
A—727	
1969-76 All	2 turns

First and Reverse Band Adjusting Screw Locknut Torque

A—904 (1969-70)	20 ft lbs
A—904 (1971-72)	35 ft lbs
A—727 (1969-72)	35 ft lbs
A—904 (1974-76 Six Cyl)	30 ft lbs
A—904 and A—727 (1973-76)	30 ft lbs

Pan Removal and Installation, Fluid and Filter Change

Refer to the Barracuda section for this operation.

U-JOINTS

All Dodge and Plymouth vehicles use a cross and roller type universal joint at both the front and rear. Two basic types of driveshafts are used; a solid, tube type and a type that incorporates an internal vibration damper inside the tube itself. On certain applications, the driveshaft may be found to incorporate an inertia-type ring at the front universal joint. Servicing of all driveshafts is identical.

Cross and Roller Bearing-Type Joint Disassembly

1. To disassemble the joint, remove the four bolts that hold the two bearing assemblies to the companion flange and knock the bearings off the flange.
2. To remove the bearings from the yoke, first remove the bearing retainer lock washers or C-washers, then pressing on one of the bearings, drive the bearing in toward the center of the joint.

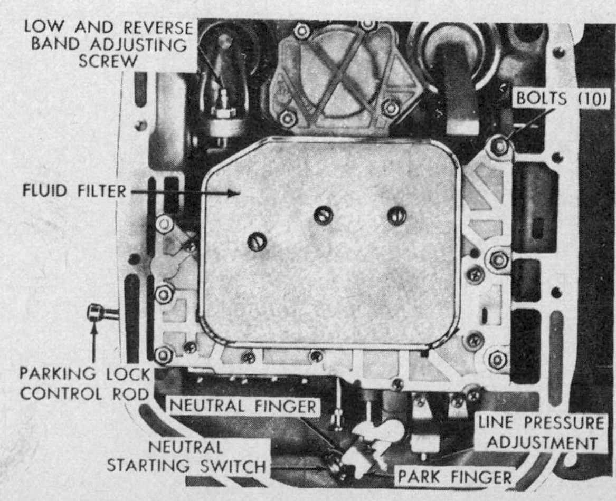

Low and reverse band adjusting screw (except 1974-76 A-904 six-cylinder applications) (© Chrysler Corp)

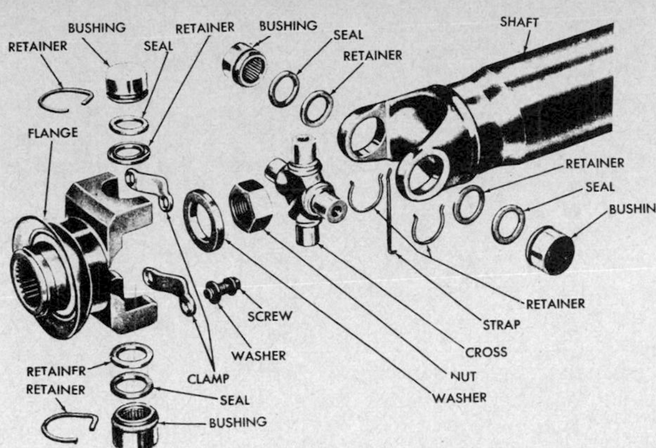

Exploded view—cross and bearing type universal joint (rear shown)
(© Chrysler Corp)

This will force the cross to push the opposite bearing out of the universal joint yoke. After it has been pushed all the way out of the yoke, pull up the cross slightly and pack some washers under it. Then press on the end of the cross from which the bearing was just removed to force the first bearing out of the yoke.

3. Perhaps the easiest way to reassemble is to start both bearing retainers into the yoke at the same time, hold the cross carefully in the fingers and squeeze both bearings in a vise or heavy C-clamp. Driving the bearings into place usually cocks the little rollers, greatly reducing the life of the bearings.
4. Reinstall the locking devices.

REAR AXLE

Five different rear axle assemblies have been used on intermediate and full-sized Dodge and Plymouth models. A 7¼ in. (ring gear diameter) unitized carrier axle is used on most 1969-70 six cylinder applications. An 8¼ in. unitized carrier axle is installed in many 1969-76 models equipped with the heavy-duty six cylinder or small block (318, 340, 360) V8 engines. An 8¾ in. removable carrier axle is used through 1974 with the heavy-duty six cylinder all small block V8's, and the 383 V8. Starting 1974, a 9¼ in. unitized carrier axle is installed in models equipped with the 400 or 440 V8. A 9¾ in. unitized carrier axle is used on 1969-72 intermediates equipped with the high-performance 426 Hemi or 440 V8s.

These axles can be visually identified as follows: The 7¼ in. axle has a 9 bolt rear cover with a filler plug. The 8¼ in. axle has a 10 bolt rear cover without a filler plug. The 8¾ in. axle has a welded rear cover. The 9¼ and 9¾ in. axles have a 10 bolt rear cover with a filler plug.

Axle Shaft, Bearing, and Seal

Removal and Installation

Because the axle shafts are slightly different from one rear axle assembly to another, individual service procedures are required for each axle shaft assembly. Two very important points to remember when servicing any rear axle assembly are:

1. Always elevate *both* rear wheels when performing any rear axle service, or when using the engine or other means to rotate the axle.
2. On those cars that are equipped with a Sure-Grip differential, you must never rotate one axle shaft without rotating the other. If it is necessary to rotate one of the axle shafts, *both* shafts must be in position and both must be rotated. Otherwise, alignment of the axle shafts will be very difficult.

7¼ In. Axle

NOTE: *Whenever this axle assembly is serviced, both the brake support plate gaskets and the inner axle shaft oil seal must be renewed.*

1. Support the rear of the car and remove the rear wheels.
2. Detach the clips which secure the brake drum to the axle shaft studs and remove the brake drum.
3. Disconnect the brake lines at the wheel cylinders and block off the lines.
4. Through the access hole in the axle shaft flange, remove the shaft retaining nuts.
5. Attach a suitable puller to the axle shaft flange and remove the axle shaft.
6. Remove the brake assembly from the axle housing.
7. Remove the axle shaft oil seal from the axle housing.

Caution Never use a torch, or other heat source as an aid in removing any axle shaft components as this will result in serious damage to the axle asembly.

8. Place the axle shaft housing retaining collar in a vise. With a chisel, cut deeply into the retaining collar at 90° intervals. Remove the bearing with a suitable puller.
9. To assemble and install the axle shaft, replace the retainer plate, bearing, and bearing retainer collar on the axle shaft, using a suitable press or puller.
10. Insert new axle shaft oil seals in the axle housing and lightly grease the outside diameter of the bearing.
11. Replace the foam gasket on the studs of the axle housing and install the brake support plate assembly on the axle housing studs. Refit the outer gasket.
12. Very carefully slide the axle shaft assembly through the oil seal and engage the splines of the differential side gear. Using a non-metallic hammer, lightly tap the end of the axle shaft to position the axle shaft bearing in the recess of the axle housing. *Install* the retainer plate over the axle housing studs and torque the securing nuts to 35 ft lbs.
13. Reconnect the brake lines to the wheel cylinders and bleed the hydraulic system.
14. Install the brake drum and retaining clips.
15. Refit the rear wheels and lower the car.

8¼ and 9¼ In. Axle—C-clip type (1972-76)

1. Raise the vehicle and remove the wheels. Drain the oil from the rear axle.
2. Remove the differential cover, if not already removed.
3. Remove the differential pinion shaft lockscrew and the differential pinion shaft.
4. Push the flanged end of the axle shaft toward the center of the vehicle and remove the C-lock from the end of the shaft.
5. Remove the axle shaft from the housing being careful not to damage the oil seal. The axle shaft may not slide easily out of the housing. If so, obtain an axle puller.
6. The axle bearing will come out with the axle and will have to be replaced at an automotive repair shop.
7. Pry the axle seal loose from the bore and tap a new seal into place.
8. Installation is the reverse of removal. Use new gaskets for reassembly.

NOTE: *Mid 1972 and later models with an 8¼ in. axle no longer used a paper gasket under the rear axle cover. Instead of the paper gasket, a bead of gel type non sticking seal-*

ant is now used in production. The sealant should be applied as follows:

1. Scrape away any remains of the paper gasket.
2. Clean the cover surface with mineral spirits. Any axle lubricant on the cover or axle housing will prevent the sealant from taking.
3. Apply a 1/16-3/32 in. bead of sealant to the clean, dry, cover flange. Apply the bead in a continuous bead along the bolt circle of the cover, looping inside the bolt holes.
4. Allow the sealant to air dry.
5. Clean the carrier gasket flange and air dry. Install the cover. If, for any reason, the cover is not installed within 20 minutes of applying the sealant, remove the sealant and start over.

8¾ and 9¾ In. Axles

NOTE: *Whenever this axle assembly is serviced, both the brake support plate gaskets and the inner shaft oil seal must be removed.*

1. Jack up the rear of the car and remove the rear wheels.
2. Detach the clips which secure the brake drum to the axle shaft studs, and remove the brake drum.
3. Through the access hole in the axle shaft flange, remove the axle shaft retaining nuts. The right-side axle shaft has a threaded adjuster in the retainer plate and a lock under one of its studs which should be removed at this time.
4. Remove the parking brake strut.
5. Attach a suitable puller to the axle shaft flange and remove the axle shaft.
6. Remove the brake assembly from the axle housing.
7. Remove the axle shaft oil seal from the axle housing.

Caution It is advisable to position some sort of a protective sleeve over the axle shaft seal surface. Never use a torch or other heat source as an aid in removing any axle shaft components as this will result in serious damage to the axle assembly.

8. Wipe the axle housing seal bore clean. Install a new axle shaft oil seal.
9. Place the axle shaft housing retaining collar in a vise. With a chisel, cut deeply into the retaining collar at 90° intervals. Remove the bearing with a suitable puller.
10. Remove the bearing roller retainer flange by cutting off the lower edge with a chisel.
11. Grind or file a section off the flange of the inner bearing cone and remove the bearing rollers.
12. Pull the bearing roller retainer down as far as possible and cut off with side cutters.
13. Remove the roller bearing cup with its protective sleeves.
14. To prevent damage to the seal journal when the bearing cone is removed, protect the journal with a single wrap of shim stock that is 0.002 in. thick and is held in place by a rubber band.
15. Using a suitable puller, remove the bearing cone. Remove the seal in the bearing retainer plate and replace it with a new seal.
16. To assemble the axle, first install the retainer plate and seal assembly on the axle shaft.
17. Grease the wheel bearings and install them.
18. Install a new axle shaft bearing cup, cone and collar on the shaft by using a suitable puller. Check the axle seal journal for imperfections and if necessary, polish with no. 600 crocus cloth.
19. Thoroughly clean the axle housing flange face and brake support. Install a new rubber asbestos gasket onto the axle housing studs. Next, install the brake support plate assembly on the left side of the axle housing.
20. Lightly grease the outside edge of the bearing cup. Install the bearing cup in the bearing bore.
21. Replace the foam gasket on the studs of the left-side axle housing and very carefully slide the axle shaft assembly through the oil seal and engage the splines of the differential side gear.
22. Using a non-metallic hammer, lightly tap the end of the axle shaft to position the axle shaft bearing in the recess of the axle housing. Install the recess of the housing studs and, starting with the bottom securing nut, torque the nuts to 30-35 ft lbs.
23. Repeat step 19 for the right-side axle housing.
24. At the right side of the axle housing, back off the threaded adjuster until the inner face of the adjuster is flush with the inner face of the retainer plate. Very carefully slide the axle shaft assembly through the oil seal and engage the splines of the differential side gear. Repeat step 22.
25. Mount a dial indicator on the left brake support. Turn the adjuster clockwise until both wheel bearings are seated and there is zero end-play in the axle shafts. Back off the adjuster about four notches to establish an end-play of 0.008-0.018 in. on 8¾ in axles and 0.008-0.012 for the 9¾ in.
26. Lightly tap the end of the left axle shaft with a non-metallic hammer. This will seat the right wheel bearing cup against the adjuster. Turn the axle shaft several times so that a true end-play reading is obtained.
27. Remove one retainer plate nut and install the adjuster lock. If the lock tab does not mate with the notch in the adjuster, turn the adjuster slightly until it does. Refit the nut and torque it to 30–35 ft lbs.
28. Recheck the axle shaft end-play. If it is not within 0.008-0.018 in., repeat the adjustment. When the adjustment is complete, remove the dial indicator.
29. Install the parking brake strut. Refit the brake drum and retaining clips.

JACKING, HOISTING

Jack car at front lower control arm and at rear under axle housing.

To lift at frame, use adapters so that contact will be made at points shown. Lifting pads must extend beyond sides of supporting structure.

FRONT SUSPENSION

All Chrysler vehicles utilize a torsion-bar front suspension. The front torsion bar attachments are a part of the lower control arms; the rear fastenings are incorporated into the engine rear support crossmember. Compression-type lower ball joints are located in the steering arms on intermediates through 1972 and full size cars through 1973. 1973 Satellite, Charger and Coronet models use screw-in type lower ball joints. All 1974 and later models utilize serviceable lower ball joints which are *pressed* into the lower control arms. When servicing the front suspension, it should be kept in mind that rubber bushings must not be lubricated at

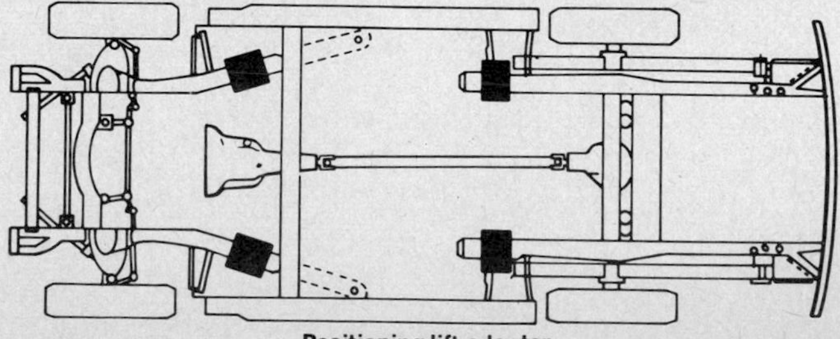

Positioning lift adapter

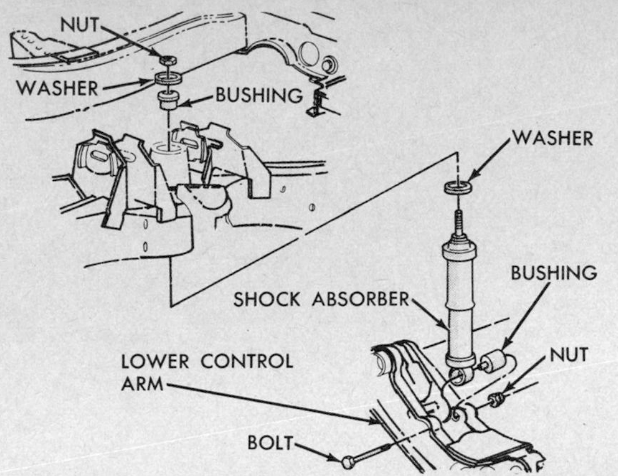

Front shock absorber replacement—1969-73 Fury, Polara, Monaco; 1973-76 Satellite, Coronet, Charger, 1975-76 Fury
(© Chrysler Corp)

TORQUE SPECIFICATION

A	200 IN. LB.	D	125 FT. LB.
B	52 FT. LB.	E	145 FT. LB.
C	85 FT. LB.	F	160 FT. LB.
		G	95 FT. LB.

1973-76 Satellite, Coronet, Charger, 1975-76 Fury lower control arm assemblies (© Chrysler Corp)

any time. Any front suspension adjustments or servicing that is required on any part that contains rubber should be tightened with the suspension at the proper height and with the full vehicle weight on the point in question (if possible).

Front Shock Absorbers

Removal and Installation

1. Remove the washer and nut from the upper end of the shock absorber. Be sure to note the positions of all small parts.
2. Jack the vehicle until the wheels are off the floor. Remove the shock absorber lower attaching bolt.
3. Fully compress the shock absorber by pulling upward. Pull the shock firmly and remove it from the vehicle.
4. Check the shock absorber bushings, if they are worn or scored, replace them. Remove and install the bushings with a press or a drift and hammer. To ease installation, lubricate with water. Do not use oil to ease installation.
5. To install the shock, compress it fully. Insert the mount through the upper bushing, replace the retainer and nut, and torque it to 25 ft lbs. Be sure that all of the retainers are installed with the concave side in contact with the rubber.
6. Position and align the lower mount of the shock absorber. Install the bolt (on some models it must be installed from the rear) with a nut and finger-tighten it. Lower the vehicle and torque the bolt to 50 ft lbs with the full weight of the vehicle on the wheels.

Lower Ball Joint

Inspection

1. Raise the front of the vehicle by placing a floor jack under the lower control arm. Position the lifting point of the jack as close to the wheel as possible.
2. Have an assistant raise and lower the tire and wheel assembly and observe any movement at the lower ball joint.
3. On intermediate models through 1972 and full size models through 1973, replace the ball joint if the axial (up and down) play exceeds 0.070 in. On 1973 and later Satellite, Charger and Coronet models, as well as 1974 and later Fury, Polara and Monaco models, replace the joint if axial play exceeds 0.020 in.

Removal

Intermediates through 1972, Full Size through 1973

The lower ball joint is integral with the steering arm and is not serviced separately.

1. Raise the vehicle on a hoist so the front suspension will drop to the downward limit of its travel.
2. Place a jack stand under the lower control arm.
3. Lower the vehicle onto the jack stand.
4. Remove the tire, wheel, and brake drum from the vehicle as an assembly. If equipped with disc brakes, remove the tire and wheel, remove the brake pads, and remove the caliper from the steering knuckle and position it out of the way with the brake line attached. Remove the rotor from the spindle.
5. Remove the two lower and upper bolts that attach the steering arm-ball joint assembly to the brake assembly mounting plate and move the backing plate out of the way.

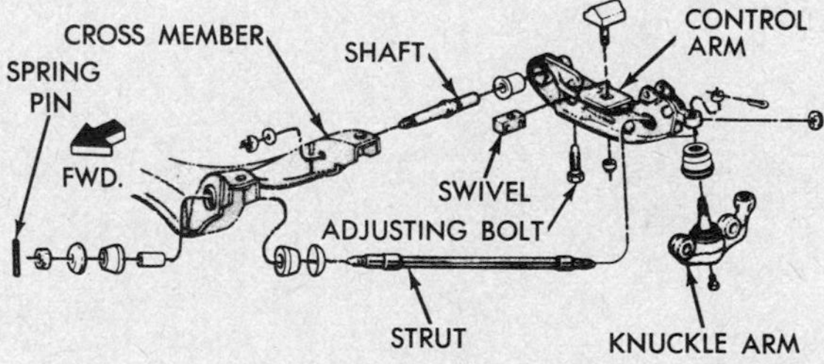

Lower control arm—Belvedere, Satellite, Coronet and Charger
(© Chrysler Corp)

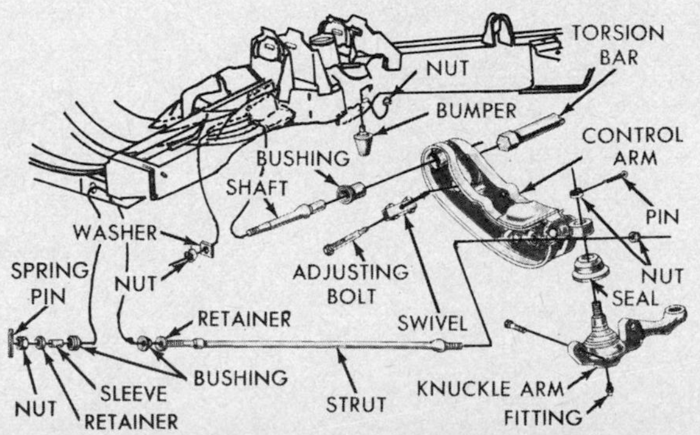

Lower control arm—Fury, Polara and Monaco
(© Chrysler Corp)

6. Using a suitable tool, disconnect the tie-rod end from the steering arm.
7. Remove the ball joint stud retaining nut and cotter pin.
8. Using a suitable tool, separate and remove the ball joint from the lower control arm.

Installation

Intermediates through 1972, Full Size through 1973

1. Position ball joint-steering arm assembly on the steering knuckle and install the two retaining bolts.
2. Insert the ball joint stud in the lower control arm and install the retaining nut and cotter pin.
3. Position the tie-rod end in the steering knuckle and install the retaining nut and cotter pin.
4. Place a load on the torsion bar by turning the adjusting bolt in a clockwise direction. *Note: Loading the torsion bar is only necessary if it was removed.*
5. Install the tire, wheel and brake drum assembly. If equipped with disc brakes, install the rotor, caliper, brake pads and tire and wheel assembly.
6. Lower vehicle and install upper control arm rebound bumper if so equipped and if it was removed.
7. Check and adjust front suspension height as required.

Removal

All 1974-76 Models and 1973 Intermediates

Lower ball joints on these models may be serviced separately.

Removing ball joint stud—1973-76 intermediates and 1974-76 full size models (© Chrysler Corp)

1. Place the ignition switch in the "Off" or "Unlocked" position.
2. Remove the rebound bumper.
3. Raise the vehicle on a hoist so that the front suspension drops to the downward limit of its travel. Position jackstands beneath the front frame for extra support.
4. Remove the wheel and tire assembly.
5. Remove the caliper from its mounts and tie it up out of the way so that there is no strain on the flexible brake hose.
6. Remove the hub and rotor assembly, splash shield, lower shock absorber mounting nut, retainer and insulator.
7. Off-load the torsion bars by rotating the adjusting bolts counterclockwise.
8. Remove the upper and lower ball joint stud cotter pins and nuts. Using a ball joint press tool, slide the tool over the upper stud until the tool rests on the steering knuckle.
9. Then turn the threaded portion of the tool so that it locks snugly against the lower stud. Tighten the tool enough to load the lower ball joint stud, and then strike the steering knuckle arm with a hammer to loosen the stud. Under no circumstances should you attempt to force the stud from the knuckle using the tool alone.
10. On all 1974-76 models, use a press to press the ball joint out of the lower control arm. On 1973 intermediates, unscrew the ball joint from the lower control arm.

Installation

All 1974-76 Models and 1973 Intermediates

1. On all 1974-76 models, use a ball joint press to press the new ball joint into the lower control arm. On 1973 intermediates, screw in the ball joint and tighten to 125 ft lbs.
2. Place a new seal over the ball joint (as necessary). Using an adapter tool, press the retainer portion of the seal down over the ball joint housing until it locks into position.
3. Insert the ball joint stud through the opening in the knuckle arm and install the stud retaining nuts. Tighten to 85 ft lbs. Install the cotter pins and lubricate the ball joint.
4. Load the torsion bar by rotating the adjusting bolt clockwise.
5. Install the shock absorber retaining nut, retainer and insulator, splash shield, hub and rotor assembly, and brake caliper. Install the wheel and tire assembly.
6. Adjust the front wheel bearings.
7. Remove the jackstands and lower the car. Install the rebound bumper. Adjust the front suspension height.

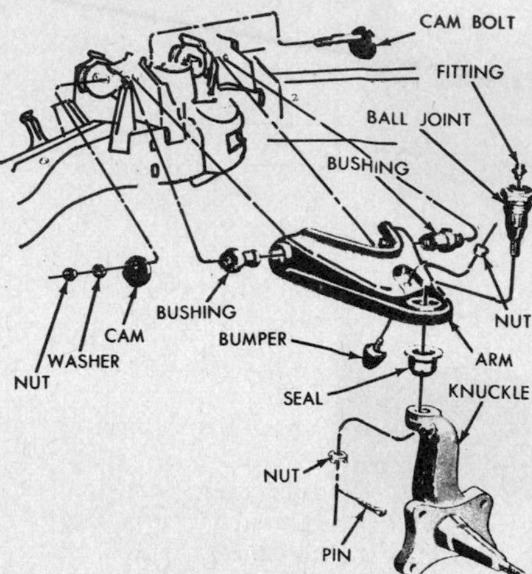

Upper control arm—1969-73 Fury, Polara, and Monaco (© Chrysler Corp)

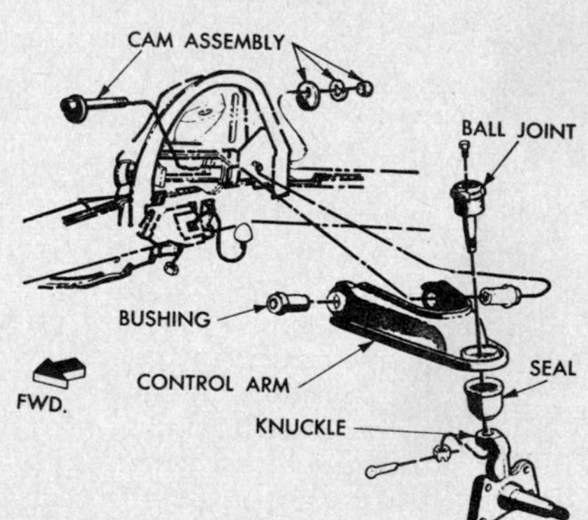

Upper control arm 1969-72 Belvedere, Satellite, Coronet and Charger (© Chrysler Corp)

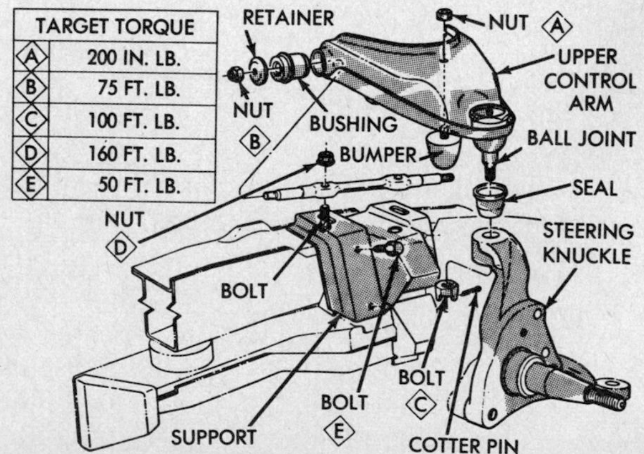

1973-76 Satellite, Coronet, Charger, 1975-76 Fury upper control arm assemblies (© Chrysler Corp)

Upper Ball Joint

Replacement

1. Raise the vehicle by placing a floor jack under the lower control arm. Place the lifting point of the jack as close as possible to the wheel.
2. Remove the wheel, tire and drum as an assembly. On models with disc brakes, remove the tire and wheel, remove the disc brake pads, remove the disc brake caliper from the steering knuckle and position the caliper out of the way with the brake line attached. Remove the brake rotor from the steering knuckle.
3. Remove the nut that attaches the upper ball joint to the steering knuckle and, using a suitable tool, loosen the ball joint stud from the steering knuckle.
4. Unscrew the upper ball joint from the upper control arm and remove it from the vehicle.
5. Position new ball joint on the upper control arm, screw the ball joint into the control arm until it bottoms on the control arm and tighten the ball joint to a minimum of 125 ft lbs.

NOTE: when installing a ball joint, make certain the ball joint threads engage those of the upper control arm squarely if the original control arm is being used.

6. Position a new seal on the ball joint stud and install the seal in the ball joint making sure the seal is fully seated on the ball joint housing.
7. Position ball joint stud in the steering knuckle and install the retaining nut.
8. Lubricate ball joint and, if replacement ball joint is equipped with knock-off type grease fitting, break off that portion of the fitting over which the lubrication gun was installed.
9. If equipped with disc brakes, install the rotor, caliper and brake pads. Install the tire and wheel.
10. Lower the vehicle and adjust front suspension height as required.

Front Suspension Height

1969-74

1. Check to make sure that the vehicle is fully loaded with fuel, that the tire pressures are correct, and that the vehicle is positioned on a level floor.
2. Clean road dirt from the bottom of the steering knuckle arm assemblies. Clean the lowest area of the height-adjusting blades directly below the center of the lower control arm inner pivot assembly.
3. Bounce vehicle at least five times and release on a downward motion.

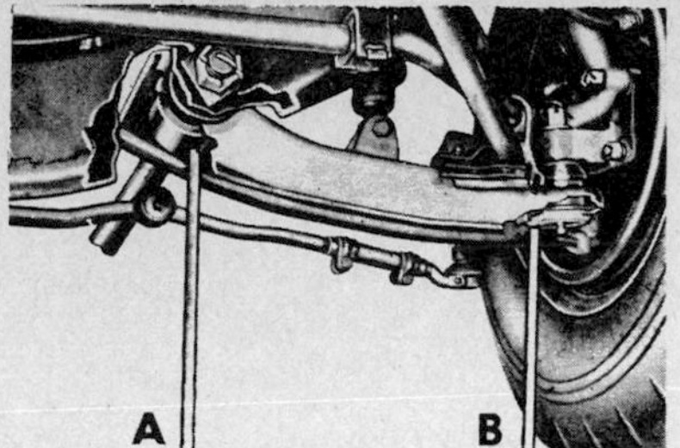

Checking front suspension height at ball joint and lower control arm
(© Chrysler Corp)

4. Check the distance from the bottom of one adjusting blade to the floor (refer to illustration measurement A) and from the lowest point of the steering knuckle arm at the centerline on the same side of the vehicle (measurement B). Be sure to measure only one side at a time.
5. The difference in measurement between A and B is the front suspension height.
6. Refer to the specifications and make adjustments as necessary. Do this by rotating the torsion bar adjusting bolt clockwise to increase the height and counterclockwise to decrease the height. After each adjustment, bounce the vehicle as was done previously before checking the height. Both sides must be measured even though only one side may have been adjusted. Be sure that height does not vary more than ⅛ in. from side to side.

1975-76

1. Jounce the car several times, releasing it on the downward motion.
2. Measure the distance between the lowest point of the lower control arm torsion bar anchor (at a point one inch forward of the rear face of the anchor) and the ground. This is measurement "A".
3. Compare measurement "A" with the figure given under "Front End Height" in the "wheel Alignment Specifications" chart at the beginning of this car section.
4. Adjust, if necessary, by rotating the torsion bar adjusting bolt clockwise to increase front end height, or rotating counterclockwise to decrease the height.
5. Check the adjustment on both sides. Maximum variation of front end height is ⅛ in.

Torsion Bars

Removal and Installation

NOTE: Torsion bars are not interchangable side-for-side. Do not mix them.

1. Remove the upper control arm rebound bumper (if so equipped).
2. If the vehicle is jacked on a hoist, be sure that it is lifted on the body in such a manner that the front suspension is under no load. If the vehicle is to be lifted with a floor jack, at the center crossmember, first place a support between the jack and the crossmember. The front suspension must be under no load.
3. Remove all load from the torsion bars by rotating the anchor adjusting bolts counterclockwise.
4. At the torsion bar rear anchor, remove the lockring.
5. Using an appropriate tool, remove the torsion bar from its attachments.

Caution The torsion bar may be under some load so be careful when removing it. Heat must never be used to ease bar removal.

6. It may be necessary to move the rear balloon seal out of the way to ease removal of the torsion bar. Slide the torsion out through the rear of the anchor. Be careful not to damage the balloon seal at removal.

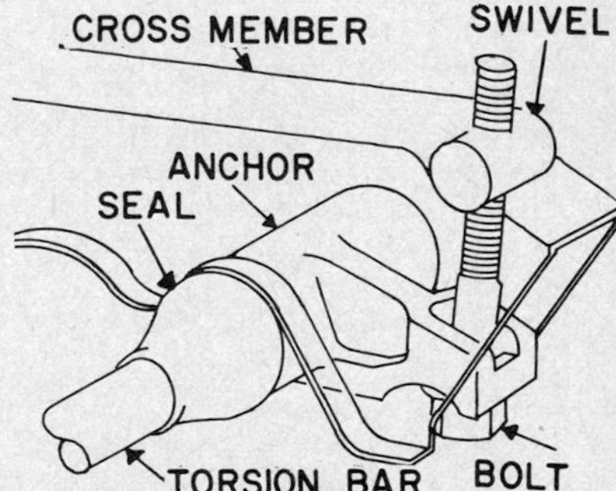

Torsion bar adjustment bolt
(© Chrysler Corp)

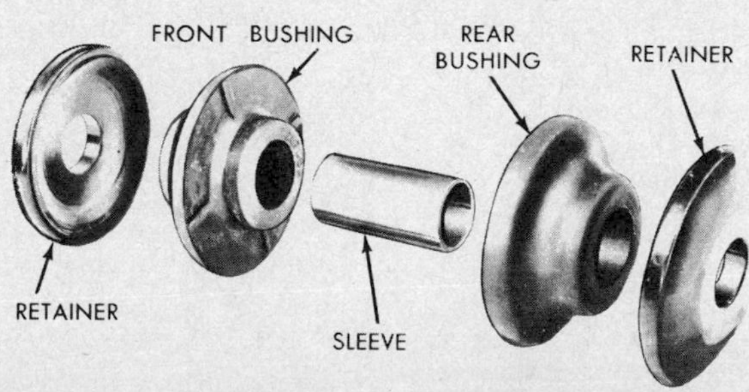

Crossmember strut bushing
(© Chrysler Corp)

7. Inspect the torsion bar and lightly dress all sharp edges. Coat the area of repair with a rust preventive. Thoroughly clean the entire bar and lubricate it lightly to ease installation.
8. To begin replacement, slide the torsion bar into the rear anchor. Slide the balloon (if so equipped) seal over the bar with the cupped end toward the rear of the bar.
9. Lightly grease the hex ends of the bar. Insert the torsion bar through the hex opening of the lower control arm. Replace the lockring in the rear anchor.
10. Fully pack the ring opening in the rear anchor with grease.
11. Install the balloon seal on the rear anchor so the seal lip engages with the anchor groove.
12. Rotate the adjusting bolt clockwise to load the torsion bar. Lower the vehicle and adjust the front suspension height. Replace the upper control arm rebound bumper and torque it to 16 ft lbs.

Lower Control Arm and Steering Knuckle

Removal and Installation

1. Remove the wheel/tire and drum (or disc) as an assembly.
2. Remove the shock absorber at the bottom attachment and swing it up out of the way. Remove the torsion from its attachment at the lower control arm.
3. Using a puller, remove the tie rod end from the steering knuckle arm. Be careful not to damage the seal during this operation. At this point, it is a good idea to match-mark the wheel alignment cam to act as an aid in assembly.
4. Remove the sway bar link from the lower control arm (or strut attaching straps). Remove the knuckle arm-to-brake support bolts and remove the knuckle arm. Position the brake support assembly to one side.
5. With a puller, remove the ball joint stud from the lower control arm. Be sure not to damage the seal during this operation.
6. At the forward end of the crossmember, remove the strut spring, pin, nut, and retainer, taking note of their relative positions. Remove the nut and washer from the lower control arm shaft.
7. Using a non-metallic object, tap the end of the lower control arm shaft to aid in shaft removal from the crossmember. Take off the lower control arm, strut, and shaft as an assembly.
8. To begin installation (on some models), insert a new strut bushing into the crossmember with a twisting motion. Use water as a lubricant to aid installation—grease or oil must not be used. Position the strut bushing inner retainer on the strut and install the control arm, strut, and shaft assembly. Replace the shaft bushing retainer and finger-tighten the nut.
9. Replace the lower control arm shaft washer and finger-tighten the nut.
10. Replace the lower ball joint stud into the lower control arm and torque it to specifications. Install the cotter pin.
11. Install the brake support to the steering knuckle and replace the two upper bolts with nuts. Finger-tighten them only.
12. Install the steering knuckle on the steering knuckle arm and insert the two lower bolts with nuts. Torque the upper bolts to 55 ft lbs and the lower bolts to 120 ft lbs. Inspect the tie rod end seal and replace it if necessary. Install the tie rod end to the steering knuckle arm and torque it to 40 ft lbs. At this point, install the cotter pin.
13. Connect the shock absorber and finger-tighten it.
14. Replace the torsion bar assembly.
15. Install the wheel/tire/brake assembly.
16. Lower the vehicle. Adjust the front suspension height. Torque the strut nut at the crossmember of 52 ft lbs and insert the strut pin. Torque the lower control arm shaft nut to specifications and complete the installation of the shock absorber.
17. Align the front end as necessary.

Wheel Bearing Adjustment

1. The wheel must be rotated while the bearing adjusting nut is tightened. 1969-72 models should be adjusted to 90 in. lbs, and 1973-76 models to 240-300 in. lbs.
2. Place the lock over the nut so that one pair of slots align with the cotter pin hole.
3. Back the nut and lock assembly off one slot. Install the cotter pin. This adjustment should yield zero to .003 in. end-play.
4. Clean the grease cap. Coat, but do not fill, the cap with grease. Install it on the hub.
5. Lower car and road test.

REAR SUSPENSION

All Dodge and Plymouth models utilize rear springs of the semi-elliptical leaf type. They are engineered to operate with little or no camber under conditions of small loads (including no load). Heavy-duty springs are offered as an option on all models. They increase the stability of the vehicle under conditions of heavy load. All vehicles equipped with leaf springs are constructed with zinc interleaves between the normal leaves. They have the purpose of reducing spring corrosion and lengthening spring life.

Shock absorbers used on Chrysler vehicles are not used to support vehicle load. Their sole purpose is to control ride motion.

Rear Shock Absorbers

Removal and Installation

1. Jack up the vehicle under the axle assembly in such a manner as to relieve the load from the shock absorbers.
2. Remove the nut attaching the shock to the spring mounting plate stud and withdraw bolt.
3. At the upper mount, remove shock attaching bolt and the shock.
4. To install the shock, position it so that the upper bolt may be inserted. Hand-tighten (only) the shock absorber bolt.
5. Align the shock with the spring mounting plate stud and install the bolt and nut. Hand-tighten only.
6. Lower the vehicle to the ground. Torque the lower nut to 50 ft lbs and the upper nut to 70 ft lbs.

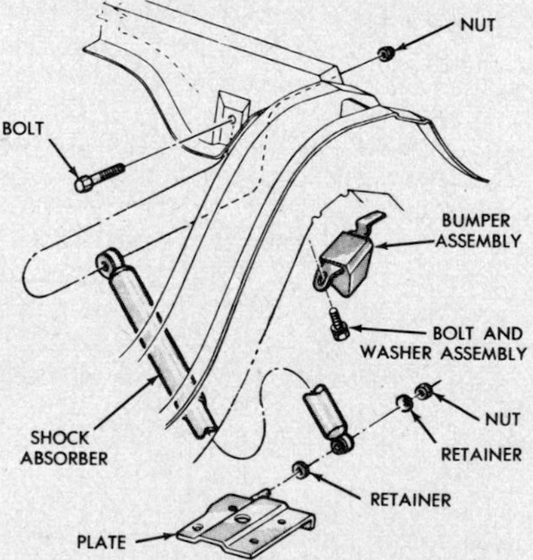

Rear shock absorber installation—Satellite, Coronet, Charger, and 1975-76 Fury
(© Chrysler Corp.)

Rear Springs

Removal and Installation

1. Jack up the vehicle and remove the wheels. Position the jack stands under the axle in such a manner so as to relieve the weight on the rear springs.
2. Disconnect the rear shock absorbers at the bottom attaching bolts. Lower the axle assembly to allow the rear springs to hang free.

Caution 1974 and later full-size models have preloaded rear springs. A special spring stretcher (tool no. C-4211) must be installed before releasing either end of the spring. Do not try to remove the spring without the stretcher; its sudden release could cause serious injury.

3. Remove the U-bolt nuts and withdraw the bolts and spring plates. Remove the nuts securing the front spring hanger to the body mounting bracket.
4. Remove the rear spring hanger bolts and allow the spring to drop enough to allow the front spring hanger bolts to be removed.
5. Remove the front pivot bolt from the front spring hanger.
6. Remove the shackle nuts and remove the shackle from the rear spring.
7. To begin installation, assemble the shackle and bushings in the rear of the spring and hanger. Start the shackle bolt nuts. Do not lubricate the rubber bushings to ease installation. Do not tighten the bolt nut.
8. Install the front spring hanger to the front spring eye and insert the pivot bolt and nut. Do not tighten them.
9. Install the rear spring hanger to the body bracket and torque the bolts to 30 ft lbs.
10. With the aid of a helper, raise the spring and insert the bolts in the spring hanger mounting bracket holes. Install the nuts and torque them to 30 ft lbs.
11. Position the axle assembly so it is correctly aligned with the spring center bolt.
12. Position the center bolt over the lower spring plate. Insert the U-bolt and nut. Torque the bolt to 45 ft lbs and connect the shock absorbers.
13. Lower the vehicle. Torque the pivot bolts to 85 ft lbs. Torque the shackle nuts to 30 ft lbs.
14. After this operation, drive the vehicle. Return to the shop, check the front suspension height, and make adjustments as necessary.

BRAKES

Information on brake adjustments, lining replacement, disc brakes, bleeding procedure, master and wheel cylinder overhaul can be found in the Unit Repair Section.

A tandem-type master cylinder is used on all models. This design divides the brake hydraulic system into two independent and hydraulically separated halves.

Details and repair procedures on this tandem system may be found in the Unit Repair Section.

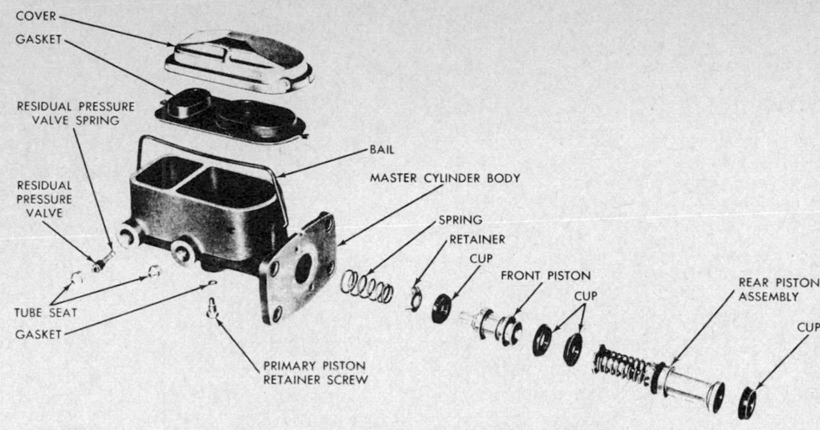

Dual type master cylinder used with disc brakes
(© Chrysler Corp)

Master Cylinder R & R

1. Disconnect front and rear brake tubes from master cylinder.

NOTE: on drum brake master cylinders, residual pressure valves will keep cylinder from draining, but front brake outlet (rearmost) must be plugged on disc brake master cylinders.

2. Remove nuts that attach master cylinder to cowl panel or power brake unit.
3. On manual drum brakes, disconnect pedal pushrod from brake pedal.
4. Slide master cylinder straight out from cowl or power brake unit.
5. Install the master cylinder in the reverse order of removal. Bleed the brake system after installation is finished.

Power Brake

Various types of power brakes are used. One is the vacuum-type, using a master cylinder and pedal linkage of the reaction type. A vacuum cylinder is combined with a conventional master cylinder.

Another is a tandem-diaphragm-type, consisting of a self-contained vacuum hydraulic power unit.

The basic elements are vacuum power chamber with a front and rear shell, a center plate, front and rear diaphragm, pushrod and diaphragm return spring.

A control valve integral with the diaphragms regulates the amount of application.

Removal and Installation

1. Remove the nuts that attach the master cylinder to the brake booster and position the master cylinder out of the way without disconnecting the lines. Use care not to kink the brake lines.
2. Disconnect the vacuum hose from the brake booster.
3. Working under the dash, remove the nut and bolt that attach the brake booster pushrod to the brake pedal. On linkage-type brake boosters, remove the lower pivot retaining bolt.
4. Remove the four brake booster attaching nuts and washers.
5. Remove the booster assembly from the vehicle.
6. Reverse the above procedure to install. The power brake unit is serviced as an assembly only. Do not discard the old unit; it is needed as a trade-in on a rebuilt booster assembly.

Parking Brake Adjustment

NOTE: Adjust the service brakes properly before adjusting the parking brake.

1. Release parking brake lever and loosen cable adjusting nut to ensure cable is slack. Before loosening cable adjusting nut, clean threads with wire brush and lubricate.
2. Tighten cable adjusting nut until a slight drag is felt while rotating wheel. Loosen cable enough to allow both wheels to rotate freely. Back off cable adjusting nut two full turns.
3. Apply and release parking brake several times. Test to see that rear wheels rotate freely without grabbing.

Disc Brakes

Disc brakes have been available on front wheels of some models. These include both fixed and floating caliper types from several different manufacturers. Sliding caliper disc brakes were introduced on all models starting in 1974. Complete service procedures are covered in the Unit Repair Section.

STEERING

A worm and recirculating ball-type steering gear is used with the manual steering system.

The worm shaft is supported at each end by ball-type thrust bearings.

The sector shaft includes an integral sector gear which meshes with helical grooves on the worm shaft ball nut.

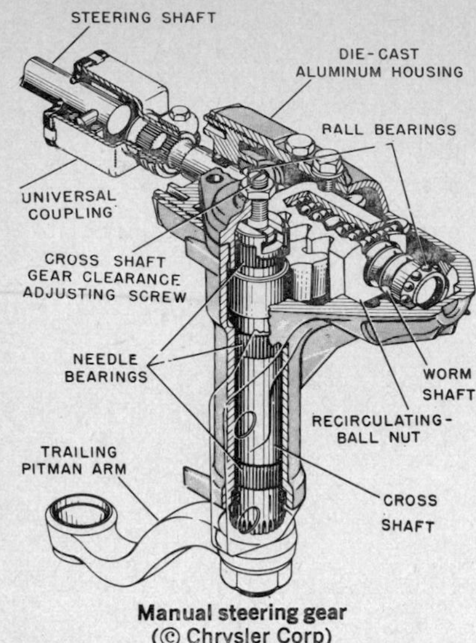

Manual steering gear
(© Chrysler Corp)

The sector shaft is supported, and rotates, in two needle bearings in the housing and one in the housing cover.

Constant-Control power steering is an option on all models. Hydraulic power is provided by a vane-type, belt-driven pump. A double-groove pump pulley is used.

Some power steering pumps were equipped by the factory with oil coolers. These were used on vehicles with high-performance engines and/or special axle ratios.

Turn Signal Switch R & R

1969

1. Remove the steering wheel.
2. If applicable, remove the horn wires and/or turn a signal lever.
3. Tie a piece of string to the turn signal wires. Remove the turn signal switch while holding the other end of the string to prevent the wires from falling inside the steering column.
4. To install the switch, reverse the removal procedure.

1970-76

1. Remove the steering wheel.
2. Remove the three screws which fasten the turn signal switch to the steering column.
3. Remove the turn signal lever.
4. Unfasten the moulded wiring connector from the turn signal switch and withdraw the switch.
5. Installation is the reverse of removal.

Power Steering Pump

Removal and Installation

NOTE: Before beginning removal, take careful note of the exact hose routing. Hoses must be routed and installed in the exact same manner as they were removed. Read the entire procdure before beginning pump service.

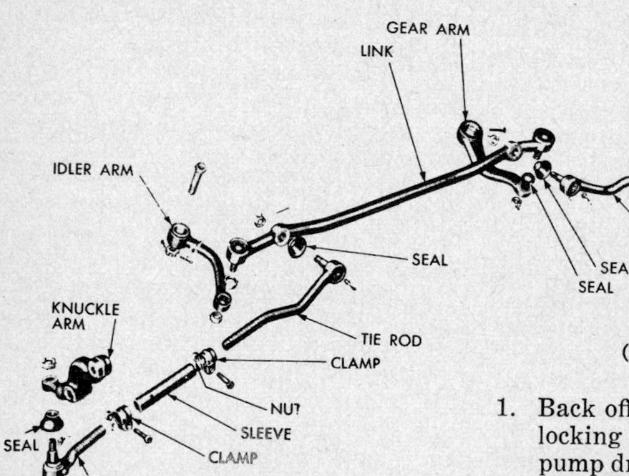

Steering linkage
(© Chrysler Corp)

1. Back off the pump mounting and locking bolts and remove the pump drive belt.
2. Disconnect all hoses at the pump.
3. Remove the pump bolts and the pump with the bracket.
4. To install a pump, place it in position and install the mounting bolts.
5. Install the pump drive belt and adjust it to specifications. Torque the mounting bolts to 25–30 ft lbs.
6. Connect the pressure and return hoses. On the 1.06 cu in. pump, install a new pressure hose O-ring.
7. Fill the pump with power steering fluid.
8. Turn on the motor and rotate the steering wheel from stop to stop at least ten times. This will tend to bleed the system. Check the pump oil level and fill as required.
9. The torque of the pump-end hose fitting is 24 ft. lbs. The gear end fitting torque is 160 in. lbs. Be certain that hoses are at least two inches from exhaust manifolds and are not kinked or twisted.

Steering Wheel

Removal and Installation

NOTE: Be careful when removing the steering wheel from those vehicles equipped with collapsible columns. A sharp blow or excessive pressure on the column could cause it to collapse; this renders it unfit for further use.

1. Disconnect the battery.
2. Remove the center, padded assembly with a screwdriver.
3. Remove the large center nut. Using a puller, pull the steering wheel from the column.
4. To install the wheel, reverse the removal procedure. Torque the steering wheel nut to 28 ft lbs.

INSTRUMENT PANEL

Ignition Switch Replacement

1969

1. Disconnect the push-on connector from the rear of the ignition switch, directly behind the ignition lock cylinder.
2. Remove the bezel nut that attaches the ignition switch to the rear of the instrument panel.
3. Remove the ignition switch.
4. Position a new ignition switch under the instrument panel and install and tighten the bezel nut.
5. Connect the wiring to the rear of the switch.

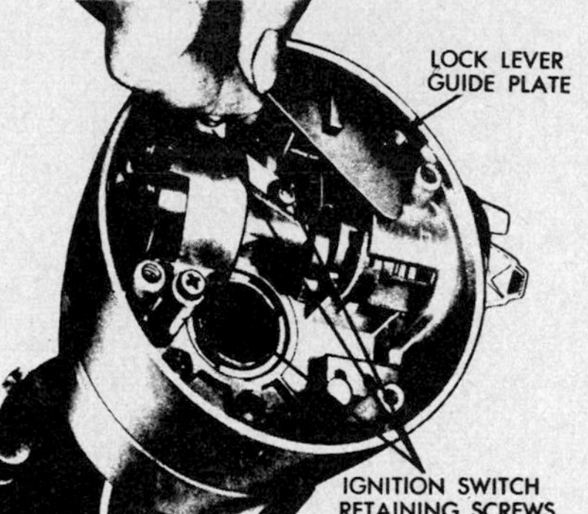

Removing lock lever guide plate—standard column (© Chrysler Corp)

Ignition Lock Cylinder Replacement

1969

1. Insert the ignition key into the lock cylinder.
2. Insert a piece of stiff wire into the small hole in the front face of the cylinder and apply pressure to the wire.
3. Turn the ignition key counterclockwise toward the ACC position.

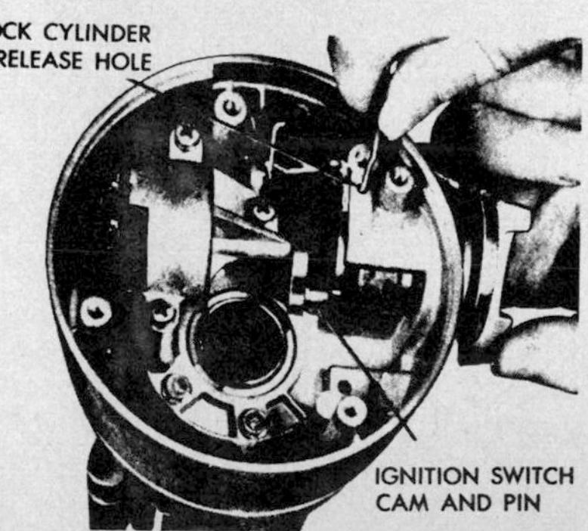

Removing ignition lock cylinder—standard column (© Chrysler Corp)

4. Pull the lock cylinder and key from the instrument panel.
5. Insert a new lock cylinder into the instrument panel and it will lock itself in place.

Ignition Switch and/or Ignition Lock Cylinder Replacement

1970-76 Standard Steering Column

1. Disconnect the negative battery cable. Remove the steering wheel.
2. Remove the screw that attaches the turn signal lever to the steering column.
3. Remove the three screws that attach the upper bearing retainer to the turn signal switch.
4. Pull the turn signal switch as far upward as possible.
5. Using snap-ring pliers, remove the upper bearing housing snap-ring from the steering shaft.
6. Remove the screw that attaches the ignition key light assembly to the upper bearing housing.
7. Using care not to damage any components, pry the upper bearing housing off the steering shaft by lifting upward on alternate sides of the bearing housing with screwdrivers.
8. Lift upward as far as possible on the steering shaft lock plate and place a screwdriver or other object under it to hold it in the raised position. If this operation does not provide adequate working room under the lock plate, it will be necessary to press out the pin that attaches the lock plate to the steering shaft and remove the lock plate from the steering shaft. If the ignition switch is being replaced, the lock plate must be removed.
9. Using an offset screwdriver, remove the two screws that attach the lock lever guide plate to the steering column.
10. With the ignition lock cylinder in the "Lock" position and the ignition key removed, insert a stiff wire into the lock cylinder release hole in the steering column. Push in on the wire to release the spring-loaded lock retainer and pull the lock cylinder out of the steering column.
11. If the ignition switch is being replaced, remove the two screws that attach the ignition key buzzer switch to the steering column and the three screws that attach the ignition switch to the steering column. Lift off the ignition switch out of the housing.
12. Reverse the above procedure for installation.

1970-76 Tilt Steering Column

1. Disconnect the negative battery cable.
2. Remove the steering wheel.
3. Remove the three attaching screws and remove the shaft lock cover.
4. Remove the screws that attach the tilt control lever and the turn signal lever to the steering column and then remove the levers.
5. Push in the hazard warning knob and unscrew the knob from the turn signal switch. Remove the ignition key lamp assembly.
6. Using a suitable tool, depress the lock plate to gain access to the lock plate retaining snap-ring. Remove the snap-ring from the steering shaft.
7. Remove the lock plate, cancelling cam, and spring.
8. Remove the three turn signal switch attaching screws, place the shift lever in the Low (L) position, and pull the switch and wires as far upward as possible.
9. With the ignition lock cylinder in the "Lock" position, insert a small screwdriver into the lock release slot in the housing cover.
10. Press down with the screwdriver to release the spring latch at the bottom of the slot and pull the lock cylinder from the housing. The following steps are for ignition switch replacement only.
11. Remove the three screws that attach the upper steering column housing to the steering column and remove the housing.
12. Install the column tilt control lever and move the column to the full "Up" position.
13. Insert a screwdriver into the slot

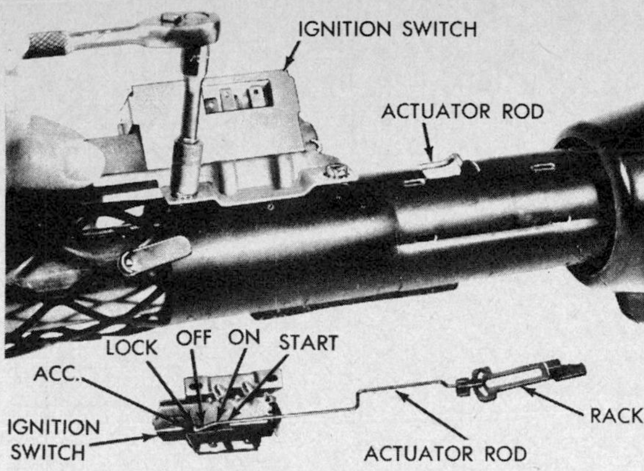

Removing ignition switch—tilt column
(© Chrysler Corp)

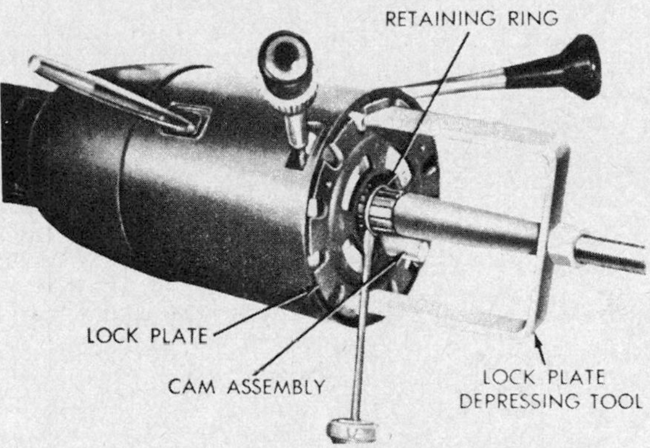

Removing lock plate retaining ring—tilt column
(© Chrysler Corp)

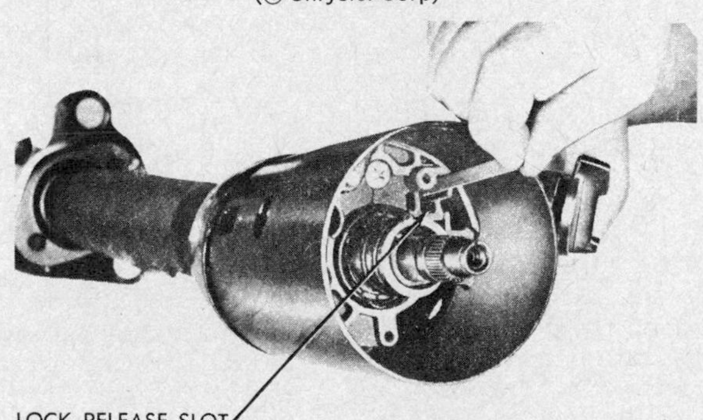

Removing ignition lock cylinder—tilt column
(© Chrysler Corp)

in the spring retainer and press the retainer in approximately 3/16 in. Turn the retainer approximately 1/8 turn to the left until the ears align with the grooves in the housing. Remove the spring retainer, spring, and guide.

14. Push the steering shaft inward to enable removal of the inner race and seat. Remove the race and seat.
15. Make sure the ignition switch is in the "Lock" position, then remove the wire connector from the ignition switch and remove the screws that attach the ignition switch to the outside of the steering column.
16. Lift the ignition switch from the column and twist it to disengage the switch actuating rod from the rack. Remove the switch.
17. To install the ignition lock cylinder, insert the cylinder into the housing with the cylinder in the "Lock" position and the key *removed.*
18. Move the cylinder into the housing until it contacts the switch actuator. Move the switch actuator rod up and down to align the parts. When the parts are aligned, the cylinder will move inward and lock into place. The following steps are for ignition switch installation only.
19. With the ignition switch in the "Lock" position, insert the actuating rod into the steering column.
20. Twist the switch and rod assembly as required to engage the actuating rod with the rack. Make sure the ignition lock cylinder is in the "Lock" position.
21. Install the ignition switch mounting screws but do not tighten them.
22. Move the ignition switch downward, away from the steering wheel, and tighten the switch mounting screws. Make sure that the ignition switch has not moved out of the lock detent.
23. Attach the switch wiring connector.

Headlight Switch R & R

1969-70 Belvedere, Satellite and Coronet; 1969-71 Fury, Polara and Monaco

1. Disconnect the multiple connector from the rear of the headlight switch. On models with air conditioning, it may be necessary to disconnect the ducts to gain access to the wiring.
2. Remove the two screws that attach the headlight switch to the dash and remove the headlight switch from the vehicle.
3. Reverse above procedure to install.

1969-70 Charger

1. Disconnect the negative battery cable.
2. Remove the instrument cluster. See "Instrument Cluster Removal and Replacement."
3. Disconnect the wiring connector from the rear of the headlight switch.
4. Disconnect the two vacuum hoses from the heater switch to gain access to the headlight switch mounting screws.
5. Remove the headlight switch mounting screws and remove the switch.
6. Reverse the above procedure to install the new switch.

1971-76 Coronet, Charger, Satellite, and 1975-76 Fury; 1972-74 Fury, 1972-76 Polara, Monaco, and 1975-76 Gran Fury

1. Disconnect the negative battery cable.
2. On cars equipped with air conditioning, disconnect the air duct from the spot cooler on the instrument panel.
3. Reach up under the instrument panel and depress the headlight switch control knob release button on the headlight switch.
4. While depressing the release button, pull the headlight switch control knob and shaft from the front of the instrument panel.
5. Disconnect the electrical leads from the rear of the switch.
6. Using a spanner wrench, remove the spanner nut that attaches the front of the headlight switch to the front of the instrument panel.
7. Remove the headlight switch from the rear of the instrument panel.
8. Reverse the above procedure to install the new switch.

WINDSHIELD WIPERS

Motor R & R

1969-70 Fury, Polara and Monaco

1. Remove the windshield wiper arm and blade assemblies. On 1969-70 models insert a 0.090 in. pin in the hole in the base of the wiper arm to release the assemblies from the pivots.
2. Remove the windshield lower moulding.
3. Remove the cowl grille.
4. Remove the nut that attaches the wiper link to the wiper motor drive pin or crank and disconnect the link from the motor.
5. Disconnect the wiper motor wiring at the multiple connector.
6. Remove the nuts that attach the wiper motor to the cowl panel and remove the motor through the cowl grille opening.

1969-70 Belvedere, Satellite, Coronet and Charger and All 1971-76 with Non-Concealed Wipers

1. Disconnect the negative battery cable.

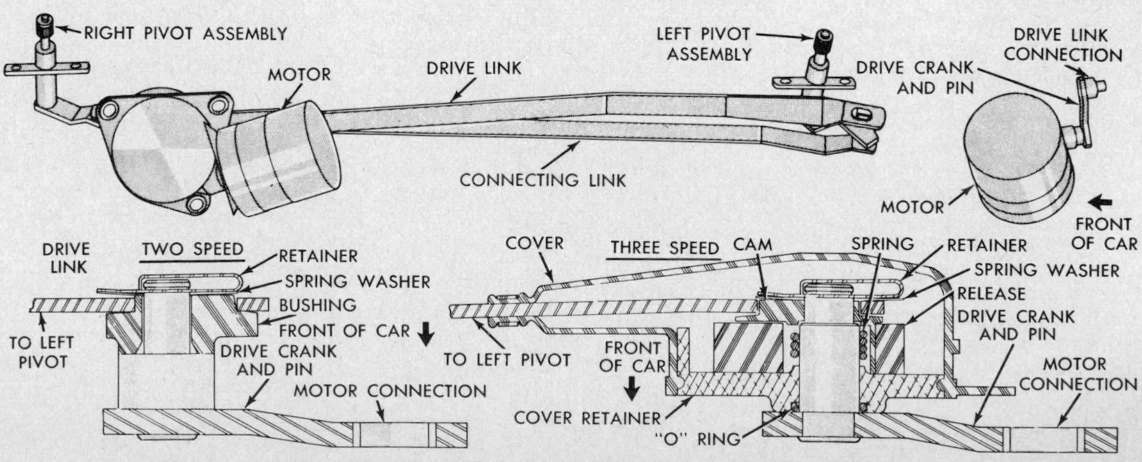

Windshield wiper system—Fury, Polara and Monaco (© Chrysler Corp)

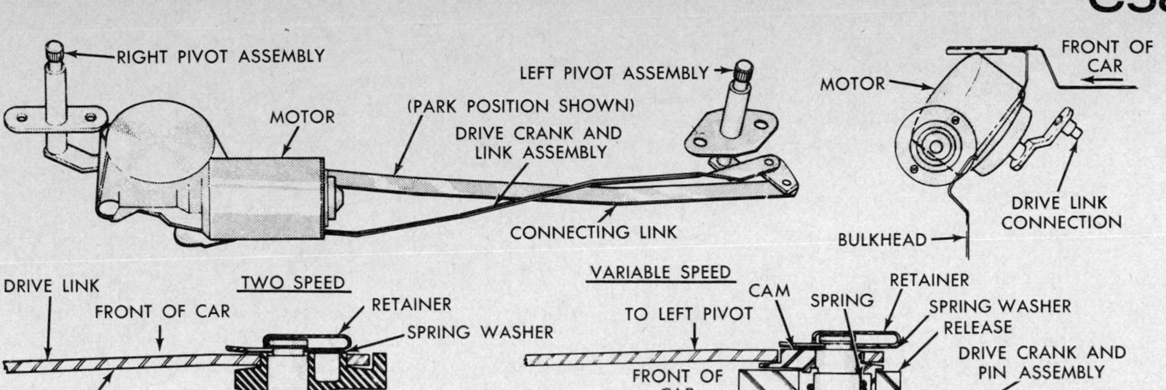

Windshield wiper system—Satellite, Belvedere, Coronet and Charger (© Chrysler Corp)

2. Disconnect the wiper motor wiring at the multiple connector.
3. On models without air conditioning, working under the dash, remove the nut that attaches the drive link to the wiper motor and disconnect the drive link from the motor. Remove the nuts that attach the wiper motor to the studs in the cowl panel and remove the motor from the vehicle.
4. Remove the wiper motor mounting nuts. Work the motor off the mounting studs far enough to gain access to the nut that attaches the drive link to the wiper motor. *Do not force or pry the wiper motor off the mounting studs as this could damage the wiper drive link.* Using a ½ in. open end wrench, remove the motor crank arm nut. Remove the arm from the wiper motor and remove the motor from the vehicle.

1971-76 All Models with Concealed Wipers

1. Disconnect the negative battery cable.
2. Lift the latch on each wiper arm and remove the arms and blades as an assembly.
3. Remove the cowl screen.
4. Remove the drive crank retaining nut and drive crank.
5. Disconnect the lead wires from the wiper motor.
6. Remove the three wiper motor mounting bolts and remove the motor from the vehicle.
7. Reverse the above procedure to install. When installing the wiper arms and blades, make sure the wiper motor is in the Park position.

Linkage and Pivots

1969-70 Belvedere, Satellite, Coronet and Charger

If car is air-conditioned, remove glove compartment to gain access to right pivot retainer.

1. Disconnect the negative battery cable. Remove the wiper arm and blade assemblies.
2. Remove the link retaining clip from the right pivot.
3. Remove wiper motor mounting nuts and pull motor out far enough to remove drive link from drive crank arm.
4. From under the panel, remove left pivot mounting nuts and right pivot retainer.
5. Remove the two links and left pivot as an assembly from under the panel or through the glove compartment.

1969 Fury, Polara and Monaco

1. Remove the wiper arm and blade assemblies.
2. Remove the windshield lower moulding.
3. Remove the cowl grille.
4. To remove the right pivot, disconnect the connecting link from the pivot, remove the bolts that attach the pivot to the cowl and remove the pivot.
5. To remove the left pivot, disconnect the connecting link from the right pivot. Disconnect the drive crank from the wiper motor. Remove the bolts that attach the left pivot to the cowl and remove the pivot and links through the cowl opening.

1970 Fury, Polara and Monaco

1. Remove the wiper arm and blade assemblies.
2. Remove the cowl screen.
3. Remove the crank arm nut and crank arm from the wiper motor.
4. Remove the bolts that attach the right and left pivots to the body.
5. Remove the pivots and linkage from the vehicle as an assembly through the cowl opening.

1971-76 All Models with Non-Concealed Wipers

1. Remove the wiper arm and blade assemblies.
2. If equipped with air conditioning, remove the left spot cooler duct to gain access to the left wiper pivot. Remove the glove box to gain access to the right wiper pivot.
3. Insert a wide blade screwdriver between the wiper link and the pivot crank arm and gently pry the link and plastic bushing from the pivot.
4. Remove the three wiper motor mounting nuts and move the motor outward on the mounting studs to gain access to the motor crank arm nut. Remove the crank arm nut and disconnect the crank arm from the wiper motor.
5. Remove the nut that attaches the pivot to the body of the vehicle and remove the pivot.

1971-76 All Models with Concealed Wipers

1. Insert a 0.090 in. pin in the base of each wiper arm and remove the arm and blade assemblies from the wiper pivots.
2. Remove the cowl screen.
3. Remove the crank arm retaining nut and crank arm from the wiper motor.
4. Remove the bolts that attach the right and left pivots to the body of the vehicle.
5. Remove the links and pivots as an assembly through the cowl opening.
6. Reverse the above procedure to install.

RADIO

R & R

1969-70 Charger

1. Disconnect battery.
2. Remove radio finish plate.
3. On air conditioned vehicles, remove lower center air duct, left air duct, and upper center duct.
4. Remove radio mounting bracket.

5. Remove two screws mounting radio to front of instrument panel.
6. Disconnect antenna and speaker leads.
7. Remove radio from under panel. Reverse procedure to install.

1969-70 Coronet, Belvedere, and Satellite

1. Disconnect battery.
2. Remove radio upper trim panel.
3. Remove radio finish plate.
4. Remove radio rear mounting nut from mounting bracket.
5. Disconnect electrical wiring and antenna lead.
6. Remove two mounting screws from front of instrument panel.
7. Remove radio from instrument panel.

1969-70 Polara and Monaco

1. Disconnect battery.
2. Remove automatic temperature control, if so equipped.
3. Remove radio bezel.
4. Remove two radio mounting bolts at front of instrument panel.
5. Remove air conditioner duct, if so equipped.
6. Disconnect electrical leads and antenna lead.
7. Loosen radio mounting bracket stud nut and slide radio and stud towards front of car from mounting bracket.
8. Carefully remove radio from under panel to avoid damaging electrical leads from main harness or automatic temperature control aspirator tube. Reverse procedure to install.

1969-74 Fury, 1971-76 Polara, Monaco, and 1975-76 Gran Fury

1. Disconnect battery.
2. Remove nine lamp panel mounting screws, lower lamp panel assembly slightly, disconnect lamp harness from main harness, and remove lamp panel from instrument panel.
3. Remove steering column cover.
4. Remove radio trim bezel mounting screws and bezel.
5. Remove center lower air conditioner duct, if so equipped.
6. Disconnect electrical leads and antenna lead at radio.
7. Remove radio support mounting bracket.
8. Remove two radio mounting bolts.
9. Move radio down through bottom of instrument panel carefully to avoid damage to vacuum hoses and electrical leads. Reverse procedure to install.

1971-76 Satellite, Coronet, Charger, and 1975-76 Fury

1. Disconnect the negative battery cable.
2. Remove the ash tray (1971 models only).
3. Remove the radio control knobs and retaining nuts. On 1972 models remove the rear radio support brackets.
4. Disconnect the lead wires from the radio and remove the radio from the vehicle.

HEATER

Heater Assembly R & R—Non Air-Conditioned Cars

1969-70 Belvedere, Satellite, Coronet and Charger

1. Drain radiator and disconnect battery. Remove the glove box.
2. On models equipped with a console, the console must be moved rearward before the heater assembly can be removed. From inside the console storage area, remove the two console mounting bolts and the two screws from the front sides of the console. Remove the two shift indicator bezel screws, move the transmission selector lever to the Drive position, and turn the bezel sideways and allow it to rest on the console. Remove the two screws from the rear of the gear selector mounting bracket and disconnect the back up light switch wiring. Remove the gear indicator light bulb, then move the console rearward.
3. Disconnect heater hoses at bulkhead. Plug hose fittings on heater to prevent spilling coolant on trim when removing heater.
4. From under instrument panel remove heater to cowl support bracket.
5. Remove defroster hoses and disconnect wiring from heater motor resistor.
6. Disconnect fresh air vent control and shut off door cables at heater from under instrument panel. Reaching through glove box, disconnect temperature control door cable.
7. From inside engine compartment, remove three nuts that mount heater to bulkhead.
8. Rotate heater assembly until mounting studs are up and carefully remove heater from under instrument panel.
9. Reverse procedure to install.

1969-74 Fury, 1969-76 Polara and Monaco, and 1975-76 Gran Fury

NOTE: This is the removal procedure for the heater housing that attaches to the passenger compartment side of the firewall. Do not remove the part of the housing that attaches to the engine side of the firewall.

1. Disconnect battery and drain radiator.

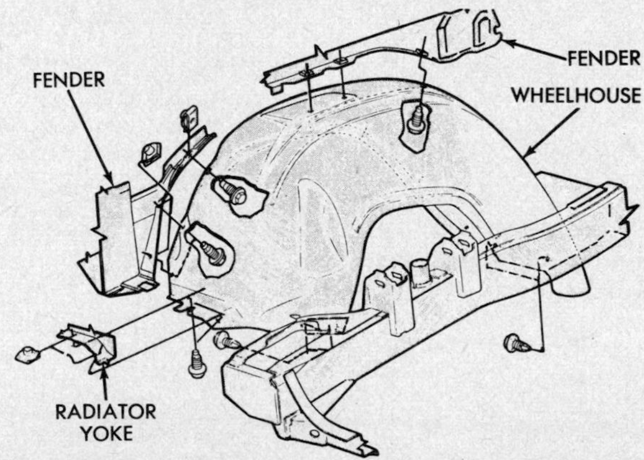

Inner fender shield attaching points—1969-73 Fury, Polara, and Monaco
(© Chrysler Corp)

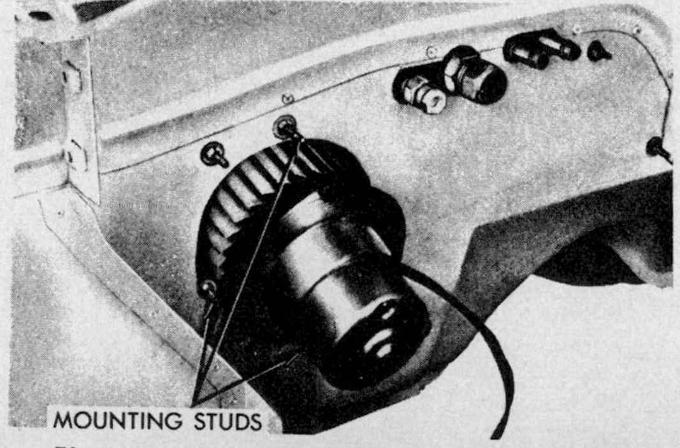

Blower motor removal—1969-76 Coronet, Belvedere, Charger, Satellite, 1975-76 Fury
(© Chrysler Corp)

2. Disconnect heater hoses at dash panel. Plug hose fittings on heater to prevent spilling coolant on trim.
3. Slide front seat back to allow room.
4. Disconnect radio antenna.
5. Disconnect electrical conductors from blower motor resistor block on face of housing.
6. Remove vacuum hoses from trunk lock if so equipped.
7. Remove control cables from defroster door crank and heat shut off door crank.
8. Remove bottom retaining nut from support bracket and swing bracket up and out of way.
9. In engine compartment remove four retaining nuts from studs on engine side housing.
10. Remove locating bolt from bottom center of passenger side housing.
11. Roll or tip housing out from under instrument panel.
12. Remove temperature control cable retaining clip and cable from heat shut off door crank.

1971-76 Satellite, Coronet Charger, and 1975-76 Fury

1. Disconnect the negative battery cable.
2. Drain the cooling system.
3. Disconnect the heater hoses from the heater core tubes at the dash panel. Plug the core tubes to prevent spilling coolant on the interior of the car.
4. Remove the three mounting nuts from the studs around the blower motor, the one nut from the heater housing near the center of the instrument panel, and remove the flange and air seal.
5. Disconnect the antenna lead wire from the radio and position it out of the way.
6. Remove the screw that attaches the housing to the support rod for the plenum. It is located on the right-side of the housing above the outside air opening.
7. Disconnect the three air door cables.
8. Disconnect the wires from the blower motor resistor.
9. Tip the heater assembly down and out from under the dash.

Blower Motor R&R—Non Air-Conditioned Cars

1969-76 Belvedere, Satellite, Coronet, Charger, and 1975-76 Fury

1. Remove heater assembly as outlined in Heater Assembly Removal.
2. Disconnect wiring from blower motor to heater assembly.
3. Remove motor cooler tube.
4. Remove heater back plate assembly from heater.
5. Remove fan from motor shaft.
6. Remove blower motor from back plate.

1969-74 Fury, 1969-76 Polara, Monaco, and 1975-76 Gran Fury

The blower motor is mounted to the engine side housing under the right front fender, between the inner fender shield and the fender. The inner fender shield must be removed to service the blower motor.

1. Raise the hood and remove all brackets and clips that attach to the inner fender shield under the hood.
2. Raise the car on a hoist and remove the right front tire and wheel assembly.
3. From under the fender, remove the bolts that attach the inner fender shield to the fender.
4. Remove the fender shield from the vehicle.
5. Disconnect the blower motor wiring at the multiple connector.
6. Remove the nuts that attach the blower motor to the heater housing and remove the blower motor.

Heater Core R&R—Non Air-Conditioned Cars

1969-70 Belvedere, Satellite, Coronet and Charger

1. Remove the heater assembly.
2. Remove the heater cover plate.
3. Remove the screws that attach the heater core to the heater assembly and remove the core.

1969-74 Fury, 1969-76 Polara, Monaco, and 1975-76 Gran Fury

1. Remove the heater assembly.
2. From inside the heater assembly, remove the two retaining nuts from the right-side of the heater core.
3. Remove the four heater core attaching screws from the outside of the heater housing.
4. Remove the heater core locating metal screw from the top of the heater housing.
5. Carefully pull the heater core from the heater housing.

1971-76 Belvedere, Satellite, Coronet, Charger and 1975-76 Fury

1. Remove the heater assembly.

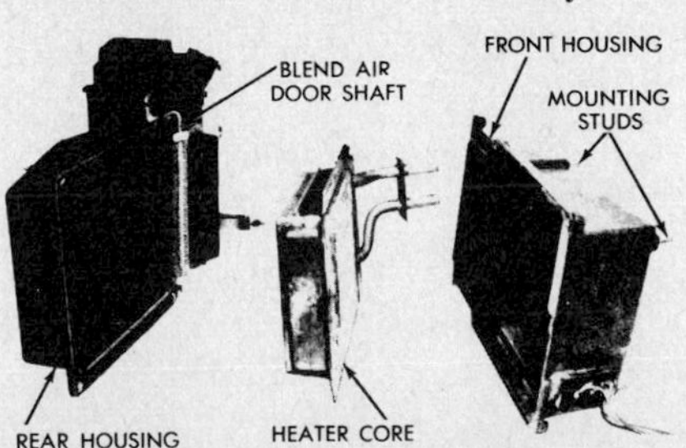

Heater core removal—1974-76 Monaco, 1974 Fury, and 1975-76 Gran Fury
(© Chrysler Corp.)

2. Remove the screws that attach the front cover to the heater housing.
3. Cut sponge rubber plenum-to-housing air seal in two places, where the front cover separates the cover from the housing.
4. Remove the one core tube retaining screw from behind the heater housing, between the heater core tubes.
5. Remove the sponge rubber gaskets from the heater core tubes. Remove the heater core from the heater housing.

Air Conditioner Heater Core Removal

1969-70 Charger, Coronet, Belvedere and Satellite

The heater core is positioned behind a separate cover attached to the evaporator case. It is located just forward of the instrument panel.

1. Disconnect the battery and drain the cooling system. Remove the air cleaner and disconnect the heater hoses.
2. Remove the distribution housing, glove box, and the heater core intake-outlet tube assembly.
3. Remove the fresh air intake hose. Disconnect the floor air actuator rod.
4. Disconnect the actuator vacuum hoses. Remove the fresh air door housing assembly.
5. Remove the defroster hoses. Disconnect the resistor block and bypass switch electrical connections.
6. Extract the screws holding the water bypass valve to the heater cover. Remove the operating link attaching screw.
7. At its mounting bracket, disconnect the air conditioning door actuator and remove the supporting braces.
8. Remove the retainer spring clips and screws securing the cover to the case.
9. Pull the lower edge of the cover rearward; lift the assembly 3/8 in. This will release the cover lip from the case. Lower the assembly and remove it from the right side.
10. To begin the installation procedure, install the water bypass valve to the heater core (if it was removed). Be sure to use new O-rings on the intake and outlet tubes.
11. Place the heater core into the evaporator case. Install the cover by hooking the cover lip on the evaporator case and rolling it down into position. Replace the retainer spring clips and screws.
12. Install the water bypass valve to the heater cover. Connect the linkage to the air conditioning door.

13. Replace the air conditioning door actuator with its vacuum hoses. Be sure to replace the hose with the red stripe to the rod side. Install the two support braces.
14. Replace all electrical connections to the resistor block.
15. Connect the vacuum hoses to the floor air actuator and the fresh air recirculating actuator. Be sure the hose with the red stripe is facing the rod side. Replace the fresh air recirculating door housing. Connect the floor air actuator rod to its linkage.
16. Connect the fresh air recirculating air intake hose.
17. Replace the heater core intake-outlet tube assembly. Use a drop of water on the O-rings to ease installation. Replace the temperature control valve capillary tube in the heater core cover.
18. Open the air conditioning door about 1 in. Install the distribution housing.
19. Replace the flexible hoses to the instrument panel outlets.
20. Replace the glove box.
21. Connect the heater hoses and fill the cooling system with the proper amount and type of antifreeze.
22. Install the air cleaner and connect the battery. Test the operation of the heater.

1969-71 Fury, VIP, Polara, and Monaco

The air conditioning heater core is located in the front cover of the passenger side housing. To remove only the heater core, the air conditioning system need not be discharged.

1. Disconnect the battery and drain the cooling system. Disconnect the heater hoses and remove the air cleaner.
2. Plug the heater core tubes to prevent coolant loss when the core is removed.
3. Take off the steering column cover and remove the left spot cooler duct.
4. At the linkage on the left side of the housing, disconnect the two actuator rods. Remove the two cover retaining screws.
5. Remove the screws securing the heat duct in position and remove the duct. With the duct removed, the screws in the bottom of the front cover lip will be exposed. Remove them.
6. Remove the glove box. Remove the center spot cooler duct, the air distribution housing, and the right spot cooler duct.
7. Working in the glove box opening, remove the top retaining screws and the screws from the right side of the housing.
8. At the resistor block, disconnect all electrical connections. Disconnect the vacuum hoses from the recirculating housing actuator.
9. Take off the nut at the housing end of the cover support bracket. Swing the bracket upward and carefully roll the front cover and heater core outward. Remove it from under the instrument panel.
10. To begin installation, replace the heater core in the front cover. Position the core and cover on the evaporator housing. While holding the front cover in position, swing the support bracket downward over the stud on the front cover face. Install its retaining nut.
11. Working in the glove box opening, replace the top housing and right-side screws.
12. Working under the instrument panel, install the screws that retain the housing in position.
13. Replace the heat distribution duct to the housing bottom and connect the actuator rods.
14. Connect all the vacuum hoses to their actuators; install all electrical connections to the resistor block.
15. Through the glove box opening, install the air distribution housing, the center spot cooler duct, and the right spot cooler duct.
16. Replace the steering column cover and the left spot cooler duct. Replace the glove box assembly.
17. From this point, reverse the removal procedure. Be sure to fill cooling system with proper type and amount of antifreeze.

1971-76 Satellite, Coronet, Charger, and 1975-76 Fury

NOTE: this procedure requires evacuation of the refrigerant system which requires special tools and training.

1. Remove the air cleaner and disconnect the battery.
2. Drain the cooling system. Disconnect the heater hoses at the dash panel. Plug the core tubes to prevent spillage.
3. Discharge refrigerant from the system.
4. Disconnect the refrigerant lines at the dash panel (use two wrenches for this procedure). Leave the expansion valve attached to the line. Plug all refrigerant openings.
5. Disconnect the blower motor electrical connections. Remove the motor cooling tube and the blower motor.
6. Remove the glove box assembly.
7. Take the appearance shield from the lower edge of the instrument panel.
8. Remove the left spot cooler duct and the air distribution housing.
9. Disconnect all wires from the blower motor resistor, and the antenna wire from the radio bottom.

Evaporator and heater core mounting—1973-76 Satellite, Coronet, Charger, 1975-76 Fury
(© Chrysler Corp)

10. Remove the radio.
11. Disconnect the vacuum harness from the control switch rear.
12. Remove the water valve cable from the bracket on the housing left end.
13. In the engine compartment, remove the nuts from the housing mounting studs.
14. Remove the rubber drain tube.
15. Remove the support bracket from the plenum-to-housing panel.
16. Remove the unit from beneath the instrument panel.
17. With the unit removed from the vehicle, remove the plenum air seal.
18. Remove the vacuum hose from the fresh air door actuator and bypass door actuator. Remove the air seal from the evaporator core tubes and heater.
19. Remove the 18 screws securing the front and rear covers; extract one screw from between the evaporator core tubes. Pull the housings apart.
20. Extract the three screws from the evaporator core access plate; remove the plate. With access now clear to the two evaporator core mounting screws, remove them. In addition, remove the four screws securing the evaporator core to the front cover; remove the core.
21. Carefully lift the left housing half seal from the rear cover. Do not remove the entire seal; the lower portion acts as a water seal.
22. Remove the two core retaining screws from the mounting plate. From the back of the rear cover, remove one screw from between the core tubes. Lift the heater core from the housing.
23. To begin assembly and installation, place the heat door in the up position. Place the heater core into the rear cover. Install its retaining screws.
24. Apply rubber cement to the bottom of the raised portion of the housing seal; carefully replace it in its original position over the heater core.
25. Insert the evaporator core into the front cover and replace its four securing screws.
26. Place the front and rear covers

together. Make sure the cover seal is seated properly. Replace the 18 securing screws (and the screw between the evaporator core tubes at the back of the rear cover).

27. Replace the air seal over the heater and evaporator core tubes.
28. Connect all vacuum hoses to their respective actuators. Connect the hose with the red tracer to the actuator rod side.
29. Install the evaporator core access cover plate to the housing front and replace its three sheet metal screws.
30. Apply rubber cement to the plenum air seal and install it in position.
31. Position the housing up under the instrument panel. Connect the housing-to-plenum support bracket.
32. In the engine compartment, install four retaining nuts on the housing mounting studs; torque to 24 in. lbs.
33. Install the vacuum harness to the control switch rear. Install the water valve control cable in its retaining bracket.
34. Install the radio.
35. Install all blower motor resistor wiring. Plug the antenna lead into the radio bottom.
36. Replace the center outlet air distribution housing. Replace the left spot coller duct.
37. Replace the appearance shield at the instrument panel bottom.
38. Replace the glove box.
39. Replace the blower motor and connect its wiring. Install the blower motor cooling tube and replace the evaporator drain tube.
40. Connect the refrigerant lines to the evaporator core tubes. Freely lubricate fittings and O-rings with refrigerant oil. Use two wrenches to avoid twisting the tubes.
41. Connect the heater hoses to the core tubes. Fill the cooling system.
42. Sweep the system. Evacuate the system. Charge the system and check for leaks.

1972-73 Polara, Monaco, and Fury

To remove only the heater core, it is not necessary to discharge the air conditioning system. The heater core is positioned in the rear housing of the passenger-side unit.

1. Disconnect the battery and drain the cooling system. Remove the air cleaner and disconnect the heater hoses. Plug the heater core tubes to prevent coolant loss when the core is removed.
2. Remove the steering column cover and remove the left spot cooler duct.

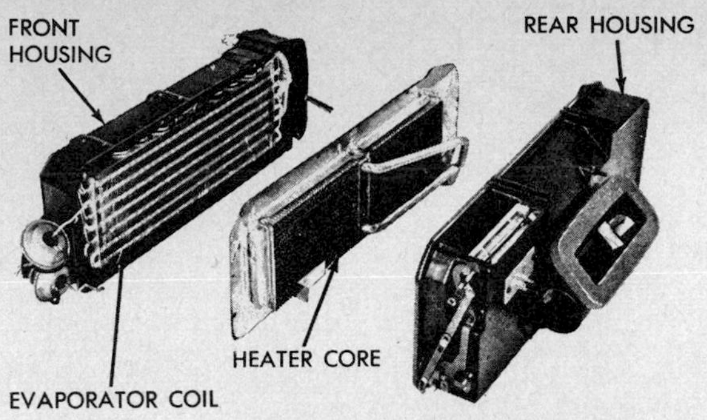

Heater and evaporator core—1972-73 Polara, Monaco and Fury
(© Chrysler Corp)

3. On the left side of the housing, remove the linkage shield and disconnect the actuator rods. Remove the screws from the housing left side.
4. Remove the screws holding the heat distribution duct and remove it. With duct removed, the screws in the bottom lip of the rear housing will become visible. Remove them.
5. Remove the glove box. In addition, remove the right spot cooler duct, the air distribution housing, and the center outlet duct.
6. Working in the glove box opening, remove the top retaining screws and the right-side housing screws. If the vehicle is Auto-Temp equipped, remove the aspirator tube from the clip first and then remove the amplifier and master compressor switches. Now remove the right-side housing screws.
7. Disconnect all electrical connections at the resistor block. On Auto-Temp equipped vehicles, remove the wires from the two plastic straps and the metal clip.
8. Remove the nut from the housing end of the support bracket. Swing the bracket upward and out of the way. Carefully roll the housing out from under the instrument panel. The heater core may be removed by pulling it out from the top. Cut the adhesive along the bottom and sides with a knife to ease removal.
9. To begin installation, scrape all remaining sealer from the heater core flange and fit a new seal. Position the heater core in the rear housing and secure with a screw at either end. Place the front housing in position; hold the rear housing in place and swing the support bracket down. Secure it in position with its retaining nut.
10. Working in the glove box opening, install the top two housing screws and the screws at the right side of the rear housing.
11. From beneath the instrument panel, install the screws along the housing bottom and the screws at the left side of the rear housing. It is not necessary to reinstall the linkage shield.
12. Replace the heat distribution duct to the housing bottom.
13. Connect the actuator rods.
14. Working in the glove box opening, connect the resistor block wires. Tighten the support bracket nuts. On Auto-Temp equipped vehicles, fasten the wires with the plastic straps and metal clip. Install the aspirator tube in the clip.
15. Replace the center outlet duct. the air distribution housing, and the right spot cooler duct.
16. Install the steering column cover, the left spot cooler duct, and the glove box assembly. On Auto-Temp equipped vehicles, install the amplifier and the master and compressor switches.
17. From this point, reverse the removal procedure. Be sure to fill the cooling system with the proper amount and type of antifreeze.

1974-76 Polara and Monaco, 1974 Fury, 1975-76 Gran Fury

NOTE: *This procedure requires evacuation of the refrigerant in the air conditioning system. Therefore, this operation should not be attempted by persons not having the special tools and training required to perform the job safely.*

1. Purge the system of refrigerant.
2. Disconnect the battery ground cable.
3. Remove the air cleaner and disconnect the heater hoses. Plug the core tubes.
4. Remove the 5/16" bolt in the center of the plumbing sealing plate.
5. Pull the refrigerant line assembly toward the front of the car.
6. Remove the two 1/4-20 Allen screws and remove the "H" valve.
7. Slide the front seat back, out of the way. Remove lap cooler and lower instrument panel cover.
8. Remove the A/C distribution duct.
9. Unplug the antenna lead from the radio.

10. Disconnect wires and vacuum lines from unit.
11. Remove the drain tube. With automatic temperature control (ATC), remove electrical connections and vacuum connector from the servo. Disconnect the amplifier wires. Disconnect the wires and vacuum hoses from the master and compressor switches. Disconnect the aspirator tube.
12. Remove the temperature control cable from the clip on the unit.
13. Remove the retaining nut from the support bracket.
14. Remove the six retaining nuts from the studs in the engine compartment.
15. Remove the housing from under the instrument panel, and place on a work table.
16. Remove the mode door and the blend air door levers from the shaft. Remove the screws and lift off the top cover.
17. Remove the 4 retaining screws and the 3 screws for the core tube seal. Lift out the core.
18. Reverse the procedure to install.

Air Conditioning Blower Motor Removal

1969-76 Coronet, Charger, Belvedere, Satellite and 1975-76 Fury

1. Working inside the engine compartment, disconnect the feed wire and ground wire. Remove the air tube (if so equipped).
2. Remove the mounting screws located on the outer surface of the mounting plate.
3. Remove the mounting plate, blower motor, and fan as an assembly.
4. To install motor, if the motor was removed from its mounting plate, be sure mounting grommets are installed at the attaching bolts. In addition, be sure the blower wheel is free and does not rub.
5. Install the blower motor assembly to the evaporator casing with the air tube opening toward the bottom. Install its retaining screws.
6. Install the air tube, ground, and feed wires.
7. Check blower motor operation.

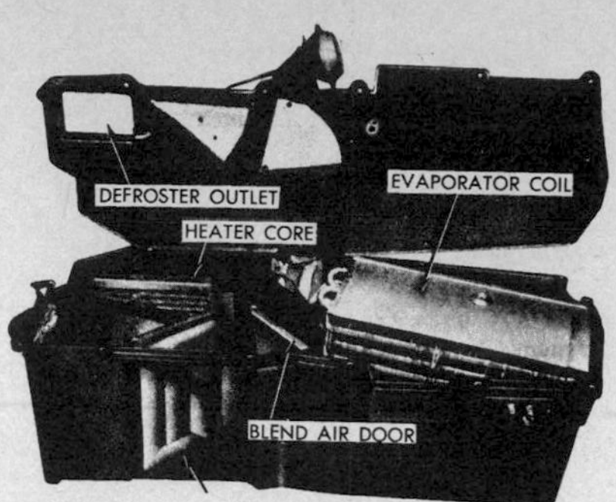

Evaporator and heater core mounting—1974 Fury, 1974-76 Polara, Monaco, and 1975-76 Gran Fury (© Chrysler Corp)

1969-74 Fury, 1972-76 Polara, Monaco, and 1975-76 Gran Fury

The blower motor is located under the right front fender between the inner fender shield and the fender. Remove the inner fender shield to provide access to the blower motor. Service consists of removing its electrical leads and attaching screws. The blower motor is not repaired; replace if defective.

SEAT BELTS

Buzzer System—1972-73

All Chrysler Corporation cars built after January 1, 1972 have front seat belts with a reminder light and buzzer system. The warning system consists of a buzzer and light, two lap belt retractor switches, a front passenger weight-sensing switch and a relay.

With only the driver in the front seat, the system will give warning when the ignition swich is on, the automatic transmission is in any gear or the parking brake is released on manual transmission models and the driver's seat belt has not been pulled out of the retractor at least ten inches.

With a passenger in the right front seat, the system will operate as for the driver alone unless the passenger's seat belt has also been extended.

Seat Belt/Starter Interlock—1974-1975

The interlock system prevents the starter from being operated until all outboard front seat occupants have fastened their seat belts. An interlock control requires that the seat belts be fastened in all outboard front seats each time the engine is started.

For the convenience of the serviceman, there is an underhood bypass switch for the system. This enables him to start the engine once, without having to sit on the seat and fasten the seat belt.

The earlier light and buzzer reminder system is retained, with coverage for the center front seat position added.

Component Locations

The underhood bypass switch is located near the electronic control unit on the firewall on all intermediate models, and located near the right hand hood hinge plate on all full-size models.

The remaining major components are situated in the following locations; Buzzer—at the right side of the instrument panel above the parking brake on intermediates, and at the left side of the brake support bracket on full-size models. Buzzer Light Fuse—fuse #2 on intermediates, and fuse #3 on full-size models. Interlock Unit—On the instrument panel to the left of the glovebox on intermediates, and above the buzzer on full-size models. Interlock System Fuse—fuse #1 on intermediates, and fuse #5 on full-size models.

Disabling the Interlock System

Since the regulation requiring the interlock system was done away with during the 1975 model year, this device may now be legally disabled. All dealers have received a service bulletin on how to properly accomplish this modification for customers requesting it. It involves disconnecting the buzzer wire (you could easily do this yourself) and making some internal wiring changes to the printed circuit board in the interlock module (the bulletin recommends that this be done by a radio repair shop).

NOTE: *Although the interlock can be disabled by disconnecting the seat sensor wires at the connectors under the seat, this is not the proper method, since it also disables the seat belt warning light. The seat belt warning light is still required.*

Ford · Mercury · Thunderbird

YEAR IDENTIFICATION

FORD

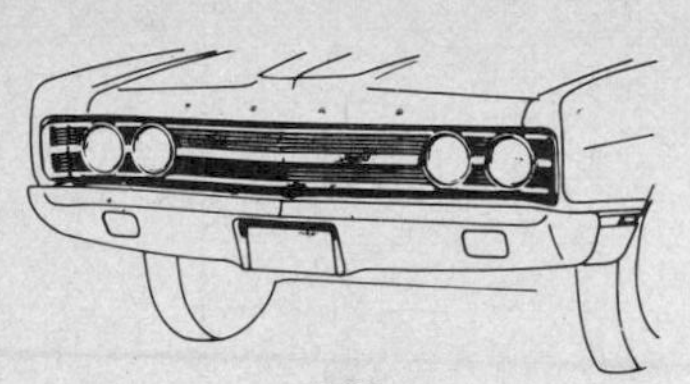
1969

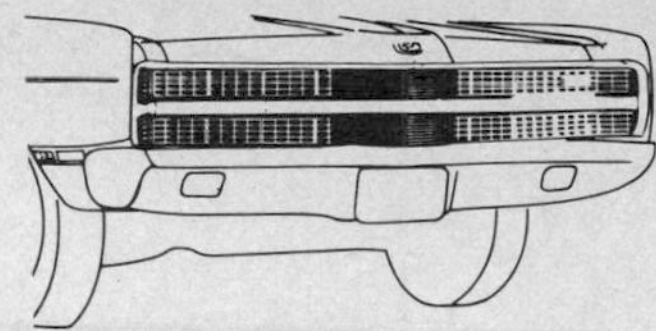
1969 LTD

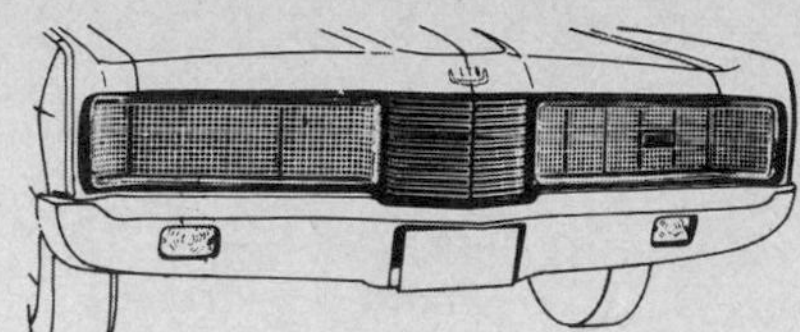
1970 LTD

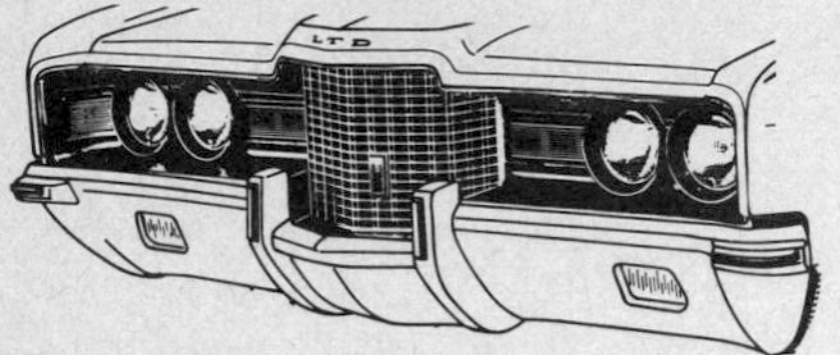
1971 LTD

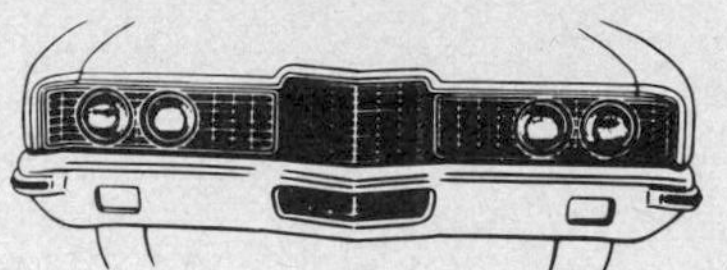
1972 Galaxie

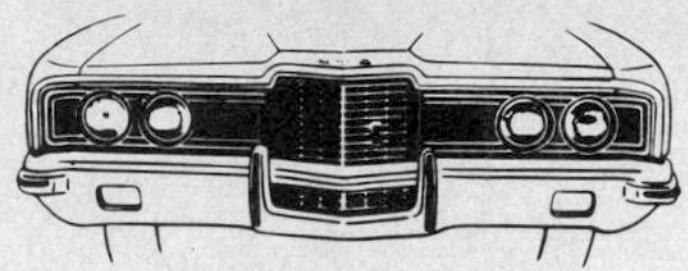
1972 LTD

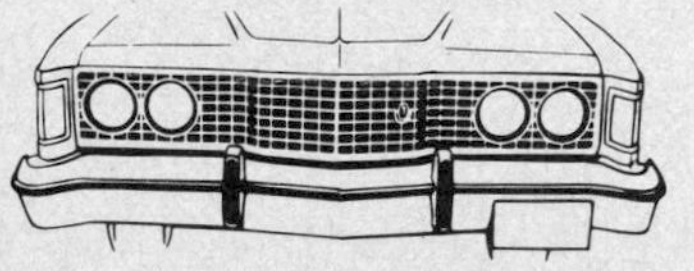
1973 Galaxie

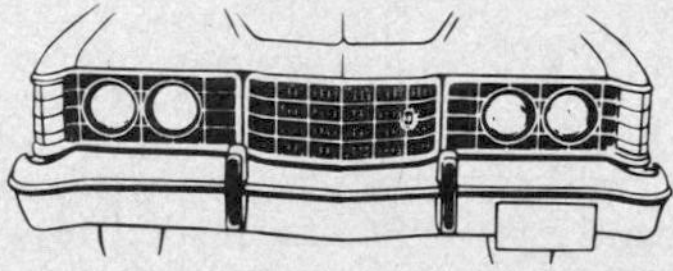
1973 LTD

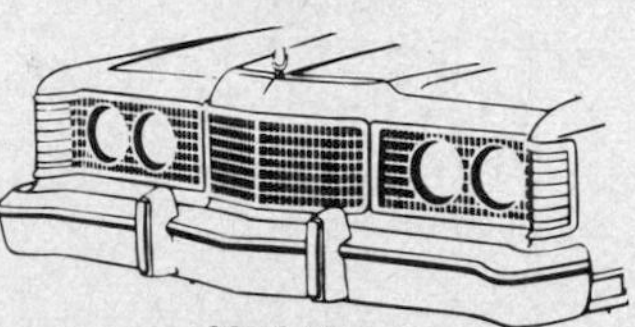
1974 LTD

1975 Ford LTD Landau

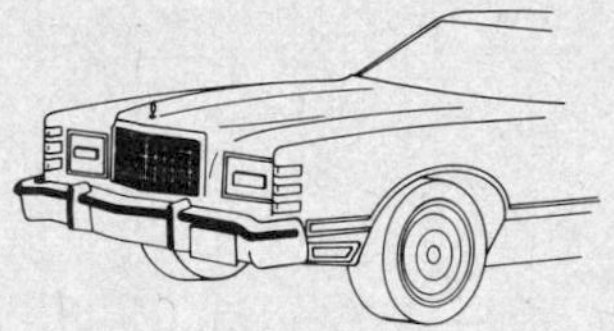
1976

THUNDERBIRD

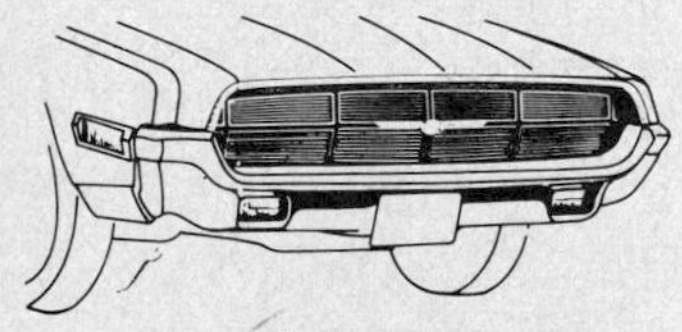
1969

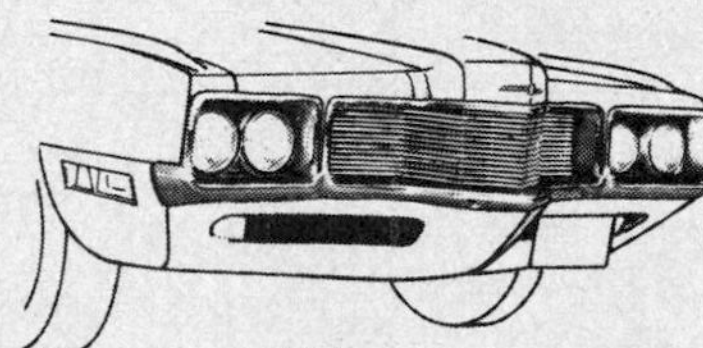
1970

1972

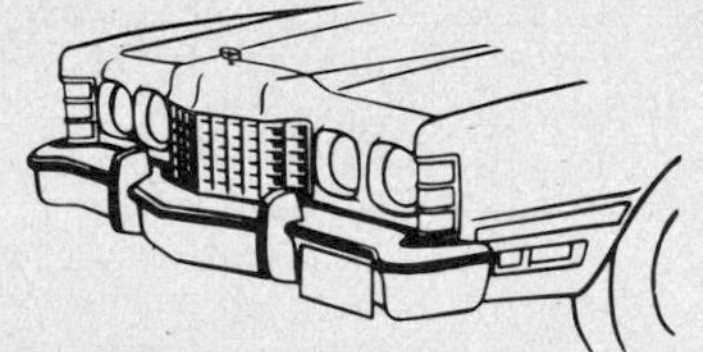
1973

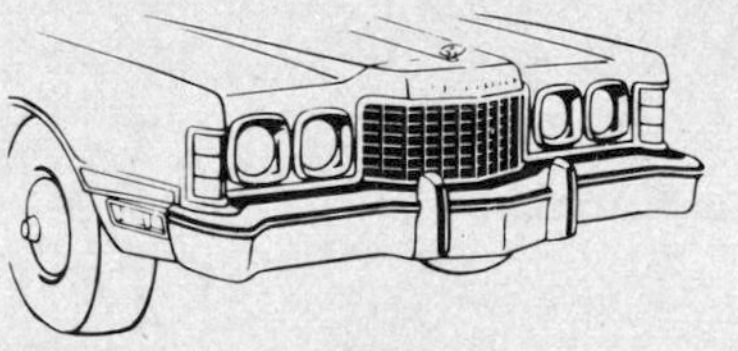
1974

1975

1976

MERCURY

1969

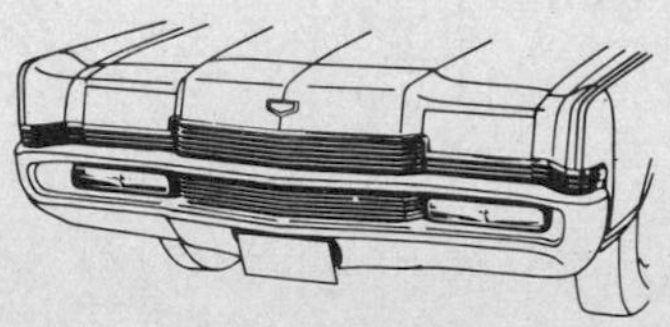
1969 Marquis

1970 Monterey

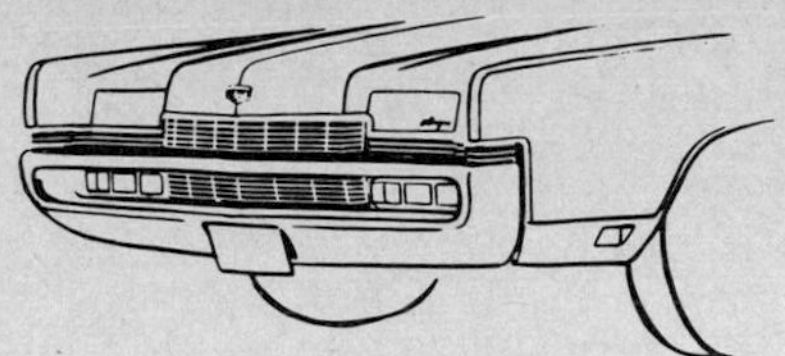
1970 Marquis Brougham

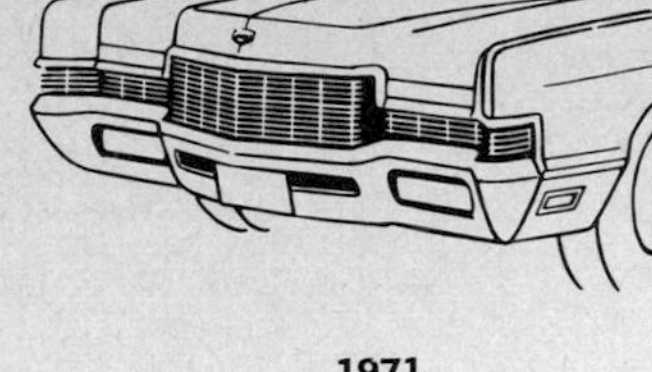
1971

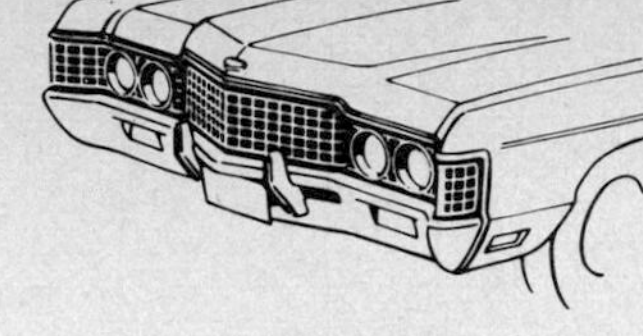
1972 Monterey

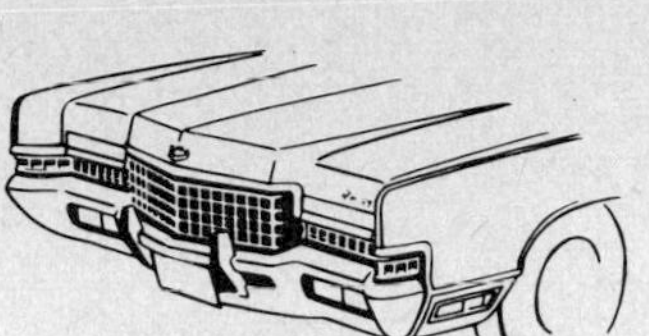
1972 Marquis

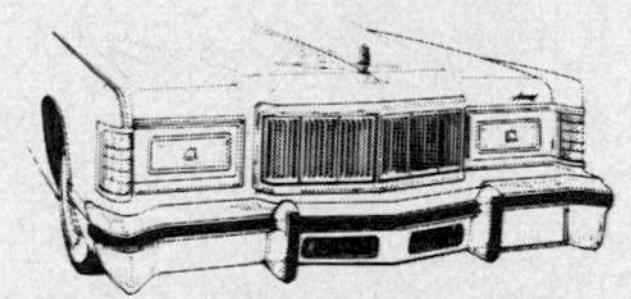
1973 Marquis

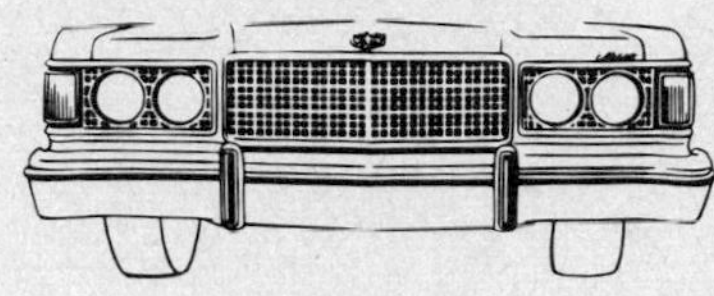
1974 Monterey

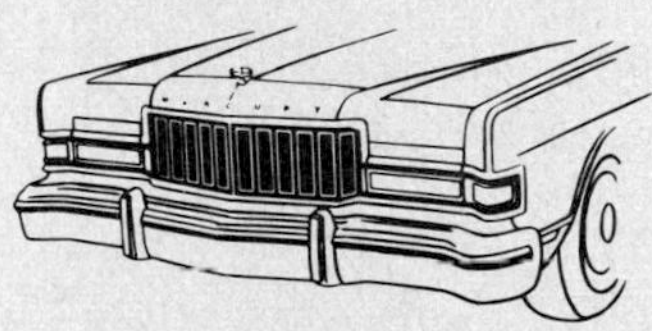
1974 Marquis

1975 Marquis

1976

FIRING ORDER

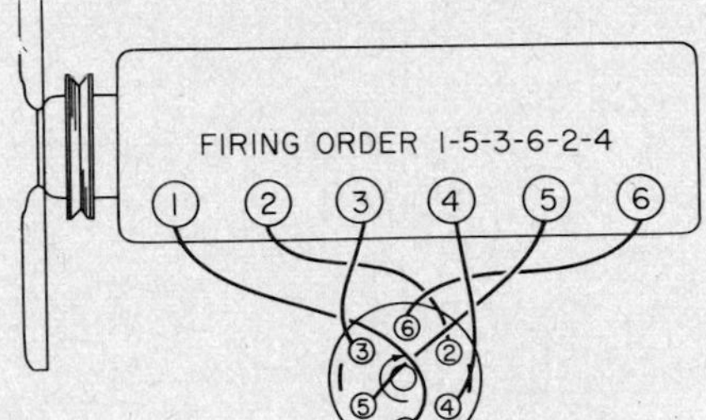

6 cyl.

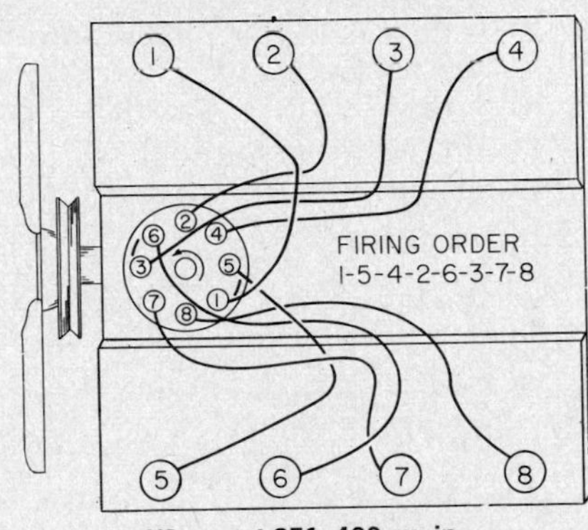

V8 except 351, 400 cu. in.

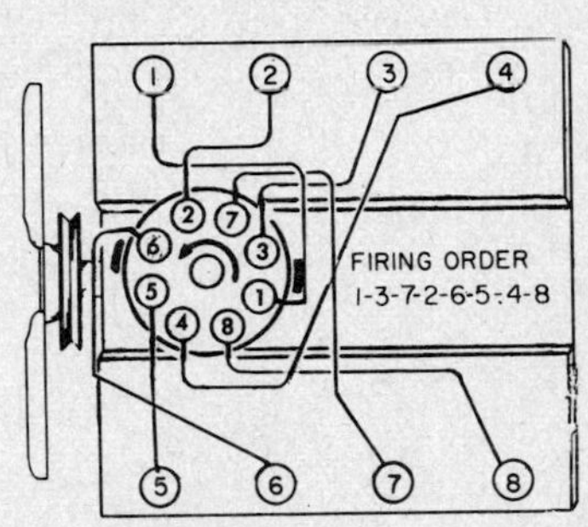

351, 400 cu. in. V8

CAR SERIAL NUMBER LOCATION AND ENGINE IDENTIFICATION

The engine number is stamped on the top surface of the engine block near the crankcase breather pipe, front left side.

The car serial number is composed of eleven digits, interpreted as illustrated. The production year code is the last digit of the model year in which the vehicle was produced. (For example, "9" = 1969). The fifth digit, a letter, represents the engine identification code. (See table.)

The serial number can be found on a plate attached to the top of the instrument panel, visible through the windshield.

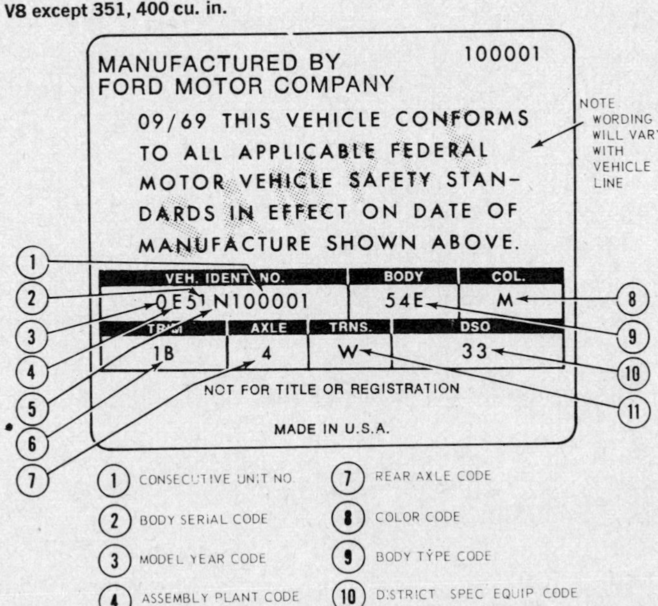

Vehicle Certification Label
(© Ford Motor Co)

Vehicle Certification Label

1970-76

The label is located on the rear of the driver's door. The upper portion contains the name of the manufacturer, the month and year of manufacture, and the certification statement. The lower portion of the label is interpreted in the illustration.

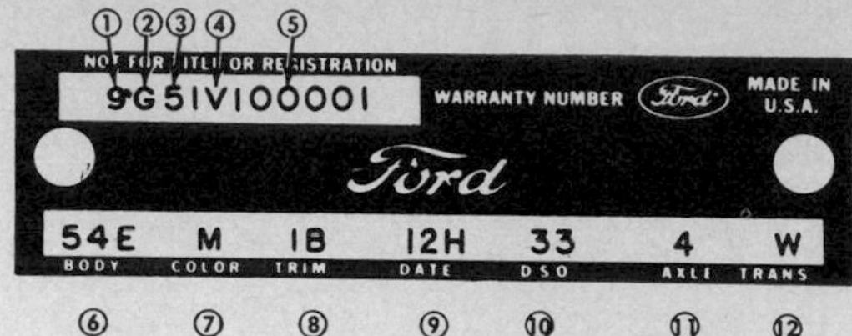

1 Model year code
2 Assembly plant code
3 Body serial code
4 Engine code
5 Consecutive unit number
6 Body type code
7 Color code
8 Trim code
9 Date code
10 District—special equipment code
11 Rear axle code
12 Transmission code

1969 serial number plate (© Ford Motor Co)

9Y83N100001

Typical vehicle identification number (VIN) tab (© Ford Motor Co)

TRANSMISSION CODES

1969-71

1. Three speed manual
5. Four speed manual—wide ratio
6. Four speed manual—close ratio

W. Automatic C4
U. Automatic C6
X. Automatic FMX
Y. Automatic MX
Z. Automatic C6 special—Police and trailer towing

1972-76

W. Automatic C4
U. Automatic C6
X. Automatic FMX
#. Automatic CW
Y. Automatic FMX
Z. Automatic C6 Special—Police trailer towing

The CW transmission is a Warner unit used on 1973-74 400 cid equipped Ford and Mercury sedans with a 2.75:1 rear axle ratio only.

ENGINE CODE

The engine code designation is the 5th digit of the vehicle identification number (V.I.N.). The V.I.N. is stamped on a plate located at the left side of the instrument panel, visible through the windshield.

Disp (Cu in.)	Carb no. bbls	Hp*	'69	'70	'71	'72	'73	'74	'75	'76
6-Cylinder Models										
240	1	103 (net)				V				
240	1	140			V					
240	1	150	V	V						
8-Cylinder Models										
302	2	140 (net)				F				
302	2	210	F	F	F					
351 W	2	153, 162 (net)				H	H	H		
351 C	2	163 (net)				H	H	H		
351 M	2	148, 150 (net)							H	H
351	2	240			H					
351	2	250		H					H	
390	2	255			Y					
390	2	265	Y	Y						
390	2	270		Y						
400	2	144, 158, 170 (net)						S	S	S
400	2	172 (net)				S	S			
400	2	260			S					
428 PI	4	360	P	P						
429	4	208, 212 (net)				N	N			
429 PI	4	N.A.				P				
429	4	320	K	K	K					
429	4	360	N	N	N					
429 PI	4	370			P					
460	4	194, 195, 218, 220, 223, 224 (net)						A	A	A
460	4	200, 208, 212 (net)				A	A			
460 PI	4	226, 267, 274, 275 (net)					C	C	C	C

PI Police Interceptor
* Net horsepower rating varies with model application

GENERAL ENGINE SPECIFICATIONS

Year	Engine No. Cyl. Displacement (cu in.)	Carburetor Type	Horsepower @ rpm ■	Torque @ rpm (ft lbs) ■	Bore and Stroke (in.)	Compression Ratio	Oil Pressure @ 2000 rpm
'69	6-240	1 bbl	150 @ 4000	234 @ 2200	4.000 x 3.180	9.2:1	35-60
	8-302	2 bbl	210 @ 4400	295 @ 2400	4.000 x 3.000	9.5:1	35-60
	8-390	2 bbl	270 @ 4400	390 @ 2600	4.050 x 3.784	9.5:1	35-60
	8-390	2 bbl	280 @ 4400	430 @ 2600	4.050 x 3.784	10.5:1	35-60
	8-428 PI	4 bbl	360 @ 5400	459 @ 3200	4.130 x 3.984	10.5:1	35-60
	8-429	2 bbl	320 @ 4400	460 @ 2200	4.360 x 3.590	10.5:1	35-60
	8-429	4 bbl	360 @ 4600	476 @ 2800	4.360 x 3.590	11.0:1	35-60
'70	6-240	1 bbl	150 @ 4000	234 @ 2200	4.000 x 3.180	9.2:1	35-60
	8-302	2 bbl	210 @ 4400	295 @ 2400	4.000 x 3.000	9.5:1	35-60
	8-351	2 bbl	250 @ 4600	355 @ 2600	4.000 x 3.500	9.5:1	35-60
	8-390	2 bbl	270 @ 4400	390 @ 2600	4.050 x 3.784	9.5:1	35-60
	8-428 PI	4 bbl	360 @ 5400	459 @ 3200	4.130 x 3.984	10.5:1	35-60
	8-429	2 bbl	320 @ 4400	460 @ 2200	4.360 x 3.590	10.5:1	35-60
	8-429	4 bbl	360 @ 4600	476 @ 2800	4.360 x 3.590	11.0:1	35-60
'71	6-240	1 bbl	140 @ 4000	230 @ 2200	4.000 x 3.180	8.9:1	35-60
	8-302	2 bbl	210 @ 4600	296 @ 2600	4.000 x 3.000	9.0:1	35-60
	8-351	2 bbl	240 @ 4600	350 @ 2600	4.000 x 3.500	8.9:1	35-60
	8-390	2 bbl	255 @ 4400	376 @ 2600	4.050 x 3.784	9.5:1	35-60
	8-400	2 bbl	260 @ 4400	400 @ 2200	4.000 x 4.000	9.0:1	50-70
	8-429	2 bbl	320 @ 4400	460 @ 2200	4.360 x 3.590	10.5:1	35-75
	8-429	4 bbl	360 @ 4600	480 @ 2800	4.360 x 3.590	10.5:1	35-75
	8-429 PI	4 bbl	370 @ 5400	450 @ 3400	4.360 x 3.590	11.0:1	35-75
'72	6-240	1 bbl	103 @ 3800	170 @ 2200	4.000 x 3.180	8.5:1	35-60
	8-302	2 bbl	140 @ 4000	239 @ 2000	4.000 x 3.000	8.5:1	35-60
	8-351 W	2 bbl	153 @ 3800	266 @ 2000	4.000 x 3.500	8.3:1	35-60
	8-351 C	2 bbl	163 @ 3800	277 @ 2000	4.000 x 3.500	8.6:1	35-60
	8-400	2 bbl	172 @ 4000	298 @ 2200	4.000 x 4.000	8.4:1	50-70
	8-429	4 bbl	208 @ 4400	322 @ 2800	4.362 x 3.590	8.5:1	35-75
	8-429	4 bbl	212 @ 4400	327 @ 2600	4.362 x 3.590	8.5:1	35-75
	8-460	4 bbl	200 @ 4400	326 @ 2800	4.362 x 3.850	8.5:1	35-75
	8-460	4 bbl	212 @ 4400	342 @ 2800	4.362 x 3.850	8.5:1	35-75
'73	8-351 W	2 bbl	153 @ 3800	266 @ 2000	4.000 x 3.500	8.3:1	35-60
	8-351 C	2 bbl	163 @ 3800	277 @ 2000	4.000 x 3.500	8.6:1	35-60
	8-400	2 bbl	172 @ 4000	298 @ 2200	4.000 x 4.000	8.4:1	50-70
	8-429	4 bbl	208 @ 4400	322 @ 2800	4.362 x 3.590	8.5:1	35-75
	8-429	4 bbl	212 @ 4400	327 @ 2600	4.362 x 3.590	8.5:1	35-75
	8-460	4 bbl	200 @ 4400	326 @ 2800	4.362 x 3.850	8.5:1	35-75
	8-460	4 bbl	212 @ 4400	342 @ 2800	4.362 x 3.850	8.5:1	35-75
'74	8-351 W	2 bbl	162 @ 4000	275 @ 2200	4.000 x 3.500	8.2:1	45-65
	8-351 C	2 bbl	163 @ 4200	278 @ 2000	4.000 x 3.500	8.0:1	45-75
	8-400	2 bbl	170 @ 3400	330 @ 2000	4.000 x 4.000	8.0:1	45-75
	8-460	4 bbl	195 @ 3800	335 @ 2600	4.362 x 3.850	8.0:1	35-65
	8-460 PI	4 bbl	275 @ 4400	395 @ 2800	4.362 x 3.850	8.8:1	35-65

GENERAL ENGINE SPECIFICATIONS

Year	Engine No. Cyl. Displacement (cu in.)	Carburetor Type	Horsepower @ rpm ■	Torque @ rpm (ft lbs) ■	Bore and Stroke (in.)	Compression Ratio	Oil Pressure @ 2000 rpm
'75-'76	8-351 M	2 bbl	148 @ 3800	243 @ 2400	4.000 x 3.500	8.0:1	45-75
	8-351 M Calif.	2 bbl	150 @ 3800	244 @ 2800	4.000 x 3.500	8.0:1	45-75
	8-400	2 bbl	158 @ 3800	276 @ 2000	4.000 x 4.000	8.0:1	45-75
	8-400 Calif.	2 bbl	144 @ 3600	255 @ 2200	4.000 x 4.000	8.0:1	45-75
	8-460	4 bbl	218 @ 4000	369 @ 2000	4.362 x 3.850	8.0:1	35-65
	8-460 Calif.	4 bbl	218 @ 4000	367 @ 2600	4.362 x 3.850	8.0:1	35-65
	8-460 T-Bird①	4 bbl	224 @ 4000	370 @ 2600	4.362 x 3.850	8.0:1	35-65
	8-460 T-Bird②	4 bbl	194 @ 3800	347 @ 2600	4.362 x 3.850	8.0:1	35-65
	8-460 T-Bird③	4 bbl	223 @ 4000	366 @ 2600	4.362 x 3.850	8.0:1	35-65
	8-460 PI	4 bbl	226 @ 4000	374 @ 2600	4.362 x 3.850	8.0:1	35-65

■ Beginning 1972, horsepower and torque are SAE net figures. They are measured at the rear of the transmission with all accessories installed and operating. Since the figures vary when a given engine is installed in different models, some are representative rather than exact.

W Windsor Design
C Cleveland Design
M Modified Cleveland Design
PI Police Interceptor

① Dual exhaust
② Single exhaust
③ California

Ford

TUNE-UP SPECIFICATIONS

- When analyzing compression test results, look for uniformity among cylinders rather than specific pressures.

Year	Engine No. Cyl Displacement (cu in.)	Engine hp	Spark Plugs Type	Spark Plugs Gap (in.)	Distributor Point Dwell (deg)	Distributor Point Gap (in.)	Ignition Timing (deg) ▲ Man Trans	Ignition Timing (deg) ▲ Auto Trans	Valves Intake Opens ■ (deg)	Fuel Pump Pressure (psi)	Idle Speed (rpm) ▲ Man Trans *	Idle Speed (rpm) ▲ Auto Trans
'69	6-240	150	BF-42	.034	35-40	.027	6B	6B	12	4-6	775/550	550
	8-302	210	BF-42	.034	24-29③	.021③	6B	6B	16	4½-6½	650	550②
	8-390	270	BF-42	.034	24-29③	.021③	6B	6B	13	4½-6½	650	550
	8-428PI	360	BF-32	.034	24-29③	.021③	—	6B	18	4½-6½	—	600
	8-429	320	BF-42	.034	26-31	.017	—	6B	16	4½-6½	—	550
	8-429	360	BF-42	.034	24-29③	.021③	6B	6B	16	4½-6½	650	550
'70	6-240	150	BF-42	.034	35-40	.027	6B	6B	12	4-6	800/500	500
	8-302	210	BF-42	.034	24-29	.021	6B	6B	16	4-6	575 800/500	575 600/500
	8-351	250	BF-42	.034	24-29	.021	10B	10B	11	5-7	575 700/500	575 600/500
	8-390	270	BF-42	.034	24-29③	.021③	6B	6B	13	5-7	750/500	600/500
	8-428PI	360	BF-32	.034	24-29	.021	—	6B	18	4½-6½	—	600/500
	8-429	320	BRF-42	.034	24-29③	.021③	—	6B	16	5-7	—	600/500
	8-429	360	BRF-42	.034	24-29③	.021③	6B	6B	16	5-7	700/500	600/500
'71	6-240	140	BRF-42	.034	33-38	.027	6B	6B	18	4-6	800/500	600/500
	8-302	210	BRF-42	.034	24-29	.021	6B	6B	16	4-6	575 800/500	575 650/500
	8-351W	240	BRF-42	.034	24-29	.021	6B	6B	11	5-7	575 775/500	575 600/500
	8-351C	240	ARF-42	.034	24-29	.021	—	6B	12	5-7	—	625/550
	8-390	255	BRF-42	.034	24-29	.021	—	6B	13	5-7	—	600/475
	8-400	260	ARF-42	.034	26-31	.017	—	10B(6B)	17	5-7	—	625/500
	8-429PI	370	ARF-42	.034	27½-29½	.020	—	10B	32	5-7	—	650/500
	8-429	320	BRF-42	.034	24-29③	.021③	—	4B	16	5-7	—	600
	8-429	360	BRF-42	.034	24-29③	.021③	4B	4B	16	5-7	700	600

Ford

TUNE-UP SPECIFICATIONS

• When analyzing compression test results, look for uniformity among cylinders rather than specific pressures.

Year	ENGINE No. Cyl Displacement (cu in.)	hp	SPARK PLUGS Type	Gap (in.)	DISTRIBUTOR Point Dwell (deg)	Point Gap (in.)	IGNITION TIMING (deg) ▲ Man Trans	Auto Trans	VALVES Intake Opens ■ (deg)	Fuel Pump Pressure (psi)	IDLE SPEED (rpm) ▲ Man Trans *	Auto Trans
'72	6-240	103	BRF-42	.034	35-39	.027	—	6B	18	4-6	—	500
	8-302	140	BRF-42	.034	26-30	.017	—	6B	16	5-7	—	575 600/500
	8-351W	153	BRF-42	.034	26-30	.017	—	6B	11	5-7	—	575 600/500
	8-351C	163	ARF-42	.034	26-30	.017	—	6B	12	5-7	—	600/500
	8-400	172	ARF-42	.034	26-30	.017	—	6B	17	5-7	—	625/500
	8-429	208	BRF-42	.034	26-30	.017	—	10B	8	5-7	—	600/500
	8-429PI	N.A.	ARF-42	.034	26-30	.017	—	10B	32	4½-6½	—	650/500
'73	8-351W	153	BRF-42	.034	26-30	.017	—	6B	11	5-7	—	575 600/500
	8-351C	163	ARF-42	.034	26-30	.017	—	6B	12	5-7	—	600/500
	8-400	172	ARF-42	.034	26-30	.017	—	6B	17	5-7	—	625/500
	8-429	208	BRF-42	.034	26-30	.017	—	10B	8	5-7	—	600/500
	8-460PI	267, 274	ARF-42	.034	26-30	.017	—	10B	32	4½-6½	—	650/500
'74	8-351W	162	BRF-42	.034④	26-30⑥	.014-.020⑥	—	6B	15	4-6		600/500
	8-351C	163	ARF-42	.044	26-30⑥	.014-.020⑥	—	14B	19½	5½-6½	—	700/500
	8-400	170	ARF-42	.044 (.054)	Electronic		—	12B	17	5½-6½	—	625/500
	8-460	195	ARF-52	.054 (.044)	Electronic		—	14B	8	5½-6½	—	650(675) 500
	8-460PI	275	ARF-52	.054	Electronic		—	10B	18	Electric	—	700/500
'75	8-351M	148, 150	ARF-42	.044	Electronic		—	8B	19½	5½-6½	—	700
	8-400	144, 158	ARF-42	.044	Electronic		—	6B⑦	17	5½-6½	—	625
	8-460	218	ARF-52	.044	Electronic		—	14B	8	6.2-7.2	—	650
	8-460PI	226	ARF-52	.044	Electronic		—	14B	18	6.2-7.2	—	650
'76	8-351M	All	ARF-42/52⑧	.044	Electronic		—	⑧	19½	5½-6½	—	650(650/675⑧)
	8-400	All	ARF-42/52⑧	.044	Electronic		—	⑧	17	5½-6½	—	650(625)
	8-460	All	ARF-52	.044	Electronic		—	8/14B⑧⑨ @ 650	8	6.2-7.2	—	650
	8-460PI	226	ARF-52	.044	Electronic		—	14B @ 650⑨	18	6.2-7.2	—	650

▲ See text for procedure
• Figure in parentheses indicates California engine
■ All figures Before Top Dead Center
* In all cases where two figures are separated by a slash, the first is for idle speed with solenoid energized and the automatic transmission in Drive, while the second is for idle speed with solenoid disconnected and automatic transmission in Neutral.
① Not used
② A/C off
③ For engines equipped with single diaphragm distributors adjust point dwell to 26-31 degrees and point gap to .017 inch

TDC Top Dead Center
W Windsor
— Not applicable

④ .044 on California models and all cars using Solid State Ignition
⑤ Not used
⑥ Solid State Ignition used on all engines nationwide on cars assembled after May, 1974.
⑦ 8B with 3.25:1 rear axle, Code 9 or R on Certification label, except in California
⑧ Depends on emission equipment, check underhood specification sticker
⑨ In Drive

B Before Top Dead Center
C Cleveland
M Modified Cleveland
N.A. Not available
PI Police Interceptor

TUNE-UP SPECIFICATIONS

• When analyzing compression test results, look for uniformity among cylinders rather than specific pressures.

Year	ENGINE No. Cyl Displacement (cu in.)	hp	SPARK PLUGS Type	Gap (in.)	DISTRIBUTOR Point Dwell (deg)	Point Gap (in.)	IGNITION TIMING (deg) ▲ Man Trans	Auto Trans	VALVES Intake Opens ■ (deg)	Fuel Pump Pressure (psi)	IDLE SPEED (rpm) ▲ Man Trans *	Auto Trans
'69	8-390	265	BF-42	.034	29	.017	6B	6B	13	4½-6½	650	550
	8-390	280	BF-42	.030	27	.021	—	6B	13	4½-6½	—	550
	8-428PI	360	BF-42	.034	29	.016	—	6B	18	4½-6½	—	600
	8-429	320	BF-42	.034	29	.017	6B	6B	16	4½-6½	650	550
	8-429	360	BF-42	.034	29	.017	6B	6B	16	4½-6½	650	550
'70	8-390	265	BF-42	.034	27	.021	10B	10B	13	5½-6½	750/500	575
	8-428PI	360	BF-32	.034	27	.021	—	6B	13	5-6	—	600
	8-429	320	BF-42	.034	27	.021	6B	6B	18	5½-6½	850/500	600
	8-429	360	BF-42	.034	27	.021	6B	6B	16	5½-6½	850/500	600
'71	8-351C	240	ARF-42	.034	27	.021	6B	6B	12	5½-6½	700/500	600 600/500
	8-351W	240	BRF-42	.034	27	.021	6B	6B	11	5½-6½	775/500	575 600/500
	8-400	260	ARF-42	.034	27①	.021①	—	10B(6B)	17	5½-6½	—	600/500
	8-429	320	BRF-42	.034	27①	.021①	—	6B	16	5½-6½	—	590 600/500
	8-429	360	BRF-42	.034	27①	0.21①	4B	4B	16	5½-6½	700	650
	8-429PI	370	AF-32	.034	27①	.021①	10B	10B	32	5½-6½	700 700/500	650 650/500
'72	8-351C	163	ARF-42	.034	28	.017	6B	6B	12	5½-6½	750/500	575/500 (625/500)
	8-400	172	ARF-42	.034	28	.017	—	8B(6B)	17	5½-6½	—	625/500
	8-429	208	BRF-42	.034	28	.017	—	10B	8	5½-6½	—	650/500
	8-429PI	N.A.	ARF-42	.034	28	.020	—	10B	32	5½-6½	—	650/500
	8-460	200	BRF-42	.034	28	.017	—	10B(6B)②	8	5½-6½	—	625/500
'73	8-351C	163	ARF-42	.034	28	.017	—	6B	12	5½-6½	—	650/500
	8-400	172	ARF-42	.034	28	.017	—	6B	17	5½-6½	—	650/500
	8-429	208	BRF-42	.034	28	.017	—	10B	8	5½-6½	—	650/500
	8-429PI	N.A.	ARF-42	.034	28	.020	—	10B	32	5½-6½	—	650/500
	8-460	200	BRF-42	.034	28	.017	—	6B	8	5½-6½	—	(625/500)
'74	8-351C	163	ARF-42	.044	28③	.017③	—	14B	19½	5½-6½	—	600/500
	8-400	170	ARF-42	.044 (.054)	Electronic		—	12B	17	5½-6½	—	625/500
	8-460	195	ARF-52	.054	Electronic		—	10B	8	5½-6½	—	625/500
'75	8-400	144, 158	ARF-42	.044	Electronic		—	12B	17	5.5-6.5	—	625
	8-460	218	ARF-52	.044	Electronic		—	14B	8	6.2-7.2	—	650
	8-460PI	226	ARF-52	.044	Electronic		—	14B	18	6.2-7.2	—	650
'76	8-351M	All	ARF-42/52④	.044	Electronic		—	④	19½	5½-6½	—	650 (650/675④)
	8-400	All	ARF-42/52④	.044	Electronic		—	④	17	5½-6½	—	650(625)
	8-460	All	ARF-52	.044	Electronic		—	8/14B④⑤ @ 650	8	6.2-7.2	—	650
	8-460PI	226	ARF-52	.044	Electronic		—	14B @ 650⑤	18	6.2-7.2	—	650

▲ See text for procedure
• Figure in parentheses indicates California engine
■ All figures Before Top Dead Center
* In all cases where two figures are separated by a slash, the first figure is for idle speed with solenoid energized and automatic transmission in Drive, while the second is for idle speed with solenoid disconnected and automatic transmission in Neutral.

① For single diaphragm distributors, the dwell is 26-31 deg and the gap is .017 in.
② For all vehicles with 3.00 axles, Code 6 or 0 on certification label, figure is 6B
③ Solid State Ignition used on all engines nationwide on cars assembled after May 1974.
④ Depends on emission equipment, check underhood specifications sticker
⑤ In Drive

Thunderbird TUNE-UP SPECIFICATIONS

● When analyzing compression test results, look for uniformity among cylinders rather than specific pressures.

ENGINE			SPARK PLUGS		DISTRIBUTOR		IGNITION TIMING (deg) ▲		VALVES	Fuel	IDLE SPEED (rpm) ▲	
Year	No. Cyl Displacement (cu in.)	hp	Type	Gap (in.)	Point Dwell (deg)	Point Gap (in.)	Man Trans	Auto Trans	Intake Opens ■ (deg)	Pump Pressure (psi)	Man Trans *	Auto Trans
'69	8-429	360	BF-42	.034	26-31	.017	—	6B	16	4½-6½	—	550
'70	8-429	360	BRF-42	.034	26-31	.017	—	6B	16	5½-6½	—	600
'71	8-429	360	BRF-42	.034	26-31	.017	—	4B	16	5½-6½	—	600
'72	8-429	208, 212	BRF-42	.034	26-30	.020	—	10B	8	5½-6½	—	650/500
	8-460	200, 212	BRF-42	.034	26-30	.020	—	10B(6B)	8	5½-6½	—	650/500
'73	8-429	208, 212	BRF-42	.034	26-30	.020	—	10B	8	5½-6½	—	650/500
	8-460	200, 212	BRF-42	.034	26-30	.020	—	6B	8	5½-6½	—	650/500
'74	8-460	195	ARF-52	.044	Electronic		—	14B	8	5½-6½		675/500
'75	8-460	194, 223, 224	ARF-52	.044	Electronic		—	14B	8	6½-7½		650
'76	8-460	All	ARF-52	.044	Electronic		—	8/14B① @ 650	8	6-7	—	650

▲ See text for procedure
● Figure in parentheses indicates California engine
■ All figures Before Top Dead Center
— Not applicable
① In Drive

* First figure is for idle speed with solenoid energized and automatic transmission in Drive, while the second figure is for idle speed with solenoid disconnected and automatic transmission in Neutral

B Before Top Dead Center

Ford CAPACITIES

ENGINE		Engine Crankcase Add 1 Qt For New Filter	TRANSMISSION Pts To Refill After Draining			Drive Axle (pts)	Gasoline Tank (gals) ■	COOLING SYSTEM (qts)	
Year	No. Cyl. Displacement (Cu. In.)		Manual 3-Speed	Manual 4-Speed	Automatic			With Heater	With A/C
'69	6-240	4	3.5	—	See	5	24.5	14.3	14.3
	8-302	4	3.5	—	chart	4.5	24.5	15.4	15.6
	8-390	4	3.5	—	below	4.5	24.5	20.1	20.5
	8-428P	4	—	—		4.5	24.5	19.7	19.7
	8-429	4	—	4.0		4.5	24.5	20.5	21.5
'70	6-240	4	3.5	—		5	24.5	14.4	14.4
	8-302	4	3.5	—		4.5	24.5	15.4	15.6
	8-351	4	3.5	—		4.5	24.5	16.5	16.9
	8-390	4	3.5	—		4.5	24.5	20.1	20.5
	8-428P	4	—	—		4.5	24.5	19.7	19.7
	8-429	4	—	—		4.5	24.5	18.6	19.0
'71	6-240	4	3.5	—		5	22.5	14.1	14.1
	8-302	4	3.5	—		4.5	22.5	15.2	15.6
	8-351	4	3.5	—		4.5	22.5	16.3	16.7
	8-390	4	—	—		4.5	22.5	20.3	26.3
	8-400	4	—	—		4.5	22.5	17.6	17.6
	8-429	4	—	—		4.5	22.5	18.8	18.8
'72	6-240	4	—	—		4	22	14.2	14.2
	8-302	4	—	—		4.5	22	15.2	15.2
	8-351	4	—	—		4.5	22	16.3	16.3
	8-400	4	—	—		5	22	17.7	18.3
	8-429	4	—	—		5	22	18.8	19.5
'73	8-351	4	—	—		4.5	22	16.3	16.3
	8-400	4	—	—		5	22	17.7	18.3
	8-429	4	—	—		5	22	18.8	19.5

Ford

CAPACITIES

Year	ENGINE No. Cyl. Displacement (Cu. In.)	Engine Crankcase Add 1 Qt For New Filter	TRANSMISSION Pts To Refill After Draining: Manual 3-Speed	Manual 4-Speed	Automatic	Drive Axle (pts)	Gasoline Tank (gals) ■	COOLING SYSTEM (qts) With Heater	With A/C
'74	8-351	4	—	—		4.5	22	16.3	①
	8-400	4	—	—		5	22	18.0	18.0
	8-460	4	—	—		5	22	19.4	19.4
'75-'76	8-351 M	4	—	—		4.5④	24.2③	17.1	17.6
	8-400	4	—	—		4.5④	24.2③	17.1	17.6
	8-460	4	—	—		5	24.2③	18.5	18.5
	8-460 PI	6②	—	—		5	24.2③	20.0	20.0

① 351W—17.1 qts.; 351C—16.3 qts
② 7.5 w/oil cooler
③ With auxiliary fuel tank: sedan—32.3 gals; wagon—29.0 gals.
④ 5 with locker or 3.25:1 ratio
■ Station wagons:
'69 to '70—20 gals
'71—22 gals
'72-'76—21 gals
M Modified Cleveland
P Police
PI Police interceptor
—— Not applicable

AUTOMATIC TRANSMISSION REFILL CAPACITIES (Pts)

Year	Code▲	Capacities
'69-'76	X, Y, #	22
'69-'76	W	20.5
'69	U, Z	26
'70-'76	U, Z	25

▲ Transmission code can be found on the serial number plate or the vehicle certification label.

Mercury

CAPACITIES

Year	ENGINE No. Cyl. Displacement (Cu. In.)	Engine Crankcase Add 1 Qt For New Filter	TRANSMISSION Pts To Refill After Draining: Manual 3-Speed	Manual 4-Speed	Automatic	Drive Axle (pts)	Gasoline Tank (gals) ■	COOLING SYSTEM (qts) With Heater	With A/C
'69	8-390	4	3.5	—	26	5	24.5	20.1	20.5
	8-428	4	—	—	26	5	24.5	19.7	19.7
	8-429	4	—	—	26	5	24.5	20.5	21.5
'70	8-390	4	3.5	—	25.5	5	24.5	20.1	20.5
	8-428	4	—	—	25.5	5	24.5	19.7	19.7
	8-429	4	—	—	25.5	5	24.5	20.5	21.5
'71	8-351	4	3.5	—	22	5	23	16.3	16.7
	8-400	4	—	—	25	5	23	17.6	17.6
	8-429	4	—	—	25	5	23	18.8	18.8
'72	8-351	4	—	—	22	4	22	15.8	16.3
	8-400	4	—	—	25.5	5	22	17.7	18.3
	8-429	4	—	—	25.5	5	22	18.8	19.5
'73-'74	8-351	4	—	—	22	4	22	15.8	16.3
	8-400	4	—	—	25.5	5	22	17.7	18.3
	8-429	4	—	—	25.5	5	22	18.8	19.5
	8-460	4	—	—	26	5	22	19.5	19.5
'75-'76	8-400	4	—	—	22	4④	24.2②	17.1	17.6
	8-460	4	—	—	25③	4④	24.2②	18.5	18.5
	8-460 PI	6①	—	—	25	4④	24.2②	20.0	20.0

■ Station Wagons:
'69—20 gals
'70 to '71—22 gals
'72 to '76—21 gals

① 7.5 with oil cooler
② With auxiliary fuel tank: sedan—32.3 gals; wagon—29.0 gals.
③ 22 for FMX
④ 5 for removeable differential carrier axle
— Not applicable

Thunderbird

CAPACITIES

Year	ENGINE No. Cyl. Displacement (Cu. In.)	Engine Crankcase Add 1 Qt For New Filter	TRANSMISSION Pts To Refill After Draining Manual 3-Speed	Manual 4-Speed	Automatic	Drive Axle (pts)	Gasoline Tank (gals)	COOLING SYSTEM (qts) With Heater	With A/C
'69	8-429	4	—	—	26	5	24	18.5	19.0
'70	8-429	4	—	—	26	5	24①	19.4	19.4
'71	8-429	4	—	—	26	5	22.5	19.4	19.4
'72-'74	8-429	4	—	—	26	5	22.5	18.8	18.8
	8-460	4	—	—	26	5	22.5	20	20
'75-'76	8-460	4	—	—	25	5	26.5	19.3②	19.3②

① With evaporative emission controls—22.5 gals ② 19.8 with Class III towing package — Not applicable

VALVE SPECIFICATIONS

Year	Engine No. Cyl. Displacement (cu in.)	Seat Angle (deg)	Face Angle (deg)	Spring Test Pressure (lbs @ in.)	Spring Installed Height (in.)	STEM TO GUIDE Clearance (in.) Intake	Exhaust	STEM Diameter (in.) Intake	Exhaust
'69	6-240	45	44	197 @ 1.30	1 11/16	.0010-.0027	.0010-.0027	.3420	.3420
	8-302	45	44	180 @ 1.23	1 21/32	.0010-.0027	.0015-.0032	.3420	.3415
	8-390	45	44	220 @ 1.38	1 13/16	.0010-.0027	.0015-.0032	.3715	.3710
	8-429	45	44	251 @ 1.33	1 13/16	.0010-.0027	.0010-.0027	.3420	.3420
'70	6-240	45	44	197 @ 1.30	1 11/16	.0010-.0027	.0010-.0027	.3420	.3420
	8-302	45	44	180 @ 1.23	1 21/32	.0010-.0027	.0015-.0032	.3420	.3415
	8-351	45	44	215 @ 1.34	1 25/32	.0010-.0027	.0010-.0027	.3420	.3415
	8-390	①	44	220 @ 1.38	1 13/16	.0010-.0027	.0015-.0032	.3715	.3710
	8-429	45	44	253 @ 1.33	1 13/16	.0010-.0027	.0010-.0027	.3420	.3420
'71	6-240	45	44	197 @ 1.30	1 11/16	.0010-.0027	.0010-.0027	.3420	.3420
	8-302	45	44	180 @ 1.23	1 21/32	.0010-.0027	.0015-.0032	.3420	.3415
	8-351③	45	44	215 @ 1.34	1 25/32	.0010-.0027	.0015-.0032	.3420	.3415
	8-351④	45	44	210 @ 1.42	1 13/16	.0010-.0027	.0015-.0032	.3420	.3415
	8-390	①	44	220 @ 1.38	1 13/16	.0010-.0027	.0015-.0032	.3715	.3710
	8-400	45	44	226 @ 1.39	1 13/16	.0010-.0027	.0015-.0032	.3420	.3415
	8-429	45	45	253 @ 1.33	1 13/16	.0010-.0027	.0015-.0032	.3420	.3415
'72	6-240	45	44	197 @ 1.30	1 11/16	.0010-.0027	.0010-.0027	.3420	.3420
	8-302	45	44	200 @ 1.31	1 11/16	.0010-.0027	.0015-.0032	.3420	.3415
	8-351③	45	44	200 @ 1.34	1 25/32	.0010-.0027	.0015-.0032	.3420	.3415
	8-351④	45	44	210 @ 1.42	1 13/16	.0010-.0027	.0015-.0032	.3420	.3415
	8-400	45	44	226 @ 1.39	1 13/16	.0010-.0027	.0015-.0032	.3420	.3415
	8-429	45	45	229 @ 1.33	1 13/16	.0010-.0027	.0010-.0027	.3420	.3420
	8-460	45	45	229 @ 1.33	1 13/16	.0010-.0027	.0010-.0027	.3420	.3420
'73-	8-351③	45	44	200 @ 1.34	1 25/32	.0010-.0027	.0015-.0032	.3420	.3415
'74	8-351④	45	44	210 @ 1.42⑤	1 13/16	.0010-.0027	.0015-.0032	.3420	.3415
	8-400	45	44	226 @ 1.39	1 13/16	.0010-.0027	.0015-.0032	.3420	.3415
	8-429	45	45	229 @ 1.33	1 13/16	.0010-.0027	.0010-.0027	.3420	.3420
	8-460	45	45	229 @ 1.33	1 13/16	.0010-.0027	.0010-.0027	.3420	.3420
'75-	8-351⑥	44½-45	45½-45¾	226 @ 1.39	1 13/16	.0010-.0027	.0015-.0032	.3420	.3415
'76	8-400	44½-45	45½-45¾	226 @ 1.39	1 13/16	.0010-.0027	.0015-.0032	.3420	.3415
	8-460	44½-45	45½-45¾	253 @ 1.33	1 13/16	.0010-.0027	.0010-.0027	.3420	.3420
	8-460 PI	44½-45	45½-45¾	315 @ 1.32	1 13/16	.0010-.0027	.0010-.0027	.3420	.3420

① Intake valve seat angle 30°
Exhaust valve seat angle 45°
② Intake valve face angle 29°
Exhaust valve face angle 44°
③ Windsor heads
④ Cleveland heads
⑤ 1974 models—226 @ 1.39
⑥ Modified Cleveland heads
PI Police interceptor

TORQUE SPECIFICATIONS

All readings in ft lbs

Year	Engine No. Cyl. Displacement (cu in.)	Cylinder Head Bolts	Rod Bearing Bolts	Main Bearing Bolts	Crankshaft Pulley or Damper Bolt	Flywheel to Crankshaft Bolts	MANIFOLD Intake	MANIFOLD Exhaust
'69	6-240	70-75	40-45	60-70	130-150	75-85	25	25
	8-302	65-72	19-24	60-70	70-90	75-85	24	14
	8-390, 428	80-90	40-45	95-105	70-90	75-85	33½	21
	8-429	130-140	40-45	95-105	70-90	75-85	27½	30½
'70	6-240	70-75	40-45	60-70	130-150	75-85	25	25
	8-302	65-72	19-24	60-70	70-90	75-85	24	14
	8-351	95-100	40-45	95-105	70-90	75-85	23-25	18-24
	8-390	80-90	③	95-105	70-90	75-85	32-35	18-24
	8-429	130-140	40-45	95-105	70-90	75-85	27½	30½
'71	6-240	70-75	40-45	60-70	130-150	75-85	25	25
	8-302	65-72	19-24	60-70	70-90	75-85	24	14
	8-351	95-100	40-45	95-105	70-90	75-85	23-25	18-24④
	8-390	80-90	40-45	95-105	70-90	75-85	32-35	18-24
	8-400	95-105	40-45	95-105	70-90	75-85	27-33	12-16
	8-429	130-140	40-45	95-105	70-90	75-85	27½	30½
'72	6-240	70-75	40-45	60-70	130-150	75-85	23-28	23-28
	8-302	65-72	19-24	60-70	70-90	75-85	23-25	12-16
	8-351W	105-112	40-45	95-105	100-130	75-85	23-25	18-24
	8-351C, 400	95-105⑤	40-45⑥	⑦	70-90	75-85	⑧	12-16
	8-429, 460	130-140	40-45	95-105	70-90	75-85	25-30	28-33
'73-'76	8-351W	105-112	40-45	95-105	100-130	75-85	23-25	18-24
	8-351C, 351M, 400	95-105⑤	40-45⑥	⑦	70-90	75-75	⑧	18-24⑨
	8-429, 460	130-140	40-45	95-105	70-90	75-85	25-30	28-33

③ 390—40-45; 428—53-58
Tighten cylinder head bolts in 3 steps: the first 20 ft. lbs. less than maximum torque, the second 10 ft. lbs. less than maximum torque, and the third maximum torque

④ 351C engine—12-16

⑤ 351 HO—120

⑥ 351 HO—40-45

⑦ ½ x 13 in. bolt—95-105
⅜ x 16 in. bolt—35-45

⑧ 5/16 in. bolt—21-25
⅜ in. bolt—27-23
¼ in. bolt—6-9

⑧ 1973-74 351—12-22
1973-74 400—12-16

⑨ 1973-74 351—12-22
1973-74 400—12-16

CRANKSHAFT AND CONNECTING ROD SPECIFICATIONS

All measurements are given in inches

Year	Engine No. Cyl. Displacement (cu in.)	CRANKSHAFT Main Brg. Journal Dia	CRANKSHAFT Main Brg. Oil Clearance	CRANKSHAFT Shaft End-Play	CRANKSHAFT Thrust on No.	CONNECTING ROD Journal Diameter	CONNECTING ROD Oil Clearance	CONNECTING ROD Side Clearance
'69	6-240	2.3982-2.3990	.0005-.0015	.004-.008	5	2.1228-2.1236	.0008-.0015	.006-.013
	8-302	2.2482-2.2490	.0005-.0015	.004-.008	3	2.1228-2.1236	.0008-.0015	.010-.020
	8-390	2.7484-2.7492	.0013-.0025	.004-.010	3	2.4380-2.4388	.0008-.0015	.010-.020
	8-428	2.7484-2.7492	.0010-.0020	.004-.010	3	2.4380-2.4388	.0020-.0030	.010-.020
	8-429	2.9994-3.0002	.0005-.0015	.004-.008	3	2.4992-2.5000	.0008-.0015	.010-.020
'70	6-240	2.3982-2.3990	.0005-.0015	.004-.008	5	2.1228-2.1236	.0008-.0026	.006-.013
	8-302	2.2482-2.2490	.0005-.0015	.004-.008	3	2.1228-2.1236	.0008-.0026	.010-.020
	8-351	2.9994-2.3002	.0013-.0025	.004-.008	3	2.3103-2.3111	.0008-.0026	.010-.020
	8-390	2.7484-2.7492	.0005-.0025	.004-.008	3	2.4380-2.4388	.0008-.0026	.010-.020
	8-428	2.7484-2.7492	.0008-.0020	.004-.008	3	2.4380-2.4388	.0008-.0026	.010-.020
	8-429	2.9994-3.0002	.0005-.0025	.004-.008	3	2.4992-2.5000	.0008-.0026	.010-.020

CRANKSHAFT AND CONNECTING ROD SPECIFICATIONS

All measurements are given in inches

Year	Engine No. Cyl. Displacement (cu in.)	Crankshaft				Connecting Rod		
		Main Brg. Journal Dia	Main Brg. Oil Clearance	Shaft End-Play	Thrust on No.	Journal Diameter	Oil Clearance	Side Clearance
'71	6-240	2.3982-2.3990	.0005-.0022	.004-.008	5	2.1228-2.1236	.0008-.0026	.006-.013
	8-302	2.2482-2.2490	.0005-.0024①	.004-.008	3	2.1228-2.1236	.0008-.0026	.010-.020
	8-351W	2.9994-3.0002	.0013-.0030	.004-.008	3	2.3103-2.3111	.0008-.0026	.010-.020
	8-351C	2.7484-2.7492	.0009-.0026	.004-.010	3	2.3103-2.3111	.0008-.0026	.010-.020
	8-390	2.7484-2.7492	.0008-.0020	.004-.008	3	2.4380-2.4388	.0010-.0030	.010-.020
	8-400	2.9994-3.0002	.0009-.0026	.004-.010	3	2.3103-2.3111	.0008-.0026	.010-.020
	8-429	2.9994-3.0002	.0005-.0025	.004-.008	3	2.4992-2.5000	.0008-.0028	.010-.020
'72	6-240	2.3982-2.3990	.0005-.0022	.004-.008	5	2.1228-2.1236	.0008-.0026	.006-.013
	8-302	2.2482-2.2490	.0005-.0024①	.004-.008	3	2.1228-2.1236	.0008-.0026	.010-.020
	8-351W	2.9994-3.0002	.0008-.0026	.004-.008	3	2.3103-2.3111	.0008-.0026	.010-.020
	8-351C	2.7484-2.7492	.0011-.0028	.004-.010	3	2.3103-2.3111	.0011-.0026	.010-.020
	8-400	2.9994-3.0002	.0011-.0028	.004-.010	3	2.3103-2.3111	.0011-.0026	.010-.020
	8-429	2.9994-3.0002	.0010-.0020②	.004-.008	3	2.4992-2.5000	.0008-.0028	.010-.020
	8-460	2.9994-3.0002	.0010-.0020②	.004-.008	3	2.4992-2.5000	.0008-.0026	.010-.020
'73-'74	8-351W	2.9994-3.0002	.0008-.0026	.004-.008	3	2.3103-2.3111	.0008-.0026	.010-.020
	8-351C	2.7484-2.7492	.0011-.0028	.004-.010	3	2.3103-2.3111	.0011-.0026	.010-.020
	8-400	2.9994-3.0002	.0011-.0028	.004-.010	3	2.3103-2.3111	.0011-.0026	.010-.020
	8-429	2.9994-3.0002	.0010-.0020②	.004-.008	3	2.4992-2.5000	.0008-.0028	.010-.020
	8-460	2.9994-3.0002	.0010-.0020②	.004-.008	3	2.4992-2.5000	.0008-.0026	.010-.020
'75-'76	8-351M	2.9994-3.0002	.0009-.0026	.004-.008	3	2.3103-2.3111	.0008-.0026	.010-.020
	8-400	2.9994-3.0002	.0009-.0026	.004-.008	3	2.3103-2.3111	.0008-.0026	.010-.020
	8-460	2.9994-3.0002	.0012-.0028③	.004-.008	3	2.4992-2.5000	.0008-.0028	.010-.020

① #1—.0001-.0018 ② #1—.010-.015 ③ #1 bearing—.0004-.0020 in.

RING GAP

All measurements are given in inches

Year	Engine	Top Compression	Bottom Compression
'69-'76	6-240, 8-302, 351, 429, 400, 460	.010-.020	.010-.020
'69	8-390	.010-.031	.010-.020
'69-'71	8-390	.010-.020	.010-.020
'69-'70	8-428	.010-.020	.010-.020

Year	Engine	Oil Control
'69-'72	6-240	.015-.055
'69-'71	8-302	.015-.069
'72	8-302	.015-.055
'70-'74	8-351, 351W	.015-.069
'72-'74	8-351C	.015-.055
'69-'71	8-390	.015-.055
'70-'74	8-351M, 400	.015-.069
'75-'76	8-351M, 400	.015-.055
'69-'70	8-428, 429	.010-.035
'71-'76	8-429, 460	.015-.055

PISTON CLEARANCE

Year	Engine	Piston-to-Bore Clearance (in.)
'69-'72	240 Six	.0014-.0022
'69-'74	302, 351W V8	.0018-.0026
'69-'71	390, 428 V8	.0015-.0023
'70-'76	351C, 351M, 400, 429, 460 V8	.0014-.0022

RING SIDE CLEARANCE

All measurements are given in inches

Year	Engine	Top Compression	Bottom Compression
'69-'76	All engines	.002-.004	.002-.004

Year	Engine	Oil Control
'69-'76	All engines	Snug

ALTERNATOR AND REGULATOR SPECIFICATIONS

	ALTERNATOR			REGULATOR						
					Field Relay			Regulator		
Year	Manufacturer	Field Current @ 12 V	Output (amps)	Manufacturer	Air Gap (in.)	Point Gap (in.)	Volts to Close	Air Gap (in.)	Point Gap (in.)	Volts @ 75°
'69	Autolite	2.9	42	Autolite	①	①	4.2-9.0	①	①	13.5-15.3
	Autolite	2.9	55	Autolite	①	①	4.2-9.0	①	①	13.5-15.3
	Autolite	2.9	65	Autolite	①	①	4.2-9.0	①	①	13.5-15.3
	Leece-Neville	2.9	65	Leece-Neville	.012	.025	6.2-7.2	.047	.019	13.9-14.9
'70-'76	Autolite②	2.9	42	Autolite	①	①	2.0-4.2	①	①	13.5-15.3
	Autolite	2.9	55	Autolite	①	①	2.0-4.2	①	①	13.5-15.3
	Autolite	2.9	61	Autolite	①	①	2.0-4.2	①	①	13.5-15.3
	Autolite	2.9	65	Autolite	①	①	2.0-4.2	①	①	13.5-15.3
	Motorcraft	2.9	70	Motorcraft	①	①	2.5-4.0	①	①	13.5-15.3
	Leece-Neville	2.9	65	Leece-Neville	.012	.025	6.2-7.2	.047	.019	13.9-14.9
	Motorcraft	2.9	90	Motorcraft	①	①	2.5-4.0	①	①	13.5-15.3

① Transistorized regulator—not adjustable
② Beginning 1974, the name Autolite has been changed to Motorcraft

BATTERY AND STARTER SPECIFICATIONS

		BATTERY			STARTER ●						
					Lock Test			No-Load Test			
Year	Engine No. Cyl. Displacement (cu in.)	Ampere Hour Capacity	Volts	Terminal Grounded	Amps	Volts	Torque (ft lbs)	Amps	Volts	RPM	Brush Spring Tension (oz)
'69	6	45	12	Neg.	670	5	15.5	70	12	9,500	40
	8-302	55②	12	Neg.	670	5	15.5	70	12	9,500	40
	8-390	45③	12	Neg.	670	5	15.5	70	12	9,500	40
	8-428	80	12	Neg.	670	5	15.5	70	12	9,500	40
	8-429	80	12	Neg.	700	5	15.5	70	12	9,500	40
'70	6	45	12	Neg.	670	5	15.5	70	12	9,500	40
	8-302, 351	55②	12	Neg.	670	5	15.5	70	12	9,500	40
	8-390	45③	12	Neg.	670	5	15.5	70	12	9,500	40
	8-428, 429	80	12	Neg.	700	5	15.5	70	12	11,000	40
'71	6	45④	12	Neg.	670	5	15.5	70	12	9,500	40
	8-302	45④	12	Neg.	670	5	15.5	70	12	9,500	40
	8-351	45③	12	Neg.	670	5	15.5	70	12	9,500	40
	8-390	55②	12	Neg.	670	5	15.5	70	12	9,500	40
	8-400	70⑤	12	Neg.	700	5	15.5	70	12	11,000	40
	8-429	80	12	Neg.	700	5	15.5	70	12	11,000	40
'72	6	45	12	Neg.	670	5	15.5	70	12	9,500	40
	8-302	45	12	Neg.	670	5	15.5	70	12	9,500	40
	8-351	45③	12	Neg.	670	5	15.5	70	12	9,500	40
	8-400	70⑤	12	Neg.	670	5	15.5	70	12	9,500	40
	8-429	80	12	Neg.	700	5	15.5	70	12	11,000	40
	8-460	85	12	Neg.	700	5	15.5	70	12	11,000	40
'73-'74	8-351	55③	12	Neg.	670	5	15.5	70	12	9,500	40
	8-400	70⑤	12	Neg.	670	5	15.5	70	12	9,500	40
	8-429	80⑥	12	Neg.	700	5	15.5	80	12	11,000	80
	8-460	85⑥	12	Neg.	700	5	15.5	80	12	11,000	80

BATTERY AND STARTER SPECIFICATIONS

Year	Engine No. Cyl. Displacement (cu in.)	BATTERY Ampere Hour Capacity	BATTERY Volts	BATTERY Terminal Grounded	STARTER ● Lock Test Amps	Lock Test Volts	Lock Test Torque (ft lbs)	No-Load Test Amps	No-Load Test Volts	No-Load Test RPM	Brush Spring Tension (oz)
'75-'76	8-351	53/80	12	Neg.	670	5	15.5	80	12	9,500	80
	8-400	70/80	12	Neg.	670	5	15.5	80	12	9,500	80
	8-460 exc. T-Bird	80	12	Neg.	—	—	—	70	12	11,000	40
	8-460 Thunderbird	77	12	Neg.	—	—	—	70	12	11,000	40

● Starter specifications in table are for 4½ in. starter. Starter specifications for all models with a 4 in. diameter starter are: 460 5 9 70 12 —— 40

① Not Used
② 70 Amp. with air conditioning
③ 70 Amp. with air conditioning
④ 55 Amp. with air conditioning
⑤ 80 Amp. with air conditioning
⑥ 77 Amp. side terminal standard on Thunderbird

BRAKE SPECIFICATIONS

All measurements are given in inches

Year	Model	MASTER CYLINDER Disc	MASTER CYLINDER Drum	WHEEL CYLINDER Front Disc	WHEEL CYLINDER Front Drum	WHEEL CYLINDER Rear	BRAKE DISC OR DRUM DIAMETER Front Disc	Front Drum	Rear
'69	Ford and Mercury Sedan	1.0	1.0	2.750	1.125	.938	11.72	11.03	11.03
	Ford and Mercury Wagon	1.0	1.0	2.750	1.094	.938	11.72	11.03	11.03
	Thunderbird	1.0	—	2.750	—	.938	11.72	—	11.03
'70-'71	Ford and Mercury	1.0	1.0	2.750	1.125	.938	11.72	11.03	11.03
	Thunderbird	1.0	—	2.750	—	.938	11.72	—	11.03
'72	Ford and Mercury	1.0	1.0	2.750	1.125	.938	11.72	11.03	11.03
	Thunderbird	1.0	—	3.100	—	.938	11.72	—	11.03
'73-'74	Ford, Mercury and Thunderbird	1.0	—	3.100	—	1.0	11.72	—	11.03
'75-'76	Ford and Mercury	1.0②	—	3.100	—	1.0④	11.80	—	11.03⑤
	Thunderbird	1.0③	—	3.100	—	1.0④	11.80	—	11.03⑤

① With power brakes—.937 in.
② With 4-wheel disc brakes—1.125 in.
③ With 4-wheel discs—1.585 in.
④ With 4-wheel discs—2.6 in.
⑤ With 4-wheel discs—11.50 in.
— Not applicable

WHEEL ALIGNMENT SPECIFICATIONS

Year	Model	CASTER Range (deg)	CASTER Pref Setting (deg)	CAMBER Range (deg)	CAMBER Pref Setting (deg)	Toe-in (in.)	Steering Axis Inclin. (deg)	WHEEL PIVOT RATIO (deg) Inner Wheel	WHEEL PIVOT RATIO (deg) Outer Wheel
'69	Ford, Mercury	0 to 2P	1P	¼N to 1¼P	¾P	⅛ to ¼	7¾	20	18⅛
	T-Bird	0 to 2P	1P	¼N to 1¼P	½P	1/16 to 5/16	7¾	20	18¼
'70-'71	Ford, Mercury	0 to 2P	1P	¼N to 1¼P	½P	1/16 to 5/16	7¾	20	19 4/25
	T-Bird	0 to 2P	1P	¼N to 1¼P	½P	1/16 to 5/16	7¾	20	19 8/25
'72	Ford, Mercury	1N to 3P	1P	½N to 1½P	½P	1/16 to 7/16	7¾	20	19 4/25
	T-Bird	1N to 3P	1P	¼N to 1¾P	¾P	1/16 to 7/16	7¾	20	17 37/50
'73	Ford, Mercury	0 to 4P	2P	1N to 1P	0	1/16 to 7/16	7¾	20	18¾
	T-Bird	½N to 3½P	1½P	¼N to 1¾P	¾P	1/16 to 7/16	7¾	20	17¾
'74	Ford	0 to 4P	2P	①	②	3/16	9½	20	18¾
	Mercury	0 to 4P	2P	③	②	3/16	9½	20	18¾
	T-Bird	½P to 3½P	2P	¼N to 1¾P	¾P	3/16	9	20	18
'75-'76	Ford, Mercury	0 to 4P	2P	③	②	3/16	9 7/16	20	18¾
	T-Bird	2½P to 5½P	4P	④	⑤	3/16	9	20	18

① Left wheel—0 to 1P
Right wheel—¼N to ¾P
② Left wheel—½P
Right wheel—¼P
③ Left wheel—½N to 1½P
Right wheel—¾N to 1¼P
④ Left wheel—0 to 2P
Right wheel—½N to 1½P
⑤ Left wheel—1P
Right wheel—½P
— Not specified
N Negative P Positive

CHARGING SYSTEM

All Ford cars use alternating-current (AC) charging systems.

This charging system requires certain precautions.

1. Reversing battery connections will cause damage to the one-way electrical valves, the rectifiers.
2. Booster battery connections must be made as follows: the negative terminal of the booster battery must be connected to the negative terminal of the car battery. The positive terminal of the booster battery must be connected to the positive terminal of the car battery.
3. Fast chargers should never be used as boosters to start AC circuit-equipped cars.
4. When servicing the battery with a fast charger, always disconnect car battery cables.
5. Never attempt to polarize an AC generator.

Complete alternator servicing data is in the Unit Repair Section.

Alternator R & R

1. Disconnect the negative battery cable.
2. Loosen the alternator mounting bolts, remove the alternator to adjusting arm bolt and remove the belt.
3. Remove the alternator mounting bolt and spacer, position the alternator so that the wire connectors can be disconnected and remove the alternator.

NOTE: on alternators with integral regulators mounted on the back of the alternator housing, press the sides of the retainer clip and remove the wire from the regulator.

4. Reverse above procedure to reinstall, applying pressure only to the front of the alternator housing when tightening the drive belt.

Regulator R & R

1. Disconnect the negative battery cable. The regulator is located behind the battery and it is necessary to remove the battery to remove the regulator.
2. Remove the regulator mounting screws, unlock the wire connectors, then with integral regulator.
3. On vehicles with integral regulator, remove the alternator to adjusting arm bolt and the drive belt.
4. Swing the alternator down, remove the terminal covers from the regulator and remove the regulator attaching nuts.
5. Press the sides of the retainer clip and remove the retaining clip and supply wire. Remove the regulator.
6. Reverse above procedure to reinstall. On electromechanical regulators, the radio suppression condenser mounts under one screw.

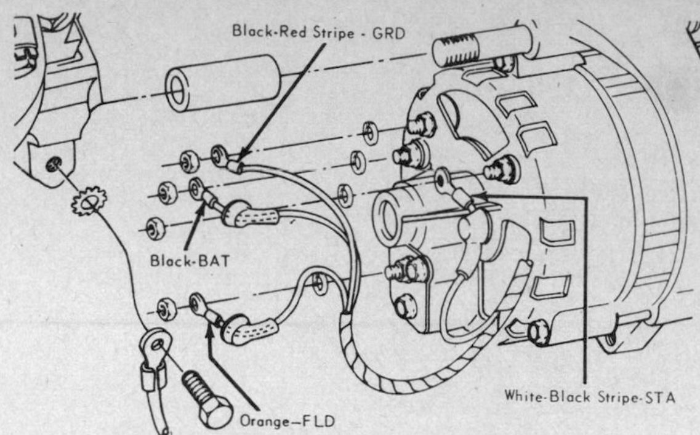

Typical alternator installation
(© Ford Motor Co)

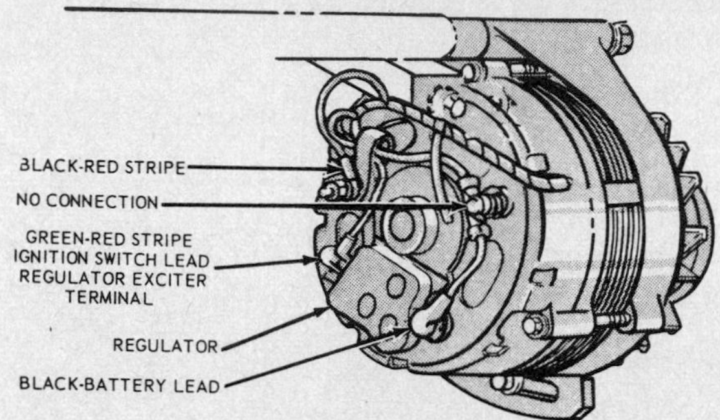

Alternator wiring harness—with integral regulator
(© Ford Motor Co)

Fuse Link

Since 1970, all Ford products have incorporated a fuse link in the charging system. The fuse link is a short length of insulated wire, several gauge sizes smaller than the system it protects. The fuse link blows out if a booster battery is hooked into the system incorrectly, or if a component of the electrical system is shorted to ground. When the fuse link blows, it leaves an open circuit in the charging system and the alternator will not charge the battery. A blown fuse link can be indentified by bare wire ends or bubbled insulation. It is located in the engine wire harness on or near the starter solenoid and is marked FUSE LINK.

STARTING SYSTEM

All models, except 1970 and later 429 and 460 V8 engined Thunderbirds, Fords and Mercurys, use positive engagement starters. These medium-duty starters have a self-contained engagement mechanism. The 429 and 460 V8 engined cars are equipped with heavy-duty, solenoid-actuated starters, to which an outboard solenoid is mounted. There is no difference in procedures for removing or installing these two types of starters.

Starting system troubleshooting and repairs may be found in the Unit Repair Section under Charging and Starting Systems.

Starter R & R

1. Disconnect the negative battery cable.
2. Disconnect the starter cable from the starter.
3. Remove the starter mounting bolts. On Thunderbird, remove the 2 front brace attaching bolts.
4. Manipulate the starter so that it can be lowered through the steering linkage. On some engine/chassis combinations this can be done by turning the steering wheel all the way to the right; on others it will be necessary to remove the idler arm bracket attaching bolts and lower the assembly away from the engine.
5. Reverse above procedure to reinstall.

Starter Drive R & R

Positive Engagement Starters

1. Loosen and remove the brush cover band and the starter drive plunger lever cover.
2. Loosen the thru-bolts enough to facilitate the removal of the drive end housing and plunger lever return spring.
3. Some drive end housings are equipped with needle bearings. If equipped, and not replacing the bearings, insert a dummy shaft through the housing to prevent

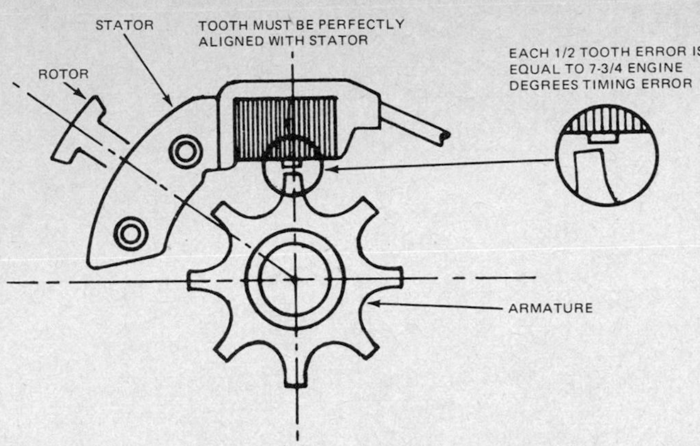

Static timing position—electronic ignition (© Ford Motor Co)

the loss of any of the bearing needles.

4. Remove the retaining pivot pin and starter drive plunger lever.
5. Remove the stop-ring and retainer from the end of the armature shaft. Remove the drive gear assembly.
6. Apply a thin coat of Lubriplate to the armature shaft splines. Install the drive gear assembly on the armature shaft and install a new stop-ring.
7. Position the starter gear plunger lever on the starter frame and install the pivot pin. Check to see that the plunger lever properly engages the starter drive assembly.
8. Install a new stop-ring retainer. Remove the dummy shaft from the drive end housing and lightly grease the needle bearings, if so equipped. Position the starter drive plunger lever return spring and the drive end housing to the starter frame.
9. Tighten the thru-bolts to 55–75 in. lbs.
10. Position the plunger lever cover and brush cover band, with its gasket, on the starter. Tighten the brush cover band retaining screw.

Solenoid-Actuated Starters

See "Unit Repair Section."

Distributor R & R

All Models

Remove the distributor cap and mark the position of tip of the rotor in relation to the body of the distributor and the engine block. Disconnect the ignition primary wires, the vacuum line(s) then take out the hold-down bolt that holds the distributor down in the block and lift it up out of the block.

Do not disturb the engine after the distributor has been removed. If the engine is cranked with the distributor removed, the engine will have to be retimed.

Ignition Retiming—Except Solid State Distributor

If the timing relationship has been disturbed, proceed to retime the ignition as follows: bring No. 1 cylinder up into the firing position. This can be checked by removing the spark plug, placing your thumb in the spark plug hole, then cranking the engine until the compression attempts to blow by your thumb. Now, slowly bring the crankshaft around until the T.D.C. mark on the crankshaft pulley lines up with the pointer. This is the approximate firing position for No. 1 cylinder.

Scribe a mark on the engine that corresponds with the position of the no. 1 spark plug wire in the distributor cap. Remove the distributor and reinstall it so that the tip of the rotor aligns with the mark on the engine.

Viewed from above, rotation of distributor for six cylinder engine is clockwise; for eight cylinder, counterclockwise.

Ignition Retiming—Solid State Distributor

1. Rotate the engine until No. 1 piston is on TDC of the compression stroke.
2. Align the correct initial timing mark with the pointer.
3. Position the distributor in the block with one of the armature segments as shown and the rotor at No. 1 firing position.
4. Be sure that the oil pump intermediate shaft properly engages the distributor shaft. Install, but do not tighten, the distributor clamp bolt.
5. Rotate the distributor to advance the timing to a point where the armature tooth is properly aligned. Tighen the clamp.
6. Connect the distributor wiring and check the timing with a timing light.

Contact Point Replacement and Adjustment

1. Unsnap the distributor cap retaining clips and position the cap clear of the breaker plate. Remove the rotor by pulling it straight up.
2. Remove the metal point shield, if so equipped.
3. Disconnect the primary lead and condenser wires from the contact point assembly. On dual-point distributors, remove the jumper strap also.
4. Remove the contact point and condenser retaining screws. Lift the contact point assembly and condenser from the distributor.
5. Lightly lubricate the distributor cam with heat-resistant lubricant.
6. Place the new contact point assembly and condenser in the distributor. Install, but do not tighten, the retaining screws.
7. On all V8 engines, place the ground wire under the contact point assembly screw farthest from the contacts. On all six-cylinder engines, this ground wire is positioned under the condenser retaining screw.
8. Turn the engine until the rubbing block on the point assembly is resting on the high point of the distributor cam lobe. Insert a feeler gauge of specified thickness between the contact points and adjust the gap. Tighten the retaining screw and remove the feeler gauge.
9. Connect the primary and condenser wires to the contact point assembly in the same order in which they were removed. On distributors equipped with a metal point shield, the wires should be positioned 180° from each other, then install the shield.
10. Install the rotor and distributor cap.
11. If a dwell meter is available, check to see that the distributor dwell is within specifications.

Ignition Timing

1. Locate the timing marks and pointer on the lower engine pulley and engine front cover.
2. Clean the marks and apply chalk or bright-colored paint to the pointer.
3. Attach a timing light according to the manufacturer's specifications.
4. Disconnect and plug all vacuum lines leading to the distributor.
5. If the recommended engine idle speed is in excess of 500 rpm, set the idle at 500 rpm for setting the timing. If the recommended idle speed is below 500 rpm, do not alter it.
6. Aim the timing light at the timing mark and pointer on the front of the engine. If the marks align when the timing light

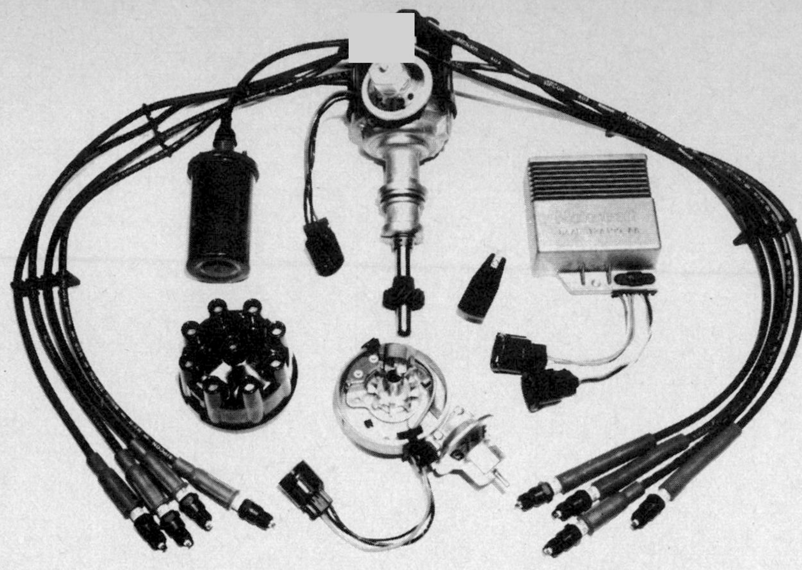

Solid state "breakerless" ignition system components (© Ford Motor Co)

flashes, remove the timing light, set the idle to its proper specification, and connect the vacuum lines at the distributor. If the marks do not align when the light flashes, loosen the distributor hold-down clamp slightly.

7. Start the engine again, and observe the alignment of the timing marks. To advance the timing, turn the distributor counterclockwise on six-cylinder engines and clockwise on V8 engines. When altering the timing, it is wise to tap the distributor lightly with a wooden hammer handle in order to move it in the desired direction. Grasping the distributor with your hand may result in a painful electric shock. When the timing marks are aligned, turn the engine off and tighten the distributor hold-down clamp.

Solid State Ignition

Beginning 1974, Ford is utilizing a solid state or "breakerless" ignition system on all 351 cubic inch and larger engines in the state of California, and on all 400 and 460 cubic inch V8s nationwide. All 1975 and later engines use this maintenance-saving ignition system. This system is unique in that it eliminates the contact breaker points, replacing them with a permanent magnet, low voltage generator.

Briefly, the system works as follows; When the ignition is on and the distributor is rotating, the low voltage generator in the distributor produces alternating current which is then sent to the electronic control module. The module senses the signal from the low voltage generator as the alternating current wave swings from positive to negative each time one of the gear teeth on the armature passes the magnetic field in the coil of the generator. When a gear tooth is directly opposite the magnetic field, the alternating current wave is at crossover (neither negative nor positive). The control module senses this and cuts off electricity (low voltage) to the coil, causing it to fire (high voltage). After the coil fires, the timing circuitry in the module redirects the low tension voltage to the coil.

Other than the low voltage generator and the control module, the rest of the system is conventional in appearance, with a conventional distributor cap and rotor. Spark advance or retard is accomplished by moving the plate for the low voltage generator in the distributor.

Complete service information for the Ford Solid State Ignition System can be found in the "Electronic Ignition" Unit Repair Section.

Tachometer Connection—Electronic Ignition

Install a tachometer alligator clip into the "Tach Test" cavity as shown. If the coil connector must be removed, grasp the wires and pull horizontally until it disconnects from the terminals.

An alligator type clip from the tachometer test lead can also be connected to the DEC (Distributor Electronic Control) without removing the connector.

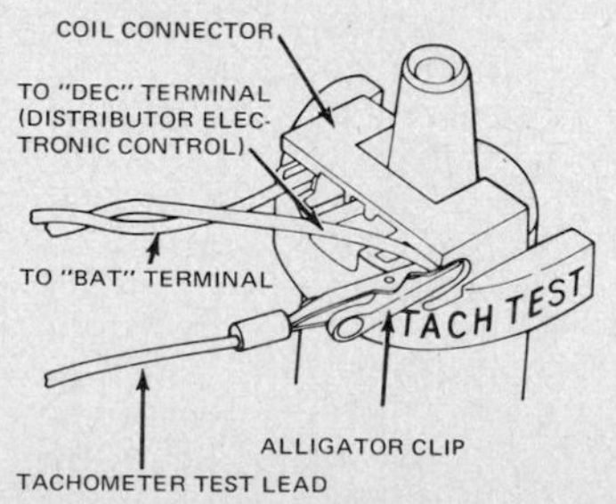

Electronic ignition tach connection (© Ford Motor Co.)

FUEL SYSTEM

Fuel Pump R & R

A single-action, permanently sealed fuel pump is used on all models. On 6-cylinder engines, the fuel pump is located on the lower left center of the engine block. The V8 fuel pump is mounted on the left side of the cylinder front cover.

1. Remove the inlet and outlet lines from the pump.
2. Remove the fuel pump retaining screws and remove the pump and gasket.
3. Clean all gasket material from the pump mounting surface on the engine, and apply a coat of oil-resistant sealer to the new gasket.
4. Position pump on engine and install retaining screws.
5. Reinstall lines, start engine and check for leaks.

NOTE: if resistance is felt while positioning the fuel pump on the block, the camshaft eccentric is in the high position. To ease installation, connect a remote engine starter switch to the engine and "tap" remote switch until resistance fades.

Fuel Filter R & R

All models use a non-serviceable inline fuel filter which is located at the carburetor fuel inlet.

1. Remove the air cleaner.
2. Loosen the hose clamp or crimp type clamp at the fuel inlet hose connection.
3. Unscrew the filter from the carburetor.
4. Disconnect the filter from the hose and discard the hose clamp.
5. Reverse the above procedure to install, using a new hose clamp. After installation, start the engine and check for fuel leakage.

Carburetor

Ford uses ten types of carburetors: Autolite (Motorcraft) 1100, Carter YF, YFA, and RBS (1-barrel), Autolite (Motorcraft) 2100 and 2150 (2-barrel), Autolite (Motorcraft) 4300, 4350, and Holley 4150 and 4150C (4-barrel).

See the applicable Carter, Holley, or Motorcraft carburetor Unit Repair Section for all carburetor adjustments not covered in this section.

Idle Speed Adjustment

1969-74

This is the procedure for adjusting all carburetors, any exceptions are listed below. Adjust with air cleaner installed.

1. Run engine at fast idle to equalize operating temperature.
2. Make sure the choke plate is fully released.
3. Turn headlights on high beam.

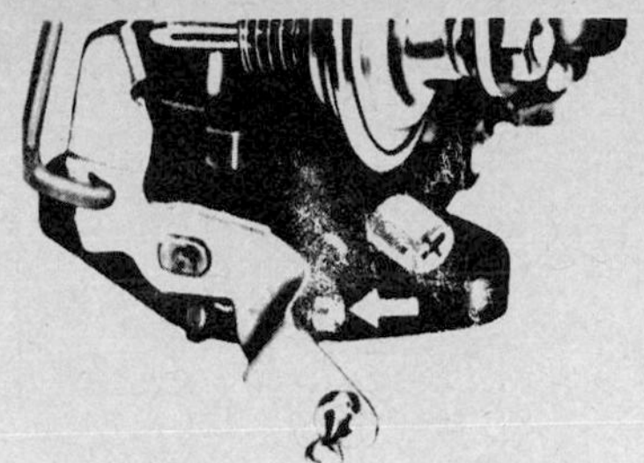
CARTER MODEL YF 1-V

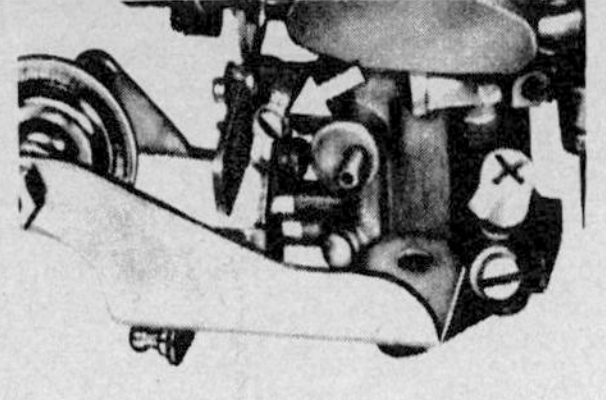
CARTER MODEL RBS 1-V

AUTOLITE MODEL 2100-D, 2-V

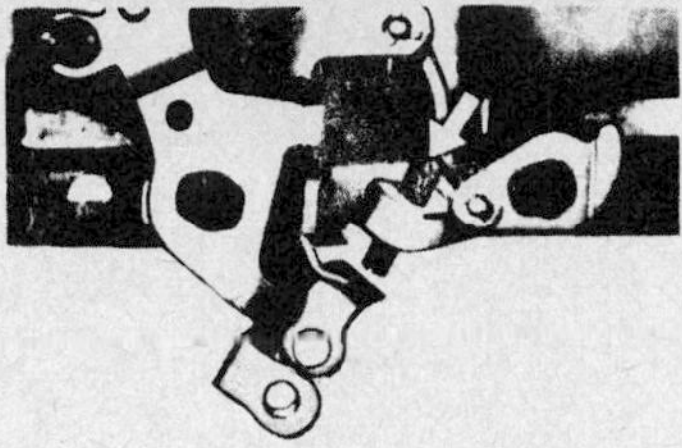
AUTOLITE MODEL 4300 4-V

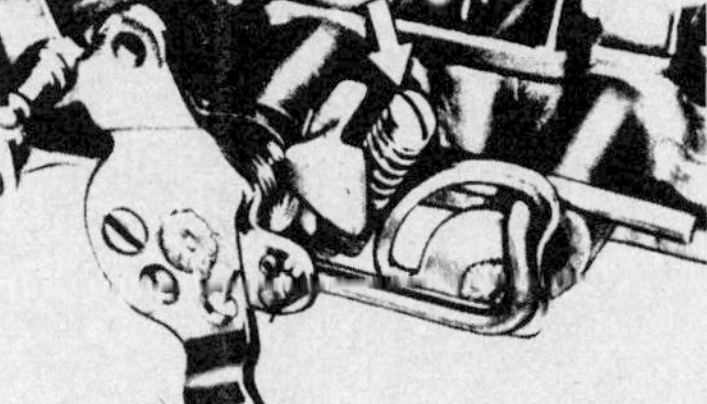
HOLLEY MODEL 4150C 4-V

ROCHESTER MODEL 4 MV

Idle speed adjusting screws (© Ford Motor Co)

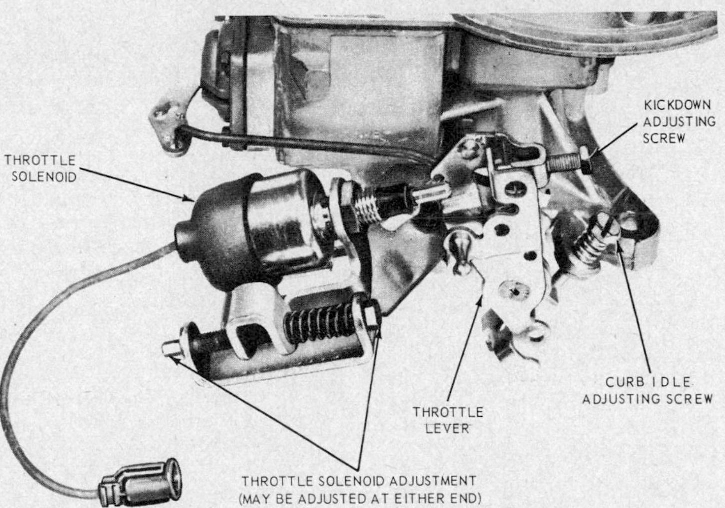

Throttle solenoid adjusting locations—Motorcraft 2100 shown; Motorcraft 4300 similar.
(© Ford Motor Co)

4. If engine is equipped with hot idle compensator valve, make sure it is fully seated in the closed position.
5. Attach tachometer of known accuracy to the engine.
6. On cars equipped with air conditioning, 1969 models (except 302 V8 engines with automatic transmission) set idle speed with air conditioner turned ON. On all 1970 and later models the idle speed is set with the air conditioner turned OFF.
7. On models equipped with a temperature sensing valve in the distributor vacuum line, remove and plug the vacuum hoses from the distributor to the valve and from the intake manifold to the valve, at the valve located in the intake manifold.
8. Make sure the dashpot is working freely and not binding.
9. If it is not possible to adjust the idle speed with the air cleaner installed, the engine idle speed must be rechecked after installing the air cleaner. On cars with vacuum controlled heat ducts in the air cleaner, the vacuum line must be plugged if the carburetor is to be adjusted with the air cleaner removed.
10. On 1969–71 model cars for which the specifications list two idle speeds, the first speed listed is obtained by turning the plunger on the electric solenoid. On 1972-74 models equipped with an electric solenoid, the higher idle speed is adjusted by turning the adjusting screw in the solenoid mounting bracket. On all models with a solenoid, the lower idle speed is obtained by putting the transmission in Park or Neutral, disconnecting the solenoid and adjusting the carburetor idle screw in the normal manner.

NOTE: with the electric solenoid disengaged, the carburetor adjusting screw must make contact with the throttle shaft to prevent the throttle plates from jamming in the throttle bore when the engine is shut off.

1975-76 351M and 400 V8

1. Set the parking brake and put the transmission in Drive. Turn the air conditioner OFF.
2. Remove the air cleaner and plug the vacuum hoses from the intake manifold to the air cleaner.
3. Disconnect the EGR valve by plugging the vacuum hose at the valve.
4. If the idle fuel mixture screws have not been previously set, be sure they are at maximum rich (full counterclockwise) against the limiter stops. Otherwise, do not disturb the mixture screws.
5. Start the engine and warm it thoroughly.
6. Set the ignition timing.
7. Adjust the idle speed to specifications with the TSP (throttle solenoid positioner) energized. Use the TSP screw in the solenoid mounting bracket. After adjustment, put the transmission in Neutral and increase the rpm slightly to clear up any loading condition. Return the engine to idle and check the speed in Drive.
8. Reconnect the EGR valve and install the air cleaner.

1975-76 460 V8

1. Warm the engine to operating temperature.
2. Check the timing with the advance line disconnected and plugged. Connect the hose after checking.
3. Set the idle rpm to specification in Drive with the solenoid positioner engaged.
4. Run the engine briefly at fast idle in Neutral and check the idle speed again in Drive.
5. Readjust the idle speed if necessary.

Dashpot Adjustment

Model	Clearance (in.) Manual	Automatic
1969 240 six	0.080	0.080
1969 302 2V	⅛	⅛
1969 351 2V	7/64	—
1969 351 4V	3/32	—
1969 390 2V	⅛	⅛
1969 390 4V	⅛	—
1969 428 Police	—	7/64
1969 429 2V	—	⅛
1969 429 4V	3/32	—
1970 240 1V	—	7/64
1971 240 1V	—	0.100
1970-72 302, 351, 400, 429 2V	—	⅛
1970-71 429 4V	—	0.100
1972 240 1V	—	7/64

NOTE: many models are equipped with a solenoid instead of a dashpot.

Fuel Mixture Adjustment

1969-74

1. On models with idle mixture limiters, adjust to obtain the highest rpm possible. Limiter caps should not be removed.

1975-76

Fuel mixture adjustment requires an artificial enrichment substance (propane). This should not be attempted unless you have the special equipment.

Dashpot Adjustment

1. With engine idle speed and mixture properly adjusted and with engine at operating temperature, loosen dashpot locknut.
2. Hold throttle in closed position and depress dashpot plunger. Measure clearance between plunger and cam. Adjust dashpot adjusting nut to give proper clearance.
3. Tighten locknut and check setting of accelerator pump.

COOLING SYSTEM

Both the 6-cylinder and V8 engines employ cooling systems that are basically similar.

In the 6-cylinder engine, coolant flows from the cylinder head, past the thermostat (if it is open) and into the radiator upper tank. In the V8 engine, coolant from each cylinder head flows through water passages in the intake manifold, then past the thermostat (if it is open) and into the radiator upper tank.

A single water pump assembly is used. The pump has a sealed bearing integral with the water pump shaft. The bearing requires no lubrication. There is a bleed hole in the water pump housing. This is not a lubrication hole.

Radiator R & R

1. Drain the cooling system.
2. Remove the upper and lower radiator hoses from the radiator.
3. On models with a fan shroud, remove the shroud attaching screws and move the shroud rearward to gain clearance.
4. If equipped with automatic transmission, remove the cooler lines from the radiator.
5. Remove radiator attaching screws and remove radiator from the car.
6. Reverse above procedure to install.
7. Fill cooling system, run engine at fast idle and check for leaks.

Water Pump R & R

1. Drain the cooling system. Disconnect the negative battery cable.
2. On cars with power steering, remove the drive belt; remove the power steering mounting retaining screws and remove the pump and bracket as an assembly and position it out of the way.
3. If vehicle is equipped with air conditioning, remove the idler pulley and drive belt from the engine.
4. Disconnect the lower radiator hose, heater hose and bypass hose from the water pump.
5. On cars with a fan shroud, remove the shroud retaining screws and position the shroud rearward over the fan.
6. Remove the fan attaching screws and remove the fan, fan spacer and shroud from the engine compartment.
7. Loosen the alternator mounting bolts and remove the belt.
8. Remove the air pump pulley and pivot bolt. Remove the air pump adjusting bracket. Swing the upper bracket aside. Detach the air conditioner compressor and lay it aside.
9. Remove any accessory mounting brackets from the water pump.
10. Disconnect the heater and lower radiator hoses from the water pump.
11. Remove the water pump mounting bolts and remove the pump from the engine.
12. Clean all gasket surfaces, and on 429 and 460 V8 remove the water pump backing plate and replace the gasket.

NOTE: the 240 6-cylinder engine originally had a one-piece gasket for the cylinder front cover and the water pump. Trim away the old gasket at the edge of the cylinder cover and replace with service gasket.

13. Remove the water pump fitting from the old pump and install it in the new pump.
14. Coat both sides of the new gasket with water resistant sealer, then install pump by reversing above procedure.

Thermostat R & R

1. Drain the radiator so that the coolant level is below the thermostat housing.
2. Remove the outlet elbow retaining bolts and position the elbow clear of the intake manifold or cylinder head sufficiently to provide access to the thermostat.
3. Remove the thermostat and old gasket. The thermostat must be rotated counterclockwise for removal.
4. Clean the mating surfaces of the outlet elbow and the engine to remove all old gasket material and sealer. Coat the new gasket with water-resistant sealer and install it on the engine. Install the thermostat in the outlet elbow. The thermostat must be rotated clockwise to lock it in position.
5. Install the outlet elbow and retaining bolts on the engine. Torque the bolts to 12–15 ft lbs.
6. Refill the radiator. Run the engine at operating temperature and check for leaks. Recheck the coolant level.

EMISSION CONTROLS

All Ford cars use positive crankcase ventilation (PCV) systems. The PCV system routes a harmful mixture of blow-by gases and condensation vapors, which were formerly dispelled into the atmosphere, through a modulating valve (PCV valve) and into the intake manifold where they combine with the carburetor air/fuel mixture and are burned in the combustion chamber. The system is closed to the atmosphere, deriving its fresh air from the air cleaner.

1969

In order to comply with stringent, federal antipollution laws, Ford Motor Company adopted the IMCO (IMproved COmbustion) emission control system. Rather than burning the exhaust gases in the exhaust manifolds, as in the Thermactor system, the IMCO system reduces carbon monoxide and hydrocarbons through more complete combustion in the combustion chambers. This is accomplished through the use of a heated air intake system which thermostatically supplies air, which has been heated by the exhaust manifold, as needed, to the air cleaner, as well as idle mixture limiter caps which prevent the air/fuel mixture from being adjusted to an overly rich condition at idle, and control of ignition timing by a dual diaphragm vacuum advance mechanism on the distributor and a ported vacuum or temperature override switch (PVS). The outer chamber of the vacuum advance is controlled by carburetor vacuum and the inner chamber by intake manifold vacuum. During normal engine operation the outer diaphragm advances ignition timing, while the inner diaphragm retards timing at idle. Three vacuum hoses are attached to the PVS switch, the top hose is connected to the carburetor, the second to the distributor, and the third to the intake manifold. When the engine is operating under normal temperature conditions, vacuum is supplied to the distributor vacuum advance by the carburetor. If the engine should overheat, the PVS switch connects intake manifold vacuum to the distributor which advances ignition timing while the engine is idling, thus speeding up the engine and lowering engine temperature.

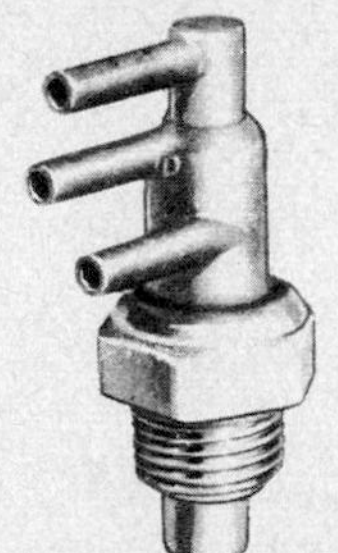

Ported Vacuum Switch (PVS)
(© Ford Motor Co)

To further aid in reducing emissions, a distributor vacuum advance (deceleration) control valve and a throttle solenoid were used on some models. The deceleration valve provides maximum intake manifold vacuum to the distributor and subsequent timing advance to prevent backfiring in the exhaust system when the vehicle is slowing down. The throttle solenoid is located on the side of the carburetor. When the ignition key is turned on, the throttle solenoid plunger extends and contacts the carburetor throttle lever, raising the idle speed of the engine. When the ignition key is turned off, the solenoid lever retracts, allowing the carburetor throttle lever to fall back on the carburetor idle speed adjusting screw. This prevents the engine from running on when the key is turned off.

1969-71

On 1969 cars with manual transmissions, and 1969-71 high-performance V8 models, the Thermactor (air injection) system was used. This system, which injects fresh air into the exhaust ports to achieve afterburning of exhaust fumes, consists of an air pump, a bypass and a check valve, and external air manifolds (not an integral part of the engine exhaust manifolds).

1970-71

The fuel evaporative emission control system was introduced on California models in 1970, and nationwide in 1971. This system eliminates pollution due to evaporating fuel by channeling the breathing of the fuel tank and by the venting of the carburetor float bowl through a canister filled with activated charcoal, condensing the fuel vapors and returning them to the fuel system.

The IMCO system of emission control was further extended in 1970 to become the Distributor Modulator (Dist-O-Vac) System. The Dist-O-Vac system incorporated all of the IMCO features but included three units of equipment which control spark advance in a more sophisticated manner. A speed sensor is located between two sections of the speedometer cable and generates a small current which increases in direct proportion to speed. A thermal switch is located in the right door pillar and activates at outside temperatures of 58°F or higher. The impulses of both are fed into the electronic control amplifier.

The distributor vacuum advance hose is connected from the carburetor, through the electronic control amplifier, to the distributor. When ambient temperature is above 58°F, the contacts in the temperature switch open and a plunger in the amplifier prevents vacuum from being supplied to the distributor. When vehicle speed reaches approximately 30 mph, the signal from the speed sensor causes the control amplifier to open the vacuum line to the distributor and ignition timing is allowed to advance in the normal manner. When the ambient temperature is below 58°F, the temperature switch closes, and normal vacuum is supplied to the distributor regardless of vehicle speed. In the event of engine overheating, the ported vacuum switch (PVS), a carryover from the IMCO system overrides the electronic control modulator by connecting intake manifold vacuum to the distributor.

1972

For 1972, the Dist-O-Vac system was replaced by two different spark control systems. The Electronic Spark Control (ESC) system is the same as the old Dist-O-Vac system except that the electronic control modulator was separated into two pieces, an amplifier and a distributor modulator valve. The amplifier judges the signals sent to it by the speed and temperature switches and tells the distributor modulator valve when to open and close and thus allow or prevent vacuum to reach the distributor. The Transmission Regulated Spark (TRS) is similar to the ESC system except that the speed sensor is replaced by a transmission switch. The switch is mounted on the side of the transmission and is hydraulically actuated on cars equipped with an automatic transmission and manually actuated on models equipped with a manual transmission. When the ambient temperature is above 55°F, the transmission switch is closed whenever the transmission is in any gear other than high gear (manual transmission), or high gear or reverse (automatic transmission).

When the transmission switch closes, it signals the distributor modulator valve to close and thus prevent carburetor vacuum from reaching the distributor. As in past systems, neither of these systems is functional below 55–58°F, and both are bypassed by the PVS if the engine should overheat.

On some 1972 models, a spark delay valve has been inserted into the vacuum advance line to the distributor. The valve closes under hard acceleration, blocking carburetor vacuum to the distributor for a predetermined period of a few seconds. The valves are color coded for identification purposes.

1973-74

1973-74 models use an Exhaust Gas Recirculation System (EGR) to control oxides of nitrogen. On V8 engines, exhaust gases travel through the exhaust gas crossover passage in the intake manifold. A portion of these gases is diverted into a spacer which is mounted under the carburetor. The EGR control valve, which is attached to the rear of the spacer, consists of a vacuum diaphragm with an attached plunger which normally blocks off exhaust gases from entering the intake manifold. The EGR valve is controlled by a vacuum line from the carburetor which passes through a ported vacuum switch. The EGR ported vacuum switch provides vacuum to the EGR valve at coolant temperatures above 125°F. The vacuum diaphragm then opens the EGR

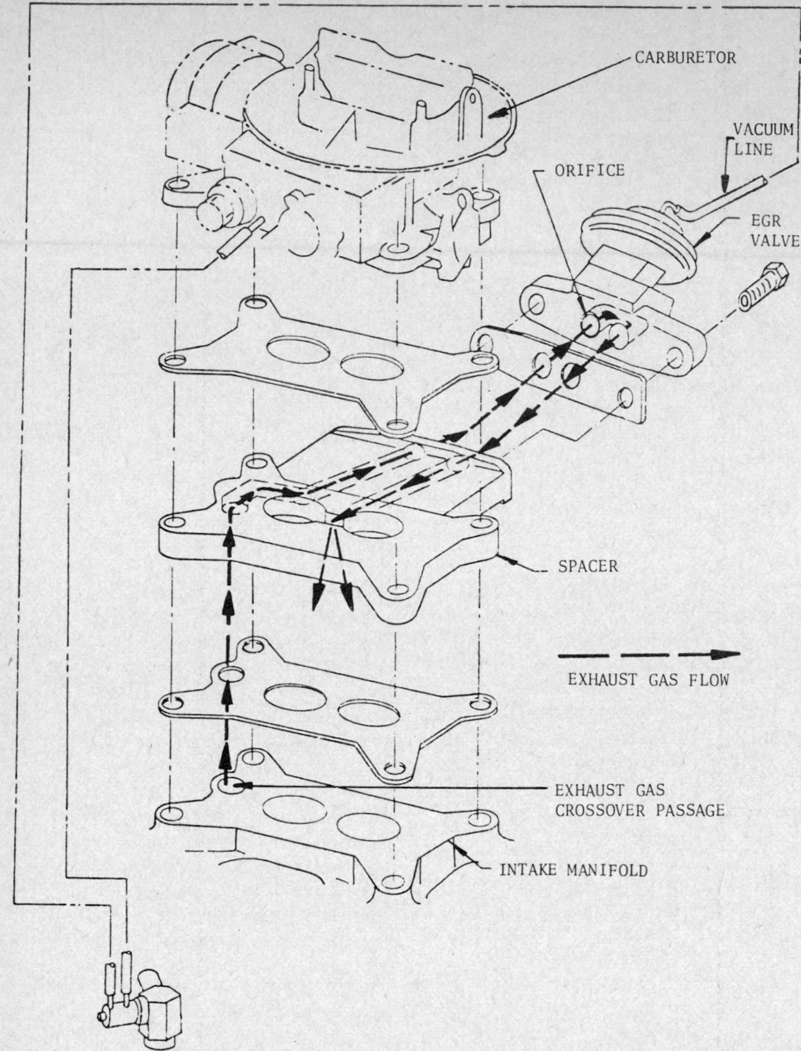

Exhaust Gas Recirculation (EGR) System (© Ford Motor Co)

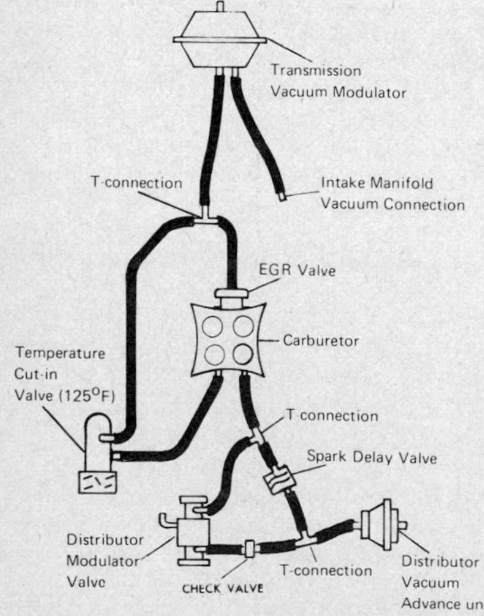

Typical vacuum hose schematic with EGR (© Ford Motor Co)

valve permitting exhaust gases to flow through the carburetor spacer and enter the intake manifold where they combine with the fuel mixture and enter the combustion chambers. The exhaust gases are relatively oxygen-free and tend to dilute the combustion charge. This lowers peak combustion temperature thereby reducing oxides of nitrogen.

All models that are equipped with a 351C, 400, 429, or 460 V8 use the new Delay Vacuum By-Pass (DVB) spark control system. This system provides two paths by which carburetor vacuum can reach the distributor vacuum advance. The system consist of a spark delay valve, a check valve, a solenoid vacuum valve, and an ambient temperature switch. When the ambient temperature is below 49°F, the temperature switch contacts are open and the vacuum solenoid is open (de-energized). Under these conditions, vacuum will flow from the carburetor, through the open solenoid, and to the distributor. Since the spark delay valve resist the flow of carburetor vacuum, the vacuum will always flow through the vacuum solenoid when it is open, since this is the path of least resistance. When the ambient temperature rises above 60°F, the contacts in the temperature switch (which is located in the door post) close. This passes ignition switch current to the solenoid, energizing the solenoid. This blocks one of the two vacuum paths. All distributor vacuum must now flow through the spark delay valve. When carburetor vacuum rises above a certain level on acceleration, a rubber valve in the spark delay valve blocks vacuum from passing through the valve for from 5 to 30 seconds. After this time delay has elapsed, normal vacuum is supplied to the distributor. When the vacuum solenoid is closed, (temperature above 60°), the vacuum line from the solenoid to the distributor is vented to atmosphere. To prevent the vacuum that is passing through the spark delay valve from escaping through the solenoid into the atmosphere, a one-way check valve is installed in the vacuum line from the solenoid to the distributor.

In order to meet 1974 California emission control standards, all 1974 Ford cars sold in that state will be equipped with a Thermactor (air injection) system to control hydrocarbons and carbon monoxide. The EGR and IMCO systems are retained, as in 1973, to control oxides of nitrogen.

1975

1975 is the year of the catalytic converter. All full size Ford, Mercury and Thunderbird models with the 351M, 400 and 460 engines are equipped with the converters. California models are equipped with two converters, while models sold in the 49 states have only one unit. The converters are needed to meet the 1975 Federal and California emission control standards.

Catalytic converters convert noxious emissions of hydrocarbons (HC) and carbon monoxide (CO) into harmless carbon dioxide and water. The units are installed in the exhaust system ahead of the mufflers and are designed, if the engine is properly tuned, to last 50,000 miles before replacement.

In addition to the converters, most 1975 Ford, Mercury and Thunderbird cars are equipped with the Thermactor air pumps (air injection system) previously mentioned. The air injection system, which afterburns the uncombusted fuel mixture in the exhaust ports, is needed with the converters to prevent an overly rich mixture from reaching the converter, and to help supply oxygen to aid in converter reaction.

Other emission control equipment for 1975 includes a carryover of the Positive Crankcase Ventilation (PCV) System, the Fuel Evaporative Control System, spacer entry exhaust gas recirculation, and all of the IMCO engine modifications first introduced in 1968.

Emission control related improvements for 1975 include standard Solid

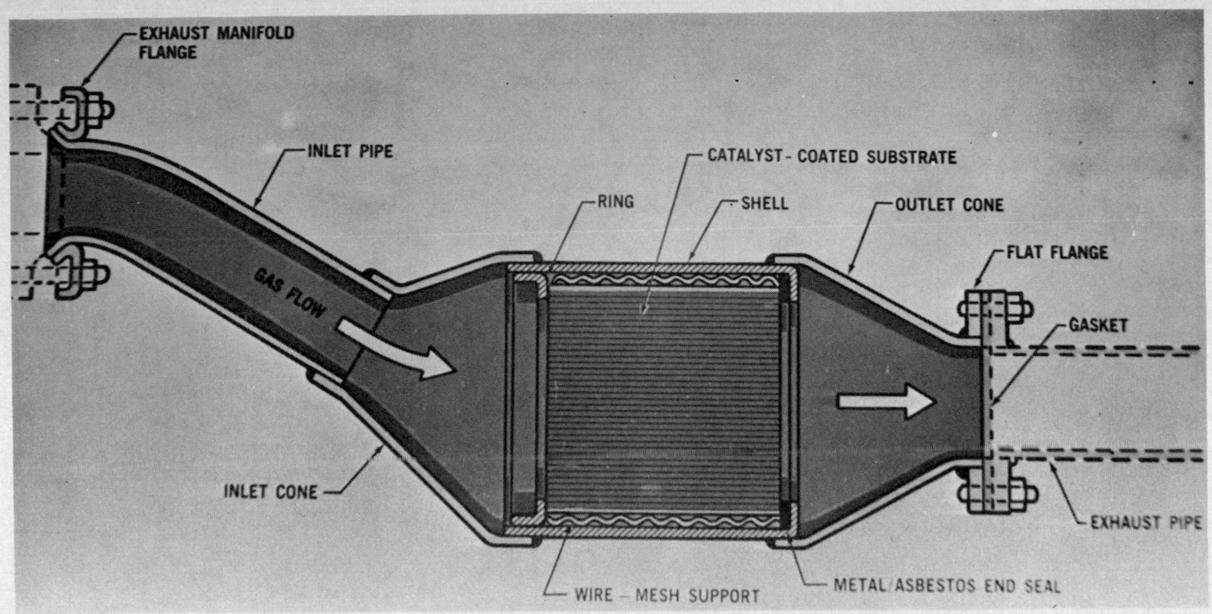

Catalytic converter (© Ford Motor Co)

CSSA system components

State (breakerless) Ignition, induction hardened exhaust valve seats, exhaust manifold redesign, vacuum operated heat riser valves, and improved carburetors with more precise fuel metering control and a mechanical high-speed bleed system.

All cars equipped with the 460 V8 engine use a Cold Start Spark Advance (CSSA) System in 1975 to aid in cold start driveability. Basically, the system will allow full vacuum advance to the distributor until the coolant temperature reaches 125°F.

1976

For 1976, the complexity of emission control equipment has been reduced on Ford products. The average number of emission control components has been reduced from 25 to 11 on most cars. All 1976 models have catalytic converters. In addition, a new proportional exhaust gas recirculation system has been introduced. Exhaust backpressure regulates the EGR valve spark port vacuum signal to modulate the recirculation of gases, matching EGR flow to engine load.

Thermactor system air by-pass valve

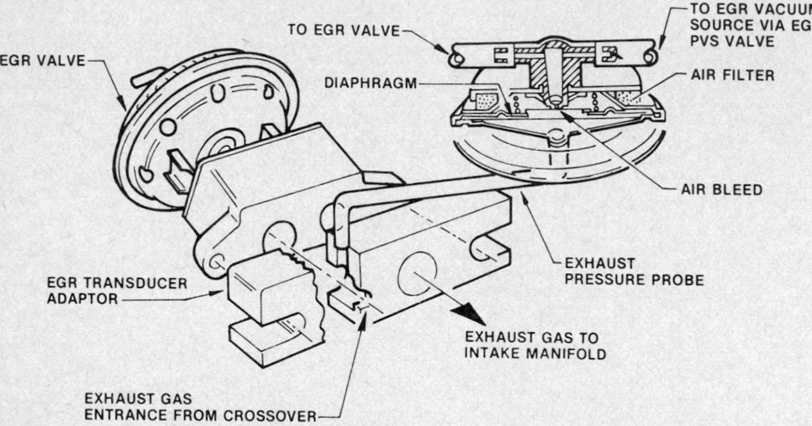

EGR valve with exhaust back pressure transducer (© Ford Motor Co)

ENGINE

The only 6-cylinder engine available on full sized Fords through 1972 is the 240 cu. in. version. The intake manifolding on this six is mounted conventionally on the right-hand side and is detachable, unlike the intake manifolding on Ford sixes in smaller cars. The 302, 351W, 351C, 351M and 400 V8 engines are the most popular engines in full sized Fords. The 302 is notably compact, about 20 in. across. The larger displacement 351W is wider and bulkier although nearly identical in layout and conformation. All have trapezoidal shaped valve covers. The 390 and 428 family of engines is recognizable by its unusual intake manifold that extends under valve covers. The engines of this family are identical in exterior appearance. These engines have been widely used in full size Fords and the 351M, a modified 351C, was introduced in 1975.

The 429 engine was the first of a new series of big block Ford engines. It has been available in two-barrel and four-barrel versions. The engine is identifiable by its great bulk, and by the tunnel port configuration noticeable in the shape of its intake manifold. A similar 460 V8 is available on the Thunderbird and Mercury from 1972 and the Ford from 1974. The 240 Six and 302 V8 were discontinued in 1973 Fords, the 351 engine becoming standard equipment. The 429 V8 was dropped after the 1973 model run.

Engine Removal

Remove or disconnect air pump equipment that interferes with removal.

1. Scribe the hood hinge outline on the underside of the hood, disconnect the hood and remove.
2. Drain the entire cooling system and oil from engine oil pan.
3. Remove the air cleaner, disconnect the battery at the cylinder head. On automatic transmission-equipped cars, disconnect oil cooler lines at the radiator.
4. Remove the upper and lower radiator hoses from the engine and, if the engine is equipped with a fan shroud, disconnect the shroud from the radiator and position it rearward. Remove the radiator from the car.
5. Remove the fan attaching screws and remove the fan, fan spacer and shroud from the engine as an assembly. Loosen and remove all drive belts. Remove the water pump pulley.
6. Disconnect the heater hoses from the engine. If the vehicle is equipped with power steering, remove the pump from the engine and position it out of the way.
7. Remove the alternator mounting bolts and ground wire from the block and remove the alternator. Disconnect the carburetor kick-down linkage and speed control wire from the engine.
8. On models with power brakes, remove the vacuum line from the engine. On cars with air conditioning, remove the compressor mounting bracket from the engine and position the compressor out of the way without disconnecting the refrigerant lines.

NOTE: if the compressor lines do not have enough slack to move the compressor out of the way without disconnecting the refrigerant lines, the air conditioning system must be evacuated, using the required tools, before the refrigerant lines can be disconnected.

9. Disconnect fuel tank line at the fuel pump and plug the line. On 460 V8 remove the automatic transmission filler tube.
10. Disconnect the coil primary wire at the coil. Disconnect wires at the oil pressure and water temperature-sending units.
11. Remove the starter and dust seal.
12. On a car equipped with a manual-shift transmission, remove the clutch retracting spring. Disconnect the clutch equalizer shaft and arm bracket at the underbody rail and remove the arm bracket and equalizer.
13. Raise the car. Remove the flywheel or converter housing upper retaining bolts through the access holes in the floor pan.
14. Disconnect the exhaust pipe or pipes at the exhaust manifold. Disconnect the right and left motor mount at the underbody bracket. Remove the flywheel or converter housing cover.
15. On a car with manual shift, remove the flywheel housing lower retaining bolts.
16. On a car with automatic transmission, disconnect throttle valve vacuum line at the intake manifold, disconnect the converter from the flywheel. Remove the converter housing lower retaining bolts.

17. Lower the car. Support the transmission and flywheel or converter housing with a jack.
18. Attach an engine lifting hook. Lift the engine up and out of the compartment and onto an adequate work stand.

Engine Installation

1. Place a new gasket over the studs of the exhaust manifold/s except on 390 and 428 engines.
2. Attach engine sling and lifting device. Then lift engine from work stand.
3. Lower the engine into the engine compartment. Be sure the exhaust manifold/s properly line up with the muffler inlet pipe/s and the dowels in the block engage the holes in the flywheel housing.
   On a car with automatic transmission, start the converter pilot into the crankshaft.
   On a car with manual-shift transmission, start the transmission main drive gear into the clutch disc. If the engine hangs up after the shaft enters, rotate the crankshaft slowly (with transmission in gear) until the shaft and clutch disc splines mesh.
4. Install the flywheel or converter housing upper bolts.
5. Install engine support insulator to bracket retaining nuts. Disconnect engine lifting sling and remove lifting brackets.
6. Raise front of car. Connect exhaust line/s and tighten attachments.
7. Position dust seal and install starter.
8. On cars with manual-shift transmissions, install remaining flywheel housing-to-engine bolts. Connect clutch release rod. Position the clutch equalizer bar and bracket and install retaining bolts. Install clutch pedal retracting spring.
9. On cars with automatic transmissions, remove the retainer holding the converter in the housing. Attach the converter to the flywheel. Install the converter housing inspection cover. Install the remaining converter housing retaining bolts.
10. Remove the support from the transmission and lower the car.
11. Connect engine ground strap and coil primary wire.
12. Connect water temperature gauge wire and the heater hose at coolant outlet housing. Connect accelerator rod at the bellcrank.
13. On cars with automatic transmission, connect the transmission filler tube bracket. Connect the throttle valve vacuum line.
14. On cars with power steering, install the drive belt and power steering pump bracket. Install the bracket retaining bolts. Adjust drive belt to proper tension.
15. Remove plug from the fuel tank line. Connect the flexible fuel line and the oil pressure sending unit wire.
16. Install the pulley, belt spacer, and fan. Adjust belt tension.
17. Install the alternator and the negative battery cable.
18. In vehicles with power brakes, connect vacuum line at intake manifold. On cars with air conditioning, install compressor on mounting bracket.
19. Install radiator. Connect radiator hoses.
20. On cars with automatic transmissions, connect oil cooler lines.
21. Install oil filter. Connect heater hose at water pump, after bleeding the system.
22. Bring crankcase to level with correct grade of oil. Run engine at fast idle and check for leaks. Install air cleaner and make final engine adjustments.
23. Install and adjust hood.
24. Road test car.

Engine Manifolds

Intake and Exhaust Manifold Removal—6-Cylinder

1. Remove the air cleaner. Remove the carburetor linkage and kick down linkage from the engine.
2. Disconnect the fuel line from the carburetor and all vacuum lines from the manifolds.
3. Remove the negative battery cable, then remove the alternator mounting bolts and remove the alternator from the engine with the wires attached.
4. Disconnect the muffler inlet pipe from the engine.
5. Remove the manifold attaching parts from the engine, and remove the two manifolds as an assembly.
6. To separate the manifolds, remove the carburetor and then remove the nuts that secure the manifolds together.
7. Clean all gasket areas and reverse above procedure to install; using all new gaskets.

Intake Manifold Removal—V8

1. Remove the compressor from its mount. Leave the refrigerant lines attached and set the compressor aside.
2. Drain the cooling system.
3. Disconnect the upper radiator hose from the thermostat housing and the bypass hose from the manifold.
4. Remove the air cleaner and ducts.
5. Remove the distributor cap and wires from the engine. Mark the position of the distributor rotor in relationship to the intake manifold, remove the primary wire from the coil, then remove the distributor hold-down bolt and the distributor. Remove the coil, vacuum solenoid valve and bracket.
6. Remove all vacuum lines from the intake manifold and remove the temperature sending unit wire.
7. Disconnect the fuel line and any vacuum lines from the carburetor.
8. Remove all carburetor linkage and kickdown linkage that attaches to the intake manifold.
9. On 390 and 428 engines, remove the valve covers, the rocker arm assemblies and the pushrods. The rocker arms should be removed by backing off each of the four bolts two turns in sequence from front to back. Keep pushrods in order so that they can be installed in their original position.
10. Remove the manifold attaching bolts and remove the manifold. If it is necessary to pry the manifold to loosen it from the engine, use care not to damage any gasket sealing surfaces.
11. Clean all gasket surfaces and firmly cement new gaskets in place. The gaskets should be securely locked in place before attempting to install the manifold.
12. Reverse procedure to reinstall.

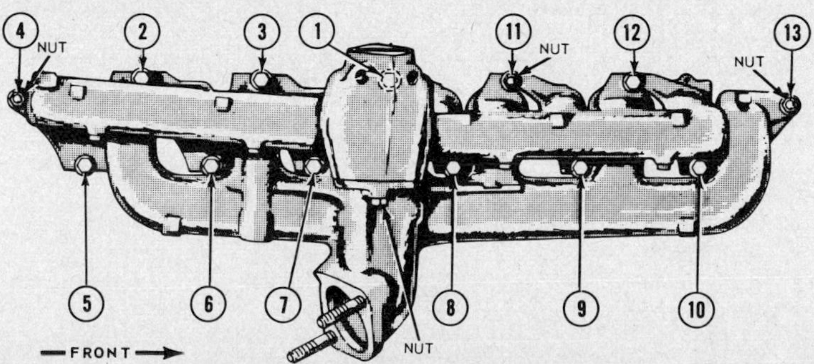

Intake and exhaust manifold torque sequence—240 six cyl. (© Ford Motor Co)

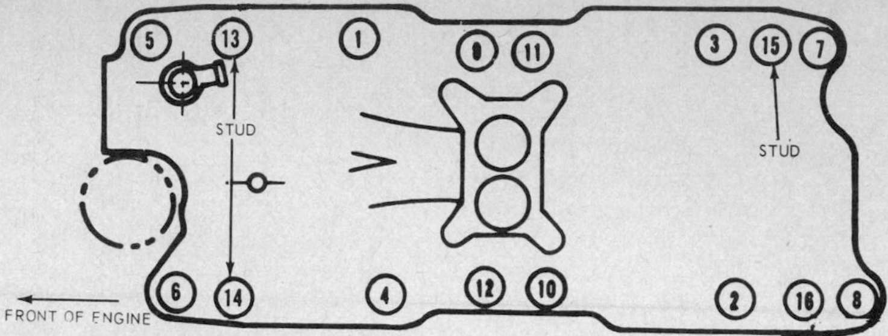

Intake manifold torque sequence—351W V8 (© Ford Motor Co)

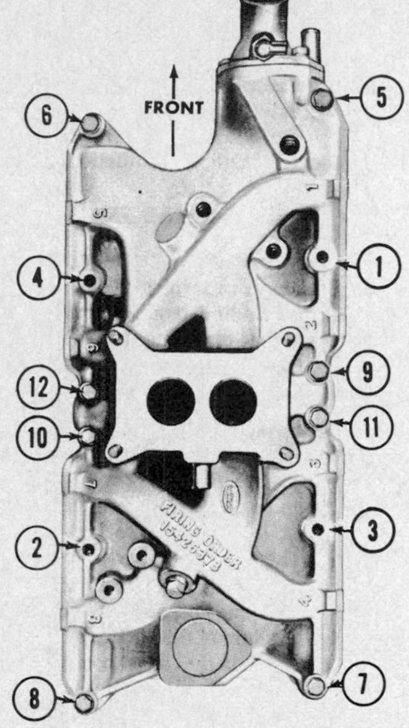

Intake manifold torque sequence—302 V8 (© Ford Motor Co)

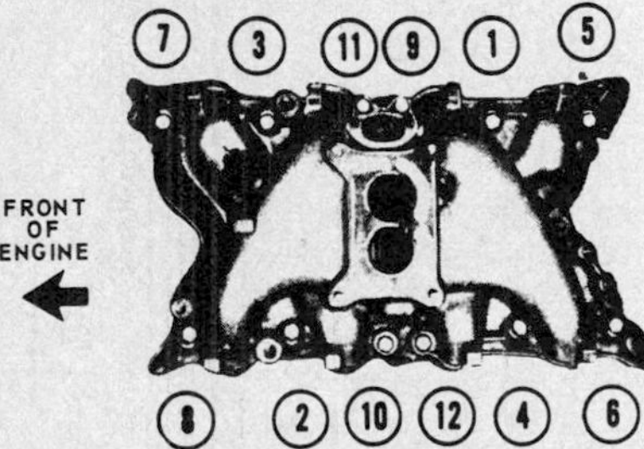

Intake manifold torque sequence—351C, 351M, 400 V8 (© Ford Motor Co)

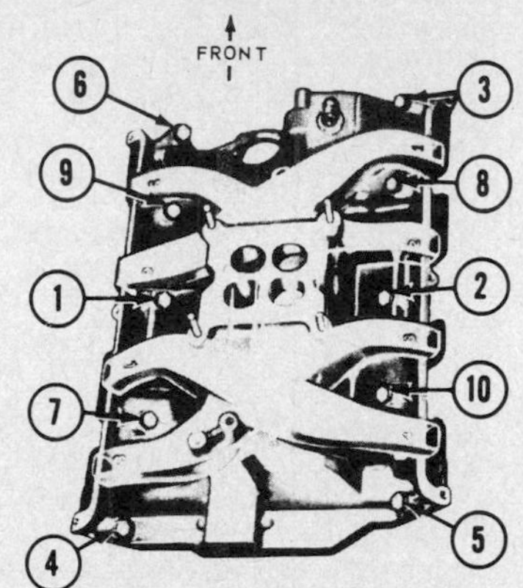

Intake manifold torque sequence—390 and 428 V8 (© Ford Motor Co)

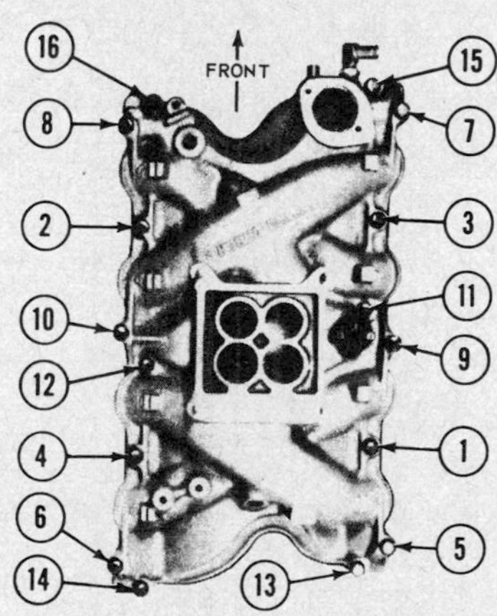

Intake manifold torque sequence—429 and 460 V8 (© Ford Motor Co)

Exhaust Manifold Removal—V8

1. If the right-side manifold is to be removed, disconnect the choke heat tube, remove the air cleaner and ducts.
2. On vehicles with 351C and 400 V8s, to remove the left manifold, remove the oil filter. If equipped with an automatic transmission remove the transmission selector lever cross-shaft from the engine block. If equipped with a manual transmission, disconnect the equalizer shaft bracket and clutch linkage from the engine.
3. Disconnect the manifolds from the muffler inlet pipes.
4. If the manifold attaching bolts are installed with locking washers, bend back the tabs on the washers.
5. Remove the manifold to cylinder head attaching bolts, and remove the manifolds from the car.
6. Clean all gasket surfaces, and reverse above procedure to install; using all new gaskets.

Valve System

All engines used in full-size Ford products are equipped with hydraulic valve lifters. Valve systems with hydraulic valve lifters operate with zero clearance in the valve train, and because of this the rocker arms are nonadjustable. The only means by which valve system clearances can be altered is by installing .060 in. over- or undersize pushrods; but, because of the hydraulic lifter's natural ability to compensate for slack in the valve train, all components of the valve system should be checked for wear if there is excessive play in the system.

Preliminary Valve Adjustment

6-Cylinder

1. Crank the engine until the TDC mark on the crankshaft damper is aligned with timing pointer on the cylinder front cover.
2. Scribe a mark on the damper at this point.
3. Scribe two more marks on the damper, each equally spaced from the first mark (see illustration).
4. With the engine on TDC of the compression stroke, (mark A aligned with the pointer) back off the rocker arm adjusting nut until there is end-play in the pushrod. Tighten the adjusting nut until all clearance is removed, then tighten the adjusting nut one additional turn. To determine when all clearance is removed from the rocker arm, turn the pushrod with the fingers. When the pushrod can no longer be turned, all clearance has been removed.
5. Repeat this procedure for each valve, turning the crankshaft 1/3 turn to the next mark each time and following the engine firing order of 1-5-3-6-2-4.

Valve locations—1969-72 240 6 cylinder

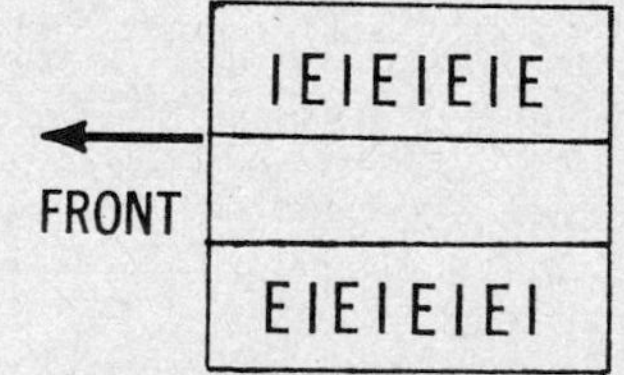

Valve locations—302, 351W, 351C, 351M, 400, 429 and 460 V8

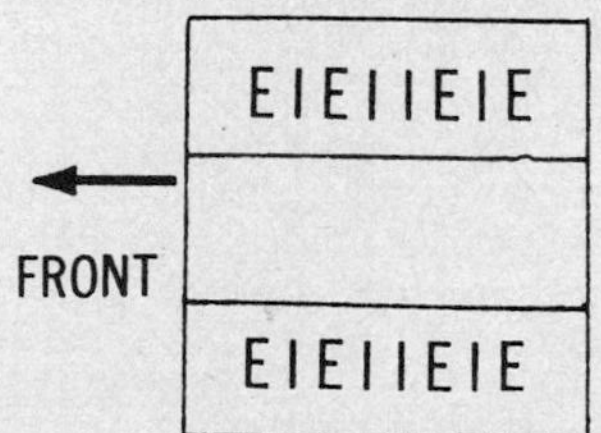

Valve locations—390 and 428 V8

All V8

NOTE: The early 302 V8 engine has rocker arm mounting studs which do *not* incorporate a positive stop shoulder on the mounting stud. These

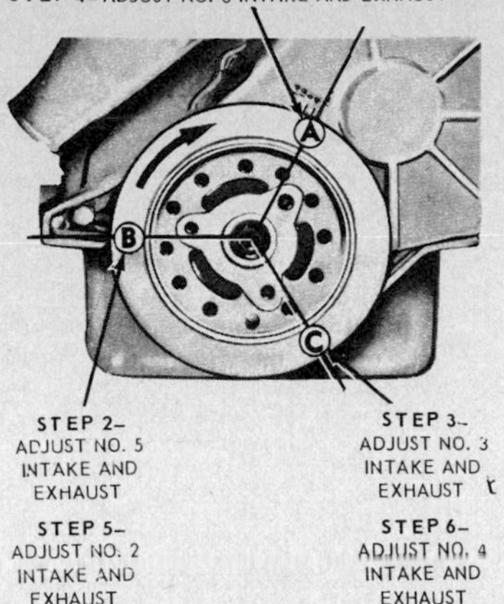

Position of crankshaft for valve adjustment —6 cylinder
(© Ford Motor Co)

engines were originally equipped with this kind of stud. However, due to production differences, it is possible some early 302 engines may be encountered that *are* equipped with positive stop rocker arm mounting studs. Before adjusting the valves, verify that the rocker arm mounting studs do not incorporate a positive stop shoulder. On studs without a positive stop, the shank portion of the stud that is exposed just above the cylinder head is the same diameter as the threaded portion, at the top of the stud, to which the rocker arm retaining nut attaches. If the shank portion of the stud is of greater diameter than the threaded portion, this identifies it as a positive stop rocker arm stud and the adjustment specifications for the 351 engine with adjusting nuts should be used. Only the 302, 351W and 1969-71 429 engines require a preliminary valve adjustment. All other V-8s use either a bolt and fulcrum (351C, 351M, 400, 460 and 1972-73 429) or rocker shafts (390 and 428). High performance versions of any of these V8s probably will be equipped with rocker arm adjusting nuts.

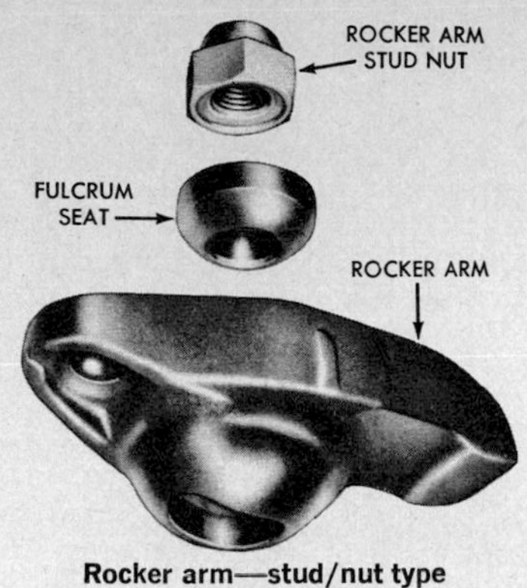

Rocker arm—stud/nut type
(© Ford Motor Co)

302, 351W and 1969-71 429
With Rocker Arm Adjusting Nuts

1. Crank the engine until #1 cylinder is at TDC of the compression stroke and the timing pointer is aligned with the mark on the crankshaft damper.
2. Scribe a mark on the damper at this point.
3. Scribe three more marks on the damper, dividing the damper into quarters.
4. With the first mark aligned with the timing pointer, adjust the valves on #1 cylinder by backing off the adjusting nut until the pushrod has free play in it. Then, tighten the nut until there is no free play in the rocker arm. This can be determined by turning the pushrod while tightening the nut; when the pushrod can no longer be turned, all clearance has been removed. After the clearance has been removed, tighten the nut an additional ¾ of a turn. (302 V8 w/o positive stop rocker arm studs).
5. Rocker arm adjusting nut tightening specifications are: 302 (with positive stop rocker arm studs) and 351W—tighten the nut until it contacts the rocker shoulder, then torque it to 18-20 ft lbs; 429—tighten the nut until it contacts the rocker shoulder then tighten the nut to 18-22 ft lbs.
6. Repeat this procedure for each valve, turning the crankshaft ¼ turn to the next mark each time and following the engine firing order.

390 and 428 with Rocker Shafts

These engines do not require a preliminary valve adjustment. In the event of cylinder head removal or some operation requiring that the valve train be disturbed, torque the rocker arm shaft supports to 40-45 ft lbs.

351C, 351M, 400, 460, and 1972-73 429

These engines use a bolt and fulcrum rocker arm and require no preliminary valve adjustment. In the event that the valve train is disturbed, install the fulcrum, oil deflector, and tighten the bolt to 18-25 ft. lbs.

Valve Guides

Valve guides on all engines are an integral part of the cylinder head casting. If valve guides become worn, they can be reamed oversize or bronze replacement bushings can be installed. Oversize valves are available with stem diameters .003, .015,

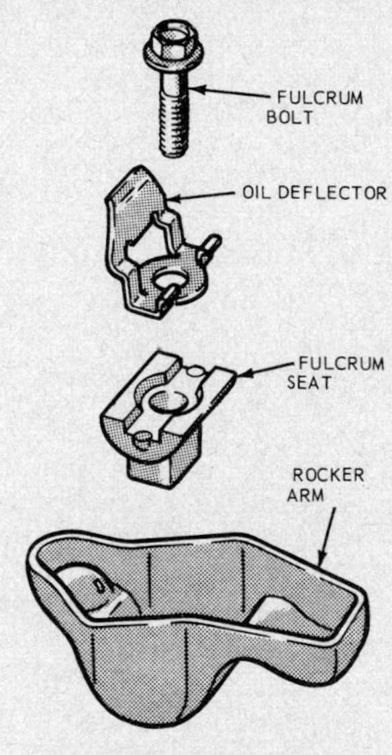

Bolt and fulcrum rocker arm
(© Ford Motor Co)

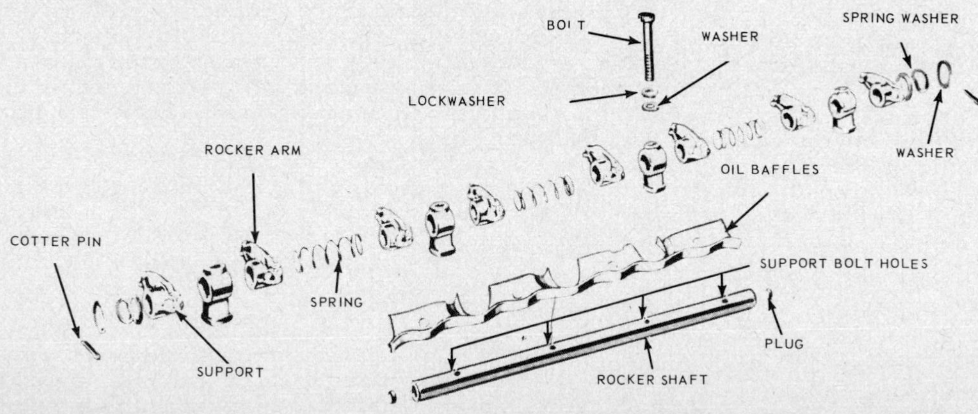

Rocker arm and shaft (© Ford Motor Co.)

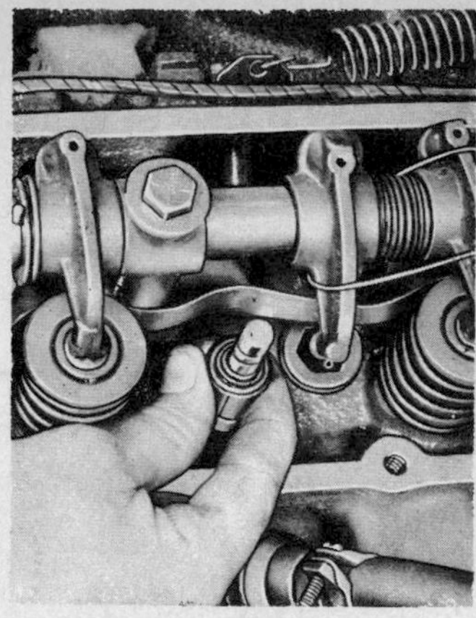

Valve stem seal removal
(© Ford Motor Co)

and .030 in. larger than standard. If the guides are to be reamed more than .003 in. oversize, they must be reamed in steps starting with .003 in. and progressing until the desired diameter is achieved.

NOTE: when valve guides become worn, the excessive clearance between the valve and the head can allow the valve to tap on the cylinder head and emit a noise very similar to the noise a defective valve lifter emits. When checking the valve system to locate a noise, and the lifters are not defective and no excessive clearances exist in the valve train, the valve guides should be checked for wear.

Frequently valves become bent or warped, or their seats become blocked with carbon or other material. Left unattended, these situations can cause burnt valves, damaged cylinder heads and other expensive trouble. To detect leaking valves early, perform this test whenever the cylinder head is removed.

1. After removing head, replace spark plugs. Removing spark plugs before removing heads eliminates breakage.
2. Place head on bench with valves, springs, retainers, and keys installed—combustion chambers up.
3. Pour enough gasoline into each combustion chamber to completely cover both valves. Watch combustion chambers for two minutes for any leakage.

Tappet Removal

To remove and replace tappets from 390 and 428 engines without removing the intake manifold, first remove rocker covers and rocker assembly. Then remove pushrods from their bores. Locate tappet or tappets to be moved by shining a light through pushrod bores. Use a magnet or claw tool to seize tappet and withdraw it through pushrod bore. It may be necessary on some tappets to move them over and draw them through a larger adjoining pushrod bore, but tappets should always be replaced in their original holes.

Cylinder Head

6-Cylinder Head Removal

1. Drain coolant and remove air cleaner. Disconnect battery cable at cylinder head.
2. Disconnect exhaust pipe at manifold.
3. Disconnect accelerator retracting spring, choke control cable and accelerator rod at carburetor.
4. Disconnect fuel line and distributor control vacuum line at the carburetor.
5. Disconnect coolant tubes from carburetor spacer. Disconnect coolant and heater hoses.
6. Disconnect distributor control vacuum line at distributor and fuel inlet line at the filter. Remove lines as an assembly.
7. On an engine equipped with positive crankcase ventilation, disconnect the emission exhaust tube.
8. Disconnect spark plug wires at the plugs and the small wire from the temperature-sending unit. On an engine equipped with a Thermactor exhaust emission control system, disconnect the air pump hose at the air manifold assembly. Unscrew the tube nuts and remove the air manifold. Disconnect the anti-backfire valve air and vacuum lines at the intake manifold. On a car equipped with power brakes, disconnect the brake vacuum line at the intake manifold.
9. Remove rocker arm cover.
10. Loosen the rocker arm stud nut so that the rocker arm can be rotated to one side. Remove valve pushrods and keep them in sequence.
11. Remove remaining cylinder head bolts, then remove cylinder head.

6-Cylinder Head Installation

1. Clean head and block surfaces.
2. Apply sealer to both sides of head gasket. Position gasket over guide studs or dowel pins.

NOTE: apply gasket sealer only to steel shim head gaskets. Steel-asbestos composite head gaskets are to be installed without any sealer.

3. Install new gasket on the exhaust pipe flange.
4. Lift the cylinder head over the guide studs and slide it carefully into place while guiding the exhaust manifold studs into the exhaust pipe flange.

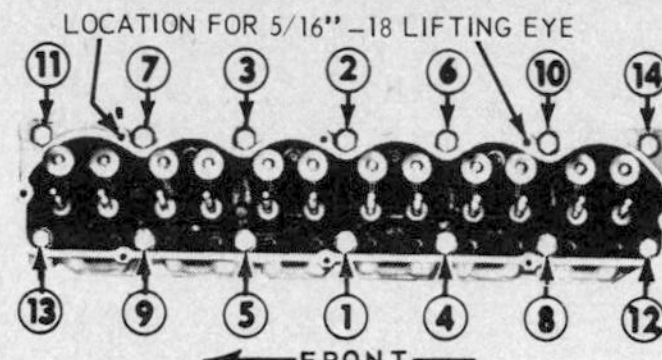

Cylinder head torque sequence—240 six cyl.
(© Ford Motor Co)

5. Coat cylinder-head attaching bolts with water-resistant sealer and install (but do not tighten), the head bolts.
6. Torque the head, in proper sequence, and in three progressive steps to specifications.
7. Lubricate both ends of the pushrods and insert them in their original bores and sockets.
8. Lubricate valve stem tips and rocker arm pads.
9. Position the rocker arms and tighten the stud nuts enough to hold the pushrods in position. Adjust the valves.
10. Install exhaust pipe-to-manifold nuts and lockwashers. Torque to 17-22 ft. lbs.
11. Connect radiator and heater hoses. Connect coolant tubes at the carburetor spacer.
12. Connect distributor vacuum line and the carburetor fuel line. Connect battery cable to cylinder head.
13. On engines equipped with positive crankcase ventilation, clean components thoroughly and install.

NOTE: on engines equipped with a Thermactor exhaust emission control system, install the air manifold assembly on the cylinder head. Connect the air pump outlet hose to the air manifold. Connect the anti-backfire valve, air and vacuum lines to the intake manifold.

14. Connect accelerator rod pull-back spring. Connect choke control cable and the accelerator rod at the carburetor.
15. Connect distributor control vacuum line at distributor. Connect carburetor fuel line at fuel filter.
16. Connect temperature - sending unit wire at sending unit. Connect spark plug wires.
17. Completely fill and bleed the cooling system.

18. Run the engine to stabilize engine temperature. Check for coolant and oil leaks.
19. Adjust engine idle mixture and speed.
20. Install valve rocker arm cover, then the air cleaner.

V8 Head, 390, 428, Removal

1. Remove intake manifold as previously described.
2. Remove any remaining accessories.
3. Disconnect the muffler inlet pipes from the manifolds.
4. Unbolt and remove heads.

V8 Head, 302, 351, 400, 429, and 460 cu. in., Removal

1. Remove the intake manifold and carburetor as an assembly.
2. Remove rocker arm covers.
3. On cars equipped with air conditioning, isolate and remove the compressor.
4. If the left cylinder head is involved on a car with power steering, remove the steering pump and bracket and remove the drive belt. Tie assembly out of the way.
5. If the left cylinder head is involved on a car equipped with a Thermactor exhaust emission control system, disconnect the hose from the air manifold on the left cylinder head.
6. If the right head is involved, remove the alternator mounting bracket bolt and spacer, ignition coil and air cleaner inlet duct from the right cylinder head.
7. If the right cylinder head is to be removed on an engine equipped with a Thermactor exhaust emission control system, remove the air pump and bracket. Disconnect the hose from the right cylinder head.
8. Disconnect the exhaust manifold/s at the exhaust pipe/s.
9. Loosen rocker arm stud nuts so that the arms can rotate to the side to clear the pushrods. Remove the pushrods. On 351 engines, remove exhaust manifold to get access to lower cylinder head bolts.
10. Remove cylinder-head bolts and lift off cylinder head.

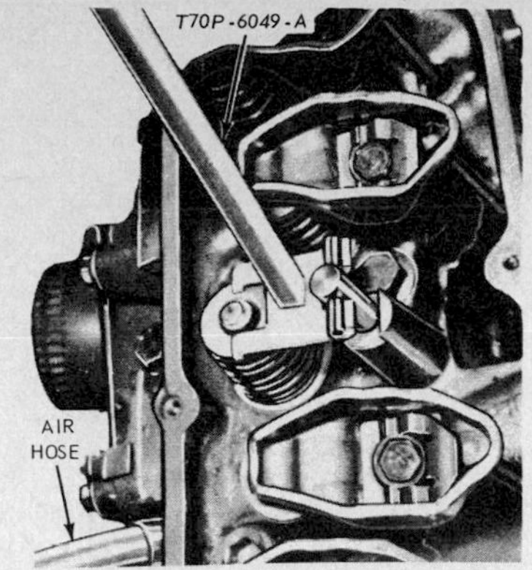

Compressing valve spring with cylinder head installed (© Ford Motor Co)

V8 Head Installation

Installation is the reverse of removal. See valve adjustment under Valve System.

Timing Case

Timing Gear Cover Removal

6-Cylinder Engines

1. Drain the cooling system and the crankcase.
2. Remove the radiator from the car.
3. Loosen and remove all engine drive belts.
4. On vehicles with power steering, disconnect the pump mounting bracket from the cylinder front cover and position the pump and bracket out of the way.
5. On models with air conditioning, remove the condenser mounting bolts and position the condenser out of the way. *Do not disconnect the refrigerant lines.*
6. Disconnect and remove the fan and fan spacer.
7. Remove any accessory drive pulleys from the crankshaft damper. Remove the capscrew and washer from the crankshaft end; then, using a puller, remove the crankshaft damper.
8. Remove the alternator adjusting arm bolt and position the arm out of the way.
9. Remove the starter cable and attaching bolts, and remove the starter.
10. Remove the engine front support insulator to intermediate support bracket nuts on both supports. Remove the engine rear support insulator to crossmember bolt and insulator to transmission extension housing bolts. Raise the transmission and remove the support insulator. Lower the transmission to the crossmember.
11. Raise the engine and place 2 in. thick blocks of wood between both supports and brackets.
12. Remove the oil pan bolts, and lower the oil pan. Reach inside the oil pan and remove the two oil pump to block bolts, and lower the pump and screen into the pan. Turn the crankshaft as required to gain clearance and remove the oil pan.
13. Remove the front cover attaching bolts and remove the cover from the engine.
14. Reverse above procedure to install.

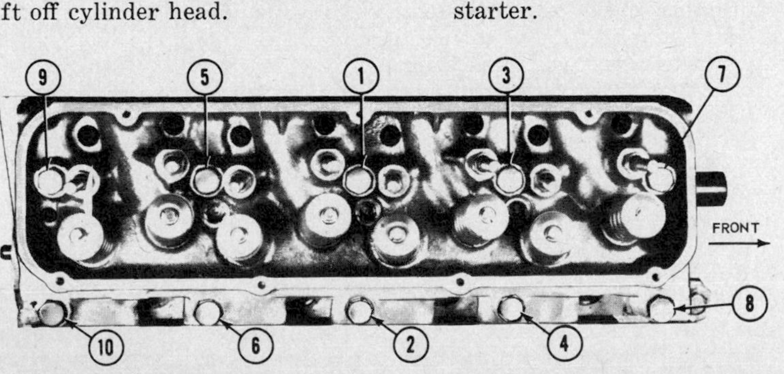

Cylinder head torque sequence—all V8 (© Ford Motor Co)

Timing Gear and/or Camshaft Replacement

6-Cylinder

1. Remove the timing case cover.
2. Mark the location of the grille center support and hood lock assembly in relation to the radiator support. Remove the grille, center support, and hood lock as an assembly.
3. Remove the air cleaner and valve cover.
4. Disconnect the fuel pump outlet line and remove the fuel pump from the engine.
5. Loosen the rocker arm nuts and position the rocker arms to the side so the pushrods can be removed. Keep the pushrods in order so that they can be returned to their original location in the engine.
6. Remove the pushrod cover from the side of the engine, and, using a magnet, remove the lifters from their bores. Keep the lifters in order so they can be returned to their original location in the engine.
7. Rotate the engine until the timing marks are aligned on the timing gears.
8. Remove the camshaft thrust plate screws.
9. Remove the camshaft by pulling it out the front of the engine. Use care not to damage the camshaft lobes or journals while removing the cam from the engine.
10. Place the camshaft/gear assembly in a press and press the cam from the gear.
11. Position new gear on camshaft and press into position.
12. Using a puller, remove the crankshaft timing gear.

13. Using a suitable tool, press the new gear onto the crankshaft.
14. Before installing the camshaft in the engine, coat the lobes with Lubriplate and the journals and all valve train components with heavy oil.
15. Reverse above procedure to install, following recommended torque settings and performing preliminary valve adjustment before starting engine.

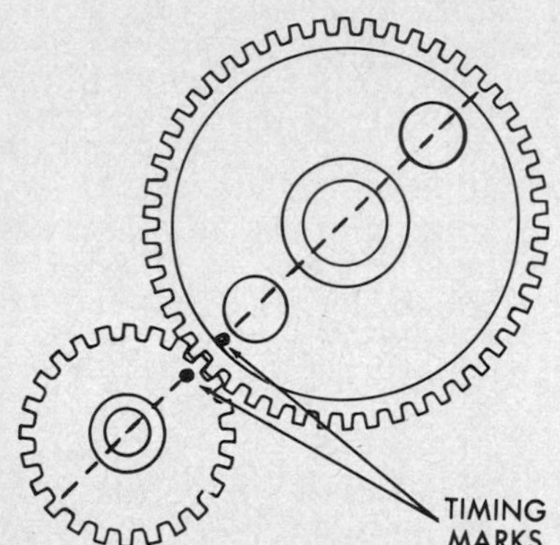

Timing mark alignment—6 cyl.

V8 Cover and Chain

Removal

1. Drain the cooling system and crankcase.
2. Disconnect the negative battery cable.
3. If equipped with a fan shroud, disconnect it from the radiator and position it rearward.
4. Remove the radiator. Remove the fuel pump.
5. Remove the fan attaching bolts, remove the fan, fan spacer and shroud from the engine.
6. Loosen and remove all engine drive belts.
7. Remove the power steering pump mounting bracket and position the pump and bracket out of the way.
8. If equipped with air conditioning, remove the compressor and condenser and position them out of the way. *Do not disconnect the refrigerant lines.*
9. Disconnect the alternator adjusting arm from the engine and position it out of the way.
10. If equipped with Thermactor, remove the pump from the engine.
11. Disconnect the heater hose and bypass hose from the water pump.
12. Remove any accessory drive pulleys from the crankshaft damper and remove the crankshaft front bolt and washer.
13. Using a puller, remove the crankshaft damper from the engine.
14. On 390 and 428 V8, use a suitable tool to pull the crankshaft sleeve away from the cylinder front cover. Remove the sleeve from the engine.
15. Remove the front cover attaching bolts and the front oil pan bolts.
16. Remove the front cover and water pump from the engine.
17. Remove the crankshaft front oil slinger.
18. To check timing chain free play, rotate the crankshaft in a clockwise direction until all slack is removed from the left side of the chain. Scribe a mark on the engine parallel to the present position of the chain. Next, rotate the crankshaft in a counterclockwise direction to remove all the slack from the right side of the chain. Force the left side of the chain outward with the fingers and measure the distance between the present position of the chain and the reference mark on the engine. If the distance exceeds ½ in., replace the chain and sprockets.
19. To replace the chain and sprockets, crank the engine until the timing marks are aligned as shown in the illustration.
20. Remove the camshaft sprocket attaching bolt and remove the chain and sprockets from the engine by sliding them forward as an assembly.

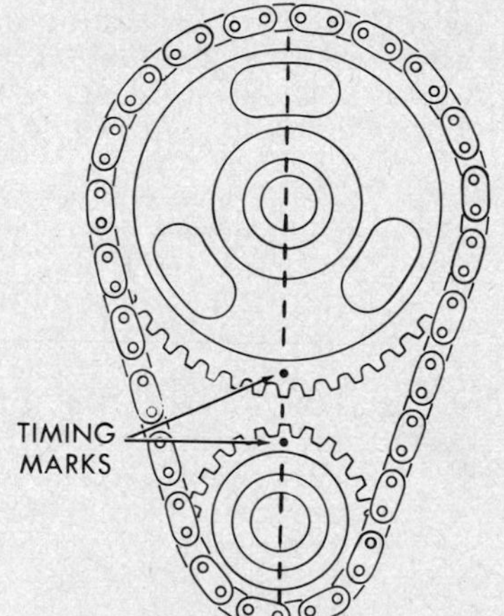

Timing mark alignment—V8

Installation

1. Position the chain and sprockets on the engine, making sure that the timing marks on the sprockets are aligned.
2. Clean all gasket surfaces. Trim away the exposed portion of the oil pan gasket flush with the front of the block.
3. Cut and position the required portion of a new gasket to the oil pan, applying sealer to both sides of it.
4. Reinstall the front cover, applying oil resistant sealer to the new gasket.
5. Install the components that were removed from the engine by reversing the removal procedure.

Timing Case Oil Seal Replacement

All Models

To replace the oil seal, it is necessary to take off the timing case cover and drive the seal out with a pin punch. Clean out the recess in the cover and install a new seal using a special driving tool.

Coat the new seal with grease to reduce friction when installing and starting the car.

V8 Camshaft Replacement

1. Remove the intake manifold.
2. Remove the cylinder front cover, timing chain and sprockets as outlined previously.
3. Remove the rocker arm covers.
4. On 390 and 428 engines it is necessary to remove the rocker arm shafts to remove the intake manifold. On all other engines with individual rocker arms, loosen the rocker arm fulcrum bolts or nuts and rotate the rocker arms to the side.
5. Remove the pushrods and lifters and keep them in order so that they can be installed in their original location.
6. Remove the camshaft thrust plate and washer if so equipped. Remove the camshaft from the front of the engine. On certain engine/chassis combinations it may be necessary to remove the grille to gain adequate clearance to remove the camshaft. Use care not to damage the camshaft lobes or journals while removing the cam from the engine.
7. Before installing the camshaft in the engine, coat the lobes with Lubriplate and the journals and all valve train components with heavy oil.
8. Reverse above procedure to install.
9. On all engines with individually mounted rocker arms, a preliminary valve adjustment must be performed before starting the engine.

Engine Lubrication

Oil Pan Removal

6 Cylinder

1. Drain crankcase and cooling system.
2. Disconnect upper hose at outlet elbow and lower hose at radiator. Remove radiator.
3. Disconnect flexible fuel line at fuel pump.
4. With automatic transmission, disconnect kickdown rod at bellcrank assembly. On car with standard transmission, disconnect clutch linkage.
5. Raise car on hoist.

6. Disconnect starter cable at starter. Remove retaining bolts and remove starter.
7. Remove nuts on both engine front support insulator-to-support bracket.
8. Remove bolt and insulator, rear support insulator-to-crossmember and insulator-to-transmission extension housing.
9. Raise transmission, remove support insulator, lower transmission to crossmember.
10. Raise engine with transmission jack and place 3-in. thick wood blocks between both front support insulators and intermediate support brackets.
11. Remove oil pan retaining bolts and oil pump mounting bolts. With oil pump in pan, rotate crankshaft as needed to remove pan.
12. Install in reverse of above.

1969 302, 351 V8
Ford and Mercury

1. Remove oil level dipstick. Drain oil pan.
2. Disconnect stabilizer bar from lower control arms, and pull ends down.
3. Remove oil pan attaching bolts and position pan on front cross-member.
4. Remove one oil inlet tube bolt and loosen the other to position tube out of way to remove pan.
5. Turn crankshaft as required for clearance to remove pan.
6. Install in reverse of above.

All V8s Except 1969 303, 351
Ford and Mercury

1. Raise car and place safety stands in position. Drain oil from crankcase. On 429 V8s, disconnect the negative battery cable. On 1970–71 429 V8s, remove bolt attaching vacuum line retaining clip to upper right side of converter housing.
2. Disconnect stabilizer bar links and pull ends down. On models equipped with a fan shroud, remove the shroud from the radiator and position it rearward over the fan. On automatic transmission equipped cars, position oil cooler lines aside.
3. Remove nuts and lockwashers from engine front support insulator-to-intermediate support bracket.
4. Install block of wood on jack and position jack under leading edge of pan.
5. Raise engine approximately 1¼ in. and insert a 1-in. block between insulators and crossmember. Remove floor jack. On 351C, 400, 429, and 460 V8s, remove the starter. On 1972-75 429 and 460 V8s remove the oil filter.
6. Remove oil pan attaching screws and lower pan to frame crossmember.
7. Turn crankshaft to obtain clearance between crankshaft counterweight and rear of pan.
8. Remove oil pump attaching bolts.
9. Position tube and screen out of the way and remove the pan.
10. Install in reverse of above.

Oil Pump

Removal and Installation

1. Remove the oil pan as under the previous "Oil Pan Removal and Installation" procedure.
2. On 302 and 351W V8 applications, remove the oil pump inlet tube and screen assembly.
3. Remove the oil pump attaching bolts. Lower the oil pump, gasket, and intermediate driveshaft from the crankcase. If not already removed, remove and clean the inlet tube and screen assembly.
4. To install, prime the oil pump by filling either the inlet or outlet port with engine oil. Rotate the pump shaft to distribute the oil within the pump body.
5. Position the intermediate driveshaft into the distributor socket. With the shaft firmly seated in the socket, the stop on the shaft should contact the roof of the crankcase. Remove the shaft and position the stop as necessary.
6. Insert the intermediate driveshaft into the oil pump. Using a new gasket, install the pump and shaft as an assembly. Do not attempt to force the pump into position if it will not seat readily. If necessary, rotate the intermediate driveshaft hex into a new position so that it will mesh with the distributor shaft.
7. Torque the oil pump attaching bolts to 12-15 ft lbs on the six-cylinder engines, 22-32 ft lbs on the 302 and 351W V8, 20-35 ft lbs on the 351C, 351M and 400 V8, and 20-25 ft lbs on the 390, 428, 429, and 460 V8.
8. Clean and install the inlet tube and screen assembly.
9. Install the oil pan as under "Oil Pan Removal and Installation."

Rear Main Bearing Oil Seal

1969 302, 351W

NOTE: the rear oil seal originally installed in these engines is a rope (fabric) type seal. However, all service replacements are of the rubber type. To remove the rope type seal and install the rubber type, the following procedure is used.

1. Drain the crankcase and remove the oil pan.
2. Remove the lower half of the rear main bearing cap and, after removing the old seal from the bottom of the seal groove with a punch.

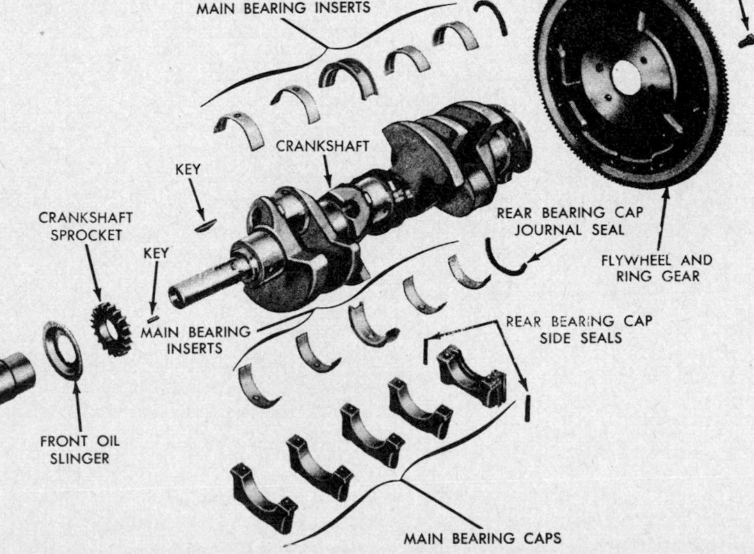

V8 crankshaft and related parts (© Ford Motor Co)

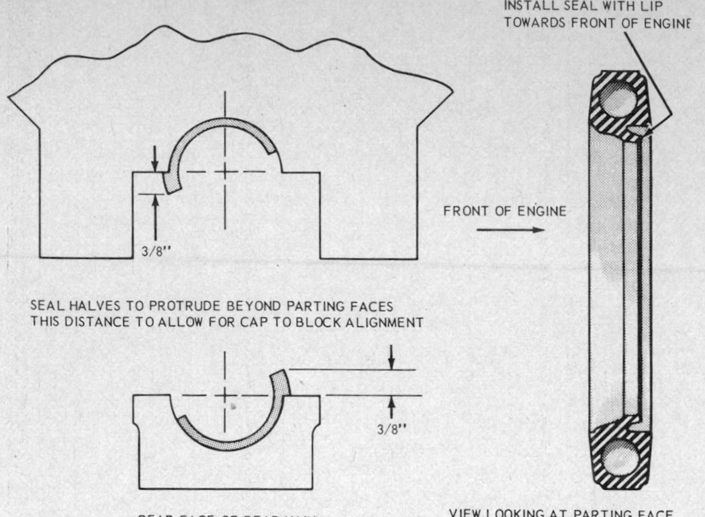

Installing split-lip type rear main oil seal (© Ford Motor Co)

3. Loosen all main bearing caps and allow the crankshaft to lower slightly.

NOTE: the crankshaft should not be allowed to drop more than 1/32 in.

4. With a 6 in. length of 3/16 in. brazing rod, drive up on either exposed end of the top half of the oil seal. When the opposite end of the seal starts to protrude, have a helper grasp it with pliers and gently pull while the driven end is being tapped.
5. After removing both halves of the rope seal and the retaining pin from the lower half of the bearing cap, follow steps four through 10 of the below procedure for 1970-75 engines to install the rubber seal.

1969 390, 428 and All 1970-76

NOTE: the rear oil seal installed in these engines is a rubber type seal.

1. Remove the oil pan and oil pump if required.
2. Loosen all main bearing cap bolts, lowering crankshaft slightly but not more than 1/32 in.
3. Remove rear main cap, and remove upper and lower halves of seal. On block half of seal, use seal removing tool or insert a small metal screw into end of seal with which to draw it out.
4. Clean seal grooves with solvent and dip replacement seal in clean engine oil.
5. Install upper seal half in its groove in block with lip toward front of engine by rotating it on seal journal of crankshaft until approximately 3/8 in. protrudes below parting surface.
6. Tighten other main caps and torque to specification.
7. Install lower seal half in rear main cap with lip to front and approximately 3/8 in. of seal protrudes to mate with upper seal.
8. Install rear main cap and torque.
9. Dip side seals in engine oil and install them. Tap seals in last half inch if necessary. Do not cut protruding ends of seals.

1969 6-Cylinder

If the rear main bearing oil seal is the only operation involved, it can be replaced in the car according to the following procedure.

NOTE: if the oil seal is being replaced in conjunction with a rear main bearing replacement, the engine must be removed from the car.

1. Remove the starter.
2. On cars equipped with automatic transmissions, remove the transmission. On cars equipped with manual shift transmissions, remove the transmission, clutch, flywheel and engine rear cover plate.
3. With an awl, punch holes in the main bearing oil seal, on opposite sides of the crankshaft and just above the bearing cap to cylinder block split line. Insert a sheet metal screw in each hole. With two large screwdrivers, pry the oil seal out.
4. Clean the oil recess in the cylinder block, main bearing cap and the crankshaft sealing surface.
5. Lubricate the entire oil seal. Then, install and drive the seal into its seat .005 in. below the face of the cylinder block with tool T-65L-6701-A.
6. The remaining procedure is the reverse of removal.

CLUTCH

Clutch Pedal Adjustment

1. Disconnect the clutch return spring from the release lever.
2. Loosen the release lever adjusting nut and locknut.
3. Move the clutch release lever rearward until the throwout bearing can be felt to lightly contact the pressure plate fingers.
4. Adjust the rod length until the rod seats in the pocket in the release lever.
5. Insert a feeler gauge of specified thickness between the adjusting nut and swivel sleeve. Tighten the nut against the feeler gauge. Correct feeler gauge thickness is 0.194 in.
6. Tighten the locknut against the adjusting nut, being careful not to disturb the adjustment.
7. Connect the clutch return spring.
8. Make a final check with the engine running at 3000 rpm, and transmission in neutral. Under this condition, centrifugal weights on release fingers may reduce the clearance. Readjust, if necessary, to obtain at least ½in. free-play while maintain ing the 3000 rpm to prevent fingers contacting release bearing.

Clutch and/or Transmission R & R

1. Raise the vehicle on a hoist.
2. Disconnect the driveshaft from the rear U-joint flange and slide the front yoke from the transmission.
3. Insert a cap or rag in the transmission extension housing to prevent fluid leakage.
4. Disconnect the speedometer cable and shifter linkage from the transmission. On models with a four-speed transmission, remove the shifter mounting bracket from the extension housing.
5. On models with a three-speed transmission, disconnect the transmission mount from the crossmember. If equipped with a four-speed transmission, remove the front parking brake cable from the crossmember and remove the crossmember from the car.
6. Remove the bolts that mount the transmission to the bellhousing. On 429 V8s, the upper left-hand transmission attaching bolt is a seal bolt. Carefully note its location so that it may be returned to its original position.
7. Move the transmission rearward until the input shaft clears the bellhousing and lower it from the car.
8. Disconnect the clutch release lever return spring.
9. If equipped with a one-piece aluminum bellhousing, remove the starter and remove the bellhousing from the engine. If equipped with a cast iron bellhousing, remove only the inspection cover from the bottom of the bellhousing.

10. Loosen the 6 pressure plate attaching bolts evenly to release spring pressure, and remove the clutch assembly from the car.
11. To install, position clutch assembly on flywheel and install each pressure plate attaching bolt finger tight.
12. Insert a transmission pilot shaft or other suitable tool to align the clutch disc with the flywheel and alternately tighten the pressure plate attaching bolts until the plate is secured to the flywheel.
13. Reverse above procedure to install transmission and driveshaft.

MANUAL TRANSMISSION

Manual Transmission Linkage Adjustment

Column Shift

1. Place the gear shift lever in the Neutral position.
2. Loosen the two gear shift adjustment nuts on the shift linkage.
3. Insert a 3/16 in. alignment tool through the first and reverse lever, the second and third gear shift lever, and the two holes in the lower casing. An alignment tool can be fabricated from 3/16 in. rod bent to an L shape. The extension that is to be inserted into the levers should be 1 in. in length from the elbow.
4. Manipulate the levers so the alignment tool will move freely through the alignment holes.
5. Tighten the two gear shift rod adjustment nuts.
6. Remove the tool and check linkage operation.

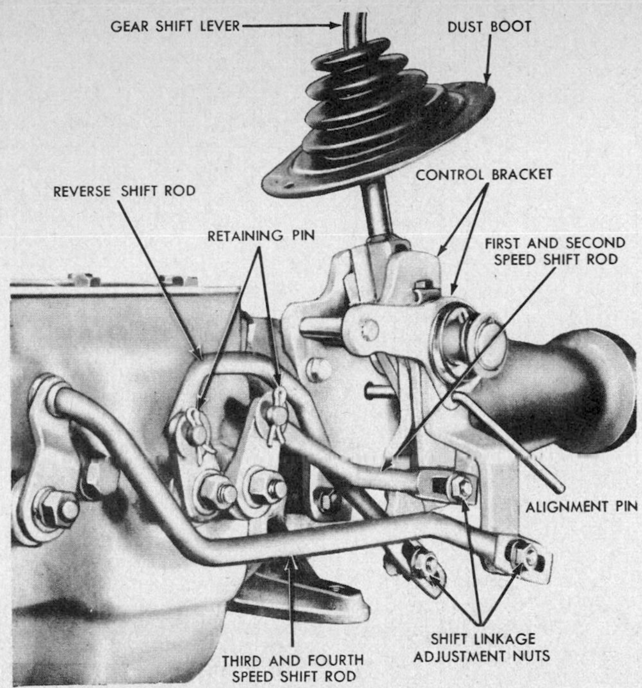

Adjusting shift linkage, 4-speed transmission (© Ford Motor Co)

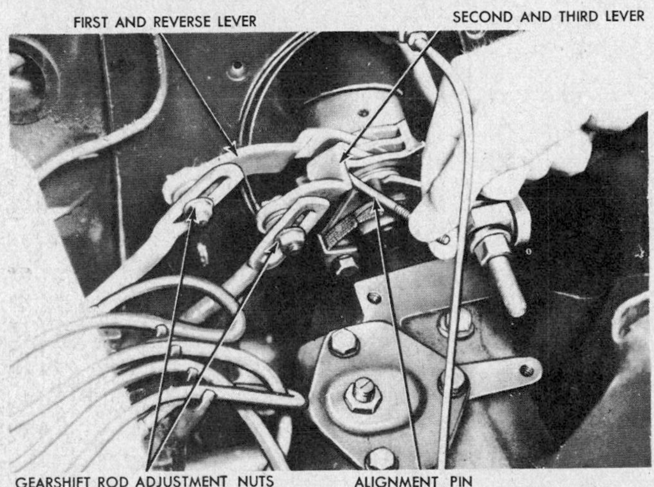

Gearshift linkage adjustment 3-speed transmission (© Ford Motor Co)

Floorshift

1. Place hand shifter lever in neutral position, then raise car on a hoist.
2. Insert a ¼ in. rod into the alignment holes of the shift levers.
3. If the holes are not in exact alignment, check for bent connecting rods or loose lever locknuts at the rod ends. Make replacements or repairs, then adjust as follows.
4. Loosen the three rod-to-lever retaining locknuts and move the levers until the ¼ in. gauge rod will enter the alignment holes. Be sure that the transmission shift levers are in neutral, and the reverse shifter lever is in the neutral detent.
5. Install shift rods and torque locknuts to 18–23 ft. lbs.
6. Remove the ¼ in. gauge rod.
7. Operate the shift levers to assure correct shifting.
8. Lower the car and road-test.

Transmission Lock Rod Adjustment

1970 and later models with floor or console shifters and manual transmissions incorporate a transmission lock rod which prevents the shifter from being moved from the reverse position when the ignition lock is in the OFF position. The lock rod connects the shift tube in the steering column to the transmission reverse lever. The lock rod cannot be properly adjusted until the manual linkage adjustment is correct.

1. With the transmission selector lever in the neutral position, loosen the lock rod adjustment nut on the transmission reverse lever.
2. Insert a .180 in. diameter rod (No. 15 drill bit) in the gauge pin hole located at the 6 o'clock position on the steering column socket casting, directly below the ignition lock.
3. Manipulate the pin until the casting will not move with the pin inserted.
4. Torque the lock rod adjustment nut to 10-20 ft. lbs.
5. Remove the pin and check the linkage operation.

AUTOMATIC TRANSMISSION

Shift Linkage Adjustment

1. With engine off, loosen clamp at shift lever so shift rod is free to slide.

   On models with a shift cable, remove the nut from the transmission manual lever and disconnect the cable from the transmission.

2. Position selector lever in D1 position (large green dot) on dual range transmissions. On select shift transmission (P R N D 2 1) position lever in D position tightly against the D stop.
3. Shift lever at transmission into D1 detent position on dual range transmissions or into D position on select shift transmissions.

NOTE: D1 position is second from rear on all dual range transmissions. D position is third from rear on all column shift select shift transmissions. D position is fourth from rear on 1969-72 console shift select shift transmissions.

4. Tighten clamp and nut.

Neutral Start Switch Adjustment

Column Shift 1969-71

1. With manual linkage properly adjusted, try to engage starter in each position on quadrant. Starter should engage only in neutral or park position.
2. Place shift lever in neutral detent.
3. Disconnect start switch wires at plug connector. Disconnect vacuum hoses, if any. Remove screws securing neutral start switch to steering column and remove switch. Remove actuator lever along with Type III switches.
4. With switch wires facing up, move actuator lever fully to the left and insert gauge pin (No. 43 drill) into gauge pin hole at point A. See accompanying figure. On Type III switch, be sure gauge pin is inserted a full ½ in.
5. With pin in place, move actuator lever to right until positive stop is engaged.
6. On Type I and Type II switches, remove gauge pin and insert it at point B. On Type III switches, remove gauge pin, align two holes in switch at point A and reinstall gauge pin.
7. Reinstall switch on steering column. Be sure shift lever is engaged in neutral detent.
8. Connect switch wires and vacuum hoses and remove gauge pin.
9. Check starter engagement as in Step 1.

Console Shift 1969-71

1. With manual linkage properly adjusted, try to engage starter at each position on quadrant. Starter should engage only in Neutral and Park positions.
2. Remove shift handle from shift lever, and console from vehicle.
3. Loosen switch attaching screws, and move shift lever back and forward until gauge pin (No. 43 drill) can be inserted fully.
4. Place shift lever firmly against neutral detent stop and slide switch back and forward until switch lever contacts shift lever.
5. Tighten switch attaching screws, and check starter engagement as in Step 1.
6. Reinstall console and shift linkage.

Column Shift 1972-76

1972-75 models which are equipped with a column mounted shift lever are not equipped with neutral start switch. Instead, an ignition lock cylinder-to-shift lever interlock prevents these models from being started in any gear other than Park or Neutral.

Lock Rod Adjustment

From 1970–71, all models with a floor or console mounted selector lever incorporated a transmission lock rod to prevent the transmission selector from being moved out of the Park position when the ignition lock is in the Off position. The lock rod connects the shift tube in the steering column to the transmission manual lever. The lock rod cannot be properly adjusted until the manual linkage adjustment is correct.

1. With the transmission selector lever in the Drive position, loosen the lock rod adjustment nut on the transmission manual lever.
2. Insert a .180 in. diameter rod (No. 15 drill bit) in the gauge pin hole in the steering column socket casting, it is located at the 6 o'clock position directly below the ignition lock.
3. Manipulate the pin so that the casting will not move when the pin is fully inserted.
4. Torque the lock rod adjustment nut to 10-20 ft. lbs.
5. Remove the pin and check the linkage operation.

Throttle Linkage Adjustment

1. Disconnect downshift lever return spring.
2. Hold throttle shaft lever wide open, and hold downshift rod against "through detent stop".
3. Adjust downshift screw to provide 0.050-0.070 in. clearance between screw and throttle shaft lever on 1969–72 models and 0.010-0.080 in. on 1973-75 models. On 240 cu. in. engine, tighten locknut.
4. Connect downshift lever return spring.

C-4 Band Adjustment

Intermediate Band

1. Clean all the dirt from the adjusting screw and remove and discard the locknut.
2. Install a new locknut on the adjusting screw using a torque wrench, tighten the adjusting screw to 10 ft lbs.
3. Back off the adjusting screw *exactly 1¾ turns.*
4. Hold the adjusting screw steady and tighten the locknut.

Low-Reverse Band

1. Clean all dirt from around the band adjusting screw, and remove and discard the locknut.
2. Install a new locknut on the adjusting screw. Using a torque wrench, tighten the adjusting screw to 10 ft lbs.
3. Back off the adjusting screw *exactly three full turns.*
4. Hold the adjusting screw steady and tighten the locknut.

C-6 Band Adjustment

Intermediate Band Adjustment

1. Raise the car on a hoist or place it on jack stands.
2. Clean the threads of the intermediate band adjusting screw.

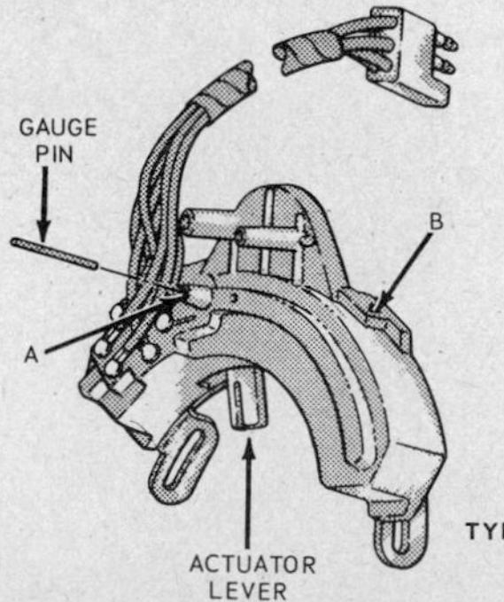

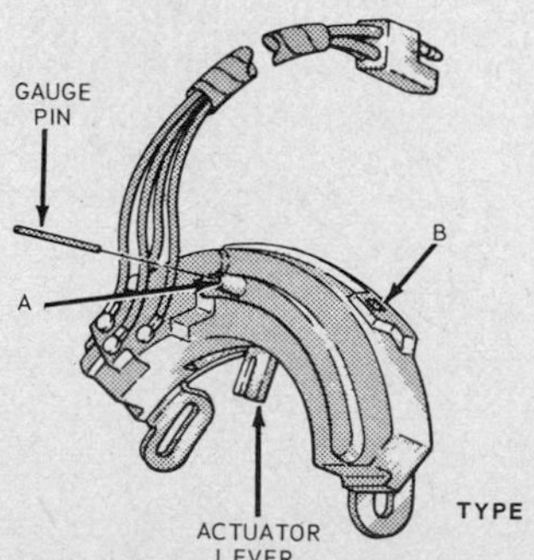

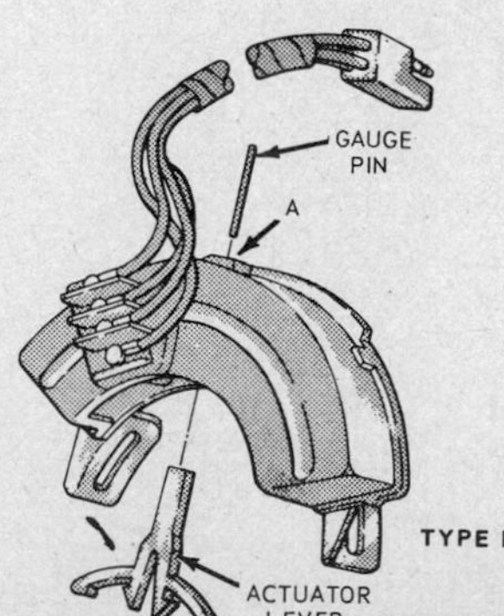

Neutral start switches—1969-70 (© Ford Motor Co)

3. Loosen the adjustment screw locknut.
4. Tighten the adjusting screw to 10 ft lbs and back the screw off *exactly 1½ turns.* Tighten the adjusting screw locknut.

FMX, MX, and CW Band Adjustment

Front Band Adjustment

1. Drain the transmission fluid and remove the oil pan, fluid filter screen, and clip.
2. Clean the pan and filter screen and remove the old gasket.
3. Loosen the front servo adjusting screw locknut.
4. Pull back the actuating rod and insert a ¼ in. spacer bar between the adjusting screw and the servo piston stem. Tighten the adjusting screw to 10 in. lbs torque. Remove the spacer bar and tighten the adjusting screw *an additional ¾ turn.* Hold the adjusting screw fast and tighten the locknut securely (20-25 ft lbs).
5. Install the transmission fluid filter screen and clip. Install pan with a new pan gasket.
6. Refill the transmission to the mark on the dipstick. Start the engine, run for a few minutes, shift the selector lever through all positions, and place it in Park. Recheck the fluid level and add fluid if necessary.

Rear Band Adjustment

On certain cars with a console floor shift, the entire console, shift lever and linkage will have to be removed to gain access to the rear band external adjusting screw.

1. Locate the external rear band adjusting screw on the transmission case, clean all dirt from the threads, and coat the threads with light oil.

NOTE: the adjusting screw is located on the upper right side of the transmission case. Access is often through a hole in the front floor to the right of center under the carpet.

2. Loosen the locknut on the rear band external adjusting screw.
3. Using torque wrench tighten the adjusting screw to 10 ft lbs torque. If the adjusting screw is tighter than 10 ft lbs torque, loosen the adjusting screw and retighten to the proper torque.
4. Back off the adjusting screw *exactly 1½ turns.* Hold the adjusting screw steady while tightening the locknut to the proper torque (35–40 ft lbs).

Pan R&R, Fluid Change

Normal maintenance and lubrication requirements do not include periodic changes of transmission fluid. A change is required only when it is necessary to replace the transmission fluid. At this time the converter, oil cooler core, and cooler lines should be throughly flushed out to remove any dirt or deposits that might clog these units later.

When filling a completely dry (no fluid) transmission and converter, install five quarts of transmission fluid and then start the engine. Shift the selector lever through all gear positions briefly and set at Park position. Check the fluid level and add enough fluid to raise the level to between the marks on the dipstick. Do not overfill the transmission.

The procedure for a partial drain and refill of the transmission fluid is as follows:

1. Raise the car on a hoist or jack stands.
2. Place a drain pan under the transmission pan.

NOTE: *On some models of the C4 transmission, the fluid is drained by disconnecting the filler tube from the transmission fluid pan.*

3. Loosen the pan attaching bolts to allow the fluid to drain.
4. When the fluid has stopped draining to the level of the pan flange, remove the pan bolts starting at the rear and along both sides of the pan, allowing the pan to drop and drain gradually.
5. When all the transmission fluid has drained, remove the pan and the fluid filter and clean them.
6. Install the fluid filter screen, a new pan gasket, and the pan on the transmission. Tighten the pan attaching bolts on C4 and C6 transmissions to 12-16 ft lbs. On FMX and CW transmissions, tighten the pan attaching bolts to 10-13 ft lbs.

NOTE: *Be sure to use Type "F" transmission fluid. The use of any other type of fluid will materially affect the service life of the transmission.*

7. Install three quarts of transmission fluid through the filler tube. If the filler tube was removed to drain the transmission, install the filler tube using a new O-ring.
8. Start and run the engine for a few minutes at low idle speed and then at the fast idle speed (about 1,200 rpm) until the normal operating temperature is reached. Do not race the engine.
9. Move the selector lever through all gear positions and place it at the Park position. Check the fluid level, and add fluid until the level is between the "add" and "full" marks on the dipstick. Do not overfill the transmission.

U-JOINTS

Rear Joint Removal—Ford and Mercury

The universal joints on all Fords, Mercurys, and 1972-76 Thunderbirds in this section are of the cross- and needle-bearing-type.

The rear universal joint has two pillow blocks which are bolted to the pinion shaft flange.

Take out the four bolts that hold the bearing blocks to the pinion shaft and gently tap off the bearing blocks.

Lower the back end of the driveshaft and the front end can be slid out of the back of the transmission together with the transmission yoke portion of the front universal joint.

Carry the assembly—the front universal joint complete, the driveshaft and the rear universal joint crossover—to the bench and remove the cross from the rear universal joint by taking out the lock rings from the inner side of the bearings. Using a large punch or an arbor press, drive one of the bearings in toward the center forcing out the opposite bearing.

When the bearing is pressed out far enough, grip it with a pair of pliers and pull it out of the driveshaft yoke.

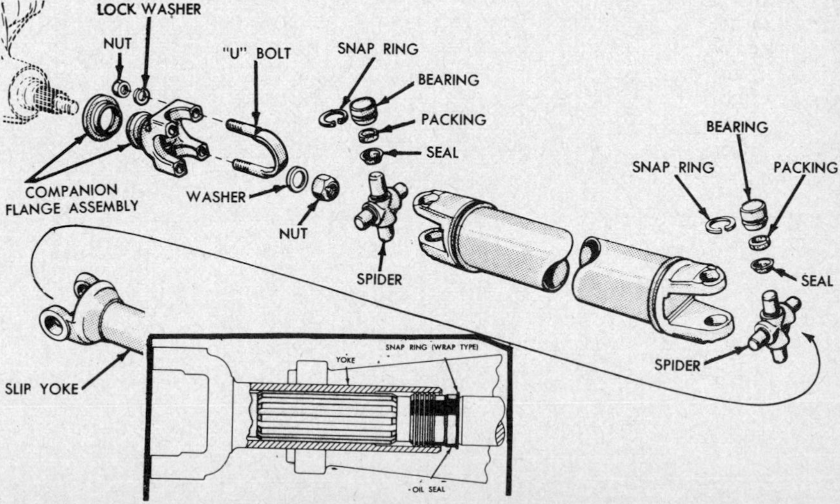

Driveshaft and universal joint (© Ford Motor Co)

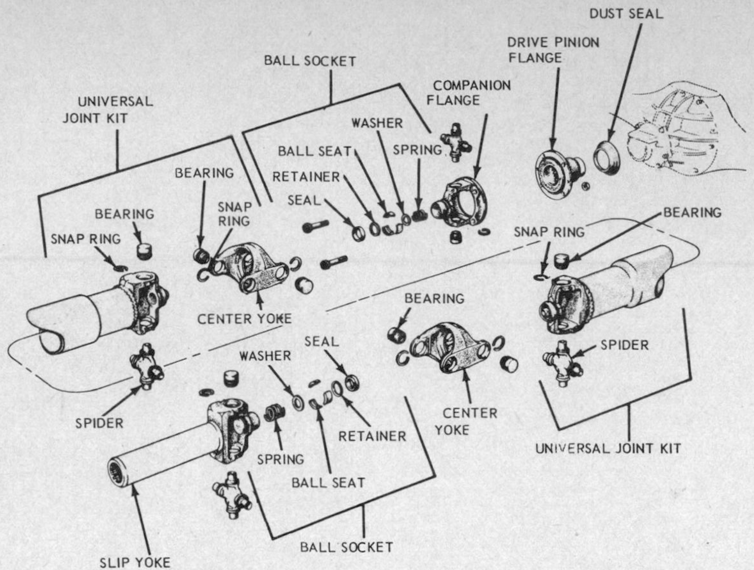

Driveshaft with double Cardan universal joints (© Ford Motor Co)

Now, drive the cross in the opposite direction until the remaining bearing has been driven out far enough for a purchase with a pair of pliers.

When both bearings have been taken out, the cross can be lifted from between the two yokes.

Front Joint Removal— Ford and Mercury

Follow the procedure given above for the rear universal joint, but leave the rear universal joint cross in place on the driveshaft if it is not to be removed.

Remove the lock rings from the inner side of two opposite bearings and press on the outer side of one of the bearings, forcing the crossover. This will force the bearing on the opposite side out of its yoke.

Remove the forced-out bearing and press the cross in the opposite direction to force the other bearing out.

Repeat this procedure on the third and fourth bearings.

When installing the new bearings in the universal joint yoke, it is possible to put them in with a driver of some type, but it is recommended that this work be done in an arbor press since a heavy jolt on the needle bearings can very easily misalign them.

Double Cardan Universal Joints

All 1969-71 Thunderbirds use a driveshaft with a double Cardan U-Joint. Each of the two Cardan joints consist of two universal joints, a centering socket yoke and a center yoke. Bearing cups are retained by injected plastic; but, repair kits contain replacement snap-rings. This driveshaft mounts to the differential pinion flange by means of a circular companion flange.

Replacement

1. Mark the position of the companion flange in relation to the pinion flange so the driveshaft may be returned to its original location.
2. Disconnect the companion flange from the pinion flange.
3. Pull the driveshaft rearward until the front yoke clears the transmission extension housing and remove the driveshaft from the car.
4. Mark the position of the spiders, the center yoke and the centering socket yoke in relation to the companion flange. *The spiders must be assembled with the bosses in their original position to provide proper clearance.*
5. If the universal joints have been previously replaced and are retained with snap-rings, remove the snap-rings.
6. Using a press or large punch, drive one of the bearing caps on the U-Joint to be replaced toward the center of the driveshaft. Remove the bearing cap opposite the cap being driven as it emerges from the driveshaft. Repeat this procedure until all the bearing caps have been removed, then, remove the spider.
7. To disassemble the ball socket from the yoke, insert a screwdriver into the centering ball socket and pry out the rubber seal. Remove the retainer, three piece ball seat, washer and spring from the ball socket.
8. Reverse above procedure to install, making sure all parts are mounted in their original location.

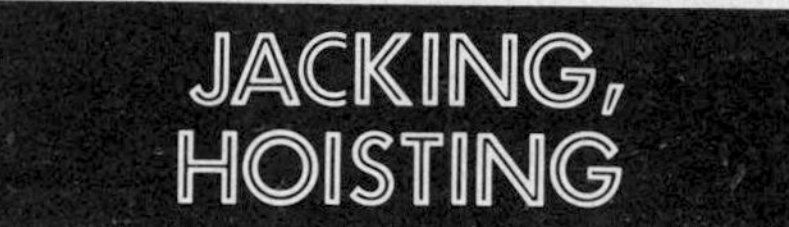

Ford, Mercury and T-Bird

1. Jack car at front spring seats of lower control arms, and at rear

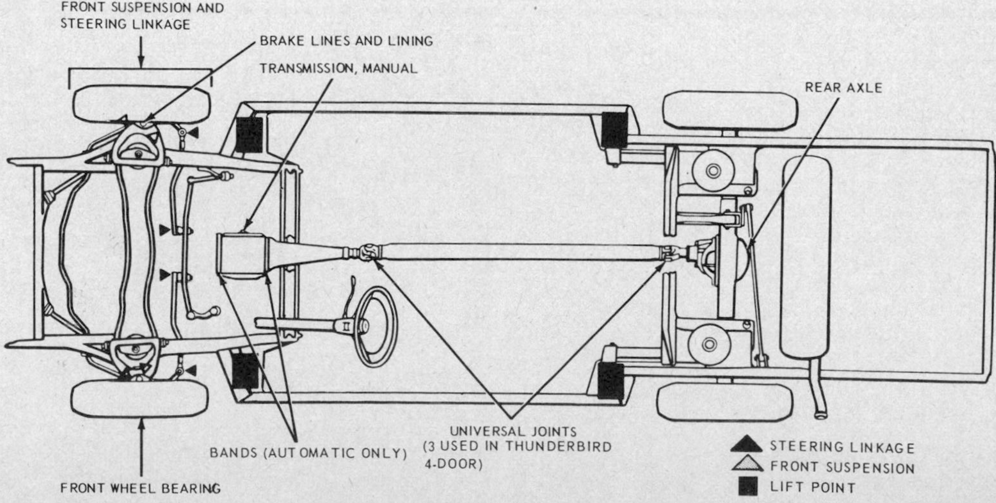

Ford hoist lifting positions (© Ford Motor Co)

axle housing close to differential case.

2. To lift at frame, use adapters so that contact will be made at points shown. Adapters should support at least 12 sq. in.

REAR AXLE

Two basic types of rear axles are used; a removable differential carrier type and an integral carrier type which occurs in two variations; a standard type and the light duty (WER) version. Some integral carrier types and all WER types use C-locks on the inside end of the axle shaft to retain it, while removable carrier axles have no C-locks. To properly identify a C-lock axle, drain the lubricant, remove the rear cover and look for the C-lock on the end of the axle shaft in the differential side gear bore.

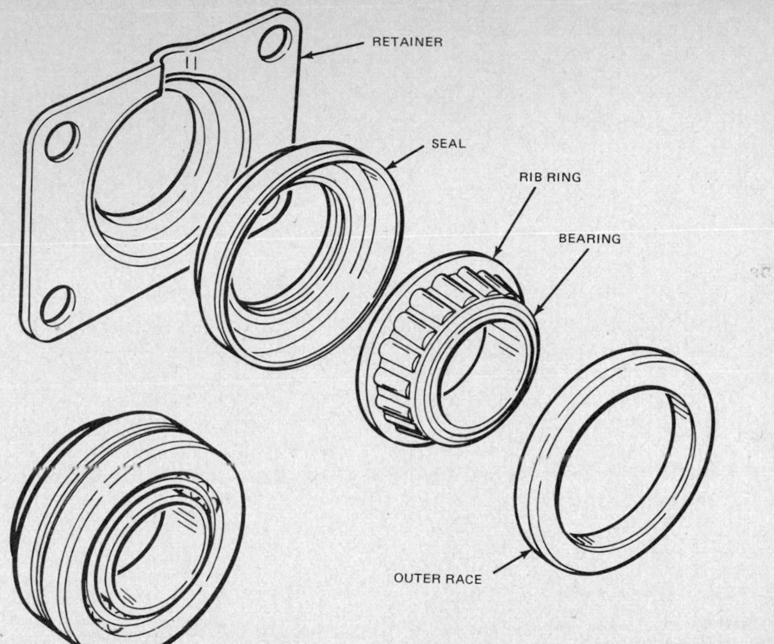

Axle shaft bearing and retainer—removable carrier axle (© Ford Motor Co)

Axle Shaft, Bearing and Seal

Removal and Installation

Removable Carrier Axles, except C-Lock Type

NOTE: *Bearings must be pressed on and off the shaft with an arbor press. Unless you have access to one, it is inadvisable to attempt any repair work on the axle shaft bearing assemblies.*

1. Remove the wheel, tire, and brake drum.
2. Remove the nuts holding the retainer plate to the backing plate. Disconnect the brake line.
3. Remove the retainer and install nuts, finger-tight, to prevent the brake backing plate from being dislodged.
4. Pull out the axle shaft and bearing assembly, using a slide hammer.

NOTE: *If end-play is found to be excessive, the bearing should be replaced. Shimming the bearing is not recommended as this ignores end-play of the bearing itself and could result in improper seating of the bearing.*

5. Using a chisel, nick the bearing retainer in 3 or 4 places. The retainer does not have to be cut, but merely collapsed sufficiently to allow the bearing retainer to be slid from the shaft.
6. Press off the bearing and install the new one by pressing it into position.
7. Press on the new retainer.

NOTE: *Do not attempt to press the bearing and the retainer on at the same time.*

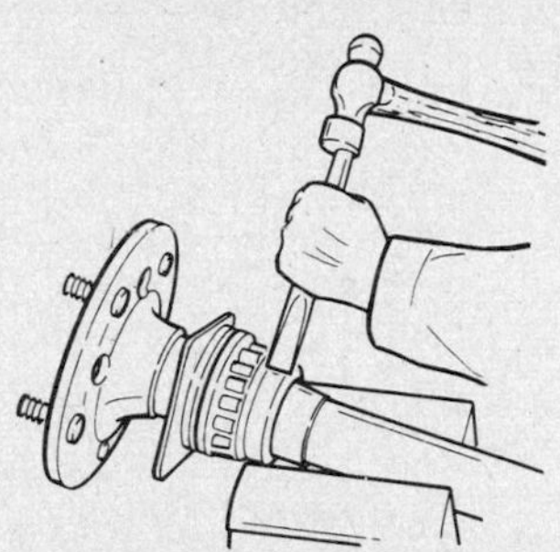

Axle shaft bearing retainer removal —removable carrier axle (© Ford Motor Co.)

Remove the differential pinion shaft lockbolt —WER axle (© Ford Motor Co.)

Remove the axle shaft C-locks —WER axle (© Ford Motor Co.)

8. Assemble the shaft and bearing in the housing, being sure that the bearing is seated properly in the housing.
9. Install the retainer, drum, wheel and tire. Bleed the brakes.

WER and C-Lock Axles

1. Jack up and support the rear of the car.
2. Remove the wheels and tires from the brake drums.
3. Place a drain pan under the housing and drain the lubricant by loosening the housing cover.
4. Remove the nuts securing the brake drums to the axle shaft flanges and remove the drums.
5. Remove the housing cover and gasket.
6. Position jackstands under the rear frame member and lower the axle housing. This is done to give easy access to the inside of the differential.
7. Working through the opening in the differential case, remove the side gear pinion shaft lockbolt and the side gear pinion shaft.
8. Push the axle shafts inward and remove the C-locks from the inner end of the axle shafts.
9. Remove the axle shafts with a slide hammer. Be sure the seal is not damaged by the splines on the axle shaft.
10. Remove the bearing and oil seal from the housing. Two types of bearings are used on some axles, one requiring a press fit and the other a loose fit. A loose fitting bearing does not necessarily indicate excessive wear.
11. Inspect the axle shaft housing and axle shafts for burrs or other irregularities. Replace any worn or damaged parts. A light

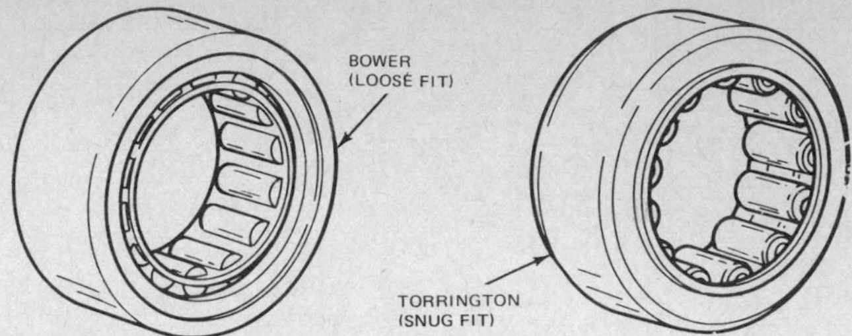

Two types of bearings used on WER axles (© Ford Motor Co.)

yellow color on the bearing journal of the axle shaft is normal, and does not require replacement of the axle shaft. Slight pitting and wear is also normal.

12. Lightly coat the wheel bearing rollers with axle lubricant. Install the bearings in the axle housing until the bearing seats firmly against the shoulder.
13. Wipe all lubricant from the oil seal bore, before installing the seal.
14. Inspect the original seals for wear. If necessary, these may be replaced with new seals, which are prepacked with lubricant and do not require soaking.
15. Install the oil seal.

Caution Installation of the seal without the proper tool can cause distortion and seal leakage. Oil seals for the right-side are marked with green stripes and the word RIGHT. Seals for the left-side are marked yellow with the word LEFT. Do not interchange seals from side to side.

16. Carefully slide the axle shafts into place. Be careful that you do not damage the seal with the splined end of the axle shaft. Engage the splined end of the shaft with the differential side gears.
17. Install the axle shaft C-locks on the inner end of the axle shafts and seat the C-locks in the counterbore of the differential side gears.
18. Rotate the differential pinion gears until the differential pinion shaft can be installed. Install the differential pinion shaft lockbolt.
19. Install the brake drum on the axle shaft flange.
20. Install the wheel and tire on the brake drum and tighten the attaching nuts.
21. Clean the gasket surface of the rear housing and install a new cover gasket and the housing cover.
22. Raise the rear axle so that it is in the running position. Add the amount of specified lubricant to bring the lubricant level to the bottom of the filler plug hole.

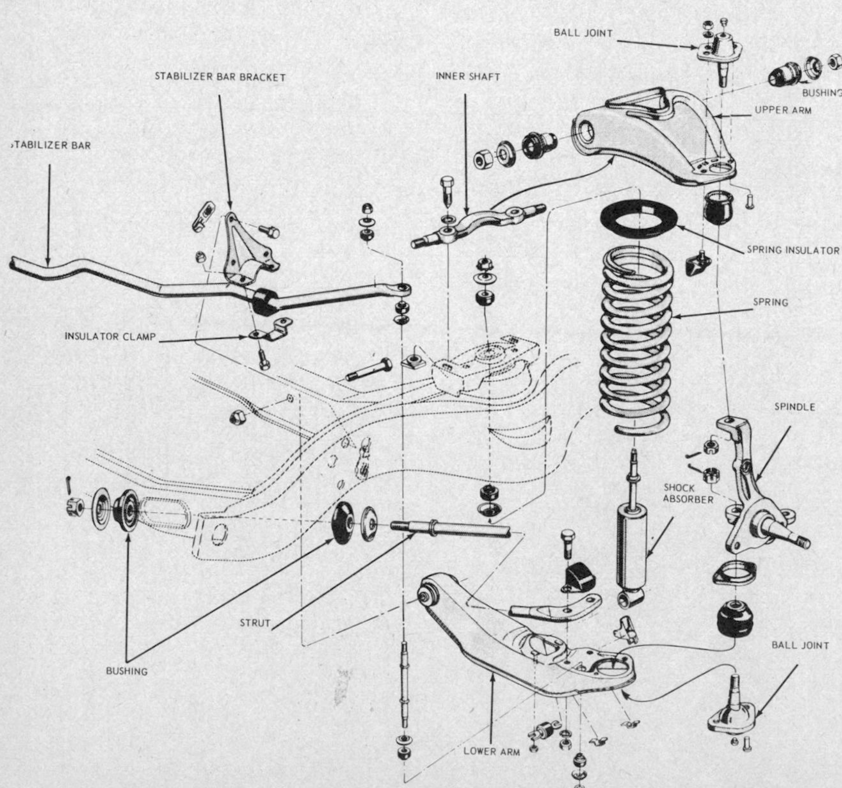

Typical front suspension—1968-70 (© Ford Motor Co)

FRONT SUSPENSION

Shock Absorber R & R

1. Remove the nut, washer, and bushing from the upper end of the shock absorber.
2. Raise the vehicle and install jackstands under the frame rails.
3. Remove the two bolts securing the shock absorber to the lower control arm and remove the shock absorber.
4. Install a new bushing and washer on the top of the shock absorber and position the unit inside the front spring. Install the two lower attaching bolts.
5. Remove the jackstands and lower the vehicle.
6. Place a new bushing and washer on the shock absorber top stud and install the attaching nut.

Coil Spring and Lower Control Arm R & R

1. Raise car and support with stands placed back of lower arms.
2. If necessary for clearance or access and equipped with drum brakes, remove the wheel and brake drum as an assembly. Remove the brake backing plate attaching bolts and remove the backing plate from the spindle. Wire the assembly back out of the way.
3. If necessary for clearance or access and equipped with disc brakes, remove the wheel from the hub. Remove two bolts and washers that hold the caliper and brake hose bracket to the spindle. Remove the caliper from the rotor and wire it back out of the way. Then, remove the hub and rotor from the spindle.
4. Disconnect lower end of the shock absorber and push it up to the retracted position.
5. Disconnect stabilizer bar link from the lower arm.
6. Remove cotter pins from the upper and lower ball joint stud nuts.
7. Remove two bolts and nuts holding the strut to the lower arm.
8. Loosen the lower ball joint stud nut two turns. Do not remove this nut.
9. Install spreader tool between the upper and lower ball joint studs.
10. Expand the tool until the tool exerts considerable pressure on the studs. Tap the spindle near the lower stud with a hammer to loosen the stud in the spindle. Do not loosen the stud with tool pressure only.

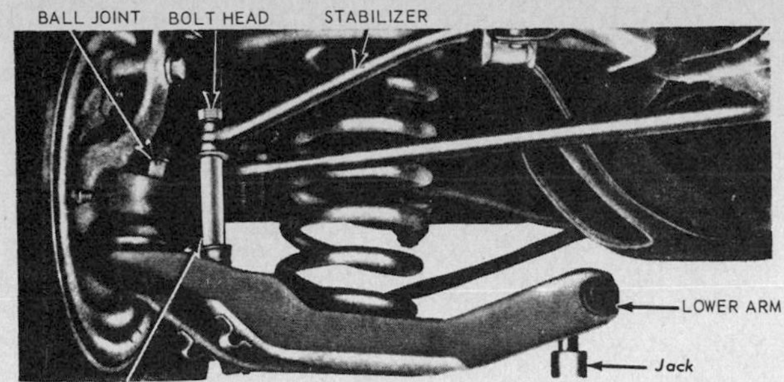

Removing front coil spring (© Ford Motor Co)

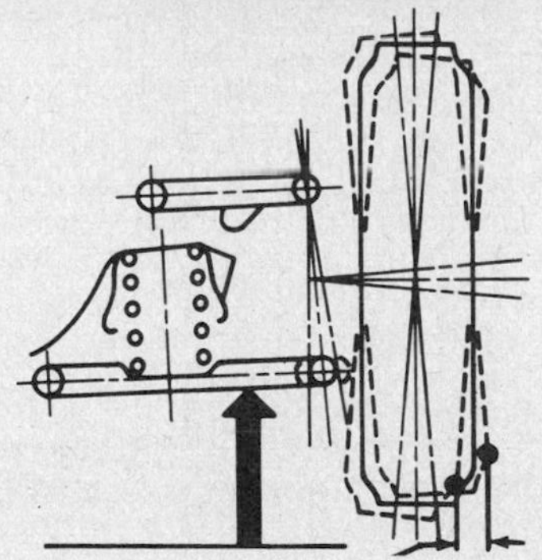
Measuring lower ball joint radial play (© Ford Motor Co)

11. Position floor jack under the lower arm and remove the lower ball joint stud nut.
12. Install a spring compressor and lower floor jack and remove the spring and insulator.
13. Remove the A-arm to crossmember attaching parts, and remove the arm from the car.
14. Reverse above procedure to install. If lower control arm was replaced because of damage, check front end alignment.

Lower Ball Joint

Inspection

1. Raise the vehicle by placing a floor jack under the lower arm; or, raise the vehicle on a hoist and place a jack stand under the lower arm and lower the vehicle onto it to remove the preload from the lower ball joint.
2. Adjust the wheel bearings.
3. Have an assistant grasp the wheel top and bottom and apply alternate in and out pressure to the top and bottom of the wheel.
4. Radial play of 1/4 in. is acceptable measured at the inside of the wheel adjacent to the lower arm.

NOTE: this radial play is multiplied at the outer circumference of the tire and should be measured only at the inside of the wheel.

Replacement

1. Raise the vehicle on a hoist and allow the front wheels to fall to their full down position.
2. Drill a 1/8 in. hole completely through each ball joint attaching rivet.
3. Use a 3/8 in. drill in the pilot hole to drill off the head of the rivet.
4. Drive the rivets from the lower arm.
5. Place a jack under the lower arm and lower the vehicle about 6 in.
6. Remove the lower ball joint stud cotter pin and attaching nut.
7. Using a suitable tool, loosen the ball joint from the spindle and remove the ball joint from the lower arm.
8. Clean all metal burrs from the lower arm and install the new ball joint, using the service part nuts and bolts to attach the ball joint to the lower arm. Do not attempt to rerivet the ball joint once it has been removed.
9. Check front end alignment.

Upper Ball Joint

Inspection

1. Raise the vehicle by placing a floor jack under the lower arm. Do not allow the lower arm to hang freely with the vehicle on a hoist or bumper jack.
2. Have an assistant grasp the bottom of the tire and move the wheel in and out.
3. As the wheel is being moved, observe the upper control arm where the spindle attaches to it. Any movement between the upper part of the spindle and the upper ball joint indicates a bad ball joint which must be replaced.

NOTE: during this check the lower ball joint will be unloaded and may move; this is normal and not an indication of a bad ball joint. Also, do not mistake a loose wheel bearing for a defective ball joint.

Replacement

1. Raise the vehicle on a hoist and allow the front wheels to fall to their full down position.
2. Drill a 1/8 in. hole completely through each ball joint attaching rivet.
3. Using a large chisel, cut off the head of each rivet and drive them from the upper arm.
4. Place a jack under the lower arm and lower the vehicle about 6 in.
5. Remove the cotter pin and attaching nut from the ball joint stud.
6. Using a suitable tool, loosen the ball joint stud from the spindle and remove the ball joint from the upper arm.
7. Clean all metal burrs from the upper arm and install the new ball joint, using the service part nuts and bolts to attach the ball joint to the upper arm. Do not attempt to rerivet the ball joint once it has been removed.
8. Check front end alignment.

Upper Control Arm

Replacement

1. Perform steps 1-12 of the above "Coil Spring and Lower Control Arm R&R" procedure.
2. Remove the upper arm inner shaft attaching bolts and remove the arm and shaft from the chassis as an assembly.
3. Reverse above procedure to install.
4. Adjust front end alignment.

Wheel Bearing Adjustment

1. Raise the front of the vehicle.
2. Remove the wheel cover and grease cap.
3. Remove the cotter pin and nut lock.
4. Back off the adjusting nut and retighten the nut to 17–25 ft. lbs. Back off the adjusting nut again 1/2 turn. Retighten the nut to 10–15 in. lbs. Install the nut lock so that the castellations are aligned with the cotter pin hole. Install the cotter pin and bend the ends around the castellations of the nut lock to prevent interference with the radio static collector in the grease cap.
5. Install the grease cap and wheel cover.
6. Lower the vehicle.

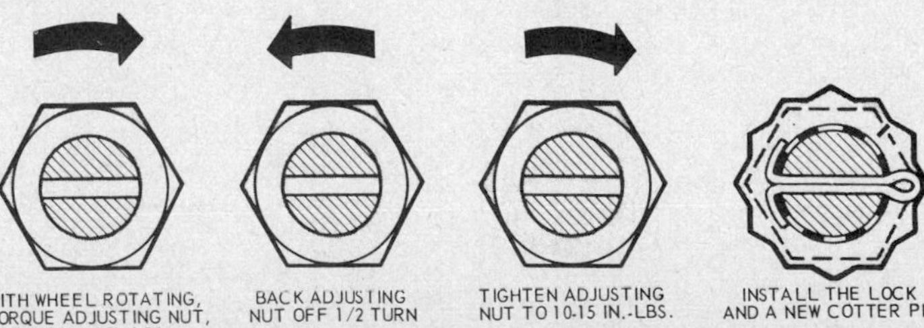

Front wheel bearing adjustment (© Ford Motor Co)

REAR SUSPENSION

The rear suspension is a coil-link design. Large, low-rate coil springs are mounted between rear axle pads and frame supports. Parallel lower arms extend forward of the spring seats to rubber frame anchor to accommodate driving and breaking forces. A third link is mounted between the axle and the frame to control torque reaction forces from the rear wheels.

Lateral (side sway) motion of the rear axle is controlled by a rubber bushed ıear track bar, linked laterally between the axle and frame.

Spring R & R

1. Place car on hoist and lift under rear axle housing. Place jack stands under frame side rails.
2. Disconnect track bar at the rear axle housing bracket.
3. On Ford/Mercury, disconnect the rear of the front-to-rear brake line from the rear brake hose at the No. 4 crossmember bracket. Remove the clip.
4. Disconnect rear shock absorbers from the rear axle housing brackets.
5. Disconnect hose from axle housing vent.
6. Install a spring compressor.
7. Lower hoist with axle housing until coil springs are released.
8. Remove spring lower retainer with bolt, nut, washer and insulator.
9. Remove spring with large rubber insulator pads from car.
10. Install in reverse of above.

Shock Absorber Replacement

Rear shock absorbers on all Fords are straddle-mounted and are held to rubber bushings at both the top and bottom connections. Simply remove the nuts from the top and bottom of the shock absorber and lift the shock absorber off the car.

BRAKES

All models have single anchor, internal expanding, self adjusting shoe brakes on the rear wheels as standard equipment. On models without disc brakes, the front brakes are identical to the rear brakes with the exception of parking brake hardware. Front disc brakes have single piston, floating or sliding calipers. All cars have dual reservoir master cylinders and brake systems in which the front and rear brake hydraulic systems are separate and independent of each other.

Starting 1975, Thunderbird and Mercury cars are available with improved brake system equipment. A new four-wheel disc brake system combined with the Sure-Track (anti-skid) system is an option on these cars. In addition, a hydraulically assisted Hydro-Boost system is available on some models instead of a vacuum assist brake system.

The Hydro-Boost system uses the power steering pump to pressurize the hydraulic system and is connected to the pump by means of normal power steering hydraulic hoses. The decision to use hydraulic assist instead of vacuum assist was made in order to conserve engine vacuum for emission control equipment and other vacuum assisted power accessories. The rear brake caliper on models with four-wheel disc brakes is of single-piston, fixed caliper design. The parking brake design marks a departure from former practice as the parking brake cable acts directly on the brake pads bringing them into contact with the brake rotor (disc). No auxiliary parking brake drum assemblies are required with this arrangement.

NOTE: procedure for brake shoe or pad replacement and adjustment as well as wheel and master cylinder overhaul, and brake bleeding can be found in the "Unit Repair Section."

Master Cylinder

Master Cylinder R & R

Standard Brakes

1. Working under the dash, disconnect the master cylinder pushrod from the brake pedal. The pushrod cannot be removed from the master cylinder.
2. Disconnect the stoplight switch wires and remove the switch from the brake pedal, using care not to damage the switch.

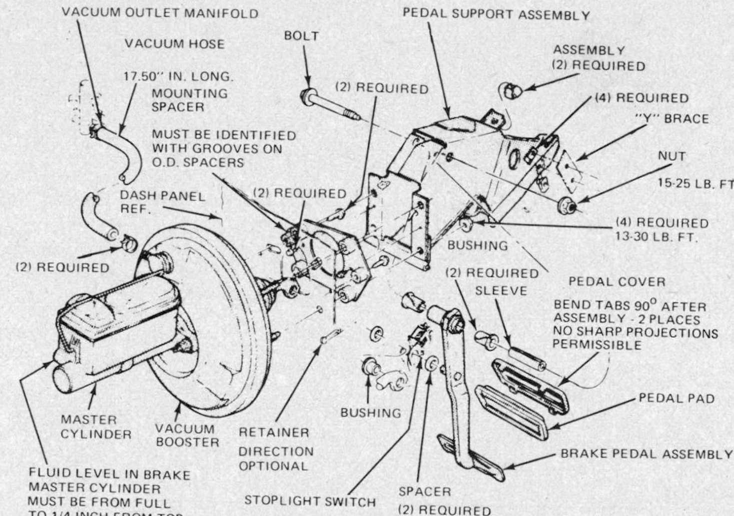

Master cylinder and vacuum booster installation—power brakes—1972-74 Thunderbird installation shown
(© Ford Motor Co)

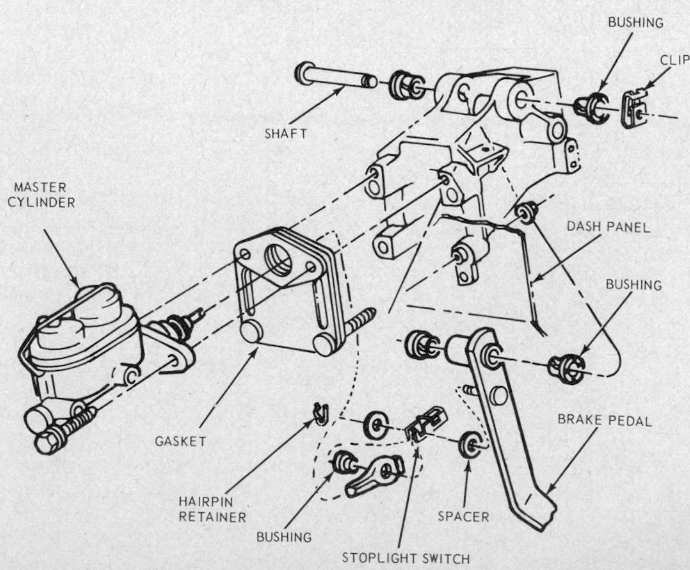

Master cylinder and brake pedal installation—non-power brakes—1969-71 Ford and Mercury installation shown
(© Ford Motor Co)

3. Disconnect the brake lines from the master cylinder.
4. Remove the attaching screws master cylinder from the car. from the firewall and remove the
5. Reinstall in reverse of above order, leaving the brake line fittings loose at the master cylinder.
6. Fill the master cylinder, and with the brake lines loose, slowly bleed the air from the master cylinder using the foot pedal.

Power Brakes (vacuum assist)

1. Disconnect the brake line from the master cylinder.
2. Remove the two nuts and lockwashers that attach the master cylinder to the brake booster.
3. Remove the master cylinder from the booster.
4. Reverse above procedure to reinstall.
5. Fill master cylinder and bleed entire brake system.
6. Refill master cylinder.

Brake Vacuum Booster R & R

1. Working from inside the car, beneath the instrument panel, remove the booster pushrod from the brake pedal.
2. Disconnect the stop light switch wires and remove the switch from the brake pedal. Use care not to damage the switch during removal.
3. Raise the hood and remove the master cylinder from the booster without disconnecting the brake lines. Carefully position the master cylinder out of the way, being careful not to kink the brake lines.
4. Remove the manifold vacuum hose from the booster.
5. Remove the booster to firewall attaching bolts and remove the booster from the car.
6. Reverse above procedure to reinstall.

Hydro-Boost Accumulator R&R

1. Open the hood and remove the 2 nuts attaching the master cylinder to the brake booster.
2. Remove the master cylinder from the Hydro-Boost accumulator.
3. Set the master cylinder aside without disturbing the hydraulic lines.
4. Disconnect the pressure, steering and return lines from the accumulator.
5. Plug the lines and ports.
6. Working below the dash, disconnect the Hydro-Boost pushrod from the brake pedal. To do this, disconnect the stoplight switch at the connector. Remove the hairpin retainer. Slide the spotlight switch from the brake pedal pin far enough to clear the switch outer pin hole. Remove the switch from the pin.
7. Loosen the Hydro-Boost attaching nuts and remove the pushrod, washers and bushing from the brake pedal pin.
8. Remove the accumlator.
9. Installation is the reverse of removal.

Parking Brake Adjustment—Rear Drum Brakes

1. Raise the vehicle on an axle hoist with the transmission in Neutral and the parking brake fully released.
2. Tighten the adjusting nut against the cable equalizer until the rear brakes drag when the wheels are turned.
3. Loosen up on the adjustment nut until the brakes are fully released.
4. Tighten the locknut (if used) to 7-10 ft lbs.

Parking Brake Adjustment—Rear Disc Brakes

1. Be sure the parking brake is fully released.
2. Place the transmission in Neutral and raise the vehicle on an axle hoist.
3. Tighten the adjuster nut until the levers on the calipers just begin to move. Loosen the nut just enough to obtain full return to the stop position.
4. Check the operation. Attempt to pull the parking brake levers rearward. If they can be pulled rearward, the parking brake is too tight.

STEERING

The steering gear on all models with manual steering is the worm and recirculating ball type. The sector shaft is straddle mounted in the cover above the gear and a housing mounted roller bearing below the gear.

All full-size Fords, Mercurys and Thunderbirds with power steering use integral type power steering. On this type of steering, hydraulic assist is provided directly to the steering gear, eliminating all hoses and hardware which was previously mounted under the chassis. The most common type of steering gear used with integral power steering is the Ford torsion bar model. The torsion bar type power steering unit includes a worm and one-piece rack piston, which is meshed with the gear teeth on the steering sector shaft. In certain limited applications a Saginaw Rotary Valve type power steering unit is

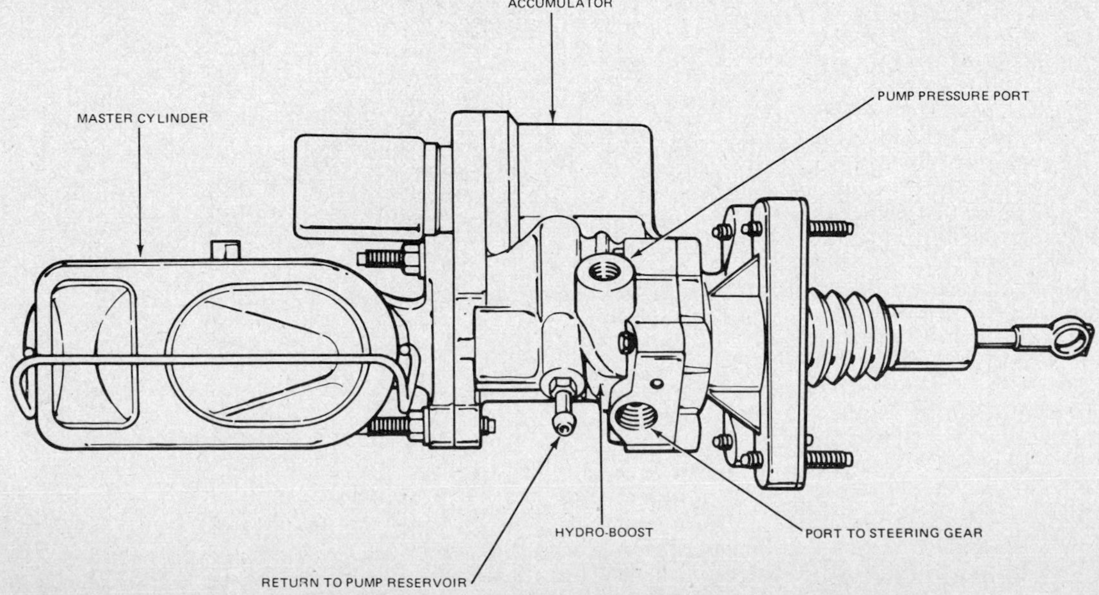

Hydro-Boost accumulator and master cylinder (© Ford Motor Co)

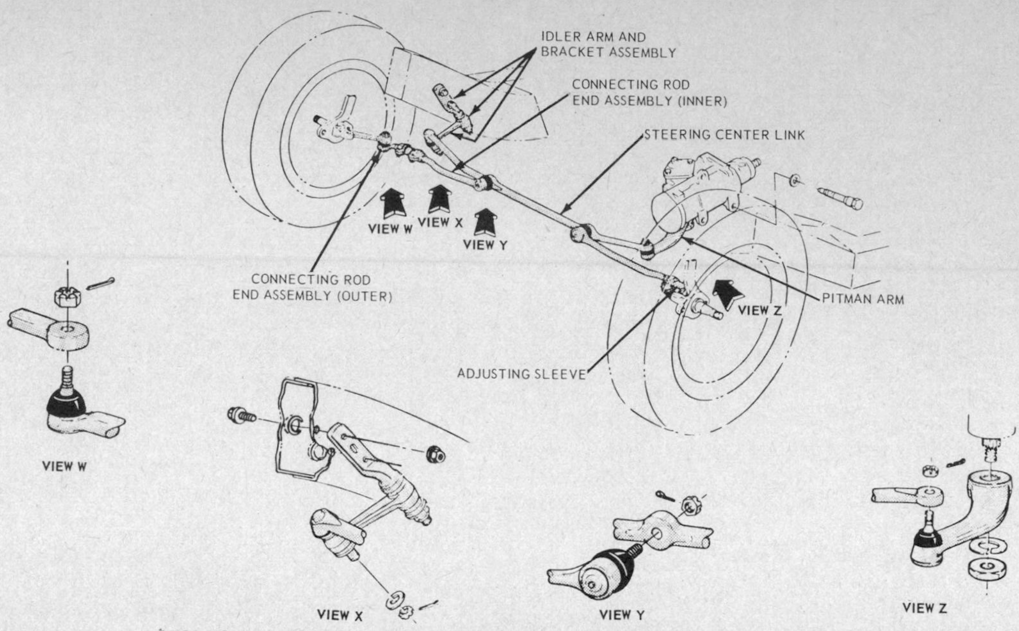

1969-76 Ford and Mercury manual or power steering linkage (© Ford Motor Co)

used. In this unit, the rack-piston nut is of one piece design and is geared to the steering sector shaft.

All adjustment and overhaul operations are contained in the Unit Repair Section of this book; listed under manual steering and power steering respectively.

Power Steering Pump R & R

1. Drain the fluid from the pump reservoir by disconnecting the fluid return hose at the pump. Then, disconnect the pressure hose from the pump.
2. Remove the mounting bolts from the front of the pump. On eight cylinder engines, there is a nut on the rear of the pump that must be removed. After removal, move the pump inward to loosen the belt tension and remove the belt from the pulley. Then, remove the pump from the car.
3. To reinstall the pump, position on mounting bracket and loosely install the mounting bolts and nuts. Put the drive belt over the pulley and move the pump outward against the belt until the proper belt tension is obtained. Measure the belt tension with a belt tension gauge for the proper adjustment. Only in cases where a belt tension gauge is not available should the belt deflection method be used. If the belt deflection method is used, be sure to check with a belt tension gauge as soon as possible, since deflection method is not accurate.
4. Tighten the mounting bolts and nuts.

Steering Wheel R & R

1. Disconnect the negative battery cable.
2. Remove the horn ring or hub cap by pushing it down and rotating it counterclockwise. Remove the retaining screws (from underside of steering wheel) and the crash pad. On both 1968-69 Thunderbirds and 1969-70 Fords and Mercurys with speed control, the switch bezels must be pried up with a thin knife blade and the center trim plate removed to gain access to the crash pad retaining screws. On later models with speed control, the switches simply snap into plastic retainers inside the crash pad. Disconnect the horn and speed control wires.
3. Remove the steering wheel nut. Install a steering wheel puller on the end of the shaft and remove the wheel.

Caution The use of a knock-off type steering wheel puller or the use of a hammer on the steering shaft will damage the column bearing and, on collapsible columns, the column itself may be damaged.

4. Lubricate the steering shaft bushing with white grease. Transfer all serviceable parts to the new steering wheel.
5. With the front wheels pointing in a straight-ahead direction, and with the alignment marks on steering wheel and the steering shaft lined up, install the steering wheel and locknut.
6. Connect the horn and speed control wires and install the horn ring or hub cap. Install the crash pad and retaining screws.
7. Connect the negative battery cable.

Turn Signal Switch R & R

1. Disconnect the negative battery cable.
2. Remove the steering wheel as outlined in the "Steering Wheel R&R" section.
3. Unscrew the turn signal lever from the side of the column. Remove the emergency flasher retainer and knob, if so equipped.
4. Locate and remove the finish cover on the steering column and disconnect the wiring connector plugs.

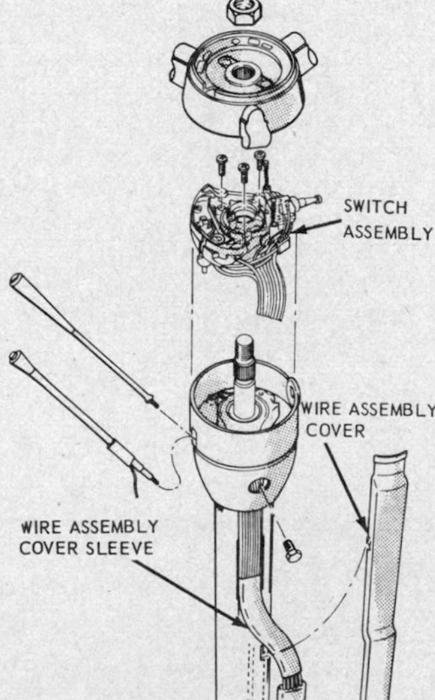

Turn signal switch—fixed column
(© Ford Motor Co)

5. On all 1969-70 Thunderbirds, and all 1969-76 models with a tilt steering column, it is necessary to separate the wires from the connector plug in order to remove the switch and wires. First note the location and color code of each wire, prior to removal, with the wire terminal removal tool. Remove the plastic cover from the wiring harness. Attach a piece of heavy cord to the switch wires to pull them down

through the column during installation.

6. Remove the retaining clips and screws from the turn signal switch and lift the switch and wire assembly from the top of the column.
7. Tape the ends of the new switch wires together and transfer the pull cord to these wires.
8. Pull the wires down through the column with the cord and attach the new switch to the column hub.
9. If the switch wires were separated from the connector plug, press the wires into their proper location. Connect the wiring connector plugs and install the finish cover on the column.
10. Install the turn signal lever. Install the emergency flasher retainer and knob, if so equipped.
11. Install the steering wheel as outlined in the "Steering Wheel R&R" section.
12. Connect the negative battery cable and test the operation of the turn signals, horn, emergency flashers, and speed control, if so equipped.

INSTRUMENT PANEL

Ignition Lock Cylinder Replacement

1969

1. Insert key and turn to Acc. position.
2. With stiff wire in hole, depress lock pin and rotate cylinder counterclockwise, then pull out cylinder.

1970-76

1. Disconnect the negative battery cable.
2. On cars with a fixed steering column, remove the steering wheel trim pad and the steering wheel. Insert a stiff wire into the hole located in the lock cylinder housing. On cars with a tilt steering wheel, this hole is located on the outside of the steering column near the emergency flasher button and it is not necessary to remove the steering wheel.
3. Place the gear shift lever in Reverse on standard shift cars and in Park on cars with automatic transmission, and turn the ignition key to the ON position.
4. Depress wire and remove lock cylinder and wire.
5. Insert new cylinder into housing and turn to the OFF position. This will lock the cylinder into position.
6. Reinstall steering wheel and pad if removed.
7. Connect negative battery cable.

Ignition Switch Replacement

1969

1. Remove cylinder as above.
2. Unscrew the bezel from the ignition switch and remove switch from panel.
3. Remove insulated plug from rear of switch.
4. Install in reverse of above.

1970-76

1. Disconnect the negative battery cable.
2. Remove the shrouding from the steering column, and detach and lower the steering column from the brake support bracket.
3. Disconnect the switch wiring at the multiple plug.
4. Remove the two nuts that retain the switch to the steering column.
5. On vehicles with column mounted gearshift lever, detach the switch plunger from the switch actuator rod and remove the switch. On vehicles with console mounted gearshift lever, remove the pin connecting the plunger to the actuator and remove the switch.
6. To re-install the switch, place both the lock mechanism at the top of the column and the switch itself in lock position for correct adjustment. To hold the column in the lock position, place the automatic shift lever in PARK or manual shift lever in reverse, and turn to LOCK and remove the key. New switches are held in lock by plastic shipping pins. To pin existing switches, pull the switch plunger out as far as it will go and push it back into the first detent. Insert a 3/32 in. diameter wire in the locking hole in the top of the switch.
7. Connect the switch plunger to the switch actuator rod.
8. Position the switch on the column and install the attaching nuts. Do not tighten them.
9. Move the switch up and down to locate mid-position of rod lash, and then tighten the nuts.
10. Remove the locking pin or wire.
11. Attach the steering column to the brake support bracket and install the shrouding.

Headlight Switch R & R

All Except 1970 Mercury and 1972-76 Thunderbird

1. Disconnect the negative battery cable. Remove the knob from the washer switch.
2. On 1971-76 Ford and 1971 and 1973-76 Mercury, remove the instrument panel pad, and instrument cluster. On 1972 Mercurys, remove the instrument panel pad only.
3. Pull the headlight switch control knob to the full ON position and press the release knob on the

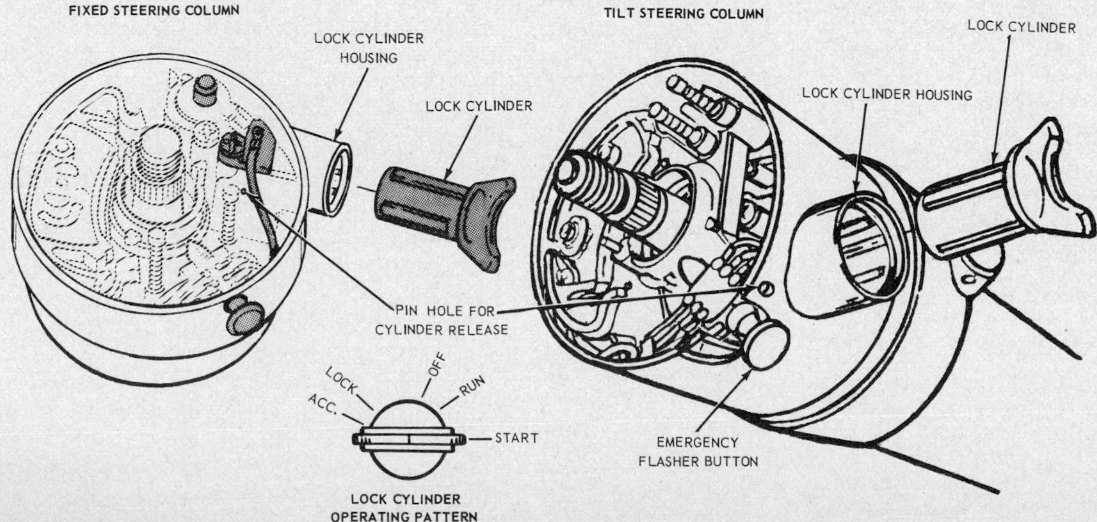

1970 and later lock cylinder replacement (© Ford Motor Co)

switch. With the knob depressed, pull the knob and shaft from the switch.

4. Remove the wire connector from the back of the switch and, if equipped with headlight doors, remove the vacuum hoses. On 1969 Mercury, remove the wire harness bracket.
5. Remove the bezel retaining nut and remove the switch from the dash. On 1971-72 Fords and 1971 Mercurys, the switch is attached to the dash with three screws instead of a bezel nut.
6. Reverse above procedure to reinstall. When installing the headlight switch control knob and shaft, turn the shaft in the switch until a distinct click is heard, locking the shaft in place.

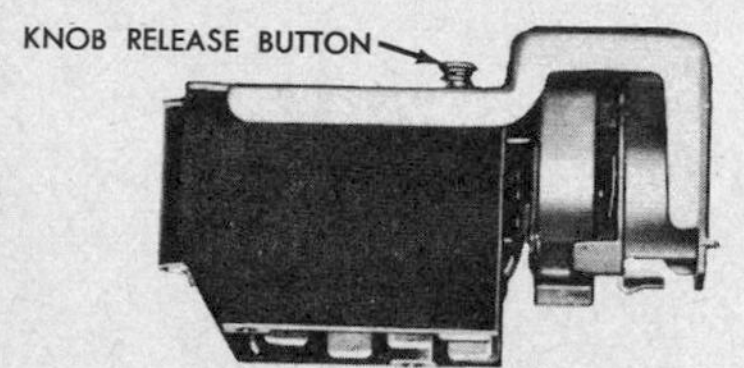

Typical headlight switch
(© Ford Motor Co)

1970 Mercury

1. Remove the battery ground cable.
2. Working under the dash, remove the wire connector from the back of the headlight switch. If equipped with headlight doors, remove the vacuum hoses from the switch.
3. Remove the four switch retaining screws and remove the switch from the dash.
4. Reverse above procedure to install.

1972-76 Thunderbird

1. Disconnect the negative battery cable.
2. Remove the cluster trim panel.
3. Remove the headlight switch mounting plate.
4. Remove the bezel nut and disconnect the multiple connector.
5. If equipped, remove the vacuum lines.
6. Remove the switch.
7. Reverse the above procedure to install.

WINDSHIELD WIPERS

Motor R & R

Ford and Mercury 1969-76, Thunderbird 1972-76

1. Disconnect the negative battery cable.
2. Remove the wiper arm and blade assemblies from the pivot shafts.
3. On 1969-70 models, remove the cowl grille. Remove the left side cowl grille.
4. Disconnect the wiper links at the wiper output pin by removing the retaining clip.
5. Disconnect the wire leads from the motor. They are located under the dash.
6. Remove the motor attaching bolts from under the dash and remove the motor.
7. Reverse procedure to install.

NOTE: before installing the wiper arms and blades, operate the wiper motor to ensure the pivot shafts are in the park position when the arms and blades are installed.

Thunderbird, 1969-71 Except 1970

This motor works by hydraulic pressure taken from the power steering system. During wiper operation, a part of the fluid supply is bypassed through the wiper motor by a valve on the motor.

1. Remove wiper arm and blade assemblies, pivot shaft nuts and bezels.
2. Remove the cowl top panel.
3. Disconnect both pivot shaft links at the wiper motor.
4. Remove carburetor air cleaner.

Caution If the engine has been running recently, watch out for hot fluid in the wiper system.

5. Disconnect the lines at the wiper motor.
6. Remove wiper motor mounting screws.
7. Disconnect the control cable from the motor, then remove the motor.
8. If replacing the wiper motor, transfer all fittings.
9. Position motor to the bracket area, connect and adjust the control cable.
10. Start the lines in the fittings, position the motor on its mount and install attaching screws. Tighten fittings.
11. Connect the links to the wiper motor arm.
12. Start engine and check operation of wiper motor. Stop engine and bring power steering reservoir to level.
13. Reinstall cowl top panel.
14. Install bezels, nuts and wiper arm assemblies. Install the air cleaner.

Thunderbird, 1970

1970 Thunderbirds used electric, two-speed wipers instead of the usual hydraulic type.

1. Disconnect the negative battery cable.
2. Disconnect the windshield washer hose. Remove the three retaining bolts and pull the cowl grille from under the two clips.
3. Disconnect the wiper motor leads from the engine side of the firewall and push the wiring and insulating grommet through the hole in the firewall.
4. Remove the four motor to dash retaining bolts.
5. Lift the wiper motor out and, at the same time, pull the wiper arm and blade assembly to the left to gain access to the wiper output pin.
6. Remove the clip and disconnect the wiper links from the motor.
7. Remove the three motor-to-mounting plate bolts and remove the motor.
8. To reinstall, first position the wire harness and grommet in the hole in the firewall, then reverse above procedure.

Linkage R & R

1. Disconnect the battery ground cable.
2. Remove the wiper arms and blades from the pivots as an assembly. On Thunderbird be sure to remove the tension arm retaining clip from the stud on the left pivot.
3. Remove the cowl grille from the car.
4. Disconnect the linkage arm from the drive arm by removing the clip.
5. Remove the pivot attaching screws from the cowl and remove the pivot from the cowl.

NOTE: on 1969-72 Fords and Mercurys, to remove the left wiper linkage, it is first necessary to loosen the attaching screws on the right wiper arm pivot.

RADIO

Removal and Installation

1969 Thunderbird

1. Disconnect battery.
2. Remove inspection cover plate beneath steering wheel.
3. If necessary remove vacuum motor on inboard tilt swing column to provide clearance. Place shift lever in any position but Park before removing motor.
4. Remove two knobs and discs from radio.
5. Remove sleeve or fader control and two hex mounting nuts from radio shafts.
6. Remove radio rear support bracket.
7. Slide radio forward and down toward inspection hole.
8. Disconnect all leads and remove radio.
9. Reverse procedure to install radio.

1969-70 Mercury

1. Disconnect battery.
2. Remove radio knobs and remove nut from radio shaft.

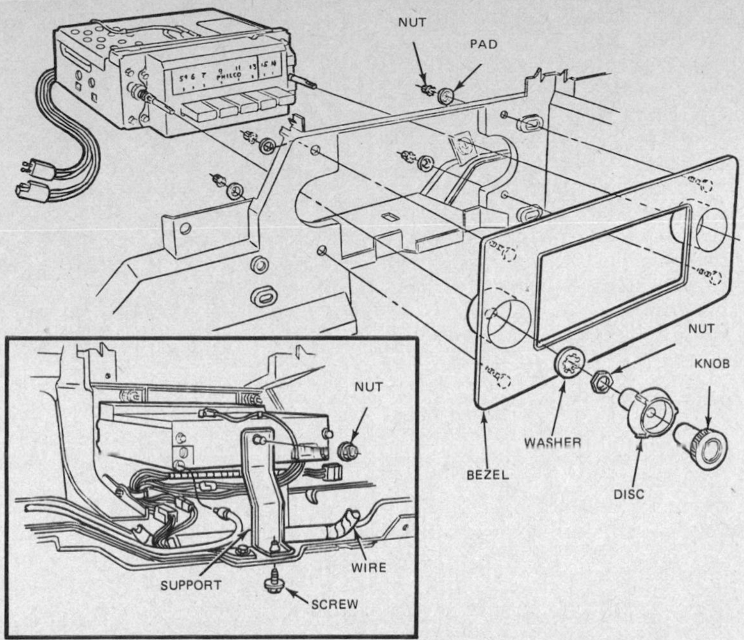

Radio installation—1972-76 Thunderbird (© Ford Motor Co)

3. Remove radio rear support nut and nut retaining radio to instrument panel.
4. Lower radio and disconnect antenna, radio, power, and speaker lead wires.
5. Remove radio. Reverse procedure to install radio.

1969-70 Ford

1. Remove radio knobs and wiper and washer knobs.
2. Remove lighter and pull off heater switch knobs.
3. Remove ten screws retaining instrument panel trim cover assembly and remove.
4. Remove lower rear radio support bolt.
5. Remove three nuts retaining radio in instrument panel and pull radio halfway out.
6. Disconnect all leads and remove radio.
7. Reverse procedure to install radio.

1970-71 Thunderbird

Use the procedure for the 1970-71 Mark III.

1971-76 Ford and Mercury

1. Disconnect the negative battery cable.
2. Remove the radio knobs and the nuts retaining the radio cover bezel.
3. Remove the bezel and the nut retaining the fader control to the bezel.
4. Remove the upper and lower radio support brackets and bolts.
5. Disconnect all leads from the radio.
6. Remove the two nuts retaining the radio to the instrument panel and remove the radio.
7. Reverse above procedure to install.

1972-75 Thunderbird

1. Disconnect the negative battery cable.
2. Remove the knobs from the radio shafts.
3. Remove the radio shaft nuts and the rear support attaching screw.
4. Disconnect the power lead, speaker wires and antenna lead, and remove the radio.
5. Remove the 2 screws attaching the twilight sentinel amplifier. Lower the amplifier.
6. Remove the air conditioning duct from beneath the radio.
7. Disconnect the radio rear support.
8. Reverse the above procedure to install.

HEATER

Vehicles Without Air Conditioning

Heater Core R & R

Ford and Mercury

1. Partially drain cooling system.
2. Remove heater hoses at core.
3. Remove retaining screws, core cover and seal from plenum.
4. Remove core from plenum.
5. Install in reverse of above, applying a thin coat of silicone to the pads.

1969-71 Thunderbird

1. Remove the hood and air cleaner.
2. Drain the cooling system.

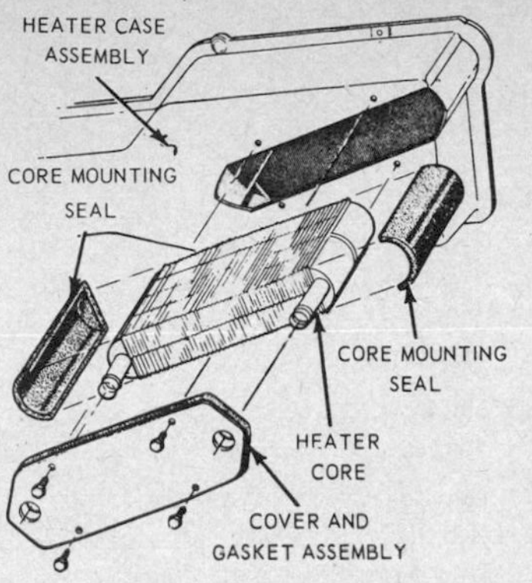

Ford heater core installation
(© Ford Motor Co)

3. Remove the heater hoses and position the hoses and hot water valve out of the way.
4. Disconnect the vacuum hose from the top of the heater case and position it out of the way.
5. Remove the transmission dip stick and tube assembly from the transmission.
6. Disconnect the blower motor lead wires.
7. Remove the heater core case cover and remove the core from the case.
8. Reverse above procedure to install.

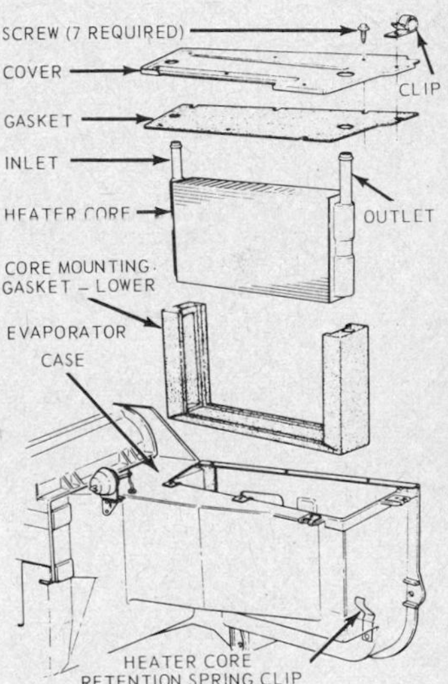

Heater core removal—1973-76
Ford and Mercury
(© Ford Motor Co)

1972-76 Thunderbird

1. Drain the coolant and disconnect the hoses from the heater core.
2. Remove the glove box and the heater air outlet register.
3. Remove the mounting screw and disconnect the temperature cable at the blend door crank arm.
4. Remove the blue and red vacuum hoses from the high-low door vacuum motor, the yellow hose from the panel-defrost door motor, and the brown hose at the tee connector to the temperature bypass door motor.

5. Disconnect the wiring connector from the resistor.
6. Remove the 10 retaining screws and the rear half of the plenum case.
7. Remove the heater core tube support bracket mounting nut.
8. Reverse the above procedure to install, taking care to reseal the plenum case halves.

Blower Motor R & R

1969-71 Thunderbird

1. Working inside the car, remove the right kick panel cover.
2. Remove the screws attaching the fresh air duct and remove the duct from the car.
3. Reach inside the cowl panel and disconnect the blower motor wire leads.
4. Still working inside the cowl panel, remove the one screw attaching the blower motor to the mounting plate. Rotate the motor mounting plate clockwise to disengage it from the heater case.
5. Remove the blower motor and wheel assembly from the car by guiding it out of the opening in the cowl panel.

1972-76 Thunderbird

1. Remove the glovebox and recirc air register and duct assembly.
2. Remove the two, blower lower housing retaining screws.
3. Disconnect the white hose from the outside recirc air door vacuum motor, and remove the vacuum motor from the blower lower housing. Leave the motor actuator connected to the door crank arm.
4. Disconnect the orange lead wire and black ground wire from the blower motor.
5. Remove the six flange screws and separate the blower lower housing from the upper housing. Remove the lower housing from the car.
6. Remove the blower motor and wheel assembly from the lower housing.
7. Reverse the above procedure to install.

1969-72 Ford and Mercury

1. Disconnect the negative battery cable.
2. Disconnect the blower motor wire leads under the hood.
3. Remove any parts mounted on the inside of the right fender apron.
4. Raise the vehicle on a hoist and remove the right front wheel.
5. Remove the fender apron-to-fender attaching bolts and lower the fender apron.
6. Insert a block of wood between the apron and the fender to gain working space.
7. Reach inside the fender apron and remove the blower motor mounting plate attaching screws.
8. Remove the blower motor, wheel and mounting plate from inside the fender as an assembly.
9. Reverse above procedure to install.

1973-76 Ford and Mercury

1. Disconnect the blower motor lead wire. This is an orange wire located at the rear of the right hood hinge.
2. Remove the mounting screw from the black ground wire located at the upper cowl. Remove both wires from the clip.
3. Remove the right front tire and wheel.
4. In order to get to the blower motor, an access hole must be cut out in the right front fender apron. The pattern for this hole has been outlined on the apron by the factory. It appears as a beaded line.
5. A small indentation or drill dimple is present 1/2 in. from the centerline of the bead. Drill a 1 in. diameter hole at this drill dimple. Be careful not to damage the heater case by overdrilling.
6. Using aircraft snips, cut along the bead to create the opening. Do not use a saber saw.
7. Remove the blower motor mounting plate screws and disconnect the cooler tube from the motor.
8. Remove the motor and wheel assembly out of the heater case and out through the access hole.
9. To install, reverse the removal procedure. Apply rope sealer to the motor mounting plate. Obtain a cover plate from your local Ford parts department, drill 8, 1/8 in. holes in the fender apron and install the cover plate.

Vehicles With Factory Air Conditioning

Heater Core R & R

1969-72 Ford and Mercury

1. Drain the cooling system.

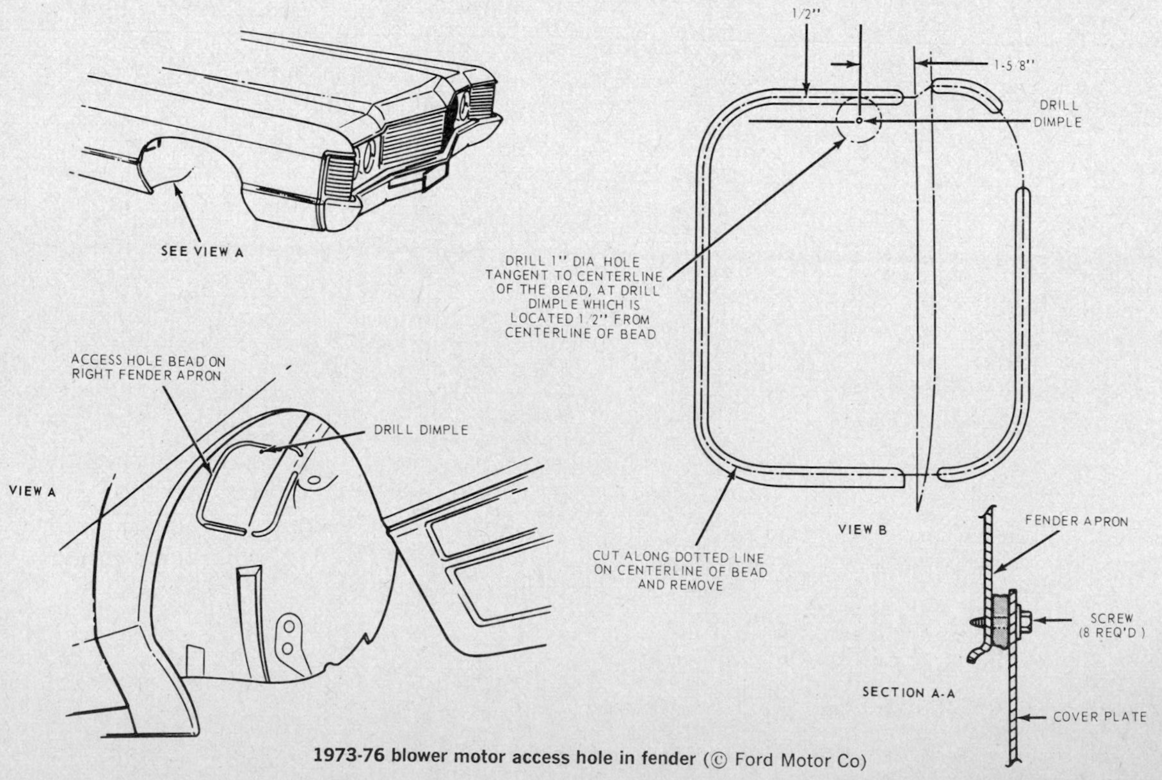

1973-76 blower motor access hole in fender (© Ford Motor Co)

2. Remove the carburetor air cleaner.
3. Remove the two screws retaining the vacuum manifold to the dash. Disconnect the vacuum hoses as necessary, taking note of their placement, and move the manifold to one side of the heater core cover.
4. Disconnect the heater hoses.
5. Remove the seven attaching screws and the heater core cover.
6. Remove the heater core and pad from the housing.
7. Reverse above procedure to install.

1973-76 Ford and Mercury

1. Drain the cooling system.
2. Disconnect the heater hoses at the heater core tubes.
3. Remove the seven screws which retain the core cover plate to the core housing and lift off the plate.
4. Pull the heater core and mounting gasket up out of the case. Remove the core mounting gasket.
5. Reverse the above procedure to install, taking care to ensure that the core and gasket seat firmly forward of the core retention spring in the case. Fill the cooling system with the recommended mixture of water and anti-freeze (coolant).

1969-71 Thunderbird

1. Drain the cooling system.
2. Remove the air cleaner. Scribe the outline of the hinges on the hood and remove the hood.
3. On models equipped with hydraulic wipers, disconnect and plug the hydraulic lines at the motor.
4. Disconnect the heater hoses.
5. Disconnect the vacuum supply hose from the top of the housing and remove the oil pressure sender unit from the engine.
6. Remove the transmission dipstick and tube assembly.
7. Disconnect the icing switch multiple connector.
8. Remove the heater-air conditioner housing front cover.
9. Remove the glove compartment liner, and disconnect the electrical and vacuum junction blocks from the inner dash panel.
10. Remove two evaporator stud nuts and remove the heater core case cover.
11. Remove the core retaining bracket and core.
12. Reverse above procedure to install.

1972-76 Thunderbird

See heater core R&R for non-air-conditioned 1972-76 Thunderbirds.

Blower Motor R & R

1969-72 Ford and Mercury

1. Remove the battery.
2. Remove the right front wheel.
3. Remove the vacuum tank bolts and fender apron bolts.
4. Move the fender apron inboard.
5. Remove the blower motor attaching screws and vent hose.
6. Pry upward on the hood hinge and remove the blower.
7. Reverse the above procedure to install.

1973-76 Ford and Mercury

For air-conditioned cars, follow the same procedure outlined under "Blower Motor R & R" for non-air-conditioned 1973-76 Ford and Mercury.

1969-71 Thunderbird

1. Disconnect the ground cable from the battery.
2. Take out the courtesy light from the lower edge of the instrument panel.

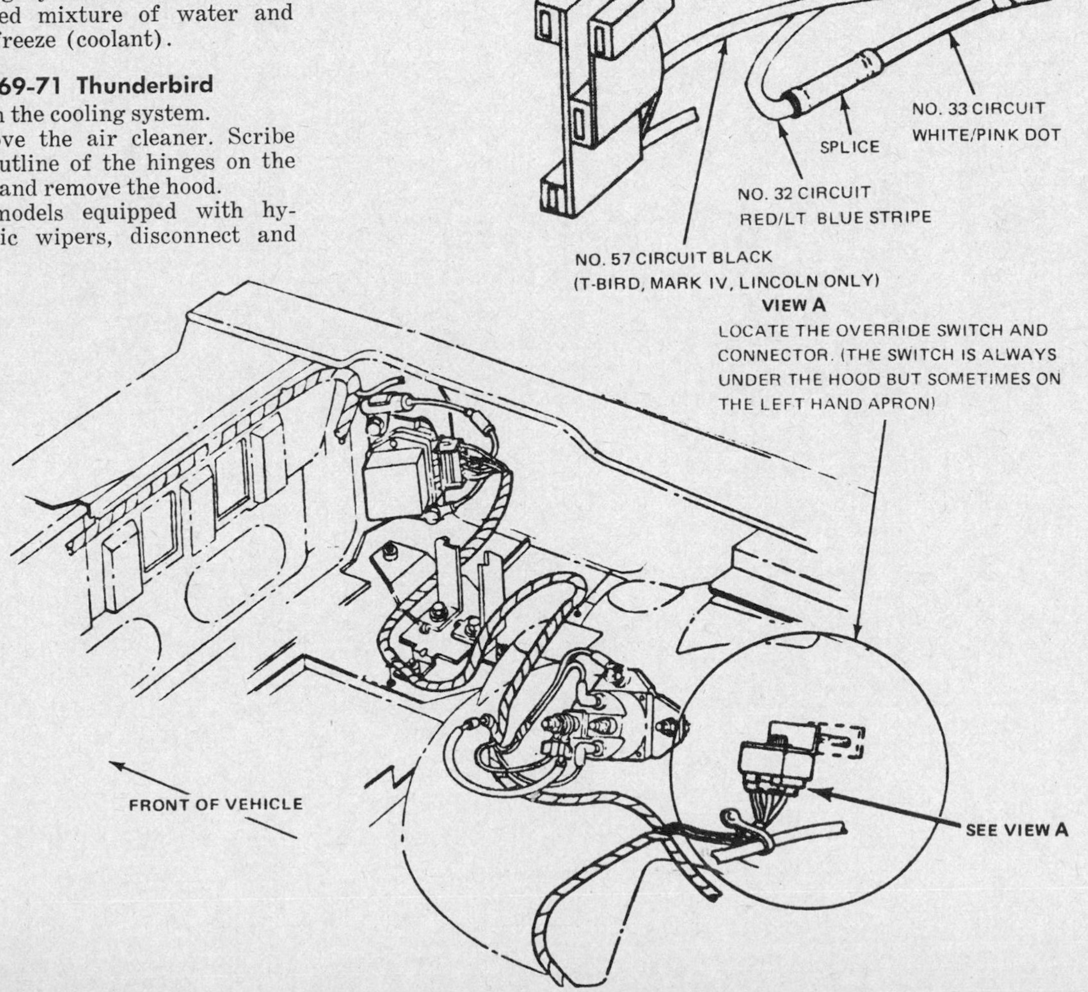

Seat belt interlock disconnect points (© Ford Motor Co)

3. Take out the glove box liner.
4. Take off the right cowl side of the trim panel.
5. Take out the six duct mounting flange screws. Reach through the recirculating door opening and take the vacuum hose from the vacuum motor and take out the duct assembly.
6. Disconnect the lead wire from the blower motor.
7. Lift out the motor and wheel assembly through the opening in the cowl side panel.
8. Take out the screw from the motor mounting plate.
9. Rotate the motor mounting plate counter-clockwise until unlocked, then lift out.
10. Reverse the above procedure to install.

1972-76 Thunderbird

See "Blower Motor R&R" for non-air-conditioned 1972-76 Thunderbirds.

SEAT BELTS

Seat Belt/Starter System Interlock System

As required by law on 1974-75 models, a starter interlock system is employed consisting of a warning light, buzzer, seat sensors, switches in the outboard belt retractors, and an electronic logic module. The starter will not engage unless the driver and the right front seat passenger sit on their seats and pull out their seat belts. Unless the driver and passenger have remained seated and buckled,. the sequence must be repeated every time the engine is started. Leaving the belts pulled all the way out will also prevent the engine from being started, as the belts must be retracted and buckled each time the engine is started. In the event of a starter interlock system failure, or to permit the use of a remote starter switch when working under the hod, a starter interlock by-pass switch is located in the engine compartment, eliminating the need to perform the buckling sequence.

NOTE: Each time the by-pass switch is operated the buckling sequence may be eliminated one time only.

Disabling the Seat Belt/ Starter Interlock

As of 29 October 1974, it is legal to disable the seat belt/starter interlock system. However the warning light portion of the system must be left operational.

1. Apply the parking brake and remove the ignition key.
2. Open the hood and locate the system emergency override switch and connector. It is always under the hood and sometimes on the left fender apron. Remove the connector.
3. Cut the white wire(s) with the pink dots (#33 circuit) and the red wire(s) wth the light blue stripe (#32 circuit).
4. Splice the two (or four) wires together and tape the splice. Use a "butt" connector if available.

NOTE: Do not cut and splice the other connector wires. If the red/yellow hash wire is spliced to any of the other wires the car will start in gear.

6. Install the connector back on the override switch. Close the hood.
7. Apply the parking brakes, buckle the seat belt, and turn the key to the "ON" position. If the starter cranks in "ON" or any gear selected, the wrong wires have been cut and spliced. Repeat steps 3-6.
8. Unbuckle the belt and try to start the car. If the car doesn't start, repeat steps 3-6. If the car starts, everything is O.K.
9. To stop the warning buzzer from operating, remove it from the connector. Tape the connector to the wiring harness so that it can't rattle.

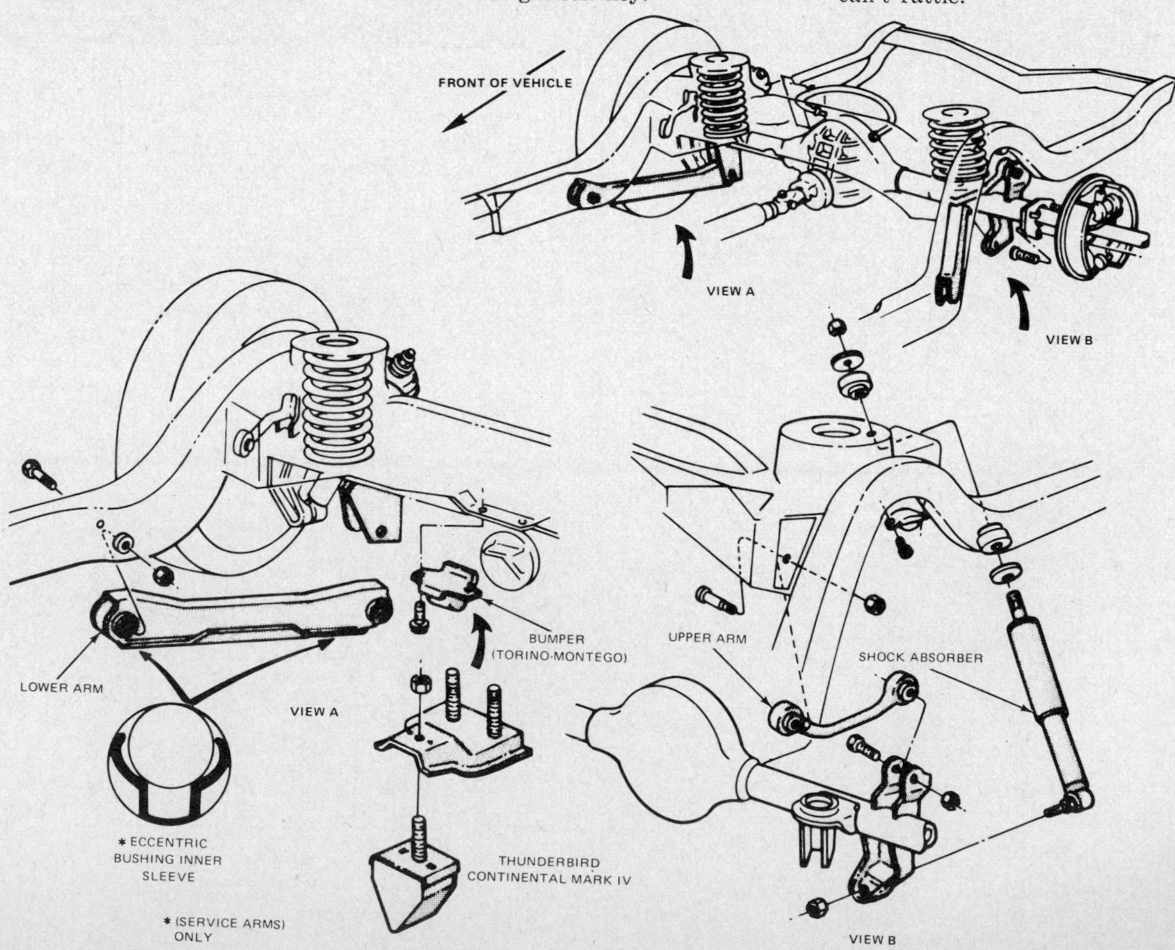

Rear suspension details (© Ford Motor Co)

INDEX

Lincoln Continental · Mark III · Mark IV

YEAR IDENTIFICATION

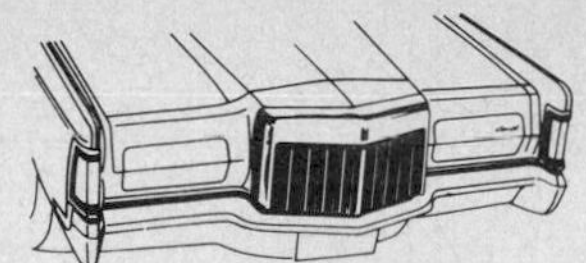
1969 Mark III

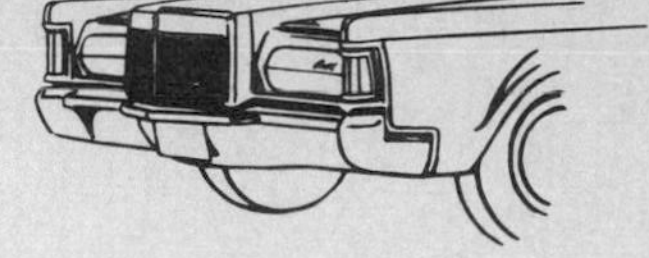
1970-71 Continental Mark III

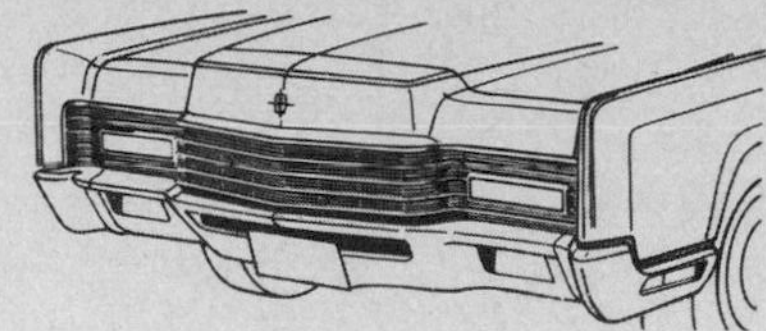
1970 Continental

1971 Continental

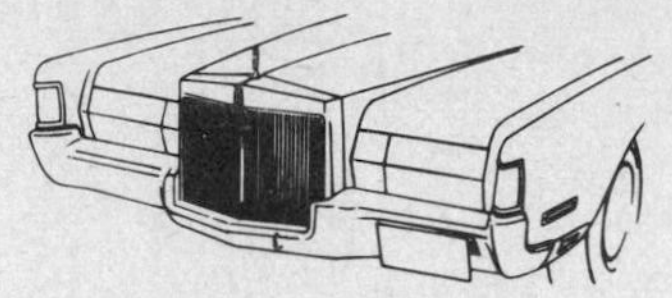
1972 Continental Mark IV

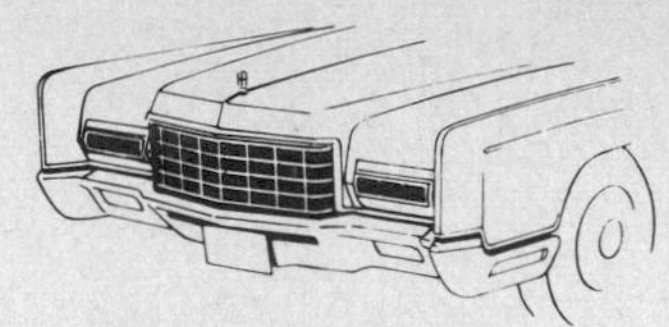
1972 Continental

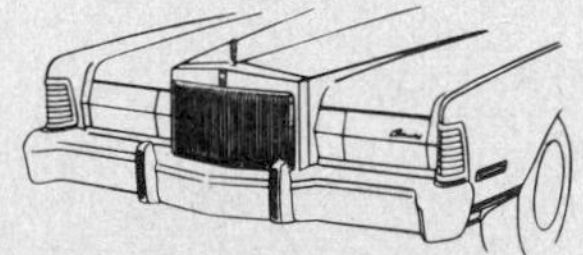
1973 Continental Mark IV

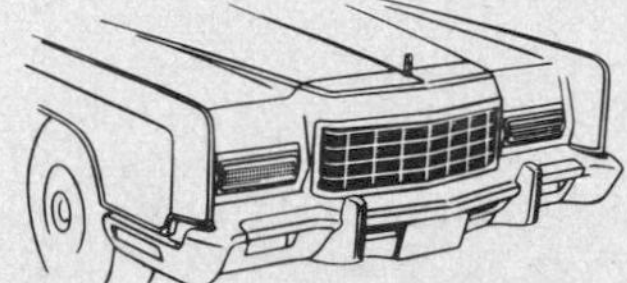
1973 Continental

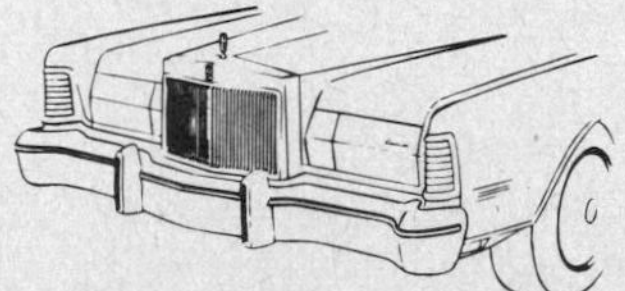
1974 Continental Mark IV

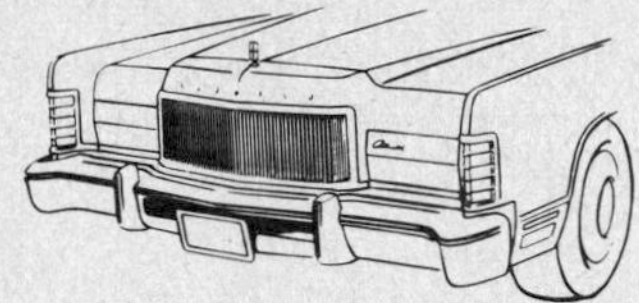
1974 Continental

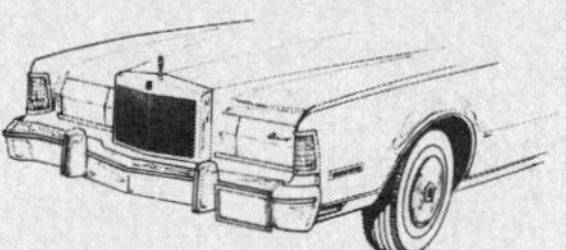
1975 Continental Mark IV

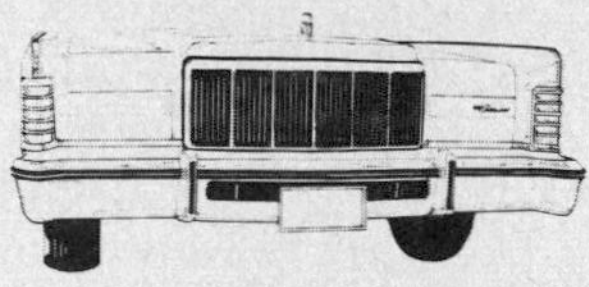
1975 Lincoln Continental

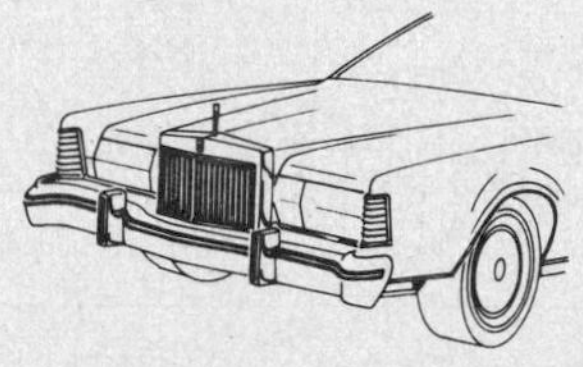
1976 Continental Mark IV

FIRING ORDER

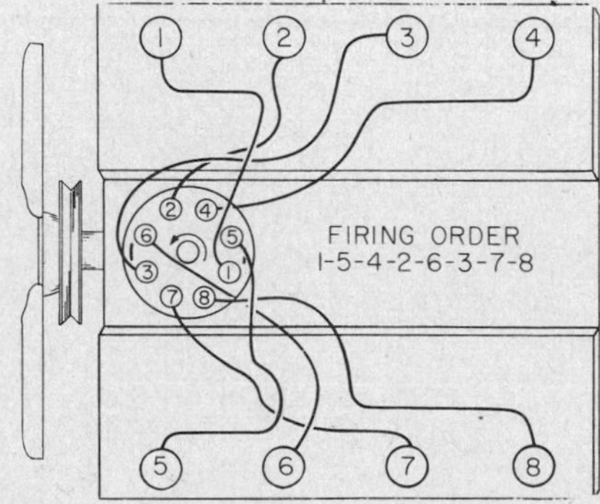

CAR SERIAL NUMBER LOCATION

1969-76

The vehicle number is stamped on an aluminum tab riveted to the top of the instrument panel, visible through the driver's side windshield. The serial number contains eleven digits. They are interpreted as follows:
First: Model year code. (9 = 1969, 0 = 1970, 1 = 1971, 2 = 1972, etc.)
Second: Assembly plant code.
Third and fourth: Body serial code.
Fifth: Engine code. (A = 460 cu. in.)
Last six: Consecutive unit number.

Vehicle Certification Label

1970-76

The vehicle certification label is attached to the left-hand door jamb. This label has, on its upper portion, the name of the manufacturer, the month and year of manfacture, and the certification statement. The label also shows the vehicle identification number, which must match that on the dashboard. See the illustration for interpretation of the label.

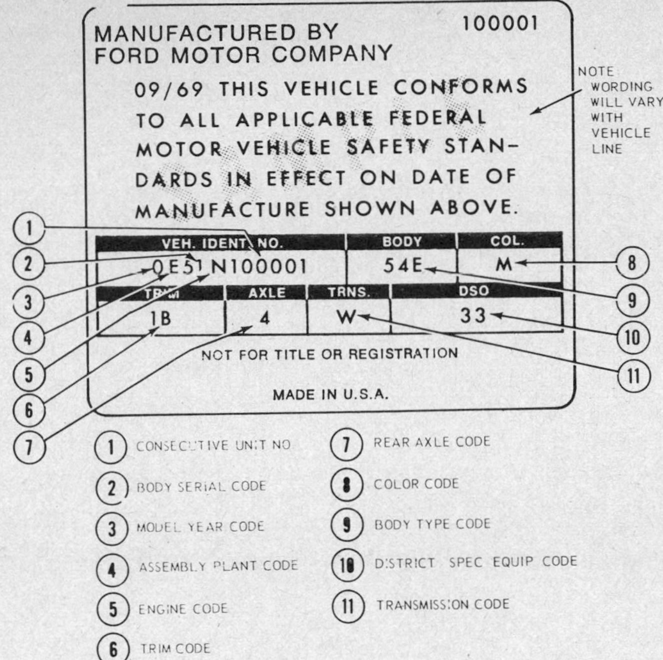

Vehicle certification label—1970-76
(© Ford Motor Co)

ENGINE CODE

The engine code designation is the 5th digit of the vehicle identification number (V.I.N.) The V.I.N. is stamped on a plate located at the left side of the instrument panel visible through the windshield

Disp	Bbl	Hp	'69	'70	'71	'72	'73	'74	'75	'76
8-Cylinder Models										
460	4	202, 208, 219 (net)*					A	A	A	A
460	4	212, 224 (net)*				A				
460	4	365	A	A	A					

*Net horsepower rating varies with model application

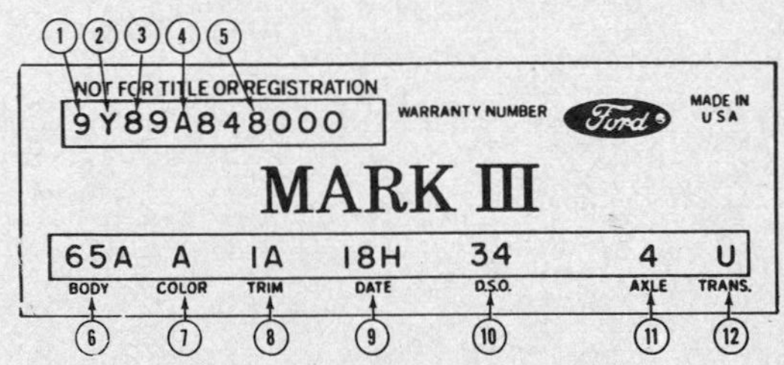

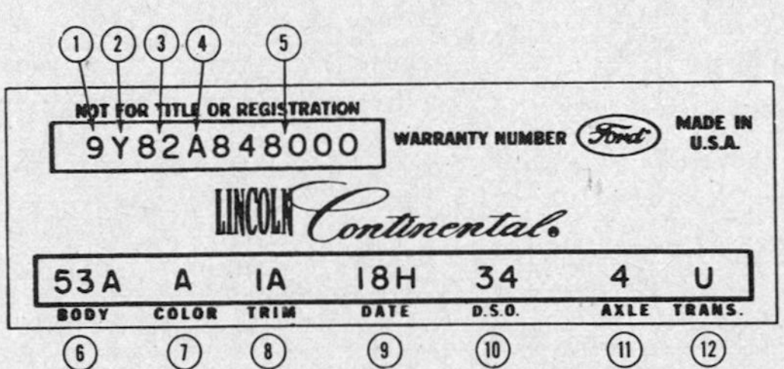

1 Model year code
2 Assembly plant code
3 Body serial code
4 Engine code
5 Consecutive unit number
6 Body type code
7 Color code
8 Trim code
9 Date code
10 District—special equipment code
11 Rear axle code
12 Transmission code

GENERAL ENGINE SPECIFICATIONS

Year	Engine No. Cyl. Displacement Cu. In.	Carburetor Type	Horsepower @ rpm ■	Torque @ rpm (ft lbs) ■	Bore and Stroke (in.)	Compression Ratio	Oil Pressure @ 2050 rpm
'69	8-460	4 bbl	365 @ 4600	500 @ 2800	4.362 x 3.850	10.50:1	55
'70	8-460	4 bbl	365 @ 4600	500 @ 2800	4.362 x 3.850	10.50:1	55
'71	8-460	4 bbl	365 @ 4600	500 @ 2800	4.362 x 3.850	10.50:1	35-75
'72	8-460	4 bbl	224 @ 4400	357 @ 2800	4.362 x 3.850	8.50:1	35-75
	8-460 Mark IV	4 bbl	212 @ 4400	342 @ 2800	4.362 x 3.850	8.50:1	35-75
'73	8-460 Continental	4 bbl	224 @ 4400	357 @ 2800	4.362 x 3.850	8.5:1	35-65
	8-460 Mark IV	4 bbl	212 @ 4400	342 @ 2800	4.362 x 3.850	8.5:1	35-65
'74	8-460 Continental	4 bbl	215 @ 4000	350 @ 2600	4.362 x 3.850	8.5:1	35-65
	8-460 Mark IV	4 bbl	220 @ 4000	350 @ 2600	4.362 x 3.850	8.5:1	35-65
'75-'76	8-460 Continental	4 bbl	206 @ 4000①	357 @ 2600②	4.362 x 3.850	8.0:1	35-65
	8-460 Mark IV	4 bbl	194 @ 4000①	347 @ 2600②	4.362 x 3.850	8.0:1	35-65

■ Beginning 1972, horsepower and torque are SAE net figures. They are measured at the rear of the transmission with all accessories installed and operating. Since the figures vary when a given engine is installed in different models, some are representative rather than exact.

① 223 @ 4000—California

② 366 @ 2600—California

TUNE-UP SPECIFICATIONS

Year	ENGINE No. Cyl Displacement (cu in.)	hp	SPARK PLUGS Type	Gap (in.)	DISTRIBUTOR Point Dwell (deg)	Point Gap (in.)	IGNITION TIMING (deg) ▲ Man Trans	● Auto Trans	VALVES Intake Opens ■ (deg)	Fuel Pump Pressure (psi)	IDLE SPEED (rpm) ▲ Man Trans	Auto Trans
'69	8-460	365	BF-42	.034	26-31	.017	—	10B	16	4½-6½	—	550①
'70	8-460	365	BF-42	.034	26-31	.017	—	10B	16	5-7	—	600
'71	8-460	365	BRF-42	.034	26-31	.017	—	4B	16	5-7	—	600
'72	8-460	224	ARF-42	.034	26-30	.017	—	10B(6B)	16	5-7	—	625/500②
'73	8-460	224	ARF-22	.034	26-30	.017	—	6B	16	5-7	—	625/500②
'74-'75	8-460 Mark IV	220	ARF-52	.044	Electronic		—	14B	8	6-7	—	650/500②
	8-460	215	ARF-52	.044	Electronic		—	14B	8	6-7	—	650/500②
'76	8-460	All	ARF-52	.044	Electronic		—	14/8B③ @ 650	8	6-7	—	650

▲ See text for procedure
● Figure in parentheses indicates California engine
■ All figures Before Top Dead Center
① A/C on

② First figure is for idle speed with solenoid energized and automatic transmission in Drive, while second figure is for idle speed with splenoid disconnected and automatic transmission in Neutral
B Before Top Dead Center
— Not applicable

CAPACITIES

Year	ENGINE No. Cyl. Displacement (cu. in.)	Engine Crankcase Add 1 Qt For New Filter	TRANSMISSION Pts To Refill After Draining Manual 3-Speed	Manual 4-Speed	Automatic	Drive Axle (pts)	Gasoline Tank (gals)	COOLING SYSTEM (qts) With Heater	With A/C
'69	8-460	4	—	—	26	5	25②	19.5④	19.5④
'70	8-460	4	—	—	26①	5	③	19.5④	19.5④
'71	8-460	4	—	—	26①	5	23	19.4	19.4
'72	8-460	4	—	—	26①	5	22.5	19.4	19.4
'73	8-460	4	—	—	26	5	22⑤	19.5	19.5
'74	8-460	4	—	—	25	5	26.5⑦	21.5	21.5
'75-'76	8-460	4	—	—	26	5	26.5⑧	⑥	⑥

① Mark III—25.5 pts
② Mark III—24 gals
③ Without evaporative emission controls:
Continental—24.5 gals
Mark III—24.1 gals
With evaporative emission controls:
Continental—23.1 gals
Mark III—22.5 gals
④ Mark III—19.4 qts
⑤ Mark IV—22.5 gals
⑥ Mark IV—20.5 qts; Lincoln—19.7 qts
⑦ Lincoln—22 gals
⑧ Lincoln—24.2 gals
— Not applicable

VALVE SPECIFICATIONS

Year	Engine No. Cyl. Displacement (cu in.)	Seat Angle (deg)	Face Angle (deg)	Spring Test Pressure (lbs @ in.)	Spring Installed Height (in.)	STEM TO GUIDE Clearance (in.) Intake	Exhaust	STEM Diameter (in.) Intake	Exhaust
'69	8-460	45	46	80 @ 1.81	1 13/16	.0010-.0027	.0010-.0027	.3420	.3420
'70	8-460	45	46	80 @ 1.81	1 13/16	.0010-.0027	.0010-.0027	.3420	.3420
'71	8-460	45	46	80 @ 1.81	1 13/16	.0010-.0027	.0010-.0027	.3420	.3420
'72	8-460	45	46	80 @ 1.81	1 13/16	.0010-.0027	.0010-.0027	.3420	.3420
'73	8-460	45	44	170 @ 1.39	1 13/16	.0010-.0027	.0010-.0027	.3420	.3420
'74-'76	8-460	45	44	80 @ 1.81	1 13/16	.0010-.0027	.0010-.0027	.3420	.3420

TORQUE SPECIFICATIONS

All readings in ft lbs

Year	Engine Displacement (cu in.)	Cylinder Head Bolts	Rod Bearing Bolts	Main Bearing Bolts	Crankshaft Pulley Bolt	Flywheel to Crankshaft Bolts	MANIFOLD Intake	Exhaust
'69-'76	8-460	130-140①	40-45	95-105	70-90	75-83	25-30	28-33

① In three steps:
Step 1—70-80
Step 2—100-110
Step 3—130-140

CRANKSHAFT AND CONNECTING ROD SPECIFICATIONS

All measurements are given in in.

Year	Engine Displacement (cu in.)	CRANKSHAFT Main Brg Journal Dia	Main Brg. Oil Clearance	Shaft End-Play	Thrust on No.	CONNECTING ROD Journal Diameter	Oil Clearance	Side Clearance
'69-'76	8-460	2.9998-3.0002	.0005-.0025	.004-.008	3	2.4992-2.5000	.0008-.0026	.010-.020

RING GAP

All measurements are given in inches

Year	Engine No. Cyl. Displacement (cu in.)	Top Compression	Bottom Compression
'69-'76	8-460	.010-.020	.010-.020

Year	Engine	Oil Control
'69-'70	8-460	.010 .035
'71-'76	8-460	.015-.055

RING SIDE CLEARANCE

All measurements are given in inches

Year	Engine	Top Compression	Bottom Compression
'69-'76	8-460	.002-.004	.002-.004

Year	Engine	Oil Control
'69-'76	8-460	Snug

PISTON CLEARANCE

Year	Engine	Piston to bore clearance (in.)
'69-'73	8-460	.0014-.0022
'74	8-460	.0022-.0030
'75-'76	8-460	.0014-.0022

ALTERNATOR AND REGULATOR SPECIFICATIONS

	ALTERNATOR			REGULATOR						
					Field Relay			Regulator		
Year	Part No. or Manufacturer	Field Current @ 12 V	Output (amps)	Part No. or Manufacturer	Air Gap (in.)	Point Gap (in.)	Volts to Close	Air Gap (in.)	Point Gap (in.)	Volts @ 75°
'69	Autolite	2.9-3.1	55	Autolite	.018	.019	2.5-4	.052	.020	13.3-15.3
'70-'71	Autolite① DOLF-10300	2.9-3.1	55	Autolite		③		—	—	13.3-14.6
	Autolite② DOAF-10300	2.8-3.3	65	Autolite		③		—	—	13.8-15.3
'72-'74	Motorcraft D2AF-10300-CA, D32F-10300-CA, D42F-10300-BA	2.9	61	Motorcraft	—	—	2.5-4	—	—	13.5-15.3
	Motorcraft D20F-10300-AA	2.9	64④	Motorcraft	—	—	2.5-4	—	—	13.5-15.3
	Motorcraft D2SF-10300-AA	2.9	55	Motorcraft	—	—	2.5-4	—	—	13.5-15.3
	Motorcraft D20F-10300-CB	2.9	61	Motorcraft	—	—	2.5-4	—	—	13.5-15.3
	Motorcraft D30F-10300-AA	2.9	70	Motorcraft	—	—	2.5-4	—	—	13.5-15.3
	Motorcraft D3VF-10300-AA	2.9	90	Motorcraft	—	—	2.5-4	—	—	13.5-15.3
'75-'76	Motorcraft D42F-10300-BA	2.9	61	Motorcraft	—	—	2.5-4	—	—	13.5-15.3
	Motorcraft D40F-10300-AA	2.9	61	Motorcraft	—	—	2.5-4	—	—	13.5-15.3
	Motorcraft D40F-10300-AA	2.9	70	Motorcraft	—	—	2.5-4	—	—	13.5-15.3
	Motorcraft D3VF-10300-AB	2.9	90	Motorcraft	—	—	2.5-4	—	—	13.5-15.3

① Integral regulator
② Opt.; required with heated back window
③ Transistor type
④ 70 amp—1973

BATTERY AND STARTER SPECIFICATIONS

Year	Engine Displacement (cu in.)	BATTERY Ampere Hour Capacity	BATTERY Volts	BATTERY Terminal Grounded	STARTER Lock Test Amps	STARTER Lock Test Volts	STARTER Lock Test Torque (ft lbs)	STARTER No-Load Test Amps	STARTER No-Load Test Volts	STARTER No-Load Test RPM	STARTER Brush Spring Tension (oz)
'69	460	85	12	Neg.	670	5	15.5	70	12	9,500	40
'70-'72	460	85	12	Neg.	Not Recommended			70	12	—	40
'73	460	77①	21	Neg.	Not Recommended			70	12	—	40
'74-'76	460	77	12	Neg.	Not Recommended			80	12	—	80

① Side Terminal

BRAKE SPECIFICATIONS

Year	Model	MASTER CYLINDER Disc	MASTER CYLINDER Drum	WHEEL CYLINDER Front Disc	WHEEL CYLINDER Front Drum	WHEEL CYLINDER Rear	BRAKE DISC OR DRUM DIAMETER Front Disc	BRAKE DISC OR DRUM DIAMETER Front Drum	BRAKE DISC OR DRUM DIAMETER Rear
'69	All exc. Mark III	1.0	—	1 15/16	—	15/16	11.96	—	11.09①
'69	Mark III	1.0	—	2 3/4	—	15/16	11.72	—	11.03②
'70-'72	All exc. Mark III, IV	1.0	—	1 15/16	—	15/16	11.72	—	11.03
	Mark III, IV	1.0	—	2.755	—	15/16	11.72	—	11.03
'73	All Models	1.0	—	3.1	—	1.0	11.72	—	11.03
'74	All Models	1.0	—	3.1	—	1.0	11.72	—	11.03
'75-'76	Lincoln	1.125	—	3.1	—	1.0⑤	11.80	—	11.03⑥
	Mark IV	1.125	—	3.1	—	2.6④	11.80	—	11.50③

① Refinishing Limit—11.150
② Refinishing Limit—11.090
③ Rear rotor diameter
④ Disc brake
⑤ 2.6 in. with rear disc brakes
⑥ 11.50 in. rotor with rear disc brakes
— Not applicable

WHEEL ALIGNMENT SPECIFICATIONS

Year	Model	CASTER Range (deg)	CASTER Pref Setting (deg) ■	CAMBER Range (deg)	CAMBER Pref Setting (deg) ▲	Toe-in (in.)	Steering Axis Inclin. (deg)	WHEEL PIVOT RATIO (deg) Inner Wheel	WHEEL PIVOT RATIO (deg) Outer Wheel
'69	Continental	2 1/4N to 3/4N	1 1/2N	0 to 3/4P	1/2P	1/16 to 3/16	7 3/4	20	17 3/4
'69-'70	Mark III	1/2P to 1 1/2P	1	0 to 1P	1/2P	1/8 to 1/4	7 3/4	20	19.3
'70	Continental	2 1/4N to 3/4N	1 1/2N	1/8P to 5/8P	1/2P	0 to 1/16	7 3/4	20	18 1/2
'71	Continental	2 1/2N to 1/2N	1 1/2N	1/4N to 1 1/4N	1/2P	0 to 1/4	7 7/8	20	18 1/2
	Mark III	0 to 2P	1	1/4N to 1 1/4P	1/2P	1/16 to 5/16	7 3/4	20	19 1/4
'72	Continental	1/2N to 2 1/2P	1 1/2P①	1/2N to 1 1/2P	1/2P②	0 to 1/4	7 3/4	20	18 7/16
'72-'74	Mark IV	0 to 2P	1P①	1/4N to 1 1/4P	1/2P③	1/16 to 5/16	7 3/4	20	17 3/4
'73-'74	Continental	1/2N to 2 1/2P	1P	1/4N to 1 1/4P	1/2P	0 to 1/4	9 1/2	20	17 3/4④
'75-'76	Mark IV	1/4P-2 3/4P	2P⑦	⑤	⑥⑧	1/16-7/16	7 3/4	20.00	18.16
	Continental	1/4P-2 3/4P	2P⑦	⑤	⑥⑧	0-1/4	9 1/2	20.00	18.16

■ Not to vary more than 1/2 degree from one side to the other unless otherwise noted
▲ Not to vary more than 1/4 degree from one side to the other unless otherwise noted
N Negative P Positive
① Maximum caster difference between wheels should not exceed 1°
② Maximum camber difference between wheels should not exceed 1°
③ Maximum camber difference between wheels should not exceed 3/4°
④ 18 1/2° on Lincoln in 1974
⑤ Left—1/4P-1 1/4P; Right—1 1/2N-1P
⑥ Left—1/2P; Right—1/4P
⑦ Maximum camber difference between wheels should not exceed ± 3/4°
⑧ Maximum caster difference between wheels should not exceed — 1/2 to + 1°

CHARGING SYSTEM

General information on alternator and regulator repair and troubleshooting is in the Unit Repair Section under the heading Charging and Starting Systems.

Alternator

Cars are equipped with alternating current generators. This charging system is different from the DC circuit, and requires certain precautions

1. Reversing battery connections will cause damage to the rectifiers.
2. Booster battery connections must be made as follows: the negative terminal of the booster battery must be connected to the negative terminal of the car battery. The positive terminal of the booster battery must be connected to the positive terminal of the car battery.
3. Fast charges should never be used as boosters to start AC circuit equipped cars.
4. Then servicing the battery with a fast charger, always disconnect car battery cables.
5. Never attempt to polarize an AC generator.
6. Complete alternator servicing data is in the Unit Repair Section.

Alternator R & R

1. Disconnect the negative battery cable.
2. Loosen the alternator mounting bolts, remove the alternator to adjusting arm bolt and remove the belt.
3. Remove the alternator mounting bolt and spacer, position the alternator so that the wire connectors can be disconnected and remove the alternator.

NOTE: on alternators with integral regulators mounted on the back of the alternator housing, press the sides of the retainer clip and remove the wire from the regulator.

4. Reverse above procedure to reinstall, applying pressure only to the front of the alternator housing when tightening the drive belt.

Regulator R & R

1. Disconnect the negative battery cable.
2. Remove the regulator mounting screws and wires, then remove the regulator.
3. On vehicles with integral regulator, remove the alternator to adjusting arm bolt and the drive belt.
4. Swing the alternator down, remove the terminal covers from the regulator and remove the regulator attaching nut.
5. Press the sides of the retainer clip and remove the retaining clip and supply wire. Remove the regulator.
6. Reverse above procedure to reinstall.

Fuse Link

Since 1970, all Ford products have incorporated a fuse link in the charging system. The fuse link is a short length of insulated wire, several gauge sizes smaller than the system it protects. The fuse link blows out if a booster battery is hooked into the system incorrectly, or if a component of the electrical system is shorted. When the fuse link blows, it leaves an open circuit in the charging system and the alternator will not charge the battery. A blown fuse link can be identified by bare wire ends or bubbled insulation. It is located in the engine wire harness on or near the starter relay and is marked FUSE LINK. Be sure that the new fuse link is an exact duplicate of the one being replaced.

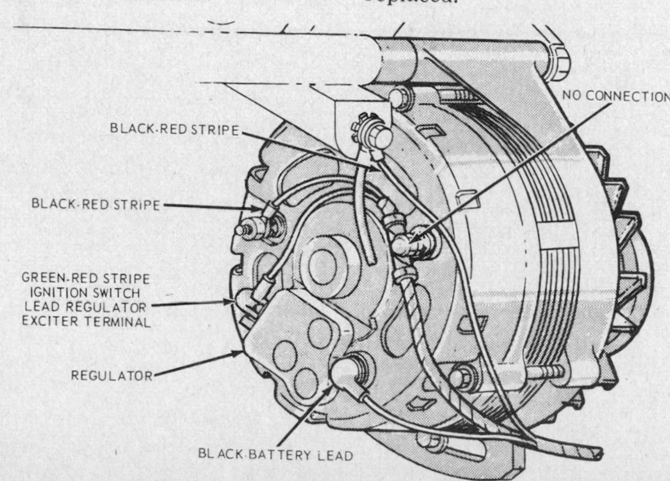

Alternator installation with integral regulator
(© Ford Motor Co)

STARTING SYSTEM

All Lincoln and Continental models use a starter which mounts an outboard solenoid.

Starter R & R

1. Disconnect the battery ground cable.
2. Raise the car on a hoist.
3. Disconnect the wires at the solenoid terminals.
4. Loosen the 2 front brace attaching bolts.
5. Remove all other brace attaching bolts and let the brace hang free.
6. Turn the front wheels to full right lock.
7. Remove the bolts securing the steering idler arm to the frame.
8. Unbolt and remove the starter.
9. Installation is the reverse of removal.

IGNITION SYSTEM

Distributor Removal

The distributor is located at the front of the engine between the cylinder banks.

1. Remove the carburetor air cleaner, the ignition primary lead and the vacuum advance lead.
2. Carefully mark the position of the rotor in relation to the body of the distributor, and mark the position of the body of the distributor relative to the engine block.
3. Remove the hold-down bolt and lift out distributor. The marks are made so that the distributor can be reinstalled without having to retime the ignition.
4. Installation is the reverse of removal. Align the tip of the rotor and the mark made on the distributor housing with the mark made on the engine during removal. If the crankshaft was turned while the distributor was removed, refer to "Ignition Retiming."

Ignition Timing

All 1974-76 engines have monolithic timing, set at the factory. The monolithic system uses a timing receptacle on the front of the engine which can be connected to digital read-out equipment, which electronically determines timing. Timing can also be adjusted in the conventional way.

1. Locate the timing mark and pointer. Mark the pointer and timing mark according to the timing specifications of your car.

2. Install a strobascopic type timing light and tachometer according to the manufacturer's specifications.
3. Disconnect the vacuum line(s) to the distributor and plug them. Loosen the distributor hold-down slightly.
4. Start the engine. If the engine idle speed is above 500 rpm (600 rpm—1974-75), it should be brought down to approximately 500 rpm (600 rpm—1974-75) before timing is attempted.
5. Check the timing mark and pointer alignment with the timing light. To advance the timing, turn the distributor clockwise.
6. Stop the engine, tighten the distributor hold-down, start the car, and check the timing. If necessary, reset the idle.

Ignition Retiming

If the timing relationship has been disturbed, retime the ignition as follows: bring No. 1 cylinder up to the firing position. This can be checked by removing the spark plug, placing your thumb in the spark plug hole and then cranking the engine until the compression is felt. Now, slowly bring the crankshaft around until the proper ignition timing mark on the crankshaft pulley lines up with the pointer. This is the approximate firing position for No. 1 cylinder.

Note the placement of the no. one spark plug wire on the distributor cap. Scribe a mark on the distributor body directly below the no. one spark plug wire. Remove the distributor cap, and install the distributor in the engine with the rotor in the No. 1 firing position. Align the mark made on the distributor housing with the tip of the rotor. Install the distributor hold-down bolt and tighten the pinch bolt until snug and the distributor housing can be turned with moderate pressure. Install the distributor cap and, working counterclockwise, check to make sure that the installation of the spark plug wires corresponds with the firing order of the engine. Check the timing with a timing light.

Contact Point Replacement and Adjustment

Through 1973

1. Unsnap the distributor cap retaining clips and position the cap clear of the breaker plate. Remove the rotor by pulling it straight up.
2. Remove the metal point shield, if so equipped.
3. Disconnect the primary lead and condenser wires from the contact point assembly. On dual-point distributors, remove the jumper strap also.
4. Remove the contact point and condenser retaining screws. Lift the contact point assembly and condenser from the distributor.
5. Lightly lubricate the distributor cam with heat-resistant lubricant.
6. Place the new contact point assembly and condenser in the distributor. Install, but do not tighten, the retaining screws.
7. On all V8 engines, except those equipped with a centrifugal advance distributor, place the ground wire under the contact point assembly screw farthest from the contacts.
8. Turn the engine until the rubbing block on the point assembly is resting on the high point of the distributor cam lobe. Insert a feeler gauge of specified thickness between the contact points and adjust the gap. Tighten the retaining screw and remove the feeler gauge.
9. Connect the primary and condenser wires to the contact point assembly in the same order in which they were removed. On distributors equipped with a metal point shield, the wire should be positioned 180 degrees (180°) from each other, then install the shield.
10. Install the rotor and distributor cap.
11. If a dwell meter is available, check to see that the distributor dwell is within specifications.

Solid State Ignition

Beginning 1974, Lincoln is utilizing a solid state or "breakerless" ignition system on 460 cubic inch V8s. This system eliminates the contact breaker points, replacing them with a permanent magnet low voltage generator.

When the ignition is on and the distributor is rotating, the low voltage generator in the distributor produces alternating current which is then sent to the electronic control module. The module senses the signal from the low voltage generator as the alternating current wave swings from positive to negative each time one of the gear teeth on the armature passes the magnetic field in the coil of the generator. When a gear tooth is directly opposite the magnetic field, the alternating current wave is at crossover (neither negative nor positive). The control module senses this and cuts off electricity (low voltage) to the coil, causing it to fire (high voltage). After the coil fires, the timing circuitry in the module redirects the low tension voltage to the coil.

Other than the low voltage generator and the control module, the rest of the system is conventional in appearance, with a standard distributor cap and rotor. Spark advance or retard is accomplished by moving the plate for the low voltage generator in the distributor.

A computer controlled timing (CCT) system is added to the electronic spark timing module, which is basically a mini-computer, monitors what gear the transmission is in, coolant temperature, manifold vacuum, and engine speed. With the information obtained from these sensors, the spark timing module, through an electronic logic circuit, determines whether to superimpose a 6° timing advance on the normal vacuum and centrifugal spark advance or a 4° time delayed retarded spark.

The distributor used with the CCT system has two separate magnetic

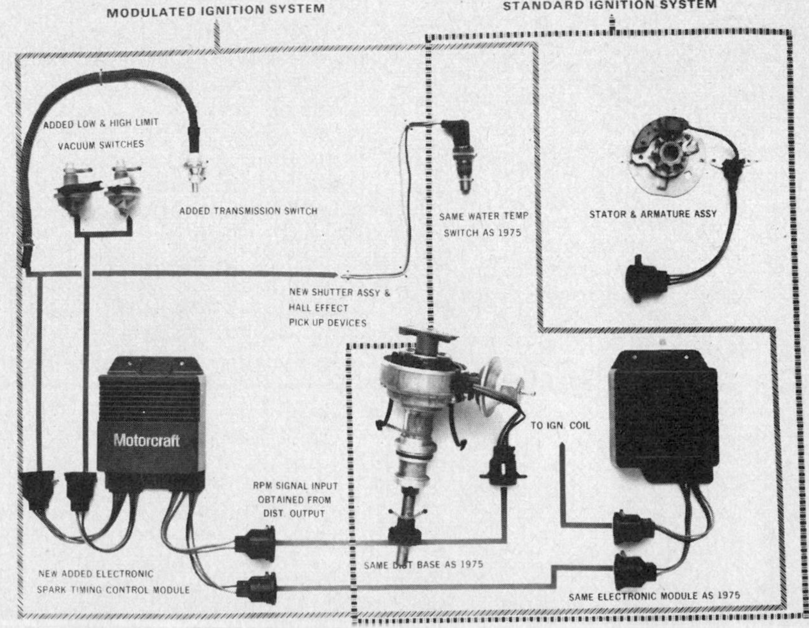

Diagram of the Computer Controlled Timing (CCT) ignition system on the 1976 Mark IV 460 V8
(© Ford Motor Co)

timing pickups; one for initial timing and the other, offset by 6 crankshaft degrees for advance timing. An instantaneous change in ignition timing can be made by the spark timing module by switching the primary ignition circuit to the second pickup.

The electronic spark timing control module is connected to the input of the various sensors and the output of the module is connected to a standard breakerless ignition module.

The time delayed 4° retard ignition is created by the spark timing module when operating from the initial advance magnetic pick-up in the distributor.

The centrifugal and vacuum advance systems operate independently of the CCT system and in the same manner as in a normal distributor.

The advance and retard conditions are instituted as follows:

a. At idle (below 800 rpm) the 6° advance is in effect when the engine is cold or overheated. Normal advance is used otherwise.
b. Between 800 and 2500 rpm, the 6° advance is used only when the transmission is in High gear and the manifold vacuum is above 7 to 12 in. Hg. Normal advance is used at all other times within this rpm range.
c. When the engine is running above 2500 rpm, the ignition timing is retarded 4° when the transmission is in High gear and the manifold vacuum is below 3 to 5 in. Hg. Otherwise, the normal ignition timing advance is used.

Tachometer Connection

The coil connector used with solid state ignition is provided with a cavity for connection of a tachometer, so that the connector doesn't have to be removed to check engine rpm.

Install a tach lead with a #60 alligator clip on its end into the cavity marked "TACH TEST" and connect the other lead to a good ground.

If the coil connector must be removed, pull it out horizontally until it is disengaged from the coil terminal.

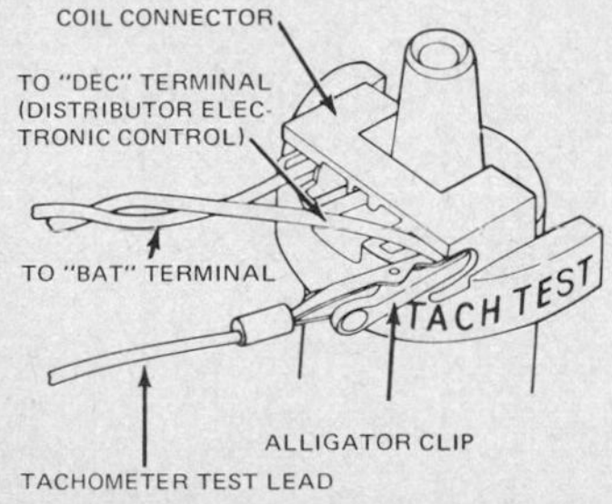

Connecting a tachometer to the coil—1975-76
(© Ford Motor Co)

FUEL SYSTEM

Fuel Pump Removal

The fuel pump is mounted on the left side of the cylinder front cover.

A separate in-line fuel filter is used. The filter cannot be serviced. Renew it in case of obstruction. This pump is spring loaded in opposition to camshaft eccentric lobe action, and is conventional.

The pump is Carter-built and cannot be serviced.

1. Disconnect the inlet and outlet lines at the fuel pump.
2. Remove the attaching bolts and lift the pump off its mount. Remove and discard the gasket.
3. Clean the mounting surfaces of the pad and pump.
4. Apply oil-resistant sealer to both sides of a new gasket. Place the new gasket on the pump flange and hold the pump against the pad. Be sure that the rocker arm is riding on the camshaft eccentric.
5. Install the bolts and connect the fuel lines.
6. Run the engine and check for leaks.

Fuel Filter R & R

1. Remove the air cleaner.
2. Loosen the hose clamp at the fuel inlet hose connection.
3. Unscrew the filter from the carburetor.
4. Disconnect the filter from the hose and discard the hose clamp.
5. Reverse the above procedure to install, using a new hose clamp. After installation, start the engine and check for fuel leakage.

Idle Speed Adjustment

1969-73

1. 1969-73 4300 Carburetor: *Adjust with air cleaner installed.* If it is not possible to adjust carburetor idle speed with the air cleaner installed, the engine idle speed must be rechecked after installing the air cleaner. On models with vacuum controlled heat ducts in the air cleaner, the vacuum line must be plugged if the carburetor is to be adjusted with the air cleaner removed.
2. Run engine at fast idle to equalize operating temperature.
3. Make sure the choke plate is fully released.
4. Turn headlights on high beam.
5. Tape hot idle compensator so that it is fully seated in the closed position.
6. On vehicles equipped with air conditioning, all models EXCEPT 1969, set the idle speed with the air conditioner turned OFF. 1969 models, set the idle speed with the air conditioner turned ON.
7. Remove and plug the vacuum line to the parking brake release, then, set the parking brake and put the transmission in the Drive position.
8. Attach a tachometer of known accuracy to the engine.
9. Adjust the idle speed screw or solenoid to obtain specified rpm. On Carter carburetors, turn the idle speed adjusting screw in to decrease speed and out to increase engine speed. On Autolite carburetors, turn the idle adjusting screw in to increase speed and out to decrease speed. On 1968-71 carburetors with an electric solenoid, turn the solenoid plunger to the right to increase idle speed and to the left to decrease it. On 1972-73 carburetors with an electric solenoid, turn the adjusting screw in the solenoid mounting bracket to adjust the idle speed.

NOTE: There are two engine idle speeds listed for cars with solenoid equipped carburetors. The first or higher speed is adjusted as explained above, the second is adjusted with the solenoid electrical lead disconnected, and the transmission in Park or Neutral, by turning the adjustment screw on the side of the carburetor.

With the solenoid disconnected, the idle adjusting screw must contact the throttle shaft or the throttle plates may become jammed in the throttle bores of the carburetor when the engine is shut off.

Autolite carburetor idle speed adjustment
(© Ford Motor Co)

1974

These cars use either the Motorcraft model 4300 4-bbl carburetor or the Carter Thermo-Quad®, which is used only on 1974 California cars.

1. Remove the air cleaner and plug the vacuum line.
2. Set the parking brake.
3. Check the throttle and choke linkage for freedom of movement.
4. Connect a tachometer.
5. Stabilize the engine temperature.
6. Set the ignition timing.
7. Be sure that the choke is fully open.
8. Place automatic transmission in Drive.

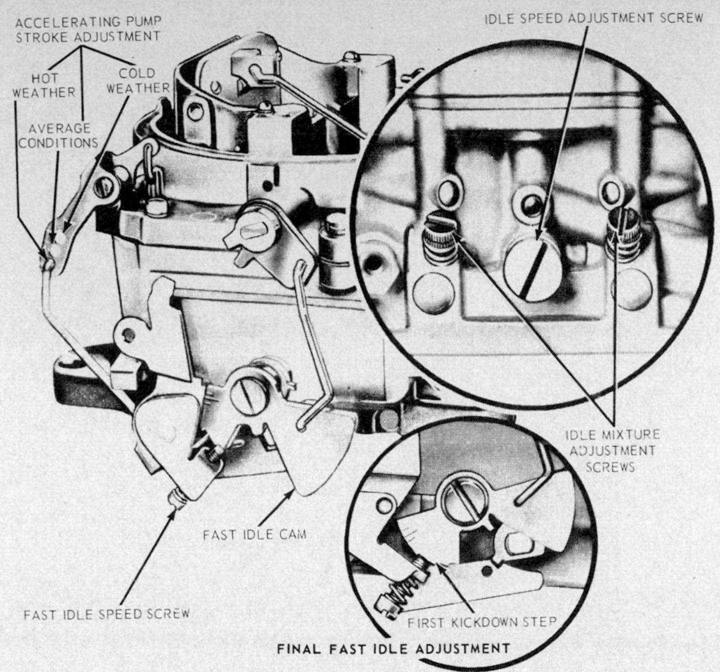

Carter carburetor adjustments
(© Ford Motor Co)

9. Turn the solenoid adjusting screw in or out to obtain the higher rpm specified.
10. Disconnect the electrical lead from the throttle solenoid positioner and place the automatic transmission in Neutral.
11. Adjust the "solenoid off" idle speed screw, located on the carburetor body, to obtain the lower specified idle speed.
12. Connect the solenoid wire and allow the plunger to extend.
13. Stop the engine, connect the vacuum line and install the air cleaner.
14. Recheck the idle speed.
15. If it is not as specified, readjust the idle to obtain the smoothest idle within the range of the limiter caps.

1975

1. Allow the engine to reach normal operating temperature. Check the timing and adjust it, as necessary.
2. Disconnect and plug the distributor vacuum hoses. Remove the top and center hoses from the CSSA coolant temperature operated vacuum valve (in the heater elbow) and connect the two hoses together.
3. Disconnect the EGR vacuum hoses from the carburetor and plug the EGR port. Remove the air cleaner and plug its vacuum hoses. Connect a tachometer.
4. Put the fast idle screw on the kickdown step of the fast idle cam. Adjust the fast idle speed to 1350 rpm. Open the throttle and then return the screw to the kickdown step of the cam.
5. Allow the fast idle speed to stabilize. If the fast idle speed is not correct, repeat step 4 until it is.
6. Install the air cleaner and its vacuum hoses. Connect the hoses to the CSSA vacuum valve and the carburetor EGR port.
7. Disconnect the antidieseling solenoid wiring. Set the low idle speed to specification with the low speed adjusting screw (transmission in Neutral).
8. Connect the antidieseling solenoid wiring. Set the curb idle speed to specification by rotating the solenoid body (transmission in Drive).
9. Shift into Neutral and increase the engine speed to 2000 rpm for 15 seconds.
10. Return the engine speed to idle Shift into Drive. Recheck the idle speed. Adjust it, if necessary, by repeating steps 7 and 8.
11. Remove the tachometer. Unplug and connect the distributor vacuum hoses.

Fuel Mixture Adjustment

1. On engines with Carter carburetors, turn the mixture screws clockwise until engine idle becomes rough, then, back out adjustment screws until engine reaches highest rpm.
2. On Autolite/Motorcraft carburetors with idle mixture limiter caps, follow the same procedure, but, final adjustment must be made with the caps installed.
3. If adjusting the idle mixture has altered engine idle speed, reset idle speed to specification.

NOTE: *This procedure does not apply to 1975 engines which require the use of propane gas to enrichen the mixture for adjustment.*

COOLING SYSTEM

A radiator, with large tanks provided on both sides of the core, is used.

On this new type of radiator, a cold fill reference mark is stamped into the metal about 2 in. below the filler cap. This radiator must be checked for fluid level when the engine is cold and not running.

Radiator Removal

1. Drain the cooling system.
2. Disconnect the upper and lower radiator hoses from the radiator.
3. Disconnect the transmission cooler lines from the radiator.
4. If the air conditioner condenser attaches to the radiator, remove the retaining bolts and position the condenser out of the way. *Do not disconnect the refrigerant lines.*
5. If equipped with a fan shroud, disconnect it from the radiator and position it rearward over the fan.
6. Remove the radiator mounting

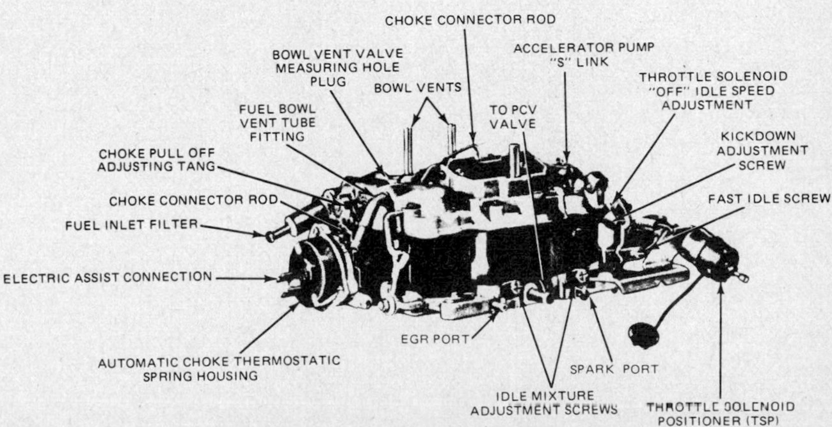

Carter Thermo-Quad® carburetor adjustment points (© Ford Motor Co)

bolts and remove the radiator from the car.

7. Reverse above procedure to install.

Water Pump Removal

1. Drain cooling system. Remove the fan shroud bolts.
2. Remove bolts retaining fan assembly to water pump.
3. Remove radiator shroud and fan.
4. On air conditioned cars, loosen compressor drive belt.
5. Loosen mounting bolts and remove alternator, power steering and air pump drive belts.
6. Remove water pump pulley.
7. Disconnect radiator lower hose, heater hose, and bypass hose at water pump.
8. Remove water pump bolts and remove water pump.
9. Install in reverse order of removal.

Thermostat R & R

1. Drain the radiator so that the coolant level is below the thermostat.
2. Remove the coolant outlet housing retaining bolts, pull the elbow away from the manifold, and remove the thermostat and its gasket.
3. Clean the coolant outlet housing and manifold gasket surfaces. Coat a new gasket with water-resistant sealer, and position the gasket on the manifold.
4. Install the thermostat into the outlet with the bridge section facing the outlet.
5. Position the coolant outlet elbow against the intake manifold. Install the retaining bolts, and torque them to specifications.
6. Fill the radiator to the cold fill level, install the cap, start the engine, and check the system for leaks.

EMISSION CONTROLS

Regardless of what other emission controls have been featured from year to year on Lincoln cars, all models feature positive crankcase ventilation (PCV) for purposes of burning the crankcase fumes, which on earlier cars had been dispelled through the road draft tube.

1969

All Lincoln cars to the present feature a distributor vacuum control valve, which is also known as a temperature sensing valve or a coolant temperature operated vacuum valve (PVS). This valve is installed in the coolant outlet elbow and features three ports which are connected by hoses to a carburetor, the intake manifold, and the distributor vacuum advance diaphragm. This valve operates during periods of higher-than-normal operating temperatures (usually associated with prolonged idle periods) to supply added vacuum from the intake manifold to the distributor, thus advancing the timing, increasing idle speed, and enhancing the operation of the cooling system.

During the 1969 model year, the Thermactor System was not used on Lincolns.

Most 1969 and later carburetors are equipped with an electrically controlled throttle solenoid, which raises engine idle speeds and reduces terminal exhaust pollutants.

1970-71

Lincoln cars used the Thermactor System in 1970, this time in combination with the other, improvements which are grouped together into what is called the IMCO (IMproved COmbustion) system. The only change in the Thermactor system for 1970 is that its air manifolds are cast as an integral part of the engine's exhaust manifolds. The Thermactor System continued to be used on all 1971 models and on those 1972 cars designed for California.

Beginning in 1970, some Lincoln cars were equipped with an Evaporative Emisson Control System, a further extension of the IMCO system. This component channels the breathing of the fuel tank and the venting of the carburetor float bowl through a canister filled with activated charcoal, with the result that pollution due to evaporating of fuel is eliminated. The Evaporative Emission Control System became standard on all models in 1971.

1972

1972 California cars are equipped with an addition to the IMCO System, an Electronic Spark Control (ESC) system. This system is composed of an electronic control amplifier, a three-way distributor modulator valve, a speed sensor (found between two sections of the speedometer cable), and a thermal switch (located in the right door pillar of the Lincoln Continental and in the left door pillar of the Continental Mark IV).

The three-way distributor modulator valve is found within the vacuum line connecting the previously discussed ported vacuum switch and the carburetor. It is vented to the atmosphere. The thermal switch is designed to react to a critical temperature range of 50–58° F (outside air temperature). The speed sensor reacts to speeds in excess of 40 mph. The thermal switch dominates over the speed sensor. The impulses from both are fed into the electronic control amplifier.

When the ambient temperature is below 49°F, the ESC system does not operate. When the outside temperature rises above 65°F, the contacts in the temperature switch close. This causes the temperature switch to pass current from the ignition switch to the amplifier. The amplifier then signals the distributor modulator to close and prevent vacuum from reaching the distributor. When the vehicle reaches a speed of 40 mph, the signal from the speed sensor causes the modulator to open and restore normal vacuum advance to the engine. If the engine should overheat at idle, the ported vacuum switch overrides the ESC system and connects intake manifold vacuum to the distributor.

1973

The 1973 emission control system consists of a new Exhaust Gas Recirculation (EGR) system, and a Delaytd Vacuum Bypass (DVB) spark advance control system.

The DVB system provides two paths by which distributor vacuum can reach the distributor vacuum advance. The system consists of a spark delay valve, a check valve, a solenoid vacuum valve, and an ambient temperature switch. When the ambient temperature is below 49°F, the temperature switch contacts are open and the vacuum solenoid is open (de-energized). Under these conditions, vacuum will flow from the carburetor, through the open solenoid, and to the distributor. Since the spark delay valve resists the flow of carburetor vacuum, the vacuum will always flow through the vacuum solenoid when it is open, since this is the path of least resistance. When the ambient temperature rises above 60°F, the contacts in the temperature switch (which is located in the door post) close. This passes ignition switch current to the solenoid, energizing the solenoid. This blocks one of the two vacuum paths. All distributor vacuum must now flow through the spark delay valve. When carburetor vacuum rises above a certain level on acceleration, a rubber valve in the spark delay valve blocks vacuum from passing through the valve for from 5 to 30 seconds. After this time delay has elapsed, normal vacuum is supplied to the distributor. When the vacuum solenoid is closed (temperature above 60°), the vacuum line from the solenoid to the distributor is vented to atmosphere. To prevent the vacuum that is passing through the spark delay valve from escaping through the solenoid into the atmosphere, a one-way check valve is installed in the vacuum line from the solenoid to the distributor.

The EGR system consists of a control valve, a temperature-controlled vacuum switch, and a special carburetor mounting spacer. A hole that is drilled in the carburetor flange on the intake manifold passes exhaust gases from the manifold crossover passage into the carburetor spacer. A plunger which is attached to the EGR valve normally prevents the exhaust gases from entering the engine. When the engine coolant temperature reaches 125°F, the EGR vacuum valve opens and connects carburetor vacuum to the EGR valve. Under high carburetor vacuum conditions, the EGR valve opens and recirculates exhaust gases into the engine. This lowers peak combustion temperature and reduces oxides of nitrogen.

The spark delay is connected into the distributor vacuum line and closes on hard acceleration to prevent carburetor vacuum from reaching the distributor. After a predetermined number of seconds, the spark delay valve opens and carburetor vacuum is again connected to the distributor.

To meet the standards of the revised California emission controls, all California engines for 1974 will be equipped with the Ford Thermactor system, Exhaust Gas Recirculation (EGR) and the Ford Improved Combustion (IMCO) system.

The Thermactor system keeps hydrocarbon and carbon monoxide emissions at the required level, while the EGR and IMCO systems are designed to reduce oxides of nitrogen.

See the "Unit Repair Section" for troubleshooting procedures for all emission control equipment.

NOTE: *On models made after 15 March 1973, the ambient temperature controls were removed from the DVB and EGR systems.*

1974

The EGR-CSC system regulates distributor spark advance and EGR valve operation, according to coolant temperature, by sequentially switching vacuum sources. The major components are:

a. 95°F EGR-PVS valve,
b. spark delay valve (SDV), and
c. a vacuum check valve.

When coolant temperature is below 85°F, the EGR-PVS valve admits carburetor EGR port vacuum (at about 2500 rpm) directly to the distributor advance diaphragm through a one-way check valve. At the same time, EGR-PVS valve shuts off carburetor EGR vacuum to the EGR valve and transmission diaphragm.

When coolant temperature is above 95°F, the EGR-PVS valve is actuated and admits carburetor EGR vacuum to the EGR valve and transmission instead of the distributor. At temperatures between 82° and 95°F, the EGR-PVS valve may be open, closed, or in midposition.

The CTAV system (Cold Temperature Actuated Vacuum) consists of an ambient temperature switch, a 3-way vacuum switch, an inline vacuum bleed and a relay. The system is used to more accurately match spark advance to engine requirements in cold ambient temperature conditions.

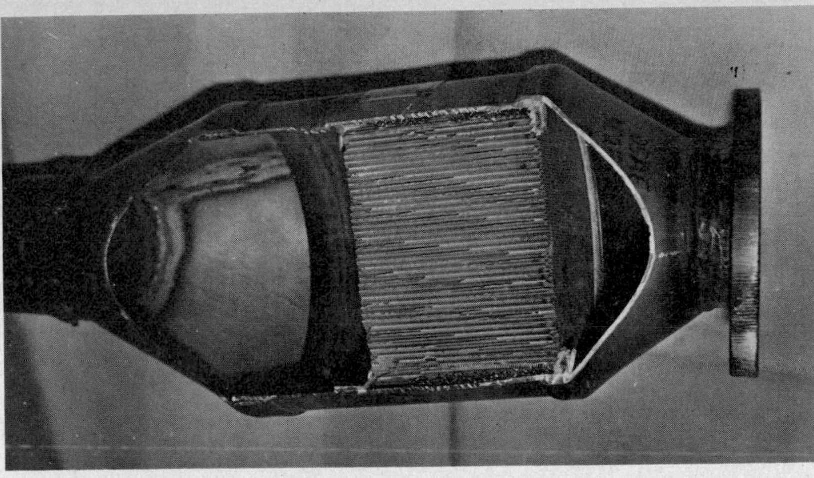

Cutaway view of the catalytic converter used on 1975-76 Lincoln and Mark IV (© Ford Motor Co)

When ambient air temperatures are below 49°F, spark port vacuum is selected for distributor modulation. When ambient temperatures reach 65°F, the system selects EGR vacuum. In between, the system selects either port, depending on the cycle it is in.

1975

Lincoln uses catalytic converters on all models for 1975. To supply air to the converter, the air injection (Thermactor) system has been modified considerably for the first time since its introduction. For information concerning both air injection changes and catalytic converters, see "Emission Control Systems" in the unit repair section.

A cold start spark advance (CSSA) system has been added to improve cold engine operation. When the coolant temperature is below 125° F. manifold vacuum is routed to the distributor vacuum unit. Above 125° F, carburetor ported vacuum is routed to the distributor through a spark delay valve and coolant temperature operated vacuum valve (PVS).

Another aid to cold engine operation is a "cold weather modulator," which is added to the heated air intake system. When the ambient temperature is below 55° F and the engine is cold, the cold weather modulator prevents the door in the air cleaner snorkle from opening to the fresh air position under hard acceleration. Above 55° F, the door works the same as in other years; i.e., opening under hard acceleration or when the engine has reached normal operating temperatures.

All 1975 engines have spacer entry EGR valves. The EGR valve is mounted on a spacer which is located beneath the carburetor. This replaces the "floor entry" system used on some 1974 engines.

Positive crankcase ventilation (PCV) and evaporative emission control systems are carryovers from previous years.

For system checks and adjustments, see "Emission Control Systems" in the Unit Repair Section.

1976

The complexity of the emission control equipment has been reduced on 1976 vehicles. The average number emission control components has been reduced from 25 to 11 on most cars. This has been accomplished through the more extensive usage of catalytic converters. There is a new exhaust gas recirculation system control system for 1976. The new proportional EGR system vacuum signal is controlled by exhaust backpressure instead of intake manifold vacuum. This relates EGR flow more accurately to engine load.

ENGINE

Engine Removal

Engine R & R is for the engine only, without the transmission attached.

1. Raise the hood, and cover or mask all parts of the car that could be scratched during R & R procedures.
2. Set the parking brake and raise the car. Put stands beneath the underbody front crossmember.
3. Drain the engine cooling system and the engine oil pan.
4. Scribe the hinge outline on the underside of the hood. Remove hood.
5. If the engine is equipped with an exhaust emission control system, remove the crankcase vent filter from the air cleaner. Re-

move carburetor air cleaner and air inlet duct assembly. Disconnect the battery ground.
6. Remove both engine radiator hoses.
7. Disconnect heater hoses at intake manifold and water pump. Disconnect power brake and power booster line from the intake manifold connection and position it to one side.
8. Disconnect heater vacuum hose from the intake manifold.
9. Disconnect automatic transmission vacuum line at the intake manifold. Disconnect all vacuum lines at the rear of the manifold.
10. Remove transmission tube slotted bracket from the right rear exhaust manifold mounting stud.
11. Disconnect battery ground strap at cylinder block.
12. Disconnect primary wires at the coil. Disconnect wires from temperature-sending unit and the fast idle solenoid (air-conditioned cars).
13. Disconnect wire from oil pressure-sending unit. Detach wiring loom from valve rocker arm cover and position it out of the way.
14. Disconnect transmission fluid lines at the radiator. Remove transmision fluid filter from underbody side member (if car is so equipped).
15. Remove fuel hose mounting bracket from radiator. Remove heat shield from fuel pump.
16. On air-conditioned cars, remove fan drive clutch to water pump pulley retaining bolts. Remove fan drive clutch, fan and compressor pulley from the car as a unit.
17. Remove fan blade and spacer assembly from water pump pulley.
18. On vehicles equipped with air conditioning, disconnect the compressor electrical lead and remove the compressor mounting bracket attaching bolts. Remove the compressor from the engine and position it out of the way without disconnecting the refrigerant lines.

Caution If the compressor refrigerant lines do not have enough slack to position the compressor out of the way without disconnecting the refrigerant lines, the air conditioning system will have to be evacuated by a trained air conditioning serviceman. Under no circumstances should an untrained person attempt to disconnect the air conditioning refrigerant lines.

19. Remove the alternator mounting bolts and position the alternator out of the way without disconnecting the wires.
20. Disconnect the transmission and accelerator linkage at the bellcrank. Secure the linkage to the dash panel for engine clearance purposes. Disconnect speed control cable.
21. Remove access cover from the converter housing. Remove underbody splash shield at lower front of transmission.
22. Remove resonator inlet pipes from the exhaust manifolds.
23. Remove the power steering pump mounting bracket from the engine and position the pump and bracket out of the way.
24. Remove the nuts and washers that hold the engine front support insulators to the underbody side members.
25. Remove the starter attaching bolts. Remove the starter.
26. Detach the oil cooler inlet and outlet transfer line retaining clip from the cylinder block. Remove the block-to-converter housing supports. Remove the converter access plate.
27. Remove the flywheel to converter retaining nuts.
28. Remove lower converter housing to cylinder block retaining bolts.
29. Install a transmission support under the transmission.
30. Remove the upper converter housing to cylinder block retaining bolts.
31. Attach engine lifting eyes to the manifolds.
32. Install lifting sling and attach to chain hoist. With plenty of help, carefully raise and remove engine from car.
33. Install by reversing removal procedure.

Intake and Exhaust Manifold(s)

Intake Manifold R & R

1. Drain the cooling system.
2. Disconnect the upper radiator hose from the thermostat housing and the bypass hose from the intake manifold.
3. Remove the air cleaner and ducts from the engine.
4. Disconnect the spark plug wires from the spark plugs and remove the distributor cap and wires from the engine as an assembly. Mark the position of the distributor rotor in relation to the intake manifold, remove the primary wire from the coil and the distributor hold-down bolt, then, remove the distributor from the engine (1969-74).
5. Remove all vacuum lines from the intake manifold and the wire from the temperature sending unit. Remove the PCV valve and hoses.
6. Disconnect all fuel and vacuum lines from the carburetor.
7. Remove all carburetor and kickdown linkage that attaches to the intake manifold. Remove the air injection supply tubes and check valve at the rear of the cylinder heads. Remove the coil and bracket.

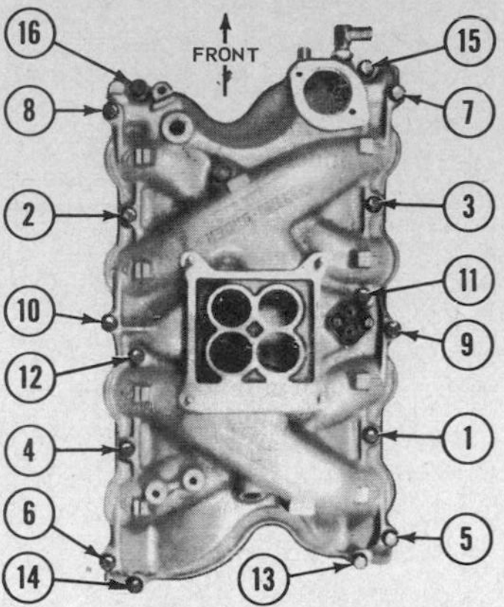

Intake manifold torque sequence
(© Ford Motor Co)

8. Remove the manifold attaching bolts and remove the manifold. If it is necessary to pry the manifold to loosen it from the engine, use care not to damage any gasket sealing surfaces.
9. Clean all gasket surfaces and cement new gaskets firmly in place. The gaskets should be firmly locked in place before attempting to install the manifold.
10. Reverse above procedure to install.

Exhaust Manifold Removal

1. Remove air cleaner and warm air duct assembly to remove right exhaust manifold.
2. Disconnect manifolds at exhaust pipe (or catalyst—1975).
3. Remove retaining bolts and washers, and remove manifolds and lifting brackets.

Valve System

Valve Guides

Lincolns use integral valve guides. Lincoln dealers offer valves with oversize stems for worn guides. To fit these, enlarge valve guide bores with valve guide reamers to an oversize that cleans up wear. If a large oversize is required, it is best to approach that size through stages by using a series of reamers of increasing diameters. This helps to maintain the concentricity of the guide bore with the valve seat. The correct valve guide to stem clearance is in front of this section. As an alternative, some local automotive machine shops will fit replacement guides that use standard stem valves.

1969-71 Rocker Assembly

Removal

1. Remove crankcase ventilation

Chilton's TIME SAVER

The following is a method for replacing valve springs, oil seals or spring retainers without removing the cylinder head.

1. **Purchase an air chuck with a spark plug hole adaptor.**
2. **Remove the valve rocker cover. Remove the rocker arm from the valve to be worked on.**
3. **Remove the spark plug from the cylinder to be worked on.**
4. **Turn the crankshaft to bring the piston of this cylinder down, away from possible contact with the valve head. Sharply tap the valve retainer to loosen the valve lock.**
5. **Then turn the crankshaft to bring the piston in this cylinder to the Exact Top of its Compression Stroke.**
6. **Screw the air chuck fitting. into the spark plug hole.**
7. **Hook up an air hose to the chuck and turn on the pressure (about 200 psi).**
8. **With a strong and constant supply of air holding the valve closed, compress the valve spring and remove the lock and retainer.**
9. **Make the necessary replacements and reassemble.**

NOTE: it is important that the operation be performed exactly as stated, in this order. The piston in the cylinder must be on exact top-center to prevent air pressure from turning the crankshaft.

regulator valve and hose from valve rocker arm cover. Remove air cleaner and duct assembly. If removing an arm assembly from the left side, take off oil filler cap and air supply hose from valve rocker cover.

2. Disconnect plug wires at spark plugs. Twist, then pull, on molded cap of wire only. Do not pull the wire. Remove wires from bracket on the valve rocker arm covers and pull wires out of the way.
3. Remove rocker arm covers.
4. Remove rocker arm stud nut, fulcrum seat, and rocker arm.

NOTE: rocker arm studs that are broken, or have bad threads, should be replaced.

If the stud is broken, flush with the head, drill and use an easy-out.

When installing the new stud, lubricate the threads, then torque to 65-75 ft. lbs.

Installation

1. Apply lubriplate to top of valve stem.
2. Lubriplate fulcrum seat and socket. Install rocker arm, fulcrum seat and stud nut. Perform preliminary valve adjustment.
3. Adjust valve clearance according to recommendations.
4. Clean rocker arm covers and cylinder head gasket surfaces.
5. Apply oil-resistant sealer to one side of new cover gaskets. Apply cemented side of gaskets in rim of covers.
6. Position covers on cylinder heads. Install and torque cover bolts to 2½-4 ft. lbs. Two minutes later, retorque attaching bolts to same specifications.
7. Route spark plug wires in brackets on valve rocker covers. Reconnect plug wires.
8. Install heater tube assembly, if disconnected, and fill cooling system.
9. On the right valve rocker arm cover, install crankcase ventilation regulator valve and hose.
10. Install air cleaner and duct, and adjust assembly, if removed. On the left rocker arm cover, install oil filler cap and air supply hose.

1972 and later Rocker Assembly

Refer to the 460 engine procedure in the Ford section.

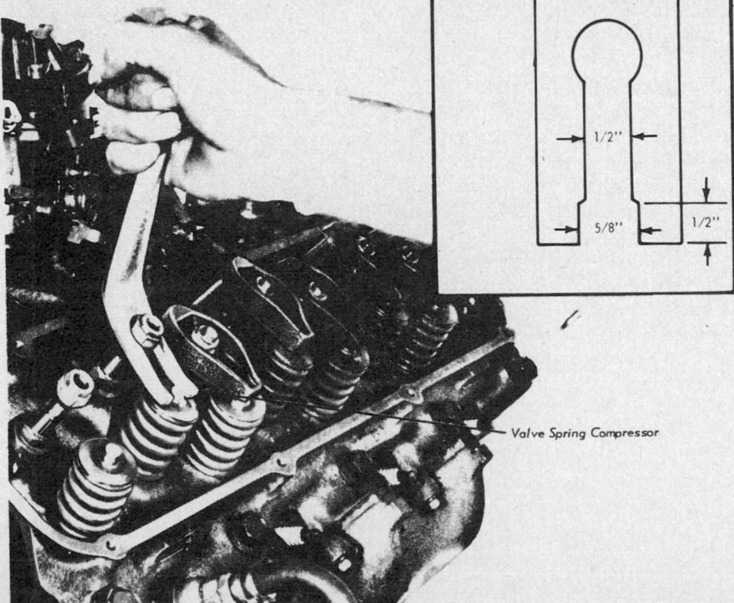

Compressing Valve Spring 1969-71 460 eng.
(© Ford Motor Co.)

Cylinder Head

Removal and Installation

1. Remove the intake manifold/carburetor assembly. See "Intake Manifold" section.
2. Disconnect the exhaust pipe or catalytic converter pipe from the exhaust manifold.
3. Loosen the A/C compressor drivebelt if necessary.
4. Loosen the alternator bolts and remove the alternator/air pump bracket from the cylinder head.
5. Set the A/C compressor out of the way without disconnecting its lines. See "Intake Manifold" for the specific procedure. Remove the compressor support bracket-to water pump muts. Remove the upper compressor bracket from the cylinder head.
6. If not equipped with A/C, remove the power steering pump bracket from the head. Position the pump and bracket out of the way without disconnecting the power steering lines.
7. Remove the valve covers and rocker assemblies, as detailed above. Remove the rockers in sequence and number them to aid in correct installation.
8. Remove the head bolts. Lift the heads and exhaust manifolds off as assemblies with a hoist.

   NOTE: *If necessary, pry the forward corners of the heads at the bosses provided on the block, in order to loosen the head gasket. Be careful not to damage the machined surfaces. Discard the gaskets.*
9. If the head is to be machined or disassembled, separate the exhaust manifolds from it.

Installation is as follows:

1. Clean the head, intake manifold,

rocker cover, and block gasket surfaces.

2. If the exhaust manifolds were separated from the head, apply graphite grease around the port areas on the manifolds and head. Install the manifold and gasket.

Cylinder head torque sequence
(© Ford Motor Co)

3. Place long cylinder head bolts in the two rear lower bolt holes of the left head. Place a long bolt in the rear lower hole on the right head. Secure the bolts with rubber bands to aid in installation.
4. Fit new head gaskets over the dowels on the block. DO NOT use sealer on the head gasket surfaces.
5. Lower the head on the block. Align the exhaust manifold studs with the exhaust or converter pipe.
6. Install the remaining cylinder head bolts. The long bolts to in the lower row of holes.
7. Tighten the bolts in proper sequence in three stages, to the figures given in the "Torque Specifications" chart.
8. Install the push rod and valve rocker assemblies in their original positions.

NOTE: *If any of the valve train components were disturbed, perform the "Preliminary Valve Adjustment" procedure in the Ford section.*

For engines through 1971, use the 1969-71 429 procedure. For 1972 and later engines, use the 460 procedure.

9. The remainder of the cylinder head installation procedure is the reverse of removal.

Timing Case Cover, Chain and Sprockets

Removal

1. Drain cooling system and crankcase.
2. Remove oil pan and oil pump.
3. Remove fan blades from water pump shaft.
4. Remove radiator (fan) shroud.
5. Disconnect all radiator hoses at engine. Disconnect oil cooler lines.
6. Remove radiator.
7. Loosen alternator and air pump. Loosen air conditioner idler pulley. Remove drive belts with water pump pulley.
8. Remove and set aside air conditioner compressor (do not open compressor lines to expose the sealed air-conditioner system to atmosphere).
9. Remove crankshaft pulley attaching bolt and washer. Remove damper and remove Woodruff key from crankshaft.
10. If necessary, disconnect power steering pressure line at pump. Drain fluid.
11. Remove steering pump.
12. Loosen by-pass hose at water pump. Disconnect heater hose at pump.
13. Disconnect and plug fuel inlet line at fuel pump. Disconnect fuel line at carburetor fuel pump. Remove fuel pump.
14. Remove front cover-to-block attaching bolts. Remove front cover and water pump as an assembly. Discard gasket.
15. If a new front cover is to be installed, change the water pump at this time.
16. Check timing chain deflection, at this time, by rotating crankshaft in a clockwise direction enough to take up the slack on the right hand side of the chain (as facing the open chain). Establish a reference mark on the block and measure from this point to the left side of the chain. This measurement when deflected should not exceed ½ in. If deflection is more than ½ in., replace chain and both sprockets.
17. If chain and sprockets are being removed, crank the engine until timing marks on the sprockets are at their closest related points and on a center line with both crankshaft and camshaft centers.
18. Remove camshaft sprocket capscrew, washer, and fuel pump eccentric. Slide off timing chain, sprockets and chain as an assembly.

Installation

1. Install chain and sprockets as an assembly with sprocket timing marks directly toward each other and on a centerline with the crankshaft and camshaft.
2. Install fuel pump eccentric, washer, and attaching cap screw. Torque camshaft sprocket attaching screw to 40-45 ft. lbs. Lubricate chain and sprockets with engine oil.
3. After cleaning mating surfaces, coat the areas with oil-resistant sealer and position gasket on cylinder block.
4. Position cover over crankshaft and slide cover on against cylinder block. Coat cover retaining screws with oil-resistant sealer and install screws. Torque attaching screws to 10-13 ft. lbs.
5. Apply Lubriplate® to oil seal rubbing surface of steering pump inner hub. Apply mixture of white lead and oil to crankshaft stub in preparing damper installation. Install power steering pump (if removed).

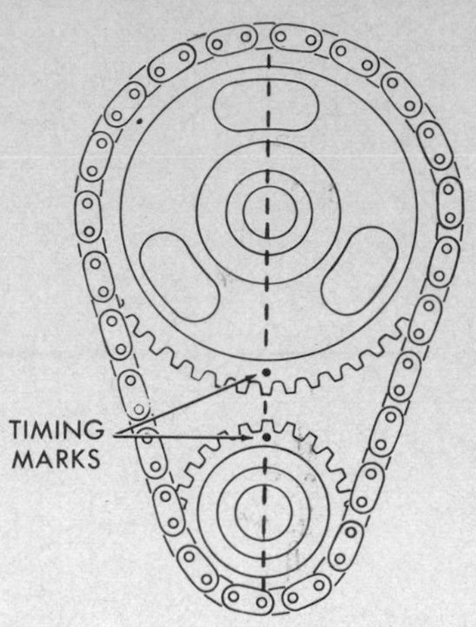

Valve timing alignment marks

6. Install crankshaft damper Woodruff key and press on crankshaft damper. Do not hammer damper into place. Install damper retainer screw and washer. Torque to 75-90 ft. lbs.
7. Coat new fuel pump gasket with oil-resistant sealer and place on fuel pump. Install fuel pump. Connect fuel lines to fuel pump.
8. Install oil pump and oil pan.
9. Install air-conditioner compressor and water pump.
10. Install water pump pulley and all drive belts.
11. Position radiator to lower support, position upper support to radiator retaining bolts. Connect air coolant hoses. Connect oil cooler lines.
12. Place fan assembly inside radiator shroud and set in position on water pump hub. Install shroud to radiator screws and tighten. Insert and tighten fan attaching screws.
13. Adjust belt tension. Tighten alternator and air pump retaining bolts and compressor idler pulley.
14. Fill and bleed cooling system Fill crankcase.
15. Run engine at fast idle and check for coolant and oil leaks. Set ignition timing.

Oil Seal R & R

The front cover oil seal should be replaced whenever the cover is removed.

1. Drive the old oil seal out with a punch.
2. Clean out the oil seal recess.
3. Coat a new oil seal with grease.
4. Install the new seal in the cover. Be sure that the seal spring is in the correct position.

Camshaft R & R

1. Remove the hood assembly. If the hood is properly aligned, index the hinges to the hood prior to removing the hood, in

order to simplify installation.

2. Remove the intake manifold, referring to the procedure under "Intake Manifold R&R."

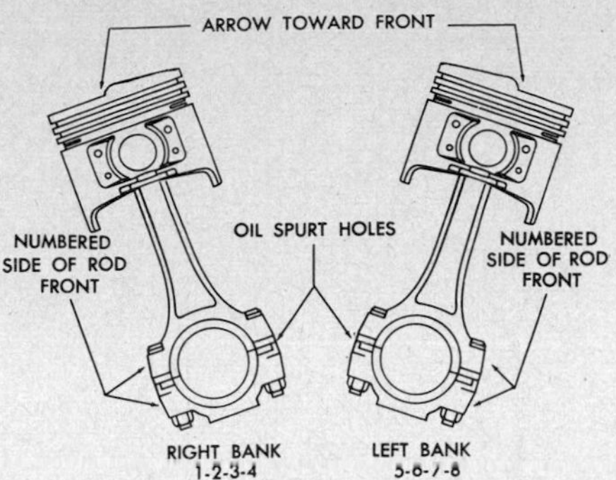

Correct piston and rod positions for 460 engines

3. Remove the distributor and the valve covers.
4. Remove the valve rocker arm shaft assemblies, push rods, and hydraulic lifters from the engine. Back off the rocker arm bolts, turn the rocker arms sideways, and remove the push rods and lifters.
5. Remove the timing chain and camshaft sprocket.
6. Remove the radiator. Remove the grille.
7. If the car is equipped with an air conditioner, cover the left front fender, lift the condenser out of the engine compartment with the lines still attached, and rest it on the covered fender.
8. Remove the camshaft from the front of the cylinder block, taking care not to damage any of the camshaft bearing surfaces.
9. Lubricate the camshaft journals and lobes with engine oil. Install the camshaft in the engine, using care to prevent damage to the camshaft bearings. Care should also be exercised to see that the rear camshaft bearing plug does not become dislodged in the process of installing the camshaft.
10. Reverse the above procedure to complete installation.

Engine Lubrication

Oil Pan Removal

1969

1. Disconnect radiator shroud.
2. Raise car on a hoist and drain crankcase.
3. Disconnect idler arm from underbody.
4. Loosen starter mounting bolts.
5. Remove cylinder block to converter housing bolts.
6. Disconnect engine front support insulators from underbody crossmember. Place floor jack under front of oil pan (block of wood between jack and oil pan). Raise engine just enough to insert 1 in. wood blocks between insulators and underbody side members. Remove floor jack.
7. Remove end attachments of front stabilizer bar and rotate ends of bar down to raise center of bar. Remove oil filter.
8. Remove oil pan mounting bolts and lower oil pan to underbody crossmember. Remove splash shield from right side of oil pan.
9. Disconnect pressure line at power steering pump. Remove bolts holding the pump to cylinder front cover and rotate pump to clear the oil pan. Remove the oil pan.
10. Install oil pan in reverse order of removal and torque attaching bolts to 6-9 ft. lbs. Torque oil pump-to-cylinder block bolts to 20-25 ft. lbs.

1970-76

1. Disconnect the negative battery cable.
2. Disconnect the fan shroud from the radiator and position it rearward over the fan.
3. Drain the crankcase and remove the oil filter.
4. On Mark III and Mark IV models, disconnect the oil cooler lines from the radiator. Remove the bolt that attaches the oil cooler line bracket to the cylinder block.
5. Remove the end attachments of the front stabilizer bar and rotate the ends downward.
6. Remove the starter attaching bolts.
7. Remove the motor mount to chassis attaching bolts and raise the engine several inches.
8. Place blocks of wood between the motor mounts and the chassis.
9. Remove the converter housing to engine block support bracket bolts and remove the brackets.
10. Remove the oil pan attaching bolts and remove the pan from the engine. On Mark III and IV models, it will be necessary to move the oil cooler lines out of position to remove the pan.
11. Clean all gasket mounting surfaces and reverse above procedure to install.

Oil Pump R & R

1. Remove the oil pan, referring to the procedure for "Oil Pan R&R."
2. Remove the oil pump mounting bolts and remove the pump from the cylinder block.
3. Prime the oil pump by filling either the inlet or outlet port with clean engine oil. Rotate the pump shaft so that the oil is evenly distributed within the pump body.
4. Install the distributor intermediate shaft within the oil pump rotor shaft. Apply oil-resistant sealer to the new oil pump mounting gasket and install the gasket on the oil pump.
5. Insert the intermediate shaft into the distributor shaft hex bore. Make sure that the intermediate shaft is properly seated. Do not attempt to force the pump into position if it does not seat readily, as the intermediate shaft hex may be misaligned with the distributor shaft. To align, rotate the intermediate shaft until it can be seated. Secure the oil pump to the cylinder block and torque the screws to 20–25 ft lbs. As you secure the oil pump, make certain that the gasket is properly installed; leakage resulting from improper gasket installation could cause loss of oil pressure and subsequent engine damage.
6. Install the oil pan and its related parts.

Rear Main Bearing Oil Seal R & R

1969

The rear main oil seal originally installed in these engines is a rope (or fabric) type seal. All service replacements, however, are of the rubber type. To remove the rope type seal and install the rubber type, the following method is used:

1. Drain the crankcase and remove the oil pan.
2. Remove the lower half of the rear main bearing cap and, after removing the old seal from the cap, drive out the pin in the bottom of the seal groove with a punch.
3. Loosen all main bearing caps, and allow the crankshaft to lower slightly. This lowering should not exceed 1/32 in.
4. Using a 6 in. length of 3/16 in. brazing rod, drive up on either exposed end of the top half of the oil seal. When the opposite end of the seal begins to protrude, grasp it with a pair of pliers and pull while continuing to tap the driven end.
5. After removing both halves of the rope seal and the retaining pin from the lower half of the bearing cap, install the new rubber seal by following steps 4-10 of the procedure for 1970-75 engines.

Rear Crankshaft Oil Seal R & R

1970-76

1. Remove the oil pan, and, if required, the oil pump.
2. Loosen all main bearing caps allowing the crankshaft to lower

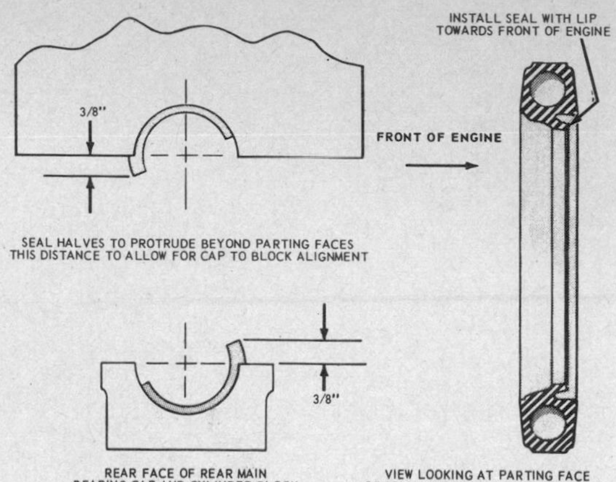

1970-76 rear main seal installation (© Ford Motor Co)

slightly.

NOTE: the crankshaft should not be allowed to drop more than 1/32 in.

3. Remove the rear main bearing cap and remove the seal from the cap and block.
4. Carefully clean the seal grooves in the cap and block with solvent.
5. Soak the new seal halves in clean engine oil.
6. Install the upper half of the seal in the block with the undercut side of the seal toward the front of the engine. Slide the seal around the crankshaft journal until ⅜ in. protrudes beyond the base of the block.
7. Repeat above procedure on lower seal, allowing an equal length of the seal to protrude beyond the opposite end of the bearing cap.
8. Install rear bearing cap and torque all main bearings to specifications. Apply sealer only to the rear of the seals.
9. Dip the bearing cap side seals in oil, then immediately install them. Do not use any sealer on the side seals. Tap the seals into place and do not clip the protruding ends.
10. Install the oil pump and pan. Fill the crankcase with oil, start engine, check for leaks.

AUTOMATIC TRANSMISSION

All Lincolns and Continentals use a Ford C6 automatic transmission. This heavy-duty three-speed unit is capable of providing automatic upshifts and downshifts through the three forward gear ratios, in addition to offering manual selection of first and second gears.

Only one band—the intermediate band—is used in this transmission. This band, along with the forward clutch, is used to obtain the intermediate gear. The adjustment of this band is the only adjustment required for the C6 transmission.

Prior to 1973, Lincoln automatic transmissions had a single-diaphragm transmission modulator valve. 1973 and later cars (because of the exhaust gas recirculation system are equipped with a dual-diaphragm transmission modulator valve.

Neutral Safety and Back-Up Light Switch Adjustment—1969

1. With manual linkage properly adjusted, try to engage starter in each position on quadrant. Starter should engage only in park or neutral positions.
2. Place shift lever in neutral detent.
3. Disconnect start switch wires at plug connector. Disconnect vacuum hoses if any. Remove screws securing neutral start switch to steering column and remove switch. Remove actuator lever along with Type III switches.
4. With switch wires facing up move actuator lever fully to the left and insert gauge pin (No. 43 drill) into gauge pin hole at point A. See accompanying figure. On Type III switch, be sure gauge pin is inserted a full ½ in.
5. With pin in place, move actuator lever to right until positive stop is engaged.
6. On Type I and Type II switches remove gauge pin and insert it at point B. On Type III switches remove gauge pin, align two holes in switch at point A and reinstall gauge pin.
7. Reinstall switch on steering column. Be sure shift lever is engaged in neutral detent.
8. Connect switch wires and vacuum hoses and remove gauge pin.

Shift Linkage Adjustment

1. If the car is equipped with a tilt wheel steering, position the column up as far as possible. With the engine off, place the selector lever against the stop in the D1 (large dot) position. Raise the car, and remove linkage splash shield.
2. Disconnect the adjustable link from the transmission manual shift lever on the transmission.
3. Be sure the transmission shift is fully engaged in D1, the second detent from the bottom. The bottom detent is L (low).
4. Loosen locknut on adjustable link, then pull down on the link to hold the selector lever against the D1 stop. Adjust the link by turning the lower end until the hole in the link aligns with the stud on the transmission manual lever. Connect it to the transmission shift lever.

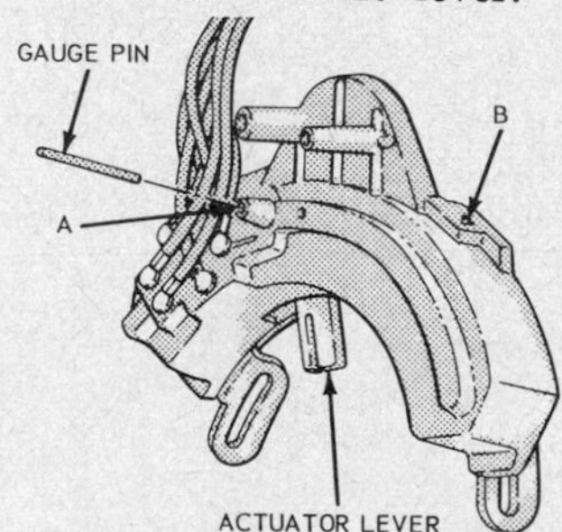

Neutral start switch—1969
(© Ford Motor Co)

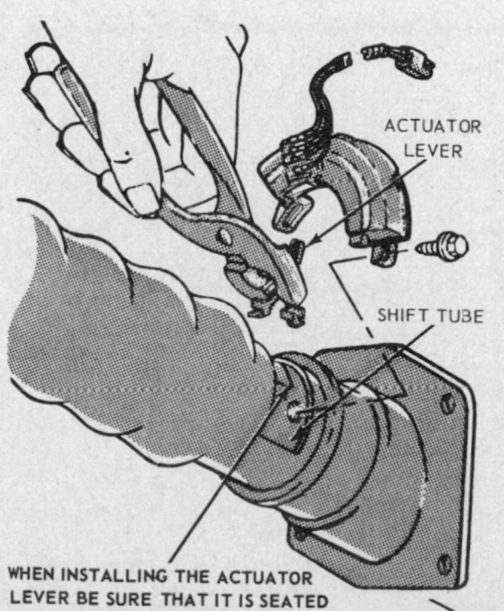

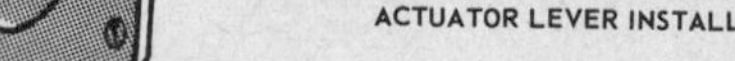

Removing or installing switch actuator (© Ford Motor Co)

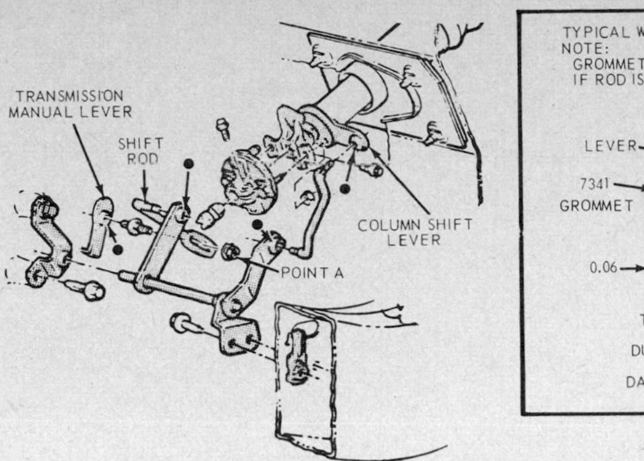

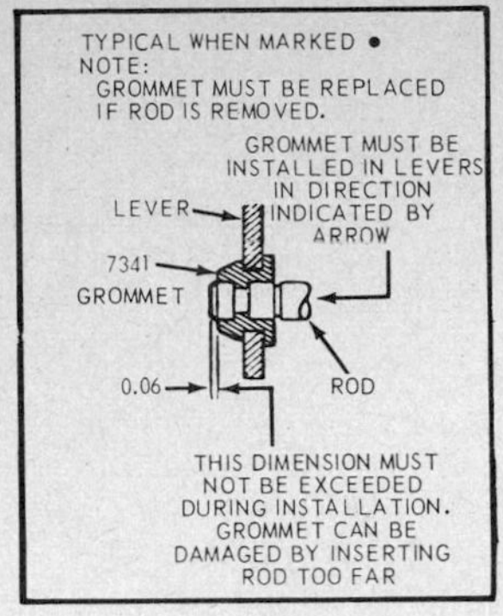

Transmission manual linkage—Lincoln Continental (© Ford Motor Co)

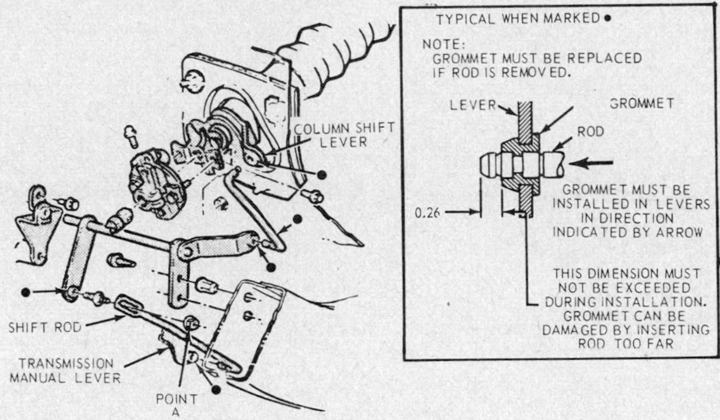

Transmission manual linkage—Mark III (© Ford Motor Co)

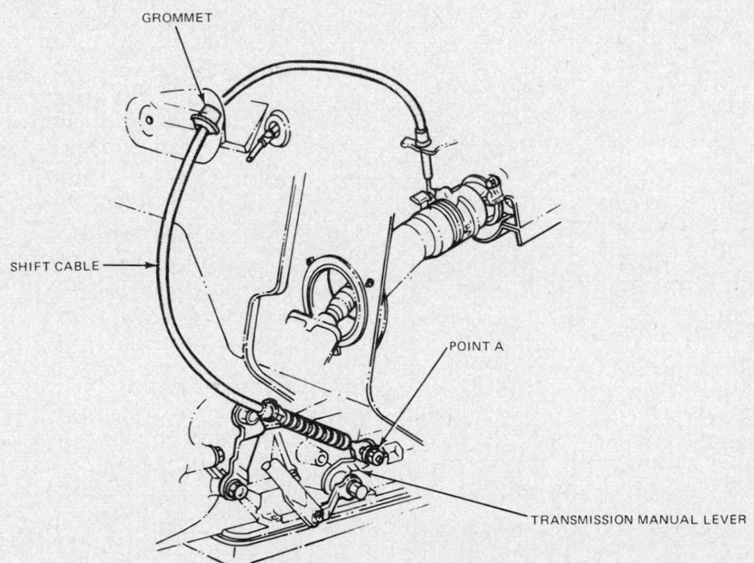

Transmission manual linkage—Mark IV (© Ford Motor Co)

Downshift Rod Adjustment

1. Loosen the locknut on the downshift rod. Disconnect rod from the ballstud on the bellcrank assembly by sliding the spring clip off the end of the rod.
2. Pull upward and hold the downshift rod against the transmission internal stop. Adjust length of rod until the hole in the rod is aligned with the ballstud on the bellcrank assembly.
3. Lengthen the downshift rod one turn and position it on the ballstud. Slide the spring clip over the end of the rod to lock the rod to the ballstud. Tighten locknut securely.
4. Be sure the bellcrank outer bracket is against the stop pin. If it is not, lengthen the downshift rod one turn. If the rod is too long, there will be no upshift.

Intermediate Band Adjustment

1. Raise the car on a hoist or place it on jack stands.
2. Clean threads of the intermediate band adjusting screw.
3. Remove the old locknut and install a new one.
4. Tighten the adjusting screw to 10 ft. lbs., and back the screw off exactly 1 turn (1971-75 models, 1 1/2 turns). Tighten the adjusting screw locknut.

Pan R & R

1. Raise the vehicle and support it securely. Place a container beneath the transmission.
2. Loosen the transmission pan bolts and allow the fluid to drain into the container. When the fluid has drained to the transmission pan flange level, remove the bolts, working from the rear, to allow the fluid to drain slowly.
3. Remove the pan and clean it. Discard the gasket.
4. Clean the filter screen.
5. Place a new gasket on the pan. Install the pan.
6. Add three quarts of type F fluid through the filler tube.
7. Run the engine, move the selector lever through all gear ranges. Check the fluid level; add fluid as necessary.

U-JOINTS

All Lincoln models are equipped with Cardan universal joints at the front end of the driveshaft. 1969 models have Cardan universal joints at the rear of the driveshaft which attached to the differential by means of a conventional pinion flange. In 1970 a companion flange was added to the rear of the driveshaft.

Each Cardan universal joint consists of two universal joints, a centering socket yoke or companion flange, and a center yoke.

Driveshaft and Universal Joint R & R

1. Mark the position of the centering socket yoke or companion flange in relation to the pinion flange so the driveshaft can be returned to its original location.
2. Disconnect the centering socket yoke or companion flange from the pinion flange. Tape the loose bearing caps to the spider.
3. Pull the driveshaft rearward until it clears the transmission extension housing and remove the driveshaft from the car. Plug the transmission extension housing to prevent leakage.

Installation is as follows:

1. Replace the rubber seals on the output shaft or the extension housing, if they are damaged.

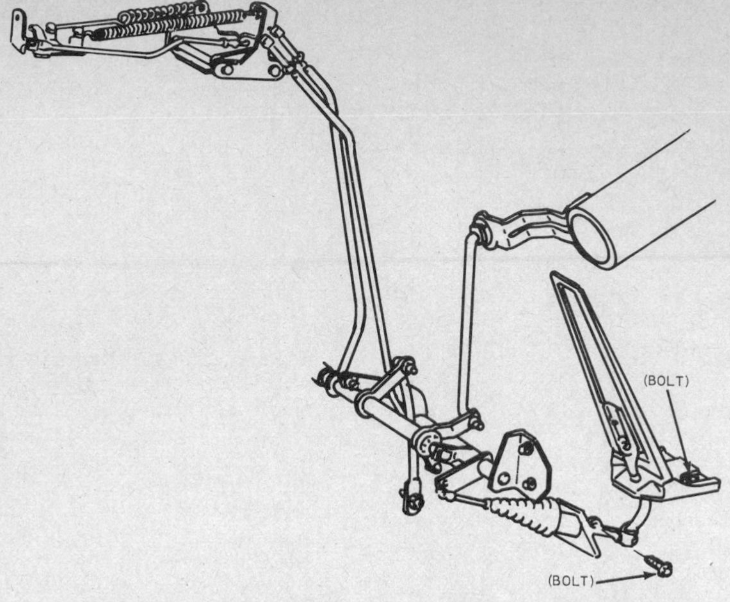

Throttle downshift linkage—1969-70 Continental (© Ford Motor Co)

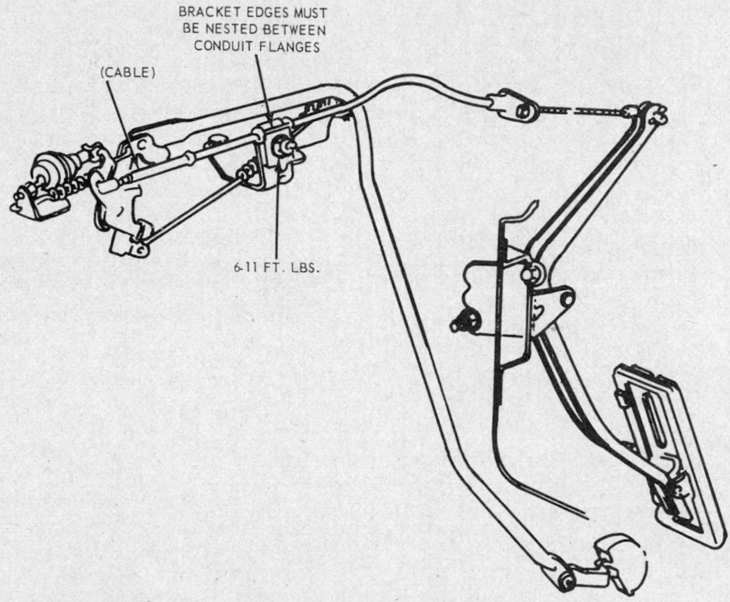

Throttle and downshift linkage—Mark III (© Ford Motor Co)

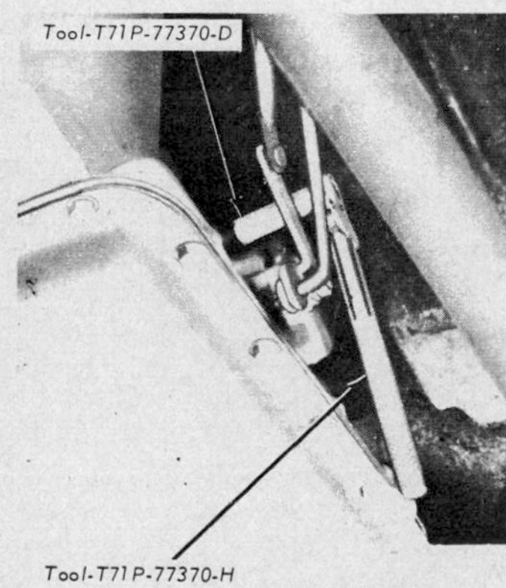

Intermediate band adjustment
(© Ford Motor Co)

2. Lubricate the yoke splines. Remove the plug from the extension housing and install the yoke. Don't bottom the yoke on the output shaft with too much force.
3. Align the matchmarks made during disassembly and install the rear joint-to-pinion flange bolts. Tighten to 70-90 ft lbs.

JACKING, HOISTING

Drive-On Hoist

Care should be exercised when driving the car on to a hoist because the body may contact the upright flanges on the hoist with subsequent damage. The approach ramp should be built up slightly if the angle of approach is too steep.

Rail-Type Hoist

The forks which contact the rear axle must be carefully positioned to avoid damage to the shock absorbers.

Forklift Hoist

The rear post fork, if not adjustable to width, may require special adapters to avoid damaging the rear shock absorbers.

Frame Contact Hoist

Particular care must be exercised when using a frame contact hoist. Specific areas marked on the underbody are designated as hoisting areas.

The lifting areas at the front of the vehicle are clearly designated by corrugated metal plates. These plates are bolted to the underbody midway between the front edge of the door and the rear edge of the front fender wheel opening. The front hoist pads or adapter arms, must be positioned on these corrugated plates.

The lifting areas at the rear of the vehicle are located at the edge of the underbody approximately 15 in. forward of the front edge of the rear wheel opening cover panel. The rear hoist pads, or adapter arms, must not be positioned forward of this point.

Floor Jack (Support)

Various acceptable jacking locations are available when it is necessary to raise any one portion of the vehicle. However, when jacking against sheet metal, a wood block 2 x 4 of suitable length should be placed betwen the jack and the sheet metal to prevent damaging or deforming the metal. Do not attempt to raise one entire side of the body by placing a jack midway between the front and rear wheels. This procedure will probably result in permanent damage.

Jacking at the Front

Each wheel can be raised independently by placing a floor jack under the spring seat pocket in the lower suspension arm.

Jacking at the Rear

Each wheel can be raised independently by placing a floor jack under the rear axle housing.

Bumper Jack

The bumper jack lifting points are at the underside edge at the front and rear bumpers.

FRONT SUSPENSION

All Lincolns and Continentals have a front suspension system in which the coil springs are supported on the lower suspension member. Each side of this independent front suspension uses two ball joints—upper and lower. Shock absorbers are positioned within the coil springs and are affixed

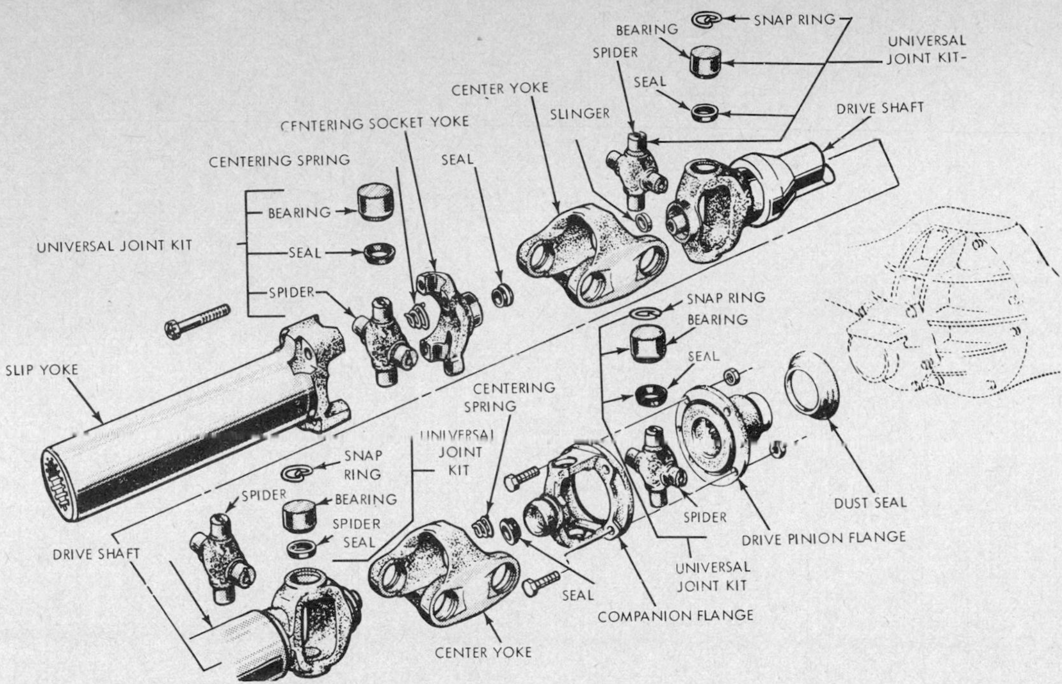

Driveshaft with Dana double Cardan universal joints (© Ford Motor Co)

to the lower suspension member and the top of the spring tower.

Front Spring and Lower Arm R & R

1969 Except Mark III

1. Raise the car. Place a support under each underbody side rail to the rear of the lower arm, in the lifting pad area.
2. Remove wheel and tire assembly, then, remove the hub and drum. On disc brake-equipped cars: remove two bolts and washers that attach the caliper to the spindle. Remove the caliper from the rotor and wire it to the underbody. Remove the hub and rotor from the spindle.
3. Loosen splash shield to provide clearance at the end of the arm when it is lowered.
4. Remove the shock absorber, and disconnect the stabilizing strut from the lower arm. Disconnect the stabilizer bar from the suspension bar.
5. Remove the cotter pin and loosen the castellated nut attaching the lower ball joint to the spindle.
6. Place a box wrench over the lower end of the ball joint remover tool between the two spindle pivot points. (The tool should seat firmly against the ends of both studs, and not against the lower stud nut.)
7. Turn the wrench until both studs are under tension, then, rap the spindle near the lower stud to loosen the stud from the spindle. Do not loosen the stud with tool pressure alone.
8. Place a jack under the outer end of the lower arm and raise the arm several inches.
9. Install spring compressor tool inside the spring with the jaws of the tool toward the center of the car.
10. Remove the nut from the ball joint stud. Lower the jack until the spindle and spring are free, and remove the spring and insulators.

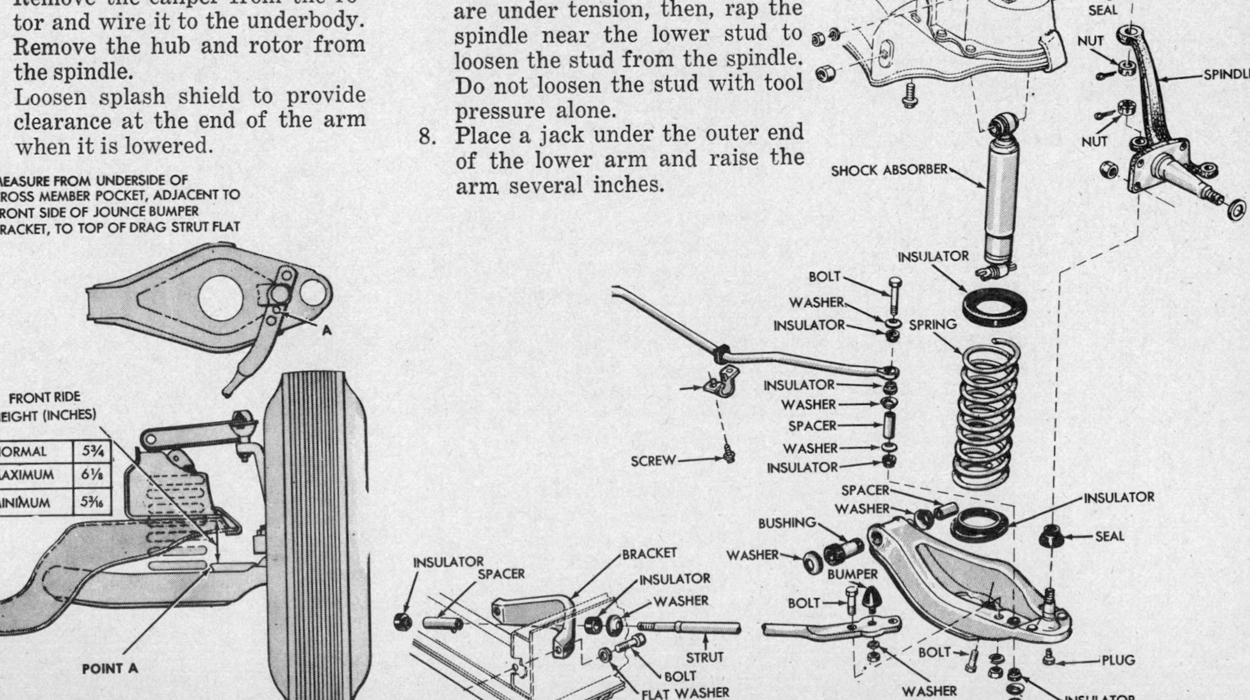

Front suspension—1969 except Mark III (© Ford Motor Co)

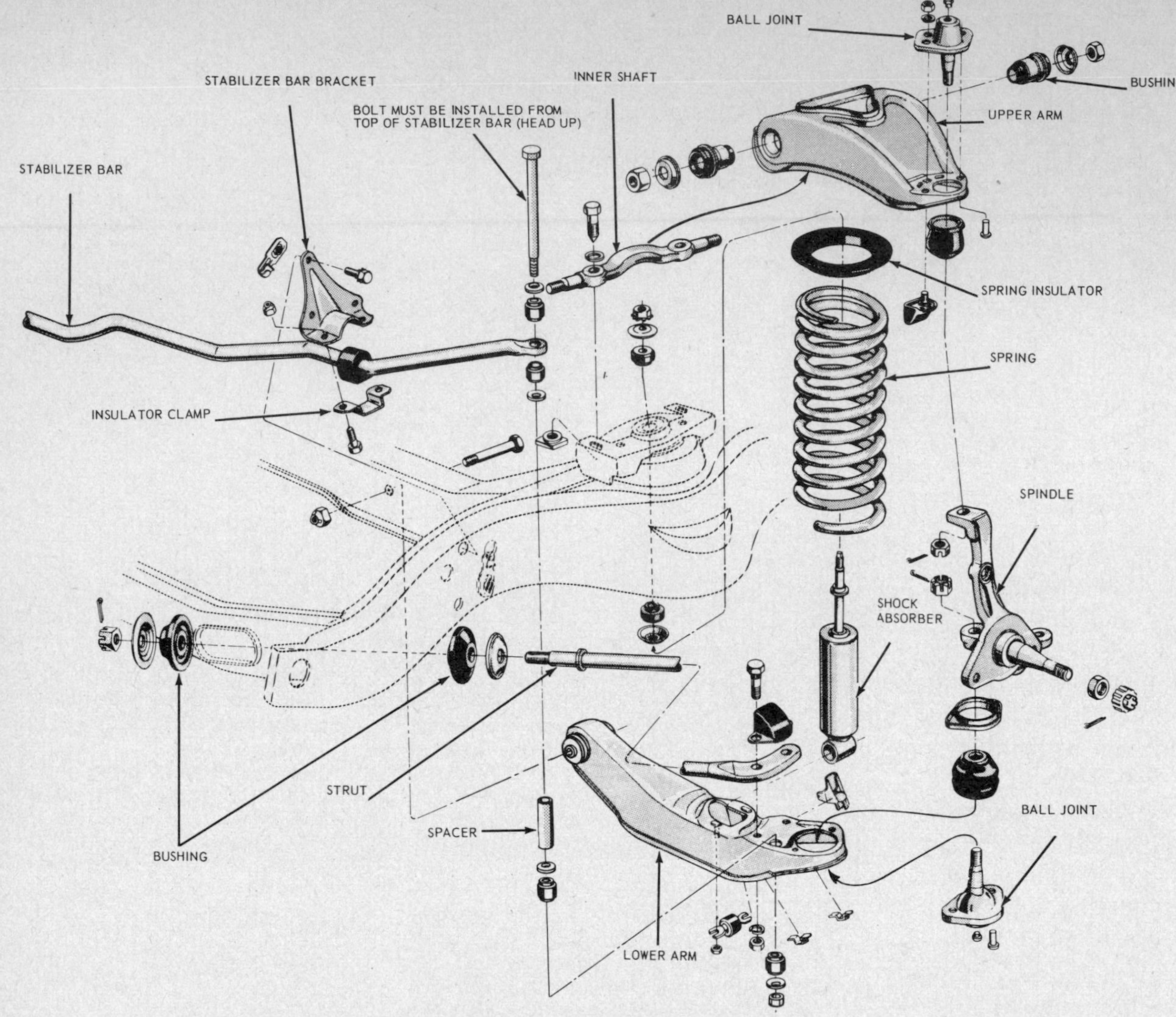

Front suspension—1970-76 Lincoln Continental, 1969-71 Mark III, and 1972-76 Mark IV
(© Ford Motor Co)

11. Remove the lower arm to cross-member nut, bolt, washers, and spacer, then remove arm.
12. Install by reversing the removal procedure.

Front Spring Removal—1969-71 Mark III, 1972-76 Mark IV and 1970-76 Continental

1. Raise vehicle and support front end of frame with jack stands.
2. Place jack under lower arm to support it.
3. Disconnect lower end of shock absorber from lower arm.
4. Remove bolts that attach strut and rebound bumper to lower arm.
5. Disconnect lower end of sway bar stud from lower arm
6. Remove nut and bolt that secures inner end of lower arm to cross-member.
7. Lower jack slowly to relieve spring pressure on lower arm then remove spring.
8. Installation is the reverse of removal.

Ball Joints

See Ford section.

Shock Absorber R & R

1969 Except Mark III

1. Remove the stud nut which is located at the upper eye of the shock absorber. Remove the upper eye stud bracket to cross-member attaching bolt and remove the stud bracket.
2. Remove the shock absorber-to-suspension lower arm attaching bolts. Lower and remove the shock absorber.
3. Examine the shock absorber unit and the rubber bushings. Replace any parts that are defective, deteriorated, or worn.
4. Fully extend the shock absorber. Position it inside the coil spring. Connect the lower end of the shock absorber to the suspension lower arm and torque the attaching nuts to 22-28 ft lbs.
5. Insert the upper bracket stud through the bushing in the shock absorber upper eye. Install the stud bracket-to-crossmember attaching bolt, but do not tighten the bolt at this time.
6. Install the upper eye bracket stud nut. Torque the nut to 40–55 ft lbs.
7. Torque the stud bracket-to-cross-member attaching bolt to 20–30 ft lbs.

1970-76 Lincoln Continental, 1969-71 Mark III, and 1972-76 Mark IV

1. Remove the nut, washer, and bushing from the shock absorber upper end.
2. Raise the vehicle and install safety stands.
3. Remove the two bolts which affix the shock absorber to the lower arm. Remove the shock absorber.
4. Place a washer and bushing on the shock absorber top stud and position the shock absorber within the coil spring. Install the two lower attaching bolts, and torque them to 8–15 ft lbs.

5. Remove the safety stands and lower the vehicle.
6. Place a bushing and washer on the shock absorber top stud and install the attaching nut. Torque this fitting to 20–28 ft lbs.

REAR SUSPENSION

In 1969, the Lincoln Continental rear suspension system used semi-elliptic leaf springs. In 1969, the newly introduced Continental Mark III came with rear coil springs, and from 1970 on, all Lincolns, Mark III, and Mark IV have used coil springs.

Rear Spring R & R

1969 except Mark III

Longitudinal leaf springs are used on these models.

They are held with a single bolt at the front, and with a shackle at the back.

Take the weight of the car on a frame in front of the rear spring. Unbolt and remove the rear shackle. Disconnect the rear shock absorber and remove the four U-bolts from each side of the spring saddle where the spring is held to the rear axle housing. Lower the spring to the ground, remove the nut that holds the front pin in the frame bracket and drive the front spring pin out.

The spring can then be slid from under the car.

Replace in reverse of the procedure which removed it.

1969-71 Mark III, 1972-76 Mark IV, 1970-76 Continental

Coil springs are used at rear suspension.

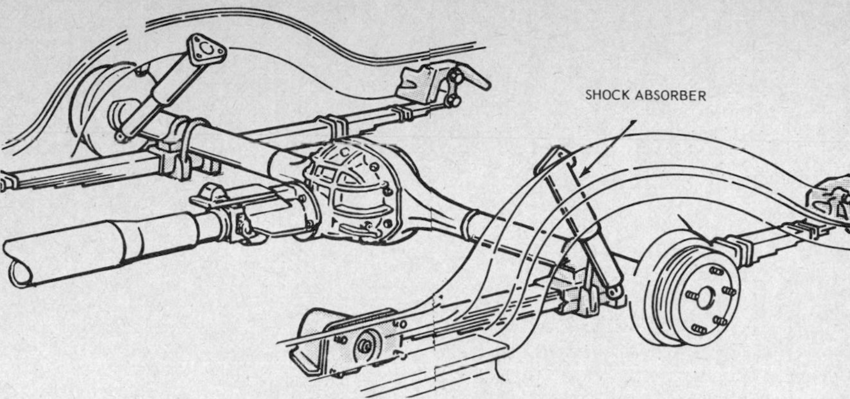

Rear suspension—1969 except Mark III

The rear suspension is a coil-link design. Large, low-rate coil springs are mounted between rear axle pads and frame supports. Parallel lower arms extend forward of the spring seats to rubber frame anchor to accommodate driving and braking forces. A third link is mounted between the axle and the frame to control torque reaction forces from the rear wheels.

Lateral (side sway) motion of the rear axle is controlled by a rubber bushed rear track bar, linked laterally between the axle and frame.

1. Place car on hoist and lift under rear axle housing. Place jack stands under frame side rails.
2. Disconnect track bar at the rear axle housing bracket.
3. Disconnect rear shock absorbers from the rear axle housing brackets.
4. Disconnect hose from axle housing vent. On Lincoln Continentals, disconnect the rear of the front-to-back brake tube from the No. 4 crossmember bracket. Remove the clip.
5. Lower hoist with axle housing until coil springs are released.
6. Remove spring lower retainer bolt, nut, washer and insulator.
7. Remove spring with large rubber insulator pads from car.
8. Install in reverse of above.

Shock Absorber R & R

1969 except Mark III

1. Lift the car and place support stands under the axle housing. Position the car with a jack to relieve tension on the shock absorbers.
2. Remove the screws which affix the shock absorber mounting plate to the crossmember.
3. Remove the attaching nut and washers from the lower end of the shock absorber.
4. Remove the shock absorber.
5. Remove the nut, outer washer, and insulator that attach the shock absorber to the mounting plate. Remove the mounting plate.
6. Transfer the mounting plate to the new shock absorber and install it on the car.

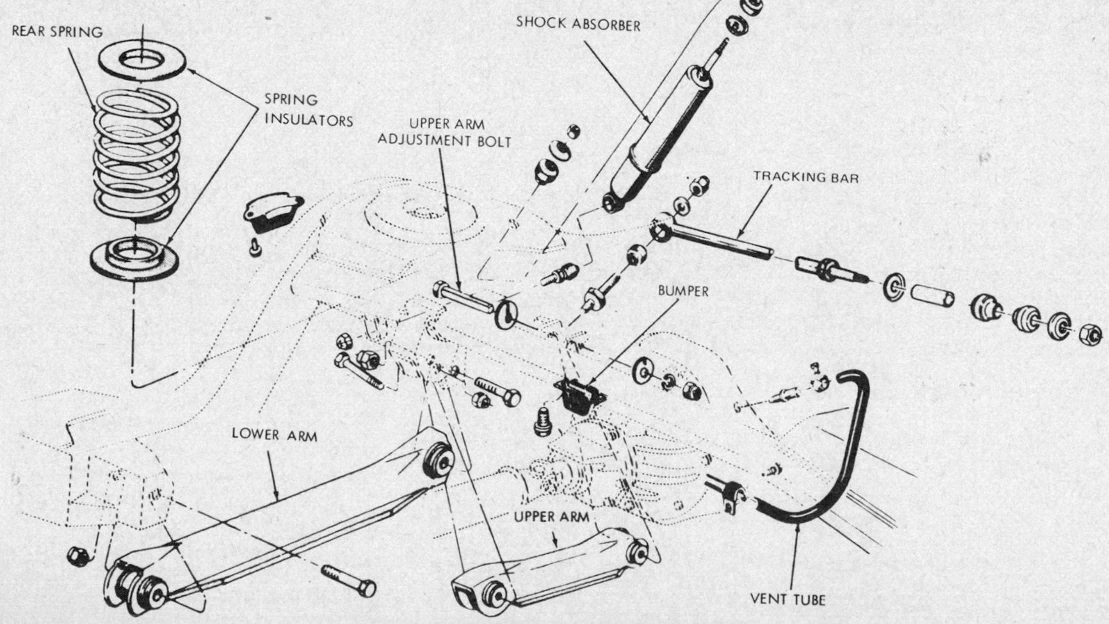

Lincoln Continental rear suspension—1970-76
(© Ford Motor Co)

1970-76 Lincoln, 1969-71 Mark III, and 1972-76 Mark IV

1. Raise the vehicle.
2. Remove the shock absorber attaching nut, washer, and insulator from the upper stud at the upper side of the spring upper seat. Compress the shock absorber to clear the hole in the spring seat and remove the inner insulator and washer from the upper attaching stud.
3. Remove the self-locking attaching nut and disconnect the shock absorber lower stud from the mounting bracket on the rear axle housing.
4. Remove the shock absorber from the car.
5. Reverse the above procedure to install the new shock absorber.

BRAKES

All Lincoln models are equipped with front power disc brakes. All rear brakes are of the conventional shoe design except 1975-76 models, which have an optional four wheel disc brake system. Also, all vehicles are equipped with dual reservoir master cylinders. The front and rear brake hydraulic systems are independent of each other. The disc brake calipers on 1969 Lincoln cars utilize dual pistons, while 1970 and later models incorporate single piston calipers. Hydro-boost power brakes were standard, starting 1975.

Master Cylinder R & R

1. Disconnect the brake lines from the master cylinder.
2. Remove the two nuts and lockwashers that attach the master cylinder to the brake booster.
3. Slide the master cylinder forward until it clears the booster pushrod, then remove the master cylinder from the car.
4. Reverse above procedure to install; but leave the brake lines loose on the master cylinder.
5. Fill the master cylinder with extra-heavy duty fluid and, using the foot pedal, slowly bleed the air from the master cylinder.
6. Tighten the brake lines, fill the master cylinder, then, bleed the brake system at the front and then the rear wheels.
7. Refill master cylinder.

Vacuum Power Brake Booster R & R

1969-74

1. Disconnect the vacuum hose from the booster.
2. Remove the two nuts and lockwashers that mount the master cylinder to the booster and move the master cylinder out of the way with the lines attached. Use care not to kink the brake lines.

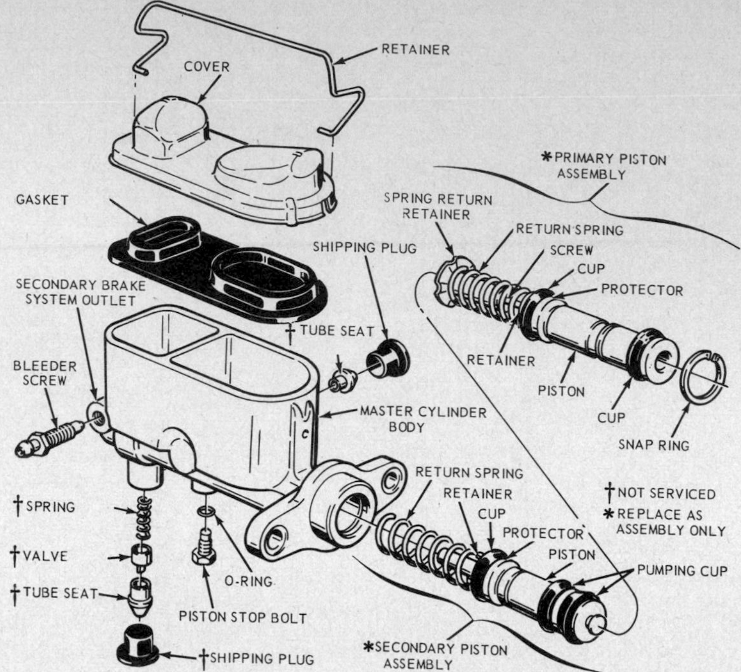

Dual type master cylinder (© Ford Motor Co)

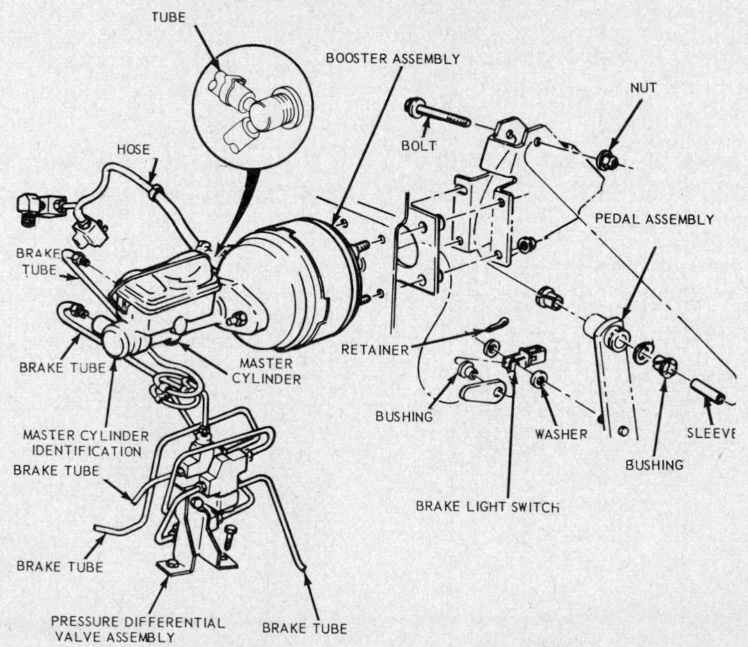

Brake pedal and booster installation (except Hydro-Boost) (© Ford Motor Co)

3. Working under the dash, disconnect and remove the stop light switch and pushrod from the brake pedal. Use care not to damage the switch during removal.
4. Remove the four booster to firewall attaching nuts from the interior side of the firewall.
5. Remove the booster from under the hood.
6. Reverse above procedure to install.

Hydro-Boost Brake Booster System

A new hydraulically powered brake booster was released as a running change in 1974 Lincoln production on April 8, 1974. The power steering pump provides the fluid pressure to operate both the brake booster and the power steering gear.

The hydro-boost assembly contains a valve which contains pump pressure while braking, a level to control the position of the valve and a boost piston to provide the force to operate a conventional master cylinder attached to the front of the booster. The hydro-boost also has a reserve system, designed to store sufficient pressurized fluid to provide at least 2 brake applications in the event of insufficient fluid flow from the power steering pump. The brakes can also

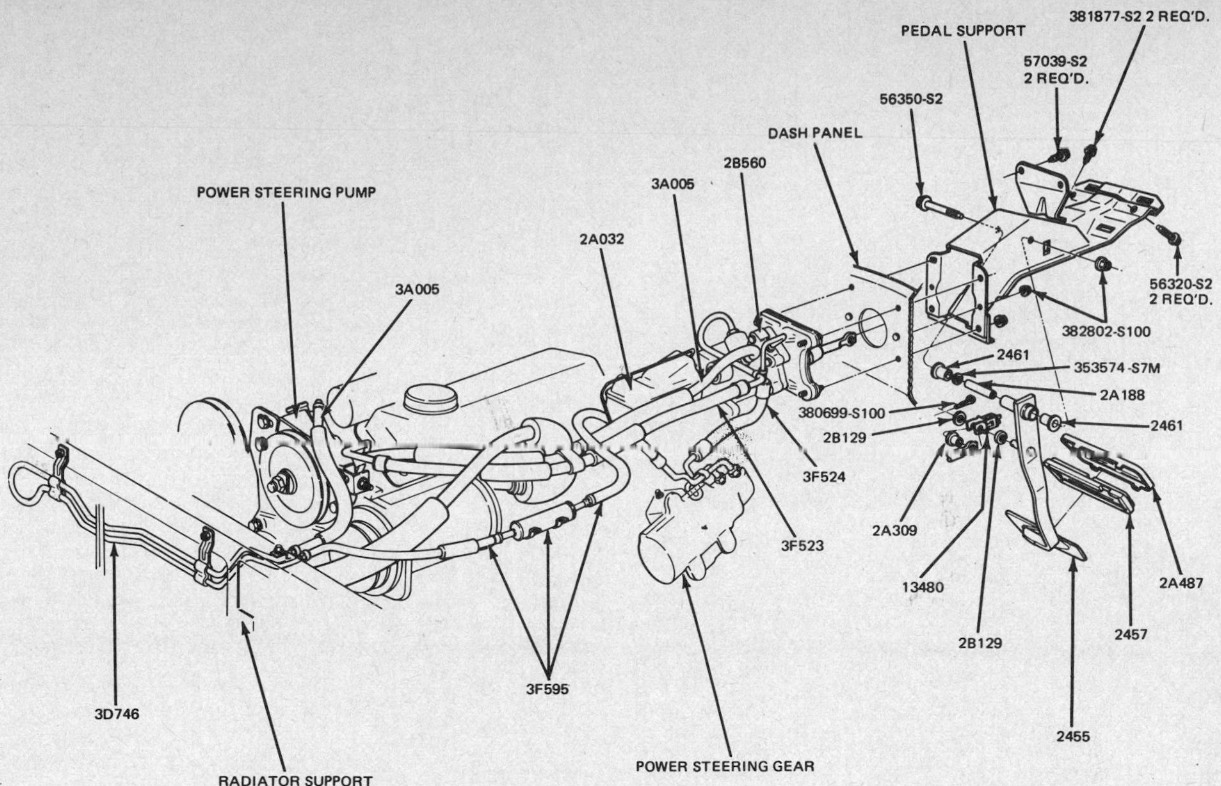

Hydro-Boost system—1974½-76 (© Ford Motor Co)

be applied manually if the reserve system is depleted.

Removal and Installation

The hydro-boost is serviced as an assembly only. Do not attempt to disassemble the booster. Before removing the hydro-boost, discharge the accumulator by making several brake applications until a hard pedal is felt.

1. Working from inside the vehicle, below the instrument panel, disconnect the pushrod from the brake pedal. Disconnect the stoplight switch wires at the connector. Remove the hairpin retainer. Slide the stoplight switch off the brake pedal far enough for the switch outer hole to clear the pin. Remove the switch from the pin. Slide the pushrod, nylon washers and bushing off the brake pedal pin.
2. Open the hood and remove the nuts attaching the master cylinder to the hydro-boost. Remove the master cylinder. Secure it to one side without disturbing the hydraulic lines.
3. Disconnect the pressure, steering gear and return lines from the booster. Plug the lines to prevent the entry of dirt.
4. Remove the nuts attaching the hydro-boost. Remove the booster from the firewall, sliding the pushrod link out of the engine side of the firewall.
5. Install the hydro-boost on the firewall and install the attaching nuts.
6. Install the master cylinder on the booster.
7. Connect the pressure, steering gear and return lines to the booster.
8. Working below the instrument panel, install the nylon washer, booster pushrod and bushing on the brake pedal pin. Install the switch so that it straddles the pushrod with the switch slot on the pedal pin and the switch outer hole just clearing the pin. Slide the switch completely onto the pin and install the nylon washer. Attach these parts with the hairpin retainer. Connect the stoplight switch wires and install the wires in the retaining clip.
9. Remove the coil wire so that the engine will not start. Fill the power steering pump and engage the starter. Apply the brakes with a pumping action. Do not turn the steering wheel until air has been bled from the booster.
10. Check the fluid level and add as required. Start the engine and apply the brakes, checking for leaks. Cycle the steering wheel.
11. If a whine type noise is heard, suspect fluid aeration.

Parking Brake Cable Adjustment

1969-73

1. Fully release the parking brake pedal.
2. Raise the car on a hoist.
3. Adjust the pedal cable to about 10 in., measured from the cable attachment at the crossmember to the cable adjusting nut.
4. Depress the parking brake pedal one notch from normal, released position.
5. Loosen locknut on equalizer rod and turn the forward nut inward toward the front of the car until a moderate drag is felt when turning the rear wheels.
6. Holding forward nut in position, tighten locknut. Lock the adjustment at the equalizer.
7. Release parking brake, and make sure that the brake shoes return to the fully released position.

1974-75—Rear Drum

1. Make sure that the parking brake is fully released.
2. Place the transmission in Neutral.
3. Raise the vehicle on an axle-type hoist.
4. Tighten the adjusting nut against the cable equalizer or cable adjusting rod to cause rear wheel brake drag. Loosen the adjusting nut until the rear brakes are fully released. There should be no brake drag. Tighten the locknut to 7-10 ft lbs.
5. Lower the vehicle and check the operation of the parking brake.

1975-76—Rear Disc

1. Fully release the parking brake. Place the transmission selector in Neutral.

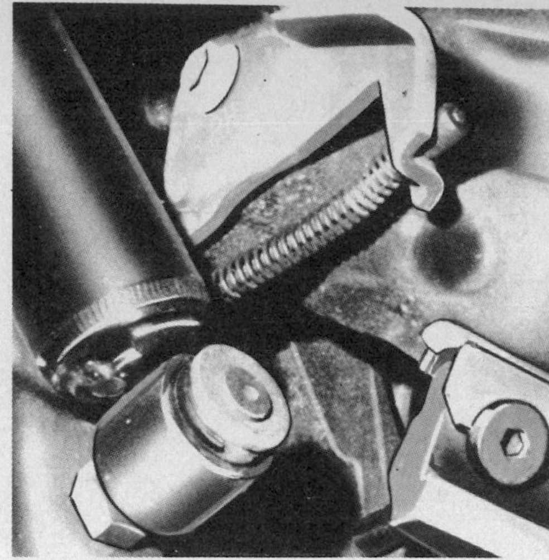

Parking brake cable at the caliper—1975-76
(© Ford Motor Co)

2. Raise the vehicle on an axle-type hoist.
3. Tighten the adjusting nut until the levers on the caliper just start to move.
4. Loosen the adjusting nut just enough to obtain complete return of the levers to the "stop" position.
5. Apply and release the parking brakes. Check the caliper levers to see if they are at full stop, by trying to pull them rearward.
6. If the levers can be moved rearward, the adjustment is too tight. Repeat the adjustment.

Brake System Service

Procedures for brake adjustment, shoe replacement, bleeding of the system, and the overhaul of wheel cylinders, calipers, and master cylinders may be found in the "Unit Repair Section."

STEERING

Steering Wheel R & R

1. Disconnect the negative battery cable.
2. If the vehicle is equipped with a horn ring, remove it by rotating it counterclockwise. If equipped with a steering wheel crash pad, remove the retaining screws from the underside of the steering wheel and then remove the crash pad. Disconnect the horn and speed control (if so equipped) wires from the inside of the steering wheel center.
3. Remove the steering wheel nut, install a steering wheel puller on the end of the shaft, and remove the steering wheel.

Caution The use of a knock-off type steering wheel puller and a hammer is inadvisable, as they may damage the steering column bearing or (in the case of the collapsible-type steering wheel the column itself.

4. With the front wheels positioned straight ahead, line up the marks on the steering wheel and column and install the steering wheel and the locknut.
5. Connect the horn and speed control wires and install the horn ring if so equipped and the crashpad and retaining screws if so equipped.
6. Connect the negative battery cable.

Procedures for the overhaul of steering gear and power steering pump may be found in the "Unit Repair Section."

Turn Signal Switch R & R

1. Disconnect the negative battery cable.
2. Remove the steering wheel as outlined in the "Steering Wheel R&R" section.
3. Unscrew the turn signal lever from the side of the column. Remove the emergency flasher retainer and knob.
4. Locate and remove the finish cover on the steering column and disconnect the wiring connector plugs.
5. On all 1969-70 and all 1969-76 Mark III models with a tilt steering column, it is necessary to separate the wires from the connector plug in order to remove the switch and wires. First note the location and color code of each wire, prior to removal. Remove the plastic cover from the wiring harness. Attach a piece of heavy cord to the switch wires to pull them down through the column during installation.
6. Remove the retaining clips and screws from the turn signal switch and lift the switch and wire assembly from the top of the column.
7. Tape the ends of the new switch wires together and transfer the pull cord to these wires.
8. Pull the wires down through the columns with the cord and attach the new switch to the column hub.
9. If the switch wires were separated from the connector plug, press the wires into their proper location. Connect the wiring connector plugs and install the finish cover on the column.
10. Install the turn signal lever. Install the emergency flasher retainer and knob, if so equipped.
11. Install the steering wheel as outlined in the "Steering Wheel R & R" section.
12. Connect the negative battery cable and test the operation of the turn signals, horn, emergency flashers, and speed control, if so equipped.

Power Steering Pump R & R

1. Drain the fluid from the pump reservoir by disconnecting the fluid return hose at the pump. Then, disconnect the pressure hose from the pump.
2. Remove the mounting bolts from the front of the pump. There is a nut on the rear of the pump that must be removed. After removal, move the pump inward to loosen the belt tension and remove the belt from the pulley. Then, remove the pump from the car.
3. To reinstall the pump, position on mounting bracket and loosely install the mounting bolts and nuts. Put the drive belt over the pulley and move the pump outward against the belt until the proper belt tension is obtained. Measure the belt tension with a belt tension gauge for the proper adjustment.
4. Tighten the mounting bolts and nuts.

Tie-Rod R & R

1. Raise the front of the vehicle and install jackstands.
2. Remove the cotter pin and nut from the tie-rod end ball stud.
3. Loosen the tie-rod sleeve clamp bolts. Remove the tie-rod end from the center link with a puller.
4. Separate the tie-rod end from the sleeve, counting the number of turns required.

Discard all of the tie-rod end assembly parts which were removed from the sleeve. Use all new parts when the tie-rod ends are replaced.

Installation is as follows:

1. Thread a new tie-rod end into the sleeve. Turn it in the same number of turns required to remove the old one. Don't tighten the sleeve clamp bolts yet.

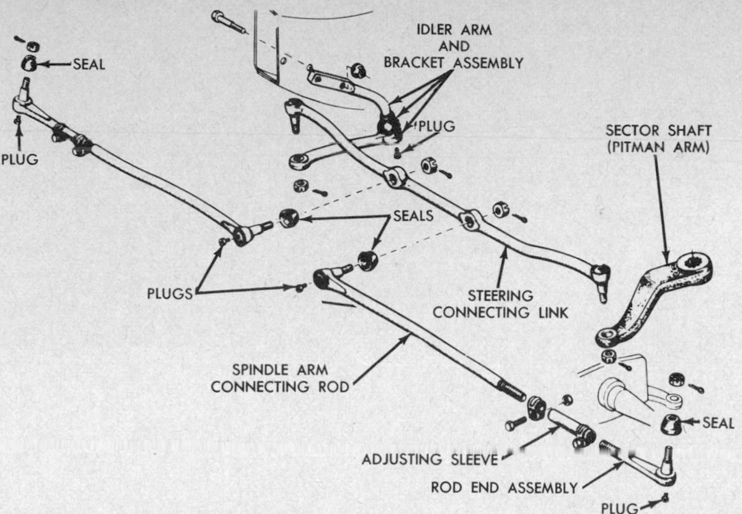

Disassembled view of typical steering linkage (© Ford Motor Co)

2. Install a new seal (if used) on the tie-rod end ball stud.
3. Install the stud and nut. Tighten to 43 ft lbs. Continue tightening the nut until the next slot aligns with the hole in the stud. Secure with a new cotter pin.
4. Check the toe-in and adjust it as necessary.
5. Loosen the sleeve clamps. Oil the clamps, bolts, sleeve, and nuts.
6. Tighten the clamp nuts to 13-18 ft lbs on Mark III models or to 20-22 ft lbs on all other models.

Idler Arm R & R

1. Raise the vehicle and support it with jackstands.
2. Remove the cotter pin and nut securing the idler arm to the center link.
3. Separate the center link and idler arm. Use a puller if necessary.
4. Remove the bolt, nuts, and washers which secure the idler arm bracket to the frame.

Installation is as follows:

1. Attach the idler arm to the center link without tightening the nut.
2. Install the idler arm bracket on the frame.
3. On all models, except 1969 Lincoln Continentals, place the idler arm and front wheels straight ahead. On 1969 Continentals, see that the seal is correctly installed on the center link.
4. Install the center link stud through the idler arm hole. Install the nut and washer. Tighten the nut to 35 ft lbs on Mark III or to 43 ft lbs on all other models.
5. Keep tightening the nut until its next slot aligns with the hole in stud. Secure with a new cotter pin.
6. Remove the jackstands and lower the vehicle. Check front end alignment.

Pitman Arm R & R

1. Raise the vehicle on a hoist and support it with jackstands.
2. Remove the cotter pin and nut which secure the pitman arm to the center link.
3. Use a puller to separate the center link from the pitman arm.
4. Remove the pitman arm securing nut and lockwasher.
5. Remove the pitman arm with a puller, after placing the front wheels in the straight ahead position.

Installation is as follows:

1. Start with the front wheels straight ahead. Place the pitman arm (pointing forward) on the steering gear sector shaft. Be sure that the blind teeth on the pitman arm and sector shaft are aligned.
2. Install the nut and lockwasher which secure the pitman arm to the sector shaft. Torque to 150-225- ft lbs on 1969-74 models or to 236-250 ft lbs on 1975-76 models.
3. Install the nut which secures the pitman arm to the center link. Torque to 43 ft lbs.
4. Tighten the nut so that its next castallation aligns with the cotter pin hole. Secure the nut with a new cotter pin.
5. Remove the jackstands and lower the car. Check front end alignment.

INSTRUMENT PANEL

Ignition Lock R & R

See Ford section

Ignition Switch R & R

See Ford Section.

Light Switch Replacement

Except Mark III and Mark IV

1. Disconnect battery.
2. Remove knob and shaft by pressing release knob button on switch housing and with knob in full on position.
3. Remove moulding nut from switch.
4. Remove junction block from switch.
5. Install in reverse of above.

Mark III

1. Disconnect battery ground cable.
2. Remove seven screws holding lower finish panel to lower side of instrument panel.
3. Remove control knob and shaft from headlight switch. This is done by pressing the release button on the underside of the switch (with shaft pulled all the way out).
4. Remove bezel and nut from headlight switch.
5. Remove two screws from switch-to-instrument panel.
6. Remove switch from panel. Disconnect wire multiple connector and vacuum hoses from the switch.
7. Install by reversing removal procedure.

Mark IV

1. Remove the instrument cluster trim panel, as explained under "Instrument Cluster R&R."
2. Remove the lighting switch mounting plate.
3. Remove the bezel nut and disconnect the multiple connector.
4. Remove the vacuum lines and the switch.
5. Reverse this procedure to install.

WINDSHIELD WIPERS

Motor R & R

1969

The wiper motor is hydraulically operated by oil pressure from the power steering pump via the steering gear.

1. Remove washer coordinator hose from bottom of wiper motor.
2. Remove oil return, feed and control lines from wiper motor.
3. Disconnect wiper control cable at the wiper motor.
4. Remove two screws holding the wiper motor to the auxiliary drive mounting plate. Remove wiper motor.
5. Install motor by reversing the removal procedure.
6. Refill the power steering system and bleed the lines.

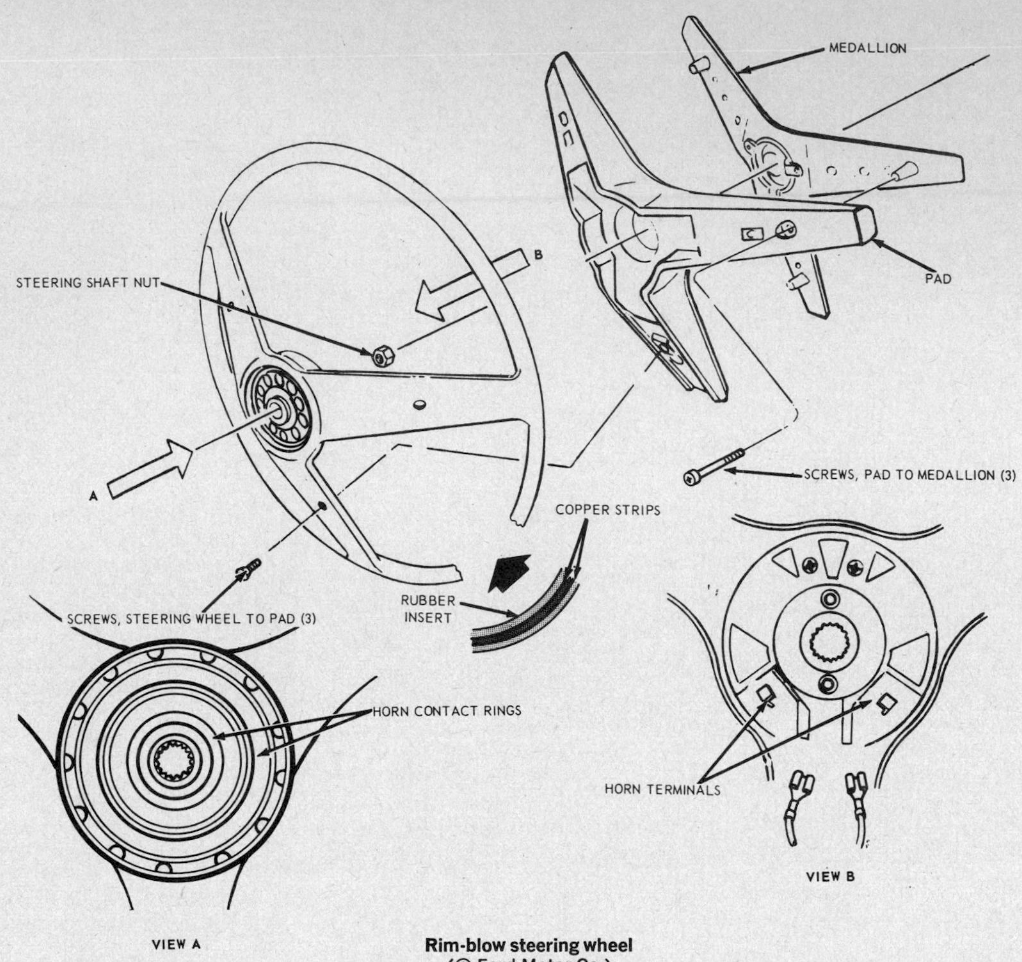

Rim-blow steering wheel
(© Ford Motor Co.)

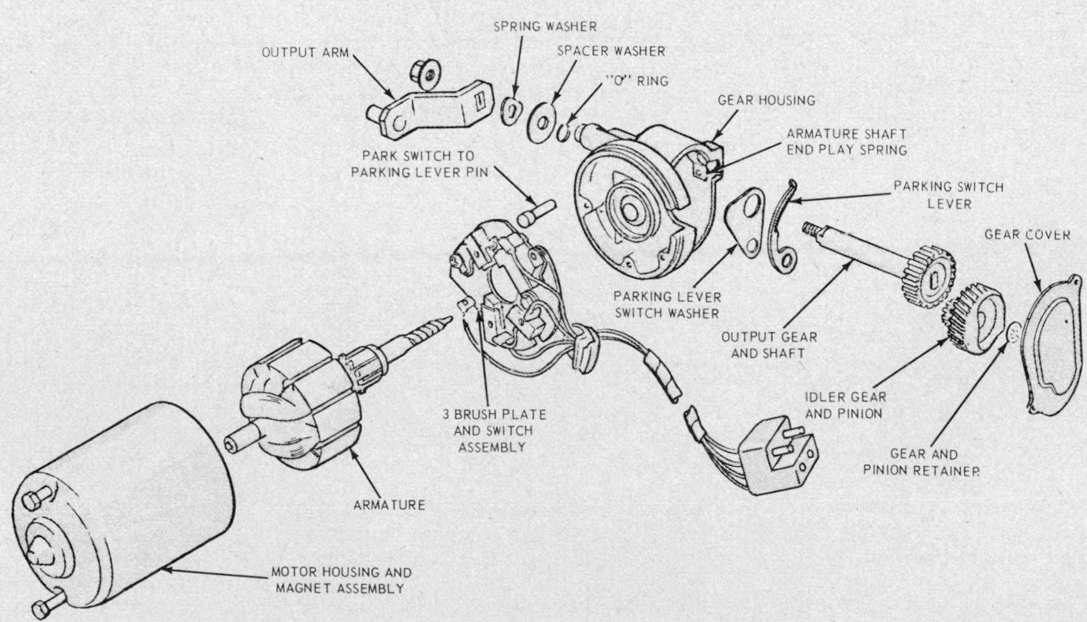

Wiper motor details
(© Ford Motor Co.)

1970-76 Continental and 1972-76 Mark IV

1. Disconnect battery.
2. Remove wiper arm and blade assemblies from pivot shafts.
3. Remove left cowl screen for access.
4. Disconnect linkage drive arm from motor output arm crank pin by removing retaining clip.
5. Disconnect two push on wire connectors from the motor.
6. From engine side of dash, remove three bolts that retain motor and remove motor. Reverse procedure to install. Be sure that output arm is in "park."

1970 Mark III

1. Disconnect battery.
2. Disconnect washer hose, remove three retaining bolts, and pull cowl top grille out from under two clips.
3. Disconnect connector plugs from wiring harness at engine side of dash panel. Push wiring and plugs along with grommet through hole in dash.
4. Remove four motor to cowl retaining bolts. Lift motor out, and at the same time pull wiper arm and blade assembly to left for access to motor crank pin clip. Remove clip and disconnect drive link from motor crank pin. Remove three retaining bolts and separate motor from mounting plate and cover and wiring harness assembly. Reverse procedure to install.

1971 Mark III

See 1971 Thunderbird.

Linkage R & R

1969

Auxiliary Drive

1. Remove both wiper arms and blades from the pivot assemblies.
2. Remove the ventilation grille and screen.
3. Remove both washer nozzles.
4. Disconnect the pivot shaft drive arm from the auxiliary drive.
5. Remove the four screws and the auxiliary drive assembly.
6. To install, reverse the removal procedure.

Wiper Pivot

1. Remove the windshield wiper arms and blades.
2. Remove the cowl top ventilation grille and screen.
3. Right hand: disconnect the drive arm from the pivot shaft assembly.
4. Left hand: disconnect the drive arm from the right hand pivot assembly and the drive arm from the auxiliary drive assembly.
5. Remove the pivot shaft retaining capscrews and nuts.
6. Remove the pivot shaft and housing from the car.
7. To install, reverse the removal procedure.

1970-76 Continental

1. Disconnect battery.
2. Remove wiper arm and blade assemblies from pivot shafts.
3. Remove cowl screens for access.
4. Disconnect left linkage arm from drive arm by removing clip.
5. Remove three bolts retaining left pivot shaft assembly through cowl opening.
6. Disconnect linkage drive arm from motor crank pin by removing clip.
7. Remove three bolts that connect drive arm pivot shaft assembly to cowl. Remove pivot shaft drivearm and right arm as an assembly. Reverse procedure to install.

1970 Mark III

1. Disconnect battery.
2. Disconnect washer hose, remove three retaining bolts, and pull cowl top grille out from under two clips.
3. Remove wiper arm and blade assemblies.
4. To remove left pivot shaft, loosen right pivot shaft retaining bolts, and remove left pivot shaft retaining bolts. Remove connecting clip, and disconnect left pivot shaft link from right pivot shaft crank pin. Work left pivot shaft and link assembly toward right and out through cowl opening.
5. To remove right pivot shaft, remove three retaining bolts and disconnect linkage from crank pin by removing clip. Lift pivot shaft assembly from cowl. Reverse procedure to install.

1971 Mark III, and 1972-76 Mark IV

1. Disconnect the battery. Remove the wiper arm and blade assemblies. Be sure to remove the tension arm retaining clip from the tension arm retaining stud on the left pivot assembly.
2. Remove the retaining screws and remove the cowl grille. Disconnect the washer hoses.
3. Remove the clip retaining the link assembly to the motor.
4. Remove the screws that attach the pivot shaft and link assembly to the cowl and remove the pivot shaft and link assembly.
5. Reverse above procedure to install. Force the linkage connecting clip into the locked position when installing.

RADIO

Radio R & R

1969 Except Mark III

1. Disconnect battery.
2. Remove eight screws in the lower control housing.
3. Disconnect lead from the speaker/s.
4. Disconnect power antenna lead.
5. Disconnect lead to the foot operated switch for AM-FM radios on cars so equipped.
6. Disconnect one two-way disconnect for power and pilot light.
7. Remove the two knobs and two bezels on the selector shafts. Remove the two nuts and two retainers on the selector shafts.
8. Remove the two screws holding the radio bracket to the lower reinforcement on the instrument panel.
9. Remove the two nuts and washers from the selector shafts. Disconnect the antenna lead and remove the radio.
10. To install, reverse the above.

1969-71 Mark III

Removal

1. Disconnect ground from battery.
2. Pull knobs off the control shafts.
3. Remove the cover plate located below the steering column.
4. Remove nut from the right radio control shaft.
5. Remove six screws and the trim applique from in front of the radio.
6. Remove the nut and washer from the right radio control shaft.
7. Remove screw attaching the front left side of the radio to the instrument panel.
8. Remove the radio support attaching screw.
9. Disconnect the radio power wires and speaker wires at the connectors.
10. Disconnect the antenna lead-in cable and remove the radio.

Installation

1. Connect the power, speaker, and antenna leads to the radio.
2. Position radio to instrument panel and install the attaching screw at the left front side of the radio.
3. Install the washer and nut on the radio right control shaft.
4. Install radio rear support attaching screw.
5. Position the trim applique to the instrument panel and install the six attaching screws.
6. Install the nut on the radio right control shaft.
7. Install the discs, felt washer and knobs on the radio control shafts.
8. Install cover plate below the steering column.

9. Connect the ground cable to the battery.
10. Check operation of radio and set the push buttons.

1970-76 Continental

1. Disconnect battery.
2. Remove map light assembly.
3. Remove right and left inspection covers.
4. Remove lower instrument panel pad.
5. Remove glove box, open ashtray, and leave it open.
6. Remove glove box switch.
7. Through glove box opening remove two nuts retaining radio finish panel to instrument panel.
8. Install cover plate below the
9. Remove two screws at top of finish panel. Position panel out and disconnect cigar lighter and light from right panel.
10. Through glove box opening remove nut from lower right corner of center finish panel.
11. Remove radio top support nut and three mounting screws. Pull radio out. Disconnect power leads and antenna cable. Remove radio.
12. Reverse procedure to install.

1972-76 Mark IV

1. Disconnect the negative battery cable.
2. Pull the radio control knobs off the radio shafts. Disconnect and lower the "twilight sentinal" amplifier.
3. Remove the nuts from both radio control shafts. Disconnect the air conditioning ducts.
4. Remove the radio rear support to panel attaching screw.
5. Disconnect the radio power wires. Disconnect the speaker wires at the connectors.
6. Disconnect the antenna lead and remove the radio.
7. Reverse the above procedure to install.

HEATER

Heater Core Removal

1969 Continental

1. Disconnect battery, remove air cleaner and drain coolant from system.
2. Disconnect hoses at heater core.
3. Remove harness clamp on top of evaporator-heater case.
4. Remove temperature blender door variable actuator.
5. Remove heater core cover plate retaining screws and cover plate.
6. Lift out heater core. Reverse procedure to install.

1969-71 Mark III

1. Remove hood and air cleaner and drain engine coolant.
2. Disconnect both hydraulic lines at wiper motor and position them to one side on 1969 Mark III.
3. Disconnect heater hoses at heater core and position hoses and water valve away from housing.
4. Disconnect vacuum supply hose on top of housing and remove oil pressure sending unit from back of engine.
5. Remove transmission dip stick and tube assembly.
6. Disconnect multiple connector leading to icing switch.
7. Remove evaporator housing front cover. On air-conditioned cars, remove the glove compartment liner and disconnect the electrical and vacuum junction blocks on the inner dash panel.
8. Remove heater core housing cover.
9. Remove heater core retaining bracket and remove heater core. Reverse procedure to install.

1970-73 Continental

1. Drain engine coolant.
2. Disconnect vacuum junction valve from dash panel and move valve and vacuum hoses away from case.
3. Disconnect speed control servo and bracket assembly if so equipped from dash panel and move it away from case.
4. Disconnect multiple connector from blower resistor and remove harness from clip on case.
5. Disconnect heater hoses from heater case and remove hose support clamp from case. Move hoses and water valve away from case.
6. Remove seven case cover to case flange attaching screws and wire harness clip.
7. Remove six cover to back plate stud nuts.
8. Remove one upper case to dash panel mounting screw.
9. Remove two case to dash panel mounting stud nuts, one on inboard mounting flange and one below case on lower flange.
10. Carefully move heater core assembly forward to clear mounting studs and lift up and out of vehicle.
11. Remove two spring clips from core tubes on front of core cover.
12. Remove three screws from core end plate and remove plate.
13. Remove heater core and mounting gasket assembly from core cover and remove gasket from core. Reverse procedure to install.

1972-76 Mark IV

1. Drain the engine coolant and disconnect the heater hoses from the heater core.
2. Remove the glove box.
3. Remove the heater air outlet register from the plenum assembly. It is held in position by two snap-rings.
4. Remove the temperature control cable assembly mounting screw, and disconnect the end of the cable from the blend door crank arm by removing the spring nut.
5. Remove the blue and red vacuum hoses from the high-low door vacuum motor, and the brown hose at the in-line tee connector to the temperature bypass door motor.
6. Disconnect the wire connector from the resistor.
7. Remove 10 screws from around the flange of the plenum case and remove the rear case half of the plenum.
8. Remove the mounting nut from the heater core tube support bracket.
9. Reinstall in the reverse procedure. To provide a positive seal between the front and rear case halves, apply body sealer around the case flanges prior to installation. Be certain that the core mounting gasket is properly installed. Reverse procedure to install.

1974-76 Continental

1. Drain the engine coolant.
2. Disconnect the heater hoses from the heater core.
3. Remove the heater core cover and gasket.
4. Lift the heater core and lower the mounting gasket out of the evaporator housing.
5. Remove the lower mounting gasket from the heater core.
6. Installation is the reverse of removal.

Heater Blower Removal

1969 Continental

The blower motor is mounted in the right fender well.

1. Remove right fender splash shield secured with six bolts.
2. Remove four screws retaining blower motor to housing.
3. Disconnect electrical leads and remove motor.
4. Remove four nuts retaining motor housing to air door assembly and remove one nut through motor opening.
5. Remove housing and disassemble boot.
6. From inside car, remove right cowl trim panel and remove three screws retaining air door assembly to cowl.
7. From under fender remove screw at top.
8. Disconnect vacuum hose and remove air door assembly. Reverse procedure to install.

1969-71 Mark III

1. Remove right cowl side trim panel.

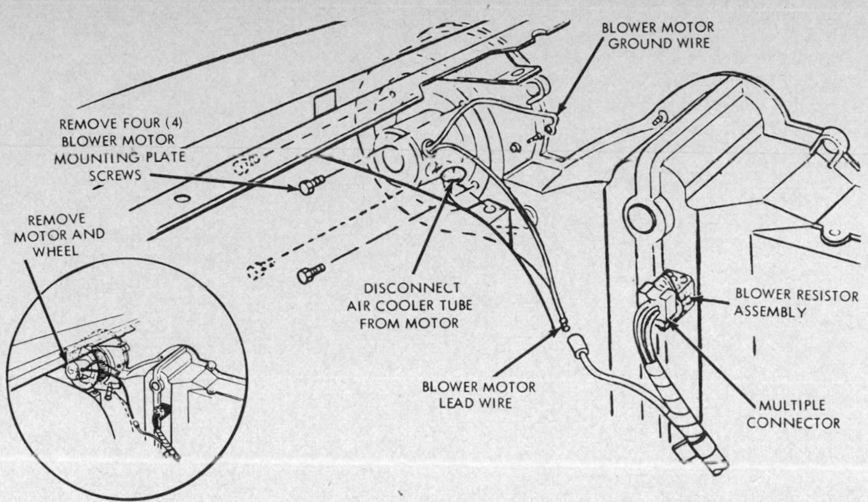

Heater blower removal—1970-76 Lincoln Continental (© Ford Motor Co)

2. Remove screws retaining duct to cowl side panel and sound baffle and remove duct.
3. Disconnect lead wire to blower motor.
4. Remove one screw from motor mounting plate, rotate motor mounting plate clockwise to unlock plate from case and remove motor and wheel assembly through opening in cowl side of panel. Reverse procedure to install.

1970-76 Continental

1. Remove hood.
2. Remove right hood hinge and right fender inner support brace as an assembly.
3. Disconnect blower motor air cooling tube from motor.
4. Disconnect motor lead wire from harness and ground wire from dash panel.
5. Disconnect rear section of right front fender panel apron from fender around wheel opening and remove two lower fender to cowl mounting screws.
6. Separate fender apron from fender wheel opening so that apron can be pushed downward away from blower motor.
7. Remove four blower motor plate screws. Move motor and wheel forward out of blower scroll and remove assembly through opening while applying pressure to fender apron to enlarge opening at hinge area. Reverse procedure to install.

1972-76 Mark IV

1. Remove the glove box for access.
2. Remove the recirculation air register and duct assembly from the blower assembly.
3. Remove the two screws that attach the blower lower housing to the dash panel.
4. Disconnect the white hose from the outside-recirc air door vacuum motor and remove the vacuum motor from the blower lower housing. It is held in place by two screws. Leave the motor actuator connected to the door crank arm.
5. Disconnect the orange blower motor lead wire from the harness connector, and disconnect the black motor ground wire.
6. Remove the six upper-to-lower blower housing flange screws.
7. Separate the blower lower housing and motor assembly from the upper housing and remove it from beneath the instrument panel.
8. Remove the blower motor and wheel assembly from the lower housing. It is held by four screws.
9. The upper flange of the recirc duct is retained to the blower upper housing with two S-clips that remained on the housing during removal. Be certain that the duct is properly installed in the two clips during reinstallation. Reverse procedure to install.

SEAT BELTS

Buzzer System—1972-73

The front seat belt warning system consists of a switch in each belt retractor, a sensor switch in the seat cushion on the passenger side, a reminder light and a warning buzzer.

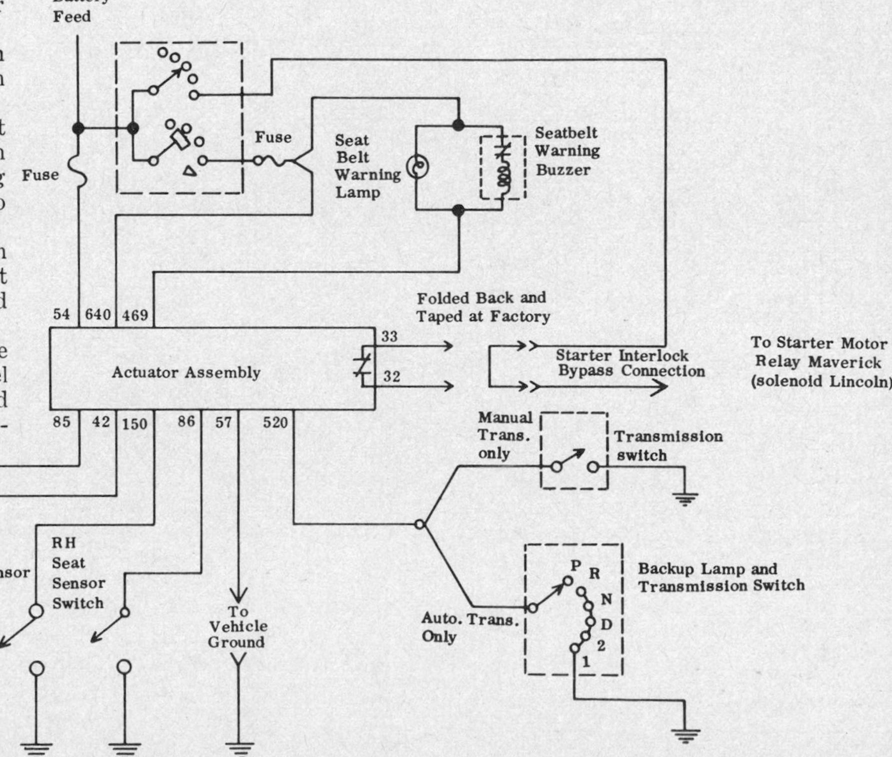

Late 1973 Lincolns have the 1974 seat belt/starter interlock system components and wiring. The interlock parts of the system are not connected, since only a light and buzzer warning system was required for 1973. (© Ford Motor Co)

The circuit wiring is routed through the ignition switch and transmission neutral safety switch on all models.

With the automatic transmission shift selector in a forward position on all models, the warning circuit (light and buzzer) is closed (activated) until the driver's seat belt is extended to open (de-activate) the circuit. The seat sensor on the passenger side reacts to weights in excess of 0-47 lbs. on the seat cushion and closes the warning circuit. Extending the passenger belt will open the circuit.

Seat Belt/Starter Interlock System —1974-75

Starting with 1974 models, a new starter interlock system is employed, consisting of a warning light, buzzer, seat sensors, switches in the outboard belt retractors, and an electronic logic module. The starter will not operate unless the driver and right front seat passenger sit on the seat and pull out their seat belts. Unless the driver or passenger has remained seated and buckled, the sequence must be repeated every time the engine is started. Leaving the belts pulled all the way out will also prevent the engine from being started as the belts must be retracted and buckled each time the engine is started.

The center seat belt is connected to the warning light and buzzer system, but not to the starter interlock. In the event of a starter interlock system failure or to permit the use of a remote starter switch when working under the hood, a starter interlock by-pass switch is located in the engine compartment, thereby eliminating the need to perform the buckling sequence.

NOTE: Each time the by-pass switch is operated the buckling sequence may be eliminated only once. The system may not be permanently by-passed.

Disabling the Seat Belt/ Starter Interlock

As of 29 October 1974, it is legal to disable the seat belt/starter interlock system. However the warning

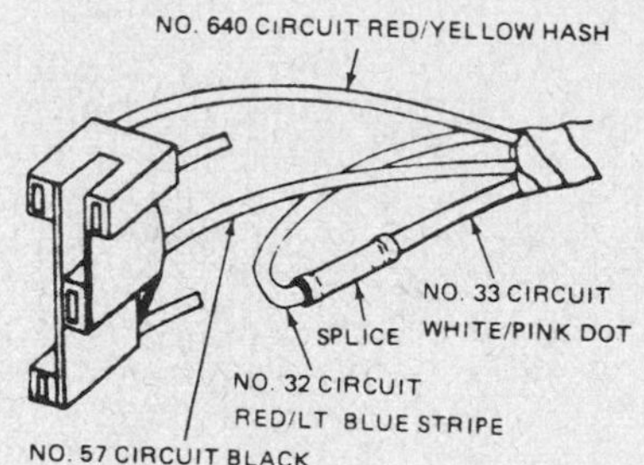

Cut and splice the seat belt/starter interlock wires as shown (© Ford Motor Co)

light portion of the system must be left operational.

1. Apply the parking brake and remove the ignition key.
2. Open the hood and locate the system emergency override switch and connector. Remove the connector.
3. Cut the white wire(s) with the pink dots (#33 circuit) and the red wire(s) with the light blue stripe (#32 circuit).
4. Splice the two (or four) wires together and tape the splice. Use a "butt" connector if available.

NOTE: Do not cut and splice the other connector wires. If the red/yellow hash wire is spliced to any of the other wires the car will start in gear.

6. Install the connector back on the override switch. Close the hood.
7. Apply the parking brakes, buckle the seat belt, and turn the key to the "ON" position. If the starter cranks in "ON" or any gear selected, the wrong wires have been cut and spliced. Repeat steps 3-6.
8. Unbuckle the belt and try to start the car. If the car doesn't start, repeat steps 3-6. If the car starts, everything is O.K
9. To stop the warning buzzer from operating, remove it from the connector. Tape the connector to the wiring harness so that it can't rattle.

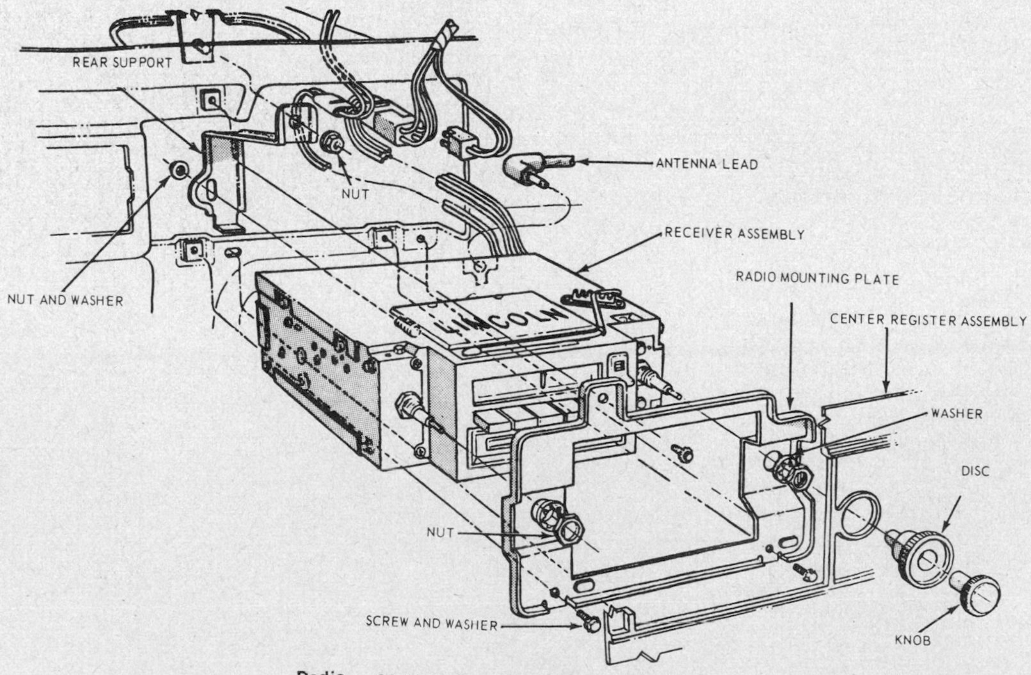

Radio —1970-76 Continental (© Ford Motor Co)

INDEX

Monza · Vega

YEAR IDENTIFICATION

1971-72

1973

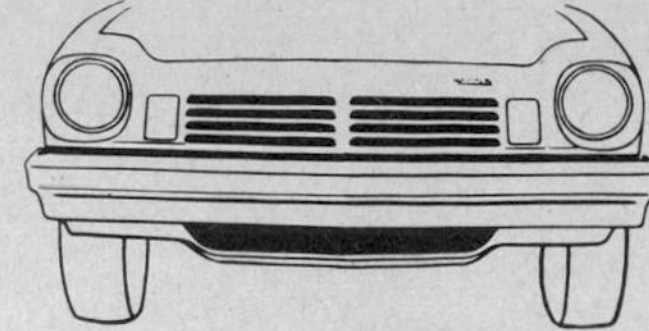
1974

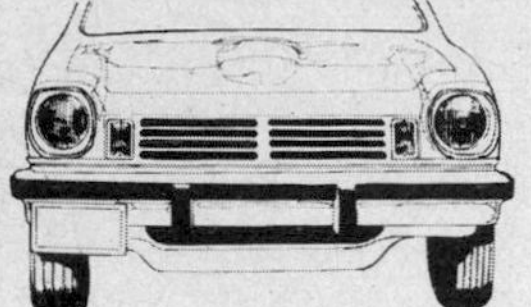
1975 Vega

1975 Monza 2 + 2

1975 Monza Town Coupe

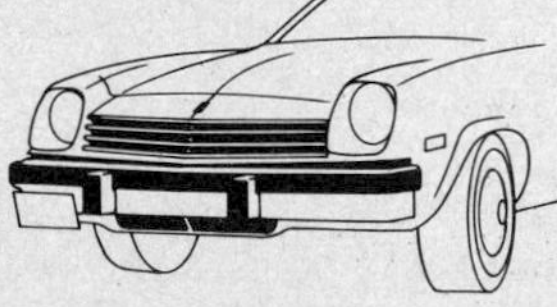
1976 Vega

1976 Monza 2 + 2

1976 Monza Town Coupe

FIRING ORDER

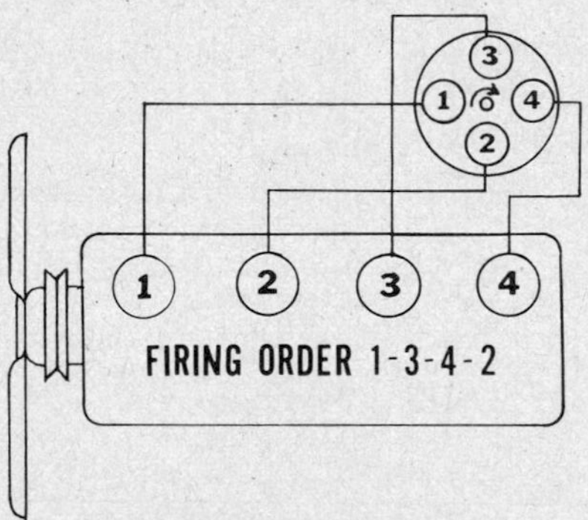

4 cylinder

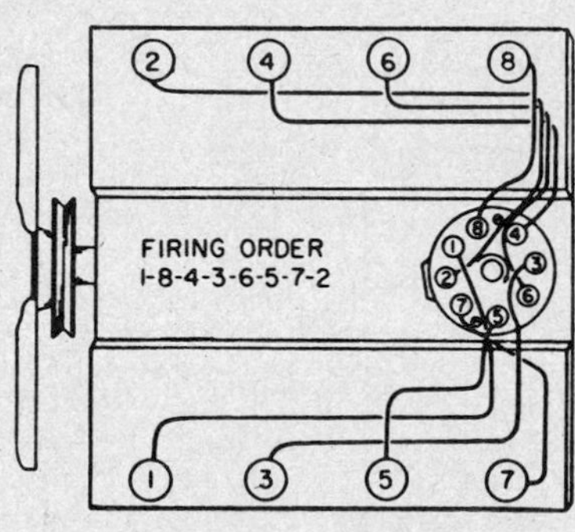

262, 305 and 350 V8

Model Identification

The vehicle serial number plate is found on top of the instrument panel and is visible through the left side of the windshield. The body number, trim code and paint number are located on the upper right side of the dash panel.

Engine Identification Number

The 4 cylinder engine identification number is located on a machined pad, on the right side of the cylinder block, above the starter motor.

The V8 engine number is located on a pad on the front right-hand side of the cylinder block.

GENERAL ENGINE SPECIFICATIONS

Year	Engine No. Cyl. Displacement (Cu. In.)	Carburetor Type	Horsepower @ rpm ■	Torque @ rpm (ft lbs) ■	Bore and Stroke (in.)	Compression Ratio	Oil Pressure @ 2000 rpm
'71	4-140	1 bbl	90 @ 4600	136 @ 2400	3.501 x 3.625	8.0:1	40
	4-140	2 bbl	110 @ 4800	138 @ 3200	3.50 x 3.625	8.0:1	40
'72	4-140	1 bbl	80 @ 4400	121 @ 2800	3.50 x 3.625	8.0:1	40
	4-140	2 bbl	90 @ 4800	121 @ 3200	3.50 x 3.625	8.0:1	40
'73	4-140	1 bbl	72 @ 4400	100 @ 2000	3.50 x 3.625	8.0:1	40
	4-140	2 bbl	85 @ 4800	115 @ 2400	3.50 x 3.625	8.0:1	40

GENERAL ENGINE SPECIFICATIONS

Year	Engine No. Cyl. Displacement Cu. In.	Carburetor Type	Horsepower @ rpm ■	Torque @ rpm (ft lbs) ■	Bore and Stroke (in.)	Compression Ratio	Oil Pressure @ 2000 rpm
'74	4-140	1 bbl	75 @ 4400	115 @ 2400	3.50 x 3.625	8.0:1	40
	4-140	2 bbl	85 @ 4400	122 @ 2400	3.50 x 3.625	8.0:1	40
'75-'76	4-140	1 bbl	75 @ 4400	115 @ 2400	3.50 x 3.625	8.0:1	40
	4-140	2 bbl	85 @ 4400①	122 @ 2400②	3.50 x 3.625	8.0:1	40
	4-122	EFI	110 @ 5600	107 @ 4800	3.501 x 3.160	8.5:1	40
	8-262	2 bbl	110 @ 3400	110 @ 1600	3.671 x 3.10	8.5:1	32-40
	8-305	2 bbl	N.A.	N.A.	3.74 x 3.48	8.5:1	32-40
	8-350	2 bbl	125 @ 3600	235 @ 2000	4.00 x 3.48	8.5:1	32-40

■ Beginning 1972, horsepower and torque are SAE net figures. They are measured at the rear of the transmission with all accessories installed and operating. Since the figures vary when a given engine is installed in different models, some are representative rather than exact.

EFI—Electronic Fuel Injection

① 80 @ 4400—Calif.

② 116 @ 2200—Calif.

TUNE-UP SPECIFICATIONS

When analyzing compression test results, look for uniformity among cylinders rather than specific pressures.

Year	ENGINE No. Cyl. Displacement (cu. In.)	ENGINE hp	SPARK PLUGS Type	SPARK PLUGS Gap (in.)	DISTRIBUTOR Point Dwell (deg)	DISTRIBUTOR Point Gap (in.)	IGNITION TIMING (deg) ▲ Man Trans	IGNITION TIMING (deg) ▲ ● Auto Trans	VALVES Intake Opens ■ (deg) ●	Fuel Pump Pressure (psi)	IDLE SPEED (rpm) ▲ Man Trans	IDLE SPEED (rpm) ▲ * Auto Trans
'71	4-140①	90	R42TS	.035	31-34	.019	6B	6B	22	3-4½	850/700	650/550
	4-140①	110	R42TS	.035	31-34	.019	6B	10B	25	3-4½	1200/700	650/550
'72	4-140①	80	R42TS	.035	31-34	.019	6B	6B(4B)	22(28)	3-4½	700	700②/550
	4-140①	90	R42TS	.035	31-34	.019	8B	8B	28	3-4½	700	700②/550
'73	4-140①	72	R42TS	.035	31-34	.019	8B	8B	22	3-4½	1000/450	750/450
	4-140①	85	R42TS	.035	31-34	.019	10B	12B	28	3-4½	1200/450	750②/450
'74	4-140①	75	R42TS	.035	31-34	.019	10B(8B)	12B(8B)	22	3-4½	1000/700	750/550
	4-140①	85	R42TS	.035	31-34	.019	10B(8B)	12B(8B)	28	3-4½	1200/700	750②/500
'75	4-122③	All	R43TSX	0.060	Electronic		12B	—	38	40	800	—
	4-140 1 bbl①	All	R-43TSX	0.060	Electronic		8B	10B	22	3-4½	1200/700	700/550
	4-140 2 bbl①	All	R-43TSX	0.060	Electronic		10B	12B	28	3-4½	1200/700	750/600
	8-262	All	R-44TX	0.060	Electronic		8B	8B	26	7-8½	800	600
	8-350	All	R44TX	0.060	Electronic		6B	6B	28	7-8½	900	600
'76	4-122③	All	R-43TS	.035	Electronic		—	—	38	40		
	4-140 1 bbl	All	R-43TS	.035	Electronic		—	—	34	3-4½	1200④/750	750/550
	4-140 2 bbl	All	R-43TS	.035	Electronic		—	—	34	3-4½	700(1000④/700)	750/600
	8-262	All	R-45TS	.045	Electronic		—	—	26	3-4½	600	600
	8-305, 350	All	See Underhood Specifications Sticker									

▲ See text for procedure

● Figure in parentheses indicates California engine

■ All figures Before Top Dead Center

* Where two figures are separated by a slash, the first figure is for idle speed with solenoid connected, while the second is for idle speed with solenoid disconnected

① Adjust mechanical valve lifter clearance to .015 in. for intake, and to .030 in. for exhaust with engine cold

② For air-conditioned vehicles, adjust idle speed to 800 rpm with A/C on

③ Adjust valve clearance to 0.014 in. (intake and exhaust) with engine cold

④ In Neutral

CAPACITIES

Year	Engine No. Cyl. Displacement (cu. in.)	Engine Crankcase Add 1 Qt For New Filter	Transmission Pts To Refill After Draining: Manual 3-Speed	Manual 4-Speed	Automatic •	Drive Axle (pts)	Gasoline Tank (gals)	Cooling System (qts): With Heater	With A/C
'71	4-140	3	2.4	3	6	2.3	11	6.5	6.5
'72	4-140	3	2.4	3	6①	2.8	11	6.5	6.5
'73	4-140	3	3	3	6②	2.8	11	8.6	9.0
'74	4-140	3	3	3	8	2.8	16	8.6	9.0
'75-'76	4-140, 4-122	3	3	3③	8	2.8	16	8.0	8.0
	8-262	4	—	3	8	2.8	18½	18	18
	8-305, 8-350	4	—	3	8	2.8	18½	18	18

- • Specifications do not include torque converter
- ① 5 pts with Turbo Hydra-Matic
- ② 8 pts with Turbo Hydra-Matic
- — Not Applicable
- ③ 3 pts for 5 speed

VALVE SPECIFICATIONS

Year	Engine No. Cyl. Displacement (cu in.)	Seat Angle (deg)	Face Angle (deg)	Spring Test Pressure (lbs @ in.)	Spring Installed Height (in.)	Stem to Guide Clearance (in.): Intake	Exhaust	Stem Diameter (in.): Intake	Exhaust
'71	4-140	46	45	75 @ 1.75	1 3/4	.0010-.0027	.0010-.0027	.3414	.3414
'72	4-140	46	45	75 @ 1.75	1 3/4	.0010-.0027	.0010-.0027	.3414	.3414
'73	4-140	46	45	75 @ 1.75	1 3/4	.0010-.0027	.0010-.0027	.3414	.3414
'74	4-140	46	45	75 @ 1.75	1 3/4	.0010-.0027	.0010-.0027	.3414	.3414
'75-'76	4-140	46	45	75 @ 1.75	1 3/4	.0010-.0027	.0010-.0027	.3414	.3414
	4-122	46	45	45 @ 1.3	1.3	.0010-.0027	.0010-.0027	.2791	.2791
	8-262	46	45	80 @ 1.70①	1.70②	.0010-.0027	.0010-.0027	.3414	.3414
	8-305	46	45	80 @ 1.70①	1.70②	.0010-.0027	.0010-.0027	.3414	.3414
	8-350	46	45	80 @ 1.70①	1.70②	.0010-.0027	.0010-.0027	.3414	.3414

① Exhaust—80 @ 1.61
② Exhaust—1.61

TORQUE SPECIFICATIONS

All readings in ft lbs

Year	Engine No. Cyl. Displacement (cu in.)	Cylinder Head Bolts	Rod Bearing Bolts	Main Bearing Bolts	Crankshaft Pulley Bolt	Flywheel to Crankshaft Bolts	Manifold: Intake	Exhaust
'71-'76	4-140	60	35	65	80	60	30	30
'75-'76	8-262	65	45	70	60	60	30	20①
'76	8-305	65	45	75	60	60	30	20①
'75-'76	8-350	65	45	75	60	60	30	20①

① Inside bolts—30 ft. lbs

CRANKSHAFT AND CONNECTING ROD SPECIFICATIONS

All measurements are given in inches

Year	Engine No. Cyl. Displacement (cu in.)	CRANKSHAFT Main Brg. Journal Dia	Main Brg. Oil Clearance	Shaft End-Play	Thrust on No.	CONNECTING ROD Journal Diameter	Oil Clearance	Side Clearance
'71-'72	4-140	2.2983-2.2993	.0029-.0003	.002-.008	4	1.999-2.000	.0007-.0027①	.0085-.0135
'73-'74	4-140	2.2983-2.2993	.0003-.0020②	.002-.007	4	1.999-2.000	.0007-.0038①	.0085-.0135
'75-'76	4-122	2.3004	⑤	.002-.008	4	1.999-2.000	.0007-.0027	.0009-.0013
	4-140	2.3004	.0003-.0029	.002-.008	4	1.999-2.000	.0007-.0027	.0009-.0013
	8-262	2.4502③	④	.002-.007	5	2.098-2.099	.0013-.0035	.008-.014
	8-305	2.4502③	④	.002-.007	5	2.098-2.099	.0013-.0035	.008-.014
	8-350	2.4502③	④	.002-.007	5	2.098-2.099	.0013-.0035	.006-.016

① Maximum service clearance = .004 in.
② .0003-.0027 for No. 2, 3, 4, 5
③ No. 5—2.4508 in.
④ No. 1—.0008-.0020 in.
No. 2, 3, 4—.0011-.0023 in.
No. 5—.0017-.0033 in.
⑤ No. 1, 2, 3, 5—.0008-.0034
No. 4—.002-.0029

RING GAP

All measurements are given in inches

Year	Engine	Top Compression	Bottom Compression
'71-'76	4-140, 4-122	.015-.025	.009-.019
'75-'76	8-262, 8-350	.010-.020	.010-.020
'76	8-305	.010-.020	.010-.020

Year	Engine	Oil Control
'71-'76	4,140, 4-122	.010-.030
'75-'76	8-262	.010-.025
'75-'76	8-350	.015-.055
'76	8-305	.015-.025

RING SIDE CLEARANCE

All measurements are given in inches

Year	Engine	Top Compression	Bottom Compression
'71-'76	4-140	.0012-.0027	.0012-.0027
'75-'76	8-262	.0012-.0032	.0012-.0032
'75-'76	8-350	.0012-.0032	.0012-.0027
'76	8-305	.0012-.0032	.0012-.0027

Year	Engine	Oil Control
'71-'76	4-140	.000-.005
'75-'76	8-262	.002-.007
'75-'76	8-350	.000-.005
'76	8-305	.002-.007

PISTON CLEARANCE

Year	Engine	Piston to Bore Clearance (in.)
'75-'76	4-122	.0020-.0030②
'71-'76	4-140	.0018-.0028①
'75-'76	8-262	.0008-.0018②
'75-'76	8-350	.0007-.0017
'76	8-305	.0008-.0018②

① Measured 1.50 in. from top of piston
② Measured 1.75 in. from top of piston

ALTERNATOR AND REGULATOR SPECIFICATIONS

	ALTERNATOR			REGULATOR						
					Field Relay			Regulator		
Year	Part No. or Manufacturer	Field Current @ 12 V	Output (amps)	Part No. or Manufacturer	Air Gap (in.)	Point Gap (in.)	Volts to Close	Air Gap (in.)	Point Gap (in.)	Volts @ 75°
'71-'76	1100545	4-4.5	32	—	Integral	—	—	—	—	13.8-14.8
	1100559	4-4.5	32	—	Integral	—	—	—	—	13.8-14.8
	1102854	4-4.5	37	—	Integral	—	—	—	—	13.8-14.8
	1100546	4-4.5	55	—	Integral	—	—	—	—	13.8-14.8
	1100560	4-4.5	55	—	Integral	—	—	—	—	13.8-14.8
	1100950	4-4.5	42	—	Integral	—	—	—	—	13.8-14.8
	1102471	4-4.5	42	—	Integral	—	—	—	—	13.8-14.8
	1102854	4-4.5	37	—	Integral	—	—	—	—	13.8-14.8

— Not applicable

BATTERY AND STARTER SPECIFICATIONS

		BATTERY			STARTER						
					Lock Test			No-Load Test			
Year	Engine (No. Cyl.) Displacement (cu in.)	Ampere Hour Capacity	Volts	Terminal Grounded	Amps	Volts	Torque (ft lbs)	Amps	Volts	RPM	Brush Spring Tension (oz)
'71-'73	4-140	45	12	Neg.	Not Recommended			50-75	9	6,500-10,000	—
'74-'76 (Vega)	4-140, 4-122	①	12	Neg.	Not Recommended			50-75	9	6,500-10,000	—
'75-'76	8-262	③	12	Neg.	Not Recommended			55-80	9	3,500-6,000	—
'75-'76 (Monza)	4-140	②	12	Neg.	Not Recommended			50-75	9	6,500-10,000	—
'75-'76	8-350	③	12	Neg.	Not Recommended			55-80	9	3,500-6,000	—
'76	8-305	③	12	Neg.	Not Recommended			55-80	9	3,500-6,000	—

① 2300 watts cranking power @ 0°F.; 2600 watts cranking power @ 0°F. w/H.D. battery (80 amp.)
② 2500 watts @ 0°F.
③ 3200 watts @ 0°F.

BRAKE SPECIFICATIONS

All measurements are given in inches

		MASTER CYLINDER		WHEEL CYLINDER			BRAKE DISC OR DRUM DIAMETER		
				Front			Front		
Year	Model	Disc	Drum	Disc	Drum	Rear	Disc	Drum	Rear
'71-'75	All	.75	—	1.875	—	.75	9.88	—	9.0
'76	Vega	.75	—	1.875	—	.688	9.88	—	9.0
	Monza	.88	—	2.500	—	.688	9.74	—	9.5

— Not applicable

WHEEL ALIGNMENT SPECIFICATIONS

		CASTER		CAMBER				WHEEL PIVOT RATIO (deg)	
Year	Model	Range (deg)	Pref Setting (deg)	Range (deg)	Pref Setting (deg)	Toe-in (in.)	Steering Axis Inclin. (deg)	Inner Wheel	Outer Wheel
'71-'73	All	1¼N to ¼N	¾N	¼N to ¾P	¼P	3/16 to 5/16	8.55	—	—
'74	All	1¾N to ¼P	¾N	¾N to 1¼P	¼P	3/16 to 5/16	8.55	—	—
'75-'76	All	1¾N to ¼P	¾N	¾N to 1½P	½P	3/16 to 5/16	8.55	—	—

— Not specified

CHARGING SYSTEM

A 10-SI Series Delcotron alternator is used. This unit features a non-adjustable, integral solid-state regulator mounted inside the slipring end frame. Testing and overhaul procedures for the integrated charging system are found in the Unit Repair Section.

Caution Observe the following precautions when servicing a Delcotron:

1. When installing a battery, be certain that the ground polarity of the battery and the generator and regulator are matched correctly.
2. Make sure that the correct terminals are connected when jumping the battery.
3. When charging the battery, make sure that the correct leads are connected to the battery terminals.
4. Never operate the generator on an open circuit. Be sure all connections in the circuit are tight.
5. Do not short across or ground any of the terminals on the generator or regulator.
6. Never polarize an AC system.
7. Do not use test lamps of more than 12 V for checking diode continuity.
8. Avoid long soldering times when replacing diodes or transistors; prolonged heat will damage them.
9. Always disconnect the battery ground terminal when servicing an AC system. This will prevent accidentally reversing polarity.

Alternator R & R

1. Disconnect the battery.
2. Disconnect the alternator wiring.
3. Remove the alternator brace bolt and V-belt.
4. Remove the pivot mount bolt and the alternator.
5. Installation is the reverse of the removal procedure. Adjust the belt tension.

STARTING SYSTEM

The starter is a solenoid actuated Delco-Remy unit similar to other Chevrolet starters used in the past except that the 1975 starter has no "R" terminal. The HEI system does not use the solenoid to coil wire. See the Unit Repair Section for testing and overhaul procedures.

Starter R & R

1. Disconnect the battery ground cable and all wiring at the solenoid terminals. Install each nut on the terminal from which it was removed, as these nuts are not interchangeable.
2. Loosen the front starter bracket and remove the two mounting bolts.
3. Remove the front bracket bolt and rotate the bracket out of the way.
4. Remove the starter from the car, lowering the front end first.
5. To install, reverse the removal procedure. Tighten the mounting bolts, and then install the brace.

IGNITION SYSTEM

The 140 cu in. distributor is mounted in the cylinder head at the rear of the engine and is driven by the camshaft. An unusual feature of this unit is a cup, mounted at the lower end of the driveshaft. This cup is under full engine oil pressure when the engine is running, acting as a vibration damper to reduce driveshaft oscillations. If this cup is not installed after the distributor has been disassembled, engine oil pressure will be lost.

A replaceable cam lubricator is installed, which should be changed each time the points are replaced.

The Cosworth-Vega distributor is mounted in its own housing which is bolted to the right side of the cylinder head directly behind the belt cover. The distributor is a magnetic pulse unit without conventional breaker points. Switching is controlled by an external, transistorized pulse amplifier. Operation and troubleshooting for this unit can be found in the Electronic Ignition chapter of the Unit Repair section.

A short belt driven off the right camshaft gear turns a shaft which drives the distributor through gears. The distributor additionally functions as an engine speed sensor for input to the electronic fuel injection.

The V8 distributor is mounted at the rear of the engine, gear driven off the camshaft.

Electronic ignition is standard equipment on all 1975 and later models, eliminating the need for point replacement.

Two types of HEI distributor are used. V8 distributors combine all ignition components in one unit. The coil is in the distributor cap and connects directly to the rotor. The 6-cylinder distributor has an externally mounted coil. Both units operate in the same manner, except that the module and pick-up coil replace the conventional breaker points. The module automatically controls the dwell, stretching it with increased engine speed. The system also has a longer spark duration due to the greater amount of energy stored in the primary coil. This is necessary to fire leaner mixtures.

The centrifugal and vacuum advance mechanisms are basically the same type of unit as on a conventional ignition distributor.

The electronic module is serviced by complete replacement.

WARNING: *Do not remove the spark plug wires with the engine running. Severe shock could result.*

Timing Light Connections—HEI System

Timing light connections should be made in parallel using an adaptor at the distributor No. 1 terminal.

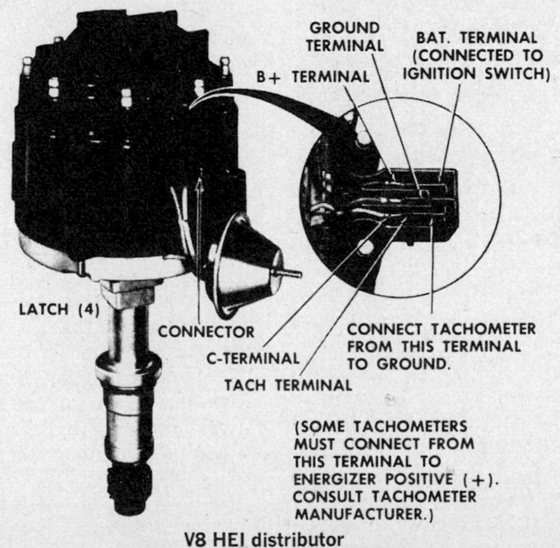

V8 HEI distributor
(© Chevrolet Div., G.M. Corp)

Tachometer Connections—HEI System

There is a "tach" terminal on the V8 distributor cap and on the 4 cylinder coil. Connect the tachometer to this terminal and ground. Follow the tachometer manufacturers instructions.

Caution *Grounding the tach terminal could damage the HEI ignition module.*

Distributor Removal

1. Release the cap hold-down screws and remove the cap. On electronic ignition, disconnect the wiring harness connectors at the side of the cap and remove the cap.
2. Disconnect the vacuum line and the primary lead.
3. Mark the distributor housing and the engine in line with the rotor centerline with chalk.
4. Remove the hold-down clamp and distributor.

NOTE: avoid turning the engine while the distributor is removed.

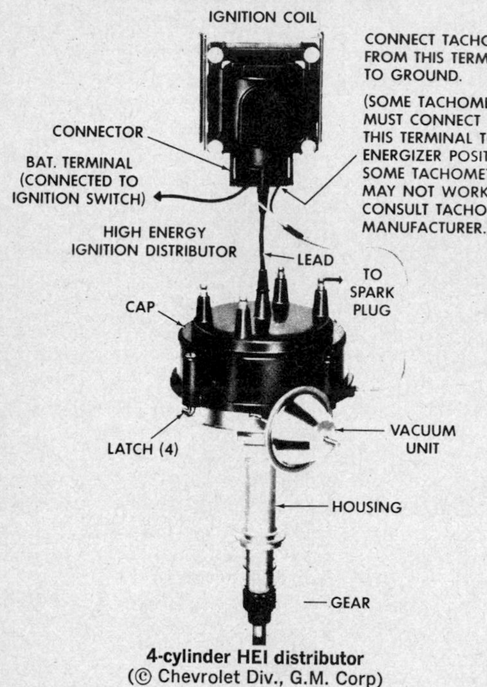

4-cylinder HEI distributor
(© Chevrolet Div., G.M. Corp)

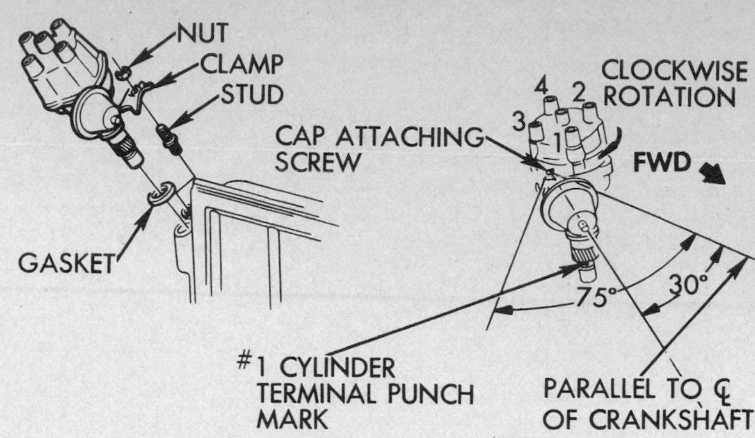

Distributor alignment—4 cylinder (© Chevrolet Div., G.M. Corp)

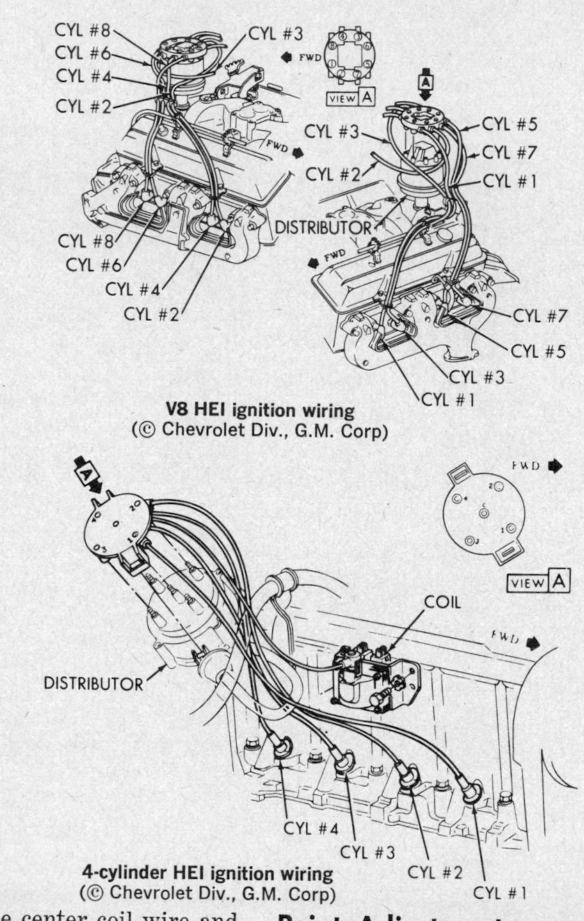

V8 HEI ignition wiring
(© Chevrolet Div., G.M. Corp)

4-cylinder HEI ignition wiring
(© Chevrolet Div., G.M. Corp)

Distributor Installation

1. Turn the rotor approximately ⅛ turn clockwise past the alignment mark.
2. Push the distributor into position, moving the rotor to mesh the gears.
3. Install the clamp bolt.
4. Connect the vacuum line and the primary lead.
5. Install the cap and, if necessary, adjust the timing.

Installation—Engine Disturbed

1. Remove No. 1 spark plug and place a finger over the plug hole. Remove the center coil wire and crank the engine until compression is felt in No. 1 cylinder. Rotate the engine until the timing pointer is aligned with the proper mark.
2. Install the distributor with the vacuum advance pointing toward the front of the engine and the punchmarks on the drive gear in line with the No. 1 cap tower.
3. Install the hold-down clamp and rotate the distributor slightly so that the points are just open. Tighten the clamp bolt.
4. Install the rotor, cap and vacuum line.
5. Connect the primary lead.
6. Check and adjust the ignition timing.

Point Adjustment

Inspect the points for alignment and pitting. If necessary, clean the points with a point file. All the roughness need not be removed. To set the gap, rotate the crankshaft until one of the distributor cam lobes is directly opposite the rubbing block of the point arm (gap at maximum separation). Measure the gap, and if it is not within specifications, loosen the contact point assembly attaching screw and move the assembly to obtain the specified gap. This is done by inserting a screwdriver in the slot formed by the contact points and the breaker plate and levering the points as required. Tighten the attaching screw.

Check the dwell angle. Check the ignition timing, adjusting it if necessary.

Ignition Timing

The timing marks are on a plate mounted on the front of the block and the timing notch is on the crankshaft pulley.

Timing is set as follows:

1. Bring the engine to normal operating temperature, shut the engine off, and connect a timing light to no. 1 spark plug or no. 1 plug tower on HEI. Clean the timing plate and mark the notch in the pulley with chalk.
2. Disconnect and plug the vacuum line to the distributor.
3. On 4-cylinder engines disconnect the fuel tank line from the evaporative emission canister.
4. If equipped, disconnect the electrical lead from the idle stop solenoid on the carburetor.
5. Start the engine and adjust the carburetor idle screw for an idle speed of 700 rpm or less for 1971-72 models, 1000 rpm or less for 1973-75 4-cylinder models.

NOTE: The idle solenoid is turned to adjust the idle speed on single barrel carburetor models.

6. Aim the timing light at the timing marks. If the notch does not align with the correct value on the scale, loosen the distributor clamp locknut and slowly turn the distributor to adjust.
7. Tighten the clamp locknut. Adjust the carburetor idle speed screw to give the specified idle speed with the solenoid disconnected.
8. Reconnect the idle stop solenoid lead. Increase the engine speed to allow the solenoid to extend and then adjust the solenoid plunger screw to obtain the idle speed specified with the solenoid connected.
9. Shut the engine off and connect the vacuum and evaporative emission line.

FUEL SYSTEM

Two types of carburetors are used through 1972. Base engines are equipped with a Rochester MV one barrel carburetor. While the base Monza 2 + 2 engine uses a Holley, the optional engine is equipped with a Rochester 2GV two barrel carburetor. The MV one barrel continues to be used on the base engine beginning 1973, but the optional engine is equipped with a Holley 5210-C two barrel. The 262 V8 in the Monza 2 + 2 uses a Rochester 2 bbl. 1973-75 carburetors are all equipped with a tube takeoff for vacuum supply to the EGR valve. There are variations on each carburetor for manual and automatic transmission applications. Each has an integral fuel filter.

The electric fuel pump is an integral part of the fuel tank unit assembly, which includes the fuel gauge metering unit. The fuel pump is energized by the ignition switch when the key is in the start or on position. After the engine starts, the pump receives current through the oil pressure safety switch as long as there is approximately 2 psi oil pressure.

The Cosworth Vega uses electronic fuel injection with an additional inline electric fuel pump.

Fuel Pump R & R (Integral Unit)

1. Disconnect the battery ground cable and siphon the fuel from the tank.
2. Disconnect the gauge sending-unit and pump wires at the rear harness connector.
3. Raise the car. Disconnect the fuel line at the gauge connection.
4. On 1971 models, disconnect the tank vent lines to the vapor separator, which is mounted on the top of the tank. On later models, disconnect the tank vent line to the vapor separator, which is mounted in the tank.
5. Disconnect the gauge wire ground screw from the floorpan.
6. Remove the tank strap bolts and, very carefully, lower the tank.
7. Use the special wrench, or a suitable substitute, to unscrew the retaining cam ring. Do not strike any part of the tank with a metal tool, such as a hammer; there is a danger of explosion from sparks.
8. Remove the gauge sending-unit and fuel pump assembly.
9. Remove the flat wire conductor from the plastic clip on the fuel tube.
10. While squeezing the clamp, pull the pump straight back ½ in. for access to the terminals. Remove the two nuts, lockwashers, and wires from the pump.
11. Squeeze the clamp and pull the pump straight back to completely remove it from the sending unit.

Caution Be careful not to bend the circular support bracket.

12. Slide the replacement pump through the circular support bracket until it rests against the rubber coupling. Be sure that the rubber isolator and saran strainer, supplied in the service package, are attached to the pump.
13. Attach the two pump terminals, using lockwashers and nuts. Be sure that the flat conductor is attached to the terminal farthest away from the float arm.
14. Squeeze the clamp and push the pump into the rubber coupling.
15. Replace the flat wire conductor in the plastic clip on the fuel tube.
16. Install the pump and gauge unit into the tank opening. Tighten the cam ring.
17. Install the fuel tank using a reverse of the removal procedure.

Fuel Filter R & R

Both paper and bronze filters are used on all models.

1. Disconnect the fuel line at the intake fuel filter nut on the carburetor.
2. Remove the intake fuel filter nut.
3. Remove the filter element and spring.
4. Install the element spring and element. Bronze filters are installed with the conical section facing out and with a gasket between the filter element and the fuel intake nut.
5. Install the nut using a new gasket and tighten. Do not overtighten this nut, as it is easily stripped.
6. Install fuel line and tighten the connector.

Carburetor Adjustments

The only carburetor adjustment given here is for idle speed. The idle mixture screw(s) is equipped with a sealed limiter cap(s). Mixture should not be adjusted, except after carburetor overhaul or repair, since it is factory-set to ensure the lowest possible level of exhaust emissions.

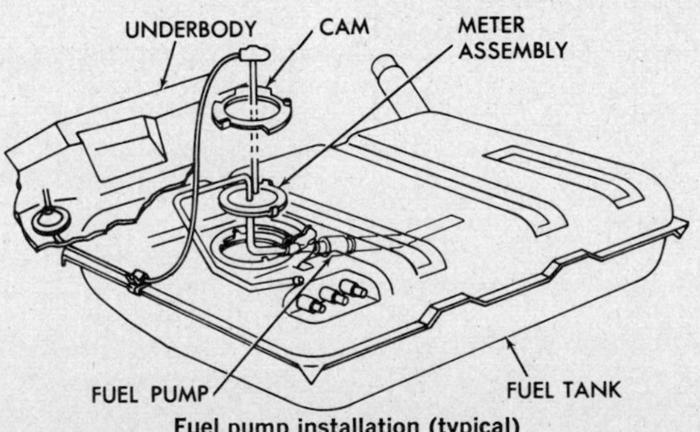

Fuel pump installation (typical)
(© Chevrolet Div., G.M. Corp)

Idle stop solenoid adjustment
(© Chevrolet Div., G.M. Corp)

1971-72

1. The engine must be at normal operating temperature and the air cleaner in place. Air conditioning should be on in 1971 models; off in later models.
2. Detach the fuel tank line from the top of the evaporative emission canister.
3. Disconnect the distributor vacuum line and plug the carburetor hose.
4. Disconnect the electrical connector at the idle stop solenoid on the carburetor.
5. Start the engine and adjust the carburetor idle speed screw to obtain the idle speed specified in the "Tune-Up Specifications Chart" (for speed with the solenoid disconnected).
6. Reconnect the idle stop solenoid electrical lead. Speed up the engine to allow the solenoid plunger to extend, then adjust the solenoid plunger screw to obtain the idle speed specified in the "Tune-Up Specifications Chart" (for speed with the solenoid connected).
7. Stop the engine and reconnect the vacuum line and the evaporative emission canister line.

1973-74

Follow steps 1 through 4 of the 1971-72 procedure, then proceed as follows.

Rochester MV 1-bbl

1. Start the engine and, using a 1/8 in. allen wrench, adjust the idle speed to the figure given in the "Tune-Up Specifications Chart" (for speed with the solenoid disconnected).
2. Check the dwell and ignition timing. Check the idle speed again.
3. Reconnect the electrical wire to the solenoid.
4. Adjust the idle speed (for speed with solenoid connected) by turning the body of the solenoid itself.

Holley 5210-C 2-bbl

1. Start the engine and adjust the idle speed screw for the speed listed in the "Tune-Up Specifications Chart" (speed with solenoid disconnected).
2. Check the dwell and ignition timing. Check the idle speed again.
3. Reconnect the electrical wire to the solenoid.
4. Adjust the screw on the throttle lever (not the same screw as step 1). Set the idle speed to the figure given in the "Tune-Up Specifications Chart" (for speed with the solenoid connected).

1975-76
All Carburetors

1. The engine should be at normal operating temperature, air cleaner ON, choke open and air conditioner OFF.
2. Set the parking brake.
3. Disconnect the fuel tank hose from the vapor canister.
4. Disconnect and plug the vacuum hose. Check and adjust the timing. Reconnect the vacuum hose on Rochester 1MV and 2GC carburetors.
5. Disconnect the electrical connector at the idle stop solenoid.
6. Place automatic transmissions in Drive and manual transmissions in Neutral. On Rochester 1MV carburetors, turn the hex screw in the end of the solenoid body with a 1/8 in. allen wrench to set the low idle speed. On Holley 5210-C and Rochester 2GC models set the low idle speed with the idle screw.
7. Reconnect the electrical connector and crack the throttle slightly.
8. Turn the solenoid in or out to set the curb idle speed.
9. Reconnect the vapor line to the canister.

Throttle Linkage Adjustment

The throttle linkage is the cable type, and is not adjustable. The throttle linkage should be checked for correct operation and binding. Have an assistant hold the accelerator pedal to the floor and check to see that the throttle valves are wide-open.

COOLING SYSTEM

Engine cooling is of conventional design and utilizes an impeller type water pump to circulate the coolant. The system is pressurized and utilizes a thermostat to maintain operating temperature. The intake manifold is water heated to provide an even intake temperature. Only early 1971 models have an engine block-drain plug. All 1971 models and models built after March 1973 have a radiator drain petcock. The 1972 models have neither a block drain plug nor a radiator petcock. To drain the cooling system on these models, either the lower radiator hose must be removed or the coolant must be siphoned out.

There are two radiators: a standard type and a larger heavy duty radiator equipped with a fan shroud.

Radiator R & R

1. Drain the radiator.
2. On models with the heavy duty radiator, remove the fan shroud as described below.
3. Disconnect the intake and outlet hoses.
4. Remove the two screws which secure the fan guard to the radiator support, then remove the support and the two radiator pads.

NOTE: on vehicles with the heavy duty radiator, remove the two upper brackets (instead of the single support).

5. Lift the radiator up and out of the lower brackets.
6. To install, reverse the removal procedure.

Fan Shroud R & R

1. Remove the two screws which secure the shroud to the upper radiator brackets.
2. Remove the screw which holds the two halves of the shroud together at the lower left-hand corner.
3. Remove the left and right sections of the shroud from the clips at the bottom of the radiator.
4. To install, reverse the above procedure.

Water Pump R & R

4 Cylinder

The pump bearings are permanently lubricated during manufacture and do not require periodic maintenance other than keeping the air vent (top of housing) and drain holes (bottom of housing) free of dirt and grease.

The pump components cannot be serviced separately and, in the event of pump failure, the complete assembly must be replaced as a unit, as follows:

1. Raise the hood and install a bolt through the hood hold-open link. tightening the bolts to 20 ft. lbs.
2. Disconnect the negative battery cable.
3. Remove the fan and spacer.

Caution No attempt should be made to repair a bent or damaged fan. The fan assembly must be in proper balance and an improperly balanced fan may cause extensive damage.

4. Loosen, but do not remove, the two lower timing belt cover retaining screws. The holes in the cover are slotted so that the cover is easily removed.
5. Remove the two upper timing belt cover retaining screws and remove the cover.
6. Drain the coolant.
7. Loosen the water pump bolts to relieve the tension on the timing belt.
8. Remove the hoses from the water pump.
9. Remove the water pump bolts, pump and gasket.
10. Thoroughly clean the old gasket material from the pump and block.
11. To install, position the water pump on the block using a new gasket and loosely install the water pump bolts. Make sure that the V grooves of the belt are aligned with the grooves in the water pump.

NOTE: use an anti-seize compound on the water pump bolt threads.

12. A special tool is available to adjust the timing belt. It fits into the round hole in the square lug to the upper right (facing) of the water pump and bears against the pump housing midway between the bolt holes. If this tool is available, apply 15 ft lbs of torque against the water pump (and belt). If the tool is not available, apply a force to the pump in a similar manner. Tighten the pump bolts to 15 ft lbs.
13. Install the radiator and heater hoses to the pump.
14. Install the timing belt cover, lowering the cover lower screw slots over the screws. Loosely tighten the screws against the cover.
15. Install the two upper timing cover screws, then tighten the upper and lower screws to 50 in. lbs.
16. Install the fan spacer and fan, tightening the bolts to 20 ft lbs.
17. Fill the cooling system, connect the battery negative cable, start the engine and check for leaks.
18. Remove the bolt from the hood hold-open link and close the hood.

V8

1. Drain the coolant from the radiator.
2. Loosen the fan pulley bolts.
3. If necessary, remove the alternator with the drive belt and brackets.
4. If necessary, remove the air pump with the drive belt and brackets.
5. Disconnect the lower radiator hose and the heater hose at the water pump.
6. Remove the fan and pulley.
7. Remove the pump-to-cylinder block and power steering-to-pump bolts and remove the water pump and old gasket.
8. Installation is the reverse of removal. Use a new gasket coated with sealer. Adjust the alternator and air pump drive belt tension. Fill the cooling system, run the engine and check for leaks.

Thermostat R & R

The thermostat is located in a housing at the cylinder head water outlet adjacent to the intake manifold. On V8 engines, the thermostat is in the water outlet housing in the front of the intake manifold.

4 Cylinder

1. Drain the cooling system.
2. Disconnect the upper radiator hose at the engine.
3. If the alternator is attached to the water outlet, loosen the swivel bolt attachment and move it out of the way.
4. Unbolt the housing and remove the housing, gasket, and thermostat.
5. Replace the thermostat and housing, using a new gasket.
6. Install the alternator and adjust the drive belt. The adjustment procedure is outlined further on in this section.
7. Replace the radiator hose, fill the cooling system, start the engine, and check for leaks.

V8

1. Drain the coolant to a level below that of the water outlet housing.
2. Remove the radiator upper hose.
3. Remove the housing bolts and remove the water outlet housing and gasket.
4. Remove the thermostat.
5. Installation is the reverse of removal. Use a new gasket.

EMISSION CONTROLS

Positive Crankcase Ventilation

All models use the Positive Crankcase Ventilation System (PCV).

Some unburned fuel and combustion products leak past the rings during combustion. These gases travel into the crankcase where, if they are not removed, they will combine with the oil to form sludge and also build excessive pressure inside the crankcase. The PCV system removes these gases from the crankcase and routes them to the intake manifold where they are combined with the raw air fuel mixture and reburned in the combustion chamber.

The crankcase gases are drawn from the crankcase by intake manifold vacuum. There is a PCV valve in the line between the crankcase and the intake manifold which regulates the flow of the gases.

Evaporative Emission Control

The Evaporative Emission Control system (EEC) is used on all 1971–76 models. This system limits the amount of gasoline vapor discharged into the air from the gas tank and carburetor. The fuel tank has a non-vented cap. As vapors are generated in the fuel tank, they flow through a liquid vapor separator to a canister where they are stored. Vapors generated by the carburetor after the engine is turned off are also routed to this canister. From the canister, the vapors are routed back to the carburetor where they are burned when the engine is started.

Controlled Combustion System

The Controlled Combustion System (CCS) is used on all 1971-76 models. Essentially the CCS increases combustion efficiency through carburetor and distributor calibrations and by increasing engine operating temperatures.

Carburetors are calibrated leaner and initial ignition timing is retarded. The vacuum advance curve is also altered to decrease emissions.

The CCS also incorporates a higher engine operation temperature. A 195° thermostat is used. Engines that run hotter provide more complete vaporation of fuel and reduce quench area in the combustion chamber. Quench area is the relatively cool area near the cylinder wall and combustion chamber surfaces. Fuel in these areas does not burn properly because of the lower temperatures. This incomplete burning increases emissions.

The CCS uses a thermostatically controlled air cleaner called the Auto-Therm air cleaner. It is designed to keep the temperature of the air entering the carburetor at approximately 100°F. This allows the lean carburetor to work properly, minimizes carburetor icing, and improves engine warm-up characteristics. A sensor unit located on the clean air side of the air filter senses the temperature of the air passing over it and regulates the vacuum supplied to a vacuum diaphragm in the inlet tube of the air cleaner. The colder the air, the greater the amount of vacuum supplied to the vacuum diaphragm. The vacuum diaphragm, depending on the vacuum supplied to it, opens or closes a damper door in the inlet tube of the air cleaner. If the door is open it allows air from the engine compartment to go to the carburetor. If the door is closed, air flows from the heat stove located on the exhaust manifold into the carburetor. In this way, heated air is supplied to the carburetor during cold days and when first starting the engine and warming it up.

Air Injection Reactor System

AIR is used on all 1972 models except non-California cars with single-barrel carburetors. 1975 California cars with the 140 cu. in. engine, Cosworth Vega, and Monza V8 also use an air pump.

The Air Injection Reactor (AIR) system was used to treat exhaust emissions. It consists of an air pump, a diverter valve, and tubes and hoses used to inject the air into the exhaust manifolds. The pump, driven by the engine, compresses air which is routed to the exhaust port of each cylinder. The air provides oxygen to further burn any unburned gases that are left over from the combustion process.

The diverter valve closes during engine overrun and deceleration and dumps the output from the air pump to the atmosphere. This prevents backfire due to air being injected when an overly rich mixture is present in the exhaust port.

Air Pump R & R

1. Disconnect the output hose.
2. Hold the pump from turning by squeezing the drive belt.
3. Loosen the pulley bolts.
4. Loosen the alternator so the belt can be removed.
5. Remove the pulley.
6. Remove the pump mounting bolts and the pump.
7. Install the pump with the mounting bolts hand-tight.
8. Install the pulley and tighten the bolts hand-tight.
9. Install and adjust the drive belt as outlined in the "Engine" portion of this section.
10. Squeeze the drive belt to prevent the pump from turning.
11. Torque the pulley bolts to 25 ft lbs. Tighten the pump mountings.
12. Check and adjust the belt tension again, if necessary.
13. Reconnect the hose.

Transmission Controlled Spark System

The Transmission Controlled Spark (TCS) is used on all 1971–72 models and on all 1973 85 hp engines with manual transmissions. It is also used on all 1973-74 cars built for California with manual transmissions and the Cosworth Vega.

The TCS system is used to prevent vacuum advances when the transmission is in low forward gear. The TCS system consists of a temperature-sensing switch, a transmission switch, an idle stop solenoid, and a vacuum advance solenoid.

On 1971–72 cars, the vacuum advance solenoid is normally open, providing full vacuum to the distributor. When the vacuum advance solenoid is energized, the vacuum to the distributor is turned off and the advance unit is vented to the atmosphere.

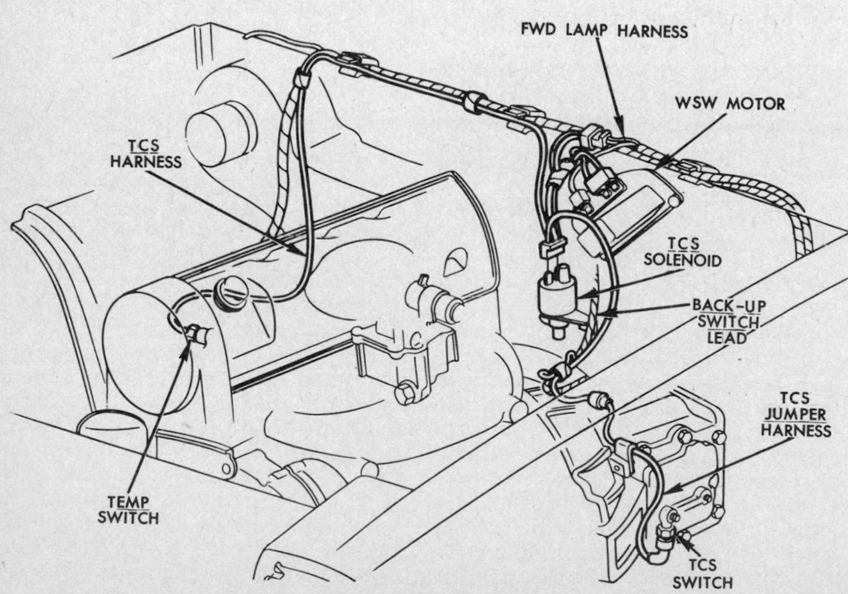

1973-74 TCS electrical components—4 cylinder
(© Chevrolet Div., G.M. Corp)

The transmission switch is located on the transmission and senses when the transmission is in one of the lower gears. When in a lower gear, the switch activates the vacuum advance solenoid, shutting off vacuum advance. There is also an engine-temperature-sensing switch which overrides the transmission switch. It will allow vacuum advance in the lower gears when engine temperature is below 82° F. There is always vacuum advance in high gear and reverse.

On 1972 California models equipped with an automatic transmission, the transmission switch is a dummy switch and will not energize the solenoid. These engines have vacuum advance only when engine temperature is below 82° F.

An idle stop solenoid is used to prevent afterrun when the ignition is turned off. Afterrun is caused by the higher operating temperatures of today's engines and the wider throttle plate openings necessary for emission controls. The loss of spark from turning off the ignition is usually sufficient to stop the engine. However, if the engine has high enough cylinder temperatures, enough air-fuel mixture can pass the wide throttle plate opening and be ignited without the spark plug and the engine will continue to run even after the key is turned off. The idle solenoid is attached to the carburetor to solve this problem. The solenoid has an adjustable plunger and is electrically operated. When the ignition is turned on, the plunger is extended and contacts the carburetor throttle lever, opening the throttle plate wide enough for the engine to idle properly. When the ignition is turned off, the plunger retracts and the throttle lever falls back on the lever stop. When the throttle lever is on its stop the throttle plate opening is very small and will not allow enough air-fuel mixture to pass to run the engine with the ignition off.

On 1973-74 cars, the vacuum advance solenoid is normally closed, when (de-energized), venting the vacuum advance circuit to the atmosphere and shutting off vacuum to the distributor advance unit.

When the key is turned on the idle stop solenoid is energized, the plunger extends to touch the throttle lever and maintains idle speed. As long as the engine temperature remains below 93°F, the vacuum advance solenoid is energized and the distributor receives a vacuum supply. The vacuum advance unit functions to give good start-up and drive-away characteristics. When the engine temperature reaches approximately 93°F, the temperature switch breaks the circuit, causing the vacuum advance solenoid to de-energize and cut off the vacuum supply. When the engine overheats, the temperature switch completes the circuit to activate the instrument panel warning lamp. Under normal driving conditions, the transmission switch controls the vacuum advance solenoid. In the lower gears, the switch is open and the solenoid de-energized. In high gear, the switch is closed and energizes the solenoid to open the vacuum port to the distributor and permits the advance unit to function. The idle stop solenoid operates as before.

Exhaust Gas Recirculation

Exhaust Gas Recirculation (EGR) is used in 1973-74 on all models.

EGR is used to reduce oxides of nitrogen (NO_x) that are formed at high operating temperatures.

EGR operates by introducing small amounts of relatively inert exhaust gas into the intake manifold, lowering the peak combustion temperature. The amount of exhaust gas introduced is regulated by the EGR valve. The EGR valve is vacuum modulated. The vacuum to operate the valve is supplied by an orifice just above the throttle valve in the carburetor.

When there is a high vacuum during heavy acceleration, the valve opens to allow exhaust gas into the intake manifold. At idle or cruising speeds the valve is closed and no exhaust gas is introduced into the intake manifold.

EGR Valve R & R

1. Disconnect the vacuum line at the top of the valve.
2. Remove the valve-to-manifold retaining bolts.
3. Remove the EGR valve from the manifold.
4. Reinstall the EGR valve on the manifold.
5. Tighten the clamp bolt to 25 ft lb. Bend the lock tab over the bolt head.
6. Reconnect the vacuum line to the valve.

Catalytic Converter System

The 1975 Vega and Monza 2 + 2 are equipped with catalytic converters nationwide (including California. It is located between the front and rear exhaust pipes on the right-hand side of the car. A major benefit from the catalytic converter is a large reduction in pollutants, while allowing carburetor settings that provide smoother power, and more spark advance for increased fuel economy and better overall performance.

NOTE: *Unleaded fuel must be used with catalytic converters.*

In addition to the catalytic converters, a restricted fuel inlet is used, which will only accept the smaller fuel nozzles, used to dispense unleaded fuel.

For further information concerning emission controls, consult the "Emission Control Systems" Unit Repair Section.

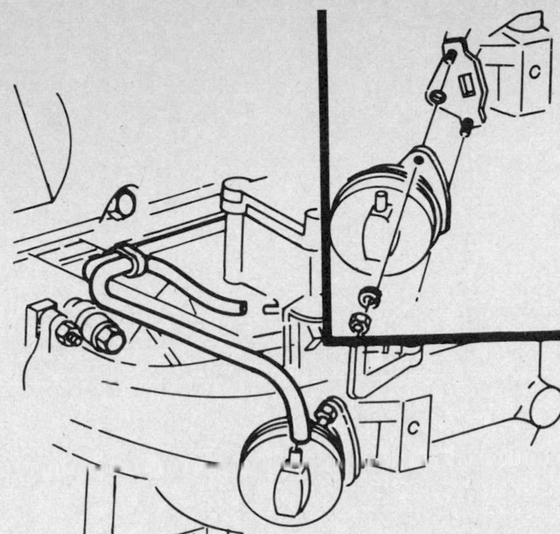

EGR valve mounting—4 cylinder (© Chevrolet Div., G.M. Corp)

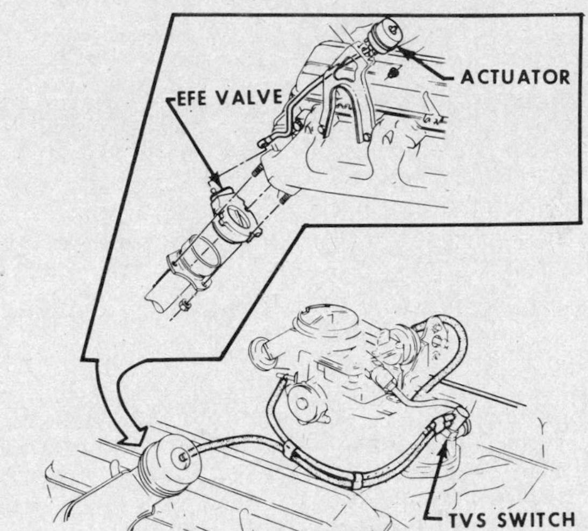

V8 EFE system
(© Chevrolet Div., G.M. Corp)

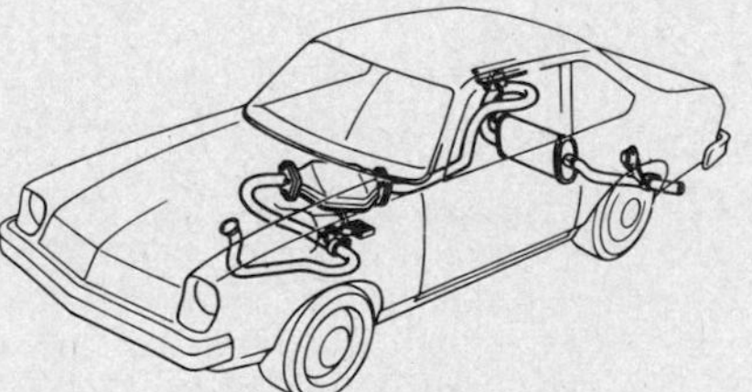

Schematic of typical catalytic exhaust system
(© Chevrolet Div., G.M. Corp)

Catalytic Converter R & R

Caution *Catalytic converter operating temperatures are extremely high, often reaching well over 1000°F. Use extreme care servicing cars equipped with catalytic converters.*

To remove the catalytic converter, disconnect it from the front and rear exhaust pipes. The catalytic converter should be installed so that the fill plug is downward and at the front of the car.

Early Fuel Evaporation (EFE)

Early Fuel Evaporation is used on all V8 models. The system consists of an EFE valve at the exhaust manifold flange, an actuator and a thermal vacuum switch (TVS). The TVS is mounted in the water outlet housing and directly controls vacuum in response to coolant temperatures.

The actuator closes the EFE valve when coolant temperatures are below 180°F., routing hot gases to the base of the carburetor. When coolant temperatures reach 180°F., vacuum to the actuator is cut off releasing an internal spring in the actuator and opening the EFE valve.

For testing, see the Emission Controls Unit Repair Section.

ENGINE

The standard 4 cylinder Vega engine is a single overhead camshaft, four-cylinder design using a die cast aluminum cylinder block and a cast iron cylinder head. The iron-plated aluminum pistons ride directly on

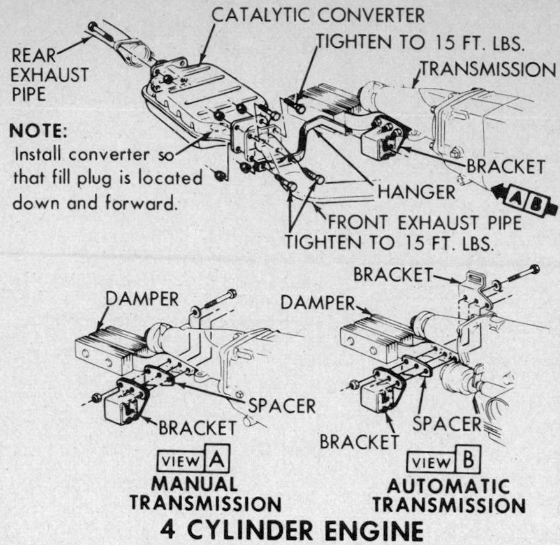

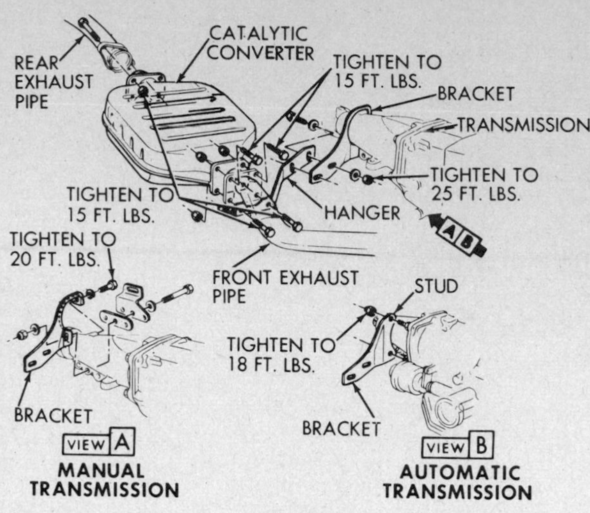

Catalytic converter installation
(© Chevrolet Div., G.M. Corp)

honed and electrochemically treated aluminum bores. The cylinder block is cast of an alloy containing silicon which, after suitable etching, provides a proper bore surface for the pistons and rings.

The valve train is completely contained in the head, with a straight-line vertical valve configuration. The camshaft is driven by a timing belt which in turn is driven from a front crankshaft pulley.

The limited production Cosworth Vega uses the basic Vega engine block with a shorter stroke, forged steel crankshaft. Unlike the standard cast iron head, the Cosworth cylinder head is cast aluminum. The dual overhead cams, water pump, and fan are belt driven in a similar manner to the standard engine. The cylinder head is a crossflow design with intake and exhaust manifolds on opposite sides of the head. Each cylinder is serviced by two intake and two exhaust valves.

The Monza 2 + 2 is optionally available with the 262 cu in. V8 engine nationwide in 1974 and in 49 states in 1975. The 350 cu in. V8 is available in California in 1975. The 305 V8 is added in 1976. This engine is very similar in design to other small block Chevrolet engines.

Engine R & R

4 Cylinder

1. Raise the hood and install a bolt in the hold-open link.
2. Disconnect the battery cables.
3. Drain the cooling system and disconnect the hoses at the radiator.
4. Disconnect the heater hoses at the water pump and at the heater inlet (bottom hose).
5. Disconnect the following emission hoses:
   a. PCV at the cam cover.
   b. The canister vacuum hose at the carburetor.
   c. PCV vacuum hose at the intake manifold.
   d. Bowl vent at the carburetor.
   e. TCS at the rear of the carburetor.
6. Remove the radiator shroud, radiator, fan, fan spacer and air cleaner.
7. Disconnect the following electrical leads:
   a. Alternator.
   b. Ignition coil.
   c. Starter solenoid.
   d. Oil pressure sending unit.
   e. Temperature sending unit.
   f. TCS switch at the transmission.
   g. TCS solenoid on the firewall.
   h. Ground strap at the firewall.
8. Disconnect:
   a. Powerglide throttle valve linkage or Turbo Hydra-Matic detent cable.
   b. Fuel line at the rubber hose, rearward of the carburetor.
   c. Automatic transmission vacuum modulator and air conditioning vacuum line at the intake manifold.
   d. Throttle cable at the manifold bellcrank.
9. On cars with air conditioning, disconnect the compressor at the front support, rear support, rear lower bracket and remove the drive belt from the compressor.

NOTE: Do not disconnect any air conditioning lines or fittings.

10. Being careful not to crimp or bend the hoses, move the compressor slightly forward, allowing the front of the compressor to rest on the frame forward brace. Secure the rear of the compressor to the engine compartment so that it does not interfere with the engine removal.
11. If so equipped, disconnect the power steering pump and position it out of the way.
12. Raise the car on a hoist.
13. Disconnect the exhaust pipe at the exhaust manifold.
14. Remove the engine flywheel lower cover or the torque converter underpan.
15. On vehicles equipped with automatic transmission:
    a. Mark the converter-to-flywheel relationship for reassembly.
    b. Remove the converter to flywheel retaining bolts and install a coverter safety strap, to keep the converter from falling out.
    c. Remove the converter housing to engine retaining bolts.
    d. Loosen the engine front mount retaining bolts at the frame attachment and lower the vehicle on the hoist.
    e. Install a floor jack under the transmission and an engine lifting adapter to raise the engine slightly from its mounts.
    f. Remove the engine front mount retaining bolts.
    g. Remove the engine from the vehicle. Pull the engine forward enough to clear the transmission while slowly lifting the engine.
16. On vehicles with manual transmission:
    a. Remove the flywheel housing to engine retaining bolts.
    b. Proceed with Step 15 above. parts d, e, f, and g.

To install engine:

17. Install two guide pins into the upper bolt holes in the engine block. Guide pins can be fabricated by cutting the heads off two bolts and sawing screwdriver slots into them.
18. Lower the engine into place, aligning the engine with the transmission.

19. Install the front mount bolts hand-tight.
20. Install the converter or clutch housing-to-engine bolts, replacing the guide pins. Remove the torque converter retaining strap, if one was used.
21. Torque the clutch housing-to-engine bolts to 25 ft lbs and the converter housing-to-engine bolts to 35 ft lbs.
22. After checking to make sure that the front engine mounts are aligned and not making metal-to-metal contact, tighten them to 20 ft lbs.
23. Align the previously made converter and flywheel marks, and torque the bolts to 35 ft lbs.
24. Install the flywheel dust cover or torque converter underpan.
25. Connect the exhaust pipe at the manifold.
26. If so equipped, install the air conditioning compressor and power steering pump. Adjust the alternator belt.
27. Reconnect:
    a. the accelerator cable,
    b. the automatic transmission vacuum modulator line and the air conditioning vacuum line,
    c. the fuel line, and
    d. the Powerglide transmission throttle valve linkage or the Turbo Hydra-Matic detent cable.
28. Attach the following electrical connections:
    a. alternator
    b. coil
    c. starter solenoid
    d. oil pressure switch
    e. temperature switch
    f. TCS transmission switch
    g. TCS solenoid
    h. engine ground strap
29. Replace the air cleaner and install these hoses:
    a. vent tube at the air cleaner base
    b. carburetor bowl vent
    c. PCV vacuum line
    d. vacuum canister hose
30. Install the radiator, radiator panel or shroud, spacer, and fan.
31. Connect the heater and radiator hoses. Fill the cooling system.
32. Connect the battery cables. Start the engine and check for leaks. Remember to remove the bolt from the hood hold-open link.

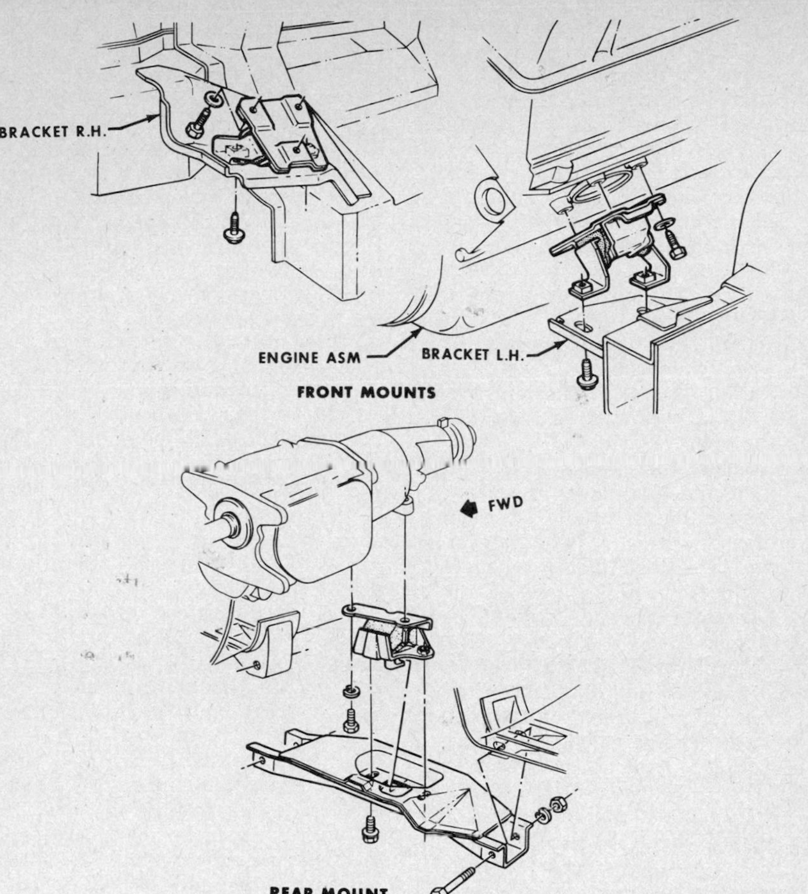

V8 engine mounts
(© Chevrolet Div., G.M. Corp)

V8

1. Raise the hood and install a bolt in the hold-open link.
2. Disconnect the battery cables.
3. Raise and support the car.
4. Drain the coolant, engine and transmission.
5. Disconnect the exhaust pipes at the manifold.
6. Remove the flywheel or converter underpan.
7. On automatic transmissions, remove the converter-to-flywheel retaining bolts and install a converter retaining strap.
8. Remove the accessible converter housing or flywheel housing-to-engine bolts.
9. Remove the transmission cooler lines from the retaining clips on the side of the engine.
10. Remove the engine front mounting bolts at the frame brackets and lower the car.
11. Remove the radiator panel or shroud.
12. Remove the radiator and fan.
13. Disconnect the heater hose from the water pump and manifold.
14. Remove the air cleaner.
15. Disconnect the electrical leads from:
    - alternator
    - distributor
    - starter solenoid
    - oil pressure switch
    - engine temperature switch
    - temperature gauge switch
    - choke secondary pull-off solenoid.
16. Unclip the wiring harness from the rocker cover and position it out of the way.
17. Disconnect the automatic transmission vacuum modulator and air conditioning vacuum line from the manifold.
18. Disconnect the rubber fuel line at the rear of the engine.
19. Disconnect the following:
    - canister vacuum hose at the carburetor
    - accelerator at the carburetor and manifold bracket
    - air conditioning blower delay lead at the rear of the engine.
20. On air conditioned cars, remove the compressor from its mount. Do not disconnect any fittings. Secure the compressor to the fender.
21. Disconnect the power steering pump and lay it aside.
22. Install a floor jack under the transmission.
23. Install a hoist on the engine and raise the engine slightly to take the weight off the engine mounts. Remove the remaining engine to transmission bolts.
24. Remove the engine from the car.

To install the engine:

25. Install transmission-to-engine guide pins made from 3/8 in. bolts with the heads cut off, into the engine.
26. Install the engine, aligning the engine with the transmission housing.
27. Align the engine mounts with the frame brackets and lower the engine onto the brackets. Loosely install the engine mount bolts.

28. Remove the guide pins and install the engine-to-housing bolts. Remove the lifting equipment.
29. Remove the support from transmission and raise and support the car.
30. Remove the converter retaining strap and install and tighten the engine-to-housing bolts.
31. Tighten the engine front mount bolts.
32. Install the converter to the flywheel.
33. Install the flywheel cover or converter underpan.
34. Install the transmission cooler lines in the clips on the side of the block.
35. Connect the exhaust pipe at the manifold and lower the car.
36. Install the air conditioning compressor and power steering pump. Adjust the drive belts.
37. Connect the following:
    - canister vacuum hose to carburetor
    - Accelerator cable at carburetor and manifold bracket
    - air conditioning blower delay lead at side of engine
    - Fuel line to rubber hose at rear of engine
    - air conditioning in vacuum line.
38. Install the electrical harness in the clip in the rocker cover and connect the following:
    - alternator
    - distributor
    - starter solenoid
    - oil pressure switch
    - engine temperature switch
    - temperature gauge switch
    - choke secondary pull-off solenoid.
39. Connect the heater hose at the water pump and at the manifold.
40. Install the radiator, fan, radiator panel or shroud, fill the cooling system, add engine oil and fill the transmission.
41. Install the air cleaner.
42. Connect the battery cables, start the engine and check for leaks.

Manifolds

Intake Manifold R & R

4 Cylinder

1. Raise the hood and install a bolt through the hold-open link.
2. Disconnect the negative battery cable.
3. Drain the cooling system.
4. Remove the EGR tube retaining clamps from both the intake and exhaust manifolds. Remove the EGR tube by carefully driving it off.
5. Disconnect the heater hose at the fitting on the intake manifold.
6. Disconnect the vent tube at the base of the air cleaner, then remove the air cleaner.
7. Remove the air cleaner silencer.
8. Disconnect:
    a. The choke rod at the carburetor.
    b. PCV valve at the cam cover.
    c. Fuel line at the carburetor.
    d. The carburetor bowl vent line at the carburetor.
    e. Throttle linkage and the transmission throttle valve linkage.
    f. Power steering pump brace at the manifold.
9. Remove the alternator to thermostat housing through-bolt and loosen the alternator swivel bolt. Move the alternator aside to gain access to the manifold bolt.
10. Remove the four intake manifold bolts and remove the manifold.
11. Remove from the manifold:
    a. The carburetor and carburetor linkage.
    b. Pipe plug.
    c. Vacuum fittings.
    d. Hot water nipple.
12. Install the items removed in Step 10 above to the new manifold.
13. Clean the gasket surfaces on the manifold and the cylinder head.
14. Position a new gasket over the dowels on the cylinder head, then carefully install the manifold. Make sure that the gasket remains in place.
15. Install the manifold bolts, tightening to 30 ft. lbs. The stud goes in the hole nearest No. 3 intake port.
16. Connect the power steering pump brace to the manifold.
17. Install the alternator to thermostat housing through bolt and adjust the belt tension.
18. Connect:
    a. The choke rod at the carburetor.
    b. The PCV valve at the cam cover.
    c. Fuel line at the carburetor.
    d. Carburetor bowl vent line at the carburetor.
    e. The throttle and transmission throttle valve linkage.
    f. Vacuum connections at the carburetor.
19. Install the air cleaner silencer and secure it to the heat stove tube.
20. Install the air cleaner. Connect the vent tube at the base of the air cleaner.
21. Connect the heater hose to the intake manifold fitting and fill the cooling system.
22. Raise the car. Install the EGR tube on the intake and exhaust manifolds.
23. Install the EGR tube retaining clamps. Lower the car.
24. Connect the negative battery cable and start the engine. Check for leaks and adjust the carburetor.

V8

1. Remove the air cleaner.
2. Drain the radiator.
3. Disconnect:
    a. Battery cables at the battery.
    b. Upper radiator and heater hoses at the manifold.
    c. Crankcase ventilation hoses as required.
    d. Fuel line at the rubber hose.
    e. Accelerator linkage at the pedal lever.
    f. Vacuum hose at the distributor.
    g. Power brake hose at the accelerator bracket.
    h. Ignition coil and temperature sending switch wires.
    i. Air diverter valve line.
    j. Choke pull-off lead.
    k. Air conditioning bracket or power steering brace.
    l. Choke hot and cold air pipes.
4. Remove the distributor cap and scribe the rotor position relative to distributor body.
5. Remove the distributor.
6. If applicable, remove the Delcotron upper bracket.
7. Remove the air pump.
8. Remove the manifold to head attaching bolts, then remove the manifold and carburetor as an assembly.
9. If the manifold is to be replaced, transfer the carburetor (and mounting studs), and other applicable equipment to the new manifold.
10. Before installing the manifold, thoroughly clean the gasket and seal surfaces of the cylinder heads and manifold.
11. Install the manifold end seals, folding the tabs if applicable, and the manifold/head gaskets, using a sealing compound around the water passages. Make sure the gaskets are firmly cemented in place before installing the manifold.

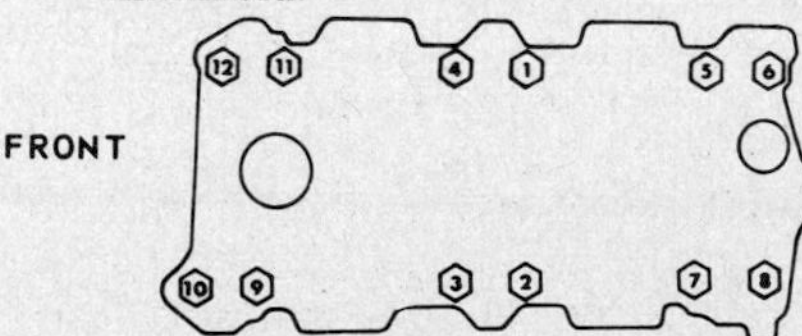

Intake manifold torque sequence—V8

12. When installing the manifold, care should be taken not to dislocate the end seals. It is helpful to use a pilot in the distributor opening. Tighten the manifold bolts to the proper torque in the sequence illustrated.
13. Install the ignition coil.
14. Install the distributor with the rotor in its original location as indicated by the scribe line. If the engine has been disturbed, refer to "Distributor R&R."
15. If applicable, install the Delcotron upper bracket and adjust the belt tension.

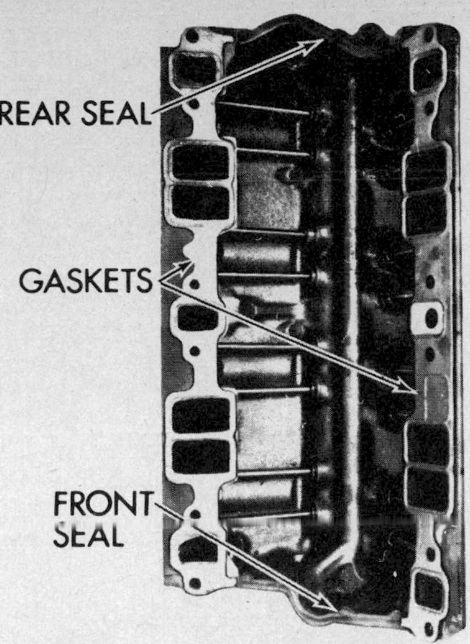

V8 intake manifold gasket and seals
(© Chevrolet Div., G.M. Corp)

16. Install the air pump. Adjust all drive belts.
17. Connect all components disconnected in Step 3 above.
18. Fill the cooling system, start the engine, check for leaks and adjust the ignition timing and carburetor idle speed and mixture.

Exhaust Manifold R & R

4 Cylinder Except Cosworth Vega

1. From under the car, disconnect the exhaust pipe from the manifold.
2. Remove the intake manifold as described above.
3. Disconnect the oil dipstick bracket at the exhaust manifold.
4. Remove the exhaust manifold bolts, then remove the manifold and carburetor heater assembly.
5. Install the carburetor heater assembly on the new manifold.
6. Install the exhaust manifold and manifold bolts (loosely). The upper bolts are shorter.
7. Tighten the manifold bolts to 30 ft. lbs.
8. Connect the exhaust pipe to the manifold.
9. Connect the oil dipstick bracket to the exhaust manifold.
10. Install the intake manifold.

Cosworth Vega

1. Disconnect the exhaust pipe from the manifold.
2. Disconnect the air injection tubes.
3. Disconnect the oil dipstick tube from the manifold.
4. Remove the retaining bolts and remove the manifold, being careful not to damage the temperature sensor or its wiring.
5. Install the exhaust manifold bolts hand tight. Gradually tighten the bolts from the inside out.
6. Connect the exhaust pipe to the manifold.
7. Install the oil dipstick tube on the manifold.
8. Install the air injection tubes.

V8

1. If equipped with AIR, remove the air injector manifold assembly. The ¼ in. pipe threads in the manifold are straight threads. Do not use a ¼ in. tapered pipe tap.
2. Disconnect the battery.
3. If applicable, remove the air cleaner pre-heater shroud.
4. Remove the air conditioning compressor. Do not disconnect any lines. Remove the A/C bracket.
5. Remove the exhaust pipe flange nuts, then hang the pipe with wire.
6. Remove the manifold mounting bolts (end bolts first), then remove the manifold.
7. To install, clean the mating surfaces, then install the manifold with the center bolts first. Install the end bolts, then tighten all bolts to the specified torque.
8. To complete installation, reverse Steps 1 through 4.

Valve System

The standard 4 cylinder valve train is an overhead camshaft operating mechanical valve tappets (hydraulic starting 1976). The Cosworth Vega uses two overhead camshafts operating mechanical valve tappets with 4 valves per cylinder. The 262, 305, 350 cu in. V-8s use a single camshaft operating hydraulic lifters.

Valve Lash Adjustment

4 Cylinder Except Cosworth Vega

1. Mark the locations of No. one and four spark plug wires on the side of the distributor with chalk. (Refer to the firing order illustration.)
2. Remove the distributor cap, air cleaner, and valve cover.
3. Turn the engine until the rotor points to the No. one position and the points are open. The No. one intake and exhaust, No. two intake and No. three exhaust valves are adjusted at this position. The intake valve is the front valve for each cylinder, and the exhaust valve is the rear one.
4. Insert the correct size feeler gauge between the camshaft lobe and the valve tappet. If the clearance is between 0.014 and 0.017 in. for intakes or 0.029 and 0.032 in. for exhausts, no adjustment is necessary. This is due to the fact that the adjusting mechanism only allows adjustments in increments of 0.003 in.

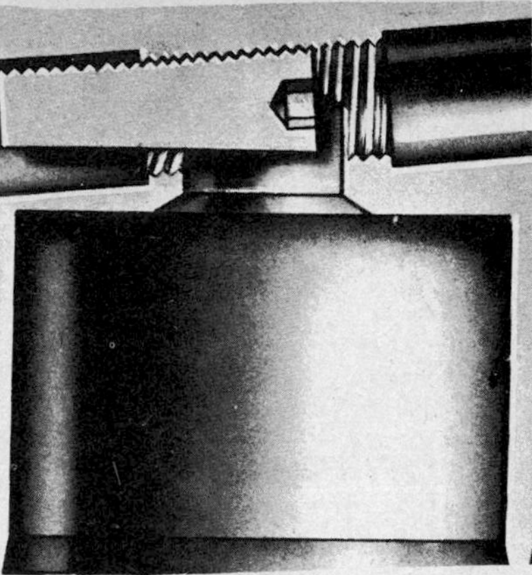

Valve tappet and adjusting screw assembly 4-cylinder (© Chevrolet Div., G.M. Corp)

5. If lash is 0.003 in. or more out of adjustment, insert a 1/8 in. allen wrench into the tappet adjusting screw and turn it one full turn. Turning clockwise tightens; turning counterclockwise loosens.
6. Check the lash again and adjust further if necessary. Always turn the adjuster screw one full turn. You can feel the flat spot by pressing down on the tappet while adjusting.
7. Turn the engine so that the rotor points to no. four. Adjust no. two exhaust, no. three intake, and no. four intake and exhaust valves in this position.
8. Replace the valve cover, air cleaner, and distributor cap.

V8

V8 engines require no periodic valve adjustment. For initial adjustment procedures after overhaul of cylinder head or removal of valve train, see the Camaro section.

Valve Guides

4 Cylinder

Valves with oversize stems are available in three sizes: 0.003 in. o/s, 0.015 in. o/s and 0.030 in. o/s. Remove the cylinder head and remove the camshaft from the head. Remove the valves. Ream the valve guides with an appropriate oversize reamer.

V8

Valve guides are integral with the cylinder head. Valve guide bores may be reamed to accommodate oversize valve stems or the guides may be knurled (if wear permits) to allow the retention of standard size valves. Maximum allowable valve stem to guide bore clearance is listed in the specifications.

4 cylinder (except Cosworth) valve arrangement

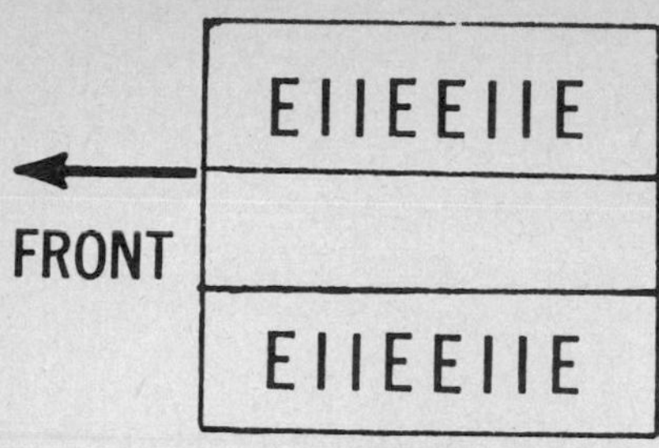

V8 valve arrangement

Cylinder Head

Cylinder Head R & R

4 Cylinder

NOTE: Cylinder head gasket R&R does not require separating the intake and exhaust manifolds from the cylinder head.

1. Remove the timing belt cover and camshaft cover. Drain the cooling system.
2. Remove the timing belt and camshaft sprocket.
3. Remove the intake and exhaust manifolds.
4. Disconnect the water hose at the thermostat housing (outlet).
5. Remove the cylinder head bolts, then the head and gasket.

NOTE: If the head sticks, bump the starter a few times to loosen it with compression. Do not insert any tools between the head and block to pry them apart.

6. Using a new gasket (smooth side up), carefully position the cylinder head on the block.
7. Install the cylinder head bolts finger-tight. Use an anti-seize compound on the threads. Install the lifting bracket under the second head bolt from the front on the spark plug side. The 6-3/8 in. bolts are installed on the manifold side and the 5-5/8 in. bolts are installed on the spark plug side.
8. Tighten the head bolts to 60 ft. lbs. (in steps), using the illustration.
9. Connect the water hose to the thermostat housing.
10. Install the intake and exhaust manifolds.
11. Install the timing bolt and sprocket.
12. Install the front cover and camshaft cover.

V8

1. Drain the coolant.
2. Remove the intake manifold.
3. Remove the exhaust manifolds.
4. Back off the rocker arm nuts and pivot the rocker arms out of the way so that the pushrods can be removed. Identify the pushrods so that they can be reinstalled in their original locations.
5. Remove the cylinder head bolts and cylinder heads.
6. Install using new gaskets. The head gasket is installed with the bead up.

NOTE: coat a STEEL gasket on both sides with sealer. If a STEEL ASBESTOS gasket is used, do not apply sealer. Clean the bolt threads, apply sealing compound and install the bolts finger tight.

7. Tighten the head bolts a little at a time in the sequence illustrated.
8. Install the exhaust and intake manifolds as described previously.
9. Adjust the valves as explained in the Camaro section. Fill the cooling system.

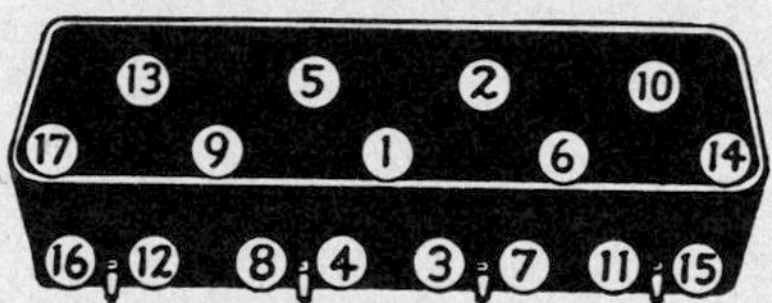

V8 cylinder head torque sequence

Rocker Arm R & R—V8

Rocker arms are removed by removing the adjusting nut. Be sure to adjust valve lash after replacing rocker arms.

NOTE: when replacing an exhaust rocker, move an old intake rocker to the exhaust rocker arm stud and install the new rocker arm on the intake stud.

Rocker arm studs that have damaged threads or are loose in the cylinder heads may be replaced with new studs available in 0.003 in. and 0.013 in. oversize or the bores may be tapped and screw-in replacement studs used. Do not attempt to install an oversize stud without reaming the stud bore. Studs are press-fit. Lubricate the press-fit area of the stud with hypoid axle lubricant.

NOTE: if engine is equipped with the AIR exhaust emission control system, the interfering components of the system must be removed. Disconnect the lines at the air injection nozzles in the exhaust manifolds.

Timing Cover, Belt, or Chain, and Camshaft

Front Cover R & R

4 Cylinder

1. Raise the hood and install a bolt in the hood hold-open link.
2. Disconnect the negative battery cable.
3. Remove the fan and spacer.
4. Loosen the two lower cover retaining screws.
5. Remove the two top cover retaining screws and remove the cover, lifting it until the slots clear the lower screws.
6. To install, position the cover, lowering it until the slots are over the lower screws. Loosely tighten the lower screws.
7. Install the upper screws, then tighten all four screws to 50 in. lbs.
8. Install the spacer and fan, tightening the bolts to 20 ft. lbs.
9. Connect the battery cable and remove the bolt from the hood hold-open link.

V8

NOTE: the timing case cover oil seal may be replaced without removing the case cover.

After gaining access to the oil seal, pry the old seal out of the cover with a screwdriver. Then, lubricate the new seal and drive it into place with a seal installer tool.

1. Remove the fan belt, fan, and pulley.
2. Remove the radiator and shroud.
3. Remove the accessory drive pulley and the torsional damper retaining bolt.
4. Remove the damper from the crankshaft.
5. Remove the water pump.
6. Remove the front cover bolts and remove the front cover and gasket.
7. Clean the gasket mating surfaces.
8. Remove any oil pan gasket material that may still be adhering to the oil pan-engine block joint face.
9. Apply a 1/8 in. bead of silicone sealant or the equivalent to the

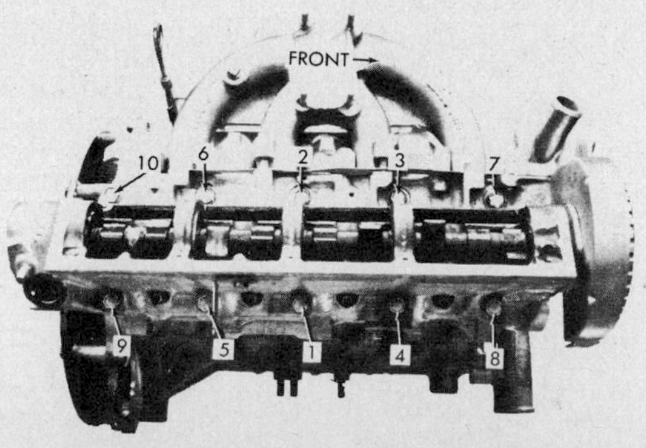

4 cylinder head torque sequence
(© Chevrolet Div., G.M. Corp)

joint formed by the oil pan and cylinder block, as well as to the entire oil pan front lip.

10. Coat the cover gasket with gasket sealer and install it on the front cover.
11. Loosely install the front cover on the block. Install the 4 top bolts loosely (about 3 turns). Install two ¼-20x½ in. screws in the hole at each side of the front cover and apply a bead of sealant on the bottom of the seal and install it on the cover.
12. Tighten the screws evenly while aligning the dowel pins and holes in the front cover.
13. Remove the ¼-20x½ in. screws and install the rest of the cover screws.
14. Further installation is the reverse of removal. Refill the engine with oil.

Timing Belt and Sprocket R & R

4 Cylinder except Cosworth Vega

NOTE: This entire procedure isn't necessary to remove only the camshaft sprocket. This can be done simply by removing the upper timing belt cover bolts and pulling the cover forward. It isn't necessary to adjust the timing belt tension.

1. Raise the hood and install a bolt in the hood hold-open link.
2. Disconnect the negative battery cable.
3. Loosen the air conditioner and alternator as necessary and remove the drive belts.
4. Remove the crankshaft pulley and four pulley-to-sprocket bolts. Remove the pulley and damper or washer as applicable.

NOTE: it is not necessary to remove the pulley if only the camshaft sprocket is being removed.

5. Drain the engine coolant and loosen the water pump bolts to relieve the tension on the timing belt.
6. Remove the timing belt lower cover.
7. Remove the timing belt.
8. Align one of the holes in the camshaft timing sprocket with the head bolt behind the sprocket. Using a socket on the head bolt to keep the sprocket from rotating, remove the sprocket retaining bolt and washer.

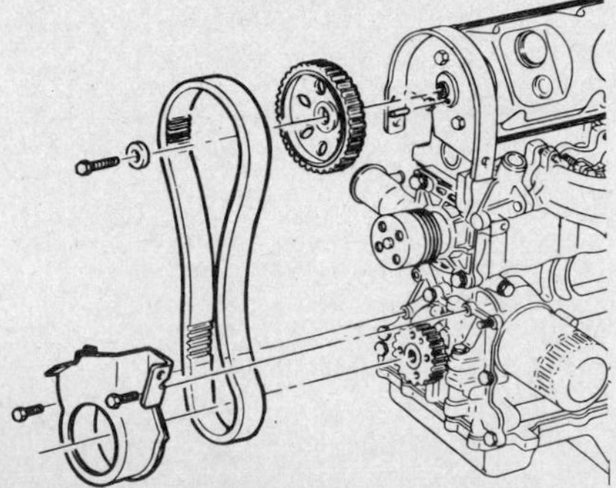

Timing belt and sprockets
(© Chevrolet Div., G.M. Corp)

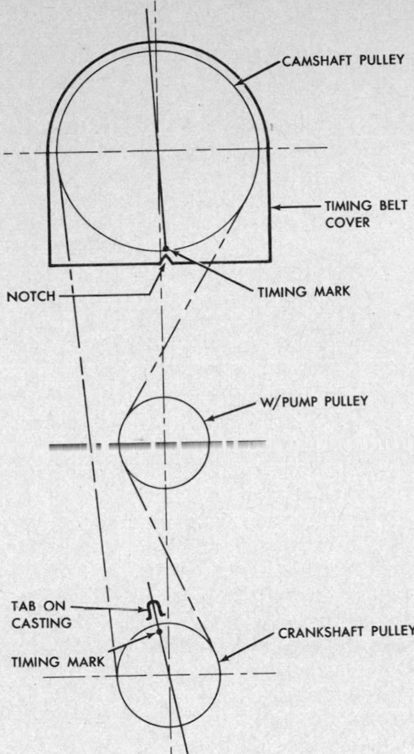

Timing sprocket alignment marks
(© Chevrolet Div., G.M. Corp)

9. Remove the camshaft sprocket.
10. The crankshaft sprocket may be removed.
11. Pull the crankshaft sprocket with an installation tool. Make sure that the timing mark is facing out and that the key is installed.
12. To install the camshaft sprocket, align the dowel in the camshaft with the locating hole in the end of the camshaft.
13. Install the sprocket retaining bolt, tightening to 80 ft. lbs.
14. Align the timing mark on the camshaft sprocket with the notch on the timing belt upper cover and the crankshaft sprocket timing mark with the cast rib on the oil pump cover.
15. Install the timing belt on the crankshaft sprocket, then with the back of the belt positioned in the water pump track, install the belt on the camshaft sprocket. Make sure that both sprockets maintain their indexed positions.
16. Install the lower timing belt cover, using anti-seize compound on the threads of the bolts and tightening them to 50 in. lbs.
17. Adjust the timing belt tension as described under Water Pump R&R above, Steps 11 and 12.
18. Fill the cooling system.
19. Install the accessory drive pulley to the crankshaft sprocket, aligning the tang on the pulley with the keyway on the crankshaft. Install the damper locating dowel in the locating hole of the sprocket.
20. Loosely install the four sprocket bolts, then install the crankshaft (center) bolt. Tighten the crankshaft bolt to 80 ft. lbs. and the four sprocket bolts to 15 ft. lbs.
21. Install the alternator and air conditioning compressor as applicable and adjust the belts.
22. Install the engine front cover, fan and fan spacer.
23. Connect the battery cable and remove the bolt from the hood hold-open link.

V8 Timing Chain Replacement

To replace the chain, remove the radiator core, water pump, the harmonic balancer, and the crankcase front cover. This will allow access to the timing chain. Crank the engine until the timing marks on both sprockets are nearest each other and in line between the shaft centers. Then take out the three bolts that hold the camshaft gear to the camshaft. This gear is a light press fit on the camshaft and will come off easily. It is located by a dowel.

The chain comes off with the camshaft gear.

A gear puller will be required to remove the crankshaft gear.

Without disturbing the position of the engine, mount the new crankshaft gear on the shaft, and mount the chain over the camshaft gear. Arrange the camshaft gear in such a way that the timing marks will line up between the shaft centers and the camshaft locating dowel will enter the dowel hole in the cam sprocket.

Place the cam sprocket, with its chain mounted over it, in position on the front of the car and pull up with the three bolts that hold it to the camshaft. Do not drive the camshaft sprocket onto the shaft. The expansion plug at the rear of the block could be dislodged.

After the gears are in place, turn the engine two full revolutions to

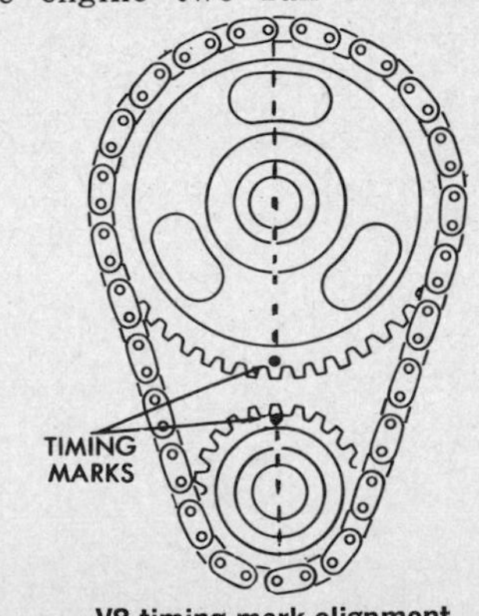

V8 timing mark alignment

make certain that the timing marks are in correct alignment between the shaft centers.

End-play of the V8 camshaft is zero.

Camshaft Cover R & R—4 Cylinder

1. Raise the hood and install a bolt in the hood hold-open link.
2. Disconnect the negative battery cable.
3. Remove the air cleaner and the vent tube (at cam cover).
4. Remove the PCV valve from the cam cover.
5. Remove the cam cover screws and the cover.
6. To install, reverse the above procedure. The gasket is reusable. The oil filler cap is at the forward end of the cover. Tighten the cam cover screws to 35 in. lbs.

Camshaft R & R

4 Cylinder except Cosworth Vega

NOTE: A special valve tappet depressing tool is necessary for camshaft removal. This tool is only available through Chevrolet.

1. Remove the hood.
2. Remove the camshaft timing sprocket.
3. Remove the three screws securing the camshaft seal and retainer assembly and timing cover to the cylinder head.
4. Inspect the seal, prying it out and replacing it if necessary.
5. Remove the camshaft cover.
6. Disconnect the fuel line at the carburetor.
7. Remove:
   a. Idle solenoid from its bracket.
   b. The choke coil, cover and rod assembly.
   c. Ignition distributor.
8. Raise the vehicle on a hoist, disconnect the front engine mounts at the body attachment, raise the front of the engine and install wood blocks, about 1-½ in. thick, between the engine mounts and the body.
9. Install camshaft removal tool on the cylinder head to hold down the lifters so that the camshaft may be removed.
   a. Position the tool so that the attaching holes are aligned with the lower cam cover bolt holes and the tappet levers of the tool are aligned to depress both valves of each cylinder.
   b. Back off the bolts in the bottom of the tool so that they are not contacting the bosses beneath the tool.
   c. Install the tool attaching bolts, tightening them securely.
   d. Tighten the bolts in the bottom of the tool until they just touch the bosses of the cylinder head. Before depressing the tappets, rotate the crankshaft pulley timing mark 90° clockwise from the timing mark on the tab. This assures that the pistons are not at TDC and will prevent valve-to-piston contact.
   e. Grease the ball end of the lever depressing bolts and tighten the bolts to depress the tappets.

NOTE: torque the lever bolts to 10 ft. lbs. If more tightening is required, check to see that the tool is properly installed, then proceed cautiously to prevent damaging the depressing lever.

10. Slide the camshaft forward until it clears the head.

NOTE: the camshaft bearings may be removed. It is not necessary to remove the camshaft end plug. Gently tap out the bearings, starting at the forward end. Tap out the rear bearing slowly into the distributor housing, being careful not to unseat the end plug. Crush the rear bearing to remove it from the distributor housing. Install, starting with the rear bearing. The oil holes in the bearings must align with the oil holes in the case. On the first two bearings the oil holes are at 11 o'clock (as seen from the front of the engine) and the oil groove in the number one bearing toward the front of the engine.

11. Install the camshaft with the journals seated in the bores.
12. With the car up on a hoist, raise the front of the engine and remove the wood blocks from the engine mounts.
13. Install the front engine mounts, then lower the vehicle.
14. Using a new gasket, install the timing belt upper cover and retainer plate and seal assembly. Tighten the retaining bolts to 15 ft. lbs.
15. Using a dial indicator, measure the camshaft end-play. If it is not 0.004-0.012 in., select a camshaft retainer (according to cam locator thickness) which will provide more or less end-play as required.
16. Remove the tappet depressing tool by first releasing the tappet depressing lever bolts, and then removing the tool attaching bolts.
17. Install:
   a. Camshaft timing sprocket.
   b. The timing belt.
   c. Front engine cover.
   d. Distributor.
   e. Vehicle hood.
18. Adjust the valve tappets.
19. Install the camshaft cover.
20. Install and adjust the carburetor choke coil, cover and rod assembly.
21. Connect the carburetor fuel line.
22. Install the idle solenoid to the bracket.
23. Check and adjust the ignition timing.

V8

1. Drain the cooling system and remove the radiator. Remove the hood.
2. Remove the water pump and the timing case cover.
3. Turn the crankshaft until the timing marks on the camshaft and crankshaft gears are aligned.
4. Remove the valve covers and loosen each rocker arm nut enough to turn the rocker to the side and remove the pushrods. Keep the pushrods in order when they are removed from the engine.
5. Remove the distributor cap and mark the position of the rotor relative to the distributor body and the position of the distributor body relative to the engine. Remove the distributor.
6. Remove the intake manifold, then remove the valve lifters from the engine. Keep the lifters in order when they are removed from the engine.
7. Remove the fuel pump.
8. Remove the timing chain and sprockets from the engine.
9. Install two 5/16 in. 18x4 bolts in the holes in the front of the cam and carefully slide it out of the engine.

NOTE: On some engine and model combinations it will be necessary to disconnect the motor mounts and jack up the front of the engine or remove the grille from the car in order to gain adequate clearance in front of the engine to get the camshaft out of the engine.

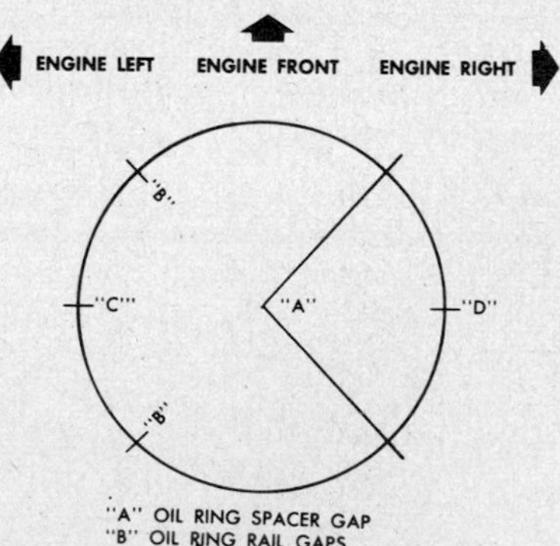

Ring gap locations (© Chevrolet Div., G.M. Corp)

10. Installation is the reverse of removal.

Piston & Rod Installation

NOTE: 4 cylinder oversize pistons were not supplied initially, since there was no mechanical means available for duplicating the cylinder bore electrochemical etching process. A me-

chanical honing process has been perfected and oversize pistons are now available.

The F on the 4 cylinder piston must face toward the front of the engine. On V8s, install the piston with the tang on the connecting rod bearing on the side away from the camshaft. Be sure that the pistons and rods are installed in their original locations or in the cylinder to which it was fitted.

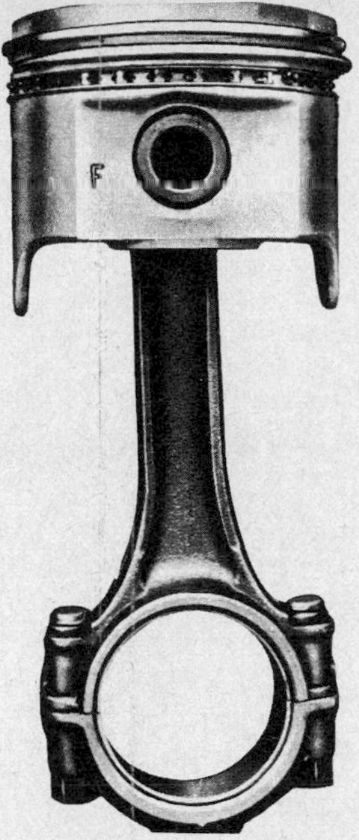

Piston marking (© Chevrolet Div., G.M. Corp)

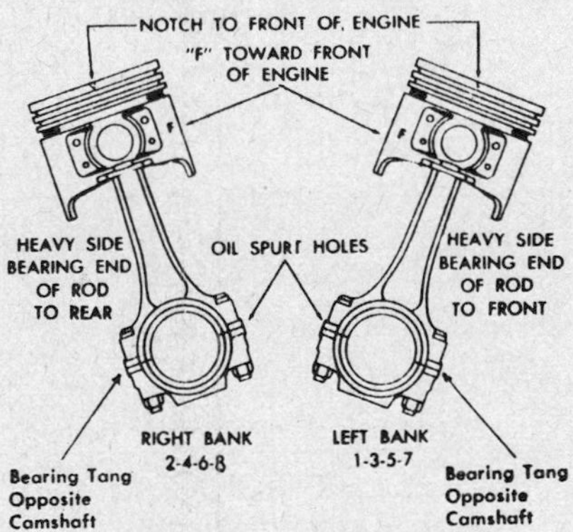

Piston-to-rod relationship—V8

Lubrication

Oil Pan and Baffle R & R—4 Cylinder

1. Raise the vehicle and drain the engine oil. Raise the front of the engine, being careful not to distort the pan.
2. Support the engine with a jack and remove the frame crossmember and both front crossmember braces.
3. Disconnect the steering idler arm at the frame side rail. On vehicles with air conditioning, disconnect the idler arm at the relay rod.
4. Mark the position of the steering linkage pitman arm to the steering gear pitman shaft and remove the pitman arm.

NOTE: do not rotate the steering gear pitman shaft while the linkage is disconnected, because the steering wheel alignment will be changed.

5. Remove the flywheel cover or converter underpan.
6. Remove the oil pan bolts, tap the oil pan to break the seal, then remove the pan.
7. Remove the pick-up screen-to-support retaining bolt and the pick-up screen-to-baffle support bolts, then remove the support from the baffle.
8. Remove the bolt which secures the oil drain back tube to the baffle, then rotate the baffle 90° toward the left side of the car and remove the baffle from the pick-up screen.
9. The oil pump screen and pick up tube may be removed as follows:
   a. Remove the two self-locking mounting bolts (in block).
   b. Lightly tap on the U section of the pick-up tube to remove the tube from the casting.
   c. If damaged, the tube and screen assembly are replaced as a unit.
   d. Apply sealing compound to the pick-up tube sealing surface.
   e. Install the tube into its bore, using an open end wrench on the tube boss, tapping the wrench with a mallet. Make sure that the retaining brackets are aligned with the bolt holes.
   f. Using anti-seize compound on the threads, install the retaining bolts. Tighten the bolts to 25 ft. lbs.
10. Install the oil pan and baffle in the reverse order of removal. Use sealing compound on the oil pump gasket surface. Tighten the oil pan bolts to 15 ft. lbs. See Steering Linkage R&R for correct pitman arm and idler arm installation procedure. Tighten frame crossmember and brace bolts to 35 ft. lbs.

Oil Pan R & R—V8

1. Disconnect the battery.
2. Raise the car and drain the oil.
3. Disconnect the exhaust crossover pipe.
4. Remove the converter housing underpan and splash shield.
5. Scribe marks on each side of the frame crossmember and support the engine. Remove the frame crossmember.
6. Disconnect the steering idler arm at the frame side rail.
7. Disconnect the starter brace and remove the starter.
8. Remove the oil pan bolts and remove the oil pan.
9. Installation is the reverse of removal. Use new gaskets with sealer as a retainer and be sure to match the scribe marks when installing the crossmember. Fill the engine with oil.

Oil Pump R & R

4 Cylinder

1. Remove:
   a. Front engine cover.
   b. Accessory drive pulley.
   c. Timing belt.
   d. Timing belt lower cover.
   e. Crankshaft sprocket.
2. Raise the vehicle on a hoist and drain the engine oil.
3. Remove the oil pan and baffle.
4. Remove the oil pump bolts and the pump.
5. Inspect the oil pump for wear. The pump gears and body are not serviced separately. Replacement of the entire oil pump is required. Check the pressure regulator for free operation.
6. When installing, clean all gasket surfaces. Be sure that the pump drive key is installed properly. Use anti-seize compound on the threads of the pump mounting bolts, tightening them to 15 ft. lbs. The stud is installed in the upper right (facing pump) and tightened to 30 ft. lbs. Install the oil pan before tightening the timing cover bolts.

V8

1. Remove the oil pan.
2. Remove the bolt holding the oil pump to the rear main bearing cap.
3. Remove the pump and the extension shaft.
4. Installation is the reverse of removal. Align the slot on the top of the extension shaft with the drive tang on the lower end of the distributor driveshaft. The installed position of the oil pump screen should be parallel to the oil pan rails.

Oil Pump (Front Cover) Seal R & R—4 Cylinder

1. Remove the following:

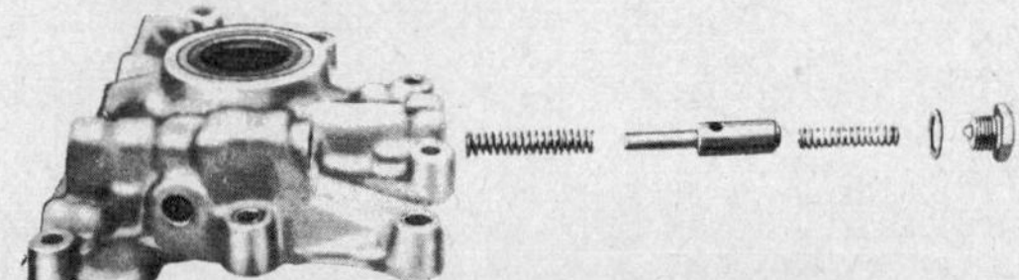

Oil pump pressure regulator (4 cylinder)
(© Chevrolet Div., G.M. Corp)

a. Engine front cover.
b. Accessory drive pulley.
c. Timing belt.
d. Timing belt lower cover.
e. Crankshaft timing sprocket.

2. Pry out the old seal, being careful not to damage the housing seal surfaces.
3. Coat the lips of the new seal with oil and apply sealing compound to the outside diameter of the seal.
4. Install the seal with the closed end outward.
5. Install all components removed in Step 1 above.

Rear Main Oil Seal R & R

4 Cylinder

NOTE: This repair can be made without removing the engine, but the transmission must be removed so that the crankshaft can be lowered.

1. Remove the oil pan and baffle.
2. Remove the rear main bearing cap and discard the lower seal.
3. Loosen the remaining bearing caps to allow the crankshaft to be lowered.
4. Push the upper seal on one end enough so that the other end can be grasped with pliers. Pull out the upper seal.
5. Cut and form a new braided fabric upper seal in the bearing cap. Taper the end of the seal and insert a piece of soft wire through the seal about ¼ in. from the end. Wrap the wire around the seal to form a secure attachment.
6. Thread the wire through the upper seal groove, then start the seal and pull it into position.
7. Tighten all the bearing caps except the rear cap to 65 ft. lbs.
8. Cut the seal flush to 1/64 in. below the bearing edge, making a clean cut and leaving no raveled edges.
9. Install and cut a seal in the rear main bearing cap.
10. Install the rear main bearing cap and measure the clearance with Plastigage, tightening the cap bolts to 65 ft. lbs. If the bearing clearance is within specifications, the seal is properly seated.
11. Install the bearing cap, tightening to 65 ft. lbs.
12. Install rear main bearing cap side sealant. This is available in a kit, complete with plunger applicator, from Chevrolet. Force the compound firmly into place to ensure that there are no air bubbles.
13. Install the oil pan and baffle.

V8

The rear main bearing seal may be replaced without removing the crankshaft. Seals should only be replaced as a pair. Fabrication of a seal installation tool will prevent damaging the bead on the cylinder block. The seal lips should face the front of the engine when properly installed.

1. Remove the oil pan and pump, and remove the rear main bearing cap.
2. Pry the lower seal out of the bearing cap with a screwdriver, being careful not to gouge the cap surface.
3. Remove the upper seal by lightly tapping on one end with a brass pin punch until the other end can be grasped and pulled out with pliers.
4. Clean the bearing cap, cylinder block, and crankshaft mating surfaces with solvent. Inspect all these surfaces for gouges, nicks, and burrs.
5. Apply light engine oil to the seal lips and bead, but keep the seal ends clean.
6. Insert the tip of the installation tool between the crankshaft and the seal seat of the cylinder block. Place the seal between the tip of the tool and the crankshaft, so that the bead contacts the tip of the tool.
7. Be sure that the seal lip is facing the front of the engine, and work the seal around the crankshaft, using the installation tool to protect the seal from the corner of the cylinder block.

NOTE: do not remove the tool until the opposite end of the seal is flush with the cylinder block surface.

8. Remove the installation tool, being careful not to pull the seal out at the same time.
9. Using the same procedure, install the lower seal into the bearing cap. Use your finger and thumb to lever the seal into the cap.
10. Apply sealer to the cylinder block only where the cap mates to the surface. Do not apply sealer to the seal ends.
11. Install the rear cap and torque the bolts to specifications. Install the oil pan and pump.

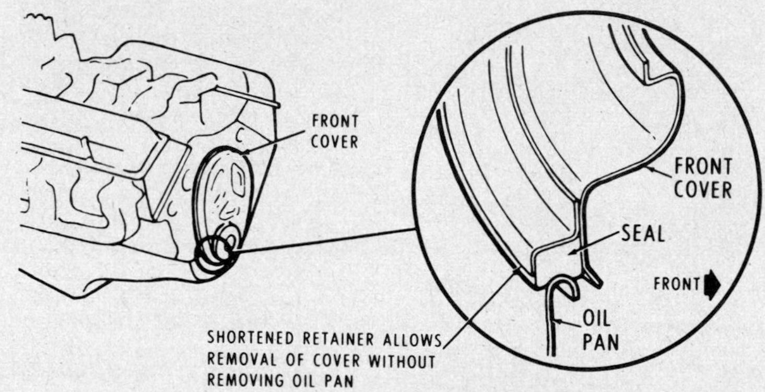

Oil seal installation—V8
(© Chevrolet Div., G.M. Corp)

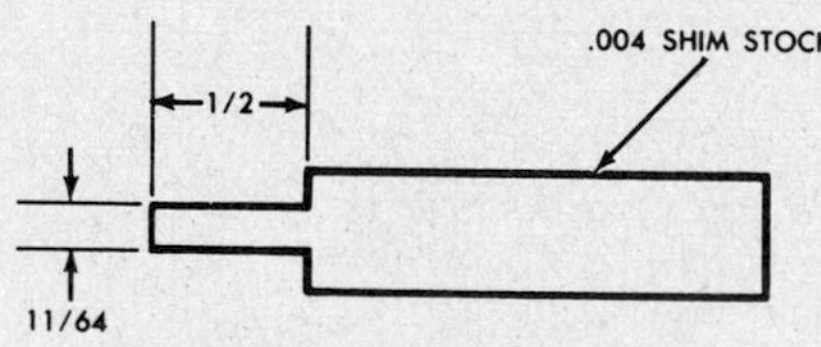

Oil seal installation tool
(© Chevrolet Div., G.M. Corp)

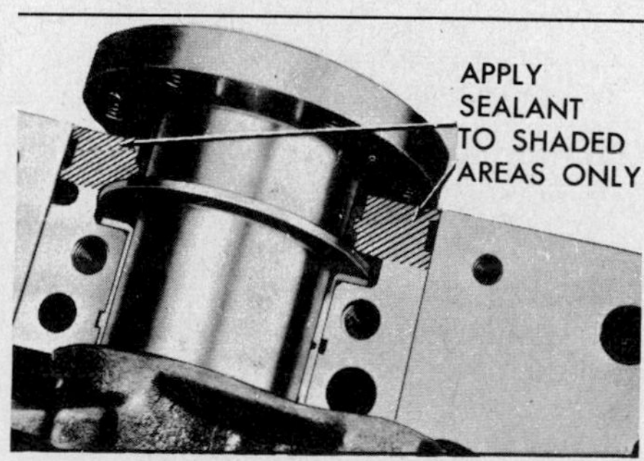

Sealant application—V8
(© Chevrolet Div., G.M. Corp)

CLUTCH

Clutch Pedal Free Travel Adjustment

Adjustment for normal clutch wear is accomplished by turning the clutch fork ball stud counterclockwise to give .90 ± .25 in. lash at clutch pedal.

1. Remove ball stud cap and loosen locknut on ball stud end located to the right of the transmission on the clutch housing.
2. Adjust ball stud to obtain .90 ± .25 in. free travel.
3. Tighten locknut to 25 ft lbs. being careful not to change adjustment and install ball stud cap.
4. Check operation of clutch.

Clutch Cable Replacement

1. Remove clutch fork cover at side of housing.
2. Disconnect return spring and clutch cable at clutch shift fork.
3. Remove clip and pin retaining cable to pedal arm.

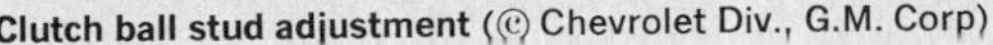

Clutch ball stud adjustment (© Chevrolet Div., G.M. Corp)

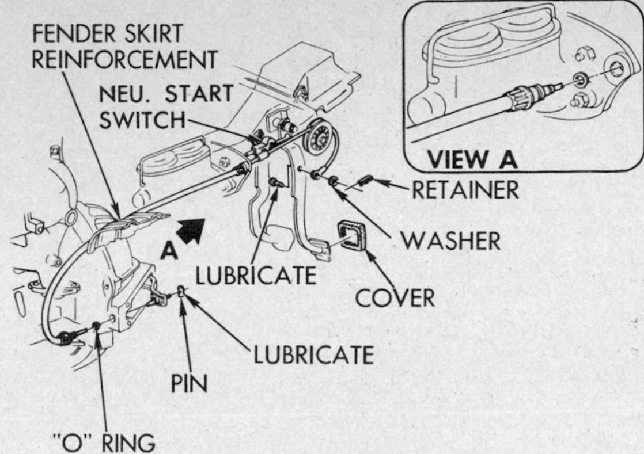

Clutch control cable (© Chevrolet Div., G.M. Corp)

4. Pull cable assembly through reinforcement and disengage from fender skirt reinforcement.
5. Push new cable through body reinforcement and around pulley. Secure cable end to pedal arm with pin, washer and clip.

NOTE: lubricate retaining pin with graphite type grease.

6. Route cable over fender skirt reinforcement and down to the clutch fork lever. Install cable end in fork lever as previously outlined under adjustment procedures.
7. Install clutch fork cover and tighten retaining screws to 80 in. lbs.

Clutch Disc R & R

1. Raise vehicle on hoist.
2. Remove transmission as outlined in this section.
3. Remove clutch fork cover then disconnect clutch return spring and control cable from clutch fork.
4. Remove main drive gear oil seal from clutch release bearing sleeve.
5. Remove flywheel housing lower cover.
6. Remove flywheel housing from engine.
7. To remove the release bearing from clutch fork and sleeve, slide lever off ball stud against spring action. If necessary to replace ball stud, remove cap, locknut and stud from housing.
8. If assembly marks on clutch assembly and flywheel are not distinguishable, remark with paint or center-punch.
9. Loosen clutch cover to flywheel, attaching bolts one turn at a time until spring pressure is released, to avoid bending clutch cover flange.
10. Support the pressure plate and cover assembly then remove the bolts and clutch assembly.

Caution Do not disassemble the clutch cover, spring and pressure plate for repair. If defective replace complete assembly.

11. Index alignment marks on clutch assembly and flywheel. Place driven plate on pressure plate with long end of splined end facing forward, damper springs inside pressure plate, and insert a dummy clutch gear shaft through the cover and driven plate.
12. Position the complete assembly against the flywheel and insert the dummy shaft into the pilot bearing in the crankshaft.
13. Index the alignment marks and install clutch cover to flywheel bolts finger-tight.

Caution Tighten all bolts evenly and gradually until tight to avoid possible clutch distortion. Torque bolts 18 ft. bs. and remove dummy shaft.

14. Lubricate the clutch fork ball socket and the fingers at the release bearing with a high melting point grease such as graphite grease.
15. Lubricate the recess on the inside of the throwout bearing collar and the fork groove with a light coat of graphite grease. Install fork in housing but not on stud.
16. Install bearing on sleeve, then position clutch fork over bearing in housing and slide fork onto ball stud.
17. Install flywheel housing and lower cover. Tighten bolts to 25 ft. lbs.
18. Install transmission as outlined previously.
19. Adjust clutch as previously outlined.
20. Lower and remove vehicle from hoist.

MANUAL TRANSMISSION

The 1971-72 three and four-speed manual transmissions available on the Vega are both fully synchronized in all forward gears and have floor mounted shift controls. The three-speed transmission first-reverse synchronizer sleeve has gear teeth on the outside diameter which enable it to function as a reverse gear when engaged with the reverse idler gear. The reverse gear on the four-speed transmission is similar to that of the three-speed except that the reverse teeth are on the first-second synchronizer. The control lever on this transmission has a reverse lockout feature.

The Opel-made transmissions used in 1971-72 were replaced with Saginaw three and four-speed units in 1973. These are fully synchronized and are similar to those used throughout the Chevrolet line.

A 5-speed is optional on 1975-76 models with 4 cylinder engines. The unit is a Borg-Warner T-50.

Shift Mechanism Adjustment

1971-72 Four-Speed

The reverse gearshift blocker adjustment can only be made on the four-speed transmission. This adjustment is made at the selector shaft on the left side of the transmission.

1. Shift into second gear.
2. Adjust the selector ring so that the shift lever finger ball has equal clearance on both sides in the intermediate lever hole.
3. Back off the selector ring a quarter turn and tighten the locknut.

Linkage Adjustment

1973-76 Three and Four-Speed

1. Turn the ignition switch to "Off" and place the shift lever in neutral.
2. Raise the car.
3. Loosen the lock nuts on the control rods. Position the transmission side cover levers in their neutral detents.
4. With the floor shift lever in neutral, align the shifter levers and insert a gauge pin into the levers and bracket.
5. Tighten the First/Reverse (First/Second on four-speed) control rod lock nut against its swivel.

6. Tighten the Second/Third (Third/Fourth on four-speed) control rod lock nut against its swivel.
7. On four-speeds, tighten the Reverse control rod lock nut against its swivel.

NOTE: All lock nuts are tightened to 120 in. lbs.

8. Remove the gauge pin and check shifter operation.

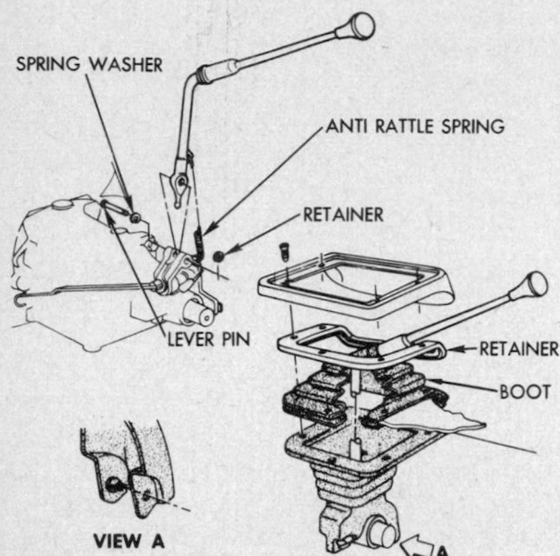

1971-72 shift control lever installation
(© Chevrolet Div., G.M. Corp)

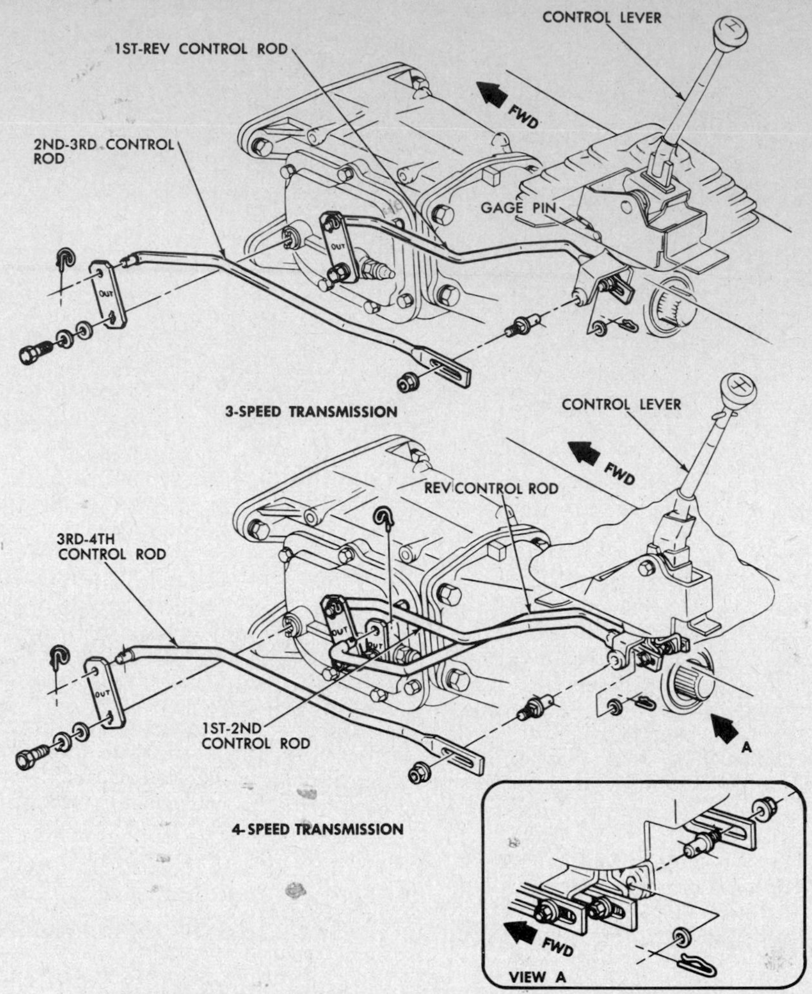

1973-76 three and four-speed linkage (© Chevrolet Div., G.M. Corp)

Gearshift Lever Control Wire Replacement

1971-72 Four-Speed

1. Remove gearshift lever from vehicle.
2. Carefully remove gearshift lever knob (by pulling) and loosen set screw.
3. Drive out spiral pins.
4. Take off shift finger and pull Bowden control wire out of gearshift lever. Thrust spring may also be removed at this time.

NOTE: before installation, oil sliding surface of stop sleeve on shift finger tube.

5. Install new control wire through gearshift lever and fasten new control wire with clamp sleeve so that the cutout of the stop sleeve shows toward the left. Insert spiral pin (long pin).

NOTE: spiral pin must not protrude on either side.

6. With set screw, clamp Bowden control wire tight so that pull ring is positioned on gearshift lever tube and clamping block on pull ring.

NOTE: do not put tension on Bowden cable. Pull knob should have approximately 1/16 in. free travel.

7. With short spiral pin, attach shift finger.
8. Install gearshift lever knob and adhere to a distance of .30 in.

Transmission R & R

1971-72

1. Place transmission shift lever in neutral and pull the boot up.
2. Unhook the antirattle coil spring. Remove the shift finger (lower end of the lever) pin retaining clip and pin. Remove shift lever.
3. Raise the vehicle and drain the lubricant from transmission.
4. Remove driveshaft assembly.
5. Disconnect the speedometer cable, TCS switch and back-up lamp switch.
6. Remove crossmember-to-transmission mount bolts.
7. Support engine with an appropriate jack stand and remove crossmember-to-frame bolts. Remove crossmember from vehicle.
8. Remove transmission to clutch housing upper retaining bolts and install guide pins in holes.
9. Remove lower bolts, then slide transmission rearward and remove from vehicle.

NOTE: inspect throwout bearing support gasket located beneath lip of support. If defective, replace gasket before installing transmission.

10. Lightly lubricate inside diameter of clutch drive gear seal and install seal on drive gear.
11. Position new gasket to face of clutch housing. The gasket can be temporarily retained by a small amount of grease.
12. Position transmission to clutch housing and slide forward, piloting clutch gear in to pilot bearing.

NOTE: make certain main drive gear splines are clean and dry.

13. Install transmission-to-clutch housing retaining bolts and lockwashers.
14. Position crossmember to frame and loosely install retaining bolts. Install crossmember-to-transmission mount bolts. Tighten all retaining bolts to specifications. Remove engine support.

Caution Check position of engine in front mounts and align as required.

15. Connect speedometer cable, back-up lamp switch and TCS switch.
16. Install driveshaft assembly.
17. Fill transmission to proper level. Lower vehicle.
18. Lubricate shift finger bolt and spherical end of shaft. Install shift lever in shift housing and install bolt. Secure with retaining clip.
19. Install shift lever spring. Position shift lever boot and bezel to floor pan. Install retaining screws.

20. Check operation of transmission.

1973-76

1. Raise the car and drain the transmission.
2. Remove the driveshaft.
3. Disconnect the speedometer cable, TCS switch, and the back-up light switch. Remove the damper.
4. Detach the control rods and levers from the transmission, tie them together, and position them out of the way.
5. Remove the crossmember-to-transmission mounting bolts.
6. Support the engine and remove the crossmember-to-frame bolts. Remove the crossmember.
7. Remove the top transmission-to-clutch housing bolts and install guide pins in the holes.
8. Remove the lower bolts and pull the transmission back and out of the car.
9. Guide the input shaft through the throwout bearing and into the pilot bearing.
10. Install the transmission retaining bolts and lockwashers. Tighten the bolts to 40 ft lbs.
11. Position the crossmember on the frame and install the retaining bolts hand-tight.
12. Install the crossmember-to-transmission bolts and then tighten all bolts to 28 ft lbs.
13. Remove the engine support.
14. Install the transmission control rods to the shifter. Adjust the linkage as previously outlined.
15. Connect the speedometer cable, TCS switch, and back-up light switch.
16. Install the driveshaft.
17. Fill the transmission to the level of the filler plug.
18. Lower the car and check transmission operation.

AUTOMATIC TRANSMISSION

Several automatic transmissions have been available on the Vega. The aluminum Powerglide consists of a three-element torque converter which drives through a two-speed planetary gear-set. The Torque Drive transmission is essentially a Powerglide without the automatic shifting mechanisms. Torque Drive was dropped after 1972. A three-speed Turbo Hydra-Matic 350 transmission became available in 1972. Beginning February 1973, a Turbo Hydra-Matic 250 was introduced to replace the 350; the 350 is still used with the 350 V8. The 250 is similar to the 350, except that the intermediate clutch assembly has been replaced by an externally adjustable intermediate band assembly. Powerglide was dropped in mid-1973.

Neutral Safety Switch Adjustment

1. Remove four screws securing floor console.
2. Disconnect the electrical plugs on the back-up, neutral start, and seat belt buzzer (1973-75) contacts of the neutral safety switch.
3. Place shift lever in Neutral.
4. Remove two screws securing shift indicator plate.
5. Remove two screws securing shift lever curved cover.
6. Remove two screws securing neutral start switch to lever assembly.

NOTE: screws are hidden beneath lever cover.

7. Tilt switch assembly to right as you lift switch out of lever hole.
8. Make sure shift lever is in Neutral before installing switch assembly.
9. Assemble switch assembly to control lever bracket by inserting drive tang into hole in neutral start switch lever.

NOTE: When installing the same neutral switch, align the contact support slot with the service adjustment hole in the switch and insert a 3/32 in. drill to hold the switch in neutral. Remove the drill after the switch is fastened to the shift lever mounting bracket.

10. Tighten two mounting screws securing switch assembly to lever bracket.
11. Install curved shift lever cover and secure with two screws.
12. Install shift indicator plate and attach with two screws.
13. Moving control lever out of Neutral will shear the switch plastic locating pin.
14. Plug electrical connectors into switch assembly; apply parking brake and start vehicle—check for starting in Neutral and Park only. Also check for back-up lamps on in reverse.
15. Turn off ignition and install console cover securing with four screws.

Shift Linkage Adjustment

1971-72 Powerglide, Torque Drive

This adjustment gives about 0.05 in. overtravel in each gear shift position to provide full engagement.

1. Loosen the two shift rod adjusting nuts at the swivel. The swivel is attached to the floorshift lever lower lever.
2. Turn the shift lever on the transmission all the way clockwise. This is the Park detent position. Turn the lever counterclockwise two detents to the neutral detent position.
3. Make sure that the floorshift is in the neutral position.
4. Push forward lightly on the floorshift assembly lower lever until the floorshift lever can be felt against its neutral detent. Hold the lower lever in place.
5. Hold a 0.073 in. thick spacer in front of the swivel. Tighten the front adjusting nut to clamp the spacer between the nut and swivel.
6. Pull out the spacer and lightly pull back on the floorshift assembly lower lever. Tighten the rear adjusting nut.

1972 Turbo Hydra-Matic 350

Use the Powerglide and Torque Drive procedure, substituting the following steps:

4. Pull back lightly on the floorshift assembly lower lever until the floorshift lever can be felt to be against its neutral detent. Hold the lower lever in place.
5. Hold a 0.073 in. thick spacer between the nut and swivel.
6. Pull the spacer out and pull lightly forward on the floorshift assembly lower lever. Tighten the front adjusting nut.

NOTE: Late 1972 models and all 1973 and later models are equipped with slotted control rods. Adjustment of this linkage is given later.

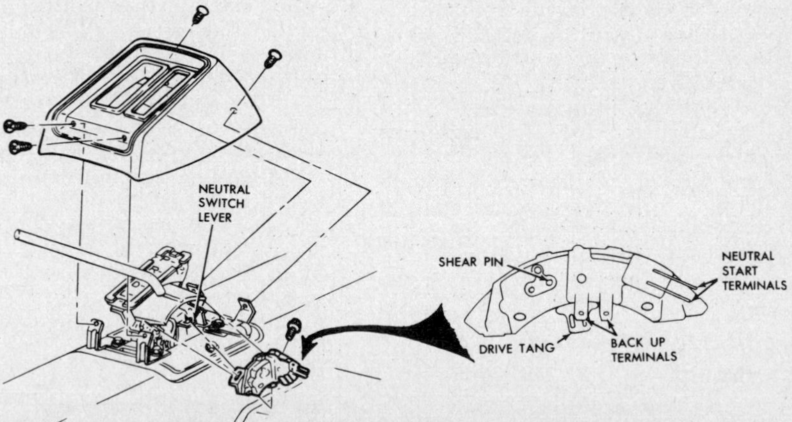

1971-72 neutral safety switch adjustment—1973-76 switch has two additional terminals for seat belt alarm (© Chevrolet Div., G.M. Corp)

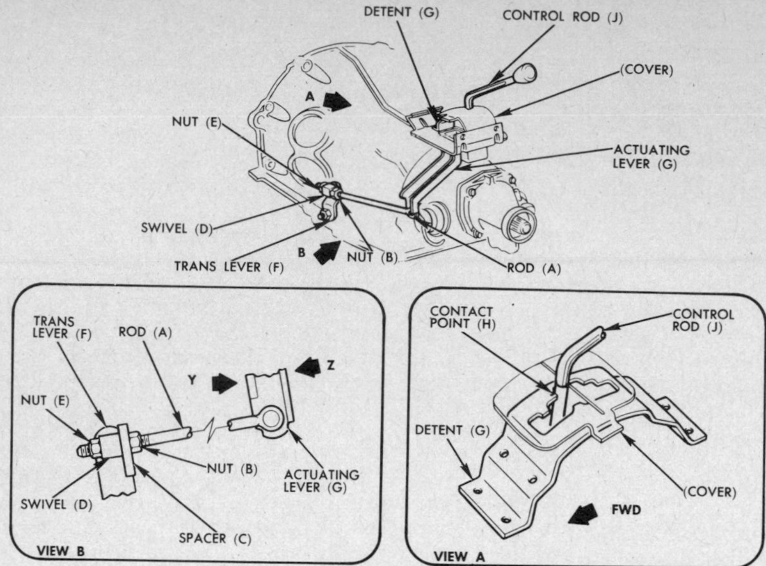

1972 Turbo Hydra-Matic 350 linkage adjustment (© Chevrolet Div., G.M. Corp)

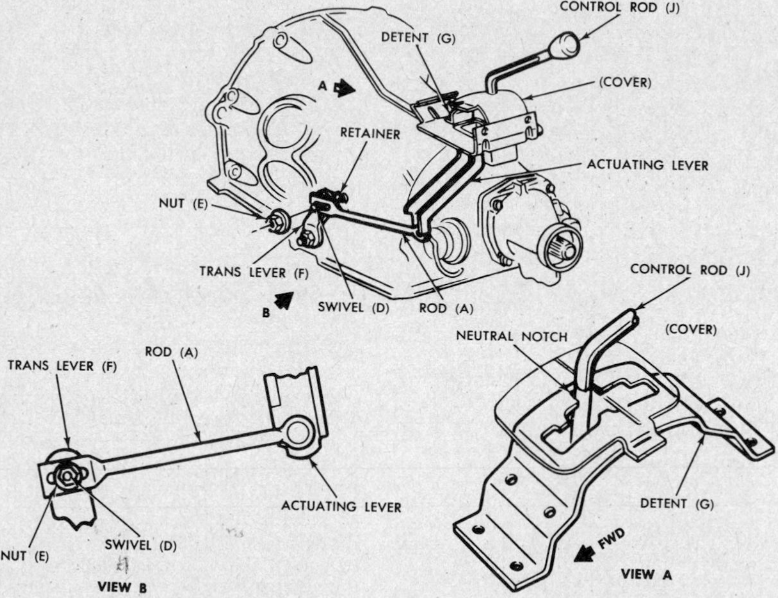

1973-76 Turbo Hydra-Matic linkage (© Chevrolet Div., G.M. Corp)

1973-76 Turbo Hydra-Matic 250 and 350

1. Loosen the nut and swivel at the transmission lever.
2. Set the transmission lever in Neutral by moving it counterclockwise to the L1 detent and then clockwise three detent positions to Neutral.
3. Position the shift lever in the Neutral notch of the detent plate.
4. Place the flat of the swivel into the slot of the control rod. Install the washer and cotter pin.
5. Tighten the locknut to 120 in lbs. Adjust the neutral safety switch, if necessary.

Throttle Valve Linkage Adjustment

Powerglide

1. Hold the accelerator pedal all the way down.
2. Unclip and detach the rear end of the throttle valve control rod (horizontal rod).
3. The bellcrank lever stud should be all the way forward in the slot at the front of the throttle valve control rod.
4. Hold the lever at the transmission against its internal stop.
5. If the rear end of the throttle valve control rod does not align with the hole in the lever, pull out the retaining clip from the sleeve in the center of the rod. Adjust the sleeve to lengthen or shorten the rod.

NOTE: The sleeve is adjustable one turn at a time.

6. Install the throttle valve control rod in the lever hole and attach the clip.

Detent Cable Adjustment

Turbo Hydra-Matic 250 and 350

1. Remove the air cleaner.
2. Insert a screwdriver on each side of the snap-lock on the bracket at the front of the transmission and pry up to release the lock.
3. Compress the lock tabs and disconnect the snap-lock assembly from the bracket.
4. Position the carburetor lever in the wide open throttle position.
5. Hold the carburetor lever in position and push the snap-lock on the cable down until the top is flush with the cable.

NOTE: The cable should not be lubricated.

6. Install the air cleaner.

Low Band Adjustment

Powerglide, Torque Drive

1. Position the shift lever in neutral.
2. Remove the protective cap from the adjusting screw.
3. Loosen the locknut ¼ turn and hold it with a wrench during the entire adjusting procedure.
4. Tighten the adjusting nut to 70 in. lbs, using a 7/32 allen wrench.
5. Back off the adjusting nut exactly three turns for a band used less than 6,000 miles. Back off exactly four turns for a band used 6,000 miles or more.
6. Torque the locknut to 15 ft lbs. and replace the cap.

Intermediate Band Adjustment

Turbo Hydra-Matic 250

1. Position the shift lever in Neutral.
2. Loosen the locknut and tighten the adjusting screw to 30 in lbs.
3. Back the screw out three turns and then tighten the locknut to 15 ft lbs.

Pan R & R, Fluid and Filter Change

The fluid should be drained with the transmission warm.

1. Support the transmission at the vibration damper. If necessary, remove the crossmember.
2. Prepare a large pan to catch the transmission fluid.
3. Loosen all the pan screws, then pull one corner down to drain most of the fluid.
4. Remove the pan screws and empty out the pan. The pan can be cleaned out with solvent but it must be dried thoroughly before replacement. Be very careful not to leave any lint or threads from rags in the pan.
5. Remove the filter or strainer retaining bolt (two on Turbo Hydra-Matic 250 and 350). A reuseable strainer is used on two-speed transmissions and the Turbo Hydra-Matic 250. The strainer may be cleaned in solvent and air-dried thoroughly.

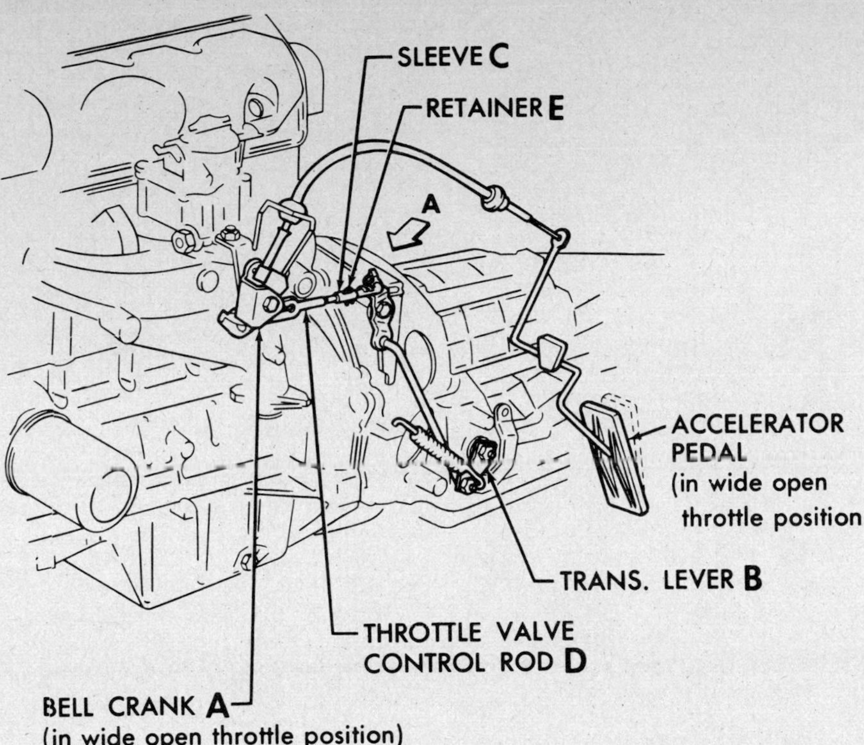

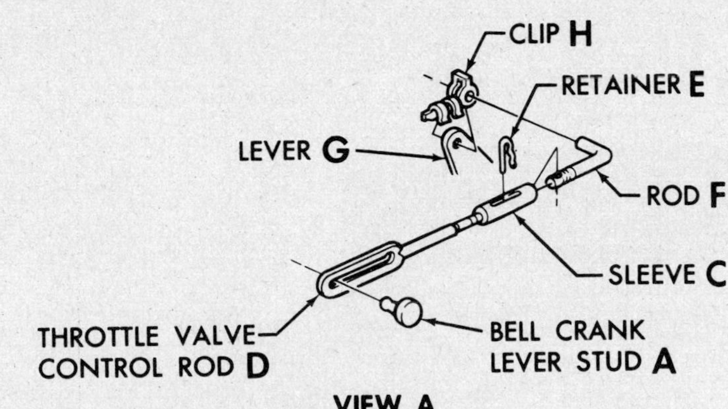

Powerglide throttle valve linkage adjustment (© Chevrolet Div., G.M. Corp)

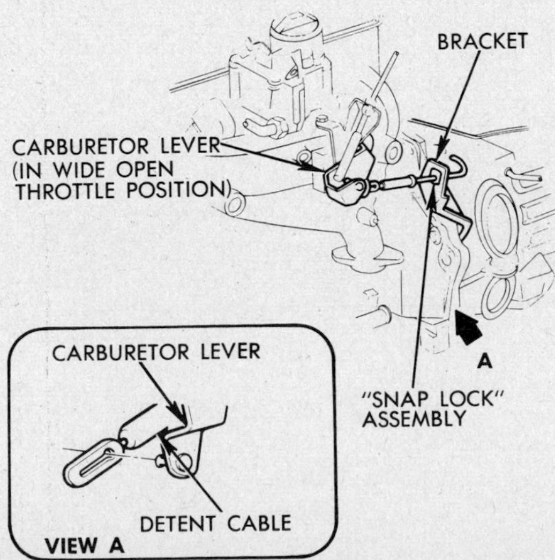

Turbo Hydra-Matic 350 and 250 detent cable adjustment (© Chevrolet Div., G.M. Corp)

Filters are to be replaced. Use a new gasket on all other models.

6. Install the new filter or cleaned strainer.
7. Install the pan with a new gasket. Tighten the bolts evenly (12 ft lbs) in a criss-cross pattern.
8. Replace the crossmembers if removed.
9. Add DEXRON or DEXRON II transmission fluid through the dipstick tube. Add 5 pts for Turbo Hydra-Matic 250, and 3 for the 350, Torque Drive, and Powerglide.
10. Start the engine and let it idle. Do not race the engine. Shift through all the indicator positions, holding thhe brakes. Check the fluid level with the engine idling in Park. The level should be between the two dimples on the dipstick, about ¼ in. below the ADD mark. Add fluid as necessary.
11. Check the fluid level after the car has been driven enough to thoroughly warm up the transmission. The level should be at the FULL mark on the dipstick. If the transmission is overfilled, the excess must be drained off. Overfilling causes aerated fluid, resulting in transmission slippage and probable damage.

U-JOINTS

U-Joint R & R

1. Raise and support the car. Mark relationship of shaft to companion flange and disconnect the rear universal joint by removing trunnion bearing U-bolts. Tape bearing cups to trunnion to prevent losing the bearing rollers.
2. Withdraw driveshaft front yoke from transmission by moving shaft rearward and passing it under the axle housing. Cover the transmission opening to prevent fluid or oil loss.
3. Inspect yoke seal in the transmission extension, replace if necessary.
4. Insert driveshaft front yoke into transmission extention, making sure that output shaft splines mate with driveshaft yoke splines.
5. Align driveshaft with companion flange using reference marks established in removal procedure. Remove the tape from the U-joint, install the U-bolts to the rear axle flange, and torque them to 15 ft lbs.

REAR AXLE

Vega and Monza axles are the Chevrolet "C-type" with C-locks retaining the axle shafts. All axles are

Removing or installing the differential pinion shaft lockpin (© Chevrolet Div., G.M. Corp)

hypoid type, semi-floating with an integral gear carrier and a removable cover plate.

Vegas use a 6½ in. ring gear and the Monza uses a 7½ in. ring gear.

Axle Shaft R & R

1. Raise and support the car.
2. Remove the wheel and brake drum.
3. Clean all dirt from the carrier area.
4. Drain the lubricant from the carrier by removing the cover.
5. Remove the differential pinion shaft lockscrew and remove the differential pinion shaft.
6. Push the flanged end of the shaft toward the center of the car and remove the C-lock from the groove in the axle shaft.
7. Pull the axle shaft from the housing. Be careful not to damage the oil seal.
8. Slide the axle shaft into place.
9. Be sure that the splines on the axle shaft engage with the splines in the differential side gears. Be sure the oil seal is not damaged.
10. Install the axle shaft C-lock. Push the shaft outward so that the C-lock seats in the counterbore of the differential side gear.
11. Install the differential pinion shaft and lockscrew.
12. Further installation is the reverse of removal. Fill the axle with fresh lubricant.

Oil Seal/Axle Bearing Replacement

1. Remove the axle shaft.
2. If replacing the seal only, insert the button end of the axle shaft behind the steel case of the oil seal and pry the seal out of the bore.
3. When removing the bearings, use a slide hammer with care.
4. Lubricate a new bearing with hypoid axle lubricant, and install it with a driver.
5. Lubricate the cavity between the seal lips with high melting point wheel bearing grease and install the seal in the axle housing nntil it is flush with the end of the housing.
6. Install the axle shaft.

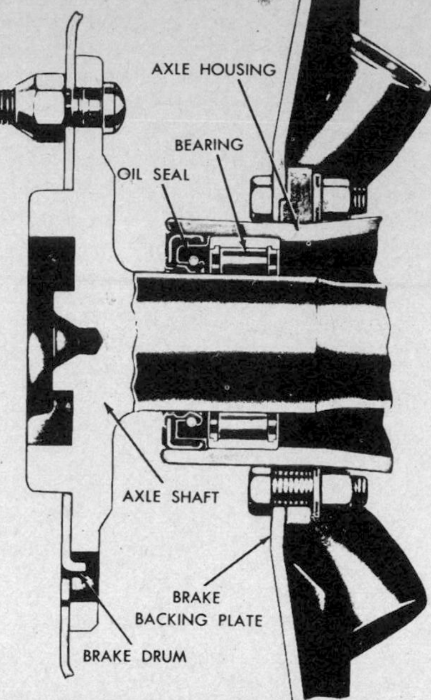

Axle shaft bearing and seal (© Chevrolet Div., G.M. Corp)

JACKING, HOISTING

The illustration shows the correct jacking and hoist lifting positions.

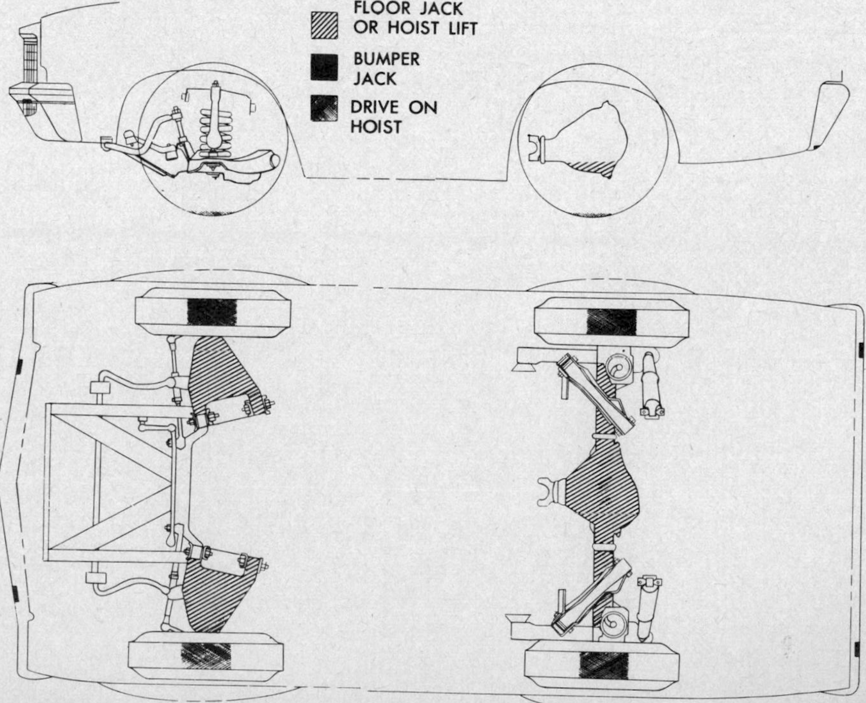

Lift points (© Chevrolet Div., G.M. Corp)

FRONT SUSPENSION

Vega and Monza suspension utilizes unequal length A-arms with coil springs. V8 models use longer coil springs. The lower control arm bolts to the front end sheet metal with cam bolts which adjust the camber and caster. The upper ball joint is riveted to the upper control arm and the lower ball joint is pressed into the lower control arm.

Shock Absorber R & R

1. Pry out the access plug in the engine compartment so that the upper mount is visible.
2. Raise the front of the car and safely support it.
3. Turn the wheels for clearance.
4. Hold the upper shock stud with a

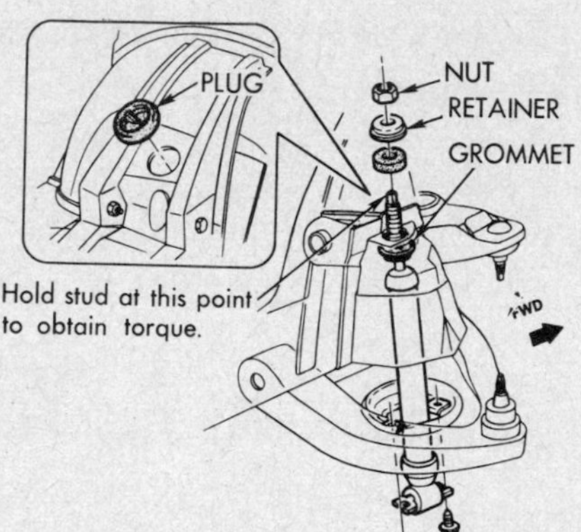

Front shock absorber mounting (© Chevrolet Div., G.M. Corp)

wrench. Loosen and remove the locknut.
5. Unbolt the lower end and pull the shock down and out.
6. Place the lower retainer and rubber grommet on the shock stud.
7. Put the shock in place and tighten the lower bolts. Torque to 20 ft lbs.
8. Place the upper grommet, retainer, and nut on the shock stud.
9. Hold the stud with a wrench and tighten the nut. Torque to 120 in. lbs.

Ball Joint and Tie-Rod End Inspection

1971-74

1. Raise the front of the car and support it under the lower control arm. Make sure that the wheel bearings are properly adjusted before making this check.
2. Turn the wheels straight ahead.
3. Grasp and shake the wheel from side to side, horizontally. If there is noticeable looseness, the tie-rod ends are worn.
4. Grasp the top and bottom of the tire and rock it by pushing in on the top and pulling out on the bottom, then pulling out on the top and pushing in on the bottom. A ¼ in. play indicates worn ball joints.

1975-76

The lower ball joints incorporate wear indicators. They can be inspected visually; when the ½ in. diameter grease fitting is flush with, or inside the cover surface, replace the ball joint. Inspect the grease fitting with the car supported on its wheels so that the lower ball joint is in a loaded condition. Normal protrusion of the grease fitting is .050 in. beyond the cover surface.

Ball joint tightness can also be checked using the preceding procedure.

Ball Joint R & R

Upper

1. Jack up the front of the car and support it under the crossmember braces. Remove the wheel.
2. Place a hydraulic jack under the lower control arm.
3. Remove the cotter pin from the ball joint stud. Loosen, but do not remove the nut.
4. The stud may now be pressed out upward. There is a special tool available to do this.
5. Remove the ball joint by grinding off the rivets, or removing the heads of the rivets with a cold chisel.
6. Bolt the new ball joint on, using the nuts and bolts supplied with the replacement joint.
7. Install the stud to the steering knuckle and torque the nut to 30 ft lbs. If the cotter pin hole does not align, tighten the nut ½ of a turn further to line it up. Install a new cotter pin.
8. Install the wheel and lower the car.

Lower

1. Repeat steps one through four of the upper ball joint procedure.
2. The stud may now be pressed out downward. A special tool is available for this purpose.
3. The old joint must be pressed out of the control arm. A tool is available for this operation.
4. Press in the new joint, positioning it so that the grease bleed vent in the rubber boot is facing inward.
5. Install a lubrication fitting in the new joint.
6. Install the stud to the steering knuckle and torque the nut to 60 ft lbs. If the cotter pin hole does not align, tighten it 1/6 of a turn further. Do not loosen the nut to install the cotter pin.
7. Install the wheel and lower the car.

Front spring removal
(© Chevrolet Div., G.M. Corp)

Spring R & R

1. Raise the front of the car and support it with jackstands placed under the front crossmember braces.
2. Remove the wheel, shock absorbers, and stabilizer bar.
3. Support the lower control arm outer end with a hydraulic floor jack and a block of wood.
4. Securely fasten the spring to the lower control arm with a heavy chain.
5. To detach the tie rod, remove the cotter pin and nut, and tap on the steering arm (not the tie-rod end) with a hammer. Hold another hammer behind the steering arm to take the force of the tapping. The tie rod should then fall free.
6. Remove the lower ball joint stud from the steering knuckle as described in the "Lower Ball Joint R&R" procedure.
7. Very cautiously lower the jack until the spring is fully expanded.
8. Place the spring in its pads on the lower control arm and shock tower. Secure it with a chain as in step four.
9. Carefully raise the jack.
10. Place the lower ball joint stud in the steering knuckle. Torque the stud nut to 60 ft lbs. If the cotter pin does not align, tighten it further 1/6 of a turn and insert a new cotter pin.
11. Install the tie-rod end to the steering arm. Torque the nut to 35 ft lbs. If the cotter pin hole does not align, tighten further up to a maximum of 50 ft lbs. Insert a new cotter pin.
12. Replace the shock absorber as described in "Shock Absorber R&R." Do not attach the top end of the shock at this point.

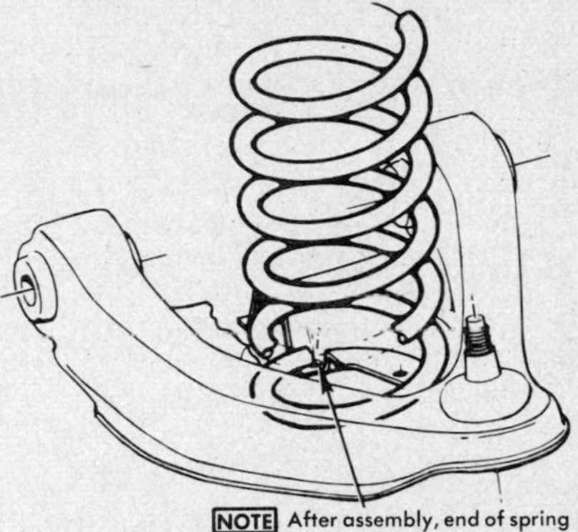

Front spring positioning
(© Chevrolet Div., G.M. Corp)

13. Install the stabilizer bar. Tighten the bracket bolts to 30 ft lbs and the control arm bolts to 10 ft lbs.
14. Replace the wheel and lower the car. Install the upper end of the shock absorber.

Wheel Bearing Adjustment

1. Jack up the front of the car and support it with jackstands.
2. Remove the dust cap with a pair of slip-joint pliers.
3. Remove and discard the cotter pin. Loosen the spindle nut. Tighten it snugly to seat the bearings, and then loosen the nut again.
4. Rotate the wheel and tighten the spindle nut to 12 ft lbs. which is roughly equivalent to finger tightness.
5. Back the nut off one flat and insert a new cotter pin. If the hole does not line up, back the nut off ½ flat or less to align the hole.
6. Check that the wheel turns freely, and then lock the cotter pin.
7. Bearing end-play should be between 0.001 and 0.008 in. (1971-73) or 0.001-0.005 in. (1974-76). Tap the dust cap back on and lower the car.

Lower Control Arm R & R

1. Raise the front of the car.
2. Remove shock absorber as previously outlined.
3. Remove ball stud from steering knuckle.
4. Remove coil spring using the preceding procedure.
5. Remove the inner pivot cam nuts and bolts.

NOTE: mark the position of the cam bolts before loosening nuts. This step will aid in assembly.

6. Remove the control arm.
7. Install the control arm.

NOTE: be sure that the control arm bushings have the metal caps installed.

8. Install the cam bolts through the control arm bushings.

NOTE: the front cam bolt (camber) must be installed with the head toward the front of the vehicle and the rear cam bolt (caster) must be installed with the head toward the rear of the vehicle.

9. Install the inner cams to the cam bolt.
10. Install the lockwasher and nut.
11. Align the cam bolts with the marks made before removal.
12. Install the coil spring.
13. Install the shock absorber.
14. Lower vehicle to the floor.
15. Check front alignment.

Upper Control Arm R & R

1. Raise vehicle on a hoist and remove the wheel.
2. Support the lower control arm with a floor jack.
3. Remove upper ball stud nut and remove ball stud from steering knuckle.
4. Remove control arm pivot bolts and remove control arm from vehicle.
5. Install upper control arm to vehicle at inner pivot.

NOTE: the inner pivot bolts must be installed with the bolt heads to the front (on the front bushing) and to the rear, (on the rear bushing).

6. Install the inner pivot nuts.
7. Position the control arm in a horizontal plane and tighten the inner pivot nuts.
8. Install ball stud to steering knuckle. Tighten nut and install cotter pin.
9. Install tire and wheel assembly and lower vehicle.

Steering Knuckle R & R

1. Raise vehicle on a hoist and support the lower control arm with a jackstand.

NOTE: this keeps the coil spring compressed.

2. Remove the tire and wheel assembly.
3. Remove the disc brake caliper.

NOTE: secure the caliper to the suspension using wire. Do not allow the caliper to hang by the brake hose. Insert a piece of wood (about the same thickness as a brake disc) between the shoes to hold the piston in the caliper bore.

4. Remove the hub and disc.
5. Remove the splash shield.
6. Remove the tie rod end from the steering knuckle.
7. Remove the cotter pins from the upper and lower ball studs and loosen the ball stud nuts.
8. Install a spare wheel stud nut on either the upper or lower ball stud and press the ball stud from the steering knuckle.
9. Using a spare nut as in Step 8 press the other ball stud from the steering knuckle.
10. Remove ball stud nuts and remove the steering knuckle.
11. Place steering knuckle in position and insert the upper and lower ball studs into knuckle bosses.
12. Install ball stud nuts and tighten to 60 ft. lbs. Install cotter pin.

NOTE: if necessary, tighten to the next slot to insert cotter pin. Never back off on a ball stud nut to align cotter pin.

13. Install splash shield to the steering knuckle.
14. Install the tie rod end to the steering knuckle. Torque to 35 ft lbs.
15. Install the hub and disc, bearings and nut. Install cotter pin.
16. Install the brake caliper.
17. Install the wheels, remove the jackstand and lower the car.

REAR SUSPENSION

Vegas (1971-75)) use a coil spring rear suspension with upper and lower control arms.

A new torque arm rear suspension is used on Monza 2 + 2s, and 1976 Vegas using lower control arms and a track bar to control lateral movement. A torque arm is used to control rear axle wind-up. A stabilizer bar is standard and the upper control arms have been eliminated.

Shock Absorber R & R

1. Raise the vehicle and support the rear axle.
2. Remove upper attaching bolts and lower attaching nut, retainer, and cushion on early 1971 models or the through-bolt on later models.
3. Remove the shock absorber.
4. Install retainer and rubber grommet onto shock.

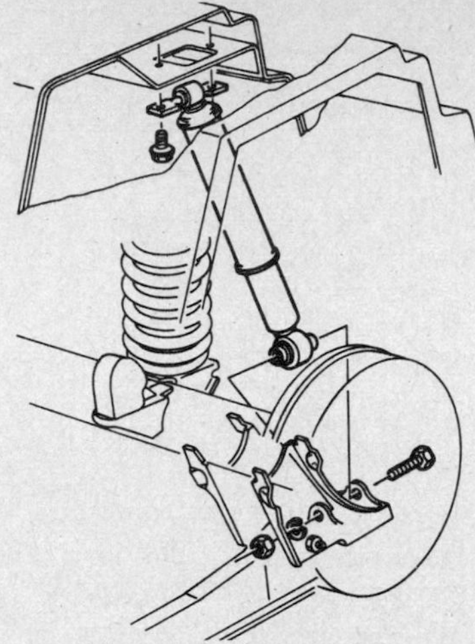

Rear shock absorber mounting
(© Chevrolet Div., G.M. Corp)

5. Place shock absorber into installed position and install upper retaining bolts. Torque to 18 ft. lbs.
6. On early models, install cushion, retainer and nut onto lower shock absorber attachment.
7. On later models, install the through bolt and a rubber grommet on each side of the shock eye. Torque the nut to 80 ft lbs.
8. Lower the car.

Rear Spring R & R

1. Raise vehicle and support the rear axle, with a hydraulic jack.
2. Disconnect both shock absorbers from lower brackets.
3. Lower axle and remove springs and spring insulators.

NOTE: one or both springs may be removed at this point.

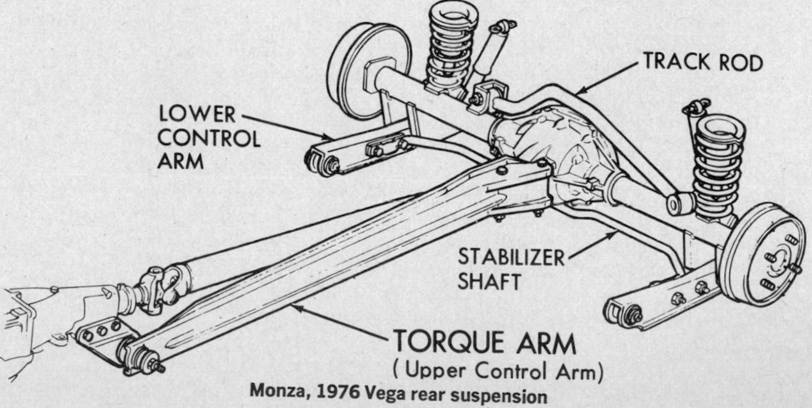

Monza, 1976 Vega rear suspension
(© Chevrolet Div., G.M. Corp)

Caution When lowering axle do not stretch brake hose running from frame to axle.

4. Install insulators on top and bottom of springs and position on axle.
5. Raise axle and reconnect shock absorbers. Torque the bottom stud or bolt nuts to 80 in. lbs.
6. Lower the vehicle.

Upper Control Arm R & R

If both control arms are to be replaced, remove and replace one control arm at a time to prevent the axle from rolling or slipping sideways.

1. Raise vehicle on hoist and support the rear axle.
2. Remove control arm front and rear bolts and remove arm.
3. Press out the bushing.
4. Before bushing installation, observe that holes in control arm have different diameters.
5. Install small end of bushing in largest hole.
6. Press bushing into control until bushing flange seats on control arm.
7. Install control arm front and rear attaching bolts. Torque to 60 ft. lbs.

NOTE: car must be at curb height when tightening pivot bolts.

8. Remove support from axle.
9. Lower vehicle and remove from hoist.

Lower Control Arm R & R

Caution If both control arms are to be replaced, remove and replace one control arm at a time to prevent the axle from rolling or slipping sideways.

1. Raise vehicle on hoist.
2. Support rear axle.
3. Disconnect stabilizer bar if so equipped.
4. Remove control arm front and rear attaching bolts and remove control arm.
5. Replacement of these bushings is the same procedure as that described for the Upper Control Arm above.
6. Place control arm into position and install front and rear bolts. Torque to 80 ft. lbs.
7. Attach stabilizer bar and restraint cable, if so equipped.
8. Remove support from axle.
9. Lower vehicle.

BRAKES

Front disc brakes are standard equipment on all models with power brakes available beginning 1975. The disc is 10 in. in diameter and 0.5 in. thick. Hub and disc are one-piece and the assembly is mounted to a one-piece steering knuckle and steering arm. The disc caliper design is similar to the single-piston Delco-Moraine disc brake used on other Chevrolet vehicles.

Rear brakes are drum-type, 9 in. in diameter. Unlike most other brake designs, the rear brakes are not automatically adjusted when the brakes are applied, but are adjusted when the parking brake is applied. For this reason, consistent parking in gear without using the parking brake is not recommended.

The tandem master cylinder pushrod is not adjustable, thus eliminating a pedal free travel adjustment.

Both front and rear hydraulic systems are routed to and from a distribution valve. Any significant change in the pressure difference between the front and rear systems moves a piston which activates a warning light switch, indicating pressure failure in one of the systems.

Master Cylinder R & R

1. Disconnect the master cylinder from the brake pedal by detaching the clip and pin.
2. Disconnect the two hydraulic lines at the master cylinder, plugging or covering the ends of the lines.
3. Remove master cylinder attaching nuts and remove the master cylinder.
4. Reverse the removal procedure to install. Torque the mounting nuts to 24 ft lbs.
5. Bleed the hydraulic system.

Front Disc Brake Caliper R & R

1. Raise the front of the vehicle and remove the front wheel.
2. Remove and discard the two mounting pin stamped nuts.

NOTE: it is not necessary to disconnect the hydraulic line when removing the caliper. Do not let the weight of the caliper assembly hang on the hydraulic line.

3. Remove the two caliper mounting pins.
4. Lift the caliper off the disc.
5. Remove the shoes (pads) by sliding them to the mounting sleeve opening.
6. The mounting sleeves and bushing assemblies may be removed for inspection.
7. To install, position the sleeves with bushings into the caliper grooves with the shouldered end toward the outside.
8. Install the inner shoe and slide the shoe ears over the sleeve, then install the outer shoe in the same manner.
9. Position the caliper on the vehicle.

NOTE: if new shoes are being installed, remove half of the brake fluid in the master cylinder.

10. Install the mounting pins, head end to the outside.
11. Install new stamped retaining nuts with a socket that just seats on the outer edge of the nut.
12. Install the front wheels and lower the vehicle.

Brake Disc R & R

1. Raise the vehicle and remove the wheel and caliper as described above.
2. Remove the dust cap with pliers.
3. Remove the cotter pin and nut from the spindle.
4. Pull on the disc to loosen the outer bearing, then remove the outer bearing.
5. Remove the disc and clean the spindle.
6. The inner bearing may be knocked out (use a brass drift or wooden hammer handle) for inspection or replacement.

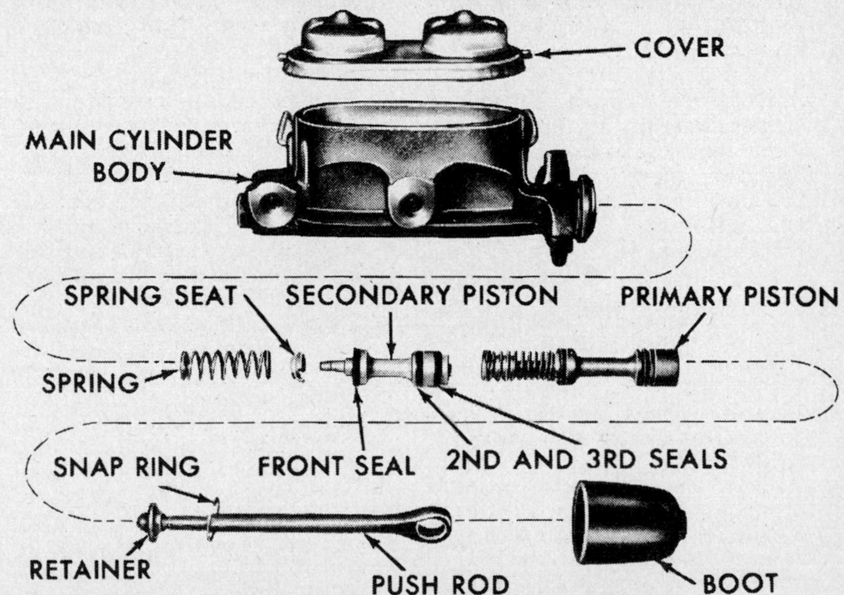

Brake master cylinder (© Chevrolet Div., G.M. Corp)

7. Clean the bearings and bearing surfaces.
8. Grease the bearings, using a disc brake wheel bearing lubricant.
9. Install the inner bearing and a new dust seal, tapping them carefully into the disc.
10. Install the brake disc onto the spindle and insert the outer bearing and washer.
11. Adjust the wheel bearings as outlined under "Wheel Bearing Adjustment."
12. Replace the dust cap and brake caliper.

Power Booster R & R

1. Remove the vacuum hose from the check valve.
2. Remove the master cylinder-to-power booster nuts.
3. Remove the brake line distribution and switch mounting bolt from the fender skirt.
4. Pull forward on the master cylinder until the cylinder clears the power booster.
5. Carefully remove the master cylinder with the brake lines attached and set the master cylinder aside. Support the cylinder so that there is no stress on the brake lines. The master cylinder should be moved the minimum distance necessary.
6. Unbolt the power booster from the firewall.
7. Remove the brake pedal pushrod from the pedal pin.
8. Remove the power brake booster.
9. Installation is the reverse of removal. Be sure the brake lines are properly routed to provide sufficient clearance.

Parking Brake Adjustment

1. Raise and support the rear of the car.
2. Apply the parking brake one notch from the fully released position.
3. Loosen the adjusting locknut and tighten the adjusting nut until a slight drag is felt when the rear wheels are rotated.
4. Tighten the locknut securely.
5. The rear wheels should rotate freely when the parking brake is fully released.
6. Lower the vehicle.

Parking Brake Cable R & R

1. Raise and support the car.
2. Disconnect the equalizer from the cables.
3. Free the cable from the underbody tabs and remove the cable retainers (two per cable).
4. Remove the rear wheels and drums.
5. Remove the parking brake cable from the parking brake lever.

NOTE: do not let the lever swing forward, causing the brakes to self-adjust.

6. Remove the pull-back spring and remove the brake shoes with the strut and adjuster assembly attached.
7. Compress the conduit locking fingers at the backing plate entry hole and withdraw the cable.
8. To install, push the cable through the hole in the backing plate and make sure the locking fingers are fully expanded.
9. Connect the cable end to the parking brake lever.
10. Install both shoes on the backing plate with the lower spring under the shoe anchor, guiding the adjusting lever and assembly into position.
11. Engage the leading and trailing shoes with the wheel cylinder links and the parking brake lever with the leading shoe.
12. Install the pull back spring on the leading shoe.
13. Install the drums and wheels.
14. Route the cable through the underbody retainers and tabs, bending the tabs to secure the cable in position.
15. Install the equalizer to the cables and to the parking brake lever rod. Install the adjusting nut and locknut.
16. Adjust the parking brake as described above.
17. Lower the vehicle.

STEERING

Tie Rod R & R

1. Place vehicle on hoist.
2. Remove cotter pins from ball studs and remove special nuts.
3. To remove outer ball stud, tap on steering arm at tie rod end with a hammer while using a heavy hammer or similar tool as a backing.
4. Remove inner ball stud from relay rod using same procedure as described in Step 3.
5. To remove tie rod ends from tie rod, loosen clamp bolts and unscrew end assemblies.
6. If the tie rod ends were removed, lubricate the tie rod threads with chassis lube and install ends on tie rod making sure both ends are threaded an equal distance from the tie rod.
7. Make sure that threads on ball studs and in ball stud nuts are perfectly clean and smooth. Check condition of ball stud seals; replace if necessary.

NOTE: if threads are not clean and smooth, ball studs may turn in tie rod ends when attempting to tighten nut.

8. Install ball studs in steering arms and relay rod.
9. Install ball stud nut, tighten and install new cotter pins. Lubricate tie rod ends.
10. Remove vehicle from hoist.
11. Adjust toe-in.

Caution Before tightening the tie rod adjusting sleeve clamp bolts, be sure that the following conditions have been met:

a. The sleeve clamps must be positioned between the locating dimples at either end of the sleeve.
b. The clamps must be positioned within the angular travel as illustrated.

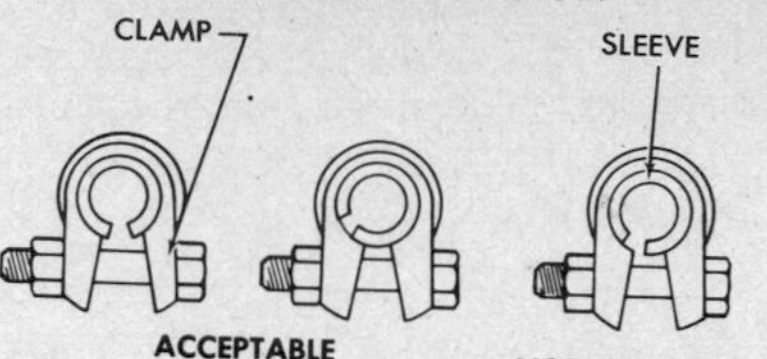

Tie-rod clamp installation
(© Chevrolet Div., G.M. Corp)

c. The relationship of the clamp slot with the slit in the sleeve should be maintained as shown.
d. Both inner and outer tie rod ends must rotate for full travel in the same direction. The position of each tie rod end must be maintained as the clamps are tightened to ensure free movement of each joint.
e. All procedures for alignment, adjustment and assembly of tie rods applies to each side.

Relay Rod R & R

1. Raise the front of the car and support with jackstands.
2. Remove inner ends of the tie rods from relay rod.
3. Remove the cotter pins from the pitman and idler arm ball studs at the relay rod. Remove the nuts.
4. Remove the relay rod from the pitman and idler arms by tapping on the relay rod ball stud bosses with a hammer, while using a heavy hammer as a backing.
5. Remove the relay rod from the vehicle.
6. Make sure that threads on the ball studs and in the ball stud nuts are perfectly clean and smooth. Check condition of ball stud seals; replace if necessary.

NOTE: if threads are not clean and smooth, ball studs may turn in sockets when attempting to tighten nut.

7. Install the relay rod to the idler arm and pitman arm ball studs, making certain the seals are in place. Install and torque the nut and then install the cotter pin. Tighten nut to 35 ft. lbs.
8. Install the tie rods to the relay rod. Lubricate the tie rod ends.
9. Remove the vehicle from the hoist.

10. Adjust toe-in and align steering wheel.

Idler Arm R & R

1. Place vehicle on a hoist.
2. Remove the cotter pin and special nut from ball stud at the relay rod. Remove the ball stud from the relay rod by tapping on the relay rod boss with a hammer, while using a heavy hammer as a backing.
3. Remove the idler arm to frame bolts and remove the idler arm assembly.
4. Position the idler arm on the frame and install the mounting bolts (special plain washers under bolt heads). Torque the nuts to 30 ft. lbs.
5. Make sure that the threads on the ball stud and in the ball stud nut are perfectly clean and smooth. Check condition of ball stud seal; replace if necessary.

NOTE: if threads are not clean and smooth, ball stud may turn in the socket when attempting to tighten nut.

6. Install the idler arm ball stud in the relay rod, making certain the seal is positioned properly; install the nut and cotter pin, tightening to 35 ft. lbs.
7. Lower the car.

Pitman Arm R & R

1. Raise the front of the car and support it with jackstands.
2. Remove the cotter pin and special nut from ball stud at the relay rod. Remove the ball stud from the relay rod by tapping on the relay rod boss with a hammer, while using a heavy hammer as a backing.
3. Remove the pitman arm to pitman shaft nut. Mark relationship of the arm to the shaft and then remove the pitman arm.
4. Install the pitman arm on the pitman shaft, aligning the marks made during removal. Install and torque the nut.
5. Make sure that the threads on the ball stud and in the ball stud are perfectly clean and smooth. Check condition of ball stud seal; replace if necessary.

NOTE: if threads are not clean and smooth, ball stud may turn in the socket when attempting to tighten nut.

6. Install the pitman arm ball stud to the relay rod, making certain the seal is positioned properly. Install the nut and cotter pin.
7. Lower the car.

Pitman Shaft Seal Replacement

A faulty seal may be replaced without removal of steering gear from car by removing pitman arm and proceeding as follows:

1. Rotate the steering wheel from stop to stop, counting the total number of turns. Then turn back exactly half-way, placing the gear on center (the wormshaft flat should be at the 12 o'clock position).
2. Remove the three self-locking bolts attaching side cover to the housing and lift the pitman shaft and side cover assembly from the housing.
3. Pry the pitman shaft seal from the gear housing using a screwdriver and being careful not to damage the housing bore.

Caution Inspect the lubricant in the gear for contamination. If the lubricant is contaminated in any way, the gear must be removed from the vehicle and completely overhauled as outlined in the Unit Repair Section of this manual.

4. Coat the new pitman shaft seal with steering gear lubricant. Position the seal in the pitman shaft bore and tap into position using a suitable size socket.
5. Remove the lash adjuster locknut. Remove the side cover from the pitman shaft assembly by turning the lash adjuster screw clockwise.
6. Place the pitman shaft in the steering gear such that the center tooth of the pitman shaft sector enters the center tooth space of the ball nut.
7. Fill the steering gear housing with 9 oz. of steering gear lubricant.
8. Install a new side cover gasket on the gear housing.
9. Install the side cover onto the lash adjuster screw by reaching through the threaded hole in the side cover with a small screwdriver and turning the lash adjuster screw counter-clockwise.
10. Install the side cover bolts and torque to 18 ft. lbs.
11. Install the lash adjuster screw locknut, perform steering gear adjustment and install the pitman arm.

Steering Wheel R & R

Standard Wheel

1. Disconnect the battery ground cable.
2. Remove the two screws from the back of the wheel, allowing the shroud (horn actuator bar) to be removed.
3. Set the wheel straight ahead. Mark the relationship of the wheel to the shaft and remove the snap-ring (1975 and later) and nut.
4. Remove the steering wheel with a puller, using the two threaded holes in the wheel.
5. Install the wheel, aligning the previously made marks. Make sure that the turn signal switch is in the neutral position. Torque the nut to 30 ft lbs.
6. Make sure that the lower horn insulator, eyelet, and spring are in place.

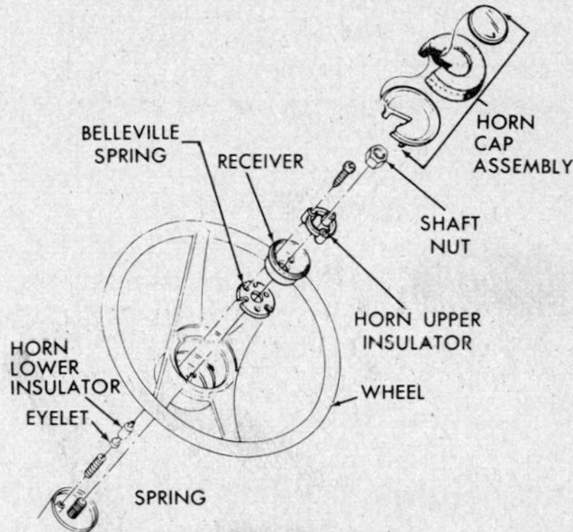

Optional steering wheel assembly, 1975 and later models have a snap-ring in front of the nut (© Chevrolet Div., G.M. Corp)

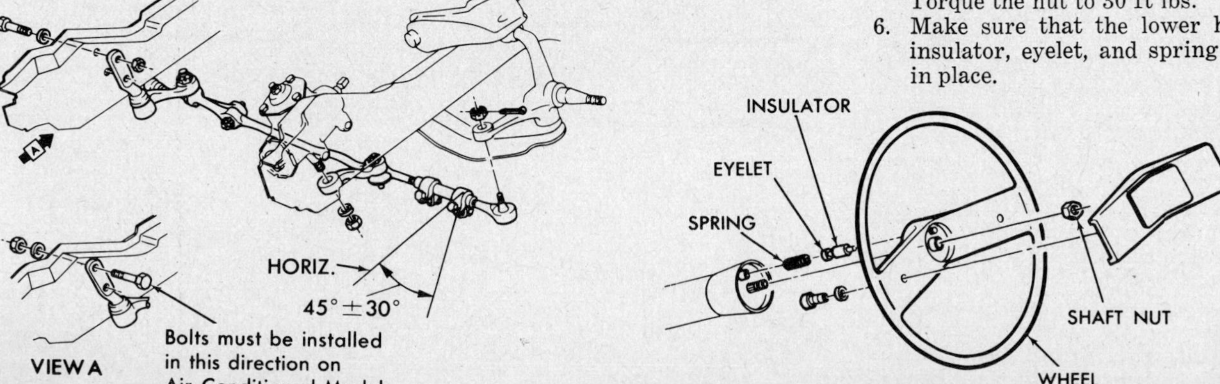

Steering linkage (© Chevrolet Div., G.M. Corp)

Standard steering wheel assembly, 1975 and later models have a snap-ring in front of the nut © Chevrolet Div., G.M. Corp)

7. Position the shroud, seating the pin on the right side of the wheel in the hole in the shroud.
8. Replace the two screws in the rear of the wheel. Connect the battery cable.

GT and Sport Wheel

1. Disconnect the battery ground cable.
2. Pry off the horn button. Set the wheel in the straight ahead position.
3. Mark the relationship of the wheel to the shaft.
4. Remove the three screws and the upper horn insulator, receiver, and round belleville spring. Remove the snap-ring (1975 and later) and nut.
5. Remove the steering wheel with a puller, utilizing the two threaded holes in the wheel.
6. Replace the wheel, aligning the marks previously made. Make sure that the turn signal switch is in the neutral position. Torque the nut to 30 ft lbs.
7. Make sure that the lower horn insulator, eyelet, and spring are in place.
8. Install the belleville spring, receiver, upper horn insulator, and the three screws.
9. Install the horn button and connect the battery cable.

Turn Signal Switch R & R

Standard column

1. Remove the steering wheel as outlined above.
2. Loosen the three captive screws and lift the cover off the shaft.
3. The lockplate must be depressed with a special tool. Depress the lockplate and remove the wire snap-ring from the shaft.
4. Remove the cancelling cam, upper bearing pre-load spring, and thrust washer from the shaft.
5. Remove the turn signal lever screw and the lever.
6. Push the hazard knob in and unscrew it.
7. Unplug the switch connector from the column and wrap the upper part of the connector with tape.
8. Remove the three switch mounting screws and pull the switch straight up. Guide the wiring connector through the column.
9. Tape the new switch connector. Feed the connector down through the column housing and under the mounting bracket.
10. Install the three switch mounting screws.
11. Replace the hazard flasher knob and the turn signal lever. The turn signal switch should be in neutral and the hazard flasher knob out.
12. Place the thrust washer, upper bearing preload spring, and cancelling cam on the shaft.
13. Place the lockplate and a new snap-ring on the shaft. Press the lockplate down as in step three and install the new snap-ring.
14. Replace the cover and its three screws.
15. Install the steering wheel.

Tilt Column

1. Remove the steering wheel.
2. Remove the cover from the steering shaft. The screws have plastic retainers on the back of the cover. It is not necessary to completely remove the screws.
3. Remove the turn signal lever screw and lever.
4. Push the hazard warning knob in and remove the knob.
5. Depress the shaft lockplate and remove the retaining snap-ring. Remove the lockplate.
6. Slide the turn signal cancelling cam and upper bearing preload spring off the end of the shaft.
7. Remove the column mounting bracket and gently lower the column. Support the column.
8. Remove the signal switch wire protective cover and strip the wires from the protector. Do not damage the wires. Disconnect the switch connector from the bracket. Tape the wires close to the connectors to facilitate removal.
9. Remove the switch mounting screws and pull the switch straight up, guiding the wiring harness through the column.
10. Tape a new turn signal switch wiring harness and connector and feed the harness through the housing. Push the hazard warning switch in to aid in installation.
11. Reinstall the protective signal switch wire cover.
12. Install the column bracket and raise the column into position.
13. Install the mounting screws and clip the connector to the bracket on the steering column jacket.
14. Install the hazard warning knob and turn signal level.
15. Be sure the switch is in the neutral position and the hazard warning knob is out. Slide the upper bearing preload spring and cancelling cam onto the shaft.
16. Install the lockplate on the end of the shaft. Compress the lockplate and install a new snap-ring.
17. Reinstall the cover on the end of the shaft.
18. Install the steering wheel.

Power Steering Pump R & R

1. On 1975-76 Monzas, remove the radiator and fan shroud.
2. Disconnect the pressure and return hoses at the pump. Cap the

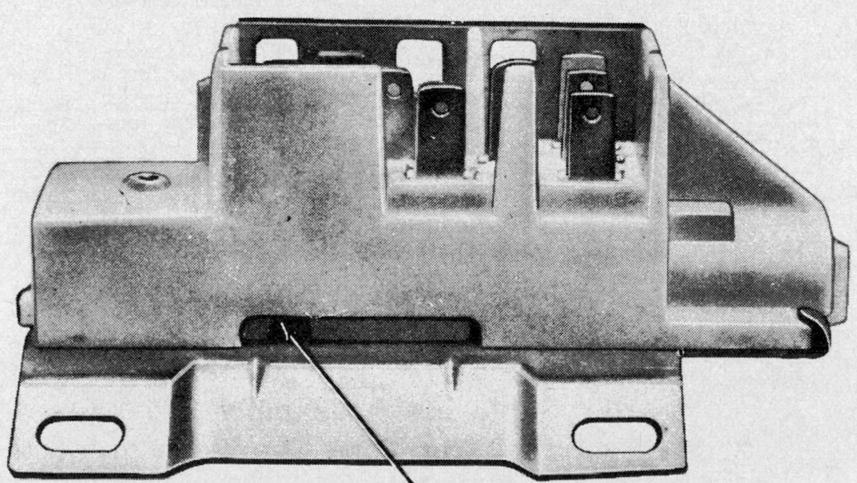

Ignition switch in lock (© Chevrolet Div., G.M. Corp)

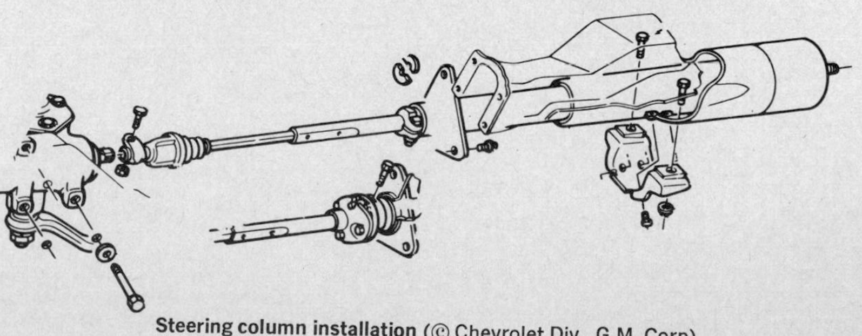

Steering column installation (© Chevrolet Div., G.M. Corp)

ends to prevent leakage and contamination.
3. Remove the drive belt.
4. Unbolt and remove the pump.
5. Reverse the removal procedure to install the pump.
6. Fill the reservoir. Turn the pulley counterclockwise to bleed the pump until no more bubbles appear in the reservoir.
7. Install the drive belt and adjust its tension.

INSTRUMENT PANEL

There are two basic instrument panel designs used on Vega models. The standard cluster consists of a full-panel-width speedometer with fuel gauge, clock and indicator lights. The optional GT model has a separate 7,000 rpm tachometer and 130 mph speedometer units, surrounded by a fuel gauge, clock, water temperature gauge and ammeter.

The speedometer cable and instruments are removed from the front of the panel. All indicator bulbs are ¼ turn twist-in type and are removed from the rear.

Descriptive and diagnostic information on dash gauges and indicators is contained in the "Unit Repair Section."

Ignition Switch R & R

The ignition switch is mounted on top of the column jacket under the dashboard, completely inaccessible unless the steering column is lowered. The energy-absorbing column is fragile when disconnected and should not be subjected to any shock or excess pressure. Since the column will distort under its own weight, make sure that it is fully supported along its entire length while it is disconnected from the dashboard.

1. Disconnect the battery ground cable.
2. Remove the steering wheel.
3. On manual steering columns, remove the pot joint coupling clamp bolt.
4. On power steering columns, remove the flexible coupling pinch bolt.
5. Move the front seat back out of the way.
6. Remove the three floor pan bracket screws.
7. Remove the two column-to-instrument panel nuts and carefully lower the column far enough to allow the harness plugs to be disconnected.
8. Disconnect the turn signal and ignition switch harnesses.
9. Place the ignition switch in LOCK position.
10. Remove the two switch screws and the switch assembly.
11. When installing, make sure that the switch is in LOCK position.
12. Install the rod to the switch and the switch to the column. Do not use mounting screws longer than the original ones because they could interfere with the ability of the column to collapse.

NOTE: the following is a mandatory column installation procedure, and must be followed exactly to prevent severe column damage.

13. On power steering models, place the pot joint clamp over the lower end of the pot joint and assemble the intermediate shaft assembly (pot joint, intermediate shaft and flex coupling) to the steering gear stub shaft, aligning the flat on the stub shaft with the flat in the pot joint.
14. Position the column in the vehicle.
15. On manual steering models, place the pot joint clamp over the lower end of the pot joint and assemble the pot joint to the steering gear wormshaft with the flat in the pot joint. On power steering models, align the steering shaft flat with the flat in the flex coupling. When the shaft is bottomed against the coupling reinforcement, install and tighten bolt to 30 ft lbs.
16. Connect the turn signal and ignition switch wiring harnesses.
17. Loosely install the steering column bracket to instrument panel stud nuts.
18. Align the pot joint clamp with the groove across the end of the pot joint. Install bolt and nut, tightening nut to 55 ft. lbs.

NOTE: bolt must pass through the shaft undercut.

19. With the vehicle on the ground, tighten instrument panel nuts to 19 ft lbs.
20. Slide the toe plate down the column to the floorboard and install the three screws.

NOTE: on power steering models, alignment flange on the toe plate must be engaged with the front of the toe pan before driving screws. On manual steering models, no side load is allowed during installation of the attaching screws. A side load could cause misalignment.

21. On manual steering models: remove the alignment spacers. The minimum allowable clearance between the O.D. of the steering shaft and the I.D. of the column jacket lower plastic bushing after installation is 0.18 in.
22. Install the steering wheel.
23. Connect the battery ground cable.

Ignition Lock Cylinder R & R

1. Place the lock cylinder in the "On" position.
2. Remove the turn signal switch as previously described.
3. Insert a thin-bladed screwdriver into the rectangular slot inside the column housing. Keep the screwdriver to the right side of the slot and break the housing casting flash loose. Depress the spring latch at the lower end of the lock cylinder. The lock cylinder can be removed with the latch depressed.
4. Place the key part way into the new lock cylinder assembly. If the key is in all the way, the sleeve assembly cannot be installed. Place the wave washer and antitheft ring onto the cylinder.
5. Make sure that the plastic keeper in the sleeve assembly is protruding. Align the lock cylinder lock bolt, the antitheft ring tab, and the slot in the sleeve.
6. Push the sleeve onto the cylinder. Push the key all the way in and rotate the cylinder clockwise.

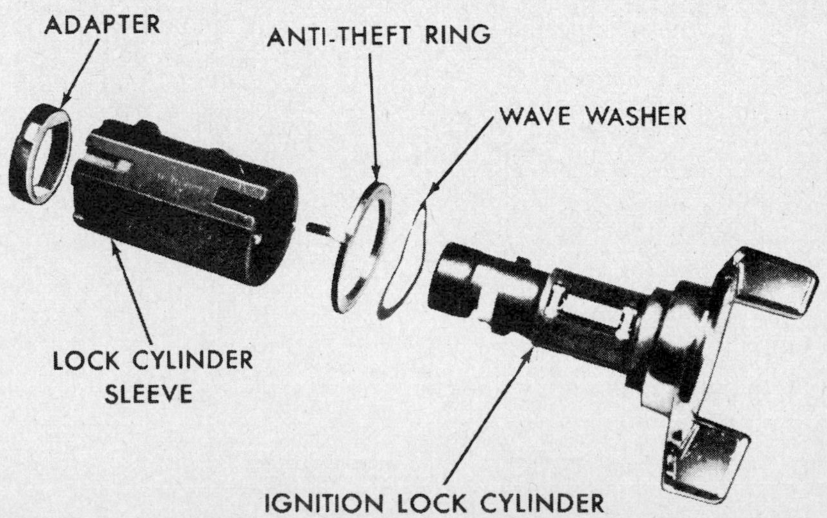

Ignition lock assembly (© Chevrolet Div., G.M. Corp)

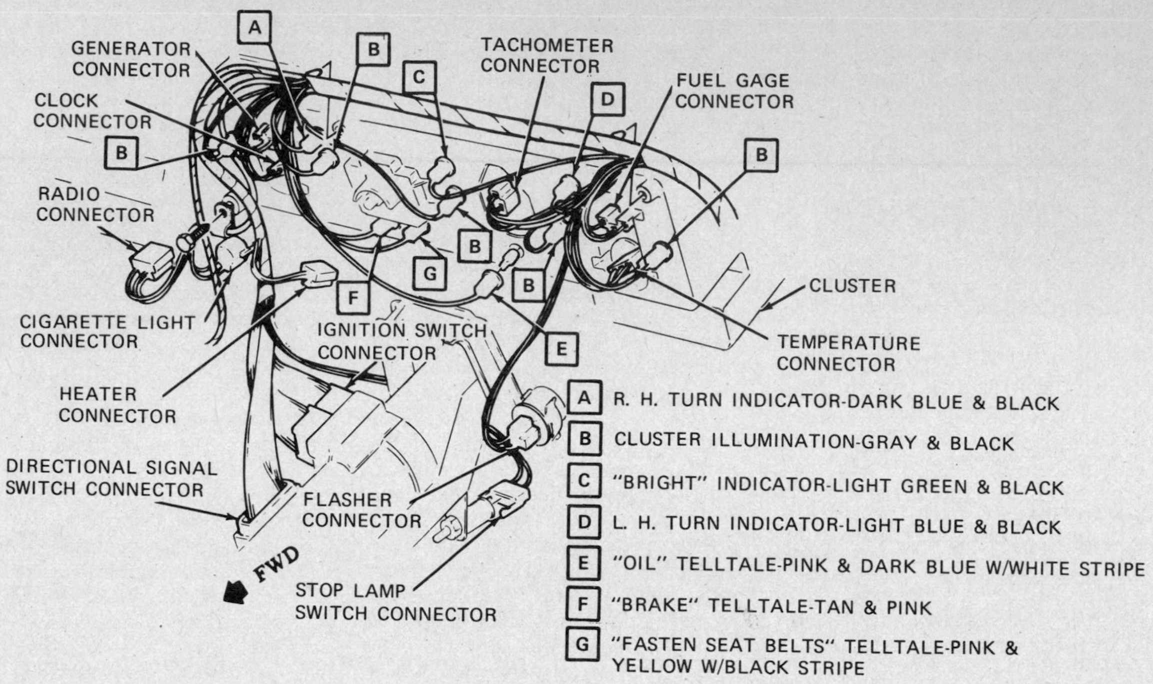

Instument cluster wiring—1975 Vega GT and Monza 2 + 2
(© Chevrolet Div., G.M. Corp.)

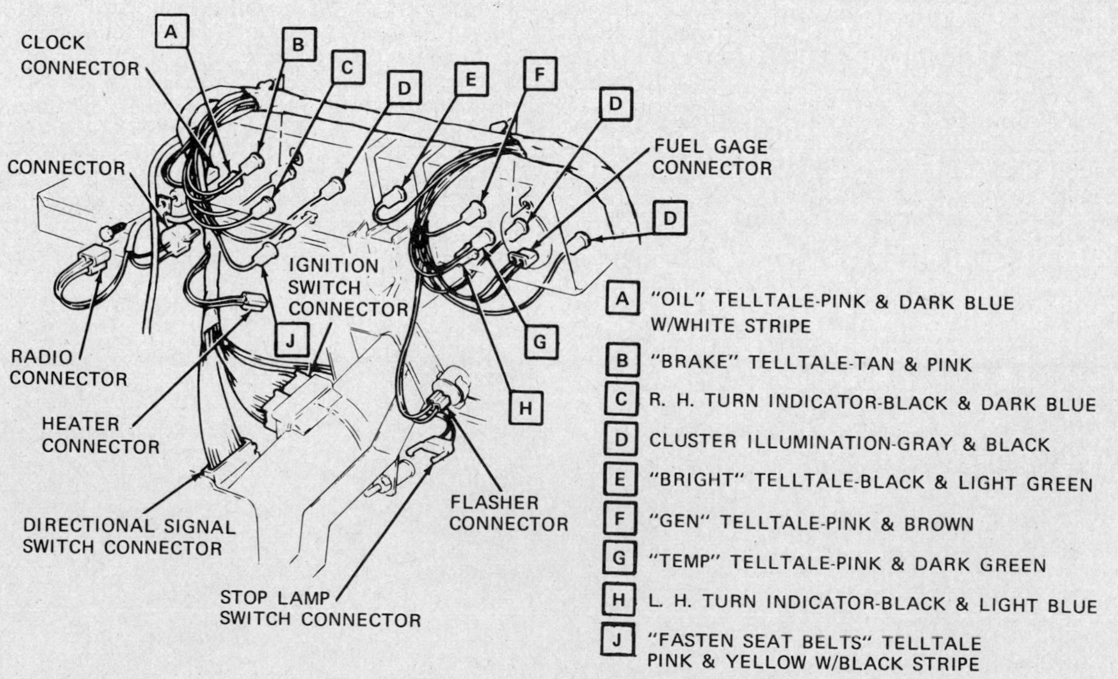

Instrument cluster wiring—standard 1975 Vega
(© Chevrolet Div., G.M. Corp.)

7. Clamp the tabs of the lock in a padded vise.
8. Place the adaptor ring on the cylinder with the serrations out. The adaptor ring tab should be against the step in the sleeve. The key must be free to rotate 120°.
9. Tap the adaptor into place so that the cylinder extends through it about 1/16 in.
10. Use a small, flat-tipped punch, at least ⅛ in. in diameter, to stake the cylinder over the adaptor ring in four places just outside the four dimples.
11. Check the lock for proper operation.
12. Hold the sleeve and turn the tabs clockwise against the stop. Insert the assembly into the housing, aligning the key on the sleeve with the slot in the housing bore.
13. Hold a 0.070 in. drill bit between the lock rim and the housing. Turn the cylinder counterclockwise while pushing in lightly.
14. When the cylinder is felt to go into place, push the cylinder in until the retainer pops into place, securing the cylinder.
15. Remove the drill. Check the operation of the lock.
16. Install the turn signal switch and the steering wheel.

Headlight Switch R & R

1. Disconnect the battery ground cable.
2. Pull the light switch to ON position.
3. Reach up under the instrument panel and depress the switch retainer button while pulling on the knob.
4. Remove the knob and shaft, then remove the ferrule nut with a large screwdriver.
5. Disconnect the multi-contact connector, prying gently with a small screwdriver.
6. Connect the new switch and reverse the removal procedure to complete the replacement.

WINDSHIELD WIPERS

Motor R & R

1. Raise hood.
2. Reaching through cowl opening, loosen the two transmission drive link attaching nuts to motor crankarm.
3. Remove transmission drive link from motor crankarm.
4. Disconnect wiring.
5. Remove three motor attaching screws.
6. Remove motor while guiding crankarm through hole.
7. To install, reverse the removal procedure.

Wiper Linkage R & R

1. Remove the wiper arms and blades.
2. Disconnect the wiring from the motor.
3. Loosen, but do not remove, the drive link-to-motor crank arm attaching nuts. Disconnect the motor crank arm from drive link.
4. Remove the wiper linkage after removing the snap-ring, washer and nut.
5. Install the linkage in the plenum chamber with the shaft extending through the attaching opening.
6. Using Loctite® or the equivalent on both hex nuts. Hand start the hex nut 2 full turns and tighten the nut to 12-18 ft lbs. The nut must be tightened within 3 minutes after applying the adhesive.
7. Repeat Step 6 for the other shaft.
8. Install the snap-ring on the right and left shafts.
9. The wiper motor should be in park. Connect the transmission drive link to the motor crank arm.
10. Connect the wiring and install the wiper arms and blades.

RADIO

Radio R & R

Vega

1. Remove battery ground cable.
2. Remove knobs, controls, washers and nuts from radio bushings.
3. Disconnect antenna lead, power connector, and speaker connectors from rear of receiver.
4. Remove two screws securing radio mounting bracket to instrument panel lower reinforcement and lift out radio receiver.
5. To install, reverse the removal procedure.

Monza

1. Disconnect the battery ground cable.
2. Remove the clock set stem knob and instrument panel bezel.
3. Remove the glove compartment.
4. Remove the radio knobs and nuts.
5. Remove the instrument panel pad.
6. Remove the lower screws from the radio mounting bracket.
7. On air conditioned cars, remove the left lap cooler and duct.
8. Remove the steering column mounting bracket and lower and support the steering column.
9. Remove the 3 screws from the top of the instrument cluster.
10. Remove the 3 bolts from the reinforcement on the instrument panel carrier.
11. Disconnect the speedometer drive cable from the speedometer head.
12. Pull the instrument panel slightly forward and disconnect the electrical and antenna leads.
13. Remove the radio from the instrument panel.
14. Installation is the reverse of removal.

HEATER

Blower Motor R & R

1. Disconnect the battery ground cable.
2. Disconnect the blower motor lead wire. Disconnect the motor cooling tube on air-conditioned models.
3. Scribe the blower motor flange to case position.
4. Remove the blower to case attaching screws and remove the blower wheel and motor assembly. Pry the flange gently if the sealer is retaining the assembly.
5. Remove the blower wheel retaining nut and separate the motor and wheel.

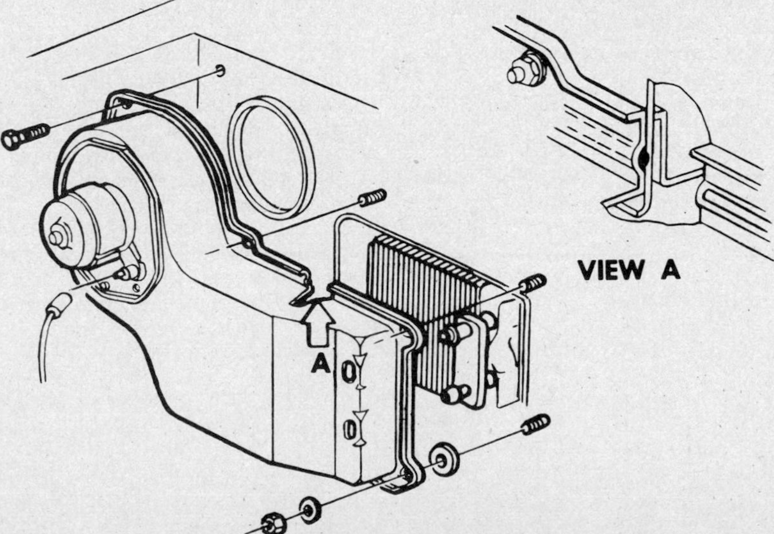

Heater installation (© Chevrolet Div., G.M. Corp)

6. To install, reverse Steps 1-5, lining up the match-marks on the motor flange and case which were made at removal.

NOTE: assemble the blower wheel to the motor with the open end of the blower away from the motor. Reseal the motor flange, if necessary.

Heater Core R & R

W/O Air Conditioning

1. Disconnect the battery ground cable.
2. Disconnect the blower motor lead wire.
3. Place a pan under the vehicle. Disconnect the heater hoses at the core connections and secure the ends of the hoses in a raised position.
4. Remove the coil bracket to dash panel stud nut and move the coil out of the way.
5. Remove the blower intake to dash panel screws and nuts and remove the blower intake, blower motor and wheel as an assembly.
6. Remove the core retaining strap screws and remove the core from the vehicle.
7. To install, reverse Steps 1-6.

NOTE: be sure that the blower intake sealer is intact, replace if necessary.

Air Conditioned Models

1. Disconnect the battery ground cable.
2. Disconnect the heater hoses at the core and plug them.
3. Remove the firewall selector stud nuts.
4. Disconnect the left-side flexible dash outlet hose from the center distributor duct.
5. Remove the right-side dash outlet assembly.
6. Remove the instrument bezel and center outlet as an assembly.
7. Remove the ash tray and retainer.
8. Remove the radio as previously outlined.
9. Remove the control-to-dash screws and lower the control assembly.
10. Remove the cigarette lighter. Remove the screw retaining the right side of the dash reinforcement.
11. Pry out the center duct-to-dash clip. Remove the center duct-to-selector duct screws and remove the center duct. Turn the duct clockwise and pull down and to the left to remove.
12. Remove the defroster duct-to-selector duct screw. Remove the remaining selector duct-to-dash screws and pull the duct back far enough to allow the electrical and vacuum lines to be disconnected.
13. Disconnect the lines and the control cable and remove the selector duct assembly.
14. Pry off the temperature door bellcrank, being careful not to bend the arm or damage the selector case.
15. Remove the temperature door. Remove the backing plate and temperature door cable retainer screws.
16. Remove the heater core and backing plate as an assembly. Remove the core retaining straps and withdraw the core.
17. Reverse the removal procedure to install the core.

SEAT BELTS

Warning System

1972-73

The seat belt warning system consists of lap belt retractor switches, a pressure-sensitive switch underneath the right-hand front passenger's seat, a warning lamp and a buzzer.

On manual transmission-equipped cars, the circuit is wired through the ignition switch, the parking brake warning light switch, and a relay, which is located between the instrument cluster wiring and the switch on the parking brake. A diode is used to prevent feedback into the parking brake warning circuit.

On cars having automatic transmissions, the seat belt warning circuit is wired through the ignition switch and the combination back-up lamp/neutral safety switch.

With the ignition key in the "RUN" position, on the driver's side and/or a weight of 40-50 lbs on the passenger's seat (pressure-sensitive switch), energizes the circuit when the parking brake is released (M/T) or the gear selector placed in a forward drive range (A/T).

A warning light will glow and a buzzer will sound with the circuit energized, unless the seat belts are withdrawn from the retractors and fastened over the laps of the two outboard front seat occupants.

Seat Belt/Starter Interlock System

1974-75

As required by law, all 1974 and some 1975 Chevrolet passenger cars cannot be started until the front seat occupants are seated, then fasten their seat belts. If the proper sequence is not followed, e.g., the occupants fasten their seat belts and then sit on them, the car cannot be started.

If, after the car is started, the seat belts are unfastened, a warning buzzer and light are activated in a similar manner to that described above for 1972-73 models.

The shoulder harness and lap belt are permanently fastened together, so that they both must be worn. The shoulder harness uses an inertia-lock reel to allow freedom of movement under normal driving conditions.

NOTE: This type of reel locks up when the car decelerates rapidly, as during a crash.

The lap belts use the same ratchet-type retractors that the 1972-73 models use.

The switches for the interlock system have been removed from the lap belt retractors and placed in the belt buckles. The seat sensors remain the same as those used in 1972-73.

For ease of service, the car may be started from outside, by reaching in and turning the key, but without depressing the seat sensors.

In case of system failure, an override switch is located under the hood. This is a "one start" switch and it must be reset each time it is used.

Disabling the Interlock System

Since the requirement for the interlock system was dropped during the 1975 model year, those systems installed on cars built earlier may now be legally disabled. The seat belt warning light is still required.

1. Disconnect the negative battery cable.
2. Locate the interlock harness connector with orange, yellow and green leads under the left side of the instrument panel on or near the fuse block. 1974 Vegas have the connector under the parking brake cable cover.
3. Cut and tape the ends of the green wire on the body side of the connector.
4. Remove the buzzer from the fuse block or connector.

INDEX

Oldsmobile · Cutlass · F-85 · 4-4-2 · Omega · Starfire

YEAR IDENTIFICATION

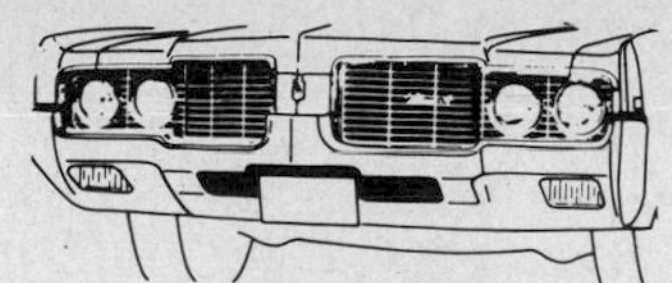
1969 88

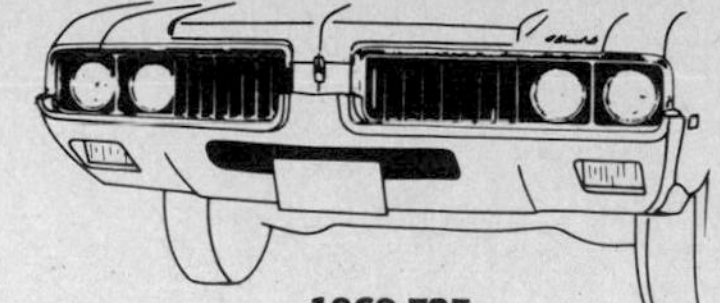
1969 F85

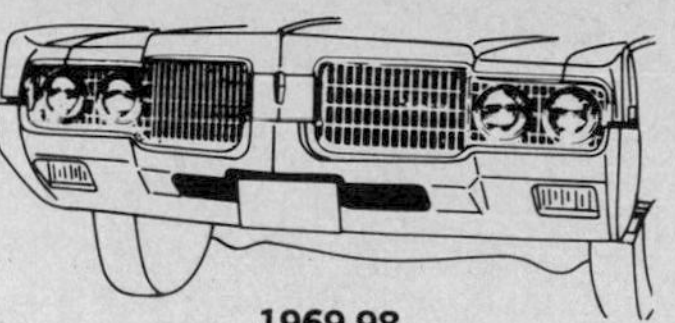
1969 98

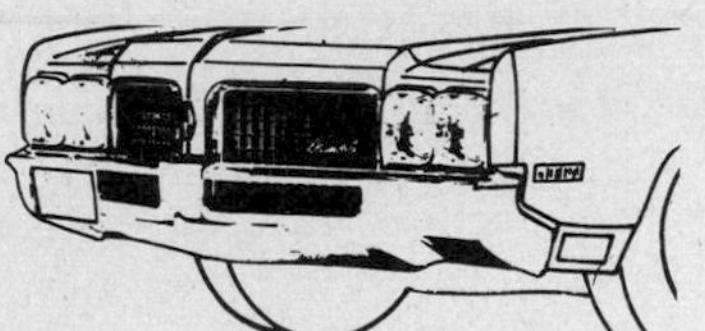
1970 Delta 88

1970 F85

1970 98 Series

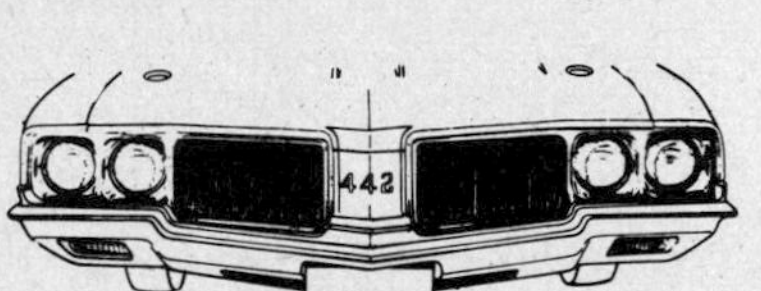

1970 4-4-2

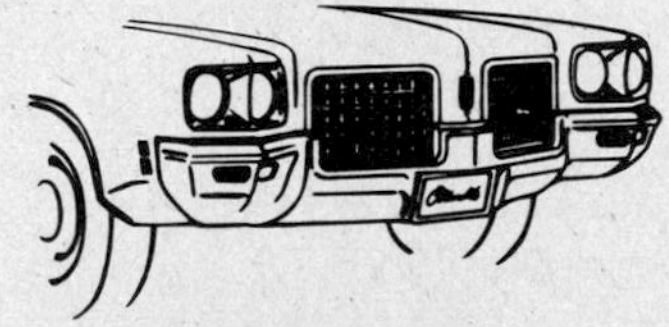
1971 Delta 88

1971 98

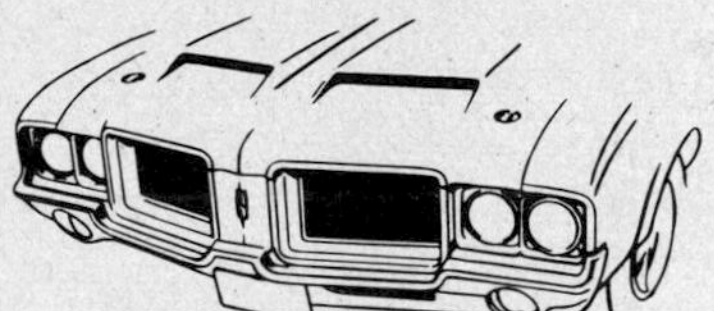
1971 4-4-2

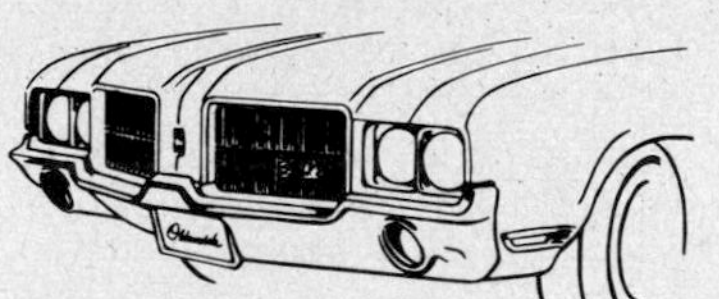
1971 Cutlass Supreme

1972 Delta 88

1972 98

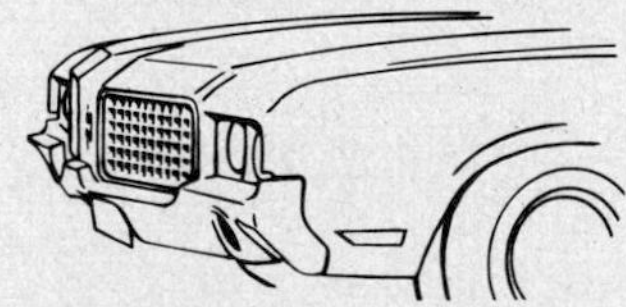
1972 Cutlass Supreme

1972 Cutlass S

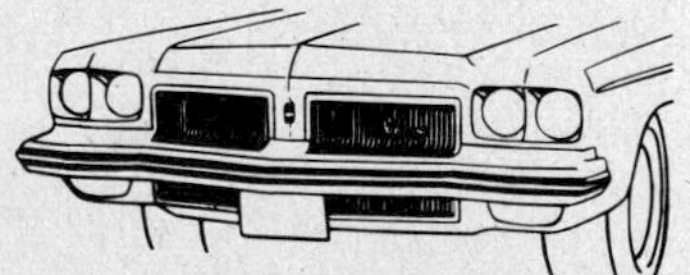
1973 Delta 88

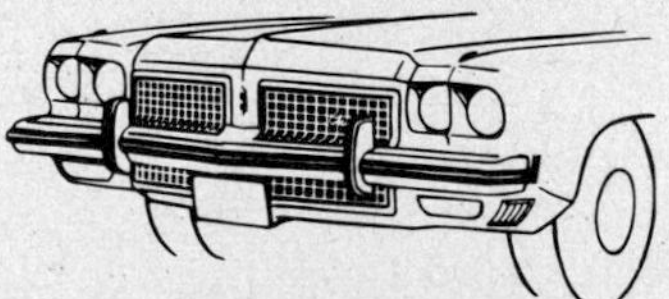
1973 98

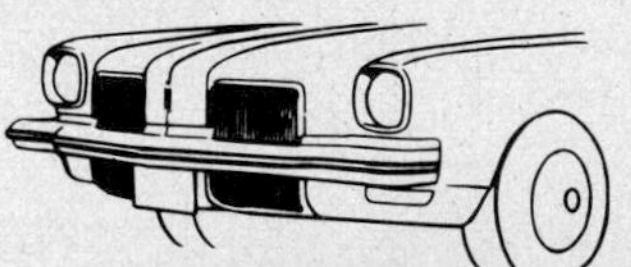
1973 Cutlass Supreme

1973 Cutlass S

1973 Omega

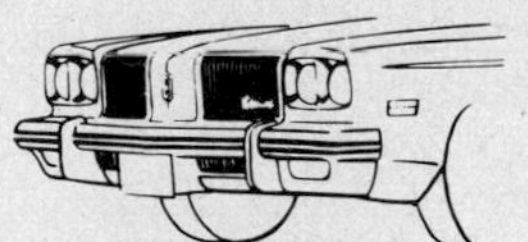
1974 Delta 88

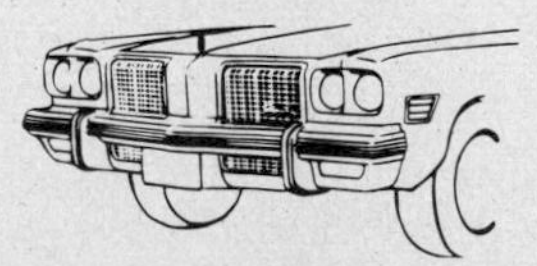
1974 98

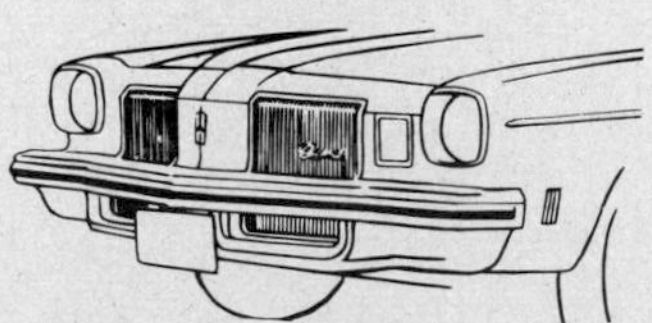
1974 Cutlass

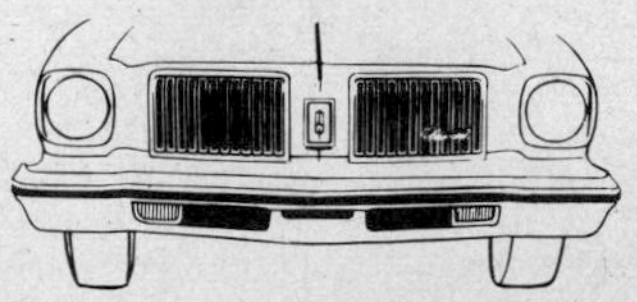
1974 Omega

1975 Delta 88

1975 98

1975 Cutlass S

1975 Omega

1975 Starfire

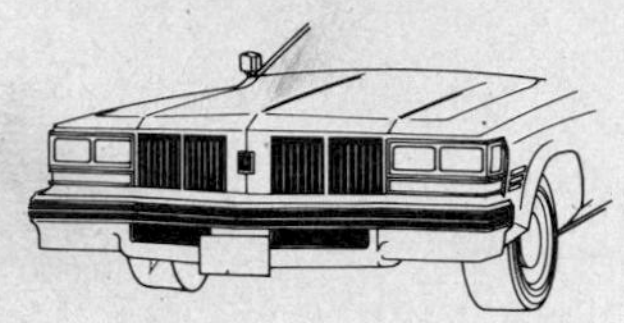
1975 Delta 88

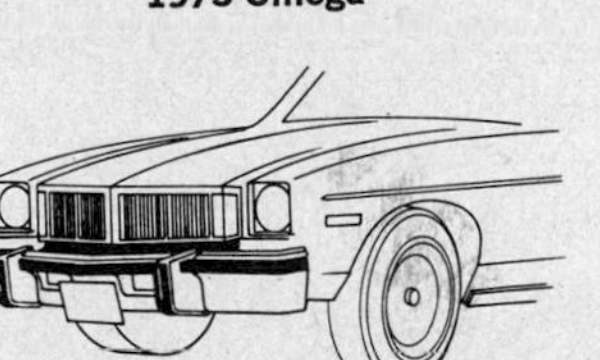
1976 Brougham

1976 98 Regency Sedan

1976 Starfire

1976 Cutlass

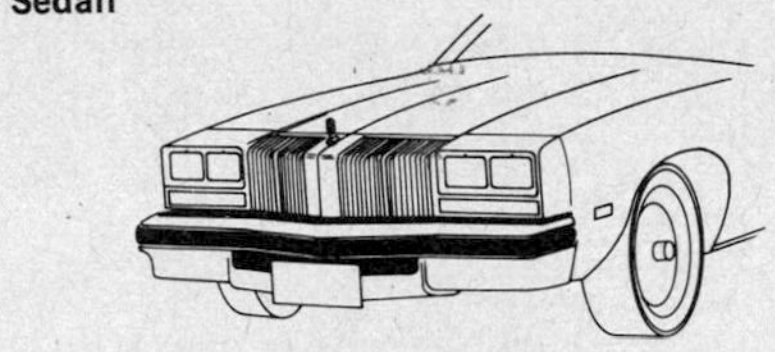
1976 Cutlass S

CAR SERIAL NUMBER LOCATION

Left side of instrument panel, visible through windshield.

1969-71

First digit—Oldsmobile Division (3)
Second digit indicates series
Third digit or letter indicates engine
Fourth and fifth digits indicate body type
Sixth digit indicates year
Seventh digit (letter) indicates plant
Eighth to thirteenth digits—sequential serial number

1972-76

First digit—Oldsmobile Division (3)
Second digit (letter)—series
Third and fourth digits—body type
Fifth digit (letter)—engine code
Sixth digit—year
Seventh digit (letter)—plant code
Eighth to thirteenth digits—sequential serial number

FIRING ORDER

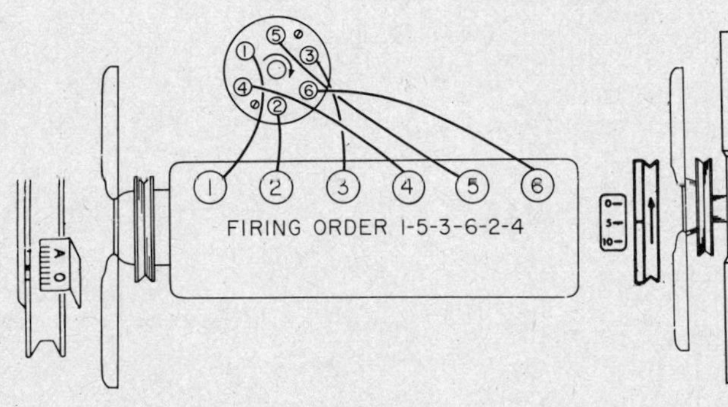

Inline 6 cylinder

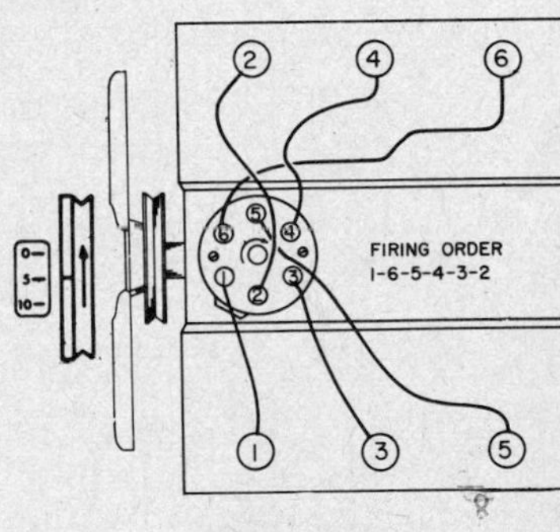

V6 engine

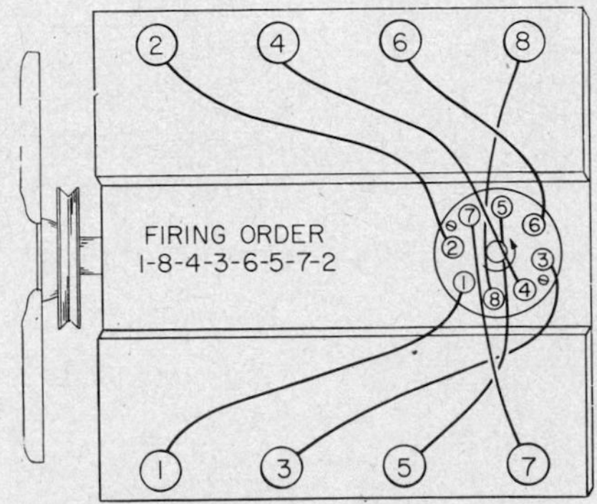

350 (except 1975-76 Omega), 400, 455 V8

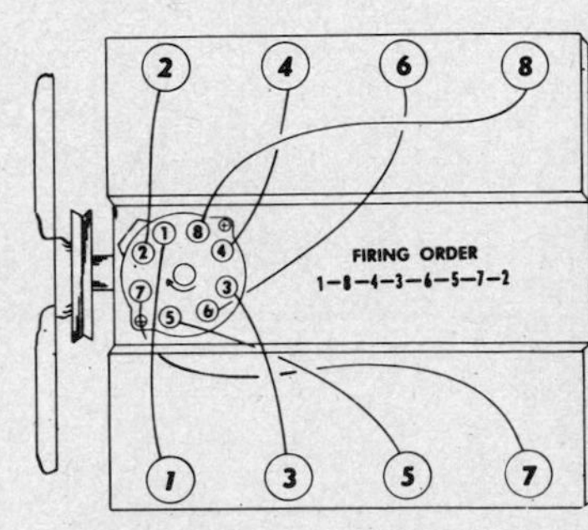

1975-76 Omega 350 V8

ENGINE IDENTIFICATION CODE

The engine identification code is stamped on a machined pad located on the right side of the cylinder block directly behind the distributor on six cylinder models through 1971, and located on tape attached directly to the front of the oil filter tube on all V8 models and 1973 and later six cylinder models.

Disp	Bbl	Hp	'69	'70	'71	'72	'73	'74	'75	'76
6-Cylinder Models										
231	2	110							FP FS FR	FN FO FJ
250	1	100 (net)					CCA CCB CCC CCD	CCA CCB CCC CCD	CJU CJT CJL	CCD CCF CCC
250	1	145			VB VF					
250	1	155	VA VB VE VF	VB VF						
8-Cylinder Models										
260	2	110							QA QB QC QD QK QN QE QJ QP TE TJ TP TT	QA QB QC QD QN QP QT TE TJ TP TT
350	2	145 (net)					QS QT			
350	2	160 (net)				QA QB QC	QN QQ QP QO QS QT			
350	4	160, 180, 200# (net)					QB QC QD QL QO QU QW TB TC TL TO	QB QC QL QO QU QW TB TC TL TO	QL QO QU QW QX TL TO TW TX	Q2 Q3 Q4 Q5 TO TL TX TW TY
350	4	180 (net)				QD QE QJ QK	QA QE QJ QK			
350	2	240			QA QI QJ TC TD TE					

Disp	Bbl	Hp	'69	'70	'71	'72	'73	'74	'75	'76
8-Cylinder Models										
350	2	250	QA QB QI QJ TB TC TD TL	QA QI QJ TC TD TL						
350	2	260	QB QN QO QP							
350	4	310	QN QP QV	QN QP QV						
350	4	325	QX	QD QX						
350	4①	165							RW RX RS RT	PE PF PM,PN PA,PB
350	2①	145								
400	4	325	QR QS QW							
400	4	350	QU							
400	4	360	QT							
400	4	190							YM YH YL	
455	4	210, 230# (net)						UA UB UC UD UL UN UR VA VB VC VD VL	UB UC UD UE UP VB VC VD VE VP	
455	4	225, 250 (net)				US UT UU UV	UA UB UD US UT UV UU			
455	4	230 (net)								
455	4	270 (net)				UA UB UD UE				
455	4	275 (net)						UV, UX		
455	2	280			UC UD UE					

ENGINE IDENTIFICATION CODE (con't.)

Disp	Bbl	Hp	'69	'70	'71	'72	'73	'74	'75	'76
8-Cylinder Models										
455	4	300 (net)				UL UN UO				
455	2	310	UC UD UJ	UC UD UJ						
455	2	320		TX TY						
455	4	320			TD TN TQ TU TV TW UN UO					
455	4	340			TB TL TS TT					
455	4	350			US UT					
455	4	365	UN UO	TP TQ TU TV TW UN UO TS TT						
455	4	370								
455	4	390	UL							

\# With dual exhaust
① 1975-76 Omega only

GENERAL ENGINE SPECIFICATIONS

Year	Engine No. Cyl. Displacement (cu. in.)	Carburetor Type	Horsepower @ rpm ■	Torque @ rpm (ft lbs) ■	Bore and Stroke (in.)	Compression Ratio	Oil Pressure @ 2000 rpm
'69	6-250	1 bbl	155 @ 4200	240 @ 2000	3.875 x 3.530	8.50:1	30-45
	8-350	2 bbl	250 @ 4400	355 @ 2600	4.057 x 3.385	9.00:1	30-45
	8-350	4 bbl	310 @ 4800	390 @ 3200	4.057 x 3.385	10.25:1	30-45
	8-350	4 bbl	325 @ 5400	360 @ 3600	4.057 x 3.385	10.50:1	30-45
	8-400	4 bbl	325 @ 4600	440 @ 3000	3.870 x 4.250	10.50:1	35-50
	8-400	4 bbl	350 @ 4800	440 @ 3200	3.870 x 4.250	10.50:1	35-50
	8-400	4 bbl	360 @ 5400	440 @ 3600	3.870 x 4.250	10.50:1	35-50
	8-455	2 bbl	310 @ 4200	490 @ 2400	4.126 x 4.250	9.00:1	30-45
	8-455	4 bbl	365 @ 4600	510 @ 3000	4.126 x 4.250	10.25:1	30-45
	8-455	4 bbl	390 @ 5000	500 @ 3200	4.126 x 4.250	10.25:1	30-45

GENERAL ENGINE SPECIFICATIONS

Year	Engine No. Cyl. Displacement (cu. in.)	Carburetor Type	Horsepower @ rpm ■	Torque @ rpm (ft lbs) ■	Bore and Stroke (in.)	Compression Ratio	Oil Pressure @ 2000 rpm
'70	6-250	1 bbl	155 @ 4200	240 @ 2000	3.875 x 3.530	8.50:1	30-45
	8-350	2 bbl	250 @ 4400	355 @ 2600	4.057 x 3.385	9.00:1	30-45
	8-350	4 bbl	310 @ 4800	390 @ 3200	4.057 x 3.385	10.25:1	30-45
	8-350	4 bbl	325 @ 5400	360 @ 3600	4.057 x 3.385	10.50:1	30-45
	8-455	2 bbl	310 @ 4200	490 @ 2400	4.125 x 4.250	9.00:1	30-45
	8-455	2 bbl	320 @ 4200	500 @ 2400	4.126 x 4.250	10.25:1	30-45
	8-455	4 bbl	365 @ 4600	510 @ 3000	4.126 x 4.250	10.25:1	35-45
	8-455	4 bbl	365 @ 5000	500 @ 3200	4.126 x 4.250	10.50:1	35-50
	8-455	4 bbl	370 @ 5200	500 @ 3600	4.126 x 4.250	10.50:1	35-50
	8-455	4 bbl	390 @ 5000	500 @ 3200	4.126 x 4.250	10.25:1	30-45
'71	6-250	1 bbl	145 @ 4200	230 @ 2000	3.875 x 3.530	8.00:1	30-45
	8-350	2 bbl	240 @ 4200	350 @ 2400	4.057 x 3.385	8.50:1	30-45
	8-350	4 bbl	260 @ 4600	360 @ 3200	4.057 x 3.385	8.50:1	30-45
	8-455	2 bbl	280 @ 4000	445 @ 2000	4.126 x 4.250	8.50:1	30-45
	8-455	4 bbl	320 @ 4400	460 @ 2800	4.126 x 4.250	8.50:1	30-45
	8-455	4 bbl	340 @ 4600	460 @ 3200	4.126 x 4.250	8.50:1	30-50
	8-455	4 bbl	350 @ 4700	460 @ 3200	4.126 x 4.250	8.50:1	30-50
'72	8-350	2 bbl	160 @ 4000	275 @ 2400	4.057 x 3.385	8.50:1	30-45
	8-350①	2 bbl	175 @ 4000	295 @ 2600	4.057 x 3.385	8.50:1	30-45
	8-350	4 bbl	180 @ 4000	275 @ 2800	4.057 x 3.385	8.50:1	30-45
	8-350①	4 bbl	200 @ 4400	300 @ 3200	4.057 x 3.385	8.50:1	30-45
	8-455	4 bbl	225 @ 3600	360 @ 2600	4.126 x 4.250	8.50:1	30-50
	8-455①	4 bbl	250 @ 4200	370 @ 2800	4.126 x 4.250	8.50:1	30-50
	8-455	4 bbl	270 @ 4400	370 @ 3200	4.126 x 4.250	8.50:1	30-50
	8-455	4 bbl	300 @ 4700	410 @ 3200	4.126 x 4.250	8.50:1	30-50
'73	6-250	1 bbl	100 @ 3600	175 @ 1600	3.875 x 3.530	8.50:1	30-45
	8-350	2 bbl	160 @ 3800	275 @ 2400	4.057 x 3.385	8.50:1	30-45
	8-350	4 bbl	180 @ 3800	275 @ 2800	4.057 x 3.385	8.50:1	30-45
	8-455	4 bbl	225 @ 3600	360 @ 2600	4.126 x 4.250	8.50:1	30-50
	8-455	4 bbl	250 @ 4000	370 @ 2800	4.126 x 4.250	8.50:1	30-50
'74	6-250	1 bbl	100 @ 3600	175 @ 1600	3.875 x 3.530	8.0:1	30-45
	8-350	4 bbl	160 @ 3800	275 @ 2400	4.057 x 3.385	8.50:1	30-45
	8-350	4 bbl	180 @ 3800	275 @ 2800	4.057 x 3.385	8.50:1	30-45
	8-350①	4 bbl	200 @ 4200	300 @ 3200	4.057 x 3.385	8.50:1	30-45
	8-455	4 bbl	210 @ 3600	350 @ 2400	4.126 x 4.250	8.50:1	30-50
	8-455①	4 bbl	230 @ 4000	370 @ 2800	4.126 x 4.250	8.50:1	30-50
'75-'76	6-231	2 bbl	110 @ 4000	175 @ 2000	3.800 x 3.400	8.00:1	37
	6-250	1 bbl	100 @ 3600	175 @ 1600	3.875 x 3.530	8.50:1	36-41
	8-260	2 bbl	110 @ 3400	205 @ 1600	3.550 x 3.385	8.50:1	30-45
	8-350②	2 bbl	145 @ 3200	270 @ 2000	3.800 x 3.850	8.00:1	37
	8-350②	4 bbl	165 @ 3800	260 @ 2200	3.800 x 3.850	8.00:1	37
	8-350	4 bbl	160 @ 3800	275 @ 2400	4.057 x 3.385	8.50:1	30-45
	8-400	4 bbl	190 @ 3400	315 @ 2000	4.121 x 3.750	8.00:1	50-60
	8-455	4 bbl	190 @ 3400	350 @ 2400	4.126 x 4.250	8.50:1	30-45

■ Beginning 1972, horsepower and torque are SAE net figures. They are measured at the rear of the transmission with all accessories installed and operating. Since the figures vary when a given engine is installed in different models, some are representative rather than exact.

① Dual exhaust
② Omega only
③ 1975 only

F-85, Cutlass, Omega, Starfire, Vista Cruiser, 442

TUNE-UP SPECIFICATIONS

When analyzing compression test results, look for uniformity among cylinders rather than specific pressures.

Year	ENGINE No. Cyl Displacement (cu in.)	hp	SPARK PLUGS Type	Gap (in.)	DISTRIBUTOR Point Dwell (deg)	Point Gap (in.)	IGNITION TIMING (deg) ▲ Man Trans * ●	Auto Trans	VALVES Intake Opens ■ (deg) ●	Fuel Pump Pressure (psi)	IDLE SPEED (rpm) ▲ Man Trans ●	Auto Trans
'69	6-250	155	R-46N	.035	31-34	.019	TDC	4B	16	3½-4½	775/400	625/400
	8-350	250	R-45S	.030	28-32	.016	6B	6B	16	5½-7	675/400	600/400
	8-350	310	R-44S	.030	28-32	.016	8B	8B	16	5½-7	675	575
	8-350	325	R-44S	.030	28-32	.016	12B	—	40	5½-7	850	—
	8-400	325	R-44S	.030	28-32	.016	—	8B	21	5½-7	—	550
	8-400	350	R-44S	.030	28-32	.016	2B	—	50	5½-7	750	—
	8-400	360	R-43S	.030	28-32	.016	14B	14	56	5½-7	850	650
'70	6-250	155	R-46T	.035	31-34	.019	TDC	4B	16	4-5	830-750	630-600
	8-350	250	R-46S	.030	28-32	.016	10B	10B	16	5½-6½	750	575
	8-350	310	R-45S	.030	28-32	.016	10B	10B	16	5½-6½	650	575
	8-350	325	R-43S	.030	28-32	.016	14B	14B	40	5½-6½	750	625
	8-455	320	R-45S	.030	28-32	.016	—	8B	20	5½-6½	—	575
	8-455	365(3)	R-44S	.030	28-32	.016	—	12½	20	5½-6½	—	600
	8-455	365(4)	R-45S	.030	28-32	.016	—	8B	24	5½-6½	—	575
	8-455	365(5)	R-44S	.030	28-32	.016	12B	12B	24(2)	5½-6½	700	650
	8-455	370(5)	R-44S	.030	28-32	.016	8B	8B	56	5½-6½	700	650
'71	6-250	145	R-46TS	.035	31-34	.019	4B	4B	16	4-5	600(8)	575(8)
	8-350	240	R-46S	.040	28-32	.016	10B	10B	14	5½-6½	750	600
	8-350	260	R-45S(6)	.040	28-32	.016	10B	12B	14(2)	5½-6½	750	600
	8-455	280	R-46S	.040	28-32	.016	—	8B	20	5½-6½	—	600
	8-455	320	R-46S	.040	28-32	.016	—	8B	20	5½-6½	—	600
	8-455	340	R-45S	.040	28-32	.016	10B	10B	24(2)	5½-6½	750	600
	8-455	350	R-45S	.040	28-32	.016	12B	10B	56	5½-6½	750	600
'72	8-350	160	R-46S	.040	28-32	.016	8B	8B(6B)	16(22)	5½-6½	750	650/550
	8-350	180	R-46S	.040	28-32	.016	8B	12B	16(22)	5½-6½	750	600
	8-455	250	R-46S	.040	28-32	.016	10B	8B	30(7)	5½-6½	750	600
	8-455	270	R-46S	.040	28-32	.016	10B	8B	30(7)	5½-6½	750	600
	8-455	300	R-45S	.040	28-32	.016	12B	10B	56	5½-6½	750	650
'73	6-250	100	R-46T	.035	33	.019	6B	6B	16	4-5	700/450	600/450
	8-350	160	R-46S	.040	30	.016	—	14B	22	5½-6½	—	650/550
	8-350	180	R-46S	.040	30	.016	—	12B	22	5½-6½	—	650/550
	8-350	180	R-45S	.040	30	.016	—	12B	22	5½-6½	1000/600	—
	8-455	225	R-45S	.040	30	.016	10B	8B	28	5½-6½	1000/750	650/550
'74	6-250	100	R-46T	.035	33	.019	8B	8B	16	4-5	850/450	600/450
	8-350	160, 180	R-46S	.040	30	.016	—	12B	22	5½-6½	—	650/550
	8-350	200	R-46S	.040	30	.016	—	14B	22	5½-6½	—	650/550
	8-455	210	R-46S	.040	30	.016	—	8B	22	5½-6½	—	650/550
	8-455	230	R-46SX	.080	Electronic		—	8B	22	5½-6½	—	650/550
'75	6-231	110	R-44SX	.060	Electronic		12B	12B	17	4½-5¾	800/600	650/500
	6-250	100	R-46TX	.060	Electronic		10B	10B	16	4-5	800/425	600/425
	8-260	110	R-46SX	.080	Electronic		16B	18B(16B)(9)	22	5½-6½	750	650/550
	8-350(10)	145	R-45TSX	.060	Electronic		—	12B	19	4½-5¾	—	600
	8-350(10)	165	R-45TSX	.060	Electronic		—	12B	19	4¼-5¾	—	600
	8-350	170	R-46SX	.080	Electronic		—	20B	16	5½-6½	—	600/650
	8-455	190	R-46SX	.080	Electronic		—	16B	20	5½-6½	—	650/550 (600)

F-85, Cutlass, Omega, Starfire, Vista Cruiser, 442 TUNE-UP SPECIFICATIONS (cont'd)

When analyzing compression test results, look for uniformity among cylinders rather than specific pressures.

Year	ENGINE No. Cyl Displacement (cu in.)	hp	SPARK PLUGS Type	Gap (in.)	DISTRIBUTOR Point Dwell (deg)	Point Gap (in.)	IGNITION TIMING (deg) ▲ Man Trans	* ● Auto Trans	VALVES Intake Opens ■ (deg) ●	Fuel Pump Pressure (psi)	IDLE SPEED (rpm) ▲ Man Trans	● Auto Trans
'76	6-231	110	R-44SX	.060	Electronic		12B	12B	17	4½-5½	800/600	650
	6-250	100	R-46TX	.060	Electronic		10B	10B	16	4-5	850/425	550/425 (600/425)
	8-260	110	R-46SX	.080	Electronic		16B	18B(16B)⑨	22	5½-6½	750	550/650 (600/650)⑪
	8-350⑩	145	R-46TSX	.060	Electronic		—	12B	19	4½-5¾	—	600
	8-350	170	R-46SX	.080	Electronic		—	20B	16	5½-6½	—	550/650 (600/550)⑪
	8-455	190	R-46SX	.080	Electronic		—	16B	20	5½-6½	—	550/650 (600/650)⑪

▲ See text for procedure
■ All figures Before Top Dead Center
● Figure in parentheses indicates California engine
* Set timing (1968-74) with carburetor adjusted to the following speeds:

All V8	Without A/C	With A/C
1969 350 Cu. In.	850	1000
1969 400 Cu. In.	850	1250
1970-74 V8	1100	850

① Not used
② Figure is 30 degrees for manual transmission
③ Cutlass
④ Vista Cruiser
⑤ 442
⑥ R-46S for automatic transmission
⑦ Figure is 44 degrees for manual transmission
⑧ Without A/C
550—automatic transmission
500—manual transmission
⑨ 14B—Omega, California
⑩ Omega only
⑪ The second figure is for cars with A/C only (see text)
B Before Top Dead Center
TDC Top Dead Center
— Not applicable
N.A. Not Available

Oldsmobile 88, 98 TUNE-UP SPECIFICATIONS

When analyzing compression test results, look for uniformity among cylinders rather than specific pressures.

Year	ENGINE No. Cyl Displacement (cu in.)	hp	SPARK PLUGS Type	Gap (in.)	DISTRIBUTOR Point Dwell (deg)	Point Gap (in.)	IGNITION TIMING (deg) ▲ Man Trans	* ● Auto Trans	VALVES Intake Opens ■ (deg) ●	Fuel Pump Pressure (psi)	IDLE SPEED (rpm) ▲ Man Trans	● Auto Trans
'69	8-350	250	45S	.030	28-32	.016	6B	6B	16	5-7	675/400	600/400
	8-455	310	45S	.030	28-32	.016	6B	6B	20	5-7	675/400	600/400
	8-455	365	44S	.030	28-32	.016	—	8B	20	5-7	—	575
	8-455	390	43S	.030	28-32	.016	—	10B	24	5½-6½	—	575
'70	8-350	250	R-46S	.030	28-32	.016	8B	8B	16	5½-6½	675	575
	8-455	310	R-46S	.030	28-32	.016	8B	8B	20	5½-6½	675	575
	8-455	365	R-45S	.030	28-32	.016	—	8B	20	5½-6½	—	575
'71	8-350	240	R-46S	.040	28-32	.016	—	10B	14	5½-6½	—	600
	8-455	280	R-46S	.040	28-32	.016	—	8B	20	5½-6½	—	600
	8-455	320	R-46S	.040	28-32	.016	—	8B	20	5½-6½	—	600
'72	8-350	160	R-46S	.040	28-32	.016	—	8B	16	5½-6½	—	650/600
	8-350	180	R-46S	.040	28-32	.016	—	12B	22	5½-6½	—	600
	8-455	225	R-46S	.040	28-32	.016	—	8B	20	5½-6½	—	650/600
'73	8-350	160	R-46S	.040	30	.016	—	12B	16	5½-6½	—	700/550
	8-455	225	R-46S	.040	30	.016	—	8B	20	5½-6½	—	650/550
'74	8-350	180	R-46S	.040	30	.016	—	12B	16	5½-6½	—	650/550
	8-455	210	R-46S	.040	30	.016	—	8B	20	5½-6½	—	650/550
	8-455	230	R-46SX	.080	Electronic		—	8B	20	5½-6½	—	650/550

Oldsmobile 88, 98 TUNE-UP SPECIFICATIONS

When analyzing compression test results, look for uniformity among cylinders rather than specific pressures.

Year	ENGINE No. Cyl Displacement (cu in.)	hp	SPARK PLUGS Type	Gap (in.)	DISTRIBUTOR Point Dwell (deg)	Point Gap (in.)	IGNITION TIMING (deg) ▲ Man Trans	* ●	Auto Trans	VALVES Intake Opens ■ (deg) ●	Fuel Pump Pressure (psi)	IDLE SPEED (rpm) ▲ Man Trans	●	Auto Trans
'75	8-350	170	R-46SX	.080	Electronic		—		20B	16	5½-6½	—		650/550
	8-400	180	R-45TSX	.040	Electronic		—		16B	30	5-6½	—		650
	8-455	190	R-46SX	.080	Electronic		—		16B	20	5½-6½	—		650/550
'76	8-350	170	R-46SX	.080	Electronic		—		20B	16	5½-6½	—		550/650 (600/650)①
	8-455	190	R-46SX	.080	Electronic		—		16B	20	5½-6½	—		550/650 (600/650)①

① The second figure is for cars with A/C only (see text)

▲ See text for procedure

* Set timing with (1969-74) carburetor adjusted to the following speeds:

Year	Without A/C	With A/C
1969	850	1250
1970-1974	1100	850

■ All figures are in degrees Before Top Dead Center

● Figures in parentheses apply to California engines. Where two figures appear separated by a slash, the first is idle speed with solenoid energized, the second is idle speed with solenoid disconnected.

B Before Top Dead Center

— Not applicable

Oldsmobile F-85, Cutlass, Vista Cruiser, Omega, Starfire CAPACITIES

Year	ENGINE No. Cyl. Displacement (Cu. In.)	Engine Crankcase Add 1 qt For New Filter	TRANSMISSION Pts To Refill After Draining Manual 3-Speed	Manual 4-Speed	Automatic ●	Drive Axle (pts)	Gasoline Tank (gals)	COOLING SYSTEM (qts) With Heater	With A/C
'69	6-250	4	3.5	——	6	3.7	20②	12.2	12.2
	8-350	4	3.5	2.25	6	3.7	20②	15.2	15.7
	8-400	4	3.5	——	8	3.7	23	15.2	15.7
'70	6-250	4	3.5	——	6	3.7	20②	12.2	12.2
	8-350	4	3.5	2.25	6	3.7	20②	15.2	15.7
	8-455	4	3.5	2.25	6	3.7	20②	17.5	18
'71	6-250	4	3.5	——	6	4.25	20③	12.2	12.2
	8-350	4	3.5	2.25	6	4.25	20③	15.2	15.7
	8-455	4	3.5	——	6	4.25	20③	17.5	18
'72	8-350	4	3.5	2.25	6	4.25①	20②	15.2	15.7
	8-455	4	——	——	6	4.25①	23	17	17.5
'73	6-250	4	3.5	——	6	4.25	21	12.5	——
	8-350	4	3.5	2.25	6	4.25①⑤	22④	15.9⑦	⑥⑦
	8-455	4	——	2.25	6	4.25①⑤	22	17.0⑧	18⑧
'74	6-250	4	3.5	——	6	4.25	21	15.5	——
	8-350	4	——	——	6	4.25⑤	22④	20.0⑨	20.0⑩
	8-455	4	——	——	6	5.50	22	21.0⑪	21.5⑪
'75-'76	6-231	4	——	2.5	6	2.75	18.5	13.3	13.8⑫
	6-250	4	3.5	——	6	4.25	22④	17.0⑬	17.0⑩
	8-260	4	3.5	——	6	4.25	22④	23.5⑨	23.5⑩⑪
	8-350	4	——	——	6	4.25⑤	22④	20.0⑨	22.5⑩
	8-455	4	——	——	6	5.50	22	21.0⑪	21.5⑪

● Specifications do not include torque converter
① Limited slip differential—5.4 pts
② Station wagon 23 gals
③ Station wagon 22 gals
④ Omega 21 gals
⑤ Vista Cruiser—5.5 pts
⑥ Omega—16.5 qts
Cutlass—16 qts
⑦ Heavy duty cooling—21 qts
⑧ Heavy duty cooling—22 qts
⑨ Omega—18.5 qts
⑩ Omega—19.5 qts
⑪ Heavy duty cooling—22.5 qts
⑫ California—14.25 qts
⑬ Omega—15.5 qts
—— Not applicable

Oldsmobile 88, 98

CAPACITIES

Year	ENGINE No. Cyl. Displacement (Cu. In.)	Engine Crankcase Add 1 qt For New Filter	TRANSMISSION Pts To Refill After Draining Manual 3-Speed	Manual 4-Speed	Automatic ●	Drive Axle (pts)	Gasoline Tank (gals)	COOLING SYSTEM (qts) With Heater	With A/C
'69	8-350	4	4.9	—	6	3.7	25	17.5	18
	8-455	4	4.9	—	6	5.3	25	17.5	18
'70	8-350	4	4.9	—	6	3.7	25	17.5	18
	8-455	4	4.9	—	6	5.3	25	17.5	18
'71	8-350	4	—	—	6	4.3	24①	17.5	18
	8-455	4	—	—	6	5.4	24①	17.5	18
'72	8-350	4	—	—	6	4.3	24②	16.2	16.7
	8-455	4	—	—	6	5.4	24②	17	17.5
'73	8-350	4	—	—	6	4.3	26	16.2④	16.2④
	8-455	4	—	—	6	5.4	26③	17.0⑤	17.5⑤
'74	8-350	4	—	—	6	4.3	26	21⑤	21⑤
	8-455	4	—	—	6	5.5	26③	21⑥	21.5⑥
'75-76	8-350	4	—	—	6	5.5	26	20⑤	20⑤
	8-400	5	—	—	6	5.5	26③	21.5⑦	22⑦
	8-455	4	—	—	6	5.5	26③	21⑥	21.5⑥

● Specifications do not include torque converter
① 22.7 gals with station wagon
② 23 gals on station wagon
③ 22 gals on station wagon
④ With heavy duty cooling system—21.5 qts
⑤ With heavy cooling system—22.5 qts
⑥ With heavy duty cooling system—23.5 qts
⑦ With heavy duty cooling—24 qts
— Not applicable

Oldsmobile 442

CAPACITIES

Year	ENGINE No. Cyl. Displacement (Cu. In.)	Engine Crankcase Add 1 qt For New Filter	TRANSMISSION Pts To Refill After Draining Manual 3-Speed	Manual 4-Speed	Automatic ●	Drive Axle (pts)	Gasoline Tank (gals)	COOLING SYSTEM (qts) With Heater	With A/C
'69	8-400	4	4.9	2.25	8	3.69	20	16.2	17.2
'70	8-455	4	5	2.25	8	3.69	20	16.2	17.2
'71	8-455	4	4.5	2.5	6	4.26	20	16.2	17.2

● Specifications do not include torque converter

VALVE SPECIFICATIONS

Year	Engine No. Cyl. Displacement (cu in.)	Seat Angle (deg)	Face Angle (deg)	Spring Test Pressure (lbs @ in.)	Spring Installed Height (in.)	STEM TO GUIDE Clearance (in.) Intake	Exhaust	STEM Diameter (in.) Intake	Exhaust
'69	6-250	46	45	186 @ 1.27	1 21/32	.0010-.0027	.0010-.0027	.3414	.3414
	8-350	45	46	187 @ 1.27	1 21/32	.0010-.0027	.0015-.0032	.3429	.3424
	8-400	①	④	187 @ 1.27	1 21/32	.0010-.0027	.0015-.0032	.3429	.3424
	8-455	45	46	187 @ 1.27	1 21/32	.0010-.0027	.0015-.0032	.3429	.3424
'70	6-250	46	45	186 @ 1.27	1 21/32	.0010-.0027	.0010-.0027	.3414	.3414
	8-350	45	46	187 @ 1.27	1 21/32	.0010-.0027	.0015-.0032	.3429	.3424
	8-455	45	46	187 @ 1.27	1 21/32	.0010-.0027	.0015-.0032	.3429	.3424
	8-455⑧	①	④	187 @ 1.27⑤	1 21/32	.0010-.0027	.0015-.0032	.3429	.3424
'71	6-250	46	45	186 @ 1.27	1 21/32	.0010-.0027	.0010-.0027	.3414	.3414
	8-350	45	46	187 @ 1.27	1 21/32	.0010-.0027	.0015-.0032	.3424	.3424
	8-455	45	46	187 @ 1.27	1 21/32	.0010-.0027	.0015-.0032	.3429	.3424
	8-455⑧	①	④	187 @ 1.27⑤	1 21/32	.0010-.0027	.0015-.0032	.3429	.3424

VALVE SPECIFICATIONS

Year	Engine No. Cyl. Displacement (cu in.)	Seat Angle (deg)	Face Angle (deg)	Spring Test Pressure (lbs @ in.)	Spring Installed Height (in.)	STEM TO GUIDE Clearance (in.) Intake	Exhaust	STEM Diameter (in.) Intake	Exhaust
'72	8-350	⑥	⑦	187 @ 1.27	1 21/32	.0010-.0027	.0015-.0032	.3429	.3424
	8-350⑨	45	46	198 @ 1.23	1 21/32	.0010-.0027	.0015-.0032	.3429	.3424
	8-455⑩	⑥	46	187 @ 1.27	1 21/32	.0010-.0027	.0015-.0032	.3429	.3424
	8-455	①	④	206 @ 1.19	1 21/32	.0010-.0027	.0015-.0032	.3429	.3424
'73	6-250	46	45	186 @ 1.27	1 21/32	.0010-.0027	.0010-.0027	.3413	.3413
	8-350	⑫	⑬	187 @ 1.27	1 21/32	.0010-.0027	.0015-.0032	.3429	.3424
	8-455⑩⑪	⑫	⑬	187 @ 1.27	1 21/32	.0010-.0027	.0015-.0032	.3429	.3424
	8-455⑭	⑮	⑯	206 @ 1.19	1 21/32	.0010-.0027	.0015-.0032	.3429	.3424
'74	6-250	46	45	186 @ 1.27	1 21/32	.0010-.0027	.0015-.0032	.3413	.3413
	8-350	⑰	⑱	187 @ 1.27	1 31/32	.0010-.0027	.0015-.0032	.3429	.3424
	8-455⑩⑪	⑰	⑬	187 @ 1.27	1 31/32	.0010-.0027	.0015-.0032	.3429	.3424
'75-	6-231	45	45	164 @ 1.34	——	.0015-.0035	.0015-.0032	.3407	.3407
'76	6-250	46	45	186 @ 1.27	1 21/32	.0010-.0027	.0015-.0032	.3413	.3413
	8-260	⑫	⑬	186 @ 1.27	1 31/32	.0010-.0027	.0015-.0032	.3427	.3424
	8-350⑲	45	46	180 @ 1.340	——	.0015-.0035	.0015-.0032	.3725	.3728
	8-350	⑫	⑬	187 @ 1.27	1 31/32	.0010-.0027	.0015-.0032	.3429	.3424
	8-400㉑	①	⑳	61 @ 1.59	1 19/32	.0016-.0033	.0021-.0038	.3416	.3411
	8-455	⑫	⑬	187 @ 1.27	1 31/32	.0010-.0027	.0015-.0032	.3429	.3424

① Intake 30°, exhaust 45°
② ③ Not used
④ Intake 30°, exhaust 46°
⑤ With air induction—302 @ 1.17
⑥ Intake 45°, exhaust 30°
⑦ Intake 46°, exhaust 30°
⑧ 4-4-2
⑨ California cars only
⑩ Oldsmobile 98
⑪ Oldsmobile 88
⑫ Intake 45°. exhaust 31°
⑬ Intake 44°; exhaust 30°
⑭ Cutlass
⑮ Intake 31°; exhaust 45°
⑯ Intake 30°; exhaust 44°
⑰ Intake 45°; exhaust 31°
⑱ Not Used
⑲ Omega only
⑳ Intake 29°; exhaust 44°
㉑ 1975 only

TORQUE SPECIFICATIONS

All readings in ft lbs

Year	Engine	Cylinder Head Bolts	Rod Bearing Bolts	Main Bearing Bolts	Crankshaft Pulley Bolt	Flywheel to Crankshaft Bolts	MANIFOLD Intake	Exhaust
'69-'74	6-250	95	35	65	Press fit	60	25	30④
	8-All	80①⑤	42	120②	160 min	③	35①⑥	25
'75-'76	6-231	75	40	115	140⑦	55	45	25
	6-250	95	35	65	Press fit	60	⑩	⑪
	8-350⑨	80	40	115	140⑦	60	45	28
	8-260, 350, 455	85①	42	120②	160⑦	③	40①	25
	8-400⑫	95	43	100⑧	160	95	40	30

① To obtain accurate torque readings, all bolts must be clean and lightly coated with engine oil
② 8-260, 350—80 on No. 1-4, 120 on No. 5
③ A.T. 60 ft lbs.; M.T. 90 ft lbs. (1970-76), 80 ft. lbs. (1969)
④ This refers to those bolts holding the exhaust manifold to the cylinder head
⑤ 1973-74—85 ft lbs
⑥ 1973-74—40 ft lbs
⑦ Minimum
⑧ 120 ft lbs on rear main
⑨ Omega only
⑩ Intake manifold integral with cylinder head
⑪ Inner bolts—30 ft lbs.; outer bolts—20 ft lbs.
min minimum
⑫ 1975 only

CRANKSHAFT AND CONNECTING ROD SPECIFICATIONS

All measurements are given in inches

Year	Engine No. Cyl. Displacement (cu in.)	Crankshaft: Main Brg. Journal Dia	Crankshaft: Main Brg. Oil Clearance	Crankshaft: Shaft End-Play	Crankshaft: Thrust on No.	Connecting Rod: Journal Diameter	Connecting Rod: Oil Clearance	Connecting Rod: Side Clearance
'69	6-250	2.2988	.0003-.0029	.002-.006	7	1.999-2.000	.0007-.0040	.0085-.0135
	8-350	2.4990	.0005-.0021①	.004-.008	3	2.1238-2.1248	.0009-.0031③	.002-.013
	8-400, 455	2.9998	.0005-.0021②	.004-.008	3	2.4988-2.4998	.0004-.0033	.002-.013
'70-'73	6-250	2.3004	.0003-.0029	.002-.006	7	1.999-2.000	.0007-.0027	.007-.016
	8-350	2.4990⑥	.0005-.0021①	.004-.008	3	2.1238-2.1248	.0004-.0033⑦	④
	8-455	2.9998	.0005-.0021②	.004-.008	3	2.4988-2.4998	.0004-.0033	④⑤
'74	6-250	2.2988	.0035⑧	.002-.006	7	1.999-2.000	.0035	.009-.014
	8-350	2.4990⑨	.0005-.0021①	.004-.008	3	2.1238-2.1248	.0004-.0033	.006-.020
	8-455	2.9998	.0005-.0021②	.004-.008	3	2.4988-2.4998	.0004-.0033	.006-.020
'75-'76	6-231	2.4995	.0004-.0015	.004-.008	2	2.000	.0002-.0023	.006-.014
	6-250	2.2999	.0003-.0029	.002-.006	7	1.999-2.000	.0007-.0027	.007-.016
	8-260	2.5000	.0005-.0021①	.004-.008	3	2.1238-2.1248	.0005-.0026	.006-.020
	8-350⑩	2.9995	.0004-.0015	.002-.006	3	1.9991-2.000	.0005-.0026	.006-.027
	8-350	2.4990⑨	.0005-.0021①	.004-.008	3	2.1238-2.1248	.0004-.0033	.006-.020
	8-400⑪	3.0000	.0002-.0017	.003-.009	4	2.250	.0005-.0025	.012-0.17
	8-455	2.9998	.0005-.0021②	.004-.008	3	2.4988-2.4998	.0004-.0033	.006-.020

① No. 5—.0015-.0031
② No. 5—.0020-.0034
③ 1969—.0005-.0026
④ 1970—.002-.013; 1971—.002-.011; 1972-73—.006-.020
⑤ 1970-73 W-30—.002-.021
N.A. Not Applicable
⑥ 1973—2.50 in.
⑦ 1973—.0005-.0026
⑧ No. 1—.0020 in. max.
⑨ No. 1—2.4988-2.4998 in.
⑩ Omega only
⑪ 1975 only

RING SIDE CLEARANCE

All measurements are given in inches

Year	Engine	Top Compression	Bottom Compression
'69-71	6-250	.0020-.0038	.0020-.0038
'69-'71	All 8 cylinders	.0018-.0033	.0018-.0038
'72-'76	8-350, 455	.0020-.0040	.0020-.0040
'73-'76	6-250	.0012-.0027	.0012-.0032
'75-'76	6-231, 8-350 (Omega)	.0030-.0050	.0030-.0050
'75	8-400	.0015-.0050	.0015-.0050

Year	Engine	Oil Control
'69-'76	6-250	.000-.005
'69	8-350	.0001-.0051
'69	8-400	.0006-.0096
'70-'76	8-350	.0006-.0096
'69-'76	8-455	.0021-.0031
'75-'76	6-231, 8-350 (Omega)	.0035-.0095
'75	8-400	.0015-.0050

RING GAP

All measurements are given in inches

Year	Engine	Top Compression	Bottom Compression
'69-'71	6-250, 350	.010-.020	.010-.020
'69	8-400	.010-.020	.010-.020
'69-'71	8-455	.013-.023	.013-.023
'72-'76	8-350, 455	.010-.023	.010-.023
'73-'76	6-250	.010-.020	.010-.020
'75-'76	6-231, 8-350 (Omega)	.015-.023	.013-.023
'75	8-400	.019	.015

Year	Engine	Oil Control
'69-'76	All engines	.015-.055

PISTON CLEARANCE

Year	Engine	Piston-to-Bore Clearance (in.)
'69	6-250	.0025
	8-350	.0075-.0125
	8-400, 455	.0010-.0020
'70-'74	6-250	.0025
	8-350, 455	.0010-.0020①
'75-'76	6-231, 8-350②	.0013-.0029
	6-250	.0025
	8-260	.0010-.0020
	8-350, 455	.0010-.0020
	8-400③	.0029-.0037

① 1972 W-30 (option 455 cu in. V8)—.0025-.0035 in.
② Omega only
③ 1975 only

ALTERNATOR AND REGULATOR SPECIFICATIONS

	Alternator			Regulator						
					Field Relay			Regulator		
Year	Part No. or Manufacturer	Field Current @ 12 V	Output (amps)	Part No. or Manufacturer	Air Gap (in.)	Point Gap (in.)	Volts to Close	Air Gap (in.)	Point Gap (in.)	Volts @ 75°
'69-'70	1100767	2.2-2.6	37	1119515	.015	.030	6.3-8.3	.060	.014	13.5-14.4
	1100880	2.2-2.6	37	Transistor type, integral with alternator, no adjustment						
	1100734	2.2-2.6	42	1119515	.015	.030	6.3-8.3	.060	.014	13.5-14.4
	1100878	2.2-2.6	42	1119515	.015	.030	6.3-8.3	.060	.014	13.5-14.4
	1100907	2.2-2.6	55	1119515	.015	.030	6.3-8.3	.060	.014	13.5-14.4
'71-'72	1100566	2.2-2.6	37	1119515	Not Adjustable					13.5-14.4
	1102440	2.2-2.6	37	1119515	Not Adjustable					13.5-14.4
	1100888	2.2-2.6	37	1119515	Not Adjustable					13.5-14.4
	1100934	2.2-2.6	37	Transistor type, integral with alternator, no adjustment						
	1100567	2.2-2.6	42	1119515	Not Adjustable					13.5-14.4
	1102439	2.2-2.6	55	1119515	Not Adjustable					13.5-14.4
	1100568	2.2-2.6	55	1119515	Not Adjustable					13.5-14.4
	1100569	2.2-2.6	55	1119515	Not Adjustable					13.5-14.4
	1100935	2.2-2.6	55	Transistor type, integral with alternator, no adjustment						
	1100570	2.2-2.6	61	1119515	Not Adjustable					13.5-14.4
	1100553	2.2-2.6	63	1119515	Not Adjustable					13.5-14.4
	1102435	2.2-2.6	42	1119515	Not Adjustable					13.5-14.4
	1102437	2.2-2.6	55	1119515	Not Adjustable					13.5-14.4
	1102463	2.2-2.6	61	1119515	Not Adjustable					13.5-14.4
'73-'74	1100497	2.2-2.6	37	Transistor type, integral with alternator, no adjustment						
	1100934	2.2-2.6	37	Transistor type, integral with alternator, no adjustment						
	1102367	2.2-2.6	55	Transistor type, integral with alternator, no adjustment						
	1100537	2.2-2.6	42	Transistor type, integral with alternator, no adjustment						
	1102368	2.2-2.6	61	Transistor type, integral with alternator, no adjustment						
	1100554	2.2-2.6	63	Transistor type, integral with alternator, no adjustment						
'75-'76	1102394, 1102483 1102399, 1102481	2.2-2.6	37	Transistor type, integral with alternator, no adjustment						
	1102493	2.2-2.6	42	Transistor type, integral with alternator, no adjustment						
	1102495, 1102488	2.2-2.6	55	Transistor type, integral with alternator, no adjustment						
	1102549	2.2-2.6	61	Transistor type, integral with alternator, no adjustment						
	1102550	2.2-2.6	63	Transistor type, integral with alternator, no adjustment						

BATTERY AND STARTER SPECIFICATIONS

Year	Engine Displacement (cu in.)	BATTERY: Ampere Hour Capacity ●	BATTERY: Volts	BATTERY: Terminal Grounded	STARTER Lock Test: Amps	Lock Test: Volts	Lock Test: Torque (ft lbs)	No-Load Test: Amps	No-Load Test: Volts	No-Load Test: RPM	Brush Spring Tension (oz)
'69-'74	6-250, 231	44	12	Neg.	Not Recommended			50-80	9-10.5	6,000-10,000	35
	8-350	62	12	Neg.	Not Recommended			50-80	9-10.5	5,000-6,000	35
	8-400, 455	70, 73, 75	12	Neg.	Not Recommended			50-80	9-10.5	5,000-6,000	35
'75-'76	6-231	2500, 3200	12	Neg.	Not Recommended			—	—	—	35
	6-250	2300	12	Neg.	Not Recommended			—	—	—	35
	8-260	3200	12	Neg.	Not Recommended			—	—	—	35
	8-350	3200, 3750	12	Neg.	Not Recommended			—	—	—	35
	8-400, 455	3500, 3750	12	Neg.	Not Recommended			—	—	—	35

— Not specified
● Cranking power in watts given starting 1975

BRAKE SPECIFICATIONS

All measurements are given in inches

Year	Model	MASTER CYLINDER: Disc	MASTER CYLINDER: Drum	WHEEL CYLINDER Front: Disc	WHEEL CYLINDER Front: Drum	WHEEL CYLINDER: Rear	BRAKE DISC OR DRUM DIAMETER Front: Disc	Front: Drum	Rear
'69	All except 88, 98 Series	1⅛	1.0	2 15/16	1⅛	15/16②	10 29/32	9½	9½
	88, 98 Series	1⅛	1.0	2 15/16	1 3/16	1.0	11 13/16	9½	9½③
'70	All except 88, 98 Series	1⅛	1.0	2 15/16	1⅛	⅞①④	11	9½	9½
	88, 98 Series	1⅛	1.0	2 15/16	1 3/16	15/16	11 29/32	11	11
'71-'74	F-85/Cutlass, 442, Std. Sta. Wag., Vista Cruiser, Omega	⑤	1.0	2 15/16	1⅛	⅞②	11	9½	9½
	88, 98 Series	1⅛	—	2 15/16	—	15/16	11 29/32	—	11
	Custom Cruiser	1⅛	—	2 15/16	—	1.0	11 29/32	—	12
'75-'76	Starfire	¾	—	1⅞	—	¾	9.80	—	9.0
	Omega	⑤	—	2 15/16	—	⅞	11.00	—	9.5
	Cutlass, Vista Cruiser	⑤	—	2 15/16	—	⅞②	11.00	—	9.5
	88, 98 Series	1⅛	—	2 15/16	—	15/16	11.88	—	11.0
	Custom Cruiser	1⅛	—	2 15/16	—	1.0	11.88	—	12.0

① 13/16 on F-85, 442 with disc brakes
② 1.0 on Vista Cruiser
③ 11 with disc brakes
④ 15/16 on Std. Sta. Wagon
⑤ Non-power disc brakes—1.0 in.; power disc brakes 1⅛ in.
⑥ 11 in.; '76
— Not applicable

WHEEL ALIGNMENT SPECIFICATIONS

Year	Model	CASTER: Range (deg)	CASTER: Pref Setting (deg)	CAMBER: Range (deg)	CAMBER: Pref Setting (deg)	Toe-in (in.)	Steering Axis Inclin. (deg)	WHEEL PIVOT RATIO (deg): Inner Wheel	WHEEL PIVOT RATIO (deg): Outer Wheel
'69	F-85 Series	½N to 2N	1¼N①	¼N to ½P	⅛P	⅛ to 3/16	9	20	18⅗
	88 & 98 Series	½N to 1½N	1¼N①	¼N to ½P	⅛P	⅛ to 3/16	11	20	18 3/10④
'70	F-85 Series	½N to 2N	1¼N①	¼N to ½P	⅛P	⅛ to 3/16	9	20	18⅗
	88 & 98 Series	½N to 1½N	1¼N①	¼N to ½P	⅛P	⅛ to 3/16	11	20	18 3/10④
'71-'72	F-85 Series	¾N to 1¾N	1¼N	¾N to ¾P*	¼P*	1/16N to 1/16P	8	20	19②
	88 & 98 Series	½P to 1½P	1P	¾N to ¾P*	¼P*	1/16N to 1/16P	10½③	20	18½

WHEEL ALIGNMENT SPECIFICATIONS

Year	Model	CASTER Range (deg)	CASTER Pref Setting (deg)	CAMBER Range (deg)	CAMBER Pref Setting (deg)	Toe-in (in.)	Steering Axis Inclin. (deg)	WHEEL PIVOT RATIO (deg) Inner Wheel	WHEEL PIVOT RATIO (deg) Outer Wheel
'73	Omega	½N to 1½P	½P	½N to 1P	½P	1/16 to 5/16	9	N.A.	N.A.
	Cutlass	¾N to 1¾N	1¼N	⑤	⑤	1/16	10½	20	19②
	88 & 98 Series	0 to 2P	1P	¾N to ¾P*	¼P*	1/16 to 1/16	9½	20	18½
'74	Omega	½N to 1½P	½P	½N to 1P	¼P	1/16 to 5/16	9	N.A.	N.A.
	Cutlass	1N to 1P	0	⑥	⑥	0 to 1/8	10½	20	19②
	Cutlass Salon	1P to 3P	2P	⑥	⑥	0 to 1/8	10½	20	19②
	88, 98 Series	0 to 2P	1P	⑥	⑥	1/16 to 3/16	9½	20	18½
'75-'76	Starfire	¼N to ¼P	¾N	¾N to ¾P	¼P	0 to 1/8	9	N.A.	N.A.
	Omega	0 to 2P⑧	1P⑦	0 to ½P	¾P	0 to 1/8	10½	N.A.	N.A.
	Cutlass	1½P to 2½P	2P	⑥	⑥	0 to 1/8	10½	20	19②
	88, 98 Series	1P to 2P	1½P	⑥	⑥	0 to 1/8	10½	20	18½

* Left side camber to be ½° more positive than right side
① Power steering—¾N
② Power steering—18
③ 9.6 for 1972 88 & 98 Series
④ 17 7/10 for power steering
⑤ 1°P—LH; ½°N—RH: ± ¾°
⑥ 1P ± ½—LH; ½P ± ½—RH
⑦ 1N with manual steering
⑧ 2N to 0 with manual steering
N Negative P Positive
N.A. Not available

CHARGING SYSTEM

The charging system consists of the Delco-Remy Delcotron AC generator and a conventional relay-type regulator. Starting in 1969, the Delcotron offered as standard equipment in the 442 model was equipped with a built in transistorized regulator unit. This regulator is a completely electronic sealed unit and cannot be adjusted. A capacitor mounted in the end frame keeps down high voltages and suppresses radio noise. All 1973-75 models have this integral alternator/regulator as standard equipment.

See "Charging and Starting Systems" in the Unit Repair Section for charging system test and component overhaul procedures.

Alternator

Removal

NOTE: Before removing the alternator, disconnect the battery ground cable.

1. Disconnect the wiring from the alternator.
2. Remove the mounting bolts and drive belt.
3. Lift out the alternator.

Installation

To install, reverse the removal procedure, connect the battery ground cable and tighten the alternator belt. Determine belt tension at a point halfway between the pulleys by pressing on the belt with moderate thumb pressure. If the distance between the pulleys (measured at the pulley center) is 13–16 in., the belt should deflect ½ in. at the halfway point or ¼ in. if the distance is 7–10 in. If the deflection is found to be too little or too much, make the proper adjustments.

Regulator

All 4-4-2 models through 1971 and all 1973-76 models are equipped with a generator containing a built-in transistorized regulator. This is a completely sealed unit that cannot be adjusted or disassembled. All other models are equipped with a conventional, externally mounted regulator which should be removed and installed in the following manner:

Removal

1. Disconnect the electrical connector from the regulator.
2. Remove the attaching screws and the regulator.

Installation

To install, reverse the removal procedure.

STARTING SYSTEM

See "Charging and Starting Systems" in the Unit Repair Section for starter motor service procedures, including overhaul and starter drive replacement.

Starter R & R

1969 Except 400 Cu. In. Engine

1. Disconnect battery.
2. Noting positions of wires, disconnect starter wiring.
3. If equipped with manual transmission, remove flywheel cover.
4. Remove upper support attaching bolt.
5. Remove two mounting bolts and remove starter. If equipped with dual exhausts, it may be necessary to remove the left-hand exhaust pipe.
6. Install by reversing the above procedure.

1969 400 Cu. In. Engine

1. Disconnect battery.
2. Disconnect clutch return spring at clutch release yoke.
3. Disconnect exhaust pipe from left manifold.

4. Loosen upper and remove lower starter to block brace bolts.
5. Remove two starter to brace block bolts.
6. Move starter forward and downward, then disconnect wires from three starter terminals. In 4-4-2 models equipped with automatic transmissions, it may be necessary to remove the flyweel housing cover.
7. Remove starter.
8. Install by reversing the above procedure.

1970-76—All (except V6)

1. Disconnect battery and carefully hoist car.
2. Remove upper support attaching bolts.
3. Remove flywheel housing cover.
4. Remove two starter mounting bolts.
5. Lower starter, disconnect wiring, and remove starter. If equipped with dual exhausts, it may be necessary to remove the left-hand exhaust pipe.
6. Install by reversing the above procedure.

V6—1975-76

1. Disconnect the battery and raise the car.
2. Disconnect and plug the oil cooler lines from the transmission.
3. Remove the upper support bolts.
4. Take off the flywheel housing cover.
5. Unfasten the two starter securing bolts and lower the starter.
6. Disconnect the wiring after noting its position for installation.

Starter installation is the reverse of removal. Check the transmission fluid level.

Starter Drive Removal and Installation

1. Remove the bolt which holds the field leads to the solenoid motor terminal and disconnect the leads. Remove the two solenoid attaching bolts, rotate, and remove the solenoid.
2. Remove the two through-bolts, end frame, and field frame assembly.
3. Pull both brush holder pivot pins and lift out each pair of brush holder assemblies. Disconnect the leads and brushes.
4. Remove the shift lever pivot bolt, plunger, shift lever, and armature from the drive housing.
5. Remove the drive assembly from the armature by first using a tool (such as a ½ in. pipe coupling) to disengage the snap-ring retainer from the snap-ring. After removing the snap-ring and retainer, slide the drive assembly off of the armature shaft.
6. Inspect all parts for wear or damage and replace where necessary. When cleaning all parts, be sure not to use any degreasing or high temperature method on the armature, field coils, and drive assembly.

To assemble:

7. Lubricate the armature shaft and install the drive assembly with the pinion out.
8. Slide the snap-ring retainer onto the shaft with the recessed side out.
9. Use a block of wood and a hammer to get the new snap-ring started on the shaft. Install the snap-ring in the shaft groove.
10. Slide the thrust collar onto the shaft, move the snap-ring retainer up to the snap-ring, and squeeze the retainer and thrust collar together with two pair of pliers. The retainer should be forced over the snap-ring.
11. Lubricate the drive frame bushing and shift lever linkage and install the shift lever in the drive end frame.
12. Install the armature and spacers into the drive end frame, making sure that the shift lever is in place.
13. Assemble the brushes and leads to the brush holders. Place the brush holders and springs in the field frame and install the pivot pins.
14. Install the field frame over the armature, spreading the brush holders to prevent damage.
15. Lubricate the commutator end frame bushing and install the frame.
16. Install the through-bolts.
17. Move the armature toward the commutator end frame. Measure the clearance between the snap-ring retainer and drive end housing with feeler gauges. It should be 0.000-0.050 in. Use spacers to adjust the clearance.

IGNITION SYSTEM

Distributors with contact points on V8 engines have a window in the cap so that the point gap (dwell angle) may be adjusted with an Allen wrench while the engine is running. When installing a new contact point set, only the gap is adjusted; the spring tension and point alignment are pre-adjusted.

A high energy ignition (HEI) was offered as an option on some engines in 1974 and made standard equipment beginning 1975. The HEI distributor replaces the points and condenser with a timing wheel, magnetic pick-up, and control module. On V6 and V8 engines, the coil is built into the distributor cap; on inline sixes, the coil is mounted separately. For further description, as well as service procedures for HEI, see the "Electronic Ignition" unit repair section.

Distributor Removal

All Engines

1. Remove distributor cap, primary (or feed) wire and vacuum line at the distributor.
2. Scribe a mark on the distributor body, locating the position of the rotor, and scribe another mark on the distributor body and engine block, showing the position of the body in the block.
3. Remove the hold-down screw and lift the distributor out of the block.

Note: Do not crank the engine with the distributor removed; this will change the timing.

Distributor Installation

If engine has *not* been disturbed (cranked) after removing the distributor, perform the following procedure for installation:

NOTE: Design of the V6 engine requires a special distributor. The distributor may be serviced in the regular way and should cause no more problems than any other distributor, if the firing plan is thoroughly understood. This particular form requires that the original pattern of spark plug wiring be used. The engine will not run in balance if number one spark plug wire is inserted into number six distributor cap tower, even though each wire in the firing sequence is advanced to the next distributor tower. There is a difference between the firing intervals of each succeeding cylinder through the 720° engine cycle.

1. Turn the rotor clockwise until it is about ⅛ turn past the locating mark previously made on the distributor housing.
2. Push the distributor down into the block. It may be necessary to turn the rotor slightly until the shaft engages in the block. The mark on the distributor housing must line up with the mark made on the engine block.
3. Tighten the hold-down bolt until it is snug and then connect the vacuum advance line.
4. Connect the primary wire to the coil or, on HEI, connect the feed wire and install the distributor cap.
5. Check the timing and adjust it as necessary. Tighten the hold-down bolt.

If engine has been disturbed (cranked) after removing distributor, perform the following procedure for installation:

1. Crank the engine until no. one piston is at the top of its compression stroke. The compression stroke can be determined by removing the spark plug from the no. one cylinder and placing your thumb over the hole while an assistant slowly cranks the engine. Crank until compression is felt at the hole and then continue cranking slowly until the timing mark on the crankshaft pulley lines up with the 0° timing mark.
2. Position the distributor in the block but do not allow it to engage with its drive gear. Observe the position of the vacuum control unit on the distributor. If the distributor is located correctly, the vacuum unit will be positioned normally so that the vacuum hose can be easily connected to it.
3. Position the distributor rotor so that it aligns with the no. one spark plug in the distributor cap.
4. Press firmly downward on the distributor housing while an assistant kicks the starter over a few times. This will assure the distributor shaft engaging the oil pump shaft, thereby allowing the distributor to fully contact the engine block.
5. Install the hold-down clamp and tighten the bolt until it is snug.
6. Turn the distributor slightly until the points just open, then tighten the bolt.
7. Install the distributor cap.
8. Attach all wires and the vacuum advance hose.
9. Check the timing and adjust it as necessary.

Contact Point Replacement

V8 Engines

1. Remove the distributor cap and rotor.
2. Beginning with 1970 models, V8 distributors were equipped with a two-piece metal shield to suppress radio static. Remove the two attaching screws and the shield.
3. Remove the two wiring terminals from the retainer.
4. Remove the mounting screws and lift out the contact points and condenser.
5. Install the new contact points and condenser and tighten the mounting screws.
6. Install the primary and condenser wire terminals in the retainer. If the replacement point set has a snap-lock type retainer, the terminals can be pushed in to provide plenty of clearance between the shield (if so equipped) and the terminals to prevent accidental short circuiting. If the contact points have a screw type retainer, insufficient clearance may exist between the terminals and the shield, possibly causing a short circuit. To prevent this possibility, insert terminals in the retainer and bend them slightly toward the distributor cam. Make sure the wiring does not interfere with the other components.
7. Inspect the cam lubricator wick and replace or rotate it if it is worn out or dry. Using a feeler gauge, check and adjust the point gap.
8. If so equipped, install the two-piece shield and tighten the mounting screws.
9. Install the rotor, making sure that the round peg goes in the round hole and the square peg into the square hole.
10. Install the distributor cap.
11. Set the points to specifications with a dwell meter while the engine is running.

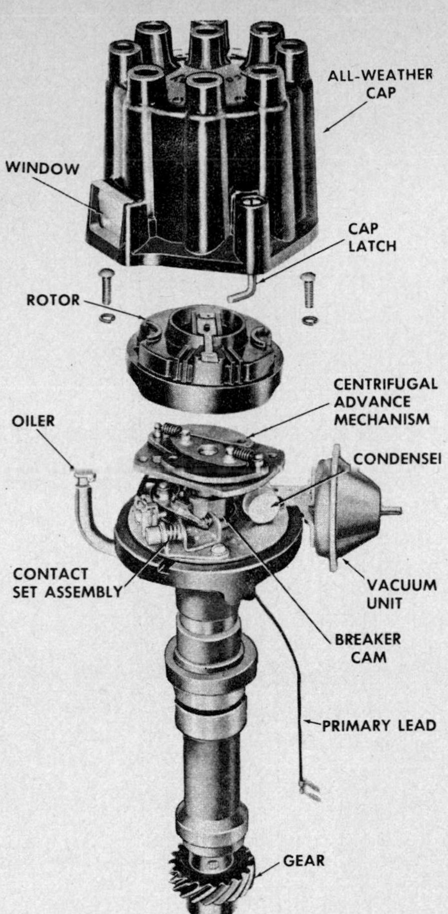

Distributor details, externally adjusted type—V8
(© Oldsmobile Div, G.M. Corp)

Inline 6

1. Remove the distributor cap retaining screws and lift off the distributor cap. Remove the rotor.
2. Disconnect the primary and condenser leads from the quick-disconnect terminal.
3. Remove the attaching screw and lift the contact point set from the distributor.
4. Withdraw the condenser retaining screw and remove the condenser.
5. Install the new condenser and tighten its retaining screw.
6. Install the new point set but do not fully tighten its attaching screw.
7. Connect the condenser and primary leads to the quick-disconnect terminal.
8. If necessary, align the contacts by bending the stationary contact bracket only. *Never bend the movable contact arm to correct alignment.*
9. Attach a remote starter switch to the electrical system. Crank the engine, rotating the distributor cam until the rubbing block of the movable contact arm rests on a peak of the cam lobe. It is also possible to turn the engine manually.
10. Insert the proper thickness feeler gauge between the contact points. If necessary, increase or decrease the gap by inserting a screwdriver in the "V" notch of the stationary contact base and using the screwdriver to move the stationary contact.
11. Tighten the point set attaching screw and recheck the gap setting.
12. Install the new rotor and replace the distributor cap. Check the point dwell and the ignition timing.

Ignition Timing

1. Disconnect the vacuum advance hose from the distributor and plug it. Disconnect the line from the charcoal canister.
2. Remove the air cleaner and tape over the vaccum hose fitting (if so equipped) on the V6 and V8 manifold.
3. Connect the tachometer and adjust the engine speed to specifications.

NOTE: If the car is equipped with electronic ignition and a tachometer, the in-tachometer wire (usually purple) going to the coil must be disconnected before connecting an external tachometer.

4. Connect a timing light, loosen the distributor mounting bolt, and turn the distributor until the specified timing is obtained. See the "Tune-Up" specifications chart for the proper engine speed for checking timing.
5. The inline six-cylinder timing indicator has an "0" marking signifying TDC. The marks represent 2, 4, 6, and 8° before TDC. The V8 indicator has four V-shaped slots each representing 4°.

6. Tighten the mounting bolt and recheck timing to see if it changed during tightening.
7. Unplug the vacuum advance hose and connect it to the distributor.
8. Remove the tape from the vacuum hose fitting and install and connect the hose, if so equipped.
9. Install the V6 and V8 air cleaner.

Timing Light and Tachometer Hook-Up for HEI

1. Use an adapter between the No. 1 spark plug and No. 1 spark plug lead, when connecting a timing light. Connect the timing light to the adapter; DO NOT pierce the spark plug lead. Because of the higher voltage used in the HEI system, any break in the insulation will cause electricity to jump to the nearest ground, making the No. 1 plug misfire.

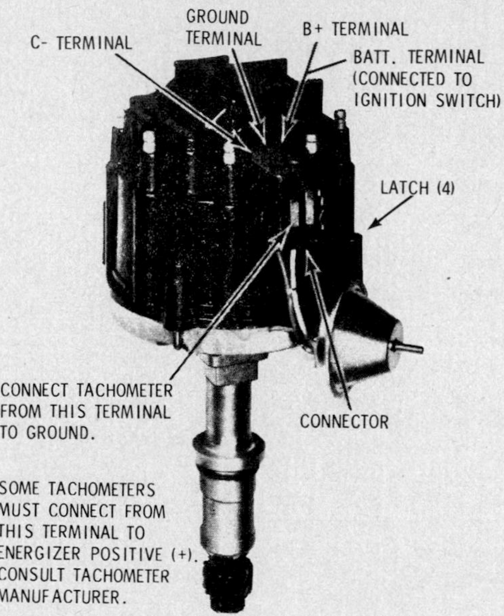

HEI distributor connections
(© Oldsmobile Div., GM Corp.)

2. The rest of the timing adjustment procedure is the same as for conventional breaker point ignition, except that timing should not have to be adjusted as frequently, since there is no rubbing block or cam wear.
3. The tachometer terminal is next to the ignition switch connector on the cap of V6 and V8 distributors or next to the ignition switch connector on the coil on inline six engines.
4. Most new tachometers can be used. Tachometers without a relay can't be used. Check the tach's instructions if you aren't sure. If you don't have the instructions, hook up the tach and check the readings on both the high and low rpm scales. If they agree the tach is OK; if they don't, use another tach.
5. There is no way of adjusting dwell, since this is controlled by the electronic module.
6. If you want to crank the engine without starting it, disconnect the ignition switch wire at the distributor cap (V8 or V6) or at the coil (inline 6).
7. No periodic lubrication is necessary.
8. Do not pull on the spark plug leads with the wiring harness in the locked position. Use a small screwdriver to release the tab from the lock.

FUEL SYSTEM

Gas tank capacities may be found in the Capacities table at the beginning of this section. See "Dash Gauges and Indicators" in the Unit Repair Section for a discussion of fuel gauge operation.

Fuel Pump Removal

1. Disconnect the fuel lines.
2. Remove the two mounting bolts.
3. Remove the pump and gasket.

Installation is the reverse of removal.

Fuel Filter

All carburetors have a fuel filter which is integral with the carburetor body. To replace the filter element, remove the fuel inlet line, then remove the inlet fitting and pull out the filter element. Be careful when tightening the brass fitting because the threads are easily stripped.

Idle Speed and Mixture Adjustments

1969-70 1-bbl

Adjust only with the air cleaner removed.

1. Run the engine to attain the normal operating temperature and remove the air cleaner. Disconnect the air vacuum hose from the base of the carburetor and plug the fitting.
2. Disconnect the vacuum advance hose from the distributor and plug the end of the hose. Plug the carburetor hot idle compensator so it is closed.
3. Apply the parking brake and set blocks in front of the rear wheels.
4. If so equipped, turn off the air conditioner.
5. If the car has an automatic transmission, place the selector lever in Drive, or in neutral if it has a manual transmission.
6. The choke must be fully opened and the fast idle cam follower must be off the cam.
7. The solenoid wire must be connected and the throttle stop screw should not touch the throttle lever.
8. Adjust the idle mixture to obtain the highest rpm possible. Adjust the throttle solenoid plunger to obtain an idle speed 25 rpm above the higher of the two idle speeds in the tune-up specifications.
9. Turn the idle mixture screw inward to lower the idle speed to the correct rpm.
10. Disconnect the solenoid wire and adjust the throttle stop screw to obtain the lower of the two idle speeds in the specifications.

1971 and 1973-76 1-bbl

NOTE: 1971 and some later models are equipped with a CEC solenoid. This solenoid does not function as an idle speed solenoid and it should not be adjusted during a routine carburetor adjustment.

1. Run the engine to the normal operating temperature, making sure that the choke is fully open.
2. Set the parking brake and block the drive wheels.
3. Disconnect the fuel tank hose from the vapor canister and the EGR valve hose.
4. Disconnect the distributor vacuum hoses from the CEC solenoid and plug the hose leading to the carburetor.
5. Set the dwell and timing.
6. Turn off the air conditioner and place automatic transmissions in Drive and manual transmissions in Neutral.
7. Connect a tachometer to the engine and, on 1971 models, turn the idle speed adjusting screw to obtain the correct speed.
8. On 1973-74 Omegas with a six cylinder engine, turn the *throttle* stop solenoid plunger inward or outward to obtain the higher of the two idle speeds listed in

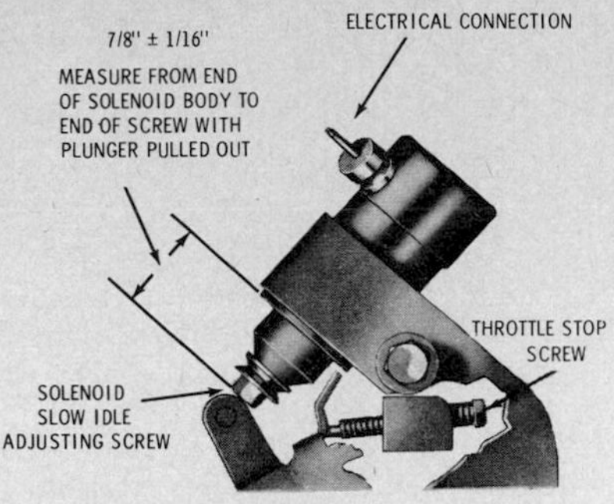

Adjusting throttle closing solenoid—1-bbl
(© Oldsmobile Div, G.M. Corp)

the specifications tables by turning the large hex nut. Disconnect the lead wire from the solenoid and insert a 1/8 in. allen wrench into the end of the solenoid to obtain the lower of the two idle speeds listed. On models with an automatic transmission, this shut-off speed adjustment should be made with the transmission in Park.

9. Idle mixture is set at the factory and should not require adjustment.

1969 2-bbl

Adjust only with the air cleaner removed.

1. Run the engine to the normal operating temperature. Plug the carburetor hot idle compensator.
2. Remove the air cleaner, disconnect the vacuum hose from the intake manifold, and plug the fitting.
3. Disconnect the vacuum hose from the distributor and plug the hose.
4. Apply the parking brake, block the drive wheels, and turn off the air conditioning.
5. Make sure that the choke is fully open and the fast idle screw is on the clearance step of the cam.
6. Adjust the idle mixture screws to obtain the highest possible idle speed.
7. On 1968–69 models without a throttle solenoid, adjust the idle speed screw to obtain an idle speed that is 25 rpm above the figure listed in the tune-up specifications.
8. On 1968–69 models with a throttle solenoid, adjust the solenoid plunger to obtain an idle speed that is 25 rpm above the higher of the two idle speeds listed in the specifications.
9. On all 1968–69 models turn the idle mixture screws inward to lower the idle speed to the correct rpm.
10. On all 1968–69 models equipped with a throttle solenoid, disconnect the solenoid wire and adjust the throttle stop screw to obtain the lower of the two idle speeds listed in the tune-up specifications.

1969 4-bbl

Adjust only with the air cleaner removed.

1. Remove the air cleaner and the air cleaner vacuum hose.
2. Disconnect and plug the vacuum hose from the distributor.
3. Run engine to the normal operating temperature. Tape the carburetor hot idle compensator closed.
4. Apply the parking brake and block the drive wheels.
5. If so equipped, turn off the air conditioner.
6. Make sure the choke is opened fully and the fast idle cam follower is off the cam steps. Place the car in Drive (automatic) or neutral (manual).
7. Adjust the idle mixture screws to obtain highest possible rpm.
8. Adjust the idle speed screw to obtain idle speed 25 rpm higher than figure in tune-up specifications table.
9. Turn the idle mixture screws inward to lower the idle speed to the correct rpm.

1970-74 2-bbl and 4-bbl

Adjust with air cleaner removed.

1. Warm up engine and leave it running.
2. Remove air cleaner, disconnect air cleaner hose at the intake manifold and plug the fitting.
3. Make sure the choke is open and the air conditioner is off. Set the parking brake and block the drive wheels.
4. Disconnect the hoses from the vapor canister and the EGR valve, depending on equipment. Plug the hoses, except on 1970-72 models which are equipped with 4-bbl carburetors. On 1973-75 4-bbl models, plug the holes.
5. Disconnect the distributor vacuum hose at the distributor and plug the hose.
6. Set the dwell and timing.
7. On models without a throttle solenoid or vacuum actuator, turn the idle speed adjusting screw inward or outward to obtain the idle speed listed in the specifications.
8. On models with a throttle solenoid or vacuum actuator, turn the solenoid plunger inward or outward to obtain the higher of the two idle speeds listed in the tune-up specifications. After this adjustment has been made, disconnect the electric lead from the solenoid or the vacuum hose from the vacuum actuator. Plug the vacuum hose after disconnecting it. On models with an automatic transmission, place the transmission in Park. Adjust the throttle stop screw to obtain an idle speed which corresponds with the lower of the two idle speeds listed in the specifications.

NOTE: idle mixture screws have been preset at the factory and capped. Remove the caps only in the case of major overhaul, throttle body removal or when all other possible causes of poor idle condition have been thoroughly checked.

9. To adjust the idle mixture, stop the engine, connect a CO (carbon monoxide) meter to the exhaust system and turn the idle mixture screws until they are lightly seated. Back out the idle mixture screws 6 full turns, then start engine and adjust the screws equally to obtain a good idle at the specified rpm with a maximum CO reading of 0.6 percent on the 1971 2-barrel models and 0.3 percent on 1972-73 models, 0.3 percent on 1971-73 4-barrel and 0.2 percent on 1974-75 models. Temporarily install the air cleaner and check that the CO concentration does not exceed the specified level, readjusting idle mixture screws if necessary.
10. Install new idler limiter caps.
11. Reinstall and reconnect everything which was removed or disconnected in Steps 1 through 5.

1975-76 Idle Speed—2-bbl and 4-bbl

1. Run the engine until it reaches normal operating temperature.
2. Remove the air cleaner and disconnect its vacuum hose from the intake manifold. Plug the manifold fitting.
3. Make sure that the choke is opened and that the A/C is turned off. Apply the parking brake and block the drive wheels.
4. Disconnect and plug the vapor canister and EGR valve vacuum lines.
5. Adjust the timing to specifications.
6. Adjust the curb idle by doing the following:
   a. 231-V6—(vacuum line connected to the distributor) adjust the anti-dieseling solenoid (energized) screw to the specified idle rpm.
   b. 260-V8—(vacuum line connected to the distributor; except California with A/T)

260 V8 antidieseling solenoid

adjust the curb idle screw to obtain specified rpm. On cars with manual transmissions, depress the dashpot and turn it to obtain 0.040 in clearance between its stem and the throttle lever.

c. Omega 350-V8—(vacuum line connected to the distributor) adjust the curb idle screw to the specified rpm. Adjust the dashpot, on California cars, by turning it toward the throttle lever until it just touches it, then 2½ more turns toward the lever.

d. 400-V8—(vacuum line connected to the distributor) turn the curb idle screw to obtain specified rpm.

e. 350-V8 (except Omega) and 455-V8—(distributor vacuum line disconnected and plugged) turn the curb idle screw to obtain specified rpm.

7. On 231-V6 engines, adjust the antidieseling solenoid in Neutral (M/T) or Drive (A/T) with the solenoid wiring disconnected, to the lower of the two idle speed figures in the "Tune-Up Specifications" chart.
8. On 260, 350 (except Omega) and 455 V8s, adjust the idle speed-up solenoid, on cars with air conditioning, as follows:
   a. Turn the A/C on.
   b. Disconnect the compressor wiring at the compressor.
   c. Place the transmission in Drive, with the parking brake applied and the drive wheels blocked.
   d. Adjust the idle speed to 650 rpm.
   e. Reconnect the compressor wiring.
9. Install the air cleaner and all vacuum hoses that were disconnected. Remove the tachometer and the timing light.

1975-76 Idle Mixture—2-bbl and 4-bbl

Idle mixture is preset at the factory and should not normally require adjustment. However, in cases of high idle emissions, carburetor overhaul, or poor idle quality (which can't be traced to other causes), it is possible to remove the limiter caps and adjust the mixture.

2-bbl—231 V6, 350 V8 (Omega) and 400 V8

1. Allow the engine to reach normal operating temperature. Apply the parking brake, block the drive wheels, and place the transmission in Neutral (M/T) or Drive (A/T).
2. Disconnect the vapor canister hose at the air cleaner. Disconnect and plug the EGR valve and distributor vacuum unit.
3. Adjust the idle rpm to specifications.
4. Cut the tabs off the limiter caps.
5. Turn the mixture screws outward equally until maximum rpm is obtained. If a speed of at least 80 rpm above curb idle can't be obtained, reset the idle speed screw until it can. If the mixture screws aren't balanced or if the carburetor was overhauled, seat the mixture screws *lightly* and back each out 5 full turns.
6. Turn the mixture screws back in, equally, until the specified idle speed is obtained.
7. Disconnect the tachometer and reconnect all vacuum lines.

2-bbl—260 V8

1. Allow the engine to reach normal operating temperature. Remove the air cleaner, disconnect the air cleaner vacuum hose from the manifold, and plug the fitting.
5. Disconnect the EGR valve vacuum hose from the carburetor. Leave the distributor vacuum hose connected.

NOTE: On cars with manual transmissions the distributor vacuum hose comes from the same carburetor port. Disconnect the EGR hose while leaving the distributor vacuum hoses connected. On California cars the distributor has no vacuum hose.

6. Connect a timing light and set the timing to specifications.
7. Remove the limiter caps. Back each mixture screw out as follows:
   Manual transmission—6 turns
   Automatic transmissions—5 turns
8. Set the engine idle to the following initial specifications:
   Manual transmission—1075 rpm
   Automatic (in Drive)—610 rpm
   California Automatic (in Drive)—700 rpm
9. Turn each mixture screw ½-turn at-a-time until the specified curb idle speed is reached.
10. Adjust the A/C idle speed-up solenoid, if so equipped, and the throttle closing dashpot, as outlined under "1975-76 Idle Speed 2-bbl and 4-bbl".
11. Connect all vacuum hoses which were removed and install the air cleaner. Disconnect the timing light and tach.

4-bbl—350 V8 and 455 V8

1. Allow the engine to reach normal operating temperature. Remove the air cleaner; disconnect and plug its vacuum hoses.
2. Make sure that the choke is opened and the A/C turned off. Apply the parking brake and block the drive wheels.
3. Disconnect the vacuum hoses from the EGR valve and vapor canister. Don't disconnect the distributor hose.
4. Break the tabs off the idle mixture screws.
5. Connect a tachometer. Connect a vacuum gauge to the intake manifold.
6. Turn the idle mixture screws out equally until the idle speed will go no higher. Note the vacuum gauge reading.

NOTE: If the carburetor has been overhauled or if the mixture screws aren't balanced, lightly seat both screws and then turn each out 3 full turns (4 full turns—California).

7. Set the idle speed to 580 rpm (625 rpm—California).
8. Adjust the idle speed to specifications by turning the mixture screws in equally. The vacuum gauge reading should not drop more than 2 in. Hg from the figure obtained in step 6. If it does, repeat the procedure.
9. On California cars, check the CO level with an accurate CO meter. The level should be less than 0.5%. If not, repeat the procedure.
10. Install the air cleaner and connect all vacuum hoses.

COOLING SYSTEM

Detailed information on cooling system capacity is in the Capacities table.

Information on the water temperature light or gauge is in the Unit Repair Section.

Radiator R & R

All—Except 1975-76 Omega

1. Drain the cooling system.
2. Remove the upper radiator baffle and slide the shroud back over the fan, if so equipped.
3. Unfasten the upper and lower hoses from the radiator.
4. Disconnect the overflow hose and the optional coolant recovery system hose, if so equipped.
5. On models equipped with an automatic transmission, disconnect and cap the lines which run to the oil cooler.
6. Unfasten the radiator's securing bolts and withdraw the radiator upward to disengage it from its supports. Remove the radiator from the car.

NOTE: It may be necessary to rotate the fan blades in order to keep them out of the way.

Installation is performed in the reverse order of removal. Refill the cooling system.

1975-76 Omega

NOTE: On models with air conditioning, it will be necessary to dis-

charge the A/C system in order to remove the radiator. Unless you have the special tools and knowledge necessary for this task, it is recommended that it be left to qualified service personnel only.

1. Disconnect the battery and drain the radiator.
2. Remove the upper radiator baffle and slide the shroud back over the fan.
3. On models with an automatic transmission, disconnect and cap the oil cooler lines.
4. Remove the upper and lower radiator hoses. Disconnect the coolant recovery system hose.
5. On models with A/C, discharge the system. To gain working clearance, disconnect the upper A/C condenser line. See the "NOTE" at the beginning of this procedure.
6. Unfasten its mounting bolts and lift the radiator out of the car.

Installation is the reverse of removal. Check the coolant and transmission fluid levels.

Water Pump R & R

1. Drain the cooling system.
2. Unfasten the heater, bypass, and lower radiator hoses from the pump.
3. Loosen the drive belts. Remove the fan and pulley, complete with the fan clutch, if so equipped.

NOTE: Keep the fan in an upright position during removal to prevent the silicone fluid from leaking out of the fan clutch.

4. Unfasten the bolts which secure the water pump and remove it.

NOTE: On six-cylinder engines, pull the pump straight out, to prevent impeller damage.

Installation is performed in the following order:

1. Apply a thin coating of sealer to the pump housing gasket mounting surface.
2. Place a *new* gasket on the housing.
3. Install the pump assembly. Lightly oil the self-tapping bolts and tighten them to 13 ft lbs.
4. Torque the 5/16 in. bolts to the following specifications:
   1969—25 ft lbs
   1970-76—10 ft lbs
5. Install the fan assembly and tighten the bolts which secure it to the pump to 20 ft lbs.

NOTE: On 1970-73 models which have a clutch-operated fan, torque the bolts to 15 ft lbs, on 1974-76 models, tighten the bolts to 20 ft lbs.

6. Install the drive belts and adjust their tension.
7. Refill the cooling system.

Thermostat R & R

1. Remove the hoses from the thermostat housing.
2. Remove the bolts, water outlet, and gasket from the thermostat housing.
3. Install the new thermostat and gasket in the engine. The thermostat may be etched with the word "front"; if so, "front" must face the radiator.
4. Connect the hoses and refill the cooling system.

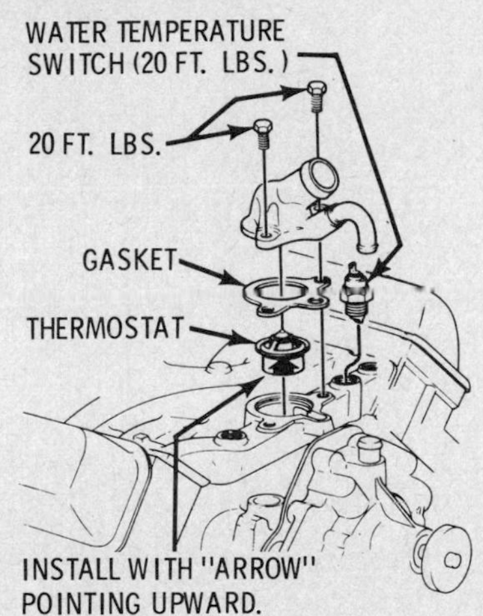

Typical thermostat installation
(© Oldsmobile Div., GM Corp.)

EMISSION CONTROLS

NOTE: See "Emission Control Systems" in the Unit Repair Section, for testing and adjustment of the various system components.

1969

Crankcase Ventilation System

The Positive Crankcase Ventilation (PCV) system used on all Oldsmobiles is designed to reburn crankcase blowby vapors by utilizing manifold vacuum to draw them through a hose connected between the valve cover and the base of the carburetor. This feeds the vapors back into the combustion chambers.

The hose contains a spring-loaded PCV valve, which ensures proper operation of the engine at the two extremes of operation—full throttle, and idle. When the engine is idling, the very high manifold vacuum draws the PCV valve plunger. against spring tension, toward the front of the valve, enabling it to restrict the flow of gases through the system. Thus, the blowby vapors and air remain a very small part of the mixture flow, permitting efficient combustion, in spite of the tremendous vacuum available to draw material from the crankcase. When the throttle is opened all the way, negligible vacuum is available, and so the tension of the spring forces the rear of the valve plunger to seal off against the back of the valve, thus keeping fuel vapors from entering the crankcase.

The crankcase vent cap is sealed off, and connected through a hose to the air cleaner. Thus the vapors which would normally escape to the atmosphere at full throttle are drawn into the carburetor with the inrushing air.

Thermostatic Vacuum Switch

A thermostatic vacuum switch was available on 1969 models equipped with air conditioning or on 400 and some 455 cu in. engines. This switch advances ignition timing when coolant temperatures rise above 220° F thereby allowing the engine to run cooler.

Controlled Combustion System (CCS)

The Controlled Combustion System, standard equipment for all engines, consists of a special air cleaner assembly including a temperature sensor, vacuum motor (actually a spring-operated diaphragm), control damper assembly, and vacuum hoses. This system improves engine warm-up and fuel economy by directing heated air from the exhaust manifold into the air cleaner when engine compartment temperatures are 85° F or below. When the temperature inside the air cleaner reaches 100° F, a temperature sensor shuts off vacuum to the vacuum motor and the control damper opens, allowing underhood air to mix with the heated air to keep air temperature at a constant 100° F. When the car is undergoing full throttle operation, only outside air enters the air cleaner. On 4-4-2 models with the W-30 engine, there is no temperature sensor in the left air cleaner snorkle. It is controlled by manifold vacuum instead. This left snorkle stays closed until full throttle when vacuum drops to a reading of 6-8 in. Hg.

Throttle Closing Solenoid

In 1969, all one-barrel carburetors were equipped with a throttle closing solenoid to prevent engine run-on once the ignition is turned off. Some two-barrels were so equipped but no four-barrels. The solenoid plunger extends when the ignition switch is turned on to raise engine idle speed and retracts when the switch is turned off to prevent the engine from running on.

1970

In 1970, the list of emission control devices grew with the addition of TCS and the evaporative control system.

Crankcase Ventilation System

For 1970, the crankcase ventilation system remains unchanged from preceding years.

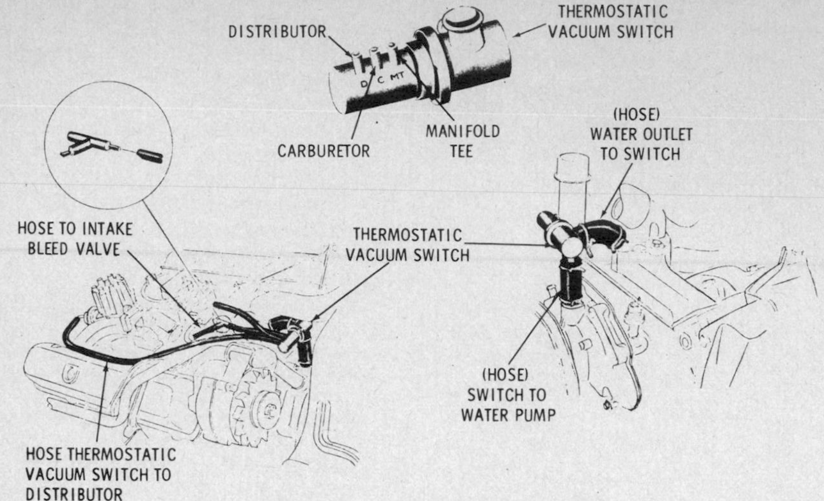

Thermostatic vacuum switch
(© Oldsmobile Div, G.M. Corp)

Thermostatic Vacuum Switch

All F-85/Cutlass models (including 4-4-2) equipped with the 455 cu in. engine (except some W-30 cars) used a thermostatic vacuum switch to advance engine timing for cooling engine operation during idle.

Controlled Combustion System (CCS)

This system remains unchanged from 1969 models.

Throttle Closing Solenoid

Remains unchanged from 1969. Continued as standard equipment on all one-barrel carburetors but no longer used on two-barrels.

Transmission-Controlled Spark (TCS)

TCS is new for 1970, consisting of a temperature switch (6 cyl only), a solenoid valve, and a transmission switch. This system allows vacuum-controlled spark advance to the distributor only when the transmission is in high gear or when a six-cylinder's engine temperature is below 85°F or above 220° F. A vacuum line runs from the carburetor to the TCS solenoid (mounted on the intake manifold) and on to the vacuum advance unit on the distributor. A pressure-sensitive switch is located on the side of the transmission case (automatic transmission) and is electrically connected to the TCS solenoid at the intake manifold.

When the transmission is in any other gear than high gear, the transmission switch is closed and the circuit to the TCS solenoid is complete. This causes the solenoid to close and prevents carburetor vacuum from reaching the distributor. When the transmission enters high gear, hydraulic pressure opens the transmission switch, and the circuit to the solenoid opens. This permits carburetor vacuum to pass to the distributor and advance the spark. On six-cylinder engines, the temperature sending switch is electrically connected to the solenoid through a relay. At engine temperatures below 85° F or above 220° F, this switch opens up and stops current from reaching the solenoid, thereby permitting vacuum to pass through to the distributor and advancing the spark. The system used on models that are equipped with a manual transmission is identical, except that the transmission switch is manually actuated by the transmission linkage.

Evaporative Control System

California law requires that all 1970 model cars sold in that state be equipped with an evaporative control system as a means of preventing fuel vapor loss to the atmosphere. The system consists of a special fuel tank, a liquid/vapor separator, a carbon canister, and a special gas cap. A gas tank baffle limits tank capacity by 1 gal to provide room for expansion of fuel. The liquid/vapor separator is mounted to the underbody near the tank. Its purpose is to separate the liquid fuel from the vapors.

A vapor line connects to the separator output and runs to the front of the car where it attaches to a carbon-filled canister mounted on the front fender inner panel. Fuel vapors from the separator are stored here and then withdrawn by manifold vacuum through a hose to the intake manifold where they are reburned.

Caution The pressure/vacuum cap used with this system cannot be replaced by a cap of any other design.

1971

The distributor vacuum control switch (replaces thermostatic vacuum switch) and limiter caps for the idle mixture screws are new for 1971. The other equipment is carried on from 1970.

Distributor Vacuum Control Switch

This switch combines the functions of a TCS solenoid with those of a thermostatic vacuum switch. All cars having air conditioning, heavy-duty cooling systems, and all F-85 models (Cutlass, 4-4-2) equipped with the 455 cu in. engine use this switch assembly, while all other models use a TCS solenoid. This vacuum control switch allows vacuum to reach the distributor when the transmission is in third or fourth gear or when coolant temperatures are high at idle. Operating the car in first or second gear energizes the solenoid which raises the solenoid plunger to block off port C thereby shutting off the vacuum supply from the carburetor. By blocking off port C, port V (vent) is opened to the atmosphere to drain any vacuum that might be present in the vacuum advance unit. In third or fourth gear, the transmission switch opens and current to the solenoid stops and the solenoid plunger drops to seal off the vent port (V). This allows vacuum from the carburetor to enter the switch at port C and out port D (distributor) to the distributor vacuum advance. When coolant temperatures reaches 210° F, expansion within the intake manifold moves the plunger upward to seal off the vent (V) port and opening up the manifold (MT) port to manifold vacuum. At 218–224° F, full manifold vacuum is directed to port D (distributor) and on to the vacuum advance unit on the distributor. This advances the spark and cools coolant temperatures, regardless of transmission position.

Limiter Caps

Beginning in 1971, limiter caps (plastic caps) were placed over the idle mixture screws on the carburetor. Mixture is pre-set at the factory and no further adjustment is required.

Evaporative Control System

In 1971, this system was standard for all models, not just California cars. The system remains basically the same as that used in 1970.

1972

1972 cars contain the same emission control equipment as 1971 cars with the following exceptions:

Transmission-Controlled Spark Solenoid

For 1972, this switch is used only on Cutlass models equipped with 350 cu in. two-barrel engines and no air conditioning. On all other models equipped with TCS, the vacuum cut-off solenoid is contained in the distributor vacuum control switch.

Idle Solenoid

The two-barrel and four-barrel carburetors are now equipped with an idle solenoid or a vacuum actuator. Both controls help to create a higher idle speed as a means of reducing emissions.

1973

Exhaust Gas Recirculation

All 1973 models are equipped with Exhaust Gas Recirculation (EGR). This system routes a portion of the engine exhaust gases back into the engine to dilute the incoming air/fuel mixture. By reducing the amount of combustible material in the combustion chamber, peak combustion temperature and the corresponding formation of oxides of Nitrogen (NO_x) are lowered.

An internal intake manifold passage conducts gases from the intake manifold crossover passage to the air/fuel passages in the manifold on V8 engines. In 6-cylinder engines, a drilled hole passes the exhaust gases to the intake manifold. The EGR control valve is attached to the intake manifold and normally blocks the exhaust gases from entering the engine. The EGR valve contains a spring-loaded diaphragm which is controlled by carburetor vacuum. On V8s, the EGR valve vacuum hose contains a low-temperature cut-off valve which blocks carburetor vacuum from the control valve until the ambient temperature around the intake manifold has reached 50-60°F. The black and white plastic cut-off valve must always be installed with the side marked "EGR" facing the EGR valve.

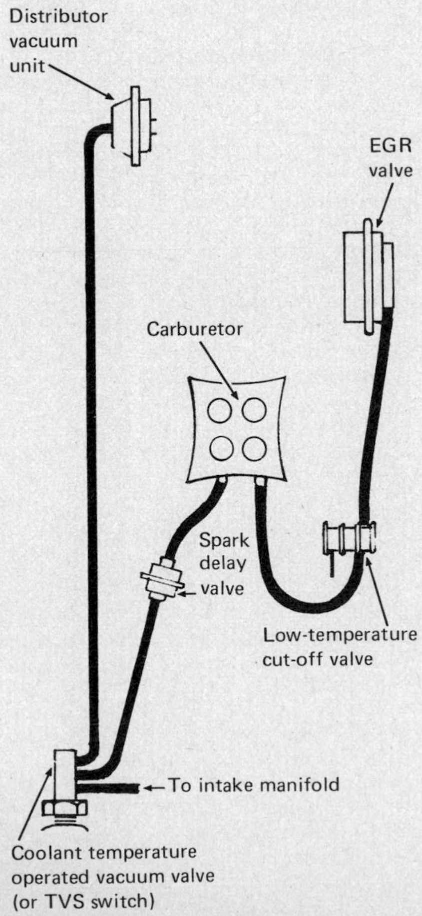

Models equipped with a 350 2-bbl engine use the same port on the carburetor as a source for both EGR and distributor vacuum.

V8s made on or after 15 March 1973 have a black plastic cover over the EGR low temperature cut-off valve, so that the valve is dependent upon engine, rather than air, temperature. Engines with 4-bbl carburetors and automatic transmissions have a large cover which is held in place by a strap around the oil filler tube. All other engines have a smaller cover which is held in place by a retainer fastened under a bolt on the water outlet.

NOTE: If the retainer is removed, coat the threads of the bolt with sealer and torque it to 20 ft lbs upon installation.

1973 350 4 bbl and 455 V8 emission controls

Thermal Vacuum Switch

All V8 engines are equipped with a Thermal Vacuum Switch (TVS). Vacuum hoses from the carburetor, intake manifold, and distributor connect to this switch which is controlled by engine coolant temperature. During normal engine operation, vacuum from the carburetor passes through the TVS to the distributor. If the engine should overheat while idling, the TVS connects intake manifold vacuum to the distributor which helps to lower the coolant temperature.

On models equipped with a 350 2-bbl engine, the intake manifold vacuum hose to the TVS contains a vacuum reducing valve. The purpose of this valve is to limit the amount of vacuum supplied to the distributor by the intake manifold to 9 in. Hg. This valve is required on this engine because of the fact that the distributor and EGR valve normally share the same vacuum port on the carburetor. Since the vacuum from this source is divided between two sources, the distributor is calibrated to operate on a maximum of about 7 in. Hg.

Thermal Check and Delay Valve

All 350 and 455 cu in. 4-bbl carburetor engines, except for the 350 engine equipped with manual transmission, have a thermal check and delay valve. This valve is in the vacuum line which runs between the carburetor spark port and the TVS.

When the underhood (or engine block) temperature is below 50°F full carburetor-ported vacuum is supplied to the distributor vacuum unit. Above 50°F, the valve blocks full vacuum for up to 40 seconds.

If ported vacuum drops, the valve opens, causing the distributor vacuum advance to be retarded. As vacuum increases, the valve closes, blocking full vacuum again.

Cars made from 15 March 1973 have a cover over the valve so that it is more dependent upon engine block temperature. For a description of the cover, see the section which describes the EGR system, above.

Air Injection Reactor

All six-cylinder engines are equipped with Air Injection Reactor (AIR). A belt-driven air pump supplies air to an injection manifold which has a nozzle positioned behind each exhaust valve. Injection of air at this point causes combustion of any unburned hydrocarbons in the exhaust manifold rather than allowing them to escape into the atmosphere. An antibackfire (diverter) valve controls the flow of air from the pump to prevent backfires resulting from an overly rich mixture under closed throttle conditions. A check valve functions to prevent hot exhaust gas backflow into the pump and hoses in case of pump failure or when the antibackfire valve is working.

Combined Emission Controls

All Omegas equipped with a six-cylinder engine and a manual transmission are equipped with a CEC valve. This system is basically a Transmission Controlled Spark (TCS) system. The CEC solenoid is mounted on the side of the carburetor and the carburetor vacuum line to the distributor passes through it. This switch, which is normally closed, is energized to allow vacuum advance only under the following conditions: when engine coolant temperature is below 93° F, for a period of 20 seconds after the engine is started, or when the transmission is in third gear. When any of the above conditions exist, a complete circuit is made from the ignition switch through either the temperature switch, time-delay relay, or transmission switch to the CEC solenoid. This energizes the solenoid and causes its plunger to extend, uncovering the carburetor vacuum port to the distributor and raising the idle speed of the engine.

Controlled Combustion System

All 1973 models are equipped with the Controlled Combustion System (CCS). This system is described above under "1968–69."

1974

Exhaust Gas Recirculation

The 1974 exhaust gas recirculation (EGR) system remains basically the same as that used on cars made after 15 March 1973 (see above). However, a backpressure transducer valve

1974-75 EGR valve with backpressure transducer valve (BPV) is used on California V8s

(BPV) has been added to the EGR system used on V8 engines which are sold in California.

The bottom of the BPV diaphragm is open to exhaust pressure. At idle, the lack of exhaust backpressure allows the spring above the diaphragm to open an air bleed, which prevents vacuum from reaching the EGR valve. When there is backpressure in the exhaust system, i.e., above idle, the diaphragm is forced up against the spring, closing the air bleed, which allows the EGR valve to get normal vacuum.

By preventing EGR from occurring at idle, the idle quality is improved on California cars, which have a greater amount of exhaust gases recirculating than cars made for the rest of the nation.

On 1974 inline six-cylinder engines, a thermostatically controlled vacuum switch (valve) controls the EGR valve's vacuum supply. When coolant temperature is below 100°F, the switch is closed, blocking vacuum to the EGR valve; above 100°F, the switch opens, allowing the EGR valve to function. The vacuum switch is threaded into the water outlet.

TCS System—Inline 6 Engine

The transmission controlled spark system, used on Omega models with six-cylinder engines and manual transmissions, is similar to the CEC system used in 1973.

The only difference is that the CEC solenoid has been replaced by a vacuum advance solenoid, which is attached to the coil bracket.

The transmission switch, temperature switch, and time-delay relay remain as before.

Distributor Vacuum Valve

A distributor vacuum valve (DVV) is used on all 350 and 455 cu in. engines sold in California and on some of the 455 cu in. engines which are sold nationally.

The DVV switches the distributor vacuum advance unit's vacuum source from the carburetor spark port to the EGR port. Below 7 in. Hg, the vacuum unit operates from the spark port. Above 7 in. Hg, the vacuum supply is switched by the DVV from the spark port to the EGR port.

The distributor vacuum valve (DVV) is used on some V8s in 1974-75

Other Emission Control Systems

The rest of the emission control systems used on 1974 Oldsmobile V8 engines remain the same as those described above for 1973.

1975

Catalytic Converter

All 1975 Oldsmobiles use catalytic converters to reduce hydrocarbon/carbon monoxide (HC/CO) emissions. See the Emission Control Unit Repair section for details.

Early Fuel Evaporation (EFE)

The early fuel evaporation (EFE) system is basically a vacuum-operated heat riser valve.

When the engine is cold, the EFE valve is closed by a vacuum motor, forcing the exhaust gases up around a plate underneath the carburetor, which heats the incoming mixture to aid in quicker warm-ups.

When the engine is warm, the vacuum for the EFE vacuum motor is blocked off, and spring tension pulls the heat valve to the opened position.

Vacuum to the EFE vacuum motor is controlled by either a coolant temperature operated vacuum valve, or by an oil temperature sensor and solenoid, depending upon engine application.

EFE is not used on some 350 and 455 cu in. V8 engines.

Early fuel evaporation (EFE) valve and vacuum motor

Dual Vacuum Break Choke

A dual vacuum break choke is used on inline six and 4-bbl V8 engines.

The secondary vacuum break pulls the choke to almost wide-open position, once the engine has reached a specified temperature. Vacuum to the secondary break is controlled by a coolant temperature operated vacuum valve (V8) or by a solenoid and electrical thermoswitch on inline sixes.

When the coolant temperature is below the specified level, vacuum is blocked to the secondary choke break. As soon as the specified temperature is reached, vacuum is sent to the break, which, in turn, opens the choke plate.

Thermostatic Air Cleaner Thermal Valve

The thermostatic air cleaner (TAC) thermal valve is located on the air cleaner housing. When the engine is cold, the valve restricts the vacuum supplied to the air cleaner door vacuum motor which slows the operation of the door down. Under wide-open throttle conditions, the door does not "jump" to the full cold air position, thus eliminating the flat spot during cold engine acceleration.

At normal operating temperatures, the thermal valve opens and the air cleaner vacuum motor is allowed to operate in the usual manner.

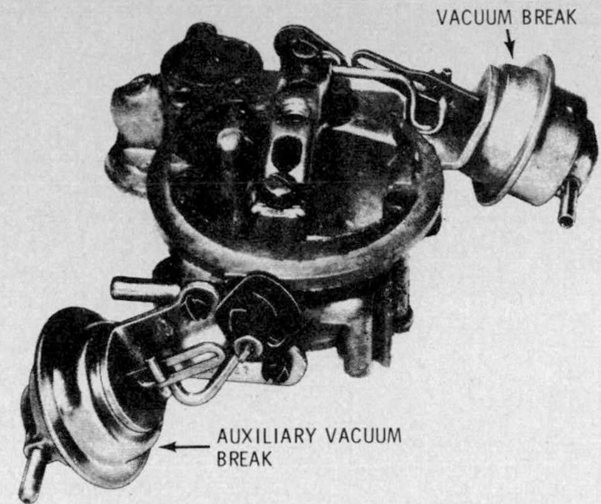

Some 1975-76 carburetors have two choke vacuum breaks (© Oldsmobile Div., GM Corp.)

Temperature Compensated Spark Advance

All V6 engines and most V8s have a temperature compensated spark advance to improve cold engine operation, and fuel economy.

When the engine is below a specified temperature, a coolant temperature operated vacuum valve supplies full manifold vacuum to the distributor vacuum advance unit.

When the coolant goes above the specified temperature, the vacuum valve switches the direct manifold vacuum supply off. This leaves only a manifold vacuum line which has a spark delay valve in it running to the distributor; reducing the amount of vacuum advance at normal operating temperature.

Other Emission Control Systems

Most of the other emission control systems remain as they were in 1974, except for the folowing changes:

1. Air injection (AIR) is used on some engines.
2. Transmission controlled spark (TCS) is not used on any engine at all this year.
3. The EGR temperature valve and its cover have been moved to above the water pump on some V8s.
4. The bowl vent on 4-bbl carburetors is opened to the charcoal canister when the engine is shut off. This helps to improve hot starting characteristics.

EGR temperature sensor is located under black metal cover which is just above water pump

AIR System Component R & R

Air Injection Pump

1. Unfasten the air supply hose(s) from the pump.
2. Compress the pump drive belt to keep the pump pulley from rotating.
3. Unfasten the pulley securing bolts and remove the drive belt, together with the pulley.
4. Remove the bolts which secure the pump to its mounting bracket.
5. Withdraw the pump assembly from the bracket.

Caution Never clamp the pump in a vise or pry on the pump housing. The housing is made of aluminum and distorts easily.

Installation of the pump is performed in the following order:

1. Install the pump on its mounting bracket, but do not tighten the mounting bolts.
2. Install the pulley and finger-tighten its mounting bolts.
3. Install and adjust the drive belt. Do not pry on the pump housing during adjustment.
4. Keep the pump pulley from turning by compressing the drive belt and tighten the pulley bolts to 9 ft lbs.
5. Connect the hose(s) to the pump.
6. Tighten the pump mounting bolts to 25 ft lbs and recheck belt tension.

Diverter (By-Pass) Valve

1. Disconnect the vacuum signal line from the diverter valve.
2. Unfasten the valve exhaust hose(s).
3. Loosen the securing screws and remove the valve from the air pump or elbow.

Installation is performed in the reverse order of removal. Use a new gasket and tighten the valve attaching screws to 7 ft lbs.

Centrifugal Filter Fan R & R

NOTE: Never attempt to clean the filter fan. It is impossible to remove the fan without destroying it.

1. Remove the air pump from the car, as detailed above.
2. Gently pry the outer disc off and pull off the remaining portion. Be careful that no fragments from the fan enter the pump air intake.
3. Install a new filter fan pulling it into place with the pump pulley and attaching bolts.
4. Alternately torque the bolts so that the fan is drawn down *evenly*. Be sure that the outer edge of the fan fits into the pump housing.

Caution Never hammer or press the fan into place; damage to it and the pump will result.

5. Install the pump on the car.

NOTE: For the first 20-30 miles of operation, the fan may squeal until its lip has worn in. This is normal and does not indicate a damaged pump.

EGR Valve R & R

1. Unfasten the vacuum signal hose from the top of the EGR valve.
2. On V8, V6, and 1975-76 inline six models, remove the two EGR valve securing bolts.
3. On 1973-74 inline 6 models, remove the clamping bolt and clamp from the manifold. If the car has power brakes, it will be necessary to remove the vacuum fitting and hose clamp from the manifold before removing the EGR valve clamp.
4. Remove the EGR valve from the manifold.
5. Discard the old gasket.

Installation of the EGR valve is performed in the reverse order of removal. Use a new gasket and torque the valve securing bolt(s) to 25 ft lbs.

EGR Valve Cleaning

Caution Do not clamp the EGR valve in a vise or wash it in solvents; permanent damage to the valve will result.

Recessed Valve

1. Remove the EGR valve.
2. Clean the base of the EGR valve with a wire brush, being sure to remove all of the exhaust deposits from the base.
3. Insert the valve portion into a regular spark plug cleaning machine.
4. Clean the valve with a 30 second blast of abrasive.
5. Unseat the valve by depressing the diaphragm spring and repeat step 4.
6. Repeat steps 4 and 5 until all of the deposits have been removed from the valve.
7. Use compressed air to remove any abrasive material which may remain on the EGR valve.

8. Install the valve on the manifold.

Protruding Valve

1. Remove the EGR valve.
2. Tap lightly on the sides and end of the EGR valve with a plastic hammer while holding the valve in your hand. Remove all exhaust deposits from the valve seat in this manner.
3. Use a wire wheel to buff the exhaust deposits from around the valve mounting surfaces.
4. Remove any exhaust deposits from the valve outlet area with a screwdriver.
5. Check the EGR valve to be sure that all of the deposits have been removed and install it on the manifold.

Thermostatically Controlled Air Cleaner

Vacuum Motor R & R

1. Remove the air cleaner assembly from the carburetor.
2. Detach the line from the vacuum motor.
3. Drill out the two retaining strap spot welds with a 1/16 in. drill.
4. Remove the retaining strap. Enlarge the holes, if necessary to do so.

NOTE: Use care not to damage the air cleaner snorkel.

5. Cock the motor to one side to unhook its linkage from the air door and lift the motor out.

Installation of a new motor is performed in the following order:

1. Drill a 7/64 in. hole at a point midway between the two holes previously drilled for the spot welds.
2. Connect the vacuum motor linkage to the air door assembly.
3. Secure the vacuum motor with the sheet metal screw and strap supplied with the motor service package.

NOTE: Once the sheet metal screw has been installed in the 7/64 in. hole, be sure that it does not interfere with the air door assembly. Use a shorter screw or shorten the existing one, as required.

4. Connect the vacuum line to the motor and install the air cleaner assembly on the carburetor.

NOTE: Be sure that the vacuum hose is not pinched during installation.

Thermal Sensor R & R

1. Remove the air cleaner assembly from the carburetor.
2. Detach the vacuum lines from the sensor.
3. Pry the tabs up on the sensor retaining clip and remove the sensor and gasket.

NOTE: Be careful to note the position of the sensor.

Sensor installation is performed in the reverse order of removal. Be sure to install the sensor in its original position.

ENGINE

Engine Removal

All Models

1. Disconnect the negative battery cable. Remove the air cleaner assembly and heat pipe.
2. Scribe the outline of the hood hinges on the hood and remove the hood.
3. Drain the cooling system and disconnect the radiator and heater hoses from the engine.
4. Disconnect the engine ground strap from the cylinder head. Remove the fan shroud.
5. Disconnect and tag all vacuum lines and electrical leads from the engine.
6. Disconnect the throttle linkage. Disconnect the fuel line from the fuel pump. Remove clutch equalizer on M/T Omegas, and Starfires.
7. If the car is equipped with an automatic transmission, disconnect the cooler lines from the radiator. If equipped with power steering or air conditioning, remove the pump and bracket or compressor and bracket from the engine *without disconnecting the lines.*

Caution Disconnecting the air conditioner lines could result in personal injury or damage to the A/C system.

8. Remove the radiator. Remove the fan, if necessary to gain working clearance. Raise the car.
9. Disconnect the exhaust pipes from the exhaust manifolds. Remove the motor mount thru-bolts. Remove the starter.
10. On models equipped with an automatic transmission, remove the torque converter cover. Turn the crankshaft pulley to gain access to the three torque converter-to-flywheel attaching bolts and remove the bolts.
11. Remove the transmission or clutch housing-to-engine bolts, place a jack under the transmission, and raise the transmission several inches.
12. Attach a chain hoist to the engine and remove the engine from the car.
13. Reverse the above procedure to install the engine.

Engine Manifolds

Intake Manifold Removal

V6 and 1975-76 Omega 350 V8

1. Disconnect the battery and drain the cooling system.
2. Remove the air cleaner assembly.
3. Disconnect the upper radiator hose from the intake manifold.
4. Disconnect the accelerator and downshift (A/T) linkages from the carburetor. Remove the linkage bracket from the manifold.
5. Disconnect the following:
   a. Power brake line from manifold
   b. Fuel line from carburetor
   c. Choke pipe from housing
   d. Transmission modulator line
   e. Antidieseling solenoid wire (if used)
   f. Distributor leads
   g. Vacuum lines from distributor, TVS, and EFE
   h. Coolant by-pass hose from manifold
6. On V6 engines remove the distributor cap and rotor to gain access to the left-hand front manifold bolt. Remove the spark plug leads, as well.
7. Remove the throttle linkage springs.
8. Unfasten the bolts and remove the intake manifold.

Intake manifold bolt tightening sequence—231 V6
(© Oldsmobile Div., GM Corp.)

Installation is the reverse of removal. Use a new gasket and seals. Coat the ends of the seals with a non-hardening silicone sealer. The pointed end of the seal should be a snug fit aginst the block and head. When installing the manifold, start with the Nos. 1 and 2 bolts, slowly tightening them until *snug*. Continue with the rest of the bolts in the sequence illustrated, tightening them in several stages to the correct torque specification.

Intake manifold bolt tightening sequence —1975-76 Omega 350 V8
(© G.M. Corp)

1975 400 V8

1. Drain the coolant from the radiator and from both sides of the block. It is possible to drain the block through the radiator drain, by hoisting the rear of the car 15-18 in. off the ground.
2. Remove the air cleaner assembly, complete with all hoses.
3. Without removing the radiator hose, remove the outlet elbow bolts, and set the elbow out of the way.
4. Disconnect the vacuum lines and electrical leads from the various emission control devices.
5. Remove the spark plug lead harness from the intake manifold.
6. Disconnect the power brake vacuum line at the carburetor. Disconnect the distributor vacuum solenoid hose from the carburetor.
7. Unfasten the fuel line from the carburetor.
8. Remove the PCV hose from the manifold.
9. Separate the accelerator cable from the carburetor. Remove the throttle control bracket screws.
10. Remove the EGR valve assembly.
11. Unfasten its bolts and remove the intake manifold. Be careful not to lose the O-ring which goes between the manifold and the timing chain cover.

Installation is the reverse of removal. Use new intake manifold gaskets, securing them with the plastic retainers. Use a new O-ring between the manifold and timing chain cover, if the old one was lost or damaged. Tighten the manifold bolts to specifications in several stages.

All Other V8 Models

1. Remove the carburetor air cleaner, drain the radiator.
2. Disconnect the upper radiator hose, by-pass hose, and heater hose from the manifold.
3. Disconnect the throttle linkage, vacuum and gas lines from the carburetor.
4. Remove the bolts that hold the intake manifold to the two cylinder heads.
5. The coil can be left on the intake manifold if the wires are disconnected (1969-74).
6. Remove the generator and air conditioning compressor brackets if necessary.

Caution Do not disconnect the A/C lines. Severe personal injury or damage to the A/C system could result.

7. Disconnect the temperature gauge wire.

NOTE: On the 400 cu. in. engine it may be necessary to remove the distributor to provide clearance for manifold removal. On the 455 cu. in. engine it will be necessary to remove the oil filler tube.

Install in the reverse order of removal, tightening all bolts first to 15 ft. lbs., then to the figure specified in the torque chart, in the sequence illustrated. Coat all gasket surfaces with sealer.

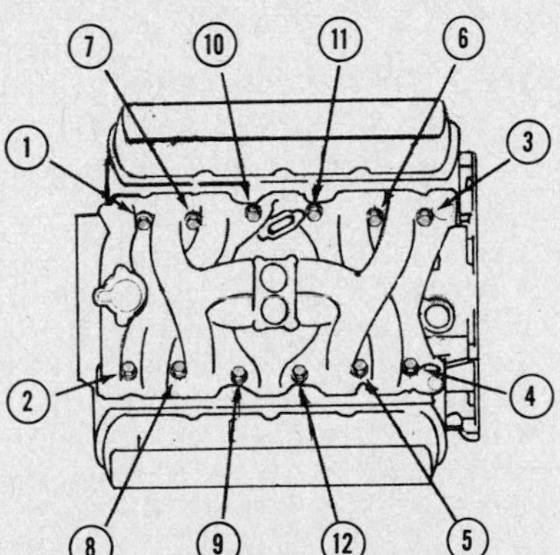

Intake manifold bolt tightening sequence—260, 350 (except 1975-76 Omega), and 455
(© Oldsmobile Div, G.M. Corp)

Exhaust Manifold Removal
V6 and 1975-76 Omega 350 V8

1. Raise the car and support it securely with jackstands.
2. Disconnect the crossover pipe if necessary.
3. When removing the left manifold from the Omega, remove the left front engine mount thru-bolt and loosen the right thru-bolt. Raise the engine.
4. When removing the exhaust manifolds from the Starfire, disconnect the choke tube on the right side and the EFE pipe on the left side.
5. Remove the exhaust pipe-to-manifold flange bolts and the manifold-to-head bolts.
6. Remove the manifold(s).

Installation is the reverse of removal. Torque the manifold bolts to specification.

1975-76 Inline 6

1. Remove the air cleaner assembly.
2. Remove the power steering pump and/or the air injection pump brackets. Leave the power steering pump hoses connected and set the pump out of the way.
3. Remove the EFE valve bracket.
4. Disconnect the throttle linkage and springs.
5. Disconnect the exhaust pipe from the manifold flange.
6. Unfasten the manifold bolts and remove the exhaust manifold. Discard the gasket.

Installation is as follows:

1. Clean the manifold and cylinder head gasket surfaces. Put a new gasket on the manifold.
2. Clean and oil all the exhaust manifold-to-head bolts. Hold the manifold in place while loosely installing the bolts.
3. Torque all exhaust manifold-to-head bolts in the sequence shown, in several stages to the correct torque specifications.
4. The rest of installation is the reverse of removal.

260, 350 (Except '75 Omega) and 455 V8

1. Disconnect the negative battery cable and remove the air cleaner.
2. Remove the bolts from the exhaust manifold flanges on both sides and take off the crossover pipe.
3. On the right side, remove generator and bracket.
4. Remove the hot air pipe and shroud if so equipped.
5. Disconnect the exhaust pipe from the manifold.
6. Remove the bolts that hold the exhaust manifold to the cylinder head and lift off the exhaust manifolds.

On some models with the 455 cu. in. engine, the starter will have to be removed to work on the left-hand exhaust manifold. On air-conditioned models with the 455 cu in. and 350 cu in (1971-76) engines, the front wheel will have to be removed in order to gain access to the right-hand manifold through the opening in the fender inner panel. When installing, tighten the manifold-to-head attaching bolts to 25 ft. lbs. torque 1969-73 models, tightening those in the center first. On 1974-76 engines, tighten the bolts to the following specifications:

5/16 in.—25 ft lbs
⅜ in.—35 ft lbs
7/16 in.—50 ft lbs

1975 400 V8

Tab locks are used on front and rear pairs of bolts on each exhaust manifold. When removing bolts, straighten tabs from beneath car using long handled screw driver. When installing tab locks, bend tabs against sides of bolt not over top of bolt.

Left-Side Manifold

1. If the car is equipped with power steering, disconnect the power steering pump but leave it attached to its hoses and pull it up out of the way.
2. Remove the generator belt, the generator and the mounting bracket as an assembly.
3. From underneath the vehicle, disconnect the exhaust crossover pipe flange.
4. If the car is equipped with power brakes, the rear bolts of the manifold are difficult to reach but they can be removed with a box wrench.
5. Remove the bolts that hold the manifold to the left cylinder head and take off the manifold.

Right-Side Manifold

From underneath the vehicle, disconnect the upper flange from the right manifold. This is the upper flange where the cross manifold, exhaust pipe and right manifold join.

From underneath the vehicle, remove the bolts that hold the manifold to the head on the back two flanges. The front flange can be removed from the top of the car with a box wrench.

Combination Manifold

Inline 6 Models through 1974

This engine uses a combined intake and exhaust manifold, equipped with thermostatic heat-riser valve.

1. Remove the air cleaner assembly.
2. Detach the throttle cable and lever at the bellcrank. Unfasten the throttle return spring.
3. Detach the fuel and vacuum lines from the carburetor.
4. Remove the PCV hose and valve from the grommet on the valve cover. Disconnect the air supply hose from the check valve on the air injection manifold (right-hand side of engine), if so equipped.
5. Detach the downpipe from the exhaust manifold flange. Discard the old packing.
6. Unfasten the manifold securing bolts and remove the clamps.
7. Remove the manifold assembly and throw the old gasket away.
8. If it is necessary to separate the manifolds, unfasten the single bolt and two nuts at the center of the assembly.

Installation is performed in the reverse order of removal.

Before reinstalling the manifold, thoroughly clean out the ports to prevent turbulence, particularly in the intake manifold. Use a new gasket and packing during installation.

1975-76 Inline 6

These inline 250 cu in. sixes use a cylinder head which has the intake manifold cast integrally with it. The intake manifold is removed along with the cylinder head and cannot be separated from it.

Valve System

Hydraulic lifters are used on all engines. These lifters are not interchangeable. To remove hydraulic lifters, first remove intake manifold and rocker assemblies, then pull out lifters.

Hydraulic lifters operate normally under conditions of zero valve lash.

Rocker arm lubrication is provided by means of oil feed through the pushrods on V8 engines.

Valve guides are not replaceable, but may be reamed to 0.003 in., 0.005 and 0.013 in. oversize. Occasionally a valve guide bore will be oversize as manufactured. These are marked on the inboard side of the cylinder heads on the machined surface just above the intake manifold. To ream a 0.010 in. oversize valve guide bore, use the 0.013 in. oversize reamer. Service valves are available in five different stem diameters: Standard, 0.003 oversize, 0.005 oversize, 0.010 oversize and 0.013 oversize.

Rocker Arm Replacement

V8—260, 350, 455 (Except '75-'76 Omega)

Remove the valve covers. Remove the two bolts that attach the rocker arm pivot to the cylinder head. Remove the rocker arms in pairs. Install the pairs of rocker arms for each cylinder only when the lifters are off the cam lobe and the valves are closed. Lubricate all pivot and rocker arm wear points with white grease. Torque the hardened flanged retaining bolts to 25 ft. lbs.

Inline 6 and 400 V8

1. Remove the valve cover.
2. Remove the attaching nut from the rocker arm to be removed, and lift the rocker arm nut, ball, and the rocker arm from the engine.
3. If more than one rocker arm is being removed, repeat step two until all the arms have been removed. Keep the nuts, balls, and arms in order when they are removed so they can be installed in their original location.
4. Install the rocker arm and ball on their stud after coating wear points with white grease.
5. Make sure the pushrod is installed in the lifter and the end of the rocker arm, and tighten the rocker arm attaching nut finger-tight.
6. Adjust the valves on inline-6 only.

1975-76 V6 and Omega 350 V8

1. Remove the rocker arm cover.
2. Remove the rocker arm shaft assembly bolts and the assembly.
3. Remove the nylon arm retainers by breaking them below their head with a chisel.
4. Remove the rocker arms.

Installation is performed in the following order:

NOTE: Each pair of rocker arms must be installed so that the external rib on each arm points away from the rocker arm shaft bolt that is located between each pair of rocker arms.

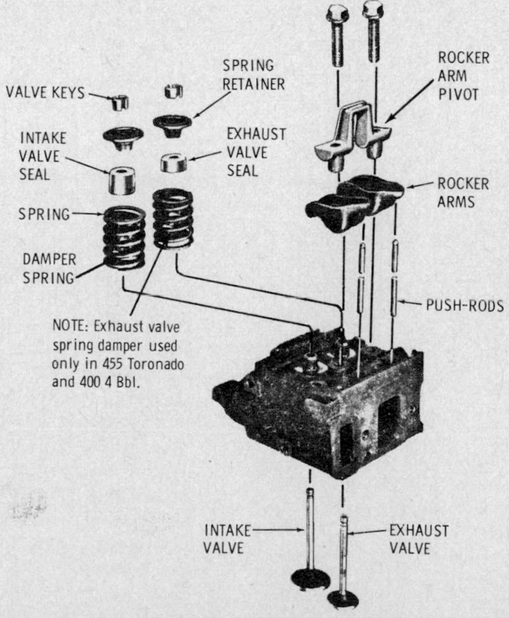

Valve and cylinder head assembly—V8, except 1975 400 and 1975-76 Omega 350
(© Oldsmobile Div, G.M. Corp)

On V6 engines, the service replacement rocker arms are marked "R" and "L" for right and left side installation; don't interchange.

1. Install the rocker arms on the shaft and lubricate them with oil.
2. Center each arm on the 1/4 in. hole in the shaft. Install new nylon rocker arm retainers in the holes using a 1/2 in. drift.
3. Locate the push rods in the rocker arms and insert the shaft-to-cylinder head bolts. Tighten the bolts a little at a time until they are tight.
4. Install the rocker cover and use a new gasket.

Valve Adjustment

V8 and V6

These valves cannot be adjusted. If there is excessive clearance in the valve train, look for worn pushrods, rocker arms, valve springs, or collapsed or stuck valve lifters.

Inline 6

1. Remove the distributor cap from the distributor and crank the engine until no. 1 piston is at top dead center (TDC). TDC can be determined in the following manner:
   a. Remove the spark plug from no. 1 cylinder.
   b. Place your thumb over the spark plug hole while an assistant cranks the engine.
   c. When no. 1 piston begins its compression stroke, compression at the spark plug hole will try to force your thumb outward.
   d. Observe the crankshaft pulley and turn the engine (preferably by hand) until the timing mark on the pulley aligns with the "0" (TDC) mark on the indicator. No. 1 piston is now at TDC.
   e. At this time, look at the rotor. The pointer on the rotor should be pointing to the no. 1 cylinder tower in the cap and the points should be open.
2. The valves on no. 1 cylinder can now be adjusted. Loosen the rocker arm adjusting nut until the pushrod can be rotated (lash) and then tighten the nut until all lash is removed and the pushrod can't be rotated. Tighten the adjusting nut an additional full turn to center the lifter plunger.
3. Using a socket wrench, turn the crankshaft pulley ¼ turn in the direction of engine rotation (counterclockwise when viewed from the rear). By turning the crankshaft, piston no. 5 is now at TDC and its valves can be adjusted. After adjusting no. 5,

Valve adjustment—inline 6
(© Oldsmobile Div., GM Corp.)

turn the crankshaft another ¼ turn to bring piston no. 3 to TDC and adjust its valves. Follow the firing order (1-5-3-6-2-4, from front to rear) and adjust the valves for cylinder no. 6 and then no. 2 and no. 4, making sure that the crankshaft is turned ¼ turn after each cylinder is adjusted.
4. Install the distributor cap and the rocker arm cover.

Cylinder Head

Cylinder Head Removal and Installation

Caution Do not disconnect the A/C lines. Severe personal injury or system damage could result.

V8 Except '75-'76 Omega 350

1. Drain the cooling system.
2. Remove the intake manifold and carburetor as an assembly.
3. Remove exhaust manifolds.
4. Loosen or remove any accessory brackets which interfere.
5. Remove the valve cover. Loosen any accessory brackets which are in the way.
6. Remove rocker arm bolts, pivots, rocker arms and pushrods. Scribe the pivots and identify the rocker arms and pushrods so that they may be installed in their original locations.

NOTE: On some models equipped with a 455 cu in. engine and air conditioning, disconnect the right motor mount and jack up the right front corner of the engine to remove the no. 8 pushrod. When the above models are also equipped with power brakes, it is necessary to disconnect the booster and turn it sideways to remove no. 7 pushrod.

7. Remove cylinder head bolts and cylinder head(s).
8. Install in the reverse order of removal. It is recommended that the head gasket be coated on both sides with sealer. Dip head bolts in oil before installing. Tighten all head bolts in the correct sequence to 60-70 ft. lbs., then again in sequence to the specified torque. See Specifications at the beginning of this section for correct head bolt torque. Retorque the bolts after engine is warmed-up.

1975 400 cu in. V8 (© Oldsmobile Div., GM Corp.)

260, 350 (except 1975-76 Omega), 400, 455 V8
(© Oldsmobile Div., GM Corp.)

1975-76 V6 and Omega 350 V8

1. Disconnect the battery.
2. Drain the coolant.
3. Remove the air cleaner.
4. Remove the air conditioning compressor, *but do not disconnect any lines.*
5. Remove the intake manifold.
6. When removing the right cylinder head, loosen the alternator belt and remove the alternator.
7. When removing the left cylinder head, remove the dipstick, power brake hose, power steering pump and AIR pump if so equipped.
8. Disconnect the plug wires.
9. Disconnect exhaust manifold from the head being removed.
10. Remove the rocker arm cover and rocker shaft assembly. Lift out the push rods.

NOTE: When removing the head on Omega models, it will be necessary to disconnect the crossover pipe, remove its support, remove the left front engine mount thrubolt, and raise the engine to gain working clearance.

11. Remove the cylinder head bolts.
12. Remove the cylinder head and gasket.
13. Reverse the above steps to install. Torque the head bolts to specifications in three steps.

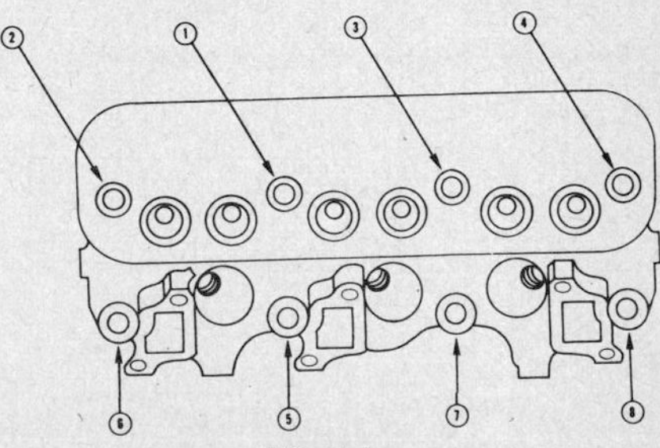

V6 engine
(© Buick Div, G.M. Corp)

1975-76 Omega 350 V8
(© G.M. Corp)

Inline 6

1. Drain cooling system (including block) and remove manifold assembly and valve mechanism.
2. Remove fuel and vacuum line from retaining clip and disconnect wires from temperature sending units and EFE solenoid (1975-76).
3. Disconnect upper radiator hose and battery ground strap.
4. Remove coil.
5. Remove cylinder head bolts, then head and gasket.

NOTE: Place the cylinder head on two blocks of wood, so that it is not damaged.

Install in the reverse order of removal. See Specifications at the beginning of this section for correct head bolt torque and tightening sequence. Use sealer on the head bolts prior to installation. Do not use gasket sealer when using a composition steel-asbestos head gasket. Retorque the head bolts after the engine has warmed up.

Inline 6 cylinder—through 1974

Field experience indicates the need for quick replacement data on worn, loose or thread damaged valve rocker arm studs.

1. **Place a thin-walled socket and a flat washer over the bad stud.**
2. **Turn the stud nut on until the stud pulls free of the cylinder head.**
3. **Unless the bad stud was loose, a standard stud can be replaced. If the stud was loose in the head, oversize studs and appropriate reamers are available from the dealer.**
4. **While cleaning or reconditioning the hole, chill the new stud (in the household refrigerator or the soda dispenser).**
5. **Run the engine until it is warm, then lightly tap the new stud into the cylinder head stud hole.**

NOTE: carefully measure the exposed length of the corresponding studs. If the new stud is inserted to a greater depth than necessary, it may damage the head.

Cylinder head/intake manifold—1975-76 inline 6
(© Oldsmobile Div., GM Corp.)

Timing Case and Camshaft

Front Cover R & R

V8 Engines Except '75-'76 Omega 350 and '75 400

The timing case cover and the water pump housing are a one-piece casting.

1. Drain the cooling system and disconnect the radiator and heater hoses, remove the radiator core, the fan blades and pulley.
2. Remove the vibration damper and crankshaft pulley.
3. Place a jack under the engine, take a light load on the jack and remove the two bolts that attach the front of the engine to the frame.
4. Drain the oil and remove the oil pan (see Engine Lubrication section).
5. Remove the front cover attaching bolts and remove the cover, timing indicator and water pump from the front of the engine.
6. Install in the reverse order of removal using a new gasket with sealing compound. Tighten self-tapping water pump attaching screws to 13 ft. lbs., 5/16 in. front cover attaching bolts to 25 ft. lbs. and the four bottom bolts (cover plate) to 35 ft. lbs. Torque the pulley hub bolt to 160 ft lbs, crankshaft pulley bolts to 20 ft lbs (10 ft lbs for 1972-76), and fan bolts to 20 ft lbs.

1975-'76 V6 and Omega 350 V8

1. Drain cooling system and remove radiator, shroud, fan, pulleys, and belts.
2. Remove crankshaft pulley, fuel pump and distributor.
3. Remove Delcotron and power steering pump, if necessary.
4. Loosen and slide rearward front clamp on thermostat by-pass hose. Remove harmonic balancer.
5. Remove bolts attaching timing chair cover to cylinder block and oil pan to timing chain cover bolts. Remove timing chain cover assembly and gasket. Clean cover thoroughly, being careful not to damage the gasket surface.
6. Turn the crankshaft so that the timing marks on the sprockets are adjacent to each other on a line with the shaft centers.
7. Remove crankshaft oil slinger.
8. Remove bolt, special washer, distributor drive gear, and fuel pump eccentric from camshaft.
9. Pry camshaft and crankshaft sprockets forward until camshaft sprocket is free. Then remove both sprockets and chain.
   If oil seal appears worn or has been leaking, replace as follows:
10. Use a punch to drive out the old seal and retaner. Drive from front to rear of the timing chain cover.
11. Coil new packing around opening so that ends are at top. Drive in retainer. Stake the retainer in at least three places. Size the packing by rotating a hammer handle, etc. around the packing until the balancer hub fits through the packing.
    If engine has been disturbed since chain and sprockets were removed:
12. Turn crankshaft until No. 1 piston is at top dead center.
13. Mount sprocket temporarily and turn camshaft so that timing mark is straight down.
14. Assemble chain and sprockets and mount on shafts with their timing marks closest to each other.
15. Mount slinger on sprocket with the concave side to the front.
16. Reinstall fuel pump eccentric, distributor drive gear, special washer, and bolt on camshaft. Reinstall Woodruff key with oil groove forward.
17. Remove oil pump cover and pack the space around the oil pump gears full of petroleum jelly, leaving no air spaces. Reinstall oil pump cover with new gasket. This step is very important. If it

is not done the oil pump will not begin to pump oil as soon as the engine is started.

18. Reinstall timing chain cover with new gasket.

Keep engine speed low for a short time after installation of a new oil seal.

1975 400 V8

1. Perform steps 1 and 2 of the "V8 Engines Except '75-'76 Omega 350 and '75 400" timing chain cover removal procedure.
2. Remove the water and fuel pumps.
3. Remove the 4 oil pan-to-timing chain cover bolts.
4. Remove all the cover-to-block bolts and nuts. Remove the cover-to-intake manifold bolt.
5. Pull the cover forward, enough to clear its mounting studs, and remove it.
6. Pull the O-ring out of its intake manifold water passage.
7. Remove the timing chain cover gasket. Clean the gasket surfaces on the block and cover thoroughly.
8. Replace the front oil pan gasket, if damaged. Cement it to the oil pan.

Installation is the reverse of removal. Use a new cover gasket and manifold O-ring. Tighten the cover-to-oil pan bolts to 12 ft lbs. harmonic balancer to 160 ft lbs, and the fan bolts to 20 ft lbs. Refill the cooling system and check for leaks.

Inline 6 Engines

1. Remove the crankshaft pulley. Remove the oil pan.
2. Remove the timing case cover attaching bolts.
3. Remove the cover and gasket. Pry the old seal out of the front side of the cover with a large screwdriver.
4. Install the new seal so that the open end of the seal is toward the inside of the cover. When reinstalling, be careful that cover is positioned to center seal on the shaft.
5. Tighten the screws and the two bolts inside the engine to 6-7½ ft. lbs.

Front Cover Oil Seal —All Engines

Removal and Installation (Cover not removed)

1. Remove belts.
2. Remove pulley and hubs.
3. Carefully pry out old seal with screwdriver or thin punch, using care not to damage shaft surface.
4. Coat outside diameter of new seal with proper sealer.
5. Drive in seal with proper tool, using care not to distort it nor damage mating surfaces or shaft.
6. Reinstall removed parts and adjust belts.

Timing Gear Replacement

Inline 6 Cylinder Engine

Timing gears are arranged so that (unless deliberately disturbed) the valve timing will remain as set at the factory. Unless the gears are badly worn or seriously damaged, the valve timing will remain constant within reasonable limits.

If it becomes necessary to remove the timing gear, proceed in the following order:

1. Remove the camshaft.
2. Place the camshaft and gear assembly in an arbor press. Using an adapter, press the camshaft from the gear.

Caution The thrust plate should be positioned so that the Woodruff key and shaft do not damage it during removal.

3. If the crankshaft gear requires replacement, remove it with a gear puller. Replace it using a drift of the proper size.

Installation is performed in the reverse order of removal. The clearance between the camshaft and the thrust plate should be 0.001-0.005 in. Install the camshaft as outlined below.

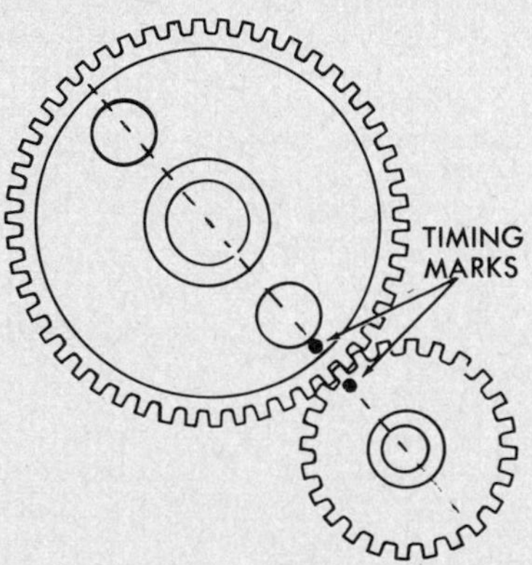

Timing marks—Inline 6 cylinder

Timing Chain Replacement and Valve Timing

On all Oldsmobile engines, except the inline 6, a chain is used to drive the camshaft. The construction is such that the chain can be worn even badly without seriously affecting the valve timing. If the chain is worn badly enough to cause the timing to jump or it becomes necessary to replace either the chain or the sprockets or both, proceed as follows:

V8 Except '75-'76 Omega 350

1. Remove the timing case cover and take off the camshaft gear.

NOTE: the fuel pump operating cam is bolted to the front of the camshaft sprocket and the sprocket is located on the camshaft by means of a dowel.

2. Remove the oil slinger, timing chain, and the camshaft sprocket. If the crankshaft sprocket is to be replaced, remove it also at this time.
3. Reinstall the crankshaft sprocket being careful to start it with the keyway in perfect alignment since it is rather difficult to correct for misalignment after the gear has been started on the shaft. Turn the timing mark on the crankshaft gear until it points directly toward the center of the camshaft. Mount the timing chain over the camshaft gear and start the camshaft gear up on to its shaft with the timing marks as close as possible to each other and in line between the shaft centers. Rotate the camshaft to align the shaft with the new gear.

A dowel pin is used for alignment. Secure the camshaft gear and check to see that the mark on the crankshaft sprocket and the mark on the camshaft sprocket are as described above. Valves timed in this manner are correct regardless of which piston is at top center. It may be necessary, however, to retime the ignition since there is a possibility it will be 180° out of position.

Timing marks—except Inline 6 cylinder

V6 Engine and '75-'76 Omega 350 V8

1. Remove the timing chain cover.
2. Make sure that the timing marks on the crankshaft and the camshaft sprockets are aligned. This will make installing the parts easier.

NOTE: It is not necessary to remove the timing chain dampers (tensioners) unless they are worn or damaged and require replacement.

3. Remove the front crankshaft oil slinger.
4. Remove the bolt and the special washer that hold the camshaft distributor drive gear and fuel pump eccentric at the forward end of the camshaft. Remove the eccentric and the gear from the camshaft.

5. Alternately pry forward the camshaft sprocket and then the crankshaft sprocket until the camshaft sprocket is pried from the camshaft.
6. Remove the camshaft sprocket, sprocket key, and timing chain from the engine.
7. Pry the crankshaft sprocket from the crankshaft.

Install as follows:

1. If the engine has not been disturbed proceed to Step 4 for installation procedures.
2. If the engine has been disturbed turn the crankshaft so that the No. 1 piston is at top dead center.
3. Temporarily install the sprocket key and the camshaft sprocket on the camshaft. Turn the camshaft so that the index mark of the sprocket is downward. Remove the key and sprocket from the camshaft.
4. Assemble the timing chain and sprockets. Install the keys, sprockets, and chain assembly on the camshaft and crankshaft so that the index marks of both the sprockets are aligned.

NOTE: It will be necessary to hold the spring loaded timing chain damper out of the way while installing the timing chain and sprocket assembly.

5. Install the front oil slinger on the crankshaft with the inside diameter against the sprocket (concave side toward the front of the engine).
6. Install the fuel pump eccentric on the camshaft and the key, with the oil groove of the eccentric forward.
7. Install the distributor drive gear on the camshaft. Secure the gear and eccentric to the camshaft with the retaining washer and bolt.
8. Torque the bolt to 40-55 ft lbs.

Camshaft R & R

Inline 6 Engine

1. Remove the valve lifters and the crankcase front cover.
2. Remove the radiator, evaporator (A/C only), and grille from the front of the car.
3. Remove the fuel pump.
4. Align the timing gear marks on the crankshaft and the camshaft gears, then remove the thrust plate bolts.
5. Remove the camshaft and gear assembly from the engine. Support the shaft during removal to prevent damage to the camshaft bearing.
6. Check the camshaft journals with a micrometer to determine if they are out-of-round. If the journals exceed .001 in. out-of round, replace the camshaft. Check the assembly for signs of wear or damage.
7. Insert the camshaft and gear assembly in the engine, being careful not to damage the shaft.
8. Turn the crankshaft and camshaft gears so that the valve timing marks align. Push the camshaft into position and install and torque the thrust plate bolts to 7 ft lbs.
9. Check camshaft and crankshaft gear run-out with a dial indicator. Camshaft gear run-out should not exceed .004 in. and crankshaft gear run-out should not be above .003 in.
10. If run-out is excessive, clean off any burrs from the shaft and make another measurement. If run-out is still excessive, replace the gear.
11. Using a dial indicator, check the backlash at several points between the camshaft and crankshaft gear teeth. Backlash should be .004–.006 in.
12. Install the fuel pump.
13. Install the grille, radiator, A/C condenser, and crankcase front cover.
14. Install the valve lifters.

1969-70 V8

1. Disconnect the battery.
2. Drain and remove the radiator.
3. Remove the grille and any other obstructing sheet metal.
4. If the car is air conditioned, move the condenser out of the way but *do not disconnect any of the refrigerant lines.*
5. Remove the fuel pump and crankcase front cover.
6. Remove the oil slinger, timing chain and gears.
7. To facilitate proper installation of the distributor, mark the exact location of the distributor in relation to the block. Remove the distributor.
8. Remove the intake manifold.
9. Remove the rocker arm assemblies, pushrods, and lifters.
10. Carefully remove the camshaft from the block.
11. Inspect the camshaft assembly for excessive wear or damage.
12. Liberally coat camshaft with heavy engine oil prior to installation.
13. Carefully insert the camshaft into the engine.
14. Install the lifters, pushrods, rocker arm assemblies, and valve covers.
15. Install the intake manifold.
16. Install the timing chain and gears, oil slinger, and front cover.
17. Install the fuel pump, radiator, air conditioning condenser, and any front-end sheet metal that may have been removed.
18. Install the distributor to agree with the location markings made before removal.

1971-76 V8 Except Omega 350

1. Disconnect the battery.
2. Drain and remove the radiator.
3. Disconnect the fuel line at the fuel pump.
4. Disconnect the throttle cable.
5. Remove the generator belt, loosen the generator bolts, and move the generator to one side.
6. Remove the power steering pump from its brackets and move it out of the way.
7. Remove the air conditioning compressor from its brackets and move the compressor out of the way *without disconnecting the lines.*
8. Disconnect the hoses from the water pump.
9. Disconnect the electrical and vacuum connections.
10. Mark the distributor as to location in the block. Remove the distributor.
11. Raise the car and drain the oil pan.
12. Remove the exhaust crossover pipe and starter motor.
13. Disconnect the exhaust pipe at the manifold.
14. Remove the harmonic balancer and pulley.
15. Support the engine and remove the front motor mounts.
16. Remove the flywheel inspection cover.
17. Remove the engine oil pan.
18. Support the engine by placing wooden blocks between the exhaust manifolds and the front crossmember.
19. Remove the engine front cover.
20. Remove the valve covers.
21. Remove the intake manifold, oil filler pipe, and temperature sending switch.
22. Mark the lifters, pushrods, and rocker arms as to location so that they may be installed in the same position. Remove these parts.
23. If the car is equipped with air conditioning, remove the condenser attaching bolts and move the condenser to one side.

NOTE: Do not remove the A/C lines from the condenser.

24. Remove the fuel pump eccentric, camshaft gear, oil slinger, and timing chain.
25. Carefully remove the camshaft from the engine.
26. Inspect the shaft for signs of excessive wear or damage.
27. Liberally coat camshaft and bearings with heavy-weight engine oil and insert them into the engine.
28. Align the timing marks on the camshaft and crankshaft gears. See "Timing Chain Replacement and Valve Timing" for details.
29. Install the distributor using the locating marks made during removal. If any problems are en-

countered, see "Distributor Installation" in the "Ignition" Section.

30. To install, reverse the removal procedure but pay attention to the following points:
    a. Install the timing indicator before installing the power steering pump bracket.
    b. Install the flywheel inspection cover after installing the starter.
    c. Replace the engine oil and radiator coolant.

V6 Engine and Omega 350 V8

1. Remove the engine, if necessary to gain working clearance.
2. Remove the intake manifold and carburetor assembly.
3. Remove the distributor.
4. Remove the fuel pump.
5. Remove the alternator, drive belts, cooling fan, fan pulley, and water pump.
6. Remove the crankshaft pulley and the vibration damper.
7. Remove the oil pump.
8. Remove the timing chain cover.
9. Remove the timing chain and the camshaft sprocket, along with the distributor drive gear and the fuel pump eccentric.
10. Remove the rocker arm assemblies.

NOTE: The push rods need not be removed. But if they are, be sure that they are replaced in their original positions.

11. Lift the tappets up so that they are not in contact with the camshaft. Use wire clips or clip-type clothes pins to hold the tappets up.
12. Carefully guide the camshaft forward out of the engine. Avoid marring the bearing surfaces.
13. Install in reverse order of the above procedure.

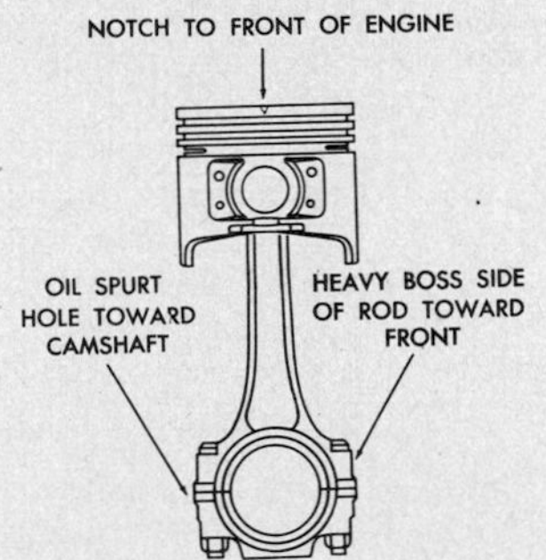

Piston and rod assembly—Inline 6 cylinder

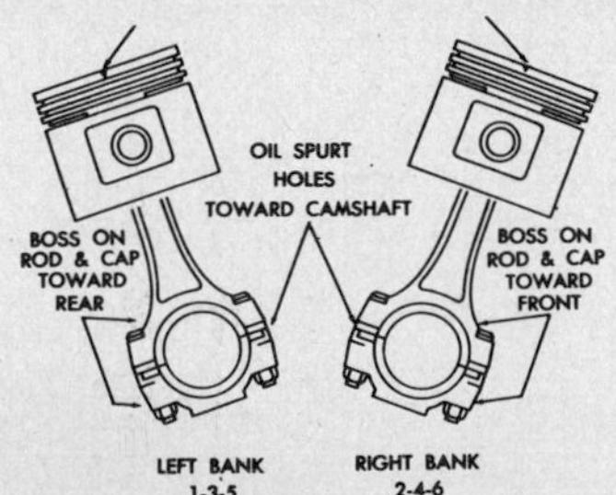

Piston and rod assembly—V6

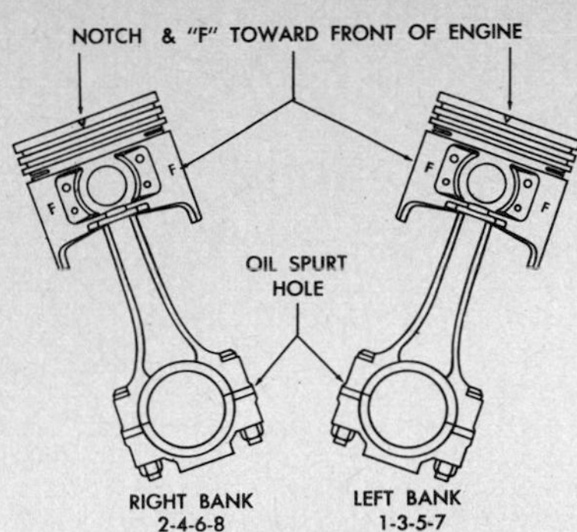

Piston and rod assembly—V8

Engine Lubrication

Oil Pan R & R

All 1969-70 Olds and F-85 with 350 and 455 Cu. In. Engines; All 1970-76 V8 F-85, Cutlass, Olds, and Omega Except 1970-72 455 Cutlass

1. Disconnect the negative battery cable and remove the dipstick.
2. On 1969-76 88 and 98 models, remove the upper radiator support and fan shroud attaching screws.
3. Raise the car on a hoist and drain the crankcase.
4. On F-85, Cutlass, 442 and Vista Cruiser models, disconnect the exhaust pipe from the right exhaust manifold. On 88 and 98 models lower the relay rod by disconnecting the idler arm or pitman arm.
5. Disconnect the engine mounts and carefully jack the front of the engine up as far as possible using a suitable tool. The special lifting tool bolts to the front of the block.
6. Remove crossover pipe and starter.
7. Remove oil pan attaching bolts, rotate the crankshaft until the No. 1 crankshaft throw is up, then remove the oil pan.
8. When installing, apply sealer to both sides of pan gasket and install on block. Install the front and rear (rubber) seals. Install the pan, tightening 5/16 in. bolts to 15 ft. lbs. and 1/4 in. bolts to 10 ft. lbs.
9. Reverse Steps 1 through 6 to complete installation.

1969 400 Cu. In.; 1970-72 F-85, Cutlass—455 Cu. In. Cu. In.

1. Disconnect the negative battery cable and disconnect the fan shroud.
2. Raise the car on a hoist and drain the crankcase.
3. Remove the driveshaft.
4. Disconnect the exhaust pipe and starter.
5. Install a rear engine support bar and remove the flywheel housing inspection cover.
6. Disconnect modulator line, speedometer cable, oil cooler lines, solenoid wire and linkage.
7. Remove transmission crossmember, transmission and flywheel.
8. Raise the front of the engine.
9. Remove the right engine mount and raise the engine 2 in. Install a wedge block.
10. Loosen the left engine mount-to-block bolts enough to allow for the removal of the oil pan bolts.
11. Remove the oil pan bolts, free the pan from the block and disconnect the oil pump.
12. Remove the oil pan and pump.
13. To install, clean all gasket surfaces and apply sealer to both sides of the pan gaskets. Install the gaskets on the block.
14. Install front and rear (rubber) seals.
15. Hold the oil pan in approximate position and install the oil pump, tightening bolts to 35 ft. lbs.
16. Install the oil pan, tightening 5/16 in. bolts to 15 ft. lbs. and 1/4 in. bolts to 10 ft. lbs.
17. Install the flywheel.
18. Remove the wedge block and tighten engine mount to engine block bolts to 50 ft. lbs.
19. Remove front engine support tool and install the transmission.
20. Install transmission crossmember and remove the rear engine support tool.
21. Connect modulator lines, speedometer cable, oil cooler lines, solenoid wire and linkage.
22. Connect the starter and exhaust pipe.
23. Install the driveshaft.
24. Lower car and fill the crankcase.
25. Connect the fan shroud and connect the battery negative cable.

1975-76 V6

1. Raise the car and support it with jackstands.
2. Drain the oil.
4. Remove the flywheel/torque converter cover.
5. Remove the crossover pipe.
6. Remove the oil pan bolts and the oil pan.

Installation is the reverse of removal. Apply non-hardening silicone sealer to several places around the oil pan gasket, before installing it on the block.

Inline 6 Engine

1. Disconnect battery negative cable, fuel flex line at the fuel pump and starter leads at the starter. On 1969 models, to remove the pan the engine must be removed, so refer to engine removal procedures.
2. Remove upper radiator support and bracket to upper hose. On cars with air conditioning, remove the fan and clutch assembly.

3. Remove front motor mount bracket to motor mount bolts.
4. Raise the car on a hoist and drain crankcase.
5. Disconnect automatic transmission linkage and remove flywheel cover and starter.
6. Disconnect exhaust pipe at the manifold.
7. Position timing mark notch at the 6 o'clock position.
8. Raise the engine with a jack at the crankshaft damper and remove the right engine mount with bracket.
9. Remove the oil pan attaching bolts and the oil pan. It may be necessary to raise the engine further to get the pan out. Be careful not to damage cowl mounted parts.
10. To install, reverse the above procedure. Use new gaskets.

Oil Pump

V6, V8, and Inline 6

On these engines, the oil pump is mounted to the bottom of the block and is accessible only by removing the oil pan.

On V8 engines, remove the oil pan, then unbolt and remove the oil pump and screen as an assembly. On the OHV 6 the pickup tube has a bolt-attached bracket.

Rear Main Bearing Oil Seal

V6 and V8—Except '75 400 V8

The crankshaft need not be removed to replace the rear main bearing upper oil seal.

1. Drain the crankcase and remove the oil pan and rear main bearing cap.
2. Using a blunt-ended tool, drive the upper seal into its groove on each side until it is tightly packed. This is usually ¼-¾ in.
3. Cut pieces of new seal 1/16 in. longer than required to fill the grooves and install, packing into place.
4. Carefully trim any protruding seal, being sure not to scratch or damage the bearing surface.
5. Install a new seal in the bearing cap and install cap, tightening bolts to 120 ft. lbs. Install the oil pan.

1975 400 V8

1. Remove the oil pan, baffle, and oil pump.
2. Remove the rear main bearing cap.
3. Make a seal tool.
4. Insert the tool against one end of the oil seal in the block and drive the seal gently into the groove ¾ in. Repeat on the other end of the seal.
5. Form a new seal in the cap. Cut four pieces ⅜ in. long from this seal.

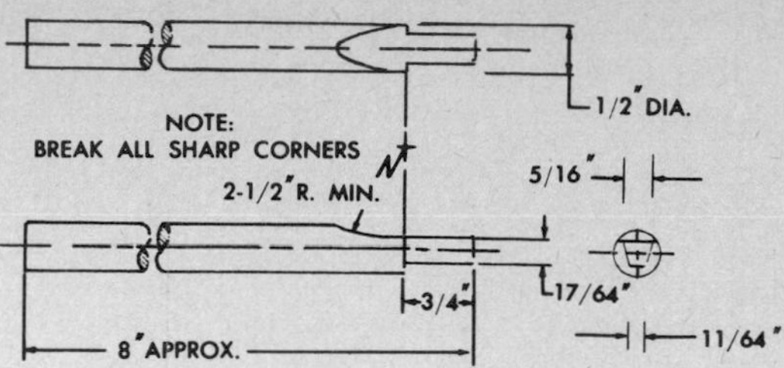

Fabricate an oil seal remover as illustrated—1975 400 V8
(© Oldsmobile Div., GM Corp.)

6. Work two of the pieces into each of the gaps which have been made at the end of the seal in the block. Do not cut off any material to make them fit.
7. Form a new seal in the bearing cap.
8. Apply a 1/16 in. bead of sealer across to the external cork groove.
9. Reassemble the cap and torque to specifications.

Inline 6 Engine

The rear main bearing oil seal is of moulded design and can be replaced (both halves) without removal of the crankshaft.

NOTE: always replace both halves as a unit. Install with the lip facing toward front of the engine.

1. With oil pan and pump removed, remove the rear main bearing cap.
2. Remove oil seal from the groove by lifting the end tab, then clean seal groove.
3. Lubricate the lip and O.D. of a new seal with engine oil. Keep oil off the parting line surface.
4. Insert seal into cap and roll into place with fingers. Use light pressure on the seal to prevent cutting the O.D. of the seal with the sharp edges of the groove. Be sure the tabs of the seal are properly located in the cross grooves.
5. To remove upper half of seal, use a small hammer to tap a brass pin punch on one end of seal until it protrudes far enough to be removed with pliers.
6. Lubricate the lip and O.D. of a new seal with engine oil. Keep oil off parting line surface. Gradually push with a hammer handle, while turning crankshaft, until seal is rolled into place. Be careful that seal bead on O.D. of seal is not cut.
7. Install rear main bearing cap (with new seal) and torque to specifications. Be sure cross seal tabs are in place and properly seated.

CLUTCH

Clutch Pedal Adjustment

1969-72—All

The clutch pedal should be adjusted so that there is ¾ to 1 in. free-play at the clutch pedal before the throwout bearing engages the clutch fingers. This adjustment is made under the car at the adjustable clutch rod just in front of the throwout fork. Loosen the jam nut and turn the adjusting screw until the desired clearance is obtained, then tighten the jam nut.

1973-76—Omega, Cutlass

The clutch pedal free-play should be adjusted to the following specifications, which are measured from the center of the clutch pedal pad:

Cutlass—¾-1 in.
Omega—⅞-1½ in.

To adjust free-play, proceed in the following manner:

1. Loosen the locknut on the push rod swivel.
2. Detach the pedal return spring.
3. Turn the equalizer assembly until the clutch pedal seats against the rubber bumper on the dash brace.
4. Push the outer end of the clutch fork rearward, so that the throwout bearing just contacts the clutch plate.
5. Remove the retaining clip from the lower push rod swivel and install the swivel in the *upper* gauge hole. Install the retaining clip.
6. Lengthen the push rod until there is no lash.
7. Remove the retaining clip and reinstall the swivel in the *lower* hole on the equalizer lever.
8. Tighten the locknut against the swivel. Be sure that the rod length remains unchanged.
9. Install the pedal return spring and check pedal free-play.

Starfire—1975-76

Adjustment for normal clutch wear is accomplished by turning the clutch fork ball stud counterclockwise to give 0.688 to 1.125 in. lash at clutch pedal.

1. Remove the ball stud cap and loosen the locknut on ball stud end located to the right of the transmission on the clutch housing.
2. Adjust the ball stud to obtain 0.69 to 1.13 in. free travel.
3. Tighten the locknut to 30 ft lbs. being careful not to change adjustment and install ball stud cap.

4. Check the operation of clutch.

Clutch R & R

Omega and Cutlass

1. Remove the transmission.
2. Detach the clutch return spring and clutch release rod assembly.
3. Withdraw the throwout bearing.
4. Without removing the starter from the engine, remove the flywheel housing.

NOTE: The release yoke, boot and ball stud will remain in the housing.

5. Scribe a mark opposite the "X" mark on the flywheel cover.
6. Loosen the pressure plate evenly, one turn at a time.

Clutch installation is performed in the following order:

Caution Do not lubricate the splines as the lubricant will be forced on to the damper, resulting in clutch rattle.

1. Install the clutch disc/cover assembly and finger-tighten its securing bolts.

NOTE: Align the mark made during removal with the "X" mark on the flywheel cover.

2. Use a clutch arbor or an old input shaft to align the disc by inserting it through the disc and into the pilot bearing.
3. Tighten every other bolt until the cover assembly is within ¼ in. of the flywheel.
4. Repeat step 3 for the three remaining bolts.
5. Tighten the first three bolts to the torque figure given below and then tighten the remaining three bolts to the same figure.
   1969-70—17 ft lbs
   1971-76—30 ft lbs
6. Remove the arbor. Lubricate the inside groove of the throwout bearing and the release yoke ball stud with wheel bearing grease.
7. Install the throwout bearing.
8. Install the flywheel housing and the transmission. Adjust clutch free-play as outlined above.

Starfire

1. Raise vehicle on hoist.
2. Remove transmission as outlined in this section.
3. Remove clutch fork cover then disconnect clutch return spring and control cable from clutch fork.
4. Remove main drive gear oil seal from clutch release bearing sleeve.
5. Remove flywheel housing lower cover.
6. Remove flywheel housing from engine.
7. To remove the release bearing from clutch fork and sleeve, slide lever off ball stud against spring action. If necessary to replace ball stud, remove cap, locknut and stud from housing.
8. If assembly marks on clutch assembly and flywheel are not visible remark with paint or centerpunch.
9. Loosen clutch cover-to-flywheel attaching bolts one turn at a time until spring pressure is released, to avoid bending clutch cover flange.
10. Support the pressure plate and cover assembly then remove the bolts and clutch assembly.

Caution Do not disassemble the clutch cover, spring and pressure plate for repair. If defective replace complete assembly.

11. Index alignment marks on clutch assembly and flywheel. Place driven plate on pressure plate with long end of splined end facing forward, damper springs inside pressure plate, and insert a dummy clutch gear shaft through the cover and driven plate.
12. Position the complete assembly against the flywheel and insert the dummy shaft into the pilot bearing in the crankshaft.
13. Index the alignment marks and install clutch cover to flywheel bolts finger-tight.

Caution Tighten all bolts evenly and gradually until tight to avoid possible clutch distortion. Torque bolts 18 ft. lbs. and remove dummy shaft.

14. Lubricate the clutch fork ball socket and the fingers at the release bearing with a high melting point grease such as graphite grease.
15. Lubricate the recess on the inside of the throwout bearing collar and the fork groove with a light coat of graphite grease. Install fork in housing but not on stud.
16. Install bearing on sleeve, then position clutch fork over bearing in housing and slide fork onto ball stud.
17. Install flywheel housing and lower cover. Tighten bolts to 30 ft lbs.
18. Install transmission as outlined.
19. Adjust clutch as previously out-outlined.
20. Lower and remove vehicle from hoist.

MANUAL TRANSMISSION

See the Capacities Table at the beginning of this section for manual transmission refill capacities. For manual transmission overhaul procedures, see the Unit Repair Section.

Transmission Removal

1. Disconnect throttle linkage and raise car. If applicable, disconnect T.C.S. switch.
2. Remove driveshaft.
3. Install engine support bar with appropriate adapter. Remove the catalytic converter and/or brackets, if they are in the way.
4. On console equipped floorshifts, disconnect shifter assembly at transmission, allowing this unit to remain in car. On regular floorshifts, remove floor pan seal. Insert a feeler gauge between the shift lever and its point of attachment. This will release a pin allowing the lever to be removed. Remove the shifter with transmission.
5. Disconnect parking brake cables and remove cross support bar.
6. Disconnect speedometer cable and back-up light switch.
7. Remove transmission upper and lower bolts.

Caution During removal, use aligning studs to support the transmission, otherwise

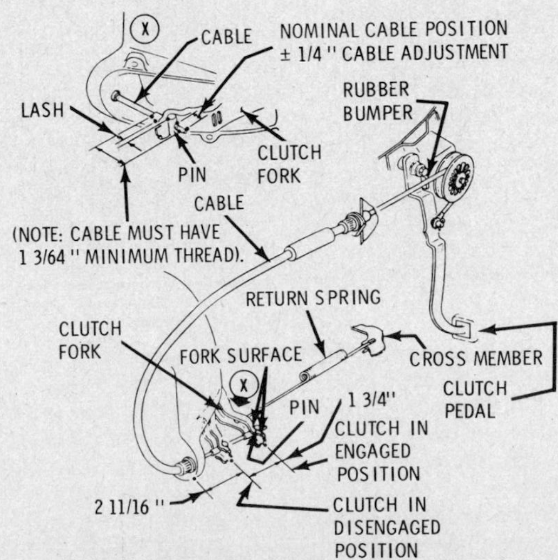

Starfire clutch cable installation and adjustment
(© Oldsmobile Div., GM Corp.)

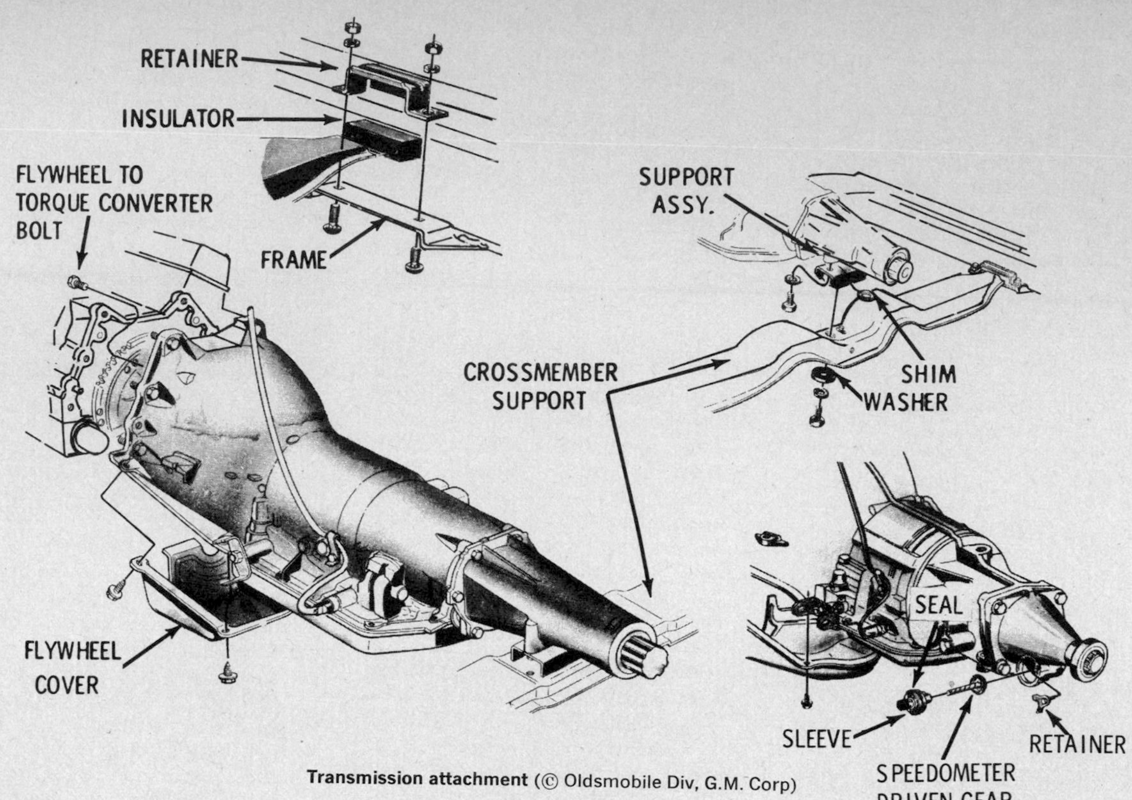

Transmission attachment (© Oldsmobile Div, G.M. Corp)

distortion of the clutch driven plate will result.

8. Slide transmission rearward and remove. On models equipped with dual exhaust, it may be necessary to disconnect left exhaust pipe at the manifold.
9. Install by reversing procedure above.

Shift Linkage Adjustment

3-Speed Column Shift

1. With the transmission in reverse and the car raised on a hoist, loosen the swivel bolts on the shift rods at the transmission.
2. Check that the shift rods move freely in the swivels, then push up on the reverse shift rod until the detent in the column is felt and tighten the swivel bolt for the first-reverse rod to 20 ft. lbs.
3. With transmission in neutral, insert a 3/16 in. rod through the second-third shift lever and into the alignment hole. Tighten the swivel bolt for the second-third shift lever to 20 ft. lbs.
4. Lower the car and check the shift operation.
5. Place transmission in Reverse and the ignition in LOCK position. Check that the key can be removed, the wheel not turned and the transmission will not shift out of Reverse.
6. Turn the ignition to RUN position and place the transmission in second gear. Check that the ignition key cannot be removed and that the steering wheel will turn.

Cutlass 3- and 4-Speed Floor Shift

The linkage adjustment procedure is the same as that described above for the column shift type, with the exception that the shift levers are aligned with a ¼ in. rod.

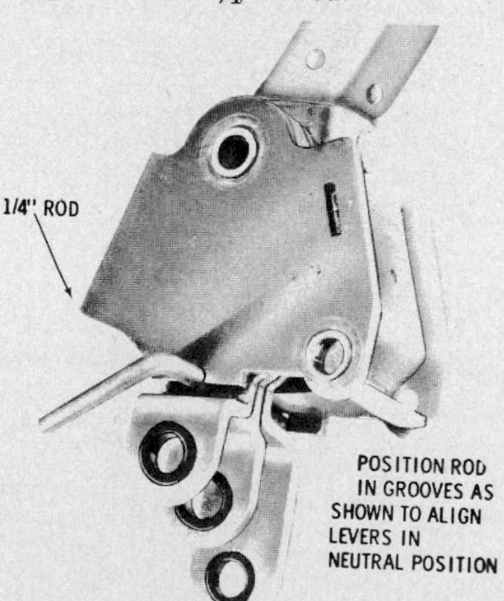

Adjusting shift linkage—4-speed (© Oldsmobile Div, G.M. Corp)

Omega 3-Speed Floorshift

1. Place the shift lever in Neutral and raise the car with a hoist.
2. Loosen the swivel nuts on the shift rods and detach the rods from the shifter assembly.
3. Insert a ¼ in. pin in the locating gauge hole on the shifter.
4. Adjust the swivel so that free pin length is obtained.
5. Tighten the swivel nuts and attach the shift rods back to the shifter.
6. Position the shift lever in Reverse and turn the ignition key to LOCK.
7. Loosen the equalizer clamp screw and pull the backdrive rod down lightly against the stop.
8. Torque the clamp screw to 23 ft lbs.
9. Lower the car and perform steps 5-6 of the "1969-74 3-Speed Column Shift" adjustment above.

Starfire 4-Speed Floorshift

1. Turn the ignition switch to "Off" and place the shift lever in Neutral.
2. Raise the car.
3. Loosen the locknuts on the control rods. Position the transmission side cover levers in their neutral detents.
4. With the floor shift lever in Neutral, align the shifter levers and insert a gauge pin into the levers and bracket.
5. Tighten the First/Second control rod locknut against its swivel.
6. Tighten the Third/Fourth control rod locknut against its swivel.
7. Tighten the Reverse control rod locknut against its swivel.

NOTE: All locknuts are tightened to 12 ft lbs.

8. Remove the gauge pin and check shifter operation.

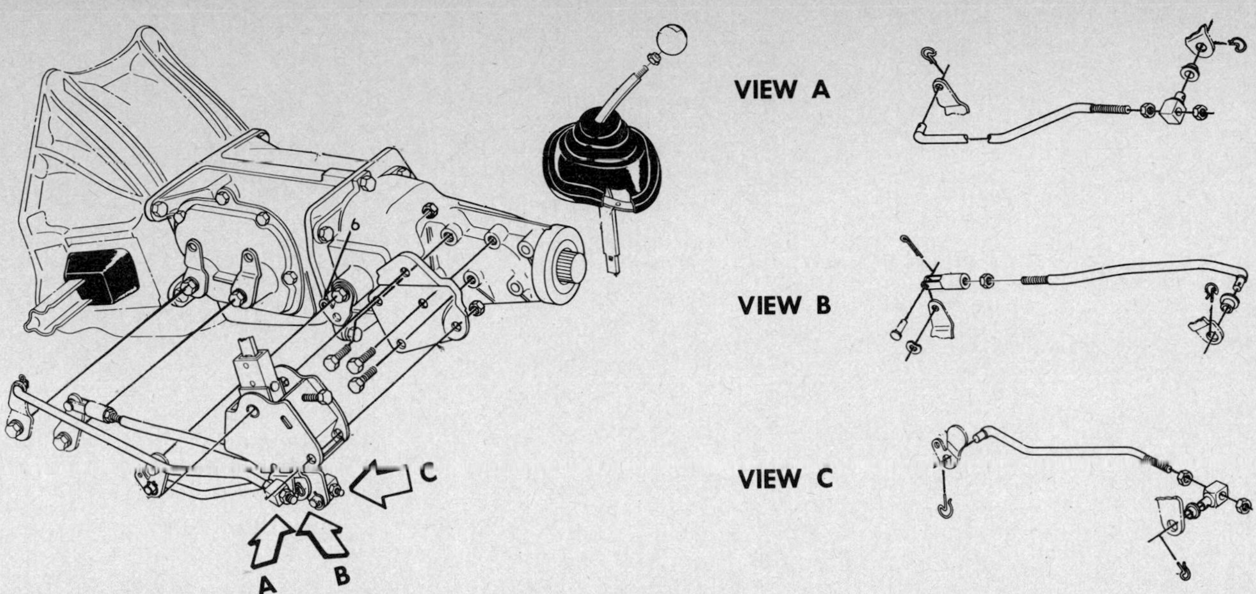

Floor shift control linkage details
(© Oldsmobile Div, G.M. Corp)

AUTOMATIC TRANSMISSION

Shift Linkage Adjustment

Turbo Hydra-Matic and Jetaway

The proper linkage adjustment is obtained by positioning the shift lever in the Neutral or Drive position at the column or console, whichever the case, and positioning the manual lever in the Neutral or Drive position at the transmission. See the illustrations for procedure.

Neutral Safety Switch

1969-76 Column-Mounted Switch
1971-76 Console-Mounted Switch

1. Place the gear selector in the appropriate range:
   1969-70 Column—Drive (D)
   1971-76 Column—Neutral (N)
   1971-76 Console—Park (P)
2. Loosen the switch securing screws.

NOTE: Remove the center console first, if necessary.

3. Fit a 0.090 in. gauge pin into the outer hole on the switch cover.
4. Move the switch until the gauge pin drops into the alignment hole on the inner slide.

Tighten the switch securing screws; then remove the gauge pin.

NOTE: Do not overtighten the switch securing screws (20 in. lbs maximum).

1969-70 Console-Mounted Switch

1. Remove the center console assembly.
2. Position the gear selector lever against the neutral stop.
3. Adjust the switch so that the car will start only when the gear

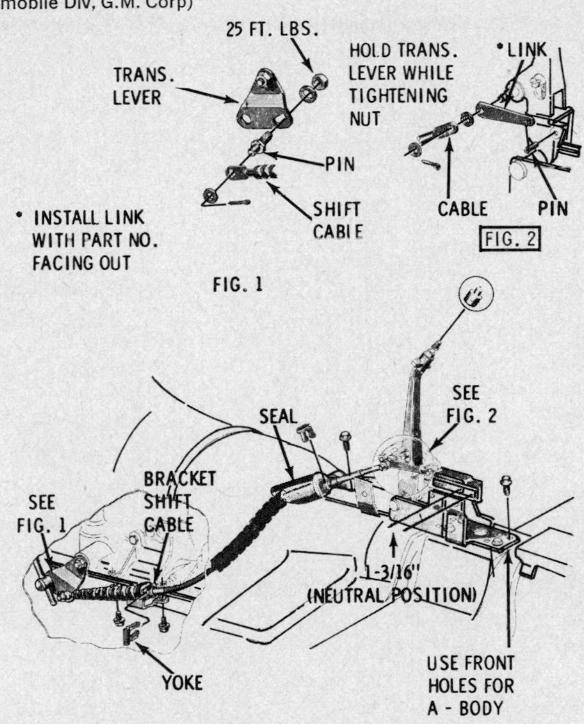

SHIFT CABLE ADJUSTMENT

1. Loosen shift rod clamp screw, loosen pin in transmission manual lever.
2. Place shift lever in "P" position, place transmission manual lever in "P" position and ignition key in lock position.
3. Pull shift rod lightly against lock stop and tighten clamp screw.
4. Move pin in manual transmission lever to give "free pin" fit and tighten attaching nut.
5. Check Operation:
   A. Move shift handle into each gear position and see that transmission manual lever is also in detent position.
   B. With key in "run" position and transmission in "reverse," be sure that key cannot be removed and that steering wheel is not locked.
   C. With key in "lock" position and transmission in "park," be sure that key can be removed and that steering wheel is locked.

Console shift linkage adjustment for Turbo Hydra-Matic transmission—Omega and Cutlass
(© Oldsmobile Div, G.M. Corp)

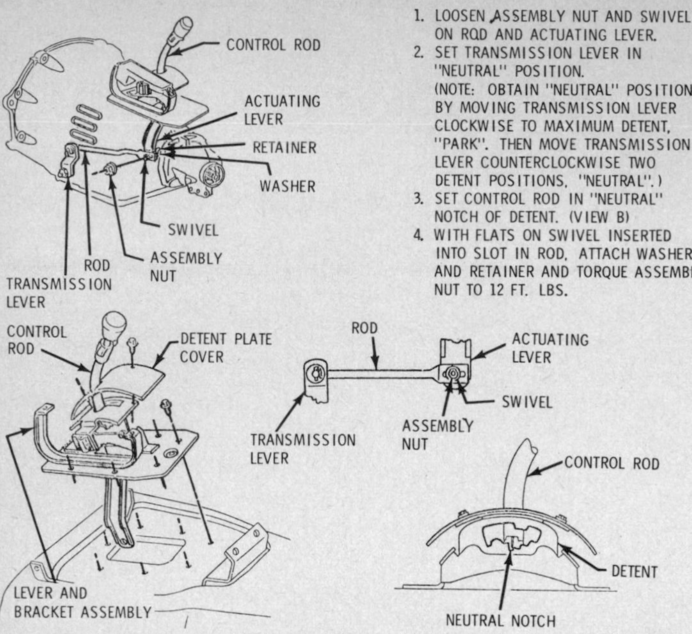

Console shift adjustment—Starfire
(© Oldsmobile Div., GM Corp.)

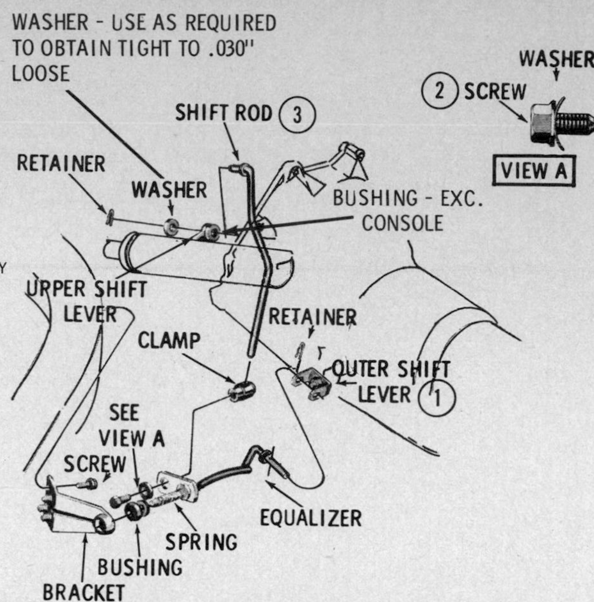

SHIFT ROD ADJUSTMENT

1. Set transmission outer lever in drive position.
2. Hold upper shift lever against drive position stop in upper steering column (do not raise lever).
3. Tighten screw in clamp on lower end of shift rod to specified torque.
4. Check Operation:
   A. With key in "run" position and transmission in "reverse" be sure that key cannot be removed and that steering wheel is not locked.
   B. With key in "lock" position and shift lever in "park," be sure that key can be removed, that steering wheel is locked, and that the transmission remains in park when the steering column is locked.

Column shift linkage adjustment for Turbo Hydra-Matic—1969-70
(© Oldsmobile Div, G.M. Corp)

selector lever is in Park (P) or Neutral (N).

Pan R & R, Fluid and Filter Change

1. Raise the car and support it securely with jackstands.
2. Place a container under the transmission pan to catch fluid.
3. Loosen the pan bolts. Remove the rear bolts, pull down the pan, and allow as much fluid to drain into the container as possible.

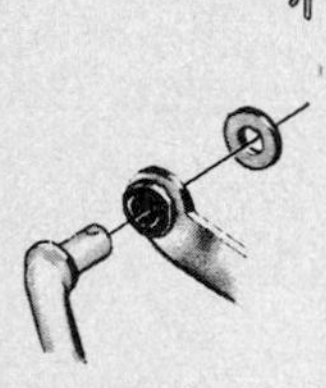

ADJUSTMENT OF MANUAL ROD

1. Set transmission outer shift lever in DRIVE position detent.
2. Loosen swivel nut. Hold manual rod up against DRIVE position stop.
3. Be sure outer shift lever is in DRIVE position detent, then tighten swivel nut.

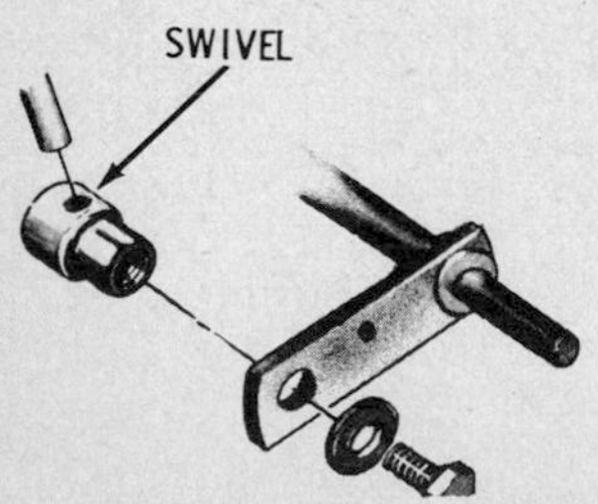

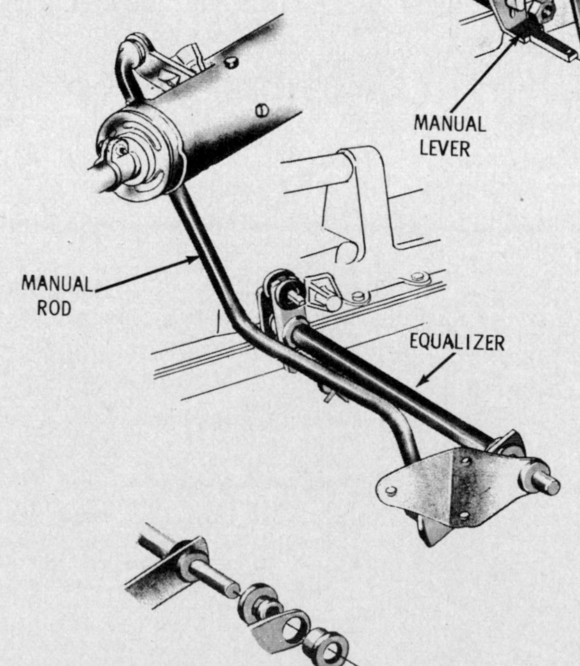

Column shift linkage adjustment for Jetaway transmission (© Oldsmobile Div, G.M. Corp)

4. Remove the rest of the bolts and lower the pan. Discard the old gasket.
5. Discard the fluid remaining in the pan. Clean the pan thoroughly with solvent and blow dry.
6. Remove the filter securing screw(s), filter, and gasket.
7. Install a new gasket and filter.
8. Install the oil pan with a new gasket. Tighten the pan securing bolts to 12 ft lbs.
9. Lower the car. Pour slightly less than the amount of fluid specified in the "Capacities" chart into the transmission through the dipstick tube.
10. Start the engine and run it at normal idle. Move the gear selector through all ranges. Place the selector in Park and apply the parking brake.

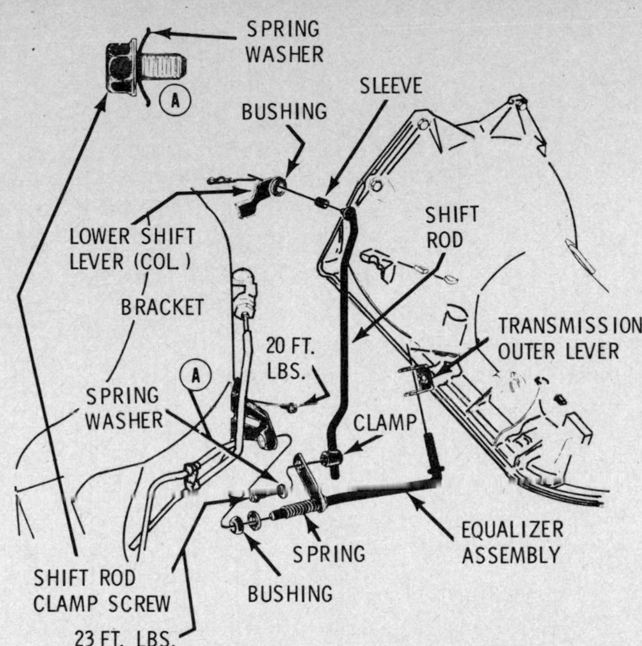

Column shift linkage adjustment—1971-76
(© Oldsmobile Div., GM Corp.)

SHIFT ROD ADJUSTMENT

1. WITH SHIFT ROD CLAMP SCREW LOOSENED, SET TRANSMISSION OUTER LEVER IN NEUTRAL POSITION.

2. HOLD UPPER SHIFT LEVER AGAINST NEUTRAL POSITION STOP IN UPPER STEERING COLUMN. (DO NOT RAISE LEVER.)

3. TIGHTEN SCREW IN CLAMP ON LOWER END OF SHIFT ROD TO SPECIFIED TORQUE.

4. CHECK OPERATION:

   A. WITH KEY IN "RUN" POSITION AND TRANSMISSION IN "REVERSE" BE SURE THAT KEY CANNOT BE REMOVED AND THAT STEERING WHEEL IS NOT LOCKED.

   B. WITH KEY IN "LOCK" POSITION AND SHIFT LEVER IN "PARK", BE SURE THAT KEY CAN BE REMOVED, THAT STEERING WHEEL IS LOCKED, AND THAT THE TRANSMISSION REMAINS IN PARK WHEN THE STEERING COLUMN IS LOCKED.

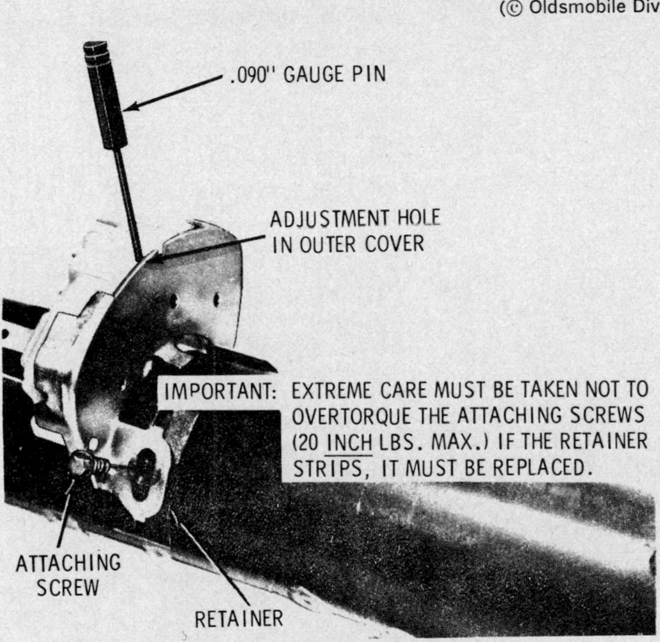

Neutral safety switch adjustment (© Oldsmobile Div, G.M. Corp)

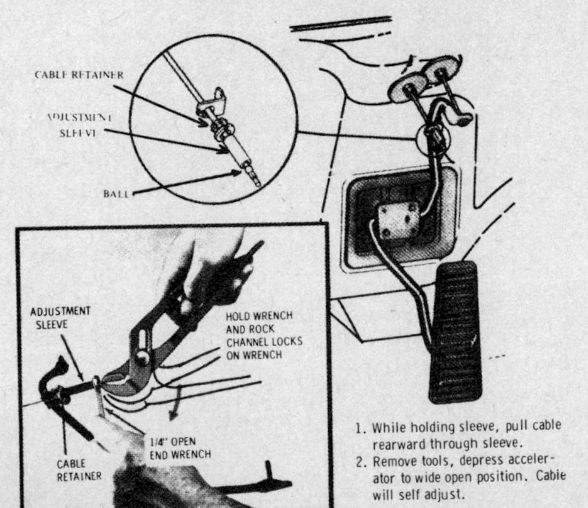

Downshift cable adjustment, Turbo Hydra-Matic 350—Cutlass V8
(© Oldsmobile Div., GM Corp.)

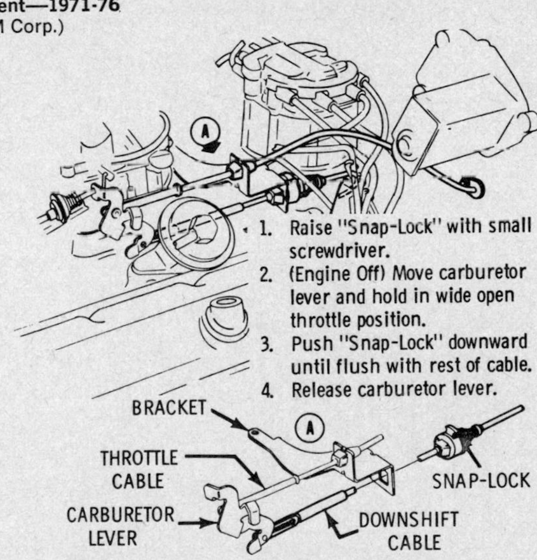

Downshift cable adjustment, Turbo Hydra-Matic 350—Omega V8
(© Oldsmobile Div., GM Corp.)

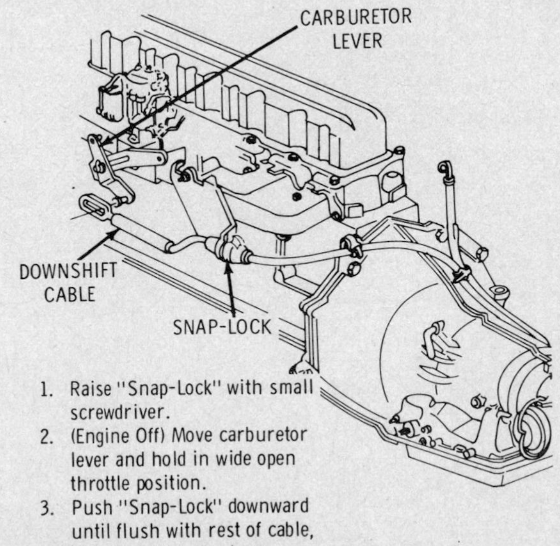

Downshift cable adjustment Turbo Hydra-Matic 350—Inline 6
(© Oldsmobile Div., GM Corp.)

11. Check the fluid level. Add fluid as necessary to bring the level between the two dimples on the dipstick or if there are no dimples, ¾ in. below "FULL," (transmission at room temperature).

Caution Overfilling the transmission will cause the fluid to foam.

U-JOINTS

Cross and bearing-type universals are used on all Oldsmobile models.

Driveshaft and Universal Joint Removal

1. Mark the companion flange and the driveshaft so they can be installed in the same position. Remove the four bolts that hold the rear universal filler blocks to the pinion shaft flange and pry the universal joint off the pinion flange, lowering the back end of the shaft to the floor.
2. Tape the bearing blocks to the universal joints so that they don't get lost or dirty.
3. The front end of the shaft can then be slid off the back of the transmission shaft and carried to the bench.
4. The bearings are held into the yokes by two lock plates, one on each side.
5. Take out the nut that holds the lock plate in position and lift off the lock plate. The bearing can then be driven from one side across to the other which will drive the opposite side bearing out. Once the opposite side bearing has been removed, drive on the cross, itself, to drive out the first bearing.
6. It is recommended, when reinstalling bearings, that an arbor press or a very heavy C-clamp be used, because driving on them distorts the outer race of the needle bearings.

Driveshaft Torque

U-bolts 16 ft. lbs. Center bearing to body 14 ft. lbs. Slip yoke nut 50-75 ft. lbs.

Constant Velocity Joint

This joint consists of two universal joints closely coupled with a coupling yoke. There is a centering ball socket between the two joints which maintains their relative position. On pre-1973 models the ball is integral with the shaft and, if damaged, the entire driveshaft must be replaced. On 1973-76 models the centering ball is a press-fit and can be replaced. The ball socket is integral with the flange yoke. The spring loaded ball seats are replaceable.

To disassemble the C.V. joint, first mark the relation of the flange yoke and driveshaft yoke, coupling ball support tube yoke. The cross bearing cups are pressed out in the usual manner, but they must be disassembled in the following sequence: rear of coupling yoke (2), differential flange yoke (2), front end of the coupling yoke (2) and driveshaft (2). Reassemble in the reverse of this order.

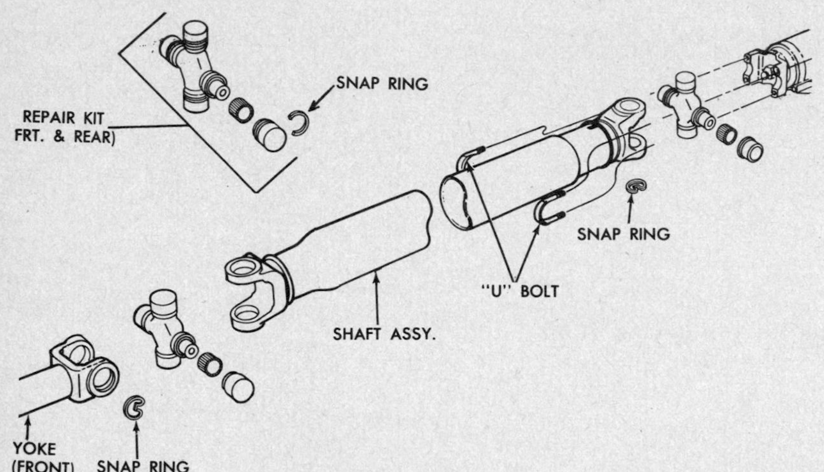

Typical driveshaft assembly
(© Oldsmobile Div, G.M. Corp)

JACKING, HOISTING

When supporting car on floor jack or floor stand, the car should be supported at the suspension points only. Under no condition should the car be supported at extreme ends of frame or side rail.

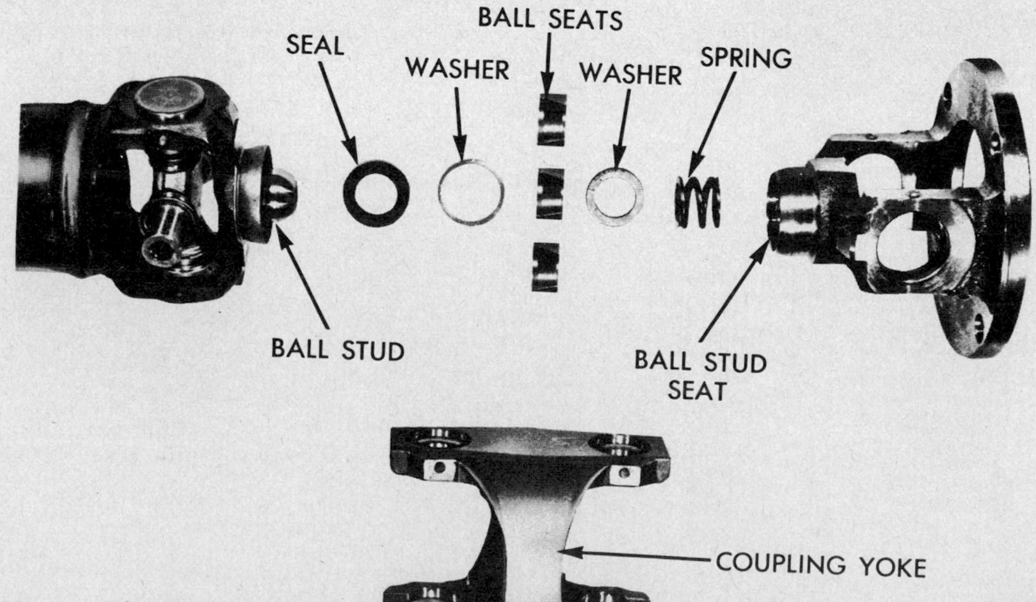

Constant velocity joint (© Oldsmobile Div, G.M. Corp)

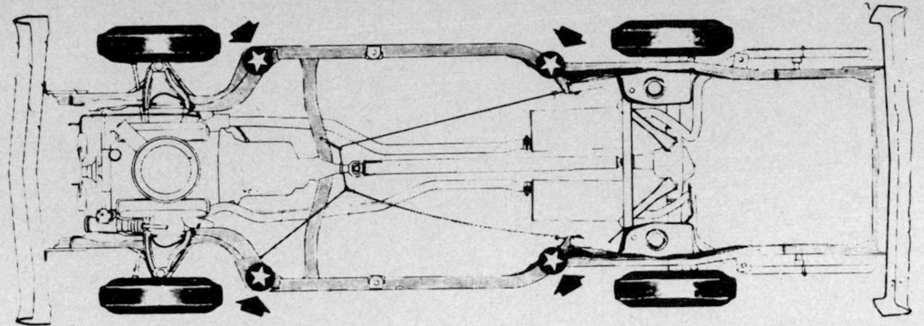
Hoist contact points—except Omega and Starfire
(© Oldsmobile Div, G.M. Corp)

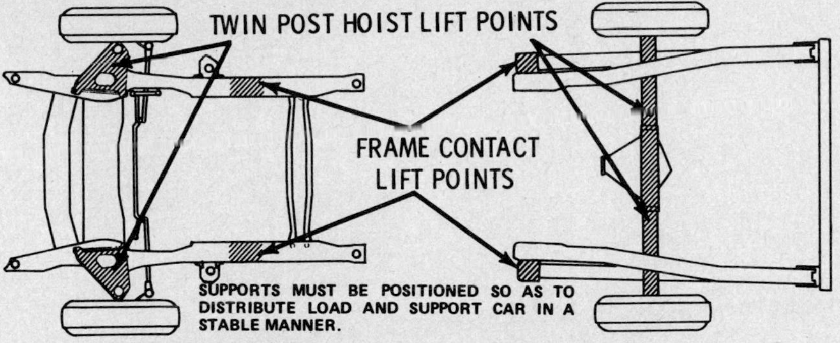

Omega hoisting points (© Oldsmobile Div, G.M. Corp)

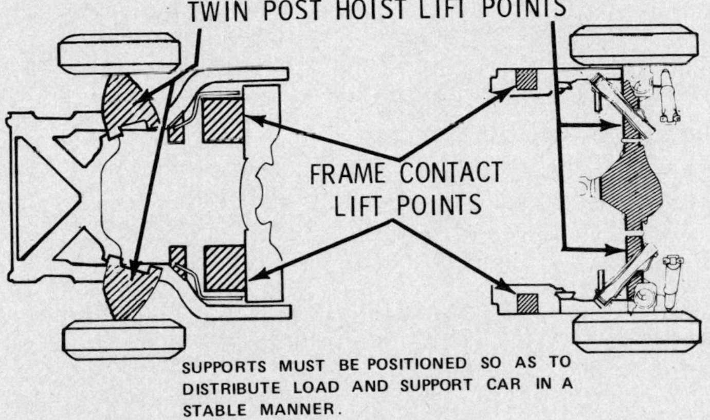

Starfire hoisting points
(© Oldsmobile Div., GM Corp.)

When using a frame contact lift on an Omega, place the contact pads on the front sub-frame just behind the center body mounts and on the rear leaf spring's front attachment bracket.

REAR AXLE

Axle, Shaft, Bearing, and Seal

Removal and Installation

These cars use two different types of drive axle, the C- and the non C-type. Axle shafts in the C-type are retained by C-shaped locks, which fit grooves at the inner end of the shaft. Axle shafts in the non C-type are retained by the brake backing plate, which is bolted to the axle housing. Bearings in the C-type axle consist of an outer race, bearing rollers and a roller cage, retained by snap-rings. The non C-type axle uses a unit roller bearing (inner race, rollers and outer race), which is pressed onto the shaft up to a shoulder. When servicing C or non C type axles, it is imperative to determine the axle type before attempting any service.

Non C-Type

Caution Before attempting any service to the drive axle or axle shafts, remove the axle carrier cover and visually determine if the axle shafts are retained by C-shaped locks at the inner end, or by the brake backing plate at the outer end. If the shafts are *not* retained by C-locks, proceed as follows.

Design allows for maximum axle shaft end-play of 0.022 in., which can be measured with a dial indicator. If end-play is found to be excessive, the bearing should be replaced. Shimming the bearing is not recommended as this ignores end-play of the bearing

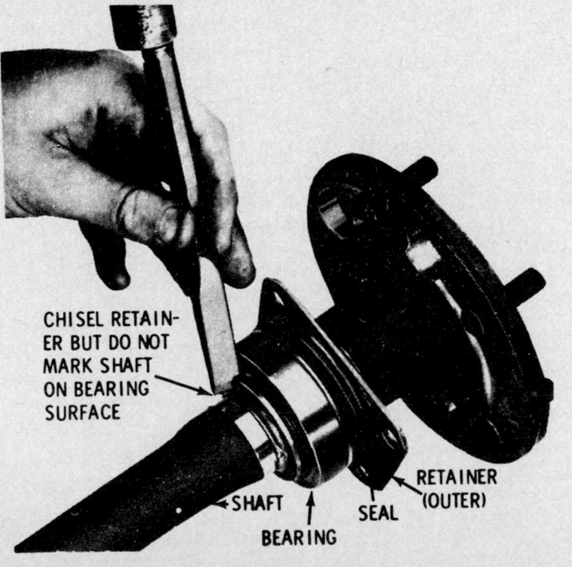

Cutting Bearing Retainer

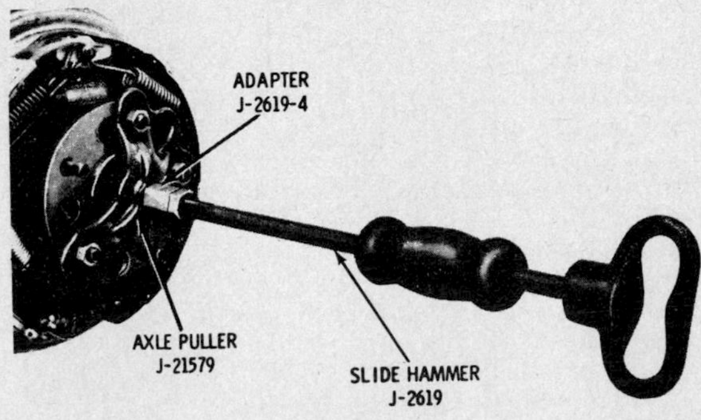

Removing Axle Shaft

itself and could result in improper seating of the bearing.

1. Remove the wheel, tire and brake drum.
2. Remove the nuts holding the retainer plate to the backing plate. Disconnect the brake line.
3. Remove the retainer and install nuts, fingertight, to prevent the brake backing plate from being dislodged.
4. Pull out the axle shaft and bearing assembly, using a slide hammer.
5. Using a chisel, nick the bearing retainer in three or four places. The retainer does not have to be cut, merely collapsed sufficiently, to allow the bearing retainer to be slid from the shaft.
6. Press off the bearing and install the new one by pressing it into position.
7. Press on the new retainer.

NOTE: do not attempt to press the bearing and the retainer on at the same time.

8. Assemble the shaft and bearing in the housing, being sure that the bearing is seated properly in the housing.
9. Install the retainer, drum, wheel and tire. Bleed the brakes.

C-Type

Caution Before attempting any service to the drive axle or axle shafts, remove the carrier cover and visually determine if the axle shaft(s) are retained by C-shaped locks at the inner ends or by a brake backing plate at the outer end. If they *are* retained by C-shaped locks, proceed as follows.

1. Raise the vehicle and remove the wheels.
2. The differential cover has already been removed (see Caution note above). Remove the differential pinion shaft lockscrew and the differential pinion shaft.
3. Push the flanged end of the axle shaft toward the center of the vehicle and remove the C-lock from the end of the shaft.
4. Remove the axle shaft from the housing, being careful not to damage the oil seal.
5. Remove the oil seal by inserting the button end of the axle shaft behind the steel case of the oil seal. Pry the seal loose from the bore.
6. Seat the legs of the bearing puller behind the bearing. Seat a washer against the bearing and hold it in place with a nut. Use a slide hammer to pull the bearing.
7. Pack the cavity between the seal lips with wheel bearing lubricant and lubricate a new wheel bearing with same.
8. Use a suitable driver and install the bearing until it bottoms against the tube. Install the oil seal.
9. Slide the axle shaft into place. Be sure that the splines on the shaft do not damage the oil seal. Make sure that the splines engage the differential side gear.
10. Install the axle shaft C-lock on the inner end of the axle shaft and push the shaft outward so that the C-lock seats in the differential side gear counterbore.
11. Position the differential pinion shaft through the case and pinions, aligning the hole in the case with the hole for the lockscrew.
12. Install the pinion shaft lockscrew.
13. Use a new gasket and install the carrier cover. Be sure that the gasket surfaces are clean before installing the gasket and cover.
14. Fill the axle with lubricant to the bottom of the filler hole.
15. Install the brake drum and wheels and lower the car. Check for leaks and road test the car.

FRONT SUSPENSION

Shock Absorber R & R —All Models

1. Remove the two bolts and lockwashers securing the shock to the lower control arm.
2. Remove the upper nut, retainer, and grommet from the shock.

NOTE: On Starfires, remove the access plug from the inner fender panel first.

3. To install, reverse the removal procedure.

Lower Ball Joint

Inspection

1969-73 Cutlass and F-85
1969-72 88 and 98

1. Jack up the car and place floor stands under the left and right control arms as near as possible to the lower ball joints. Make sure the car sits steadily on the floor stands.
2. Position a dial indicator so that its button contacts the inside lip of the wheel rim.
3. Place a 2 x 4 (about 6 in. tall) vertically between the lower control arm and the steering knuckle. Insert a pry bar between the wood and the steering knuckle nut and pry gently up and down. The dial indicator reading must not exceed .125 in. and there should be no deflection on the 1971-72 88 and 98 models. Repeat this procedure for the other side.
4. After completing this vertical check, remove the wood block and reposition the dial indicator button to contact the outer lip of the wheel rim.

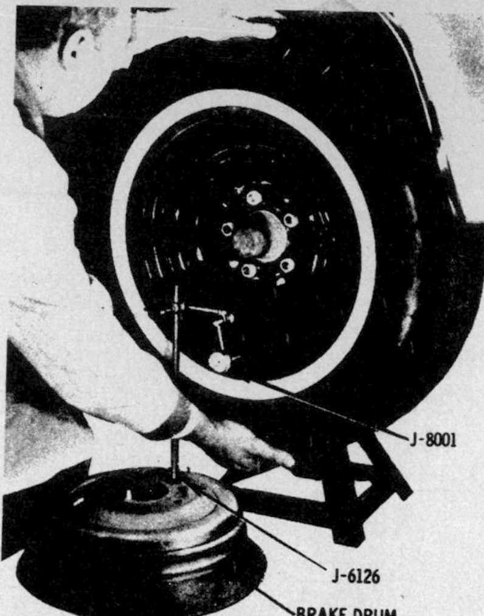

Ball joint horizontal check
(© Oldsmobile Div, G.M. Corp)

5. Push in on the top of the tire while pulling out on the bottom and observe the dial indicator reading. Reverse this push-pull procedure and check the reading. This procedure (horizontal check) enables you to check both upper and lower ball joints. The gauge reading should not exceed .125 in.
6. Do the same on the other side.

1973-74 Omega

NOTE: The lower ball joint used on the Omega is not internally preloaded but rather, is seated by the car's weight. Therefore, some looseness may be apparent when the lower control arm is raised with a jack; this looseness does not necessarily mean that the joint is defective or worn.

1. Use a jack placed underneath the lower control arm to support vehicle weight.
2. Measure the distance between the grease fitting and the threaded stud.
3. Raise the tire by means of a lever, to seat the ball stud, and measure the distance again.
4. If the difference between the two measurements is greater than 1/16 in., the ball joint is worn and should be replaced.
5. Shake the wheel and observe the end of the stud or the nut on the knuckle boss for *excessive* looseness. Replace any parts which are defective.

1973-74 88 and 98, 1974 Cutlass and All 1975-76 Models

These lower ball joints contain a visual wear indicator. The lower ball joint grease plug screws into the wear indicator which protrudes from the bottom of the ball joint housing. As long as the wear indicator extends out of the ball joint housing, the ball joint is not worn. If the tip of the wear indicator is parallel with, or recessed into the ball joint housing, the ball joint is defective.

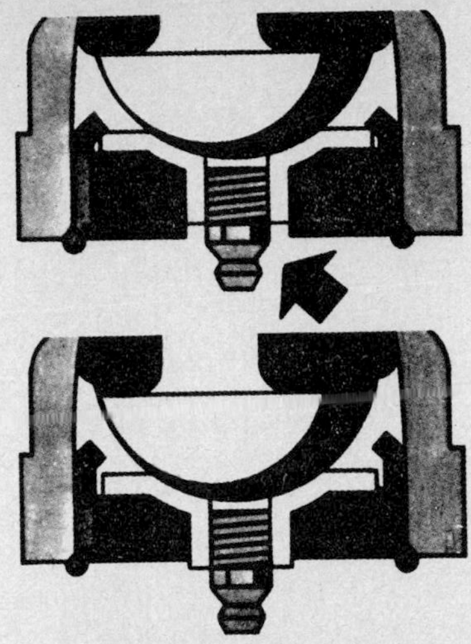

1973 and later Oldsmobile ball joint wear indicator

R & R

1. Raise car and support the frame with floor stands.
2. Remove the tire and wheel.
3. Place a floor jack under the control arm spring seat.

Caution Leave the jack under the spring seat during removal and installation, in order to keep the spring and control arm positioned.

4. Remove the cotter pin from the ball joint stud and, using an appropriate tool, separate the ball joint from the steering knuckle.
5. Raise the control arm to relieve tension and remove the stud nut.
6. If the backing plate blocks removal of the ball joint, loosen the backing plate bolts to obtain the necessary clearance.
7. Hold the brake assembly out of way by placing a wooden block between the frame and the upper control arm.
8. Using a screwdriver or chisel, remove the ball joint seal.
9. Using a suitable tool, remove the ball joint.
10. Press in a new ball joint until it bottoms on the lower control arm.

NOTE: On disc brake cars, make sure the grease purge on the seal faces away from the brakes.

11. On 1969-76 Cutlass, Omega, and F-85 models, install the ball joint stud into the steering knuckle, torque the nut to 40 ft lbs (1969), 70 ft lbs (1970-73) or 95 ft lbs (1974-76), and install the cotter pin.
12. On cars other than Cutlass and Omega models, reassemble the suspension and torque the ball joint stud nut to 70 ft lbs (1969-70) 90 ft lbs (1971-74) or to 105 ft lbs (1975-76). Install the cotter pin and bend it to the side of the nut. On the Starfire tighten the nut to 65 ft lbs.
13. If applicable, tighten the backing plate bolts.
14. Install the ball joint fitting and lube until grease appears at the seal.
15. Install the tire and wheel assembly.

Upper Ball Joint

Inspection

To inspect the upper ball joints, follow steps 1 and 4-6 of the "1969-73 Cutlass and F85/1969-72 88 and 98" lower ball joint inspection procedure.

R & R

1. Raise the front of car and place floor stands under the lower control arm between the spring seats and the ball joints.

Caution Leave the jack under the spring seat during removal and installation, in order to keep the spring and control arm positioned.

2. Remove the wheel and the speedometer cable (if so equipped) from the steering knuckle.
3. Remove the cotter pin from the upper ball joint stud and loosen the upper ball joint nut.
4. Using the appropriate tool (if available, use a ball joint remover tool), break the stud loose and remove the nut and pull stud out of knuckle. Support the steering knuckle to prevent damage to the brake line.
5. Using a 1/8 in. diameter drill bit, drill into each of the four rivet heads a depth of 1/4 in.
6. Drill off the rivet heads with a 1/2 in. diameter bit.
7. Punch out the rivets and remove the ball joint.
8. To install, place the new ball joint in the upper control arm and secure it with four bolts and nuts. Tighten the nuts to 8 ft lbs.
9. Connect the ball joint-to-steering knuckle. Torque the nut to 40 ft lbs minimum (1969-74) or to 70 ft lbs (1975-76). On Starfires, 65 ft lbs (min).

NOTE: When replacing ball joints, use only high-quality replacement parts and bolts and nuts specified to be strong enough to endure the stress.

10. Install the grease fitting and lubricate until grease appears at the seal.
11. Install the speedometer cable (if so equipped) and the wheel.

Upper Control Arm R & R

1969-70 F-85

1. Raise car and place stands under frame.
2. Remove tire and wheel.
3. Place floor jack under lower control arm spring seat.

Caution Leave the jack under the spring seat during removal and installation, in order to keep the spring and control arm positioned.

4. Remove ball joint stud from steering knuckle, by removing cotter pin and nut and with an appropriate tool, press joint loose from knuckle. For left-side arm removal, it may be necessary to move the steering gear out of the way. When installing a gear, torque bolts to 70 ft lbs.
5. Support hub assembly and remove upper arm by sliding shaft off end of bolts.

NOTE: mark or locate alignment shims for easier reassembly.

6. Attach arm assembly to frame using original shims. Torque to 55 ft lbs.
7. Install ball joint. Torque nut to 40 ft lbs (minimum). Install a grease fitting and lubricate.
8. Install hub, drum and wheel assembly and lower car to floor.

All Models Except 1969-70 F-85

1. Raise car and place stands under frame.
2. Remove tire and wheel.
3. Remove speedometer cable from knuckle where so equipped.
4. Place floor jack under lower control arm spring seat.

Caution Leave the jack under the spring seat during removal and installtion, in order to keep the spring and control arm positioned.

5. Remove ball joint stud from steering knuckle, by removing cotter pin and nut and with an appropriate tool, press joint loose from knuckle. Support hub assembly to prevent damage to the brake line.
6. Disconnect ground strap from control arm, if so equipped.
7. Loosen the pivot shaft-to-frame nuts and remove the alignment shims. Support hub assembly and remove upper arms by sliding shaft off end of bolts. On Starfires, remove the pivot bolts and remove the control arm from the car; there are no shims.

NOTE: mark or locate alignment shims for easier reassembly.

8. It is necessary to remove upper control arm attaching bolts to gain clearance to remove arm assembly. Tap bolt down with brass drift. Pry bolt up with box wrench. Using a suitable pry bar and block of wood, pry bolts from frame.
9. Remove control arm from car.
10. To reinstall, position bolts loosely in frame and install pivot shaft on bolts.

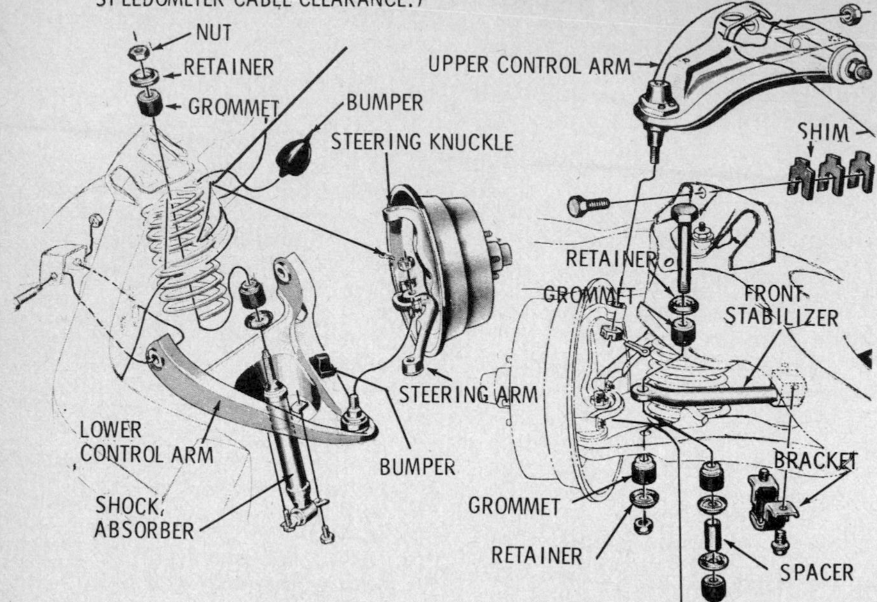

Front suspension—88 and 98 (© Oldsmobile Div, G.M. Corp)

UPPER BALL JOINT
OUTER BEARING ASSEMBLY
UPPER CONTROL ARM
HUB DUST CAP
BUSHING
SHAFT
CLAMPING RING
SEAL
SEAL
INNER BEARING ASSEMBLY
FRONT BRAKE ASSEMBLY
STEERING KNUCKLE
BUSHING
STEERING PLAIN ARM
LOWER ARM BUMPER ASSEMBLY
LOWER BALL JOINT
FRONT OF CAR
CONTROL ARM

Front suspension—F85 and Cutlass (Omega similar) (© Oldsmobile Div, G.M. Corp)

11. Install lock washers and nuts and with brass drift, drive attaching bolts into frame.
12. Install alignment shims (except Starfire) placing them in position from which they were removed. Torque nuts, 75 ft lbs (1969-71 except F-85) and 80 ft lbs for all 1972-76 models except 1972 Cutlass and F-85. Torque to 50 ft lbs for 1971-72 Cutlass and F-85 models. Torque to 65 ft lbs on Starfire.
13. Connect ball joint and torque to specifications.
14. Attach ground strap.
15. Install speedometer cable and wheel and tire and lower car to floor.

Lower Control Arm and/or Spring R & R

1. Raise front of car and support by stands under frame.
2. Remove tire and wheel.
3. Disconnect stabilizer link from lower arm, if so equipped.
4. Remove shock absorber.
5. Place floor jack under lower arm, between spring seat and ball joint. Using a spring compressor, compress spring.
6. Disconnect lower control arm ball joint from knuckle.
7. Slowly lower floor jack until spring is fully extended and remove spring.
8. To reinstall, tape insulator to top of spring.
9. While holding spring and insulator against pilot in front cross bar, tilt spring so it will pivot in lower arm. Rotate spring so bottom coil will index with edge of hole in arm spring seat. Spring should not cover any portion of hole.
10. With floor jack positioned between seat and ball joint, raise arm until ball joint is tight in knuckle. Install ball joint nut and tighten to 105 ft lbs, except for Omega, which should be tight-

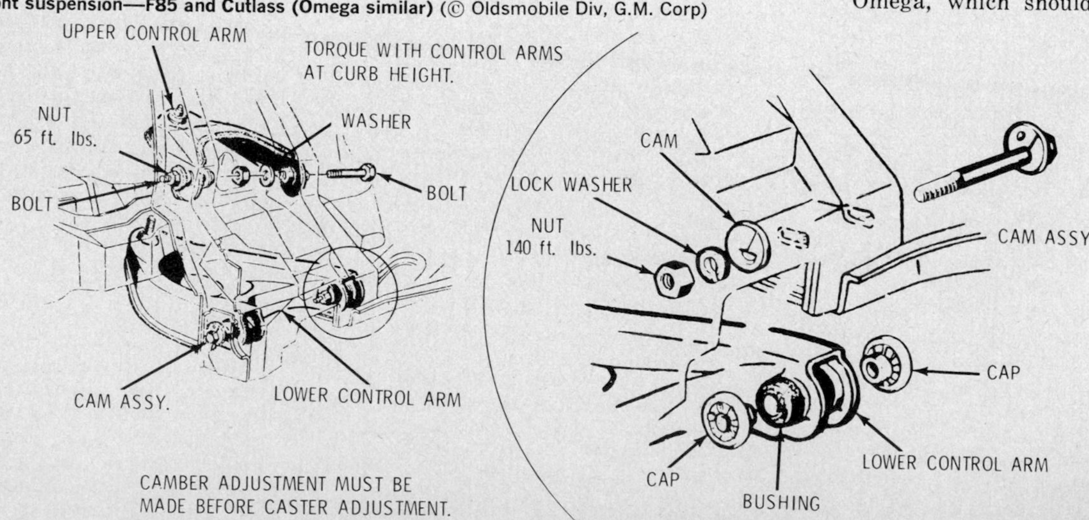

Starfire front suspension (© Oldsmobile Div., GM Corp.)

ened to 85 ft lbs. Torque to 65 ft lbs on Starfire.

11. Install shock absorber.
12. Connect stabilizer link.
13. Install wheel and lower car.

Wheel Bearing Adjustment

1. Tighten the adjusting nut to 30 ft lbs.
2. Back off on the nut ½ of a turn.
3. Finger-tighten the nut and install the cotter pin or the retaining ring.

NOTE: If the retaining ring or cotter pin cannot be installed, back off on the nut until the tabs on the clip align with the serrations on the nut. Do not back off on the nut more than 1/24 of a turn.

4. Once adjusted, the front wheel bearings should have 0.001-0.008 in. of end-play.

REAR SUSPENSION

Shock Absorber Replacement

All—Except Omega and Starfire

To replace the rear shock absorber, first raise the car and support the rear axle to prevent stretching of the brake hose. Then remove the nut from the lower end of the shock and tap the shock free from the bracket. To disconnect the shock at the top, remove the bolt or bolts and remove the shock.

NOTE: on extended station wagons, a retainer and grommet will be removed with the nut at the top.

Omega and Starfire

1. Raise the vehicle and support the rear axle housing.
2. Remove the lower shock mounting bolt from the shock absorber eye.
3. Unfasten the upper mounting bracket bolts and withdraw the shock.

Intallation is performed in the reverse order of removal, except that the upper attaching bolts should remain loose while the lower (eye) bolt is being tightened.

Upper bolts and nuts—22 ft lbs
Lower stud nut—50 ft lbs

Coil Spring Replacement

1. Disconnect the shock absorber link and raise the car enough to take the pressure off the coil spring and, reaching down through the coil spring, remove the bolt that holds the bottom of the spring to the insulating pad on the rear axle.
2. Working through the coil spring upward, take out the upper bolt that holds the spring to the frame at the top.

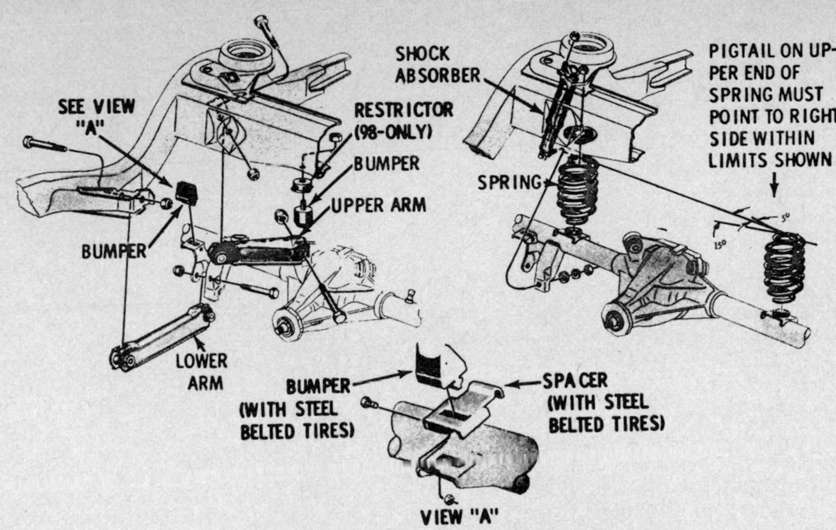

Coil spring rear suspension—except Starfire
(© Oldsmobile Div., GM Corp.)

3. If the car has been raised sufficiently, the spring can be lifted out.

Leaf Spring Replacement

88 Wagon

1. Lift the rear of the car by the axle housing and support the car on the floor stands.
2. Loosen the tailpipe and resonator if you are removing the right-side spring.
3. Remove the lower shock absorber nut and move the shock out of the way.
4. Relax the springs by lowering the lift or jack. Leave the jack under the housing for support.
5. Remove the bolts and shackles from the rear of the spring.
6. Remove the U-bolt attaching nuts.
7. Remove ONLY the nut from the front spring attachment and, while holding the spring up, remove the bolt from the front of the spring and remove the spring.
8. Remove the insulators from the spring.
9. To install, reverse the removal procedure.

NOTE: When making rear suspension repairs, replace all bolts and nuts with the specified replacement bolts.

Omega

1. Raise the rear of the car on stands.
2. Support the rear axle to take its weight off the springs.

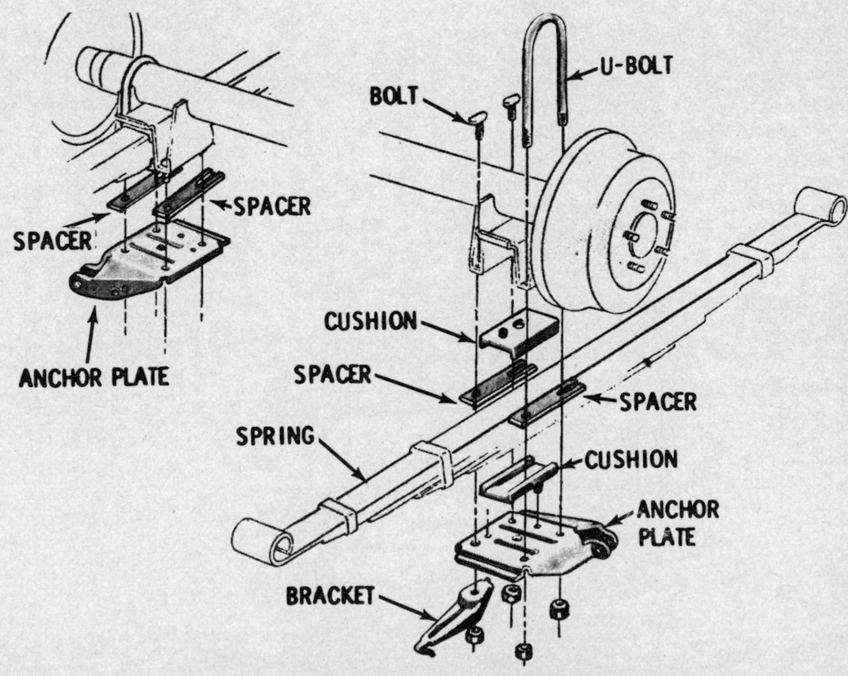

Omega leaf spring rear suspension—Custom Cruiser similar
(© Oldsmobile Div, G.M. Corp)

3. Disconnect the bottom of the shock absorber.
4. Loosen the front spring eye bolt.
5. Unbolt the spring front bracket from the underbody.
6. Lower the axle slightly and remove the front bracket from the spring.
7. Pry the parking brake cable out of its retainer bracket on the axle spring mounting plate.
8. Unbolt the spring from the axle.
9. Remove the spring plate and cushion between the axle and the spring.
10. Remove the upper bolt from the rear spring shackle. Lower the spring and remove the bottom bolt.
11. On installation, attach the front bracket to the spring eye. The head of the bolt should be toward the center of the car.
12. Assemble the shackle loosely to the rear spring eye.
13. Raise the rear end of spring and install the upper shackle bolt loosely, making sure that the parking brake cable goes under the spring.
14. Raise the front end of the spring and loosely attach the front bracket to the underbody. Make sure that the bracket tab goes into its slot.
15. Make sure that the upper and lower spring cushions are aligned properly. The upper one has locating ribs and the lower one, a locating dowel.
16. Install the spring lower mounting plate over the locating dowel and loosely install the nuts. Don't forget the parking brake cable bracket.
17. Attach the bottom of the shock absorber.
18. Attach the parking brake cable to the bracket on the lower spring plate.
19. Let the vehicle weight down on the springs. Tighten all the bolts. Torques are: rear shackle bolts —40-60 ft lbs, front bracket screws—25-35 ft lbs, front eye bolt—65-80 ft lbs, and axle bolts —35-50 ft lbs.

BRAKES

Information on brake adjustments, lining replacement, bleeding procedure, master and wheel cylinder overhaul is in the Unit Repair Section.

Information on power brakes is in the Unit Repair Section.

Parking Brake Cable Adjustment

1969-71

1. Release parking brake. Check for proper pedal clearance.
2. Adjust rear cables by tightening equalizer adjusting nut to obtain heavy drag at rear brakes.
3. Loosen equalizer adjusting nut seven full turns. Tighten locknut.

A brake pad with a warning indicator that squeals when the pad is worn to service limits is used on all 1974 and later models with disc brakes

1972-76—except Starfire

1. Depress the parking brake pedal exactly three clicks (two on Omega).
2. Loosen the nut at the rear of the equalizer adjusting nut. Then tighten the adjusting nut until the rear wheels can barely be turned backward (using two hands) but lock up when moved forward. Tighten the nut against the adjusting nut.
3. With the parking brake disengaged the rear wheels should turn freely in either direction with *no brake drag.*

Starfire

1. Raise and support the rear of the car.
2. Apply the parking brake one notch from the fully released position.
3. Loosen the adjusting locknut and tighten the adjusting nut until a slight drag is felt when the rear wheels are rotated.
4. Tighten the locknut securely.
5. The rear wheels should rotate freely when the parking brake is fully released.
6. Lower the vehicle.

Master Cylinder R & R

NOTE: Be sure that the area where the master cylinder is mounted is clean, before beginning removal.

1. Disconnect and cap or plug hydraulic lines.
2. If there is no power booster unit, remove the pushrod - to - pedal clevis pin.
3. Remove the attaching bolts and master cylinder.
4. Install in the reverse order of removal. Fill with fluid and bleed.

Power Brake Unit

The master cylinder and power booster are removed as a unit. Disconnect vacuum and hydraulic lines. Disconnect the pushrod from the brake pedal. Remove the vacuum unit mounting stud nuts and remove the assembly. Install in the reverse order of removal, tightening the mounting nuts to 28 ft. lbs. Fill the master cylinder reservoir with fluid.

Warning Switch

Whenever there is a significant difference in pressure between the front disc or drum and rear drum systems, a piston in the combination valve activates the warning light switch, thus indicating a failure in one of the hydraulic systems. In the event of combination valve malfunction, no attempt should be made to repair the valve. The complete valve assembly must be replaced.

NOTE: Bleed the hydraulic system after switch replacement.

STEERING

Horn and Steering Wheel R & R

Round center horn caps are removed by prying out. The horn pad on deluxe steering wheels is removed by either pulling down and out or by removing screws from underneath. Disconnect the battery when working on the horn.

Extreme caution must be exercised when removing the steering wheel: the energy absorbing column is held rigid by plastic fasteners which easily shear or loosen when abnormal pressure is applied. Use a steering wheel pulling tool. Carefully torque steering wheel retaining nut to 35 ft. lbs. when installing.

Special Procedure for Cars with A.C.R.S. (Air Bags)

Some 1974 and later models have an air cushion, or air bag, restraint system. One of the elements of this complex system is an air cushion module in the top of the steering wheel. The steering wheel can be removed in the manner described in this section after the module has been removed.

To remove the module:

1. Turn the ignition lock to the LOCK position.
2. Disconnect the battery ground cable and tape the end to prevent any possibility of a complete circuit.
3. Remove the 4 module-to-steering wheel screws. A special tool is available to do this.
4. Lift up the module and disconnect the horn wire.
5. Disconnect the module wire connector. A special tool is available to do this, too.

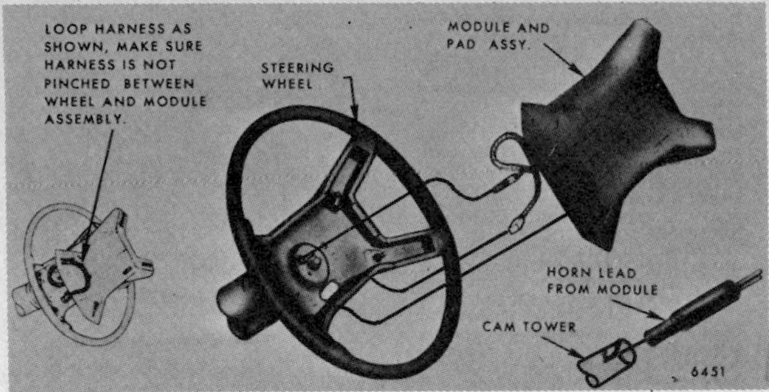

Steering wheel and module assembly—cars with air bags
(© G.M. Corp)

WARNING: The driver air cushion module should always be carried with the vinyl cover away from all parts of one's body and should always be laid on a flat surface with the vinyl side up. This is necessary so that a free space is provided to allow the air cushion to expand in case of accidental deployment.

Do not attempt to repair any portion of the module. The module must be serviced as a unit. Attempting repairs such as soldering wires, changing covers, etc. may cause accidental inflation or impair operation of the driver module and cause serious injury.

Do not dispose of a module in any way. The highly inflammable material in the module can cause serious burns if ignited. Modules must be exchanged at an authorized dealer's parts department.

To install the module:

6. Hold the module with the emblem in the lower right corner.
7. Loop the air cushion harness clockwise from the 11 o'clock position to the 6 o'clock position.
8. Install the module connector by pushing it onto the column circuit firmly. Check that it is fully seated.
9. Install the horn wire.
10. Position the module, making sure that the wiring is still in place, and install the 4 screws. Torque them to 40 in. lbs.
11. Reconnect the battery ground cable.
12. Turn the ignition lock to any position other than LOCK and check that the restraint indicator light operates correctly.

Turn Signal Switch Replacement Except Tilt and Telescopic Column

1. Disconnect the battery.
2. Remove the steering wheel.
3. Remove the cover from the shaft. Plastic keepers under the cover are not necessary for installation.
4. Depress the lockplate and remove the snap-ring from the shaft with an appropriate tool.
5. Remove the lockplate and canceling cam.
6. Remove the upper bearing preload spring.
7. Remove the turn signal lever.
8. Remove the four-way flasher knob.
9. Remove the three screws from the switch.
10. Disconnect the turn signal connector from the wiring harness.

NOTE: On 1975-76 models, it will be necessary to perform steps 10 through 13 of the "Turn Signal Switch Replacement/Tilt and Telescope Column," before proceeding with the next step.

11. Tape the turn signal wires at the connector and carefully remove the turn signal switch, wiring, and protector from the column as a unit.
12. To install, reverse the removal procedure using a new shaft snap-ring. To aid in installation of the snap-ring, use the lockplate compressing tool used during the removal procedure. When replacing screws (especially cover screws), make sure they are of the same size.

Turn Signal Switch Replacement Tilt and Telescopic Column

1. Disconnect negative battery cable.
2. Remove the steering wheel.
3. Remove the screws and lift the cover from the shaft. Plastic keepers are not necessary for installation.
4. Compress the lockplate with a suitable tool and pry the wire snap-ring from shaft.
5. Remove the lockplate and cancelling cam.
6. Remove the upper bearing preload spring.
7. Remove the turn signal lever and the four-way flasher knob.
8. Lift up on the tilt lever and position the housing in its central position.
9. Remove the switch attaching screws.
10. Remove the lower trim cap from the instrument panel and disconnect the turn signal connector from the harness.
11. Remove the four bolts securing the bracket assembly to the jacket.
12. On cars with automatic transmissions, loosen the screw holding the shift indicator needle and disconnect the clip from the link.
13. Remove the two nuts from the column support bracket while holding the column in position. Remove the bracket assembly and wire protector from the wiring, then loosely install the bracket-to-support column.
14. Tape the turn signal wires at the connector to keep them flat and parallel.
15. Carefully remove the turn signal switch and wiring from the column.
16. To install, reverse the removal procedure, making sure that screws of the same size are used.

1974 and Later Models with A.C.R.S. (Air Bags)

Follow the procedure for removing the steering wheel and air cushion module which appears previously under "Horn and Steering Wheel R & R, Special Procedure for Cars with A.C.R.S."

1. Remove the 3 screws from the retainer and cover. Carefully lift the cover and retainer from the column.
2. Carefully insert a screwdriver blade into the locking tab at the side and lift the slip-ring from the column.
3. Now proceed with Steps 3-12 of the "Turn Signal Switch Replacement Except Tilt and Telescopic Column" procedure.
4. To replace the slip-ring, align the slip-ring locating tab with the slot in the bowl and push the slip-ring into position. Make sure that all 3 locking tabs are securely positioned.
5. Install the cover and retainer, aligning the cover over the locating tab. Torque the screws to 15 in. lbs.

Steering Linkage

On all models two short tie-rods are attached to either end of a central relay rod. The pitman shaft has a vertical axis and the pitman arm rotates through a horizontal plane. The tie-rods have ball studs at each end and have an adjustable middle section which is secured with clamps.

Use a puller to remove the pitman arm from the pitman shaft. When assembling, install the pitman arm with the front wheels in the straight-ahead position and the steering wheel centered. Tighten the pitman arm retaining nut to 180 ft lbs. (1969-74); 210 ft lbs (1975-76 except Starfire; 105 ft lbs (1975-76 Starfire manual) or to 160 ft lbs (1975-76 Starfire P/S).

Whenever the tie-rod end is assembled to the tie-rod, make sure that an equal number of threads are exposed at each end of the tie rod sleeve. Tighten tie-rod clamp bolts to 19-24 ft. lbs. When disconnecting a linkage joint, never pry a wedge between the joint and the attached part. Always use a puller. When removing a tie-rod from a steering arm, loosen the ball stud nut, then tap the end of the steering arm with a hammer to free the tie-rod. Always use new seals when reassembling. Tighten tie-rod joint nuts to 45 ft. lbs.

Toe-in and steering wheel spoke alignment is obtained by turning the adjusting sleeves on the tie-rods which in turn lengthen or shorten the tie-rod assemblies.

Power Steering Pump Removal

Remove and cap the two hoses that run through the pump, loosen the clamp bolts so that the pump can be slid along its adjusting slot and take the belt off. Remove the three bolts that hold the pump bracket to the cylinder heads and lift off the pump.

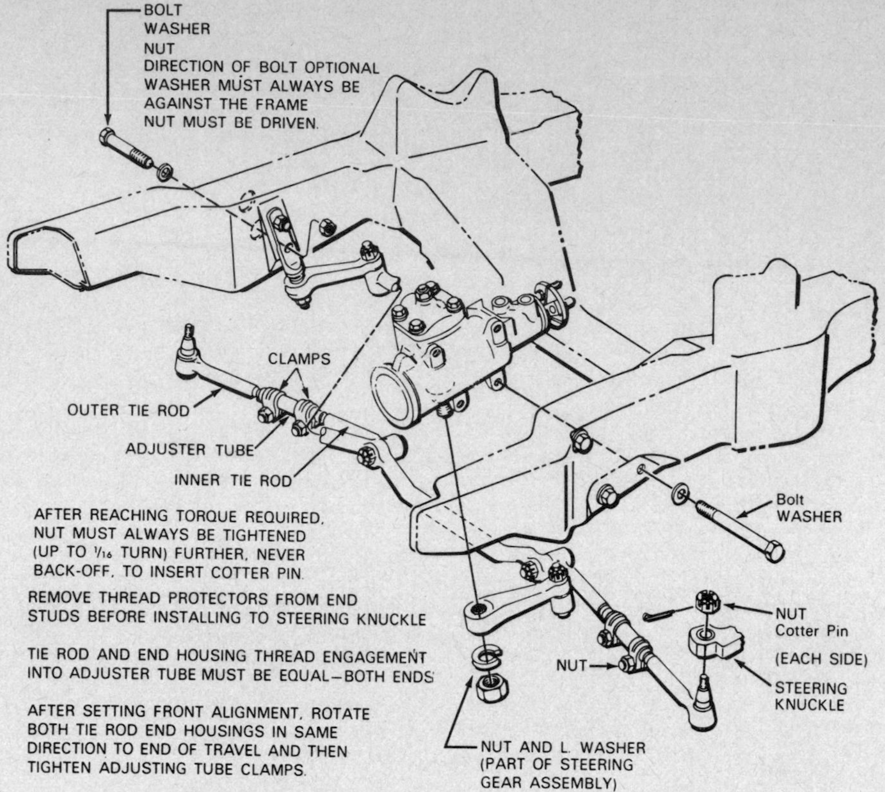

Steering linkage—all models similar (© Oldsmobile Div., GM Corp.)

INSTRUMENT PANEL

Ignition Switch and/or Lock Cylinder Replacement

Ignition Switch

1. Disconnect negative battery cable.
2. Place ignition switch in "ACC" position (1969), "RUN" position (1970) or "OFF-UNLOCKED" (1971-76)
3. Remove toe pan cover (if applicable) and loosen toe clamp bolts.
4. Remove lower instrument panel trim and toe pan trim panel.
5. Remove automatic transmission shift indicator needle.
6. Remove steering column dash bracket and let steering wheel rest on the driver's seat.
7. Remove two switch attaching screws and lift switch off actuator rod.
8. Disconnect wiring.
9. To install, check that lock cylinder is still in "ACC" (1969), "RUN" (1970) or "OFF-UNLOCKED" (1971-76) position and move sliding portion of switch until switch hole is positioned as illustrated. Hold the switch in this position with a 0.090 in. pin as illustrated.
10. Connect the wiring to the switch.
11. Position switch over actuator rod, install attaching screws (tighten to 3 ft. lbs.) and remove the 0.090 in. pin.
12. Reverse Steps 1 through 6 to complete installation.

Lock Cylinder

1. Disconnect the negative battery cable.
2. Remove the steering wheel. See the special procedure for cars equipped with air bags.

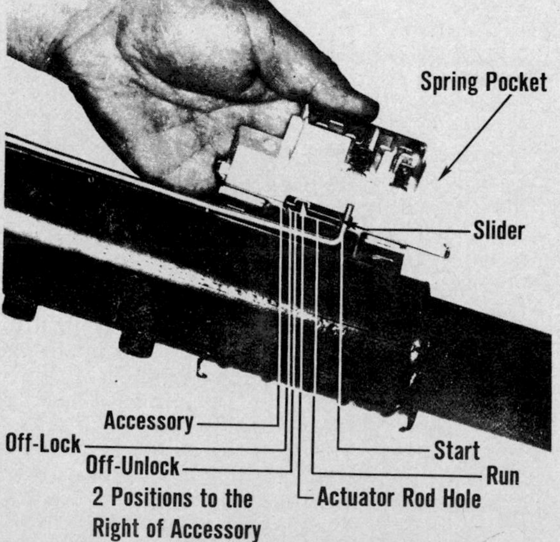

Ignition switch in "Off-Unlocked" position—1971-76
(© Oldsmobile Div, G.M. Corp)

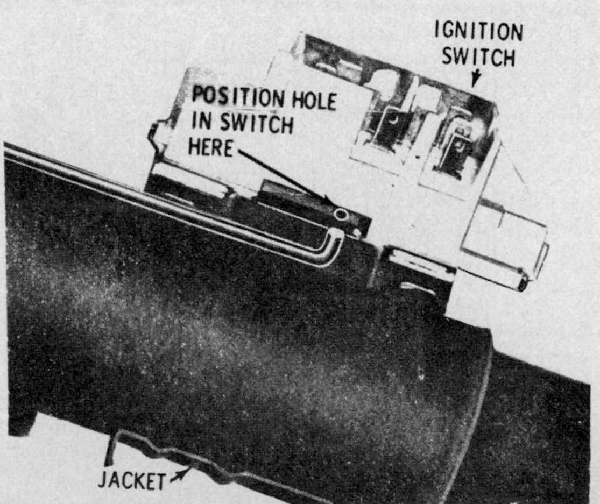

Ignition switch in "RUN" position—1970
(© Oldsmobile Div, G.M. Corp)

3. On models equipped with a tilt and travel steering column, pry up the three tabs on the plastic lock cover.

NOTE: On models with air bags, see the turn signal removal procedure for slip-ring removal.

4. On models with a standard or tilt column remove the three screws that attach the lock cover and remove it. The plastic keepers on the underside of the cover can be discarded after the cover is removed.
5. Depress the steering wheel lock plate and pry the snap-ring from the steering shaft.
6. Remove the lock plate, cancelling cam, and upper bearing spring.
7. Position the turn signal lever in the right turn position and unscrew the turn signal lever.
8. Push the hazard warning knob in and unscrew the knob.
9. Remove the turn signal switch retaining screws and pull the switch up out of the way.
10. On 1969-70 models, insert the ignition key into the cylinder and turn it to the "Acc" position. On 1971-76 models, turn the key to the "Run" position.
11. Insert a long thin screwdriver into the slot in the upper bearing housing and depress the release tab while pulling the cylinder from the column.
12. Insert the new lock cylinder into the column after aligning the key on the cylinder with the keyway in the column.
13. Press inward on the cylinder while turning it clockwise.
14. Reverse the above procedure to complete installation.

Headlight Switch Replacement

1969-76 F-85/Cutlass
1973-76 Omega
1969-74 88 and 98

1. Disconnect the battery.
2. On 1971-74 88 and 98 models and 1973-76 Cutlass models remove the left-hand control panel from the dash.
3. Pull the switch to "ON" position, then depress the spring-loaded button on the switch body and pull knob out of the switch.
4. Remove the escutcheon.
5. Remove the switch from behind the panel and disconnect the multiple connector.
6. Install in the reverse order of the above procedure.

1975-76 Starfire

1. Disconnect the negative (—) battery lead.
2. Remove the left-hand bottom air conditioning outlet.
3. Working underneath the dash, depress the switch shaft retainer. Withdraw the shaft and knob assembly.
4. Unfasten the switch bezel nut and remove the switch.
5. Disconnect the switch multiconnector by prying it with a small screwdriver at the side of the switch.

Installation is the reverse of removal.

1974-76 88 and 98

1. Disconnect the negative (—) battery lead.
2. Remove the heater/AC control assembly from the panel, but don't disconnect its leads and vacuum lines.
3. Remove the bezel nut from the switch.
4. Pull the switch out through the heater/AC control opening.
5. Disconnect the wiring and remove the switch.

Installation is the reverse of removal.

WINDSHIELD WIPERS

Motor R & R

1969 F-85

1. Disconnect the wiring and the windshield washer hoses.
2. Remove the wiper blade and arm assembly attached to the motor.
3. Remove the attaching screws.
4. Lift the left rear edge of the vent screen and loosen the two nuts securing the linkage to the crankarm.
5. Remove the motor.
6. Reverse the above steps to install. Make sure the wiper arm assemblies are installed properly.

1969-70 Oldsmobile

1. Disconnect the wiring and the washer hoses.
2. Remove the three motor attaching screws and the access hole plug.
3. Loosen the two linkage crankarm attaching nuts through the access hole.
4. Hold the motor with one hand and, with the other hand, move the wiper arm halfway through its travel. This will center the crankarm in the hole in the dash.
5. Remove the motor, guiding the crankarm through the hole.
6. Reverse the above steps to install.

1970 F-85/Cutlass

1. Remove the three cowl screen attaching screws from the left side of the cowl screen and lift the screen.
2. Loosen the two nuts securing the linkage crankarm to the pivot arm through the cowl opening.
3. Disconnect the wiring and washer hoses.
4. Remove the three motor securing screws and, guiding the crankarm through the hole in the dash, remove the motor.
5. Reverse the above steps to install.

1971-76—All Models

1. Remove the cowl screen or grille.
2. Loosen the linkage drive link-to-crankarm attaching nuts, and remove the link from the arm.
3. Disconnect the wiring and washer hoses.
4. Remove the three motor attaching screws, guide the crankarm through the hole in the dash, and remove the motor.
5. Reverse the above steps to install.

RADIO

Removal and Installation

1969-72 F-85 and Cutlass
1969-70 88 and 98
1973-76 Omega

1. Disconnect battery.
2. If equipped with air conditioning, remove cool air manifold.
3. Remove defroster manifold if necessary.
4. Remove radio knobs, washers or rear speaker control.
5. Remove radio attaching nuts and escutcheons.
6. Disconnect all wiring and antenna lead-in.
7. Remove radio support bracket attaching screw(s), if applicable.
8. Remove radio from rear of instrument panel.
9. Install by reversing removal procedure.

1971-73 88 and 98

1. Disconnect the negative battery cable.
2. Unfasten the nut which secures the radio to its mounting brace.
3. Detach the speaker and antenna leads from the radio.
4. Unfasten the radio ground strap screw.
5. Use a thin-bladed screwdriver to carefully pry out the map and flood light lens assembly.
6. Unfasten the four right-hand control panel securing screws. Withdraw the control panel from the dash.
7. Turn the radio knobs until the notch at the base of the knob appears. Insert a pointed object under the retainer and release it. Pull the knobs off the shafts.
8. Remove the inside knobs and nuts from the shafts.
9. Unfasten the nut which secures the radio attaching brace to the control panel.

Installation is the reverse of removal.

1973-76 Cutlass

1. Detach the cable from the negative battery terminal.
2. Remove the four screws which secure the steering column and separate it from the instrument panel.
3. Pull the knobs off the radio.
4. Unfasten the nuts from the front of the radio.
5. Remove its four retaining screws and then gently pull the right-hand control panel up and out.
6. Unfasten the radio support bracket screw.
7. Remove the four ashtray housing screws and take the housing off the tie-bar.
8. Disconnect the antenna and speaker wiring from the radio.
9. Withdraw the radio from behind the control panel.

Installation is the reverse of removal.

1974-76 88 and 98

1. Disconnect the negative (−) cable from the battery.
2. Detach the wiring harness and antenna lead from the radio.
3. Unfasten the throttle cable and remove the accelerator linkage, complete with support bracket.
4. Remove the screw which secures the radio bracket to the tie-bar.
5. Pull the knobs off the shafts and unfasten the securing nuts from the shafts.
6. Lower the radio and remove it from behind the dash panel.

Installation is the reverse of removal.

1975-76 Starfire

1. Disconnect the battery.
2. Remove the clock set knob.
3. Remove the screws securing the instrument cluster bezel and remove the bezel.
4. Remove the glove compartment.
5. Remove the screws securing the instrument panel crash pad and remove the pad.
6. Pull the knobs off the radio shafts and unfasten the shaft retaining nuts.
7. Remove the two bottom screws from the radio bracket.
8. On models with A/C, remove the left lap cooler and duct.
9. Remove the two steering column bracket nuts and lower the column so that it rests on the driver's seat. Remove the screw which secures the cluster to the carrier, from the steering column bracket.
10. Unfasten the instrument cluster screws, wiring, speedometer cable, and pull the cluster out toward the driver's seat.
11. Remove the lower radio support-to-dash screw.
12. Working through the cluster opening, remove the radio leads and antenna cable.
13. Remove the radio.

Installation is the reverse of removal.

HEATER

Blower Motor and Heater Core R & R For Cars without Air Conditioning

1969 Except F-85, Cutlass

To remove the heater case and core, remove the glove box. Disconnect the wiring, vacuum lines and defroster hoses from the heater case. Drain the radiator enough so that the heater hoses and gasket may be removed. Remove the blower assembly attaching screws and nuts and, from inside the car, remove the heater case. Remove the heater core from the case. Install in the reverse order of the above procedure.

To remove the blower assembly, disconnect the blower feed wire. To reach the upper sheet metal screw, construct a 3 foot length of ³⁄₈ drive extensions and a 7/16 socket, then feed the tool through the opening between the fender filler and the fender forward of the right front wheel. Use sealing compound to hold the screw when removing or installing. Remove the remaining attaching nuts and screws. Push the heater case studs back until the studs do not protrude through the dash. Remove the fender to dash panel attaching screw just over the blower assembly case and remove the two bolts from the bottom rear of the fender. Keep track of the shims. Push down on the inner fender panel and remove the blower assembly. The blower motor may be removed from the blower assembly at this point. Install in reverse order of the removal procedure.

1970 88 and 98
1973-76 Omega

To remove the heater case and core, remove the glove box. Disconnect the wiring, vacuum lines and defroster hoses from the heater case. Drain the radiator enough so that the heater hoses can be disconnected. Remove the blower assembly attaching screws and remove the heater case from inside the car. Remove the heater core from the case. Install in the reverse of the above procedure.

Blower and air inlet attachment
(© Oldsmobile Div, G.M. Corp)

To remove the blower motor, disconnect the blower feed wire. Remove the fender filler panel bolts and move the filler panel forward and inward. Remove the blower assembly attaching nuts and screws. Push the heater case studs back so that they do not protrude through the dash. Push down on the inner fender panel and remove the blower assembly. Remove the blower motor attaching screws and remove the blower. When installing, use a bead of sealer around the heater inlet.

1971-76 88 and 98

To remove the heater case and core, disconnect the battery and remove the four heater case to dash panel attaching nuts. Drain the radiator enough so that the heater hoses may be disconnected. Disconnect the control cables and vacuum hose. Remove the defroster duct to case attaching screw and the right half of the right hand dash trim panel. Remove the heater case from the car. The heater core may now be removed from the case. Install in reverse order of removal.

To remove the blower motor, disconnect the battery and remove the right front wheel. Remove the canister or battery. Remove the three filler plate to radiator support screws, the filler plate to wheelhouse attaching screws and the filler plate. Remove the blower attaching screws and the connector. Remove the blower. Installation is the reverse of the removal procedure.

1969-76 F-85, Cutlass, 422, and Vista-Cruiser

To remove the heater blower and inlet assembly, remove the right front fender filler panel. Disconnect the blower motor wiring. Remove the attaching nuts and screws and remove the heater assembly. The blower motor may be removed from the inlet assembly by removing the attaching screws. Installation is the reverse of the removal procedure.

To remove the core from the heater case, drain the radiator, disconnect the heater hoses and remove the five attaching nuts. On 1969-72 models to gain access to the lower nut it will be necessary to disconnect the right fender at the bottom and wedge it away from the body. Disconnect the wiring and the three control cables and remove the case assembly from the dash. Remove the core retainer and core. Install in reverse of the above procedure.

1975-76 Starfire

NOTE: To remove only the blower motor, perform steps 1 through 4. Skip step 3.

1. Disconnect the battery ground cable.
2. Disconnect the blower motor lead wire.
3. Place a pan under the vehicle. Disconnect the heater hoses at the core connections and secure the ends of the hoses in a raised position.
4. Remove the blower intake to dash panel screws and nuts and remove the blower intake, blower motor and wheel as an assembly.
5. Remove the core retaining strap screws and remove the core from the vehicle.
6. To install, reverse removal.

NOTE: Be sure that the blower intake sealer is intact, replace if necessary.

Blower Motor R & R for Cars with Air Conditioning

1969-76 F-85, Cutlass and 1969-70 Oldsmobile

NOTE: On models through 1972 it will be necessary to remove the inner fender (fill) panel to reach the blower.

1. Disconnect the wiring.
2. Remove the five screws securing the motor to the case.
3. Remove the motor.
4. Reverse the above steps to install.

1971-76 88 and 98

1. Raise the car and remove the right front wheel and tire.
2. Remove the charcoal canister.
3. Unfasten the bolts which attach the radiator supports to the filler panel.
4. Remove the wheel arch securing bolts.
5. Take the right-hand wheel arch filler panel off.
6. Unfasten the blower motor mounting screws, remove the motor and disconnect its wiring.

Installation is performed in the reverse order of removal.

1973-76 Omega

The blower motor removal procedure for A/C equipped Omega models is similar to that for those models without A/C. For blower motor R & R, see "Blower Motor and Heater Core Removal for Cars without Air Conditioning", above.

NOTE: The heater core removal procedure is different for Omegas with A/C, however, than for those without it. See below for details.

1975-76 Starfire

NOTE: This procedure requires discharging and changing the A/C system. Do not attempt it unless you have the special tools and knowledge necessary to perform this task.

1. Disconnect the battery.
2. Disconnect the blower relay.
3. Carefully discharge the refrigerant from the system using the special equipment required for the job. Don't allow refrigerant to come into contact with any part of your body.
4. Disconnect the O-ring and the A/C lines.
5. Remove the screws securing the blower motor. Remove the motor.

Installation is the reverse of removal. Apply a bead of sealer to the flange before installing the blower motor. Recharge the A/C system.

Heater Core R & R for Cars with Air Conditioning

1969-70 Oldsmobile

1. Working inside the car, remove the right and left duct hoses from the heater box. The hoses are sometimes stapled into place with three staples and there are tabs that snap into holes in the hoses.
2. Remove the manifold assembly from the front of the heater box.
3. Disconnect the wiring and vacuum hoses.
4. Remove the screws and/or nuts securing the heater box to the firewall. Fasteners may be located on both sides of the firewall.
5. Drain the radiator and disconnect the heater hoses from the heater core.
6. Remove the heater box and remove the core from the box by removing the top half of the heater box.
7. Reverse the above steps to install.

1971-73 Oldsmobile

1. Working inside the car, remove the air distribution hoses from the heater box. Hoses are sometimes held in place by staples. There are also tabs that snap into holes in the end of the hoses.
2. Remove the manifold from the front of the heater box. It is held in place by two screws and a tab.
3. Disconnect the wiring, vacuum hoses, and cables.
4. Disconnect the defroster manifold from the top of the heater box.
5. Working from outside the car, drain the radiator and disconnect the heater hoses.
6. Remove the heater box stud nuts and remove the heater box from the firewall.
7. Remove the heater core from the heater box.
8. Reverse the above steps to install.

1974-76 Oldsmobile

1. Drain the radiator.
2. Remove the heater case securing nuts. Disconnect the heater hoses.
3. Remove the instrument panel trim pad.
4. Remove the heater case-to-firewall bolts from inside the car.
5. Remove the bottom air duct.
6. Remove the instrument panel crash pad. Unfasten the leads from the clock and glovebox light.
7. Remove the upper right-hand trim panel.
8. Separate the air distribution manifold and defroster duct from the heater case.
9. Remove the lower dash trim panel.
10. Lift out the heater case and disconnect the hoses and cables from it.
11. Remove the core from the case.

Installation is the reverse of removal.

1969-76 F-85, Cutlass

1. Working inside the car, remove the defroster adaptor from the upper right side of the heater box.
2. Remove the manifold attached to the front of the heater box. It is secured by two screws and a metal tab. Remove the glovebox, first, if necessary.
3. Disconnect the vacuum hoses, cables, and wiring.
4. Working outside the car, drain the radiator and disconnect the heater hoses from the heater core.
5. Remove the nuts from the heater box studs and remove the heater box.
6. Remove the heater core from the heater box.
7. Reverse the above steps to install.

1973-75 Omega

1. Disconnect the battery and drain the cooling system.
2. Detach the upper heater hose at the core tube.
3. Remove all accessible heater core and case securing nuts.
4. Unfasten the right-hand front fender filler panel bolts and lower the panel, in order to gain access to the lower heater hose clamp.
5. Unfasten the hose clamp and detach the hose from the lower heater core tube.
6. Unfasten the lower nut which secures the right-hand heater case/core assembly.
7. Plug both of the core tubes to prevent coolant from leaking.
8. Remove the glovebox and its door.
9. Take the vacuum diaphragm assembly off the right-hand kickpanel.
10. Remove the outlet from the bottom of the heater case.
11. Separate the cold air duct from the heater case.

12. Unfasten the screws which secure the extension to the heater case. Remove the extension from the case.
13. Detach the cables and the wiring from the case. Remove the core and case as an assembly.
14. Remove the core from the case.

Installation is performed in the reverse order of removal.

1975-76 Starfire

NOTE: This procedure requires discharging and charging the AC system. Do not attempt it unless you have the special tools and knowledge necessary to perform this task.

1. Disconnect the battery.
2. Remove the glovebox.
3. Remove the right-hand air outlet duct.
4. Remove the instrument cluster bezel and the instrument panel crash pad.
5. Remove the left-hand air outlet deflector and feed duct.
6. Remove its retaining screws and lower the steering column so that it rests on the driver's seat.
9. Unfasten the instrument cluster screws, leads, speedometer cable, and remove the cluster. Remove the radio.
10. Remove the defroster and center distribution ducts.
11. Carefully discharge the refrigerant from the system using the special equipment required for the job. Don't allow refrigerant to come in contact with any part of your body.
12. Place a container beneath them and then remove the heater hoses from the core pipes. Plug the hoses.
13. Clean the external surfaces and fittings of the VIR assembly.
14. Disconnect the compressor intake line, oil bleed line, and condenser outlet line. Plug ALL open connections.
15. Loosen the evaporator intake and outlet connections. Remove the VIR mounting clamp screw and remove the clamp. Slide the VIR off the evaporator outlet line and then off the intake line. Remove and throw all the old O-rings away. Plug ALL open connections.
16. Remove the heater distributor/case stud-to-firewall nuts. Remove the distributor/case asbly, after disconnecting all electrical leads and vacuum hoses from it.
17. Separate the heater case from the distributor and the core from the case.

Installation is the reverse of removal. Charge the A/C system and add coolant, as required.

SEAT BELTS

Warning System

The seat belt warning system consists of lap belt retractor switches, a pressure-sensitive switch underneath the right-hand front passenger's seat, a warning lamp and a buzzer.

On manual transmission-equipped cars the circuit is wired through the ignition switch, the parking brake warning light switch and a relay, which is located between the instrument cluster wiring and the switch on the parking brake. A diode is used to prevent feedback into the parking brake warning circuit.

On cars having automatic transmissions, the seat belt warning circuit is wired through the ignition switch and the combination back-up lamp/neutral safety switch.

With the ignition key in the "RUN" position, a weight of 40-50 lbs on the seat (pressure-sensitive switch), energizes the circuit when the parking brake is released (M/T) or the gear selector placed in a forward drive range (A/T).

A warning light will glow and a buzzer will sound with the circuit energized, until the seat belts are withdrawn from the retractors and fastened over the laps of the two outboard front seat occupants.

Seat Belt/Starter Interlock System

As required by law, Oldsmobile passenger-cars cannot be started until the front seat occupants sit down and then fasten their seat belts. If the proper sequence is not followed, e.g., the occupants fasten the seat belts and then sit on them, the car cannot be started.

If, after the car is started, the seat belts are unfastened, a warning buzzer and light will be activated in a similar manner to that described above for 1972-73 models.

The shoulder harness and lap belt are permanently fastened together, so that they both must be worn. The shoulder harness uses an inertia-lock reel to allow freedom of movement under normal driving conditions.

NOTE: This type of reel locks up when the car decelerates rapidly, as during a crash.

The lap belts use the same ratchet-type retractors that the 1972-73 models use.

The switches for the interlock system have been removed from the lap belt retractors and placed in the belt buckles. The seat sensors remain the same as those used in 1972-73, except that two more have been added.

For ease of service, the car may be started from outside, by reaching in and turning the key but without depressing the seat sensors.

In case of system failure, an override switch is located under the hood. This is a "one start" switch and it must be reset each time it is used.

Disabling the Seat Belt/ Starter Interlock and Buzzer

The seat belt/starter interlock was used only on early production 1975s. A special act of Congress repealed its mandatory installation.

It is now legal to disable the seat belt/starter interlock, but *not* the warning light. To do this, proceed as follows:

1. Disconnect the negative (—) battery cable.
2. Locate the interlock harness connector, which is on or near the fuse block. The connector has orange, yellow, and green leads running to it.
3. Cut and tape the green lead on the body harness side of the interlock connector.
4. a. On Cutlass, 88, and 98 without low coolant warning and heavy duty cooling: disconnect the buzzer or beeper from the fuse panel and remove it.
   b. On Cutlass, 88, and 98 with low coolant warning and heavy duty cooling: cut the yellow wire behind the connector and tape its ends.
   c. On Omega and Starfire: remove the buzzer from its connector on the wiring harness.
5. Check the battery cable.
6. Check system operation by starting the car with the seat belt unfastened.

Oldsmobile Toronado

YEAR IDENTIFICATION

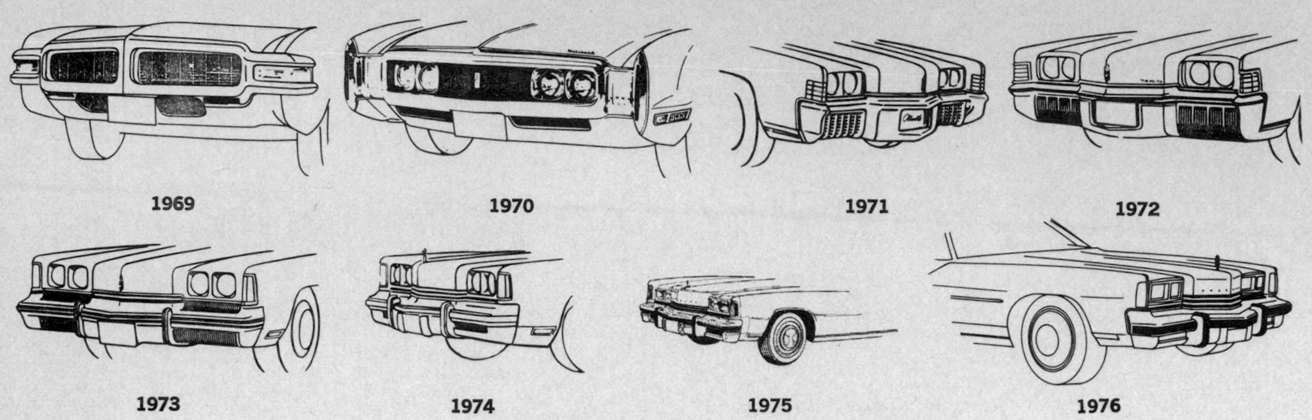

FIRING ORDER

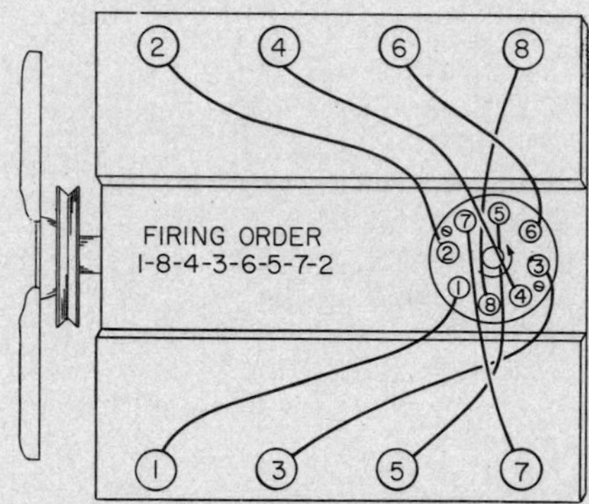

CAR SERIAL NUMBER LOCATION AND ENGINE IDENTIFICATION

Vehicle Identification Number

The vehicle identification plate is located on the left side of the dashboard, visible through the windshield.

Engine Identification

The engine identification number is found on a tape attached to the oil filler tube. All engines are 455 cu. in. displacement.

ENGINE IDENTIFICATION CODE

The engine identification code is located on tape attached directly to the front of the oil filler tube.

Disp	Bbl	Hp	'69	'70	'71	'72	'73	'74	'75	'76
455	4	215, 230 (net)					UQ UV VO VP	UO UP VO VP	UP VP	U2 VP
455	4	250 (net)					UU UV			
455	4	265 (net)				UU UV				
455	4	350			US UT					
455	4	375	US UT UV	US UT						
455	4	400	UW	UV UW						

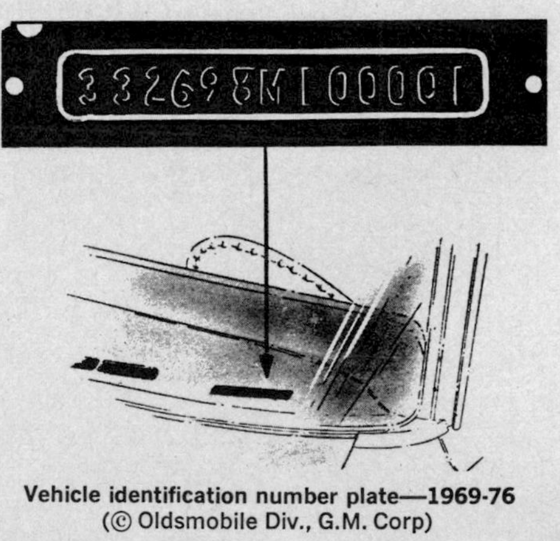

Vehicle identification number plate—1969-76
(© Oldsmobile Div., G.M. Corp)

GENERAL ENGINE SPECIFICATIONS

Year	Engine No. Cyl. Displacement Cu. In.	Carburetor Type	Horsepower @ rpm ■	Torque @ rpm (ft lbs) ■	Bore and Stroke (in.)	Compression Ratio	Oil Pressure @ 2050 rpm
'69	8-455	4 bbl	375 @ 4600	510 @ 3000	4.126 x 4.250	10.25:1	38
	8-455	4 bbl	400 @ 4800	500 @ 3200	4.126 x 4.250	10.25:1	38
'70	8-455	4 bbl	375 @ 4600	510 @ 3000	4.126 x 4.250	10.25:1	38
	8-455	4 bbl	400 @ 3200	500 @ 3200	4.126 x 4.250	10.25:1	38
'71	8-455	4 bbl	350 @ 4400	465 @ 2800	4.126 x 4.250	8.50:1	38
'72	8-455	4 bbl	265 @ 4200	375 @ 2800	4.126 x 4.250	8.50:1	38
'73	8-455	4 bbl	250 @ 4000	375 @ 2800	4.126 x 4.250	8.50:1	38
'74	8-455	4 bbl	230 @ 3800	370 @ 2800	4.126 x 4.250	8.50:1	38
'75-'76	8-455	4 bbl	215 @ 3600	370 @ 2400	4.126 x 4.250	8.50:1	38

■ Beginning 1972, horsepower and torque are SAE net figures. They are measured at the rear of the transmission with all accessories installed and operating. Since the figures vary when a given engine is installed in different models, some are representative rather than exact.

TUNE-UP SPECIFICATIONS

When analyzing compression test results, look for uniformity among cylinders rather than specific pressures.

ENGINE Year	ENGINE No. Cyl Displacement (cu in.)	ENGINE hp	SPARK PLUGS Type	SPARK PLUGS Gap (in.)	DISTRIBUTOR Point Dwell (deg)	DISTRIBUTOR Point Gap (in.)	IGNITION TIMING (deg) ▲ Man Trans ●	IGNITION TIMING (deg) ▲ * Auto Trans	VALVES Intake Opens (deg)	Fuel Pump Pressure (psi)	IDLE SPEED (rpm) ▲ Man Trans ●	IDLE SPEED (rpm) ▲ Auto Trans
'69	8-455	375	44S	.030	28-32	.016	—	8B	20B	5½-6½	—	575
	8-455	400①	44S	.030	28-32	.016	—	10B	24B	5½-6½	—	575
'70	8-455	375	45S	.030	28-32	.016	—	8B	22B	5½-6½	—	600
	8-455	400①	44S	.030	28-32	.016	—	12B	24B	5½-6½	—	600
'71	8-455	350	46S	.040	28-32	.016	—	10B	22B	5½-6½	—	600
'72	8-455	265	46S	.040	28-32	.016	—	8B	20B	5½-6½	—	650/550
'73	8-455	250	R46S	.040	30	.016	—	8B	20B	5½-6½	—	650/550
'74	8-455	250	R46S	.040	30	.016	—	10B	20B	5½-6½	—	650/550
'74	8-455	230	R46SX	.080	Electronic		—	10B	20B	5½-6½	—	650/550
'75	8-455	215	R46SX	.080	Electronic		—	12B	20B	5½-6½	—	650/550(650/600)
'76	8-455	230	R46SX	.080	Electronic		—	14B(12B)	20B	5½-6½	—	650/550(650/600)

* Set timing with carburetor adjusted to the following speeds:
1969 850 rpm
1970-1976 1100 rpm

▲ See text for procedure

● Where two figures appear separated by a slash, the first is idle speed with solenoid energized, the second is idle speed with solenoid disconnected. Figure in parentheses indicates California engine.

① Air Injection Reactor System
B Before Top Dead Center
— Not applicable

CAPACITIES

Year	ENGINE No. Cyl. Displacement (cu. in.)	Engine Crankcase Add 1 Qt For New Filter	TRANSMISSION Pts To Refill After Draining Manual 3-Speed	Manual 4-Speed	Automatic ●	Drive Axle (qts)	Gasoline Tank (gals)	COOLING SYSTEM (qts) With Heater	With A/C
'69	8-455	5	—	—	8	4	24	18	18.5
'70	8-455	5	—	—	8	4	24	18	18.5
'71	8-455	5	—	—	8	4	24	18	18.5
'72	8-455	5	—	—	8	4	25	19.5	20
'73	8-455	5	—	—	8	4	26	19.5	20
'74-'76	8-455	5	—	—	8	4	26	21	21.5

● Does not include torque converter — Not applicable

VALVE SPECIFICATIONS

Year	Engine No. Cyl. Displacement (cu in.)	Seat Angle (deg)	Face Angle (deg)	Spring Test Pressure (lbs @ in.)	Spring Installed Height (in.)	STEM TO GUIDE Clearance (in.)		STEM Diameter (in.)	
						Intake	Exhaust	Intake	Exhaust
'69	8-455	①	②	187 @ 1.27	1 21/32	.0010-.0027	.0015-.0032	.3429	.3424
'70	8-455	45	46	187 @ 1.27	1 21/32	.0010-.0027	.0015-.0032	.3429	.3424
'71	8-455	45	46	187 @ 1.27	1 21/32	.0010-.0027	.0015-.0032	.3429	.3424
'72	8-455	45	46	197 @ 1.23	1 21/32	.0010-.0027	.0015-.0032	.3429	.3424
'73	8-455	45	46	197 @ 1.23	1 21/32	.0010-.0027	.0015-.0032	.3429	.3424
'74	8-455	45	46	197 @ 1.23	1 21/32	.0010-.0027	.0015-.0032	.3429	.3424
'75-'76	8-455	45③	46③	187 @ 1.27	1 39/64	.0010-.0027	.0015-.0032	.3429	.3424

① Intake valve seat angle 30°
Exhaust valve seat angle 45°

② Intake valve face angle 30°
Exhaust valve face angle 46°

③ Exhaust valve seat 59°
Exhaust valve face 60°

TORQUE SPECIFICATIONS

All readings in ft lbs

Year	Engine No. Cyl. Displacement (cu in.)	Cylinder Head Bolts	Rod Bearing Bolts	Main Bearing Bolts	Crankshaft Pulley Bolt	Flywheel to Crankshaft Bolts	MANIFOLD	
							Intake	Exhaust
'69-'74	8-455	80	42	120	160	60	35	25
'75-'76	8-455	85	42	120	20①	60	40	25

① Balancer-to-crankshaft bolt—200-310 ft lbs

CRANKSHAFT AND CONNECTING ROD SPECIFICATIONS

All measurements are given in inches

Year	Engine No. Cyl. Displacement (cu in.)	CRANKSHAFT				CONNECTING ROD		
		Main Brg. Journal Dia	Main Brg. Oil Clearance	Shaft End-Play	Thrust on No.	Journal Diameter	Oil Clearance	Side Clearance
'69-'74	8-455	2.9998	.0005-.0021①	.004-.008	3	2.4988-2.4998	.0004-.0033	②③
'75-'76	8-455	2.9998	.0005-.0021①	.004-.008	3	2.4988-2.4998	.0004-.0033	.006-.020

① No. 5—.0020-.0034
② 1969-70—.002-.013; 1971—.002-.011; 1972-74—.006-.020
③ 1970-72 W-30—.002-.021

RING GAP

All measurements are given in inches

Year	Engine	Top Compression	Bottom Compression
'69-'71	8-455	.013-.023	.013-.023
'72-'76	8-455	.010-.023	.010-.023

Year	Engine	Oil Control
'69-'76	8-455	.015-.055

RING SIDE CLEARANCE

All measurements are given in inches

Year	Engine	Top Compression	Bottom Compression
'69-'71	8-455	.0018-.0033	.0018-.0038
'72-'76	8-455	.0020-.0040	.0020-.0040

Year	Engine	Oil Control
'69-'76	8-455	.0021-.0031

PISTON CLEARANCE

Year	Engine	Piston-to-bore Clearance (in.)
'69-'76	8-455	.001-.002

ALTERNATOR AND REGULATOR SPECIFICATIONS

	ALTERNATOR			REGULATOR						
					Field Relay			Regulator		
Year	Part No. or Manufacturer	Field Current @ 12 V	Output (amps)	Part No. or Manufacturer	Air Gap (in.)	Point Gap (in.)	Volts to Close	Air Gap (in.)	Point Gap (in.)	Volts @ 75°
'69	1100734	2.2-2.6	42	1119515	Not Adjustable					13.5-14.4
	1100777	2.2-2.6	55	1119515	Not Adjustable					13.5-14.4
'70	1100878	2.2-2.6	42	1119515	Not Adjustable					13.5-14.4
	1100907	2.2-2.6	55	1119515	Not Adjustable					13.5-14.4
'71	1100567	2.2-2.6	42	1119515	Not Adjustable					13.5-14.4
	1100570	2.2-2.6	61	1119515	Not Adjustable					13.5-14.4
'72-'74	1100573	2.2-2.6	42	Transistor type, integral with alternator, no adjustment						
	1100597	2.2-2.6	61	Transistor type, integral with alternator, no adjustment						
'75-'76	1102493	2.2-2.6	42	Transistor type integral with alternator, no adjustment						
	1102549	2.2-2.6	61	Transistor type integral with alternator, no adjustment						
	1102550	2.2-2.6	63	Transistor type integral with alternator, no adjustment						

BATTERY AND STARTER SPECIFICATIONS

		BATTERY			STARTER						
					Lock Test			No-Load Test			
Year	Engine Displacement (cu in.)	Ampere Hour Capacity •	Volts	Terminal Grounded	Amps	Volts	Torque (ft lbs)	Amps	Volts	RPM	Brush Spring Tension (oz)
'69	455	75	12	Neg.	Not Recommended			70-105	10.6	3,800	35
'70-'71	455	74	12	Neg.	Not Recommended			—	—	—	35
'72-'74	455	73	12	Neg.	Not Recommended			—	—	—	35
'75-'76	455	3500/3750	12	Neg.	Not Recommended			—	—	—	35

• Cranking power in watts given starting 1975

BRAKE SPECIFICATIONS

All measurements are given in inches

Year	Model	Master Cylinder Disc	Master Cylinder Drum	Wheel Cylinder Front Disc	Wheel Cylinder Front Drum	Wheel Cylinder Rear	Brake Disc or Drum Diameter Front Disc	Brake Disc or Drum Diameter Front Drum	Brake Disc or Drum Diameter Rear
'69	All	1⅛	1.0	2 15/16	1⅛	⅞	10.9	11.0	11.00
'70-'73	All	1⅛	—	2 15/16	—	15/16	10.88	—	11.00
'74	All	1⅛	—	2 15/16	—	15/16	11.00	—	11.00
'75-'76	All	1⅛	—	2 15/16	—	15/16	11.00	—	11.00

— Not applicable

WHEEL ALIGNMENT SPECIFICATIONS

Year	Model	Caster Range (deg)	Caster Pref Setting (deg)	Camber Range (deg)	Camber Pref Setting (deg)	Toe-in (in.)	Steering Axis Inclin.	Wheel Pivot Ratio (deg) Inner Wheel	Wheel Pivot Ratio (deg) Outer Wheel
'69	All	1½N to 2½N	2N	¼N to ½P	⅛P	0 ± 1/16	11	20	18⅕
'70	All	1½N to 2½N	2N	¼N to ½P	⅛P	0 ± 1/16	11	20	18⅕
'71-'74	All	1½N to 2½N	2N	¼N to ¾P① ¾N to ¼P②	¼P① ¼N②	0 ± 1/16	11	—	—
'75-'76	All	2N to 2P	0	1¼N to 1¾P① 1¾N to 1¼P②	¼P① ¼N②	0 ± 1/16	11	—	—

N Negative P Positive

① Left side (to be ½P more than right side)
② Right side

NOTE: Service procedures for the Charging System, Starting System, Ignition System, Fuel System, Cooling System, and Emission Controls on the Toronado can be found in the Oldsmobile section.

ENGINE

All Toronados are equipped with a 455 cu in. V8 engine. The engine is a comon design; two banks of cylinders with four cylinders in each bank, opposed at a 90° angle, with one chain driven camshaft centrally located, operating the valve train of both banks of cylinders through hydraulic lifters. The crankshaft has five main bearings, is counter-balanced, and is pressure lubricated by oil passages drilled through it. The distributor and oil pump are operated by a common shaft driven by a gear on the rear end of the camshaft. The fuel pump is driven by an eccentric mounted on the front of the camshaft.

Engine R & R

1. Drain radiator.
2. Remove hood, marking hinge for reassembly.
3. If equipped with a fan shroud, unhook the strap and remove the clips holding the seal to the venturi ring. Move the seal toward the radiator.
4. Disconnect battery.
5. Disconnect radiator hoses and cooler lines, heater hoses, vacuum hoses, engine to body ground strap, fuel hose from fuel pump, wiring and accelarator cable. Remove the air cleaner, hot air pipe, air conditioner compressor and power steering pump without disconnecting lines and set them aside.
6. Remove coil, throttle control switch bracket, radiator support and radiator.
7. Raise the car.
8. Disconnect exhaust pipes at manifold. Loosen, but do not remove, upper left flywheel cover attaching bolt (this will require 30 in. of wrench extension).
9. Disconnect wires and remove starter.
10. Remove torque converter cover and remove three bolts securing the converter to flywheel. Scribe marks on converter and flywheel for reassembly.
11. Attach a final drive supporting tool (BT-6322) to support final drive assembly.
12. Remove two attaching bolts from right output shaft support bracket and one through bolt attaching final drive to engine block on the left side. Scribe around the washers for correct reassembly.
13. Remove engine mount to crossmember nuts and front engine mount nuts. Remove the lower right engine-to-transmission attaching bolt.
14. Lower the car.
15. Support the final drive assembly with a chain stretched under and across the final drive assembly and attached to holes in the frame members.
16. Support engine by using a lifting fixture.
17. Remove five remaining transmission-to-engine bolts.
18. Using suitable lifting device, lift engine from car.

Caution If car is to be moved, install converter holding tool.

19. To install, reverse removal procedure.

Manifolds

Intake Manifold Removal and Installation

1. Remove the air cleaner. Drain the cooling system. Disconnect the upper radiator hose, the thermostat-bypass hose, and the heater hose at the rear of the intake manifold.
2. Remove the throttle cable and all fuel and vacuum lines.
3. Disconnect the ignition coil mounting bracket and the alternator and air conditioning brackets.

NOTE: Position the alternator and air conditioning compressor out of the way and secure them. Do not disconnect any refrigerant lines.

4. Before removing the intake manifold bolts, disconnect the temperature gauge electrical lead. Remove the manifold bolts and lift off the manifold with the carburetor attached.

NOTE: It is necessary to remove the oil filler tube to add clearance when removing the manifold.

5. Before installation, clean the mating surfaces of the manifold.
6. Position the intake manifold gasket correctly on the heads, making certain that the ports in the head align with the holes in the gasket.

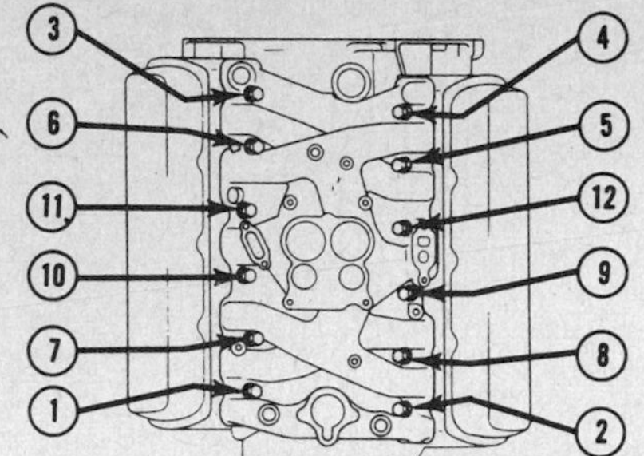

Intake manifold torque sequence (© Oldsmobile Div., G.M. Corp)

7. Install the end gaskets with the ends placed under the cylinder head.
8. Lower the intake manifold onto the engine using caution that the gaskets do not slip.
9. Connect the thermostat bypass hose to the water pump and install the manifold bolts after they have been cleaned and oiled.
10. Torque the manifold bolts to 15 ft lbs using the correct torque sequence. Then re-torque to 40 ft lbs.
11. Install the mounting brackets for the ignition coil, air conditioning and the alternator.
12. Connect the temperature gauge lead and all fuel and vacuum lines.
13. Install all disconnected hoses, spark plug wires, throttle linkage and air cleaner. Fill the cooling system.

Exhaust Manifold Removal and Installation

Left Side

1. Remove the air cleaner and the carburetor heat box on the manifold.
2. Remove the lower alternator bracket, raise the front of the car and support it securely.
3. Remove the exhaust pipe.
4. Lower the car and remove the manifold attaching bolts. Remove the manifold from above.
5. To install, reverse the removal procedure using the correct torque for the manifold attaching bolts. (See illustration for the correct torque specifications.)

Right Side

1. Raise the car and support it securely.
2. Remove the exhaust pipe and the right front wheel.
3. Remove the attaching bolts and lower the manifold down and out from under the vehicle.

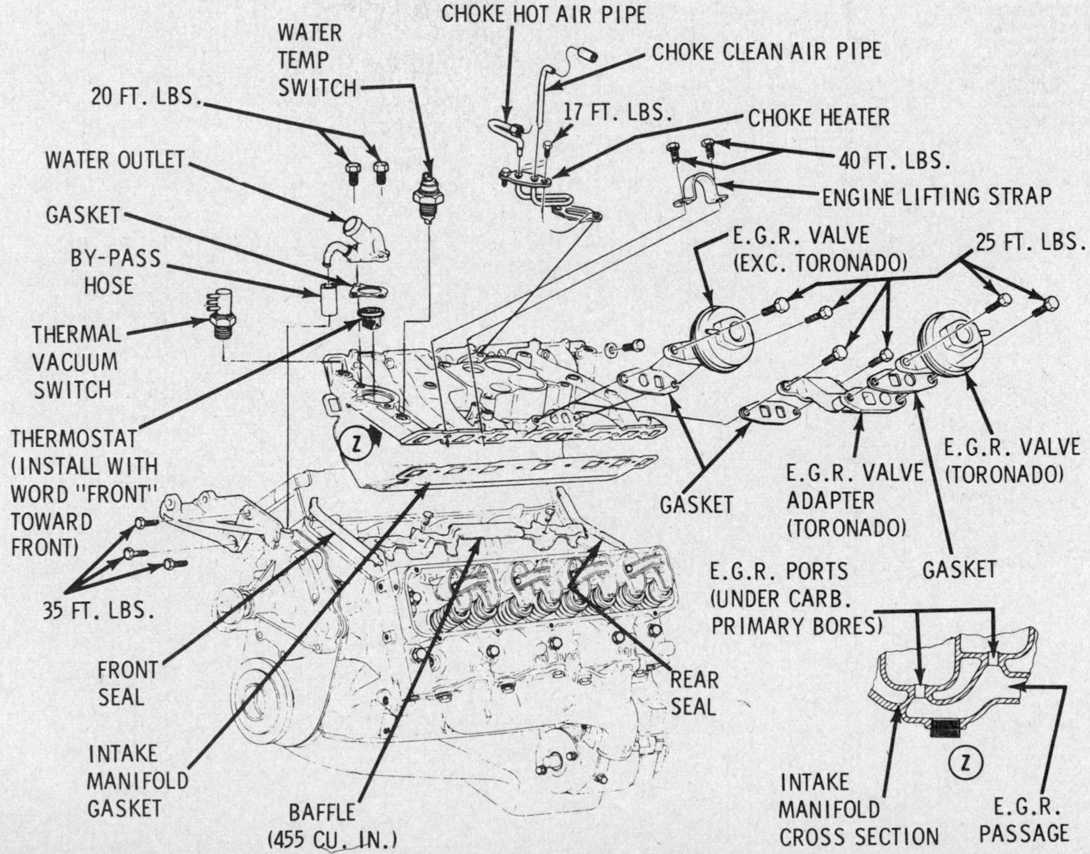

Intake manifold components (© Oldsmobile Div., G.M. Corp)

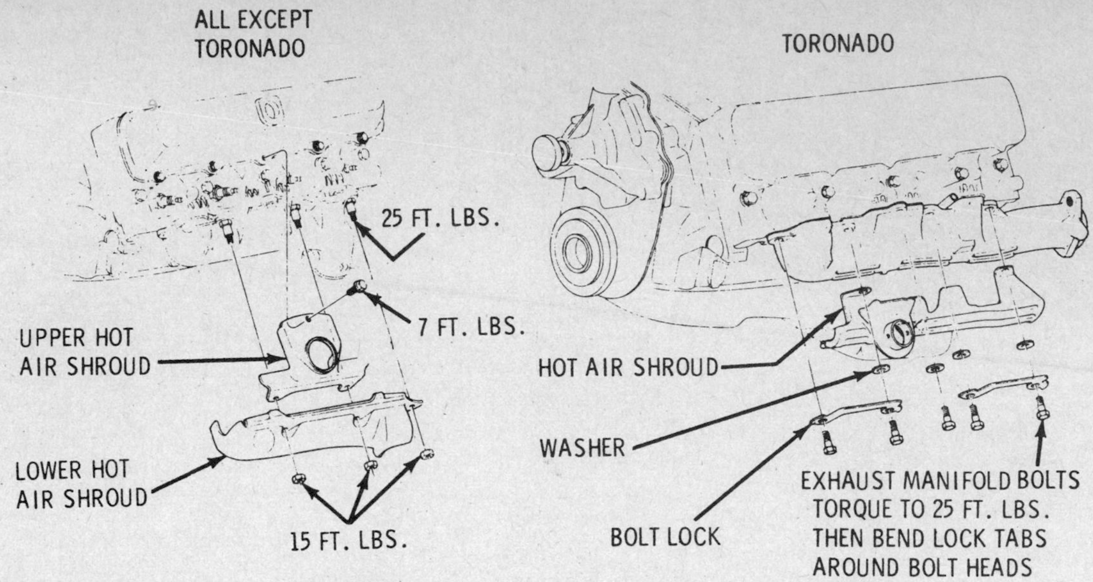

Exhaust manifold components and torque requirements (© Oldsmobile Div., G.M. Corp)

4. To install, reverse the removal procedure.

Valve System

The Toronado uses camshaft-operated hydraulic lifters. Lubricant is supplied through the pushrods to the rocker arm assembly.

Toronado engines use non-replaceable valve guides. Should the guides become worn, they must be reamed to the next oversize and larger diameter valves installed.

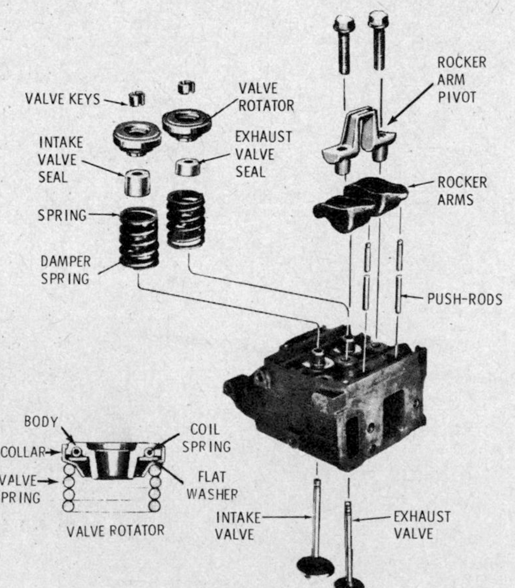

Cylinder head and valve assembly
(© Oldsmobile Div., G.M. Corp)

Valves are available in standard size, .003 in. oversize, .005 in. oversize, .010 in. oversize and .013 in. oversize. When the guides are reamed, use caution to keep the reamer straight in the valve guide bore.

Some individual oversize valves may have been installed at the factory. They are marked on the inboard side of the cylinder heads on the machined surface just above the intake manifold surface. The markings are visible after removing the air cleaner assembly. If no markings are present, then the valve guide bores are the standard size.

Rocker Arm Assembly Removal and Installation

Remove the valve cover, rocker flange bolts, rocker pivot and the rocker arms. Remove each set of rocker arms as a unit. To install, position the rocker arm assemblies and lubricate the wear points. Install the rocker pivots. Install the flange bolts and tighten to 25 ft lbs.

Cylinder Head

Cylinder Head Removal and Installation

1. Drain the radiator and the engine block.
2. Remove the intake and exhaust manifolds. (see Manifolds)
3. Remove the valve covers.

NOTE: It may be necessary to remove some accessory brackets which are in the way.

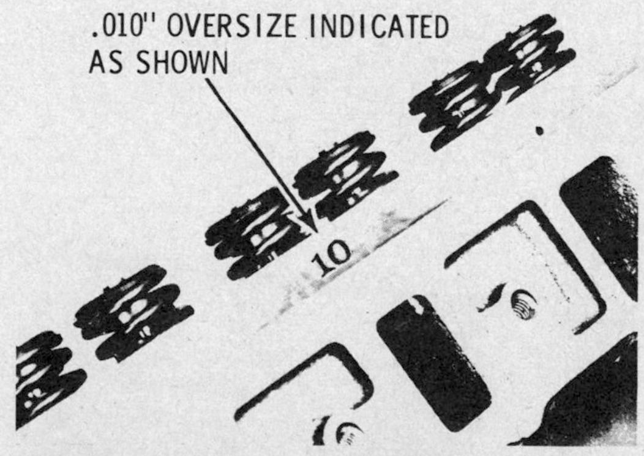

Oversize valve guide bore marking on the cylinder head
(© Oldsmobile Div., G.M. Corp)

Cylinder head bolt torque sequence
(© Oldsmobile Div., G.M. Corp)

4. Remove the engine ground strap, which is attached to the right cylinder head.
5. Remove the rocker arm bolts, rocker pivots, and rocker arms.
6. Pull out the push rods, noting the location of each.

Caution The rocker arms, rocker pivots and push rods must be replaced in their original positions.

7. Remove the cylinder head bolts and lift off the heads.
8. Before installation, the head gasket should be coated with sealer on both sides.
9. Position the cylinder heads and install the head bolts after they have been cleaned and lubricated.
10. Torque the head bolts to specifications following the sequence given.

Timing Cover, Chain, and Camshaft

Timing Cover Removal and Installation

In order to remove the front cover, on 1971-76 models, the engine must be removed from the car.

1. Drain the cooling system. Disconnect the upper and lower radiator, heater and bypass hoses.
2. Remove the radiator, belts, fan and fan pulley, crankshaft pulley and the harmonic balancer.
3. Drain the oil and remove the oil pan.
4. Remove the timing cover attaching bolts and pull off the cover. Also, remove the timing pointer and the water pump.
5. Before assembly, remove all old gaskets and install a new timing cover gasket.
6. Position the front cover, timing pointer and the water pump.
7. Lubricate the attaching bolts and install.
8. Install the harmonic balancer on the crankshaft after lubrication. Torque to 160 ft lbs.
9. Connect all cooling hoses.
10. Install the crankshaft pulley.
11. Install the fan and the fan pulley. Torque the attaching bolts to 20 ft lbs.
12. Install the drive belts and adjust.
13. Install the oil pan, fill the crankcase and the radiator.
14. Run the engine and check for leaks.

Timing Cover Oil Seal Removal and Installation

1. Remove all drive belts, crankshaft pulley and pulley hub.
2. Using an inside puller, remove the seal.

Camshaft and crankshaft gear alignment
(© Oldsmobile Div., G.M. Corp)

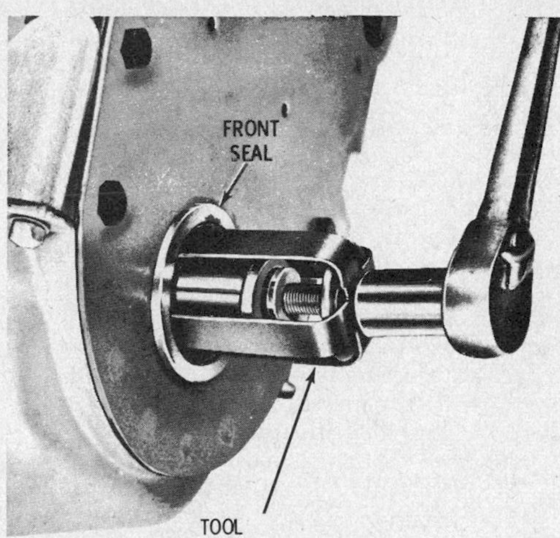

Removing the front oil seal
(© Oldsmobile Div., G.M. Corp)

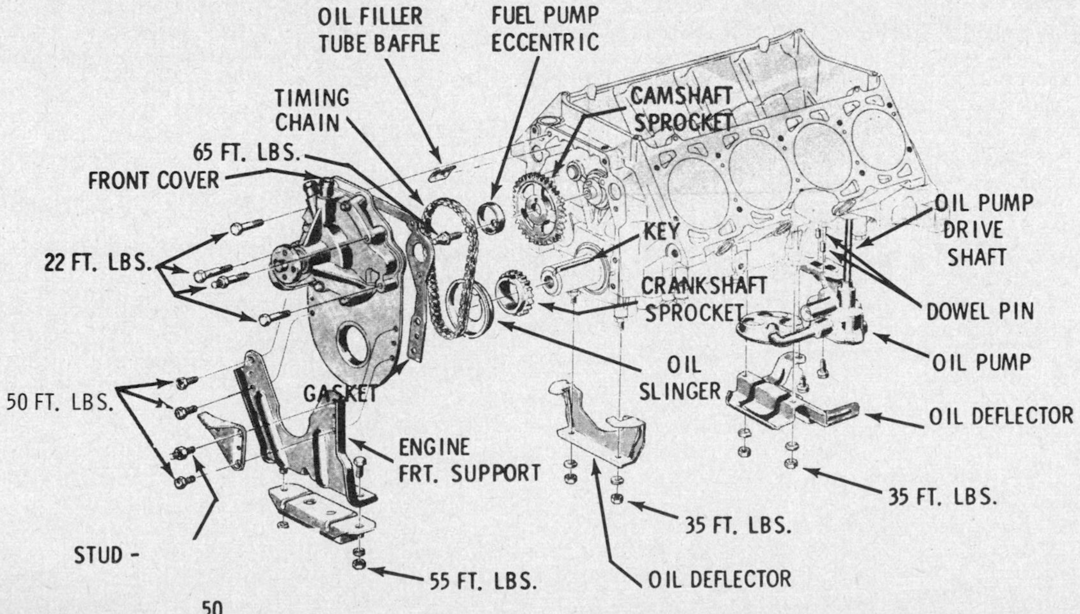

Front cover components (© Oldsmobile Div., G.M. Corp)

3. Before installing a new seal, apply sealer to the outside of the seal.
4. Install the seal making sure that it is installed straight and the sealing surface is not damaged.
5. Position the pulley hub and the crankshaft pulley and adjust the drive belts.

Timing Chain Removal and Installation

NOTE: 1971-76 models require that the engine be removed before performing the chain removal procedure.

1. Remove the front engine cover.
2. Remove the fuel pump eccentric, oil slinger, cam gear and timing chain.

Some individual oversize valves may have been installed at the factory. They are marked on the inboard side of the cylinder heads on the machined surface just above the intake manifold surface. The markings are visible after removing the air cleaner assembly. If no markings are present, then the valve guide bores are the standard size.

NOTE: It is necessary to use a puller to remove the crankshaft gear.

4. To install, align the camshaft and crankshaft gears. The camshaft gear aligning mark must be in the 6 o'clock position while the crankshaft gear must be in the 12 o'clock position.
5. Position the fuel pump eccentric with the flat side against the gear. Using a brass hammer, place the key against the gear until it bottoms.
6. Install the oil slinger and torque the attaching nut to 160 ft lbs.

Camshaft Removal and Installation

NOTE: The removal and installation of the camshaft on 1971-76 models requires the removal of the engine since the oil pan and the front cover must be removed.

1. Remove the oil pan, front cover and the distributor.

NOTE: Before removing the distributor, position the No. 1 piston at top dead center of its compression stroke.

2. Remove the valve covers and the intake manifold.
3. Remove the water temperature sensor and the oil filler tube.
4. Remove the rocker arm assemblies, the push rods and the lifters.

Caution It is important that the lifters, the push rods, and the rocker arm assemblies be replaced in their original positions.

5. Remove the fuel pump eccentric, camshaft gear, oil slinger and the timing chain.
6. Remove the camshaft by carefully withdrawing it from the front of the engine. Use caution not to damage the camshaft bearings during this procedure. Keep the camshaft parallel with the crankshaft as it is removed.
7. Before installing the camshaft, coat both the cam lobes and the bearings with camshaft grease. Install the camshaft and align the timing marks on the camshaft and crankshaft gears as outlined in the Timing Chain Removal and Installation section.
8. Install the distributor. (See Distributor Installation.)
9. Reverse the removal procedure to complete the installation.

Engine Lubrication

Oil Pan R & R

1969-70

1. Disconnect battery and remove dipstick.
2. Remove upper radiator support screws and fan shroud screws.
3. Hoist car and drain oil.
4. Disconnect engine mounts and jack front of engine up as far as possible.
5. Remove crossover pipe and starter.
6. Remove oil pan attaching bolts and remove oil pan.
7. Install in reverse order of removal, using new gaskets with sealer on both sides.

1971-76

The engine must be removed from the vehicle in order to remove the oil pan.

1. Remove engine assembly.
2. Remove dipstick.
3. Drain oil and remove filter assembly.
4. Remove the front engine mount from front cover.
5. Remove oil pan attaching bolts and remove oil pan.
6. Apply a good sealer to both sides of pan gaskets and install on block.
7. Install front and rear seal.
8. Wipe lubricant on seal area and install pan. Torque 5/16 in. bolts to 15 ft. lbs. and 1/4 in. bolts to 10 ft. lbs.
9. Reinstall mount to front cover and oil filter assembly.
10. Reinstall engine and fill crankcase as explained in charts.

Oil Pump R & R

Remove the oil pan as described above. Remove the oil baffle. Remove the oil pump to rear main bearing cap attaching bolts, then remove the pump and drive shaft extension.

Rear Main Oil Seal Replacement

Whether or not the engine must be removed from the vehicle in order to replace the rear main bearing oil seal depends upon the removal of the oil pan. See "Oil Pan R & R" above. Remove the oil pan and rear main bearing cap. Using a blunt-ended tool, drive the upper seal into its groove on each side until it is tightly packed. This is usually 1/4—3/4 in. Cut pieces of the old lower bearing cap seal 1/16 in. longer than the distance each side of the upper seal was compressed. Install these pieces into each side of the upper seal seat, packing them into place. Carefully trim any protruding seal, being sure not to scratch or damage the bearing surface. Install a new seal in the bearing cap and install the cap, tightening bolts to 120 ft. lbs. Install the oil pan.

AUTOMATIC TRANSMISSION

The Turbo Hydra-Matic transmission used on the Toronado is a fully automatic transmission used for front-wheel drive applications. It consists primarily of a three element hydraulic torque converter, dual sprocket and link assembly, compound planetary gear set, three multiple disc clutches, a sprag clutch, a roller clutch, two band assemblies and hydraulic control system.

Shift Linkage Adjustments

See illustration for linkage adjustment.

Kick-down Adjustment

1. Push forward on the switch contact so that it is flush with the switch housing.
2. Place the accelerator pedal to the wide open position. This will set the switch.
3. If there is any doubt whether the switch is working, it may be checked with a test light across the two connector poles.

Automatic Transmission Removal

1. Disconnect battery.
2. Disconnect oil cooler lines at the radiator, at transmission and speedometer cable at governor. Remove the governor and cover the opening.
3. Install engine support bar.
4. Remove nut D and the 3 upper final drive-to-transmission attaching bolts (A, B and C) as in illustration.
5. Remove the 5 transmission-to-engine bolts (A, B, C, D, and E) as in illustrations. The last bolt is removed after the car is raised.

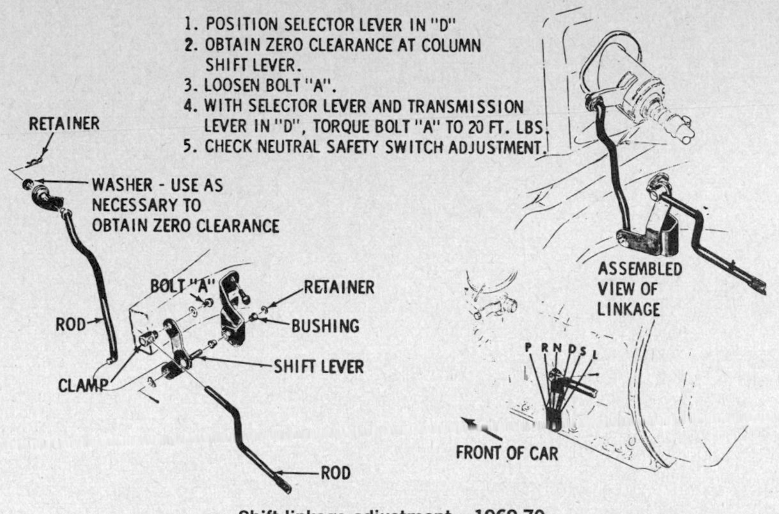

Shift linkage adjustment—1969-70
(© Oldsmobile Div., G.M. Corp)

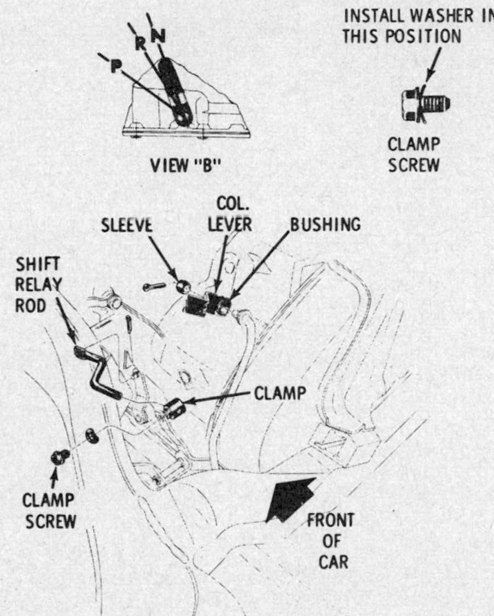

1. LOOSEN CLAMP SCREW AND BE SURE ROD IS FREE TO SLIDE IN CLAMP.
2. PLACE UPPER SHIFT LEVER AGAINST NEUTRAL STOP IN STEERING COLUMN. A DETENT WILL HOLD IT THERE.
3. SET TRANSMISSION OUTER LEVER IN NEUTRAL POSITION.
4. TIGHTEN CLAMP SCREW TO 20 FT. LBS.
5. CHECK OPERATION:
   A. WITH KEY IN "RUN" POSITION AND TRANSMISSION IN "REVERSE", BE SURE THAT KEY CANNOT BE REMOVED AND THAT STEERING WHEEL IS NOT LOCKED.
   B. WITH KEY IN "LOCK" POSITION AND SHIFT LEVER IN "PARK", BE SURE THAT KEY CAN BE REMOVED, THAT STEERING WHEEL IS LOCKED, AND THAT THE UPPER SHIFT LEVER CANNOT BE REMOVED FROM "PARK".

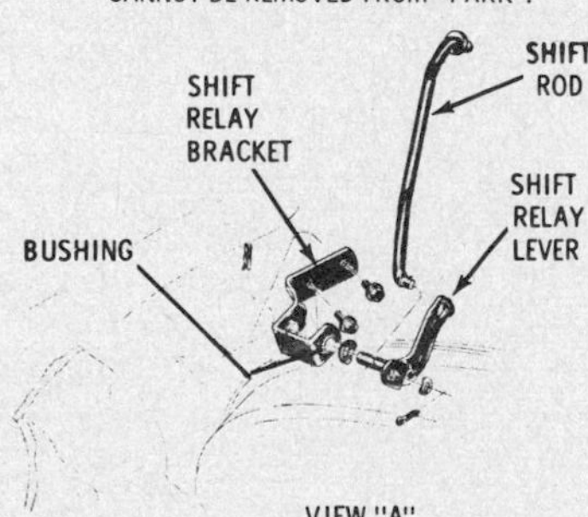

Transmission shift linkage adjustment—1971-76
(© Oldsmobile Div., G.M. Corp)

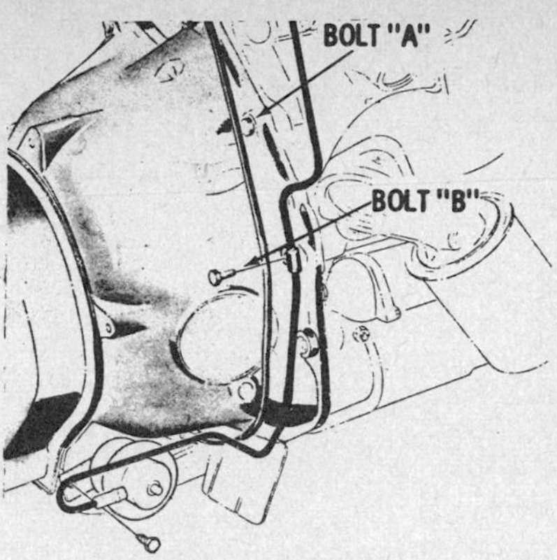

Transmission to engine attachment
(© Oldsmobile Div., G.M. Corp)

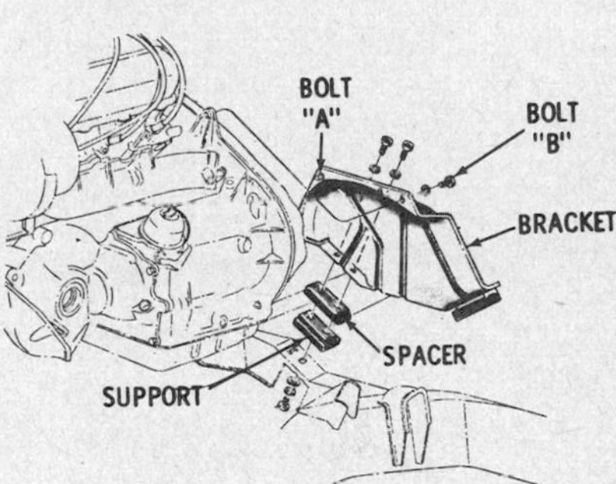

Engine mount attachment
(© Oldsmobile Div., G.M. Corp)

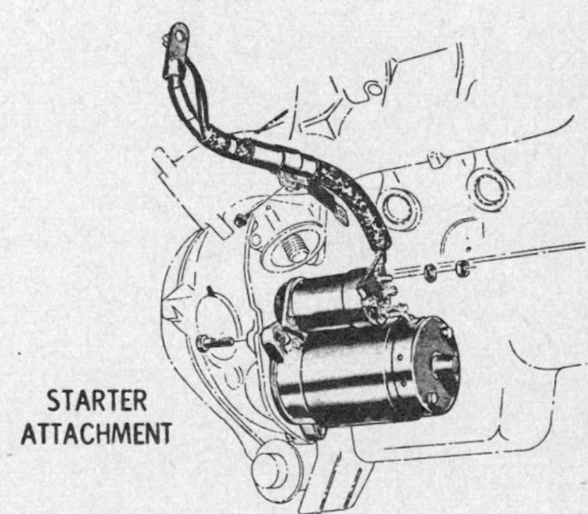

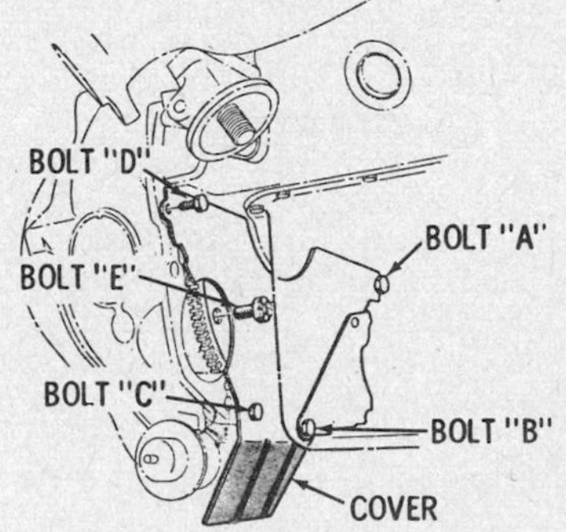

Transmission to converter attachment
(© Oldsmobile Div., G.M. Corp)

6. Raise the car on a hoist.
7. Loosen, but do not remove the upper left-hand bolt securing the flywheel cover.
8. Disconnect starter wiring, then remove starter.
9. Remove bolts B, C and D from flywheel cover plate.
10. Remove the 3 flywheel-to-converter bolts.
11. Disconnect vacuum modulator line and stator wiring.
12. Remove the remaining transmission-to-engine bolt.
13. Install transmission lift.
14. Disconnect the shift linkage.
15. Remove the 3 bolts and nut, on the right-hand side, holding the engine to the final drive.

NOTE: When the last three transmission to final drive bolts are removed, a quantity of oil will be lost.

16. Remove 3 bolts securing the engine mount bracket to the rear of the engine.
17. Remove the two bolts securing the rear engine mounts to the frame crossmember.
18. Remove the two upper engine mount brackets-to-transmission bolts A and B. (See illustration.)
19. Remove the four brackets-to-engine mount bolts.
20. Slide transmission rearward and down. Engine mount bracket will follow transmission down. Install converter holding tool J-21654.
21. After transmission is removed from car, the link assembly cover insulator can be removed or installed.

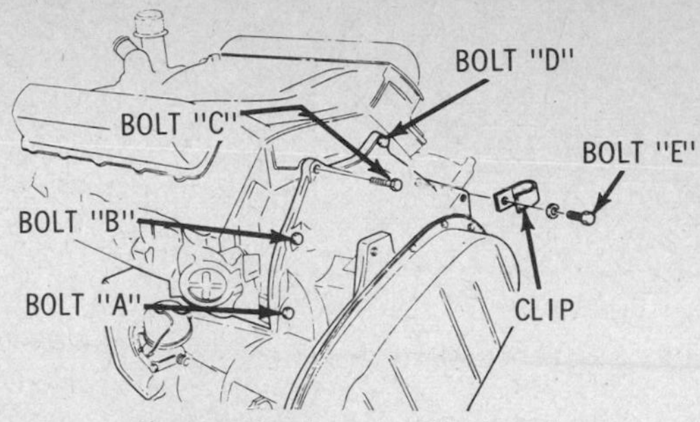

Transmission-to-engine attachment
(© Oldsmobile Div., G.M. Corp)

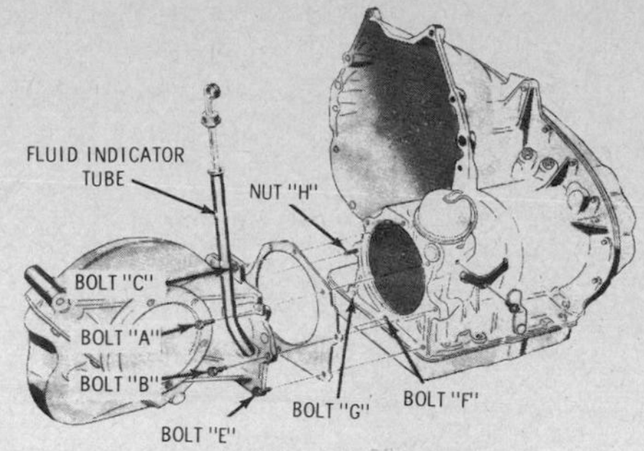

Transmission-to-final drive attachment
(© Oldsmobile Div., G.M. Corp)

Automatic Transmission Installation

When installing the transmission, the motor mount bracket must be positioned loosely on the link assembly cover until the transmission is in place. Then reverse removal procedure. Torque the bolts as follows:

Engine to torque converter housing —30 ft. lbs.
Engine bracket to transmission—55 ft. lbs.
Engine bracket to rubber mount—55 ft. lbs.
Oil cooler lines to transmission—20 ft. lbs.
Final drive to transmission nuts and bolts—25 ft. lbs.
Torque converter to flywheel bolts—30 ft lbs. (40 ft lbs—1974-76).
Flywheel housing cover—5 ft. lbs.
Starter to transmision—30 ft. lbs. (35 ft lbs—1975-76)

After the transmission is installed, check transmission fluid level.

Fluid and Filter Change

1. Raise and support the front of the car.
2. Loosen the transmission pan attaching screws and allow the fluid to drain out into a container.
3. After most of the fluid has drained, remove the remaining attaching bolts and carefully lower the pan from the transmission. Some fluid will be in the pan, so be careful not to spill it.
4. Completely drain the pan and thoroughly clean it in solvent. Discard the old pan gasket.
5. Remove the intake pipe and filter assembly. Make sure the intake pipe-to-case O-ring seal was removed with the filter assembly.
6. Install a new O-ring seal on the intake pipe and position the new filter/intake pipe assembly in the transmission.
7. Install the pan with a new gasket and tighten the attaching screws to 12 ft lbs.
8. Add four quarts of Dexron or Dexron II transmission fluid through the filler tube.
9. Start the engine with the transmission in Park and allow it to run at fast idle for one minute.
10. Check the fluid level immediately with the car parked on a level surface, with the transmission in Park and the engine at normal idle speed; not fast idle. The fluid level should appear between the two dimples below the Add mark on the dipstick. Add fluid as necessary.

Removing/installing the transmission filter and intake pipe assembly
(© Oldsmobile Div., G.M. Corp)

This procedure is for checking the fluid at room temperature. The fluid level should be up to the Full Hot mark when it is at normal operating temperature.

Drive and Driven Sprockets for the Transmission Drive

If it should be necessary to replace either the drive sprocket, chain, or driven sprocket, the three unit combination must be replaced as a set. They are matched and are serviced as a unit.

Removal

1. Remove cover housing attaching bolts.
2. Remove cover housing and gasket. Discard the gasket.
3. Using snap-ring pliers in the sprocket bearing retaining snap-rings located under the drive and driven sprockets, remove them from retaining grooves in support housings.

NOTE: Do not remove snap-rings from beneath the sprockets. Leave them in a loose position between the sprockets and the bearing assemblies.

4. Remove drive and driven sprockets, link belt, bearings and shaft pulling upward on the drive and driven sprockets until the bearings are out of the drive and driven support housings.

NOTE: It may be necessary to pry up on the sprockets. Use care not to pry on the aluminum case or chain links.

5. Remove link belt from drive and driven sprockets.
6. Remove two hook-type teflon oil seal rings from turbine shaft.
7. Inspect drive and driven sprocket bearing assemblies for rough or defective bearings.

NOTE: Do not remove bearing assemblies from drive or driven sprockets unless they need replacement.

8. If removal of bearing assembly from drive and/or driven sprockets is necessary, proceed as follows:
   A. Remove sprocket to bearing assembly retaining snap-ring using snap-ring pliers.
   B. Mount sprocket with turbine or input shaft placed in hole in work bench on two 2 x 4 x 10 in. pieces of wood.
   C. With a hammer and brass rod, drive the inner race alternately through each of the access openings until the bearing assembly is removed from the sprocket hub. Drive the sprocket, then turbine shaft and link assembly.

Inspection

1. Inspect drive sprocket teeth for nicks, burrs, scoring, galling and excessive wear. A wear pattern on the bottom of the teeth is normal.
2. Inspect drive sprocket to ball bearing retaining snap-ring for damage.
3. Inspect drive sprocket ball bearing inner race mounting surface for damage.
4. Inspect turbine shaft for open lubrication passages. Run a tag wire through the passages to make sure they are open.
5. Inspect spline for damage.
6. Inspect the bushing journals for damage.
7. Inspect the two hook-type oil seal grooves for damage or excessive wear.
8. Inspect the turbine shaft for cracks or distortion.
9. Inspect the link belt for damage or loose links

NOTE: Take particular notice of the guide links. They are the wide outside links on each side of the link assembly.

Installation

Install by reversing removal procedures.

Driven Sprocket at Input Shaft Inspection

1. Inspect driven sprocket teeth for nicks, burrs, scoring, galling and excessive wear.
2. Inspect sprocket to ball bearing retaining snap-ring for damage.
3. Inspect ball bearing inner race mounting surface for damage.
4. Inspect input shaft for open lubrication holes. Run a tag wire through the holes to make sure they are open.
5. Inspect spline for damage.
6. Inspect ground bushing journals for damage.

Sprocket Bearing Installation

1. Turn sprocket so that turbine or input shaft is pointing upward.
2. Install new sprocket bearing as follows:
   A. Install snap-ring, letter side down on the shaft.
   B. Assemble bearing assembly on turbine or input shaft.
   C. Using a drift, drive the bearing assembly onto the hub of the sprocket until it is resting on the bearing seat of the sprocket.
   D. Install sprocket to bearing assembly retaining snap-ring into groove sprocket hub.
3. Install two hook-type teflon oil seal rings onto turbine shaft.

Front Unit End-Play Check

1. Install front unit end-play checking tool, (J-22241), into driven sprocket housing so that the urethane on the tool can engage the splines and the forward clutch housing. Let the tool bottom on the main-shaft, then withdraw it approximately 1/16-1/8 in.
2. Remove two of the 5/16—18 bolts from the driven support housing.
3. Install 5/16—18 threaded slide hammer bolt with jam nut into one bolt hole in driven support housing.

NOTE: Do not thread slide hammer bolt deep enough to interfere with forward clutch travel.

4. Mount dial indicator on rod and index indicator to register with the forward clutch drum which can be reached through second bolt removed from driven support housing.
5. Push end-play tool down to remove slack.
6. Push and hold output flange outward. Place a screwdriver in case opening at parking pawl area and push upward on output carrier.

Checking front unit end-play
(© Oldsmobile Div., G.M. Corp)

THICKNESS	COLOR
.060 - .064	Yellow
.071 - .075	Blue
.082 - .086	Red
.093 - .097	Brown
.104 - .108	Green
.115 - .119	Black
.126 - .130	Purple

Front unit end-play selective washer thickness
(© Oldsmobile Div., G.M. Corp)

7. Place another screwdriver between the metal lip of the end-play tool and the drive sprocket housing. Now, push upward on the metal lip of the end-play tool and read the resulting end-play. This should be .003-.024 in. The selective washer controlling this end-play is the phenolic thrust washer located between the driven support housing and the forward clutch housing. If more or less washer thickness is required to bring the end-play within specifications, select the proper washer from the chart.

Differential

A bevel gear-type differential is used on all front-wheel drive models. This design supersedes the original planetary gear-type final drive. While unit removal and installation procedures are typical, the assembly is not interchangeable with the previous design.

Overhauling the differential assembly is not encouraged. However, reconditioning procedures are given in later paragraphs.

Output Shafts, Bearings and Seals R & R

Right Side Removal

1. Disconnect battery.
2. Hoist car.
3. Remove engine oil filter.
4. Disconnect right-hand drive axle.
5. Disconnect support from engine and brace.
6. Remove output shaft assembly.
7. If seal is to be removed, install seal remover J-943 into seal and drive seal out with a hammer.
8. If output shaft bearing is to be removed, use a press.

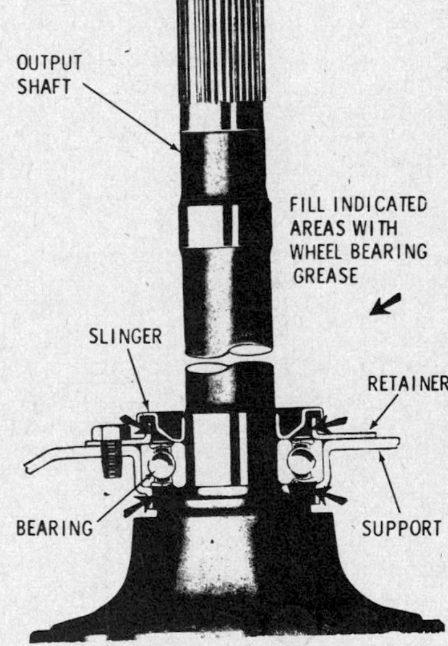

Assembly of right-hand output shaft
(© Oldsmobile Div., G.M. Corp)

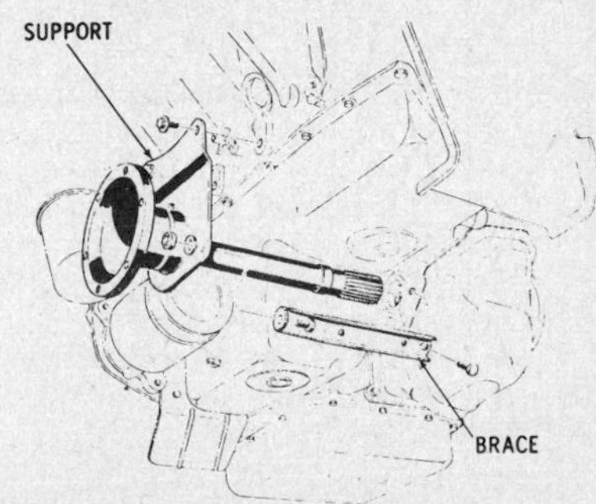

Right-hand output shaft
(© Oldsmobile Div., G.M. Corp)

Right Side Installation

1. If output bearing was removed, assemble parts as illustrated.
2. Position assembly in a press and install bearing until seated.
3. Pack area between bearing and retainer with wheel bearing grease, then install slinger.
4. If seal was removed, it can now be installed.
5. Apply special seal lubricant (Part No. 1050169) to output shaft seal, then install output shaft into final drive, indexing the splines of both units.
6. Install support to engine and brace bolts.
7. Connect drive axle to output shaft. Use new bolts.
8. Install engine oil filter.
9. Connect battery, check engine oil level and check for oil leaks.

Left Side Removal

The left-hand output shaft can normally be removed only after removing the final drive assembly from the car. However, if the left-hand axle assembly has been removed for any reason, the output shaft and seal can be removed using steps 2-3.

1. Remove left hand drive axle assembly.
2. Using a 9/16 in. socket, remove left-hand output shaft retaining bolt and left-hand shaft.
3. Drive out the left-hand output shaft seal.

Left Side Installation

1. If seal was removed, install new seal.
2. Apply special seal lubricant to seal, then insert output shaft into final drive assembly, indexing splines of output shaft with splines of final drive.
3. Install left-hand output shaft retaining bolt and torque to 45 ft. lbs.
4. Install left-hand axle.

Final Drive

Removal

1. Disconnect battery.
2. See illustration. Remove bolts A, B, and C. Nut D must be removed with a special wrench, such as MAC S-147.

NOTE: it may be necessary to remove the transmission filler tube to gain clearance.

3. Hoist the car. If a two post hoist is used, the car must be supported with floor stands at the front frame rails and the front post lowered.
4. Disconnect right and left drive axles from the output shafts.
5. Remove engine oil filter.
6. Disconnect brace from final drive, then disconnect right-hand output shaft assembly from engine.
7. Remove output shaft assembly from final drive.
8. See illustration. Remove bolt X and loosen bolts Y and Z.
9. Remove final drive cover and allow lubricant to drain.
10. Position transmission lift with adapter for final drive. Install an anchor bolt through final drive housing and lift pad.
11. See illustration. Remove bolts E, F, and G, and nut from H.
12. Move transmission lift toward front of car to disengage final drive splines from transmission. Some transmission fluid will be lost.
13. Lower transmission lift and remove final drive from lift.
14. Using a 9/16 in. socket, remove the left output shaft retainer bolt, then pull output shaft from final drive.
15. Remove transmission to final drive gasket.

Installation

1. Apply special seal lubricant (Part No. 1050169) to both output shaft seals.
2. Install the left output shaft into the final drive. Retain with bolt and torque to 40 ft. lbs. (45 ft. lbs. 1975-76)
3. Position final drive on transmission lift and install an anchor bolt through the housing and lift pad.

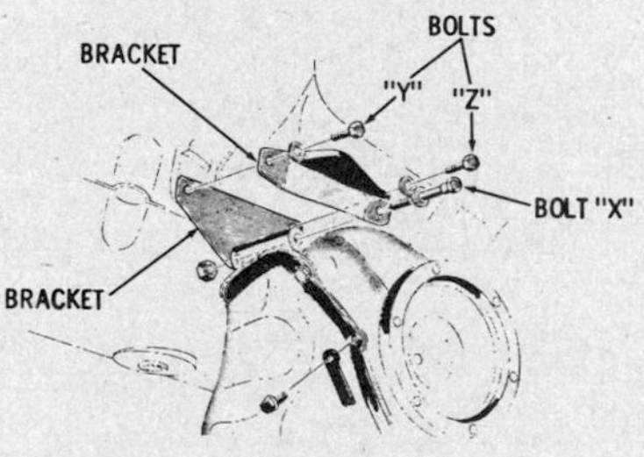

Disconnecting final drive from engine
(© Oldsmobile Div., G.M. Corp)

4. Apply a thin film of special seal lubricant on the transmission side of the new final drive to transmission gasket. Then position gasket on the transmission.
5. Raise the transmission lift. Align the two bolt studs D and H on the transmission with their mating holes in the final drive. Move final drive until it mates with the transmission.

Caution It may be necessary to rotate the left output shaft to align the splines on the final drive with the splines of the transmission output shaft.

6. Install bolts E, F, and G and nut H finger tight.
7. Install bolt X and torque to 75 ft. lbs (100 ft lbs—1974) (110 ft lbs—1975-76) Tighten and torque bolts Y and Z to 50 ft. lbs. (55 ft lbs—1975-76)
8. Loosen and remove lift from final drive.
9. Position a new cover gasket on the final drive, then install cover. Torque cover bolts to 30 ft. lbs.
10. Install right output shaft into final drive, indexing splines of output shaft with splines of final drive. Install mounting bracket and brace bolts and tighten.
11. Connect drive axles to output shafts using new bolts. Tighten the bolts to 75 ft lbs.
12. Install oil filter.
13. Raise hoist, remove stands and lower car.
14. If filler tube was removed, attach a new O-ring and install filler tube.
15. Install bolts A, B, and C and nut D. Torque all final drive to transmission bolts to 25 ft. lbs. 50 ft lbs (1974-76). Torque nuts to about 25 ft lbs. or 50 ft lbs (1974-76).
16. Connect battery.
17. Fill final drive with four and one-half pints of lubricant.

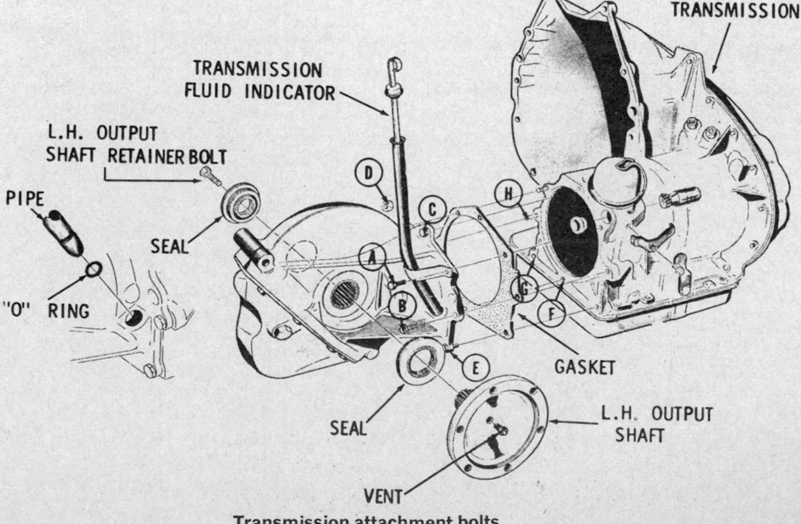

Transmission attachment bolts
(© Oldsmobile Div., G.M. Corp)

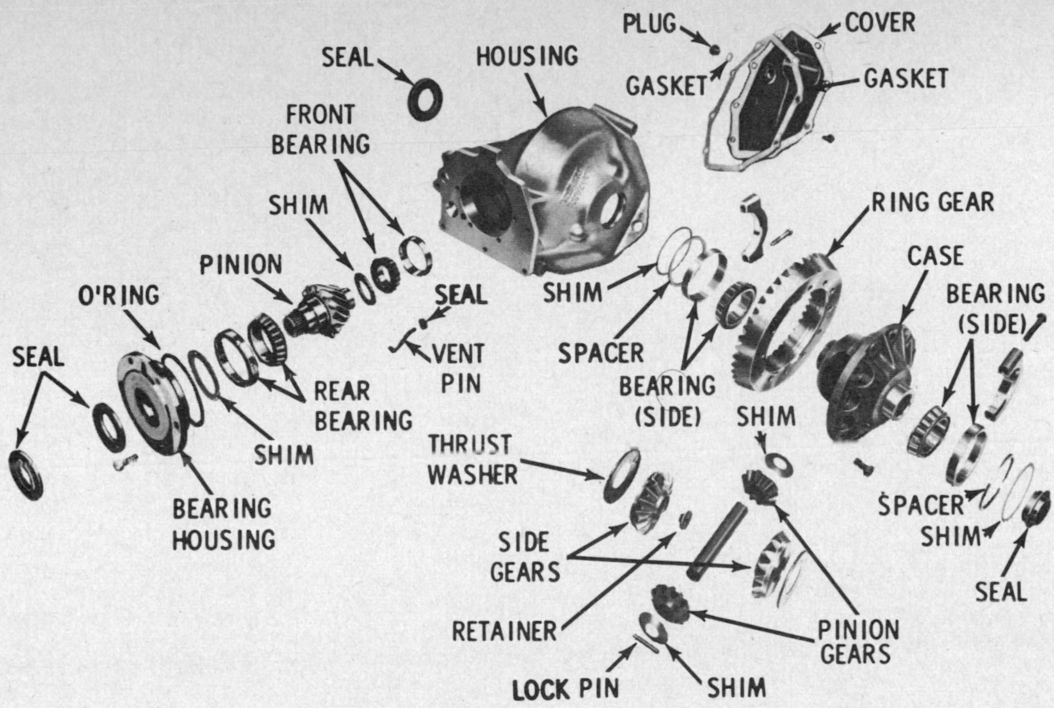

Final drive components (© Oldsmobile Div., G.M. Corp)

18. Check engine oil level. Start engine and check transmission fluid level.
19. Check for any oil leaks.

Drive Unit Disassembly

Adequate facilities are a must for this service.

1. Mount the final drive in holding fixture.
2. Use a drain pan under the assembly. Remove the drain plug. Then, remove the cover attaching screws and cover.
3. Rotate final drive until pinion points up, then check ring gear to pinion backlash with a dial indicator. Record backlash for reassembly. Check pinion and side bearing pre-load. Record pre-load reading.
4. Remove side bearing caps.

NOTE: Side bearing caps are of different size and can only be installed in their original position.

5. Install a spreader onto final drive, indexing the two guides on the spreader with the two holes on the carrier.
6. Turn the spreader screw to expand the spreader until the spacer and shims can be removed from between the small side of the bearing and the carrier. Keep the spacers and shims for reassembly.
7. Remove spreader from the carrier.
8. Remove the spacer and shims, then slide the case assembly to the left, away from the pinion gear. Remove case assembly from carrier. Check pinion bearing preload and record the reading.
9. Rotate carrier so the pinion is up.
10. Loosen set screw from adjusting nut.
11. Remove bearing housing bolts. Remove the drive pinion housing and remove the adjusting nut and housing from drive pinion. Remove rubber seal from bearing housing.
12. Remove rubber seal and vent wire from carrier.
13. With a slide hammer, remove pinion front outer race.
14. Remove the output shaft oil seals.
15. Remove the two oil seals from the adjustment nut.
16. If necessary, remove pinion rear outer race.

Pinion Bearing Removal

1. Remove the pinion front bearing and selective shim. Bearing can be removed with a press.
2. Remove the pinion rear bearing.

Final Drive Case Disassembly

1. Mark ring gear, case and case cover, then remove all but two of the case cover to ring gear bolts.

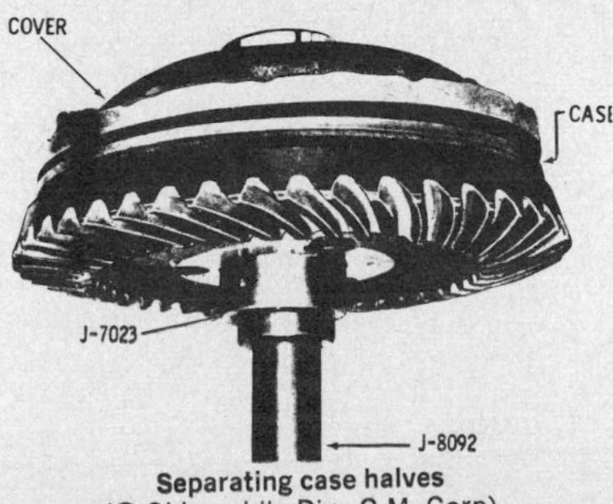

Separating case halves
(© Oldsmobile Div., G.M. Corp)

Loosen, but do not remove, two of the bolts 180° apart.

2. Jar the assembly lightly on the bench to separate the two halves of the case. Remove pinion carrier.
3. Clean all parts and examine all surfaces for wear or other damage.

Pinion Gears, Bevel-Type Removal and Installation

1. After ring gear has been removed, drive lock pin from pinion shaft.
2. Push pinion shaft out of case.
3. Rotate one pinion gear and shim toward access hole in case, then remove.

NOTE: Keep corresponding shims and pinion gear together for correct assembly.

4. Remove the other pinion and shim.
5. Remove side gears and thrust washers, keeping gears and washers in proper relationship for correct installation.

NOTE: The left-side gear has the threaded retainer that secures the (short) left output shaft. If threaded retainer is to be removed, use a brass drift to prevent trouble.

6. Upon assembling pinion and side gears into the case, lubricate components with a quality extreme pressure lubricant.
7. Place side gear thrust washers over the side gear hubs and install side gears into case. Gear with threaded retainer belongs in left side of case.
8. Position one pinion (without shims) between side gears, then rotate gears until pinion is di-

rectly opposite from loading opening in case. Place other pinion between side gears so that the pinion shaft holes are in line; then rotate gears to make sure holes in pinions line up with holes in case.

9. If holes line up, rotate pinions back to loading opening just enough to permit insertion of the pinion gear shims.
10. Install pinion shaft. Drive pinion shaft retaining lock pin into position.

Checking Pinion Depth

1. Install pinion front outer race. Drive race in until it bottoms.
2. Lubricate front bearing with final drive lubricant and install into front outer race.
3. Position tool J-21777-10 on the front bearing. Install tool J-21579 onto final drive housing and retain with two bolts. Thread screw J-21777-13 into J-21579 until tip of screw engages tool J-21777-10. Torque tool J-21777-13 to 20 in. lbs. to pre-load the bearing.
4. Remove dial indicator post from tool J-21777-9 and install discs J-21777-11 and J-21777-12. Reinstall dial indicator post.

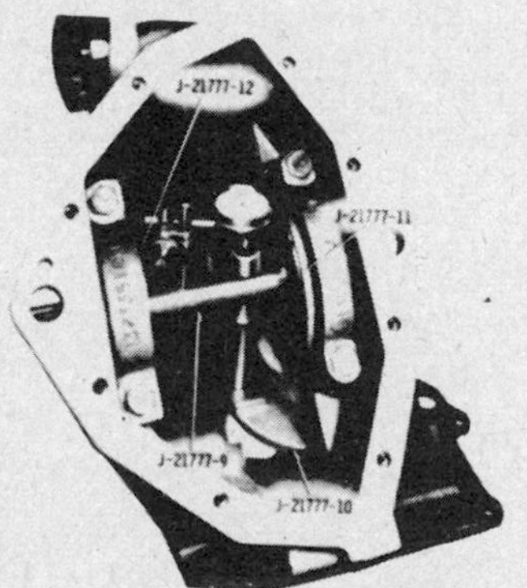

Checking pinion depth
(© Oldsmobile Div., G.M. Corp)

5. Place the gauging discs in the side bearing bores and install the side bearing caps.
6. Position the dial indicator on the mounting post of the gauge shaft with the contact button touching the indicator pad. Set dial indicator to zero, then depress the dial indicator until the needle rotates three-quarters of a turn clockwise. Tighten dial indicator.
7. Position the gauge shaft assembly in the carrier so that the dial indicator contact rod is directly over the gauging area of the gauge block, and the discs are seated fully in the side bearing bores.
8. Position gauge shaft so that the indicator rod contacts the gauging area. Rotate gauge rod back and forth until the indicator reads the greatest deflection. At the point of greatest deflection, read the pinion depth directly from the dial indicator.
9. Select the correct pinion shim to be used during assembly on the following basis:
   A. If a service pinion is being used, or a production pinion with no marking, the correct shim will have a thickness equal to the indicator gauge reading found in Step 9.
   B. If a production pinion is being used and it is marked + or —, the correct shim will be determined as follows:
   If the pinion is marked +, the shim thickness indicated by the dial indicator on the pinion setting gauge must be increased by the amount etched on the pinion. If the pinion is marked —, the shim thickness indicated on the dial must be decreased by the amount etched on the pinion.
10. Remove pinion depth checking tools and front bearing from carrier.

Final Drive Case Assembly

1. Install the pinion carrier into the case.
2. With the case and cover alignment marks indexed, insert four ring gear attaching bolts through case and cover. Align mark on ring gear with alignment marks on case and cover, then install ring gear onto case. Tighten the six attaching bolts alternately. Torque bolts to 85 ft. lbs.
3. If side bearings were removed, they can be installed now. Drive bearing on until it bottoms.
4. Install pinion rear bearing.
5. Position correct shim on drive pinion and install the drive pinion front bearing with tool J-21022 and a press.
6. Lubricate pinion bearings and install pinion into carrier.
7. Install seals into adjusting nut.
8. Install O-ring and vent pin onto face of carrier. Torque attaching nuts to 35 ft. lbs.
9. Install seal protector J-22236 over drive pinion, then install the adjusting nut over the seal protector and thread into the housing.
10. Assemble tools, as illustrated, and adjust pinion bearing preload. The preload is 2-15 in. lbs. for new bearings, and 2-5 in. lbs. for used bearings. Adjust new bearing preload to 4 in. lbs. while rotating the pinion and checking preload. Adjust until preload remains constant. When correct preload is obtained, tighten the set screw. Record preload reading as it will be used when making side bearing preload adjustment. Leave the tools on pinion for side bearing preload adjustment.

Side Bearing Preload Adjustment

Differential side bearing preload is adjusted by means of shims located between the side bearings and the carrier. One spacer is used on the right side only. Shims are used on both sides and come in thickness increments of .002 in. from .036 to .070 in. By changing the thickness of both side shims equally, ring gear and pinion backlash will not change.

1. Lubricate the side bearings with final drive lubricant.
2. Place differential in position in the carrier.
3. If the original ring gear and pinion are being used, subtract the reading obtained in Step 8 from the reading obtained in Step 3 of the Final Drive Disassembly procedure. This determines the original side bearing preload and will aid in determining whether thicker or thinner shims are needed to bring the side bearing preload to specifications.
4. Install original shim onto left side and spacer onto the right side.
5. Install the carrier spreader and apply just enough tension to allow the shim to be installed between the spacer and the carrier.
6. Release tension on the spreader, install side bearing caps, then check preload. Preload should be 10-15 in. lbs. for new bearings and 5-7 in. lbs. for old bearings over the pinion bearing preload obtained in Step 11, Final Drive Case Assembly.
7. If pre-load is not within specifications, select thicker or thinner shims to bring preload within limits.

Backlash Adjustment

1. Rotate differential case a few times to seat bearings, then mount dial indicator in order to read movement at the outer edge of one of the ring gear teeth.

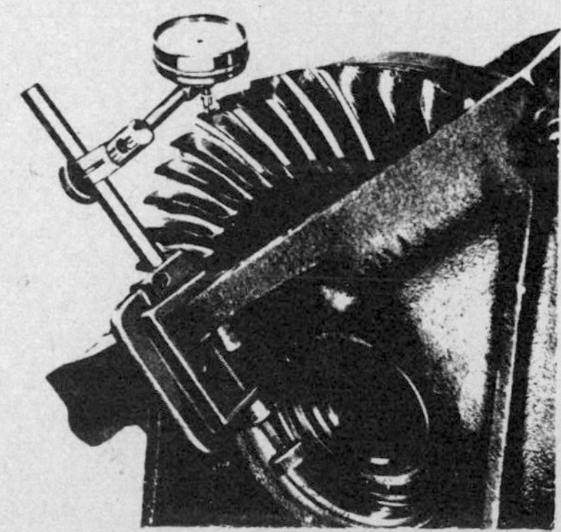

Checking backlash
(© Oldsmobile Div., G.M. Corp)

2. Check backlash at three or four points around the ring gear. Lash must not vary more than .002 in.
3. Backlash at the minimum point should be .005-.009 in. for all new gears. If original ring and pinion were installed, backlash should be set at the same reading obtained in Step 3 of Final Drive Disassembly procedure, if reading was within specifications.
4. If backlash was not within limits, correct by increasing thickness of one differential shim and decreasing thickness of other side shim the same amount. This will not disturb differential side bearing preload. For each .001 in. change in backlash desired, transfer .002 in. shim thickness. While looking into the differential from the open end (opposite the pinion) ; to decrease backlash desired, transfer .002 in. shim .001 in., decrease thickness of right shim .002 in. and increase thickness of left shim .002 in. To increase backlash .002in. increase thickness of right shim .004 in. and decrease thickness of left shim .004 in.
5. When backlash is correct, remove spreader. Install bearing caps and bolts. Torque to 65 ft. lbs.
6. Install new output shaft seals.
7. Install new gasket onto housing. Install cover, torque cover attaching bolts to 30 ft. lbs. Fill final drive to correct level.

DRIVE AXLES

Drive axles are completly flexible assemblies and consist of an axle shaft with an inner and outer constant velocity joints. Right axle shaft has a torsional damper mounted in the center. The inner constant velocity joint has complete flexibility, plus inward and outward movement. The outer constant velocity joint has complete flexibility but doesn't allow for inward and outward movement.

Drive Axle Removal —Right Side

1. Hoist car under lower control arms.
2. Remove drive axle cotter pin, nut and washer.
3. Remove oil filter.
4. Remove inner constant velocity joint attaching bolts.
5. Push inner constant velocity joint outward enough to disengage the right-hand final drive output shaft, then move rearward.
6. Remove right-hand output shaft bracket bolts to engine and final drive.
7. Remove right-hand output shaft and drive axle assembly.

Caution Care must be exercised so that constant velocity joints do not turn to full extremes, and that seals are not damaged against shock absorber or stabilizer bar.

Drive Axle Installation —Right Side

1. Carefully place righthand drive axle assembly into lower control arm and enter outer race splines into knuckle.
2. Lubricate final drive output shaft seal, with special seal lubricant part No. 1050169.
3. Install right-hand output shaft into final drive and attach the support bolts to engine and brakes. Torque the bolts to 55 ft. lbs.
4. Move right-hand drive axle assembly toward front of car and align with right-hand output shaft. Install attaching bolts and torque to 75 ft. lbs.
5. Install oil filter.
6. Install washer and nut on drive axle. Torque to 140 ft. lbs. (200 ft. lbs. 1975-76), then insert cotter pin.
7. Remove floor stands and lower hoist.
8. Check engine oil level.

Drive Axle Removal —Left Side

1. Hoist car under lower control arms.
2. Remove wheel and, if equipped with drum brakes, remove drum. If equipped with disc brakes, remove disc.
3. Remove drive axle cotter pin, nut and washer.
4. On 1969 models only, position access slot in hub assembly so that each of the attaching bolts can be removed. It will be necessary to push aside adjuster lever to remove one of the bolts.
5. On 1969 models only, install a slide hammer with adapter on the hub.
6. On 1969 models only, remove hub assembly. It will again be necessary to push aside adjuster lever for clearance for hub assembly.
7. Remove tie-rod end cotter pin and nut.

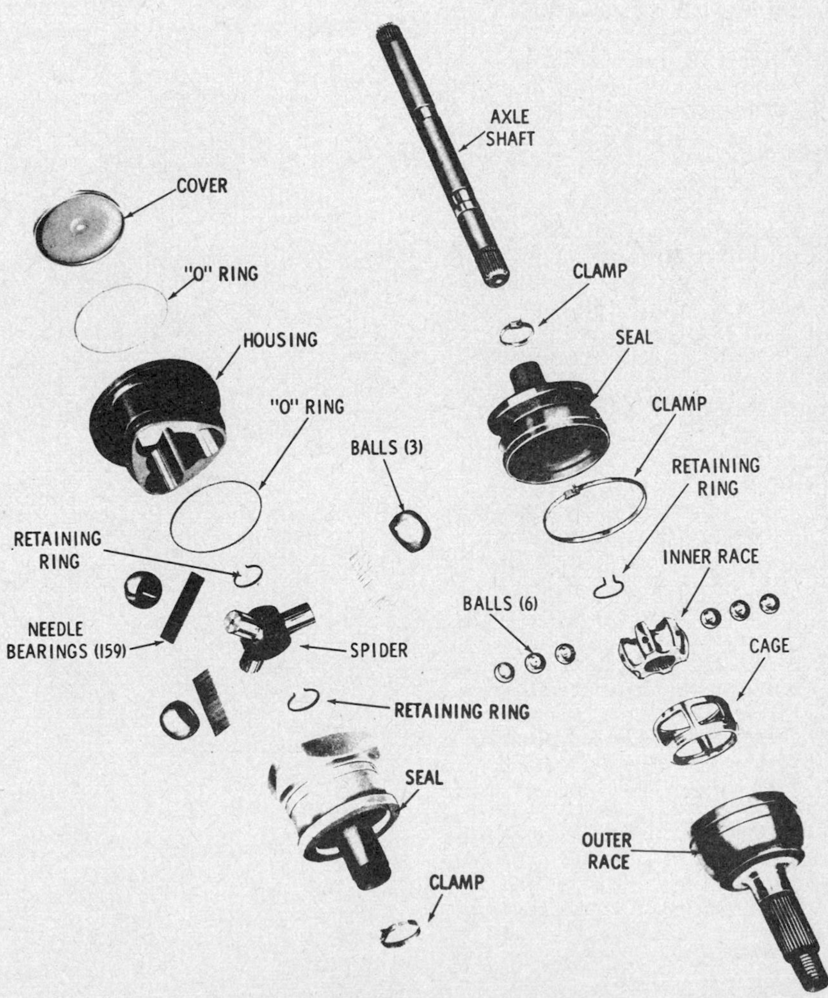

Exploded view of the left drive axle assembly
(© Oldsmobile Div., G.M. Corp)

8. Remove the tie-rod end from the knuckle with a puller.
9. Remove bolts from drive axle assembly and left output shaft. Insert a spacer between the axle shaft and lower control arm.
10. Remove upper control arm ball joint cotter pin and nut.
11. Using hammer and brass drift, drive on knuckle until upper ball joint stud is free.
12. Using puller, remove lower ball joint from knuckle. Care must be exercised so that ball joint does not damage drive axle seal.
13. Remove knuckle and support, so that brake hose is not damaged.
14. Carefully guide drive axle assembly outboard.

NOTE: Care must be exercised so that constant velocity joints do not turn to full extremes and that seals are not damaged against shock absorber or stabilizer bar.

Drive Axle Installation —Left Side

1. Carefully guide left-hand drive axle assembly onto lower control arm and into position on spacer.
2. Insert lower control ball joint stud into knuckle and attach nut. Do not torque.
3. Center left-hand drive axle assembly in opening of knuckle and insert upper ball joint stud.
4. Place brake hose clip over upper ball joint stud and install nut. Do not torque.
5. Insert tie-rod end stud into knuckle and attach nut. Torque to 45 ft. lbs. on 1969 models, 35 ft lbs. on 1970-74 models and 40 ft lbs on 1975-76 models. Install cottor pin and crimp.
6. On 1969 models, lubricate hub assembly bearing O.D. with E.P. grease and install. Torque to 65 ft. lbs.
7. Align inner constant velocity joint with output shaft and install attaching bolts. Torque to 65 ft. lbs. (75 ft lbs 1975-76)
8. Torque upper and lower ball joint stud nuts to 50 ft. lbs. upper —60 ft lbs, lower—95 ft lbs 1975-76) Install cotter pins and crimp.

NOTE: Upper ball joint cotter pin must be crimped toward upper control arm to prevent interference with outer constant velocity joint seal.

9. Install drive axle washer and nut. Torque to 60 ft. lbs. on 1969 models, 150 ft. lbs. on 1970-74 models and 200 ft lbs on 1975-76 models. Install cotter pin and crimp.
10. Install drum, if applicable, and wheel.
11. Remove floor stands and lower hoist.
12. Check camber, caster and toe-in and adjust if necessary. Refer to Front End Alignment.

Constant Velocity Joint (Out of Car)

The constant velocity joints are to be replaced as a unit and are only disassembled for repacking and replacement of seals.

Outer C. V. Joint Disassembly

1. Insert axle assembly into vise. Hold by the mid-portion of the axle shaft.
2. Remove inner and outer seal clamps.
3. Slide seal down axle shaft to gain access to C. V. joint. The seal may need to be rolled back or cut away on the right side drive axle.
4. Using snap-ring pliers, spread retaining ring until C. V. joint can be removed from axle spline.
5. Remove retaining ring.
6. Slide seal from axle shaft.
7. Remove grease from constant velocity joint.
8. Holding constant velocity joint with one hand, tilt cage and inner race so that one ball can be removed. Continue until all six balls are removed. It may be necessary to place the C.V. joint in a vise and gently tap one of the lobes with a brass drift to tip the race to remove the first ball.
9. Turn cage 90° and, with large slot in cage aligned with land in inner race, lift out.
10. With cage and inner race assembly, turn inner race 90° in line with large hole in cage. Lift short land on inner race up through large hole in cage and turn up and out to separate parts.

Outer C. V. Joint Assembly

1. Insert the short land of inner race into large hole in cage and pivot to install into cage.
2. Align inner race and pivot inner race 90° to align in outer race.
3. Insert balls into outer race one at a time until all six balls are installed. Inner race and cage will have to be tilted so that each ball can be inserted.
4. Pack constant velocity joint full of special lubricant.
5. Pack inside of seal with the same lubricant, until folds of seal are full.
6. Place small keystone clamp on axle shaft.
7. Install seal onto axle shaft.
8. Install retaining ring into inner race.
9. Insert axle shaft into splines of outer constant velocity joint

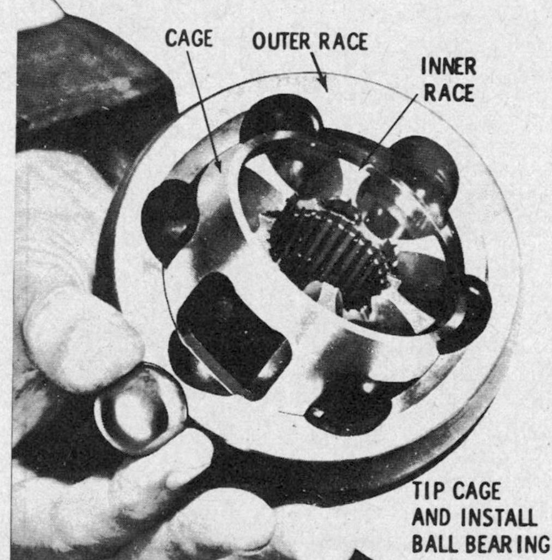

Installing the balls in the outer race
(© Oldsmobile Div., G.M. Corp)

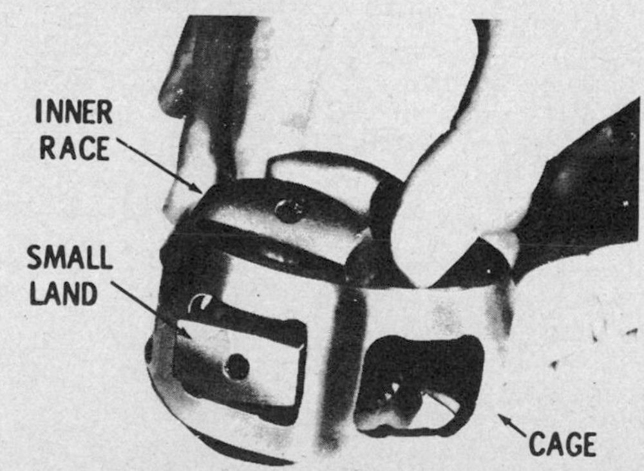

Removing or installing the inner race
(© Oldsmobile Div., G.M. Corp)

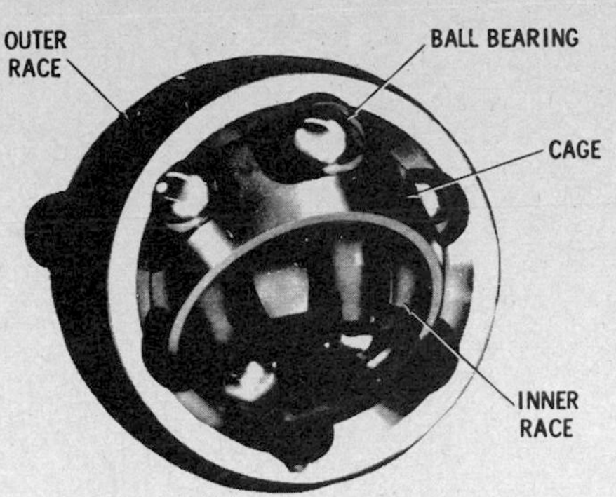

Removing the balls from the outer race
(© Oldsmobile Div., G.M. Corp)

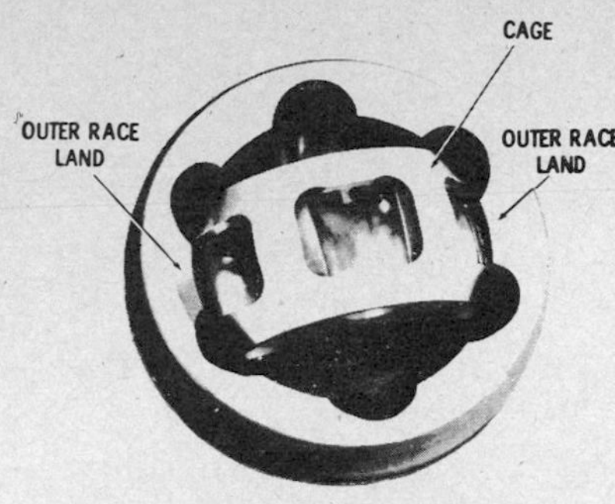

Positioning the cage
(© Oldsmobile Div., G.M. Corp)

until retaining ring secures shaft.
10. Position seal in slot of outer race.
11. Install large keystone clamp over seal and secure.

Inner C. V. Joint Disassembly

1. Place axle in a vise, clamping on the mid-portion of the axle shaft.
2. Remove the small seal clamp.
3. Remove the large end of the seal from C. V. joint with a hammer and chisel.
4. Carefully slide the seal down the axle shaft.
5. Carefully lift the housing assembly from the spider assembly and remove the O-ring from the housing outer surface. Use a rubber band to hold the three balls on the spider.
6. Remove the retaining ring from the end of the axle shaft.
7. Slide the spider assembly from the shaft.
8. Remove the inner retaining ring from the axle shaft.
9. Slide the seal off the axle shaft.
10. Remove the cover from the housing, prying with a screwdriver.
11. Remove the O-ring from the housing.
12. Remove the three balls from the spider, being careful not to lose the needle bearings. There are 53 needles per ball.

Inner C. V. Joint Assembly

1. Slide a new seal clamp onto the axle shaft, to be installed after the seal is positioned.
2. Pack the new seal full with special lubricant.
3. Position the retaining ring on the axle shaft inner slot.
4. Install the needle bearings (53) in the balls, packing with grease.
5. Install the three balls on the spider. Use a rubber band to hold them in place on the spider.
6. Position the spider assembly on the axle shaft and install the retaining ring.
7. Install a new O-ring in the outer groove in the housing.
8. Remove the rubber band from the spider assembly and push the spider assembly into the housing.
9. Lubricate the housing outer groove O-ring with seal lubricant or equivalent and slide the seal into position, lightly tapping it into place with a soft hammer and staking in six evenly spaced places. Be careful not to cut the O-ring with the metal portion of the seal.
10. Position seal into groove on the axle shaft and install the clamp.
11. Extend the axle shaft until the seal is at maximum length.
12. Fill the housing with special lubricant.
13. Install a new O-ring in the housing and lubricate the O-ring with special seal lubricant.
14. Install the cover into the housing.

Drive Axle Disassembly

1. Remove drive axle assembly.
2. Remove outer constant velocity joint seal clamps.
3. Remove inner constant velocity joint seal by prying out peened spots and driving off seal.
4. Slide seals inboard on shaft.
5. Using snap-ring pliers, spread retaining rings until both constant velocity joints can be removed from axle shaft.
6. Remove seals from axle.

Drive Axle Assembly

1. Pack seals with special lubricant.
2. Place outer constant velocity joint seal on axle, with keystone clamps in position on seal.
3. Insert axle into outer constant velocity joint until retaining ring locks axle into position.
4. Position seal and clamps and secure keystone clamps.
5. Place inner constant velocity joint seal on axle with keystone clamp in position on seal.
6. Insert axle into inner constant velocity joint until retaining ring locks axle into position.
7. Place axle assembly into press. Press seal into position and peen to secure.
8. Secure small keystone clamp with seal in position.
9. Install drive axle assembly.

FRONT SUSPENSION

The front suspension consists of control arms, stabilizer bar, shock absorbers and a right and left torsion bar. Torsion bars are used in place of conventional coil springs. The front end of the torsion bar is attached to the lower control arm. The rear of torsion bar is mounted into an adjustable arm at the torsion bar crossmember. The carrying height of the car is controlled by this adjustment.

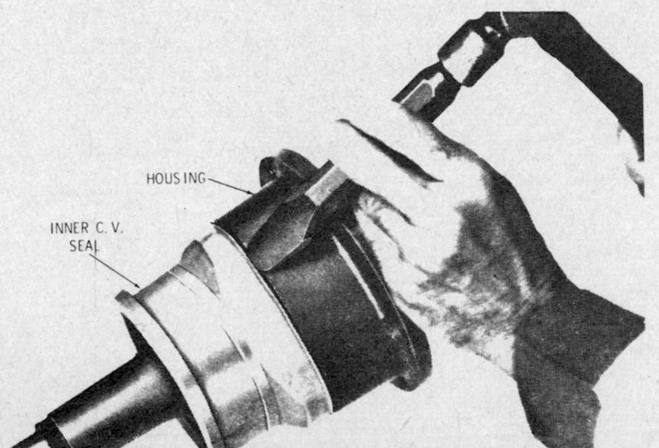

Removing the inner constant velocity joint seal with a chisel and hammer
(© Oldsmobile Div., G.M. Corp)

Removing the inner constant velocity joint housing assembly
(© Oldsmobile Div., G.M. Corp)

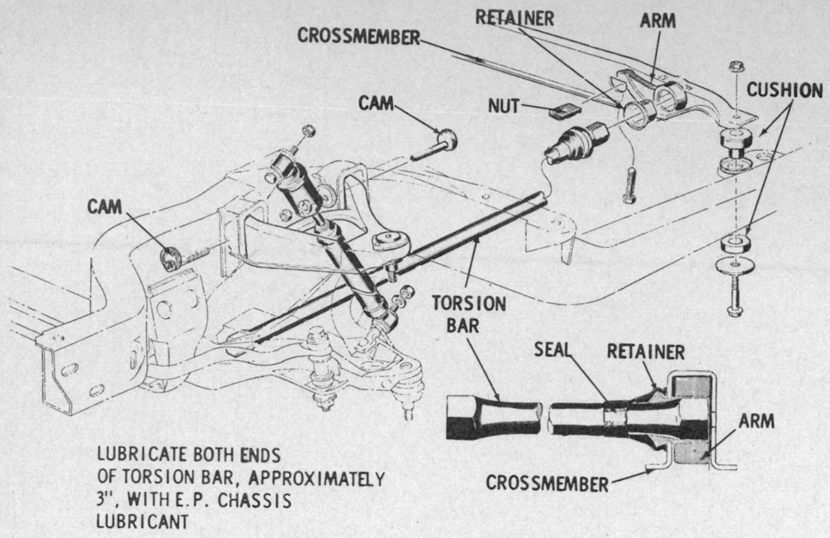

Front suspension
(© Oldsmobile Div., G.M. Corp)

Wheel Hub (Front) Removal and Installatio

1. Carefully pull drum fro hub assembly.
2. Remove drive axle cotter pi nut and washer. Remove dis if so equipped.
3. Position access slot in hub assembly so each of the attaching bolts can be removed.
4. Position spacer tool (J-22237) and install front hub puller (J-21579) and slide hammer (J-2619).
5. Remove hub assembly.
6. To install, reverse removal procedure.

NOTE: O.D. of bearing must be lubricated with E.P. chassis lubricant. Use care when installing hub assembly over drive axle splines.

Disc R & R

1. Siphon off about two-thirds of the fluid in the front reservoir of the master cylinder. Do not empty the reservoir or it will be necessary to bleed the system.
2. Hoist the car and remove the wheel.
3. Position piston compressor tool on the caliper and tighten the screw until the piston bottoms and the shoes are backed off the disc.
4. Remove the two caliper to knuckle attaching bolts and carefully lift the caliper from the disc. Support it so that the hose is not kinked or stretched.
5. Mark the hub and disc so that they will be correctly positioned when installed, then pull evenly on the disc to remove.
6. To install, reverse the above procedure. Make sure that the disc is positioned according to the marks made during removal. Tighten the caliper attaching bolts to 35 ft. lbs. and the wheel nuts to 115 ft. lbs. Fill the front reservoir of the master cylinder with new fluid and check the action of the brakes.

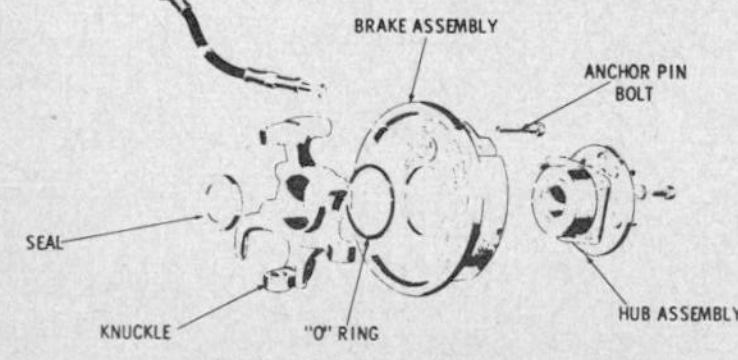

Front hub assembly—1969
(© Oldsmobile Div., G.M. Corp)

Steering Knuckle Seals R & R

Right-Hand Seal

1. Hoist car under lower control arms.
2. Remove drive axle cotter pin, nut and washer.
3. Remove oil filter element.
4. Remove inner constant velocity joint attaching bolts and push joint outward and rearward to disengage from output shaft.
5. Remove output shaft.
6. Remove drive axle assembly.
7. Pry seal from knuckle.
8. Installation is the reverse of removal.

Left-Hand Seal

1. Hoist car under lower control arms.
2. Remove wheel and drum.
3. Remove drive axle cotter pin, nut and washer.
4. Remove tie-rod end cotter pin and nut.
5. Split tie-rod.
6. Place support block between drive axle and lower control arm.
7. Remove upper control arm ball joint cotter pin and nut. Remove brake hose clip from ball joint stud.
8. Using hammer and brass drift, drive on knuckle until ball joint stud is free.

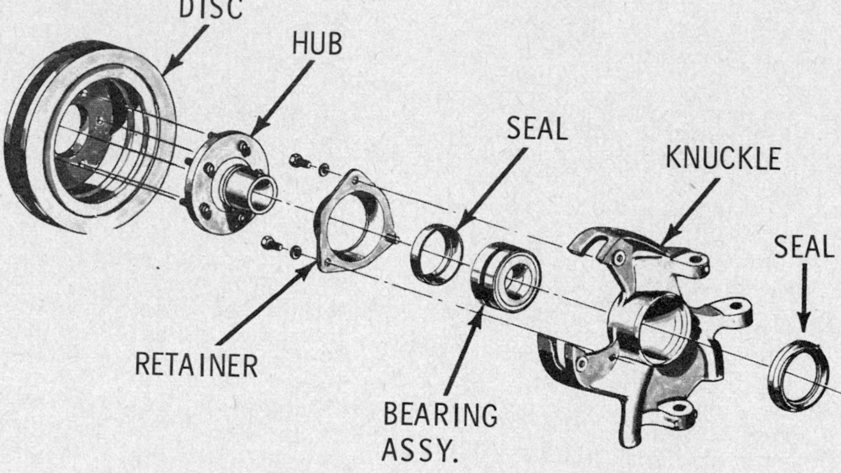

Exploded view of the hub assembly—1970-76
(© Oldsmobile Div., G.M. Corp)

9. Install spacer between lower ball joint seal and knuckle.
10. Remove lower ball joint from knuckle, using a puller.
11. Remove knuckle.
12. Pry seal from knuckle.
13. Installation is the reverse of removal.

Steering Knuckle Removal

1. Remove hub and drum or disc.
2. Remove upper ball joint cotter pin and nut.
3. Remove brake line hose clip from ball joint stud.

NOTE: Do not loosen ball joint stud.

4. Bend lock plate on anchor bolt up and remove anchor bolt of cars with drum brakes.
5. Carefully lift brake backing plate outboard over end of axle shaft and support brake hose so that it is not damaged.

NOTE: It is not necessary to remove dust shield on cars with disc brakes.

6. Place rubber pad over lower control arm torsion bar connector to protect constant velocity joint seal.
7. Using a brass drift and hammer loosen upper ball joint stud.
8. Remove cotter pin and nut from tie-rod end.
9. Using brass drift and hammer, remove tie-rod end from knuckle.
10. Remove cotter pin and nut from lower ball joint.
11. Carefully place ball joint puller adapter between ball joint seal and knuckle.
12. Remove lower ball joint from knuckle.
13. Remove knuckle.
14. The knuckle seal can be pried from the knuckle.

Steering Knuckle Installation

1. Using seal installer, install seal into knuckle. Seal should be packed with chassis grease.
2. Install lower ball joint stud into knuckle and attach nut. Do not tighten nut at this time.
3. Install tie-rod and stud into knuckle and attach nut. Do not tighten nut at this time.
4. Install upper ball joint stud into knuckle and attach nut. Do not tighten nut at this time.
5. Install backing plate onto knuckle with anchor bolt and lock plate. Do not tighten nut at this time.
6. Remove upper ball joint attaching nut and install brake line hose clip.
7. Torque ball joint nuts to a minimum of 40 ft. lbs. up to 1969, 85 ft. lbs. starting 1970. Never back off to install cotter pins.

NOTE: Cotter pin on upper ball joint must be bent up, only, to prevent interference with constant velocity joint seal.

8. Torque tie-rod end to 30 ft. lbs. and install cotter pin.
9. Torque anchor bolt to 135 ft. lbs. on drum brake models, and bend lock plate onto flat of bolt head.
10. Install drum or disc and wheel; install drive axle nut.
11. Remove floor stand and lower car.
12. Be sure to check camber, caster and toe-in, and adjust if necessary. Tighten drive axle and lug nuts to 105-110 ft. lbs.

Torsion Bar Removal

1. Hoist car and support at lift points.
2. Place torsion bar remover and installer so that center screw is seated in dimple of torsion adjusting arm.
3. Remove torsion bar adjusting bolt, counting number of turns necessary.
4. Turn center screw of tool until torsion bar is completely relaxed.
5. Disconnect stabilizer link.
6. Disconnect shock absorber from lower control arm.
7. Remove bolts from lower control arm to frame.
8. Pry lower control arm from frame and move forward until torsion bar and adjusting arm can be removed.

Torsion Bar Installation

1. Lubricate both ends of torsion bar for approximately 3 in. with extreme pressure chassis lubricant.
2. Position adjusting arm into crossmember, insert torson bar into adjusting arm and lower control arm, then position lower control arm into frame brackets and install nuts and bolts loosely.
3. Connect shock to lower control arm, tightening nut to 80 ft. lbs.
4. Connect stabilizer bar to lower control arm. Torque nut to 15 ft. lbs. and cut off bolt 1/4 in. below nut.
5. Place torsion bar remover and installer over crossmember and tighten center screw.
6. Raise hoist under lower control arms.
7. Torque lower control arm bushing nuts to 90 ft. lbs.
8. Check ride height and adjust if necessary.

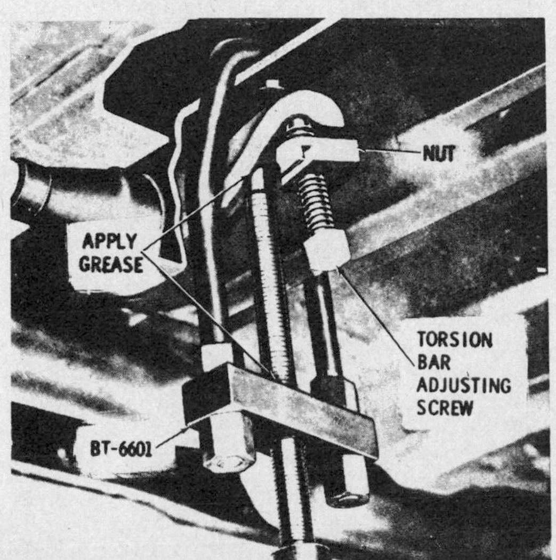

Torsion bar removal
(© Oldsmobile Div., G.M. Corp)

Upper Control Arm Removal

NOTE: The upper control arm is serviced as an assembly, less bushings.

1. Hoist car and remove wheel.
2. Remove upper shock attaching bolt.
3. Remove cotter pin and nut on upper ball joint.
4. Disconnect brake hose clamp from ball joint stud.
5. Separate upper ball joint stud from steering knuckle.
6. Remove upper control arm cam assemblies and remove control arm from car by guiding shock absorber through access hole in arm.

Upper Control Arm Installation

1. Guide upper control arm over shock absorber and install bushing ends into frame horns.
2. Install cam assemblies.

NOTE: Front cam is mounted up, rear cam is mounted down.

3. Install ball joint stud into knuckle.
4. Install brake hose clip onto ball joint stud.
5. Install ball joint nut. Torque to 50 ft. lbs. (60 ft lbs—1975-76) and insert cotter pin and crimp.

NOTE: Cotter pin must be crimped toward upper control arm to prevent interference with outer constant velocity joint seal.

6. Install upper shock, attaching bolt and nut. Torque to 75 ft. lbs, 90 ft. lbs for 1972-76 models.
7. Install wheel.
8. Lower hoist.
9. Check camber, caster and toe-in, and adjust if necessary.

Upper Control Arm Bushing Removal (On the Car)

NOTE: The upper control arm bushings can be removed and installed on or off the car.

1. Hoist car under lower control arms and remove wheel.
2. Disconnect upper shock absorber attaching bolt.
3. Remove cam assemblies from control arms.
4. Move control arms out of frame horns and attach bushing removal tools.

Upper Control Arm Bushing Installation (On the Car)

1. Install tools and press bushings into control arm.

2. Move control arm into frame horns and install cam assemblies. Front cam is installed with the bolt in the lower position. Rear cam is installed with the bolt in the upper position.
3. Connect upper shock attaching bolt. Torque to 75 ft. lbs, 90 ft. lbs on 1972-76 models.
4. Replace wheel and lower car.
5. Align front wheels.

Lower Control Arm Removal and Installation

1. Hoist car and support at lift points. Remove wheel assembly.
2. Place torsion bar remover and installer over crossmember so that center screw is seated in dimple of torsion adjusting arm.
3. Remove torsion bar adjusting bolt and nut, counting the number of turns necessary.

NOTE: This number of turns will be used when installing, to obtain initial carrying height.

4. Turn center screw of tool until torsion bar is completely relaxed.
5. Disconnect shock absorber and stabilizer link from lower control arm.
6. Remove drive axle nut.
7. Remove cotter pin and nut from lower ball joint stud.
8. Remove ball joint stud from knuckle, using puller.
9. Push drive axle in and pull knuckle outward to gain clearance, then remove lower control arm from knuckle and torsion bar.
10. Install by reversing removal procedure. Check and adjust ride height if necessary.

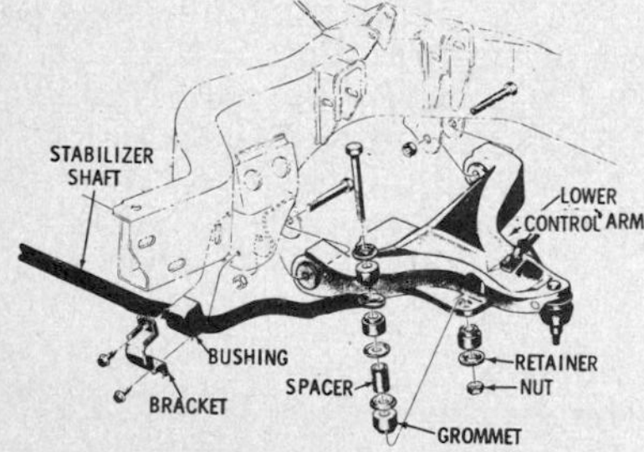

Lower control arm and related components
(© Oldsmobile Div., G.M. Corp)

Lower Control Arm Bushing Removal

1. Hoist car on a two post lift.
2. Disconnect upper shock attaching bolt.
3. Remove stabilizer link bolt and discard the bolt.
4. Place floor stands under frame horns. Lower front lift to floor.

NOTE: On 1971-76 models, the frame brace must be unbolted and moved away from the lower control arm mounts.

5. Install torsion bar removal and installation tool.
6. Remove lower control arm bushing bolts and lower control arm until free of frame horns.
7. Install bolts through rear bushing and press out bushing.

NOTE: Because of the torsion bar nut attachment to the lower control arm, it will be necessary to use a hardened ½-20 nut, to remove the front bushing.

Lower Control Arm Bushing Installation

1. Install tools and press rear bushing into lower control arm.

NOTE: Because of the torsion bar nut attachment to the lower control arm, it will be necessary to use a hardened ½-20 nut, to install the front bushing.

2. Raise lower control arm into frame horns and install bushing bolts and nuts. Do not torque.
3. Turn center bolt of tool into dimple of torsion bar arm until adjusting nut can be inserted through center frame support. Turn adjusting bolt clockwise the same number of turns needed to remove. Remove tool.
4. Raise front lift under lower control arms, and remove floor stands.
5. Connect upper shock attaching bolt and nut. Torque to 75 ft. lbs.
6. Using a new bolt, attach stabilizer link bolt to lower control arm. Torque to 14 ft. lbs. Cut the bolt off 1/4 in. below the nut.
7. Lower car and torque lower control arm bushing bolts to 75 ft. lbs, 90 ft lbs for 1972-76 cars. The frame brace on 1971-74 cars should be torqued to 55 ft lbs. (70 ft. lbs—1975-76)

Ball Joint Vertical Check

1969-72

1. Raise the car and position floor stands under the left and right lower control arm, as near as possible to each lower ball joint. Car must be stable and should not rock on floor stands.
2. Position dial indicator to register vertical movement at wheel hub.
3. Place a pry bar between the lower control arm and the outer race of the constant velocity joint and pry down on the bar. Care must be used so that the drive axle seal is not damaged. The vertical reading must not exceed .125 in.

Ball Joint Horizontal Check

1969-72

1. Place car on floor stands, as outlined in Step 1 in the Vertical Check.
2. Position dial indicator at the rim of the wheel, to indicate side play.
3. Grasp wheel with the hands, top and bottom, and push in on the bottom of the tire while pulling out at the top. Read gauge, then reverse the push-pull procedure. Horizontal deflection on the gauge should not exceed .125 in. at the wheel rim. This procedure checks both the upper and lower ball joints.

1973-76

1973-76 lower ball joints contain a visual wear indicator. The lower ball joint grease plug screws into the wear indicator which protrudes from the bottom of the ball joint housing. As long as the wear indicator extends out of the ball joint housing, the ball joint is not worn. If the tip of the wear indicator is parallel with, or recessed into the ball joint housing, the ball joint is defective.

Lower Control Arm Ball Joint Removal

1. Remove knuckle.
2. Using hack saw, saw the three rivet heads off.
3. Drill side rivets just deep enough to remove the rivet head.
4. Using hammer and punch, drive center rivet out of the control arm.

Lower Control Arm Ball Joint Installation

1. Install service ball joint into control arm and torque bolts and nut. Side bolts are torqued to 25 ft lbs while the upper nut is tightened to 45 ft lbs.
2. Install knuckle.
3. Check the nut to drive axle outer joint clearance. If necessary, grind a maximum of 1/16 in. from the nut.

Lower Control Arm Ball Joint Seal Removal

The lower ball joint seal can be installed with lower control arm either in or out of the car.

1. Remove steering knuckle. Refer to Knuckle Removal.
2. Using hammer and chisel, drive seal from ball joint.
3. Wipe grease from ball joint and stud.

Lower Control Arm Ball Joint Seal Installation

1. Position new seal over ball joint stud.
2. Lubricate jaws of seal installer and carefully slide jaw between seal and retainer.
3. Tap lightly with hammer on center bolt of tool until retainer is fully seated.
4. Install knuckle.
5. Lubricate the ball joint fitting until grease appears from seal.

Stabilizer Bar Removal

1. Remove link bolts, nuts, grommets, spacers and retainers from

lower control arm. Discard bolts.
2. Remove two bolts which attach dust shield to frame, both sides.
3. Remove bracket to frame attaching bolts and remove stabilizer bar from front of car.

Stabilizer Bar Installation

Reverse removal procedure.

NOTE: New link bolts are torqued to 14 ft. lbs., then cut off 1/4 in. from nut.

Torsion Bar Crossmember Removal

1. Raise car on a two post hoist and place floor stand under front torque boxes. Lower front hoist.
2. Disconnect parking brake cable and equalizer, and clip at torsion bar crossmember. Pull cable through the crossmember.
3. Relax torsion bars. Refer to Torsion Bar Removal.
4. Remove torsion bar with a torsion bar removal and installation tool.
5. Slide both torsion bars forward until they bottom in lower control arm nut.
6. Remove bolts from torsion bar crossmember to frame.
7. Raise torsion bar crossmember, remove rubber cushions from frame horns.
8. Disconnect hangers at muffler and tail pipes.
9. Move torsion bar crossmember to the right or left side until member clears frame, then remove.

Torsion Bar Crossmember Installation

1. Insert torsion bar crossmember above frame on right side of car and position left side over frame horn.
2. Raise crossmember so that rubber cushions can be installed.
3. Lubricate ends of torsion bars with extreme pressure chassis lubricant for about 3 in.
4. Raise crossmember up and toward rear of car. Raise torsion bars until they enter hole provided for them in crossmember.
5. Install adjuster arms into crossmember and slide torsion bars toward the rear of car until fully seated against rear edge of crossmember.
6. Install rebound cushions, bolts, washers and nuts through frame and crossmember. Torque to 40 ft. lbs.
7. Position torsion bar installation and removal tool over crossmember and tighten center bolt until nut can be inserted through crossmember.
8. Lubricate adjuster bolt with extreme pressure chassis lubricant and turn the same number of turns required to remove it.
9. Remove tool.
10. Install seals over retainers at rear of torsion bars.
11. Insert parking brake cable through crossmember. Install clip at crossmember.
12. Connect parking brake cable to equalizer.
13. Connect and tighten muffler and tail pipe hangers.
14. Hoist car and remove floor stands.
15. Lower car.
16. Check parking brake cable adjustment. Adjust as necessary.

Front End Alignment

Ride height is controlled by the adjustment setting of the torsion bar adjusting bolt. Clockwise rotation of the bolt increases the front height. It is very important that this height be considered and made correct before further steering geometry is established. Car must be on a level surface, gas tank full or a compensating weight added. Front seat must be all the way to the rear and tires inflated properly. All doors must be closed with no passengers or additional weight.

NOTE: If any excess weight other than what is mentioned above is normally carried in the car, i.e., tool boxes, salesmans samples, etc., it should remain in the car in its normal location.

1. Check rocker panel to ground dimension, as illustrated. Front and rear reading to ground should be as follows. Front to rear and side to side should be within 3/4 in.

	Front	*Rear*
1969-70	8 in.	8 in.
1971-74	8 3/4 in.	9 in.
1975-76	9 in.	9 1/4 in.

2. Align car on wheel alignment equipment as follows:
3. Raise front end and check wheel runout. Set and center the runout, then lower the car.
4. Loosen nuts on inboard side of upper control arm cam bolts.
5. Check camber and adjust if necessary by turning the front cam bolt in or out to correct 1/2 of the incorrect reading found when checked. Turn the rear cam bolt in the same direction the front bolt was turned to correct the remaining 1/2 of the incorrect setting.
6. Take the caster reading. Use camber reading scale for making this adjustment.
   A. Turn front bolt so camber changes 1/4 of the number of degrees caster change needed for correct reading.
   B. Turn the front cam bolts so camber returns to the original proper setting.
   C. Recheck caster reading.

NOTE: If you should run out of cam in the attempt to gain correct reading:

A. Turn front cam bolt so high part of cam is pointing up.

B. Turn rear cam bolt so high part of cam bolt is pointing down.

This is the location to start from. A correct setting should be obtainable with the above procedure.

   D. Torque upper control arm cam nuts to 95 ft. lbs.; hold head of bolt securely with a back-up wrench. Any movement of cam will affect final setting and you will have to recheck

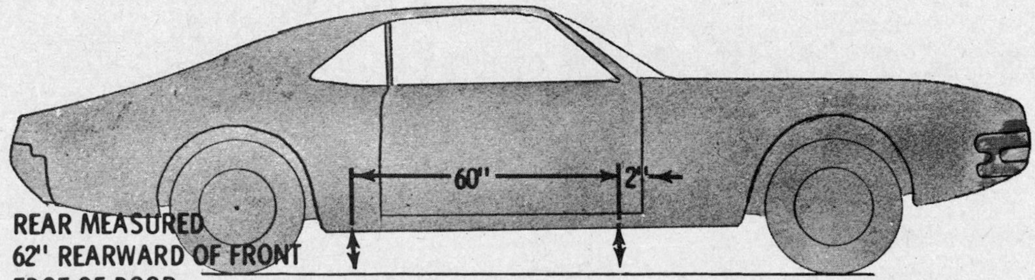

Ride height adjustment—1969-70 (© Oldsmobile Div., G.M. Corp)

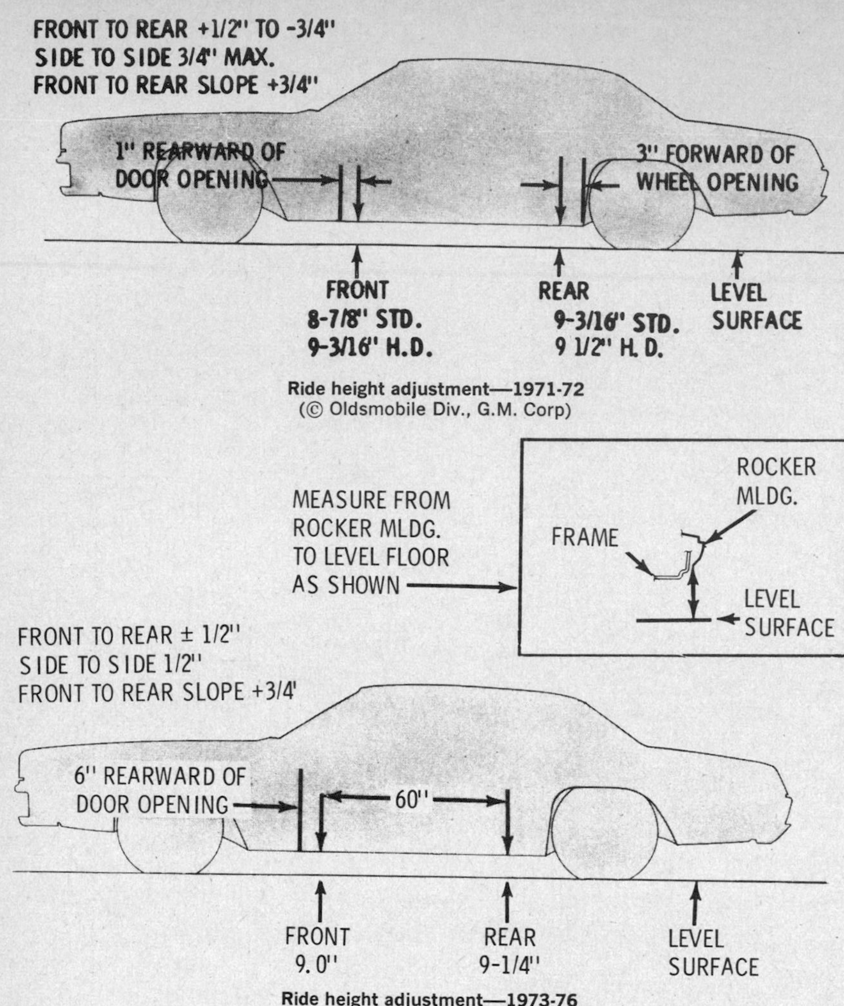

Ride height adjustment—1971-72
(© Oldsmobile Div., G.M. Corp)

Ride height adjustment—1973-76
(© Oldsmobile Div., G.M. Corp)

caster and camber adjustment.

7. Toe-in adjustment is as follows.
   A. Center steering wheel, raise car and check wheel runout.
   B. Loosen tie rod clamp nuts, and turn the tie-rod adjusting sleeves to obtain the proper toe-in setting.
   C. Tighten tie rod end nuts. Torque nuts 24 ft. lbs. Position tie rod clamps so openings of clamps are facing up. This is a very necessary setting. Interference and possible trouble with front end linkage could occur if clamps snag anything while turning.

REAR SUSPENSION

Some 1971-76 models are equipped with True-Track Braking (JL9 option). This is an electrically controlled rear brake equalizing system. The wheel speed sensors are mounted under the spindles, each with a driveshaft which runs through the spindle to attach to the grease cap.

Care must be taken when removing the rear spindle or the rear assembly not to break the sensor wiring or damage the sensor unit.

All 1971-76 models have a straight tubular axle housing instead of the I-beam drop axle used on 1969-70 models.

Rear Wheel Spindle R & R

1. Support the rear of the car with stands.
2. Remove the wheel, drum and hub assembly.
3. Disconnect the brake line fitting at the wheel cylinder.
4. If equipped with JL9, disconnect the wiring at the sensor.
5. Remove the four spindle attaching bolts and tie the backing plate out of the way.
6. On 1971-76 models, pull the spindle with a slide hammer.
7. On 1969-70 models, place a jack under the axle and remove the four bolts from the center spring clamp assembly. Remove the rubber insulator and lower the axle enough with the jack to provide working room for the spindle removal. Either drive the spindle out from behind or use a pulling tool.
8. To install, reverse the removal procedure. Install spindle with the keyway up, tightening the four bolts progressively one turn at a time. Adjust the rear wheel bearing.

Wheel Bearing Adjustment

For the rear wheel tapered roller bearings to be correctly adjusted, the following precautions should be taken:

1. The cones must be a slip fit on the spindle.
2. Inside of cones should be lubricated to make sure the cone creeps on the spindle.
3. Spindle nut must be a free-running fit on the threads.
4. Adjustment of rear wheel bearings should be made by continuously revolving the wheel while torquing the nut as follows:
   A. Torque adjusting nut to 25-30 ft. lbs. to seat all components thoroughly.
   B. Back off nut one-half turn, then retighten finger tight.
   C. If unable to insert cotter pin at this position, back off to nearest castellation.
   D. End-play should be 0.001-0.005 in.

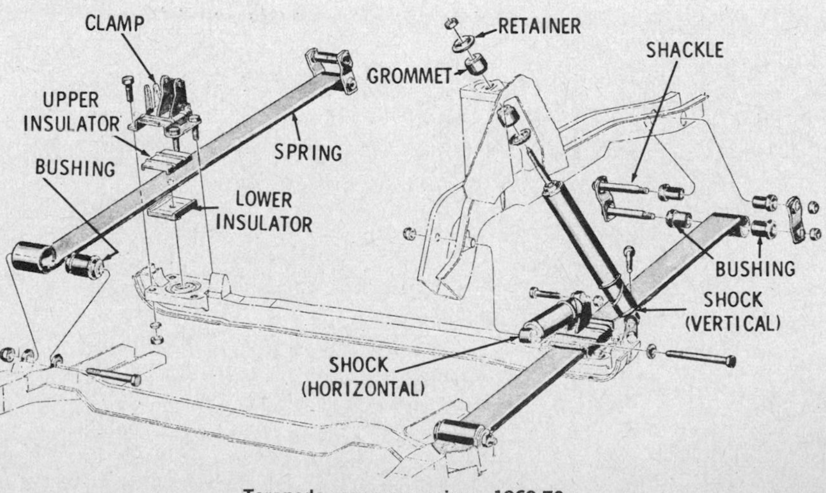

Toronado rear suspension—1969-70
(© Oldsmobile Div., G.M. Corp)

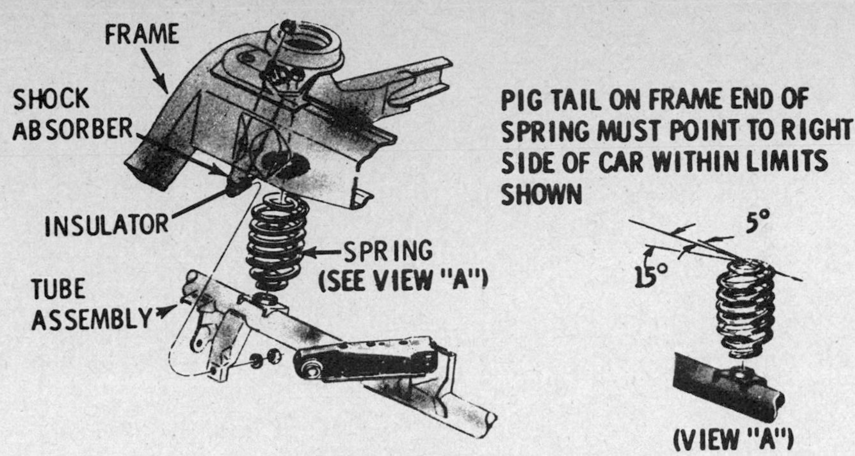

Toronado rear suspension—1971-76
(© Oldsmobile Div., G.M. Corp)

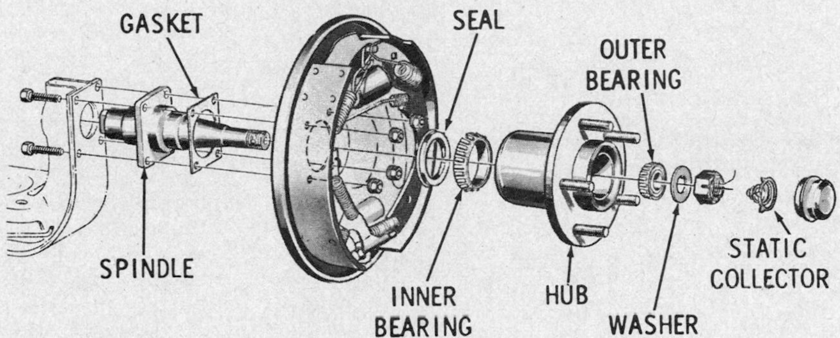

Rear hub assembly
(© Oldsmobile Div., G.M. Corp)

Rear Leaf Spring Removal

1969-70

1. Raise car and support on frame pad. With jack under axle, remove wheel.
2. Remove nut only from front of rear spring.
3. Remove two attaching nuts on rear shackle (outer). Remove rear shackle (outer).
4. Remove four attaching bolts on center clamp assembly.
5. Lift center clamp up, shock will hold it in position.
6. Lower jack until axle is free from spring.
7. Remove shackle assembly from spring and body.
8. Remove bolt from front of rear spring and remove spring.
9. If spring bushing is worn, remove and replace it.

Rear Leaf Spring Installation

1969-70

To install, reverse removal procedure.

A. Front bushing is a press fit. Replacement will require an arbor press.
B. Torque resonator bracket attaching bolts to 14 ft. lbs.
C. Torque four spring center clamp assembly bolts to 30 ft. lbs.
D. Install wheel, torque to 115 ft. lbs.
E. Remove all supports and, with car on the ground, torque rear shackle bolts to 40 ft. lbs. and front spring bolt to 75-80 ft. lbs.

Rear Coil Spring R & R

1971-76

1. With the car supported with floor stands, position a hoist under the tube assembly and raise it enough to relieve the tension on the shock absorber.
2. Disconnect the shock absorbers at the tube assembly.
3. Carefully lower the tube assembly until the springs are fully extended.

Caution Do not stretch the brake hydraulic hose.

NOTE: For 1973 and later models, the factory recommends that a spring compressor be used to compress the spring for removal and installation.

4. Remove the springs and insulators.
5. When installing, place the insulator on top of the spring and install the spring with the identification tag next to the tube assembly.
6. Hoist the tube assembly and connect the shock absorber, tightening the lower nut to 65 ft. lbs.

BRAKES

Brake adjustment, brake lining replacement, hydraulic cylinder overhaul and bleeding procedures can be found in the Unit Repair Section. Power brake overhaul procedures can be found in the Unit Repair Section.

In 1969 the single-piston disc brake an option. On 1970-76 models, the single piston Delco Moraine power front disc brakes are standard equipment. With the dual hydraulic system, a distributor assembly actuates a warning light switch whenever there is a failure in one of the hydraulic systems. Up to 1970, a balance valve in the rear system is used to proportion the hydraulic pressure to the rear wheels when more than 310 psi is required at the front (disc brake) butor and balance functions are inwheels. On 1971-76 models, the distritegrated in the combination valve assembly. Service procedures for the Delco Moraine single cylinder disc brake are found in the Unit Repaih Section.

Brake Pedal Travel

Maximum allowable brake pedal travel on 1969-70 models is 1⅞ in. In 1971-76 models maximum allowable travel is 2½ in. To bring pedal travel within specifications, adjust self-adjusting brakes by driving the car backward and forward alternately and applying the brakes. If pedal travel does not decrease, either the linings are excessively worn or the self-adjusting mechanism is frozen.

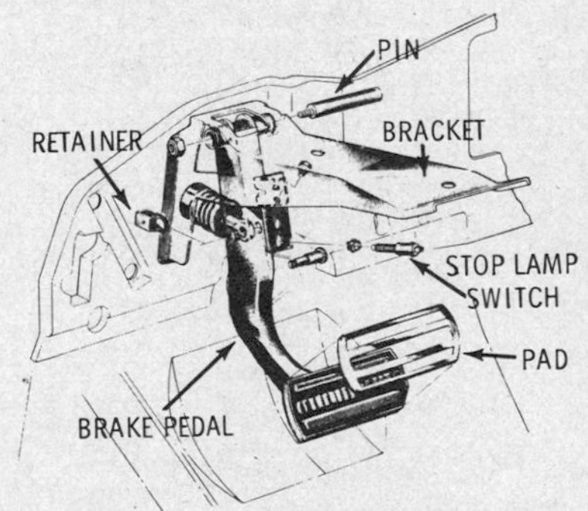

Brake pedal assembly
(© Oldsmobile Div., G.M. Corp)

Parking Brake Adjustment—1969—71

1. Release the parking brake.
2. Check hydraulic brake pedal travel, adjusting if necessary.
3. Tighten the equalizer adjusting nut until heavy resistance is felt when rotating the rear wheels forward, then back off the adjusting nut seven full turns.

Parking Brake Adjustment—1972-76

1. Depress the parking brake pedal exactly three clicks.

2. Tighten the adjusting nut until the rear wheels can just be turned rearward using 2 hands, but are locked in forward rotation.
3. With the parking brake off, the rear wheels should rotate freely in either direction with no drag.

Parking Brake Outer Cable R & R—1969-71

1. Disconnect the cable at the connector.
2. Remove the conduit bracket retainer.
3. Remove the rear wheel and brake drum.
4. Disconnect the cable from the actuating lever and install a corbin type hose clamp over the conduit retainer fingers.
5. Tap on the conduit lightly to remove it from the backing plate.
6. Install in the reverse order of removal.

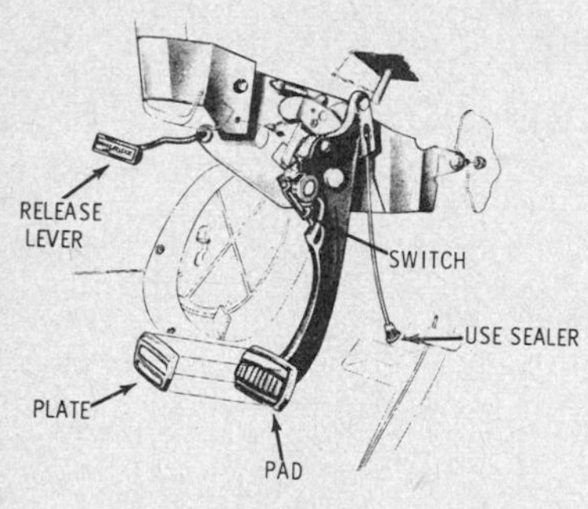

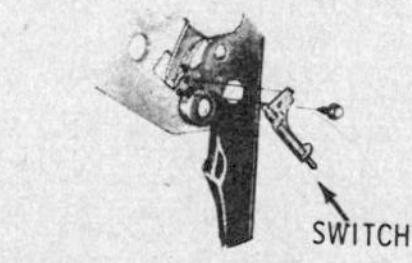

Parking brake assembly
(© Oldsmobile Div., G.M. Corp)

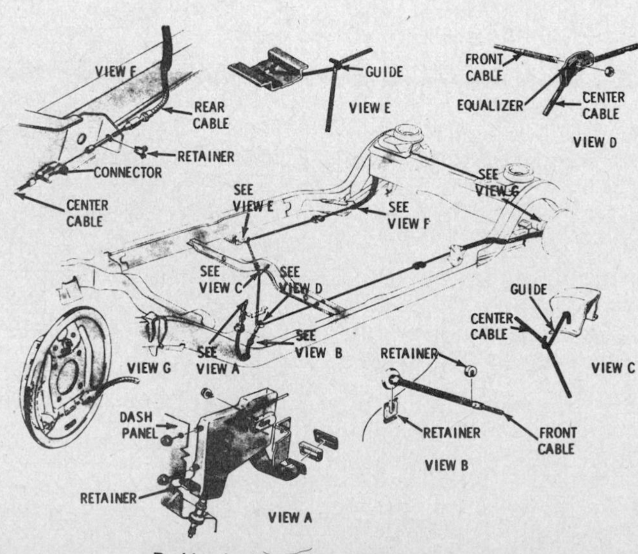

Parking brake cable—1971-74
(© Oldsmobile Div., G.M. Corp)

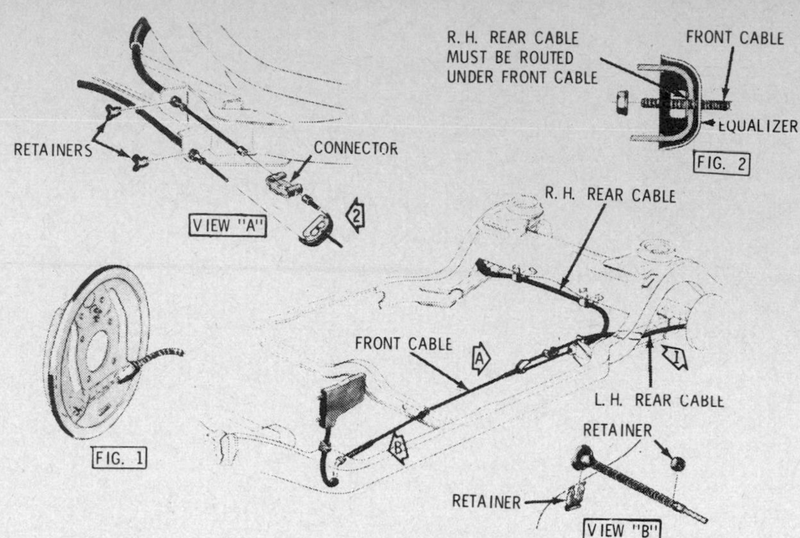

Parking brake cable routing—1975-76
(© Oldsmobile Div., G.M. Corp)

Front Parking Brake Cable R & R—1972-76

1. Raise and support the car.
2. Remove the adjusting nut from the equalizer.
3. Remove the retainer clip from the rear portion of the front cable at the frame.
4. Disconnect the front brake cable from the pedal assembly. Remove the front brake cable.
5. Installation is the reverse of removal. Adjust the parking brake.

Center Parking Brake Cable R & R—1972-74

1. Raise and support the car.
2. Remove the adjusting nut from the equalizer.
3. Unhook the connector at each end and disengage the hooks and guides.
4. Installation is the reverse of removal. Adjust the parking brake.

Rear Parking Brake Cable R & R—1972-76

1. Raise and support the car.
2. Remove the rear wheel and brake drum.
3. Loosen the adjusting nut at the equalizer.
4. Disengage the rear cable from the connector at the center cable. On 1975-76 models, remove the left rear cable from the equalizer.
5. Remove the 2 bolts attaching the cable to the backing plate.
   On 1975-76 models, push in the retaining fingers on the cable assembly at the backing plate.
6. Disengage the cable from the brake shoe lever.
7. Installation is the reverse of removal. Adjust the parking brake.

Master Cylinder R & R

1. Disconnect and plug hydraulic lines, and drain the cylinder.
2. Remove the attaching nuts and remove the master cylinder from the power unit.

Power Cylinder Removal

1. From inside the car, detach the brake pushrod from the brake pedal.
2. Detach the vacuum hose at the vacuum cylinder and disconnect the hydraulic line from the front of the slave cylinder.
3. Remove the four nuts that hold the vacuum unit up to the toeboard and remove the unit.
4. Install in reverse order of removal. Bleed system.

STEERING

The Toronado uses a parallelogram type steering linkage which connects both front wheels to the steering gear through the pitman arm. The right and left tie rods are attached to the steering arms at the wheels and to the intermediate rod by ball studs. The left end of the intermediate rod is supported by the pitman arm which is driven by the steering gear and the right end by the idler arm. The idler arm pivots on a support attached to the frame. The pitman and idler arms must be always parallel to each other.

Power Steering Pump R & R

1. Disconnect the positive battery cable.
2. Loosen the power steering pump pulley nut.
3. Remove the power steering pump belt.
4. Remove the pump hoses and seal them to prevent the entrance of foreign material.
5. Remove the pump assembly from the engine with the link attached.

NOTE: If the model is equipped with a power steering cooler, disconnect the return hose at the cooler—not at the steering gear.

6. Remove the hoses and link from the pump.
7. Installation is the reverse of removal.

Tie Rod R & R

NOTE: Any time the tie rods are replaced, the front end alignment must be checked and reset to specifications.

1. Raise the car, and remove the wheel.
2. Remove the cotter pins from the ball studs and remove the nuts.
3. Disconnect the tie rod from the steering arm with a puller.
4. Loosen the clamp bolts and unscrew the tie-rod end assemblies from the adjuster tubes.
5. Installation is the reverse of removal.

Pitman Arm R & R

1. Loosen the pitman arm nut on the pitman shaft.
2. Remove the flexible coupling bolt at the gear side of the coupling.
3. Disconnect the pitman arm from the intermediate rod by removing the cotter pin and the nut.
4. Remove the three steering gear-to-frame attaching bolts and raise the steering gear to clear the pitman arm stud. Position the steering gear sufficiently forward to allow access to the pitman arm shaft nut.
5. Remove the shaft nut and the pitman arm.
6. To install reverse the removal procedure. The pitman shaft nut should be torqued to 200 ft lbs. (210 ft lbs.—1975) with the wheels turned right. The pitman arm stud should be inserted through the intermediate rod. The nut torque is 45 ft lbs. (85 ft lbs.—1975-76). Install the cotter pin.
7. Readjust the toe-in and the steering wheel spoke alignment.

Idler Arm R & R

1. Remove the bolt and nut from the bracket which is attached to the frame crossmember. This secures one end of the idler arm.
2. Remove the cotter pin and nut. Remove the idler arm joint from the intermediate rod.
3. When installing the idler arm torque it to 45 ft lbs and install the cotter pin. The bracket bolt and nut should be torqued to 110 ft lbs.

Steering Wheel R & R

WARNING: If equipped with A.C.R.S. (Air Cushion Restraint System), do not attempt any adjustments or repairs until the disconnect procedure is complete. The system must be disconnected to prevent serious personal injury or damage to the system through accidental deployment.

To disconnect the system:

A. Turn the ignition switch to the LOCK position.

B. Disconnect the negative battery cable and tape the end to prevent any possibility of a complete circuit.

1. Disconnect the negative battery cable.
2. Pull up on the horn cap retainer assembly and remove the horn contact components.
3. Remove the contact assembly and remove the assembly from the wheel.
4. Remove the steering wheel nut. Using a puller carefully remove the wheel.
5. If the car is equipped with a tilt and telescope wheel use the following procedure.
   a. After removing the horn pad, disconnect the bayonet connector of the horn wire.
   b. Push the locking lever counterclockwise to the full release position.
   c. Scribe marks on the plate assembly in the area of the attaching screws. Remove the screws.
   d. Remove the plate assembly.
   e. Release the nut and remove the wheel.

Special Procedure for Cars with A.C.R.S. (Air Bags)

Some 1974 and later models have an air cushion, or air bag, restraint system. One of the elements of this complex system is an air cushion module in the top of the steering wheel. The steering wheel can be removed in the manner described in this section after the module has been removed.

To remove the module:

1. Turn the ignition lock to the LOCK position.
2. Disconnect the battery ground cable and tape the end to prevent any possibility of a complete circuit.
3. Remove the 4 module-to-steering wheel screws. A special tool is available to do this.
4. Lift up the module and disconnect the horn wire.
5. Disconnect the module wire connector. A special tool is available to do this, too.

WARNING: The driver air cushion module should always be carried with the vinyl cover away from all parts of one's body and should always be laid on a flat surface with the vinyl side up. This is necessary so that a free space is provided to allow the air cushion to expand in case of accidental deployment.

Do not attempt to repair any portion of the module. The module must be serviced as a unit. Attending repairs such as soldering wires, changing covers, etc. may cause accidental inflation or impair operation of the driver module and cause serious injury.

Do not dispose of a module in any way. The highly inflammable material in the module can cause serious burns if ignited. Modules must be exchanged at an authorized dealer's parts department.

To install the module:

6. Hold the module with the emblem in the lower right corner.
7. Loop the air cushion harness clockwise from the 11 o'clock position to the 6 o'clock position.
8. Install the module connector by pushing it onto the column circuit firmly. Check that it is fully seated.
9. Install the horn wire.
10. Position the module, making sure that the wiring is still in place, and install the 4 screws. Torque them to 40 in. lbs.
11. Reconnect the battery ground cable.
12. Turn the ignition lock to any position other than LOCK and check that the restraint indicator light operates correctly.

Turn Signal Switch R & R

WARNING: If equipped with A.C.R.S. (Air Cushion Restraint System), do not attempt any adjustments or repairs until the disconnection procedure is complete. The system must be disconnected to prevent serious personal injury or damage to the system through accidental deployment.

To disconnect the system:

A. Turn the ignition switch to the LOCK position.

B. Disconnect the negative battery cable and tape the end to prevent any possibility of a complete circuit.

Plastic cover
(© Oldsmobile Div., G.M. Corp)

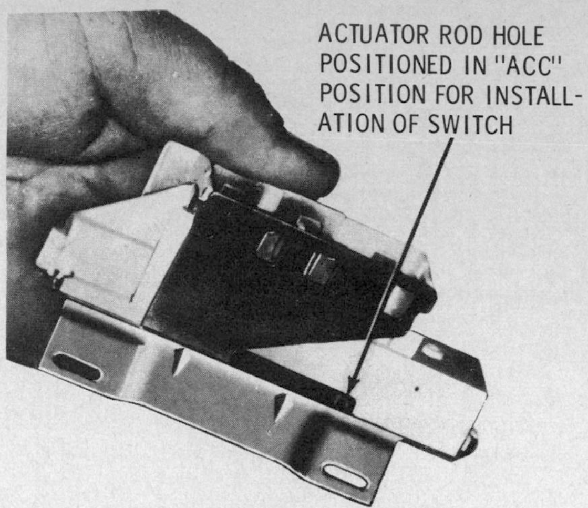

Ignition switch installation
(© Oldsmobile Div., G.M. Corp)

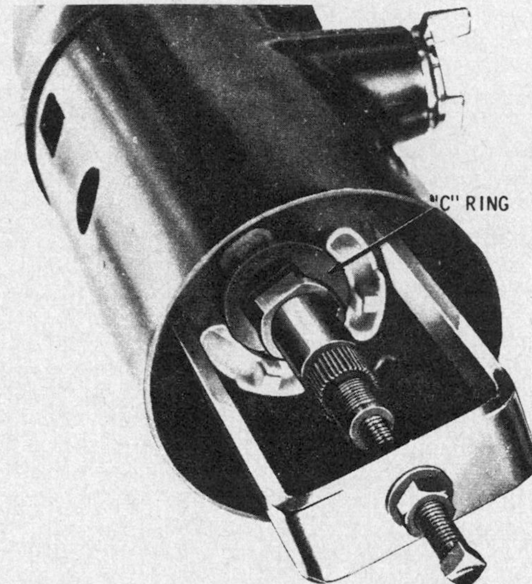

Removing the C-ring
(© Oldsmobile Div., G.M. Corp)

1. Disconnect the negative battery cable.
2. Remove the steering wheel. (See "Steering Wheel R&R.")
3. Remove the lower trim cap on the instrument panel and disconnect the turn signal connector from the harness. Wrap the connector with tape to prevent damage when removing the switch.
4. Remove the four bolts which fasten the jacket assembly to the bracket.
5. Remove the shift indicator.
6. Remove nuts from the bracket assembly while holding the column in position. Remove the bracket assembly and the wire protector from the turn signal wiring and then reinstall the nuts loosely.
7. Remove the plastic cover.
8. Using the correct puller depress the lockplate and remove the C-ring.
9. Using needle-nose pliers, remove the lockplate and the carrier assembly.
10. Release the upper bearing spring.
11. Place the signal lever in the right turn position and remove the lever. Position the tilt wheel in the center position.
12. Depress the hazard warning knob and then remove the knob.
13. Loosen and remove the three screws which fasten the switch and then carefully pull the switch and wiring from the top end of the column.

INSTRUMENT PANEL

Ignition Switch R & R

WARNING: If equipped with A.C.R.S. (Air Cushion Restraint System), do not attempt any adjustments or repairs until the disconnection procedure is complete. The system must be disconnected to prevent serious personal injury or damage to the system through accidental deployment.

To disconnect the system:

A. Turn the ignition switch to the LOCK position.

B. Disconnect the negative battery cable and tape the end to prevent any possibility of a complete circuit.

1. Disconnect the negative battery cable.
2. Place the ignition switch in "ACC" position (1969), "RUN" position (1970) or "OFF-UNLOCKED" (1971-76).
3. Remove the toe pan cover (if applicable) and loosen the toe clamp bolts.
4. Remove the lower instrument panel trim and toe pan trim panel.
5. Remove the automatic transmission shift indicator needle.
6. Remove the steering column dash bracket and let the steering wheel rest on the driver's seat.
7. Remove the two switch attaching screws and lift the switch off the actuator rod.
8. Disconnect the wiring.
9. To install, check that the lock cylinder is still in "ACC" (1969), "RUN" (1970) or "OFF-UNLOCKED" (1971-76). position and move the sliding portion of the switch until the switch hole is positioned as illustrated. Hold the switch in this position with a 0.090 in. pin as illustrated.
10. Connect the wiring to the switch.
11. Position the switch over the actuator rod, install the attaching screws (tighten to 3 ft. lbs.) and remove the 0.090 in. pin.
12. Reverse Steps 1 through 6 to complete installation.

Ignition Lock Cylinder R & R

WARNING: If equipped with A.C.R.S. (Air Cushion Restraint System), do not attempt any adjust-

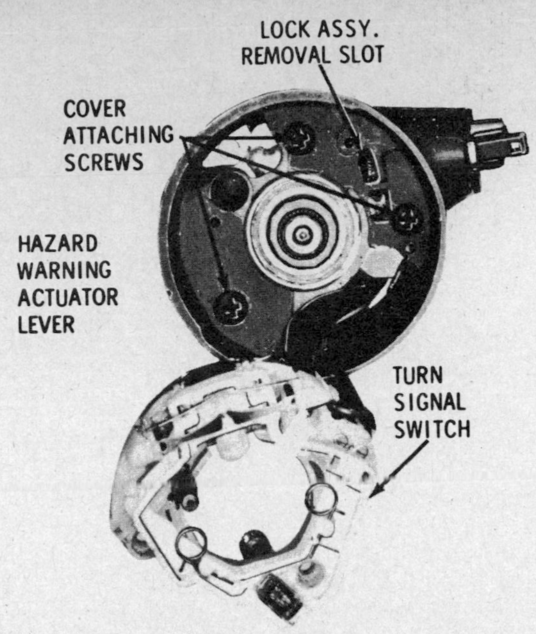

Ignition lock removal
(© Oldsmobile Div., G.M. Corp)

ments or repairs until the disconnection procedure is complete. The system must be disconnected to prevent serious personal injury or damage to the system through accidental deployment.

To disconnect the system:

A. Turn the ignition switch to the LOCK position.

B. Disconnect the negative battery cable and tape the end to prevent any possibility of a complete circuit.

1. Follow the complete procedure for the "Turn Signal Switch R&R."
2. Place the lock assembly in the "run" position and then insert a long, thin screwdriver into the slot as shown and pull outward on the lock assembly to remove it.

Headlight Switch R & R

1969-70

1. Remove lower left-hand trim panel.
2. Remove knob by first pulling the knob out to the headlight position, then depressing the spring-loaded button on switch body. Then, pull knob out of switch assembly.
3. Remove escutcheon nut.
4. Remove headlamp switch from rear of control panel.
5. Disconnect wiring and vacuum hoses.
6. Installation is the reverse of removal.

1971-73

The left hand control panel must be removed in order to remove the headlight switch.

1. Disconnect the battery.
2. Pry the floor lamp lens and lamp assembly out with a thin screwdriver.
3. Remove the screws from the left side of the lower steering trim and from the left hand trim panel.
4. Remove the nut and screw from the temperature cable on the bottom of the air conditioner or heater control.
5. Remove the ground wire attaching screw from the left hand panel lower brace.
6. Remove the four control panel attaching screws and remove the panel.
7. Remove the multiple connector from the headlight switch.
8. Pull the switch to "ON" position and push in on the small button on the switch, then pull the switch knob and shaft from the switch.
9. Remove the escutcheon from the switch and remove switch.
10. Install in reverse order of removal.

1974-76

WARNING: If equipped with A.C.R.S. (Air Cushion Restraint System), do not attempt any adjustments or repairs until the disconnection procedure is complete. The system must be disconnected to prevent serious personal injury or damage to the system through accidental deployment.

To disconnect the system:

A. Turn the ignition switch to the LOCK position.

B. Disconnect the negative battery cable and tape the end to prevent any possibility of a complete circuit.

1. Disconnect the negative battery cable.
2. Remove the heater or air conditioning control assembly as follows:
   a. With heater only, disconnect the defroster and temperature cable at the heater.
   b. With air conditioning, remove the lower trim panel and remove the nut and screw attaching the temperature cable to the control.
   c. Turn the headlight switch knob so the notch at the base of the knob can be located. Insert the pointed end of a pointed cotter key puller under the retainer to release the retainer and pull off the knob.
   d. Carefully insert the blade of a screwdriver into the slot in the lower edge of the applique and pry it from the clips in the cluster assembly.
   e. Remove the three screws attaching the control assembly to the cluster and pull the control assembly out of the panel.
3. Remove the escutcheon from the headlight switch.
4. Pull the headlight switch assembly through the heater or air conditioning control opening, disconnect the wiring connector and remove the switch.
5. Install the headlight switch in the reverse order.

WINDSHIELD WIPERS

Motor R & R

1. Raise the hood and remove the cowl screen or grille.
2. Loosen the wiper transmission drive link attaching nuts which attach to the motor crankarm. Disconnect the drive link.
3. Disconnect the wiring and the washer hoses.
4. Remove the three motor attaching screws.
5. Remove the motor while guiding the crankarm through the hole.
6. To install the unit reverse the removal procedure.

Linkage R & R

1. Remove the wiper arms and blades.
2. Remove the cowl screen or grille.
3. Loosen the linkage drive link where it connects to the motor crankarm and then disconnect the drive link from the crankarm.
4. Remove the right and left linkage-to-body attaching screws and lift the linkage assembly out through the cowl plenum chamber opening.
5. To install the unit, place the linkage assembly in the plenum chamber and install the mounting screws loosely.
6. Conect the drive link to the motor crankarm and then tighten the securing nuts.

NOTE: During installation, the motor must be in the "park" position.

7. The assemblies must be aligned before the body attaching screws are tightened.
8. Reinstall the cowl screen, wiper arms, and the blades. Check the wiper pattern and park position of the arms.

RADIO

R & R

1969-70

1. Disconnect battery.
2. Remove both lower cluster panels.
3. Remove steering column attaching nuts and lower bracket.
4. Remove shift indicator needle.
5. Disconnect speedometer cable.
6. Remove attaching nuts from cluster lower brackets, leaving brackets attached to the instrument panel.
7. Remove two upper instrument panel screws and lay cluster assembly on steering column.
8. Remove radio knobs, washers or rear seat speaker control.
9. Remove radio attaching nuts and escutcheons.
10. Disconnect all wiring and antenna lead-in.
11. Remove lower radio support bracket attaching nut.
12. Remove radio from instrument panel.
13. Install by reversing the removal procedure.

1971-76

WARNING: If equipped with A.C.R.S. (Air Cushion Restraint System), do not attempt any adjustments or repairs until the disconnection procedure is complete. The system must be disconnected to prevent serious personal injury or damage to the system through accidental deployment.

To disconnect the system:

A. Turn the ignition switch to the LOCK position.

B. Disconnect the negative battery cable and tape the end to prevent any possibility of a complete circuit.

1. Loosen the ground strap at the lower tie bar and tape the edge of the instrument panel to prevent scratching.
2. Remove the radio support bracket nut at the rear of the radio.
3. Disconnect the three lights from the bezel.
4. Remove the four bezel attaching screws and pull the bezel forward as far as possible.
5. On 1973-74 models, remove the four screws from the steering column trim cover and remove the cover. Remove the four screws securing the ash tray housing to the tie bar and remove the housing assembly.
6. On 1975-76 models, disconnect the throttle cable and remove the throttle cable lever and reinforcement.
7. Disconnect all wiring from the radio.
8. Remove the radio knobs, attaching nuts and escutcheons, then remove the radio.
9. Installation is the reverse of the removal procedure. The antenna trimmer must be adjusted when the radio is installed.

HEATER

Blower Assembly R & R

1969

1. Remove the blower feed wire.
2. Using a long extension and a 7/16 in. socket, remove the sheet metal screw which holds the heater inlet to the dash. The socket can be inserted through the opening in the fender filler plate forward of the right front wheel.
3. Remove all the remaining nuts and push the heater case studs back until they no longer come through the dash.
4. Remove three of the bolts which hold the front fender. These bolts are situated at the rear of the front fender. The removal of these should allow the fender to be moved outward and upward slightly.
5. Remove the blower motor screws and remove the motor from the heater inlet. These should be removed separately from beneath the fender.
6. Reverse the removal procedure to install. Apply sealer to the heater inlet before installation.

1970

1. Disconnect blower feed and resistor wiring.
2. Disconnect vacuum hoses from the air inlet and forced vent diaphragms.
3. Disconnect temperature cable from temperature door lever.
4. Disconnect heater hoses. Keep open ends of hoses above engine coolant level to prevent loss of coolant.
5. Remove heater assembly attaching screws.
6. Remove heater assembly from the cowl.
7. If heater core is to be removed, it can be removed at this time.
8. To install, reverse the removal procedure. Be sure to apply sealer to the mounting face of the heater assembly.

1971-74

1. Remove the right front fender filler panel.
2. Disconnect the blower electrical wiring.
3. Remove the five nuts and two screws which secure the inlet assembly to the dash.
4. Remove the inlet assembly and the blower motor. The fan may be removed from the shaft by releasing the nut and lockwasher.
5. To install, reverse the removal procedure.

1975-76

1. Disconnect the negative battery cable.
2. Raise the car and remove right front tire and wheel.
3. Cut the inner fender liner with a linoleum knife to form a flap that folds down toward the inside of the car.
4. Remove the blower motor attaching screws and remove the motor assembly through the opening in the fender liner.
5. Transfer the ground wire and lead wire with condenser to the new motor.
6. Install the motor through the opening in the fender liner and install the attaching screws.
7. Test the blower motor operation.
8. Drill a hole in the flap at the opposite end from the fold and install a 5/16 in. self-tapping screw with a large washer. Close the flap and drill two more holes at the corners of the flap and install two 5/16 in. self-tapping screws with large washers. Use a sealer along the edge of the flap.
9. Install the wheel and tire and lower the vehicle.

Heater Core R & R

1969-70

1. Remove the glove box.
2. Disconnect the wiring, vacuum lines, and the defroster hoses from the heater case.
3. Drain the radiator below the level of the heater. Remove the heater hoses and gasket.
4. Remove the blower assembly screws and also the heater case from inside the car.
5. Separate the heater core from the case.
6. To install, reverse the removal procedure.

1971-73

1. Disconnect the battery and drain the radiator and disconnect the heater hoses.
2. Remove the four attaching nuts.

NOTE: In order to gain access to one of the nuts, it may be necessary to disconnect the right front fender at the bottom and block the fender away from the body so that the nut may be removed through the opening.

3. Disconnect the wiring, the three control cables, and the defroster duct.

RADIO TROUBLE DIAGNOSIS

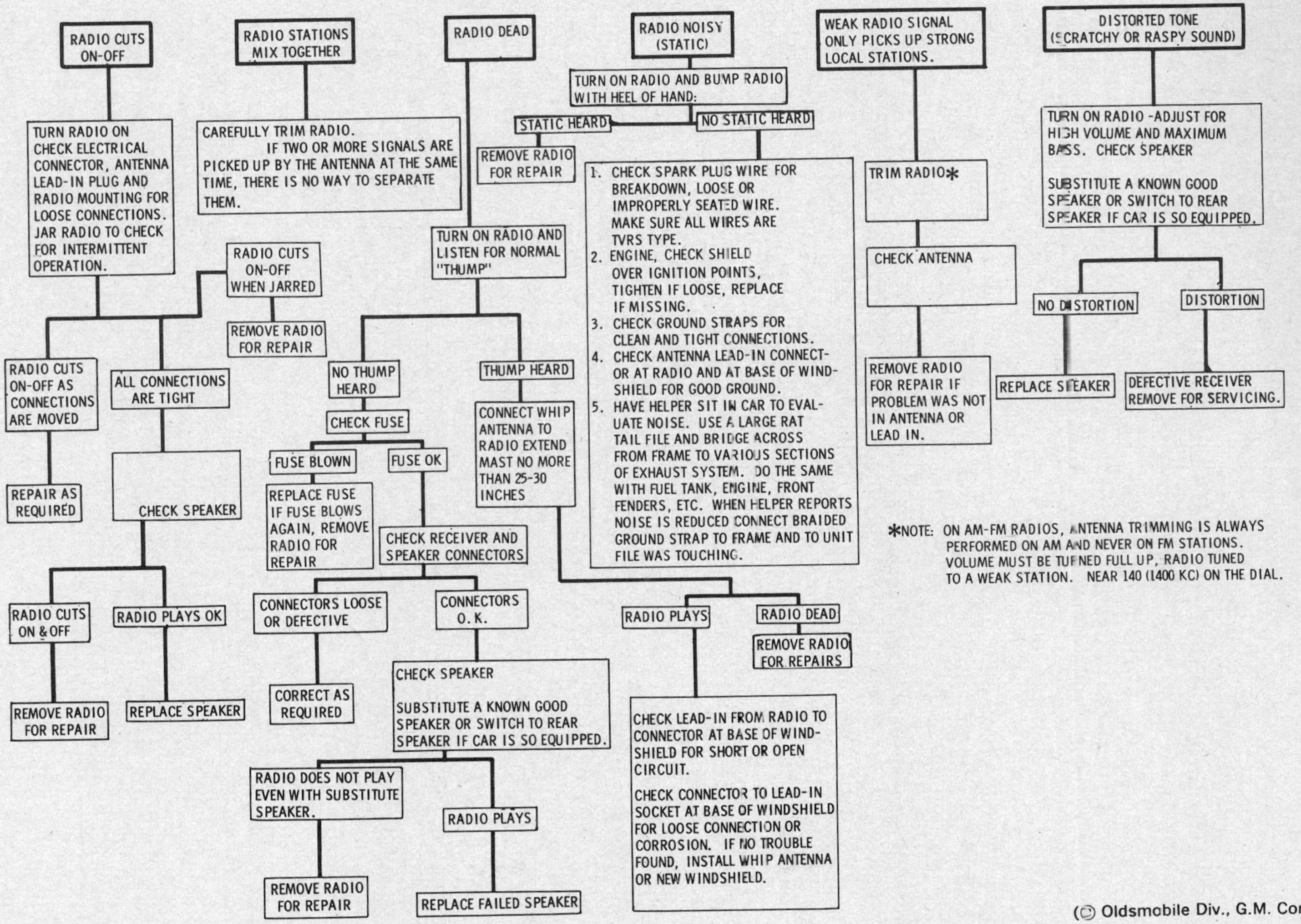

RADIO CUTS ON-OFF
- TURN RADIO ON CHECK ELECTRICAL CONNECTOR, ANTENNA LEAD-IN PLUG AND RADIO MOUNTING FOR LOOSE CONNECTIONS. JAR RADIO TO CHECK FOR INTERMITTENT OPERATION.
  - RADIO CUTS ON-OFF AS CONNECTIONS ARE MOVED → REPAIR AS REQUIRED
  - ALL CONNECTIONS ARE TIGHT → CHECK SPEAKER
    - RADIO CUTS ON & OFF → REMOVE RADIO FOR REPAIR
    - RADIO PLAYS OK → REPLACE SPEAKER
  - RADIO CUTS ON-OFF WHEN JARRED → REMOVE RADIO FOR REPAIR

RADIO STATIONS MIX TOGETHER
- CAREFULLY TRIM RADIO. IF TWO OR MORE SIGNALS ARE PICKED UP BY THE ANTENNA AT THE SAME TIME, THERE IS NO WAY TO SEPARATE THEM.

RADIO DEAD
- TURN ON RADIO AND LISTEN FOR NORMAL "THUMP"
  - NO THUMP HEARD → CHECK FUSE
    - FUSE BLOWN → REPLACE FUSE IF FUSE BLOWS AGAIN, REMOVE RADIO FOR REPAIR
    - FUSE OK → CHECK RECEIVER AND SPEAKER CONNECTORS
      - CONNECTORS LOOSE OR DEFECTIVE → CORRECT AS REQUIRED
      - CONNECTORS O. K. → CHECK SPEAKER
        SUBSTITUTE A KNOWN GOOD SPEAKER OR SWITCH TO REAR SPEAKER IF CAR IS SO EQUIPPED.
        - RADIO DOES NOT PLAY EVEN WITH SUBSTITUTE SPEAKER. → REMOVE RADIO FOR REPAIR
        - RADIO PLAYS → REPLACE FAILED SPEAKER
  - THUMP HEARD → CONNECT WHIP ANTENNA TO RADIO EXTEND MAST NO MORE THAN 25-30 INCHES
    - RADIO PLAYS → CHECK LEAD-IN FROM RADIO TO CONNECTOR AT BASE OF WINDSHIELD FOR SHORT OR OPEN CIRCUIT.
      CHECK CONNECTOR TO LEAD-IN SOCKET AT BASE OF WINDSHIELD FOR LOOSE CONNECTION OR CORROSION. IF NO TROUBLE FOUND, INSTALL WHIP ANTENNA OR NEW WINDSHIELD.
    - RADIO DEAD → REMOVE RADIO FOR REPAIRS

RADIO NOISY (STATIC)
- TURN ON RADIO AND BUMP RADIO WITH HEEL OF HAND:
  - STATIC HEARD → REMOVE RADIO FOR REPAIR
  - NO STATIC HEARD →
    1. CHECK SPARK PLUG WIRE FOR BREAKDOWN, LOOSE OR IMPROPERLY SEATED WIRE. MAKE SURE ALL WIRES ARE TVRS TYPE.
    2. ENGINE, CHECK SHIELD OVER IGNITION POINTS, TIGHTEN IF LOOSE, REPLACE IF MISSING.
    3. CHECK GROUND STRAPS FOR CLEAN AND TIGHT CONNECTIONS.
    4. CHECK ANTENNA LEAD-IN CONNECTOR AT RADIO AND AT BASE OF WINDSHIELD FOR GOOD GROUND.
    5. HAVE HELPER SIT IN CAR TO EVALUATE NOISE. USE A LARGE RAT TAIL FILE AND BRIDGE ACROSS FROM FRAME TO VARIOUS SECTIONS OF EXHAUST SYSTEM. DO THE SAME WITH FUEL TANK, ENGINE, FRONT FENDERS, ETC. WHEN HELPER REPORTS NOISE IS REDUCED CONNECT BRAIDED GROUND STRAP TO FRAME AND TO UNIT FILE WAS TOUCHING.

WEAK RADIO SIGNAL ONLY PICKS UP STRONG LOCAL STATIONS.
- TRIM RADIO*
  - CHECK ANTENNA
    - REMOVE RADIO FOR REPAIR IF PROBLEM WAS NOT IN ANTENNA OR LEAD IN.

DISTORTED TONE (SCRATCHY OR RASPY SOUND)
- TURN ON RADIO - ADJUST FOR HIGH VOLUME AND MAXIMUM BASS. CHECK SPEAKER
  SUBSTITUTE A KNOWN GOOD SPEAKER OR SWITCH TO REAR SPEAKER IF CAR IS SO EQUIPPED.
  - NO DISTORTION → REPLACE SPEAKER
  - DISTORTION → DEFECTIVE RECEIVER REMOVE FOR SERVICING.

*NOTE: ON AM-FM RADIOS, ANTENNA TRIMMING IS ALWAYS PERFORMED ON AM AND NEVER ON FM STATIONS. VOLUME MUST BE TURNED FULL UP, RADIO TUNED TO A WEAK STATION. NEAR 140 (1400 KC) ON THE DIAL.

4. Disconnect the right half of the right trim panel. If equipped with air conditioning, remove the instrument panel tie bar.
5. The case assembly may be removed from under the dash. The core may be separated from the case if it is defective.

1974-76

1. Disconnect the battery.
2. Drain the radiator below the heater hose level and disconnect the heater hoses.
3. Remove the four heater case-to-dash panel attaching nuts.
4. Remove the instrument panel trim cover.
5. Remove the two heater case-to-cowl attaching bolts from inside the car.
6. If equipped with air conditioning, remove the lower air duct.
7. Remove the instrument panel pad.
8. Disconnect the electrical leads at the glove box and clock.
9. Remove the right upper trim panel on the right side.
10. If equipped with air conditioning, disconnect the manifold from the heater case.
11. Disconnect the defroster duct from the heater case.
12. Disconnect the lower dash trim panel.
13. Disconnect the temperature cable, defroster cable, and vacuum hoses from the heater case.
14. Remove the heater case from the dash.
15. Separate the heater core from the case.
16. Install in the reverse order.

SEAT BELTS

Seat Belt/Starter Interlock System—1974-75

The seat belt starter interlock system consists of an electronic module, seat sensor switches, seat buckle switches, interlock relay and an override relay.

The electronic module receives signals from the seat sensor switches and the buckle switches to monitor the proper belt buckling sequence. If the proper sequence is followed, the module opens the interlock relay and allows the engine to be started. It is located underneath the right-hand front seat cushion.

The 3 seat sensor switches (one for each front seat position) are normally open and are located in the seat cushion.

The seat belt buckle switches on the outboard buckles are normally open, while the center buckle switch is normally closed.

The interlock relay is located near the fuse block and the points are open when the coil is energized.

For emergencies, an override relay is provided. Two fuses protect the interlock system, the "Clk-Ltr-Ctsy-Lt" and "Gauges-Trans" fuses.

Disabling the Interlock System

It is now legal to disconnect the seat belt interlock and the seat belt warning buzzer, but not the seat belt warning light. Disconnect the interlock and buzzer as follows:

1. Disconnect the negative battery cable.
2. Locate the interlock harness connector with orange, yellow and green wires under the left side of the instrument panel on or near the fuse block.
3. Cut and tape the green wire on the body harness side of the connector.
4. If not equipped with the low coolant warning and heavy duty cooling system, disconnect and remove the buzzer from the fuse panel.
5. If equipped with the low coolant warning and heavy duty cooling system, cut the yellow wire behind the connector and tape the ends.
6. Reconnect the battery and check the operation of the system.

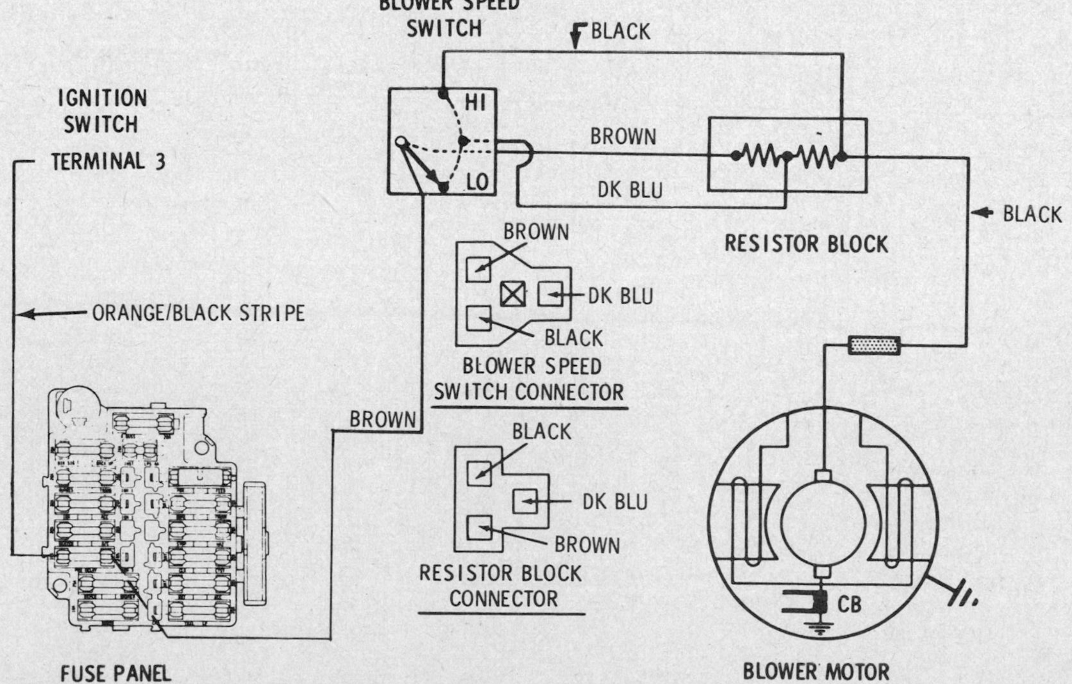

Heater wiring schematic
(© Oldsmobile Div., G.M. Corp.)

INDEX

Pontiac · Grand Prix

YEAR IDENTIFICATION

1969 Pontiac

1969 Grand Prix

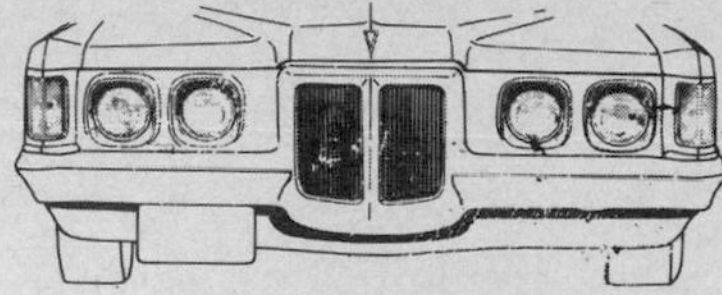

1970 Grand Prix

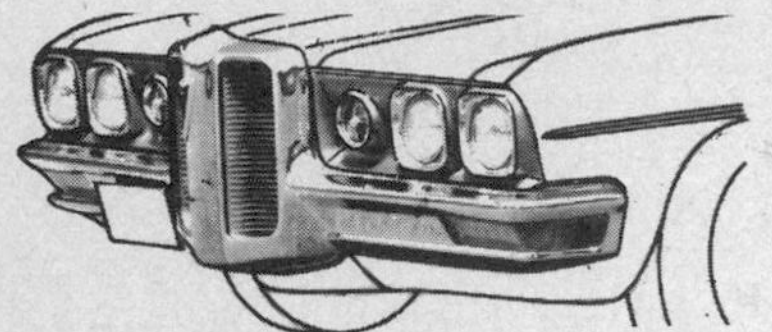

1970 Catalina

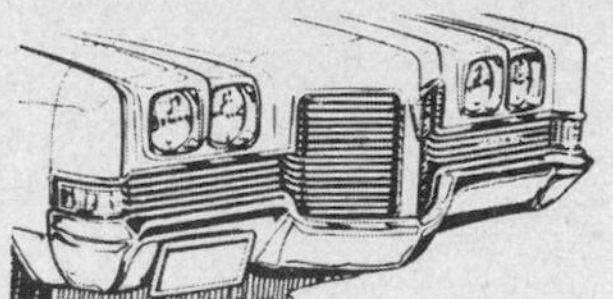

1971 Pontiac

1971 Grand Prix

1972 Pontiac

1972 Grand Prix

1973 Catalina

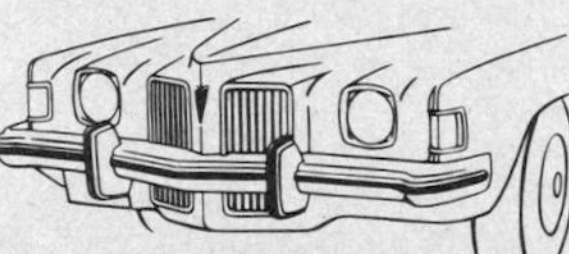

1973 Grand Prix

1974 Catalina

1974 Grand Prix

1974 Grand Ville

1975 Grand Prix

1975 Grandville Brougham, Grand Safari

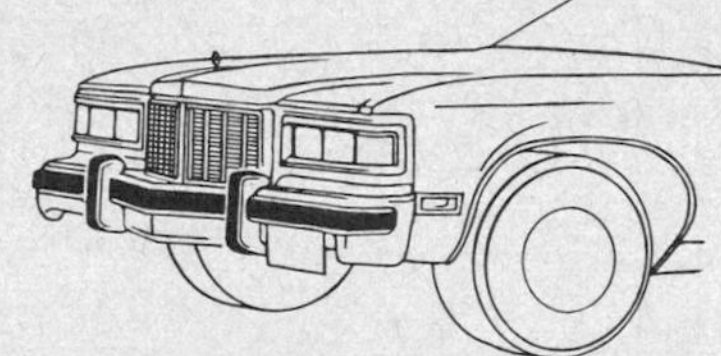

1976 Bonneville Brougham

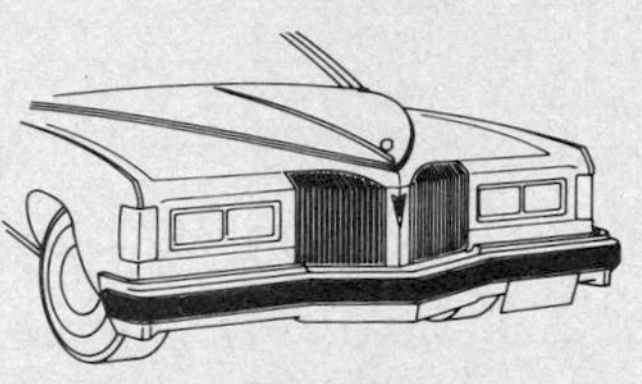

1976 Grand Prix

FIRING ORDER

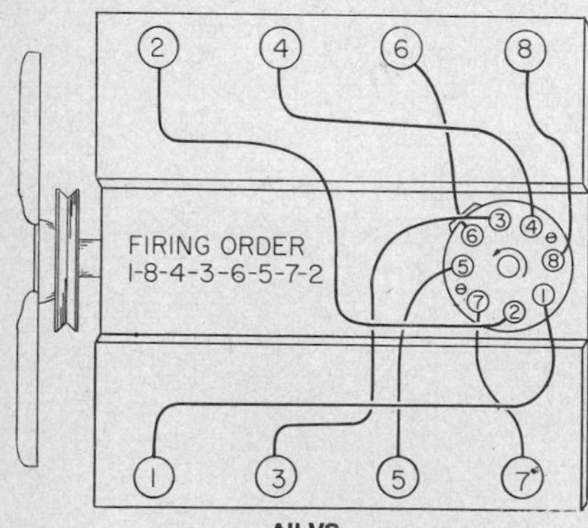

All V8

CAR SERIAL NUMBER LOCATION

Car serial number is located on the upper left-hand side of the instrument panel, visible through the windshield. The number is interpreted as follows:

Through 1971

First digit: Car division
Second and third digits: Series number
Fourth and fifth digits: Body style code
Sixth digit: Year manufactured
Seventh digit: Plant
Eighth digit: Engine used (1 = V8)
Ninth to thirteenth digits—sequential serial number

1972 and later

First digit: 2, for Pontiac division
Second digit: Series letter
Third and fourth digits: Body style
Fifth digit: Engine identification letter
Sixth digit: Last digit of model year
Seventh digit: Assembly plant letter
Eighth through thirteenth digits: Sequential serial number

2 | 52 | 69 | 8 | P | 100001

DIVISION
SERIES
BODY STYLE CODE NO.
PLANT
YEAR

Typical 1969-71 vehicle serial number
(© Pontiac Div., G.M. Corp)

Engine serial number location
(© Pontiac Div., G.M. Corp)

ENGINE IDENTIFICATION

Engine identification is made by a letter/number code located on the machined face of the cylinder block, below and in front of the right-hand cylinder head on all V8 engines.

Disp.	Bbl.	Hp.	1969	1970	1971	1972	1973	1974	1975	1976
8 Cylinder Models										
350	2	255		W7 X7						
350	2	250			WR XR YU					
350	2	150, 175# (net)					Y7 ZR			
400	2	265	YA① YB YF	YB	WS XX					
400	2	290	WA① WB① YC① WD WE YD	WE YD						
400	2	175, 200# (net)				XX ZX		AH YH YJ	YH	
400	2	170, 185# (net)					Y1 Y4 YZ ZK			
400	4	340	XZ							
400	4	350	WX XH	WX XH						
400	4	330		XZ						
400	4	300			WK WT YS	YS				
400	4	200, 250# (net)								
400	4	200, 230# (net)					Y3 YN YT ZN			
400	4	200, 225# (net)						AT YT YZ ZT	YT ZT YM	
428	4	390	WJ WL XG YK XE①							
428	4	360	YL① WG XJ XK YH							
428	4	370	WF XF							
455	2	280			WG YG					
455	2	185, 200# (net)				YH ZH				
455	4	360		YH						
455	4	370		WG XF						
455	4	325			WJ YC					

ENGINE IDENTIFICATION—cont'd

Disp.	Bbl.	Hp.	1969	1970	1971	1972	1973	1974	1975	1976
455	4	220, 250# (net)				YA YC				
455	4	215, 250# (net)					YA YC YD YK ZA ZC	AU YR YU YW YX YY ZU ZW ZX	YW YU ZU ZW	
455SD	4	310 (net)					Y8			

① Early production small valve engine with 30° intake valve angle
\# With dual exhaust

GENERAL ENGINE SPECIFICATIONS

Year	Engine No. Cyl. Displacement (Cu. In.)	Carburetor Type	Horsepower @ rpm ■	Torque @ rpm (ft lbs) ■	Bore and Stroke (in.)	Compression Ratio	Oil Pressure @ 2050 rpm
'69	8-400	2 bbl	265 @ 4600	397 @ 2400	4.1212 x 3.750	8.6:1	35
	8-400	2 bbl	290 @ 4600	428 @ 2500	4.1212 x 3.750	10.5:1	35
	8-400	4 bbl	340 @ 4800	445 @ 2900	4.1212 x 3.750	10.5:1	35
	8-428	4 bbl	360 @ 4600	472 @ 3200	4.1212 x 4.000	10.5:1	35
	8-428	4 bbl	390 @ 5200	465 @ 3400	4.1212 x 4.000	10.75:1	35
'70	8-350	2 bbl	255 @ 4600	355 @ 2800	3.8762 x 3.750	8.8:1	35
	8-400	2 bbl	265 @ 4600	397 @ 2400	4.1212 x 3.750	8.8:1	35
	8-400	2 bbl	290 @ 4600	428 @ 2500	4.1212 x 3.750	10.0:1	35
	8-400	4 bbl	330 @ 4800	445 @ 2900	4.1212 x 3.750	10.0:1	35
	8-455	4 bbl	360 @ 4300	500 @ 2700	4.1522 x 4.210	10.0:1	35
	8-455 HO	4 bbl	370 @ 4600	500 @ 3100	4.1522 x 4.210	10.25:1	35
'71	8-350	2 bbl	250 @ 4400	350 @ 2400	3.8762 x 3.750	8.0:1	35
	8-400	2 bbl	265 @ 4400	400 @ 2400	4.1212 x 3.750	8.2:1	35
	8-400	4 bbl	300 @ 4800	400 @ 3600	4.1212 x 3.750	8.2:1	35
	8-455	2 bbl	280 @ 4400	455 @ 2000	4.1522 x 4.210	8.2:1	35
	8-455	4 bbl	325 @ 4400	455 @ 3200	4.1522 x 4.210	8.2:1	35
'72	8-400	2 bbl	175 @ 4000	310 @ 2400	4.1212 x 3.750	8.2:1	35
	8-400 DE	2 bbl	200 @ 4000	325 @ 2400	4.1212 x 3.750	8.2:1	35
	8-400	4 bbl	200 @ 4000	295 @ 2800	4.1212 x 3.750	8.2:1	35
	8-400 DE	4 bbl	250 @ 4400	325 @ 3200	4.1212 x 3.750	8.2:1	35
	8-455	2 bbl	185 @ 4000	350 @ 2000	4.1522 x 4.210	8.2:1	35
	8-455 DE	2 bbl	200 @ 4000	370 @ 2000	4.1522 x 4.210	8.2:1	35
	8-455	4 bbl	220 @ 3600	350 @ 2400	4.1522 x 4.210	8.2:1	35
	8-455 DE	4 bbl	250 @ 3600	370 @ 2400	4.1522 x 4.210	8.2:1	35
'73	8-350	2 bbl	150 @ 4000	270 @ 2000	3.8762 x 3.750	7.6:1	55-60①
	8-350 DE	2 bbl	175 @ 4400	280 @ 2400	3.8762 x 3.750	7.6:1	55-60①
	8-400	2 bbl	170 @ 3600	320 @ 2000	4.1212 x 3.750	8.0:1	55-60①
	8-400 DE	2 bbl	185 @ 4000	320 @ 2400	4.1212 x 3.750	8.0:1	55-60①
	8-400	4 bbl	200 @ 4000	310 @ 2400	4.1212 x 3.750	8.0:1	55-60①
	8-400 DE	4 bbl	230 @ 4400	325 @ 3200	4.1212 x 3.750	8.0:1	55-60①
	8-455	4 bbl	215 @ 3600	350 @ 2400	4.1522 x 4.210	8.0:1	55-60①
	8-455 DE	4 bbl	250 @ 4000	370 @ 2800	4.1522 x 4.210	8.0:1	55-60①
	8-455S.D. DE	4 bbl	310 @ 4000	390 @ 3600	4.1522 x 4.210	8.4:1	75-80①

GENERAL ENGINE SPECIFICATIONS (con't.)

Year	Engine No. Cyl. Displacement (Cu. In.)	Carburetor Type	Horsepower @ rpm ■	Torque @ rpm (ft lbs) ■	Bore and Stroke (in.)	Compression Ratio	Oil Pressure @ 2050 rpm
'74	8-400	2 bbl	175 @ 3600	315 @ 2000	4.1212 x 3.750	8.0:1	55-60①
	8-400	4 bbl	200 @ 4000	320 @ 2400	4.1212 x 3.750	8.0:1	55-60①
	8-400 DE	4 bbl	225 @ 4400	330 @ 2800	4.1212 x 3.750	8.0:1	55-60①
	8-455	4 bbl	215 @ 3600	355 @ 2400	4.1522 x 4.210	8.0:1	55-60①
	8-455 DE	4 bbl	250 @ 4000	380 @ 2800	4.1522 x 4.210	8.0:1	55-60①
'75-'76	8-400	2 bbl	175 @ 3600	315 @ 2000	4.1212 x 3.750	7.6:1	55-60①
	8-400	4 bbl	200 @ 4000	320 @ 2400	4.1212 x 3.750	7.6:1	55-60①
	8-455	4 bbl	215 @ 3600	355 @ 2400	4.1522 x 4.210	7.6:1	55-60①

■ Beginning 1972, horsepower and torque are SAE net figures. They are measured at the rear of the transmission with all accessories installed and operating. Since the figures vary when a given engine is installed in different models, some are representative rather than exact.

HO High output
DE Dual exhaust
S.D. Super Duty
① Above 2600 rpm

TUNE-UP SPECIFICATIONS

When analyzing compression test results, look for uniformity among cylinders rather than specific pressures.

ENGINE			SPARK PLUGS		DISTRIBUTOR		IGNITION TIMING (deg) ▲		VALVES	Fuel	IDLE SPEED ● (rpm) ▲	
Year	No. Cyl Displacement (cu in.)	hp	Type	Gap (in.)	Point Dwell (deg)	Point Gap (in.)	Man Trans ●	Auto Trans	Intake Opens ■ (deg) ●	Pump Pressure (psi)	Man Trans	Auto Trans
'69	8-400	265	R-46S	.035	28-32	.016	9B	9B	22	5-6½	850	650
	8-400	290	R-46S	.035	28-32	.016	9B	9B	30/22	5-6½	850	650
	8-400	340	R-46S	.035	28-32	.016	9B	9B	30/22	5-6½	1000	650
	8-428	360	R-45S③	.035	28-32	.016	9B	9B	23/30	5-6½	1000	650
	8-428	390	R-44S	.035	28-32	.016	9B	9B	23/30	5-6½	1000	650
'70	8-350	255	R-46S	.035	28-32	.016	9B	9B	22	5-6½	800	650
	8-400	265	R-46S④	.035	28-32	.016	9B	9B	30/22	5-6½	800	650
	8-400	290	R-46S④	.035	28-32	.016	9B	9B	30/22	5-6½	800	650
	8-400	330	R-46S	.035	28-32	.016	9B	9B	30	5-6½	950	650
	8-455	360	R-45S	.035	28-32	.016	9B	9B	31/23	5-6½	950	650
	8-455	370	R-45S	.035	28-32	.016	9B	9B	23	5-6½	950	650
'71	8-350	250	R-47S	.035	28-32	.016	12B	12B	26B/30B	5-6½⑤	800	600
	8-400	265	R-47S	.035	28-32	.016	—	8B	26B	5-6½⑤	—	600
	8-400	300	R-46S	.035	28-32	.016	12B	12B	23B	5-6½⑤	1000/600①	700
	8-455	280	R-46S	.035	28-32	.016	—	12B	30B	5-6½⑤	—	650
	8-455	325	R-46S	.035	28-32	.016	—	12B	23B	5-6½⑤	—	650
	8-455	335	R-46S	.035	28-32	.016	12B	12B	31B	5-6½⑤	1000/600①	700
'72	8-400	175	R-46TS	.035	28-32	.016	—	10B	26	5-6½	—	625
	8-400	200	R-45TS	.035	28-32	.016	8B	10B	23	5-6½	1000/600①	700/500①
	8-400	250	R-45TS	.035	28-32	.016	10B	10B	23	5-6½	1000/600①	700/500①
	8-455	185	R-45TS	.035	28-32	.016	—	10B	30	5-6½	—	625
	8-455	200	R-45TS	.035	28-32	.016	—	10B	23	5-6½	—	625
	8-455	220	R-45TS	.035	28-32	.016	—	10B	23	5-6½	—	650/500①
	8-455	250	R-45TS	.035	28-32	.016	—	10B	23	5-6½	—	650/500①
'73	8-350	150	R-46TS	.040	28-32	.016	—	12B	26/30⑦	5-6½	—	650
	8-350	175	R-46TS	.040	28-32	.016	—	12B	26/30⑦	5-6½	—	650
	8-400	170	R-46TS	.040	28-32	.016	—	12B	26	5-6½	—	650
	8-400	185	R-46TS	.040	28-32	.016	—	12B	26	5-6½	—	650
	8-400	200	R-45TS	.040	28-32	.016	—	12B	26	5-6½	—	650
	8-400	230	R-45TS	.040	28-32	.016	—	12B	26	5-6½	—	650
	8-455	215	R-45TS	.040	28-32	.016	—	12B	23	5-6½	—	650

TUNE-UP SPECIFICATIONS

When analyzing compression test results, look for uniformity among cylinders rather than specific pressures.

	ENGINE		SPARK PLUGS		DISTRIBUTOR		IGNITION TIMING (deg) ▲		VALVES	Fuel	IDLE SPEED ● (rpm) ▲	
Year	No. Cyl Displacement (cu in.)	hp	Type	Gap (in.)	Point Dwell (deg)	Point Gap (in.)	Man Trans ●	Auto Trans	Intake Opens ■ (deg) ●	Pump Pressure (psi)	Man Trans	Auto Trans
	8-455	250	R-45TS	.040	28-32	.016	—	12B	23	5-6½	—	650
	8-455 S.D.	310	R-45TS	.040	28-32	.016	—	12B	42	5-6½	—	750/500①
'74	8-400 2 bbl	175	R-46TS	.040	29-31	.016	—	12B (10)	26	5-6½	—	650 (625)
	8-400 4 bbl	All	R-45TS	.040	29-31	.016	—	12B (10)	30	5-6½	—	650 (625)
	8-455 4 bbl	All	R-45TS	.040	29-31	.016	—	12B (10)	23	5-6½	—	650 (625)
'75	8-400 2 bbl	All	R-46TSX	.060	Electronic		—	16B	26	5-6½	—	650
	8-400 4 bbl	All	R-45TSX	.060	Electronic		—	16B (12)	30	5-6½	—	650
	8-455	All	R-45TSX	.060	Electronic		—	16B (10)	23	5-6½	—	650 (625)
'76	8-350 2 bbl	155	R-46TSX	.060	Electronic		—	16B	22	7-8½	—	—
	8-350 4 bbl	175	R-45TSX	.060	Electronic		—	16B	26	7-8½	—	—
	8-400 2 bbl	170	R-46TSX	.060	Electronic		—	16B	26	7-8½	—	550⑥
	8-400 4 bbl	185	R-45TSX	.060	Electronic		—	16B	30	7-8½	—	575⑥
	8-455	200	R-45TSX	.060	Electronic		—	16B (12)	23	7-8½	—	550(600)⑥

▲ See text for procedure
● Figure in parentheses indicates California engine
■ All figures are in degrees Before Top Dead Center. Where two figures appear, the first represents timing with manual transmission, the second with automatic transmission.
① Lower figure indicates idle speed with solenoid disconnected
② Not used
③ AC-R-44S with manual transmission
④ AC-R-45S with automatic transmission
⑤ 6½-8 with A/C
⑥ 675 rpm with air conditioning on and compressor clutch wires disconnected
⑦ Lower figure for manual transmission, higher for automatic
B Before Top Dead Center
— Not applicable
S.D. Super Duty

Pontiac

CAPACITIES

Year	ENGINE No. Cyl. Displacement (Cu. In.)	Engine Crankcase Add 1 Qt For New Filter	TRANSMISSION Pts To Refill After Draining Manual 3-Speed	4-Speed	Automatic ●	Drive Axle (pts)	Gasoline Tank (gals) ▲	COOLING SYSTEM (qts) With Heater	With A/C
'69	8-400	5	2.8	—	19	4.5	26.5	18	18
	8-428	5	2.8	—	19	4.5	26.5	17.2	17.2
'70	8-350	5	2.8	—	6	4.5	26	19.6	19.6
	8-400	5	2.8	—	7.5	4.5	26	18	18
	8-455	5	2.8	—	7.5	4.5	26	17.2	17.2
'71	8-350	5	2.8	—	6	4.5	23.5	20.2	21
	8-400	5	2.8	—	7.5	4.5	23.5	18.6	19.6
	8-455	5	2.8	—	7.5	4.5	23.5	17.9	19
'72	8-400	5	—	—	7.5	5.5	25	18.6	19.6
	8-455	5	—	—	7.5	5.5	25	17.9	19
'73	8-350	5	—	—	7.5	4.25①	25.8	21.9	23.3
	8-400	5	—	—	7.5	4.25①	25.8	21.9	24.3
	8-455	5	—	—	7.5	4.25①	25.8	21.2	22.2
'74	8-400	5	—	—	7.5	4.25①	25.8	21.9	24.3
	8-455	5	—	—	7.5	4.25①	25.8	21.2	22.2
'75-'76	8-400	5	—	—	7.5	5.31②	25.8	21.6	22.4
	8-455	5	—	—	7.5	5.31②	25.8	19.8	22.3

● '70 and later specifications do not include torque converter
— Not applicable
① 5 pts with 8.875 in. ring gear
② 4.25 pts with 8.50 in. ring gear
▲ Station wagon fuel tank (gals)

'69-'70	24
'71	22.5
'72	23
'73-'76	22

Grand Prix

CAPACITIES

Year	ENGINE No. Cyl. Displacement (Cu. In.)	Engine Crankcase Add 1 Qt For New Filter	TRANSMISSION Pts To Refill After Draining Manual 3-Speed	4-Speed	Automatic ●	Drive Axle (pts)	Gasoline Tank (gals)	COOLING SYSTEM (qts) With Heater	With A/C
'69	8-400	5	2.8	—	19	4.5	21.5	18.7	18.7
	8-428	5	2.8	—	19	4.5	21.5	17.5	17.5
'70	8-400	5	2.8	—	7.5	3①	24.5	18.7	21.1
	8-455	5	2.8	—	7.5	3①	24.5	17.5	19.9
'71	8-400	5	2.8	2.5	7.5	3①	23.5	18.6	19.6
	8-455	5	2.8	—	7.5	3①	23.5	17.9	19
'72	8-400	5	—	—	7.5	3①	26	18.7	19.7
	8-455	5	—	—	7.5	3①	26	18.1	19.2
'73	8-400	5	—	—	7.5	4.25	25	23.1	22.9
	8-455	5	—	—	7.5	4.25	25	21.3	22.5
'74	8-400	5	—	—	7.5	4.25	25	23.1	22.9
	8-455	5	—	—	7.5	4.25	25	21.3	22.5
'75-'76	8-400	5	—	—	7.5	5.31	25	21.6	24.0
	8-455	5	—	—	7.5	5.31	25	20.2	22.2

● '70 and later specifications do not include torque converter
① 5 pts with 8.875 in. ring gear
—— Not applicable

VALVE SPECIFICATIONS

Year	Engine No. Cyl. Displacement (cu in.)	Seat Angle (deg) ■	Face Angle (deg) ●	Spring Test Pressure▲ (lbs @ in.)	Spring Installed Height (in.)	STEM TO GUIDE Clearance (in.) Intake	Exhaust	STEM Diameter (in.) Intake	Exhaust
'69	8-400	45	44	63 @ 1.58	1 37/64	.0016-.0033	.0021-.0038	.3416	.3411
	8-428③	30	29	63 @ 1.58	1 37/64	.0016-.0033	.0021-.0038	.3416	.3411
	8-428④	45⑥	44	66 @ 1.56	1 9/16	.0016-.0033	.0021-.0038	.3416	.3411
	8-428⑤ HO	30	29	83 @ 1.59	1 19/32	.0016-.0033	.0021-.0038	.3416	.3411
'70	8-350	45	44	63 @ 1.58	1 37/64	.0016-.0033	.0021-.0038	.3416	.3411
	8-400	45	44	63 @ 1.58	1 37/64	.0016-.0033	.0021-.0038	.3416	.3416
	8-455⑦	30	29	63 @ 1.58	1 37/64	.0016-.0033	.0021-.0038	.3416	.3411
	8-455⑧	45	44	66 @ 1.56	1 9/16	.0016-.0033	.0021-.0038	.3416	.3411
	8-455 HO	30	45	66 @ 1.56	1 9/16	.0016-.0033	.0021-.0038	.3416	.3411
'71	8-350	45	44	61 @ 1.59	1 19/32	.0016-.0033	.0021-.0038	.3416	.3411
	8-400 2 bbl	45	44	61 @ 1.59	1 19/32	.0016-.0033	.0021-.0038	.3416	.3411
	8-400 4 bbl	30	29	65 @ 1.57	1 9/16	.0016-.0033	.0021-.0038	.3416	.3411
	8-455 2 bbl	45	44	61 @ 1.59	1 19/32	.0016-.0033	.0021-.0038	.3416	.3411
	8-455 4 bbl	30	29	65 @ 1.57	1 9/16	.0016-.0033	.0021-.0038	.3416	.3411
'72	8-400 2 bbl	45	44	61 @ 1.59	1 19/32	.0016-.0033	.0021-.0038	.3416	.3411
	8-400 4 bbl	30	29	65 @ 1.57	1 9/16	.0016-.0033	.0021-.0038	.3416	.3411
	8-455 2 bbl	45	44	61 @ 1.59	1 19/32	.0016-.0033	.0021-.0038	.3416	.3411
	8-455 4 bbl	30	29	65 @ 1.57	1 9/16	.0016-.0033	.0021-.0038	.3416	.3411
'73	8-350	45	44	61 @ 1.59	1 19/32	.0016-.0033	.0021-.0038	.3416	.3411
	8-400 2 bbl	45	44	61 @ 1.59	1 19/32	.0016-.0033	.0021-.0038	.3416	.3411
	8-400 4 bbl	30	29	65 @ 1.57	1 9/16	.0016-.0033	.0021-.0038	.3416	.3411
	8-455 2 bbl	45	44	61 @ 1.59	1 19/32	.0016-.0033	.0021-.0038	.3416	.3411
	8-455 4 bbl	30	29	65 @ 1.57	1 9/16	.0016-.0033	.0021-.0038	.3416	.3411
	8-455 S.D.	45	44	70 @ 1.82	1 9/16	.0016-.0033	.0021-.0038	.3416	.3416

VALVE SPECIFICATIONS (con't.)

Year	Engine No. Cyl. Displacement (cu in.)	Seat Angle (deg) ■	Face Angle (deg) ●	Spring Test Pressure▲ (lbs @ in.)	Spring Installed Height (in.)	STEM TO GUIDE Clearance (in.) Intake	Exhaust	STEM Diameter (in.) Intake	Exhaust
'74	8-400	30	29	65 @ 1.57	1 9/16	.0016-.0033	.0021-.0038	.3416	.3411
	8-455 2 bbl	45	44	61 @ 1.59	1 19/32	.0016-.0033	.0021-.0038	.3416	.3411
	8-455 4 bbl	30	29	65 @ 1.57	1 9/16	.0016-.0033	.0021-.0038	.3416	.3411
'75-'76	8-400 2 bbl	45	44	65 @ 1.57	1 9/16	.0016-.0033	.0021-.0038	.3416	.3411
	8-400 4 bbl	45	44	65 @ 1.57	1 19/32	.0016-.0033	.0021-.0038	.3416	.3411
	8-455	45	44	65 @ 1.57	1 9/16	.0016-.0033	.0021-.0038	.3416	.3411

■ Intake valve seat angles are shown. All exhaust valve seat angles are 45° unless otherwise indicated.
● Intake valve face angles are shown. All exhaust valve face angles are 44° unless otherwise indicated.
①② Not used
③ With automatic transmission only
④ Standard 428 with manual transmission and 428 HO with automatic
⑤ 428 HO with manual transmission only
⑥ 428 HO with automatic transmission—
intake valve seat angle 30°
intake valve face angle 29°
⑦ With manual transmission
⑧ With automatic transmission
HO High output
S.D. Super Duty

▲INNER SPRING TEST PRESSURE

Year	Engine	Pressure
'69	8-400	35 @ 1.54
	8-428⑪	35 @ 1.54
	8-428⑫	38 @ 1.52
	8-428⑬ HO	45 @ 1.52
'70	8-350	35 @ 1.54
	8-400	35 @ 1.54
	8-455⑭	35 @ 1.54
	8-455⑮	38 @ 1.52
	8-455 HO	38 @ 1.52
'71	8-350	33 @ 1.55
	8-400 2 bbl	33 @ 1.55
	8-400 4 bbl	37 @ 1.53
	8-455 2 bbl	33 @ 1.55
	8-455 4 bbl	37 @ 1.53
'72	8-400 2 bbl	33 @ 1.55
	8-400 4 bbl	37 @ 1.53
'73	8-350	33 @ 1.55
	8-400 2 bbl	33 @ 1.55
	8-400 4 bbl	37 @ 1.53
	8-455	37 @ 1.53
	8-455 S.D.	40 @ 1.75
'74-'76	8-400 2 bbl	33 @ 1.55
	8-400 4 bbl	37 @ 1.53
	8-455	37 @ 1.53

⑪ With automatic only
⑫ Standard 428 with manual transmission and 428 HO with automatic transmission
⑬ 428 HO with manual transmission only
⑭ With manual transmission
⑮ With automatic transmission

CRANKSHAFT AND CONNECTING ROD SPECIFICATIONS

All measurements are given in inches

Year	Engine No. Cyl. Displacement (cu in.)	CRANKSHAFT Main Brg. Journal Dia	Main Brg. Oil Clearance	Shaft End-Play	Thrust on No.	CONNECTING ROD Journal Diameter	Oil Clearance	Side Clearance
'69	8-400	3.000	.0018	.006	4	2.250	.0015	.009
	8-428	3.250	.0018	.006	4	2.250	.0015	.009
'70	8-350	3.000	.0002-.0017	.0035-.0085	4	2.250	.0005-.0025	.012-.017②
	8-400	3.000	.0002-.0017	.0035-.0085	4	2.250	.0005-.0025	.012-.017
	8-455	3.250	.0005-.0021	.0035-.0085	4	2.250	.0005-.0026	.012-.017
'71-'76	8-400	3.000	.0002-.0017	.0035-.0085④	4	2.250	.0005-.0025	.012-.017
	8-455	3.250	.0005-.0021③	.0035-.0085④	4	2.250	.0010-.0031⑤	.012-.017⑥

① Not used
② Total for two rods
③ .0010-.0026 in 455 S.D. engine, .0004-.0020 on No. 1 cylinder
④ 1972 and later models—0.003-0.009 in.
⑤ .0015-.0031 in 455 S.D. engine
⑥ .019-.027 in 455 S.D. engine

TORQUE SPECIFICATIONS

All readings in ft lbs

Year	Engine	Cylinder Head Bolts	Rod Bearing Bolts	Main Bearing Bolts	Crankshaft Pulley Bolt	Flywheel to Crankshaft Bolts	MANIFOLD Intake	MANIFOLD Exhaust
'69-'76	All	95	43②	100①	160	95	40	30

① Rear main—120   ② 63 ft lbs on 455 S.D. engine

RING GAP

All measurements are given in inches

Year	Engine No. Cyl.	Compression Top	Compression Bottom
'69	All engines	.010-.030	.010-.030
'70-'76	8-350, 400	.019	.015
'70-'76	8-455	.021	.015

Year	Engine No. Cyl.	Oil Control
'69-'76	All engines	0.35

RING SIDE CLEARANCE

All measurements are given in inches

Year	Engine	Top Compression	Bottom Compression
'69-'76	All engines	.0015-.0050	.0015-.0050

Year	Engine	Oil Control
'69-'76	All engines	.0015.0050

PISTON CLEARANCE

Year	Engine No. Cyl. Displacement (cu. in.)	Piston-to-Bore Clearance (in.)
'69	8-400	.0025-.0031
	8-428	.0030-.0036
'70-'72	8-350	.0025-.0033
	8-400	.0025-.0033
	8-455	.0025-.0033
	8-400 Ram Air	.0055-.0061
'73	8-350	.0029-.0037
	8-400	.0029-.0037
	8-455	.0025-.0033
	8-455 S.D.	.0060-.0068
'74-'76	8-400	.0029-.0037
	8-455	.0021-.0029

ALTERNATOR AND REGULATOR SPECIFICATIONS

	ALTERNATOR			REGULATOR						
					Field Relay			Regulator		
Year	Part No.	Field Current @ 12 V	Output (amps)	Part No.	Air Gap (in.)	Point Gap (in.)	Volts to Close	Air Gap (in.)	Point Gap (in.)	Volts @ 75°
'69	1100699	1.9-2.3	42	1119511	.015	.030	2.3-3.7	.057	.015	13.5-14.4
	1100700	1.9-2.3	55	1119511	.015	.030	2.3-3.7	.057	.015	13.5-14.4
	1100800	1.9-2.3	55	1119511	.015	.030	2.3-3.7	.057	.015	13.5-14.4
	1100801	1.9-2.3	42	1119511	.015	.030	2.3-3.7	.057	.015	13.5-14.4

ALTERNATOR AND REGULATOR SPECIFICATIONS (con't.)

Year	Alternator Part No.	Alternator Field Current @ 12 V	Alternator Output (amps)	Regulator Part No.	Field Relay Air Gap (in.)	Field Relay Point Gap (in.)	Field Relay Volts to Close	Regulator Air Gap (in.)	Regulator Point Gap (in.)	Volts @ 75°
'70	1100704	2.2-2.6	37	1119515	.015	.030	2.3-3.7	.057	.015	13.5-14.4
	1100700	2.2-2.6	55	1119515	.015	.030	2.3-3.7	.057	.015	13.5-14.4
	1100895	2.2-2.6	61	1119515	.015	.030	2.3-3.7	.057	.015	13.5-14.4
	1117765	4.1-4.6	62	1116368	Transistorized Regulator					13.6-14.2
'71-'74	1100927	4-4.5	37	——	Transistorized Regulator					13.6-14.2
	1100928	4-4.5	55	——	Transistorized Regulator					13.6-14.2
	1101015	4-4.5	80	——	Transistorized Regulator					13.6-14.2
'75	1102481	4-4.5	37	——	Transistorized Regulator					13.6-14.2
	1102482	4-4.5	55	——	Transistorized Regulator					13.6-14.2
	1101027	4-4.5	80	——	Transistorized Regulator					13.6-14.2

—— Not applicable

BATTERY AND STARTER SPECIFICATIONS

Year	Model	Battery Ampere Hour • Capacity	Battery Volts	Battery Terminal Grounded	Starter Lock Test Amps	Lock Test Volts	Lock Test Torque (ft lbs)	No-Load Test Amps	No-Load Test Volts	No-Load Test RPM	Brush Spring Tension (oz)
'69	Std.	61	12	Neg.	Not Recommended			Not Recommended			35
	H.D.②	70	12	Neg.	Not Recommended			Not Recommended			35
	Grand Prix	61	12	Neg.	Not Recommended			Not Recommended			35
'70	350 Std.	53	12	Neg.	Not Recommended			Not Recommended			35
	400 Std.; 350, 400 Opt.①	61	12	Neg.	Not Recommended			Not Recommended			35
	455 Std.; 350, 400 Opt. H.D.②	62	12	Neg.	Not Recommended			Not Recommended			35
	455 H.D. ②	76	12	Neg.	Not Recommended			Not Recommended			35
'71	350 Std.	53	12	Neg.	Not Recommended			Not Recommended			35
	400 Std.; 350, 400 Opt.①	61	12	Neg.	Not Recommended			Not Recommended			35
	455 Std.; 350, 400 H.D.①	62	12	Neg.	Not Recommended			Not Recommended			35
	455 H.D. ②	76	12	Neg.	Not Recommended			Not Recommended			35
'72-'73	350 Std.	53	12	Neg.	Not Recommended			Not Recommended			35
	400 Std.	61	12	Neg.	Not Recommended			Not Recommended			35
	455 Std.; 400 H.D.	62	12	Neg.	Not Recommended			Not Recommended			35
	455 H.D.	73	12	Neg.	Not Recommended			Not Recommended			35
	455③	80	12	Neg.	Not Recommended			Not Recommended			35
'74	400 Std.	2900	12	Neg.	Not Recommended			Not Recommended			35
	400 H.D.	3250	12	Neg.	Not Recommended			Not Recommended			35
	455	3250	12	Neg.	Not Recommended			Not Recommended			35
	455③	3750	12	Neg.	Not Recommended			Not Recommended			35
'75-'76	400 Std.	3200	12	Neg.	Not Recommended			Not Recommended			35
	400 H.D.; 455 Std.	3500	12	Neg.	Not Recommended			Not Recommended			35
	455 H.D.	4000	12	Neg.	Not Recommended			Not Recommended			35
	Maintenance free option	3750	12	Neg.	Not Recommended			Not Recommended			35

① Standard w/AC and/or rear window defogger
② Heavy Duty option
③ Maintenance free; Std. Grand Prix SJ
• Cranking power in watts beginning 1974

H.D. Heavy Duty
Std. Standard
Opt. Optional
Eng. Energizer

BRAKE SPECIFICATIONS

Year	Model	Master Cylinder Disc	Master Cylinder Drum	Wheel Cylinder Front Disc	Wheel Cylinder Front Drum	Wheel Cylinder Rear	Brake Disc or Drum Diameter Front Disc	Brake Disc or Drum Diameter Front Drum	Brake Disc or Drum Diameter Rear
'69	Catalina, Executive, Bonneville	1.13	1.0	2.94	1.12	.94	11.68	11.00	11.0
	Grand Prix	1.00	—	1.12	—	.94	10.90	—	11.0
'70	Catalina, Executive, Bonneville	1.13	1.0	2.94	1.12	.94	11.75	11.00	11.0
	Grand Prix	1.13	—	2.94	—	.88	11.00	—	9.5
'71-'76	Catalina, Grand Ville, Bonneville	1.13	—	2.94	—	.94	11.75②	—	11.0
	Grand Prix	1.13	—	2.94	—	.88	11.00	—	9.5③
	Station Wagons	1.13	—	2.94	—	.94①	11.75②	—	12.0

— Not applicable
① 1973 and later—1.0
② 1973 and later—11.88
③ 1975 and later—11.0

WHEEL ALIGNMENT SPECIFICATIONS

Year	Model	Caster Range (deg)	Caster Pref Setting (deg)	Camber Range (deg)	Camber Pref Setting (deg)	Toe-in (in.)	Steering Axis Inclin.	Wheel Pivot Ratio (deg) Inner Wheel	Wheel Pivot Ratio (deg) Outer Wheel
'69-'70	All	1N to 2N	1½N	0 to ½P	¼P	0 to ⅛	8½	20	18
'71	Grand Prix	1N to 2N	1½N	½N to ½P	0	1/16 to 3/16	8½	20	18
	Catalina, Grand Ville & Bonneville	½P to 1½P	1P	¼P to 1¼P	¾P	⅛ to ¼	8½	20	18
'72	Grand Prix	1N to 2N	1½N	¼N to ¾P	¼P	0 to ⅛	9	20	18
	Catalina, Grand Ville & Bonneville	1N to 2N	1½N	¼N to ¾P	¼P	0 to ⅛	8½	20	18
'73-'74	Grand Prix	2½P to 3½P	3P	½P to 1½P (LH)	1P	0 to ⅛	10½	20	18 13/16 (LH)
				0 to 1P (RH)	½P				19 3/16 (RH)
	Pontiac	½P to 1½P	1P	½P to 1½P (LH)	1P	0 to ⅛	10½	20	18½
				0 to 1P (RH)	½P				
'75-'76	Grand Prix	2½P to 3½P	3P	½P to 1½P (LH)	1P	0 to ⅛	10⅓	——	——
				0 to 1P (RH)	½P				
	Pontiac	1P to 2P	1½P	½P to 1P (LH)	1P	0 to ⅛	10⅓	——	——
				0 to 1P (RH)	½P				

—— Not specified
N Negative P Positive
LH lefthand side RH righthand side

CHARGING SYSTEM

Alternator R & R

1. Disconnect positive battery cable.
2. Remove two terminal plug leads from alternator.
3. Loosen adjusting bolts.
4. Remove V-belt and through-bolt.
5. Remove alternator.
6. To install, reverse removal procedure. Tighten all bolts to 30 ft. lbs., except slotted adjuster bolt (20 ft. lbs.).

Voltage Regulator R & R through 1970

Removal

1. Disconnect the battery cables.
2. Disconnect the wiring from the voltage regulator.
3. Remove the screws holding the regulator to the firewall or front bulkhead depending on the car.

Installation

1. Reverse the removal procedures to install.

Voltage Regulator R & R 1971 and later

The voltage regulator is inside the alternator. For R&R procedures see "Starting and Charging Systems" in the "Unit Repair Section."

STARTING SYSTEM

All starters are 12 volt with the shift lever mechanism and solenoid plunger enclosed in the drive housing. The solenoid is attached to the housing.

A more detailed discussion of starters and their troubles can be found in the Unit Repair Section under Starting and Charging Systems.

Starter R & R

1. Disconnect positive cable from battery.
2. Raise front of car and support on stands.
3. Pull cable and wire loom down to hang free.
4. Disconnect brace, starting 1971.
5. Remove mounting screws and starter motor with cable and solenoid wires.
6. Remove wires from starter.
7. To reinstall reverse the above, first installing the wires to solenoid.

Starter Drive R & R

1. Disconnect the field straps from the solenoid and remove the starter through bolts.
2. Remove the commutator end frame, field frame and armature from the drive housing.
3. To remove the overrunning clutch from the armature shaft:
   a. Slide the thrust collar from the end of the armature shaft.
   b. Slide a standard ½ in. pipe coupling (or an old pinion of suitable size) onto the armature shaft so that it butts against the snap-ring retainer. Tap the end of the pipe with a hammer, driving the retainer off of the snap-ring.
   c. Remove the snap-ring from the groove in the armature shaft.
   d. Slide the retainer and clutch from the armature shaft.
4. To reassemble, reverse the above procedure, being sure to:
   a. Slide the snap-ring, after it has been forced onto the armature shaft, past the grease groove to the snap-ring groove.
   b. Use two pairs of pliers at the same time, on opposite sides of the armature shaft, and grip the retainer and the thrust collar and squeeze until the retainer is forced over the snap-ring.

IGNITION SYSTEM

Distributor

An external adjustment distributor is used. The cap has a window for adjusting dwell time (cam angle) with the cap in place.

Adjustment of dwell is made on the car while the engine is operating or may be set statically with a feeler gauge.

The point set has the breaker lever spring tension and point alignment pre-set and is serviced as an assembly. Only the dwell angle requires adjustment after replacement.

Under part throttle operation, manifold vacuum is enough to actuate the vacuum control diaphragm. This causes the movable plate to advance the spark and aid fuel economy. During acceleration, or on a heavy pull, the vacuum is insufficient to move the plate. The plate is spring-loaded, through the vacuum control diaphragm, and remains in the retarded position.

The centrifugal advance is conventional and operates through two spring-loaded weights.

On 1970 and later Pontiacs, the radios are more sensitive to ignition interference due to the antenna in the windshield. To combat this all distributors have a Radio Frequency Interference Shield (R.F.I.) covering the circuit breaker plate assembly. Shield must be removed to install points or condenser, but dwell angle may be set through an opening in the shield.

A unitized point and condenser set was introduced in 1974. It was installed as original equipment in some cases. The R.F.I. shield isn't required when the unitized point and condenser set is used.

Removal

1. Disconnect coil wire connector.
2. Remove distributor cap.
3. Crank engine so that rotor points to No. 1 cylinder plug tower and timing mark on crankshaft pulley are indexed with pointer.

NOTE: Observe the position of the rotor and make marks on the distributor housing and on the block that line up with tip of the rotor. Make sure these marks line up upon reassembly. If the engine is disturbed, these marks can be used for reassembly.

4. Remove distributor vacuum line.
5. Remove distributor hold-down bolt and clamp. Do not disturb the engine after the distributor has been removed.
6. Lift the distributor out of its bore. Notice the slight rotation of the rotor as the distributor is removed from the block.

Installation

Installation procedure is the reverse of the removal procedure. However, before inserting the distributor into the block, the rotor should be moved slightly to one side. This is necessary because of the helical cut of the gears. As the distributor seats in its bore, the rotor will rotate slightly so that the reference marks will once again be in line. Retime the engine with a timing light.

Installation If Engine Has Been Disturbed

1. With no. 1 piston on the compression stroke, rotate the crankshaft until the pulley timing mark indexes with the stationary mark at TDC.
2. Replace the distributor to block gasket.
3. Install the distributor in the block so that the vacuum diaphragm faces the left side of the engine. The rotor should point toward the contact in the cap for no. 1 cylinder. Move the rotor slightly to the side because as the distributor is pressed into its bore it will rotate a small amount.
4. Install the distributor clamp and clamp bolt.
5. Install the vacuum line, rotor, cap, and coil wire.
6. It is necessary to retime the engine with a timing light.

Ignition Timing

Timing marks are located on the front engine cover and on the harmonic balancer.

1. Disconnect and plug the distributor vacuum advance hose from the distributor.
2. Make sure the dwell is adjusted.

NOTE: It may be necessary to put a small amount of white paint or chalk on the timing marks to make them more visible.

3. Connect a timing light to no. 1 cylinder.
4. Loosen the distributor clamp.
5. Start the engine and rotate the distributor until the correct marks line up. Tighten the distributor clamp and recheck the timing.
6. Reconnect the vacuum hose.

Contact Point Replacement and Adjustment

1. Remove the distributor cap and the rotor.
2. Remove the R.F.I. shield, if so equipped.
3. Remove the screws holding the points in place.
4. Remove the condenser lead and primary lead from the points.
5. Install a new set of points and tighten the attaching screws. Adjust the point gap if the point set isn't preset.
6. Connect the condenser and primary leads, to the points.
7. Apply a very small amount of grease to the breaker cam.
8. Install the R.F.I. shield; the half covering the points should be installed first. You don't need the shield if the unitized point and condenser set is being used.
9. Install the rotor and distributor cap.
10. Set the dwell.

Transistor Ignition

This system consists of a special distributor, and a special ignition coil. The distributor is similar in external appearance to the standard V8 distributor, but the internal construction bears little resemblance to the contact-point unit. An iron timer core replaces the breaker cam. This eight-lobed timer rotates inside a magnetic pick-up assembly, which replaces the contact points and condenser. The magnetic pick-up assembly consists of a ceramic permanent magnet, a steel pole piece, and a pick-up coil.

The magnetic pick-up assembly is mounted over the distributor shaft bearing, and is rotated by the vacuum advance unit to provide automatic spark advance. Centrifugal advance is provided by the rotating timer core, which is attached to normal advance weights. Troubleshooting is found in the Unit Repair Section.

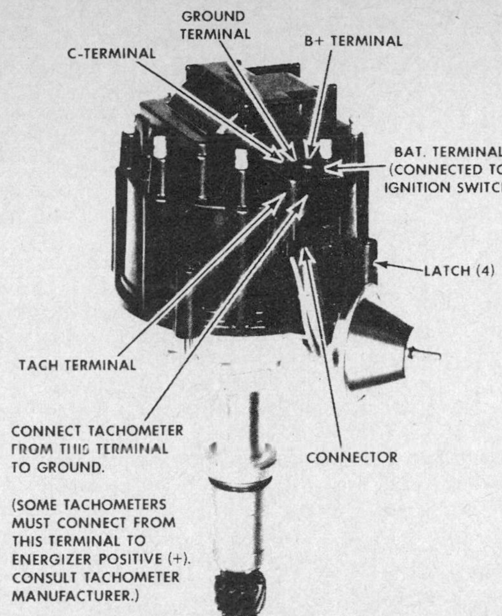

High Energy Ignition system distributor
(© Pontiac Div., G.M. Corp)

Unitized Ignition System—1971-74

A new unitized ignition system is optional on late 1971 and all 1972-74 Grand Prix SJ, Grand Ville and Grand Safari models having the 455 cu. in. V8 with four-barrel carburetor. This system replaces the ignition coil, distributor, amplifier, wiring and spark plug wires used with previous transistorized systems. The conventional contact points and condenser have been eliminated in this system, thus making it unnecessary to perform any tune-up jobs other than spark plug replacement, ignition timing adjustment and idle speed adjustment. Removal, installation, and timing procedures are the same as those given for conventional distributors with the exception of disconnecting the primary lead wires. On models with a transistorized distributor, disconnect the primary wires at the push-on connector.

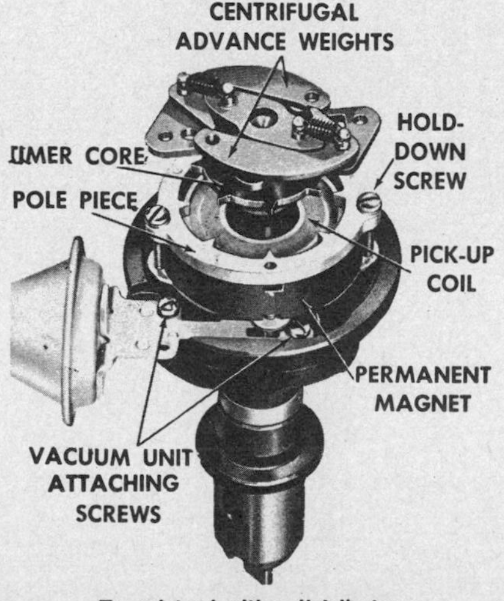

Transistor ignition distributor
(© Pontiac Div, G.M. Corp)

During the 1974 model year, the unitized distributor was replaced by the similar HEI (High Energy Ignition) distributor used on other GM products. This system is standard on all models beginning 1975.

High Energy Ignition System—1975 and Later

Starting 1975, Pontiac is using electronic ignition on all its models. It is triggered by a magnetic pulse, and transistor controlled. It operates as follows: When a cog of the timer core, rotating inside the pole piece, lines up with a cog of the pole piece, an induced voltage inside the pickup coil signals the module to trigger the coil primary circuit. The primary current decreases and high voltage is produced in the secondary winding of the coil and directed through the rotor to fire the plugs. There is a capacitor in the distributor for radio noise suppression.

Connecting a Tachometer to the HEI System

This system may not be compatible with all tachometers, so check the instruction sheet for the tachometer before attempting to hook it up to a car with electronic ignition. There is a terminal on the distributor which is marked TACH; connect a tachometer from this terminal to a suitable ground. Some tachometers may connect from this terminal to the battery positive terminal.

Troubleshooting of the Ignition System can be found in the "Unit Repair Section" under "Electronic Ignition Systems."

FUEL SYSTEM

A disposable-type fuel pump is used. When a fuel pump failure is noted, a pump assembly replacement is in order.

Information covering operation and troubles of the fuel gauge will be found in the Unit Repair Section.

Fuel Pump Removal

1. From the left front side of the engine, disconnect the input and output lines from the fuel pump.
2. Remove the bolts which hold the fuel pump to the timing case cover and lift off the pump.

NOTE: on models equipped with power steering it is possible, but somewhat difficult, to reach the mounting bolts with the steering pump in place. It may pay to slack off on the power steering pump, remove its mounting bolts and, with it still connected to its lines, lift it up out of the way.

Fuel Filter

Paper and Bronze Types

1. Disconnect fuel line connection at inlet of carburetor.
2. Remove inlet fuel filter nut from carburetor using a box wrench.
3. Remove filter element and spring.
4. If a bronze element, blow through cone end—element should allow air to pass freely.
5. Install element spring and new element into carburetor. Bronze elements are installed with small section of cone facing outward.
6. Install new gasket on fitting nut and install nut.
7. Install fuel line and tighten securely. Start engine and check for leaks.

Idle Stop Solenoid

The idle stop solenoid is used on some 4 bbl V8 engines to prevent after-run when the ignition is turned off. After-run is caused largely by the higher engine operating temperatures and wider throttle plate openings necessary for emission controls. Ordinarily, when the ignition is shut off, the loss of spark is enough to stop the engine. However, if the engine has high enough cylinder temperatures, enough air-fuel mixture can pass the wide throttle plate opening and be ignited without the spark plug, and the engine will continue running even after the key is turned off. The idle solenoid is attached to the carburetor to solve this problem. The solenoid has an adjustable plunger and is electrically operated. When the ignition is turned on, the plunger is extended and contacts the carburetor throttle lever, opening the throttle plate wide enough for the engine to idle properly. When the ignition is turned off, the plunger retracts and the throttle lever falls back on the lever stop. When the throttle lever is on its stop the throttle plate opening is very small and will not allow enough air-fuel mixture to pass to run the engine with the ignition off.

Hot Idle Compensator

The hot idle compensator is used with automatic transmissions. Its purpose is to offset the enrichening effects caused by changes in air density and fuel vapors generated during hot engine operation. It is in a chamber on the float bowl casting. The compensator is a temperature-sensitive device which opens and closes a passage leading from the atmosphere to an orifice below the throttle valve. At normal operating temperatures the valve is closed blocking the passage. During very hot engine operation, low air density and excessive fuel vapors in the carburetor enter the engine manifold causing a rich mixture and attendant rough idling and stalling. At a predetermined temperature the compensator opens and allows enough air to enter the carburetor to offset the rich mixture and maintain a smooth idle. When the engine cools the compensator closes and operation returns to normal.

Idle Speed and Mixture Adjustments

1969

Adjust with air cleaner installed.

1. Turn in idle mixture screws until lightly seated, then back out 4 turns (2-BBL.) or 6 turns (4-BBL.).
2. Connect a tachometer, start engine and allow it to warm up to normal operating temperature.
3. Use the idle mixture screws to obtain the smoothest idle after setting the correct idle with the idle speed screws.
4. Place fast idle lever on top step of cam and adjust fast idle speed.

1970

Adjust with air cleaner installed.

1. On California cars, remove fuel filler cap.
2. Disconnect and plug distributor vacuum advance hose.
3. Plug hot idle compensator on all automatic transmission V8's with Quadrajet (4MV). Also plug compensator on all V8 2-BBL. with automatic and A/C.

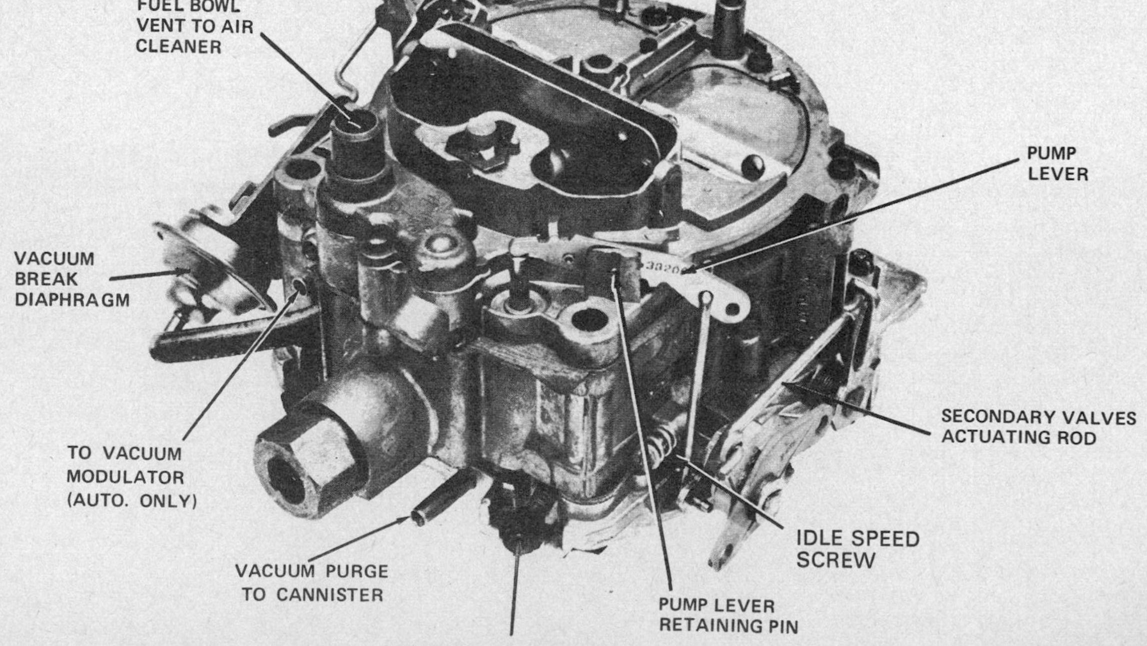

4 bbl carburetor idle mixture and idle speed screws (© Pontiac Div, G.M. Corp)

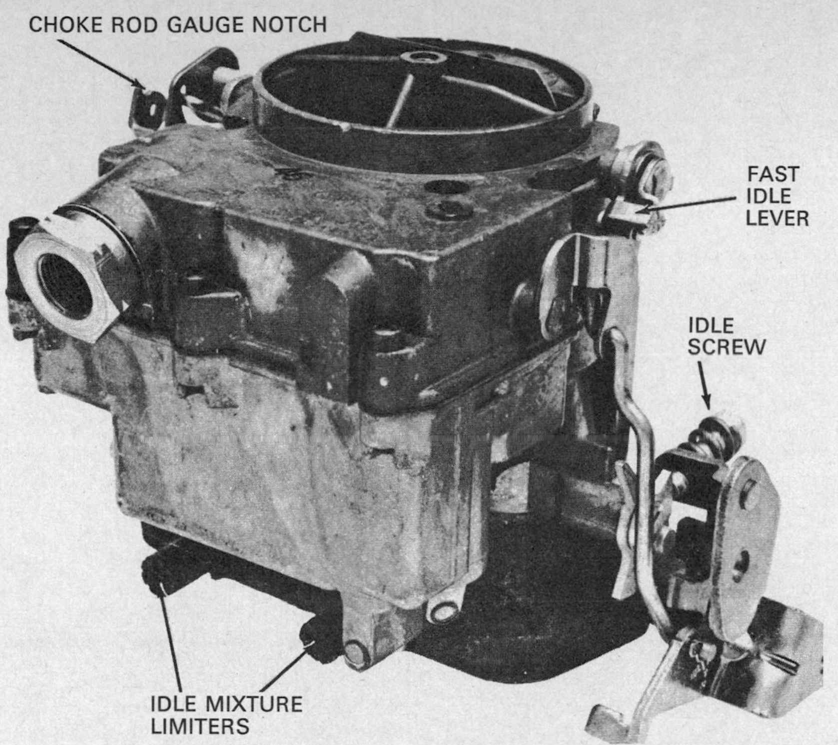

2 bbl carburetor idle mixture and idle speed screws (© Pontiac Div, G.M. Corp)

4. With automatic in Drive, Manual in Neutral, adjust curb idle speed as follows:
5. Back out mixture screws 3-5 turns from lightly seated positions.
6. Adjust carburetor idle speed screw to obtain 850 rpm for manual 350 and 400 2-BBL., 1,050 rpm for manual 400 and 455 4-BBL., or 675 rpm for all automatic 350, 400, 455 engines.
7. Lean mixture screws equally (turn in) to obtain 800 rpm for manual 350 and 400 2-BBL., 950 rpm for manual 400 and 455 4-BBL., or 650 rpm for all automatic 350, 400, 455 engines.

1971-72

Adjust with air cleaner installed.

The Combination Emission Control (C.E.C.) valve was introduced in 1971. This valve is energized through the transmission switch to increase idle speed under conditions of high gear deceleration and to provide full vacuum spark advance during high gear operation. The valve is de-energized at curb idle and in the lower gears to prevent carburetor vacuum from reaching the distributor and advancing ignition timing under these conditions, the result of which is lower exhaust emission. *The valve need not be adjusted unless the solenoid or throttle body is removed, or the carburetor overhauled.*

1. Disconnect carburetor "EVAP" hose from vapor storage canister.
2. Disconnect and plug carburetor-to-vacuum (distributor vacuum) solenoid hose at solenoid. Disconnect throttle solenoid wire on 4-BBL. manual transmission engines.
3. Set dwell and timing (in that order) at specified idle speed.
4. Adjust carburetor speed screw to obtain specified idle speed, automatic in Drive, manual in Neutral.
5. On 4-BBL. manual transmission models, reconnect throttle solenoid wire, manually extend solenoid screw and adjust to specified idle rpm.
6. Place automatic in Park, manual in Neutral and check fast idle speed with screw on top step of cam. Adjust fast idle screw to obtain 1,700 rpm.

NOTE: 2 BBL. carburetors are not adjustable for fast idle.

7. Reconnect distributor vacuum and vapor storage hoses.

Idle Mixture If Carburetor Is Rebuilt

If the carburetor has been overhauled, or the plastic locks removed from the mixture screws, the following procedure must be used to adjust idle speed and mixture.

1. Turn in mixture screws until lightly seated, then back out 3½ turns.
2. Start engine and adjust carburetor idle speed screw to obtain a speed 25 rpm above specified idle (automatic), 75 rpm higher for 2-BBL. V8 (manual), or 100 rpm higher for 4-BBL. V8 (manual).
3. Turn mixture screws in equally until specified idle speed is obtained. At this point a CO meter should be employed to adjust mixture. A reading of 0.2% or less must be maintained.
4. Shut off engine and install new limiter caps, with tabs against full rich stops.
5. Adjust fast idle speed, as described previously.

1973-75

Idle Speed

1. Disconnect and plug the carburetor hose from the vapor canister.
2. Disconnect and plug the distributor and EGR valve vacuum hoses. Plug any open vacuum tubes on the carburetor. Make sure that the hot idle compensator valve is plugged.
3. Check the dwell and timing.
4. Disconnect the idle stop solenoid wire.
5. Adjust the carburetor idle speed screw to the low rpm specified in the Tune-Up Specifications chart.
6. Reconnect the solenoid wire and adjust the solenoid plunger screw to obtain the specified idle speed.

NOTE: You might have to work the throttle linkage by hand first, since the solenoid isn't always powerful enough to move it.

7. On four-barrel carburetors, check the fast idle speed with the fast idle speed screw on the top step of the fast idle cam. Adjust the speed by turning the fast idle screw. Fast idle speed is 1,500 rpm for all engines.

NOTE: The fast idle speed screw is not the same one used in Step 5. You can't make this adjustment on two-barrel carburetors.

Idle Mixture

1. Set the parking brake and block the wheels.
2. Disconnect and plug the carburetor hose from the vapor canister in the engine compartment. Disconnect and plug the distributor vacuum hose.
3. If the idle mixture limiter caps are intact and a CO meter is available, attempt to obtain an idle setting of 0.2% CO by adjusting the mixture screws. If this doesn't work, remove the caps and proceed to the next step.

NOTE: The engine must be at normal operating temperature.

4. Remove the idle mixture limiter caps. If you have a CO meter, adjust the mixture screws equally to get a reading of 0.2% CO.
5. Run the screws in until they are lightly seated, then back them out six turns for 1973 and seven for 1974, and five for 1975.
6. Turn the air conditioner off, place the automatic transmission in Drive (block the wheels),

place the manual transmission in Neutral, leave the air cleaner off and plug the air cleaner manifold vacuum fitting. Adjust the idle speed screw or the idle stop solenoid to obtain the following temporary idle speed.

Engine	*Year*	*rpm*
8-350, 2 bbl.	1973	700
8-400, 2 bbl.	1973	700
8-400, 455, 4 bbl.	1973	700
8-400, 2 bbl.	1974	720
8-400, 2 bbl., Calif.	1974	690
8-400, 4 bbl.	1974	720
8-400, 4 bbl., Calif.	1974	685
8-455, 4 bbl.	1974	680
8-455, 4 bbl., Calif.	1974	675
8-400, 2 bbl.	1975	730
8-400, 4 bbl.	1975	690 (665-Wagon)
8-400, 4 bbl. Calif.	1975	660
8-455, 4 bbl.	1975	720
8-455, 4 bbl. Calif.	1975	745

7. Turn the mixture screws in equally to get the highest idle speed. Then set the speed back to that listed in Step 6.
8. Turn the mixture screws in equally until the engine speed drops to the normal idle speed given in the Tune-Up Specifications chart.
9. Install the air cleaner. If the idle speed changes, adjust the mixture screws slightly to compensate.

COOLING SYSTEM

The cooling system consists of the radiator cap, radiator, hoses, waterpump, cooling fan, thermostat, and passages for water circulation in the block.

A cross-flow radiator is used instead of a conventional down-flow and center type. With the cross-flow design, coolant flows horizontally through the core and the tanks are located on each side.

Advantages of the cross-flow radiator are improved cooling capability, more effective cooling surface area, and a low silhouette.

Automatic transmission radiators have oil coolers built into the right-hand tank, air-conditioned and high-performance models have greater cooling capacity than standard. The drain cock is located at the inside, lower left-hand corner of the radiator.

Radiator R & R

1. Drain the radiator.
2. On Grand Prix, remove the fan.
3. Disconnect the upper and lower radiator hoses.
4. If equipped with automatic transmission, disconnect the cooling lines and plug them to prevent excessive fluid loss.
5. Remove the radiator upper bracket bolts and remove the bracket.
6. Remove the radiator and shroud assembly by lifting straight up.
7. Reverse the above steps to install the radiator.

Water Pump R & R

This is a centrifugal type waterpump. It is die cast, with sealed bearings, and is pressed together. Therefore, it is serviced as a unit.

NOTE: It is sometimes more convenient to remove the radiator than to leave it in place. This depends on the working space available and the options on the car such as air conditioning and power steering.

1. Disconnect the battery and drain the radiator.
2. Loosen the alternator and remove the fan belt.
3. Remove the power steering and air conditioning belts, if so equipped.
4. Remove the fan and water pump pulley.
5. Remove the front alternator bracket.
6. Remove the heater hose and radiator hose at the pump.
7. Remove the water pump retaining bolts and remove the pump.
8. Install the pump by reversing above steps. Make sure the gasket surfaces are clean and smooth. Always use a gasket sealer on both sides of the gasket. Torque the retaining bolts to 15 ft lbs.

Thermostat R & R

1. Drain coolant to below thermostat level.
2. Disconnect the upper hose and remove water outlet assembly.
3. Replace by reversing the above steps. Clean gasket surfaces and use a gasket sealer and a new gasket. Torque attaching bolts to 30 ft. lbs.
4. Refill to 3 in. below filler neck and bleed cooling system.

EMISSION CONTROLS

There are three types of emissions to be controlled: crankcase emissions, carburetor and gas tank vapor emissions, and exhaust emissions. See the "Unit Repair Section" for troubleshooting and repair information.

1969

A new concept, Combustion Control System, (C.C.S.), utilizes engine modifications. Essentially the C.C.S. increases combustion efficiency through carburetor and distributor calibrations and by increasing engine operating temperature.

Carburetors are calibrated leaner and initial ignition timing is retarded. Another carburetor feature is the idle fuel mixture limiting orifice. It is located at the base of the idle mixture screw and makes sure that, even if the idle mixture screw is turned out too far, the fuel enrichment will not greatly affect exhaust emissions.

The C.C.S. also incorporates a higher engine operation temperature. A 195° thermostat is used. Engines with higher operating temperatures provide more complete vaporation of the fuel and reduce quench area in the combustion chamber. Quench area is the relatively cool area near the cylinder wall and combustion chamber surfaces. Fuel in these areas does not burn properly because of the lower temperatures. This incomplete burning increases emissions.

The C.C.S. uses a thermostatically controlled air cleaner called the Auto-Therm air cleaner. It is designed to keep the temperature of the air entering the carburetor at approximately 100°. This allows the lean carburetor to work properly, minimizes carburetor icing, and improves engine warm-up characteristics. A sensor unit located on the clean air side of the air filter senses the temperature of the air passing over it and regulates the vacuum supplied to a vacuum diaphragm in the inlet tube of the air cleaner. The colder the air, the greater the amount of vacuum supplied to the vacuum diaphragm. The vacuum diaphragm, depending on the vacuum supplied to it, opens or closes a damper door in the inlet tube of the air cleaner. If the door is open it allows air from the engine compartment to go to the carburetor. If the door is closed, air flows from the heat stove located on the exhaust manifold into the carburetor, in this way heated air is supplied to the carburetor during cold days and when first starting the engine and warming it up.

1970

The more stringent 1970 laws require tighter control of emissions. Crankcase emissions are controlled by the Closed Positive Crankcase Ventilation System, and exhaust emissions by the engine Controlled Combustion System (C.C.S.), in conjunction with the new Transmission Controlled Spark System (T.C.S.).

In addition, cars sold in California are equipped with an Evaporation Control System that limits the amount of gasoline vapor discharged into the atmosphere (usually from the carburetor and fuel tank).

The T.C.S. system consists of a transmission switch, a solenoid valve, and a temperature switch. Under normal conditions, the system permits the vacuum distributor (spark) advance to operate only in high gear (both manual and automatic transmissions) and reverse.

The transmission switch is located on the transmission and senses when the transmission is in one of the lower gears. When in a lower gear, the switch activates the vacuum solenoid valve. This valve is located in the vacuum line that runs from the carburetor to the distributor, and it prevents vacuum from going to the distributor advance when it is activated. There is also an engine-temperature sensing switch which overrides the transmission switch. It will allow vacuum advance in the lower gears when engine temperature is below 85° or above 220°. There is always vacuum advance in high gear and reverse.

1971

In 1971, the Combination Emission Control System (C.E.C.) was introduced. It uses the C.C.S. of 1969 and incorporates several but not all of the features in the T.C.S. of 1970. Although distributor vacuum advance is eliminated in the lower gears, as in the T.C.S. system, it is eliminated in a different manner. A C.E.C. solenoid valve is used to regulate distributor vacuum advance and the T.C.S. valve is eliminated.

The C.E.C. solenoid valve is mounted on the carburetor. Vacuum from the intake manifold passes through a port at the base of the solenoid before it reaches the distributor. When the solenoid receives an electrical signal from the transmission or temperature switches, the plunger extends, opening the solenoid's vacuum port, which allows vacuum to the distributor. At the same time the plunger head contacts the carburetor throttle lever increasing engine speed. When the solenoid is de-energized the spring-loaded plunger returns to its unextended position closing the vacuum port and allowing the throttle lever to rest against the idle speed adjusting screw.

The C.E.C. solenoid valve is energized by two switches and one relay.

The time delay relay is used to energize the C.E.C. solenoid and provide vacuum advance for the first 15 seconds after the ignition is turned on. This happens regardless of engine temperature. After the 15 seconds, the solenoid is again regulated by the temperature switch and the transmission switch.

One of the controlling switches is an engine temperature switch. It allows vacuum advance in all gears, by energizing the C.E.C. solenoid, when engine temperature is below 82° or above 220°. Between these temperatures, the C.E.C. solenoid is controlled by the transmission switch.

The other switch is the transmission switch. When the transmission is in the lower gears, this switch keeps the C.E.C. solenoid in the de-energized position eliminating vacuum advance. In high gear, the solenoid is energized by the transmission switch, and vacuum advance is supplied.

Engine dieseling is controlled by use of lower throttle plate openings (lower idle speeds).

On A/C, automatic transmission cars, a solid-state timing device engages the A/C compressor for about three seconds after the ignition is turned off. The load from the compressor effectively stalls the engine and prevents dieseling or over-run.

An evaporation control system was added to all cars in 1971. This system limits the amount of gasoline vapor discharged into the air from the gas tank and carburetor. The fuel tank has a non-vented cap. As vapors are generated in the fuel tank, they flow through a liquid vapor separator to a canister where they are stored. From the canister the vapors are routed to the carburetor where they are burned when the engine is running.

1972

All models use the new Speed Control Spark System, (S.C.S.).

Every engine and transmission combination uses the Auto-therm air cleaner, P.C.V. system, and the evaporation control system of 1971.

The S.C.S. system uses a solenoid valve in the vacuum line running between the carburetor and the distributor. This valve is the same as the Transmission Controlled Spark Valve used in 1970. The difference in this system is that the valve is regulated by vehicle speed using a speed control spark switch, instead of by a transmission switch. The S.C.S. solenoid valve is energized below 38 mph in any gear, under normal operating temperature, allowing no vacuum advance. Above 38 mph, in any gear, or any time engine temperature is higher or lower than normal operating temperature, the solenoid valve is de-energized allowing full vacuum advance to the distributor.

Normally S.C.S. engine operating temperatures range from 95° to 230°. An engine temperature sensing switch is located in the head and de-energizes the solenoid until operating temperature is reached regardless of vehicle speed.

1973

The Controlled Combustion System (C.C.S.) is standard on all engines. The Air Injection Reactor (A.I.R.) is used on all 350 engines with manual transmissions and 350/400 California engines. A combination of the Transmission Controlled Spark and Exhaust Gas Re-Circulation (E.G.R.) is found on all V8 engines.

E.G.R. is a system used to reduce nitrous oxide (NO_x) emissions. It functions by allowing a small amount of exhaust gas into the air fuel mixture in the intake manifold, under certain conditions.

The EGR-TCS system consists of a temperature switch which senses when the engine temperature is under 71° or over 230°, a second temperature switch sensing engine temperature between 140° and 230°, an EGR solenoid, a vacuum advance solenoid, a transmission switch, and a time delay relay.

The under 71° and over 230° switch is mounted on the left cylinder head. The 140° to 230° switch is mounted in the right cylinder head. The time delay relay is mounted on the vacuum advance solenoid.

The 71° to 230° switch grounds the circuit for the solenoids below 71° and above 230°. The 140° switch passes current to the transmission switch when engine temperature is between 140° and 230°. The transmission switch then grounds the circuit for the solenoids in first gear only. Between 71° and 140° the temperature switches are both open and the solenoids are in the normal positions.

The vacuum advance solenoid is normally closed, allowing no vacuum advance. The EGR solenoid is normally open, allowing exhaust gas recirculation.

Below 71° there is a complete circuit and both solenoids are energized, allowing vacuum advance and cutting off EGR.

From 71° to 140° there is an open circuit, the solenoids return to their normal positions and vacuum advance is cut off and EGR is allowed.

From 140° to 230°, in first gear, there is an open circuit and the solenoids are in their normal positions. The time delay relay maintains the open circuit for 33 to 55 seconds after the transmission shifts into second gear. However, after the time delay in second and third gear, the solenoids are energized to allow vacuum advance and cut off EGR.

Over 235° the solenoids are energized, vacuum advance occurs and there is no EGR.

1973½

A mid-year redesign of the emission control system was necessitated by newly-announced Federal standards. On cars equipped with A.I.R., air is not supplied to nos. 3 and 6 cylinders. This is done by internal changes in the cylinder heads. Mid-year A.I.R. cylinder heads can usually be identified by the absence of

1976 PONTIAC EMISSION CONTROL SYSTEMS

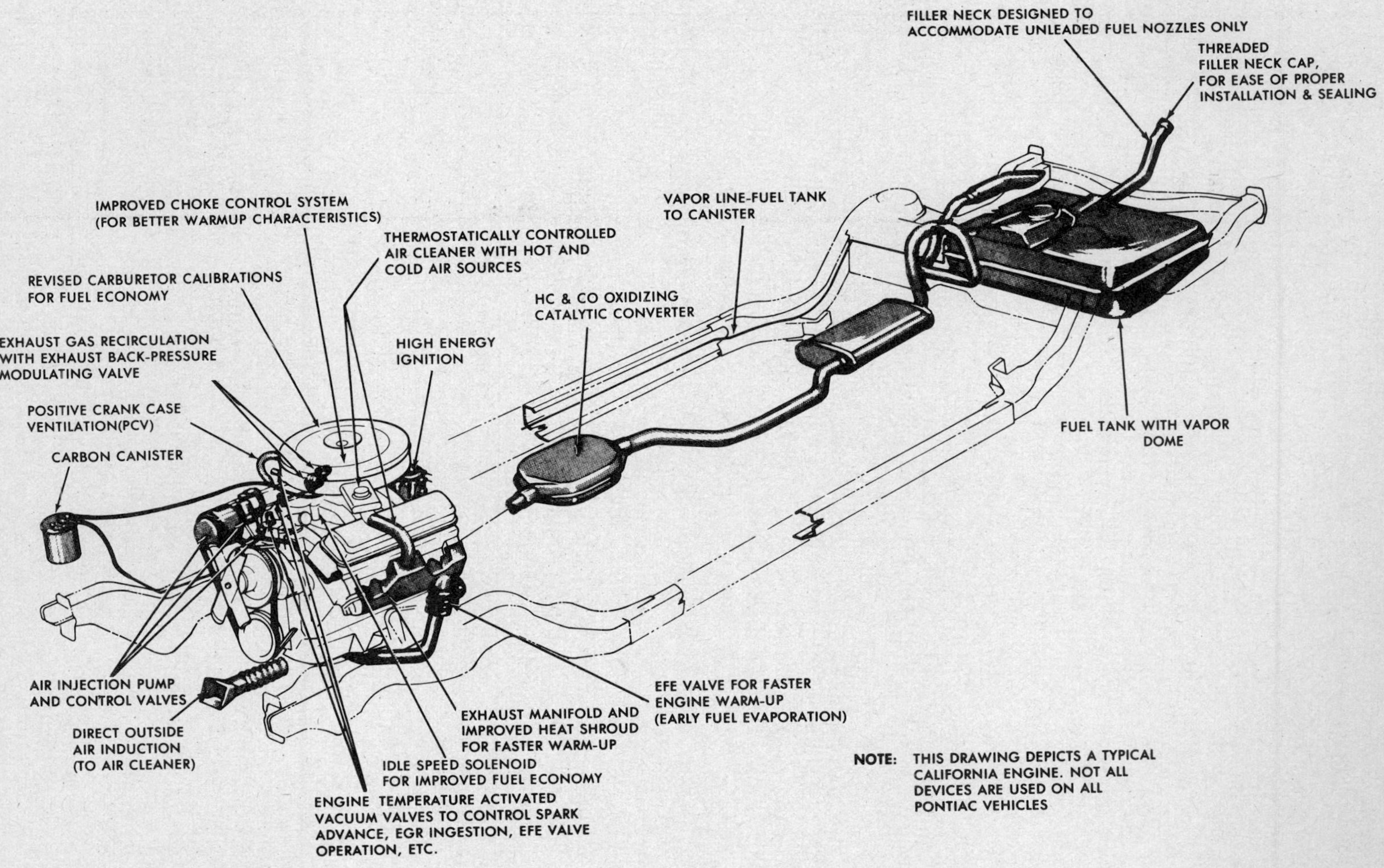

NOTE: THIS DRAWING DEPICTS A TYPICAL CALIFORNIA ENGINE. NOT ALL DEVICES ARE USED ON ALL PONTIAC VEHICLES

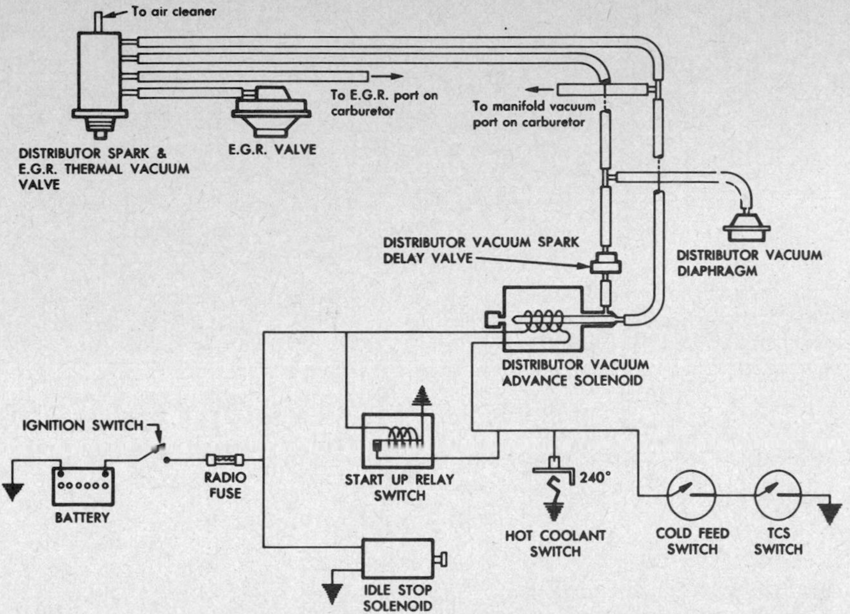

1974 emission control system—schematic diagram
(© Pontiac Div., G.M. Corp)

a drilled passage and metal sealing ball at the nos. 3 and 6 cylinder locations.

The new engines have a relocated vacuum source for the air cleaner. Vacuum is supplied through a tee in the hose feeding vacuum to the distributor vacuum spark thermal valve.

The mid-year EGR system operates basically on the same principle as the 1973 system, except for two major differences:

1. The EGR and TCS systems now work completely independent of each other.
2. A new EGR thermal vacuum valve is used to sense the temperature of the intake manifold coolant. Below 95°F, no EGR; above 95°F, ported EGR.

In the TCS system, full vacuum advance is provided below 62°F. When the temperature rises above 62°F, the distributor vacuum spark thermal valve closes and from this point on the distributor solenoid must be energized to get vacuum advance. The upper temperature limit for vacuum advance cut-in is now 240°F.

The Start-Up Relay Switch gives full advance (ported for manual transmission) in any gear for 20 seconds after all engine starts. After the 20 seconds has elapsed, the switch breaks ground and the distributor solenoid is de-energized, shutting off the vacuum advance.

1974

The A.I.R. system is carried over from 1973 and is used on all 400 cu in 2 bbl California engines.

The EGR/TCS system is once again together, as in pre-1973½ systems, and consists of a thermal vacuum valve, vacuum advance solenoid, EGR valve, hot coolant switch, cold feed switch and a time-delay relay for engine starting. The system is found on all V8s.

On the EGR/TCS system, the distributor spark-EGR thermal vacuum valve senses the temperature of the air/fuel mixture inside the intake manifold. Below 62°F, EGR is off and full vacuum advance is provided. When the temperature rises above 62°F, EGR is on (operated by a port above the throttle blade, so that it only comes on above idle). From this point on the distributor vacuum advance solenoid must be energized by the other components and switches to provide vacuum advance.

When the cylinder head metal temperature goes above 125°, 140°, 155°F (depending on use), the cold feed switch closes. This sends the 12V current to the TCS switch looking for a ground. The TCS switch provides a ground only when the transmission shifts into high gear. There is no time delay after shifting into high gear.

Any time the coolant temperature goes over 240°F, the hot coolant switch provides a ground for the distributor solenoid. Since the hot coolant switch will ground whether the TCS switch does or not, vacuum advance will be supplied to the distributor in any gear when the coolant temperature reaches 240°F or above.

There is a distributor vacuum spark delay valve on some models, between the distributor solenoid and the distributor acting as a restrictor on vacuum supplied to the distributor. This merely slows down the rate vacuum is initially supplied to the distributor. Full vacuum is eventually supplied.

The function of the start-up relay switch is identical to 1973½.

1975

The Controlled Combustion System (C.C.S.) is continued on all non-California engines. It introduces preheated carburetor intake air during engine warmup.

The Air Injection Reactor (A.I.R.), or air pump system is continued in some applications.

E.G.R. (Exhaust Gas Recirculation) is used with the exhaust gas introduced into the intake mixture in the intake manifold and modulated by an exhaust backpressure modulating valve.

A hot air choke is used to provide quick response to engine warmup.

All models have high energy ignition (H.E.I.) to prevent any possible catalyst damage caused by ignition miss. Refer to the "Electronic Ignition" Unit Repair Section for details.

Oxidizing catalytic converters are used on all models to control hydrocarbons and carbon monoxide. Refer to the "Emission Control" Unit Repair Section for details on this system.

All engines have outside air intakes. The cooler outside air improves driveability.

The Early Fuel Evaporation System has a heat valve in the exhaust manifold which, during warm-up, forces the exhaust gases to flow under the carburetor heating the mixture. When the engine reaches normal temperature the valve opens and exhaust gases are routed normally.

The Evaporative Emission Control System is carried over from the previous year.

ENGINE

In 1970 Pontiac increased the displacement of its largest engine by bringing the bore and stroke out to 4.15 in. by 4.21 in. for 455 cu. in., and then introduced a small bore 350 cu. in. version of their 400 V8 for their base Catalina engine. In 1971, Pontiac retained the 1970 engines, modifying them to operate on low-lead fuel. No premium-fuel engines have been offered by Pontiac since 1970.

Engine Removal and Installation

1. Disconnect battery cables and remove battery.
2. Drain cooling system.
3. Scribe alignment marks around hood hinges and remove hood.
4. Disconnect engine wiring and all ground straps. Disconnect the thermal feed switch from the left rear cylinder head on all 1973 and later cars.
5. Remove air cleaner and fan shroud, then disconnect radiator and heater hoses.
6. Remove the radiator.
7. Remove power steering pump and A/C compressor from

brackets and swing units aside without disconnecting hoses.

Caution If the compressor refrigerant lines do not have enough slack to position the compressor out of the way without disconnecting the refrigerant lines, the air conditioning system will have to be removed by a trained air-conditioning specialist. Under no conditions should an untrained person attempt to disconnect the air conditioning refrigerant lines. These lines contain pressurized Freon, which can be extremely dangerous to the untrained.

8. Remove fan and fan pulley.
9. Disconnect accelerator linkage or cable and remove bracket.
10. Disconnect transmission vacuum modulator line (automatic) and power brake vacuum line.

Caution Do not bend the metal transmission modulator line.

11. Jack up car and support on axle stands.
12. Drain engine oil, disconnect fuel lines at pump and exhaust pipes from manifolds.
13. Disconnect starter wires and remove starter motor on manual transmission cars.
14. If equipped with automatic transmission: remove converter cover and three converter retaining bolts. Slide converter rearward.
15. If equipped with manual transmission: disconnect clutch linkage and remove cross-shaft and flywheel housing cover.
16. Remove four lower bellhousing bolts—two per side.
17. Disconnect auto transmission filler tube support and starter wire shield.
18. Remove the two front motor mount bolts, then lower car to floor.
19. Support auto transmission with a wood-padded jack, then remove the two remaining bellhousing bolts from above.
20. Jack up auto transmission slightly, attach a chain hoist and remove the engine.
21. To install, reverse removal Procedure. Note that there are dowel pins in the block that have matching holes in the bellhousing. These dowel pins must be in almost perfect alignment with their holes before the engine and bellhousing will go together. Do not lower the engine completely while the jack is supporting the transmission.

Manifolds

Exhaust Manifold Removal

Tab locks are used on front and rear pairs of bolts on each exhaust manifold. When removing bolts, straighten tabs from beneath car using long handled screw driver. When installing tab locks, bend tabs against sides of bolt not over top of bolt.

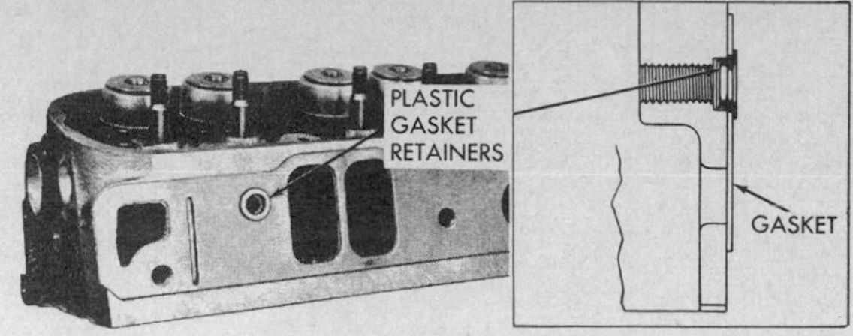

Plastic manifold retainers
(© Pontiac Div, G.M. Corp)

Left-Side Manifold

1. If the car is equipped with power steering, disconnect the power steering pump but leave it attached to its hoses and pull it up out of the way.
2. Remove the alternator belt, the alternator and the mounting bracket as an assembly.
3. From underneath the vehicle, disconnect the exhaust crossover pipe flange.
4. If the car is equipped with power brakes, the rear bolts of the manifold are difficult to reach but they can be removed with a box wrench.
5. Remove the bolts that hold the manifold to the left cylinder head and take off the manifold.

Right-Side Manifold

From underneath the vehicle, disconnect the upper flange from the right manifold. This is the upper flange where the cross manifold, exhaust pipe and right manifold join.

From underneath the vehicle, remove the bolts that hold the manifold to the head on the back two flanges. The front flange can be removed from the top of the car with a box wrench.

Intake Manifold Removal

All Models

1. Drain coolant from petcocks on radiator and on each side of block. Remove the EGR valve where necessary before removing the manifold.

NOTE: most of the coolant can be drained from block through radiator drain by raising rear end of car approximately 15-18 in. off floor.

2. Remove air cleaner.
3. Remove water outlet fitting bolts and position fitting out of way, leaving radiator hose attached.
4. Disconnect heater hose from fitting.
5. Disconnect electrical wires and vacuum hoses from all emission switches and solenoids.
6. Remove spark plug wire brackets from manifold.
7. On cars equipped with power brakes, remove power brake vacuum pipe from carburetor.
8. Disconnect distributor to carburetor vacuum hoses.
9. Disconnect fuel line connecting carburetor and fuel pump.
10. Disconnect crank case vent hose from intake manifold.
11. Disconnect throttle rod from carburetor.
12. Remove screws retaining throttle control bracket assembly.
13. Remove intake manifold retaining bolts and nuts, and remove manifold and gaskets. Make sure that O-ring seal between intake manifold and timing chain cover is retained and installed during assembly.
14. Reverse procedure to install. Use plastic gasket retainers, as shown, to prevent manifold gaskets from slipping out of place.

Valve System

All V8 engines use a ball pivot type valve train and hydraulic valve lifters.

Rocker Arm R & R

1. Remove the valve covers.
2. Remove the rocker arm nut and rocker arm ball.
3. Lift the rocker arm off the rocker arm stud. Always keep the rocker arm assemblies together and assemble them on the same stud.
4. Remove the pushrod from its bore. Make sure the rods are returned to their original bore, with the same end in the block.
5. Reverse the removal procedure to install the rocker arms and adjust the valve on any rocker arm removed before installing the valve cover.

Valve Guides

Pontiac engines have integral valve guides. Pontiac offers valves with oversize stems for worn guides (0.001, 0.003 and 0.005 in. being available for most engines). To fit these, enlarge valve guide bores with valve guide reamers to an oversize that cleans up wear. If a large oversize is required, it is best to approach that size in stages by using a series of reamers of increasing diameter. This helps to maintain the concentricity of the guide bores with the valve seats.

Compressing valve spring—air chuck method
(© Pontiac Div, G.M. Corp)

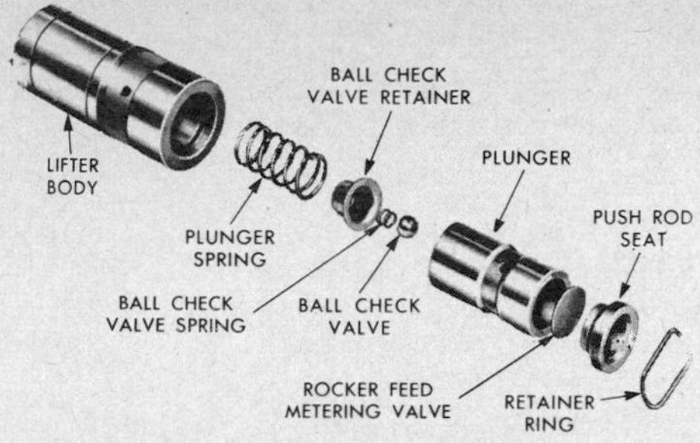

Hydraulic lifter
(© Pontiac Div, G.M. Corp)

As an alternate procedure, some local automotive machine shops fit replacement guides that use standard stem valves.

The following is a method for replacing valve springs, oil seals or spring retainers without removing the cylinder head.

1. **Obtain a spark plug hole air chuck adaptor from an auto parts store.**
2. **To this adaptor add an air chuck so that the hose from an air compressor can be attached. This assembly will be used later to pressurize the cylinder.**
3. **Remove the valve rocker cover. Remove the rocker arm from the valve to be worked on.**
4. **Remove the spark plug from the cylinder to be worked on.**
5. **Turn the crankshaft to bring the piston of this cylinder down, away from possible contact with the valve head. Sharply tap the valve retainer to loosen the valve lock.**
6. **Then turn the crankshaft to bring the piston in this cylinder to the Exact Top of its Compression Stroke.**
7. **Screw in the chuck-equipped tool.**
8. **Hook up an air hose to the chuck and turn on the pressure (about 200 lbs.).**
9. **With a strong and constant supply of air holding the valve closed, compress the valve spring and remove the lock and retainer.**
10. **Make the necessary replacements and reassemble.**

NOTE: it is important that the operation be performed exactly as stated, in this order. The piston in the cylinder must be on exact top-center to prevent air pressure from turning the crankshaft.

Hydraulic Valve Lifter Removal

Remove the rocker cover and the intake manifold, then take off the pushrod cover. Loosen the rocker arm ball nut and lift the rocker arm off the pushrod. The pushrods can be pulled up through the cylinder head and the lifters can then be pulled up out of their bores. Tool J-3049 (hydraulic valve lifter remover) may facilitate removal of the lifters. The lifters must be returned to the bores from which they were taken.

Caution The hydraulic lifter is a complete assembly, matchmated at the factory, and the bore of one lifter positively cannot be used in the body of another. These parts should not be mixed.

NOTE: the rear-most pushrod on the left bank cannot be lifted out on some cars. However, the pushrod can be lifted up far enough to permit removal of the hydraulic lifter.

Cylinder Head

Cylinder Head Removal

1. Drain the cooling system including the block. Remove intake manifold, valley cover, and rocker arm cover.
2. Loosen all rocker arm retaining nuts and pivot rockers off pushrods.
3. Remove pushrods and place in order. The pushrods must be replaced in the same position with the same end in the block.
4. On all but the left head of the 455 S.D. engine, remove the exhaust pipe-to-manifold attaching bolts. In order to remove the left head of the 455 S.D., it is necessary to remove the exhaust manifold attaching nuts and drop the manifold. Remove the inner panel of the carburetor heat stove from the two center cylinder head bolts.
5. Remove battery ground strap and engine ground strap on left head; engine ground strap and automatic transmission oil filler tube bracket on right head.
6. Remove cylinder head bolts and head, with exhaust manifold attached.

NOTE: left head must be maneuvered to clear power steering and power brake units.

Cylinder Head Installation

1. Check head surface for straightness, then place a new head gasket on block.

NOTE: bolts are of three different lengths on all V8s. When bolts are properly installed, they will project an equal distance from head.

2. Install all bolts and tighten evenly to specified torque. Tighten to specifications in three stages.
3. Install pushrods in original positions.

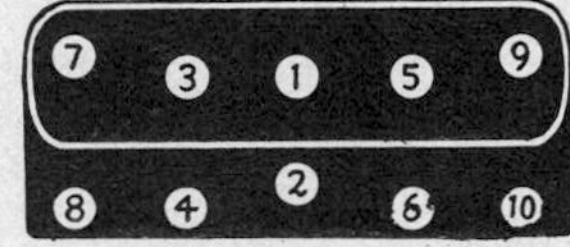

V8 cylinder head tightening sequence

4. Position rocker arms over pushrods. Tighten the rocker arm ball retaining nut to 20 ft lbs.
5. Replace rocker arm cover.
6. Replace valve tappet cover.
7. Replace ground straps, oil filler tube bracket, intake manifold.
8. Install exhaust pipe flange nuts. On 455 S.D. engine, install left head exhaust manifold, with new gasket.

Stud Removal

Pressed-in Studs

Caution This procedure can be used *only* on engines with pressed-in rocker studs. Some special high performance engines have screwed-in rocker studs which are easily identified by their hex head lower portion. All 1974 and later engines have screwed-in studs. Another common stud-securing procedure on standard engines is "pinning" pressed-in studs by drilling through the stud boss and stud and inserting an interference-fit roll pin. Make sure any such pins are removed before attempting the following procedure.

1. Disconnect battery and drain cooling system.
2. Remove rocker cover.
3. Pack oily rags around stud holes and engine openings.
4. Remove rocker arm and pushrod, then file two slots 3/32-1/8 in. deep on opposite sides of the stud. The top of the slots should be ¼-⅜ in. below thread travel.
5. Place a spacer washer over the stud, then position stud remover on stud and tighten Allen screws.
6. Place a spacer over the remover, then thread a 7/8 in. nut on stud remover and turn in until stud pulls from head.
7. If an oversize stud is to be used (0.005 in. oversize studs are available), ream stud hole to the proper size, then clean chips from area.
8. To install, coat press-pit area of stud with axle lube, then press or hammer into place. If possible use Pontiac Tool J-23342. Cool the stud in dry ice to facilitate installation.

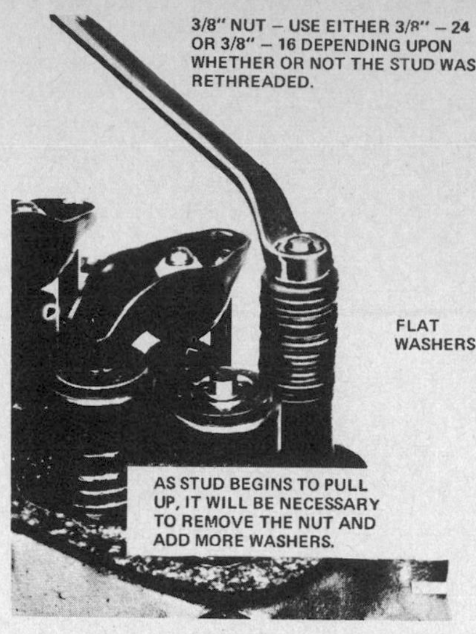

Rocker arm stud removal
(© Pontiac Div, G.M. Corp)

Timing Cover, Chain, and Camshaft

Timing Case Cover R & R and Seal Replacement

1. Drain radiator and cylinder block.
2. Loosen alternator adjusting bolts.
3. Remove fan, fan pulley, accessory drive belts, and water pump.
4. Disconnect radiator hoses.
5. Remove fuel pump.
6. Remove harmonic balancer bolt and washer.
7. Remove harmonic balancer.

NOTE: do not pry on rubber-mounted balancers. If only seal is to be replaced, proceed to Step 12.

8. Remove front four oil pan to timing cover bolts.
9. Remove timing cover bolts and nuts and cover to intake manifold bolt.
10. Pull cover forward and remove.
11. Remove O-ring from recess in intake manifold, then clean all gasket surfaces.
12. To replace seal, pry it out of the cover using a screwdriver. Install the new seal with lip inwards.

NOTE: seal can be replaced with cover installed.

13. To install, reverse removal procedure, making sure all gaskets are replaced. Tighten four oil pan bolts to 12 ft. lbs., harmonic balancer bolt to 160 ft. lbs., and fan pulley bolts to 20 ft. lbs.

Timing Chain and Sprocket R & R

1. Remove the timing case cover and fuel pump cam.
2. Turn the crank and camshaft (if the chain is broken) until the two timing marks are in line.
3. Using a puller, draw the sprocket off the front of the crankshaft.
4. Arrange the new chain on the sprocket and set the sprocket up over the camshaft by looping the chain over the crank sprocket. That way, when the cam sprocket engages its key, the timing marks are in line.
5. Secure the camshaft sprocket in this position, with pump cam in place.

NOTE: when reassembling the timing case cover, extra care should be taken to make sure that the oil seal between the bottom of the timing case cover and the front of the oil pan is still a good one. Plenty of gasket cement should be used, at this point, to prevent oil leaks.

Camshaft R & R

1. Drain cooling system and remove air cleaner.
2. Disconnect all water hoses, vacuum lines and spark plug wires.
3. Disconnect accelerator linkage, temperature gauge wire, and fuel lines. Remove the radiator.
4. Remove hood latch brace.
5. Remove PCV hose, then remove rocker covers. Remove the water pump.

NOTE: on air-conditioned models, remove alternator and bracket.

6. Remove distributor, then remove intake manifold.
7. Remove valve tappet cover.
8. Loosen rocker arm nuts and pivot rockers out of the way.

V8 timing marks
(© Pontiac Div., G.M. Corp)

9. Remove pushrods and lifters (keep them in proper order).
10. Remove harmonic balancer, fuel pump, and four oil pan to timing cover bolts.
11. Remove timing cover and gasket, then remove fuel pump eccentric and bushing.
12. Align timing marks, then remove timing chain and sprockets.
13. Remove camshaft thrust plate.
14. Remove camshaft by pulling straight forward, being careful not to damage cam bearings in the process.

NOTE: it may be necessary to jack up the engine slightly to gain clearance, especially if motor mounts are worn.

15. Install new camshaft, with lobes and journals coated with heavy (SAE 50-60) oil, into the engine, being careful not to damage cam bearings.

NOTE: most specialty cams come with a special "break-in" lubricant for the lobes and journals; if such lubricant is available, use it instead of heavy oil.

16. Install camshaft thrust plate and tighten bolts to 20 ft. lbs.
17. To install, reverse steps 1-12, tightening sprocket bolts to 40 ft. lbs., timing cover bolts and nuts to 30 ft. lbs., oil pan bolts to 12 ft. lbs., and harmonic balancer bolt to 160 ft. lbs.

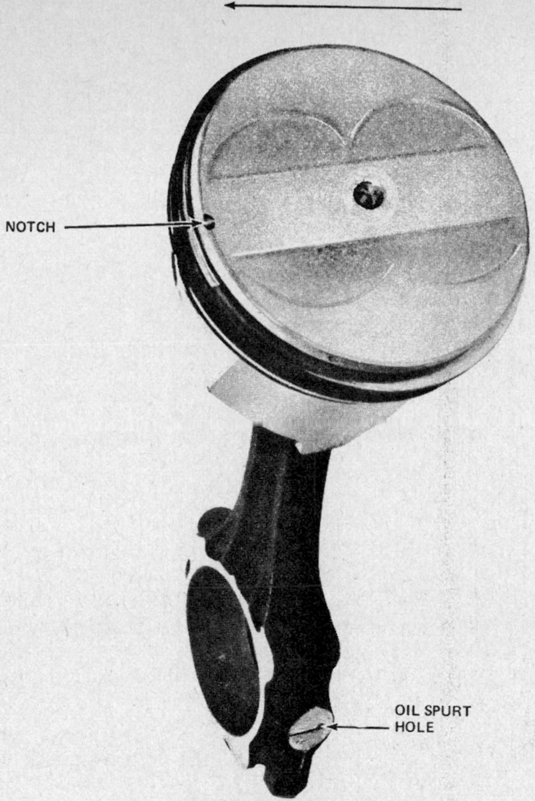

Piston and rod assembly
(© Pontiac Div, G.M. Corp)

Piston and Connecting Rod Installation

The letter F, or the notch in the edge of the piston, goes to the front of the engine in all cases. The oil spurt holes on the connecting rod lower ends must face the camshaft. Some 1973, and all 1974 and later, engines don't have these holes. These connecting rods have three dimples on one side of the rod and a single dimple on the connecting rod cap. The dimples must face to the rear on the right bank, and forward on the left.

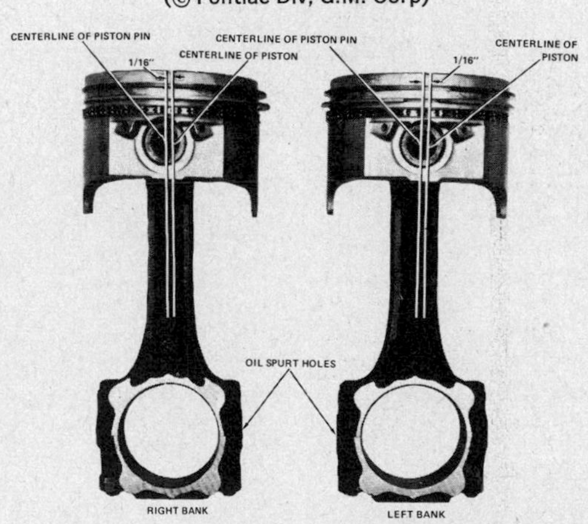

Piston and rod assembly
(© Pontiac Div, G.M. Corp)

Lubrication

A spur, gear type oil pump circulates the oil under pressure. Maximum oil pressure is regulated by a spring-loaded, ball type pressure regulator valve. Oil is supplied to the crankshaft, connecting rods, camshaft bearings, and valve train, under pressure. There are also metering jets for each cylinder wall, timing chain, and sprockets.

Oil Pan Removal and Installation

1. Disconnect battery cables.
2. Remove fan shroud and the power steering belt, then tilt the steering pump upward.
3. On A/C cars made in 1969, and all cars starting 1970, remove fan and pulley.
4. Disconnect engine ground straps. Drain radiator starting 1970.
5. On A/C cars, remove compressor from brackets and swing aside WITHOUT DISCONNECTING HOSES.
6. Check all wiring, fuel lines and hoses for clearance, and disconnect the thermal feed switch from the left rear cylinder head, on 1973 and later models, as the engine must be raised. Disconnect the radiator hose at the water pump.
7. Jack up car and drain engine oil.
8. Disconnect steering idler arm from frame on all cars up to 1970. On Grand Prix models starting 1971, both this operation and the removal of the Pitman arm from the steering box are necessary.
9. Remove exhaust crossover pipe on single-exhaust cars; disconnect manifold flanges on dual-exhaust cars. Wire pipes out of the way to gain working room.
10. Remove flywheel housing cover, starter motor, and motor bracket (on 1969 and later models).
11. Attach a hoist to the front of the engine.
12. Support engine on hoist and remove front motor mount bolts and mounts.

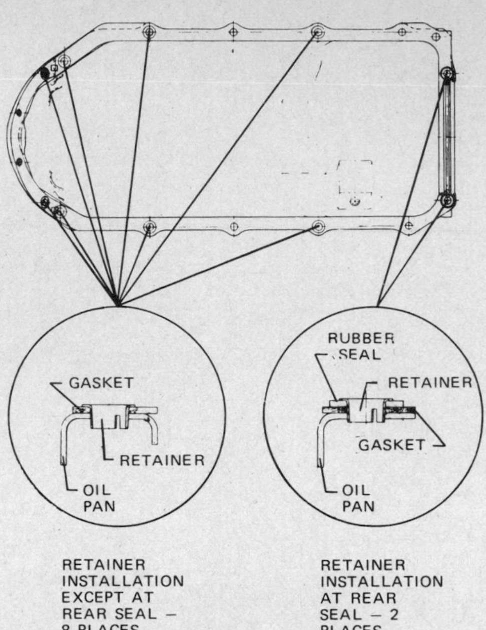

1972 and later oil pan gasket installation
(© Pontiac Div., G.M. Corp)

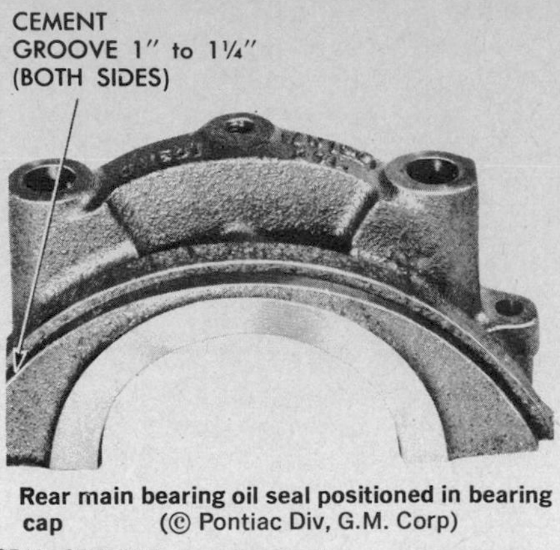

Rear main bearing oil seal positioned in bearing cap (© Pontiac Div, G.M. Corp)

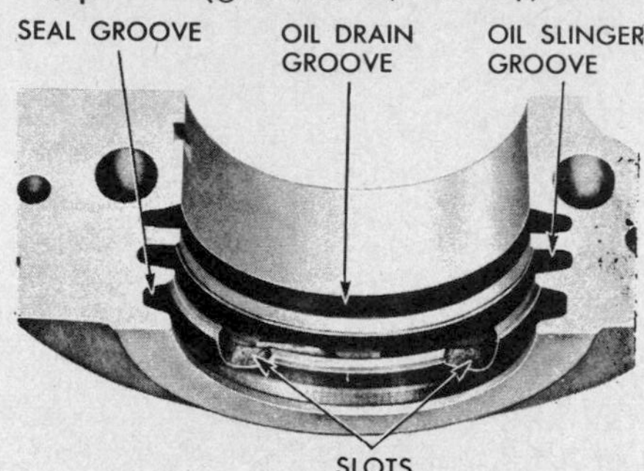

Rear main bearing cap
(© Pontiac Div., G.M. Corp)

13. Loosen rear motor mount at transmission or, better still, remove it entirely and allow extension housing to rest on crossmember.
14. Remove oil pan bolts, then raise engine straight up about 4½ in. until top of transmission is hitting floor pan. On some 1969 and later models, it also helps to move engine forward about 1½ in.
15. Rotate oil pan forward to clear oil pump, then remove oil pan.
16. Place wood blocks between engine and motor mount brackets for safety.
17. To install, reverse removal procedure. Clean all gasket surfaces thoroughly. Use gasket cement and a new gasket.

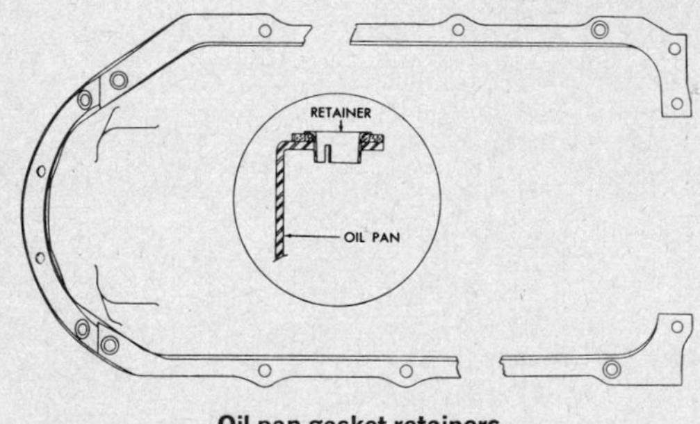

Oil pan gasket retainers
(© Pontiac Div., G.M. Corp)

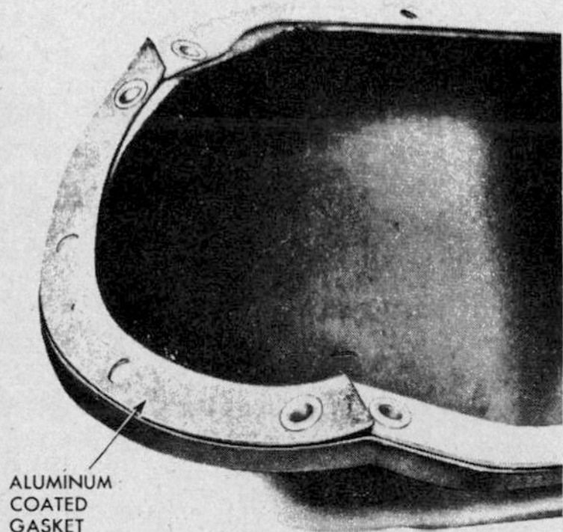

Front oil pan gasket overlapping side gaskets
(© Pontiac Div, G.M. Corp)

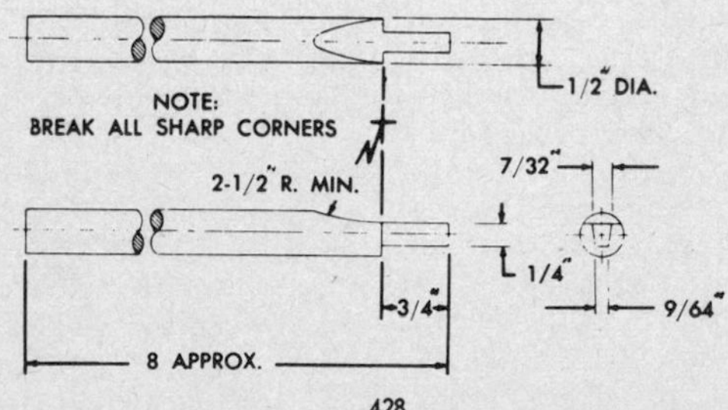

Upper rear main bearing seal tool—the lower one is for 428 and 455
(© Pontiac Div., G.M. Corp)

Rear Main Bearing Oil Seal R & R

1. Remove the oil pan, baffle, and oil pump.
2. Remove the rear main bearing cap.
3. Make a seal tool as illustrated.
4. Insert the tool against one end of the oil seal in the block and drive the seal gently into the groove ¾ in. Repeat on the other end of the seal.
5. Form a new seal in the cap. Cut four pieces ⅜ in. long from this seal.
6. Work two of the pieces into each of the gaps which have been

Forming a new crankshaft seal
(© Pontiac Div., G.M. Corp)

made at the end of the seal in the block. Do not cut off any material to make them fit.

7. Form a new seal in the bearing cap.
8. Apply a 1/16 in. bead of sealer from the center of the seal across to the external cork groove.
9. Reassemble the cap and torque to specifications.

Oil Pump R & R

1. Remove engine oil pan.
2. Remove pump attaching screws and carefully lower the pump, while removing the pump drive shaft.
3. Reinstall in reverse order.

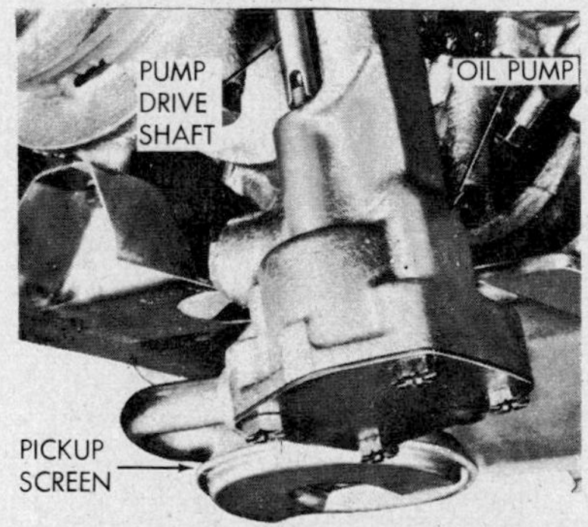

Oil pump and pump drive shaft
(© Pontiac Div, G.M. Corp)

CLUTCH

The clutch is a single plate, dry disc, diaphragm spring type. The clutch is composed of the driven plate, the pressure plate and the release mechanism. The pressure plate is spring operated which holds the driven plated (disc) against the flywheel. The springs in the pressure plate also act as release levers when the clutch is disengaged.

See the Astre, Firebird section for adjustment and R&R Procedures. No manual transmissions, are available after 1971.

MANUAL TRANSMISSION

There are four types of manual transmissions offered in full size Pontiacs. In 1969, all full size models used a three speed Saginaw unit. In 1970, there were three different types of transmissions available. They were: a three speed Dearborn unit, standard in all full size Pontiacs except the Grand Prix; a three speed Muncie standard in the Grand Prix, and a four speed Muncie available only in the Grand Prix. The four speed Muncie was available in wide and close ratios in 1970; the code letters were painted on top of the case, DJ for the wide ratio and DP for the close ratio. In 1971, the four speed used in the Grand Prix was only available with a wide ratio, code letters WT.

See the Astre, Firebird section for R&R and linkage adjustment. No manual transmissions are available after 1971.

Step-by-step repair procedures are covered in the Unit Repair Section.

AUTOMATIC TRANSMISSION

Full size Pontiacs use three types of automatic transmissions. Two three-speed Turbo Hydra-matic transmissions plus a two speed automatic are used. The M-35 (two speed), and M-38 (Turbo Hydra-Matic 350 three speed), are used with 350 cu. in. and smaller engines, while the M-40 (Turbo Hydra-Matic 400 three Speed), is used with all 400 cu. in. and larger engines. The M-35 was not offered after 1971. The M-38 can be readily identified by its downshift cable between the accelerator linkage and the transmission. The M-40 uses an electrical downshift switch at the accelerator pedal.

Throttle Valve (TV) Linkage Adjustments

Caution Satisfactory linkage operation can not prevail if binding or excessive wear exists.

1970-72 M-35 Two-Speed

1. Remove air cleaner.
2. Disconnect accelerator linkage at carburetor.
3. Disconnect return spring and T.V. rod return spring.
4. Pull upper T.V. rod forward until through detent. At same time, open throttle at carburetor to full throttle position. Full throttle must be reached at the same time the ball stud contacts end of slot in upper T.V. rod.
5. If necessary, adjust upper swivel. Tolerance is ± 1/32 in.
6. Reconnect return springs and linkage, then install air cleaner.

Selector Lever Linkage Adjustment

All Turbo-Hydramatic and M-35 Two-Speed Column

1. Loosen screw on adjusting swivel clamp.
2. Place gearshift lever in Park and lock ignition.
3. Place transmission shift lever in Park detent (rotate clockwise, see illustrations).
4. Push up on gearshift control rod until lash is taken up in steering column lock mechanism, then tighten screw on swivel clamp to 20 ft. lbs.

All Turbo-Hydramatic Console

1. Disconnect shift cable from transmission shift lever by removing nut from pin.
2. Adjust back drive linkage (as in Step 4, above).
3. Unlock ignition and rotate transmission shift lever counterclockwise two detents.
4. Place console lever in Neutral and move against forward Neutral stop.
5. Assemble shift cable and pin to transmission shift lever so that no binding exists, then tighten nut to 30 ft. lbs. (20 ft. lbs.—1970-76).

Downshift Cable Adjustment —1969-71

1. With engine off and throttle butterflies closed (off fast idle), position retainer against insert (from inside car).
2. To adjust, grasp accelerator pedal lever to wide open throttle position. Check for full cable travel.

Low Band Adjustment Two Speed (M-35)

1. Place shifter lever in neutral and raise the vehicle.
2. Remove the adjusting screw protecting cap.
3. Loosen the adjusting screw locknut 1/4 turn.

Caution Be sure to hold the adjusting screw locknut ¼ turn loose during the adjusting procedure.

4. Tighten the adjusting screw to 70 in. lbs and then back off exactly four complete turns for a band with 6,000 miles or more of use; three turns for a band with less than 6,000 miles of use.
5. Tighten the locknut, and install the protective cap.

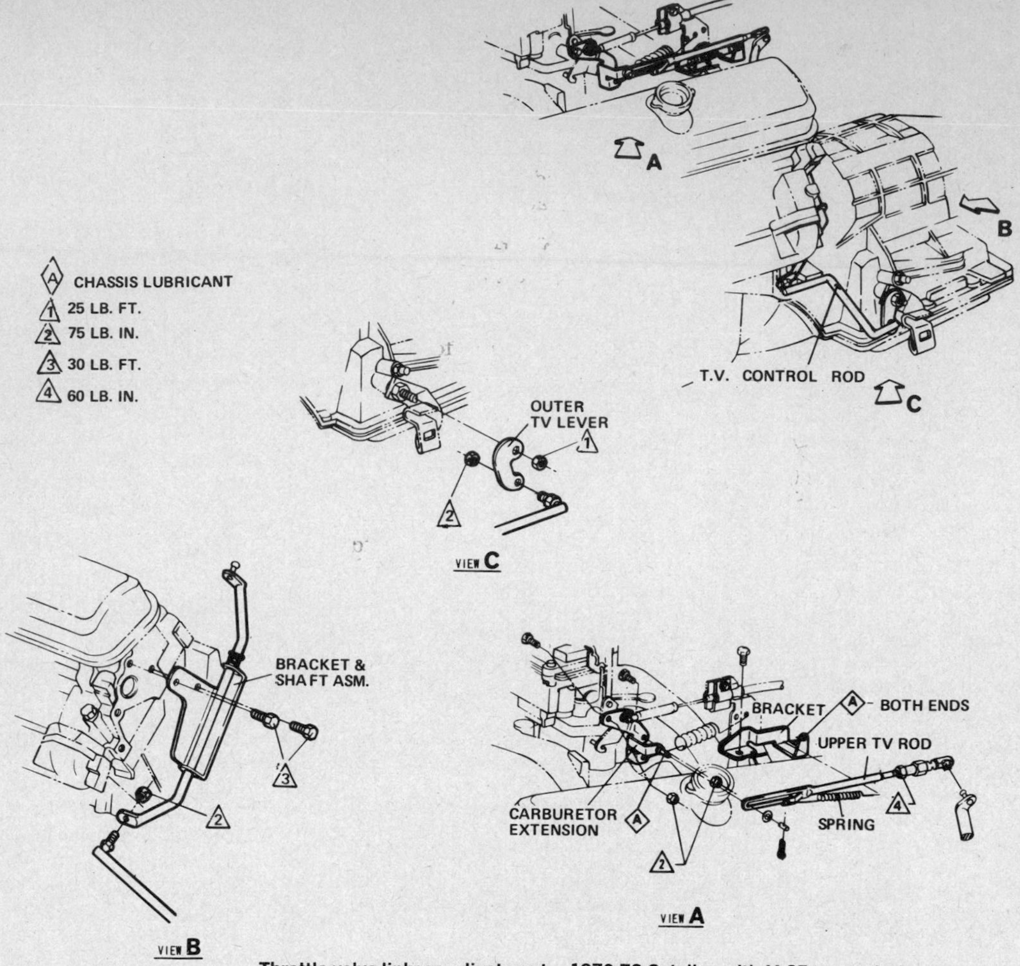

Throttle valve linkage adjustment—1970-72 Catalina with M-35 transmission
(© Pontiac Div., G.M. Corp)

Neutral Start Switch Adjustment

1969-70

Caution After the switch has been adjusted, before starting the engine to test the shifting pattern, make sure the brakes are securely locked. This is necessary because a misadjusted neutralizer switch will allow the engine to start in any of the forward or reverse gears.

1. Place the shifter lever in Park.
2. Loosen the switch retaining screws. Make sure the switch drive tang is engaged in the shifter tube slot and that it stays engaged during adjustment.
3. Rotate the switch in its slot until it is in the Park position and tighten the screws.
4. After observing the above caution, check the shifter pattern by placing the shifter lever in neutral. If the transmission does not shift into neutral, place the lever back in Park and rotate the switch slightly until the shift pattern is correct.
5. If it is possible to move the shift lever a large distance without having the transmission respond, check for a worn switch drive tang or bad electrical contacts inside the switch. In either case replace the switch.

1972 and later Floorshift, 1971 and later Column Shift

NOTE: This procedure applies to all switches with an adjusting pin hole in the back.

1. Place the shift lever in Neutral, except for 1971 models which must be placed in Drive. 1972 floorshift models must be in Park.

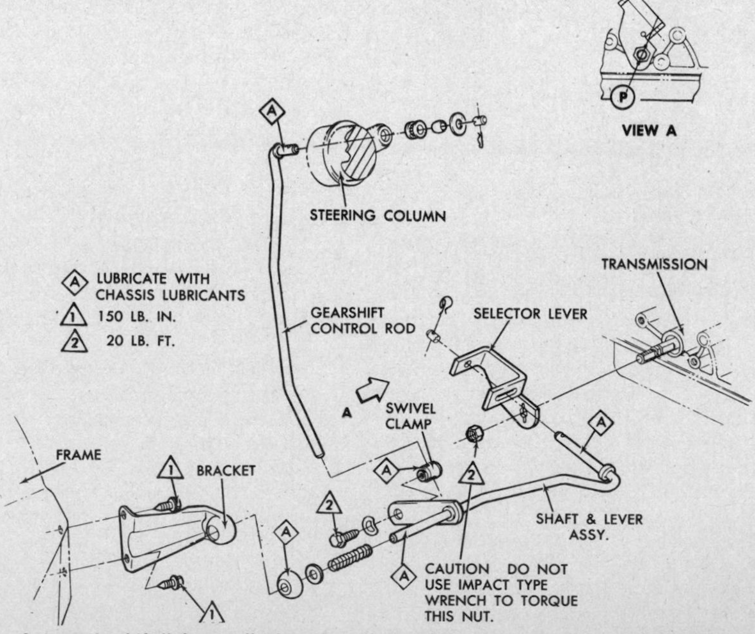

Automatic shift linkage adjustment—column shift (© Pontiac Div., G.M. Corp)

2. Loosen the switch mounting screws.
3. Move the switch until you can insert a 0.092 in. diameter adjusting pin into the hole in the back of the switch about 3/8 in.
4. Tighten the screws and remove the pin.
5. Step on the brake pedal and check that the engine will start only in Neutral or Park.

Pan R & R, Fluid and Filter Change

1. Let the engine warm up to normal operating temperature, then raise the car on a lift. On the M-35 transmission, remove the drain plug and let the fluid drain into a suitable container. On all others, remove the pan attaching bolts and let the fluid drain over the edge of the pan, being careful not to let the hot fluid spill.
2. Remove the pan on the M-35. Discard the pan gasket on all models.
3. The M-35 has a suction screen which should be cleaned and reused. Remove the two retaining bolts, the screen and gasket. Clean and replace them using a new gasket.
4. On all other models, the filter is not reused. When the pan has been removed, remove the filter retaining bolts, filter and gasket (M-38). On the M-40 transmission, the intake pipe is removed along with the transmission and the O ring gasket discarded.
5. Make sure all the old gasket material has been removed, then install the new gasket and filter.
6. Replace the pan and gasket. Add 3 pints of Dexron transmission fluid for the M-35 or 7½ for all others.
7. Start the car in Park with the parking brake on and let it idle. Shift through all the indicator positions and back to Park. The fluid level should be between the two dimples below the ADD mark. Be very cautious not to overfill. Check the level again after the transmission is throughly warm. The level should then be at FULL HOT.

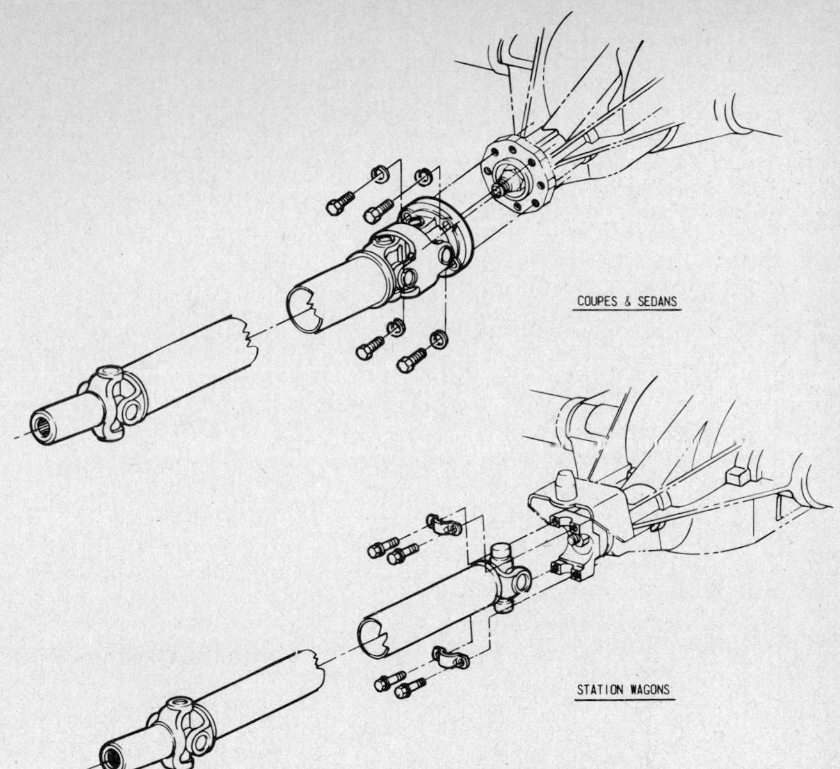

1971 and later Pontiac U-joint and driveshaft construction. Grand Prix is similar to station wagon
(© Pontiac Div., G.M. Corp)

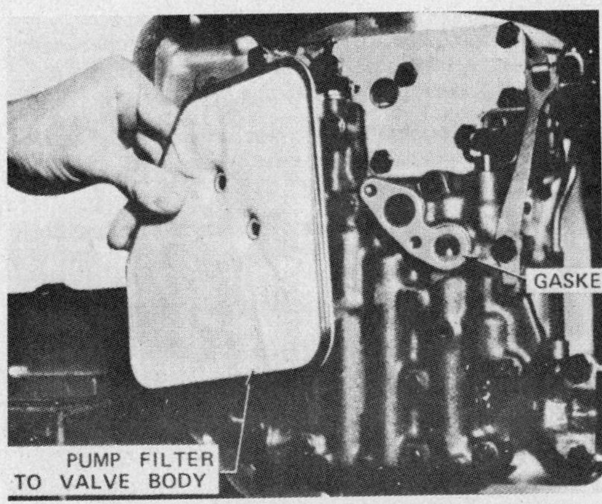

Removing the Turbo Hydra-Matic 350 transmission filter
(© Pontiac Div., G.M. Corp)

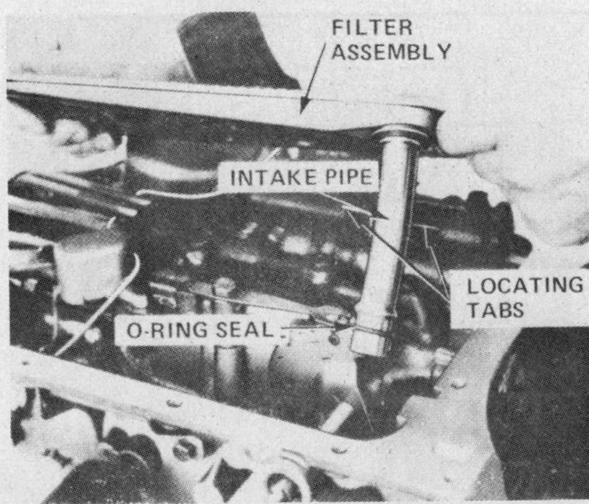

Removing the filter, intake pipe and O ring on Turbo Hydra-Matic 400 transmission
(© Pontiac Div., G.M. Corp)

U-JOINTS

Two basic designs are used; one is a typical solid shaft with two joints. Starting 1971, a new double Cardan constant velocity joint is used at the rear on all Pontiac models except the Grand Prix and station wagons.

There are two types of cross-and-bearing U-joints. One type held with a C-shaped lock ring; the other held with a lock plate.

Driveshaft R & R

1. Mark the driveshaft rear yoke

and the differential flange to assure correct alignment upon reassembly.

2. Remove the bolts and straps (or four bolts on double cardan U-joint) from the differential flange. If the bearing cups are loose, tape them together so the needle rollers don't fall out.
3. Remove the driveshaft assembly by first sliding the driveshaft forward to disengage the differential flange, then sliding the shaft downward and rearward to disengage the front splined yoke from the transmission output shaft.
4. Installation is the reversal of removal. Be sure to align the match mark made before disassembly.

U-Joint R & R All Front and Single Cardan Rear U-Joints

Removal

1. Remove the driveshaft.

NOTE: The universal may have snap-rings that are used to retain the bearing cups in the yokes. These snap-rings may be located at the outside of each yoke or in a groove at the base or open end of each bearing cap. In both cases, there are four snap-rings for each universal joint and they must be removed before proceeding further.

2. Support the splined yoke (front universal) or the journal (rear universal) in such a manner that will allow the fixed yoke on the driveshaft to be moved. Support the opposite end so that the driveshaft will be in a horizontal position.
3. Using a piece of pipe or similar tool with a large enough diameter, apply force to the fixed yoke until the bearing is almost completely pushed out of the yoke and into the pipe. Remove the bearing completely by inserting a spacer (tool # J9522-5) between the seal and the bearing cup and finish pressing the bearing out of its yoke, or by tapping around the circumference of the exposed portion of the bearing with a punch and small hammer.

NOTE: The plastic which retains factory-installed bearings will be sheared when the bearing cup is pressed out. Be sure to remove the remains of the plastic retainer from the ears of the yoke. It is easier to remove the remains if a small pin or punch is first driven through the injection holes in the yoke. Failure to remove all of the plastic remains may prevent the bearing cups from being pressed into place and the bearing retainers from being properly seated.

4. Remove the rest of the bearings following the same procedure.

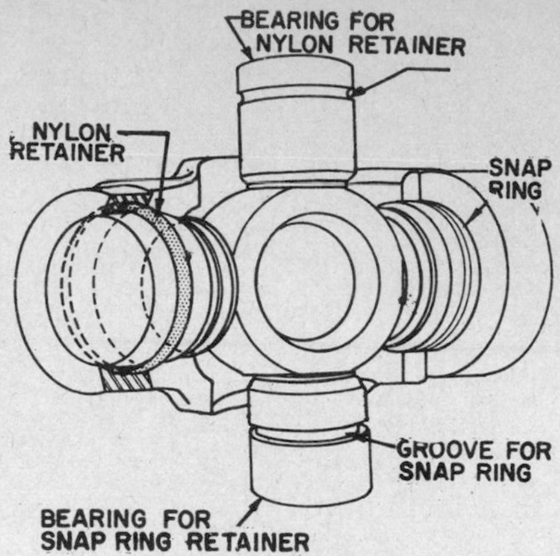

U-joint locking methods
(© Pontiac Div., G.M. Corp)

Installation

1. Install a bearing ¼ of the way into one side of the splined yoke (front universal) or fixed yoke (rear universal).
2. Insert the journal into the yoke so that an arm of the journal seats into the bearing.
3. Press the bearing in the remaining distance and snap the bearing retainer into place.
4. Install the opposite bearing. Do not allow the bearing rollers to jam. Continually check for free movement of the journal in the bearings as they are pressed into the yoke.
5. Install the rest of the bearings in the same manner.

Installing snap-ring retainer
(© Pontiac Div., G.M. Corp)

Double Cardan Constant-Velocity Rear U-Joint R & R

Removal

1. Using a punch, mark the link yoke and the adjoining yokes before disassembly to ensure proper reassembly and driveshaft balance.

NOTE: It is easier to remove the universal joint bearings from the flange yoke first. The first pair of flange yoke universal joint bearings to be removed is the pair in the link yoke.

2. With the driveshaft in a horizontal position, solidly support the link yoke (a 1 7/8 in. pipe will do).
3. Apply force to the bearing cup on the opposite side with a 1⅛ in. pipe or a socket the size of the bearing cup. Use a hammer, vise, or press to apply force. Force the cup inward as far as possible.

NOTE: In the absence of a press, a heavy vise may be used, but make sure that the universal to be removed is at a right angle to the jaws of the vise. Do not cock the bearing cups in their bores.

4. Remove the pieces of pipe and complete the removal of the protruding bearing cup by tapping around the circumference of the exposed portion of the bearing with a small hammer.
5. Reverse the position of the pieces of pipe and apply force to the exposed journal end. This will force the other bearing cup out of its bore and allow removal of the flange.

NOTE: There is a ball joint located between the two universals. The ball portion of this joint is on the inner end of the flange yoke. Prior to 1973, the ball was not replaceable. Beginning 1973, the ball, as well as the ball seat parts, is replaceable. Care must be taken not to damage the ball. The ball portion of this joint is on the driveshaft. To remove the seat, pry the seal out with a screwdriver.

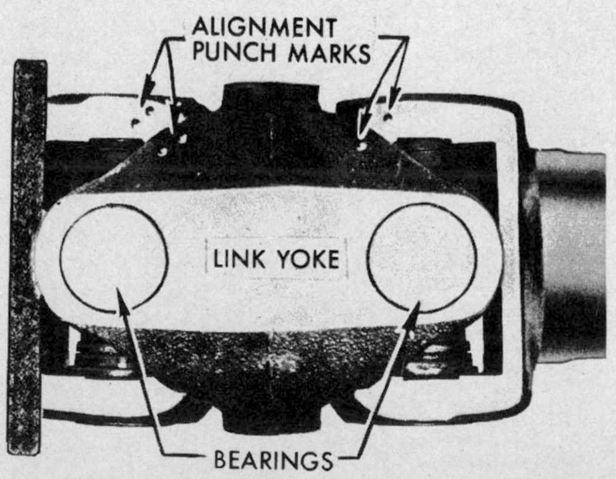

Match marks for double cardan joint
(© Pontiac Div., G.M. Corp)

THIS NOTCH IDENTIFIES
DRIVE SHAFT WITH
REPLACEABLE BALL.

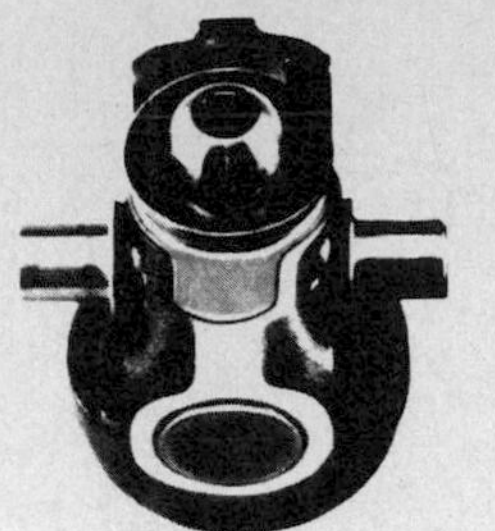

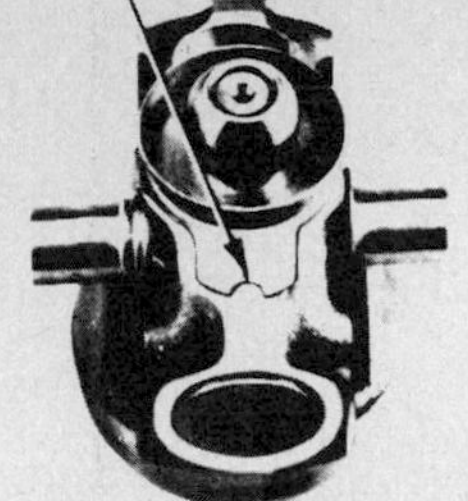

SOLID BALL REPLACEABLE BALL

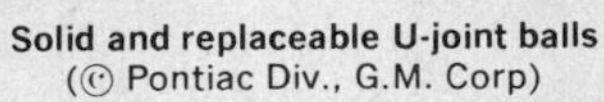

Solid and replaceable U-joint balls
(© Pontiac Div., G.M. Corp)

6. To remove the journal from the flange, use steps two through five.
7. Remove the universal joint bearings from the driveshaft using the steps from two through five. The first pair of bearing caps that should be removed is the pair in the link yoke.

Installation

1. Examine the ball stud seat and ball stud for scores or wear. Worn seats can be replaced with a kit. A worn ball, however, requires the replacement of the entire propeller shaft yoke and flange assembly. Clean the ball seat cavity and fill it with grease. Install the spring, washer, ball seats, and spacer, if removed.
2. Install the universal joints opposite the order in which they were disassembled.
3. Install a bearing ¼ of the way into one side of the yoke.
4. Insert the journal into the yoke so that an arm of the journal seats into the bearing.
5. Press the bearing in the remaining distance and install its snapring.
6. Install the opposite bearing. Do not allow the bearing rollers to jam. Continually check for free movement of the journal in the bearings as they are pressed into the yoke.
7. Install the rest of the bearings in the same manner.

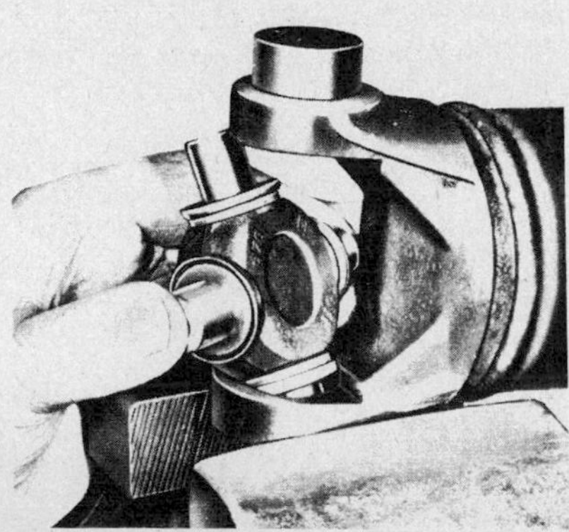

Journal installation
(© Pontiac Div., G.M. Corp)

REAR AXLE

For axle shaft, bearing and seal removal and installation procedures, refer to the Astre section.

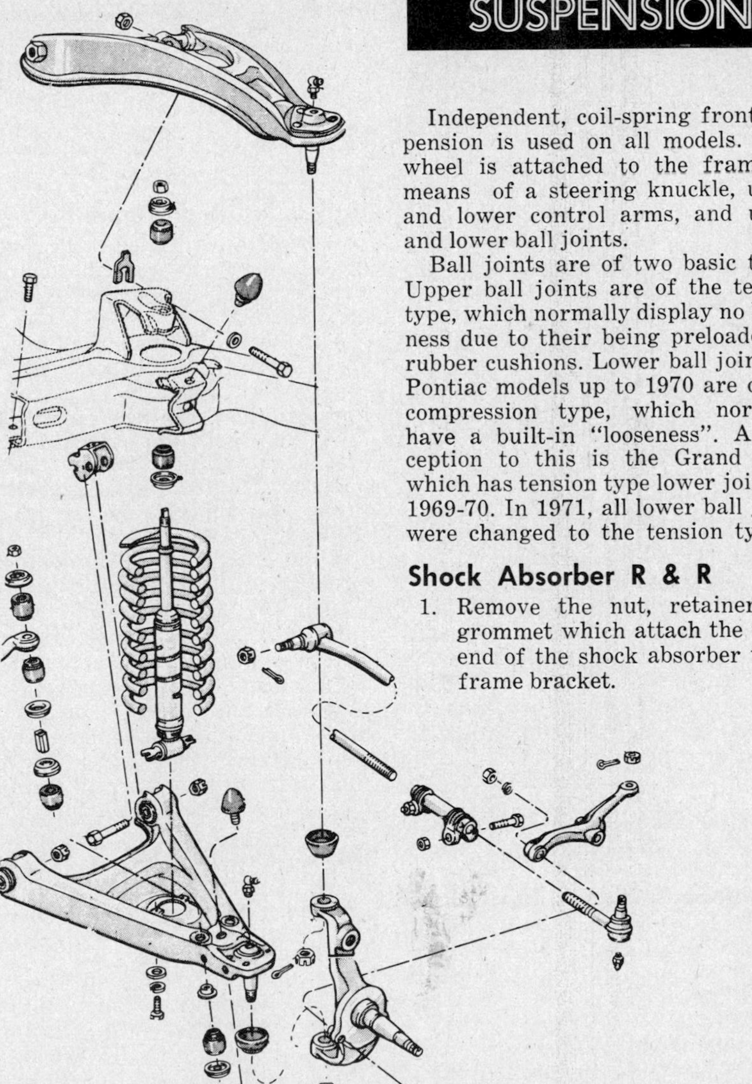

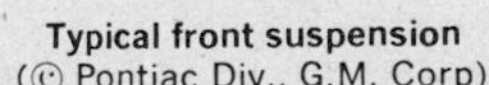

Typical front suspension
(© Pontiac Div., G.M. Corp)

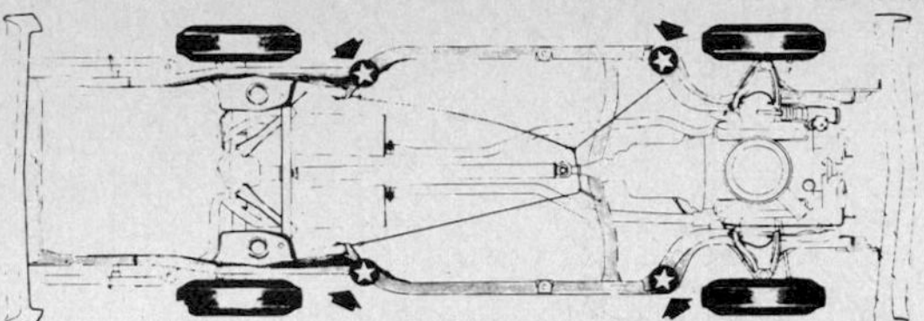

Hoist contact lifting points

JACKING, HOISTING

Jack car at front spring seats of lower control arms and, at rear, at axle housing.

When using frame lift, use side rails at points shown on diagram. Be sure that adapters are properly supporting these designated areas.

FRONT SUSPENSION

Independent, coil-spring front suspension is used on all models. Each wheel is attached to the frame by means of a steering knuckle, upper and lower control arms, and upper and lower ball joints.

Ball joints are of two basic types. Upper ball joints are of the tension type, which normally display no looseness due to their being preloaded by rubber cushions. Lower ball joints on Pontiac models up to 1970 are of the compression type, which normally have a built-in "looseness". An exception to this is the Grand Prix, which has tension type lower joints in 1969-70. In 1971, all lower ball joints were changed to the tension type.

Shock Absorber R & R

1. Remove the nut, retainer and grommet which attach the upper end of the shock absorber to the frame bracket.

NOTE: The shock absorber stud may turn while loosening the nut. If necessary, use pliers or a wrench to hold the top of the stud while removing the nut, do not grasp the shaft as any marks on the shaft will cause rapid failure of the shock.

2. Raise the car to allow removal of the shock down through the lower control arm.
3. Remove the two shock absorber lower attaching screws and remove the shock through the lower control arm.
4. Reverse the above steps to install. Make sure all grommets and washers are in the correct position. Tighten the stud nut until it bottoms at the end of the threads.

Ball Joint Inspection

1969-72

NOTE: Before performing this inspection, make sure the wheel bearings are adjusted correctly and that the A-arm bushings are in good condition.

1. Jack the car up under the front lower control arm at the spring seat.
2. Raise the car until there is 1-2 in. of clearance under the wheel.
3. Insert a bar under the wheel and pry upward. If the wheel raises more than 1/8 in. the ball joints are worn. Determine if the upper or lower ball joint is worn by visual inspection while prying on the wheel.

NOTE: Due to the distribution of forces in the suspension, the lower ball joint is usually the defective joint.

1973 and later

Beginning 1973, lower ball joints contain a visual wear indicator. The lower ball joint grease plug screws into the wear indicator which protrudes from the bottom of the ball joint housing. As long as the wear indicator extends out of the ball joint housing, the ball joint is not worn. If the tip of the wear indicator is parallel with, or recessed into the ball joint housing, the ball joint is defective.

Alternate Ball Joint Inspection Method

Upper—Tension Type

1. Disengage the ball stud from the steering knuckle, weight of car being supported by a jack under the spring seat on the side being checked.
2. Install stud nut onto stud and check torque required to rotate ball stud.
3. If torque is less than 1/2 ft. lb., the joint must be replaced.

Lower—Compression Type

1. Place a jack under lower control arm spring seat and jack up car.
2. Pry wheel and tire up and down (or remove wheel and hub to eliminate wheel bearing play) and measure play in joint using a dial indicator or a standard inspection station ball joint checking device.
3. If play exceeds 0.050 in., the ball joint must be replaced.

Lower—Tension Type

1. Place a jack under the lower control arm spring seat and jack up car.
2. Remove grease fitting from lower ball joint.
3. Remove hub and backing plate, or caliper, assembly.
4. Separate lower ball stud from steering knuckle using a pry bar and hammer.

NOTE: make sure seal is not damaged.

5. Place probe of dial indicator into grease fitting hole until it touches base of ball joint.
6. Preload and zero indicator, then pull up and down on threaded portion of stud and measure play.
7. If play exceeds 0.050 in., the ball joint must be replaced.

Ball Joint Replacement

Ball joints are riveted to the control arms at the factory except on Grand Prix beginning 1969 and all 1971 and later models.

The service joint comes with specially hardened bolts and nuts that replace the rivets. It is extremely important that only these special fasteners are installed—standard bolts are not strong enough for this application. Tighten service bolts to 9 ft. lbs. for upper joints, 16 ft. lbs. for lower joints.

All 1971 and later and 1969 and later Grand Prix models have their lower ball joints pressed into the control arms. The entire control arm can be removed and the joint pressed out using various spacers and a large bench vise, or the old joint can be pressed from the arm while in the car using a screw-type remover. The new joint must be pressed into place, in any case, to avoid damage.

Upper Ball Joint R & R

Removal

1. Raise the car and support the lower control arm.
2. Remove the ball joint stud nut and cotter pin. Using a ball joint removing tool, break the taper holding the steering knuckle to the ball joint stud and move the steering knuckle out of the way.
3. Remove the rivets securing the ball joint to the control arm by chiseling or drilling the rivet heads and drive out the rivets with a punch.
4. Remove the ball joint from the control arm.

Installation

1. Install the new ball joint assembly using the special bolts supplied with the ball joint. Torque to 9 ft lbs.
2. Insert the ball stud in the steering knuckle and tighten the nut to 40 ft lbs. (50 ft lbs., 1975-76) Insert a new cotter pin.
3. Install the wheel and tire.
4. Lower the car.

NOTE: It may be necessary to adjust the wheel alignment after installing a new ball joint.

Lower Ball Joint R & R All 1969-70 Except Grand Prix

Removal

NOTE: Jack the car securely under the lower control arm.

1. Remove the hub and backing plate assembly or, if equipped with disc brakes, hub and brake caliper.
2. Remove the ball joint stud from the steering knuckle using a ball joint removal tool.
3. Remove the ball joint assembly from the lower control arm by chiseling or drilling the rivet heads and drive out the rivets with a punch.

Installation

1. Installation is the same as the upper ball joint installation procedures.

Models 1971 and Later, All Grand Prix

Removal

1. Raise the car under the lower control arm.
2. Remove the hub and backing plate or, if equipped with disc brakes, the rotor and caliper assembly, remove the stud nut and cotter pin.
3. Remove the ball joint stud from the steering knuckle using a ball joint removal tool.
4. Pry the ball joint seal and retainer off the joint.
5. Press the ball joint out of the lower control arm. This is a very heavy press fit.

Installation

1. Press, do not hammer, a new ball joint into place and reverse steps 1 to 4 to install.

Front Spring R & R

1. Jack up car and support on jack stands at frame side rails.
2. Remove shock absorber.
3. Disconnect stabilizer bar at lower control arm.
4. Support lower control arm with a hydraulic floor jack, then

remove the two inner control arm to front crossmember bolts.
5. Carefully lower the control arm, allowing the spring to relax.
6. Reach in and remove spring.
7. To install, reverse removal procedure. Tighten pivot bolts to 110 ft. lbs., nuts to 80 ft. lbs. (1972-74—bolts to 120 ft lbs; nuts to 90 ft lbs) (1975-76, bolts to 105 ft lbs; nuts to 95 ft lbs.) with car resting on wheels.

Wheel Bearing Inspection and Adjustment

Inspection

1. Raise the car and support it under the front lower control arm.
2. Spin the wheel to check for unusual noise. Bad wheel bearings sometimes squeal or sound as though there is sand in the bearing.
3. If the bearings are noisy or loose, they should be cleaned, inspected, and repacked before adjustment.
4. To check for loose bearings, grip the tire at top and bottom and move the wheel in and out. Movement less than 0.001 in. or greater than 0.005 in. indicates improper adjustment or excessive wear.

Adjustment

1. Lift the wheel off the ground by jacking under the lower control arm.
2. Remove the dust cap from the hub.
3. Remove the cotter pin and discard.
4. Snug up the spindle nut to seat the bearings (12 ft. lbs.). Then back off the nut 1/4-1/2 turn.
5. Retighten the nut by hand until it is finger-tight.
6. Loosen the nut until the nearest hole in the spindle lines up with a slot in the spindle nut, and insert a new cotter pin. When the bearing is properly adjusted there will be 0.001-0.005 in. endplay.

NOTE: Under no circumstances is the final bearing nut adjustment to be even finger-tight.

7. Replace the dust cover and lower the car.

REAR SUSPENSION

The rear wheels are fastened to the axle shafts within a solid axle housing. The axle housing is connected to the frame by a four-link suspension system, consisting of two upper and two lower control arms pivoted in rubber at each end. These control arms locate the axle with relation to the frame and oppose torque reaction under acceleration and braking.

Two coil springs are mounted between seats in the frame and on the axle housing. Shock absorbers are direct double-action hydraulic units and are mounted between the axle housing and the frame.

Rubber bumpers are mounted near the outer ends of the axle housing and at the center of the frame cross member to prevent metal-to-metal contact during bottoming of the suspension.

Shock Absorber R & R

1. Raise the car at the axle housing. Remove the wheel on station wagons.
2. Remove the nut, retainer, and grommet, or nut, and lock washer, as equipped, which attach the lower end of the shock absorber to its mounting.
3. Remove the two shock absorber upper attaching screws and remove the shock absorber.
4. Reverse the removal procedures to install.

Rear Leaf Spring Replacement 1971 and later Station Wagon

1. Jack up car at axle housing. Make sure you don't crush exhaust pipe.
2. Support car at both frame side rails, using axle stands.
3. Remove nut and lockwasher from lower shock stud.
4. Move shock out of the way.
5. Remove spring anchor plate nuts, then remove anchor plate and cushion.
6. Jack axle housing up and remove upper cushion.
7. Loosen upper and lower spring shackle nuts.
8. Loosen front spring eye bolt.

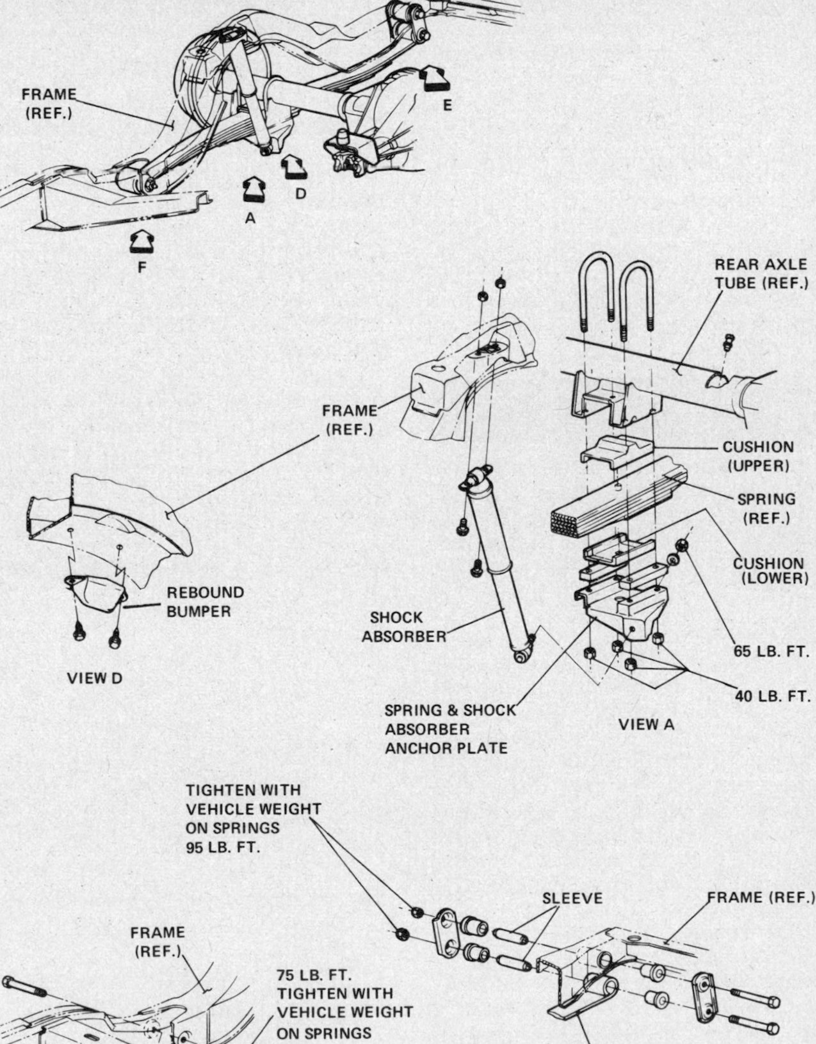

1971-76 Pontiac station wagon leaf spring rear suspension (© Pontiac Div., G.M. Corp)

9. Remove front eye bolt and carefully lower spring.
10. Support spring and remove lower shackle pin.
11. Remove spring.
12. To install, reverse removal procedure. Tighten front eye bolt to 75 ft. lbs., shackle nuts to 95 ft. lbs., anchor plate nuts to 40 ft. lbs., and lower shock nut to 65 ft. lbs.

Rear Coil Spring Replacement

1. Raise the rear of the car. Place jackstands under the frame side rails.
2. Remove the clip attaching the brake hose to the rear crossmember on Pontiacs. On 1972 and later Grand Prix, remove the clip and disconnect the brake hose.
3. Support the rear axle housing with a floor jack. On 1973 and later Grand Prix, make sure to support the nose of the axle housing.
4. Disconnect the bottom of the shock absorbers.
5. On 1973 and later Grand Prix, disconnect the upper control arms at the axle.
6. Carefully lower the rear axle until the springs are fully extended.
7. Remove the springs.
8. On installation, make sure that the end of the bottom spring coil is to the rear of the car. The brake system will have to be bled of air on 1973 and later Grand Prix.

BRAKES

Information on brake adjustment, lining replacement, bleeding procedure, master and wheel cylinder overhaul can be found in the Unit Repair Section.

Disc Brakes

Single-piston, sliding caliper disc brakes have been available as optional equipment on most models (standard with high performance packages). These brakes have a vented, cast-iron rotor with two braking surfaces. Beginning 1971, power disc brakes are standard on all Grand Prix and full-size Pontiac models. Drum brakes are no longer available on the frontwheels.

Disc brakes need no adjustment because, during operation, the application and release of hydraulic pressure causes the piston and caliper to move only slightly. In the released position, the pads do not move very far from the rotor; thus, as pads wear down, the piston simply moves farther out of the caliper bore and the caliper repositions itself on its mounting bolts to maintain proper pad-to-rotor clearance.

A metering valve in the front brake circuit prevents the discs from operating until about 75 psi exists in the system. This enables the rear drum brakes to operate in synchronization with the front discs and reduces the possibility of unequal brake application and premature lock-up. A proportioning valve in the rear brake circuit of some models accomplishes the same. Starting 1971, all functions of the two separate valves are performed by either a two- or three-element combination valve. The two-function valve is used on all wagons and sedans except Grand Prix, which uses a three-function valve. Disc brake pads should be examined for wear every 12,000 miles. 1974 and later Pontiacs employ a disc brake pad wear indicator. As the lining material wears down, a steel sensor approaches the rotor. When enough lining material has worn away, the sensor makes contact with the rotor causing noise which is audible to the driver. See the Unit Repair Section of this manual for service procedures.

Master Cylinder Removal

The master cylinder is located in the engine compartment just above the steering column.

From under the dash, disconnect the brake pedal from the master cylinder on Bendix power brakes and non-power brakes. Delco power booster pushrods are not connected to the master cylinder. From under the hood, disconnect the hydraulic lines and the stoplight wire.

Remove the bolts which hold the master cylinder to the cowl panel and lift off the master cylinder.

The unit is installed in reverse order of removal. Bleed the brakes after installation.

Power Brake Booster R & R

1. Remove the vacuum hose from the front housing. Remove the master cylinder and position it away from the booster. It is not necessary to disconnect the lines from the master cylinder if it is not to be repaired.
2. Remove the clevis pin retainer from the brake pedal inside the car.
3. Remove the nuts from the vacuum cylinder studs under the dash and remove the vacuum power section.
4. Reverse the removal procedure to install the booster.

Parking Brake Adjustment

1. Jack up both rear wheels.
2. Apply parking brake, 5-7 notches through 1970, 4-8 notches for 1971-72, 8 notches for 1973-74 models, from full release. 1975 and later models should be adjusted 3 notches from full release, except the station wagons which should be 6 notches.
3. Loosen equalizer rear locknut. Adjust forward nut until a light to moderate drag is felt when rear wheels are rotated.
4. Tighten the locknut.
5. Fully release the parking brake and rotate rear wheels; no drag should be felt.

STEERING

The manual steering gear is the recirculating ball nut type. The steering shaft, worm shaft, and worm nut are all in line. The steering shaft and worm shaft are separated by a flexible coupling. This coupling permits

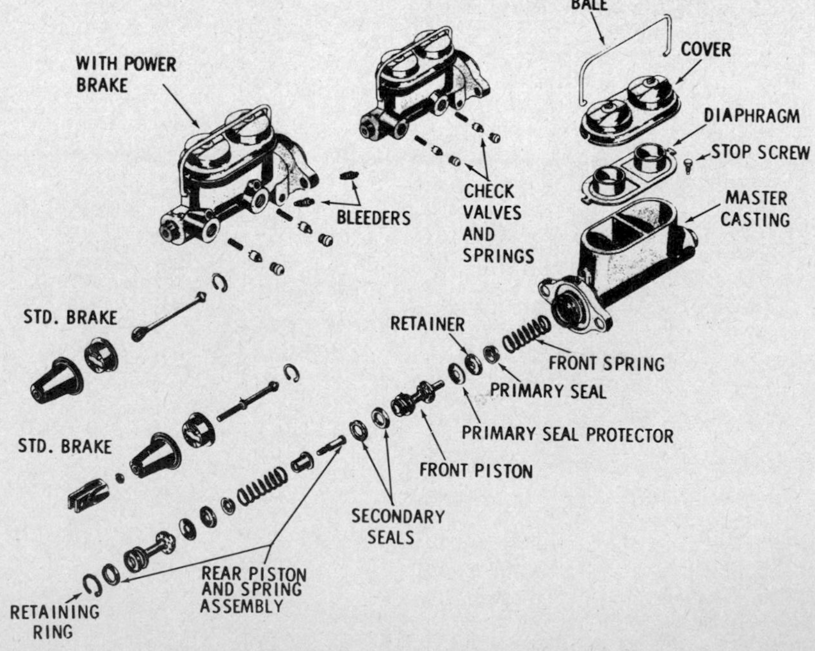

Dual type master cylinder (Delco) (© Pontiac Div., G.M. Corp)

the gear to be removed independently of the steering shaft and steering column.

All Pontiacs use a variable-ratio power steering gear. The gear is the recirculating ball type incorporating a wormshaft and a rack-piston. A rotary valve is contained in the gear housing, eliminating the need for separately mounted valve and cylinder assemblies.

Hydraulic pressure for the power steering is provided by a constant-displacement vane type pump. It is located on the front of the engine and is belt-driven off the engine crankshaft pulley.

See the "Unit Repair Section" for rebuilding procedures.

Tie-Rod End R & R

1. Loosen the tie-rod adjuster sleeve clamp nuts.
2. Remove the tie-rod stud nut cotter pin and nut.
3. Remove the tie-rod stud from the steering arm or intermediate rod. This is a taper fit. Removal is accomplished by using a ball joint removal tool or by hitting the arm or rod sharply with a hammer while prying on the tie rod. If the ball joint is to be reused the removal tool must be used.
4. Unthread the tie rod from the adjuster sleeve. Outer tie rods have right-hand threads and inner tie rods have left-hand threads. Count the number of turns the tie rod must be rotated to remove it from the adjusting sleeve. This will allow a reasonably accurate realignment upon reassembly.
5. Reverse the removal procedures to install. Clean rust and dirt from the threads. Check the alignment and adjust if necessary.

Power Steering Pump R & R

1. Disconnect the hoses at the pump. Plug the lines and the pump to prevent loss of fluid.
2. Remove the drive pulley attaching nut.
3. Loosen the bracket-to-pump mounting bolts and remove the drive belt.
4. Slide the pulley from the shaft. Do not hammer on the pulley.
5. Remove the bracket-to-pump mounting bolts and remove the pump.
6. Reverse the removal steps to install.

Steering Wheel R & R

1. On deluxe models, remove the screws holding the trim cover to the wheel or, if equipped with a horn button, lift the button off.
2. Remove the steering wheel nut from the steering shaft.
3. Position the wheels in the straight-ahead position and make match marks on the steering shaft and steering wheel.
4. Using a puller, remove the steering wheel.

Caution Don't pound on the steering wheel or the steering shaft. The collapsible column could be damaged enough to require replacement.

5. Disconnect the horn wire insulator by rotating the insulator counterclockwise to unlock position and then pull up.
6. Reverse the removal procedures to install. Make sure the match marks are lined up when installing the wheel.

Turn Signal Switch R & R

1. Remove the steering wheel.
2. Loosen the three cover screws and lift cover off the shaft. Do not remove the screws completely.
3. Depress the lockplate downward and remove the snap-ring.
4. Slide the upper bearing spring and turn signal cam off the shaft. Remove the thrust washer.
5. Remove the turn signal lever screw and lever.
6. Push the hazard warning switch in and remove the knob.
7. Lower the steering column and disconnect the switch wiring.

Caution The steering column must be supported at all times to prevent damage.

8. Remove the turn signal switch mounting screws and pull the switch straight up with the wire protector and remove it from the housing.
9. Reverse the removal procedures to install.

INSTRUMENT PANEL

Ignition Switch Replacement

1. Disconnect battery.
2. Loosen toe pan screws on steering column.
3. Remove column to instrument panel trim plates and attaching nuts.
4. Lower column and disconnect switch wire connectors.

Caution The steering column must be supported at all times to prevent damage.

5. Remove switch attaching screws and remove switch.
6. To replace move key lock to LOCK position.
7. Move actuator rod hole in switch to LOCK position.
8. Install switch with rod in hole.
9. Position and reassemble steering column in reverse of disassembly procedure.

Switch Adjustment—Standard Column

1. Place switch in OFF position.
2. Position switch on column, then move slider to extreme left (toward wheel).
3. Move slider back two positions to the right of ACCESSORY positon.
4. Place key in any run position and shift transmission into any position but Park for automatics. Put it in Reverse for manual.
5. Position lock toward ACCESSORY with a light finger pressure and secure switch.

Switch Adjustment—Tilt Column

1. Place key in ACCESSORY positon; leave key in lock.

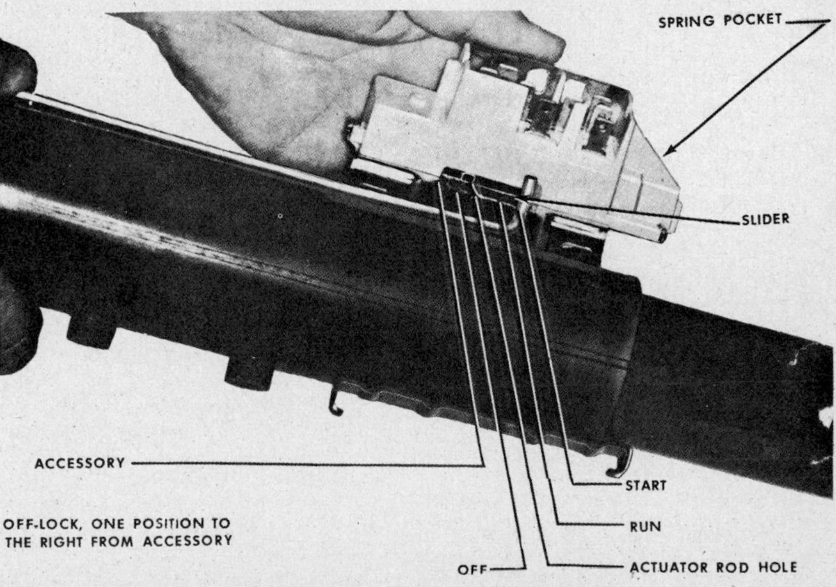

Installing ignition switch (© Pontiac Div., G.M. Corp)

2. Loosen switch mounting screws.
3. Push switch upward toward wheel to make certain it is in ACCESSORY detent.
4. Hold key in full counter clockwise ACCESSORY position and tighten switch mounting screws.
5. Switch is properly adjusted if: it will go into ACCESSORY position, the key can be removed when in lock, and switch will go into START position.

Lock Cylinder Replacement

1. Remove steering wheel.
2. Pull turn signal switch up far enough to allow access to spring latch slot.
3. Place key in RUN position, insert a thin screwdriver into the slot next to the switch mounting screw boss and depress spring latch.

NOTE: There is a casting flash over this slot if the lock has not been removed before. It is sometimes necessary to use substantial force to remove it. Be careful not to damage anything beneath the flash when penetrating the slot.

4. Remove lock from housing.
5. To install, first hold lock cylinder sleeve and rotate knob clockwise against stop.

Caution If lock cylinder is forced beyond its normal latched position, complete disassembly of upper bearing assembly will be necessary to free it.

6. Lay a 1 1/16 in. drill on housing surface next to housing bore.
7. Insert cylinder into housing bore, aligning keyway, and push in to abutment.
8. Rotate knob counterclockwise, pushing in slightly, until cylinder mates with sector.
9. Push in until spring latch pops into groove, then remove drill.

Headlight Switch Replacement

1. Disconnect the battery. Pull the knob all the way out. From under dash depress button on switch and remove knob and shaft.
2. Remove retaining nut.
3. Remove wire connector from switch and remove switch.
4. Reverse procedure to install.

WINDSHIELD WIPERS

Motor R & R

1. Disconnect electrical and hose connections at wiper.
2. Disconnect wiper crank from wiper transmission linkage, through cowl opening.
3. Remove wiper motor mounting screws, then remove the motor from the firewall.
4. Install by reversing removal procedure. Motor must be in park position.

Linkage R & R

1. Remove arm and blade assemblies.
2. Remove the air intake grille.
3. Remove wiper linkage retaining screws.
4. Loosen retainer holding linkage which connects with wiper motor crank.
5. Remove wiper linkage.
6. Install by reversing removal procedure. Be sure wiper blades are in park position after they are installed.

RADIO

Removal & Installation

1969-70

1. Disconnect battery.
2. Remove lower air conditioning duct if equipped.
3. Remove two radio control knobs and hex nuts.
4. Remove ash tray and bracket.
5. Remove upper air conditioning duct, if so equipped.
6. Disconnect all radio connections.
7. Remove screws holding radio brace to lower edge of instrument panel and remove radio.
8. Reverse procedure to install.

1971-76 Pontiac

1. Disconnect battery, then remove radio knobs and hex nuts.
2. Remove upper and lower instrument panel trim plates and lower front radio bracket.
3. Remove glove box and disconnect radio connections.
4. Loosen side brace screw and slide radio toward front seat.
5. To install, reverse removal procedure.

1971-72 Grand Prix

1. Disconnect battery and remove lower A/C duct.
2. Remove control knobs and hex nuts, then remove support bracket bolt.
3. Disconnect electrical leads and remove radio.
4. To install, reverse removal procedure.

1973-76 Grand Prix

1. Disconnect the battery.
2. Remove the knobs, bezels, and right-hand hex nut from the radio.
3. Remove the four retaining screws and the radio trim plate.
4. Remove the two side (one front beginning 1974) retaining screws and the radio mounting bracket retaining screw (below radio).
5. Remove radio and bracket as an assembly; disconnect radio connections and antenna lead-in while radio is pulled out.
6. Reverse the above steps to install.

HEATER

Cars w/o A/C

1969 Pontiac

Blower Motor R & R

1. Remove fender skirt.
2. Disconnect power lead.
3. Remove retaining screws.
4. Remove motor.
5. To install, reverse removal procedure.

Heater Core R & R

Same as 1970-76 Pontiac.

1970-76 Pontiac

Blower Motor and Impeller

1. Jack up front of car and remove right front wheel.
2. Cut access hole along stamped outline on right fender skirt, using an air chisel.
3. Disconnect blower power wire.
4. Remove blower.
5. To install, reverse removal procedure, covering access hole with a metal plate secured with sealer and sheet metal screws.

Heater Core R & R

1. Drain radiator.
2. Disconnect heater hoses at air inlet assembly.

NOTE: the water pump hose goes to right-hand heater core pipe, the other hose (from rear of right cylinder head) goes to the left-hand heater core pipe.

3. Remove nuts from core studs on firewall (under hood). Remove the glove compartment.
4. From inside the car, remove the defroster nozzle retaining screw from the heater case and pull the heater assembly from the firewall.
5. Disconnect control cables, vacuum hoses and wires, then remove heater assembly.
6. Remove the core.
7. To install, reverse removal procedure, making sure core is properly sealed during installation.

Grand Prix

Blower Motor R & R

1. Disconnect power wire.
2. Remove motor retaining screws.
3. Remove motor.
4. To install, reverse removal procedure.

Heater Core R & R

Same as 1970-76 Pontiac.

Cars With A/C

1969 Pontiac and Grand Prix

Blower

1. Remove the hoses from the inner fender panel.
2. Remove the rocker molding.
3. Loosen the lower rear fender retaining screws to allow the bottom of the fender to move.
4. Remove the inner panel.
5. Remove the blower motor or inlet duct retaining screws.
6. Remove the motor feed wire and cooling tube.
7. Remove the motor and impeller.
8. Reverse the above steps to install.

Heater Core and Case Assembly

1. Drain the coolant.
2. Remove the heater case-to-cowl attaching nuts. It may be necessary to drill a 1 in. hole in the fender skirt to gain access to the lower nut.
3. Remove the two water hoses attached to the heater core.
4. Remove the lower duct and outlet assembly.
5. Remove the glove box.
6. Remove the defroster duct attaching screw.
7. Remove the screws retaining case to the dash.
8. Remove the core and case assembly.
9. Disconnect the cables and wires.
10. Match-mark the heater cam and bracket and remove as an assembly.
11. Remove the case half screws and separate the case halves.
12. Remove the core screws and remove the core.
13. Reverse the above steps to install.

1970-76

Blower—Grand Prix

1. Working under the hood, disconnect the blower motor feed wire.
2. Remove the blower motor or duct retaining screws as required.
3. Remove the motor or duct.
4. Reverse the above steps to install.

Blower—1973 Grand Prix w/o V.I.R.

On some 1973 Grand Prix models without the V.I.R. (Valves In Receiver) system, removal and replacement of the blower motor may be hindered by the position of the POA (evaporator pressure regulator valve) valve-to-compressor tube. If this tube is positioned so that the blower motor cannot be removed:

1. Disconnect the blower motor feed wire and cooling tube.
2. Remove the six blower retaining screws.
3. Loosen the fitting on the POA valve-to-compressor tube at the POA valve just enough to allow the tube to be turned (approx. ¼ to ½ turn).

Caution This procedure should be done only by a trained air-conditioning specialist. Escaping refrigerant (Freon) could cause severe injury, even blindness.

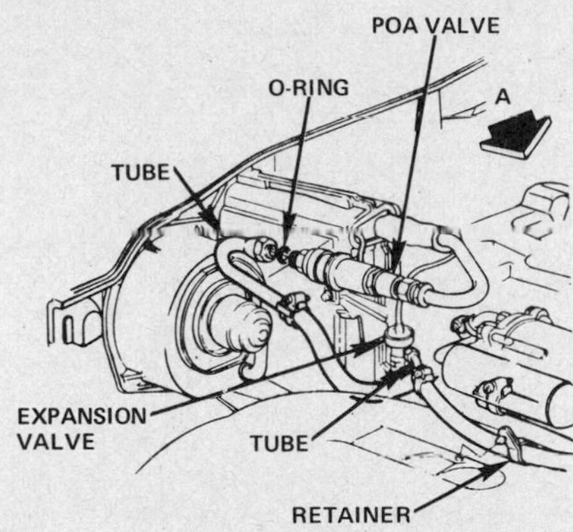

POA valve location
(© Pontiac Div., G.M. Corp)

4. Reposition the lower portion of the tube to allow clearance when removing the blower motor. Retighten the fiting to 20-33 ft lb.
5. Remove the blower motor and impeller.
6. To install, reverse the removal procedure.

Blower—Pontiac

1. Remove the right-hand front wheel.
2. Cut an access hole ¾ of the way along the outline stamped in the right inner fender panel.
3. Disconnect the blower feed wire.
4. Remove the blower motor.
5. Plug the hole in the inner fender panel and reverse the above steps to install.

Heater Core—Grand Prix

1. Drain the radiator.
2. Disconnect the heater hoses.
3. Remove the retaining nuts from the core case studs on the engine side of the dash.
4. Remove the glove box.
5. Remove the defroster duct retaining screw from the heater case and pull the heater assembly from the firewall.
6. Disconnect the heater control cables and wires.
7. Remove the core tube seal and core assembly retaining strips and remove the core.
8. Reverse the above steps to install.

Heater Core—Pontiac

1. Drain the coolant.
2. Disconnect the hoses from the heater core. Plug the tubes to prevent damage to the carpeting on removal.
3. Remove the three nuts and one screw holding the core and case assembly in place.
4. Remove the glove box and upper and lower instrument panel trim plates.
5. Remove the radio.
6. Remove the cold air duct.
7. Remove the heater outlet duct.
8. Remove the screw holding the defroster duct to the heater case.
9. Disconnect the temperature control cable at the heater case.
10. Disconnect the vacuum hoses. Remove the core and case assembly.
11. Remove three screws to take the core out of the case.
12. Reverse the procedure on installation.

SEAT BELTS

Buzzer System—1973

The front seat belt warning system consists of a switch in each belt retractor, a sensor switch in the seat cushion on the passenger side, a reminder light and a warning buzzer. The circuit wiring is routed through the ignition switch and parking brake warning switch on manual transmission models or through the ignition switch and transmission switch on models equipped with automatic transmissions.

With the ignition switch on and the parking brake released with manual transmissions or with the shift selector in a forward position on automatic transmission models, the warning circuit (light and buzzer) is closed (activated) until the driver's seat belt is extended to open (de-activate) the circuit. The seat sensor on the passenger side will react to weights in excess of 47 lbs. on the seat cushion and close the warning circuit. Extending the passenger belt will open the circuit.

Seat Belt/Starter Interlock System--Beginning 1974

All Pontiacs are equipped with the sequential interlock seat belt system. The sequential interlock system requires the driver and right front seat occupant to first sit in their seats, then fasten their seat belts before the engine can be started. The middle seat position on cars equipped with a front bench seat is not included in the interlock system. The seat sensors are similar to those found in the 1973 buzzer systems.

Engine restarting is possible without interference from the interlock system if the driver has not left his seat. In the event of system malfunction, an emergency by-pass switch

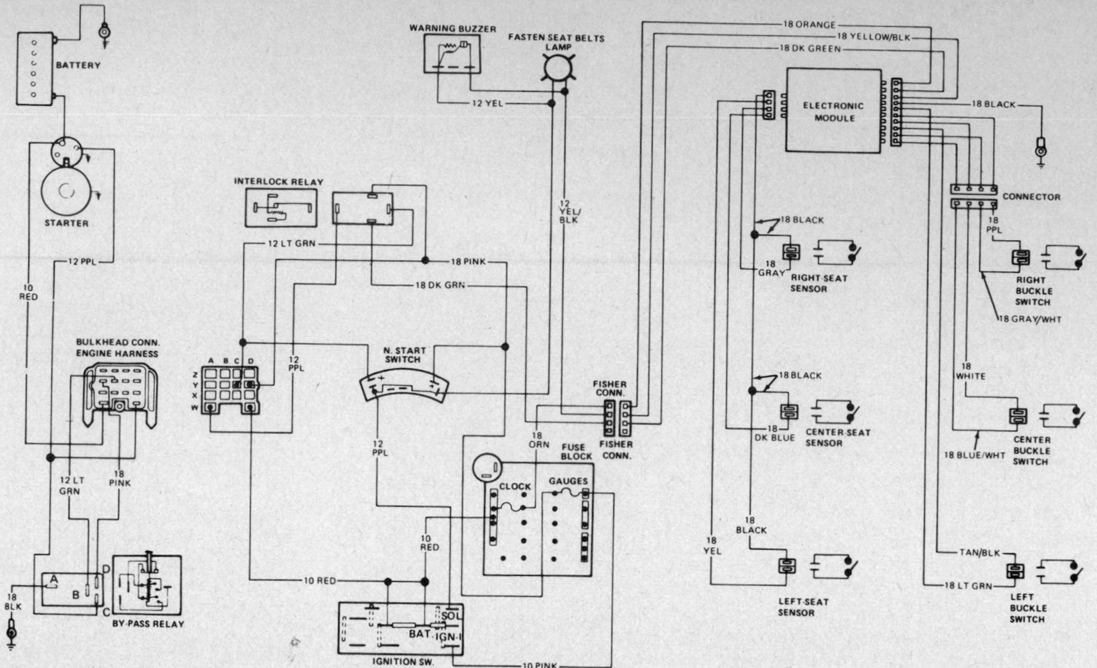

Seat belt/starter interlock schematic (© Pontiac Div., G.M. Corp)

under the hood permits starting when the ignition key is in the ON position.

The buzzer/warning light system will be activated if a front seat belt is not fastened at an occupied front seat after the car is started and moved into forward gear.

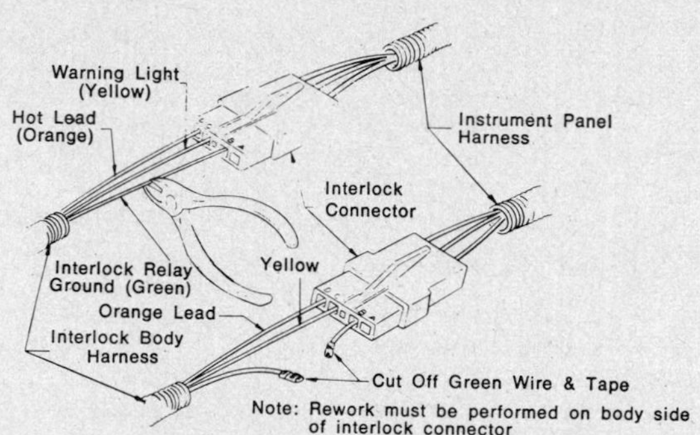

Disabling the seat belt interlock system (© Pontiac Div., G.M. Corp)

Disabling the Interlock System

Since the requirement for the interlock system was dropped during the 1975 model year, those systems installed on cars built earlier may now be legally disabled. The seat belt warning light is still required.

1. Disconnect the negative battery cable.
2. Locate the interlock harness connector under the left side of the instrument panel on or near the fuse block.
3. Cut and tape the ends of the green wire on the body side of the connector.
4. Remove the buzzer from the fuse block or connector.

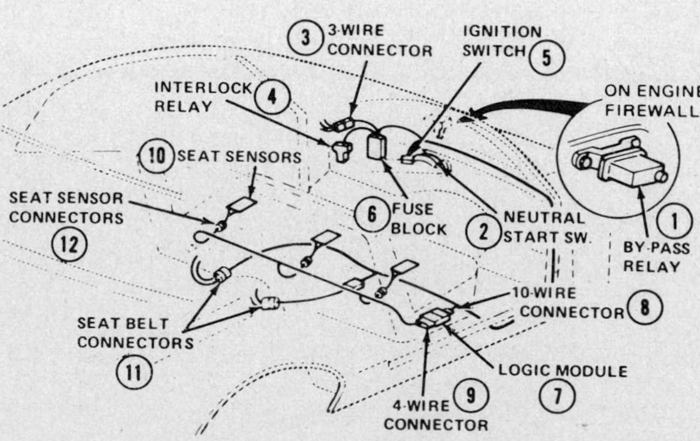

Starter interlock component locations (© Pontiac Div., G.M. Corp.)

Volkswagen—Types 1,2,3,4

INTRODUCTION

In 1932, Ferdinand Porsche produced prototypes for the NSU company of Germany which eventually led to the design of the Volkswagen. The prototypes had a rear mounted, air-cooled engine, torsion bar suspension, and the spare tire mounted at an angle in the front luggage compartment. In 1936, Porsche produced three Volkswagen prototypes, one of which was a 995 cc, horizontally opposed four cylinder automobile. Passenger car development was sidetracked during World War II, when all attention was on military vehicles. In 1945, Volkswagen production began and 1,785 Beetles were built. The Volkswagen convertible was introduced in 1949, the same year that only two Volkswagens were sold in the United States. 1950 marked the beginning of the sunroof models and the transporter series. The Karmann Ghia was introduced in 1956, and still remains in the same basic styling format. The 1500 Sqareback was introduced in the United States in 1966 to start the Type 3 series. The Type 4 was imported into the U.S.A. beginning with the 1971 model.

Type numbers are the way Volkswagen designates its various groups of models. The Type 1 group contains the Beetle, Super Beetle, the Karmann Ghia, and the "Thing". Type 2 vehicles are the Delivery Van, the Micro Bus, the Kombi and the Campmobile. The Type 3 designation is for the Fastback and the Squareback sedans. The Type 4 is for the 411 and 412 sedans and wagon. These type numbers will be used throughout the book when it is necessary to refer to models.

An explanation of the terms suitcase engine and upright fan engine is, perhaps, necessary. The upright fan engine refers to the engine used in the Type 1 and 2 (1970–71) vehicles. This engine has the engine cooling fan mounted on the top of the engine and is driven by the generator. The fan is mounted vertically in contrast to a horizontally mounted fan as found on the Chevrolet Corvair engine. The suitcase engine is a comparatively new engine and was designed as a more compact unit to fit in the Type 3, 4 and 1972 and later Type 2 engine compartments. On this engine, the cooling fan is mounted on the crankshaft giving the engine a rectangular shape similar to that of a suitcase.

MODEL IDENTIFICATION

Basic Body Types

Type 1 Beetle (left) and Super Beetle (right)

Type 1 Super Beetle Convertible (Model 15)

Type 1 Karmann Ghia (Model 14)

Type 1 Karmann Ghia Convertible (Model 14)

Type 1 Thing (Model 181)

Type 2 Bus (Model 22)

Type 2 Van (Model 21)

Type 2 Campmobile (Model 23)

Type 3 Fastback (Model 31)

Type 3 Squareback (Model 36)

Type 4 411 4-Door Sedan (1971-72 Model 41)

Type 4 412 4-Door Sedan (1973-74 Model 41)

Type 4 411 Station Wagon (1971-72 Model 46)

Type 4 412 Station Wagon (1973-74 Model 46)

SERIAL NUMBER IDENTIFICATION

Vehicle (Chassis) Number

The first two numbers are the first two digits of the car's model number and the third digit stands for the car's model year. For example a 0 as the third digit means that the car was produced during the 1970 model year, a 1 would signify 1971, and so forth.

The chassis number is on the frame tunnel under the back seat in the Type 1, 3, and 4. In the Type 2, the chassis number is on the right engine cover plate in the engine compartment and behind the front passenger's seat. All models also have an identification plate bearing the chassis number on the top of the instrument panel at the driver's side. This plate is easily visible through the windshield and aids in rapid identification.

Another identification plate bearing the vehicle's serial number and paint, body, and assembly codes, is found in the luggage compartment of Type 1, 3 and 4 vehicles.

Engine Number

On Type 1 and 2 vehicles, which have the upright engine cooling fan housing, the engine number is on the crankcase flange for the generator support. The number can readily be seen by looking through the center of the fan belt.

On Type 3 and 4 suitcase engines, the number is along the crankcase joint between the oil cooler and the air cleaner. The engine can be identified by the letter or pair of letters preceding the serial number. Engine specifications are listed according to the letters and model year.

Transmission Identification

Transmission identification marks are stamped into the bellhousing or on the final drive housing.

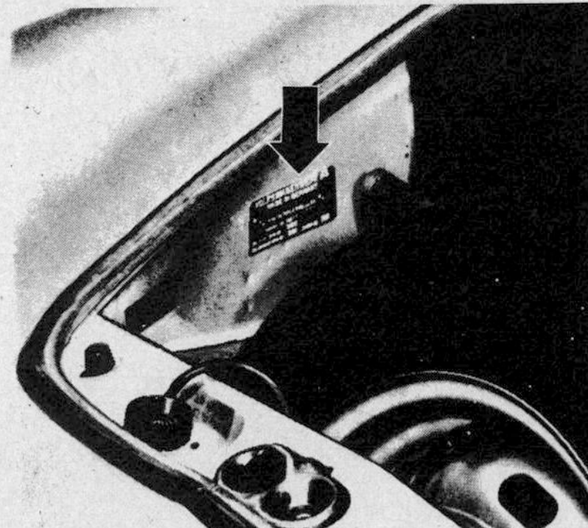
Identification plate in luggage compartment (Karmann Ghia shown)

Engine number location on the "suitcase" engine

Chassis number location on dashboard (Karmann Ghia shown)

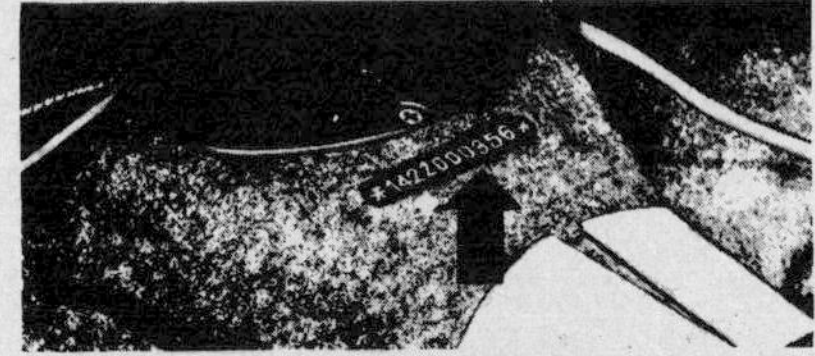
Chassis number location under rear seat (Karmann Ghia shown)

Engine number location on the "upright fan" engine

CHASSIS NUMBER CHART

Model Year	Vehicle	Model No.	Chassis Number From			Chassis Number To		
1970	Beetle	113	110	2000	001	110	3100	000
	Karmann Ghia	14	140	2000	001	140	3100	000
	Beetle Convertible	15	150	2000	001	150	3100	000
	Van	21	210	2000	001	210	2300	000
	Bus	22	220	2000	001	220	2300	000
	Camper, Kombi	23	230	2000	001	230	2300	000
	Type 3 Fastback	31	310	2000	001	310	2500	000
	Type 3 Squareback	36	360	2000	001	360	2500	000
1971	Beetle/Super Beetle	111/113	111	2000	001	111	3200	000
	Karmann Ghia	14	141	2000	001	141	3200	000
	Beetle Convertible	15	151	2000	001	151	3200	000
	Van	21	211	2000	001	211	2300	000
	Bus	22	221	2000	001	221	2300	000
	Camper, Kombi	23	231	2000	001	231	2300	000
	Type 3 Fastback	31	311	2000	001	311	2500	000
	Type 3 Squareback	36	361	2000	001	361	2500	000
	411 2 Door	41	411	2000	001	411	2100	000
	411 4 Door	42	421	2000	001	421	2100	000
	411 Wagon	46	461	2000	001	461	2100	000
1972	Beetle/Super Beetle	111/113	112	2000	001	112	3200	000
	Karmann Ghia	14	142	2000	001	142	3200	000
	Beetle Convertible	15	152	2000	001	152	3200	000
	Van	21	212	2000	001	212	2300	000
	Bus	22	222	2000	001	222	2300	000
	Camper, Kombi	23	232	2000	001	232	2300	000
	Type 3 Fastback	31	312	2000	001	312	2500	000
	Type 3 Squareback	36	362	2000	001	362	2500	000
	411 2 Door	41	412	2000	001	412	2100	000
	411 4 Door	42	422	2000	001	422	2100	000
	411 Wagon	46	462	2000	001	462	2100	000
1973	Beetle	11	113	2000	001	113	3200	000
	Super Beetle	13	133	2000	001	133	3200	000
	Karmann Ghia	14	143	2000	001	143	3200	000
	Beetle Convertible	15	153	2000	001	153	3200	000
	Thing	181	183	2000	001	183	3200	000
	Van	21	213	2000	001	213	2300	000
	Bus	22	223	2000	001	223	2300	000
	Camper, Kombi	23	233	2000	001	233	2300	000
	Type 3 Fastback	31	313	2000	001	313	2500	000
	Type 3 Squareback	36	363	2000	001	363	2500	000
	412 2 Door	41	413	2000	001	413	2100	000
	412 4 Door	42	423	2000	001	423	2100	000
	412 Wagon	46	463	2000	001	463	2100	000
1974	Beetle	11	114	2000	001	114	3200	000
	Super Beetle	13	134	2000	001	134	3200	000
	Karmann Ghia	14	144	2000	001	144	3200	000
	Beetle Convertible	15	154	2000	001	154	3200	000
	Thing	181	184	2000	001	184	3200	000
	Van	21	214	2000	001	214	2300	000
	Bus	22	224	2000	001	224	2300	000
	Camper, Kombi	23	234	2000	001	234	2300	000
	412 2 Door	41	414	2000	001	414	2100	000
	412 4 Door	42	424	2000	001	424	2100	000
	412 Wagon	46	464	2000	001	464	2100	000
1975	Beetle	11	115	2000	001	115	3200	000
	Beetle Convertible	15	155	2000	001	155	3200	000
	Thing	181	185	2000	001	185	3200	000
	Van	21	215	2000	001	215	2300	000
	Bus	22	225	2000	001	225	2300	000
	Camper, Kombi	23	235	2000	001	235	2300	000

TUNE-UP SPECIFICATIONS

Year	Code	Type	Common Designation	Spark Plugs Type	Spark Plugs Gap (in.)	Distributor Point Dwell (deg)	Distributor Point Gap (in.)	Ignition Timing (deg) MT	Ignition Timing (deg) AT	Fuel Pump Pressure (psi) @ 4000 rpm	Compression Pressure (psi)	Idle Speed (rpm) MT	Idle Speed (rpm) AT	Valve Clearance (in.) Cold In	Valve Clearance (in.) Cold Ex
1970	B	1, 2	1600	W145T1 L88A	.024	44-50	.016	TDC②	TDC②	3.5	114-142	800-900	900-1000	.006	.006
	U	3	1600	W145T1 L88A	.024	44-50	.016	TDC②	TDC②	28	114-142	800-900	900-1000	.006	.006
1971	AE	1, 2	1600	W145T1 L88A	.024	44-50	.016	5ATDC①	5ATDC①	3.5	114-142	800-900	900-1000	.006	.006
	U	3	1600	W145T1 L88A	.024	44-50	.016	TDC②	TDC②	28	114-142	800-900	900-1000	.006	.006
	W	4	1700	W175T2	.024	44-50	.016	27BTDC③	27BTDC③	28	128-156	800-900	900-1000	.006	.006
1972	AE	1	1600	W145T1 L88A	.024	44-50	.016	5ATDC①	5ATDC①	3.5	107-135	800-900	900-1000	.006	.006
	AH (Calif. only)	1	1600	W145T1 L88A	.024	44-50	.016	5ATDC①	5ATDC①	3.5	107-135	800-900	900-1000	.006	.006
	CB	2	1700	W145T2 N88	.024	44-50	.016	5ATDC①	—	5.0	100-135	800-900	—	.006	.006
	U, X	3	1600	W145T1 L88A	.024	44-50	.016	5BTDC②	5BTDC②	28	107-135	800-900	900-1000	.006	.006
	EA	4	1700	W175T2	.024	44-50	.016	27BTDC③	27BTDC③	28	128-156	800-900	900-1000	.006	.006
1973	AK	1	1600	W145T1 L88A	.024	44-50	.016	5ATDC ①④	5ATDC ①④	3.5	107-135	800-900	900-1000	.006	.006
	AH, AM (Calif. only and Thing)	1	1600	W145T1 L88A	.024	44-50	.016	5ATDC ①④	5ATDC ①④	3.5	107-135	800-900	900-1000	.006	.006
	CB	2	1700	W145T2 N88	.024	44-50	.016	10ATDC①	—	5.0	100-135	800-900	—	.006	.008
	CD	2	1700	W145T2 N88	.024	44-50	.016	—	5ATDC①	5.0	100-135	—	900-1000	.006	.008
	U, X	3	1600	W145T1 L88A	.024	44-50	.016	5BTDC②	5BTDC②	28	107-135	800-900	900-1000	.006	.006
	EA	4	1700	W175T2 N88	.024	44-50	.016	27BTDC③	27BTDC③	28	128-156	800-900	900-1000	.006	.006
	EB (Calif. only)	4	1700	W175T2 N88	.024	44-50	.016	27BTDC③	27BTDC③	28	107-135	800-900	900-1000	.006	.006

TUNE-UP SPECIFICATIONS (Con't)

Year	Code	Type	Common Designation	Spark Plugs Type	Spark Plugs Gap (in.)	Distributor Point Dwell (deg)	Distributor Point Gap (in.)	Ignition Timing (deg) MT	Ignition Timing (deg) AT	Fuel Pump Pressure (psi) @ 4000 rpm	Compression Pressure (psi)	Idle Speed (rpm) MT	Idle Speed (rpm) AT	Valve Clearance (in.) Cold In	Valve Clearance (in.) Cold Ex
1974	AK	1	1600	W145T1 L88A	.024	44-50	0.16	7½BTDC ②	7½BTDC ②	3.5	107-135	800-900	900-1000	.006	.006
	AH, AM (Calif. only and Thing)	1	1600	W145T1 L88A	.024	44-50	0.16	5ATDC①	5ATDC①	3.5	107-135	800-900	900-1000	.006	.006
	AW	2	1800	W175T2 N88	.024	44-50	.016	10ATDC①	5ATDC①	5.0	85-135	800-900	900-1000	.006	.008
	EA	4	1700	W175T2 N88	.024	44-50	.016	27BTDC③	—	28	128-156	800-900	—	.006	.006
	EC	4	1800	W175T2 N88	.024	44-50	.016	—	7½BTDC ②	28	85-135	—	900-1000	.006	.006
1975	AJ	1	1600	W145M1 L288	.024	44-50	.016	5ATDC⑤	TDC⑤	28	85-135	875	875	.006	.006
	ED	2	1800	W145M2 N288	.024	44-50	.016	5ATDC⑤	5ATDC⑤	28	85-135	900	900	.006	.006

① At idle, throttle valve closed (Types 1 & 2), vacuum hose(s) on

② At idle, throttle valve closed (Types 1 & 2), vacuum hose(s) off

③ At 3,500 rpm, vacuum hose(s) off

④ From March 1973, vehicles with single diaphragm distributor (one vacuum hose); adjust timing to 7½° BTDC with hose disconnected and plugged. The starting serial numbers for those type 1 vehicles using the single diaphragm distributors are # 113 2674 897 (manual trans.) and 113 2690 032 (auto. stick shift)

⑤ Carbon canister hose at air cleaner disconnected; at idle; vacuum hose(s) on

MT Manual Transmission
AT Automatic Transmission
BTDC Before Top Dead Center
ATDC After Top Dead Center

ENGINE IDENTIFICATION CHART

Engine Code Letter	Type Vehicle	First Production Year	Last Production Year	Engine Type	Common Designation
B	1, 2	1967	1970	Upright Fan	1600
AE	1, 2	1971	1972	Upright Fan	1600
AH (Calif.)	1	1972	1974	Upright Fan	1600
AK	1	1973	1974	Upright Fan	1600
AM (181)	1	1973	1974	Upright Fan	1600
AJ	1	1975	In Production	Upright Fan	1600
CB	2	1972	1973	Suitcase	1700
CD	2	1973	1973	Suitcase	1700
AW	2	1974	1974	Suitcase	1800
ED	2	1975	In Production	Suitcase	1800
U	3	1968	1973	Suitcase	1600
X	3	1972	1973	Suitcase	1600
W	4	1971	1971	Suitcase	1700
EA	4	1972	1974	Suitcase	1700
EB (Calif.)	4	1973	1973	Suitcase	1700
EC	4	1974	1974	Suitcase	1800

GENERAL ENGINE SPECIFICATIONS

Year	Engine Code	Displacement (cc)	Horsepower @ rpm	Torque @ rpm (ft lbs)	Bore x Stroke (in.)	Ratio Compression	Oil Pressure @ rpm (psi)
1970	B	1584	57/4400	82/3000	3.37 x 2.72	7.5:1②	42
1971–72	AE	1584	46/4000	72/2000	3.37 x 2.72	7.3:1	42
1971–74	AK	1584	46/4000	72/2000	3.37 x 2.72	7.3:1	42
1972–74	AH①, AM	1584	46/4000	72/2000	3.37 x 2.72	7.5:1	42
1972–73	CB	1679	63/4800	81/3200	3.54 x 2.60	7.3:1	42
1973	CD	1679	59/4200	82/3200	3.54 x 2.60	7.3:1	42
1970–73	U	1584	65/4600	87/2800	3.37 x 2.72	7.7:1	42
1972–73	X	1584	52/4000	77/2200	3.37 x 2.72	7.3:1	42
1971	W	1679	85/5000	99.5/3500	3.54 x 2.60	8.2:1	42
1972–74	EA	1679	76/4900	95/2700	3.54 x 2.60	8.2:1	42
1973	EB①	1679	69/5000	87/2700	3.54 x 2.60	7.3:1	42
1974	EC	1795	72/4800	91/3400	3.66 x 2.60	7.3:1	42
1974	AW	1795	65/4200	92/3000	3.66 x 2.60	7.3:1	42
1975	AJ	1584	48/4200	73.1/2800	3.37 x 2.72	7.3:1	42
1975	ED	1795	67/4400	90/2400	3.66 x 2.60	7.3:1	42

① California only
② Type 2—7.7:1

FIRING ORDERS

A general firing order diagram is shown because distributor positioning varies from model to model. All VW distributors have a scribed notch on the housing which locates the No. 1 rotor position. The firing order of all VW engines is 1-4-3-2. Correct re-wiring of the distributor cap would then begin at the No. 1 notch and proceed clockwise in the firing order.

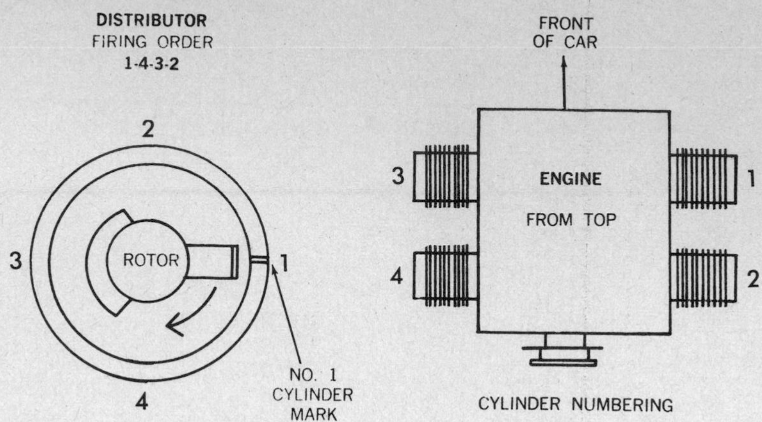

Ignition Firing order

CAPACITIES CHART

Year	Type and Model	Engine Displacement (cc)	Engine Crankcase (qts) With Filter	Engine Crankcase (qts) Without	Transaxle (pts) Manual	Transaxle (pts) Automatic Conv.	Transaxle (pts) Automatic Final Drive	Gasoline Tank (gals)
1970–75	1, 111, 114	1600	—	2.5	6.3	7.6	6.3①	10.6
1970–74	1, 113	1600	—	2.5	6.3	7.6	6.3①	11.1
1970–71	2, All	1600	—	2.5	7.4	12.6②	3.0	15.8
1972–75	2, All	1700, 1800	4.4	3.7	7.4	12.6②	3.0	15.8
1970–73	3, All	1600	—	2.5	6.3	12.6②	2.1	10.6
1971–74	4, All	1700, 1800	4.4	3.7	5.3	12.6②	2.1	13.2

Conv—Torque Converter ① 5.3 when changed ② 6.3 when changed

CRANKSHAFT AND CONNECTING ROD SPECIFICATIONS

(All measurements are given in inches)

Year	Type Engine	Crankshaft: Main Bearing Journal Dia No. 1, 2, 3	Main Bearing Journal Dia No. 4	Main Bearing Oil Clearance No. 1, 3	Main Bearing Oil Clearance No. 2	Main Bearing Oil Clearance No. 4	Crankshaft End-Play	Thrust on No	Connecting Rods: Journal Dia	Oil Clearance	Endplay
1970–75	1, 2, 3 1600	2.1640-2.1648	1.5739-1.5748	0.0016-0.004	0.001-0.003	0.002-0.004	0.0027-0.005	1 at flywheel	2.1644-2.1653	0.0008-0.0027	0.004-0.016
1971–75	2, 4 1700, 1800	2.3609-2.3617	1.5739-1.5748	0.002-0.004	0.0012-0.0035	0.002-0.004	0.0027-0.005	1 at flywheel	2.1644-2.1653	0.0008-0.0027	0.004-0.016

VALVE SPECIFICATIONS

Year	Vehicle Type Displacement	Seat Angle (deg) Intake	Seat Angle (deg) Exhaust	Face Angle (deg) Intake	Face Angle (deg) Exhaust	Valve Seat Width (in.) Intake	Valve Seat Width (in.) Exhaust	Spring Test Pressure (lbs @ in.)	Valve Guide Inside Dia (in.) Intake	Valve Guide Inside Dia (in.) Exhaust	Stem to Guide Clearance (in.) Intake	Stem to Guide Clearance (in.) Exhaust	Stem Diameter (in.) Intake	Stem Diameter (in.) Exhaust
1970–75	1, 2, 3 1600	45	45	45	45	0.05-0.10	0.05-0.10	117.7-134.8 @ 1.22	0.3150-0.3157	0.3150-0.3157	0.009-0.010	0.009-0.010	0.3125-0.3129	0.3113-0.3117
1971–75	2, 4 1700, 1800	30	45	30	45	0.07-0.08	0.078-0.098	168-186 @ 1.14	0.3150-0.3157	0.3534-0.3538	0.018	0.014	0.3125-0.3129	0.3507-0.3511

CARBURETOR SPECIFICATIONS

(All measurements are in metric units)

Year	Type/ Common Designation	Engine Code	Carburetor (Solex)	Venturi Diameter (mm)	Main Jet	Air Correction Jet	Pilot Jet	Aux. Fuel Jet	Aux. Air Jet	Power Fuel Jet	Needle Valve Washer Thickness (mm)	Accelerator Pump Injection Quantity (cc³ stroke)	Throttle Valve Gap (mm)	Fuel Level (mm)
1970	1/1600, 2/1600	B	30 PICT-3	24	x 112.5	125Z-MT 140Z-AT 140Z-Bus	65	45.0	130	100/100	1.5	1.05-1.35	—	19.5-20.5
1971	1/1600	AE	34 PICT-3	26	x 130	75Z/80Z	g60	47.5	90	100/100	0.5	1.45-1.75	—	17.19
	2/1600	AE	34 PICT-3	26	x 125	60Z	g57.5	42.5	90	95/95	0.5	1.45-1.75	—	17-19
1972	1/1600	AE	34 PICT-3	26	x 130	75Z/80Z	g60	47.5	90	100/100	0.5	1.45-1.75	—	17-19
	1/1600	AH (Calif. only)	34 PICT-3	26	x 127.5/x 130	75Z/80Z	g55	42.5	90	100	0.5	1.3-1.6	—	17-19
	2/1700	CB	Left 34 PDSIT-2	26	x 137.5	155	55	45.0	0.7	—	0.5	0.8-1.0	0.6	12-14
			Right 34 PDSIT-3	26	x 137.5	155	55	—	—	—	0.5	0.8-1.0	0.6	12-14

CARBURETOR SPECIFICATIONS

(All measurements are in metric units)

Year	Type/ Common Designation	Engine Code	Carburetor (Solex)	Venturi Diameter (mm)	Main Jet	Air Correction Jet	Pilot Jet	Aux. Fuel Jet	Aux. Air Jet	Power Fuel Jet	Needle Valve Washer Thickness (mm)	Accelerator Pump Injection Quantity (cc³ stroke)	Throttle Valve Gap (mm)	Fuel Level (mm)
1973	1/1600	AK	34 PICT-3	26	x 127.5/x 127.5	75Z/80Z	g55	42.5	90	100	0.5	1.3-1.6	—	17-19
	1/1600	AH, AM (Calif. only and Thing)	34 PICT-3	26	x 112.5	75Z/70Z	g55	42.5	90	100	0.5	1.3-1.6	—	17-19
	2/1700	CB (man. trans.)	Left 34 PDSIT-2	26	x 130	140	55	45.0	0.7	—	1.0	0.6-0.8	0.6	12-14
			Right 34 PDSIT-3	26	x 130	140	55	—	—	—	1.0	0.6-0.8	0.6	12-14
	2/1700	CD (AT)	Left 34 PDSIT-2	26	x 132.5	155	50	45.0	0.7	—	1.0	0.7-1.2	0.6	12-14
			Right 34 PDSIT-3	26	x 132.5	155	50	—	—	—	1.0	0.7-1.2	0.6	12-14
1974	1/1600	AK	34 PICT-3	26	x 127.5/x 127.5	75Z/80Z	g55	42.5	90	100	0.5	1.3-1.6	—	17-19
	1/1600	AH, AM (Calif. only and Thing)	34 PICT-4	26	x 127.5	75Z-MT 70Z-AT	g55	42.5	90	100	0.5	1.1-1.7	—	17-19
	2/1800	AW	Left 34 PDSIT-2	26	x 130	175	52.5	45.0	0.7	—	1.0	1.3-1.7	0.7	12-14
			Right 34 PDSIT-3	26	x 130	175	52.5	—	—	—	1.0	1.3-1.7	0.7	12-14
1975						—All Electronic Fuel Injection—								

MT—Manual Transmission
AT—Automatic Transmission
— Not Applicable

PISTON AND RING SPECIFICATIONS

(All measurements in inches)

Year	Type, Engine Displacement	Piston Clearance	Ring Gap			Ring Side Clearance		
			Top Compression	Bottom Compression	Oil Control	Top Compression	Bottom Compression	Oil Control
1970–75	1, 2, 3 1600	0.0016-0.0023	0.012-0.018	0.012-0.018	0.010-0.016	0.0027-0.0039	0.002-0.0027	0.0011-0.0019
1971–75	2, 4 1700, 1800	0.0016-0.0023	0.014-0.021	0.012-0.022	0.010-0.016	0.0023-0.0035	0.0016-0.0027	0.0008-0.0019

TORQUE SPECIFICATIONS

(All readings in ft lbs)

Year	Type Vehicle	Cylinder Head Nuts	Rod Bearing Bolts	Generator Pulley	Crankshaft Pulley Bolt	Flywheel to Crankshaft Bolts	Fan to Hub	Hub to Crank-shaft	Crankcase Half Nuts		Drive Plate to Crank-shaft	Spark plugs	Oil Strainer Cover
									Sealing Nuts	Non-Sealing Nuts			
1970–75	1	23	22-25	40-47	29-36	253	—	—	18	14	—	25	5
1970–71	2/1600	23	22-25	40-47	29-36	253	—	—	18	14	—	25	5
1972–75	2/1700, 1800	23	24	—	—	80	14	23	23	14	61	22	9
1970–73	3	23	22-25	40-47	94-108	253	—	—	18	14	—	25	5
1971–74	4	23	24	—	—	80	14	23	23	14	61	22	9

TORQUE SEQUENCES

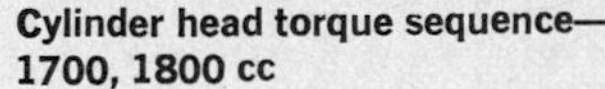

Cylinder head torque sequence—
1700, 1800 cc

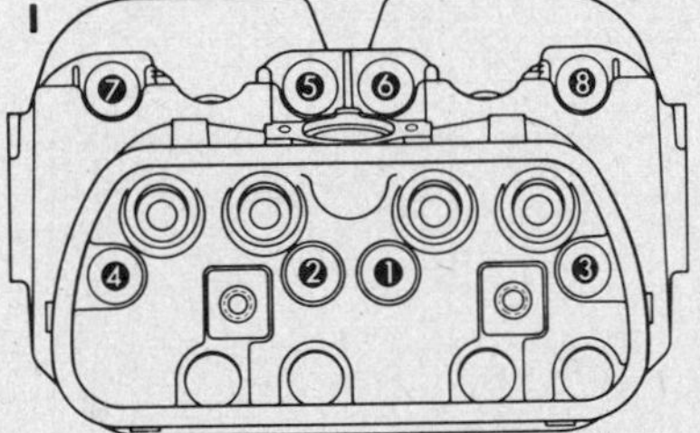

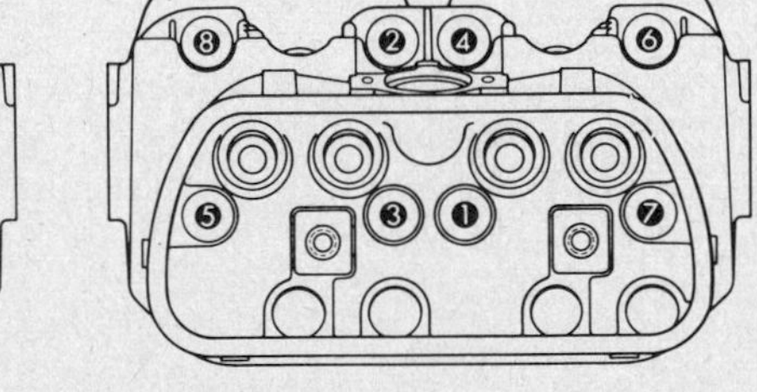

For 1600cc engines, the cylinder head nuts should initially be tightened to 7 ft-lbs in order I, then tightened to the recommended torque in order II

ALTERNATOR, GENERATOR, AND REGULATOR SPECIFICATIONS

Year	Type	Generator	Alternator			Regulator	
		Maximum Output (Amps)	Maximum Output (Amps)	Stator Winding Resistance (Ohms)	Exciter Winding Resistance (Ohms)	Load Current (Amps)	Regulating Voltage Under Load (Volts)
1970-73	1	30	—	—	—	25①	12.5-14.5
1973-75	1	—	50	0.13 ± 0.013	4.0 ± 0.4	25-30	13.8-14.9②
1970-71	2/1600	38	—	—	—	25①	12.5-14.5
1972-73	2/1700	—	55	0.13 ± 0.013	4.0 ± 0.4	25-30	13.8-14.9②
1974-75	2/1800	—	55	0.13 ± 0.013	4.0 ± 0.4	25-30	13.8-14.9②
1970-73	3	30	—	—	—	25①	12.5-14.5
1971-74	4	—	55	0.13 ± 0.013	4.0 ± 0.4	25-30	13.8-14.9②

① @ 2000-2500 generator rpm ② @ 2000 engine rpm — Not Applicable

STARTER SPECIFICATIONS

Starter Number	Lock Test Amps	Lock Test Volts	No-Load Test Amps	No-Load Test Volts	No-Load Test rpm	Brush Spring Tension (oz)
111 911 023A	270–290	6	25–40	12	6700–7800	42
311 911 023B	250–300	6	35–45	12	7400–8100	42
003 911 023A	250–300	6	35–50	12	6400–7900	42

BRAKE SPECIFICATIONS

(All measurements are given in in.)

Year	Model	Master Cylinder Bore	Wheel Cylinder Bore Front Disc	Wheel Cylinder Bore Front Drum	Wheel Cylinder Bore Rear	Drum Diameter Front	Drum Diameter Rear	Brake Disc Thickness	Brake Disc Thickness after Machining (minimum)
1970–75	Type 1	0.750	1.575 ⑤ ③	0.874 ⑥	0.687	9.059 ④ +0.008	9.055 +0.008	0.372-0.374	0.335
1970	Type 2	0.875	—	1.000	0.875	9.843 +0.008	9.843 +0.008	—	—
1971–75	Type 2	0.938	2.126	—	0.874	—	9.920 +0.008	0.511	0.472
1970–73	Type 3	0.750	1.654	—	0.874	—	9.768 +0.008	0.372-0.374①	0.335②
1970–74	Type 4	0.750	1.654	—	0.874	—	9.768 +0.008	0.433	0.393

① 1972–74—thickness 0.433
② 1972–74—thickness after machining 0.393
③ Karmann Ghia—1971–74
④ Super Beetle—9.768 + 0.008
⑤ Ate—1.575 in.; Girling 1.591 in.
⑥ Super Beetle—0.937

WHEEL ALIGNMENT SPECIFICATIONS

Year	Model	Front Axle Caster Range (deg)	Front Axle Caster Pref Setting (deg)	Front Axle Camber Range (deg)	Front Axle Camber Pref Setting (deg)	Front Axle Toe-in (in.)	Rear Axle Camber Range (deg)	Rear Axle Camber Pref Setting (deg)	Rear Axle Toe-in (deg)
1970–75	Type 1	±1°	+3° 20′	±20′	+30′	+0.071-+0.213	±40′	−1°	0′±15′
1971–74	Type 1①	±35′	+2°	+20′ −40′	+1°	+0.071-+0.231	±40′	−1° ③	0′±15′
1970–75	Type 2	±40′	+3°	±20′	+40′	0.0-+0.136	±30′	−50′	+10′±20′
1970–73	Type 3	±40′	+4°	±20′	+1° 20′	+0.118-+0.260	±40′	−1° 20′	0′±15′②
1971–74	Type 4	±35′	+1° 45′	+25′ −30′	+1° 10′	+0.024-+0.165	±30′	−1°	+10′±15′

① Super Beetle
② Squareback given; Sedan 5′±15′
③ Model 181 (Thing); +20′

FUSES

Type 1

Circuit	Fuse
Left parking, side marker, and tail lights	8 amps
Right parking, side marker, and tail lights	8 amps
Left low beam	8 amps
Right low beam	8 amps
Left high beam	8 amps
Right high beam, high beam indicator	8 amps
License plate light	8 amps
Emergency flasher system	8 amps
Interior lights	16 amps
Windshield wiper, rear window defogger, fresh air fan	16 amps
Horn, stop lights, ATF warning light	8 amps
Fuel gauge, turn signals, brake warning light, oil pressure, turn sinal and generator warning lights	8 amps

Type 2

Circuit	Fuse
Left tail and side marker lights	8 amps
Right tail and marker lights, license light, parking lights	8 amps
Left low beam	8 amps
Right low beam	8 amps
Left high beam, high beam indicator	8 amps
Right high beam	8 amps
Accessories	8 amps
Emergency flasher, front interior light	8 amps
Rear interior light, buzzer alarm, auxiliary heater	16 amps
Windshield wipers, rear window defogger	16 amps
Turn signals, warning lamps for alternator, oil pressure, fuel gauge, kickdown, and back-up lights	8 amps
Horn, stop lights, brake warning light	8 amps

Type 3

Circuit	Fuse
Right tail light, license plate light, parking and side marker light, luggage compartment light	8 amps
Left tail light	8 amps
Left low beam	8 amps
Right low beam	8 amps
Left high beam, high beam indicator	8 amps
Right high beam	8 amps
Electric fuel pump	8 amps
Emergency flasher, interior light	8 amps
Buzzer	16 amps
Windshield wipers, fresh air fan, rear window defogger	16 amps
Stop lights, turn signals, horn, brake warning light, back-up lights	8 amps
Accessories	8 amps

Type 4

Circuit	Fuse
Parking lights, left tail and left rear side marker lights	8 amps
Right tail light, right rear side marker light, license plate light, selector lever console light	8 amps
Left low beam	8 amps
Right low beam	8 amps
Left high beah	8 amps
Right high beam, high beam indicator	8 amps
Fuel pump	8 amps
Interior light, emergency flasher, buzzer	8 amps
Cigarette lighter, heater	16 amps
Window wiper, fresh air fan, heater, rear window defogger	16 amps
Turn signals, back-up lights, warning lights for alternator, oil pressure, fuel gauge	8 amps
Horn, brake warning light, stop lights	8 amps

TYPE 4 ENGINE AND TRANSMISSION ASSEMBLY CENTERING SPECIFICATIONS

Offset between vehicle center and engine/transmission unit center	1.0 in
Center of left measuring hole to center of right measuring hole	44.3±0.04 in.
Center of left measuring hole to center of rib on transmission	23.1±0.02 in.
Center of right measuring hole to center of rib on transmission	21.2±0.02 in.

UNLOADED REAR TORSION BAR SETTINGS

Type	Model	Transmission	Setting	Range
1	all	all	20° 30′	+50′
2	221, 223, 226	Manual	21° 10′	+50′
2	222	Manual	23°	+50′
2③	221, 223	all	20°	+50′
2④	222	all	23°	+50′
3	311	Manual	23°	+50′
3	311	\utomatic	24°	+50′
3	361	all	21° 30′	+50′

③ From chassis 212 2 000 001 (1972-up)
④ From chassis 212 2 000 001 (1972-up)

IGNITION SYSTEM

This section gives specific procedures on how to tune-up your Volkswagen and is intended to be as complete and basic as possible. Later in this book, there is another, more generalized section for tune-ups that includes troubleshooting and diagnosis.

CAUTION: *When working with a running engine, make sure that the transmission is in Neutral (unless otherwise specified) and the parking brake is fully applied. When the ignition is turned on and the engine running, do not grasp the ignition wires, distributor cap, or coil wire, as a shock in excess of 20,000 volts may result. Whenever working around the distributor, even if the engine is not running, make sure that the ignition is switched off.*

Spark Plugs

Before attempting any work on the cylinder head, it is very important to note that the cylinder head is aluminum. It is extremely easy to damage threads in the cylinder head. Care must be taken not to cross-thread the spark plugs or any bolts or studs. Never overtighten the spark plugs, bolts, or studs.

CAUTION: *To prevent seizure, always lubricate the spark plug threads with liquid silicon or Never-Seez.*

To avoid cross-threading the spark plugs, always start the plugs in their threads with your fingers. Never force the plugs into the cylinder head. Do not use a wrench until you are certain that the plug is correctly threaded.

VW spark plugs should be cleaned and regapped every 6,000 miles and replaced every 12,000.

Removal and Installation

To install the spark plugs, remove the spark plug wire from the plug. Grasp the plug connector and, while removing, do not pull on the wire. Using a 13/16 in. spark plug socket, remove the old spark plugs. Examine the threads of the old plugs; if one or more of the plugs have aluminum clogged threads, it will be necessary to rethread the spark plug hole. See the following section for the necessary information.

Obtain the proper heat range and type of new plug. Set the gap by bending the side electrode only. Do not bend the center electrode to adjust the gap. The proper gap is listed in the "Tune-Up Specifications" chart. Lubricate the plug threads.

Start each new plug in its hole using your fingers. Tighten the plug several

Set plug gap (a) to 0.024 in. for longer service

turns by hand to assure that the plug is not cross-threaded. Using a wrench, tighten the plug just enough to compress the gasket. Do not overtighten the plug. Consult the torque specifications chart.

Rethreading Spark Plug Hole

It is possible to repair light damage to spark plug hole threads by using a spark plug hole tap of the proper diameter and thread. Plenty of grease should be used on the tap to catch any metal chips. Exercise caution when using the tap as it is possible to cut a second set of threads instead of straightening the old ones.

If the old threads are beyond repair, then the hole must be drilled and tapped to accept a steel bushing or Heli-Coil. **It is necessary to remove the cylinder head to rethread the spark plug holes. Bushing kits, Heli-Coil kits, and spark plug hole taps are available at most auto parts stores. Heli-Coil information is contained in the "Engine Rebuilding" section of this book.**

Breaker Points and Condenser

Removal and Installation

1. Release the spring clips which secure the distributor cap and lift the cap from the distributor. Pull the rotor from the distributor shaft.

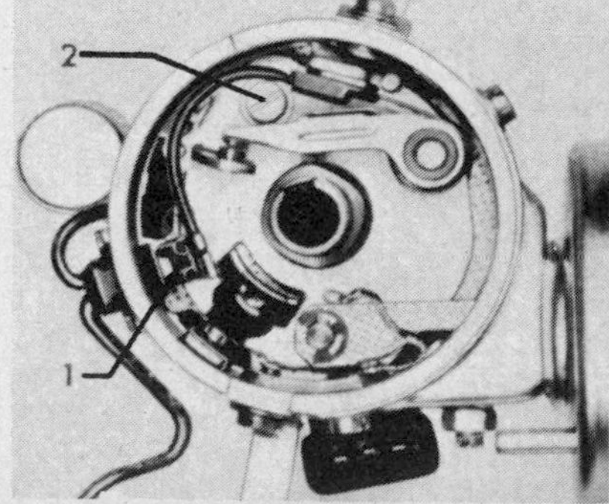

Breaker point removal is accomplished by disconnecting snap connection (1) and removing attaching screw (2)

2. Disconnect the points wire from the condenser snap connection (1) inside the distributor.
3. Remove the locking screw (2) from the stationary breaker point.
4. To remove the condenser which is located on the outside of the distributor, remove the screw which secures the condenser bracket and condenser connection to the distributor.
5. Disconnect the condenser wire from the coil.
6. With a clean rag, wipe the excess oil from the breaker plate.

NOTE: *Make sure that the new point contacts are clean and oil free.*

7. Installation of the points and condenser is the reverse of the above; however, it will be necessary to adjust the point gap, (or dwell), and check the timing. Lubricate the point cam with a small amount of lithum or white grease. Set the dwell, or gap, before the ignition timing.

Point Gap Adjustment

1. Remove the distributor cap and rotor.
2. Turn the engine by hand until the fiber rubbing block on the movable breaker point rests on a high point of the cam lobe. The point gap is the maximum distance between the points and must be set at the top of a cam lobe.

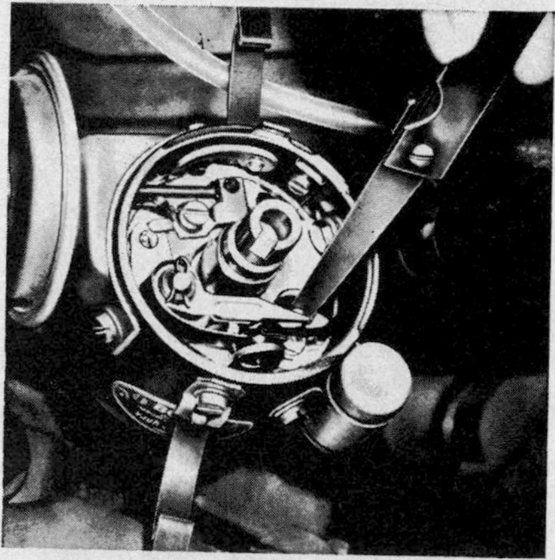

Checking point gap with feeler gauge

3. Using a screwdriver, loosen the locking screw of the stationary breaker point.
4. Move the stationary point plate so that the gap is set as specified and then tighten the screw. Make sure that the feeler gauge is clean. After tightening the screw, recheck the gap.

Dwell Angle

1. Setting the dwell angle with a dwell meter achieves the same effect as setting the point gap but offers better accuracy.

NOTE: *The dwell must be set before setting the timing. Setting the dwell will alter the timing, but when the timing is set, the dwell will not change.*

2. Attach the positive lead of the dwell meter to that coil terminal which has a

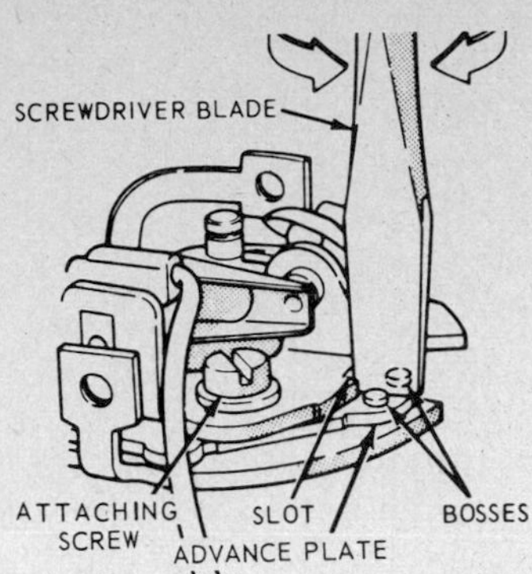

Adjusting point gap by moving stationary arm with screwdriver

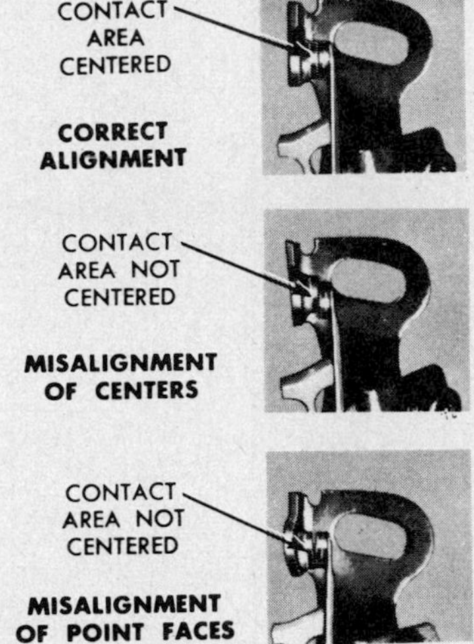

Breaker point alignment guide

wire leading to the distributor. The negative lead should be attached to a good ground.

3. Remove the distributor cap and rotor. Turn the ignition ON and turn the engine over using a starter or a starter button. Read the dwell from the meter and open or close the points to adjust the dwell.

NOTE: *Increasing the gap decreases the dwell and decreasing the gap increases the dwell.*

Dwell specifications are listed in the "Tune-Up Specifications" chart.

4. Reinstall the cap and rotor and start the engine. Check the dwell and reset it if necessary.

Ignition Timing

Dwell or point gap must be set before the timing is set. Also, the idle speed must be set to specifications.

NOTE: *The engine must be warmed up before the timing is set (oil temperature of 122°F–158°F).*

1. Remove the No. 1 spark plug wire from the distributor cap and attach the timing light lead. Disconnect the vacuum hose if so advised by the "Tune-Up Specifications" chart (and re-adjust the idle speed if necessary).

2. Start the engine and run it at the specified rpm. Aim the timing light at the crankshaft pulley on upright fan engines and at the engine cooling fan on the suitcase engines. The rubber plug in the fan housing will have to be removed before the timing marks on the suitcase engine can be seen.

3. Read the timing and rotate the distributor accordingly.

NOTE: *Rotate the distributor in the opposite direction of normal rotor rotation to advance the timing. Retard the timing by turning the distributor in the normal direction of rotor rotation.*

4. It is necessary to loosen the clamp at the base of the distributor before the distributor can be rotated. It may also be necessary to put a small amount of white paint or chalk on the timing marks to make them more visible.

Valve Lash

Preference should be given to the valve clearance specified on the engine fan housing sticker, if they differ from those in the "Tune-Up Specifications" chart.

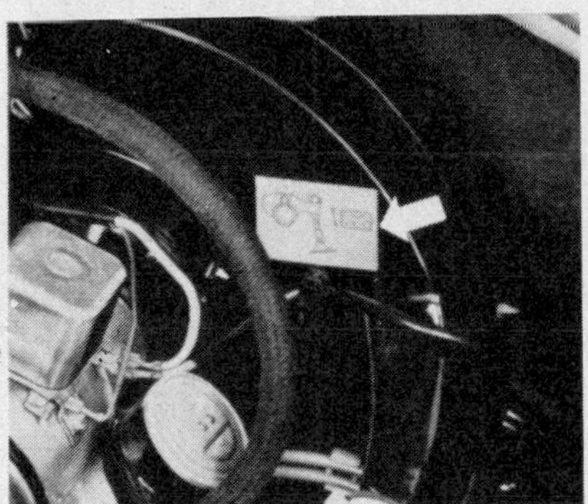

Valve clearance sticker location—Type 1, 2/1600

NOTE: *The engine must be as cool as possible before adjusting the valves.*

Adjust the valves as follows:

1. Remove the distributor cap and turn the engine until the rotor points to the No. one spark plug wire post in the distributor cap. To bring the piston to exactly top dead center (TDC) on the compression stroke, align the crankshaft timing marks on TDC.

2. Remove the rocker arm covers. At TDC, the pushrods should be down and there should be clearance between the rocker arms and valve stems of both valves of the subject cylinder.

3. With the proper feeler gauge, check the clearance between the adjusting screw and the valve stem of both valves for the No. 1 cylinder. If the feeler gauge slides in snugly without being forced, the clearance is correct. It is better that the clearance is a little loose than a little tight.

No. 1 piston at Top Dead Center—Type 1, 2/1600

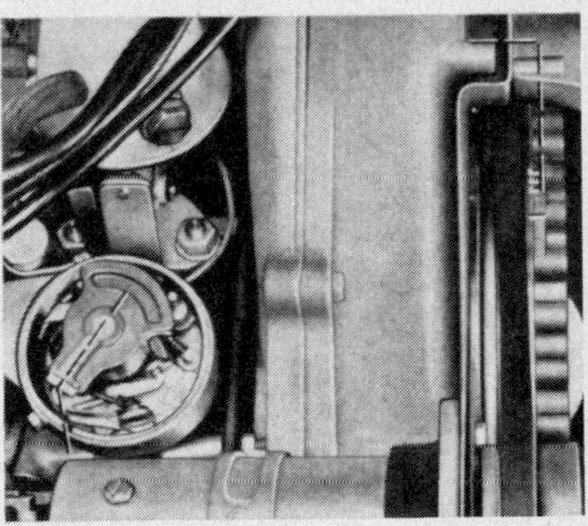

No. 1 piston at Top Dead Center—Type 3

4. If the clearance is incorrect, the lock-nut must be loosened and the adjusting screw turned until the proper clearance is obtained. After tightening down the lock nut, it is then advisable to recheck the clearance. It is possible to alter the adjustment when tightening the lock-nut.

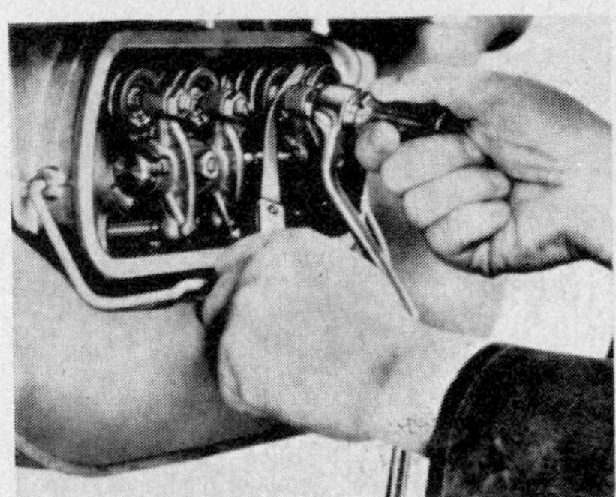

Checking valve clearance with feeler gauge

5. The valves are adjusted in a 1–2–3–4 (exact opposite of firing [1–4–3–2] order) sequence. To adjust cylinders 2 through 4, the distributor rotor must be pointed at the appropriate distributor cap post 90° apart from each other. Align the crankshaft timing marks for each cylinder, remembering that the piston must be at TDC on the compression stroke when the valves are adjusted.

NOTE: *Always use new valve cover gaskets.*

Ignition timing Type 1

Type	Engine number from – to	Ignition setting	Marking	Speed rpm	Remarks
1/1600	B 6 000 001 - B 6 440 900	0°			Vacuum hose <u>off</u>
1/1600 - M 9	B 6 000 002 - B 6 440 899				Vacuum hoses <u>on</u>
1/1600*) 1/1600*) 1/1600*) 18/1600*)	AE 000 001 - AE 999 999 AK 000 001 - AH 000 001 - AM 000 001 -	5° <u>after</u> TDC (see note 1 on page 1)		850 ± 50	Vacuum hoses <u>on</u>
1/1600**) 1/1600**)	AK 120 009 - AH 090 024 -	7.5° before TDC			Vacuum hose <u>off</u>

Ignition timing Type 2

Type	Engine number from – to	Ignition setting	Marking	Speed rpm	Remarks
2/1600	B 5 000 001 - B 5 230 000	0°		850 ± 50	Vacuum hose <u>off</u>
2/1600	AE 0 000 002 -	5° <u>after</u> TDC (see note 1 on page 1)			
2/1700	CB 000 001 - 062 000	5° <u>after</u> TDC		900 ± 50	Vacuum hoses <u>on</u>

*) Double acting vacuum
**) Single acting vacuum

Explanation of M-equipment listed in the table:
M 9 = Automatic Stick Shift
M 27 = Exhaust gas recirculation (Automatic Stick Shift / California)

Timing mark identification—Types 1, 2, 3 and 4

Ignition timing Type 2 (Cont'd)

Type	Engine number from	to	Ignition setting	Marking	Speed rpm	Remarks
2/1700	CB 062 001 -		10° after TDC		900 ± 50	Vacuum hoses on
2/1700-M 249	CD 000 001		5° after TDC		950 ± 50	
Ignition timing Type 3						
3/1600	U 0 000 001 -	U 0 502 000	0°		850 ± 50	Vacuum hose off
3/1600 3/1600-M 27	U 5 000 000 - X 0 000 001 -	U 5 057 000 X 0 004 000	5° before TDC (see note 1 on page 1)			Vacuum hoses off
3/1600 3/1600-M 27	U 5 057 001 - X 0 004 001 -		5° before TDC			Vacuum hose off
Ignition timing Type 4						
4/1700 4/1700 4/1700-M 27	W 0 000 001 - EA 000 001 - EB 000 001 -		27° before TDC		3500	Vacuum hose or hoses off

Explanation of M-equipment listed:

M 249 = Automatic transmission

M 27 = Exhaust gas recirculation (automatic transmission / California)

Timing mark identification—Types 1, 2, 3 and 4

Adjustments

Carburetor Idle Speed and Mixture

A carburetor adjustment should be performed as the last step of a tune-up. Prior to making any carburetor adjustments, the engine should be at operating temperature (122–158°F oil temperature) and the automatic choke should be fully open and off of the fast idle cam. Shut off the engine and connect a tachometer. Connect the hot lead to the distributor side of the ignition coil and the ground wire to an engine bolt or other good metal to metal connection. Keep the wire clear of the fan.

NOTE: *An improper carburetor adjustment may have an adverse effect on exhaust emission levels. If any doubt exists, check your state laws regarding the adjusting of emission control equipment.*

Solex 30 PICT-3 (1970 Type 1 and Type 2 Models)

1. Start the engine and bring it to operating temperature. Make sure the car is in neutral.
2. Using the idle speed (bypass) screw, adjust the idle speed to that specified in the "Tune-up Specifications" chart.

NOTE: *The bypass screw adjustment is the only adjustment that should be made to the 30 PICT-3 carburetor. Do not attempt to adjust the mixture or idle speed by turning the throttle valve adjustment screw, as increased exhaust emissions or poor driveability would result.*

Solex 34 PICT-3 (1971–74 Type 1 Models, 1971 Type 2 Models)

1. Start the engine and bring it to operating temperature. Make sure the car is in neutral.

Solex 34 PICT-3 Idle Adjustments

1. Throttle valve adjustment
2. Volume control (mixture) screw
3. Bypass (idle speed) screw

2. Shut off the engine. On 1971 models, turn out the throttle valve adjustment screw until it clears the fast idle cam. Then turn in the screw until it makes contact with the fast idle cam. Finally, turn the throttle valve adjusting screw in another one-quarter turn.
3. Slowly turn in the idle mixture (volume control) screw until it bottoms. Then, carefully counting the complete revolutions of the screwdriver, turn it out 2½ to 3 turns.
4. With a tachometer connected to the engine as previously described, start the engine.
5. Using the idle speed (bypass) screw, adjust the idle speed to specifications. Then, using the idle mixture (volume control) screw, adjust until the fastest idle is obtained. Observing the tachometer, turn the volume control screw until the engine speed drops by 20–30 rpm.
6. Finally, using the bypass screw, adjust the idle to specifications.

Dual Carburetor Engines (1972 Models)

Adjusting the carburetors on the dual carb models requires the use of a Uni-Syn or similar device to measure air-flow. This device measures the vacuum created inside the carburetor and gives a way of adjusting the carburetors equally. An adapter is necessary to use the Uni-Syn on the VW carburetors. A small frozen juice can with both ends removed will do.

1. Remove the right-hand connecting rod of the carburetor linkage system. This is the rod which connects the center bell crank with the right-hand carburetor.
2. Remove the air cleaner.
3. With the engine running and the Uni-Syn in place, balance the carburetors by turning the idle speed screws. Disregard the idle speed when balancing the carburetors.

NOTE: *It is easier to balance the carburetors first and adjust the idle speed later.*

4. Adjust the idle speed to specifications by turning both idle speed screws an equal amount until the proper speed is reached. Recheck the balance and idle speed in that order.
5. Next, adjust the volume control screw for each carburetor. Slowly turn the screw clockwise until the engine speed begins to drop, then turn the screw counterclockwise until the engine runs smoothly once again. Turn the screw ¼ turn farther in the counterclockwise direction.
6. Recheck the idle speed adjustment.
7. Reinstall the carburetor linkage and recheck the carburetor balance. If the balance is off, adjust the length of the linkage to restore balance. Lubricate the linkage pivot points with lithium grease.

Type 2 Twin Carb Adjustments—34 PDSIT-2 (left carburetor shown)

1. Synchronizing screw
2. Central idling system left end piece
3. Central idling system left end connecting hose
4. Central idling (idle speed) adjusting screw
5. Central mixture control screw
6. Throttle linkage ball socket

Type 2 With Air Pump (1973–74 Models)

Idle speed is set at the center adjusting screws. If a satisfactory idle cannot be obtained and all other conditions are correct (ignition timing, valve clearance, and choke fully open), use the following procedure to adjust the idle speed.

NOTE: *Since the idle mixture will be adjusted, it is necessary that the CO level be checked with an exhaust analyzer as part of this procedure.*

1. Connect the tachometer and exhaust analyzer to the engine.
2. Disconnect the throttle rod from the right side carburetor.
3. Remove the vacuum *retard* hose from the distributor.
4. Unplug the cut-off valve wire at the center idle system. Disconnect and plug the air pump hose.
5. Turn the idle mixture screws on both carburetors all the way in.

CAUTION: *Do not force the screws or the tips will be distorted.*

Turn both screws out 2½ turns.

6. Start the engine and set the idle speed at 500–700 rpm (CO level 3–5%) by equally adjusting both mixture screws.
7. Disconnect the idle cut-off wire at one carburetor and note the decrease in idle speed. Repeat this operation on the other carburetor. The idle speed decrease should be the same for both sides. If not, readjust the mixture screws.
8. Connect the cut-off valve at the center idle system and install the air pump hose.
9. Race the engine for a moment and then adjust the idle speed with center idle system screws (CO level 1–3%).

Fuel Injection Idle Speed

The idle speed is adjusted by a screw located on the left side of the intake air distributor. To adjust the idle speed,

Fuel Injection Idle speed adjustments—Type 3

a. slower
b. faster
c. tighten locknut

Fuel Injection idle speed adjustment—Type 4

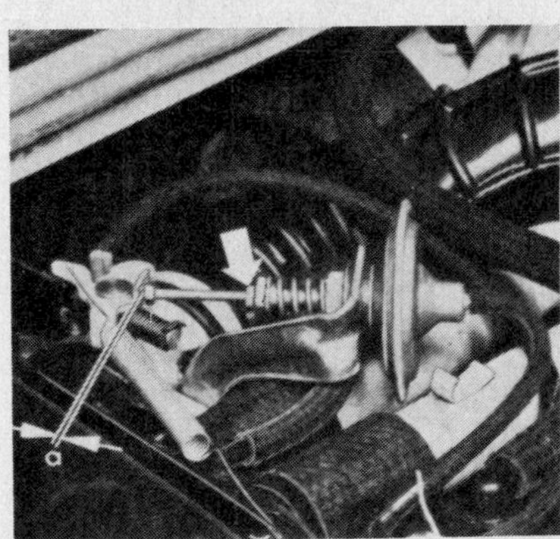

Idling speed regulator dashpot adjustment—Type 4

loosen the lock nut (Type 3 only) and turn the screw with a screwdriver until the idle speed is adjusted to specification.

On Type 4 models equipped with automatic transmission, the idling speed regulator dashpot must also be adjusted. With the car idling in neutral at 900 rpm, firmly apply the parking brake, block the front wheels, and place the transmission in drive. Under this load, the car should idle at 600–700 rpm. Check that clearance "a" between the end of the dashpot plunger and the bracket is 0.002–0.004 in. Adjust as necessary with the M5 bolt indicated by the arrow (see illustration).

ENGINE ELECTRICAL

Distributor

Removal and Installation

1. Take off the vacuum hose(s) at the distributor.
2. Disconnect the coil wire and remove the distributor cap.
3. Disconnect the condenser wire.
4. Bring No. 1 cylinder to top dead center (TDC) on the compression stroke by rotating the engine so that the rotor points to the No. 1 spark plug wire tower on the distributor cap and the timing marks are aligned at 0°. Mark the rotor-to-distributor relationship. Also, match mark the distributor housing-to-crankcase relationship.
5. Unscrew the distributor retaining screw on the crankcase and lift the distributor out.
6. If the engine has been rotated since the distributor was removed, bring the No. 1 cylinder to TDC on the compression stroke and align the timing marks on 0°. Align the match marks and insert the distributor into the crankcase. If the match marks are gone, have the rotor pointing to the No. 1 spark plug wire tower upon insertion.
7. Replace the distributor retaining screw and reconnect the condenser and coil wires. Reinstall the distributor cap.
8. Retime the engine.

Distributor Driveshaft

Removal and Installation

1. On carbureted engines remove the fuel pump.
2. Bring the engine to TDC on the compression stroke of No. 1 cylinder. Align the timing marks at 0°.
3. Remove the distributor.
4. Remove the spacer spring from the driveshaft.
5. Grasp the shaft and turn it slowly to the left while withdrawing it from its bore.
6. Remove the washer found under the shaft.

CAUTION: *Make sure that this washer does not fall down into the engine.*

7. To install, make sure that the engine is at TDC on the compression stroke for No. 1 cylinder with the timing marks aligned at 0°.
8. Replace the washer and insert the shaft into its bore.

NOTE: *Due to the slant of the teeth on the drive gears, the shaft must be rotated slightly to the left when it is inserted into the crankcase.*

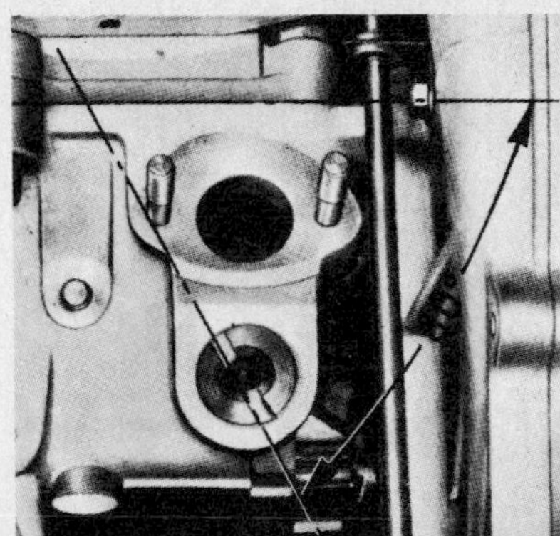

Type 3 distributor driveshaft alignment

Type 4 timing mark and rotor alignment

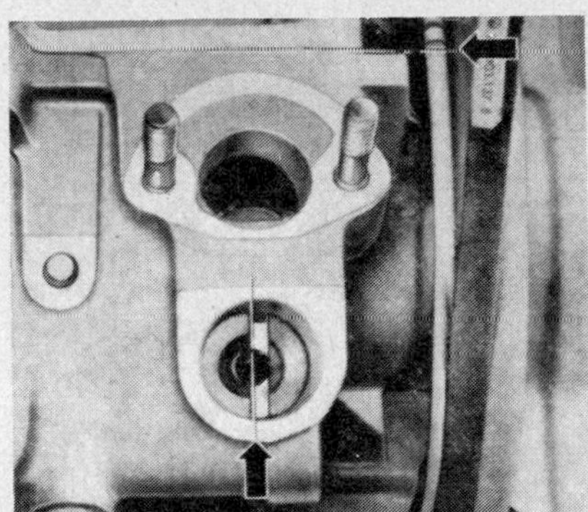

Type 1 and 2/1600 distributor driveshaft alignment

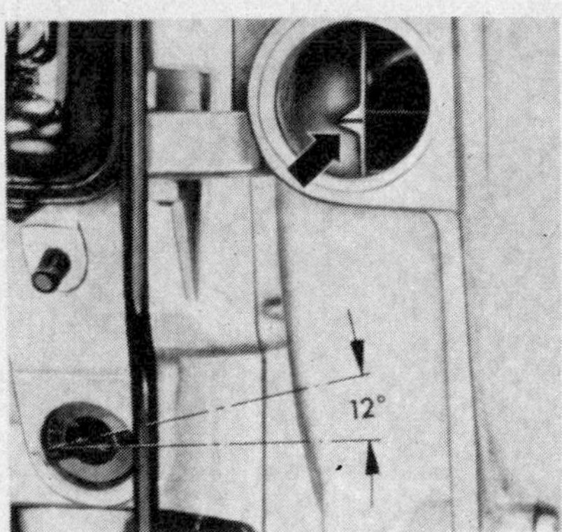

Type 4 distributor driveshaft alignment

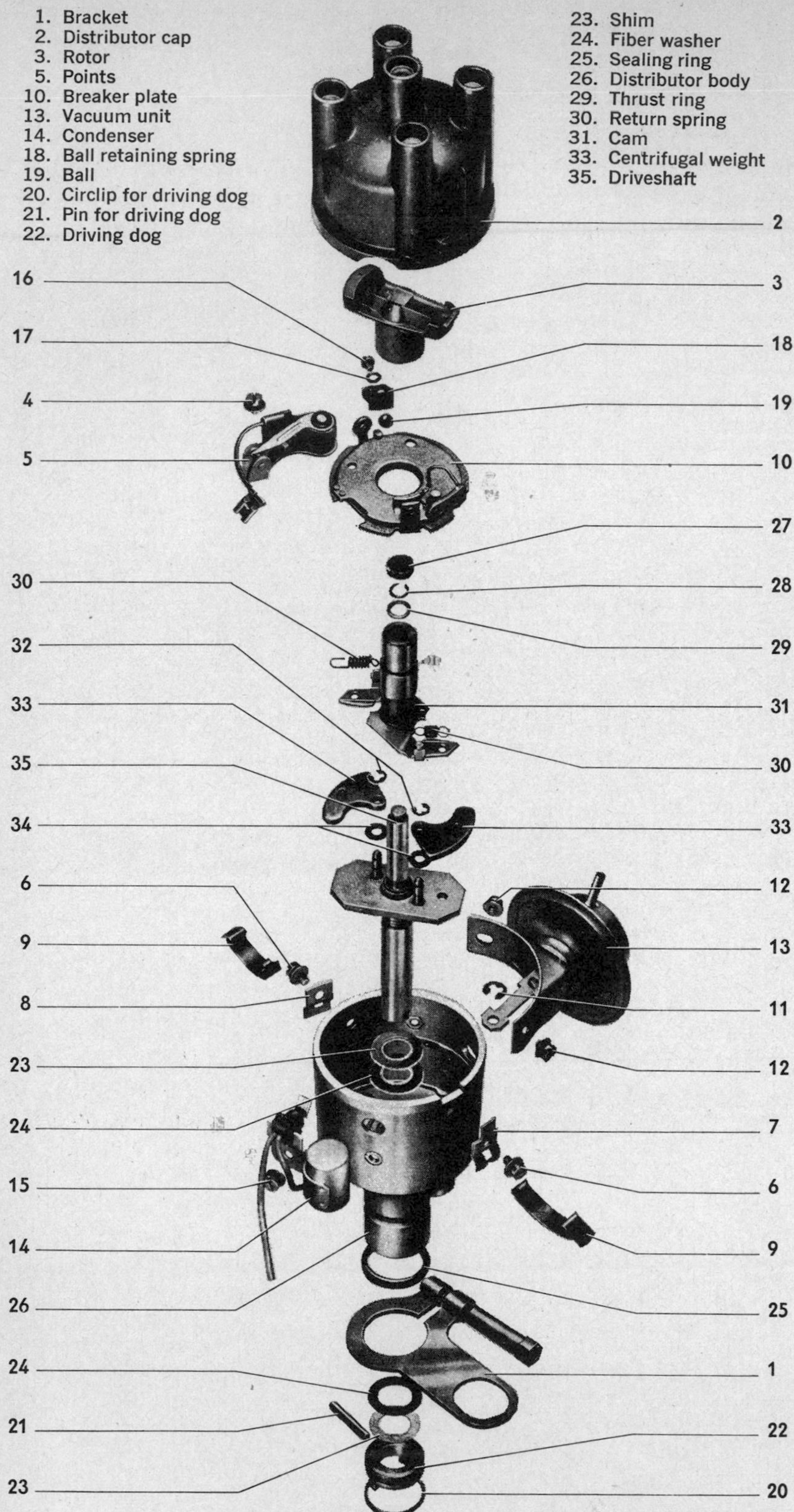

Distributor with vacuum and centrifugal advance

9. When the shaft is properly inserted, the offset slot in the drive shaft of Type 1 and 2/1600 engines will be perpendicular to the crankcase joint and the slot offset will be facing the crankshaft pulley. On Type 3, the slot will form a 60° angle with the crankcase joint and the slot offset will be facing the oil cooler. On Type 4 engines, and Type 2/1700 and 2/1800 engines, the slot should be about 12° out of parallel with the center line of the engine and the slot offset should be facing outside the engine.

10. Reinstall the spacer spring.

11. Reinstall the distributor and fuel pump, if removed.

12. Retime the engine.

CHARGING SYSTEM

Alternator Precautions

1. Battery polarity should be checked before any connections, such as jumper cables or battery charger leads, are made. Reversing the battery connections will damage the diodes in the alternator. It is recommended that the battery cables be disconnected before connecting a battery charger.
2. The battery must never be disconnected while the alternator is running.
3. Always disconnect the battery ground lead before working on the charging system, especially when replacing an alternator.
4. Do not short across or ground any alternator or regulator terminals.
5. If electric arc welding has to be done to the car, first disconnect the battery and alternator cables. Never start the car with the welding unit attached.

Removal and Installation

Types 1 and 2/1600

1. Disconnect the battery.
2. Disconnect the leads from the generator, noting their position on the generator.
3. Remove the air cleaner and the carburetor.
4. Separate the generator pulley halves, noting the number and position of the pulley shims, and remove the belt from the pulley.
5. Remove the retaining strap from the generator.
6. Remove the cooling air thermostat.
7. Remove the hot air hoses from the fan housing, take out the fan housing screws, and lift off the housing.
8. The generator, fan, and fan cover may be removed as an assembly.
9. Remove the fan from the generator by unscrewing the special nut and pulling the fan off the keyed generator shaft. Note the position of any shims found on Type 2 generators, from chassis number 219000001, as these shims are used to maintain a gap of 0.047 in. between the fan and the fan cover. The Type 1 gap is 0.08 in.
10. Reverse the above steps to install. When reinstalling the generator, the cooling air intake slot in the fan cover must face downward and the generator pulley must align with the crankshaft pulley.

Type 3

1. Remove the cooling air intake cover and disconnect the battery.
2. Loosen the fan belt adjustment and remove the fan belt. Removal of the belt

2. Distributor cap
3. Rotor
6. Points
8. Vacuum unit
9. Condenser
10. Holding spring
16. Ball retaining spring
17. Ball
18. Breaker plate
22. Return spring
23. Distributor cam
25. Flyweight
27. Circlip for drive dog
28. Pin for drive dog
29. Drive dog
30. 0.1 mm compensating washer
32. Distributor shaft
33. Distributor housing
34. Rubber sealing ring
35. Fuel injection trigger contacts

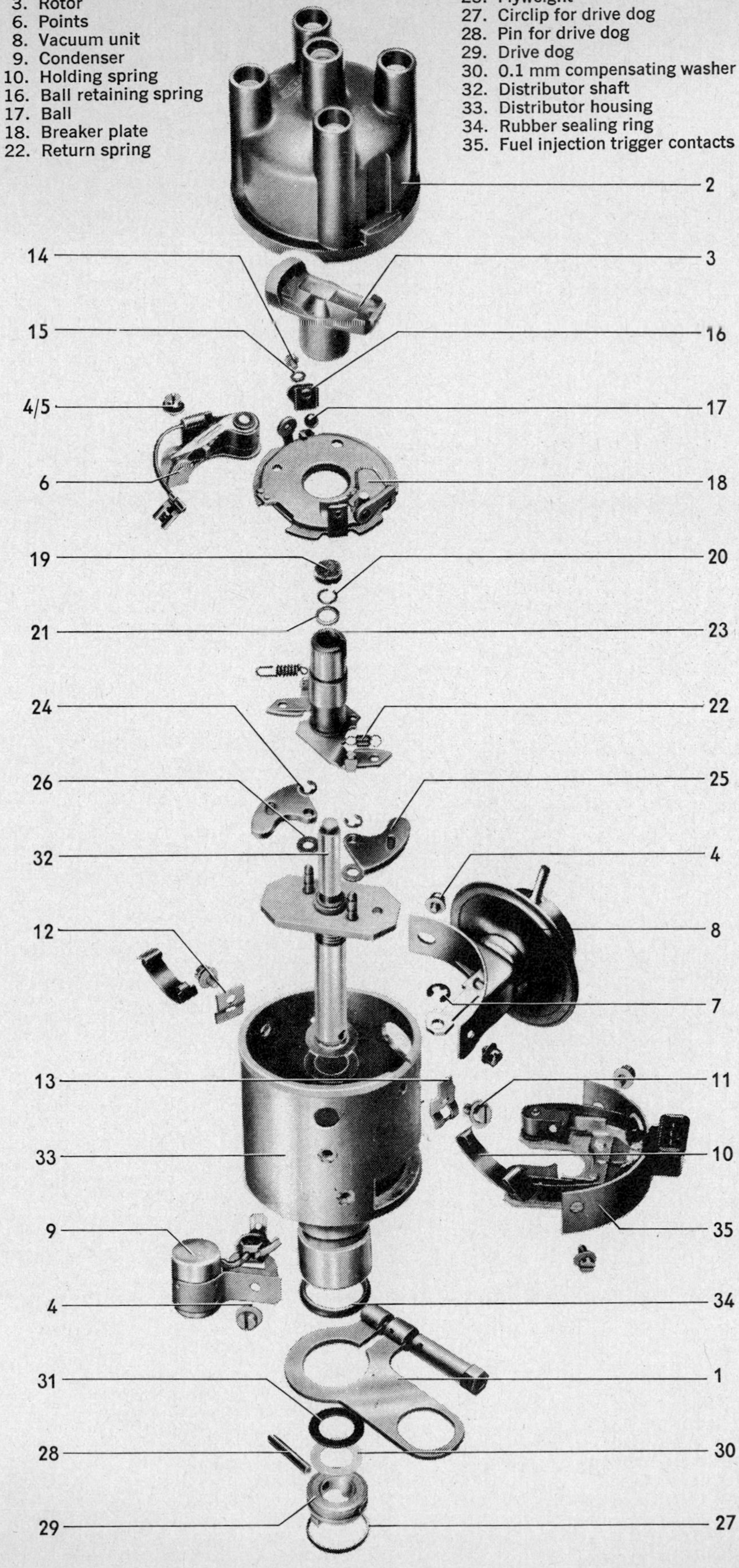

Fuel injection distributor

is accomplished by removing the nut in the center of the generator pulley and removing the outer pulley half.

3. Remove the two nuts which hold the generator securing strap in place and then remove the strap.

4. Disconnect the generator wiring.

5. Remove the generator.

6. Installation is the reverse of the above. Install the generator so that the mark on the generator housing is in line with the notch on the clamping strap. The generator pulley must be aligned with the crankshaft pulley. Make sure that the boot which seals the generator to the air intake housing is properly placed.

Alignment of Type 3 generator

Type 4

The factory procedure recommends removing the engine to remove the alternator. However, it is possible to reach the alternator by first removing the right heater box which will provide access to the alternator.

1. Disconnect the battery.

2. The following is the alternator removal and installation procedure after removing the engine; however, all bolts and connections listed below must be removed, except the engine cooling fan, if the right heater box is removed to gain access to the alternator.

3. Remove the engine.

4. Remove the dipstick, if necessary, and the rear engine cover plate.

5. Remove the fan belt.

6. Remove the lower alternator bolt and the alternator cover plate.

7. Disconnect the wiring harness from the alternator.

8. Remove the allen-head screws which attach the engine cooling fan, then remove the fan.

9. Remove the rubber elbow from the fan housing.

NOTE: *This elbow must be in position upon installation because it provides cooling air for the alternator.*

10. Remove the alternator adjusting bracket.

11. Remove the alternator.

12. Installation is the reverse of the above. Make sure that the belt is properly adjusted.

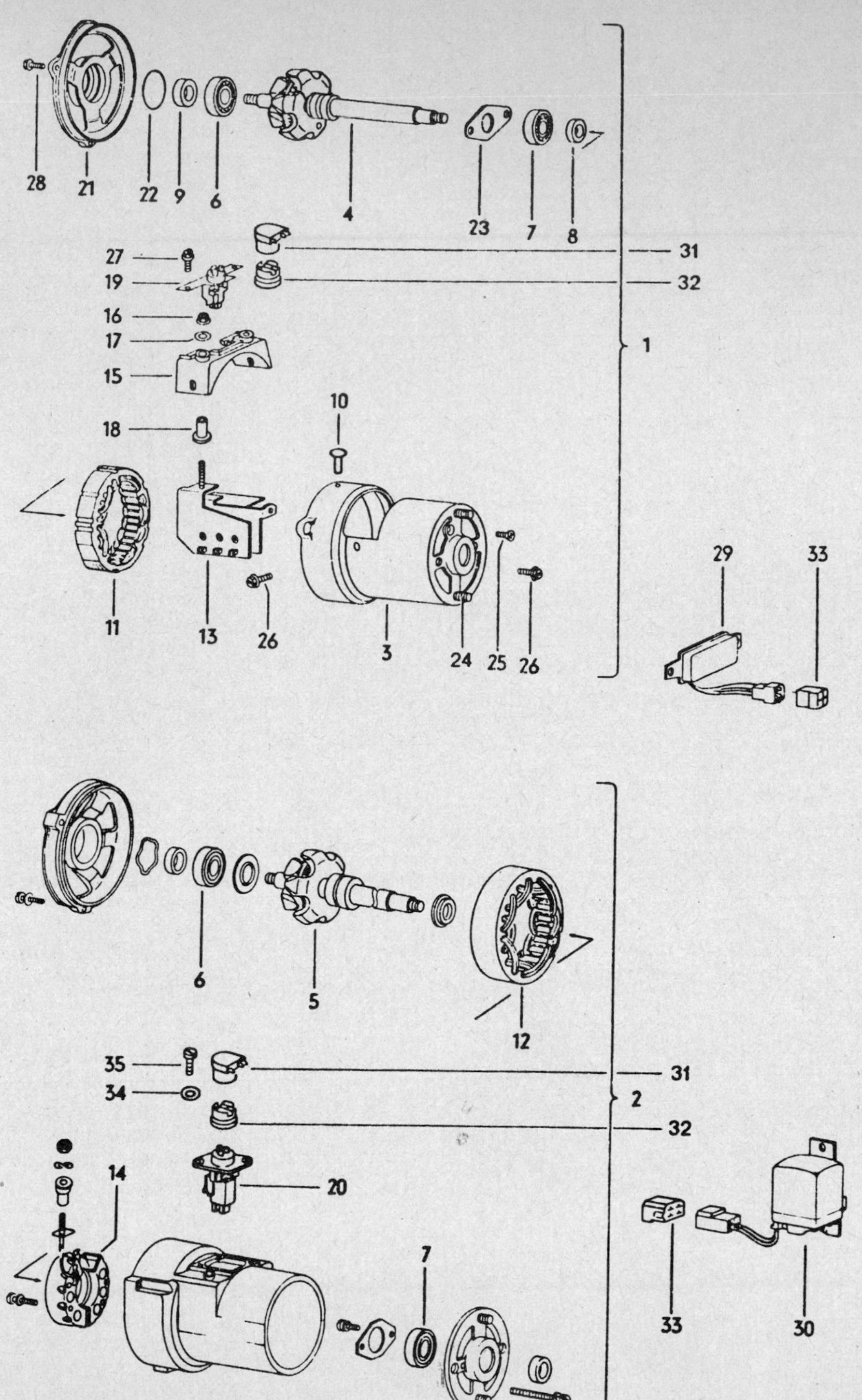

Exploded view of 50 amp alternator used in Type 1/1600 models

1. Motorola alternator
2. Bosch alternator
3. Housing
4. Claw-pole rotor
5. Claw-pole rotor
6. End plate ball bearing
7. Ball bearing
8. Fan end spacer ring
9. Drive end spacer ring
10. Rotor locating plate
11. Stator winding
12. Stator winding
13. Diode carrier
14. Diode carrier
15. Diode carrier retainer
16. B+ terminal nut
17. B+ terminal insulating washer
18. B+ terminal insulating bushing
19. Brush holder
20. Carbon brush holder plate
21. End plate
22. O-ring
23. Retaining plate
24. Fan cover bolt
25. Diode carrier screw
26. Retaining plate screw
27. Brush holder cover screw
28. End plate screw
29. Voltage regulator
30. Voltage regulator
31. Boot
32. Terminal sleeve housing
33. Terminal pin housing
34. Spring washer
35. Screw

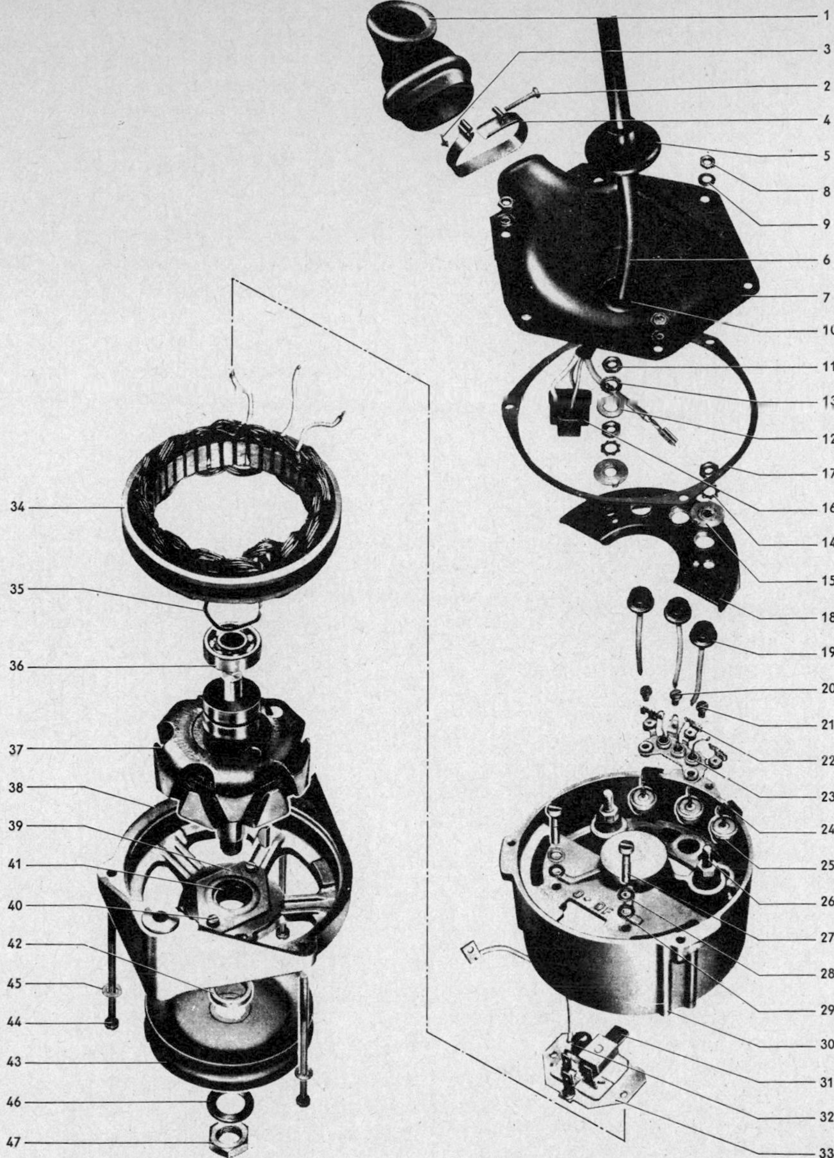

1. Elbow
2. Screw for hose clip
3. Threaded portion for hose clip
4. Cable hose clamp
5. Rubber grommet
6. Alternator wiring harness
7. Intake cover for alternator
8. Hex nut
9. Lockwasher
10. Rubber grommet for intake cover
11. B+ connection hex nut
12. Washer
13. Washer
14. Star washer
15. Contact disc
16. Three pin plug
17. Intake cover gasket
18. Positive diode carrier
19. Positive diodes
20. Screw
21. Stator winding connection screw
22. Exciter diode carrier
23. Exciter diodes
24. Seal
25. Negative diodes
26. Positive diode carrier pin
27. Brush holder screw
28. Washer
29. Spring washer
30. Alternator housing
31. Carbon brush
32. Brush retaining spring
33. Brush holder
34. Stator
35. Spring washer
36. Slip ring ball bearings
37. Claw pole rotor
38. End plate
39. Bearing end plate
40. Screw
41. Drive end ball bearing
42. Intermediate ring
43. Pulley
44. Housing bolt
45. Washer
46. Washer
47. Nut

Exploded view of 55 amp alternator used in Type 2/1700, 2/1800, and Type 4 models

1. Nut for pulley
2. Special washer
3. Shim
4. Pulley
5. End plate
6. End ring
7. Through-bolt
8. Washer
9. Screw
10. Washer
11. End plate with carbon brushes
12. Spring
13. Carbon brushes
14. Screw
15. Ball bearing
16. Splash shield
18. Splash shield
19. Retaining plate
20. Woodruff key
21. Splash shield
22. Armature
23. Armature flange
24. Gasket
25. Field coil
26. Housing
27. Field screw

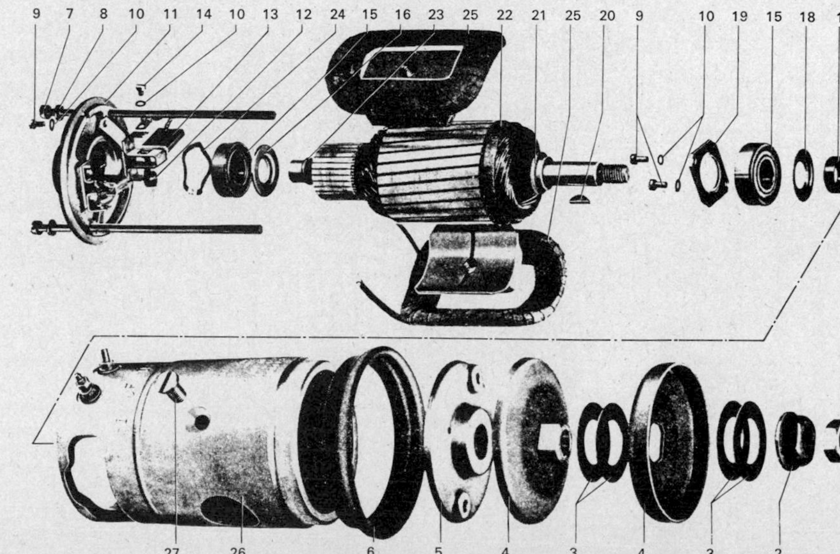

Exploded view of typical generator—Type 3 shown

Generator Belt Adjustment

Type 1, 2/1600, and 3

Belt adjustment is performed by removing the nut in the center of the generator pulley and removing or installing shims between the generator pulley halves. Removing shims tightens the belt and installing shims loosens the belt.

Alternator belt tension adjustment

Alternator Belt Adjustment

1. Remove the insert in the cover plate and loosen the bolt in the slotted hole.
2. Move the alternator left or right to adjust the tension and then tighten the bolt. Tension is correct if the bolt can be deflected no more than ½ in. at the midpoint of the pulleys.

Voltage Regulator

Removal and Installation

Type 1 and 3

The regulator is located under the rear seat on the left side. It is secured to the frame by two screws. Take careful note of the wiring connections before removing the wiring from the regulator. Disconnect the battery before removing the regulator.

CAUTION: *Interchanging the connections on the regulator will destroy the regulator and generator.*

Type 2 and 14 (Karmann Ghia)

Disconnect the battery. The regulator is located in the engine compartment and is secured in place by two screws. Take careful note of the wiring connections before removing the wiring from the regulator.

Type 4

Disconnect the battery and do not disconnect any other wiring until the engine is turned off. Make careful note of the wiring connections. The regulator is located near the air cleaner and is mounted either on the air cleaner or on the firewall. It is secured by two screws.

Voltage Adjustment

Volkswagen voltage regulators are sealed and cannot be adjusted. A malfunctioning regulator must be replaced as a unit.

Removal and Installation

1. Disconnect the battery.
2. Disconnect the wiring from the starter.
3. The starter is held in place by two bolts. Remove the upper bolt through the engine compartment. Remove the lower bolt from underneath the car.
4. Remove the starter from the car.
5. Before installing the starter, lubricate the outboard bushing with grease. Apply sealing compound to the mating surfaces between the starter and the transmission.
6. Place the long starter bolt in its hole in the starter and locate the starter on the transmission housing. Install the other bolt.
7. Connect the starter wiring and battery cables.

Solenoid Replacement

1. Remove the starter.
2. Remove the nut which secures the connector strip at the end of the solenoid.
3. Take out the two retaining screws on the mounting bracket and withdraw the solenoid after it has been unhooked from its actuating lever.
4. When replacing a defective solenoid with a new one, care should be taken to see that the distance (a) in the accompanying diagram is 19 mm when the magnet is drawn inside the solenoid.

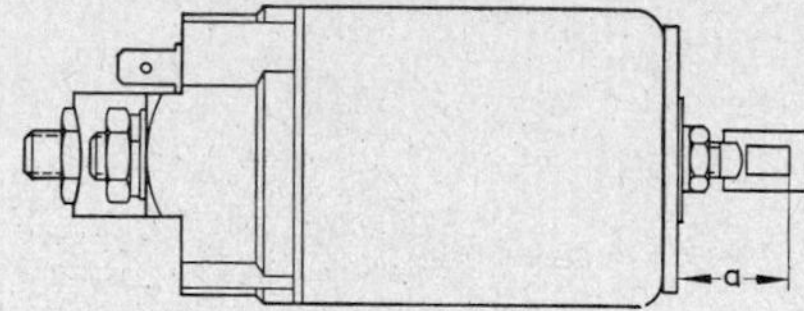

Solenoid adjustment

5. Installation is the reverse of removal. In order to facilitate engagement of the actuating rod, the pinion should be pulled out as far as possible when inserting the solenoid.

Battery

The electrical system of the Volkswagen is a negative grounded type. In most VW models, the battery is located under the right-hand side of the rear seat. In Karmann Ghia, Type 2 and 4 models, it is located in the engine compartment.

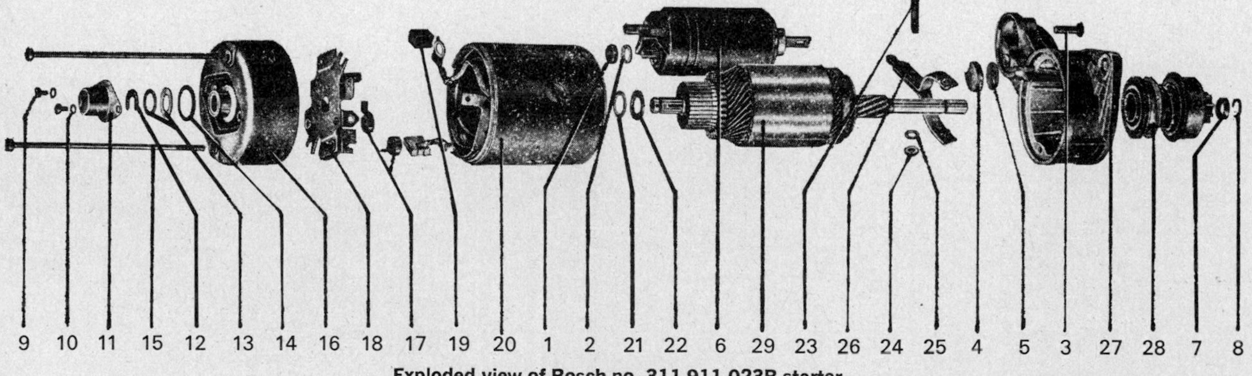

Exploded view of Bosch no. 311 911 023B starter

1. Nut
2. Lockwasher
3. Screw
4. Rubber seal
5. Disc
6. Solenoid switch
7. Stop-ring
8. Circlip
9. Screw
10. Washer
11. End cap
12. C-washer
13. Shim
14. Sealing ring
15. Housing screw
16. End plate
17. Spring
18. Brush holder
19. Rubber grommet
20. Housing
21. Insulating washer
22. Thrust washer
23. Pin
24. Nut
25. Lockwasher
26. Operating lever
27. Drive end plate
28. Drive pinion
29. Armature

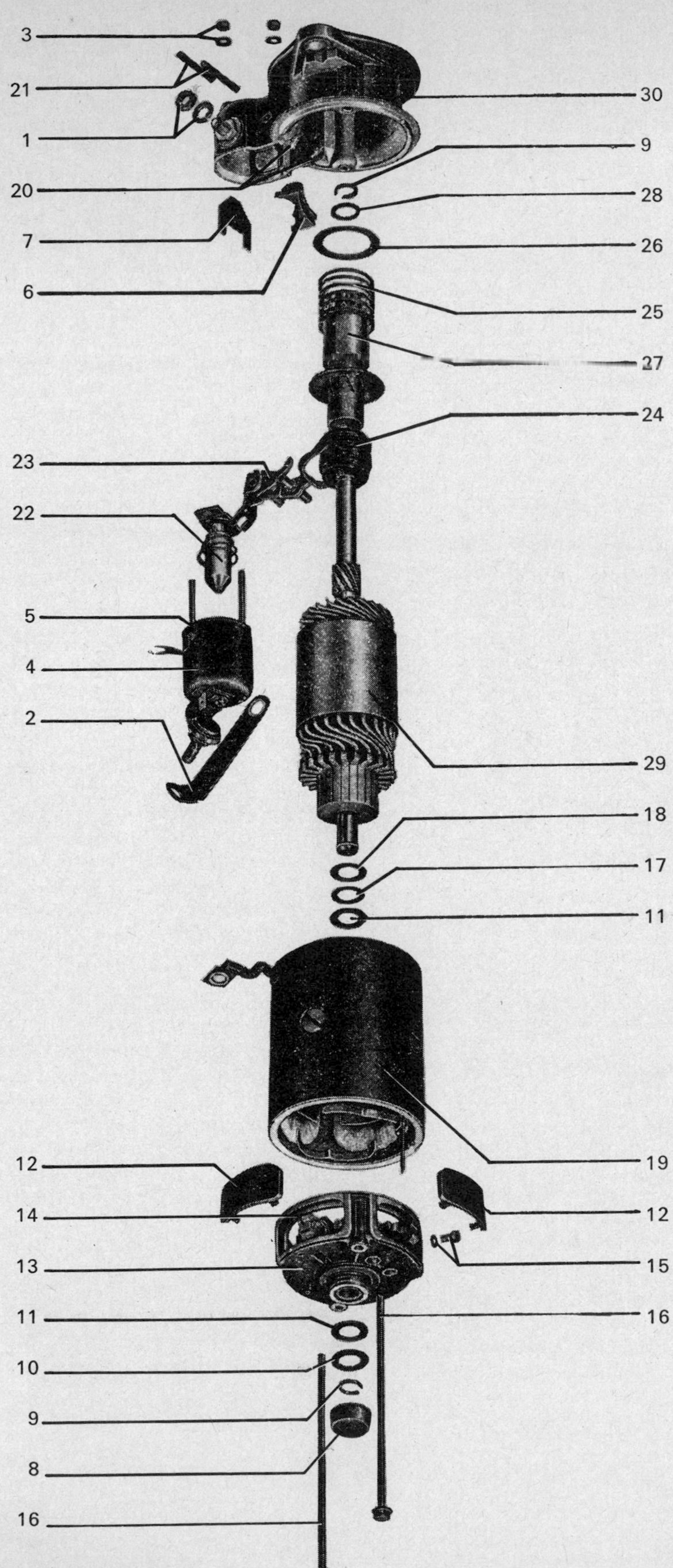

Exploded view of VW no. 111 911 023A starter

1. Nut and lockwasher
2. Connecting strip
3. Nut and lockwasher
4. Solenoid
5. Insulating disc
6. Seal
7. Insulating plate
8. Cap
9. Circlip
10. Steel washer
11. Bronze washer
12. Brush inspection cover
13. Commutator end plate
14. Brush holder
15. Screw and lockwasher
16. Housing screws
17. Dished washer
18. Steel washer
19. Housing and field windings
20. Spring clip
21. Pin
22. Solenoid core
23. Linkage
24. Bushing
25. Spring
26. Washer
27. Drive pinion
28. Dished washer
29. Armature
30. Mounting bracket

Removal and Installation

1. Disconnect the battery cables. Note the position of the battery cables for installation. The small diameter battery post is the negative terminal. The negative battery cable is usually black.
2. Undo the battery holddown strap and lift the battery out of its holder.
3. Install the battery in its holder and replace the clamp. Reconnect the battery cables.

ENGINE MECHANICAL

The Volkswagen engine is a flat four cylinder design. This four cycle, overhead valve engine has two pairs of horizontally opposed cylinders. All VW engines are air cooled.

The Type 1 and 2/1600 engine is known as an upright fan engine, that is, the engine cooling fan is mounted vertically on top of the engine and is driven by the generator shaft. The Type 2/1700, Type 2/1800, Type 3 and 4 engine, although of the same basic design, i.e. flat four, has the cooling fan driven by the crankshaft and is therefore mounted on the front of the engine. This type of engine is known as the suitcase engine. The upright fan engine is carbureted, while the suitcase engine is available carbureted in the Type 2/1700, 2/1800 or fuel injected in the Type 3 and fuel injected in the Type 4.

Because it is air cooled, the VW engine is slightly noisier than a water cooled engine. This is due to the lack of water jacketing around the cylinders which provides sound deadening on water cooled engines. In addition, air cooled engines tend to run at somewhat higher temperatures, necessitating larger operating clearances to allow more room for the expansion of the parts. These larger operating clearances cause an increase in noise level over a water cooled engine.

The crankshaft of all Volkswagen engines is mounted in a two piece crankcase. The halves are machined to very close tolerances and line bored as a pair and, therefore, should always be replaced in pairs. When fitting them, it is necessary to coat only the mating surfaces with sealing compound and tighten them down to the correct torque. No gasket is used.

The pistons and cylinders are identical on any particular engine. However, it is not possible to interchange pistons and cylinders between engines. The four pistons each have three rings, two compression rings and one oil scraper. Each piston is attached to its connecting rod with a fully floating piston pin.

Each pair of cylinders shares a detachable cylinder head made of light aluminum alloy casting. The cylinder head contains the valves for both cylinders. Shrunk-in valve guides and valve seats are used.

Engine Removal and Installation

Type 1, 2, and 3

The Volkswagen engine is mounted on the transmission, which in turn is attached to the frame. In the Type 1 and 2 models, there are two bolts and two studs attaching the engine to the transmission. Type 3 engines have an extra mounting at the rear of the engine. Type 3 engines with automatic transmissions have front and rear engine and transmission mounts. At the front, the gearbox is supported by the rear tubular crossmember; at the rear, a crossmember is bolted to the crankcase and mounted to the body at either end.

When removing the engine from the car, it is recommended that the rear of the car be about 3 ft off the ground. Remove the engine by bringing it out from underneath the car. Proceed with the following steps to remove the engine.

1. Disconnect the battery ground cable.
2. Disconnect the generator wiring.
3. Remove the air cleaner. On Type 1 engines, remove the rear engine cover plate. On Type 2/1600 cc engines, remove the rear crossmember.
4. Disconnect the throttle cable and remove the electrical connections to the automatic choke, coil, electromagnetic cutoff jet, and the oil pressure sending unit.
5. Disconnect the fuel hose at the front engine cover plate and seal it to prevent leakage.
6. On Type 3 models, remove the oil dipstick and the rubber boot between the oil filter and the body.
7. Remove the cooling air intake bellows on Type 3 engines after loosening the clip that secures the unit.
8. On Type 3 models, remove the warm air hose.
9. On Type 3 fuel injected engines, remove and plug the pressure line to the left fuel distributor pipe and to the return line on the pressure regulator. Disconnect the fuel injection wiring harness.
10. Raise the car and support it with jackstands.
11. Remove the flexible air hoses between the engine and heat exchangers, disconnect the heater flap cables, unscrew the two lower engine mounting nuts, and slide a jack under the engine. On Type 2 engines, remove the two bolts from the rubber engine mounts located next to the muffler.

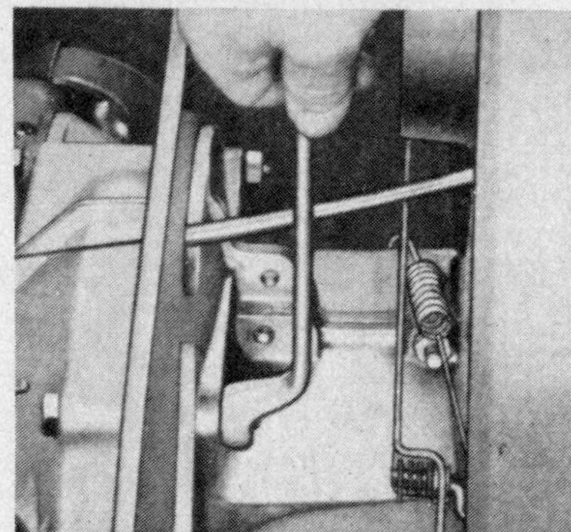

Removing upper engine mounting bolts

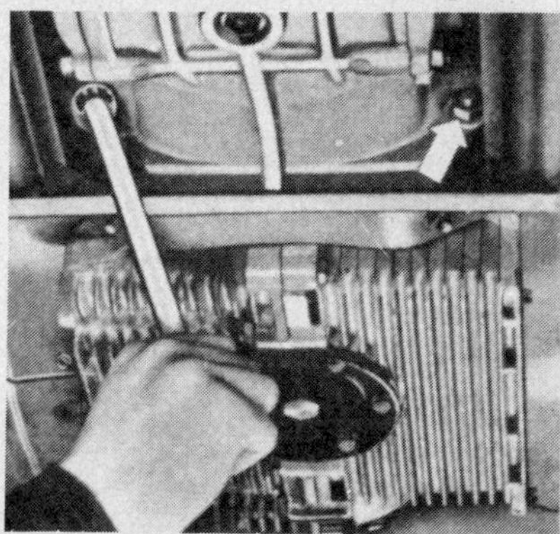

Removing lower engine mounting bolts

12. On Type 1 Automatic Stick Shift models, disconnect the control valve cable and the manifold vacuum hoses. Disconnect the ATF suction line and plug it. On Type 3 fully automatic transmission models, disconnect the vacuum hose and the kickdown cable.
13. On all Automatic Stick Shift and fully automatic models, remove the four bolts from the converter drive plate through the holes in the transmission case. After the engine is removed, hold the torque converter on the transmission input shaft by using a strap bolted to the bellhousing.
14. Raise the jack until it just contacts the engine and have an assistant hold the two upper mounting bolts so that the nuts can be removed from the bottom.
15. When the engine mounts are disconnected and there are no remaining cables or wires left to be disconnected, move the engine toward the back of the car so that the clutch or converter plate disengages from the transmission.
16. Lower the engine out of the car.
17. Installation is the reverse of the above. When the engine is lifted into position, it should be rotated using the generator pulley so that the clutch plate hub will engage the transmission shaft splines. Tighten the upper mounting bolts first. Check the clutch, pressure plate, throwout bearing, and pilot bearing for wear.

On Type 3, synthetic washers are used to raise the engine about 3 mm when the rear engine mounting is attached and tightened. Use only enough washers in the rear mount so that the engine is lifted no more than 3 mm. Care should be used when installing the rear intake housing bellows of the Type 3 engine.

Type 4

1. Disconnect the battery.
2. Remove the cooling air bellows, warm air hoses, cooling air intake duct, and air cleaner. On sedans, remove the cooling air fan. On station wagons, remove the dipstick tube rubber boot and the dipstick.
3. Disconnect the fuel injection wiring.
4. Disconnect the coil wires and remove the coil and its bracket.
5. Disconnect the oil pressure switch and the alternator wiring.
6. Disconnect the vacuum hose for the intake air distributor.
7. Disconnect the accelerator cable.
8. Working through the access hole at the upper right corner of the flywheel housing, remove the three screws which secure the torque converter to the drive plate. Remove the ATF oil dipstick and the rubber boot.
9. Remove the two upper engine mounting bolts.

Access hole for torque converter bolts—Type 4

Engine carrier screw location upon installation of engine—Type 4

10. Jack up the car and, working beneath the car, remove the muffler shield and the heat exchanger.
11. Disconnect the starter wiring.
12. Remove the heater booster exhaust pipe.
13. Remove the two lower engine mounting nuts.
14. Jack up the engine slightly and remove the four engine carrier screws.

NOTE: *Do not loosen the mountings on the body or the engine-transmission assembly will have to be recentralized in the chassis.*

Checking that engine carrier is vertical and parallel to the fan housing—Type 4

15. Remove the engine from the car.
16. Reverse the removal procedures to install the engine. Install the engine on the lower engine mounting studs and then locate the engine in the engine carrier. When installing the engine in the carrier, lift the engine up so that the four screws are at the top of the elongated holes and tighten them in this position. If it is necessary to raise or lower the engine for adjustment purposes, use the threaded shaft. After the engine is installed, make sure that the rubber buffer is centered in the rear axle carrier. Make sure that the engine carrier is vertical and parallel to the engine fan housing. Readjust it if necessary by moving the brackets on the side members.

Cylinder Head

Removal and Installation

In order to remove the cylinder head from either pair of cylinders, it is necessary to lower the engine.

1. Remove the valve cover and gasket. Remove the rocker arm assembly. Unbolt the intake manifold from the cylinder head. The cylinder head is held in place by eight studs. Since the cylinder head also holds the cylinders in place in the VW engine, and the cylinders are not going to be removed, it will be necessary to hold the cylinders in place after the head is removed.
2. After the rocker arm cover, rocker arm retaining nuts, and rocker arm assembly have been removed, the cylinder head nuts can be removed and the cylinder head lifted off.
3. When reinstalling the cylinder head, the head should be checked for cracks both in the combustion chamber and in the intake and exhaust ports. Cracked heads must be replaced.
4. Spark plug threads should be checked. New seals should be used on the pushrod tube ends and they should be checked for proper seating.
5. The pushrod tubes should be turned so that the seam faces upward. In order to ensure perfect sealing, used tubes should be stretched slightly before they are reinstalled.
6. Install the cylinder head. Using new rocker shaft stud seals, install the pushrods and rocker shaft assembly.

NOTE: *Pay careful attention to the orientation of the shaft as described in the "Rocker Shaft" section.*

7. Torque the cylinder head in three stages. Adjust the valve clearance. Using a new gasket, install the rocker cover. It may be necessary to readjust the valves after the engine has been run a few minutes and allowed to cool.

Valve Guides and Valve Seats

On all air-cooled VW engines, the valve guides and valve seats are shrunk-fit into the cylinder head. This usually involves freezing the seat or guide with liquid nitrogen or some other refrigerant to about 200°F below zero, and heating up the cylinder head to approximately 400°F. Due to the extreme temperatures required to shrink-fit these items, and because of the extra care needed when working with metals at these extreme temperatures, it is advised that this operation be referred to an experienced repair shop.

On types 1, 2/1600, and 3, install the rocker shaft with the chamfer out and the slot up

Cylinder Head Overhaul

See the "Engine Rebuilding" section at the end of this book.

Rocker Shafts

Rocker Shaft Removal and Installation

1. Before the valve rocker assembly can be reached, it is necessary to undo the clip that retains the valve cover and then remove the valve cover.
2. Remove the rocker arm retaining nuts, the rocker arm shaft, and the rocker arms. Remove the stud seals.

On Types 2/1700, 2/1800, and 4, install the rocker shaft with the chamfer out and the slots down

3. Before installing the rocker arm mechanism, be sure that the parts are as clean as possible.
4. Install new stud seals. On Type 1, 2/1600, and 3, install the rocker shaft assembly with the chamfered edges of the rocker shaft supports pointing outward and the slots pointing upward. On Type 4 and Type 2/1700, 2/1800 models, the chamfered edges must point outward and the slots must face downward.
5. Tighten the retaining nuts to the proper torque. Use only the copper colored nuts that were supplied with the engine.
6. Make sure that the ball ends of the push rods are centered in the sockets of the rocker arms.
7. Adjust the valve clearance. Install the valve cover using a new gasket.

Intake Manifold

Removal and Installation

Single Carburetor Engines

1. Disconnect the battery.
2. Disconnect the generator wiring.

1. Cylinder head cover
2. Gasket
3. Nut
4. Spring washer
5. Rocker shaft
6. Clip
7. Thrust washer
8. Spring washer
9. Rocker arm
10. Adjusting screw
11. Nut
12. Support
13. Stud seal
14. Nut
15. Washer

16a. Type 1, Type 2/1600 cylinder head
16b. Type 3 cylinder head
17. Thermostat link
18. Valve cotter
19. Spring cap
20. Valve spring
21. Oil deflector ring
22. Intake valve
23. Exhaust valve
24. Intake valve guide
25. Exhaust valve guide
26. Pushrod tube
27. Sealing ring
28. Pushrod

Cylinder head exploded view—Types 1/1600, 2/1600, 3/1600

3. Remove the generator. It will be necessary to loosen the fan housing and tilt it back to gain clearance to remove the generator.

4. Disconnect the choke and the accelerator cable.

5. On some models it will be necessary to remove the carburetor from the manifold.

6. Unbolt the manifold from the cylinder head and remove the manifold from the engine.

7. Reverse the above to install. Always use new gaskets.

Intake Manifold

Removal and Installation

Fuel Injection Engines

1. Remove the air cleaner.

2. Remove the pressure switch which is mounted under the right pair of intake manifold pipes. Disconnect the injector wiring.

3. Remove the fuel injectors by removing the two nuts which secure them in place. On Type 3, do not separate the pair of injectors; they can be removed as a pair and must be left in the injector plate. See Step 7 for proper injector installation.

4. After removing the intake manifold outer cover plate, remove the two screws which secure the manifold inner cover plate.

5. The manifold may be removed by removing the two nuts and washers which hold the manifold flange to the cylinder head.

6. Installation is the reverse of the above. The inner manifold cover should be installed first, but leave the cover loose until the outer cover and manifold are in place. Always use new gaskets.

7. Connect the fuel hoses to the injectors, if removed, after assembling the injectors with the injector retainer plate in place. Make sure that the sleeves are in place on the injector securing studs. Carefully slip the injectors into the manifold and install the securing nuts. Never force the injectors in or out of the manifold. Reconnect the injector wiring.

Intake Air Distributor

Removal and Installation

Fuel Injected Engines

The intake air distributor is located at the center of the engine at the junction of the intake manifold pipes.

NOTE: *It is not necessary to remove the distributor if only the manifold pipes are to be removed.*

1. Remove the air cleaner and pressure switch which are located under the right pair of manifold pipes.

2. Push the four rubber hoses onto the intake manifold pipes.

3. Remove the accelerator cable and the throttle valve switch.

4. Disconnect the accelerator cable.

5. Disconnect the vacuum hoses leading to the ignition distributor and the pressure sensor and disconnect the hose running to the auxiliary air regulator.

6. Remove those bolts under the air distributor which secure the air distributor to the crankcase and remove the air distributor.

7. Installation is the reverse of removal.

Mufflers, Tailpipes, Heat Exchangers

Removal and Installation

Muffler, Type 1 and 2

1. Working under the hood, disconnect the pre-heater hoses.

2. Remove the pre-heater pipe protection plate on each side of the engine. The plates are secured by three screws.

3. Remove the crankshaft pulley cover plate.

4. Remove the rear engine cover plate from the engine compartment. It is held in place by screws at the center, right, and left sides.

5. Remove the four intake manifold preheat pipe bolts. There are two bolts on each side of the engine.

6. Disconnect the warm air channel clamps at the left and right side of the engine.

7. Disconnect the heat exchanger clamps at the left and right side of the engine.

8. Remove the muffler from the engine.

9. Installation is the reverse of the above. Always use new gaskets to install the muffler.

Muffler, Type 3

The muffler is secured to the heat exchangers with clamps and, on some models, to the body with bolts at the top and at the ends.

Muffler, Type 4

The muffler is secured to the left and right heat exchangers by three bolts. There is a bracket at the left end of the muffler. Always use new gaskets when installing a new muffler.

Heat Exchangers, Type 1, 2, and 3

1. Disconnect the air tube at the outlet end of the exchanger.

2. Remove the clamp which secures the muffler to the exchanger.

3. Loosen the clamp which secures the exchanger to the heater hose connection at the muffler.

1. Tail pipe
2. Retaining ring
3. Seal
4. Nut
5. Clamp
6. Bolt
7. Muffler
8. Seal
9. Heater hose
10. Hose clamp
11. Rubber grommet
12. Connecting pipe
13. Gasket
14. Gasket
15. Gasket
16. Self-locking nut
17. Clamp
18. Heat exchanger
19. Bolt
20. Pin
21. Circlip
22. Link
23. Pin
24. Pin
25. Heater flap lever
26. Return spring
27. Damper pipe
28. Bolt
29. Washer
30. Lockwasher
31. Bolt
32. Damper pipe bracket
33. Bracket clamp
34. Bolt
35. Clamp
36. Tailpipe

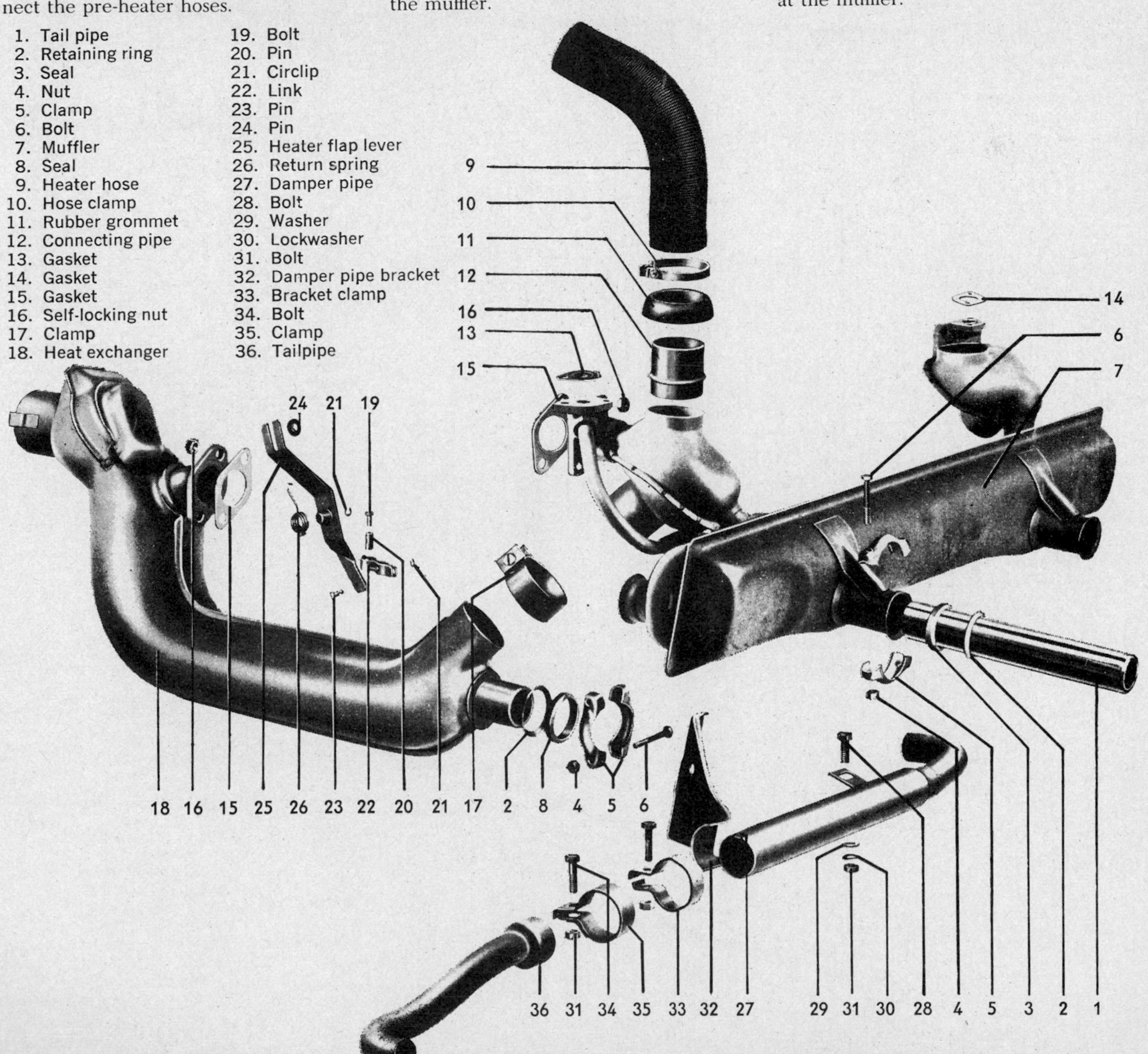

Exhaust system—Type 1, 2/1600

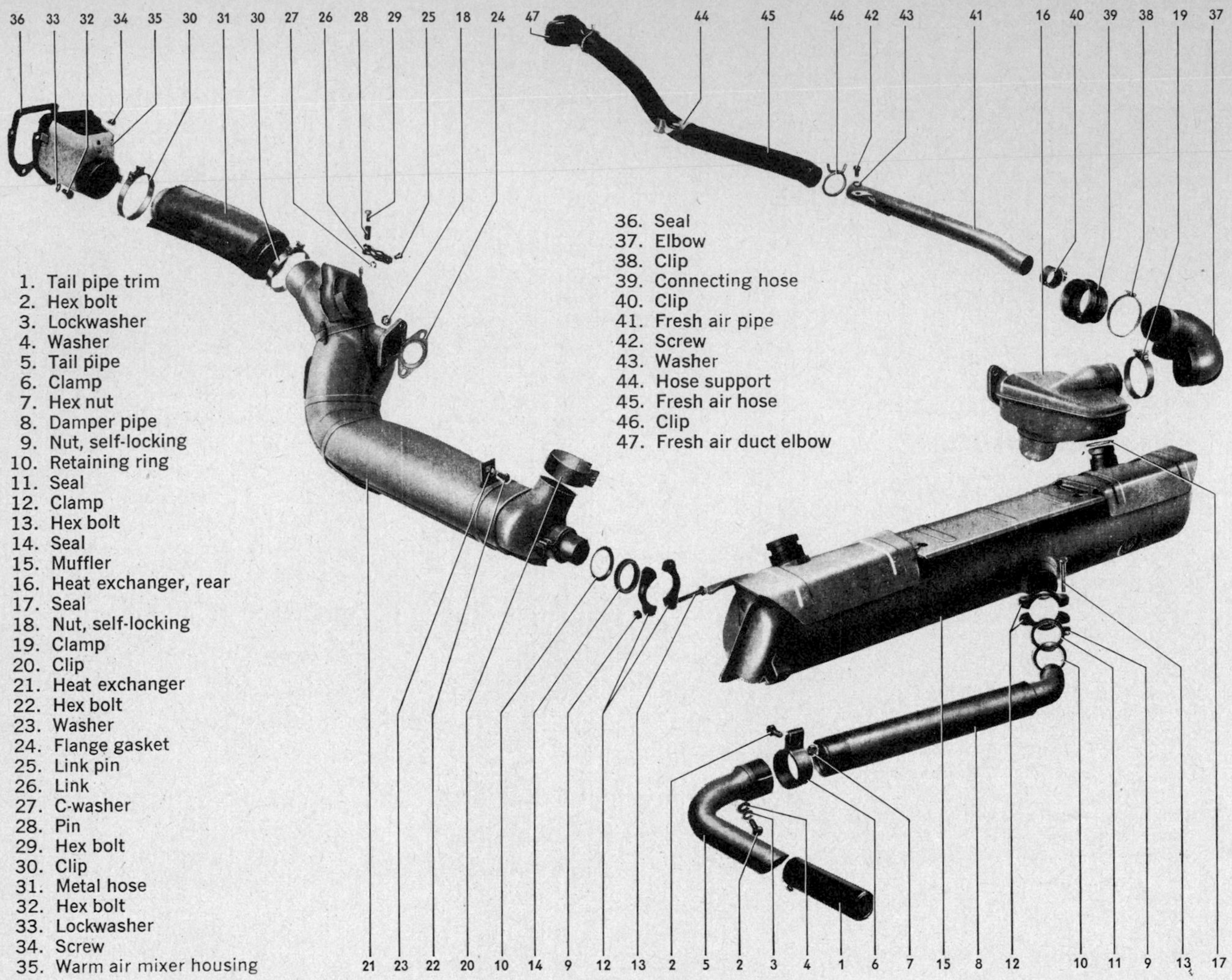

1. Tail pipe trim
2. Hex bolt
3. Lockwasher
4. Washer
5. Tail pipe
6. Clamp
7. Hex nut
8. Damper pipe
9. Nut, self-locking
10. Retaining ring
11. Seal
12. Clamp
13. Hex bolt
14. Seal
15. Muffler
16. Heat exchanger, rear
17. Seal
18. Nut, self-locking
19. Clamp
20. Clip
21. Heat exchanger
22. Hex bolt
23. Washer
24. Flange gasket
25. Link pin
26. Link
27. C-washer
28. Pin
29. Hex bolt
30. Clip
31. Metal hose
32. Hex bolt
33. Lockwasher
34. Screw
35. Warm air mixer housing
36. Seal
37. Elbow
38. Clip
39. Connecting hose
40. Clip
41. Fresh air pipe
42. Screw
43. Washer
44. Hose support
45. Fresh air hose
46. Clip
47. Fresh air duct elbow

Exhaust system—Type 3

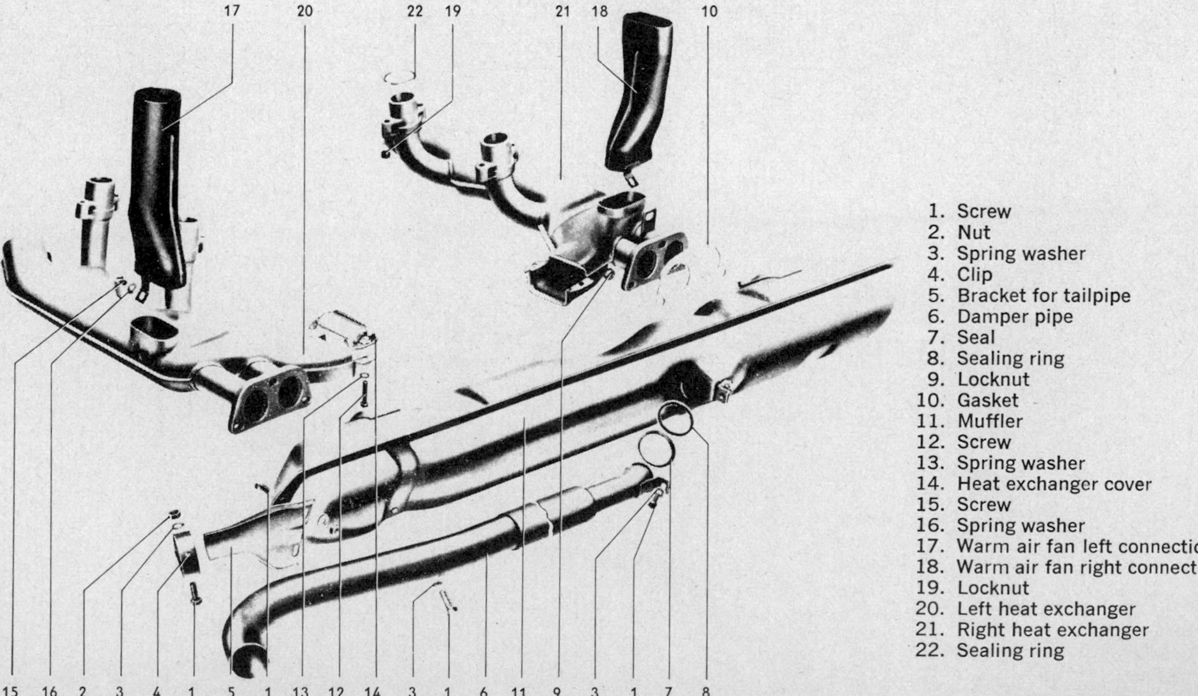

1. Screw
2. Nut
3. Spring washer
4. Clip
5. Bracket for tailpipe
6. Damper pipe
7. Seal
8. Sealing ring
9. Locknut
10. Gasket
11. Muffler
12. Screw
13. Spring washer
14. Heat exchanger cover
15. Screw
16. Spring washer
17. Warm air fan left connection
18. Warm air fan right connection
19. Locknut
20. Left heat exchanger
21. Right heat exchanger
22. Sealing ring

Exhaust system—Type 2/1700, 2/1800, and Type 4

4. Remove the two nuts which secure the exchanger to the forward end of the cylinder head.

5. Remove the heater flap control wire.

6. Reverse the above to install. Always use new gaskets.

Heat Exchangers, Type 4

1. Disconnect the air hose at the outlet of each exchanger.

2. Disconnect the warm air tube at the outside end of the exchanger.

3. Disconnect the three bolts which secure each exchanger to the muffler.

4. Remove the four nuts, two at each exhaust port, which secure the exchanger to the cylinder head.

5. Installation is the reverse of the above. Always use new gaskets.

Tailpipes, Type 1 and 2

Loosen the clamps on the tailpipes and apply penetrating oil. Work the pipe side-to-side while trying to pull the tailpipe out of the muffler.

NOTE: *It is often difficult to remove the tailpipes without damaging them.*

Tailpipe and Resonator, Type 3

Loosen the clamp at the resonator-to-muffler connection. Remove the bolt at the bend of the tail pipe and remove the resonator and tailpipe assembly. To remove the tailpipe from the resonator, loosen the clamp which secures the tailpipe to the resonator and work them apart.

Tailpipe, Type 4

Remove the bolt which secures the pipe to the muffler. Remove the bolt which secures the pipe to the body and remove the pipe.

Pistons and Cylinders

Pistons and cylinders are matched according to their size. When replacing pistons and cylinders, make sure that they are properly sized.

NOTE: *See the "Engine Rebuilding" section for cylinder refinishing.*

Cylinder Removal and Installation

1. Remove the engine. Remove the cylinder head, pushrod tubes, and the deflector plate.

2. Slide the cylinder out of its groove in the crankcase and off of the piston. Matchmark the cylinders for reassembly. The cylinders must be returned to their original bore in the crankcase. If a cylinder is to be replaced, it must be replaced with a matching piston.

3. Cylinders should be checked for wear and, if necessary, replaced with another matched cylinder and piston assembly of the same size.

Matchmarking pistons

4. Check the cylinder seating surface on the crankcase, cylinder shoulder, and gasket, for cleanliness and deep scores. When reinstalling the cylinders, a new gasket, if required, should be used between each cylinder and the crankcase.

Installing a cylinder

5. The piston, as well as the piston rings and pin must be oiled before reassembly.

6. Be sure that the ring gaps are of the correct dimension. Stagger the ring gaps around the piston, but make sure that the oil ring gap is positioned up when the pistons are in position on the connecting rods.

7. Compress the rings with a ring compressor, oil the cylinder wall, and slide the cylinder onto the piston. Make sure that the cylinder base gasket is in place.

8. Install the deflector plates.

9. Install the pushrod tubes using new gaskets. Install the pushrods. Make sure that the seam in the pushrod tube is facing upward.

10. Install the cylinder head.

Piston Removal and Installation

NOTE: *See the "Engine Rebuilding" section for piston ring procedures.*

1. Remove the engine. Remove the cylinder head and, after matchmarking the cylinders, remove the cylinders.

2. Matchmark the pistons to indicate the cylinder number and which side points toward the clutch.

3. Remove the circlips which retain the piston pin.

4. Heat the piston to 176 F. To heat the piston, boil a clean rag in water and wrap it around the piston. Remove the piston pin after the piston has been heated.

5. Remove the piston from the connecting rod.

6. Before installing the pistons, they should first be cleaned and checked for wear. Remove the old rings. Clean the ring grooves using a groove cleaner or a broken piece of ring. Clean the piston with solvent but do not use a wire brush or sand paper. Check for any cracks or scuff marks. Check the piston diameter with a micrometer and compare the readings to the specifications. If the running clearance between the piston and cylinder wall is 0.008 in (0.2 mm) or greater, the cylinder and piston should be replaced by a set of the same size grading. If the cylinder shows no sign of excessive wear or damage, it is permissible to install a new piston and rings of the appropriate size.

7. Place each ring in turn in its cylinder bore and check the piston ring end-gap. If the gap is too large, replace the ring. If the gap is too narrow, file the end of the ring until the proper gap is obtained.

Checking piston ring end-gap

8. Insert the rings on the piston and check the ring side clearance. If the clearance is too large, replace the piston. Install the rings with the marking "Oben" or "Top" pointing upward.

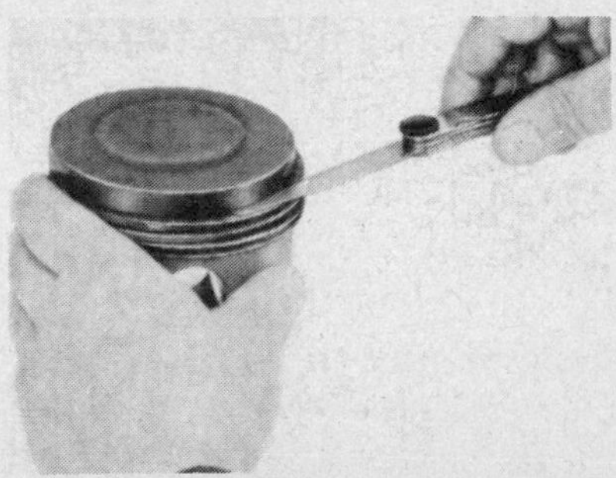

Checking piston ring side clearance

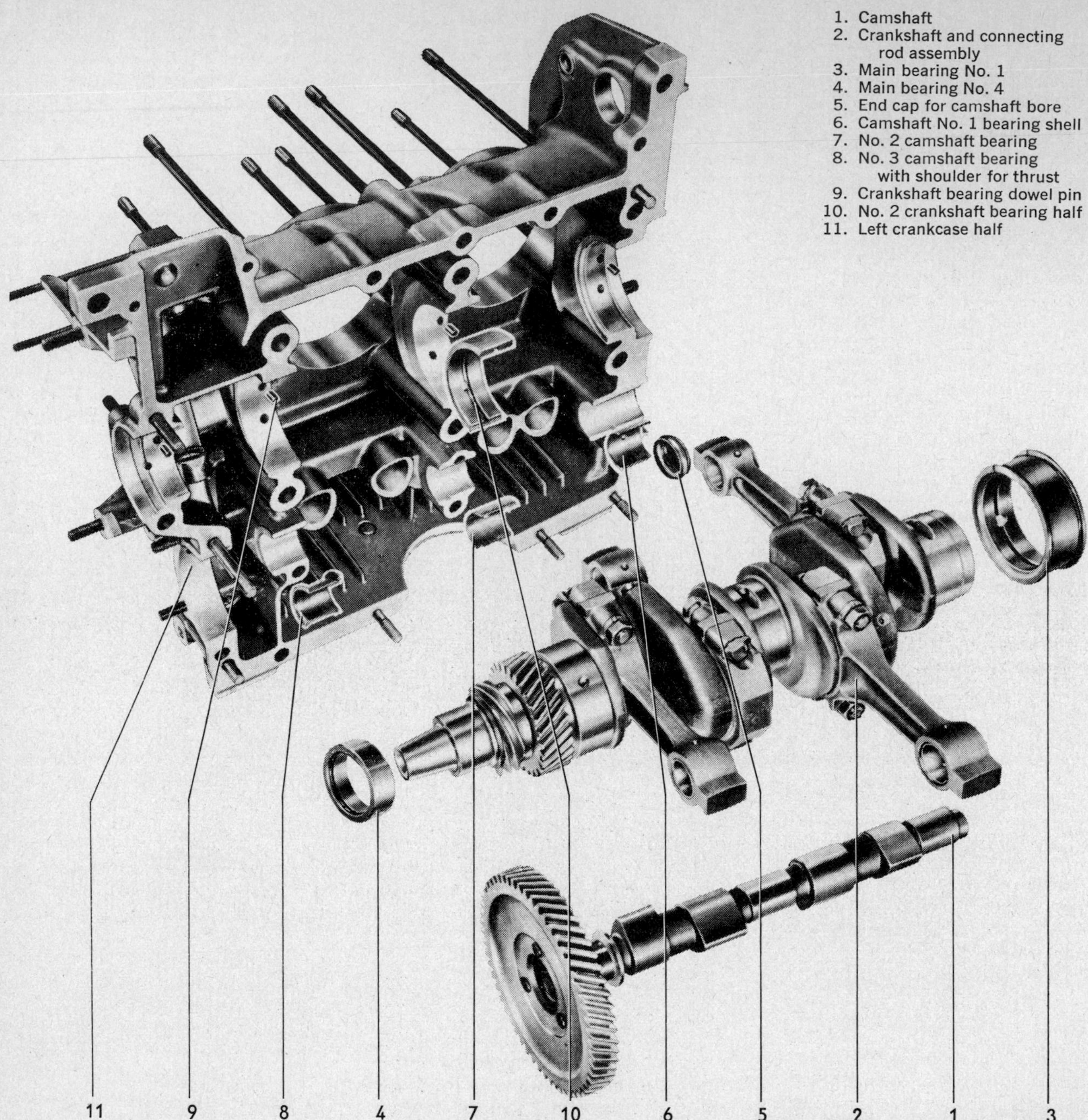

Crankcase half assembly—Type 2/1700, 2/1800, and Type 4

9. If new rings are installed in a used piston, the ring ridge at the top of the cylinder bore must be removed with a ridge reamer.

10. Install the piston and piston pin on the connecting rod from which it originally came. Make sure that the piston is facing the proper direction.

11. Install the cylinders and the cylinder heads.

Crankcase

Disassembly and Assembly

1. Remove the engine.

2. Remove the cylinder heads, cylinders, and pistons.

3. Remove the oil strainer, oil pressure switch, and the crankcase nuts. Remove the flywheel and oil pump. The flywheel is held in place by the bolt, (Type 4 has five bolts), at the center of the flywheel. Matchmark the flywheel so that it can be replaced in the same position.

4. Keep the cam followers in the right crankcase half in position by using a retaining spring.

5. Use a rubber hammer to break the seal between the crankcase halves.

CAUTION: *Never insert sharp metal tools, wedges, or any prying device between the crankcase halves. This will ruin the gasket surface and cause serious oil leakage.*

6. After the seal between the crankcase halves is broken, remove the right hand crankcase half, the crankshaft oil seal and the camshaft end plug. The camshaft and crankshaft can now be lifted out of the crankcase half.

7. Remove the cam followers, bearing shells, and the oil pressure relief valve.

8. Before starting reassembly, check the crankcase for any damage or cracks.

9. Flush and blow out all ducts and oil passages. Check the studs for tightness. If the tapped holes are worn install a Heli-Coil.

10. Install the crankshaft bearing dowel pins and bearing shells for the crankshaft and camshaft. Make sure that

Check dowel pins for tightness

the bearing shells with thrust flanges are installed in the proper journal.

11. Install the crankshaft and camshaft after the bearings have been well lubricated. When installing the camshaft and crankshaft, make sure that the timing marks on the timing gears are aligned.

12. Install the oil pressure relief valve.

13. Oil and install the cam followers.

14. Install the camshaft end plug using sealing compound.

15. Install the thrust washers and crankshaft oil seal. The oil seal must rest squarely on the bottom of its recess in the crankcase. The thrust washers at the flywheel end of the crankshaft are shims used to set the crankshaft end-play.

16. Spread a thin film of sealing compound on the crankcase joining faces and place the two halves together. Torque the nuts in several stages. Tighten the 8 mm nut located next to the 12 mm stud of the No. 1 crankshaft bearing first. As the crankcase halves are being torqued, continually check the crankshaft for ease of rotation.

Tighten the 8mm nut located next to the 12mm stud of the no. 1 crankcase bearing first on Type 1, 2/1600, and 3 models

17. Crankshaft end-play is checked when the flywheel is installed. It is adjusted by varying the number and thickness of the shims located behind the flywheel. Measure the end-play with a dial indicator mounted against the flywheel, and attached firmly to the crankcase.

Camshaft and Timing Gears

Removal and Installation

1. Removal of the camshaft requires splitting the crankcases. See "Crankcase Disassembly". The camshaft and its bearing shells are then removed from the crankcase halves.

2. Before reinstalling the camshaft, it should be checked for wear on the lobe surfaces and on the bearing surfaces. In addition, the riveted joint between the camshaft timing gear and the camshaft should be checked for tightness.

3. The camshaft should be checked for a maximum run-out of 0.0008 in.

4. The timing gear should be checked for the correct tooth contact and for wear.

5. If the camshaft bearing shells are worn or damaged, new shells should be fitted. The camshaft bearing shells should be installed with the tabs engaging the notches in the crankcase. It is usually a good idea to replace the bearing shells under any circumstances. Before installing the camshaft, the bearing journals and cam lobes should be generously coated with oil.

6. When the camshaft is installed, care should be taken to ensure that the timing gear tooth marked (0) is located between the two teeth of the crankshaft timing gear marked with a center punch.

7. The camshaft end-play is measured at the No. 3 bearing. End-play is 0.0015–0.005 in. (0.04–0.12 mm) and the wear limit is 0.006 in. (0.16 mm).

Aligning valve timing marks on gears

Crankshaft

Crankshaft Pulley Removal and Installation

On the Type 1 and 2/1600, the crankshaft pulley can be removed while the engine is still in the car. However, in this instance it is necessary for the rear cover plate of the engine to be removed. Remove the cover plate after taking out the screws in the cover plate below the crankshaft pulley. Remove the fan belt and the crankshaft pulley securing screw. Using a puller, remove the crankshaft pulley. The crankshaft pulley should be checked for proper seating and belt contact. The oil return thread should be cleaned and lubricated with oil. The crankshaft pulley should be installed in the reverse sequence. Check for oil leaks after installing the pulley.

On the Type 3, the crankshaft pulley can be removed only when the engine is out of the car and the muffler, generator, and cooling air intake housing are removed. After these parts have been removed, take out the plastic cap in the pulley. Remove the crankshaft pulley retaining bolt and remove the pulley.

Type 4 and Type 2/1700 removal is the same as the Type 3. However, the pulley is secured by three socket head screws and a self locking nut.

Types 2/1700, 2/1800, and Type 4 engine fan bolts

Installation for Type 2/1700, 2/1800, 3 and 4 engines is the reverse of removal. When installing, use a new paper gasket between the fan and the crankshaft pulley. If shims are used, do not forget them. Don't use more than two shims. When inserting the pulley, make sure that the pin engages the hole in the fan. Ensure that the clearance between the generator belt and the intake housing is at least 4 mm and that the belt is parallel to the housing.

Flywheel Removal and Installation

Types 1, 2/1600, and 3

1. The flywheel is attached to the crankshaft with a gland nut and is located by four dowel pins. An oil seal is recessed in the crankcase casting at No. 1 main bearing. A needle bearing, which supports the main driveshaft, is located in the gland nut. Prior to removing the flywheel, it is necessary to remove the clutch pressure plate and the clutch disc.

2. Loosen the gland nut and remove it, using a 36 mm wrench.

3. Before removing the flywheel, matchmark the flywheel and the crankshaft.

4. Installation is the reverse of removal. Before installing the flywheel,

check the flywheel teeth for any wear or damage. Check the dowel pins for correct fit in the crankshaft and in the flywheel.

5. Adjust the crankshaft end-play and check the needle bearing in the gland nut for wear.

Type 2/1700, 2/1800 and 4

Removal and installation is similar to the Type 1, 2/1600, and 3 except that the flywheel is secured to the crankshaft by five socket head screws.

Crankshaft Oil Seal (Flywheel End)

Replacement

This seal is removed after removing the flywheel. After the flywheel is removed, inspect the surface on the flywheel joining flange where the seal makes contact. If there is a deep groove or any other damage, the flywheel must be replaced. Remove the oil seal by prying it out of its bore. Before installing a new seal, clean the crankcase oil seal recess and coat it thinly with a sealing compound. Be sure that the seal rests squarely on the bottom of its recess. Make sure that the correct side of the seal is facing outward, that is, the lip of the seal should be facing the inside of the crankcase. Reinstall the flywheel after coating the oil seal contact surface with oil.

NOTE: *Be careful not to damage the seal when sliding the flywheel into place.*

Crankshaft Removal and Installation

NOTE: *See the "Engine Rebuilding" section for crankshaft refinishing procedures.*

1. Removal of the crankshaft requires splitting the crankcase. See "Crankcase Disassembly".

2. After the crankcase is opened, the crankshaft can then be lifted out.

3. The crankshaft bearings are held in place by dowel pins. These pins must be checked for tightness.

4. When installing the bearings, make sure that the oil holes in the shells are properly aligned. Be sure that the bearing shells are seated properly on their dowel pins. Bearing shells are available in three undersizes. Measure the crankshaft bearing journals to determine the proper bearing size. Place one half of the No. 2 crankshaft bearing in the crankcase. Slide the No. 1 bearing on the crankshaft so that the dowel pin hole is toward the flywheel and the oil groove faces toward the fan. The No. 3 bearing is installed with the dowel pin hole facing toward the crankshaft web.

5. To remove the No. 3 main bearing, remove the distributor gear circlip and the distributor drive gear. Mild heat (176° F) must be applied to remove the gear. Next slide the spacer off of the crankshaft.

6. The crankshaft timing gear should now be pressed off the crankshaft after mild heating.

7. When the timing gear is reinstalled, the chamfer must face towards the No. 3 bearing. The No. 3 bearing can then be replaced. When removing and installing the gears on the crankshaft, be careful not to damage the No. 4 bearing journal.

8. When all of the crankshaft bearings are in place, lift the crankshaft and the connecting rod assembly into the crankcase and align the valve timing marks.

9. Install the crankcase half and reassemble the engine.

Connecting Rods

Removal and Installation

NOTE: *See the "Engine Rebuilding" section for additional information.*

1. After splitting the crankcase (See "Crankcase Disassembly"), remove the crankshaft and the connecting rod assembly.

2. Remove the connecting rods, clamping bolts, and the connecting rod caps.

3. Inspect the piston pin bushing. With a new bushing, the correct clearance is indicated by a light finger push fit of the pin at room temperature.

4. Reinsert the new connecting rod bearings after all parts have been thoroughly cleaned.

5. Assemble the connecting rods on the crankshaft, making sure that the rods are oriented properly on the crankshaft. The identification numbers stamped on the connecting rods and connecting rod caps must be on the same side. Note that the marks on the connecting rods are pointing upward, while the rods are pointing toward their respective cylinders. Lubricate the bearing shells before installing them.

6. Tighten the connecting rod bolts to the specified torque. A slight pre-tension between the bearing halves, which is likely to occur when tightening the connecting rod bolts, can be eliminated by gently striking the side of the bearing cap with a hammer.

7. Do not install the connecting rod in the engine unless it swings freely on its journal.

8. Using a peening chisel, secure the connecting rod bolts in place.

9. Failure to swing freely on the journal may be caused by improper side clearance, improper bearing clearance, or failure to lubricate the rod before assembly.

Forge marks on connecting rods must face up

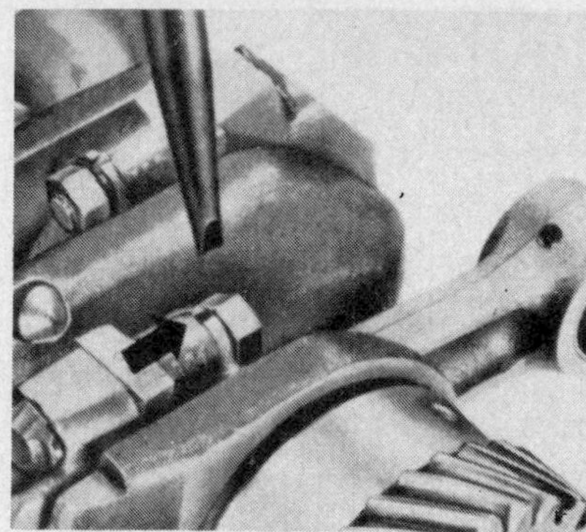

Staking the connecting rod bolt

Tapping the connecting rod cap to relieve pre-tension

Measuring the connecting rod side clearance

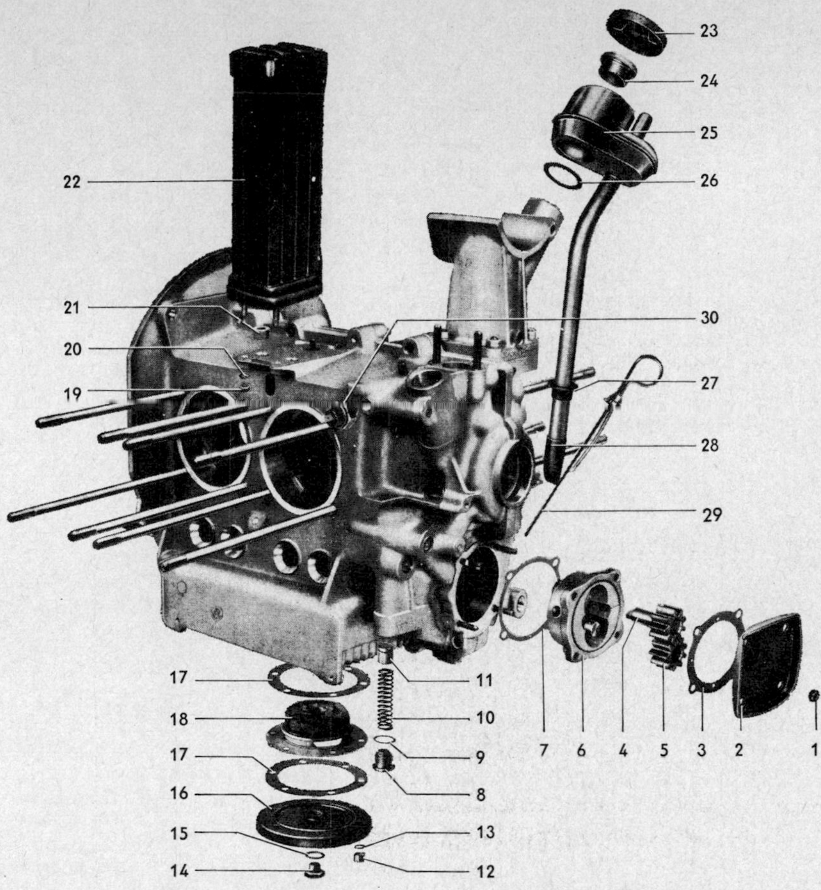

Lubricating System—Types 1, 2/1600

1. Sealing nut
2. Oil pump cover
3. Pump cover gasket
4. Driveshaft
5. Oil pump gear
6. Oil pump housing
7. Housing gasket
8. Plug
9. Seal
10. Spring
11. Relief valve piston
12. Cap nut
13. Seal
14. Oil drain plug
15. Seal
16. Oil strainer cover
17. Gasket
18. Oil strainer
19. Nut
20. Lockwasher
21. Oil cooler seal
22. Oil cooler
23. Oil filler neck cap
24. Breather gland nut
25. Oil filler and breather assembly
26. Seal
27. Grommet
28. Breather rubber valve
29. Dipstick
30. Oil pressure switch

LUBRICATION

Oil Strainer

Removal and Installation

The oil strainer can be easily removed by removing the retaining nuts, washers, oil strainer plate, strainer, and gaskets. The Type 2/1700, 2/1800 and Type 4 strainer is secured by a single bolt at the center of the strainer. Once taken out, the strainer must be thoroughly cleaned and all traces of oil gaskets removed prior to installing new ones. The suction pipe should be checked for tightness and proper position. When the strainer is installed, be sure that the suction pipe is correctly seated in the strainer. If necessary, the strainer may be bent slightly. The measurement from the strainer flange to the tip of the suction pipe should be 10 mm. The measurement from the flange to the bottom of the strainer should be 6 mm. The cap nuts on Types 1, 2/1600, and 3 must not be overtighened. The Type 4 and Type 2/1700, 2/1800 have a spin-off replaceable oil filter as well as the strainer in the crankcase. The oil filter is located at the left rear corner of the engine.

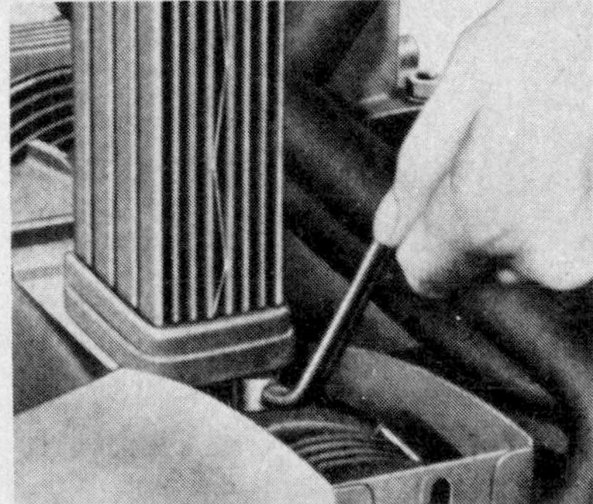

Removing oil cooler mounting

Oil Cooler

Removal and Installation

The Type 1 and 2/1600 oil cooler is located under the engine cooling fan housing at the left side of the engine. The Type 3 cooler is located at the same position but is mounted horizontally. The Type 4 and Type 2/1700, 2/1800 coolers are mounted near the oil filter, at the left corner of the engine.

The oil cooler may be removed without taking the engine out of the car. On Types 1 and 2/1600, the engine fan housing must be removed. On the Type 3, the cooler is accessible through the left-hand cylinder cover plate. The Type 4 and Type 2/1700, 2/1800 cooler is accessible through the left side engine cowling, working either in the engine compartment or from underneath the car.

The oil cooler can be removed after the three retaining nuts have been taken off. The gaskets should be removed along with the cooler and replaced with new gaskets. If the cooler is leaking, check the oil pressure relief valve. The studs and bracket on the cooler should be checked for tightness. Make certain that the hollow ribs of the cooler do not touch one another. The cooler must not be clogged with dirt. Clean the contact surfaces on the crankcase, install new gaskets, and attach the oil cooler. Types 3, 4 and 2/1700, 2/1800 have a spacer ring between the crankcase and the cooler at each securing screw. If these rings are omitted, the seals may be squeezed too tightly, resulting in oil stoppage and resultant engine damage.

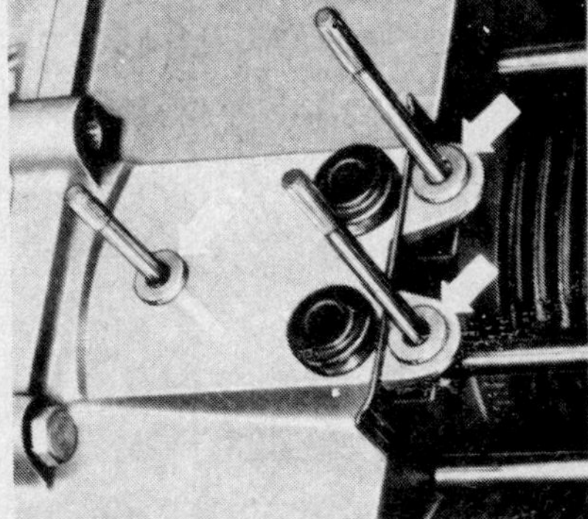

Oil cooler spacers on suitcase engines

Oil Pump

Removal and Installation

1. On Types 1 and 2/1600, the pump can be removed while the engine is in the car, but it is first necessary to remove the cover plate, the crankshaft pulley, and the cover plate under the pulley.

2. On Types 3, 4 and 2/1700, 2/1800 the oil pump can be taken out only after

1. Sealing nut
2. Oil pump cover
3. Cover gasket
4. Drive shaft
5. Oil pump gear
6. Oil pump housing
7. Housing gasket
8. Plug
9. Seal
10. Spring
11. Relief valve piston
12. Cap nut
13. Seal
14. Oil drain plug
15. Seal
16. Oil strainer cover
17. Gasket
18. Oil strainer
19. Bolt
20. Plate under oil cooler
21. Spacer
22. Oil cooler seal
23. Oil cooler
24. Washer
25. Lockwasher
26. Nut
27. Seal
28. Oil pressure switch connection
29. Gland nut for connection
30. Oil pressure switch
31. Plastic plug
32. Spring
33. Washer
34. Sleeve
35. Gland nut
36. Oil breather
37. Seal
38. Valve for cleaner
39. Nut
40. Lockwasher
41. Oil filler neck
42. Gasket
43. Dipstick
44. Boot
45. Clamp

Lubricating System—Type 3

1. Oil filter cover
2. Oil filter
3. Nut
4. Spring washer
5. Oil filter seal
6. Oil vent
7. Seal
8. Oil dipstick
9. Dipstick
10. Bellows
11. Nut
12. Spring washer
13. Oil filler
14. Gasket
15. Nut
16. Spring washer
17. Oil pump housing
18. Pump housing seal
19. Locknut
20. Spring washer
21. Oil pump cover
22. Pump cover sealing ring
23. Oil pump gear
24. Driveshaft
25. Oil pressure switch
26. Screw
27. Sealing ring
28. Spring
29. Piston for oil relief valve
30. Screw
31. Sealing ring
32. Spring
33. Piston for oil pressure control valve
34. Nut
35. Sealing ring
36. Oil strainer closing cover
37. Seal
38. Oil strainer
39. Closing screw
40. Sealing ring
41. Nut
42. Spring washer
43. Washer
44. Oil cooler
45. Oil cooler sealing ring
46. Oil filter
47. Nut
48. Spring washer
49. Oil filter intermediate flange
50. Seal

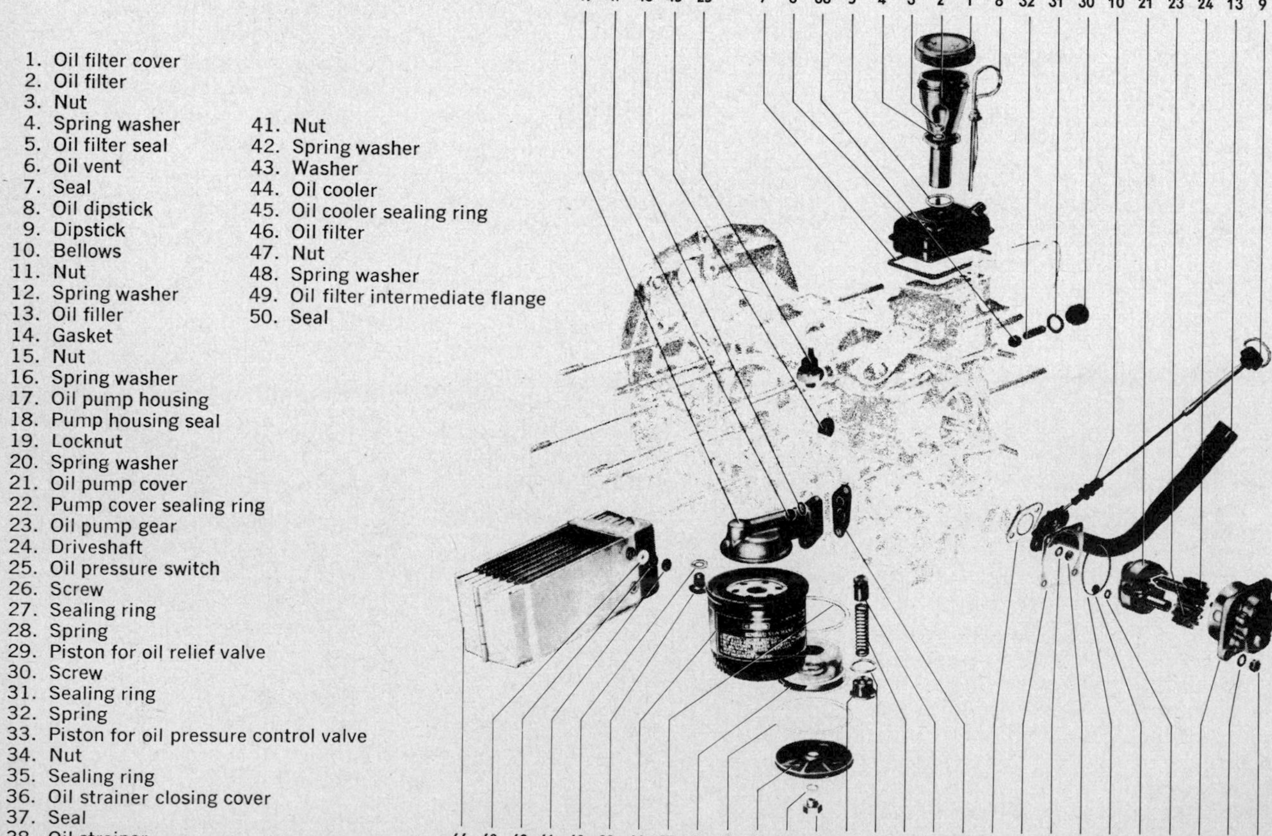

Lubricating System—Types 2/1700, 2/1800, 4

the engine is removed from the car and the air intake housing, the belt pulley fan housing, and fan are dismantled.

3. On the Automatic Stick Shift models, the torque converter oil pump is driven by the engine oil pump.

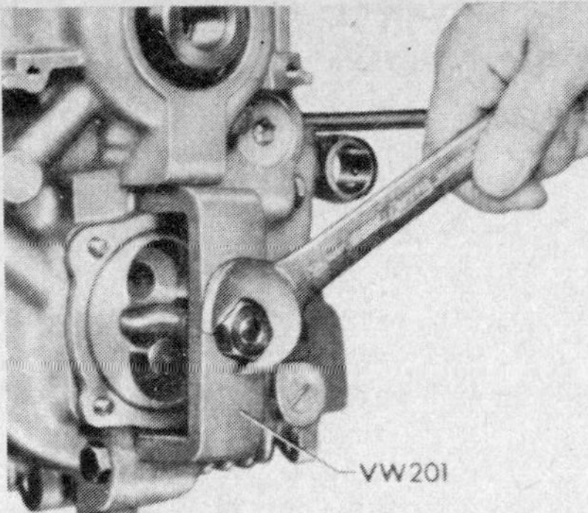

Removing oil pump housing—Types 1, 2/1600, 3

4. On Type 1, 2/1600 and 3 remove the nuts from the oil pump cover and then remove the cover and its gasket. Remove the gears and take out the pump with a special extractor that pulls the body out of the crankcase. Care should be taken so as not to damage the inside of the pump housing.

5. On Type 4 and Type 2/1700, 2/1800 engines, remove the four pump securing nuts and, prying on either side of the pump, pry the pump assembly out of the crankcase.

6. To disassemble the pump, the pump cover must be pressed apart.

Disassembling Types 2/1700, 2/1800, and type 4 oil pump

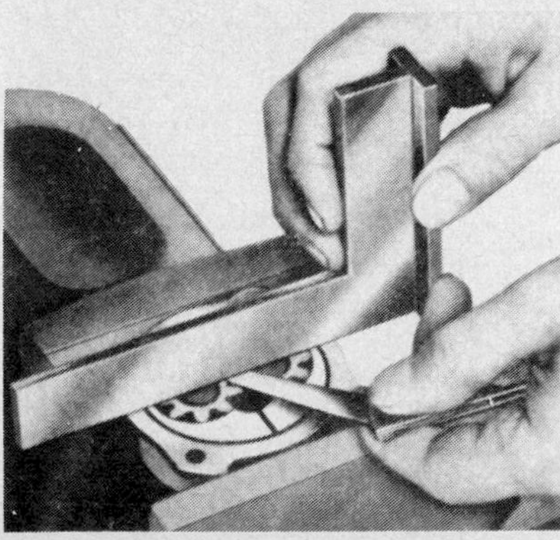

Checking oil pump end-play

7. Prior to assembly, check the oil pump body for wear, especially the gear seating surface. If the pump body is worn, the result will be loss of oil pressure. Check the driven gear shaft for tightness and, if necessary, peen it tightly into place or replace the pump housing. The gears should be checked for excessive wear, backlash, and end-play. Maximum end-play without a gasket is 1 mm (0.004 in.). The end-play can be checked using a T-square and a feeler gauge. Check the mating surfaces of the pump body and the crankcase for damage and cleanliness. Install the pump into the crankcase with a new gasket. Do not use any sealing compound.

8. Turn the camshaft several revolutions in order to center the pump body opposite the slot in the camshaft.

9. On Type 1, 2/1600, and 3 the cover may now be installed.

10. On Type 4 and Type 2/1700, 2/1800 models, the pump was installed complete.

11. Tighten the securing nuts.

Oil Pressure Relief Valve

Removal and Installation

The oil pressure relief valve is removed by unscrewing the end plug and removing the gasket ring, spring, and plunger. If the plunger sticks in its bore, it can be removed by screwing a 10 mm tap into it.

On 1600 cc engines, the valve is located to the left of the oil pump. On Automatic Stick Shift models, it is located in the oil pump housing. On 1700 and 1800 engines, the valve is located beside the oil filter.

Before installing the valve, check the plunger for any signs of seizure. If necessary, the plunger should be replaced. If there is any doubt about the condition of the spring, it should also be replaced. When installing the relief valve, be careful that you do not scratch the bore. Reinstall the plug with a new gasket.

Type 4 and Tye 2/1700, 2/1800 engines have a second oil pressure relief valve located just to the right of, and below the oil filler.

COOLING SYSTEM

Fan Housing Removal and Installation

Type 1 and 2/1600

1. Remove the two heater hoses and the generator strap.

2. Pull out the lead wire from the coil. Remove the distributor cap and take off the spark plug connectors.

3. Remove the retaining screws that are located on both sides of the fan housing. Remove the rear hood.

4. Remove the outer half of the generator pulley and remove the fan belt.

5. Remove the thermostat securing screw and take out the thermostat.

6. Remove the lower part of the carburetor pre-heater duct.

7. The fan housing can now be removed with the generator. After removal, check the fan housing for damage and for loose air deflector plates.

8. Installation is the reverse of the above.

9. Make sure that the thermostat connecting rod is inserted into its hole in the cylinder head. The fan housing should be fitted properly on the cylinder cover plates so that there is no loss of cooling air.

Fan Removal and Installation

Type 1 and 2/1600

1. Remove the generator and fan assembly as described in the "Generator Removal and Installation" section.

2. While holding the fan, unscrew the fan retaining nut and take off the fan, spacer washers, and the hub.

3. To install, place the hub on the generator shaft, making sure that the woodruff key is securely positioned.

4. Insert the spacer washers. The clearance between the fan and the fan cover is 0.06–0.07 in. Place the fan into position and tighten its retaining nut. Correct the spacing by inserting the proper number of spacer washers. Place any extra washers between the lockwasher and the fan.

5. Reinstall the generator and the fan assembly.

Fan Housing and Fan Removal and Installation

Type 3

1. Remove the crankshaft pulley, the rear fan housing half, and the fan.

2. Unhook the linkage and spring at the right-hand air control flap.

3. Remove the screws for the front half of the housing and remove the housing.

4. Install the front half and ensure the correct sealing of the cylinder cover plates.

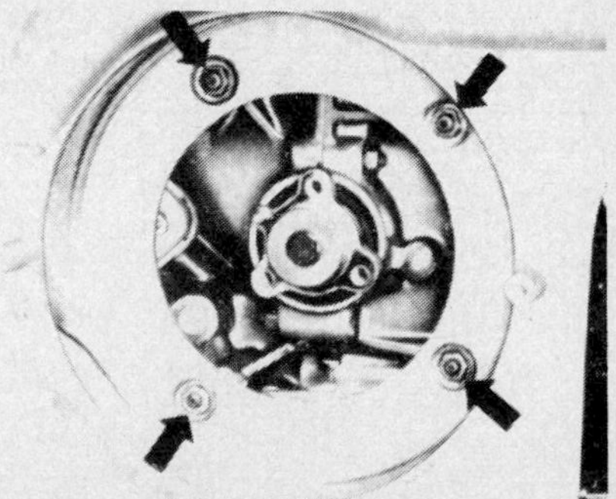

Type 3 fan housing nuts

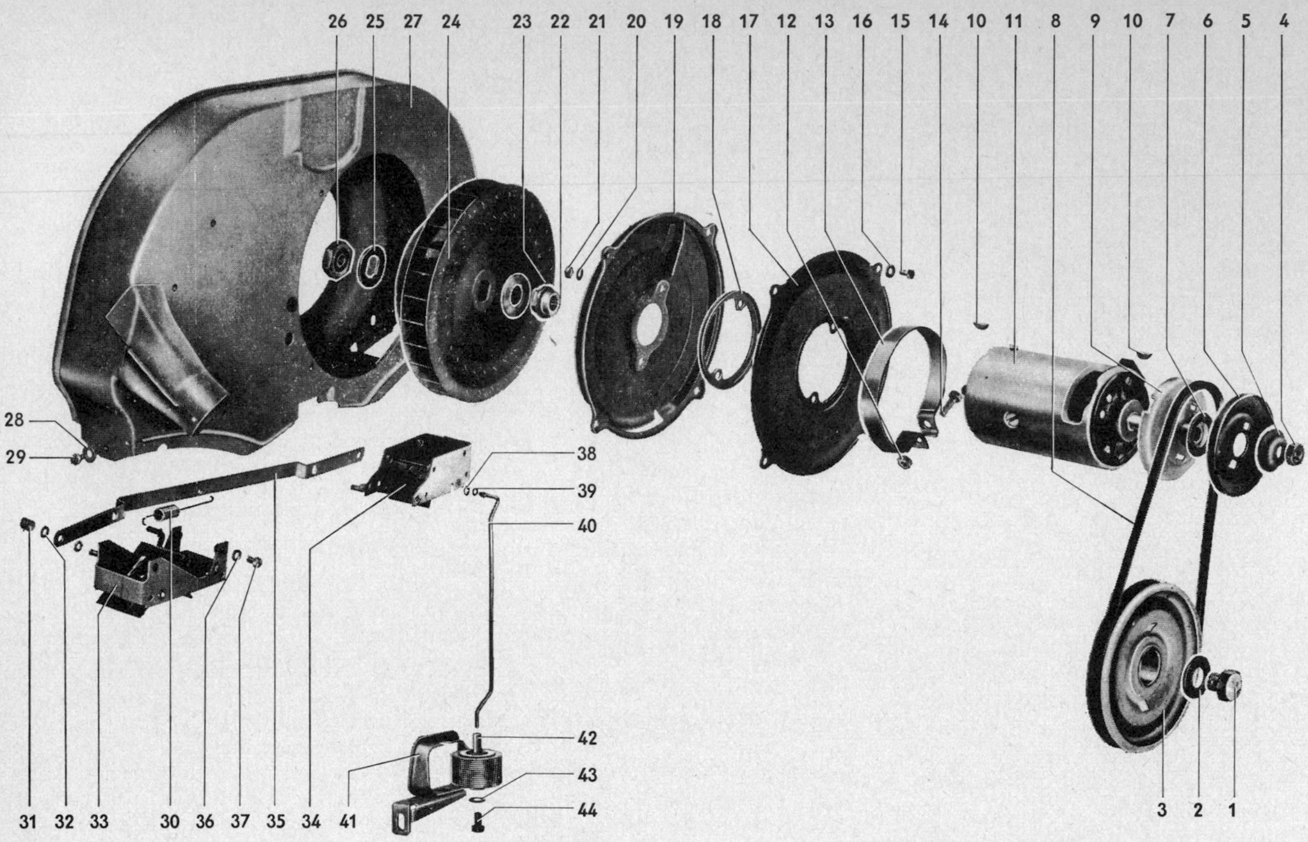

Cooling System—Types 1, 2/1600

1. Pulley bolt
2. Dished washer
3. Crankshaft pulley
4. Pulley nut
5. Special washer
6. Rear pulley half
7. Spacer washer
8. V-belt
9. Front pulley half
10. Woodruff key
11. Generator
12. Nut
13. Strap
14. Bolt
15. Bolt
16. Lockwasher
17. Outer fan cover
18. Reinforcement flange
19. Inner fan cover
20. Lockwasher
21. Nut
22. Fan hub
23. Shim
24. Fan
25. Lockwasher
26. Special nut
27. Cheese head screw
28. Washer
29. Cheese head screw
30. Return spring
31. Spring
32. Washer
33. Left cooling air regulator
34. Right cooling air regulator
35. Cooling air regulator connecting rod
36. Washer
37. Cheese head screw
38. Lockwasher
39. Washer
40. Connecting rod
41. Thermostat bracket
42. Thermostat
43. Lockwasher
44. Bolt

5. Replace and tighten the two lower mounting screws slightly.

6. Turn the two halves of the fan housing to the left until the left crankcase half is contacted by the front lug.

7. Fully tighten the two lower mounting screws.

8. Loosen the nuts at the breather support until it can be moved.

9. Insert and tighten the mounting screws of the upper fan housing half. Tighten the breather support nuts fully.

10. Connect the linkage and spring to the right-hand air control flap.

11. Install the fan and the rear half of the fan housing.

Type 4

1. Remove the engine. Remove the fan belt.

2. Remove the allen head screws and remove the belt pulley and fan as an assembly.

NOTE: *It is not necessary to remove the alternator to remove the fan housing.*

3. Remove the spacer and the alternator cover plate.

4. Disconnect the cooling air regulating cable at the shaft.

5. Remove the nuts and remove both halves of the fan housing at the same time.

6. Installation is the reverse of the above.

Air Flap and Thermostat Adjustment

Type 1 and 2

1. Loosen the thermostat bracket securing nut and disconnect the thermostat from the bracket.

2. Push the thermostat upwards to fully open the air flaps.

3. Reposition the thermostat bracket so that the thermostat contacts the bracket at the upper stop, and then tighten the bracket nut.

Engine cooling air thermostat

4. Reconnect the thermostat to the bracket.

Type 3

1. Loosen the clamp screw on the relay lever.

2. Place the air flaps in the closed posi-

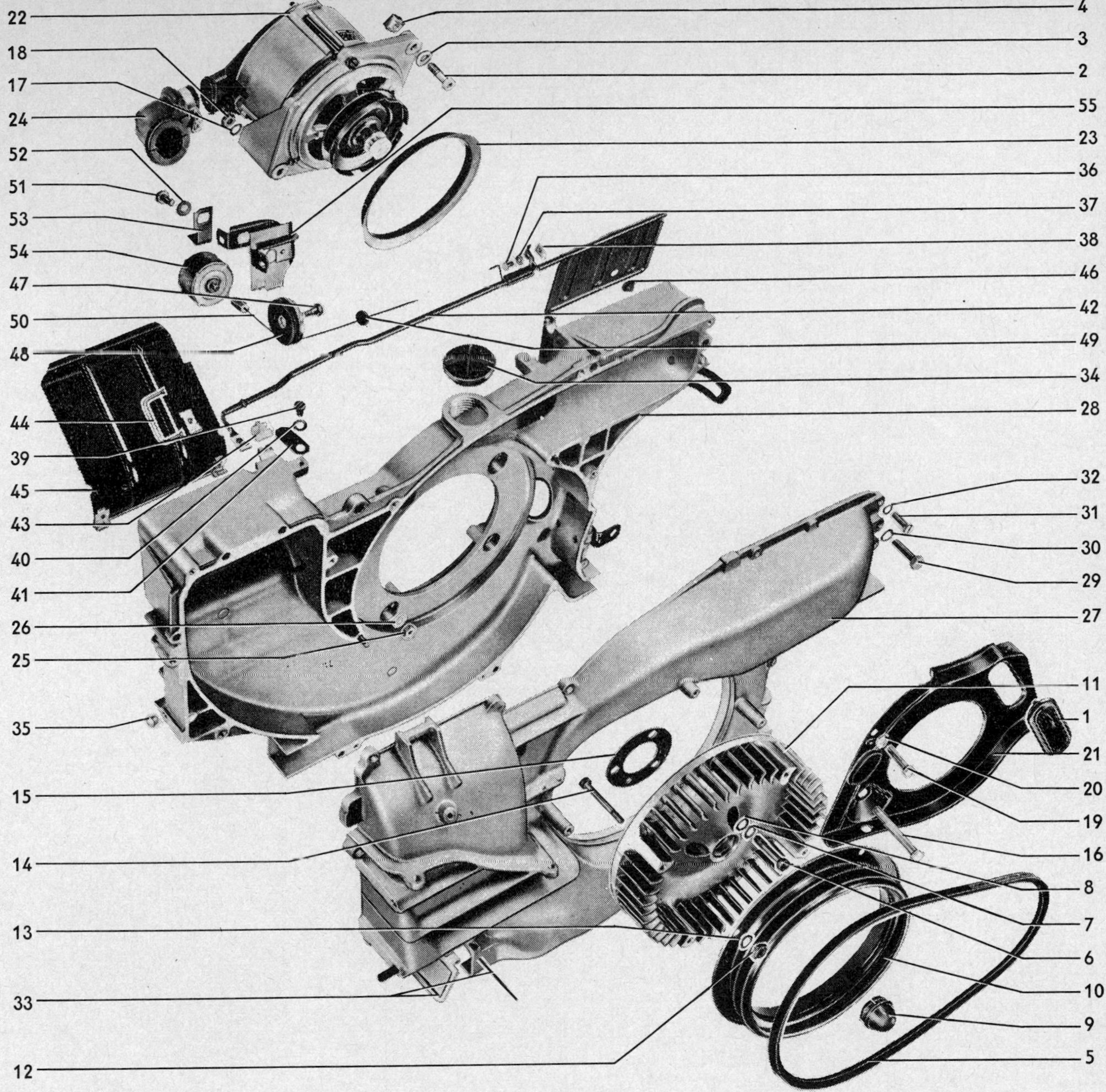

Cooling System—Types 2/1700, 2/1800, 4

1. Cover plate insert
2. Socket head capscrew
3. Spring washer
4. Nut
5. Belt
6. Socket head capscrew
7. Spring washer
8. Flat washer
9. Cap
10. Crankshaft pulley
11. Fan
12. Nut
13. Spring nut
14. Socket head capscrew
15. Spacer
16. Bolt
17. Spring washer
18. Nut
19. Screw
20. Spring washer
21. Alternator cover plate
22. Alternator
23. Alternator sealing ring
24. Alternator elbow
25. Nut
26. Spring washer
27. Fan housing—rear half
28. Fan housing—front half
29. Bolt
30. Spring washer
31. Screw
32. Spring washer
33. Air non-return flap
34. Inspection hole cover
35. Plug
36. Bolt
37. Washer
38. Nut
39. Screw
40. Spring washer
41. Shaft retaining spring
42. Right flap and shaft
43. Bearing
44. Flap link
45. Left flap
46. Plug
47. Bolt
48. Cooling air control cable roller
49. Sealing washer
50. Cooling air control cable
51. Bolt
52. Washer
53. Thermostat washer
54. Thermostat
55. Thermostat bracket

1. Hose clip
2. Bellows
3. Hose clip
4. Hex bolt
5. Lockwasher
6. Cooling air intake housing
7. Seal
8. Rubber plug
9. Cooling air intake housing cover
10. Cap
11. Bolt
12. Lockwasher
13. Crankshaft pulley
14. Dowel pin
15. Shim
16. Gasket
17. Pulley nut
18. Special washer
19. Rear pulley half
20. Spacer washer
21. Belt
22. Front pulley half
23. Hex bolt
24. Washer
25. Hex bolt
26. Lockwasher
27. Washer
28. Engine mounting tube
29. Rear fan housing half
30. Fan
31. Hex bolt
32. Washer
33. Front fan housing half
34. Nut
35. Washer
36. Center support
37. Hex bolt
38. Lockwasher
39. Washer
40. Throttle valve shaft
41. Left throttle valve
42. Right throttle valve
43. Spring
44. Lockwasher
45. Valve rod
46. Hex bolt
47. Pin
48. C-washer
49. Washer
50. Intermediate lever
51. Connecting rod
52. Thermostat
53. Washer
54. Hex bolt
55. Thermostat bracket

Cooling System—Type 3

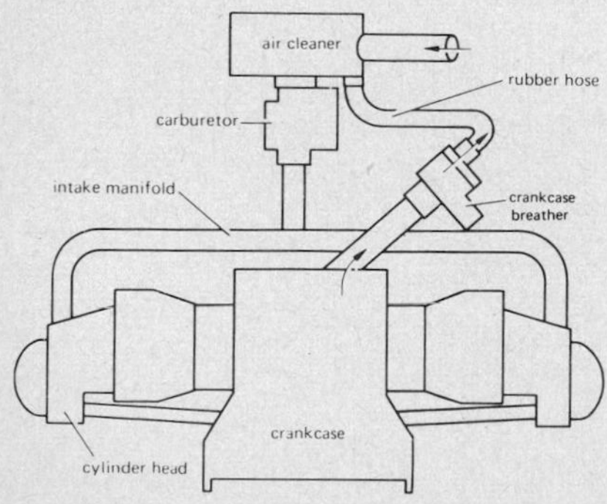

Crankcase ventilation system—Types 1, 2/1600

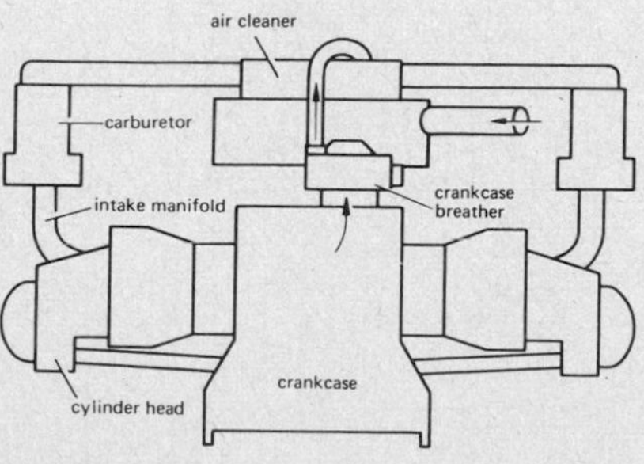

Crankcase ventilation system—Types 2/1700, 2/1800

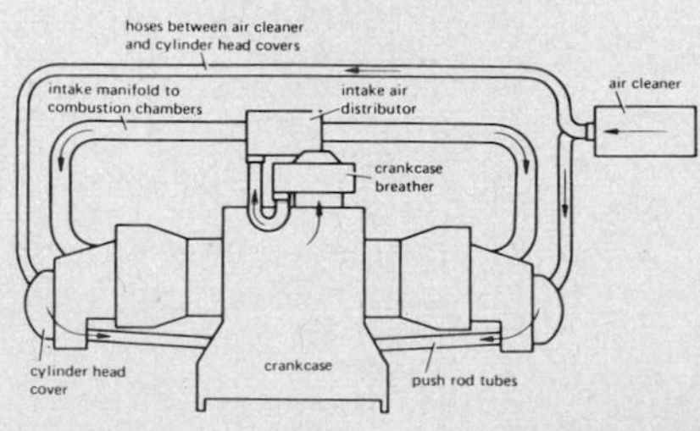

Crankcase ventilation system—Types 3, 4

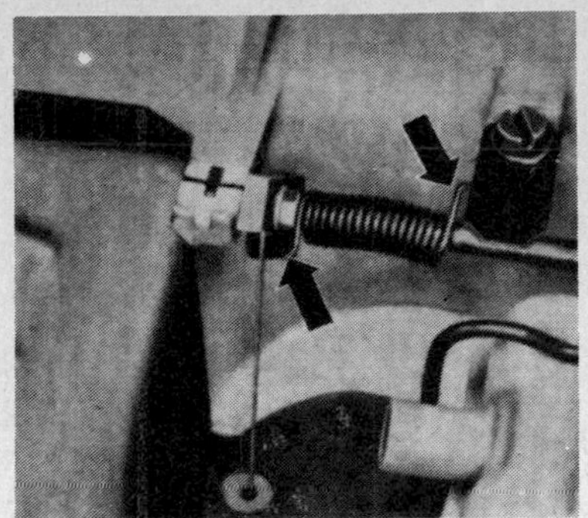

Type 4 air flap cable control

tion. Make sure that the flaps close evenly. To adjust a flap, loosen its securing screw and turn it on its shaft.

3. With the flaps closed, tighten the clamp screw on the relay lever.

Type 4

1. Loosen the cable control.
2. Push the air flaps completely closed.
3. Tighten the cable control.

EMISSION CONTROLS

Crankcase Ventilation System

All models are equipped with a crankcase ventilation system. The purpose of the crankcase ventilation system is twofold. It keeps harmful vapors from escaping into the atmosphere and prevents the buildup of crankcase pressure. Prior to the 1960s, most cars employed a vented oil filler cap and road draft tube to dispose of crankcase vapors. The crankcase ventilation systems now in use are improvement over the old method and, when functioning properly, will not reduce engine efficiency.

Type 1 and 2 crankcase vapors are recirculated from the oil breather through a rubber hose to the air cleaner. The vapors then join the air/fuel mixture and are burned in the engine. Fuel injected cars mix crankcase vapors into the air/fuel mixture to be burned in the combustion chambers. Fresh air is forced through the engine to evacuate vapors and recirculate them into the oil breather, intake air distributor, and then to be burned.

The only maintenance required on the crankcase ventilation system is a periodic check. At every tune-up, examine the hoses for clogging or deterioration. Clean or replace the hoses as required.

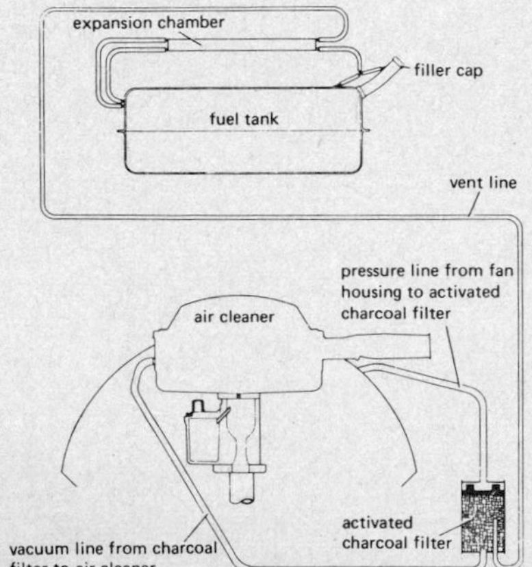

Typical Evaporative Emission Control System

Evaporative Emission Control System

Required by law since 1971, this system prevents raw fuel vapors from entering the atmosphere. The various systems for different models are similar. They consist of an expansion chamber, activated charcoal filter, and connecting lines. Fuel vapors are vented to the charcoal filter where hydrocarbons are deposited on the element. The engine fan forces fresh air into the filter when the engine is running. The air purges the filter and the hydrocarbons are forced into the air cleaner to become part of the air/fuel mixture and burned.

Maintenance of this system consists of checking the condition of the various connecting lines and the charcoal filter at 10,000 mile intervals. The charcoal filter, which is located under the engine compartment, should be replaced at 48,000 mile intervals.

Air Injection System

1973–74 Type 2 vehicles are equipped with the air injection system, or air pump as it is sometimes called. In this system, an engine driven air pump delivers fresh air to the engine exhaust ports. The additional air is used to promote afterburning of any unburned mixture as they leave the combustion chamber. In addition, the system supplies fresh air to the intake manifold during gear changes to provide more complete combustion of the air/fuel mixture.

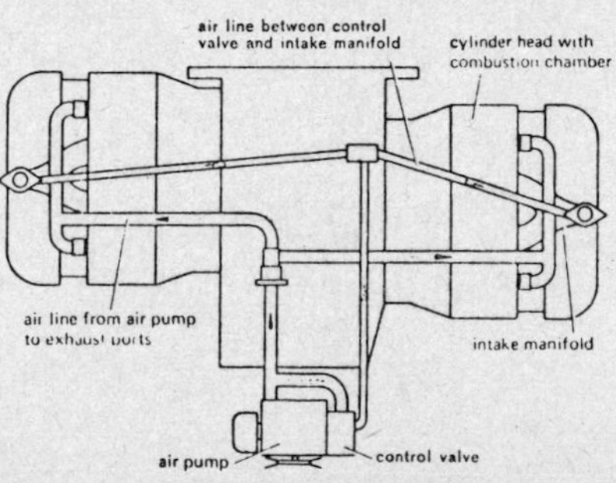

Air injection (exhaust manifold afterburning) System—1973 Type 2/1700

Check the air pump belt tension and examine the hoses for deterioration as a regular part of your tune-up procedure. The filter element in the pump should be replaced every 18,000 miles or at least every two years.

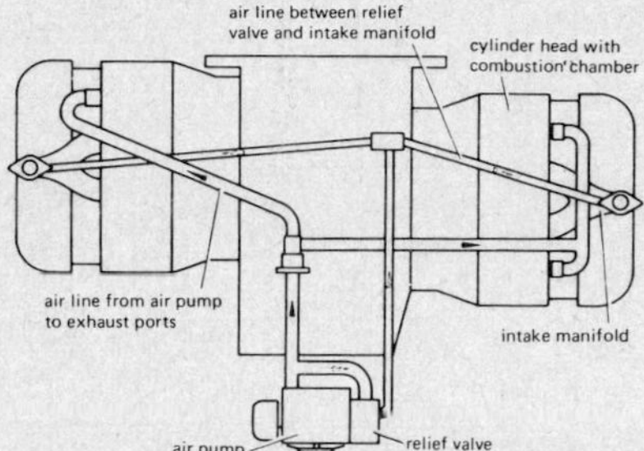

Air injection (Exhaust Manifold Afterburning) System—1974 Type 2/1800

Exhaust Gas Recirculation System

In order to control exhaust emissions of oxides of nitrogen (NO_x), an exhaust gas recirculation (EGR) system is employed on 1972 Type 1 and Type 3 models equipped with automatic transmission and sold in California, on 1973 Type 1 and Type 3 models equipped with automatic transmission sold nationwide, on all 1973–75 Type 2 models, on all 1974 Type 4 models equipped with automatic transmission, and on all 1974–75 Type 1 models. The system lowers peak flame temperature during combustion by introducing a small (about 10%) percentage of relatively inert exhaust gas into the intake charge. Since the exhaust gas contains little or no oxygen, it cannot react with nor influence the air/fuel mixture.

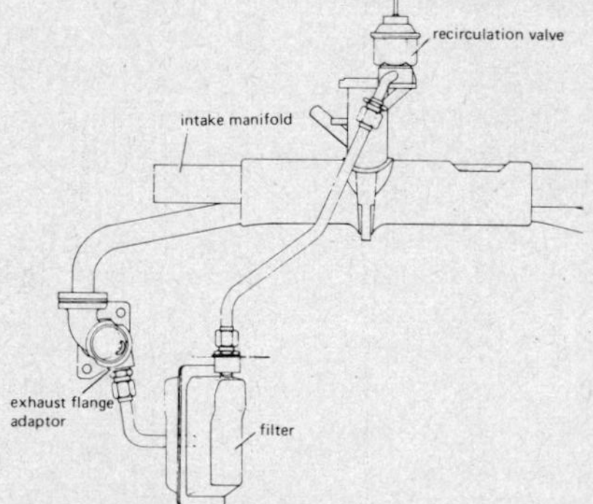

Exhaust Gas Recirculation System—1973-74 Type 1

However, the exhaust gas does (by volume) take up space in the combustion chambers (space that would otherwise be occupied by a heat-producing, explosive air/fuel mixture), and does serve to lower peak combustion chamber temperature. The amount of exhaust gas directed to the combustion chambers is infinitely variable by means of a vacuum operated EGR valve. For system specifics, see the vehicle type breakdown under "General Description".

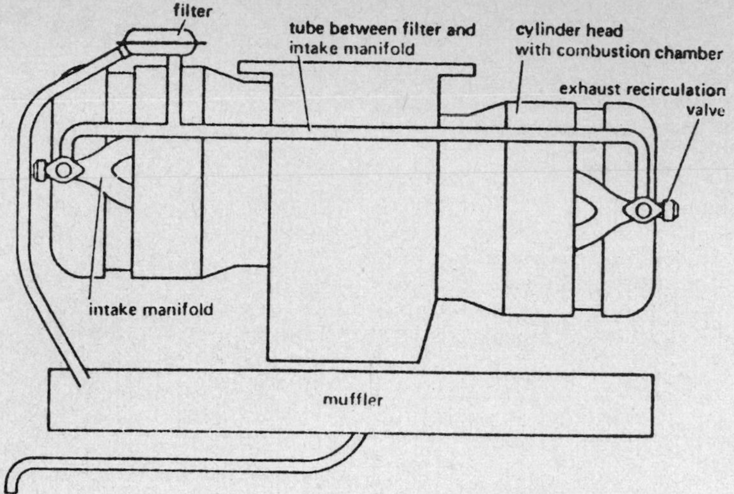

Exhaust Gas Recirculation System—1973 Type 2/1700

General Description

Type 1

For 1972, EGR is used only on automatic stick shift models sold in California. Exhaust gas is drawn from the left hand rear exhaust flange and then cooled in a cooling coil. From here, the gas is filtered in a cyclone filter and finally channelled to the intake manifold, via the EGR valve. The valve permits exhaust gas recirculation during part throttle applications, but not during idling or wide open throttle.

All 1973 models (nationwide) equipped with the automatic stick shift transmission use an EGR system. As in '72, the gas is drawn from the left rear exhaust flange. However, instead of the cooling coil and cyclone filter, a replaceable element type filter is used. The remainder of the system remains unchanged from 1972.

All 1974 Type 1 cars, regardless of equipment, are equipped with EGR. The system uses the element type filter and EGR valve which recirculates exhaust gasses during part throttle applications as before. However, to improve driveability, all California models use a two stage EGR valve (one stage in the 49 states), and California models equipped with an automatic use an electric throttle valve switch to further limit exhaust gas recirculation to part throttle applications (EGR permitted only between 12° to 72° on a scale of 90° throttle valve rotation).

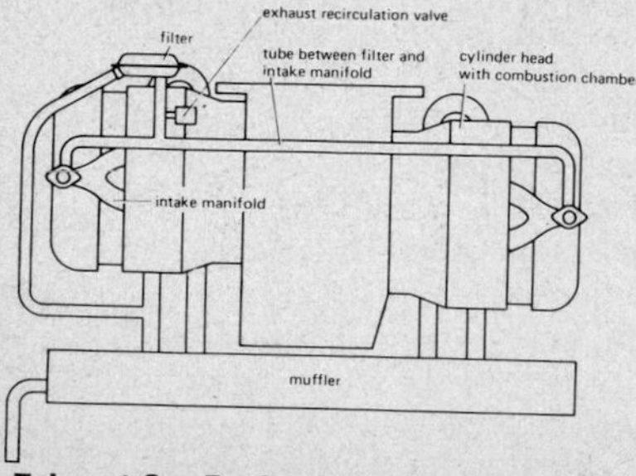

Exhaust Gas Recirculation System—1974
Type 2/1800

EGR is installed on all 1975 models. All applications use the element type filter and single stage EGR valve. Recirculation occurs during part throttle applications as before. The system is controlled by a throttle valve switch which measures throttle position, and an intake air sensor which reacts to engine vacuum. Beginning in 1975, an odometer actuated EGR reminder light (on the dashboard) is used to inform the driver that it is time to service the EGR system. The reminder light measures elapsed mileage and lights at 15,000 mile internals. A reset button is located behind the switch.

Type 2

Type 2 models use an EGR system beginning in 1973. All models use two valves; one at each manifold. Exhaust gas is taken from the muffler, cleaned in a replaceable element type filter, then directed to both intake manifolds, via the

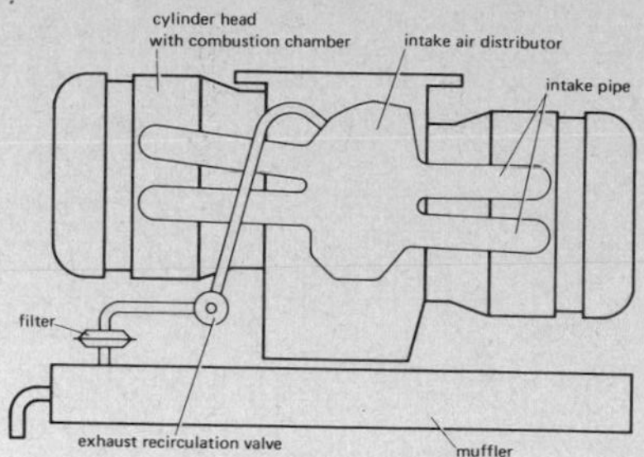

Exhaust Gas Recirculation System—1974
Type 4

EGR valves. On models equipped with manual transmission, recirculation is vacuum controlled and occurs *both* during part *and* full throttle applications. On models equipped with the automatic, recirculation is controlled both by throttle position and engine compartment (ambient) temperature. When the ambient temperature exceeds 54°F, a sensor switch (located above the battery) opens, permitting EGR during part throttle applications.

All 1974 Type 2 models use EGR, but there are three different systems used. All models use one central EGR valve. Exhaust gas is taken from #4 exhaust port, cleaned in an element type filter, and then directed to both intake manifolds via the single EGR valve. Models equipped with manual transmission and sold in the 49 states use a single stage EGR valve which allows recirculation according to the vacuum signal in the left carburetor during part throttle applications. Models equipped with manual transmission and sold in California use a two stage EGR valve which recirculates exhaust gasses during part throttle openings in two steps. During the first stage, EGR is controlled by the vacuum in the

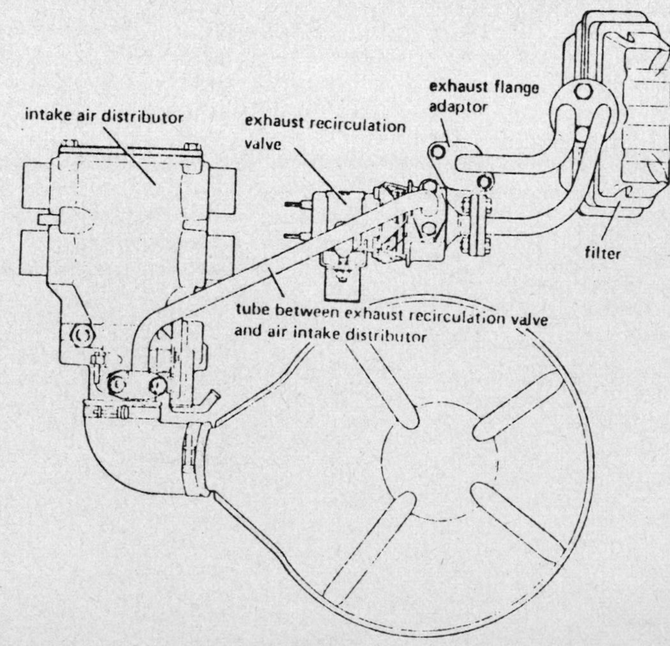

Exhaust Gas Recirculation System—1973 Type 3

left carburetor. The second stage controls EGR according to the throttle position of the right carburetor. Finally, all models equipped with automatic transmission (nationwide) use a single stage EGR valve which controls recirculation according to throttle valve position and engine cooling air temperature. When the cooling system air reaches 185° F, a sensor switch (located between the coil and distributor) opens, permitting EGR during part throttle applications.

All 1975 Type 2 models utilize an EGR system. A single stage EGR valve and element type filter are used on all applications. Recirculation occurs during part throttle openings, and is controlled by throttle position, engine vacuum, and engine compartment temperature (54° F cutoff as in 1973). At 15,000 mile intervals, a dash mounted EGR service reminder light is activated to warn the driver that EGR service is now due. A reset button is located behind the switch.

Type 3

EGR is first used in the 1972 Type 3 models destined for California and equipped with automatic transmission. Exhaust gas is drawn from the front right hand exhaust flange to the EGR valve via a container and cyclone filter. The EGR valve then delivers the exhaust gasses to the intake air distributor under the following conditions; Under part throttle (not full throttle or idling) conditions when the ambient air temperature reaches 65°F *and* only first or second gears are selected.

All 1973 Type 3 models equipped with automatic transmission use an EGR system. The exhaust gasses are cleaned in a replaceable element type filter in 1973 instead of the cyclone filter and container of the previous year. The EGR valve then delivers the gasses according to an electromagnetic valve which permits recirculation above 54°F.

Type 4

EGR appears only on 1974 models (nationwide) equipped with automatic transmission. On this system, exhaust gas is drawn from the muffler to a single EGR valve via an element type filter. The gasses are delivered to the intake air distributor under part throttle conditions.

Replace the filter and check the EGR valve every 24,000 miles.

EGR Valve Checking

Type 1 and 3

1. Remove the EGR valve.
2. Reconnect the vacuum hose and place the valve on the base.
3. Start the engine. If it doesn't stall, the vacuum line between the valve base and the intake manifold is clogged and must be cleaned.
4. Run the engine at 2000–3000 rpm. The closing pin of the EGR valve should pull in 0.15 in. (4 mm) and immediately return to its original position at idle. Replace the EGR valve if it doesn't operate correctly.
5. Install the EGR valve using new seals.

Type 2

1. Remove the EGR valve.
2. Inspect the valve for cleanliness.
3. Check the valve for freedom of movement by pressing in on the valve pin.
4. Connect the valve to the vacuum hose of another engine or vacuum source and start the engine. At 1500–2000 rpm the valve pin should be pulled in and when the speed is reduced it should return to its original position. Replace the EGR valve if it doesn't operate correctly.
5. Replace the washer and install the valve.
6. Repeat this operation on the second valve.

Throttle Regulator (Positioner)

1970–71 Type 1 and 2 vehicles equipped with manual transmission, and 1972 Type 1 models with manual transmission sold in California use a throttle regulator which holds the throttle slightly open during deceleration to prevent an excessively rich mixture. The throttle regulator consists of two parts, connected by a hose. The operating part is mounted at the carburetor. The control section is located on the left side of the engine compartment.

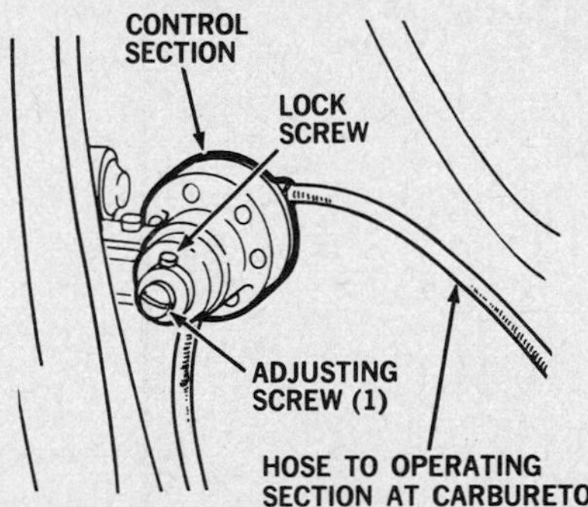

Throttle valve positioner used on 1970-71 models showing adjusting screw (1)

Adjustment

1. The engine must be at operating temperature, with the automatic choke fully open.
2. Start the engine. Turn the regulator adjusting screw clockwise until the control rod just starts to move the throttle valve lever. The stop collar on the control rod will be against the regulator body. Engine speed should be 1,700–1,800 rpm.
3. If speed is too high, shorten the control rod.
4. After adjustment, tighten the locknuts on the control rod.
5. Turn the regulator adjusting screw counterclockwise until an idle speed of 850 rpm is obtained.
6. Increase the engine speed to 3,000 rpm, then release the throttle valve lever. The engine should take 3–4 seconds to return to idle.

Incorrect throttle regulator adjustment may cause erratic idle, excessively high idle speed, and backfiring on deceleration.

Catalytic Converter System

All 1975 Type 1 and 2 models sold in California are equipped with a catalytic converter. The converter is installed in the exhaust system, upstream and adjacent to the muffler.

Catalytic converters change noxious emissions of hydrocarbons (HC) and carbon monoxide (CO) into harmless carbon dioxide and water vapor. The reaction takes place inside the converter at great heat using platinum and palladium metals as the catalyst. If the engine is operated on lead-free fuel, they are designed to last 50,000 miles before replacement.

Deceleration Control

All 1975 Type 2 models, as well as those 1975 Type 1 models equipped with manual transmission, are equipped with deceleration control to prevent an overly rich fuel mixture from reaching the catalyst. During deceleration, a vacuum valve (manual transmission) or electrical transmission switch (automatic transmission) opens, bypassing the closed throttle plate and allowing air to enter the combustion chambers.

FUEL SYSTEM

Mechanical Fuel Pump

There are two types of fuel pumps. They are identified by the cover on the top of the pump. The fuel filter screen is found under this cover.

Type 1 has a fuel pump with the cover secured by four screws. The Type 2 fuel pump has a cover secured by a single screw.

The removal and installation procedures for both mechanical fuel pumps are the same.

Removal and Installation

1. Disconnect the fuel lines at the pump and plug them to prevent leakage.

1. Screw
2. Washer
3. Screw
4. Upper pump cover
5. Gasket
6. Cut-off valve spring
7. Cut-off valve diaphragm
8. Fuel filter plug
10. Fuel filter
14. Inspection cover
16. Operating lever spring
17. Operating lever
18. Pump diaghragm with spring and guide halves attached
19. Pump housing
21. Pushrod
22. Intermediate flange

Exploded view of fuel pump—1970-72 Type 1 models

2. Remove the two securing nuts.

3. Remove the fuel pump. If necessary, the pushrod, gaskets, and intermediate flange may also be removed.

4. When installing the fuel pump, it is necessary to check the fuel pump pushrod stroke. This is done by measuring the distance that the pushrod projects above the intermediate flange when both gaskets are in place. The rod must project ½ in.

5. Fill the cavity in the lower part of the fuel housing with grease.

6. Using new gaskets, install the fuel pump and tighten the two securing nuts.

7. Install the fuel hoses.

Testing and Adjusting

The maximum fuel pump pressure developed by the Type 1 and 2 fuel pump is 3.5 psi, at 3,400 rpm for the Type 1 and 3,800 rpm for the Type 2.

All fuel pumps deliver 400 cc of fuel per minute.

The only adjustment possible is performed by varying the thickness of the fuel pump flange gaskets. Varying the thickness of the gaskets will change the stroke of the fuel pump pushrod. This adjustment is not meant to compensate for a pump in bad condition; therefore, do not attempt to vary the height of the pushrod to any great extent.

The fuel pumps used on 1970–72 models may be disassembled for cleaning or repairs. 1973 and later mechanical pumps are permanently sealed and must be replaced if found defective.

Electric Fuel Pump

The Type 3 and Type 4 have an electric pump. The fuel pump is located near the front axle.

Type 3 electric fuel pump location

Removal and Installation

1. Disconnect the fuel pump wiring. Pull the plug from the pump but do not pull on the wiring.

2. Disconnect the fuel hoses and plug them to prevent any leakage.

3. Remove the two nuts which secure the pump and then remove the pump.

4. Reconnect the fuel pump hoses and wiring and install the pump on the vehicle.

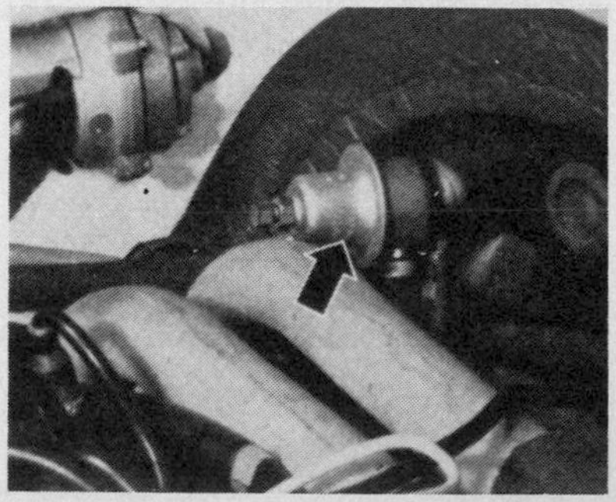

Fuel pressure regulator with locknut and adjusting screw at the left end of the regulator

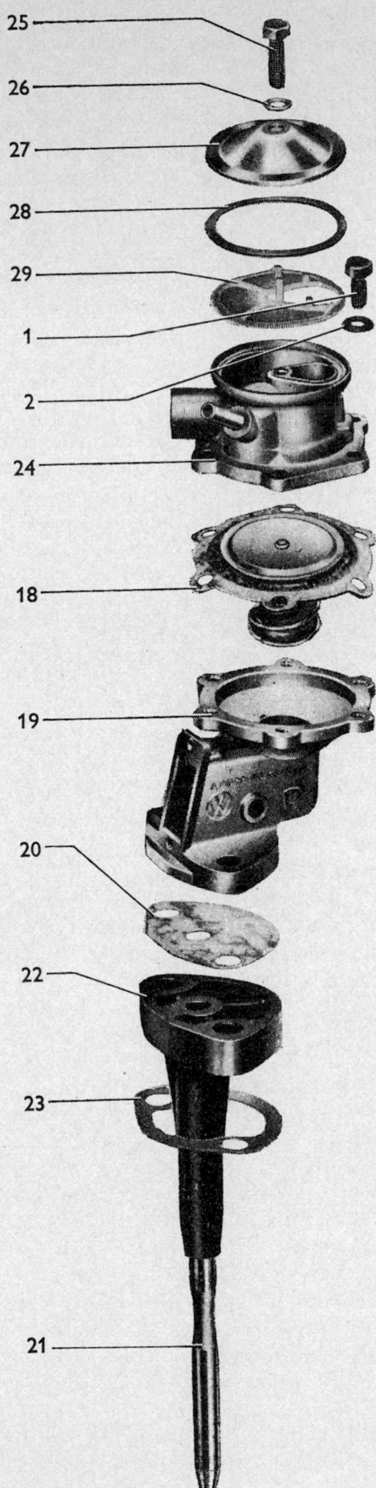

Exploded view of fuel pump—1970 Type 2 models, 1971 unit similar

18. Pump diaphragm with spring and guide halves attached
21. Pushrod
22. Intermediate flange
27. Fuel filter cover
28. Fuel filter cover gasket
29. Fuel filter screen

Adjustments

Electric fuel pump pressure is 28 psi. Fuel pump pressure is determined by a pressure regulator which diverts part of the fuel pump output to the gas tank when 28 psi is reached. The regulator, located on the engine firewall, has a screw and lock nut on its end. Loosen the lock nut and adjust the screw to adjust the pressure. Do not force the screw in or out if it does not turn.

CARBURETORS

Carburetors are used on all Type 1 and 2 models. A single downdraft unit is used on all Type 1 models and on 1970–71 Type 2 models. Beginning with the 1972 model year, the Type 2 utilizes twin carburetion.

Removal and Installation

Type 1 and 2/1600

1. Remove the air cleaner.
2. Disconnect the fuel hose.
3. Disconnect the vacuum hoses.
4. Remove the automatic choke cable and remove the wire for the electromagnetic pilot jet.
5. Disconnect the accelerator cable at the throttle valve lever.
6. Remove the two nuts securing the carburetor on the intake manifold and then remove the carburetor from the engine.
7. Using a new gasket, install the carburetor on the manifold.
8. Reconnect the fuel and vacuum hoses, the automatic choke cable, and the wiring for the pilot jet.
9. Reconnect the throttle cable and adjust it so that at full throttle there is a gap of 0.04 in. between the throttle valve lever and its stop on the lower portion of the carburetor body.

NOTE: *Open the throttle valve by hand and tighten the adjustment*

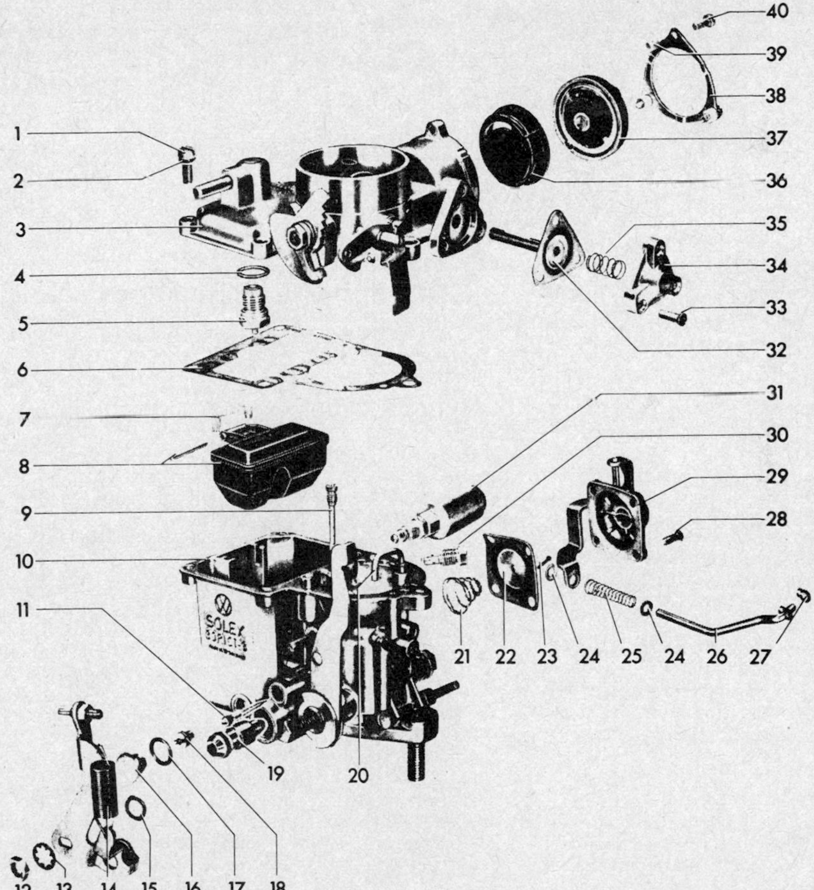

Exploded view of Solex 30 PICT-3 carburetor used on 1970 Type 1 and 2 models

1. Carburetor screw, upper part
2. Spring washer
3. Carburetor upper part
4. Float needle valve washer
5. Float needle valve
6. Washer
7. Float pin retainer
8. Float and pin
9. Air correction jet
10. Carburetor lower part
11. Volume control screw
12. Nut
13. Lock washer
14. Accelerator cable spring
15. Spring
16. Plug
17. Plug seal
18. Main jet
19. By-pass air screw
20. Accelerator pump injector tube
21. Pump diaphragm spring
22. Pump diaphgragm
23. Cotter pin
24. Washer
25. Connecting rod spring
26. Connecting rod
27. Clip
28. Screw
29. Pump cover
30. Pilot jet
31. By-pass mixture cut-off valve
32. Vacuum diaphragm
33. Screw
34. Vacuum diaphragm cover
35. Vacuum diaphragm spring
36. Cap (plastic)
37. Automatic choke
38. Cover retaining ring
39. Cover spacer
40. Retaining ring screw

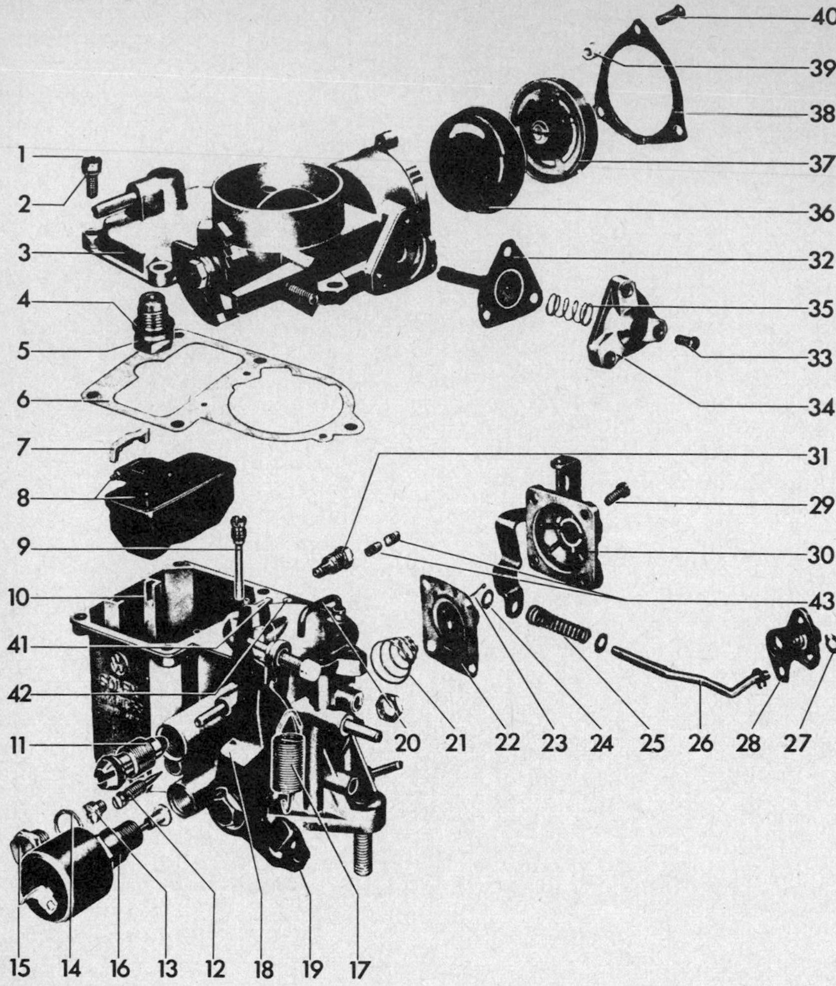

Exploded view of Solex 34 PICT-3 carburetor used on 1971-74 Type 1 models and 1971 Type 2/1600

1. Carburetor screw, upper part
2. Spring washer
3. Carburetor upper part
4. Float needle valve washer
5. Float needle valve
6. Washer
7. Float pin retainer
8. Float and pin
9. Air correction jet and emulsion tube
10. Carburetor lower part
11. By-pass screw
12. Volume control screw
13. Main jet
14. Plug washer
15. Plug
16. By-pass air cut-off valve
17. Return spring
18. Fast idling lever
19. Throttle valve lever and stop screw
20. Accelerator pump injection pipe
21. Diaphragm spring
22. Accelerator pump diaphragm
23. Cotter pin
24. Washer
25. Connecting rod spring
26. Connecting rod
27. Clip
28. Bell crank lever
29. Countersunk head screw
30. Pump cover
31. Pilot jet
32. Vacuum diaphragm
33. Countersunk head screw
34. Vacuum diaphragm cover
35. Vacuum diaphragm spring
36. Plastic cap
37. Insert with spring and heater element
38. Cover retaining ring
39. Retaining ring spacer
40. Retaining ring screw
41. Pilot air drilling
42. Auxiliary air drilling
43. Auxiliary fuel jet and plug

screw, then have an assistant open the throttle and recheck the adjustment.

Overhaul

All Types

Efficient carburetion depends greatly on careful cleaning and inspection during overhaul, since dirt, gum, water, or varnish in or on the carburetor parts are often responsible for poor performance.

Overhaul your carburetor in a clean, dust-free area. Carefully disassemble the carburetor, referring often to the exploded views. Keep all similar and look-alike parts segregated during disassembly and cleaning to avoid accidental interchange during assembly. Make a note of all jet sizes.

When the carburetor is disassembled, wash all parts (except diaphragms, electric choke units, pump plunger, and any other plastic, leather, fiber, or rubber parts) in clean carburetor solvent. Do not leave parts in the solvent any longer than is necessary to sufficiently loosen the deposits. Excessive cleaning may remove the special finish from the float bowl and choke valve bodies, leaving these parts unfit for service. Rinse all parts in clean solvent and blow them dry with compressed air or allow them to air dry. Wipe clean all cork, plastic, leather, and fiber parts with a clean, lint-free cloth.

Blow out all passages and jets with compressed air and be sure that there are no restrictions or blockages. Never use wire or similar tools to clean jets, fuel passages, or air bleeds. Clean all jets and valves separately to avoid accidental interchange.

Check all parts for wear or damage. If wear or damage is found, replace the defective parts. Especially check the following:

1. Check the float needle and seat for wear. If wear is found, replace the complete assembly.
2. Check the float hinge pin for wear and the float(s) for dents or distortion. Replace the float if fuel has leaked into it.
3. Check the throttle and choke shaft bores for wear or an out-of-round condition. Damage or wear to the throttle arm, shaft, or shaft bore will often require replacement of the throttle body. These parts require a close tolerance of fit; wear may allow air leakage, which could affect starting and idling.

NOTE: *Throttle shafts and bushings are not included in overhaul kits. They can be purchased separately.*

4. Inspect the idle mixture adjusting needles for burrs or grooves. Any such condition requires replacement of the needle, since you will not be able to obtain a satisfactory idle.
5. Test the accelerator pump check valves. They should pass air one way but not the other. Test for proper seating by blowing and sucking on the valve. Replace the valve if necessary. If the valve is satisfactory, wash the valve again to remove breath moisture.
6. Check the bowl cover for warped surfaces with a straight edge.
7. Closely inspect the valves and seats for wear and damage, replacing as necessary.
8. After the carburetor is assembled, check the choke valve for freedom of operation.

Carburetor overhaul kits are recommended for each overhaul. These kits contain all gaskets and new parts to replace those that deteriorate most rapidly. Failure to replace all parts supplied with the kit (especially gaskets) can result in poor performance later.

Some carburetor manufacturers supply overhaul kits of three basic types: minor repair; major repair; and gasket kits. Basically, they contain the following:

Minor Repair Kits:

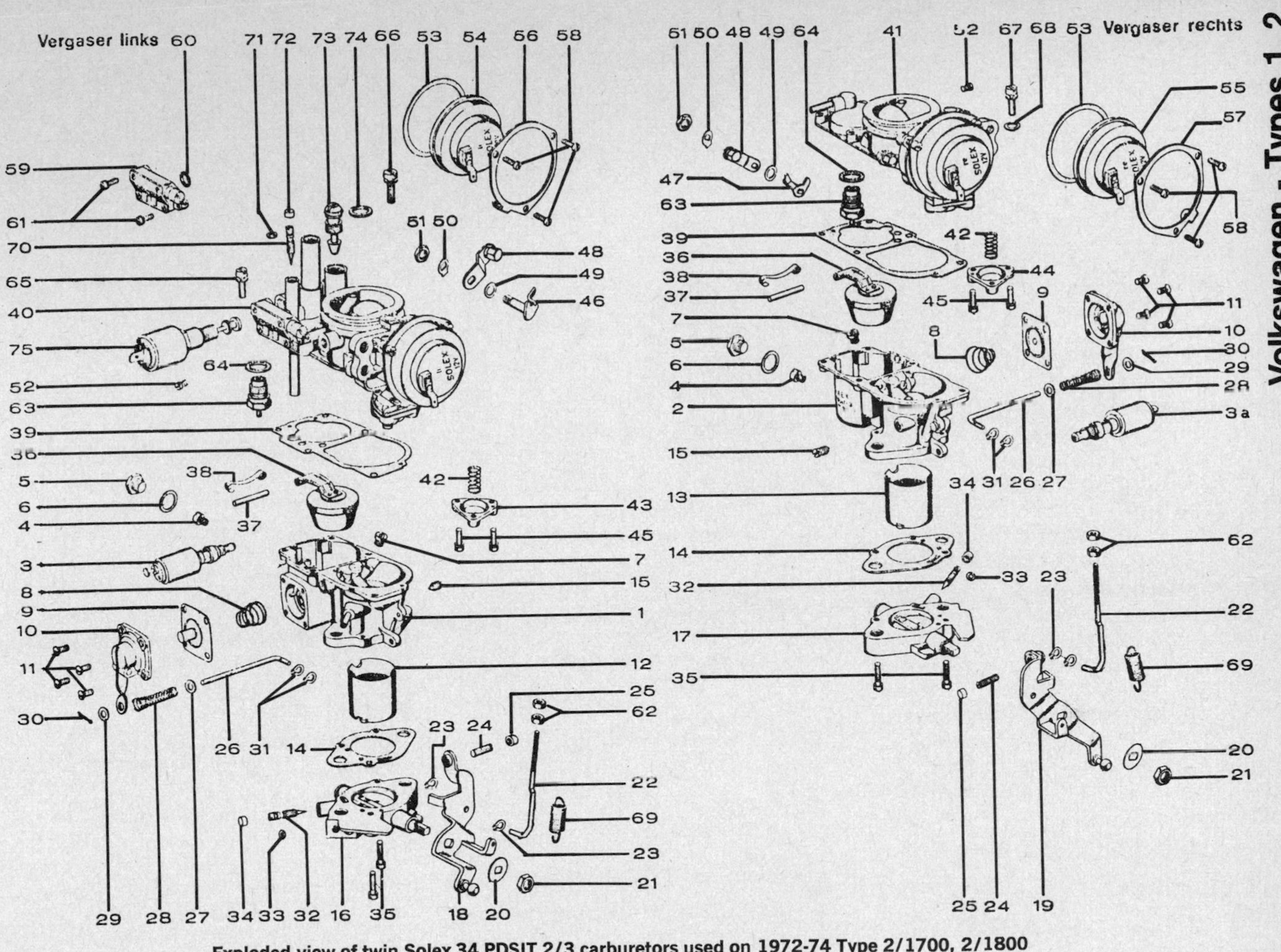

Exploded view of twin Solex 34 PDSIT 2/3 carburetors used on 1972-74 Type 2/1700, 2/1800

1. Carburetor body—34 PDSIT-2
2. Carburetor body—34 PDSIT-3
3. Electromagnetic idling cutoff valve—34 PDSIT-2
3a. Electromagnetic idling cutoff valve—34 PDSIT-3
4. Main jet
5. Main jet cover plug
6. Main jet cover plug seal
7. Air correction jet
8. Pump diaphragm spring
9. Pump diaphragm
10. Accelerator pump cover
11. Screws
12. Venturi—34 PDSIT-2
13. Venturi—34 PDSIT-3
14. Throttle body gasket
15. Venturi setscrew
16. Throttle body—34 PDSIT-2
17. Throttle body—34 PDSIT-3
18. Throttle arm—34 PDSIT-2
19. Throttle arm—34 PDSIT-3
20. Special washer
21. Nut
22. Connecting rod
23. Circlip
24. Throttle valve opening adjusting screw
25. Plug
26. Connecting link
27. Washer
28. Connecting link spring
29. Washer
30. Cotter pin
31. Circlip
32. Idle mixture screw
33. O-ring
34. Plug
35. Throttle body screws
36. Float
37. Float pin
38. Float pin retainer
39. Gasket
40. Carburetor upper part (air horn) with idle mixture enrichment—34 PDSIT-2
41. Carburetor upper part (air horn)—34 PDSIT-3
42. Vacuum diaphragm spring
43. Vacuum diaphragm cover—34 PDSIT-2
44. Vacuum diaphragm cover—34 PDSIT-3
45. Screws
53. Choke heating element gasket
54. Choke heating element—34 PDSIT-2
55. Choke heating element—34 PDSIT-3
56. Choke cover retaining ring—34 PDSIT-2
57. Choke cover retaining ring—34 PDSIT-3
58. Screws
59. Idle mixture enrichment unit
60. O-ring
61. Screws
62. Connecting rod locknuts
63. Float valve
64. Float valve washer
65. Screws
66. Screws
67. Screws
68. Washer
69. Throttle return spring
70. Idle mixture screw
71. O-ring
72. Plug
73. Idle speed adjusting screw
74. O-ring
75. Central idling system electromagnetic cutoff valve

Vergaser links—left carburetor (34 PDSIT-2)
Vergaser rechts—right carburetor (34 PDSIT-3)

All gaskets
Float needle valve
Volume control screw
All diaphragms
Spring for the pump diaphragm
Major Repair Kits:
All jets and gaskets
All diaphragms
Float needle valve
Volume control screw
Pump ball valve
Main jet carrier
Float
Complete intermediate rod
Intermediate pump lever
Complete injector tube
Some cover hold-down screws and washers
Gasket Kits:
All gaskets

After cleaning and checking all components, reassemble the carburetor, using new parts and referring to the exploded view. When reassembling, make sure that all screws and jets are tight in their seats, but do not overtighten as the tips will be distorted. Tighten all screws gradually, in rotation. Do not tighten needle valves into their seats: uneven jetting will result. Always use new gaskets. Be sure to adjust the float level when reassembling.

Throttle Linkage Adjustment

Type 1 and 2/1600

1. Have an assistant hold the accelerator pedal to the floor at wide open throttle. Measure the distance (a) between the throttle valve lever and the stop on the carburetor body. Proper distance (a) is 0.04 in.
2. Loosen the cable adjusting screw found in the bottom on the throttle lever.
3. The throttle lever has a rigid cylinder attached to its end. Move the rigid portion in or out of the end of the throttle lever to obtain the proper adjustment and tighten the adjusting screw. The proper adjustment is reached when there is a gap of 0.04 in. between the throttle valve lever and its stop on the lower portion of the carburetor body. See the note at the end of the "Carburetor Removal and Installation" procedure.

Accelerator Pump Adjustment

Improper accelerator pump adjustment is characterized by flat spots during acceleration or a severe hesitation when the throttle is first depressed.

1. Remove the carburetor from the engine and remove the upper half of the carburetor.
2. Support the carburetor securely in a vise without damaging the carburetor body.

Full-throttle clearance (distance a) should be 0.04 in. on single carburetor engines

Measuring accelerator pump output

3. Fill the float chamber with gasoline and attach a rubber tube to the injector tube. Place the open end of the tube into a millileter measuring tube.
4. Move the throttle lever several strokes until all of the air is forced out of the tube. Move the throttle lever an additional ten full strokes and measure the quantity of gas in the measuring tube. Multiply the accelerator pump quantity injected specification by 10 and compare this figure to the amount of gas in the measuring tube.
5. To decrease the amount injected, reduce the number of washers between the cotter pin and the pump lever. To increase the amount, increase the number of washers. If varying the number of washers will not yield enough adjustment, move the cotter pin in the connecting link.

Float and Fuel Level Adjustment

A properly assembled carburetor has a preset float level. For the float level to be correct the fiber washer under the needle valve seat must be installed and be of the proper thickness. See the "Carburetor Specifications Chart".

The only way tc adjust the float level, if it is absolutely necessary, and still retain proper seating of the needle in the needle valve seat, is to vary the thickness of the fiber washer beneath the seat.

Throttle Valve Gap

Carburetor Removed

1. Remove the carburetor from the car.

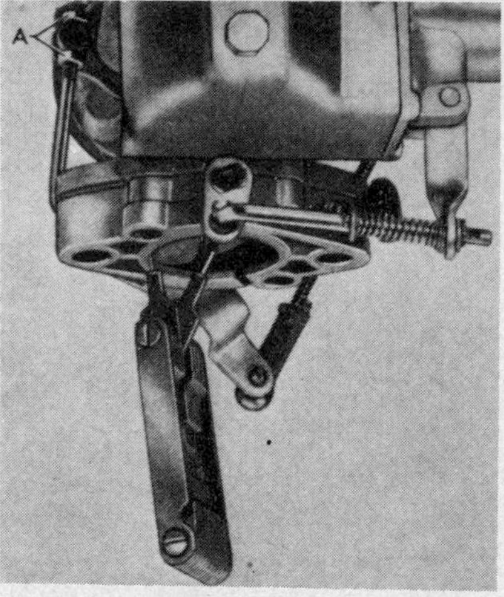

Adjusting throttle valve gap with adjusting nuts (A)

2. Loosen the two nuts on the automatic choke connecting rod and insert a 0.028 in. wire gauge or drill between the throttle valve and the side of the venturi.
3. Move the two nuts up or down on the connecting rod until the throttle valve gap is adjusted and tighten the two nuts.

NOTE: *The choke valve must be closed for proper adjustment.*

Carburetor Installed

1. Back out the idle speed screw until the throttle valve is completely closed.
2. Turn the idle speed screw until it just touches the throttle lever.
3. Close the choke valve.
4. Place a 0.09 in. drill or wire gauge between the idle screw and the throttle valve lever. Adjust the two nuts on the automatic choke connecting rod either up or down until the drill can be easily pulled out.
5. It will be necessary to rebalance the carburetors on dual carburetor models.

Fast Idle Adjustment

1. The fast idle speed is adjusted by means of a screw located at the upper end of the throttle valve arm. This screw rests against a cam with steps cut into its edge.
2. To adjust the fast idle, start the engine and rotate the cam so that the fast idle screw is resting against the highest step on the fast idle cam. The fast idle

speed should be approximately 1500 rpm.

3. Turn the fast idle screw either in or out until the proper idle speed is obtained.

4. On dual carburetor engines it is necessary to adjust the fast idle on only one of the carburetors. There is a direct mechanical connection between the two carburetors and if one carburetor is adjusted the other will automatically be adjusted.

Accelerator Cable Replacement

1. Disconnect the cable from the accelerator pedal.

2. Disconnect the cable from the throttle lever.

3. Pull the cable from the accelerator pedal end and then remove it from the car.

4. Grease the cable before sliding it into its housing.

5. Slide the cable into its housing and push it through its guide tubes. It may be necessary to raise the car and start the cable into the segments of guide tube found under the car.

6. Install one cable end into the accelerator cable. Slip the other end into the throttle valve lever and adjust the cable.

NOTE: *Make sure that the rubber boot at the rear end of the cable is properly seated so that water will not enter the guide tubes.*

Electronic Fuel Injection (Non-Air Flow Controlled)

The Bosch Electronic fuel injection system used on all Type 3 models, and on 1971–74 Type 4 models (except 1974 models equipped with an automatic), consists of two parts. One part consists of the actual injection components: the injectors, the fuel pump, pressure regulator, and related wiring and hoses. The second part consists of the injection controls and engine operating characteristics sensors: a manifold vacuum sensor that monitors engine load, trigger contacts used to determine when and which pair of injectors will operate, three temperature sensors used to control air fuel mixture enrichment, a cold starting valve for additional cold starting fuel enrichment, a throttle valve switch used to cut off fuel during deceleration, and the brain box used to analyze information about engine operating characteristics and, after processing this information, to control the electrically operated injectors.

It is absolutely imperative that no adjustments other than those found in the following pages be performed. The controls for this fuel injection system are extremely sensitive and easily damaged when subject to abuse. Never attempt to test the control box without proper training and the proper equipment. The dealer is the best place to have any needed work performed.

CAUTION: *Whenever a fuel injection component is to be removed or installed, the battery should be disconnected and the ignition turned OFF.*

It is not recommended that the inexperienced mechanic work on any portion of the fuel injection system.

Air Flow Controlled Electronic Fuel Injection

1974 Type 4 models equipped with automatic transmission, as well as all 1975 Type 1 and Type 2 models, are equipped with an improved system known as the Air Flow Controlled Electronic Fuel Injection System. With this system, some of the electronic sensors and wiring are eliminated, and the control box is smaller. Instead, fuel is metered according to intake air flow.

Electronic Control Box

All work concerning the control box is to be performed by the dealer. Do not remove the control box and take it to a dealer because the dealer will not be able to test it without the vehicle. Do not disconnect the control box unless the battery is disconnected and the ignition is OFF.

Fuel Injectors

There are two types of injectors. One type is secured in place by a ring that holds a single injector. The second type of injector is secured to the intake manifold in pairs by a common bracket.

Removal and Installation

Single Injectors

1. Remove the nut which secures the injector bracket to the manifold.

2. If the injector is not going to be replaced, do not disconnect the fuel line. Disconnect the injector wiring.

3. Gently slide the injector bracket up the injector and pull the injector from the intake manifold. Be careful not to damage the inner and outer rubber sealing rings. These sealing rings are used to seal the injector to the manifold and must be replaced if they show any sign of deterioration.

4. Installation is the reverse of removal. Be careful not to damage the injector tip or contaminate the injector with dirt.

Paired Injectors

1. Disconnect the injector wiring.

2. Remove the two nuts which secure the injector bracket to the manifold.

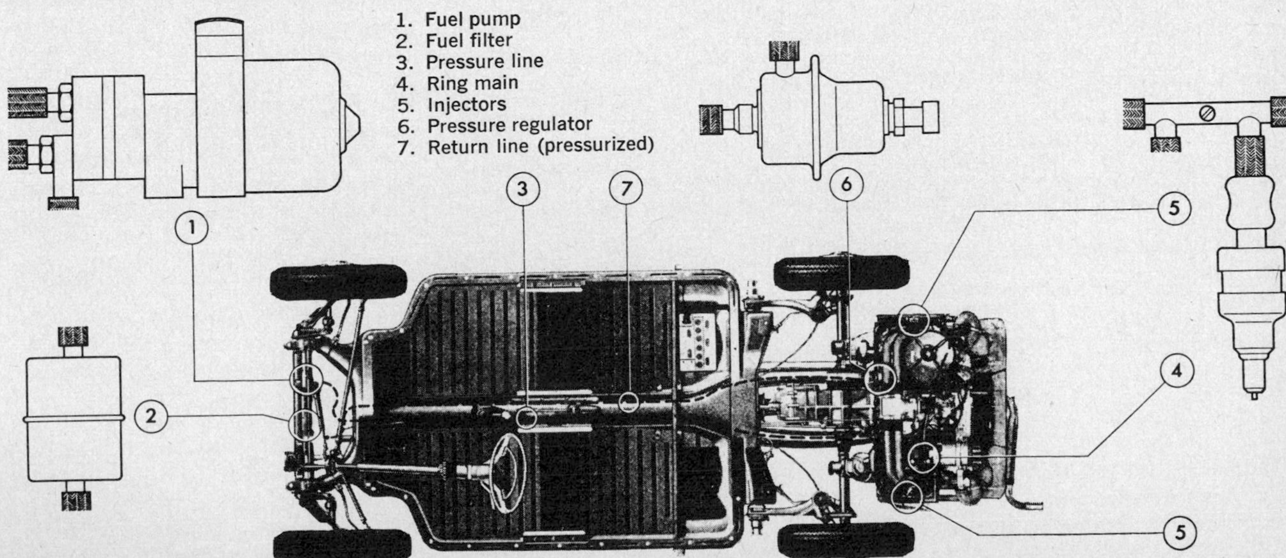

Location of fuel injection components—Type 3

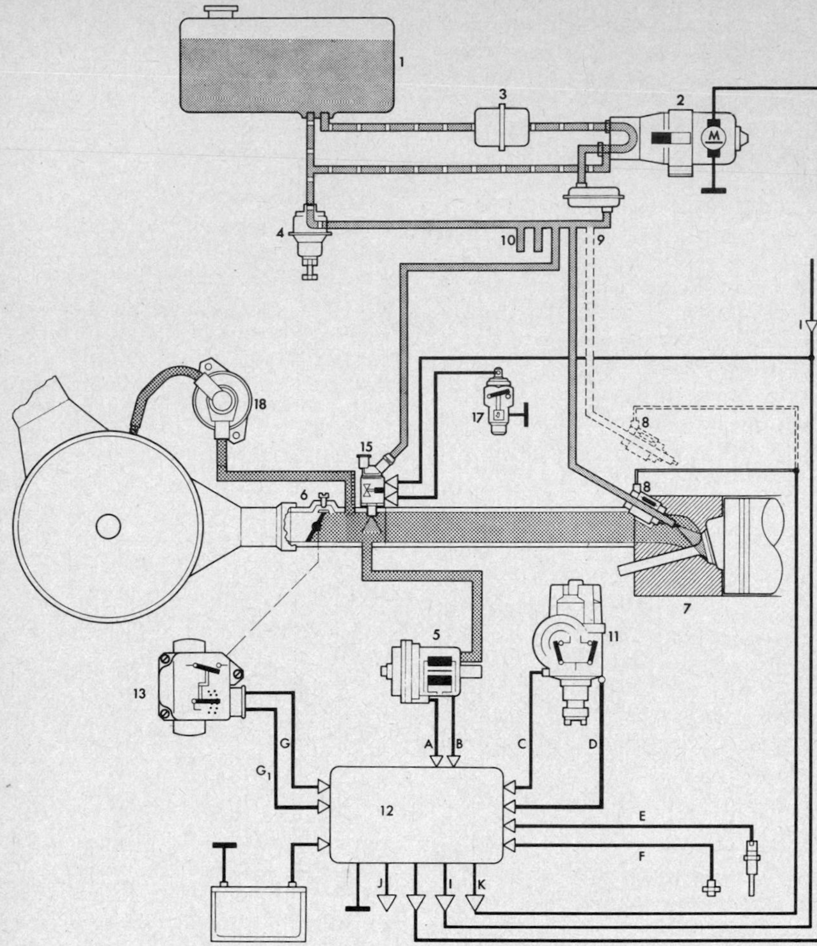

Schematic of fuel injection system—1970 and later 49 states models, 1970-71 California models

1. Fuel tank
2. Fuel pump
3. Fuel filter
4. Pressure regulator
5. Pressure sensor
6. Intake air distributor
7. Cylinder head
8. Injectors
9. Fuel distributor pipe
10. Fuel distributor pipe with connection for cold starting device
11. Distributor with trigger contacts (distributor contact I, distributor contact II)
12. Control unit
13. Throttle valve switch with acceleration enrichment
15. Cold starting valve
17. Thermostat for cold starting device
18. Auxiliary air regulator

A + B. from pressure sensor (load condition signal)
C + D. from distributor contacts (engine speed and releasing signal)
E + F. from temperature sensors (warmup signal)
G. from throttle valve switch (fuel supply cut-off when coasting)
G1. Acceleration enrichment
I. from starter, terminal 50 solenoid switch (signal for enrichening mixture when starting)
J. to the injectors, cylinders 1 and 4
K. to the injectors, cylinders 2 and 3

Slide the bracket up the injector. Do not disconnect the fuel lines if the injector is not going to be replaced.

3. Gently slide the pair of injectors out of their bores along with the rubber sealing rings, injector plate, and the inner and outer injector locating bushings. It may be necessary to remove the inner bushings from the intake manifold after the injectors are removed since they sometimes lodge within the manifold.

NOTE: *There are two sleeves that fit over the injector bracket studs. Be careful not to lose them.*

4. Upon installation, place the injector bracket, the outer locating bushings, the injector plate, and the inner locating bushings on the pair of injectors in that order.

5. Gently slip the injector assembly into the manifold and install the bracket nuts. Be careful not to damage the injector tips or contaminate the injectors with dirt.

6. Reconnect the injector wiring.

Throttle Valve Switch

Removal and Installation

1. Remove the air filter.
2. The switch is located on the throttle valve housing. Disconnect the throttle valve return spring.
3. Remove the throttle valve assembly but do not disconnect the bowden wire for the throttle valve or the connecting hoses to the ignition distributor.
4. Remove the throttle valve, switch securing screws and remove the switch.
5. Reverse the above steps to install. It will be necessary to adjust the switch after installation.

Throttle valve switch—1971 Type 4 models showing securing screws (a) and direction of adjustment (b)

Adjustment (Non-Air Flow Controlled Only)

The throttle valve switch is used to shut off the fuel supply during deceleration. The switch is supposed to operate when the throttle valve is opened 2°. A degree scale is stamped into the attachment plate for adjustment purposes.

1. Completely close the throttle valve.
2. Loosen the switch attaching screws and turn the switch carefully to the right until it hits its stop.
3. Turn the switch slowly to the left until it can be heard to click and then note the position of the switch according to the degree scale.
4. Continue to turn the switch another 2°. The distance between any two marks on the degree scale is 2°.

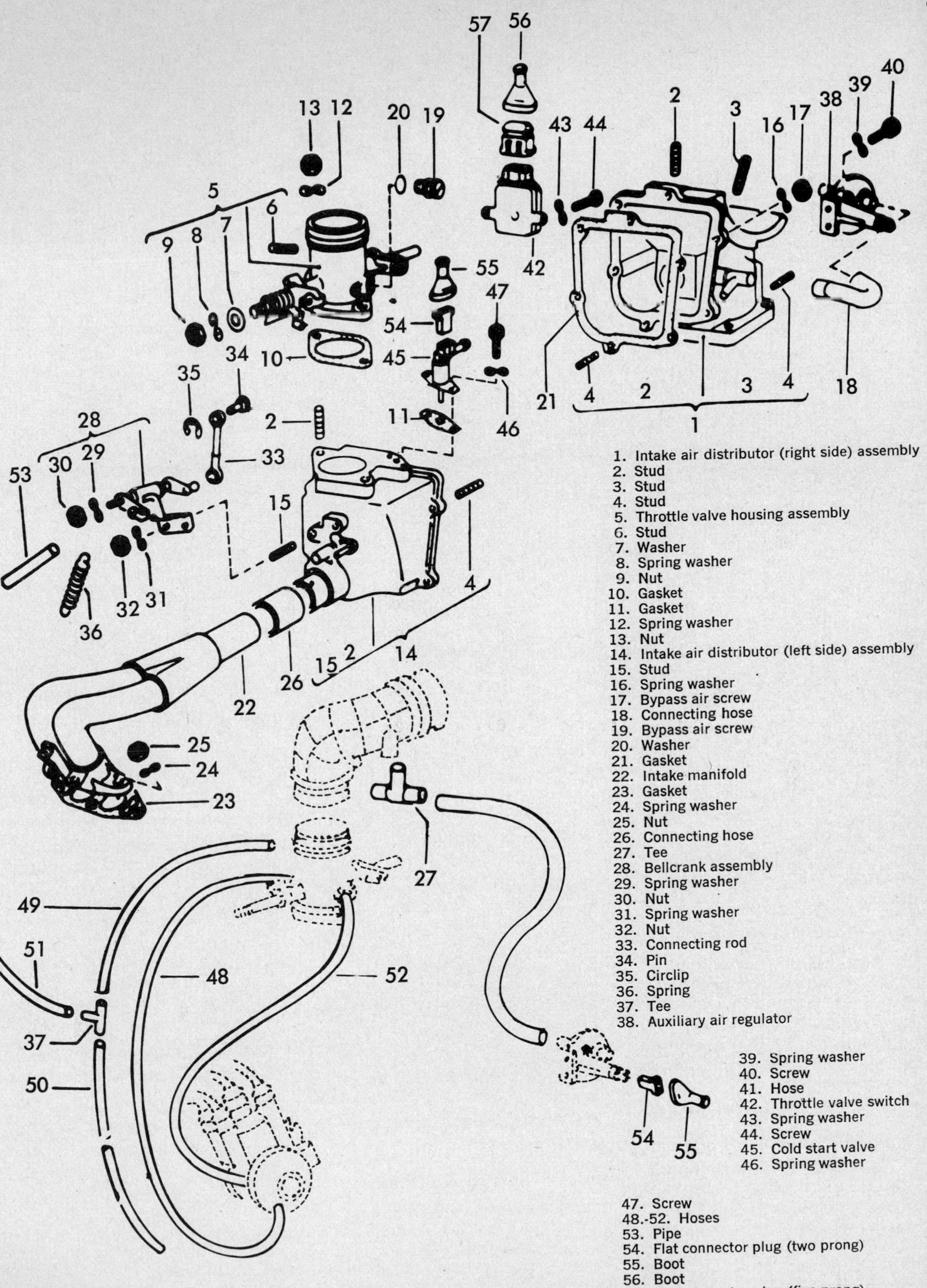

1. Intake air distributor (right side) assembly
2. Stud
3. Stud
4. Stud
5. Throttle valve housing assembly
6. Stud
7. Washer
8. Spring washer
9. Nut
10. Gasket
11. Gasket
12. Spring washer
13. Nut
14. Intake air distributor (left side) assembly
15. Stud
16. Spring washer
17. Bypass air screw
18. Connecting hose
19. Bypass air screw
20. Washer
21. Gasket
22. Intake manifold
23. Gasket
24. Spring washer
25. Nut
26. Connecting hose
27. Tee
28. Bellcrank assembly
29. Spring washer
30. Nut
31. Spring washer
32. Nut
33. Connecting rod
34. Pin
35. Circlip
36. Spring
37. Tee
38. Auxiliary air regulator
39. Spring washer
40. Screw
41. Hose
42. Throttle valve switch
43. Spring washer
44. Screw
45. Cold start valve
46. Spring washer
47. Screw
48.-52. Hoses
53. Pipe
54. Flat connector plug (two prong)
55. Boot
56. Boot
57. Flat connector plug (five prong)

Exploded view of components for air flow controlled electronic fuel injection system used in 1975 Type 1 and Type 2 vehicles—Type 1 system shown; Type 2 similar

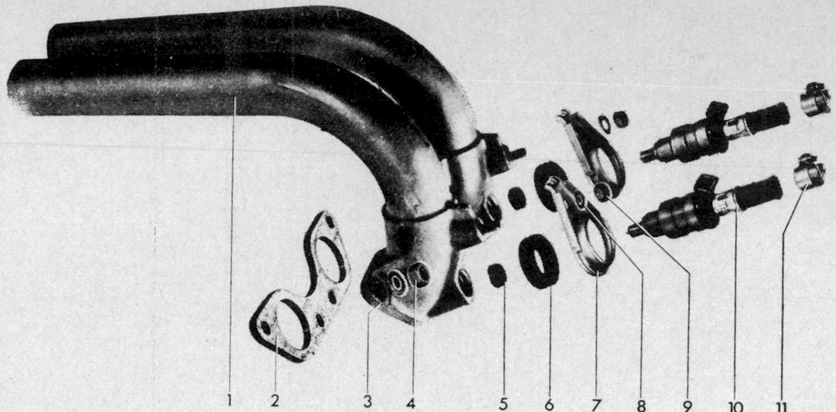

Individually mounted fuel injectors

1. Intake manifold
2. Intake manifold gasket
3. Lock washer
5. Inner sealing bushing
6. Outer sealing bushing
7. Retainer
8. Lock washer
9. Nut
10. Fuel injector
11. Hose connection with clamp

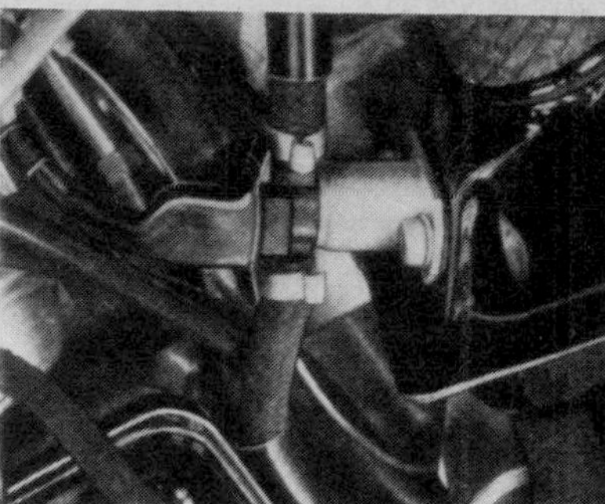

Cold start valve location

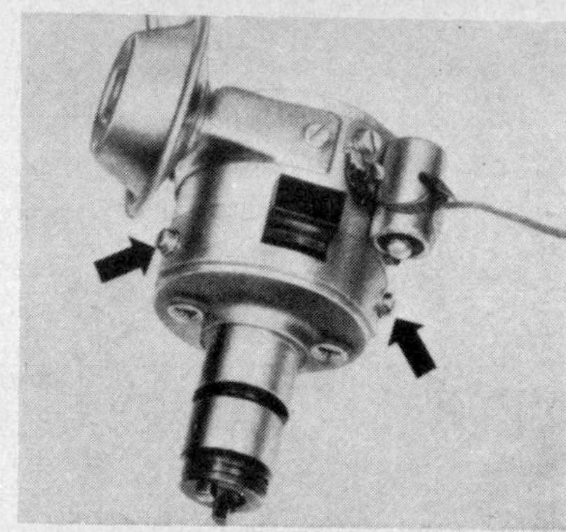

Removing trigger contacts

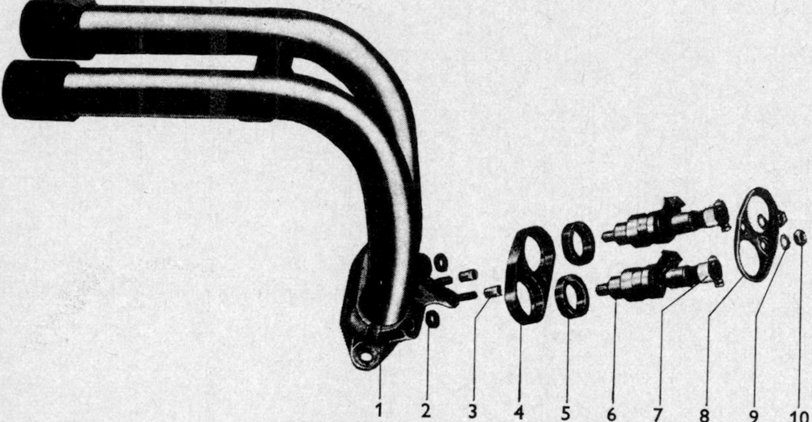

Paired fuel injectors

1. Intake manifolds with injector seats
2. Injector inner locating sealing bushings
3. Sleeves
4. Injector plate
5. Injector outer locating bushings
6. Electromagnetic fuel injector
7. Hose connection with clamp
8. Injector retainer
9. Lock washer
10. Nut

Fuel pressure regulator test gauge installation

5. Tighten the screws and recheck the adjustment.

Cold Start Valve

Removal and Installation

The cold start valve is located near the thermo-switch and is secured to the air intake distributor by two screws. This valve sometimes jams open and causes excessive consumption, rough idle, and low power output.

Trigger Contacts (Non-Air Flow Controlled Only)

Removal and Installation

The trigger contacts are located in the base of the distributor and are secured by two screws. These contacts are supplied in pairs and are not adjustable. Do not attempt to replace just one set of contacts.

One set of contacts controls a pair of injectors and tells the injectors when to fire.

Throttle valve switch on 1970-73 Type 3, 1972-74 Type 4

Fuel Pressure Regulator

Removal and Installation

Disconnect the hoses from the regulator and remove the regulator from its bracket. The fuel pump pressure is adjustable; however, lack of fuel pressure is usually due to other defects in the system and the regulator should be adjusted only as a last resort.

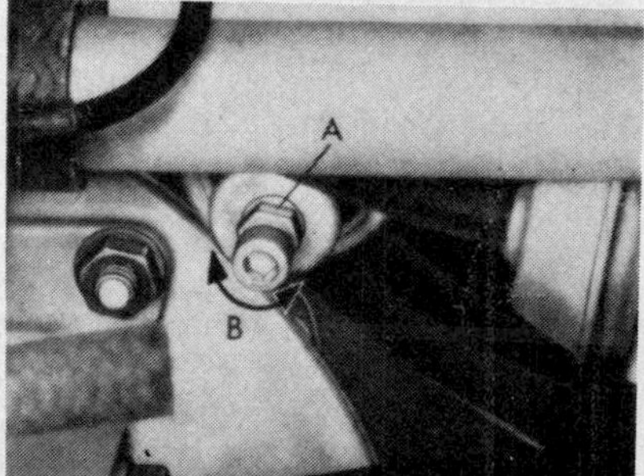

Fuel pressure regulator adjustment—Type 3

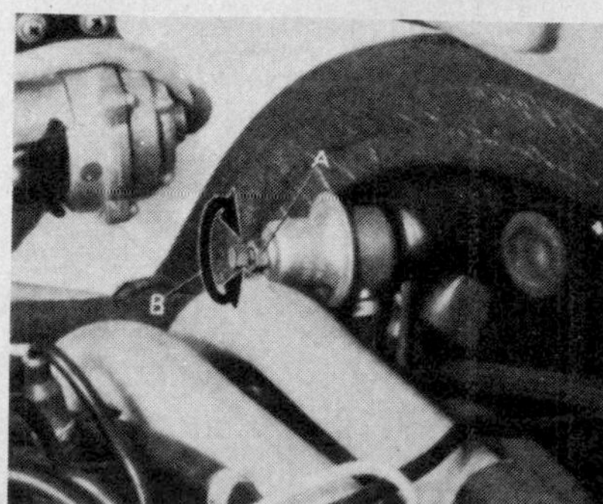

Fuel pressure regulator adjustment—Type 4

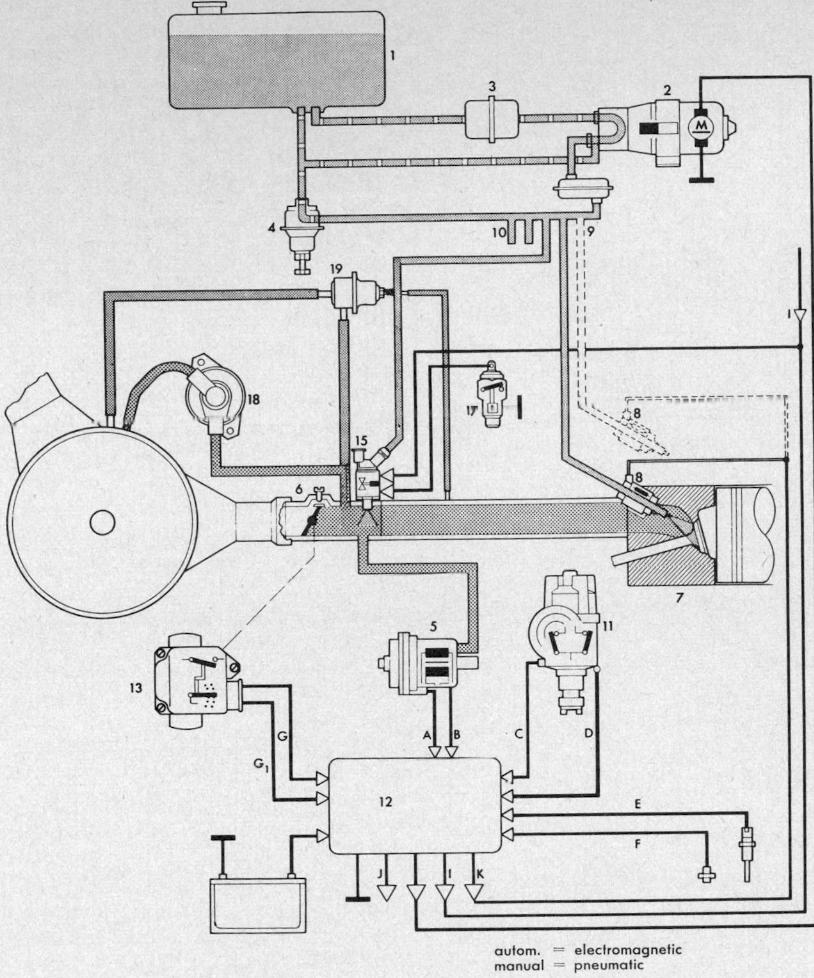

Schematic of fuel injection system 1972-74 California models

1. Fuel tank
2. Fuel pump
3. Fuel filter
4. Pressure regulator
5. Pressure sensor
6. Intake air distributor
7. Cylinders head
8. Injectors
9. Fuel distributor pipe
10. Fuel distributor pipe with connection for cold starting device
11. Distributor with trigger contacts (contacts I and II)
12. Electronic control unit
13. Throttle valve switch with acceleration enrichment
14. Pressure switch
15. Cold starting valve
17. Thermostat for cold starting device
18. Auxiliary air regulator
19. Deceleration mixture control valve

A + B. from pressure sensor (load condition signal)
C + D. from distributor contacts (engine speed and releasing signal)
E + F. from temperature sensors (warmup signal)
G. from throttle valve switch (full throttle signal, Type 3 only)
G1. Acceleration enrichment
I. from starter, terminal 50 solenoid switch (signal for enrichening mixture when starting)
J. to the injectors, cylinders 1 and 4
K. to the injectors, cylinders 2 and 3

Adjustment

1. Remove the air cleaner.
2. Connect a fuel pressure gauge as shown.
3. Start the engine and operate at idle.
4. Loosen locknut "A" and adjust fuel pressure to 28 psi with screw "B".

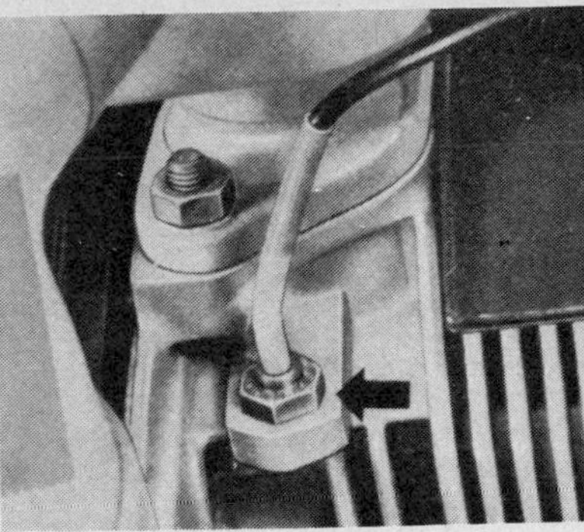

Cylinder head temperature sensing switch

Thermoswitch location

Temperature Sensor

Testing, Removal and Installation

The air temperature sensor is located in the air distributor housing and may be unscrewed from the housing. The second temperature switch is located in the cylinder head on the left side. It is removed with a special wrench. To test these switches, attach an ohmmeter and measure the resistance of the switch as the temperature is raised gradually to 212°. As the temperature rises, the resistance of the first switch should drop from about 200 ohms to 80 ohms. The cylinder head switch resistance should drop from about 1700 ohms to 190 ohms at 212°.

The third switch is actually a thermoswitch and is an ON/OFF type switch. Below 41° it is ON to activate the cold starting valve. The switch is located next to the distributor and may be removed with a 24 mm wrench.

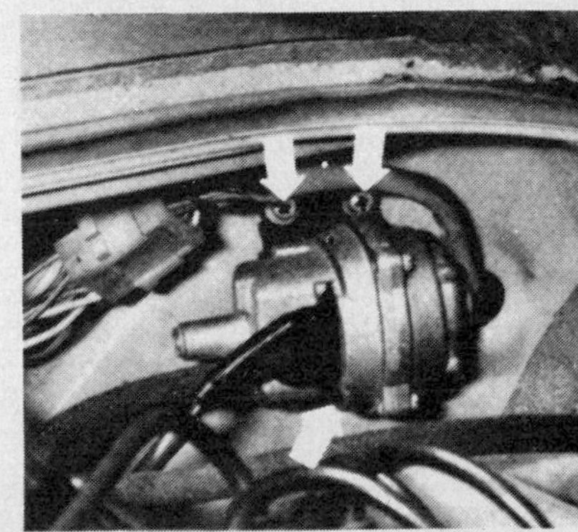

Pressure sensor retaining screws

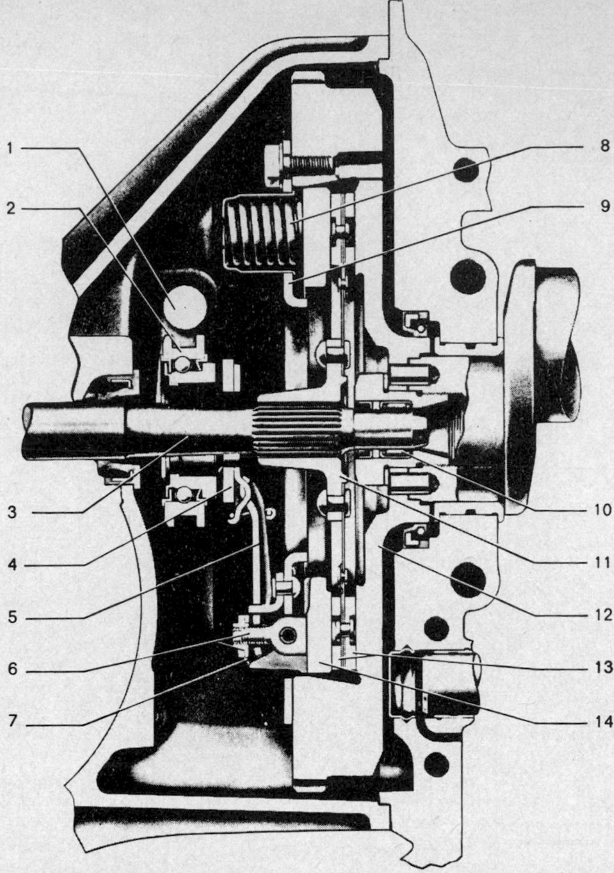

Cross-sectional view of clutch assembly—Type 1, 2/1600 with manual transmission

1. Operating shaft
2. Release bearing
3. Main driveshaft
4. Release plate
5. Release lever
6. Bolt and special nut
7. Release lever spring
8. Thrust spring
9. Cover
10. Needle bearing for gland nut
11. Driven plate
12. Flywheel
13. Lining
14. Pressure plate

Pressure Sensor (Non Air-Flow Controlled Only)

Removal and Installation

1. The sensor is secured to the firewall by two screws. Remove the screws and disconnect the wiring.

2. Remove the pressure connection and immediately plug the connection into the sensor.

3. Always keep the connection plugged as the bellows inside the sensor is sensitive to the smallest pieces of dirt. Reverse the above steps to install.

4. Do not disassemble the sensor. There are no adjustments possible for the sensor.

NOTE: *Do not reverse the square electrical plug when reconnecting the sensor wiring.*

Troubleshooting

There are very few items to check without the special tester used by the dealer.

It is possible to check the fuel pressure by inserting a fuel pressure gauge in the line after the pressure regulator. Insert the gauge using a T-fitting. Turn on the key and check the pressure. If the pressure is low, check for leaking injectors, restricted lines, clogged fuel filters, damaged pressure regulator, bad fuel pump, water in the gas and resultant corrosion of the injectors, or a leaking or jammed cold start valve.

CLUTCH

Removal and Installation

Manual Transmission

1. Remove the engine.

2. Remove the pressure plate securing bolts one turn at a time until all spring pressure is released.

3. Remove the bolts and remove the clutch assembly.

NOTE: *Notice which side of the clutch disc faces the flywheel and install the new disc in the same direction.*

4. Before installing the new clutch, check the condition of the flywheel. It should not have excessive heat cracks and the friction surface should not be scored or warped. Check the condition of the throw out bearing. If the bearing is worn, replace it.

5. Lubricate the pilot bearing in the end of the crankshaft with grease.

6. Insert a pilot shaft, used for centering the clutch disc, through the clutch disc and place the disc against the flywheel. The pilot shaft will hold the disc in place.

7. Place the pressure plate over the disc and loosely install the bolts.

NOTE: *Make sure the correct side of the clutch disc is facing outward. The disc will rub the flywheel if it is incorrectly positioned.*

8. After making sure that the pressure plate aligning dowels will fit into the pressure plate, gradually tighten the bolts.

9. Remove the pilot shaft and reinstall the engine.

10. Adjust the clutch pedal free-play.

Automatic Stick Shift

1. Disconnect the negative battery cable.

2. Remove the engine.

3. Remove the transaxle.

4. Remove the torque converter by sliding it off of the input shaft. Seal off the hub opening.

5. Mount the transaxle in a repair stand or on a suitable bench.

6. Loosen the clamp screw and pull off the clutch operating lever. Remove the transmission cover.

7. Remove the hex nuts between the clutch housing and the transmission case.

NOTE: *Two nuts are located inside the differential housing.*

8. The oil need not be drained if the clutch is removed with the cover opening up and the gearshift housing breather blocked.

9. Pull the transmission from the clutch housing studs.

10. Turn the clutch lever shaft to disengage the release bearing.

11. Remove both lower engine mounting bolts.

12. Loosen the clutch retaining bolts gradually and alternately to prevent distortion. Remove the bolts, pressure plate, clutch plate, and release bearing.

13. Do not wash the release bearing. Wipe it dry only.

14. Check the clutch plate, pressure plate, and release bearing for wear and damage. Check the clutch carrier plate, needle bearing, and seat for wear. Replace the necessary parts.

15. If the clutch is wet with ATF, replace the clutch carrier plate seal and the clutch disc. If the clutch is wet with transmission oil, replace the transmission case seal and clutch disc.

16. Coat the release bearing guide on the transmission case neck and both lugs on the release bearing with grease. Insert the bearing into the clutch.

17. Grease the carrier plate needle bearing. Install the clutch disc and pres-

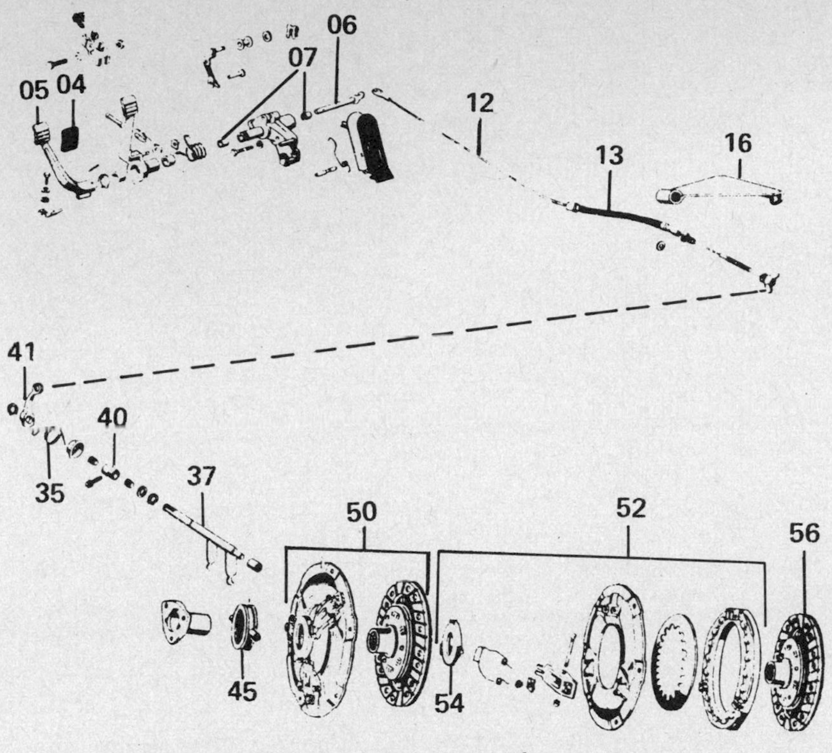

Clutch Control—Type 1

4. Clutch pedal pad
5. Clutch pedal
6. Clutch pedal shaft
7. Bushings for pedal cluster
12. Clutch cable
13. Clutch cable sleeve
16. Angle plate for clutch cable
35. Clutch return spring
37. Clutch cross shaft
40. Bushing—operating shaft
41. Clutch operating lever
45. Clutch release bearing
50. Clutch
52. Pressure plate
54. Clutch release plate
56. Clutch disc

sure plate using a pilot shaft to center the disc on the flywheel.

18. Tighten the pressure plate retaining bolts evenly and alternately. Make sure that the release bearing is correctly located in the diaphragm spring.

19. Insert the lower engine mounting bolts from the front. Replace the sealing rings if necessary. Some units have aluminum sealing rings and cap nuts.

20. Push the transmission onto the converter housing studs. Insert the clutch lever shaft behind the release bearing lugs. Push the release bearing onto the transmission case neck. Tighten the bolts which hold the clutch housing to the transmission case.

21. Install the clutch operating lever.

22. It is necessary to adjust the basic clutch setting. The clutch operating lever should contact the clutch housing. Tighten the lever clamp screw slightly.

23. First adjust dimension (a) to 0.335 in. Adjust dimension (b) to 3.03 in. Finally adjust dimension (c) to 1.6 in. by repositioning the clutch lever on the clutch shaft. Tighten the lever clamp screw.

24. Push the torque converter onto the support tube. Insert it into the turbine shaft by turning the converter.

25. Check the clutch play after installing the transaxle and engine.

Clutch Cable Adjustment

Manual Transmission

1. Check the clutch pedal travel by measuring the distance the pedal travels toward the floor until pressure is exerted against the clutch. The distance is ⅜ to ¾ in.

2. To adjust the clutch, jack up the rear of the car and support it on jackstands.

3. Remove the left rear wheel.

4. Adjust the cable tension by turning the wing nut on the end of the clutch cable. Turning the wing nut counterclockwise decreases pedal free-play, turning it clockwise increases free-play.

5. When the adjustment is completed, the wings of the wing nut must be horizontal so that the lugs on the nut engage the recesses in the clutch lever.

6. Push on the clutch pedal several times and check the pedal free-play.

7. Install the wheel and lower the car.

Automatic Stick Shift clutch assembly

1. Torque converter
2. One-way clutch support
3. Gasket
4. Circlip for carrier plate
5. Ball bearing
6. O-ring for stud
7. Converter housing
8. Spring washer
9. Socket head screw
10. Seal
11. Clutch carrier plate
12. Needle bearing
13. Seal/carrier plate
14. Clutch plate
15. Diaphragm clutch pressure plate
16. Spring washer
17. Socket head screw
18. Release bearing
19. Seal/converter
20. O-ring/one-way clutch support

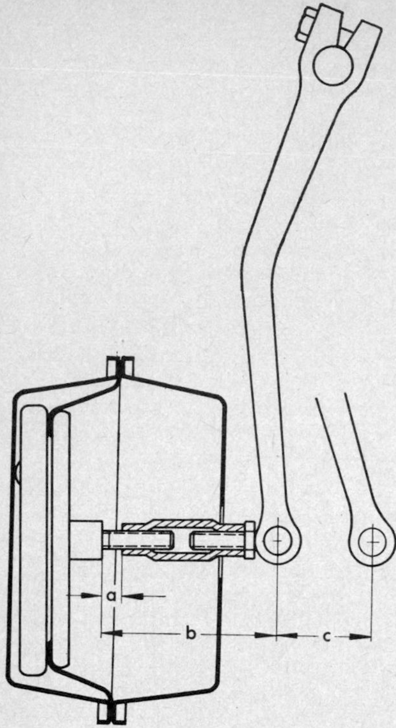

Automatic Stick Shift basic clutch adjusting dimensions

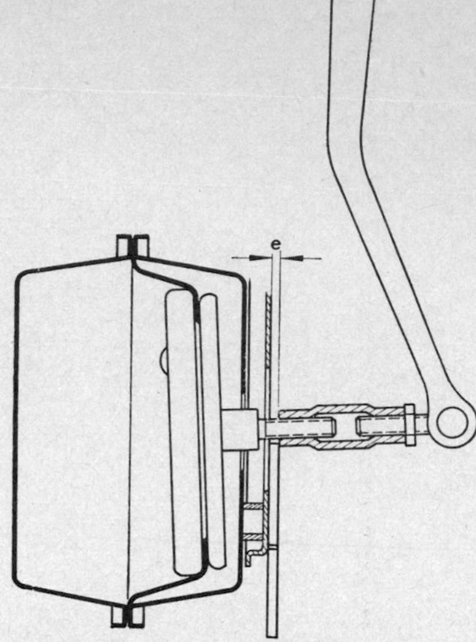

Checking clutch adjustment—Automatic Stick Shift

Adjusting Automatic Stick Shift Clutch—(d) is 0.25 in., measured between locknut and turnbuckle

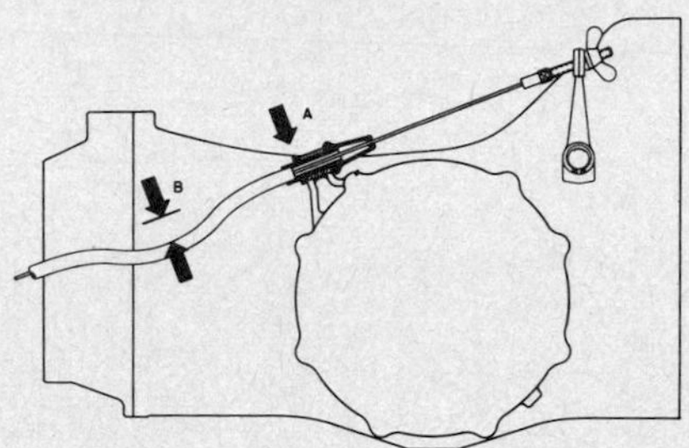

For smooth clutch action, dimension B should be 1.0-1.7 in. Adjust cable to provide slight sag at point B by installing spacer washers at point A

Automatic Stick Shift

The adjustment is made on the linkage between the clutch arm and the vacuum servo unit. To check the clutch play:

1. Disconnect the servo vacuum hose.
2. Measure the clearance between the upper edge of the servo unit mounting bracket and the lower edge of the adjusting turnbuckle. If the clearance (e) is 0.16 in. or more, the clutch needs adjustment.
3. Reconnect the vacuum hose.

To adjust the clutch:

1. Disconnect the servo vacuum hose.
2. Loosen the turnbuckle locknut and back it off completely to the lever arm. Then turn the servo turnbuckle against the locknut. Now back off the turnbuckle 5–5½ turns. The distance between the locknut and the turnbuckle should be 0.25 in.
3. Tighten the locknut against the adjusting sleeve.
4. Reconnect the vacuum hose and road test the vehicle. The clutch is properly adjusted when Reverse gear can be engaged silently and the clutch does not slip on acceleration. If the clutch arm contacts the clutch housing, there is no more adjustment possible and the clutch plate must be replaced.

The speed of engagement of the Automatic Stick Shift clutch is regulated by the vacuum operated valve rather than by the driver's foot. The adjusting screw is on top of the valve under a small protective cap. Adjust the valve as follows:

1. Remove the cap.
2. To slow the engagement, turn the adjusting screw ¼–½ turn clockwise. To speed engagement, turn the screw counterclockwise.
3. Replace the cap.
4. Test operation by shifting from Second to First at 44 mph without depressing the accelerator. The shift should take exactly one second to occur.

Clutch pedal free play (a)

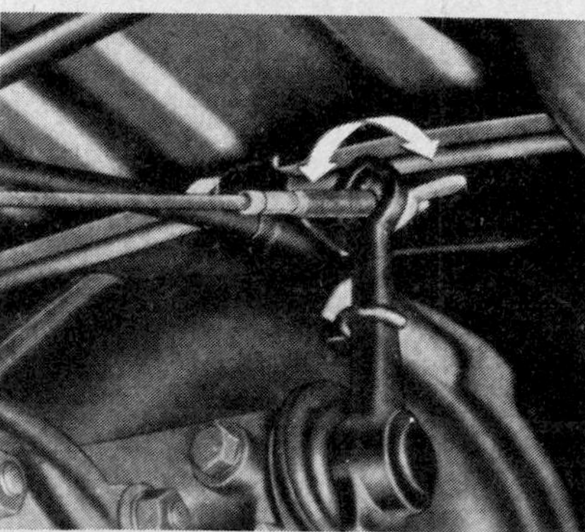

Wing nut for clutch cable adjustment

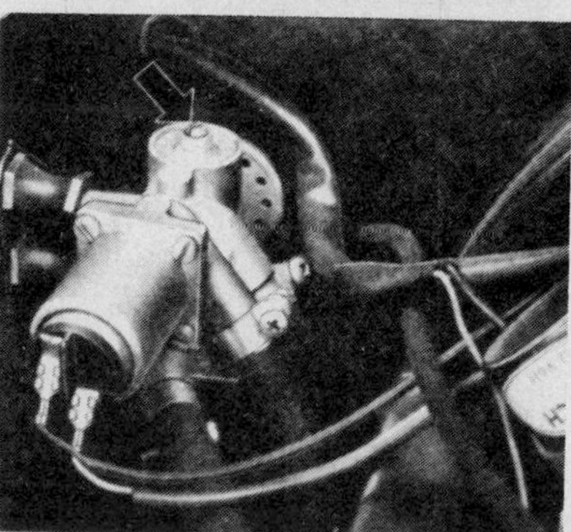

Speed of engagement adjusting screw

Clutch Cable Replacement

1. Jack up the car and remove the left rear wheel.
2. Disconnect the cable from the clutch operating lever.
3. Remove the rubber boot from the end of the guide tube and off the end of the cable.
4. On Type 1, unbolt the pedal cluster and remove it from the car. It will also be necessary to disconnect the brake master cylinder push rod and throttle cable from the pedal cluster. On Type 2, remove the cover under the pedal cluster, then remove the pin from the clevis on the end of the clutch cable. On Type 3, remove the frame head cover and remove the pin from the clevis on the end of the clutch cable.
5. Pull the cable out of its guide tube from the pedal cluster end.
6. Installation is the reverse of the above.

NOTE: *Grease the cable before installing it and readjust the clutch pedal free-play.*

TRANSAXLE

Manual Transaxle

Removal and Installation

1. Disconnect the negative battery cable.

2. Remove the engine.

3. Remove the socket head screws which secure the drive shafts to the transmission. Remove the bolts from the transmission end first and then remove the shafts.

NOTE: *It is not necessary to remove the drive shafts entirely from the car if the car does not have to be moved while the transaxle is out.*

Socket head screws securing axle driveshafts

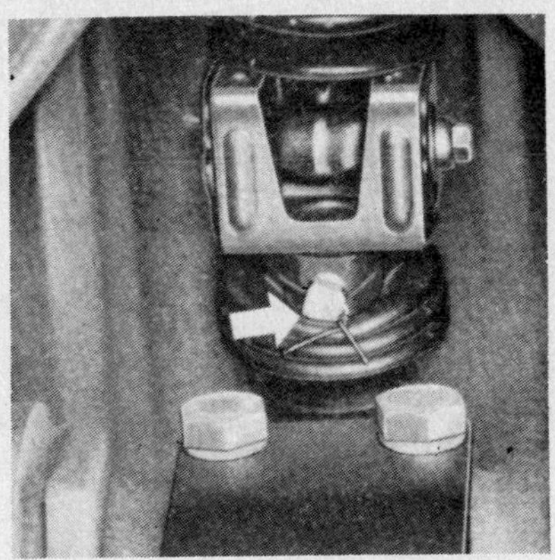

Shift linkage coupling

4. Disconnect the clutch cable from the clutch lever and remove the clutch cable and its guide tube from the transaxle. Loosen the square head bolt at the shift linkage coupling located near the rear of the transaxle. Slide the coupling off the inner shift lever. There is an access plate under the rear seat to reach the coupling on Type 1 and 3. It is necessary to work under the car to reach the coupling on Type 2 models.

5. Disconnect the starter wiring.

6. Disconnect the back-up light switch wiring.

7. Remove the front transaxle mounting bolts.

8. Support the transaxle with a jack and remove the transmission carrier bolts.

Front transaxle mounting bolts

9. Carefully lower the jack and remove the transaxle from the car.

10. To install, jack the transaxle into position and loosely install the bolts.

11. Tighten the transmission carrier bolts first, then tighten the front mounting nuts.

12. Install the drive shaft bolts with new lockwashers. The lockwashers should be positioned on the bolt with the convex side toward the screw head.

13. Reconnect the wiring, the clutch cable, and the shift linkage.

NOTE: *It may be necessary to align the transmission so that the driveshaft joints do not rub the frame.*

14. Install the engine.

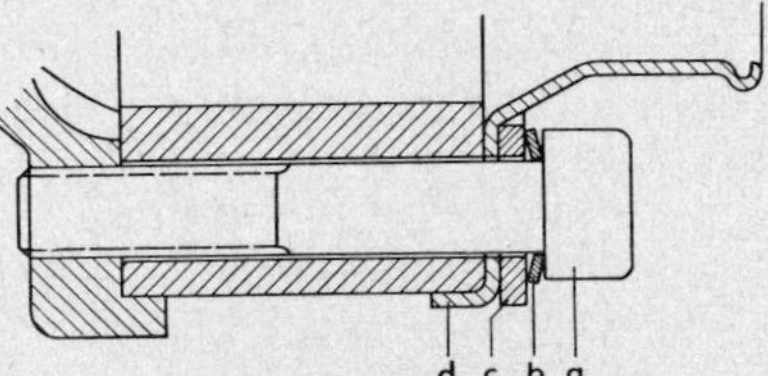

Drive axle bolts and washer positioning

a. Socket head screws
b. Lock washer
c. Spacer
d. Protective cap

Automatic Stick Shift Transaxle

Removal and Installation

1. Disconnect the negative battery cable.

2. Remove the engine.

3. Make a bracket to hold the torque converter in place. If a bracket is not used, the converter will slide off the transmission input shaft.

4. Detach the gearshift rod coupling.

5. Disconnect the drive shafts at the transmission end. If the driveshafts are not going to be repaired, it is not necessary to detach the wheel end.

6. Disconnect the ATF hoses from the transmission. Seal the open ends. Disconnect the temperature switch, neutral safety switch, and the back-up light switch.

7. Pull off the vacuum servo hose.

8. Disconnect the starter wiring.

9. Remove the front transaxle mounting nuts.

10. Loosen the rear transaxle mounting bolts. Support the transaxle and remove the bolts.

11. Lower the axle and remove it from the car.

12. With the torque converter bracket still in place, raise the axle into the car.

13. Tighten the nuts for the front transmission mounting. Insert the rear mounting bolts but do not tighten them at this time.

14. Replace the vacuum servo hose.

15. Connect the ATF hoses, using new washers. The washers are seals.

16. Connect the temperature switch and starter cables.

17. Install the drive shafts, using new washers. Turn the convex sides of the washers toward the screw head.

18. Align the transaxle so that the inner drive shaft joints do not rub on the frame fork and then tighten the rear mounting bolts.

19. Insert the shift rod coupling, tighten the screw, and secure it with wire.

20. Remove the torque converter bracket, and install the engine.

21. After installing the engine, bleed the ATF lines if return flow has not started after 2–3 minutes.

Shift Linkage Adjustment

1. The Volkswagen shift linkage is not adjustable. When shifting becomes difficult or there is an excessive amount of play in the linkage, check the shifting mechanism for worn parts. Make sure the shift linkage coupling is tightly connected to the inner shift lever located at the rear of the transaxle under the rear seat. Worn parts may be found in the shift lever mechanism and the supports for the linkage rod sometimes wear out.

2. The gear shift lever can be removed after the front floor mat has been lifted.

3. After the two retaining screws have been removed from the gear shift lever ball housing, the gear shift lever, ball housing, rubber boot, and spring are removed as a unit.

CAUTION: *Carefully mark the position of the stop plate and note the position of the turned up ramp at the side of the stop plate. Normally the ramp is turned up and on the right hand side of the hole.*

4. Installation is the reverse of removal.

5. Lubricate all moving parts with grease.

6. Test the gear shift pattern. If there is difficulty in shifting, adjust the stop plate back and forth in its slotted holes.

DriveShaft and Constant Velocity U-Joint

Removal and Installation

1. Remove the bolts which secure the joints at each end of the shaft, tilt the shaft down, and remove the shaft.
2. Loosen the clamps which secure the rubber boot to the axle and slide the boot back on the axle.
3. Drive the stamped steel cover off of the joint with a drift.

NOTE: *After the cover is removed, do not tilt the ball hub as the balls will fall out of the hub.*

4. Remove the circlip from the end of the axle and press the axle out of the joint.
5. Reverse the above steps to install. The position of the dished washer is dependent on the type of transmission. On automatic transmissions, it is placed between the ball hub and the circlip. On manual transmissions, it is placed between the ball hub and the shoulder on the shaft. Be sure to pack the joint with grease.

NOTE: *The chamfer on the splined inside diameter of the ball hub faces the shoulder on the driveshaft.*

AUTOMATIC TRANSMISSION

Removal and Installation

NOTE: *The engine and transmission must be removed as an assembly on the Type 4 and Type 2/1700, 2/1800.*

1. Remove the battery ground cable.
2. On the sedan, remove the cooling air intake duct with the heating fan and hoses. Remove the cooling air intake connection and bellows, then detach the hoses to the air cleaner.
3. On the station wagons, remove the warm air hoses and air cleaner. Remove the boot between the dipstick tube and the body and the boot between the oil filler neck and the body. Disconnect the cooling air bellows at the body.
4. Disconnect the wires at the regulator and the alternator wires at the snap-connector located by the regulator. Disconnect the auxiliary air regulator and the oil pressure switch at the snap connectors located by the distributor.
5. Disconnect the fuel injection wiring on Type 3 and 4 models. There are 12 connections and they are listed as follows:
   a. Fuel injector cylinder 2, 2-pole, protective gray cap
   b. Fuel injector cylinder 1, 2-pole, protective black cap
   c. Starter, 1-pole, white
   d. Throttle valve switch, 4-pole
   e. Distributor, 3-pole
   f. Thermo switch, 1-pole, white
   g. Cold start valve, 3-pole
   h. Temperature sensor crankcase, 2-pole
   i. Ground connection, 3-pole, white wires
   j. Temperature sensor for the cylinder head, 1-pole
   k. Fuel injector cylinder 3, 2-pole, protective black cap
   l. Fuel injector cylinder 4, 2-pole, protective gray cap
6. Disconnect the accelerator cable.
7. Disconnect the right fuel return line.
8. Raise the car.
9. Disconnect the warm hoses from the heat exchangers.
10. Disconnect the starter wires and push the engine wiring harness through the engine cover plate.
11. Disconnect the fuel supply line and plug it.
12. Remove the heater booster exhaust pipe.
13. Remove the rear axles and cover the ends to protect them from dirt.
14. Remove the selector cable by unscrewing the cable sleeve.
15. Remove the wire from the kick-down switch.
16. Remove the bolts from the rubber transmission mountings, taking careful note of the position, number, and thickness of the spacers that are present.

CAUTION: *These spacers must be reinstalled exactly as they were removed. Do not detach the transmission carrier from the body.*

17. Support the engine and transmission assembly in such a way that it may be lowered and moved rearward at the same time.
18. Remove the engine carrier bolts and the engine and transmission assembly from the car.
19. Matchmark the flywheel and the torque converter and remove the three attaching bolts.
20. Remove the engine-to-transmission bolts and separate the engine and transmission.

CAUTION: *Exercise care when separating the engine and transmission as the torque converter will easily slip off the input shaft if the transmission is tilted downward.*

21. Installation is as follows. Install and tighten the engine-to-transmission bolts after aligning the match marks on the flywheel and converter.
22. Making sure the match marks are aligned, install the converter-to-flywheel bolts.
23. Make sure the rubber buffer is in place and the two securing studs do not project more than 0.7 in. from the transmission case.
24. Tie a cord to the slot in the engine compartment seal. This will make positioning the seal easier.
25. Lift the assembly far enough to allow the accelerator cable to be pushed through the front engine cover.
26. Continue lifting the assembly into place. Slide the rubber buffer into the locating tube in the rear axle carrier.

Engine carrier bolts positioned at the top of their elongated holes

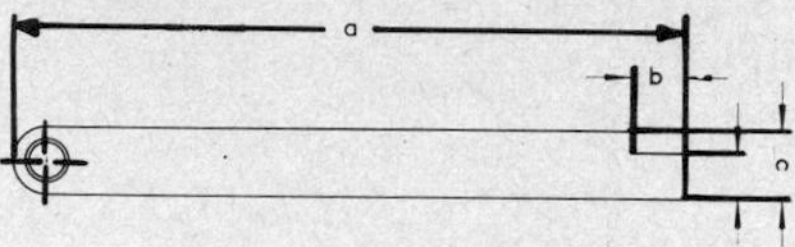

Buffer alignment gauges

a. 5.095 in.
b. 0.472 in.
c. 0.590 in.
d. 0.393, 0.433, and 0.472 in.

27. Insert the engine carrier bolts and raise the engine until the bolts are at the top of their elongated slots. Tighten the bolts.

NOTE: *A set of three gauges must be obtained to check the alignment of the rubber buffer in its locating tube. The dimensions are given in the illustration as is the measuring technique. The rubber buffer is centered horizontally when the 11 mm gauge can be inserted on both sides. The buffer is located vertically when the 10 mm gauge can be inserted on the bottom side and the 12 mm gauge can be inserted on the top side. See Steps 28 and 29 for adjustment procedure.*

28. Install the rubber transmission mount bolts with spacers of the correct thickness. The purpose of the spacers is to center the rubber buffer vertically in its support tube. The buffer is not supposed to carry any weight; it absorbs torsional forces only.
29. To locate the buffer horizontally in its locating tube, the engine carrier must be vertical and parallel to the fan housing. It is adjusted by moving the engine carrier bolts in elongated slots. Further travel may be obtained by moving the brackets attached to the body. It may be necessary to adjust the two rear suspension wishbones with the center of the transmission after the rubber buffer is

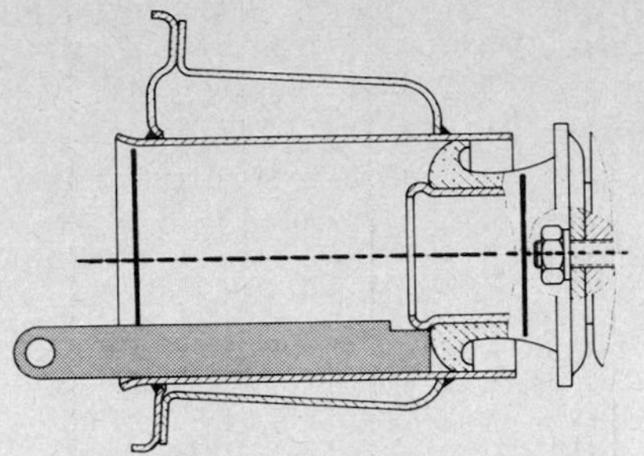
Measuring procedure or centering the buffer

Checking the position of the engine carrier

horizontally centered. Take the car to a dealer or alignment specialist to align the rear suspension.

30. Adjust the selector lever cable.

31. Connect the wire to the kickdown switch.

32. Install the rear axles. Make sure the lockwashers are placed with the convex side out.

33. Reconnect the fuel hoses and heat exchanger hoses. Install the pipe for the heater booster.

34. Lower the car and pull the engine compartment seal into place with the cord.

35. Reconnect the fuel injection and engine wiring. Push the starter wires through the engine cover plate and connect the wires to the starter.

36. Install the intake duct with the fan and hoses, also the cooling air intake.

Pan Removal and Installation

1. Some models have a drain plug in the pan. Remove the plug and drain the transmission oil. On models without the plug, loosen the pan bolts 2–3 turns and lower one corner of the pan to drain the oil.

2. Remove the pan bolts and remove the pan from the transmission.

NOTE: *It may be necessary to tap the pan with a rubber hammer to loosen it.*

3. Use a new gasket and install the pan. Tighten the bolts loosely until the pan is properly in place, then tighten the bolts fully, moving in a diagonal pattern.

NOTE: *Do not overtighten the bolts.*

4. Refill the transmission with ATF.

5. At 5 minute intervals, retighten the pan bolts two or three times.

Filter Service

The Volkswagen automatic transmission has a filter screen secured by a screw to the bottom of the valve body. Remove the pan and remove the filter screen from the valve body.

CAUTION: *Never use a cloth that will leave the slightest bit of lint in the transmission when cleaning transmission parts. The lint will expand when exposed to transmission fluid and clog the valve body and filter.*

Clean the filter screen with compressed air.

Front (Second) Band Adjustment

Tighten the front band adjusting screw to 7 ft lbs. Then loosen the screw and tighten it to 3.5 ft lbs. From this position, loosen the screw exactly 1¾ to 2 turns and tighten the locknut.

Rear (First) Band Adjustment

Tighten the rear band adjusting screw to 7 ft lbs. Then loosen the screw and retighten it to 3.5 ft lbs. From this position, loosen the screw exactly 3¼ to 3½ turns and tighten the locknut.

Kickdown Switch Adjustment

Type 3

1. Disconnect the accelerator cable return spring.

2. Move the throttle to the fully open position. Adjust the accelerator cable to give 0.02–0.04 in. clearance between the stop and the end of the throttle valve lever.

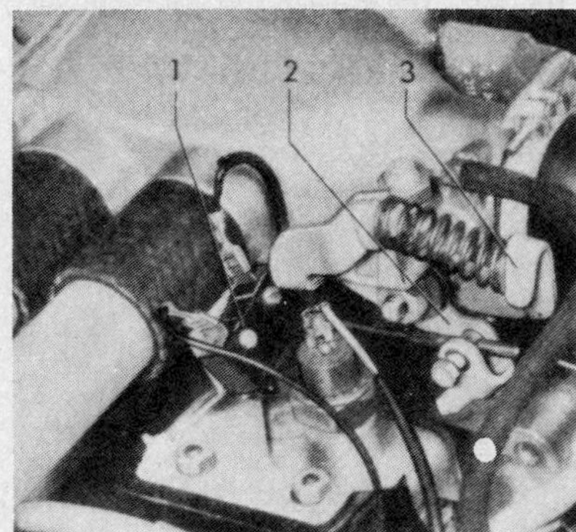

Kickdown Switch—Type 3
1. Kickdown switch
2. Accelerator cable lever
3. Throttle valve lever

3. When the accelerator cable is adjusted and the throttle is moved to the fully open position, the kickdown switch should click. The ignition switch must be ON for this test.

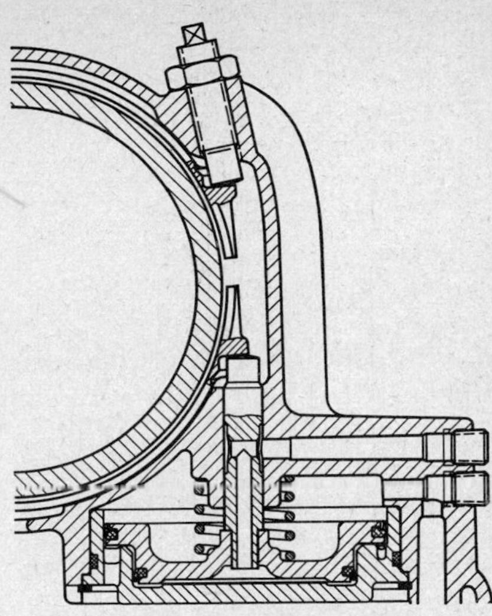
Rear band assembly adjustment screw at top

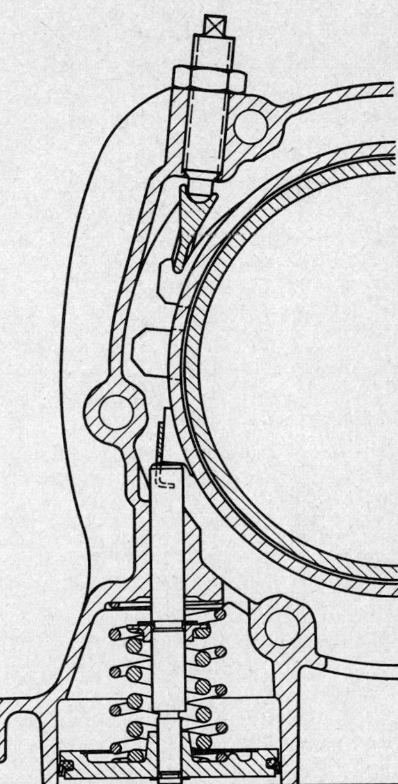
Front band assembly adjustment screw at top

4. To adjust the switch, loosen the switch securing screws and slide the switch back and forth until the test in Step 3 is satisfied.

5. Reconnect the accelerator cable return spring.

Type 4

The Type 4 switch is not adjustable.

Shift Linkage Adjustment

Make sure the shifting cable is not kinked or bent and that the linkage and cable are properly lubricated.

1. Move the gear shift lever to the Park position.

2. Loosen the clamp which holds the front and rear halves of the shifting rod

together. Loosen the clamping bolts on the transmission lever.

3. Press the lever on the transmission rearward as far as possible. Spring pressure will be felt. The manual valve must be on the stop in the valve body.

4. Holding the transmission lever against its stop, tighten the clamping bolt.

5. Holding the rear shifting rod half, push the front half forward to take up any clearance and tighten the clamp bolt.

6. Test the shift pattern.

Diagonal Arm Suspension—Types 1, 2, 3

Diagonal Arm Removal and Installation

1. Remove the wheel shaft nuts.

CAUTION: *Do not raise the car to remove the nuts. They can be safely removed only if the weight on the car is on its wheels.*

2. Disconnect the driveshaft of the side to be removed.

3. Remove the lower shock absorber mount. Raise the car and remove the wheel and tire.

4. Remove the brake drum, disconnect the brake lines and emergency brake cable, and remove the backing plate.

5. Matchmark the torsion bar plate and the diagonal arm with a cold chisel.

6. Remove the four bolts and nuts which secure the plate to the diagonal arm.

7. Remove the pivot bolts for the diagonal arm and remove the arm from the car.

NOTE: *Take careful note of the washers at the pivot bolts. These washers are used to determine alignment and they must be put back in the same place.*

8. Remove the spring plate hub cover.

9. Using a steel bar, lift the spring plate off of the lower suspension stop.

10. On Type 1, remove the five bolts at the front of the fender. On all others, remove the cover in the side of the fender.

11. Remove the spring plate and pull the torsion bar out of its housing.

NOTE: *There are left and right torsion bars designated by an (L) or (R) on the end face. (Coat any rubber bushings with talcum powder upon installation. Do not use graphite, silicon, or grease.*

Pressing transmission lever back as far as possible

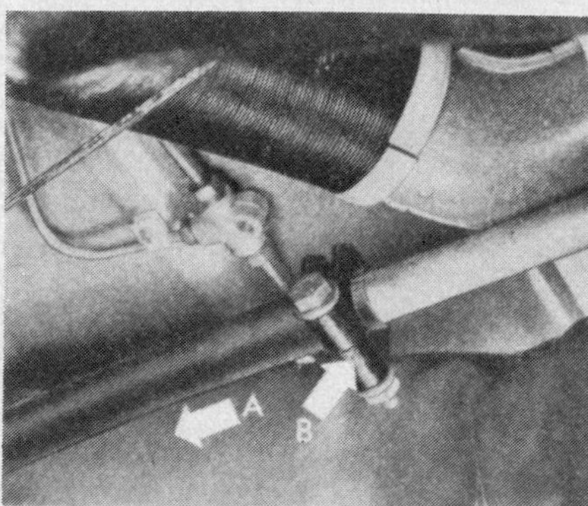

Clamp securing shift linkage rod halves

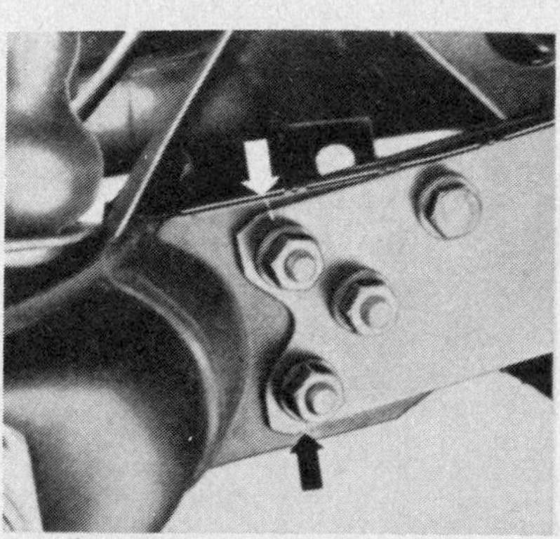

Matchmarking torsion bar and diagonal arm with cold chisel

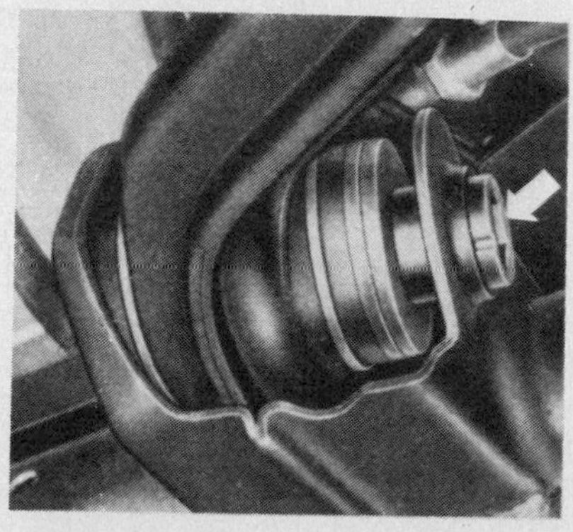

Proper positioning of diagonal arm pivot bolt with both spacer washers on the outside

12. To install, insert the torsion bar, outer bushing, and spring plate. The torsion bar is properly adjusted when the spring plate, with no load, is the specified number of degrees below a horizontal position.

13. Using two bolts, loosely secure the spring plate hub cover. Place a thick nut between the leaves of the spring plate.

14. Lift the spring plate up to the lower suspension stop and install the remaining bolts into the hub cover. Tighten the hub cover bolts.

15. Install the diagonal arm pivot bolt and washers and peen it with a chisel. There must always be at least one washer on the outside end of the bolt.

16. Align the chisel marks and attach the diagonal arm to the spring plate.

17. Install the backing plate, parking brake cable, and brake lines.

18. Reconnect the shock absorber. Install the brake drum and wheel shaft nuts.

19. Reconnect the drive shaft. Bleed the brakes.

20. Install the wheel and tire.

21. Check the suspension alignment.

A-Arm Suspension—Type 4

A-Arm Removal and Installation

1. Raise the car and place it on jackstands. Securely block up the A-arm.

CAUTION: *The A-arm must be securely supported when the shock absorber is disconnected to prevent the spring tension from being released suddenly. The shock absorber is the lower stop for the suspension.*

2. Disconnect the driveshaft.

3. Disconnect the handbrake cable at the brake lever and remove it.

4. Disconnect the brake lines and the stabilizer bar if equipped.

5. With the vehicle on the ground or the A-arm securely supported, remove the lower shock absorber mounting bolt.

6. Slowly release the A-arm and remove the coil springs.

7. Mark the position of the brackets or the eccentric bolts, whichever are removed, with a chisel. Remove the nuts which secure the brackets in the rear axle carrier, or the pivot bolts in the bonded rubber bushings, and remove the A-arm.

8. Loosely install the A-arm. If the pivot bolts were removed, install them loosely. If the eccentric bolts and brackets were removed, install them, aligning the chisel marks, and then tighten them.

9. Insert the coil spring and slowly compress it into place. Install the lower shock absorber mount.

10. Reverse Steps 1–4 to complete.

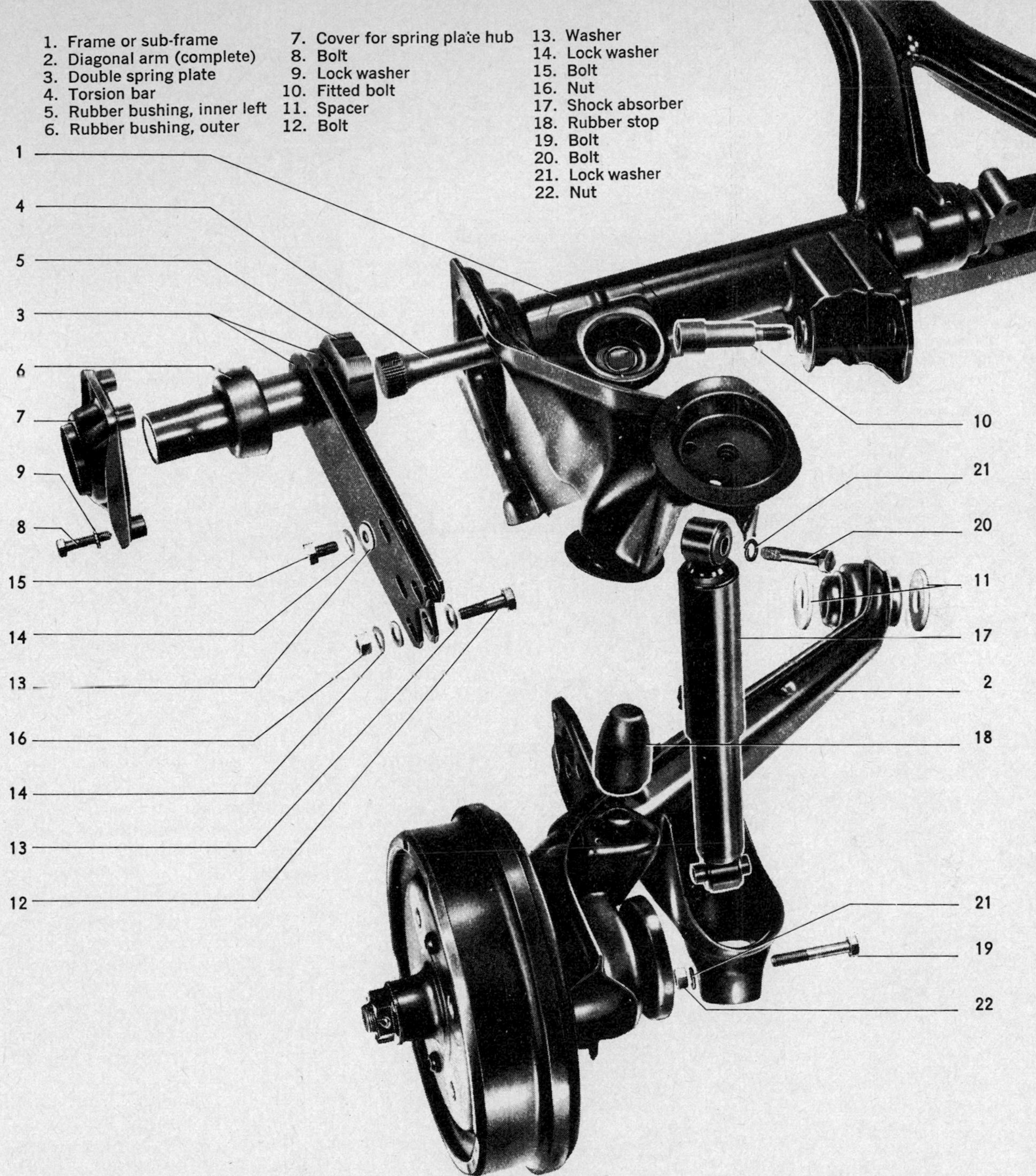

Diagonal arm rear suspension—Types 1, 2, and 3

Shock Absorber Removal and Installation

Diagonal Arm Suspension

The shock absorber is secured at the top and bottom by a through bolt. Raise the car and remove the bolts. Remove the shock absorber from the car.

A-Arm Suspension

The shock absorber is the lower stop for the suspension.

CAUTION: *The A-arm must be securely supported when the shock absorber is disconnected to prevent the spring tension from being released suddenly.*

Leaving the car on the ground or raising the car and securely supporting the A-arm, remove the lower shock absorber through bolt. To gain access to the upper shock mounting, remove the access panel for each shock located at the sides of the rear luggage shelf. Remove the self locking nut from the shock absorber shaft and remove the shock. Installation is the reverse of removal.

Rear Suspension Adjustments

Type 1, Diagonal Arm Suspension

The only adjustment is the toe-in adjustment. The adjustment is performed by varying the number of washers at the diagonal arm pivot. There must always

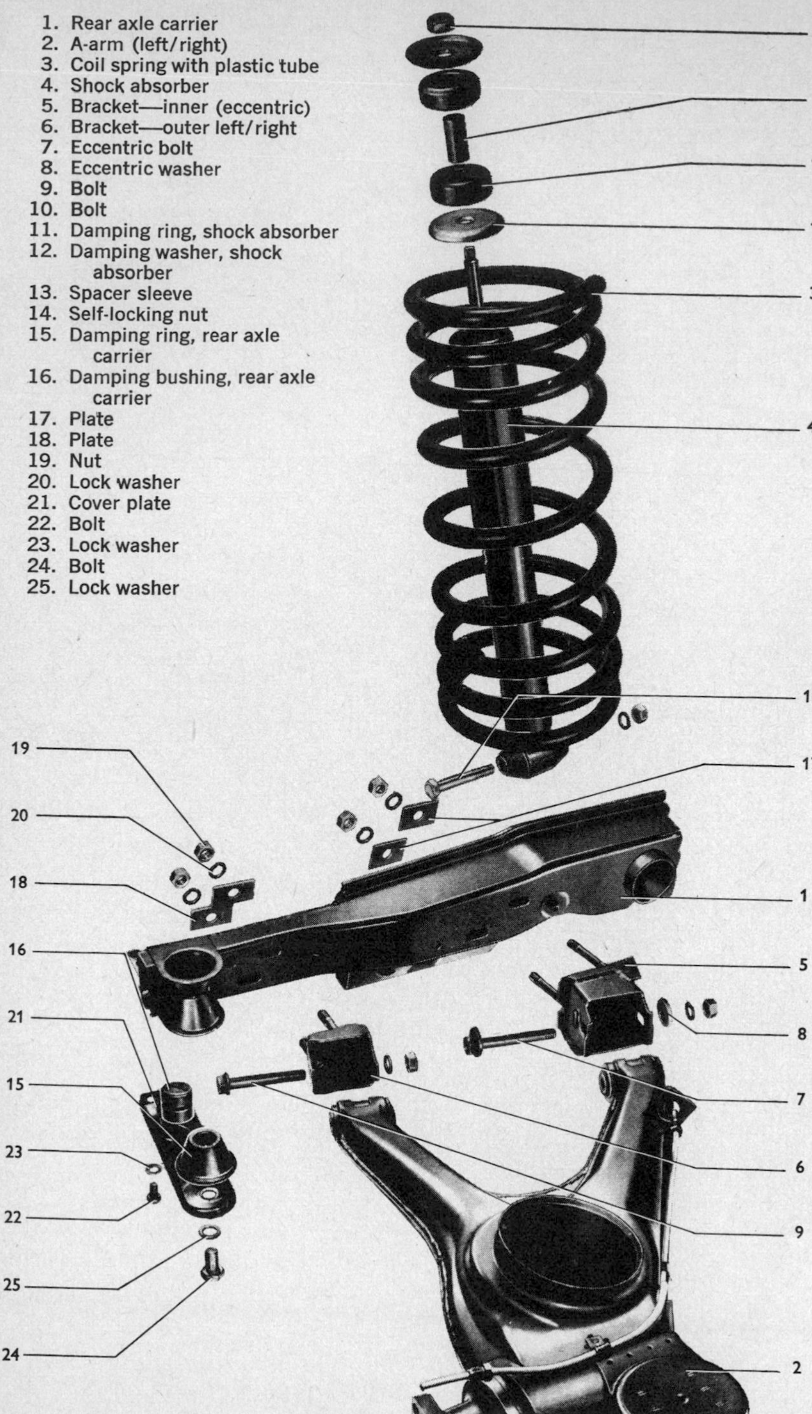

A-Arm rear suspension—Type 4

be one washer located on the outboard side of the pivot.

Type 2, 3, Diagonal Arm Suspension

The transmission and engine assembly position in the vehicle is adjustable. It is necessary that the assembly be correctly centered before the suspension is aligned. It may be adjusted by moving the engine and transmission brackets in their elongated slots.

The distance between the diagonal arms may be adjusted by moving the washers at the A-arm pivots. The washers may be positioned only two ways. Either both washers on the outboard side of the pivot or a single washer on each side of the pivot. To adjust the distance, position the diagonal arms and move the washers in the same manner at both pivots.

The wheel track angle may be adjusted by moving the diagonal arm flange in the elongated slot in the spring plate.

The toe-in adjusted by positioning the washers and the diagonal arm pivot.

Type 4, A-Arm Suspension

The toe-in is adjusted by the eccentric A-arm pivot bolts.

The rubber buffer centralization procedure is given in the "Type 4 Transaxle Removal and Installation" procedure.

The track width can be adjusted by loosening the A-arm mounting bracket bolts and moving the brackets in or out to the proper position.

FRONT SUSPENSION

Torsion Bar Suspension—Types 1, 2, 3 (Except Super Beetle and 1971–75 Beetle Convertible)

Torsion Bar Removal and Installation

1. Jack up the car and remove both wheels and brake drums.
2. Remove the ball joint nuts and remove the left and right steering knuckles. A forked ball joint removing tool is available at an auto parts store.

   CAUTION: *Never strike the ball joint stud.*
3. Remove those arms attached to the torsion bars on one side only. To remove the arms, loosen and remove the arm set-screw and pull the arm off the end of the torsion bar.
4. Loosen and remove the set-screw which secures the torsion bar to the torsion bar housing.
5. Pull the torsion bar out of its housing.
6. To install, carefully note the number of leaves and the position of the countersink marks for the torsion bar and the torsion arm.
7. Align the countersink mark in the center of the bar with the hole for the set-screw and insert the torsion bar into its housing. Install the set screw. Install the torsion arm.
8. Reverse Steps 1–3 to complete.

Torsion Arm Removal and Installation

1. Jack up the car and remove the wheel and tire.
2. Remove the brake drum and the steering knuckle.
3. If the lower torsion arm is being removed, disconnect the stabilizer bar. To remove the stabilizer bar clamp, tap the wedge shaped keeper toward the outside of the car or in the direction the narrow end of the keeper is pointing.
4. On Type 1 and 2, back off on the set-screw locknut and remove the set-

1. Nut
2. Spring washer
3. Washer
4. Bolt
5. Nut
6. Spring washer
7. Bolt
8. Support for axle
9. Bolt
10. Spring washer
11. Plate
12. Rubber packing, upper
13. Rubber packing, lower
14. Bolt
15. Spring washer
16. Lock washer
17. Dust cap
18. Clamp nut for wheel bearing
19. Socket hd. screw for clamp nut
20. Thrust washer
21. Outer tapered roller bearing
22. Brake drum
23. Oil seal
24. Inner tapered roller bearing
25. Bolt
26. Spring washer
27. Front wheel brake and backing plate
28. Steering knuckle
29. Retainer, small
30. Retainer, large
31. Clip, small
32. Clip, large
33. Plate, small
34. Plate, large
35. Rubber mounting, small
36. Rubber mounting, large
37. Stabilizer bar
38. Self-locking nut
39. Washer, small
40. Washer, large
41. Eccentric bushing for camber adjustment
42. Upper ball joint
43. Lower ball joint
44. Ring for rubber boot
45. Boot for lower joint
46. Boot for upper joint
47. Ring for rubber boot
48. Plug
49. Locknut
50. Setscrew for torsion bar
51. Torsion arm, upper
52. Torsion arm, lower
53. Pin
54. Pin for shock absorber
55. Nut
56. Lock washer
57. Lock washer
58. Nut
59. Plate for damper bushing
60. Damper bushing
61. Pin for buffer
62. Buffer
63. Tube
64. Shock absorber
65. Sleeve for rubber bushing
66. Rubber bushing
67. Torsion bar—10 leaf
68. Seal for upper torsion arm
69. Seal for lower torsion arm
70. Needle bearing, upper
71. Needle bearing, lower
72. Grease fitting
74. Axle
75. Bolt

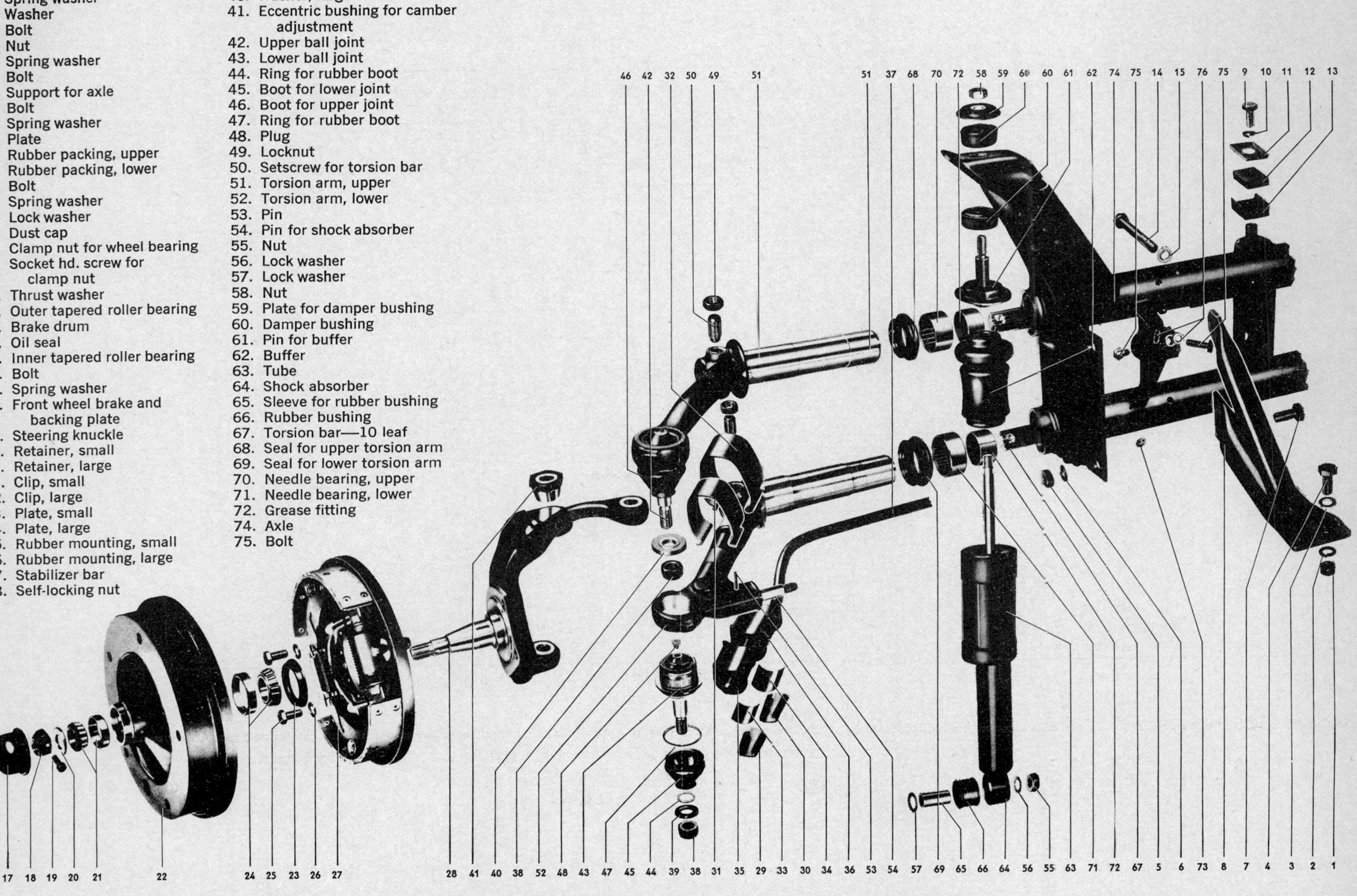

Torsion bar front suspension—Types 1 (Beetle, Karmann Ghia, Thing), 2 and 3

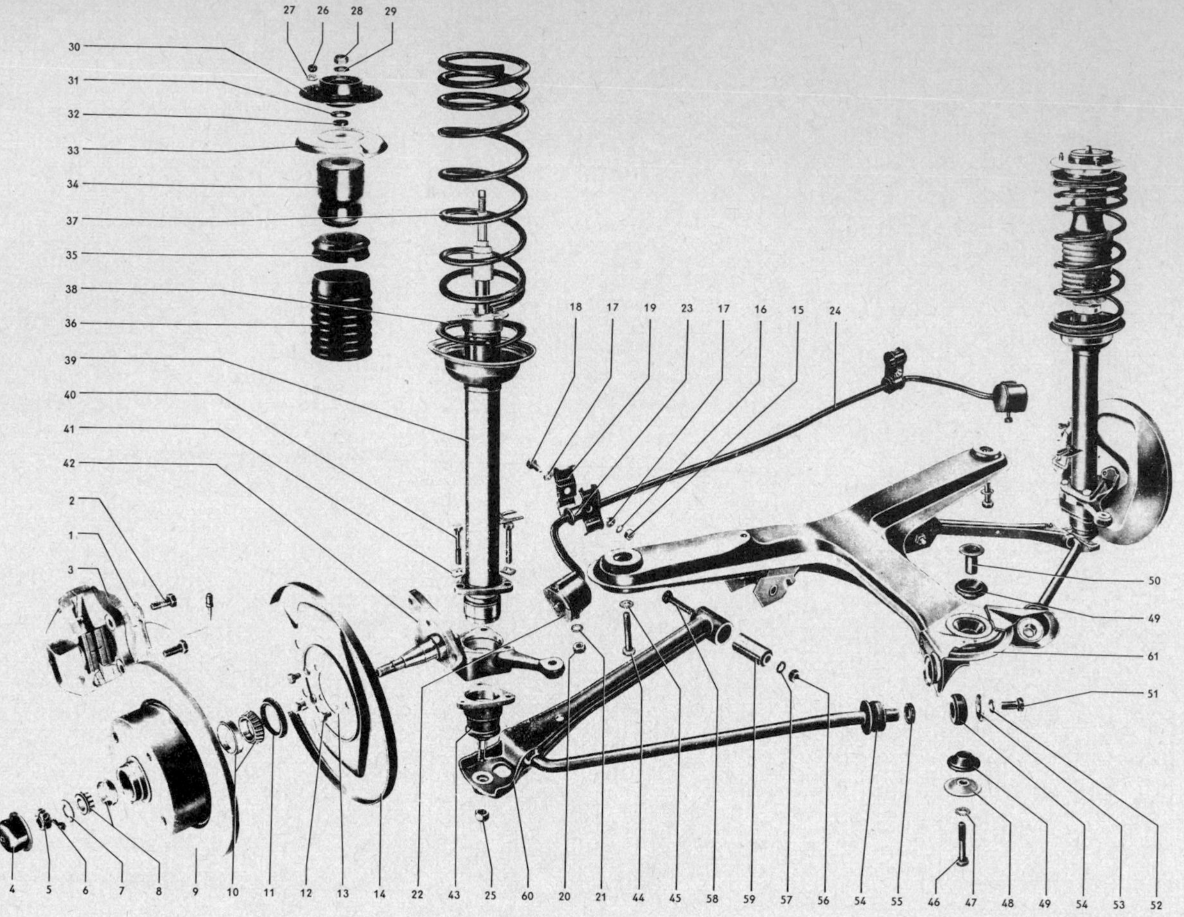

Strut type front suspension—Type 4, Type 1 Super Beetle and 1971-75 Beetle convertible

1. Lockplate
2. Bolt
3. Caliper
4. Hub cap
5. Wheel bearing locknut
6. Allen screw for locknut
7. Thrust washer
8. Outer taper roller bearing
9. Brake disc
10. Inner taper roller bearing
11. Oil seal
12. Bolt
13. Spring washer
14. Splash shield for disc
15. Nut
16. Spring washer
17. Washer
18. Bolt
19. Clamp for stabilizer bar
20. Nut
21. Spring washer
22. Stabilizer mounting for control arm
23. Rubber bushing for clamp
24. Stabilizer bar
25. Self-locking nut
26. Self-locking nut
27. Washer
28. Self-locking nut
29. Washer, small
30. Suspension strut bearing
31. Sealing plate
32. Spacer ring
33. Spring plate
34. Rubber stop for shock absorber
35. Retaining ring for protective tube
36. Protective tube for shock absorber
37. Coil spring
38. Damping ring, coil spring
39. Shock absorber
40. Bolt
41. Lock washer
42. Steering knuckle
43. Ball joint
44. Bolt
45. Lock washer
46. Bolt
47. Lock washer
48. Seat for damping ring
49. Damping ring for front axle carrier
50. Spacer sleeve
51. Bolt
52. Spring washer
53. Plate for damping ring
54. Damping ring for radius rod
55. Locating ring for radius rod
56. Nut
57. Spring washer
58. Bolt
59. Bushing for track control arm
60. Track control arm
61. Front axle carrier

screw. On Type 3, remove the bolt and keeper from the end of the torsion bar.

5. Slide the torsion arm off the end of the torsion bar.

6. Reverse the above steps to install. Check the camber and toe-in settings.

Strut Suspension—Type 1 Super Beetle, 1971–75 Beetle Convertible, and all Type 4

Suspension Strut Removal and Installation

1. Jack up the car and remove the wheel and tire.

2. If the left strut is to be removed, remove the speedometer cable from the steering knuckle.

3. Disconnect the brake line from the bracket on the strut.

4. At the base of the strut, bend down the locking tabs for the three bolts and remove the bolts.

5. Push down on the steering knuckle and pull the strut out of the knuckle.

6. Remove the three nuts which secure the top of the strut to the body. Before removing the last nut, support the strut so that it does not fall out of the car.

7. Reverse the above steps to install the strut. Always use new nuts and locking tabs during installation.

Track Control Arm Removal and Installation

1. Remove the ball joint stud nut and remove the stud from the control arm.

2. Disconnect the stabilizer bar from the control arm.

3. Remove the nut and eccentric bolt at the frame. This is the pivot bolt for the control arm and is used to adjust camber.

4. Pull the arm downward and remove it from the vehicle.

5. Reverse the above steps to install. Make sure the groove in the stabilizer bar bushing is horizontal.

6. Realign the front end.

Shock Absorber Removal and Installation

Torsion Bar Suspension (Types 1, 2, and 3)

1. Remove the wheel and tire.
2. Remove the nut from the torsion arm stud and slide the lower end of the shock off of the stud.
3. Remove the nut from the shock absorber shaft at the upper mounting and remove the shock from the vehicle.
4. The shock is tested by operating it by hand. As the shock is extended and compressed, it should operate smoothly over its entire stroke with an even pressure. Its damping action should be clearly felt at the end of each stroke. If the shock is leaking slightly, the shock need not be replaced. A shock that has had an excessive loss of fluid will have flat spots in the stroke as the shock is compressed and extended. That is, the pressure will feel as though it has been suddenly released for a short distance during the stroke.
5. Installation is the reverse of Steps 1–3.

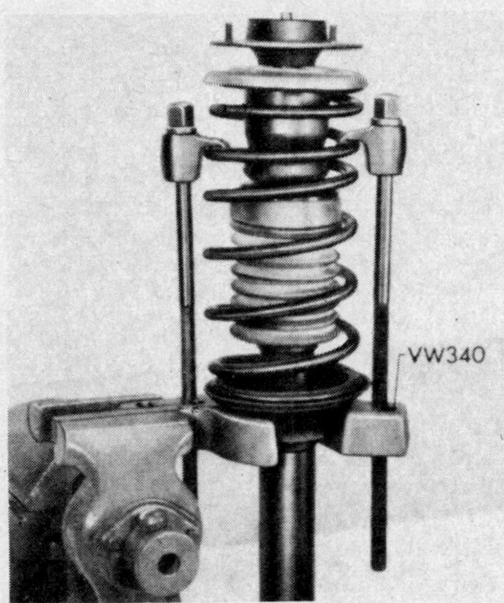

Compressing coil spring of strut type suspension

Strut Suspension (Super Beetle and Type 4)

In this type suspension system, the shock absorber is actually the supporting vertical member.

1. Remove the strut as outlined above.
2. It is necessary to disassemble the strut to replace the shock absorber. To remove the spring, it must be compressed. The proper type compressor is available at an auto parts store.
3. Remove the nut from the end of the shock absorber shaft and slowly release the spring. The strut can now be disassembled. Testing is the same as the torsion bar shock absorber.
4. Reverse the above steps to install.

Ball Joint Removal and Installation

Vehicles with strut suspension have only one ball joint on each side located at the base of the strut in the track control arm. Vehicles with torsion bar suspension have two ball joints on each side located at the end of each torsion arm.

Torsion Bar Suspension

1. Jack up the car and remove the wheel and tire.
2. Remove the brake drum and disconnect the brake line from the backing plate.
3. Remove the nut from each ball joint stud and remove the ball joint stud from the steering knuckle. Remove the steering knuckle from the car. A ball joint removal tool is available at an auto parts store. Do not strike the ball joint stud.

A notched ball joint on a car with a torsion bar suspension indicates that it is oversized

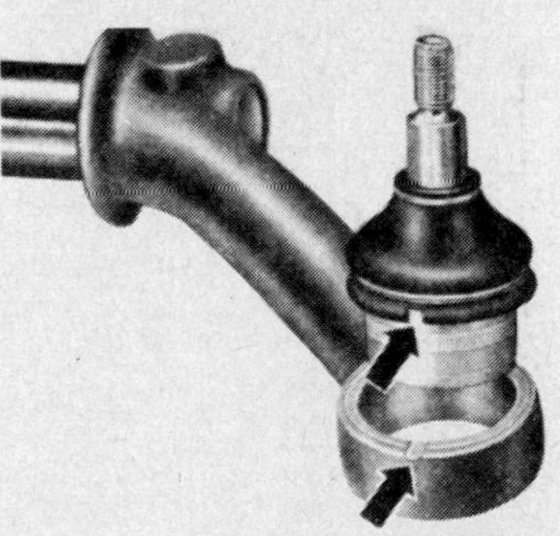

Align the square notch in the ball joint with the notch in the torsion arm upon installation

4. Remove the torsion arm from the torsion bar.
5. Remove the ball joint from the torsion arm by pressing it out.
6. Press a new ball joint in, making sure that the square notch in the joint is in line with the notch in the torsion arm eye.

   NOTE: *Ball joints are supplied in different sizes designated by V-notches in the ring around the side of the joint. When replacing a ball joint, make sure that the new part has the same number of V-notches. If it has no notches, the replacement joint should have no notches.*

7. Reverse Steps 1–4 to complete the installation.

Strut Suspension

1. Jack up the car and remove the wheel and tire.
2. Remove the nut from the ball joint stud and remove the stud from the track control arm.
3. Bend back the locking tab and remove the three ball joint securing screws.
4. Pull the track control arm downward and remove the ball joint from the strut.
5. Reverse the above steps to install.

Ball Joint Inspection

Torsion Bar Suspension

1. A quick initial inspection can be made with the vehicle on the ground.
2. Grasp the top of the tire and vigorously pull the top of the tire in and out. Test both sides in this manner.
3. If the ball joints are excessively worn, there will be an audible tap as the ball moves around in its socket. Excess play can sometimes be felt through the tire.
4. A more rigorous test may be performed by jacking the car under the lower torsion arm and inserting a lever under the tire.
5. Lift up gently on the lever so as to pry the tire upward.
6. If the ball joints are worn, the tire will move upward ⅛–¼ in. or more.
7. If the tire displays excessive movement, have an assistant inspect each joint, as the tire is pryed upward, to determine which ball joint is defective.

Strut Suspension

1. Raise the car and support it under the frame. The wheel must be clear of the ground.
2. With a lever, apply upward pressure to the track control arm.
3. Apply the pressure gently and slowly; it is important that only enough pressure is exerted to check the play in the ball joint and not compress the suspension.
4. Using a vernier caliper, measure the distance between the control arm and the lower edge of the ball joint flange. Record the reading.
5. Release the pressure on the track control arm and again measure the distance between the control arm and the lower edge of the ball joint flange.
6. Record the reading.
7. Subtract the higher reading from the lower reading. If the difference is more than 0.10 in., the ball joint should be replaced.

   NOTE: *Remember that even in a new joint there will be measurable play because the ball in the ball joint is spring loaded.*

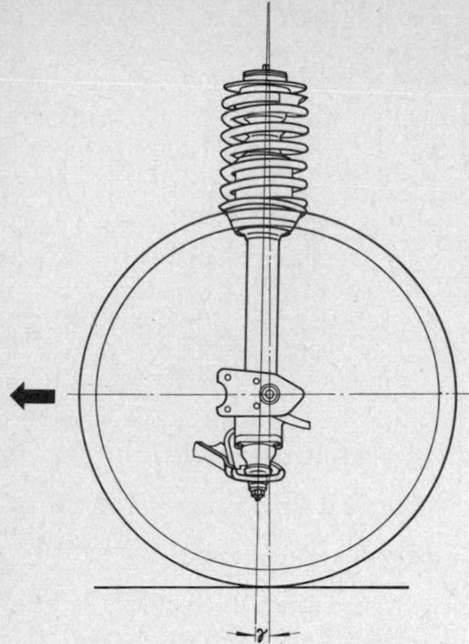

Caster—strut suspension shown

γ = Caster angle

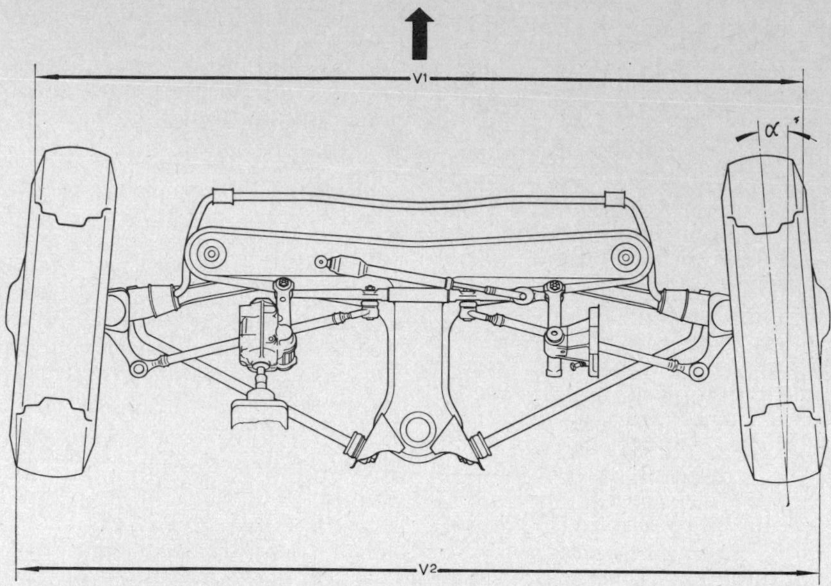

Toe-in—strut suspension shown

V_1—distance between the rims on the forward side of the tire
V_2—distance between the rims on the rear side of the tire
α—the angle of toe-in, measured in degrees for one wheel only
If V_2 is larger than V_1, the wheels are said to have toe-in

Front End Alignment

Caster Adjustment

Caster is the forward or backward tilt of the spindle. Forward tilt is negative caster and backward tilt is positive caster. Caster is not adjustable on either the torsion bar or the strut suspensions.

Camber Adjustment

Camber is the tilt of the top of the wheel, inward or outward, from true vertical. Outward tilt is positive, inward tilt is negative.

Torsion Bar Suspension

The upper ball joint on each side is mounted in an eccentric bushing. The bushing has a hex head and it may be rotated in either direction using a wrench.

Strut Suspension

The track control arm pivots on an eccentric bolt. Camber is adjusted by loosening the nut and rotating the bolt.

Toe-in Adjustment

Toe-in is the adjustment made to make the front wheels point slightly into the front. Toe-in is adjusted on both types of front suspensions by adjusting the length of the tie-rod sleeves.

STEERING

Steering Wheel Removal and Installation

1. Disconnect the negative battery cable.
2. Remove the center emblem. This emblem will gently pry off the wheel, or is attached by screws from the back of the steering wheel.
3. Remove the nut from the steering shaft. This is a right-hand thread.

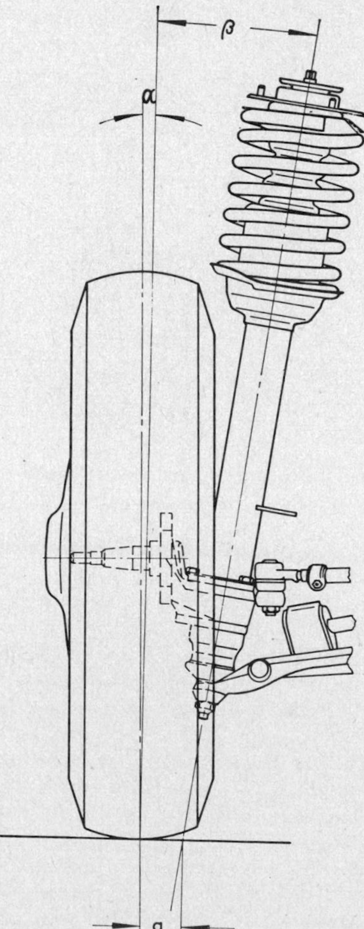

Camber—strut suspension shown

Angle α = camber
β = steering pivot angle
a = steering roll radius

NOTE: *Mark the steering shaft and steering wheel so that the wheel may be installed in the same position on the shaft.*

4. Using a steering wheel puller, remove the wheel from the splined steering shaft. Do not strike the end of the steering shaft.
5. Reverse the above steps to install. Make sure to align the match marks made on the steering wheel and steering shaft. The gap between the turn signal switch housing and the back of the wheel is 0.08–0.12 in. (distance "a").

Turn Signal Switch Removal and Installation

1. Disconnect the negative battery cable.
2. Remove the steering wheel.
3. Remove the four turn signal switch securing screws.
4. Disconnect the turn signal switch wiring plug under the steering column.
5. Pull the switch and wiring guide rail up and out of the steering column.

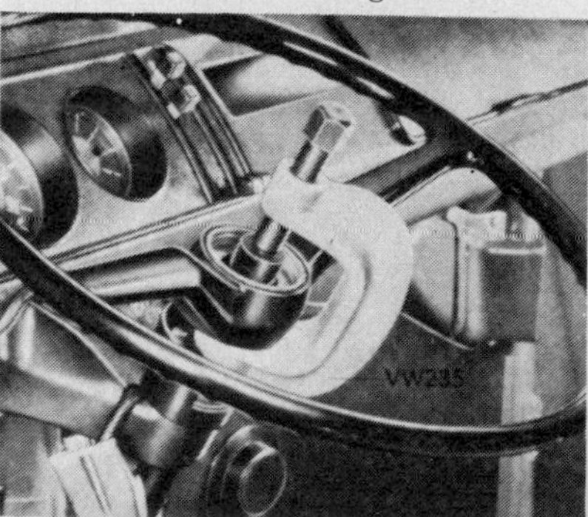

Steering wheel removal—Type 2

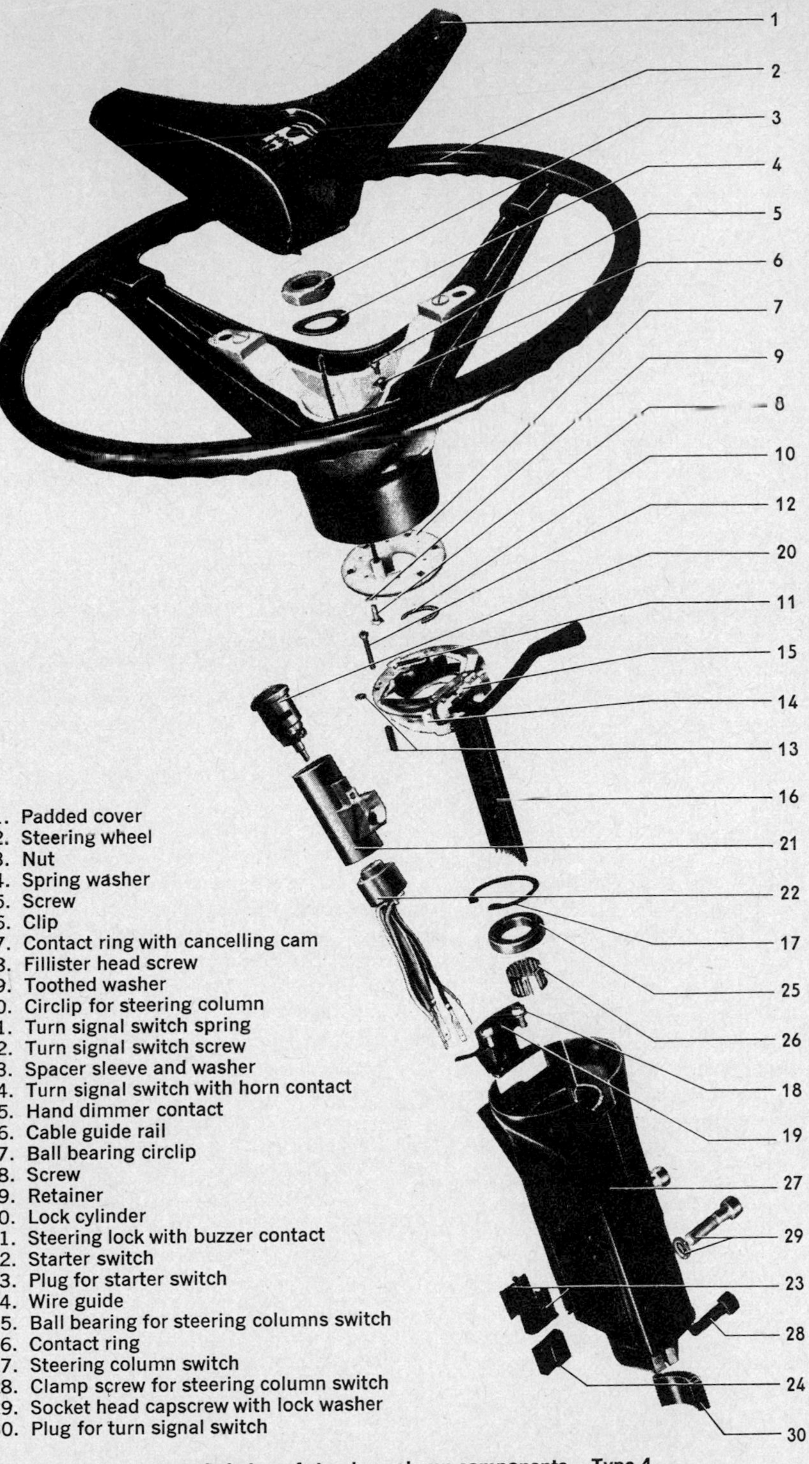

1. Padded cover
2. Steering wheel
3. Nut
4. Spring washer
5. Screw
6. Clip
7. Contact ring with cancelling cam
8. Fillister head screw
9. Toothed washer
10. Circlip for steering column
11. Turn signal switch spring
12. Turn signal switch screw
13. Spacer sleeve and washer
14. Turn signal switch with horn contact
15. Hand dimmer contact
16. Cable guide rail
17. Ball bearing circlip
18. Screw
19. Retainer
20. Lock cylinder
21. Steering lock with buzzer contact
22. Starter switch
23. Plug for starter switch
24. Wire guide
25. Ball bearing for steering columns switch
26. Contact ring
27. Steering column switch
28. Clamp screw for steering column switch
29. Socket head capscrew with lock washer
30. Plug for turn signal switch

Exploded view of steering column components—Type 4

Turn signal switch retaining screws

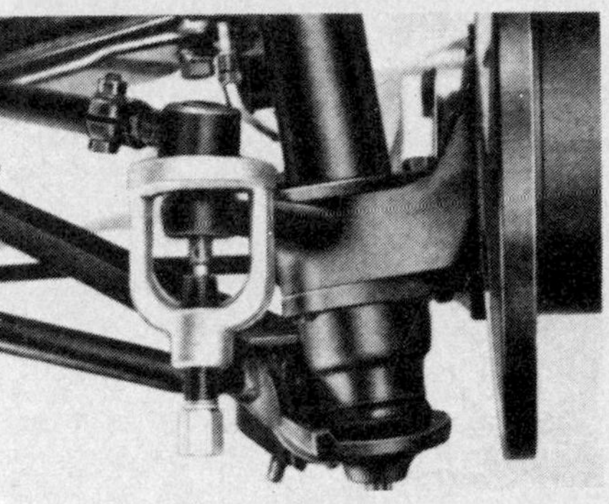

Removing tie-rod end from steering knuckle

Correct gap (a) between steering wheel and column

6. Reverse the above steps to install. Make sure the spacers located behind the switch, if installed originally, are in position. The distance between the steering wheel and the steering column housing is (distance "a") 0.08–0.12 in. Install the switch with the lever in the central position.

Steering Linkage Removal and Installation

1. All tie-rod ends are secured by a nut which holds the tapered tie-rod end stud into a matching tapered hole. There are several ways to remove the tapered stud from its hole after the nut has been removed.

2. First, there are several types of removal tools available from auto parts stores. These tools include directions for their use. One of the most commonly available tools is the fork shaped tool which is a wedge that is forced under the tie-rod end. This tool should be used with caution because instead of removing the tie-rod end from its hole it may pull the ball out of its socket, ruining the tie-rod end.

3. It is also possible to remove the tie-rod end by holding a heavy hammer on one side of the tapered hole and striking the opposite side of the hole sharply with another hammer. The stud will pop out of its hole, usually.

CAUTION: *Never strike the end of the tie-rod end stud. It is impossible to remove the tie-rod end in this manner.*

4. Once the tie-rod end stud has been removed, turn the tie-rod end out of the adjusting sleeve.

5. On the pieces of the steering linkage that are not used to adjust the toe-in, the tie-rod end is welded in place and it will be necessary to replace the whole assembly.

6. When reassembling the steering linkage, never put lubricant in the tapered hole.

Manual Steering Gear Adjustment

There are two types of steering gear boxes. The first type is the roller type, identified by the square housing cover secured by four screws, one at each corner. The second type is the worm and peg type, identified by an assymetric housing cover with the adjusting screw located at one side of the housing cover.

Roller Type—Types 1, 3, 4

Disconnect the steering linkage from the pitman arm and make sure the gearbox mounting bolts are tight. Have an assistant rotate the steering wheel so that the pitman arm moves alternately 10° to the left and then 10° to the right of the straight ahead position. Turn the adjusting screw in until no further play can be felt while moving the pitman arm. Tighten the adjusting screw locknut and recheck the adjustment.

Worm and Peg Type—Type 2 Models (1970–72)

Have an assistant turn the steering wheel back and forth through the center position several times. The steering wheel should turn through the center position without any noticeable binding.

To adjust, turn the adjusting screw inward while the assistant is turning the steering wheel. Turn the screw in until the steering begins to tighten up. Back out the adjusting screw until the steering no longer binds while turning through the center point and tighten the adjusting screw locknut.

The adjustment is correct when there is no binding and no perceptible play.

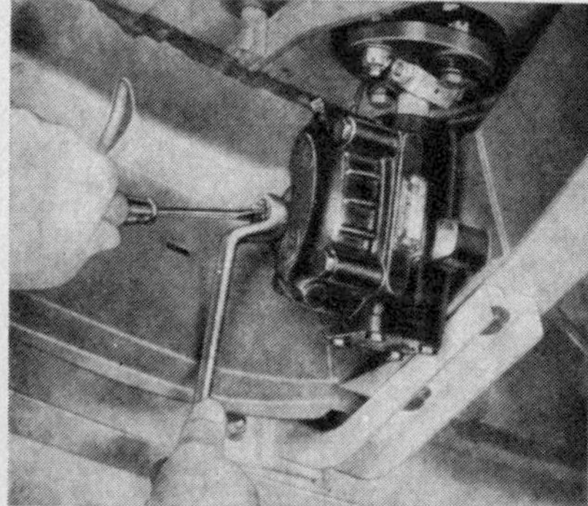

Adjusting worm and peg steering gear—roller type similar

BRAKES

Brake Adjustment

Disc brakes are self adjusting and cannot be adjusted by hand. As the pads wear, they will automatically compensate for the wear by moving closer to the disc, maintaining the proper operating clearance.

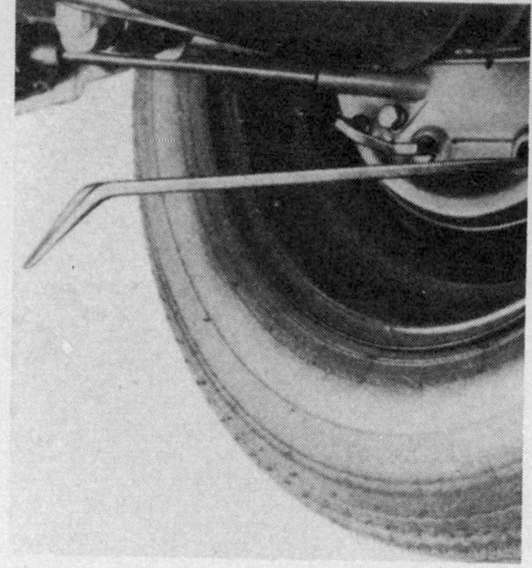

Adjusting drum brakes through access hole in backing plate—rear brakes shown

Drum brakes, however, must be manually adjusted to take up excess clearance as the shoes wear.

1. To adjust drum brakes, both front and rear, it is necessary to jack up the car and support it on a jackstand. The wheel must spin freely.
2. On the backing plate there are four inspection holes with a rubber plug in each hole. Two of the holes are for checking the thickness of the brake lining and the other two are used for adjustment.

   NOTE: *There is an adjustment for each brake shoe. That means that on each wheel it is necessary to make two adjustments, one for each shoe on that wheel.*
3. Remove the adjustment hole plugs and, using a screwdriver or brake adjusting tool, insert the tool into the hole.
4. Turn the star wheel until a slight drag is noticed as the wheel is rotated by hand.
5. Back off on the star wheel 3–4 notches so that the wheel turns freely.
6. Perform the same adjustment on the other shoe.

   NOTE: *One of the star wheels in each wheel has left-hand threads and the other star wheel has right-hand threads.*
7. Repeat the above procedure on each wheel with drum brakes.

Master Cylinder

Removal and Installation

1. Drain the brake fluid from the master cylinder reservoir.

   CAUTION: *Do not get any brake fluid on the paint, as it will dissolve the paint.*
2. On Type 3, remove the master cylinder cover plate.
3. Pull the plastic elbows out of the rubber sealing rings on the top of the master cylinder.
4. Remove the two bolts which secure the master cylinder to the frame and remove the cylinder. Note the spacers on the Type 1 between the frame and the master cylinder.
5. To install, bolt the master cylinder to the frame. Do not forget the spacers on the Type 1.
6. Lubricate the elbows with brake fluid and insert them into the rubber seals.
7. If necessary, adjust the brake pedal free travel. On Type 1, 3, and 4, adjust the length of the master cylinder pushrod so that there is 5–7 mm of brake pedal free-play before the pushrod contacts the master cylinder piston. On Type 2, the free-play is properly adjusted when the length of the pushrod, measured between the ball end and the center of the clevis pin hole, is 4.17 in.
8. Refill the master cylinder reservoir and bleed the brakes.

Master Cylinder Overhaul

1. Remove the master cylinder from the car.
2. Remove the rubber sealing boot.
3. Remove the stop screw and sealing ring on the top of the unit.
4. Insert a screwdriver in the master cylinder piston, exert inward pressure, and remove the snap-ring from its groove in the end of the unit. The internal parts are spring loaded and must be kept from flying out when the snap-ring is removed.
5. Carefully remove the internal parts of the unit and make note of their order and the orientation of the internal parts. If parts remain in the cylinder bore, they may be removed with a wire hook or very gentle application of low pressure air to the stop screw hole. Cover the end of the cylinder bore with a rag and stand away from the open end of the bore when using compressed air.
6. Use alcohol or brake fluid to clean the master cylinder and its parts.
7. It may be necessary to hone the cylinder bore, or clean it by lightly sanding it with emery cloth. Clean thoroughly after honing or sanding. Lubricate the bore with brake fluid before reassembly.
8. Holding the master cylinder with the open end downward, place the cup washer, primary cup, support washer, spring retainer, and spring onto the front brake circuit piston and insert the piston vertically into the master cylinder bore.
9. Assemble the rear brake circuit piston, cup washer, primary cup, support washer, spring retainer, stop sleeve, spring, and stroke limiting screw and insert the assembly into the master cylinder.
10. Install the stop washer and snapring.
11. Install the stop screw and seal, making sure the hole for the screw is not blocked by the piston. If the hole is

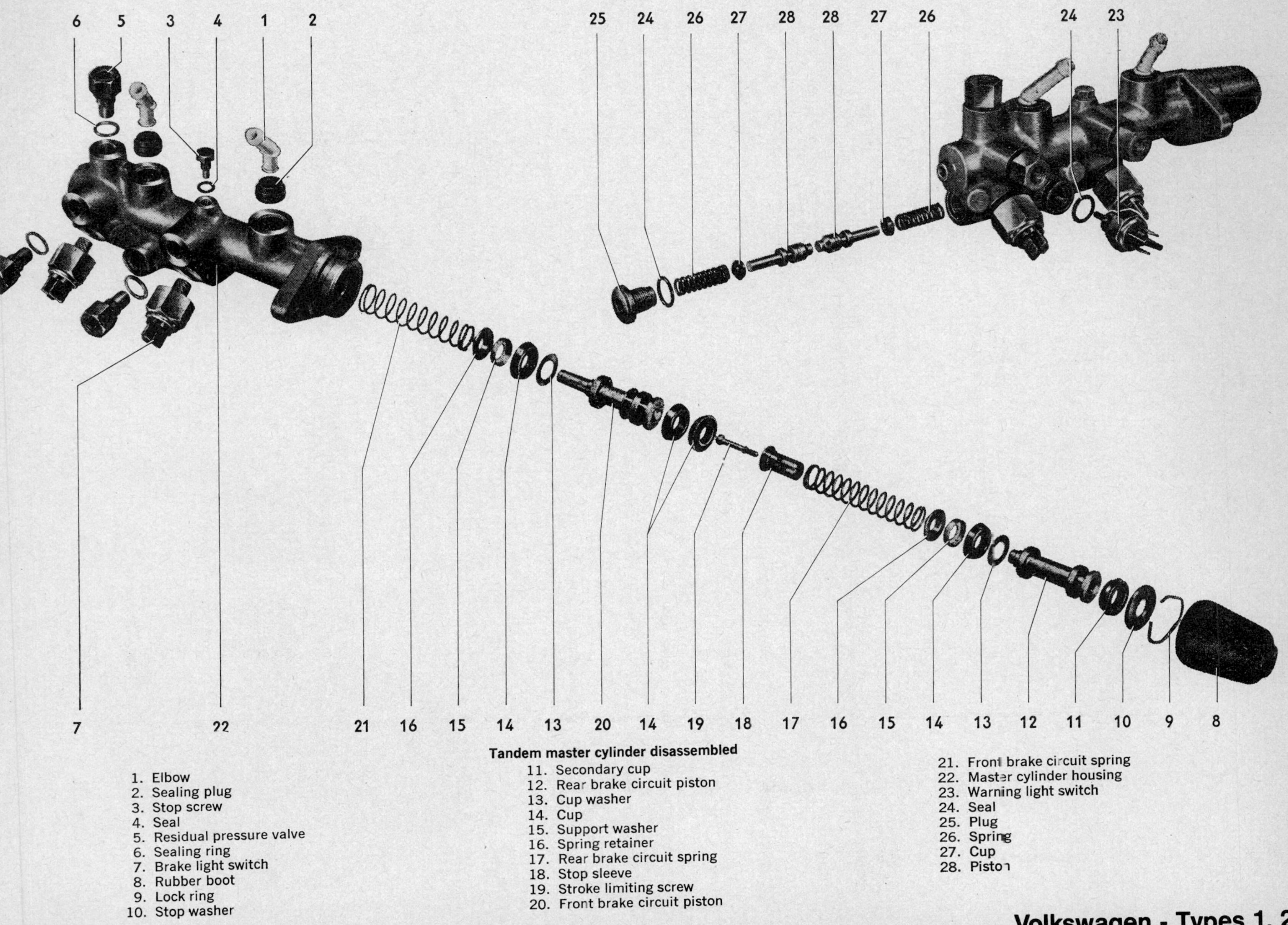

Tandem master cylinder disassembled

1. Elbow
2. Sealing plug
3. Stop screw
4. Seal
5. Residual pressure valve
6. Sealing ring
7. Brake light switch
8. Rubber boot
9. Lock ring
10. Stop washer
11. Secondary cup
12. Rear brake circuit piston
13. Cup washer
14. Cup
15. Support washer
16. Spring retainer
17. Rear brake circuit spring
18. Stop sleeve
19. Stroke limiting screw
20. Front brake circuit piston
21. Front brake circuit spring
22. Master cylinder housing
23. Warning light switch
24. Seal
25. Plug
26. Spring
27. Cup
28. Piston

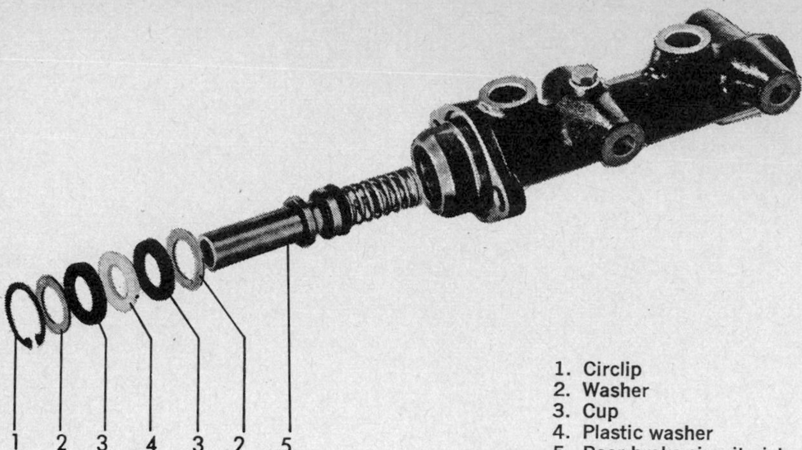

Type 2 brake servo disassembled

blocked, it will be necessary to push the piston further in until the screw can be turned in.

NOTE: *Some Type 2 vehicles have a brake servo and the order of assembly of the additional seals is illustrated.*

12. Install the master cylinder and bleed the brakes.

Hydraulic System Bleeding

The hydraulic brake system must be bled any time one of the lines is disconnected or air enters the system.

Manual Bleeding

This method requires two people: one to depress the brake pedal and the other to open the bleeder nipples.

1. Remove the reservoir caps and fill the reservoir.
2. Attach a bleeder hose and a clear container as outlined in the pressure bleeding procedure.
3. Have the assistant depress the brake pedal to the floor several times and then have him hold the pedal to the floor. With the pedal to the floor, open the bleeder nipple until the fluid flow ceases and then close the nipple. Repeat this sequence until there are no more air bubbles in the fluid.

NOTE: *As the air is gradually forced out of the system, it will no longer be possible to force the brake pedal to the floor.*

Periodically check the master cylinder for an adequate supply of fluid. Keep the master cylinder reservoir full of fluid to prevent air from entering the system. If the reservoir does run dry during bleeding, it will be necessary to rebleed the entire system.

Front Disc Brakes

Brake Pad

Removal and Installation

1. Loosen but do not remove the reservoir cover.
2. Jack up the car and remove the wheel and tire.
3. Using a punch, remove the two pins which retain the disc brake pads in the caliper.

NOTE: *If the pads are to be reused, mark the pads to insure that they are reinstalled in the same caliper and on the same side of the disc. Do nót invert the pads. Changing pads from one location to another can cause uneven braking.*

4. If the pads are not going to be reused, force a wedge between the disc and the pad and pry the piston back into the caliper as far as possible.
5. Using compressed air, blow away the brake dust. Pull the old pad out of the caliper and insert a new one.
6. Now insert the wedge between the disc and pad on the opposite side and force that piston into the caliper. Remove the old pad and insert a new one.
7. If the old pads are to be reused, it is not necessary to push the piston into the caliper. Pull the pads from the caliper and reinstall the pads when necessary.
8. Install a new brake pad spreader spring and insert the retaining pins. Be

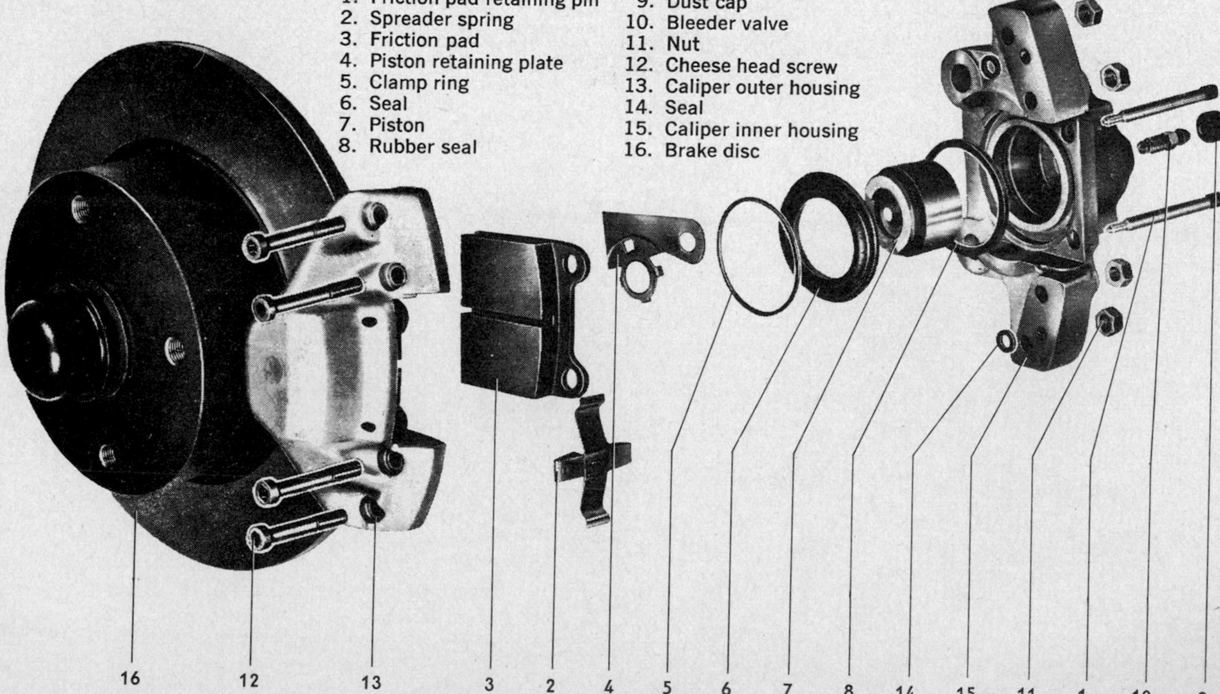

Front disc brake assembly—Types 1 (Karmann Ghia) and 3

careful not to shear the split clamping bushing from the pin. Insert the pin from the inside of the caliper and drive it to the outside.

9. Pump the brake pedal several times to take up the clearance between the pads and the disc before driving the car.

10. Install the wheel and tire and carefully road test the car. Apply the brakes gently for 500 to 1000 miles to properly break in the pads and prevent glazing them.

Brake Caliper

Removal and Installation

1. Jack up the car and remove the wheel and tire.
2. Remove the brake pads.
3. Disconnect the brake line from the caliper.
4. Remove the two bolts which secure the caliper to the steering knuckle and remove the caliper from the vehicle.
5. Reverse the above steps to install the caliper and bleed the brakes after the caliper is installed.

Overhaul

Clean all parts in alcohol or brake fluid.

1. Remove the caliper from the vehicle.
2. Remove the piston retaining plates.
3. Pry out the seal spring ring using a small screwdriver. Do not damage the seal beneath the ring.
4. Remove the seal with a plastic or hard rubber rod. Do not use sharp edged or metal tools.

Clamping a caliper piston in place and applying compressed air to the brake hose port

5. Rebuild one piston at a time. Securely clamp one piston in place so that it cannot come out of its bore. Place a block of wood between the two pistons and apply air pressure to the brake fluid port.

CAUTION: *Use extreme care with this technique because the piston can fly out of the caliper with tremendous force.*

6. Remove the rubber seal at the bottom of the piston bore using a rubber or plastic tool.
7. Check the bore and piston for wear, rust, and pitting.
8. Install a new seal in the bottom of the bore and lubricate the bore and seal with brake fluid.
9. Gently insert the piston, making sure it does not cock and jamb in the bore.
10. Install the new outer seal and new spring ring.
11. Install the piston retaining plate.
12. Repeat the above procedure on the other piston. Never rebuild only one side of a caliper.

Brake Disc

Removal and Installation

1. Jack up the car and remove the wheel and tire.
2. Remove the caliper.
3. On Type 2, remove the three socket head bolts which secure the disc to the hub and remove the disc from the hub. Sometimes the disc is rusted to the hub. Spray penetrating oil on the seam and tap the disc with a lead or brass hammer. If it still does not come off, screw three 8 mm by 40 screws into the socket head holes. Tighten the screws evenly and pull the disc from the hub.
4. On Type 1, 3, and 4, remove the wheel bearing cover. On the left side it will be necessary to remove the small clip which secures the end of the speedometer cable to the cover.
5. Unscrew the wheel bearing nut and remove the nut and outer wheel bearing.
6. Pull the disc off of the spindle.
7. To remove the wheel bearing races, see the "Wheel Bearing Removal and Installation" procedure.
8. Installation is the reverse of the above. Make sure the wheel bearing is properly adjusted.

Inspection

Visually check the rotor for excessive scoring. Minor scores will not affect the performance; however, if the scores are over 1/32 in., it is necessary to replace the disc or have it resurfaced. The disc must be 0.02 in. over the wear limit to be resurfaced. The disc must be free of surface cracks and discoloration (heat bluing). Hand spin the disc and make sure that it does not wobble from side to side.

Front Wheel Bearings

Removal and Installation

1. Jack up the car and remove the wheel and tire.
2. Remove the caliper and disc (if equipped with disc brakes) or brake drum.
3. To remove the inside wheel bearing, pry the dust seal out of the hub with a screwdriver. Lift out the bearing and its inner race.
4. To remove the outer race for either the inner or outer wheel bearing, insert a long punch into the hub opposite the end from which the race is to be removed. The race rests against a shoulder in the hub. The shoulder has two notches cut into it so that it is possible to place the end of the punch directly against the back side of the race and drive it out of the hub.
5. Carefully clean the hub.
6. Install new races in the hub. Drive them in with a soft faced hammer or a large piece of pipe of the proper diameter. Lubricate the races with a light coating of wheel bearing grease.
7. Force wheel bearing grease into the sides of the tapered roller bearings so that all the spaces are filled.
8. Place a small amount of grease inside the hub.
9. Place the inner wheel bearing into its race in the hub and tap a new seal into the hub. Lubricate the sealing surface of the seal with grease.
10. Install the hub on the spindle and install the outer wheel bearing.
11. Adjust the wheel bearing and install the dust cover.
12. Install the caliper (if equipped with disc brakes).

Adjustment

The bearing may be adjusted by feel or by a dial indicator.

To adjust the bearing by feel, tighten the adjusting nut so that all the play is taken up in the bearing. There will be a slight amount of drag on the wheel if it is hand spun. Back off fully on the adjusting nut and retighten very lightly. There should be no drag when the wheel is hand spun and there should be no perceptible play in the bearing when the wheel is grasped and wiggled from side to side.

To use a dial indicator, remove the dust cover and mount a dial indicator against the hub. Grasp the wheel at the side and pull the wheel in and out along the axis of the spindle. Read the axial play on the dial indicator. Screw the adjusting nut in or out to obtain 0.001–0.005 in. of axial play. Secure the adjusting nut and recheck the axial play.

Front Drum Brakes

Brake Drum

Removal and Installation

1. Jack up the car and remove the wheel and tire.
2. On the left side, remove the clip which secures the speedometer cable to

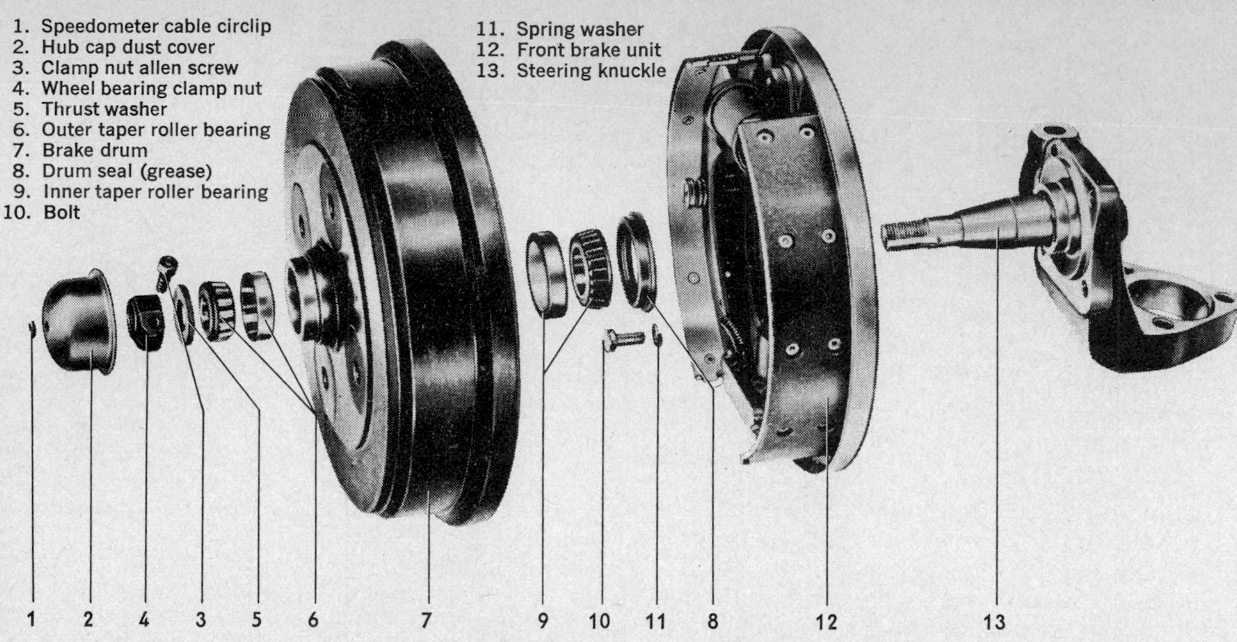

Exploded view of Type 1 front wheel bearings

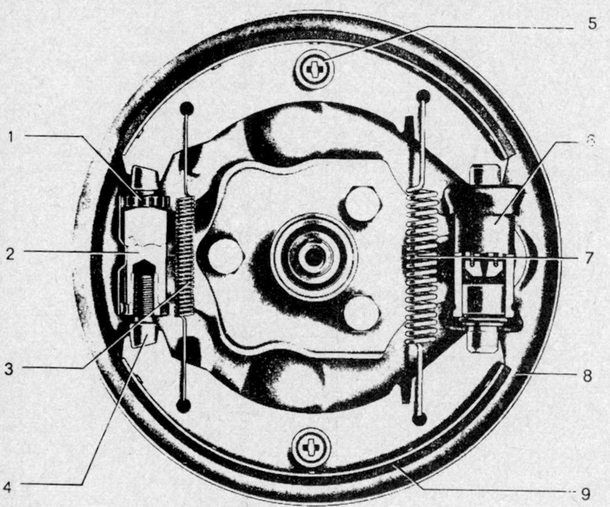

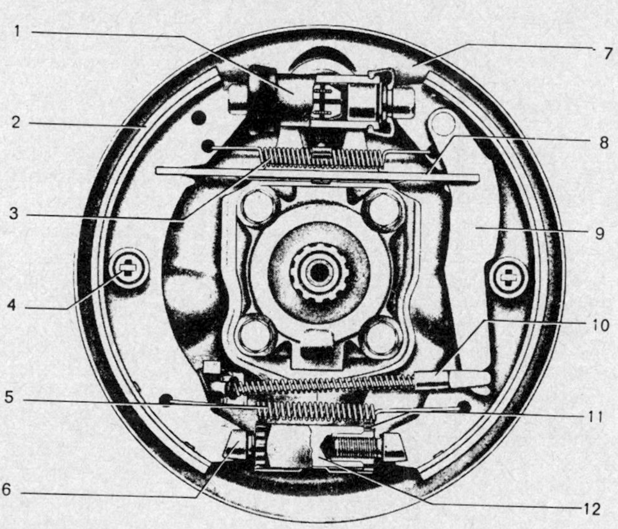

Front and rear drum brakes—Type 1

FRONT
1. Adjusting screw
2. Anchor block
3. Front return spring
4. Adjusting nut
5. Guide spring with cup and pin
6. Cylinder
7. Rear return spring
8. Back plate
9. Brake shoe with lining

REAR
1. Cylinder
2. Brake shoe with lining
3. Upper return spring
4. Spring with cup and pin
5. Lower return spring
6. Adjusting screw
7. Back plate
8. Connecting link
9. Lever
10. Brake cable
11. Adjusting nut
12. Anchor block

the wheel bearing dust cover. Remove the dust cover.

3. Remove the wheel bearing adjusting nut and slide the brake drum off of the spindle. It may be necessary to back off on the brake shoe star wheels so that there is enough clearance to remove the drum.

4. Installation is the reverse of removal. Adjust the wheel bearings after installing the drum.

CAUTION: *Do not forget to readjust the brake shoes if they were disturbed during removal.*

Inspection

If the brake drums are scored or cracked, they must be replaced or machined. If the vehicle pulls to one side or exhibits a pulsating braking action, the drum is probably out of round and should be checked at a machine shop. The drum may have a smooth even surface and still be out of round. The drum should be free of surface cracks and dark spots.

Brake Linings

Removal and Installation

Type 1

1. Jack up the car and remove the wheel and tire.

2. Remove the brake drum.

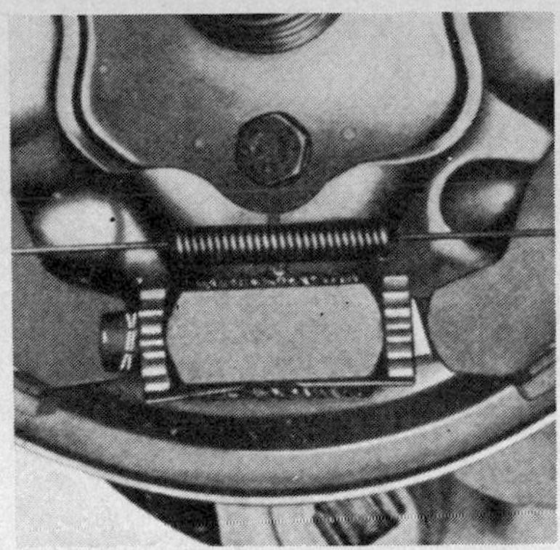

The notched adjusters must be positioned as shown

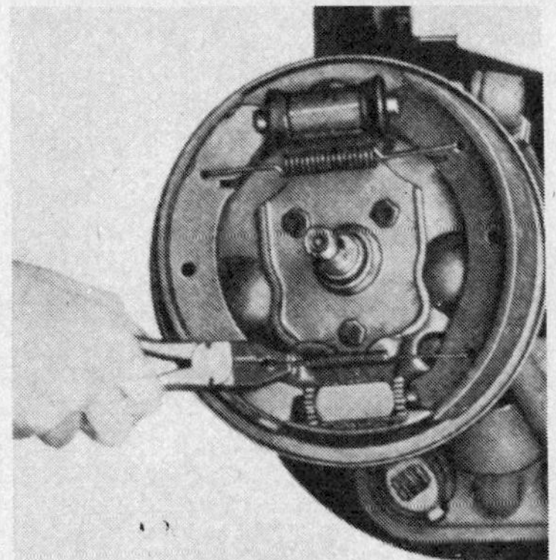

For proper installation, Type 1 brake shoes must have notches in shoes on wheel cylinder side

3. Remove the small disc and spring which secure each shoe to the backing plate.

4. Remove the two long springs between the two shoes.

5. Remove the shoes from the backing plate.

6. If new shoes are being installed, remove the adjusters in the end of each wheel cylinder and screw the star wheel up against the head of the adjuster. When inserting the adjusters back in the wheel cylinders, notice that the slot in the adjuster is angled and must be positioned as illustrated.

7. Position new shoes on the backing plate. The slot in the shoes and the stronger return spring must be at the wheel cylinder end.

8. Install the disc and spring which secure the shoe to the backing plate.

9. Install the brake drum and adjust the wheel bearing.

Type 2

1. Remove the brake drum.

2. Pry the rear brake shoe out of the adjuster, as illustrated, and detach the return springs. Remove the forward shoe.

3. If new shoes are to be installed, screw the star wheel up against the head of the adjuster.

4. Install the rear brake shoe.

5. Attach the return spring to the front brake shoe and then to the rear shoe.

Removing Type 2 front brake drum

6. Position the front brake shoe in the slot of the adjusting screw and lever it into position in the same manner as it was removed. Make sure that the return springs doe not touch the brake line between the upper and lower wheel cylinders.

7. Install the brake drum and adjust the wheel bearings.

Wheel Cylinder

Removal and Installation

1. Remove the brake shoes.

2. On Type 1, disconnect the brake line from the rear of the cylinder. On Type 2, disconnect the brake line from the rear of the cylinder and the transfer line from the front of the cylinder.

3. Remove the bolts which secure the cylinder to the backing plate and remove the cylinder from the vehicle.

4. Reverse the above steps to install and bleed the brakes.

Overhaul

1. Remove the wheel cylinder.

2. Remove the brake adjusters and remove the rubber boot from each end.

NOTE: *The Type 2 cylinder has only one rubber boot, piston, and cup. The rebuilding procedures are the same.*

3. On Type 1, push in on one of the pistons to force out the opposite piston and rubber cup. On Type 2, remove the piston and cup by blowing compressed air into the brake hose hole.

4. Wash the pistons and cylinder in clean brake fluid or alcohol.

5. Inspect the cylinder bore for signs of pitting, scoring, and excessive wear. If it is badly scored or pitted, the whole cylinder should be replaced. It is possible to remove the glaze and light scores with crocus cloth or a brake cylinder hone. Before rebuilding the cylinder, make sure the bleeder screw is free. If the bleeder is rusted shut or broken off, replace the entire cylinder.

6. Dip the new pistons and rubber cups in brake fluid. Place the spring in the bore and insert the rubber cups into the bore against the spring. The concave side of the rubber cup should face inward.

7. Place the pistons in the bore and install the rubber boot.

8. Install the cylinder and bleed the brakes after the shoes and drum are in place. Make sure that the brakes are adjusted.

Rear Drum Brakes

Brake Drum

Removal and Installation

Type 1, 2, 3

1. With the wheels still on the ground, remove the cotter pin from the slotted nut on the rear axle and remove the nut from the axle.

Removing rear brake drum using puller—Types 1, 2, and 3

CAUTION: *Make sure the emergency brake is now released.*

2. Jack up the car and remove the wheel and tire.

3. The brake drum is splined to the rear axle and the drum should slip off the axle. However, the drum sometimes rusts on the splines and it is necessary to remove the drum using a puller.

4. Before installing the drum, lubricate the splines. Install the drum on the axle and tighten the nut on the axle. Line up a slot in the nut with a hole in the axle and insert a cotter pin. Never loosen the nut to align the slot and hole.

Type 4

The drum is held in place by the wheel lugs. Jack up the car and remove the wheel and tire. After the wheel is removed, there are two small screws that secure the drum to the hub and they must be removed before the drum will slip off the hub.

Inspection

Inspection is the same as given in the "Front Drum Brake" section.

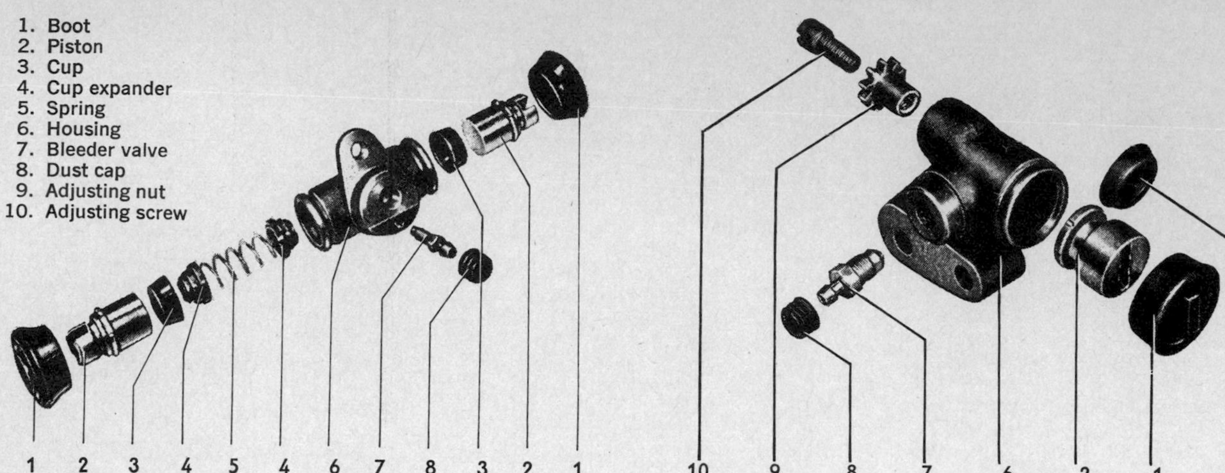

Front wheel cylinders disassembled—Type 1 (left), Type 2 (right)

Brake Lining

Removal and Installation

1. Remove the brake drum.
2. Remove both shoe retaining springs.

Rear wheel brake assembly—Parking brake cable disconnected

3. Disconnect the lower return spring.
4. Disconnect the hand brake cable from the lever attached to the rear shoe.
5. Remove the upper return spring and clip.
6. Remove the brake shoes and connecting link.
7. Remove the emergency brake lever from the rear shoe.
8. Lubricate the adjusting screws and the star wheel against the head of the adjusting screw.
9. Reverse Steps 1–7 to install the shoes.
10. Adjust the brakes.

Wheel Cylinder

Removal and Installation

Remove the brake drum and brake shoes. Disconnect the brake line from the cylinder and remove the bolts which secure the cylinder to the backing plate. Remove the cylinder from the vehicle.

Overhaul

Overhaul is the same as given in the "Front Drum Brake" section.

Parking Brake

Cable Adjustment

Brake cable adjustment is performed at the handbrake lever in the passenger compartment. There is a cable for each rear wheel and there are two adjusting nuts at the lever.

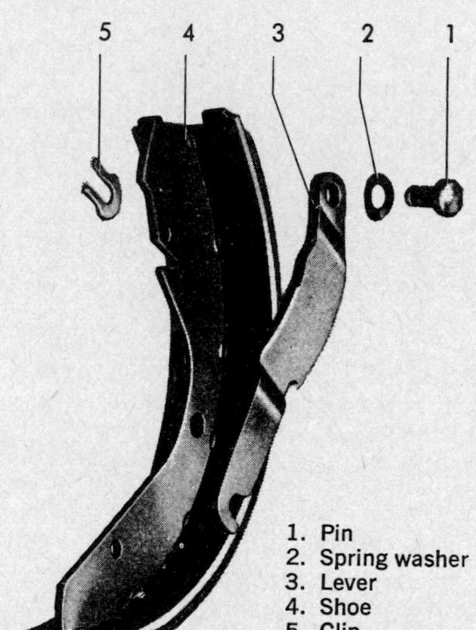

Parking brake lever attachment to rear shoe

To adjust the cable, loosen the locknut. Jack up the rear wheel to be adjusted so that it can be hand spun. Turn the adjusting nut until a very slight drag is felt as the wheel is spun. Then back off on the adjusting nut until the lever can be pulled up three notches.

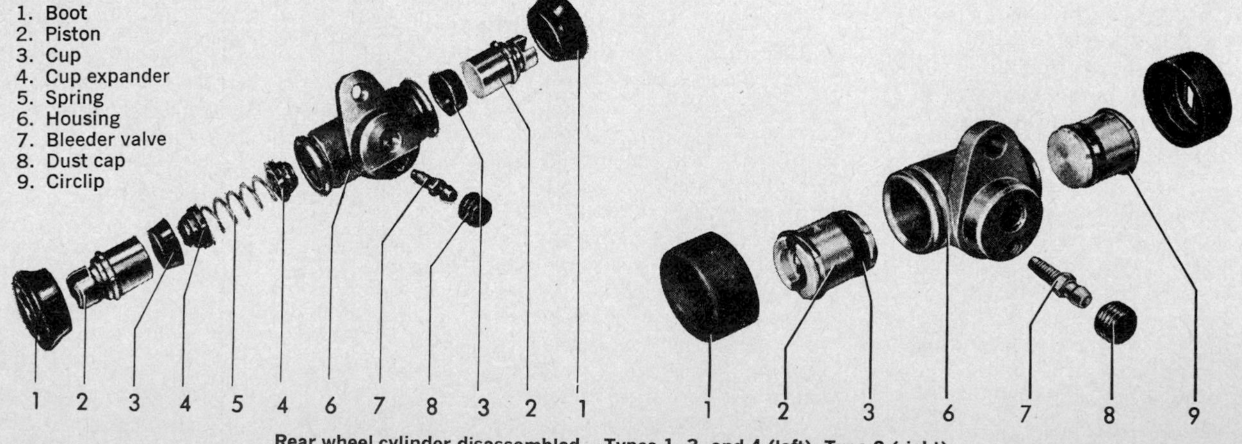

Rear wheel cylinder disassembled—Types 1, 3, and 4 (left), Type 2 (right)

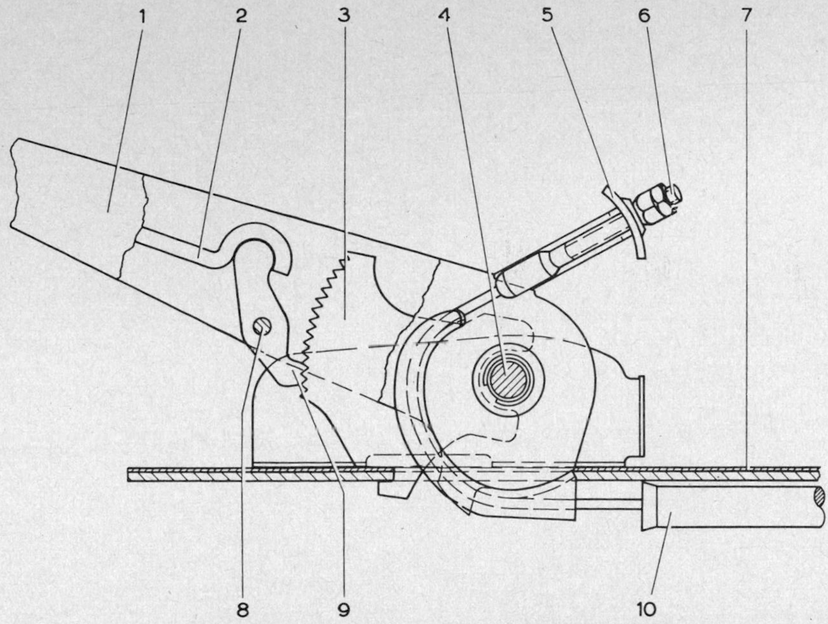

Parking brake hand lever and cable end assembly

1. Hand brake lever
2. Pawl rod
3. Ratchet segment
4. Lever pin
5. Cable compensator
6. Brake cable
7. Frame
8. Pawl pin
9. Pawl
10. Cable guide tube

CAUTION: *Never pull up on the hand-brake lever with the cables disconnected.*

Cable

Removal and Installation

1. Disconnect the cables at the hand-brake lever by removing the two nuts which secure the cables to the lever. Pull the cables rearward to remove that end from the lever bracket.
2. Remove the brake drum and detach the cable end from the lever attached to the rear brake shoe.
3. Remove the brake cable bracket from the backing plate and remove the cable from the vehicle.
4. Reverse the above steps to install and adjust the cable.

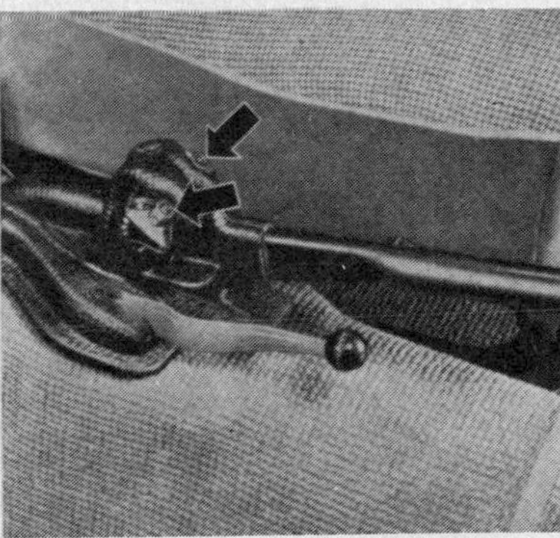

Parking brake cable adjusting nuts

CHASSIS ELECTRICAL

Heater

The Volkswagen heating system has no electrical blower. The engine cooling fan blows air over the engine and out through the cooling ducts. If the heater flaps are opened, then a portion of the heated air from the engine is diverted to the passenger compartment. An auxiliary gas heater is optional on Types 1, 2, and 3, and standard on Type 4.

Procedures for removing the heat exchangers and heater flap assemblies are given in Chapter Three.

Cable for Heater Outlet

Removal and Installation

Types 1, 2, 3

1. Remove the rear air outlet, hose, and heater pipe as an assembly.
2. Remove the hose from the outlet and from the pipe.
3. Remove the pin which attaches the cable to the flap in the heater pipe.

NOTE: *The pin is push-fit.*

4. Remove the heater pipe from the outlet.
5. Bend up the tabs which secure the cable shielding to the outlet.
6. Disconnect the opposite end from the heater controls and remove the cable.
7. Reverse the above steps to install.

Windshield Wipers

Motor Removal and Installation

Type 1

1. Disconnect the battery ground cable.
2. Loosen the clamp screws and remove the wiper arms.
3. Remove the wiper bearing nuts as well as the washers. Take off the outer bearing seals.
4. Remove the back of the instrument panel from the luggage compartment.
5. Disconnect the cable from the wiper motor.
6. Remove the glove compartment box.
7. Remove the screw which secures the wiper frame to the body.
8. Remove the frame and motor with the linkage.

NOTE: *The ball joints at the ends of the linkage may be slipped apart by gently popping the ball and socket apart with a screwdriver. Always lubricate the joints upon reassembly.*

9. Remove the lock and spring washers from the motor driveshaft and remove the connecting rod. Matchmark the motor and frame to ensure proper realignment when the motor is reinstalled.
10. Remove the nut located at the base of the motor driveshaft, and the nut at the side of the driveshaft, and remove the motor from the frame.
11. To install, reverse the above steps and heed the following reminders.
12. The pressed lug on the wiper frame must engage the groove in the wiper bearing. Make sure that the wiper spindles are perpendicular to the plane of the windshield.
13. Check the linkage bushings for wear.
14. The hollow side of the links must face toward the frame with the angled end of the driving link toward the right bearing.
15. The inner bearing seal should be placed so that the shoulder of the rubber molding faces the wiper arm.

Type 2

1. Disconnect the ground wire from the battery.
2. Remove both wiper arms.
3. Remove the bearing cover and nut.
4. Remove the heater branch connections under the instrument panel.
5. Disconnect the wiper motor wiring.
6. Remove the wiper motor securing screw and remove the motor.
7. Reverse the above steps to install.

Type 3

1. Disconnect the negative battery cable.

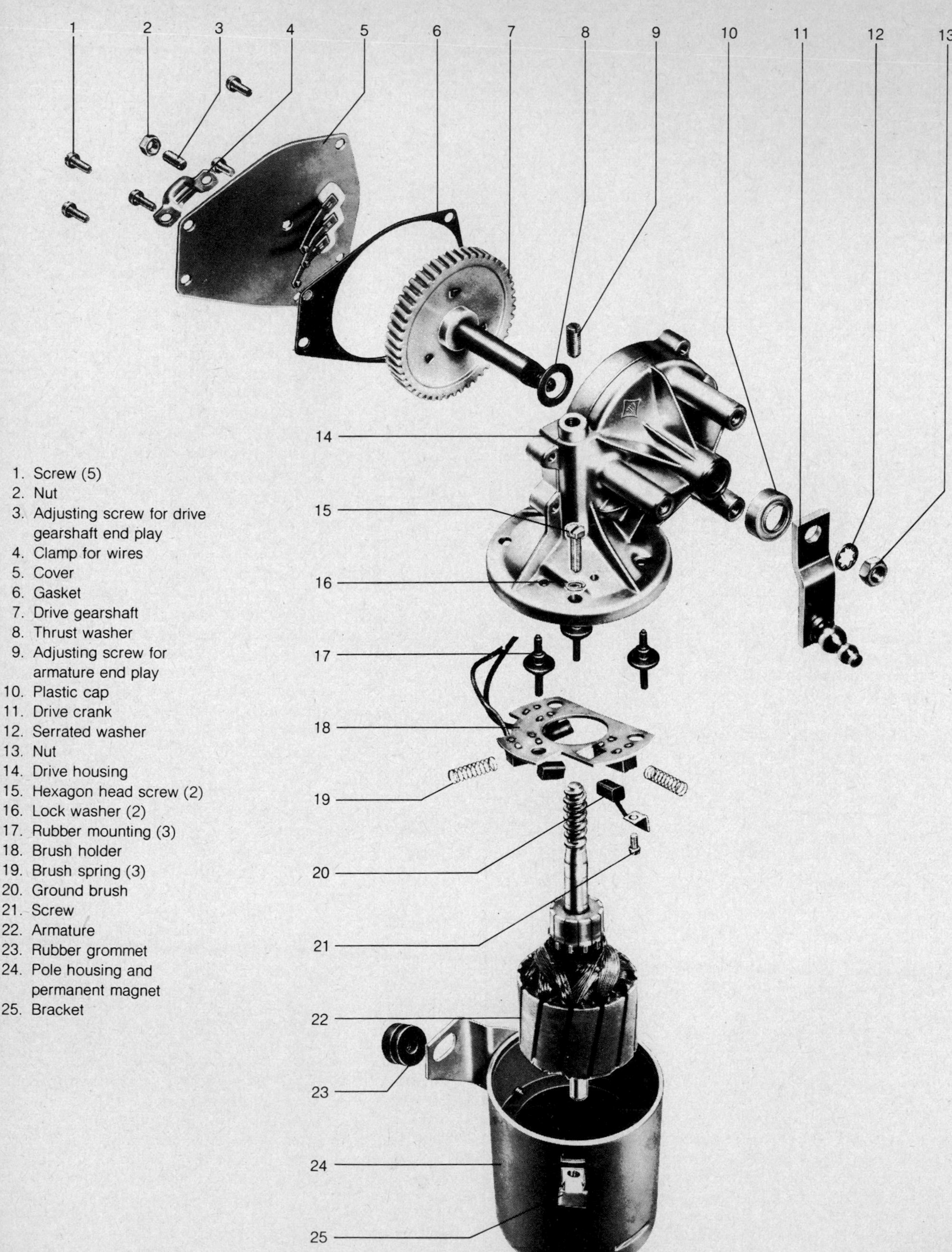

Exploded view of windshield wiper motor and drive.

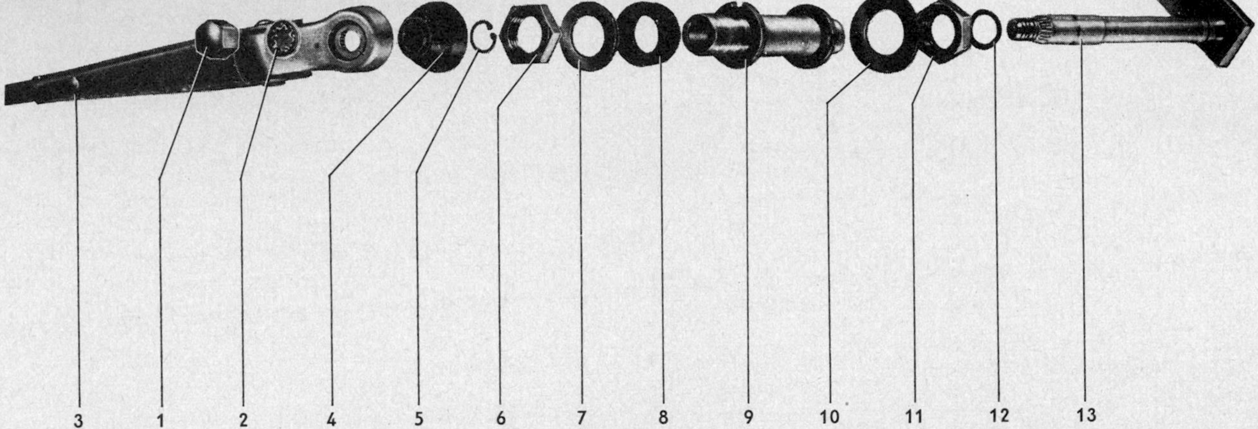

Type 4 wiper shaft assembly

2. Remove the ashtray and glove compartment.
3. Remove the fresh air controls.
4. Remove the cover for the heater and water drainage hoses.
5. Disconnect the motor wiring.
6. Remove the wiper arms.
7. Remove the bearing covers and nuts, washers, and outer bearing seals.
8. Remove the wiper motor securing screws and remove the motor.
9. Reverse the above steps to install.

Type 4

1. Disconnect the negative battery cable.
2. Remove the wiper arms.
3. Remove the bearing cover and remove the nut under it.
4. Remove the steering column cover and the hoses running between the fresh air control box and the vents.
5. Remove the clock but do not disconnect the wiring.

Typical wiper linkage ball joint—Type 4 shown

6. Remove the left fresh air and defroster vent. Disconnect the air hose from the vent.
7. Disconnect the wiring for the motor at the windshield wiper switch. Remove the ground wire from the motor gear cover.
8. Remove the motor securing screw and remove the motor frame and motor assembly downward and to the right.
9. Reverse the above steps to install.

Linkage Removal and Installation

The windshield wiper linkage is secured at the ends by a ball and socket type joint. The ball and joint may be gently pryed apart with the aid of a screwdriver. Always lubricate the joints with grease before reassembly.

Wiper Arm Shaft

1. Remove the wiper arm.
2. Remove the bearing cover or the shaft seal depending on the type.
3. On Type 4, remove the shaft circlip.
4. Remove the large wiper shaft bearing securing nut and remove the accompanying washer and rubber seal.
5. Disconnect the wiper linkage from the wiper arm shaft.
6. Working from inside the car, slide the shaft out of its bearing.

NOTE: *It may be necessary to lightly tap the shaft out of its bearing. Use a soft face hammer.*

7. Reverse the above steps to install.

Instrument Cluster

Speedometer

Removal and Installation

1. Disconnect the negative battery cable.

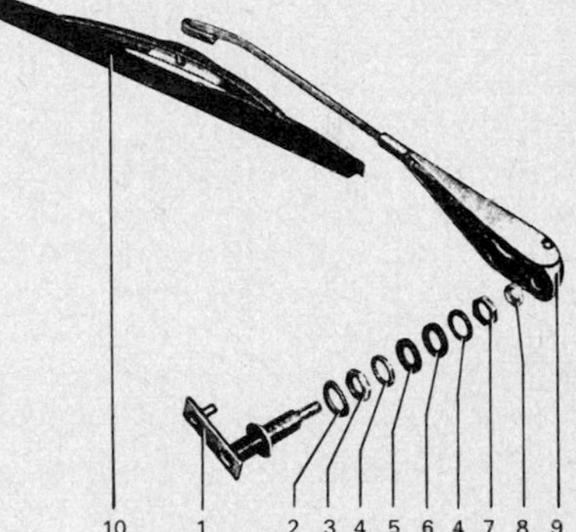

Type 1, 2, 3 wiper shaft assembly

1. Wiper shaft with crank
2. Spring washer
3. Brass nut
4. Washer
5. Inner bearing seal
6. Outer bearing seal
7. Nut
8. Wiper shaft seal
9. Bracket and arm
10. Windshield wiper blade

2. Disconnect the speedometer light bulb wires.
3. Unscrew the knurled nut which secures the speedometer cable to the back of the speedometer. Pull the cable from the back of the speedometer.
4. Using a 4 mm allen wrench, remove the two knurled nuts which secure the speedometer brackets. Remove the brackets.
5. Remove the speedometer from the dashboard by sliding it out toward the steering wheel.
6. Reverse the above steps to install. Before fully tightening the nuts for the speedometer brackets, make sure the speedometer is correctly positioned in the dash.

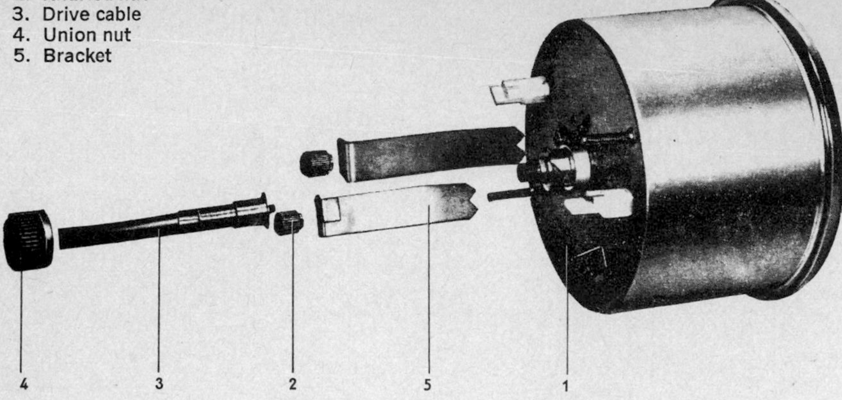

Speedometer and brackets—Type 1

Fuel Gauge and Clock Assembly

Removal and Installation

1. Disconnect the negative battery cable.
2. Disconnect the wiring from the back of the assembly.
3. Remove the knurled nuts and brackets which secure the assembly in the dash. Use a 4 mm allen wrench.
4. Remove the assembly by gently sliding it toward the steering wheel and out of the dash.
5. The fuel gauge is secured into the base of the clock by two screws. Remove the screws and slip the fuel gauge out of the clock.
6. Reverse the above steps to install. Make sure the clock and fuel gauge assembly is properly centered in the dash before fully tightening the nuts.

Ignition Switch

Removal and Installation

1. Disconnect the steering column wiring at the block located behind the instrument panel and pull the column wiring harness into the passenger compartment.
2. Remove the steering wheel.
3. Remove the circlip on the steering shaft.
4. Disconnect the negative battery cable.
5. Insert the key and turn the switch to the ON position. On Type 3 vehicles it is necessary to remove the fuse box.
6. Remove the three securing screws and slide the switch assembly from the steering column tube.

NOTE: *It is not necessary to remove the turn signal switch at this time. If it is necessary to remove the switch from the housing, continue with the disassembly procedure.*

7. Remove the turn signal switch.
8. After removing the wiring retainer, press the ignition switch wiring block upward and out of the housing and disconnect the wiring.
9. Remove the lock cylinder and the steering lock mechanism.
10. Remove the ignition switch screw and pull the ignition switch rearward.
11. Reverse the above steps to install. When reinstalling the turn signal switch, make sure the lever is in the center position.

NOTE: *The distance (a) between the steering wheel and the ignition switch housing is 2–3 mm (0.08–0.12 in.).*

Ignition Lock Cylinder

Removal and Installation

1. Proceed with Steps 1–8 in the "Ignition Switch" procedure.
2. With the key in the cylinder and turned to the ON position, pull the lock cylinder out far enough so the securing pin can be depressed through a hole in the side of the lock cylinder housing. Use a steel wire to depress the pin.
3. As the pin is depressed, pull the lock cylinder out of its housing.
4. To install the lock cylinder, gently push the cylinder into its housing. Make sure the pin engages correctly and that the retainer fits easily in place. Do not force any parts together; when they are correctly aligned, they will fit easily together.

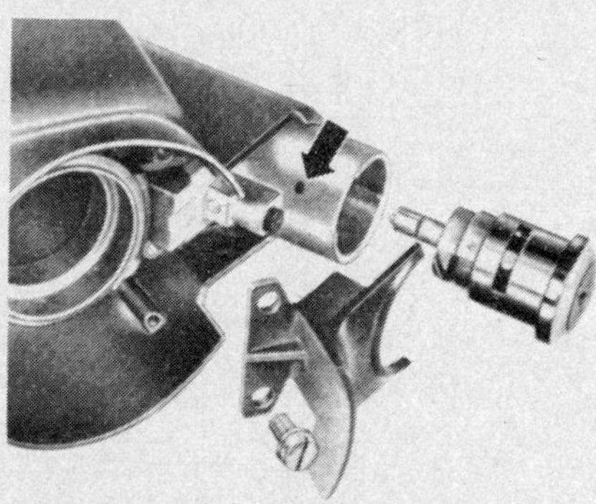

Access hole for depressing lock cylinder retaining pin

LIGHT BULB SPECIFICATIONS

Bulb	Type 1	Type 2	Type 3	Type 4
Sealed beam unit	12.8V;50/40W	12.8V;50/40W	12.8V;50/40W	12.8V;37.5/50W
Turn signal	12V;21W	12V;21W	12V;21W	——
Stop/tail light	12V;21/5W	12V;21/5W	12V;21/5W	12V;32/4 cp
License plate	12V;10W	12V;10W	12V;5W①	12V;6 cp
Back-up light	12V;25W	12V;25W	12V;25W	12V;25W
Interior light	12V;10W	12V;10W	12V;10W	10V;10W
Parking light	12V;4W	12V;4W	12V;4W	——
Warning light	12V;2W	12V;1.2W	12V;2W	12V;1.2W
Side marker light	12V;2 cp	12V;2 cp	12V;2 cp	12V;2 cp
Turn signal, parking light	——	——	——	32/4 cp

V—Volts
W—Watts
cp—Candle Power
① Squareback Sedan—12V;10W

INDEX

Volkswagen Dasher · Rabbit · Scirocco

INTRODUCTION

The Dasher is a unique VW. Most of its features are the opposite of those traditionally associated with VW cars, such as air cooling, rear engine, and torsion bar suspension. It is front wheel drive with a water-cooled, in-line, overhead camshaft engine. Suspension is by coil springs, with McPherson strut spring/shock units at the front. Steering is by rack and pinion, and radial ply tires are standard equipment. The front suspension is designed with negative roll radius. This safety feature keeps the car straight when drag on the front tires is not equal, as would happen with one wheel on wet pavement and one wheel on dry pavement.

The Rabbit and the Scirocco share most of the Dasher's unique features. The most striking difference is that the engine is mounted transversely. The rear wheels are suspended by trailing arms connected by a torsion beam and shock absorber/strut units.

MODEL IDENTIFICATION

Rabbit

Scirocco

Dasher

SERIAL NUMBER IDENTIFICATION

Vehicle Identification Plate

The Dasher vehicle identification plate is riveted to the inner right fender. On the Rabbit and Scirocco, the plate is on top of the body crossmember above the grille. On the plate are the date of manufacture and the chassis number.

Chassis Number

The chassis number is located on the driver's side windshield pillar and is visible through the windshield. The Dasher chassis number is also stamped on the firewall over the windshield washer reservoir. The Rabbit and Scirocco chassis number is also on top of the right suspension strut mounting. It also appears on the vehicle identification plate.

Engine Number

The engine number is stamped on the left side (front on the Rabbit and Scirocco) of the engine block between the fuel pump and the distributor.

GENERAL ENGINE SPECIFICATIONS

Year, Model	Engine Cu in Displacement (cc)	Carburetor Type	Horsepower @ rpm (SAE)	Torque @ rpm (ft lbs) (SAE)	Bore x Stroke (in)	Compression Ratio	Oil Pressure @ rpm (psi)
1974-75 Dasher	89.7 (1,471)	2 bbl Solex	75 @ 5,800	81 @ 4,000	3.01 x 3.15	8.5:1	40 @ 2,500
1975 Scirocco, Rabbit	89.7 (1,471)	2 bbl Zenith	70 @ 6,000	81 @ 3,500	3.01 x 3.15	8.2:1	40 @ 2,500

TUNE-UP SPECIFICATIONS

Year, Model	Engine Cu in. Displacement	Spark Plugs		Distributor		Ignition Timing (deg) ●	Intake Valve Opens (deg)	Compression Pressure (psi)	Idle Speed (rpm)	Valve Clearance (in)	
		Type	Gap (in.)	Point Dwell (deg)	Point Gap (in)					In	Ex
1974 Dasher	89.7 (1,471)	W175 T30 N8Y	0.024-0.028	44-50 ①	0.016	3 ATDC @ idle	4 BTDC	142-184	850-1000	0.008-0.012	0.016-0.020
1975 Dasher	89.7 (1,471)	W200 T30 N8Y	0.024-0.028	44-50	0.016	3 ATDC @ idle	4 BTDC	142-184	850-1000	0.008-0.012	0.016-0.020
1975 Scirocco, Rabbit	89.7 (1,471)	W200 T30 N8Y	0.024-0.028	44-50	0.016	3 ATDC @ idle	4 BTDC	142-184	900-1000	0.008-0.012	0.016-0.020

① 47-53°—California
● Vacuum hose ON

FIRING ORDER

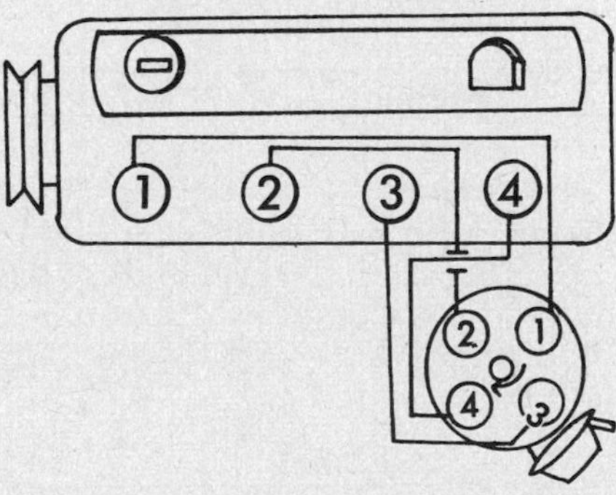

Firing order: 1-3-4-2

CAPACITIES

Year	Model	Engine Displacement Cu in (cc)	Engine Crankcase (qts)		Transmission (pts)		Drive Axle (pts)	Gasoline Tank (gals)	Cooling System (pts)
			With Filter	Without Filter	Manual	Automatic			
1974-75	Dasher	89.7 (1,471)	3.7	3.1	3.4①	12.8②	3.0	12.1③	12.7
1975	Scirocco, Rabbit	89.7 (1,471)	3.7	3.2	2.6	12.8②	1.6	12.1	13.6

① At change, initial amount 4.2 pts.
② Dry refill; normal refill is 6.4 pts.
③ Doesn't include 1.3 gal reserve.

CRANKSHAFT AND CONNECTING ROD SPECIFICATIONS

All measurements are given in inches.

Model	Crankshaft				Connecting Rod		
	Main Brg. Journal Dia.	Main Brg. Oil Clearance	Shaft End-Play	Thrust on No.	Journal Diameter	Oil Clearance	Side Clearance (max.)
1974-75 Dasher	2.126	0.001-0.003	0.003-0.007	3	1.811	0.001-0.003	0.015
1975 Scirocco, Rabbit	2.126	0.001-0.003	0.003-0.007	3	1.811	0.001-0.003	0.015

NOTE: **Main and connecting rod bearings are available in three undersizes.**

VALVE SPECIFICATIONS

Model	Seat Angle (deg)	Spring Test Pressure (lbs. @ in.)	Stem to Guide Clearance (in.)		Stem Diameter (in.)	
			Intake	Exhaust	Intake	Exhaust
1974-75 Dasher	45	96-106① @ 0.92 in.	0.001-0.002	0.001-0.002	0.314	0.313
1975 Scirocco, Rabbit	45	96-106① @ 0.92 in.	0.001-0.002	0.001-0.002	0.314	0.313

① Outer spring, inner spring test pressure is 46-51 lbs. @ 0.72 in.

NOTE: **Exhaust valves must be ground by hand.**

PISTON AND RING SPECIFICATIONS

(All measurements in inches)

Model	Piston Clearance	Ring Gap			Ring Side Clearance		
		Top Compression	Bottom Compression	Oil Control	Top Compression	Bottom Compression	Oil Control
1974-75 Dasher	0.001-0.003	0.001-0.002	0.001-0.002	0.001-0.002	0.001-0.002	0.001-0.002	0.001-0.002
1975 Scirocco, Rabbit	0.001-0.003	0.001-0.002	0.001-0.002	0.001-0.002	0.001-0.002	0.001-0.002	0.001-0.002

NOTE: **Three piston sizes are available to accommodate over bores up to 0.040 in.**

TORQUE SPECIFICATIONS

(All readings in ft lbs)

Model	Cylinder Head Bolts	Rod* Bearing Bolts	Main Bearing Bolts	Crankshaft Pulley Bolt	Flywheel To Crankshaft Bolts	Manifold	
						Intake	Exhaust
1974-75 Dasher	56①	30	47	58	36	18	18
1975 Scirocco, Rabbit	54①	33	47	58	54②	18	18

① Cold, 62 ft. lbs. warm.
② Pressure plate to crankshaft bolts.
* Always use new bolts.

TORQUE SEQUENCES

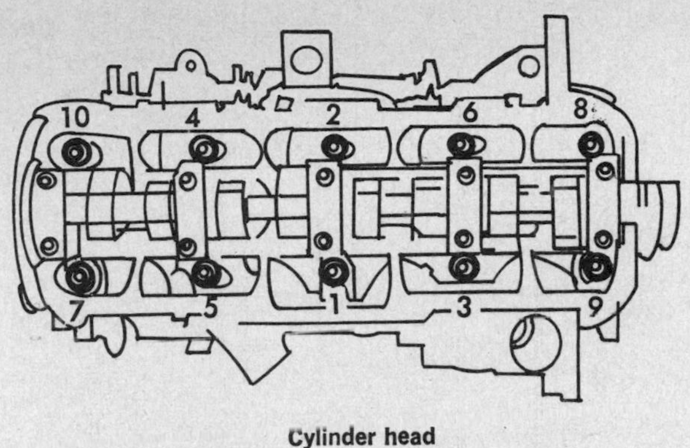

Cylinder head

BRAKE SPECIFICATIONS

(All measurements are given in in.)

Year	Model	Master Cylinder Bore	Wheel Cylinder Bore		Brake Disc or Drum Diameter	
			Front	Rear	Front	Rear
1974-75	Dasher	0.82	1.73	N.A.	9.41	7.87
1975	Scirocco, Rabbit	N.A.	N.A.	N.A.	N.A.	7.09

N.A. Not Available

WHEEL ALIGNMENT

Year	Model	CASTER*		CAMBER		Toe-in (in.)	Steering Axis Inclination* (deg)
		Range (deg)	Pref Setting (deg)	Range (deg)	Pref Setting (deg)		
1974-75	Dasher	0-1	0°30′	0°5′-0°55′	0°30′	0.08	10°30′
1975	Scirocco, Rabbit	1°30′-2°30′	2°	0°-1′	0°30′		−25′ to +5′

*Not adjustable

IGNITION SYSTEM

VW recommends a tune-up, including new points and plugs, at 10,000 mile intervals.

Spark Plugs

The firing order is 1–3–4–2, with No. 1 cylinder at the front (right on the Rabbit and Scirocco) of the engine.

1. Grasp the spark plug boot and pull it straight out. Don't pull on the wire.
2. Place the spark plug socket firmly on the plug and screw the spark plug out.

NOTE: *The cylinder head is aluminum alloy, which is easily stripped of threads. Remove the plugs only when the engine is cold.*

If removal is difficult, loosen the plug only slightly and drip penetrating oil onto the threads.

3. Inspect the plugs and clean or discard them. The recommended spark plug gap is listed in the "Tune-Up Specifications" chart.
4. Torque the new spark plugs to 22 ft lbs. Install the ignition wire boots firmly.

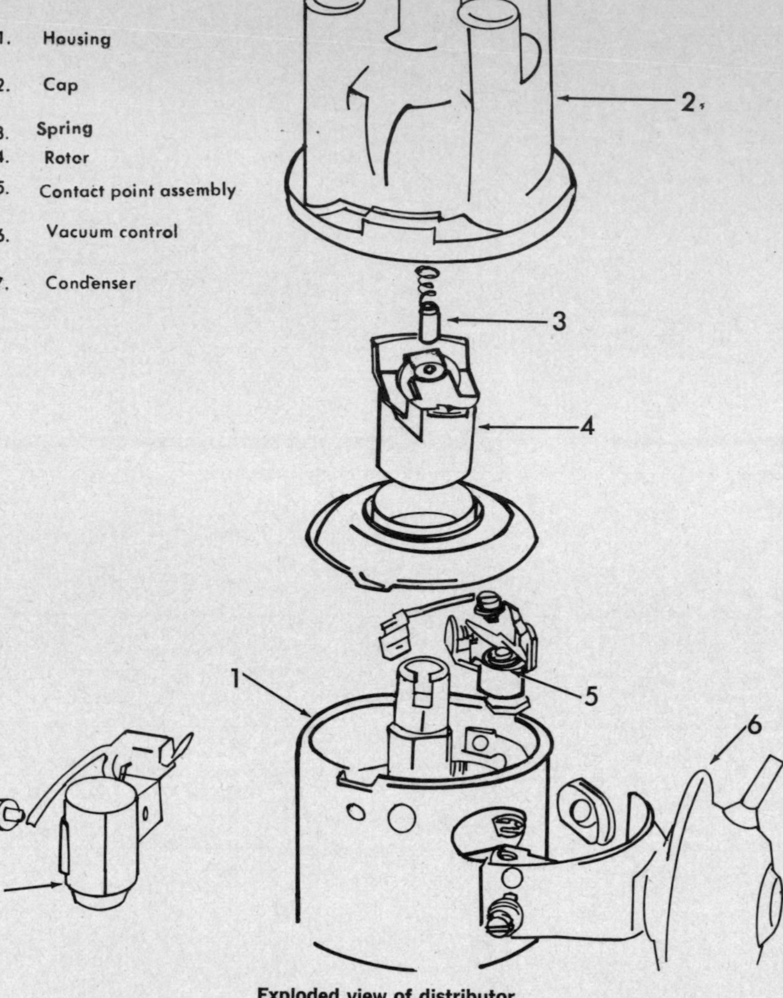

Exploded view of distributor

Breaker Points and Condenser

Snap off the two retaining clips on the distributor cap. Remove the cap and examine it for cracks, deterioration, or carbon tracking. Replace the cap, if necessary, by transferring one wire at a time from the old cap to the new one. Examine the rotor for corrosion or wear and replace it if questionable. Remove the dust shield. Check the points for pitting and burning. Slight imperfections on the contact surface may be filed off with a point file. It is best to replace the breaker point set. Always replace the condenser when you replace the point set.

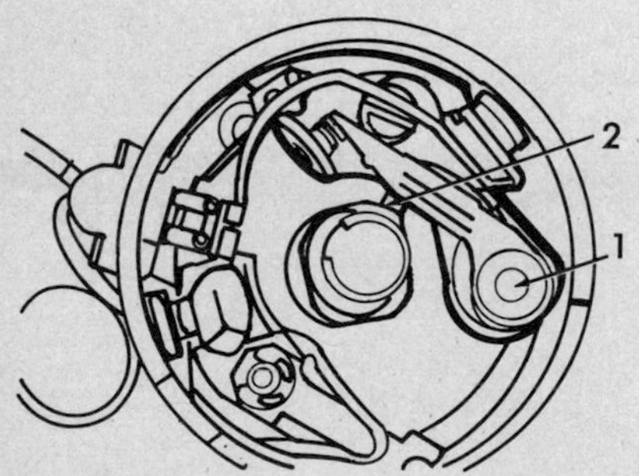

Breaker points and condenser—Lubricate at (1) with a drop of engine oil and at (2) with silicone (high melting point) grease

To replace the breaker points:

1. Remove the rotor.
2. Unsnap the point connector from the terminal at the side of the distributor. Remove the retaining screw, and lift out the point set.
3. Install the new point set, making sure that the pin on the bottom engages the hole in the breaker plate.
4. Install the wire connector and the retaining screws (hand-tight).
5. Turn the engine until the breaker arm rubbing block is on the high point of one of the cam lobes.
6. A 0.016 in. feeler gauge should just slip through the points. If the gap is incorrect, pivot a screwdriver in the point set notch and the two projections on the breaker plate to bring it within specifications.
7. When the gap is correct, tighten the retaining screw.
8. Lubricate the distributor cam with silicone grease.
9. Install the dust cover, rotor and distributor cap.
10. Check the dwell angle and the ignition timing.
11. The condenser is mounted on the outside of the distributor. Undo the mounting screw and the terminal block to replace.

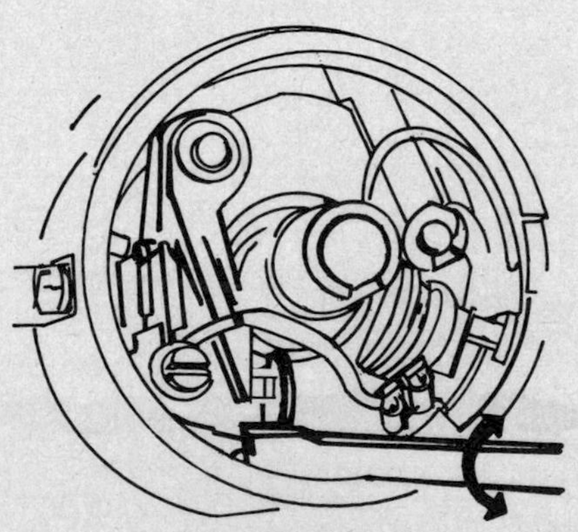

Adjusting point gap

Dwell Angle

The dwell angle or cam angle is the number of degrees that the distributor cam rotates while the points are closed. There is an inverse relationship between dwell angle and point gap. Increasing the point gap will decrease the dwell angle and vice versa. Checking the dwell angle with a meter is a far more accurate method of measuring point opening than the feeler gauge method.

After setting the point gap to specification with a feeler gauge, check the dwell angle. Attach the dwell meter. The negative lead is grounded and the positive lead is connected to the primary wire, Terminal No. 1 that runs from the coil to the distributor. Start the engine, let it idle and reach operating temperature, and observe the dwell on the meter. The reading should fall within the allowable range. If it does not, the gap will have to be reset. Dwell can also be checked with the engine cranking.

Ignition Timing

Ignition timing is always adjusted after the points are gapped (dwell angle changed), since altering the dwell affects the timing.

1. Attach a timing light. Hook-up a dwell/tachometer.

2. Locate the timing mark opening in the clutch or torque convertor housing at the rear of the engine directly behind the distributor. The 0°T mark stands for TDC or 0°. The 3 mark to the right means 3° ATDC. Mark them with chalk so that they will be more visible. Don't disconnect the vacuum line.

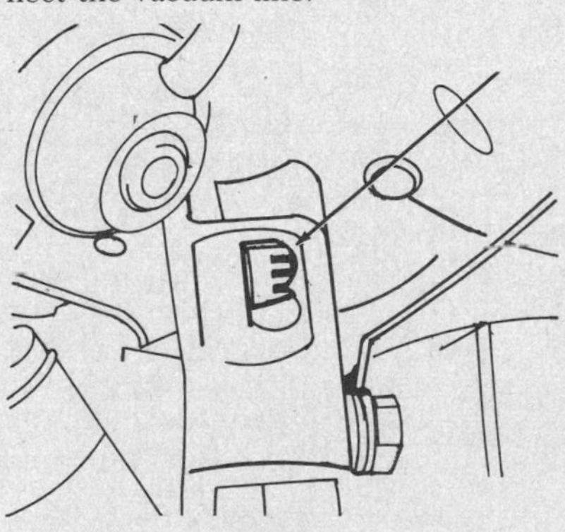

Timing window

3. Start the engine and allow it to reach normal operating temperature. The engine should be at normal idle speed.

4. Shine the timing light at the marks.

5. The 3° line and the V-shaped pointer should be aligned.

6. If not, loosen the distributor hold down bolt and rotate the distributor very slowly to align the marks.

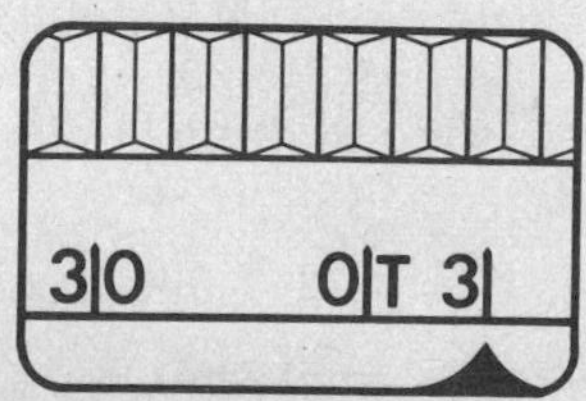

Timing mark aligned at 3° ATDC

7. Tighten the mounting nut when the ignition timing is correct.

8. Recheck the timing when the distributor is secured.

Valve Lash

The valve clearances should be checked every 20,000 miles in firing order, with the engine at normal operating temperature.

1. Remove the camshaft cover and the distributor cap.

2. Set the engine at TDC on No. 1 cylinder by aligning the 0°T mark on the flywheel with the pointer and aligning the distributor rotor with the No. 1 cylinder mark on the rim of the distributor body.

NOTE: *Always turn the crankshaft in the normal direction of rotation. There is a hole in the body behind the front license plate through which a wrench can be used on the crankshaft on the Dasher.*

3. The valve clearances of cylinder No. 1 should be checked when the valves of No. 4 cylinder overlap, i.e. when both No. 4 cylinder valves move in opposite directions simultaneously. You may have to move the crankshaft slightly to find this position. When this happens, the exhaust valve is closing and the intake opening. Check and note the clearance of both the intake and exhaust valves for No. 1 cylinder. Use a feeler gauge between each valve tappet and camshaft lobe.

4. Turn the crankshaft 180° (90° at the distributor rotor) in the normal direction of rotation. Check and note the valve clearances of cylinder No. 3 at the overlap position of cylinder No. 2.

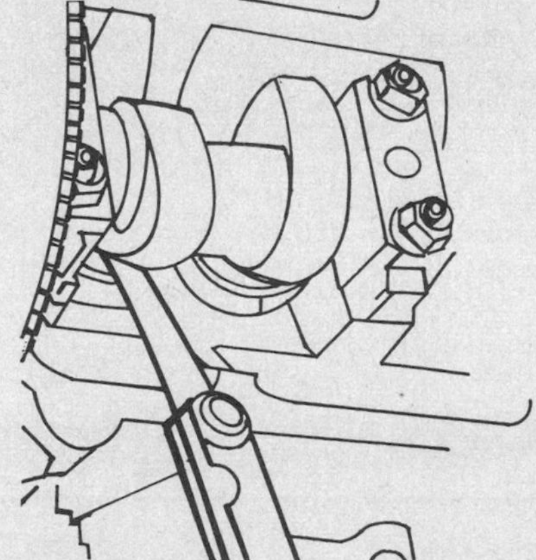

Checking valve clearance with a feeler gauge

5. Turn the crankshaft 180°. Check and note the valve clearances of cylinder No. 4 at the overlap position of cylinder No. 1.

6. Turn the crankshaft 180°. Check and note the valve clearances of cylinder No. 2 at the overlap position of cylinder No. 3.

7. Now the crankshaft has been turned two complete revolutions (one for the distributor rotor) and all the valve tappet to camshaft lobe clearances have been noted. Compare the noted clearances with those listed in the Tune-Up Specifications Chart. Normal wear usually results in the clearances becoming too small. Adjustment is made by replacing the tappet clearance disc in the top of each tappet. These are available in 26 sizes ranging from 3.0 mm (0.119 in) to 4.25 mm (0.166 in) in increments of 0.05 mm (0.002 in). The thickness of each disc is marked on the bottom.

NOTE: *If a valve clearance deviates 0.002 in or less from the specified clearance, it need not be adjusted.*

8. To remove a tappet clearance disc, turn the cylinder to TDC and press down the tappet so that the disc can be lifted out. Dealers have special tools that make this operation much easier. Once the disc is removed, check its size and determine what size will be needed to produce the required adjustment.

NOTE: *Before depressing the tappets, turn them so their openings are at right angles to the camshaft.*

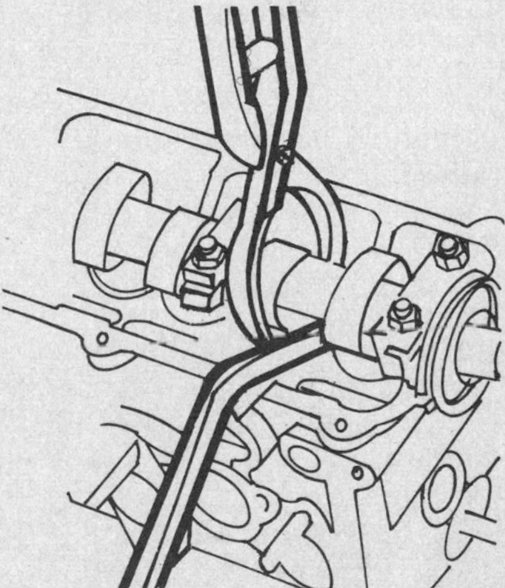

Using special tools to depress the tappet and remove the tappet clearance disc

9. Install the required disc and turn the tappet back to its normal direction. When all the clearances have been corrected, check them again to catch any possible error caused by worn discs.

Carburetor

The Dasher carburetor is a Solex 32/35 DIDTA two barrel unit with a vacuum operated secondary barrel. The Rabbit and Scirocco use a Zenith 32/32–2B2 two barrel carburetor with a vacuum operated secondary barrel and dual floats.

Idle Speed Adjustment

1. Start the engine and run it until normal operating temperature is reached.

2. Hook-up a tachometer to the engine and observe the idle speed.

3. If the idle speed is not as specified, turn the curb idle screw to correct it.

Make sure that you are turning the correct screw. Do not mistake the idle mixture screw for the curb idle screw.

Idle Mixture Adjustment

This adjustment should only be performed with a CO meter. Notice that the Dasher California idle mixture screw is in a different location.

Rabbit and Scirocco idle speed adjustment screw

All 1974 Dasher Models Except California

1. Run the engine until it reaches normal operating temperature.
2. Ignition timing should be correctly set at 3° ATDC.
3. Idle speed should be 900–950 rpm.
4. Adjust the CO level with idle mixture screw to 0.4–1.6%.

1974 California Dasher Models and all 1975 Dasher Models

1. Run the engine until it reaches normal operating temperature.
2. Disconnect the hose that connects the air injection pump and the air manifold at the pump and plug it.
3. Ignition timing should be adjusted to 3° ATDC and idle speed set at 900–950 rpm.
4. Adjust the CO level with the idle mixture screw to 1.5%.

Carburetor mixture adjustment screw location—except California Dasher models

Carburetor mixture adjustment screw location—California Dasher models

5. Unplug and connect the air injection pump hose. The CO level should now fall below 1%.

1975 Rabbit, Scirocco

1. Run the engine until it reaches normal operating temperature.
2. Check that ignition timing and idle speed are as specified.
3. Adjust the CO level with the idle mixture screw to 2%.

Rabbit and Scirocco idle mixture adjustment screw

ENGINE ELECTRICAL

Distributor

The distributor is a single breaker point unit. It has both centrifugal and vacuum advance mechanisms. A vacuum retard system works only at idle.

The distributor is gear driven by an intermediate shaft which also drives the fuel pump. The distributor shaft also turns the oil pump.

Removal and Installation

1. Disconnect the coil high tension wire from the distributor.
2. Detach the smaller primary wire.
3. Unsnap the clips and remove the distributor cap.
4. Turn the engine until the rotor aligns with the index mark on the outer edge of the distributor. This is the No. 1 position. Matchmark the bottom of the distributor housing and its mounting flange on the engine.

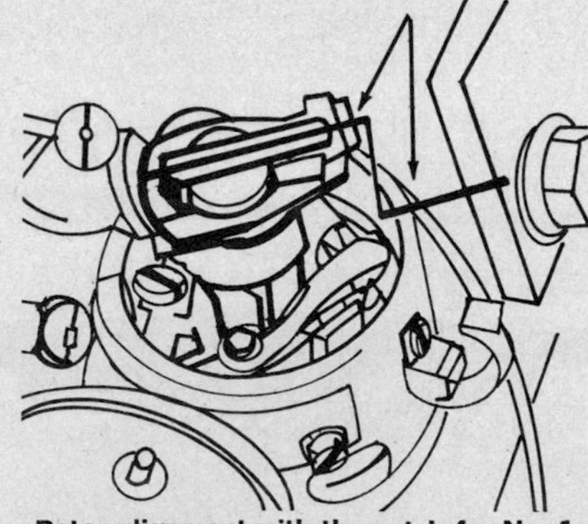

Rotor alignment with the notch for No. 1 cylinder

5. Loosen and remove the hex bolt and lift off the retaining flange. Lift the distributor straight out of the engine.

If the engine has not been disturbed while the distributor was out i.e., the crankshaft was not turned, then reinstall the distributor in the reverse order of removal. Carefully align the match marks.

If the engine has been rotated while the distributor was out, then proceed as follows:

1. Turn the crankshaft so that No. 1 piston is on its compression stroke and the 0°T timing mark is aligned with the V-shaped pointer.
2. Turn the distributor so that the rotor points approximately 15° before the No. 1 cylinder position on the distributor.
3. Insert the distributor into the engine block. If the oil pump drive doesn't engage, remove the distributor and, using a long screwdriver turn the pump shaft so that it is parallel to the centerline of the crankshaft.

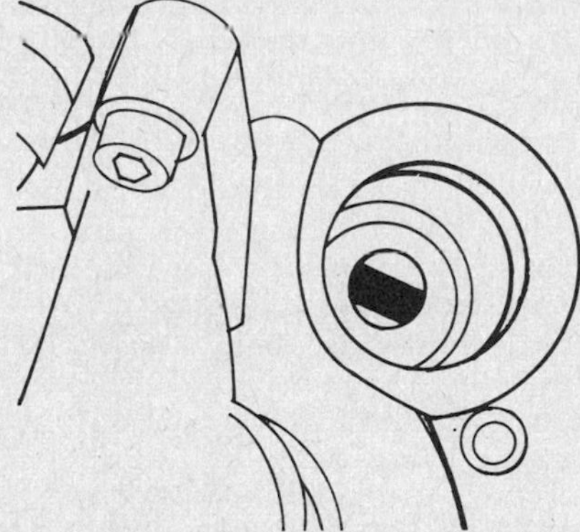

The oil pump drive should be parallel to the crankshaft

4. Install the distributor, aligning the match marks. Tighten the retaining nut.
5. Install the cap. Adjust the ignition timing.

CHARGING SYSTEM

Alternator Precautions

An alternating current (AC) generator (alternator) is used. Unlike the direct current (DC) generators used in many older cars, there are several precautions which must be strictly observed in order to avoid damaging the unit. They are:

1. Reversing the battery connections will result in damage to the diodes.
2. Booster batteries should be connected from negative to negative, and positive to positive.
3. Never use a fast charger as a booster to start cars with AC circuits.
4. When servicing the battery with a fast charger, always disconnect the car battery cables.
5. Never attempt to polarize an AC generator.
6. Avoid long soldering times when replacing diodes or transistors. Prolonged heat is damaging to AC generators.
7. Do not use test lamps of more than 12 volts (V) for checking diode continuity.
8. Do not short across or ground any of the terminals on the AC generator.
9. The polarity of the battery, generator, and regulator must be matched and considered before making any electrical connections within the system.
10. Never operate the AC generator on an open circuit. Make sure that all connections within the circuit are clean and tight.
11. Disconnect the battery terminals when performing any service on the electrical system. This will eliminate the possibility of accidental reversal of polarity.
12. Disconnect the battery ground cable if arc welding is to be done on any part of the car.

Removal and Installation

The alternator and voltage regulator are combined in one housing. No voltage adjustment can be made with this unit. The regulator can be replaced without removing the alternator; just unbolt it from the rear.

1. Disconnect the battery cables.
2. Remove the multi-connector retaining bracket and unplug the connector from the rear of the alternator.
3. Loosen and remove the top mounting nut and bolt.
4. Using a socket inserted through the timing belt cover (it is not necessary to remove the cover), loosen the lower mounting bolt.

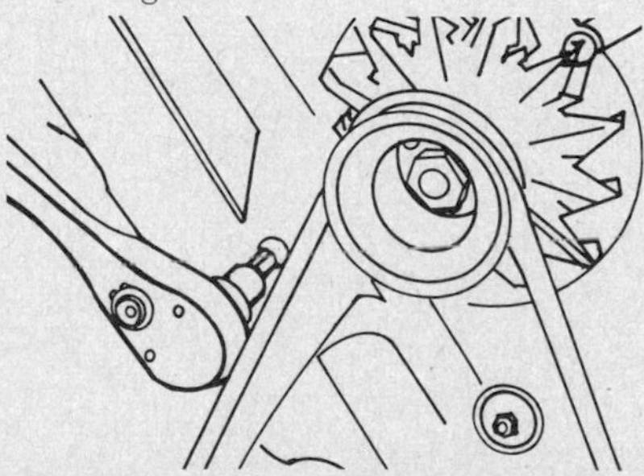

Removing the lower alternator bolt through the timing cover

5. Swing the alternator over and remove the alternator belt.
6. Remove the lower nut and bolt. Don't lose the spacers or rubber isolators.
7. Remove the alternator.

NOTE: *Remember when installing the alternator that it is not necessary to polarize an AC generating system.*

8. Install the alternator with the lower bolt. Don't tighten it at this point.
9. Install the alternator belt over the pulleys.
10. Loosely install the top mounting bolt and pivot the alternator until the belt is correctly tensioned.
11. Tighten the top and bottom bolts to 14 ft lbs.
12. Connect the alternator and battery wires.

Belt Replacement and Tensioning

1. Loosen the top alternator mounting bolt.
2. Using a socket inserted through the timing belt cover (you don't need to remove the cover), loosen the lower mounting bolt.
3. Using a pry bar, such as a large screwdriver or ratchet handle, swing the alternator over and remove the belt.
4. Slip the new belt over the pulleys.
5. Pry the alternator over until the belt deflection midway between the crankshaft pulley and the alternator pulley is ⅜–9/16 in. (10–15 mm).
6. Securely tighten the mounting bolts.

Removal and Installation

1. Disconnect the battery ground cable.
2. Raise the front of the car.
3. Mark with tape and then disconnect the two small wires from the starter solenoid. One wire connects to the ignition coil and the second to the ignition switch through the wiring harness.

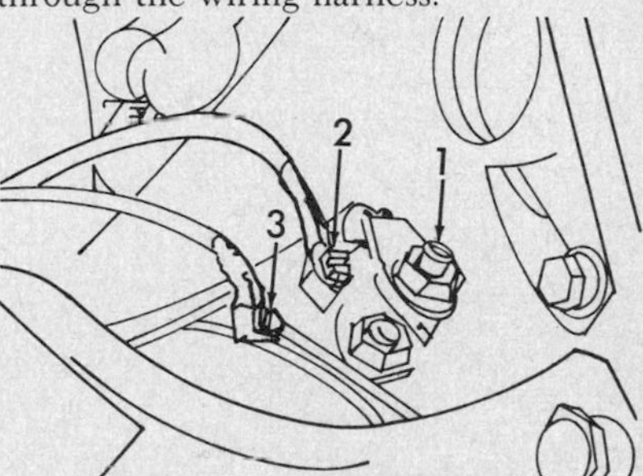

Starter electrical connections—(A) solenoid, (B) coil, (C) positive battery cable

4. Disconnect the large cable.
5. Remove the two starter retaining nuts.
6. Unscrew the bolt. Pull the starter straight out and to the front.
7. Installation of the starter is carried out in reverse order of removal.

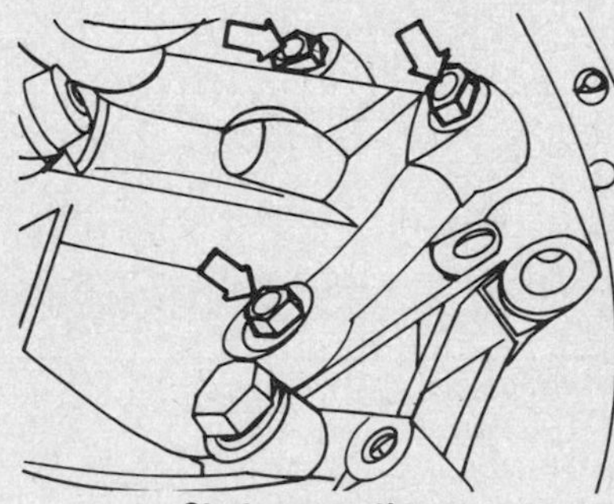

Starter mountings

Overhaul

Use the following procedure to replace brushes or starter drive.

1. Remove the solenoid.
2. Remove the end bearing cap.
3. Loosen both of the long housing screws.
4. Remove the lockwasher and spacer washers.

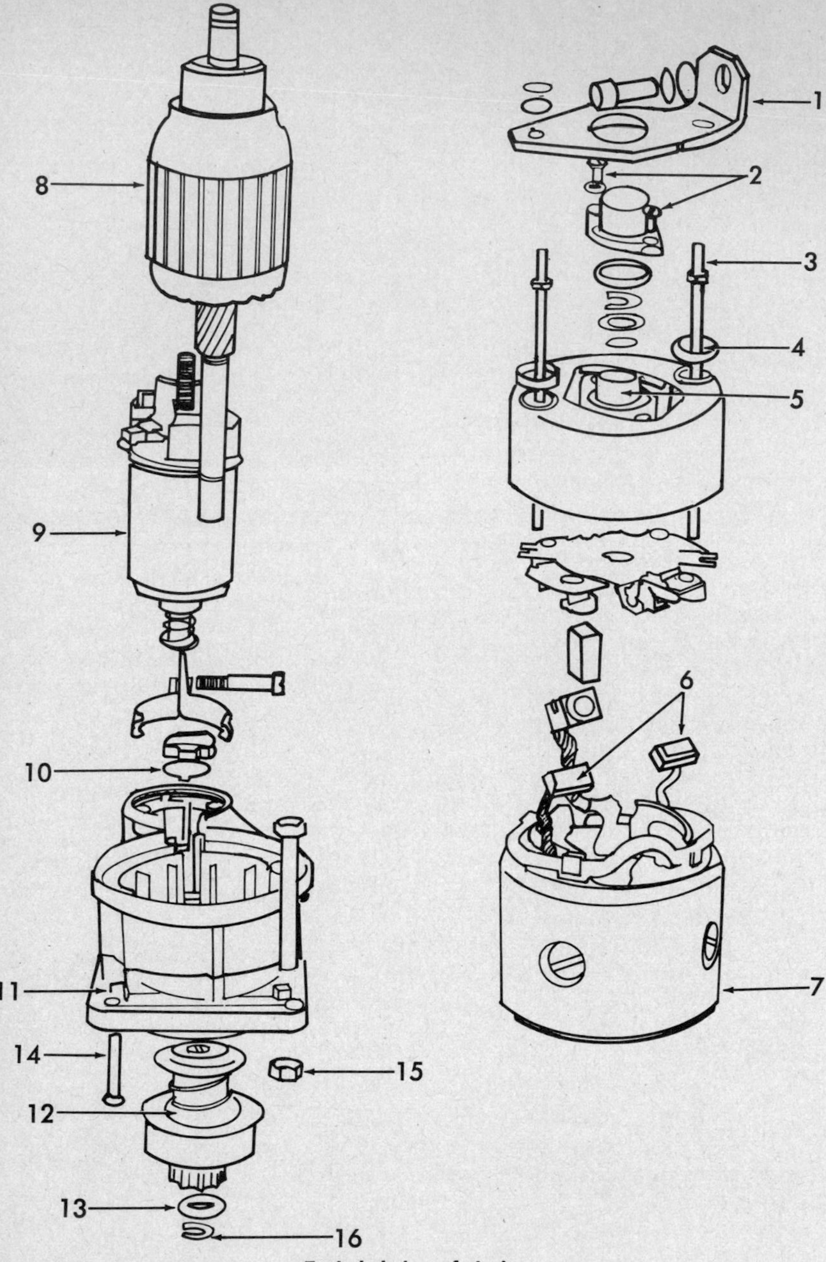

Exploded view of starter

1. Mounting bracket
2. End cap screws
3. Housing screws
4. Cupped washer
5. End plate bushing
6. Brushes
7. Field coil housing
8. Armature
9. Solenoid
10. Disc
11. Mounting housing
12. Drive pinion
13. Stop ring
14. Solenoid bolt
15. Starter bolt and nut
16. Circlip

5. Remove the long housing screws and remove the end cover.

6. Pull the two field coil brushes out of the brush housing.

7. Remove the brush housing assembly.

8. Loosen the nut on the solenoid housing, remove the sealing disc, and remove the solenoid operating lever.

9. Loosen the large screws on the side of the starter body and remove the field coil along with the brushes.

NOTE: *If the brushes require replacement, the field coil and brushes and/or the brush housing and its brushes must be replaced as a unit.*

10. If the starter drive is being replaced, push the stop ring down and remove the circlip on the end of the shaft. Remove the stop-ring and remove the drive.

11. Assembly of the starter is carried out in the reverse order of disassembly. Use a gear puller to install the stop-ring in its groove. Use a new circlip on the shaft.

Solenoid Replacement

1. Remove the starter.
2. Remove the nut which secures the connector strip on the end of the solenoid.
3. Take out the two retaining screws on the mounting bracket and pull out the solenoid after it has been unhooked from the operating lever.
4. Installation is the reverse of removal. In order to facilitate engagement of the lever, the pinion should be pulled out as far as possible when inserting the solenoid.

ENGINE MECHANICAL

The engine is an inline four cylinder unit with single overhead camshaft. It is inclined 30° to the right (to the rear in the Rabbit and Scirocco). The crankshaft runs in five bearings with thrust taken on the center bearing. The cylinder block is cast iron. A steel reinforced rubber belt drives the intermediate shaft and camshaft. The intermediate shaft drives the oil pump, distributor and fuel pump.

The cylinder head is lightweight aluminum alloy. The intake and exhaust manifolds are mounted on the same side of the cylinder head. The valves are opened and closed by camshaft lobes operating on cupped cam followers which fit over the valves and springs. This design results in lighter valve train weight and fewer moving parts.

Engine Removal and Installation

Dasher Without A/C

The engine and transmission are lifted off the mounts and the transmission then detached and left in the car. This procedure requires an overhead chain hoist, floor jack, and a helper or two. It is not necessary to remove the hood, but it would be a good idea.

1. Disconnect the battery cables.
2. Remove the exhaust manifold heater hose and breather hose from the air cleaner.
3. Remove the air cleaner assembly.
4. Pull the clip off the accelerator cable and detach the cable.
5. Loosen the upper adjustment nut on the clutch cable and detach it.
6. Disconnect the fuel line from the fuel pump, plug it, and place it out of the way.
7. Disconnect the wiring from the alternator.
8. Detach the clip and remove the heater cable.
9. Disconnect the front engine mount and remove the mount bracket.

10. Drain the coolant from the radiator. The plug is located near the lower hose. Drain the cylinder block at the plug near the starter.

11. Disconnect the electrical wire from the coil and distributor, oil pressure and temperature sending units, fan and the thermal switch on the radiator.

12. Disconnect the radiator and heater hoses from the engine. Detach the heater valve cable.

13. Loosen the radiator shroud retainers. Remove the mounting bolts and nuts and lift out the radiator and fan.

14. Raise the front of the car and safely support it.

15. Remove the starter.

16. Disconnect the exhaust pipe from the manifold.

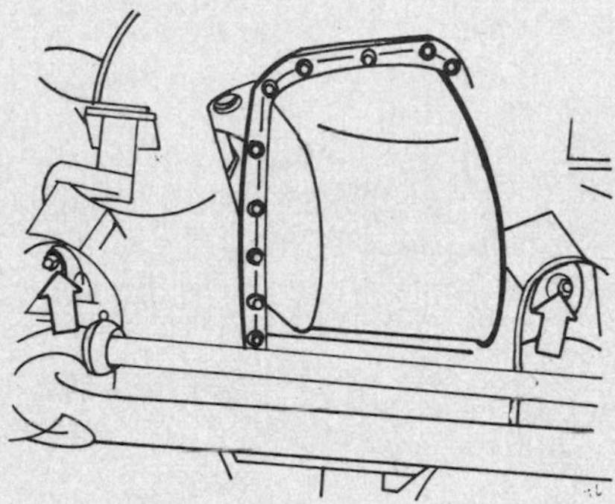

Dasher engine side mounts

17. Detach the engine side mounts.

18. Loosen the upper engine-to-transmission bolts. Remove the lower bolts. If the car is equipped with an automatic transmission, remove the three torque converter-to-flywheel bolts by working through the starter hole. Use a bar to hold the flywheel.

19. Support the transmission with a floor jack.

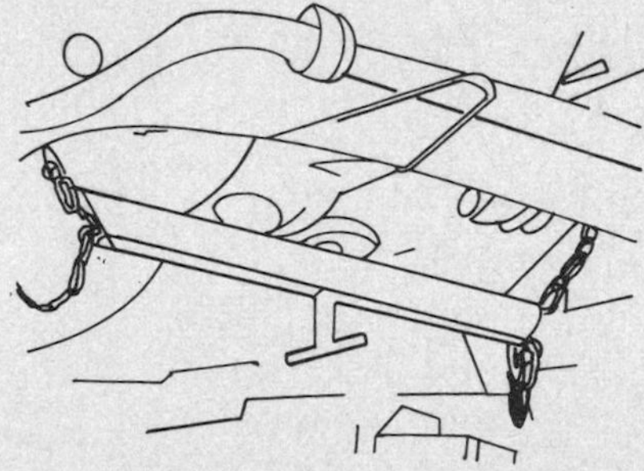

A fixture of this type can be arranged to support the Dasher transmission, or a floor jack can be used

20. Lower the car slowly and carefully until the wheels are on the ground.

21. Attach the hoist to the engine lift points.

22. Raise the engine/transmission until the transmission touches the steering.

23. Adjust your jack or support so that the transmission is held firmly.

24. Remove the upper engine-to-transmission bolts.

25. Pry the engine and transmission apart and remove the intermediate plate. Install a bar or cable to the torque converter housing on automatic cars to prevent the converter from falling out.

26. Remove the engine by slowly lifting and turning simultaneously.

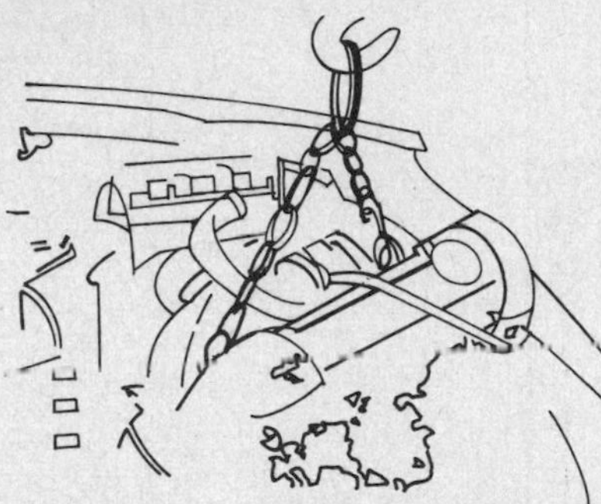

Lifting the Dasher engine out of the car. Note how it must be turned for removal

CAUTION: *Do this very carefully to avoid damaging the driveshafts or transmission.*

27. Installation is the reverse of removal. Be careful not to damage the input shaft of the transmission during installation. Install new torque converter mounting bolts. Tighten the torque converter bolts to 25 ft lbs, engine to transaxle bolts to 40 ft lbs, and the engine mount bolts to 32 ft lbs.

Dasher with A/C

On air-conditioned models, it is necessary to lower the engine, transmission, and front suspension from the car as a unit.

1. Raise the car, allowing the front wheels to hang down. Disconnect the battery ground cable.
2. Drain the coolant.
3. Disconnect all connections between engine, transmission, and body as explained for models without A/C.
4. Remove the radiator.
5. Disconnect the gearshift rod coupling at the transmission.
6. Detach the front engine mount at the engine block.
7. Use a removal tool to separate the tie rod ends from the steering levers.
8. Push the brake pedal down about 1½ in. and fasten it in place to keep the system from draining. Disconnect and plug the brake lines at the brackets on the wheel housing.
9. Attach a framework to a sturdy floor jack to keep the assembly steady and clamp it to the crossmember. Lift slightly and disconnect both coil spring units from the wheel housings. Unbolt the crossmember.
10. Disconnect the backup light switch wire and lower the engine, transmission, and front suspension assembly.
11. On installation, tighten the coil spring units to the body to 16 ft lbs, and the crossmember to the body to 33 ft lbs.

Rabbit and Scirocco With Manual Transmission

The engine and transmission are removed as an assembly. You don't have to remove the hood, but it might make the job easier.

1. Disconnect the battery ground cable.
2. Drain the coolant by unbolting the lower water pump flange or by removing the hoses.
3. Remove the radiator with the air ducts and fan.
4. Detach all the electrical wires connecting the engine to the body.
5. Disconnect and plug the fuel line at the fuel pump. Detach the coolant hoses at the left end of the engine. Disconnect the accelerator cable and remove the air cleaner.
6. Disconnect the speedometer cable from the transmission. Detach the clutch cable.
7. Remove the engine support to the right of the starter.
8. Remove the headlight caps inside the engine compartment.
9. Unbolt the driveshafts from the transmission and wire them up.
10. Unbolt the exhaust pipe from the manifold and unbolt the exhaust pipe brace.
11. Unbolt the transmission rear mount from the body (alongside the tunnel).
12. Detach the ground strap from the transmission and body.
13. Remove the shift linkage.
14. Attach a chain sling to the alternator bracket and the lifting eye at the left end of the engine. Lift the engine and transmission slightly.
15. Detach the engine carrier from the body and remove the left transmission carrier.
16. Lift the engine/transmission assembly carefully out of the car.
17. To separate the engine and transmission, turn the flywheel to align the lug on the flywheel (to the left of TDC) with the pointer in the opening. Remove the cover plate over the driveshaft flange and remove the engine to transmission bolts and the transmission housing cover plate.

To install the engine:

18. To attach the transmission to the engine, the recess in the flywheel edge must be at 3:00 O'Clock (facing the left end of the engine). Torque the engine to transmission bolts to 40 ft lbs. Lift the engine/transmission assembly into place and loosely attach the left transmission carrier to the transmission. Align the assembly, then bolt the engine and transmission carrier to the body. Torque the 10 mm bolts to 29 ft lbs. Torque the driveshaft flange bolts to 32 ft lbs. Refill the cooling system.

Rabbit and Scirocco With Automatic Transmission

The engine and transmission are removed as an assembly. You don't have to remove the hood, but it might make the job easier.

1. Disconnect both battery cables.
2. Drain the coolant by unbolting the lower water pump flange or by removing the hoses.
3. Remove the radiator with the air ducts and fan.
4. Remove the air cleaner.
5. Detach the speedometer cable from the transmission.
6. Detach all electrical wires connecting the engine to the body. Detach the coolant hoses.
7. Remove the screws holding the accelerator cable bracket to the carburetor float bowl, shift into P, detach the end of the gearshift selector cable from the transmission, detach the accelerator cable from the carburetor and from the pedal at the transmission, and remove the two bracket bolts behind this linkage on the transmission.
8. Unbolt the exhaust pipe from the manifold.
9. Remove the rear transmission mount.
10. Remove the converter cover plate and remove the three torque converter to drive plate bolts.
11. Attach a chain sling to the alternator bracket and the lifting eye at the left end of the engine. It may be necessary to remove the alternator. Lift the engine and transmission slightly.
12. Detach the engine front mounting support; remove the left transmission carrier and the right engine carrier.
13. Lift the engine/transmission assembly carefully out of the car.
14. The transmission can now be detached from the engine.

To install the engine:

15. The engine to transmission bolts should be torqued to 40 ft lbs. Lift the engine/transmission assembly into place and install the left transmission carrier, tightening first the body, then the transmission bolts. Lower the assembly to attach the engine carrier to the body, tightening the bolts to 40 ft lbs. Install the engine mounting support. Torque converter bolts should be torqued to 21 ft lbs and drive shaft bolts to 32 ft lbs. Refill the cooling system. Check the adjustment of transmission and carburetor linkages.

Cylinder Head

Removal and Installation

The engine should be cold before the cylinder head can be removed. The head is retained by 10 allen head bolts. It can be removed without removing the intake and exhaust manifolds.

1. Disconnect the battery ground cable.
2. Drain the cooling system.
3. Remove the air cleaner. Disconnect the fuel line.
4. Disconnect the radiator, heater, and choke hoses.
5. Disconnect all electrical wires. Remove the spark plug wires.
6. Separate the exhaust manifold from the exhaust pipe.
7. Disconnect the EGR line from the exhaust manifold. Remove the EGR valve and filter from the intake manifold.
8. Remove the carburetor.
9. Disconnect the air pump fittings.
10. Remove the timing belt cover and belt.
11. Loosen the cylinder head bolts in the reverse of the tightening sequence.
12. Remove the bolts and lift the head straight off.
13. Install the new cylinder head gasket with the word TOP or OBEN up.
14. Install bolts No. 7 and 8 first, these holes are smaller and will properly locate the gasket and cylinder head.
15. Install the remaining bolts. Tighten them in three stages in the sequence shown. Cylinder head bolt torque (cold) is 55 ft. lbs.

NOTE: *After approximately 300 miles, retighten the cylinder head bolts. Torque them hot to 61 ft lbs.*

16. Install the remaining components in the reverse order of removal.

Overhaul

Valve guides are a shrink fit. Always install new valve seals when doing a valve job. Valve seats are not replaceable, the cylinder head should be replaced if the valve pocket depth exceeds 0.354 in. [9 mm] for intake valves and/or 0.378 in. [9.6 mm] for exhaust valves.

Intake Manifold

Removal and Installation

1. Remove the air cleaner. Drain the cooling system.
2. Disconnect the accelerator cable.
3. Disconnect the EGR valve connections.
4. Detach all electrical leads.
5. Disconnect the coolant hoses.

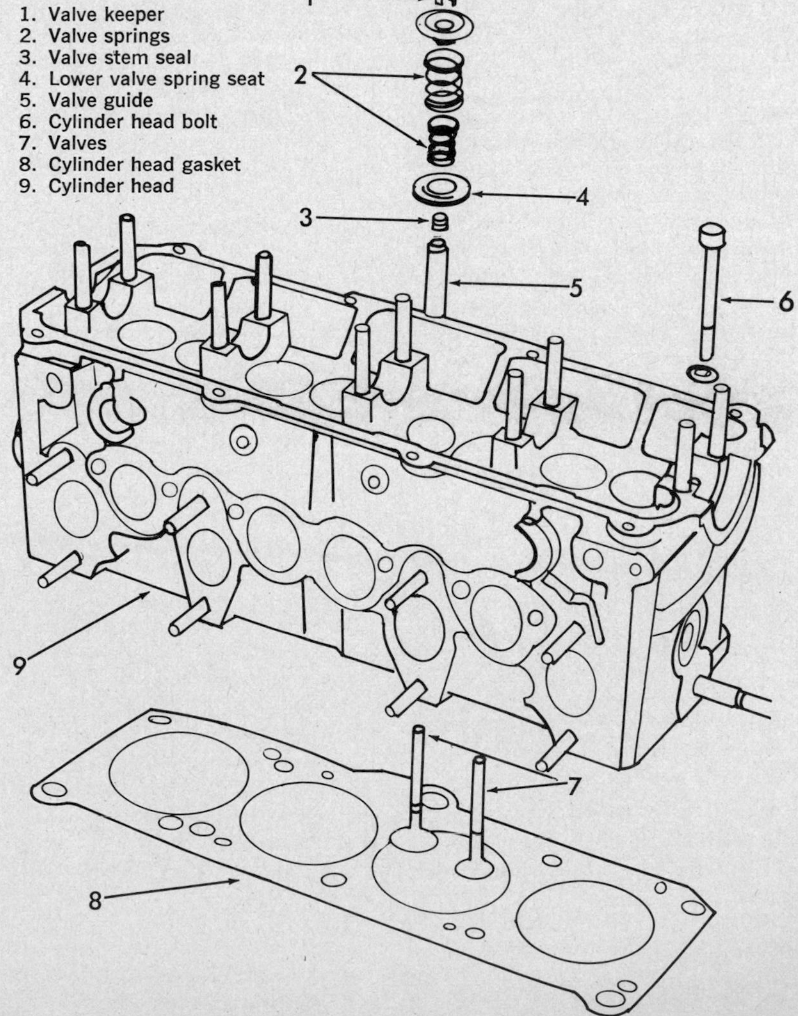

Exploded view of cylinder head showing valve train components

6. Disconnect the fuel line from the carburetor.

7. Remove the vacuum hoses from the carburetor.

8. Loosen and remove the six retaining bolts and lift off the manifold.

9. Install a new gasket. Install the manifold and tighten the bolts from the inside out. Tightening torque is 18 ft. lbs.

10. Install the remaining components in the reverse order of removal. Refill the cooling system.

Exhaust Manifold

1. Disconnect the EGR tube from the exhaust manifold.

2. Remove the interfering air pump components.

3. Remove the air cleaner hose from the exhaust manifold.

4. Disconnect the intake manifold support.

5. Separate the exhaust pipe from the manifold.

6. Remove the eight retaining nuts and remove the manifold.

7. Clean the cylinder head and manifold mating surfaces.

8. Using a new gasket, install the exhaust manifold.

9. Tighten the nuts to 18 ft. lbs. Work from the inside out.

10. Install the remaining components in the reverse order of removal. Use a new manifold flange gasket.

Timing Belt Cover

Removal and Installation

1. Loosen the alternator mounting bolts.

2. Pivot the alternator and slip the drive belt off the sprockets.

3. Unscrew the cover retaining nuts and remove the cover. Don't lose any of the washers or spacers.

4. Reposition the spacers on the studs and then install the washers and nuts.

5. Install the alternator belt and adjust its tension.

Timing Belt

NOTE: *The timing belt is designed to last for more than 60,000 miles and does not normally require tension adjustments. If the belt is removed or replaced, the basic valve timing must be checked and the belt retensioned.*

Removal, Installation, and Tensioning

1. Remove the timing belt cover.

2. While holding the large hex on the tension sprocket, loosen the pulley locknut.

3. Release the tensioner from the timing belt.

4. Slide the belt off the three toothed sprockets and remove it.

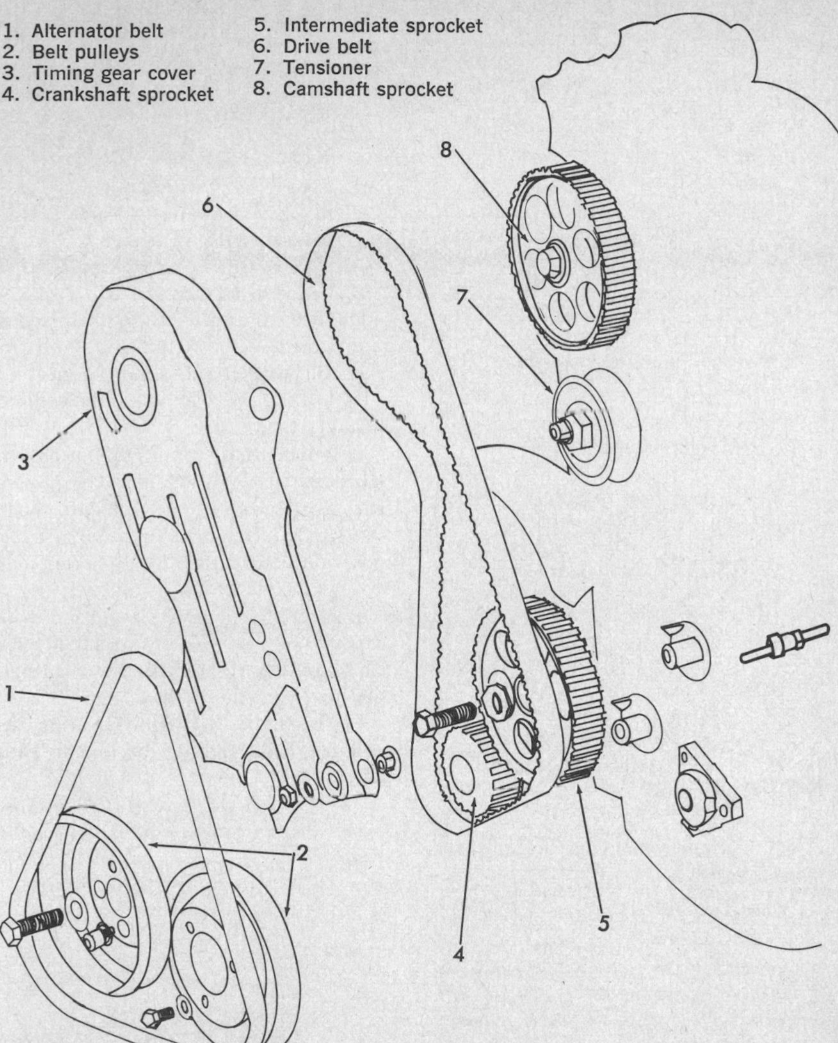

Exploded view of camshaft drive arrangement

Turn the tensioner (R) toward (a) to tighten the belt and toward (b) to loosen. Check the tension at (c)

5. Turn the crankshaft until No. 1 cylinder is at TDC. At this point, the 0°T mark will be aligned with the pointer on the bell housing.

6. Align the timing mark on the rear face of the camshaft pulley with the camshaft cover gasket on the left.

7. Align the V-notch in the crankshaft pulley with the dot mark on the intermediate shaft. The distributor rotor should be pointing to the No. 1 cylinder mark on the rim of the distributor.

0°T or TDC mark on the flywheel

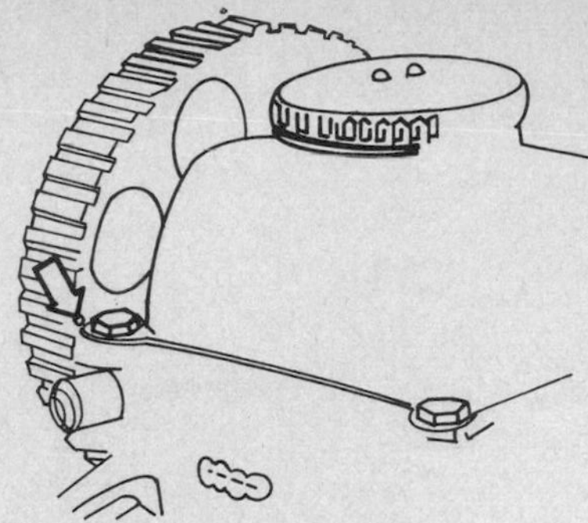

Camshaft sprocket alignment

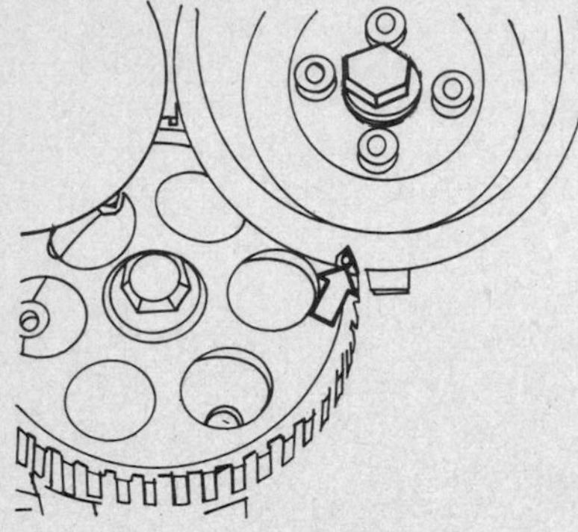

Crankshaft pulley and intermediate shaft sprocket alignment

CAUTION: *If the timing marks are not correctly aligned, valve timing will be incorrect. Poor performance and serious engine damage can result from improper valve timing.*

8. Install the belt on the sprockets.
9. Adjust the tensioner by turning the large tensioner hex to the right. Tension is correct when you can just twist the belt 90° with two fingers at the midpoint. Tighten the locknut to 32 ft. lbs.
10. Install the timing belt cover and check the ignition timing.

Timing Sprockets

Removal and Installation

The camshaft, intermediate shaft, and crankshaft sprockets are located by keys on their respective shafts and each is retained by a bolt. To remove any or all of the pulleys, first remove the timing belt cover and belt.

NOTE: *When removing the crankshaft pulley, don't remove the four allen head bolts which hold the outer belt pulley to the timing belt sprocket.*

1. Remove the center bolt.
2. Gently pry the sprocket off the shaft.
3. If it is stubborn, use a gear puller. Don't hammer on the sprocket.
4. Remove the sprocket and key.
5. Install in the reverse order of removal.
6. Tighten the center bolt to 58 ft. lbs.
7. Install the timing belt, check the valve timing, tension the belt, and install the cover.

Camshaft

Removal and Installation

1. Remove the timing belt.
2. Remove the camshaft sprocket.
3. Remove the air cleaner.
4. Remove the camshaft cover.
5. Unscrew and remove the No. 1, 3, and 5 bearing caps (No. 1 is at the front).
6. Unscrew the No. 2 and 4 bearing caps, diagonally and in increments.
7. Lift the camshaft out of the cylinder head.
8. Lubricate the camshaft journals and lobes with assembly lube or gear oil before installing it in the cylinder head.
9. Replace the camshaft oil seal with a new one whenever the cam is removed.
10. Install the No. 1, 3, and 5 bearing caps and tighten the nuts to 14 ft. lbs. The caps should be installed so they read right side up from the driver's seat.
11. Install the No. 2 and 4 bearing caps and diagonally tighten the nuts to 14 ft. lbs.

NOTE: *If checking end play, install a dial indicator so that the feeler touches the camshaft snout. Endplay should be no more than 0.006 in. [0.15 mm.].*

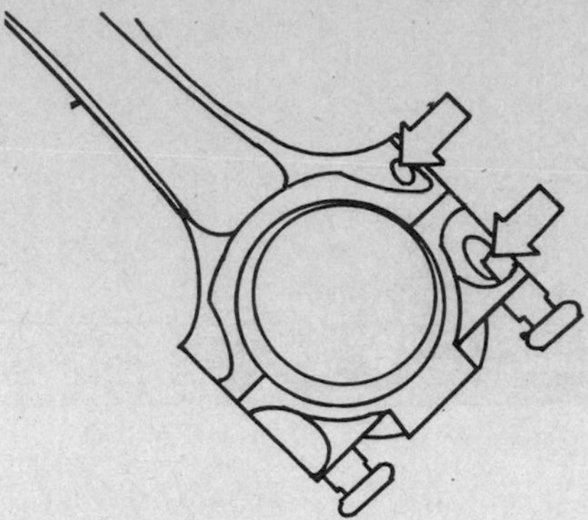

The connecting rod and cap alignment casting grooves must face the intermediate shaft

12. Replace the seal in the No. 1 bearing cap. If necessary, replace the end plug in the cylinder head.
13. Install the camshaft cover.
14. Install the camshaft pulley and the timing belt.
15. Check the valve clearance.

Pistons and Connecting Rods

The pistons must be installed in the block with the arrow at the edge of the

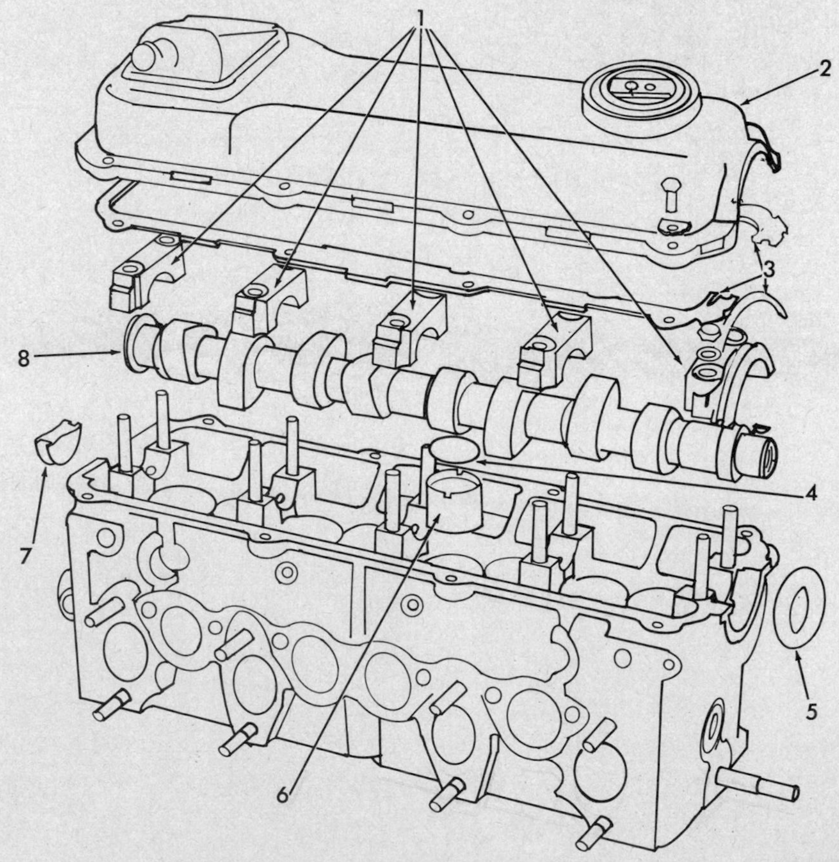

Exploded view of camshaft assembly

1. Camshaft bearing caps
2. Camshaft cover
3. Gasket
4. Valve adjusting disc
5. Oil seal
6. Cam follower
7. End plug
8. Camshaft

crown facing to the front of the car. The connecting rod and cap alignment casting grooves must face the intermediate shaft. New connecting rod bolts must always be used. The pistons must be heated to 140°F in an oven before the piston pins can be pressed in. Three piston oversizes are available to accomodate overbores up to 0.040 in.

There is a piston size code stamped on the cylinder block above the water pump.

ENGINE LUBRICATION

The lubrication system is a conventional wet-sump design. The gear type oil pump is driven by the intermediate shaft. A pressure relief valve limits pressure and prevents extreme pressure from developing in the system. All oil is filtered by a full flow replaceable filter. A bypass valve assures lubrication in the event the filter becomes plugged. The oil pressure switch is located at the end of the cylinder head gallery [the end of the system] to assure accurate pressure readings.

Oil Pan

Removal and Installation

Dasher

1. Drain the oil pan.
2. Support and slightly raise the engine with an overhead hoist.
3. Gradually loosen the engine crossmember mounting bolts. Remove the left and right side engine mounts.
4. Lower the crossmember very carefully.
5. Loosen and remove the allen head, oil pan retaining bolts.
6. Lower the pan from the car.
7. Install the pan using a new gasket and sealer.
8. Tighten the retaining bolts to 7 ft. lbs. in a crosswise pattern.
9. Raise the crossmember. Tighten the crossmember bolts to 42 ft. lbs. and the engine mounting bolts to 32 ft. lbs.
10. Refill the engine with oil. Start the engine and check for leaks.

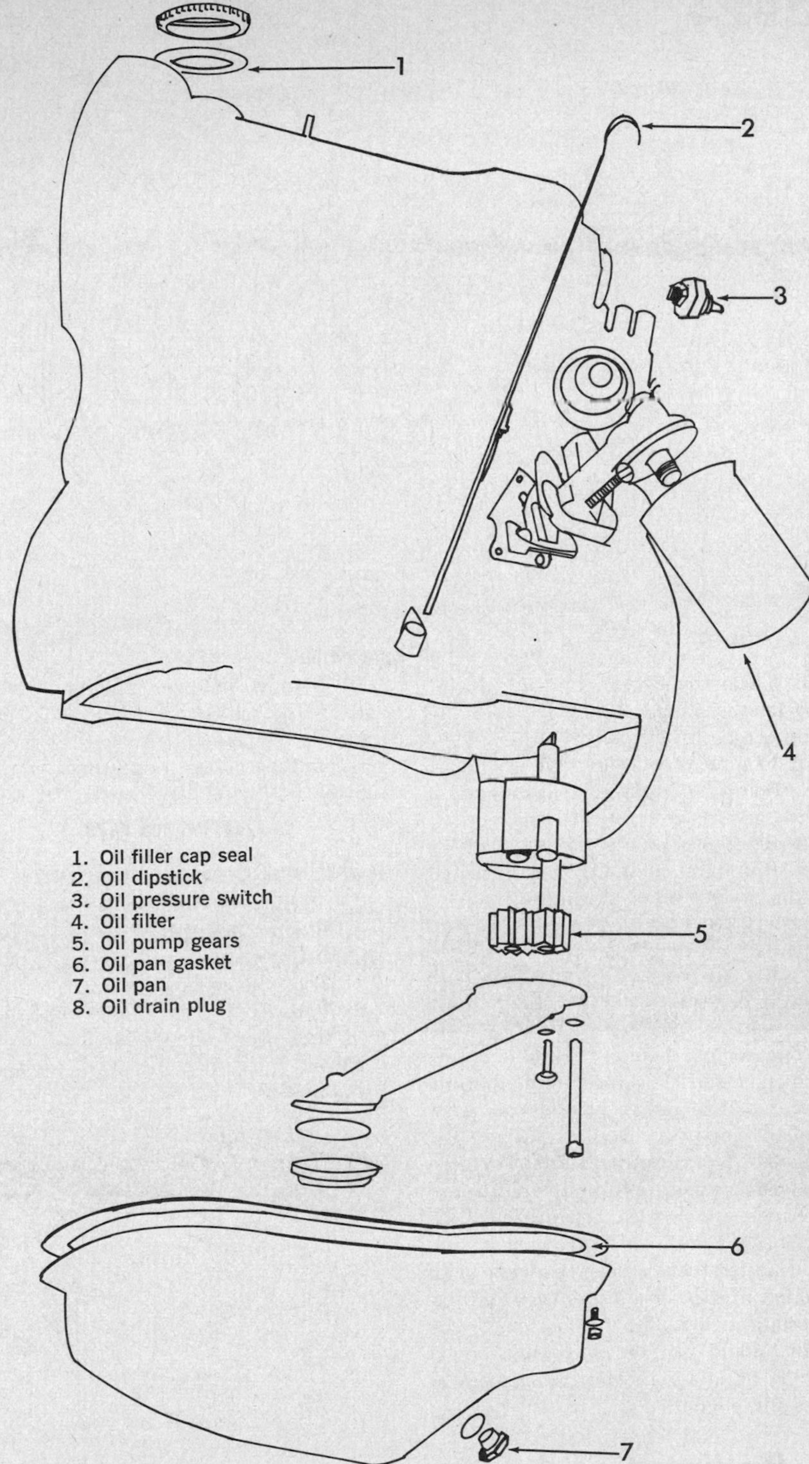

Lubrication system components

Rear Main Oil Seal

Replacement

The rear main oil seal is located in a housing on the rear of the cylinder block. To replace the seal on the Dasher, it is necessary to remove the transmission and perform the work from underneath the car or remove the engine and perform the work on an engine stand or work bench.

See "Transmission Removal and Installation." On the Rabbit and Scirocco, the engine should be removed from the car.

1. Remove the transmission and flywheel.
2. Using a screwdriver, very carefully pry the old seal out of the support ring.
3. Remove the seal.
4. Lightly oil the replacement seal and then press it into place using a circular piece of flat metal. Be careful not to damage the seal or score the crankshaft.
5. Install the flywheel and transmission. Flywheel-to-engine bolts are tightened to 36 ft. lbs.

Oil Pump

Removal and Installation

1. Remove the oil pan.
2. Remove the two mounting bolts.
3. Pull the oil pump down and out of the engine.
4. Unscrew the two bolts and separate the pump halves.
5. Remove the driveshaft and gear from the upper body.

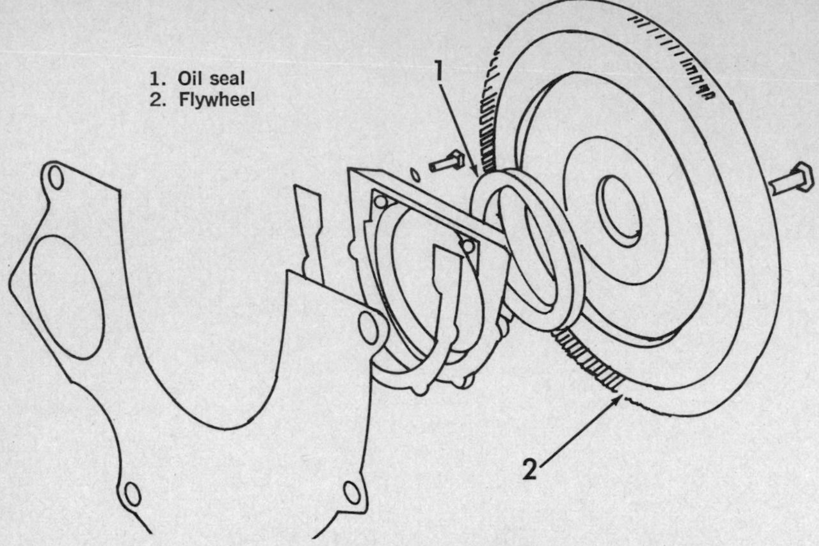

Rear main oil seal assembly

6. Clean the bottom half in solvent. Pry up the metal edges to remove the filter screen for cleaning.

7. Examine the gears and driveshaft for wear or damage. Replace them if necessary.

8. Reassemble the pump halves.

9. Prime the pump with oil and install in the reverse order of removal.

COOLING SYSTEM

The cooling system consists of a belt driven, external water pump, thermostat, radiator, and thermostatically controlled electric cooling fan. When the engine is cold the thermostat is closed and blocks the water from the radiator so the coolant is circulated only through the engine. When the engine warms up, the thermostat opens and the radiator is included in the coolant circuit. The thermostatic switch is in the bottom of the radiator and turns the electrical fan on at 199°F, off at 186°F. This reduces power loss and engine noise.

Radiator and Fan

Removal and Installation

Dasher

1. Drain the cooling system.
2. Remove the inner shroud mounting bolts.
3. Disconnect the lower radiator hose.
4. Disconnect the thermostatic switch lead.
5. Remove the lower radiator shroud.
6. Remove the lower radiator mounting units.
7. Disconnect the upper radiator hose.
8. Detach the upper radiator shroud.
9. Disconnect the heater and intake manifold hoses.
10. Remove the side mounting bolts and lift the radiator and fan out as an assembly.
11. Installation is the reverse of removal.

Thermostat

Removal and Installation

The thermostat is located in the bottom radiator hose neck on the water pump.

1. Drain the cooling system.
2. Remove the two retaining bolts from the lower water pump neck.

NOTE: *It isn't necessary to disconnect the hose.*

3. Move the neck, with the hoses attached, out of the way.
4. Remove the thermostat.
5. Install a new seal on the water pump neck.
6. Install the thermostat with the spring end up.
7. Replace the water pump neck and tighten the two retaining bolts.

Water Pump

Removal and Installation

1. Drain the cooling system.
2. Remove the alternator and drive belt.
3. Remove the timing belt cover.
4. Disconnect the lower radiator hose, engine hose, and heater hose from the water pump.
5. Remove the four pump retaining bolts. Notice where the different length bolts are located.
6. Turn the pump slightly and lift it out of the engine block.
7. Installation is the reverse of removal. Use a new seal on the mating surface with the engine.

EMISSION CONTROLS

Crankcase Ventilation

The crankcase ventilation system keeps harmful vapor byproducts of com-

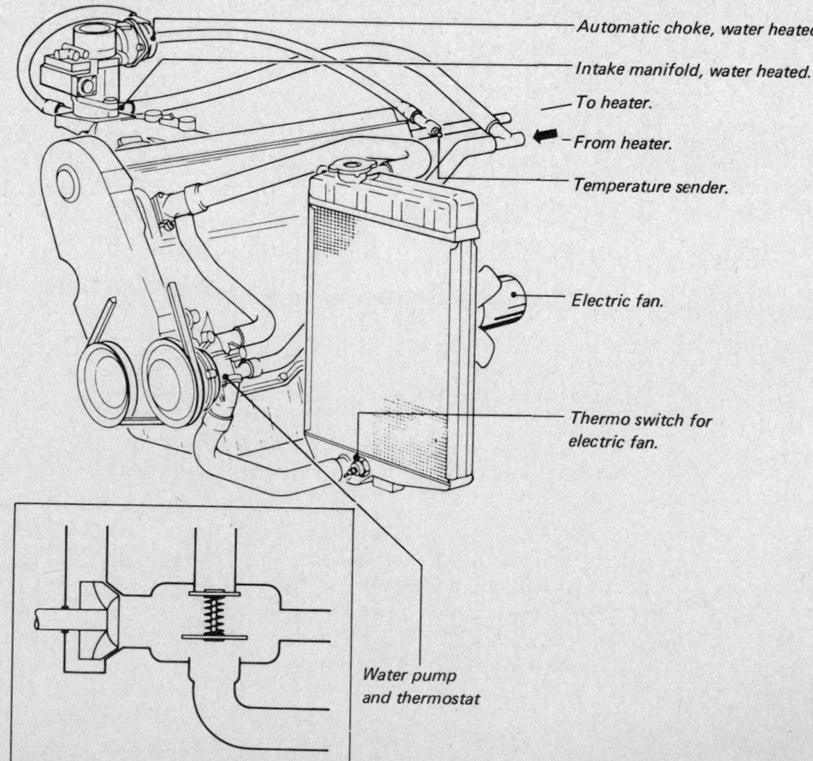

Cooling system connections and thermostat location

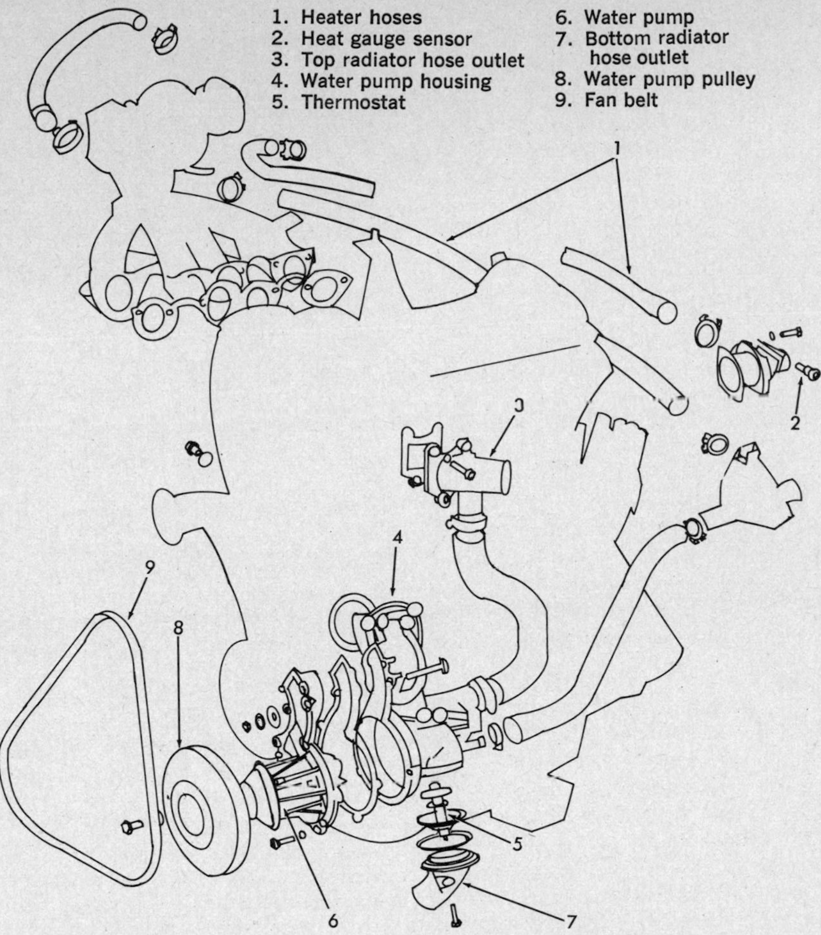

Exploded view of Dasher cooling system

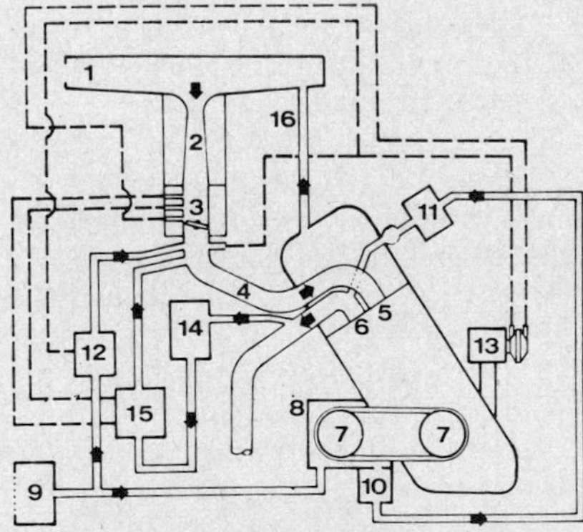

Emission control system schematic. The arrows indicate flow

1. Air cleaner
2. Carburetor venturi
3. Throttle valve
4. Intake manifold
5. Cylinder head intake port
6. Cylinder head exhaust port
7. Belt drive for air pump
8. Air pump
9. Air pump filter
10. Pressure relief valve
11. Check valve
12. Diverter valve
13. Distributor
14. EGR filter
15. EGR valve
16. Crankcase ventilation

bustion from escaping into the atmosphere and prevents the building of crankcase pressure which can lead to oil leaking. Crankcase vapors are recirculated from the camshaft cover through a hose to the air cleaner. Here they are mixed with the air/fuel mixture and burned in the combustion chamber.

Service

The only maintenance required on the crankcase ventilation system is a periodic check. At every tune up, examine the hoses for clogging or deterioration. Clean or replace the hoses as necessary.

Evaporative Emission Control System

This system prevents the escape of raw fuel vapors [unburned hydrocarbons or HC] into the atmosphere. The system consists of a sealed carburetor, unvented fuel tank filter cap, fuel tank expansion chamber, an activated charcoal filter canister and connector hoses. Fuel vapors which reach the filter deposit hydrocarbons on the surface of the charcoal filter element. Fresh air enters the filter when the engine is running and forces the hydrocarbons to the air cleaner where they join the air/fuel mixture and are burned.

Service

Maintenance of the system requires checking the condition of the various connector hoses and the charcoal filter at 10,000 mile intervals. The charcoal filter should be replaced at 50,000 mile intervals.

Dual Diaphragm Distributors

The purpose of the dual diaphragm distributor is to improve exhaust emissions during one of the engine's dirtier operating modes—idling. The distributor has a vacuum retard diaphragm, in addition to a vacuum advance diaphragm.

Testing

1. Connect a timing light to the engine. Check the ignition timing.
2. Remove the retard hose from the distributor and plug it. Increase the engine speed. The ignition timing should advance. If it doesn't, then the vacuum unit is faulty and must be replaced.

Exhaust Gas Recirculation (EGR)

To reduce NOx (oxides of nitrogen) emissions, metered amounts of exhaust gases are added to the air/fuel mixture. The recirculated exhaust gas lowers the peak flame temperature during combustion. Exhaust gas from the manifold passes through a filter where it is cleaned. The vacuum operated EGR valve controls the volume of this exhaust gas which is allowed into the intake manifold. There is no EGR at idle, partial at slight throttle and full EGR at mid-throttle. California models are equipped with a dual chamber EGR valve.

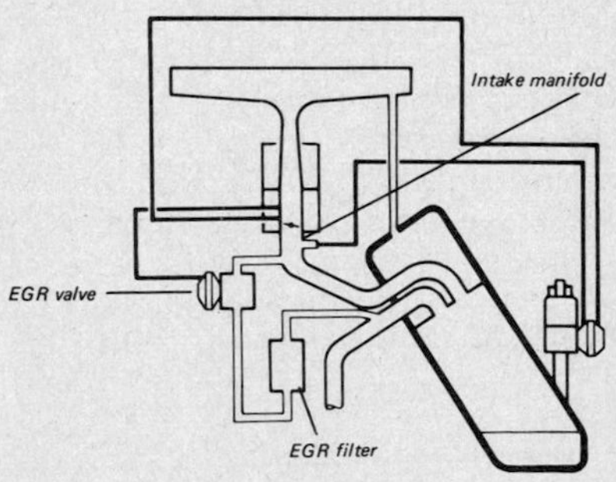

EGR system schematic

Testing

All Models Except California

1. Disconnect the vacuum line from the EGR valve.
2. Disconnect the vacuum hose from the distributor vacuum unit.
3. Start the engine and allow it to idle.
4. Connect the distributor vacuum hose to the EGR valve. The engine should stumble or stall.

5. If the idle stays even, the EGR line is clogged or the EGR valve is defective.

California Models

1. Disconnect both vacuum lines from the EGR valve.
2. Disconnect the hose from the distributor vacuum unit.
3. Start the engine and let it idle.
4. Connect the distributor vacuum line to each EGR connector. The engine should stumble or stall.

NOTE: *The right connector should affect the engine less than the left.*

5. If the idle stays even during Step 4, the EGR line is clogged or the valve is defective. If the idle remains steady during only one vacuum line connection, the EGR valve is defective.

Maintenance

The only required maintenance is that the EGR filter be replaced at 20,000 mile or two year intervals.

1. Disconnect the filter EGR line fittings.
2. Remove the filter and discard.
3. Install the new filter into the EGR lines and securely tighten the fittings.

Removal and Installation

EGR Valve

1. Disconnect the vacuum hose from the EGR valve.
2. Unbolt the EGR line fitting on the opposite side of the valve.
3. Remove the two retaining bolts and lift the EGR valve from the intake manifold.
4. Install the EGR valve in the reverse order of removal. Use a new gasket at the intake manifold.

Air Injection

The air injection system, or air pump, is installed on 1974 California models and all 1975 Dashers. This system includes a belt-driven air pump, filter, check valve, anti-backfire valve or gulp valve, and connecting hoses and air lines. The system reduces exhaust emissions by pumping fresh air to the exhaust manifold where it combines with the hot exhaust gas to burn away excess hydrocarbons and reduce carbon monoxide.

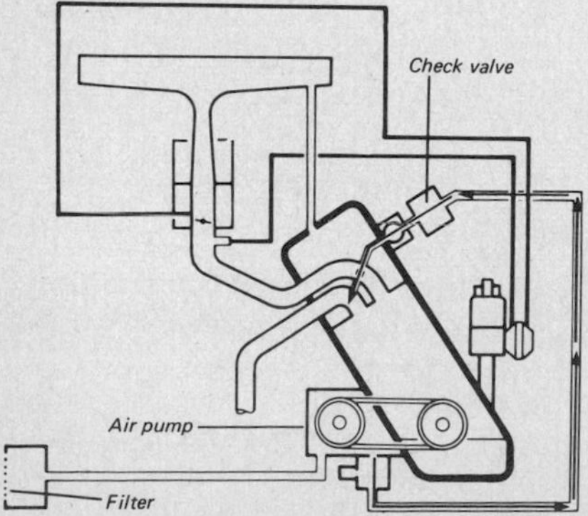

Air injection system schematic. The arrows indicate air flow

Maintenance

Required maintenance on the air pump involves visually checking the pump, control valves, hoses and lines every 10,000 miles. Clean the air pump filter element at this interval. The filter element should be replaced every 20,000 miles or two years.

Testing and Service

Air Pump System

1. Remove and clean the air mainfold.
2. Blow compressed air into the anti-backfire valve in the direction of the air flow.
3. Clean or replace the air pump filter.
4. Start the engine.
5. Exhaust gas should flow equally from each air inlet.
6. With the engine idling, block the relief valve air outlet - only a slight pressure should be felt if the system is operating properly.

Anti-Backfire Valve

1. Disconnect the air pump filter line from the anti-backfire valve.
2. Briefly disconnect the anti-backfire valve vacuum line with the engine running. There should be a noticeable vacuum.
3. Replace the anti-backfire valve if the engine backfires.

FUEL SYSTEM

Fuel Pump

Cleaning

The filter screen can be removed from the pump and cleaned.

1. Remove the center cover screw.
2. Remove the screen and gasket. Clean the screen in a safe solvent.
3. Replace the screen.
4. Install a new gasket and replace the cover.

NOTE: *Make sure the depression in the pump cover engages the projection on the body of the pump.*

Removal and Installation

The pump cannot be repaired and must be replaced when defective.

1. Disconnect and plug both fuel lines.
2. Remove the two allen head retaining bolts.
3. Remove the fuel pump and its plastic flange.
4. Replace the pump in the reverse order of removal. Use a new flange seal.

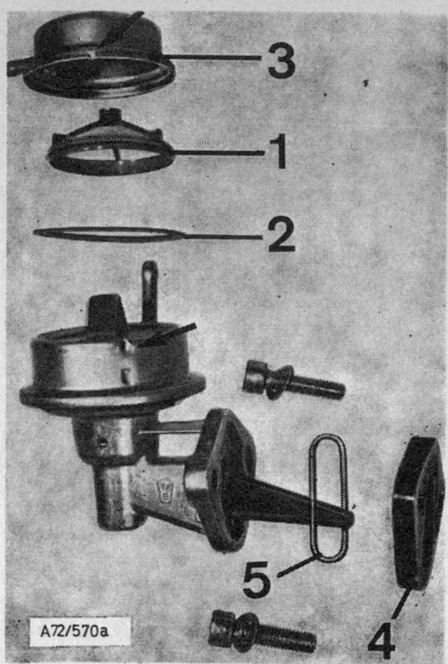

Exploded view of fuel pump

1. Screen
2. Gasket
3. Cover
4. Plastic flange
5. Flange seal

Carburetor

All Dasher models use a Solex 32/35 DIDTA carburetor with a vacuum controlled secondary throttle valve. The California model differs in some respects such as EGR vacuum pickup, and different idle system, but the carburetors are basically the same. The Rabbit and Scirocco use a Zenith 32/32–2B2 two barrel carburetor with a vacuum operated secondary barrel and dual floats.

Removal and Installation

1. Remove the air cleaner.
2. Disconnect the fuel line, being careful not to spill any fuel on the hot engine components.
3. Drain some of the coolant and then disconnect the choke hoses. If you are quick, you can detach and plug the hoses without draining the coolant.
4. Disconnect the distributor and EGR valve vacuum lines.
5. Disconnect the electrical lead for the idle cut-off valve.
6. Remove the clip which secures the throttle linkage to the carburetor. Detach the linkage, being careful not to lose any washers or bushings.
7. Unbolt the carburetor from the manifold and remove it.
8. Use a new gasket when replacing the carburetor. Don't overtighten the nuts.

Automatic Choke Adjustment

Dasher

The standard adjustment on all versions of the automatic choke is with the two notches aligned with the notch on the housing. To adjust, loosen the three clamping screws and move the outer part of the choke unit.

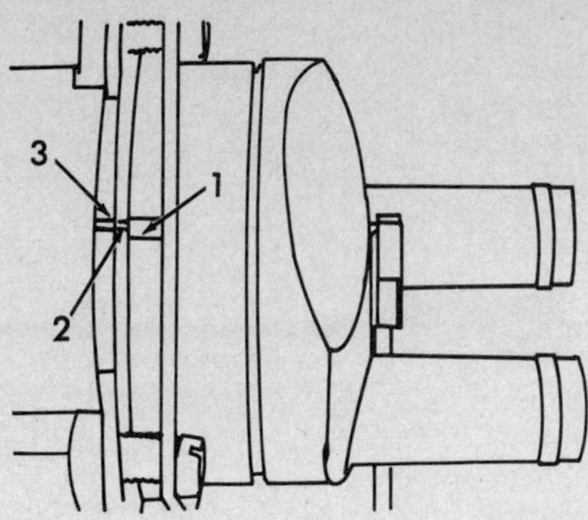

The Dasher automatic choke is correctly adjusted when (1) the choke cover, (2) the adjusting ring, and (3) the mark on the carburetor housing are aligned

Internal Choke Adjustment

Dasher

If after performing the automatic choke adjustment, the choke doesn't operate correctly, use the following procedure.

1. Remove the choke cover with the coolant hoses attached and place it out of the way.
2. The control notch should be 180° opposite the adjusting notch. If not turn it with a screwdriver.
3. Reassemble the choke cover and adjust the choke.

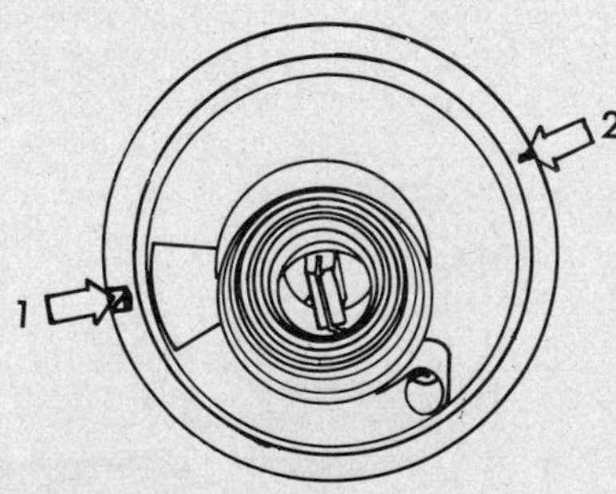

Dasher internal choke adjustment—(1) the adjusting notch, and (2) the control notch

Throttle Gap Adjustment

Dasher

This adjustment is made with the carburetor removed.

1. Close the choke tightly. The stop lever should rest on the highest step of the stepped washer, holding the throttle open slightly.
2. Check the gap between the lower edge of the throttle valve and the housing wall with a drill. The measurement should be:

   California 0.0255 in. [0.65 mm]
   All Others 0.0314 in. [0.80 mm]
3. Adjust the primary gap by means of the two bolts on the connecting rod.
4. The secondary throttle should only be adjusted when it is definitely incorrectly adjusted.

   a. Loosen the adjusting screw until the throttle valve closes.
   b. Turn the screw in ½ turn and lock.
   c. Adjust idle mixture after this adjustment.

Rabbit, Scirocco

This adjustment is made with the carburetor removed.

1. Close the choke valve fully.
2. Use a drill to check the primary throttle valve opening. Insert the drill between the lower edge of the throttle valve and the inner side of the carburetor bore. The gap should be 0.018–0.020 in.
3. Adjust the gap by turning the linkage screw.

Throttle gap adjusting screw, Rabbit and Scirocco

Fast Idle Cam Adjustment

Rabbit, Scirocco

This is set at the factory and need not be adjusted unless disturbed. To adjust, remove the plastic cap and tighten the screw ¼ turn beyond the point at which it just contacts the fast idle cam.

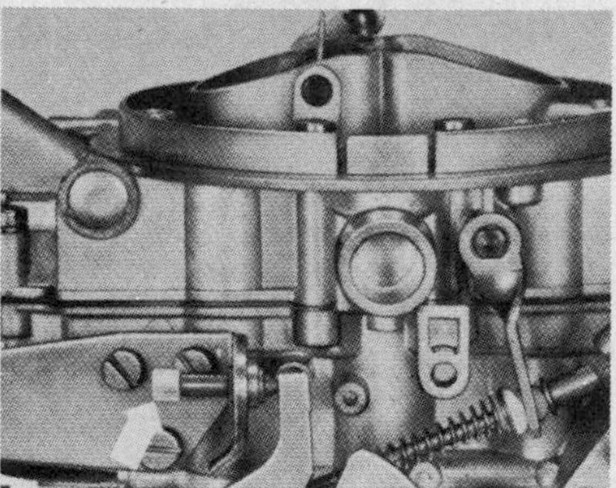

Fast idle cam adjusting screw, Rabbit and Scirocco

Choke Gap Adjustment

Rabbit, Scirocco

1. Remove the automatic choke cover.
2. Open the choke valve all the way. Push the vacuum unit rod in to the stop.
3. Check the gap between the upper edge of the choke valve and the inner side of the carburetor bore. It should be 0.130–0.147 in.
4. Adjust the gap by turning the screw on the choke vacuum unit.

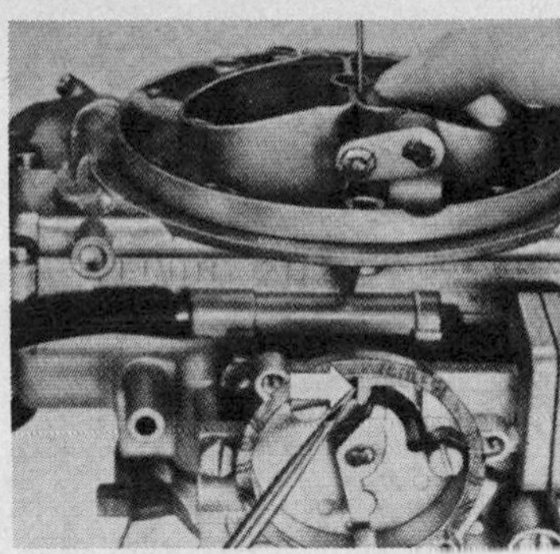

Measuring choke gap on the Rabbit and Scirocco carburetor

Fuel Level Adjustment

Dasher

This adjustment is made with the carburetor installed on the engine. Incorrect fuel level can cause stalling or high-speed miss.

1. Idle the engine for one minute.
2. Stop the engine. Remove the air cleaner.
3. Detach the fuel line.
4. Remove the five carburetor cover mounting screws.
5. Plug the fuel inlet with a finger and lift off the carburetor cover and gasket. Set them to the side, leaving the linkages attached.
6. Using a sliding T-scale, measure the distance from the top of the carburetor cover (air horn) to the upper edge of the float. It should be 0.61–.69 in.
7. The measurement may be corrected by varying the thickness of the fiber sealing ring under the float needle valve.

Rabbit, Scirocco

1. Remove and invert the top of the carburetor.
2. The distance between the bottom of the float and the gasket surface of the top of the carburetor should be 1.102 in. for the primary float and 1.118 in. for the secondary.
3. Adjust by bending the float arm.

Throttle Linkage Adjustment

Throttle linkage adjustments are not normally required. However, it is a good idea to make sure that the throttle valve[s] in the carburetor open all the way when the accelerator pedal is held in the wide-open position. Only the primary throttle valve will open; the secondary throttle is vacuum operated.

Overhaul

Efficient carburetion depends greatly on careful cleaning and inspection during overhaul since dirt, gum, water, or varnish in or on the carburetor parts are often responsible for poor performance.

Overhaul the carburetor in a clean, dust-free area. Carefully disassemble the carburetor, referring often to a diagram. Keep all similar and look-alike parts segregated during disassembly and cleaning to avoid accidental interchange during assembly. Make a note of all jet sizes.

Jet identification for the main body of the Zenith 32/32-2B2 carburetor

1. Secondary full load enrichment
2. Primary air correction jet
3. Secondary air correction jet
4. Primary idle air and fuel jets*
5. Secondary idle air and fuel jets*
6. Primary auxiliary air and fuel jets*

* The fuel jets are below the air jets

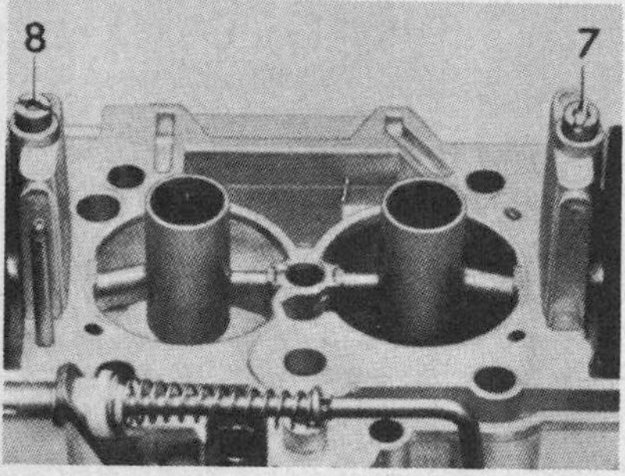

The primary main jet (7) and the secondary main jet (8) are mounted in the top of the carburetor Zenith 32/32-2B2

When the carburetor is disassembled, wash all parts (except diaphragms, electric choke units, pump plunger, and any other plastic, leather, fiber, or rubber parts) in clean carburetor solvent. Do not leave parts in the solvent any longer than is necessary to sufficiently loosen the deposits. Excessive cleaning may remove the special finish from the float bowl and choke valve bodies, leaving these parts unfit for service. Rinse all parts in clean solvent and blow them dry with compressed air or allow them to air dry. Wipe clean all cork, plastic, leather, and fiber parts with a clean, lint-free cloth.

Blow out all passages and jets with compressed air and be sure that there are no restrictions or blockages. Never use wire or similar tools to clean jets, fuel passages, or air bleeds. Clean all jets and valves separately to avoid accidental interchange.

Check all parts for wear or damage. If wear or damage is found, replace the defective parts. Especially check the following:

1. Check the float needle and seat for wear. If wear is found, replace the complete assembly.
2. Check the float hinge pin for wear and the float(s) for dents or distortion. Replace the float if fuel has leaked into it.
3. Check the throttle and choke shaft bores for wear or an out-of-round condition. Damage or wear to the throttle arm, shaft, or shaft bore will often require replacement of the throttle body. These parts require a close tolerance of fit; wear may allow air leakage, which could adversely affect starting and idling.

NOTE: *Throttle shafts and bushings are not included in overhaul kits. They can be purchased separately.*

4. Inspect the idle mixture adjusting needles for burrs or grooves. Any such condition requires replacement of the needle, since you will not be able to obtain a satisfactory idle.
5. Test the accelerator pump check valves. They should pass air one way but not the other. Test for proper seating by blowing and sucking on the valve. Replace the valve if necessary. If the valve is satisfactory, wash the valve again to remove breath moisture.
6. Check the bowl cover for warped surfaces with a straightedge.
7. Closely inspect the valves and seats for wear and damage, replacing as necessary.
8. After the carburetor is assembled, check the choke valve for freedom of operation.

Carburetor overhaul kits are recommended for each overhaul. These kits contain all gaskets and new parts to replace those that deteriorate most rapidly. Failure to replace all parts supplied with the kit (especially gaskets) can result in poor performance later.

Some carburetor manufacturers supply overhaul kits of three basic types: minor repair; major repair; and gasket kits. Basically, they contain the following:

Minor Repair Kits:
All gaskets
Float needle valve
Volume control screw
All diaphragms
Spring for the pump diaphragm

Major Repair Kits:
All jets and gaskets
All diaphragms
Float needle valve
Volume control screw
Pump ball valve
Float
Complete intermediate rod
Intermediate pump lever
Some cover hold-down screws and washers

Gasket Kits:
All gaskets

After cleaning and checking all components, reassemble the carburetor, using new parts and referring to the exploded view. When reassembling, make sure that all screws and jets are tight in their seats, but do not overtighten, as the tips will be distorted. Tighten all screws gradually, in rotation. Do not tighten needle valves into their seats; uneven jet-

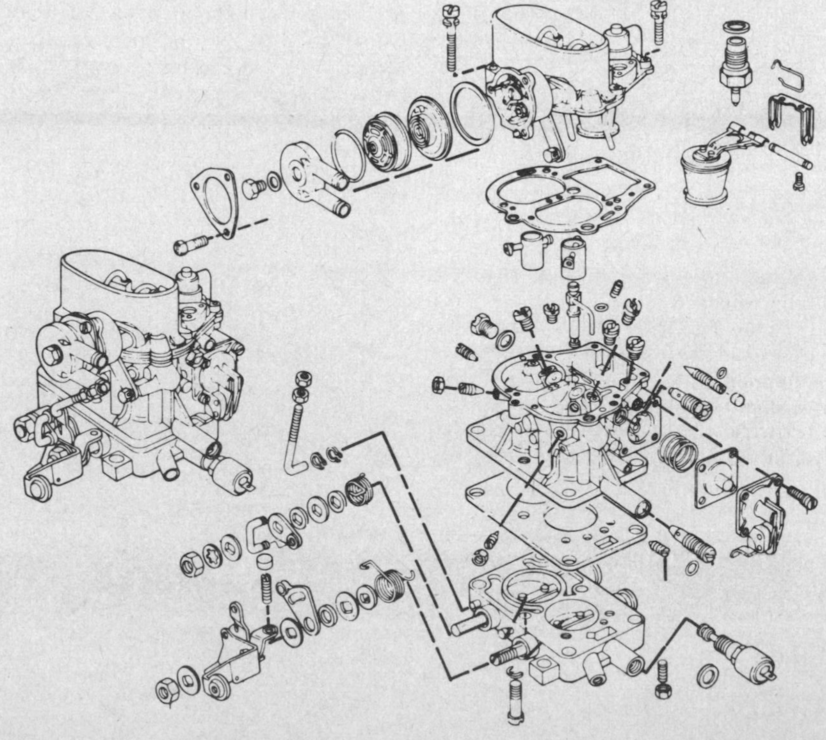

Exploded view of Solex 32/35 DIDTA carburetor

ting will result. Always use new gaskets. Be sure to adjust the float level when reassembling.

MANUAL TRANSMISSION

Transaxle Removal and Installation

Dasher

1. Disconnect the battery ground cable.
2. Disconnect the exhaust pipe from the manifold and its bracket on the transaxle.
3. Remove the square-headed bolt on the shift linkage.
4. Press the shift linkage coupling off.
5. Disconnect the clutch cable.
6. Disconnect the speedometer cable.
7. Detach the axle shafts from the transaxle.
8. Remove the starter.
9. Remove the inspection plate.
10. Remove the engine-to-transaxle bolts.
11. Remove the transaxle crossmember.
12. Support the transaxle with a jack.
13. Pry the transaxle out from the engine.
14. Lift the transaxle out of the car with an assistant.
15. Install the transaxle in the reverse order of removal. Tighten the engine-to-transaxle bolts to 40 ft. lbs. and axle driveshaft bolts to 25 ft. lbs.

Rabbit, Scirocco

The engine and transaxle may be removed together as explained under Engine Removal and Installation or the transaxle may be removed alone, as explained here.

1. Disconnect the battery ground cable.
2. Support the left end of the engine at the lifting eye.
3. Remove the left transmission mount (between the transmission and the firewall).
4. Turn the engine until the lug on the flywheel (to the left of the TDC mark) aligns with the flywheel timing pointer.
5. Detach the speedometer drive cable, backup light wire, and clutch cable.
6. Remove the engine to transmission bolts.
7. Disconnect the shift linkage.
8. Detach the transmission ground strap.
9. Remove the starter.
10. Remove the engine mounting support near the starter.
11. Remove the rear transmission mount.

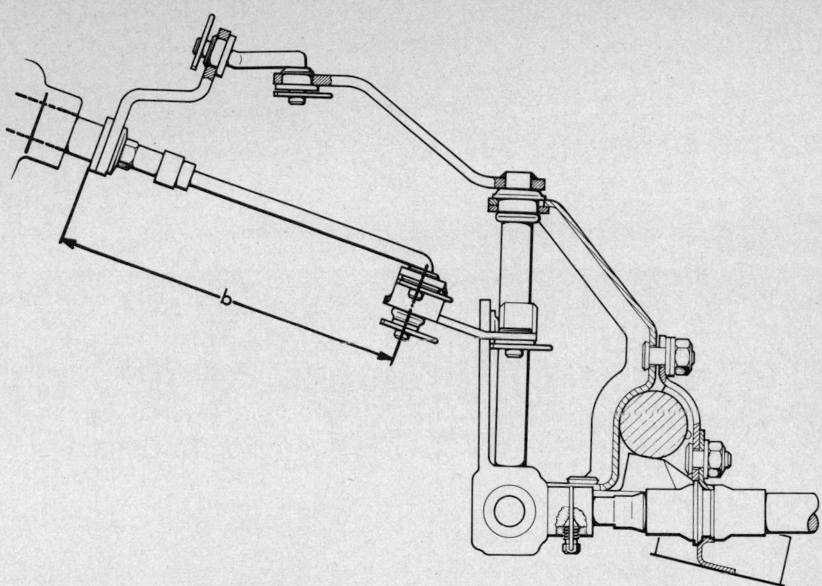

The long rod on the Rabbit and Scirocco shift linkage is to be adjusted to a length (b) of 6.42-6.50 in.

12. Unbolt and wire up the driveshafts.
13. From underneath, remove the bolts for the large cover plate, but don't remove it. Unbolt the small cover plate on the firewall side of the engine. Remove the engine to transmission nut immediately below the small plate.
14. Press the transmission off the dowels and remove it from below the car.

To install the transaxle:

15. The recess in the flywheel edge must be at 3:00 o'clock (facing the left end of the engine). Tighten the engine to transmission bolts to 47 ft lbs. Tighten the engine mounting support bolts to 47 ft lbs. Tighten the driveshaft bolts to 32 ft lbs.
16. Check the adjustment of the shift linkage.

Shift Linkage Adjustment

Dasher

1. Shift into neutral.
2. Remove the round floor cover.
3. Loosen the nuts and move the bearing housing so that the shift lever inclines approximately 5° to the rear.
4. Tighten the nuts.
5. Shift into second gear.
6. Loosen the stop plate bolts.
7. Adjust the plate so that the shift lever has ⅜–⅝ in. lateral movement at the shift knob.

NOTE: *Moving the plate to the right increases play; moving the plate to the left decreases play.*

8. Tighten the bolts. Check the shift pattern and make sure that reverse engages easily.

Rabbit, Scirocco

1. Adjust the long rod over the left driveshaft coupling to a length of 6.42–6.50 in.

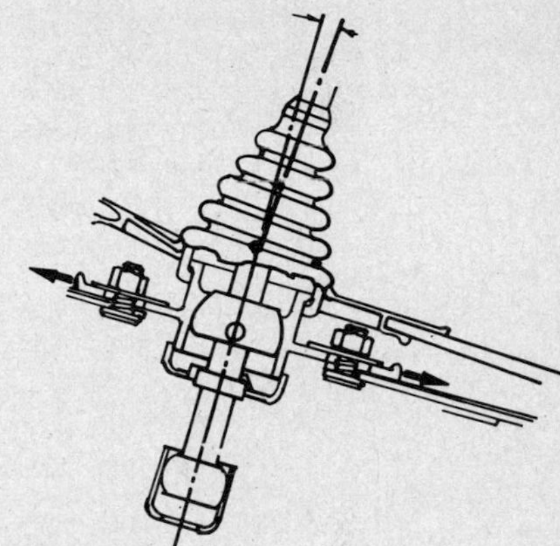

Dasher manual transmission neutral shift lever adjustment

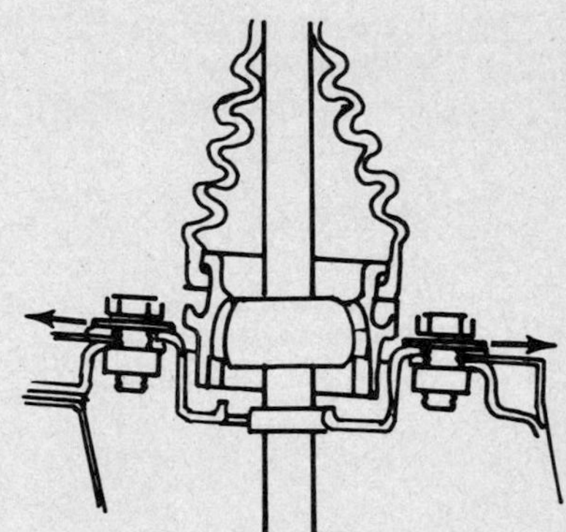

Dasher manual transmission second gear shift lever adjustment

2. Adjust the short angled rod that attaches to the final drive housing to a length of 1.18–1.25 in.
3. Make the lower part of the floorshift lever vertical (in the side to side plane) in the first gear position by loosening the bearing plate that supports the end of the long shift rod that connects to the bottom of the floorshift lever. Tighten the mounting nuts when the lever is vertical.

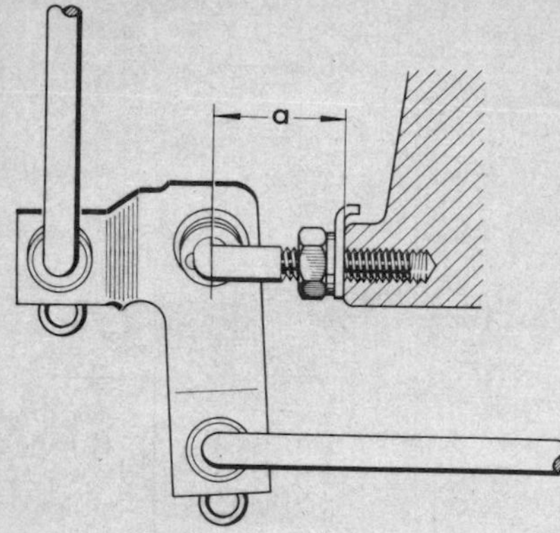

The short angled rod on the Rabbit and Scirocco shift linkage is to be adjusted to a length (a) of 1.18- 1.25 in.

4. Make the lower part of the floorshift lever vertical (in the fore and aft plane) in the Neutral position by pulling up the boot and loosening the two lever plate bolts. Move the plate until the lever is vertical.

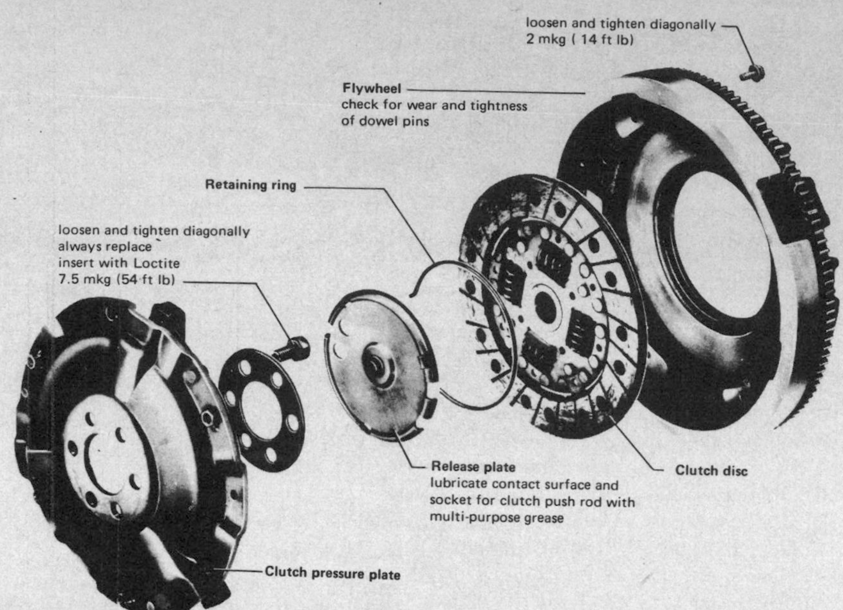

The Rabbit and Scirocco clutch, the pressure plate is bolted to the crankshaft and the clutch is actuated by a pushrod working on the release plate

CLUTCH

Pedal Free Play Adjustment

Clutch pedal free play should be ⅝ in. Pedal free play is the distance the pedal can be depressed before the linkage starts to act on the throwout bearing.

1. Adjust the clutch pedal free play by loosening the two nuts on the cable near the oil filter on the Dasher. On the Rabbit and Scirocco, the cable adjustment point is on the front of the transmission.

2. After obtaining the correct free play, tighten the adjusting nuts.

Removal and Installation

Dasher

1. Remove the transaxle.
2. Match mark the flywheel and pressure plate if the pressure plate is being reused.
3. Gradually loosen the pressure plate bolts one or two turns at a time in a crisscross pattern to prevent distortion.
4. Remove the pressure plate and disc.
5. Check the clutch disc for uneven or excessive lining wear. Examine the pressure plate for cracking, scorching, or scoring. Replace any questionable components.
6. Install the clutch disc and pressure plate. Use a dummy shaft to keep the disc centered.
7. Gradually tighten the pressure-plate-to-flywheel bolts in a criss-cross pattern. Tighten the bolts to 24 ft. lbs.
8. Install the throwout bearing.
9. Install the transaxle on the engine.
10. Replace the transaxle.

Rabbit, Scirocco

These cars use a type of clutch more common to motorcycles than to cars. The pressure plate is bolted to the flywheel and the flywheel bolted to the pressure plate; in other words, these two parts have switched places. The clutch release lever and bearing are in the left end of the transmission. The clutch is actuated by a release rod which passes through a hollow transmission shaft.

1. Remove the transmission.
2. Attach a toothed flywheel holder and gradually loosen the flywheel to pressure plate bolts one or two turns at a time in a crisscross pattern to prevent distortion.
3. Remove the flywheel and the clutch disc.
4. Use a screwdriver to remove the release plate retaining ring. Remove the release plate.
5. Lock the pressure plate in place and unbolt it from the crankshaft. Loosen the bolts one or two turns at a time in a crisscross pattern to prevent distortion.
6. On installation, use new bolts to attach the pressure plate to the crankshaft. Use a thread locking compound and torque the bolts in a diagonal pattern to 54 ft lbs.
7. Lubricate the clutch disc splines with multi-purpose grease. Lubricate the release plate contact surface and pushrod socket with multi-purpose grease. Install the release plate, retaining ring, and clutch disc.
8. Install a dummy shaft to align the clutch disc.
9. Install the flywheel, tightening the bolts one or two turns at a time in a crisscross pattern to prevent distortion. Torque the bolts to 14 ft lbs.
10. Replace the transmission.

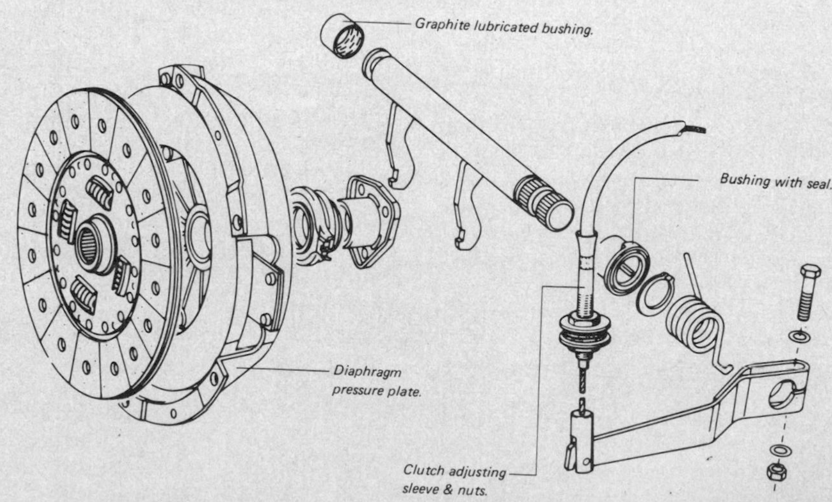

Dasher clutch components, the adjusting sleeve and nuts are adjacent to the oil filter in the engine compartment

AUTOMATIC TRANSMISSION

Transaxle Removal and Installation

Dasher

The transaxle can be lowered from the car, leaving the engine in place.

1. Disconnect the battery ground cable.

2. Raise the car on a chassis hoist.

3. Remove the lockplates and remove the axle shaft bolts. Wire the shafts up.

4. Disconnect the vacuum hose. Remove the torque converter guard plate. Disconnect the kickdown switch wire.

5. Use pliers to unscrew the speedometer cable nut.

6. Support the transaxle.

7. Remove the upper engine to transaxle bolts.

8. Remove the starter and remove the three torque converter bolts through the starter opening.

9. Unbolt the small crossmember at the rear of the transmission.

10. Lower the transaxle slightly.

11. Detach the shift linkage cable at the transmission.

12. Remove the lower engine to transaxle bolts.

13. Separate the transaxle from the engine and lower it. Secure the torque converter in the transmission with a strap. Reverse the procedure on installation. Torque the engine to transaxle bolts to 40 ft lbs and the torque converter bolts to 20–23 ft lbs. New torque converter bolts and washers must be used. Torque the axle shaft bolts to 28 ft lbs.

14. Check the shift linkage adjustment.

Rabbit, Scirocco

The engine and transaxle may be removed together as explained under Engine Removal and Installation or the transaxle may be removed alone, as explained here.

1. Disconnect both battery cables.

2. Disconnect the speedometer cable at the transmission.

3. Support the left end of the engine at the lifting eye. Attach a hoist to the transaxle.

4. Unbolt the rear transmission carrier from the body then from the transaxle. Unbolt the left side carrier from the body.

5. Unbolt the right driveshaft and wire it up.

6. Remove the starter.

7. Remove the three converter to drive plate bolts.

8. Shift into P and disconnect the floorshift linkage at the transmission.

9. Remove the accelerator and carburetor cable bracket at the transmission.

10. Unbolt the left side transmission carrier from the transmission.

11. Unbolt the front transmission mount from the transmission.

12. Unbolt the bottom of the engine from the transmission. Lift the transaxle slightly, swing the left driveshaft up, remove the rest of the bolts, pull the transmission off the mounting dowels, and lower the transaxle out of the car. Secure the converter so it doesn't fall out.

CAUTION: *Don't tilt the torque converter.*

To install the transaxle:

13. Push the transmission onto the mounting dowels and install two bolts. Lift the unit until the left driveshaft can be installed and install the rest of the bolts. Torque them to 39 ft lbs.

14. Tighten the front transmission mount bolts to 39 ft lbs. Install the left side transmission carrier to the transmission.

15. Connect the accelerator and carburetor cable bracket. Connect the floorshift linkage.

16. Tighten the torque converter to drive plate bolts to 22 ft lbs. Torque the driveshaft bolts to 32 ft lbs.

17. Install the rear transmission carrier and make sure that the left side carrier is aligned in the center of the body mount. Bolt the left side carrier to the body.

18. Connect the speedometer cable and the battery cables.

Pan Removal and Installation, Strainer Service

Dasher

VW recommends that the automatic transmission fluid be replaced every 30,000 miles, or 20,000 miles if used for trailer towing, mountain driving, or other severe service.

1. Four (4) quarts of automatic transmission fluid (Type A or Dexron) **and a pan gasket are required.**

2. Slide a drain pan under the transmission. Jack up the front of the car and support it.

3. Remove the drain plug and allow all the fluid to drain.

4. Remove the pan retaining bolts and drop the pan.

5. Discard the old gasket and clean the pan with solvent.

6. Unscrew and clean the circular oil strainer.

7. Install the oil strainer, but don't tighten the bolt too much - specified torque is only 4 ft lbs.

8. Using a long-necked funnel, refill the transmission with about 2¾ qts. of fluid. Check the level with the dipstick. Run the car for a few minutes and check again.

Rabbit, Scirocco

1. Remove the drain plug and let the fluid drain into a pan.

2. Remove the pan bolts and take off the pan.

3. Discard the old gasket and clean the pan out. Be very careful not to get any threads or lint from rags into the pan.

4. The manufacturer says that the filter needn't be replaced unless the fluid is very dirty and burnt smelling. Take it easy, the specified torque for the strainer screws is 2 ft lbs.

5. Replace the pan with a new gasket and tighten the bolts, in a cross-cross pattern, to 14 ft lbs.

6. Using a long-necked funnel, pour in 2½ qts of Dexron **automatic transmission fluid through the dipstick tube. Start the engine and shift through all the transmission ranges with the car stationary. Check the level on the dipstick with the lever in Neutral. It should be up to the lower end of the dipstick. Drive the car until it is warmed up and recheck the level.**

Linkage Adjustment

Check the cable adjustment as follows:

1. Run the engine at 1000–1200 rpm with the parking brake on.

2. Select Reverse—a drop in engine speed should be noticed.

3. Select Park—engine speed should increase. Pull the shift lever against Reverse, the engine speed shouldn't drop.

4. Move the shift lever to Neutral—an increase in engine speed should be noticed.

5. Shift the lever into Drive—a noticeable drop in engine speed should result.

6. Shift into 1—the lever must engage without having to overcome any resistance.

7. To adjust the cable—Shift into Park. Remove the cover from the bottom of the shift lever case under the car on the Dasher. Loosen the cable clamp. On the Rabbit and Scirocco, loosen the cable clamp at the transmission end of the cable.

8. Press the lever on the Dasher transmission against spring tension all the way to the stop at the rear. Press the Rabbit and Scirocco transmission lever all the way to the left.

9. Hold the lever in place and tighten the cable clamp.

Transmission Cable Adjustment

Rabbit, Scirocco

1. At the carburetor, make sure that the throttle is closed, the choke is off, and the fast idle cam is out of action. Detach the cable end at the transmission.

2. Press the lever at the transmission end of the cable toward the cable.

3. You should be able to insert the ca-

ble end into the transmission lever without moving the lever.

4. Adjust the cable length to correct.

Kickdown Switch Check

Dasher

1. Turn the ignition switch ON.
2. Floor the accelerator - you should hear an audible click from the solenoid on the transmission.
3. Replace the solenoid if no sound is heard.

First Gear [Front] Band Adjustment

Dasher

NOTE: *The transmission must be horizontal when band adjustments are performed. The first gear band has a narrow point adjusting screw, the second gear band a wide screw.*

1. Tighten the first gear band adjusting screw to 7.2 ft. lbs. [86 in lbs].
2. Loosen the screw and tighten it again to 3.5 ft. lb. [42 in. lb].
3. Turn the screw out 3¼–3½ turns and then tighten the locknut.

Second Gear [Rear] Band Adjustment

Dasher, Rabbit, Scirocco

NOTE: *The transmission must be horizontal when band adjustments are performed. The first gear band has a narrow point adjusting screw, the second gear band a wide screw.*

1. Tighten the second gear band adjusting screw to 7.2 ft. lb. [86 in. lb].
2. Loosen the screw and tighten it again to 3.6 ft. lb. (43 in. lb).
3. Turn the screw out 2½ turns and then tighten the locknut.

Neutral Start Switch

The combination neutral start and backup light switch is mounted inside the shifter housing.

DRIVE AXLES

Halfshaft Removal and Installation

Dasher

1. With the car on the ground, remove the front axle nut.

NOTE: *Use a long breaker bar with an extension [length of pipe].*

2. Raise and support the car.
3. Remove the allen head bolts retaining the axle shaft to the transaxle.

NOTE: *If you are removing the right axle shaft, detach the exhaust pipe from the manifold and the transaxle bracket.*

4. Pull the axle shaft out and up and place it on top of the transaxle.
5. Turn the steering wheel all the way to the side of the shaft being removed. Pull the axle shaft from the steering knuckle.
6. Installation is the reverse of removal. Tighten the transaxle bolts to 25 ft. lbs. The axle nut is tightened to 180–216 ft. lbs.

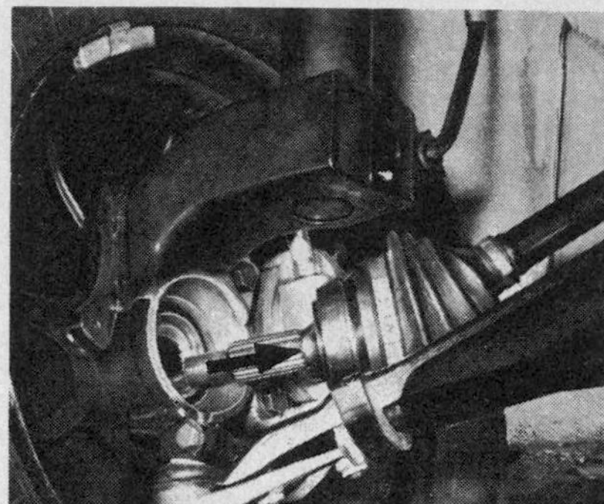

Pulling the Dasher axle shaft from the steering knuckle

REAR SUSPENSION

The Dasher rear suspension has a rear axle beam containing a full length torsion bar. A trailing arm is welded to the axle beam tube on each side. The trailing arms mount to the unit body in rubber bushings. A coil spring provides the suspension at each wheel. A Panhard rod locates the axle against side forces.

The Rabbit and Scirocco rear suspension uses an exposed cross-chassis torsion beam connecting two trailing arms. Coil spring/shock absorber units are mounted to the body and to the trailing arms.

Shock Absorbers

Removal and Installation

Dasher

1. With the car on the ground, remove the lower shock mounting bolt and nut.
2. Raise and support the car.
3. Unscrew and remove the upper retaining bolt.
4. Remove the shock absorber.
5. Install the upper retaining bolt and tighten the bolt to 43 ft. lb.
6. Insert the lower retaining bolt and nut. Tighten to 43 ft. lb.

FRONT SUSPENSION

The front suspension is a simple strut design. It consists of a lower control arm, ball joint, and suspension strut. In a McPherson strut design, such as this, the shock absorber strut serves as a locating member of the suspension as well as a damper. A shock absorber insert is located inside the strut. A coil spring is used. A stabilizer bar is used to reduce front body roll on the Dasher.

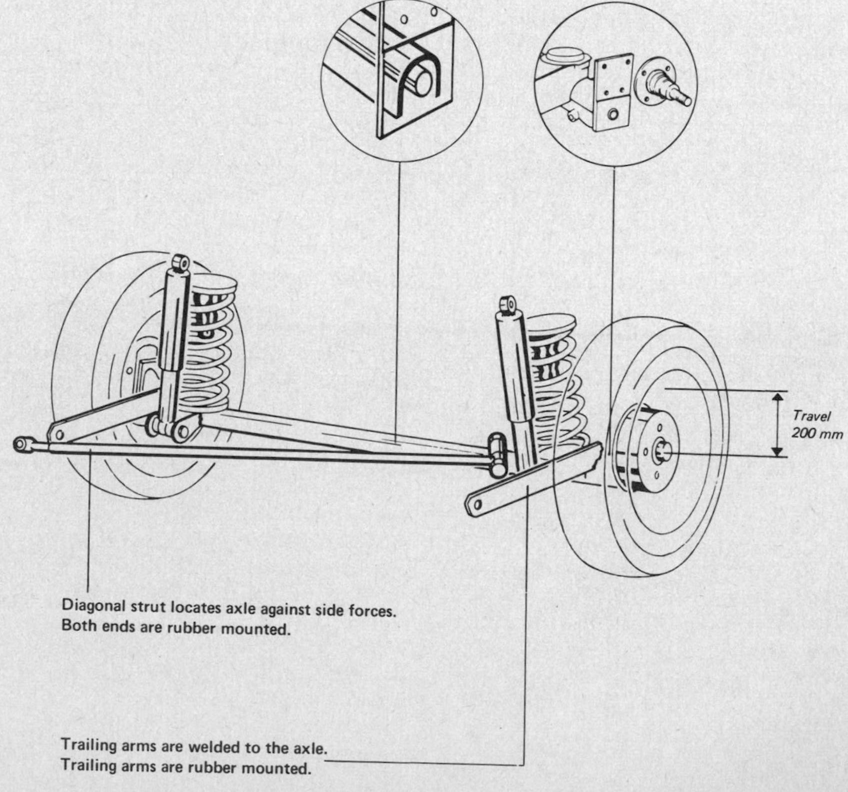

Dasher rear suspension

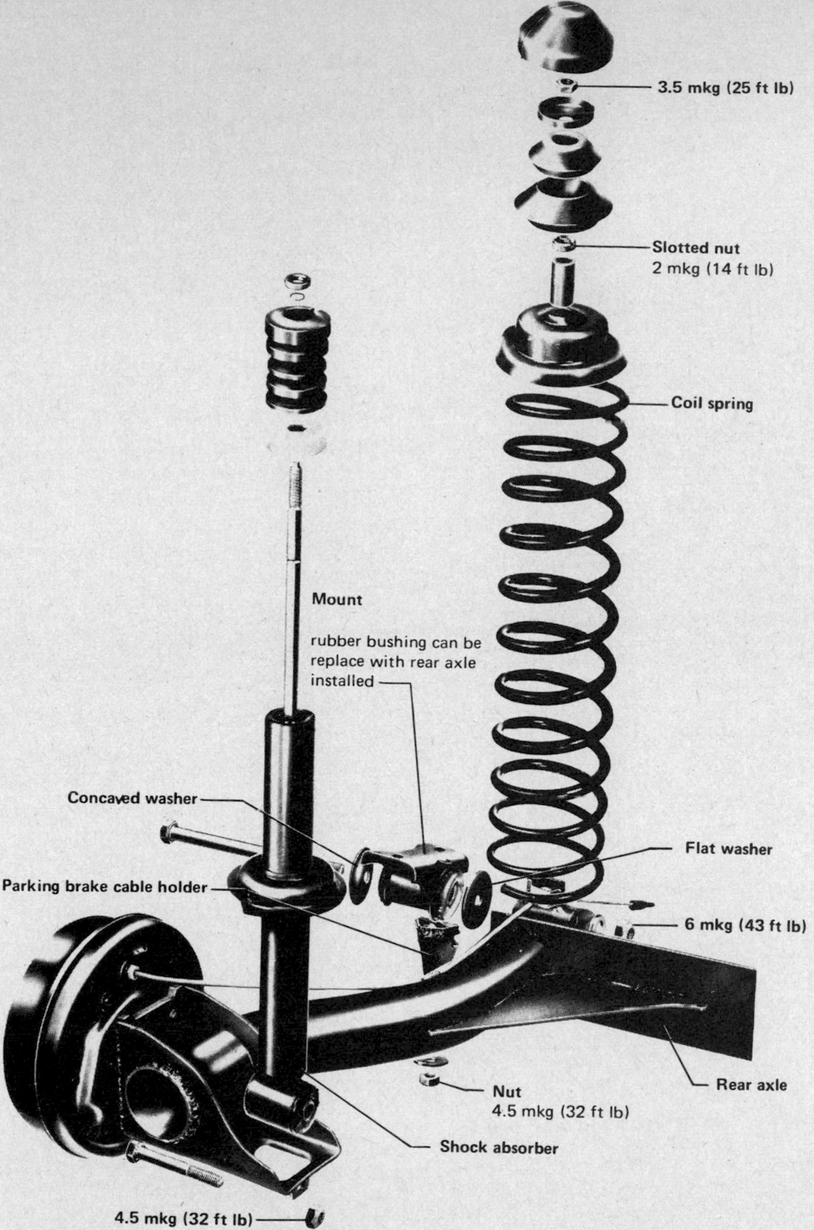

Exploded view of the Rabbit and Scirocco rear suspension

Ball Joint

Removal and Installation

1. Jack up the front of the car and support it on stands.
2. Matchmark the ball joint-to-control arm position on the Dasher.
3. Remove the retaining bolt and nut.

4. Pry the lower control arm and ball joint down and out of the strut.
5. Remove the two ball joint-to-lower control arm retaining nuts and bolts on the Dasher. Drill out the rivets on the Rabbit and Scirocco; enlarge the holes to 21/64 in.
6. Remove the ball joint assembly.
7. Install the Dasher ball joint in the reverse order of removal. If no parts were installed other than the ball joint, align the match marks made in Step 2. No camber adjustment is necessary if this is done. Pull the ball joint into alignment with pliers. Tighten the two control arm bolts to 47 ft lb and the strut-to-ball-joint bolt to 18 ft lb.

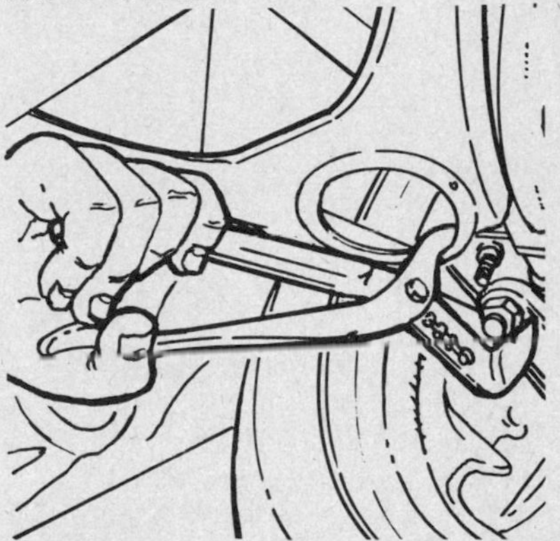

Pulling the Dasher ball joint into alignment on installation

8. On the Rabbit and Scirocco, bolt the new ball joint in place. Torque the bolts to 18 ft lbs. Tighten the retaining bolt for the ball joint stud to 21 ft lbs.

Shock Absorber

Removal and Installation

Since the shock absorber cartridge is contained within the strut assembly, it is necessary to remove the strut and then compress the coil spring in order to remove the shock.

Strut

Removal and Installation

1. With the car on the ground, remove the front axle nut. Loosen the wheel bolts.

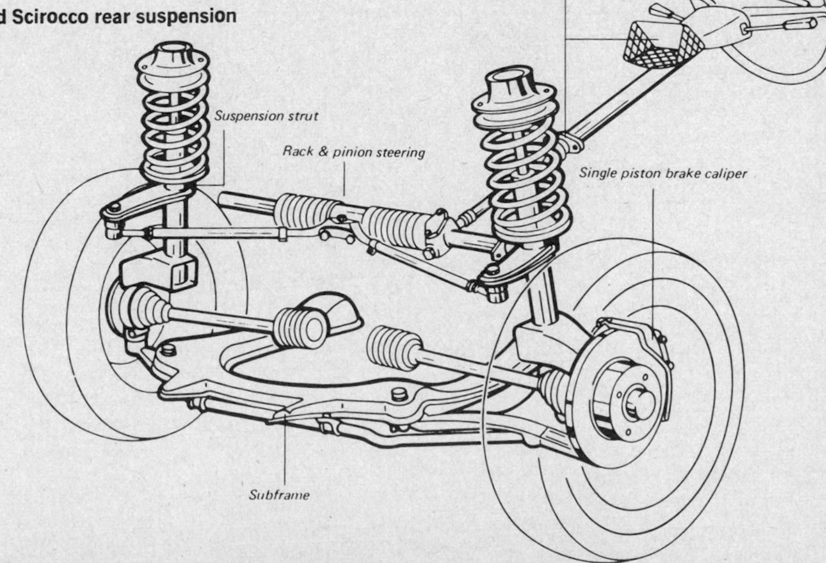

Dasher front suspension and steering components

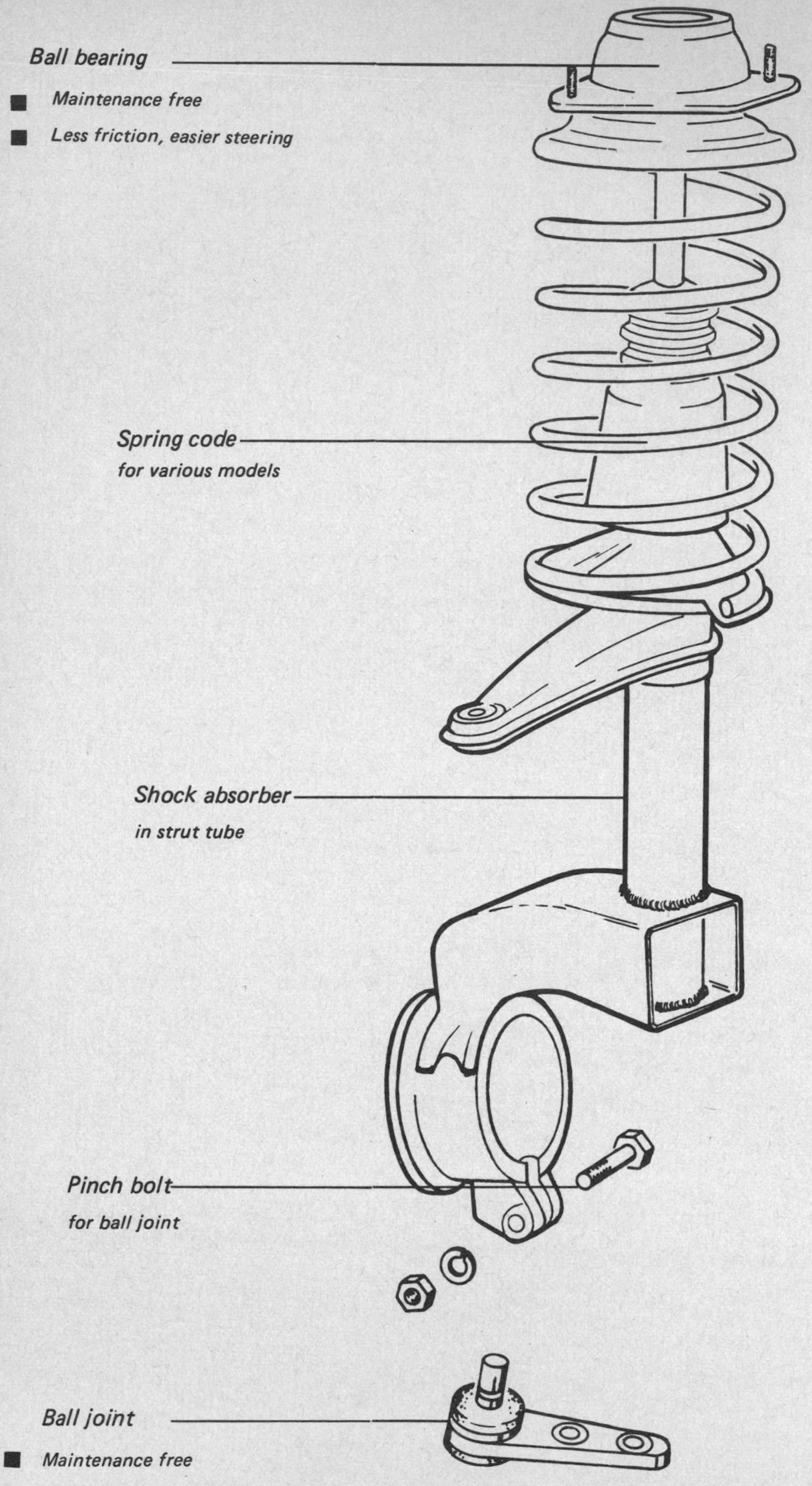

Ball bearing

- *Maintenance free*
- *Less friction, easier steering*

Spring code
for various models

Shock absorber
in strut tube

Pinch bolt
for ball joint

Ball joint

- *Maintenance free*

A pinch bolt holds the ball joint to the combination strut and steering knuckle

2. Raise and support the front of the car. Remove the wheels.
3. Remove the brake caliper from the strut and hang it with wire. Detach the brake line clips from the strut.
4. At the tie-rod end, remove the cotter pin, back off the castellated nut, and pull the end off the strut with a puller.
5. Loosen the stabilizer bar bushings and detach the end from the strut being removed.
6. Remove the ball joint.
7. Pull the axle driveshaft from the strut.
8. Remove the upper strut-to-fender retaining nuts.
9. Pull the strut assembly down and out of the car.
10. Installation is the reverse of removal. The Dasher axle nut is tightened to 180–216 ft lbs, lower control arm to strut bolt to 16 ft lb, caliper to strut bolts to 44 ft lb and stabilizer to control arm bolts to 7 ft. lb. The Rabbit and Scirocco axle nut is tightened to 173 ft lbs, ball joint stud retaining bolt to 21 ft lbs, strut to body bolts to 14 ft lbs, and caliper mounting bolts to 44 ft lbs.

Coil Spring

Removal and Installation

To remove the spring, the strut must be mounted in a large vise, the spring compressed, the retaining nut and cover removed, and the spring slowly released. A special tool is needed to remove the shock absorber retainer, after which the shock absorber is easily removed. Assembly is the reverse of removal.

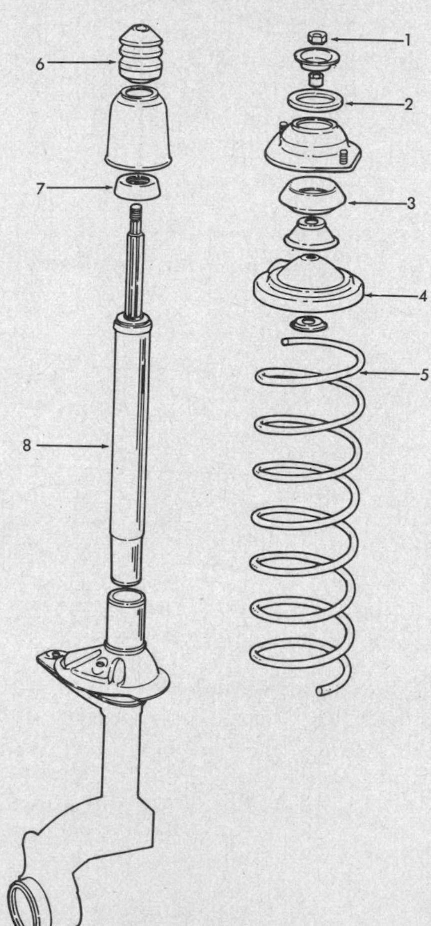

Dasher strut exploded view

1. Suspension strut nut
2. End collar
3. Rubber damper
4. Coil spring cap
5. Coil spring
6. Bumper
7. Threaded cap
8. Shock absorber

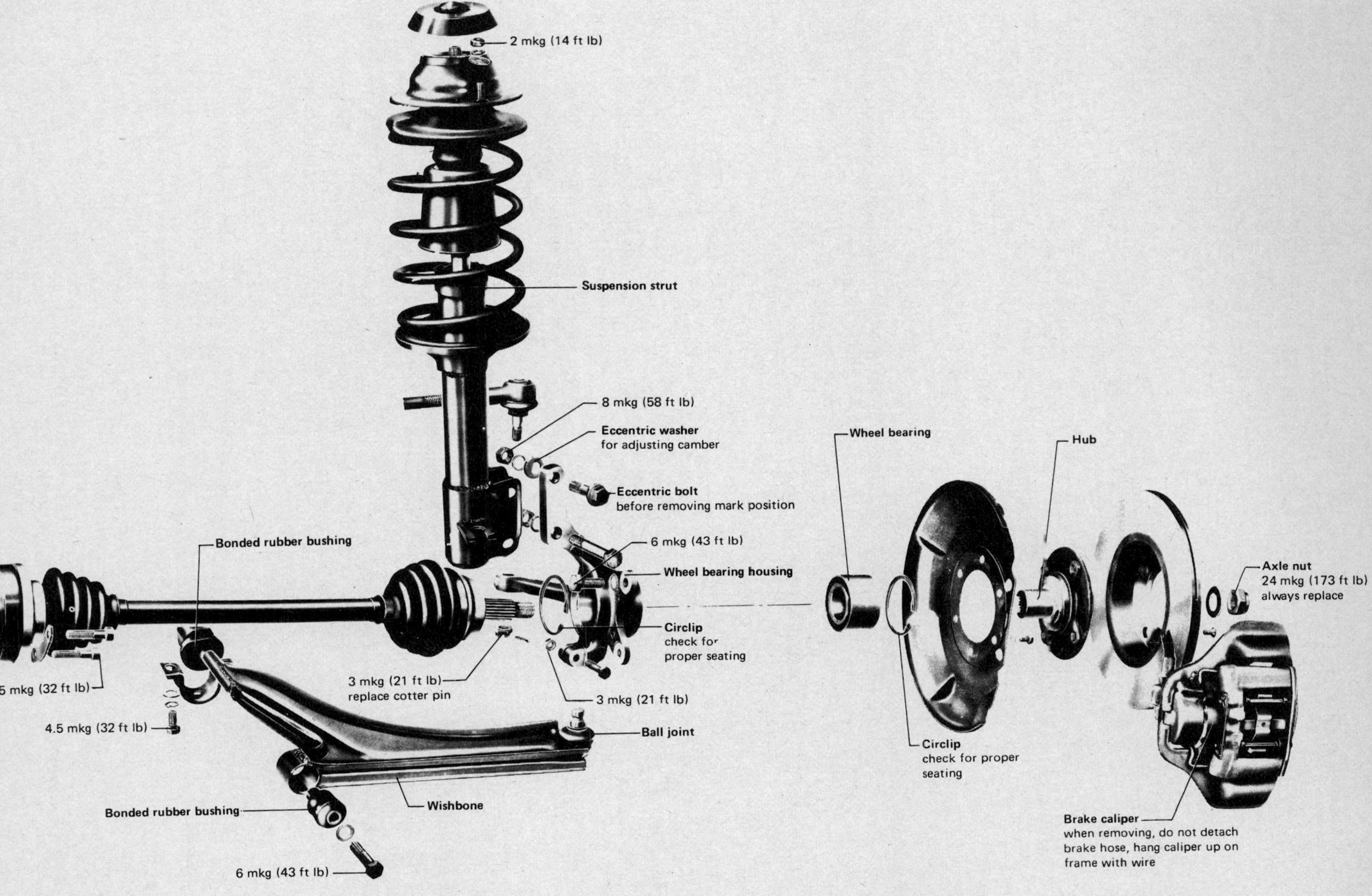

Exploded view of the Rabbit and Scirocco front suspension

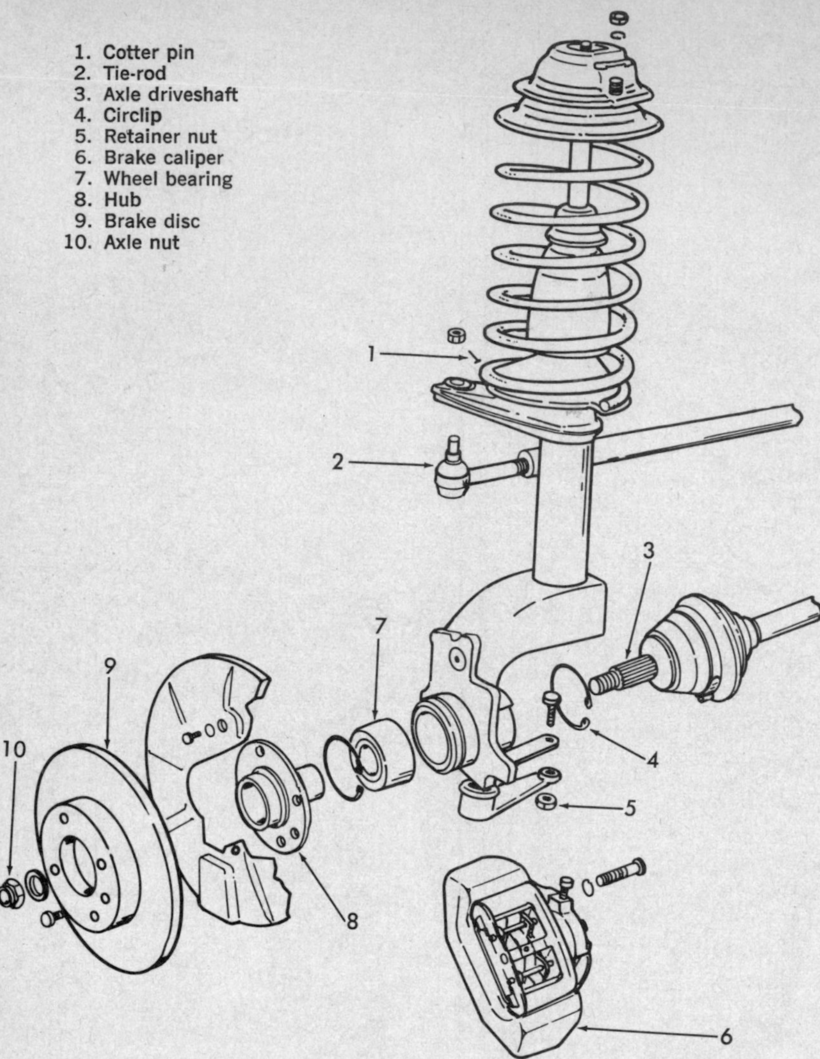

Dasher strut installation details

Front End Alignment

Camber Adjustment

Dasher

Camber is adjusted by loosening the two ball joint-to-lower control arm bolts, and moving the ball joint in or out as necessary.

Rabbit, Scirocco

Camber is adjusted by loosening the nuts of the two bolts holding the top of the wheel bearing housing to the bottom of the strut, and turning the top eccentric bolt. The range of adjustment is 2°.

Caster

Other than the replacement of damaged suspension components, caster is not adjustable.

Toe-In Adjustment

Dasher

Toe-in is checked with the wheels straight ahead. The left tie rod is adjustable. Loosen the nuts and clamps and adjust the length of the tie rod for correct toe-out. If the steering wheel is crooked, remove and align it.

Rabbit, Scirocco

Toe-in is checked with the wheels straight ahead. Only the right tie-rod is adjustable, but replacement left tie-rods are adjustable. Replacement left tie-rods should be set to the same length as the original. Toe-in should be adjusted only with the right tie-rod. If the steering wheel is crooked, remove and align it.

STEERING

The Dasher has rack and pinion steering gear with center mounted tie-rods. This allows very little toe-in change during suspension travel. A steering damper reduces road shock transmittal to the steering wheel.

The Rabbit and Scirocco have rack and pinion steering with end mounted tie-rods. No periodic maintenance is required on either rack and pinion steering system.

Steering Wheel

Removal and Installation

1. Grasp the center cover pad and pull it from the wheel.
2. Loosen and remove the steering shaft nut.
3. Pull the wheel off the shaft. A puller isn't normally needed.
4. Disconnect the horn wire.
5. Replace the wheel in the reverse order of removal. Tighten the nut to 36 ft lb.

Turn Signal and Headlight Dimmer Switch Replacement

1. Disconnect the battery ground cable.
2. Remove the steering wheel.
3. Remove the switch retaining screws.
4. Pry the switch housing off the column.
5. Disconnect the electrical plugs at the back of the switch.
6. Remove the switch housing.
7. Replace in the reverse order of removal.

Ignition Switch and Steering Lock

Removal and Installation

1. Remove the steering wheel and turn signal switch. Remove the steering column shaft covers.
2. The lock is clamped to the steering column with special bolts whose heads shear off on installation. These must be drilled out in order to remove the switch.
3. On replacement, make sure that the lock tang is aligned with the slot in the steering column.

Steering Gear

Dasher

Removal and Installation

1. Pry off the lock plate and remove both tie-rod mounting bolts from the steering rack, inside the engine compartment. Pry the tie rods out of the mounting pivot.
2. Remove the lower instrument panel trim.
3. Remove the shaft clamp bolt, pry off the clip, and drive the shaft toward the inside of the car with a brass drift.
4. Remove the steering gear mounting bolts.
5. Turn the wheels all the way to the right and remove the steering gear through the opening in the right wheelhousing.
6. For installation, temporarily install the tie-rod mounting pivot to the rack

with both mounting bolts. Remove one bolt, install the tie-rod, and replace the bolt. Do the same on the other tie-rod. Make sure to install the lock plate. Torque the tie-rod bolts to 39 ft lbs, the mounting pivot bolt to 15 ft lbs, and the steering gear to body mounting bolts to 15 ft lbs.

Steering Linkage

Tie-Rod Removal and Installation

Dasher

1. Raise the car and remove the front wheels.
2. Disconnect the outer end of the steering tie-rod from the steering knuckle by removing the cotter pin and nut and pressing out the tie-rod end. A small puller or press is required to free the tie-rod end.
3. Under the hood, pry off the lock plate and remove the mounting bolts from both tie-rod inner ends. Pry the tie-rod out of the mounting pivot.
4. First install the mounting pivot to the rack with both mounting bolts. Remove one bolt, install the tie-rod, and replace the bolt. Do the same on the other tie-rod. Be sure to install the lock plate. The inner tie-rod end bolts should be torqued to 40 ft lbs.
5. If you are replacing the adjustable left tie-rod, adjust it to the same length as the old one. Check the toe-in when the job is done.
6. Use new cotter pins when installing the outer tie-rod ends. Torque the nut to 28 ft lbs.

BRAKES

The hydraulic system is a dual circuit type that has the advantage of retaining 50% braking effectiveness in the event of failure in one system. The circuits are arranged so that you always have one front and one rear brake for a more controlled emergency stop. The right front and left rear are in one circuit; the left front and right rear are in the second circuit.

There is also a brake failure switch and a proportioning valve.

The brake failure unit is a hydraulic valve/electrical switch which warns of brake problems by the warning light on the instrument panel. A piston inside the switch is kept centered by one brake system pressure on one side and the other system pressure on the opposite side. Should a failure occur in one system, the piston would go to the "failed" side and complete an electrical circuit to the warning lamp. This switch also functions as a parking brake reminder light and will go out when the parking brake is released. The proportioning valve, actually two separate valves on manual transmission Dasher sedans, provides balanced front-to-rear braking during hard stops.

Extreme brake line pressure will overcome the spring pressure on the piston within the valve causing it to proportionately restrict pressure to the rear brakes. In this manner, the rear brakes are kept from locking. The proportioner doesn't operate under normal braking conditions.

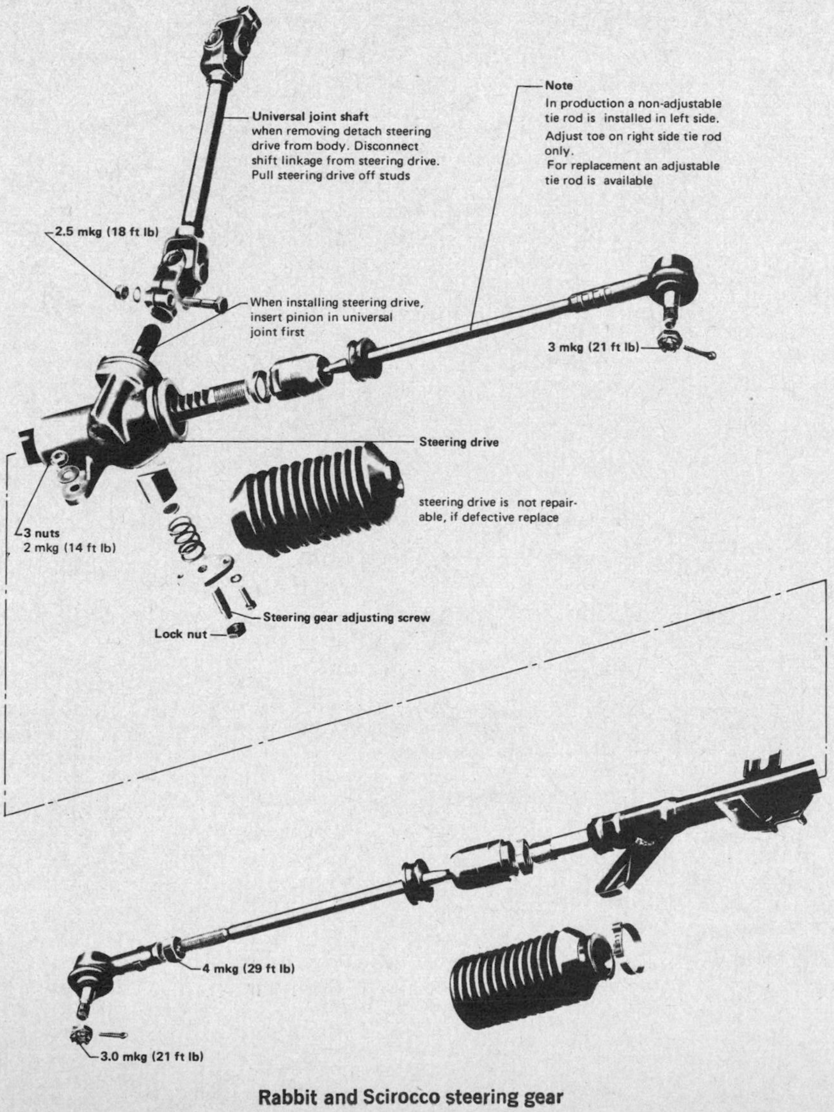

Adjustment

The front disc brakes require no adjustment, as disc brakes automatically adjust themselves to compensate for pad wear. The rear drum brakes must be adjusted whenever free travel is one third or more of the total pedal travel.

NOTE: *On all models except manual transmission Dasher sedans, it is necessary to push the brake proportioning lever toward the rear axle to relieve the pressure in the right rear brake line.*

1. Raise the rear of the car. Place the jack under the center of the Dasher torsion bar/axle. The jack pad should be at least 4 in. square, otherwise you may damage the axle. Raise the Rabbit and Scirocco on a chassis lift.
2. Block the front wheels and release the parking brake. Step on the brake pedal hard to center the linings.
3. Remove the rubber plug from the rear of the backing plate on each wheel.
4. Insert a brake adjusting tool or wide-bladed screwdriver and turn the adjuster wheel clockwise until the brakes drag as you turn the wheel in the forward direction.
5. Turn the adjuster in the opposite direction until you just pass the point of drag.
6. Repeat on the other wheel.
7. Lower the car and road test. Readjust, if necessary.

Master Cylinder

Removal and Installation

1. To prevent brake fluid from spilling

Rabbit and Scirocco steering gear

out and damaging the paint, place a protective cover over the fender.

2. Disconnect and plug the brake lines.

3. Disconnect the electrical plug from the sending unit for the brake failure switch.

4. Remove the two master cylinder mounting nuts.

5. Lift the master cylinder and reservoir out of the engine compartment being careful not to spill any fluid on the fender. Empty out and discard the brake fluid.

CAUTION: *Do not depress the brake pedal while the master cylinder is removed.*

6. Position the master cylinder and reservoir assembly onto the studs for the booster and install the washers and nuts. Tighten the nuts to no more than 10 ft. lbs.

7. Remove the plugs and connect the brake lines.

8. Bleed the entire brake system.

Overhaul

1. Remove the master cylinder from the booster.

2. Firmly mount the master cylinder in a vise. Use clean rags to protect the cylinder from the vise jaws.

3. Grasp the plastic reservoir and pull it out of the rubber plugs. Remove the plugs.

4. In the center of the cylinder there is a stop screw; remove it. Discard the stop screw seal, there should be a new one in the rebuilding kit.

5. At the end of the master cylinder is a snap-ring (circlip); remove it, using snap-ring pliers.

6. Shake out the secondary piston assembly. If the primary piston remains lodged in the bore, it can be forced by applying compressed air to the open line fitting.

7. Disassemble the secondary piston. The two secondary springs will be replaced with those in the rebuilding kit. Save the washers and spacers.

8. Carefully clamp the secondary piston. Slightly compress the spring and screw out the stroke limiting bolt.

9. Remove the secondary piston stop sleeve bolt, spring, spring seat, and support washer.

10. Replace all the parts with those supplied in the overhaul kit.

11. Clean all metal parts in alcohol and dry them with compressed air.

12. Check every part you are reusing. Pay close attention to the cylinder bores. If there is any scoring or rust, hone the cylinder or replace it.

13. Lightly coat the bores and cups with brake fluid. Assemble the cylinder components.

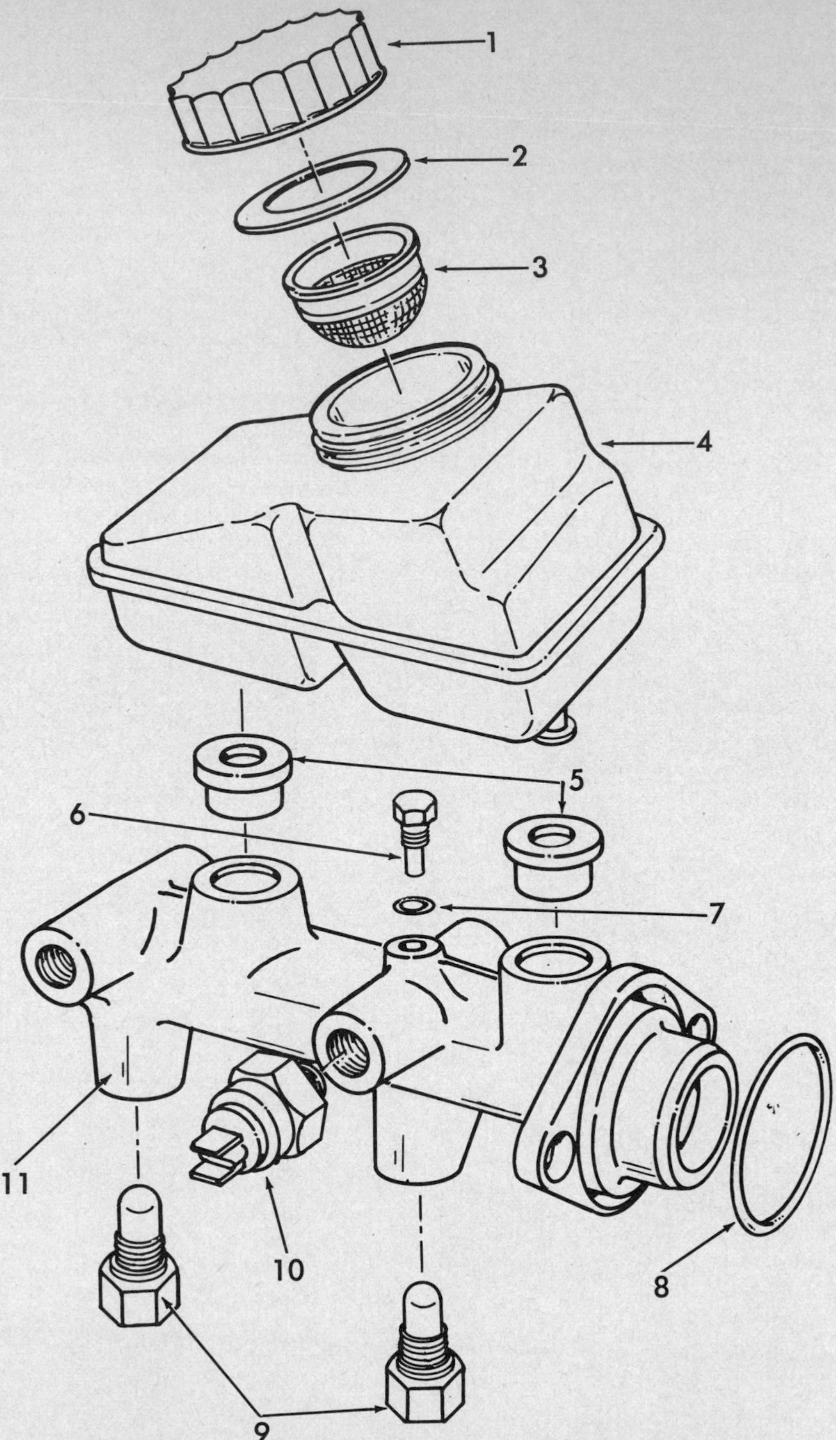

Master cylinder external components

1. Reservoir cap
2. Washer
3. Filter screen
4. Reservoir
5. Master cylinder plugs
6. Stop screw
7. Stop screw seal
8. Master cylinder seal
9. Residual pressure valves
10. Warning light sender unit
11. Brake master cylinder housing

14. Install the primary piston assembly, notice that the primary spring is conically shaped. Be sure that you aren't using the secondary spring.

15. Using a plastic rod or other nonmetallic tool, push the primary piston assembly into the housing until the stop bolt (with new seal) can be screwed in and tightened.

16. Assemble the secondary piston. Fasten the spring, spring seat, primary cup, and stop sleeve to the piston with the stroke limiting bolt.

17. Assemble the remaining master cylinder components in the reverse order of disassembly. Ensure that the snap-ring is fully seated and that the piston cups are properly positioned.

18. Install and tighten the brake failure warning sending unit.

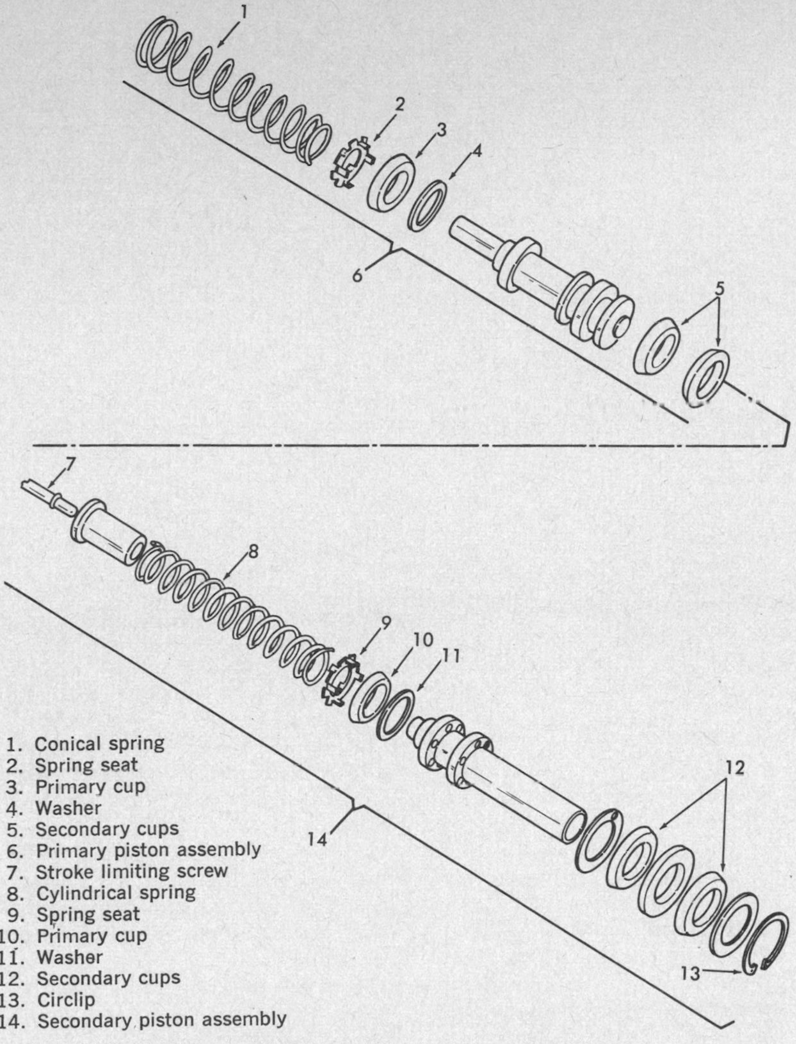

Master cylinder internal components

Proportioning Valve

Dasher manual transmission sedans are equipped with two proportioning valves mounted under the master cylinder on a bracket attached to the brake booster. Sedans with automatic transmission (from serial number 324143626) and all station wagons (from serial number 3243045522), as well as all Rabbit and Scirocco, are equipped with one valve located near the right rear wheel. This valve is activated by a spring connected to the rear axle torsion bar beam.

Neither type of brake pressure regulator is repairable. They must be replaced if defective. The double valves can be easily checked.

Have an assistant firmly depress the brake pedal. Hold your hand on the valves and have your helper release the pedal. If the valves are working, you should feel a slight knock in both valves as the pistons return. The valve can be adjusted by varying spring tension. Greater spring tension results in more hydraulic pressure at the rear brakes.

Bleeding

Anytime a brake line has been disconnected the hydraulic system should be bled. The brakes should also be bled when the pedal travel becomes unusually long ("soft pedal") or the car pulls to one side during braking. The proper bleeding sequence is: right rear wheel, left rear wheel, right front caliper, and left front caliper.

NOTE: *If the system has been drained, first refill it with fresh brake fluid. Following the bleeding sequence, open each bleeder valve by ½ to ¾ of a turn and pump the brake pedal until fluid runs out of the valve. Bleed the system after this is done.*

1. Remove the bleeder valve dust cover and install a rubber bleeder hose.
2. Insert the other end of the hose into a container about 1/3 full of brake fluid.
3. Have your assistant pump the brake pedal several times until the pedal pressure increases.
4. Hold the pedal under pressure and then start to open the bleeder valve about ½ to ¾ of a turn. At this point, have your assistant depress the pedal all the way and then quickly close the valve. The helper should allow the pedal to return slowly.

NOTE: *Keep a close check on the brake fluid in the reservoir and top it up as necessary throughout the bleeding process.*

5. Keep repeating this procedure until no more air bubbles can be seen coming from the hose in the brake fluid.
6. Remove the bleeder hose and install the dust cover.
7. Continue the bleeding at each wheel in sequence.

NOTE: *Don't spill any brake fluid; it has a detrimental effect on paint. Any fluid accidentally spilled on the body should be immediately flushed off with water.*

Front Disc Brakes

Single piston floating caliper disc brakes are used. In this design, the single piston forces one pad against the rotating disc brakes. Counter pressure forces against the floating frame and the frame then pushes the second pad into the disc. The advantages of the floating caliper are better heat dissipation, simpler repairs, fewer leaks, and less sensitivity to variance-in-disc thickness and parallelism.

Brake Pads

Removal and Installation

Brake pads should be replaced when there is no visible clearance between the pads and the cross-spring or when they are worn to a thickness of 0.08 in.

1. Jack up the front of the car and support it on stands. Remove the wheels.
2. Pry the clip out of both retaining pins.
3. While pressing down on the cross-spring, push the pad retaining pins out with a drift or small screwdriver.
4. Reference mark positions of the brake pads if they are being reused.
5. Remove the cross-spring from the caliper.
6. Remove the inner brake pad. VW has a special tool for this purpose, but by using a small drift or punch you can pry the pad out of the caliper until it can be gripped by a pair of pliers and removed.
7. The outer brake pad is positioned in a notch. Use a flat, smooth piece of hardwood or metal to press the floating caliper frame and piston cylinder outward.
8. Grip the outer pad and remove it.
9. Siphon out about half of the brake fluid in the reservoir to prevent it from overflowing when the piston is pushed in and new thicker pads are inserted. Press the piston back into the cylinder with the flat piece of wood or metal.

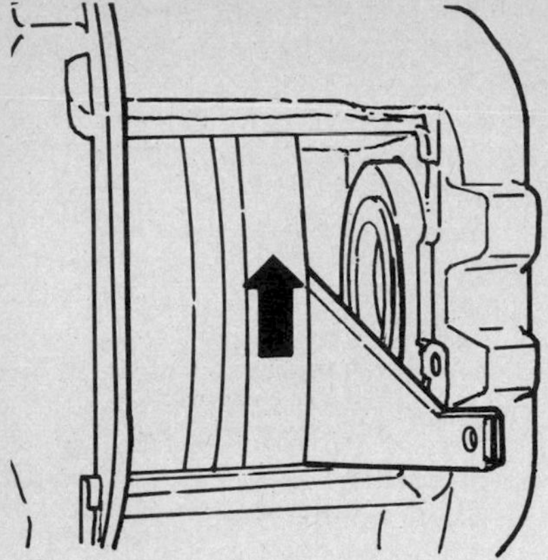

Checking that the piston is at the correct 20° angle

10. Check that piston is at the proper 20° angle. You can make a gauge out of stiff cardboard.

11. Install the brake pads into the caliper.

NOTE: *Replace used pads in the side of the caliper from which they were removed. When installing new pads always replace the pads on the opposite wheel at the same time.*

12. Position the cross-spring in the caliper and then carefully tap the pad retaining pins into place with a small hammer. Install the pin clip.

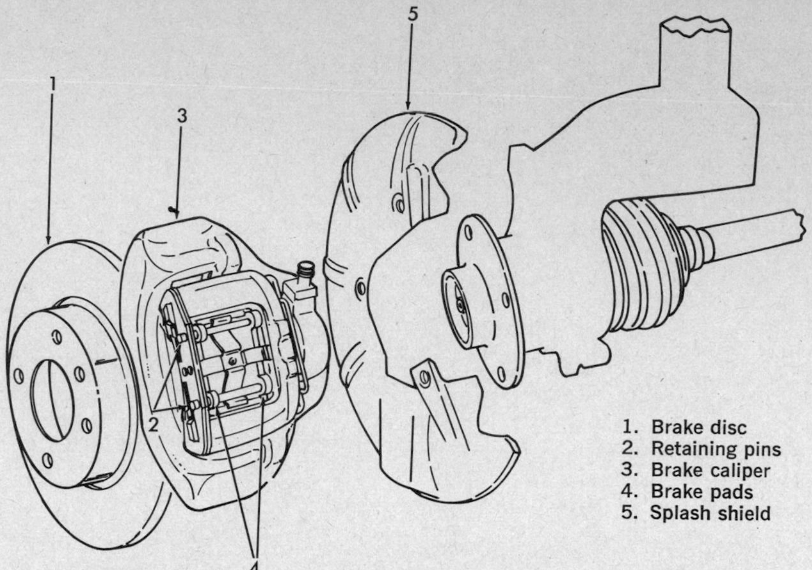

Caliper and disc mounting

Calipers

Removal and Installation

1. Jack up and support the front of the car.
2. Remove the brake pads.
3. If you are removing the caliper for overhaul, disconnect and plug the brake line at the caliper. If not, do not remove the hose—hang it by a wire.
4. Remove the two caliper-to-strut retaining bolts and remove the caliper.
5. Install the caliper using the reverse of the removal procedure. Tighten the two retaining bolts to 43 ft. lbs.
6. Bleed the brakes.

Overhaul

1. Remove the caliper.
2. Mount the caliper in a soft-jawed vise or place cloths over the jaws to protect the caliper.
3. Pry the fixed mounting frame off the floating frame.
4. Separate the caliper cylinder from the floating frame by prying it and the guide spring off the frame. Use a brass drift to lightly tap on the cylinder and place a piece of wood under the piston to protect it.
5. Using pliers remove the piston clamp ring. Remove and discard the rubber dust cover, a new one should be supplied with the rebuilding kit.
6. Remove the piston from the cylinder. If it is stubborn, remove the bleeder screw and blow it out with compressed air.

CAUTION: *Hold the piston over a block of wood when doing this as the piston will fly out with considerable force.*

7. When the piston pops out of the caliper, remove the rubber seal with a wood or plastic pin to avoid damaging the seal groove.
8. Clean all metal parts in alcohol. Never use a mineral based solvent such as gasoline, kerosene, acetone or the like. These solvents deteriorate rubber parts. Inspect the pistons and their bores. They must be free of scoring and pitting. Replace the cylinder if there is any damage.
9. Discard all rubber parts. The caliper rebuilding kit includes new boots and seals which should be used as the caliper is reassembled.
10. Lightly coat the cylinder bore, piston, and seal with brake assembly paste or fresh brake fluid.
11. Using a vise, install the piston into the cylinder.
12. Position the guide spring in the groove of the brake cylinder and using a brass drift install the cylinder on the floating frame.
13. Place the mounting frame in the guide spring and slip it onto the floating frame. The fixed frame has two grooves which position it over the raised ribs of the floating frame.
14. Install the caliper and bleed the brakes.

Brake Disc

Inspection

Brake discs may be checked for lateral run-out while on the car. This check will

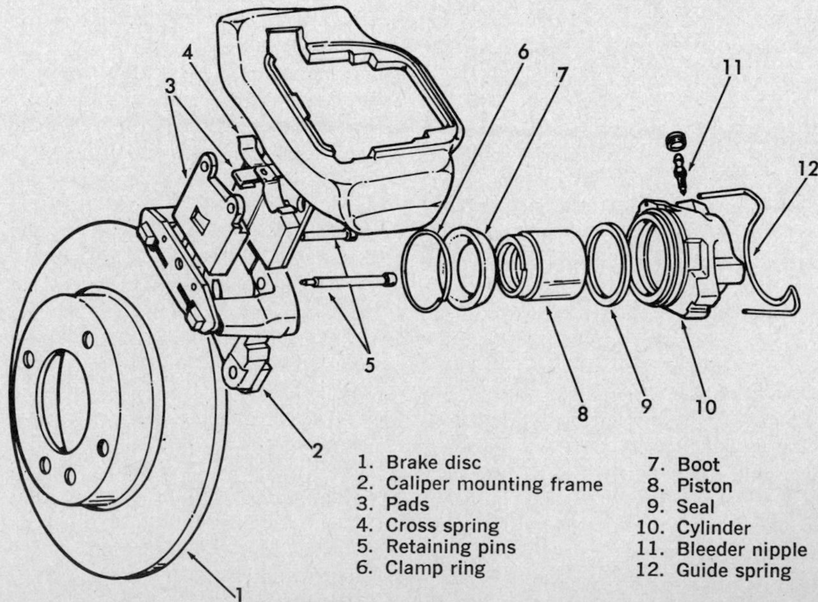

Caliper exploded view

require a dial indicator gauge and stand to mount it on the caliper. VW has a special tool for this purpose which mounts the dial indicator to the caliper, but it can also be mounted on the shaft of a C-clamp attached to the outside of the caliper.

1. Remove the wheel and reinstall the wheel bolts (tightened to 65 ft. lbs.) to retain the disc to the hub.
2. Mount the dial indicator securely to the caliper. The feeler should touch the disc about ½ in. below the outer edge.
3. Rotate the disc and observe the gauge. Radial run-out (wobble) must not exceed 0.004 in. A disc which exceeds this specification must be replaced or refinished.
4. Brake discs which have excessive radial runout, sharp ridges, or scoring can be refinished. First grinding must be done on both sides of disc to prevent squeaking and vibrating. Discs which have only light grooves and are otherwise acceptable can be used without refinishing.

The standard disc is 0.47 in thick. It should not be ground to less than 0.39 in. (0.41 for Rabbit and Scirocco).

Removal and Installation

1. Loosen the wheel bolts. Remove the hub cap.
2. Jack up the front of the car and place it on stands. Remove the wheel(s).
3. Remove the caliper.
4. Remove the disc-to-hub retaining screw.
5. Grip the disc with both hands and give it a sharp pull to remove it. A stubborn disc should be removed with a puller. Never strike the disc with a hammer. Be careful not to get grease on the disc.
6. The disc is installed in the reverse order of removal. Don't forget to install the retaining screw. Install the caliper and bleed the brakes.
7. Install the wheel and lower the car. Tighten the wheel bolts diagonally to 65 ft lbs.

Front Wheel Bearings

There is no front wheel bearing adjustment. The bearing is pressed into the steering knuckle. Axle nut torque is 180–216 ft lbs for the Dasher and 174 ft lbs for the Rabbit and Scirocco. The axle nut should be tightened only with the wheels resting on the ground.

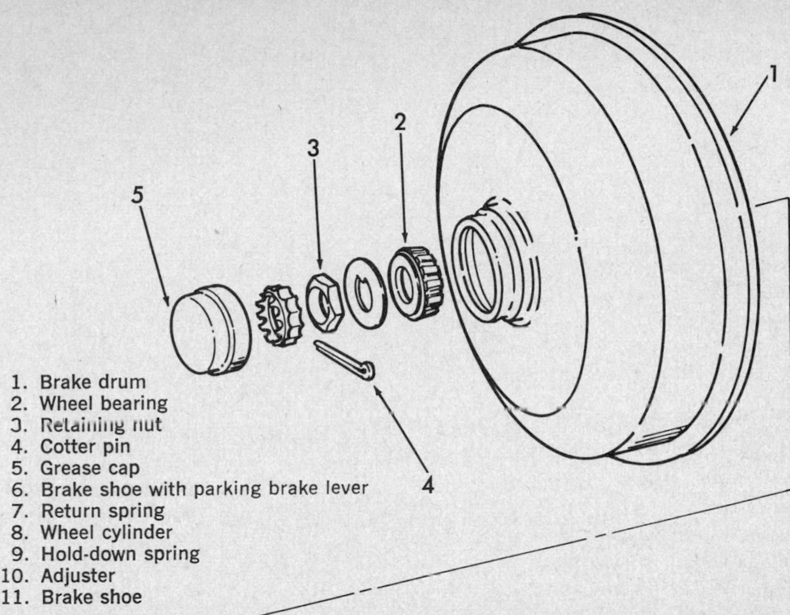

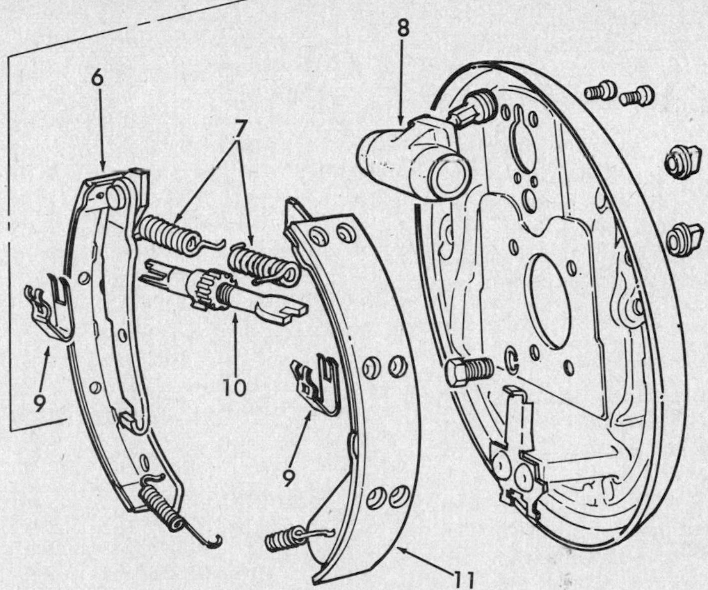

Dasher rear brake, drum, and wheel bearing assembly, the Rabbit and Scirocco are similar but there is no inner wheel bearing snap-ring

Rear Drum Brakes

Brake Drums

Removal and Installation

1. Loosen the wheel bolts.
2. Jack up the rear of the car and support it on stands. Remove the wheel(s).
3. Pry off the hub cap.
4. Remove and discard the cotter pin.
5. Remove the castellated nut, hex nut, and washers.
6. Pull off the brake drum. Be careful not to lose the inner race of the outer bearing.

NOTE: *If the brake drum is stubborn, remove the rubber cover at the backing plate and back off the brake adjuster with an adjusting tool or wide-bladed screwdriver. If this doesn't work, use a puller. Never heat the drum or beat on it with a hammer.*

7. Check the brake drum for any cracks, scores, grooves, or an out-of-round condition. Replace a drum that shows cracking. Smooth out light scoring with fine emery cloth. If scoring is extensive have the drum turned. Never have a drum turned more than 0.030 in (0.020 for the Rabbit and Scirocco).
8. The stub axle bearings in the brake drum must be pressed out for replacement. Always use new seals on reassembly. The outer bearing race is retained by a snap-ring (circlip) on the Dasher.
9. After greasing the bearings and installing them in the drum with new seals, place the drum onto the stub axle.
10. Install the washer and the hex nut. Tighten the nut and then loosen it. Retighten the nut slightly so that the washer between the nut and the bearing can just be moved with a screwdriver. Correct bearing play is 0.001–.003 in.
11. Install the castellated nut and insert a new cotter pin. Fill the hub cap with grease and install it.
12. Install the wheel and lower the car.

Brake Shoes

Removal and Installation

1. Remove the brake drum.
2. Using pliers, disconnect the lower spring.
3. Disconnect the anchor spring and pins from each shoe.
4. Detach the parking brake cable by pressing back the spring with needle-nosed pliers and then disconnecting the cable at the lever.
5. Remove the second lower spring.
6. Raise one brake shoe from the bottom and remove the adjusting mechanism.
7. Lift the brake shoes and remove the upper springs. Remove both brake shoes.
8. Clean and inspect all brake parts. Spray solvents which do not affect linings are available for brake cleaning. Do not spray rubber parts with solvent.
9. Check the wheel cylinders for boot condition and leaking.
10. Inspect the replacement shoes for nicks or burrs; lubricate the backing plate contact points with Lubriplate, **lubricate the brake cable, lever and adjuster, and then assemble.**
11. Reverse the removal procedure for assembly. When completed, install the drum and make an initial adjustment by turning the adjuster wheel until a slight drag is felt between the shoes and drum, and back off about ¼ turn. Adjust the brakes.

Wheel Cylinders

Removal and Installation

1. Remove the brake shoes.
2. Loosen the brake line on the rear of the cylinder, but do not pull the line away from the cylinder or it may bend.
3. Remove the bolts and lockwashers that attach the wheel cylinder to the backing plate and remove the cylinder.
4. Position the new wheel cylinder on the backing plate and install the cylinder attaching bolts and lockwashers.
5. Attach the brake line.
6. Install the brakes and bleed the system.

Overhaul

1. Remove the brakes.
2. Place a bucket or some newspapers under the brake backing plate to catch the brake fluid that will run out of the wheel cylinder.
3. Remove the boots from the ends of the wheel cylinders.
4. Push one piston toward the center of the cylinder to force the opposite piston and cup out the other end of the cylinder. Reach in the open end of the cylinder and push the spring, cup, and piston out of the cylinder.
5. Remove the bleeder screw from the rear of the cylinder, on the back of the backing plate.

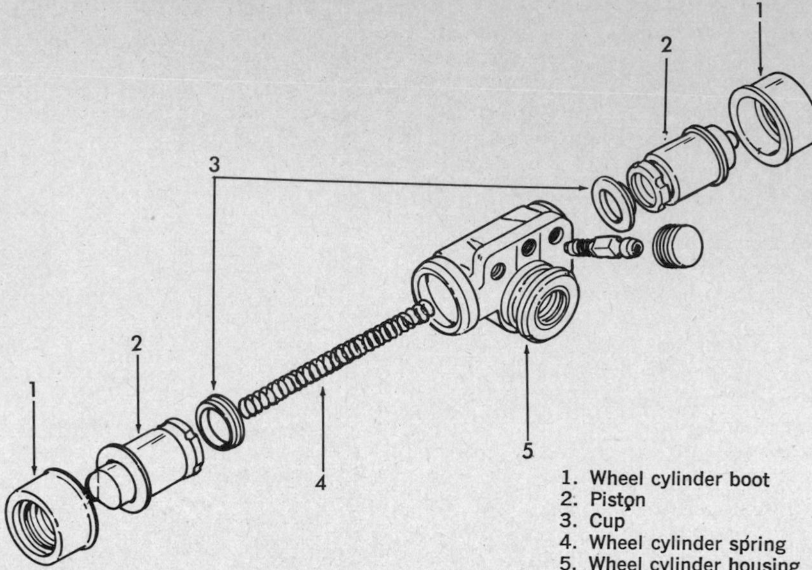

Exploded view of the wheel cylinder

6. Inspect the inside of the wheel cylinder. If it is scored in any way, the cylinder must be honed with a wheel cylinder hone or fine emery paper, and finished with crocus cloth if emery paper is used. If the inside of the cylinder is excessively worn, the cylinder will have to be replaced, as only 0.003 in. of material can be removed from the cylinder walls. Whenever honing or cleaning wheel cylinders, keep a small amount of brake fluid in the cylinder to serve as a lubricant.
7. Clean any foreign matter from the pistons. The sides of the pistons must be smooth for the wheel cylinders to operate properly.
8. Clean the cylinder bore with alcohol and a lint-free rag. Pull the rag through the bore several times to remove all foreign matter and dry the cylinder.
9. Install the bleeder screw and the return spring in the cylinder.
10. Coat new cylinder cups with new brake fluid and install them in the cylinder. Make sure they are square in the bore or they will leak.
11. Install the pistons in the cylinder after coating them with new brake fluid.
12. Coat the insides of the boots with new brake fluid and install them on the cylinder. Install and bleed the brakes.

Rear Wheel Bearings

Rear wheel bearing adjustment is covered under Brake Drum Removal and Installation.

PARKING BRAKE

Cable

Adjustment

Dasher parking brake adjustment is made at the cable compensator, which is attached to the lever push rod. On the Rabbit and Scirocco, adjustment is made at the cable end nuts on top of the handbrake lever.

1. Block the front wheels. Raise the rear of the car.
2. Apply the parking brake so that the lever is on the second notch.

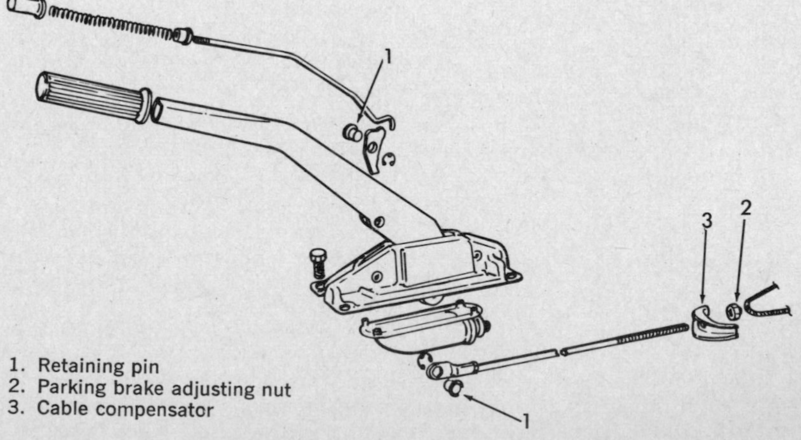

Dasher parking brake linkage and adjusting point

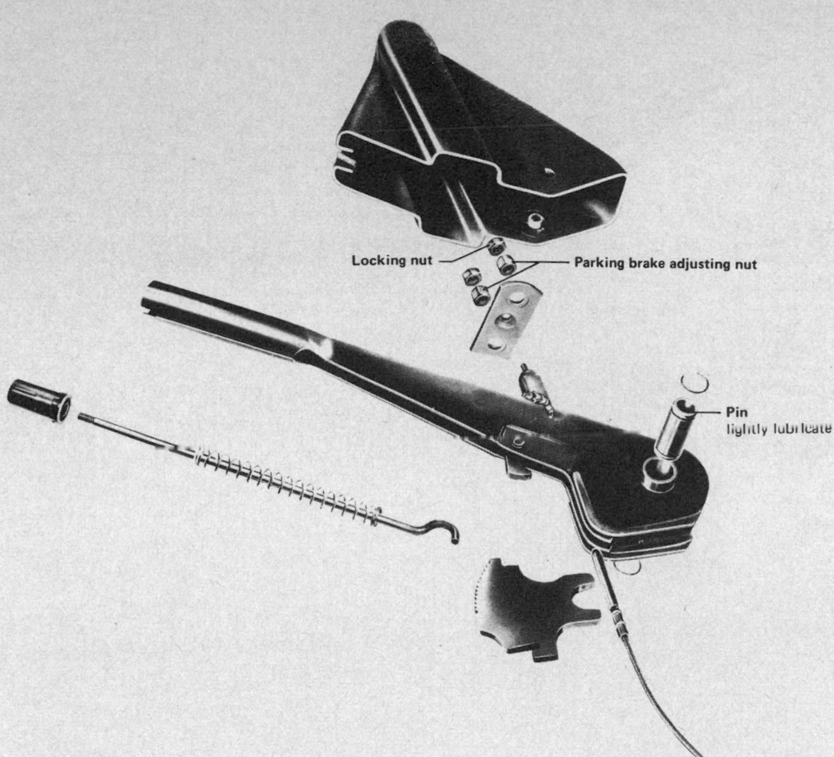

Rabbit and Scirocco parking brake, only one of the two brake cables is shown here

3. The Dasher adjustment is made directly under the passenger compartment.

4. Tighten the compensator nut or adjusting nuts until both rear wheels can just be turned by hand. On the Rabbit and Scirocco, you shouldn't be able to turn them at all.

5. Release the parking brake lever and check that both wheels can be easily turned.

6. Lubricate the Dasher compensator with chassis grease.

CHASSIS ELECTRICAL

Heater

The heater core and blower are contained in the heater assembly which is removed and disassembled to service either component. The heater assembly is located in the passenger compartment under the center of the dash.

Removal and Installation

Dasher

1. Disconnect the battery ground cable.
2. Drain the cooling system.
3. Remove the windshield washer container from its mounts. Remove the ignition coil.
4. Disconnect the two hoses from the heater core connections at the firewall.
5. Unplug the electrical connector.
6. Remove the heater control knobs on the dash.
7. Remove the two retaining screws and remove the controls from the dash complete with brackets.
8. Pull the cable connection off the electric motor.
9. Disconnect the cable from the lever on the round knob.
10. Using a screwdriver, pry the retaining clip off the fresh air housing [the front portion of the heater].
11. Remove the fresh air housing complete with the controls.
12. Detach the left and right air hoses.
13. Remove the heater-to-dash panel mounting screws and lower the heater assembly.
14. Pull out the two pins and remove the heater cover. Unscrew and remove the fan motor.
15. Separate the heater halves to remove the heater core.
16. Installation is the reverse of removal. Refill the cooling system.

Windshield Wiper Motor

Removal and Installation

Dasher

1. Unplug the multi-connector from the wiper motor.
2. Remove the three motor-to-linkage bracket retaining screws.
3. Carefully pry the motor crank out of the two linkage arms.
4. Remove the motor from the car.
5. Install the motor in the reverse order of removal. The crank arm should be at a right angle to the motor.

Rabbit, Scirocco

When removing the wiper motor, leave the mounting frame in place. Do not remove the wiper drive crank from the motor shaft—if it must be removed for any reason, matchmark the shaft, motor, and crank for reinstallation.

1. Access is with the hood open. Disconnect the battery ground cable.
2. Detach the connecting rods from the motor crank arm.
3. Pull off the wiring plug.
4. Remove the 4 mounting bolts. You may have to energize the motor for access to the top bolt.
5. Remove the motor. Reverse the procedure for installation.

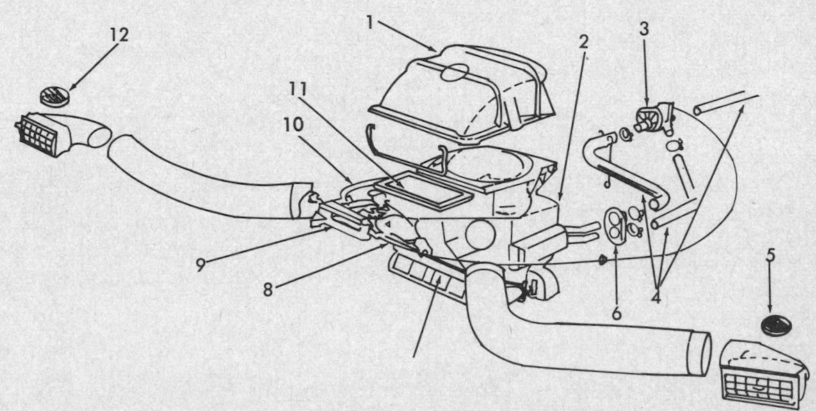

Dasher heater assembly

1. Heater cover
2. Main heater assembly
3. Heater valve
4. Heater hoses
5. Vent for side windows
6. Double grommet
7. Control flap cable
8. Heater valve cable
9. Heater controls
10. Cutoff flap cable
11. Fresh air housing
12. Vent for side windows

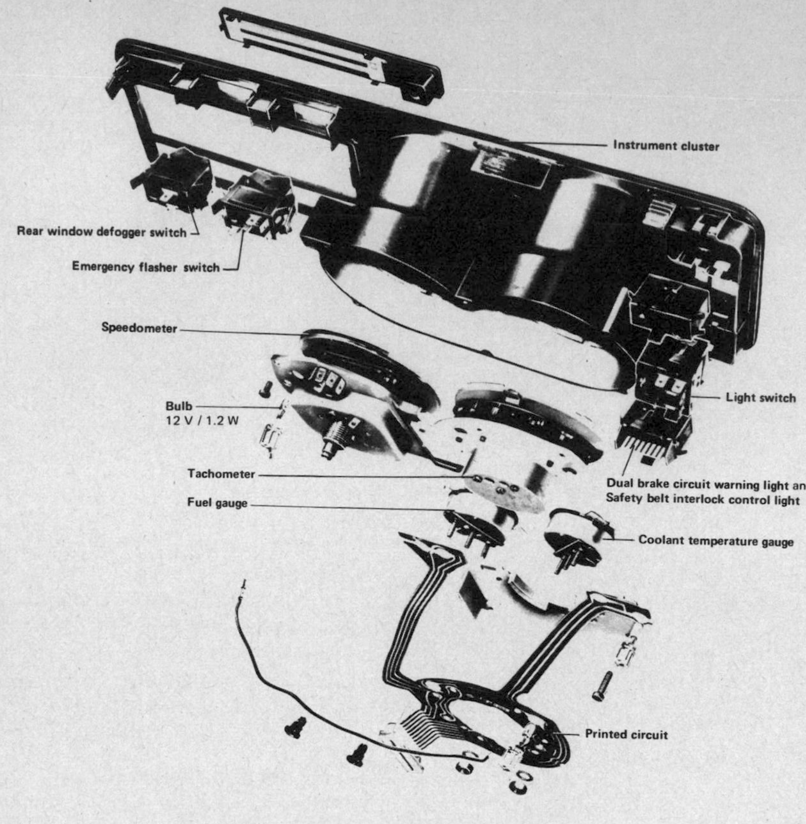

Exploded view of Rabbit and Scirocco instrument cluster

Instrument Cluster

Removal and Installation

Dasher

1. Disconnect the battery ground cable.
2. Unscrew the speedometer cable from the rear of the cluster.
3. Using needle-nosed pliers, detach the retaining springs on either side of the cluster.
4. Pivot the instrument cluster out of the dash.
5. Disconnect the multi-connector plug at the rear of the cluster.
6. Remove the cluster from the dash.
7. Installation is the reverse of removal.

Rabbit, Scirocco

1. Disconnect the battery ground cable.
2. Remove the fresh air controls trim plate.
3. Remove the radio or glove box.
4. Unscrew the speedometer drive cable from the back of the speedometer. Detach the electrical plug.
5. Remove the attaching screw inside the radio/glove box opening.
6. Remove the instrument cluster. Reverse the procedure for installation.

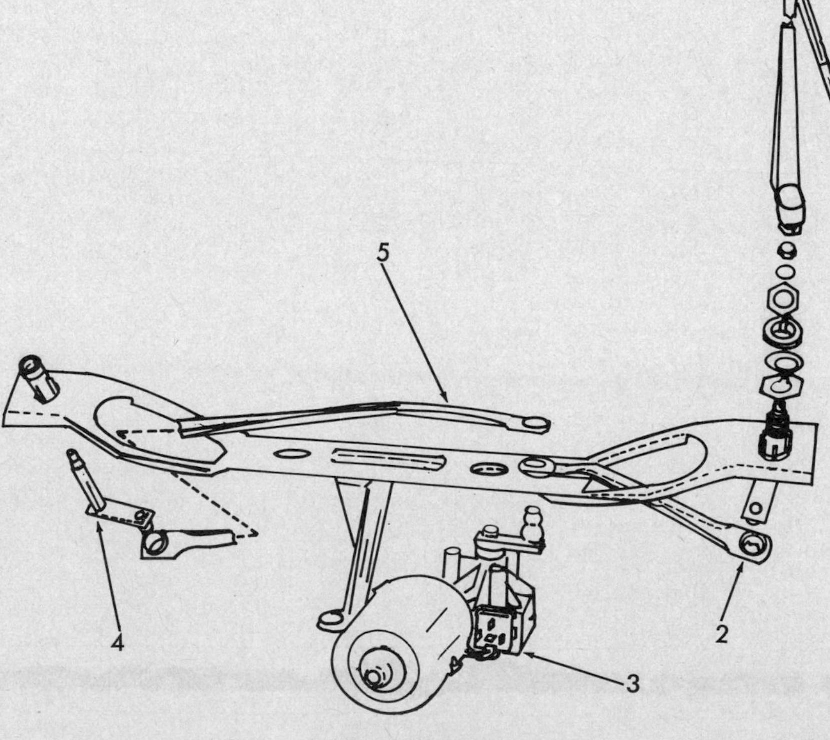

Dasher windshield wiper system components

1. Wiper arm
2. Left linkage rod
3. Wiper motor with crank
4. Wiper shaft
5. Right linkage rod

Jeep INDEX

MODEL IDENTIFICATION

1974 Cherokee

1975-76 Cherokee

1968-70 Jeepster

1974 Wagoneer

1971-73 Commando

CJ Series

1975-76 Wagoneer

FIRING ORDER

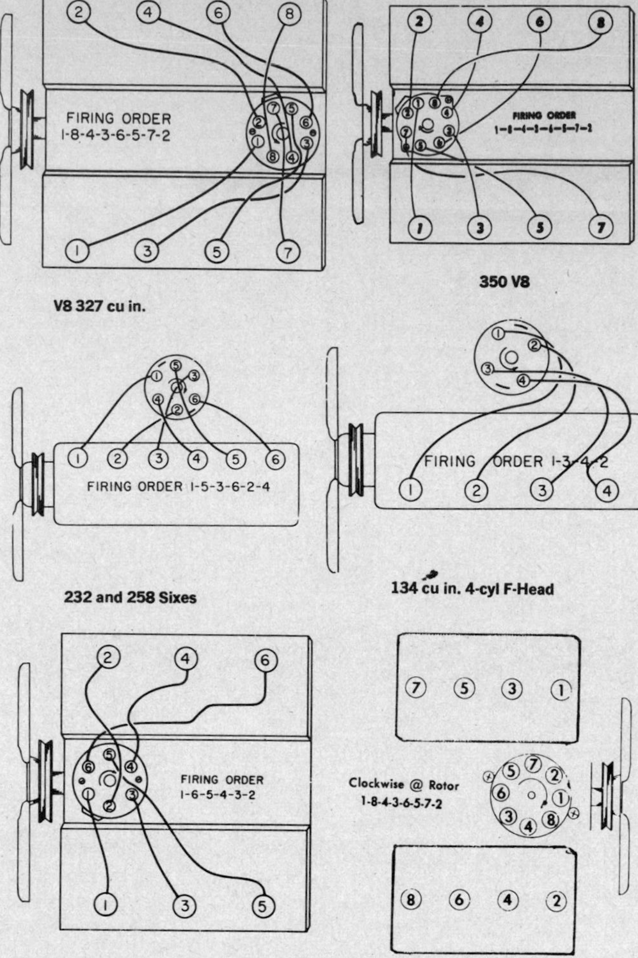

V8 327 cu in.

350 V8

232 and 258 Sixes

134 cu in. 4-cyl F-Head

225 V6

V8 (304, 360, 401 cu in.)

Vehicle Serial Number

The vehicle serial number is on a metal plate mounted on the firewall under the hood. It is on the left side for models CJ-5, CJ-5A, CJ-6, CJ-6A, DJ-5, DJ-6, and the Jeepster. The serial number plate is on the left front door body hinge pillar on the Wagoneer and Cherokee.

Axle and Transmission Identifying Numbers

Axles on Jeep vehicles have a model number cast into the axle differential housing near or on one of the reinforcing webs. A tag installed under one of the gear cover screw heads lists the number of teeth on the gear and also on the pinion. In some cases, the axle ratio is also listed.

Manual transmissions are identified by the manufacturer's model number on a metal plate attached to the transmission case cover. Starting 1972, automatic transmissions have a serial number on a plate on the right side.

ENGINE IDENTIFICATION CODE

The engine identification code is located at the front of the block above the water pump on 1968-71 four cylinder engines; stamped on a boss between the No. 2 and No. 3 spark plugs on 1968-76 232 and 258 sixes; at the right block deck between the front two spark plugs on 1968-71 225 V6 engines; on the alternator bracket on 1968 327 V8 engines; and stamped on a tab on the right valve cover on 1971-76 304, 360, and 401 V8 engines. Beginning 1972, the engine code is the eighth digit of the vehicle identification number.

Disp	Bbl	Hp	'68	'69	'70	'71	'72	'73	'74	'75	'76
4-Cylinder—(Kaiser)											
134	1	75	4J	4J	SF	F					
6-Cylinder—(Buick)											
225	2	160	PH	PH	SH	HC					
6-Cylinder—(AMC)											
232	1	100 (net)					E	E	E	E	E
232	1	145	1L	1L	3L	E					
258	1	110 (net)					A	A	A	A	A
258	1	150				A					
8-Cylinder—(AMC)											
304	2	150 (net)					H	H	H	H	H
304	2	210				H					
327	2	250	E								
327	4	270	E								
8-Cylinder—(Buick)											
350	2	230	KPO	KRO	KSO	KTO					
8-Cylinder—(AMC)											
360	2	175 (net)					N	N	N	N	N
360	2	245				N					
360	4	195 (net)						P	P	P	P
401	4	215 (net)							Z	Z	Z

GENERAL ENGINE SPECIFICATIONS

Year	Engine Cu In. Displacement	Carburetor Type	Horsepower @ rpm ■	Torque @ rpm (ft lbs) ■	Bore and Stroke (in.)	Compression Ratio	Oil Pressure @ 30 mph (psi)
'68-'71	4-134	1 bbl	75 @ 4000	114 @ 2000	3.125 x 3.375	7.4:1/6.9:1/7.8:1	35
'68-'71	6-232	1 bbl	145 @ 4300	215 @ 1600	3.750 x 3.500	8.5:1	50
'71	6-258	1 bbl	150 @ 3800	240 @ 1800	3.750 x 3.895	8.0:1/7.6:1	37
'68-'71	6-225	2 bbl	160 @ 4200	235 @ 2400	3.750 x 3.400	9.0:1	33
'68-'69	8-327	2 bbl	250 @ 4700	340 @ 2600	4.000 x 3.250	8.7:1	55
'69-'71	8-350	2 bbl	230 @ 4400	350 @ 2400	3.800 x 3.850	9.0:1	37
'71	8-304	2 bbl	210 @ 4400	300 @ 2600	3.750 x 3.440	8.4:1	37
'71	8-360	2 bbl	245 @ 4400	365 @ 2600	4.080 x 3.440	8.5:1	37
'72-'73	6-232	1 bbl	100 @ 3600	185 @ 1800	3.895 x 3.500	8.0:1/7.6:1	37
'72-'73	6-258	1 bbl	110 @ 3500	195 @ 2000	3.750 x 3.500	8.0:1/7.6:1	37
'72-'75	8-304	2 bbl	150 @ 4200	245 @ 2500	3.750 x 3.440	8.4:1	37
'72-'73	8-360	2 bbl	175 @ 4000	285 @ 2400	4.080 x 3.440	8.5:1	37
'72-'73	8-360	4 bbl	195 @ 4400	295 @ 2900	4.080 x 3.440	8.5:1	37
'74-'76	6-232	1 bbl	100 @ 3600	185 @ 1800	3.750 x 3.500	8.0:1	37
	6-258	1 bbl	110 @ 3500	195 @ 2000	3.750 x 3.900	8.0:1	37
	8-360	2 bbl	175 @ 4000	285 @ 2400	4.080 x 3.440	8.3:1	37
	8-360	4 bbl	195 @ 4400	295 @ 2900	4.080 x 3.440	8.3:1	37
	8-401	4 bbl	215 @ 4200	320 @ 2800	4.165 x 3.680	8.4:1	37

■ Beginning in 1972, horsepower and torque are SAE net figures. They are measured at the rear of the transmission with all accessories installed and operating. Since the figures vary when a given engine is installed in different models, some are representative rather than exact.

TUNE-UP SPECIFICATIONS

When analyzing compression test results, look for uniformity among cylinders rather than specific pressures.

Year	ENGINE No. Cyl Displacement (cu. in.)	hp	SPARK PLUGS Type	SPARK PLUGS Gap (in.)	DISTRIBUTOR Point Dwell (deg)	DISTRIBUTOR Point Gap (in.)	IGNITION TIMING (deg) ▲	VALVES Intake Opens (deg) ■	Fuel Pump Pressure (psi)	IDLE SPEED (rpm) ● Man Trans	IDLE SPEED (rpm) ● Auto Trans
'68-'71	4—134	75	J8	.030	40	.020	5B	9	3	600	N.A.
'68-'71	6—232	140	N-14Y	.035	32	.016	①	12½	5	650⑤	700⑤
'71	6—258	150	N-14Y	.035	32	.016	5B	12½	4-5½	600	700
'68-'71	6—225	160	44S	.035	30	.016	5B	24	5	550	N.A.
'68-'69	8—327	250	H-14Y	.035	30	.016	②	12½	4½	550③	500③
'69-'71	8—350	230	H-14Y	.035	30	.016	④	24	5	650⑤	700⑤
'71	8—304	210	N-12Y	.035	30	.016	2½B	18½	4-5½	650	700
'71	8—360	245	N-12Y	.035	30	.016	2½B	18½	4-5½	650	750
'72	6—232	100	N-12Y	.035	32	.016	5B⑥	12½	4-5	700	600
'72	6—258	110	N-12Y	.035	32	.016	3B⑥	12½	4-5	700	600
'72	8—304	150	N-12Y	.035	30	.016	5B⑥	14¾	5-6½	750	650
'72	8-360	175	N-12Y	.035	30	.016	5B⑥	14¾	5-6½	750	650
'73-'74	6-232	100	N-12Y	.035	32	.016	5B⑥	12½	4-5	700⑦	—
'73-'74	6-258	110	N-12Y	.035	32	.016	3B⑥	12½	4-5	700⑦	550
'73-'74	8-304	150	N-12Y	.035	30	.016	5B⑥	14¾	5-6½	750	700
'73-'74	8-360	175	N-12Y	.035	30	.016	5B⑥	14¾	5-6½	750	700

TUNE-UP SPECIFICATIONS

When analyzing compression test results, look for uniformity among cylinders rather than specific pressures.

Year	ENGINE No. Cyl Displacement (cu. in.)	hp	SPARK PLUGS Type	SPARK PLUGS Gap (in.)	DISTRIBUTOR Point Dwell (deg)	DISTRIBUTOR Point Gap (in.)	IGNITION TIMING (deg) ▲	VALVES Intake Opens (deg) ■	Fuel Pump Pressure (psi)	IDLE SPEED (rpm) • Man Trans	IDLE SPEED (rpm) • Auto Trans
'73-'74	8-360	195	N-12Y	.035	30	.016	5B⑥	14¾	5-6½	750	700
'74	8-401	225	N-12Y	.035	30	.016	5B⑥⑧	25½	5-6½	700⑨	700
'75	6-232	100	N-12Y	.035	Electronic		5B	12½	4-5	700	—
	6-258	110	N-12Y	.035	Electronic		3B	12½	4-5	650	550(600)
	8-304	150	N-12Y	.035	Electronic		5B	14¾	5-6½	750	—
	8-360	All	N-12Y	.035	Electronic		2½B	14¾	5-6½	750	700
	8-401	225	N-12Y	.035	Electronic		2½B	25½	5-6½	750	700
'76	All				See underhood specifications sticker						

▲ With vacuum advance disconnected
■ All figures before TDC (BTDC)
• With manual transmission in Neutral and automatic transmission in Drive, California figures in parentheses
B Before top dead center (BTDC)
① W/o emission control, 5B on dist. model 1110340, 0 on dist. model 110444, 0 w/ emission control
② 5B w/o emission control, 0 w/ emission control
③ 650/700 rpm w/o emission control
④ 0 on dist. model 1111330, 1111474, and 1111938, 5B on model 11116964
⑤ 100 rpm less w/o emission control
⑥ At 550 rpm in 1973; 700 rpm in 1974
⑦ 700 rpm for CJ, 600 rpm Commando and Wagoneer
⑧ 2.5° B on heavy-duty engine (painted red)
⑨ 625 rpm on heavy-duty engine (painted red)

CAPACITIES

Model	Engine Crankcase (add 1 qt for new filter)	TRANSMISSIONS Manual (add 1 pt for overdrive) 3-Speed	4-Speed	Automatic (pts) •	Front Drive Axle (pts)	Transfer Case (pts)	Rear Drive Axle (pts)	Gas Tank (gal)	Cooling System (qts) With Heater
4—134①	4	1½	—	22	—	—	2	15	12
4—134②	4	3	—	22	2½	3½	3	15	12
6—225	4	2½	6½	19	2½	3¼	3	20	13
8—327	5	2½	6½	22	2½	3¼	3	N.A.	19
8—350	4	2½	6½	22	2½	3	3	N.A.	15
6—232	5	2½	6½	22	2½⑥	3¼	3	16④	10½
6—258	5	2½	6½	22	2½⑥	3¼③	3	16④	10½
8—304	4	2¾	6½	22	2½⑥	3¼③	3	16④	14⑤
8—360	4	2¾	6½	22	2½⑥	3¼③	3	22④	14
8—401	4	—	—	22	2½⑥	③	3	22	14

① 2-wheel drive
② 4-wheel drive
③ 3.5 pts with Quadra-Trac and 1 pt more with reduction unit
④ 1972-74—22 gals Wagoneer and Cherokee; 15.5 gals CJ
⑤ 13 qts in 1974-76
⑥ 3 pts with Dana Model 44 (front or rear); Dana Model 30 given

VALVE SPECIFICATIONS

Year	Engine No. Cyl. Displacement (cu in.)	Seat Angle (deg) •	Face Angle (deg) ■	Spring Test Pressure (lbs @ in.)	Spring Installed Height (in.)	STEM TO GUIDE Clearance (in.) Intake	STEM TO GUIDE Clearance (in.) Exhaust	STEM Diameter (in.) Intake	STEM Diameter (in.) Exhaust
'68-'71	4-134	45①	46②	73 @ 1 27/32	⑥	.0014	.0035	.373	.371
	6-232	45③	45③	90 @ 1 13/16	2 13/64⑦	.0020	.0020	.373	.373
	6-258	45③	44	195 @ 1 7/16	N.A.	.0020	.0020	.372	.372
	6-225	45④	45④	⑤	1 23/32	.0020	.0025	.3407	.3407
'68-'69	8-327	45③	45③	88 @ 1 13/16	2 13/64⑦	.0020	.0020	.372	.372
	8-350	45④	45④	75 @ 1 11/16	1 23/32	.0025	.0025	.372	.372
'71	8-304	45	44½	195 @ 1 7/16	N.A.	.0020	.0020	.372	.372
	8-360	45	44½	195 @ 1 7/16	N.A.	.0020	.0020	.372	.372
'72-'76	6-232	44½	44	100 @ 1 13/16⑨	2 15/64⑦⑧	.0020	.0020	.372	.372
	6-258	44½	44	100 @ 1 13/16⑨	2 15/64⑦⑧	.0020	.0020	.372	.372

VALVE SPECIFICATIONS

Year	Engine No. Cyl. Displacement (cu in.)	Seat Angle (deg) •	Face Angle (deg) ■	Spring Test Pressure (lbs @ in.)	Spring Installed Height (in.)	STEM TO GUIDE Clearance (in.)		STEM Diameter (in.)	
						Intake	Exhaust	Intake	Exhaust
	8-304	44½	44	84 @ 1 13/16⑨	2 7/32⑦⑧	.0020	.0020	.372	.372
	8-360	44½	44	84 @ 1 13/16⑨	2 7/32⑦⑧	.0020	.0020	.372	.372
'74-'76	8-401	44½	44	84 @ 1 13/16⑨	2 7/32⑦⑧	.0030	.0030	.372	.372

- • Exhaust valve seat angle given; all intake valve seat angles are 30° unless otherwise noted
- ■ Exhaust valve face angle given; all intake valve face angles are 29° unless otherwise noted
- —— Not applicable
- N.A. Not available
- ① Intake valve seat angle 45°
- ② Intake valve face angle 46°
- ③ Intake valve angle 30°
- ④ Intake valve angle 45°
- ⑤ Intake: 64 @ 1 11/16; exhaust 64 @ 1 5/8
- ⑥ Free length of intake spring 1 31/32 in.; exhaust 2½ in.
- ⑦ Free length
- ⑧ 1974 and later only; other years N.A.
- ⑨ Without rotators

CRANKSHAFT AND CONNECTING ROD SPECIFICATIONS

All measurements are given in inches

Engine No. Cyl. Displacement (cu in.)	CRANKSHAFT				CONNECTING ROD		
	Main Brg. Journal Dia	Main Brg. Oil Clearance	Shaft End-Play	Thrust on No.	Journal Diameter	Oil Clearance	Side Clearance
4-134	2.333	.0019	.005	1	1.9375	.0014	.007
6-225	2.4995	.0009	.006	2	2.0000	.0021	.010
6-232	2.4988	.0012	.005	3	2.0952	.0008	.009①
6-258	2.4986-2.5001	.001-.002	.002-.007	3	2.0934-2.0955	.001-.002	.003-.010①
8-327	2.4991	.0018	.005	1	2.2486	.0015	.010
8-350	2.9995	.0010	.006	3	2.0000	.0012	.010
8-304	2.7489-2.7474②	.001-.002③	.003-.008	3	2.0934-2.0955	.001-.002	.006-.018
8-360	2.7489-2.7474②	.001-.002③	.003-.008	3	2.0934-2.0955	.001-.002	.006-.018
8-401	2.7489-2.7474②	.001-.002③	.003-.008	3	2.2464-2.2485	.001-.002	.006-.018

- ① .005-.014 from 1972-on
- ② Rear main, 2.7479-2.7464
- ③ Rear Main, .002-.003

TORQUE SPECIFICATIONS

All readings in ft lbs

Engine No. Cyl. Displacement (cu in.)	Cylinder Head Bolts	Rod Bearing Bolts	Main Bearing Bolts	Crankshaft Pulley Bolt	Flywheel to Crankshaft Bolts	MANIFOLD	
						Intake	Exhaust
4-134	60-70	35-45	65-75	60-70	35-41	29-35	29-35
6-232, 258	95-115	26-30	75-85	18-28	95-120	37-47③	20-30③
6-225	65-80	30-40	95-120	140-160	50-65	25-35	15-20
8-327	58-62	46-50	①	70-80	100-110	20-25	20-25
8-350	②	35	110	140-180	60	50	18
8-304, 360	100-120	26-30	90-105	18-28	95-120	37-47	20-30
8-401	100-120	35-40	90-105	18-28	95-120	37-47	20-30

- ① 80-85; rear only 50-55
- ② Metal gasket 75; composition 80
- ③ 18-28 for 1974-'75

CYLINDER HEAD BOLT TIGHTENING SEQUENCE

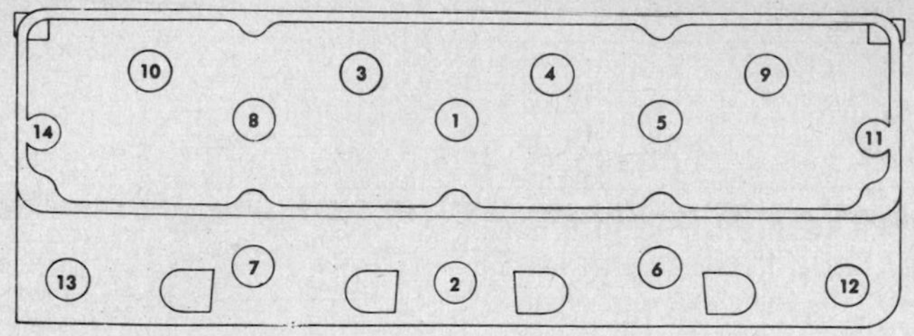

304, 360, 401 V8s

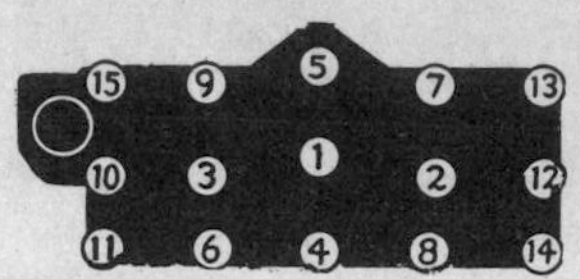

134 cu in. 4-cyl F-Head

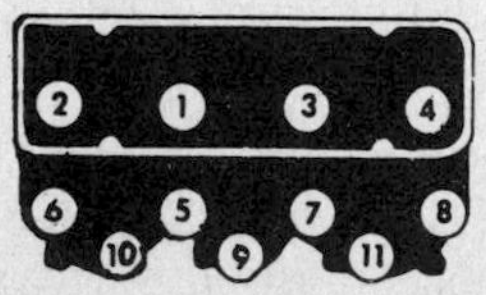

225 V6

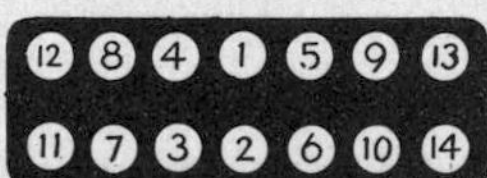

232 and 258 Sixes

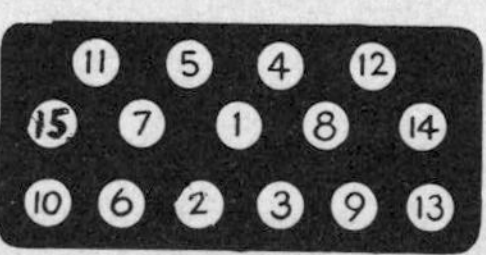

327 V8

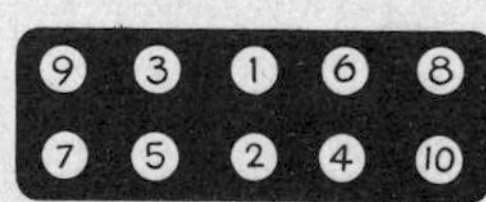

350 V8

RING GAP

All measurements are given in in.

Engine	Top Compression	Bottom Compression	Oil Control
4-134	.007-.015①	.007-.015①	.007-.015①
6-225	.010-.020	.010-.020	.015-.035
6-232	.010-.020	.010-.020	.010-.025②
6-258	.010-.020	.010-.020	.010-.025②
8-327	.010-.020	.010-.020	.015-.055
8-350	.010-.020	.010-.020	.015-.035
8-304	.010-.020	.010-.020	.010-.025
8-360	.010-.020	.010-.020	.015-.045
8-401	.010-.020	.010-.020	.015-.055

① The maximum ring gap for the 4-134 engine with standard bore can be as high as .045 in.
② Ring gap for oil control ring in 1973 is .015-.055

RING SIDE CLEARANCE

All measurements are given in in.

Engine	Top Compression	Bottom Compression	Oil Control
4-134	.002-.004	.0015-.0035	.001-.0025
6-225	.002-.0035	.003-.0035	.0015-.0085
6-232	.0015-.003	.0015-.003	.001-.008
6-258	.0015-.003	.0015-.003	.001-.008
8-304	.0015-.0035	.0015-.0035	.0011-.008
8-327	.002-.004	.002-.004	.000-.005
8-350	.003-.005	.003-.005	.0035-.0095
8-360	.0015-.003	.0015-.0035	.000-.007
8-401	.0015-.003	.0015-.0035	.000-.007

PISTON CLEARANCE

(All measurements are in inches)

Engine No. Cyl. Displacement (cu. in.)	Piston to Bore Clearance
4-134	.0025
6-225	①
6-232	.0009-.0017②
6-258	.0009-.0017
8-304	.0010-.0018
8-327	③
8-350	④
8-360	.0012-.0020
8-401	.0010-.0018

① Top Land—.0265 in.-.0345 in.
Skirt Top—.0005 in.-.0011 in.
Skirt Bottom—.0005 in.-.0021 in.
② Skirt Bottom
③ Top Land—.028 in.-.032 in.
Skirt Top—.0009 in.-.0025 in.
Skirt Bottom—.0009 in.-.0015 in.
④ Top Land—.0270 in.-.0360 in.
Skirt Top—.0008 in.-.0014 in.
Skirt Bottom—.0013 in.-.0029 in.

ALTERNATOR AND REGULATOR SPECIFICATIONS

Make	ALTERNATOR Model No.	Field Current Draw @ 12 V-Amps	Output (Amps)	REGULATOR Model No.	Type	Regulated Voltage	Regulated Amperage
Motorola	A12NW528 A12NW526	1.2-1.7	35	R2K1	Transistorized	14.2-14.6	35
Motorola	A12NAM453 A12NAM451-S A12NW526 A12NW525 A12NW527	1.2-1.7	35	TVR-12-W14	Transistorized	14.2-14.6	35
Motorola	ALK6312	2.4-2.5	35	VSC-62437	Transistorized	14.2	35
	A12NAM460	2.0-2.6	35	R2AM4	Transistorized	15.0	35
	A12NAM555	1.8-2.4	55	R2AM4	Transistorized	15.0	55
Motorola	——	1.8-2.5	37/51	8RD-2001①	Transistorized	14.2	37/51

① 8RH-2003 in 1974

GENERATOR AND REGULATOR SPECIFICATIONS

Make	GENERATORS—6 VOLT Model No.	Output Amps	Brush Spring Tension (oz)	REGULATORS—6 VOLT Model No.	Regulated Voltage	Regulated Amperage	Cutout Relay Closing Voltage
Auto-Lite	GDZ4817	35	35-53	VRP-6003	7.1-7.3	49	6.3-6.8 @ 1000 rpm
	GDZ6001	35	35-53	VRP-4007 VBO-4601			
	GGW4801	45	35-53	VBO-4601C	7.1-7.3	49	6.3-6.8 @ 1000 rpm
	GGW7404	45	18-36				
Delco-Remy	1102811		28	1972063	6.9-7.4	42-47	5.9-6.7

Make	GENERATORS—12 VOLT Model No.	Output Amps	Brush Spring Tension (oz)	REGULATORS—12 VOLT Model No.	Regulated Voltage	Regulated Amperage	Cutout Relay Closing Voltage
Auto-Lite	GJC-7002	30	18-36	VRX-6009	14.3-14.7	39	12.6-13.6 @ 1325 rpm
	GJP-7202	35	18-36	VBO-4201E-4A	14.3-14.7	39	12.6-13.6 @ 1325 rpm
	GJP-7402A	35	18-36				
	GJP-7401A	35	18-36				
Delco-Remy	1102096	35	28	1972029	14.2-14.4	36	11.8-13.5
Prestolite	GJP-7402B	35	18-36	VBO-4201IE-4A	14.2-14.4	36	12.6-13.6 @ 1325 rpm

BATTERY AND STARTER SPECIFICATIONS

Model	Battery: Ampere Hour Capacity	Battery: Volts	Battery: Terminal Grounded	Starter Lock Test: Amps	Starter Lock Test: Volts	Starter Lock Test: Torque (ft lbs)	Starter No-Load Test: Amps	Starter No-Load Test: Volts	Starter No-Load Test: RPM	Starter: Brush Spring Tension (oz)
Universal, Dispatcher 4 Cyl	100	6	Neg.	335	2.0	6.0	65	5.0	4,300	42-53
			Neg.	600	3.0	15.0	60	5.0	6.000	24
Universal, Dispatcher 4 Cyl	50	12	Neg.	170/280	4.0	1.5/6.2	50	10.0	4,400/5,300	31-47
			Neg.	435	5.8	10.5	75	10.3	6,900	35
Jeepster 4 Cyl	50	12	Neg.	405	—	9.0	50	10.0	5,300	32-40
232 6 Cyl (to 1971)	50/70	12	Neg.	405	4.0	9.0	60	10.0	4,200	32-40
V6	50	12	Neg.	—	—	—	75	10.6	6,200	32-40
327V8	60	12	Neg.	405	4.0	9.0	60	10.0	4,200	32-40
350V8	60/70	12	Neg.	300-360	3.5	9.0	65-100	10.6	3,600-5,100	35
232, 258 6 Cyl ('72-'76)	50	12	Neg.	600	4.3	6.5	65	12.0	9,250	40
304V8	50/70	12	Neg.	600	3.4	13	65	12.0	9,250	40
360V8, 401V8	60/70	12	Neg.	600	3.4	13	65	12.0	9,250	40

BRAKE SPECIFICATIONS

(All measurements are given in inches)

Year	Model	Master Cylinder: Disc	Master Cylinder: Drum	Wheel Cylinder Front: Disc	Wheel Cylinder Front: Drum	Wheel Cylinder: Rear	Brake Disc or Drum Diameter Front: Disc	Brake Disc or Drum Diameter Front: Drum	Brake Disc or Drum Diameter: Rear
'68-'71	CJ	—	1	—	1	13/16	—	10	10
'72	CJ	—	1	—	1⅛	15/16	—	10	10
'68-'71	Wagoneer	—	1	—	1⅛	1	—	11	11
'72-'73	Wagoneer	—	1	—	1⅛	15/16	—	11	11
'68-'71	Jeepster	—	1	—	1	13/16	—	10①	10①
'72-'73	Commando	—	1	—	1⅛	15/16	—	11	11
'73-'76	CJ	—	1	—	1⅛	15/16	—	11	11
'74-'76	Wagoneer, Cherokee	1⅛	1	2 15/16	1⅛	15/16	12	11	11

— Not applicable
① 11 in. with Bendix brakes

WHEEL ALIGNMENT

Model	Caster: Pref. Setting (deg)	Camber: Pref. Setting (deg)	Toe-In (in.)	King-Pin Inclination (deg)	Wheel Pivot Ratio: Inner Wheel	Wheel Pivot Ratio: Outer Wheel
CJ-5, CJ-6, DJ-5, DJ-6, CJ-5A, CJ-6A, CJ-7	3	1°30′	3/64-3/32	7½①	20	20
Jeepster, Commando	3	1°30′	3/64-3/32	7½	N.A.	N.A.
Wagoneer, Cherokee	3②	1°30′	3/64-3/32	7½①	N.A.	N.A.

N.A. Not available
① 8½° in 1974-'75
② 4° in 1974

NOTE: Jeep vehicles have, in the past, used a variety of engines made by other manufacturers. The only engines covered in detail in this section are the F4, the American Motors 327 V8, and the Buick 225 V6. For specific procedures concerning the 350 V8, refer to the Buick Special section. For specific procedures concerning the 232 and 258 in-line sixes and the 304, 360, and 401 V8, refer to the American Motors section. Specifications for all of the engines are given at the beginning of this section.

CHARGING SYSTEM

CAUTION: Since the AC generator and regulator are designed for use on only one polarity system, the following precautions must be observed:

a. The polarity of the battery, generator and regulator must be matched and considered before making any electrical connections in the system.

b. When connecting a booster battery, be sure to connect the negative battery terminals together and the positive battery terminals together.

c. When connecting a charger to the battery, connect the charger positive lead to the battery positive terminal. Connect the charger negative lead to the battery negative terminal.

d. Never operate the AC generator on open circuit. Be sure that all connections in the circuit are clean and tight.

e. Do not short across or ground any of the terminals on the AC generator.

f. Do not attempt to polarize the AC generator.

g. Do not use test lamps of more than 12 V for checking diode continuity.

h. Avoid long soldering times when replacing diodes or transistors. Prolonged heat is damaging to these units.

i. Disconnect the battery ground terminal when servicing any AC system. This will prevent the possibility of accidentally reversing polarity.

DC Generator Polarity

CAUTION: Whenever the circuits to the generator, the regulator or the battery have been disconnected, it is best to apply the following procedure:

Before the engine is started, momentarily short the Bat to the Gen terminals of the regulator with a screwdriver. This gives a momentary surge of current from the battery to the generator and correctly polarizes the generator with regard to the battery.

Failure to polarize the generator before starting the engine may severely damage the regulator because

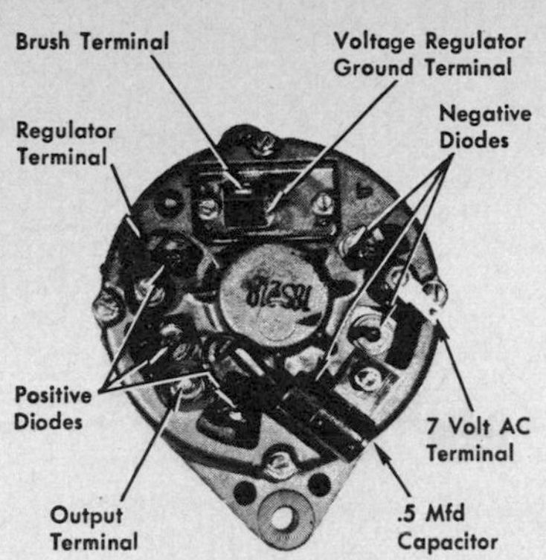

Wire locations for alternator hook-up
(© Kaiser Willys Corp)

reversed polarity causes vibration, arcing, and burning of the relay points.

Alternator R & R

Unfasten the bolt holding the tension bar to the alternator. Push the alternator in toward the engine to release the drive belt. Unfasten the mounting bolt to release the alternator from the engine.

When reinstalling, adjust the drive belt to allow ½ in. play on the longest run between pulleys.

Regulator R & R

232, 258, 304, 327, 360 and 401 Engines

Disconnect the plug from the regulator. Remove the attaching sheet metal screws and lift off the regulator. Install in the reverse of removal.

STARTING SYSTEM

Starter Removal

232 and 258 Engines

Remove the oil filler pipe and disconnect the battery and solenoid leads from the starter. From underneath the vehicle, remove the bolts that attach the starter to the bellhousing and lift out the starter.

Install in the reverse of removal.

304 V8, 360 V8, 401 V8

Disconnect the battery lead and solenoid lead from the starter. From underneath the vehicle, remove the attaching bolts and lift out the starter. Install in the reverse of removal.

225 V6

Disconnect the negative battery cable from the battery. Note the locations of the wiring connections and disconnect the electrical leads from the starter. Remove the capscrew which secures the starter motor to the angle bracket on the side of the engine. Remove the two capscrews which secure the drive end of the

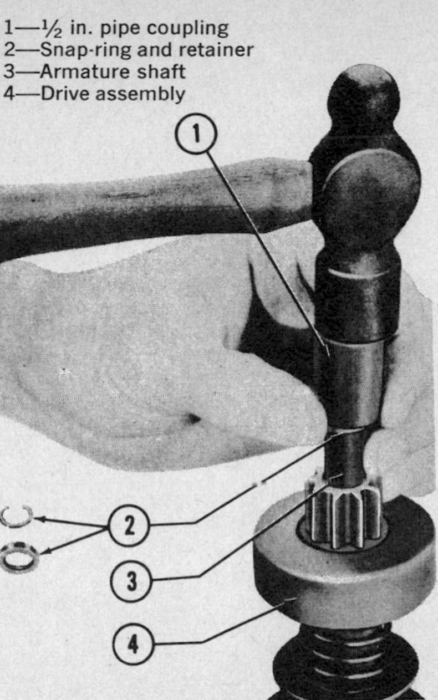

Removing the starter drive assembly from the armature shaft on a 327 V8 and 225 V6 starter

starter motor to the cylinder block and remove the starter. Install the starter in the reverse order of removal.

327 V8

Disconnect the negative battery cable from the battery. Loosen the exhaust pipe clamp at the right exhaust manifold and slide it away from the manifold. Remove the exhaust pipe-to-manifold nuts and remove the pipe and heat valve from the right bank exhaust manifold. Remove the 7 bolts which secure the exhaust manifold to the engine. Remove the manifold from the top of the engine compartment. Disconnect the electrical leads from the starter motor. Remove the two bolts which hold the starter motor to the flywheel housing. Remove the starter motor from the bottom of the engine compartment.

Starter Drive R & R

F4

The starter drive on the F4 starter is not to be removed. If it is defective, the whole starter unit must be replaced.

225 V6

1. Remove the thru-bolts.
2. Remove the starter drive housing.
3. Slide the two-piece thrust collar off the end of the armature shaft.
4. Slide a standard ½ in. pipe coupling, or other spacer, onto the shaft so that the end of the coupling butts against the edge of the retainer.
5. Tap the end of the coupling with a hammer, driving the retainer toward the armature end of the snap-ring.

6. Remove the snap-ring from its groove in the shaft with pliers. Slide the retainer and the starter drive from the armature.

To install the unit:

1. Lubricate the drive end of the shaft with silicone lubricant.
2. Slide the drive gear assembly onto the shaft, with the gear facing outward.
3. Slide the retainer onto the shaft with the cupped surface facing away from the gear.

1—Retainer
2—Snap-ring
3—Thrust collar
4—Drive assembly
5—Retainer
6—Groove in armature shaft
7—Snap-ring

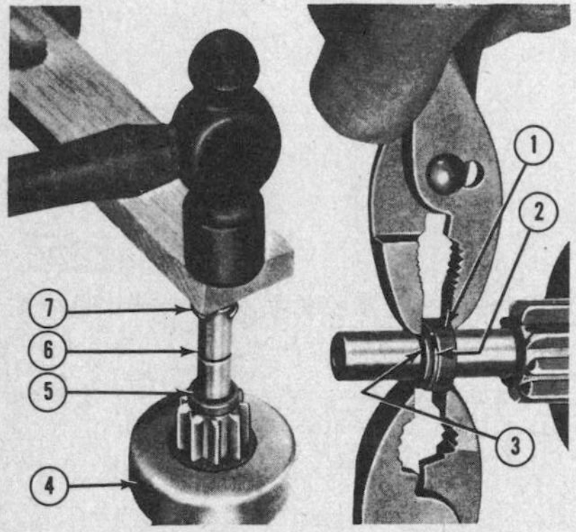

Installing the starter drive stop retainer and thrust collar on the armature shaft on a 327 V8 and 225 V6 starter

4. Stand the whole starter assembly on a block of wood with the snap-ring positioned on the upper end of the shaft. Drive the snap-ring down with a small block of wood and a hammer. Slide the snap-ring into its groove.
5. Install the thrust collar onto the shaft with the shoulder next to the snap-ring.
6. With the retainer on one side of the snap-ring and the thrust collar on the other side, squeeze them together with a pair of pliers until the ring seats in the retainer. On models without a thrust collar, use a washer. Remember to remove the washer before installing the starter in the engine.

327 V8

1. Slide the thrust collar off the armature shaft.
2. Using a standard ½ in. pipe connector, drive the snap-ring retainer off the shaft.
3. Remove the snap-ring from the groove, and then remove the drive assembly.

To install the unit:

1. Lubricate the drive end and splines with Lubriplate.
2. Install the clutch assembly onto the shaft.
3. Install the snap-ring retainer with the cupped surface facing toward the end of the shaft.
4. Install the snap-ring into the groove. Use a new snap-ring if necessary.
5. Install the thrust collar onto the shaft with the shoulder against the snap-ring.
6. Force the retainer over the snap-ring in the same manner as was used for the 225 V6 starter (Step 6 in the above procedure).

IGNITION SYSTEM

Distributor Removal

F4, 225 V6 and 327 V8

1. Remove the high-tension wires from the distributor cap terminal towers, noting their positions to assure correct reassembly. For diagrams of firing orders and distributor wiring, refer to the front of this section.
2. Remove the primary lead from the terminal post at the side of the distributor.
3. Disconnect the vacuum tube if there is one.
4. Unlatch the two distributor cap retaining hooks and remove the distributor cap.
5. Note the position of the rotor in relation to the base. Scribe a mark on the base of the distributor and on the engine block to facilitate reinstallation. Align the marks with the direction the metal tip of the rotor is pointing.
6. Remove the screw that holds the distributor to the engine.
7. Lift the distributor assembly from the engine.

Distributor Installation

F4, 225 V6 and 327 V8

1. Insert the distributor shaft and assembly into the engine. Line up the mark on the distributor and the one on the engine with the metal tip of the rotor. Make sure that the vacuum advance diaphragm is pointed in the same direction as it was pointed originally. This will be done automatically if the marks on the engine and the distributor are lined up with the rotor.

NOTE: On the F4 the distributor shaft fits into a slot in the end of the oil pump shaft.

2. Install the distributor hold-down bolt and clamp. Leave the screw loose enough so that you can move the distributor with heavy hand pressure.
3. Connect the primary wire to the distributor side of the coil. Install the distributor cap on the distributor housing. Secure the distributor cap with the spring clips or the screw type retainers, whichever is used.
4. Install the spark plug wires. Make sure that the wires are pressed all of the way into the top of the distributor cap and firmly onto the spark plugs.

NOTE: Design of the V6 engine requires a special form of distributor cam. The distributor may be serviced in the regular way and should cause no more problems than any other distributor, if the firing plan is thoroughly understood. The distributor cam is not ground to standard six cylinder indexing intervals. This particular form requires that the original pattern of spark plug wiring be used. The engine will not run in balance if number one spark plug wire is inserted into number six distributor cap tower, even though each wire in the firing sequence is advanced to the next distributor tower. There is a difference between the firing intervals of each succeeding cylinder through the 720° engine cycle.

5. Adjust the point cam dwell and set the ignition timing.

If the engine has been turned while the distributor has been removed, or if the marks were not drawn, it will be necessary to initially time the engine. Follow the procedure below.

Distributor Installation, Engine Disturbed

F4, 225 V6 and 327 V8

1. It is necessary to place the No. 1 cylinder in the firing position to correctly install the distributor. To locate this position, some engines have marks placed on the flywheel while other engines have marks placed on the timing gear covers and crankshaft pulleys. The flywheel marks may be viewed through a covered opening directly in back of the starting motor by loosening the hole cover and sliding it to one side.
2. Remove the No. 1 cylinder spark plug. Turn the engine until the piston in No. 1 cylinder is moving up on the compression stroke. This can be determined by placing your thumb over the spark plug hole and feeling the air being forced out of the cylinder. Stop turning F-head engines when either the 5° mark on the flywheel is in the middle of the flywheel inspection opening, or the marks on the crankshaft pulley and the timing gear cover are in alignment.
3. Oil the distributor housing lightly where the distributor bears on the cylinder block.
4. Install the distributor so that the rotor, which is mounted on the shaft, points toward the No. 1 spark plug terminal tower position when the cap is installed. Of

course you won't be able to see the direction in which the rotor is pointing if the cap is on the distributor. Lay the cap on the top of the distributor and make a mark on the side of the distributor housing just below the No. 1 spark plug terminal. Make sure that the rotor points toward that mark when you install the distributor.

5. When the distributor shaft has reached the bottom of the hole, move the rotor back and forth slightly until the driving lug on the end of the shaft enters the slot, which is cut in the end of the oil pump gear on the F4, or when the drive gears of the distributor and cam mesh on the other engines, and until the distributor assembly slides down into place.

On models that have a gear on the end of the distributor shaft and a gear on the end of the oil pump drive, these gears have to mesh with the same teeth as originally installed when the distributor is inserted into the engine. Once again, the marks that were placed on the engine and the base of the distributor housing come into play. If the distributor shaft gear and the oil pump drive gear are but one tooth off from what they are supposed to be, the engine will not run correctly.

6. When the distributor is correctly installed, the breaker points should be in such a position that they are just ready to break contact with each other. This is accomplished by rotating the distributor body after it has been installed in the engine. Once again, line up the marks that you made before the distributor was removed from the engine.
7. Install the distributor hold-down screw and the hold-down bracket. Be sure that the models that have vacuum advance units are free to turn in the mounting socket. Note that the vacuum advance control of some distributors is connected directly to the plate on which the points are mounted. When this is the case, the plate must be free to turn rather than the distributor body.
8. Install the spark plug into the No. 1 spark plug hole and continue from Step 3 of the distributor installation procedure.

Contact Point Replacement and Adjustment

F4

1. Pry the distributor cap hold-down clips loose from the cap and remove the cap and rotor.
2. Loosen the nut which holds the condenser lead and spring arm of the points assembly and remove the lead.
3. Remove the condenser and points assembly hold-down screws and remove the assembly and condenser from the distributor.
4. Install the new points assembly and condenser in the reverse order of removal.
5. Turn the engine until the fiber block on the breaker arm is resting on one of the cam lobes at the highest point.
6. Loosen the lock screw and turn the adjusting eccentric until the proper gap is obtained. Tighten the lock screw.
7. Replace the rotor and cap and start the engine to check the ignition timing and point dwell. Make any necessary adjustments to obtain the correct timing and dwell.

225 V6 With Prestolite Distributor

1. Remove the distributor cap from the distributor. Remove the rotor.
2. The condenser and primary leads are retained by breaker point spring tension. Relieve the spring tension to remove the leads.
3. Remove the contact set retaining screw and remove the contact set.
4. Remove the condenser screw and remove the condenser.
5. Install the new parts by reversing the removal procedure. Relieve the spring tension of the breaker point spring to install the primary and condenser leads.
6. Rotate the crankshaft until the distributor cam holds the distributor points to a wide-open position. Check the gap between the points. Then, slightly loosen the contact set mounting screw and adjust the contact point gap to the proper specification. Tighten the mounting screw when the correct gap is obtained. Check the point dwell with a dwell meter and make any necessary readjustments.

225 V6 With Delco Distributor

1. Remove the distributor cap by inserting a screwdriver in the upper slotted end of the cap retainers, press down and turn 90° counterclockwise. Push the distributor cap aside and remove the rotor. Disconnect the condenser and primary leads from their terminal by loosening the retaining screw. If there is no retaining screw, simply slip the leads out.
2. Loosen the two screws and lock washers which hold the contact point set in place. Remove the point set.
3. Slide the new point set over the boss on the breaker plate and under the two screw heads. Tighten the two screws and lockwashers.
4. Install the condenser and primary leads. The leads must be properly positioned so that they will not come in contact with the bottom of the base or rotor.
5. Install the rotor and distributor cap.
6. If the engine does not readily start, position the contact arm rubbing block on a peak of a cam lobe of the distributor cam, insert a 1/8 in. allen wrench in the adjusting screw and turn the screw in (clockwise) until the contact points just close. Then back the screw out (counterclockwise) 1/2 turn to obtain a point gap of about 0.016 in. for a preliminary setting.
7. Connect a dwell meter and check and adjust the point dwell with the engine running, adjusting the points with the allen wrench inserted through the adjustment window in the side of the distributor cap.
8. Check and adjust the ignition timing.

327 V8

1. Remove the distributor cap, condenser, and primary leads which are attached to the nylon terminal.
2. Loosen the two base screws and remove the points and condenser.
3. When installing the points, make sure the pilot hole is properly positioned, over the hole in the breaker plate.
4. Install the new condenser, then attach the primary and condenser leads to the nylon terminal.
5. Reverse the lubricator and make sure that the terminal leads will not touch the rotor.
6. Install the rotor, making sure that the round and square holes are lined up with their respective dowels.
7. Adjust the point dwell to specifications by turning the allen screw on the point assembly through the window in the side of the cap.

Ignition Timing

All Engines

1. Locate the timing marks on the crankshaft pulley and the front of the timing case cover.
2. Clean off the timing marks, so that you can see them.
3. Use chalk or white paint to color the mark on the scale that will indicate the correct timing, when aligned with the mark on the pulley or the pointer. It is also helpful to mark the notch in the pulley or the tip of the pointer with a small dab of color.
4. Attach a tachometer to the engine.

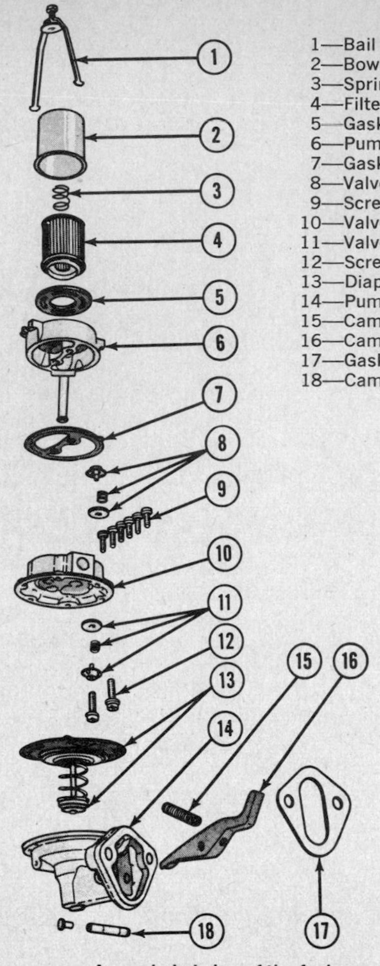

An exploded view of the fuel pump installed on the F-Head engine and pre-1971 Six showing the fuel filter

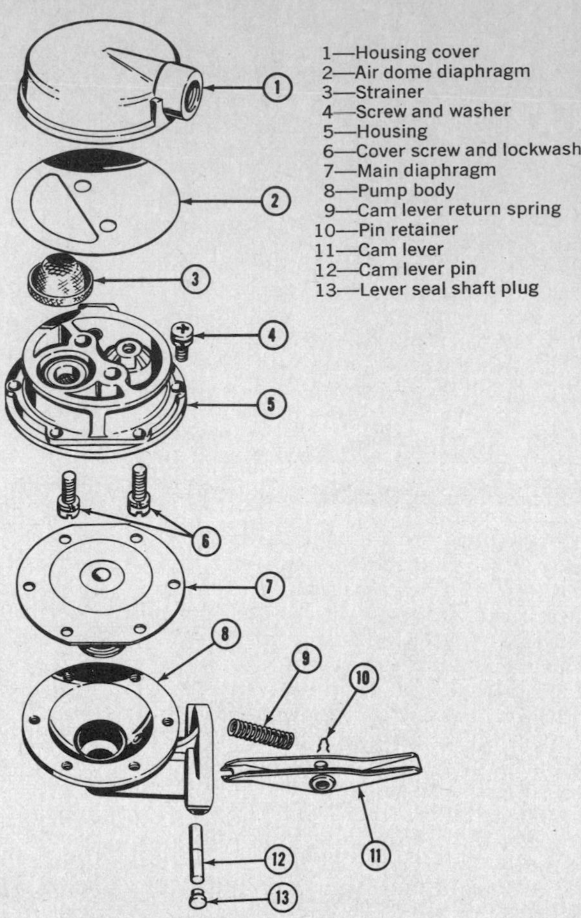

An exploded view of the 327 V8 fuel pump showing the fuel strainer inside the pump

5. Attach a timing light to the engine.
6. Disconnect the vacuum lines to the distributor at the distributor and plug the vacuum lines. Disconnect the TCS switch if so equipped. Loosen the distributor lock-bolt just enough so that the distributor can be turned with a little resistance.
7. Check to make sure that all of the wires clear the fan and then start the engine.
8. Adjust the idle to the correct specification.
9. With the timing light aimed at the pulley and the marks on the engine, turn the distributor in the direction of rotor rotation to retard the spark, and in the opposite direction of rotor rotation to advance the spark. Align the marks on the pulley and the engine with the flashes of the timing light.
10. When the marks are aligned, tighten the distributor lockbolt and recheck the timing to make sure that the distributor did not move when the lockbolt was tightened.
11. Turn off the engine and remove the tachometer and timing light.

FUEL SYSTEM

Fuel Pump Removal and Installation

All Engines

1. Disconnect the fuel lines leading to the carburetor and from the fuel tank.
2. Remove the two attaching bolts that hold the fuel pump to the engine and lift the fuel pump off of the engine.
3. Before installing the fuel pump, make sure that all of the mating surfaces are clean.
4. Cement a new gasket to the mating surface of the fuel pump.
5. Position the fuel pump on the cylinder block so that the cam lever of the pump rests on the camshaft.
6. Secure the pump to the engine with the two bolts and lock washers.
7. Connect the fuel lines to the fuel pump.

Fuel Filter Removal and Installation

The inline fuel filter on a 225 V6 is located between the fuel pump and the carburetor. It is removed by loosening the clamps at both ends and removing the filter from the fuel line. Replace the fuel filter in the opposite manner.

The F4 and pre-1971 232 Six have a sediment type bowl with a filter element inside mounted on top of the fuel pump. To change the filter element in the fuel pump, unscrew the tension nut on the filter bail, allow the bail to swing down out of the way, lift off the bowl and remove the element. Reassemble the fuel pump-mounted filter in the reverse manner.

The 327 V8 fuel pump has a strainer within the pump, under the upper housing cover and air dome diaphragm. Disassemble the fuel pump to clean the strainer only if it is suspected of being clogged.

Carburetor Adjustments

Idle Mixture Adjustment

F4

Turn the idle adjustment screw ¾ to 1¾ turns open from the fully closed position for normal adjustment setting.

For a richer mixture, turn this screw out. For a leaner mixture, turn this screw in.

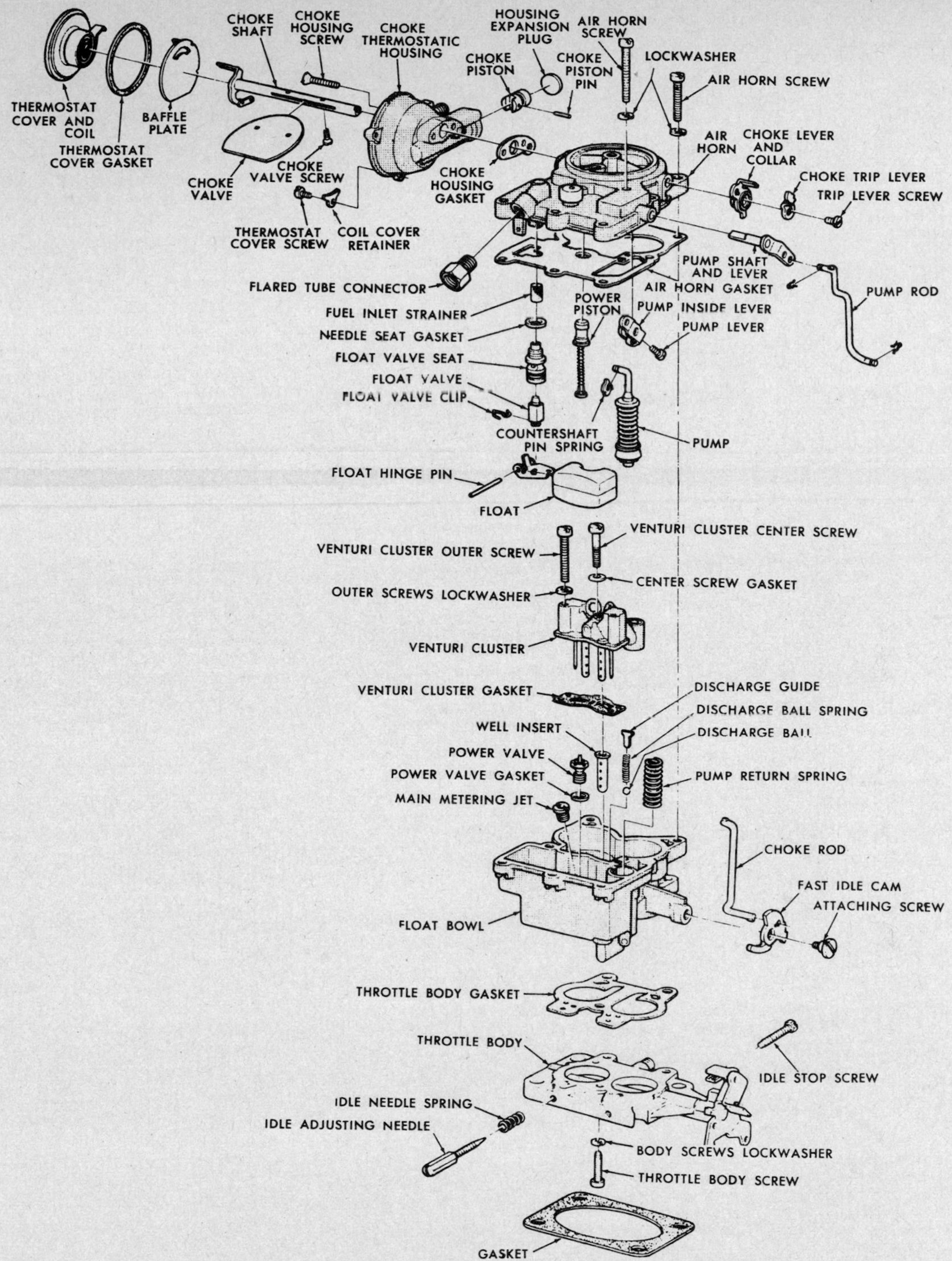

An exploded view of a Rochester 2G carburetor installed on the 225 V6 and 350 V8

Turn the screw until highest rpm is reached and the engine is idling smoothly.

225 V6

NOTE: The initial adjustment of the mixture screws is ¾ to 1¾ turns off their seats. Do not tighten the screws down into their seats to avoid damaging the tips of the needles.

1. Run the engine until it reaches normal operating temperature.
2. Adjust the curb idle speed to the correct specification.
3. Turn the mixture screw(s) (one at a time) in (clockwise) until the engine speed starts to drop off due to too lean a mixture. Then, turn the mixture screw(s) out (counterclockwise), past the starting point, until the engine speed starts to drop off due to too rich a mixture. Next, turn the mixture screw(s) in again to a point midway between the two extremes to obtain the fastest idle speed. It is best to set the adjustment screw on the richer side of the midpoint than on the leaner side.
4. After performing Step 3 on both mixture screws, check and adjust the curb idle speed, as necessary.

327 V8

1. With the air cleaner installed, connect a tachometer to the engine.
2. Gently seat both mixture screws, then back them out exactly one turn.

NOTE: All adjustments of dual mixture screws must be made equally.

3. Start the engine and allow it to warm up to operating temperature.

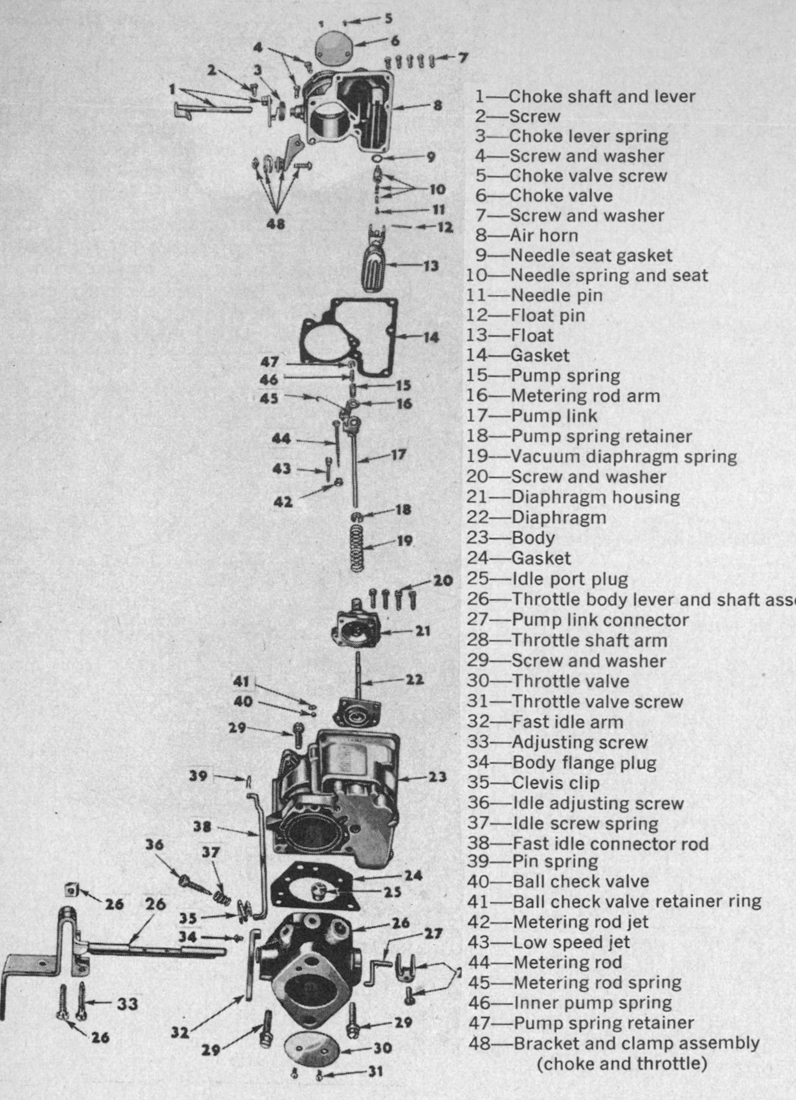

1—Choke shaft and lever
2—Screw
3—Choke lever spring
4—Screw and washer
5—Choke valve screw
6—Choke valve
7—Screw and washer
8—Air horn
9—Needle seat gasket
10—Needle spring and seat
11—Needle pin
12—Float pin
13—Float
14—Gasket
15—Pump spring
16—Metering rod arm
17—Pump link
18—Pump spring retainer
19—Vacuum diaphragm spring
20—Screw and washer
21—Diaphragm housing
22—Diaphragm
23—Body
24—Gasket
25—Idle port plug
26—Throttle body lever and shaft assembly
27—Pump link connector
28—Throttle shaft arm
29—Screw and washer
30—Throttle valve
31—Throttle valve screw
32—Fast idle arm
33—Adjusting screw
34—Body flange plug
35—Clevis clip
36—Idle adjusting screw
37—Idle screw spring
38—Fast idle connector rod
39—Pin spring
40—Ball check valve
41—Ball check valve retainer ring
42—Metering rod jet
43—Low speed jet
44—Metering rod
45—Metering rod spring
46—Inner pump spring
47—Pump spring retainer
48—Bracket and clamp assembly (choke and throttle)

An exploded view of the Carter Model YF carburetor installed on the F-Head engine
(© Kaiser Willys Corp)

4. Adjust the throttle stop screw to obtain 600 rpm for 1967 models, keeping both manual and automatic transmissions in Neutral. On A/C cars, set the speed to 600 rpm, with the A/C turned on.
5. Turn the mixture screws counterclockwise until the engine speed drops off, then slowly turn the screws equal amounts clockwise until the speed picks up. Continue past this point until the speed begins to fall off again, then back out the screws to again obtain the fastest idle. This mid-range adjustment is called the "lean best idle" speed.
6. Readjust the idle stop screw, if necessary, to obtain the specified idle. If the idle speed changed more than 50 rpm during mixture adjustment, readjust the idle speed.
7. Disconnect the tachometer.

Dashpot Adjustment

Some carburetors are equipped with a dashpot to prevent stalling. The dashpot adjustment procedure for these carburetors is as follows:

1. Be sure that the throttle valves are closed tightly and that the diaphragm stem is fully depressed.
2. Measure the clearance between the dashpot stem and the throttle lever with a feeler gauge.
3. If the clearance is not correct, adjust it by loosening the locknut and rotating the dashpot until the proper clearance is obtained. Tighten the locknut.

On the 327 V8 engine with the Holley 4 bbl carburetor, the dashpot is adjusted to 5/32 in. clearance on the model 2209 and 3/32 in. on the model 4160.

On the 225 V6, the dashpot is adjusted with the engine at curb idle. Loosen the dashpot locknut and turn the dashpot assembly until the dashpot plunger contacts the throttle lever without the plunger being de-

1—Thermostat housing cover screw
2—Thermostat housing cover clamp
3—Thermostat housing cover
4—Thermostat housing cover gasket
5—Choke shaft nut, lockwasher and spacer
6—Choke lever link and piston assembly
7—Choke shaft
8—Choke plate screw
9—Choke rod retainer (upper)
10—Choke rod seal retainer
11—Choke rod felt seal
12—Diaphragm cover screw and lockwasher
13—Diaphragm cover
14—Diaphragm spring
15—Diaphragm assembly
16—Diaphragm check ball
17—Diaphragm housing gasket
18—Pump discharge nozzle screw
19—Pump discharge nozzle gasket
20—Pump discharge nozzle
21—Pump check weight
22—Pump check ball
23—Choke plate
24—Diaphragm housing
25—Secondary diaphragm housing screw and lockwasher
26—Choke rod
27—Lower choke rod retainer and washer
28—Choke housing shaft
29—Choke housing gasket
30—Fast idle cam
31—Choke housing
32—Choke housing screw and lockwasher

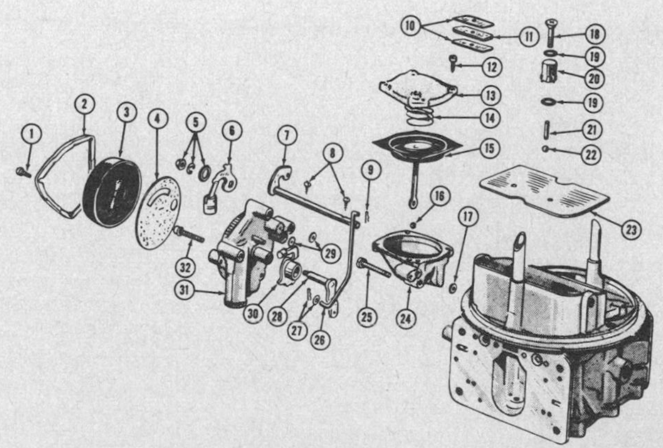

An exploded view of the main body of a Holley 4160 carburetor used on the 327 V8
(© Kaiser Willys Corp)

1—Secondary metering body plate gasket
2—Secondary metering body plate
3—Secondary metering body gasket
4—Secondary metering body
5—Metering body screw (clutch type)
6—Float retainer
7—Float spring
8—Float and lever assembly
9—Baffle plate
10—Fuel level sight plug
11—Fuel level sight plug gasket
12—Secondary fuel bowl
13—Fuel valve seat O-ring gasket
14—Fuel inlet valve and seat assembly
15—Fuel valve seat adjusting nut gasket
16—Fuel valve seat adjusting nut
17—Fuel valve seat lockscrew gasket
18—Fuel valve seat lockscrew

An exploded view of the secondary fuel bowl and metering body of a Holley 4160 used on the 327 V8
(© Kaiser Willys Corp)

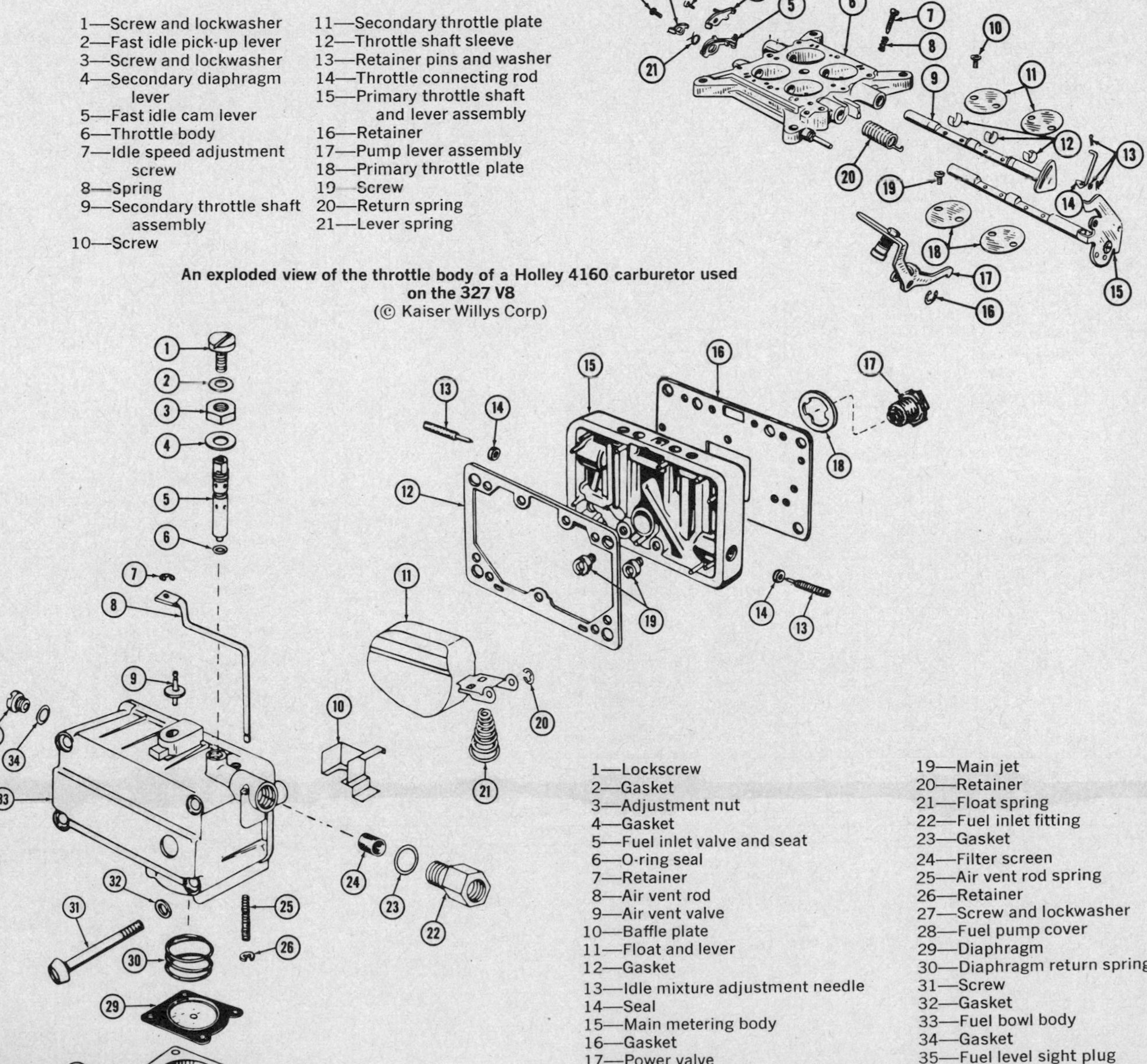

1—Screw and lockwasher
2—Fast idle pick-up lever
3—Screw and lockwasher
4—Secondary diaphragm lever
5—Fast idle cam lever
6—Throttle body
7—Idle speed adjustment screw
8—Spring
9—Secondary throttle shaft assembly
10—Screw
11—Secondary throttle plate
12—Throttle shaft sleeve
13—Retainer pins and washer
14—Throttle connecting rod
15—Primary throttle shaft and lever assembly
16—Retainer
17—Pump lever assembly
18—Primary throttle plate
19—Screw
20—Return spring
21—Lever spring

An exploded view of the throttle body of a Holley 4160 carburetor used on the 327 V8
(© Kaiser Willys Corp)

1—Lockscrew
2—Gasket
3—Adjustment nut
4—Gasket
5—Fuel inlet valve and seat
6—O-ring seal
7—Retainer
8—Air vent rod
9—Air vent valve
10—Baffle plate
11—Float and lever
12—Gasket
13—Idle mixture adjustment needle
14—Seal
15—Main metering body
16—Gasket
17—Power valve
18—Gasket
19—Main jet
20—Retainer
21—Float spring
22—Fuel inlet fitting
23—Gasket
24—Filter screen
25—Air vent rod spring
26—Retainer
27—Screw and lockwasher
28—Fuel pump cover
29—Diaphragm
30—Diaphragm return spring
31—Screw
32—Gasket
33—Fuel bowl body
34—Gasket
35—Fuel level sight plug

An exploded view of the fuel bowl and main metering body of a Holley 4160 carburetor used on the 327 V8
(© Kaiser Willys Corp)

pressed. Then turn the dashpot assembly 2½ turns against the throttle lever, depressing the dashpot plunger. Tighten he locknut.

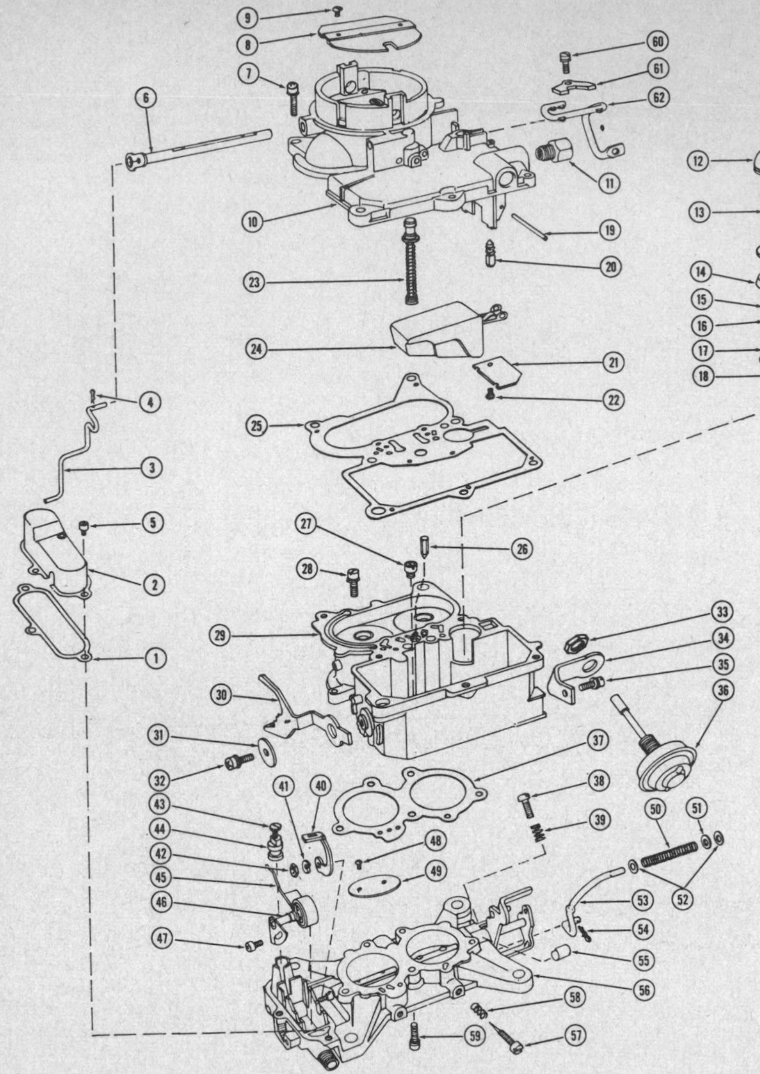

An exploded view of the Holley 2209 carburetor installed on the 327 V8 engine
(© Kaiser Willys Corp)

1—Thermostat housing cover gasket
2—Thermostat cover and guide assembly
3—Choke rod
4—Choke rod retainer
5—Thermostat housing cover screw
6—Choke shaft and lever assembly
7—Air horn-to-main body screw
8—Choke plate
9—Choke plate screw
10—Air horn and plugs assembly
11—Fuel inlet fitting
12—Acceleration pump stem seal
13—Acceleration pump assembly
14—Acceleration pump cup
15—Acceleration pump cup liner
16—Acceleration pump cup retainer
17—Acceleration pump return spring
18—Acceleration pump inlet valve
19—Float hinge pin
20—Fuel inlet needle assembly
21—Fuel bowl baffle
22—Fuel bowl baffle screw
23—Power valve piston assembly
24—Float assembly
25—Main body gasket
26—Pump discharge valve
27—Main jet
28—Throttle body-to-main body screw and lockwasher
29—Main body and plugs assembly
30—Fast idle cam
31—Fast idle cam washer
32—Fast idle cam screw
33—Dashpot nut
34—Dashpot bracket
35—Dashpot bracket screw and lockwasher
36—Dashpot assembly
37—Throttle body gasket
38—Throttle stop screw
39—Throttle stop screw spring
40—Fast idle and dechoke lever
41—Lockwasher
42—Nut
43—Choke piston screw
44—Choke piston
45—Choke piston link
46—Choke thermostat assembly
47—Choke thermostat assembly lock screw
48—Throttle plate screw
49—Throttle plate
50—Pump drive spring
51—Pump link washer
52—Pump drive spring retainer
53—Pump operating link
54—Pump operating link retainer
55—Throttle shaft bearing ribbon
56—Throttle body and shaft assembly
57—Idle adjusting needle
58—Idle adjusting needle spring
59—Throttle body to main body screw and lockwasher
60—Clamp retainer screw
61—Pump rod clamp
62—Pump rod

COOLING SYSTEM

Radiator Removal and Installation

1. Drain the radiator by opening the drain cock and removing the radiator pressure cap.
2. Remove the upper and lower hose clamps and hose at the radiator. On vehicles with an automatic transmission, disconnect the oil cooler lines. Plug the lines to prevent dirt from entering the transmission oil.
3. Remove the cap screws, lock washers, and flat washers that hold the radiator to the radiator support.
4. Remove the radiator.
5. Install the radiator in the reverse order of removal.

Water Pump Removal and Installation

F4

1. Drain the coolant from the system by opening the petcock.
2. Remove the fan belt, fan, and fan pulley.
3. Remove the bolts which attach the water pump to the block and remove the pump.
4. Install the pump in the reverse order of removal, using a new gasket.

225 V6

1. Drain the cooling system.
2. Remove the fan belt and the fan and pulley from the hub on the water pump.
3. Disconnect the hoses from the water pump.
4. Remove the capscrews which secure the water pump to the engine and remove the pump from the vehicle.
5. Clean all of the mating surfaces, install new gaskets with sealer applied and install the water pump in the reverse order of removal.

327 V8

1. Open the petcock and drain the radiator.
2. Remove the radiator fan shroud by removing the two attaching bolts and nuts.
3. Loosen the alternator at the support.
4. Remove the fan belt.
5. Remove the fan, fan hub, and the fan pulley which are attached by four capscrews and lockwashers.
6. Remove the four nuts and lockwashers from the water pump

mounting studs in the timing chain cover.
7. Remove the water pump and its gasket.
8. Install the water pump in the reverse order of removal, using a new gasket.

Thermostat Removal and Installation

F4

The thermostat is located in a housing on the top front of the cylinder head. To remove it, drain the cooling system, unscrew and remove the two bolts which hold the housing to the head, lift the housing, and remove the thermostat. Remove the gasket and replace it with a new one, installing the thermostat in the reverse order of removal.

225 V6

The thermostat is located in the thermostat housing of the intake manifold. Replace it as for the F4 engine.

327 V8

The thermostat is located in the water outlet manifold, enclosed by the thermostat housing. Remove it in the same manner as for the F4.

EMISSION CONTROLS

F4, 327 V8 and 225 V6

The F4, 327 V8 and 225 V6 have an AIR (air injection reactor) type exhaust emission control system along with a closed PCV (positive crankcase ventilation) system.

The AIR system consists of a belt driven air pump which directs compressed air through connecting hoses to a steel distribution manifold into stainless steel injection tubes in the exhaust port adjacent to each exhaust valve stem. This air, with its normal oxygen content, reacts with the hot but incompletely burned exhaust gases and permits further combustion in the exhaust port or manifold.

Between the air pump and the injection manifold on the F4, there is an anti-backfire diverter valve. The valve remains closed except when the throttle is closed rapidly from an open position. To check the valve for proper operation, remove the large hose that connects the check valve with the anti-backfire valve, accelerate the engine, and allow the throttle to close rapidly. If a momentary interuption of rushing air is audible, the valve is operating satisfactorily. The diverter valve diverts the air coming from the air pump into the atmosphere when sudden deceleration occurs. This prevents combustion from taking place in the exhaust manifold where it could do damage.

On the 327 V8 and 225 V6, there is an anti-backfire valve which is known as a gulp valve. It differs from the diverter valve in that when there is sudden deceleration, the gulp valve allows fresh air to be "gulped" into the intake manifold so that more complete combustion can take place.

ENGINE

Engine Removal and Installation

NOTE: This operation requires discharging the air conditioning system. This requires special tools and skills. For safety reasons, it should not be attempted by untrained persons.

F4

1. Drain the cooling system.
2. Disconnect the battery ground cable.
3. Remove the air cleaner and disconnect the breather hose at the oil filter.
4. Disconnect the choke and throttle controls.
5. Disconnect the fuel line and windshield wiper hose at the fuel pump.
6. Remove the radiator stay bar, if so equipped.
7. Remove the radiator and heater hoses.
8. Remove the fan blades, fan hub, radiator, and shroud.
9. Remove the starter motor.
10. Disconnect:
    a. The alternator or generator.
    b. The ignition primary wire at coil.
    c. The oil pressure and temperature sending units.
    d. The exhaust pipe from manifold.
    e. The engine ground strap.
11. Attach a lifting device to the engine. Unbolt and remove the front engine supports.
12. Remove the flywheel housing bolts.
13. Pull the engine forward until the clutch clears the flywheel housing. Lift the engine from the vehicle.
14. Install the engine by reversing the removal procedure.

V6

1. Remove the hood if necessary.
2. Disconnect the battery ground cable.
3. Remove the air cleaner.
4. Drain the coolant.
5. Disconnect the radiator hoses.
6. Remove the radiator support bars.
7. On the Universal series, remove the radiator. On the Jeepster series, disconnect the headlamp wiring from the block on the left fender, the horn wiring from the horn, the oil cooler lines if equipped with automatic transmission, and remove the front fenders, radiator, and grille as a unit.
8. Disconnect the engine wiring from the connectors on the firewall.
9. Remove the starter motor.
10. Disconnect the fuel hoses at the right frame rail. Plug the hoses.
11. Disconnect the throttle and choke.
12. Disconnect the exhaust pipes.
13. Place a jack under the transmission and support the weight.
14. Remove the front motor mount bolts.
15. Support the engine with a lifting device.
16. Remove the flywheel housing bolts.
17. Raise the engine slightly and slide the engine forward until the engine is free of the transmission shaft. Remove the engine.
18. Install in reverse order of the above procedure.

327 and 350 V8

1. Remove the hood.
2. Remove the air cleaner.
3. Drain the radiator and cylinder block.
4. Disconnect the radiator and heater hoses.
5. If equipped with an automatic transmission, disconnect the oil cooler lines at the radiator. Remove the radiator.
6. Remove the fan, belt, and hub.
7. Drain the engine oil and remove the filter.
8. Disconnect the temperature-sender lead, pressure-sender lead, coil, starter solenoid, and alternator and distributor leads.
9. Disconnect the accelerator cable at the carburetor throttle shaft lever and at the cable support bracket.
10. Disconnect the heater system vacuum valve hose at the intake manifold.
11. Disconnect the flexible fuel line from the frame-to-crankcase at the frame end. Plug the end of the hose.
12. Disconnect the exhaust pipes at both manifolds.
13. Remove the air conditioning compressor (if so equipped). Do not disconnect the hoses.
14. If equipped with a manual transmission, disconnect the linkage at the clutch. Disconnect the clutch cross-shaft support brackets at the flywheel housing and frame.
15. Install a suitable lifting fixture on the engine.
16. Support the transmission on a jack.
17. Remove the nuts from the engine-to-front support brackets.

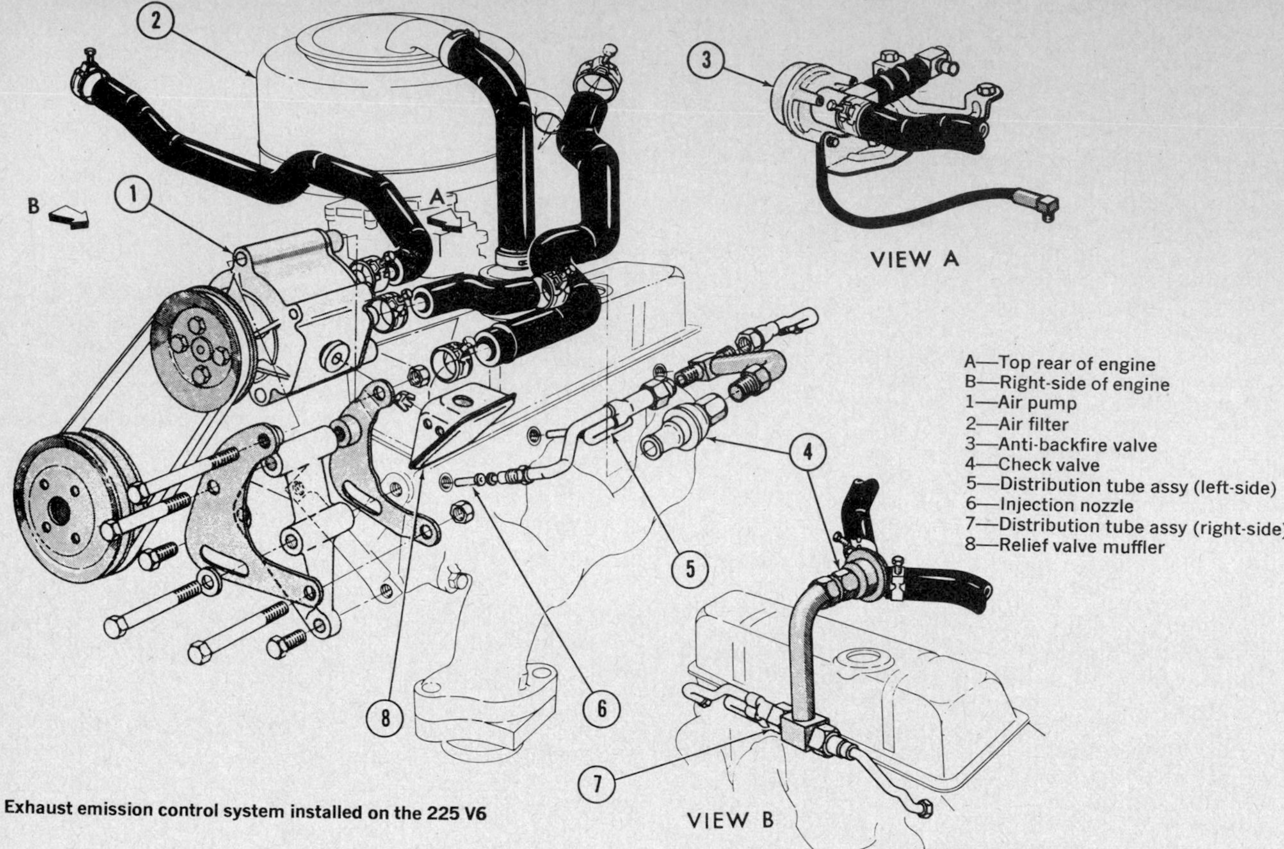

Exhaust emission control system installed on the 225 V6

18. With a manual transmission, remove the cap screws from the transmission-to-clutch housing. With an automatic transmission, remove the cap screws attaching the transmission housing-to-flywheel housing adaptor.
19. Pull the engine forward and upward until free from the transmission or clutch.
20. Install by reversing the removal procedure.

232, 258 OHV 6

NOTE: This operation requires discharging the air conditioning system. This requires special tools and skills for safety reasons. It should not be attempted by untrained persons.

1. Remove the hood after marking the hinge locations. The hood need not be removed on the CJ series.
2. Remove the air cleaner.
3. Drain the coolant. Disconnect the radiator hoses. Disconnect automatic transmission cooler lines from the radiator. If there is a radiator shroud, remove it, then remove the radiator.
4. Remove the fan.
5. Remove and set aside the power steering pump and belt. Do not disconnect the hydraulic lines.
6. Bleed the compressor refrigerant charge. See the note at the start of this procedure. Remove the condenser and receiver assembly.
7. Disconnect all wires, lines, linkage, and hoses from the engine.
8. Drain the oil and remove the filter.
9. Remove both engine front support cushion-to-frame retaining nuts.
10. Disconnect the exhaust pipe at the support bracket and the manifold.
11. Support the engine with the lifting equipment.
12. Remove the front support cushion and bracket assemblies from the engine.
13. Remove the transfer case lever boot, the floor mat, and the transmission access cover.
14. On automatic transmissions, remove the upper bolts holding the bellhousing to the engine adaptor plate. On manual transmissions, remove the upper bolts holding the clutch housing to the engine.
15. Remove the starter.
16. On automatics, remove the two adaptor plate inspection covers. Mark the relationship of the converter to the flex plate and remove the converter-to-flex plate bolts. Remove the rest of the bolts holding the bellhousing to the adaptor plate. On manual transmissions, remove the clutch housing lower cover and the rest of the bolts holding the clutch housing to the engine.
17. Support the transmission with a floor jack and remove the engine by pulling it forward and upward.

To install the engine:

18. Lower the engine into place and align it with the bellhousing or clutch housing. Make sure the manual transmission clutch shaft aligns with the splines of the clutch driven plate.
19. On automatics, install the bellhousing-to-engine adaptor plate bolts. On manuals, install the clutch housing-to-engine bolts. Torque the bolts to 25–28 ft lbs at the top and 40–45 ft lbs at the bottom.
20. Remove the floor jack.
21. Align the marks made in step 16 and install the converter-to-flex plate bolts, torquing them to 21–23 ft lbs.
22. Install the two engine adaptor plate inspection covers or the clutch housing lower cover.
23. Replace the starter.
24. Install the front support cushion and bracket assemblies to the engine, torquing the bolts to 25–30 ft lbs. Lower the engine onto the frame supports. Install the front support cushion retaining nuts, torquing them to 25–30 ft lbs.
25. Connect the exhaust pipe at the support bracket and manifold. A new manifold seal is advisable.
26. Install the oil filter.
27. Replace all the items removed in step seven.
28. Replace the air conditioning condenser and receiver assembly and recharge the system.
29. Replace the power steering pump

and belt. Install the fan and tighten the bolts to 15–25 ft lbs.

30. Replace and reconnect the radiator. Replace the oil cooler lines. Fill the cooling system.
31. Fill the crankcase and replace the air cleaner. Install the transmission access cover, floor mat, and transfer case lever boot. Replace the hood.

304, 360 and 401 V8

NOTE: This operation requires discharging the air conditioning system. This requires special tools and skills. For safety reasons, it should not be attempted by untrained persons.

The engine is removed without the transmission and bellhousing.

1. On the Commando, Cherokee, and Wagoneer, the hood must be removed. Mark the hinge locations at the hood panel for alignment during installation. Remove the hood from the hinges.
2. Remove the air cleaner assembly.
3. Drain the cooling system and disconnect the upper and lower radiator hoses. If equipped with automatic transmission, disconnect the cooler lines from the radiator.

NOTE: If the vehicle is equipped with a radiator shroud, it is necessary to separate the shroud from the radiator to facilitate removal and installation of the radiator and engine fan.

4. Remove the radiator.
5. Remove the engine fan.
6. If equipped with power steering, remove the pump from the engine and lay it aside. Do not disconnect the hoses.
7. If equipped with air conditioning, turn both service valves clockwise to the front seated position. Bleed the compressor refrigerant charge by slowly loosening the service valve fittings. Disconnect the condenser and evaporator lines from the compressor. Disconnect the receiver outlet at the disconnect coupling. Remove the condenser and receiver assembly.
8. Remove the battery and tray only if required.
9. On Wagoneers and Cherokees, remove the heater core housing and charcoal canister from the firewall.
10. Disconnect all wires, lines, linkage, and hoses which are connected to the engine.
11. If equipped with automatic transmission, disconnect the transmission filler tube bracket from the right cylinder head. Do not remove the filler tube from the transmission.
12. Remove both engine front support cushion-to-frame retaining nuts.
13. Support the weight of the engine with a lifting device.
14. On CJ and Commando models, remove the transfer case shift lever boot, floor (if so equipped), and transmission access cover.
15. Remove the upper bolts which secure the transmission bellhousing to the engine adapter plate on vehicles equipped with automatic transmission. If equipped with manual transmission, remove the upper bolts which secure the clutch housing to the engine.
16. Disconnect the exhaust pipes at the exhaust manifolds and support bracket.
17. Remove the starter motor.
18. Support the transmission with a floor jack.
19. If equipped with automatic transmission, remove the two engine adapter plate inspection covers. Mark the assembled position of the converter and flex plate and remove the converter-to-flex plate cap screws. Remove the remaining bolts which secure the transmission bellhousing to the engine adapter plate.
20. If equipped with manual transmission, remove the clutch housing lower cover and the remaining bolts which secure the clutch housing to the engine.
21. Remove the engine by pulling upward and forward.

NOTE: If equipped with power brakes, care must be taken to avoid damaging the power unit while removing the engine.

To install the engine:

22. Lower the engine slowly into the engine compartment and align with the transmission bellhousing (automatic transmission) or clutch housing (manual transmission). On manual transmissions, make certain the clutch shaft is aligned properly with the splines of the clutch driven plate.
23. Install the transmission bellhousing-to-engine adapter plate bolts (automatic transmission) or the clutch housing to engine bolts (manual transmission). Tighten the bolts to the specified torque. Remove the floor jack which was used to support the transmission.
24. If equipped with automatic transmission, align the marks previously made on the converter and flex plate, install the converter-to-flex plate cap screws and tighten to the specified torque.
25. Install the two engine adapter plate inspection covers (automatic transmission) or the clutch housing lower cover (manual transmission).
26. Install the starter motor.
27. Lower the engine onto the frame supports, remove the lifting device and install the front support cushion retaining nuts. Tighten the nuts to the specified torque.
28. Connect the exhaust pipes at the exhaust manifolds and support bracket.
29. If equipped with automatic transmission, connect the transmission filler tube bracket to the right cylinder head.
30. On Wagoneers and Cherokees, install the heater core housing and charcoal canister to the firewall.
31. If removed, install the battery and tray.
32. Connect all wires, lines, linkage and hoses which were previously disconnected from the engine.
33. If removed, install the air conditioning condenser and receiver assembly. Connect the receiver outlet to the disconnect coupling. Connect the condenser and evaporator lines to the compressor. Purge the compressor of air.

Caution Both service valves must be open before the air conditioning system is operated.

34. If equipped with power steering, connect the power steering pump to the engine.
35. Install the engine fan and tighten the retaining bolts to the specified torque.
36. Install the radiator and connect the upper and lower hoses. If equipped with automatic transmission, connect the cooler lines.
37. Fill the cooling system to the specified level.
38. Install the air cleaner assembly.
39. Start the engine. Check all connections for leaks. Stop the engine.
40. If removed, install and align the hood assembly.
41. If removed, install the transmission access cover, floor mat and transfer case shift lever boot.

Manifolds

F4

The intake manifold is cast as an integral part of the cylinder head.

The exhaust manifold is removed by removing the five nuts from the manifold studs, removing the two bolts that hold the manifold to the exhaust pipe, and lifting the manifold off of the mounting studs. Remove the center and two end gaskets from the cylinder block. Install in the reverse order of removal, using new gaskets.

NOTE: On engines with the AIR exhaust emission control devices, the rubber hose leading from the air pump to the air injection manifold must be disconnected in order to remove the exhaust manifold.

1—Gasket
2—Guide bolts

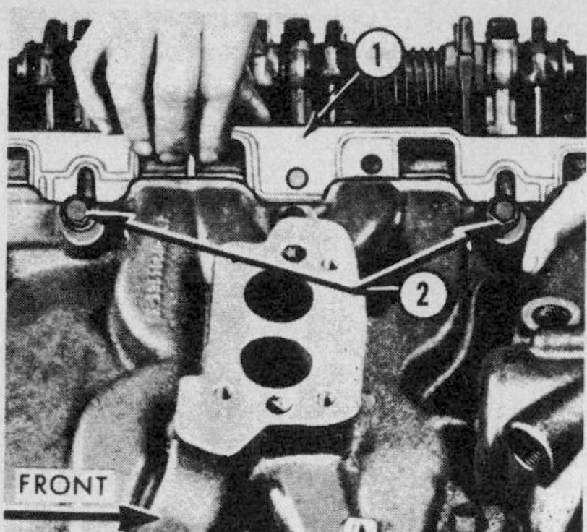

Installing the intake manifold-to-cylinder head gasket on the 225 V6

1—Long bolt
2—Open bolt hole

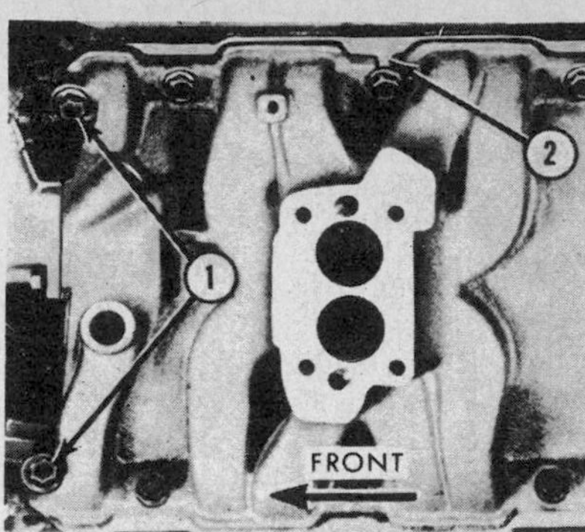

Installation and positioning of the intake manifold and attaching bolts on the 225 V6

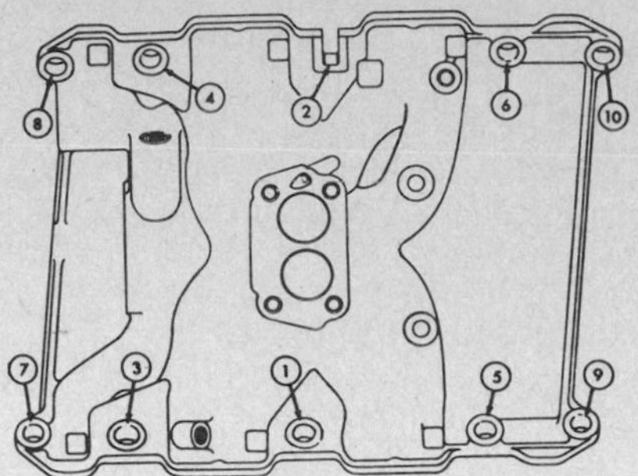

Intake manifold bolt tightening sequence—225 V6

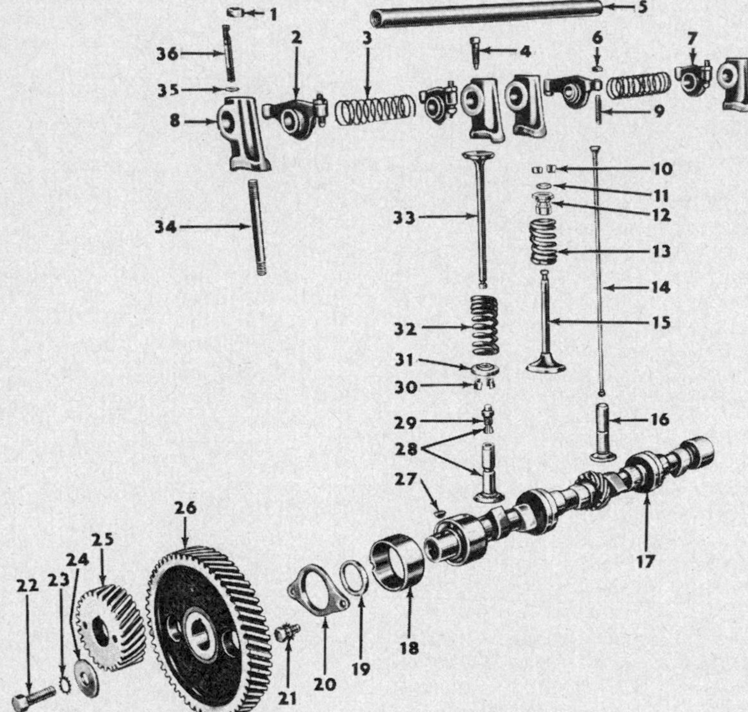

Valve system for the F-Head engine (© Kaiser Willys Corp)

1—Nut
2—Left rocker arm
3—Rocker arm shaft spring
4—Rocker shaft lock screw
5—Rocker shaft
6—Nut
7—Right rocker arm
8—Rocker arm shaft bracket
9—Intake valve tappet adjusting screw
10—Intake valve upper retainer lock
11—Oil seal
12—Intake valve spring upper retainer
13—Intake valve spring
14—Intake valve push rod
15—Intake valve
16—Intake valve tappet
17—Camshaft
18—Camshaft front bearing
19—Camshaft thrust plate spacer
20—Camshaft thrust plate
21—Bolt and lock washer
22—Bolt
23—Lock washer
24—Camshaft gear washer
25—Crankshaft gear
26—Camshaft gear
27—Woodruff key No. 9
28—Exhaust valve tappet
29—Tappet adjusting screw
30—Spring retainer lock
31—Roto cap assembly
32—Exhaust valve spring
33—Exhaust valve
34—Rocker shaft support stud
35—Washer
36—Rocker arm cover stud

Intake Manifold Removal and Installation

327 V8

1. Disconnect the water outlet tube and remove the distributor.
2. Take off the air cleaner.
3. Disconnect all throttle linkage at the carburetor.
4. Disconnect the vacuum lines, the coil, and the ignition primary leads.
5. Remove the bolts which hold the intake manifold to both the cylinder heads and lift off the manifold.
6. Remove all gaskets and replace with new ones.
7. Replace the intake manifold in the reverse order of removal.

225 V6

1. Disconnect the crankcase vent hose, exhaust manifold line, choke heat tube, distributor vacuum hose, and the fuel line at the carburetor.
2. Disconnect the two distributor leads from the ignition coil.
3. Disconnect the wiring harness from the coolant temperature sending unit.
4. Remove the 10 capbolts which attach the intake manifold to the cylinder heads.
5. Remove the intake manifold and carburetor as an assembly.
6. Clean all the mating surfaces of the intake manifold and cylinder heads, removing all traces of gasket material.
7. Install a new rubber intake manifold seal at the front and rear rails of the cylinder block. Be sure that the pointed ends of the seals fit snugly against the block and cylinder heads.
8. Set the intake manifold in place on the cylinder block between the cylinder heads. Thread two capbolts through the manifold into each cylinder head as guide bolts. Lift the manifold slightly and insert each of the two gaskets into position between the manifold and corresponding cylinder head. Be certain that the gasket is installed with its 3 apertures aligned with the ports of the head and manifold. One gasket should be installed in position on the right-side and the other gasket reversed and installed on the left-side.
9. Install the manifold attaching bolt in the open bolt hole at the right center side of the intake manifold. During manufacture, this open bolt hole is held to close tolerances so that the bolt in this location serves to locate the manifold front and rear.
10. Install the remaining intake

manifold attaching bolts. The longer bolts are installed in the two forward holes on either side.

11. Tighten the intake manifold bolts to the proper torque in the proper sequence.
12. Assemble the remaining components to the engine in the reverse order of removal.

Exhaust Manifold Removal and Installation

225 V6 and 327 V8

Disconnect the exhaust pipe at the flange, remove the bolts which hold the manifold to the cylinder head, and lift off the manifold.

Install in the reverse order of removal.

Valve System

F4

The intake valves are located in the cylinder head and are operated by the gear driven camshaft through push rods and rocker arms. The exhaust valves are located in the block, stems down, and are operated directly by the tappets. The intake valves are adjusted by adjusting nuts on the rocker arms and the exhaust valves are adjusted by adjusting screws on the tappets. Both the intake and exhaust valve guides are replaceable.

225 V6 and 327 V8

The valve arrangement is an overhead type operated by a camshaft through pushrods and rocker arms. The valves are not adjustable. The valve guides are replaceable.

Rocker Arm Shaft Removal and Installation

1. Remove the cap screws which hold the valve cover in place and remove the valve cover and the gasket.
2. On the F4, remove the nuts which hold the rocker arm shaft to the mounting studs and lift off the rocker arm shaft. On the 327 V8 and 225 V6, remove the rocker arm retaining cap screws and remove, the rocker arm shafts.
3. If the pushrods are removed, replace them in the same positions from which they were removed.
4. Install the rocker arm shafts in the reverse order of removal, using a new gasket under the valve covers.

Valve Adjustment

Only the F4 engine requires periodic valve adjustments. All the others have self-adjusting hydraulic lifters. Valve clearance can be properly adjusted only when the lifter is on the heel or low portion of the cam. The exhaust valves (in the block) are adjusted by turning the adjusting screw in or out of the lifter to obtain the proper clearance between the end of the adjusting screw and the stem of the valve. The intake valves (in the head) are adjusted by turning the rocker arm screw at the pushrod end to obtain the proper clearance between the rocker arm and the valve stem. The engine must be cold for proper valve adjustment.

Cylinder Head

Cylinder Head Removal and Installation

F4

1. Drain the coolant.
2. Remove the upper radiator hose. Remove the carburetor.
3. On early engines, remove the bypass hose from the front of the cylinder head.
4. Remove the rocker arm cover.
5. Disconnect the oil line.
6. Remove the rocker arm attaching stud nuts and rocker arm shaft assembly.
7. Remove the cylinder head bolts. One head bolt is located below the carburetor mounting, inside the intake manifold.
8. Lift off the cylinder head.
9. Remove the pushrods and valve lifters.
10. Reverse the procedure for installation.

225 V6

1. Remove the intake manifold.
2. Remove the rocker cover.
3. Remove the exhaust pipes at the flanges.
4. Remove the alternator in order to remove the right head.
5. Remove the dipstick and power steering pump, if so equipped, in order to remove the left head.
6. Remove the valve cover and the rocker assemblies. Mark these parts so that they can be reinstalled in exactly the same positions.
7. Unbolt the head bolts and lift off the cylinder head(s). It is very important that the inside of the engine be protected from dirt. The hydraulic lifters are particularly susceptible to being damaged by dirt.
8. To install, use the reverse procedure.

327 V8

The cylinder heads have two holes to assist head location. Maximum out-of-true is 0.006 in. for the entire length of head; 0.001 in. every 1 in. Make sure the rear rocker arm bolts are properly installed, otherwise no oil will get to the rockers.

1. Remove the oil filler tube, rocker covers, power steering pump, alternator, exhaust manifolds, and air conditioner. Swing the air conditioner out of the way without disconnecting its hoses.
2. Remove the rockers and pushrods.
3. Disconnect the water hoses, fuel lines, wiring, vacuum lines; remove the distributor and intake manifold.
4. Remove the cylinder head bolts and lift off the heads carefully, making sure all ground straps, etc. have been disconnected.

There are two locating dowels on the cylinder block to assist in gasket alignment during installation. Apply a commercial sealing compound to both sides of the head gasket. The word "top" and "A.M." should always face upward when installing the gasket. Tighten the head bolts to 58-62 ft lbs in three steps in the sequence illustrated. The rest of installation is the reverse of removal.

Timing Cover, Gear/Chain, and Camshaft

Timing Cover Removal and Installation

F4

1. To remove the timing gear cover, it is necessary to remove the radiator, fan, and the pulleys.
2. Remove the bolts, nuts, and lockwashers from the timing gear cover.
3. Remove the cover, timing pointer, and cover gasket from the engine. Discard the gasket.
4. Install in the reverse order of removal, using a new cover gasket.

225 V6

1. Remove the water pump and crankshaft pulley.
2. Remove the two bolts which attach the oil pan to the timing chain cover.
3. Remove the 5 bolts which attach the timing chain cover to the engine block.
4. Remove the cover and gasket.
5. Install the front cover in the reverse order of removal, using new gaskets.

327 V8

The timing chain cover on the 327 V8 is a cast iron affair that contains the water pump. Remove the timing chain cover as follows:

1. Drain the cooling system and remove the radiator and shroud. Remove the fan and pulley.
2. Remove the nut which secures the vibration damper to the crankshaft and remove the damper. Use a new cork washer when reinstalling the vibration damper.
3. Remove the heater hose from the hose adapter going into the housing.
4. Unscrew the cap screws which

hold the timing chain cover to the block.
5. Remove the cover and gasket.
6. Replace in the reverse order of removal, using a new gasket.

Timing Gear Cover Oil Seal Removal and Installation

F4

1. The timing gear cover has to be removed from the engine to replace the oil seal.
2. Pry out the old seal with a screwdriver.
3. Install the new seal by tapping it gently into place.
4. Install the timing gear cover in the reverse order of removal, using a new gasket.

225 V6

1. Remove the timing chain cover.
2. Remove the crankshaft front oil seal.
3. From the rear of the timing chain cover, coil new packing around the crankshaft hole in the cover so that the ends of the packing are at the top. Drive in the new packing with a punch. It will be necessary to ream out the hole to obtain clearance for the crankshaft vibration damper hub.
4. Assemble the timing chain cover to the engine in the reverse order of removal.

327 V8

The timing chain cover oil seal can be replaced without removing the whole cover assembly from the engine. This is accomplished through the use of a special threaded tool that fits over the crankshaft and threads the seal onto it. When the tool is pushed down against the crankshaft, the seal pops out. The new seal is placed over the crankshaft, into position, and then tapped into place.

If the tool is not available, the timing chain cover has to be removed and the seal replaced in the manner outlined for the F4.

Timing Gear/Chain Removal and Installation

F4

1. Remove the timing gear cover.
2. Remove the oil slinger and spacer from the crankshaft.
3. Using a gear puller, remove the timing gears and the woodruff keys.
4. Install the gears in the reverse order of removal, lining up the alignment marks on both gears and using a new cover gasket.

225 V6

1. Remove the timing chain cover.
2. Make sure that the timing marks on the crankshaft and the camshaft sprockets are aligned. This will make installing the parts easier.

NOTE: It is not necessary to remove the timing chain dampers (tensioners) unless they are worn or damaged and require replacement.

3. Remove the front crankshaft oil slinger.
4. Remove the bolt and the special washer that hold the camshaft distributor drive gear and fuel pump eccentric at the forward end of the camshaft. Remove the eccentric and the gear from the camshaft.
5. Alternately pry forward the camshaft sprocket and then the crankshaft sprocket until the camshaft sprocket is pried from the camshaft.
6. Remove the camshaft sprocket, sprocket key, and timing chain from the engine.
7. Pry the crankshaft sprocket from the crankshaft.

Install as follows:

1. If the engine has not been disturbed proceed to Step 4 for installation procedures.
2. If the engine has been disturbed turn the crankshaft so that No. 1 piston is at top dead center.
3. Temporarily install the sprocket key and the camshaft sprocket on the camshaft. Turn the camshaft so that the index mark of the sprocket is downward. Remove the key and sprocket from the camshaft.
4. Assemble the timing chain and sprockets. Install the keys, sprockets, and chain assembly on the camshaft and crankshaft so that the index marks of both the sprockets are aligned.

NOTE: It will be necessary to hold the spring loaded timing chain damper out of the way while installing the timing chain and sprocket assembly.

5. Install the front oil slinger on the crankshaft with the inside diameter against the sprocket (concave side toward the front of the engine).
6. Install the fuel pump eccentric on the camshaft and the key, with the oil groove of the eccentric forward.
7. Install the distributor drive gear on the camshaft. Secure the gear and eccentric to the camshaft with the retaining washer and bolt.
8. Torque the bolt to 40-55 ft lbs.

327 V8

To remove the timing chain, the fuel pump has to be removed.

1. Remove the timing chain cover and gasket.
2. Remove the crankshaft oil slinger from the crankshaft.
3. Remove the fuel pump eccentric from the face of the camshaft sprocket by removing the retain-

1—Puller
2—Camshaft gear

Removing the timing gears with a gear puller on the F-Head engine (© Kaiser Willys Corp)

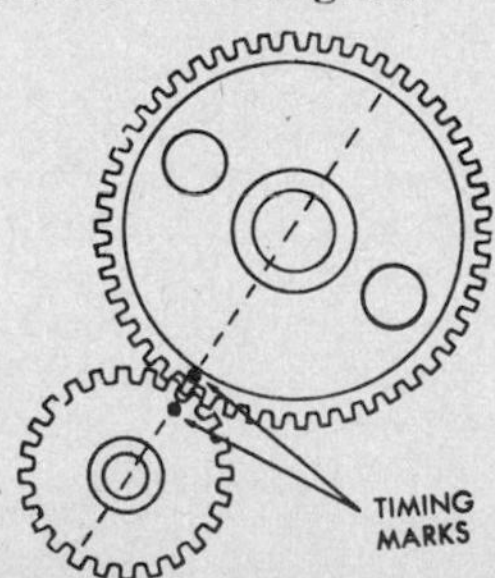

Alignment of the timing marks on the timing gears of the F-Head engine (© Willys Corp)

1—Camshaft sprocket timing mark
2—Crankshaft sprocket timing mark

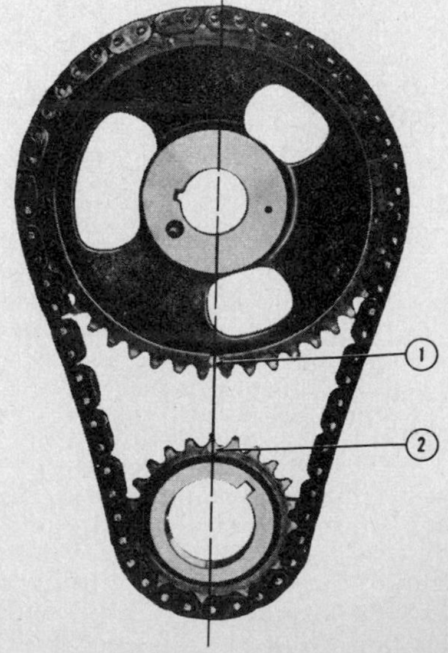

Timing chain sprocket alignment marks (© Kaiser Willys Corp)

ing bolt, lockwasher, and flat washer.

4. Pry the camshaft sprocket and crankshaft sprocket forward a little at a time until the camshaft sprocket is free of the camshaft.
5. Remove the timing chain from both sprockets.
6. Continue prying the crankshaft sprocket forward until it is free from the crankshaft.
7. Install the timing chain and sprockets in the reverse order of removal, making sure that the alignment marks on the sprockets are aligned.

Camshaft Removal and Installation

F4

1. Remove the timing gear cover, the timing gears, and the camshaft thrust plate.
2. Remove the cylinder head, pushrods, and exhaust valves.
3. Remove the distributor and the oil pump.
4. Lift the valve tappets off of the camshaft and use common, clip type clothes pins on the shank of each lifter to hold them up off of the camshaft.
5. Remove the camshaft thrust plate attaching screws and remove the thrust plate and spacer.
6. Pull the camshaft forward out of the cylinder block, using care to prevent damage to the bearing surfaces.
7. Before installing the camshaft, lubricate it generously with clean engine oil.
8. Carefully slide the camshaft into place. Do not allow the rear of the camshaft to strike sharply against the expansion plug installed in the rear end of the bore.
9. Install the camshaft thrust plate. Slide the thrust plate spacer onto the end of the camshaft with the beveled inner edge of the spacer facing the camshaft.
10. Install the timing gears.
11. Turn the crankshaft until the marks on the timing gears are aligned.
12. With a new gasket installed, and the wider side of the shaft on top (nearer the top of the cylinder block) insert the oil pump into the opening on the left side of the block.
13. Insert a long bladed screwdriver into the distributor hole and engage the slot in the end of the oil pump shaft. Turn the shaft until the slot is positioned at what would be roughly the nine-thirty position on a clock face.
14. Remove the screwdriver and, looking down into the distributor hole, observe the position of the slot in the end of the oil pump shaft to make certain it is properly positioned.
15. Replace the screwdriver and, while turning the screwdriver clockwise to guide the oil pump driveshaft gear into engagement with the camshaft gear, press against the oil pump to force it into place.
16. Remove the screwdriver and again observe the position of the slot. If the installation was properly made, the slot will be in a position roughly equivalent to 11 o'clock on a clock face with the wider side of the shaft still on the top. If the slot is improperly positioned, remove the oil pump assembly and repeat the operation.
17. Replace the oil pump attaching screws.
18. Replace the distributor, the valves, and the cylinder head.
19. Replace the timing gear cover.

225 V6

1. Remove the engine.
2. Remove the intake manifold and carburetor assembly.
3. Remove the distributor.
4. Remove the fuel pump.
5. Remove the alternator, drive belts, cooling fan, fan pulley, and water pump.
6. Remove the crankshaft pulley and the vibration damper.
7. Remove the oil pump.
8. Remove the timing chain cover.
9. Remove the timing chain and the camshaft sprocket, along with the distributor drive gear and the fuel pump eccentric.
10. Remove the rocker arm assemblies.

NOTE: The pushrods need not be removed. But if they are, be sure that they are replaced in their original positions.

11. Lift the tappets up so that they are not in contact with the camshaft. Use wire clips or clip-type clothes pins to hold the tappets up.
12. Carefully guide the camshaft forward out of the engine. Avoid marring the bearing surfaces.
13. Install in reverse order of the above procedure.

327 V8

1. Detach the battery cable.
2. Drain the radiator and both banks of the cylinder block. Remove the radiator, the hoses, and the thermostat housing.
3. Remove the distributor, complete with spark plug wires and the coil, from the intake manifold.
4. Remove the intake manifold as a complete assembly.
5. Take off the valve cover and take out the valve train, including the hydraulic tappets.

NOTE: Keep the valve train components in proper order. They must be returned to their original place during assembly.

6. Remove the power steering pump from its bracket, without disconnecting the hoses. Set it out of the way.
7. Remove the fan assembly and then the fuel pump. Unfasten the heater hose at the water pump.
8. Unbolt the alternator bracket and set it out of the way, complete with the alternator. Do not disconnect the alternator wiring.
9. Remove the crankshaft pulley and the vibration damper.
10. Remove the water pump and the cylinder head water distribution manifold.
11. With the timing marks in vertical alignment, remove the front cover, distributor/oil pump drive gear, fuel pump eccentric, sprockets, and the timing chain.
12. Unfasten the hood latch upper support bracket attachment screws. Move the bracket, as necessary, to permit withdrawal of the camshaft.
13. Use care during camshaft removal, so that the journal bearings are not damaged.
14. Inspect all parts for wear and damage. Replace them as required.

Installation of the cam is the reverse of removal. Install the timing chain and cover as outlined above. Adjust the belt tension and fill up the cooling system.

NOTE: Lubricate the camshaft, tappets, and the valve train with a suitable engine oil supplement. Add the remaining supplement to the crankcase, and leave it in the engine for at least the first 1000 miles. It does not require draining until the next regular oil change.

Piston Removal

F4

1. Remove the cylinder head and the oil pan.
2. Remove the ridge from the tops of the cylinder bores, using a ridge reamer.
3. Remove the oil pan and, one at a time, remove the connecting rod caps and push the piston assemblies out the top of the block. Number all pistons, connecting rods, and caps on removal.

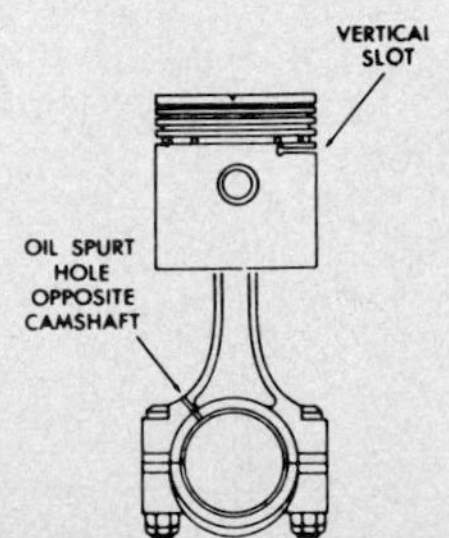

Piston to rod assembly of the F-Head engine

4. Remove the old rings with a ring expander.
5. Release the piston pin lockscrews and force out the pins.
6. Check the cylinder bores for distortion, taper, and other evidence of excessive wear. Bore and hone as necessary.

225 V6

1. Remove the intake manifold, cylinder head (s) and the oil pan.
2. Examine the cylinder bores. If the bores are worn so that a shoulder or ridge exists at the top of the piston ring travel, remove the ridges with a ridge reamer.
3. Mark the cylinder number on all of the pistons, connecting rods and caps. Starting at the front end of the crankcase, the cylinders in the right bank are numbered 2-4-6, and in the left bank are numbered 1-3-5.
4. Remove the cap and lower connecting rod bearing half from the No. 1 connecting rod.
5. Push the piston and the rod assembly up and away from the crankshaft and remove it from the top of the cylinder bore. Install the cap and the lower bearing half on the connecting rod to avoid mixing the parts.
6. Remove each of the connecting rod and piston assemblies as described above.

327 V8

1. Drain the cooling system and remove the cylinder head assembly as outlined in the applicable section above.
2. Use a ridge reamer to remove the ridge at the top of the cylinder wall. Each cylinder must be done separately with the piston at the bottom of its stroke.
3. Drain the oil and remove the oil pan.
4. Remove the connecting rod bearing caps and inserts from below.

NOTE: The rods and caps have the number of the cylinder to which they were assembled stamped on them. It is important that they be kept in the order in which they were removed.

5. Withdraw the piston and connecting rod assemblies through the *top* of the cylinder bore. Use care not to scratch the connecting rod journals or the cylinder walls with the rod bolts.

Piston Ring Replacement

F4

When new rings are installed without reboring the cylinders, the cylinder wall glaze should be broken by honing.

New piston rings should be checked for end-gap and clearance in the cylinder bores and ring grooves. When fitting new rings, compression ring side-clearance should be no more than 0.006 in. for four-cylinder engines. Any clearance greater than this indicates a need for a new piston. End-gap of compression rings is checked by pushing the ring to the bottom of the bore in which it will operate. Compression ring end-gap should be at least 0.007 in. for four-cylinder engines.

Piston pins should be a push-fit. If they are excessively loose, the piston must be replaced.

When assembling the rod and piston assemblies to the four-cylinder engine, the T-slot in the piston should be on the left side. The oil spurt hole should face to the right, away from the camshaft and the T-slot.

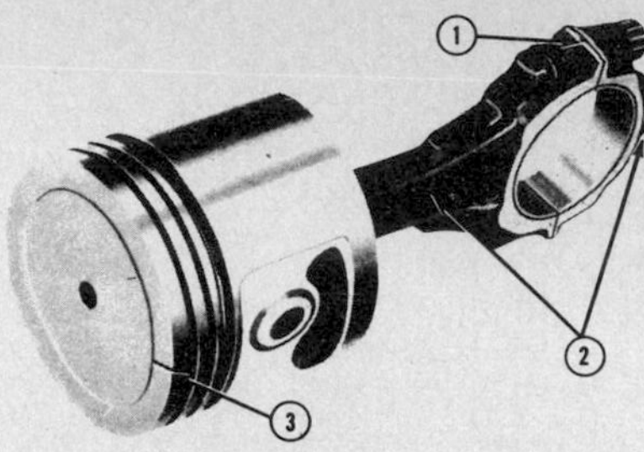

Piston and rod assembly for the right bank in the 225 V6

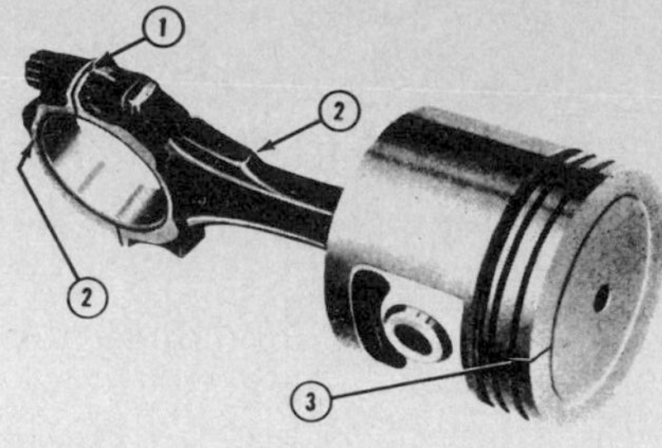

Piston and rod assembly for the left bank in the 225 V6

225 V6

When new piston rings are to be installed without reboring the cylinders, the cylinder wall glaze should be removed by honing.

New compression rings should be checked for the correct gap in the cylinders and for side clearance on the pistons. The flexible oil rings are not checked for gap. Make sure that the cylinder bores and piston ring grooves are clean, dry, and free of carbon and burrs.

Check the piston for ring groove wear at the inner portion of the lower land of the groove. Wear takes place in the form of a step on the lower land of the ring groove. If the piston grooves have worn enough that relatively high steps exist on the lower lands, the piston should be replaced because the steps will interfere with the proper operation of the new rings and the ring clearances will be excessive.

Install the piston rings onto the piston, using a ring expander. Install the oil control ring rail spacer and the oil ring rails first, in that order, in the bottom groove of the piston. The gap of the oil control ring assembly is positioned toward the center of the engine when assembled on the piston and installed in the engine block. Install the compression rings in the two upper grooves. If a single chrome-plated compression ring is used, the chrome ring must be installed in the top groove.

All compression rings are marked with a dimple, a letter "T", a letter "O", or the word "TOP" to identify the side of the ring which must face toward the top of the piston.

327 V8

1. Clean the carbon from the oil ring grooves, the oil drain openings and the pin boss. Use care not to remove any metal from the ring grooves or lands, as this will change clearance.
2. Measure the ring clearances and the cylinder bore taper.
3. Remove the glaze from the cylinder bore wall with an *expanding* hone. Ten strokes (down and return) are sufficient to clean the walls; more than ten will change clearances.

Caution Never use a rigid hone to remove cylinder glaze; it will destroy cylinder taper.

4. Install the oil control rings on the pistons, first. Then install the compression rings with the top side (which is marked) up. Use a ring tool on the compression ring to prevent distortion and breakage.

Piston rings should be arranged with the end gaps 120° apart, with no gap being placed over the pin boss.

Piston Replacement

F4

1. Assemble the piston to the rod by pushing in and locking the pin.
2. Using a ring expander, install the piston rings. Install the bottom (oil) ring first, center ring second, and top ring last.
3. Coat all the bearing surfaces and rings, and the piston skirt, with engine oil.
4. Turn down the crankpin of the cylinder being worked on.
5. Make sure that the gaps in the rings are not in line.
6. Using a ring compressor, install the piston and rod assembly into the cylinder and carefully tap down until the rod bearing is solidly seated on the crankpin.
7. Install the cap and lower bearing

Installation of the piston in the 327 V8; notches and "F" face toward the front of the engine

shell. Torque to the specified figure.

8. Install all piston assemblies in the same manner.
9. Install the cylinder head and oil pan.

225 V6

1. When the piston and connecting rod assembly is properly installed, the oil spurt hole in the connecting rod will face the camshaft. The rib on the edge of the bearing cap will be on the same side as the conical boss on the connecting rod web. These marks on the rib and boss will be toward the other connecting rod on the same crankpin. The notch on the piston will face the front of the engine.
2. Be certain that the cylinder bores, pistons, connecting rod bearings and crankshaft journals are clean. Coat all the bearing surfaces with engine oil.
3. Before installing a piston and connecting rod assembly into its bore, rotate the crankshaft so that the corresponding crankpin is moved downward, away from the cylinder bore.
4. Remove the bearing cap from the connecting rod. With the upper bearing half seated in the connecting rod, install connecting rod guides on the cap bolts. Lengths of rubber hose covering the bolts do a good job.
5. Be sure that the gap in the oil ring faces upward toward the center of the engine. The gaps of the compression rings are not to be aligned with each other or with the oil ring gap.
6. Lubricate the piston and rings with engine oil. Compress the rings around the piston with a suitable ring compressor. Install the piston and connecting rod assembly from the top of the cylinder bore.
7. Install the connecting rod bearing cap with the lower half of the bearing shell in place on the

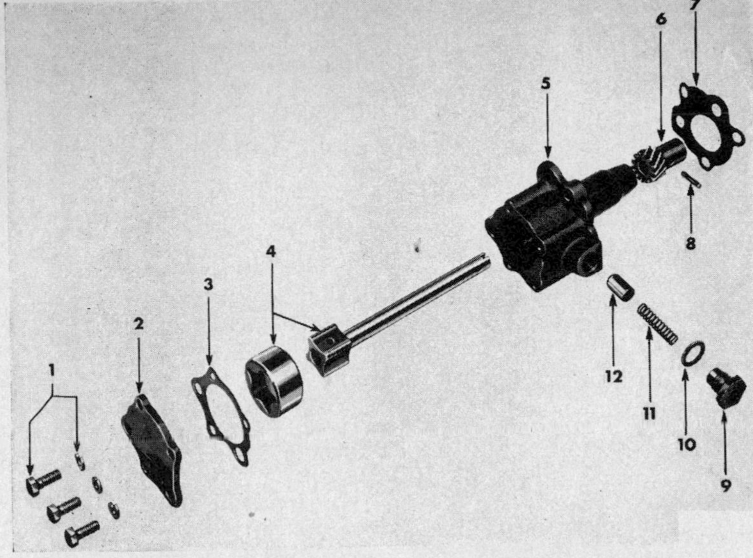

1—Cover screw
2—Cover
3—Cover gasket
4—Shaft and rotors
5—Body assembly
6—Driven gear
7—Pump gasket
8—Gear retaining pin
9—Relief valve retainer
10—Relief valve retainer gasket
11—Relief valve spring
12—Relief valve plunger

An exploded view of an F-Head engine oil pump (© Kaiser Willys Corp)

Checking the clearance between the rotors of an F-Head engine oil pump (© Kaiser Willys Corp)

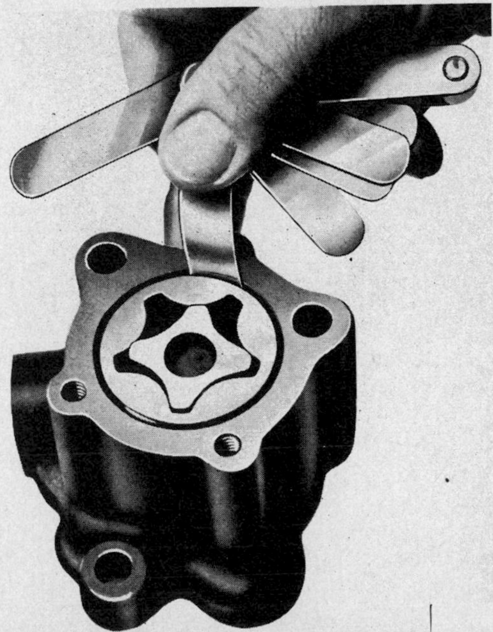

Checking the clearance between the outer rotor and the housing of an F-Head engine oil pump (© Kaiser Willys Corp)

connecting rod. Tighten the nuts to the proper torque.

8. Install the other piston and connecting rod assemblies in the same manner.
9. Check the end clearance between the connecting rods on each crankpin with a feeler gauge.
10. Assemble the oil pan, cylinder head(s) and intake manifold in the reverse order of removal.

327 V8

On engines using split-skirt pistons, the slit in the skirt must be installed opposite the oil squirt hole in the connecting rod. Solid skirt pistons are assembled so that the boss, or dimple, (and, in some instances, the letter F) at the top of the piston is on the same side of the connecting rod as the boss. This will be found on the connecting rod channel about halfway up the rod.

The piston and rod assemblies are united to the engine from the top and the dimple, or dot, on the top of the piston goes toward the front. On those engines having split-skirt pistons, the slit in the skirt of the piston goes to the left side of the engine.

Piston pins are a press fit in the connecting rod, hand fit in the piston at 68°F. Before assembly, clean the ring grooves using a broken ring or commercial groove cleaner. Piston-to-cylinder bore clearance at top land should be 0.028-0.032 in.; at skirt top 0.0009-0.0025 in.; at skirt bottom 0.0009-0.0015 in.

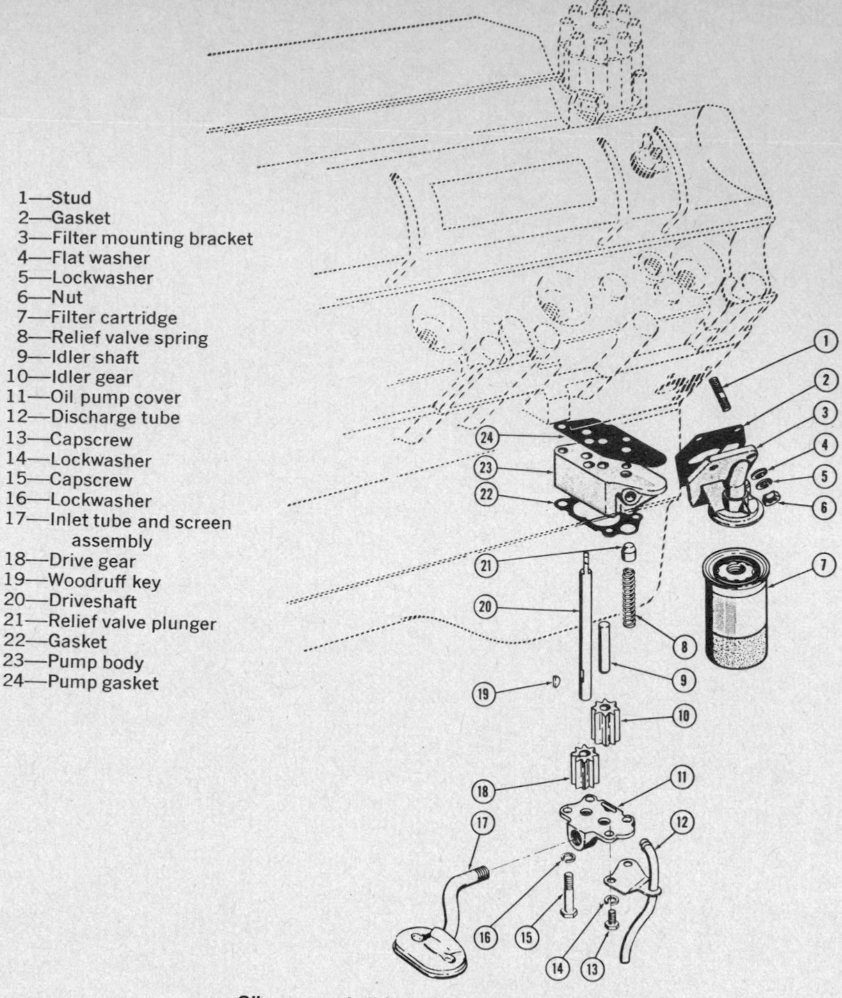

Oil pump and oil filter assembly on the 327 V8
(© Kaiser Willys Corp)

Lubrication System

Oil Pan Removal and Installation

Due to the variety of engines used in Jeep vehicles, oil pan removal and installation procedures range from simply removing the attaching bolts to removing the front end components for access. On the Commando and CJ series with the 232 or 258 OHV 6, the engine right support must be unbolted from the block and the engine raised by means of a jack under the bellhousing.

Oil Pump Removal and Installation

F4

1. Set No. 1 piston at TDC for reference for reinstalling the oil pump without greatly disturbing the ignition timing.
2. Remove the distributor cap and note the position of the distributor rotor. If the distributor is already removed, sight through the distributor hole before removing the oil pump. The slot should be near the vertical position.
3. Remove the capscrews and lockwashers which attach the oil pump to the engine.
4. Carefully slide the oil pump and its drive shaft out of the cylinder block.
5. Check the clearance between the lobes of the rotors: it should be 0.010 in. Check the clearance between the outer rotor and the pump housing; it should be 0.012 in.
6. Remove the gasket, clean the mating surfaces, and install a new gasket.
7. If the distributor was left in the engine and was not disturbed, install the oil pump, engaging the distributor shaft without disturbing the position of the rotor. If the distributor was removed along with the oil pump, refer to the "Camshaft Removal and Installation" procedure for exact details on installing the oil pump and distributor.

225 V6

1. Remove the oil filter.
2. Disconnect the lead from the oil pressure indicator switch in the filter by-pass valve cap.
3. Remove the screws which attach the oil pump cover assembly to the timing chain cover.
4. Remove the cover assembly and slide out the oil pump.
5. Install the oil pump in the reverse order of removal. Replenish the crankcase oil supply to the proper level.

327 V8

The oil pump is driven by the distributor drive shaft. Oil pump removal and installation does not, however, affect distributor timing because the drive gear remains in mesh with the camshaft gear.

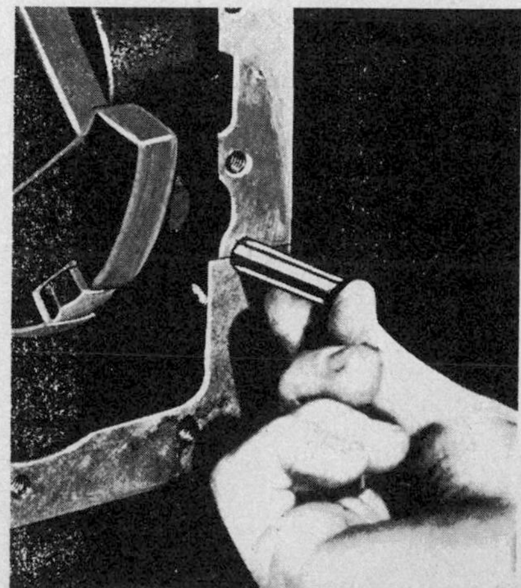

Installing the rear main bearing cap side packing

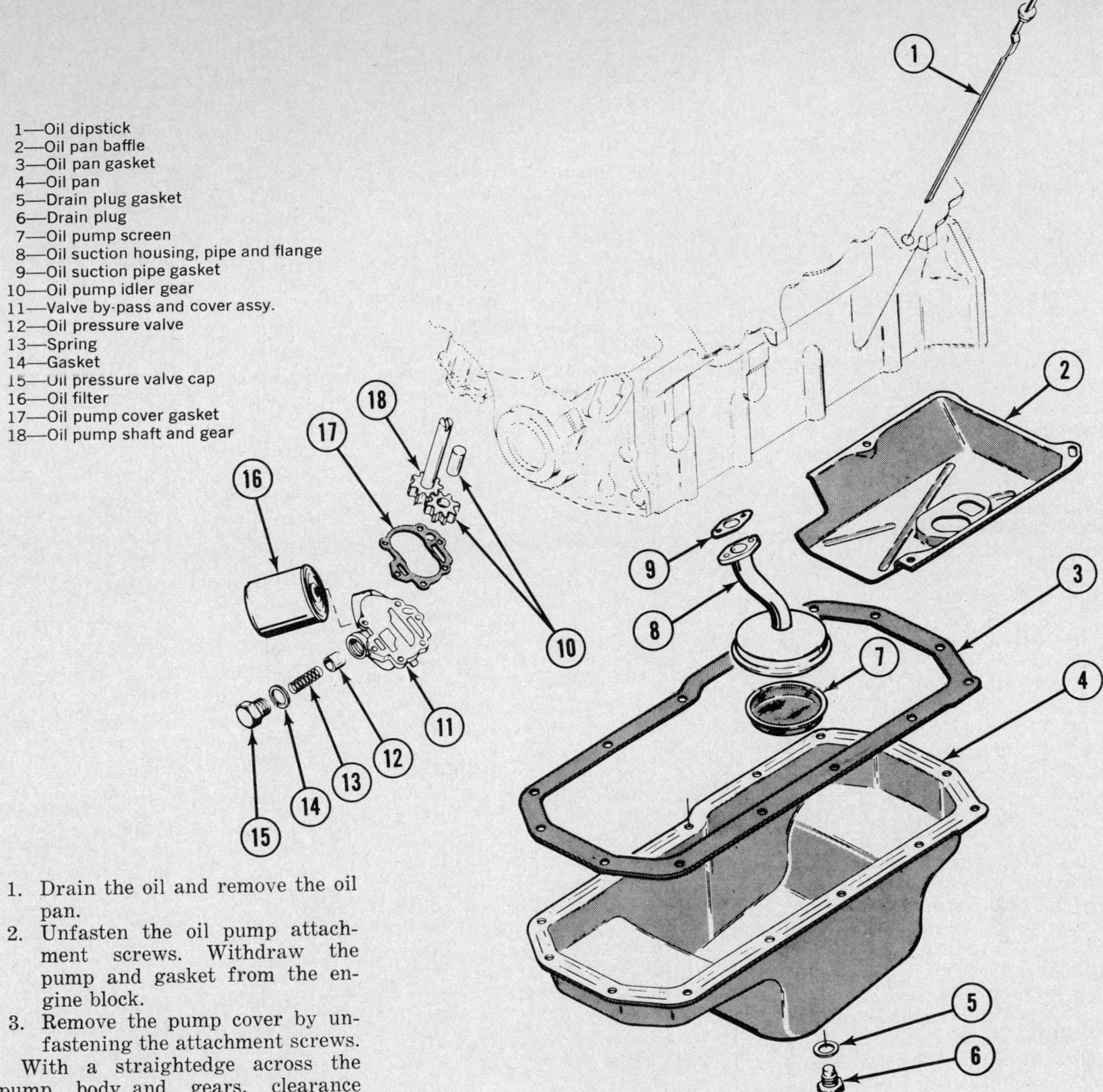

Oil pump and pan assemblies on the 225 V6

1. Drain the oil and remove the oil pan.
2. Unfasten the oil pump attachment screws. Withdraw the pump and gasket from the engine block.
3. Remove the pump cover by unfastening the attachment screws.

With a straightedge across the pump body and gears, clearance should be 0.000-0.004 in. (gears should project above body). Do not disturb the location of the tube in the pump body if possible. Now, measure the clearance between gears and wall of gear cavity opposite point of gear mesh; should be 0.008 in. The oil pressure relief valve is set at the factory to 60 psi and is not adjustable.

Installation is the reverse of removal.

Rear Main Seal Removal and Installation

F4

1. Drain the oil from the engine and remove the oil pan.
2. Remove the screws and lockwashers that attach the rear main bearing cap to the cylinder block.
3. Remove the bearing cap with a lifting bar to pry the cap off of the mounting dowels. Do not apply too much pressure to the cap. Lift the cap off a little at a time from one side to the other until the cap is removed.
4. Remove the two pieces of rear main bearing cap packing out of position between the side of the bearing cap and the cylinder block.
5. Remove the lower half of the oil seal from the bearing cap and install a new half.

NOTE: Coat the seal with oil to facilitate installation.

6. Remove the upper half of the seal by pushing it out with a suitable tool.
7. Coat the new seal with oil and, using a wire to pull it around the crankshaft, install the new upper half of the seal.

NOTE: For better sealing, make the joints of the seal off-set from the joints of the rear main bearing cap and the cylinder block.

8. Reinstall the bearing cap, being careful not to bend the dowel pins and making sure that the seal is inserted correctly. Tighten to the correct torque.
9. Apply a small amount of plastic type gasket cement to the rubber packings to be inserted into the holes between the bearing cap and the crankcase. Insert the packings in these holes. Do not trim the packings. They are trimmed to the correct length at the time of manufacture. They will protrude about 1/4 in. from the crankcase. When the oil pan is installed, it will force them

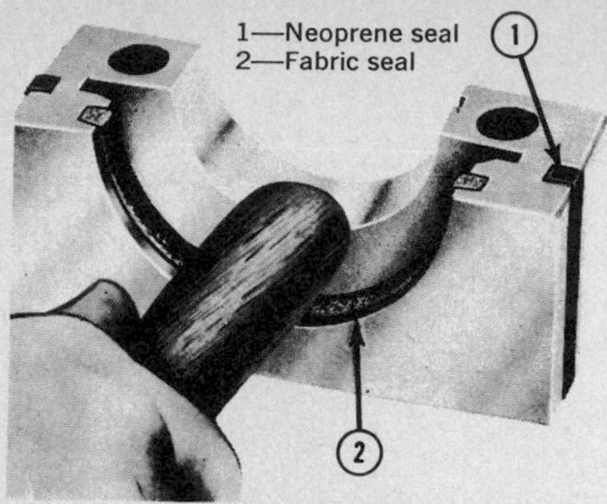

Installing the packing in the rear main oil seal of the 225 V6

tightly into the holes and seal any spaces between the bearing cap and the crankcase.

10. Reinstall the oil pan and fill the crankcase with the correct amount of oil.

225 V6

1. Remove the oil pan and the crankshaft. When the rear main bearing cap is removed, remove the fabric packing type seal from the radius portion of the cap and the neoprene seals from the grooves on the side of the cap.
2. With an ice pick or similar tool pry the upper half of the seal from the block.
3. Place the new seal in the groove in the rear main bearing cap with both ends protruding above the parting surface of the cap. Force the seal into the groove by rubbing down with a hammer handle or similar tool until the seal projects above the groove no more than 1/16 in. Cut the ends off flush with the mating surface of the cap with a razor blade. Lubricate the seal with engine oil just before installing it in the engine.
4. Lubricate all of the main bearings and install the crankshaft. Install all the main bearing caps and tighten them to the correct torque.
5. Dip the neoprene main bearing cap side seals in kerosene (any light oil will do) for 1½ minutes. This will cause the seals to swell; so you will have to work quickly. Install the seals into tne bearing cap grooves. The protruding ends of the seals should then be squirted with kerosene (or oil), wiped off, and peened over with a hammer to be sure of a seal at the upper mating surface of the cap and cylinder block.

NOTE: Do not cut the seals to length before installing them.

6. Attach the connecting rods to the crankshaft and install the oil pan in the reverse order of removal.

327 V8

1. Remove the oil pan and the crankshaft. When the rear main bearing is removed, remove the fabric packing type seal from the radius portion of the cap and the neoprene seals from the grooves on the side of the cap. Remove the upper half of the seal from the cylinder block.

NOTE: If difficulty is encountered in removing the rear main bearing cap because of the grip of the seals, use a long bolt with a slide hammer to remove the cap.

2. Position the new seal in the groove in the rear main bearing cap with both ends protruding above the mating surface of the cap. Force the seal into the groove by rubbing it down with a hammer handle or similar tool. Cut any excess packing off flush with the mating surface of the cap. Install the upper half of the seal in the cylinder block in the same manner.
3. Dip the side seals in kerosene or any light oil, and install them immediately in the side grooves of the rear main bearing cap. Work quickly as the neoprene side seals will swell when exposed to oil.

NOTE: The neoprene side seals are supplied in the correct length and should not be trimmed to fit.

4. Install the side seals in the cap first, then, after installing the crankshaft, install the cap to the cylinder block. Use care not to damage the side seals.
5. When installing the rear main bearing cap, carefully add a thin film of Permatex No. 1 ® on the mating surface of the bearing cap from the oil relief groove rearward. Do not put any sealer on the main seal end.
6. Connect the connecting rods to the crankshaft and install the oil pan in the reverse order of removal.

CLUTCH

Removal

All Models Except 350 V8 and 225 V6

1. Remove the transmission.
2. Disconnect the clutch linkage.
3. Mark the clutch pressure plate and engine flywheel so the clutch will be reassembled in the same position.
4. Remove the clutch pressure plate bracket bolts alternately, a little at a time, to prevent distortion.
5. Remove the pressure plate assembly and driven plate from the flywheel.

225 V6 and 350 V8

1. Mark the universal joint and transmission shaft companion flange for proper indexing at the time of installation. Remove the two U-bolts and disconnect the driveshaft at the front joint. Slide the driveshaft rearward as far as possible and tie it to one side.
2. Disconnect the shift linkage from the transmission.
3. Disconnect the speedometer cable at the transmission.
4. Loosen all three exhaust pipe ball joints to permit the transmission and the rear of the engine to be lowered.
5. Remove the two bolts holding the transmission mounting pad to the transmission support. Leave the mounting pad bolted to the transmission.
6. With a padded jack under the engine, raise the unit until the transmission mounting pad just clears the transmission support.
7. Remove the four bolts holding the transmission support to the body members. Remove the support, then lower the jack to allow

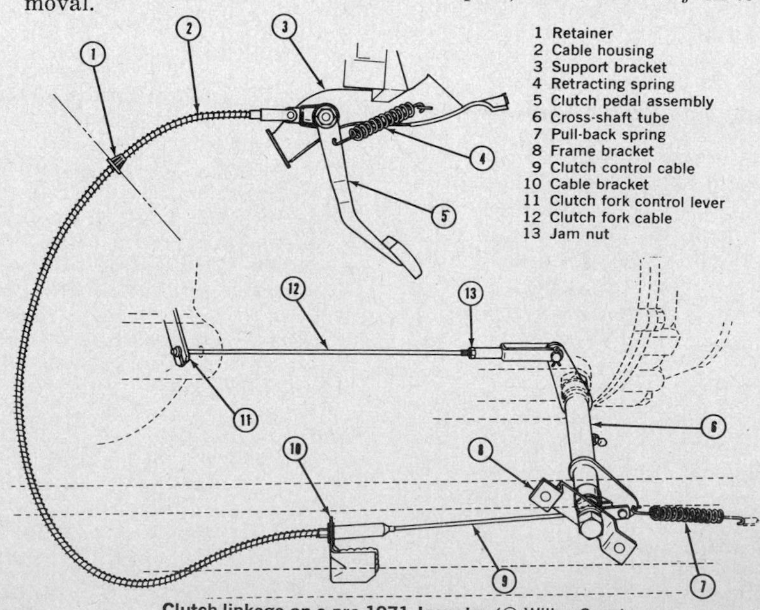

Clutch linkage on a pre-1971 Jeepster (© Willys Corp)

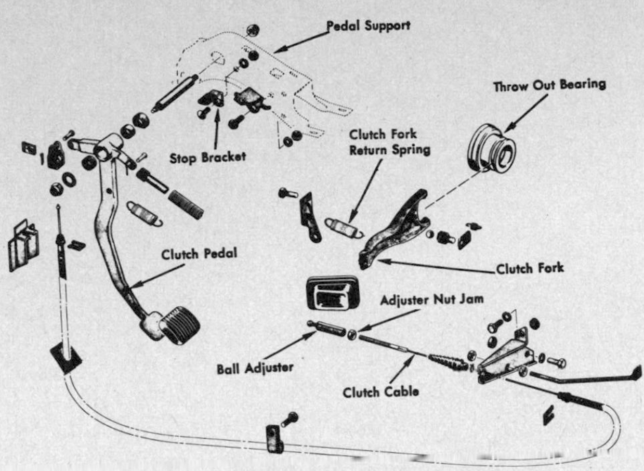

Clutch linkage for 1972 Commandos and CJs
(© Jeep Corp)

the transmission to clear the underbody.

8. Remove the upper left transmission-to-flywheel housing bolt and install a guide pin. Remove the lower right bolt and install a guide pin.
9. Remove the other two transmission attaching bolts. Slide the transmission back until the drive gear shaft disengages the clutch disc and clears the flywheel housing. Lower the transmission.
10. Remove the pedal return spring from the clutch fork.
11. Remove the flywheel housing.
12. Remove the throw-out bearing.
13. Disconnect the clutch fork from the ball stud.
14. Mark the clutch cover and flywheel to assure proper balance on reassembly.
15. Loosen the clutch cover-to-flywheel bolts one turn at a time until spring pressure is released.
16. Support the pressure plate and cover assembly while removing the last bolts, then remove the cover assembly and driven plate.

Installation

All Models Except 350 V8 and 225 V6

NOTE: The clutch release bearing is lubricated during assembly and need not be lubricated at any other time.

1. Put a very small amount of light grease in the flywheel pilot bushing. Install the driven plate with short end of hub toward flywheel. Place the pressure plate assembly in position.
2. Using a clutch plate aligning arbor or a spare transmission mainshaft, align the driven plate splines. Tighten the pressure plate screws evenly to 40 ft lbs. Remove the aligning arbor.
3. Assemble the flywheel housing to the engine. Make sure that the clutch release bearing carrier return spring is hooked in place. Reverse the order of the clutch assembly removal procedure to complete installation.

225 V6 and 350 V8

Install the clutch by reversing the removal procedure. Use a clutch aligning pilot or a spare main drive gear through the hub of the driven plate and into the pilot bushing. Be sure to align the clutch cover-to-flywheel index marks.

Clutch Linkage Adjustment

Universal (CJ) Series, Jeepster

Adjust the linkage at the turnbuckle on the cable from the clutch fork control lever so that the clutch pedal can be depressed 1 in. before clutch disengagement starts.

Wagoneer through 1971

1. Disconnect the adjustable rod from the clutch pedal.
2. Adjust the clutch pedal stop bolt for a positive over-center action. This is done by turning the stop bolt in or out to obtain clutch pedal travel of ¼–½ in. before the over-center spring assists the pedal to the floorboard. The pedal need not be the same height as the brake pedal.
3. Adjust the rod from the brake pedal to the cross-shaft so that proper angle is obtained between the arm of the cross-shaft and the top of the left frame rail. For the 350 V8, the correct angle is 30°. For the 327 V8 and the 232 OHV 6, the correct angle is 49°. This angle may be measured with a protractor.
4. Adjust the cross-shaft to throw-out lever link so that the clutch pedal can be depressed 1 in. before clutch engagement starts.

1972 Models

All vehicles equipped with 232, 258 OHV6, 304 V8, and 360 V8 engines utilize a cable-actuated linkage. To adjust the cable, follow this procedure:

1. Lift the clutch pedal up against the support bracket stop.
2. Disconnect the clutch fork return spring.
3. Loosen the ball adjusting nut for some cable slack.
4. Turn the ball adjusting nut until slack is taken up and the clutch throw-out bearing contacts the pressure plate fingers.
5. Back off adjusting nut ¾ turn to provide proper free-play and then tighten the jam nut.
6. Connect the clutch fork return spring.

If the clutch cable adjustment does not provide satisfactory disengagement, the pedal height may be adjusted by following these steps:

1. Lift the pedal up against the support bracket stop.
2. Adjust the stop to provide 7 in. clearance between the pedal and the floorpan by turning the stop-screw located on top of the support bracket directly behind the instrument cluster.
3. Readjust the clutch control cable.

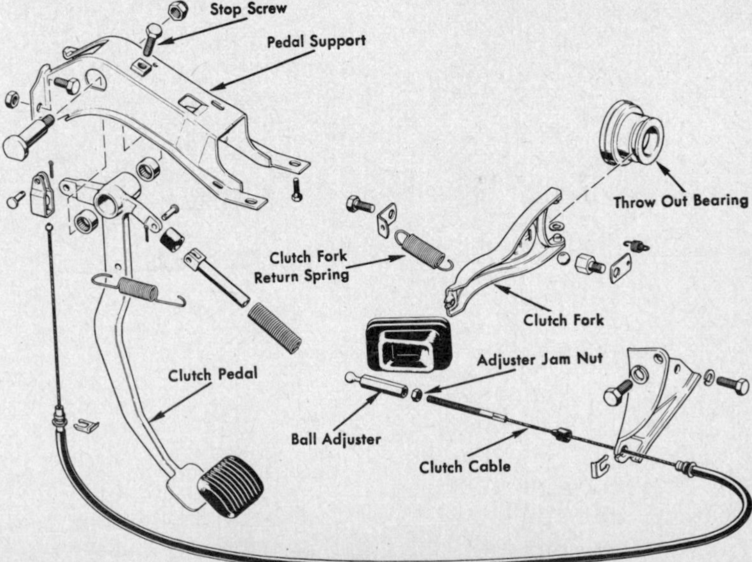

Clutch linkage on a 1972 Wagoneer (© Jeep Corp)

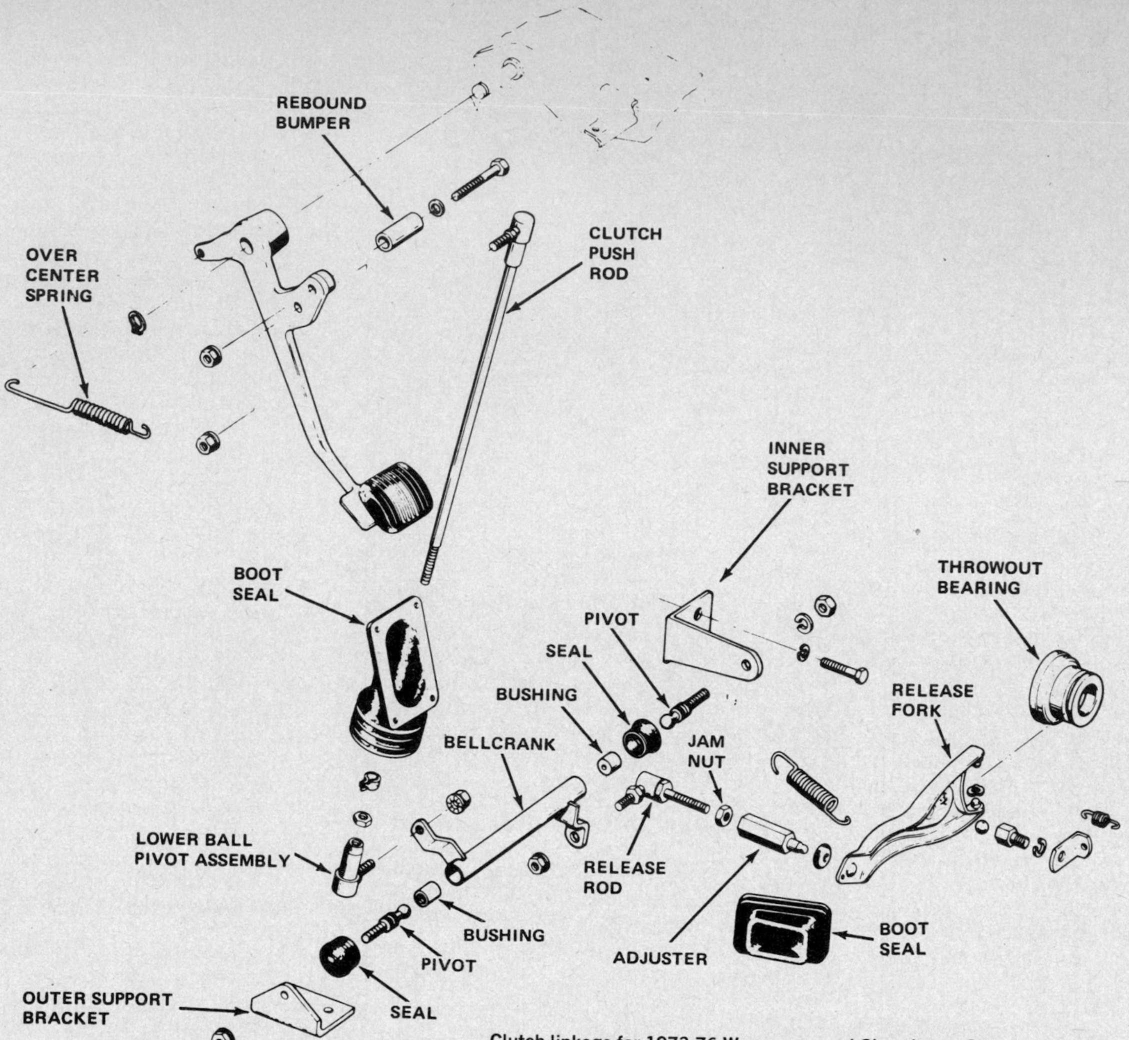

REBOUND
BUMPER
OVER
CENTER
SPRING
CLUTCH
PUSH
ROD
INNER
SUPPORT
BRACKET
THROWOUT
BEARING
BOOT
SEAL
PIVOT
SEAL
RELEASE
FORK
BUSHING
JAM
NUT
BELLCRANK
LOWER BALL
PIVOT ASSEMBLY
RELEASE
ROD
BUSHING
BOOT
SEAL
PIVOT
ADJUSTER
OUTER SUPPORT
BRACKET
SEAL

Clutch linkage for 1973-76 Wagoneers and Cherokees (© Jeep Corp)

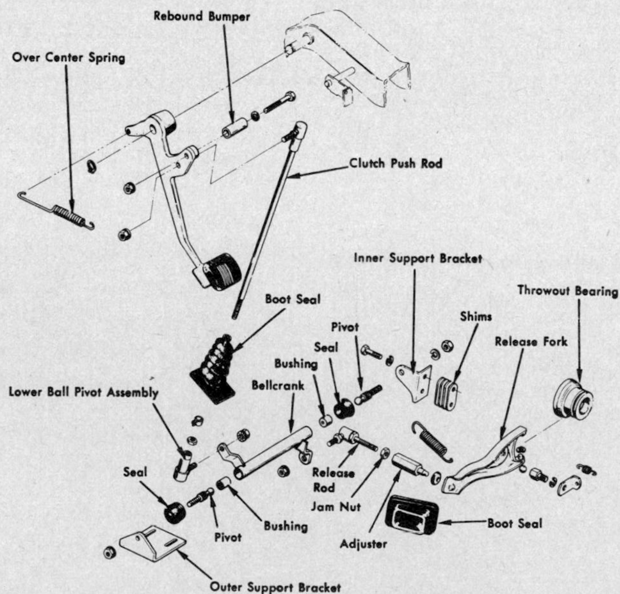

Rebound Bumper
Over Center Spring
Clutch Push Rod
Inner Support Bracket
Throwout Bearing
Boot Seal
Shims
Pivot
Release Fork
Seal
Bushing
Bellcrank
Lower Ball Pivot Assembly
Seal
Release
Rod
Jam Nut
Bushing
Pivot
Adjuster
Boot Seal
Outer Support Bracket

Clutch linkage for 1973-76 Commandos and CJs
(© Jeep Corp)

Clutch Linkage Adjustment (1973-76) All Models

1. Adjust the bellcrank outer support bracket to provide about 1/8 in. of bellcrank end-play.
2. Lift the clutch pedal up against the pedal stop.
3. On the clutch pushrod (pedal-to-bellcrank), adjust the lower ball pivot assembly on or off of the rod as required to position the bellcrank inner lever parallel to the front face of the clutch housing (slightly forward from vertical).
4. Adjust the clutch fork release rod (bellcrank-to-release fork) to obtain the maximum specified clutch pedal free-play as follows: CJ-5/CJ-6, 3/4-1/2 in.; Cherokee and Wagoneer, 5/8-3/8 in.

MANUAL TRANSMISSION

Transmission Removal and Installation

The transmission and transfer case can be removed as a unit. These instructions apply to both three and four-speed transmissions, and also generally to two-wheel drive models which have no transfer case.

Universal (CJ) Series through 1971

1. Drain the transmission and transfer case.
2. Remove the floor pan inspection plate.
3. Remove the shift lever and hous-

ing, or disconnect the remote control rods, depending on the model.

4. If the vehicle has a power take-off, remove the shift lever.
5. Disconnect the front and rear driveshafts from the transfer case. Disconnect the power take-off driveshaft.
6. Disconnect the speedometer cable.
7. Disconnect the handbrake cable.
8. Disconnect the clutch release cable or rod.
9. Place the jacks under the engine and transmission, protecting the oil pan with a wooden block.
10. Remove the rear crossmember.
11. Unbolt the transmission from the flywheel housing.
12. Force the transmission to the right to disengage the clutch control lever tube ball joint.
13. Lower the jacks. Slide the transmission and transfer case rearward until the clutch shaft clears the flywheel housing.
14. Lower the transmission jack. Remove the assembly from beneath the vehicle.
15. To install, reverse the procedure.

Jeepster through 1971

The procedure for these models is the same as that for the Universal series, with the substitution of the following steps:

2. Remove the right front seat, floor mat, and floorboard center section. Disconnect the back-up switch wires.
10. Remove the rear crossmember. Remove the transmission and transfer case stabilizer brackets.

Wagoneer through 1971

The procedure for these models is the same as that for the Universal series, with the substitution of the following step:

2. Remove the transmission access cover.

All Models—1972 and Later

1. Remove the shift lever knobs, trim rings, and boots.
2. On three-speed floorshift models, remove the floor covering. Remove the floor pan section from above the transmission. Remove the shift control and lever assembly. On four-speed models, remove the shift control housing cap, washer, spring, shift lever, and pin.
3. Remove the transfer case shift lever and bracket.
4. Raise the vehicle on a lift.
5. Disconnect the column shift rods.
6. Remove the front driveshaft and disconnect the front of the rear driveshaft. Disconnect the vacuum line and electrical lead on a Quadra-Trac unit.
7. Disconnect the clutch cable, if so equipped and remove the cable mounting bracket from the transfer case.
8. Disconnect the speedometer cable, TCS switch, and back-up light switch. Disconnect the parking brake cable if it is connected to the crossmember.
9. On models equipped with V8 engines, disconnect and lower the exhaust pipes from the exhaust manifolds.
10. Support the transmission with a floor jack.
11. Unbolt the crossmember from the frame. Unbolt the transmission from the clutch housing.
12. Lower the transmission slightly and move it to the rear to disengage the clutch shaft. Remove the unit.

To replace the transmission:

13. Place the wave washer and throw-out bearing and sleeve assembly in the fork. Center the bearing over the release levers.
14. Slide the transmission into place, being careful to align the transmission splines with those on the clutch plate. Bolt the transmission to the clutch housing and torque the bolts to 55 ft lbs.
15. Bolt the crossmember to the frame. Torque the bolts to 30–35 ft lbs. Remove the jack.
16. On models equipped with V8 engines, connect the exhaust pipes to the exhaust manifolds.
17. Connect the speedometer cable, back-up light switch, TCS switch, parking brake cable, clutch cable and cable mounting bracket.
18. Install the driveshafts. Flange bolts should be torqued to 25–45 ft lbs.
19. Replace the column shift linkage.
20. Lower the vehicle.
21. Replace the transfer case shift lever and bracket.
22. On four-speeds, install the lever pivot pin, shift lever, spring, washer, and control housing cap. On three-speeds, install the shift control and lever assembly. Set the gears and the cover in the neutral position. Install the cover, placing the shift forks into the sleeves. Torque the cover bolts to 8–15 ft lbs.
23. Replace the floor covering, boots, trim rings, and shift lever knobs.

Shift Linkage Adjustment

Universal (CJ) Series—Column Shift

1. Disconnect the shift rods at the transmission.
2. Put the transmission lever in the neutral position. *NOTE: Lock the gearshift levers in the neutral positions by putting a ¼ in. dia rod through the gearshift levers and housing at the bottom of the steering column.*
3. Adjust the length of the shift rods and reconnect them.
4. If shifting from first to second is difficult or the transmission hangs in first gear, shorten the first-reverse rod one turn at a time until the condition is corrected.

Jeepster—Console Shift

1. Remove the plug from the hole in the left side of the console. If there is no hole, cut a 1 1/8 in. dia. hole or remove the console.
2. Lift the shift tower rubber cover and remove the plug in the shift tower. Move the selector lever to the neutral position.
3. Loosen the adjusting nuts at the transmission.
4. Insert a 3/16 in. dia rod through the holes in the console and shift tower, and through the aligning holes in the two shift levers. Check to see that the transmission shift levers are in neutral positions.
5. Torque the adjusting nuts to 15–20 ft lbs.
6. Remove the adjusting rod, replace the plugs, and check the shifting action. If the selector lever interferes with the console, relocate the console.

Wagoneer—Column Shift

1. Put the selector lever in Neutral position.
2. Loosen the shift rod adjusting nuts at the transmission. Place the shift levers in Neutral position.
3. Insert a 3/16 in. dia. rod through the remote control shift levers and housing at the bottom of the steering column.
4. Torque the adjusting nuts to 15–20 ft lbs. Remove the adjusting rod.

Transfer Case Removal

The transfer case can also be removed as a separate unit.

Jeepster

1. Drain the transmission and transfer case.
2. Remove the transfer case shift lever.
3. Disconnect the driveshafts.
4. Disconnect the speedometer cable.
5. Disconnect the brake cable (directly under the transfer case).
6. Disconnect the clutch cables from the cross-shaft.
7. Disconnect the clutch control cross-shaft ball joint at frame.
8. Remove the transfer case stabilizer bracket.
9. Remove the bolts securing the transfer case to the transmission. Slide the transfer case rearward to remove it.
10. Reinstall in the reverse order of the above steps.

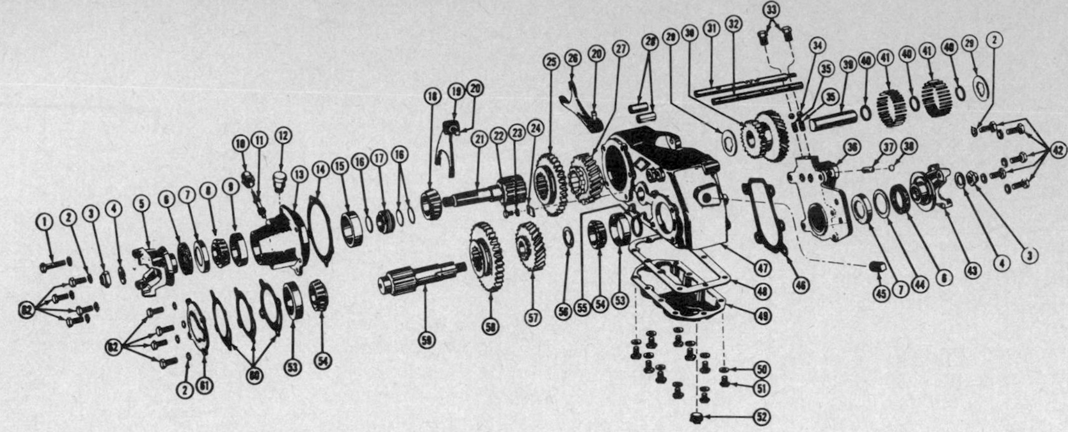

Spicer Model 20 transfer case (© Willys Corp)

1 Long bolt
2 Lock washer
3 Nut
4 Flat washer
5 Rear propeller shaft yoke
6 Felt seal
7 Yoke oil seal
8 Cone and roller
9 Bearing cup
10 Speedometer driven gear sleeve
11 Speedometer driven gear
12 Breather
13 Rear bearing cap
14 Rear bearing cap gasket
15 Bearing cup
16 Shims
17 Speedometer drive gear
18 Cone and roller
19 Outer shift fork
20 Shift fork bolt
21 Rear output shaft
22 Bolt
23 Lock washer
24 Lock plate
25 Mainshaft sliding gear
26 Inner shift fork
27 Mainshaft gear
28 Shift rod caps
29 Thrust washer
30 Intermediate gear
31 Inner shift rail
32 Outer shift rail
33 Poppet plug
34 Poppet ball
35 Poppet spring
36 Shift rail housing
37 Shift rail interlock
38 Plug
39 Intermediate shaft
40 Bearing spacer
41 Needle bearings
42 Bolt
43 Front propeller shaft yoke
44 Oil seal gasket
45 Oil fill plug
46 Shift rail housing gasket
47 Case
48 Bottom cover gasket
49 Bottom cover
50 Lock washer
51 Bolt
52 Oil drain plug
53 Bearing cup
54 Cone and roller
55 Thrust washer
56 Thrust washer
57 Front output shaft gear
58 Front output shaft sliding gear
59 Front output shaft
60 Shims
61 Cover plate
62 Bolt

Wagoneer, Cherokee (Model 20 Transfer Case)

This procedure is the same as that detailed above for the removal of the Jeepster transfer case with the substitution of the following steps:

5. Disconnect the parking brake spring from the fuel tank flange. Remove the clevis pin from the brake cable connnecting bracket.
6. Remove exhaust pipe bracket bolts.
7. Delete Step 7.
8. Delete Step 8.

Universal (CJ) Series

1. Drain the transmission and transfer case.
2. Disconnect the brake cable.
3. Disconnect the driveshafts.
4. Disconnect the speedometer cable.
5. Disconnect the transfer case shift levers.
6. Remove the cover plate on the rear of the transfer case. Remove the cotter key, nut, and washer from the transmission mainshaft.
7. If possible, remove the transfer case main drive gear from the transmission mainshaft.
8. Remove the transfer case mounting bracket bolts and nuts.
9. Unbolt the transmission from the transfer case.
10. Remove the transfer case. If the main drive gear has not been removed in Step 7, proceed as follows: Brace the end of the transmission mainshaft so that it cannot move in the transmission, pull the transfer case to the rear to remove. Be careful that the transmission mainshaft bearing, which bears in both housings, remains in the transmission case.
11. Installation is the reverse of the removal procedure.

Quadra-Trac Models

Complete assembly removal is normally not required except when the front output shaft, front annular bearing, transmission output shaft seals, or the transfer case (front housing) require servicing. To service the chain, drive sprocket, differential unit, diaphragm control system, needle bearing, thrust washer, or the rear output shaft, just the rear case cover has to be removed, not the entire unit.

To remove the transfer case from the vehicle, proceed as follows:

1. Lift and support the vehicle.
2. Mark the front and rear output shaft yokes and universal joints to provide alignment references to be used during assembly. Disconnect the front drive shaft rear universal joint from the transfer case front yoke.
3. Disconnect the rear propeller shaft front universal joint from the transfer case rear yoke.
4. Remove the bolts which attach the exhaust pipe bracket to the transfer case.
5. Mark the diaphragm control vacuum hoses for identification during assembly, then disconnect the diaphragm control vacuum hoses, Lock-Out indicator switch wire, and the speedometer cable.
6. Disconnect the parking brake cable guide from the pivot on the right frame side.
7. Remove the two transfer case-to-transmission bolts which enter from the front side. Install a 7/16-14×5 in. guide pin into the upper hole. Remove the two transfer case-to-transmission bolts which enter from the rear. Install a 7/16-14×5 in. guide pin into the upper hole.
8. Move the transfer case assembly backward until the unit is free of the transmission output shaft and guide pins.
9. Lower the assembly from the vehicle.
10. Remove all gasket material from the rear of the transmission.

To install the complete assembly:

11. Position a new gasket onto the rear of the transmission.
12. Install 7/16-14×5 in. guide pins in the upper threaded holes in the transmission adapter and the transfer case.
13. Lift the transfer case assembly and move it forward to the transmission. The drive hub splines must align with the transmission output shaft. Slight rotation of the transfer case rear output shaft yoke may be necessary. Do not install any attaching bolts until the transfer case assembly is positioned against the transmission gasket.

14. Install the rear and front attaching bolts.
15. Attach the exhaust pipe support bracket to the transfer case.
16. Align and attach the front and rear propeller shafts.
17. Connect the Lock-Out indicator switch wire and diaphragm control vacuum hoses.
18. Connect the parking brake cable guide to the pivot bracket on the right frame side.
19. Install the proper type and amount of lubricant and lower the vehicle.

Transfer Case Disassembly

The transfer case can be disassembled as follows:

1. Remove the rear bearing cap assembly.
2. Remove the bottom cover.
3. Remove the lockplate bolt, lockwasher, and lock plate.
4. Drive the intermediate shaft out the rear of the case using a dummy shaft. This tool allows the two sets of needle bearings and three spacers to remain in position as the shaft is withdrawn. The aligner should be centered in the intermediate gear assembly to avoid interference from the thrust washers.
5. Remove the intermediate gear through the bottom of the case.
6. Remove the front output shaft yoke. Remove the felt oil seal, the oil seal gasket and front oil seal.
7. Remove the rear cover. *CAUTION: When removing the rear cover, care should be exercised to avoid damaging the gasket and shim separating the cover plate from the transfer case.*
8. Using a soft-faced hammer, drive the rear bearing cup from the case.
9. Loosen and remove the inner shift fork bolt. Tap the underdrive and direct shift rail to the rear of the case to remove the shift rail cap. Tap the inner rail out the front of the case. The main gear and inner shift fork can then be removed. *NOTE: Front refers to the transmission side of the transfer case.*
10. Remove the shift rail housing assembly from the case and outer shift rail.
11. Wedge the front bearing cone and roller assembly from its seat on the output shaft. Drive the front bearing cone out of the case. Loosen the snap-ring and slide the shaft through the rear of the case. *NOTE: A snap-ring is used on early models only. Current models use a thrust washer on each side of the bearing.*
12. With the shaft removed, the output shaft sliding gear can be lifted from the outer fork. The fork can then be turned and the shift rail fork bolt removed.

Transfer Case Assembly

NOTE: Design changes have been incorporated in the mainshaft, intermediate, and output shaft gears on silent type transfer cases. These late design gears are not interchangeable with early type gears. Should replacement be required, individual gears should be replaced with the identifying numbers on each.

1. Slide the front-wheel drive shift rail partially into the case. Place the front-wheel drive shift fork on the rail with the shift rod fork bolt hole aligned with the countersunk hole on the rail. Replace the shift rail fork bolt and torque to 12–15 ft lbs and replace the safety wire.
2. Place the front-wheel drive shift fork in the proper position in the case. Set the front output shaft sliding gear in the shift fork with the gear facing the front of the transfer case.
3. Install the rear cone and roller on the front output shaft.
4. Hold the output shaft gear in place and insert the output shaft.
5. Install the thrust washer and snap-ring. *NOTE: A snap-ring is used on early models only. Current models use a thrust washer on each side of the bearing.*
6. Install the front cone and roller on the front output shaft.
7. Install the front and rear bearing cup.
8. Install the shift rail housing gasket, shift rail housing, lockwashers, and bolts, and torque to 28–30 ft lbs.
9. Replace the rear cover shim set, rear cover plate, lockwashers, and bolts (28–32 ft lbs).
10. Check the output shaft bearing adjustment using a dial indicator. Position the shaft in the extreme rear position, set the dial indicator on zero, and pry the output shaft forward. A reading of 0.001–0.003 in. should be obtained. This clearance can be altered by changing the rear cover shims. Shims for this adjustment are available as follows: 0.003 in., 0.010 in., 0.031 in.
11. Position the outer shift rail so it will allow the shift rail interlocks to enter the detents in the rod as the inner shift rail is inserted in the shift rod housing.
12. Start the inner drive shift rail into the case along with its shift fork. Place the mainshaft gear on the fork with the gear facing the front of the transfer case. Push the shift rail into the case and through the fork until the countersunk hole on the rod aligns with the shift fork bolt hole. Replace the bolt and torque to 12–15 ft lbs.
13. Place the thrust washers with the tang aligned to the groove in the case. The rear thrust washer can be held in place by just starting the intermediate shaft into the case. The front thrust washer can be held with heavy grease.
14. Position the intermediate gear in the case. Using a soft-faced hammer, drive the intermediate shaft into the intermediate gear. Install the intermediate shaft lockplate, lockwasher, and bolt. Torque to 12–15 ft lbs.
15. Install the rear bearing cap assembly. Torque the long bolt and four short bolts 28–32 ft lbs.
16. Tap the shift rail cups about 3/8 in. into the case.
17. Install the lower cover gasket, the lower cover, lockwashers, and bolts (torque to 12–15 ft lbs).
18. Replace the oil seal gasket and felt oil seal.
19. Install the front and rear propeller shaft yokes (225–250 ft lbs).

Quadra-Trac Rear Case Cover Removal and Disassembly

Most Quadra-Trac components can be serviced without removing the complete unit from the vehicle. To gain access to the rear output shaft, drive sprocket and thrust washer, chain, differential and needle bearing, or the diaphragm control system, just the rear cover has to be removed.

1. Lift and support the vehicle.
2. If the vehicle is equipped with a reduction unit, continue on to the next step for the reduction unit removal procedure. If the vehicle is not equipped with a reduction unit, proceed to Step 7.
3. Loosen all the bolts that attach the reduction unit to the transfer case cover.
4. Move the reduction unit backward just enough to allow the oil to drain from the unit.
5. Loosen the cable retaining bolt at the shift control lever. Loosen the cable clamp bolt and remove the control cable from the clamp bracket and control lever.
6. When the oil has drained, remove the bolts which hold the reduction unit to the transfer case cover. Move the reduction unit rearward to clear the transmission output shaft and pinion cage which is attached to the transfer case drive sprocket. The pinion cage will remain with the transfer case assembly.

NOTE: The pinion cage should not be removed if the transfer case cover assembly is to be removed, but may be removed for inspection or replacement if the transfer case cover assembly is to remain in the vehicle. Removal of the pinion cage involves

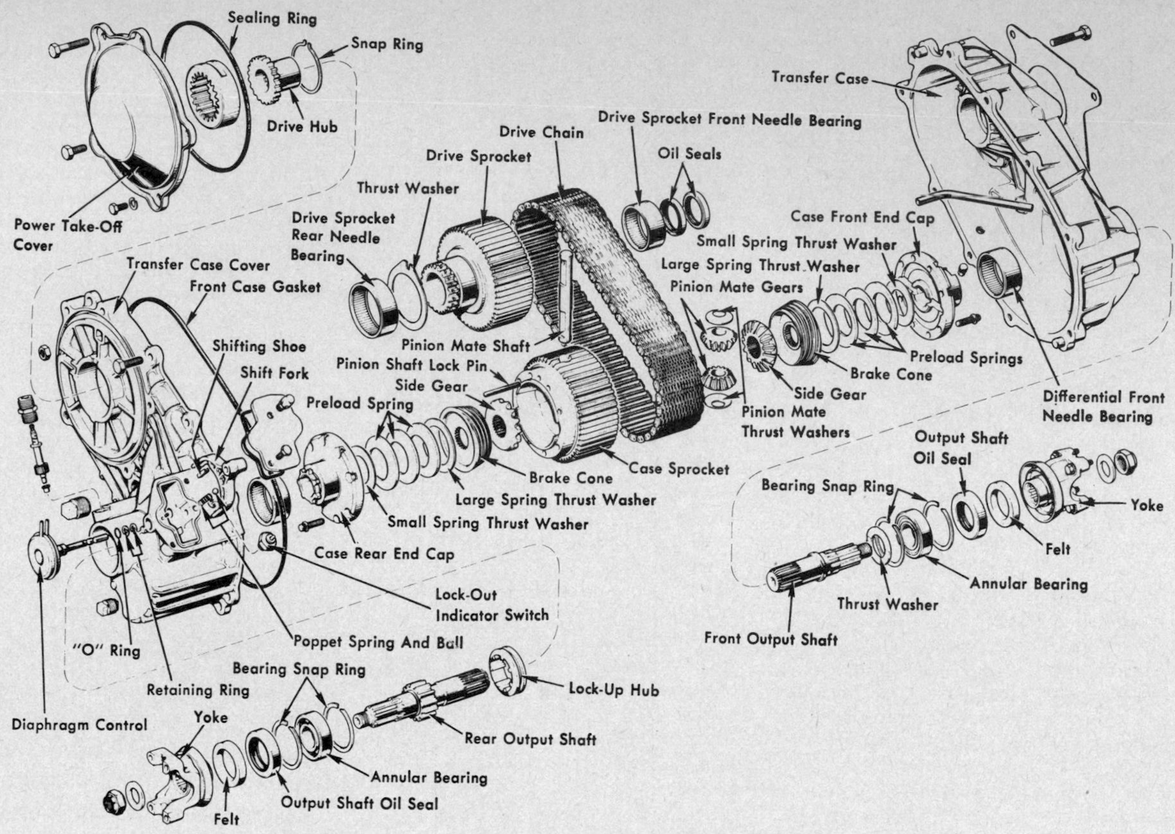

Exploded view of a Quadra-Trac transfer case (© Jeep Corp)

only removing the snap-ring which holds the cage to the sprocket and sliding the cage backward.

7. Remove the transfer case drain plug and allow the unit to drain.
8. Mark the rear output shaft yoke and universal joint to provide an alignment reference during reassembly. Disconnect the rear propeller shaft front universal joint from the transfer case rear yoke.
9. Mark the diaphragm control vacuum hoses for identification during reassembly, then disconnect them. Also remove the lock-up indicator switch wire and the speedometer cable. Remove the indicator switch.
10. Disconnect the parking brake cable guide from the pivot on the right frame side.
11. Remove the bolts which attach the case cover assembly to the case (front housing). Carefully slide the cover assembly backward off the front output shaft and the transmission output shaft.
12. To disassemble the unit, remove the rear output shaft yoke.
13. If the unit is *not* equipped with a reduction unit, remove the power take-off cover from the rear of the transfer case cover. Remove the sealing ring from the transfer case cover.
14. Using a piece of wood 2 in. × 4 in. and 6 in. long, position the cover and sprocket.
15. If *not* equipped with a reduction unit, remove the drive hub and sleeve from the drive sprocket rear splines by expanding the internal snap-ring. The ring expanding tabs are accessible through a slot in the outside edge of the drive sleeve.

    If equipped with a reduction unit, remove the pinion cage snap-ring and carrier. Lift the case cover from the drive sprocket and differential. The cover, rear output shaft, bearings and seal, drive sprocket rear needle bearing, and lock-up hub can now be serviced without any further disassembly of other components.
16. Slide the drive sprocket toward the differential unit and remove the chain. The differential unit may now be serviced without any further disassembly of other components.

Quadra-Trac Assembly and Rear Case Cover Installation

1. Position the drive sprocket on a block of wood 2 in. × 4 in. and 6 in. long.
2. Place the differential assembly about 2 in. from the drive sprocket and with the front end of the differential on the bench.
3. Position the drive chain around the drive sprocket and the differential assembly. Be sure that the chain is properly engaged with the sprocket and differen-

Quadra-Trac case cover positioned for disassembly (© Jeep Corp)

Differential and drive sprockets positioned for chain installation (© Jeep Corp)

Drive chain positioned around the differential and drive sprockets (© Jeep Corp)

tial teeth and that the slack is removed from the chain.

4. Insert the rear output shaft into the differential.
5. Shift the lock-up hub rearward in the case cover. Lubricate the drive sprocket thrust washer and insert it in position on the case cover.
6. Carefully align the case cover and position it onto the drive sprocket and differential. The output shaft may have to be slightly rotated to align it with the lock-up hub. Be sure that the drive sprocket thrust washer stays positioned correctly.
7. If equipped with a reduction unit, install the pinion cage onto the drive sprocket rear splines. Install the snap-ring. Be sure that the snap-ring seats properly in the groove.

   If the vehicle is *not* equipped with a reduction unit, assemble the drive hub, drive sleeve, and snap-ring, then install them onto the drive sprocket rear splines. Be sure the snap-ring seats properly.
8. Rotate the drive sleeve or pinion cage to be sure the drive sprocket thrust washer did not come out of position. No binding should be present.
9. If *not* equipped with a reduction unit, install the power take-off sealing ring and cover and tighten the screws.
10. Install the speedometer gear on the rear output shaft.
11. Install the rear output shaft oil seal and the rear yoke and nut. Tighten the nut.
12. Clean the groove which the front oil seal gasket fits into and install the seal.
13. Install two 3/8 in.-16 × 2 in. long pilot studs into the transfer case front cover housing.
14. Insert the oil tube into the case bore at the front output shaft bearing boss. Insert a 6 in. length of 5/16 in. rod into the tube. The rod will be used as a pilot to align the tube with the case cover.
15. Lift the cover assembly and align the tube pilot with the hole in the cover. Move the assembly forward over the pilot studs.
16. Move the cover assembly forward to mesh with the front output shaft and transmission output shaft. It may be necessary to rotate the rear output shaft slightly to allow the two sets of splines to engage.
17. After the cover assembly has been moved forward and is evenly touching the front half of the case, remove the pilot studs and install the rear cover attaching bolts. Tighten the bolts alternately and evenly.
18. Install the Lock-Out indicator switch and connect the Lock-Out switch wire, diaphragm control vacuum hoses, and the speedometer cable.
19. Install the rear drive shaft.
20. Install the parking brake cable guide to the pivot on the right frame side.
21. Install the reduction unit, if so equipped.
22. Install the proper type and amount of lubricant and lower the vehicle.

NOTE: Use 8 oz of "Special Quadra-Trac" limited slip differential lubricant additive mixed with SAE 30 non-detergent motor oil. 3.5 pints of the mixture is required to fill the transfer case without a reduction unit, 4.5 pints with a reduction unit.

Warner T14(A), T15(A) 3 Speed Transmission

Transmission Disassembly

1. Separate the transfer case by removing the five capscrews.
2. Remove the cover and gasket. Disassemble the floorshift housing cover by removing the shift rails, poppet balls, springs, and shift forks.
3. Remove the nut, flat washer, transfer case drive gear, adaptor, and spacer.
4. Remove the main drive gear bearing retainer and gasket.
5. Remove the main drive gear and mainshaft bearing snap-rings.
6. Pull out the main drive gear and mainshaft bearings.
7. Remove the main drive gear.
8. Remove the mainshaft assembly through the cover opening.
9. On remote-shift models, remove the roll pins from the lever shafts and housing. From inside the case, slide the levers and interlock assembly out. Remove the forks and lever assemblies.
10. Remove the lockplate from the slots in the reverse idler shaft and countershaft.
11. Drive the countershaft out to the rear with a dummy shaft. Remove the countergear and the two thrust washers. Remove the spacer washers, rollers, and spacer from the gear.
12. Drive the reverse idler shaft out to the rear. Remove the gear, washers, and roller bearings.
13. Remove the clutch hub snap-ring and the second-third synchronizer assembly.
14. Remove second and reverse gears.
15. Remove the clutch hub snap-ring and the low synchronizer assembly.
16. Remove low gear.

Synchronizer Disassembly and Assembly

1. Remove the springs. The low synchronizer has only one spring; second-third, two.
2. Mark the sleeve and hub before separating.
3. Remove the hub.
4. Remove the three shifter plates from hub.
5. Inspect all parts for wear.
6. Assemble in the reverse order of disassembly. On the second-third unit, make sure that the spring openings are 120° from each other, with spring tension opposed.

NOTE: if a synchronizer assembly is replaced on a floor-shift unit, the shift fork operating the synchronizer being replaced must have the letter "A" just under the shaft hole on the side opposite the pin.

Inspection

1. Wash all parts in solvent.
2. Air dry.
3. Check the case bearing and shaft bores. Check for cracks or burrs.
4. Check all gears and bronze blocking rings for cracks, and chipped, worn, or cracked teeth If any gears are replaced, also replace the meshing gears.
5. Check all bearings and bushings for wear or damage.
6. Check to see that the synchronizer sleeves slide freely on the clutch hubs.

Transmission Assembly

1. Place the reverse idler gear with the dummy shaft, roller bearing, and thrust washers in the case. Install the reverse idler shaft.
2. Assemble the countershaft cen-

1—Clutch hub
2—Shifter plate
3—Synchronizer spring (1)
4—Clutch sleeve

Low synchronizer assembly
(© Kaiser Willys Corp)

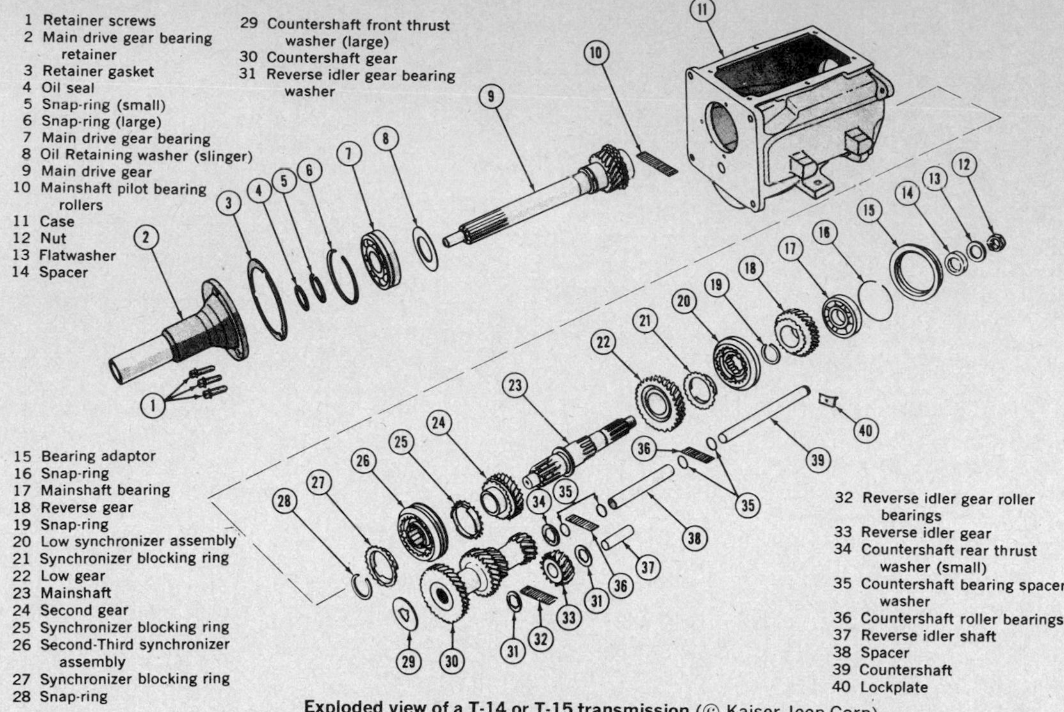

Exploded view of a T-14 or T-15 transmission (© Kaiser Jeep Corp)

ter spacer, four bearing spacers, and bearing rollers in the countershaft gear.

3. Install the large countergear thrust washer in front of case. Position the small thrust washer on the countergear hub with the lip facing the groove in the case. Holding the countergear in position, push in the countershaft from the rear.
4. Install the lockplate in the slots of the reverse idler shaft and the countershaft.
5. Install to mainshaft:
   a. low gear.
   b. bronze blocking ring.
   c. low synchronizer assembly.
   d. largest snap-ring that fits in groove.
   e. second gear.
   f. bronze blocking ring.
   g. second-third synchronizer assembly.
   h. largest snap-ring that fits in groove.
   i. reverse gear.
6. Install the mainshaft assembly through the top of the case.
7. Install the bronze blocking ring to the second-third synchronizer assembly.
8. On remote-shift units, install new O-rings on the shifter lever shafts and install the shafts into the case.

NOTE: T-15 interlock levers are marked as to location. T-14 levers have no marks and are interchangeable.

9. Depress the interlock lever while installing the shift fork into the shift lever and synchronizer clutch sleeve. Install the poppet spring. Install the tapered pins securing the shafts in the case.
10. Install the main drive gear roller bearings.
11. Install the main drive gear and oil slinger into the case with cutaway portion of the gear toward the countergear. Install the main drive gear to the mainshaft.
12. Using the bearing installer and thrust yoke tool, install the main drive gear and mainshaft bearings. Drive the bearings into position. The thrust yoke is needed to prevent damage to the synchronizer clutch.
13. Install the main drive gear and mainshaft bearing snap-rings. The mainshaft bearing snap-ring is 0.010 in. thicker than the main drive gear bearing snap-ring.
14. Install the mainshaft rear bearing adaptor, spacer, transfer case drive gear, flat washer, and nut. Torque the nut to 130–170 ft lbs.
15. Replace the main drive gear bearing retainer oil seal. Install the retainer and gasket. Align the oil drain holes in the retainer and gasket.
16. Install the case cover gasket. On remote-shift units, install the cover gasket with the vent holes to the left side.
17. Position the gear train and floor-shift assembly in neutral. Insert the shifter forks into the clutch sleeves. Install and torque the bolts to 8–15 ft lbs.

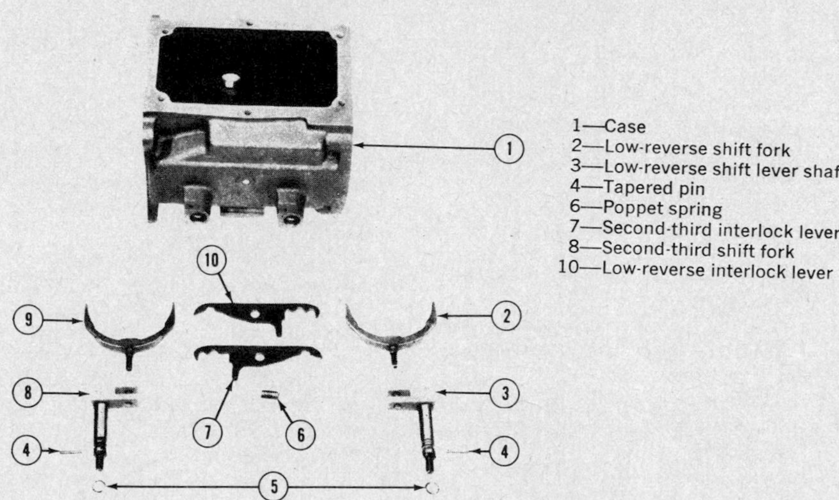

Remote shift interlock assembly for T-14 or T-15 transmission (© Kaiser Willys Corp)

Warner T86 and T90 3 Speed Transmission

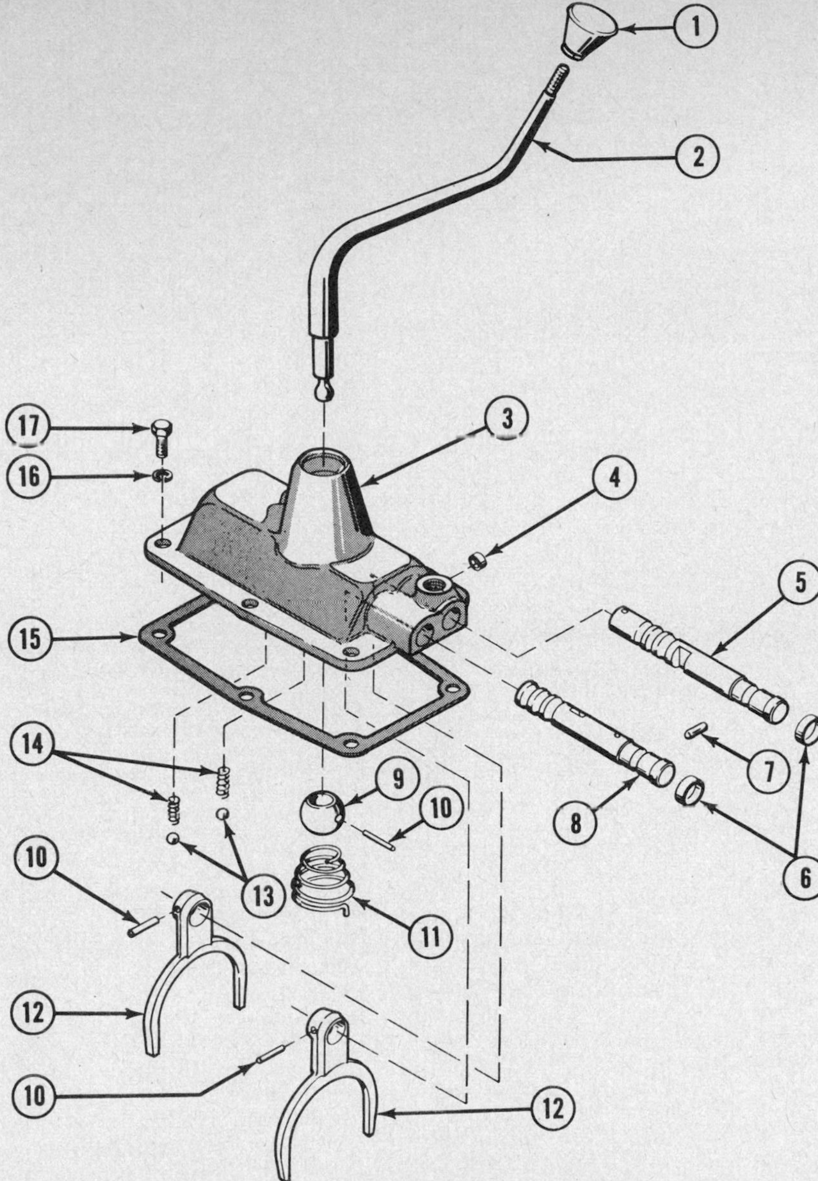

Floor shift control housing assembly (© Kaiser Willys Corp)

1—Shift lever knob
2—Shift lever
3—Control housing
4—Plug
5—Shift rail (second-third)
6—Shift rail cap
7—Interlock plunger
8—Shift rail (low-reverse)
9—Shift lever fulcrum ball
10—Pin
11—Shift lever support spring
12—Shift fork
13—Poppet ball
14—Poppet spring
15—Gasket
16—Lockwasher
17—Bolt

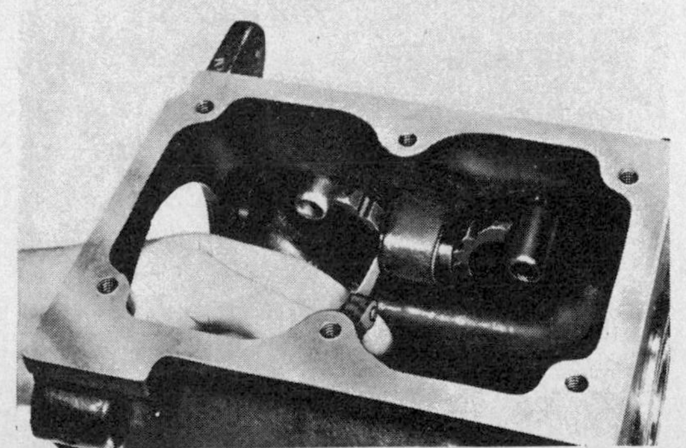

Measuring the interlock sleeve clearance (© Kaiser Willys Corp)

Disassembly

1. Drain the lubricant and flush out the case.
2. If a transfer case is involved, remove its rear cover.
3. If a power take-off is involved, remove the shift unit which replaces the cover.
4. Remove the cotter pin, nut, and washer, and remove the transfer case main drive gear.
5. Remove the transmission shift cover.
6. Loop a piece of wire around the mainshaft just back of the second-speed gear. Twist the wire and attach one end to the right front cover screw, the other end to the left cover screw. Tighten the wire to prevent the mainshaft from pulling out of the case when the transfer case is removed. Should the mainshaft come out, the synchronizer parts will drop into the bottom of the case.
7. Remove the five screws holding the transfer case to the rear face of the transmission.
8. Support the transfer case, then tap lightly on the end of the transmission mainshaft to separate the two units. The transmission mainshaft bearing should slide out of the transfer case and stay with the transmission.
9. Remove the three screws and washers in the front main drive gear bearing retainer, then remove the retainer and gasket.
10. Remove the two hollow-head screws that support the oil collector.
11. Remove the lockplate from the reverse idler shaft and the countershaft at the rear of the case.
12. Drive the countershaft out the rear of the case with a dummy shaft and a brass drift.
13. Remove the loop of wire previously twisted around the mainshaft for support.
14. Remove the mainshaft rear bearing adaptor, then remove the mainshaft assembly from the case. The assembly may be removed through the rear opening of the case. Remove the main drive gear.
15. Remove the countershaft gear set and three thrust washers from the bottom of the case, then dismantle the countershaft gear assembly.
16. Remove the reverse idler shaft and gear by driving the shaft out with a brass drift.
17. On column-shift models, check the clearance between the ends of the interlock sleeve and the

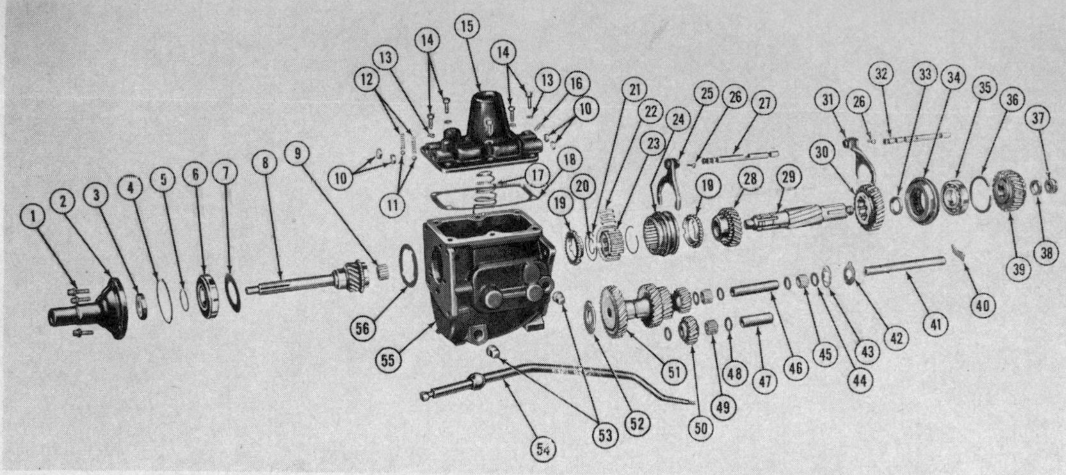

T-90, T-86 three-speed transmission, floor shift (© Kaiser Willys Corp)

1—Bearing retainer screws
2—Main drive gear bearing retainer
3—Bearing retainer oil seal
4—Bearing snap-ring
5—Main drive gear snap ring
6—Main drive gear bearing
7—Front bearing oil retaining washer
8—Main drive gear
9—Pilot roller bearing
10—Shift rail cap
11—Poppet ball
12—Poppet spring
13—Lock washer
14—Shift housing bolt
15—Control housing
16—Interlock punger
17—Shift lever spring
18—Shift tower gasket
19—Blocking ring
20—Clutch hub snap ring
21—Synchronizer spring
22—Synchronizer plate
23—Clutch hub
24—Clutch sleeve
25—High and intermediate clutch fork
26—Shift fork pin
27—High and intermediate shift rail
28—Second speed gear
29—Main shaft
30—Low and Reverse sliding gear
31—Low and Reverse shift fork
32—Low and Reverse shift rail
33—Bearing spacer
34—Rear bearing adapter
35—Rear bearing
36—Rear bearing snap ring
37—Nut
38—Washer
39—Transfer case drive gear
40—Lock plate
41—Countershaft
42—Rear countershaft thrust washer (steel)
43—Rear countershaft thrust washer (bronze)
44—Countershaft bearing washer
45—Countershaft bearing
46—Countershaft center bearing spacer
47—Reverse idler gear shaft
48—Reverse ider gear bearing washer
49—Reverse idler gear roller bearings
50—Reverse idler gear
51—Countershaft gear
52—Countershaft front thrust washer
53—Plug
54—Shift lever
55—Transmission case
56—Retainer gasket

notched surface of each shift lever. The correct clearance is 0.001–0.007 in. Several sizes of interlock sleeves are available for adjustment.

Assembly

Assemble the transmission in the reverse order of disassembly, giving the following points particular attention.

1. The countershaft gear set, when assembled in the case, should have 0.012–0.018 in. end-play. This clearance is controlled by the selective thickness of the rear steel thrust washer.
2. Assemble the large bronze washer at the front of the case with the lip entered in the slot in the case.
3. The bronze-faced steel washer is placed next to the gear at the rear end, and the steel washer next to the case.
4. To assemble the countershaft bearing rollers, use a dummy shaft. Use grease and a loading sleeve to facilitate reassembly of the countershaft gear components.
5. In assembling the mainshaft gears, low and reverse gear is installed with the shift shoe groove toward the front.
6. In assembling the synchronizer unit, install the two springs in the high and intermediate clutch hub with spring tension opposed. Place the right, lipped end of a spring in the slot of the hub and place the spring in the hub. Turn the hub around and make the same installation with the other spring, starting with the same slot. Install the three synchronizer shifting plates into the three slots in the hub, with the smooth sides of the plates out. Hold the plate in position and slip the second and direct clutch sleeve over the hub, with the long beveled edge toward the long part of the clutch hub. Install the completed assembly onto the mainshaft with the beveled edge of the clutch sleeve toward the front end of the shaft.
7. When installing the mainshaft, be sure the bearing rollers are in place in the pilot bore of the clutch gear.
8. Be sure that the countershaft and reverse idler shaft lockplate are in position and completely recessed into the indents of the transfer case.

Warner T98, T18 4 Speed Transmission

Disassembly

1. Remove the transmission transfer case adaptor plate and gasket.
2. Remove the transmission control housing assembly.
3. Mark the two blocking rings, third and high synchronizing gear, and third and high synchronizing sleeve. Also mark the blocking ring, low and second synchronizing gear, and low and second synchronizer sleeve.
4. Slide the low-speed gear toward the rear of the transmission case.
5. Disengage the reverse gearshift arm from the reverse idler gear and remove the reverse gearshift arm from the reverse mounting pin.
6. Move the low-speed gear back into neutral position.
7. Remove the rear bearing retainer. Remove the snap-ring from the main drive pinion (clutch shaft) and the outer race of the drive pinion ball bearing.
8. Remove the main drive pinion ball bearing and oil slinger.
9. Remove the snap-ring from the outer bearing race of the transmission mainshaft ball bearing, then, with a bearing puller, pull the bearing.
10. Separate the mainshaft assembly from the main drive pinion.
11. Lift the mainshaft assembly from the case.
12. Remove the main drive pinion from the case.

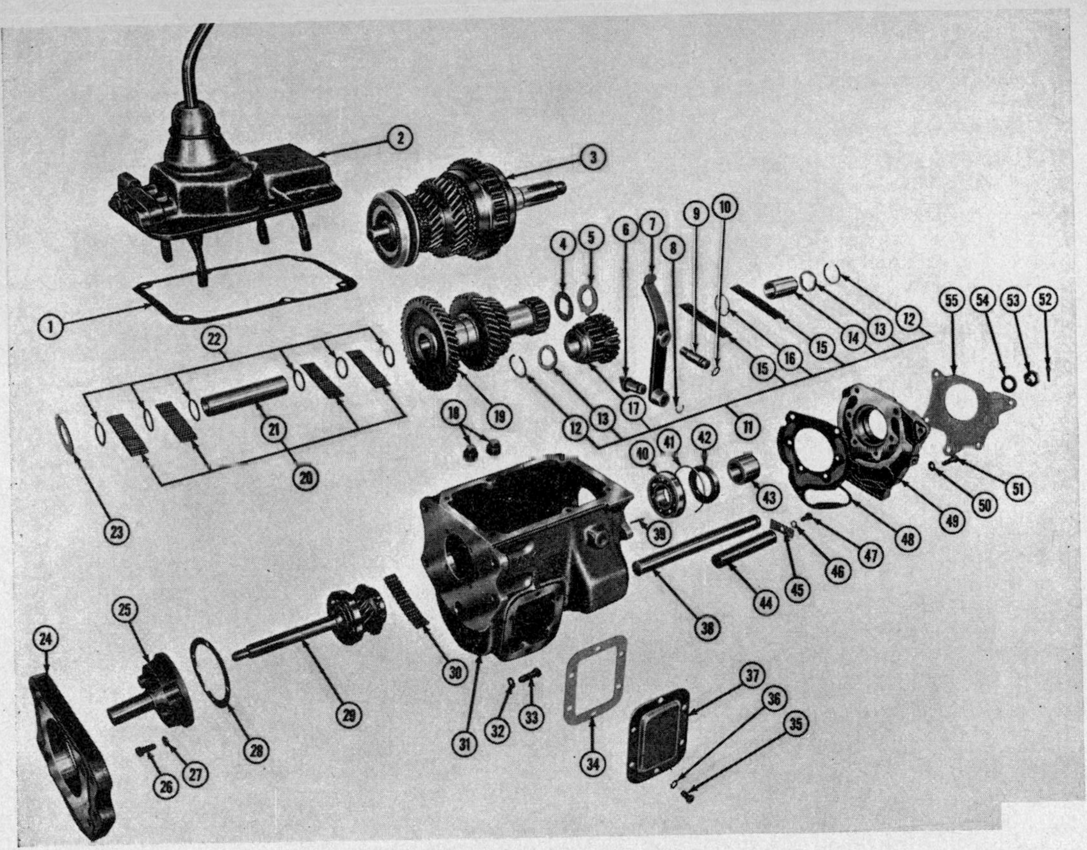

Warner T-18 and T-98 transmission (© Kaiser Willys Corp)

1—Control housing gasket
2—Control housing assembly
3—Mainshaft assembly
4—Thrust washer
5—Thrust washer
6—Reverse shifting shoe
7—Reverse shifting arm
8—C-washer
9—Reverse shifting arm pivot
10—O-ring
11—Reverse idler gear assembly
12—Snap-ring
13—Thrust washer
14—Sleeve
15—Bearing rollers
16—Spacer
17—Reverse idler gear
18—Pipe plug
19—Countershaft gears
20—Bearing rollers
21—Spacer
22—Spacer
23—Thrust washer
24—Bellhousing-to-transmission adapter plate
25—Bearing retainer
26—Bearing retainer bolt
27—Bearing retainer lockwasher
28—Bearing retainer gasket
29—Main drive gear
30—Bearing rollers
31—Transmission case
32—Adapter plate lockwasher
33—Adapter plate capscrew
34—Side opening cover gasket
35—Side opening cover bolt
36—Side opening cover lockwasher
37—Side opening cover
38—Countershaft
39—Shifting arm pivot taper pin
40—Bearing
41—Snap-ring
42—Oil seal
43—Spacer
44—Reverse-idler gear shaft
45—Lock plate
46—Lock plate lockwasher
47—Lock plate bolt
48—Gasket
49—Adapter plate
50—Adapter plate lockwasher
51—Adapter plate bolt
52—Cotter key
53—Nut
54—Washer
55—Gasket

13. Remove the mainshaft pilot rollers from the drive pinion.
14. Mark the relation between the synchronizer gears and splines on the mainshaft.
15. Disassemble the mainshaft by removing the snap-ring holding the third and high synchronizer assembly onto the mainshaft.
16. Remove the snap-ring holding the second-speed synchronizer onto the mainshaft.
17. Slide the second-speed synchronizer and second-speed gear from the mainshaft.
18. Remove the two remaining snap-rings, spacer, and thrust washer from the mainshaft.
19. Remove the two large lockrings and push the synchronizer gear out of the sleeve.
20. If the second-speed synchronizer assembly is to be disassembled, wrap the assembly in a cloth to prevent losing the lock balls and springs. Push the gear out of the sleeve in a direction opposite the shift fork groove. Remove the cloth and lift the balls, springs, and plates out of the gear.
21. Remove the lockplate for the countershaft and the reverse idler gear shaft.
22. With a pry bar in the slot of the reverse idler gear shaft, loosen the shaft. Slip the reverse idler shaft out of the housing and gear. Lift the reverse idler gear from the case.
23. To remove the countershaft, use a dummy shaft, (1⅛ x 9.850 in.) to displace the countershaft and keep the countergear components intact. After the countershaft has been pushed entirely out of the countergear and case, remove the gear.
24. Completely disassemble the countergear assembly.
25. To disassemble the reverse idler gear assembly, remove one of the snap-rings and tap out the washer, both sets of bearing rollers, center spacer, and sleeve. Remove the remaining snap-ring.

Assembly

Assemble in the reverse order of disassembly. Pay particular attention to the following:

1. Install the countershaft from the rear, with the bronze front thrust washer and the steel-backed bronze rear thrust washer installed with the lugs engaged in the notches in the end of the gear cluster. Do not seat the countershaft until the reverse idler gear and shaft have been installed.
2. Install the reverse idler shaft

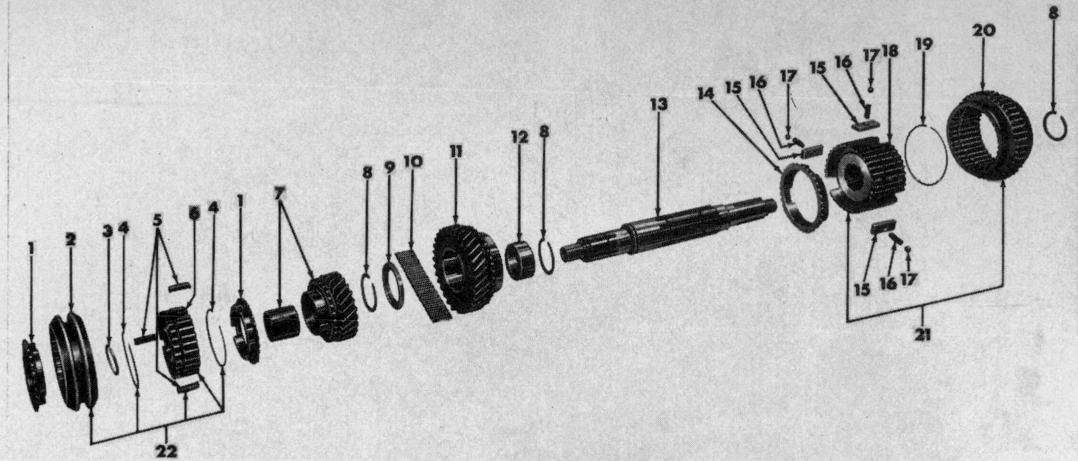

Four-speed mainshaft assembly (© Kaiser Willys Corp)

1—Blocking ring
2—Direct and third clutch sleeve
3—Snap ring
4—Spring
5—Shifting plate
6—Direct and third clutch hub
7—Third speed gear assembly
8—Snap ring
9—Thrust washer
10—Bearing rollers
11—Second speed gear
12—Spacer
13—Mainshaft
14—Blocking ring
15—Shifting plate
16—Poppet spring
17—Ball
18—Low and second clutch hub
19—Retaining ring
20—Low and second speed gear
21—Second speed synchronizer assembly
22—Direct and third synchronizer assembly

until the lockplate slot is adjacent to the countershaft slot. Insert the lock-plate and tap the shafts together.

3. Assemble the second-speed synchronizer by installing the low-second hub into low-second gear. Install the retaining ring in the gear. Slide the hub out of the gear until the holes in the hub are clear of the gear. Install the shifter plates and springs. Push the hub back into the gear. Push a shifter plate toward the center of the gear while installing the ball. Repeat for the other two balls. Push the hub into the gear until the balls snap into position.
4. Assemble the third-fourth synchronizer by installing the springs with the tension opposed. Place the right, lipped end of one spring in a hub slot. Place the spring in hub. Turn the hub around and repeat the operation with the other spring. Install the three synchronizer shifting plates in the hub with the smooth side of the plates out. Slip the clutch sleeve over the hub with the long beveled edge toward the long part of the hub. Install the two blocking rings.
5. Assemble the mainshaft, placing the threaded end up. Install the snap-ring and thrust washer with the recessed side covering the snap-ring. Install the bearing rollers around the shaft and hold them with a rubber band. Install the spacer. Install the second gear, tapered shoulder up. Install the snap-ring and blocking ring. Install the second-speed synchronizer and snap-ring. Install third gear, tapered shoulder to front. Install the third-fourth synchronizer assembly and snap-ring.
6. Install the main drive gear assembly and bearings in front of the case and mainshaft assembly through the top of the case. Temporarily install the bearing retainer.
7. Install the mainshaft bearing snap-ring; press the bearing into the case. Remove the bearing retainer. Install the oil slinger and snap-ring. Press the main drive gear bearing into the case. Use the thickest snap-ring that will fit in the groove.
8. Measure the space between the main drive gear bearing retainer and the case. Install a gasket 0.003–0.005 in. thicker than this measurement.

Warner T85 3 Speed Transmission

Disassembly

1. With the transmission drained and mounted in an adequate stand, remove the cap screws, washers, and side cover assembly of the transmission.
2. Remove the four cap screws and washers which hold the mainshaft rear bearing retainer extension to the case and move the extension away from the case about ½ in. Then rotate the retainer to expose the countershaft end and lock key.
3. From the front of the transmission, drive the countershaft to

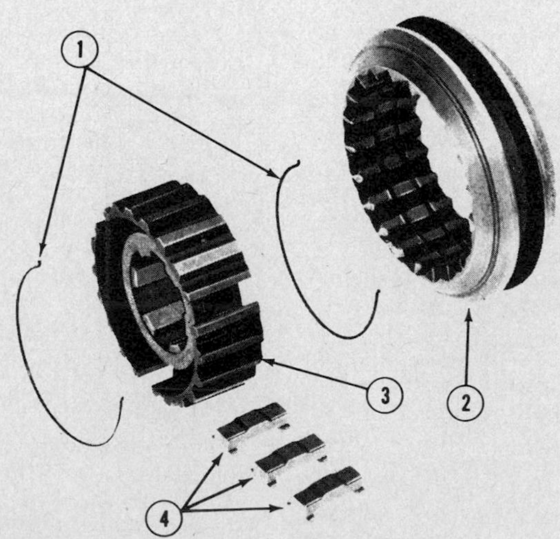

Second and third gear synchronizer assembly (© Kaiser Willys Corp)

1—Synchronizer spring (2)
2—Clutch hub
3—Cutch sleeve
4—Shifter plate

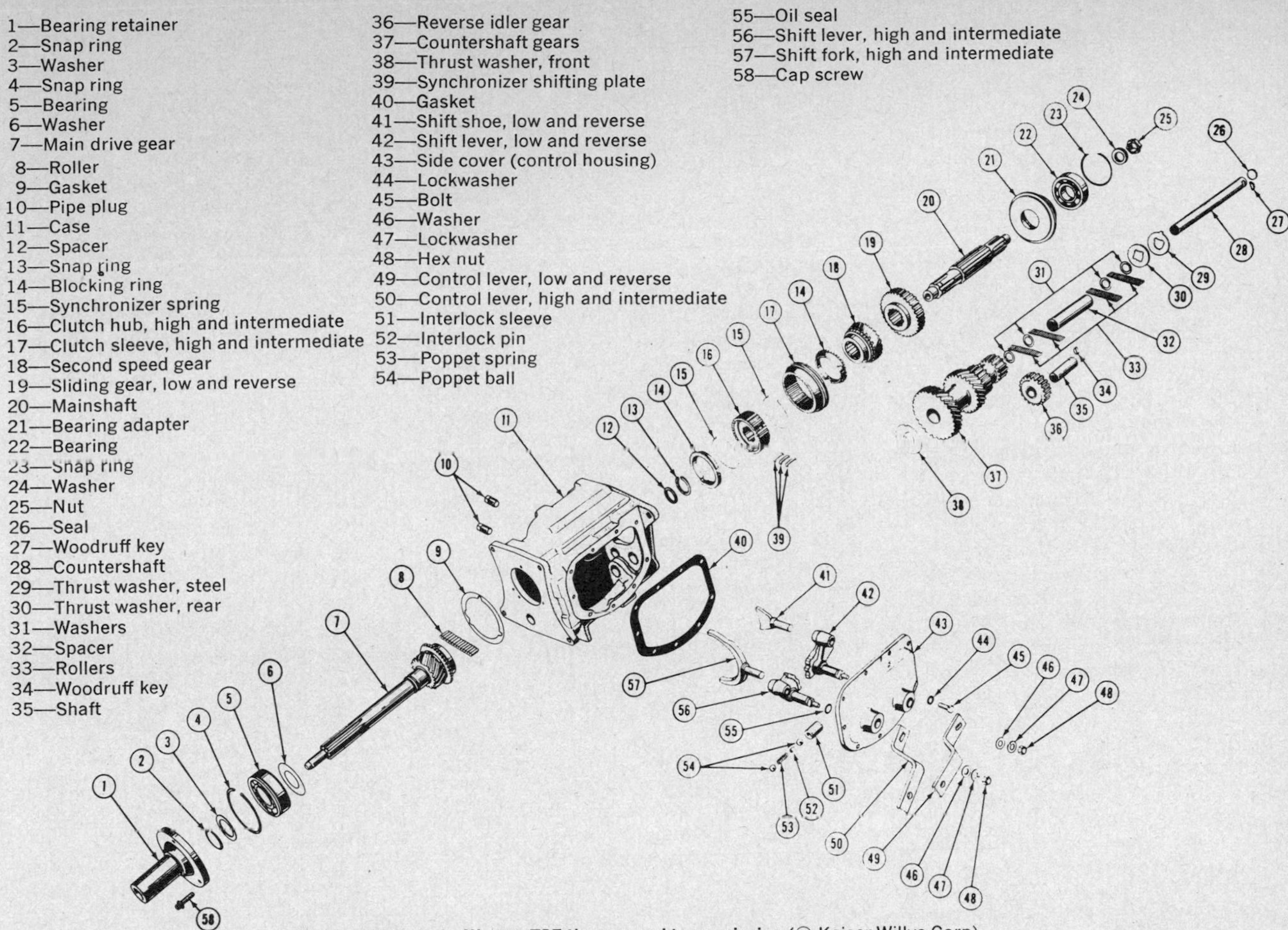

Exploded view of a Warner T85 three speed transmission (© Kaiser Willys Corp)

the rear, using a countershaft dummy.

4. Work the countershaft all the way out of the cluster, end spacers, rollers and roller bearing spacer.
5. Leave the dummy shaft in place in the countershaft gear cluster to keep the bearings and spacers in location.
6. Lower the countergear cluster down into the bottom of the case, then remove the rear bearing retainer extension, gasket, and mainshaft assembly from the transmission case.
7. Remove the mainshaft front bearing rollers from inside the main drive gear.
8. Remove the bearing spacing washer from the front end of the mainshaft.
9. Remove the attaching cap screws and washers, then the main drive gear bearing retainer from front of the case.
10. Remove the main drive gear bearing snap-ring from the front side of the main drive gear bearing.
11. With the transmission case upended (front up) press the main drive gear out of the bearing.
12. Remove the oil retainer from the main drive gear.
13. Tap the main drive gear bearing out through the front of the case and remove the main drive gear bearing snap-ring from the shaft.
14. Using a brass drift, drive the reverse idler shaft to the rear of the case to clear the lock key.
15. Remove the lock key and, from the rear of the case, drive the idler gear shaft into the case, then remove the idler gear and shaft from the case.
16. Lift out the countergear, dummy shaft, and washers from the case.
17. Remove the synchronizing ring from the front side of the second and third-speed clutch. Remove the clutch hub retaining snap-ring from the front end of the mainshaft.
18. Remove the second- and third-speed clutch sleeve from the clutch hub, then remove the clutch hub from the mainshaft.
19. Remove the two clutch key springs and three clutch keys from the clutch hub.
20. Remove the rear synchronizer ring and second-speed gear from the mainshaft.
21. Remove the first and reverse sliding gear from the mainshaft.
22. Remove the speedometer driven gear lock plate-to-extension bolt and lock washer, then remove the lock plate.
23. Insert a screwdriver in the lock-plate slot in the fitting and pry the fitting and shaft from the extension.
24. Remove the mainshaft rear bearing front snap-ring from the rear bearing retainer extension and tap the mainshaft and rear bearing out of the retainer extension.
25. Remove the snap-ring from the rear of the speedometer drive gear.
26. Remove the speedometer drive gear, detent ball and speedometer gear front snap-ring.
27. Remove the mainshaft rear bearing rear snap-ring.
28. Using a press, press the mainshaft rear bearing toward the rear of the shaft until loose and remove it.
29. Remove the seal from the rear bearing retainer.

Assembly

1. Assemble by reversing the above procedure.

AUTOMATIC TRANSMISSION

All current Jeep vehicles use the General Motors Turbo Hydra-Matic 400 automatic transmission. The 327 V8 used a Borg Warner AS-8F unit.

Transmission Removal

Models Prior to 1972

1. Disconnect the battery ground strap. Release the parking brake. Raise and support the vehicle.
2. Drain and remove the transfer case.
3. Disconnect:
   a. Electrical lead case connector.
   b. Vacuum line at modulator.
   c. Oil cooler lines.
   d. Shift linkage.
4. Remove the exhaust pipe assembly from the muffler and the exhaust manifolds.
5. Remove the handbrake cable plate from the crossmember.
6. Support the transmission with a jack.
7. Remove the crossmember.
8. Remove the converter dust shield from the transmission case.
9. Remove the bolts, the torque coverter to the flex plate.
10. Lower the transmission until the jack is barely supporting it.
11. Remove the transmission mounting bolts.
12. Raise the transmission to its normal position, slide it rearward, and lower it away from the vehicle.

Caution Keep the rear of the transmission lower than the front to avoid dropping the converter.

13. Installation is the reverse of removal.

1972 and Later Models

1. Remove the bolt holding the transmission dipstick tube to the engine.
2. Remove the shift lever carpet trim ring.
3. Remove the top cover and lever on the Model 20 transfer case.
4. Remove the rear driveshaft after making chalk marks so that it can be replaced in the same position.
5. Remove the exhaust pipe clamp bolt, shift lever, downshift wire, and speedometer cable.
6. Place a jack under the transmission.
7. Remove the rear crossmember.
8. Remove the exhaust pipe.
9. Disconnect the transfer case end of the front driveshaft after making chalk marks so that it can be replaced in the same position.
10. Detach the oil cooler lines and the vacuum line. On Quadra-Trac transfer cases, remove the diaphragm control hoses and electrical leads.
11. Remove the converter housing splash pan. Mark the relationship between the converter and the flywheel and unbolt the converter from the flywheel.
12. Unbolt the converter housing from the engine and remove the transmission.

To install:

13. Replace the transmission and bolt the converter housing to the engine. Torque the bolts to 28 ft lbs.
14. Align the marks made in step 11 and bolt the converter to the flywheel. Torque the bolts to 33 ft lbs.
15. Replace the converter splash pan.
16. Connect the oil cooler and vacuum lines. Install the vacuum lines and electrical leads on Quadra-Trac transfer cases.
17. Replace the front driveshaft, aligning the marks made in step 9. The flange bolts should be torqued to 25–45 ft lbs.
18. Replace, but do not tighten down, the exhaust pipe.
19. Replace the crossmember and torque the bolts to 30–35 ft lbs. Remove the jack.
20. Tighten the exhaust pipe. Replace the exhaust pipe clamp bolt.
21. Replace the shift lever, speedometer cable, and downshift wire.
22. Replace the rear driveshaft, aligning the marks made in Step 4. The flange bolts should be torqued to 25-45 ft lbs.
23. Install the top cover and shift lever on the transfer case.
24. Replace the carpet trim ring and the dipstick tube-to-engine bolt.

Linkage Adjustment

Cable-Operated Linkage

1. Disconnect the control cable at the transmission lever and place the transmission shift lever in Neutral.
2. Place the control lever in neutral position.
3. Loosen the two nuts at the upper end of the control cable housing and move the housing up or down until the cable exactly matches the position of the lever on the transmission.
4. Lock the nuts on the housing and connect the cable to the lever.

Rod-Operated Linkage

1. Remove the adjusting block from the transmission shift lever.
2. Make sure that the transmission lever is in Neutral position.
3. Place the selector lever in the Neutral position and hold firmly against the stop.
4. Loosen the locknuts on the adjusting block. Install the block on the transmission lever without moving the lever. Tighten the locknuts to 6–12 ft lbs.
5. Check the shifting operation. If the console interferes with the shift selector lever, reposition the console.

Neutral Safety Switch Adjustment

1. Make certain the shift linkage is correctly adjusted.
2. Set the handbrake and the footbrake. Put the handlever on the steering column in the Drive position. Hold the ignition key (or starter button) on and slowly move the handlever toward neutral until the starter cranks and the engine runs.
3. Without moving the lever further, press the accelerator to determine whether or not the transmission is really in neutral.
4. If all is correct, the engine will have started when the handlever got to the Neutral position, and the transmission will not be in gear.
5. Adjust the neutral safety switch by turning it and its mounting bracket until the above conditions have been met.

U-JOINTS

Driveshaft and U-Joints

The drive of four-wheel drive Universal and Jeepster models from the transfer case to the front and rear axles is through two tubular driveshafts. Each driveshaft has two cross and roller universal joints. Two-wheel drive models drive through a single driveshaft with two universal joints. Each driveshaft has a splined slip joint at one end to allow for variations in length.

Jeepster V6 models have a front driveshaft made up of two shafts with three universal joints and one slip joint. The shorter of the two shafts, directly ahead of the transfer case, has a shaft support bearing.

Wagoneer models use several types and sizes of driveshafts, depending upon various transmission and equipment options. These are divided into two basic types. The first is that with two cross and roller joints and a slip joint. The second has a cross and roller joint at one end, and a ball and trunnion universal joint at the other end. Automatic transmission Wagoneer models have the slip joint end of the front driveshaft at the axle rather than at the transfer case, as on all other models.

Cross and Roller Universal Joint

Snap-Ring Type Disassembly and Repair

1. Remove the snap-rings.
2. Press on the end of one bearing until the opposite bearing is pushed from the yoke arm.
3. Turn the joint over. Press the first bearing back out of the arm

1 Grease cover
2 Gasket
3 Thrust washer
4 Spring washer
5 Centering button
6 Bearing ball
7 Bearing roller
8 Universal joint body
9 Trunnion pin
10 Clamp
11 Dust cover
12 Clamp
13 Breather
14 Ballhead
15 Tube
16 Tube yoke
17 Seal retainer
18 Bearing seal
19 Cross
20 Bearing cup
21 Bearing roller
22 Cup retainer ring
23 Roller retainer
24 Tie link
25 Bearing block retainer

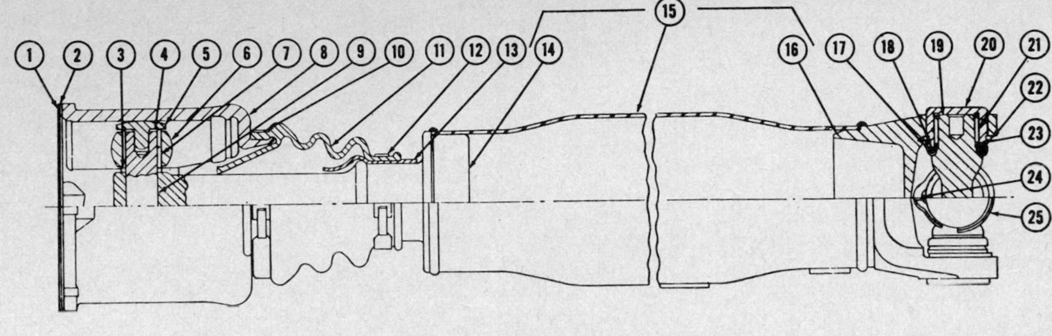

Ball and trunnion type rear driveshaft (© Willys Corp)

by pressing on the exposed end of the journal shaft. Repeat this operation for the other two bearings, then lift out the journal assembly by sliding it to one side.

4. Wash all parts in solvent and inspect for wear. Replace all worn parts.
5. Install new gaskets on the journal assembly. Make certain that the grease channel in each journal trunnion is open.
6. Pack the bearing cones one-third full of grease and install the rollers.
7. Assemble in the reverse order of disassembly. If the joint binds when assembled, tap the arms lightly to relieve any pressure on the bearings at the end of the journal.

U-Bolt Type Disassembly and Repair

Remove the attaching U-bolts to release one set of bearing races. Slide the driveshaft into the yoke flange to remove the races. The rest of the disassembly and repair procedure is the same as that given above for the snap-ring type of cross and roller joint. The correct U-bolt torque is 15–20 ft lbs.

Ball and Trunnion Universal Joint

Disassembly and Repair

1. Clamp the shaft firmly in a vise.
2. Bend the grease cover lugs away from the universal joint body. Remove the cover and gasket.
3. Remove the two clamps from the dust cover. Push the joint body toward the driveshaft tube. Remove two each: centering buttons, spring washers, ball and roller bearings, and thrust washers, from the trunnion pin.
4. Press the trunnion pin from ballhead.
5. If the ballhead is bent out of alignment or if the trunnion pin bore is worn or damaged, replace the driveshaft.

To reassemble:

6. Secure the larger end of the dust cover to the joint body with the larger of two clamps. Install the smaller clamp. Fit the cover over the ballhead shaft.
7. Push the universal joint cover toward the driveshaft tube. Press the trunnion pin into the centered position. If the trunnion pin is not centered, imbalance will result.
8. Install the thrust washers, ball and roller bearings, spring washer, and centering buttons on the trunnion pin. Compress the centering buttons. Move the joint body to hold the buttons in place.
9. Insert the breather between the dust cover and the ballhead shaft, along the length of the shaft. The breather must extend no more than ½ in. beyond the dust cover. Tighten the clamp screw to secure the cover to the shaft. Cut away any portion of dust cover protruding under the clamps.
10. Pack the raceways around the ball and roller bearings with about 2 oz of universal joint grease.
11. Position the gasket and grease cover on the body. Bend the lugs of the cover into the notches of the body. Move the body back and forth to distribute grease in the raceways.

FRONT SUSPENSION

Live Front Axle

On four-wheel drive models, caster is adjusted by placing shims between the spring pads on the front axle housing and the top of the spring.

This method should only be used where it is necessary to adjust both sides of the vehicle the same amount. In the event the caster angle is incorrect because of sag of the front leaf springs, it is advisable to replace the springs rather than use caster wedges. Camber cannot be adjusted.

Solid Front Axle

Universal models with two-wheel drive have a solid front axle. The axle may be either of tubular construction or a forged I-beam. Springs may be slung either under or over the axle. Standard caster and camber are built into the front axle. Camber cannot be changed, but caster can be adjusted by placing tapered shims between the springs and spring seats.

Shock Absorber Removal and Installation

1. Raise the vehicle.
2. Remove the lock nuts and washers (cotter pins on older models) that hold the upper and lower mounting eyes to the mounting pins.
3. Pull the shock absorber eyes and the rubber bushings from the mounting pins.
4. To install the shock absorber, first install the rubber bushings and shock absorber eyes, then install the washers and locknuts or cotter pins.
5. Tighten the locknuts securely.

NOTE: If a shock absorber is removed from the vehicle and turned upside down, it will lose its prime and become inoperative.

Steering Knuckle Pivot Pins and Bearings

Removal and Installation

Closed Knuckle Type

1. Raise the side of the vehicle that is to be worked on and remove the hub and brake drum assembly, wheel bearings, axle shaft,

spindle, and the steering tie-rod.
2. Remove the eight screws that hold the oil seal retainer in place.
3. Remove the four screws that hold the lower pivot pin bearing cap.
4. Remove the four screws that hold the upper bearing cap and remove the bearing cap.
5. The steering knuckle can now be removed from the axle.
6. Lift out the bearings and inspect, clean, and replace all worn parts.
7. Install in the reverse order of removal.

NOTE: When installing the steering knuckle, sufficient shims must be placed under the top bearing cap to obtain the correct preload on the bearing. The preload should be 12-16 lbs and checked with a spring scale hooked in the hole in the knuckle arm for the tie-rod socket.

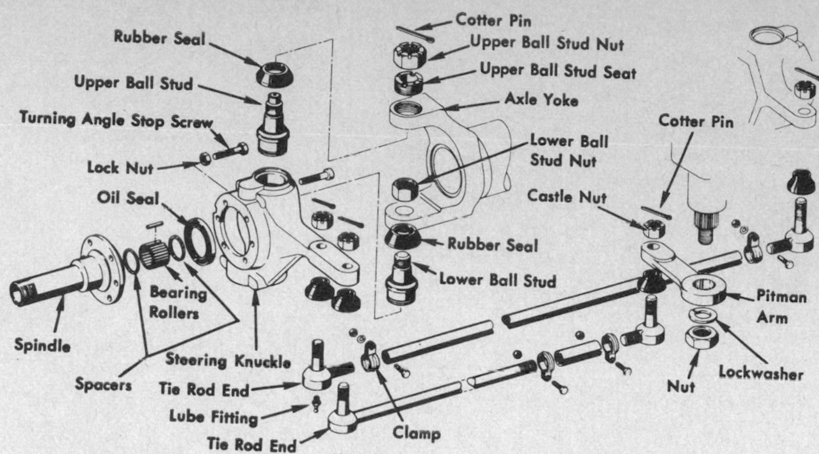

Open knuckle front axle, Commando and CJ—1971-on; Wagoneer and Cherokee—1974-76
(© Jeep Corp)

Open Knuckle Type

1. Replacement of the ball joints, or ball stud, as they will be called from here on, requires the removal of the steering knuckle. To remove the steering knuckle, first remove the wheel, brake drum, and hub as an assembly. Remove the brake assembly from the spindle. Position the brake assembly on the front axle in a convenient place. Remove the snap-ring from the axle shaft.
2. Remove the spindle and bearing assembly. It may be necessary to tap the spindle with a soft mallet to disengage it from the steering knuckle.
3. Slide the axle shaft out through the steering knuckle.
4. Disconnect the steering rods from the knuckle arm.
5. Remove the lower ball stud nut.
6. Remove the cotter pin from the upper stud. Loosen the upper stud until the top edge of the nut is flush with the top end of the stud.
7. Use a lead hammer to unseat the upper and lower studs from the yoke. Remove the upper nut and the knuckle assembly.
8. Remove the ball stud seat from the upper hole in the axle yoke. It is threaded in the hole. There are special wrenches available for removing the seat.
9. Securely clamp the knuckle assembly in a vise with the upper ball stud pointed down.
10. Using a large socket or drift, of approximately the same size as the ball stud, and a mallet, drive the lower stud out of the knuckle.

NOTE: Throughout this procedure, where a ball stud is either removed or installed, a hydraulic press or a two-jawed gear puller can be used and, if at all possible, should be used to make the job easier. However it is possible to complete the job using a mallet, a drift, and a large socket the same size as the ball studs.

11. Place the socket on the bottom surface of the upper ball stud. Place the drift through the hole where the lower ball stud was and place it on the socket. Drive the upper ball stud out of the knuckle with a mallet.
12. Before installing the lower ball stud, run the lower ball stud nut onto the stud just far enough so the head of the stud is flush with the top edge of the nut.
13. Invert the knuckle in the vise. Position the lower ball stud in the knuckle with the nut in place. Place the same size socket over the nut and drive the ball stud into place with the drift and mallet.
14. Use the same procedure for installing the upper ball stud. The drift will not be needed to install the upper ball stud.

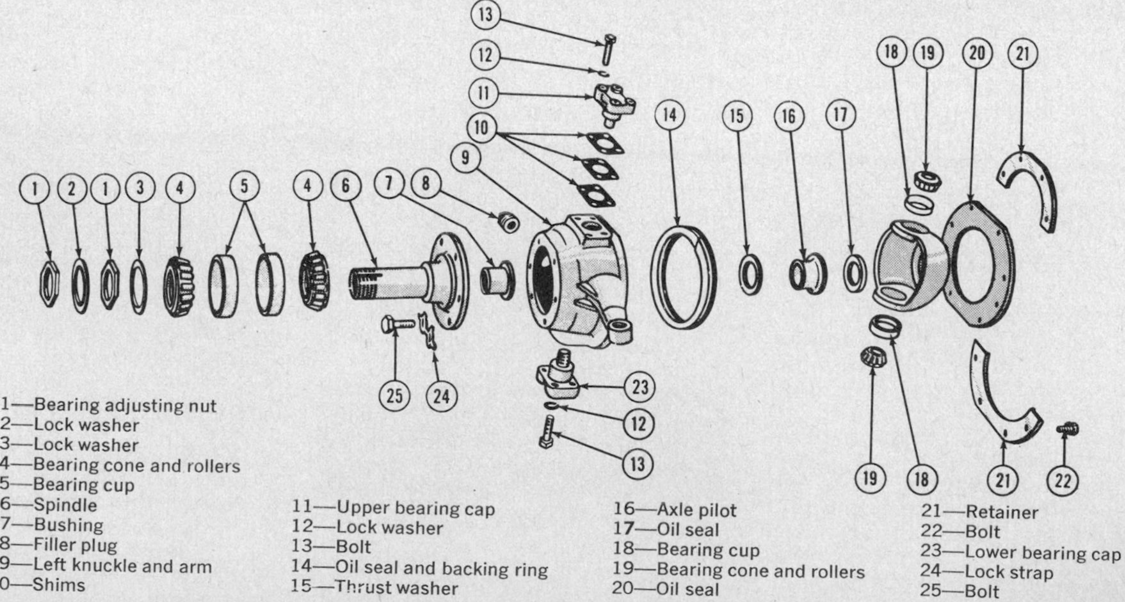

Closed knuckle front axle, Commando and CJ—pre-1971; Wagoneer—pre-1974
(© Kaiser Willys Corp)

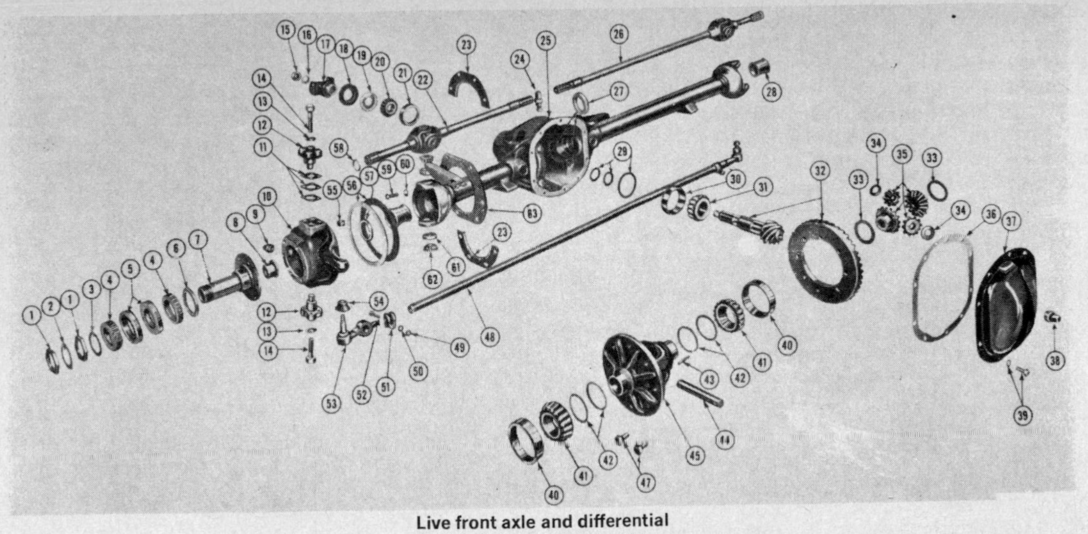

Live front axle and differential
(© Kaiser Willys Corp)

1—Nut
2—Lock washer
3—Bearing lock washer
4—Wheel bearing cap
5—Cone and rollers
6—Oil seal
7—Spindle
8—Spindle bushing
9—Filter plug
10—Right knuckle and arm
11—Shims
12—Pivot pin
13—Lock washer
14—Cap screw
15—Nut
16—Washer
17—Universal joint yoke
18—Oil seal
19—Oil slinger
20—Cone and rollers
21—Bearing cup
22—Right axle shaft with universal joint
23—Knuckle oil seal retainer
24—Housing breather
25—Front axle housing
26—Axle shaft with universal joint
27—Oil seal
28—Axle shaft guide
29—Shim pack
30—Bearing cup
31—Cone and rollers
32—Ring gear and pinion
33—Thrust washer
34—Thrust washer
35—Differential gears
36—Housing cover gasket
37—Housing cover
38—Fill plug
39—Screw and lock washer
40—Bearing cup
41—Cone and rollers
42—Shims
43—Lock pin
44—Pinion shaft
45—Differential case
47—Bolts
48—Steering tie-rod
49—Tie-rod clamp nut
50—Lock washer
51—Tie-rod socket clamp
52—Screw
53—Tie-rod socket
54—Dust cover
55—Nut
56—Oil seal and backing ring
57—Thrust washer
58—Snap-ring
59—Stop bolt
60—Nut
61—Bearing cup
62—Cone and rollers
63—Gasket

15. Install the upper ball stud seat into the axle yoke. Use a new one if the old one shows evidence of wear. The top of the seat should be flush with the top of the yoke.
16. Install the knuckle assembly onto the axle yoke. Install the lower stud nut. Tighten it to 70-90 ft lbs.
17. Install the upper stud nut and tighten it to 100 ft lbs. Install the cotter pin. If the cotter pin holes do not align, tighten the nut until the pin can be installed. Do not loosen the nut to align the holes.
18. Install the axle shaft, spindle and bearing assembly, and brake assembly. Connect the steering rods. Install the drum and hub, and wheel assembly. Adjust the wheel bearings. Check the turning angle. Adjust the stop screw to permit the proper turning angle of 31°.

Springs

Removal and Installation

Prior to 1972

1. Raise the vehicle with a jack under the axle and place a jackstand under the frame side rail. Then lower the axle jack so that the load is relieved from the spring and the wheels rest on the floor.
2. Remove the nuts which secure the spring clip bolts. Remove the spring plate and clip bolts. Free the spring from the axle by raising the axle jack.
3. Remove the pivot bolt nut and drive out the pivot bolt. Disconnect the shackle either by removing the lower nuts and bolts on the rubber-bushed shackles, or by removing the threaded bushings on the U-shackles.
4. To replace, first install the pivot bolt. Then, connect the shackle using the following procedures.
5. On bronze-bushed pivot bolts, install the bolt and nut and tighten the nut. Then back it off two cotter pin slots and install the cotter pin. The nut must be drawn up tightly but must be sufficiently loose to allow the spring to pivot freely. Otherwise the spring might break.
6. On rubber-bushed pivot bolts and locknuts (or lockwasher and nut), only tighten the bolt enough to hold the bushings in position until the vehicle is lowered from the jack.
7. Connect the shackle. On rubber-bushed shackles install the bolts as in Step 6 above. For U-shackles, insert the shackle through the frame bracket and eye of the spring. Holding the U-shackle tightly against the frame, start the upper bushing on the shackle, taking care that when it enters the thread in the frame it does not cross-thread. Screw the bushing on the shackle tightly against the spring eye and thread the bushing in approximately half way. Then, alternately from top bushing to lower bushing, turn them in until the head of the bushing is snug against the frame bracket and the bushing in the spring eye is 1/32 in. away from the spring as measured from the inside of the hexagon head to the spring. Lubricate the bushing and then try the flex of the shackle, which must be free. If a shackle is tight, rethread the bushings on the shackle.
8. Move the axle into position on the spring by lowering or raising the axle jack Install the spring clip bolts, spring plate, lockwashers, and nuts. Torque the nuts to 50-55 ft lbs. Avoid over-tightening. Be sure the spring is free to move at both ends.
9. Remove both jacks. On rubber bushed shackles and pivot bolts, allow the weight of the vehicle to seat the bushings in their operating positions. Then torque the nuts to 27-30 ft lbs.

1972 and Later

1. Raise the vehicle with a jack under the axle. Place a jackstand

under the frame side rail. Then lower the axle jack so the load is relieved from the spring and the wheels rest slightly on the floor.

2. Disconnect the shock absorber from the spring clip plate.
3. Remove the nuts which secure the spring clips (U-bolts). Remove the spring plate and spring clips. Free the spring from the axle by raising the axle.
4. Remove the pivot bolt nut and drive out the pivot bolt. Disconnect the shackle from the shackle bracket by removing the lock nut, lock nut and bolt or nut, or lockwasher and bolt.
5. With the spring removed, the spring shackle and/or shackle plate may be removed from the spring by removing the lock nut, lock nut and shackle bolt or nut, or lockwasher and shackle bolt.
6. Inspect the bushings in the eye of the main spring leaf and the bushings of the spring shackle for excessive wear. Replace if necessary.
7. The spring can be disassembled, for replacing an individual spring leaf, by removing the clips and the center bolt.
8. To install the spring on the vehicle with the bushings in place and the spring shackle attached to the springs, position the spring in the pivot hanger and install the pivot bolt and lock nut. Only tighten the lock nut enough to hold the bushings in position until the vehicle is lowered from the jack.
9. Position the spring and install the shackle, shackle bolts, shackle plate if applicable, lockwasher, and nut. Only finger tighten the nuts at this time.
10. Move the axle into position on the spring by lowering the axle jack. Place the spring center bolt in the axle saddle hole. Install the spring clips, spring plate, lockwashers and nuts. Torque the 7/16 in. nuts to 36-42 ft lbs and the ½ in. nuts to 45-65 ft lbs.

NOTE: Be sure that the center bolt is properly centered in the axle saddle.

11. Connect the shock absorber.
12. Remove the axle and allow the weight of the vehicle to seat the bushings in their operating positions. Then torque the 7/16 in. spring pivot bolt nuts and spring shackle nuts to 25-40 ft lbs. Torque the ⅝ in. shackle nuts to 55-75 ft lbs.

Front Axle Universal Joints

Three types of constant velocity universal joints are used on Jeep four-wheel drives. The first is the Bendix type universal joint, the second the Rzeppa type, and the third the Spicer type.

Removal

1. Remove the wheel.
2. Remove the hub dust cap.
3. Remove the axle shaft driving flange bolts.
4. Apply and hold the foot brakes. Remove the axle shaft flange with a puller.
5. Release the lip on the lockwasher, remove the outer nut, lockwasher, adjusting nut, and bearing lockwasher. Use a special wrench for these nuts.
6. Remove the wheel hub and drum assembly with the bearings.
7. Remove the hydraulic brake tube, backing plate screws, spindle, axle shaft and universal joint assembly.
8. Install in the reverse order of removal.

Repair

Bendix Joint

The factory no longer supplies replacement component parts for the Bendix universal joint. Rebuilding these universals requires complex shop equipment and is economically unfeasible. However, the complete universal joint assembly may be replaced.

If the assembly falls apart upon removal from the vehicle, reassemble as follows:

1. Place the differential half of the axle shaft in a vise, with the ground portion above the jaws.
2. Install the center ball in the socket in the shaft, with the hole and groove toward you.
3. Drop the center ball pin into the drilled passage in the wheel half of the shaft.
4. Place the wheel half of the shaft on the center ball. Then slip three balls into the raceways.
5. Turn the center ball until the groove lines up with the raceway for the remaining ball. Slip the ball into the raceway and straighten up the wheel end of the shaft.
6. Turn the center ball until the center ball pin drops into the hole in the ball.
7. Install the retainer pin and prick punch both ends to lock it in place.
8. After reassembly, grasp both ends of the shaft and twist the ends back and forth. Should excessive wear be indicated by backlash or lost motion, the assembly should be replaced.

Rzeppa Joint

1. To dismantle the Rzeppa joint, remove the three screws (some axles have no screws) that hold the front axle shaft to the joint itself, and pull the shaft out of the splined inner race. To take out the axle shaft retainer, remove the retainer ring on the shaft. Push down on the various points of the inner race and cage until the balls can be removed with the help of a small screwdriver.
2. There are two large elongated holes in the cage. Turn the cage so that the two bosses in the spindle shaft will drop into the elongated holes in the cage. The cage can then be lifted out.
3. To remove the inner race, turn it so that one of the bosses will drop into an elongated hole in this cage, then shift the race to one side and lift it out.

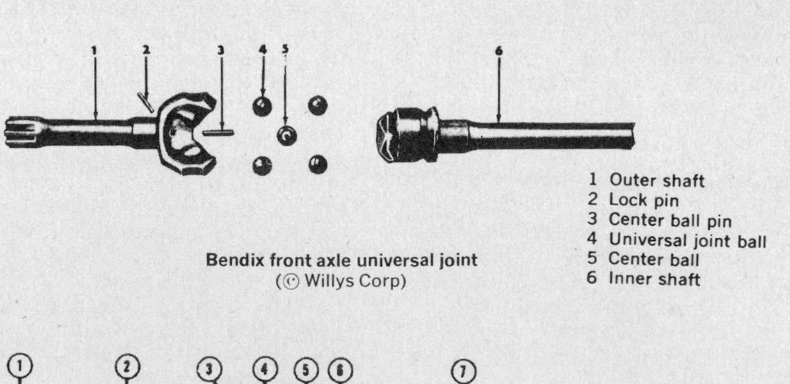

Bendix front axle universal joint
(© Willys Corp)

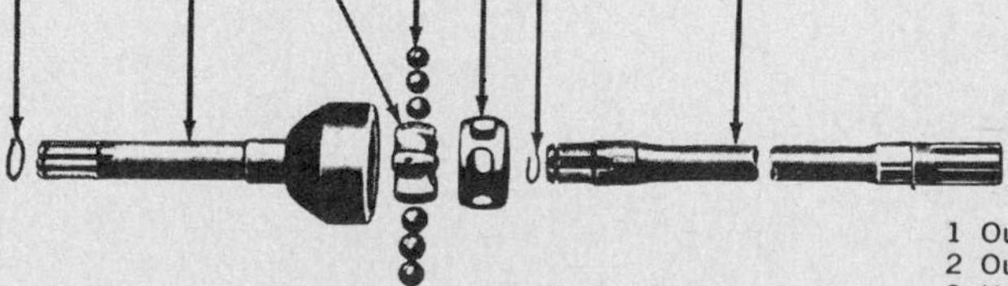

Rzeppa front axle universal joint
(© Willys Corp)

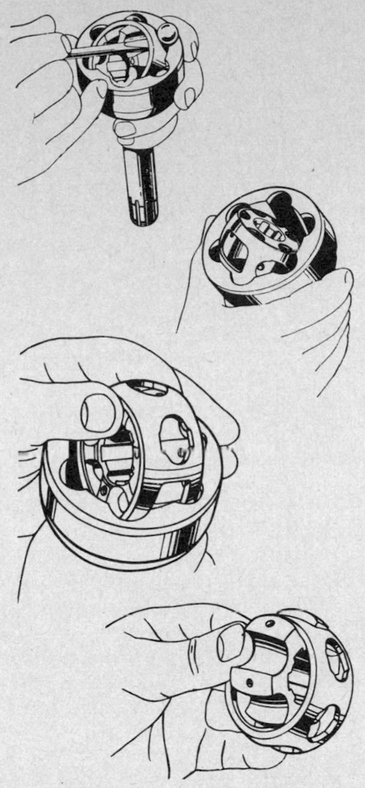
Disassembly of Rzeppa joint (© Willys Corp)

4. Reverse the procedure to reassemble.

Spicer Joint

The Spicer universal joint is a cross and roller unit with needle bearings. It is quite similar in design to the Spicer driveshaft universal joint. Disassembly is as follows:

1. Remove the snap-rings.
2. Press on the end of one bearing until the opposite bearing is pushed from the yoke arm.
3. Turn the joint over. Press the first bearing back out of the arm by pressing on the exposed end of the journal shaft. Repeat this operation for the other two bearings, then lift out the journal assembly by sliding it to one side.
4. Wash all parts in solvent and inspect for wear. Replace all worn parts.
5. Install new gaskets on the journal assembly. Make certain that the grease channel in each journal trunnion is open.
6. Pack the bearing cones one-third full of grease and install the rollers.
7. Assemble in the reverse order of disassembly. If the joint binds when assembled, tap the arms lightly to relieve any pressure on the bearings at the end of the journal.

DRIVE AXLES

NOTE: The following procedures apply to both front and rear drive axles.

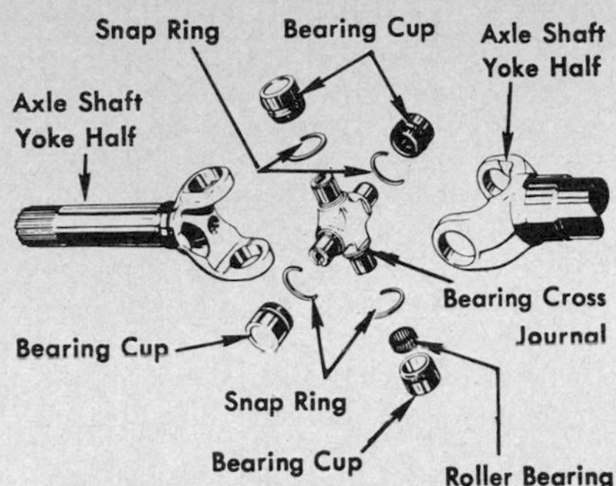

Spicer front axle universal joint (© Willys Corp)

Axle Shaft End-Play Adjustment

1. Remove the wheel and tire and, using a puller, remove the brake drum from the tapered shaft. (Do not use a knock-off puller, as the bearing or other parts may be damaged.)
2. Disconnect the brake line from the wheel cylinder.
3. Remove the backing plate.
4. To reduce the axle play, remove the shims; to increase end-play, add shims.
5. To measure the results, reinstall the backing plate and thoroughly tighten the retaining bolts. A dial gauge can be set up to ascertain exact bearing play.
6. Reconnect the brake line and bleed air from the brake system.
7. Reinstall the hub and drum, wheel and tire.
8. Recommended end-play is 0.012–0.020 in.

On this construction, with the tapered roller bearing, end-play adjust-

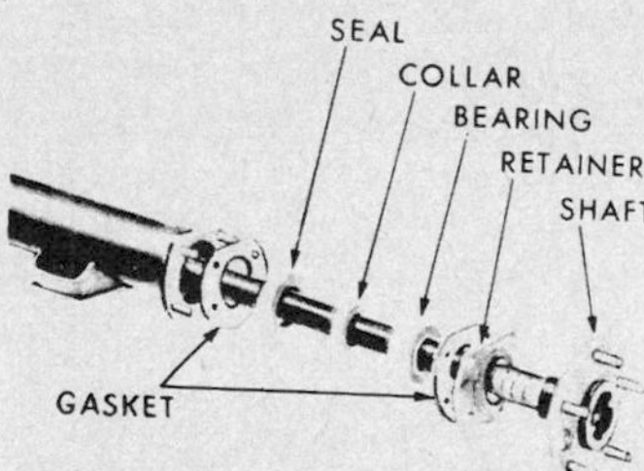

Adjusting the axle shaft end-play

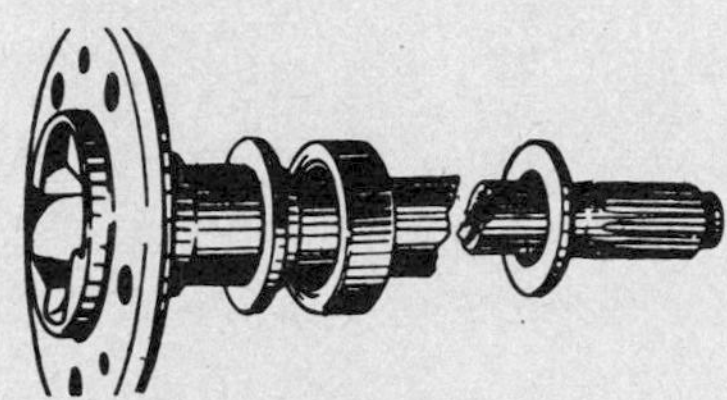
Arrangement of oil seals on rear axle shaft

ment is accomplished by adding or removing shims from behind the backing plate.

Axle Shaft and/or Bearing Replacement

1. Remove the wheel and tire and, using a puller, remove the brake drum from the tapered shaft. (Do not use a knock-off puller, as the bearing or other parts may be damaged.)
2. Disconnect the brake line from the wheel cylinder.
3. Remove the backing plate. Note the thickness of the shims used, to aid in reassembly.
4. Remove the axle shaft and bearing. (Drum, without axle key and nut on about halfway, may be used as an inertia puller.)
5. Press off the old and press on the new bearing cone.
6. Install a new seal, as required.
7. Place the axle shaft in the proper position and drive in the cone. Do not use a hammer and punch to locate the cone, as damage may occur.
8. Check axle shaft end-play. A dial gauge can be set up to measure the clearance. It is necessary that the axle shaft be entirely against the center block or a false reading will be obtained.
9. To reduce axle play, remove shims. To increase end-play, add shims.
10. Reassemble in reverse order and bleed brakes as needed.
11. Recommended end-play is 0.012–0.020 in.

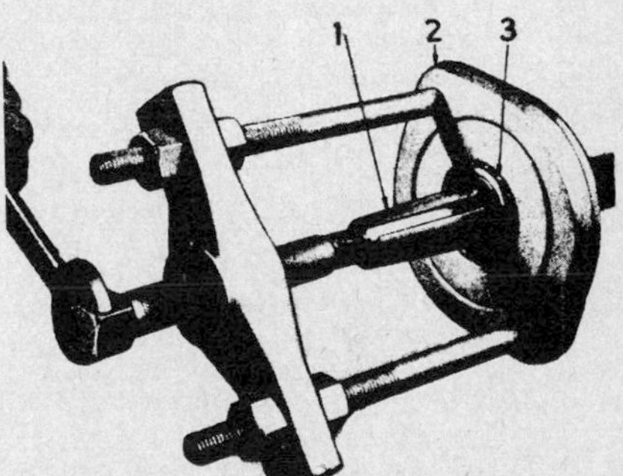

Using screw-type puller to remove bearing cone from rear axle

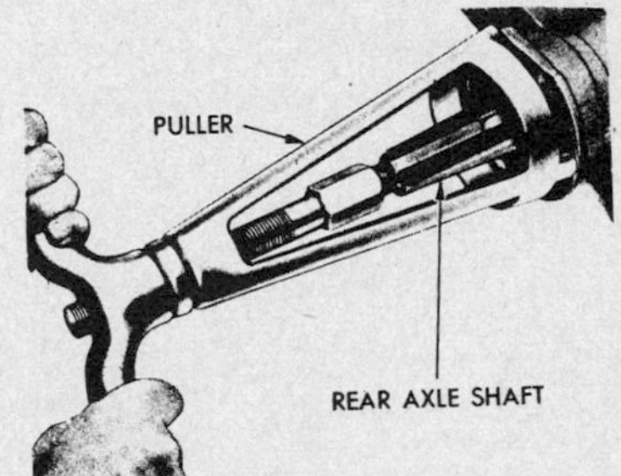

Using screw-type puller to remove rear axle shaft and bearing

Axle Outer Oil Seal Replacement

1. Remove the wheel and tire and, using a puller, remove the brake drum from the tapered shaft. (Do not use a knock-off puller, as bearing or other parts may be damaged.)
2. Disconnect the brake line from the wheel cylinder.

3. Remove the backing plate.
4. These backing plate bolts also hold the oil seal, which can now be replaced. Replace the shims, as removed, unless bearing is to be adjusted at the same time.
5. Reinstall in the reverse order of above.

BRAKES

Master Cylinder

All Jeep brake systems are actuated hydraulically through either a single or a dual master cylinder. Some models are equipped with a power booster that is integral with the master cylinder and mounted on the engine firewall.

To remove the master cylinder, disconnect and plug the brake lines, disconnect the wires from the stoplight switch, remove the attaching nuts, and lift out the assembly.

Installation is the reverse of the removal procedure. Make certain that all parts are clean. Bleed the brakes.

Power Booster

Power-assisted brakes are optional on some Jeep models. A Bendix single-diaphragm unit is used and it operates by utilizing manifold vacuum and atmospheric pressure to reduce pedal travel and effort. Free-play is factory set and not adjustable.

Removal

1. Clean the master cylinder and booster unit.
2. Remove the cotter and clevis pins securing the booster pushrod to the pedal linkage.
3. Disconnect the vacuum hose from the booster check valve.
4. Disconnect the fluid lines from the master cylinder. Plug the ends and catch any escaping fluid. *Do not reuse brake fluid.*
5. Disconnect the stoplight wires from the switch.
6. Remove the attaching nuts, booster unit assembly, and block spacers.
7. Remove the attaching nuts and separate the master cylinder from the booster.

Installation

To install the booster unit, reverse the removal procedure and bleed the brakes.

CAUTION: Do not pressure-bleed power-assisted brake systems.

Parking Brakes

The parking brake is operated by a foot pedal and a hand release lever. When the pedal is depressed, the rear brakes are actuated via an adjustable

1 Primary outlet—to front wheel brakes
2 Secondary outlet—to rear wheel brakes

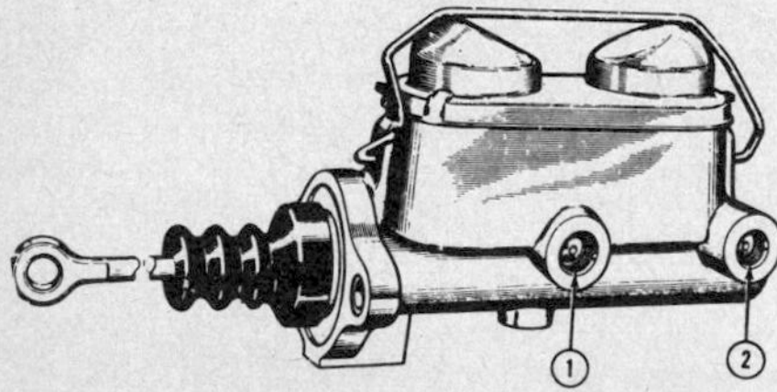

Master cylinder brake line outlets
(© Willys Corp)

1 Pedal link
2 Mounting bracket
3 Power section
4 Master cylinder

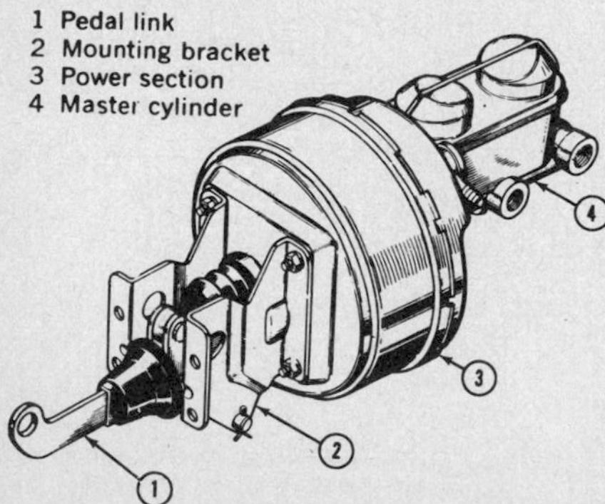

Brake booster unit and master cylinder
(© Willys Corp)

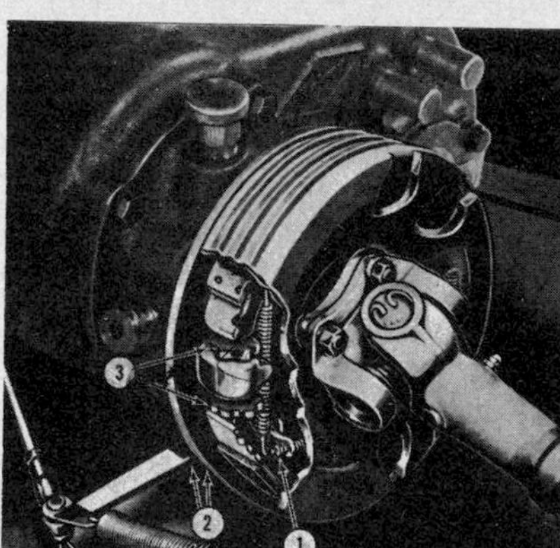

Transmission brake adjustment
(© Kaiser Willys Corp)
1—Ball nut
2—3/32 in. clearance
3—Adjusting screw

Brake bleeding and adjusting fixtures, models prior to 1972
(© Kaiser Willys Corp)
1—Adjusting cam
2—Brake hydraulic hose
3—Bleeder screw
4—Adjusting cam

Some J-series vehicles may be equipped with a transmission brake mounted at the rear output bearing housing on the transfer case.

Parking Brake Adjustment

1. Make certain the service brakes are in adjustment.
2. Raise the rear wheels.
3. Disengage the parking brake pedal.
4. Loosen the locknut on the brake cable adjusting rod.
5. Spin the wheels and tighten the rod until the brakes drag slightly.
6. Back off the adjustment until the wheels spin freely.
7. Tighten the locknut.

Transmission Brake Adjustment

1. Release the transmission brake pedal.
2. Rotate the transmission brake drum until the holes line up with the adjusting screws.
3. Turn the adjusting screws until the shoes are snug in the drum.
4. Back off the adjustment screws seven notches.
5. Make certain there is 3/32 in. clearance between the drum backing plate and the operating lever.

NOTE: If the clearance is incorrect, remove the drum and adjust the ball nut on the operating link until correct clearance is obtained.

STEERING

Steering Connecting Rod

The steering connecting rod is of the ball and socket type. All ball seat springs are identical except for their location. The ball joints must be loose enough to allow free movement, yet tight enough to prevent end-play.

Steering connecting rods used on 1974-75 models consist of a rod threaded at the left end, with an integral ball-stud end assembly at the right end. A turnbuckle and a removable ball-stud end at the threaded end complete the connecting rod assembly. The end having the integral ball-stud end assembly attaches to the tie-rod. The threaded end with the turnbuckle and removable ball-stud end assembly is attached to the pitman arm of the steering gear.

If the connecting rod is found to be damaged or worn, it must be replaced as an assembly. However, the ball-stud end assembly can be replaced separately.

Removal and Installation

Models Through 1973

1. Remove the cotter pins and nuts from both ends.
2. Remove the rod.
3. Inspect all parts and replace

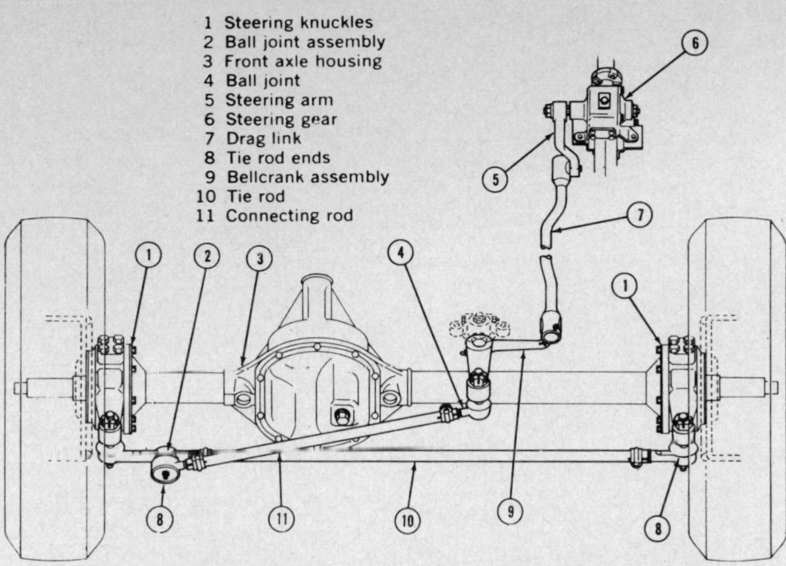

Jeepster and Commando steering linkage prior to 1972 (© Willys Corp)

kle and a removable ball-stud end complete the tie-rod assembly. The threaded end of the tie-rod has right-hand threads which accept the turnbuckle. The ball-stud tie-rod end screws into the turnbuckle. A large boss is located on the tie-rod about 8 in. from the unthreaded end. A tapered hole machined into the boss accepts the steering connecting rod end. The steering damper is connected to a stud which is mounted on a bracket that is either welded or clamped at the center of the tie-rod.

Removal and Installation

Models Through 1973

1. Remove cotter pins and nuts at both ends.
2. Using a puller or expansion fork, remove the tie rods from the steering knuckle arms.
3. Separate the joint seals and remove the socket assembly by loosening the clamp bolt nuts and unscrewing the unit.
4. Inspect all parts and replace as necessary.
5. Install by reversing the removal procedure. Use new seals and cotter pins, then torque the nuts to 38–42 ft lbs. If the steering arm was removed, torque the nut to 70–90 ft lbs for models with drag link steering, and 110–140 ft lbs for all others.

1974-76 Models

1. Remove the cotter pins and retaining nuts at both ends of the tie-rod, and from the end of the connecting rod where it attaches to the tie-rod.
2. Remove the nut attaching the steering damper pushrod to the tie-rod bracket and move the damper aside.
3. Remove the tie-rod ends from

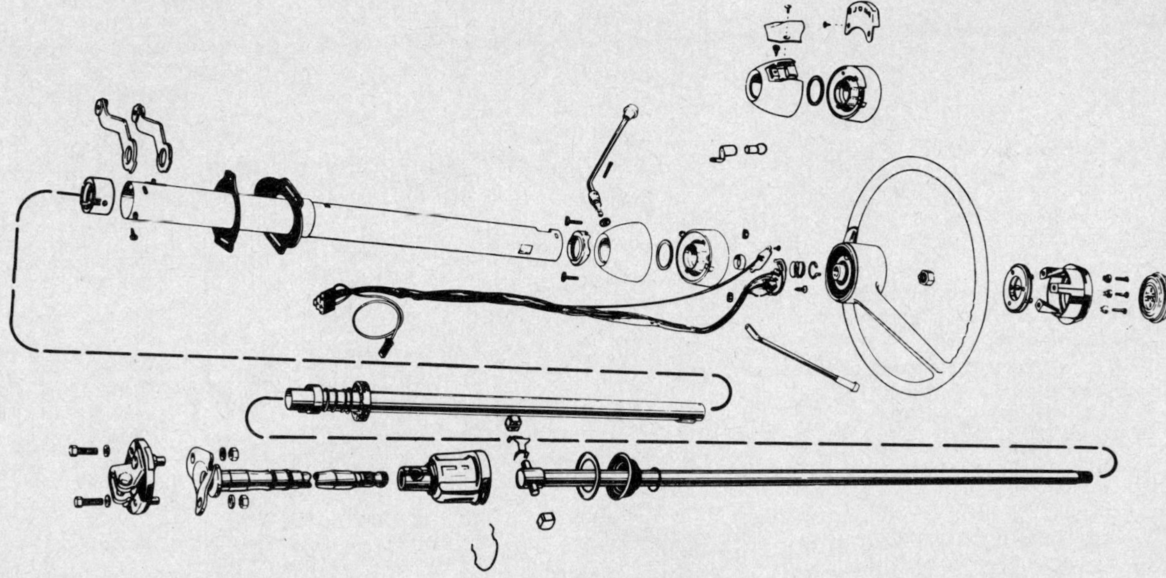

Exploded view of a Wagoneer steering column (© Jeep Corp)

them as necessary. *NOTE: Ball joints on late-model vehicles cannot be disassembled for service or inspection.*

4. Locate wheels in the straight-ahead position.
5. Locate the steering arm parallel to the centerline of the vehicle.
6. Align the steering arm and gear-shaft at the high point and then install the steering connecting rod with nuts and new cotter pins.

1974-76 Models

The steering connecting rod can be removed by removing the cotter pins and nuts from both ends, and then removing the rod. The steering connecting rod ball joints cannot be disassembled for service.

When installing the steering connecting rod, place the wheels in the straight-ahead position and place the steering arm parallel to the centerline of the vehicle. Have the steering gear steering arm properly indexed, with the line marks on the steering arm and gear shaft and the steering gear on the center of its high point. With the steering arm so positioned, install the connecting rod.

Tie Rods

The tie rods are a three-piece construction consisting of the rod and two ball and socket assemblies. Right-hand and left-hand threads on the rods provide toe-in adjustment without removing the rod.

NOTE: Early production F4-134 4×2 vehicles are equipped with a divided type tie rod connecting the steering knuckles. On these vehicles, each wheel must be adjusted independently.

The tie-rod used on 1974-75 models consists of a solid rod threaded on one end with an integral ball-stud end assembly at the other end. A turnbuc-

the steering arms and the connecting rod using a puller or expansion fork tool.

NOTE: After removal, the tie-rod ends can be removed from the tie-rod by loosening the turnbuckle clamp bolts and unscrewing the ends.

4. Attach the tie-rod ends to the steering arms. Tighten the nuts to 50 ft lbs and use new cotter pins to secure the nuts.
5. Attach the connecting rod to the tie-rod. Tighten the nut to 50 ft lbs and use a new cotter pin to secure the nut.
6. Attach the steering damper to the tie-rod bracket.
7. Adjust the toe-in as necessary.

Power Steering Pump Removal and Installation

Before working on the power steering pump, clean the exterior of the pump and the reservoir assembly.

NOTE: On all engines except the pre-1971 232 Six, the power steering pump need not be removed to service the pressure relief/flow control valve. The valve is located under a cap on the 327 V8 power steering pump and behind a pressure union on all the other engines, except the pre-1971 232 Six with a Thompson pump. The pressure relief valve in the Thompson unit is removed after the pump has been disassembled.

1. Loosen the drive belt tension adjustment bolt and remove the belt.
2. Place a receptacle under the pump/reservoir assembly and disconnect the pressure and return hoses from the pump. Fluid will drain out of the pump and hoses. Lay the ends of the hoses up higher than the steering gear to prevent all of the fluid from draining out. Cover the ends of the hoses to prevent dirt from entering.
3. Remove either the bolts that hold the pump to the mounting bracket or the bolts that hold the bracket and pump to the engine, whichever is easiest. Remove the pump from the engine.
4. Install the pump in the reverse order of removal and install the correct type and amount of fluid.

Steering Wheel Removal and Installation

CJ Models

1. Disconnect the negative battery cable.
2. Locate the front tires to a straight ahead position.
3. Remove the horn button by pulling it from the center of the steering wheel.

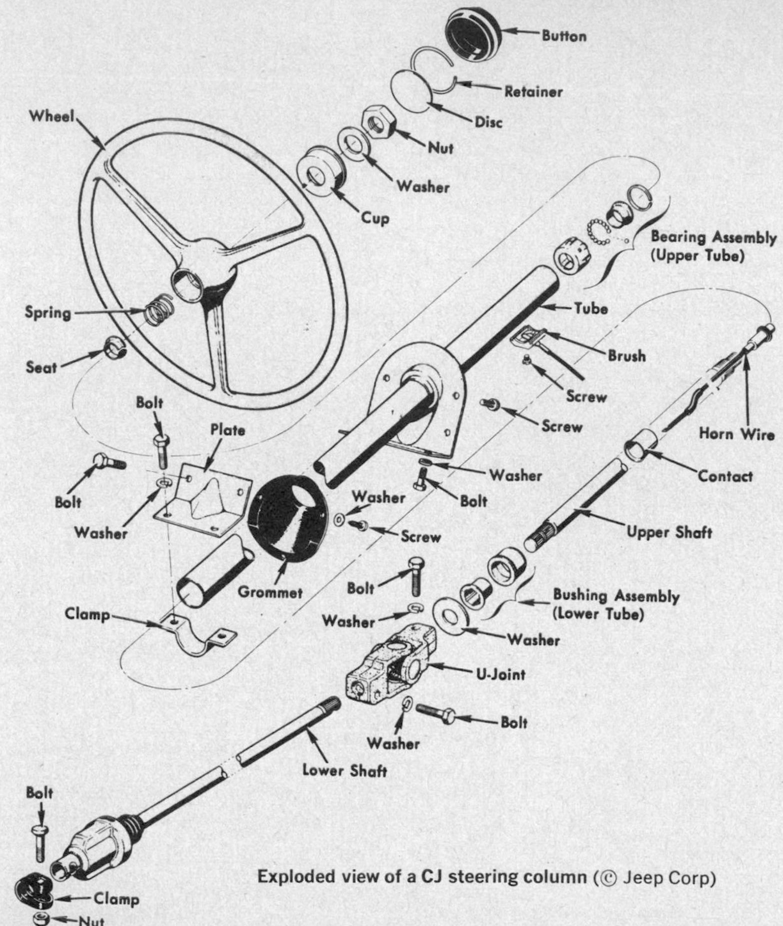

Exploded view of a CJ steering column (© Jeep Corp)

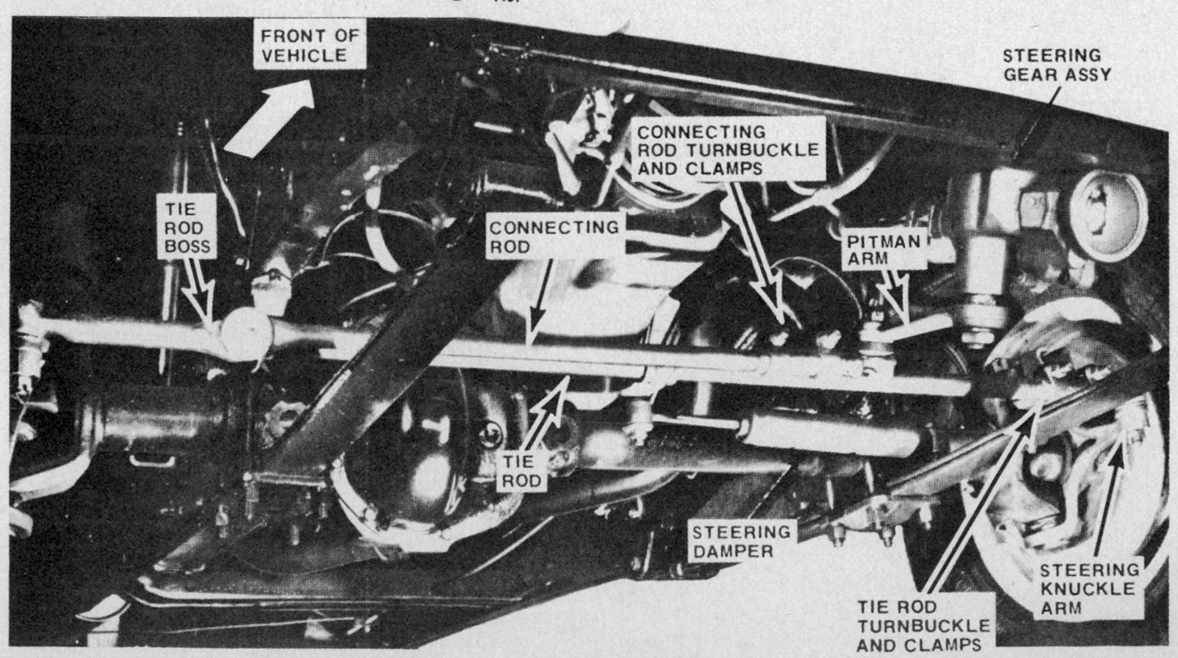

Steering linkage for 1974-76 Wagoneers and Cherokees (© Jeep Corp)

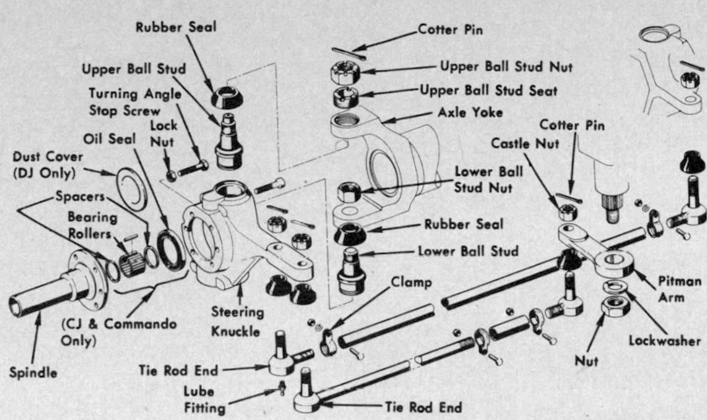

Steering knuckle (open type) and steering linkage for 1972-73 vehicles
(© Jeep Corp)

4. Remove the steering wheel nut and the horn button contact cup.
5. Scribe a line mark on the steering wheel and the steering shaft. Release the turn signal assembly from the steering post.
6. Using a puller, remove the steering wheel and spring, if present.
7. Install the steering wheel in the reverse order of removal. Line up the marks that were scribed on the steering wheel and the steering shaft.

Commando

1. Disconnect the negative battery cable.
2. Pull the horn button from the center of the steering wheel.
3. Remove the steering wheel nut and washer.
4. Remove the three attaching screws in the wheel cavity and remove the horn button receiver bushing, receiver, and spring.
5. Scribe a line mark on the steering wheel and the steering shaft and use a puller to remove the steering wheel.
6. Replace the steering wheel in the reverse order of removal, aligning the marks that were scribed.

Wagoneer, Cherokee

1. Disconnect the negative battery cable. Place the front wheels in a straight-ahead position.
2. Remove the steering wheel spoke horn cover attaching screws from the under side of the steering wheel spoke and remove the horn cover.
3. Disconnect the horn wire from the switch in the steering wheel cavity by gently pulling and wiggling the quick disconnect connector.
4. Remove the steering wheel nut and washer.
5. Scribe a line mark on the steering wheel and the steering shaft and use a puller to remove the steering wheel.
6. Install the steering wheel in the reverse order of removal, aligning the scribe marks.

INSTRUMENT PANEL

Turn Signal Switch Removal and Installation

CJ

The turn signal switch unit is secured to the steering column with two Allen head screws. To remove the unit, remove the Allen head screws. Replace in reverse order of removal.

Commando

1. Remove the steering wheel.
2. Remove the direction signal lever.
3. Disconnect the direction signal harness from the frame harness and remove the wires from each plastic connector.
4. Remove the wires by inserting a narrow blade screwdriver into the terminal end of the connector. Insert the blade into the narrowest part of the opening to depress the retaining tang and pull the wire out of the connector.
5. Remove the harness loom.
6. Remove the two retaining screws from the direction switch and the two screws from the 4-way flasher switch.
7. Pry out the horn contact button.
8. Remove the two bowl attaching screws and allow the bowl to slide down the column.
9. Tape the disconnected wires together. Fold some of the wires back to flatten the bulge.
10. Attach a wire or heavy string to the turn signal harness and pull the harness out from the top of the steering column.
11. Install in the reverse order of removal.

Wagoneer, Cherokee

1. Disconnect the battery and remove the steering wheel.
2. Loosen the anti-theft cover retaining screws and lift the cover from the column. It is not necessary to completely remove the screws.
3. Depress the lock plate and pry the round wire snap ring from the steering shaft groove. Remove the snap ring, lock plate, directional signal canceling cam, upper bearing preload spring, and the thrust washer from the steering shaft.
4. Place the directional signal actuating lever in the right turn position and remove the lever.
5. Depress the hazard warning light switch and remove the button by turning it counterclockwise.
6. Remove the direction signal wire harness connector block from its mounting bracket on the side of the steering column. On vehicles with automatic transmissions, use a stiff wire to depress the lock tab which retains the shift quadrant light wire in the connector block.
7. Remove the direction signal switch retaining screws and pull the switch and wire harness from the column.
8. Install in the reverse order of removal.

Ignition Switch Removal and Installation

Wagoneer, Cherokee

1. Disconnect the battery.
2. Remove the steering wheel.
3. Loosen the anti-theft cover retaining screws and lift the cover from the column.
4. Depress the lock plate and remove the round wire snap ring from the steering shaft groove.
5. Remove the lock plate, direction signal cancelling cam, upper bearing preload spring, and thrust washer from the steering shaft.
6. Place the direction signal actuating lever in the right turn position and remove the lever.
7. Depress the 4-way flasher switch and remove the button by turning it in a counterclockwise direction.
8. Place the automatic transmission shift lever in the Park position. Remove the shift lever by driving out the pivot pin with a 1/4 in. punch.
9. Remove the direction signal wire harness connector block from its mounting bracket on the right side of the lower column. Use a stiff wire, such as a paper clip, to depress the lock tab which retains the shift quadrant light wire in the connector block.
10. Remove the direction signal switch retaining screws and pull the direction signal switch and wire harness from the column.
11. Use a small wire with a right angle bend to remove the buzzer switch and clip as an assembly. Place the lock in the RUN posi-

tion. Hook the bend of the wire into the loop of the clip at the top of the switch at the base of the housing and pull up and out on the clip.

12. Place the key in the LOCK position and using a small flat screwdriver, depress the lock cylinder retaining tab.
13. Remove the lock cylinder.
14. To remove the ignition switch, remove the two mounting screws and disconnect the switch from the remote rod. Remove the harness connector and remove the switch from the vehicle.
15. To install the switch with the actuator rod disconnected, position the switch on the column and move the slider to extreme left (Accessory position). The left side of the switch is toward the steering wheel.
16. Install the actuator rod in the slider and install the switch to the steering column being careful not to move the slider out of position.
17. Tighten the retaining screws.
18. Reassemble and install the lock cylinder and the steering column in the reverse order of removal.

CJ and Commando

1. Press the main switch body toward the instrument panel, compressing the spring until the notched bezel is free to be turned counterclockwise and removed.
2. Pull back the main switch body and lower it from under the instrument panel so that the wiring harness plug can be removed from the prong connection.
3. Install the switch in the reverse order of removal with the key installed in the OFF position and pointing straight up and down. The word STARTER should be at the top when the switch is installed in the dash.

Head Light Switch Removal and Installation

To replace the old push-pull type head light switch, use an allen wrench to loosen the set screw and remove the knob. Remove the retaining nut and remove the switch through the back of the instrument panel. Install in reverse order.

To replace the new style push-pull switch, first disconnect the wire connector plug from the switch. Pull the control knob out to the second position. From behind the instrument panel, depress the knob release button and pull the knob out of the switch. Remove the retaining nut and bezel and remove the switch through the back of the panel. Replace in reverse order.

To replace the two-position rocker type switch found in the Commandos, first disconnect one of the battery cables. Remove the control panel by depressing the clip springs located on each side of the panel while at the same time, pushing away from the panel. Remove the circuit breaker and the attached wires. Remove the screws which hold the switch to the panel and remove the switch. Replace in reverse order.

WINDSHIELD WIPERS

Vacuum Operated Wiper, CJ

Motor Removal and Installation

On the early CJ models, the windshield wiper motor was vacuum actuated and mounted at the top of the windshield. To remove it, disconnect the vacuum hose, remove the wiper arm assembly, remove the attaching bolts, and remove the motor assembly from the windshield. Replace in the reverse order.

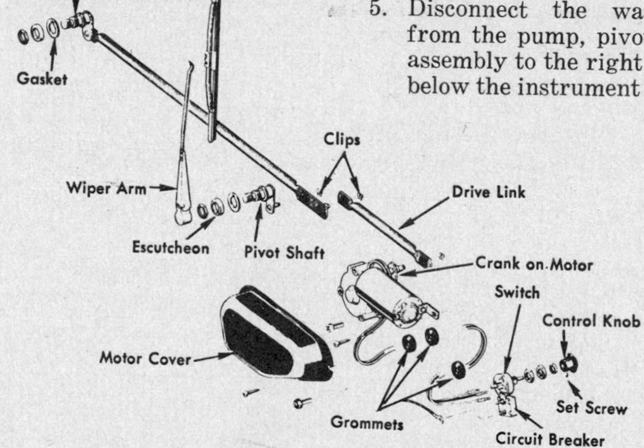

Windshield wiper compo s for late model CJs (© Jeep Corp)

Electric Wiper Motor

Removal and Installation

CJ

1. Remove the plastic hole plug at the extreme left of the bottom of the windshield frame air duct and disconnect the drive link from the motor crank.
2. Disconnect the wires from the back of the control switch.
3. Remove the motor cover then remove the motor.
4. Install the wiper motor in the reverse order of the removal procedure.

Commando

1. Disconnect the wire harness plug and the speedometer cable from the instrument cluster.
2. Remove the instrument cluster from the instrument panel by depressing the retainer springs at each corner.
3. Remove the three motor-to-brake and clutch pedal mounting bracket screws.
4. Disconnect the wiper drive link from the motor crank.
5. Disconnect the washer hoses from the pump, pivot the motor assembly to the right and drop it below the instrument panel.

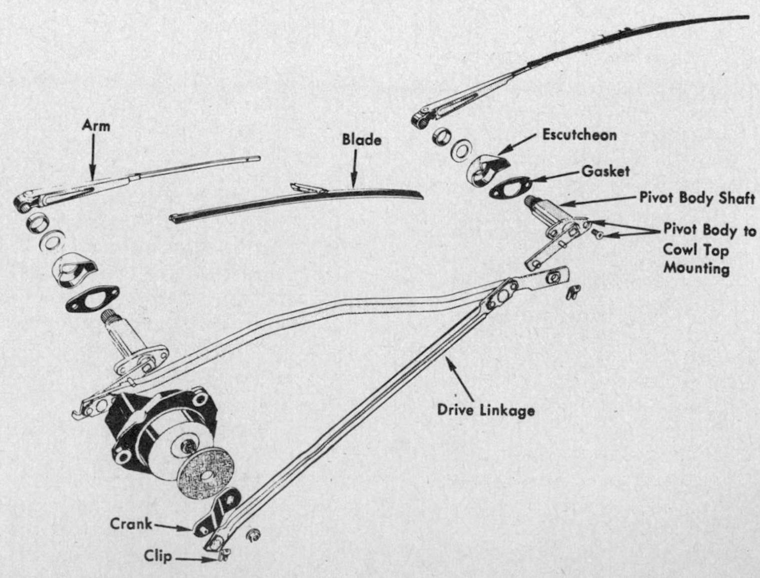

Windshield wiper components for late model Wagoneers (© Jeep Corp)

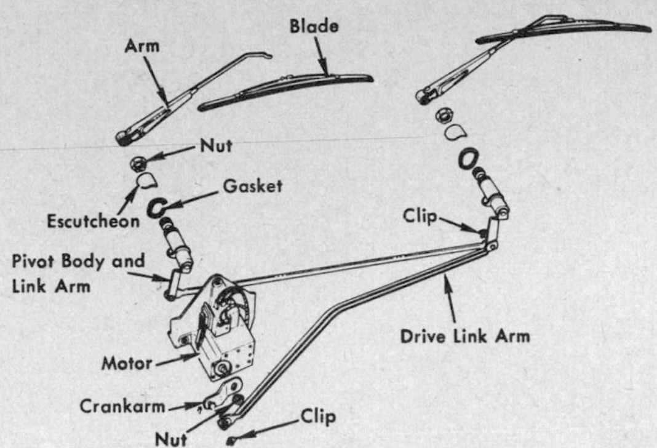

Windshield wiper components for late model Commandos (© Jeep Corp)

6. Mark the wires for identification and disconnect the wire harness from the motor and washer pump.
7. Remove the motor.
8. Install in the reverse order.

Wagoneer, Cherokee

1. Disconnect the wiper drive link from the crank under the instrument panel.
2. Mark the wires for identification at the motor under the hood.
3. Disconnect the motor and washer pump wires at the motor under the hood.
4. Remove the motor-to-dash mounting screws and remove the motor.
5. Install the motor in the reverse order of removal.

RADIO

Removal and Installation

Commando

1. Pull off the control knobs.
2. Remove the two attaching nuts.
3. Remove the antenna lead.
4. Disconnect the rear support strap from the radio, push the radio back far enough to clear the back of the instrument panel and lower the radio far enough to disconnect the speaker leads.
5. Remove the fused wire and remove the radio. Replace the radio in the reverse order of removal.

Wagoneer, Cherokee

1. Open the glove box door and remove the liner and lock striker.
2. Remove the antenna lead.
3. Disconnect the fused wire from the fuse panel.
4. Disconnect the rear support bracket from the radio.
5. Pull off the radio control knobs and remove the radio attaching nuts.
6. Push the radio back to clear the dash panel and remove the radio through the glove box.

HEATER

Heater Core Removal and Installation

CJ

1. Drain the cooling system.
2. Remove the screws that hold the two halves of the duct together and separate the two halves.
3. Remove the screws that hold the heater core to the duct and remove the core.
4. Install the core in the reverse order of removal.

Wagoneer, Cherokee

1. Drain the cooling system.
2. Disconnect the temperature control cable at the heater unit.
3. Remove the heater hoses at the heater unit.
4. Disconnect the heater resistor.
5. Remove the nuts that hold the heater core and duct to the firewall and remove the core and duct assembly.

NOTE: Two of the nuts are located on the inside of the vehicle.

6. Remove the screws that hold the two halves of the duct together and remove the heater core from the duct.
7. Assemble and install the heater core and duct in the reverse order of removal and disassembly.

Blower Motor Removal and Installation

The blower motor is removed from the vehicle simply by removing the attaching screws that hold it to the heater housing and lifting out the motor and fan assembly. Install the blower assembly in the reverse order of removal.

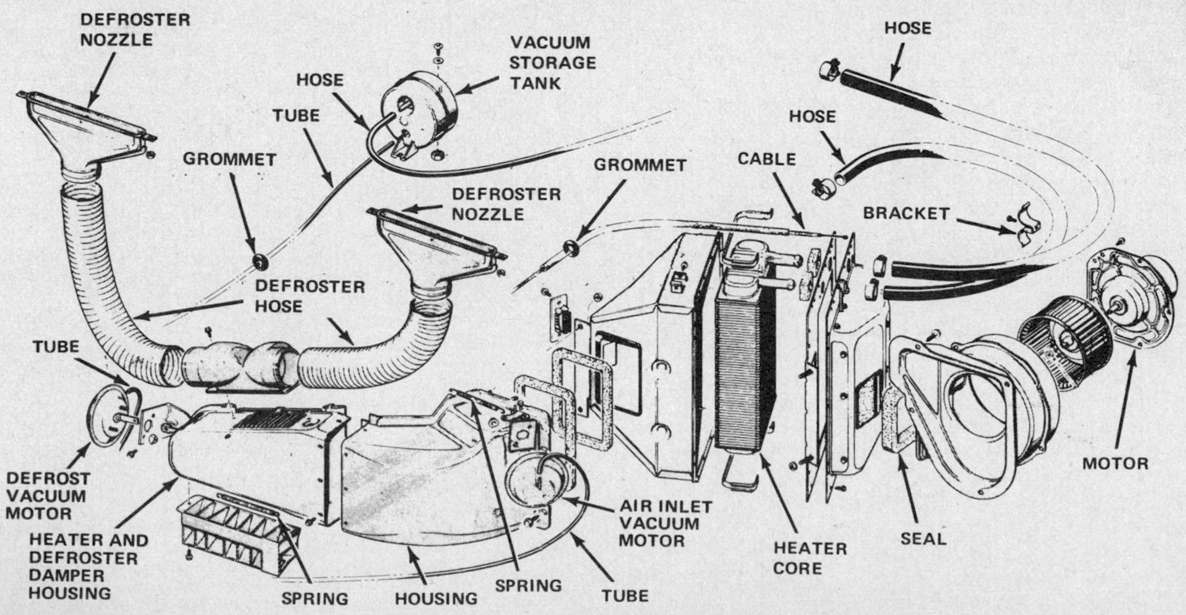

1975-76 Cherokee and Wagoneer heater/defroster
(© Jeep Corp)

Drive Axles, Differential

Introduction

The rear axle must transmit power through 90°. To accomplish this, straight cut bevel gears or spiral bevel gears were used. This type of gear is satisfactory for differential side gears, but since the centerline of the gears must intersect, they rapidly became unsuited for ring and pinion gears. The lowering of the driveshaft brought about a variation of the bevel gear, which is called the hypoid gear. This type of gear does not require a meeting of the gear centerlines and can therefore be underslung, relative to the centerline of the ring gear.

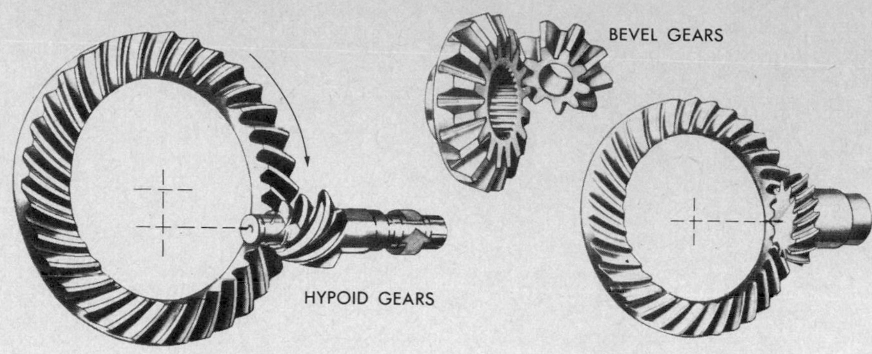

Hypoid gear application
(© Chevrolet Div., G.M. Corp)

Bevel gear application
(© Chevrolet Div., G.M. Corp)

Gear Ratios

The drive axle of a vehicle is said to have a certain axle ratio. This number (usually a whole number and a decimal fraction) is actually a comparison of the number of gear teeth on the ring gear and the pinion gear. For example, a 4.11 rear means that theoretically, there are 4.11 teeth on the ring gear and one tooth on the pinion. Actually, on a 4.11 rear, there are 37 teeth on the ring gear and nine teeth on the pinion gear. By dividing the number of teeth on the pinion gear into the number of teeth on the ring gear, the numerical axle ratio (4.11) is obtained. This also provides a good method of ascertaining exactly which axle ratio one is dealing with.

Differential Operation

The differential is an arrangement of gears that permits the rear wheels to turn at different speeds when cornering and divides the torque between the axle shafts. The differential gears are mounted on a pinion shaft and the gears are free to rotate on this shaft. The pinion shaft is fitted in a bore in the differential case and is at right angles to the axle shafts.

Power flow through the differential is as follows. The drive pinion, which is turned by the driveshaft, turns the ring gear. The ring gear, which is bolted to the differential case, rotates the case. The differential pinion forces the pinion gears against the side gears. In cases where both wheels have equal traction, the pinion gears do not rotate on the pinion shaft, because the input force of the pinion gear is divided equally between the two side gears. Consequently the pinion gears revolve with the pinion shaft, although they do not revolve on the pinion shaft itself. The side gears, which are splined to the axle shafts, and meshed with the pinion gears, rotate the axle shafts.

When it becomes necessary to turn a corner, the differential becomes effective and allows the axle shafts to rotate at different speeds. As the inner wheel slows down, the side gear splined to the inner wheel axle shaft also slows down. The pinion gears act as balancing levers by maintaining equal tooth loads to both gears while allowing unequal speeds of rotation at the axle shafts. If the vehicle speed remains constant, and the inner wheel slows down to 90 percent of vehicle speed, the outer wheel will speed up to 110 percent.

GENERAL DRIVE AXLE DIAGNOSTIC GUIDE

(Also see following text for further differential diagnosis.)

CONDITION	POSSIBLE CAUSE	CORRECTION
Rear Wheel Noise	(a) Loose Wheel.	(a) Tighten loose wheel nuts.
	(b) Spalled wheel bearing cup or cone.	(b) Check rear wheel bearings. If spalled or worn, replace.
	(c) Defective or brinelled wheel bearing.	(c) Defective or brinelled bearings must be replaced. Check rear axle shaft end-play.
	(d) Excessive axle shaft end-play.	(d) Readjust axle shaft end play.
	(e) Bent or sprung axle shaft flange.	(e) Replace bent or sprung axle shaft.
Scoring of Differential Gears and Pinions	(a) Insufficient lubrication.	(a) Replace scored gears. Scoring marks on the pressure face of gear teeth or in the bore are caused by instantaneous fusing of the mating surfaces. Scored gears should be replaced. Fill rear axle to required capacity with proper lubricant.
	(b) Improper grade of lubricant.	(b) Replace scored gears. Inspect all gears and bearings for possible damage. Clean and refill axle to required capacity with proper lubricant.
	(c) Excessive spinning of one wheel.	(c) Replace scored gears. Inspect all gears, pinion bores and shaft for scoring, or bearings for possible damage.
Tooth Breakage (Ring Gear and Pinion)	(a) Overloading.	(a) Replace gears. Examine other gears and bearings for possible damage. Avoid future overloading.
	(b) Erratic clutch operation.	(b) Replace gears, and examine remaining parts for possible damage. Avoid erratic clutch operation.
	(c) Ice-spotted pavements.	(c) Replace gears. Examine remaining parts for possible damage. Replace parts as required.
	(d) Improper adjustment.	(d) Replace gears. Examine other parts for possible damage. Be sure ring gear and pinion backlash is correct.

Rear Axle Noise	(a) Insufficient lubricant.	(a) Refill rear axle with correct amount of the proper lubricant. Also check for leaks and correct as necessary.
	(b) Improper ring gear and pinion adjustment.	(b) Check ring gear and pinion tooth contact.
	(c) Unmatched ring gear and pinion.	(c) Remove unmatched ring gear and pinion. Replace with a new matched gear and pinion set.
	(d) Worn teeth on ring gear or pinion.	(d) Check teeth on ring gear and pinion for contact. If necessary, replace with new matched set.
	(e) End-play in drive pinion bearings.	(e) Adjust drive pinion bearing preload.
	(f) Side play in differential bearings.	(f) Adjust differential bearing preload.
	(g) Incorrect drive gearlash.	(g) Correct drive gear lash.
	(h) Limited-Slip differential—moan and chatter.	(h) Drain and flush lubricant. Refill with proper lubricant.
Loss of Lubricant	(a) Lubricant level too high.	(a) Drain excess lubricant.
	(b) Worn axle shaft oil seals.	(b) Replace worn oil seals with new ones. Prepare new seals before replacement.
	(c) Cracked rear axle housing.	(c) Repair or replace housing as required.
	(d) Worn drive pinion oil seal.	(d) Replace worn drive pinion oil seal with a new one.
	(e) Scored and worn companion flange.	(e) Replace worn or scored companion flange and oil seal.
	(f) Clogged vent.	(f) Remove obstructions.
	(g) Loose carrier housing bolts or housing cover screws.	(g) Tighten bolts or cover screws to specifications and fill to correct level with proper lubricant.
Overheating of Unit	(a) Lubricant level too low.	(a) Refill rear axle.
	(b) Incorrect grade of lubricant.	(b) Drain, flush and refill rear axle with correct amount of the proper lubricant.
	(c) Bearings adjusted too tightly.	(c) Readjust bearings.
	(d) Excessive wear in gears.	(d) Check gears for excessive wear or scoring. Replace as necessary.
	(e) Insufficient ring gear-to-pinion clearance.	(e) Readjust ring gear and pinion backlash and check gears for possible scoring.

Limited-Slip Differential Operation

Limited-slip differentials provide driving force to the wheel with the best traction before the other wheel begins to spin. This is accomplished through clutch plates or cones. The clutch plates or cones are located between the side gears and inner wall of the differential case. When they are squeezed together through spring tension and outward force from the side gears, three reactions occur. Resistance on the side gears causes more torque to be exerted on the clutch packs or clutch cones. Rapid one-wheel spin cannot occur, because the side gear is forced to turn at the same speed as the case. Most important, with the side gear and the differential case turning at the same speed, the other wheel is forced to rotate in the same direction and at the same speed as the differential case. Thus driving force is applied to the wheel with the better traction.

Differential Diagnosis

The most essential part of rear axle service is proper diagnosis of the problem. Bent or broken axle shafts or broken gears pose little problem, but isolating an axle noise and correctly interpreting the problem can be extremely difficult, even for an experienced mechanic.

Any gear driven unit will produce a certain amount of noise, therefore, a specific diagnosis for each individual unit is the best practice. Acceptable or normal noise can be classified as a slight noise heard only at certain speeds or under unusual conditions. This noise tends to reach a peak at 40-60 mph, depending on the road condition, load, gear ratio and tire size. Frequently, other noises are mistakenly diagnosed as coming from the rear axle. Vehicle noises from tires, transmission, driveshaft, U-joints and front and rear wheel bearings will often be mistaken as emanating from the rear axle. Raising the tire pressure to eliminate tire noise (although this will not silence mud or snow treads), listening for noise at varying speeds and road conditions and listening for noise at drive and coast conditions will aid in diagnosing alleged rear axle noises.

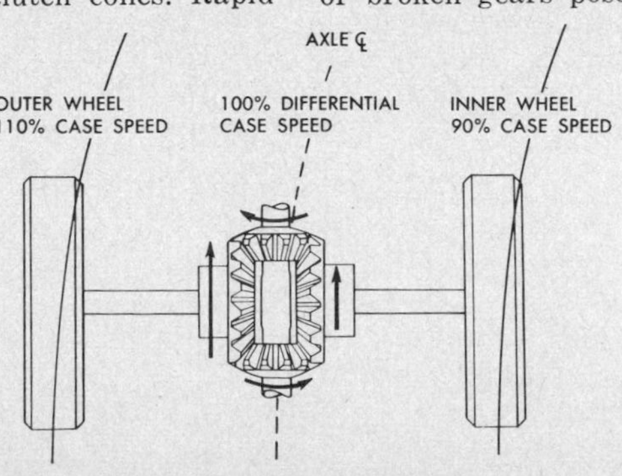

Differential action during cornering
(© Chevrolet Div., G.M. Corp)

External Noise Elimination

It is advisable to make a thorough road test to determine whether the noise originates in the rear axle or whether it originates from the tires, engine transmission, wheel bearings or road surface. Noise originating from other places cannot be corrected by overhauling the rear axle.

Road Noise

Brick roads or rough surfaced concrete, may cause a noise which can be mistaken as coming from the rear axle. Driving on a different type of road, (smooth asphalt or dirt) will determine whether the road is the cause of the noise. Road noise is usually the same on drive or coast conditions.

Tire Noise

Tire noise can be mistaken as rear axle noises, even though the tires on the front are at fault. Snow tread and mud tread tires or tires worn unevenly will frequently cause vibrations which seem to originate elsewhere; *temporarily, and for test purposes only,* inflate the tires to 40-50 lbs. This will significantly alter the noise produced by the tires, but will not alter noise from the rear axle. Noises from the rear axle will normally cease at speeds below 30 mph on coast, while tire noise will continue at lower tone as car speed is decreased. The rear axle noise will usually change from drive conditions to coast conditions, while tire noise will not. Do not forget to lower the tire pressure to normal after the test is complete.

Engine and Transmission Noise

Engine and transmission noises also seem to originate in the rear axle. Road test the vehicle and determine at which speeds the noise is most pronounced. Stop the car in a quiet place to avoid interfering noises. With the transmission in neutral, run the engine slowly through the engine speeds corresponding to the car speed at which the noise was most noticeable. If a similar noise was produced with the car standing still, the noise is not in the rear axle, but somewhere in the engine or transmission.

Front Wheel Bearing Noise

Front wheel bearing noises, sometimes confused with rear axle noises, will not change when comparing drive and coast conditions. While holding the car speed steady, lightly apply the footbrake. This will often cause wheel bearing noise to lessen, as some of the weight is taken off the bearing. Front wheel bearings are easily checked by jacking up the wheels and spinning the wheels. Shaking the wheels will also determine if the wheel bearings are excessively loose.

Rear Axle Noises

If a logical test of the vehicle shows that the noise is not caused by external items, it can be assumed that the noise originates from the rear axle. The rear axle should be tested on a smooth level road to avoid road noise. It is not advisable to test the axle by jacking up the rear wheels and running the car.

True rear axle noises generally fall into two classes; gear noise and bearing noises, and can be caused by a faulty driveshaft, faulty wheel bearings, worn differential or pinion shaft bearings, U-joint misalignment, worn differential side gears and pinions, or mismatched, improperly adjusted, or scored ring and pinion gears.

Rear Wheel Bearing Noise

A rough rear wheel bearing causes a vibration or growl which will continue with the car coasting or in neutral. A brinelled rear wheel bearing will also cause a knock or click approximately every two revolutions of the rear wheel, due to the fact that the bearing rollers do not travel at the same speed as the rear wheel and axle. Jack up the rear wheels and spin the wheel slowly, listening for signs of a rough or brinelled wheel bearing.

Differential Side Gear and Pinion Noise

Differential side gears and pinions seldom cause noise, since their movement is relatively slight on straight ahead driving. Noise produced by these gears will be more noticeable on turns.

Pinion Bearing Noise

Pinion bearing failures can be distinguished by their speed of rotation, which is higher than side bearings or axle bearings. Rough or brinelled pinion bearings cause a continuous low pitch whirring or scraping noise beginning at low speeds.

Side Bearing Noise

Side bearings produce a constant rough noise, which is slower than the pinion bearing noise. Side bearing noise may also fluctuate in the above rear wheel bearing test.

Gear Noise

Two basic types of gear noise exist. First, is the type produced by bent or broken gear teeth which have been forcibly damaged. The noise from this type of damage is audible over the entire speed range. Scoring or damage to the hypoid gear teeth generally results from insufficient lubricant, improper lubricant, improper breakin, insufficient gear backlash, improper ring and pinion gear alignment or loss of torque on the drive pinion nut. If not corrected, the scoring will lead to eventual erosion or fracture of the gear teeth. Hypoid gear tooth fracture can also be caused by extended overloading of the gear set (fatigue fracture) or by shock overloading (sudden failure). Differential and side gears rarely give trouble, but common causes of differential failure are shock loading, extended overloading and differential pinion seizure at the cross-shaft, resulting from excessive wheel spin and consequent lubricant breakdown.

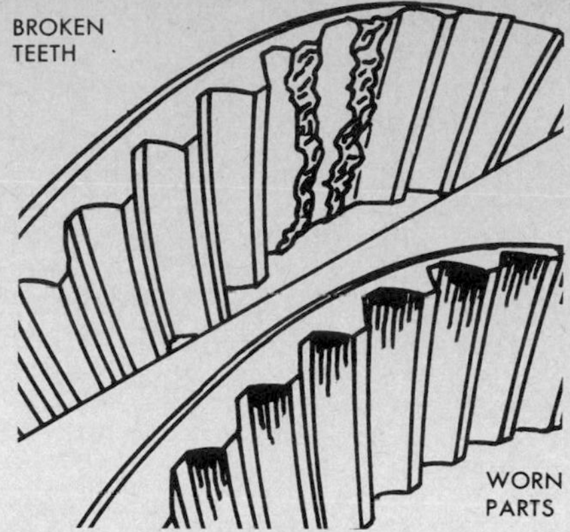

Two types of damage which cause gear noise (© Chevrolet Div., G.M. Corp)

The second type of gear noise pertains to the mesh pattern between the ring and pinion gears. This type of abnormal gear noise can be recognized as a cycling pitch or whine audible in either drive, float or coast conditions. Gear noises can be recognized as they tend to peak out in a narrow speed range and remain constant in pitch, whereas bearing noises tend to vary in pitch with vehicle speeds. Noises produced by the ring and pinion gears will generally follow the pattern below.

A. Drive Noise: Produced under vehicle acceleration.

B. Coast Noise: Produced while the car coasts with a closed throttle.

C. Float Noise: Occurs while maintaining constant car speed (just enough to keep speed constant) on a level road.

NOISE DIAGNOSIS CHART

PROBLEM	CAUSE
1. Identical noise in Drive or Coast conditions	1. Road noise Tire noise Front wheel bearing noise
2. Noise changes on a different type of road	2. Road noise Tire noise
3. Noise tone lowers as car speed is lowered	3. Tire noise
4. Similar noise is produced with car standing and driving	4. Engine noise Transmission noise
5. Vibration	5. Rough rear wheel bearing Unbalanced or damaged driveshaft Unbalanced tire Worn universal joint in driveshaft Misaligned drive shaft at companion flange Excessive companion flange runout
6. A knock or click approximately every two revolutions of rear wheel	6. Brinelled rear wheel bearing
7. Noise most pronounced on turns	7. Differential side gear and pinion wear or damage
8. A continuous low pitch whirring or scraping noise starting at relatively low speed	8. Damaged or worn pinion bearing
9. Drive noise, coast noise or float noise	9. Damaged or worn ring and pinion gear
10. Clunk on acceleration or deceleration	10. Worn differential cross-shaft in case
11. Clunk on stops	11. Insufficient grease in driveshaft slip yoke
12. Groan in Forward or Reverse	12. Improper differential lubricant
13. Chatter on turns	13. Improper differential lubricant Worn clutch plates
14. Clunk or knock during operation on rough roads.	14. Excessive end-play of axle shafts to differential cross-shaft

D. Drive, Coast and Float Noise: These noises will vary in tone with speed and be very rough or irregular if the differential or pinion shaft bearings are worn.

Bearing Diagnosis

This section will help in the diagnosis of bearing failure and the causes. Bearing diagnosis can be very helpful in determining the cause of rear axle failure.

When disassembling a rear axle, the general condition of all bearings should be noted and classified where possible. Proper recognition of the cause will help in correcting the problem and avoiding a repetition of the failure.

Some of the common causes of bearing failure are:

a. Abuse during assembly or disassembly.
b. Improper assembly methods.
c. Improper or inadequate lubrication.
d. Bearing contact with dirt or water.
e. Wear caused by dirt or metal chips.
f. Corrosion or rust.
g. Seizing due to overloading.
h. Overheating.
i. Frettage of the bearing seats.
j. Brinelling from impact or shock loading.
k. Manufacturing defects.
l. Pitting due to fatigue.

To avoid damage to the bearing from improper handling, it is best to treat a used bearing the same as a new bearing. Always work in a clean area with clean tools. Remove all outside dirt from the housing before exposing a bearing and clean all bearing seats before installing a bearing.

Caution Never spin a bearing, either by hand or with compressed air, as this will lead to almost certain bearing failure.

Limited-Slip Differential Diagnosis

Lubrication

The use of proper lubricant is very important in limited-slip type drive axles. The forces applied when cornering tend to apply the clutch pack or clutch cones. The use of the wrong lubricant can cause the clutch services to grab and chatter while turning. Always follow the manufacturer's recommendations regarding drive axle lubrication. When chatter is encountered, the differential lubricant should be drained and refilled with the specified lubricant.

Testing

The clutch operation on all limited-slip type axles can be tested as follows. Refer to the manufacturer in question.

American Motors "Twin-Grip"

1. With the engine off and the transmission in neutral, jack up one rear wheel.
2. Block the other wheel to prevent it from moving.
3. With a socket and torque wrench on the axle shaft nut, turn the raised wheel forward.
4. The torque required to move the wheel should be 70–100 ft lbs for 8⅞ in. axles or 80 120 ft lbs for 7-9/16 in. axles.
5. A breakaway torque which is less than the specified figure, indicates a need for repair or replacement.

Cadillac Controlled Differential

This unit should not be serviced. If a malfunction exists that cannot be cured by changing the fluid, remove the unit and install a new one.

Chrysler Corp. Sure-Grip

1. Place the vehicle on a hoist with the engine off and the automatic transmission in Park (manual transmission in low gear).
2. Attempt to rotate the wheel by hand, by gripping the tire.
3. If it is extremely difficult, if not impossible, to rotate either wheel the Sure-Grip differential can be assumed to be performing satisfactorily.
4. If it is relatively easy to continuously turn either rear wheel, the unit should be removed and replaced.

Caution The Sure-Grip differential is serviced as a unit only. Under no circumstances should the unit be disassembled and reinstalled.

Ford Motor Company Equa-Lok

1. Jack up one rear wheel and remove the wheel cover.
2. Block the other wheel front and rear to prevent the car from moving.
3. Using a 200 ft lbs capacity torque wrench on one of the wheel lug nuts, measure the torque required to continuously rotate the wheel. The breakaway torque reading can be disregarded. The minimum torque to continuously rotate the wheel should be as follows.

   All axles except integral carrier type: 75 ft lbs

   Integral carrier type axles: 50 ft lbs
4. If the minimum torque is not as specified, the differential should be checked for improper assembly.

Ford Motor Company Traction-Lok

1. Follow the procedure for the Ford Motor Company Equa-Lok rear. The minimum torque to continuously rotate the wheel (disregarding the breakaway torque) should be at least 40 ft lbs.

General Motors Corp. (except Cadillac) Positraction

1. Place the transmission in neutral.
2. Raise one rear wheel off the floor and block the other rear wheel (front and rear) to prevent the car from moving.
3. Install a torque wrench and extension on the lug nut and note the torque required to continuously rotate one rear wheel. Disregard the breakaway torque figure, as this may be a great deal higher.
4. The minimum torque to continuously rotate the rear wheel should be at least 35 ft lbs. If it is not, the rear axle is in need of service.

General Diagnosis

Improper operation of a limited-slip type rear axle is generally indicated by clutch slippage or grabbing, which will sometimes produce a whirring or chatter sound. Occasionally, this condition is induced by improper lubrication. Check the unit for the wrong type of lubricant or lubricant which has broken down or become contaminated. Replace the lubricant with the type specified by the manufacturer.

During normal operation, i.e., straight-ahead driving, both wheels are rotating at equal speeds, and the driving force is distributed equally between both wheels. When cornering, the inside wheel delivers extra driving force, causing slippage in both clutch packs. Therefore, if the wheel rotation of both rear wheels is not equal, the unit will constantly be functioning as if the car were cornering. This will cause constant slippage and lead to eventual failure of the unit. It is important that there be no excessive differences in wheel and tire size, wear pattern, or tire pressures between both rear wheels. Swerving on acceleration is an indication of one or more of the above conditions. Before attempting an overhaul or replacement operation, check both rear wheels for identical tire sizes, tire pressure, tire tread depth, and wear pattern.

Drive Axle Disassembly Analysis

Testing the Gear Tooth Contact Pattern

Once it has been established that

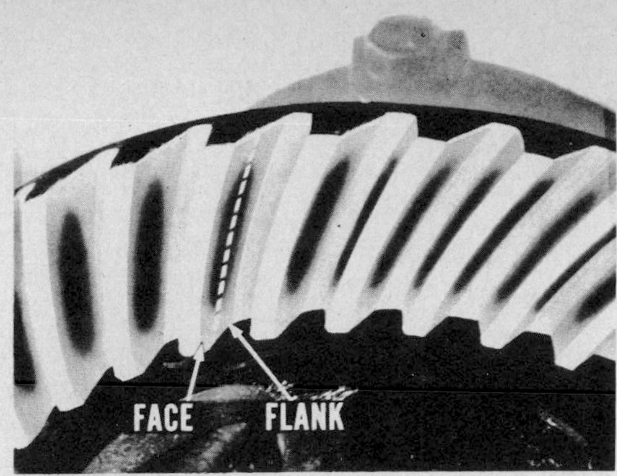

Gear tooth face and flank showing oval gear tooth contact pattern
(© Chrysler Corp)

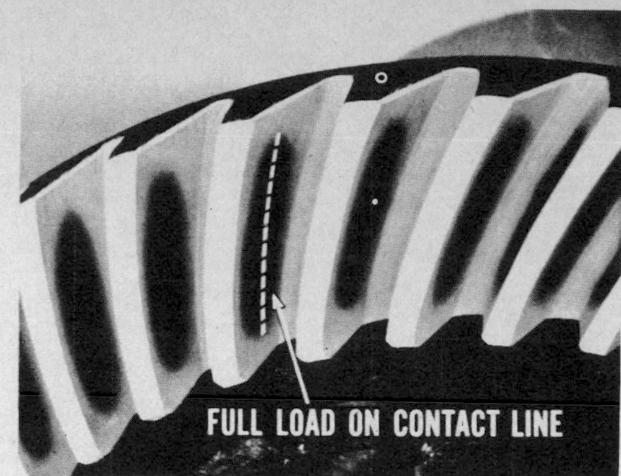

Gear tooth contact pattern showing load centered on gear tooth
(© Chrysler Corp)

the differential is indeed in need of service, the worst procedure is to simply plunge ahead and remove the differential and disassemble the parts. Prior to disassembly, a tooth contact pattern test should be made. However, it is worthwhile to first know the nomenclature associated with hypoid gear teeth.

The thick end of the tooth is called the heel and the thin end of the tooth is called the toe. The base half of the tooth is called the flank and the other end of the tooth is known as the face. The imaginary line at the halfway point between the face and flank is known as the pitch line. The space between the meshed pinion and ring gear teeth is known as backlash.

A gear tooth contact pattern can be made with the carrier in or out of the housing depending on the type of carrier. On integral carrier models, the lubricant must be drained and the rear cover removed. The ring gear will now be exposed and the test can be made with the carrier still in the housing. On removable carrier models, drain the lubricant and remove the carrier from the housing. The test can be made on the bench.

Unlike simple spur gears, hypoid gear teeth leave a complex pattern on the ring gear. When hypoid gears turn, the line contact between pinion and ring gear teeth has the same wiping motion as with spur gear teeth. Because of the complicated movement of hypoid gear teeth, the contact area takes an oval shape as opposed to the rectangular shape left by spur gear teeth. Actually, the tooth contact test shows where each gear tooth has been wiped by the movement of the contact line, so that you can tell whether the gears are set correctly. With a properly adjusted ring and pinion (with properly adjusted pinion depth and backlash) the tooth contact will be close to center. In this case, the load is borne by the strongest part of the tooth. If the gear setting is off, the contact line may reach any part of the edge of a tooth, and the metal will be overloaded at that point. When overload occurs, rapid deterioration of the gears will follow.

Preparing the Test

Coat the drive gear teeth with red or white lead. The white lead will show the pattern in better contrast on new gears. If either lead is not available, substitute a metallic base artists' oil color such as zinc white or titanium white. The tooth coating material must be smooth and firm enough to spread without running. A consistency somewhat like toothpaste works well. If it is necessary to thicken the material, add a small amount of cup grease.

NOTE: prussian blue dye does not work well, since the blue tends to smear the pattern.

Thoroughly clean the ring gear and pinion before applying the testing material. Any gear lube left on the teeth will make the pattern quite unreadable. Coat the drive and coast sides of all the ring gear teeth, but leave the pinion gear teeth clean. Do not apply the coating too thickly as the pattern will be smeared.

Because the axle gears are normally easy to rotate, turning resistance must be applied to produce pressure between the pinion and ring gear teeth to make a legible pattern. On a removable carrier type axle, insert a large screwdriver between the carrier housing and the differential case rim. Apply the load squarely against the case rim while prying out against the upper or lower section of the carrier housing. On integral carrier models, apply the parking brake to a point where it requires approximately 50 ft lbs to turn the pinion with a torque wrench. Since the

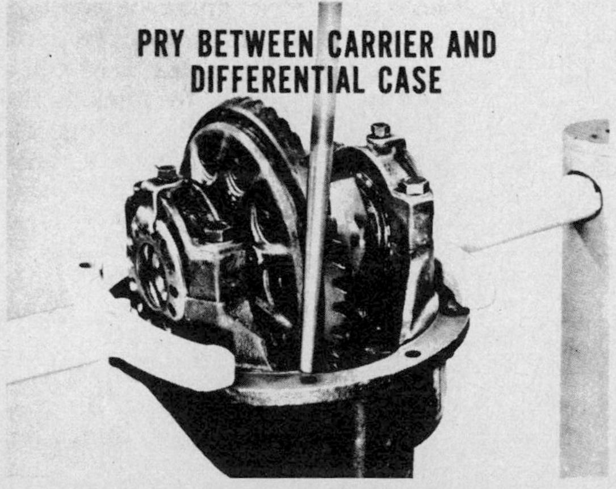

Applying a load to the differential case
(© Chrysler Corp)

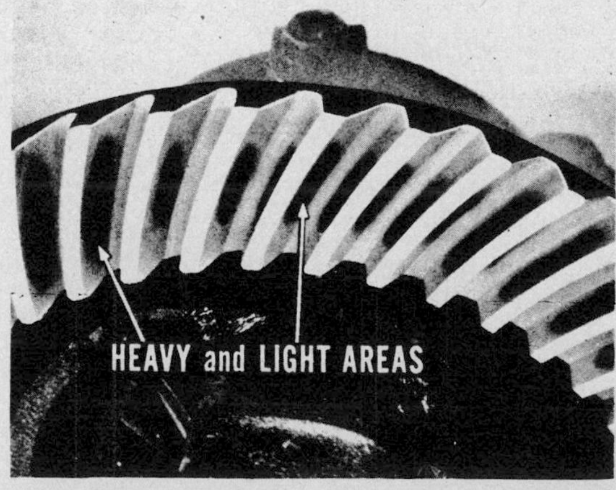

Excessive run-out will cause an uneven pattern
(© Chrysler Corp)

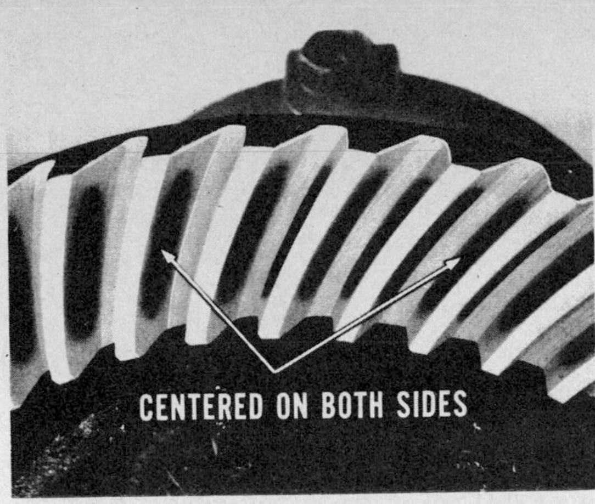

Gear tooth contact pattern showing load centered on gear tooth
(© Chrysler Corp)

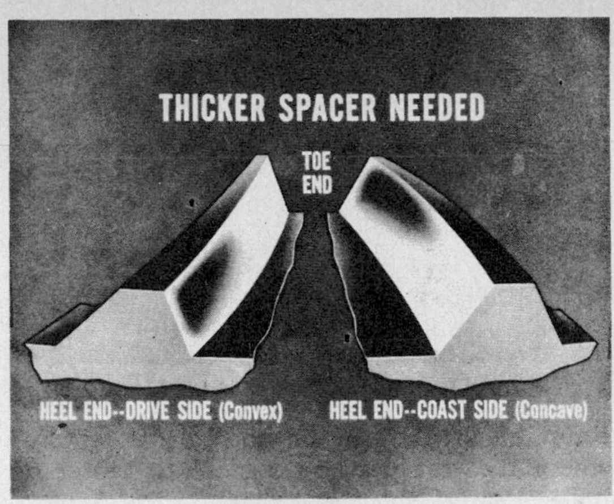

Tooth contact patterns high on the tooth side
(© Chrysler Corp)

shape and position of the contact pattern will vary, depending on the load, try to use the same load for each test or the results can be misleading. This is especially true when testing after an overhaul.

Once the gears have a load applied, obtain a tooth contact pattern by rotating the ring gear and pinion one complete turn in each direction. This will produce a constant pattern on the coast and drive side of each tooth. Do not rotate the ring gear more than one revolution in each direction as this will tend to obscure the pattern.

NOTE: if the pattern does not look right on the first try, recoat the gear teeth and try again.

Making a good gear tooth test takes a little practice; so if it is not right, try again.

Interpreting Gear Tooth Contact Patterns

The tooth contact pattern should be the same on every tooth. If the pattern shows heavy and light areas on different teeth, check the ring gear and differential case for excessive run-out.

Note: run-out can be cured in many cases by removing the ring gear from the case, rotating it 90° or 180°, and remounting it.

Since you can only apply test load pressure to the gears, the contact pattern will be less distinct toward the tooth ends. But, when the ring gear and pinion are under operating loads in the vehicle, the tooth contact area spreads out, especially towards the heel end of the tooth. For this reason, do not try to "get by" with a tooth contact pattern that is centered, but favors the heel end of the teeth. This will only lead to overloading at the heel ends of the gear teeth. On the other hand, a contact pattern which is reasonably centered, but favors the toe end of the teeth, is acceptable.

Assuming that the tooth contact pattern is even on all teeth, the main problem is to get the most distinct part of the pattern centered on both the drive and coast sides of the ring gear teeth. The contact patterns should be nearly opposite each other on both sides of each tooth. In some cases, the pattern will be centered on the drive side and off center on the coast side, or vice versa. The off center pattern can be moved to a more acceptable position by slightly altering the backlash. This procedure will not seriously affect the other pattern. More often, however, the pattern will be off center on both sides of the teeth. The basic cause of this condition is an improperly adjusted pinion.

Adjusting Pinion Depth

It is necessary to understand that an incorrect pinion depth setting moves the contact pattern away from the center on both sides of the tooth in opposite directions. This means that when you install a thicker or thinner washer under the pinion head you bring the pattern into the center of the tooth from opposite ends.

When the contact pattern is high on the heel end of the drive side and low on the toe end of the coast side, a thicker washer is needed to bring the pinion in, toward the center of the drive gear. Increasing the thickness of the spacer washer will bring the pattern in, toward the center of the drive gear teeth, and also will move the pattern down from the tooth face. However, this movement is less than the in-or-out movement.

When tooth contact is low on the toe end of the drive side and high on the heel end of the coast side, the pin-

A thicker spacer moves the pattern in and down
(© Chrysler Corp)

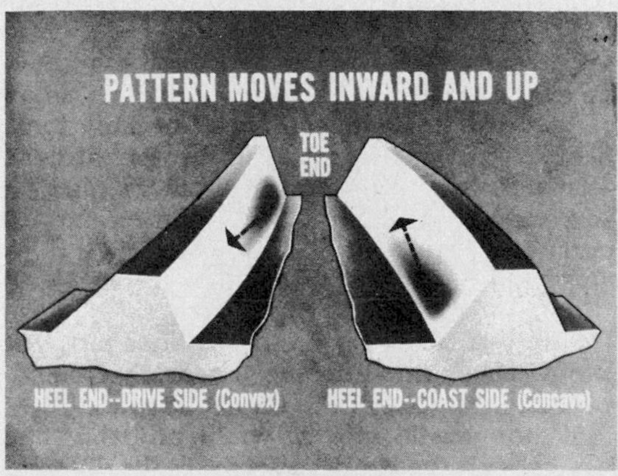

A thinner spacer will move the pattern up and inward
(© Chrysler Corp)

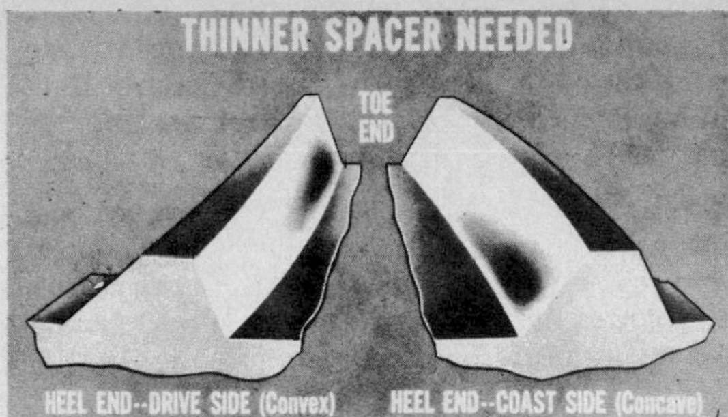

Gear contact pattern low on tooth side
(© Chrysler Corp)

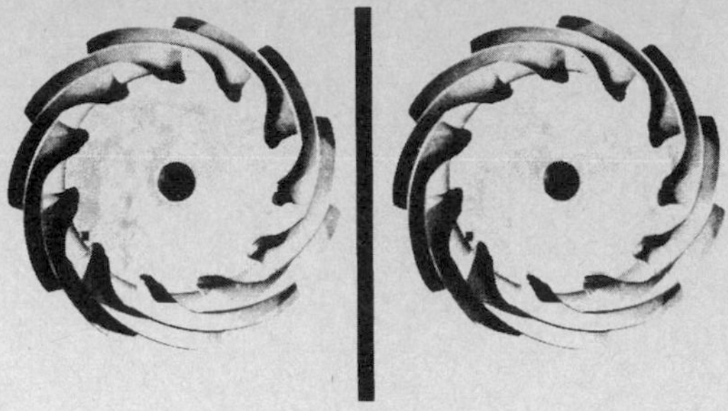

One example of pinion markings
(© Chrysler Corp)

ion must be moved out, by installing a thinner washer under the pinion head. This will move the pattern inward toward the center, and will also result in slight movement of the pattern up from the tooth flank.

A factory service facility will use special tools and gauge blocks to determine the thickness of the spacer under the pinion head. In the absence of such specialized equipment, the following procedure may be used. Bear in mind that with the "hit-or-miss" method, each time you are wrong with the pinion depth, the unit must be disassembled, the spacer thickness changed, and the unit must be completely set up again.

Gather a handful of spacers to cover any thickness and several collapsible pinion spacers (if the unit uses them). Assemble the unit following the procedures in the overhaul section. If the original gear set is being reused, and the tooth contact pattern is reasonably correct, install a new spacer of the same thickness as the old one. This will provide a reasonable starting point. If the gear contact pattern test indicates a need for movement of the pinion, use a new spacer 0.001–0.002 in. thicker or thinner, depending on the direction the pinion must go. If a new gear set is being used, the thickness of the spacer will have to be determined in the following manner. Compare the markings on the old and new pinion. It will usually be marked with a number preceded by a plus (+) or minus (−) sign. This number indicates the production deviation from the nominal pinion, which are known as "zero pinions." In service, zero pinions are rare. Assume that the old pinion is marked with a plus two (+2). Assume that the new pinion is marked with a +3. By comparing the pinion markings, find the numerical difference between the two pinions, in this case +1. With a micrometer, measure the thickness of the original spacer. We will assume that the old spacer is 0.030 in. thick. If the numerical difference between pinions is a positive number (+1) the spacer should be 0.001 in. thinner than the original spacer, or 0.029 in. total. If the numerical difference is a negative number (say, −1) then the spacer should be increased by 0.001 in., to 0.031 in. total. This will only provide a reasonable beginning point.

It is rare that this method works out the first time. Assemble the pinion, differential, and ring gear with the spacer of calculated thickness. The side bearing preload, backlash, pinion nut torque, and pinion rotating torque must all be set correctly. Obtain a gear tooth pattern on the ring gear teeth and analyze the results. Small deviations from the acceptable pattern can usually be made by varying the backlash within the limits of specifications. If the gear tooth contact pattern is off, the unit must be disassembled and another spacer installed. This spacer must be of suitable thickness to compensate for the contact pattern test.

NOTE: without special tools, there is absolutely no way of determining exactly how much to increase or decrease the thickness of the pinion shim; it must be estimated.

After estimating the thickness of the new shim, assemble the unit again, setting all preloads and backlash. Check the contact pattern again and act accordingly. If the unit uses a collapsible spacer, be sure a new one is installed each time it is disassembled. Crushed spacers can not be used again. It is well to note that the unit may have to be assembled and disassembled several times before an acceptable contact pattern is obtained.

Adjusting Backlash

The tooth contact pattern can be altered slightly, by varying the backlash adjustment within the limits of the specifications. The backlash adjustment can be used to alter a pattern which is slightly off center on either side of the tooth, but should not be used as a substitute for pinion depth adjustment. This adjustment must always be made after the pinion depth has been adjusted.

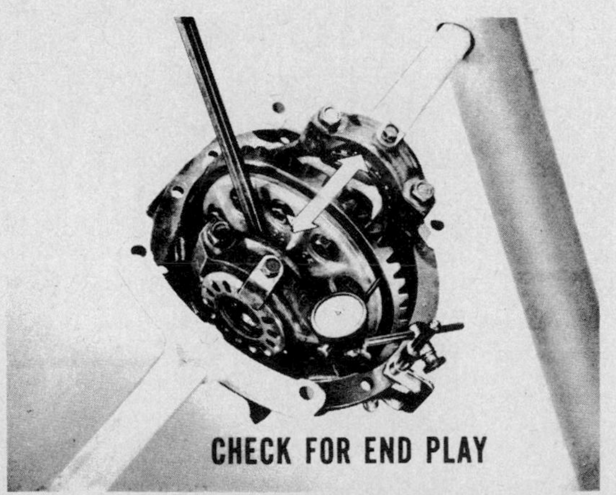

Checking differential bearing end-play
(© Chrysler Corp)

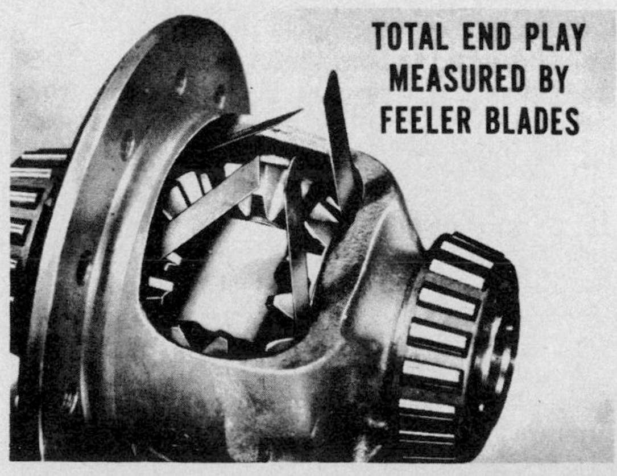

Checking total differential end-play
(© Chrysler Corp)

Unit Repair Section

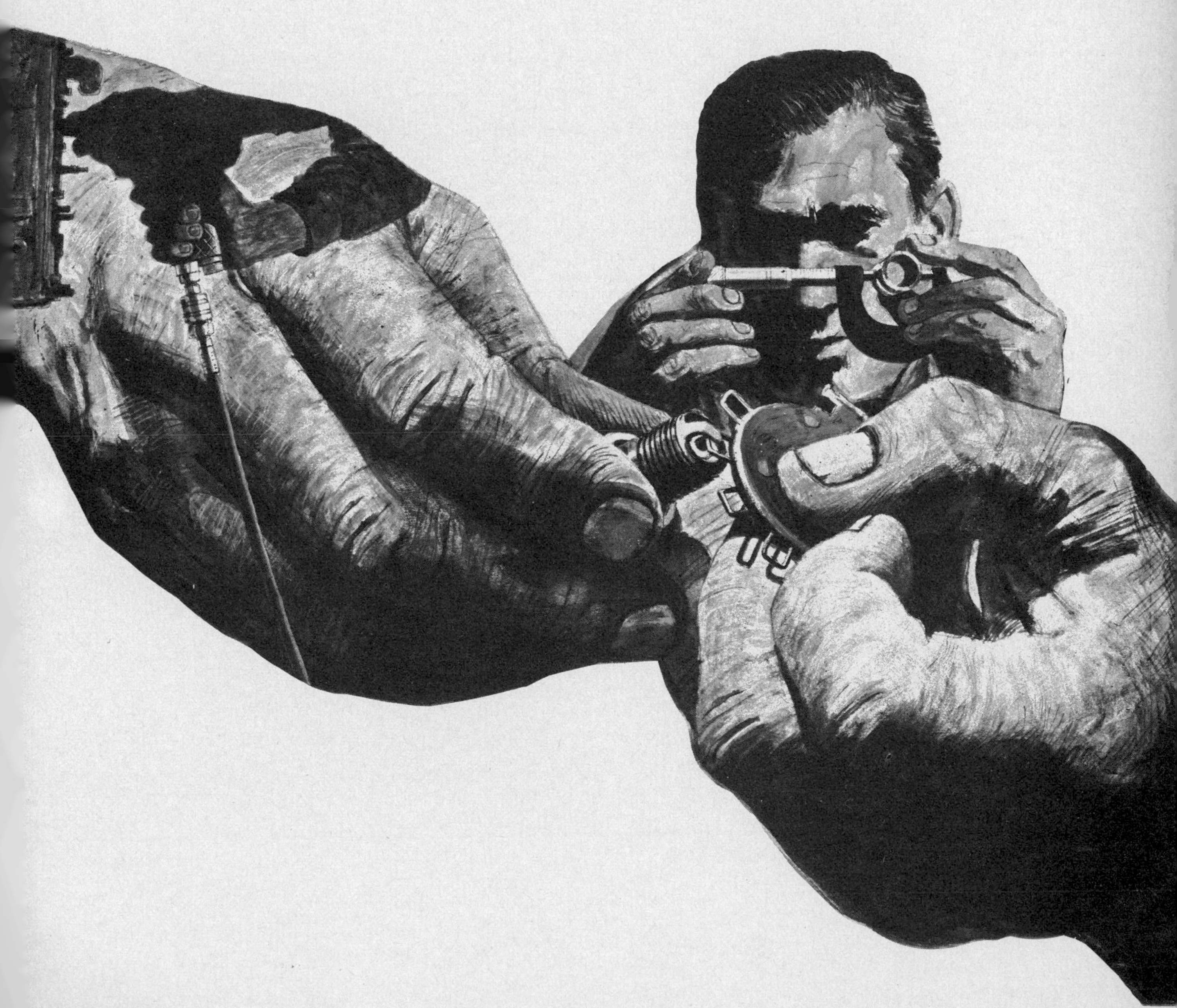

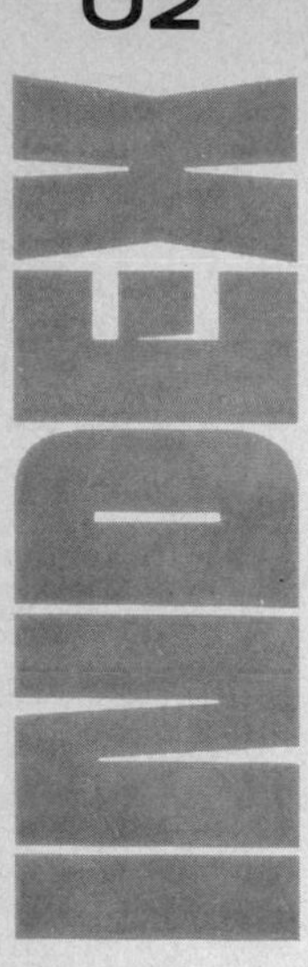

Charging and Starting Systems

Testing the Battery

Selection of Battery

The modern car battery (with very few exceptions) is a 12-volt lead-acid unit having a particular ampere hours capacity, depending upon the required work load (radio, air conditioning, electric windows, tailgate, telephone, etc.).

Batteries come in different forms as specified and designed by the car manufacturer and are matched to the car's electrical needs.

The prime purpose of the battery is to supply a source of energy for cranking the car engine. It also provides the necessary power for the ignition system. A battery can, for a limited time, supply adequate current to satisfy electrical demands during periods when requirements exceed generator output.

Replacing a Battery

The most convenient and popular way to store new batteries is in a dry state. They are charged (with special equipment) at the time of manufacture. A dry charged unit will hold this charge almost indefinitely, in the absence of moisture.

Before deciding on a particular battery, consider some of the essentials that may put the replacement battery in a different category from that of the unit originally supplied with the vehicle. When the original battery wears out, resistance in the wiring circuits is probably much increased, and the starter may be less efficient, along with the ignition system. There is also the likelihood that electrical accessories have been added.

All of the above reasons are justification for choosing a battery of greater capacity than the one supplied by the manufacturer.

Preparation

After the electrical needs have been considered, and a selection made, place the new battery on a bench or work table. Never activate a battery installed in the car. Remove vent caps from all the cells.

Fill each cell carefully, using sulfuric acid and distilled water (electrolyte) at a strength of 1.250-1.265 specific gravity to about ⅜ in. above the top of the separators, or to indicated level mark.

Place a battery type thermometer in one of the center cells. Check specific gravity of the electrolyte with a battery hydrometer. The battery temperature must be above 80°F. and specific gravity must be above 1.250 prior to installing the battery.

In charging 12-volt batteries, set charging rate at 35 amperes (6-volt batteries at 70 amperes) until electrolyte has reached 80° F. and electrolyte gravity is 1.250 or higher. Lower charging rates also may be used to obtain 80° F. and 1.250 specific gravity. When charging, do not allow electrolyte temperature to exceed 125° F. Normally, 10-15 minutes charging will be sufficient; however, in colder climates a little longer is O.K.

When the battery is removed from the charger, top up if necessary, with electrolyte, and replace the vent plugs.

When installing, make sure that both ends of the battery cables are clean and securely tightened, observing correct polarity.

Start engine and make sure that the generator is charging with lights and all accessories on.

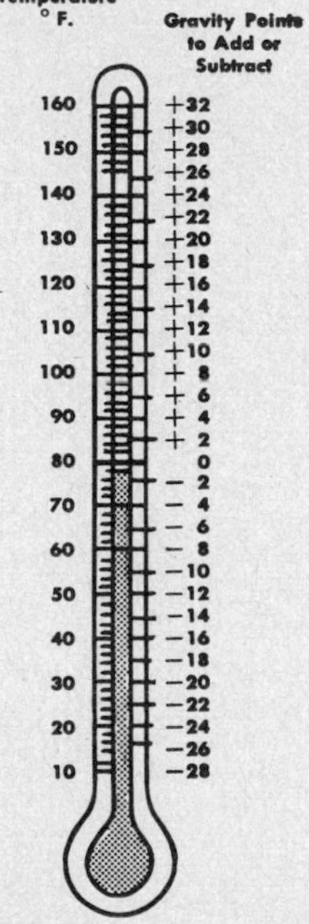

Hydrometer temperature correction chart (© Chrysler Corp)

Caution Be careful not to install or charge the battery with cables reversed. Damage to battery and generator can result, especially if the car is equipped with an alternator or transistorized radio.

Caution Because electrolyte is extremely corrosive to metals and many other materials, do not pour into sinks or drains. If battery acid is spilled on battery during filling or charging, or on bench or clothing, immediately flush it off with generous amounts of water and baking soda or ammonia.

Battery Troubles—Causes

1. Battery too small for the job (accessories, etc.).
2. Tired battery (worn out).
3. Corroded battery connections.
4. Generator not charging.
5. Generator charging rate too low.
6. Regulator defective.
7. Regulator out of adjustment.
8. Regulator has poor ground.
9. Alternator inoperative.
10. Loose generator or alternator drive belt.
11. Constant drain of current due to short circuit.

Battery Troubles—Corrections

1. Battery capacity may be less than requirements demand. Additional accessories, too frequent use of starter, low operational speeds, require a greater source of electrical supply. Install a larger capacity battery.
2. Either age or abuse is the usual cause of a tired battery. No amount of charging will offer more than temporary relief. Install a new battery of proper capacity if plates are sulfated.
3. Corroded battery posts and connections result from the chemical reaction between dissimilar metals and battery electrolyte. Excessive corrosion at a battery post is usually an indication of the failure of a seal between the post and the battery cover. Clean post and cable clamp, seal post-to-battery cover with rubber cement or other plastic material, then coat post with petroleum jelly, install cable clamp and tighten.
4. Generator not charging can be caused by a defective generator or other system component. Check entire charging system and correct the fault.
5. Low generator charging rate may be caused by a loose drive belt, loose or poor battery post connections, high resistance in charging circuit or a poor or improperly adjusted regulator.
6. Regulator may be defective because of burned points in the regulator or any open circuit in the control system.
7. Regulator out of adjustment.
8. A possible cause of trouble in DC systems is a poor regulator ground in any of the externally grounded (Type A) field circuit or, in heavy-duty (Type B) circuits, the internally grounded field within the generator.
9. The alternator may be inoperative because of damaged diodes, poor internal connections, open, grounded, or shorted field circuit, grounded or shorted stator windings.
10. A loose generator drive belt will cause low, or partial charging. Correct by adjusting drive belt.
11. A constant drain of current from the battery may be caused by frayed insulation on any live wire in the electrical system. This can cause a short circuit.

There is also the possibility of a light (in the trunk, glove box, under the hood. etc.) or other electric accessory remaining on after the ignition is turned off. To correct the situation:

First, with a sensitive ammeter, determine whether or not there is a current drain by opening the circuit at either battery post connection, hooking the ammeter in series, and checking for current drain.

Second, if the meter registers a drain, isolate the leak by reconnecting the battery, then, one by one, check each circuit at the fuse block. This is a tedious but unavoidable procedure and consists of removing each fuse and testing that circuit with the prods of an ammeter (in series). The circuit which activates the meter is the guilty one; identify the trouble spot by elimination. Correct the trouble by correcting the short or replacing the switch or other electrical component.

In the event that the fuse block test does not indicate the trouble, check the circuits which are protected with circuit breakers, (headlamps, parking lamps, seat and window controls, etc.).

Specific Gravity Test—Hydrometer

Before attempting any electrical checks, it is important to check the condition of the battery.

While not technically exact, a practical measurement of the chemical condition of the battery is indicated by measuring the specific gravity of the acid (electrolyte) contained in each cell. The electrolyte in a fully charged battery is usually between 1.260 and 1.280 times as heavy as pure water at the same temperature (80°F.). Variations in the specific gravity readings for a fully charged battery may differ. Therefore, it is most important that all battery cells produce an equal reading.

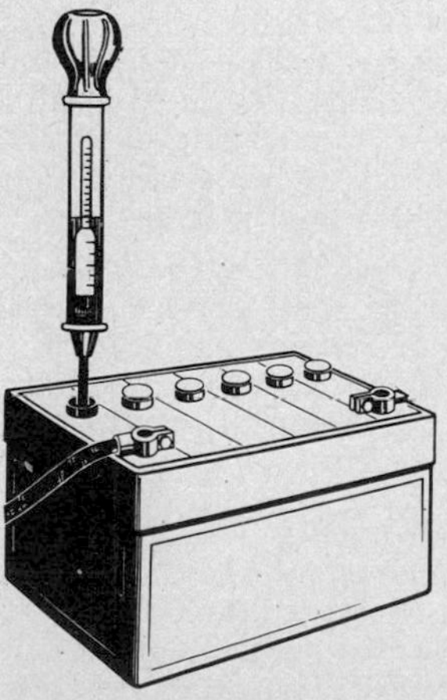

Testing battery specific gravity

As a battery discharges, a chemical change takes place within each cell. The sulfate factor of the electrolyte combines chemically with the battery plates, reducing the weight of the electrolyte. A reading of the specific gravity of the acid, or electrolyte, of any partially charged battery, will therefore be less than that taken in a fully charged one.

The hydrometer is the instrument in general use for determining the specific gravity of liquids. The battery hydrometer is readily available from many sources, including local auto replacement parts stores. The following chart gives an indication of specific gravity value, related to battery charge condition. If, after charging, the specific gravity between any two cells varies more than 50 points (.050), the battery is probably bad.

Specific Gravity Reading	*Charged Condition*
1.260-1.280	Fully charged
1.230-1.250	Three-quarter charged
1.200-1.220	One-half charged
1.170-1.190	One-quarter charged
1.140-1.160	Just about flat
1.110-1.130	All the way down

Testing Battery Polarity

Battery polarity is very important, especially since the introduction of AC generators. Permanent damage to the diodes of alternators (AC generators) will result from reversing polarity.

To determine battery polarity, turn the voltmeter selector to the high reading scale. Connect voltmeter leads to the battery posts. If the gauge needle moves in the correct direction, the positive lead of the meter is on the positive (+) post of the battery. If the gauge needle moves in the wrong direction, polarity is reversed.

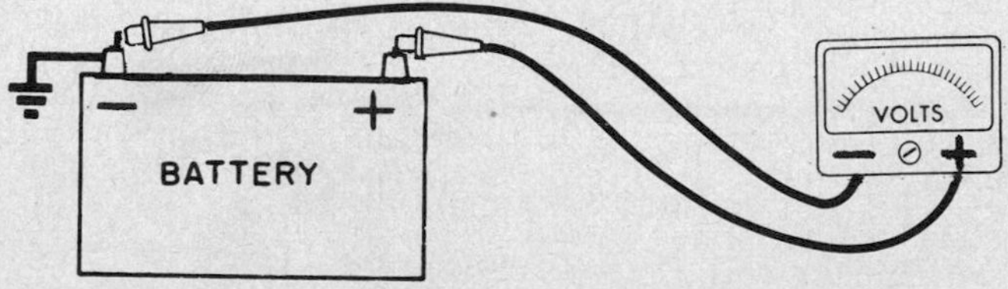

Battery polarity test

Testing the Delco "Sealed Top" Battery

Some GM cars come equipped with a "sealed top" battery which does not require the usual maintenance. Because the battery has a greater amount of electrolyte and a reduced need for water, the top of the battery has no filler caps and is sealed. A small vent is provided at one edge of the battery top.

There are two types of sealed batteries used: one has a charge indicator eye and the other does not. Both types may be tested in the following manner:

The Delco "sealed top" battery
(© Oldsmobile Div., G.M. Corp)

1. Check the condition of the battery case. If the case is damaged so that loss of electrolyte is possible, the battery must be replaced.
2. If the battery has a charge indicator eye, check the following:
   a. If the eye is dark, the battery has enough electrolyte. If the eye is light, the electrolyte level is too low and the battery must be replaced.
   b. If a green dot appears in the middle of the eye, the battery is sufficiently charged; go on to Step 4. If there is no green dot visible, charge the battery as in Step 3.
3. Charge the battery if there is no green dot visible in the eye, or if it is the type without an eye, at the following rates:

Amps	*Time*
75	40 min
50	1 hr
25	2 hr
10	5 hr

Caution Do not charge the battery for more than 50 ampere-hours. If the green dot appears or electrolyte squirts out of the vent, stop the charge and go on with Step 4.

4. Either disconnect the high-tension coil wire or the engine harness (electronic ignition) and crank the starter motor for 15 seconds, to remove the surface charge.
5. Connect a voltmeter and a 230

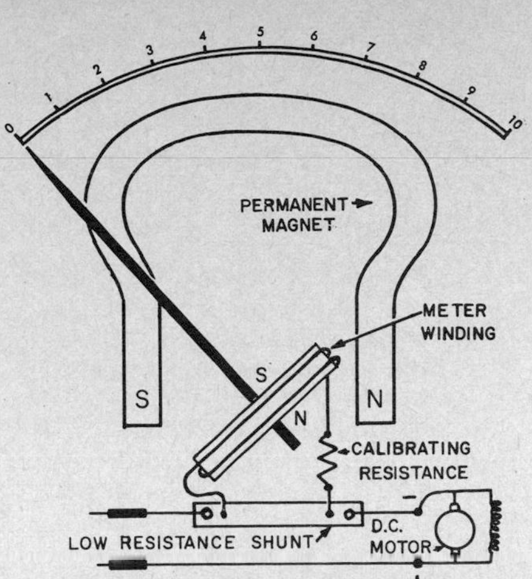

Ammeter circuit

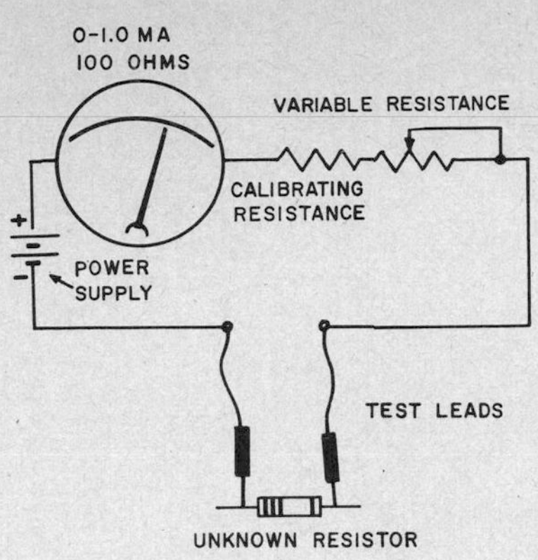

Ohmmeter circuit

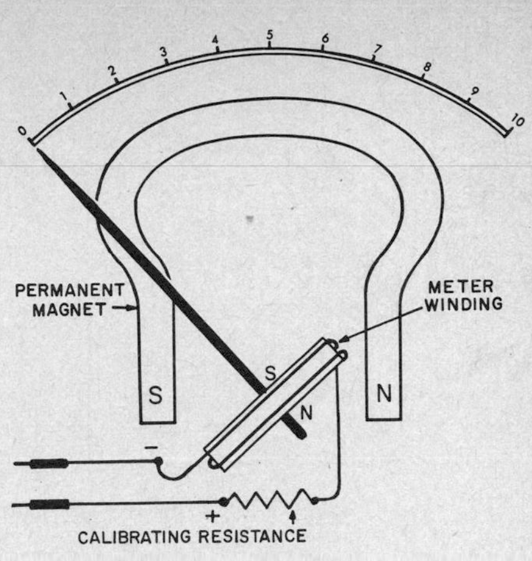

Voltmeter circuit

amp load across the battery terminals.

6. Take a voltmeter reading after the load has been connected for 15 seconds, then disconnect the load.
7. Consult the following chart. If the battery voltage is that specified (or more) for the given ambient temperature, the battery is good. If the voltage falls below that specified, then the battery is bad and must be replaced.

Ambient Temperature (°F)	*Minimum Voltage*
70 (or above)	9.6
60	9.5
50	9.4
40	9.3
30	9.1
20	8.9
10	8.7
0	8.5

Know Your Instruments

Ohmmeter

An ohmmeter is used to measure electrical resistance in a unit or circuit. The ohmmeter has a self-contained power supply. In use, it is connected across (or in parallel with) the terminals of the unit being tested.

Ammeter

An ammeter is used to measure current (amount of electricity) flowing through a unit, or circuit. Ammeters are always connected in the line (in series) with the unit or circuit being tested.

Voltmeter

A voltmeter is used to measure voltage (electrical pressure) pushing the current through a unit, or circuit. The meter is connected across the terminals of the unit being tested. The meter reading will be the difference in pressure (voltage drop) between the two sides of the unit.

Boost Charging Rates

12-volt Battery: 1,000 ampere/minutes (50 amps. x 20 min.)

6-volt Battery: 1,800 ampere/minutes (60 amps. x 30 min.)

NOTE: *Not all charger clips will fit the newer side-terminal batteries. If your clips don't fit, adapters are available from your local jobber.*

Testing the Starting Motor

Testing the Starter Circuit

The starter circuit should be divided and tested in four separate phases:

1. Cranking voltage check.
2. Amperage draw.
3. Voltage drop—grounded side.
4. Voltage drop—battery side.

NOTE: The battery must be in good condition for this test to have significance. To accurately check battery condition, use equipment designed to measure its capacity under a load. Instructions accompanying the equipment should be followed.

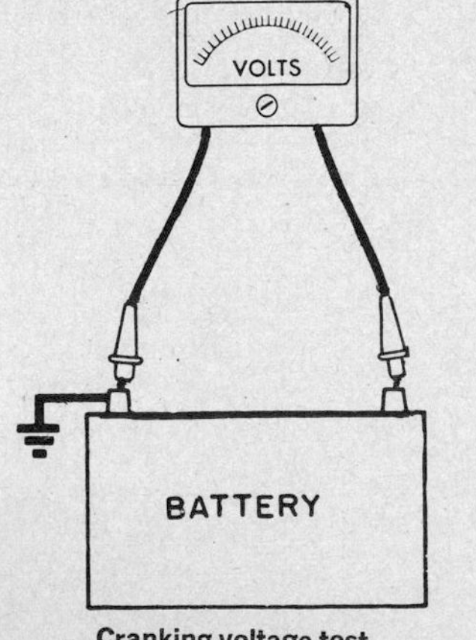

Cranking voltage test

Cranking Voltage

Turn voltmeter selector to 8-10 volt scale for cars equipped with 6-volt systems, and to the 16-20 volt scale for cars equipped with 12-volt systems.

Connect voltmeter leads to the battery posts (observe polarity and reverse meter leads if necessary). Remove the high tension wire from the distributor cap and ground it to prevent starting. Now, turn the key. Observe both voltmeter reading and cranking speed. The cranking speed should be even, and at a satisfactory rate of speed, with a voltmeter reading of 4.8 volts or more for 6-volt systems, and at least 9.6 volts for 12-volt systems.

Amperage Draw

The amount of current the starter motor draws is usually (but not always) associated with the mechanical problems involved in cranking the engine. (Mechanical trouble in the engine, frozen or worn starter parts, misaligned starter or starter components, etc.) Because starter motor amperage draw is directly influenced by anything restricting the free turning of the engine, or starter, it is important that the engine and all components be at operating temperatures.

Starter current indicator

To measure starter current draw, remove the high tension wire from the center of the distributor cap and ground it.

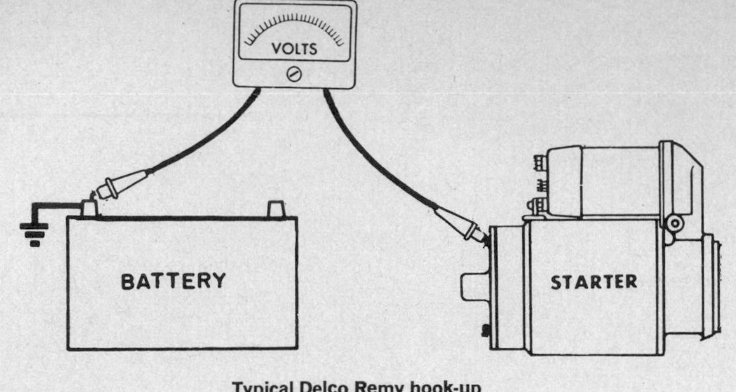

Typical Delco Remy hook-up

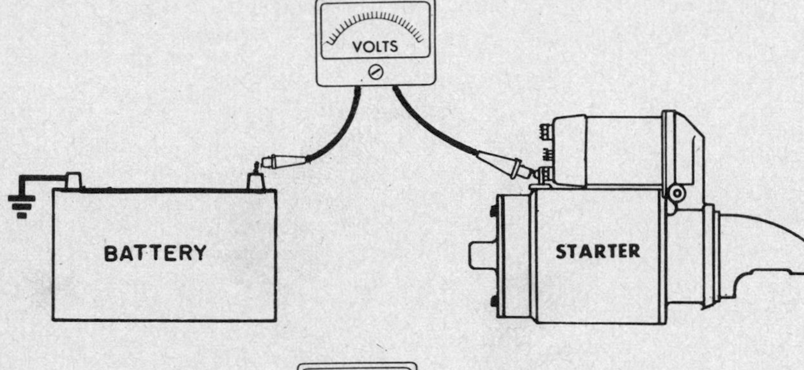

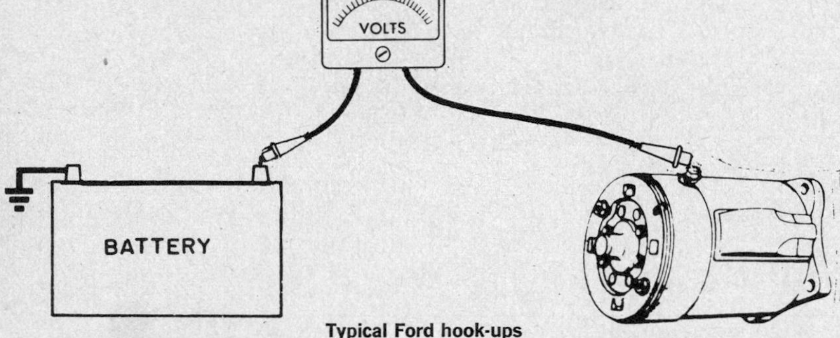

Typical Ford hook-ups

NOTE: *On cars with electronic ignition, disconnect the control box from the distributor (harness).*

A very simple and inexpensive starter current indicator is available at auto stores. This indicator is an induction type gauge and shows, without disconnecting any wires, starter current draw.

Place the yoke of the meter directly over the insulated starter supply cable (cable must be straight for a minimum of 2 in.). Close the starter switch for about 20 seconds, watch the meter dial and record the average reading. If the indicator swings in the wrong direction, reverse the position of the meter. On 6-volt systems, normal draw for small to medium size engines is 150 to 225 amperes. Larger and high compression engines may draw as much as 400 amperes. On 12-volt systems, the current draw should be about one-half the amount registered for the 6-volt system.

More accurate but complex equipment is available from many name brand manufacturers. This equipment consists of a combination voltmeter, ammeter, and carbon pile rheostat. When using this equipment, follow the equipment manufacturer's procedures and recommendations.

High amperage and lazy performance would suggest an excessively tight engine, friction in the starter or starter drive, grounded starter field or armature.

Normal amperage and lazy performance suggest high resistance, or possibly poor connections somewhere in the starter circuit.

Low amperage and lazy or no performance suggest battery condition poor, bad cables or connections along the line.

Voltage Drop—Grounded Side

With a voltmeter on the 3-volt scale, without disconnecting any wires, connect negative test lead of the voltmeter to a prod secured in the grounded battery post. The positive test lead is connected to a cleaned, bare metal portion of the starter motor housing. Close the starter switch and note the voltmeter reading. If the reading is the same as battery reading, the ground circuit is open somewhere between the battery and the starter. In many cases the reading will be very small. The reading shown will indicate voltage drop (loss) between battery ground post and starter housing. The drop should not exceed 0.2 volt. If the voltage drop is above the specified amount, the next step is to isolate and correct the cause. It can be a bad cable or connection anywhere in the battery-to-starter ground circuit. A check of this type should progress along the various points of possible trouble, between the battery ground post and the starter motor housing, until the trouble spot has been located.

NOTE: due to the design of the Chrysler reduction gear starter, testing is limited to measuring voltage drop to starter cable connection.

Voltage Drop—Battery Side

Bad starter cranking may result from poor connections or faulty components of the battery or hot phase of

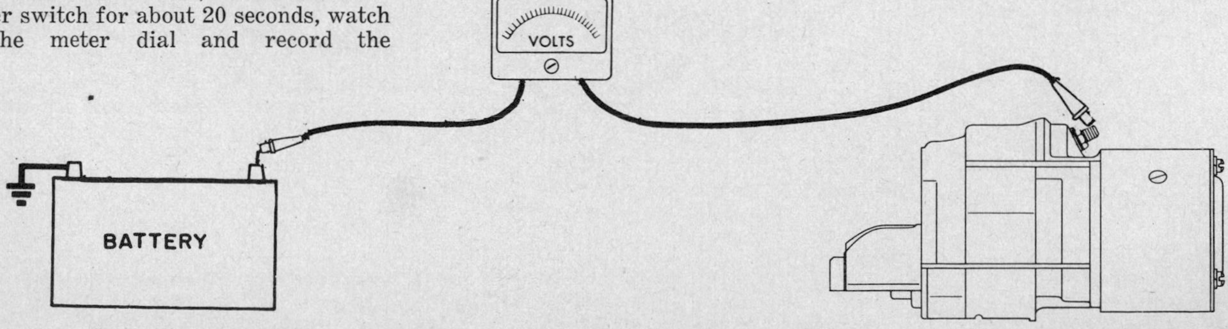

Typical Chrysler hook-up

the starter motor circuit. To check this phase of the circuit, without disconnecting any wires, connect one lead of a voltmeter to a prod secured in the hot post of the battery and the other voltmeter lead to the field terminal of the starting motor. The meter should be set to the 16-20 volt scale. Before closing the starter switch, the voltmeter reading will be that of the battery. After closing the starter switch, change the selector on the voltmeter to the 3-volt scale. With a jumper wire between the relay battery terminal and the relay starter switch terminal, crank the engine. If the starting motor cranks the engine, the relay (solenoid) is operating.

While the engine is being cranked, watch the voltmeter. It should not register more than 0.5 volt. If more than this, check each part of the circuit for voltage drop to isolate the trouble, (high resistance).

Without disturbing the voltmeter-to-battery hook-up, move the free voltmeter lead to the battery terminal of the relay (solenoid), and crank the engine. The voltmeter should show no more than 0.1 volt.

If this reading is correct, move the same voltmeter lead to the starting motor terminal of the relay (solenoid). While the engine is being cranked, the voltmeter should show no more than 0.3 volt. If it does, the trouble lies in the relay.

If the reading is correct, the trouble is in the cable or connections between the relay and the starting motor.

Starter Motor And System Service

Diagnosis

Starter Won't Crank the Engine

1. Dead battery.
2. Open starter circuit, such as:
   A. Broken or loose battery cables.
   B. Inoperative starter motor solenoid.
   C. Broken or loose wire from starter switch to solenoid.
   D. Poor solenoid or starter ground.
   E. Bad starter switch, (ignition, dash button or carburetor).
   F. Defective seat belt interlock system—1974-75 cars only.
3. Defective starter internal circuit, such as:
   A. Dirty or burnt commutator.
   B. Stuck, worn or broken brushes.
   C. Open or shorted armature.
   D. Open or grounded fields.
4. Starter motor mechanical faults, such as:
   A. Jammed armature end bearings.
   B. Bar bearing, allowing armature ture to rub fields.
   C. Bent shaft.
   D. Broken starter housing.
   E. Bad starter worm or drive mechanism.
   F. Bad starter drive or flywheel driven gear.
5. Engine hard or impossible to crank, such as:
   A. Hydrostatic lock, water in combustion chamber.
   B. Crankshaft seizing in bearings.
   C. Piston or ring seizing.
   D. Bent or broken connecting rod.
   E. Seizing of connecting rod bearing.
   F. Flywheel jammed or broken.
   G. In some remote cases, an incandescent particle in the combustion chamber of a hot engine will prevent starting. This condition acts like a low battery or ignition timing so far advanced that the engine kicks back. The piston refuses to pass over top center. A two or three minute wait is generally enough to cool the troubled spot and temporarily clear the fault.

Starter Spins Free, Won't Engage

1. Sticking or broken drive mechanism.

Magnetic Switches

Magnetic switches serve only to make contact for the starter motor. Usually, such switches are located on the inner fender panel, although they are found mounted on the starter in a few cases.

Magnetic Switches with Two Control Terminals

On this type of magnetic switch current is supplied from the ignition switch or transmission neutral button to one of the magnetic switch control terminals. The other control terminal is connected to the transmission neutral safety switch (on the transmission) where it is grounded.

Magnetic Switches with Ignition Resistor By-Pass Terminals

Used with 12-volt systems. All normally use a magnetic switch with a single control terminal. The second terminal is an ignition resistor by-pass terminal.

Solenoids Without Relays

This type of starter solenoid is always mounted on the starter. Makes electrical contact for the starter and pulls the starter and drive clutch into mesh with the flywheel. The Chrysler reduction gear starter has this solenoid embodied in the starter housing.

There is only one control terminal on the solenoid.

The ignition by-pass terminal is usually marked R or IGN, if it is used.

Solenoids With Separate Relays

The solenoid itself is always mounted on the starter. In addition to making contact for the starter, it also pulls the starter drive clutch gear into mesh with the flywheel. A single control terminal is used on the solenoid itself. The relay is usually found mounted to the inner fender panel or on the firewall.

Solenoids With Built-In Relays

These units are always mounted on the starter and are connected, through linkage, to the starter drive clutch. The relay portion is a square box built into and integral with the front end of the solenoid assembly.

Neutral Safety Switches

The purpose of the neutral safety switch is to prevent the starter from cranking the engine except when the transmission is in Neutral or Park.

NOTE: *Fords starting 1971 and Cadillacs starting 1974 with a column mounted automatic transmission selector and steering column lock do not have a neutral safety switch; instead the key can only be turned to the*

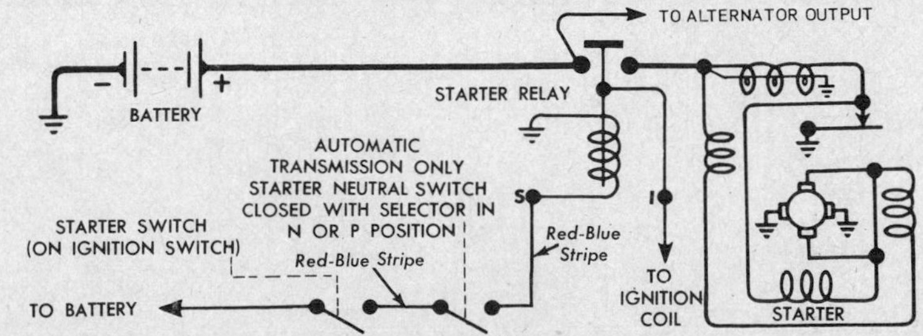

Ford positive engagement starter circuit (© Ford Motor Co)

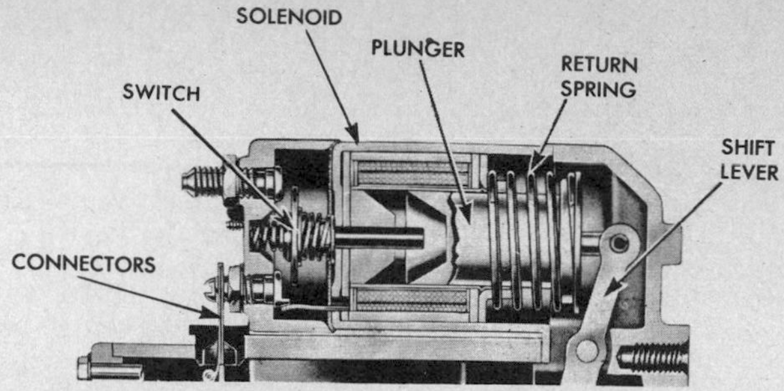

Starter solenoid mounted on starter motor

"START" position when the selector is in Park or Neutral.

On some cars, the neutral safety switch is located on the transmission. It serves to ground the solenoid or magnetic switch, whichever is used.

On other cars the neutral safety switch is located either at the bottom of the steering column, where it contacts the shift mechanism, on the steering column, underneath the dash, or on the shift linkage (console).

NOTE: *Some recent cars with manual transmissions have a safety switch mounted on the clutch linkage to prevent starter operation unless the pedal is depressed.*

On most cars, the neutral safety switch and the back-up light switch are combined into a single switch mechanism.

See the car sections for specific details.

Troubleshooting Neutral Safety Switches—Quick Test

If the starter fails to function and the neutral safety switch is to be checked, a jumper can be placed across its terminals. If the starter then functions the safety switch is defective.

In the case of neutral safety switches with one wire, this wire must be grounded for testing purposes. If the starter works with the wire grounded, the switch is defective.

Neutral Safety Switch—Back-Up Light Switch

When the neutral safety switch is built in combination with the back-up light switch, the easiest way to tell which terminals are for the back-up lights is to take a jumper and cross every pair of wires. The pair of wires which light the back-up lamps should be ignored when testing the neutral safety switch. Once the back-up light wires have been located, jump the other pair of wires to test the neutral safety switch. If the starter functions only when the jumper is placed across these two wires, the neutral safety switch is defective or requires adjustment.

Reduction-Gear Starter Motor

(Chrysler Corporation)

The housing is die-cast aluminum. A 3.5 to 1 reduction, combined with the starter to ring gear ratio, results in a total gear reduction of about 45 to 1.

NOTE: the high-pitched sound is caused by the higher starter speed.

The positive shift solenoid is enclosed in the starter housing and is energized through the ignition switch. When ignition switch is turned to start, the solenoid plunger engages drive gear through a shifting fork. At the completion of travel, the plunger closes a switch to revolve the starter.

The tension of the spring-type shifting prevents a butt-tooth lock up and motor will not start before total shift.

An overrunning clutch prevents motor damage if key is held on after engine starts.

No lubrication is required due to Oilite bearings.

1975 and later Chrysler Corporation cars with large V-8s (360 cu. in. and up) use a larger reduction gear starter motor. It is similar to the previous models but is more powerful and has a 2:1 gear reduction rather than the 3.5:1 unit. The clutch drive unit in the new starter has been enlarged to handle the increased load as have the rest of the components. While the new starter is outwardly similar to the old one, parts are not interchangeable; however removal, installation, disassembly and assembly procedures are unchanged.

Disassembly

1. Support assembly in a vise equipped with soft jaws. Do not clamp. Care must be used not to distort or damage the die cast aluminum.
2. Remove the thru-bolts and the end housing.
3. Carefully pull the armature up and out of the gear housing, and the starter frame and field assembly. Remove the steel and fiber thrust washer.

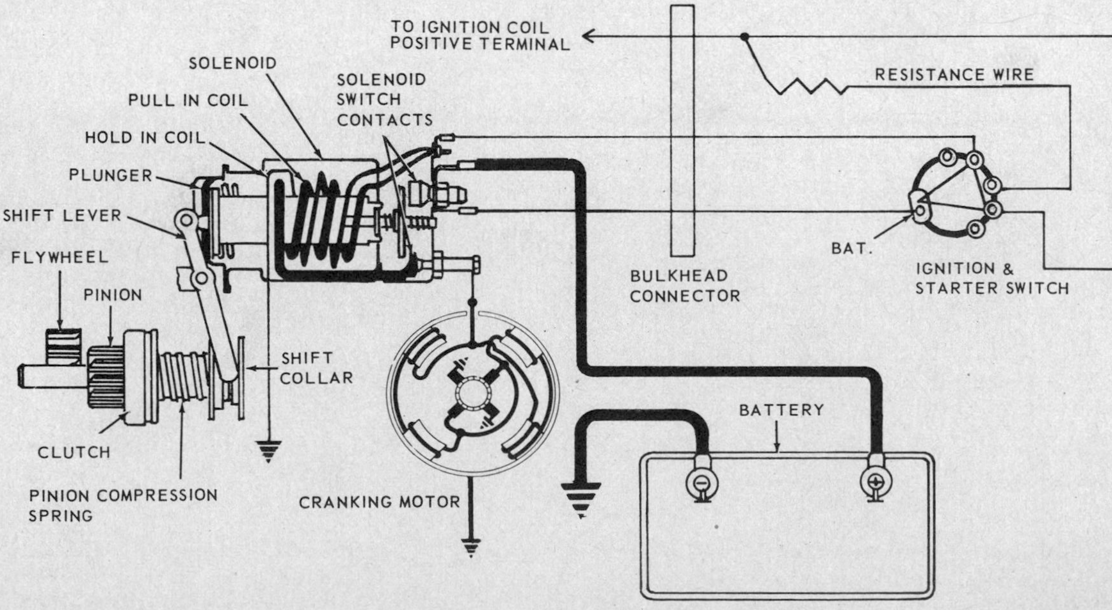

G.M. starter circuit (© G.M. Corp)

NOTE: on eight cylinder engines the starting motors have the wire of the shunt field coil soldered to the brush terminal. Six cylinder engines have the four coils in series and do not have a wire soldered to the brush terminal. One pair of brushes is connected to this terminal. The other pair of brushes is attached to the series field coils by means of a terminal screw. Carefully pull the frame and field assembly up just enough to expose the terminal screw and the solder connection of the shunt field at the brush terminal. Place two wood blocks between the starter frame and starter gear housing to facilitate removal of the terminal screw and unsoldering of the shunt field wire at the brush terminal.

4. Support the brush terminal with

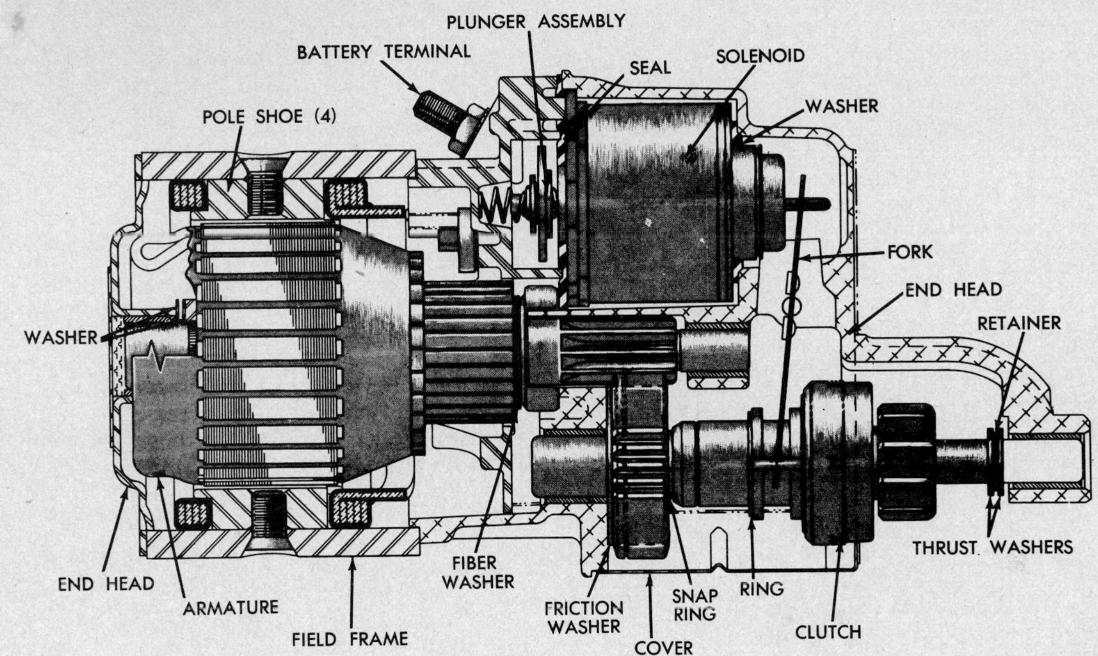

Reduction gear starter motor (© Chrysler Corp)

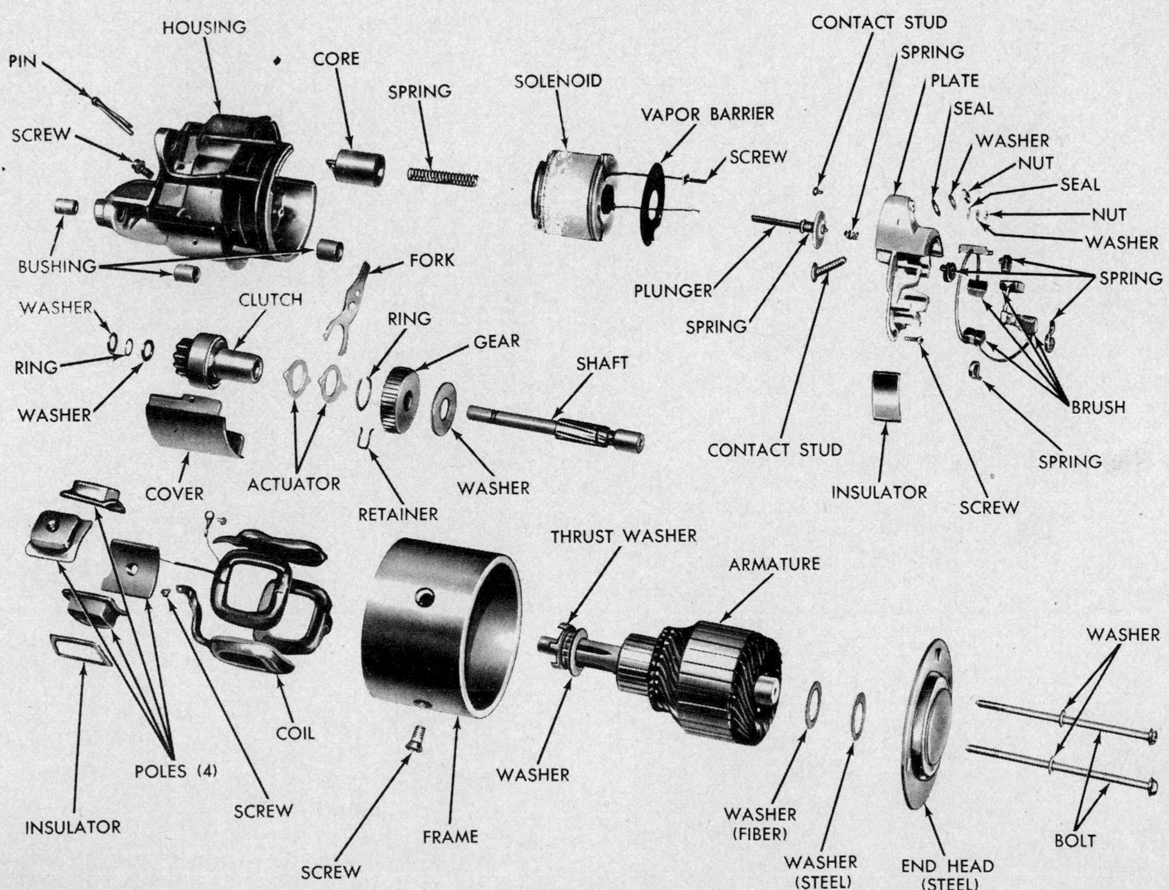

Reduction gear motor—exploded view (© Chrysler Corp)

a finger behind terminal and remove screw.
5. On eight cylinder engine starters unsolder the shunt field coil lead from the brush terminal and housing.
6. The brush holder plate with terminal, contact and brushes is serviced as an assembly.
7. Clean all old sealer from around plate and housing.
8. Remove the brush holder attaching screw.
9. On the shunt type, unsolder the solenoid winding from the brush terminal.
10. Remove 11/32 in. nut, washer and insulator from solenoid terminal.
11. Remove brush holder plate with brushes as an assembly.
12. Remove gear housing ground screw.
13. The solenoid assembly can be removed from the well.
14. Remove nut, washer and seal from starter battery terminal and remove terminal from plate.
15. Remove solenoid contact and plunger from solenoid and remove the coil sleeve.
16. Remove the solenoid return spring, coil retaining washer, retainer and the dust cover from the gear housing.
17. Release the snap-ring that locates the driven gear on pinion shaft.

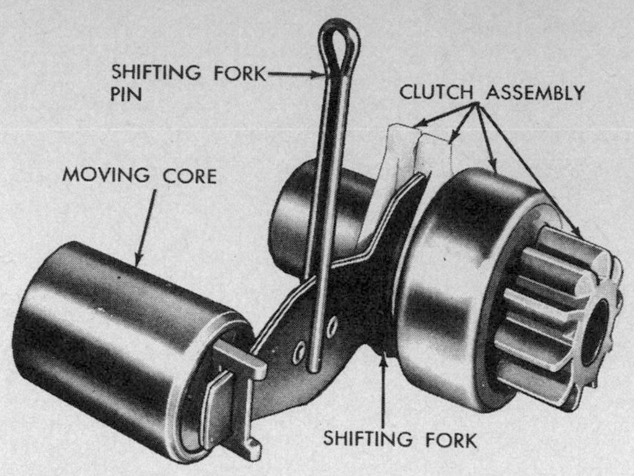

Shift fork and clutch arrangement—reduction gear motor
(© Chrysler Corp)

CAUTION: *The snap-ring is under tension; to prevent it from flying off, place a cloth over it prior to removal.*

18. Release front retaining ring.
19. Push pinion shaft toward the rear and remove snap-ring, thrust washers, clutch and pinion, and two shift fork nylon actuators.
20. Remove driven gear and friction washer.
21. Pull shifting fork forward and remove moving core.
22. Remove fork retainer pin and shifting fork assembly. The gear housing with bushings is serviced as an assembly.

Replacement of Brushes

1. Brushes that are worn more than one-half the length of new brushes, or are oil-soaked, should be replaced.
2. When resoldering the shunt field and solenoid lead, make a strong, low-resistance connection using a high-temperature solder and resin flux. Do not use acid or acid-core solder. Do not break the shunt field wire units when removing and installing the brushes.

Starter Clutch and Pinion Gear Inspection

1. Do not immerse the starter

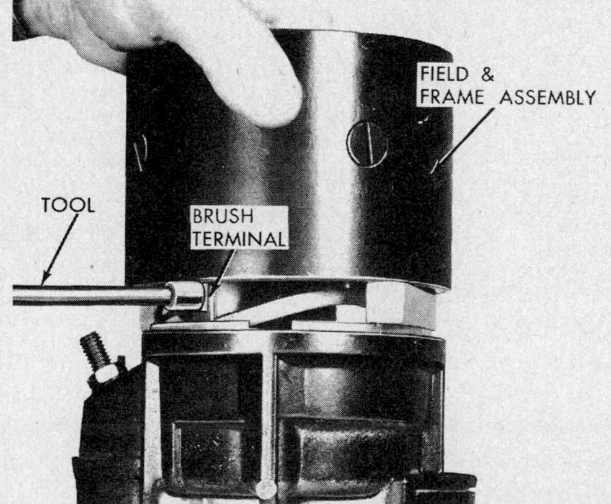

Removing terminal screw—reduction gear motor
(© Chrysler Corp)

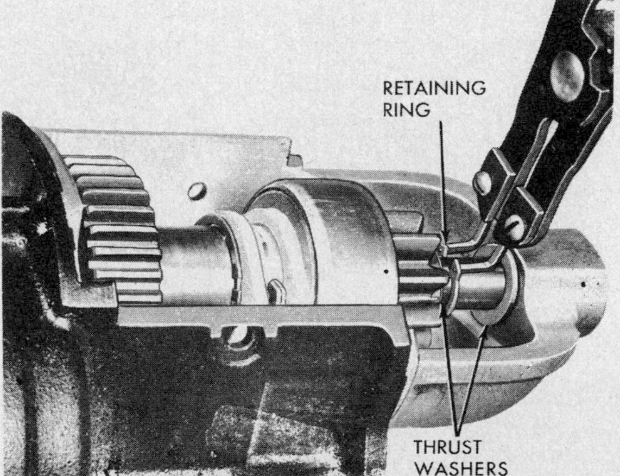

Removing retainer ring—reduction gear motor
(© Chrysler Corp)

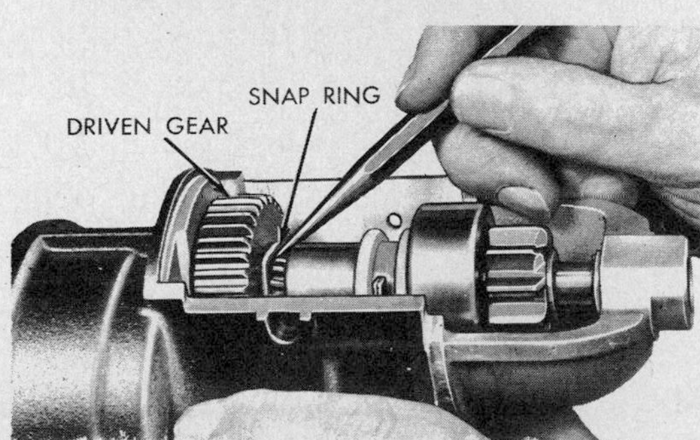

Removing drive gear snap-ring—reduction gear motor
(© Chrysler Corp)

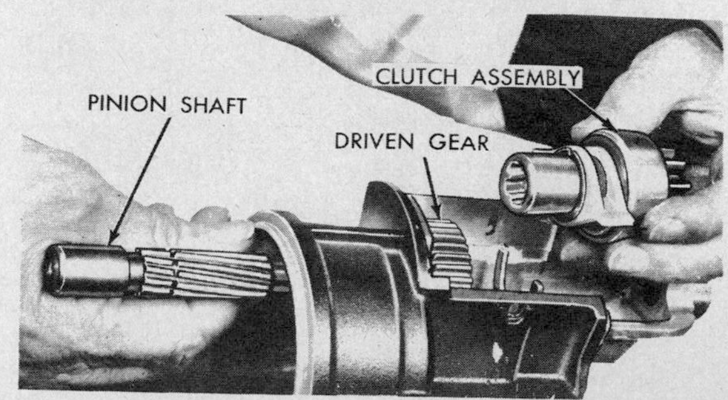

Removing clutch assembly—reduction gear motor
(© Chrysler Corp)

clutch unit in a cleaning solvent. The outside of the clutch and pinion must be cleaned with a cloth so as not to wash the lubricant from the inside of the clutch.

2. Rotate the pinion. The pinion gear should rotate smoothly and in one direction only. If the starter clutch unit does not function properly, or if the pinion is worn, chipped, or burred, replace the starter clutch unit.

Commutator Inspection

1. Inspect the commutator and the surface contacted by the brushes when the starter is assembled, for flat spots, out-of-roundness, or excessive wear.
2. Reface the commutator if necessary, removing only a sufficient amount of metal to provide a smooth, even surface.
3. Using light pressure, clean the grooves of the face of the commutator with a pointed tool. Neither remove any metal or widen the grooves.

Assembly

1. The shifter fork consists of two spring steel plates held together by two rivets. Before assembling the starter, check the plates for side movement. After lubricating between the plates with a small amount of SAE 10 engine oil, they should have about 1/16 in. side movement to insure proper pinion gear engagement.
2. Position the shift fork in the drive housing and install the shifting fork retainer pin. One tip of the pin should be straight and the other bent at a 15 degree angle away from the housing. The fork and retainer pin should operate freely after bending the tip of the pin.
3. Install the solenoid moving core and engage the shifting fork.
4. Place the pinion shaft into the drive housing and install the friction washer and drive gear.
5. Install the clutch and pinion assembly, thrust washer, and retaining washer.
6. Engage the shifting fork with the clutch actuators.

Caution The friction washer must be positioned on the shoulder of the splines of the pinion shaft before the driven gear is positioned.

7. Install the driven gear snap ring.
8. Install the pinion shaft retaining ring.
9. The starter solenoid return spring can now be inserted in the movable core.
10. Install the solenoid contact plunger assembly into the solenoid and reform the double wires so they can be curved around the contactor. This will allow the terminal stud to enter the brush holder properly.

Caution The contactor must not touch these double wires after assembly is complete.

11. Assemble the battery terminal stud in the brush holder.
12. Position the seal on the brush holder plate.
13. Run the solenoid lead wire through the hole in the brush holder and attach the solenoid stud, insulating washer, flat washer, and nut.
14. Wrap the solenoid lead wire tightly around the brush terminal post and solder it.
15. Fix the brush holder to the solenoid attaching screws.
16. Gently lower the solenoid coil and brush plate into the gear housing.
17. Position the brush plate assembly into the starter gear housing, install the nuts, and tighten.
18. Solder the shunt coil lead wire to the starter brush terminal.
19. Install the brush terminal screw.
20. Position the field frame on the gear housing and start the armature into the housing, carefully engaging the splines on the shaft with the reduction gear by rotating the armature.
21. Install the fiber thrust washer and the steel washer on the armature shaft.
22. Replace the starter end housing and starter through bolts; tighten securely.

Direct Drive Starter Motor

(Chrysler Corporation)

NOTE: *The direct drive starter was last used in 1973.*

Disassembly

1. Remove through bolts and tap commutator end head from frame.
2. Remove thrust washers from armature shaft.
3. Lift brush holder springs and remove brushes from holders.
4. Remove brush holder plate.
5. Disconnect the field coil wires at the solenoid connector, and remove the solenoid screws.

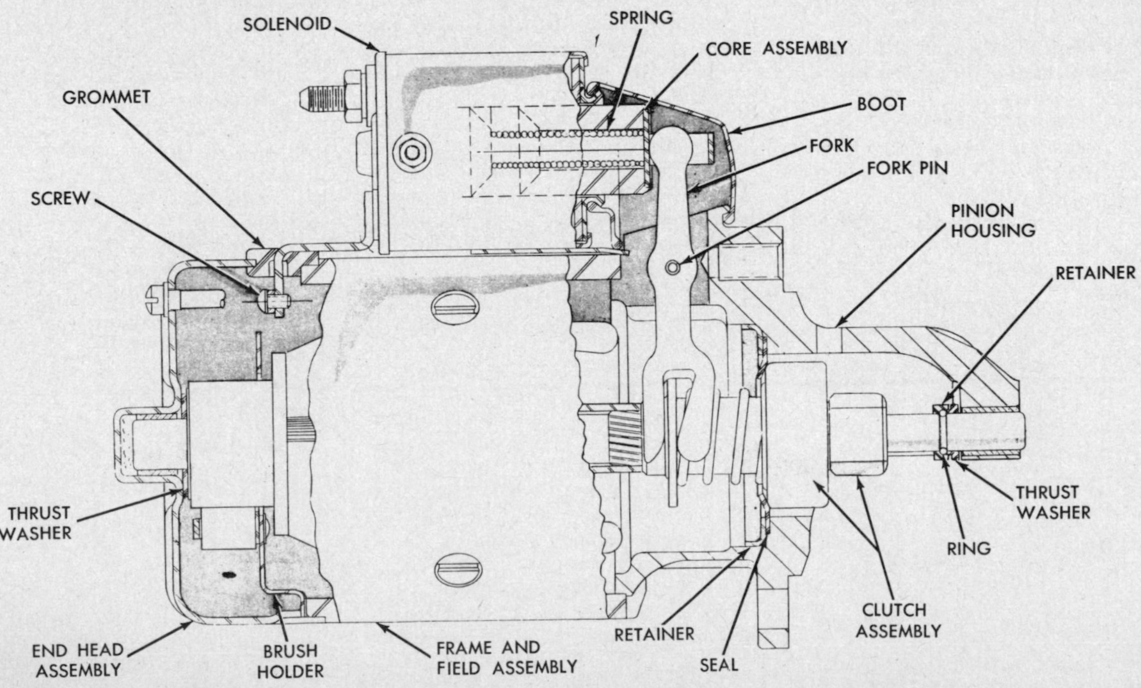

Chrysler direct drive starter motor (© Chrysler Corp)

Chrysler direct drive motor—exploded view (© Chrysler Corp)

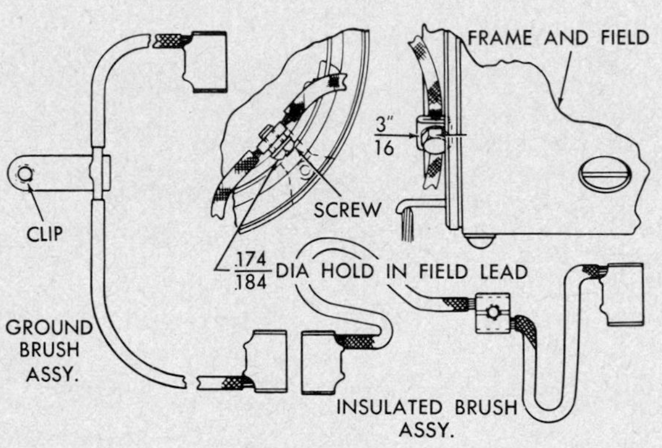

Brush lead arrangement—Chrysler direct drive motor (© Chrysler Corp)

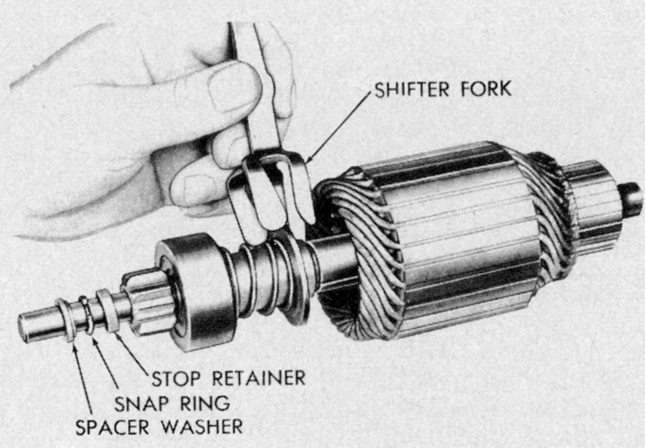

Removing shift fork—direct drive motor (© Chrysler Corp)

6. Remove solenoid and boot.
7. Drive out shift fork pivot pin.
8. Remove drive end pinion housing and spacer washer.
9. Remove shift fork from starter drive.
10. Slide overrunning clutch pinion gear toward commutator, drive stop retainer toward clutch pinion gear and remove the now-exposed snap-ring.
11. Remove overrunning clutch drive from armature shaft.
12. If field coils are good, stop disassembly at this point. If field coils must be replaced, remove ground brushes terminal screw and remove brushes, terminal and shunt wire. Remove pole shoe screws, using a ratchet-type impact driver and special wide screwdriver blade, then remove field coils.
13. Replacement of the brushes, inspection of the starter clutch and pinion, and inspection of the commutator procedures are the same as the reduction-gear starter procedures.

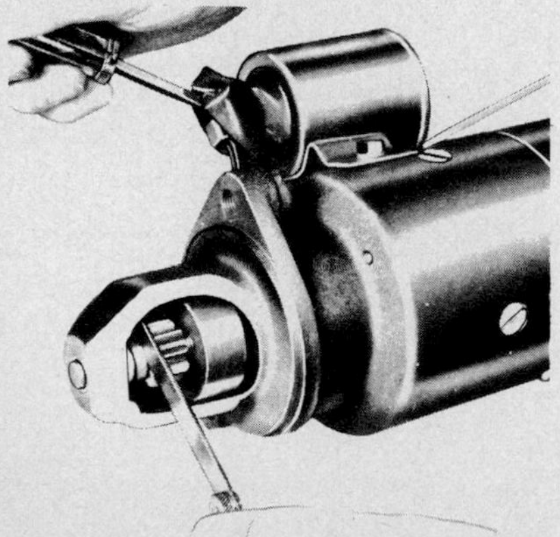

Checking drive pinion clearance—direct drive motor (© Chrysler Corp)

Assembly

1. Install field coils into frame, if removed.
2. Lubricate armature shaft and splines with engine oil.
3. Install starter drive, stop retainer, lock ring and spacer washer.
4. Install shift fork, with *narrow* leg of fork toward commutator.
5. Install pinion housing onto armature shaft, indexing shift fork with slot in housing.
6. Install shift fork pivot pin.
7. With clutch drive, shift fork, and pinion housing assembled onto the armature, slide armature into frame until pinion housing indexes with slot.
8. Install solenoid and boot, tightening bolts to 60-70 in. lbs.
9. Connect field coil wires to solenoid connector, making sure they do not touch frame.
10. Install brush holder plate, indexing tang in frame hole.
11. Place brushes in holders, making sure field coil wires do not interfere.
12. Install thrust washers on commutator end of armature shaft to obtain a maximum of 0.010 in. end-play.
13. Install commutator end head and through bolts. Tighten bolts to 40-50 in. lbs.
14. Measure drive gear pinion clearance; it should be 1/8 in. Adjust by moving solenoid fore and aft as required.

Autolite Positive Engagement Starter Motor

(Ford Motor Co.)

This starting motor is a series-parallel wound, four pole, four brush unit. It is equipped with an overrunning clutch drive pinion, which is engaged with the flywheel ring gear

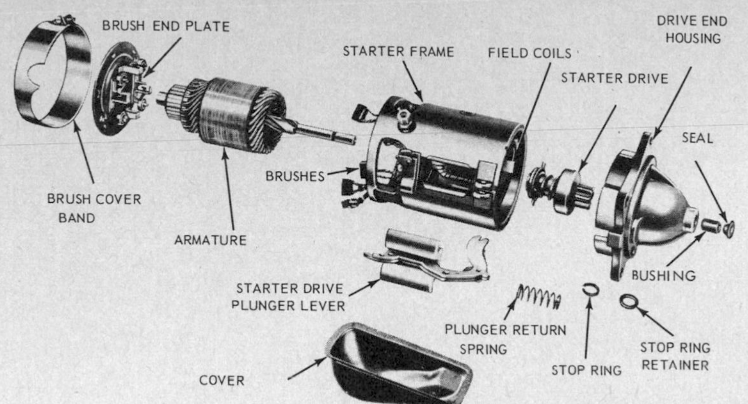

Exploded view Ford positive engagement starter motor
(© Ford Motor Co)

by an actuating lever, operated by a movable pole piece. This pole piece is hinged to the starter frame and can drop into position through an opening in the frame.

Three conventional field coils are located at three pole piece positions. The fourth field coil is designed to serve also as an engaging coil and a hold-in coil for the operation of the drive pinion.

When the ignition switch is turned to the start position, the starter relay is energized and current flows from the battery to the starter motor terminal. This prime surge of current first flows through the starter engaging coil, creating a very strong magnetic field. This magnetism draws the movable pole piece down toward the starter frame, which then causes the lever attached to it to move the starter pinion into engagement with the flywheel ring gear.

When the movable pole shoe is fully seated, it opens the field coil, grounding contacts, and the starter is then in normal operation. A holding coil is used to hold the movable pole shoe in the fully seated position during the engine cranking operation.

Cars equipped with automatic transmissions have a starter neutral switch circuit control. This is to prevent operation of the starter if the selector lever is not in Neutral or Park.

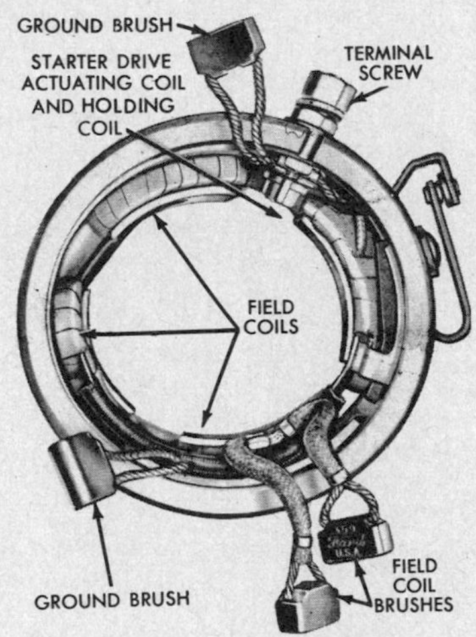

Autolite field coil assembly

This type starter is used on both Ford and late-model American Motors products.

Disassembly

1. Remove brush cover band and starter drive gear actuating lever cover. Observe the brush lead locations for reassembly, then remove the brushes from their holders.

NOTE: factory brush length is ½ in.; wear limit is ¼ in.

2. Remove the through bolts, starter drive gear housing and the drive gear actuating lever return spring.
3. Remove the pivot pin retaining the starter gear actuating lever and remove the lever and the armature.
4. Remove the stop ring retainer. Remove and discard the stop ring holding the drive gear to the armature shaft; then remove the drive gear assembly.
5. Remove the brush end plate.
6. Remove the two screws holding the ground brushes to the frame.
7. On the field coil that operates the starter drive gear actuating lever, bend the tab up on the field retainer and remove the field coil retainer.
8. Remove the three coil retaining screws. Unsolder the field coil leads from the terminal screw, then remove the pole shoes and

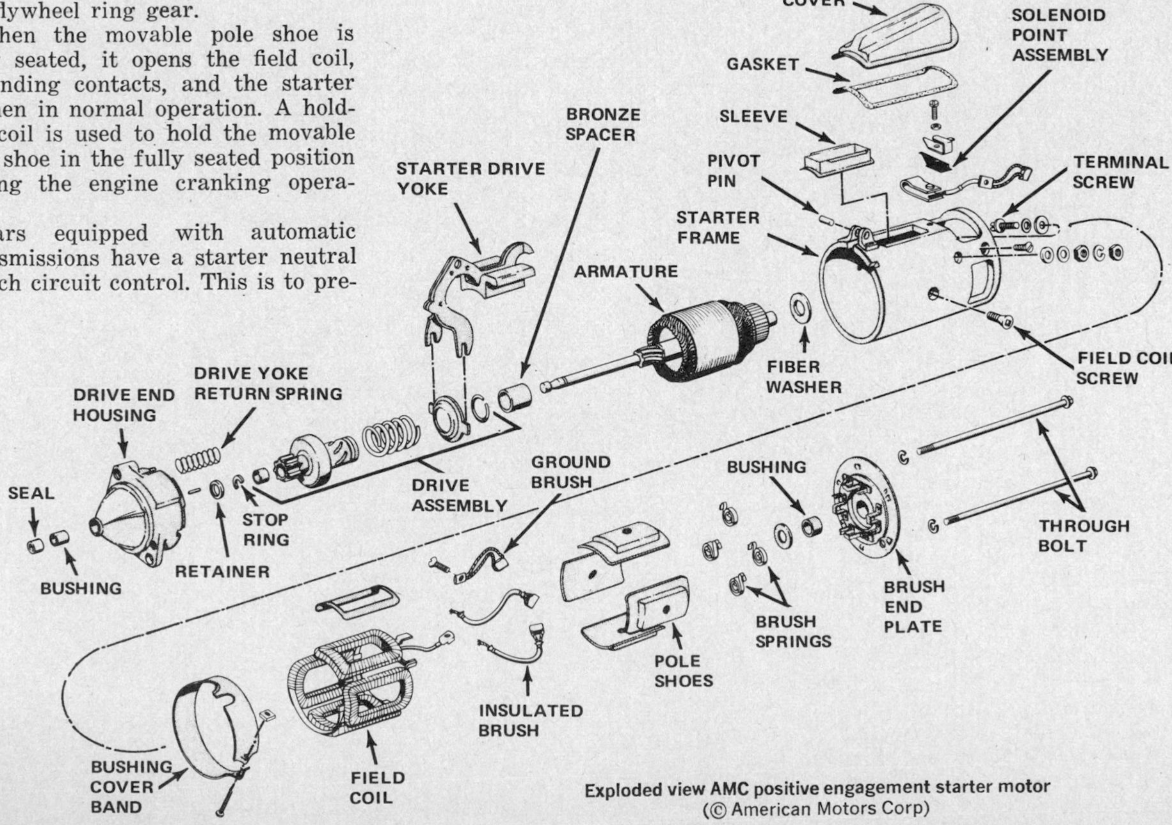

Exploded view AMC positive engagement starter motor
(© American Motors Corp)

coils from the frame (use a 300 watt iron).
9. Remove the starter terminal nut, washer, insulator and terminal from the starter frame.
10. Check the commutator for runout. If the commutator is rough, has flat spots, or is more than 0.005 in. out of round, reface the commutator. Clean the grooves in the commutator face.
11. Inspect the armature shaft and the two bearings for scoring and excessive wear. Replace if necessary.
12. Inspect the starter drive. If the gear teeth are pitted, broken, or excessively worn, replace the starter drive.

Assembly

1. Install starter terminal, insulator, washers and retaining nut in the frame. (Be sure to position the slot in the screw perpendicular to the frame end surface.)
2. Position coils and pole pieces, with the coil leads in the terminal screw slot, then install the retaining screws. As the pole screws are tightened, strike the frame several sharp hammer blows to align the pole shoes. Tighten, then stake the screws.
3. Install solenoid coil and retainer and bend the tabs to hold the coils to the frame.
4. Solder the field coils and solenoid wire to the starter terminal, using rosin-core solder and a 300 watt iron.
5. Check for continuity and ground connections in the assembled coils.
6. Position the solenoid coil ground terminal over the nearest ground screw hole.
7. Position the ground brushes to the starter frame and install retaining screws.
8. Position the brush end plate to the frame, with the end plate boss in the frame slot.
9. Lightly Lubriplate the armature shaft splines and install the starter drive gear assembly on the shaft. Install a new retaining stop ring and stop ring retainer.
10. Position the fiber thrust washer on the commutator end of the armature shaft, then position the armature in the starter frame.
11. Position the starter drive gear actuating lever to the frame and starter drive assembly, and install the pivot pin.

NOTE: fill drive gear housing bore ¼ full of grease.

12. Position the drive actuating lever return spring and the drive gear housing to the frame, then install and tighten the through bolts. Do not pinch brush leads between brush plate and frame. Be sure that the stop ring retainer is properly seated in the drive housing.
13. Install the brushes in the brush holders and center the brush springs on the brushes.
14. Position the drive gear actuating lever cover on the starter and install the brush cover band with a new gasket.
15. Check starter no-load amperage draw.

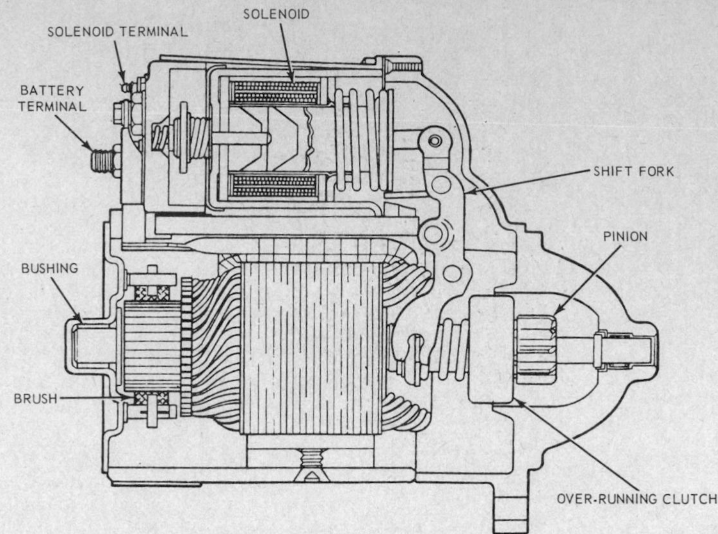

Ford solenoid actuated starter motor (© Ford Motor Co)

Autolite Solenoid Actuated Starter Motor

(Ford Motor Co.)

This starter motor, usually used with late-model 429 and 460 engines, is a four-brush, four-field, four-pole wound unit. The frame encloses a wound armature, which is supported at the drive end by caged needle bearings and at the commutator end by a sintered copper bushing. The four pole shoes are retained to the frame by one pole screw apiece, and on each pole shoe is wound a ribbon-type field coil connected in series-parallel.

The solenoid is mounted to a flange on the starter drive housing, which encloses the entire shift mechanism and solenoid plunger. The solenoid, following standard industry practice, utilizes two windings—a pull-in winding and a hold-in winding.

Disassembly

1. Disconnect the copper strap from the solenoid starter terminal, remove the remaining screws and remove the solenoid.
2. Loosen the retaining screw and slide the brush cover band back

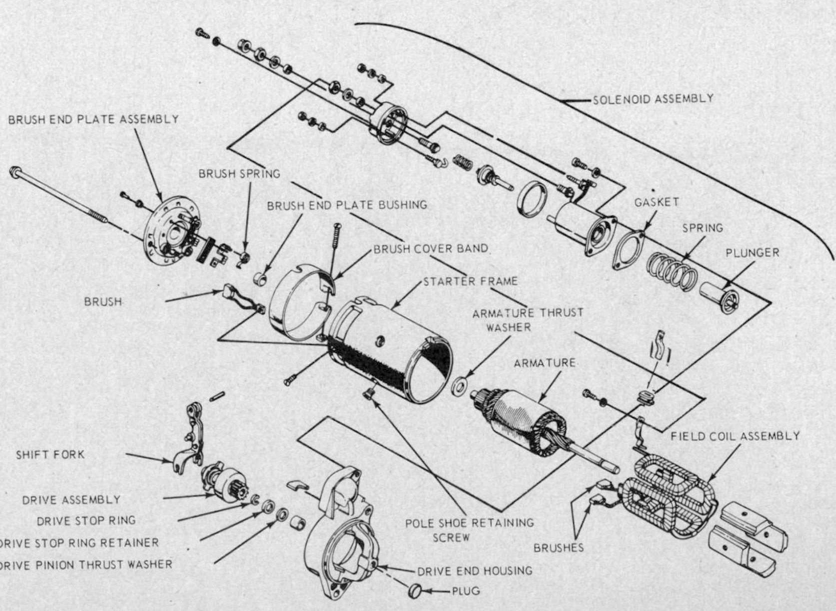

Ford solenoid actuated starter motor (© Ford Motor Co)

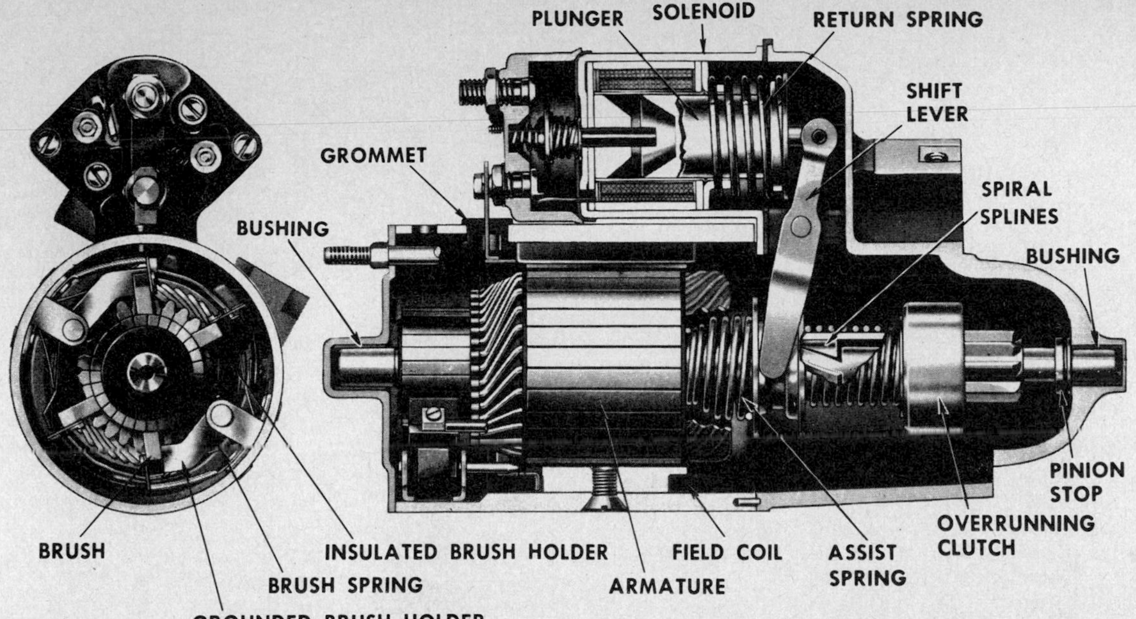

Typical Delco-Remy starter motor using an assist spring—light duty Chevrolet illustrated
(© Chevrolet Div., G.M. Corp)

far enough to gain access to the brushes.

3. Remove the brushes from their holders, then remove the through bolts and separate the drive end housing from the frame and brush end plate.

NOTE: factory brush length is ½ in., wear limit ¼ in.

4. Remove the solenoid plunger and shift fork. These two items can be separated from each other by removing the roll pin.
5. Remove the armature and drive assembly from the frame. Remove the drive stop ring and slide the drive off the armature shaft.
6. Remove the drive stop ring retainer from the drive housing.
7. Inspection of the commutator, armature and bearings, and pinion gear procedures is the same as the positive engagement starter procedures.

Assembly

1. Lubricate the armature shaft splines with Lubriplate, then install drive assembly and a new stop ring.
2. Lubricate shift lever pivot pin with Lubriplate, then position solenoid plunger and shift lever assembly in the drive housing.
3. Place a new retainer in the drive housing. Apply a small amount of Lubriplate to the drive end of the armature shaft, then place. armature and drive assembly into the drive housing, indexing the shift lever tangs with the drive assembly.
4. Apply a small amount of Lubriplate to the commutator end of the armature shaft, then position the frame and field assembly to the drive housing.
5. Position the brush plate assembly to the frame, making sure it properly indexes. Install through bolts and tighten to 45-85 in. lbs.
6. Install brushes into their holders and make sure leads are not touching any interior starter components.
7. Place the rubber gasket between the solenoid mount and the frame surface.
8. Place the starter solenoid in position with metal gasket and spring, install heat shield (if so equipped) and install solenoid screws.
9. Connect copper strap and install cover band.

Delco-Remy Starter Motor

(General Motors Corp.)

There are many different versions of the Delco-Remy starter, depending upon application. In general, six-cylinder engines use a unit having four field coils in series between the terminal and armature. Standard V8 engines use, depending on displacement, one of three types: one has two field coils in series with the armature and parallel to each other; another has two field coils in parallel between the field terminal and ground, and another has three field coils in series with the armature and one field connected between the motor terminal and ground. Heavy-duty starter motors, such as used on some of the largest G.M. high-output engines (over 400 cu. in.) have series compound windings. On the 1975 and later Delco starter, the terminal that connects the starter solenoid to the ignition coil has been removed as it is unnecessary with the High Energy Ignition System.

In spite of these differences, all Delco-Remy starters are disassembled and assembled in essentially the same manner.

Disassembly

1. Detach the field coil connectors from the motor solenoid terminal.

NOTE: on models so equipped, remove solenoid mounting screws.

2. Remove the through bolts.
3. Remove commutator end frame, field frame and armature assembly from drive housing.
4. Remove the overrunning clutch from the armature shaft as follows:
   a. Slide the two-piece thrust collar off the end of the armature shaft.
   b. Slide a standard ½ in. pipe coupling or other spacer onto the shaft so that the end of the coupling butts against the edge of the retainer.
   c. Tap the end of the coupling with a hammer, driving retainer towards armature end of snap-ring.
   d. Remove snap-ring from its groove in the shaft using pliers. Slide retainer and clutch from armature shaft.
5. Disassemble brush assembly from field frame by releasing the V-spring and removing the support pin. The brush holders, brushes and springs now can be pulled out as a unit and the leads disconnected.
6. On models so equipped, separate

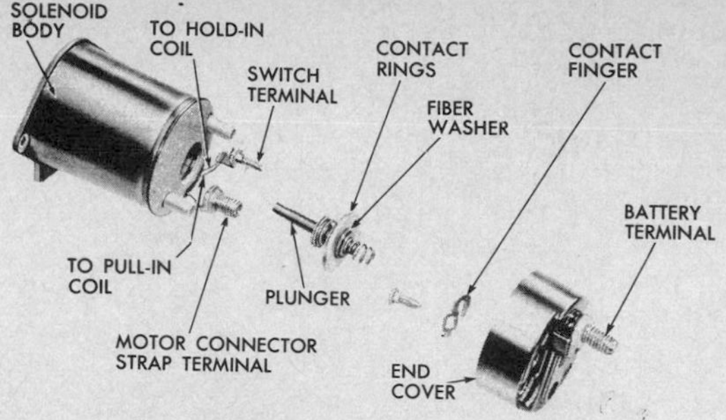

Delco-Remy starter solenoid
(© Chevrolet Div., G.M. Corp)

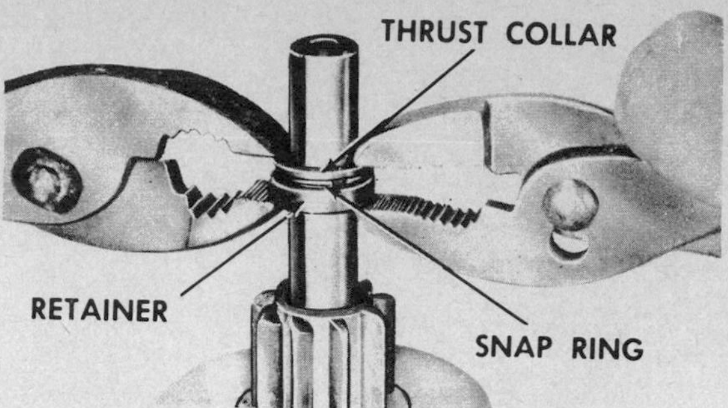

Forcing snap ring into retainer—Delco-Remy motor
(© Chevrolet Div., G.M. Corp)

solenoid from lever housing.

Cleaning and Inspection

1. Clean parts with a rag, but do not immerse the parts in a solvent. Immersion in a solvent will dissolve the grease that is packed in the clutch mechanism and damage the armature and field coil insulation.
2. Test overrunning clutch action. The pinion should turn freely in the overrunning direction and must not slip in the cranking direction. Check pinion teeth to see that they have not been chipped, cracked, or excessively worn. Replace the unit if necessary.
3. Inspect the armature commutator. If the commutator is rough or out of round, it should be turned down and undercut.

Caution Undercut the insulation between the commatator bars by 1/32 in.

This undercut must be the full width of the insulation and flat at the bottom; a triangular groove will not be satisfactory. Some starter motor models use a molded-armature commutator design and no attempt to undercut the insulation should be made or serious damage may result to the commutator.

Assembly

1. Install brushes into holders. Install solenoid, if so equipped.
2. Assemble insulated and grounded brush holder together using the V-spring and position the assembled unit on the support pin. Push holders and spring to bottom of support and rotate spring to engage the slot in support. At-

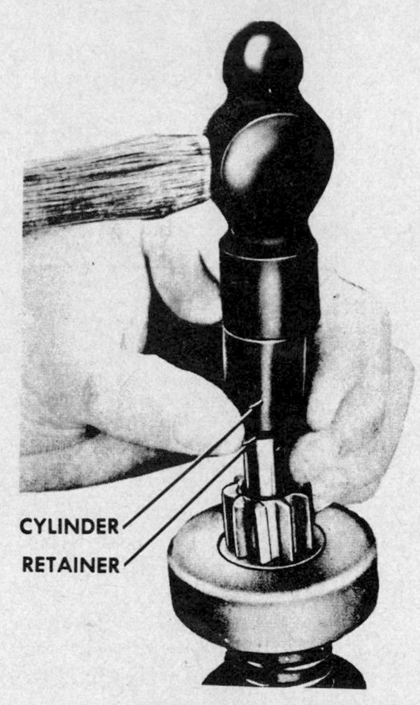

Driving retainer off snap ring —Delco-Remy motor
(© Chevrolet Div., G.M. Corp)

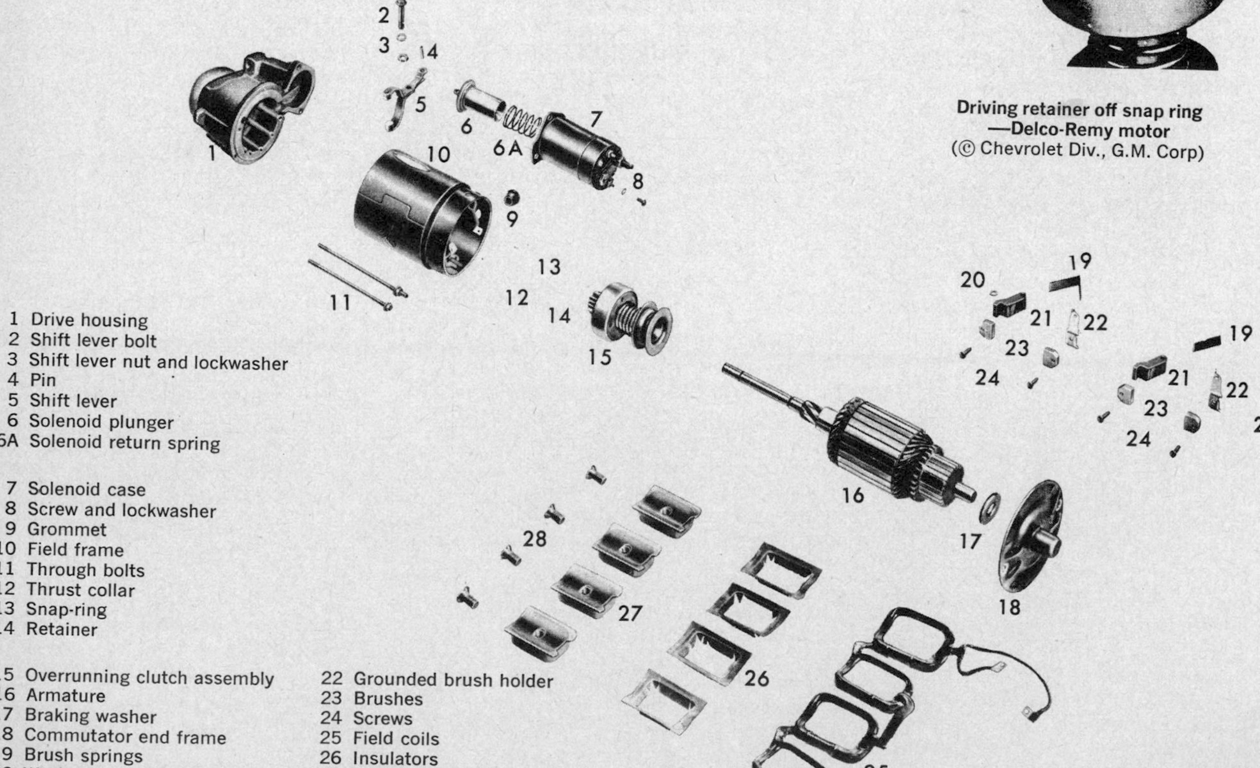

1 Drive housing
2 Shift lever bolt
3 Shift lever nut and lockwasher
4 Pin
5 Shift lever
6 Solenoid plunger
6A Solenoid return spring

7 Solenoid case
8 Screw and lockwasher
9 Grommet
10 Field frame
11 Through bolts
12 Thrust collar
13 Snap-ring
14 Retainer

15 Overrunning clutch assembly
16 Armature
17 Braking washer
18 Commutator end frame
19 Brush springs
20 Washer
21 Insulated brush holders
22 Grounded brush holder
23 Brushes
24 Screws
25 Field coils
26 Insulators
27 Pole shoes
28 Screws

Typical Delco-Remy starter motor exploded view—light duty Chevrolet illustrated
(© Chevrolet Div., G.M. Corp)

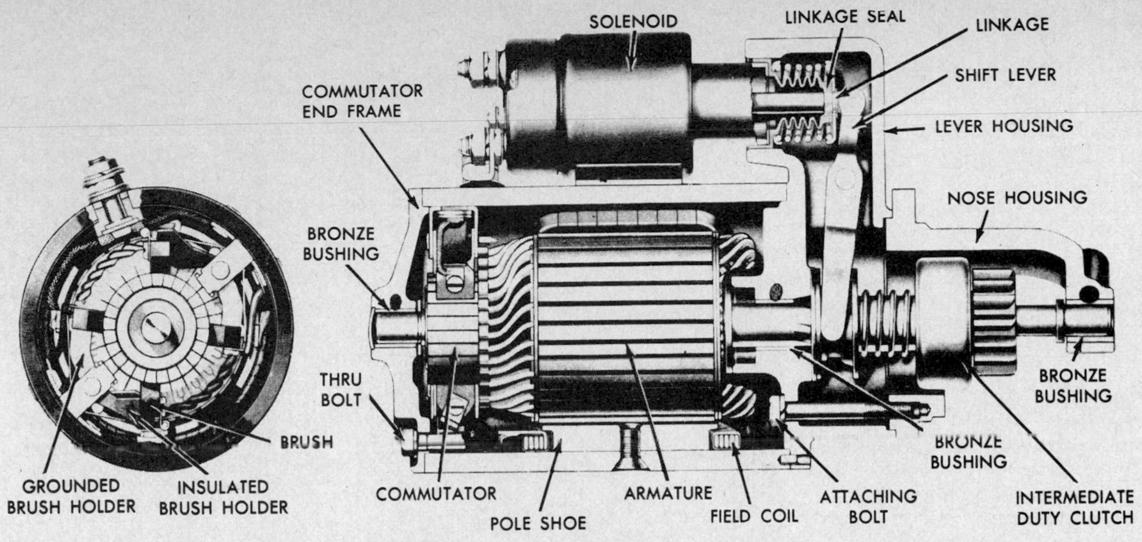

Typical Delco-Remy starter motor as used on intermediate models—Chevrolet application illustrated (© Chevrolet Div., G.M. Corp)

tach ground wire to grounded brush and field lead wire to insulated brush, then repeat for other brush sets.

3. Assemble overrunning clutch to armature shaft as follows:
   a. Lubricate drive end of shaft with silicone lubricant.
   b. Slide clutch assembly onto shaft with pinion outward.
   c. Slide retainer onto shaft with cupped surface facing away from pinion.
   d. Stand armature up on a wood surface, commutator downwards. Position snap-ring on upper end of shaft and drive it onto shaft with a small block of wood and a hammer. Slide snap-ring into groove.
   e. Install thrust collar onto shaft with shoulder next to snap-ring.
   f. With retainer on one side of snap-ring and thrust collar on the other side, squeeze together with two sets of pliers until ring seats in retainer. On models without thrust collar, use a washer. Remember to remove washer before continuing.

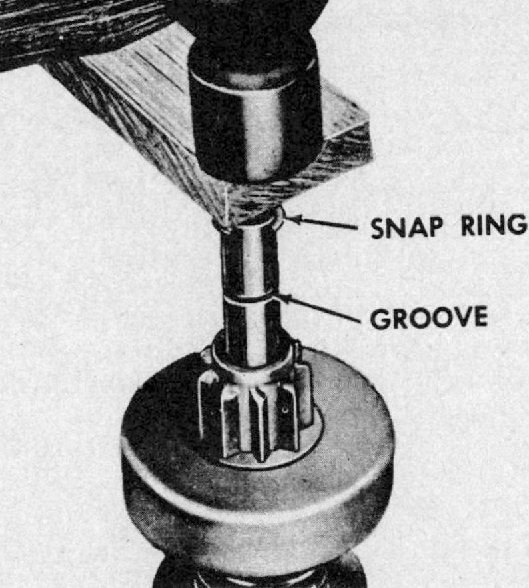

Forcing snap ring over armature shaft—Delco-Remy motor
(© Chevrolet Div., G.M. Corp)

4. Lubricate drive end bushing with silicone lubricant, then slide armature and clutch assembly into place, at the same time engaging shift lever with clutch.
5. Position field frame over armature and apply sealer (silicone) between frame and solenoid case. Position frame against drive housing, making sure brushes are not damaged in the process.
6. Lubricate commutator end bushing with silicone lubricant, place a leather brake washer on the armature shaft and slide commutator end frame onto shaft. Install through bolts and tighten to 65 in. lbs.
7. Reconnect field coil connector/s to the solenoid motor terminal. Install solenoid mounting screws, if so equipped.
8. Check pinion clearance; it should be 0.010-0.140 in. on all models.

AC Generator (Alternator) And System Service

Preliminary Charging System Inspection

NOTE: before performing any tests on the charging systems, these precautions should be taken to ensure the accuracy of the tests in this section.

1. Check the condition of the alternator belt and tighten it if necessary.
2. Clean the battery cable connections at the battery. Make sure that the connections between the battery wires and the battery clamps are good. Reconnect the negative terminal only, and proceed to the next step.
3. With the key off, insert a test light between the positive terminal on the battery and the disconnected positive battery terminal clamp. If the test light comes on, there is a short in the electrical system of the car. The short has to be repaired before proceeding. If the light fails to glow, reconnect the clamp and proceed to the next step.

NOTE: alternators with transistorized regulators sometimes draw a slight current even when the key is turned off. To properly check these systems for a short, the regulator must be disconnected. Also, on cars equipped with an electric clock, disconnect the lead wire from the clock.

4. Check the charging system wiring for breaks or shorts.
5. Check the battery to make sure that it is fully charged and in good condition.

Chrysler Isolated Field Alternator (Electronic Regulator)

The Chrysler isolated field alternator replaced the grounded brush alternator in 1970 and derived its name from its construction. Both of the brushes are insulated from ground and there is no heat sink connection, thereby isolating the internal field.

Troubleshooting

NOTE: see the "Preliminary Charging System Inspection" section before proceeding further. Make sure that the continuous running blower, if equipped, is disconnected. This blower will run with the key turned on even if the blower controls are off unless disconnected.

Fusible Links

Chrysler Corporation cars have a single fusible link which is connected between the starter relay and the junction block. Failure of this link will cause all electrical systems to stop functioning.

Charging System Operation

NOTE: if the current indicator is to give an accurate reading, the battery cables must be of the same gauge and length as the original equipment.

1. With the engine running and all electrical systems off, place a current indicator over the positive battery cable.
2. If a charge of about 5 amps is recorded, the charging system is working. If a draw of about 5 amps is recorded the system is not working. The needle moves toward the battery when a charge condition is indicated and away from the battery when a draw condition is indicated. If a draw is indicated, proceed to the next testing procedure. If an overcharge of 10-15 amps is indicated, check for a faulty regulator.

Ignition Switch-to-Regulator Circuit Check

1. Disconnect the regulator wires at the regulator.
2. Turn the key on but do not start the engine.
3. Using a voltmeter or test light, check for voltage across the I and F terminals. If there is current present, the circuit is good. If there is no current, check for bad connections, a bad ballast resistor, a bad ammeter, broken wires, or bad ground at the alternator or voltage regulator. Also, check for voltage from the I wire to ground; current should be present. Check for voltage from the F terminal to ground; current should be present.

Isolation Test

This test determines whether the regulator or alternator is bad if everything else in the circuit was OK.

1. Disconnect, at the alternator, the wire that runs between one of the alternator field connections and the voltage regulator.
2. Run a jumper wire from the disconnected alternator terminal to ground.
3. Connect a voltmeter to the battery. The positive voltmeter lead connects to the positive battery terminal, and the negative lead goes to the negative terminal. Record the reading.

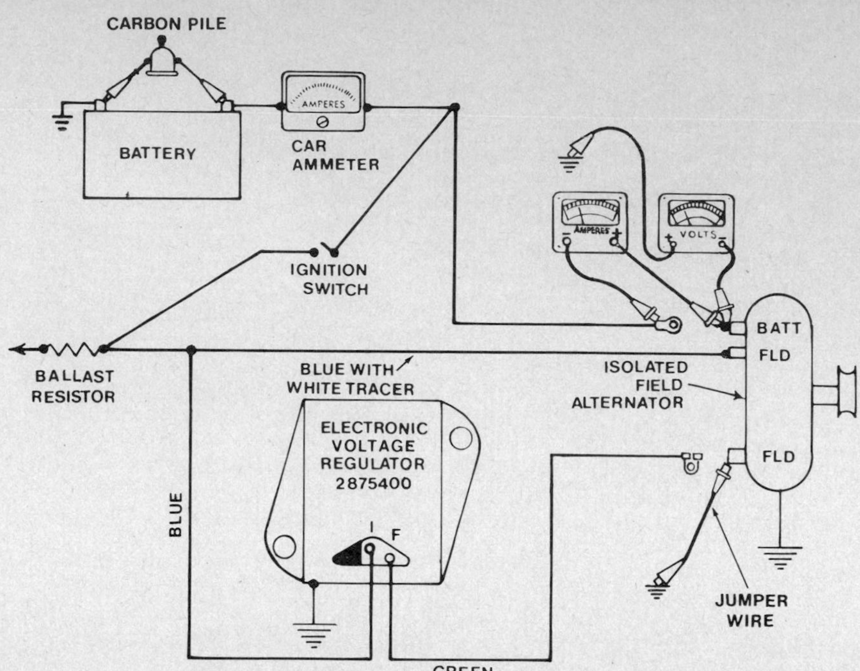

Current output test hook-up—Chrysler isolated field alternator

4. Make sure that all electrical systems are turned off. Start the engine. Do not race the engine.
5. Gradually raise engine speed to 1500–2000 rpm. There should be an increase of one to two volts on the voltmeter. If this is true, the alternator is good and the voltage regulator should be repaired. If there is no voltage increase, the alternator is faulty.

NOTE: the following tests require the use of a carbon pile and an ammeter.

Charging Circuit Resistance Test—beginning 1970

1. Disconnect battery ground cable.
2. Disconnect the lead from the alternator output (BATT.) terminal.
3. Hook up an ammeter as follows:
   a. Connect the positive lead to the alternator output terminal.
   b. Connect the negative lead to the lead just disconnected from the alternator output terminal.
4. Hook up voltmeter as follows:
   a. Connect the positive voltmeter lead to the lead just disconnected from the alternator output terminal.
   b. Connect the negative voltmeter lead to the positive battery post.
5. Disconnect the lead from the alternator field (FLD.) terminal.
6. Connect a jumper wire between alternator field terminal and ground.
7. Hook up a tachometer to the engine.
8. Connect the battery ground cable, then connect carbon pile to battery terminals.
9. Start the engine and allow to idle.
10. Slowly adjust the engine speed and carbon pile until the ammeter registers 20 amps.
11. The voltmeter reading will now show the voltage drop in the charging circuit. There should not be more than 0.7 volt drop.
12. If the voltage drop exceeds 0.7 volt, stop the engine, clean and tighten all circuit connections, then repeat the test.

Current Output Test—beginning 1970

1. The ammeter and carbon pile hookup should remain the same as for the circuit resistance test.
2. Connect the voltmeter negative lead to the battery negative post.
3. Move the positive voltmeter lead to the alternator "BATT" post.
4. Start the engine and adjust speed to 1250 rpm.

CAUTION: *Reduce the engine speed to idle immediately after starting the engine. Adjust the carbon pile and engine speed incrementally until 1250 rpm is reached.*

5. Note voltmeter and ammeter readings. Maintain a 15 volt reading by adjusting the carbon pile control.
6. Compare ammeter reading with manufacturer's specifications. The reading should be no less than specified, 3 amps.
7. If below specifications, internal trouble is indicated. Remove the alternator for further testing.

Electronic Voltage Regulator Test—beginning 1970

1. Make sure battery terminals are clean and battery is charged.
2. Connect the positive lead of a test voltmeter to ignition Terminal No. 1 of the ballast resistor. On 1975 and later Dart and Valiant, connect the positive lead of the voltmeter to the terminal on the ballast resistor which has a blue or black wire connected to it. On all other 1975 and later models, connect the voltmeter to the battery.

NOTE: *Don't remove the connector from the ballast resistor terminal.*

3. Connect the negative voltmeter lead to a good *body* ground.
4. Start engine and allow it to idle at 1250 rpm, all lights and accessories turned off. Voltage should be as follows:

Ambient Temp. ¼ in. from Regulator	*Voltage*
-20°F.	14.3-15.3
80°F.	13.8-14.4
140°F.	13.3-14.0

5. If the voltage is *below* specifications, check the following:
   a. Voltage regulator ground—check voltage drop between regulator cover and ground.
   b. Harness wiring—disconnect regulator plug (ign. switch off), then turn on ign. switch and check for battery voltage at the terminal having the blue and green leads. *Wiring harness must be disconnected from the regulator when checking individual leads.* If no voltage is present in either lead, the problem is in the car wiring or alternator field.
6. If Step 5 tests showed no malfunctions, install a new regulator and repeat Step 4.
7. If voltage is *above* specifications (Step 4), or fluctuates, check the following:
   a. Ground between regulator and body, and between body and engine.
   b. Ignition switch circuit between switch and regulator.
8. If voltage is still more than ½ volt above specifications, install a new regulator and repeat Step 4.

Field-Loads Relay Test

On all Chrysler Corporation cars beginning 1975 except Dart and Valiant, the charging system wiring circuit has been redesigned to protect the battery from overcharging by the addition of an ignition switch operated field-loads relay. This unit reduces voltage drop between charging system components, making the regulator more sensitive to battery requirements and decreasing the possibility of overcharging.

1. Disconnect the wiring harness connector at the voltage regulator. Ground the negative lead of the voltmeter.
2. Turn the ignition switch on but don't start the engine.
3. Measure the voltage at the terminals of the disconnected wiring harness connector with the positive lead of the voltmeter. Voltage here should be the same as at the battery.
4. If there is battery voltage at the terminals, the unit is working properly.
5. If battery voltage is not obtained, check all wiring and connections for damage. If they are alright, the unit must be replaced.

Chrysler Alternator (Electro-Mechanical Regulator)

The alternator that was used in 1969 was the grounded brush alternator with an electro-mechanical voltage regulator. This alternator has one brush connected to the single field terminal and the other brush grounded to the housing. In this system, the field circuit is grounded at the alternator through the ground brush.

Troubleshooting

NOTE: before performing any tests, see the "Preliminary System Inspection" section. This will help ensure the accuracy of the tests. Make sure the continuous running blower, if equipped, is disconnected.

Fusible Link

Check the condition of the fusible link as described in the "Isolated Field Alternator" section.

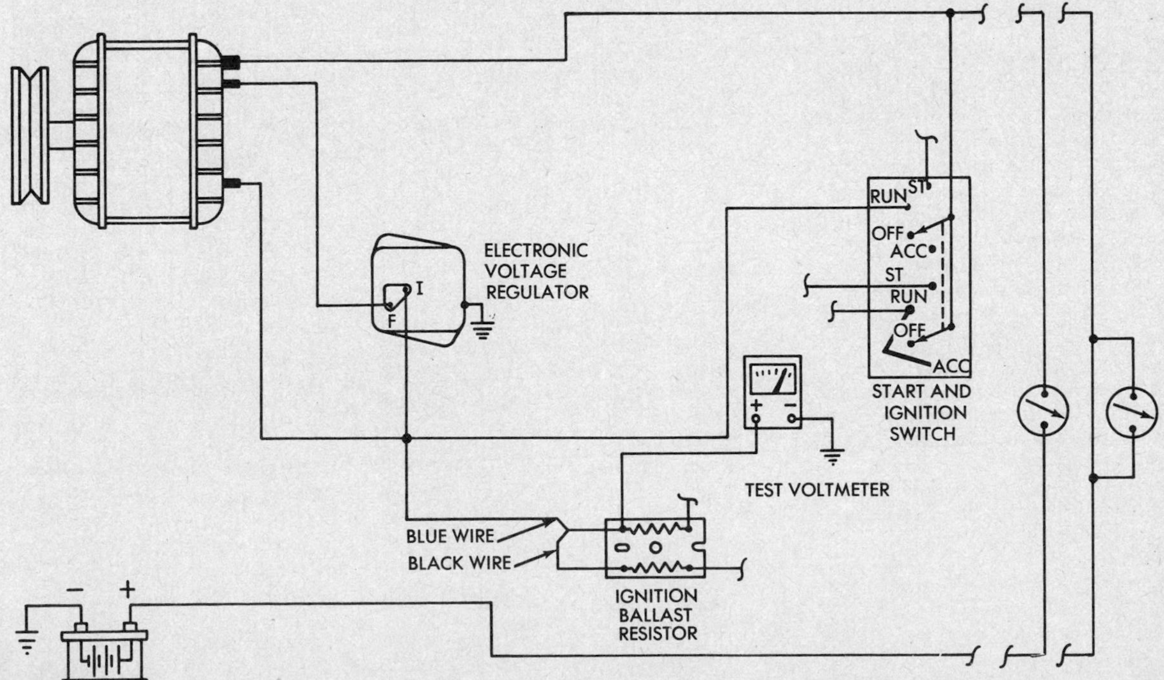

Voltage Regulator Test hook-up; right ammeter gauge for Monaco, Fury, Chrysler and Imperial, left for all other models
(© Chrysler Corp)

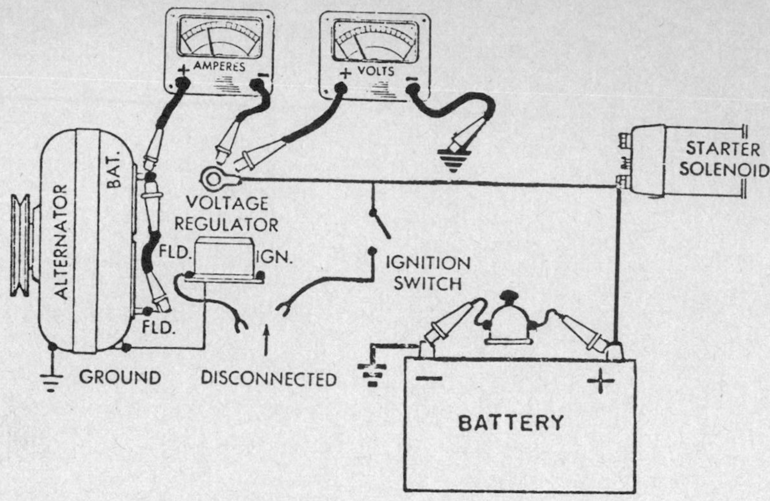

Current output test hook-up—1969 Chrysler design

Charging System Operation

Check the operation of the system as described in the "Isolated Field Alternator" section.

Ignition Switch-to-Regulator Circuit Check

1. Disconnect the ignition wire from its voltage regulator terminal.
2. Turn on the ignition switch but do not start the engine.
3. Using a voltmeter or a test light, check for voltage between the ignition wire and ground. If no voltage is found, trace the wire back, checking for a break or short in the wire, a bad indicator bulb, resistor wire, or ammeter.

Isolation Test

This test determines whether the regulator or the alternator is bad, if the rest of the circuit is OK.

1. Disconnect the regulator field terminal at the alternator.
2. With a jumper wire, connect the alternator field terminal to the alternator battery terminal.
3. Connect the positive lead from a voltmeter to the positive terminal of the battery, and connect the negative lead to the negative terminal. Record the reading on the voltmeter.
4. Connect the red lead of a tachometer to the distributor terminal on the coil and the black lead to ground.
5. Start the engine, making sure all electrical systems are turned off. Do not race the engine upon starting.
6. Gradually increase engine speed to 1500–2000 rpm. The voltmeter reading should increase above the previously recorded battery voltage reading by at least one to two volts. If there is no increase, the alternator is not working correctly. If there is an increase, the voltage regulator needs to be repaired.

NOTE: the following tests require the use of a carbon pile and an ammeter.

Current Output Test—1969

1. Disconnect battery ground cable.
2. Disconnect the BATT. lead from the alternator BATT. terminal.
3. Connect a test ammeter in series between the alternator BATT. terminal and the lead just disconnected from it.
4. Connect the positive lead of a test voltmeter to the BATT. lead and the negative voltmeter test lead to ground.
5. Disconnect the FLD. lead from the alternator and the ignition lead from the regulator IGN. terminal.
6. Connect a jumper wire between the alternator FLD. terminal and the alternator BATT. terminal.
7. Connect a tachometer to the engine and reconnect the negative battery cable.
8. Connect a carbon pile rheostat between the two battery terminals.
9. Start engine and allow it to idle. Adjust carbon pile and engine speed until 1250 rpm and 15 volts are attained. *Do not exceed* 16 volts.
10. The ammeter should now read specified output for the particular alternator. A reading 5-7 amps. less than specified may indicate an open rectifier; a considerably less than normal reading could mean a shorted rectifier.
11. If reading is within limits, remove test gear and reconnect all leads to original terminals. If reading is outside of limits, remove alternator for bench tests.

Voltage Regulator Test

Upper Contacts

1. With the battery ground cable disconnected at the battery and the BATT. lead disconnected from the alternator output terminal, hook up an ammeter as follows:
   a. Connect the ammeter positive lead to the alternator output terminal.
   b. Connect the ammeter negative lead to the lead just disconnected from the alternator output terminal.
2. Hook up a voltmeter as follows:
   a. Disconnect the ignition wire at the IGN. terminal of the regulator. Install a pushbutton switch in series with the IGN. terminal and the wire just disconnected.
   b. Connect the negative voltmeter lead to ground.
   c. Connect the positive voltmeter lead to the IGN. terminal of the regulator or to the regulator side of the test switch.
3. Connect a tachometer to the engine.
4. Hook up the ground cable to the battery.
5. Hook up a carbon pile (load control turned to the off position) between the battery posts.
6. With engine operating at 1250 rpm, adjust carbon pile and/or turn on headlights; watch the voltmeter and ammeter. A 15 amp. output must be obtained.

Caution Voltmeter reading must not exceed 15 volts. Continue to run the engine at this setting until the regulator has reached operating temperature (15 min.)

7. No current output indicates a low set regulator or a blown fuse wire inside regulator (between upper stationary contact and IGN. terminal).
8. If output is O.K. after 15 minutes, adjust engine rpm to 1250 again and adjust carbon pile to obtain 15 amps.
9. Measure and record temperature of regulator about 1/4 in. from cover.
10. Momentarily open and close the test switch several times and observe the voltmeter; it now reads the upper contact setting (see chart).
11. If regulator is within specifications, proceed to the *Lower Contacts* test. If not, remove regulator cover and adjust upper contacts (see *Regulator Adjustments*).

Lower Contacts

1. Keep the same hook-up as used for upper contact test.

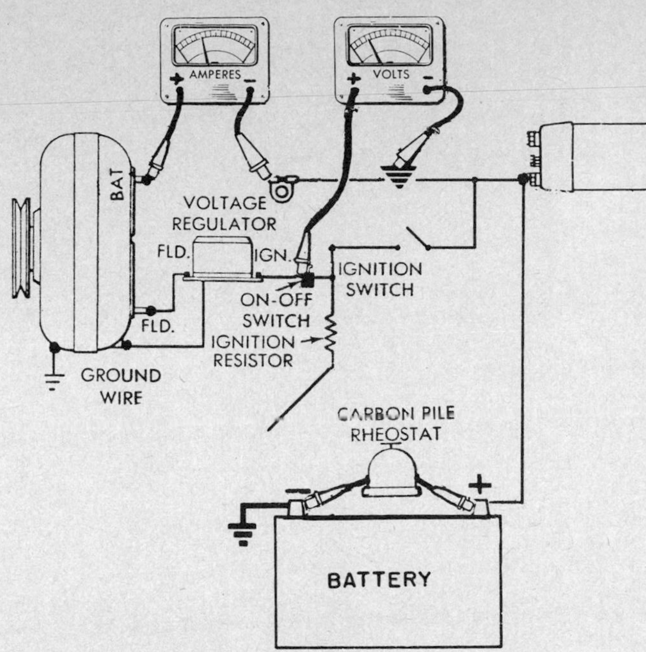

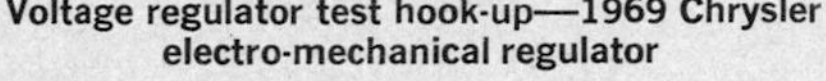
Voltage regulator test hook-up—1969 Chrysler electro-mechanical regulator

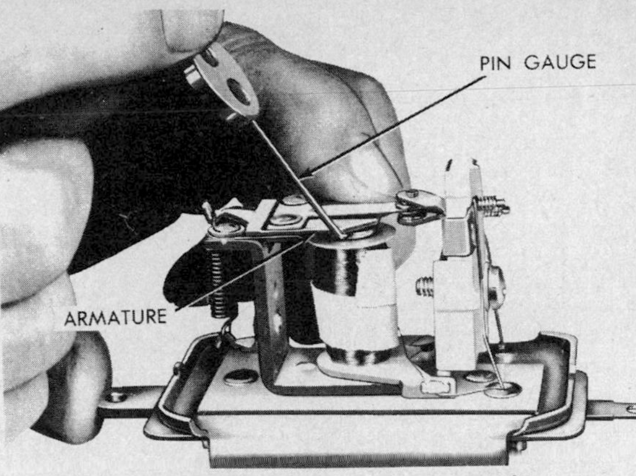

Checking air gap on Chrysler regulator to 1969
(© Chrysler Corp)

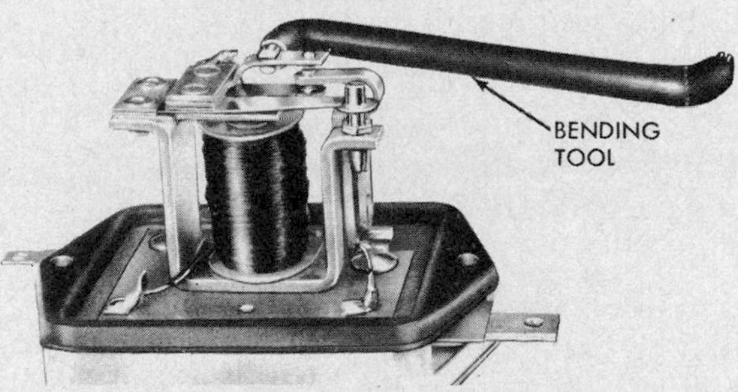

Bending upper contact arm to obtain upper contact point gap of 0.014 in.—Essex Wire built regulator
(© Chrysler Corp)

2. Increase engine speed to 2200 rpm, then turn off all lights and accessories and/or adjust carbon pile to decrease output to 7 amps.
3. Again take a regulator temperature reading and turn the test switch on and off a few times.
4. The test voltmeter now will register an increase in voltage over that recorded for the upper contacts. This increase should not be less than 0.2 volt, or greater than 0.7 volt. If the voltage increase is not within these limits, it indicates that the air gap/contact clearance must be adjusted (see *Regulator Adjustments*). If the reading is less than 0.2 volt greater than upper contact voltage, charge the battery and retest.
5. Reduce engine speed to idle, stop engine and reconnect all terminal leads to their original positions.

Regulator Adjustments—1969

Upper Contact Voltage—Chrysler Regulator

Upper contact voltage is set by bending the regulator lower spring hanger *down* to increase voltage, *up* to decrease voltage. The bending tool must be insulated properly in order to prevent grounding and regulator damage. The regulator must be installed, correctly connected and retested after each adjustment of the lower spring hanger. *Cover must be on.*

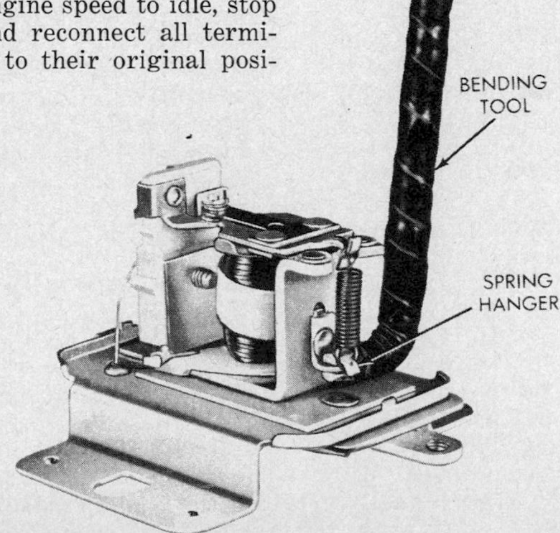

Adjusting upper contact voltage—Chrysler built regulator to 1969
(© Chrysler Corp)

Lower Contact Voltage—Chrysler Regulator

If the adjustment of the upper contact voltage does not bring the regulator within specifications, measure the lower contact point gap. Gap should be 0.014 in. ± 0.002. This gap is adjusted by bending the lower *stationary* contact bracket, making sure points remain in alignment. If the lower contact gap is correct, and voltage still is out of specification, adjust the air gap, as follows:

1. Connect a 1½-volt self-powered test light in series between the IGN. and FLD. terminals of the regulator.
2. Insert a 0.048 in. wire gauge between the regulator armature and the core of the voltage coil.
3. Press down on the armature, not the contact reed, until the armature hits the wire gauge. At this point, the upper contacts should just open and the test light should be dim.
4. Insert a 0.052 in. wire gauge between the armature and voltage coil coil, next to the armature stop pin. (After removing 0.048 in. gauge).
5. Press down on the armature until it hits the wire gauge. The upper contacts should remain closed and the test light should be bright.

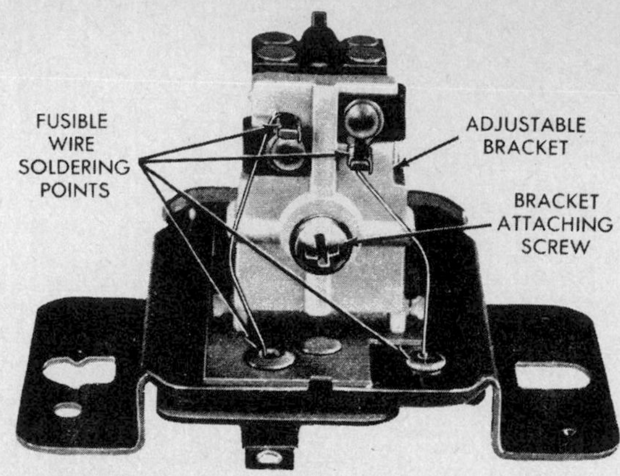

Chrysler voltage regulator to 1969, showing fusible wires and bracket adjusting screw
(© Chrysler Corp)

Bending stationary contact arm to obtain proper air gap —Essex Wire built regulator
(© Chrysler Corp)

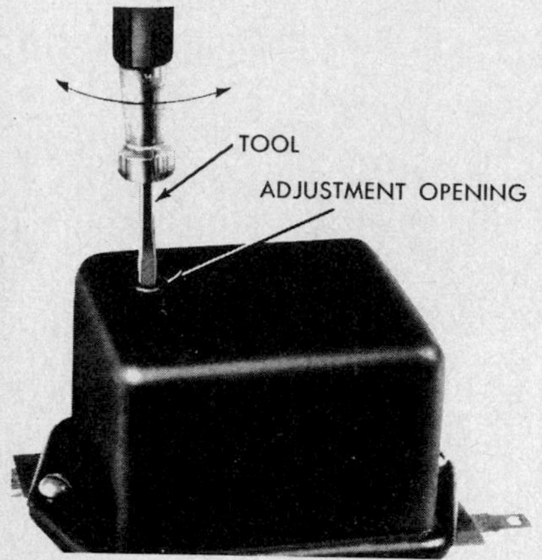

Lower contact voltage adjustment—Essex Wire built regulator (© Chrysler Corp)

6. If an adjustment is required, loosen the stationary contact bracket screw and move bracket up and down as necessary to obtain the proper air gap. Following are guidelines for this adjustment:

Voltage Difference	*Air Gap Min.**	*Air Gap Max.#*
0.7 volt	0.045	0.048
0.2 volt	0.052	0.055

* Contacts open, test light dim.
\# Contacts closed, test light bright.

Lower Contact Voltage—Essex Wire Regulator

Lower contact voltage is adjusted by turning the adjustment screw, accessible through the cover opening. Turning clockwise increases voltage, turning counterclockwise decreases voltage.

Upper Contact Point Gap—Essex Wire Regulator

Measure the upper contact point gap; it should be 0.014 in. ± 0.004. Adjust gap by bending armature upper contact bracket with an insulated tool, making sure contacts remain in alignment. If upper contact gap is correct, and voltage still is out of specifications, adjust air gap, as follows:

1. Connect a 1½-volt self-powered test light in series between the IGN. and FLD. terminals of the regulator.
2. Insert a 0.032 in. wire gauge between the regulator armature and voltage core coil.
3. Press down on armature until it hits the gauge. At this point, lower contacts should just open and test light should be dim.
4. Check that a 0.042 in. gauge cannot be inserted between the armature and voltage core. This must not be possible, or air gap must be readjusted.

NOTE: if voltage difference is greater than 0.7 volt, reduce air gap; if less than 0.2 volt, increase air gap.

Chrysler Overhaul and Internal Testing

Alternator disassembly, repair and assembly procedures are basically the same for all Chrysler alternators, including the Isolated Field type used for the first time in 1970. Certain variations in design, or in-production modifications, could require slightly different procedures that should be obvious upon inspection of the unit being serviced. An example of this is the new isolated field alternator, which has two FLD. terminals.

Disassembly

To prevent damage to the brush assemblies they should be removed before proceeding with the disassembly of the alternator. The insulated brush is mounted in a plastic holder that positions the brush vertically against one of the slip rings.

1. Remove the retaining screw, flat washer, nylon washer and field terminal and carefully lift the plastic holder containing the spring and brush assembly from the end housing.
2. The ground brush is positioned horizontally against the remaining slip ring and is retained in the holder that is integral with the end housing. Remove the retaining screw and lift the clip, spring and brush assembly from the end housing.

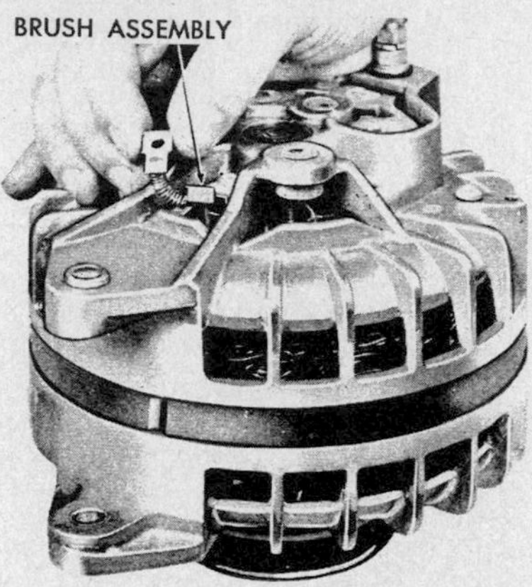

Insulator brush
(© Chrysler Corp)

Caution The stator is laminated, don't burr the stator or end housings.

3. Remove the through bolts and pry between the stator and drive end housing with a thin blade screwdriver. Carefully separate the drive end housing, pulley and rotor assembly from the stator and rectifier housing assembly.
4. The pulley is an interference fit on the rotor shaft. Remove with a puller and special adapters.
5. Remove the three nuts and washers and, while supporting the end frame, tap the rotor shaft with a plastic hammer and separate the rotor and end housing.
6. The drive end ball bearing is an interference fit with the rotor shaft. Remove the bearing with puller and adapters.

NOTE: further dismantling of the rotor is not advisable, as the remainder of the rotor assembly is not serviced separately.

7. Remove the DC output terminal nuts and washers and remove terminal screw and inside capacitor (on units so equipped).

NOTE: the heat sink is also held in place by the terminal screw.

8. Remove the insulator.

NOTE: three positive rectifiers are

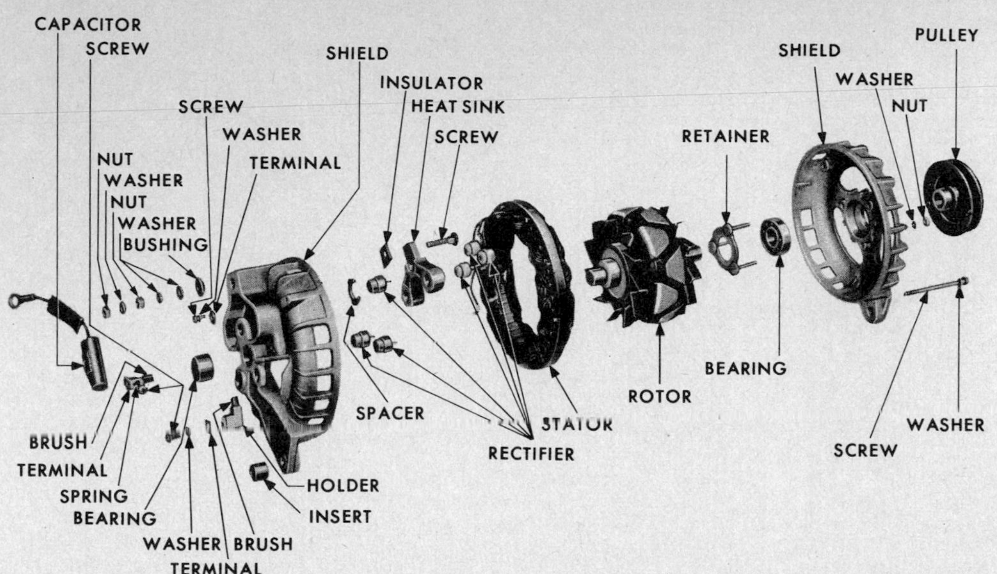

Alternator—typical 1969 Chrysler

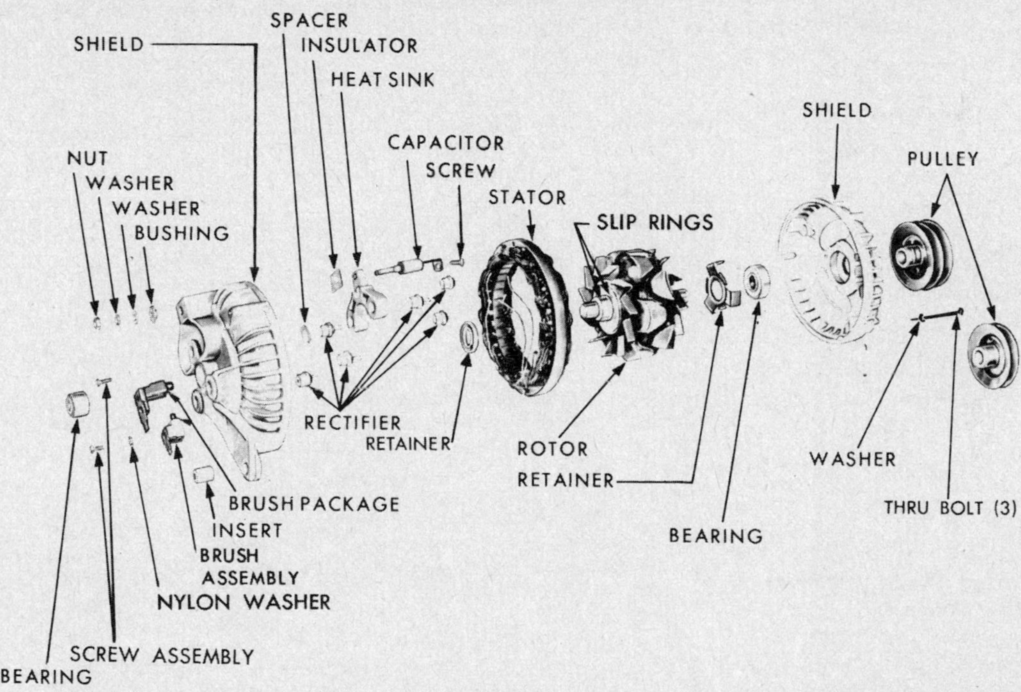

Chrysler isolated field alternator—1970-74 (© Chrysler Corp)

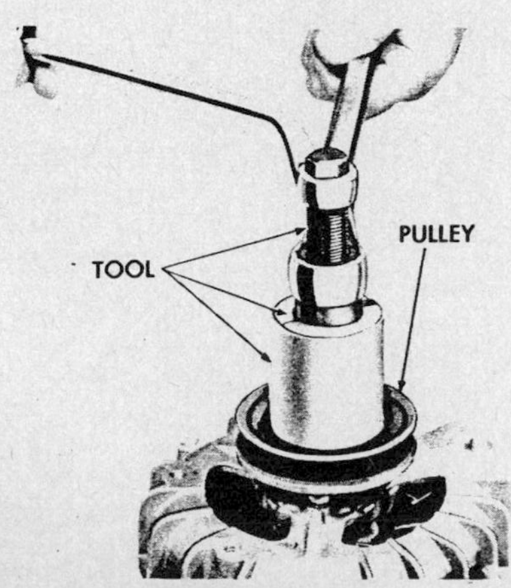

Removing the pulley
(© Chrysler Corp)

pressed into the heat sink and three negative rectifiers in the end housing. When removing the rectifiers, it is necessary to support the end housing and/or heat sink to prevent damage to these castings. Another caution is in order relative to the diode rectifiers. Don't subject them to unnecessary jolting. Heavy vibration or shock may ruin them.

A. Cut rectifier wire at point of crimp.

B. Support rectifier housing.

NOTE: the factory tool is cut away and slotted to fit over the wires and around the bosses in the housing. Be sure that the bore of the tool completely surrounds the rectifier, then press the rectifier out of the housing.

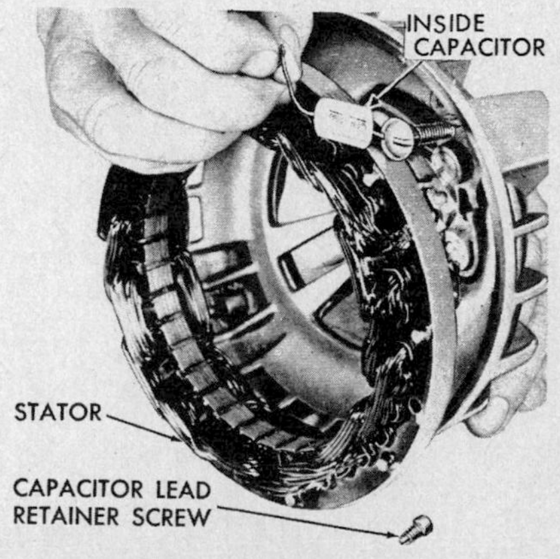

Inside capacitor
(© Chrysler Corp)

NOTE: the roller bearing in the rectifier end frame is a press fit. To protect the end housing it is necessary to support the housing with a tool when pressing out the bearing.

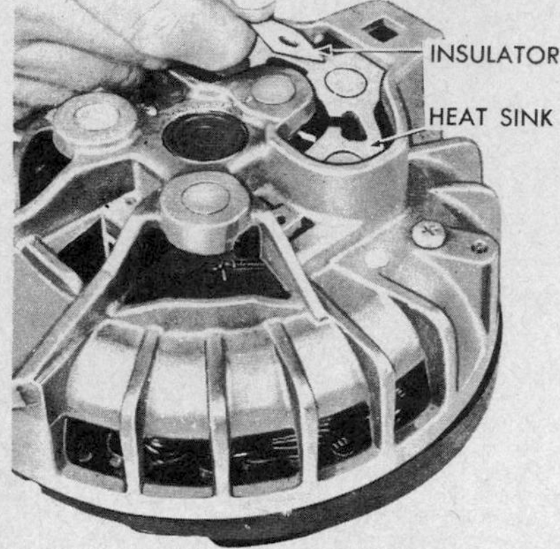

Heat sink and insulator
(© Chrysler Corp)

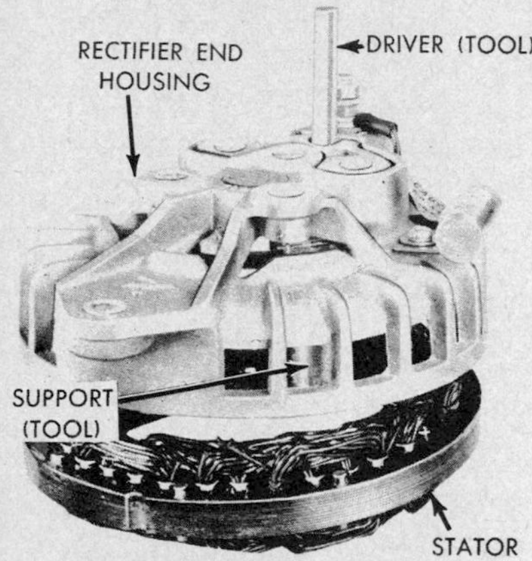

Removing a rectifier
(© Chrysler Corp)

Bench Tests

Testing Silicon Diode Rectifiers With Ohmmeter

Preferred method—rectifiers open in all three phases.

Disassemble the alternator and separate the wires at the Y-connection of the stator.

There are six diode rectifiers mounted in the back of the alternator. Three of them are marked with a plus (+), and three are marked with a minus (—). These marks indicate diode case polarity.

To test, set ohmmeter to its lowest range. If case is marked positive (+), place positive meter probe to case and negative probe to the diode lead. Meter should read between 4 and 10 ohms. Now, reverse leads of ohmmeter, connecting negative meter probe to positive case and positive meter probe to wire of rectifier. Set meter on a high range. Meter needle should move very little, if any (infinite reading). Do this to all three positive diode rectifiers.

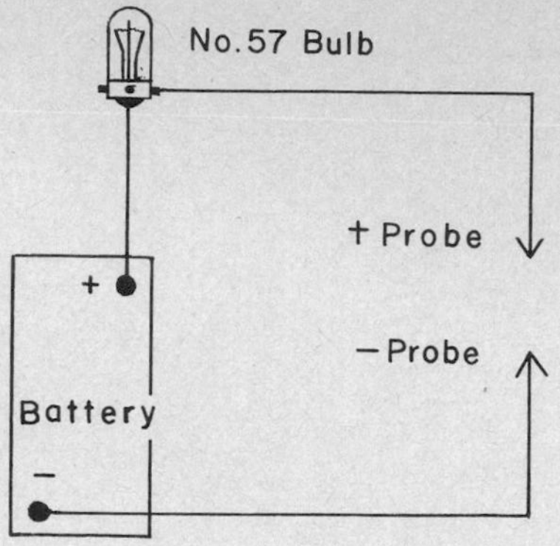

The test light method of testing diodes
(© Chrysler Corp)

The three with minus (—) marks on their cases are checked the same way as above. Only now the negative ohmmeter probe is connected to the case for a reading of 4 to 10 ohms. Reverse leads as above for the other part to test.

If a reading of 4 to 10 ohms is obtained in one direction and no reading (infinity) is read on the ohmmeter in the other direction, diode rectifiers are good. If either infinity or a low resistance is obtained in both directions on a rectifier, it must be replaced.

If meter reads more than 10 ohms when ohmmeter positive probe is connected to positive on diode, and negative probe to negative, replace diode rectifier.

NOTE: with this test, it is necessary to determine the polarity of the ohmmeter probes. This can be done by connecting the ohmmeter to a DC voltmeter. The voltmeter will read up-scale when the positive probe of the ohmmeter is connected to the positive side of the voltmeter and the negative probe of the ohmmeter is connected to the negative side of the voltmeter.

Alternate method—test light.

Make up a tester as shown in the sketch. Be sure that the lead from the center of the diode rectifiers is disconnected.

To test rectifiers with plus (+) case, touch positive probe of tester to case and minus (—) probe to lead wire of rectifier. Bulb should light if rectifier is good. If bulb does not light, replace rectifier.

Now reverse tester probe connections to rectifier. Bulb should not light. If bulb does light, replace rectifier.

For testing minus (—) marked cases, follow above procedure, except that now bulb should light with negative probe of tester touching rectifier case and positive probe touching lead wire.

Rectifier is good if the bulb lights when tester probes are connected one way, and does not light when tester connections are reversed.

Rectifier must be replaced if the bulb does not light either way. Also, replace rectifier if bulb lights both ways.

NOTE: the usual cause of an open or blown diode or rectifier is a defective capacitor or a battery that has been installed in reverse polarity. If the battery is installed properly and the diodes are open, test the capacitor.

Capacitor capacity:
(int. installed)
............158 microfarad, min.
(ext. installed) .... .5 microfarad

Alternator Bench Tests

Field Coil Draw

1. Connect a jumper between one FLD terminal and the positive terminal of a fully charged 12 volt battery.
2. Connect the positive lead of a test ammeter to the other field (FLD) terminal and the negative test lead to the negative battery terminal.
3. Slowly rotate the rotor by hand and observe the ammeter. The proper field coil draw is 2.3–2.7 amps at 12 volts.

Field Circuit Ground Test

1. Touch one test lead of a 110 volt AC test bulb to one of the alternator brush (field) terminals and the other test lead to the end shield.
2. If the lamp lights, remove the field brush assemblies and separate the end housing by removing the three thru-bolts.
3. Place one test lead on a slip ring and the other on the end shield.
4. If the lamp lights, the rotor assembly is grounded internally and must be replaced.
5. If the lamp does not light, the cause of the problem was a grounded brush.

Grounded Stator

1. Disconnect the diode rectifiers from the stator leads.
2. Test from stator leads to stator core, using a 110-volt test lamp. Test lamp should not light. If it does, stator is grounded and must be replaced.

Low Output

(About 50% output accompanied with a growl-hum caused by a shorted phase or a shorted rectifier.)

Perform Steps 1, 2 and 3 (rectifier open in all three phases). If the rectifiers are found to be within specifications, replace the stator assembly.

Current Output Too High (No Control) Caused by Open Rectifier or Open Phase

Perform Steps 1, 2 and 3 (rectifier

open in all three phases). If the rectifier tests satisfactorily, inspect the stator connections before replacing the stator.

Assembly

1. Support the heat sink or rectifier end housing on circular plate.
2. Check rectifier identification to be sure the correct rectifier is being used. The part numbers are stamped on the case of the rectifier. They are also marked, red for positive and black for negative.
3. Start the new rectifier into the casting and press it in squarely.

Caution Do not start rectifier with a hammer or it will be ruined.

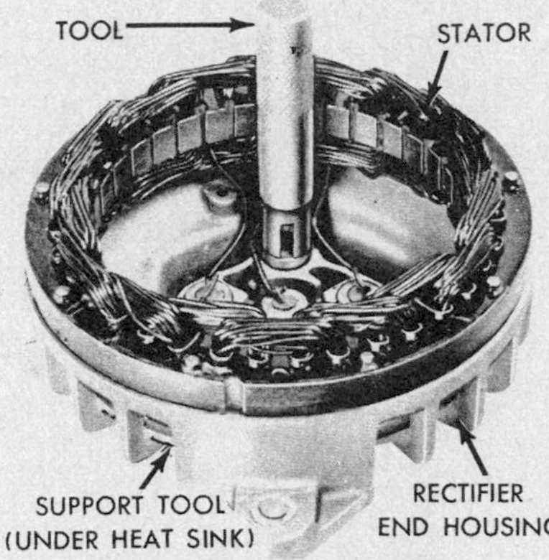

Installing diode rectifier
(© Chrysler Corp)

4. Crimp the new rectifier wire to the wires disconnected at removal, or solder (using a heat sink with rosin core solder).
5. Support the end housing on tool so that the notch in the support tool will clear the raised section of the heat sink, then press the bearing into position with tool SP-3381, or equivalent.

NOTE: new bearings are pre-lubricated, additional lubrication is not required.

6. Insert the drive end bearing in the drive end housing and install the bearing plate, washers and nuts to hold the bearing in place.
7. Position the bearing and drive end housing on the rotor shaft and, while supporting the base of the rotor shaft, press the bearing and housing in position on the rotor shaft with an arbor press and arbor tool.

Caution Be careful that there is no cocking of the bearing at installation; or damage will result. Press the bearing on the rotor shaft until the bearing contacts the shoulder on the rotor shaft.

8. Install pulley on rotor shaft. Shaft of rotor must be supported so that all pressing force is on the pulley hub and rotor shaft.

NOTE: Do not exceed 6,800 lbs. pressure. Pulley hub should just contact bearing inner race. Do not use a hammer.

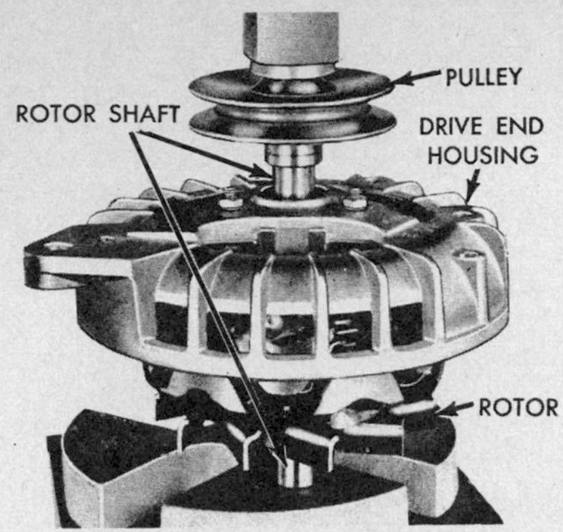

Installing the pulley
(© Chrysler Corp)

9. Some alternators will be found to have the capacitor mounted internally. Be sure the heat sink insulator is in place.
10. Install the output terminal screw with the capacitor attached through the heat sink and end housing.
11. Install insulating washers, lockwashers and locknuts.
12. Make sure the heat sink and insulator are in place and tighten the locknut.
13. Position the stator on the rectifier end housing. Be sure that all of the rectifier connectors and phase leads are free of interference with the rotor fan blades and that the capacitor (internally mounted) lead has clearance.
14. Position the rotor assembly in the rectifier end housing. Align the through bolt holes in the stator with both end housings.
15. Enter stator shaft in the rectifier end housing bearing, compress stator and both end housings manually and install through bolts, washers and nuts.
16. Install the insulated brush and terminal attaching screw.
17. Install the ground screw and attaching screw.
18. Rotate pulley slowly to be sure the rotor fan blades do not hit the rectifier and stator connectors.

Delcotron 5.5 Series 1D and 6.2 Series 2D (General Motors Corporation)

Description

The Delcotron continuous output AC generator consists of two major parts—the stator and the rotor. The stator is composed of many turns of wire on the inside of a laminated core that is attached to the generator frame. The rotor is mounted on bearings at each end. Two brushes carry current through slip rings to the field coils, which are wound on the rotor shaft.

The 5.5 Series 1D Delcotron is similar in operation to the 6.2 Series 2D perforated stator Delcotron. Where differences exist, the two units are mentioned separately.

Six diodes, mounted on internal heat sinks, change the AC current output into DC current. This current is controlled by the regulator. The regulator is a double-contact unit combined with a field relay or a triple-contact unit containing an indicator lamp relay as well as the field relay and voltage relay. Transistor regulators were also used in production intermittently.

On high-output Delcotron units, the regulator incorporates a field discharge diode.

Delcotron rated output is stamped on the case
(© Oldsmobile Div., G.M. Corp)

Troubleshooting

NOTE: *See the "Preliminary Charging System Inspection" section before proceeding further. Make sure that the continuous running blower, if equipped, is disconnected. This blower will run with the key on and even if the blower control is off, it is not disconnected.*

Indicator Light Circuit Check:

Check the indicator light for normal operation:

Ignition Switch Condition	Light Condition	Engine Condition
Off	Off	Stopped
On	On	Stopped
On	Off	Running

If the alternator light is operating properly, proceed to the next section. If one of the following conditions exists, proceed as directed:

A. *Ignition Switch off, light stays on:* disconnect leads from number 1 and 2 terminals. If the light remains on, there is a short between these two leads. If the lamp goes out, replace the rectifier bridge.

B. *Ignition switch on, light off, engine not running:* This condition can

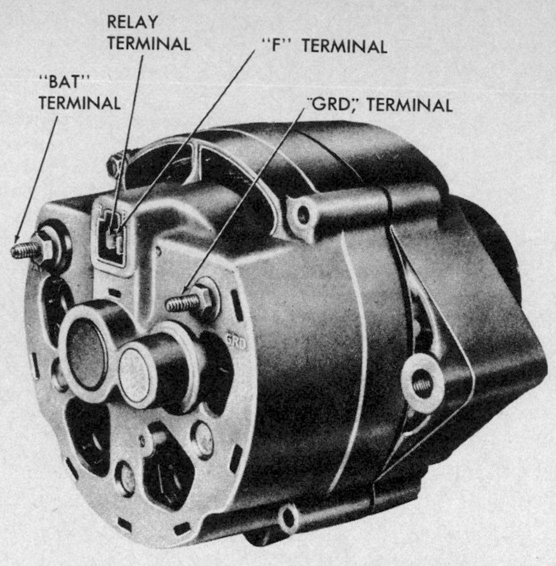

5.5" ALUMINUM DELCOTRON

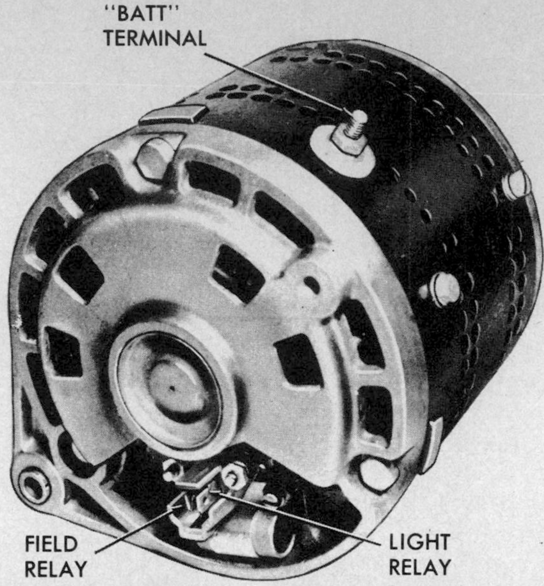

6.2" PERFORATED STATOR DELCOTRON

5.5 and 6.2 Delcotron models (© Chevrolet Div., G.M. Corp)

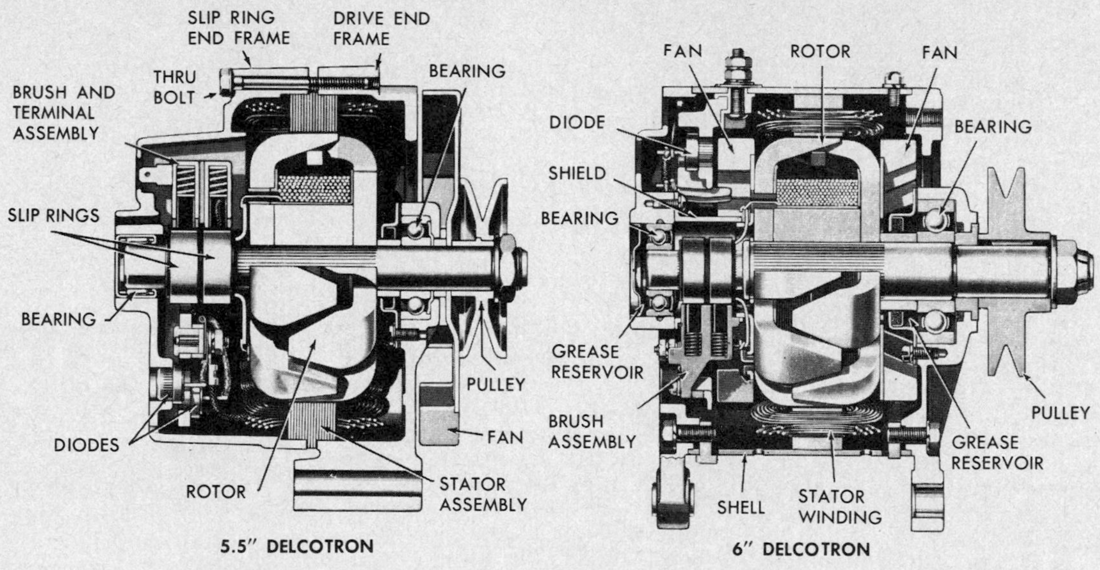

5.5 and 6.2 Delcotron models—cross sectional views (© Chevrolet Div., G.M. Corp)

be caused by the defects listed in A., by reversal of number 1 and 2 leads at the alternator, or by an open circuit. If the circuit is open proceed as follows:

1. Connect a voltmeter from no. 2 alternator terminal to ground. If a reading is obtained, proceed to the next step. If a zero reading is obtained, repair the circuit between no. 2 terminal and the battery. If the light comes on, no further testing is necessary.
2. With the ignition switch on and with no. 1 and 2 terminals disconnected at the alternator, momentarily ground no. 1 terminal lead.

Caution *Do not ground no. 2 Lead.* If the light still doesn't light, check for a blown fuse or fusible link, burned out bulb, defective bulb socket, or an open no. 1 lead circuit between generator and ignition switch.

3. If the lamp lights, remove the ground at no. 1 terminal, and with no. 1 and 2 terminals connected to the alternator, insert a screwdriver into the test hole at the back of the alternator to ground the winding.
4. If the light does not come on, check the connection between the wiring harness and no. 1 terminal of the alternator. If the connection is alright, disassemble the alternator and check the brushes, slip rings, and field winding.
5. If a light now comes on, and a reading was obtained in step 1, replace the regulator.

C. *Switch on, Light on, Engine Running.* The causes for this condition are covered in Charging System Tests, Low Charging Rate.

Fusible Links

There are four fusible links on all GM cars.

1. The 14 gauge wire that runs from the junction block to the positive battery terminal serves as a fusible link.
2. There is a second link in the circuit between the horn relay and the ignition switch.
3. A third link is in the wire running to the No. 3 voltage regulator terminal. It's purpose is to protect the regulator contacts and the alternator field circuit.
4. The fourth link is connected between the main junction block and the horn relay.

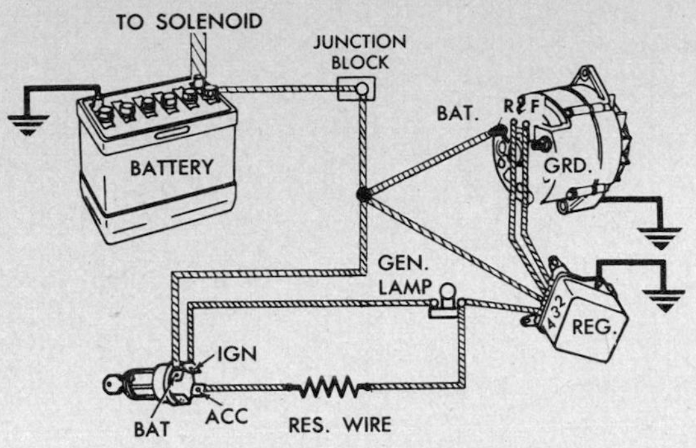

Typical Delcotron circuit diagram
(© Chevrolet Div., G.M. Corp)

These links must be inspected before proceeding with troubleshooting.

Charging System Operation

NOTE: *If the current indicator is to give an accurate reading, the battery cables must be the same gauge and length as the original equipment.*

1. With the engine running and all electrical systems turned off, place a current indicator over the positive battery cable.
2. If a charge of about 5 amps is recorded, the charging system is working. If a draw of about 5 amps is recorded, the system is not working. The needle moves toward the battery when a charge condition is indicated, and away from the battery when a draw condition is indicated. If a draw is indicated, proceed with further testing. If an excessive charge (10–15 amps) is indicated, check for an overcharge, caused by a faulty regulator.

Indicator Light Circuit Testing

The indicator light is important in AC charging systems, for it provides initial field excitation current to the alternator. The light goes out when the field relay closes, which applies battery current to both sides of the bulb. If the light does not go on when key is turned, the bulb could be faulty, there could be an open circuit in the wiring or a positive diode in the alternator could be shorted to ground.

1. Disconnect plug from regulator and connect a test light between terminal No. 4 (in plug) and ground. Turn on ignition switch and observe the light. If light does not go on, check bulb, socket or wiring between switch and regulator plug. If light goes on, check regulator, wiring between regulator F terminal and alternator, or Delcotron itself.
2. Disconnect jumper wire at ground end and reconnect to F terminal in plug. Turn on ignition for a second and note light. If light goes on, problem is in regulator. If light does not go on, problem is in wire between F terminals (regulator and alternator).
3. Disconnect light at plug F terminal and reconnect the free end to F terminal at alternator. Turn on ignition switch for a second and note light. If light goes on, the problem is an open circuit in the wire connecting the regulator and alternator F terminals. If light does not go on, the alternator field windings are defective.

If the indicator light does not extinguish when engine is started, check for a loose drive belt, faulty field relay, faulty alternator, open parallel resistance wire (usually shows up at idle). If the light stays on with the key turned off, an alternator positive diode is shorted to ground.

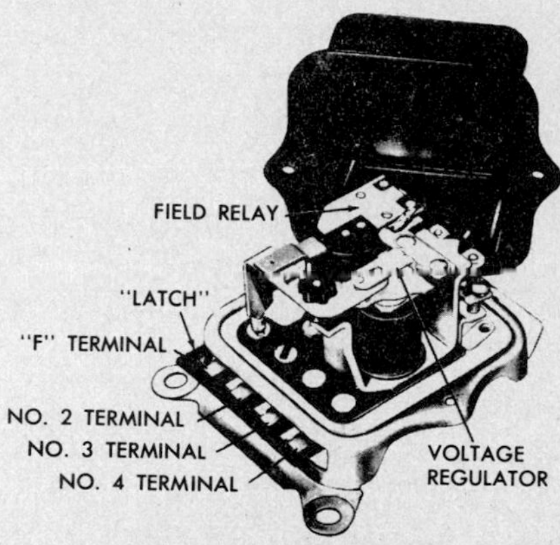

Mechanical voltage regulator
(© Chevrolet Div., G.M. Corp)

Isolation Test

1. Disconnect the wiring harness from the voltage regulator. With a jumper wire connect the F wire to the no. 3 wire in the wire harness plug.
2. Connect a voltmeter across the battery terminals, the positive voltmeter lead to the positive battery terminal, and the negative lead to the negative terminal. Record the reading.
3. Start the engine. Do not race the engine.
4. Gradually raise engine speed to 1500-2000 rpm. The reading on the voltmeter should increase one to two volts over the initial reading. If there is no increase in the reading, repair the alternator. If there is an increase in the voltmeter reading, replace the regulator.

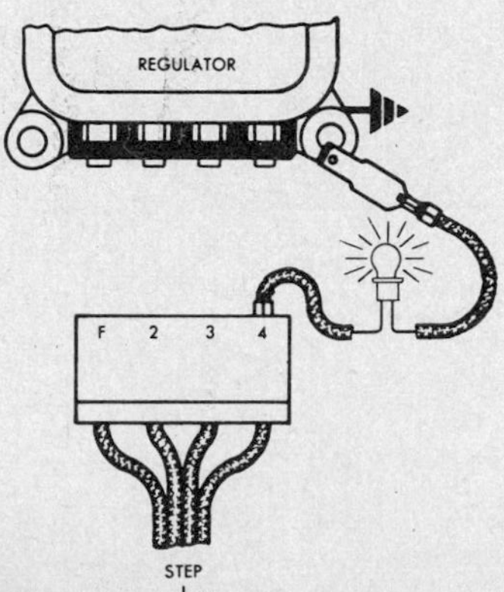

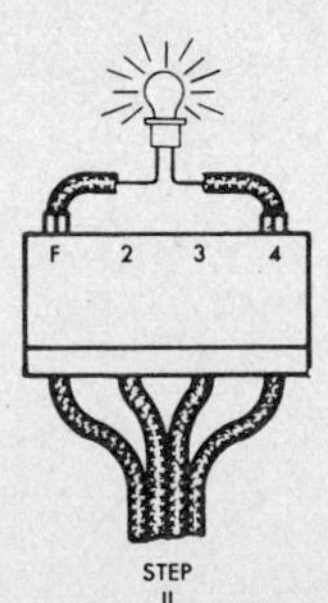

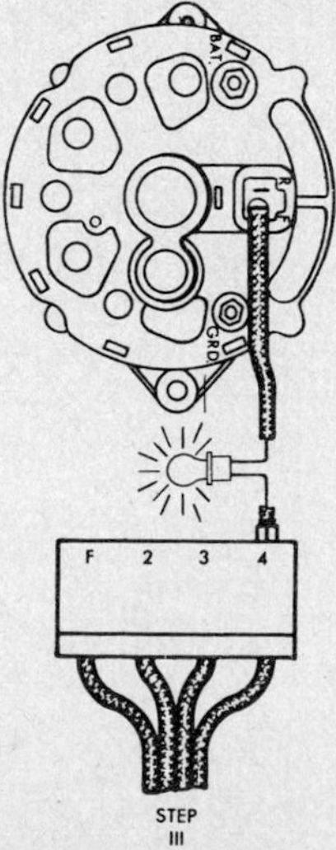

Initial field excitation circuit test hook-ups (© Chevrolet Div., G.M. Corp)

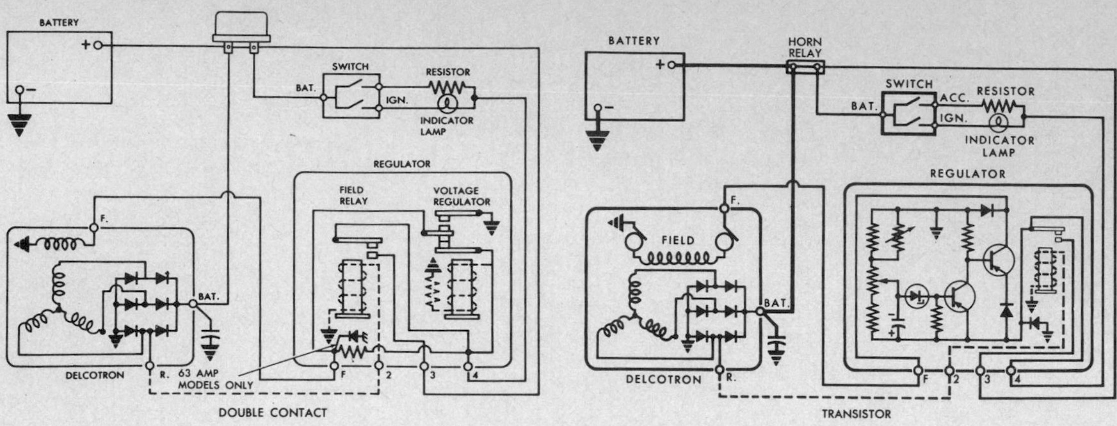

Voltage regulator circuit diagrams (© Chevrolet Div., G.M. Corp)

Field Relay Test

1. Connect a voltmeter between the No. 2 terminal and the ground on the regulator.
2. Turn ignition switch on; do not start the engine. Voltmeter should read battery voltage.
3. If voltmeter reads zero, check circuit connecting regulator terminal No. 2 and Delcotron R terminal.
4. Start engine and run at 1,500-2,000 rpm. If voltage exceeds closing voltage (field relay), and light remains on, field relay is faulty and must be checked.

Field Relay Adjustment

1. Connect a voltmeter between No. 2 regulator terminal and ground.

Adjusting field relay closing voltage
(© Chevrolet Div., G.M. Corp)

2. To adjust, connect a 50 ohm rheostat between wiring harness terminal No. 3 and regulator terminal No. 2, after disconnecting the spade lug on the end of the No. 2 regulator terminal wire. Connect a voltmeter between regulator terminal No. 2 and ground, then turn the resistor to "open" position, turn off ignition switch and slowly decrease resistance until relay closes (noting voltage at this point). Voltage can be adjusted by bending heel iron as illustrated.

Field Circuit Resistance Testing

The resistance wire is an integral part of the ignition wiring harness. The wire cannot be soldered; any connections must be made using crimp-type connectors. Resistance is 10 ohms, 6¼ watts.

1. Connect a voltmeter between the wiring harness terminal No. 4 and ground.

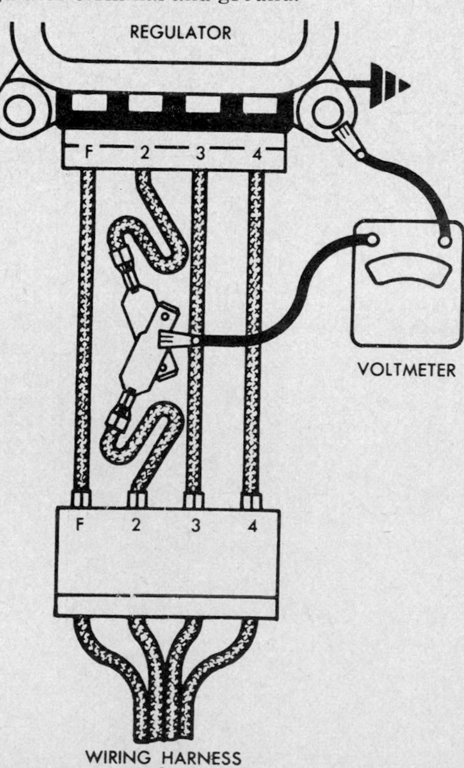

Testing field relay
(© Chevrolet Div., G.M. Corp)

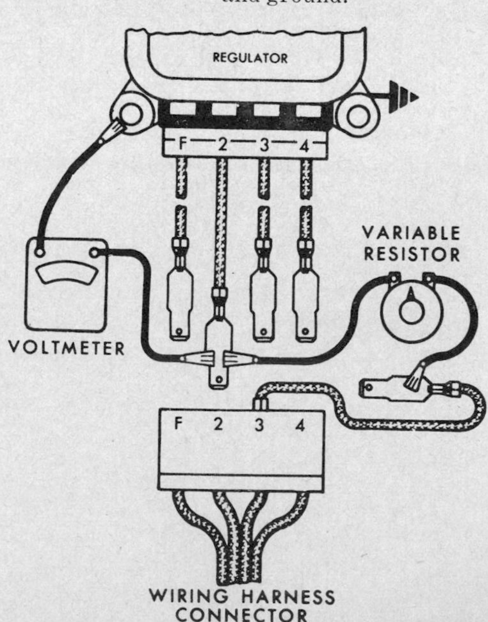

Testing field relay closing voltage
(© Chevrolet Div., G.M. Corp)

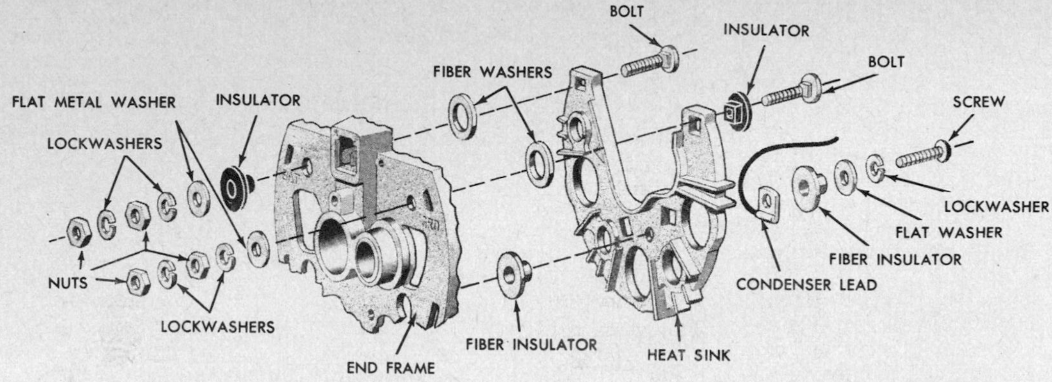

Heat sink assembly—5.5 Delcotron (© Chevrolet Div., G.M. Corp)

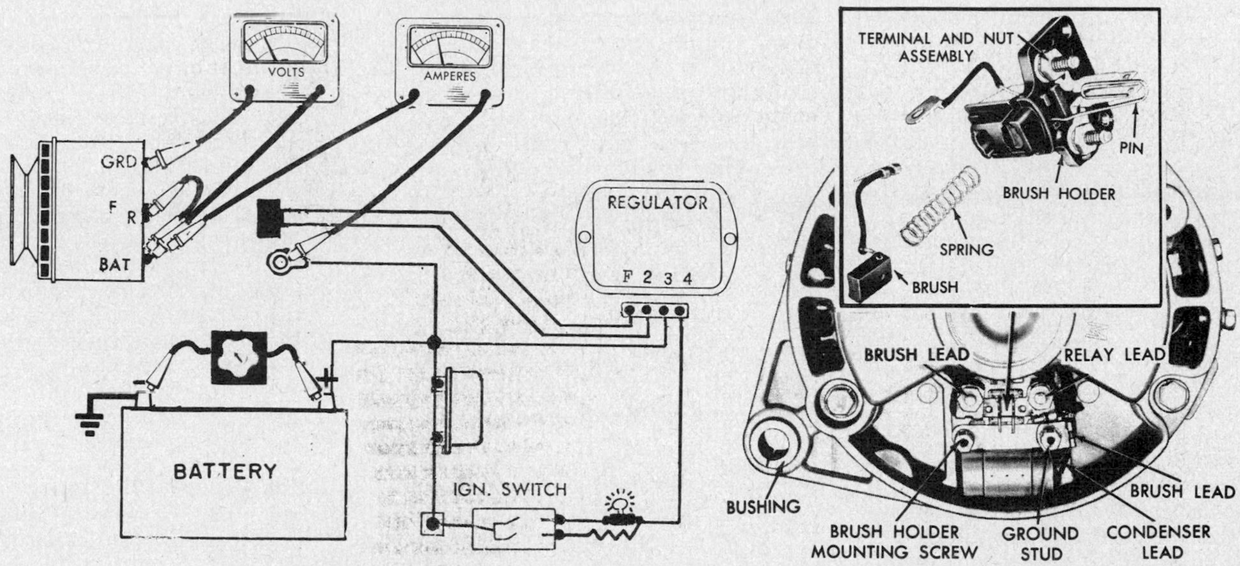

Delcotron output test hook-up

Brush assembly 6.2 Delcotron (© Chevrolet Div., G.M. Corp)

2. Turn on ignition switch, needle must indicate or resistor is open.

Delcotron Current Output Test

NOTE: disconnect battery ground cable while making test connections, then reconnect cable after completing Step 5. Disconnect battery ground cable again before removing test set-up. This test yields the same information as the isolation test but requires the use of an ammeter and a carbon pile.

1. Disconnect lead from BAT. terminal of Delcotron.
2. Hook an ammeter to the lead just disconnected, and to the BAT. terminal of the Delcotron.
3. Hook up the voltmeter leads to the BAT. terminal and a good ground on the alternator.
4. Disconnect the lead from the FR. terminal of the Delcotron.
5. Hook up a jumper wire between BAT. and F terminals of the Delcotron.
6. With a carbon pile load control hooked up to the battery posts, start the engine and set engine to 1,500 rpm, while adjusting carbon pile to obtain 14 volts. With a 6.2 in. alternator, only 600-800 rpm is required.

Caution Be careful not to exceed the recommended regulator voltage setting. This is controlled by the carbon pile load.

7. Ammeter should read within 10% of rated output, as stamped on frame of each unit.

Alternator Overhaul (5.5 and 6.2 Delcotron)

Disassembly—5.5 Series 1D

1. Remove four bolts.
2. Separate drive end frame and rotor from stator assembly by prying with screwdriver. Note that separation is between stator frame and drive end frame.
3. Place tape over slip ring end frame bearing to seal dirt.
4. Lightly clamp rotor in vise to remove shaft nut.

Caution Do not distort rotor by overtightening vise.

5. After nut removal, take off washer, pulley, fan and collar.
6. Separate drive end frame from rotor shaft.
7. Remove three stator lead attaching nuts and separate stator from end frame.
8. Remove screws, brushes and holder assembly.
9. Remove BAT., GND., and attaching screw terminals, then remove heat sink.

Disassembly—6.2 Series 2D

1. Clamp drive end mounting flange in a vise, remove the two screws that secure the cover to the brush holder and remove the cover.
2. Remove the nut that holds the indicator light wire to the blade connector post; disconnect wire lead from post.
3. Remove the two screws that hold the condenser and brush holder to rear end frame, then remove brush holder. Allow condenser to remain with alternator.
4. Remove three slip ring end frame bolts and tab nuts, then carefully pry end frame and case apart, working evenly around the circumference.
5. Remove the three drive end frame bolts and tab nuts, then remove end frame, rotor and pulley as an assembly.
6. Remove shaft nut, washer, pulley and Woodruff key from rotor

shaft, then slide rotor from end frame.
7. Remove drive end frame bearing retainer plate and bearing from end frame.
8. Bearing can be removed, if necessary, at this time. Use puller to prevent damage.
9. Disconnect the three stator leads by cutting between coils and diodes.

NOTE: diode leads can be cleaned and unsoldered, *if* proper heat sinks are used to prevent diode damage.

10. Remove heat sink-to-case retaining screws, then remove heat sinks. Insulated heat sink (BATT. terminal) holds positive diode.

Diode Tests

All diodes are marked with either a + or — on the head or are marked with *red* paint for + diodes, *black* paint for — diodes to identify the polarity of the case. On a generator to be used with a negative ground system, the negative case diodes are mounted into the slip ring end frame and the positive case diodes are mounted into the insulated heat sink. Diodes with a negative case have positive polarity leads, whereas positive case diodes have negative polarity leads.

Diodes can be checked for shorts or opens with an ohmmeter.

With the stator leads disconnected, connect one ohmmeter test prod to the diode lead and the other test prod to the heat sink. Reverse the test prods and note the ohmmeter readings. The meter should read high ohms in one direction, low ohms in the other. If both readings are the same, either both high or both low, the diode is faulty and must be replaced. A 1½ volt test light also will indicate a faulty diode. It will light in one direction and not in the other if the diode is good. If it lights in both directions, or in neither direction, the diode is bad.

Diode Replacement

Early Delcotrons had screwed-in diodes, as does the extremely heavy-duty 6.6 Series 4D Delcotron. Models covered here use pressed-in diodes exclusively. If there is any doubt about the year and model of the Delcotron being serviced, note the diode construction—screwed-in diodes have hexagonal heads and the later, pressed-in, units have straight sides with no hex head. Old-style, screwed-in diodes have both right- and left-hand threads. Plus (+) diodes have left-hand and minus (—) have right-hand threads.

5.5 Series 1D

1. Support end frame on a deep socket with a larger inside diameter than the diode outside diameter.
2. Carefully *press* out the diode with a brass drift and an arbor press, or a large bench vise. Be extremely careful so as not to distort the end frame.
3. Select a new diode (red or black), noting that the red (+) diodes go into the heat sink and the black (—) diodes into the end frame.
4. Support end frame on a flat, smooth surface around diode hole and carefully *press* the new diode into position. Diode must be square when starting or both diode and frame will be ruined.

6.2 Series 2D

1. Cut leads connected to diode stem as close as possible to stem, then support end frame as for 5.5 Delcotron and press out diode.
2. Select diode with proper color marking (same as for 5.5 Delcotron), then press new diode into position.
3. Scrape enough insulation from diode stem and leads to ensure good contact, then install a sleeve over diode and place the T-clip from diode package over diode stem.
4. Place the flexible lead and stator lead (if applicable) into the T-clip, crimp clip and solder with rosin core solder only, using heat sinks (pliers) to avoid destroying diode.
5. Tape the leads together to prevent vibration damage.

Rotor Checks—All Models

The rotor may be checked electrically for grounded, open, or shorted field coils.

To check for grounds, connect a

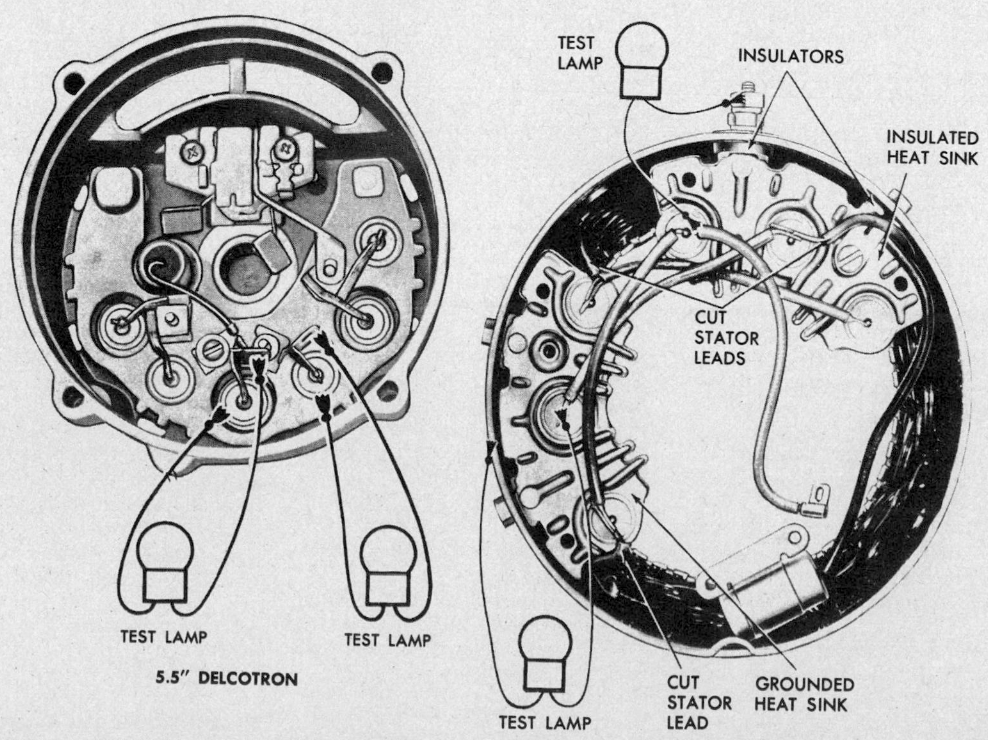

Testing diodes (© Chevrolet Div., G.M. Corp)

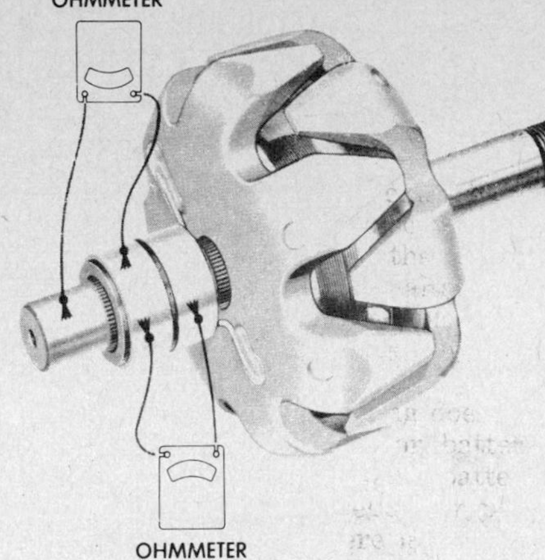

Checking rotor for grounds or opens —all Delcotron models
(© Chevrolet Div., G.M. Corp)

110-volt test light from either slip ring to the rotor shaft or to the laminations. If the lamp lights, the field windings are grounded.

To check for opens, connect the leads of a 110-volt test light to each slip ring. If the lamp fails to light, the windings are open.

The windings are checked for short-circuits by connecting a battery and ammeter in series with the two slip rings. Note the ammeter reading.

An ammeter reading greater than that specified in the charts preceding each car section of this manual indicates shorted windings.

Since the field windings are not serviced separately, the rotor assembly must be replaced if the windings are defective.

Stator Checks—All Models

Stator windings may be checked for grounded, open, or shorted windings. If a 110-volt test lamp lights when connected from any stator lead to the stator frame, the windings are grounded. If the lamp fails to light when successively connected between each pair of stator leads, the windings are open.

A short circuit in the stator windings is difficult to locate without laboratory equipment, due to the low resistance of the windings. However, if all other electrical checks are normal and the generator fails to supply the rated output, shorted stator windings are indicated.

Slip Ring Servicing and Replacement—All Models

Slip rings which are rough or out of round should be trued in a lathe to .001 in. maximum indicator reading. Remove only enough material to make the rings smooth and round. Finish with 400 grit or finer polishing cloth and blow away all dust.

Slip rings which must be replaced can be removed from the shaft with a gear puller, after the leads have been unsoldered. The new assembly should be pressed on with a sleeve which just fits over the shaft; this will apply all the pressure to the inner slip ring collar and prevent damage to the outer slip ring. Only pure tin solder should be used when reconnecting field leads.

Brush Replacement—All Models

The extent of brush wear can be determined by comparison with a new brush. If brushes are one-half worn, they should be replaced.

1. Remove brush holder assembly from end frame by removing two holder assembly screws.
2. Place springs and brushes in the holder and insert straight wire or pin into holes at bottom of holder to retain brushes.

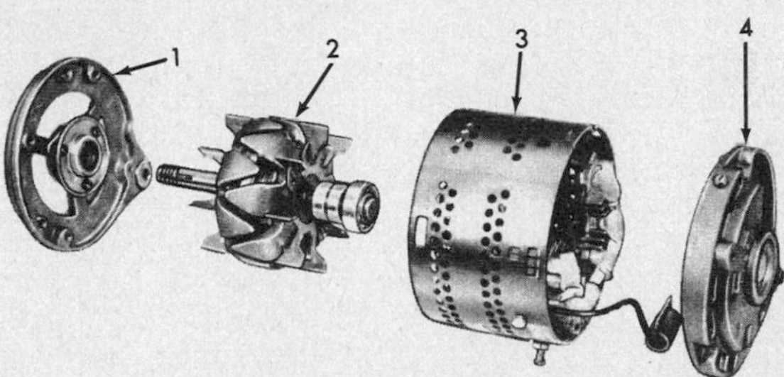

6.2 Delcotron assembly sequence: 1) drive end frame 2) rotor 3) stator 4) end frame
(© Chevrolet Div., G.M. Corp)

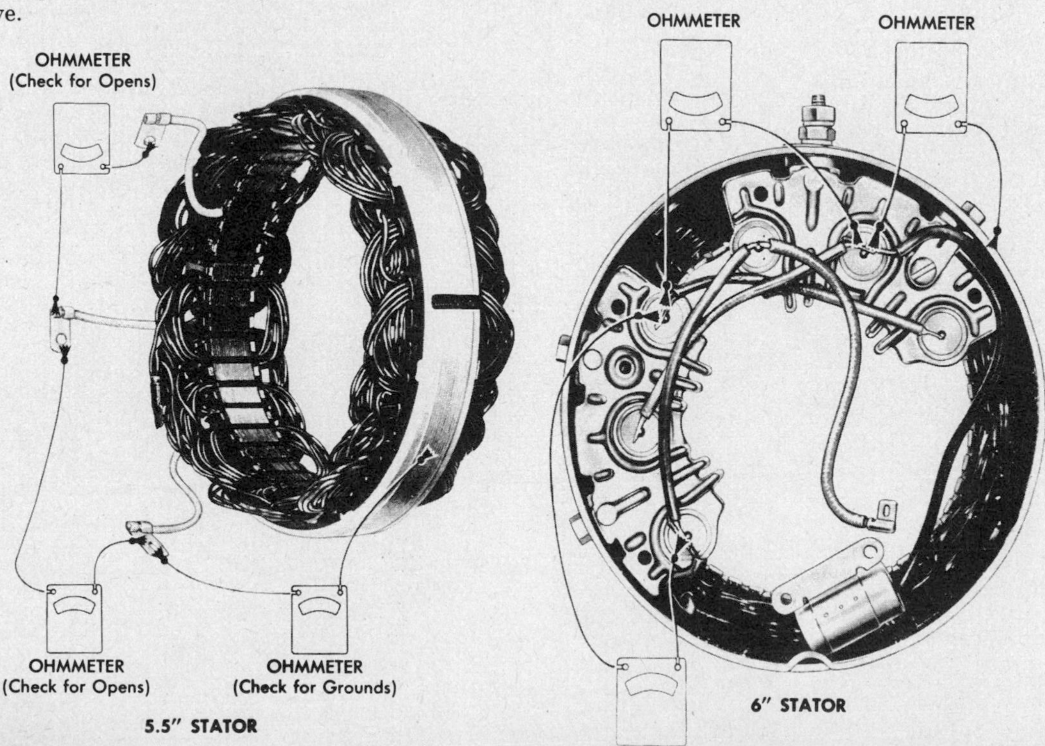

Checking stator for grounds or opens—all Delcotron models
(© Chevrolet Div., G.M. Corp)

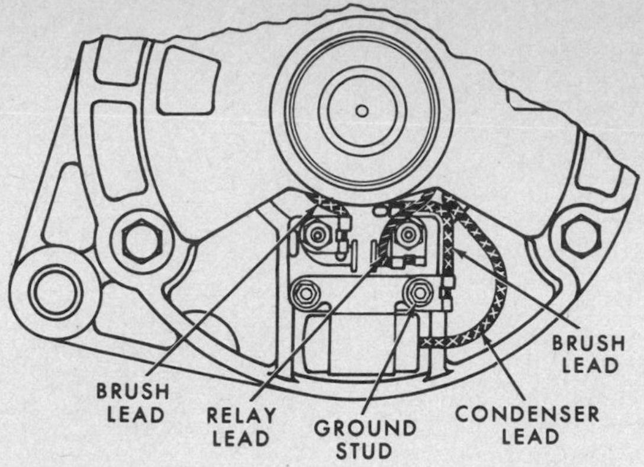

Brush lead arrangement after assembly—6.2 Delcotron
(© Chevrolet Div., G.M. Corp)

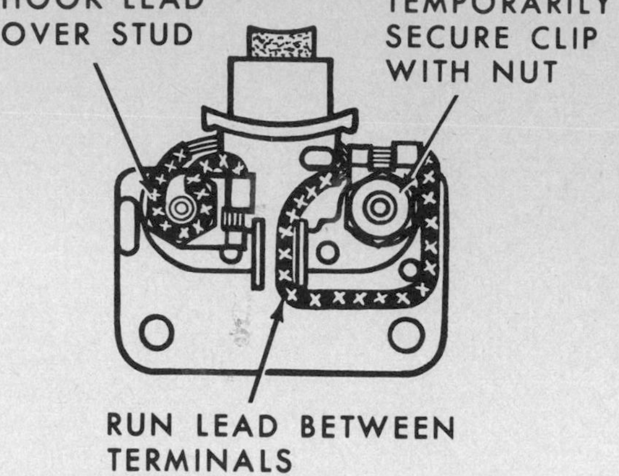

Brush lead arrangement during assembly—6.2 Delcotron
(© Chevrolet Div., G.M. Corp)

3. Attach holder assembly onto end frame.

Assembly—5.5 Series 1D

1. Install stator assembly into slip ring end frame and locate diode connectors over the relay, diode and stator leads. Tighten terminal nuts.
2. Install rotor into drive end frame.
3. Install fan, spacer, pulley washer and nut.
4. Install Allen wrench (5/16 in.) into end of shaft to hold drive shaft, then tighten pulley nut to 40-50 ft. lbs. using a crowsfoot wrench (15/16 in.) and torque wrench.
5. Assemble slip ring end frame and stator assembly to drive end frame and rotor.
6. Install four through bolts and tighten securely.

Assembly—6.2 Series 2D

1. Install stator assembly into slip ring end frame and locate diode connectors over the relay, diode and stator leads. Tighten terminal nuts.

Brush assembly—5.5 Delcotron
(© Chevrolet Div., G.M. Corp)

2. Install the front frame over the rotor.
3. Install fan, spacer, Woodruff key, pulley, washer and nut.
4. Clamp pulley in a padded-jaw vise and tighten shaft nut to 50-60 ft. lbs.

Caution Do not clamp rotor, or segments will be distorted.

5. Position rotor and drive end frame assembly into slip ring end frame and stator. Install through bolts and tighten securely.
6. Push the brushes into the holder and secure the leads.
7. Attach brush assembly and condenser to the end frame with left-hand hex stud only.
8. Arrange the leads with the right-hand brush lead connected under the right-hand hex stud.
9. Attach terminal cover with two screws, making sure not to pinch the leads.

Delcotron 10-SI Series 100 (General Motors Corp.)

This system is an integrated AC generating system containing a built-in voltage regulator. Removal and replacement is essentially the same as for the standard AC generator.

The regulator is mounted inside the slip ring end frame. All regulator components are enclosed in an epoxy molding, and the regulator cannot be adjusted. Rotor and stator tests are the same as for the 5.5 Delcotron, covered previously.

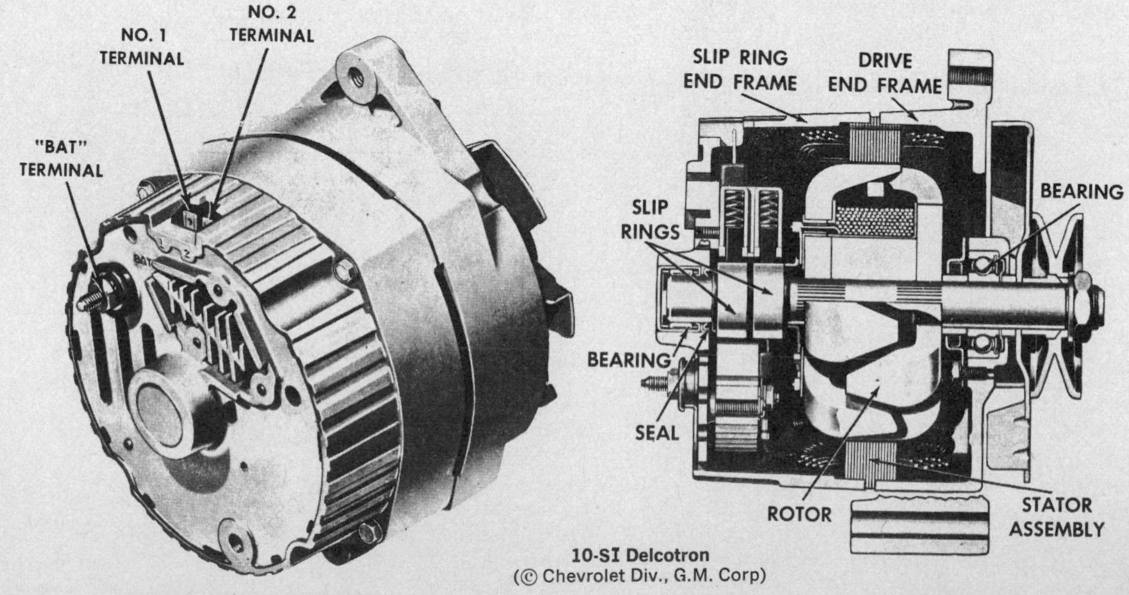

10-SI Delcotron
(© Chevrolet Div., G.M. Corp)

This alternator is also used in some American Motors cars, starting 1975.

Troubleshooting

NOTE: *See the "Preliminary Charging System Inspection" section before proceeding further. Make sure that the continuous running blower, if equipped, is disconnected. This blower will run with the key on even if the blower control is off, unless disconnected.*

Charging System Test—Low Charging Rate

1. After battery condition, drive belt tension, and wiring terminals and connections have been checked, charge the battery fully and perform the following test:
2. Connect a test voltmeter between the alternator BAT. terminal and ground, ignition switch on. Connect the voltmeter in turn to alternator terminals No. 1 and No. 2, the other voltmeter lead being grounded as before. A zero reading indicates an open circuit between the battery and each connection at the alternator. If this test discloses no faults in the wiring, proceed to Step 3.
3. Connect the test voltmeter to the alternator BAT. terminal (the other test lead to ground), start the engine and run at 1,500-2,000 rpm with all lights and electrical accessories turned on. If the voltmeter reads 12.8 volts or greater, the alternator is good and no further checks need be made. If the voltmeter reads less than 12.8 volts, ground the field winding by inserting a screwdriver into the test hole in the end frame.

Caution Do not force tab more than ¾ in. into end frame.

a. If voltage increases to 13 volts or more, the regulator unit is defective.
b. If voltage does not increase significantly, generator is defective.

Charging System Test—High Charging Rate

1. With the battery fully charged, connect a voltmeter between alternator terminal no. 2 and ground. If the reading is zero, no. 2 circuit from the battery is open.
2. If no. 2 circuit is OK, but an obvious overcharging condition still exists, proceed as follows:
   a. Remove the alternator and separate the end frames.
   b. Connect a low-range ohmmeter between the brush lead clip and the end frame, as illustrated (test no. 1), then reverse the lead connections. If both readings are zero, either the brush lead clip is grounded or the regulator is defective. A grounded brush lead clip can be due to a damaged insulating sleeve or

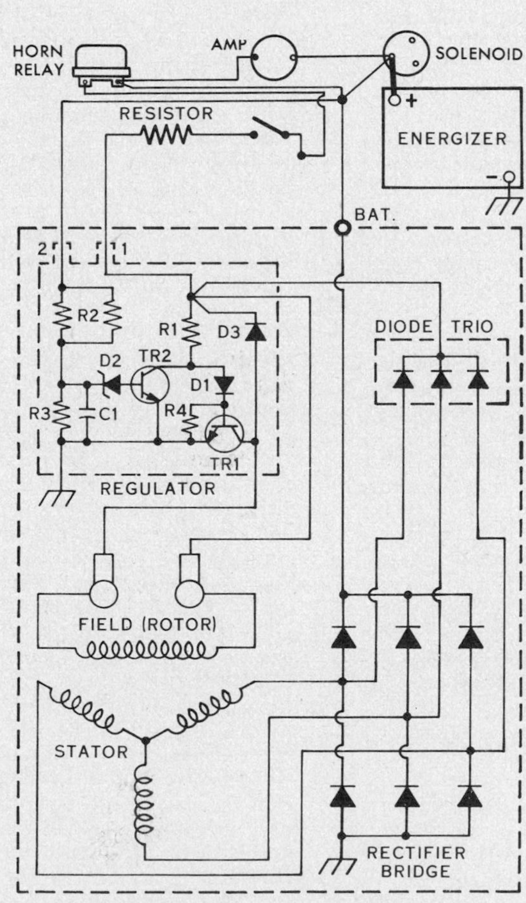

10-SI charging circuit schematic
(© Chevrolet Div., G.M. Corp)

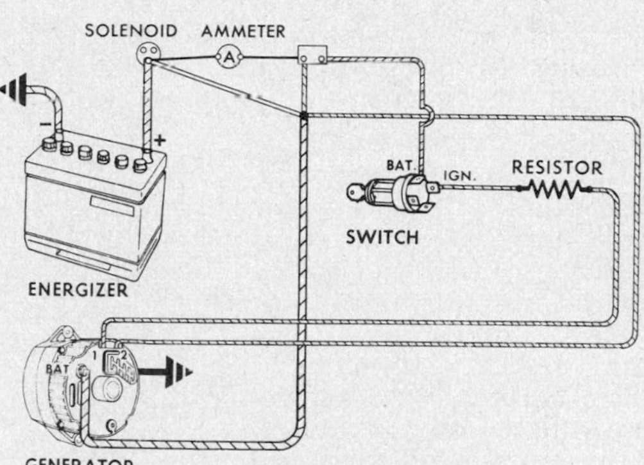

10-SI basic wiring diagram
(© Chevrolet Div., G.M. Corp)

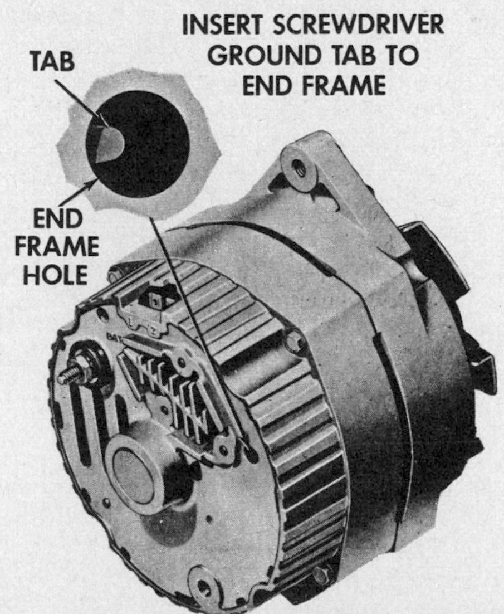

10-SI Delcotron end view
(© Chevrolet Div., G.M. Corp)

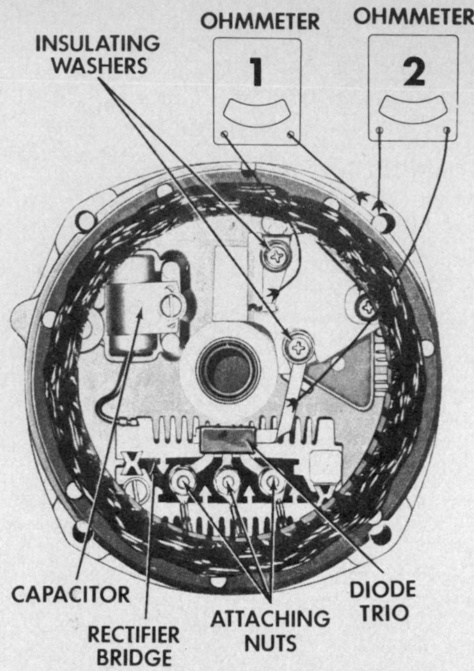

Brush lead clip ground test— 10-SI Delcotron
(© Chevrolet Div., G.M. Corp)

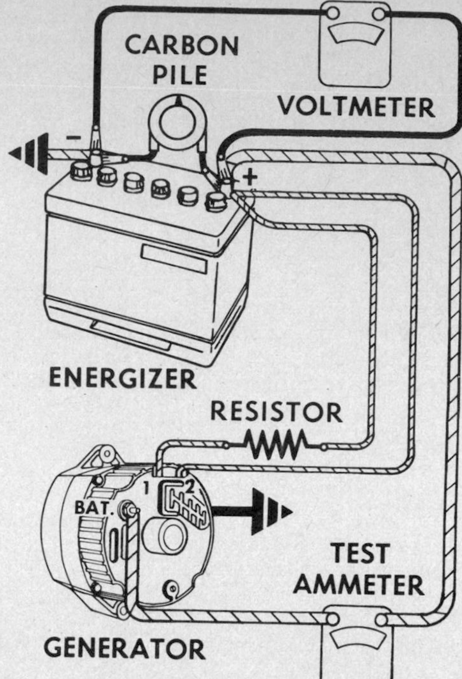

10-SI Delcotron output test hook-up
(© Chevrolet Div., G.M. Corp)

omission of the insulating washer.

Alternator Output Test

1. Connect a test voltmeter, ammeter and 10 ohm 6 watt resistor into the charging circuit. Do not connect the carbon pile to the battery posts at this time.
2. Increase alternator speed and observe voltmeter—if voltage is uncontrolled with speed and increases to 16 volts or more, check for a grounded brush lead clip as covered previously. If brush lead clip is not grounded, the voltage regulator is faulty and must be replaced.
3. Connect the carbon pile load to the battery terminals.
4. Operate the alternator at moderate speed and adjust the carbon pile to obtain maximum alternator output as indicated on the ammeter. If output is within 10% of rated output as stamped on the alternator frame, alternator is O.K. If output is not within specifications, ground the alternator field by inserting a screwdriver into the test hole in the end frame. If output now is within 10% of rating, replace the voltage regulator; if still not within specifications, check field winding, diode trio, rectifier bridge and stator, as described later. Dissasembly of alternator up to and including Step 6 is necessary.

Disassembly and Assembly

1. Place alternator in a vise, clamped by the mounting flange only.
2. Remove the four through bolts and separate the slip ring end frame and stator assembly from the drive end and rotor assembly, using a screwdriver to pry the two sections apart. Use the slots provided for the purpose.

NOTE: *Scribe matchmarks on the parts to aid in assembly.*

3. Place a piece of tape over the slip ring end frame bearing to prevent entry of dirt; also tape shaft at slip ring end to prevent scratches.
4. Clean brushes, if they are to be reused, with trichloroethylene or carbon tetrachloride solvent. Use these solvents only in an adequately ventilated area.
5. Remove the stator lead nuts and separate the stator from the end frame.
6. Remove the screw that secures the diode trio and remove diode trio.

NOTE: at this point, test the rotor, rectifier bridge, stator and diode trio if these tests are necessary.

7. Remove the rectifier bridge hold-down screw and the BAT. terminal screw, then disconnect condenser lead. Remove rectifier bridge from end frame.
8. Remove the two securing screws and brush holder and regulator assemblies. Note the insulating sleeves over the screws.
9. Remove the retaining screw and condenser from the end frame.
10. Remove the slip ring end frame bearing, if it is to be replaced, using the procedure given later in this section.
11. Remove the pulley nut, washer, pulley, fan and spacer from the rotor shaft, using a 5/16 in. Allen key to hold the shaft while loosening the nut.
12. Remove rotor and spacers from drive end frame assembly.
13. Remove drive end frame bearing retainer plate, screws, plate, bearing, and slinger from end frame, if necessary.
14. To assemble, reverse order of disassembly. Pulley nut must be tightened to 40-50 ft. lbs.

Cleaning and Inspection

1. Clean all metal parts, except stator and rotor assemblies, in solvent.
2. Wipe off bearings and inspect them for pitting or roughness.
3. Inspect rotor slip rings for scoring. They may be cleaned with 400 grit sandpaper (not emery), rotating the rotor to make the rings concentric. Maximum out-of-true is 0.001 in. If slip rings are deeply scored, the entire rotor must be replaced as a unit.
4. Inspect brushes for wear; minimum length is ¼ in.

Diode Trio Initial Testing

1. Before removing this unit, connect an ohmmeter between the brush lead clip and the end frame. The lowest reading scale should be used for this test.
2. After taking a reading, reverse the lead connections. If the meter reads zero, the brush lead clip is probably grounded, due to omission of the insulating sleeve or insulating washer.

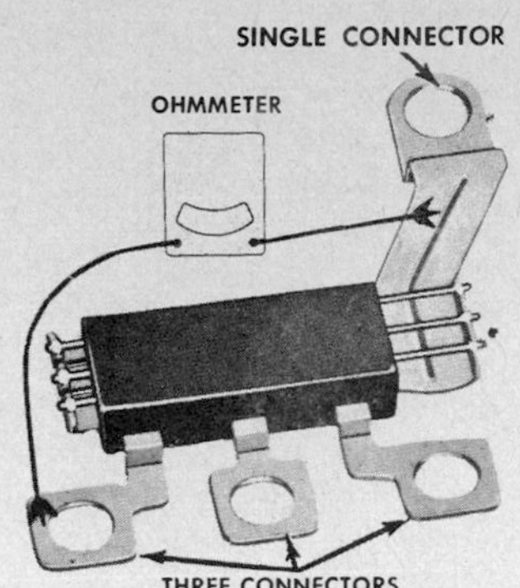

Testing diode trio—10-SI AC generator
(© Pontiac Motor Div., G.M. Corp)

Diode Trio Removal

1. Remove the three nuts which secure the stator.
2. Remove stator.
3. Remove the screw which secures the diode trio lead clip, then remove diode trio.

NOTE: The position of the insulating washer on the screw is critical; make sure it is returned to the same position on reassembly.

Diode Trio Testing

1. Connect an ohmmeter, on lowest range, between the single brush connector and one stator lead connector.
2. Observe the reading, then reverse the meter leads. Repeat this test with each of the other two stator lead connectors. The readings on each of these tests should NOT be identical, there should be one low and one high reading for each test. If this is not the case, replace the diode trio.

Caution Do not use high voltage on the diode trio.

Rectifier Bridge Testing

1. Connect an ohmmeter between the heat sink (ground) and the base of one of the three terminals. Then, reverse the meter leads and take a reading. If both readings are identical, the bridge is defective and must be replaced.
2. Repeat this test with the remaining two terminals, then between the INSULATED heat sink (as opposed to the GROUNDED heat sink in previous test) and each of the three terminals. As before, if any two readings are identical, on reversing the meter leads, the rectifier bridge must be replaced.

Brush holder—10-SI generator
(© Pontiac Motor Div., G.M. Corp)

Rectifier Bridge Removal

1. Remove the attaching screw and the BAT. terminal screw.
2. Disconnect the condenser lead.
3. Remove the rectifier bridge.

NOTE: The insulator between the insulated heat sink and the end frame is extremely important to the operation of the unit. It must be replaced in exactly the same position on reassembly.

Caution Do not use high voltage to test the rectifier bridge.

Brush and/or Voltage Regulator R & R

1. Remove two brush holder screws and stator lead to strap nut and washer, brush holder screws and one of the diode trio lead strap attaching screws.

NOTE: The insulating washers must be replaced in the same position on reassembly.

2. Remove brush holder and brushes. The voltage regulator may also be removed at this time, if desired.
3. Brushes and brush springs must be free of corrosion and must be undamaged and completely free of oil or grease.
4. Insert spring and brushes into holder, noting whether they slide freely without binding. Insert wooden or plastic toothpick into bottom hole in holder to retain brushes.

NOTE: The brush holder is serviced as a unit; individual parts are not available.

5. Reassemble in reverse order of disassembly.

Slip Ring End Frame Bearing and Seal R & R

1. With stator removed, press out bearing and seal, using a socket or similar tool that fits inside the end frame housing. Press from outside to inside, supporting the frame inside with a hollow cylinder (large, deep socket) to allow the seal and bearing to pass.
2. The bearings are sealed for life and permanently lubricated. If a bearing is dry, do not attempt to repack it, as it will throw off the grease and contaminate the inside of the generator.
3. Using a flat plate, press the new bearing from the outside toward the inside. A large vise is a handy press, but care must be exercised so that end frame is not distorted or cracked. Again, use a deep socket to support the inside of the end frame.
4. From inside the end frame, insert seal and press flush with housing.
5. Install stator and reconnect leads.

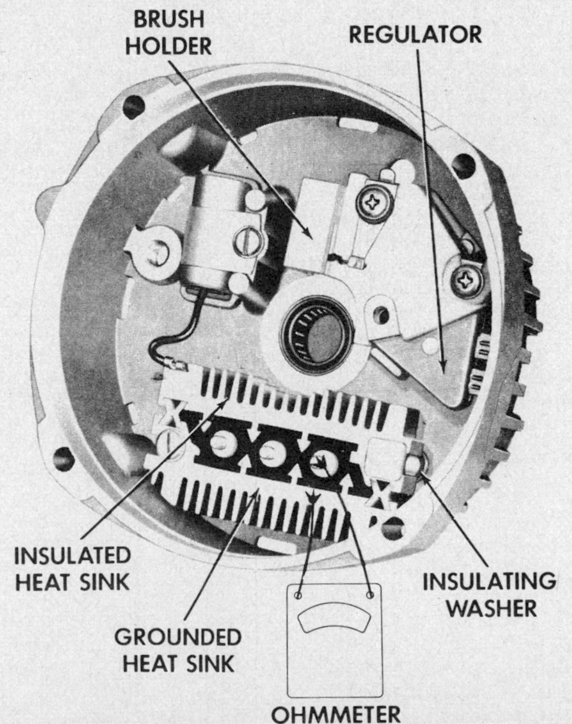

Rectifier bridge testing—10-SI Delcotron
(© Chevrolet Div., G.M. Corp)

Ford-Autolite (Ford Motor Co.) with Electro-Mechanical Regulator

The Ford-Autolite charging system is a negative ground system. It includes an alternator, an electro-mechanical regulator, a charge indicator, and a storage battery.

Caution Some 1974 and later Continental Mark IVs and Thunderbirds may have two alternators. The second alternator is a high voltage (120 volt) unit which is used to operate a special heated windshield and rear window. This alternator and its wiring are completely isolated from the regular charging system, and all of its connections are marked with warning tags. DO NOT attempt to service the alternator or its wiring and DO NOT confuse its wiring with that of the regular charging system. Because this system can produce a severe electrical shock, its service should be left to an authorized facility.

Troubleshooting

NOTE: See the "Preliminary Charging System Inspection" section before proceeding further.

Charging System Tests Using a Voltmeter

This test series will determine which element of the charging system is malfunctioning.

1. Connect the leads of a voltmeter to the battery clamps.
2. Check the voltage.
3. Connect a tachometer and run the engine at about 1,500 RPM with no electrical load.
4. The voltage should increase 1 V but should not be more than 2 V above the previously recorded voltage.
5. With the engine running, turn on the heater and/or air conditioner blower motor (high speed) and the headlights (high beam).
6. Increase the engine speed to 2000 RPM.
7. The voltmeter should now indicate a minimum of 0.5 V above the first recorded battery voltage.
8. If the voltmeter indicates more than 2 volts above the battery voltage, stop the engine and check the regulator and alternator ground connections. Clean and tighten these connections and repeat the test.
9. If the overvoltage condition still exists, disconnect the wiring plug from the regulator and repeat the test.
10. If the overvoltage condition ceases replace the voltage regulator and repeat the test. If the

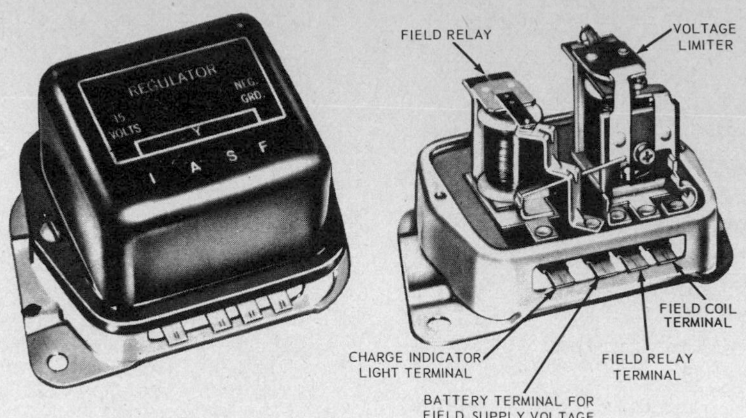

External electro-mechanical regulator
(© Ford Motor Co)

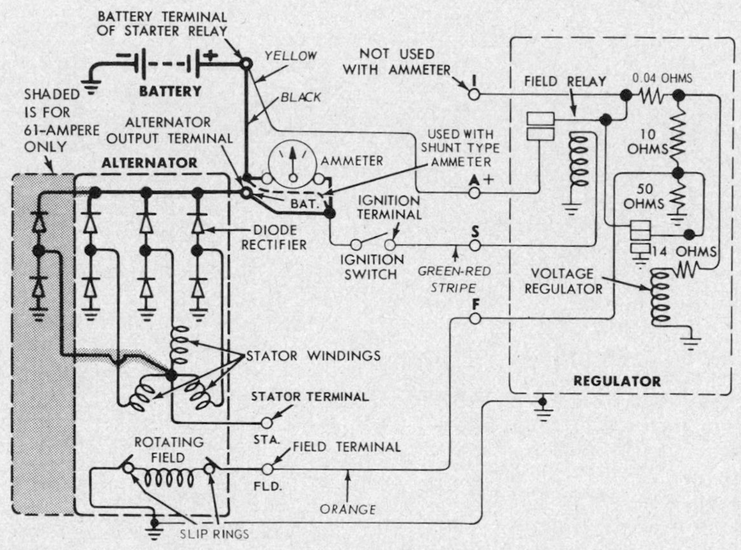

Charging system schematic with electro-mechanical regulator and charging light
(© Ford Motor Co)

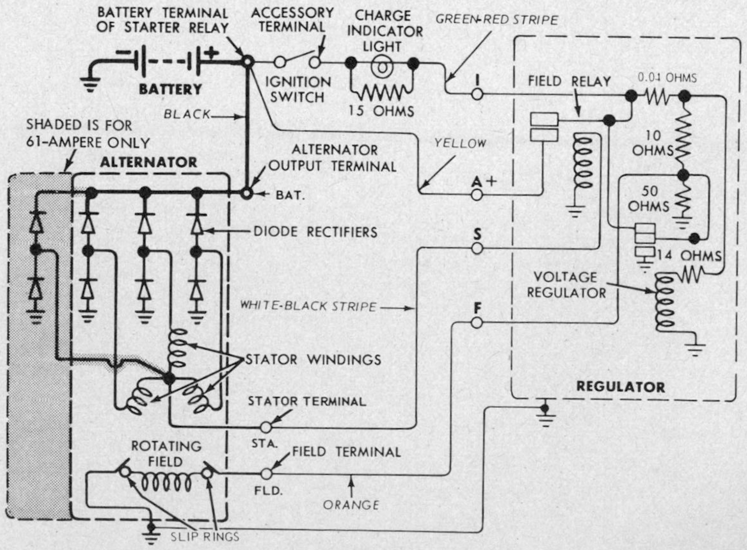

Charging system schematic with electro-mechanical regulator and charging light
(© Ford Motor Co)

problem is in the regulator, replacing it should provide a normal reading.

11. If overvoltage still exists with the regulator plug disconnected, repair the short in the wiring harness between the alternator and regulator; then replace the regulator and wiring plug and repeat the test.
12. If the voltmeter reading does not increase 1 V check for battery voltage at the alternator battery terminal and the regulator plug 'A' terminal. If there is no voltage, repair the wiring and repeat the test.
13. If the voltage does not increase by 1 V, the field circuit must be checked to determine if it is grounding. The field circuit should be checked with the regulator wiring plug disconnected and an ohmmeter connected between the 'F' terminal of the plug and the battery ground. There should be between 4 and 250 ohms resistance.
14. Check for an open wire in the regulator by connecting an ohmmeter between the 'I' and 'F' terminals of the regulator. There should be no resistance between the two terminals. If there is about 10 ohms, the connector wire inside the regulator is shorted.

Field Circuit and Alternator Tests

1. If the field circuit is ok, disconnect the regulator wiring plug at the regulator and connect the jumper wire from the 'A' to the 'F' terminals on the plug.
2. Repeat the test procedure. If there is still a problem (under voltage), remove the jumper wire and leave the plug disconnected.
3. Connect a jumper wire to the FLD and BAT terminals on the alternator and repeat the test. If the tests are now satisfactory, repair the wiring harness between the alternator and regulator. If there is no defect in the harness, replace the alternator, and repeat the test.

CHARGING NO LOAD VOLTAGE
CHARGING VOLTAGE UNDER LOAD
BATTERY NO LOAD VOLTAGE
12 13 14 15
OVERVOLTAGE
OVERCHARGE
VOLTMETER TEST
TYPICAL VOLTAGE BANDS SHOWN

Voltmeter readings isolation test
(© Ford Motor Co)

Diode Tests on Car

1. Disconnect the electric choke and voltage regulator plug.
2. Connect a jumper between the 'A' and 'F' terminals of the plug; connect a voltmeter to the battery clamps, start the engine and let it run at idle.
3. Read and record the voltmeter reading; move the voltmeter lead to the 'S' terminal in the wiring harness and note the reading.
4. If the voltmeter reads ½ of battery voltage, the diodes are ok.
5. If the voltmeter reads approximately 1.5 V, the alternator has a shorted negative diode, or a grounded stator winding.
6. If the voltmeter reads about 1.5 V less than battery voltage, the alternator has a shorted positive diode.
7. If the voltmeter reads 1.0-1.5 V less than ½ battery voltage, there is an open positive diode; if it is 1.0-1.5 V more than ½ battery charge, there is an open negative diode.

After the test is complete, reconnect the choke.

Fusible Links

1. Check the fusible link located between the starter relay and the alternator. Replace the link if it is burned or open.
2. Ford, Mercury, Torino, Montego, Maverick, Comet, Bobcat, and Pinto all have two fusible links between the starter relay and the alternator. Be sure to check both of them for damage.

Charging System Operation

NOTE: if the current indicator is to give an accurate reading, the battery cables must be of the same gauge and length as the original equipment.

1. With the engine running, and all electrical systems turned off, place a current indicator over the positive battery cable.
2. If a charge of about 5 amps is recorded, the charging system is working. If a draw of about 5 amps is recorded, the system is not working. The needle moves toward the battery when a charge condition is indicated, and away from the battery when a draw condition is indicated. If a draw is indicated, continue to the next testing procedure. If an overcharge of 10-15 amps is indicated, check for a faulty regulator or a bad ground at the regulator or the alternator.

Testing the Ignition Switch to Regulator Circuit

1. Disconnect the regulator wiring harness from the regulator.
2. Turn on the key. Using a test light or voltmeter, check for voltage between the I wire and ground. Check for voltage between the A wire and ground. If voltage is present at this part of the system, the circuit is OK. If there is no voltage at the I wire,

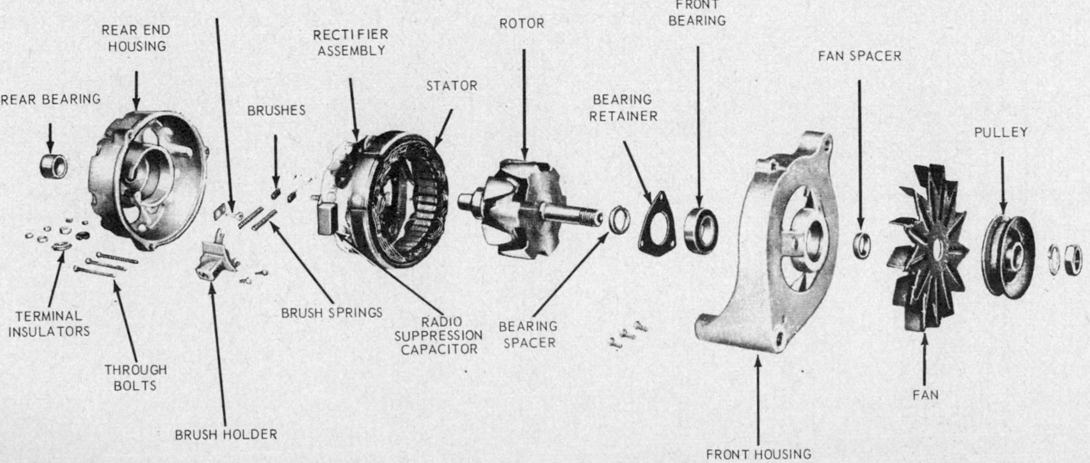

Typical disassembled Autolite alternator—except 65 amp unit (© Ford Motor Co)

check for a burned-out charge indicator bulb, a burned-out resistor, or a break or short in the wiring. If there is no voltage present at the A wire, check for a bad connection at the starter relay or a break or short in the wire.

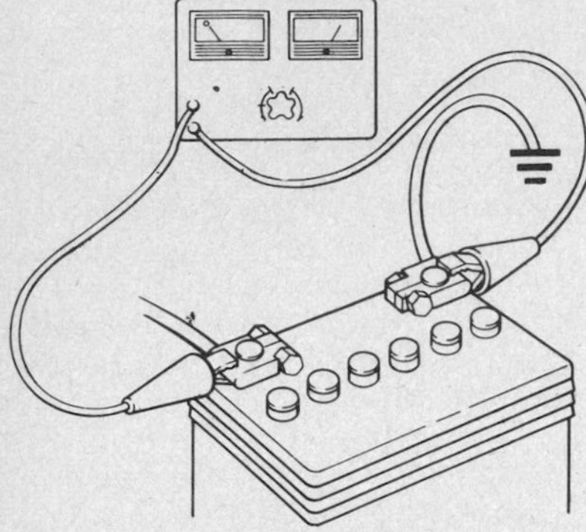

Voltmeter connections isolation test and ignition circuit test
(© Ford Motor Co)

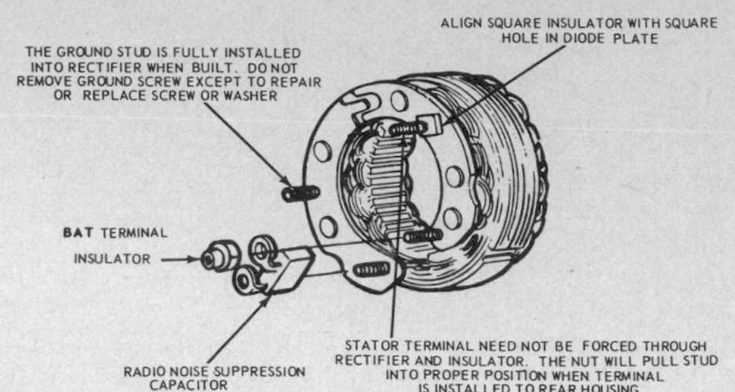

Terminal insulators—fiber circuit board
(© Ford Motor Co)

Overhaul—Autolite

Disassembly—Except 65 AMP Autolite

1. Mark both end housings with a scribe mark for assembly.
2. Remove the three housing through bolts.
3. Separate the front housing and rotor from the stator and rear housing.
4. Remove the nuts from the rectifier to rear housing mounting studs, and remove the rear housing.
5. Remove the brush holder mounting screws and the holder, brushes, springs, insulator, and terminal.
6. If replacement is necessary, press the bearing from the rear end housing, supporting housing on inner boss.
7. If rectifiers are to be replaced, carefully unsolder the leads from the terminals.

Caution Use only a 100-watt soldering iron. Leave the soldering iron in contact with the diode terminals only long enough to remove the wires. Use pliers as temporary heat sinks in order to protect the diodes.

8. There are various types of rectifier assembly circuit boards installed in production. One type has the circuit board spaced away from the diode plates and the diodes are exposed. Another type consists of a single circuit board with integral diodes; and still another has integral diodes with an additional booster diode plate containing two diodes. This last type is used only on the eight-diode, 61-amp. 1971 and later Autolite alternator. To disassemble, use the following procedures:
   a. Exposed Diodes—remove the screws from the rectifier by rotating bolt heads 1/4 turn clockwise to unlock, then unscrewing.
   b. Integral Diodes—press out the stator terminal screw, making sure not to twist it while doing this. Do not remove grounded screw.
   c. Booster Diodes—press out the stator terminal screw about 1/4 in., then remove the nut from the end of the screw and lift screw from circuit board, making sure not to twist it as it comes out.
9. Remove the drive pulley and fan. On alternator pulleys with threaded holes in the outer end of the pulley, use a standard puller for removal.
10. Remove the three screws that hold the front bearing retainer, and remove the front housing.
11. If the bearing is to be replaced, press from housing.

Cleaning and Inspection

1. The rotor, stator, diode rectifier assemblies, and bearings are not to be cleaned with solvent. These parts are to be wiped off with a clean cloth. Cleaning solvent may cause damage to the electrical parts or contaminate the bearing internal lubricant. Wash all other parts in solvent and dry them.
2. Rotate the front bearing on the driveshaft. Check for any scraping noise, looseness or roughness that indicates that the bearing is excessively worn. As the bearing is being rotated, look for excessive lubricant leakage. If any of these conditions exist, replace the bearing. Check rear bearing and rotor shaft.
3. Place the rear end housing on the slip ring end of the shaft and rotate the bearing on the shaft. Make a similar check for noise, looseness or roughness. Inspect the rollers and cage for damage. Replace the bearing if these con-

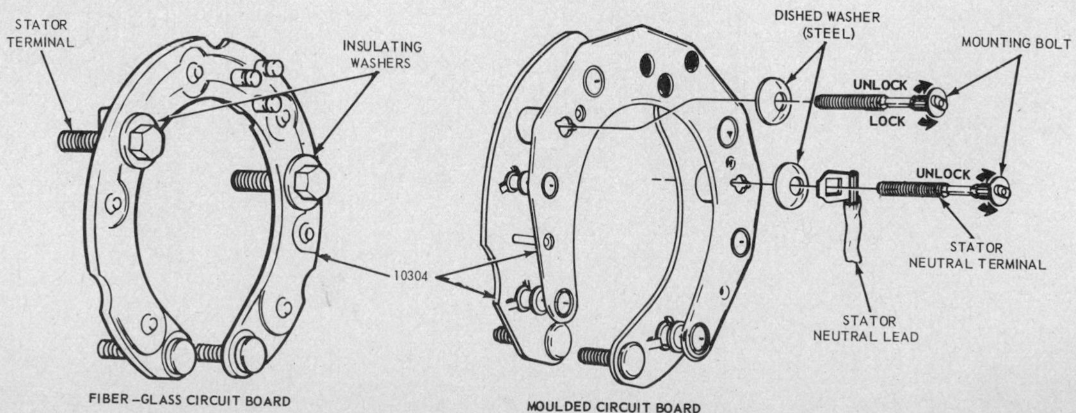

Rectifier assembly (© Ford Motor Co)

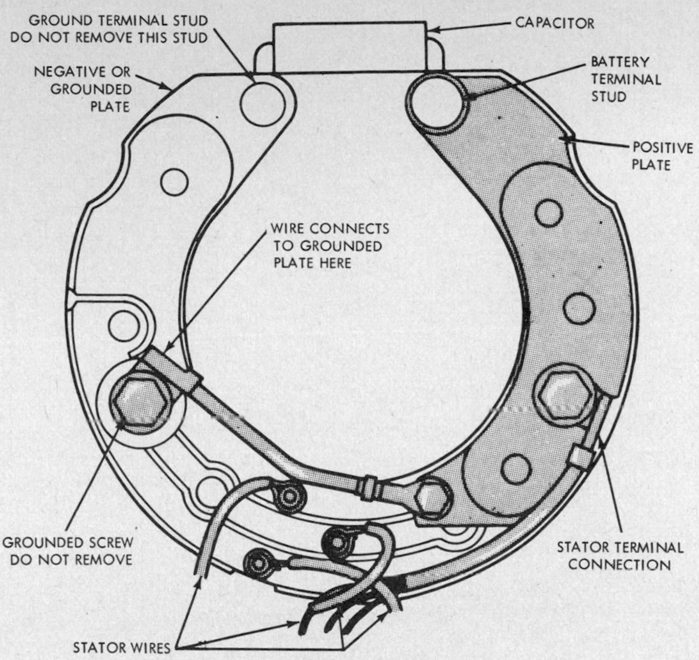

Rectifier terminal locations—61 amp booster diode model
(© Ford Motor Co)

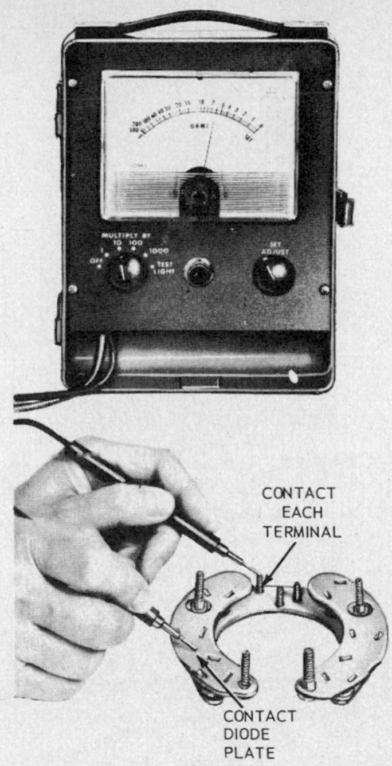

Testing diodes—all except 65 Amp Autolite
(© Ford Motor Co)

ditions exist, or if the lubricant is missing or contaminated.

4. Check both the front and rear housings for cracks.
5. Check all wire leads on both the stator and rotor assemblies for loose soldered connections, and for burned insulation. Solder all poor connections. Replace parts that show burned insulation.
6. Check the slip rings for damaged insulation and runout. If the slip rings are more than 0.0005 in. out of round, take a light cut (minimum diameter limit 1.22 in.) from the face of the rings to true them. If the slip rings are badly damaged, the entire rotor will have to be replaced, as they are serviced as a complete assembly.
7. Replace any parts that are burned or cracked. Replace brushes that are worn to less than 5/16 in. in length. Replace the brush spring if it has less than 7-12 oz. tension.

Field Current Draw Test

NOTE: alternator must be removed from the car.

1. Connect a test ammeter between the alternator frame and the positive post of a 12-volt test battery.
2. Connect a jumper wire between the negative test battery post and the alternator field terminal.
3. Observe the ammeter:
   a. Little or no current flow indicates high brush resistance, open field windings, or high winding resistance.
   b. Current in excess of specifications (approximately 2.9 amps. for most models) indicates shorted or grounded field windings, or brush leads touching.

NOTE: sometimes the alternator produces current output at low engine speeds, but ceases to put out at higher speeds. This can be caused by centrifugal force expanding the rotor windings to the point where they short to ground. Place in a test stand and check field current draw while spinning alternator.

Diode Tests

Disassemble the alternator. Disconnect diode assembly from stator and make tests as illustrated. To test one set of diodes, contact one ohmmeter probe to the diode plate and contact each of the three stator lead terminals with the other probe. Reverse the probes and repeat the test. All six tests (eight for 1971-74 61 amp. Autolite eight-diode models) should show a reading of about 60 ohms in one direction and infinite ohms in the other. If two high readings, or two low readings, are obtained after reversing probes the diode is faulty and must be replaced.

Stator Tests

Disassemble the stator from the alternator assembly and rectifiers. Connect test ohmmeter probes between each pair of stator leads. If the ohmmeter does not indicate equally between each pair of leads, the stator coil is open and must be replaced.

Connect test ohmmeter probes between one of the stator leads and the stator core. The ohmmeter should not show any reading. If it does show continuity, the stator winding is grounded and must be replaced.

NOTE: When doing any type of stator test, don't touch the metal probe or stator leads; this will throw the readings off.

Assembly—Except 65 AMP Autolite

1. Press the front bearing into the front housing boss, putting pressure on outer race only. Install bearing retainer.
2. If the stop ring on the driveshaft was damaged, install a new stop ring. Push the new ring onto the shaft and into the groove.

Caution Do not open the stop ring with snap-ring pliers, as it will be rendered useless.

3. Position the front bearing spacer on the driveshaft against the stop ring.
4. Place the front housing over the shaft, with the bearing positioned in the front housing cavity.
5. Install fan spacer, fan, pulley, lockwasher and retaining nut and tighten nut to 60-100 ft. lbs. holding the drive shaft with an Allen key.
6. If rear bearing was removed, press a new one into rear housing.
7. Assemble brushes, springs, terminal and insulator in the brush holder, retract the brushes and insert a short length of 1/8 in. rod or stiff wire through the hole in the holder to hold the brushes in the retracted position.
8. Position the brush holder assem-

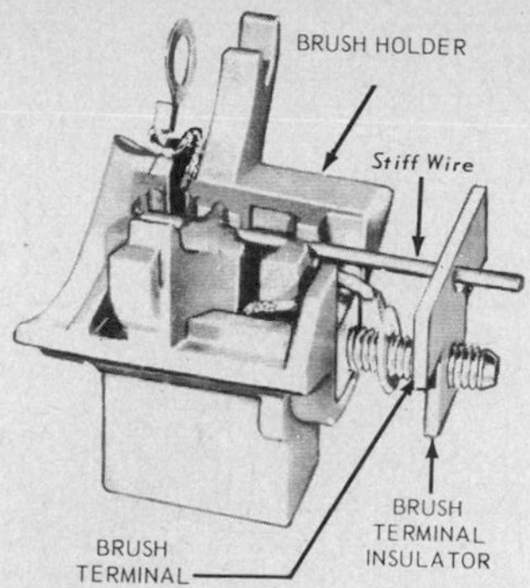

Autolite brush holder assembly
(© Ford Motor Co)

bly in the rear housing and install mounting screws. Position brush leads as illustrated to prevent shorting.

9. Wrap the three stator winding leads around the circuit board terminals and solder them using only rosin core solder and a 100-watt iron. Position the stator neutral lead eyelet on the stator terminal screw and install the screw in the rectifier assembly.

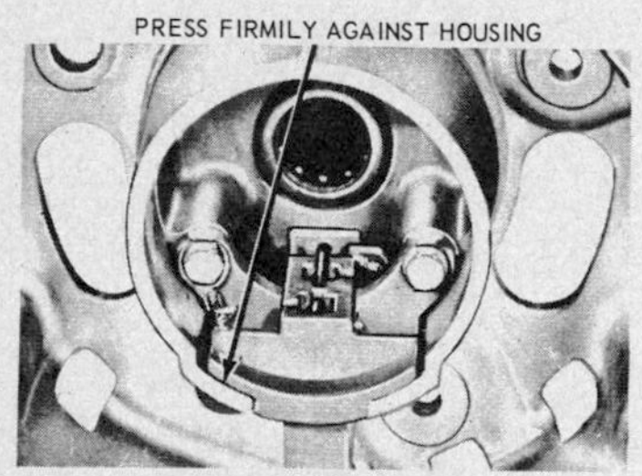

Brush lead positioning
(© Ford Motor Co)

10. A. Exposed Diodes—insert the special screws through the wire lug, dished washers and circuit board. Turn 1/4 turn counterclockwise to lock in place.
    B. Integral Diodes—insert the screws straight through the holes.

NOTE: the dished washers are to be used on *molded* circuit boards only. Using these washers on a *fiber* board will result in a serious short circuit, as only a flat insulating washer between the stator terminal and the board is used on fiber circuit boards.

    C. Booster Diodes—position the stator wire terminal on the stator terminal screw, then position screw on rectifier. Position square insulator over the screw and into the square hole in the rectifier, rotate terminal screw until it locks, then press it in finger-tight. Position the stator wire, then press the terminal screw into the rectifier and insulator with a vise.

11. Place the radio noise suppression condenser on the rectifier terminals. With molded circuit board, install the STA and BAT terminal insulators. With fiber circuit board, place the square stator terminal insulator in the square hole in the sectifier assembly, then position BAT terminal insulator.

Position the stator and recti-

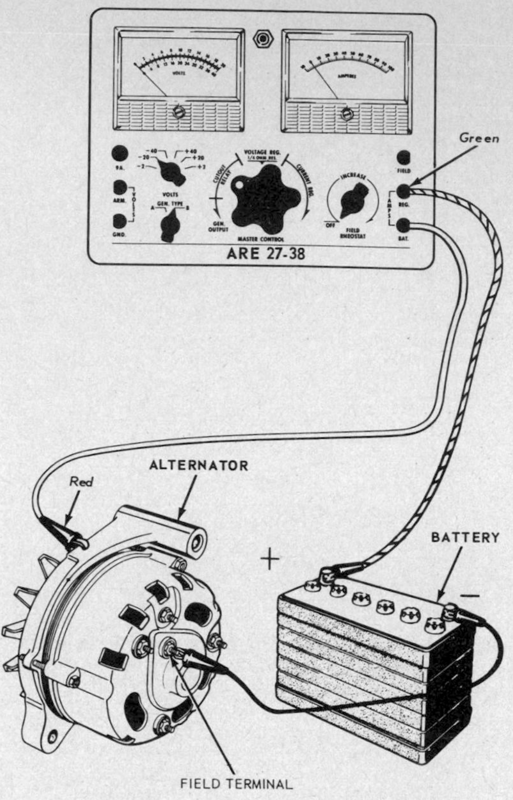

Alternator field current test hook-up
(© Ford Motor Co)

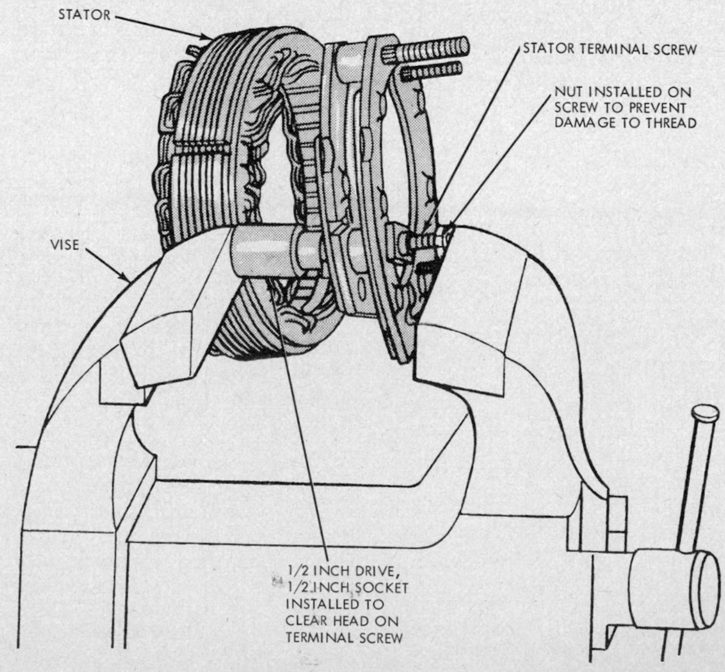

Stator terminal screw removal—61 amp booster diode model
(© Ford Motor Co)

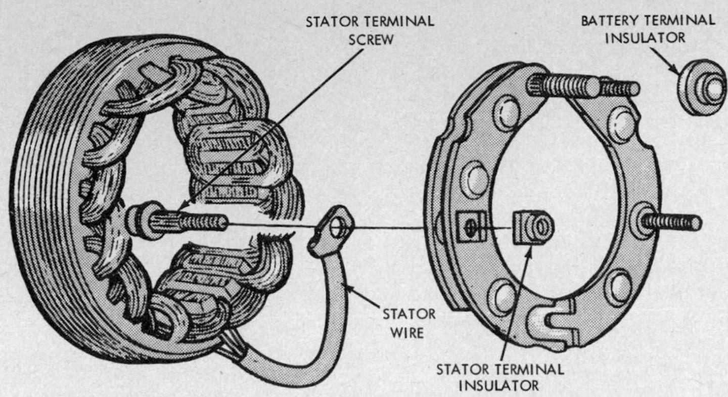

Stator and rectifier assembly—61 amp booster diode model
(© Ford Motor Co)

fier assembly in the rear housing, making sure that all terminal insulators are seated properly in the recesses. Position STA, BAT and FLD insulators on terminal bolts; install nuts.

12. Clean the rear bearing surface of the rotor shaft with a rag, then position rear housing and stator assembly over rotor. Align matchmarks made during disassembly and install through bolts. *Remove brush retracting wire and place a dab of silicone sealer over the hole.*

Disassembly—65 AMP Autolite through 1972

1. Remove the brush holder and cover assembly from the rear housing.
2. Mark both end housings and the stator.
3. Remove the three housing through bolts.
4. Separate the front housing and rotor from the stator and rear housing.
5. Remove the drive pulley nut, lockwasher, flat washer, pulley, fan, fan spacer and rotor from the front housing.
6. Remove the three screws that hold the front bearing retainer and remove the retainer. If the bearing is damaged or has lost its lubricant, support the housing close to the bearing boss and press out the bearing.
7. Remove all the nut and washer assemblies and insulators from the rear housing and remove the rear housing from the stator and rectifier assembly.
8. If necessary, press the rear bearing from the housing, supporting the housing on the inner boss.
9. Unsolder the three stator leads from the rectifier assembly, and separate the stator from the assembly. Use a 200-watt soldering iron.

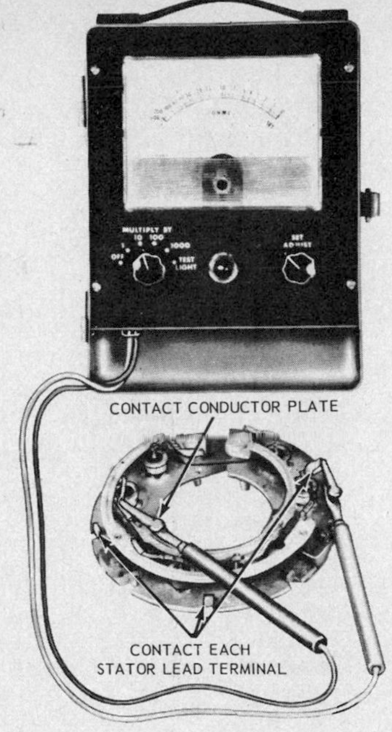

Testing diodes—65 amp Autolite
(© Ford Motor Co)

10. Perform a diode test and an open and grounded stator coil test.

Cleaning and Inspection

Nicks and scratches may be removed from the rotor slip rings by turning down the slip rings. Do not go beyond the minimum diameter limit of 1.22 in. If the slip rings are badly damaged, the entire rotor must be replaced. The rectifier also is serv-

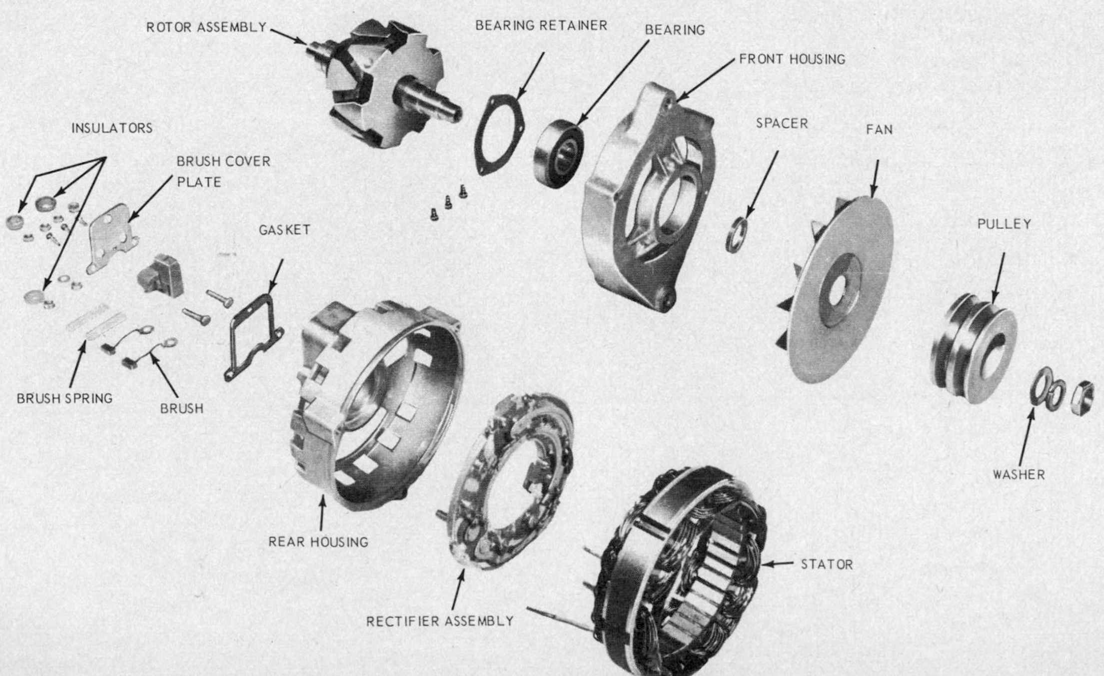

Disassembled view of 65 amp Autolite alternator (used through 1972)
(© Ford Motor Co)

iced as an assembly. See Lower Ampere Alternator Section for test procedures.

Assembly—65 AMP Autolite

1. If the front bearing is being replaced, press the new bearing into the bearing boss, putting pressure on the outer race only. Install the bearing retainer and tighten the retainer screws until the tips of the retainer touch the housing.
2. Position the rectifier assembly to the stator, wrap the three stator leads around the diode plate terminals and solder them using a 200-watt soldering iron.
3. If the rear housing bearing was removed, press in a new bearing from the inside of the housing, putting pressure on the outer race only.
4. Install the BAT-GRD insulator, and position the stator and rectifier assembly in the rear housing.
5. Install the STA (purple) and BAT (red) terminal insulators on the terminal bolts and install the nut and washer assemblies. *Make certain that the shoulders on all insulators, both inside and outside of the housing, are seated properly before tightening the nuts.*
6. Position the front housing over the rotor and install the fan spacer, fan, pulley, flat and lockwashers and nut on the rotor shaft.
7. Wipe the rear bearing surface of the rotor shaft with a clean rag.
8. Position the rotor with the front housing into the stator and rear housing assembly, and align the matchmarks made during disassembly. Seat the machined portion of the stator core into the step in both housings and install the through bolts.
9. If the field brushes have worn to less than $3/8$ in., replace both brushes. Hold the brushes in position by inserting a stiff wire into the brush holder.
10. Position the brush holder assembly into the rear housing and install the three mounting screws. Remove the brush retracting wire and put a dab of silicone cement over the hole.

Brush Replacement—65 AMP Autolite

1. Remove the brush holder and cover assembly from the rear housing.
2. Remove the terminal bolts from the brush holder and cover assembly, then remove the brush assemblies.
3. Position the new brush terminals on the terminal bolts and assemble the terminals, bolts, brush holder washers and nuts. The insulating washer mounts under the FLD terminal nut. The entire brush and cover assembly also is available for service.
4. Depress the brush springs in the brush holder cavities and insert the brushes on top of the springs. Hold the brushes in position by inserting a stiff wire in the brush holder as shown. Position the brush leads as shown.
5. Install the brush holder and cover assembly into the rear housing. Remove the brush retracting wire and put a dab of silicone cement over the hole.

Disassembly—Side Terminal Alternator

1. Matchmark both end housings and the stator to aid in assembly.
2. Remove the 4 housing thru-bolts. Separate the front housing /rotor assembly from the rear housing/stator assembly. Use the screwdriver slots provided for this purpose.

Caution Do not separate the rear housing and stator at this point.

3. Remove the drive pulley nut with a socket and an allen wrench.
4. Withdraw the lockwasher, pulley, cooling fan, and spacer from the rotor shaft.
5. Pull the rotor shaft assembly out of the front housing. Take the spacer off the shaft.
6. Unfasten the 3 screws which secure the bearing to the front housing. Remove the bearing by pressing it out of the housing, while it is being supported close to the bearing boss.

NOTE: *It is only necessary to remove the bearing if it is damaged or has lost its lubricant.*

7. Use a *200-watt* soldering iron to unsolder the 3 stator leads from the rectifier.

Caution Using a hotter iron or a soldering gun will damage the rectifier.

8. Remove the stator from the housing.
9. Use the 200-watt soldering iron to unsolder the brush holder lead from the rectifier.
10. Unfasten the screw which secures the capacitor lead to the rectifier.
11. Unfasten the 4 screws which secure the rectifier to the rear housing.
12. Remove the two terminal nuts, complete with insulators, from the outside of the housing.

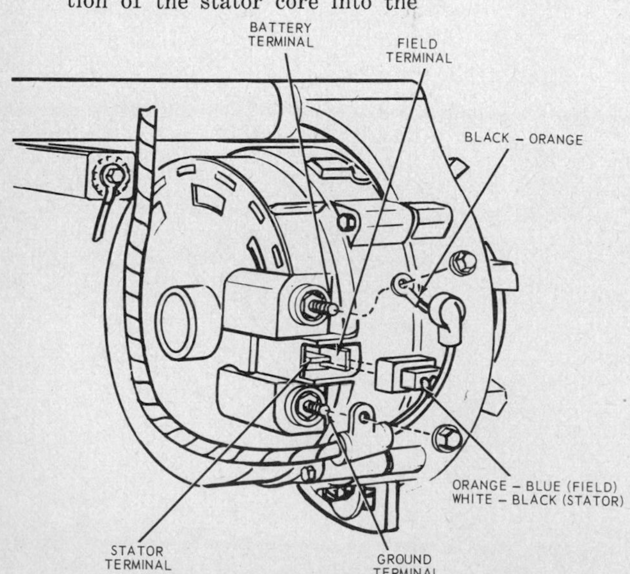

Wiring connections—Ford side terminal alternator
(© Ford Motor Co)

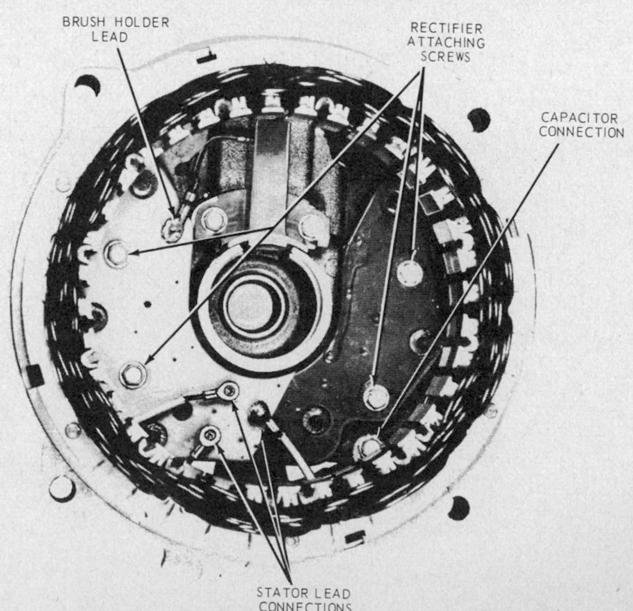

Stator lead connections—Ford side terminal alternator
(© Ford Motor Co)

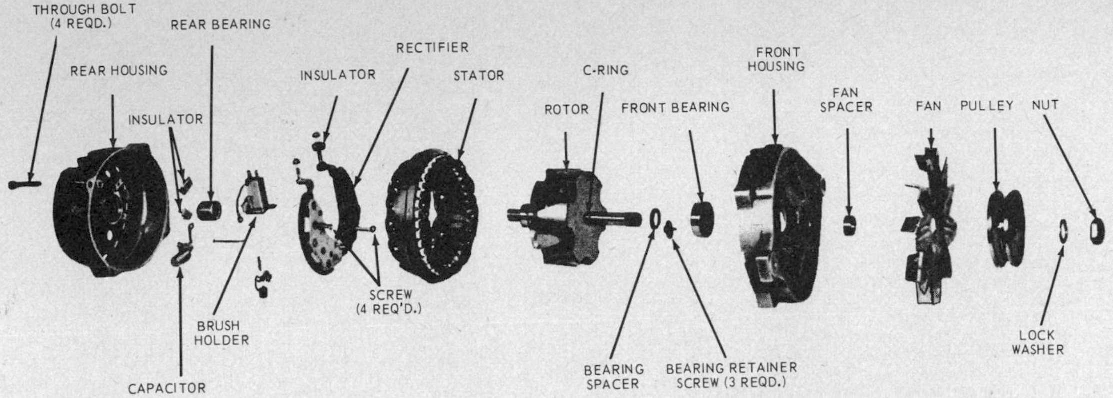

Ford side terminal alternator—exploded view (© Ford Motor Co)

13. Withdraw the rectifier assembly from the housing.
14. Unfasten the two brush holder securing screws and withdraw it, with brushes, from the housing. Clean off any sealer remaining on the housing or brush holder.
15. Remove the screw which secures the capacitor to the housing and remove the capacitor.
16. Remove the bearing from the rear housing, as necessary, in the same manner as detailed for the front bearing in Step 6.

Cleaning and Inspection

Do not clean the rotor, stator, or the bearings in solvent; wipe them with a clean cloth instead.

Inspect for damaged or worn parts, and replace as necessary.

Proper installation of brush holder and rectifier insulators —Ford side terminal alternator
(© Ford Motor Co)

Assembly—Side Terminal Alternator

1. If it is to be replaced, press a new bearing into the front housing, being careful to apply pressure to its outer race only.
2. Secure the bearing with its retaining screws.
3. Fit the inner spacer on the rotor shaft, then install the shaft through the front housing and bearing.
4. Place the spacer, fan, pulley, and lockwasher on the front of the rotor shaft.
5. Tighten the retaining nut to 60-100 ft lbs, while holding the shaft with an allen wrench.
6. If it was to be replaced, press the new bearing in, from the inside of the rear housing, so that it is flush with the boss on its outer surface.
7. Place the brush terminal on the brush holder, and install the springs and brushes in the holder. Temporarily retract the brushes with a stiff piece of wire.
8. Place the brush holder in the rear housing and loosely secure it with its attaching screws. Slide the brush holder toward the shaft opening and tighten the screws.
9. Secure the capacitor to the rear housing with its retaining screw.
10. Lay the two rectifier insulators over the two bosses on the rear housing. The insulator tabs fit into the recesses at the ends of the bosses.
11. Position the insulator on the terminal (large) marked "BAT" on the rectifier. Install the rectifier in the rear housing. Fit the external insulator over the "BAT" terminal. Finger-tighten the nuts on the "BAT" and "GRD" terminals.
12. Loosely install the 4 rectifier securing screws.
13. First tighten the "BAT" and "GRD" terminal nuts and then tighten the rectifier securing screws.
14. Connect the capacitor lead to the rectifier and install its securing screw.
15. Push the end of the brush holder lead on the rectifier pin and solder it using a *200-watt* soldering iron.
16. Align the matchmarks that you made on the stator and rear housing during disassembly. Push the ends of the 3 stator leads over the pins on the rectifier and solder them securely, using a *200-watt* soldering iron.

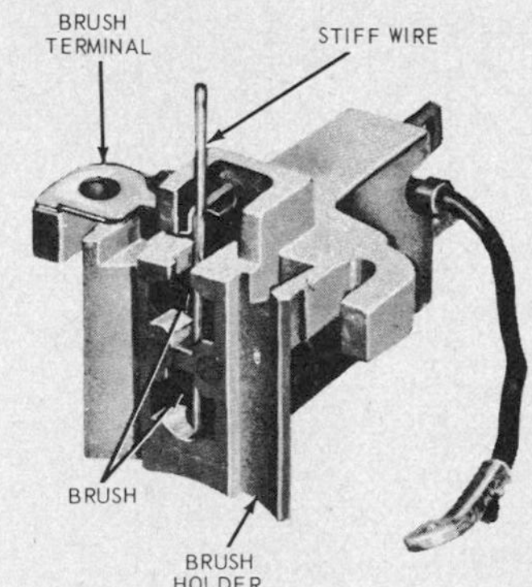

Brush holder—Ford side terminal alternator
(© Ford Motor Co)

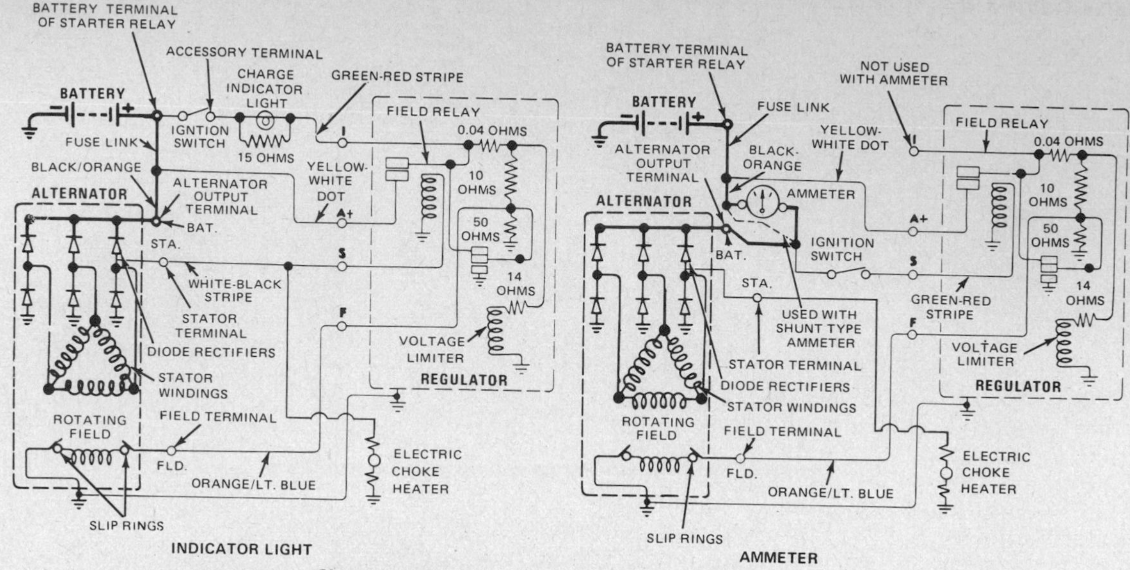

Charging circuit—Ford 90 amp side terminal alternator
(© Ford Motor Co)

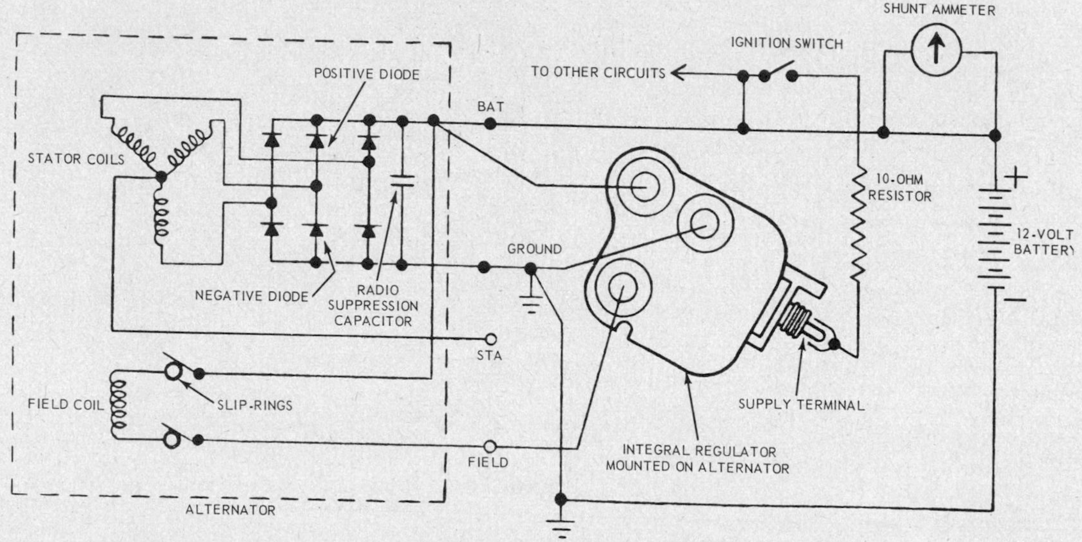

Charging system schematic with integral regulator (© Ford Motor Co)

17. Assemble the front housing and rotor to the rear housing and stator, by aligning the matchmarks made during disassembly. Insert the thru-bolts, tightening the two opposing bolts first and then the two remaining bolts.
18. Rotate the fan and pulley to check for any binding in the alternator.
19. Withdraw the wire which was inserted to keep the brushes retracted.
20. Seal the hole with a small amount of waterproof cement. Do not allow cement to run down the hole.

Brush Replacement—Side Terminal Alternator

1. Perform Steps 1 and 2 of the side terminal alternator disassembly procedure above; note the Caution.
2. Use a *200-watt* soldering iron to unsolder the brush holder lead from the rectifier.

Caution Do not use a hotter iron or a soldering gun; damage to the rectifier will result.

3. Unfasten the brush holder retaining screws. Lift the holder out of the housing.
4. Clean any sealing compound out of the housing and brush holder.

Installation is performed in the following order:

1. Place the brush holder with new brushes installed in the rear housing.
2. Insert a stiff piece of wire to retract the brushes through the hole, in the rear housing, which is provided for this purpose.
3. Loosely install the brush holder securing screws. Push the holder toward the rotor shaft and tighten the screws.
4. Push the brush holder lead connector over the rectifier pin and solder it in place with a *200-watt* soldering iron.
5. Perform Steps 17-19 of the side terminal alternator assembly procedure given above.

Autolite Alternator with Integral Regulator

Description

In 1969-70, some vehicles were equipped with an Autolite alternator having an integral regulator mounted to the rear end housing. The regulator is a hybrid unit featuring use of solid state integrated circuits. These circuits may consist of transistors, diodes and resistors. The unusual feature of this type of microelectronic circuit is that the entire circuit is within a silicone crystal approximately ⅛ in. square. Because of the small size of the circuit, it is not repairable or adjustable and must be replaced as a unit if found to be defective. It should be noted that the

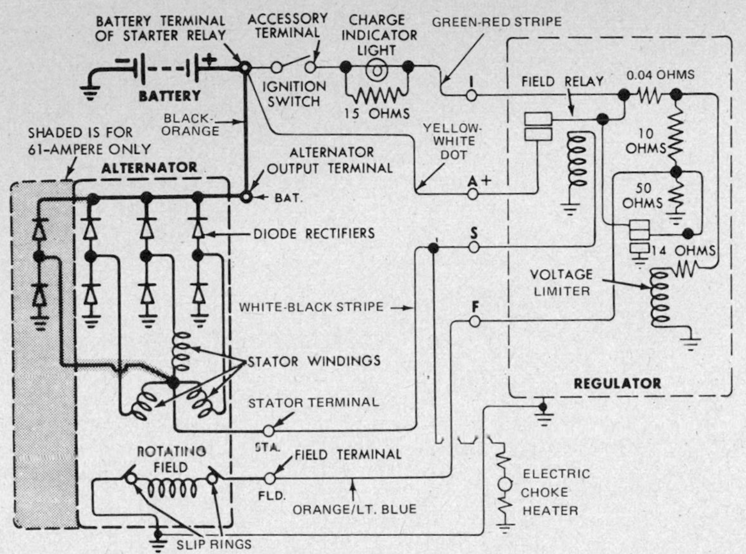

Charging system schematic with transistor regulator and charging light (© Ford Motor Co)

size of the regulator housing is dictated only by the fact that some means of connecting the regulator to the alternator is necessary. Overhaul is the same as for other Autolite alternators.

Troubleshooting

NOTE: see the "Preliminary Charging System Inspection" section before proceeding further.

Fusible Links

1. Check the fusible link located between the starter relay and the alternator. Replace the link if it is burned or open.

Output Test

1. Place transmission in Neutral or Park.
2. Remove the positive battery cable and install a battery adapter switch in the line.
3. Attach one lead of a test voltmeter to the negative battery post and the other test lead to the circuit side of the adapter switch.
4. Connect a test ammeter to each side of the adapter switch, so that charging current will go through the ammeter when the switch is opened.
5. Connect a jumper wire between the alternator frame and the integral regulator field terminal (cover plug removed).
6. Close adapter switch, start engine and open adapter switch.
7. Running engine at 2,000 rpm, observe voltmeter and ammeter. At 15 volts indicated, the ammeter should read 50-57 amps. If so, and there is still a no-charge condition, the regulator is probably faulty and must be replaced. An output 2-8 amps. below 50 amps. usually indicates an open diode rectifier, while an output 10-15 amps. below minimum specifications usually indicates a shorted diode. An alternator with a shorted diode usually will whine at idle speed.

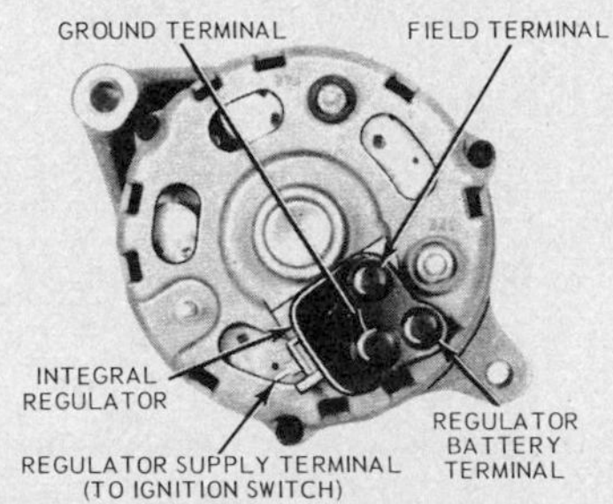

Alternator with integral regulator (© Ford Motor Co)

Field Test (Voltmeter)

1. Turn ignition switch to OFF position.
2. Remove wire from regulator supply terminal.
3. Remove cover plug from regulator field terminal and connect one test voltmeter lead to this terminal. A ¼ ohm resistor should be in the circuit.
4. Connect the other test voltmeter lead to a good engine ground.

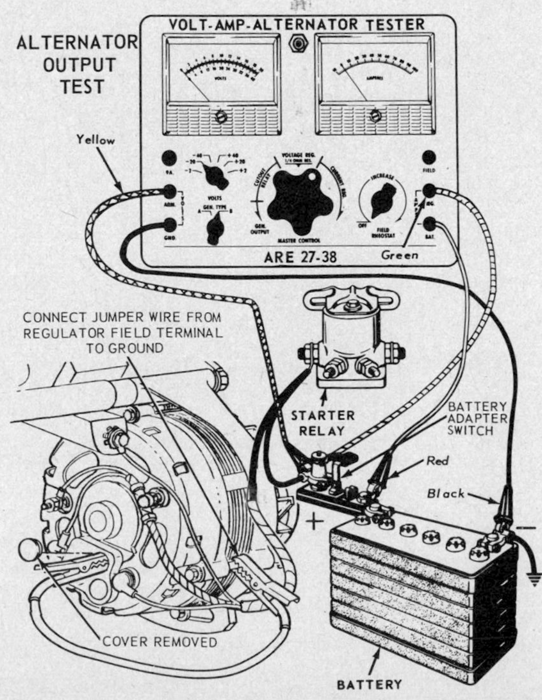

Output test hook-up—integral regulator alternator (© Ford Motor Co)

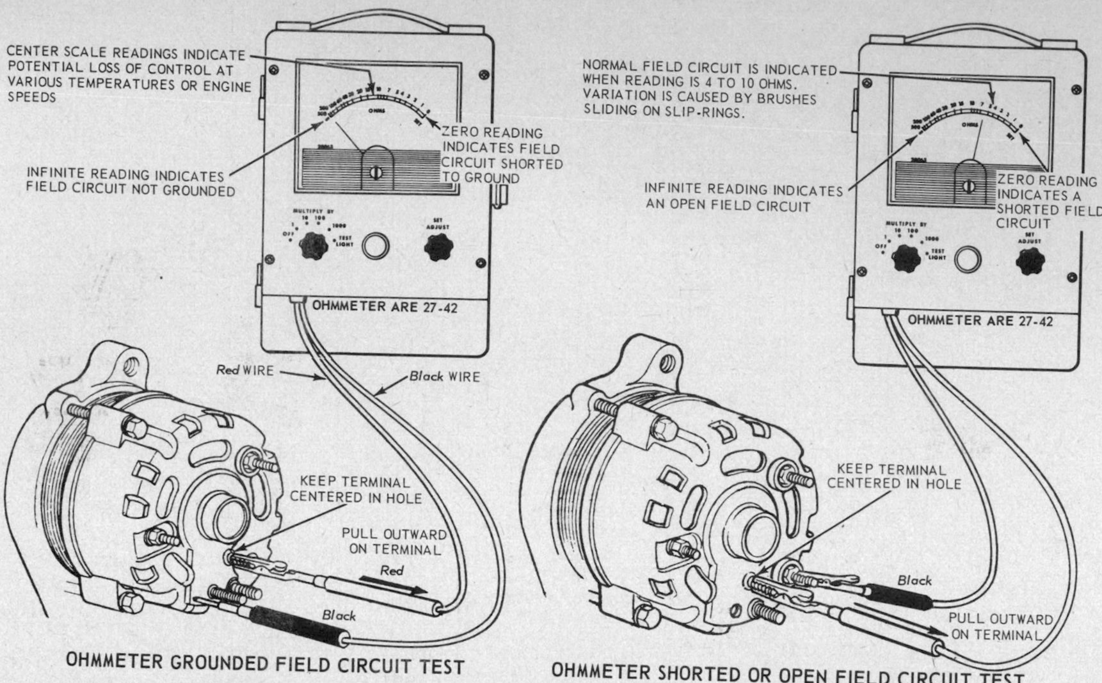

Field circuit test hook-ups with ohmmeter—integral regulator alternator (© Ford Motor Co)

5. The voltmeter should read 12 volts. If *no* voltage is present, the field circuit is open or grounded.
6. If voltmeter reads more than 1 volt, but still less than battery voltage, there is probably a partial ground in the alternator field circuit and the circuit should be checked with an ohmmeter.

Field Test (Ohmmeter)

1. Disconnect battery ground cable; remove alternator from car.
2. Remove the regulator from the alternator (covered later).
3. Make the ohmmeter tests as illustrated. If any of the tests indicates a field circuit problem, disassemble the alternator to further isolate the trouble.
   a. Contact each ohmmeter probe to a slip ring. Resistance should be 4-5 ohms. A higher reading indicates a damaged slip ring soldered connection or a broken wire. A lower reading indicates a shorted wire or slip ring assembly.
   b. Contact one ohmmeter probe to a slip ring and the other probe to the rotor shaft. Any reading other than infinite ohms indicates a short to ground. If neither of these tests (A and B) isolates the trouble, the brushes or brush assembly are the probable cause.

Voltage Limiter Test

1. Check the battery specific gravity. If it is not at least 1.230, charge the battery or install a charged battery for the test.
2. Make sure all lights and accessories are turned off, including such items as dome lights and radio.
3. Make the test connections as illustrated.
4. Place transmission in Neutral or Park, close battery adapter switch and start the engine.
5. Open the battery adapter switch and operate engine at 2,000 rpm for 5 minutes. The voltmeter should read 13.3-15.3 volts.
6. If voltage does not rise above 12 volts, perform a regulator supply voltage test to determine whether or not the regulator is getting voltage from the battery. Before replacing a regulator, check the wiring of the entire charging system for shorts, opens, or high resistance connections.

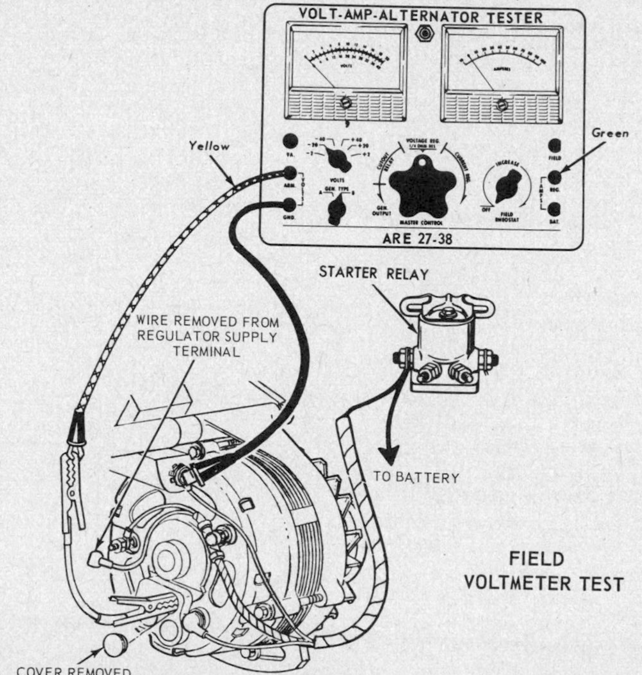

Field voltmeter test hook-up—integral regulator alternator (© Ford Motor Co)

Regulator Supply Voltage Test

The regulator is "turned on" by the application of battery voltage through a 10 ohm resistor wire. If the supply circuit is defective, the regulator will not function and the alternator will not put out current.

1. Connect a 12-volt test light or

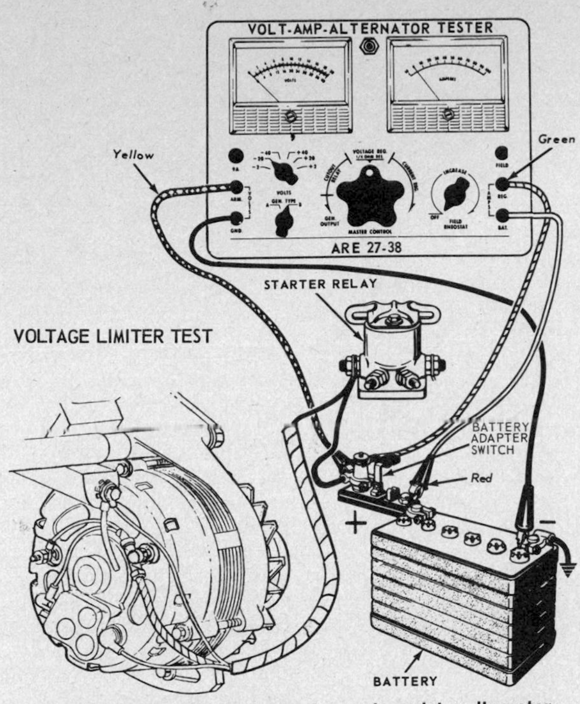

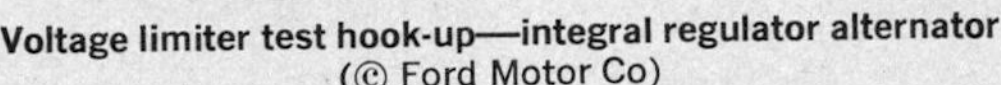
Voltage limiter test hook-up—integral regulator alternator
(© Ford Motor Co)

VOLT-AMP-ALTERNATOR TESTER
Yellow
ARE 27-38
WIRE REMOVED FROM REGULATOR SUPPLY TERMINAL
SUPPLY VOLTAGE TEST
NO. 12 COPPER WIRE SOLDERED TO CLIP

Supply voltage test hook-up—integral regulator alternator
(© Ford Motor Co)

voltmeter between the regulator supply lead and ground.

2. Turn on the ignition switch. The test light should glow or the volmeter indicate. If not, the supply circuit should be checked back to the battery, especially the resistance wire.

Overhaul

The overhaul procedures for the alternator are the same as for the Ford Autolite electro-mechanical alternator.

The Motorola System

The Motorola alternator is designed to pass all the DC current through an isolation diode, or diodes, mounted in an external aluminum heat sink.

Due to the nature of the alternator, residual magnetism is at near zero when the unit is at rest. It is, therefore, necessary to provide some small current to excite the field prior to generating current. With Motorola, this priming current is supplied by means of a 75 ohm resistance unit between the ignition coil and the alternator (inside the regulator). It is quite important that this resistance unit be checked and found satisfactory before proceeding with subsequent tests.

The charge indicator light on some cars operates in the same way as this resistor by furnishing the necessary initial field starting current. If this resistor circuit is open (a burned out indicator lamp) on some models, the alternator will not function. On later models, a resistor is placed in parallel with the bulb to provide excitation current if the bulb burns out.

The regulator is a sealed unit and should require no adjustment. It is therefore, recommended that nonfunctioning regulators be replaced.

Troubleshooting

NOTE: see the "Preliminary Charging System Inspection" section before proceeding further.

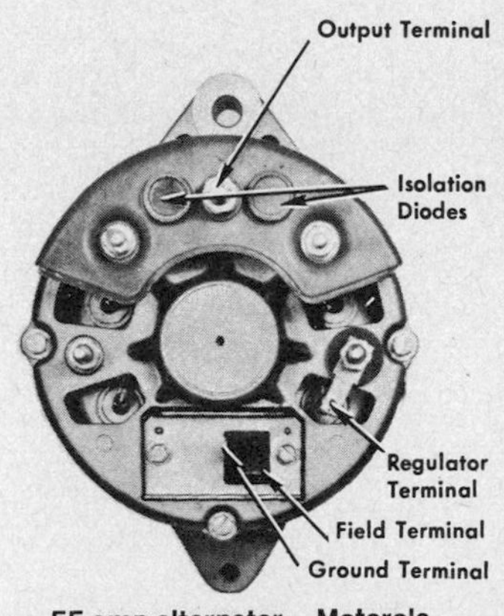

55 amp alternator—Motorola
(© American Motors Corp)

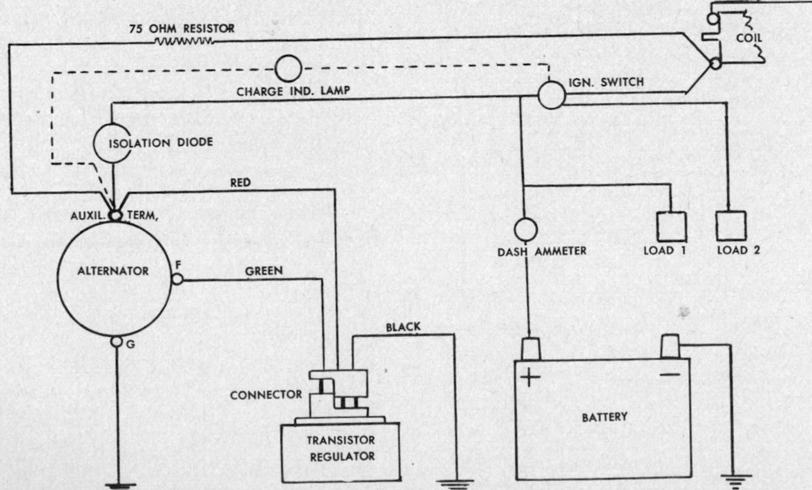

Typical Motorola alternator system charging circuit
(© American Motors Corp)

Fusible Link Test

There are many fuse links in the car, however, the fuse link located in the wiring between the battery terminal of the horn relay to the main wire harness is the only one that concerns the charging system. This link protects the entire wiring harness. If it fails, all the electrical systems will fail to function.

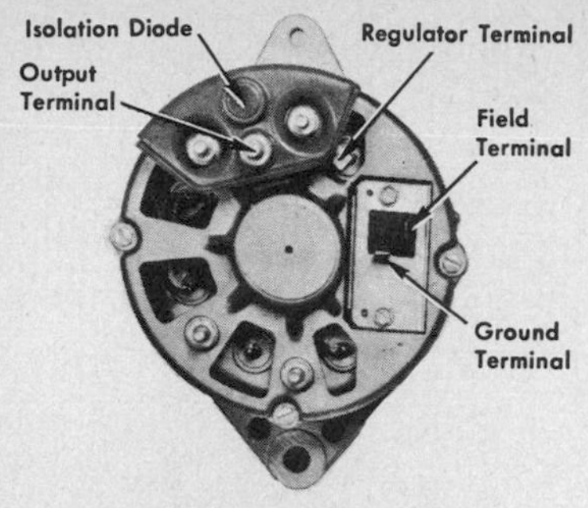

35 amp alternator—Motorola
(© American Motors Corp)

Charging System Operation

NOTE: if the current indicator is to give an accurate reading, the battery cables must be of the same gauge and length as the original equipment.

1. With the engine running and all electrical systems off, place a current indicator over the positive battery cable.
2. If a charge of about 5 amps is recorded, the charging system is working. If a draw of about 5 amps is recorded, the system is not working. The needle moves toward the battery when a charge condition is indicated, and away from the battery when a draw condition is indicated. If a draw is indicated, continue to the next testing procedure. If an overcharge of 10-15 amps is indicated, check for a faulty regulator, or a bad ground at the regulator or the alternator.

Testing the Ignition Switch to Regulator Circuit

1. Disconnect the regulator wires from the regulator.
2. Turn on the key. Using a test light or voltmeter, check for current between the voltage supply wire and ground. This wire is usually orange and has another wire connected to it, usually blue or orange with a tracer.
3. If current is present, this part of the system is OK. If no voltage is present, check for broken or shorted wiring, a bad indicator bulb, a bad fuse in the fuse panel, or a bad connection at the ignition switch or on the battery side of the starter relay.

Isolation Test

This test determines whether the regulator or the alternator is faulty, after the rest of the circuit is found to be in good working order.

1. Disconnect the regulator wiring harness from the regulator.
2. Connect a jumper wire from the voltage supply wire from the battery, orange, to the field wire for the alternator, green.
3. Connect a voltmeter to the battery. The positive voltmeter lead goes to the positive terminal and the negative lead to the negative terminal. Record the reading on the voltmeter.
4. Turn off all of the electrical systems and start the engine. Do not race the engine.
5. Gradually increase engine speed to 1500-2000 rpm. The voltmeter reading should increase above the previously recorded battery voltage reading by at least one to two volts. If there is no increase, the alternator is not working correctly. If there is an increase the voltage regulator needs to be replaced.

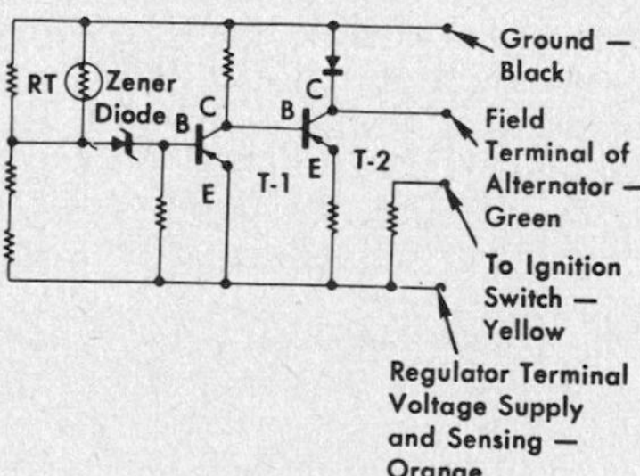

Voltage regulator circuit. RT is a thermistor that regulates voltage according to temperature
(© American Motors Corp)

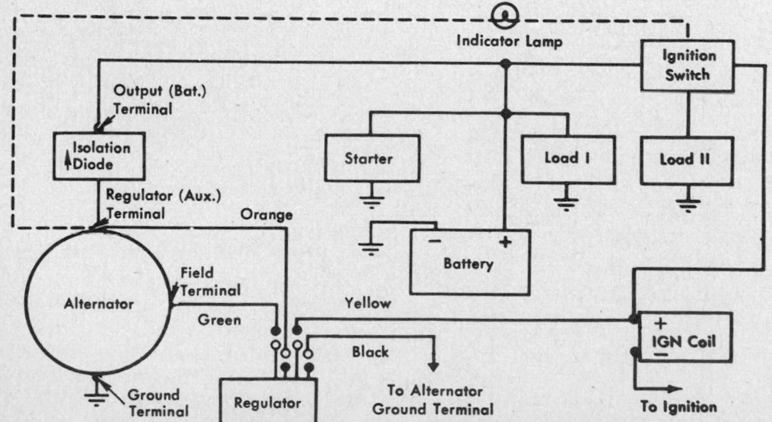

Motorola circuit diagram—1970 American Motors illustrated
(© American Motors Corp)

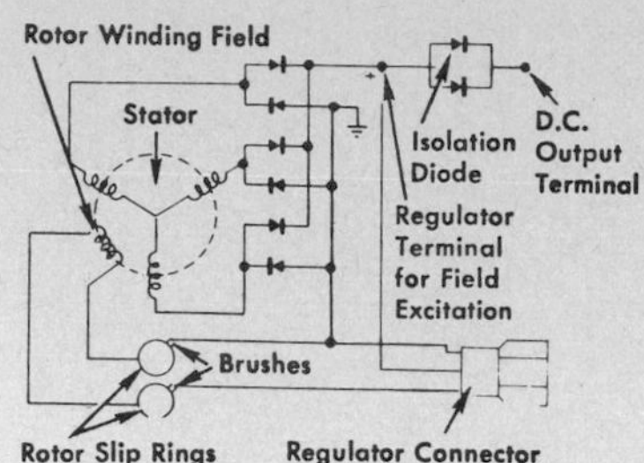

Alternator circuit—40 and 55 amp models
(© American Motors Corp)

Field Current Draw Test

1. With battery disconnected, disconnect the wires from the alternator output terminal and the alternator field terminal.
2. With a field rheostat in the open position, connect its leads to the disconnected alternator output wire and to the positive lead of the test ammeter.
3. Connect the negative ammeter lead to the alternator field terminal.
4. Connect the positive voltmeter lead to the alternator field terminal.
5. Connect the negative voltmeter lead to the alternator ground terminal.
6. Reconnect the battery.
7. Start and run the engine at fast idle.
8. Adjust field rheostat to closed position, then note the voltmeter and ammeter readings.
9. Adjust field rheostat control to the open position.
10. Compare the readings obtained in Step 8 with manufacturers' specifications.
11. If readings are zero, there is an indication of trouble in the field coil, or the connections between field coil and slip ring.
12. If readings are low, there is probable trouble in the slip rings or brushes.
13. If readings are high, the field coil is probably shorted.
14. If readings are normal, on an alternator which failed to produce its rated output, the probable cause lies in the stator or diodes. Replace the alternator in this case.

Alternator Output Test beginning 1971 (Alternator In Car)

1. Connect a voltmeter to the battery.
2. Start the engine and turn the lights on low beam.
3. Run the engine at 1000 RPM and observe the voltage reading for two minutes. If the voltage remains above 13 V, the alternator and regulator are ok. If not, proceed to the Regulator Bypass Test to determine which component is at fault.

Field Draw (Amperage) Test, beginning 1971

This test determines if there is an open or short circuit in the alternator brush circuit.

1. Disconnect the voltage regulator.
2. Connect an ammeter between the positive battery post and the green wire leading to the insulated brush terminal of the alternator. Ground the black wire.
3. Turn the alternator rotor slowly by hand. The ammeter should indicate between 1½ and 3 amperes. If the reading varies, the slip rings require cleaning. If the amperage is too high, remove the brush assembly and do continuity and isolation tests on it. Check the rotor field windings if the field draw is too low or high after testing the brush assembly and cleaning the slip rings.

Alternator Output (Regulator Bypass) Test, beginning 1972

This test will determine whether the alternator or voltage regulator is at fault for a no or low charge condition.

1. Disconnect the voltage regulator and perform the Field Draw Test. After completing it, disconnect the ammeter.
2. Connect the voltmeter to the battery and start the engine and run it at idle.
3. Connect an ammeter between the battery positive post and the insulated brush on the alternator.
4. Observe the voltage reading while slowly increasing the engine RPM. If 16 volts can be obtained, the alternator is not bad. Do not exceed sixteen volts or component damage may occur. It may take a few minutes for a dead battery to achieve a reading of 16 volts.
5. If the reading does not reach 16 volts then the fault is in the alternator.

Diode Trio Test, beginning 1971 (on car)

This test will check the field diode assembly for marginal defects which may not affect alternator performance but may cause the dash indicator light to glow.

1. Do the Regulator Bypass Test. If 16 volts can not be obtained from the alternator, this test's results will not be valid.
2. Start and idle the engine. Connect a voltmeter to the alternator (if no reading is obtained, switch the test leads).
3. Turn on the lights and blower (heater) unit and let them operate for about 2 minutes, then turn them off.

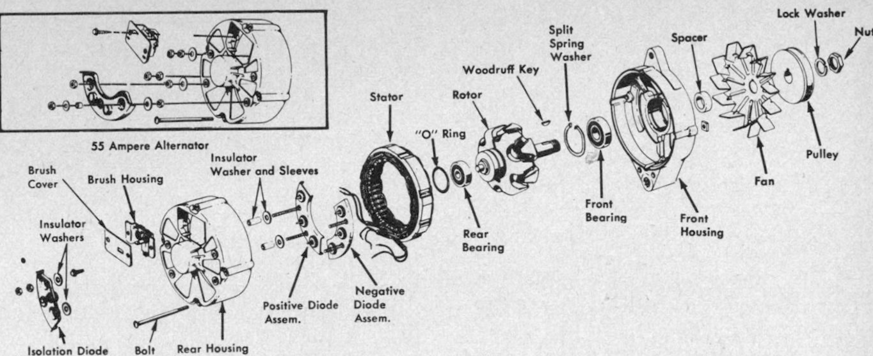

Motorola alternator—exploded view
(© American Motors Corp)

4. Check the meter reading. A good diode will read from zero to 0.2 volts. A reading above this indicates that the diodes are deteriorating. It is not necessary to replace them until the reading is above 0.6 volts.
5. If the meter pulsates, either the diode trio, the positive diode, or the soldered connections between them is beginning to break down. In either case the alternator will have to be disassembled and the diode tested.
6. If the reading is over 0.6 V. but the alternator output is alright, remove the diode trio for a bench test.
7. If the reading is less than 0.6 V. and the diode trio appears to be functioning properly, and the indicator light still glows, check the wiring connections for corrosion.

Alternator Disassembly

1. Remove the two self-tapping screws and the cover. Pull the brush assembly straight up to clear the locating pins, then lift out the brush assembly.
2. Remove the two locknuts and remove the isolation diode assembly from the rear housing on models through 1971.
3. Scribe a matchmark across the front housing, stator, and rear housing. Remove the four thru-bolts and nuts, then carefully separate the rear housing and strator from the front housing using two screwdrivers in the slots provided.

Caution Do not insert screwdrivers deeper than 1/16 in., to avoid damaging stator winding.

4. Remove the four locknuts and insulating washers that hold the stator and diode assembly, then separate the assembly from the rear housing. Avoid bending the stator wires—do not unsolder the wires without using pliers as a heat sink.

Starting 1971, AMC dropped the isolation diode and switched to a field diode. Two types are used: the board type and the potted type.

To remove the board type:

a. Remove the diode assembly attaching nuts.
b. Separate the stator from the end housing.
c. Unsolder the lead at each positive diode and remove the attaching nut and withdraw the diode.

To remove the potted type:

a. Separate the stator and diode assemblies from the rear housing.
b. Unsolder the leads at the diode trio and withdraw the unit.

To install the board type, use pliers as a heat sink between the solder point and the positive diode; use a rosin core solder and only as much heat as is necessary.

To install the potted type, make sure that the diode connections are toward the outside of the alternator. Use only as much heat as necessary and a rosin core solder.

5. There is no reason to remove the rotor from the front housing unless there is a defect in the field coil or front bearing. Front and

Separating Motorola alternator housing
(© American Motors Corp)

rear bearings are lubricated for life and sealed and, as a rule, do not go bad unless the drive belt has been adjusted with too much tension. If the rotor must be removed, use a puller to remove the front drive pulley, then unseat the split-ring washer using long-nose pliers through the front housing to compress the washer while pulling on the rotor. Tap the rotor shaft lightly to remove the rotor and front bearing, then reach in and remove the split-ring washer. Bearings must be removed using a puller and new bearings must be pressed into place.

Bench Tests

Isolation Diode Circuit Test through 1971

Excessive leakage through the isolation diode will discharge the battery. The rate of discharge depends upon the degree of leakage. Normal and tolerable leakage is less than .001 amperes.

1. To check isolation diode leakage, connect the regulator to the battery. Do not operate the alternator.
2. Measure the voltage from auxiliary terminal F to ground terminal G. The voltage appearing at the auxiliary terminal should not exceed 0.1 volt. Voltage greater than this indicates leakage through the isolation diode. Check the isolation diode with a commercial diode tester, or with a 12-volt DC test lamp.

Isolation diode—35 amp models
(© American Motors Corp)

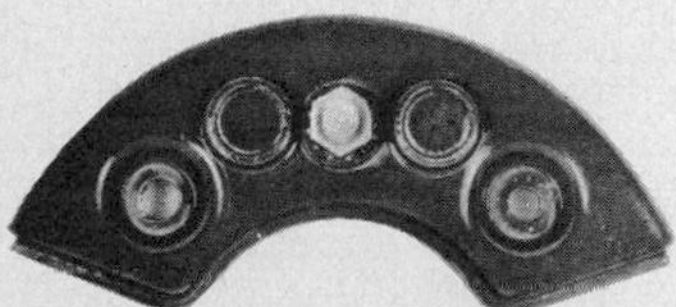

Isolation diodes—55 amp models
(© American Motors Corp)

Isolation Diode Test through 1971

If a commercial diode tester is not available, use a 12-volt DC test lamp only, otherwise diodes can be damaged.

1. Connect the test lamp to output terminal and auxiliary terminal. Then reverse the test probes. Test lamp should light in one direction only. If test light lights in both directions, the isolation diode is shorted. If lamp won't light in either direction, the diode is open.

Rotor Leakage Test

This is a check of the field coil for leakage or shorts to rotor poles. An ohmmeter or test lamp (12V or 120V) may be used.

1. Remove the brush assembly to gain access to rotor slip rings.
2. Connect ohmmeter or test lamp probes to one of the slip rings and the ground terminal, points G and P.

Ohmmeter resistance should be infinite or test lamp should not light. If condition is contrary, leakage or a short exists between field coil and rotor.

Repeat test after rotor has been removed from the alternator to pinpoint findings.

Rotor leakage test points

Stator Coil Leak and Continuity Test

This check is for shorts or leakage between stator coil windings. The 30 and 40 amp. alternators use a Wye-Type winding. 45 ampere models use a Delta type winding.

Wye Type (30, 37, and 40 Amp Models)

1. Separate winding ends. An ohmmeter or 12-volt DC test lamp may be used.
2. Connect one lead of the ohmmeter or test lamp to point 1. Connect the other test lead to point 2 and then to point 3. Ohmmeter reading should be infinite or the test lamp should not light.
3. Connect test leads to points 2 and 3. Ohmmeter reading should be infinite, or the test lamp should not light.

In test 2 or test 3, if the test results are contrary, excess leakage or a short exists between stator windings; replace the stator.

4. Check continuity by measuring the resistance of each winding in the stator with an ohmmeter, between test points, 1 to 1A, 2 to 2A and 3 to 3A.

   Resistance should be very low (about 0.1 ohm).

Never replace stator until all other components have been checked and proven satisfactory.

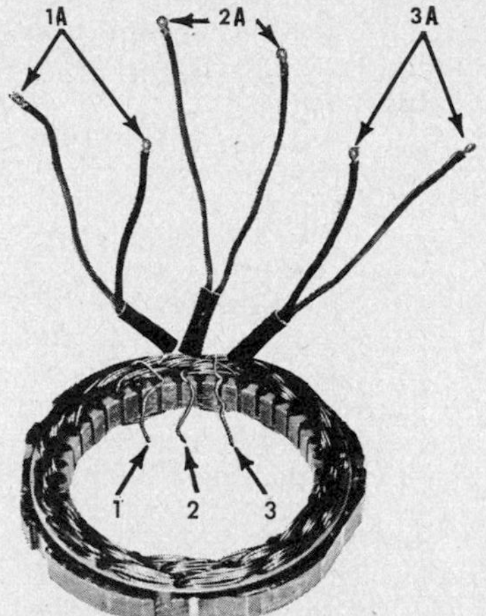

Stator coil test points (Wye type)

Delta Type (45, 55, and 62 Amp Models)

1. Separate stator winding ends. An ohmmeter or 12-volt DC test lamp may be used.
2. Connect one lead of the ohmmeter or test lamp to point 4. Connect

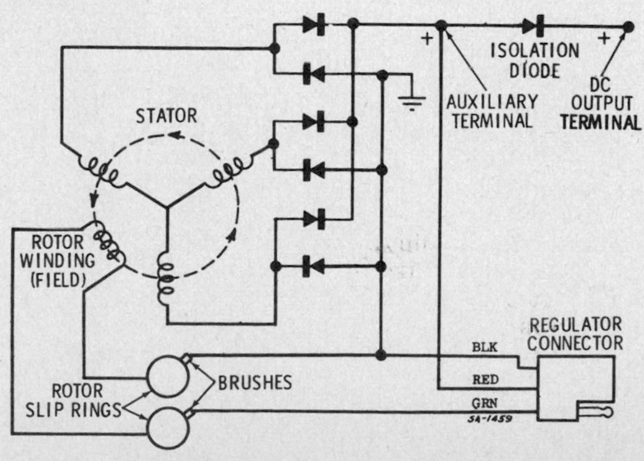

Wye-type circuit (used through 1970)

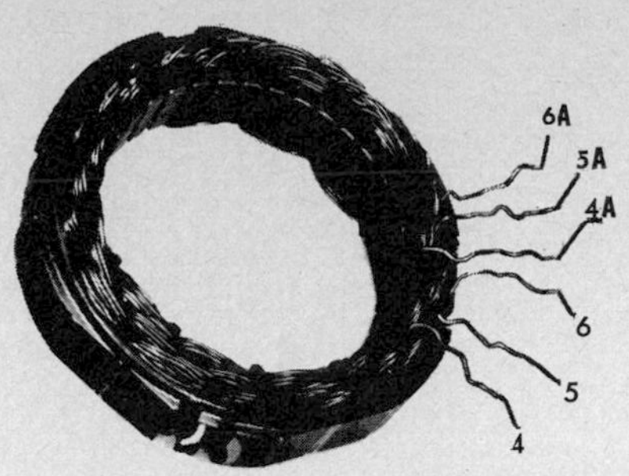

Stator coil test points (delta type)

the other test lead to point 5 and then to point 6. Ohmmeter reading should be infinite or the test lamp should not light.
3. Connect test leads to test points 5 and 6. Ohmmeter reading should be infinite, or the test lamp should not light.

In test 2 or test 3, if the test results are contrary, excess leakage or a short exists between stator windings; replace the stator.

4. Check continuity by measuring the resistance of each winding in the stator with an ohmmeter placed between test points 4 to 4A, 5 to 5A and 6 to 6A.
   Resistance should be very low (about 0.1 ohm).

Never replace stator until all other components have been checked and proven satisfactory.

Out-of-Circuit Rectifier Diode Test

If a commercial diode tester is not available, check the diodes with a 12-volt DC test lamp only.

Caution When unsoldering the stator wires from the rectifier diode assembly, provide a heat sink to the diode terminal with a pair of longnosed pliers.

1. Connect test lamp probes to diode terminal and diode plate stud, then reverse test lamp probes. The test light should light in one direction but not in the other.
   If the test lamp lights in both directions, the diode is shorted. If test lamp does not light in either direction, the diode is open.
   Test the remaining diodes of the assembly in the same manner. Replace entire assembly if one of the diodes is found to be bad.

NOTE: *Starting 1974, use a diode tester that draws a one amp (maximum) at 12 volts to test the diode trio, and a tester that draws 20 amps at 12 volts to test the rectifier diodes. Keep the test connections hooked up for at least two minutes.*

Brush Assembly Isolation Test, beginning 1971

1. Connect an ohmmeter to the field terminal and bracket. Resistance should be infinite. If not, the brush assembly is shorted and must be replaced.

Brush Assembly Continuity Test, beginning 1971

1. Connect an ohmmeter to the field terminal and insulated brush. Make sure there is a good contact. The resistance reading should be zero.
2. Connect an ohmmeter to the bracket and grounded brush; resistance here should also be zero. Wiggle the connections to the brushes to make sure that the connections are not loose; readings should not vary.

Diode Trio Test, beginning 1971

This test requires a device that draws a one amp load at 12 volts. An ohmmeter may be used to determine whether the diode is defective or not, but a one amp load is necessary for testing diodes that show intermittant failure causing the indicator bulb to glow.

1. Unsolder the wire at the diode trio. Set up the test apparatus and attach it to a 12 V source.
2. Attach the negative clip to the threaded stud of the trio.
3. Attach the positive clip to one of the diode terminals. The test light should light. Keep it on for one to three minutes, if the light flickers or goes out, the diode is defective.

Alternator Assembly

1. Clean the bearing and the inside of the bearing hub in the front housing, then gently seat the bearing using a socket of appropriate size and a small hammer.
2. Insert the split-ring washer into the hub of the front housing and seat the washer in its groove. Be extremely careful doing this, because the bearing seal is easily damaged.
3. The front bearing now must be seated against the shoulder on the rotor shaft. Install the fan and pulley spacer, then the Woodruff key, fan and pulley. Using a 7/16 in. socket or equivalent tool to fit inside the rear bearing race, apply pressure to drive the bearing against the shoulder of the rotor shaft.
4. Assemble the front and rear housing assemblies by hand, making certain that the rear bearing is properly seated in the rear housing hub and that the diode wires are not touching the rotor at any point.
5. Align the matchmarks made during disassembly, then spin the rotor to make sure sufficient clearance exists between it and the diode wires. Install the through bolts and tighten them evenly, using only a hand wrench. Continue assembly in reverse of disassembly.

The Prestolite System

Prestolite alternators incorpoate an *isolation diode*, mounted as a component part of the internal positive heat sink assembly. Such alternators are almost identical to late model Motorola units in operation. Test procedures for the Motorola alternator also apply to the diode-equipped Prestolite.

Troubleshooting

NOTE: see the "Preliminary Charging System Inspection" section before proceeding further.

For troubleshooting procedures see the Motorola Troubleshooting section.

Alternator Disassembly—Diode Type

1. Remove the two brush mounting screws and cover, then tip the brush assembly away from the alternator and remove.
2. Matchmark the rear housing, stator and drive end housing, then remove the four retaining screws. The stator and rear housing are removed as a unit

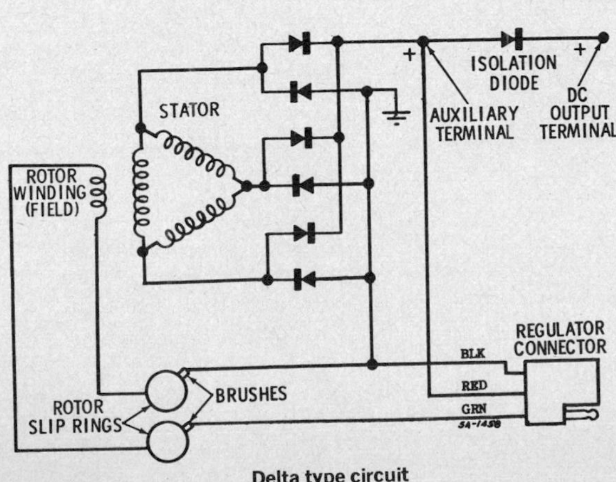

Delta type circuit

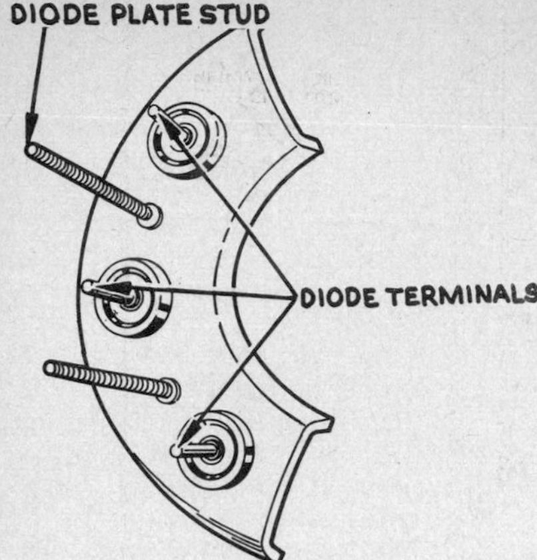

Rectifier diode test points (positive or negative)

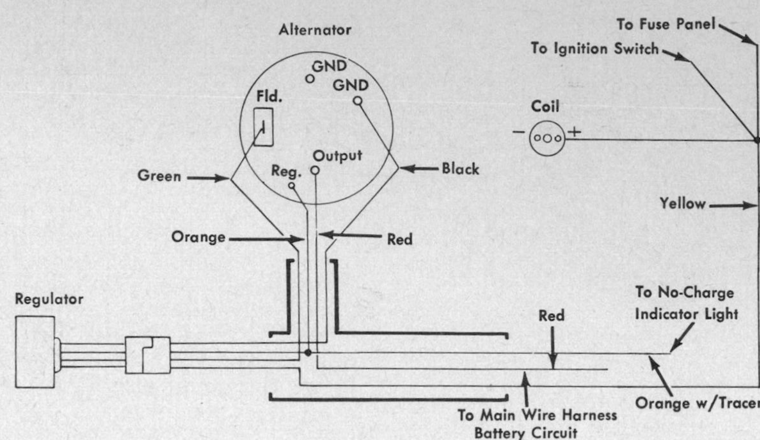

Prestolite wiring diagram

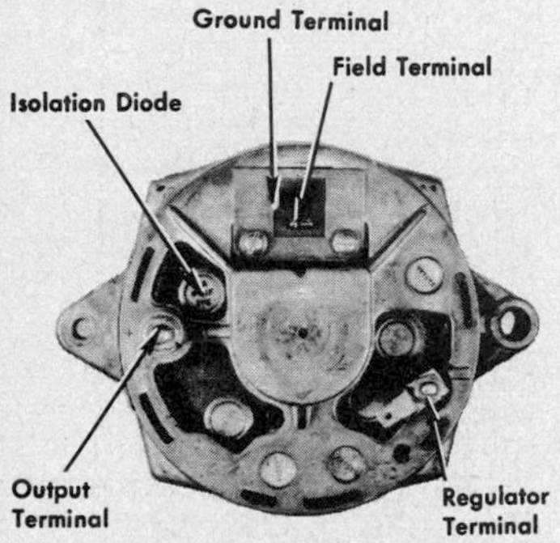

Prestolite alternator—diode type
(© American Motors Corp)

by tapping lightly with a fiber hammer to separate them from the front housing.

3. The rotor should not be removed unless it or the front bearing is defective. To remove the rotor under these conditions, first remove the pulley nut and pulley (using a two-jaw puller), then remove the fan, Woodruff key and spacer. The rotor is removed from the front housing using a three-jaw puller. (Such a puller is made by Snap-On Tool Corp. — part No. CG 253).

4. The front bearing is easily removed, after taking out the retaining ring, by pressing it out in a large vise using sockets to support the housing from the rear.

Stator Coil Test—Diode Type

1. Using a No. 57 bulb, connected in series with a 12-volt battery, as a test light, touch one test lead to the connection of the three stator windings and the other test lead to each stator lead that is connected to the diodes. If the bulb does not light, the winding is open.
2. To test for a grounded stator, use a 110-volt test lamp. First disconnect the diodes from the stator leads, then touch one test lead to the stator core and the other test lead to each of the three stator leads. If the test lamp lights, the winding is grounded.

NOTE: if all other components are O.K. and alternator still does not work, it can be assumed that the stator windings are internally shorted. This type of short is impossible to detect by using the previous test.

Diode tests are the same as for the Motorola alternator.

Alternator Assembly—Diode Type

1. Press the front bearing into the front housing, making sure the dust seal faces the rotor. Install the bearing retaining snap-ring, then press the shoulder of the shaft against the inner bearing race using a tool that fits over the shaft and against the race. Install the spacer, Woodruff key, fan and pulley, then install lockwasher and pulley nut.
2. Install the diode heat sink, negative diodes and stator. Solder any stator to diode connections that were unsoldered, using pliers as a heat sink to prevent overheating.
3. Install the rotor and front drive housing to stator and rear housing, aligning matchmarks made during disassembly. Install the four retaining screws, then the brush holder assembly and retaining screws.
4. Make sure the stator leads and brush holder assembly clear the rotor and that the rotor can be spun by hand without binding.

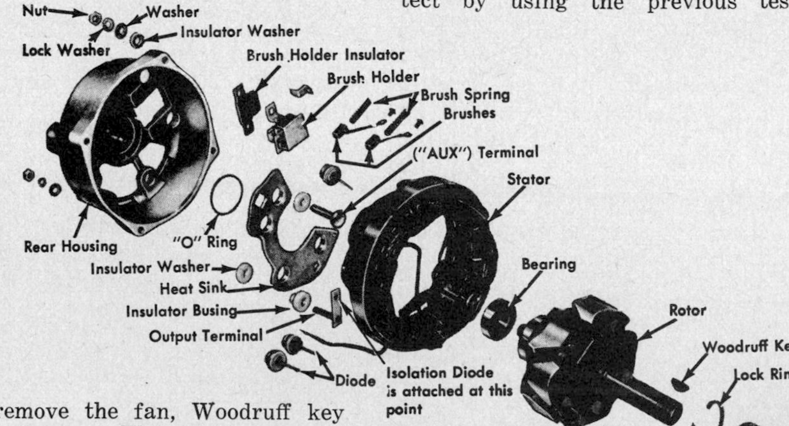

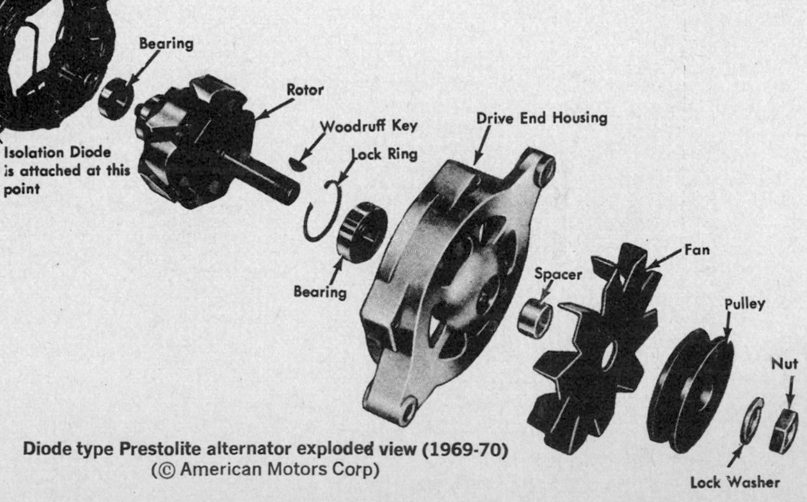

Diode type Prestolite alternator exploded view (1969-70)
(© American Motors Corp)

Electronic Ignition Systems

INDEX

Introduction

Why Electronic Ignition?

The recent rise to prominence of electronic ignition systems is due to the superiority of electronic ignition over conventional ignition systems in several major areas. These systems with the exception of the early Ford-Autolite Breaker Point System, totally remove one area of maintenance from the ignition system; the troublesome ignition points and condenser. Since the electronic ignition system produces a higher voltage than the conventional system, the electronic ignition system can usually fire a fouled spark plug. In the area of high performance, the electronic ignition system is far superior in that its voltage does not deteriorate as quickly at high engine speeds as the conventional ignition system.

As automotive antipollution laws become stricter, the maintenance-free electronic ignition systems are gaining favor among automotive manufacturers. Since these systems do not contain ignition points which wear, ignition performance does not deteriorate with mileage. This, plus the fact that these systems can usually fire a fouled plug, helps to keep down exhaust emissions after a car leaves the factory. Evidence of the manufacturer's acceptance of these systems is the fact that all 1973 and later Chrysler Corporation cars as well as all 1975 domestic cars have electronic ignition as standard equipment.

The best way to understand the operation of these systems is to compare the electronic systems to the conventional system and see where they differ.

Conventional Ignition System Operation

The conventional ignition system consists of two circuits, the primary circuit and the secondary circuit. The primary circuit includes the battery, the ignition switch, the primary side of the coil, and the ignition points and condenser. The secondary circuit consists of the secondary side of the coil, and the spark plugs and wires.

The 12 volts (V) of the automotive electrical system cannot, by itself, produce enough current to fire a spark plug and ignite the air/fuel mixture in the cylinders. It is the job of the ignition coil to increase the ignition system voltage to the required level (10,000-20,000V).

When the ignition points in the distributor are closed, the primary ignition circuit is energized. Current flows from the battery, through the ignition switch, through the primary (outer) coil windings, to the ignition points, where the system is grounded. As current passes through the primary windings in the coil, a magnetic field builds up around these windings.

When the distributor cam rotates and the ignition points open, an open circuit occurs in the primary circuit and current stops flowing through it. When this open circuit occurs, the magnetic field that was built up around the primary windings in the coil collapses and the magnetic lines of force cut through the secondary (inner) windings in the coil. These magnetic lines of force cutting through the secondary windings in the coil induce a very high electrical current into the secondary circuit. This high-voltage surge leaves the coil through the large coil wire and travels through the center tower in the distributor cap to the distributor rotor. The turning rotor directs the voltage surge to the proper sparkplug, where the voltage jumps the spark plug gap and completes the secondary circuit.

The higher the voltage supplied to the spark plug (up to a certain point), the better the ability of the plug to fire. One way to increase the voltage available to the plugs is to increase the amount of current in the primary circuit of the ignition system. It is very logical that the higher the current in the primary circuit, the higher the voltage in the secondary circuit will be when the primary circuit collapses. However, the more voltage that is used in the primary circuit, the quicker the points will pit and burn as they open. In fact, the

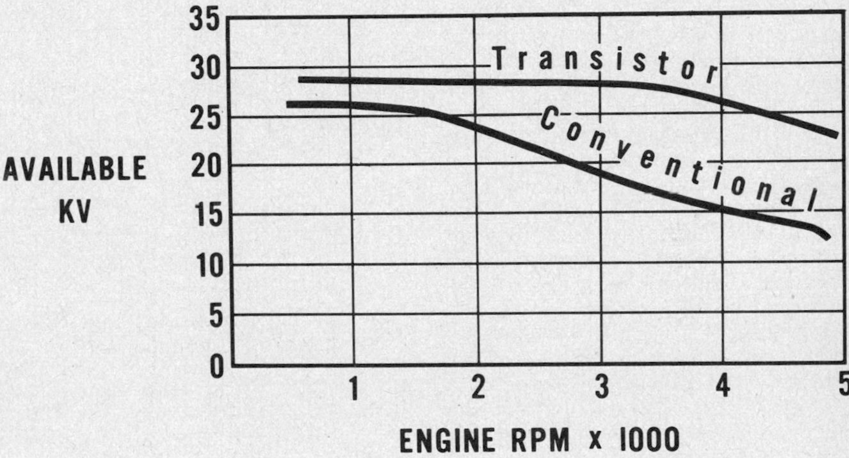

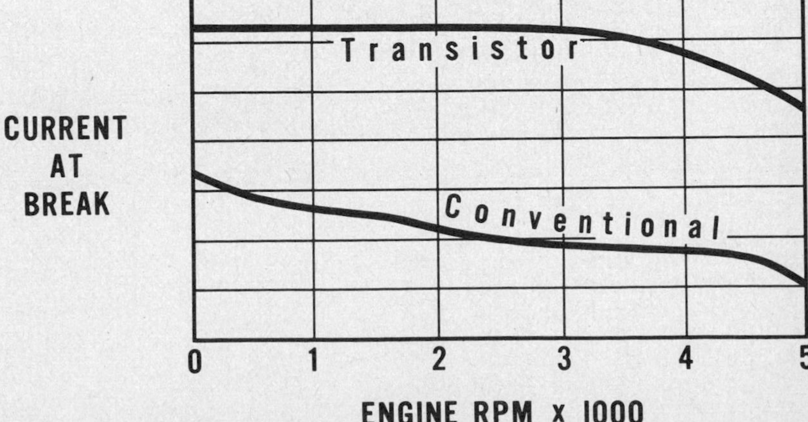

Comparison of conventional and transistor ignition system coil output and break current (© Ford Motor Co)

points are so sensitive to high current that full battery current (12 V) is only applied to the points during starting. The remainder of the time that the engine is running, the current from the ignition switch to the primary side of the coil passes through resistance wire which limits the amount of current supplied to the ignition points. While the ignition condenser serves to limit the amount of arcing between the points when they open, it cannot handle high current loads. When the ignition points become pitted or burned, two things happen: it becomes very difficult for current to pass from one contact to the other when the points are closed, and the gap between the open points (which determines how long the magnetic field from the collapsed primary circuit will have to cut into the coil secondary windings) gradually diminishes.

Since the ignition points open and close 16,000 times each minute at 4,000 rpm (8 cylinder, 4 cycle engine), any weak links in the system become very critical.

In the following pages you will find explanations of how American auto manufacturers have designed electronic ignition systems which minimize or eliminate the weak spots in the ignition system.

Ford-Autolite Breaker Point System

This transistorized system uses conventional breaker points, but does not use a condenser. The only external components that serve to distinguish this system from a conventional ignition are an external ballast resistor, a tachometer connecting block, a cold-start relay and an amplifier (transistor switching device).

As was mentioned in the earlier discussion of conventional ignition systems, the major hurdle to increasing primary ignition circuit voltage is that the points burn very easily. This system uses a transistor to bypass that weakness.

The design of the main transistor in this system allows it to conduct current from the wire running into it to the wire running out of it—if it is connected to a complete electrical circuit. However, as the current passes through the transistor, it breaks that current down into two paths, one of high voltage and one of low voltage. This transistor is called a PNP transistor because of it's three component parts. The top part of the transistor is called a collector (C), the middle part the base (B), and the lower part the emitter (E). The two currents that form inside the transistor are the high current one, or power current, which runs from E to C and the low current, or the switching current, which runs from B to E.

As is shown in the accompanying illustration, the power current is connected to the primary side of the ignition coil and the switching current is connected to the ignition points. This allows high current to energize the primary circuit in the coil while permitting a much smaller current to pass through the points.

In order for the transistor to pass current, both the power circuit and the switching circuit must make a complete circuit. This has made adaptation of this transistor system to an automotive ignition system relatively simple.

When the ignition key is turned on and the breaker points are closed, current passes from the battery, through the ignition switch, to the amplifier which contains the PNP transistor. As the current from the battery passes through the transistor, the two transistor circuits are connected as follows: the power current is connected to the coil, and the switching current is connected to the points. Since the points are closed, both transistor circuits are complete and the primary side of the ignition coil builds up a magnetic field. When the ignition points open, the switching circuit in the transistor (B to E) opens causing the transistor to stop passing current. When the transistor stops passing current, the primary ignition circuit breaks down, and the induction of the magnetic field from the primary circuit in the coil into the secondary circuit in the coil takes place. However, since the initial voltage in the primary circuit in the coil was much higher than in a conventional system, the voltage buildup in the coil will be much quicker and will rise to a higher level than in a conventional ignition system.

The other components of the system, all of which are contained in the amplifier housing with the PNP transistor, are a condenser, a zener diode, a toroid, a base-to-emitter resistor, and a collector resistor.

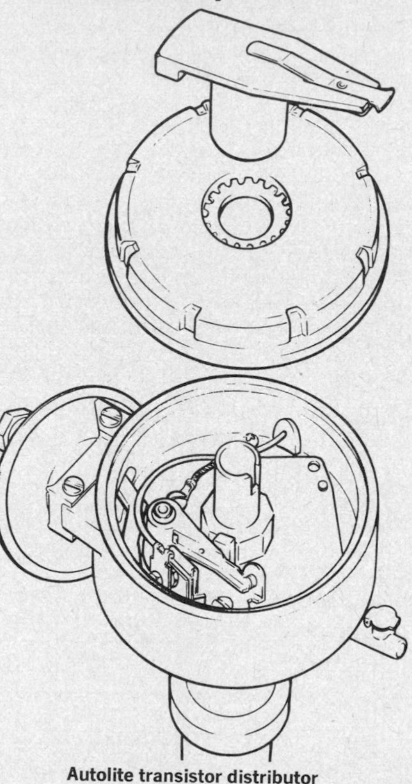

Autolite transistor distributor (© Ford Motor Co)

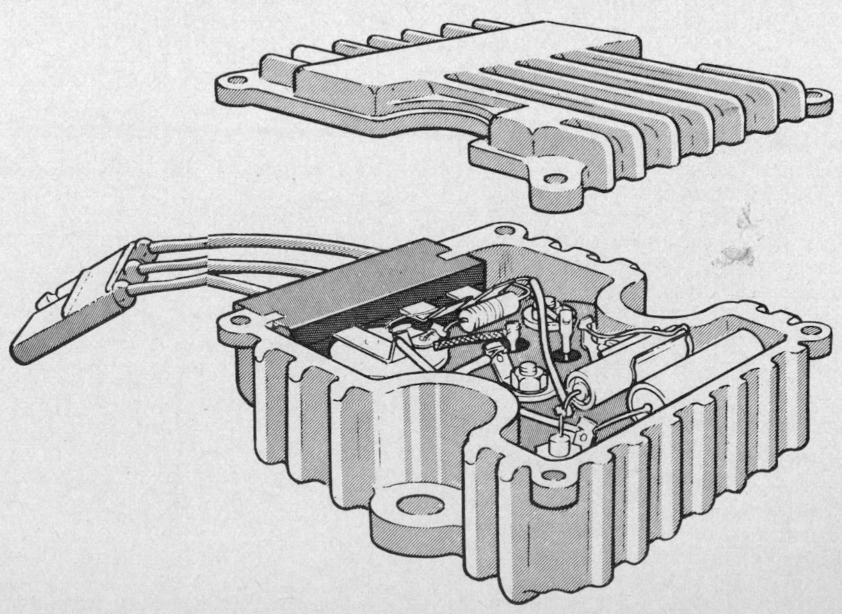

Autolite amplifier assembly (© Ford Motor Co)

The base resistor is similar to the conventional ignition resistor wire and is located between the distributor and the transistor (heat sink). It provides an 8.0 ohm resistance which is necessary for current limitation and it should not be replaced with any other wire, resistance or otherwise. To do so would result in immediate transistor destruction.

The collector and emitter resistors both are located in a ballast resistor block made of white ceramic for electrical and thermal insulation. Both resistors serve the same purpose —limiting system current and control of voltages within their respective circuits. The two resistors are in series in the collector-emitter circuit, together with the ignition coil, toroid and transistor. The emitter resistor also is in series with the base resistor, the toroid, and the transistor, in the base-emitter circuit. The transistor and emitter resistance therefore are common to both circuits. The combined resistances in each circuit permit a base current of approximately 1.0 amp. and a collector current of approximately 12 amps.

A tach block is included in the circuit for attaching tachometer and dwellmeter leads. In the conventional system, these leads are connected to the distributor primary lead and ground, but in the transistorized circuit, the connection of the leads in this manner would jump the contact gap, contributing to a current buildup in the base circuit and in the collector circuit which would overheat and burn out the transistor. The area surrounding the collector terminal is colored *red* for the meter red lead while the area surrounding the emitter terminal is colored *black* for the meter black lead.

A cold start relay is incorporated into the circuit at the starter relay, interrupting the conventional battery-to-coil lead. The purpose of this is to furnish additional current to the coil primary windings during situations when the starter draw is excessive. The cold start relay contacts normally are closed; only opening during the cranking cycle. However, when the available battery voltage drops below

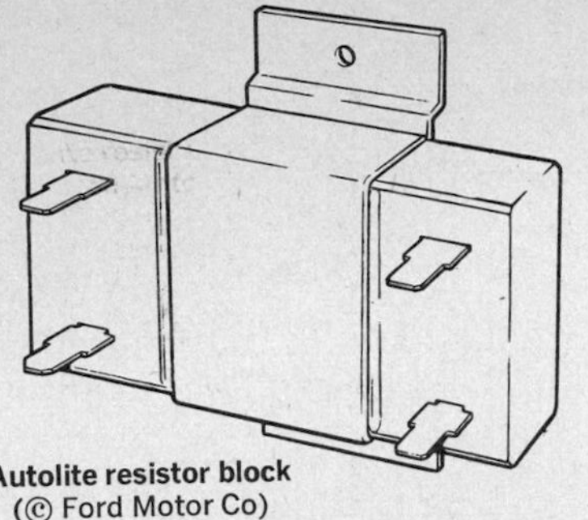

Autolite resistor block
(© Ford Motor Co)

a predetermined value during the cranking cycle, they again close, bypassing the ignition resistor and furnishing full battery current to the system.

The distributor differs from the conventional distributor only in the absence of the condenser and in the highly polished breaker cam. Because one of the big advantages of the transistor ignition is long breaker point life, wear on the rubbing block must be reduced to a minimum. Because the current at the breaker points is so small, the amount of pitting that occurs during normal operation is hardly measurable and point life should be indefinite. The points should be set to .020 in. gap and Chevron O.H.T. grease used for cam lubrication.

When testing the transistor ignition distributor in a test machine, incorporate a condenser into the primary-to-ground circuit using a jumper wire. This will prevent point pitting or oxidation during testing.

Caution When connecting an in-car tachometer to the Ford System, always shunt the tachometer leads that go to the coil IGN terminal and ignition switch with a 10 in. length of Ford ignition resistor wire, part No. COLF-12250-A, to prevent tachometer damage. The higher current draw of the transistor system can ruin a tach if this precaution is not taken.

Troubleshooting

Ignition problems are caused by a failure in the primary or secondary circuit, or incorrect ignition timing. Isolate the trouble as follows:

1. Remove the coil high tension lead from the distributor cap.
2. Disconnect the brown wire from the starter relay "I" terminal and the red and blue wire from the starter relay "S" terminal.
3. Turn the ignition switch on.
4. While holding the high tension lead approximately ¼ in. from

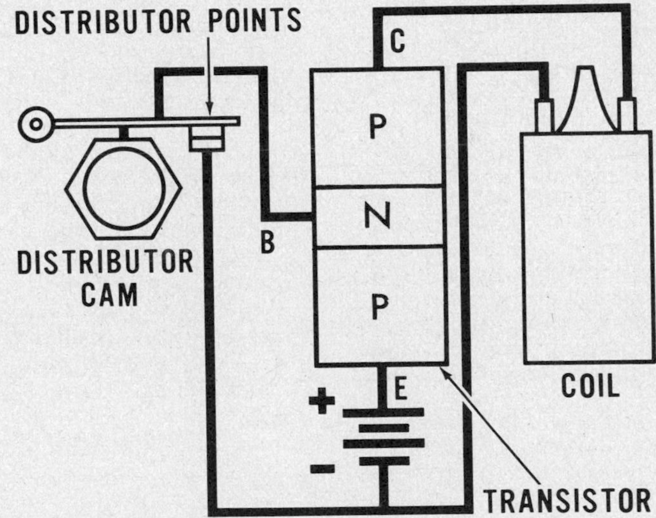

Primary ignition circuit connected to PNP transistor (© Ford Motor Co)

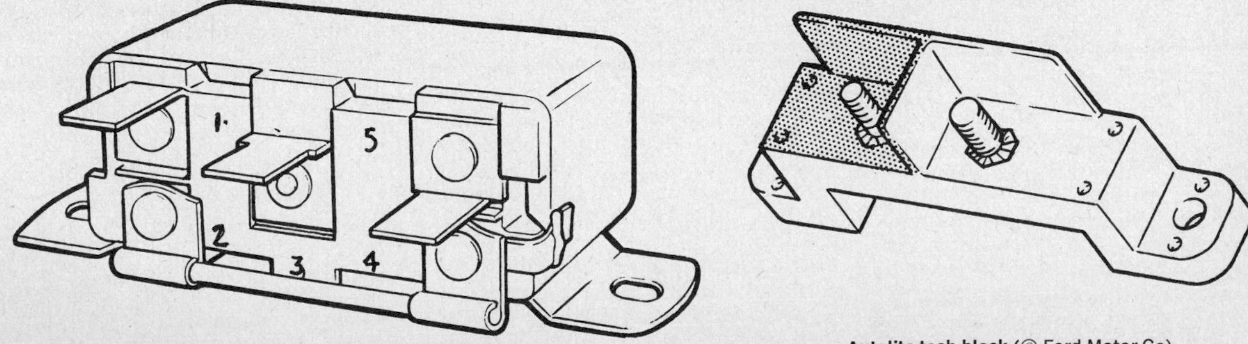

Autolite cold start relay (© Ford Motor Co)

Autolite tach block (© Ford Motor Co)

the engine block, crank the engine by using remote starter switch between the starter relay "S" and battery terminals.

If the spark is good, the trouble lies in the secondary (high voltage) circuit. If there is no spark or a weak spark, the trouble is in the primary (low voltage) circuit.

A breakdown or energy loss in the primary circuit can be caused by:

1. Defective primary wiring.
2. Improperly adjusted, contaminated or defective distributor points.
3. Defective amplifier assembly.

The trouble can be isolated by performing a primary circuit test.

A breakdown or energy loss in the secondary circuit can be caused by:

1. Fouled or improperly adjusted spark plugs.
2. Defective high voltage wiring.
3. High voltage leakage across the coil distributor cap or rotor.

To isolate a problem in the secondary circuit, turn the ignition switch off, remove the remote starter switch from the starter relay, install the coil high tension lead in the distributor cap, the red and blue wire to the starter relay (this goes on the "S" terminal) and the brown wire to the starter relay (this goes on the "I" terminal) and perform a secondary circuit test.

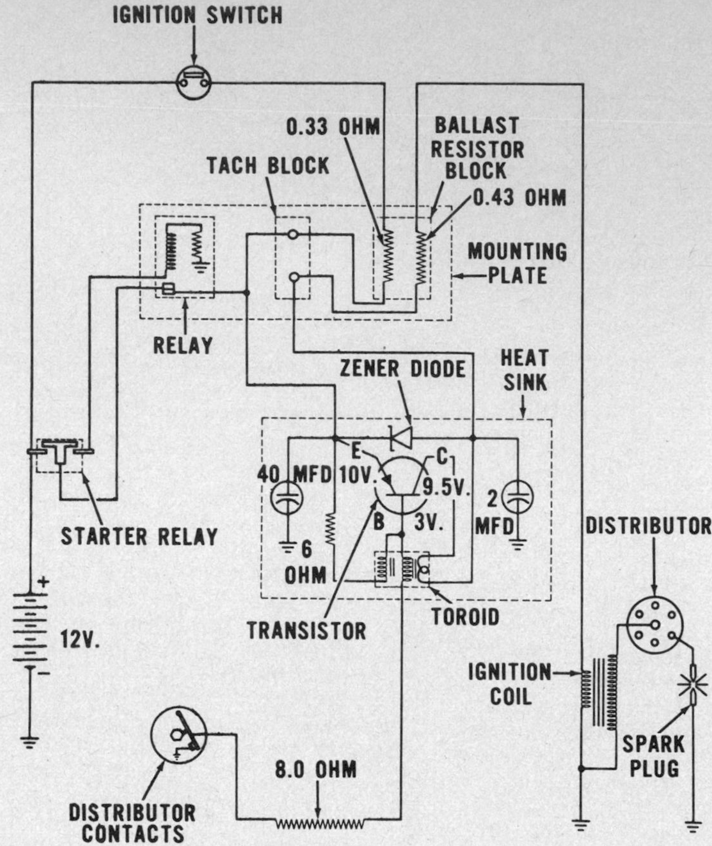

Ford-Autolite transistor ignition schematic (© Ford Motor Co)

Primary Circuit Tests

Caution Do not use any other procedure, conventional short-cut, or connect test equipment in any other manner than described, or extensive damage can be caused to the transistor ignition system.

Connect a dwell meter to the tachometer block. Connect the black lead to the black (large) terminal and the red lead to the red (small) terminal.

With the remote starter switch installed and the ignition switch on, ground the coil high tension wire and crank the engine and observe the dwell reading.

0° Dwell

1. The distributor points are contaminated or are not closing.
2. An open circuit in the distributor lead to the amplifier.

To determine which item listed is causing the trouble, proceed as follows:

Disconnect the distributor lead at the bullet connector and connect a voltmeter red lead to the red (small) tach block terminal and the voltmeter black lead to the distributor lead from the distributor. *Do not connect the voltmeter to the lead from the amplifier.* Crank the engine and note the voltmeter reading.

If a steady indication of voltage is obtained, the trouble is in the distributor lead to the amplifier. Absence of any voltage indication on the voltmeter shows that there is an open circuit between the distributor lead and the breaker point ground.

0-45° Dwell

1. The transistor and the primary circuit are functioning properly.
2. The trouble could be in the secondary circuit.

45° Dwell

1. No power from the ignition switch.
2. The distributor points are closed and not opening.
3. Defective amplifier assembly.

To determine which of the three items listed is causing the trouble, proceed as follows:

Disconnect the distributor lead at the bullet connector, and crank the engine. If the dwellmeter indicates 0° dwell, the distributor points are not opening. If 45° dwell is indicated, the amplifier is malfunctioning or there is no power from the ignition switch.

Use a voltmeter or test light to determine if the transistor (amplifier assembly) is at fault. Connect the voltmeter to the red-green lead terminal of the ballast resistor and to ground. Crank the engine.

Absence of any voltage indication on the voltmeter shows there is an open circuit, or no power between the ignition switch and the amplifier. The ballast resistor could be defective. Replace it with a good ballast resistor, and repeat the test.

A steady indication of voltage on the voltmeter indicates either a defective amplifier or the coil to amplifier lead is defective or improperly connected to the ballast resistor. Proceed as follows:

1. Disconnect the amplifier at the quick disconnect.
2. Connect an ohmmeter across the outside terminals of the amplifier side of the quick disconnect.
3. Reverse the ohmmeter leads.

If a very high resistance is obtained one way and a very low or *zero* resistance is obtained the other way, the amplifier is not defective. Check the coil to amplifier wiring for a loose connection or defective wiring.

After a repair has been made, run through the test again to check for any other malfunctions.

Secondary Circuit Tests

Use conventional system test procedures.

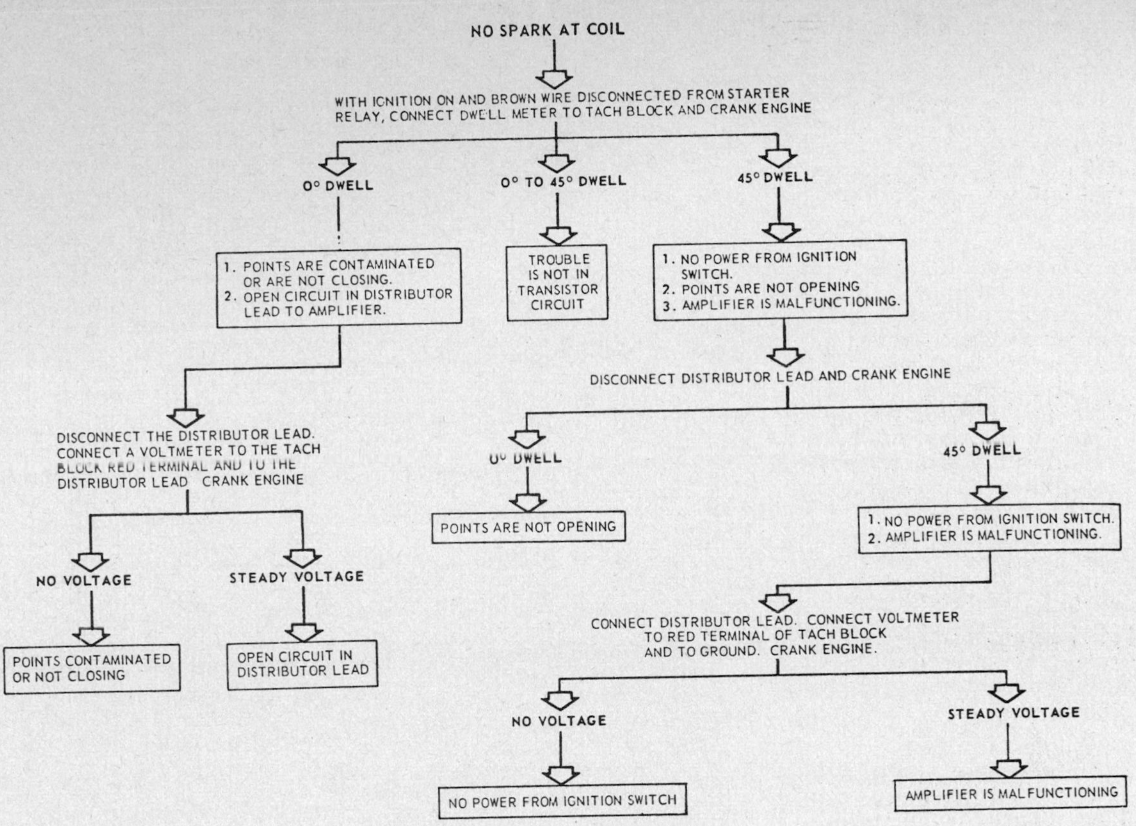

Autolite transistor ignition troubleshooting chart (© Ford Motor Co)

Ford-Motorcraft Solid-State Ignition System

The Ford-Motorcraft Solid-State Ignition System is a pulse triggered, breakerless, transistor controlled ignition system available on some late model 1973 460 V8 Lincolns; all 1974 models sold in the 49 states with a 400 or 460 V8; all 1974 six-cylinder and V8 models sold in California; and is standard equipment on all 1975 Ford Motor Company models. The system utilizes most of the standard ignition components, but substitutes an amplifier module and magnetic pick-up assembly for the conventional ignition contact points.

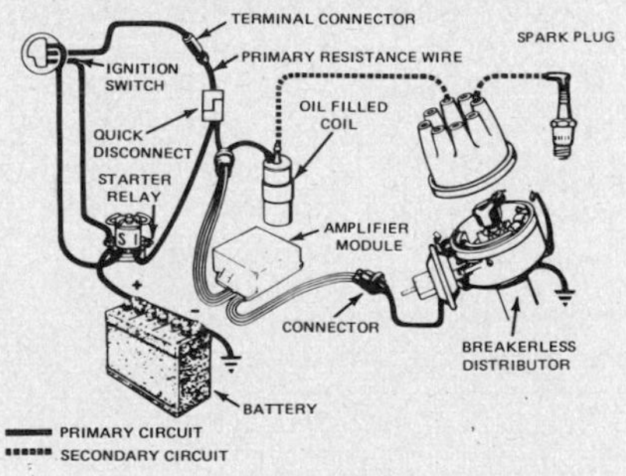

Ford-Motorcraft Solid-State Ignition System —basic wiring
(© Ford Motor Co)

Operation

With the ignition switch "on", the primary circuit is on and the ignition coil is energized. When the armature "spokes" approach the magnetic pick-up coil assembly, they induce a voltage which tells the amplifier to turn the coil primary current off. A timing circuit in the amplifier module will turn the current on again after the coil field has collapsed. When the current is "on", it flows from the battery through the ignition switch, the primary windings of the ignition coil, and through the amplifier module circuits to ground. When the current is off, the magnetic field built up in the ignition coil is allowed to collapse, inducing a high voltage into the secondary windings of the coil. High voltage is produced each time the field is thus built up and collapsed.

The high voltage flows through the coil high tension lead to the distributor cap where the rotor distributes it to one of the spark plug terminals in the distributor cap. This process is repeated for every power stroke of the engine.

Ignition system troubles are caused by a failure in the primary and/or the secondary circuit; incorrect ignition timing; or incorrect distributor advance. Circuit failures may be caused by shorts, corroded or dirty terminals, loose connections, defective wire insulation, cracked distributor cap or rotor, defective pick-up coil assembly or amplifier module, defective distributor points, fouled spark plugs, or by improper dwell angle.

If an engine starting or operating trouble is attributed to the ignition system, start the engine and verify the complaint. On engines that will not start, be sure that there is gasoline in the fuel tank and that fuel is reaching the carburetor. Then locate the ignition system problem by an oscilloscope test or by a spark intensity test.

Primary Circuit Testing

A breakdown or energy loss in the primary circuit can be caused by: defective primary wiring, loose or corroded connections, inoperative or defective magnetic pick-up coil assembly, or defective amplifier module.

A complete test of the primary circuit consists of checking the circuits in the ignition coil, the magnetic pick-up coil assembly and the amplifier module. Wiring harness checks will be included as a part of basic component circuit tests.

Always inspect connectors for dirt, corrosion or poor fit before assuming you have spotted a possible problem.

Troubleshooting

Make sure that the battery is fully charged before beginning tests. Perform a Spark Intensity Test. If no spark is observed, make sure that the high tension coil wire is good. Disconnect the three-way and four-way connectors at the electronic module.

The first trouble isolation test will be conducted on the harness terminals, with the electronic module disconnected from the circuit. The pin numbers shown in the schematic correspond to those shown in the trouble isolation test table.

Make the following tests using a sensitive volt-ohmmeter. These tests will direct you to the proper follow-up test to determine the actual problem.

If the circuit checks good at all these test points, connect a known good electronic module in place of the vehicle module and again perform the spark intensity test. If the substitution corrects the malfunction again reconnect the vehicle module and perform the spark intensity test. If the malfunction still exists, the problem is in the module and it must be replaced. If the problem is gone, it may be in the wiring connectors.

If the substitute module does not correct the problem, reconnect the original module and make repairs elsewhere in the system.

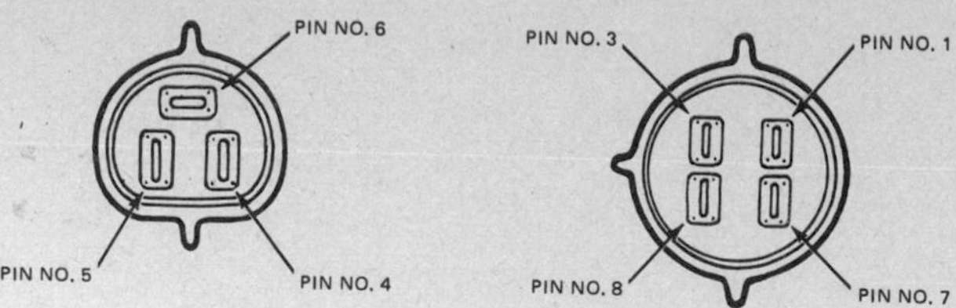

Electronic Module Connectors—harness side
(© Ford Motor Co)

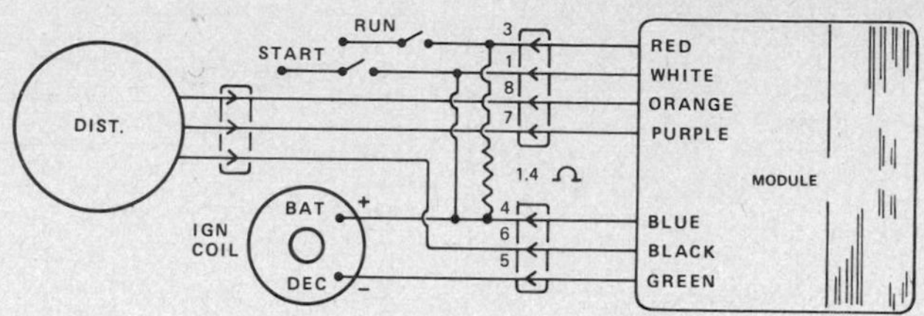

Electronic Module Schematic—solid-state ignition
(© Ford Motor Co)

Module Bias Test

Measure the voltage at Pin 3 to engine ground with the ignition key "on". If the voltage observed is less than battery voltage, repair the voltage feed wiring to the module for running conditions (re-wire).

Battery Source Test

1. Connect the voltmeter leads from the battery terminal at the coil to engine ground, without disconnecting the coil from the circuit.
2. Install a jumper wire from the DEC terminal of the coil to a good engine ground.
3. Turn the lights and all accessories off.
4. Turn the ignition switch "on".
5. If the voltmeter reading is between 4.9 and 7.9 volts, the primary circuit from the battery is satisfactory.
6. If the voltmeter reading is less than 4.9 volts, check the following:
   a. The primary wiring for worn insulation, broken strands, and loose or corroded terminals.
   b. The resistance wiring for defects.
7. If the voltmeter reading is greater than 7.9 volts, the resistance wire should be replaced after verifying a defect.

Cranking Test

Measure the voltage at Pin 1 to engine ground with the engine cranking. If the voltage observed is not 8 to 12 volts, repair the voltage feed to the module for starting conditions (white wire).

Starting Circuit Test

If the reading is not between 8 and 12 volts, the ignition by-pass circuit is open or grounded from either the starter solenoid or the ignition switch to Pin 5. Check the primary connections at the coil.

Distributor Hardware Test

1. Disconnect the three-wire weatherproof connector at the distributor pigtail.
2. Connect a D.C. voltmeter on a 2.5 volt scale to the two parallel blades. With the engine cranking, the meter needle should oscillate.
3. Remove the distributor cap and check for visual damage or misassembly.
   a. Sintered iron armature (6 or 8-toothed wheel) must be tight on the sleeve, and the roll pin aligning the armature must be in position.
   b. Sintered iron stator must not be broken.
   c. Armature must rotate when the engine is cranked.
4. If the hardware is alright, but the meter doesn't oscillate, replace the magnetic pick-up assembly.

TROUBLE ISOLATION TESTS

	TEST VOLTAGE BETWEEN	SHOULD BE	IF NOT, CONDUCT
KEY ON	Pin # 3 and Engine Ground	Battery Voltage	Module Bias Test
	Pin # 5 and Engine Ground	Battery Voltage	Battery Source Test
CRANKING	Pin # 1 and Engine Ground	8 to 12 volts	Cranking Test
	Pin # 5 and Engine Ground	8 to 12 volts	Starting Circuit Test
	Pin # 7 and Pin # 8	½ volt A.C. or D.C. volt wiggle	Distributor Hardware Test

	TEST RESISTANCE BETWEEN	SHOULD BE	IF NOT, CONDUCT
KEY OFF	Pin # 7 and Pin # 8 Pin # 6 and Engine Ground Pin # 7 and Engine Ground Pin # 8 and Engine Ground	400 to 800 ohms 0 ohms more than 70,000 ohms more than 70,000 ohms	Magnetic Pick-up (Stator) Test
	Pin # 3 and Coil Tower Pin # 5 and Pin # 4	7000 to 13000 ohms 1.0 to 2.0 ohms	Coil Test
	Pin # 5 and Engine Ground	more than 10.0 ohms	Short Test
	Pin # 3 and Pin # 4	1.0 to 2.0 ohms	Resistance Wire

Ford-Motorcraft Solid-State Ignition System Diagnosis
(© Ford Motor Co)

Magnetic Pick-Up Tests

1. Resistance of pick-up coil mea-

sured between two parallel pins in the distributor connector must be 400-800 ohms.
2. Resistance between the third blade (ground) and the distributor bowl must be zero ohms.
3. Resistance between either parallel blade and engine ground must be greater than 70,000 ohms.
4. If any test fails, the distributor stator assembly is defective and must be replaced.
5. If the above readings are not the same as measured in the original test, check for a defective harness. If the readings are the same, proceed.
6. If these tests check alright, the signal generator portion of the distributor is working properly.

Ignition Coil Test

The breakerless ignition coil must be diagnosed separately from the rest of the ignition system.

1. Primary resistance must be 1.0-2.0 ohms, measured from the BAT to the DEC terminals.
2. Secondary resistance must be 7,000-13,000 ohms, measured from the BAT or DEC terminal to the center tower of the coil.
3. If resistance tests are alright, but the coil is still suspected, test the coil on a coil tester by following the test equipment manufacturer's instructions for a standard coil. If the reading differs from the original test, check for a defective harness.

Module Test—1975 Only

1. Unplug the electronic module connector, but don't remove the existing module from the car.
2. Connect a module which is known to be good to the connector. There is no need to attach the module to the car in order to have it work.
3. Start the engine; if it starts and operates correctly go on to the next step. If it won't start and run the trouble is somewhere else. Check and repair the wiring and other systems, as required.
4. If the engine started in step 3, reconnect the original module and try to start the engine again. If the engine won't start, replace the module.
5. If the engine starts in step 4, the original module is not defective. Check all the wiring and connections in the ignition system.

Short Test

If the resistance from Pin 5 to ground is less than 10 ohms, check for a short to ground at the DEC terminal of the ignition coil or in the connection wiring to that terminal.

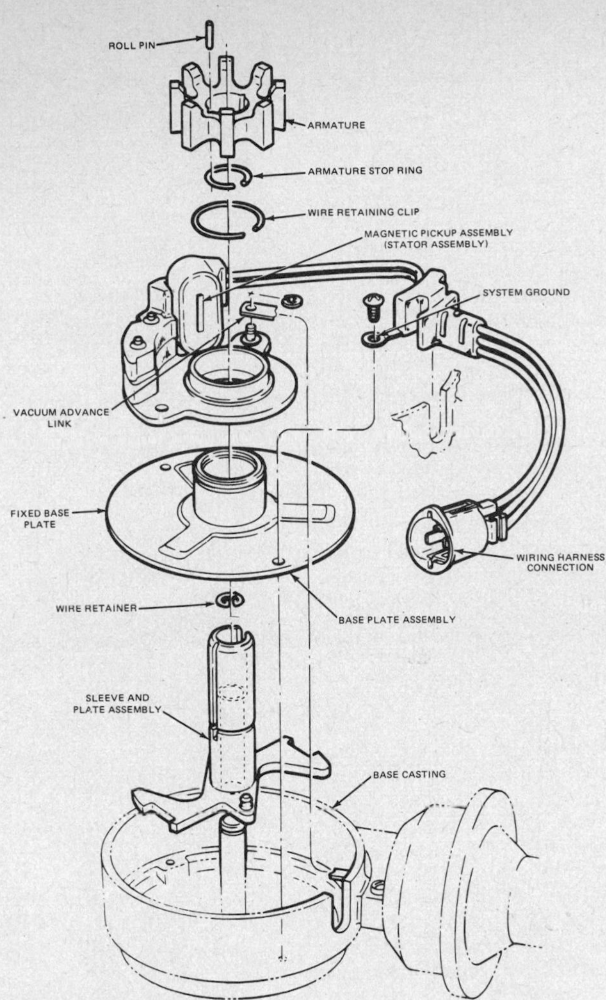

Ford-Motorcraft Solid-State Ignition distributor disassembled
(© Ford Motor Co)

Resistance Wire Test

Replace the resistance wire if it is out of specifications (See "Ignition Resistor Wire").

Adjustments

The air gap between the armature and magnetic pick-up coil in the distributor is not adjustable, nor are there any adjustments for the amplifier module. Inoperative components are simply replaced. Any attempt to connect components outside the vehicle may result in component failure.

Component Replacement

Magnetic Pick-up Assembly Removal and Installation

1. Remove the distributor cap and rotor and disconnect the distributor harness plug.
2. Using a small gear puller or two screwdrivers, lift or pry the armature from the advance plate sleeve. Remove the roll pin.
3. Remove the large wire retaining clip from the base plate annular groove.
4. Remove the snap-ring which secures the vacuum advance link to the pick-up assembly.
5. Remove the magnetic pick-up assembly ground screw and lift the assembly from the distributor.
6. Lift the vacuum advance arm off the post on the pick-up assembly and move it out against the distributor housing.
7. Place the new pick-up assembly in position over the fixed base plate and slide the wiring in position through the slot in the side of the distributor housing.
8. Install the fine wire snap-ring securing the pick-up assembly to the fixed base plate.
9. Position the vacuum advance arm over the post on the pick-up assembly and install the snap-ring.
10. Install the grounding screw through the tab on the wiring harness and into the fixed base plate.
11. Install the armature on the advance plate sleeve making sure that the roll pin is engaged in the matching slots.
12. Install the distributor rotor cap.
13. Connect the distributor wiring plug to the vehicle harness.

Delco-Remy Magnetic Pulse System

Components

The Delco-Remy magnetic pulse, fully transistorized ignition system uses a magnetic pulse distributor having no breaker points. This system switches power electronically rather than with ignition contact points. Instead of the familiar cam and breaker plate assembly, this distributor uses a rotating iron timer core and a magnetic pickup assembly. The magnetic pickup assembly consists of a bearing plate on which are sandwiched a ceramic ring-type permanent magnet, two pole pieces and a pick-up coil. The pole pieces are doughnut shaped steel plates with accurately spaced internal teeth, one tooth for each cylinder of the engine.

A critically important part is the iron timer core. It has a number of equally spaced projections or vanes and is attached to, and rotates with, the distributor shaft.

The transistor control unit, the switchbox of the system, is mounted in an aluminum case and contains three transistors, a zener diode, a condenser and five small resistors The zener diode is a circuit protection device. Remaining components control and switch ignition-coil current electronically; there are no moving parts in the control unit.

The ignition coil is of standard design except for a special winding. The external primary resistor is a ceramic type, similar to those used on various conventional systems.

Operation

The ignition primary circuit is connected from the battery, through the ignition switch, through the ignition pulse amplifier assembly, through the primary side of the ignition coil, and back to the amplifier housing where it is grounded externally. The secondary circuit is the same as in conventional ignition systems: the secondary side of the coil, the coil wire to the distributor, the rotor, the spark plug wires and the spark plugs.

The magnetic pulse distributor is also connected to the ignition pulse amplifier. As the distributor shaft rotates, the distributor rotating pole piece turns inside the stationary pole piece. As the rotating pole piece turns inside the stationary pole piece, the eight teeth on the rotating pole piece align with the eight teeth on the stationary pole piece eight times during each distributor revolution (two crankshaft revolutions since the distributor runs at one-half crankshaft speed). As the rotating pole piece teeth move close to, and align with, the teeth on the stationary pole piece, the magnetic rotating pole piece induces voltage into the magnetic pole piece through the stationary pole piece. This voltage pulse is sent to the ignition pulse amplifier from the magnetic pole piece. When the pulse enters the amplifier, it signals the ignition pulse amplifier to interrupt the ignition primary circuit. This causes the primary circuit to collapse and begins the induction of the magnetic lines of force from the primary side of the coil into the secondary side of the coil. This induction provides the required voltage to fire the spark plugs.

The advantages of this system are that the transistors in the ignition pulse amplifier can make and break the primary ignition circuit much faster than conventional ignition points, and higher primary voltage can be utilized since this system can be made to handle higher voltage without adverse effects, whereas ignition breaker points cannot. The shorter switching time of this system allows longer coil primary circuit saturation time and longer induction time when the primary circuit collapses. This increased time allows the primary circuit to build up more current and the secondary circuit to discharge more current.

ROTOR
CENTRIFUGAL ADVANCE
ROTATING POLE PIECE
STATIONARY POLE PIECE
MAGNETIC PICKUP ASSEMBLY
VACUUM ADVANCE
DISTRIBUTOR HOUSING
DRIVE GEAR

Delco-Remy pulse distributor exploded view
(© Chevrolet Div., G.M. Corp)

CAP
VACUUM UNIT
PICK-UP COIL LEADS
HOUSING
GEAR

Delco-Remy magnetic pulse distributor
(© Chevrolet Div., G.M. Corp)

Troubleshooting

Cautions

1. Don't use 18 volts or 24 volts for emergency starting.
2. Never crank engine with coil high-tension lead or more than three spark plug leads disconnected.
3. Don't short circuit between coil positive terminal and ground.
4. On any repair that necessitates replacement of control unit or ignition resistor, perform complete charging system check before releasing the unit. Basic cause of trouble may be high or uncontrolled charging rate.

Engine Surge or Intermittent Miss

Since there are so many possible causes for this problem, all other possible defects must be ruled out before the specialized components of the

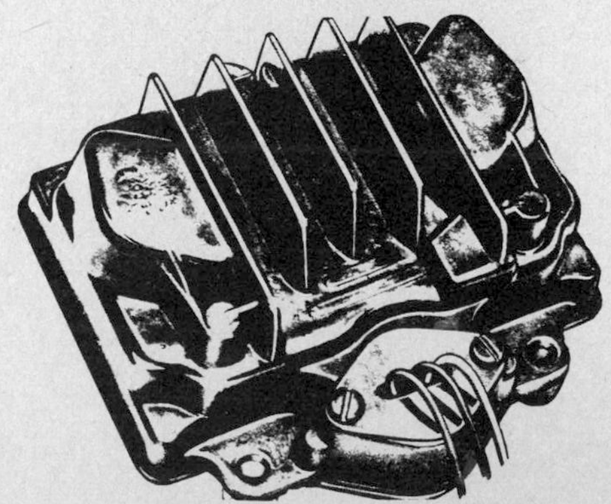

Delco-Remy amplifier unit
(© Chevrolet Div., G.M. Corp)

electronic ignition system are judged defective.

As a general rule, a miss or surge that is caused by an ignition problem will be much more pronounced than a similiar problem that is caused by carburetion. Also, carburetion is usually affected by temperature more than the ignition system is. A carburetor or intake manifold vacuum leak is often compensated for by the choke when the engine is cold. When the engine warms up and the choke is released, the engine surge will show up.

If the ignition system is found to be the source of the problem, first check all connections in the system to make sure that they are *clean and tight.* Check the coil and spark plug high-tension wires with an ohmmeter to be sure they have the correct resistance. Check the inside and outside of the distributor cap and the tower on the ignition coil for cracks which would allow the high voltage intended for the spark plugs to short to ground.

If none of the above checks uncovers a defective component, the distributor pick-up coil leads may be reversed in the connector, or the pick-up coil itself may have an intermittent open.

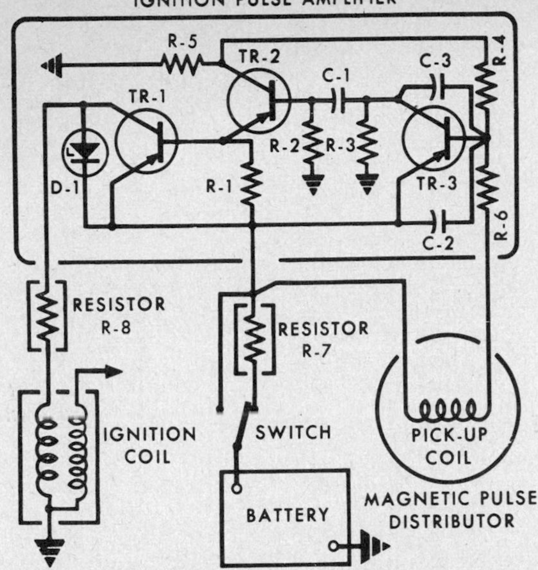

Delco-Remy amplifier schematic
(© Chevrolet Div., G.M. Corp)

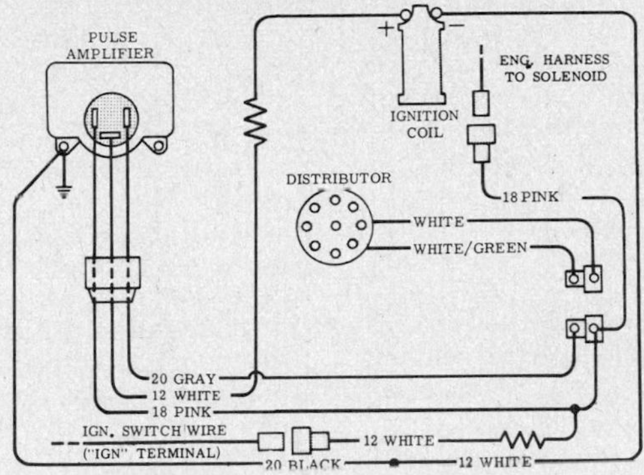

Delco-Remy circuit diagram
(© Chevrolet Div., G.M. Corp)

Engine Will Not Start or Is Hard to Start

1. Disconnect a spark plug wire from one spark plug and hold the wire 1/4 in. from a good ground with a pair of insulated pliers.
2. Crank the engine over and observe whether a spark jumps from the plug wire to ground.
3. *If spark occurs,* the problem is not in the ignition system.
4. *If spark does not occur,* reconnect the spark plug wire that was disconnected and connect a tachometer between the positive (+) coil primary terminal and the pink wire in the three-wire connector to the ignition pulse amplifier.
5. Crank the engine over and observe the tachometer.
6. *If the tachometer needle deflects* while cranking the engine, perform "Ignition Distributor Test" to locate the problem.
7. *If the tachometer needle does not deflect* while cranking the engine, perform "Circuit Resistance Test" to pinpoint the problem.

Circuit Resistance Test

Ignition Distributor Check

1. Disconnect the distributor leads from the engine wiring harness.
2. Connect the two leads of an ohmmeter to the distributor leads at the connector.
3. Rotate the magnetic pick-up assembly in the distributor through full vacuum advance travel and read the ohmmeter. If the reading is not within a range of 500-700 ohms, replace the magnetic pick-up assembly.
4. If the reading is within the 500-700 ohms range, disconnect one ohmmeter lead from the distributor connector and connect it to a good ground. If the reading is less than infinity (needle moves to end of scale), replace the magnetic pick-up assembly.
5. If the reading is infinite, and there was no spark when the spark plug wire was disconnected from the plug, the amplifier is defective.

Delcotronic Capacitive Discharge System

Components

The capacitive discharge ignition system consists of a magnetic pulse distributor, an ignition pulse amplifier, and a special ignition coil and distributor cap. The coil and distributor cap are red to distinguish them from standard coils and distributor caps. The ignition pulse amplifier contains transistors, diodes, resistors, capacitors, a thyristor, and a transformer. These components are mounted on a printed circuit board in the amplifier housing.

System Operation

The magnetic pulse distributor used in this system is similar to the one used in the previously described Delco-Remy Magnetic Pulse Ignition system. The system functions in a much different way, however. In the Magnetic Pulse Distributor System, the ignition primary circuit is connected through the ignition pulse amplifier and, upon receiving a signal from the distributor, the primary circuit is broken and the induction of high voltage into the secondary circuit takes place. In the capacitive discharge system, the ignition primary circuit is energized when the distributor signals the ignition pulse amplifier to discharge 300 V that the amplifier has been storing in its capacitor. When this voltage is discharged into the primary circuit and the capacitor is completely drained of current, an open circuit occurs in the primary system and this causes the collapse of the primary circuit which causes the induction of high voltage into the secondary circuit.

Battery voltage is connected to the ignition pulse amplifier. The ignition pulse amplifier receives this current (12V) and, through the transformer contained in the amplifier, increases this current to 300 V. Since battery voltage is DC, and the transformer used in this application can only increase AC current; the amplifier also contains a circuit to convert the DC battery voltage to AC. After converting the current to AC, and increasing it to 300 V, the amplifier sends the current to its capacitor where it is stored.

During this sequence of events, the ignition coil primary side is not energized.

When the teeth on the pole pieces in the distributor align (thus sending a current pulse to the ignition pulse amplifier), the capacitor in the amplifier is connected to the primary side of the ignition coil, discharging its current into it. When the capacitor is connected to the primary of the coil and is discharging current, a complete circuit exists. When the capacitor is completely drained of current, however, it causes an open circuit in the ignition primary. This open circuit causes the ignition primary circuit to collapse, which brings about the induction of the magnetic lines of force from the primary side of the coil across the ignition coil secondary windings. This causes high voltage to be induced into the secondary circuit which fires the spark plugs.

This system has all of the advantages of the Magnetic Pulse Distributor System, plus the extra advantage of containing a transformer. The use of a transformer permits the system to operate on a minimum current drain on the battery. This is due to the transformer's ability to greatly increase the current that is supplied to it. Thus, ignition primary current can be increased (which means higher secondary current) without

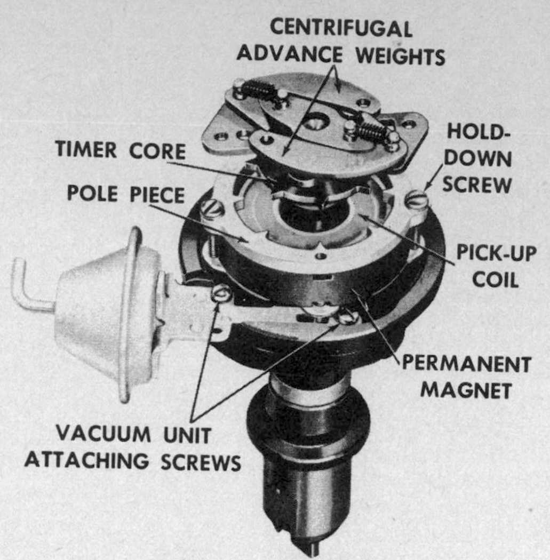

C-D distributor—Delcotronic System
(© Oldsmobile Div., G.M. Corp)

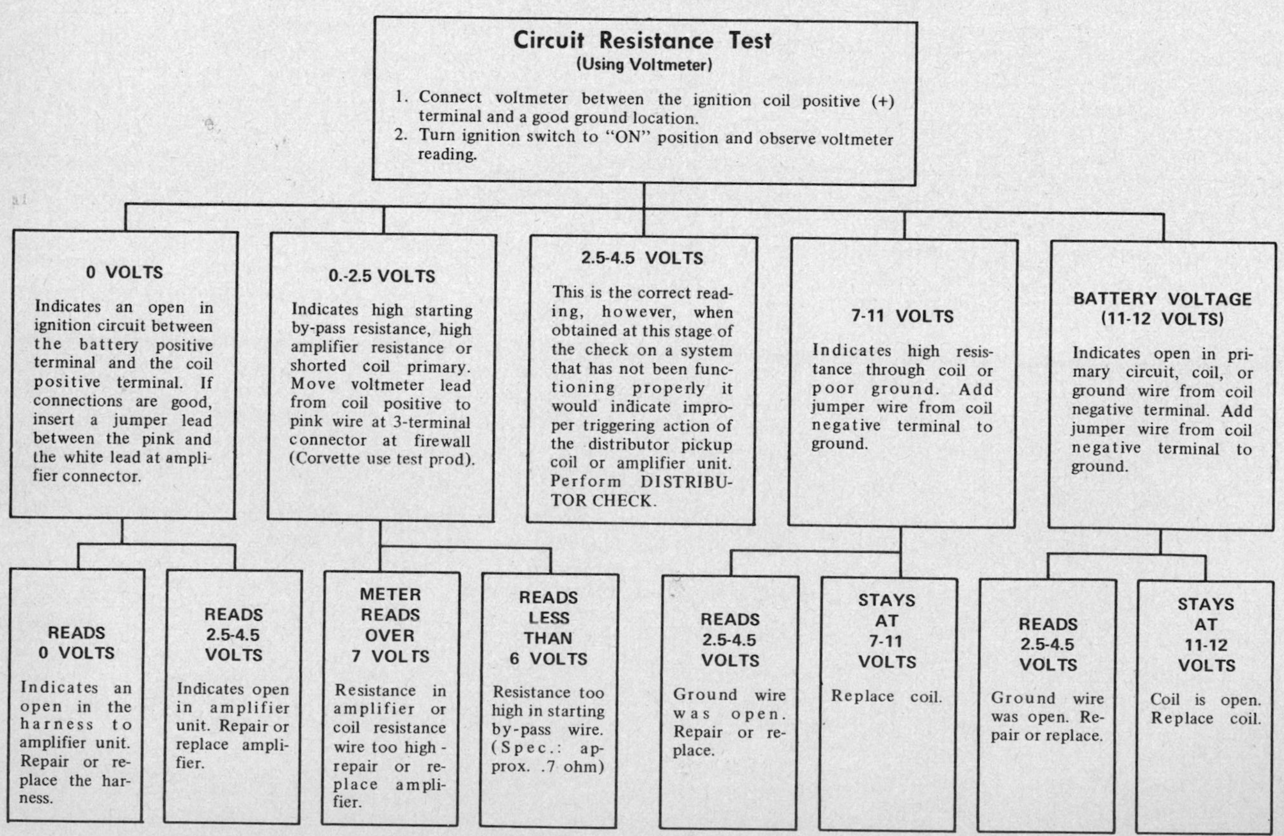

Magnetic Pulse System (© Chevrolet Div., G.M. Corp)

imposing the extra load on the battery that the Magnetic Pulse System does.

Amplifier Operation

Transistor Q2 and accompanying circuitry momentarily supplies voltage through the primary of transformer T1. This voltage is increased through transformer action and a much higher voltage is induced in the secondary. The four diodes, CR3, 4, 5 and 6 form a full wave rectifier which has the capability of delivering maximum DC voltage from the transformer T1 secondary. It is this voltage that charges the capacitor C1.

The following is a list of the parts, and their function, used in the amplifier as illustrated in the schematic.

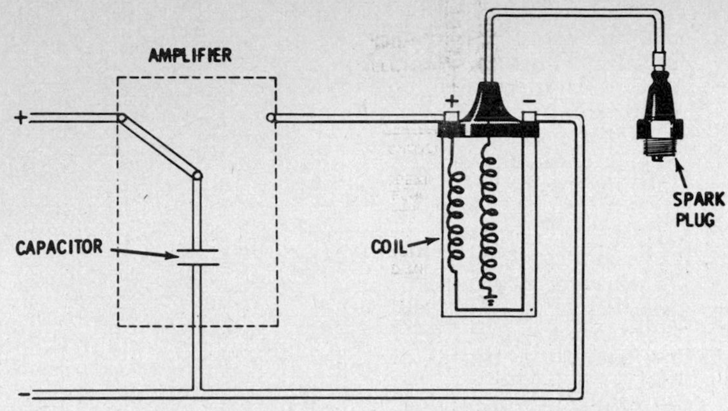

Battery voltage is connected to the transformer while the capacitor is being charged mechanical linkage is used to show electrical connection

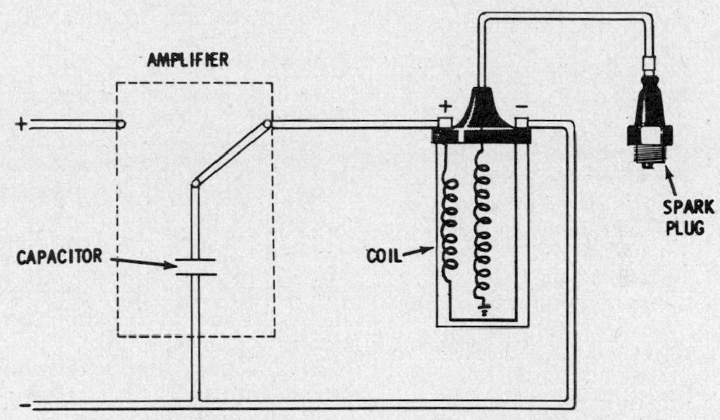

Capacitor discharging into primary ignition circuit mechanical linkage is used to show electrical connection

Transistor

Q1 Initiates turn-on and turn-off of Q5.

Q2 Turns T1 primary on and off.

Q3 Turns Q2 on and off with engine running.

Q4 Triggers Thyristor THY.

Q5 When on, it turns off Q3 and Q4.

Diode

CR1 Blocks 3 line current through CR2.

CR2 (Zener) Clips T1 primary voltage to limit secondary output to approximately 300 volts across C1.

CR3, CR4, CR5, CR6 Provide full wave rectification of T1 secondary voltage.

CR7 Provides proper bias to Q2.

CR8 Clips FB voltage of T1 to limit reverse voltage across E-B of Q2.

CR9 Provides proper biasing of THY.

CR10 Eliminates reverse voltage across THY, allows ignition coil primary to partially recharge C1.

CR12 Provides proper biasing of THY.

CR13 With C7 and R17 reduces rate of voltage increases across THY.

Protects amplifier in case of battery reverse polarity,

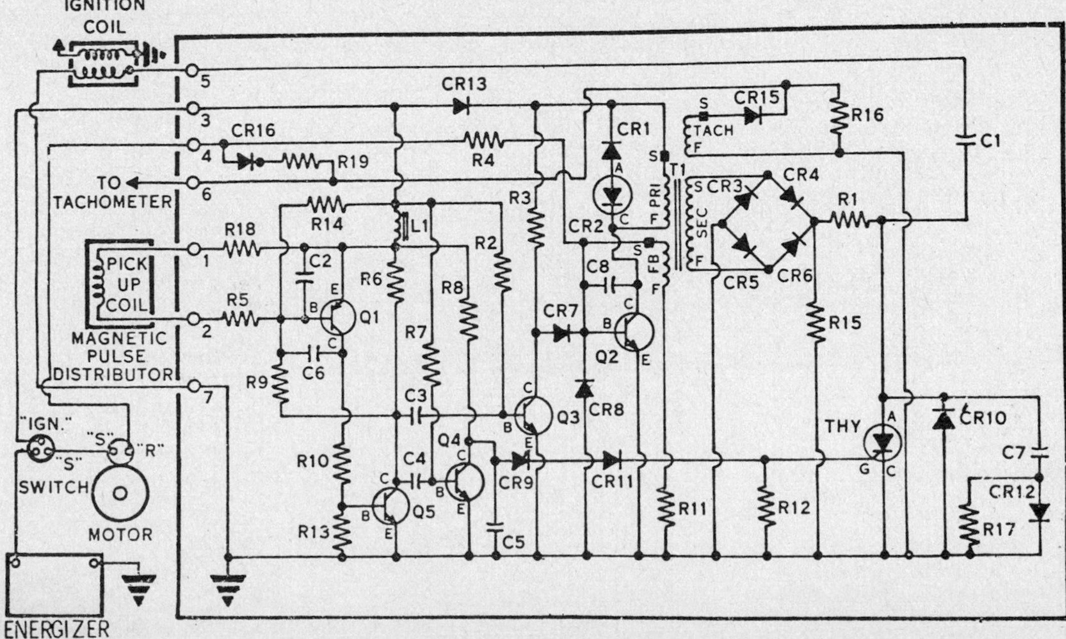

Delcotronic Capacitor Discharge System schematic (© Oldsmobile Div., G.M. Corp)

or lead reversal.

CR15 Half wave rectified T1 tachometer winding voltages for proper tachometer operation.

CR16 With R19 prevents erroneous tachometer reading during cranking.

Resistor

R1 Prevents T1 secondary rectified voltage from being shorted to ground when THY is on.

R2 Provides proper biasing of Q3.

R3 Limits current through Q3.

R4 Provides proper biasing of Q2.

R5 Prevents damage to amplifier if #2 lead is grounded.

R6 Limits current through Q5.

R7 Provides proper biasing of Q4.

R8 Limits current through Q4.

R9 Provides feed back for Q1, holds Q1 on after pick up coil voltage has ceased.

R10 Provides signal to Q5 when Q1 turns on.

R11 Limits current through Q2 from winding of T1.

R12 Provides bias to THY.

R13 Biases B-E of Q5.

R14 Biases E-B of Q1.

R15 Allows C1 to bleed off during shut-down.

R16 Provides proper voltage to tachometer.

R17 Reduces rate of voltage change imposed on THY when C7 discharges.

R18 Prevents damage to amplifier if #1 lead is grounded.

R19 With CR16 prevents erroneous tachometer reading during cranking.

Capacitor

C1 Stores charge from T1 to energize ignition coil primary.

C2 Protects Q1 from transient voltages.

C3 Turns Q3 off.

C4 Turns Q4 off.

C5 Protects Q4 from transient voltages.

C6 Protects Q1 from transient voltages.

C7 With CR12 and R17 reduces rate of voltage increase across THY.

C8 Reduces radio noise.

Transformer

T1 Steps up voltage to charge C1; provides voltage to operate tachometer; provides feed back voltage to operate Q2.

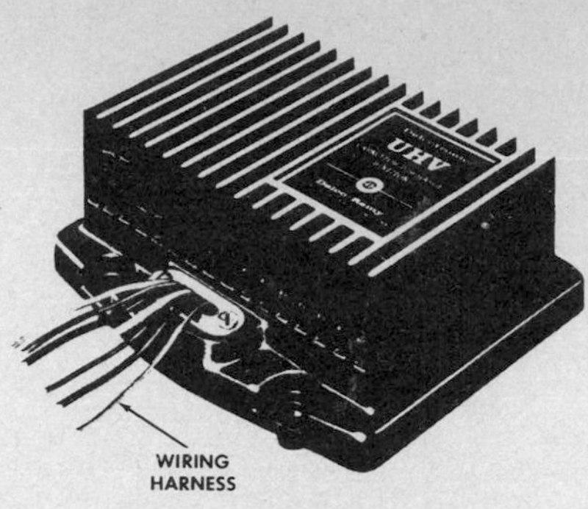

Delcotronic amplifier unit
(© Oldsmobile Div., G.M. Corp)

Thyristor

THY Discharges C1 through primary of ignition coil.

Troubleshooting

Faulty engine performance will be evidenced by one of the following conditions:

a. Engine will not run.
b. Engine will start but not run.
c. Engine will miss or surge.

When troubleshooting the system, use care to avoid accidental shorts and grounds, which may cause instant damage to the amplifier and wiring.

NOTE: the special coil used in this system cannot be tested with a conventional coil tester.

Engine Will Not Run

To determine if the ignition system is operating, hold one spark plug lead about ¼ in. from the engine block and crank the engine. If sparking occurs, the trouble most likely is not ignition. If sparking does not occur, and the vehicle fuel system is satisfactory, check the ignition system. The spark plugs, wiring, distributor cap and rotor can be checked in the conventional manner. Only the coil requires a different procedure. The ignition coil can be checked for primary and secondary winding continuity with an ohmmeter as follows: with leads disconnected from coil, connect ohmmeter across primary terminals. If reading is infinite, winding is open. To check secondary, connect ohmmeter to high voltage (center tower) and coil case. An infinite reading means coil secondary is open.

NOTE: when checking secondary, use middle or high resistance range on ohmmeter.

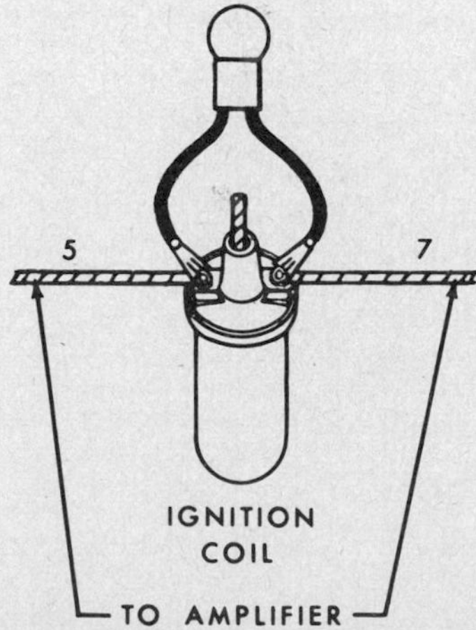

Amplifier test hook-up
(© Oldsmobile Div., G.M. Corp)

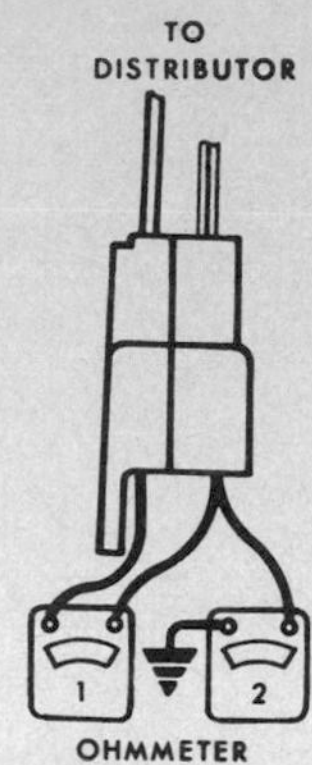

Distributor test hook-up
(© Oldsmobile Div., G.M. Corp)

Amplifier

1. Temporarily connect a jumper lead between the amplifier housing to a good ground. If the engine will not start and run, the amplifier is not properly grounded. Correct as required.
2. Connect a 12-volt, 2-candlepower bulb to the primary terminals of the ignition coil.
3. Crank the engine.
   a. If the bulb flickers on and off, the amplifier is operating properly. In this case, recheck the secondary system for the cause of the "no run" condition.
   b. If the bulb does not flicker on and off, proceed to next test.

Distributor

1. Insure that the two distributor leads are connected to the distributor connector body as illustrated.
2. With the distributor connector disconnected from the harness connector, connect an ohmmeter (1) to the two terminals of the distributor connector as shown.
3. Connect a vacuum source to the distributor, and observe the ohmmeter reading throughout the vacuum range. (The distributor need not be removed from the engine.)
4. Any reading outside the 550-750 ohm range indicates a defective pickup coil in the distributor.
5. Remove one ohmmeter (2) lead from the connector body and

connect to ground.

6. Observe the ohmmeter reading throughout the vacuum range.
7. Any reading less than infinite indicates a defective pickup coil.
8. Reconnect the harness connector to the distributor connector.

Continuity

Carefully inspect all wiring connections to ensure that they are clean and tight. If satisfactory, disconnect the amplifier No. 3 and No. 4 leads from the two connectors. Proceed as follows:

1. Connect a voltmeter from ground to the No. 4 connector lead.
2. Turn switch to "Start" position.
3. If reading is zero, circuit is open between connector body and battery.
4. If reading is obtained, connect voltmeter from ground to the No. 3 connector lead.
5. Turn switch to the run position.
6. If reading is zero, circuit is open between connector body and switch.
7. If reading is obtained, replace amplifier.

Engine Will Start But Not Run

If the engine starts, but then stops when the switch is returned to the run position, check as follows:

1. Ensure that the leads are properly connected in the No. 3 lead connector body.
2. If satisfactory, connect a voltmeter from ground to the terminal connection inside the connector.
3. Turn switch to run position.
4. If reading is zero, lead between connector and ignition switch is open.
5. If reading is obtained, replace amplifier.

Engine Miss or Surge

The vehicle fuel system should be checked in the usual manner. If satisfactory, check the ignition system as follows:

Timing, Spark Plugs, Wiring, Distributor Cap and Ignition Coil

Checks in these areas should be made in the same manner as for a conventional ignition system. In particular, the spark plugs should be checked in the usual manner. Plugs should be gapped to 0.045 in. Also the timing, the high-voltage wiring, the ignition coil tower, and the distributor cap inside and out should be inspected for evidence of arcing or leakage to ground. The ignition coil can be checked for primary and secondary winding continuity with an ohmmeter, as follows: disconnect coil leads and connect ohmmeter across primary terminals. If reading is infinite (no reading) winding is open.

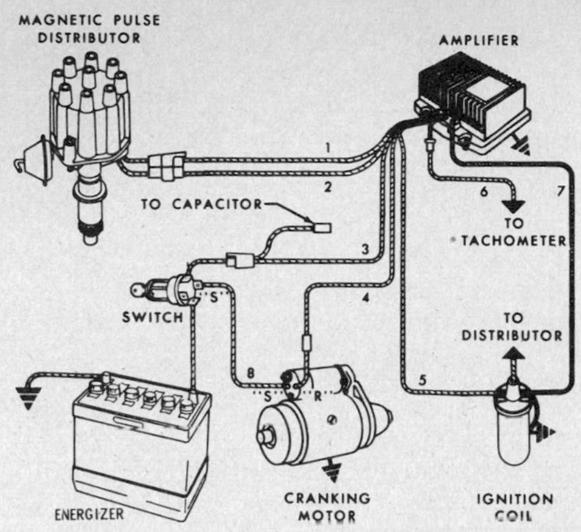

Delcotronic System wiring diagram
(© Oldsmobile Div., G.M. Corp)

To check secondary, connect ohmmeter to high voltage (center tower) and coil case. An infinite reading means coil secondary is open.

NOTE: when checking secondary, use middle or high resistance range on ohmmeter.

Amplifier

A poorly grounded amplifier can cause an engine miss or surge. To check, temporarily connect a jumper lead from the amplifier housing to a good ground. If the engine performance improves, the amplifier is poorly grounded. Correct as required.

If no defects up to this point have been found, and the secondary system (plugs, wiring, distributor cap and coil) have been thoroughly checked, the most likely cause of the engine condition is a defective amplifier.

C-D Distributor Removal

1. Disconnect the harness connector.
2. Remove distributor cap.

NOTE: if necessary to remove secondary wires from cap, mark position on cap tower for lead to No. 1 cylinder. This will aid in reinstalling of leads.

3. Remove vacuum hose line from vacuum advance unit.
4. Remove distributor clamp.
5. Note position of rotor, then pull distributor up until rotor just stops turning counterclockwise and again note position of rotor.
6. To install, reverse removal procedure.

NOTE: to ensure correct timing of the distributor, the distributor must be installed with the rotor correctly positioned as noted in Step 5.

7. If the engine has been turned after the distributor was removed, it will be necessary to crank the engine until the slot on the harmonic balancer indexes with the 0° timing mark on the engine front cover. If both valves of the No. 1 cylinder are closed, the piston will be on top dead center of the firing stroke.

Distributor Disassembly

1. Remove screws securing rotor; remove rotor.
2. Remove centrifugal weight springs, if necessary.
3. Remove centrifugal weights.
4. Remove roll pin.
5. Remove drive gear and washer.
6. Remove drive shaft.
7. Remove weight support and timer core from drive shaft.
8. Remove screws securing magnetic core assembly; remove assembly.
9. Remove connector from primary lead by disengaging leads from connector.
10. Remove coil assembly.
11. Remove retaining ring which secures magnetic core support plate and remove plate.
12. Remove brass washer and felt.
13. Remove vacuum advance unit.
14. To assemble, reverse disassembly procedure.

C-D Amplifier Removal

1. Disconnect negative battery cable.
2. Disconnect the following leads from the amplifier harness assembly:
   a. Tachometer pickup
   b. Harness ground
   c. Coil wires
   d. Distributor connector
   e. Connectors at fuse panel
   f. Connector at junction block
3. Remove three retaining nuts from amplifier assembly and remove amplifier.
4. To install, reverse removal procedure.

No adjustments can be made to the C-D ignition system, and no periodic maintenance is required.

Delco-Remy Unit Ignition System

This system is almost identical to the Delco-Remy Magnetic Pulse System. The ignition primary circuit passes through the electronic module (called the ignition pulse amplifier in Delco-Remy system) and is interrupted when a signal is sent to the control module from the distributor. The main difference between the two systems is that, in the Unitized System, the ignition coil and control module are attached to the distributor body, making a compact, one-piece ignition system. It is optional equipment on some 1973-74 model Pontiacs with V8 engines.

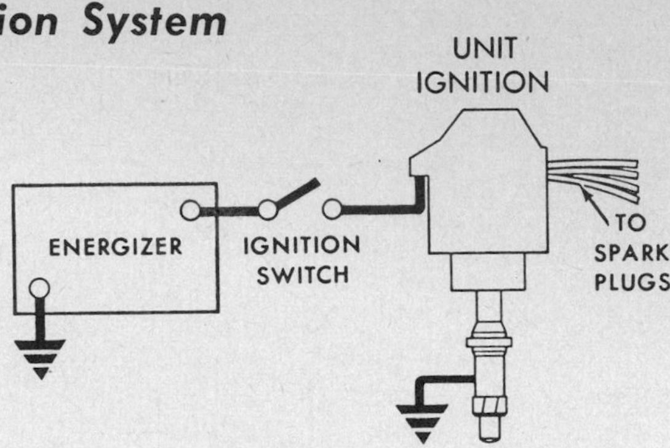

Unit Ignition System wiring diagram
(© Pontiac Div., G.M. Corp)

Delco-Remy High Energy Ignition (HEI) System

Components

The Delco-Remy High Energy Ignition (HEI) System is a breakerless, pulse triggered, transistor controlled, inductive discharge ignition system available as an option on 1974 model Oldsmobiles, Buicks, and Cadillacs with V8 engines. Starting 1975, HEI is used on all GM passenger car engines as standard equipment.

It is similar in operation to the Magnetic Pulse System and is identical to the Unit Ignition System except for the arrangement of components within the distributor. There are only nine external electrical connections; the ignition switch feed wire, and the eight spark plug leads. On V8 engines, the ignition coil is located within the distributor cap, connecting directly to the rotor. The major difference between the HEI System and the Unit Ignition System is that the HEI System is a full 12 volt system, while the Unit Ignition System incorporates a resistance wire to limit the voltage to the coil except during periods of starter motor operation.

Operation

The magnetic pick-up assembly located inside the distributor contains a permanent magnet, a pole piece with internal teeth, and a pick-up coil. When the teeth of the rotating timer core and pole piece align, an induced voltage in the pick-up coil signals the electronic module to open the coil primary circuit. As the primary current decreases, a high voltage is induced in the secondary windings of the ignition coil, directing a spark through the rotor and high voltage leads to fire the spark plugs. The dwell period is automatically controlled by the electronic module and is increased with increasing engine rpm. The HEI System features a longer spark duration which is instrumental in firing lean and EGR diluted fuel/air mixtures. The condenser (capacitor) located within the HEI distributor is provided for noise (static) suppression purposes only and is not a regularly replaced ignition system component.

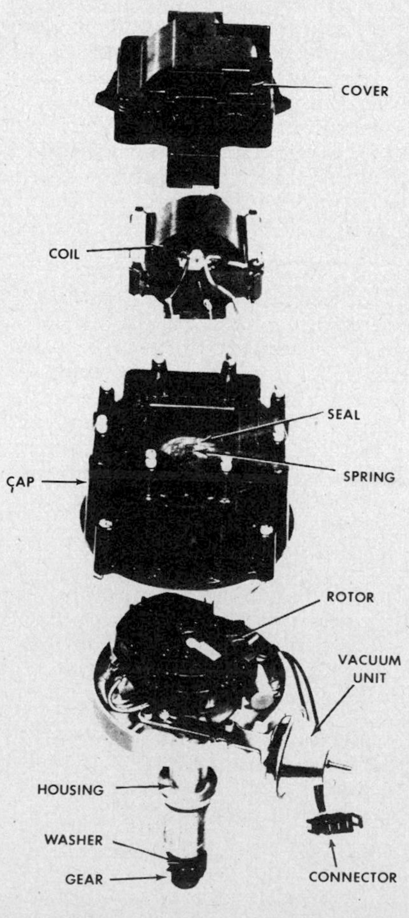

HEI distributor internal parts
(© Buick Div., G.M. Corp)

Major Repair Operations (distributor in engine)

Ignition Coil Replacement V6 and V8 Engines

1. Disconnect the feed and module wire terminal connectors from the distributor cap.
2. Remove the ignition set retainer.
3. Remove the 4 coil cover-to-distributor cap screws and the coil cover.
4. Remove the 4 coil-to-distributor cap screws.
5. Using a blunt drift, press the coil wire spade terminals up out of distributor cap.
6. Lift the coil up out of the distributor cap.
7. Remove and clean the coil spring, rubber seal washer and coil cavity of the distributor cap.
8. Coat the rubber seal with a dielectric lubricant furnished in the replacement ignition coil package.
9. Reverse the above procedures to install.

Four and Six Cylinder Engines

On 4 and 6 cylinder engines, a separate ignition coil is used. To remove and install it, proceed as follows:

1. Remove the ignition switch-to-coil lead from the coil.
2. Unfasten the distributor leads from the coil.
3. Remove the screws which secure the coil to the engine and lift it off.

Installation is the reverse of removal.

Distributor Cap Replacement All Engines

1. Remove the feed and module wire terminal connectors from the distributor cap.
2. Remove the retainer and spark

UNIT IGNITION SYSTEM TROUBLESHOOTING

Insure that black and pink leads are connected as shown in Fig. 1. Tighten both bolts, Fig. 1. Loose bolts may cause poor performance and radio interference.

ON THE VEHICLE

ENGINE WILL NOT RUN

1. Check ignition switch connector, Fig. 1.
2. Connect voltmeter from ignition switch connector to ground.
3. Turn on ignition switch.
4. If reading is zero, circuit is open between connector and ignition switch. Repair if needed.
5. If reading is battery voltage, hold one spark lead with insulating pliers about 1/4 in. from dry area of engine block while cranking engine.

If sparking occurs, trouble most likely is not ignition. Check fuel system.

If no spark, follow procedure under "On the Bench," with Unit Ignition System initially either on or off the engine.

ENGINE WILL START BUT NOT RUN, AND ENGINE MISS OR SURGE.

1. Insure that fuel system is satisfactory.
2. Check spark plug leads for arcing or leakage to ground.
3. Check spark plugs.

If no defects are found, follow procedure under "On the Bench" with Unit Ignition System initially either on or off the vehicle.

ON THE BENCH

1. Disassemble unit (Fig. 2).
2. Inspect coil, eight inserts, shell and rotor for arc-over or leakage.

1. Connect ohmmeter, Fig. 3.
2. Parts A and B each should be practically zero. If infinite on either reading, replace coil.
3. Part C should be 6000-9000 ohms. If outside range, replace coil.
4. Part D should be infinite. If not, replace coil.

1. Connect test stand vacuum source to vacuum unit.
2. Connect ohmmeter Parts A and B, Fig. 4.
3. Observe ohmmeter throughout vacuum range.
4. If Part A reads less than 650 ohms, or more than 850 ohms at any time, replace pickup coil, per Step 7 below.
5. If Part B reads other than infinite at any time, replace pickup coil, per step 7 below.
6. If vacuum unit is inoperative, replace per Step 7 below.
7. Remove unit from engine, drive pin from gear, remove rotor and shaft assembly from housing, remove shim and then "C" washer to replace pickup coil or vacuum unit (Fig. 5).

If no defects have been found, remove two attaching screws and replace module.

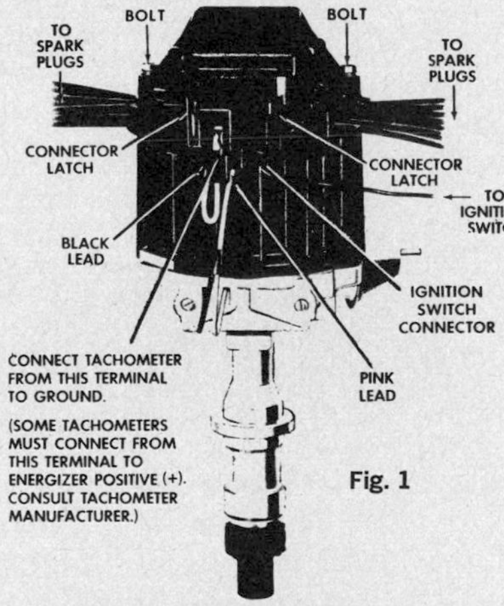

BOLT
BOLT
TO SPARK PLUGS
TO SPARK PLUGS
CONNECTOR LATCH
CONNECTOR LATCH
TO IGNITION SWITCH
BLACK LEAD
IGNITION SWITCH CONNECTOR
CONNECT TACHOMETER FROM THIS TERMINAL TO GROUND.
(SOME TACHOMETERS MUST CONNECT FROM THIS TERMINAL TO ENERGIZER POSITIVE (+). CONSULT TACHOMETER MANUFACTURER.)
PINK LEAD

Fig. 1

Unit Ignition System test hook-up
(© Pontiac Div., G.M. Corp)

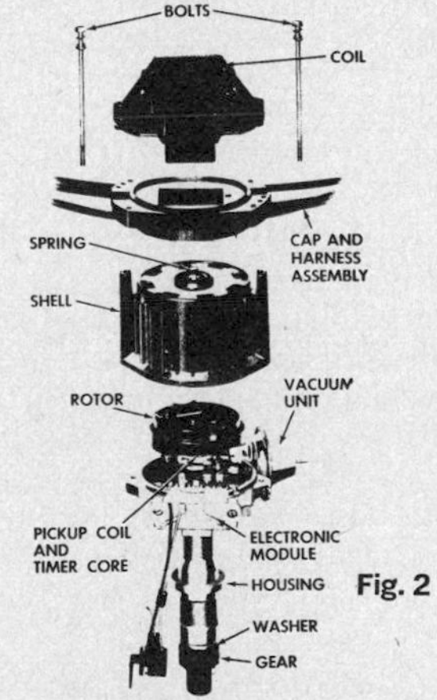

Fig. 2

Unit Ignition System exploded view
(© Pontiac Div., G.M. Corp)

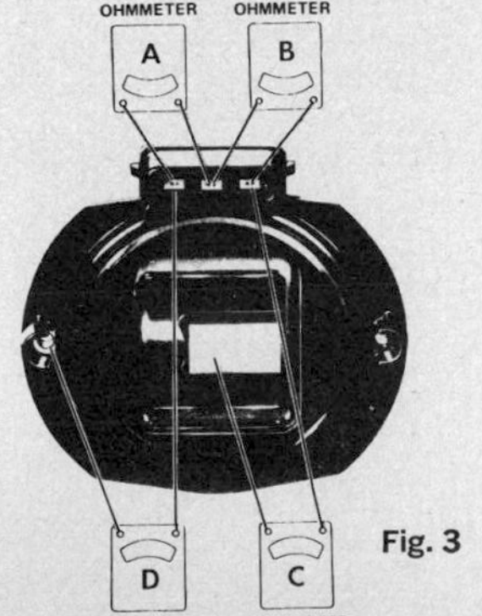

Fig. 3

Coil test hook-up—Unit Ignition System
(© Pontiac Div., G.M. Corp)

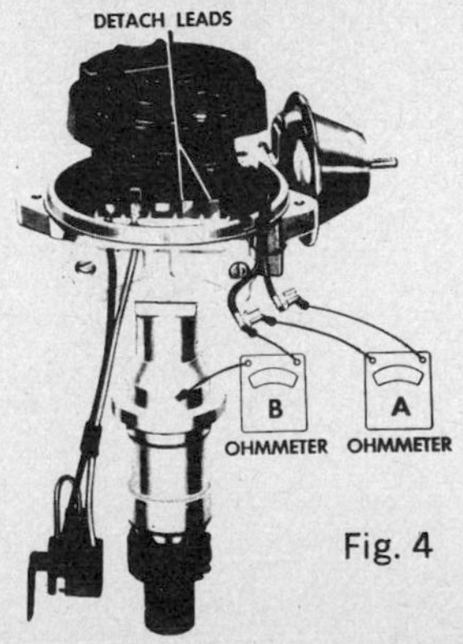

Fig. 4

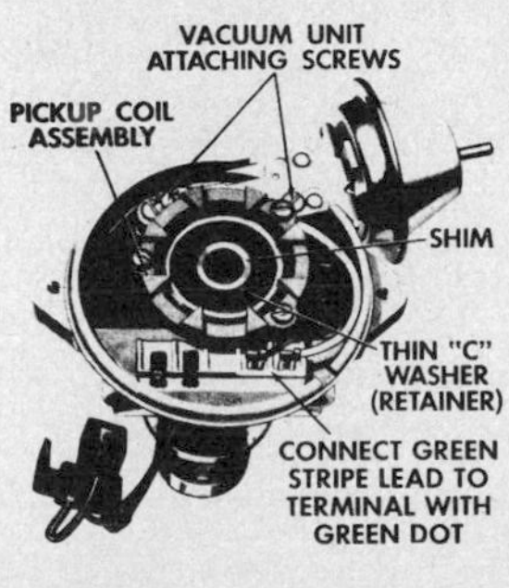

Fig. 5

plug wires from the cap.
3. Depress and release the 4 distributor cap-to-housing retainers and lift off the cap assembly.
4. Remove the 4 coil cover screws and cover (V8 and V6 only).
5. Using a finger or a blunt drift, push the spade terminals up out of the distributor cap (V8 and V6 only).
6. Remove all 4 coil screws and lift the coil, coil spring and rubber seal washer out of the cap coil cavity (V8 and V6 only).
7. Using a new distributor cap, reverse the above procedures to assemble being sure to clean and lubricate the rubber seal washer with dielectric lubricant.

Rotor Replacement
All Engines

1. Disconnect the feed and module wire connectors from the distributor.
2. Depress and release the 4 distributor cap to housing retainers and lift off the cap assembly.
3. Remove the two rotor attaching screws and rotor.
4. Reverse the above procedure to install.

Vacuum Advance Replacement
All Engines

1. Remove the distributor cap and rotor as previously described.
2. Disconnect the vacuum hose from the vacuum advance unit. Remove the module.
3. Remove the two vacuum advance retaining screws, pull the advance unit outward, rotate and disengage the operating rod from its tang.
4. Reverse the above procedure to install.

Module Replacement
All Engines

1. Remove the distributor cap and rotor as previously described.
2. Disconnect the harness connector and pick-up coil spade connectors from the module (note their positions).
3. Remove the two screws and module from the distributor housing.
4. Coat the bottom of the new module with dielectric lubricant. Reverse the above procedure to install. Be sure that the leads are installed correctly.

Distributor Removal
All Engines

1. Disconnect the ground cable from the battery.
2. Disconnect the feed and module terminal connectors from the distributor cap. (Don't use a screwdriver).

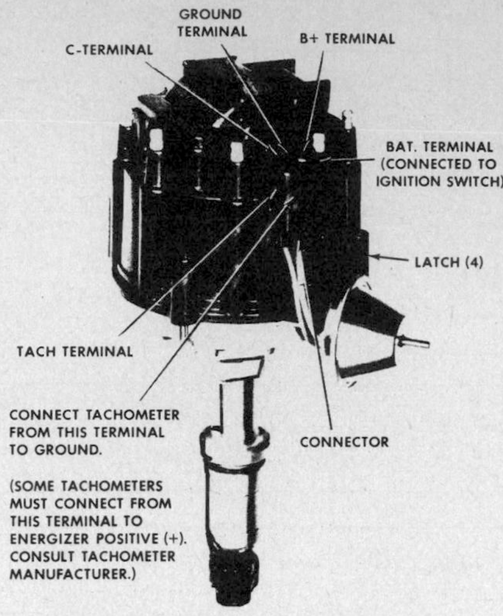

High Energy Ignition System distributor
(© Oldsmobile Div., G.M. Corp)

3. Disconnect the hose at the vacuum advance.
4. Depress and release the 4 distributor cap-to-housing retainers and lift off the cap assembly.
5. Using crayon or chalk, make locating marks on the rotor and module and on the distributor housing and engine for installation purposes.
6. Loosen and remove the distributor clamp bolt and clamp, and lift distributor out of the engine. Noting the relative position of the rotor and module alignment marks, make a second mark on the rotor to align it with the one mark on the module.

Distributor Installation
All Engines

1. With a new O-ring on the distributor housing and the second mark on the rotor aligned with the mark on the module, install the distributor, taking care to align the mark on the housing with the one on the engine. It may be necessary to lift the distributor and turn the rotor slightly to align the gears and the oil pump driveshaft.
2. With the respective marks aligned, install the clamp and bolt finger-tight.
3. Install and secure the distributor cap.
4. Connect the feed and module connectors to the distributor cap.
5. Connect a timing light to the engine and plug the vacuum hose.
6. Connect the ground cable to the battery.
7. Start the engine and set the timing.
8. Turn the engine off and tighten the distributor clamp bolt. Disconnect the timing light and unplug and connect the hose to the vacuum advance.

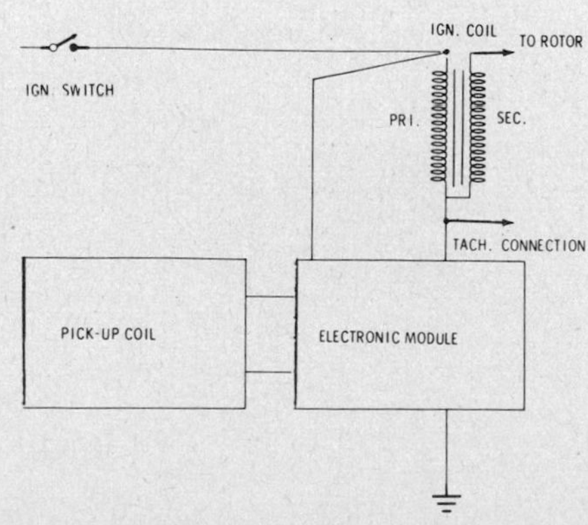

HEI System—basic wiring
(© Oldsmobile Div., G.M. Corp)

Service Procedures (distributor removed)

Driven Gear Replacement
All Engines

1. With the distributor removed, use a ⅛ in. pin punch and tap out the driven gear roll pin.
2. Hold the rotor end of shaft and rotate the driven gear to shear any burrs in the roll pin hole.
3. Remove the driven gear from the shaft.
4. Reverse the above procedure to install.

Mainshaft Replacement
All Engines

1. With the driven gear and rotor removed, gently pull the mainshaft out of the housing.
2. Remove the advance springs, weights and slide the weight base plate off the mainshaft.
3. Reverse the above procedure to install.

Pole Piece, Magnet or Pick-up Coil Replacement
All Engines

1. With the mainshaft out of its housing, remove the 3 retaining screws, pole piece and magnet and/or pick-up coil.
2. Reverse the removal procedure to install making sure that the pole piece teeth do not contact the timer core teeth by installing and rotating the mainshaft. Loosen the 3 screws and realign the pole piece as necessary.

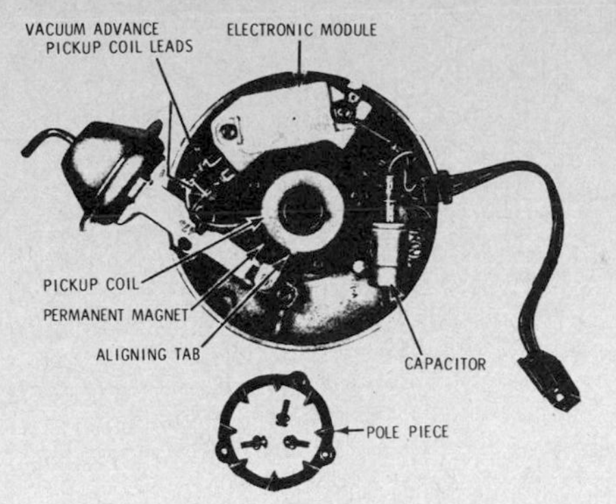

HEI System—pole piece removal
(© Oldsmobile Div., G.M. Corp)

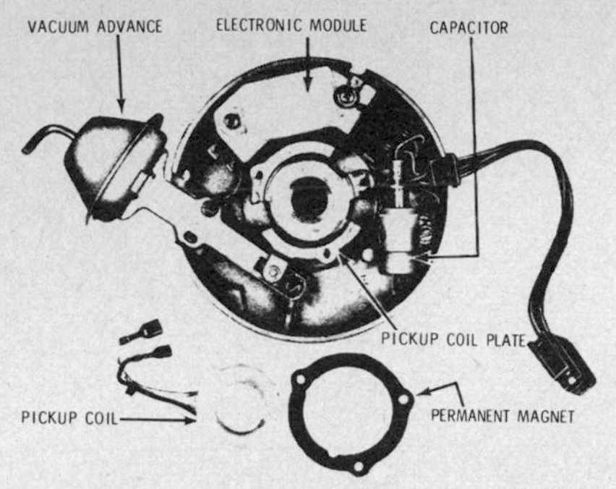

HEI System—coil and magnet removal
(© Oldsmobile Div., G.M. Corp)

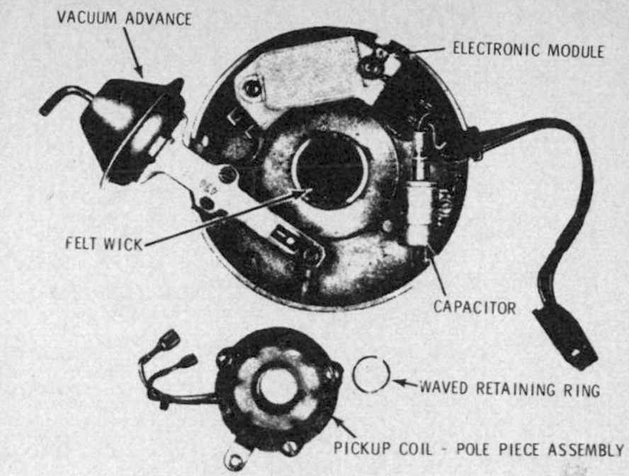

HEI System—pick-up coil removal
(© Oldsmobile Div., G.M. Corp)

HIGH ENERGY IGNITION DIAGNOSIS

ENGINE WILL NOT START

Use fiber or plastic spark plug wire removing tool to remove one spark plug lead. Hold the lead 1/4" from dry area of engine block while cranking engine.

- SPARK JUMPS
  - Problem is not ignition distributor. Check fuel system.
- SPARK DOES NOT JUMP
  - Connect 12 volt test lamp to ground and to "BAT" terminal lead on distributor, ignition switch ON.
    - LAMP OFF
      - Repair open in pink wire from ignition switch to distributor.
    - LAMP ON
      - (go to Remove cap and coil assembly by turning 4 latches. Inspect cap and rotor for arc-over.)

ENGINE RUNS, BUT RUNS ROUGH

If an ignition oscilloscope is available go to next page.

- ENGINE ROUGH AT IDLE ONLY
  - Problem is not ignition. Check:
    1. vacuum hoses for leaks
    2. carburetor mounting bolts (15 ft.-lb).
    3. idle speed and timing
- ENGINE ROUGH AT ALL SPEEDS
  - Remove cap and coil assembly by turning 4 latches. Inspect cap and rotor for arc-over.
    - ARC-OVER
      - Replace cap or rotor as required.
    - NO ARC-OVER
      - Connect ohmmeter, Step 1, Figure A. Reading should be zero or nearly zero.
        - READING HIGH
          - Replace coil
        - READING NORMAL
          - Connect ohmmeter, Step 2, Figure A. Use high scale. Reading should be high, but less than infinite
            - READING INFINITE
              - Replace coil
            - READING NORMAL
              - Remove coil and inspect for arc-over at spring and seal.
                - ARC-OVER
                  - Replace cap, coil or seal as required.
                - NO ARC-OVER
                  - Connect test stand vacuum source to vacuum advance unit.
                    - VACUUM ADVANCE INOPERATIVE
                      - Replace vacuum advance.
                    - VACUUM ADVANCE OPERATES
                      - Connect ohmmeter Step 1, Figure B. Operate vacuum advance through range. Ohmmeter should read infinite at all positions.
                        - READING NOT INFINITE
                          - Replace pick-up coil
                        - READING NORMAL
                          - Connect ohmmeter, Step 2, Figure B. Should read 650 to 850 ohms in all vacuum advance positions.
                            - READING NOT NORMAL
                              - Replace pick-up coil.
                            - READING NORMAL
                              - If no defects have been found at this time, replace module.
- ENGINE ROUGH AT PART THROTTLE AND HIGHER SPEEDS. OK AT IDLE AND OFF. IDLE.
  - Replace module.

INSTRUCTIONS
1. Insure that ignition switch feed ("BAT") connector is properly attached.
2. Insure that all spark plug leads are properly connected.

INSURE THAT PROPER FUEL IS BEING DELIVERED TO ENGINE. CHECK ALL VACUUM HOSES FOR LEAKS.

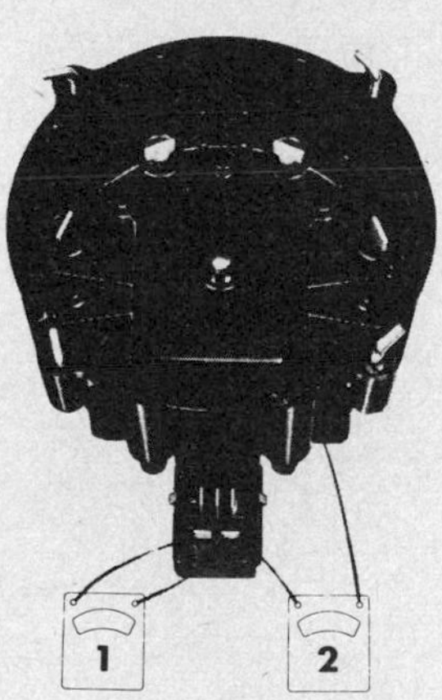

1 2

Figure A

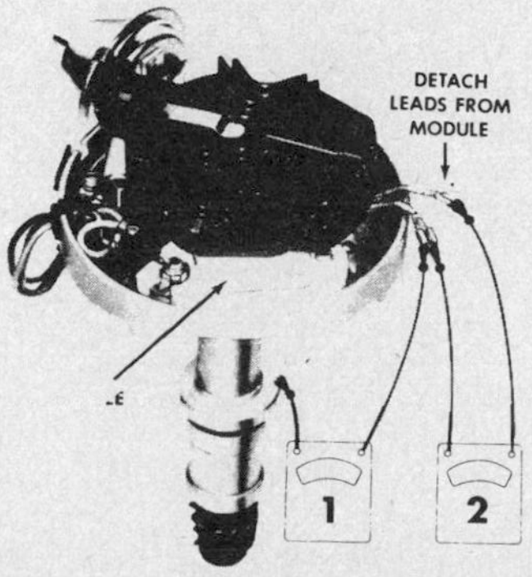

DETACH LEADS FROM MODULE

1 2

Figure B

(© Oldsmobile Div., G.M. Corp)

Chrysler Electronic Ignition

Components

This system consists of a special pulse-sending distributor, an electronic control unit, a two-element ballast resistor, and a special ignition coil.

The distributor does not contain breaker points or a condenser, these parts being replaced by a distributor reluctor and a pick-up unit.

Operation

The ignition primary circuit is connected from the battery, through the ignition switch, through the primary side of the ignition coil, to the control unit where it is grounded. The secondary circuit is the same as in conventional ignition systems: the secondary side of the coil, the coil wire to the distributor, the rotor, the spark plug wires, and the spark plugs.

The magnetic pulse distributor is also connected to the control unit. As the distributor shaft rotates, the distributor reluctor turns past the pick-up unit. As the reluctor turns past the pick-up unit, each of the eight teeth on the reluctor pass near the pick-up unit once during each distributor revolution (two crankshaft revolutions since the distributor runs at one-half crankshaft speed). As the reluctor teeth move close to the pick-up unit, the magnetic rotating reluctor induces voltage into the magnetic pick-up unit. This voltage pulse is sent to the ignition control unit from the magnetic pick-up unit. When the pulse enters the control unit, it signals the control unit to interrupt the ignition primary circuit. This causes the primary circuit to collapse and begins the induction of the magnetic lines of force from the primary side of the coil into the secondary side of the coil. This induction provides the required voltage to fire the spark plugs.

The advantages of this system are that the transistors in the control unit can make and break the primary ignition circuit much faster than conventional ignition points can, and higher primary voltage can be utilized, since this system can be made to handle higher voltage without adverse effects, whereas ignition breaker points cannot. The quicker switching time of this system allows longer coil primary circuit saturation time and longer induction time when the primary circuit collapses. This increased time allows the primary circuit to build up more current and the secondary circuit to discharge more current.

TROUBLESHOOTING CHRYSLER ELECTRONIC IGNITION

Condition	*Possible Cause*	*Correction*
ENGINE WILL NOT START (Fuel and carburetion known to be OK)	a) Dual Ballast	Check resistance of each section: Compensating resistance: .50-.60 ohms @ 70°-80°F Auxiliary Ballast: 4.75-5.75 ohms Replace if faulty. Check wire positions.
	b) Faulty Ignition Coil	Check for carbonized tower. Check primary and secondary resistances: Primary: 1.41-1.79 ohms @ 70°-80°F Secondary: 9,200-11,700 ohms @ 70°-80°F Check in coil tester.
	c) Faulty Pickup or Improper Pickup Air Gap	Check pickup coil resistance: 400-600 ohms Check pickup gap: .010 in. feeler gauge should not slip between pickup coil core and an aligned reluctor blade. No evidence of pickup core striking reluctor blades should be visible. To reset gap, tighten pickup adjustment screw with a .008 in. feeler gauge held between pickup core and an aligned reluctor blade. After resetting gap, run distributor on test stand and apply vacuum advance, making sure that the pickup core does not strike the reluctor blades.
	d) Faulty Wiring	Visually inspect wiring for brittle insulation. Inspect connectors. Molded connectors should be inspected for rubber inside female terminals.
	e) Faulty Control Unit	Replace if all of the above checks are negative. Whenever the control unit or dual ballast is replaced, make sure the dual ballast wires are correctly inserted in the keyed molded connector.
ENGINE SURGES	a) Wiring	Inspect for loose connection and/or broken conductors in harness.
SEVERELY (Not Lean	b) Faulty Pickup Leads	Disconnect vacuum advance. If surging stops, replace pickup.
Carburetor)	c) Ignition Coil	Check for intermittent primary.
ENGINE MISSES (Carburetion OK)	a) Spark Plugs	Check plugs. Clean and regap if necessary.
	b) Secondary Cable	Check cables with an ohmmeter, or observe secondary circuit performance with an oscilloscope.
	c) Ignition Coil	Check for cabonized tower. Check in coil tester.
	d) Wiring	Check for loose or dirty connections.
	e) Faulty Pickup Lead	Disconnect vacuum advance. If miss stops, replace pickup.
	f) Control Unit	Replace if the above checks are negative.

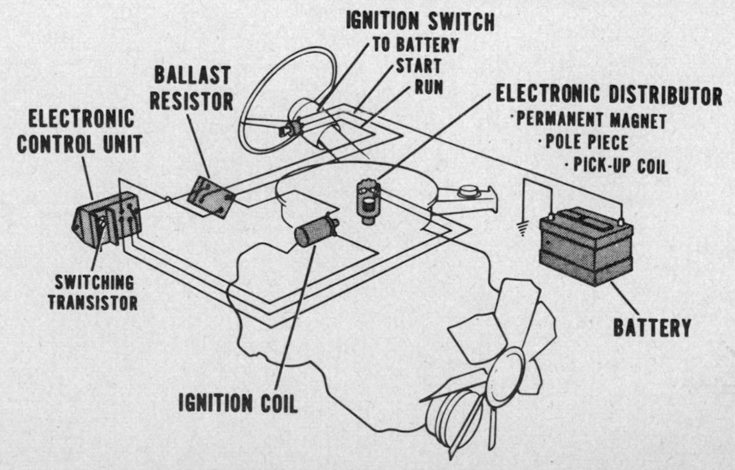

Chrysler system wiring diagram (© Chrysler Corp)

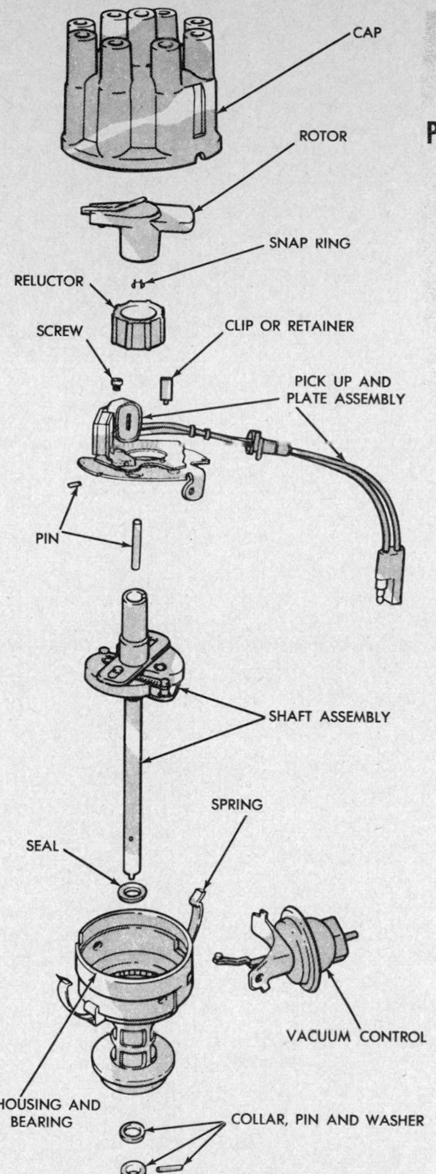

Chrysler Electronic Ignition distributor disassembled—V8 (© Chrysler Corp)

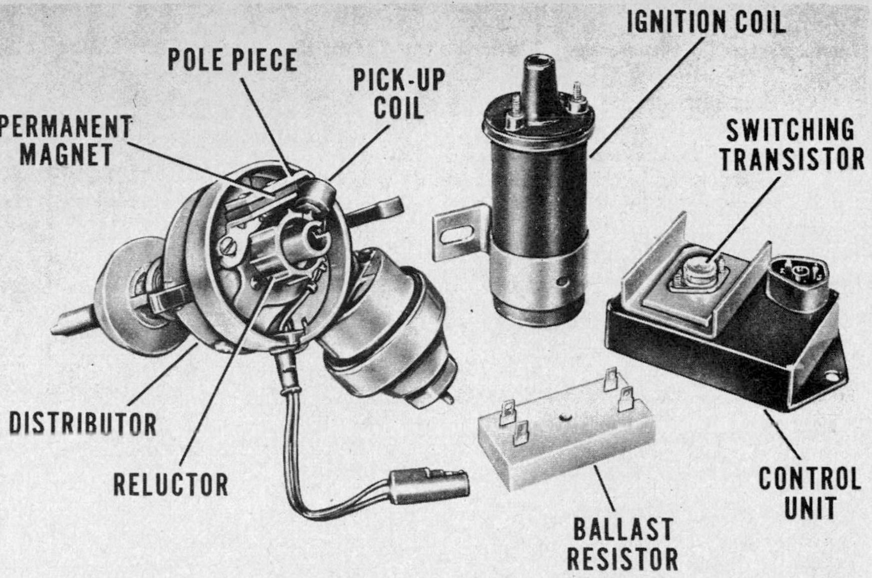

Chrysler system components (© Chrysler Corp)

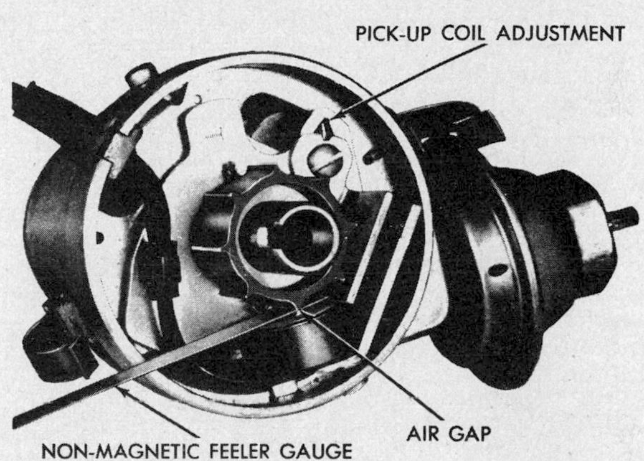

Air gap adjustment—Chrysler Electronic Ignition distributor (© Chrysler Corp)

Pick-Up Coil Replacement

1972-74

1. Remove the distributor.
2. Remove the pick-up coil mounting screw.
3. Remove the wires from the retainers on the upper plate and distributor housing.
4. Remove pick-up coil from the upper plate.
5. Position the pick-up coil on the pivot of the upper plate and install the mounting screw. Do not tighten.
6. Insert the wires into the appropriate retainers in the distributor.
7. Install the distributor.
8. Set the air gap.

1975

1. Remove the distributor from the engine.
2. Using two small pry-bars or screwdrivers (maximum 7/16 in. wide), pry the reluctor off the shaft from the bottom.

Caution Do not damage the teeth on the reluctor.

3. Unfasten the vacuum advance-to-distributor housing screws. Remove the vacuum unit, after disconnecting the arm from the upper plate.
4. Unfasten the pick-up coil wires from the distributor housing.
5. Unfasten the two screws which secure the lower plate to the distributor housing. Lift out the lower plate together with the upper plate and pick-up coil.
6. Separate the upper and lower plates by depressing the retaining clip on the underside of the plate and slide it away from the stud. The pick-up coil will come off with the upper plate; they cannot be separated; they must be serviced as an assembly.

Installation is the reverse of removal. Place a small amount of distributor grease on the support pins on the lower plate.

Air Gap Adjustment

1. Align one reluctor tooth with the pick-up coil tooth.
2. Loosen the pick-up coil hold-down screw.
3. Insert a 0.008 in. nonmagnetic feeler gauge between the reluctor tooth and the pick-up coil tooth.
4. Adjust the air gap so that contact is made between the reluctor tooth, the feeler gauge, and the pick-up coil tooth.
5. Tighten the hold-down screw.
6. Remove the feeler gauge.

NOTE: *No force should be required in removing the feeler gauge.*

7. Check the air gap with a 0.010 in. feeler gauge. A 0.010 in. feeler gauge should not fit into the air gap.

CAUTION: *A 0.010 in. feeler gauge can be forced into the air gap. DO NOT FORCE THE FEELER GAUGE INTO THE AIR GAP.*

8. Apply vacuum to the vacuum unit and rotate the governor shaft. The pick-up pole should not hit the reluctor teeth. The gap was not properly adjusted if any hitting occurs. If hitting occurs on only one side of the reluctor, the distributor shaft is probably bent, and the governor and shaft assembly should be replaced.

AMC Breakerless Inductive Discharge (BID) Ignition

Components

The AMC breakerless inductive discharge (BID) ignition system consists of five components:

Control unit
Coil
Breakerless distributor
Ignition cables
Spark plugs

The control unit is a solid-state, epoxy-sealed module with waterproof connectors. The control unit has a built-in current regulator, so no separate ballast resistor or resistance wire is needed in the primary circuit. Battery voltage is supplied to the ignition coil positive (+) terminal when the ignition key is turned to the "ON" or "START" position; low voltage is also supplied by the control unit.

The coil used with the BID system requires no special service. It works just like the coil in a conventional ignition system.

The distributor is conventional, except for the lack of points, condenser and cam. Advance is supplied by both a vacuum unit and a centrifugal advance mechanism. A standard cap, rotor, and dust shield are used.

In place of the points, cam, and condensor, the distributor has a sensor and trigger wheel. The sensor is a small coil which generates an electromagnetic field when excited by the oscillator in the control unit.

Standard spark plugs and ignition cables are used.

Operation

When the ignition switch is turned on, the control unit is activated. The control unit then sends an oscillating signal to the sensor which causes the sensor to generate a magnetic field. When one of the trigger wheel teeth enters this field, the strength of the oscillation in the sensor is reduced. Once the strength drops to a predetermined level, a demodulator circuit operates the control unit's switching

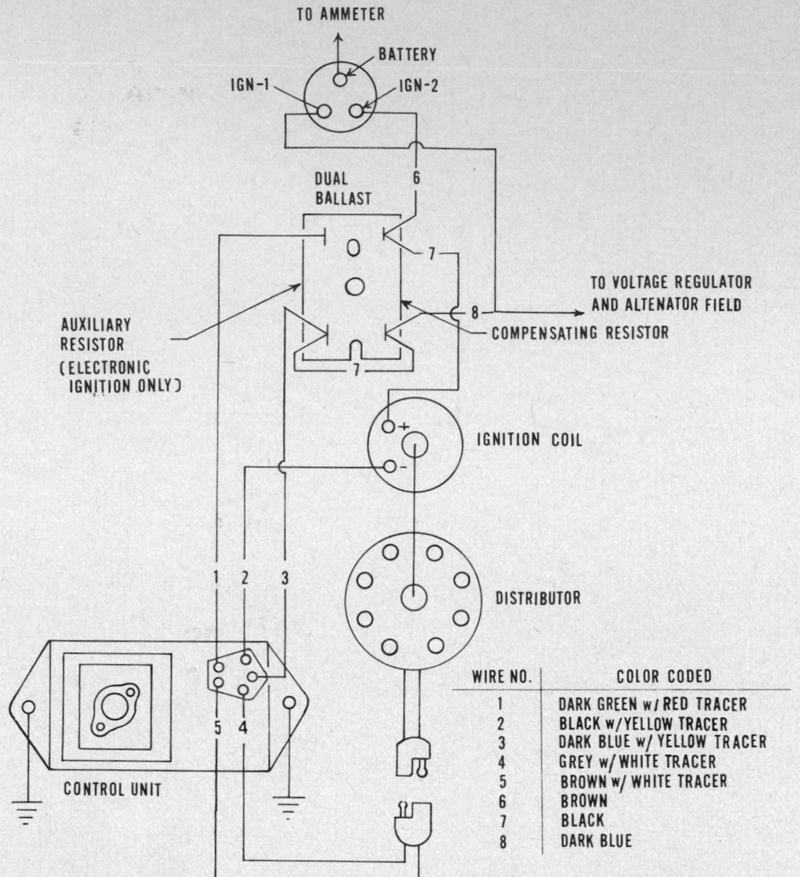

WIRE NO.	COLOR CODED
1	DARK GREEN w/ RED TRACER
2	BLACK w/YELLOW TRACER
3	DARK BLUE w/ YELLOW TRACER
4	GREY w/ WHITE TRACER
5	BROWN w/ WHITE TRACER
6	BROWN
7	BLACK
8	DARK BLUE

Chrysler system schematic
(© Chrysler Corp)

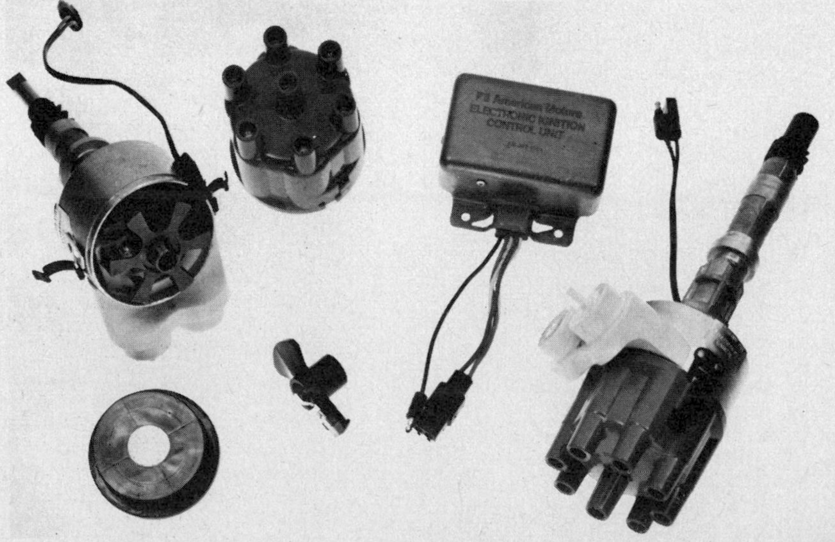

Components of the BID electronic ignition system (© AMC)

transistor. The switching transistor is wired in series with the coil primary circuit; it switches the circuit off when it gets the demodulator signal.

From this point on, the BID ignition system works in the same manner as a conventional ignition system.

Troubleshooting

1. Check all of the BID ignition system electrical connections.
2. Disconnect the coil-to-distributor high tension lead.
3. Hold the end of the lead ½ in. away from a ground. Crank the engine. If there is a spark, the trouble is not in the ignition system.
4. If there was no spark in step 3, connect a test light with a No. 57 bulb between the positive coil terminal (+) and a good ground. Have an assistant turn the ignition switch to "ON" and "START" (Do not start the engine). The bulb should light in both positions; if it doesn't, the fault lies in the battery-to-coil circuit. Check the ignition switch and related wiring.
5. If the test light lit in step 4, disconnect the coil-to-distributor leads at the connector and connect the test light between the positive (+) and negative (−) coil terminals.
6. Turn the ignition switch on. If the test light doesn't come on, check the control unit's ground lead. If the ground lead is in good condition, replace the control unit.
7. If the bulb lights in step 6, leave the test light in place and short the terminals on the coil-to-distributor connector together with a jumper lead, (connector separated) at the coil side of the connector. If the light stays on, replace the control unit.
8. If the test light goes out, remove it. Check for a spark, as in step 2, each time that the coil-to-distributor connector terminals are shorted together with the jumper lead. If there is a spark, replace the control unit; if there is no spark, replace the coil.

Coil Testing

Test the coil with a conventional coil checker or an ohmmeter. Primary resistance should be 1-2 ohms and secondary resistance should be 8-12 kilohms. The open output circuit should be more than 20 kilovolts. Replace the coil if it doesn't meet specifications.

Sensor Testing

Check the sensor resistance by connecting an ohmmeter to its leads. Resistance should be 1.8 ohms (±10%)

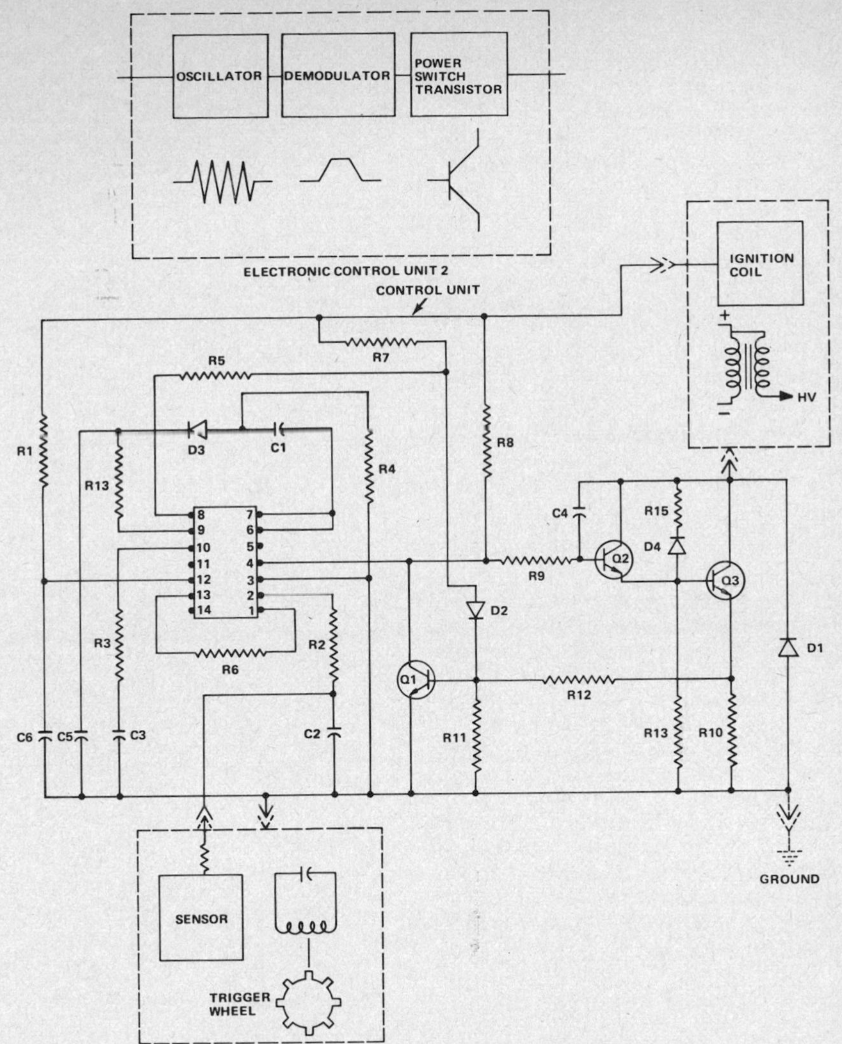

BID ignition system schematic (© AMC)

at 77° F. Replace the sensor if it doesn't meet these specifications.

Distributor Overhaul

NOTE: *If you must remove the sensor from the distributor for any reason, it will be necessary to have the special sensor positioning gauge in order to align it properly during installation.*

1. Scribe matchmarks on the distributor housing, rotor, and engine block. Disconnect the leads and vacuum lines from the distributor. Remove the distributor. Unless the cap is to be replaced, leave it connected to the spark plug cables and position it out of the way.
2. Remove the rotor and dust cap.
3. Place a small gear puller over the trigger wheel, so that its jaws grip the inner shoulders of the wheel and not its arms. Place a thick washer between the gear puller and the distributor shaft to act as a spacer; do not press against the smaller inner shaft.

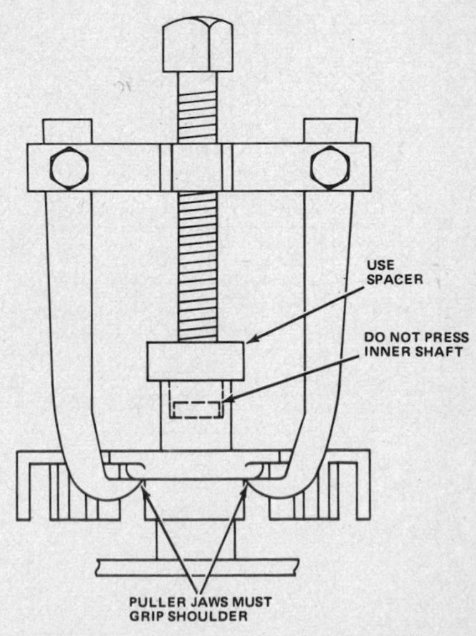

Removing the trigger wheel (© AMC)

4. Loosen the sensor hold-down screw with a small pair of needle-nosed pliers; it has a tamper-proof head. Pull the sensor lead grommet out of the distributor body and pull out the leads from around the spring pivot pin.
5. Release the sensor securing spring by lifting it. Make sure that it clears the leads. Slide the sensor off the bracket. *Remember, a special gauge is required for sensor installation.*
6. Remove the vacuum advance unit securing screw. Slide the vacuum unit out of the distributor. Remove it only if it is to be replaced.
7. Clean and dry the vacuum unit and sensor backets. Lubrication of these parts is not necessary.

BID distributor assembly is as follows:

1. Install the vacuum unit, if it was removed.
2. Assemble the sensor, sensor guide, flat washer, and retaining screw. Tighten the screw only far enough to keep the assembly together; don't allow the screw to project below the bottom of the sensor.

NOTE: *Replacement sensors come with a slotted-head screw to aid in assembly. If the original sensor is being used, replace the tamper-proof screw with a conventional one. Use the original washer.*

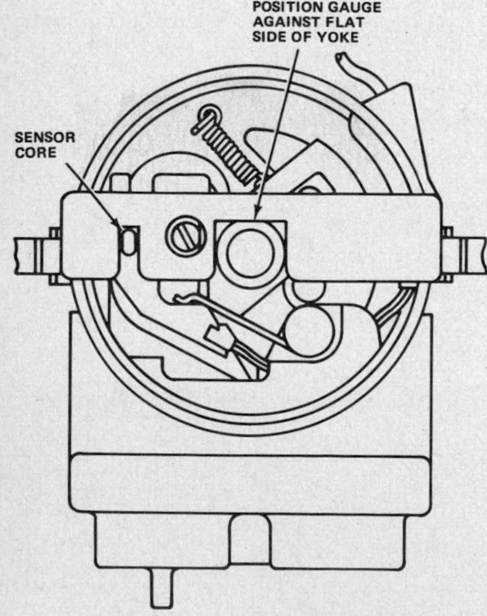

Using the special gauge to align the sensor coil (© AMC)

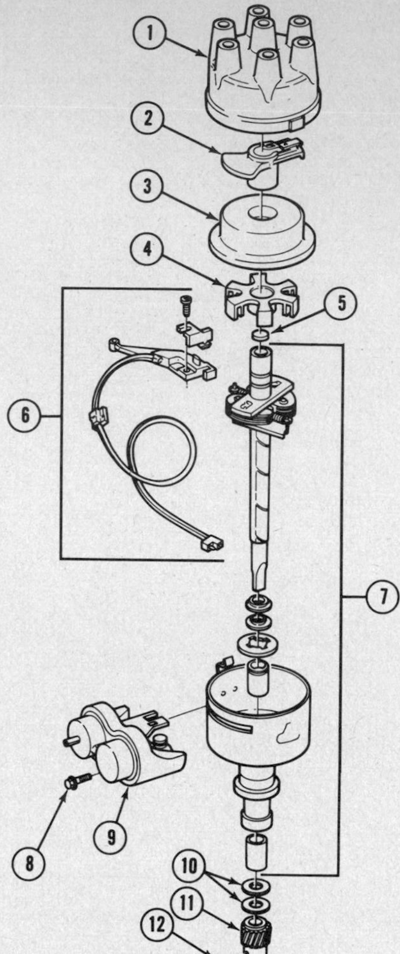

BID distributor components (© AMC)

1 Cap
2 Rotor
3 Dust shield
4 Trigger wheel
5 Felt lubricator
6 Sensor assembly
7 Distributor body
8 Vacuum unit screw
9 Vacuum advance unit
10 Shim
11 Drive gear
12 Pin

3. Secure the sensor on the vacuum advance unit bracket, making sure that the tip of the senor is placed in the notch on the summing bar.
4. Position the spring on the sensor and route the leads around the spring pivot pin. Fit the sensor lead grommet into the slot on the distributor body. Be sure that the lead can't get caught in the trigger wheel.
5. Place the special sensor positioning gauge over the distributor shaft, so that the flat on the shaft is against the large notch on the gauge. Move the sensor until the sensor core fits into the small notch on the gauge. Tighten the sensor securing screw with the gauge in place (through the round hole in the gauge).
6. It should be possible to remove and install the gauge without any side movement of the sensor. Check this and remove the gauge.
7. Position the trigger wheel on the shaft. Check to see that the sensor core is centered between the trigger wheel legs and that the legs don't touch the core.
8. Bend a piece of 0.050 in. gauge wire, so that it has a 90° angle and one leg ½ in. long. Use the gauge to measure the clearance between the trigger wheel legs and the sensor boss. Press the trigger wheel on the shaft until it just touches the gauge. Support the shaft during this operation.
9. Place 3 to 5 drops of SAE 20 oil on the felt lubricator wick.
10. Install the dust shield and rotor on the shaft.
11. Install the distributor on the engine using the matchmarks made during removal and adjust the timing. Use a new distributor mounting gasket.

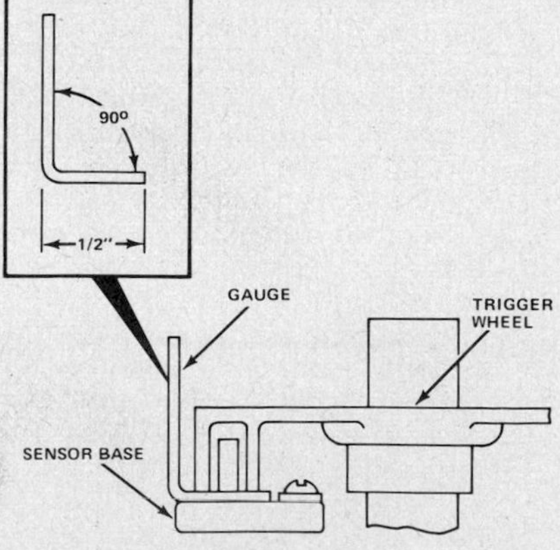

Fabricate a gauge to measure trigger wheel clearance (© AMC)

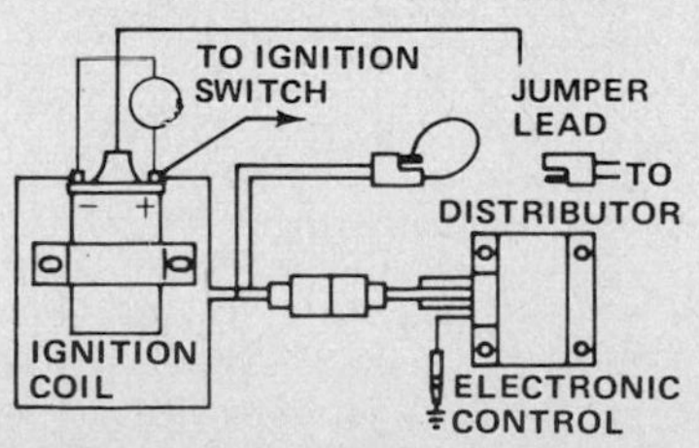

Carburetors

Carburetor Functions, Principles, and Circuits

Functions

Gasoline is the source of fuel for power in the automobile engine and the carburetor is the mechanism which automatically mixes liquid fuel with air in the correct proportions to provide the desired power output from the engine. The carburetor performs this function by metering, atomizing, and mixing fuel with air flowing through the engine.

A carburetor also regulates the volume of air-to-fuel mixture which enters the engine. It is the carburetor's regulation of the mixture flow which gives the operator control of the engine speed.

Metering

The automotive internal combustion engine operates efficiently within a relatively small range of air-to-fuel ratios. It is the function of the carburetor to meter the fuel in exact proportions to the air flowing into the engine, so that the optimum ratio of air-to-fuel is maintained under all operating conditions. Regulations governing exhaust gas emissions have made the proper metering of fuel by the carburetor an increasingly important factor. Too rich a mixture will result in poor economy and increased emissions, while too lean a mixture will result in loss of power and generally poor performance.

Carburetors are matched to engines so that metering can be accomplished by using carefully calibrated metering jets which allow fuel to enter the engine at a rate proportional to the engine's ability to draw air.

Atomization

The liquid fuel must be broken up into small particles so that it will more readily mix with air and vaporize. The more contact the fuel has with the air, the better the vaporization. Atomization can be accomplished in two ways: air may be drawn into a stream of fuel which will cause a turbulence and break the solid stream of fuel into smaller particles; or a nozzle can be positioned at the point of highest air velocity in the carburetor and the fuel will be torn into a fine spray as it enters the air stream.

Distribution

The carburetor is the primary device involved in the distribution of fuel to the engine. The more efficiently fuel and air are combined in the carburetor, the smoother the flow of vaporized mixture through the intake manifold to each combustion chamber. Hence, the importance of the carburetor in fuel distribution.

Principles

Vacuum

All carburetors operate on the basic principle of pressure difference. Any pressure less than atmospheric pressure is considered vacuum or a low pressure area. In the engine, as the piston moves down on the intake stroke with the intake valve open, a partial vacuum is created in the intake manifold. The farther the piston travels downward, the greater the vacuum created in the manifold. As vacuum increases in the manifold, a difference in pressure occurs between the carburetor and cylinder. The carburetor is positioned in such a way that the high pressure above it, and the vacuum or low pressure beneath it, causes air to be drawn through it. Fuel and air always move from high to low pressure areas.

Venturi Principle

To obtain greater pressure drop at the tip of the fuel nozzle so that fuel will flow, the principle of increasing the air velocity to create a low pressure area is used. The device used to increase the velocity of the air flowing through the carburetor is called a venturi. A venturi is a specially designed restriction placed in the air flow. In order for the air to pass through the restriction, it must accelerate causing a pressure drop or vacuum as it passes.

Carburetor Circuits

Float Circuit

The float circuit includes the float, float bowl, and a needle valve and seat. This circuit controls the amount of gas allowed to flow into the carburetor.

As the fuel level rises, it causes the float to rise which pushes the needle valve into its seat. As soon as the valve and seat make contact, the flow of gas is cut off from the fuel inlet. When the level of fuel drops, the float sinks and releases the needle valve from its seat which allows the gas to flow in. In actual operation, the fuel is maintained at practically a constant level. The float tends to hold the needle valve partly closed so that the incoming fuel just balances the fuel being withdrawn.

Idle and Low Speed Circuit

When the throttle is closed or only slightly opened, the air speed is low and practically no vacuum develops in the venturi. This means that the fuel nozzle will not feed. Thus, the carburetor must have another circuit to supply fuel during operation with a closed or slightly opened throttle.

This circuit is called the idle and low speed circuit. It consists of passages in which air and gas can flow beneath the throttle plate. With the throttle plate closed, there is high vacuum from the intake manifold. Atmospheric pressure pushes the

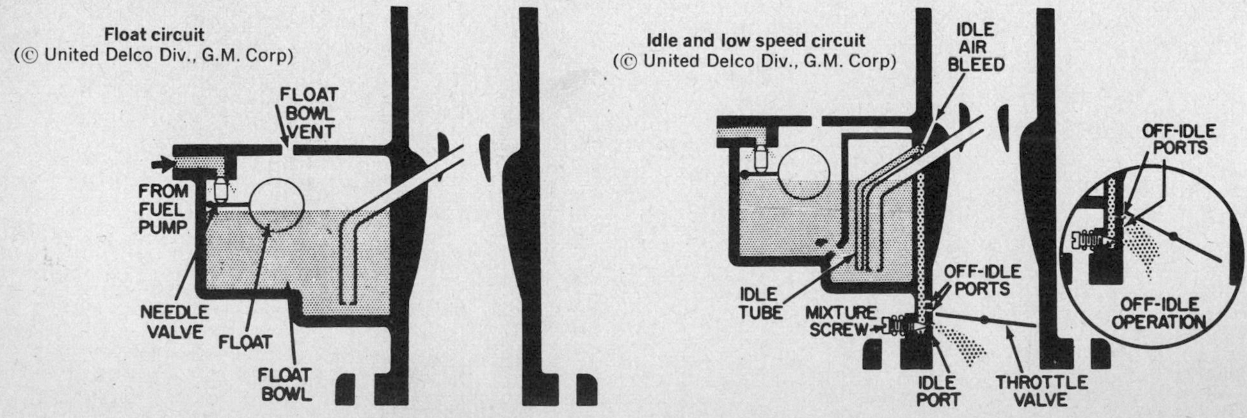

Float circuit
(© United Delco Div., G.M. Corp)

Idle and low speed circuit
(© United Delco Div., G.M. Corp)

air/fuel mixture through the passages of the idle and low speed circuit and past the tapered point of the idle adjustment screw, which regulates engine idle mixture volume.

High Speed Partial Load Circuit

When the throttle plate is opened sufficiently, there is little difference in vacuum between the upper and lower part of the air horn. Thus, little air/fuel mixture will discharge from the low speed and idle circuit. However, under this condition enough air is moving through the air horn to produce vacuum in the venturi to cause the main nozzle or high speed nozzle to discharge fuel. The circuit from the float bowl to the main nozzle is called the high speed partial load circuit. A nearly constant air/fuel ratio is maintained by this circuit from part to full-throttle.

High Speed Full Power Circuit

For high-speed, full-power, wide-open throttle operation, the air/fuel mixture must be enriched; this is done either mechanically or by intake manifold vacuum.

Full Power Circuit (Mechanical)

This circuit includes a metering rod jet and a metering rod. The rod has two steps of different diameters and is attached to the throttle linkage.

When the throttle is wide open, the metering rod is lifted bringing the smaller diameter of the rod into the jet. When the throttle is partly closed, the larger diameter of the metering rod is in the jet. This restricts fuel flow to the main nozzle but adequate amounts of fuel do flow for part-throttle operation.

Full Power Circuit (Vacuum)

This circuit is operated by intake manifold vacuum. It includes a vacuum diaphragm linked to a valve on a metering rod.

When the throttle is opened so that intake manifold vacuum is reduced, the spring raises the diaphragm. This allows the metering rod to be lifted so that its smaller diameter clears the jet, thus allowing more fuel to flow in.

Accelerator Pump Circuit

For acceleration, the carburetor must deliver additional fuel. A sudden inrush of air is caused by rapid acceleration or applying full throttle.

When the throttle is opened, the pump lever pushes the plunger down and this forces fuel to flow through the accelerator pump circuit and out the pump jet. This fuel enters the air passage through the carburetor to supply additional fuel demands.

Choke

When starting an engine, it is necessary to increase the amount of fuel delivered to the intake manifold. This increase is controlled by the choke.

The choke consists of a valve in the top of the air horn controlled mechanically by an automatic device. When the choke valve is closed, only a small amount of air can get past it. When the engine is cranked, a fairly high vacuum develops in the air horn. This vacuum causes the main nozzle to discharge a heavy stream of fuel. The quantity delivered is sufficient to produce the correct air/fuel mixture needed for starting the engine. The choke is released either manually or by heat from the engine.

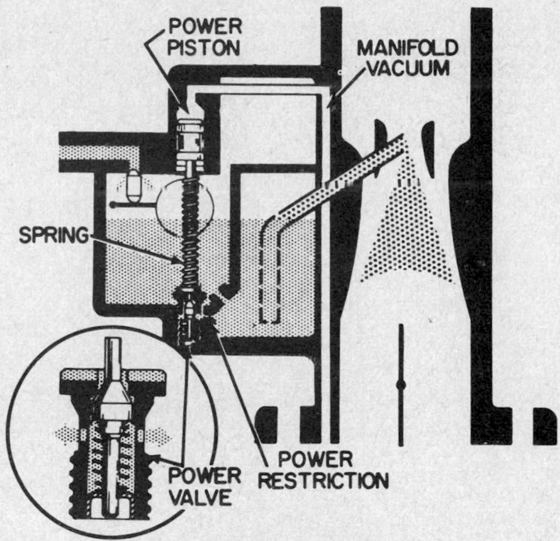

Power circuit
(© United Delco Div., G.M. Corp)

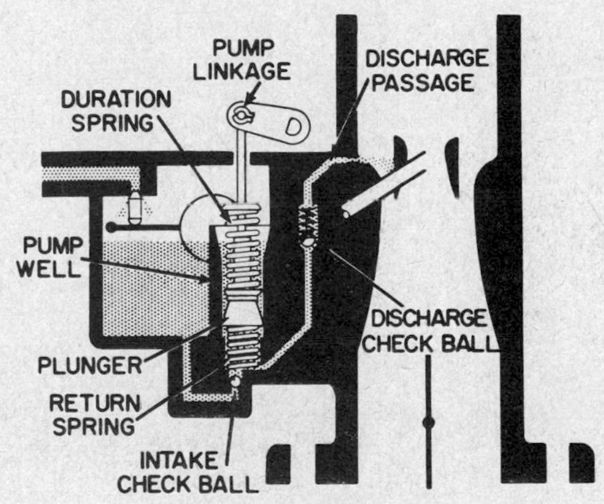

Accelerator pump circuit
(© United Delco Div., G.M. Corp)

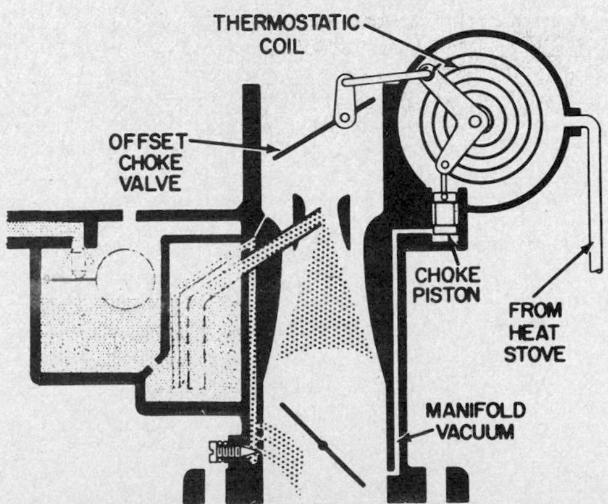

Choke system
(© United Delco Div., G.M. Corp)

TROUBLESHOOTING

NOTE: Carburetor problems cannot be isolated effectively unless all other engine systems are functioning correctly and the engine is properly tuned.

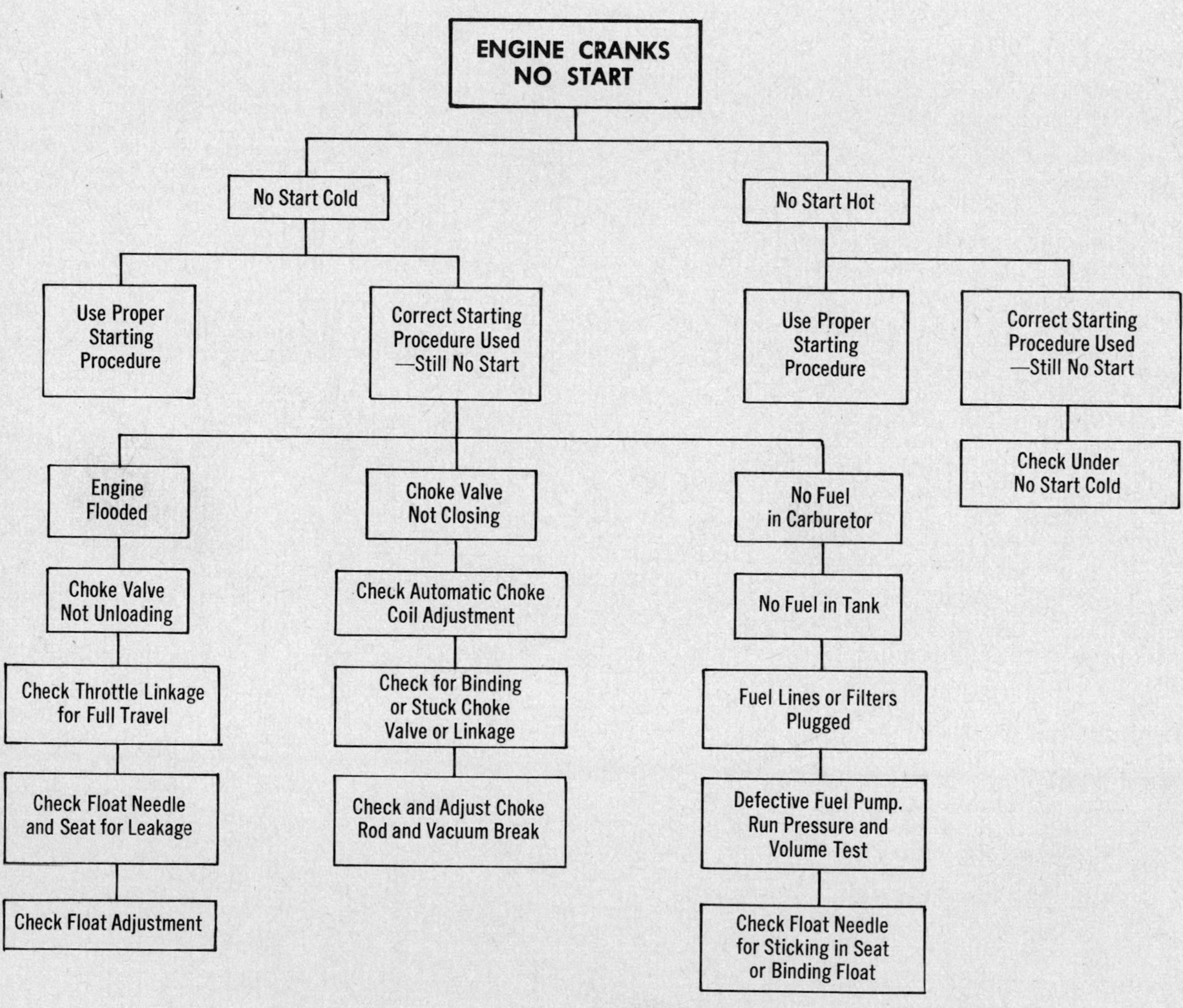

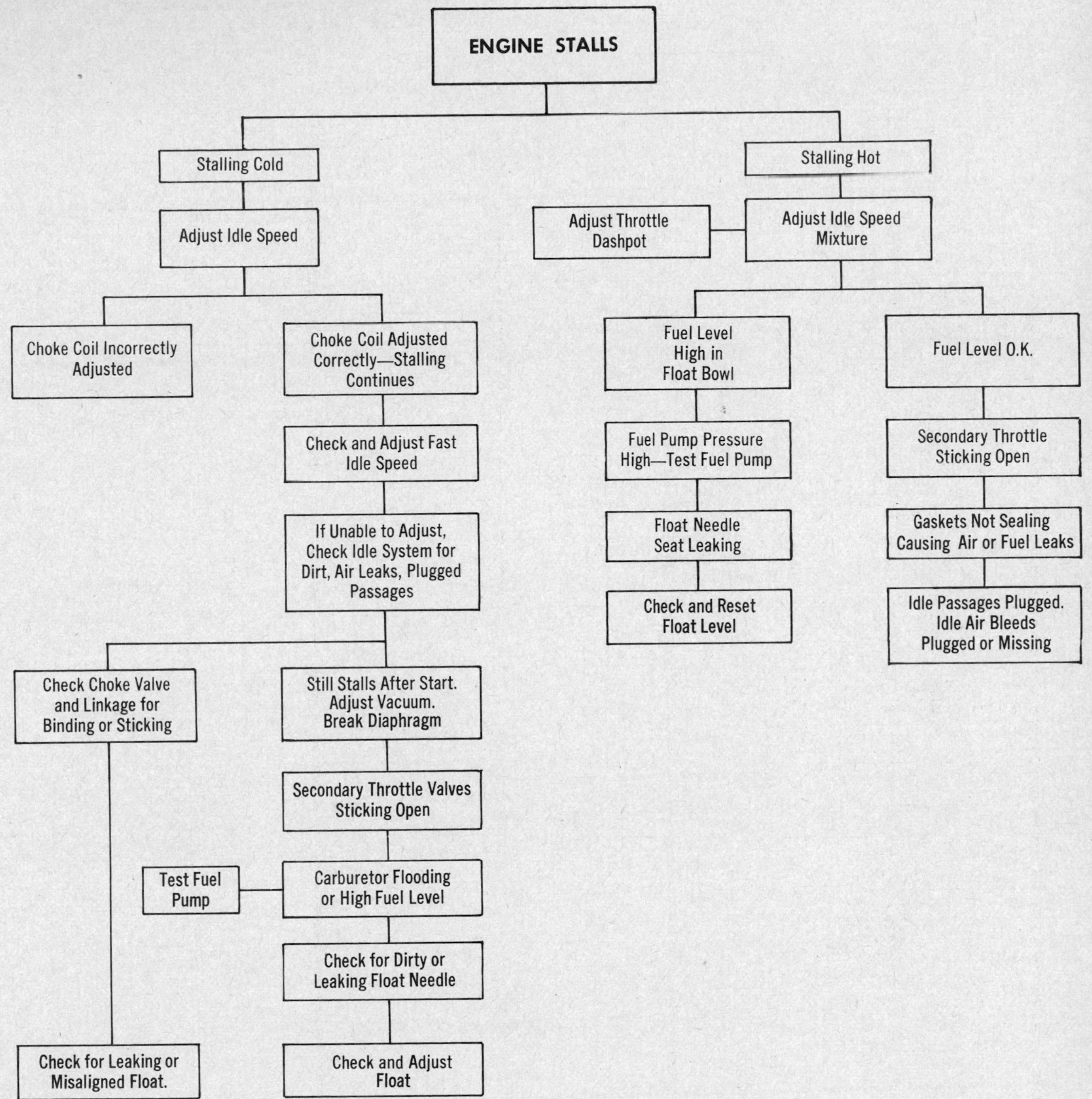
ENGINE STALLS
Stalling Cold
Adjust Idle Speed
Choke Coil Incorrectly Adjusted
Choke Coil Adjusted Correctly—Stalling Continues
Check and Adjust Fast Idle Speed
If Unable to Adjust, Check Idle System for Dirt, Air Leaks, Plugged Passages
Check Choke Valve and Linkage for Binding or Sticking
Still Stalls After Start. Adjust Vacuum. Break Diaphragm
Secondary Throttle Valves Sticking Open
Test Fuel Pump
Carburetor Flooding or High Fuel Level
Check for Dirty or Leaking Float Needle
Check for Leaking or Misaligned Float.
Check and Adjust Float
Stalling Hot
Adjust Throttle Dashpot
Adjust Idle Speed Mixture
Fuel Level High in Float Bowl
Fuel Pump Pressure High—Test Fuel Pump
Float Needle Seat Leaking
Check and Reset Float Level
Fuel Level O.K.
Secondary Throttle Sticking Open
Gaskets Not Sealing Causing Air or Fuel Leaks
Idle Passages Plugged. Idle Air Bleeds Plugged or Missing

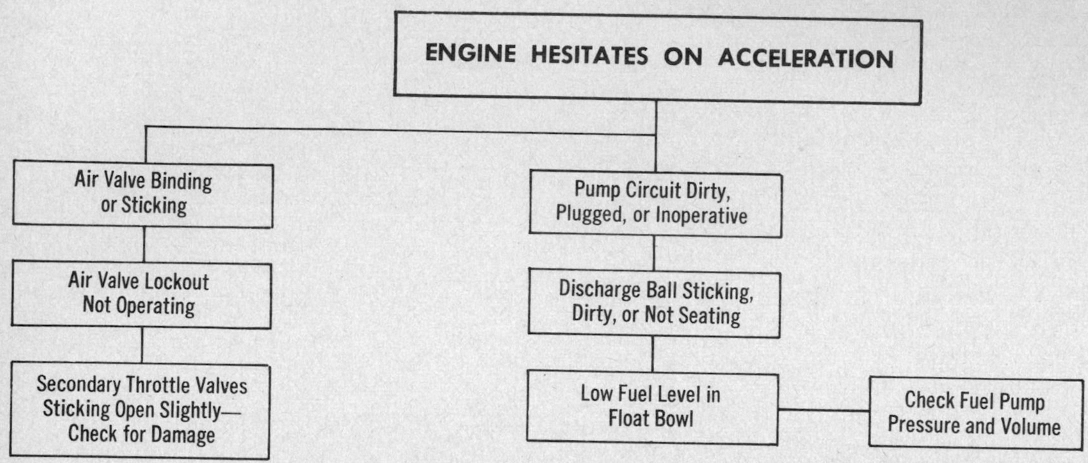

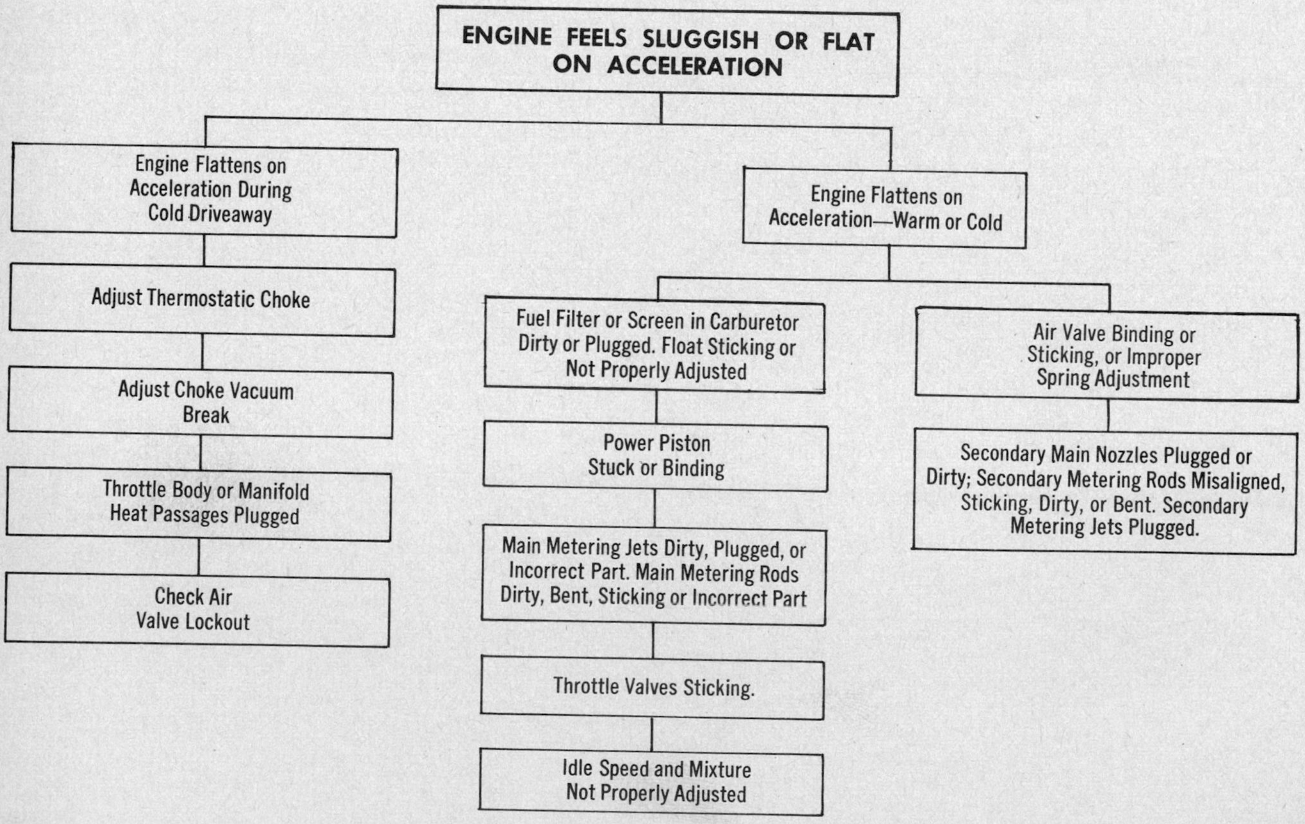

ENGINE FEELS SLUGGISH OR FLAT ON ACCELERATION

Engine Flattens on Acceleration During Cold Driveaway

Adjust Thermostatic Choke

Adjust Choke Vacuum Break

Throttle Body or Manifold Heat Passages Plugged

Check Air Valve Lockout

Engine Flattens on Acceleration—Warm or Cold

Fuel Filter or Screen in Carburetor Dirty or Plugged. Float Sticking or Not Properly Adjusted

Power Piston Stuck or Binding

Main Metering Jets Dirty, Plugged, or Incorrect Part. Main Metering Rods Dirty, Bent, Sticking or Incorrect Part

Throttle Valves Sticking.

Idle Speed and Mixture Not Properly Adjusted

Air Valve Binding or Sticking, or Improper Spring Adjustment

Secondary Main Nozzles Plugged or Dirty; Secondary Metering Rods Misaligned, Sticking, Dirty, or Bent. Secondary Metering Jets Plugged.

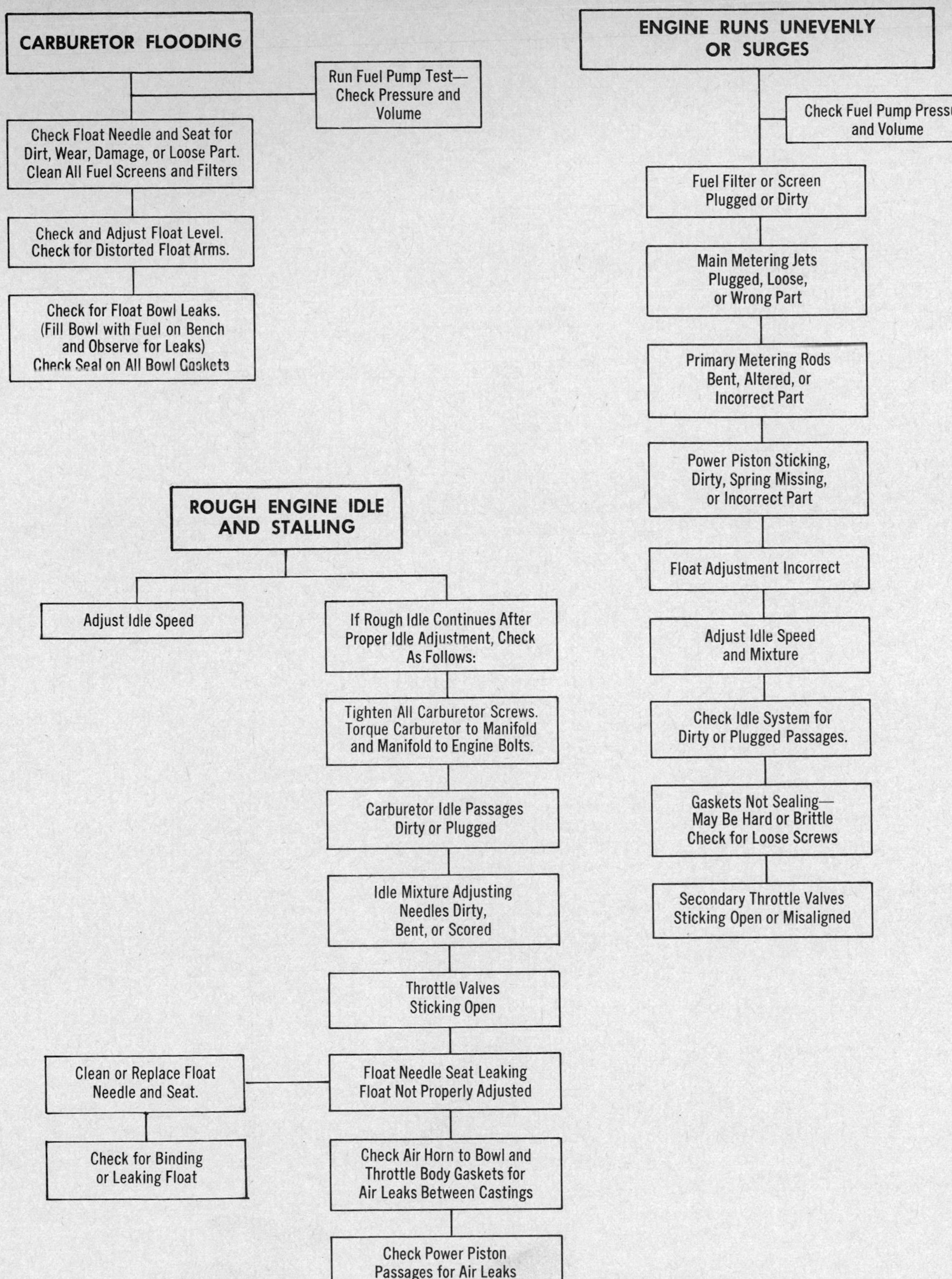
CARBURETOR FLOODING
Run Fuel Pump Test—Check Pressure and Volume
Check Float Needle and Seat for Dirt, Wear, Damage, or Loose Part. Clean All Fuel Screens and Filters
Check and Adjust Float Level. Check for Distorted Float Arms.
Check for Float Bowl Leaks. (Fill Bowl with Fuel on Bench and Observe for Leaks) Check Seal on All Bowl Gaskets
ROUGH ENGINE IDLE AND STALLING
Adjust Idle Speed
If Rough Idle Continues After Proper Idle Adjustment, Check As Follows:
Tighten All Carburetor Screws. Torque Carburetor to Manifold and Manifold to Engine Bolts.
Carburetor Idle Passages Dirty or Plugged
Idle Mixture Adjusting Needles Dirty, Bent, or Scored
Throttle Valves Sticking Open
Float Needle Seat Leaking Float Not Properly Adjusted
Clean or Replace Float Needle and Seat.
Check for Binding or Leaking Float
Check Air Horn to Bowl and Throttle Body Gaskets for Air Leaks Between Castings
Check Power Piston Passages for Air Leaks
ENGINE RUNS UNEVENLY OR SURGES
Check Fuel Pump Pressure and Volume
Fuel Filter or Screen Plugged or Dirty
Main Metering Jets Plugged, Loose, or Wrong Part
Primary Metering Rods Bent, Altered, or Incorrect Part
Power Piston Sticking, Dirty, Spring Missing, or Incorrect Part
Float Adjustment Incorrect
Adjust Idle Speed and Mixture
Check Idle System for Dirty or Plugged Passages.
Gaskets Not Sealing—May Be Hard or Brittle Check for Loose Screws
Secondary Throttle Valves Sticking Open or Misaligned

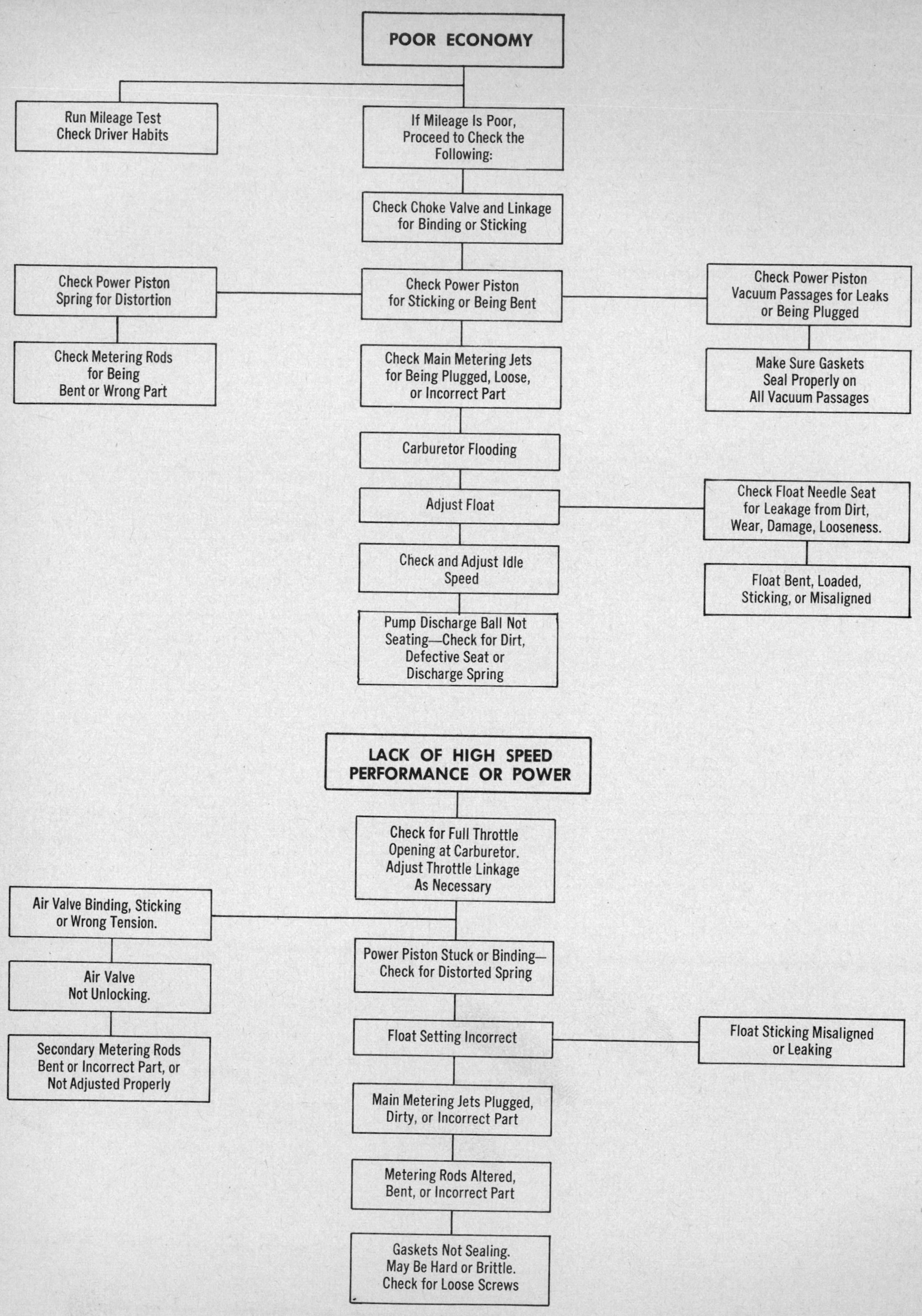
POOR ECONOMY
Run Mileage Test
Check Driver Habits
If Mileage Is Poor,
Proceed to Check the
Following:
Check Choke Valve and Linkage
for Binding or Sticking
Check Power Piston
Spring for Distortion
Check Power Piston
for Sticking or Being Bent
Check Power Piston
Vacuum Passages for Leaks
or Being Plugged
Check Metering Rods
for Being
Bent or Wrong Part
Check Main Metering Jets
for Being Plugged, Loose,
or Incorrect Part
Make Sure Gaskets
Seal Properly on
All Vacuum Passages
Carburetor Flooding
Adjust Float
Check Float Needle Seat
for Leakage from Dirt,
Wear, Damage, Looseness.
Check and Adjust Idle
Speed
Float Bent, Loaded,
Sticking, or Misaligned
Pump Discharge Ball Not
Seating—Check for Dirt,
Defective Seat or
Discharge Spring
LACK OF HIGH SPEED
PERFORMANCE OR POWER
Check for Full Throttle
Opening at Carburetor.
Adjust Throttle Linkage
As Necessary
Air Valve Binding, Sticking
or Wrong Tension.
Power Piston Stuck or Binding—
Check for Distorted Spring
Air Valve
Not Unlocking.
Float Setting Incorrect
Float Sticking Misaligned
or Leaking
Secondary Metering Rods
Bent or Incorrect Part, or
Not Adjusted Properly
Main Metering Jets Plugged,
Dirty, or Incorrect Part
Metering Rods Altered,
Bent, or Incorrect Part
Gaskets Not Sealing.
May Be Hard or Brittle.
Check for Loose Screws

CARTER CARBURETORS

Model BBS

Introduction

The BBS series carburetor is a standard Ball and Ball single throat model. It uses a CAP (Cleaner Air Package), CAS (Cleaner Air System), and ECS (Evaporation Control System) on its newer models. It also uses a spring staged choke which is a device incorporated into the choke mechanism which limits the choke blade closing torque when cranking the engine at temperatures below zero. Thus, the spring staging of the choke is a better match for the engine's starting requirements at low temperatures.

Float Level Adjustments

1. Invert the main body so that the weight of each float is forcing the needle against the seat.
2. If the proper gauge is not available, measure from the surface of the bowl to the crown of each float at the center.
3. Adjustment is listed in the specifications chart.
4. To adjust, bend the lip of the float lever in or out until adjustment is correct.

NOTE: On the ECS BBS carburetor, it is necessary to check or set the accelerator pump travel before checking the bowl vent valve opening.

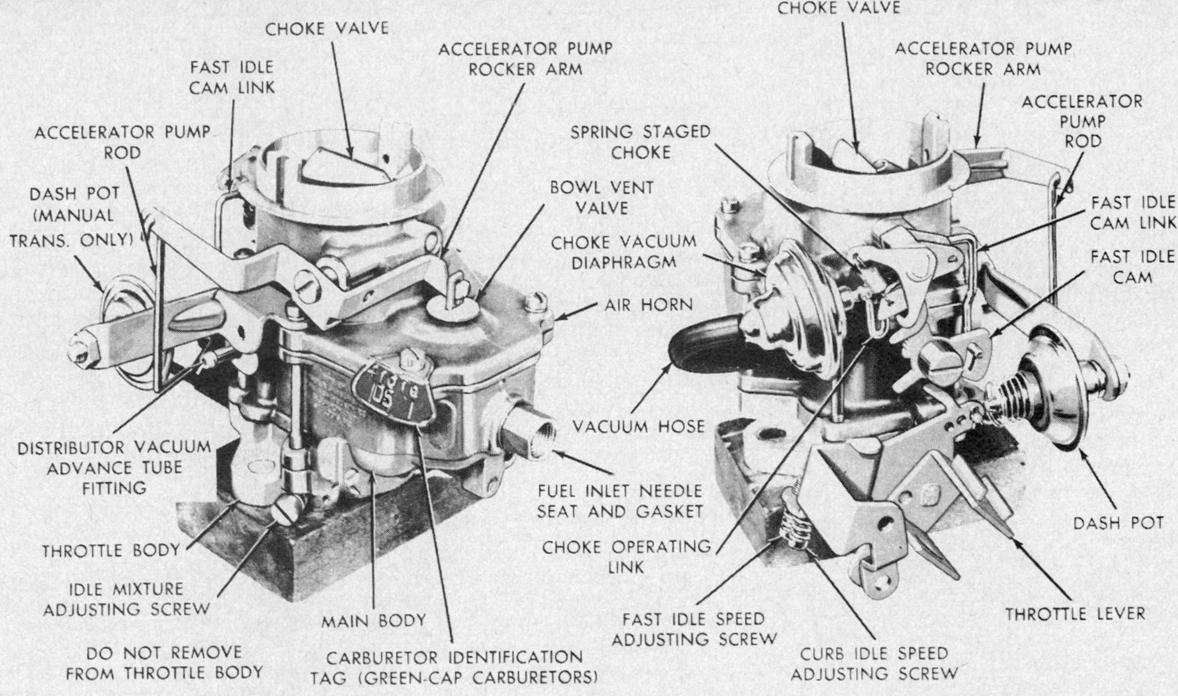

BBS carburetor assembly

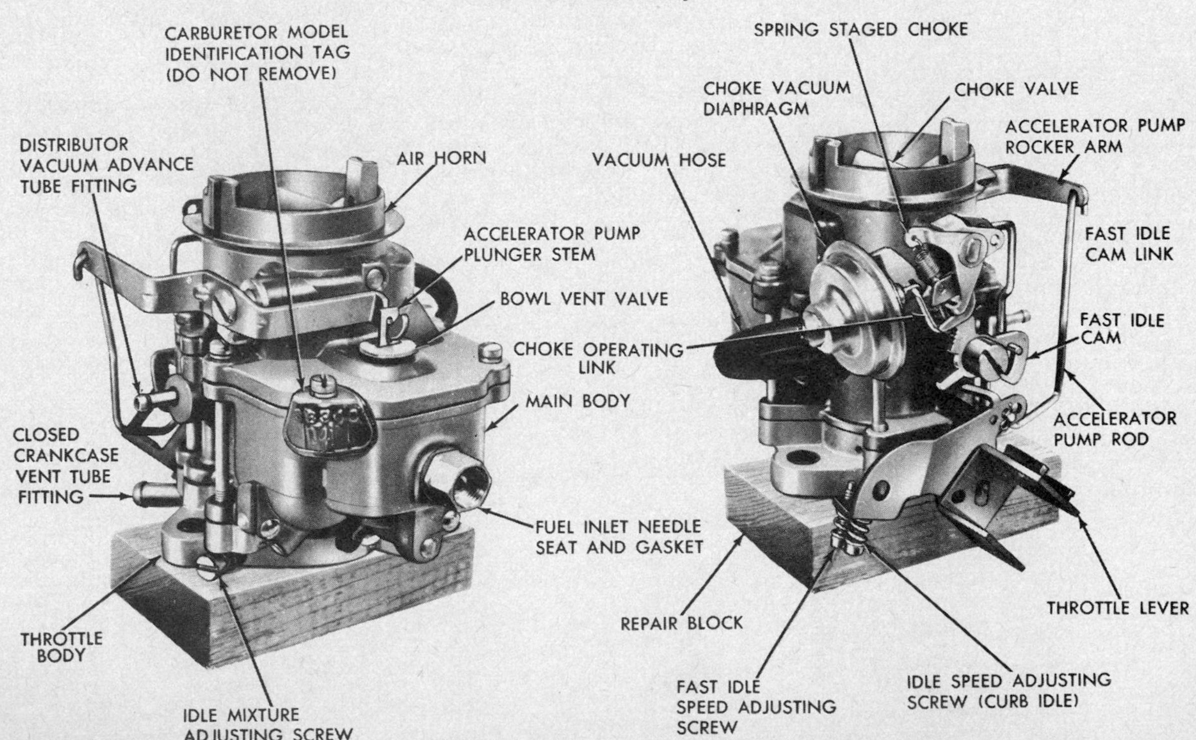

BBS carburetor assembly

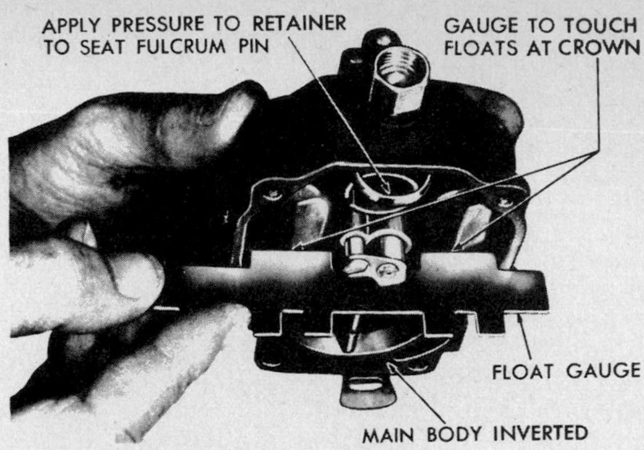

BBS float level adjustment

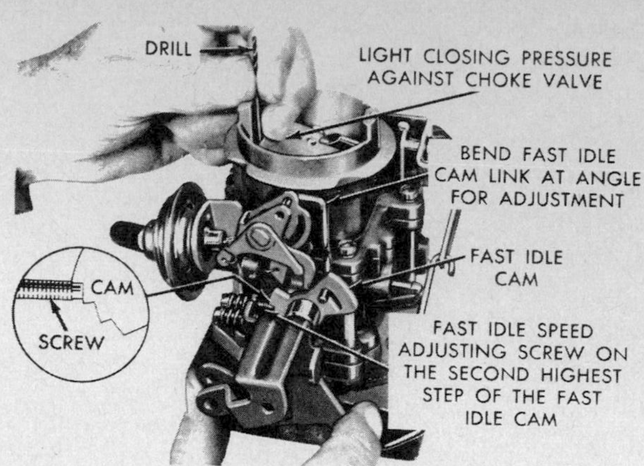

BBS fast idle cam adjustment

Pump and Bowl Vent Adjustment (CAS)

1. Back off the idle adjusting screw.
2. Open the choke valve so that when the throttle valve is closed, the fast idle adjusting screw will not contact the fast idle cam.
3. Be sure that the pump operating rod is in the center hole in the throttle lever.
4. Make sure that the bowl vent clip on the pump stem is in the center groove.
5. Close the throttle valve tightly.
6. Insert a drill of the specified size between the bowl vent and the air horn.
7. To adjust, bend the pump operating rod at the lower angle.

Pump and Bowl Vent Adjustment (ECS)

1. With the throttle valve at curb idle, measure the distance from the top of the casting to the top of the bowl vent valve stem.
2. See specifications for the distance.
3. If an adjustment is necessary, bend the lower tang on the bowl vent valve operating lever at the pivot until the correct opening has been obtained.

Accelerator Pump Adjustment

1. Be sure that the accelerator pump rod is in the outer hole of the throttle lever.
2. Close the throttle valve to curb idle.
3. Place a straightedge on the air cleaner mounting surface.
4. Measure the distance between the straight edge and the top of the accelerator pump plunger.
5. See the Specifications Chart for the proper distance.
6. If an adjustment is necessary, bend the accelerator pump until the correct pump angle has been obtained.

Fast Idle Cam Adjustment

1. With the fast idle speed adjusting screw contacting the second highest step on the fast idle cam, move the choke valve toward the closed position with light pressure on the choke shaft lever.
2. Insert the specified gauge between the top of the choke valve and the wall of the air horn. Refer to the Specifications Chart.
3. An adjustment will be necessary if a slight drag is not obtained as the drill shank is being removed.
4. Adjust by bending the fast idle link at an angle, until the correct valve opening has been obtained.

Choke Vacuum Kick Adjustment

NOTE: The test can be made on or off the vehicle.

1. If the adjustment is to be made with the engine running, back off the fast idle speed screw until the choke can be closed to the kick position with the engine at curb idle. (Note the number of screw turns required so that the fast idle can be returned to the original adjustment.)
2. If an auxiliary vacuum source is to be used, open the throttle valve (engine not running) and move the choke to the closed position. Release the throttle first, then release the choke.

   When using an auxiliary vacuum source, disconnect the vacuum hose from the carburetor and connect it to the hose from the vacuum supply with a small length of tube to act as a fitting. Removal of the hose from the diaphragm may require sufficient force to damage the system. Apply a vacuum of 15 or more in. of mercury.
3. Insert the gauge between the top of the choke valve and the wall of the air horn. Refer to the Specifications Chart.
4. Apply sufficient closing pressure on the lever to which the choke rod attaches, to provide a minimum choke valve opening without distortion of the diaphragm link.

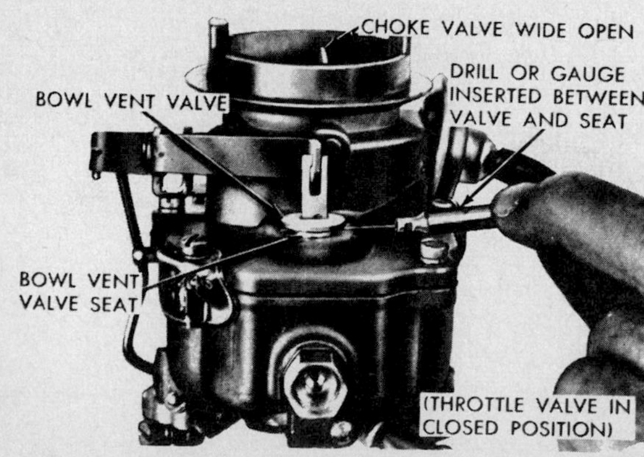

BBS pump and bowl vent adjustment

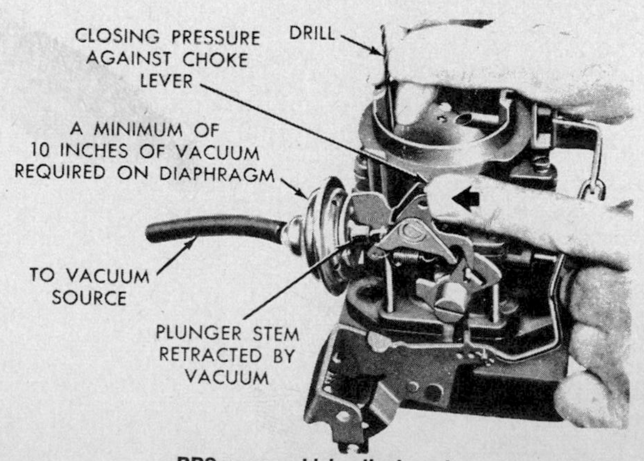

BBS vacuum kick adjustment

NOTE: The cylindrical stem of the diaphragm extends as the internal spring is compressed: This spring must be fully compressed for proper measurement of the vacuum kick adjustment.

5. Adjustment is necessary if a slight drag is not obtained when removing the gauge. Shorten or lengthen the diaphragm link to obtain the correct choke valve opening. Length changes should be made by carefully opening or closing the U-bend provided in the link. Improper bending causes contact between the U-section and the diaphragm assembly.

NOTE: Do not apply a twisting or bending force to diaphragm.

6. After completing adjustments, reinstall the vacuum hose on the correct carburetor fitting.
7. Return the fast idle screw to its original location if it was disturbed. Make the following check. With no vacuum applied to the diaphragm, the choke valve should move freely between the open and closed positions. If the movement is not free, examine the linkage for misalignment or interferences caused by the bending operation.

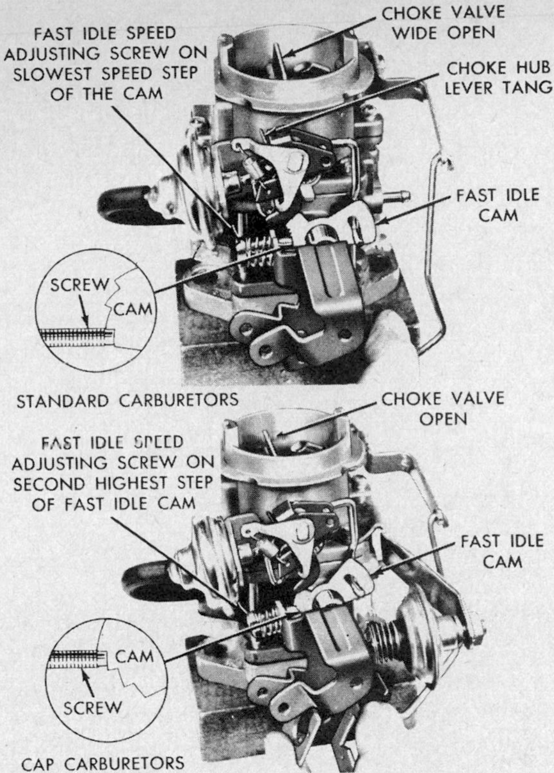

BBS fast idle speed adjustment (on the vehicle)

Choke Unloader (Wide Open Kick) Adjustment

1. With the throttle valve in the wide open position, insert a drill gauge between the upper edge of the choke valve and the inner wall of the air horn. Refer to the Specifications Chart.
2. With a finger lightly pressing against the shaft lever, a slight drag should be felt as the drill is being withdrawn.
3. Adjust by bending the unloader tang on the throttle lever until the correct opening has been obtained.

Fast Idle Speed Adjustment (On the Vehicle)

1. With the engine off and transmission in Neutral, open the throttle slightly.
2. On standard carburetors, close the choke valve about 20 degrees, then allow the throttle to close. The fast idle speed screw should be turned in or out to secure the specified speed.
3. On the CAP carburetors, close the choke valve until the fast idle screw can be positioned on the second highest speed step of the fast idle cam.
4. Start engine and let the idle speed stabilize. Turn the fast idle speed screw in or out to obtain a fast idle of 1800 RPM.
5. To provide the correct throttle closing torque, reposition the fast idle speed screw on the cam after each adjustment.

Spring Staged Choke Adjustment

1. Push the hub lever to the closed choke position.
2. There should be between 0.010-0.040 in. distance between the shaft and the hub levers.
3. If an adjustment is necessary, bend the hub lever tang until the correct opening has been obtained.

Choke Adjustment

1. Loosen the mounting post locknut.
2. Turn the mounting post with a screwdriver until the index mark on the disc is positioned as listed in the specifications chart.
3. Hold in this position with a screwdriver and tighten with the locknut.

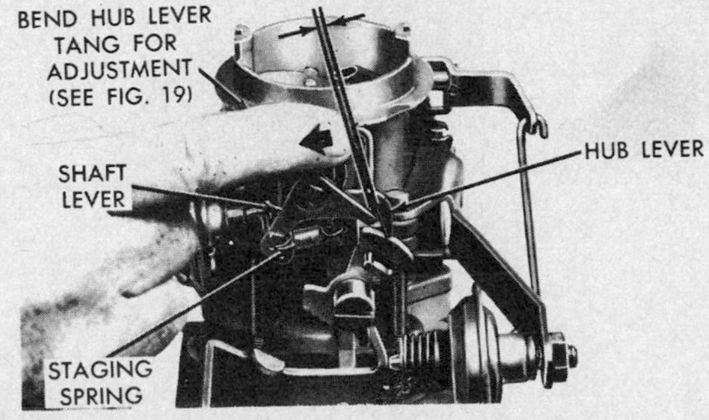

BBS spring staged choke adjustment

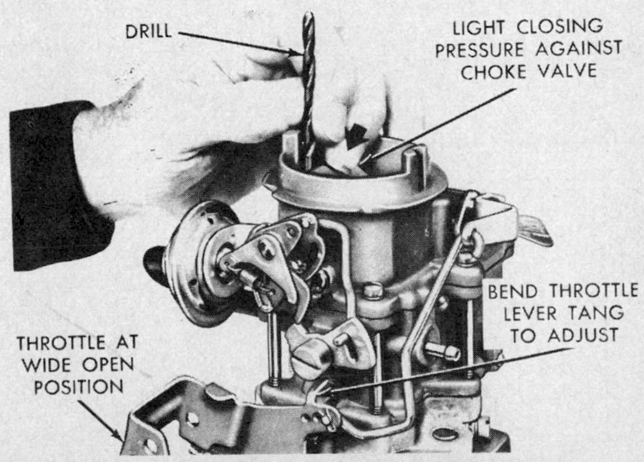

BBS choke unloader adjustment (wide open kick)

CARTER BBS SPECIFICATIONS

DODGE AND PLYMOUTH

Year	Model ②	Float Level (in.)	Accelerator Pump Travel (in.)	Bowl Vent (in.)	Choke Unloader (in.)	Fast Idle Cam Position ①	Choke Vacuum Kick ①
1969	4601S	1/4	—	1/16	3/16	48	35
	4602S	1/4	—	1/16	3/16	48	35
1970	4715S	1/4	—	1/32	3/16	48	35
	4716S	1/4	—	1/32	3/16	48	48
	4717S	1/4	5/16	9/32	3/16	48	35
	4718S	1/4	5/16	9/32	3/16	48	48
1971	4955S	1/4	5/16	17/64	3/16	48	35
	4956S	1/4	5/16	17/64	3/16	48	35

① Indicates the drill bit number.
② Model numbers located on tag or casting
Note: Automatic choke setting 2 Rich for all BBS

Model BBD

Introduction

The BBD carburetor is a two barrel unit. It has been equipped with CAP (Cleaner Air Package) and CAS (Cleaner Air System) packages and now uses ECS (Evaporation Control System) on the newer models. It is also equipped with a dashpot on some applications.

Accelerator Pump Adjustment

Except 1 1/4 in. Bore Units

1. Back off the idle adjusting screw. Open the choke valve so that the fast idle cam allows the throttle valves to finally close. Be sure that the pump connector rod is installed in the center hole of the throttle lever.
2. With the throttle valves closed tightly, measure the distance between the top of the air horn and the end of the pump plunger shaft. If the dimension is not as specified, bend the pump connector rod at an angle on the rod until the correct setting is obtained.

1 1/4 in. Bore Units beginning 1974

1. Back off the idle adjusting screw. Open the choke valve so that the fast idle cam allows the throttle valves to close. Be sure that the accelerator pump "S" link is in the outer hole of the pump arm.
2. Turn the idle adjusting screw in two complete turns after it contacts the stop.
3. With the throttle valves closed tightly, measure the distance between the top of the air horn and the top of the pump plunger shaft. If the dimension is not as specified, loosen the pump arm adjusting lockscrew (near the plunger shaft) and rotate the sleeve to obtain the correct dimension.

Fast Idle Cam Position Adjustment

1. With the fast idle speed adjusting screw contacting the second highest speed step on the fast idle cam, move the choke valve toward the closed position with light pressure on the choke shaft lever.

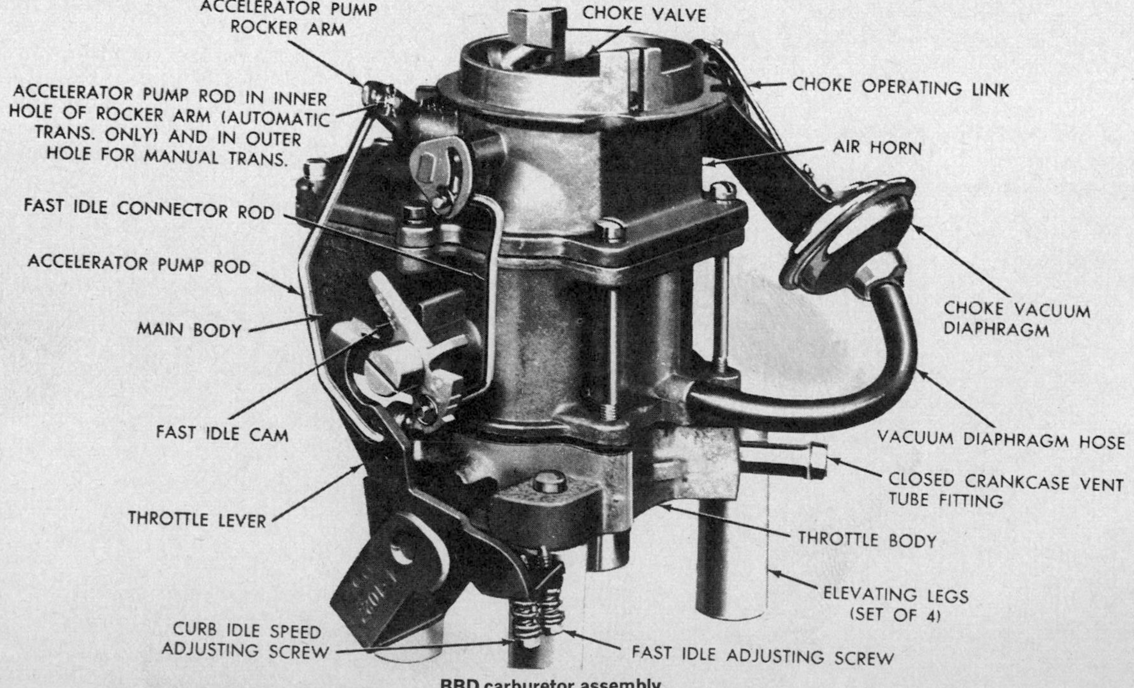

BBD carburetor assembly

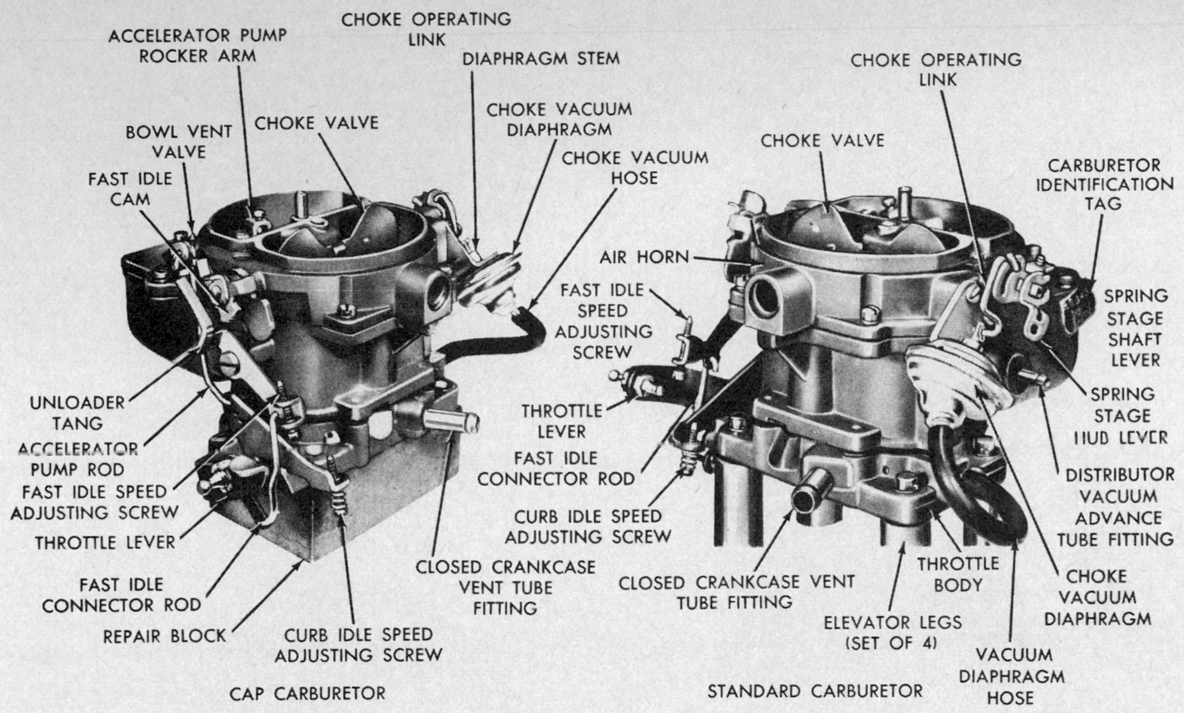

BBD carburetor assembly

2. Insert the specified drill (refer to Specifications), between the choke valve and the wall of the air horn. An adjustment will be necessary if a slight drag is not obtained as the drill is being removed.
3. If an adjustment is required, bend the fast idle connector rod at the lower angle. On 1969 units, bend the stop on the choke shaft.

Accelerator Pump & Bowl Vent (ECS)

1 1/4 in. bore units through 1973

1. Back off the idle speed adjusting screw to completely close the throttle valves. Open the choke valve so that the fast idle cam allows the throttle valves to seat in the bores.
2. Be sure that the accelerator pump operating rod is in the medium stroke hole in the throttle lever.
3. Close the throttle valves tightly. Measure the distance between the air cleaner gasket surface and the top of the accelerator pump rod. This measurement should be .200 in.
4. To adjust the pump travel, bend the accelerator pump operating rod at a lower angle, until the correct pump travel has been obtained.

Choke Unloader (Wide Open Kick)

1. Hold the throttle valves in the wide open position. Insert the specified drill (see Specifications) between the upper edge of the choke valve and the inner wall of the air horn.
2. With a finger lightly pressing against the valve, a slight drag should be felt as the drill is being withdrawn. If an adjustment is necessary, bend the unloader tang on the throttle lever until the correct opening has been obtained.

Fast Idle Speed (On Vehicle)

1. With the engine off and the transmission in Park or Neutral position, open the throttle slightly.
2. Close the choke valve until the fast idle screw can be positioned on the second highest speed step (highest speed step, 1974) of the fast idle cam.

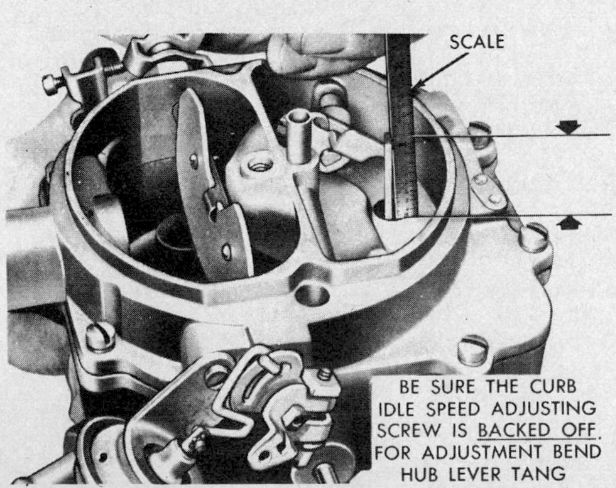

BBD accelerator pump adjustment

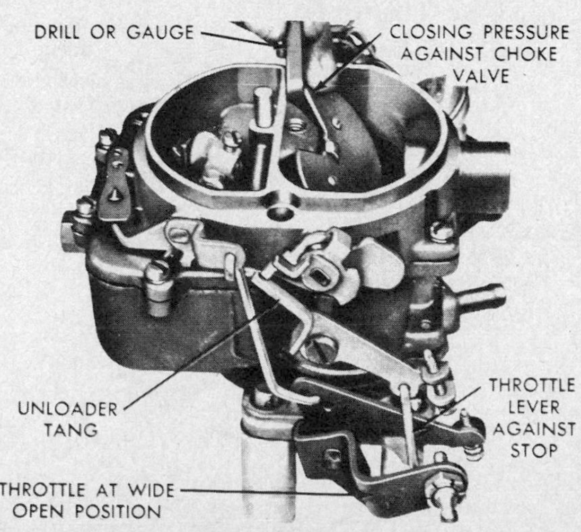

BBD choke unloader adjustment (wide open kick)

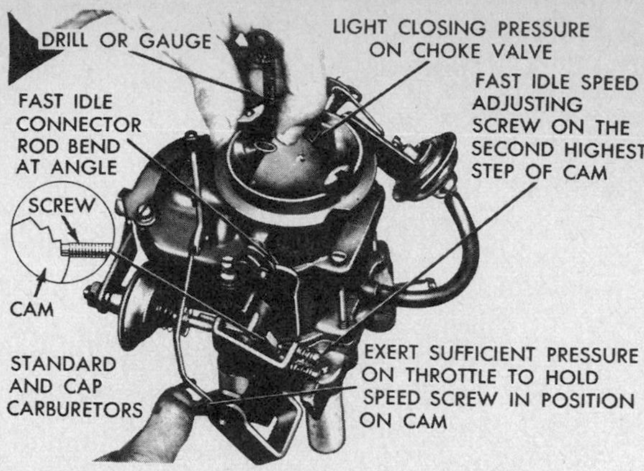

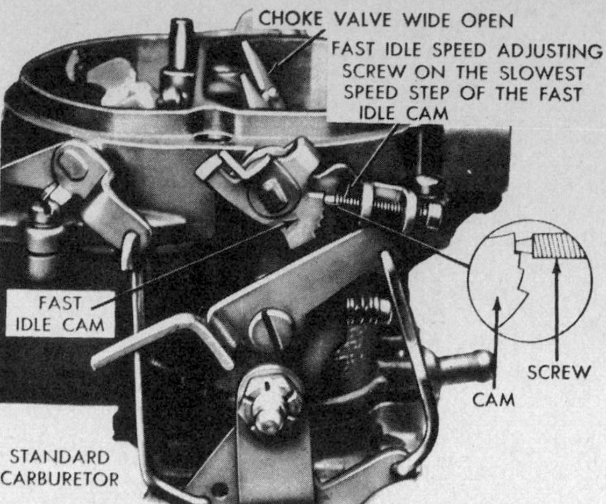

BBD fast idle cam position adjustment

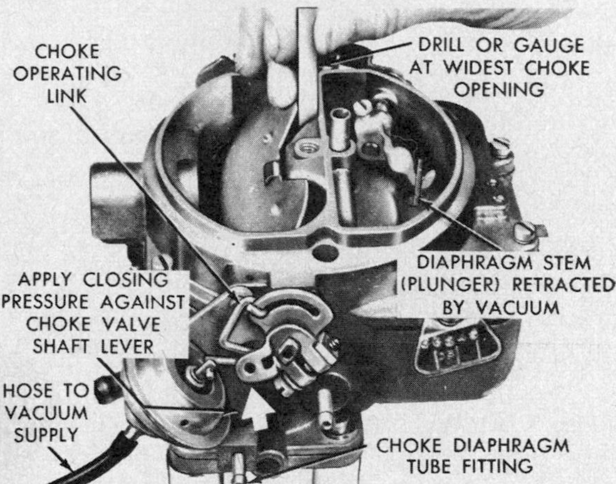

BBD vacuum kick adjustment

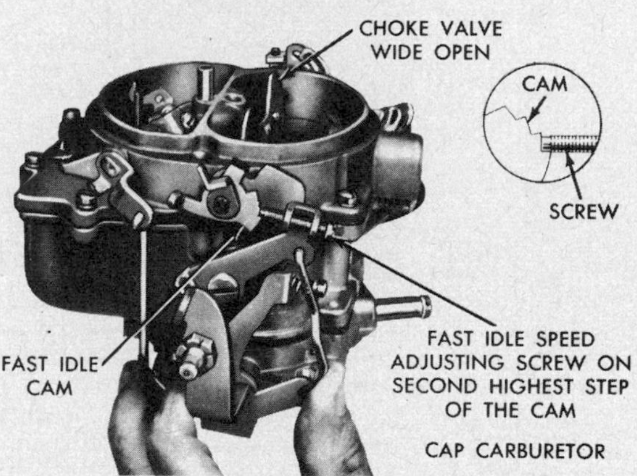

BBD fast idle adjustment on the vehicle

3. Start the engine and let the idle stabilize. Turn the fast idle speed screw in or out to obtain the specified speed.
4. Stopping the engine between adjustments is not necessary. However, reposition the fast idle speed screw on the cam after each speed adjustment to provide the correct throttle closing torque.

Vacuum Kick Adjustment

1. If the adjustment is to be made with the engine running, disconnect the fast idle linkage to allow the choke to close to the kick position with engine at curb idle. If an auxiliary vacuum source is to be used, open the throttle valves (engine not running) and move the choke to the closed position. Release the throttle first, then release the choke.
2. When using an auxiliary vacuum source, disconnect the vacuum hose from the carburetor and connect it to the hose from the vacuum supply with a small length of tube to act as a fitting. Removal of the hose from the diaphragm may require sufficient force to damage the system. Apply a vacuum of 10 (15 beginning 1973) or more in. of mercury.

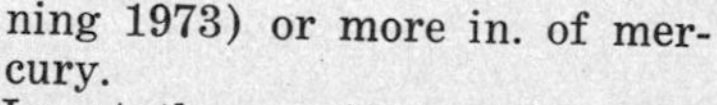

3. Insert the specified drill (refer to Specifications) between the choke valve and the wall of the air horn. Apply sufficient closing pressure on the lever to which the choke rod attaches to provide a minimum choke valve opening without distortion of the diaphragm link. Note that the cylindrical stem of the diaphragm will extend as the internal spring is compressed. This spring must be fully compressed for proper measurement of the vacuum kick of adjustment.
4. An adjustment will be necessary if a slight drag is not obtained as the drill is being removed. Shorten or lengthen the diaphragm link to obtain the correct choke opening. Length changes should be made carefully by bending (opening or closing) the bend provided in the diaphragm link.

Caution Do not apply twisting or bending force to the diaphragm.

5. Reinstall the vacuum hose on the correct carburetor fitting. Return the fast idle linkage to its original condition if it was disturbed, as suggested in Step 1.
6. Make the following check: With no vacuum applied to the diaphragm, the choke valve should move freely between the open and closed positions. If its movement is not free, examine the linkage for misalignment or interference caused by the bending operation. Repeat the adjustment if necessary to provide proper link operation.

Float Level

1. Invert the carburetor so that the weight of the floats is the only force on the needle and seat.
2. Use a T-scale to check the float level. Measure the area from the surface of the fuel bowl to the crown of each float at center.
3. To adjust, hold the floats on the bottom of the bowl and bend the float lip to give the specified dimension.

Bowl Vent Adjustment

1½ in. bore units

1. Open the choke valve so that the fast idle cam allows the valves to close to curb idle.
2. Be sure that the pump operating rod is in the long stroke hole in the throttle lever. Remove the bowl vent valve cover if it was

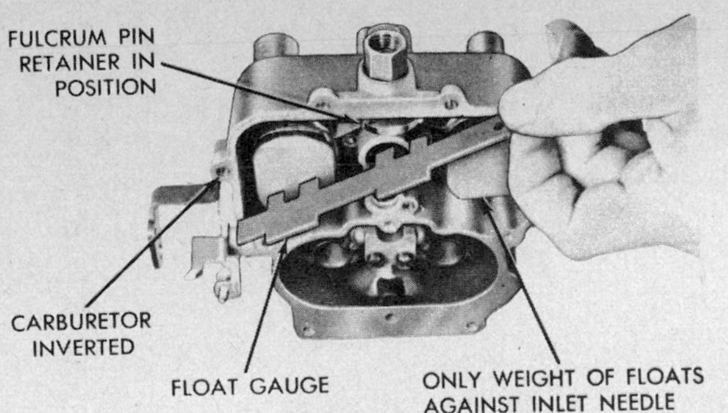

BBD float level adjustment

not previously done.

3. On ECS units, close the throttle valves tightly. Using a narrow ruler, measure the distance from the top of the bowl vent valve to the top of the air horn casting.

On CAS units, with the throttle valves closed (curb idle), there should be the specified clearance between the bowl vent valve and the seat on the air horn. Measure at the outermost or the longest dimension.

4. To adjust, bend the lift arm until the correct clearance has been obtained.

Dashpot Adjustment

1. Make sure that the curb idle speed and mixture are correct.
2. Start the engine and move the throttle lever so that the tab is just touching the dashpot.
3. The engine speed should be 2000 rpm for models through 1971 and 2500 rpm for later models.
4. Adjustment is made by loosening the locknut and turning the dashpot.

CARTER BBD SPECIFICATIONS

CHRYSLER, DODGE AND PLYMOUTH

Year	Model ④	Float Level (in.)	Accelerator Pump Travel (in.)	Bowl Vent (in.)	Choke Unloader (in.)	Choke Vacuum Kick ①	Fast Idle Cam Position ①	Fast Idle Speed (rpm)	Automatic Choke Adjustment
1969	4605S	1/4	—	1/16	1/4	20	41	1500	Index
	4606S	1/4	—	1/16	1/4	41	41	1600	Index
	4607S	1/4	—	1/16	1/4	20	41	1300	Index
	4608S	1/4	—	1/16	1/4	28	41	1700	Index
	4613S	5/16	1	1/16	1/4	20	30	1600	2 Rich
	4614S	5/16	1	1/16	1/4	20	30	1600	2 Rich
	4474S	5/16	1	1/16	1/4	20	30	1600	2 Rich
1970	4721S	1/4	—	1/32	1/4	20	41	1600	Index
	4722S	1/4	—	1/32	1/4	20	41	2000	Index
	4723S	1/4	—	15/64	1/4	20	41	1600	Index
	4724S	1/4	—	15/64	1/4	20	41	2000	Index
	4725S	11/32	1	1/32	1/4	20	28	1700	2 Rich
	4726S	11/32	1	1/32	1/4	28	28	1700	2 Rich
	4727S	11/32	1	1/8	1/4	20	28	1700	2 Rich
	4728S	11/32	1	3/16	1/4	28	28	1700	2 Rich
	4894S	11/32	1	1/32	1/4	28	28	1700	2 Rich
	4895S	1/4	—	1/32	1/4	20	41	1700	Index
1971	4957S	1/4	0.200②	13/64	1/4	20	41	1600	Index
	4958S	1/4	0.200②	13/64	1/4	20	41	1900	Index
	4961S	5/16	1	3/16	1/4	20	20	1900	2 Rich
	4962S	5/16	1	3/16	1/4	28	28	1700	2 Rich
1972	6149S	1/4	0.225③	15/64	1/4	25	41	1700	Fixed
	6150S	1/4	0.225③	15/64	1/4	25	41	1900	Fixed
	6151S	1/4	0.225③	15/64	1/4	25	41	1800	Fixed
	6152S	1/4	0.225③	15/64	1/4	25	41	2000	Fixed
1973	6316SA	1/4	0.242③	—	1/4	24	41	1700	Fixed
	6317SA	1/4	0.242③	—	1/4	30	41	1700	Fixed
	6343SA	1/4	0.242③	—	1/4	24	41	1700	Fixed
	6344SA	1/4	0.242③	—	1/4	24	41	1700	Fixed
1974	6464S	1/4	0.500③	—	.325	25	41	1700	Fixed
	6465S	1/4	0.500③	—	.325	35	41	1500	Fixed
	6466S	1/4	0.500③	—	.325	25	41	1700	Fixed
	6467S	1/4	0.500③	—	.325	35	41	1500	Fixed

CARTER BBD SPECIFICATIONS

CHRYSLER, DODGE AND PLYMOUTH

Year	Model ④	Float Level (in.)	Accelerator Pump Travel (in.)	Bowl Vent (in.)	Choke Unloader (in.)	Choke Vacuum Kick ①	Fast Idle Cam Position ①	Fast Idle Speed (rpm)	Automatic Choke Adjustment
1975	8000S	¼	0.500	—	0.280	0.130	0.070	1500	Fixed
	8064S	¼	0.500	—	0.310	0.070	0.070	1500	Fixed
	8001S	¼	0.500	—	0.310	0.110	0.070	1500	Fixed
	8003S	¼	0.500	—	0.310	0.110	0.070	1500	Fixed
	8066S	¼	0.500	—	0.280	0.130	0.070	1500	Fixed
	8062S	¼	0.500	—	0.310	0.110	0.070	1500	Fixed

① Indicates the drill bit number.
② Throttle closed
③ At idle
④ Model numbers located on the tag or casting

Model YF

Introduction

The YF carburetor is a single barrel downdraft carburetor with a diaphragm type accelerator pump and diaphragm operated metering rods.

Float Adjustment

1. Invert the air horn assembly and check the clearance from the top of the float to the surface of the air horn with a T-scale. The air horn should be held at eye level when gauging and the float arm should be resting on the needle pin.
2. Do not exert pressure on the needle valve when measuring or adjusting the float. Bend the float arm as necessary to adjust the float level.

Caution Do not bend the tab at the end of the float arm as it prevents the float from striking the bottom of the fuel bowl when empty.

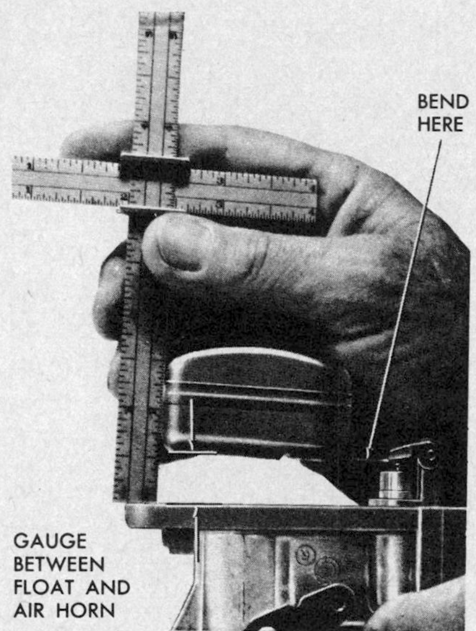

YF float level adjustment

Accelerator Pump Adjustment

1. Seat the throttle valve in the bore of the carburetor.
2. Press down on the upper end of the diaphragm shaft until it bottoms.
3. The metering rod arm should now contact the pump lifter link at the outer end nearest the springs.
4. To make the adjustment, bend the pump connector link at its lower angle.

Metering Rod Adjustment

1. Back out the idle speed adjusting screw until the throttle plate is seated fully in its bore.
2. Press down on the upper end of the diaphragm shaft until the diaphragm bottoms in the vacuum chamber.
3. The metering rod should contact the bottom of the metering rod well and lifter link at the outer

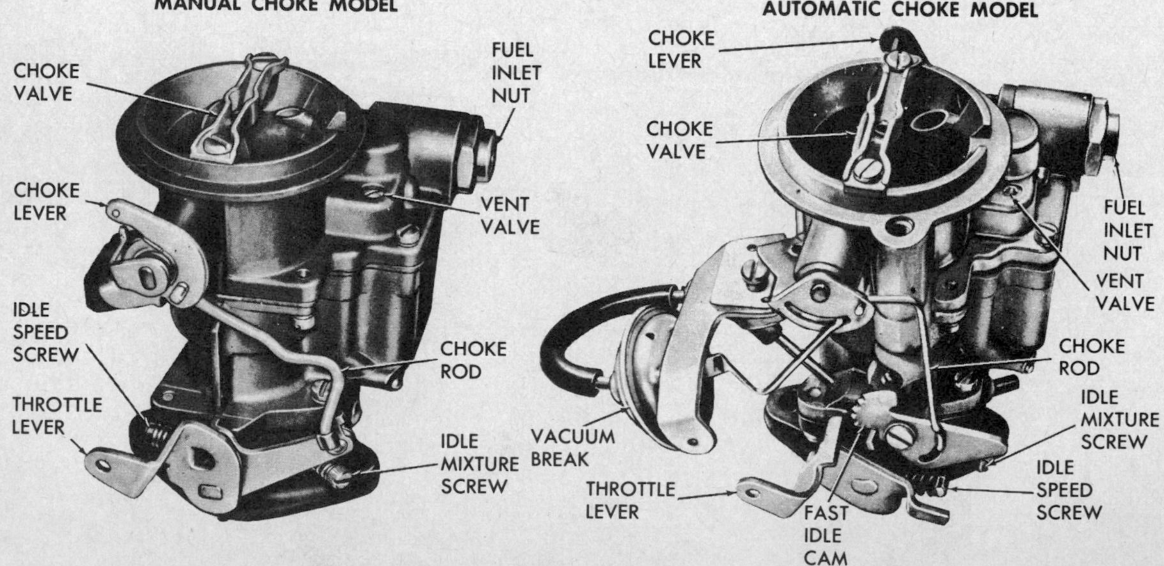

Carter YF carburetor

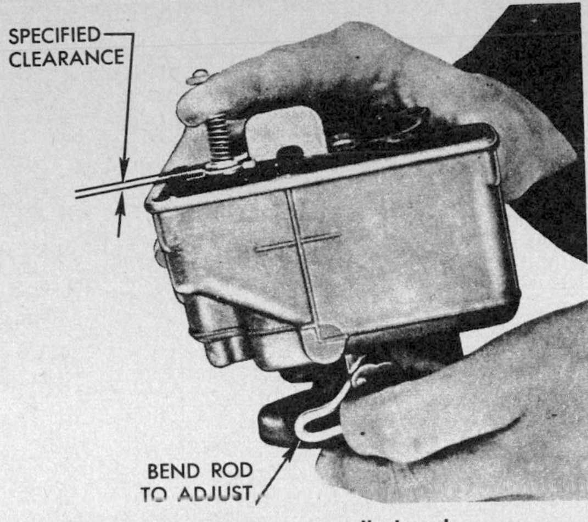

YF accelerator pump adjustment

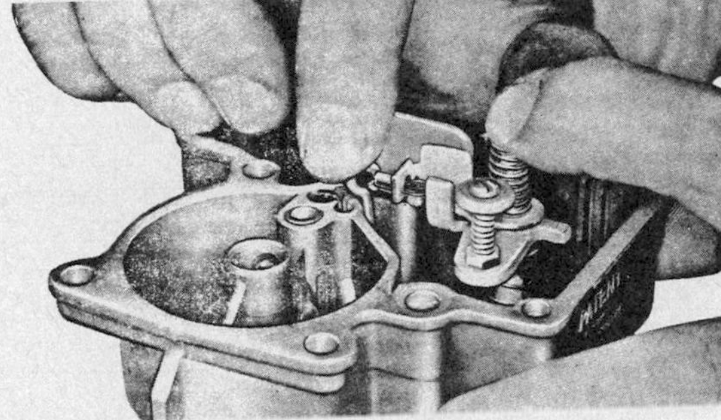
YF metering rod adjustment

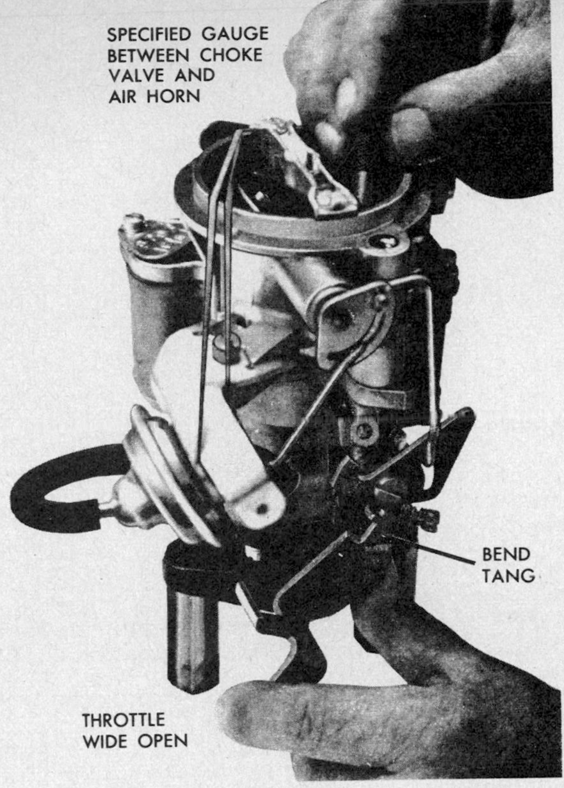

YF choke unloader adjustment

end nearest the springs and at the supporting link.

4. On models not equipped with an adjusting screw, adjust by bending the lip of the metering rod arm to which the metering rod is attached.
5. On models with an adjusting screw, turn the screw until the metering rod just bottoms in the body casting. For final adjustment, turn the screw one additional turn clockwise.

Idle Vent Adjustment

1. This adjustment should not be made until the accelerator pump and metering rod adjustments have been completed. Install the bowl cover and air horn assembly.
2. With the throttle valve tightly closed, the specified clearance should exist between the idle vent valve and the inside of the bowl cover.
3. Adjust the idle vent screw as required.

Fast Idle Cam Adjustment

1. Open the throttle wide enough to allow full closing of the choke valve. Be sure that the fast idle screw is not contacting the fast idle cam.
2. Close the throttle valve and the fast idle cam should revolve to the fast idle position.
3. On 1969-70 Fords, the clearance is measured between the throttle valve and the throttle bore on the side opposite the idle port.
4. On 1971 and later Ford models, the clearance is measured between the lower edge of the choke valve and the air horn wall.
5. On models other than Ford with automatic choke, the index mark on the fast idle cam should line up with the upper edge of the tang on the throttle lever. If adjustment is necessary, bend the fast idle tang to achieve correct alignment.

Choke Unloader Adjustment

1. With the throttle valve held wide open and the choke valve held in the closed position, bend the unloader tang on the throttle lever to obtain the specified clearance between the lower edge of the choke valve and the air horn wall.

Automatic Choke Adjustment

1. Loosen the choke cover retaining screws.
2. Turn the choke over so that the index mark on the cover lines up with the specified mark on the choke housing.

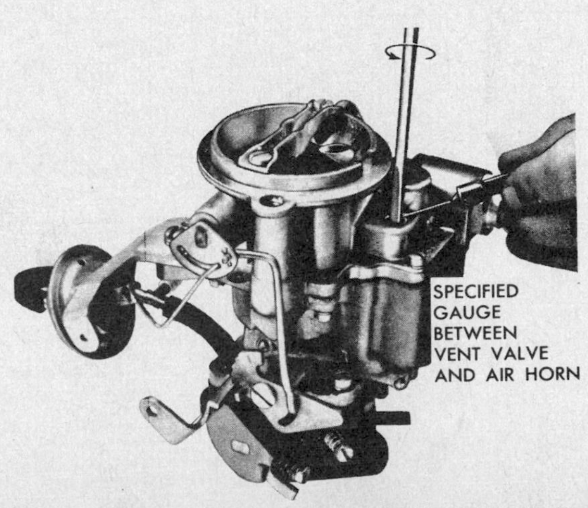

YF idle vent adjustment

CARTER YF SPECIFICATIONS

AMERICAN MOTORS

Year	Model ①	Float Level (in.)	Idle Vent (in.)	Fast Idle Cam (in.)	Unloader (in.)	Choke
1970	4767S	29/64	0.052	2300 RPM	0.300	Index
	4768S	29/64	0.052	2300 RPM	0.325	Index
	4769S	29/64	0.055	2300 RPM	0.300	Index
	4770S	29/64	0.055	2300 RPM	0.300	Index
	4978S	29/64	0.055	2300 RPM	0.300	1 Rich
1971	6038S	29/64	—	2300 RPM	0.300	Index
	6093S	29/64	—	2300 RPM	0.300	Index
	6094S	29/64	—	2300 RPM	0.300	1 Rich
	6095S	29/64	—	2300 RPM	0.300	Index
	6096S	29/64	—	2300 RPM	0.300	1 Rich
1972	6199S	29/64	—	1600 RPM	0.300	Index
	6200S	29/64	—	1600 RPM	0.300	Index
1973	All	29/64	—	Index mark	0.275	1 Rich
1974	All	0.476	—	0.190	0.275	1 Rich
1975	All	0.476	—	0.190	0.275	1 Rich

FORD

Year	Model ①	Float Level (in.)	Idle Vent (in.)	Fast Idle Cam (in.)	Unloader (in.)	Choke
1969	C8AF-BF	7/32	—	0.035	0.280	Index
	C8DF-G	7/32	—	0.046	0.280	Index
	C8DF-H	7/32	—	0.040	0.280	1 Lean
1970	D0AF-A	3/8	—	0.029	0.250	Index
	D0AF-B	3/8	—	0.025	0.250	1 Lean
	D0DF-L	3/8	—	0.036	0.250	Index
	D0DF-M	3/8	—	0.031	0.250	Index
	D0DF-N	7/32	—	0.035	0.280	Index
	D0DF-R	7/32	—	0.036	0.280	1 Rich
	D0DF-S	7/32	—	0.035	0.280	Index
	D0DF-T	3/8	—	0.031	0.250	Index
	D0DF-U	7/32	—	0.036	0.280	1 Rich
	D0DF-V	3/8	—	0.036	0.250	Index
1971	D1DF-EA	3/8	—	0.105	0.250	Index
	D1DF-GA, HA	3/8	—	0.170	0.250	Index
	D1DF-JA, LA	3/8	—	0.140	0.250	Index
	D1DF-KA, MA	3/8	—	0.140	0.250	Index
	D1DF-PA	3/8	—	0.190	0.250	Index
	D1DF-RA	3/8	—	0.220	0.250	Index
1972	D2DF-AA	3/8	—	0.105	0.280	Index
	D2DF-BA	3/8	—	0.170	0.250	Index
	D2DF-CA	3/8	—	0.170	0.250	Index
	D2DF-DA	3/8	—	0.140	0.250	1 Rich
	D2DF-EA	3/8	—	0.140	0.250	1 Rich
	D2AF-JA	3/8	—	0.220	0.250	1 Lean
1973	D3DF-AA	3/8	—	0.170	0.250	Index
	D3DF-CA	3/8	—	0.140	0.250	1 Rich

CARTER YF SPECIFICATIONS

FORD

Year	Model ①	Float Level (in.)	Idle Vent (in.)	Fast Idle Cam (in.)	Unloader (in.)	Choke
1974	D4DE-JA	3/8	—	0.140	0.250	1 Rich
	D4DE-JB	3/8	—	0.140	0.250	Index
	D4DE-ABA	3/8	—	0.170	0.250	Index
	D4DE-KA	3/8	—	0.140	0.250	1 Rich
	D4DE-KB	3/8	—	0.140	0.250	Index
	D4DE-EA	3/8	—	0.140	0.250	Index
1975	D5DE-EA	3/8	—	0.140	0.250	2 Rich
	D5DE-MA	3/8	—	0.140	0.250	2 Rich
	D5DE-ZA	3/8	—	0.140	0.250	2 Rich
	D5DE-DA	3/8	—	0.140	0.250	2 Rich
	D5DE-GA	3/8	—	0.140	0.250	2 Rich

① Model number located on the tag or casting

Model RBS

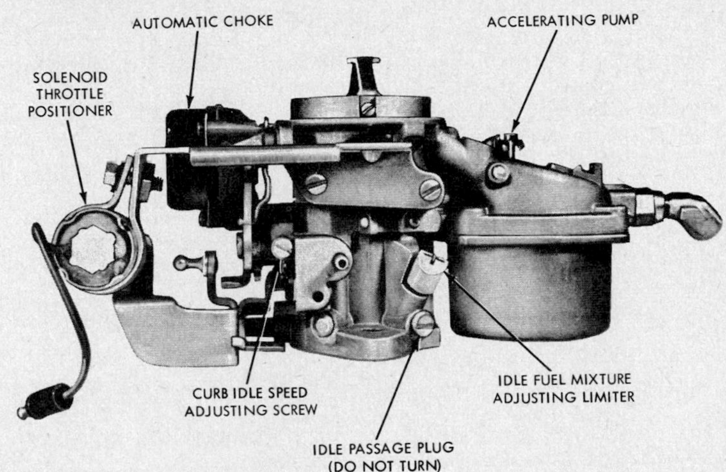

RBS carburetor assembly

Introduction

The Carter RBS is a single barrel carburetor made from aluminum casting. It is equipped with a vacuum piston automatic choke. The 1973 and later models use an EGR (Exhaust Gas Recirculation) system.

Float Level Adjustment

1. After removing the bowl and the bowl gasket, invert the carburetor so that only the weight of the float is pressing down on the needle and seat assembly.
2. Measure the vertical distance from the casting to the projections at the outer ends of the float.
3. Measure both ends of the float and, if adjustment is necessary, it can be done by holding the lip end of the float bracket with needle nose pliers and bending the float bracket at its narrowest point.

Float Drop Adjustment

With the air horn upright and the float hanging free, measure the vertical distance from the main body casting surface of the fuel bowl to the outer ends of the float on the top side. Adjust by bending the tab at the end of the float arm. The proper setting is 1.250 in.

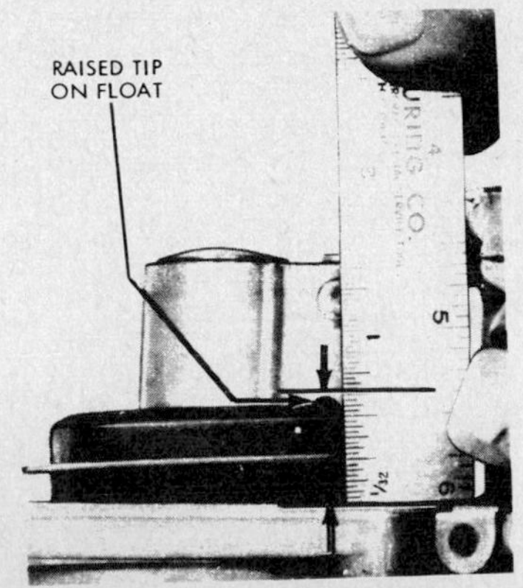

RBS float level adjustment

Accelerator Pump Adjustment

NOTE: The accelerator pump adjustment must be made before adjusting the bowl vent or the choke unloader.

Back out the curb idle adjusting

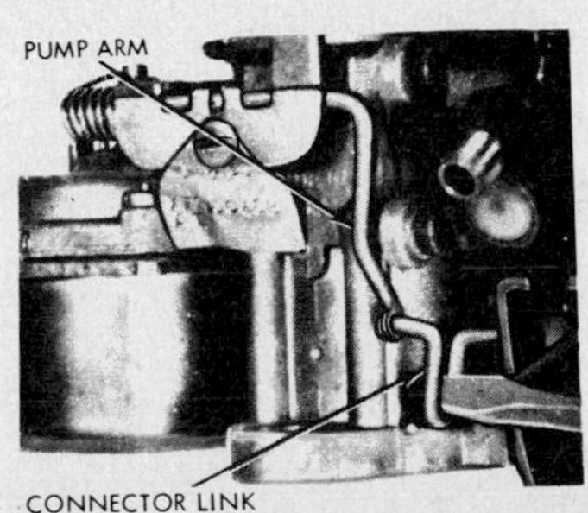

RBS accelerator pump adjustment 1970-1974

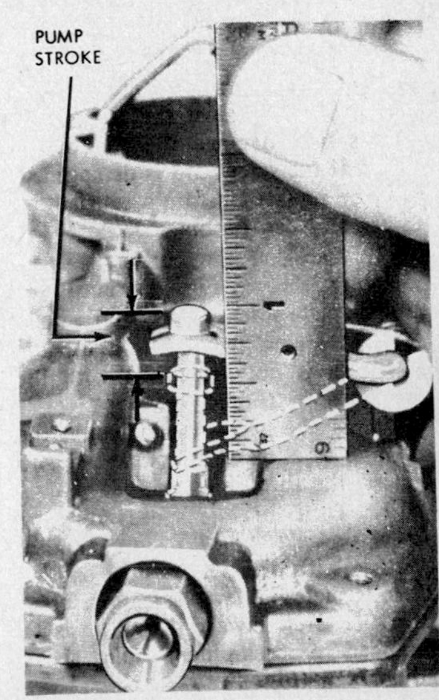

RBS accelerator pump adjustment

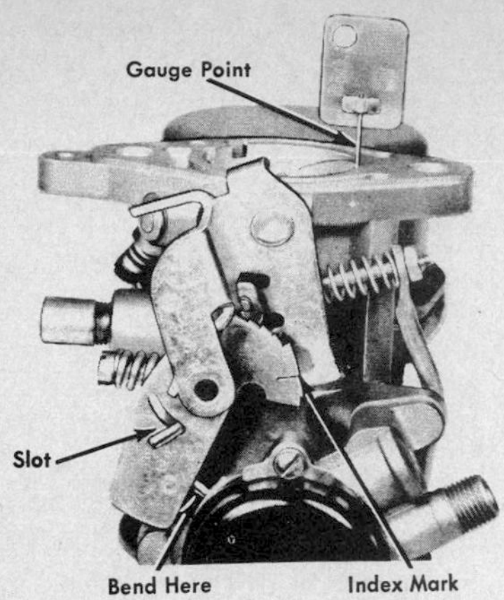

RBS fast idle cam adjustment

screw and hold the choke valve wide open so that the throttle valve is completely closed. Turn the pump adjusting nut until the specified clearance is obtained between the shoulder on the pump shaft and the pump arm. This procedure may be used through 1969.

On later models 1970 and up, the pump stroke is measured as the difference in height between the measured height with the throttle valve fully closed and fully open. To adjust, open or close the pump connector link at the offset portion.

Bowl Vent Adjustment

After adjusting the accelerator pump stroke, close the throttle valve completely and measure the distance between the vent valve and the carburetor casting. To adjust, bend the

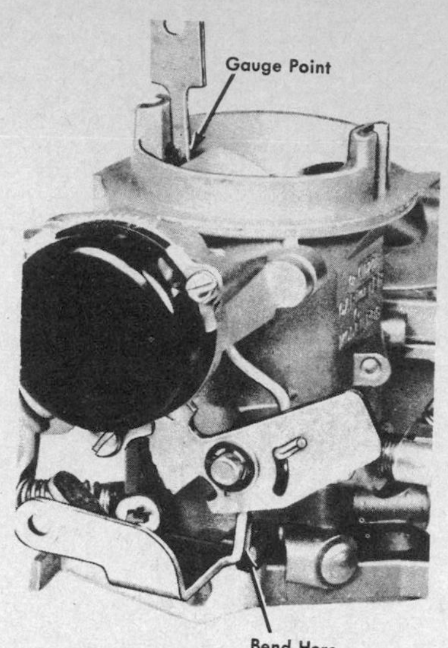

RBS choke unloader adjustment

connector rod at the accelerator pump end.

Fast Idle Cam Adjustment

Through 1970

With the choke valve tightly closed and the choke connector rod in the upper end of the slot in the cam, align the cam index with the center of the fast idle tang. Adjust by bending the choke connector rod at the offset portion.

Beginning 1971

Place the fast idle screw on the second step of the fast idle cam and against the shoulder of the high step. Specified clearance should exist between the lower edge of the choke valve and the air horn wall. If adjustment is needed, bend the choke plate connecting rod.

Choke Unloader Adjustment

With the throttle valve wide open, the clearance between the upper edge of the valve and the inner air horn wall should be to specification. If it is not, adjust by bending the tang on the throttle lever.

Fast Idle Speed Adjustment

1. Revolve the fast idle cam until the tang on the throttle lever is aligned with the mark on the cam.
2. Proper clearance should exist between the throttle valve and the carburetor bore on the idle port side.
3. If adjustment is required, close the choke valve fully and put the fast idle connector rod against the end of the slot in the cam. Bend the connector rod at the offset portion to align the marks.

Automatic Choke Adjustment

1. Loosen the choke cover retaining screws.
2. Turn the choke cover so that the index mark on the cover lines up with the specified mark on the choke housing.

CARTER RBS SPECIFICATIONS

AMERICAN MOTORS

Year	Model ①	Float Level (in.)	Bowl Vent (in.)	Accelerator Pump (in.)	Fast Idle (rpm)	Fast Idle Throttle Plate (in.)	Choke Unloader (in.)	Choke
1969	4634S	9/16	5/64	1/64	2000	0.035	3/16	2 Rich
	4666S	9/16	5/64	1/64	2000	0.035	1/8	2 Rich

FORD MOTOR CO.

Year	Model ①	Float Level (in.)	Bowl Vent (in.)	Accelerator Pump (in.)	Fast Idle (rpm)	Fast Idle Throttle Plate (in.)	Choke Unloader (in.)	Choke
1970	D0ZF-C	9/16	—	0.400③	See Text	0.040	0.250	Index
	D0ZF-D	9/16	—	0.400③	See Text	0.046	0.252	1 Rich
	D0ZF-F	9/16	—	0.400③	See Text	—	0.252	1 Rich
1971	D1ZF-HA, LA	9/16	—	0.400③	0.115②	—	0.250	Index
	D1ZF-NA, KA	9/16	—	0.400③	0.115②	—	0.250	1 Rich
1972	D2OF-LA	9/16	—	0.400③	0.115②	—	0.250	Index
	D2OF-MA	9/16	—	0.400③	0.115②	—	0.250	1 Rich
	D2OF-SA	9/16	—	0.400③	0.115②	—	0.250	1 Rich
1973	D3OF-BA	9/16	—	0.420③	0.115②	—	0.250	Index
	D3OF-CA	9/16	—	0.400③	0.115②	—	0.250	Index
1974	D4DE-BB	9/16	—	—	0.115②	—	0.250	Index
	D4DE-SB	9/16	—	—	0.115②	—	0.250	Index
	D4DE-AAA	9/16	—	—	0.115②	—	0.250	1 Lean
	D4DE-AB	9/16	—	—	0.115②	—	0.250	Index

① Model numbers located on a tag or on the casting ② At kickdown ③ Closed throttle.

Model WCD

Introduction

This is a two barrel carburetor using a single needle valve even though two floats are provided. On several of these units, the floats operate independently of each other so that the highest float always controls the fuel level. This is necessary when the carburetor is mounted with the float centerline parallel to the centerline of the engine.

Float Adjustment

(Lateral)

1. Invert the bowl cover.
2. Remove the bowl cover gasket.
3. Place the float gauge directly under the floats with the notched portions of the gauge fitted over the edges of the casting.
4. The sides of the float should barely touch the vertical uprights of the float gauge. A gauge is normally included in a rebuilding kit.
5. Adjustment is made by bending the arms of the floats.

RBS float level adjustment

(Vertical)

1. With the float gauge in the same position as for the lateral adjustment, the floats should just clear the horizontal portion of the gauge.
2. The vertical distance between the top center of the float and the machined surface of the casting must be 7/32 in.
3. Adjust by bending the float arms as required.
4. To install the bowl cover gasket, remove the floats, install the gasket, and reinstall the floats.

Pump Adjustment

1. Install the pump connector link in the outer hole (long stroke) of the pump arm with the ends extending away from the countershaft arm.
2. Back out the throttle lever set screw until the throttle valves seat in the carburetor bores.
3. Be sure that the fast idle adjustment screw does not hold the throttle open.
4. Hold a straightedge across the top of the dust cover boss at the pump arm.
5. The flat on top of the pump arm should be parallel to the straightedge.
6. Adjust by bending the throttle connector rod to the upper angle.

RBS pump adjustment

Metering Rod Adjustment

1. Complete the pump adjustment.
2. Back out the throttle lever set screw to allow the valves (throttle) to seat in the bores of the carburetor.
3. Loosen the metering rod clamp screw.
4. With the metering rod in place, press down on the vacumeter link until the metering rods bottom in the carburetor body casting.
5. While holding the rods in a downward position, revolve the metering rod arm until the finger on the arm contacts the lip of the vacumeter link.
6. Hold in place and carefully tighten the clamp screw.

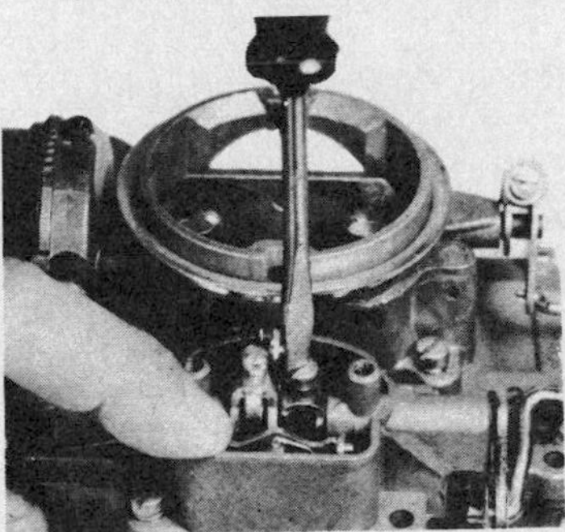

RBS metering rod adjustment

Fast Idle Cam Adjustment

1. Loosen the choke lever clamp screw on the choke shaft.
2. Insert a 0.010 in. feeler gauge between the lip of the fast idle cam and the boss of the flange casting.
3. Hold the choke valve tightly closed and take the slack out of the linkage by pressing the choke lever toward the closed position.
4. With the choke valve in the closed position, tighten the fast idle adjusting screw to obtain the specified clearance.
5. Be sure that the fast idle adjusting screw is on the high step of the cam or index mark while making this adjustment.

RBS fast idle cam adjustment

Choke Unloader Adjustment

1. With the throttle valves wide open, there should be clearance between the upper edge of the choke valve and the inner wall of the air horn.
2. Adjust by bending the unloader lip on the throttle shaft lever.
3. Adjustment is 3/16 in.

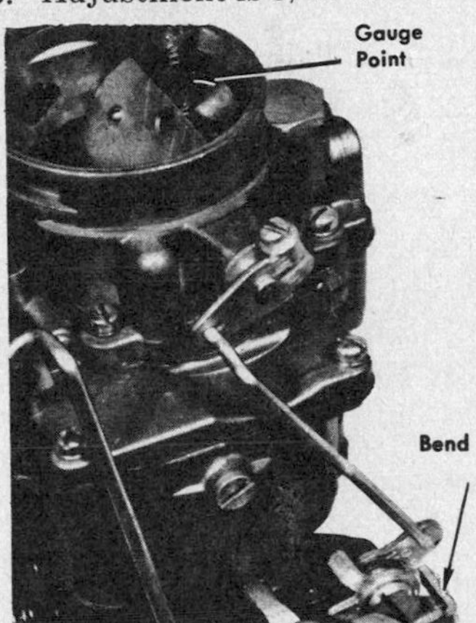

RBS choke unloader adjustment

Automatic Choke Adjustment

1. Loosen the choke cover retaining screws.
2. Turn the cover so that the index mark on the cover lines up with the specified mark on the choke housing.
3. See the Specifications Chart for the proper mark alignment.

CHOKE SPECIFICATIONS

Year	Model ①	Choke
1969	4667S	Index
	4668S	Index
1970	4816S	Index
	4817S	Index
	4950S	Index

① Model numbers located on the tag or the casting

Model WGD

Introduction

The WGD carburetor is the same basic carburetor as the WCD, the only difference being that the WGD has only one float. The choke is operated by a thermostatic coil. This carburetor is used mainly on 1972 Pontiacs. It carries model number 6311S.

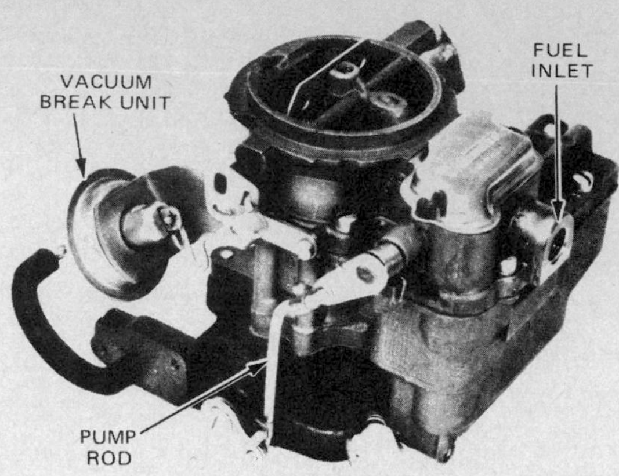

WGD carburetor assembly

Float Adjustment

1. With the air horn inverted, check to see that the float is parallel with the outer edge of the air horn casting.
2. Adjust by bending the float arm. Next, place the gauge between the air horn and the center of the float. The distance should be 5/16 in.

WGD float level adjustment

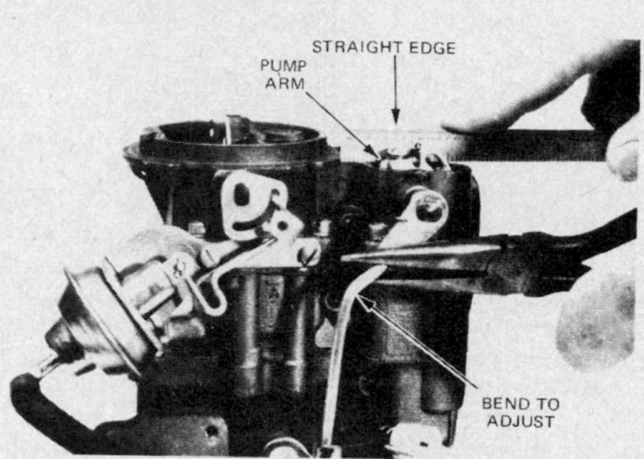

WGD pump adjustment

3. Adjust the float level by bending the float arm until the float touches the gauge. The float should not have excessive clearance at the hinge pin and must operate freely.

NOTE: When adjusting the float, care must be exercised to avoid pressing the flared tip needle into the needle seats as a false setting will result. Allow only the float weight to seat the needle when gauging.

Pump Adjustment

1. Back out the throttle stop screw.
2. Turn the fast idle cam to "hot" position and fully close the throttle valves.
3. Place a 1/4 in. gauge or a similar straightedge across the dust cover boss. The dust cover boss should be parallel with the top surface of the pump arm.
4. Adjust by bending the pump rod at the offset.

Metering Rod Adjustment

NOTE: This adjustment should be made after the pump adjustment. No metering rod gauges are necessary.

1. Back out the throttle screw and fully close the throttle valves. Press down on the vacuum piston link until the metering rods bottom.
2. While holding the rods down and the metering arm tongue against the lip of the vacuum piston link, carefully tighten the metering arm set screw.

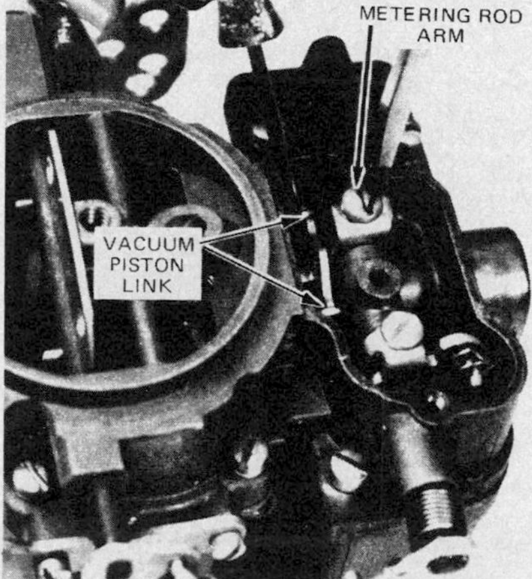

WGD metering rod adjustment

Fast Idle Cam Adjustment

1. Open the throttle to clear the fast idle cam and close the choke valve.
2. With the choke valve held fully closed and the stop on the fast idle cam against the casting, there should be 0.005 in. minimum clearance between the inner and outer choke levers.
3. Adjust by bending the outer lever lug as required.

NOTE: With the choke fully closed, the tang on the fast idle cam must clear the stop on the throttle body flange.

Unloader Adjustment

1. Hold the choke closed lightly.
2. Fully open the throttle, forcing the choke valve open.
3. Check the clearance between the upper edge of the choke valve and the wall of the air horn. The

WGD choke unloader adjustment

WGD fast idle cam adjustment

clearance should be 3/16 in.

4. Adjust by bending the unloader arm as required.

Fast Idle Speed Adjustment

1. With the carburetor on the engine, rotate the fast idle cam until the fast idle tang contacts the cam's high step.
2. With the engine at normal operating temperature, adjust the fast idle tang to obtain an engine speed of 1500 rpm.

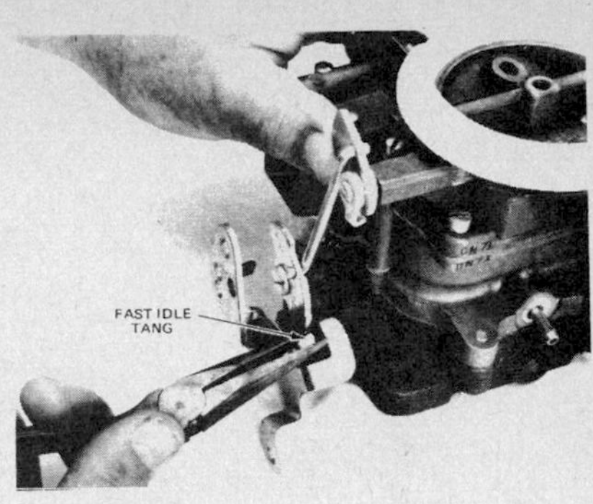

WGD fast idle speed adjustment

Model AVS

Introduction

The AVS carburetor is very similar to the AFB carburetor. AVS means Air Valve Secondary. It employs a spring loaded air valve located above the secondary fuel nozzles. This system gives smooth response whenever the secondaries are opened. Venturi clusters are used in the primary side for fuel control in the idle and economy ranges.

Float Alignment

1. The sides of the float should be parallel to the edge of the casting with minimum clearance between the lever and the air horn lugs without binding.
2. To adjust, bend the float arm lever.

Float Level Adjustment

1. With the air horn inverted, the air horn gasket in place, and the float needle seated, slide the float gauge between the top of the float, at the outer edge, and the air horn gasket. Refer to the Specifications Chart.
2. Check the other float in the same manner.
3. Adjust by bending the float arm. After bending the arm, recheck the float alignment.

Float Drop Adjustment

1. The dimension listed in the Specifications Chart should exist between the tops of the floats, at the outer end, and the air horn gasket.
2. To adjust, bend the stop tabs on the float brackets.

Pump Adjustment

1. With the throttle valves closed tightly, the dimension listed in the Specifications Chart should be from the top of the air horn to the top of the pump plunger shaft with the throttle connector rod in the inner hole of the pump arm.
2. To adjust, bend the throttle connector rod at an angle.

Fast Idle Cam Adjustment

1. With the fast idle speed adjusting screw contacting the second highest speed step on the fast idle cam, move the choke valve

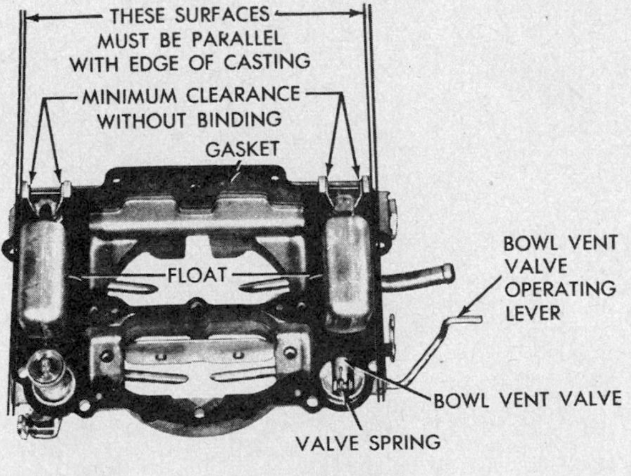

AVS float alignment

GASKET IN PLACE FLOAT FLOAT GAUGE GAUGE OUTER END OF FLOAT

AVS float level adjustment

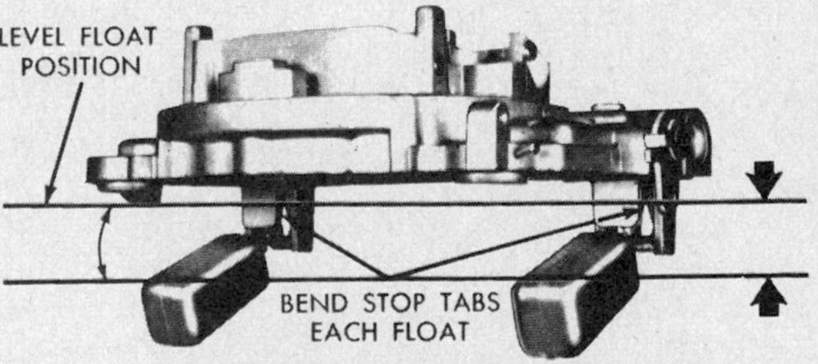

AVS float drop adjustment

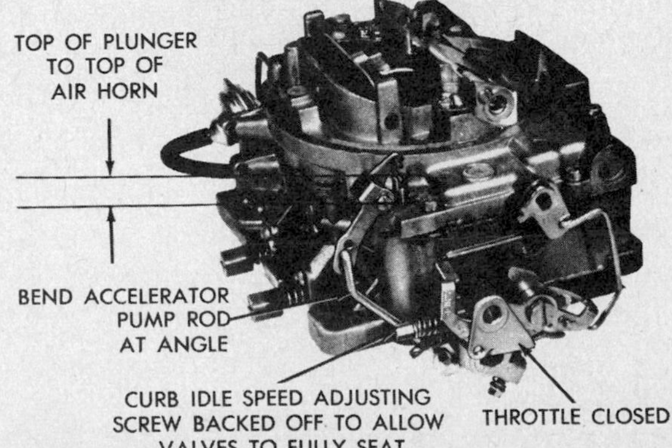

AVS pump adjustment

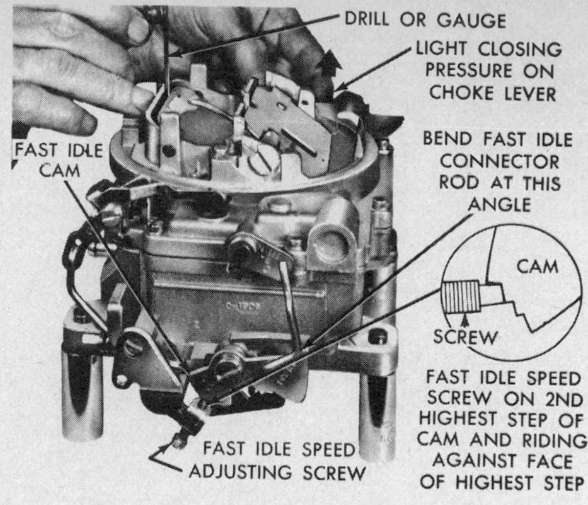

AVS fast idle cam adjustment

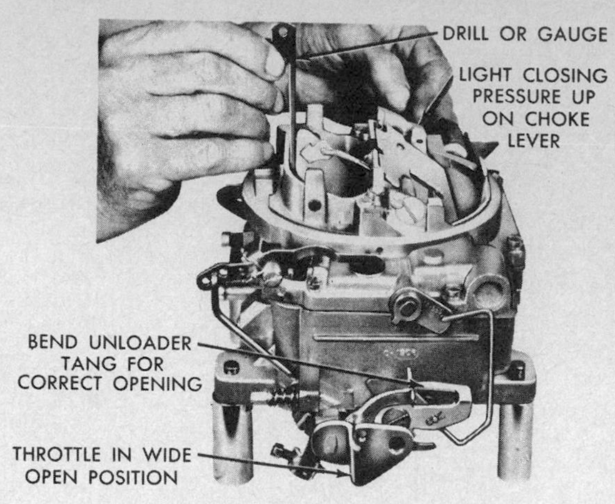

AVS choke unloader adjustment

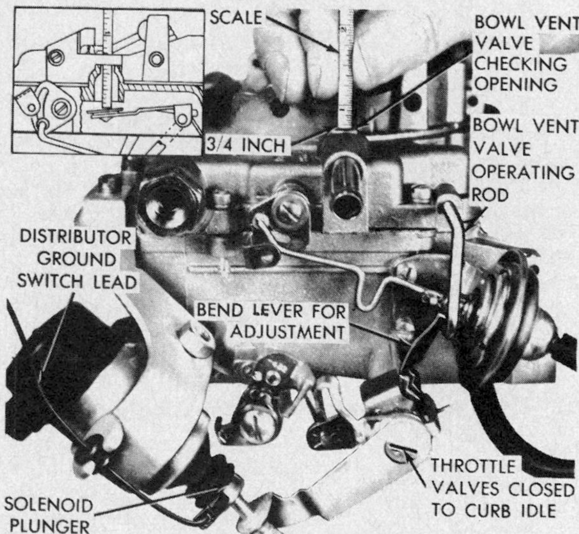

AVS bowl vent adjustment

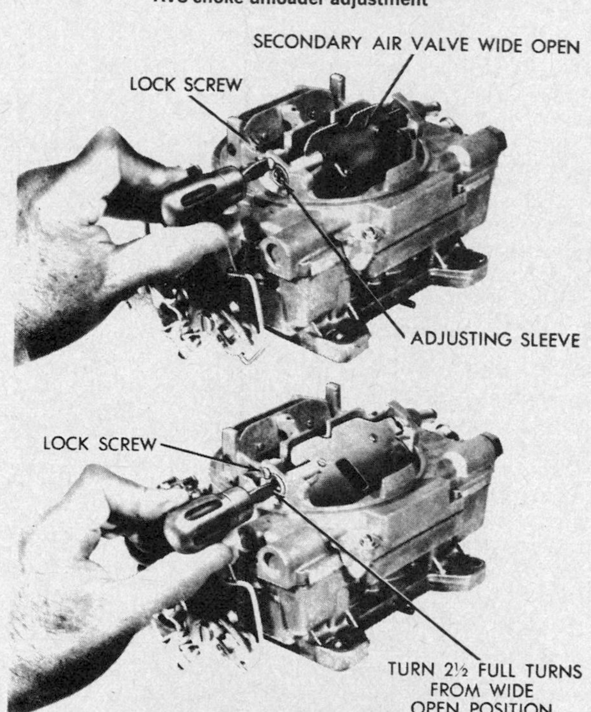

AVS secondary air valve adjustment

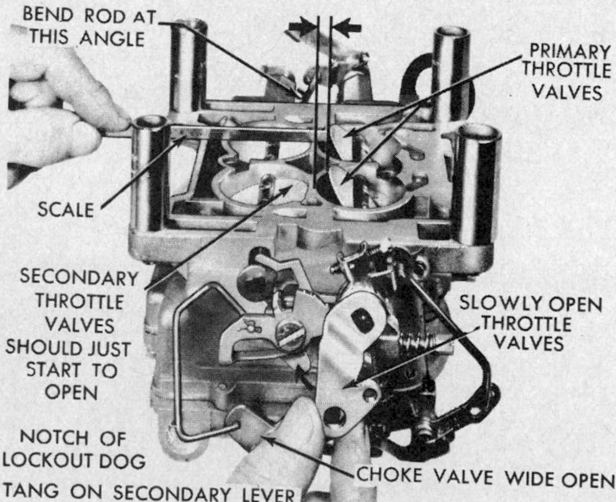

AVS secondary throttle lockout

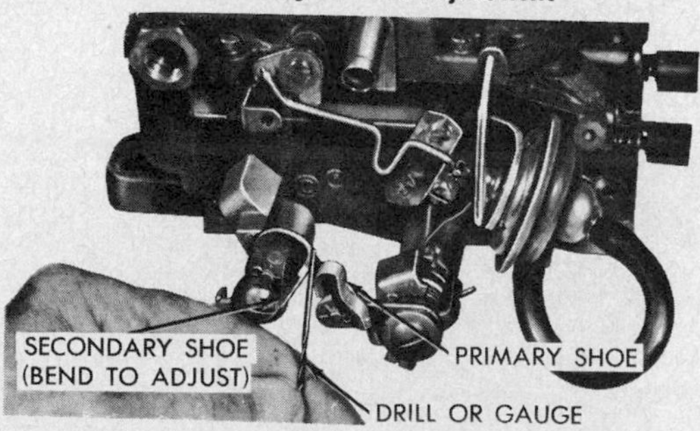

AVS closing shoe adjustment

toward the closed position with light pressure on the choke shaft lever.

2. Insert the drill gauge between the choke valve and the wall of the air horn. Refer to the Specifications Chart.
3. An adjustment will be necessary if a slight drag is not obtained as the drill is beginning to be removed.
4. Adjust by bending the fast idle connector rod at an angle.

Choke Unloader Adjustment

1. With the throttle valves wide open there should be ¼ in. clearance between the upper edge of the choke valve and the inner wall of the air horn.
2. To adjust, bend the unloader tang on the fast idle cam.

Bowl Vent Adjustment

CAS Equipped

1. With the throttle valves tightly closed, insert a drill gauge between the air horn and the valve at the smallest opening. Refer to the Specifications Chart.
2. Adjust by bending the tang on the pivot end of the lever.

ECS Equipped

1. Remove the bowl vent valve and check the hole plug in the air horn.
2. With the throttle valves at closed curb idle position, insert a narrow ruler down through the hole. Allow the ruler to rest lightly on top of the valve.
3. Measure from the top of the valve to the top of the air horn casting at the opening. Refer to the Specifications Chart.
4. Adjust by bending the bowl vent operating lever.
5. Install the plug and rap lightly on the seat, using a hammer.

Secondary Air Valve Adjustment

1. Loosen the lock screw and allow the air valve to position itself at the wide open position.
2. From the wide open position, turn the slotted sleeve 2½ turns counterclockwise.
3. Hold the sleeve in this position with your fingers, then tighten the lock screw securely.
4. Check the valve for freedom of movement.

Secondary Throttle Lever Adjustment

1. Block the choke valve in the wide open position and invert the carburetor.
2. Slowly open the primary throttle valves until the specified measurement is obtained between the lower edge of the primary valve and the bore opposite the idle port. Refer to the Specifications Chart.
3. At this measurement, the secondary valves should just start to open.
4. Adjust by bending the secondary throttle operating rod at the angle.

Closing Shoe Adjustment

1. With the primary and secondary throttle valves closed, bend the secondary closing shoe to obtain 0.020 in. clearance between the positive closing shoes on the primary and secondary throttle levers.
2. To adjust, bend the shoe on the secondary lever.

Secondary Throttle Lockout

1. Crack the throttle valves and manually open and close the choke valve. The tang on the secondary throttle lever should freely engage in the notch of the lockout dog.
2. To adjust, bend the tang on the secondary throttle lever.

CARTER AVS SPECIFICATIONS

CHRYSLER, DODGE, PLYMOUTH, AND IMPERIAL

Year	Carb. Model ①	Float Level (in.)	Float Drop (in.)	Accelerator Pump (in.)	Bowl Vent (in.)	Fast Idle Cam (in.) ②	Secondary Throttle Lever (in.)
1969	4611S	7/32	1/2	7/16	1/8	50	21/64
	4612S	7/32	1/2	7/16	1/8	50	21/64
	4615S	5/16	1/2	7/16	1/8	50	21/64
	4616S	5/16	1/2	7/16	1/8	50	21/64
	4617S	7/32	1/2	7/16	1/8	50	11/32
	4618S	7/32	1/2	7/16	1/8	50	3/8
	4638S	5/16	1/2	7/16	1/8	50	21/64
	4639S	7/32	1/2	7/16	1/8	50	21/64
	4640S	7/32	1/2	7/16	1/8	50	1/8
	4682S	5/16	1/2	7/16	1/8	50	21/64
	4711S	5/16	1/2	7/16	1/8	50	21/64
1970	4732S*	5/16	1/2	7/16	3/64	50	19/64
	4734S*	5/16	1/2	7/16	3/64	50	19/64
	4736S*	5/16	1/2	7/16	3/64	50	19/64
	4737S*	7/32	1/2	7/16	3/64	50	23/64
	4738S	7/32	1/2	7/16	3/64	50	23/64
	4739S	7/32	1/2	7/16	3/64	50	23/64
	4740S	7/32	1/2	7/16	3/64	50	23/64
	4741S	7/32	1/2	7/16	3/64	50	23/64
	4933S	7/32	1/2	7/16	3/64	50	19/64
	4934S	7/32	1/2	7/16	1/8	50	19/64
	4935S	7/32	1/2	7/16	1/8	50	19/64
	4936S	7/32	1/2	7/16	3/4	50	19/64
	4937S	7/32	1/2	7/16	3/4	50	19/64
1971	4966S	7/32	1/2	7/16	3/4	50	23/64
	4967S	7/32	1/2	7/16	3/4	50	23/64
	4968S	7/32	1/2	7/16	3/4	50	23/64
	6125S	7/32	1/2	7/16	3/4	50	23/64

① Model numbers are located on a tag or on the casting
② Indicates drill bit number.
NOTE: Accelerator pump adjustment is 7/16 in. for all AVS carburetors. Choke setting on all models through 1970 is on the index except when marked (*) which is 2 notches rich. 1971 models should be 2 rich.

Model TQ

Introduction

The TQ (Thermo Quad) has a fuel bowl made of phenolic resin. This acts as a heat insulator. Fuel is kept 20 degrees cooler than in metal carburetors. It also has a suspended design metering system which aids in cooling. All the calibration points are in the upper aluminum casting or air horn and are in effect suspended in the cavities in the main body.

Float Adjustment

1. With the bowl cover inverted, the gasket installed, and the floats resting on the seated needle, the dimension of each float from the bowl cover gasket to the bottom side of the float should be as shown in the specifications chart.

Secondary Throttle Linkage

1. Block the choke valve in the wide open position and invert the carburetor.
2. Slowly open the primary throttle valves until the secondary valves start to open. Measure between the lower edge of the primary valve and its bore.
3. If it is necessary to adjust, bend the rod until the correct dimension is obtained.

Secondary Air Valve Opening

1. With the air valve in the closed position, the opening along the air valve at its long side must be at its maximum and parallel

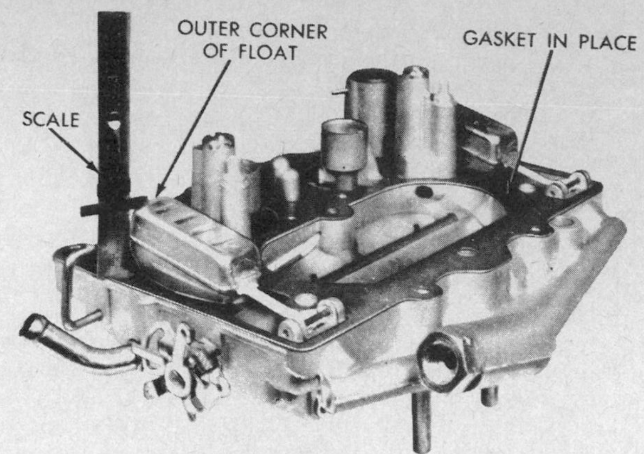

TQ float adjustment

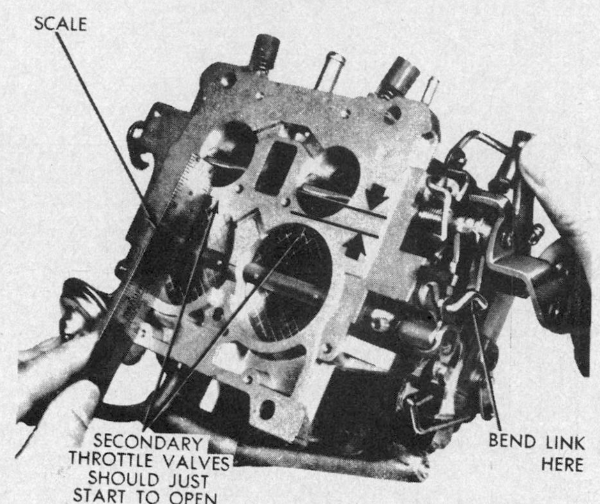

TQ secondary throttle adjustment

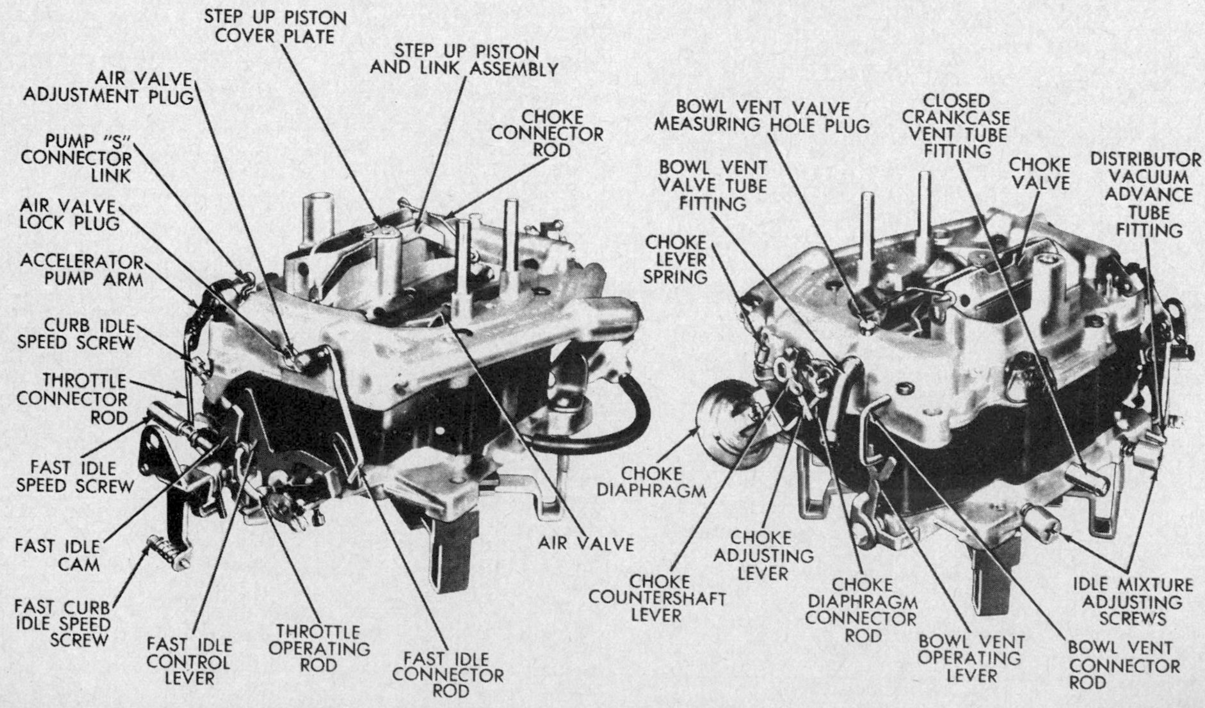

TQ carburetor assembly

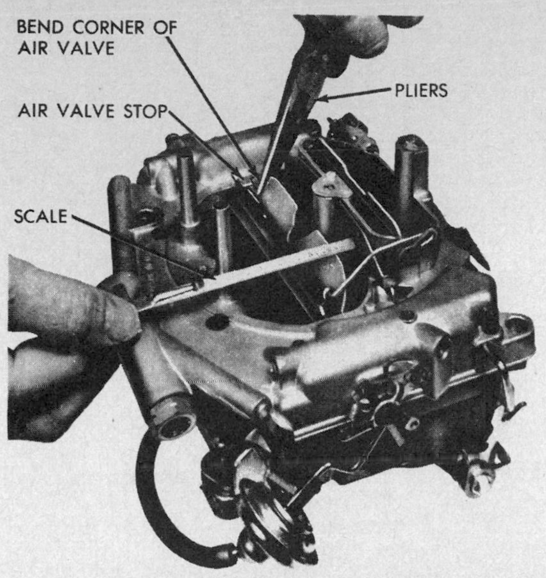

TQ secondary air valve adjustment

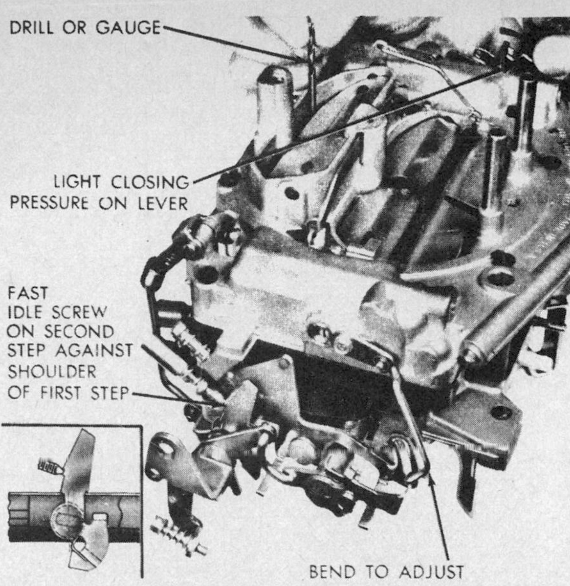

TQ adjusting fast idle cam and linkage

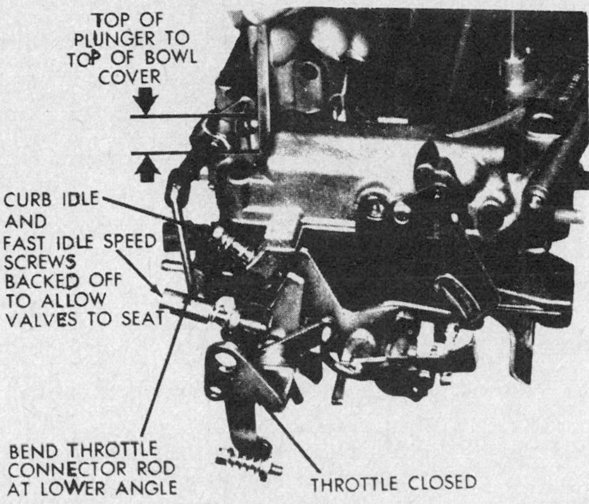

TQ accelerator pump adjustment

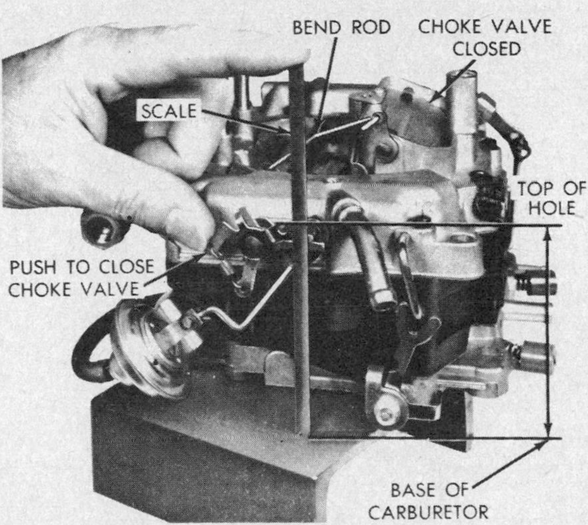

TQ choke control lever

with the air horn gasket surface.

2. With the air valve wide open, the opening of the air valve at the short side and the air horn must match the dimensions in the Specifications Charts. The corner of the air valve is notched for adjustment. Bend the corner with a pair of pliers to give proper opening.

Accelerator Pump Adjustment

1. Move the choke valve wide open to release the fast idle cam.
2. Back off the idle speed adjusting screw until the throttle valves are seated in the bores.
3. Be sure that the throttle connector rod is in the center hole of the pump arm.
4. Close the throttle valve tightly and measure the distance between the top of the bowl cover and the end of the plunger shaft. The dimension should be as shown in the Specifications Chart.
5. Bend the throttle connector rod at the lower angle to adjust. On manual transmission models the second stage adjustment is made by bending the second stage stop lever until the correct travel is obtained.

Choke Control Lever

1. Remove the choke assembly stainless steel cup and gasket.
2. Close the choke by pushing on the choke lever with the throttle partly open.
3. Measure the vertical distance from the top of the rod hole in the control lever down to the carburetor base. The dimensions should be as shown in the Specifications Chart.
4. To adjust, bend the link which connects the two choke shafts.

Vacuum Kick Adjustment

1. With the engine running, back off the fast idle speed screw until the choke can be closed to the kick position at idle.
2. Count the number of screw turns so that the fast idle can be turned back to the original adjustment.
3. Insert the specified drill between the long side, lower edge, of the choke valve and the air horn wall.
4. Apply sufficient pressure on the choke control lever to provide a minimum choke valve opening. The spring connecting the control lever to the adjustment lever must be fully extended for proper adjustment.
5. Bend the tang as shown to change contact with the end of the diaphragm rod. Do not adjust the diaphragm rod. A slight drag should be felt as the drill is being removed.

Fast Idle Cam and Linkage

1. With the fast idle screw on the second fastest step of the cam against the shoulder of the first step, there should be 0.110 in. (.100 beginning 1974) between the air horn wall and edge of the choke valve.

2. To adjust, bend the fast idle connector rod.

Secondary Throttle Lockout

1. Move the choke control lever to the open choke position.
2. Measure the clearance between the lockout lever and the stop.
3. Bend the tang on the fast idle control lever to provide the proper clearance. The reading should be as illustrated for models through 1972, and 0.060 to 0.090 in. beginning 1973.

Bowl Vent Valve Adjustment

1. Remove the bowl vent valve checking hole plug in the bowl cover.
2. With the throttle valve in the idle position insert a narrow ruler down through the hole.
3. Allow the ruler to rest lightly on the top of the valve. Measure from the top of the valve to the top of the bowl cover at the opening. The correct dimension should be 13/16 in.
4. Bend the bowl vent operating lever at the notch to adjust.
5. Install a new plug.

Fast Idle Speed Cam

1. With the engine off and the transmission in Park or Neutral, open the throttle slightly.
2. Close the choke valve until the fast idle screw can be positioned on the second step of the cam against the shoulder of the first step.
3. Start the engine and adjust the screw to obtain the specified fast idle speed.

Choke Unloader Adjustment

1. Hold the throttle valves in the wide open position and insert the specified drill between the long side of the choke valve and inner wall of the air horn.
2. With a finger pressing lightly against the choke control lever, a slight drag should be felt as the drill is being withdrawn.
3. To adjust, bend the tang on the fast idle control lever.

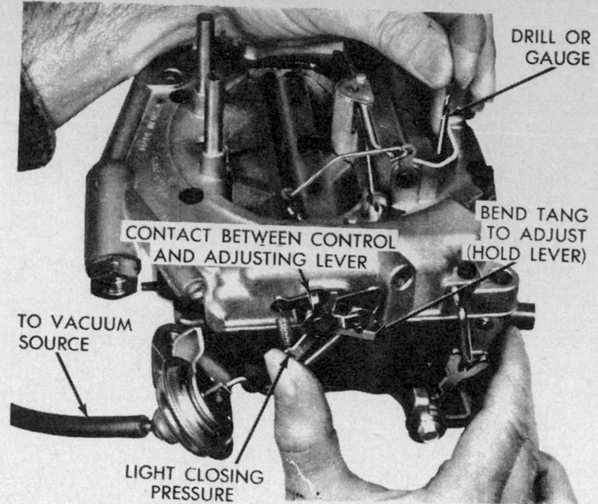

TQ vacuum kick adjustment

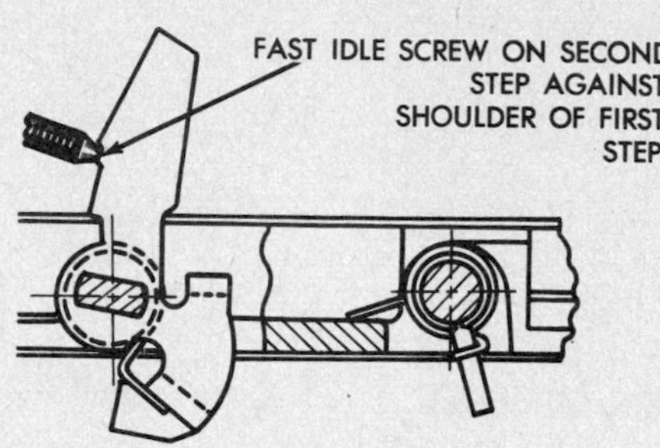

TQ fast idle cam adjustment

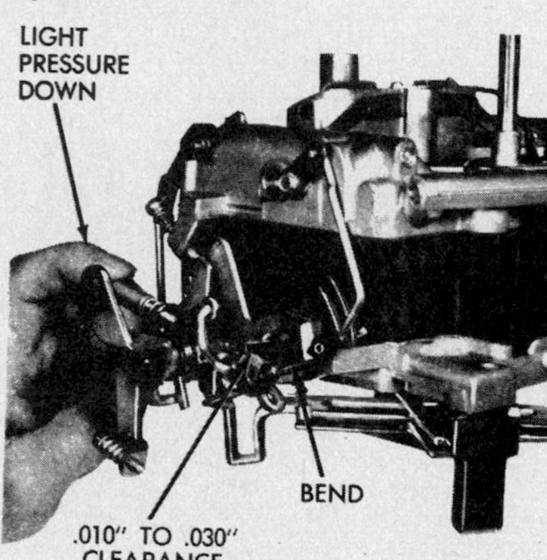

Adjusting the TQ secondary throttle lockout

Secondary Air Valve Spring Tension

1. Loosen the air valve lock plug and allow the air valve to position itself in the wide open position.
2. With a long screwdriver that will enter the center of tool C-4152 positioned on the air valve adjustment plug, turn the plug counterclockwise until the air valve contacts the stop lightly, then an additional 1¼ turn.
3. Hold the adjustment plug with the screwdriver and tighten the lock plug with the tool. Make sure the adjustment does not move and that the air valve moves freely.

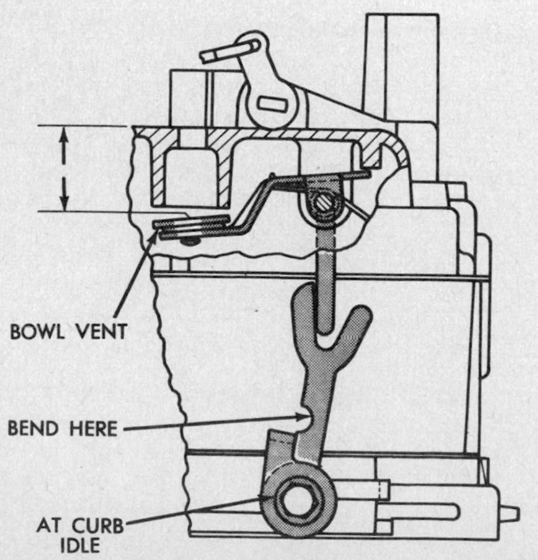

TQ bowl vent adjustment

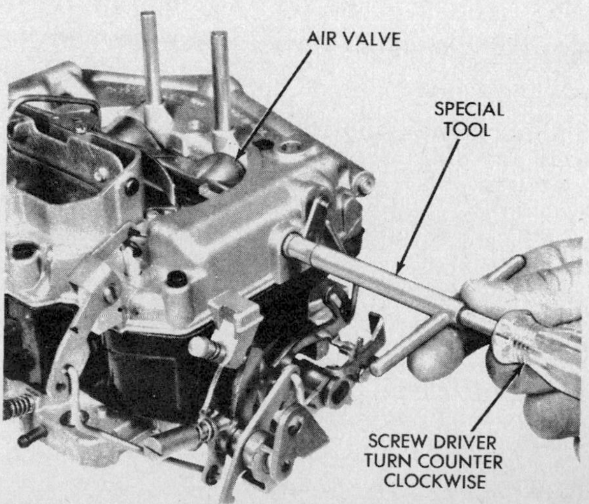

TQ air valve spring tension adjustment

CARTER TQ SPECIFICATIONS

CHRYSLER, DODGE, PLYMOUTH, IMPERIAL

Year	Model ①	Float Setting (in.)	Secondary Throttle Linkage (in.)	Secondary Air Valve Opening (in.)	Secondary Air Valve Spring (turns)	Accelerator Pump (in.)	Choke Control Lever (in.)	Choke Unloader (in.)	Vacuum Kick (Drill Size)	Fast Idle Speed (rpm)
1971	4972S	1	11/32	31/64	1 1/4	31/64	5 41/64	0.190	35	1800
	4973S	1	11/32	31/64	1 1/4	31/64	5 41/64	0.190	35	1800
1972	6090S	1	②	31/64	1	31/64	3 3/8	0.190	28	1900
	6138S	1	②	29/64	1	9/16	3 3/8	0.190	21	1900
	6139S	1	②	29/64	1	31/64	3 3/8	0.190	28	1900
	6140S	1	②	31/64	1	9/16	3 3/8	0.190	21	1900
	6165S	1	②	31/64	1	9/16	3 3/8	0.190	21	2000
	6166S	1	②	31/64	1	31/64	3 3/8	0.190	28	2100
1973	6318S	1 1/16	②	29/64	1 1/4	35/64	3 3/8	0.190	21	1300
	6319S	1 1/16	②	29/64	1 1/4	31/64	3 3/8	0.190	21	1800
	6320S	1 1/16	②	31/64	1 1/4	35/64	3 3/8	0.190	21	1300
	6321S	1 1/16	②	31/64	1 1/4	31/64	3 3/8	0.190	21	1800
	6322S	1 1/16	②	31/64	1 1/4	31/64	3 3/8	0.190	21	1700
	6324S	1 1/16	②	31/64	1 1/4	31/64	3 3/8	0.190	21	1800
	6339S	1 1/16	②	29/64	1 1/4	35/64	3 3/8	0.190	21	1700
	6340S	1 1/16	②	29/64	1 1/4	31/64	3 3/8	0.190	21	1800
	6341S	1 1/16	②	29/64	1 1/4	35/64	3 3/8	0.190	21	1700
	6342S	1 1/16	②	29/64	1 1/4	31/64	3 3/8	0.190	21	1700
	6410S	1 1/16	②	31/64	1 1/4	31/64	3 3/8	0.190	21	1700
	6411S	1 1/16	②	31/64	1 1/4	31/64	3 3/8	0.190	21	1700
1974	6488S	1	②	1/2	1 1/4	35/64	3 3/8	.310	21	1800
	6452S	1	②	1/2	1 1/4	35/64	3 3/8	.310	4	1900
	6453S	1	②	1/2	1 1/4	31/64	3 3/8	.310	21	1900
	6454S	1	②	1/2	1 1/4	35/64	3 3/8	.310	4	1900
	6455S	1	②	1/2	1 1/4	31/64	3 3/8	.310	21	1900
	6489S	1	②	1/2	1 1/4	31/64	3 3/8	.310	21	2000
	6496S	1	②	1/2	1 1/4	31/64	3 3/8	.310	21	2000
	6456S	1	②	1/2	1 1/4	35/64	3 3/8	.310	4	1700
	6457S	1	②	1/2	1 1/4	31/64	3 3/8	.310	21	1800
	6459	1	②	1/2	1 1/4	31/64	3 3/8	.310	21	1800
	6460S	1	②	1/2	1 1/4	31/64	3 3/8	.310	21	1700
	6461S	1	②	1/2	1 1/4	31/64	3 3/8	.310	21	1700
	6462S	1	②	1/2	1 1/4	31/64	3 3/8	.310	21	1700
	6463S	1	②	1/2	1 1/4	31/64	3 3/8	.310	21	1700
1975	9004S	29/32	2	1/2	1 1/4	35/64	3 3/8	0.310	0.100	1600
	9002S	29/32	2	1/2	1 1/4	35/64	3 3/8	0.310	0.100	1600
	9046S	29/32	2	1/2	1 1/4	35/64	3 3/8	0.310	0.100	1800
	9008S	29/32	2	1/2	1 1/4	35/64	3 3/8	0.310	0.100	1800
	9053S	29/32	2	1/2	1 1/4	35/64	3 3/8	0.310	0.100	1800
	9009S	29/32	2	1/2	1 1/4	35/64	3 3/8	0.310	0.100	1600
	9010S	29/32	2	1/2	1 1/4	35/64	3 3/8	0.310	0.100	1600
	9011S	29/32	2	1/2	1 1/4	35/64	3 3/8	0.310	0.100	1600
	9012S	29/32	2	1/2	1 1/4	35/64	3 3/8	0.310	0.100	1800

① Model numbers located on the tag or on the casting
② Adjust link so primary and secondary stops both contact at same time

NOTE: All choke settings are fixed except 1971 which is 2 notches rich

Model AFB

Introduction

The Carter AFB carburetor has four barrels. All the major castings are of aluminum and the venturi assemblies are rcplaceable. For better performance in cornering and stopping, one fuel bowl feeds the primary and secondary on the left. The other bowl feeds the primary and secondary on the right. Thermostatic spring coil chokes are used on most models.

Float Alignment

1. Sight down the side of the float to determine if it is parallel to the outer edge of the air horn casting.
2. To adjust, bend the float lever accordingly.
3. Apply pressure on the end of the float with your fingers while supporting the float lever with your thumb.
4. After aligning the float, remove as much clearance as possible between the arms of the float lever and the lugs on the air horn by bending the float lever.
5. The arms of the float lever should be parallel to the inner surfaces of the lugs on the air horn. The floats must operate freely without excess clearance on the hinge pin.

Float Level Adjustment

1. With the air horn inverted, the bowl cover in place, and the needle seated, clearance between the top of the float (at outer edge) and the air horn gasket should be as listed in the Specifications Chart.
2. To adjust, bend the float arm. Adjust both floats and recheck the float alignment.

Float Drop Adjustment

1. With the bowl cover held in the upright position, measure between the outer end of each float, the distance between the top of the floats and the bowl cover gasket as listed in the Specifications Chart.
2. To adjust, bend the tabs on the float brackets.

Pump Adjustment

1. Back out the idle speed screw until the throttle valve seats in the carburetor bores.
2. With the throttle connector rod in the center hole (medium stroke) of the pump arm, the distance from the top of the bowl cover to the top of the pump plunger shaft should be as listed in the Specifications Chart.

To adjust, bend the throttle connector rod at its offset angle.

NOTE: Some models require the throttle connector rod to be placed in the inner hole (long stroke) or the outer hole (short stroke). In such cases the chart will indicate the proper hole connection.

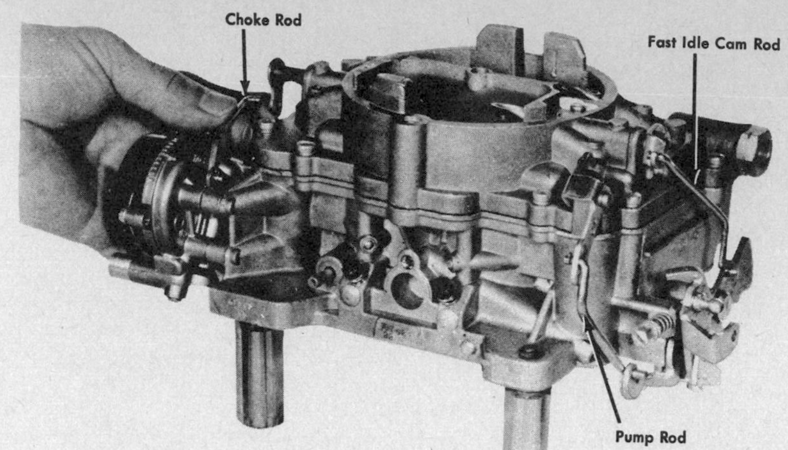

AFB carburetor assembly

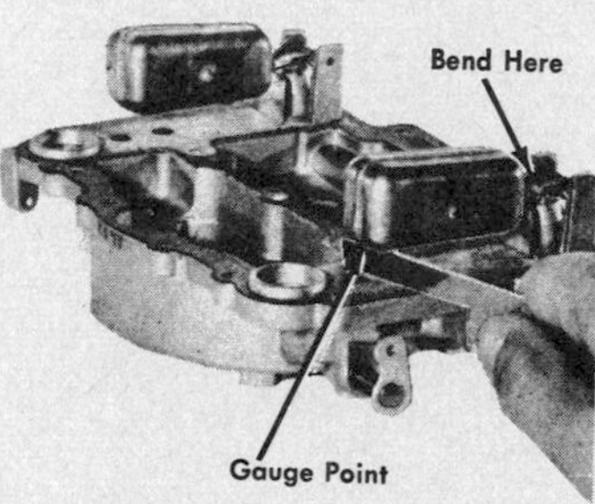

AFB float level adjustment

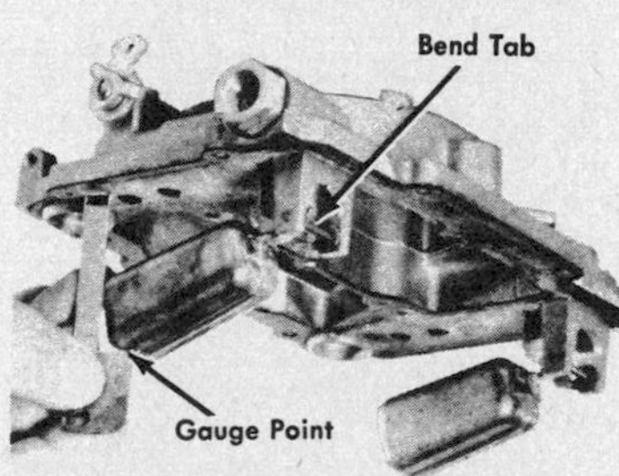

AFB float drop adjustment

AFB pump adjustment

AFB fast idle linkage adjustment

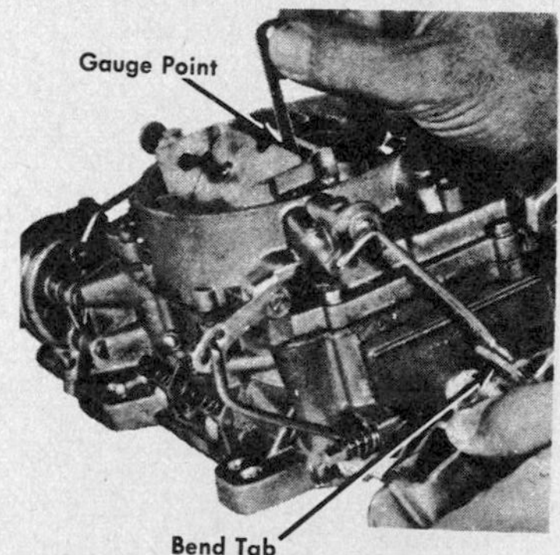

AFB choke unloader adjustment

Fast Idle Linkage Adjustment

1. With the choke valve tightly closed and the lug on the outer choke shaft lever contacting the stop on the inner choke shaft lever, align the center of the fast idle screw with the index mark on the cam.
2. To adjust, bend the fast idle connector rod. On some models it may be necessary to bend the stop lug on the fast idle cam.

Fast Idle Throttle Valve Clearance

1. Close the choke valve.
2. Tighten the fast idle and adjusting screw on the index mark on the cam until the clearance between the throttle valve and the carburetor bore (side opposite the idle port) is as listed in the Specifications Chart.

Fast Idle Speed Cam Position Adjustment

1. With the fast idle speed adjusting screw contacting the second highest speed step on the fast idle cam, move the choke valve toward the closed position with light pressure on the choke shaft lever.
2. Insert a drill gauge between the choke valve and the wall of the air horn. Refer to the Specifications Chart.
3. Adjustment is necessary if a slight drag is not obtained as the drill is being removed.
4. Adjust by bending the fast idle connector rod at the angle.

Choke Unloader Adjustment

1. With the throttle wide open, the clearance between the upper edge of the choke valve and the inner wall of the air horn should be as listed in the Specifications Chart.
2. To adjust, bend the unloader tang on the throttle shaft lever.

Secondary Throttle Lever Adjustment

1. Block the choke valve wide open. The secondary throttle valves should just start to open when the primary throttle valves are opened to the clearance (listed in the Specifications Chart) between the lower edge of the throttle valve and the carburetor bore.
2. To adjust, bend the throttle connecting rod.

AFB secondary throttle lever adjustment

Secondary Throttle Lockout

1. Crack the throttle valves and manually open and close the choke valve.
2. The tang on the secondary throttle lever should freely engage in the notch of the lockout dog.
3. To adjust, bend the tang on the throttle lever. Refer to the Specifications Chart.

Bowl Vent Valve Adjustment

1. With the throttle valves tightly closed, insert the drill gauge between the air horn and the valve at the smallest opening. Refer to the Specifications Chart.
2. Adjust by bending the adjusting tang on the pivot end of the lever.

ECS Equipped

1. Remove the bowl vent valve and checking the hole plug in the air horn.
2. With the throttle valves in the closed curb idle position, insert a narrow ruler down through the hole.
3. Allow the ruler to rest lightly on top of the valve.
4. Measure from the top of the valve to the top of the air horn casting at the opening. Refer to the Specifications Chart.
5. Adjust by bending the bowl vent valve operating lever.
6. Install a new plug and rap lightly to seat it, using a hammer.

Automatic Choke Adjustment

1. Loosen the choke cover retaining screws.
2. Turn the choke cover so that the index mark on the cover lines up with the specified mark on the choke housing.

CARTER AFB SPECIFICATIONS

CHRYSLER PRODUCTS

Year	Carb. Model ①	Float Level (in.)	Float Drop (in.)	Accelerator Pump Travel (in.)	Fast Idle ②	Choke Unloader (in.)	Secondary Throttle Lever (in.)	Secondary Throttle Lockout (in.)	Bowl Vent (in.)	Choke
1969	4619S	7/32	3/4	7/16	—	—	17/64	0.020	—	—
	4620S	7/32	3/4	7/16	50	1/4	17/64	0.020	5/32	2 Rich
	4621S	7/32	3/4	7/16	50	1/4	17/64	0.020	5/32	2 Rich
1970	4742S	7/32	3/4	7/16	—	—	17/64	0.020	—	—
	4745S	7/32	3/4	7/16	50	1/4	17/64	0.020	3/4③	2 Rich
	4746S	7/32	3/4	7/16	50	1/4	17/64	0.020	3/4③	2 Rich
1971	4969S	7/32	3/4	31/64	—	1/4	17/64	0.020	3/4③	—
	4970S	7/32	3/4	31/64	50	1/4	17/64	0.020	3/4③	—
	4971S	7/32	3/4	31/64	50	—	17/64	0.020	—	—

AMERICAN MOTORS

Year	Carb. Model ①	Float Level (in.)	Float Drop (in.)	Accelerator Pump Travel (in.)	Fast Idle ②	Choke Unloader (in.)	Secondary Throttle Lever (in.)	Secondary Throttle Lockout (in.)	Bowl Vent (in.)	Choke
1969	4660S	11/32	2	21/64	—	5/32	7/16	0.015	—	2 Rich
	4661S	11/32	2	21/64	—	5/32	7/16	0.015	—	Index
	4662S	11/32	2	21/64	—	5/32	7/16	0.015	—	Index
	4663S	11/32	2	21/64	—	5/32	7/16	0.015	—	Index
	4664S	11/32	2	21/64	—	5/32	7/16	0.015	—	Index
	4665S	11/32	2	21/64	—	5/32	7/16	0.015	—	Index

① Model numbers are located on a tag or on the casting
② Indicates drill bit number. See Mechanic's Data.
③ At curb idle
④ Place the connector rod in the inner hole

Holley Carburetors

Model 1920

On these units, the choke valve in the carburetor bore is connected to a well-type automatic choke.

Some models are equipped with a spring-staged choke, which is a device incorporated in the choke mechanism to limit choke valve closing torque when cranking the engine at temperatures below zero. The spring-staging of the choke is suited for starting mixture requirements at both low and moderate temperatures.

The accelerator pump is a diaphragm, spring-driven type operated by a lever connected to the throttle shaft.

A two-stage power valve, mounted in the metering body and actuated by manifold vacuum, delivers additional fuel for full power and high speed operation.

Float Level Adjustment

NOTE: Do not allow the float tab to contact the float needle head during the adjustment procedure as the rubber tip of the needle can be compressed, giving a false reading.

Units through 1972

1. With the carburetor inverted, slide the special float gauge into position and test the setting on the "touch" leg of the gauge. The float should just touch the gauge.
2. Reverse the gauge and test the "no touch" leg. The float should just clear the gauge.
3. To adjust, bend the float tab which touches the head of the fuel inlet needle, using needle nose pliers.
4. This adjustment corresponds to a wet fuel level of 27/32 in., measured through the economizer opening from the top of the bowl.

Units beginning 1973

1. With the carburetor inverted, measure from the top of the float to the upper wall of the main body with the gauge against the cast rib, approximately 2 in. from the float hinge pin.
2. Be sure that the gauge is parallel with the top of the float. Refer to the Specifications Chart for the proper dry float setting.
3. Adjust by bending the float tab which touches the head of the fuel needle using needle nosed pliers.

Float Bowl Vent Valve Adjustment

1. With the throttle valve closed,

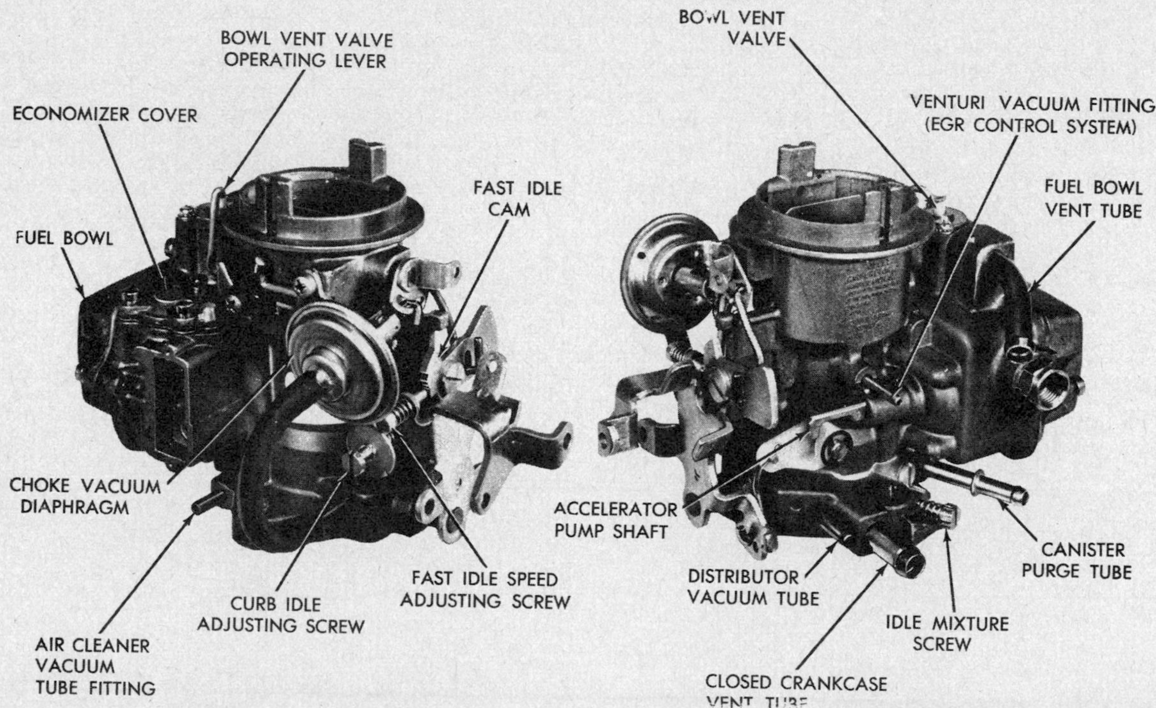

Carburetor assembly—Holley 1920

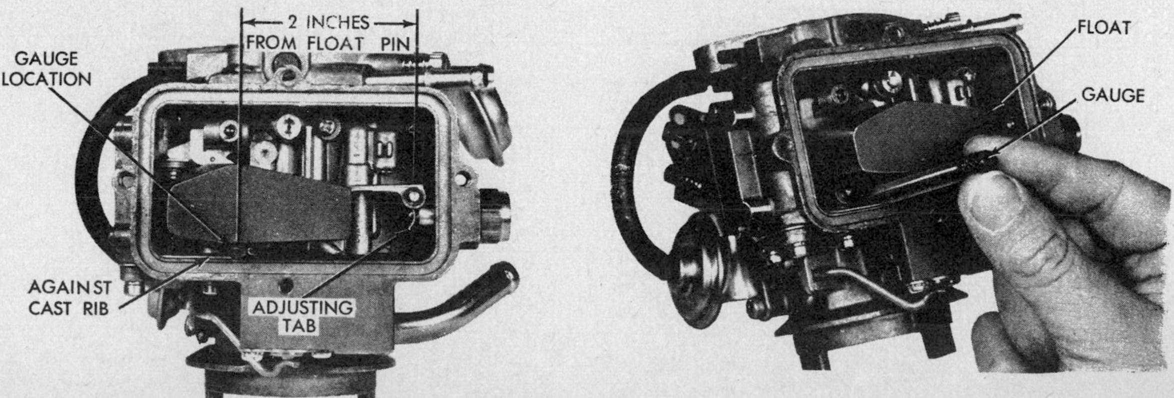

Adjusting the float level

the bowl vent should be adjusted so that the shank of a drill of the size listed in the Specifications Chart can be inserted between the bowl vent stem and the bowl vent rod.

2. Adjust by bending the bowl vent operating lever up or down as required.
3. Be sure that the vent rod does not bind in the guide after adjusting.

Fast Idle Cam Position and Choke Unloader Adjustment

1. With the fast idle speed adjusting screw contacting the second highest step on the fast idle cam, move the choke valve toward the closed position with light pressure on the choke shaft lever.
2. Insert the specified gauge between the top of the choke valve and the wall of the air horn. Refer to the Specifications Chart.
3. Adjust by bending the fast idle link at the lower angle, until the correct valve opening has been obtained.

NOTE: When the correct fast idle cam position adjustment has been made, the choke unloader (wide open kick) adjustment has also been obtained. No further adjustment is required.

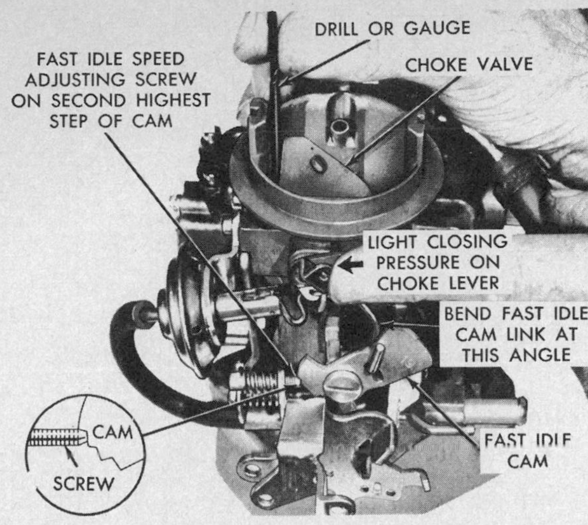

Fast idle cam position adjustment

Choke Vacuum Kick

NOTE: The test can be made on or off the vehicle.

1. If adjustments are to be made with the engine running, back off the fast idle speed screw until the choke can be closed to the kick position with the engine at curb idle.
2. Note the number of screw turns required so that fast idle can be returned to its original adjustment.
3. If an auxiliary vacuum source is to be used, open the throttle valve (engine not running) and move the choke to the closed position. Release the throttle first, then release the choke.

When using an auxiliary vacuum source, disconnect the vacuum hose from the carburetor and connect it to the hose from the vacuum supply with a small length of tube to act as a fitting. Removal of the hose from the diaphragm may damage the system. Apply a vacuum of 15 or more in. of mercury.

4. Insert the gauge between the top of the choke valve and the wall of the air horn. Refer to the Specifications Chart.
5. Apply sufficient closing pressure on the lever to which the choke rod attaches to provide a minimum choke valve opening without distortion of the diaphragm link.

NOTE: The cylindrical stem of the diaphragm extends as the internal spring is compressed. This spring must be fully compressed for proper measurement of the vacuum kick adjustment.

6. Adjustment is necessary if a slight drag is not obtained when removing the gauge. Shorten or lengthen the diaphragm link to obtain the correct choke valve opening. Length changes should be made by carefully opening or closing the U-bend in the link.

NOTE: Do not apply a twisting or bending force to the diaphragm.

7. After completion of adjustment, reinstall the vacuum hose onto the correct carburetor fitting.
8. Return the fast idle screw to its original location if disturbed. Make the following check. With no vacuum applied to the diaphragm, the choke valve should move freely between the open and closed positions. If the movement is not free, examine the linkage for misalignment or interferences caused by the bending operation.

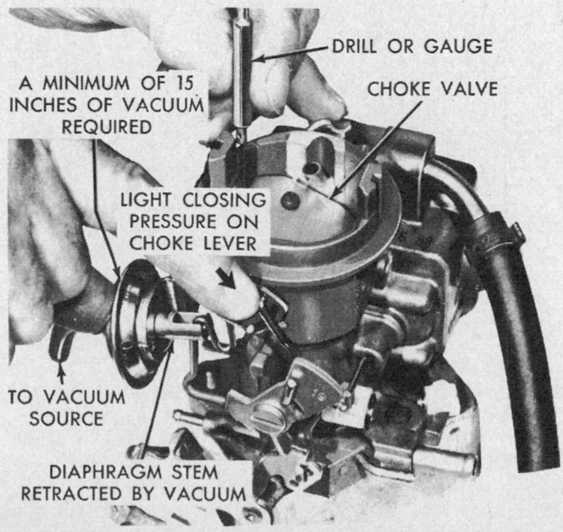

Adjusting the choke vacuum kick

Well-Type Automatic Choke

1. To function properly, it is important that all parts be clean and move freely. Other than an occasional cleaning, the choke requires no attention. However, it is important that the choke control unit work freely in the well and at the choke shaft.
2. Move the choke rod up and down to check for free movement on the pivot. If the unit binds, a new choke unit should be installed.

NOTE: This type of choke is serviced only as a unit. Do not attempt to repair or change the setting.

When installing the choke unit, be certain that the coil housing does not contact the sides of the well in the exhaust manifold. Any contact at this point will affect choke operation. Do not lubricate any parts of the choke or the control unit. This causes an accumulation of dirt which will result in binding of the mechanism.

Spring Staged Choke Adjustment

1. To test the adjustment on carburetors equipped with this feature, press against the choke lever firmly.
2. Measure the clearance between the hub lever and the shaft lever.
3. If the clearance is not within 0.010 in. and 0.025 in., bend the fast idle rod slightly until the normal clearance is obtained.

Model 1931

This carburetor has a one-piece main body and throttle body casting, together with a large capacity fuel bowl cover, to maintain a stable fuel level for the best performance on turns. The large capacity fuel bowl is designed to efficiently handle vapor loaded fuels and fuel vapors.

The automatic choke is mounted in a heat sink on the exhaust manifold and is connected to the carburetor by a choke rod.

Float Adjustment

1. Invert the carburetor fuel bowl cover and check the float setting at both ends.
2. If float adjustment is necessary, the float may be raised by pushing on the center of the float.

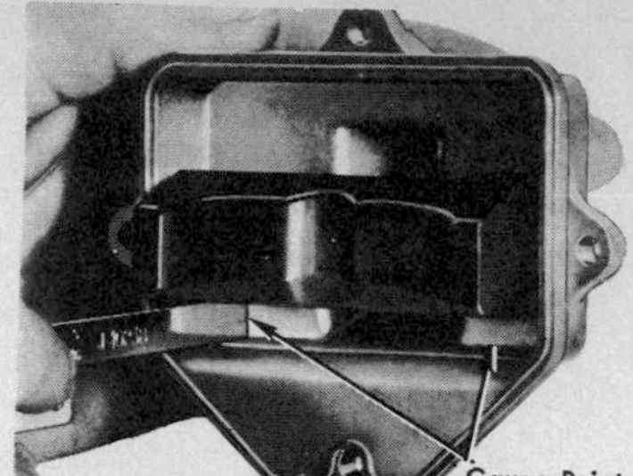

Float adjustment

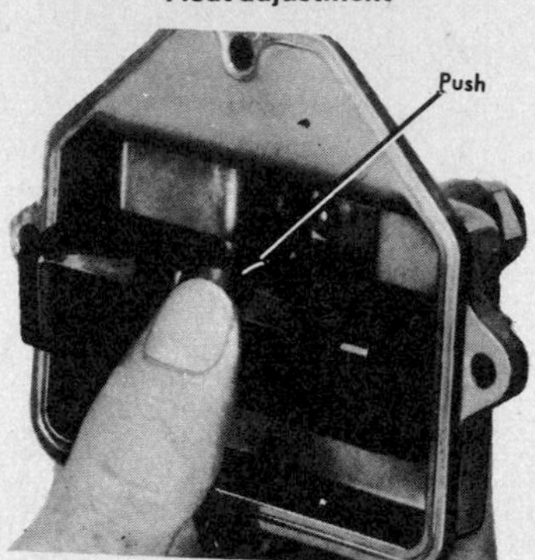

Raising the float

Caution During float adjustment, do not allow the float tab to contact the fuel inlet needle as the resilient tip of the needle can be damaged or compressed, resulting in an improper float setting

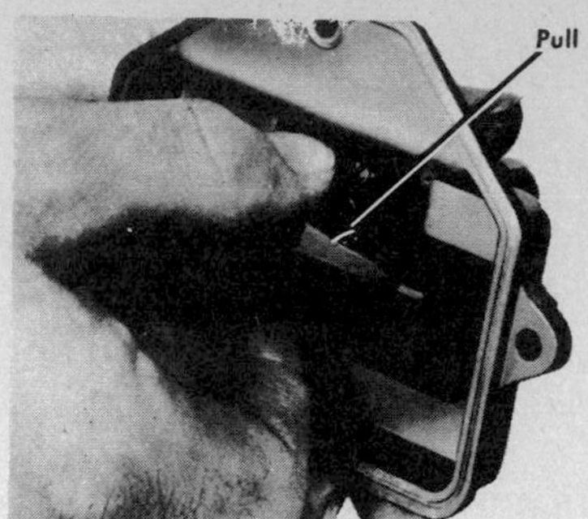

Lowering the float

and a leaky needle and seat.

If the proper gauge is not available, measure the distance between the roof of the float cover and the top of the float. If the setting is not as listed in the Specifications Chart, adjust as required.

Fast Idle Adjustment

1. With the fast idle screw resting on the second step of the fast idle cam and the engine at normal operating temperature, screw it in clockwise.
2. Adjust by bending the tab on the throttle lever.

Choke Unloader Adjustment

1. With the throttle valve held in the wide open position and the choke plate rotated toward the closed position, the distance be-

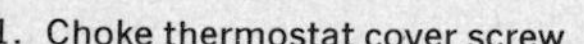

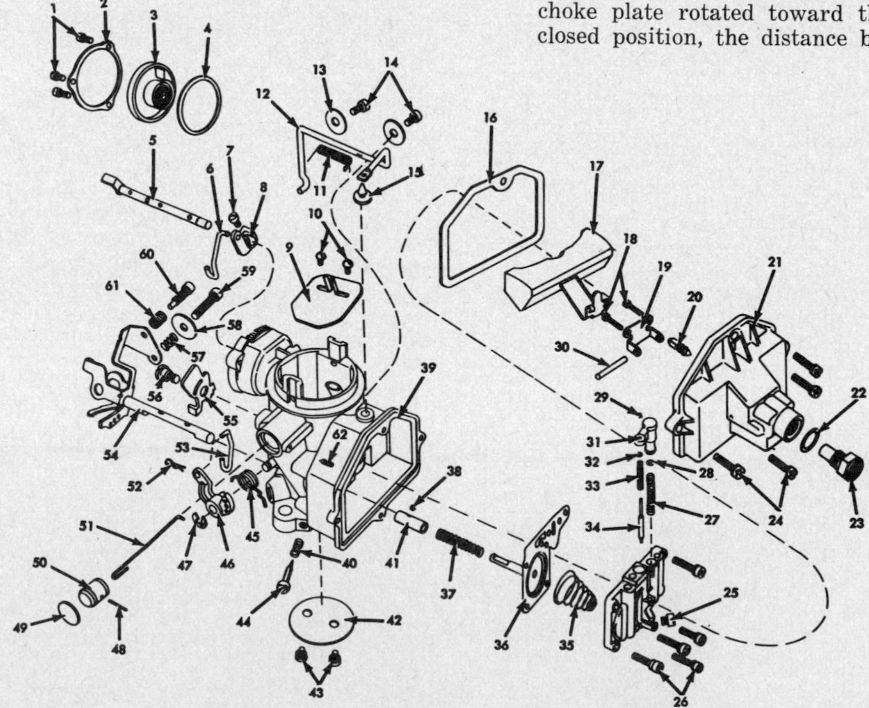

Disassembled view—Holley 1931

1. Choke thermostat cover screw
2. Choke thermostat cover retainer
3. Choke thermostat cover assembly
4. Choke thermostat cover gasket
5. Choke shaft assembly
6. Fast idle connector rod
7. Choke lever screw
8. Choke lever
9. Choke plate
10. Choke plate screws
11. Bowl vent rod spring
12. Bowl vent rod
13. Vent rod retainer washer
14. Vent rod retainer screws
15. Bowl vent valve
16. Fuel bowl gasket
17. Foat assembly
18. Float shaft bracket screws
19. Float shaft retaining bracket
20. Fuel inlet needle
21. Float bowl
22. Fuel inlet fitting gasket
23. Fuel inlet fitting
24. Float bowl screws
25. Main jet
26. Metering block screws
27. Power valve piston spring
28. Power valve piston spring washer
29. Power valve retainer
30. Float shaft pin
31. Power valve piston
32. Power valve spring washer
33. Power valve spring
34. Power valve
35. Pump return spring
36. Pump diaphragm assembly
37. Pump override spring
38. Pump push rod sleeve ball
39. Main body
40. Idle mixture needle spring
41. Pump push rod sleeve
42. Throttle plate
43. Throttle plate screws
44. Idle mixture adjustment needle
45. Pump return spring
46. Pump operating cam lever
47. Pump operating cam lever retainer
48. Choke piston pin
49. Choke piston plug
50. Choke piston
51. Choke piston link
52. Pump link retainer
53. Pump link
54. Throttle shaft assembly
55. Fast idle cam
56. Fast idle cam screw
57. Throttle stop screw spring
58. Vent rod operating washer
59. Throttle stop screw
60. Fast idle adjusting screw
61. Fast idle adjusting screw spring
62. Choke piston stop screw

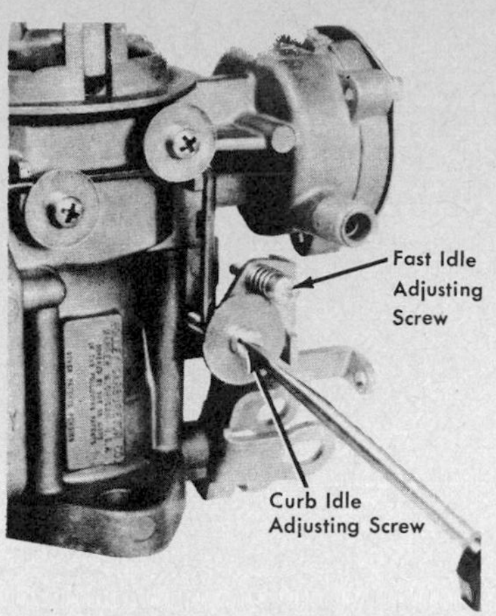

Fast and curb idle speed adjusting screws

tween the top edge of the choke plate and the flat portion of the air horn can be referred to in the Specifications Chart.

2. Adjust by bending the tab on the throttle lever.

Choke Piston Stop Adjustment

1. Hold the choke piston against the stop screw with a wire inserted in the slot above the choke piston link.
2. Rotate the choke plate toward the closed position until the link is firm. The distance between the top edge of the choke plate and the flat portion of the air horn should be 3/16 in.
3. Adjust by turning the piston stop screw in or out as required.

Automatic Choke Adjustment

1. The adjustment is made by loosening the choke cover screws and rotating the cover in the desired direction as indicated by an arrow on the cover.
2. The choke should be set to the mark specified in the Specifications Chart for all normal driving.
3. Never set the choke more than two graduations in either direction of the specified setting.

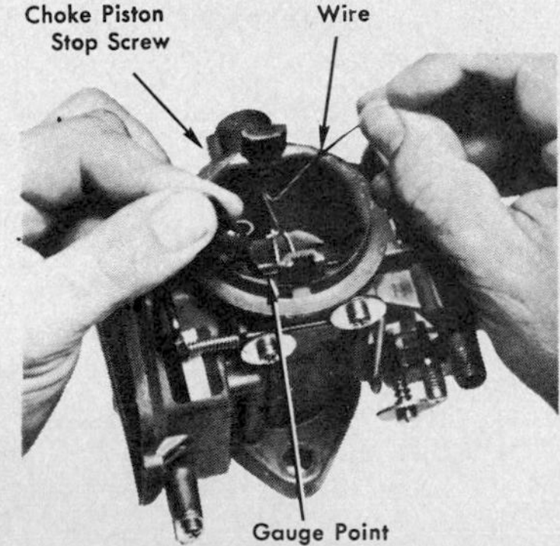

Automatic choke adjustment

Bowl Vent Adjustment

1. With the throttle set at curb idle, the clearance between the vent valve and the seat should be as listed in the Specifications Chart.

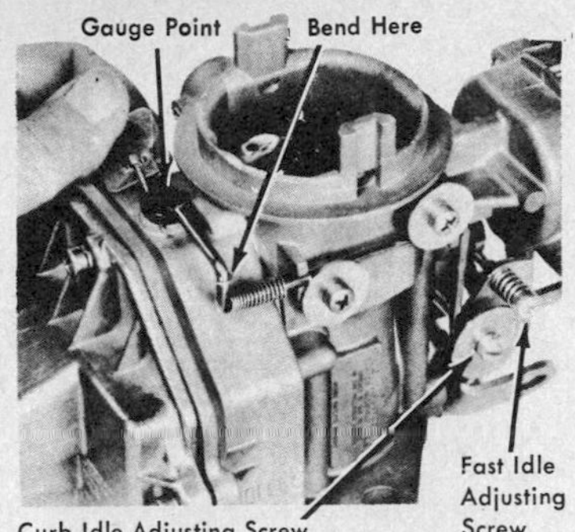

Bowl vent adjustment

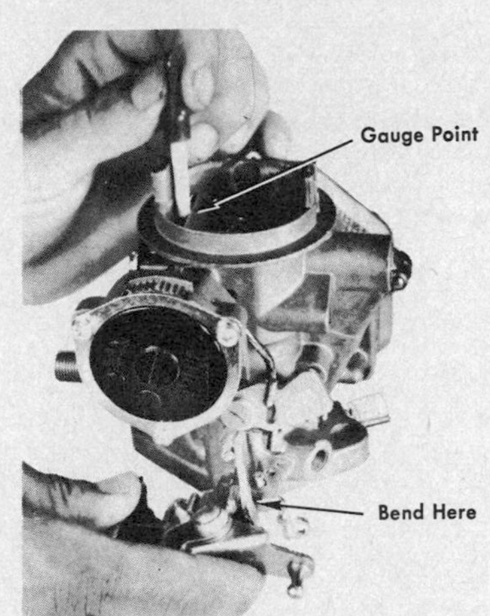

Unloader adjustment

2. If an adjustment is necessary, bend the vent rod at the horizontal portion above the fuel bowl. Check the operation of the vent rod for binding.

Accelerator Pump Adjustment

1. The accelerator link is set in the middle hole in the throttle lever for normal driving conditions.
2. If a richer pump discharge is required, place the pump link in the outer hole of the throttle lever. For a leaner pump discharge, place the pump link in the inner hole of the throttle lever.

Model 1945

The model 1945 carburetor is a concentric downdraft single barrel carburetor with an internal float bowl which completely surrounds the venturi. The unit uses dual nitrophyl floats which permit operation at extreme angles.

Float Adjustment

1. Remove the float bowl cover and invert the bowl. Hold the retaining spring in place.
2. Place a straightedge across the surface of the bowl. It should just clear the toes of the floats by the specified measurement.
3. If adjustment is necessary, bend the float tang to obtain the correct adjustment.

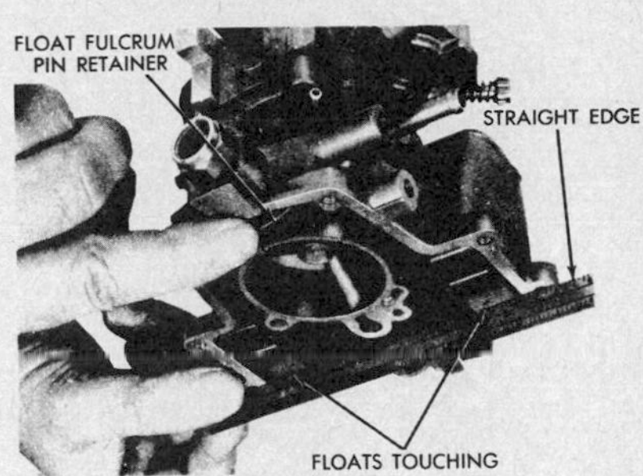

Checking the float adjustment

Fast Idle Adjustment

1. Remove the air cleaner and disconnect the vacuum lines to the heated air control and the OSAC (Orifice Spark Advance Control) valve. If there is no OSAC valve, disconnect the hose to the distributor and the EGR hose. Cap all carburetor vacuum fittings.
2. With the engine off, transmission in Neutral and the parking brake set, open the throttle and close the choke.
3. Close the throttle. This will place the fast idle speed screw on the highest step.
4. Move the fast idle cam until the screw drops to the second highest speed step.

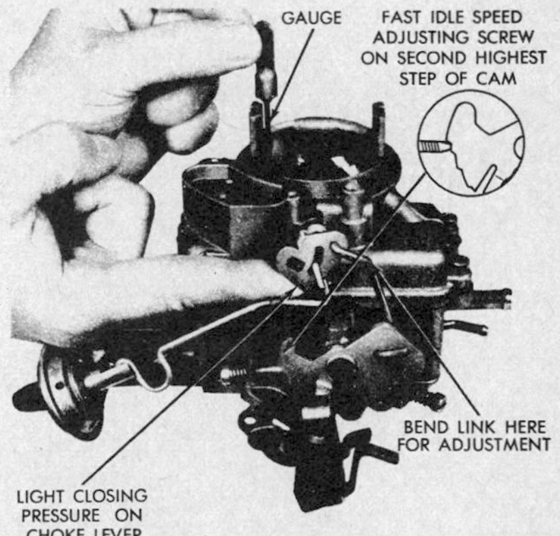

Checking the fast idle adjustment

5. Start the engine and stabilize the engine speed. Rotate the idle speed screw to obtain the specified setting. See Specifications Chart.

Choke Unloader Adjustment

1. Hold the throttle valves wide-open and insert the specified gauge between the upper edge of the choke valve and the inner wall of the air horn.

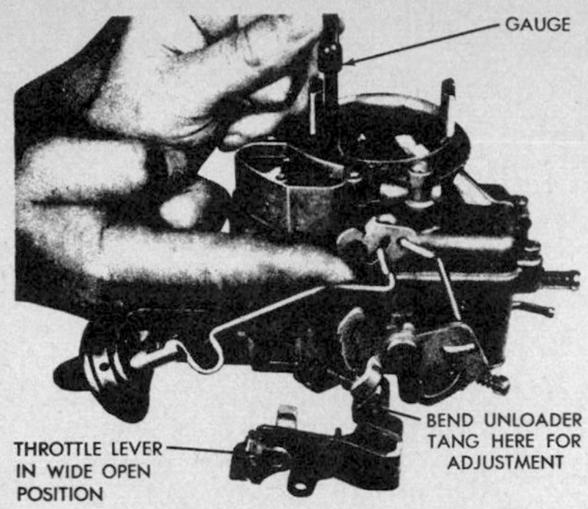

Choke unloader adjustment

2. Place slight pressure against the control lever and attempt to remove the gauge. There should be a slight drag as the gauge is being withdrawn. If adjustment is necessary, bend the unloader tang on the throttle lever until the correct opening has been obtained.

Choke Vacuum Kick Adjustment

1. With the engine running, back off the fast idle screw to allow the choke to close to the kick position with the engine at curb idle. Note the number of turns. If the adjustment is made with the engine stopped, open the throttle and move the choke to the closed position. Release the throttle first and then the choke.
2. If an auxiliary vacuum source is used, disconnect the vacuum hose from the carburetor and connect it to the hose from the vacuum supply with an extra length of tube. Apply a vacuum of 15 or more in. of mercury.
3. Insert the correct gauge (see Specifications Chart) between the choke valve and the wall of the air horn. Close and hold the choke rod lever with light pressure. The cylindrical stem of the diaphragm will extend as the internal spring is compressed. This spring must be fully compressed for proper measurement of the vacuum kick.

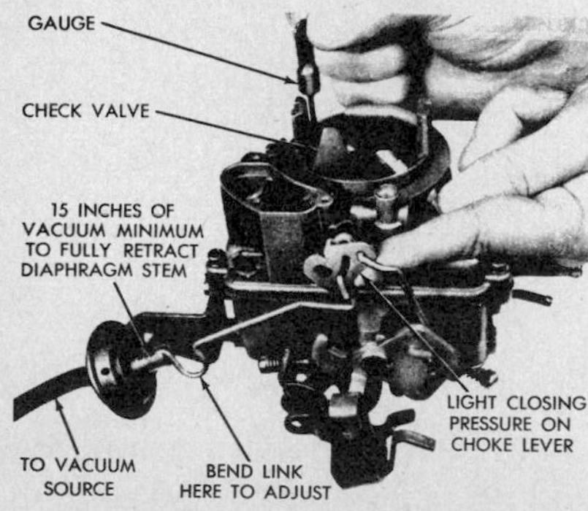

Choke vacuum kick adjustment

4. If adjustment is necessary, shorten or lengthen the diaphragm link to obtain the correct opening.

Caution Do not twist or bend the diaphragm.

5. Install the vacuum hose on the correct carburetor fitting and connect the fast idle linkage.
6. Check the operation in the following manner. With no vacuum applied to the diaphragm, the choke valve should move freely between the open and closed positions. If there is binding, examine the linkage for misalignment or interferences caused by bending.

Model 2209

This carburetor has a large capacity side inlet fuel bowl with a separate throttle body and gasket to create a thermal barrier which reduces heat transfer to the fuel. The automatic choke is part of the throttle body and is connected to the choke plate by a choke rod.

Float Level Adjustment

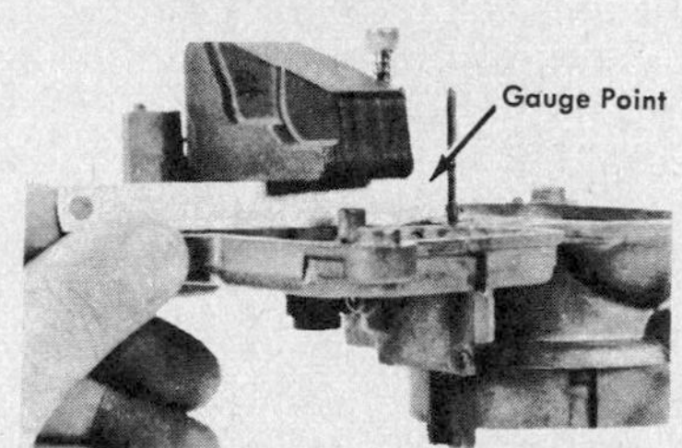

Float level adjustment

1. Check the float setting with float dry and the air horn inverted.
2. Measure the distance between the float and the air horn.
3. If the dimension is not as listed in the Specifications Chart, adjust by bending the float tab as required.

Checking Float Drop

1. With the air horn held upright, the bottom surface of the float should be parallel with the air horn, as shown.
2. Adjust by bending the float drop tab.

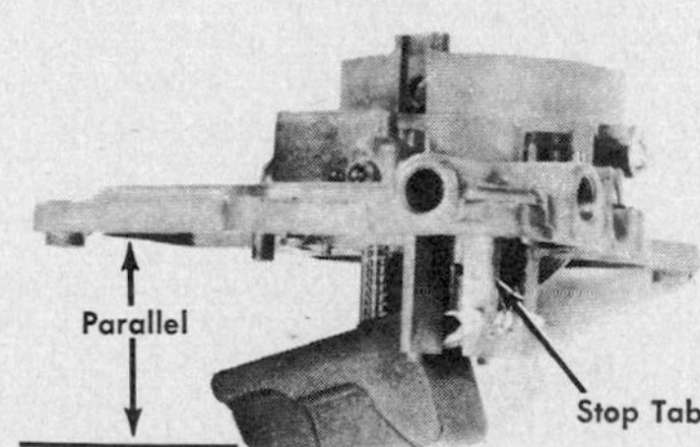

Checking the float drop

Choke Unloader Adjustment

1. With the throttle held in the wide open position, there should be the clearance listed in the Specifications Chart between the top edge of the choke plate and the air horn wall as shown.
2. Adjust by bending the tab on the fast idle cam.

Choke unloader adjustment

Choke Adjustment

1. Set the automatic choke on the index mark for all normal driving.
2. If a richer or leaner mixture is desired during the warm-up period, the choke can be reset by rotating the choke thermostat shaft clockwise for a richer mixture and counterclockwise for a leaner mixture.

Choke adjustment

3. Never set the choke more than two graduations in either direction from the specified mark listed in the Specifications Chart.

Fast Idle Adjustment

1. With the throttle stopped on the high step of the fast idle cam, the fast idle speed should be as listed in the Specifications Chart with the engine at normal temperature.
2. Adjust by bending the tab on the throttle lever.

Fast idle adjustment

Accelerator pump adjustment

Accelerator Pump Adjustment

1. The accelerator pump operating link is set in the inner hole of the pump lever for all normal driving conditions.
2. If a leaner pump discharge is required, set the link in the outer hole.

Model 2210

This carburetor is a two-barrel unit but can be considered as two carburetors built side by side into one unit, utilizing the same fuel and air inlets. Each throat of the carburetor has its own throttle valve and main metering systems and are supplemented by the float, accelerating, idle, and power systems. The 1970 version is equipped with a distributor ground switch which retards the distributor when the carburetor is at curb idle, resulting in better emission control.

The 1971 version is equipped with a hot idle compensator valve which is a thermostatically operated air bleed to relieve an over-rich condition at idle. Units beginning 1971 have a bowl vent valve tube which works in conjunction with the vent valve. In 1973, an extra port for use with the (EGR) Exhaust Gas Recirculation system was added.

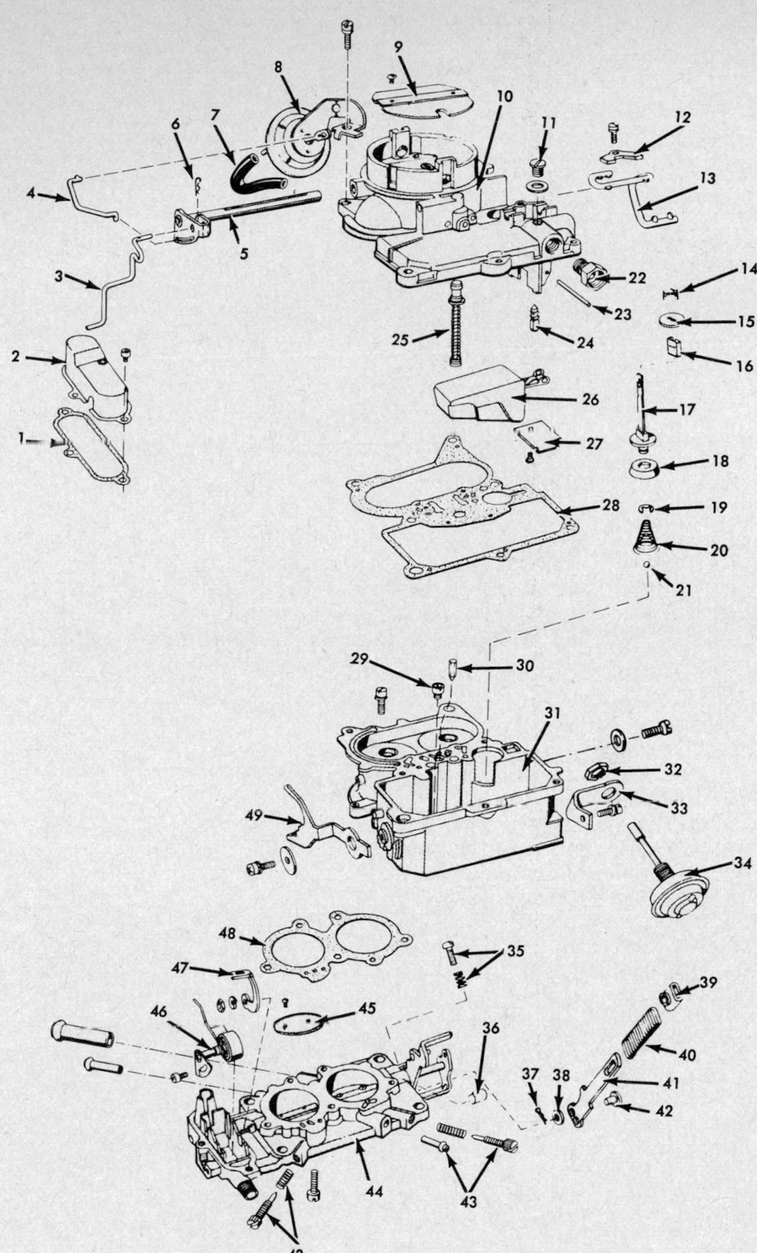

Disassembled view—Holley 2209 Carburetor

1. Thermostat housing cover gasket
2. Thermostat cover and guide assembly
3. Choke rod
4. Choke diaphragm rod
5. Choke shaft and lever assembly
6. Choke rod retainer
7. Vacuum hose
8. Choke diaphragm
9. Choke plate
10. Air horn assembly
11. Screw plug
12. Pump rod clamp
13. Pump rod
14. Bowl vent spring
15. Bowl vent washer
16. Bowl vent adjustment clip
17. Accelerator pump shaft
18. Pump cup
19. Pump cup retainer
20. Pump return spring
21. Pump inlet check valve (ball)
22. Fuel inlet fitting
23. Float hinge pin
24. Fuel inlet needle
25. Power valve piston assembly
26. Float assembly
27. Fuel bowl baffle
28. Main body gasket
29. Main jet
30. Pump discharge check needle
31. Main body
32. Dashpot locknut
33. Dashpot bracket
34. Dashpot
35. Throttle stop screw and spring
36. Throttle shaft bearing
37. Pump link retainer
38. Pump link washer
39. Nylon slide
40. Pump override spring
41. Pump link
42. Pump link pin
43. Idle mixture adjusting needle and spring
44. Throttle body
45. Throttle plate
46. Choke thermostat assembly
47. Choke unloader lever
48. Throttle body gasket
49. Fast idle cam

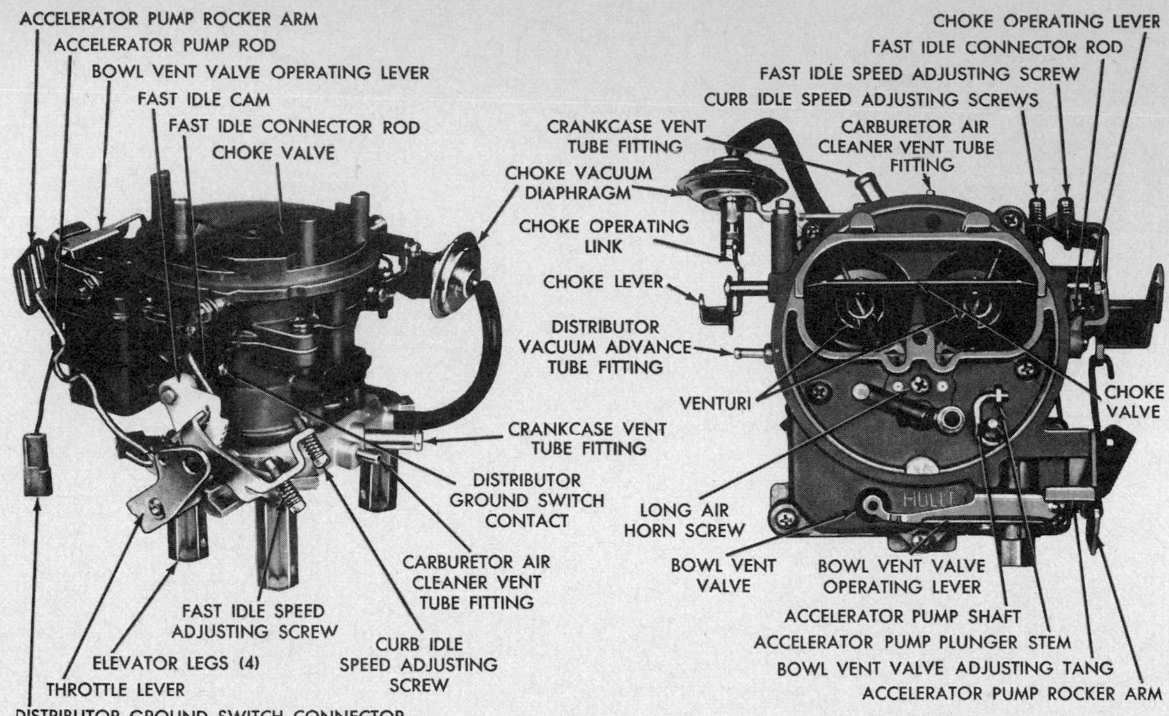

Carburetor assembly—Holley 2210

Float Adjustment

1. Invert the air horn so that the weight of the float only is forcing the needle against the seat.
2. Measure the clearance between the top of the float and the float stop.
3. Be sure the drill gauge is perfectly level when measuring. Adjust by bending the float lip toward or away from the needle, using a narrow blade screwdriver, until the correct clearance of the setting has been obtained.

Float Drop Adjustment

1. Check the float drop by holding the air horn in an upright position.
2. The bottom edge of the float should be parallel to the underside surface of the air horn.
3. Adjust by bending the tang on the float arm.

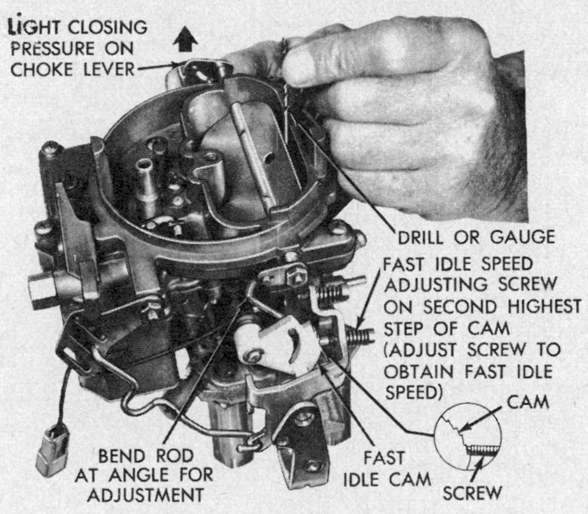

Fast idle cam position adjustment

Fast Idle Cam Position Adjustment

1. With the fast idle speed adjusting screw contacting the second highest step on the fast idle cam, move the choke valve toward the closed position with light pres-

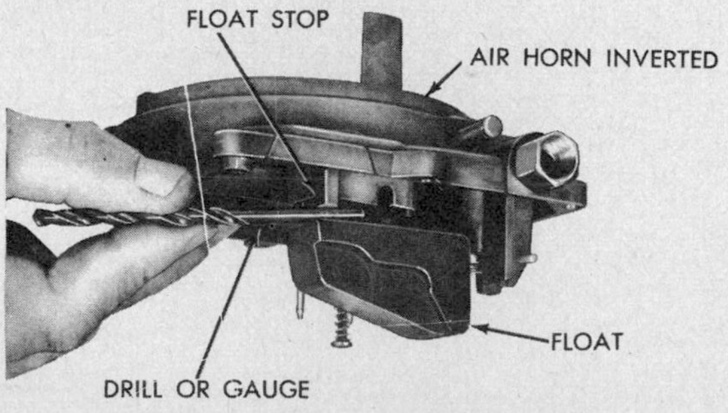

Checking the float adjustment

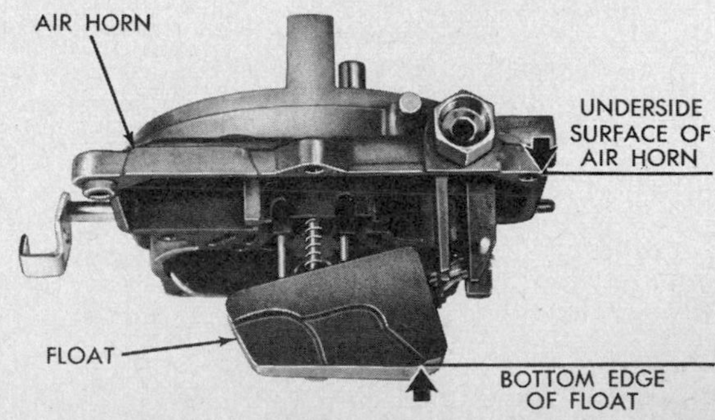

Checking the float drop

sure on the choke shaft lever.

2. Insert the specified gauge between the top of the choke valve and the wall of the air horn. Refer to the Specifications Chart.
3. An adjustment will be necessary if a slight drag is not obtained as the drill shank is being removed.
4. Adjust by bending the fast idle link at the angle.

Choke Vacuum Kick Adjustment

NOTE: The test can be made on or off the vehicle.

1. If the adjustment is to be made with the engine running, disconnect the fast idle linkage to allow the choke to close to the kick position.
2. If an auxiliary vacuum source is to be used, open the throttle valve (engine not running) and move the choke to the closed position. Release the throttle first, then release the choke.

When using an auxiliary vacuum source, disconnect the vacuum hose from the carburetor and connect it to the hose from the vacuum supply with a small length of tube to act as a fitting. Removal of the hose from the diaphragm may require forces which could damage the system. Apply a vacuum of 10 or more in. of mercury.

3. Insert the gauge between the top of the choke valve and the wall of the air horn. Refer to the Specifications Chart.
4. Apply sufficient closing pressure on the lever to which the choke rod attaches, to provide a minimum choke valve opening without distortion of the diaphragm link.

NOTE: The cylindrical stem of the diaphragm extends as the internal spring is compressed. This spring must be fully compressed for proper measurement of the vacuum kick adjustment.

5. Adjustment is necessary if a slight drag is not obtained when removing the gauge. Shorten or lengthen the diaphragm link to obtain the correct choke valve opening. Length changes should be made by carefully opening or closing the U-bend provided in the link. Improper bending causes contact between the U-section and the diaphragm assembly.

NOTE: Do not apply a twisting or bending force to diaphragm.

6. After completing adjustments, reinstall the vacuum hose on the correct carburetor fitting.
7. Return the fast idle linkage to its original location if it was disturbed. Make the following check. With no vacuum applied to the diaphragm, the choke valve should move freely between the open and closed positions. If the movement is not free, examine the linkage for misalignment or interferences caused by the bending operation.

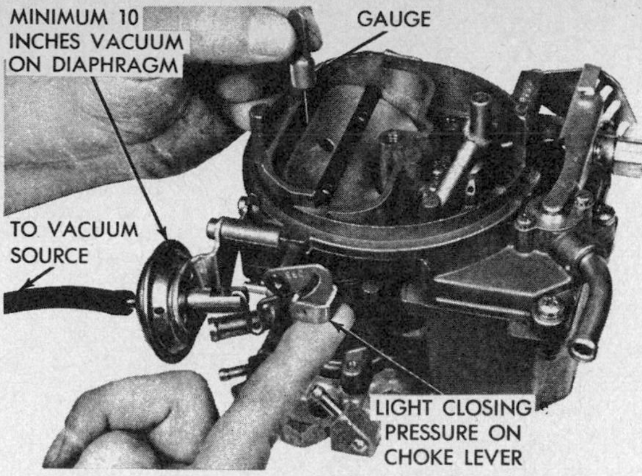

Vacuum kick adjustment

2. Open the choke valve so that the fast idle cam allows the throttle valves to be completely seated in the bores.
3. Be sure that the pump connector rod is installed in the correct slot of the accelerator pump rocker arm. The slot for manual transmissions is next to the retaining nut.

Choke Unloader (Wide Open Kick) Adjustment

1. With the throttle valve in the wide open position, insert a drill gauge between the upper edge of the choke valve and the inner wall of the air horn. Refer to the Specifications Chart.
2. With a finger lightly pressing against the shaft lever, a slight drag should be felt as the drill is being withdrawn.
3. Adjust by bending the unloader tang on the throttle lever until the correct opening has been obtained.

Accelerator Pump Adjustment

1. Back off the curb idle speed adjusting screw.

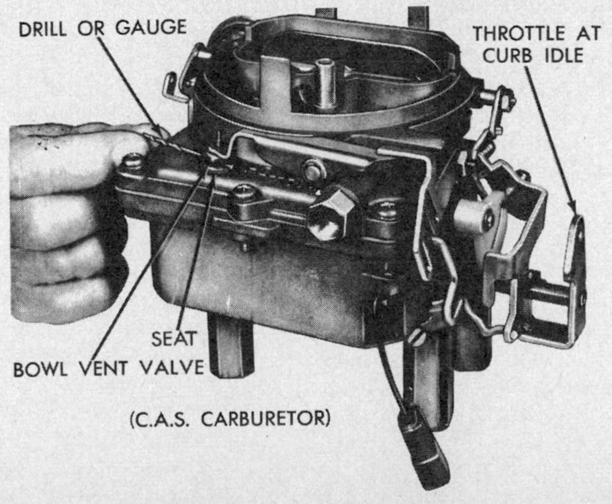

Choke unloader adjustment

4. Close the throttle valves tightly. Measure the distance between the top of the air horn and the end of the plunger shaft. Refer to the Specifications Chart.
5. Adjust pump travel by bending the pump operating rod at the loop of the rod, until the correct setting has been obtained.

Bowl Vent Valve Clearance Adjustment

1. With the throttle valves at curb idle, it should be possible to insert a gauge between the bowl vent valve plunger stem and the operating rod. Refer to the Specifications Chart.
2. Adjust by bending the tang on the pump lever to change the arc of contact with the throttle lever.

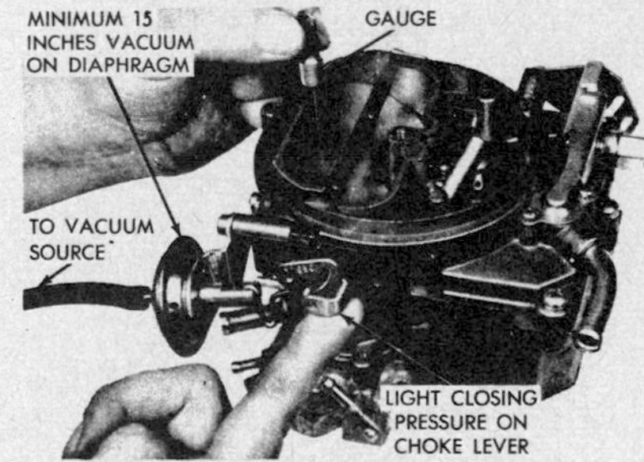

Adjusting the vacuum kick

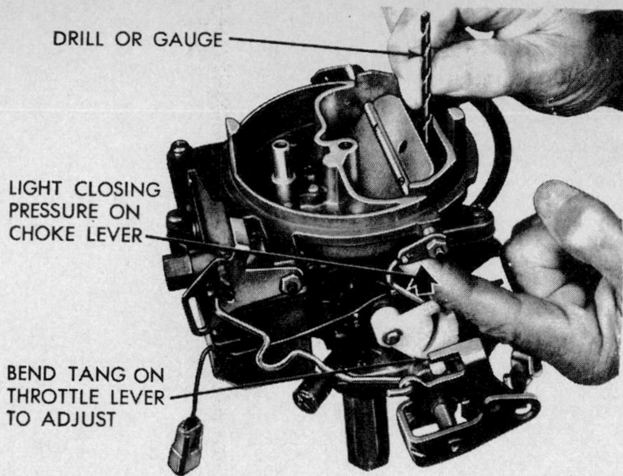

Bowl vent valve adjustment

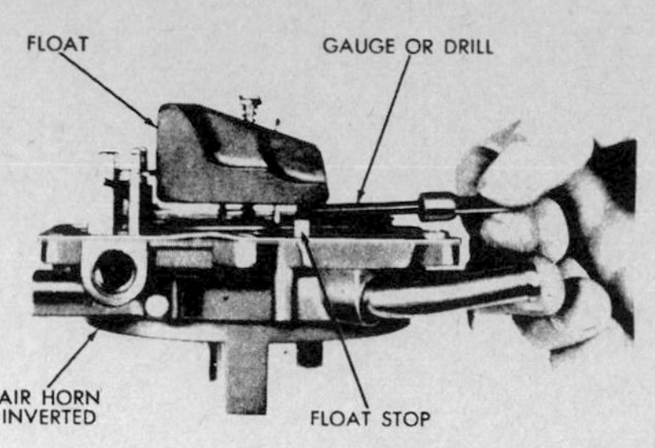

Adjusting the float

Model 2245

The model 2245 carburetor is a two barrel unit used on Chrysler products with 360 or 400 cubic inch engines. The carburetor uses 4 fuel metering systems. The Idle and idle enrichment System provides the correct mixture for idle and high-speed performance; the Accelerator Pump System furnishes additional fuel during acceleration; the Main Metering System gives an economical mixture for normal cruising conditions; and the Power Enrichment System enriches the mixture when high power output is desired.

Float Adjustment

1. Invert the air horn so that the weight of the float is forcing the metering needle against its seat.
2. Measure the distance from the top of the float and the float stop. The clearance should be the same as given in the Specifications Chart. Make certain that the gauge is level when making the measurement.
3. If adjustment is necessary, bend the float adjusting tab toward or away from the needle until the correct clearance is obtained. A narrow-bladed screwdriver may be used to bend the tab.
4. Check the float drop by holding the air horn upright. The bottom edge of the float should be parallel to the underside of the air horn. If an adjustment is necessary, bend the tang on the float arm.

Fast Idle Cam Position Adjustment

1. Position the fast idle speed adjusting screw on the second highest notch on the fast idle cam. Move the choke valve toward the closed position by applying light pressure on the choke shaft lever.
2. Insert the correct gauge (see Specifications Chart between the top of the choke valve and the wall of the air horn. An adjustment will be necessary if there is not a slight drag when the gauge is removed.
3. If an adjustment is necessary, bend the fast idle connector rod at the angle.

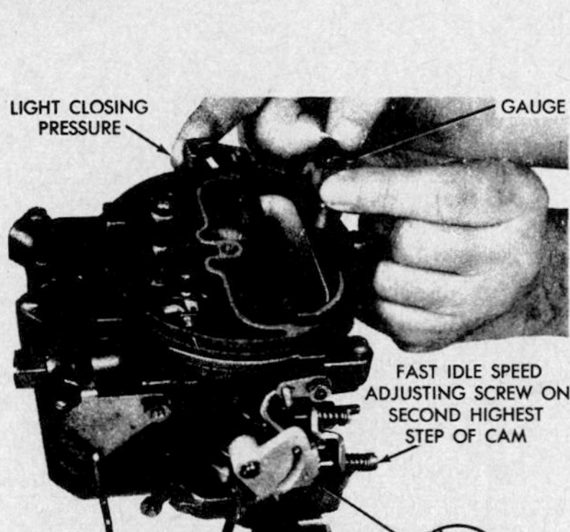

Adjusting the fast idle cam

Vacuum Kick Adjustment

1. The adjustment must be made with some type of vacuum source. If the adjustment is made with the engine running, disconnect the fast idle linkage to allow the choke to close to the kick position with the engine at curb idle. If an auxiliary vacuum source is to be used, open the throttle valves and move the choke to the closed position. Release the throttle first and then the choke.
2. If an auxiliary vacuum source is used, disconnect the vacuum hose from the carburetor and connect it to the hose from the vacuum supply with a small length of extra hose. Apply a vacuum of 15 or more in. of mercury.
3. Insert the correct gauge (see Specifications Chart) between the top of the choke valve and the wall of the air horn. Apply pressure to the choke rod without distorting the diaphragm link. The cylindrical stem of the diaphragm will extend as the internal spring is compressed. This spring must be fully compressed for proper measurement of the vacuum kick adjustment.
4. If a slight drag is not felt when the gauge is removed, adjustment is necessary. Adjust the diaphragm link to obtain the correct choke valve opening. Adjustments can be made by carefully opening or closing the U-bend in the lnik.

Caution Do not twist or bend the diaphragm.

5. Connect the vacuum hose to the correct carburetor fitting. Replace the linkage.
6. Make the following check. With no vacuum source attached to the diaphragm, the choke valve should move freely between open and closed positions. If the movement is not free, examine the linkage for misalignment or interferences caused by the bending operation.

Choke Unloader (Wide Open Kick) Adjustment

1. Place the throttle valves in the wide-open position and insert the proper gauge (see Specifications Chart) between the upper edge of the choke valve and the inner wall of the air horn.
2. While holding pressure on the shaft lever, a slight drag should be felt as the gauge is removed.
3. If an adjustment is necessary, bend the unloader tang on the throttle lever until the correct opening has been obtained.

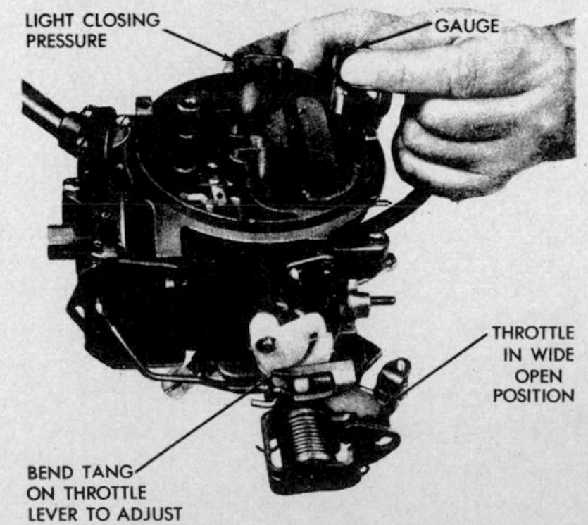

Adjusting the choke unloader

Accelerator Pump Adjustment

1. Back off the curb idle adjusting screw and open the choke valve so that the fast idle cam allows the throttle valves to be completely seated in their bores.

NOTE: Make certain that the pump connector rod is placed in the correct slot of the accelerator pump rocker arm. On manual transmission models, it is the first slot next to the retaining nut.

2. Close the throttle valves and measure the distance from the top of the air horn to the end of the plunger shaft. See Specifications Chart.
3. If adjustment is needed, bend the pump operating rod at its loop until the correct setting has been obtained.

Bowl Vent Valve Clearance

1. With the throttle valves set at curb idle, insert the specified gauge between the bowl vent valve plunger stem and the operating rod.
2. If the gauge does not fit, bend the tang on the pump lever until the correct clearance has been obtained.

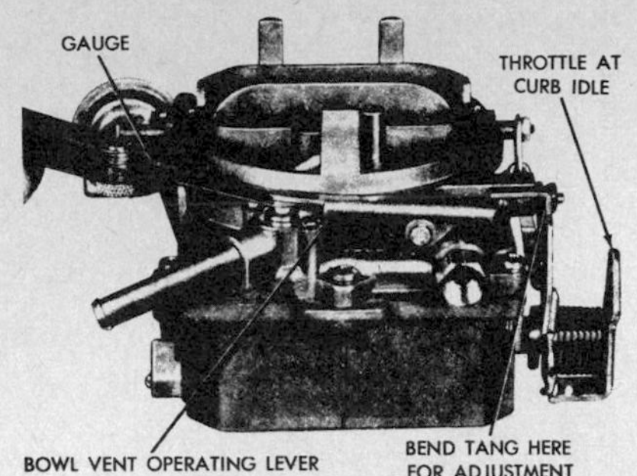

Adjusting the bowl vent clearance

Model 2300

The 2300 carburetor is used only in a triple installation. This sytem utilizes two types of Holley two-barrels, one mounted in the center and the two secondaries mounted fore and aft. The secondary units contain all the regulatory systems with the exception of chokes, power enrichment valve, accelerating pump, idle system and spark advance. The throttle operation of the primary carburetor is conventional whereas the secondary units are equipped with throttle control vacuum diaphragms for the purpose of opening the secondary throttles which close mechanically. The choke used only on the primary unit is controlled by a temperature sensing choke coil mounted on the intake manifold, over the exhaust crossover passage.

The only adjustments required on the secondary units are the float level and the wet fuel level. All other adjustments are made on the primary unit.

Float Adjustment

1. Make a preliminary float adjustment by inverting the fuel bowl and turning the adjustable needle and seat until the float is centered in the bowl.
2. Do not fully tighten the lock screw. Snug the screw to temporarily retain adjustment.

NOTE: Final adjustment of the float is made on the vehicle.

Wet Fuel Level

1. With the car level and the engine idling, remove the sight plug from the fuel bowl.

NOTE: The fuel pump pressure must be at least 5 psi.

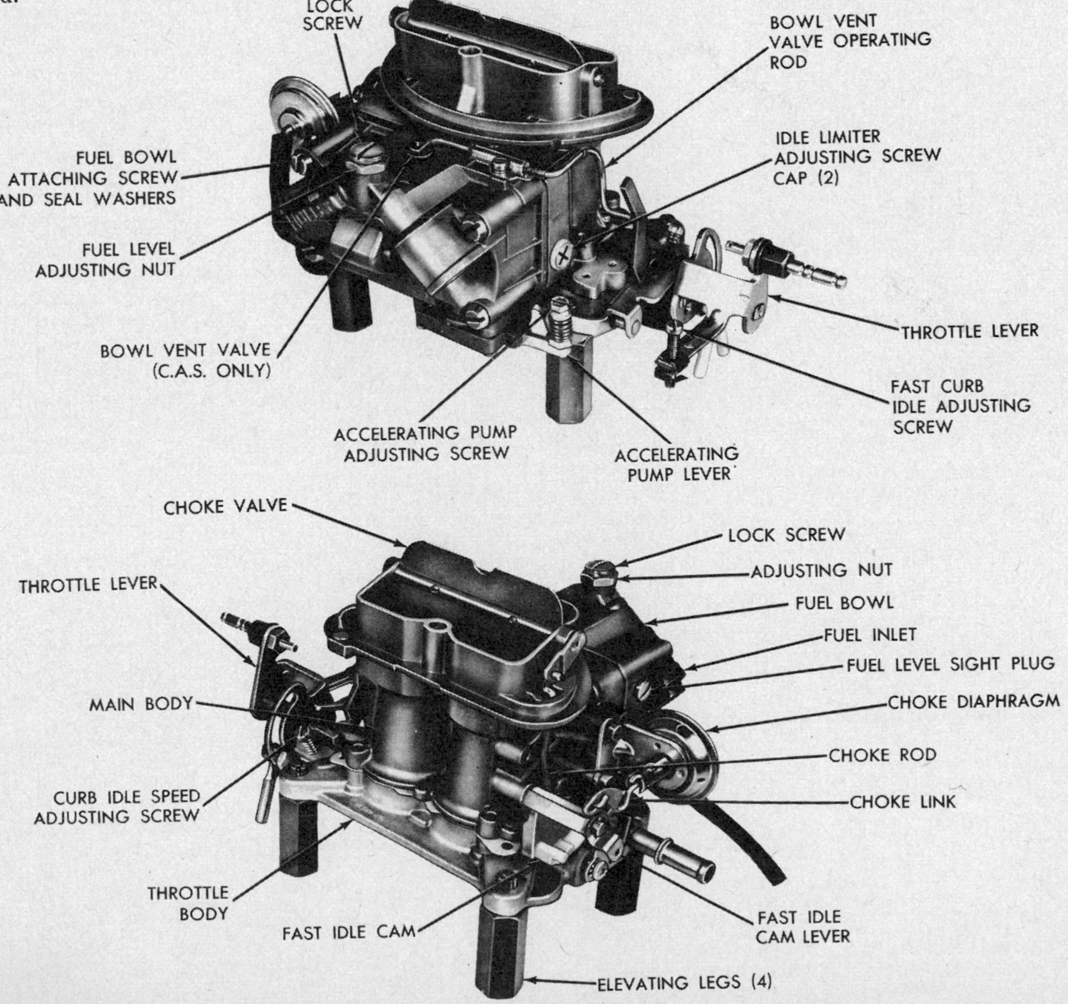

Carburetor assembly—Holley 2300

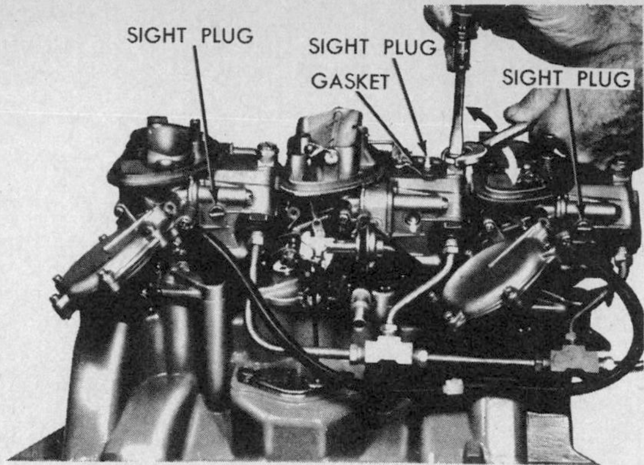

Adjusting fuel level on vehicle

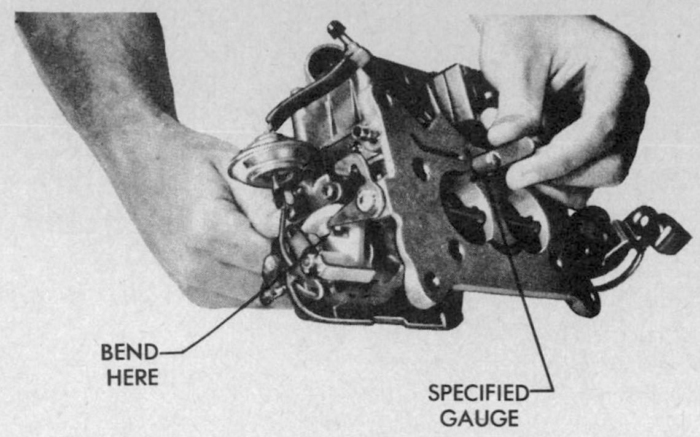

Fast idle cam adjustment, Chevrolet

2. The fuel level should be in line with the threads at the bottom of the sight plug hole. Fuel should dribble out slowly.

Caution *Use a cloth to catch the excess fuel. Discard it safely.*

3. To adjust, loosen the lock screw and turn the adjusting nut as required to raise or lower the fuel level.

Automatic Choke Control Lever Setting

Adjustment of the choke control lever is necessary to provide the correct relationship between the choke valve, the thermostatic coil spring, and the fast idle cam. It should be checked and adjusted (if necessary), as preparation of the choke system linkage before making the Vacuum Kick, Cam Position, or Unloader adjustment. These three adjustments must be made after adjustment of the choke control lever.

NOTE: Improper bending of the choke rod will result in binding.

Chevrolet

1. Close the choke rod by applying slight pressure on the choke control lever; the thermostatic choke rod should be even with the top of the choke rod hole.
2. Adjust by bending the choke rod at the upper angle.

Chrysler

1. Open the throttle to mid-position; close the choke valve by applying slight pressure on the choke control lever.
2. The top of choke rod hole in the control lever should be 3 49/64 in. above the choke pad with the carburetor on the engine, or 1 23/32 in. above the carburetor base with the carburetor on a bench.
3. Adjust by bending the choke shaft rod.

Fast Idle Cam Position Adjustment

Chevrolet

1. With the throttle slightly open, close the choke plate positioning fast idle lever against the top step of the fast idle cam.
2. Adjust the fast idle screw to obtain the clearance listed in the Specifications Chart between the throttle valve and the bore on the idle transfer slot side of the carburetor.
3. Adjust by bending the idle lever.

Chrysler

1. With the fast idle speed adjusting screw contacting the second highest step on the fast idle cam, move the choke valve toward the closed position with light pressure on the choke control lever.
2. Insert the specified gauge between the top of the choke valve and the wall of the air horn. Refer to the Specifications Chart.
3. An adjustment will be necessary if a slight drag is not obtained as the drill shank is being removed.
4. Adjust by bending the cam position adjusting tang.

Choke Unloader Adjustment (Wide Open Kick)

Chevrolet

1. Hold the throttle lever in the wide open throttle position with a rubber band.
2. Hold the choke valve toward the closed position against the unloader tang of the throttle shaft, then measure the opening between the choke valve lower edge and the main body. Refer to the Specifications Chart.
3. Adjust by bending the choke rod (at the off-set bend).

Chrysler

1. Hold the throttle valves in the wide-open position.
2. Insert the specified drill between the upper edge of the choke valve and the inner wall of the air horn. Refer to the Specifications Chart.

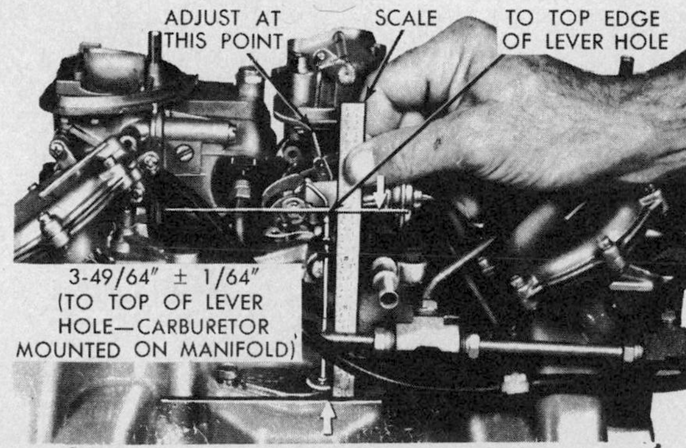

Adjusting the choke control lever

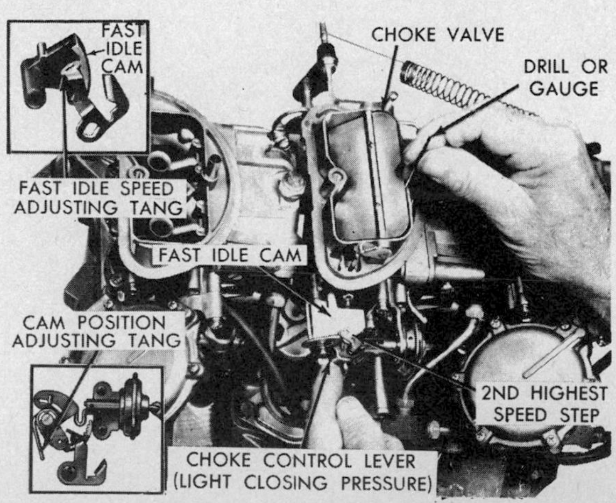

Fast idle cam position adjustment, Chrysler

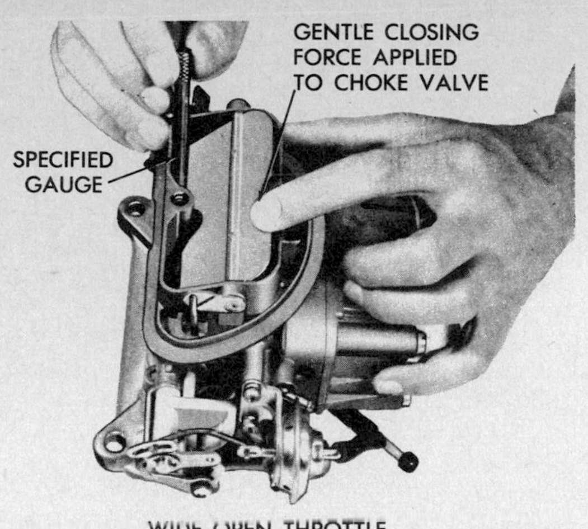

Choke unloader adjustment—wide open kick, Chevrolet

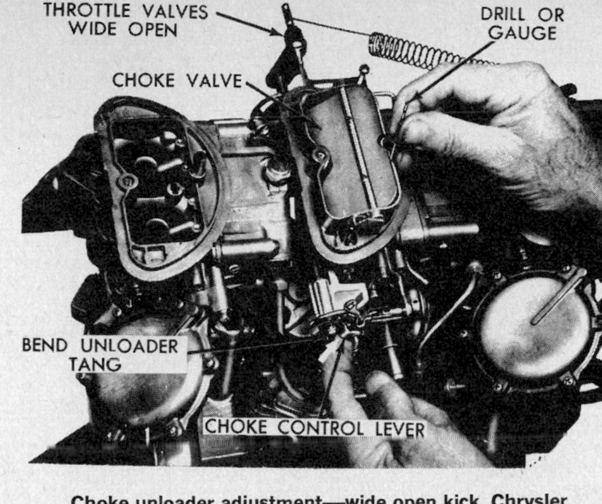

Choke unloader adjustment—wide open kick, Chrysler

3. With a finger lightly pressing against the choke control lever, a slight drag should be felt as the drill is being withdrawn.
4. Adjust by bending the indicated tang until the correct opening has been obtained.

Choke Vacuum Kick Adjustment

Chevrolet

1. With the choke valve closed, hold the vacuum break against the stop.
2. Measure the distance between the choke valve lower edge and the main body. Refer to the Specifications Chart.

Chrysler

NOTE: The test can be made on or off the vehicle.

1. If adjustment is to be made with the engine running, position the fast idle tang (cam position adjustment) to allow the choke to close to the kick position.
2. If an auxiliary vacuum source is to be used, open the throttle valve (engine not running) and move the choke to the closed position. Release the throttle first, then release the choke.

When using an auxiliary vacuum source, disconnect the vacuum hose from the carburetor and connect it to the hose from the vacuum supply with a small length of tube to act as a fitting. Removal of the hose from the diaphragm may require forces which damage the diaphragm. Apply a vacuum of 10 or more in. of mercury.

3. Insert the gauge between the top of the choke valve and the wall of the air horn. Refer to the Specifications Chart.
4. Apply sufficient closing pressure on the lever to which the choke rod attaches to provide a minimum choke valve opening without distortion of the diaphragm link.

NOTE: The cylindrical stem of the diaphragm extends as the internal spring is compressed for proper measurement of the vacuum kick adjustment.

5. Adjustment is necessary if a slight drag is not obtained when removing the gauge. Shorten or lengthen the diaphragm link to obtain the correct choke valve opening. Length changes should be made by carefully opening or closing the U-bend provided in the link. Improper bending causes contact between the U-section and the diaphragm assembly.

NOTE: Do not apply a twisting or bending force to the diaphragm.

6. After completion of adjustment, reinstall the vacuum hose onto the correct carburetor fitting.
7. Return the fast idle screw to its original location if it was disturbed. Make the following check. With no vacuum applied to the diaphragm, the choke valve should move freely between the open and closed positions. If the movement is not free, examine the linkage for misalignment or interferences caused by the bending operation.

Fast Idle Speed Adjustment (On Vehicle)

Chrysler

1. Open the throttle slightly with the engine off. Close the choke

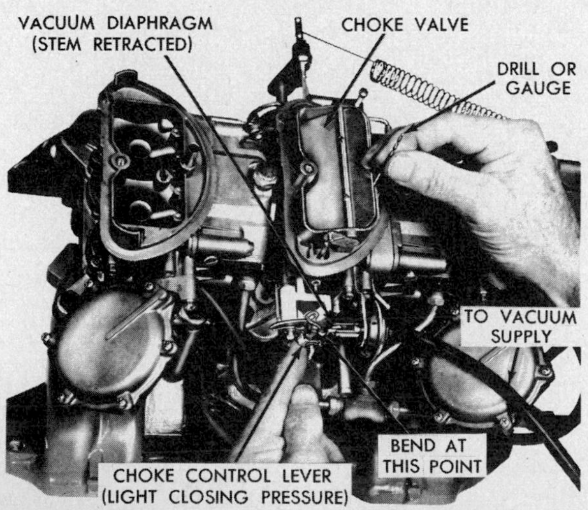

Choke vacuum kick adjustment, Chrysler

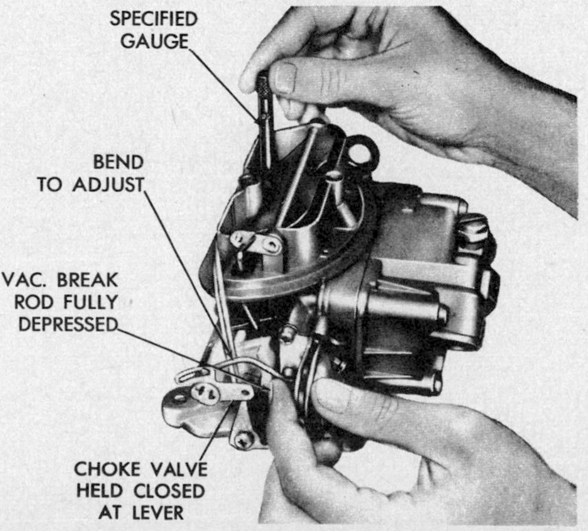

Choke vacuum kick adjustment, Chevrolet

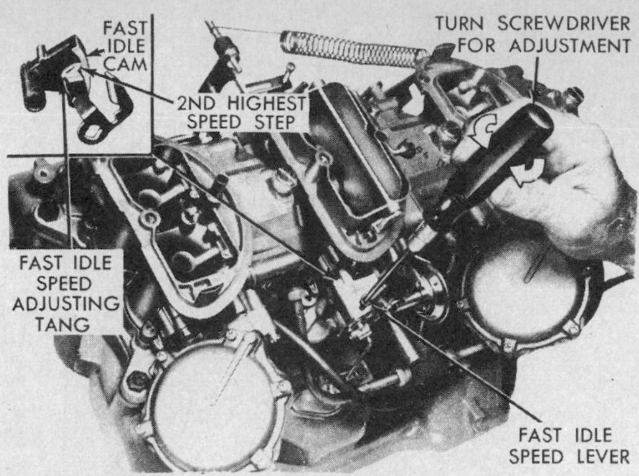

Fast idle speed adjustment on the vehicle

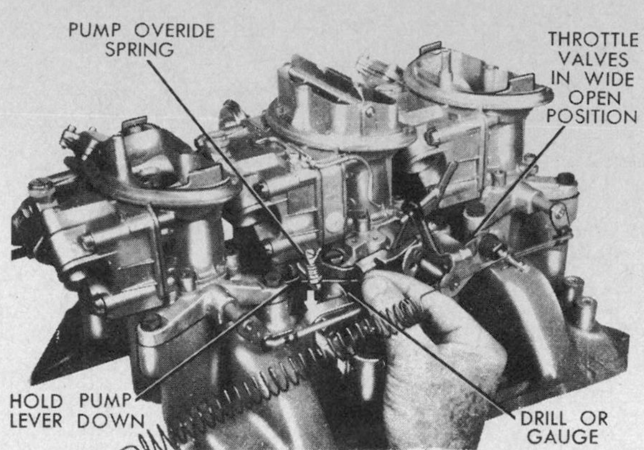

Checking the accelerator pump lever adjustment, Chrysler

valve until the fast idle screw tang can be positioned on the second highest-speed step of the fast idle cam.

2. Start the engine and determine the stabilized speed.
3. Bend the fast idle tang by use of a screwdriver placed in the tang slot to secure the specified speed. Refer to the Specifications Chart.

NOTE: Bend it only in a direction perpendicular to the contact surface of the cam. Movement in any other direction changes the cam position adjustment. Bend it only when the tang is clear of the cam. Stopping the engine between adjustments is not necessary. However, reposition the fast idle tang on the cam after each speed adjustment to provide correct throttle closing torque.

Accelerator Pump Adjustment

1. With the throttle lever in the wide open position and the pump lever fully compressed (down), measure the clearance between the spring adjusting nut and the arm of the pump lever. Refer to Specifications Chart. It should be a minimum of 0.015 in. and a maximum of 0.063 in.
2. Adjust by turning the nut or screw as required while holding the opposite end. (The pump operating lever is not threaded.) There should be no free movement of the pump lever when the throttle is at curb idle.

Bowl Vent Valve Adjustment

1. With the throttle valves at fast curb idle, insert the drill gauge between the bowl vent valve and the bowl vent rod with the fast curb idle speed properly set. Refer to the Specifications Chart.
2. Adjust by bending the rod to change the arc of contact with the throttle lever, until the correct clearance has been obtained.

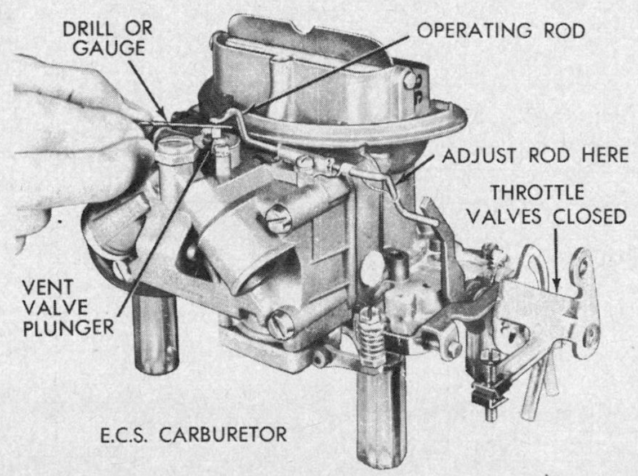

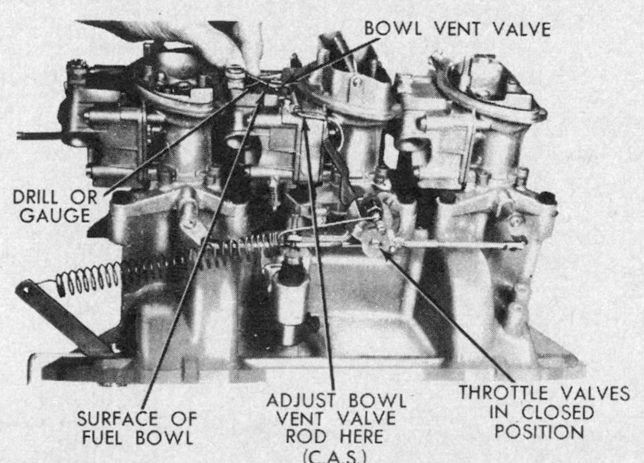

Checking the bowl vent valve adjustment

HOLLEY ONE AND TWO BARREL SPECIFICATIONS

Year	Carb. Part No. ⑦	Float Level Dry (in.)	Accelerator Pump Adjustment (in.)	Bowl Vent Clearance (in.)	Fast Idle On Car (rpm)	Choke Unloader Clearance (in.)	Choke
AMERICAN MOTORS							
1969	4294A	5/16	⑥	1/16	1600⑧	15/64	1 Rich
CHEVROLET							
1969-70	R4055-A	0.350	0.015	0.085	2200	0.250	⑥
	R4056-A	0.350	0.015	0.085	2200	0.250	⑥
	A3659-A	0.350	—	—	—	—	—

HOLLEY ONE AND TWO BARREL SPECIFICATIONS

CHRYSLER PRODUCTS

Year	Carb. Part No. ⑦	Float Level (in.)	Accelerator Pump Adjustment (in.)	Bowl Vent Clearance (in.)	Fast Idle (rpm)	Choke Unloader Clearance (in.)	Vacuum Kick Drill Size (in.)	Cam Position Drill Size (in.)	Choke
1969	R-4161-A	See Text	⑥	3/32	1600②	9/32	#39	#52	2 Rich
	R-4162-A	See Text	⑥	3/32	1800②	9/32	#50	#52	2 Rich
	R-4163-A	See Text	⑥	3/32	1600②	9/32	#39	#52	2 Rich
	R-4164-A	See Text	⑥	3/32	1800②	9/32	#50	#52	2 Rich
	R-4165-A	See Text	⑥	3/32	1700②	9/32	#39	#52	—
	R-4391-A	9/16	0.015	0.080-0.125	2200	5/32	—	—	See Text
	R-4392-A	9/16	0.015	0.080-0.125	1800	5/32	—	—	See Text
	R-4393-A	3/4	—	—	—	—	—	—	—
	R-4394-A	3/4	—	—	—	—	—	—	—
1970	R-4351-A	See Text	⑥	3/32	1600②	⑤	#39	#52	2 Rich
	R-4352-A	See Text	⑥	3/32	1800②	⑤	#50	#52	2 Rich
	R-4353-A	See Text	⑥	3/32	1600②	⑤	#39	#52	2 Rich
	R-4354-A	See Text	⑥	3/32	1800②	⑤	#50	#52	2 Rich
	R-4355-A	See Text	⑥	3/32	1700②	⑤	#39	#52	2 Rich
	R-4363-A	See Text	⑥	3/32	1700②	⑤	#39	#52	2 Rich
	R-4371-A	0.200	—	5/64	1700②	11/64	#28	#35	2 Rich
	R-4175-AF	③	—	—	—	—	—	—	—
	R-4144-A	③	0.015	0.101	1800	5/32	#50	#53	2 Rich
	R-4365-AR	③	—	—	—	—	—	—	—
	R-4374-A	③	0.015	0.101	2200	5/32	#28	#53	2 Rich
	R-4375-A	③	0.015	0.101	2200	5/32	#28	#53	2 Rich
	R-4376-A	③	0.015	0.101	1800	5/32	#50	#53	2 Rich
	R-4382-AF	③	—	—	—	—	—	—	—
	R-4383-AR	③	—	—	—	—	—	—	—
1971	R-4655-A	See Text	—	1/32	1600	9/32	#39	#52	2 Rich
	R-4656-A	See Text	—	1/32	1900	9/32	#39	#52	2 Rich
	R-4659-A	See Text	—	1/32	1800	9/32	#39	#52	2 Rich
	R-6363-A	See Text	—	1/64	2000	9/32	—	—	2 Rich
	R-6364-A	See Text	—	1/64	1900	9/32	—	—	2 Rich
	R-4373-A	0.200	9/16	5/64	1700	11/64	0.141	0.110	2 Rich
	R-4665-A	0.200	9/16	0.015	1800	1/4	#28	#35	2 Rich
	R-4666-A	0.200	9/16	0.015	1800	1/4	#30	#35	2 Rich
	R-4669-A	③	0.015-0.063	0.102	1800	5/32	0.141	0.060	2 Rich
	R-4670-A	③	0.015-0.063	0.102	1800	5/32	0.700	0.060	2 Rich
	R-4671-A	③	—	—	—	—	—	—	—
	R-4672-A	③	—	—	—	—	—	—	—
	R-4789-A	③	—	—	—	—	—	—	—
	R-4790-A	③	—	—	—	—	—	—	—
	R-4791-A	③	0.015	0.101	2600	5/32	#28	#53	On Index
	R-4792-A	③	0.015	0.101	2800	5/32	#39	#53	On Index
1972	R-6153-A	See Text	—	0.015	2000	⑤	0.100	0.064	Fixed
	R-6154-A	See Text	—	0.015	2000	⑤	0.100	0.064	Fixed
	R-6155-A	See Text	—	0.015	2000	⑤	0.100	0.064	Fixed
	R-6156-A	See Text	—	0.015	1900	⑤	0.100	0.064	Fixed
	R-6159-A	See Text	—	0.015	1900	⑤	0.100	0.064	Fixed
	R-6363-A	See Text	—	0.015	2000	⑤	0.100	0.064	Fixed
	R-6364-A	See Text	—	0.015	1900	⑤	0.100	0.064	Fixed
	R-6365-A	See Text	—	0.015	2000	⑤	0.100	0.064	Fixed

HOLLEY ONE AND TWO BARREL SPECIFICATIONS

CHRYSLER PRODUCTS

Year	Carb. Part No. ⑦	Float Level (in.)	Accelerator Pump Adjustment (in.)	Bowl Vent Clearance (in.)	Fast Idle (rpm)	Choke Unloader Clearance (in.)	Vacuum Kick Drill Size (in.)	Cam Position Drill Size (in.)	Choke
	R-6366-A	See Text	—	0.015	2000	⑤	0.100	0.064	Fixed
	R-6162-A	0.180	0.285	0.015	1900	0.170	0.100	0.064	Fixed
	R-6164-A	0.180	0.250	0.015	2000	0.170	0.100	0.064	Fixed
	R-6368-A	0.180	0.285	0.015	1900	0.170	0.100	0.110	Fixed
	R-6370-A	0.180	0.285	0.015	2000	0.170	0.100	0.110	Fixed
	R-6404-A	③	0.015-0.063	0.015	1800	0.150	0.070	0.060	Fixed
	R-6405-A	③	—	—	—	—	—	—	—
	R-6406-A	③	—	—	—	—	—	—	—
1973	R-6447-A	0.260	—	0.015	2000	⑤	0.100	0.065	Fixed
	R-6448-A	0.260	—	0.015	1700	⑤	0.080	0.045	Fixed
	R-6593-A	0.260	—	0.015	2000	⑤	0.100	0.065	Fixed
	R-6594-A	0.260	—	0.015	1700	⑤	0.100	0.065	Fixed
	R-6595-A	0.260	—	0.015	2000	⑤	0.100	0.065	Fixed
	R-6596-A	0.260	—	0.015	1700	⑤	0.100	0.065	Fixed
	R-6452-A	0.180	0.250	0.015	1900	0.170	0.150	0.110	Fixed
	R-6454-A	0.180	0.250	0.015	1800	0.170	0.150	0.110	Fixed
	R-6472-A	0.180	0.250	0.015	1800	0.170	0.150	0.110	Fixed
	R-6575-A	0.180	0.250	0.015	1900	0.170	0.150	0.110	Fixed
1974	R-6721-A	3/64	11/16	—	1600	0.250	0.140	0.080	Fixed
	R-6722-A	3/64	13/16	—	1800	0.250	0.090	0.080	Fixed
	R-6723-A	3/64	11/16	—	1600	0.250	0.140	0.080	Fixed
	R-6724-A	3/64	3/4	—	1800	0.250	0.080	0.080	Fixed
	R-6725-A⑨	3/64	3/4	—	1600	0.250	0.140	0.080	Fixed
	R-6726-A⑨	3/64	3/4	—	1800	0.250	0.090	0.080	Fixed
	R-6731-A	0.180	0.255	0.015	1800	0.170	0.150	0.110	Fixed
	R-6990-A	0.180	0.255	0.015	1600	0.170	0.150	0.110	Fixed
	R-7139-A	0.180	0.255	0.015	1600	0.170	0.150	0.110	Fixed
1975	R-7329-A	3/64	2-7/32	—	1700	0.250	0.130	0.080	Fixed
	R-7017-A	3/64	2-7/32	—	1600	0.250	0.130	0.080	Fixed
	R-7018-A	3/64	2-21/64	—	1700	0.250	0.090	0.080	Fixed
	R-7019-A⑨	3/64	2-7/32	—	1600	0.250	0.130	0.080	Fixed
	R-7020-A⑨	3/64	2-21/64	—	1700	0.250	0.090	0.080	Fixed
	R-7029-A	3/64	2-7/32	—	1600	0.250	0.130	0.080	Fixed
	R-7210-A	3/64	2-21/64	—	1700	0.250	0.090	0.080	Fixed
	R-7226-A	3/16	1/4	0.015	1600	0.170	0.150	0.110	Fixed
	R-7211-A	3/16	1/4	0.015	1600	0.170	0.150	0.110	Fixed
	R-7027-A	3/16	1/4	0.015	1600	0.170	0.150	0.110	Fixed

① Not used
② Engine hot and on the highest step of the cam
③ Center the float in the bowl with the bowl inverted for preliminary adjustment; then set wet level to bottom of sight plug opening
④ Not used
⑤ Unloader automatically set when the fast idle cam is adjusted
⑥ Seasonal setting, the long stroke hole for winter, the short stroke hole for summer
⑦ Located on the tag attached to the carburetor or on the casting
⑧ Engine hot and screw on the second step of the cam
⑨ California equipment
—— Not applicable

HOLLEY 5210 SPECIFICATIONS

CHEVROLET Monza, Vega

Year	Carb. Part No. ①	Float Level (Dry) (in.)	Float Drop (in.)	Pump Position	Fast Idle Cam (in.)	Choke Plate Pulldown (in.)	Fast Idle Setting (rpm)	Choke Setting
1973	R-6477A	0.420	1	#3	0.140	0.300	2000	1 Rich
	R-6478A	0.420	1	#2	0.140	0.300	2200	2 Rich
	R-6580A	0.420	1	#2	0.140	0.300	2200	2 Rich
	R-6581A	0.420	1	#3	0.140	0.300	2000	1 Rich
1974②	338179③	0.420	1	#3	0.140	0.300	2000⑥	2½ Rich
	338181③④	0.420	1	#3	0.140	0.300	2000⑥	2½ Rich
	338168⑤	0.420	1	#2	0.140	0.300	2200⑥	3½ Rich
	338170⑤④	0.420	1	#2	0.140	0.300	2200⑥	3½ Rich
1975	348659, 348663,	0.420	1	#2	0.110	0.325	1600⑥	3 Rich
	348661, 348665④	0.420	1	#2	0.110	0.275	1600⑥	3 Rich
	348660, 348664	0.420	1	#2	0.110	0.300	1600⑥	4 Rich
	348662, 348666④	0.420	1	#2	0.110	0.275	1600⑥	4 Rich

Pontiac Astre

Year	Carb. Part No.	Float Level (Dry) (in.)	Float Drop (in.)	Pump Position	Fast Idle Cam (in.)	Choke Plate Pulldown (in.)	Fast Idle Setting (rpm)	Choke Setting
1975	Manual	0.420	1	#3	0.140	0.300	2000⑥	2½ Rich
	Automatic	0.420	1	#2	0.140	0.400	2200⑥	3½ Rich

① Located on tag attached to the carburetor, or on the casting or choke plate
② Beginning 1974, GM identification numbers are used in place of the Holley numbers
③ Manual transmission
④ Used on California cars
⑤ Automatic transmission
⑥ With no vacuum to the distributor

Model 5210

The Holley 5210 is a two barrel carburetor with a new automatic choke system which is activated by a water heated thermostatic coil. It also has an exhaust gas recirculation system with the valve located in the intake manifold. It is used on General Motors four-cylinder engines.

Float Level

1. With the carburetor air horn inverted, and the float tang resting lightly on the inlet needle, insert the specified drill bit between the air horn and the float.
2. Bend the float tang if an adjustment is needed.

Float Drop

1. With the air horn right side up, measure between the air horn and the top of the float.
2. Bend the float tang if an adjustment is needed.

Fast Idle Cam Adjustments

1. Place the fast idle screw on the second step of the fast idle cam and against the shoulder of the first step.
2. Place the specified drill or gauge on the downstream side of the choke plate.
3. To adjust, bend the choke lever tang.

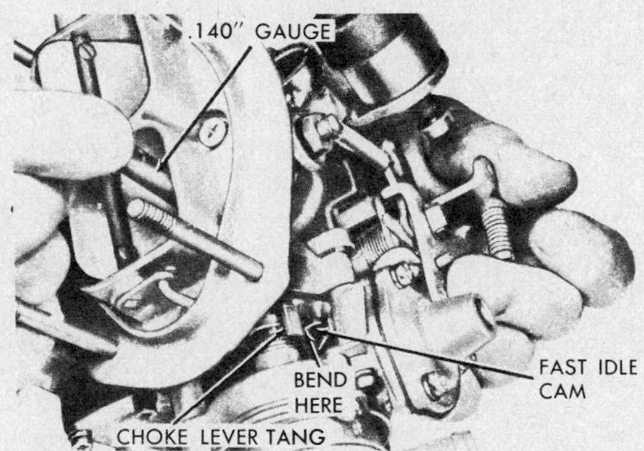

Adjusting fast idle cam

Adjusting fast idle

Choke Plate Pulldown Adjustment

1. Remove the three hex headed screws and ring which retain the choke cover.

Caution Do not remove the choke water housing screw if adjusting on the car. Pull the choke water housing and bimetal cover assembly back out of the way.

2. Push the diaphragm shaft against the stop.
3. Insert the specified size drill bit on the downstream side of the primary choke plate.
4. Take the slack out of the linkage and turn the adjusting screw with a 5/32 in. Allen wrench.

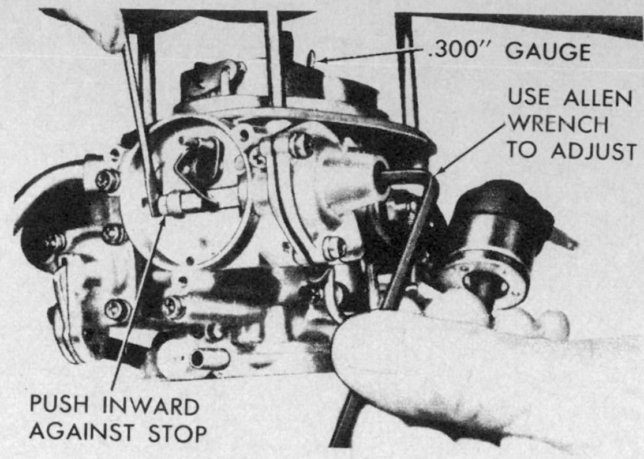

Choke plate pulldown adjustment

Fast Idle Adjustment

1. Engine temperature must be normal.
2. Position the fast idle screw on the top step (second step beginning 1975) of the fast idle cam.
3. Adjust the fast idle to specifications.
4. Adjustments are made by turning the fast idle screw in or out.

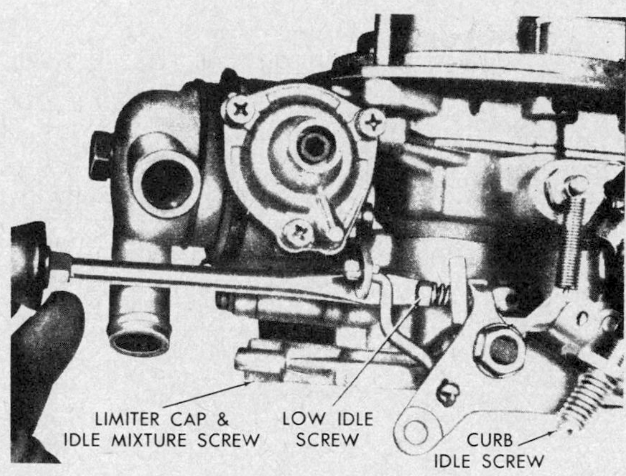

Idle adjustment

Model 4150, 4160

The 4150 and 4160 are four barrel carburetors which contain all the basic systems in the primary sides. The secondary sides of these units contain a fuel transfer and bypass system which richens the mixture when needed.

Some 4150 models have a central fuel inlet whereas other units have a side inlet.

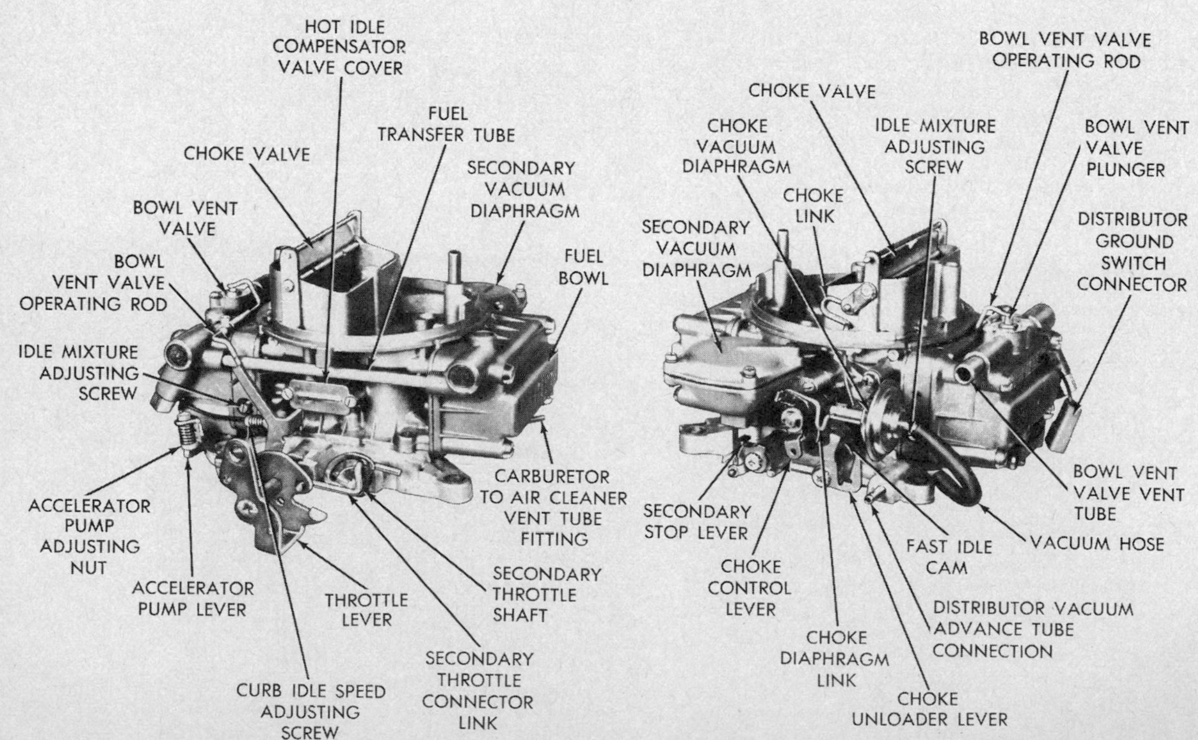

Carburetor assembly—Holley 4160

Model 4160 Adjustments (Chrysler Products)

Bowl Vent Valve Adjustment

1. With the throttle valves at curb idle, it should be possible to insert a 0.015 in. gauge between the bowl vent valve plunger stem and the operating rod.
2. If an adjustment is necessary, bend the rod to change the arc of contact with the throttle lever until the correct clearance has been obtained.

Accelerator Pump Adjustment

1. With the throttle valves open wide and the pump lever held down, it should be possible to insert a 0.015 in. feeler gauge between the adjusting nut and the lever.
2. If an adjustment is necessary, adjust the pump override screw until the correct clearance has been obtained.
3. There must be no free movement of the pump lever when the throttle is at curb idle.

Choke Lever Adjustment

1. Open the throttle to the mid position.
2. Close the choke valve by exerting slight pressure on the choke control lever.
3. The top of the choke rod hole in the control lever should be 2¾ in. above the choke assembly with the carburetor on the engine. With the carburetor on the bench, the measurement should be 1-9/16 in. above the carburetor base.
4. To adjust, bend the choke shaft rod at the top bend.

Caution Improper bending will cause binding of the rod. Check for free movement between the open and closed position.

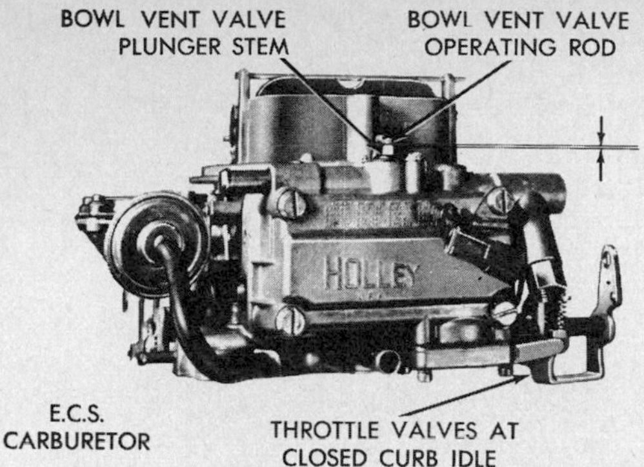

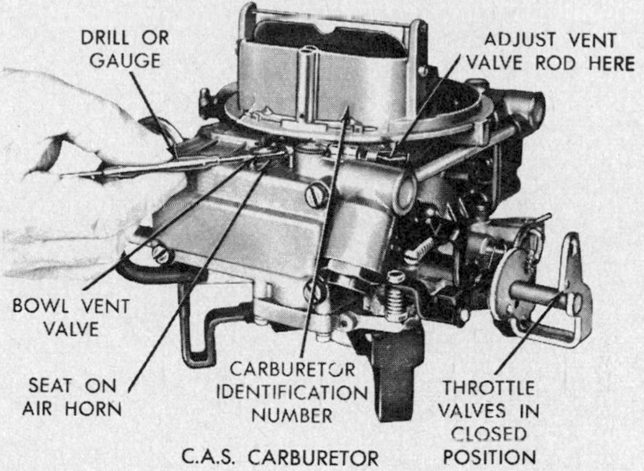

Checking the bowl vent valve clearance, Chrysler

Choke Unloader Adjustment (Wide Open Kick)

1. Adjust the choke control lever.
2. Hold the throttle valves in the wide-open position. Insert the specified drill between the upper edge of the choke valve and the inner wall of the air horn.
3. With a finger pressed against the choke control lever, a slight drag should be felt as the drill is being withdrawn. If an adjustment is to be made, bend the flat tang that contacts the bottom of the fast idle cam until the correct opening has been obtained.

Fast Idle Speed Adjustment

1. With the engine off and the transmission in Neutral, open the throttle slightly.
2. Close the choke valve until the fast idle screw tang can be positioned on the second highest step of the fast idle cam.
3. Start the engine and determine the stabilized speed. Bend the fast idle tang by use of a screwdriver placed in the tang slot to secure the specified speed.

Caution Bend only in a direction perpendicular to the contact surface of the cam. Move-

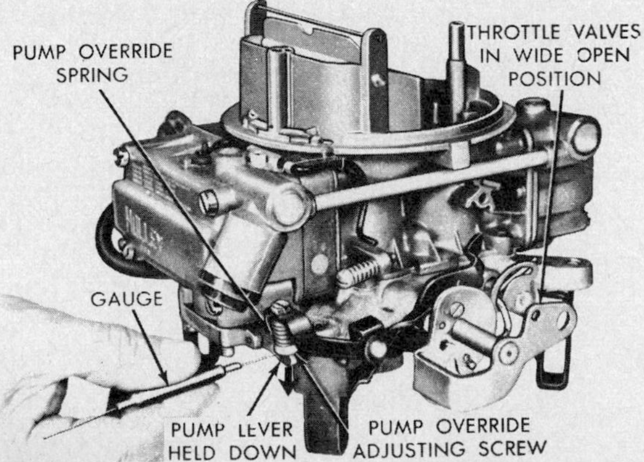

Checking accelerator pump lever clearance, Chrysler

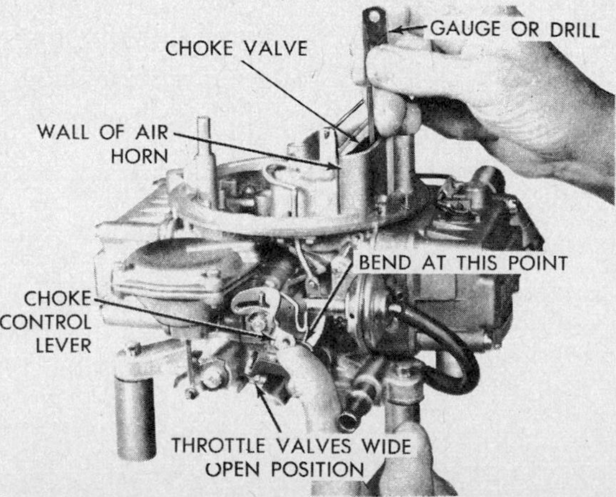

Choke unloader adjustment, Chrysler

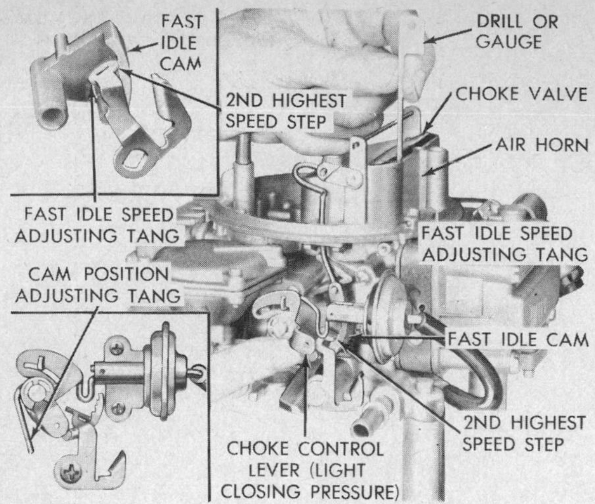

Fast idle cam position adjustment, Chrysler

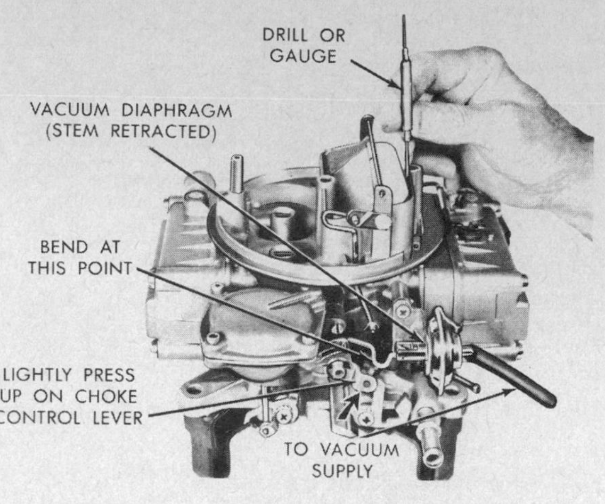

Vacuum kick adjustment, Chrysler

ment in any other direction will change the cam position adjustment described earlier.

4. Reposition the fast idle tang on the cam after each speed adjustment, to provide the correct throttle closing torque.

Fast Idle Cam Position Adjustment

1. Adjust the choke control lever.
2. With the fast idle speed adjusting tang contacting the second highest speed step on the fast idle cam, move the choke valve toward the closed position with light pressure on the choke control lever.
3. Insert a 0.060 in. drill between the choke valve and the wall of the air horn. An adjustment will be necessary if a slight drag is not obtained as the drill is being removed.
4. To adjust, bend the adjusting tang until the correct choke valve opening has been obtained.

Vacuum Kick Adjustment

1. Start the engine and position the fast idle tang to allow choke closure to the kick position.
2. Insert the specified drill between the choke valve and the wall of the air horn. Apply sufficient closing pressure on the lever to which the choke rod attaches to provide a minimum choke valve opening without distortion of the diaphragm link.

NOTE: The cylindrical stem of the diaphragm will extend as an internal spring is compressed. This spring must be fully compressed for proper measurement of the vacuum link adjustment.

4. An adjustment will be necessary if a slight drag is not obtained as the drill is being removed. Shorten or lengthen the diaphragm link to obtain the correct choke opening. Length changes should be made by carefully opening or closing the bend provided in the diaphragm link.

Caution Do not apply twisting or bending force to the diaphragm.

5. With no vacuum applied to the diaphragm, the choke valve should move freely between the open and closed positions. If the movement is not free, examine the linkage for misalignment or interference caused by the bending operation. Repeat the adjustment if necessary to provide the proper link operation.

Model 4150, 4160 Adjustments (General Motors)

Float Adjustment

1. A preliminary float adjustment can be made by inverting the primary fuel bowl and turning the adjustable needle seat until the top of the float is the specified distance from the top of the fuel bowl.
2. Repeat Step 1 for the secondary float.

Secondary Throttle Valve Stop Screw

1. Back off the adjustment screw until the throttle plates are fully closed.
2. Turn the adjustment screw until it just touches the throttle lever and then make ½ turn more to position the valves.

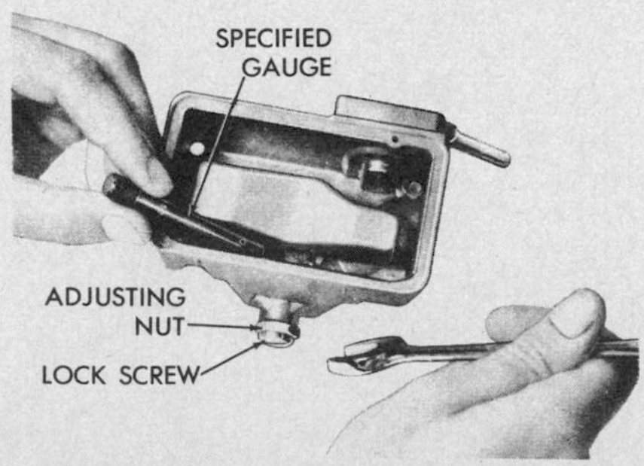

Preliminary float adjustment, GM

Air Vent Valve Adjustment

1. Back off the idle speed screw until the throttle valves are fully closed.
2. Check the clearance between the choke valve and the seat.
3. Bend the air valve rod to adjust.
4. Turn the idle screw in until contact is made with the throttle lever, then turn the screw in 1½ additional turns for preliminary idle speed adjustments.

Fast Idle Cam Adjustment

1. Open the throttle slightly, close the choke plate, and position the fast idle lever against the top step of the fast idle cam.
2. Adjust the fast idle to give the 0.025 in. opening on the throttle plates on the idle transfer slot side of the carburetor.
3. Bend the fast idle lever to adjust.

Accelerator Pump Adjustment

1. Hold the throttle lever in the wide-open position with a rubber band; hold the pump lever fully compressed down; then measure the clearance between the spring adjusting nut and the arm of the pump lever.
2. Clearance should be 0.015 in.; adjust by turning the nut or screw as required while holding the opposite end.
3. After the adjustment is made, rotate the throttle lever to fully closed and partly open again. Any movement of the throttle lever should be noticed at the operating lever spring end, indicating the correct pump tip-in.

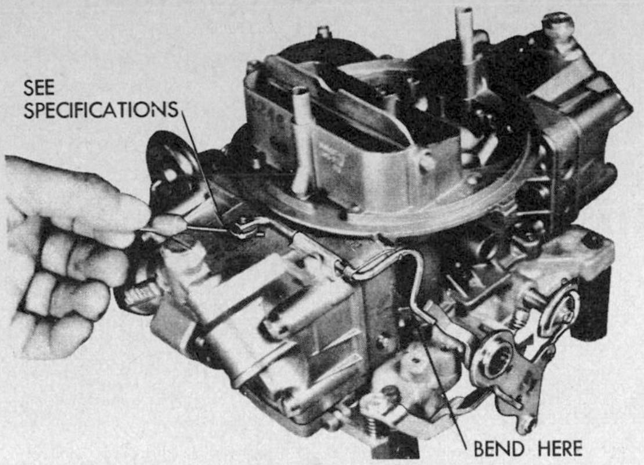

Air vent valve adjustment, GM

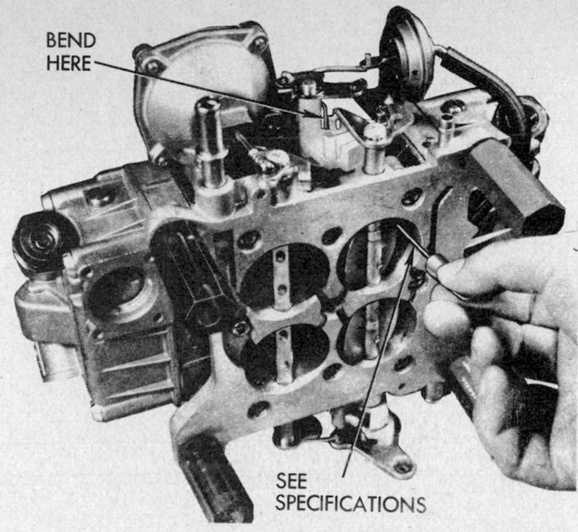

Fast idle cam adjustment, GM

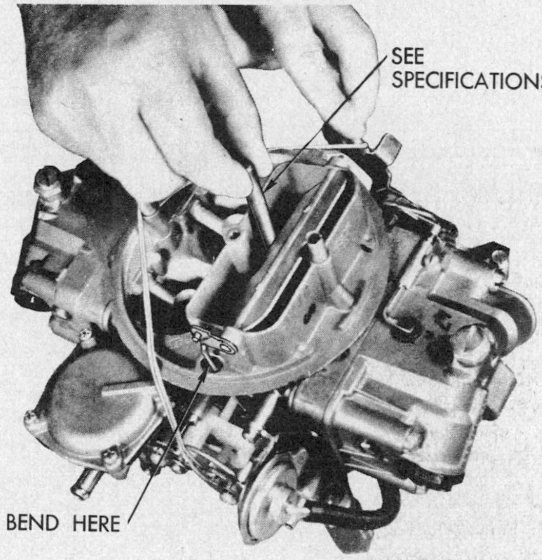

Choke unloader adjustment, GM

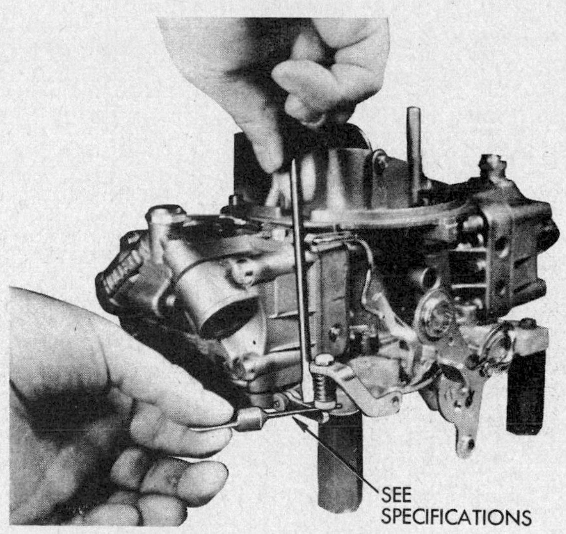

Accelerator Pump adjustment, GM

Choke Unloader Adjustment

1. Hold the throttle lever in the wide-open position with a rubber band.
2. Hold the choke valve toward the closed position against the unloader tang of the throttle shaft, then measure the opening between the choke valve lower edge and the main body.
3. To adjust, bend the choke rod at the offset end. Recheck after adjusting.

Vacuum Break Adjustment

1. Hold the choke valve closed with a rubber band attached to the linkage.
2. Hold the vacuum break in against the stop.
3. Measure the distance between the choke valve lower edge and the main body.
4. Bend the vacuum break link to adjust.

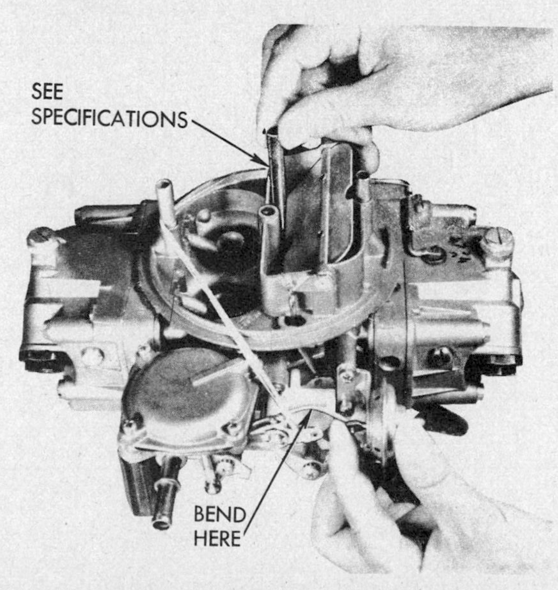

Vacuum break adjustment, GM

HOLLEY 4150 and 4160 SPECIFICATIONS

CHEVROLET

Year	Carb. Part No. ①	Float Level (Dry) (in.)	Accelerator Pump Lever Adjustment (in.)	Choke Setting (in.)	Choke Unloader Clearance (in.)	Bowl Vent Clearance (in.)	Fast Idle On Car (rpm)	Choke Vacuum Break (in.)
1969-70	R4053-A	⑥	0.015	⑧	0.350	—	2200	0.300
	R4296-A	⑥	0.015	⑧	0.350	—	2200	0.350
	R4346	⑥	0.015	⑧	0.350	—	2200	0.300
	R4492-A	⑥	0.015	⑧	0.350	—	2200	0.350
	R4557-A	⑥	0.015	⑧	0.350	—	2200	0.350
1971	R4800-A	⑩	0.015	1.320⑪	0.350	—	2200	0.350
	R4801-A	⑩	0.015	1.320⑪	0.350	—	2200	0.350
	R4802-A	⑩	0.015	1.320⑪	0.350	—	2200	0.350
	R4803-A	⑩	0.015	1.320⑪	0.350	—	2200	0.350
1972	R6238-A	⑩	0.015	1.320⑪	0.350	—	2350	0.350
	R6239-A	⑩	0.015	1.320⑪	0.350	—	2350	0.350
1968	R-3918-A	⑦	0.015	See Text	5/32	50 Drill	1400⑨	—
1969	R-4166-A	⑦	0.015	See Text	5/32	5/64	1400⑤	—
	R-4440-A	⑦	0.015	See Text	5/32	5/64	1500⑨	—
1970-71	R-4360-A	⑦	0.015	2 Rich	25 Drill	72 Drill	1600	46 Drill
	R-4366-A	⑦	0.015	2 Rich	25 Drill	5/64	1600	46 Drill
1971	R-4668-A	⑦	0.015	2 Rich	25 Drill	0.015	1700	46 Drill
	R-4735-A	⑦	0.015	2 Rich	25 Drill	0.015	1700	46 Drill
	R-6191-A	⑦	0.015	2 Rich	25 Drill	0.015	1800	18 Drill
	R-6193-A	⑦	0.015	2 Rich	25 Drill	0.015	1800	18 Drill
1972	R-6160-A	⑫	0.015	Fixed	0.150	0.015	1600	0.080
	R-6252-A	⑫	0.015	Fixed	0.150	0.015	1800	0.140
	R-6253-A	⑫	0.015	Fixed	0.150	0.015	1600	0.080
	R-6254-A	⑫	0.015	Fixed	0.150	0.015	1800	0.140
	R-6255-A	⑫	0.015	Fixed	0.150	0.015	1600	0.080
	R-6256-A	⑫	0.015	Fixed	0.150	0.015	2000	0.140
	R-6257-A	⑫	0.015	Fixed	0.150	0.015	1800	0.080
	R-6290-A	⑫	0.015	Fixed	0.150	0.015	1500	0.080

CHRYSLER PRODUCTS

Year	Carburetor Part No. ①	Float Level (Dry) (in.)	Minimum Pump Clearance (in.)	Choke Setting	Choke Unloader Clearance (in.)	Bowl Vent Valve Clearance (in.)	Fast Idle Speed (rpm)	Vacuum Kick (in.)
1969	R-4166-A	⑦	0.015	See Text	5/32	5/64	1400⑤	—
	R-4440-A	⑦	0.015	See Text	5/32	5/64	1500⑨	—
1970	R-4360-A	⑦	0.015	2 Rich	25 Drill	72 Drill	1600	46 Drill
	R-4366-A	⑦	0.015	2 Rich	25 Drill	5/64	1600	46 Drill
1971	R-4668-A	⑦	0.015	2 Rich	25 Drill	0.015	1700	46 Drill
	R-4735-A	⑦	0.015	2 Rich	25 Drill	0.015	1700	46 Drill
	R-6191-A	⑦	0.015	2 Rich	25 Drill	0.015	1800	18 Drill
	R-6193-A	⑦	0.015	2 Rich	25 Drill	0.015	1800	18 Drill

CHRYSLER PRODUCTS

HOLLEY 4150 and 4160 SPECIFICATIONS

Year	Carburetor Part No. ①	Float Level (Dry) (in.)	Minimum Pump Clearance (in.)	Choke Setting	Choke Unloader Clearance (in.)	Bowl Vent Valve Clearance (in.)	Fast Idle Speed (rpm)	Vacuum Kick (in.)
1972	R-6160-A	⑫	0.015	Fixed	0.150	0.015	1600	0.080
	R-6252-A	⑫	0.015	Fixed	0.150	0.015	1800	0.140
	R-6253-A	⑫	0.015	Fixed	0.150	0.015	1600	0.080
	R-6254-A	⑫	0.015	Fixed	0.150	0.015	1800	0.140
	R-6255-A	⑫	0.015	Fixed	0.150	0.015	1600	0.080
	R-6256-A	⑫	0.015	Fixed	0.150	0.015	2000	0.140
	R-6257-A	⑫	0.015	Fixed	0.150	0.015	1800	0.080
	R-6290-A	⑫	0.015	Fixed	0.150	0.015	1500	0.080

① Located on tag attached to carburetor, or on the casting or choke plate
② Not used
③ Not used
④ Not used
⑤ No. 5 Step on cam
⑥ Primary 0.350 in., secondary 0.500 in.
⑦ Primary 15/64 in., secondary 17/64 in.
⑧ Top of rod even with bottom of hole
⑨ No. 2 Step on cam
⑩ Float centered in bowl
⑪ Not used
⑫ Primary 0.110 in., secondary 0.204 in.

Ford, Autolite, Motorcraft Carburetors

Models 1100, 1101, and 1250

These carburetors are essentially the same as far as adjustments are concerned and, therefore, will be grouped together for easier reference.

The Model 1100 carburetor is used on Ford six cylinder cars through 1969 and is essentially the same as the Model 1101 carburetor. Both carburetors consist of two major assemblies, the upper body and the throttle body. The 1100 carburetor is equipped with a hydraulically operated dashpot, and the 1101 is equipped with an externally mounted pneumatic dashpot.

The model 1250 is a single barrel downdraft carburetor designed for use on the 1600 cc Pinto engine. It is equipped with a diaphragm type accelerator pump and a water heated thermostatic choke.

Choke Plate Pulldown

Model 1250

1. Remove the thermostatic spring and the water housing.

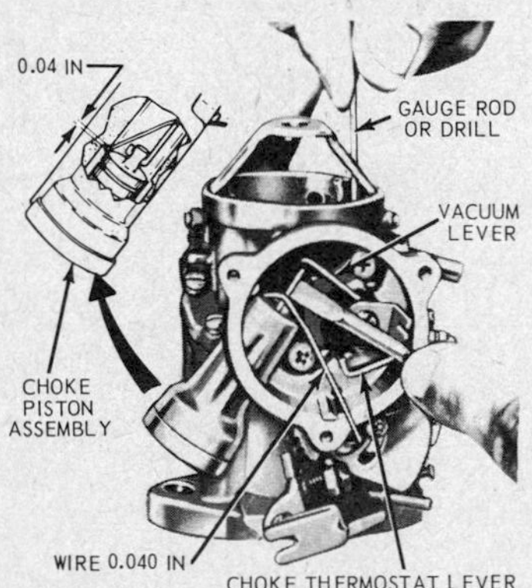

Choke plate pulldown adjustment
(© Ford Motor Co)

2. Push in on the vacuum piston until the vacuum inner bleed slot is fully exposed.
3. Take a length of 0.040 in. wire and insert it into this slot. Raise the piston to trap the wire.
4. Partially open the throttle valve so that the choke plate may be moved toward the closed position.
5. Close the choke plate until its movement is stopped.
6. Check the clearance between the bottom of the choke plate and the inside wall of the carburetor body.
7. If the specified clearance is not present, bend the extension of the choke thermostat lever to adjust it.

Models 1100 and 1101

1. Position the fast idle adjusting screw on the highest step of the fast idle cam.
2. Insert a gauge of the proper dimension between the lower edge of the choke plate and the air horn wall.
3. If needed, adjust by turning the plastic nut on the choke plate pulldown rod until it contacts the swivel on the choke lever assembly.

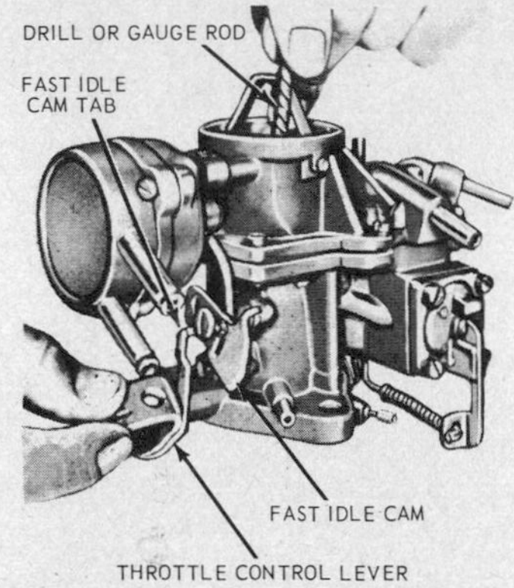

Dechoke adjustment—Autolite 1 barrel
(© Ford Motor Co)

Dechoke

1. Open the throttle valve fully and measure the clearance between the bottom of the choke plate and the carburetor body.
2. If adjustment is necessary, bend the tang on the fast idle cam.

Accelerator Pump Stroke

1. Back out the throttle stop screw so that the throttle plate may be fully closed.
2. Depress the plunger of the accelerator pump diaphragm and check the clearance between the operating lever and the plunger with the proper gauge.

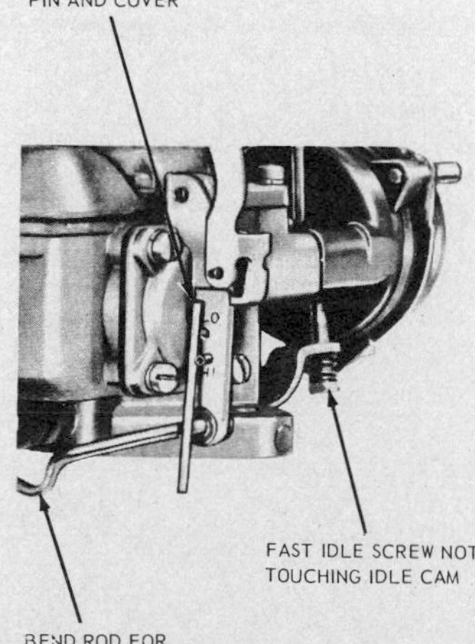

Accelerator pump adjustment
(© Ford Motor Co)

3. To adjust, bend the gooseneck of the pump push rod. Closing the gooseneck will lengthen the stroke and expanding it will shorten the stroke.
4. Reset the throttle valve stop screw.

Fast Idle

1. After adjusting the choke plate pulldown, hold the choke plate in the closed position.
2. Make sure the fast idle tab is on the second step of the fast idle cam.
3. Install the thermostatic spring and water housing. Locate the spring in the center slot and accurately align the marks on the housing.
4. Connect a tachometer to the engine.
5. Run the engine until the normal operating temperature is reached.
6. Put the fast idle tab on the second step of the fast idle cam and check engine speed. If adjustment is needed, bend the tab which contacts the fast idle cam.

Float Level

Model 1250

1. Disconnect all connections to the carburetor upper body including the fuel line, decel valve hose, choke fast idle pivot screw, and the thermostatic housing. Remove the upper carburetor body.
2. With the upper carburetor body held so that the float hangs down, measure the distance from the bottom of the float to the upper body gasket. To adjust, bend the tab which contacts the needle valve and seat assembly.
3. Invert the carburetor so that the float rests on the carburetor body. Again measure the distance from the bottom of the float to the body gasket. Adjust by bending the tab which rests on the needle valve housing.

Models 1100 and 1101

1. Remove the upper carburetor body and the gasket from the lower carburetor section.

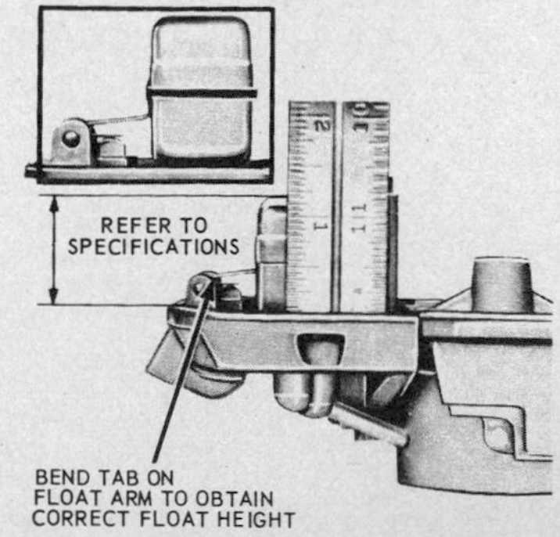

Float level adjustment—Autolite 1100, 1101
(© Ford Motor Co)

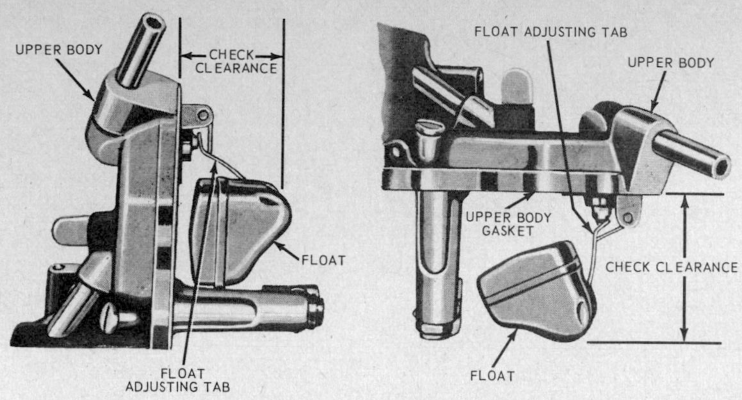

Adjusting float level—Model 1250
(© Ford Motor Co)

2. Measure the distance from the upper body gasket surface to the top of the float. This should be done with the carburetor sitting on the air cleaner gasket surface.
3. Adjust by bending the float arm tab.

Caution Do not apply pressure to the fuel inlet needle as this will damage the Viton® tip of the needle.

Vent Valve Adjustment

1. Adjust the vent valve only after the accelerator pump has been properly adjusted.
2. Set the linkage in the hot idle position.
3. The groove in the vent valve should now be even with the open end of the vent.
4. Bend the arm on the vent valve actuating lever to align the groove with the edge of the bore.

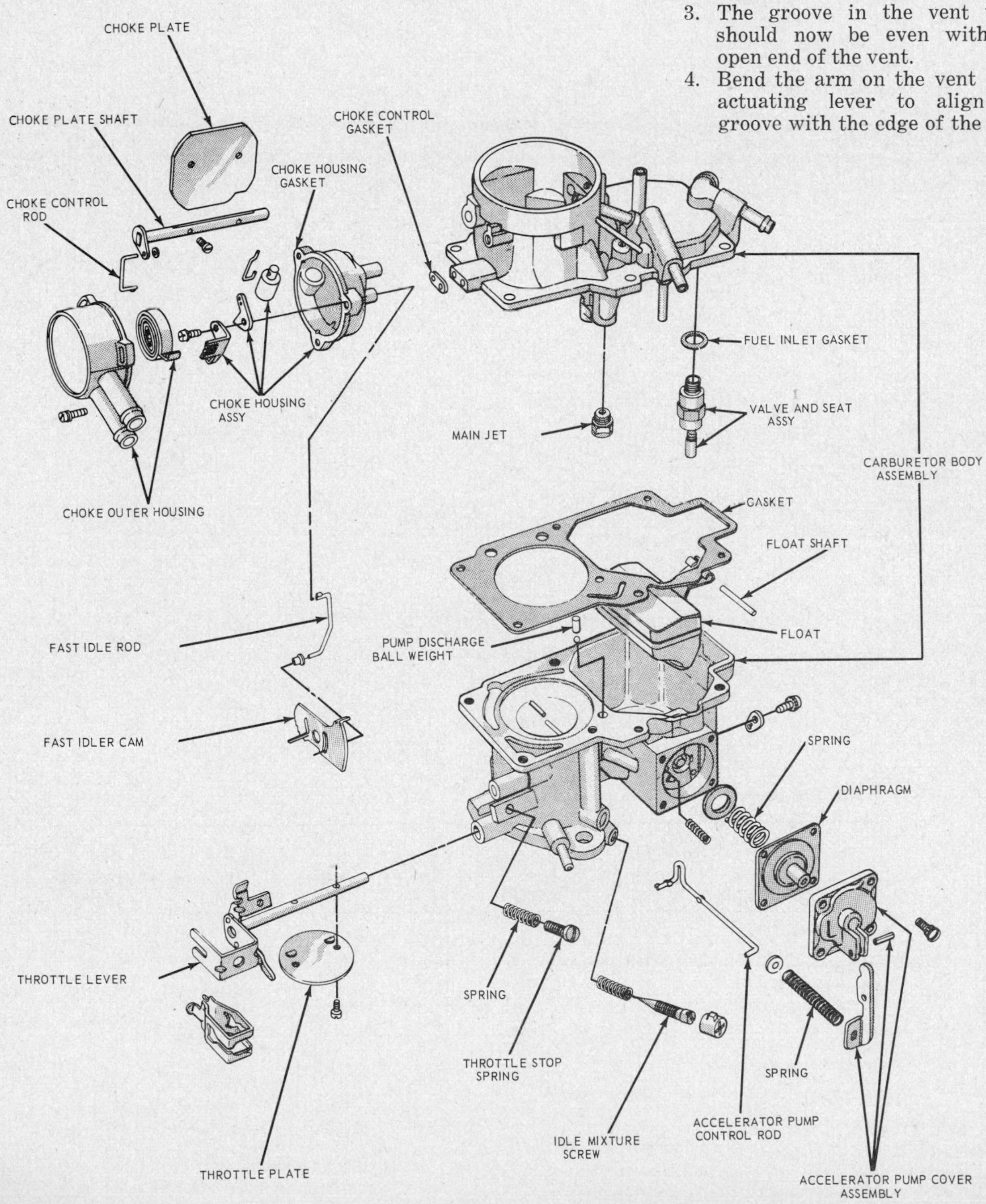

Disassembled Model 1250 carburetor (© Ford Motor Co)

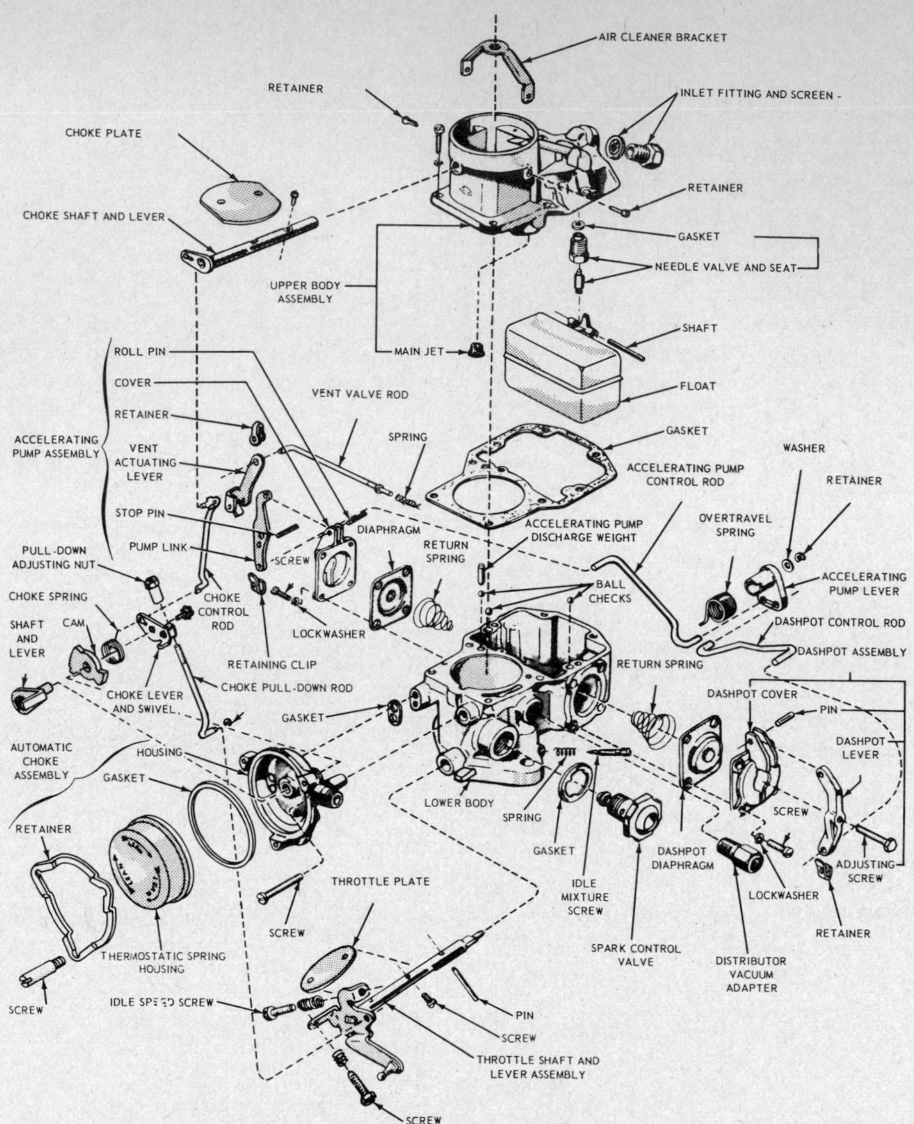

Exploded view—Model 1100 (© Ford Motor Co)

FORD, AUTOLITE, MOTORCRAFT MODEL 1100,1101, SPECIFICATIONS

Ford Products

Year	(9510)* Carburetor Identification	Float Level (in.)	Pump (in.)①	Fast Idle (rpm)	Choke Plate Pulldown (in.)②	Dechoke (in.)③	Choke Setting
1969	C8OF-B	1 3/32	0.190	1500	0.130	1/4	1 Lean
	C9DF-B	1 3/32	0.150	1500	0.150	1/4	3 Lean
	C8AF-E	1 3/32	0.190	1500	0.200	0.160	3 Lean
	C9OF-A	1 3/32	0.190	1500	0.200	0.160	3 Lean
	C9OF-B	1 3/32	0.190	1500	0.200	0.160	1 Lean
	C9OF-J	1 3/32	0.190	1500	0.200	0.160	1 Lean
	C9OF-K	1 3/32	0.190	1500	0.200	0.160	3 Lean

* Basic carburetor number
① Given in inches with pin in high position and throttle valve fully seated
② ± 0.010
③ Minimum clearance between choke valve and air horn wall with throttle valve wide open

FORD, AUTOLITE, MOTORCRAFT MODEL 1250 SPECIFICATIONS

Pinto

Year	(9510)* Carburetor Identification	Float Level (in.)	Pump (in.)	Fast Idle (rpm)	Choke Plate Pulldown (in.)	Dechoke (in.)	Choke Setting
1971	711-BDA	①	0.085	1700	0.120	0.210	Index
	711-BDB	①	0.070	1700	0.075	0.210	Index
1972	721F-KFA	②	0.070	1700	0.075	0.210	Index
1973	731F-KAA	②	0.085	——	0.075	——	Index

* Basic carburetor number
① Body vertical—1.100-1.200
Body horizontal—1.350-1.370
② Body vertical—1.200

Models 2100, 2150, 4100

The Model 2100 and 2150 two barrel carburetor and the 4100 four barrel carburetor are basically the same in construction. Adjustments are performed in the same manner for all carburetors.

The air horn assembly covers the main body and houses the choke plate and the internal fuel bowl vents. The throttle plate, accelerator pump assembly, power valve assembly, and fuel bowl are contained in the main body. The automatic choke is also attached to the main body. On the 2100 and 2150 two barrel, each bore contains a main and booster venturi, a main fuel discharge, an accelerating pump discharge, an idle fuel discharge, and a throttle plate. The four barrel 4100 model has vacuum operated throttle plates and a main fuel discharge in each secondary bore.

Float Level (Dry)

The dry float level measurement is a preliminary check and must be followed by a wet float level measurement with the carburetor mounted on the engine.

1. With the air horn removed and the fuel inlet needle seated lightly,

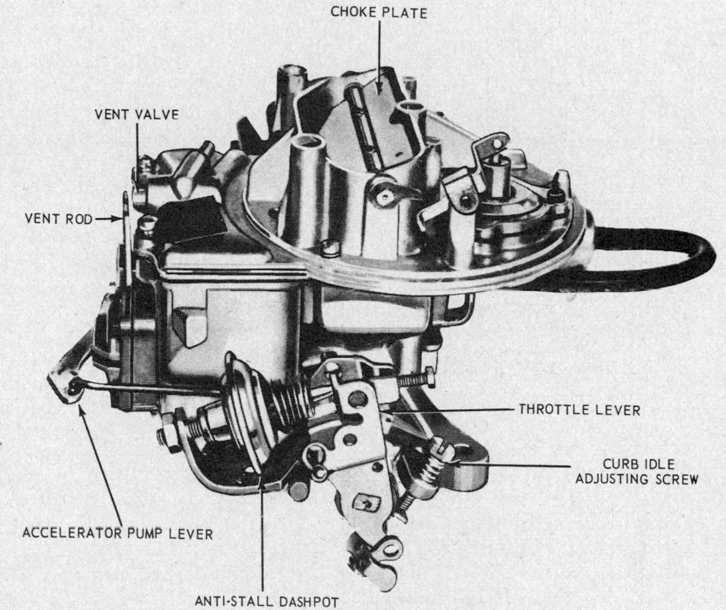

Model 2100 two barrel carburetor
(© Ford Motor Co)

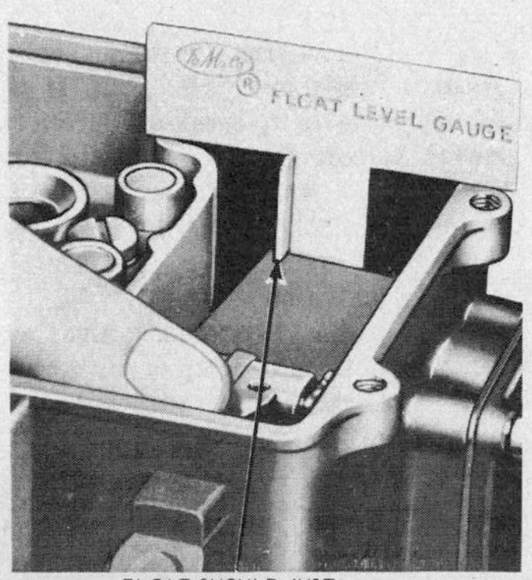

Checking float level (dry)
(© Ford Motor Co)

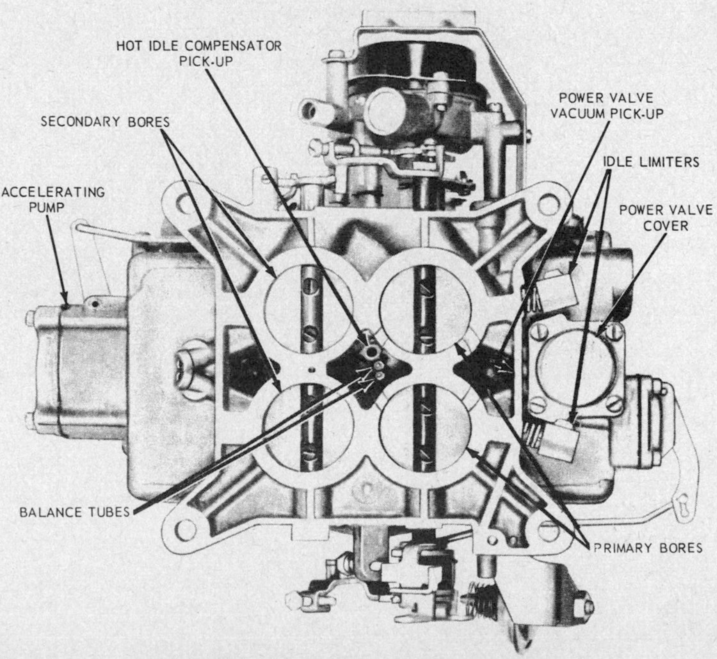

Bottom view—model 4100 four barrel carburetor
(© Ford Motor Co)

gently raise the float and measure the distance between the main body gasket surface (gasket removed) and the top of the float.

2. If necessary, bend the float tab to obtain the correct level.

Float Level (Wet)

1. Remove the screws that hold the air horn to the main body and break the seal between the air horn and main body. Leave the air horn and gasket loosely in place on top of the main body.
2. Start the engine and allow it to idle for at least three minutes.
3. After the engine has idled long enough to stabilize the fuel level, remove the air horn assembly.

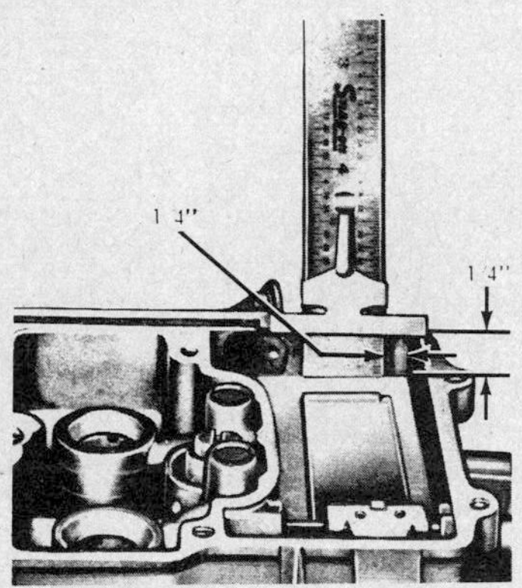

Fuel level measurement (wet)
(© Ford Motor Co)

4. With the engine idling, use a T-scale to measure the distance from the top of the fuel bowl machined surface to the surface of the fuel. The scale must be held at least ¼ in. away from any vertical surface to ensure proper measurement.
5. If any adjustment is required, stop the engine to avoid a fire from fuel spraying on the engine.
6. Bend the float tab upward to raise the level and downward to lower the level.

Caution Be sure to hold the fuel inlet needle off its seat when bending the float tab so as not to damage the Viton® tip.

7. Each time the float level is changed, the air horn must be temporarily positioned and the engine started to stabilize the fuel level before again checking it.

Choke Plate Pulldown

Model 2100 through 1974

1. Loosen the screws on the choke cover and rotate the cover ¼ turn clockwise (rich), then tighten the screws.
2. Operate the throttle to allow full closing of the choke plate.
3. Press down on the choke modulator arm until the choke modulator diaphragm is bottomed and then measure the distance from the lower edge of the choke plate to the inside air horn wall.
4. Adjustment is achieved by turning the diaphragm stop screw on the underside of the air horn.
5. Turn the screw clockwise to decrease clearance and counterclockwise to increase clearance.

NOTE: Do not reset the choke cover until the fast idle cam adjustment is made.

Model 2150 beginning 1975

1. Remove the air cleaner assembly.
2. Set the throttle on the top step of the fast idle cam.
3. Noting the position of the choke housing cap, loosen the retaining screws and rotate the cap 90 degrees in the rich (closing) direction.
4. Activate the pull-down motor by manually forcing the pull-down control diaphragm link in the direction of applied vacuum or by applying vacuum to the external vacuum tube.
5. Using a drill gauge of the specified diameter, measure the clearance between the choke plate and the center of the air horn wall nearest the fuel bowl.
6. To adjust, reset the diaphragm stop on the end of the choke pulldown diaphragm.
7. After adjusting, reset the choke housing cap to the specified notch. Check and reset fast idle speed, if necessary. Install the air cleaner.

Fast Idle Cam

1. Push down on the fast idle cam lever until the fast idle screw is in contact with the second step of the fast idle cam and against the shoulder of the high step.
2. The specified clearance should be present between the lower edge of the choke plate and the air horn wall.
3. The adjustment is made by turning the fast idle cam lever screw.
4. The choke cover may now be replaced and indexed according to specification.

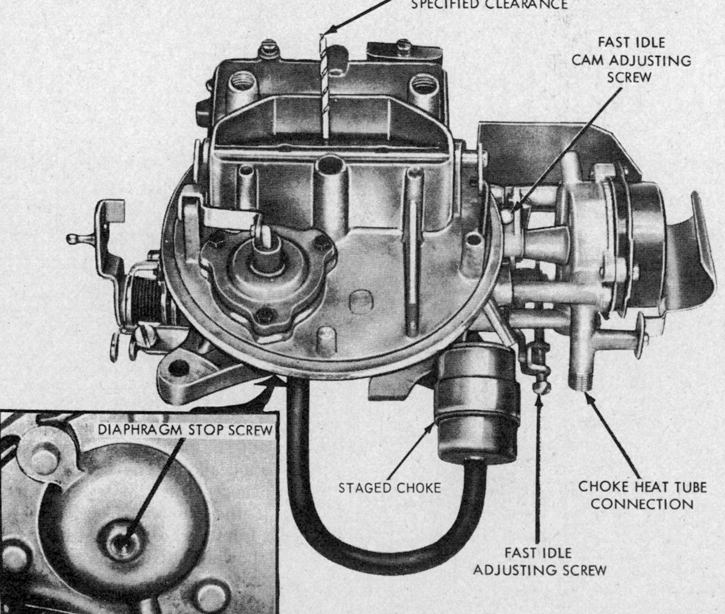

Adjusting choke plate pulldown
(© Ford Motor Co)

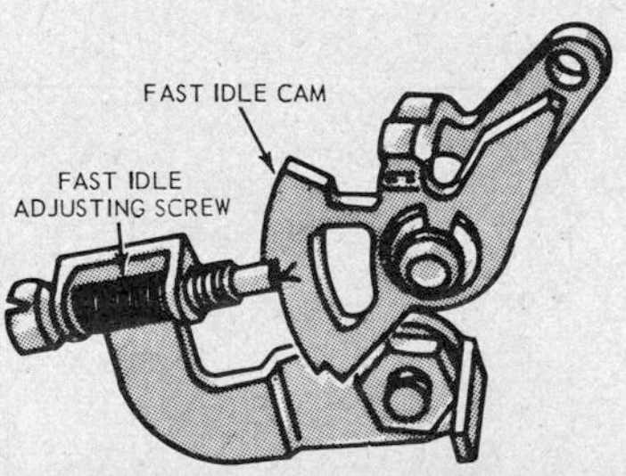

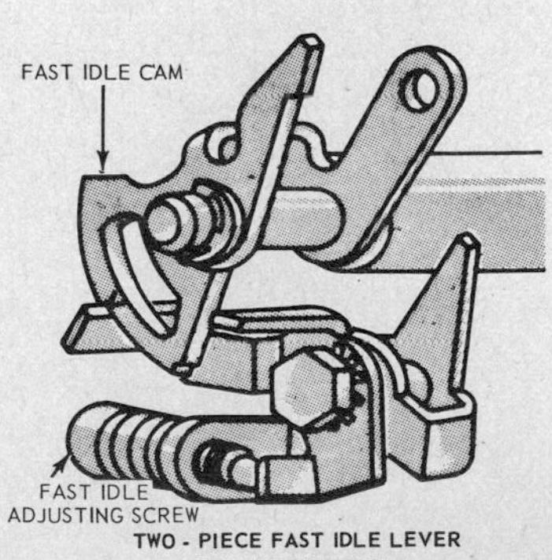

Fast idle adjustment
(© Ford Motor Co)

Choke Unloader (Dechoke)

1. With the throttle held completely open, move the choke plate to the closed position.
2. Measure the distance between the lower edge of the choke plate and the air horn wall.
3. Adjust by bending the tang on the fast idle speed lever which is located on the throttle shaft.

NOTE: Final unloader adjustment must be performed on the car and the throttle should be opened by using the accelerator pedal of the car. This is to be sure that full throttle operation is achieved.

Accelerator Pump

The accelerator pump operating rod must be positioned in the proper holes of the accelerator pump lever and the throttle over-travel lever to assure correct pump travel. If adjusting is required, additional holes are provided in the throttle over-travel lever.

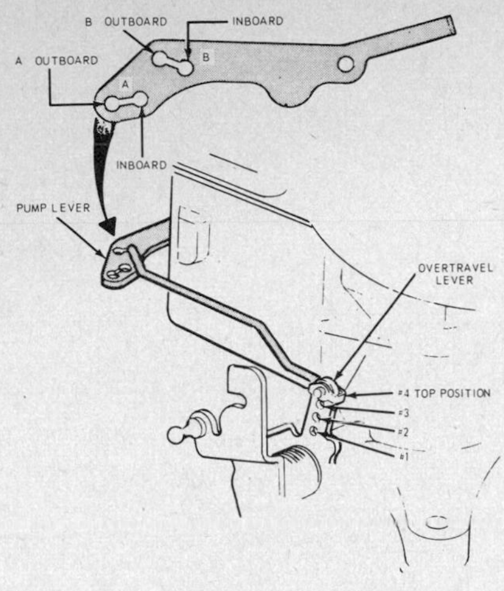

Accelerator pump stroke adjustment
(© Ford Motor Co)

Dashpot Adjustment

With the throttle set at the curb idle position, fully depress the dashpot stem and measure the distance between the stem and the throttle lever. Adjust by loosening the locknut and turning the dashpot.

Fast Idle

Adjust the fast idle setting with the engine at operating temperature. The fast idle screw should be resting against the second step of the fast idle cam. Adjust by turning the fast idle screw.

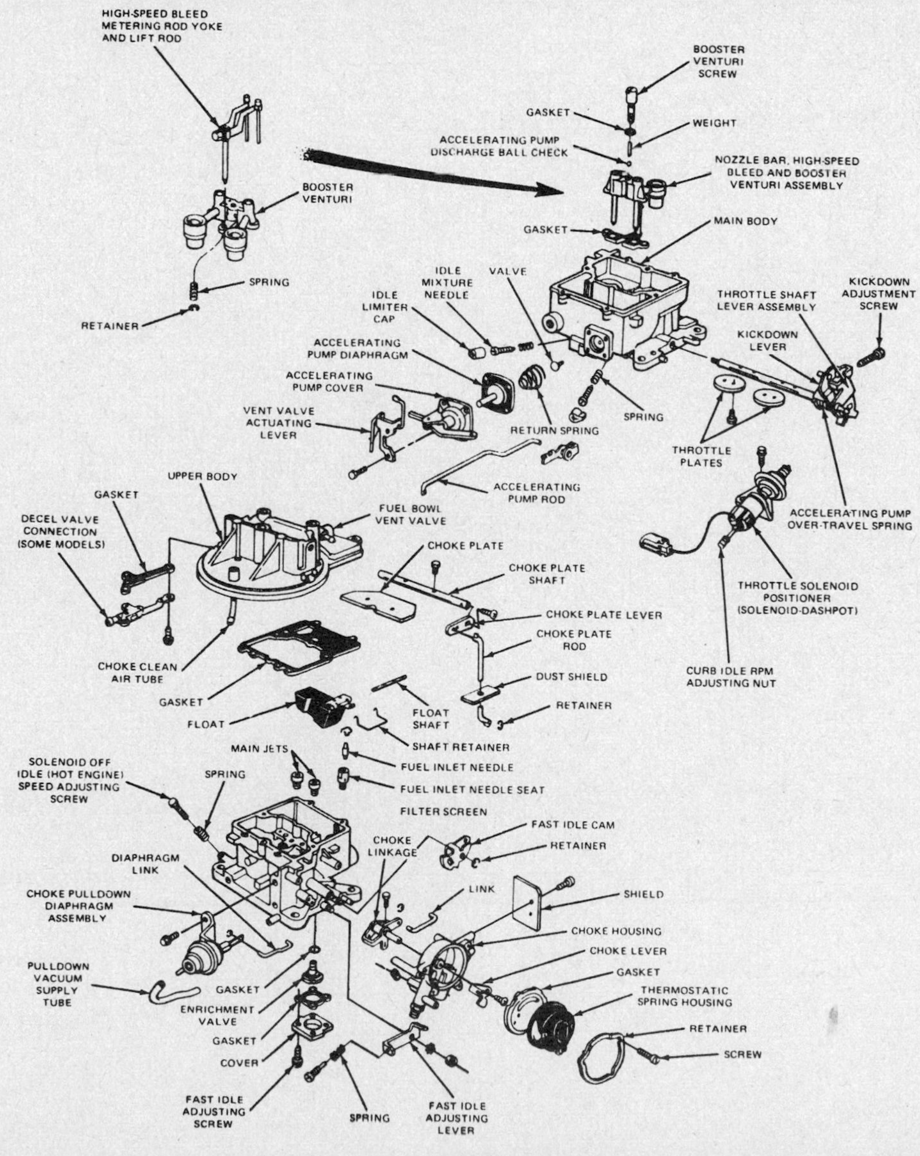

Exploded view—Motorcraft 2150-2V

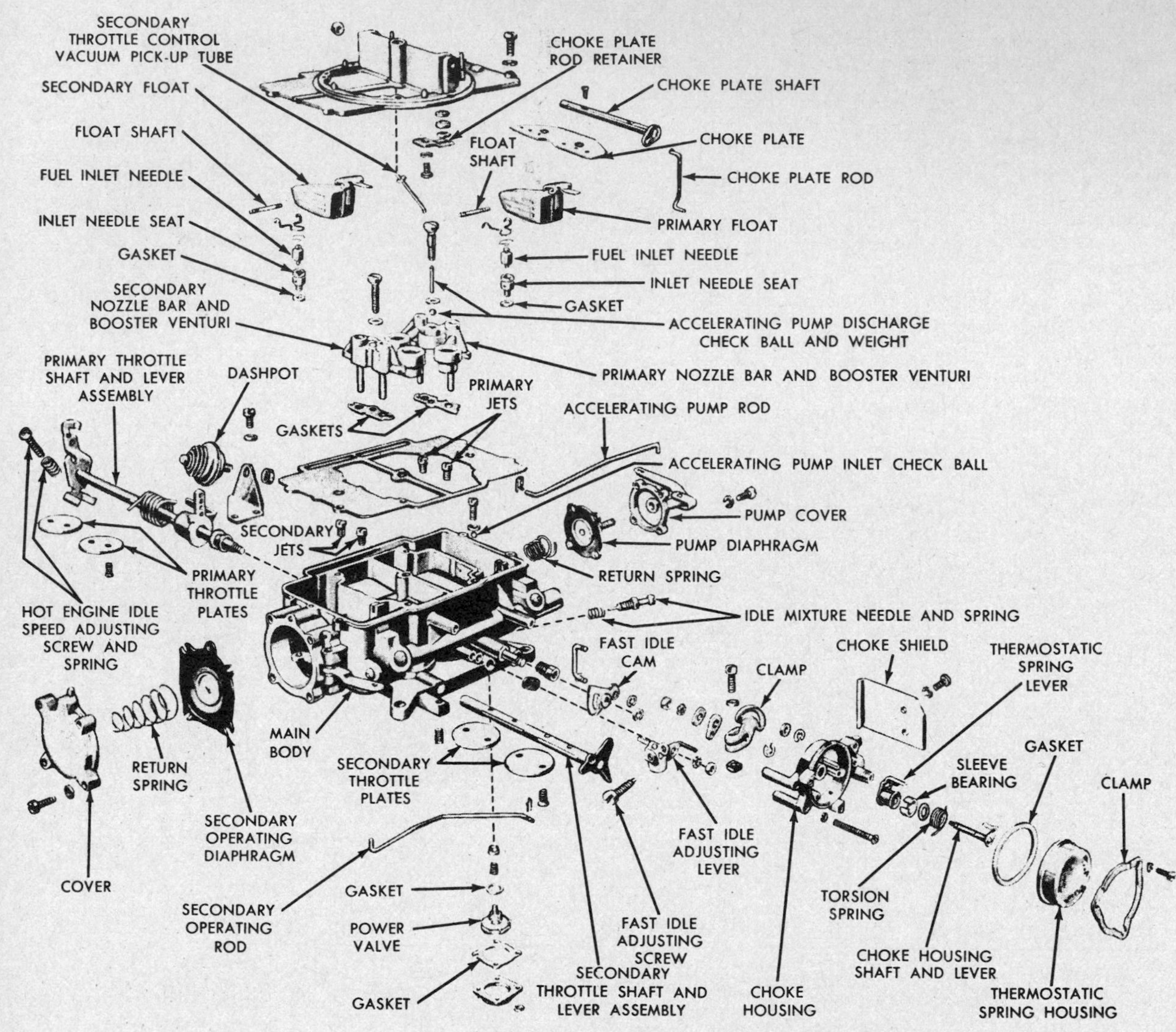

Model 4100 carburetor (© Ford Motor Co)

FORD, AUTOLITE, MOTORCRAFT MODEL 4100 SPECIFICATIONS

Ford Products

Year	(9510)* Carburetor Identification	Dry Float Level (in.) Pri.	Dry Float Level (in.) Sec.	Wet Float Level (in.) Pri.	Wet Float Level (in.) Sec.	Pump Setting Hole	Choke Plate Pulldown (in.)	Fast Idle Cam Linkage (in.)	Fast Idle (rpm)	Dechoke (in.)	Choke Setting	Dashpot (in.)
1969	C8AF-AE	17/32	1 1/16	29/32	1 1/16	3	0.140	0.120	1350	1/16	2 Rich	7/64

* Basic carburetor number

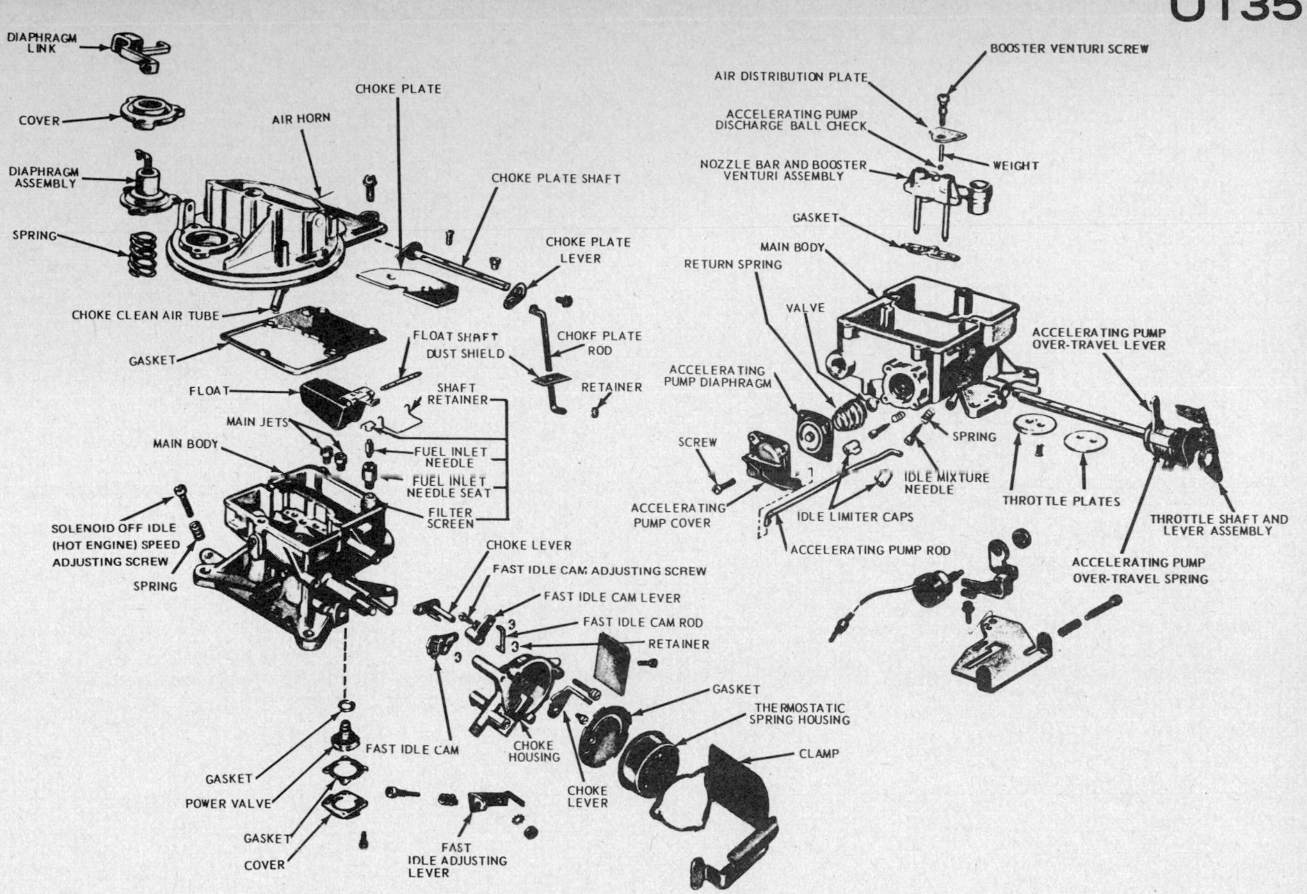

Model 2100D carburetor—disassembled (© Ford Motor Co)

FORD, AUTOLITE, MOTORCRAFT MODELS 2100, 2150 SPECIFICATIONS

American Motors

Year	Carburetor Identification	Dry Float Level (in.)	Wet Float Level (in.)	Pump Setting Hole # ①	Choke Plate Pulldown (in.)	Fast Idle Cam Linkage Clearance (in.)	Fast Idle (rpm)	Dechoke (in)	Choke Setting	Dashpot (in.)
1969	9HM2	1/2	13/16	3	0.125	0.120	1600	0.080	Index	0.140
	9HA2	1/2	13/16	3	0.140	0.120	1600	0.080	Index	0.140
	9ZA2	1/2	13/16	3	0.140	0.120	1600	0.080	Index	0.140
1970	0DA2	3/8	13/16	3	0.300	0.170	1600	0.200	2 Rich	1/8
	0DM2	3/8	13/16	3	0.260	0.170	1600	0.200	Index	1/8
	0RA2	3/8	13/16	3	0.350	0.170	1600	0.200	1 Rich	1/8
1971	1DA2	3/8	13/16	3	0.190	0.170	1600	0.200	2 Rich	1/8
	1DM2	3/8	13/16	3	0.190	0.170	1600	0.200	1 Rich	1/8
	1RA2	3/8	13/16	3	0.190	0.170	1600	0.200	2 Rich	1/8
1972	2DA2	3/8	3/4	3A	0.130	0.120	1600	0.200	2 Rich	9/64
	2DM2	3/8	3/4	3A	0.140	0.130	1600	0.200	1 Rich	7/64
	2RA2	3/8	3/4	3A	0.130	0.120	1600	0.200	2 Rich	—
1973	3DA2	3/8	3/4	3A	0.120	0.110	1600	0.250	2 Rich	—
	3DM2	3/8	3/4	3A	0.130	0.130	1600	0.250	1 Rich	9/64
	3RA2	3/8	3/4	3A	0.120	0.110	1600	0.250	2 Rich	—
1974	4DA2, 4DA2-E	25/64	25/32	3A	0.140	0.130	1600	0.250	1 Rich	—
	4DM2	25/64	25/32	3A	0.130	0.130	1600	0.250	2 Rich	9/64
	4RA2, 4RAC2	25/64	25/32	3A	0.140	0.130	1600	0.250	1 Rich	—
1975	5DA2	13/32	3/4	—	0.140	0.130	1600	0.250	1 Rich	—
	5DMS	13/32	3/4	—	0.130	0.130	1600	0.250	2 Rich	3/32
	5RAS	13/32	3/4	—	0.140	0.130	1600	0.250	1 Rich	—

Ford Products

Year	(9510)* Carburetor Identification	Dry Float Level (in.)	Wet Float Level (in.)	Pump Setting Hole #①	Choke Plate Pulldown (in.)	Fast Idle Cam Linkage Clearance (in.)	Fast Idle (rpm)	Dechoke (in)	Choke Setting	Dashpot (in.)
1969	C8AF-BD	3/8	3/4	2	0.130	0.110	1400	0.060	2 Rich	0.125
	C9AF-A	3/8	3/4	3	0.120	0.110	1400	0.060	Index	0.125
	C9OF-C	31/64	7/8	3	0.120	0.100	1600	0.060	2 Rich	—
	C9ZF-A	9/16	15/16	3	0.150	0.130	1300	0.060	1 Rich	7/64
	C9AF-B	31/64	7/8	2	0.210	0.170	1300	0.060	1 Rich	1/8
	C9AF-C	31/64	7/8	3	0.130	0.100	1500	0.060	2 Rich	1/8
	C9MF-A	31/64	7/8	3	0.150	0.120	1500	0.060	2 Rich	1/8
	C9AF-J	31/64	7/8	3	0.130	0.100	1500	0.060	2 Rich	1/8
1970	D0AF-C	7/16	13/16	3	0.150	0.130	1400	0.060	1 Rich	—
	D0AF-D	7/16	13/16	3	0.150	0.130	1500	0.060	1 Rich	1/8
	D0AF-U	7/16	13/16	3	0.150	0.130	1500	0.060	1 Rich	—
	D0AF-E	7/16	13/16	3	0.230	0.190	1300	0.190	2 Lean	—
	D0AF-F	7/16	13/16	3	0.200	0.170	1600	0.170	2 Lean	1/8
	D0AF-V	7/16	13/16	3	0.200	0.170	1600	0.170	2 Lean	—
	D0OF-K	7/16	13/16	3	0.220	0.190	1500	0.190	Index	—
	D0OF-L	7/16	13/16	3	0.190	0.130	1500	0.130	1 Rich	1/8
	D0OF-M	7/16	13/16	3	0.190	0.130	1500	0.130	1 Rich	—
1971	D1YF-DA	7/16	13/16	3	0.200	0.160	1500	0.060	Index	—
	D1MF-JA	7/16	13/16	3	0.190	0.160	1500	0.060	1 Rich	1/8
	D1MF-FA	7/16	13/16	3	0.200	0.160	1500	0.060	1 Rich	1/8
1972	D2AF-FB	7/16	13/16	3	0.140	0.130	1500	0.030	Index	1/8
	D2AF-GB	7/16	13/16	3	0.140	0.130	1500	0.030	Index	1/8
	D2AF-HA	7/16	13/16	2	0.150	0.130	1400	0.060	1 Rich	1/8
	D2GF-AA	7/16	13/16	2	0.150	0.130	1400	0.060	1 Rich	1/8
	D2GF-BA	7/16	13/16	2	0.150	0.130	1400	0.060	1 Rich	—
	D2MF-FB	7/16	13/16	4	0.180	0.150	1500	0.060	1 Rich	—
	D2OF-KA	7/16	13/16	2	0.150	0.130	1400	0.060	1 Rich	—
	D2OF-VB	7/16	13/16	3	0.190	0.160	1400	0.030	2 Rich	—
	D2WF-CA	7/16	13/16	3	0.190	0.160	1400	0.030	2 Rich	—
	D2ZF-FA	7/16	13/16	2	0.150	0.130	1400	0.060	1 Rich	—
	D2ZF-LA	7/16	13/16	3	0.240	0.210	1500	0.030	1 Rich	—
1973	D3AF-CE	7/16	13/16	3A	②	②	1500	②	1 Rich	—
	D3AF-DC	7/16	13/16	3A	②	②	1500	②	3 Rich	—
	D3GF-AF	7/16	13/16	2A	②	②	1400	②	3 Rich	—
	D3GF-BB	7/16	13/16	2A	②	②	1250	②	3 Rich	—
	D3ZF-EA	7/16	13/16	2A	②	②	1400	②	1 Rich	—
	D3AF-KA	7/16	13/16	3A	②	②	1500	②	3 Rich	—
	D3MF-AE	7/16	13/16	3A	②	②	1500	②	3 Rich	—
	D3MF-BA	7/16	13/16	3A	②	②	1500	②	3 Rich	—
1974	D4AE-DA	7/16	13/16	2A	②	②	1500	②	1 Rich	—
	D4AE-EA	7/16	13/16	2A	②	②	1500	②	3 Rich	—
	D4AE-FA	7/16	13/16	3A	②	②	1500	②	3 Rich	—
	D4AE-GA	7/16	13/16	3A	②	②	1500	②	3 Rich	—
	D4DE-LA	7/16	13/16	2A	②	②	1500	②	3 Rich	—
	D4DE-RB	7/16	13/16	2A	②	②	1500	②	3 Rich	—
	D4OE-FA	7/16	13/16	2A	②	②	1500	②	3 Rich	—
	D4AE-HB	7/16	13/16	3A	②	②	1500	②	3 Rich	—
	D4DE-NB	7/16	13/16	2	②	②	1500	②	3 Rich	—
	D4DE-PA	7/16	13/16	2	②	②	1500	②	3 Rich	—

Ford Products (con't.)

Year	(9510)* Carburetor Identification	Dry Float Level (in.)	Wet Float Level (in.)	Pump Setting Hole #①	Choke Plate Pulldown (in.)	Fast Idle Cam Linkage Clearance (in.)	Fast Idle (rpm)	Dechoke (in)	Choke Setting	Dashpot (in.)
	D40E-CA	7/16	13/16	2	②	②	1500	②	3 Rich	—
	D4ME-BA	7/16	13/16	3A	②	②	1500	②	3 Rich	—
	D4ME-CA	7/16	13/16	3A	②	②	1500	②	3 Rich	—
1975	D5ZE-AC	3/8	3/4	2	0.145	②	1500	②	2 Rich	—
	D5ZE-BC	3/8	3/4	2	0.145	②	1500	②	2 Rich	—
	D5ZE-CC	3/8	3/4	3	0.145	②	1500	②	2 Rich	—
	D5ZE-DC	3/8	3/4	2	0.145	②	1500	②	2 Rich	—
	D5DE-AA	7/16	13/16	2	0.140	②	1500	②	3 Rich	—
	D5DE-BA	7/16	13/16	2	0.140	②	1500	②	3 Rich	—
	D5DE-JA	7/16	13/16	2	0.140	②	1500	②	3 Rich	—
	D5ZE-JA	7/16	13/16	2	0.140	②	1500	②	3 Rich	—
	D50E-AA	7/16	13/16	2	0.140	②	1500	②	3 Rich	—
	D50E-DA	7/16	13/16	2	0.140	②	1500	②	3 Rich	—
	D5DE-HA	7/16	13/16	3	0.140	②	1500	②	3 Rich	—
	D5DE-UA	7/16	13/16	2	0.140	②	1500	②	3 Rich	—
	D50E-BA	7/16	13/16	3	0.125	②	1500	②	3 Rich	—
	D50E-CA	7/16	13/16	3	0.125	②	1500	②	3 Rich	—
	D50E-GA	7/16	13/16	2	0.125	②	1500	②	3 Rich	—
	D5AE-AA	7/16	13/16	3	0.125	②	1500	②	3 Rich	—
	D5AE-EA	7/16	13/16	3	0.125	②	1500	②	3 Rich	—
	D5ME-BA	7/16	13/16	2	0.125	②	1500	②	3 Rich	—
	D5ME-FA	7/16	13/16	2	0.125	②	1500	②	3 Rich	—

* Basic carburetor number for Ford products
① With link in inboard hole of pump lever
② Electric choke; see procedure in text

Model 5200

The 5200 carburetor is a two-stage, two-venturi carburetor in which the secondary venturi is the larger. The secondary system is mechanically operated. It is used with 2000, 2300 and 2800 cc Pinto, Bobcat and Mustang II engines.

Fast Idle Cam

1. Insert a 5/32 in. drill between the lower edge of the choke plate and the air horn wall.

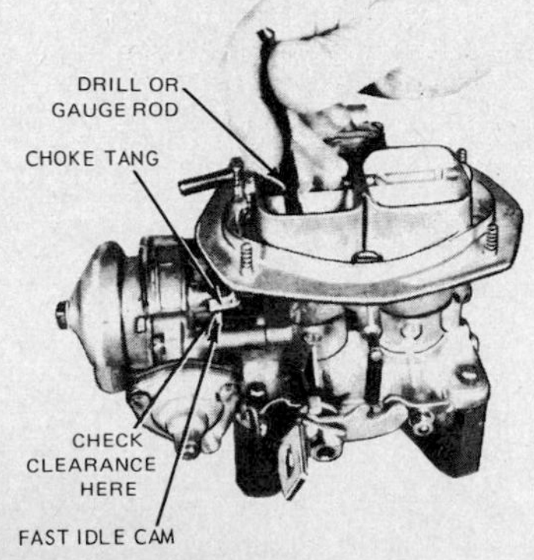

Fast idle cam adjustment
(© Ford Motor Co)

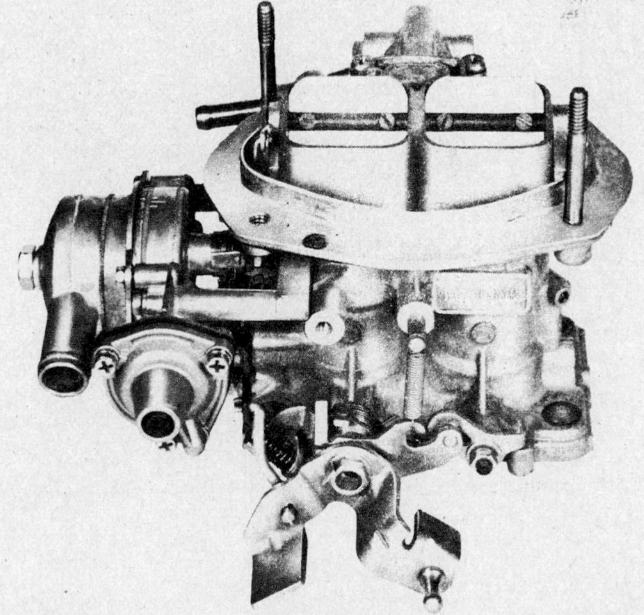
Model 5200 carburetor
(© Ford Motor Co)

2. With the fast idle screw held on the second step of the fast idle cam, measure the clearance between the tang of the choke lever and the arm on the fast idle cam.
3. Bend the choke lever tang to adjust it if it is not up to specification.

Choke Plate Pulldown

1. Remove the choke thermostatic spring cover.
2. Pull the water cover and the thermostatic spring cover assembly out of the way.
3. Set the fast idle cam on the high step.
4. Push the diaphragm stem against its stop and insert the specified gauge between the lower edge of the choke valve and the air horn wall.
5. Apply sufficient pressure to the upper edge of the choke valve to take up any slack in the choke linkage.
6. Turn the adjusting screw in or out to adjust the choke plate-to-air horn clearance.

Dechoke (Unloader) Adjustment

1. Hold the throttle in the wide open position.

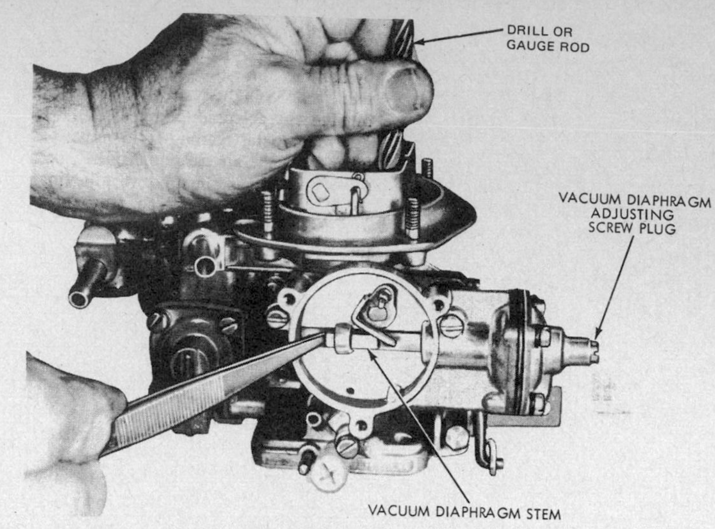

Choke plate pulldown adjustment
(© Ford Motor Co)

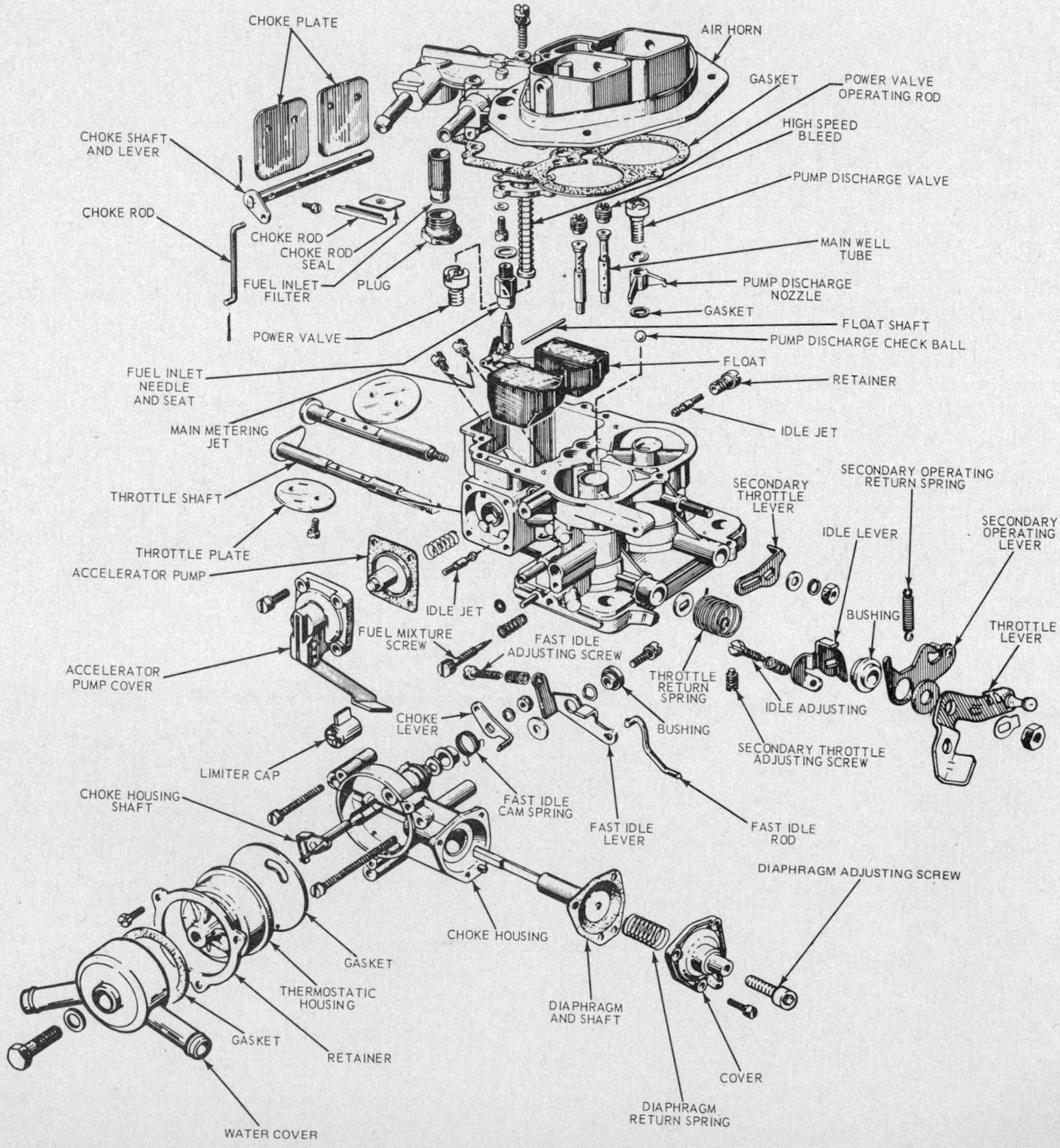

Model 5200 carburetor—exploded view (© Ford Motor Co)

2. Remove any slack from the choke linkage by applying pressure to the upper edge of the choke valve.
3. Measure the distance from the lower edge of the choke valve to the air horn wall.
4. Make adjustments by bending the tab on the fast idle lever where it touches the fast idle cam.

Fast Idle

Set the fast idle speed with the fast idle screw positioned on the second step of the fast idle cam and with the engine at operating temperature.

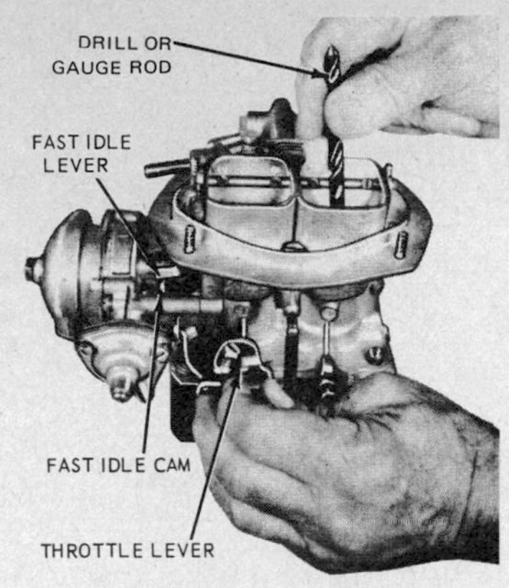

Dechoke adjustment
(© Ford Motor Co)

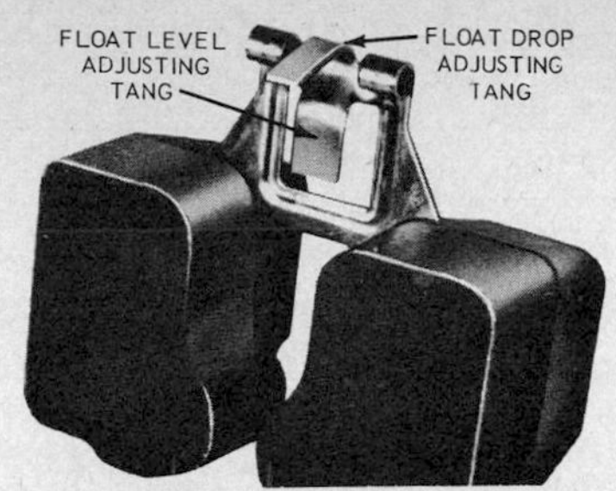

Float adjustment
(© Ford Motor Co)

Float Level Adjustment

With the bowl cover held upside down and the float tang resting

FORD, AUTOLITE, MOTORCRAFT MODEL 5200 SPECIFICATIONS

Year	(9510)* Carburetor Identification	Dry Float Level (in.)	Pump Hole Setting	Choke Plate Pulldown (in.)	Fast Idle Cam Linkage (in.)	Fast Idle (rpm)	Dechoke (in.)	Choke Setting	Dashpot
1971	D12F-AA	0.420	Lower	0.236	0.010	1800	0.256	Index	—
	D12F-BA	0.420	Lower	0.236	0.010	1600	0.256	Index	—
	D12F-CA	0.420	Lower	0.236	0.010	1800	0.256	Index	—
	D12F-DA	0.420	Lower	0.236	0.010	1800	0.256	1 Rich	—
	D12F-EA	0.420	Lower	0.236	0.010	1600	0.256	1 Rich	—
	D12F-FA	0.420	Lower	0.236	0.010	1800	0.256	1 Rich	—
1972	D22F-AB	0.420	3	0.236	0.156	1800	0.256	1 Lean	—
	D22F-BB	0.420	2	0.236	0.079	1600	0.256	1 Lean	—
	D22F-CB	0.420	3	0.236	0.156	1800	0.256	1 Lean	—
	D22F-DB	0.420	2	0.236	0.079	1600	0.256	1 Lean	—
	D22F-EA	0.420	3	0.236	0.156	1800	0.256	Index	—
	D22F-GA	0.420	3	0.236	0.156	1800	0.256	Index	—
1973	D32F-CA	0.420	2	0.158	0.158	1800	0.256	Index	—
	D32F-BD	0.420	2	0.158	0.118	1600	0.256	1 Lean	—
1974	D42E-AA	0.460	2	0.280	0.158	1800	0.255	Index	—
	D42E-BA	0.460	2	0.280	0.158	1800	0.255	1 Rich	—
	D42F-EA	0.460	2	0.236	0.158	1800	0.255	Index	—
	D42F-GA	0.460	2	0.236	0.158	1800	0.255	Index	—
	D4ZE-CA	0.430	2	0.195	0.195	1800	0.256	1 Rich	—
	D4ZE-BC	0.430	2	0.195	0.195	1800	0.255	1 Rich	—
	D4ZE-DC	0.430	2	0.195	0.195	1800	0.255	1 Rich	—
	D42E-EB	0.460	2	0.158	0.158	1800	0.255	Index	—
	D42E-CD	0.460	2	0.280	0.158	1800	0.255	Index	—
	D42E-AC	0.460	2	0.280	0.158	1800	0.255	Index	—
	D42E-KA	0.460	2	0.280	0.158	1800	0.255	1 Rich	—
1975	D52E-AA	0.460	2	0.200	0.100	1800	0.260	1 Lean	—
	D52E-BA	0.460	2	0.200	0.100	1800	0.260	1 Lean	—
	D52E-CA	0.460	2	0.200	0.100	1800	0.260	1 Lean	—
	D52E-DB	0.460	2	0.200	0.100	1800	0.260	1 Lean	—
	D5ZE-EA	0.460	2	0.200	0.100	1800	0.260	1 Lean	—
	D5ZE-FA	0.460	2	0.200	0.100	1800	0.260	1 Lean	—
	D5ZE-GA	0.460	2	0.200	0.100	1800	0.260	1 Lean	—
	D5ZE-HB	0.460	2	0.200	0.100	1800	0.260	1 Lean	—

* Basic carburetor number

lightly on the spring loaded fuel inlet needle, measure the clearance between the edge of the float and the bowl cover. To adjust the level, bend the float tang up or down as required. Adjust both floats equally.

Secondary Throttle Stop Screw

1. Turn the secondary throttle stop screw counterclockwise until the secondary throttle plate seats in its bore.
2. Turn the screw clockwise until it touches the tab on the secondary throttle lever.
3. Add ¼ turn clockwise and the stop is adjusted.

Model 4300, 4350

The model 4300 and 4350 4 barrel carburetor is composed of three main assemblies: the air horn, the main body, and the throttle body. The air horn assembly serves as the fuel bowl cover as well as the housing for the choke valve and shaft. It contains the accelerator pump linkage, fuel inlet seat, float and lever, booster venturi, and internal fuel bowl vents.

The main body houses the fuel metering passages, accelerator pump mechanism, and the power valve.

The throttle body contains the primary and secondary throttle valves and shafts, the curb idle adjusting screw, the fast idle adjusting screw, the idle mixture adjusting screws, and the automatic choke assembly.

Float Adjustment

1. Adjustments to the fuel level are best made with the carburetor removed from the engine and the carburetor cleaned upon disassembly.
2. Invert the air horn assembly and remove the gasket from the surface.
3. Use a T-scale to measure the distance from the floats to the air horn casting. Position the scale horizontally over the flat surface of both floats at the free ends and parallel to the air horn casting. Hold the lower end of the vertical scale in full contact with the smooth surface of the air horn.

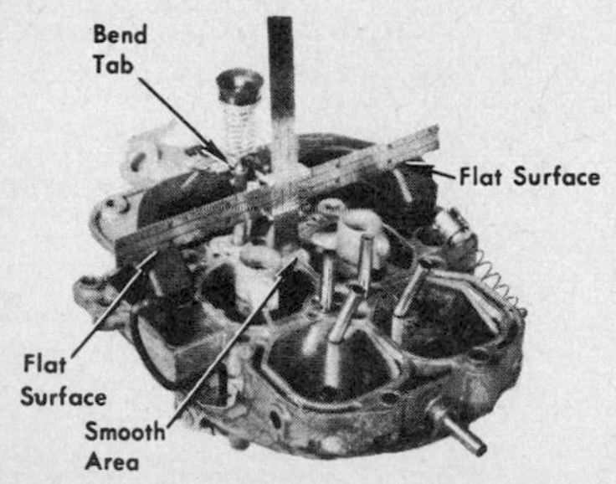

Checking float level using a T-scale
(© American Motors Co)

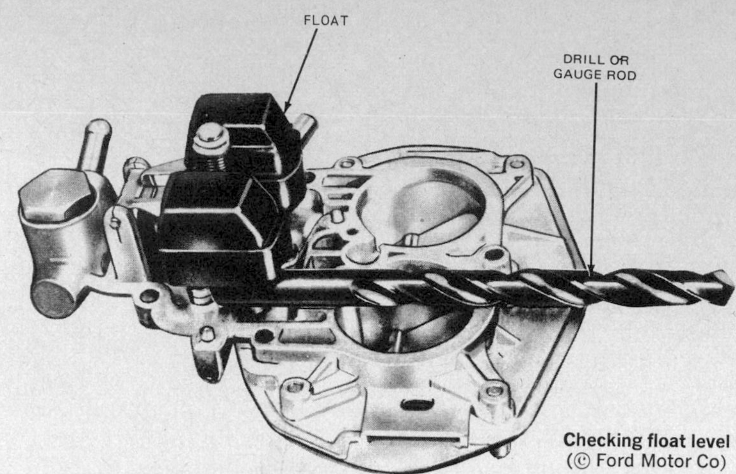

Checking float level
(© Ford Motor Co)

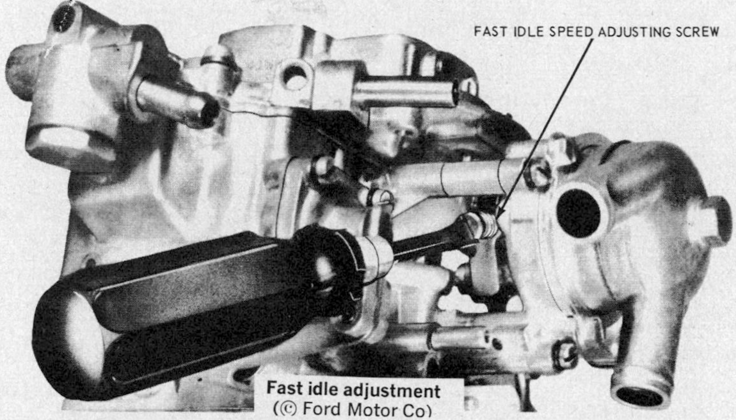

Fast idle adjustment
(© Ford Motor Co)

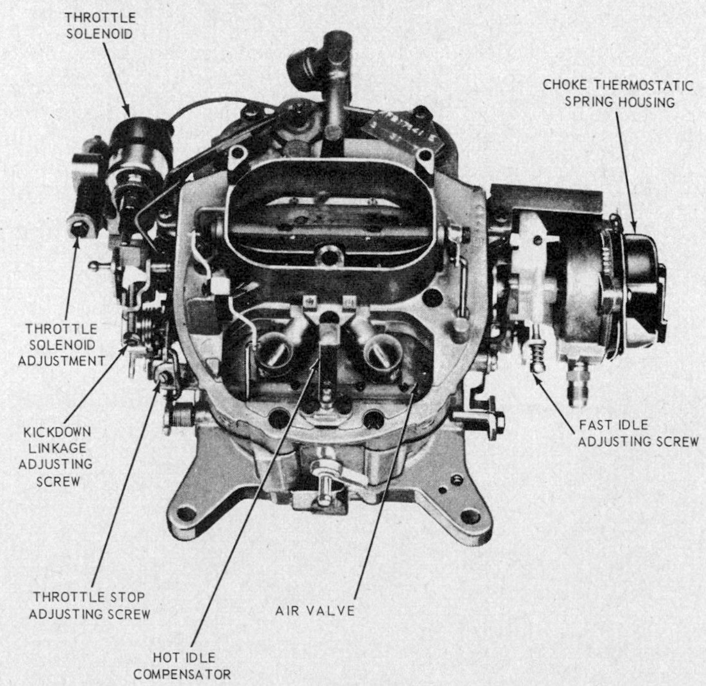

Top view—Model 4300 carburetor
(© Ford Motor Co)

Caution The end of the vertical scale must not come into contact with any gasket sealing ridges while measuring the float level.

4. The free end of each float should just touch the horizontal scale, if one float is lower than the other; twist the float and lever assembly slightly to correct.

5. Adjust the float level by bending the tab which contacts the needle and seat assembly.

NOTE: The illustrations in this section show an alternate method of adjusting the floats on the model 4300 carburetor.

The procedure includes the fabrication of a gauge and a bending device. After fabricating the gauge, it is possible to adjust it to the specified dimensions and insert it into the air horn outboard holes. Both pontoons should just touch the gauge.

A float tab bending tool is also shown and may be used in the following manner.

To raise the float: insert the open end of the bending tool to the RIGHT side of the float lever tab and between the needle and float hinge. Raise the float lever off of the needle and bend the tab downward.

To lower the float: insert the bending tool to the LEFT side of the float lever tab between the needle and float hinge, support the float lever, and bend the tab upward.

Choke Plate Pulldown

1. Remove the air cleaner and choke thermostatic spring housing.
2. Bend a wire gauge (0.036 in. diameter) at a 90 degree angle about 1/8 in. from one end.
3. Block the throttle open so that the fast idle screw does not contact the fast idle cam.
4. Insert the bent end of the wire gauge between the lower edge of the piston slot and the upper edge of the right hand slot in the choke housing.
5. Pull the choke piston lever counterclockwise until the gauge is snug in the piston slot. Hold the wire in place by exerting light pressure in a rearward direction on the choke piston lever. Check the distance from the lower edge of the choke valve to the air horn wall.
6. Adjustment is done by loosening the hex head screw (left-hand thread) on the choke valve shaft and prying the link away from the shaft. Use a drill gauge 0.010 in. under the specified clearance between the lower edge of the choke valve and the air horn wall. Hold the choke valve against the gauge and maintain a light rearward pressure on the choke lever.
7. With the choke piston snug against the 0.036 in. wire and the choke valve against the drill, tighten the hex screw on the choke valve shaft. The use of a gauge 0.010 in. undersize compensates for tolerance in the linkage.
8. Use the correct size gauge for

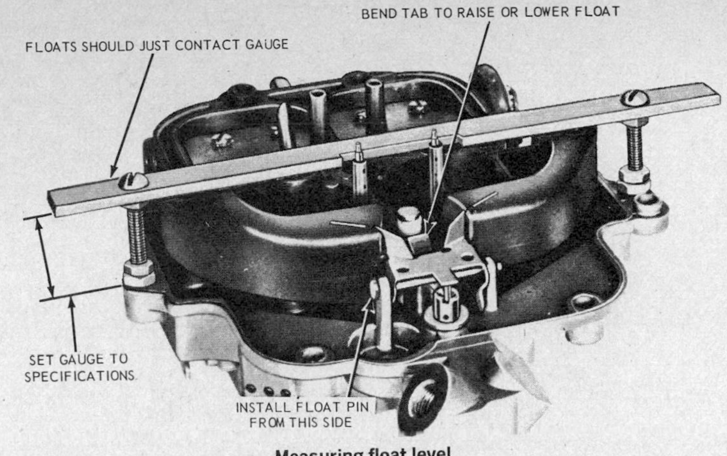

Measuring float level
(© Ford Motor Co)

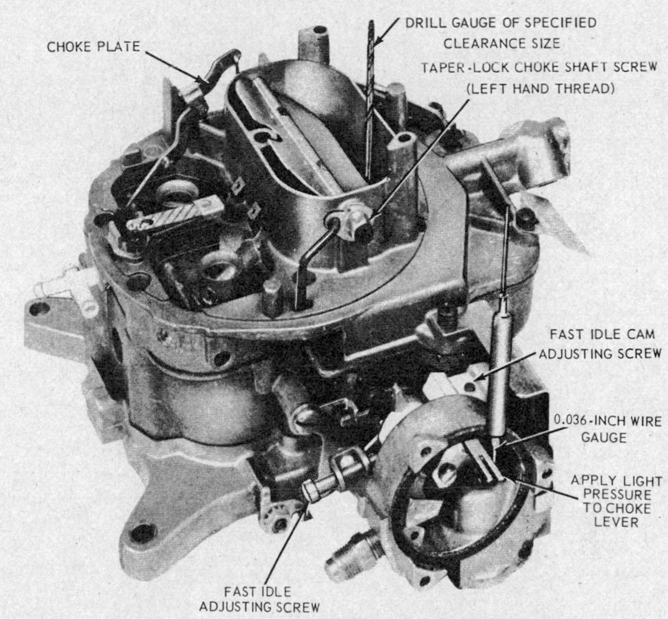

Choke plate pulldown and fast idle cam adjustment
(© Ford Motor Co)

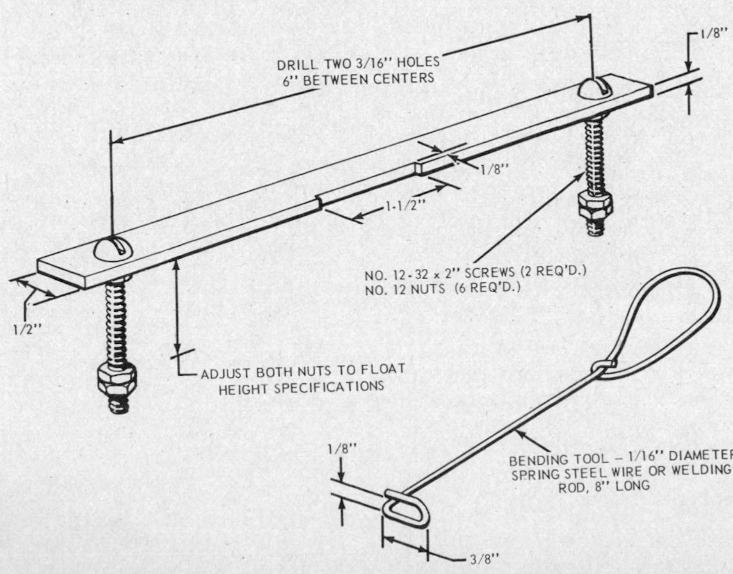

Construction of float level gauge and float arm bending tool
(© Ford Motor Co)

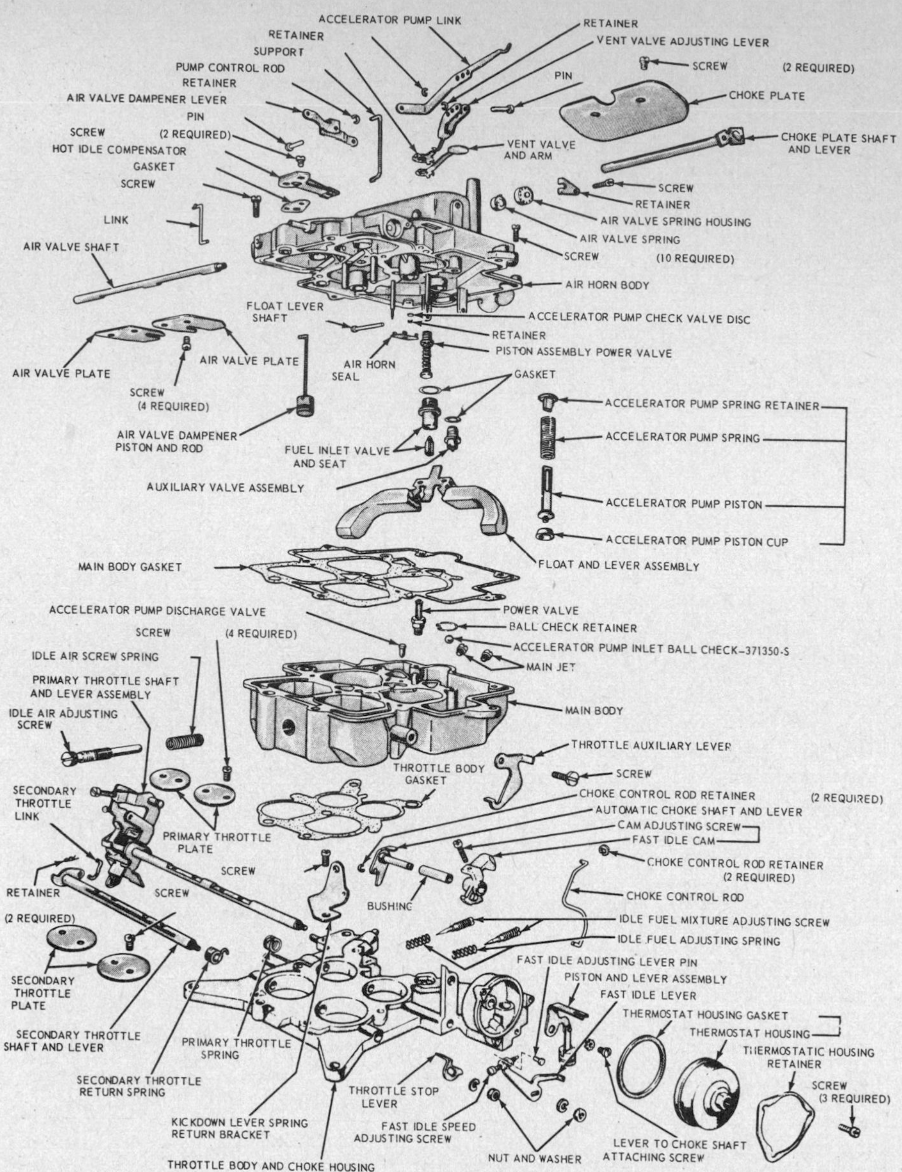

Model 4300 carburetor—disassembled
(© Ford Motor Co)

final measurement.

9. Replace the housing on the thermostatic spring.

Fast Idle Cam Adjustment

1. Loosen the screws on the choke thermostatic spring cover and rotate the housing ¼ turn counter clockwise. Tighten the screws.
2. Open the throttle and allow the choke valve to close completely.
3. Push down on the fast idle cam counterweight until the fast idle screw is in contact with the second step of the cam and against the high step.
4. Measure the clearance between the lower edge of the choke plate and the air horn wall.
5. Adjust by turning the fast idle cam adjusting screw (inward to increase clearance, outward to decrease clearance).
6. Return the housing on the thermostatic spring to its original position.

Choke Unloader (Dechoke) Adjustment

1. Open the throttle fully and hold it in this position.
2. Rotate the choke plate toward the closed position until the pawl on the fast idle speed lever contacts the fast idle cam.
3. Check the clearance between the lower edge of the choke plate and the air horn wall.
4. Adjust by bending the pawl on the fast idle speed lever forward to increase the clearance and backward to decrease the clearance.

Accelerator Pump Stroke Adjustment

Model 4300 through 1974

The accelerator pump should not need adjustment as its stroke is preset in compliance with exhaust emission control standards. If for any reason the stroke must be altered, it may be done by repositioning the external

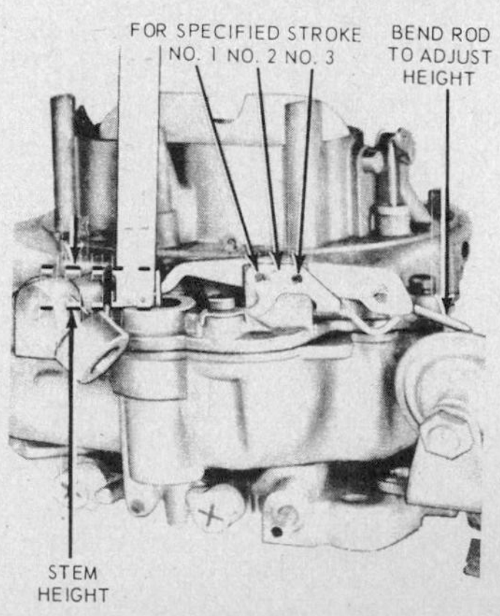

Accelerator pump adjustment
(© Ford Motor Co)

link in the desired holes.

Model 4350 beginning 1975

The accelerator pump adjustment is preset at the factory for reduced exhaust emissions. Adjustment is provided only for different engine installations. The adjustment is internal, with three piston-to-shaft pin positions in the pump piston.

To check that the shaft pin is located in the specified piston hole, remove the carburetor air horn and invert it. Disconnect the accelerator pump from the operating arm by pressing downward on the spring and sliding the arm out of the pump shaft slot. Disassemble the spring and nylon keeper retaining the adjustment pin. If the pin is not in its specified hole, remove it, reposition the shaft to the correct hole in the piston assembly and reinstall the pin. Then, slide the nylon retainer over the pin and position the spring on the shaft. Finally, compress the

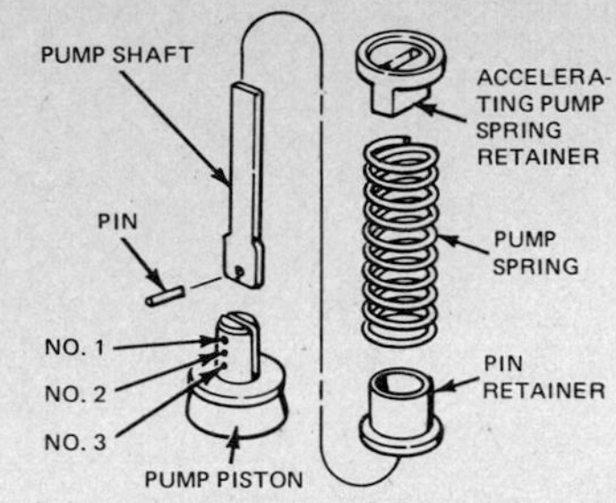

Accelerator Pump stroke adjustment—-Motorcraft 4350-4V

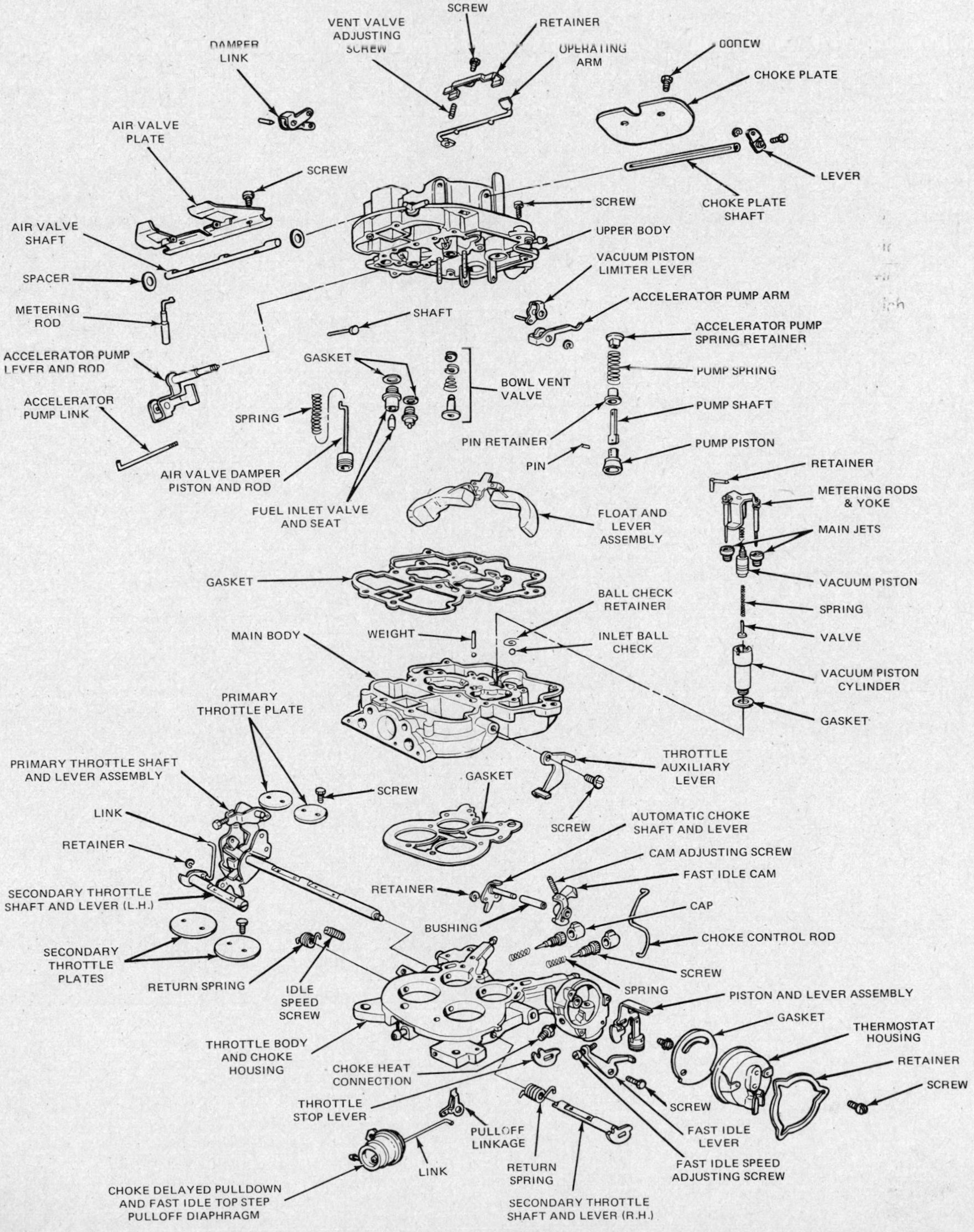

Exploded view—Motorcraft 4350-4V

spring on the shaft and install the pump on the pump arm.

NOTE: *Under no circumstances should you adjust the stroke of the accelerator pump by turning the vacuum limiter lever adjusting nut. This adjustment is preset at the factory and modification could result in poor cold driveability.*

Fast idle adjustment
(© Ford Motor Co)

Fast Idle Speed

The fast idle speed is adjusted with the engine at operating temperature and the fast idle screw on the second step of the fast idle cam. Adjust by turning the fast idle screw in or out as required.

FORD, AUTOLITE, MOTORCRAFT MODELS 4300, 4350 SPECIFICATIONS

Year	(9510)* Carburetor Identification①	Dry Float Level (in.)	Pump Setting Hole	Choke Plate Pulldown (in.)	Fast Idle Cam Linkage (in.)	Fast Idle (rpm)	Dechoke (in.)	Choke Setting	Dashpot (in.)
American Motors									
1970	0WA4	13/16	Center	0.170	0.190	1600	0.300	2 Rich	1/8
	0WM4	13/16	Center	0.190	0.200	1600	0.300	2 Rich	1/16
1971	1TA4	13/16	Center	0.190	0.200	1600	0.300	Index	1/8
	1TM4	13/16	Center	0.170	0.190	1600	0.300	Index	1/16
1972	2RA4	13/16	Center	0.190	0.190	1600	0.300	1 Rich	9/64
	2TA4	13/16	Center	0.190	0.190	1600	0.300	1 Rich	9/64
	2TM4	13/16	Center	0.190	0.190	1600	0.300	1 Rich	9/64
1973	3TA4	13/16	Center	0.190	0.160	1600	0.275	2 Rich	9/64
	3TA4 (Police)	15/16	Center	0.190	0.160	1600	0.275	2 Rich	9/64
	3TM4	13/16	Center	0.190	0.160	1600	0.275	2 Rich	9/64
1974	4TA4, 4TM4	13/16	Center	0.170	0.160	1600	0.325	2 Rich	9/64
1975	5TA4	0.90		0.140	0.160	1600	0.325	2 Rich	—
Ford Products									
1969	C8SF-H	25/32	2	0.230	0.160	1300	0.300	—	3/32
	C8VF-J	25/32	2	0.230	0.160	1300	0.300	—	3/32
	C9AF-G	25/32	2	0.270	0.220	1200	0.300	—	3/32
	C9AF-R	25/32	2	0.230	0.160	1300	0.300	—	—
	C9OF-D	13/16	2	0.160	0.100	1400	0.300	—	—
	C9OF-E	13/16	3	0.250	0.230	1400	0.300	—	—
	C9ZF-C	13/16	2	0.170	0.130	1250	0.300	—	3/32
	C9ZF-D	13/16	2	0.160	0.100	1400	0.300	—	—
	C9ZF-E	13/16	3	0.230	0.210	1300	0.300	—	1/8
	C9ZF-F	13/16	3	0.250	0.230	1400	0.300	—	—
1970	DOAF-K	49/64	2	0.220	0.170	1300	0.300	Index	0.070
	DOAF-L	25/32	2	0.250	0.220	1400	0.300	Index	0.070
	DOAF-M	1.00	3	0.160	0.120	1600	0.300	2 Rich	0.080
	DOAF-R	1.00	3	0.160	0.120	1600	0.300	2 Rich	—
	DOAF-AD	1.00	3	0.160	0.120	1600	0.300	2 Rich	0.080
	DOAF-AJ	1.00	3	0.160	0.120	1600	0.300	2 Rich	0.080
	DOAF-AE	1.00	3	0.160	0.120	1600	0.300	2 Rich	—
	DOAF-AK	1.00	3	0.160	0.120	1600	0.300	2 Rich	—
	DOAF-AB	25/32	2	0.250	0.220	1400	0.300	Index	0.070
	DOAF-AL	25/32	2	0.250	0.220	1400	0.300	Index	0.070
	DOAF-AG	25/32	2	0.220	0.170	1300	0.300	Index	0.070

Ford Products (con't.)

Year	(9510)* Carburetor Identification①	Dry Float Level (in.)	Pump Setting Hole	Choke Plate Pulldown (in.)	Fast Idle Cam Linkage (in.)	Fast Idle (rpm)	Dechoke (in.)	Choke Setting	Dashpot (in.)
	D0AF-AM	25/32	2	0.220	0.170	1300	0.300	Index	0.070
	D0AF-AN	49/64	2	0.225	0.170	1350	0.300	Index	0.070
	D0OF-B	13/16	2	0.180	0.160	1250	0.300	Index	—
	D0OF-C	13/16	2	0.200	0.180	1400	0.300	Index	0.080
	D0OF-D	13/16	2	0.180	0.160	1250	0.300	Index	—
	D0OF-H	13/16	2	0.200	0.180	1400	0.300	Index	—
	D0OF-Y	13/16	2	0.180	0.160	1250	0.300	Index	—
	D0OF-Z	13/16	2	0.180	0.160	1250	0.300	Index	—
	D0OF-AA	13/16	2	0.200	0.180	1400	0.300	Index	—
	D0OF-AB	13/16	2	0.180	0.160	1250	0.300	Index	—
	D0OF-AC	13/16	2	0.200	0.180	1400	0.300	Index	0.080
	D0OF-AD	13/16	2	0.200	0.180	1400	0.300	Index	—
	D0OF-AE	13/16	2	0.180	0.160	1250	0.300	Index	—
	D0SF-A	25/32	2	0.220	0.170	1300	0.300	Index	0.070
	D0SF-D	25/32	2	0.220	0.170	1300	0.300	Index	0.070
	D0SF-E	25/32	2	0.220	0.170	1300	0.300	Index	0.070
	D0VF-A	25/32	2	0.230	0.170	1250	0.300	Index	0.100
1971	D1AF-MA	49/64	2	0.220	—	1350	—	Index	1/16
	D10F-EA	13/16	2	0.180	0.160	1250	—	Index	—
	D10F-AAA	13/16	2	0.200	0.180	1400	—	Index	—
	D1SF-AA	49/64	2	0.220	—	1350	—	Index	1/16
	D1VF-AA	49/64	2	0.220	0.170	1250	—	1 Rich	0.100
1972	D2AF-AA	49/64	1	0.220	0.200	1350	—	2 Rich	—
	D2AF-LA	49/64	1	0.215	0.190	1900	—	2 Rich	—
	D2SF-AA	49/64	1	0.220	0.200	1350	—	2 Rich	—
	D2SF-BA	49/64	1	0.220	0.200	1350	—	2 Rich	—
	D2VF-AA	49/64	1	0.230	0.200	1250	—	Index	—
	D2VF-BA	49/64	1	0.230	0.200	1250	—	Index	—
	D2ZF-AA	13/16	1	0.200	0.180	1200	—	Index	—
	D2ZF-BB	13/16	1	0.200	0.200	1200	—	Index	—
	D2ZF-DA	13/16	1	0.200	0.200	1200	—	Index	—
	D2ZF-GA	13/16	1	0.200	0.180	1200	—	Index	—
1973	D3VF-DA	0.76	1	0.210	0.190	1350	—	Index	—
	D3ZF-AC	0.82	1	0.180	0.180	1300	—	Index	—
	D3ZF-BC	0.82	1	0.170	0.170	1300	—	INR	—
	D3ZF-DC	0.82	1	0.180	0.180	1300	—	Index	—
	D3AF-HA	0.76	1	0.210	0.200	1350	—	Index	—
	D3AF-EB	0.88	1	0.200	0.200	1900	—	Index	—
1974	D4AE-AA	3/4	1	0.230	0.200	1900	—	Index	—
	D4AE-NA, D4VE-AB	3/4	1	0.220	0.200	1250	—	Index	—
	D4TE-ATA	13/16	1	0.220	0.180	1250	—	Index	—
	D40E-AA	13/16	1	0.180	0.180	1800	—	Index	—
1975	D5VE-AD	15/16	1	②	0.160	1600	0.300	2 Rich	—
	D5VE-BA	15/16	1	②	0.160	1600	0.300	2 Rich	—
	D5AE-CA	31/32	1	②	0.160	1600	0.300	2 Rich	—
	D5AE-DA	31/32	1	②	0.160	1600	0.300	2 Rich	—

* Basic carburetor number for Ford products.

① The identification tag is on the bowl cover.

② Initial—0.160 in.
Delayed—0.190 in.

Rochester Carburetors

Model MV

The model MV carburetor is a single bore, down-draft carburetor with an aluminum throttle body, automatic choke, internally balanced venting, and a hot idle compensating system for cars equipped with automatic transmissions. Newer models are also equipped with Combination Emission Control valves (C.E.C.) and an Exhaust Gas Recirculation (EGR) system. An electrically operated idle stop solenoid replaces the idle stop screw of older models.

The MV carburetor is used on General Motors four and six cylinder cars from 1968 and service procedures apply to all MV carburetors.

Choke Rod (fast idle cam) Adjustment

NOTE: Adjust the fast idle before making choke rod adjustments.

1. Place the fast idle cam follower on the second step of the fast idle cam and hold it firmly against the rise to the high step.
2. Rotate the choke valve in the direction of a closed choke by applying force to the choke coil lever.
3. Bend the choke rod, at the point shown in the illustration, to give the specified opening between the lower edge of the choke valve and the inside air horn wall.

NOTE: Measurement must be made at the center of the choke valve.

uum break diaphragm until the plunger is fully seated.

3. When the plunger is seated, push the choke valve toward the closed position.
4. Holding the choke valve in this position, place the specified gauge between the lower edge of the choke valve and the air horn wall.
5. If the measurement is not correct, bend the vacuum break rod at the point shown in the illustration.

Choke Auxiliary Vacuum Break Adjustment (beginning 1975)

This adjustment is required in addition to the preceding vacuum break adjustment, beginning 1975.

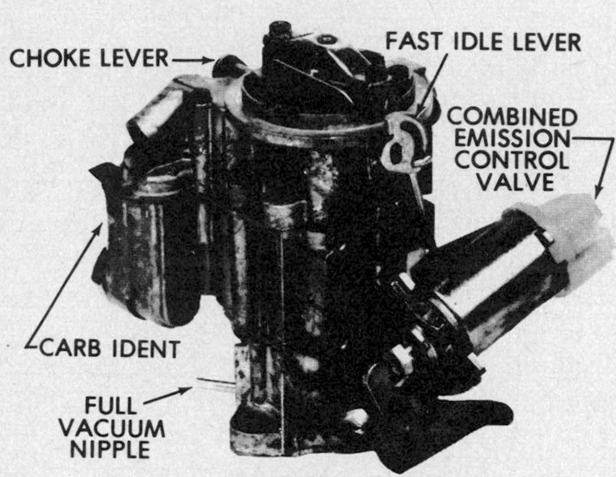

Rochester Monojet Carburetor
(© Buick Div., G.M. Corp)

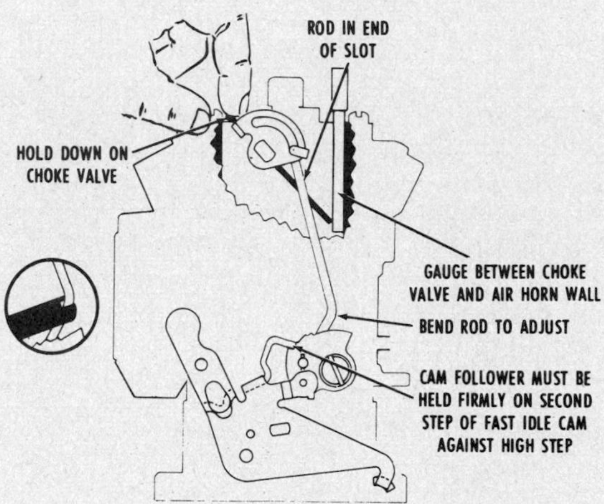

Fast Idle Cam Adjustment
(© Chevrolet Div., G.M. Corp)

Fast Idle Adjustment

NOTE: The fast idle adjustment must be made with the transmission in Neutral.

1. Position the fast idle lever on the high step of the fast idle cam.
2. Be sure that the choke is properly adjusted and in the wide open position with the engine warm.
3. Bend the fast idle lever until the specified speed is obtained.

Choke Vacuum Break Adjustment

The adjustment of the vacuum break diaphragm unit insures correct choke valve opening after engine starting.

1. Remove the air cleaner on vehicles with Therm AC air cleaner; plug the sensor's vacuum take off port.
2. Using an external vacuum source, apply vacuum to the vac-

1. Using an external source of vacuum, apply vacuum to the auxiliary vacuum break diaphram until the plunger is seated fully.
2. Place the cam follower on the highest step of the fast idle cam.
3. With the diaphragm seated, insert the specified gauge between the upper edge of the choke valve and the inner air horn wall.
4. To adjust the clearance, bend the link between the vacuum

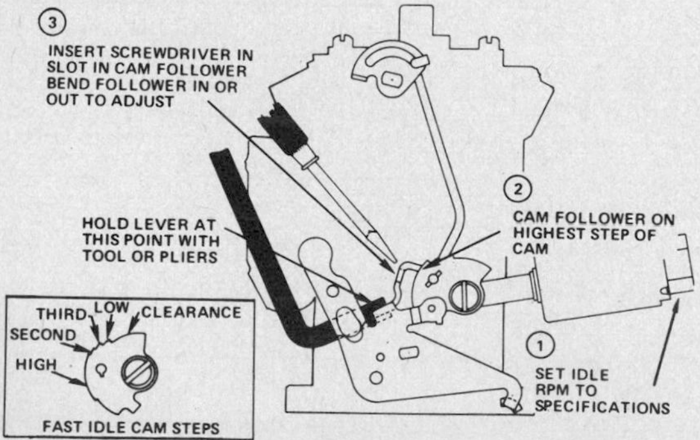

Fast Idle Adjustment
(© Chevrolet Div., G.M. Corp)

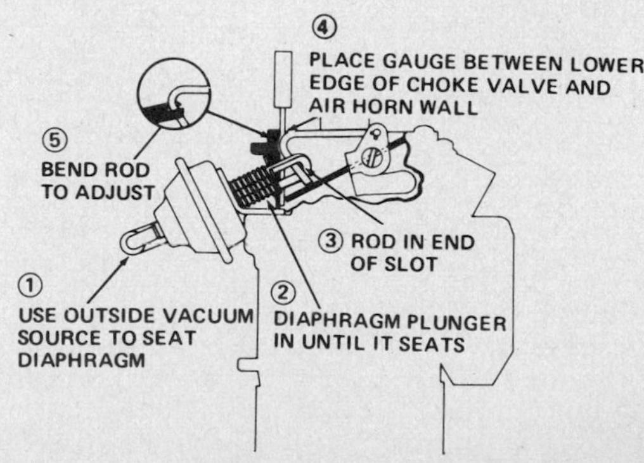

Vacuum Break Adjustment
(© Chevrolet Div., G.M. Corp)

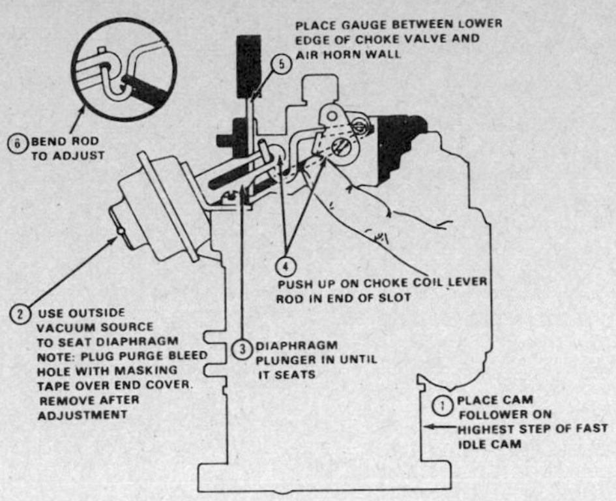

Primary vacuum break adjustment, beginning 1975

(© Chevrolet Div., G.M. Corp.)

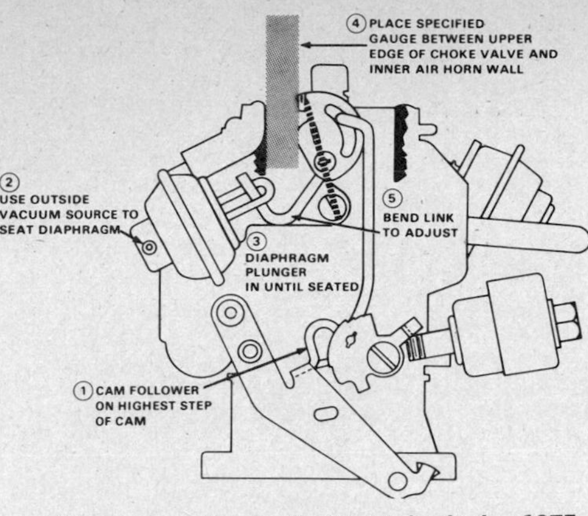

Auxiliary vacuum break adjustment, beginning 1975

(© Chevrolet Div., G.M. Corp.)

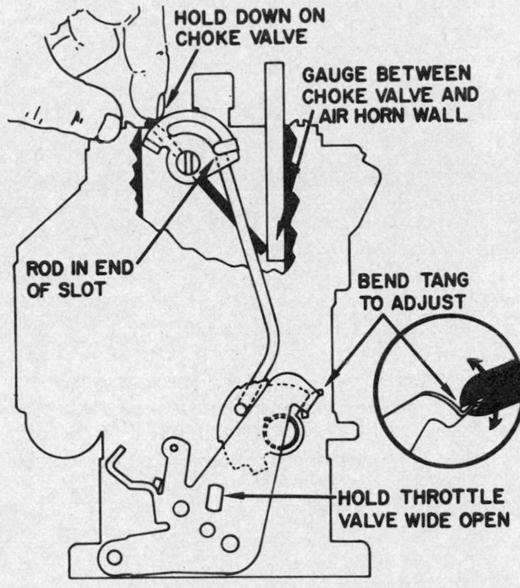

Adjusting Choke Unloader
(© Chevrolet Div., G.M. Corp)

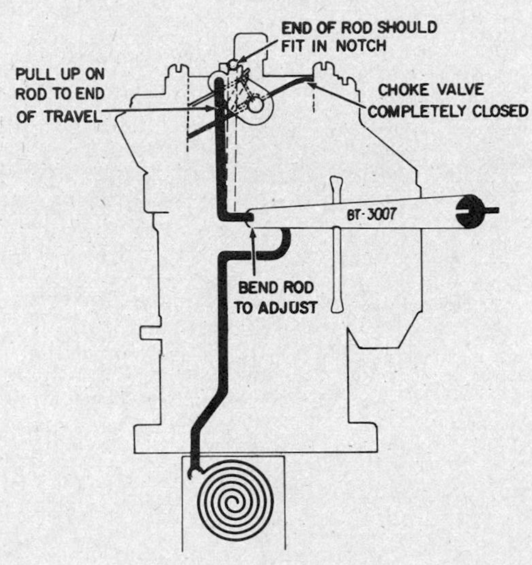

Choke Coil Rod Adjustment
(© Pontiac Div., G.M. Corp)

break and the choke lever.

NOTE: The auxiliary vacuum break diaphragm is on the same side of the carburetor as the throttle stop solenoid.

Choke Unloader Adjustment

1. Apply pressure to the choke valve and hold it in the closed position.
2. Open the throttle valve to the wide open position.
3. Check the dimension between the lower edge of the choke plate and the air horn wall; if adjustment is needed, bend the unloader tang on the throttle lever to adjust to specification.

Choke Coil Rod Adjustment

1. Disconnect the thermostatic coil rod from the upper choke lever and hold the choke valve closed.
2. Push down on the coil rod to the end of its travel.
3. The top of the rod should be even with the bottom hole in the choke lever.
4. To make adjustments, bend the rod at the point shown in the illustration.

Float Adjustment

1. Hold the float retainer in place and the float arm against the top of the float needle by pushing down on the float arm at the outer end toward the float bowl casting.
2. Using an adjustable T scale, measure the distance from the toe of the float to the float bowl gasket surface.

NOTE: The float bowl gasket should be removed and the gauge held on the index point on the float for accurate measurement.

3. Adjust the float level by bending the float arm up or down at the float arm junction.

Metering Rod Adjustments

1. Hold the throttle valve wide open and push down on the metering rod against spring tension, then remove the rod from the main metering jet.
2. In order to check adjustment, the slow idle screw must be backed out and the fast idle cam rotated so that the fast idle cam follower does not contact the steps on the cam.
3. With the throttle valve closed, push down on the power piston until it contacts its stop.
4. With the power piston depressed, swing the metering rod holder over the flat surface of the bowl casting next to the carburetor bore.
5. Insert a specified size drill between the bowl casting sealing bead and the lower surface of the metering rod holder. The drill should slide smoothly between both surfaces.
6. If adjustment is needed, carefully bend the metering rod holder up or down at the point shown. After adjustment, reinstall the metering rod.

Idle Vent Adjustment (1969 only)

1. The engine idle must be set at the specified RPM and the choke valve held wide open so that the fast idle cam follower is not contacting the cam.

NOTE: If the carburetor is off the car, a preliminary idle setting can be made by turning the idle speed screw

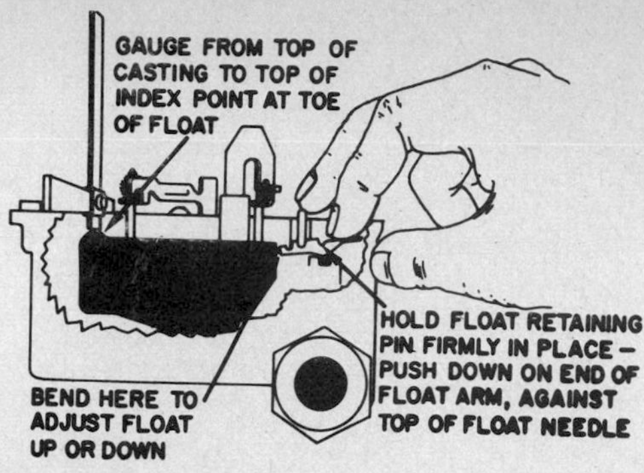

Float Level
(© Pontiac Div., G.M. Corp)

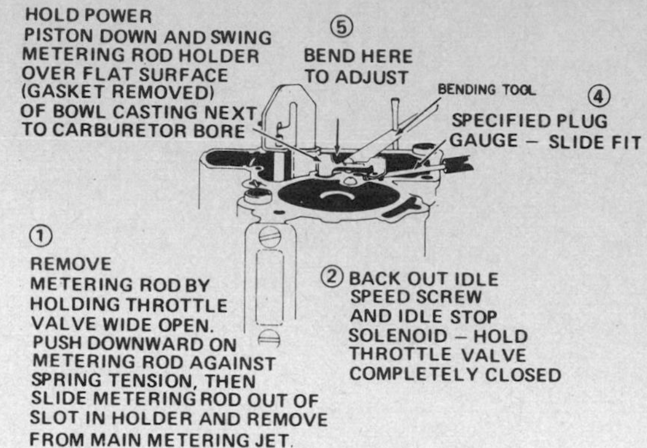

Metering Rod Adjustment
(© Chevrolet Div., G.M. Corp)

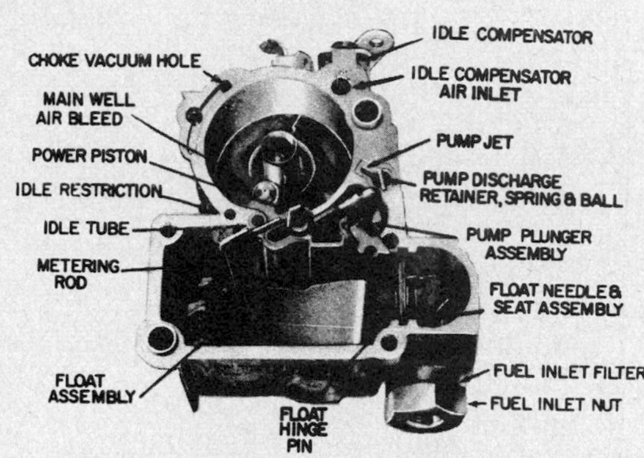

Float Bowl Assembly
(© Oldsmobile Div., G.M. Corp)

in 1½ turns from the closed throttle valve position.

2. With the throttle stop screw held against the idle stop screw, the idle vent valve should be open to specification. To check, a drill of specified size may be inserted between the top of the air horn casting and the bottom surface of the valve.
3. If adjustment is necessary, turn the slotted vent valve head with a screwdriver. Turning the head clockwise *increases* the clearance.

NOTE: On models equipped with an idle stop solenoid, the solenoid must be activated when checking and adjusting the valve.

MV CARBURETOR SPECIFICATIONS

BUICK

Year	Carburetor Identification①	Float Level (in.)	Metering Rod (in.)	Pump Rod	Idle Vent (in.)	Vacuum Break (in.)	Auxiliary Vacuum Break (in.)	Fast Idle Off Car (in.)	Choke Rod (in.)	Choke Unloader (in.)	Fast Idle Speed (rpm)
1969	7029014	1/4	0.070	—	0.050	0.245	—	—	0.170	0.350	620
	7029047	9/32	0.140	—	0.020	0.275	—	—	0.190	0.350	720
1970	7040014	1/4	0.070	—	0.050	0.245	—	—	0.170	0.350	650
	7040015	1/4	0.140	—	0.050	0.275	—	—	0.200	0.350	900
	7040017	1/4	0.070	—	—	0.230	—	0.100	0.190	0.350	900
1971	7041014	1/4	0.080	—	0.050	0.225	—	—	0.160	0.500	500
	7041017	1/4	0.080	—	0.050	0.225	—	—	0.180	0.350	550
1974	Automatic	1/4	0.080	—	—	0.300	—	—	0.245	0.500	1800②
	Manual	1/4	0.080	—	—	0.350	—	—	0.275	0.500	1800②
1975	7045012	11/32	0.080	—	—	0.200	0.215	—	0.160	0.275	1700②
	7045013	11/32	0.080	—	—	0.350	0.312	—	0.275	0.275	1800②
	7045314	11/32	0.080	—	—	0.275	0.312	—	0.230	0.275	1700②

① The Carburetor identification tag is located at the rear of the carburetor on one of the air horn screws.

② In Neutral or Park

CHEVROLET

Year	Carburetor Identification①	Float Level (in.)	Metering Rod (in.)	Pump Rod	Idle Vent (in.)	Vacuum Break (in.)	Auxiliary Vacuum Break (in.)	Fast Idle Off Car (in.)	Choke Rod (in.)	Choke Unloader (in.)	Fast Idle Speed (rpm)
1969	7029014	1/4	0.070	—	0.050	0.245	—	0.100	0.170	0.350	2400②
	7029015	1/4	0.090	—	0.050	0.275	—	0.100	0.200	0.350	2400②
	7029017	1/4	0.090	—	0.050	0.275	—	0.100	0.200	0.350	2400②
1970	7040014	1/4	0.070	—	—	0.200	—	0.110	0.170	0.350	2400②
	7040017	1/4	0.090	—	—	0.160	—	0.100	0.190	0.350	2400②
1971	7041014	1/4	0.080	—	—	0.200	—	0.100	0.160	0.350	—
	7041017	1/4	0.080	—	—	0.230	—	0.100	0.180	0.350	—
	7041023	1/16	—	—	—	0.200	—	0.110	0.120	0.350	—
1972	7042014	1/4	0.080	—	—	0.190	—	—	0.125	0.500	2400②
	7042017	1/4	0.078	—	—	0.225	—	—	0.150	0.500	2400②
	7042984	1/4	0.078	—	—	0.190	—	—	0.125	0.500	2400②
	7042987	1/4	0.076	—	—	0.225	—	—	0.150	0.500	2400②
1973	7043014	1/4	0.080	—	—	0.300	—	—	0.245	0.500	1800②
	7043017	1/4	0.080	—	—	0.350	—	—	0.275	0.500	1800②
1974	7044014	3/10	0.079	—	—	0.275	—	—	0.230	0.500	1800②③
	7044017	3/10	0.072	—	—	0.350	—	—	0.275	0.500	1800②③
	7044314	3/10	0.073	—	—	0.300	—	—	0.245	0.500	1800②③
1975	7045013	11/32	0.080	—	—	0.200	0.215	—	0.160	0.215	1800④
	7045012	11/32	0.080	—	—	0.350	0.312	—	0.275	0.275	1800④
	7045314	11/32	0.080	—	—	0.275	0.312	—	0.230	0.275	1800④

① The carburetor identification tag is located at the rear of the carburetor on one of the air horn screws.
② High step of cam.
③ Without vacuum advance.
④ 1700 rpm with automatic transmission in neutral.

CHEVROLET VEGA

Year	Carburetor Identification①	Float Level (in.)	Metering Rod (in.)	Pump Rod (in.)	Vacuum Break (in.)	Auxiliary Vacuum Break (in.)	Fast Idle Off Car (in.)	Choke Rod (in.)	Choke Unloader (in.)	Fast Idle Speed (rpm)
1971	Manual	1/16	—	—	0.200	—	0.110	0.120	0.350	2400②
	Automatic	1/16	—	—	0.140	—	0.110	0.080	0.350	2400②
1972	Manual	1/8	—	—	0.200	—	0.110	0.130	0.375	2400②
	Automatic	1/16	—	—	0.120	—	0.110	0.070	0.375	2800②
1973	Manual	0.06	—	—	0.140	—	—	0.110	0.375	2000③
	Automatic	0.06	—	—	0.120	—	—	0.085	0.375	2200③
1974	Manual	0.06	—	—	0.130	—	—	0.080	0.375	2000③
	Automatic	0.06	—	—	0.130	—	—	0.080	0.375	2200③
1975	7045025, 7045029	1/8	—	—	0.100	0.450	—	0.080	0.375	2200④
	7045024, 7045028	1/8	—	—	0.100	0.450	—	0.080	0.375	2200④

① The carburetor identification tag is located at the rear of the carburetor on one of the air horn screws.
② TCS disconnected for full vacuum advance.
③ No vacuum to distributor.
④ 2000 rpm with manual transmission.

OLDSMOBILE

Year	Carburetor Identification①	Float Level (in.)	Metering Rod (in.)	Pump Rod	Idle Vent (in.)	Vacuum Break (in.)	Auxiliary Vacuum Break (in.)	Fast Idle Off Car (in.)	Choke Rod (in.)	Choke Unloader (in.)	Fast Idle Speed (rpm)
1969	7029014	¼	0.070	—	0.050	0.245	—	—	0.170	0.350	750③
	7029057	5/16	0.120	—	0.030	0.260	—	—	0.180	0.350	750③
1970	7040014	¼	0.070	—	—	0.200	—	—	0.170	0.350	900③
	7040017	¼	0.070	—	—	0.225	—	—	0.190	0.350	750③
1971	7041014	¼	0.070	—	—	0.200	—	—	0.160	0.350	900③
	7041019	¼	0.070	—	—	0.225	—	—	0.180	0.350	750③
1973-74	Manual	¼	0.080	—	—	0.350	—	—	0.275	0.500	②
	Automatic	¼	0.080	—	—	0.300	—	—	0.245	0.500	②
1975	Manual	11/32	0.080	—	—	0.350	0.312	—	0.275	0.275	1800②
	Automatic	11/32	0.080	—	—	0.200	0.215	—	0.160	0.275	1800②

① The carburetor identification tag is located at the rear of the carburetor on one of the air horn screws.
② Preset
③ Low step of cam.

PONTIAC

Year	Carburetor Identification①	Float Level (in.)	Metering Rod (in.)	Pump Rod	Idle Vent (in.)	Vacuum Break (in.)	Auxiliary Vacuum Break (in.)	Fast Idle Off Car (in.)	Choke Rod (in.)	Choke Unloader (in.)	Fast Idle Speed (rpm)
1969	7029165	9/32	0.085	—	0.040	0.275	—	0.120	0.200	0.450	2400②
	7029166	9/32	0.085	—	0.040	0.260	—	0.130	0.180	0.450	2800②
	7029167	9/32	0.085	—	0.040	0.275	—	0.120	0.200	0.450	2600②
	7029168	9/32	0.085	—	0.040	0.260	—	0.130	0.180	0.450	2800②
1970	7040014	¼	0.100	—	—	0.200	—	—	0.170	0.350	—
	7040017	¼	0.100	—	—	0.230	—	—	0.190	0.350	—
1971	7041014	¼	0.080	—	—	0.200	—	—	0.160	0.350	—
	7041017	¼	0.078	—	—	0.225	—	—	0.180	0.350	—
1972	7042014	¼	0.080	—	—	0.200	—	—	0.160	0.500	2400②
	7042017	¼	0.080	—	—	0.230	—	—	0.180	0.500	2400②
	7042984	¼	0.080	—	—	0.200	—	—	0.160	0.500	2400②
	7042987	¼	0.080	—	—	0.230	—	—	0.180	0.500	2400②
1973	7043014	¼	0.080	—	—	0.300	—	—	0.245	0.500	2400②
	7043017	¾	0.080	—	—	0.350	—	—	0.275	0.500	2400②
1974	7044041	0.354	0.079	—	—	0.275	—	—	0.230	0.500	1800②
	7044017	0.354	0.072	—	—	0.350	—	—	0.275	0.500	1800②
	7044314	0.354	0.073	—	—	0.300	—	—	0.245	0.500	1800②
1975	7045012	11/32	0.080	—	—	0.200	0.215	—	0.160	0.275	1800②
	7045013	11/32	0.080	—	—	0.350	0.312	—	0.275	0.275	1800②
	7045014	11/32	0.080	—	—	0.257	0.312	—	0.230	0.275	1800②
	Astre Man.	1/8	—	—	—	0.130	—	—	0.080	0.375	2000③
	Astre Auto.	1/8	—	—	—	0.130	—	—	0.080	0.375	2000③

① The carburetor identification tag is located at the rear of the carburetor on one of the air horn screws.
② High step of cam.
③ No vacuum to the distributor

Model 2GC, 2GV— 1¼, 1½

This two barrel downdraft carburetor comes in two bore sizes to provide a wide variety of usage. The newer carburetors use a plastic float and a longer needle and seat to provide better fuel control.

The carburetor is used on General Motors cars and on some 1971 Chrysler Corp vehicles.

Fast Idle Adjustment

1. On 2GC and 2GV models, except on some Oldsmobile and Chrysler Corp cars, the fast idle is set automatically when the curb idle and mixture is set.
2. Some Oldsmobile 2GC carburetors have a screw to adjust the fast idle.
3. On Chrysler Corp cars, follow this procedure: with engine off and the transmission in Neutral, open the throttle slightly. Close the choke valve until the fast idle screw can be positioned on the second step of the fast idle cam. Start the engine to determine speed. Turn the fast idle screw to obtain the specified RPM.

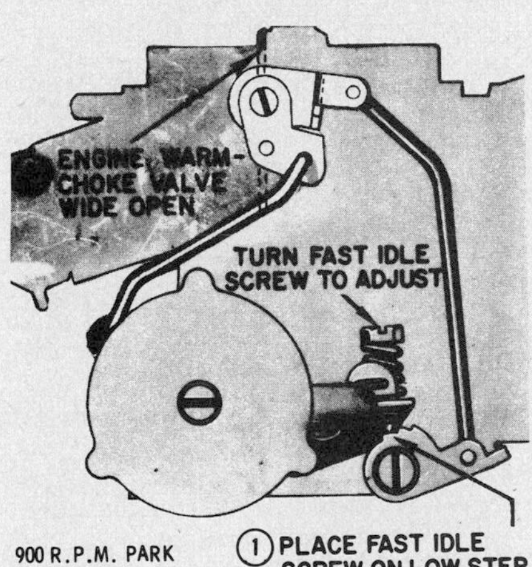

Fast Idle Speed Setting
(© Oldsmobile Div., G.M. Corp)

Choke Rod (fast idle cam)

1. Turn in the idle cam stop screw until it just contacts the bottom step of the fast idle cam. Then turn the screw one full turn.
2. Place the idle screw on the second step of the fast idle cam against the shoulder of the high step.
3. Hold the choke valve closed and check the clearance between the upper edge of the choke valve and the air horn wall.
4. Adjust the clearance by bending the tang on the choke lever.

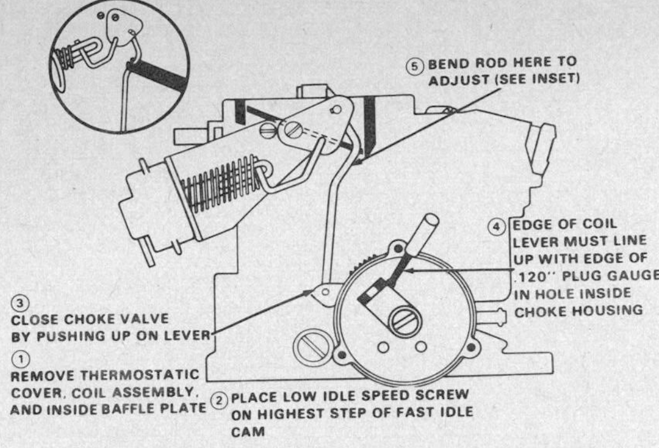

Intermediate choke rod adjustment, beginning 1975
(© Chevrolet Div., G.M. Corp.)

Intermediate Choke Rod Adjustment (Beginning 1975)

1. Remove the thermostatic cover coil, gasket, and inside baffle plate assembly.
2. Place the idle speed screw on the highest step of the fast idle cam.
3. Close the choke valve by pushing up on the intermediate choke lever.
4. The edge of the coil lever inside the choke housing must line up with the edge of the plug gauge.
5. Adjust by bending the intermediate choke rod at the first bend from the bottom of the rod.

Vacuum Break Adjustment

1. Remove the air cleaner. Vehicles with a Therm AC air cleaner should have the sensor's vacuum take-off port plugged.
2. Using an external vacuum source, apply vacuum to the vacuum break diaphragm until the plunger is fully seated.
3. When the plunger is seated, push the choke valve toward the closed position. For 1975 and later models, place the idle speed screw on the high step of the fast idle cam.
4. Holding the choke valve or coil lever inside the choke housing in the closed position, place the specified size gauge between the upper (lower, through 1974) edge of the choke valve and the air horn wall.
5. If the measurement is not correct, bend the vacuum break rod.

Auxiliary Vacuum Break (Beginning 1975)

1. Seat the auxiliary vacuum diaphragm by applying an outside source of vacuum. Tape over the vacuum bleed hole so the vacuum will not bleed down.
2. Place the idle speed screw on the high step of the fast idle cam.
3. Hold the choke coil lever inside the choke housing towards the closed choke position.
4. Rotate the inside choke coil lever until the spring in the diaphragm plunger is seated. Meas-

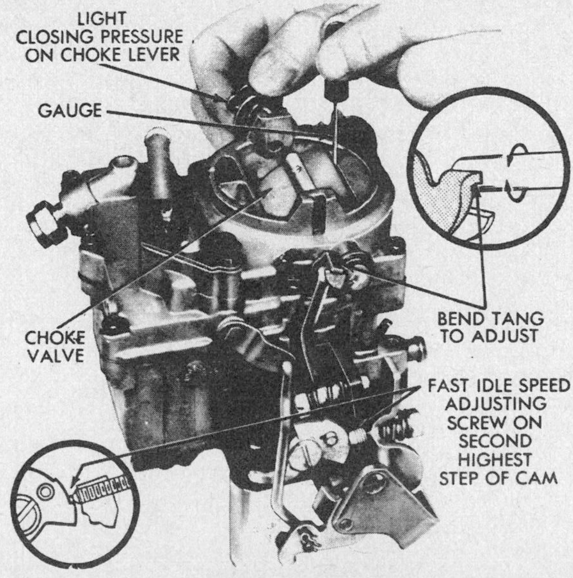

Fast Idle Cam Setting
(© Dodge Div., Chrysler Corp)

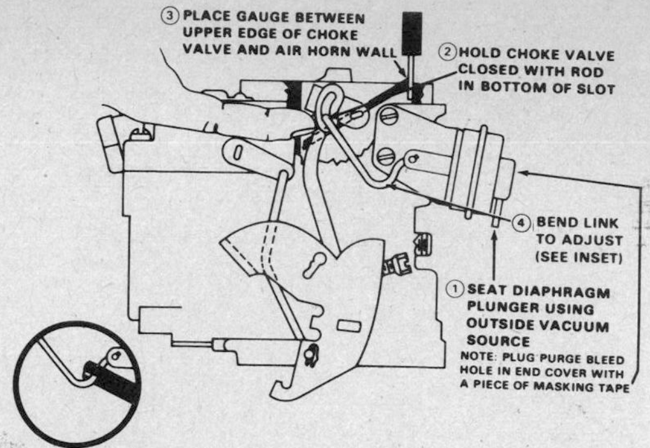

Primary vacuum break adjustment, beginning 1975
(© Buick Div., G.M. Corp.)

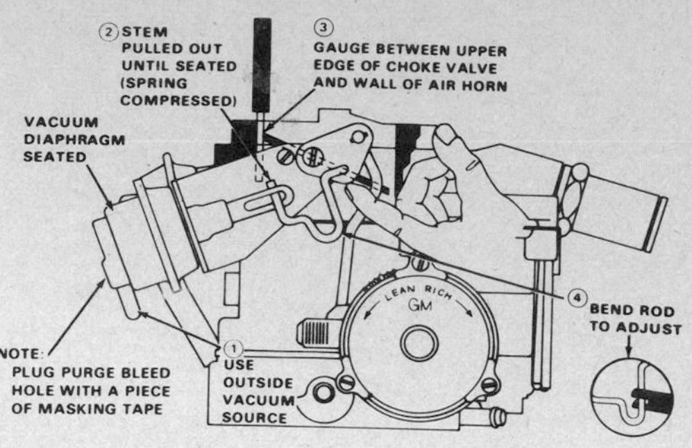

Auxiliary vacuum break adjustment, beginning 1975
(© Buick Div., G.M. Corp.)

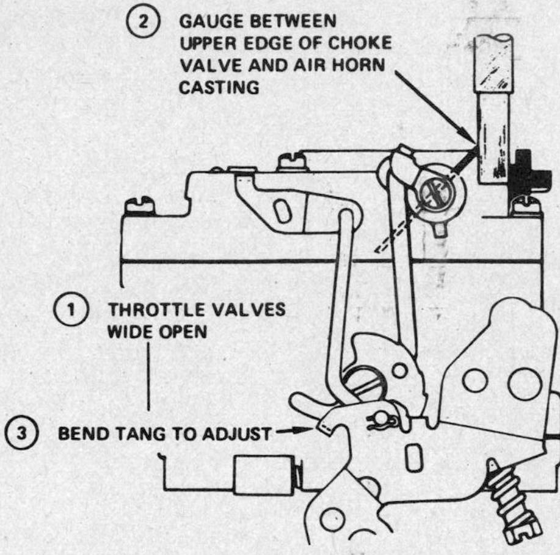

Choke Unloader Adjustment
(© Chevrolet Div., G.M. Corp)

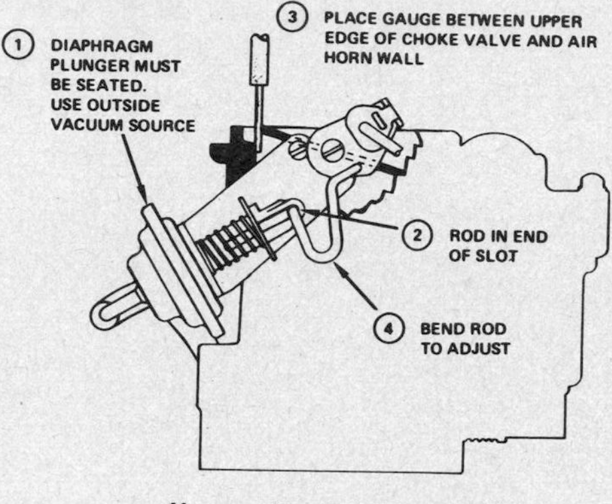

Vacuum Break Adjustment
(© Chevrolet Div., G.M. Corp)

ure the distance between the upper edge of the choke valve and the air horn wall.

5. Adjust by bending the auxiliary vacuum break rod at the bottom of the U-shaped bend. Remove the piece of tape from the auxiliary vacuum diaphragm.

Choke Unloader Adjustment

1. Hold the throttle valves wide open.
2. Close the choke valve.
3. Bend the unloader tang to obtain the proper clearance between the upper edge of the choke valve and air horn wall.

Choke Coil Rod Adjustment

1. Hold the choke valve completely open.
2. Disconnect the coil rod from the upper lever and push down on the rod to the end of its travel.
3. When the rod is all the way down, the top of the rod should line up with the bottom of the slotted hole on the choke valve linkage.
4. Adjust by bending the lever at the point shown in illustration.

Float Level

With the air horn assembly upside down, measure the distance from the air horn gasket to the lip at the toe of the float. Bend the float arm to adjust to specifications.

Float Drop

Holding the air horn assembly upright, measure the distance from the gasket to the lip at the toe of the float. If correction is necessary, bend the float tang at the rear, next to the needle and seat.

Accelerator Pump Rod

1. Back out the idle speed screw and completely close the throttle valves.
2. Place the pump gauge across the air cleaner mounting surface.
3. With the T-scale set to the specified height, the lower leg of the gauge should just touch the top of the accelerator pump rod.
4. Bend the pump rod to adjust.

Bowl Vent Valve Adjustment

NOTE: Check and adjust, if necessary, the pump rod clearance and curb idle speed before adjusting the oowl vent valve.

1. Remove the two bowl vent valve cover attaching screws in the top of the air horn and remove the cover and gasket. Remove the bowl vent valve spring.
2. Place the idle speed screw on the second step of the fast idle cam next to the highest step. In this position, the bowl vent valve should just be closed.

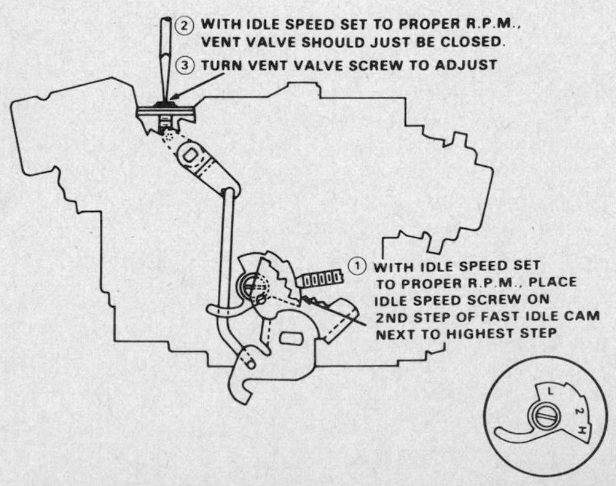

Bowl vent valve adjustment (© Buick Div., G.M. Corp.)

3. If the vent valve is just closed with the idle speed screw on the second step of the fast idle cam, rotate the fast idle cam so that the idle speed screw is on the next lower step. In this position, the vent valve should just begin to open.
4. If it is necessary to adjust the bowl vent valve, turn the adjustment screw in the top of the valve, to obtain the conditions mentioned in Steps 2 and 3.

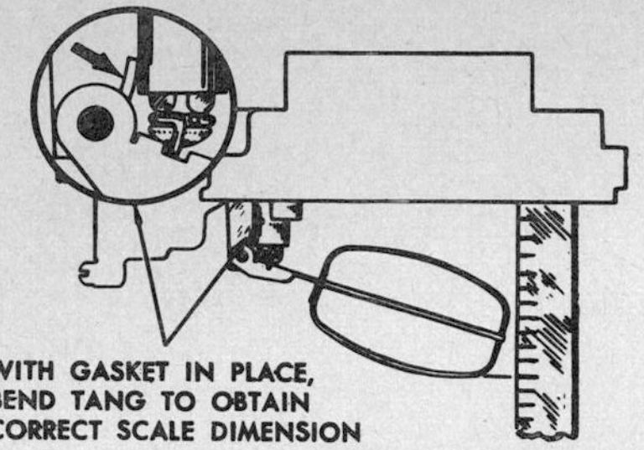

Float Drop, Metal Float

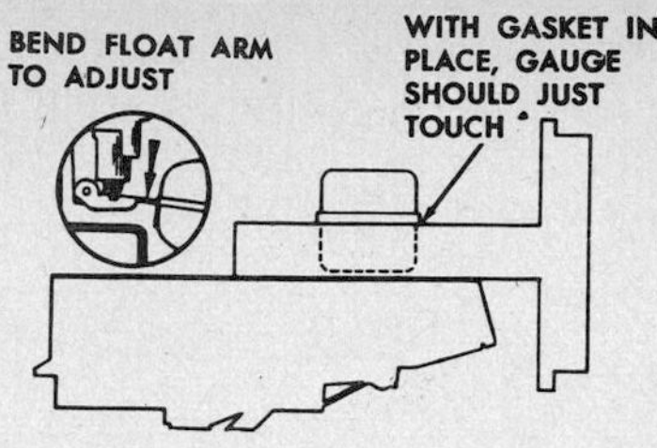

Float Level Measurement, Metal Float

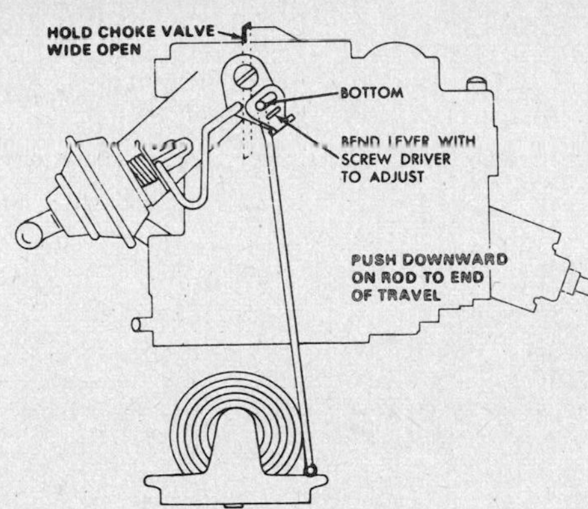

Choke Coil Rod Adjustment
(© Chevrolet Div., G.M. Corp)

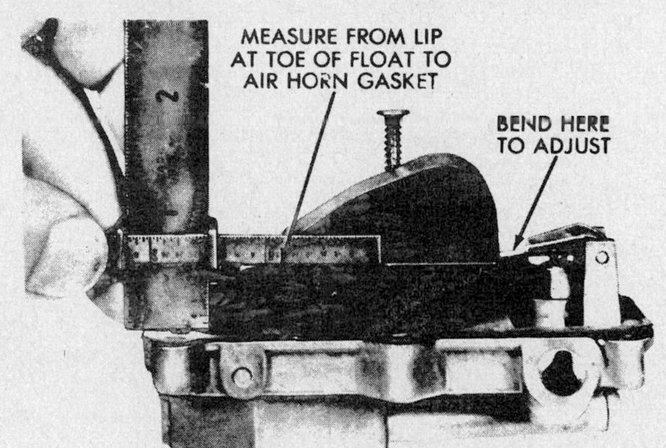

Float Level Measurement, Plastic Float
(© Dodge Div., Chrysler Corp)

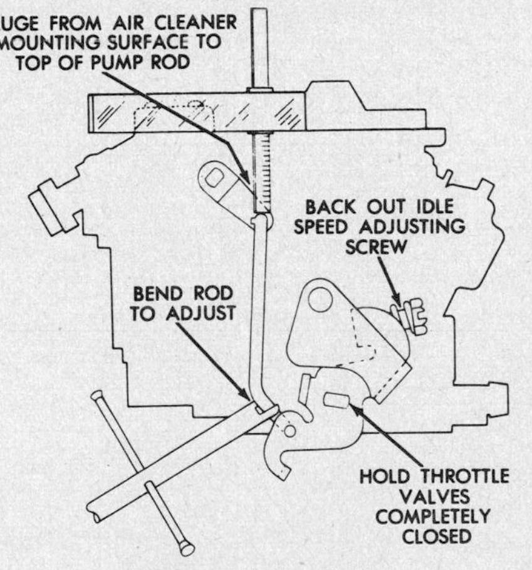

Accelerator Pump Rod
(© Dodge Div., Chrysler Corp)

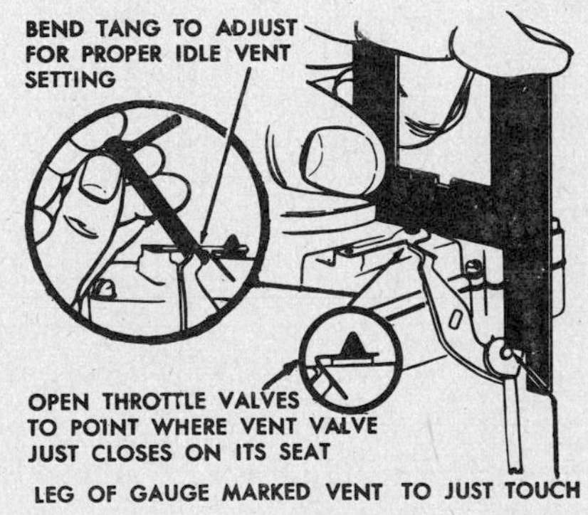

Idle Vent Adjustment

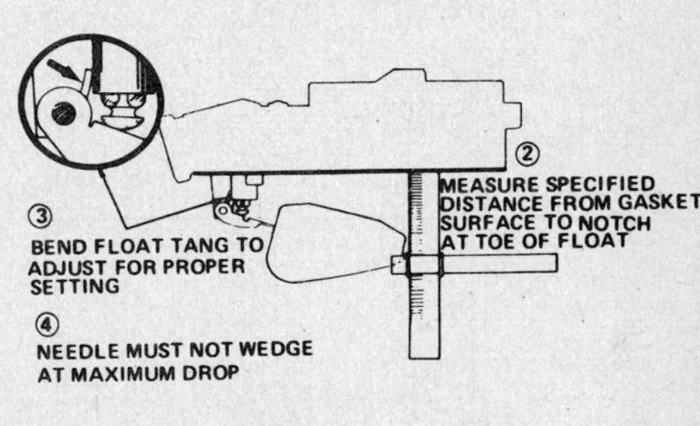

Float Drop, Plastic Float

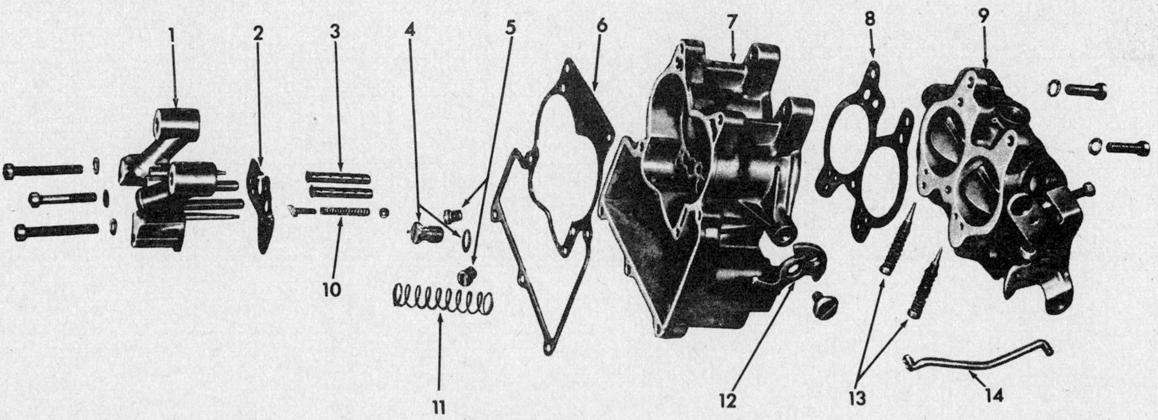

Float Bowl, Exploded View

1. Cluster assembly
2. Gasket
3. Splash shield—main well
4. Power valve assembly
5. Main jets
6. Air horn gasket
7. Bowl assembly
8. Throttle body-to-bowl gasket
9. Throttle body assembly
10. Pump discharge check assembly
11. Accelerator pump spring
12. Fast idle cam
13. Idle mixture screws
14. Choke rod

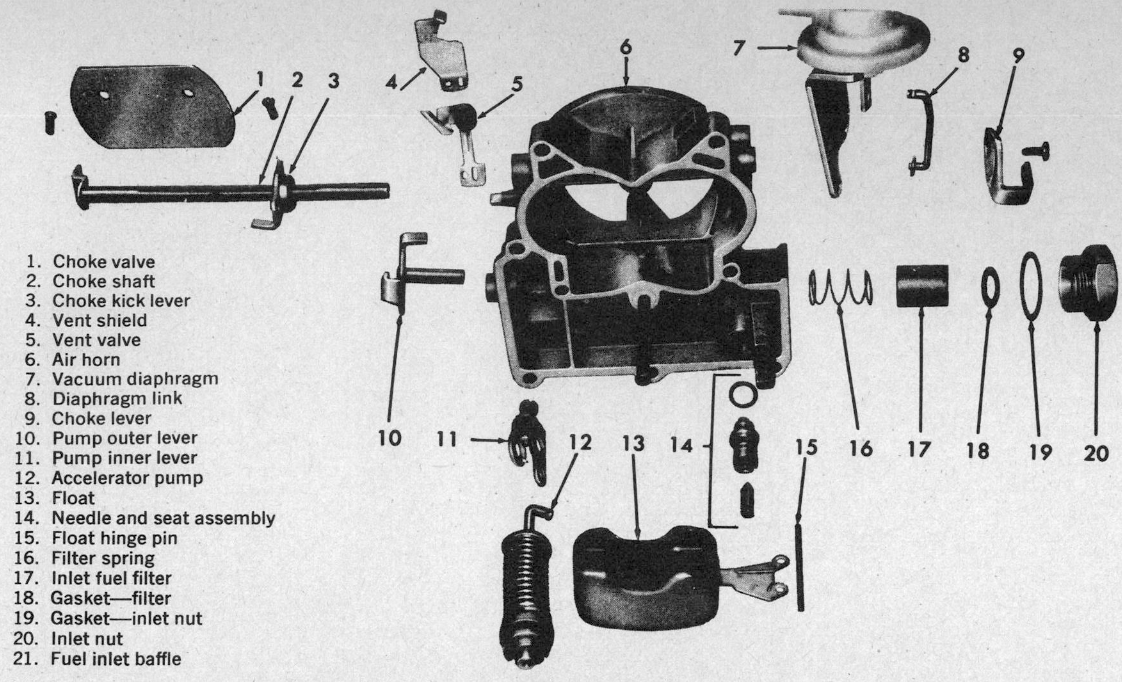

Air horn, exploded view, 2GC, 2GV

2GC, 2GV CARBURETOR SPECIFICATIONS

① The carburetor identification tag is located at the rear of the carburetor on one of the air horn screws.

BUICK

Year	Carburetor Identification①	Float Level (in.)	Float Drop (in.)	Pump (Rod (in.)	Idle Vent (in.)	Vacuum Break (in.)	Auxiliary Vacuum Break (in.)	Choke Rod (in.)	Choke Unloader (in.)	Fast Idle Speed (rpm)
1969	7029140	15/32	1 7/32	1 11/32	0.020	0.110	—	0.055	0.140	—
	7029141	15/32	1 7/32	1 11/32	0.020	0.110	—	0.055	0.140	—
1970	7040142	15/32	1 7/32	1 13/32	—	0.150	—	0.080	0.180	—
	7040143	15/32	1 7/32	1 15/32	—	0.190	—	0.100	0.200	—
	7040446	15/32	1 7/32	1 13/32	—	0.150	—	0.080	0.180	—
1971	7040143	15/32	1 7/8	1 15/32	—	0.160	0.140	0.080	0.180	—
	7041142	15/32	1 7/8	1 15/32	—	0.150	0.140	0.080	0.180	—
	7041442	15/32	1 7/8	1 15/32	—	0.150	0.140	0.080	0.180	—
1972	7042142	15/32	1 7/8	1 15/32	—	0.150	0.140	0.080	0.180	—
	7042143	15/32	1 7/8	1 15/32	—	0.160	0.140	0.080	0.180	—
	7042842	15/32	1 7/8	1 15/32	—	0.150	0.140	0.080	0.180	—
1973	7043142	15/32	1 9/32	1 15/32	—	0.140	0.120	0.080	0.180	—
	7043143	15/32	1 9/32	1 15/32	—	0.150	0.120	0.080	0.200	—
1974	7044142	15/32	1 9/32	1 15/32	—	0.140	0.120	0.080	0.180	—
	7044442	15/32	1 9/32	1 15/32	—	0.140	0.120	0.080	0.180	—
	7044141	15/32	1 9/32	1 15/32	—	0.160	0.120	0.080	0.180	—
	7044144	15/32	1 9/32	1 15/32	—	0.140	0.120	0.080	0.180	—
	7044444	15/32	1 9/32	1 15/32	—	0.140	0.120	0.080	0.180	—
1975	7045145	15/32	1 9/32	1 15/32	—	0.120	0.120	0.080	0.120	—
	7045146	15/32	1 9/32	1 15/32	—	0.120	0.120	0.080	0.120	—
	7045147	15/32	1 9/32	1 15/32	—	0.120	0.120	0.080	0.120	—
	7045148	15/32	1 9/32	1 15/32	—	0.120	0.120	0.080	0.120	—
	7045149	15/32	1 9/32	1 15/32	—	0.120	0.120	0.080	0.120	—
	7045446	15/32	1 9/32	1 15/32	—	0.120	0.120	0.080	0.120	—
	7045448	15/32	1 9/32	1 15/32	—	0.120	0.120	0.080	0.120	—
	7045449	15/32	1 9/32	1 15/32	—	0.120	0.120	0.080	0.120	—
	7045143	15/32	1 9/32	1 15/32	—	0.140	0.120	0.080	0.140	—
	7045140	15/32	1 9/32	1 15/32	—	0.140	0.120	0.080	0.140	—

2GC, 2GV CARBURETOR SPECIFICATIONS

CHEVROLET

Year	Carburetor Identification①	Float Level (in.)	Float Drop (in.)	Pump (Rod (in.)	Idle Vent (in.)	Vacuum Break (in.)	Auxiliary Vacuum Break (in.)	Choke Rod (in.)	Choke Unloader (in.)	Fast Idle Speed (rpm)
1969	7029101	27/32	1 3/4	1 1/8	0.020	0.100	—	0.060	0.215	—
	7029103	27/32	1 3/4	1 1/8	0.020	0.100	—	0.060	0.215	—
	7029110	27/32	1 3/4	1 1/8	0.020	0.100	—	0.060	0.215	—
	7029112	27/32	1 3/4	1 1/8	0.020	0.100	—	0.060	0.215	—
	7029102	3/4	1 3/4	1 13/32	0.020	0.215	—	0.085	0.275	—
	7029104	3/4	1 3/4	1 13/32	0.020	0.215	—	0.085	0.275	—
	7029127	3/4	1 3/4	1 13/32	0.020	0.215	—	0.085	0.275	—
	7029129	3/4	1 3/4	1 13/32	0.020	0.215	—	0.085	0.275	—
	7029117	3/4	1 3/4	1 13/32	0.020	0.215	—	0.085	0.275	—
	7029118	3/4	1 3/4	1 13/32	0.020	0.215	—	0.085	0.275	—
	7029119	5/8	1 3/4	1 13/32	0.020	0.215	—	0.085	0.275	—
	7029120	5/8	1 3/4	1 13/32	0.020	0.215	—	0.085	0.275	—
1970	7040110	27/32	1 3/4	1 1/8	0.020	0.100	—	0.060	0.215	—
	7040112	27/32	1 3/4	1 1/8	0.020	0.100	—	0.060	0.215	—
	7040101	27/32	1 3/4	1 1/8	0.020	0.125	—	0.060	0.160	—
	7040103	27/32	1 3/4	1 1/8	0.020	0.125	—	0.060	0.225	—
	7040114	23/32	1 3/8	1 17/32	0.020	0.200	—	0.085	0.325	—
	7040116	23/32	1 3/8	1 17/32	0.020	0.200	—	0.085	0.325	—
	7040113	23/32	1 3/8	1 17/32	0.020	0.215	—	0.085	0.275	—
	7040115	23/32	1 3/8	1 17/32	0.020	0.215	—	0.085	0.275	—
	7040118	23/32	1 3/8	1 17/32	0.020	0.215	—	0.085	0.325	—
	7040120	23/32	1 3/8	1 17/32	0.020	0.215	—	0.085	0.325	—
	7040117	23/32	1 3/8	1 17/32	0.020	0.215	—	0.085	0.325	—
	7040119	23/32	1 3/8	1 17/32	0.020	0.215	—	0.085	0.325	—
1971	7041024	1/16	—	—	—	0.140	—	0.080	0.350	—
	7041101	13/16	1 3/4	1 3/64	—	0.110	—	0.075	0.215	—
	7041110	13/16	1 3/4	1 3/64	—	0.080	—	0.040	0.215	—
	7041102	25/32	1 3/8	1 5/32	—	0.170	—	0.100	0.325	—
	7041114	25/32	1 3/8	1 5/32	—	0.170	—	0.100	0.325	—
	7041113	23/32	1 3/8	1 5/32	—	0.180	—	0.100	0.325	—
	7041127	23/32	1 3/8	1 5/32	—	0.180	—	0.100	0.325	—
	7041117	23/32	1 3/8	1 5/32	—	0.170	—	0.100	0.325	—
	7041118	23/32	1 3/8	1 5/32	—	0.170	—	0.100	0.325	—
	7041181	5/8	1 3/4	1 3/8	—	0.120	—	0.080	0.180	—
	7041182	5/8	1 3/4	1 3/8	—	0.120	—	0.080	0.180	—
1972	7042111	23/32	1 9/32	1 1/2	—	0.180	—	0.100	0.325	—
	7042113	23/32	1 9/32	1 1/2	—	0.180	—	0.100	0.325	—
	7042831	23/32	1 9/32	1 1/2	—	0.180	—	0.100	0.325	—
	7042833	23/32	1 9/32	1 1/2	—	0.180	—	0.100	0.325	—
	7042112	23/32	1 9/32	1 1/2	—	0.170	—	0.100	0.325	—
	7042114	23/32	1 9/32	1 1/2	—	0.170	—	0.100	0.325	—
	7042118	23/32	1 9/32	1 1/2	—	0.190	—	0.100	0.325	—
	7042832	23/32	1 9/32	1 1/2	—	0.170	—	0.100	0.325	—
	7042834	23/32	1 9/32	1 1/2	—	0.170	—	0.100	0.325	—
	7042838	23/32	1 9/32	1 1/2	—	0.190	—	0.100	0.325	—
	7042100	25/32	1 31/32	1 5/16	—	0.080	—	0.040	0.215	—
	7042820	25/32	1 31/32	1 5/16	—	0.080	—	0.040	0.215	—
	7042101	25/32	1 31/32	1 5/16	—	0.110	—	0.075	0.215	—
	7042821	25/32	1 31/32	1 5/16	—	0.110	—	0.075	0.215	—

2GC, 2GV CARBURETOR SPECIFICATIONS

CHEVROLET

Year	Carburetor Identification①	Float Level (in.)	Float Drop (in.)	Pump Rod (in.)	Idle Vent (in.)	Vacuum Break (in.)	Auxiliary Vacuum Break (in.)	Choke Rod (in.)	Choke Unloader (in.)	Fast Idle Speed (rpm)
1973	7043100	21/32	1 9/32	1 5/16	—	0.080	—	0.150	0.215	—
	7043101	21/32	1 9/32	1 5/16	—	0.080	—	0.150	0.215	—
	7043120	21/32	1 9/32	1 5/16	—	0.080	—	0.150	0.215	—
	7043105	21/32	1 9/32	1 5/16	—	0.080	—	0.150	0.215	—
	7043114	19/32	1 9/32	1 7/16	—	0.130	—	0.245	0.325	—
	7043113	19/32	1 9/32	1 7/16	—	0.140	—	0.200	0.250	—
	7043112	19/32	1 9/32	1 7/16	—	0.130	—	0.245	0.325	—
	7043111	19/32	1 9/32	1 7/16	—	0.140	—	0.200	0.250	—
	7043118	19/32	1 9/32	1 7/16	—	0.130	—	0.245	0.325	—
1974	7044111	19/32	1 9/32	1 9/32	—	0.140	—	0.200	0.250	1600②
	7044112	19/32	1 9/32	1 3/16	—	0.130	—	0.245	0.325	1600②
	7044113	19/32	1 9/32	1 9/32	—	0.140	—	0.200	0.250	1600②
	7044114	19/32	1 9/32	1 3/16	—	0.130	—	0.245	0.325	1600②
	7044115	19/32	1 9/32	1 9/32	—	0.140	—	0.200	0.250	1600②
	7044116	19/32	1 9/32	1 3/16	—	0.130	—	0.245	0.325	1600②
	7044118	19/32	1 9/32	1 3/16	—	0.130	—	0.245	0.325	1600②
	7044123	19/32	1 9/32	1 9/32	—	0.140	—	0.200	0.250	1600②
	7044124	19/32	1 9/32	1 3/16	—	0.130	—	0.245	0.320	1600②
1975	7045105	19/32	1 7/32	1 19/32	—	0.130	—	0.375	0.350	—
	7045106	19/32	1 7/32	1 19/32	—	0.130	—	0.380	0.350	—
	7045111	21/32	31/32	1 5/8	—	0.130	—	0.400	0.350	—
	7045112	21/32	31/32	1 5/8	—	0.130	—	0.400	0.350	—
	7045114	21/32	31/32	1 5/8	—	0.130	—	0.400	0.350	—
	7045115	21/32	31/32	1 5/8	—	0.130	—	0.400	0.350	—
	7045123	21/32	31/32	1 5/8	—	0.130	—	0.400	0.350	—
	7045124	21/32	31/32	1 5/8	—	0.130	—	0.400	0.350	—
	7045405	21/32	1 7/32	1 19/32	—	0.130	—	0.380	0.350	—
	7045406	21/32	1 7/32	1 19/32	—	0.130	—	0.380	0.350	—

① The carburetor identification tag is located at the rear of the carburetor on one of the air horn screws.

② This setting is with the low idle at 500 rpm with the clutch fan disengaged.

CHEVROLET VEGA

Year	Carburetor Identification①	Float Level (in.)	Float Drop (in.)	Pump Rod (in.)	Idle Vent (in.)	Vacuum Break (in.)	Automatic Choke	Choke Rod (in.)	Choke Unloader (in.)	Fast Idle Speed
1971	Manual	5/8	1 3/4	1 3/8	—	0.120	—	0.080	0.180	2400②
	Automatic	5/8	1 3/4	1 3/8	—	0.120	—	0.080	0.180	2400②
1972	Manual	19/32	1 7/8	1 1/16	—	0.100	—	0.080	0.215	2400②
	Automatic	19/32	1 7/8	1 1/16	—	0.085	—	0.060	0.215	2800②

① The carburetor identification tag is located at the rear of the carburetor on one of the air horn screws.

② TCS disconnected for full vacuum advance.

CHRYSLER CORP.

Year	Carburetor Identification①	Float Level (in.)	Float Drop (in.)	Pump Rod (in.)	Idle Vent (in.)	Vacuum Break (in.)	Automatic Choke	Choke Rod (in.)	Choke Unloader (in.)	Fast Idle Speed
1971	7041180	21/32	1 3/4	1 5/64	—	41 drill	—	—	29 drill	1800

① The carburetor identification tag is located at the rear of the carburetor on one of the air horn screws.

OLDSMOBILE

Year	Carburetor Identification①	Float Level (in.)	Float Level (in.)	Pump (Rod (in.)	Idle Vent (in.)	Primary Vacuum Break (in.)	Secondary Vacuum Break (in.)	Secondary Opening (in.)	Choke Rod (in.)	Choke Unloader (in.)	Fast Idle Speed (rpm)
1969	7029155	9/16	1 3/8	1 7/16	0.025	0.180	—	1 Lean	0.140	0.170	—
	7029156	9/16	1 3/8	1 7/16	0.025	0.180	—	Index	0.140	0.170	—
	7029158	9/16	1 3/8	1 7/16	0.025	0.180	—	Index	0.140	0.170	—
	7029159	9/16	1 3/8	1 7/16	0.025	0.180	—	Index	0.140	0.170	—
1970	7040154	9/16	1 3/8	1 11/32	—	0.160	—	Index	0.140	0.170	—
	7040155	9/16	1 3/8	1 11/32	—	0.160	—	1 Lean	0.140	0.170	—
	7040156	9/16	1 3/8	1 11/32	—	0.160	—	Index	0.140	0.170	—
	7040158	9/16	1 3/8	1 11/32	—	0.160	—	Index	0.140	0.170	—
	7040159	9/16	1 3/8	1 11/32	—	0.160	—	Index	0.140	0.170	—
1971	7041155	9/16	1 3/8	1 11/32	—	0.200	—	1 Lean	0.140	0.170	—
	7041156	9/16	1 3/8	1 11/32	—	0.200	—	Index	0.140	0.170	—
	7041159	9/16	1 3/8	1 11/32	—	0.215	—	Index	0.140	0.170	—
1972	7042155	17/32	1 3/8	1 3/8	—	0.200	—	1 Lean	0.160	0.170	—
	7042156	17/32	1 3/8	1 3/8	—	0.200	—	Index	0.160	0.170	—
1973	All	15/32	1 9/32	1 11/32	—	0.200	—	Index	0.160	0.250	—
1975	7045143	15/32	1 9/32	1 19/32	—	0.140	0.120	1 Rich	0.080	0.080	Preset
	7045147	7/16	1 9/32	1 19/32	—	0.120	0.120	1 Lean	0.080	0.140	1800②
	7045149	7/16	1 9/32	1 19/32	—	0.120	0.120	1 Rich	0.080	0.140	1800②
	7045160	9/16	1 7/32	1 11/32	—	0.145	0.265	1 Rich	0.085	0.180	Preset
	7045161	9/16	1 7/32	1 11/32	—	0.145	0.265	1 Rich	0.085	0.180	Preset
	7045449	7/16	1 9/32	1 19/32	—	0.120	0.120	1 Lean	0.080	0.140	Preset

① The carburetor identification tag is located at the rear of the carburetor on one of the air horn screws.
② In Park
③ In Neutral

PONTIAC

Year	Carburetor Identification①	Float Level (in.)	Float Level (in.)	Pump (Rod (in.)	Idle Vent (in.)	Primary Vacuum Break (in.)	Secondary Vacuum Break (in.)	Secondary Opening (in.)	Choke Rod (in.)	Choke Unloader (in.)	Fast Idle Speed (rpm)
1969	7028066	9/16	1 3/4	1 11/32	—	0.170	—	—	0.085	0.180	—
	7028071	9/16	1 3/4	1 11/32	—	0.160	—	—	0.085	0.180	—
	7029060	9/16	1 3/4	1 11/32	—	0.150	—	—	0.085	0.180	—
	7029062	9/16	1 3/4	1 11/32	—	0.150	—	—	0.085	0.180	—
1970	7040060	11/16	1 3/4	1 11/32	—	0.180	—	—	0.085	0.180	—
	7040062	9/16	1 3/4	1 11/32	—	0.150	—	—	0.085	0.180	—
	7040064	11/16	1 3/4	1 11/32	—	0.150	—	—	0.085	0.180	—
	7040066	11/16	1 3/4	1 11/32	—	0.170	—	—	0.085	0.180	—
	7040071	9/16	1 3/4	1 11/32	—	0.160	—	—	0.085	0.180	—
	7040072	9/16	1 3/4	1 11/32	—	0.150	—	—	0.085	0.180	—
	7040460	11/16	1 3/4	1 11/32	—	0.150	—	—	0.085	0.180	—
	7040461	11/16	1 3/4	1 11/32	—	0.150	—	—	0.085	0.180	—
	7040462	9/16	1 3/4	1 11/32	—	0.150	—	—	0.085	0.180	—
	7040463	9/16	1 3/4	1 11/32	—	0.150	—	—	0.085	0.180	—
	7040466	11/16	1 3/4	1 11/32	—	0.170	—	—	0.085	0.180	—
	7040471	9/16	1 3/4	1 11/32	—	0.160	—	—	0.085	0.180	—
1971	7041060	11/16	1 3/4	1 11/32	—	0.125	—	—	0.085	0.180	—
	7041061	11/16	1 3/4	1 11/32	—	0.125	—	—	0.085	0.180	—
	7041062	9/16	1 3/4	1 11/32	—	0.105	—	—	0.085	0.180	—
	7041063	9/16	1 3/4	1 11/32	—	0.105	—	—	0.085	0.180	—

PONTIAC

Year	Carburetor Identification①	Float Level (in.)	Float Level (in.)	Pump (Rod (in.)	Idle Vent (in.)	Primary Vacuum Break (in.)	Secondary Vacuum Break (in.)	Secondary Opening (in.)	Choke Rod (in.)	Choke Unloader (in.)	Fast Idle Speed (rpm)
	7041064	11/16	1 3/4	1 11/32	—	0.130	—	—	0.085	0.180	—
	7041070	11/16	1 3/4	1 11/32	—	0.125	—	—	0.085	0.180	—
	7041072	9/16	1 3/4	1 11/32	—	0.105	—	—	0.085	0.180	—
	7041074	11/16	1 3/4	1 11/32	—	0.130	—	—	0.085	0.180	—
	7041171	9/16	1 3/4	1 11/32	—	0.140	—	—	0.085	0.180	—
1972	7042060	5/8	1 9/32	1 11/32	—	0.122	—	—	0.085	0.180	—
	7042061	5/8	1 9/32	1 11/32	—	0.122	—	—	0.085	0.180	—
	7042062	9/16	1 9/32	1 11/32	—	0.105	—	—	0.085	0.180	—
	7042064	5/8	1 9/32	1 11/32	—	0.150	—	—	0.085	0.180	—
	7042100	25/32	1 31/32	1 5/16	—	0.080	—	—	0.040	0.215	—
	7042101	25/32	1 31/32	1 5/16	—	0.100	—	—	0.075	0.215	—
1973	7043062	21/32	1 9/32	1 5/16	—	0.167	—	—	0.085	0.180	—
	7043063	21/32	1 9/32	1 5/16	—	0.167	—	—	0.085	0.180	—
	7043071	23/32	1 9/32	1 5/16	—	0.195	—	—	0.085	0.180	—
	7043072	23/32	1 9/32	1 5/16	—	0.167	—	—	0.085	0.180	—
	7043060	21/32	1 9/32	1 5/16	—	0.157	—	—	0.085	0.180	—
	7043061	21/32	1 9/32	1 5/16	—	0.157	—	—	0.085	0.180	—
	7043066	21/32	1 9/32	1 5/16	—	0.180	—	—	0.085	0.180	—
	7043067	21/32	1 9/32	1 5/16	—	0.180	—	—	0.085	0.180	—
	7043070	23/32	1 9/32	1 5/16	—	0.157	—	—	0.085	0.180	—
1974	7043060	0.670	1 3/4	1 5/16	—	0.157	—	1 Lean	0.085	0.180	—
	7043062	0.670	1 3/4	1 5/16	—	0.167	—	1 Lean	0.085	0.180	—
	7043070	0.670	1 3/4	1 5/16	—	0.157	—	1 Lean	0.085	0.180	—
	7043071	0.670	1 3/4	1 5/16	—	0.195	—	1 Lean	0.085	0.180	—
	7043072	0.670	1 3/4	1 5/16	—	0.167	—	1 Lean	0.085	0.180	—
	7044063	0.670	1 3/4	1 5/16	—	0.157	—	1 Lean	0.085	0.180	—
	7044066	0.670	1 3/4	1 5/16	—	0.177	—	1 Lean	0.085	0.180	—
	7044067	0.670	1 3/4	1 5/16	—	0.177	—	1 Lean	0.085	0.180	—
1975	7045160	9/16	1 7/32	1 3/4	0.025	0.145	0.265	1 Rich	0.085	0.180	—
	7045162	9/16	1 7/32	1 13/16	0.025	0.145	0.260	1 Rich	0.085	0.180	—
	7045171	9/16	1 7/32	1 13/16	0.025	0.145	0.260	1 Rich	0.085	0.180	—
	7045143	15/32	1 7/32	1 13/16	0.025	0.140	0.120	1 Rich	0.080	0.180	—

① The carburetor identification tag is located at the rear of the carburetor on one of the air horn screws.

Model 2MC

The Rochester model 2MC carburetor is a two-barrel single stage carburetor which incorporates the design features of the primary side of the standard Rochester Quadrajet four-barrel carburetor.

Fast Idle

1. Place the fast idle lever on the high step of the fast idle cam.
2. Make sure that the choke valve is wide open and the engine warm.
3. Turn the fast idle screw to get the proper fast idle rpm.

Fast Idle Cam (Choke Rod) Adjustment

1. Adjust the fast idle speed.
2. Place the cam follower lever on the second step of the fast idle cam, holding it firmly against the rise of the high step.
3. Close the choke valve by pushing upward on the choke coil lever inside the choke housing.
4. Gauge between the upper edge of

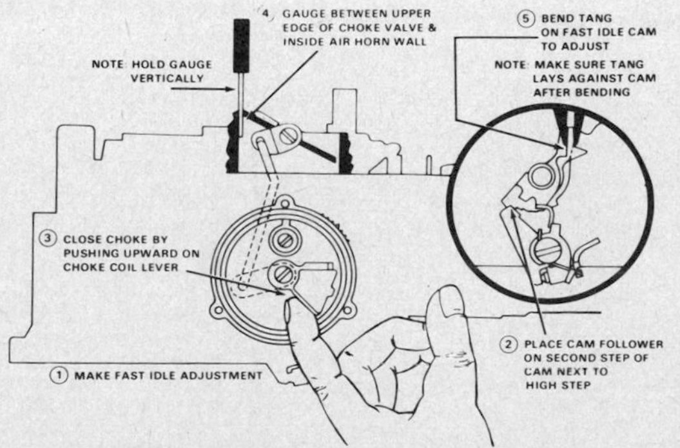

Fast idle cam (choke rod) adjustment (© Buick Div., G.M. Corp.)

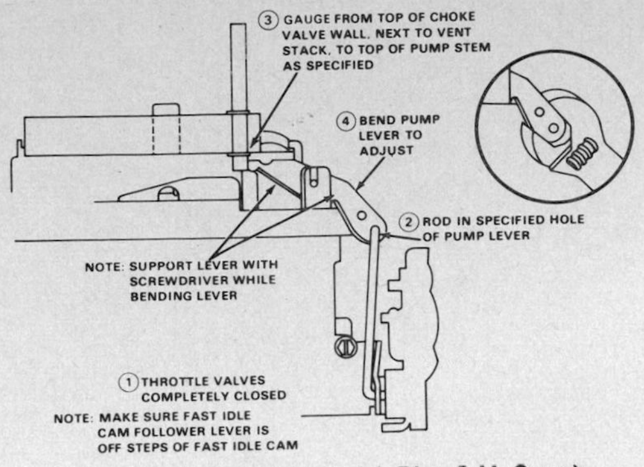

Pump adjustment (© Buick Div., G.M. Corp.)

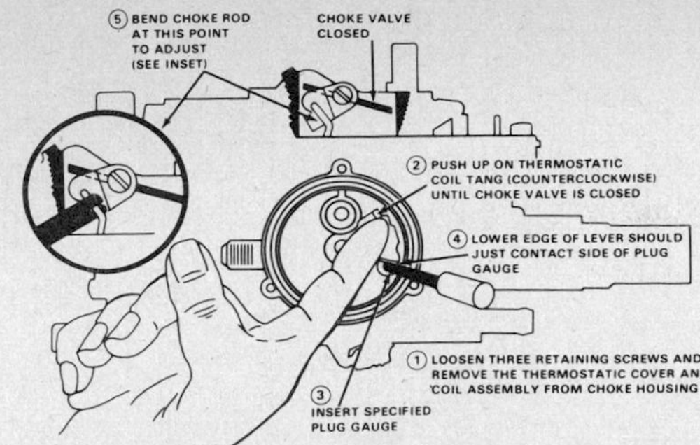

Choke coil lever adjustment (© Buick Div., G.M. Corp.)

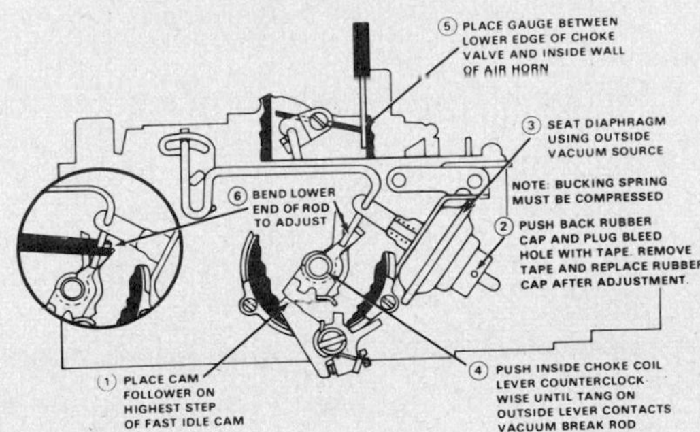

Vacuum break adjustment (© Buick Div., G.M. Corp.)

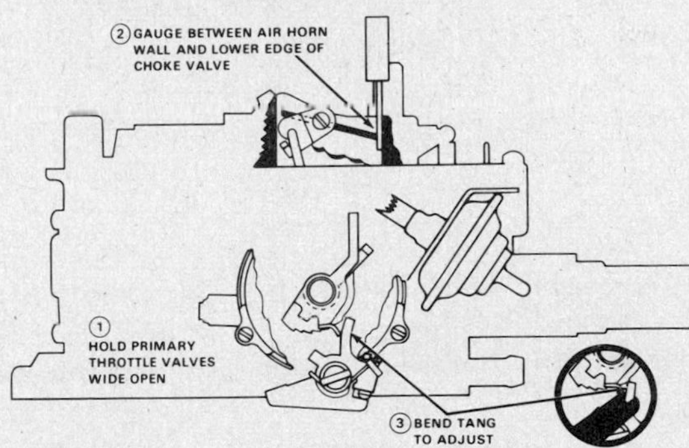

Unloader adjustment (© Buick Div., G.M. Corp.)

the choke valve and the inside of the air horn wall.

5. Bend the tang on the intermediate choke lever to adjust.

Pump Adjustment

1. With the fast idle cam follower off the steps of the fast idle cam, back out the idle speed screw until the throttle valves are completely closed.
2. Place the pump rod in the proper hole of the lever.
3. Measure from the top of the choke valve wall, next to the vent stack, to the top of the pump stem.
4. Bend the pump lever to adjust.

Choke Coil Lever Adjustment

1. Remove the choke cover and thermostatic coil from the choke housing.
2. Push up on the coil tang (counter-clockwise) until the choke valve is closed.
3. Insert a 0.120 in. plug gauge in the hole in the choke housing.
4. The lower edge of the choke coil lever should just contact the side of the plug gauge.
5. Bend the choke rod to adjust.

Vacuum Break Adjustment

1. Place the cam follower on the highest step of the fast idle cam.
2. Seat the vacuum break diaphragm by using an outside vacuum source.
3. Remove the choke cover and thermostatic coil and push up on the coil lever inside the choke housing until the tang on the vacuum break lever contacts the tang on the vacuum break plunger stem. Do not compress the backing spring for lean adjustment. Compress the backing spring for rich adjustment.
4. With the choke rod in the bottom of the slot in the choke lever, gauge between the upper edge of the choke valve and the inside wall of the air horn.
5. Bend the link rod at the vacuum break plunger stem to adjust the lean setting. Bend the link rod at the opposite end from the diaphragm to adjust the rich setting.

Unloader Adjustment

1. With the choke valve completely closed, hold the throttle valves wide open.
2. Measure between the edge of the choke valve and air horn wall.
3. Bend the tang on the fast idle lever to obtain the proper measurement.

Idle Speed-Up Solenoid Adjustment

1. With the engine at normal operating temperature and the air conditioning turned on, the solenoid should be electrically energized (plunger stem extended).
2. Adjust the plunger screw to obtain the specified idle speed.
3. Turn off the air conditioner. The solenoid plunger should move away from the tang on the throttle lever.
4. Adjust the curb idle speed with the idle speed screw, if necessary.

BUICK

Year	Carburetor Identification①	Float Level (in.)	Choke Rod (in.)	Choke Unloader (in.)	Vacuum Break Lean (in.)	Vacuum Break Rich (in.)	Pump Rod (in.)	Choke Coil Lever (in.)
1975	7045156	5/32	0.130	0.285	0.235	0.150	9/32②	0.120
	7045248	5/32	0.130	0.285	0.235	0.150	9/32②	0.120
	7045358	3/16	0.130	0.285	0.300	0.150	5/16③	0.120
	7045354	3/16	0.130	0.285	0.300	0.150	5/16③	0.120

① The carburetor identification tag is located at the rear of the carburetor on one of the air horn attaching screws.

② Inner hole.
③ Outer hole.

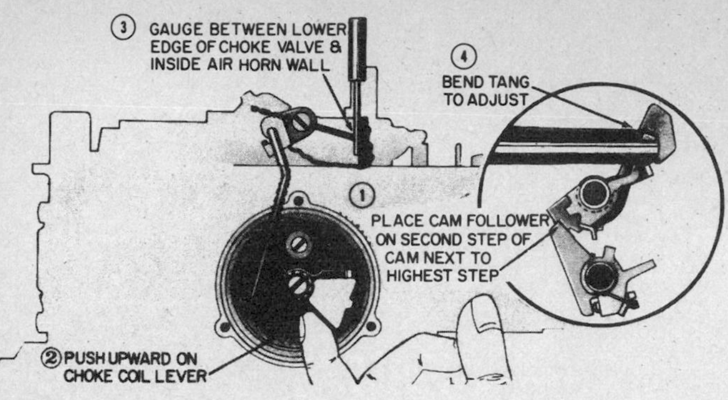

Fast Idle Cam Adjustment
(© Oldsmobile Div., G.M. Corp)

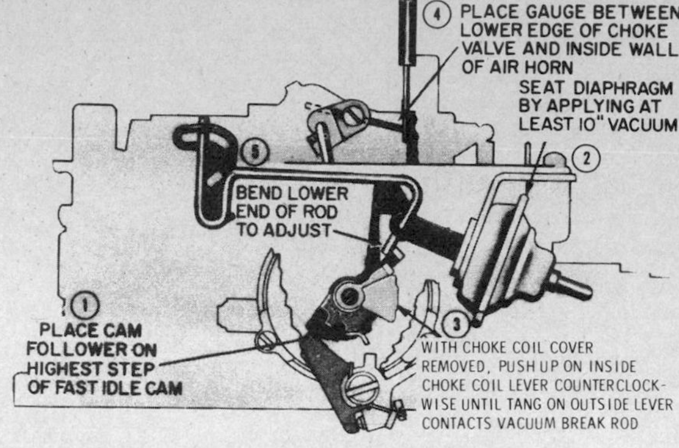

Vacuum Break Adjustment
(© Oldsmobile Div., G.M. Corp)

Primary Vacuum Break Adjustment (Beginning 1975)

1. Loosen the three retaining screws and remove the thermostatic cover and coil assembly from the choke housing.
2. Place the cam follower lever on the highest step of the fast idle cam.
3. Seat the front vacuum diaphragm using an outside vacuum source.
4. Push up on the inside choke coil lever until the tang on the vacuum break lever contacts the tang on the vacuum break plunger.
5. Place the proper size gauge between the upper edge of the choke valve and the inside of the air horn wall.
6. To adjust, turn the adjustment screw on the vacuum break plunger lever.
7. Install the vacuum hose to the vacuum break unit.

Secondary Vacuum Break (Through 1974)

1. Using an outside vacuum source, seat the auxiliary vacuum break diaphragm plunger.
2. Rotate the choke lever in the closed position until the spring loaded diaphragm plunger is fully extended.
3. Holding the choke valve closed, check the distance between the lower edge of the choke valve and the air horn wall.
4. To adjust to specifications, bend the vacuum break link.

Secondary Vacuum Break Adjustment (Beginning 1975)

1. Remove the thermostatic cover and coil assembly from the choke housing.
2. Place the cam follower on the highest step of the fast idle cam.
3. Tape over the bleed hole in the rear vacuum break diaphragm and seat the diaphragm using an outside vacuum source.
4. Close the choke by pushing up on the choke coil lever inside the choke housing.
5. With the choke rod in the bottom of the slot in the choke lever, measure between the upper edge of the choke valve and the air horn wall with a wire type gauge.

NOTE: On 1975 454 cu. in engines the choke valve should be held wide open.

6. To adjust, bend the vacuum break rod at the first bend near the diaphragm.
7. Remove the tape covering the bleed hole of the diaphragm and connect the vacuum hose.

Choke Unloader

1. Push up on the vacuum break lever to close the choke valve, and fully open the throttle valves.
2. Measure the distance from the lower (upper beginning 1975) edge of the choke valve to the air horn wall.
3. To adjust, bend the tang on the fast idle lever.

Choke Coil Rod

1. Close the choke valve by rotating the choke coil lever counterclockwise.
2. Disconnect the thermostatic coil rod from the upper lever.
3. Push down on the rod until it contacts the bracket of the coil.
4. The rod must fit in the notch of the upper lever.
5. If it does not, it must be bent on the curved portion just below the upper lever.

Secondary Closing Adjustment

This adjustment assures proper closing of the secondary throttle plates.

1. Set the slow idle as per instructions in the appropriate car section. Make sure that the fast idle cam follower is not resting on the fast idle cam and the choke valve is wide open.
2. There should be 0.020 in. clearance between the secondary throttle actuating rod and the front of the slot on the secondary throttle lever with the closing tang on the throttle lever resting against the actuating lever.

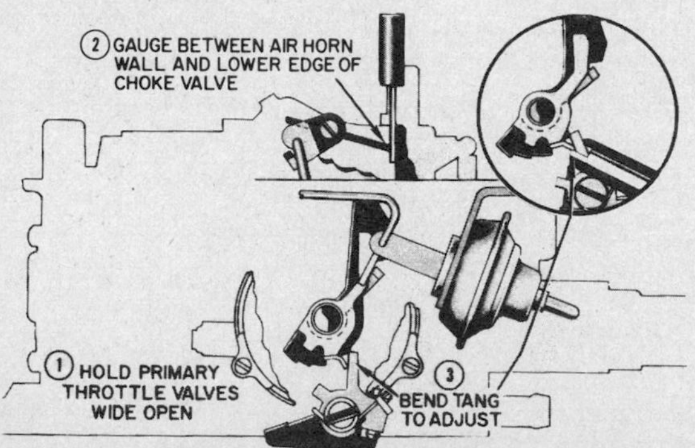

Choke Unloader Adjustment
(© Oldsmobile Div., G.M. Corp)

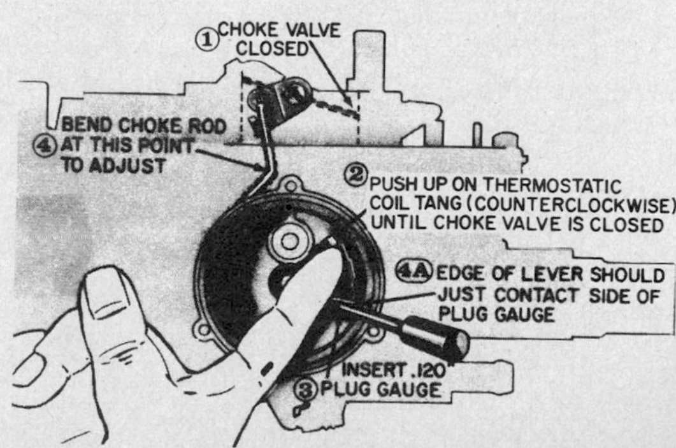

Choke Coil Rod Adjustment
(© Oldsmobile Div., G.M. Corp)

OLDSMOBILE

Year	Carburetor Identification①	Float Level (in.)	Choke Rod (in.)	Choke Unloader (in.)	Vacuum Break Lean (in.)	Vacuum Break Rich (in.)	Pump Rod (in.)	Choke Coil Lever (in.)
1975	7045297	3/16	0.130	0.300	0.300	0.150	9/32②	0.120
	7045354	3/16	0.130	0.300	0.300	0.150	5/16③	0.120
	7045358	3/16	0.130	0.300	0.300	0.150	5/16③	0.120
	7045156	5/32	0.130	0.300	0.300	0.150	9/32②	0.120
	7045598	5/32	0.130	0.300	0.300	0.150	3/16②	0.120
	7045298	5/32	0.130	0.300	0.300	0.150	3/16②	0.120
	7045356	5/32	0.130	0.300	0.300	0.150	3/16②	0.120

① The carburetor identification tag is located at the rear of the carburetor on one of the air horn attaching screws.
② Inner hole
③ Outer hole

PONTIAC

Year	Carburetor Identification①	Float Level (in.)	Choke Rod (in.)	Choke Unloader (in.)	Vacuum Break Lean (in.)	Vacuum Break Rich (in.)	Pump Rod (in.)	Choke Coil Lever (in.)
1975	7045156	5/32	0.130	0.275	0.230	0.150	9/32②	0.120
	7045297	3/16	0.130	0.275	0.275	0.180	9/32②	0.120
	7045298	5/32	0.130	0.275	0.275	0.150	9/32②	0.120
	7045598	5/32	0.160	0.275	0.230	0.150	9/32②	0.120
	7045356	5/32	0.160	0.275	0.275	0.180	9/32②	0.120

① The carburetor identification tag is located at the rear of the carburetor on one of the air horn attaching screws.
② Inner hole

Model 4MC, 4MV

The Rochester Quadrajet carburetor is a two stage, four-barrel downdraft carburetor. The designation MC or MV refers to the type of choke system the carburetor is designed for. The MV model is equipped with a manifold mounted thermostatic choke coil. The MC model has a choke housing and coil mounted on the side of the float bowl.

The primary side of the carburetor is equipped with 1⅜ diameter bores and a triple venturi with plain tube nozzles. During off idle and part throttle operation, the fuel is metered through tapered metering rods operating in specially designed jets positioned by a manifold vacuum responsive piston.

The secondary side of the carburetor contains two 2¼ bores. An air valve is used on the secondary side for metering control and supplements the primary bores.

The secondary air valve operates tapered metering rods which regulate the fuel in constant proportion to the air being supplied.

Fast Idle

1. Position the fast idle lever on the

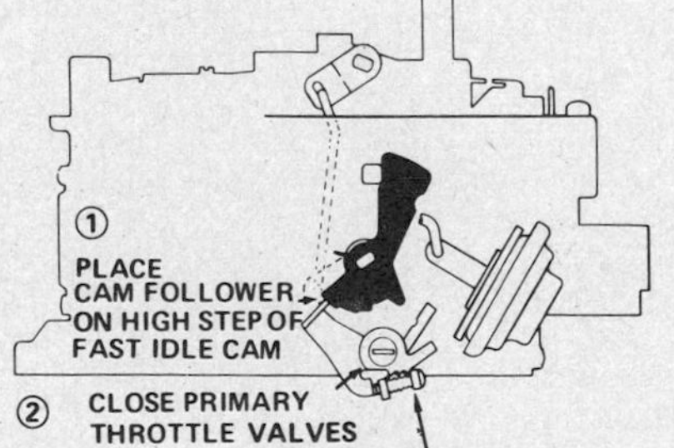

Fast Idle Adjustment
(© Chevrolet Div., G.M. Corp)

high step of the fast idle cam, the second step on the 1974 454 engine.
2. Be sure that the choke is wide open and the engine warm.
3. Turn the fast idle screw to gain the proper fast idle rpm.

Choke Rod (Fast idle cam)

1. Adjust the fast idle and place the cam follower on the second step of the fast idle cam.
2. Close the choke valve by exerting counterclockwise pressure on the external choke lever.
3. Insert a gauge of the proper size between the lower (upper beginning 1975) edge of the choke valve and the inside air horn wall.
4. To adjust models through 1974, bend the choke rod. To adjust 1975 and later models, bend the tang on the fast idle cam. Be sure that the tang rests against the cam after bending.

Primary Vacuum Break (Through 1974)

1. Fully seat the vacuum break diaphragm using an outside vacuum source.
2. Open the throttle valve enough to allow the fast idle cam follower to clear the fast idle cam.
3. The end of the vacuum break rod should be at the outer end of the slot in the vacuum break diaphragm plunger.
4. The specified clearance should register from the lower end of the choke valve to the inside air horn wall.
5. If the clearance is not correct, bend the vacuum break link at the point shown in the illustration.

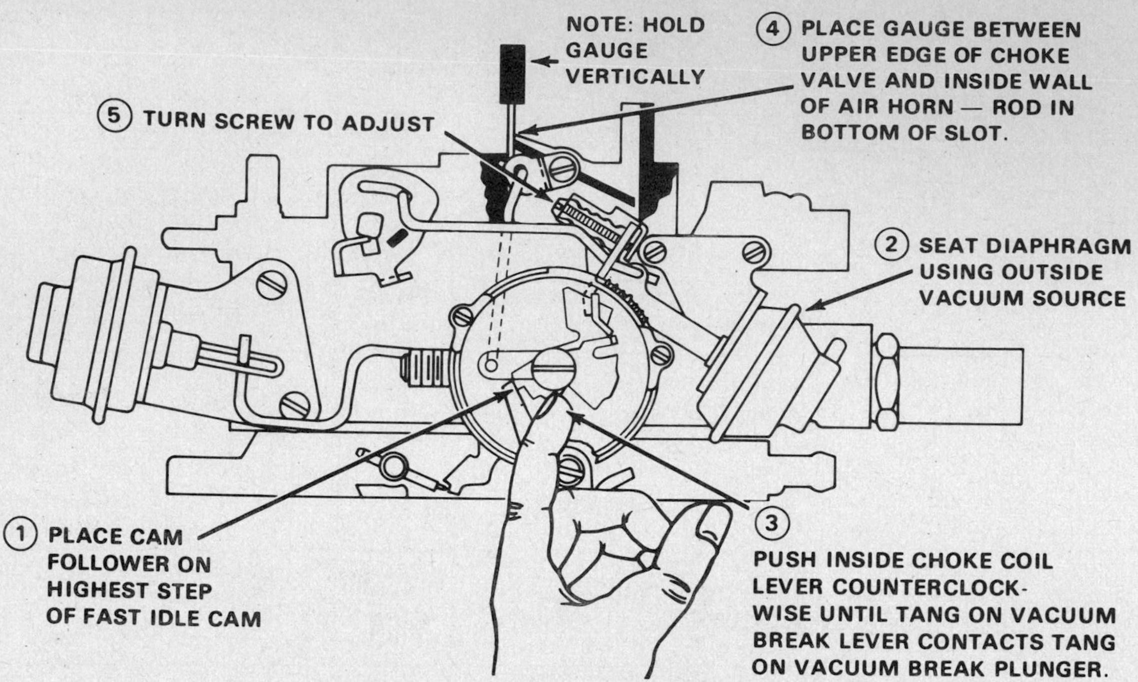

Front vacuum break adjustment, beginning 1975 (© Buick Div., G.M. Corp.)

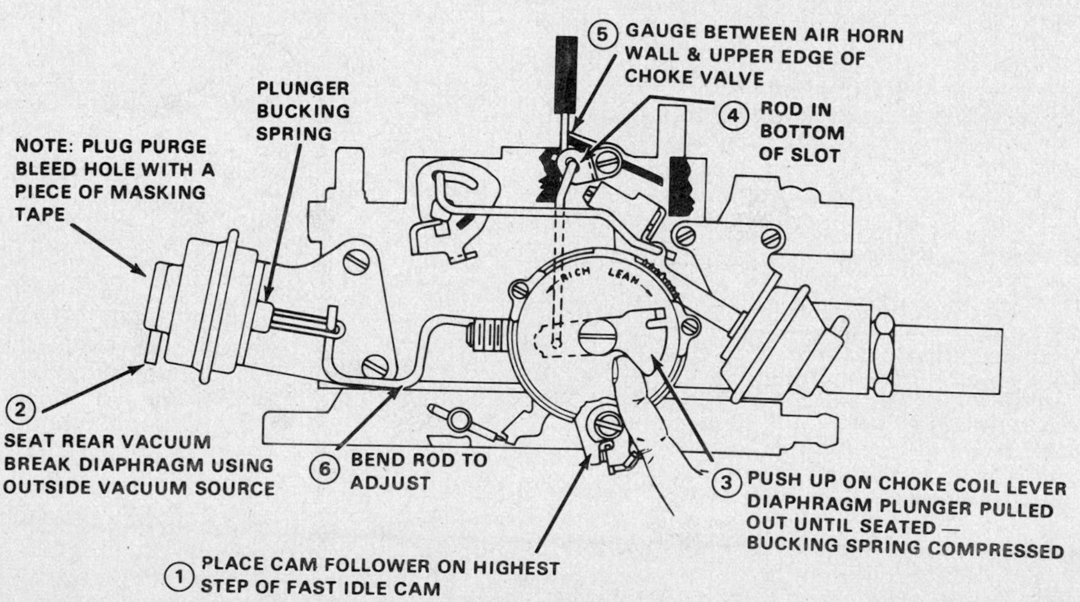

Rear vacuum break adjustment, beginning 1975 (except 454 cu in.)
(© Buick Div., G.M. Corp.)

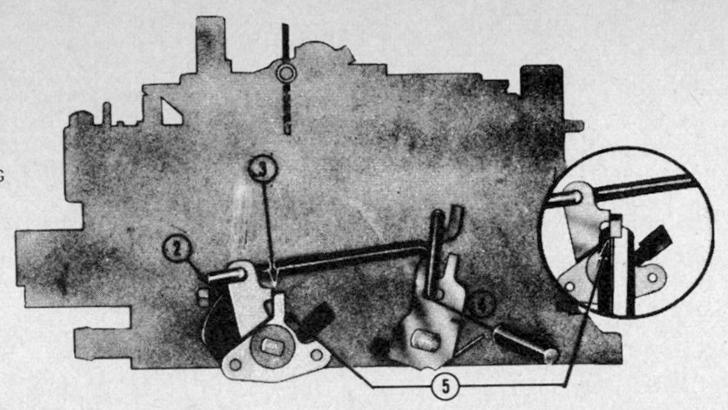

Secondary Closing Adjustments (© Odsmobile Div., G.M. Corp)

3. Bend the secondary closing tang on the primary throttle actuating rod or lever to adjust.

Secondary Opening Adjustment

1. Open the primary throttle valves until the actuating link contacts the upper tang on the secondary lever.
2. With two point linkage, the bottom of the link should be in the center of the secondary lever slot.
3. With three point linkage, there should be 0.070 in. clearance between the link and the middle tang.
4. Bend the upper tang on the secondary lever to adjust as necessary.

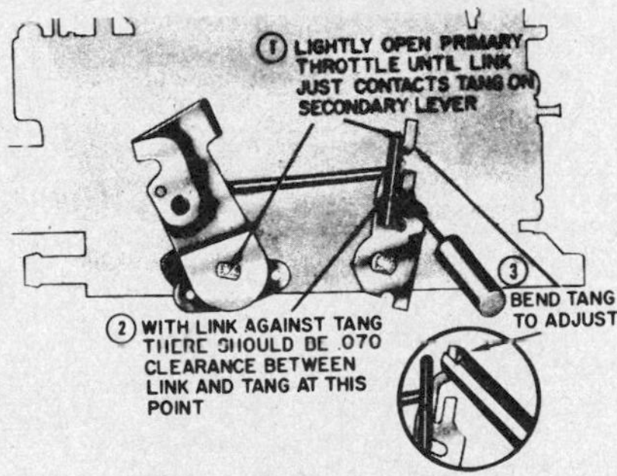

Secondary Opening Adjustments
(© Oldsmobile Div., G.M. Corp)

Float Level

With the air horn assembly upside down, measure the distance from the air horn gasket surface (gasket removed) to the top of the float at the toe (1/16 in. back from the toe on 1975 (and later models).

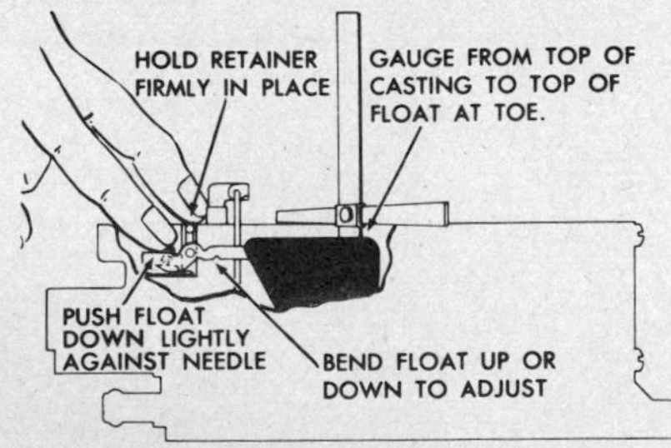

Adjusting Float Level
(© Pontiac Div., G.M. Corp)

NOTE: Make sure the retaining pin is firmly held in place and that the tang of the float is firmly against the needle and seat assembly.

Bend the float arm to adjust.

Secondary Metering Rod Adjustment

1. With the air valves fully closed, measure from the top of each metering rod to the top of the air horn casting.
2. The measurement should be 5 3/64 in., 2 7/32 in. on 1974 Cadillac; if not, correct by bending the metering rod hanger. Make sure both rods are adjusted correctly.

Accelerator Pump

1. Close the primary throttle valves by backing out the slow idle screw and making sure that the fast idle cam follower is off the steps of the fast idle cam.
2. Bend the secondary throttle closing tang away from the primary throttle lever, if necessary, to insure that the primary throttle valves are fully closed.
3. With the pump in the appropriate hole in the pump lever, measure from the top of the choke valve wall to the top of the pump stem.
4. To adjust, bend the pump lever.

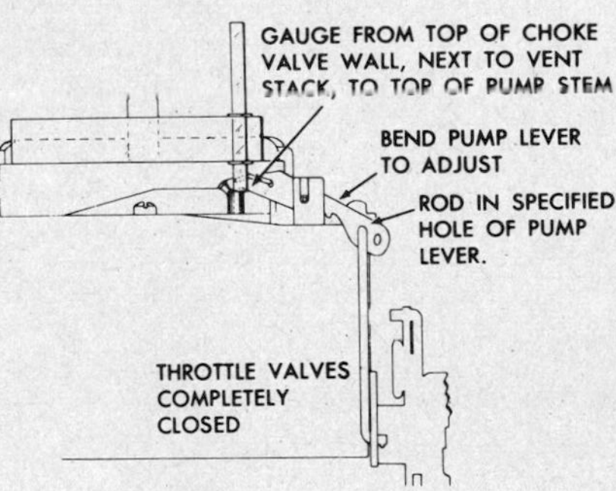

Accelerator Pump Rod Adjustment
(© Pontiac Div., G.M. Corp)

5. After adjusting, readjust the secondary throttle tang and the slow idle screw.

Idle Vent Adjustment

After adjusting the accelerator pump rod as specified above, open the primary throttle valve enough to just close the idle vent. Measure from the top of the choke valve wall to the top of the pump plunger stem. If adjustment is necessary, bend the wire tang on the pump lever.

Air Valve Spring Adjustment

To adjust the air valve spring windup, loosen the Allen head lockscrew and turn the adjusting screw counterclockwise to remove all spring tension. With the air valve closed, turn the adjusting screw clockwise

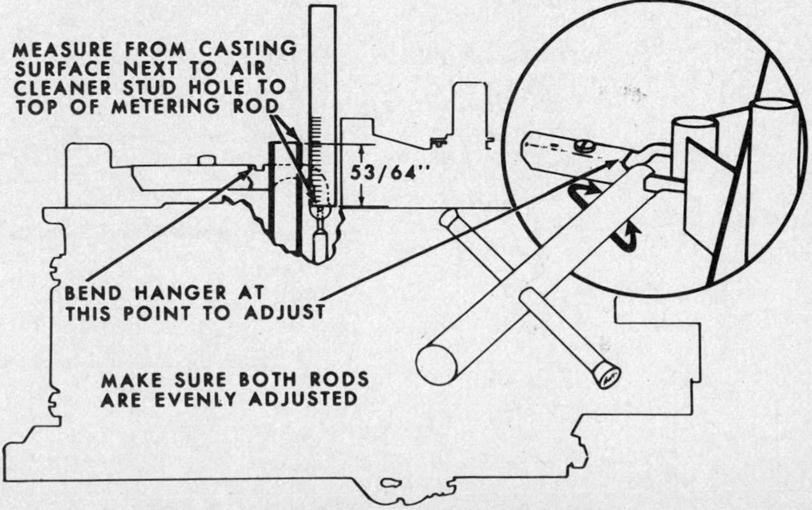

Adjusting Secondary Metering Rods (© Pontiac Div., G.M. Corp)

the specified number of turns after the torsion spring contacts the pin on the shaft. Hold the adjusting screw in this position and tighten the lock-screw.

1. Screw—cam and fast idle levers
2. Fast idle lever
3. Spring—fast idle screw
4. Screw—fast idle adjusting
5. Cam lever
6. Throttle body assembly
7. Screw—throttle body
8. Spring—idle needle
9. Idle needle
10. Rod—accelerator pump
11. Throttle lever
12. Screw—throttle lever

Throttle Body 4MV, Exploded View
(© Chevrolet Div., G.M. Corp)

Exploded View 4MV Float Bowl (© Chevrolet Div., G.M. Corp)

1. Screw—choke control
2. Hose—vacuum break
3. Vacuum break
4. Link—vacuum break
5. Clip—vacuum break rod
6. Bracket assembly—choke control
7. Cam—fast idle
8. Lever—secondary lock out
9. Lever—choke intermediate
10. Rod—choke
11. Nut—fuel inlet
12. Gasket—fuel filter
13. Gasket—fuel inlet nut
14. Filter—fuel inlet
15. Spring—fuel filter
16. Gasket—idle compensator
17. Idle compensator assembly
18. Cover—idle compensator
19. Screw—idle compensator cover
20. Spring—idle speed screw
21. Screw—idle speed
22. Jet—primary
23. Ball—pump discharge
24. Retainer—pump discharge ball
25. Spring—pump return
26. Pump assembly
27. Spring—power piston
28. Metering rod—primary
29. Power piston assembly—primary
30. Spring—metering rod primary
31. Float needle and diaphragm assembly
32. Retainer—float needle assembly
33. Screw—float needle retainer
34. Pull clip—float needle
35. Float assembly
36. Hinge pin—float assembly
37. Gasket—throttle body
38. Float bowl assembly
39. Insert—float bowl
40. Gasket—air horn
41. Baffle—float bowl

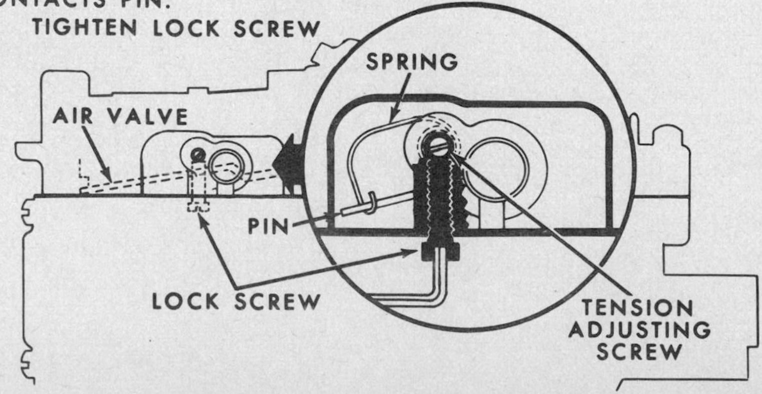

Air Valve Spring Setting (© Pontiac Div., G.M. Corp)

4MC, 4MV CARBURETOR SPECIFICATIONS

BUICK

Year	Carburetor Identification①	Float Level (in.)	Air Valve Spring (turn)	Pump (Rod (in.)	Idle Vent (in.)	Primary Vacuum Break (in.)	Secondary Vacuum Break (in.)	Secondary Opening (in.)	Choke Rod (in.)	Choke Unloader (in.)	Fast Idle Speed (rpm)
1969	7029240	3/8	5/8	13/32	1/2	0.180	—	0.020	0.130	0.325	600
	7029241	5/16	5/8	13/32	1/2	0.180	—	0.020	0.130	0.325	600
	7029242	3/8	5/8	13/32	1/2	0.180	—	0.020	0.130	0.325	600
	7029243	3/8	5/8	13/32	1/2	0.215	—	0.020	0.140	0.325	600
	7029244	5/16	5/8	13/32	1/2	0.190	—	0.020	0.130	0.325	600
	7029245	5/16	5/8	13/32	1/2	0.215	—	0.020	0.130	0.325	600
1970	7040240	3/8	1/2	9/32	—	0.180	—	0.020	0.130	0.335	720
	7040243	3/8	1/2	9/32	—	0.215	—	0.020	0.130	0.335	650
	7040244	5/16	1/2	13/32	—	0.170	—	0.020	0.130	0.335	720
	7040245	5/16	1/2	13/32	—	0.215	—	0.020	0.130	0.335	650
	7040246	5/16	1/2	9/32	—	0.200	—	0.020	0.130	0.335	650
	7040247	3/8	1/2	9/32	—	0.160	—	0.020	0.130	0.335	650
1971	7041242	3/8	1/2	1/4	—	0.200	—	0.020	0.130	0.335	800
	7041243	13/32	1/2	1/4	—	0.215	—	0.020	0.130	0.335	600
	7041245	15/32	1/2	9/32	—	0.170	—	0.020	0.130	0.335	700
	7041540	3/8	1/2	1/4	—	0.180	—	0.020	0.130	0.335	600
	7041544	15/32	1/2	9/32	—	0.170	—	0.020	0.130	0.335	600
1972	7042240	3/8	1/2	1/4	—	0.180	—	0.020	0.130	0.335	820
	7042242	3/8	1/2	1/4	—	0.200	—	0.020	0.130	0.335	700
	7042243	13/32	1/2	1/4	—	0.215	—	0.020	0.130	0.335	920
	7042244	15/32	1/2	9/32	—	0.170	—	0.020	0.130	0.335	700
	7042245	15/32	1/2	9/32	—	0.170	—	0.020	0.130	0.335	920
	7042940	3/8	1/2	1/4	—	0.180	—	0.020	0.130	0.335	700
	7042942	3/8	1/2	1/4	—	0.200	—	0.020	0.130	0.335	700
	7042944	15/32	1/2	9/32	—	0.170	—	0.020	0.130	0.335	700
1973	7043240	13/32	7/16	7/16	—	0.215	—	0.020	0.130	0.335	900
	7043243	13/32	7/16	7/16	—	0.215	—	0.020	0.130	0.335	900
	7043242	13/32	7/16	7/16	—	0.200	—	0.020	0.130	0.335	900
	7043244	15/32	11/16	0.306	—	0.170	—	0.020	0.130	0.335	900
	7043245	15/32	11/16	0.410	—	0.170	—	0.020	0.130	0.335	900
1974	7044240	13/32	7/16	1/4	—	0.215	0.160	0.070	0.130	0.335	700
	7044540	13/32	7/16	1/4	—	0.215	0.160	0.070	0.130	0.335	700
	7044242	13/32	7/16	1/4	—	0.200	0.180	0.070	0.130	0.335	700
	7044241	13/32	7/16	1/4	—	0.215	0.160	0.070	0.130	0.335	700
	7044244	15/32	11/16	0.306	—	0.170	0.150	0.070	0.130	0.335	700
	7044544	15/32	11/16	0.306	—	0.170	0.150	0.070	0.130	0.335	700
	7044546	15/32	11/16	0.306	—	0.170	0.150	0.070	0.130	0.335	700
	7044246	15/32	11/16	0.306	—	0.170	0.150	0.070	0.130	0.335	700
1975	7045240	7/16	7/16	9/32	—	0.135	0.120	②	0.095	0.240	600
	7045548	7/16	7/16	9/32	—	0.135	0.120	②	0.095	0.240	600
	7045244	5/16	3/4	15/32	—	0.130	0.115	②	0.095	0.240	600
	7045246	5/16	3/4	15/32	—	0.130	0.115	②	0.095	0.240	600
	7045544	5/16	3/4	15/32	—	0.145	0.130	②	0.095	0.240	600
	7045546	5/16	3/4	15/32	—	0.145	0.130	②	0.095	0.240	600

① The carburetor identification tag is located at the rear of the carburetor on one of the air horn screws.

② No measurement necessary; see text

CADILLAC

Year	Carburetor Identification①	Float Level (in.)	Air Valve Spring (turn)	Pump (Rod (in.)	Primary Vacuum Break (in.)	Secondary Vacuum Break (in.)	Secondary Opening (in.)	Choke Rod (in.)	Choke Unloader (in.)	Fast Idle Speed (rpm)
1969	7029230	1/4	1/2	11/32	0.230	—	0.020	0.090	0.300	—
	7029231	1/4	1/2	11/32	0.230	—	0.020	0.090	0.300	—
1970	7047030	1/4	1/2	11/32	0.230	—	0.020	0.090	0.300	—
1971	7041766	1/4	1/2	11/32	0.300	—	0.020	0.090	0.310	—
	7041777	23/64	1/2	11/32	0.300	—	0.020	0.090	0.310	—
1972	7047231	15/64	1/2	11/32	0.140	—	0.020	0.090	0.312	—
	7047232	23/64	1/2	11/32	0.140	—	0.020	0.090	0.312	—
1973	7047331	1/4	1/2	11/32	0.200	—	0.020	0.090	0.015	—
	7047332	23/64	1/2	11/32	0.205	—	0.020	0.090	0.015	—
1974	7044230	1/4	3/8	1/4	0.185	—	0.020	0.110	0.312	1200-1500②
	7044232	23/64	1/2	1/4	0.200	—	0.020	0.110	0.312	1200-1500②
	7044530	1/4	3/8	1/4	0.185	—	0.020	0.110	0.312	1200-1500②
	7044532	23/64	1/2	1/4	0.200	—	0.020	0.110	0.312	1200-1500②
	7044234	1/4	7/16	11/32	0.185	—	0.020	0.110	0.312	1200-1500②
	7044235	23/64	9/16	11/32	0.200	—	0.020	0.110	0.312	1200-1500②
	7044233	19/64	3/8	11/32	0.185	—	0.020	0.110	0.312	1200-1500②
1975	7045230	15/32	7/16	3/8	0.160	0.130	0.015	0.080	0.215	1200-1250
	7045530	15/32	1/2	3/8	0.230	0.230	0.015	0.080	0.215	1200-1250

① The carburetor identification tag is located at the rear of the carburetor on one of the air horn screws.
② On second step.

CHEVROLET

Year	Carburetor Identification①	Float Level (in.)	Air Valve Spring (turn)	Pump (Rod (in.)	Idle Vent (in.)	Primary Vacuum Break (in.)	Secondary Vacuum Break (in.)	Secondary Opening (in.)	Choke Rod (in.)	Choke Unloader (in.)	Fast Idle Speed (rpm)
1969	7029203	7/32	7/16	5/16	3/8	0.245	—	0.015	0.100	0.450	—
	7029202	7/32	7/16	5/16	3/8	0.180	—	0.015	0.100	0.450	—
	7029207	3/16	13/16	5/16	3/8	0.245	—	0.015	0.100	0.450	—
	7029215	1/4	13/16	5/16	3/8	0.245	—	0.015	0.100	0.450	—
	7029204	1/4	13/16	5/16	3/8	0.180	—	0.015	0.100	0.450	—
1970	7040202	1/4	7/16	5/16	—	0.245	—	—	0.100	0.450	—
	7040203	1/4	7/16	5/16	—	0.275	—	—	0.100	0.450	—
	7040207	1/4	13/16	5/16	—	0.275	—	—	0.100	0.450	—
	7040200	1/4	13/16	5/16	—	0.245	—	—	0.100	0.450	—
	7040201	1/4	13/16	5/16	—	0.275	—	—	0.100	0.450	—
	7040204	1/4	13/16	5/16	—	0.245	—	—	0.100	0.450	—
	7040205	1/4	13/16	5/16	—	0.275	—	—	0.100	0.450	—
1971	7041200	1/4	7/16	—	—	0.260	—	—	0.100	—	—
	7041202	1/4	7/16	—	—	0.260	—	—	0.100	—	—
	7041204	1/4	7/16	—	—	0.260	—	—	0.100	—	—
	7041212	1/4	7/16	—	—	0.260	—	—	0.100	—	—
	7041201	1/4	7/16	—	—	0.275	—	—	0.100	—	—
	7041203	1/4	7/16	—	—	0.275	—	—	0.100	—	—
	7041205	1/4	7/16	—	—	0.275	—	—	0.100	—	—
	7041213	1/4	7/16	—	—	0.275	—	—	0.100	—	—
1972	7042220	1/4	7/16	3/8	—	0.250	—	—	0.100	0.450	—
	7042216	1/4	7/16	3/8	—	0.250	—	—	0.100	0.450	—
	7042215	1/4	7/16	3/8	—	0.250	—	—	0.100	0.450	—

CHEVROLET

Year	Carburetor Identification①	Float Level (in.)	Air Valve Spring (turn)	Pump (Rod (in.)	Idle Vent (in.)	Primary Vacuum Break (in.)	Secondary Vacuum Break (in.)	Secondary Opening (in.)	Choke Rod (in.)	Choke Unloader (in.)	Fast Idle Speed (rpm)
	7042217	1/4	7/16	3/8	—	0.250	—	—	0.100	0.450	—
	7042202	1/4	1/2	3/8	—	0.215	—	—	0.100	0.450	—
	7042203	1/4	1/2	3/8	—	0.215	—	—	0.100	0.450	—
	7042902	1/4	1/2	3/8	—	0.215	—	—	0.100	0.450	—
	7042903	1/4	1/2	3/8	—	0.215	—	—	0.100	0.450	—
1973	7043202	7/32	1/2	13/32	—	0.250	—	—	0.430	0.450	—
	7043203	7/32	1/2	13/32	—	0.250	—	—	0.430	0.450	—
	7043212	7/32	1	13/32	—	0.250	—	—	0.430	0.450	—
	7043213	7/32	1	13/32	—	0.250	—	—	0.430	0.450	—
	7043200	1/4	11/16	13/32	—	0.250	—	—	0.430	0.450	—
	7043201	1/4	11/16	13/32	—	0.250	—	—	0.430	0.450	—
1974	7044202	1/4	7/8	13/32②	—	0.230	—	—	0.430	0.450	1600③-1300④
	7044203	1/4	7/8	13/32②	—	0.230	—	—	0.430	0.450	1600③-1300④
	7044206	1/4	7/8	13/32②	—	0.230	—	—	0.430	0.450	1600③-1300④
	7044207	1/4	7/8	13/32②	—	0.230	—	—	0.430	0.450	1600③-1300④
	7044223	3/8	7/16	13/32②	—	0.220	—	—	0.430	0.450	1600③-1300④
	7044201	3/8	7/16	13/32②	—	0.250	—	—	0.430	0.450	1600③-1300④
	7044500	3/8	7/16	13/32②	—	0.250	—	—	0.430	0.450	1600③-1300④
	7044208	1/4	1	13/32②	—	0.230	—	—	0.430	0.450	1600③-1300④
	7044209	1/4	1	13/32②	—	0.230	—	—	0.430	0.450	1600③-1300④
	7044210	1/4	1	13/32②	—	0.230	—	—	0.450	0.450	1600③-1300④
	7044211	1/4	1	13/32②	—	0.230	—	—	0.430	0.450	1600③-1300④
	7044502	1/4	7/8	13/32②	—	0.230	—	—	0.430	0.450	1600③-1300④
	7044503	1/4	7/8	13/32②	—	0.230	—	—	0.430	0.450	1600③-1300④
	7044506	1/4	7/8	13/32②	—	0.230	—	—	0.430	0.450	1600③-1300④
	7044507	1/4	7/8	13/32②	—	0.230	—	—	0.430	0.450	1600③-1300④
	7044221	3/8	7/16	13/32	—	0.250	—	—	0.430	0.450	1600③-1300④
	7044225	3/8	7/16	13/32	—	0.220	—	—	0.430	0.450	1600③-1300④
	7044226	1/4	3/4	13/32	—	0.230	—	—	0.430	0.450	1600③-1300④
	7044505	3/8	7/16	13/32	—	0.250	—	—	0.430	0.450	1600③-1300④
	7044526	1/4	3/4	13/32	—	0.230	—	—	0.430	0.450	1600③-1300④
1975	7045200	17/32	9/16	0.275	—	0.200	0.550	—	0.300	0.325	1000
	7045202	15/32	7/8	0.275	—	0.180	0.170	—	0.300	0.325	1600
	7045203	15/32	7/8	0.275	—	0.180	0.170	—	0.300	0.325	1600
	7045206	15/32	7/8	0.275	—	0.180	0.170	—	0.300	0.325	1600
	7045207	15/32	7/8	0.275	—	0.180	0.170	—	0.300	0.325	1600
	7045208	15/32	7/8	0.275	—	0.180	0.170	—	0.300	0.325	1600
	7045209	15/32	7/8	0.275	—	0.180	0.170	—	0.300	0.325	1600
	7045210	15/32	7/8	0.275	—	0.180	0.170	—	0.300	0.325	1600
	7045211	15/32	7/8	0.275	—	0.180	0.170	—	0.300	0.325	1600
	7045222	15/32	7/8	0.275	—	0.180	0.170	—	0.300	0.325	1600
	7045223	15/32	7/8	0.275	—	0.180	0.170	—	0.300	0.325	1600
	7045224	15/32	3/4	0.275	—	0.180	0.170	—	0.325	0.325	1600
	7045228	15/32	3/4	0.275	—	0.180	0.170	—	0.325	0.325	1600
	7045502	15/32	7/8	0.275	—	0.180	0.170	—	0.300	0.325	1600
	7045503	15/32	7/8	0.275	—	0.180	0.170	—	0.300	0.325	1600
	7045504	15/32	7/8	0.275	—	0.180	0.170	—	0.300	0.325	1600
	7045506	15/32	7/8	0.275	—	0.180	0.170	—	0.300	0.325	1600
	7044507	15/32	7/8	0.275	—	0.180	0.170	—	0.300	0.325	1600

① The carburetor identification tag is located at the rear of the carburetor on one of the air horn screws.
② Without vacuum advance.
③ With automatic transmission; vacuum advance connected and EGR disconnected and the throttle positioned on the high step of cam.
④ With manual transmission; without vacuum advance and the throttle positioned on the high step of cam.

FORD

Year	Carburetor Identification①	Float Level (in.)	Air Valve Spring	Pump Rod (in.)	Idle Vent (in.)	Vacuum Break (in.)	Secondary Opening (in.)	Choke Rod (in.)	Choke Unloader (in.)	Fast Idle Speed (rpm)
1970	DOOF-A	5/8	0.030	5/16	——	0.140	——	0.130	0.300	750②
	DOOF-B	5/8	0.030	5/16	——	0.190	——	0.166	0.300	1850③
	DOOF-E	5/8	0.030	5/16	——	0.190	——	0.166	0.300	1850③
	DOOF-F	5/8	0.030	5/16	——	0.140	——	0.130	0.300	750②
1971	DOOF-A	11/32	0.030	5/16	——	0.140	——	0.130	0.300	1800③
	DOOF-E	11/32	0.030	5/16	——	0.190	——	0.166	0.300	2000③

① The carburetor identification tag is located at the rear of the carburetor on one of the air horn screws.
② Third step of cam.
③ Second step of cam.

OLDSMOBILE

Year	Carburetor Identification①	Float Level (in.)	Air Valve Spring (turn)	Pump (Rod (in.)	Idle Vent (in.)	Primary Vacuum Break (in.)	Secondary Vacuum Break (in.)	Secondary Opening (in.)	Choke Rod (in.)	Choke Unloader (in.)	Fast Idle Speed (rpm)
1969	7029250	1/4	1/2	5/16	——	——	——	——	0.140	0.200	——
	7029251	1/4	3/4	5/16	——	——	——	——	0.140	0.200	——
	7029252	1/4	3/4	5/16	——	——	——	——	0.140	0.200	——
	7029253	1/4	3/4	5/16	——	——	——	——	0.120	0.200	——
	7029254	1/4	3/4	5/16	——	——	——	——	0.140	0.200	——
	7029255	1/4	3/4	5/16	——	——	——	——	0.090	0.200	——
1970	7040250	1/4	1/2	3/8	——	0.200	——	——	0.120	0.200	——
	7040251	1/4	3/4	3/8	——	0.200	——	——	0.120	0.200	——
	7040252	1/4	3/4	3/8	——	0.200	——	——	0.120	0.200	——
	7040253	1/4	3/4	3/8	——	0.275	——	——	0.120	0.200	——
	7040255	1/4	3/4	3/8	——	0.325	——	——	0.120	0.200	——
	7040256	1/4	3/4	3/8	——	0.325	——	——	0.120	0.200	——
	7040257	1/4	3/4	3/8	——	0.200	——	——	0.120	0.200	——
	7040258	1/4	3/4	3/8	——	0.200	——	——	0.120	0.200	——
1971	7041250	1/4	1/2	3/8	——	0.200	——	——	0.120	0.200	——
	7041251	1/4	3/4	3/8	——	0.200	——	——	0.120	0.200	——
	7041252	1/4	3/4	3/8	——	0.200	——	——	0.120	0.200	——
	7041253	1/4	3/4	3/8	——	0.200	——	——	0.120	0.200	——
	7041257	1/4	3/4	3/8	——	0.200	——	——	0.120	0.200	——
1972	7042250	1/4	1/2	3/8	——	0.230	——	——	0.120	0.200	——
	7042251	1/4	3/4	3/8	——	0.215	——	——	0.120	0.200	——
	7042252	1/4	3/4	3/8	——	0.215	——	——	0.120	0.200	——
	7042953	1/4	3/4	3/8	——	0.275	——	——	0.120	0.200	——
1973	7043256	1/4	3/4	——	——	0.200	——	——	0.120	0.300	——
	7043257	1/4	1/2	——	——	0.200	——	——	0.120	0.300	——
	7043255	1/4	3/4	——	——	0.200	——	——	0.120	0.300	——
	7043251	1/4	3/4	——	——	0.200	——	——	0.120	0.300	——
	7043253	1/4	3/4	——	——	0.275	——	——	0.120	0.300	——
	7043252	1/4	3/4	——	——	0.200	——	——	0.120	0.300	——
	7043259	1/4	3/4	——	——	0.215	——	——	0.120	0.300	——

OLDSMOBILE

Year	Carburetor Identification①	Float Level (in.)	Air Valve Spring (turn)	Pump (Rod (in.)	Idle Vent (in.)	Primary Vacuum Break (in.)	Secondary Vacuum Break (in.)	Secondary Opening (in.)	Choke Rod (in.)	Choke Unloader (in.)	Fast Idle Speed (rpm)
1974	7043250	1/4	1/2	3/8	—	0.200	—	0.070	0.120	0.300	1000②
	7043251	1/4	3/4	3/8	—	0.200	—	0.070	0.120	0.300	1000②
	7043252	1/4	3/4	3/8	—	0.200	—	0.070	0.120	0.300	1000②
	7043254	1/4	3/4	3/8	—	0.275	—	0.070	0.120	0.300	1000②
	7043255	1/4	1/2	3/8	—	0.200	—	0.070	0.120	0.300	1000②
	7043256	1/4	1/2	3/8	—	0.200	—	0.070	0.120	0.300	1000②
	7043259	1/4	3/4	3/8	—	0.215	—	0.070	0.120	0.300	1000②
	7043282	1/4	3/4	3/8	—	0.215	—	0.070	0.120	0.300	1000②
	7044557	1/4	3/4	3/8	—	0.200	—	0.070	0.120	0.300	1000②
	7044558	1/4	3/4	3/8	—	0.200	—	0.070	0.120	0.300	1000②
	7044559	1/4	3/4	3/8	—	0.275	—	0.070	0.120	0.300	1000②
1975	7045183	3/8	1/2	9/32	—	0.190	0.140	—	0.135	0.235	③
	7045250	3/8	1/2	9/32	—	0.250	0.180	—	0.170	0.300	③
	7045483	3/8	1/2	9/32	—	0.275	0.180	—	0.135	0.235	③
	7045550	3/8	1/2	9/32	—	0.275	0.180	—	0.135	0.235	③
	7045264	17/32	1/2	9/32	—	0.150	0.260	—	0.130	0.235	③
	7045184	3/8	3/4	9/32	—	0.190	0.140	—	0.135	0.235	③
	7045185	3/8	3/4	9/32	—	0.275	0.140	—	0.135	0.235	③
	7045251	3/8	3/4	9/32	—	0.190	0.140	—	0.135	0.235	③
	7045484	3/8	3/4	9/32	—	0.190	0.140	—	0.135	0.235	③
	7045485	3/8	3/4	9/32	—	0.190	0.180	—	0.160	0.235	③
	7045551	3/8	3/4	9/32	—	0.190	0.140	—	0.135	0.235	③
	7045246	5/16	3/4	3/8	—	0.130	0.115	—	0.095	0.240	③
	7045546	5/16	3/4	3/8	—	0.145	0.130	—	0.095	0.240	③

① The carburetor identification tag is located at the rear of the carburetor on one of the air horn screws.

② On low step.

③ 1800 rpm on Omega and 400 cu. in. engines with the cam follower on the highest step of the fast idle cam; 900 rpm on all others with the fast idle cam follower on the lowest step of the fast idle cam.

PONTIAC

Year	Carburetor Identification①	Float Level (in.)	Air Valve Spring (turn)	Pump (Rod (in.)	Idle Vent (in.)	Primary Vacuum Break (in.)	Secondary Vacuum Break (in.)	Secondary Opening (in.)	Choke Rod (in.)	Choke Unloader (in.)	Fast Idle Speed (rpm)
1969	7029260	3/16	1/2	9/32	3/8	0.150	—	—	0.100	0.300	—
	7029261	3/16	1/2	9/32	3/8	0.180	—	—	0.100	0.300	—
	7029262	9/32	1/2	9/32	3/8	0.245	—	—	0.100	0.300	—
	7029263	9/32	1/2	9/32	3/8	0.245	—	—	0.100	0.300	—
	7029268	9/32	1/2	9/32	3/8	0.245	—	—	0.100	0.300	—
	7029270	9/32	1/2	9/32	3/8	0.245	—	—	0.100	0.300	—
	7029273	9/32	1/2	1/4	3/8	0.245	—	—	0.100	0.300	—
	7028270	1/4	1/2	9/32	3/8	0.245	—	—	0.100	0.300	—
1970	7040262	9/32	7/16	—	—	0.400	—	—	0.100	—	—
	7040263	9/32	7/16	—	—	0.400	—	—	0.100	—	—
	7040264	9/32	7/16	—	—	0.400	—	—	0.100	—	—
	7040267	9/32	7/16	—	—	0.400	—	—	0.100	—	—
	7040268	9/32	7/16	—	—	0.400	—	—	0.100	—	—
	7040270	9/32	7/16	—	—	0.245	—	—	0.100	—	—
	7040273	9/32	7/16	—	—	0.245	—	—	0.100	—	—
	7040274	9/32	7/16	—	—	0.400	—	—	0.100	—	—

PONTIAC

Year	Carburetor Identification①	Float Level (in.)	Air Valve Spring (turn)	Pump (Rod (in.)	Idle Vent (in.)	Primary Vacuum Break (in.)	Secondary Vacuum Break (in.)	Secondary Opening (in.)	Choke Rod (in.)	Choke Unloader (in.)	Fast Idle Speed (rpm)
1971	7041262	9/32	7/16	—	—	0.240	—	—	0.100	—	—
	7041263	9/32	7/16	—	—	0.240	—	—	0.100	—	—
	7041264	9/32	7/16	—	—	0.240	—	—	0.100	—	—
	7041267	9/32	1/2	—	—	0.370	—	—	0.100	—	—
	7041268	9/32	1/2	—	—	0.430	—	—	0.100	—	—
	7041270	9/32	1/2	—	—	0.430	—	—	0.100	—	—
	7041271	9/32	7/16	—	—	0.240	—	—	0.100	—	—
	7041273	9/32	1/2	—	—	0.370	—	—	0.100	—	—
1972	7042262	1/4	7/16	13/32	—	0.290	—	—	0.100	—	—
	7042263	1/4	11/16	13/32	—	0.290	—	—	0.100	—	—
	7042264	1/4	5/8	13/32	—	0.290	—	—	0.100	—	—
	7042270	1/4	7/16	7/16	—	0.290	—	—	0.100	—	—
	7042273	1/4	7/16	7/16	—	0.290	—	—	0.100	—	—
1973	7043263	13/32	5/8	13/32	—	0.290	—	—	0.100	—	—
	7043264	13/32	1/2	13/32	—	0.290	—	—	0.100	—	—
	7043274	13/32	9/16	13/32	—	0.290	—	—	0.100	—	—
	7043262	13/32	3/8	13/32	—	0.290	—	—	0.100	—	—
	7043265	13/32	9/16	13/32	—	0.290	—	—	0.100	—	—
	7043272	13/32	3/8	13/32	—	0.290	—	—	0.100	—	—
1974	7043263	25/64	5/8	0.410	—	0.290	—	0.020	0.205	0.310	1500
	7044262	25/64	3/8	0.410	—	0.260	—	0.020	0.205	0.310	1500
	7044266	25/64	1/2	0.410	—	0.260	—	0.020	0.205	0.310	1500
	7044267	25/64	3/8	0.410	—	0.260	—	0.020	0.205	0.310	1500
	7044268	25/64	1/2	0.410	—	0.260	—	0.020	0.205	0.310	1500
	7044269	25/64	1/2	0.410	—	0.290	—	0.020	0.205	0.310	1500
	7044270	25/64	3/4	0.410	—	0.290	—	0.020	0.205	0.310	2000
	7044272	25/64	3/8	0.315	—	0.290	—	0.020	0.205	0.310	1500
	7044273	25/64	3/4	0.410	—	0.290	—	0.020	0.205	0.310	2000
	7044274	25/64	9/16	0.315	—	0.290	—	0.020	0.205	0.310	1500
	7044560	25/64	3/8	0.410	—	0.260	—	0.020	0.205	0.310	1500
	7044568	25/64	1/2	0.410	—	0.260	—	0.020	0.205	0.310	1500
1975	7045246	5/16		15/32	—	0.130	0.115	—	0.095	0.240	1800
	7045546	5/16		15/32	—	0.145	0.130	—	0.095	0.240	1800
	7045263	1/2	1/2	9/32	—	0.150	0.260	—	0.130	0.230	1800
	7045264	1/2	1/2	9/32	—	0.150	0.260	—	0.130	0.230	1800
	7045268	1/2	3/8	9/32	—	0.150	0.260	—	0.130	0.230	1800
	7045269	1/2	3/8	9/32	—	0.160	0.265	—	0.130	0.230	1800
	7045274	1/2	1/2	9/32	—	0.150	0.260	—	0.130	0.230	1800
	7045260	1/2	1/2	9/32	—	0.150	0.260	—	0.130	0.230	1800
	7045262	1/2	1/2	9/32	—	0.150	0.260	—	0.130	0.230	1800
	7045266	1/2	1/2	9/32	—	0.150	0.260	—	0.130	0.230	1800
	7045562	1/2	1/2	9/32	—	0.150	0.260	—	0.130	0.230	1800
	7045564	1/2	1/2	9/32	—	0.150	0.260	—	0.130	0.230	1800
	7045568	1/2	1/2	9/32	—	0.150	0.260	—	0.130	0.230	1800
	7045566	1/2		9/32	—	0.150	0.260	—	0.130	0.230	1800

① The carburetor identification tag is located at the rear of the carburetor on one of the air horn screws.

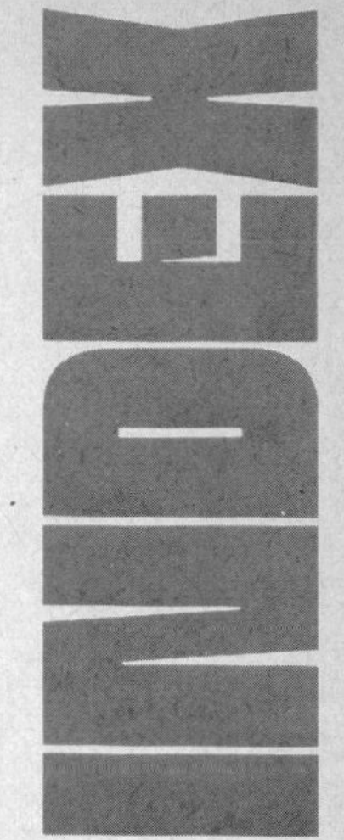

Emission Control Systems

Introduction

With emission level maintenance standards getting stricter on both the State and Federal levels, proper testing and adjustment of emission control systems are becoming increasingly important. Much confusion results from the many types and combinations of emission control systems currently in use.

To ease some of the confusion, the emission control systems section in this book has been divided into two parts. The first part is found in each of the individual car sections. It explains which system and components each make and model uses. Component R&R is also given where it is available.

The second part, below, covers testing and adjustment of the emission control systems and their individual components. Many of the components are similar (or the same) from one manufacturer to another and therefore the testing procedures are the same. Thus, one test may be used for several different manufacturers or models. Where components, although similar, differ significantly the tests are different.

For the sake of added clarity, a general description of the various types of emission control systems follows.

Positive Crankcase Ventilation (PCV) Systems

A simple valve, operated by intake manifold vacuum, is used to meter the flow of air and vapors through the crankcase. Air is drawn in through either the breather cap, on pre-1968 cars (open system), or, on cars made after 1968, through the carburetor air cleaner (closed system). When the car is decelerating or the engine is idling, high manifold vacuum closes the valve; this restricts the flow of crankcase vapor into the intake manifold. During acceleration or at a constant speed, the intake manifold vacuum drops, the valve spring forces the valve open and more vapors flow into the intake manifold from the crankcase. If a backfire occurs the valve closes, preventing the vapor in the crankcase from being ignited. If the vapor is ignited, an explosion will result.

Air Injection System

On most engines, a belt-driven air pump supplies air to an injector manifold which has a nozzle positioned behind each exhaust valve. On some engines with catalytic converters, the air from the pump is routed directly from the pump to the head pipe. Injection of air at this point causes combustion of any unburned hydrocarbons in the exhaust manifold rather than allowing them to escape into the atmosphere. An antibackfire valve controls the flow of air from the pump to prevent backfires resulting from an overly rich mixture under closed throttle conditions. A check valve, sometimes an integral part of the air injection manifold, functions to prevent hot exhaust gas backflow into the pump and hoses in case of pump failure or when the antibackfire valve is working.

On some 1975 engines, the air injection system also supplies air to aid in the operation of the catalytic converter. (see "Catalytic Converter" section.)

Thermostatically Controlled Air Cleaner

Thermostatically controlled air cleaners are used to improve operation of the engine and to prevent carburetor icing during warm-up in cold weather.

A movable door in the air cleaner snorkle allows air to be drawn in from either a manifold heat stove (cold operation) or from under the hood (normal operation). The door may be operated by a bimetallic spring or a vacuum motor. Doors of both types may use a vacuum override to provide cold air intake during periods of hard acceleration when stove-heated air is normally being supplied.

Distributor Controls

There are three basic types of distributor controls:

1. Engine vacuum controls
2. Transmission-controlled spark —transmission gear selected and/or temperature.
3. Speed-controlled spark—vehicles speed and/or temperature.

It is easier to consider these three types separately, although some of them perform similar functions and may be used in conjunction with one another.

Engine Vacuum Controls

Many small valves and solenoids fall into this class of emission controls. Some distributors are equipped with a dual-diaphragm vacuum unit which retards the spark during closed throttle deceleration and idle. On some distributors, solenoids may be used to either advance or retard the timing under predetermined conditions.

A deceleration valve may be used to provide maximum vacuum advance when the car is slowing down, by sending intake manifold vacuum to the distributor vacuum unit. By doing this, emissions may be better controlled during deceleration.

Because emission-controlled engines run hotter, it is often necessary to use a coolant temperature vacuum valve to provide additional vacuum advance when the engine is overheated. The valve is threaded into an engine coolant passage. If the engine overheats, the additional vacuum advance causes the engine speed to increase; allowing it to cool down quite rapidly. A similar valve may also be used to determine the temperature at which a TCS, SCS, or EGR system operates (see below).

A spark delay valve is installed on some engines to prevent the vacuum advance from working immediately under heavy acceleration.

On some engines a temperature activated valve may also control distributor vacuum. This valve may be part of the spark delay valve.

Transmission-Controlled Spark (TCS) System

Many variations of transmission-controlled spark (TCS) systems are used to control vehicle emissions. The basic components of these systems are: a transmission switch, which is operated either by oil pressure (automatic transmissions) or by the gear selected (manual transmission); and a vacuum solenoid. The solenoid allows vacuum to be supplied to the distributor vacuum unit or ports it into the atmosphere. Usually vacuum is supplied only in high gear and is ported in the lower gears. However, few TCS systems are quite this simple.

For example, most TCS systems use some type of temperature switch to control their operation, i.e., the system will not function below a specified air or engine temperature. In some cases it will not work above a specified temperature either. Some cars use a coolant temperature-operated vacuum valve in conjuction with the TCS system.

Various reversing and time delay relays may also be used, depending upon the needs of the engine and transmission.

Speed-Controlled Spark (SCS) Systems

Speed-controlled spark (SCS) systems perform a similar function to the transmission-controlled systems above. Many of the components are the same and used in similar way in both of the systems. The major difference lies in the switch which is activated by the speed, rather than the gear.

In its simplest form, this switch is nothing more than a centrifugal switch, connected to the speedometer drive, which completes the SCS circuit at or above a predetermined speed. A more complicated type of switch uses a small speedometer gear (or speedometer cable) driven pulse generator to send a signal to an amplifier, which, in turn, completes the SCS system circuit at predetermined speed.

Once the circuit has been completed, vacuum is allowed to flow to the distributor vacuum unit. When the circuit is not energized, vacuum is ported into the atmosphere.

Like the transmission-controlled spark systems, SCS systems use temperature switches and various relays.

Carburetor Controls

Because of the increase in engine speed necessary to control emissions at idle, dieseling has become a problem. As a result, many carburetors use a solenoid to allow the throttle to close when the ingition is shut off, thus reducing engine speed which, in turn, prevents dieseling.

To prevent dieseling on some air-conditioned cars, a signal from an amplifier engages the A/C compressor clutch momentarily when the engine is shut off. This puts a load on the engine, thus slowing it down.

Some carburetors have enrichment circuits which are controlled by coolant temperature. This provides a richer mixture when the engine is cold, making the engine less likely to stall.

Dashpots are used on many engines to reduce emissions during deceleration. This is done by slowing down throttle closing. The dashpot may be combined with the anti-dieseling solenoid in some aplications.

Compensators may also be used on the carburetor to provide a more uniform mixture under different temperature and altitude conditions.

On some vehicles, with catalytic converters, a solenoid is used to hold the throttle open slightly when the vehicle is decelerating and the engine speed is above 2,000 rpm. This prevents catalyst damage from too rich a mixture.

Evaporative Emission Control Systems

To control emissions resulting from fuel evaporation, all cars made after 1971 use a closed fuel supply system. Instead of fuel vapor being vented into the atmosphere, it goes into a vapor/liquid separator and is routed from there, either directly through a charcoal storage canister, or into the crankcase. To prevent vapor loss at other points, the carburetor has controlled vents and a PCV system (see above) is used along with the evaporative emission control system.

Exhaust Gas Recirculation (EGR)

Exhaust gas recirculation (EGR) systems are used to reduce NO_x emissions by lowering peak flame temperature during combustion. Exhaust gases are routed into the intake manifold via floor jets, intake manifold passages, and/or an EGR control valve. This valve may be located either on the intake manifold or on a special carburetor spacer.

Some EGR systems use coolant temperature-operated vacuum valves or air temperature-operated valves to determine when they function. In addition, a vacuum amplifier (mechanical) may be provided if a weak vacuum signal is being supplied to the EGR valve.

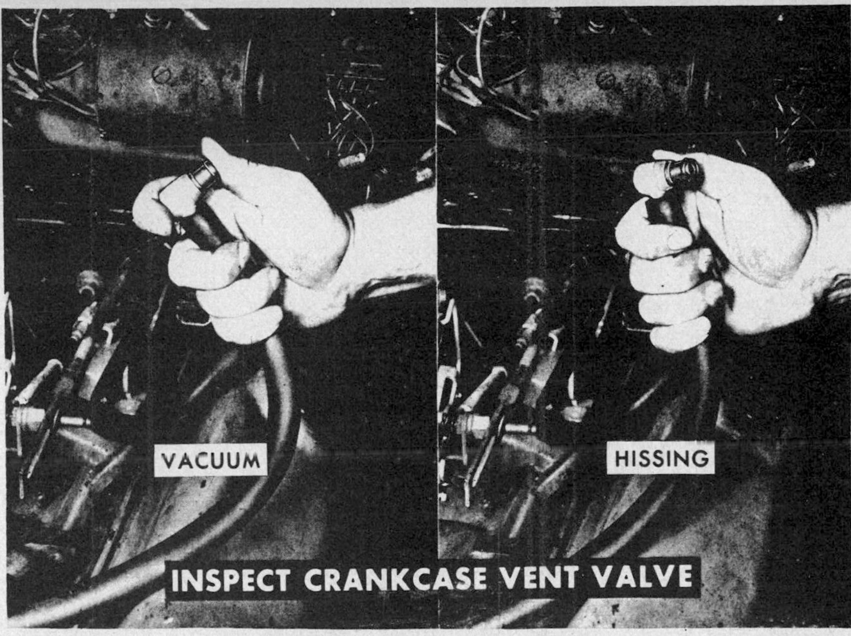

Testing PCV valve (© Chrysler Corp)

Catalytic Converters

Starting 1975, all domestic cars sold in California are equipped with catalytic converters, as are many of the cars sold in the rest of the U.S. The converters are used to oxidize hydrocarbons (HC) and carbon monoxide (CO). They are necessary because of even stricter emission standards for the 1975 models.

The catalysts are made of noble metals (platinum and palladium) which are bonded to either a monolithic (one-piece) element or to individual pellets. The catalyst causes the HC and CO to break down without taking part in the reaction; hence, a catalyst life of 50,000 miles is expected.

Some engines equipped with the converters require an air injection pump to supply air for the reaction; others will not.

Vacuum-Operated Heat Risers

Starting 1975, some Ford and GM engines have a vacuum-operated heat riser (manifold heat valve). These valves replace the bimetallic spring operated valves which have been previously used.

TROUBLESHOOTING

NOTE: For model usage, a description of, as well as, available removal and installation procedures for the components of emission control systems, consult the individual car repair sections. This section covers tests and adjustments only.

Positive Crankcase Ventilation (PCV) System

Valve Tests

1. See if any deposits are present in the carburetor passages, the oil filler cap, or the hoses. Clean these as required.
2. Connect a tachometer, as instructed by its manufacturer, to the engine.
3. With the engine idling, do one of the following:
   a. Remove the PCV valve hose from the crankcase or the oil filler connection.
   b. On cars with the PCV valve located in a grommet on the valve cover, remove both the valve and the grommet.

NOTE: If the valve and the hoses are not clogged-up, a hissing sound should be present.

4. Check the tachometer reading. Place a finger over the valve or hose opening (a suction should be felt).
5. Check the tachometer again. The engine speed should have dropped at least 50 rpm. It should return to normal when the finger is removed from the opening.
6. If the engine does not change

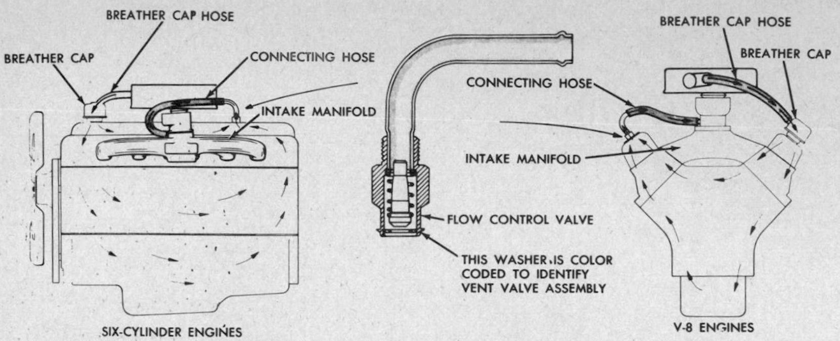

Fully closed ventilation system (© Chrysler Corp)

speed or if the change is less than 50 rpm, the hose is clogged or the valve is defective. Check the hose first. If the hose is not clogged replace, do not attempt to repair, the PCV valve.

7. Test the new valve in the above manner, to make sure that it is operating properly.

NOTE: There are several commercial PCV valve testers available. Be sure that the one used is suitable for the valve to be tested, as the testers are not universal. Follow the manufacturer's instructions.

Air Injection System

Air Pump Tests

Caution Do not hammer on, pry, or bend the pump housing while tightening the drive belt or testing the pump.

Belt Tension and Air Leaks

1. Before proceeding with the tests, check the pump drive belt tension to see if it is within specifications.
2. Turn the pump by hand. If it has seized, the belt will slip, producing noise. Disregard any chirping, squealing, or rolling sounds from inside the pump; these are normal when it is turned by hand.
3. Check the hoses and connections for leaks. Hissing or a blast of air is indicative of a leak. Soapy water, applied lightly around the area in question, is a good method for detecting leaks.

Air Output Tests

1. Disconnect the air supply hose at the antibackfire valve.
2. Connect a vacuum gauge, using a suitable adaptor, to the air supply hose.

NOTE: If there are two hoses plug the second one up.

3. With the engine at normal operating temperature, increase the idle speed and watch the vacuum gauge.
4. The air flow from the pump should be steady and fall between 2–6 psi. If it is unsteady or falls below this, the pump is defective and must be replaced.

Pump Noise Diagnosis

The air pump is normally noisy; as engine speed increases, the noise of the pump will rise in pitch. The rolling sound the pump bearings make is normal, however if this sound becomes objectionable at certain speeds, the pump is defective and will have to be replaced.

A continual hissing sound from the air pump pressure relief valve at idle, indicates a defective valve. Replace the relief valve.

If the pump rear bearing fails, a continual knocking sound will be heard. Since the rear bearing is not separately replaceable, the pump will have to be replaced as an assembly.

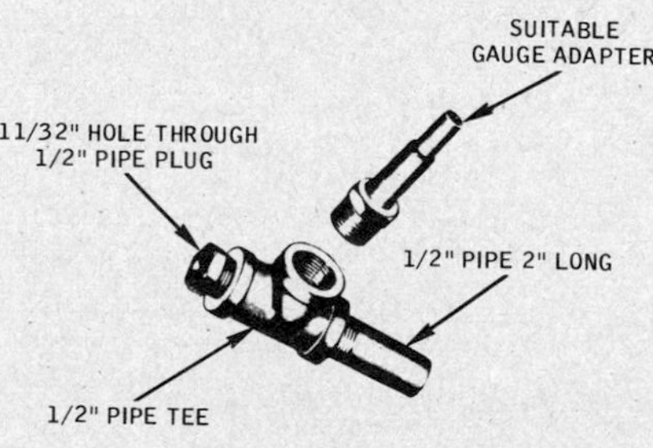

Making an air pump-to-vacuum gauge adapter

(© Ford Motor Co)

Antibackfire Valve Tests

There are different types of antibackfire valves used with air injection systems. A by-pass (diverter) valve is used on most current engines, while most older engines use a gulp type antibackfire valve. Test procedures for both types are given below.

To protect the catalyst, 1975 Ford cars have a slightly different arrangement used when the car is equipped with a catalytic converter. The bypass valve allows air to flow to the exhaust ports when high manifold vacuum is applied to it. Since there is no manifold vacuum, the by-pass valve dumps the air from the pump into the atmosphere at wide-open throttle. To prevent backfiring, during deceleration, when manifold vacuum is high, a vacuum differential valve (VDV) is used to block the vacuum signal to the by-pass valve, causing it to dump the air from the pump.

A solenoid which is connected to a temperature sensor in the air cleaner, blocks vacuum to the by-pass valve when the choke is on; shutting the entire air injection system off when the engine is cold.

On 351M and 400 cu in. engines, a coolant temperature operated vacuum valve is used to block vacuum to the by-pass valve if the engine overheats.

Gulp Valve

1. Detach the air supply hose which runs between the pump and the gulp valve.
2. Connect a tachometer and run the engine between 1,500–2,000 rpm.
3. Allow the throttle to snap closed. This should produce a loud sucking sound from the gulp valve.
4. Repeat this operation several times. If no sound is present, the valve is not working or the vacuum connections are loose.
5. Check the vacuum connections. If they are secure, replace the

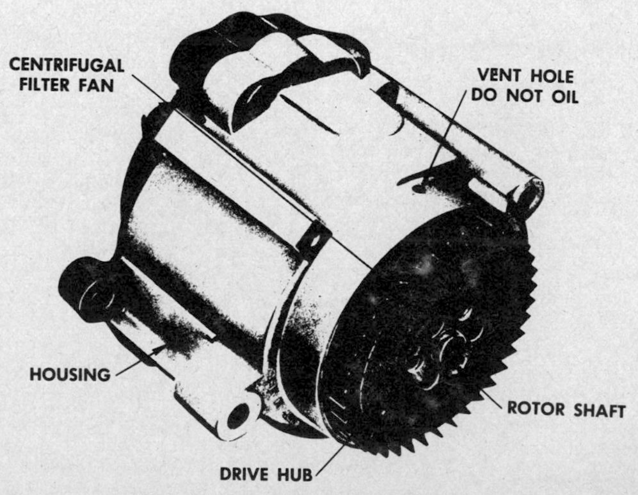

Identifying the external parts of an air pump (© G.M. Corp)

gulp valve.

By-pass (Diverter) Valve (except '75 Ford)

1. Detach the hose, which runs from the by-pass valve to the check valve, at the by-pass valve hose connection.
2. Connect a tachometer to the engine. With the engine running at normal idle speed, check to see that air is flowing from the by-pass valve hose connection.
3. Speed the engine up, so that it is running at 1,500–2,000 rpm. Allow the throttle to snap shut. The flow of air from the by-pass valve at the check valve hose connection should stop momentarily and air should then flow from the exhaust port on the valve body or the silencer assembly.
4. Repeat step three several times. If the flow of air is not diverted into the atmosphere from the valve exhaust port or if it fails to stop flowing from the hose connection, check the vacuum lines and connections. If these are tight, the valve is defective and requires replacement.
5. A leaking diaphragm will cause the air to flow out both the hose connection and the exhaust port at the same time. If this happens, replace the valve.

By-Pass Valve—1975-76 Ford

1. Allow the engine to reach normal operating temperature. Put the transmission in Neutral (N) or Park (P) and apply the parking brake.
2. Stop the engine. Remove the by-pass valve-to-check valve hose from the by-pass valve. On V6s and V8s, remove both hoses.
3. Install a tachometer and start the engine.
4. Hold your hand over the by-pass valve hose connection(s) and increase the engine speed to 1500 rpm. Air should flow from the hose connection(s).
5. Remove and plug the by-pass valve vacuum hose. Increase the engine speed to 1500 rpm. No air should flow from the hose connections. Instead, air should flow out the exhaust ports in the silencer cover.
6. If the by-pass valve fails the preceding tests, replace it.
7. Stop the engine. Remove the tachometer and reconnect all hoses. If you are going to perform the air injection decel valve test, leave the tachometer in place.

Check Valve Test

1. Before starting the test, check all of the hoses and connections for leaks.

Large canister is 1975 Ford air by-pass valve; smaller valve below it is vacuum differential valve (VDV)

2. Detach the air supply hose(s) from the check valve(s).
3. Insert a suitable probe into the check valve and depress the plate. Release it; the plate should return to its original position against the valve seat. If binding is evident, replace the valve.

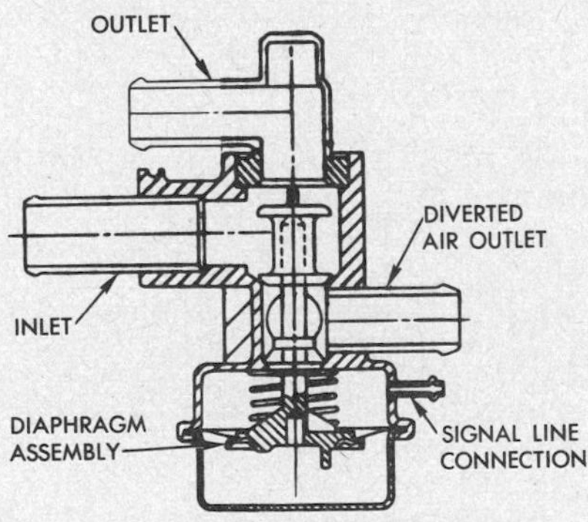

GM type air by-pass (diverter) valve

4. Repeat step three if two valves are used.
5. With the engine running at normal operating temperature, gradually increase its speed to 1,500 rpm. Check for exhaust gas leakage. If any is present, replace the valve assembly.

NOTE: Vibration and flutter of the check valve at idle speed is a normal condition and does not mean that the valve should be replaced.

1975-76 Ford Differential Vacuum Valve Test

The differential vacuum valve is only used on air injection systems on models with catalytic converters.

Perform the by-pass valve test prior to this test.

1. Allow the engine to reach normal operating temperature. Put transmission in Park (P) or Neutral (N) and apply the parking brake.
2. Stop the engine. Remove the by-pass valve-to-check valve hose at the by-pass valve end. On V6s and V8s, remove both hoses.
3. Install a tachometer and start the engine.
4. Hold your hand over the by-pass valve hose connection(s) and increase engine speed to 2500 rpm. Release the throttle. Air flow from the hose connections should stop momentarily and then start again. When the hose connection air flow stops, air should start coming out the by-pass valve silencer ports.
5. If the by-pass valve isn't working correctly in step 4, check to see that the decel valve is getting a vacuum signal.
6. If the decel valve is getting vacuum, and the by-pass valve is known to be working OK, replace the decel valve.
7. Stop the engine. Remove the test equipment and reconnect the hoses.

1975-76 Ford Air Injection System Solenoid Vacuum Valve Tests

Air injection system solenoid vacuum valves are used only on models with catalytic converters. There are two types of solenoid vacuum: type

Vacuum solenoid for VDV/air by-pass system —1975 Ford (© Ford Motor Co)

I is normally closed and type II is normally open. Check the vehicle's tune-up specifications decal to determine which type is used.

Type I (Normally Closed)

1. Allow the engine to reach normal operating temperature. Be sure that the air cleaner temperature is above 65°F.
2. Allow the engine to idle, Detach the vacuum hose from the by-pass valve. Air should flow from the by-pass valve silencer exhaust ports. Connect the by-pass valve vacuum hose.
3. If the air is exhausted out the silencer cover exhaust ports, the solenoid vacuum hose connections are OK. The vacuum supply hose should always go to the bottom solenoid fitting (type I).
4. Detach the vacuum supply hose from the solenoid. Place your finger over the end of the hose. Vacuum should be felt. It not, check the hose and manifold vacuum fitting. Reconnect the vacuum hose.
5. Unfasten the solenoid vacuum valve wiring.
6. Connect one terminal of the solenoid vacuum valve to a 12V power source. Ground the other terminal. Air should *not* come out the by-pass valve exhaust ports.
7. Disconnect the 12V power source and ground wires. Reconnect the solenoid valve wiring.
8. Air still should not come out of the by-pass valve exhaust ports.
9. If the solenoid vacuum valve doesn't operate as outlined, replace it.

Type II (Normally Open)

1. Do steps 1 through 3 of the type I solenoid vacuum valve test.

NOTE: *The vacuum supply hose should be connected to the black nozzle on type II valves.*

2. Unfasten the wiring from the solenoid vacuum valve.
3. Connect one terminal of the vacuum valve to a 12V power source. Ground the other terminal.
4. Air should flow from the by-pass valve exhaust ports.
5. Disconnect the 12V power source and ground wires. Reconnect the solenoid vacuum valve wiring.
6. Air should *stop* flowing out of the by-pass valve exhaust ports. If it dosen't operate as outlined replace the solenoid vacuum valve.

1975-76 Ford Vacuum Reservoir Check

A vacuum reservoir is required on some air injection systems when used with a catalytic converter. To check it:

1. Detach the soleniod vacuum valve-to-reservoir hose from the reservoir fitting.
2. Connect a vacuum gauge to the reservoir fitting.
3. Disconect the manifold vacuum hose from the reservoir and connect an external vacuum source in its place.
4. Apply a 14 in. Hg vacuum to the reservoir and trap it. The vacuum should not drop more than 1 in. Hg in 1 min.
5. Remove the test equipment and reconnect the vacuum lines.

Thermostatically Controlled Air Cleaner

Air Door Tests

Non-Vacuum-Operated and 1968-71 Ford Vacuum-Operated

1. Unfasten the temperature sensing valve and snorkle assembly from the air cleaner. Place it in a container of cold water. Make sure that the thermostat is completely covered with water.
2. Place a thermometer, of known accuracy, in the water. Heat the water slowly and watch the temperature.
3. At 105° F, or less, the door should be closed (manifold heat position).
4. Continue heating the water until it reaches 130° F. The door should be fully open to the outside air position.
5. If the door does not open at or near this temperature, check it for binding or a detached spring. If neither of this situations exist, the sensor is defective and must be replaced.

NOTE: This usually means that the entire snorkle assembly must be replaced.

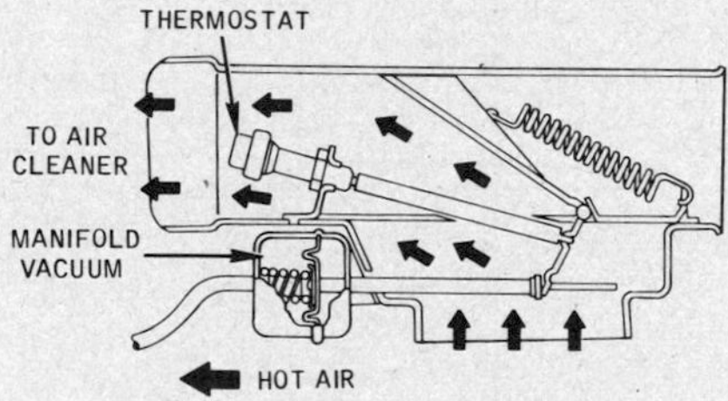

Duct and valve assembly in "heat on" position — warm-up

Vacuum-Operated Door—Except 1968-71 Ford

1. Either start with a cold engine or remove the air cleaner from the engine for at least half an hour. While cooling the air cleaner, leave the engine compartment hood open.
2. Tape a thermometer, of known accuracy, to the inside of the air cleaner so that it is near the temperature sensor unit. Install the air cleaner on the engine but do not fasten its securing nut.
3. Start the engine. With the engine cold and the outside temper-

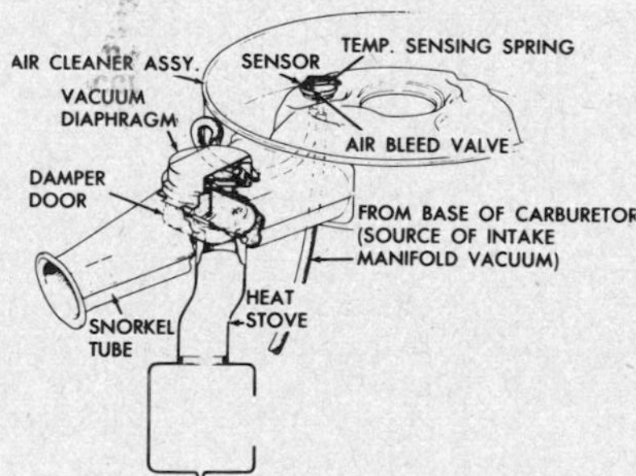

Components of the thermostatically controlled air cleaner (© G.M. Corp)

AIR INJECTION SYSTEM DIAGNOSIS CHART

Problem	*Cause*	*Cure*
1. Noisy drive belt	1a Loose belt 1b Seized pump	1a Tighten belt 1b Replace
2. Noisy pump	2a Leaking hose 2b Loose hose 2c Hose contacting other parts 2d Diverter or check valve failure 2e Pump mounting loose 2g Defective pump	2a Trace and fix leak 2b Tighten hose clamp 2c Reposition hose 2d Replace 2e Tighten securing bolts 2g Replace
3. No air supply	3a Loose belt 3b Leak in hose or at fitting 3c Defective anti-backfire valve 3d Defective check valve 3e Defective pump	3a Tighten belt 3b Trace and fix leak 3c Replace 3d Replace 3e Replace
4. Exhaust backfire	4a Vacuum or air leaks 4b Defective anti-backfire valve 4c Sticking choke 4d Choke setting rich	4a Trace and fix leak 4b Replace 4c Service choke 4d Adjust choke

ature less than 80° F., the door should be in the "heat on" position (closed to outside air).

NOTE: Due to the position of the air cleaner on some cars, a mirror may be necessary when observing the position of the air door.

4. Operate the throttle lever rapidly to ½–¾ of its opening and release it. The air door should open to allow outside air to enter and then close again, except on some 1975 Ford models with a cold weather modulator.
5. Allow the engine to warm up to normal temperature. Watch the door. When it opens to the outside air, remove the cover from the air cleaner. The temperature should be over 80°F and no more than 130°F; 115°F is about normal. If the door does not work within these temperature ranges, or fails to work at all, check for linkage or door binding.

If binding is not present and the air door is not working, proceed with the vacuum tests, given below. If these indicate no faults in the vacuum motor and the door is not working, the temperature sensor is defective and must be replaced.

Vacuum Motor Tests

1968-71 Ford

1. Detach the hose from the vacuum override motor. Connect a vacuum gauge to the hose.
2. With the engine at idle, the vacuum gauge should read 15 in. Hg or better. If it is less than this, check the vacuum lines and connections for leaks.
3. If the vacuum is at specification, install the hose back on the vacuum motor.
4. With the underhood temperature below 100°F, check the air door position. If the air door is less than halfway to the "heat on" position and no components are binding, remove the vacuum motor for bench-testing.
5. Connect the motor to an *alternate* vacuum source. If the rod on the motor moves at least ½ in., reinstall it and check for a defective thermostat bulb.
6. If the rod does not move at all or if it moves less than ½ in., the motor is defective and should be replaced.

GM, AMC, and Ford (1972-on)

NOTE: Be sure that the vacuum hose that runs between the temperature switch and the vacuum motor is not pinched by the retaining clip under the air cleaner. This could prevent the air door from closing.

1. Check all of the vacuum lines and fittings for leaks. Correct any leaks. If none are found, proceed with the test.
2. Remove the hose which runs from the sensor to the vacuum motor. Run a hose directly from the manifold vacuum source to the vacuum motor.
3. If the motor closes the air door, it is functioning properly and the temperature sensor is defective.
4. If the motor does *not* close the door and no binding is present in its operation, the vacuum motor is defective and must be replaced.

NOTE: If an alternate vacuum source is applied to the motor, insert a vacuum gauge in the line by using a T-fitting. Apply at least 9 in. Hg of vacuum in order to operate the motor.

Chrysler Corp.

1. Remove the air cleaner from the carburetor and allow it to cool to 90°F. Connect a vacuum source to the sensor as well as a vacuum gauge.
2. Apply 20 in. Hg to the sensor, the door should be in the "heat on" (up) position. If it remains in the "off" position, test the vacuum motor.
3. Connect the motor to a vacuum source. In addition to the vacuum gauge, a hose clamp and a bleed valve are necessary. Connect them in the following order:
   a. Vacuum source
   b. Hose clamp (or shut-off valve)
   c. Bleed valve
   d. Vacuum gauge
   e. Vacuum motor
4. Apply 20 in. Hg vacuum to the motor. Use the hose clamp to block the line, so that the motor will retain the vacuum. The door operating motor should retain this amount of vacuum for five minutes. Release the hose clamp.

NOTE: If the vacuum cannot be built up to the specified amount, the diaphragm has a leak and the valve will require replacement.

5. By slowly closing the bleed valve, check the operation of the door. The door should start to raise at not less than 5 in. Hg and should be fully raised at no more than 9 in. Hg.

Testing the vacuum motor—Chrysler heated air intake system (© Chrysler Corp)

6. If the vacuum motor fails any of the tests in steps 3–5, it is defective. Replace it with a new unit.
7. If the door works properly but fails to pass step two, the sensor is a fault and should be replaced.

NOTE: If the engine has a dual snorkle air cleaner, check the right side as in steps 3–5, above. However, there is no temperature sensor on the right-side door.

Cold Weather Modulator Tests

1975-76 Ford

Some 1975-76 Ford models use a cold weather modulator to prevent the air door from being opened under hard acceleration, when the temperature is below 55°F.

Check the vehicle's tune-up specifications decal, to see if the cold weather modulator is used, before beginning this test:

1. Stop the engine.
2. Cool the modulator unit in the air cleaner to below 40°F with areosol circuit test spray or equivalent.

Caution Do not spray the modulator with the engine running. If the spray is drawn into the carburetor, poisonous PHOSGENE gas will come out the tailpipe. Perform this test only in a well ventilated area.

3. Apply at least 16 in. Hg with an external vacuum source to the vacuum motor side of the modulator. Trap the vacuum.
4. The modulator must hold at least 14 in. Hg vacuum for one minute. If it doesn't, replace the modulator.
5. Use a heat gun or run the engine to warm the modulator to at least 70°F.
6. Perform step 3. This time the modulator should not hold the vacuum. Replace it, if it does.

1975 Ford cold weather modulator is mounted in the air cleaner (© Ford Motor Co.)

Distributor Controls

NOTE: Most, but not all distributors on 1975 models use manifold rather than carburetor vacuum.

Dual Diaphragm Distributor Tests

1. Connect a timing light to the engine. Check the ignition timing.
   NOTE: Before proceeding with the tests, disconnect any spark control devices, distributor vacuum valves, etc. If these are left connected, inaccurate results may be obtained.
2. Remove the retard hose from the distributor and plug it. Increase the engine speed. The timing should advance. If it fails to do so, then the vacuum unit is faulty and must be replaced.
3. Check the timing with the engine at normal idle speed. Unplug the retard hose and connect it to the vacuum unit. The timing should instantly be retarded from 4–10°. If this does not occur, the retard diaphragm has a leak and the vacuum unit must be replaced.

Timing Retard Solenoid Test

A timing retard solenoid is used on some Chrysler Corp. products up to, and including the 1971 model year.

1. Connect a timing light to the engine and check the timing.
2. Detach the solenoid ground lead near its carburetor end. Timing should advance at least 5° and there should be an increase in engine speed.

Detach the timing retard solenoid leads at the carburetor end (© Chrysler Corp)

3. Reconnect the ground lead. Timing should be retarded to the original position noted and the engine should slow down. Repeat the test several times.
4. If the timing does not behave in the manner indicated, the solenoid is defective and must be replaced; it cannot be adjusted or repaired.

Timing Advance Solenoid Test

NOTE: A timing advance solenoid is used on Chrysler products in 1972. It should not be confused with the retard solenoid, above. It is used only on the 400 cu. in. 4-bbl engine in 1973–1974.

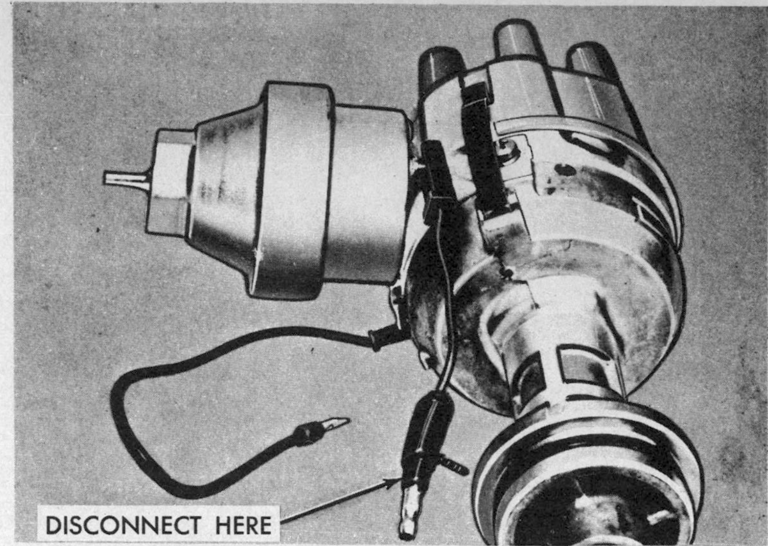

Detach the timing advance solenoid where indicated (© Chrysler Corp)

1. Attach a tachometer to the engine.
2. Detach the vacuum advance line from the distributor advance unit.
3. Run the engine at normal idle and check engine rpm with the tachometer.
4. Detach the solenoid lead wire at its connection, which is about 6 in. away from it. Run a jumper wire from the battery to the disconnected lead from the solenoid.
5. When the two leads are touched, the engine speed should increase by 50 rpm or, if a timing light is used, the timing should advance 7–8°.

NOTE: Do not touch the jumper wire to the solenoid lead for more than 30 seconds, or the solenoid will overheat.

6. If the engine speed does not increase or the timing advance, the solenoid is defective and must be replaced. Remember to reconnect it when through testing.

Deceleration Valve Tests

NOTE: Timing, idle speed and air/fuel mixture should be at proper specifications before starting this test.

1. Connect a vacuum gauge to the distributor vacuum advance line, by using a T-connection which has about the same inside diameter as the line. Do not clamp the line shut.
2. If the carburetor is equipped with a dashpot, tape its plunger down so that it cannot touch the throttle lever at idle.
3. Speed the engine up to about 2,000 rpm and retain this speed for about five seconds.
4. Release the throttle, allowing the engine to return to normal idle.
5. The vacuum reading should rise to about 15–16 in. Hg and stay there for one second. It should take about three seconds for the vacuum to return to its normal 6 in. Hg reading. These specifications do not apply to American Motors cars. See note under "De-

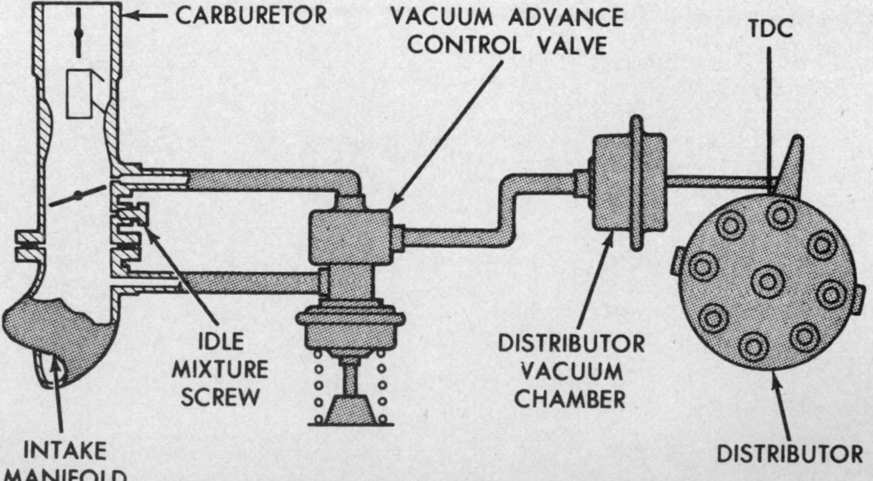

Carburetor/deceleration (control) valve/distributor relationship

celeration Valve Adjustment for American Motors Cars."

6. If the valve does not retain its high reading for about one second or if it takes over three seconds for the reading to return to normal, the valve should be adjusted, as outlined below.

To check for a leaking valve diaphragm, proceed as follows:

1. Remove the vacuum gauge and connect it to the manifold vacuum line with a T-connection.
2. Clamp the valve-to-distributor vacuum line and, with the engine at normal idle speed, check the vacuum reading.
3. Clamp the line shut between the deceleration valve and the T-connection. Check the vacuum gauge reading again.
4. If the second reading is higher than the first, the valve diaphragm is leaking and the valve should be replaced.

Deceleration Valve Adjustments

If the deceleration valve test indicated a need for adjustments, proceed as follows:

1. Remove the cover to gain access to the adjusting screw.
2. If an *increase* in valve opening time is desired, turn the adjusting screw counterclockwise.
3. If a *decrease* in time is desired, turn the adjusting screw clockwise.

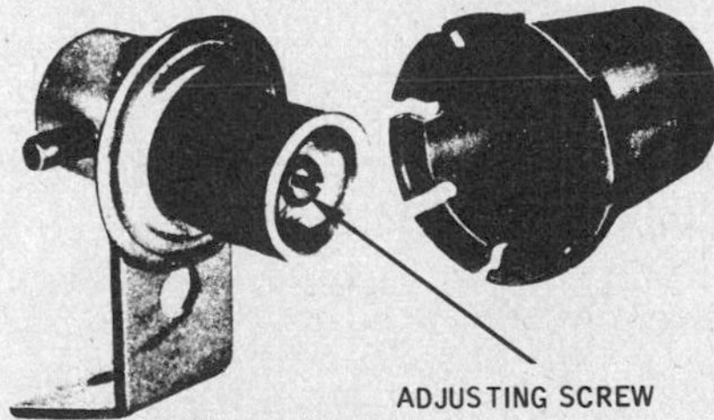

Adjustment of the deceleration valve (© Ford Motor Co)

NOTE: Each complete turn of the adjusting screw equals ½ in. Hg. Thus, if the vacuum reading at the end of three seconds is 7½ in. Hg, it will take three turns of the screw to return it to the proper 6 in. Hg reading.

4. After finishing the adjustments, retest the valve, as outlined above. If the valve cannot be adjusted to proper specifications, it is defective and must be replaced.

NOTE: On 1970 American Motors cars equipped with a deceleration valve, the test and adjustment procedures are the same, but the specifications are different. Operate the engine at 2,000 rpm for ten seconds; the vacuum reading range should fall between 4 (low)–20 (high) in. Hg.

Coolant Temperature Operated Vacuum Valve Tests

NOTE: On some cars equipped with distributor control systems, this valve also is used to override the control system under overheating conditions. If a malfunction of the distributor control system occurs, remember to check the vacuum valve.

1. Check all of the vacuum hoses for proper installation and routing.
2. Connect a tachometer to the engine.
3. Run the engine until it reaches normal operating temperature but do not allow it to overheat. Be sure that the choke is open.
4. On Chrysler Corp., cars, detach the distributor solenoid ground lead at the carburetor (if so equipped).
5. Check engine rpm with the carburetor at curb idle.
6. Detach the vacuum line from the intake manifold at the valve end. Plug this hose.

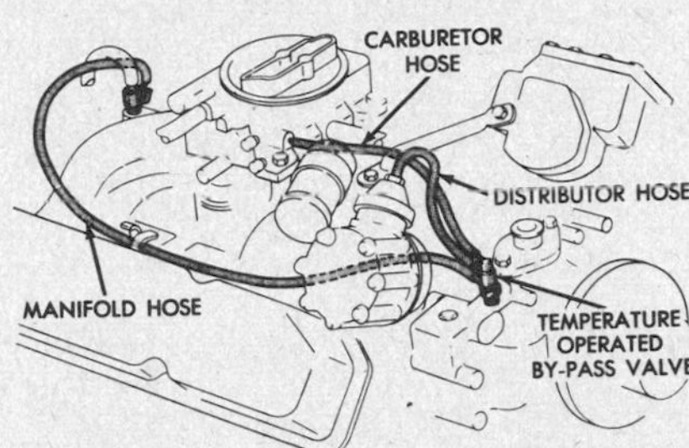

Basic hose routing for temperature-operated vacuum valve

7. Check the idle speed; there should be no change. If the idle speed drops 100 rpm or more, the valve is defective and must be replaced.
8. Check the coolant level and radiator cap. Reconnect the intake manifold hose to the temperature valve.
9. Cover the radiator to increase the coolant temperature. Then do one of the following:

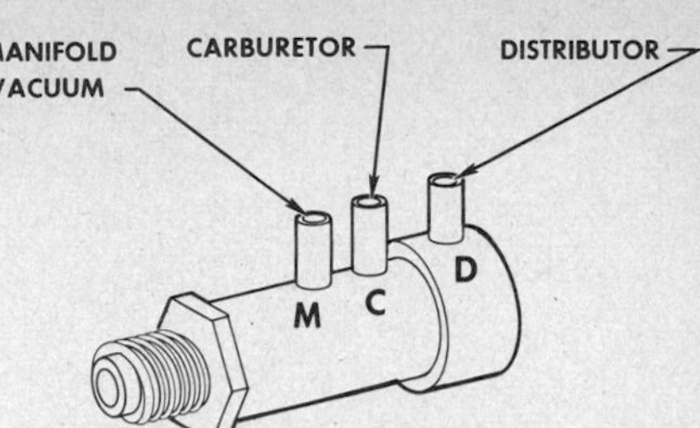

Typical GM coolant temperature-operated vacuum valve (© G.M. Corp)

a. If the car is equipped with a temperature gauge, run the engine until the gauge registers near the top of the "Normal" range.
b. On cars equipped with warning lights, run the engine until the red temperature light comes on.

Caution Do not run the engine at an abnormally high temperature for any longer than is required to test the valve. It is not necessary, nor desirable, to overheat an engine when the car uses a temperature gauge, i.e., the gauge should never be allowed to register "H" (Hot) when testing the valve.

10. If the engine speed has increased by at least 100 rpm, the valve is functioning properly. If there is little or no increase in engine speed, the valve is faulty and must be replaced.
11. Uncover the radiator and allow the car to cool by running the engine at idle.
12. On Chrysler products, remember to connect the distributor solenoid wire.

Ford Spark Delay Valve Tests

NOTE: If the distributor vacuum line contains a cut-off solenoid, it must be open during this test.

1. Detach the vacuum line from the distributor at the spark delay valve end. Connect a vacuum gauge to the valve, in its place. On some 1975 models, the valve

WITHOUT FILTER

CARBURETOR OR MODULATOR VACUUM

DISTRIBUTOR – ADVANCE SIDE

MANIFOLD VACUUM

WITH FILTER

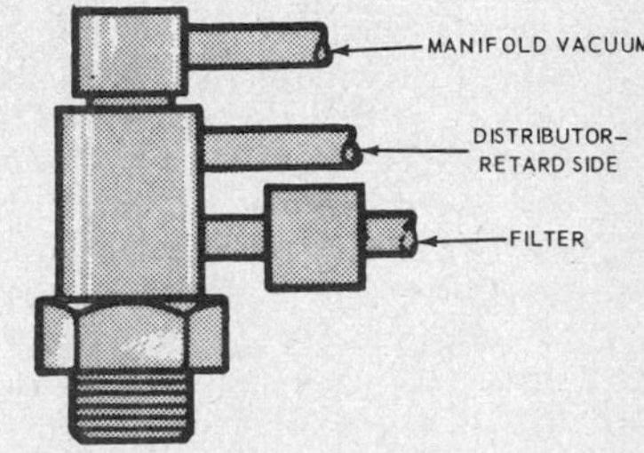

DISTRIBUTOR ADVANCE IS CONTROLLED BY CARBURETOR VACUUM

DISTRIBUTOR RETARD IS CONTROLLED BY MANIFOLD VACUUM

Typical Ford coolant temperature-operated vacuum valves (© Ford Motor Co)

Testing the Ford spark delay valve—the black side should be connected to the vacuum source

has a "CARB" nipple also; leave it alone.

2. Connect a tachometer to the engine. Start the engine and rapidly increase its speed to 2,000 rpm with the transmission in neutral.
3. As soon as the engine speed is increased, the vacuum gauge reading should drop to zero.
4. Hold the engine speed at a steady 2,000 rpm. It should take longer than two seconds for the gauge to register 6 in. Hg. If it takes less than two seconds, the valve is defective and must be replaced.
5. If it takes longer than the number of seconds specified in the chart below for the gauge to reach 6 in. Hg, disconnect the vacuum gauge from the spark delay valve. Disconnect the hose which runs from the spark delay valve to the carburetor at the valve end. Connect the vacuum gauge to this hose.
6. Start the engine and increase its speed to 2,000 rpm. The gauge should indicate 10–16 in Hg. If it does not, there is a blockage in the carburetor vacuum port or else the hose itself is plugged or broken. If the gauge reading is within specification, the valve is defective.
7. Reconnect all vacuum lines and remove the tachometer, once testing is completed.

Spark Delay Valve Color Code (Ford)

Color (With Black)	*1972 Time Delay Maximum (sec)*	*1973-76 Time Delay Maximum (sec)*
Gray	—	4
Green	20	20
Blue	15	16
Red	40	28
White	5	12
Yellow	10	14
Orange	—	24
Brown	—	5

Chrysler Orifice Spark Advance Control (OSAC) Valve

NOTE: Air temperature around the car must be above 68°F for this test because the OSAC valve has a temperature sensor in it. Valves produced from around 1 March 1973 do not have an ambient temperature sensor built into them. They may be identified by their white gasket (old OSAC valves had a black one) and a pasted-on label with the part number (3755499) on it. 1974–75 models have the OSAC valve located in the air cleaner, rather than on the firewall.

1. Check the vacuum hoses and connections for any signs of leaks or plugging.
2. Detach the vacuum line which runs from the distributor to the OSAC valve at the distributor end. Connect a vacuum gauge to this line.
3. Connect a tachometer to the engine. Rapidly open the throttle and then stabilize the engine speed at 2,000 rpm in neutral. When the throttle is rapidly opened the vacuum gauge reading should drop to zero.
4. With the engine speed at a steady 2,000 rpm, it should take about 15 seconds for the vacuum level to rise and then stabilize.

NOTE: The length of time may vary slightly with different engines; 15 seconds is an approximate figure.

5. If the vacuum level rises immediately, the valve is defective and must be replaced.
6. If there is no increase in vacuum at all, disconnect the hose which runs from the carburetor to the OSAC valve at the valve and connect a vacuum gauge to this hose. Speed the engine up to 2,000 rpm.
7. If there is no vacuum reading on the gauge, check for a clogged carburetor port, filters or hoses.
8. If there is a vacuum reading, the valve is defective and must be replaced.
9. Reconnect the vacuum hoses, after disconnecting the vacuum gauge. Disconnect the tachometer.

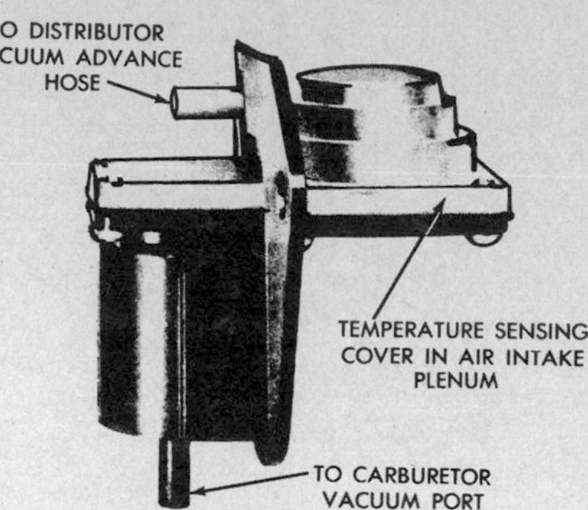

Chrysler orifice spark advance control (OSAC) valve (© Chrysler Corp)

1973-75 Oldsmobile, Vega and Buick Spark Delay Valve

NOTE: The ambient temperature must be 50°F or above, for this test. 1974 2bbl. Vegas with A/T made before Dec. 7, 1973 use a spark delay valve, as well as 1975 models.

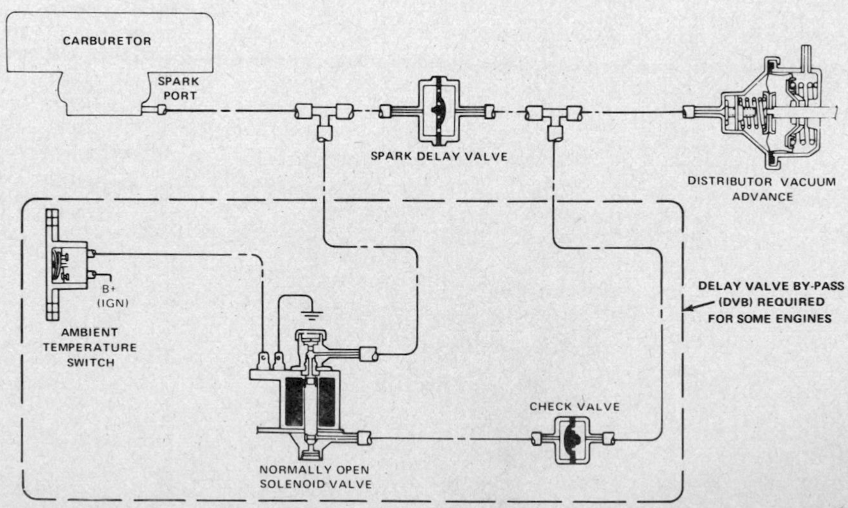

Ford spark delay valve circuit (© Ford Motor Co)

1. Disconnect the vacuum lines from the spark delay valve, after removing its cover.
2. Connect a vacuum gauge to the "TVS" port on the valve and a *hand-operated* vacuum pump (with a gauge attached) to the "CARB" port.
3. Operate the hand pump to create a vacuum. The vacuum gauge on the TVS side should show a slight hesitation before registering.
4. The gauge reading on the pump should drop slightly, taking 3-4 seconds for it to balance with the reading on the other gauge.
5. If Steps 3 and 4 are negative, replace the valve.
6. Remove the vacuum gauge from the TVS side of the valve.
7. Cover the "TVS" port on the valve with your finger and operate the pump to create a vacuum of 15 in. Hg.
8. The reading on the pump gauge should remain steady, if the valve leaks down, i.e., the gauge reading drops, replace the valve.
9. Remove your finger, the reading on the gauge should drop slowly. If the reading goes to zero rapidly, replace the valve.

   This part of the test applies only to 1973-74 models:
10. Use ice to cool the valve to below 40°F. Connect the vacuum gauge and the hand pump as in Step 2.
11. Operate the pump to create a vacuum; this time there should be no delay before the gauge readings balance. If there is a delay, replace the valve.
12. Reconnect the vacuum lines, in the correct order, to the valve after completing the test. Replace the cover.

1975 Pontiac (All V8) and Olds (V8-400) Vacuum Retard Delay Valve Tests

1. Check the vacuum retard delay valve installation. The side labeled "DIST" should face the distributor.
2. Disconnect and plug the hose which runs to the No. 1 port on the coolant temperature operated vacuum valve (located on the manifold water crossover) at its vacuum source. Plug the vacuum source.
3. Using a T-connector, hook up a vacuum gauge in the line between the spark delay valve and the distributor vacuum advance unit.
4. Stop the engine and watch the vacuum gauge.
5. It should take the gauge reading 2 to 5 seconds to drop from 15 to 5 in Hg. If the vacuum drop is within specifications, everything is OK; disconnect the vacuum gauge and connect the vacuum lines. If the vacuum drops too fast, proceed with the rest of the test.
6. Remove and plug the line which runs to the No. 2 port on the coolant temperature operated vacuum valve.
7. Repeat steps 4 and 5. If the vacuum reading now drops slowly, replace the coolant temperature operated vacuum valve. If the reading still drops rapidly, replace the delay valve (unless there is a second coolant temperature operated vacuum valve).
8. On engines with two vacuum valves, disconnect and plug the vacuum line which runs from the "D" port of the valve on the right cylinder head.
9. Repeat steps 4 and 5. If the vacuum reading now drops slowly, replace the valve on the right cylinder head. If it still drops fast replace the delay valve.
10. Remove the vacuum gauge and reconnect the vacuum lines.

1975 Pontiac Distributor Vacuum Valve (DVV)

1. Remove the hose from the distributor vacuum advance unit. Connect a vacuum gauge to the hose.
2. Using a T-connector, hook up a second vacuum gauge to the "C" or "CARB" port on the DVV.
3. At idle the gauge should register 10 in. Hg at the distributor hose.
4. Replace the DVV if the gauge registers more than 11 or less than 9 in. Hg.
5. With the engine idling in Park (P), open the throttle slowly and watch the gauges.
6. The vacuum at the distributor should remain at 10 in. Hg while that at the "CARB" port should slowly increase.
7. As the gauge at the "CARB" port goes over 10 in. Hg, the distributor gauge will read the same as the throttle is opened further. The maximum reading should be about 15 in. Hg.
8. If the DVV doesn't work right, replace it.

1974 Oldsmobile Distributor Vacuum Valve (DVV)

NOTE: The distributor vacuum valve (DVV) is used on all California V8s and on all Toronado models.

1. Remove the air cleaner from the carburetor and plug up the manifold vacuum fitting.
2. Place the transmission in Park and block the wheels.
3. Start the engine and allow it to reach normal running temperature. Be sure that the air conditioner is turned off.
4. Remove the vacuum line from the "D" port of the coolant temperature operated vacuum valve. Install a vacuum gauge on the "D" port.
5. Connect another vacuum gauge to the hose at the carburetor EGR port with a T-fitting.
6. Slowly open the throttle; the reading on the gauge connected to the "D" port should raise, and level off at one of the following:

   Toronado—8 in. Hg

   All California—7 in. Hg
7. The second gauge (at the EGR port) should then reach the same figure given in Step 6. If this does not happen, replace the DVV.
8. After completing the test, disconnect both vacuum gauges, then install the vacuum lines and the air cleaner.

1973-74 Oldsmobile Vacuum Reducing Valve Test

1. Allow the engine to warm up.
2. Disconnect the line which runs from the vacuum reducing valve to the coolant temperature operated vacuum valve at the temperature valve end. Plug the nipple on the temperature valve to prevent a vacuum leak.
3. Connect a vacuum gauge to the line, after being sure that the line is neither plugged nor pinched.
4. With the engine at idle, the vacuum gauge should register no more than 9 in Hg—1973; 11-12 in. Hg—1974; or 13—13.5 in. Hg—1975. If the reading is

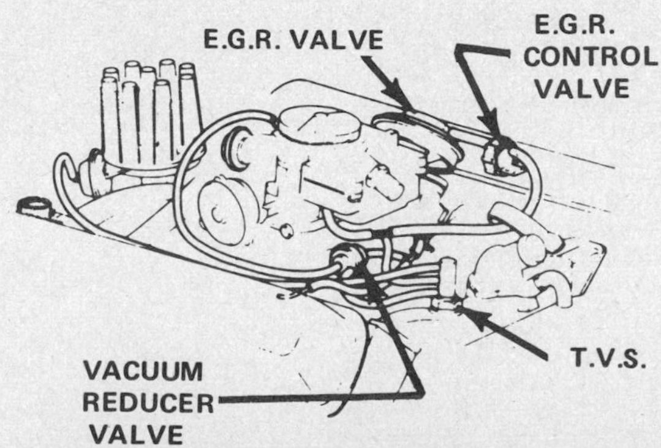

Oldsmobile vacuum reducing valve location (© G.M. Corp)

higher than this, replace the vacuum reducing valve.

Transmission Controlled Spark System Tests

Ford

NOTE: When performing the following tests, be sure that the temperature switch is kept above 65°F, expect as noted. On models equipped with a spark delay valve, the spark delay valve must be removed for this test to be valid.

Manual Transmission System Test

1. Connect a vacuum gauge between the distributor and the distributor modulator valve, using a T-connector.
2. Start the engine. With the transmission in neutral, the vacuum gauge should read zero.
3. Increase engine speed to between 1,000–1,500 rpm with the clutch pedal depressed. The vacuum reading should remain at zero.
4. With the clutch still depressed, place the transmission in high gear. Increase engine speed, as before. The vacuum gauge should now read at least 6 in. Hg. If it does not, proceed further with testing. Remember to shift into netural or stop the engine before engaging the clutch.
5. Unfasten the transmission switch lead from the distributor modulator terminal. Connect the lead in series with a low amperage test lamp and the positive side of the battery.
6. Move the gear shift lever through all of the gears. The test lamp should remain on until high gear is entered.
7. If the lamp stays on when the transmission is in high, either the switch is defective or the circuit is grounded. If it fails to come on at all, the switch is defective or the circuit has a loose wire.
8. If the transmission switch is functioning properly but the system check indicates that something is still wrong, proceed with the temperature switch test below.

Automatic Transmission System Test

1. Connect a vacuum gauge between the distributor and the distributor modulator valve using a T-connection. Start the engine.
2. When the transmission is in Park or neutral, the vacuum gauge should read zero.
3. Apply the brakes and shift into Reverse. Increase the engine speed. The gauge may or may not register a vacuum.

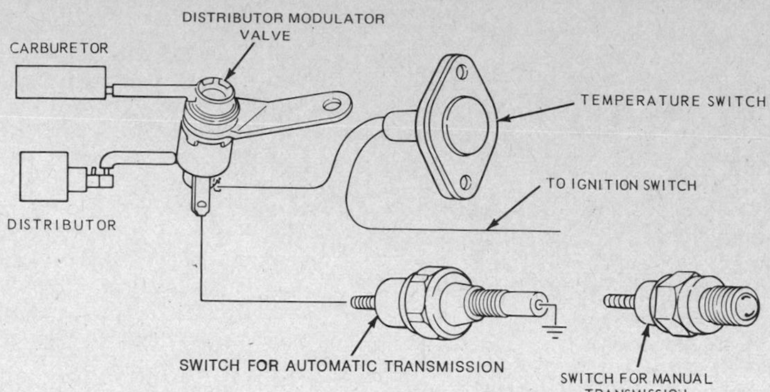

Ford transmission controlled spark system (© Ford Motor Co)

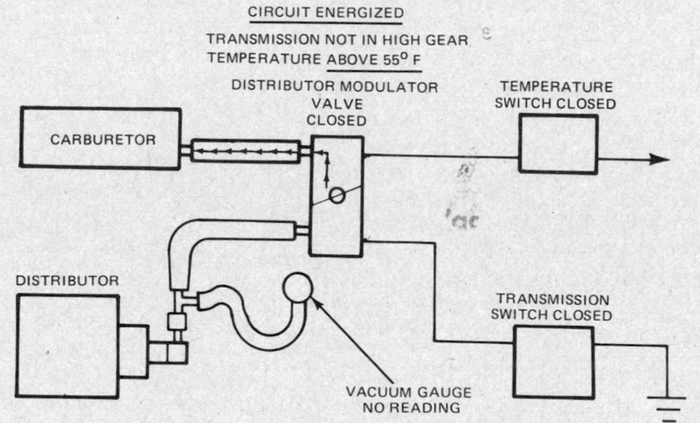

Testing the transmission-controlled spark system with the circuit energized (© Ford Motor Co)

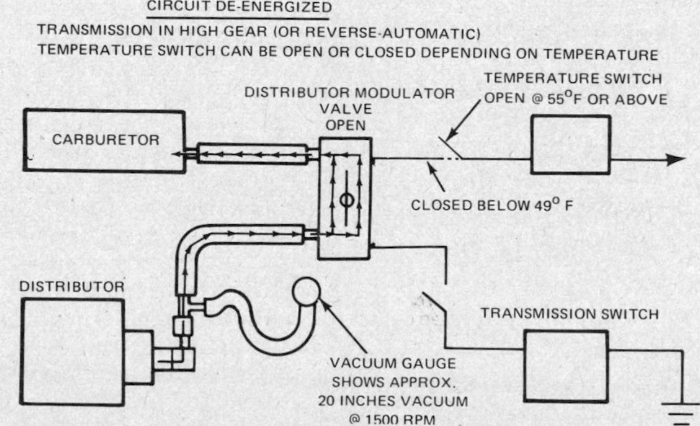

Testing the transmission-controlled spark system with the circuit de-energized (© Ford Motor Co)

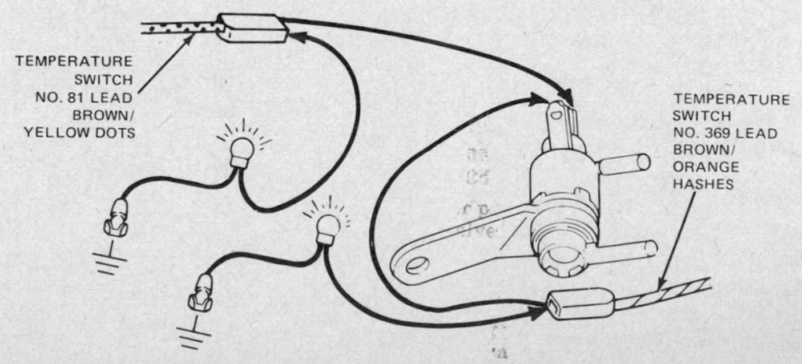

Using a test lamp to check the temperature of the transmission switch (© Ford Motor Co)

4. If no vacuum is present, detach a wire from the distributor modulator valve and shift into neutral. Increase engine speed to between 1,000–1,500 rpm. This time the gauge should definitely show a vacuum reading.
5. If vacuum still is not present, disconnect the two vacuum lines from the distributor modulator valve and join them, using a nipple, to bypass the valve. Repeat step four.
6. If there is vacuum now, proceed with the rest of the tests. If no vacuum is present, check for loose, pinched, or plugged hoses. When finished, reconnect the wire to the valve.
7. Detach the transmission switch lead from the distributor modular valve. Connect the lead in series with a test lamp and the positive terminal of the battery.
8. Start the engine and apply the brakes. Move the transmission selector through all of the positions on the quadrant.
9. The lamp should go out only when Reverse is selected. If it stays on in Reverse or fails to come on at all, either the switch is defective or the wiring is faulty.
10. If the transmission switch and wiring are in proper order, but vacuum still is not present, it will be necessary to test the temperature switch.

Temperature Switch Tests

NOTE: Cars made after 15 March 1973 do not use ambient temperature switches with TCS systems.

1. Detach the temperature switch lead from its terminal or the distributor modulator valve. Connect the lead to a grounded test lamp.
2. Remove the temperature switch from either the right or left door pillar. Warm the switch by holding it in the palm of the hand. The lamp should come on once 65°F is reached.
3. Using ice, or an aerosol spray circuit cooler, cool the switch to below 49°F. The test lamp should go out.
4. If the lamp fails to go on or off when it should, the switch is defective and must be replaced.
5. If the temperature switch is functioning properly, and no vacuum was present in the system test, the distributor modulator valve is defective.

Distributor Modulator Valve Test

1. Perform the above system test.
2. If the other components, i.e., the transmission switch and the temperature switch, are functioning properly and vacuum is present when it should not be, or vice versa, the fault probably lies in the distributor modulator valve.
3. Before replacing the valve, however, remember to check for clogged, pinched, or loose vacuum hoses, as these could result in similar symptoms.

American Motors

NOTE: All 1973 V8s and 1973 sixes from 15 March on, as well as all 1974 engines with TCS, use a coolant temperature operated vacuum valve to shut the TCS system off below 160°F.

Manual Transmission Test

The transmission-controlled spark (TCS) system used on American Motors cars equipped with manual transmissions is similar to the one used by Ford for their cars with manual transmissions.

The major difference is in the temperature switch (not used after 15 March 1973). The American Motors switch is located on the front upper crossmember and closes at 63°F. Also, American Motors refers to the "distributor modulator valve" (Ford) as the "solenoid vacuum valve."

Bearing these differences in mind, test the American Motors system in the same manner as outlined under "Ford—Manual Transmission," above.

NOTE: For the test procedures to be used when a 1972–73½ car is equipped with an automatic transmission, consult the "Speed Controlled Spark" section, below.

1973½-74 Automatic Transmission

NOTE: The spark control system used on AMC cars, equipped with automatic transmissions and made after 15 March 1973, is controlled by a switch which operates on transmission governor oil pressure. Test procedures for cars made before this date may be found in the "Speed Controlled Spark Systems" section, below.

1. Disconnect the electrical lead from the terminal of the governor pressure switch.

NOTE: The switch may easily be reached with the hood opened. On sixes, the switch is located on the right rear of the cylinder block; on V8s, it is attached to a bracket at the rear of the right-hand rocker cover.

2. Connect a 12V test light in series, between the lead and the terminal on the switch.

Caution *Use a low amperage test light, so that the switch contacts will not be damaged.*

3. Raise the car, block the front wheels (if they are not off the ground), and securely support it so that the rear wheels are free to turn.
4. Apply the service brakes. Start the engine. The test light should glow.
5. Place the gear selector in Drive (D), release the brake pedal and slowly depress the gas pedal.
6. Watch the speedometer and the test light; between 33-37 mph the switch should open and the test light should go out.
7. If the light does not go out within this speed range, adjust the switch by turning the 1/16 in. allen screw on the switch terminal. Turn the screw clockwise to increase or counterclockwise to decrease the switch cut-out speed. The switch should be adjusted to open at 35 mph.
8. If the switch cannot be adjusted to specification, replace it.
9. If the switch is working properly, but the TCS system is not working, the solenoid vacuum valve is probably defective.

Location of American Motors ambient temperature switch on the front upper crossmember (© American Motors Corp)

1973½ solenoid vacuum valve (top) and transmission governor pressure switch (bottom). —AMC V8

Chrysler

Manual Transmission

NOTE: For testing procedures to be used on Chrysler products that are equipped with an automatic transmission, see Speed Control Spark.

1. Turn the ignition switch to the "on" position. Place the transmission selector lever in the "neutral" position.
2. Disconnect the wire from the B+ terminal on the ignition system ballast resistor while holding the solenoid vacuum valve.
3. When the wire is disconnected, the valve should be felt to deenergize.
4. Reconnect the wire to the ballast resistor, the valve should be felt to energize. If the solenoid vacuum valve does not react this way, either the vacuum valve or the transmission switch is defective, or voltage is not present at the ballast resistor. Connect a

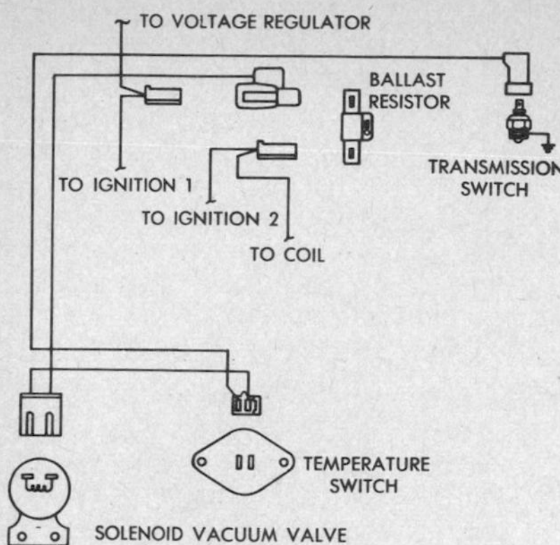

NO_x (TCS) system schematic—manual transmission (© Chrysler Corp)

test light to the B+ terminal of the resistor to check for voltage.

5. To test the solenoid vacuum valve, disconnect the wiring connector from the solenoid. Run a jumper wire from the piggyback connector on the ballast resistor to one of the terminals on the solenoid vacuum valve. Connect another jumper wire from the other terminal on the solenoid vacuum valve to a good ground. When the ignition switch is turned to the "on" position, the vacuum valve should be felt to energize. If the vacuum valve does not energize, it is defective. If the vacuum valve does energize, but did not energize in Steps 2–4, proceed to Step 6. Connect the lead wires to the vacuum valve.
6. Disconnect the lead wire from the transmission switch. Connect a jumper wire from the just disconnected switch lead to a good ground. When the ignition switch is turned to the "on" position the solenoid vacuum valve should be felt to energize. If the switch does energize when the lead wire to the switch was connected to ground, but failed to energize in Steps 2–4, the transmission switch is either defective or it has a bad ground. If the transmission switch is attached to the transmission with 180 in. lbs torque, it is correctly grounded.
7. If the vacuum valve energized in Step 5, but did not energize in Step 6, the lead wire from the ballast resistor to the vacuum valve is defective.

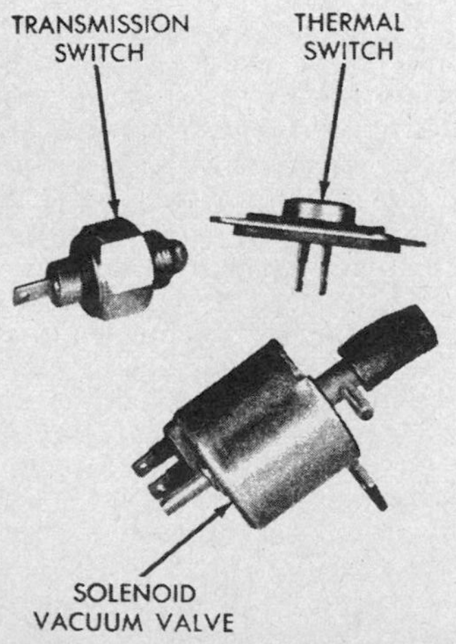

NO_x (TCS) system components—manual transmission (© Chrysler Corp)

GM Except All 1973 Pontiac Models

NOTE: The components used on the GM transmission-controlled spark (TCS) systems vary from model to model. For a description of the components used for each model, see the appropriate Car Section.

SYSTEM TEST

1. Connect a vacuum gauge to the vacuum source for the vacuum solenoid. With the transmission in neutral and the engine idling, vacuum should be present.
2. If there is no vacuum present, check for a clogged vacuum port, damaged vacuum lines or loose hose connections.
3. Disconnect the vacuum guage and reconnect the vacuum line.
4. Detach the vacuum line from the distributor vacuum unit and connect it to the vacuum gauge. This is the line which contains the vacuum advance solenoid or CEC solenoid.
5. With engine temperature above 95°F and the transmission in neutral, run the engine for at least 25 seconds. The vacuum gauge should read zero.

NOTE: All 1971 Cadillacs have a by-pass circuit to provide vacuum advance in both Park and neutral.

6. Do one of the following:
   a. Manual transmission — Depress the clutch pedal and move the shift lever through the gears. Increase engine speed in each gear, enough to cause vacuum advance. A vacuum should be present only in High gear.

   NOTE: On 1970–71 models with four-speed transmissions, vacuum should also be present in third gear.

   b. Automatic transmission — Raise the rear wheels of the car off the ground. Support the car and block the front wheels, so that it cannot roll forward. Place the transmission in Drive and speed the engine up enough so that the transmission will shift into high gear; vacuum should only be present when the transmission enters high gear, and not while it is in lower gears.

NOTE: Some cars are equipped with a time-delay device, so it may take 20–25 seconds before vacuum is present once the proper gear has been reached. Do not run the engine any longer than necessary to complete the test.

7. If no vacuum is present when it should be or if it is present when it should not be, first check the TCS system fuse (if so equipped) and then proceed with the individual tests outlined below.

VACUUM ADVANCE SOLENOID TESTS

NOTE: There are several different types of vacuum advance solenoids used on GM cars; look at the chart below to determine proper model usage.

Type A—Normally Opened

1. Disconnect the vacuum line from the vacuum advance solenoid to the distributor vacuum unit, at the distributor end. Connect a vacuum gauge to the line after making sure that it is not broken or clogged.
2. Detach the electrical leads from the solenoid. With the engine running, the vacuum gauge should register a vacuum. If it does not, the solenoid is faulty and must be replaced.
3. Using care to observe the proper polarity, connect one solenoid terminal to a 12 V power source. Using a jumper wire,

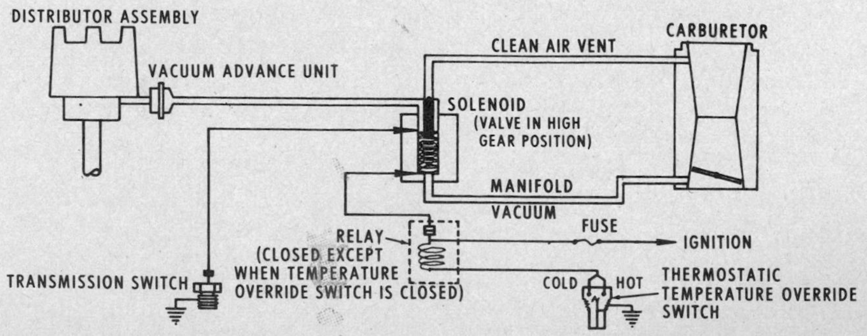

A typical transmission controlled spark system (© General Motors Corp)

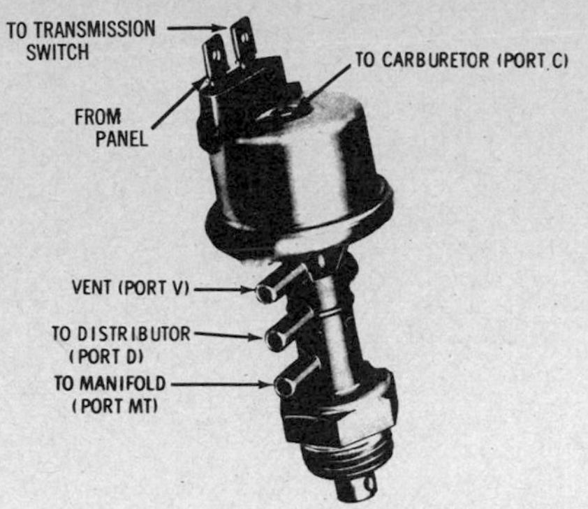

The combination vacuum advance solenoid and coolant temperature operated vacuum valve

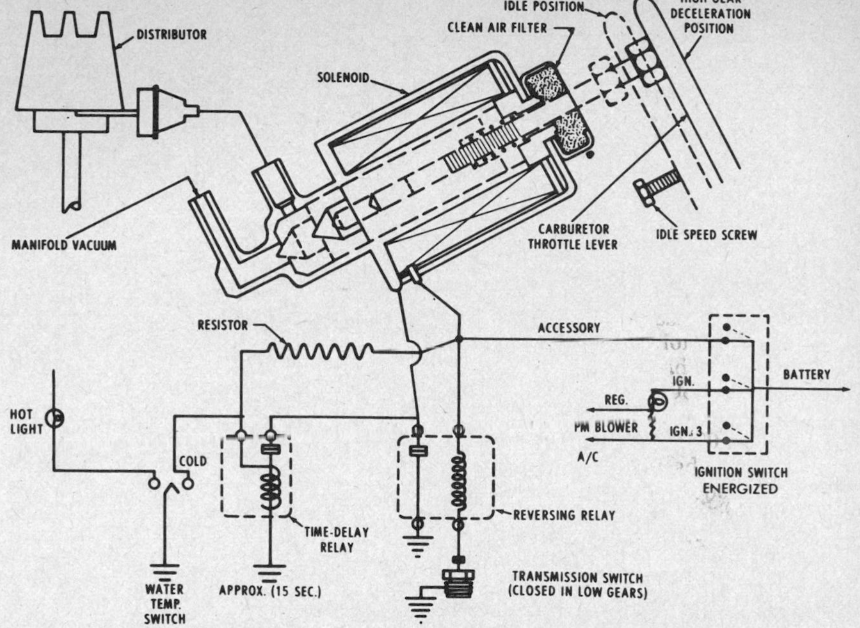

1970-71 CEC System (© G.M. Corp)

connect the transmission switch terminal on the vacuum solenoid to ground. The solenoid should energize and the vacuum gauge reading should return to zero. If vacuum is still present, the solenoid is jammed and should be replaced.

4. If the solenoid is not defective, connect it in the original manner and go on to the next appropriate test.

Type B—Normally Closed

1. Disconnect the line which runs from the vacuum advance solenoid to the distributor vacuum unit. Connect a vacuum gauge to this line, after making sure that it is neither plugged nor broken.
2. Detach both electrical leads from the solenoid. The gauge should indicate zero vacuum. If it does not, the solenoid is defective and must be replaced.
3. Using care to observe proper polarity, connect the "hot" lead of the solenoid to a 12 V power source. Ground the other lead. Vacuum should now be present in the line. If it is not, the solenoid is defective and needs to be replaced.
4. If the solenoid is not defective, connect it in the original manner and go on with the next applicable test.

Type C—CEC Solenoid and Relays

The test for the CEC solenoid is similar to that for the Type B vacuum advance solenoid, above, expect that a vacuum guage is not needed. With 12 V applied to the CEC solenoid, its plunger should extend. With no power applied to the solenoid, the plunger should retract. If it fails to do either properly, the solenoid is defective and must be replaced. If it is not defective, reconnect it.

NOTE: A defective CEC solenoid will also affect the operation of the throttle. For further details, see "Carburetor Modifications," below.

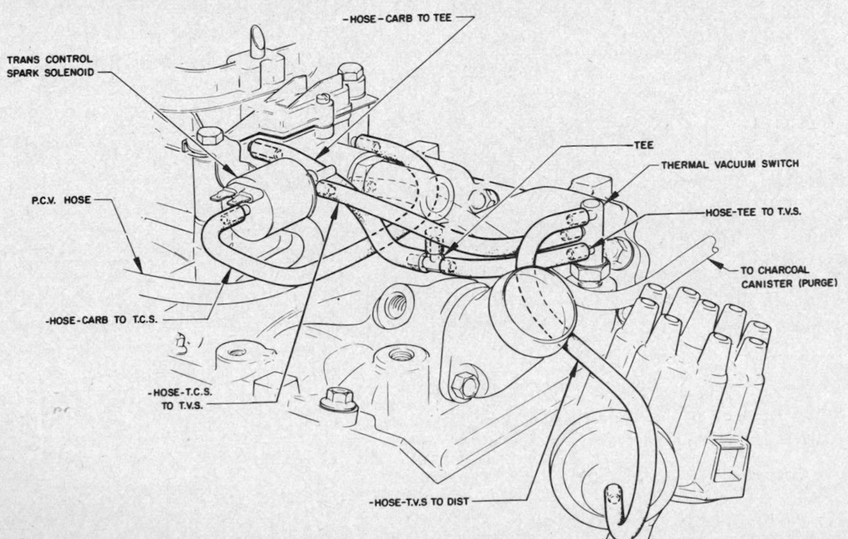

TCS system installation (© G.M. Corp)

Models made prior to 1972 which are equipped with a CEC solenoid, use a reversing relay to provide proper switching action for the solenoid. To test relay operation:

1. Bypass the relay by grounding its single wire connector.
2. If the CEC solenoid plunger will now extend, and it did not extend in the above test, the reversing relay is defective.

A time-delay relay is used on some models equipped with a CEC solenoid to provide vacuum advance for 15–20 seconds after the ignition is switched on. To check its operation, proceed as follows:

1. Disconnect the electrical lead from the temperature switch.
2. Allow the relay to cool. Turn the ignition on. The CEC solenoid should energize (plunger extend) for about 15–20 seconds and then go off.
3. If it fails to go off, detach the blue lead from the time-delay relay. If the CEC solenoid now de-energizes, then the relay is faulty and must be replaced.

If none of the CEC system components which were tested are defective, go on to the next applicable test.

VACUUM DELAY RELAY TESTS

This relay is a solid-state unit which is used on some 1972 models. (It is not used with the CEC solenoid and should not be confused with the *time*-delay relay, above.) It is located underneath the dashboard, inside the passenger compartment. To test it proceed in the following manner:

1. Turn the ignition on. Then, using a lower amperage test lamp, check to see that the relay

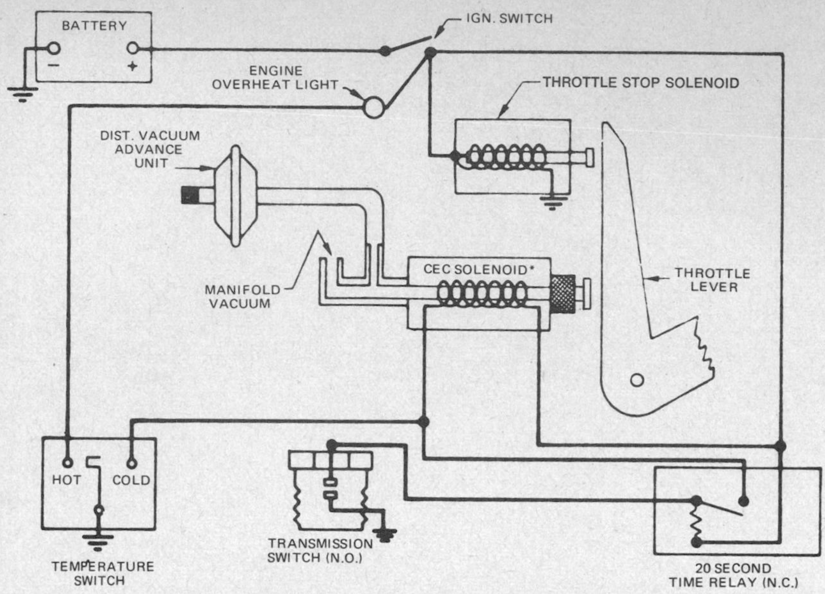

1972-73 CEC system without the reversing relay (© G.M. Corp)

is getting power. If it is not, check its wiring.

2. Disconnect and ground the black lead.
3. Wait for 26 seconds. The vacuum advance solenoid should then energize. If it does not, the relay is faulty and must be replaced. If it does, reconnect the vacuum delay relay and proceed with the next applicable test.

TEMPERATURE SWITCH TEST

1. Connect a vacuum gauge to the vacuum advance solenoid to the distributor vacuum unit.
2. Allow the engine to cool to around 75°F and then start it. The gauge should indicate the presence of a vacuum.
3. If it does not, ground the lead from the cold terminal of the temperature switch.
4. On temperature controls with an additional hot terminal, repeat step 3—this time grounding the hot terminal.
5. If vacuum is not present when either terminal is grounded, the temperature switch is defective.

The temperature sensing switch is usually threaded into the cylinder head (© G.M. Corp)

If vacuum still is not present, reconnect the temperature switch leads and vacuum line. Proceed with the next applicable test.

TCS RELAY TEST—VEGA 1971–72

1. Test the TCS relay with the engine warm and the ignition on.
2. Ground the vacuum advance solenoid with the black lead. The solenoid should energize.
3. Keep the solenoid engaged in this manner. Ground the terminal which has the green and white wire running to it.
4. The vacuum advance solenoid should de-energize. If it remains energized, the TCS solenoid is faulty and must be replaced. If it is functioning properly, remove the jumpers and proceed with the next applicable test.

Location of the Vega TCS relay (© G.M. Corp)

TRANSMISSION SWITCH TESTS

NOTE: There are several different types of transmission switches used on GM cars. Check the chart below for proper model usage and then proceed with the applicable test.

Type D—Normally Opened

This test should be performed last, once all the other TCS system components are known to be in proper working order.

1. Repeat steps 4–6 of the "System Test." There should be vacuum to the distributor in high gear.
2. If there is none, disconnect the lead from the transmission switch and ground it.
3. If vacuum is now present, i.e., the vacuum advance solenoid has energized, then the transmission switch is faulty and must be replaced.

Type E—Manual Transmission/ Normally Closed

NOTE: Some models with manual transmissions use a two-terminal transmission switch. Before proceeding with the test, ground the extra terminal.

1. Detach the switch connector at the side of the transmission.
2. Connect a test lamp in series with the switch and 12 V power source.

Caution Do not use a bulb any larger than 0.8 amp (no. 1893); the switch contacts will be damaged at a higher amperage.

Location of the manual transmission switch (© G.M. Corp)

3. With the engine and ignition off, move the gear shift lever through all of the gears. The test lamp should remain lighted in every gear except third and fourth (if so equipped).

NOTE: On 1972 models with four-speed transmissions, the lamp should remain lighted in third gear and not go out until fourth is selected.

4. If the test lamp fails to go out when it should, the switch is defective.
5. If the test lamp fails to come on at all, the switch is broken or the wiring is faulty.
6. If the switch is not defective, reconnect it when finished testing.

Type F—Automatic Transmission/ Normally Closed

NOTE: Vegas, made for sale in California in 1972, have a non-functional, dummy transmission switch when equipped with an automatic transmission.

1. Connect a test lamp as detailed in steps 1–2 of the test for type E switch above. Pay particular attention to the "Caution."
2. Raise the rear wheels of the car so they are off of the ground and support the car so that it cannot move forward.
3. Start the engine. Shift the transmission into Drive. Increase engine speed so that the transmission shifts into high gear, the test lamp should go out when the transmission enters high gear.
4. Allow the engine to return to idle and apply the brakes. Shift into Reverse. The light should go out again, except on cars equipped with Powerglide or Torque Drive.
5. In all other gears the lamp should remain on. If it does not or if it fails to go out when it should, replace the switch.

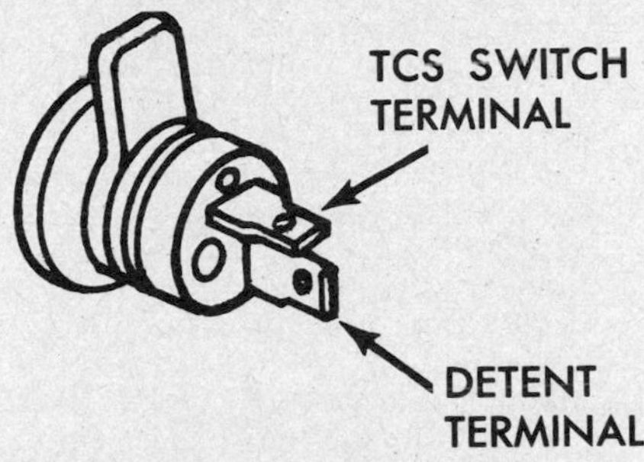

The terminals on the Turbo Hydra-Matic 400 transmission switch (© G.M. Corp)

1973 Pontiac Combination T.C.S.-E.G.R. System

System Test

1. Apply parking brake, and securely block wheels. Connect a vacuum gauge to the distributor end of the vacuum line that runs from the T.C.S. solenoid to the distributor. Observe the position of the stem under the E.G.R. valve, this should be in the closed position.
2. The engine must be "overnight" cold with the ambient temperature below 71°. If this condition cannot be duplicated, follow the instructions below, skipping step four, and then use the "Simulated Temperature Switch Test" which follows the normal testing procedures.
3. Depress accelerator to set choke and place throttle linkage on fast idle cam. Start the engine and allow throttle to remain on fast idle cam.

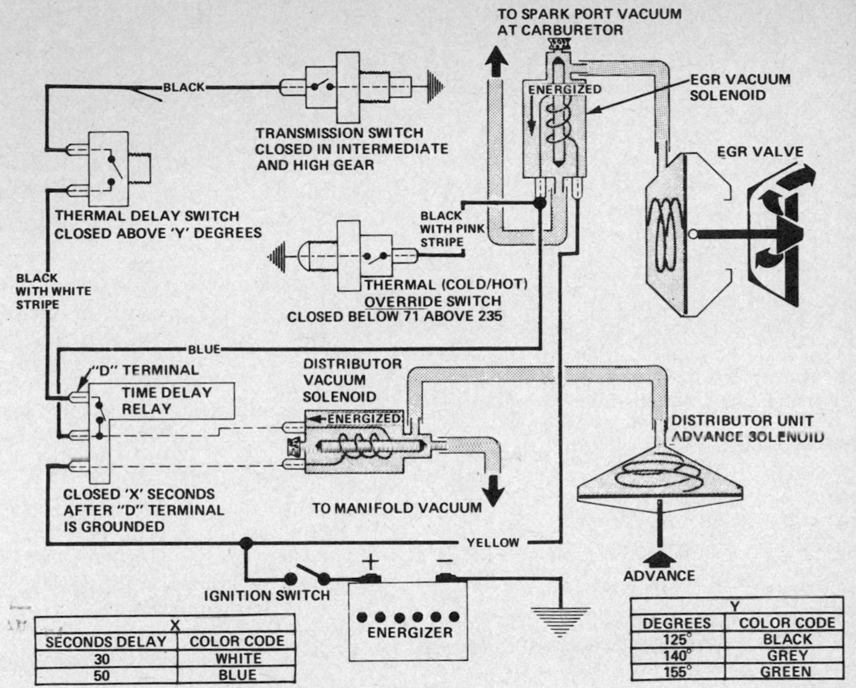

1973 Pontiac TCS-EGR system (© G.M. Corp)

4. Vacuum gauge should indicate a high manifold vacuum and E.G.R. valve should remain fully closed.
5. When the engine reaches 71°, manifold vacuum should disappear and the E.G.R. valve should open.
6. Shut off the engine. Raise the rear of the car and place it on jackstands so wheels are off the floor. Release parking brake. Put automatic transmission in Drive, manual transmission in highest gear. Place throttle on fast idle cam. Make sure automatic transmission shifts out of first gear.
7. When engine temperature reaches 140° (well before coolant flows through radiator), the E.G.R. valve should close fully, and manifold vacuum should again show on the vacuum gauge. Shift transmission out of gear for several seconds, then put it back in gear. Vacuum

VACUUM ADVANCE SOLENOID AND TRANSMISSION SWITCH USAGE

Make	*Year*	*Model*	*Test Section Used For: Vacuum Advance Solenoid*	*Transmission Switch*
Buick	1970–74	All V8	A	E, F
	1974	L6	B	D
Cadillac	1970–71	All	A	F
Chevrolet	1970	All	A	E, F
	1971	L6, V8	C	E, F
		Vega	A	E, F
	1972–73	L6	C	D
		V8	C	D
	1974	V8	B	D
	1972	Vega	A	E, F①
	1973-74	Vega	B	D
	1974	L6	B	D
Pontiac	1970–71	All	A	E, F
	1972–73	L6	C	D
	1974	L6	B	D
	1972	V8	A	E, F
	1974	V8	B	D
Oldsmobile	1971–73	V8	A	E, F
	1973	L6	C	D
	1974	L6	B	D

①—The transmission switch is not operative on Vegas sold in California when equipped with an automatic transmission.

should disappear and E.G.R. valve should open. 33–55 seconds. after the transmission shifts out of first gear, vacuum should come back and the E.G.R. valve should close.

8. Restrict the flow of air across the radiator core. Shift the transmission into neutral. Vacuum will disappear, and E.G.R. valve will open. At 235° (before temperature light comes on) vacuum should be restored and the E.G.R. valve should close.

NOTE: If the EGR valve is not operating properly, perform steps 5-7 of the GM EGR valve test, below.

Simulated Temperature Switch Test

If the other parts of the system function, but conditions would not permit testing the low temperature function, remove the temperature sensor from the rear of the left head as follows:

1. Allow engine to cool until radiator cap can be safely removed, then remove the cap.
2. Place a clean container under the drain cock and begin draining coolant.
3. Disconnect wiring and loosen switch at rear of left cylinder head to check for presence of coolant. As soon as switch can be removed without loss of coolant, close the radiator drain cock and remove the switch. Test the switch as follows:

1. Prepare a container of cold water or water and ice. Check with a thermometer to make sure temperature is below 60°.
2. Immerse the threaded portion of the switch in the water, and allow it to cool until it has reached the temperature of the water.
3. Remove the switch from the bath and immediately check for continuity between the electrical prong and the threaded portion of the switch. Replace a switch which shows no continuity under these conditions.

Symptoms and Appropriate Checks

1. System responds normally at operating temperatures but does not supply advance and deny EGR below 71° and/or above 235°. Operate engine at fast idle with transmission in neutral until normal operating temperature is reached. Jump the switch at the rear of the left cylinder head by grounding the wire which goes to the switch. If this produces vacuum and shuts off the EGR valve, replace the switch. Otherwise, check for defects in the wiring between this switch and the solenoids.
2. System responds to temperature changes, but does not provide vacuum advance and deny EGR after transmission shifts to second gear. Operate engine at fast idle with transmission in Neutral until operating temperature is reached. Ground the switch on the right side of the transmission, by grounding the wire connected to it. Keep wire grounded one minute. If this produces vacuum advance and denies EGR, replace the transmission switch. Otherwise, bypass the switch on the right cylinder head and ground the wire to the transmission switch. If this produces vacuum advance and denies EGR after one minute, replace the sensor in the right head. Otherwise, the Time Delay Relay or associated wiring is defective. Bypass each to locate the defective component.
3. System responds normally except that EGR is denied and vacuum advance established as soon as transmission shifts to second gear. Replace Time Delay Relay.
4. Only one function responds as required, or system provides EGR and denies vacuum advance at all times; check wiring. Replace if defective. Otherwise, solenoid (s) are at fault.

Speed Controlled Spark Systems

Ford Distributor Modulator System—1970-71

System Tests

Check the distributor vacuum advance on an analyzer (distributor modulator system bypassed if distributor is left in engine for test). If it is functioning correctly, proceed with the tests outlined below.

1. Disconnect the distributor vacuum advance line from the carburetor and connect a vacuum gauge to vacuum line fitting on the carburetor. Run the engine at 1,500 rpm and take a vacuum reading. Make a note of the result. Disconnect the vacuum gauge and attach the vacuum line back on the carburetor.
2. Using a short length of rubber hose to bypass the distributor modulator control box, connect the distributor vacuum advance unit directly to the carburetor. Disconnect the vacuum line from the distributor vacuum advance unit and connect it to the vacuum gauge.
3. Run the engine at 1,500 rpm again. The vacuum gauge reading should be similar to that obtained above. If it is zero or much less than in step one, check for pinched or leaking vacuum lines.
4. Remove the hose used to bypass the distributor modulator and reconnect the vacuum lines as originally found. Leave the vacuum gauge connected to the distributor vacuum line, however.
5. Raise the rear wheels off the ground and support the car so that it cannot roll forward. Run the engine at idle until normal operating temperature is reached.
6. Remove the thermal switch from the door pillar. Hold the switch in the palm of the hand long

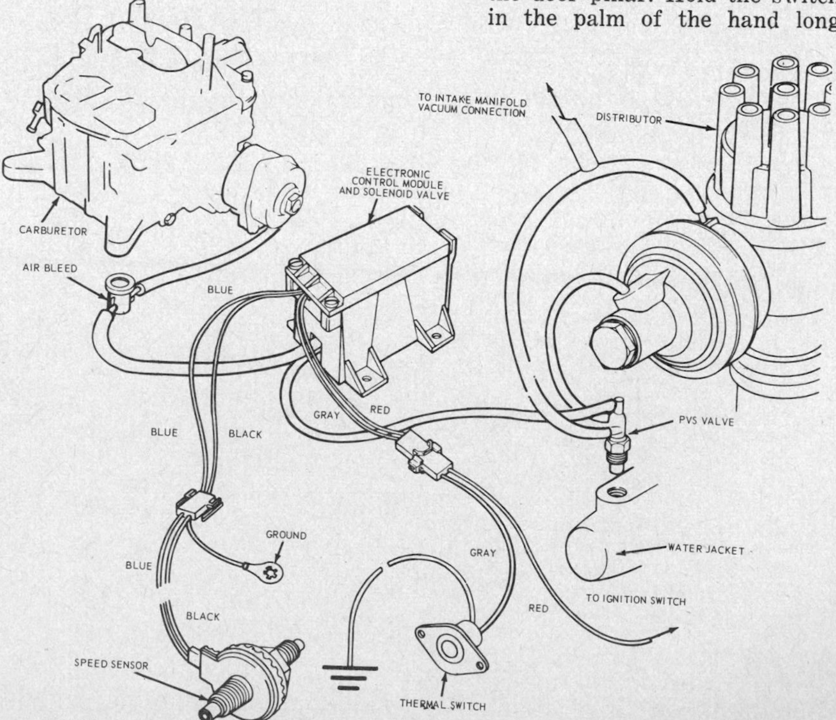

Distributor modulator system details (© Ford Motor Co)

DISTRIBUTOR MODULATOR SYSTEM TROUBLESHOOTING CHART

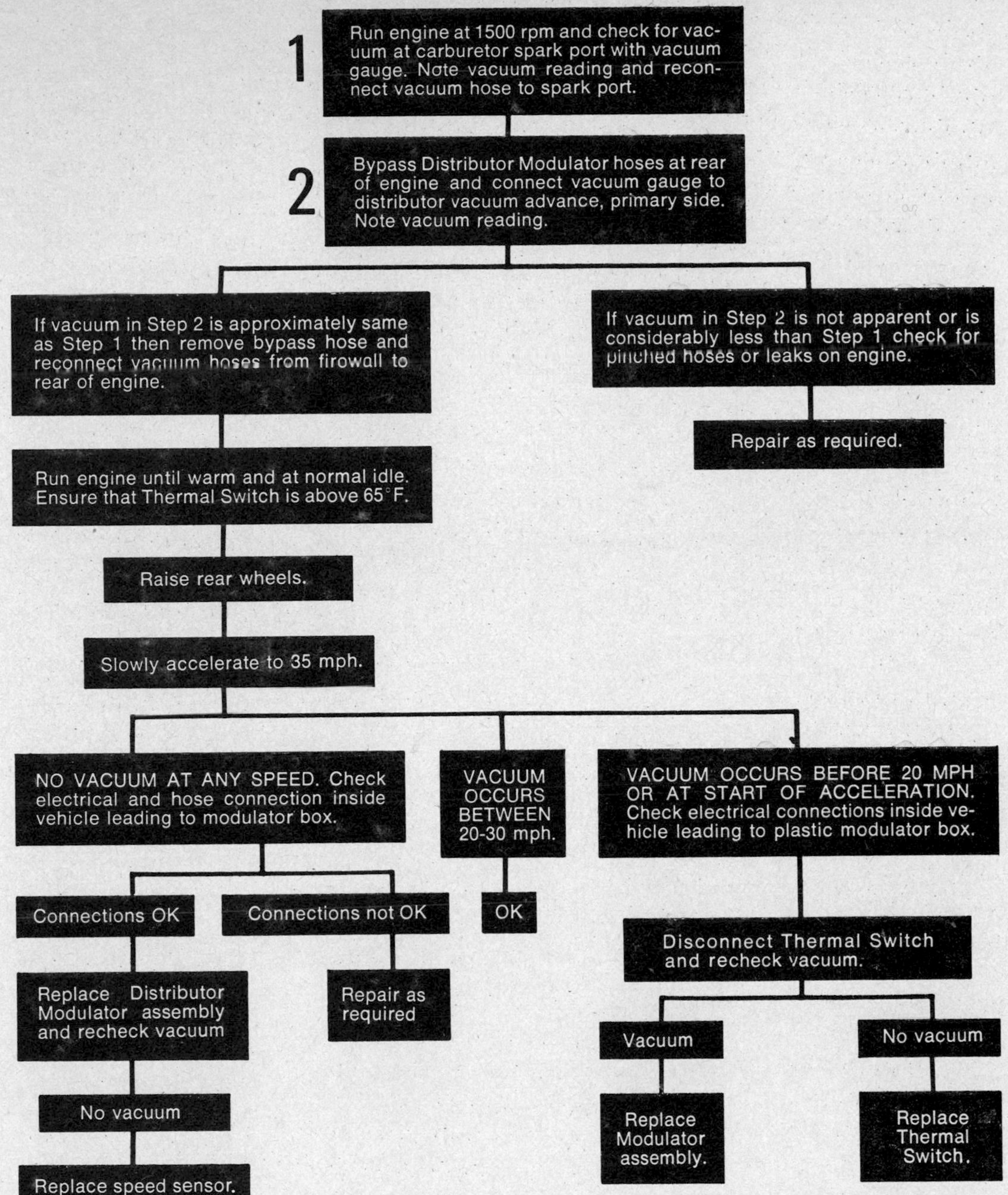

enough to bring its temperature above 60° F.

7. Place the transmission selector in Drive. Accelerate to 35 mph. By the time this speed is reached, the vacuum gauge should show a reading.
8. If the vacuum gauge shows a reading below 20–35 mph, or if it does not show a reading above 35 mph, proceed with the individual component tests as required.

NOTE: Remember to check the coolant temperature operated vacuum valve, if so equipped, as possible cause of trouble. The test procedures may be found above.

Power Supply Test

1. Switch the ignition on. Take a voltage reading at the red lead which runs to the control module.
2. If the voltmeter reads zero, check for a blown system fuse or faulty wiring.
3. If the voltmeter registers normal battery voltage, the module is getting the proper power. Proceed with the next test.

Thermal Switch Test

1. Disconnect the thermal switch at its multiconnector.
2. Connect an ohmmeter to the grey (or white) and black leads coming from the switch.
3. Warm the switch by holding it in the palm of the hand until it is above 68° F. There should be no reading (zero) on the ohmmeter. If there is a reading the switch is defective and needs to be replaced.
4. Chill the switch, using ice or cold water, to below 50° F. There should now be a reading (resistance indicated) on the meter. If there is no reading, the switch is defective and should be replaced.
5. If the temperature switch is functioning properly, proceed with the next test.

Control Module Test

1. Disconnect the thermal switch multiconnector from the module. Use a jumper lead to connect the two red wires leading from the two halves of multiconnector.
2. Attach a vacuum gauge to the distributor vacuum line fitting on the carburetor. Run the engine at fast idle and note the reading. Disconnect the gauge and reconnect the vacuum line to the port.
3. Connect the vacuum gauge to the vacuum hose that runs to the distributor vacuum advance unit.
4. Use another jumper lead to connect the grey (or white) wire, which runs from the control module to the thermal switch connector, to ground.
5. Run the engine at fast idle again and note the vacuum reading. It should be almost the same as that taken at the carburetor port.
6. If the reading is zero or lower than that at the carburetor port, the module is defective and must be replaced.
7. If the module is functioning properly, reconnect it and go on with the next test.

Speed Sensor Test

1. Detach the speed sensor leads at its multiconnector. Connect the test prods of an ohmmeter to them.
2. With the sensor at room temperature, the meter should read between 40–60 ohms.
3. Test for continuity between the black lead and the speed sensor case. There should be no meter reading.
4. The speed sensor is defective if the reading in step 2 does not fall within specifications or if a reading is obtained between the case and the black lead.

Ford Electronic Spark Control (ESC)—1972-73

This system replaces the distributor modulator system, above. The test procedures for the two systems are somewhat different and should not be interchanged, except as noted.

NOTE: Vehicles made on or after 15 March 1973 do not use a temperature switch.

System Test

1. Raise the rear wheels off the ground and support the car so it cannot roll forward.
2. Detach the vacuum hose on the primary side of the distributor vacuum advance unit. Connect a vacuum gauge to the hose.
3. Warm the temperature sensor in the palm of the hand, after removing it from its location on the door pillar (left or right, depending upon model). Be sure it is heated to above 65°F.
4. Start the engine. Place the transmission selector in Drive. Accelerate until the speed specified in the chart is reached (see below). This speed is determined by the color of the amplifier case. Wait for 40 seconds; this allows the time delay valve to work (if so equipped). At this point vacuum should be present.

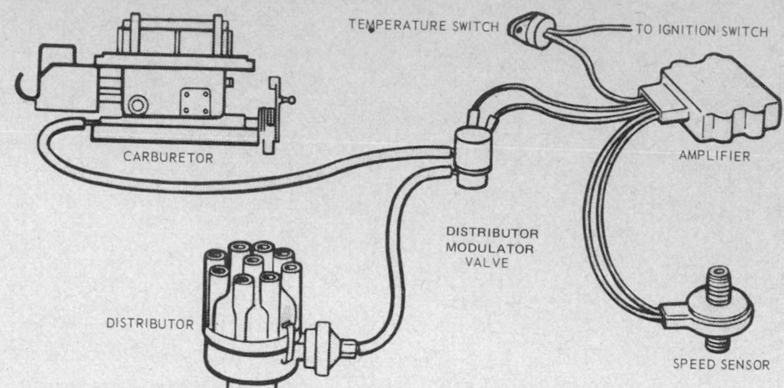

Components of the Ford ECS system (© Ford Motor Co)

Amplifier Case Color	*Vacuum Advance Cut-in Speed (mph)*
Black	23
White	28
Blue	33
Grey	35

5. If there is no vacuum, first check for a clogged carburetor vacuum port.
6. Then check the vacuum lines to see if they are pinched, clogged or misrouted.

NOTE: Remember to check the coolant temperature-operated vacuum valve, if so equipped, as a possible source of the malfunction. The test procedures for it are given above.

7. If the above checks indicate that the problem does not lie in the vacuum supply system, proceed with the ESC individual component tests.

Distributor Modulator Solenoid Test

1. Disconnect the electrical leads from the distributor modulator solenoid.
2. Increase engine speed. If there is no vacuum reading, with the gauge connected as in the System Test, the solenoid is defective and must be replaced. Reconnect the electrical leads to the distributor modulator solenoid and allow the engine to slow down.
3. If vacuum occurs below the specified cut-in speeds (see the chart in step 4, above), the solenoid

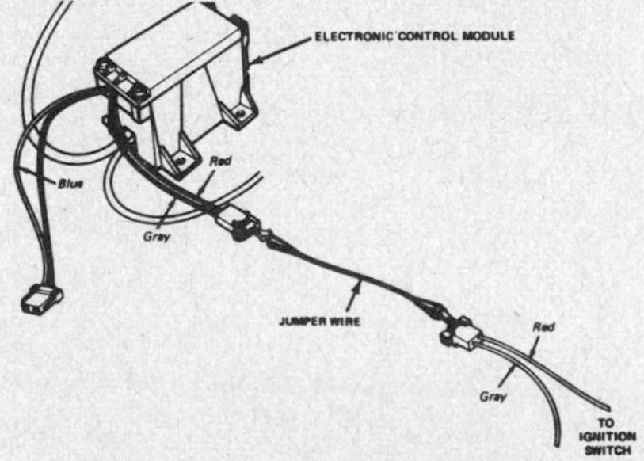

Connect the two red wires of the multiconnector by using a jumper lead
(© Ford Motor Co)

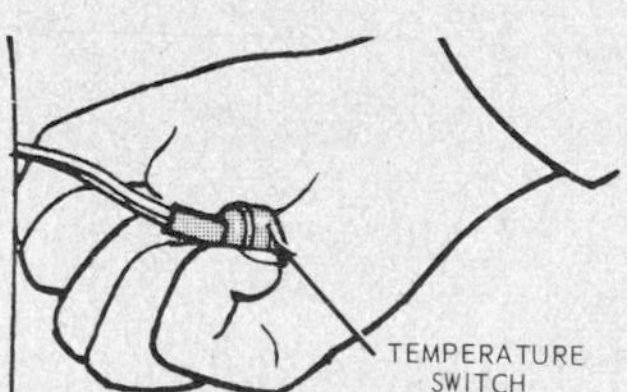

Warm the temperature switch in the palm of your hand
(© Ford Motor Co)

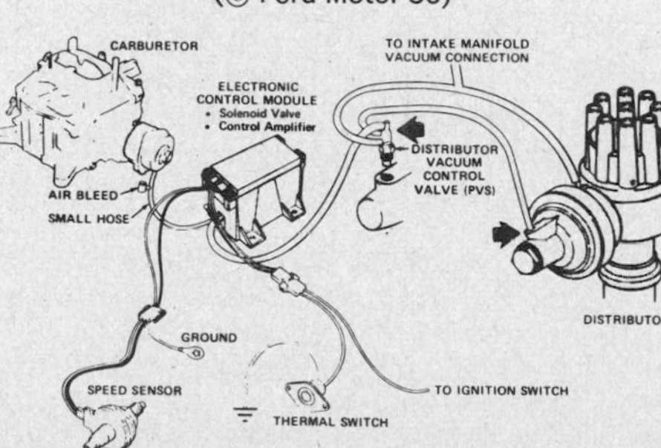

Arrows show the vacuum gauge hook-up points used during control module tests
(© Ford Motor Co)

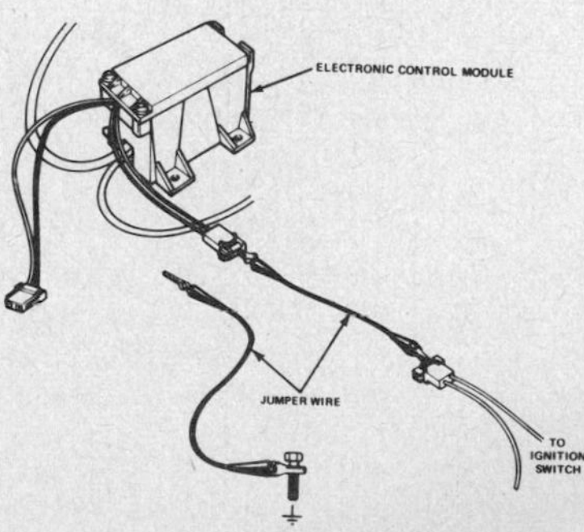

Connect the grey (or white) wire to ground by using a jumper lead
(© Ford Motor Co)

is not being energized and the trouble lies elsewhere in the system. Proceed with the next test.

Temperature Switch Tests

1. Disconnect the temperature switch at the multiconnector. Connect an ohmmeter to the switch terminals.
2. Warm the switch by placing it in the palm of the hand. The ohmmeter should show a reading. If it does not, the switch is defective.
3. Chill the switch to 49°F or below, by using ice or cold water. There should be no reading (zero) on the ohmmeter. If a resistance is indicated, the temperature switch is defective.
4. Replace the switch if defective. If it is not, proceed with the next test.

Power Supply Test

1. Ground one side of a low-amperage test lamp and connect the other side to the temperature switch connector of the instrument panel wiring (red/yellow hash lead).
2. Turn on the ignition. The lamp should light. If it fails to do so, check the wiring to the ignition switch or check the ignition switch itself.
3. If the ESC system is getting power, proceed with the next test.

Speed Sensor Test

This test is exactly the same as that for the speed sensor used in the distributor modulator system.

Perform the speed sensor test as outlined in the "Distributor Modulator" section, above.

Amplifier

If everything else in the ESC system is functioning properly, the fault lies with the amplifier module. Replace the amplifier and repeat the "System Test".

Chrysler Corp.

Automatic Transmission System Test

1. Warm the engine to normal operating temperature. Be sure the ambient temperature is well above 70°F.
2. T-connect a vacuum gauge between the distributor and the solenoid vacuum valve.
3. Raise the car on a lift, with the wheels hanging free.
4. Disconnect the vacuum line at the vacuum switch on the control unit.
5. Start the engine and run at a speed above 850 rpm. Vacuum gauge should read zero.
6. Disconnect the wire from the control unit. The vacuum gauge should read normal advance unit operating vacuum. Reconnect the wire. The gauge should drop to zero.
7. Unplug and reconnect the vacuum line to the vacuum switch. Disconnect the wire from the control unit to the speed switch. The gauge should read normal advance unit operating vacuum.
8. Place transmission in Drive. Sharp acceleration should cause the gauge reading to drop sharply to zero. Do not exceed 40 mph.
9. Accelerate above 30 mph. The gauge should read normal vacuum advance unit operating vacuum.
10. If solenoid valve did not operate during the tests, replace control unit.

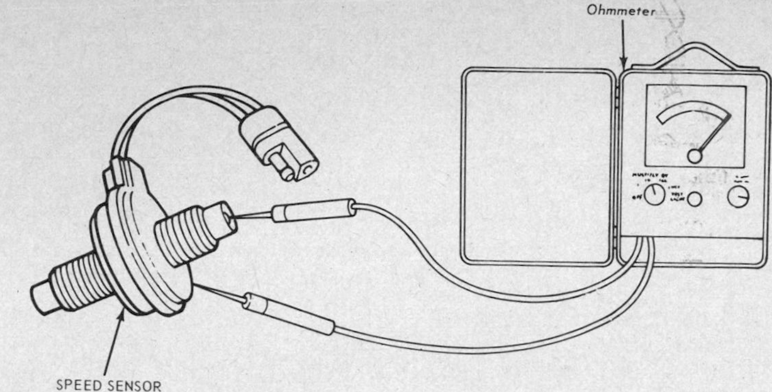

Using an ohmmeter to see if the speed sensor is grounded to the case (© Ford Motor Co)

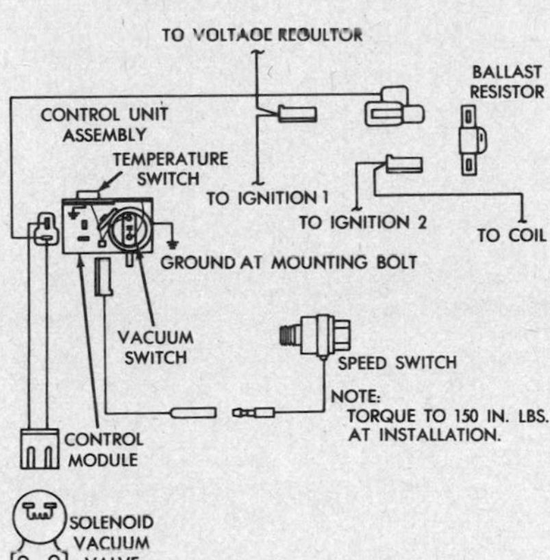

NO_x (SCS) system schematic —automatic transmission (© Chrysler Corp)

American Motors (1972-early '73) and Pontiac

NOTE: Although American Motors calls all of their spark control systems "Transmission - Controlled Spark" (TCS), the one used with automatic transmissions is really a speed-controlled spark system (SCS). American Motors cars made on or after 15 March 1973 do not use an SCS system, but have, instead, a transmision controlled spark (TCS) system. Consult the appropriate section above for system testing.

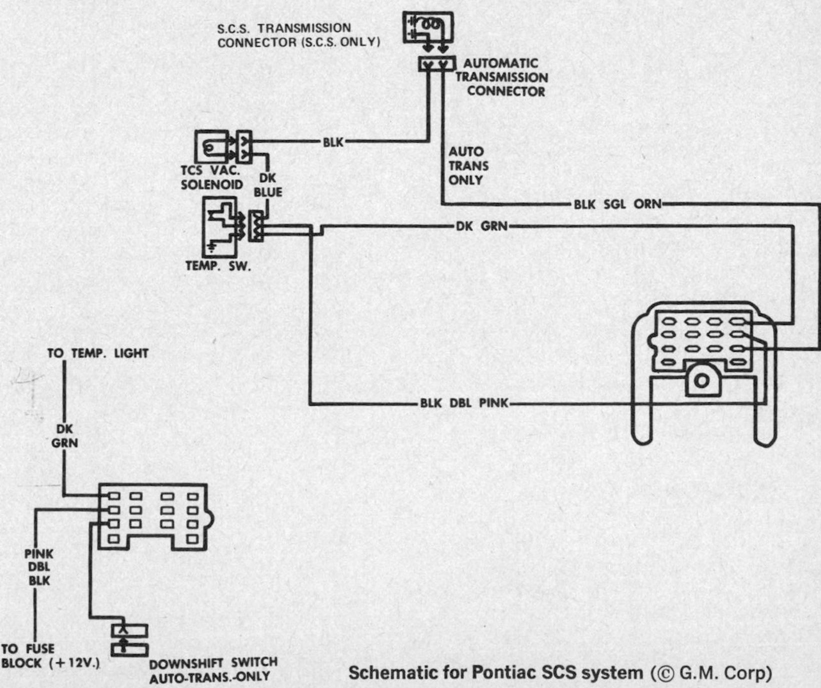

Schematic for Pontiac SCS system (© G.M. Corp)

System Test

This test should be performed with the air temperature above 65°F and the coolant temperature above 160°F (American Motors V8) or with the engine temperature between 95° and 230°F (Pontiac).

1. Raise the rear wheels off the ground and support the car so it cannot roll forward.
2. Disconnect the vacuum hose which runs between the distributor vacuum unit or the coolant temperature vacuum override valve (1972–73 American Motors) and the vacuum advance solenoid at the distributor or valve end. Connect a vacuum gauge to the hose.
3. Start the engine and shift into Drive. Accelerate to until the speedometer registers the speed specified in the chart at the end of this section.
4. Until the specified speed is reached, the vacuum reading should be zero. Once this speed is reached, vacuum should be present.
5. If no vacuum is registered at or above the specified speed, check the vacuum lines and connections first. Examine the carburetor port to be sure that it is not clogged.

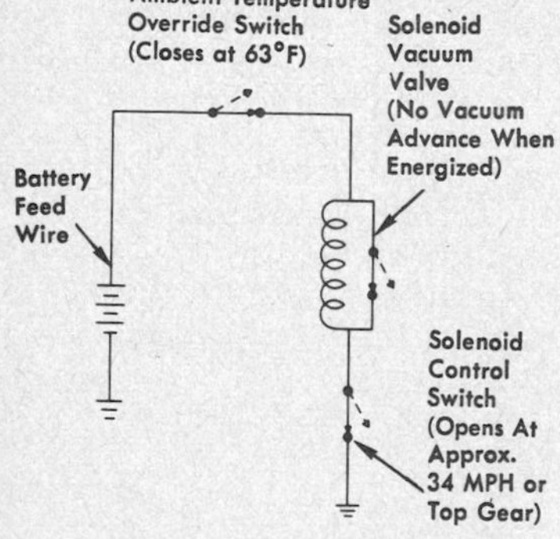

Schematic for the American Motors SCS (or TCS) system (© American Motors Corp)

NOTE: Remember to check the coolant temperature vacuum override valve, if so equipped, as its failure could cause a loss of vacuum. Test procedures for it are given earlier in this section.

6. If there is nothing wrong with the vacuum supply, disconnect the gauge, reconnect the hose and proceed with the next test.

Transmission Switch Tests

1. Leave the rear wheels of the car off the ground as in the system test above.
2. Disconnect the transmission switch leads. Connect a low-amperage test lamp in series with the switch and the positive side of the battery.

American Motors vacuum advance solenoid location
(© American Motors Corp)

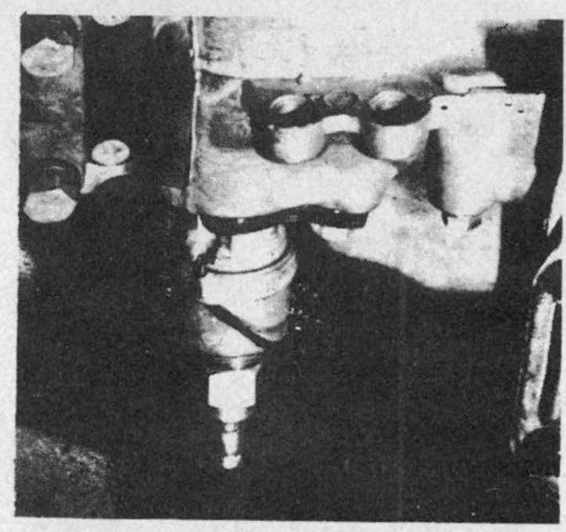

Transmission switch location on American Motors cars
(© American Motors Corp)

3. Accelerate to the specified speed (see chart below) and watch the test lamp. It should remain on until the specified speed is reached. If the lamp fails to go out or if it does not light at all, the switch is defective and must be replaced.
4. If the switch is working properly, reconnect it and go on with the next test.

Vacuum Advance Solenoid Test

1. Disconnect the vacuum advance solenoid leads. Connect a vacuum gauge to the solenoid hose as in the system test.
2. Place the transmission in neutral and start the engine. Increase engine speed. The gauge should indicate the presence of a vacuum.
3. Connect the hot lead to a 12 V power source. Ground the other lead. Increase the engine speed again. The solenoid should energize, resulting in a vacuum reading of zero.
4. Replace the vacuum advance solenoid if it is faulty. If it is not, reconnect the wiring and go on with the next appropriate test.

Ambient Temperature Override Switch—American Motors

1. Disconnect the ambient temperature switch leads.
2. Replace the switch in the circuit with a jumper wire.
3. Repeat the system test. If the vacuum gauge now reads zero or below the specified speed, i.e., the solenoid energizes, the temperature switch is defective.

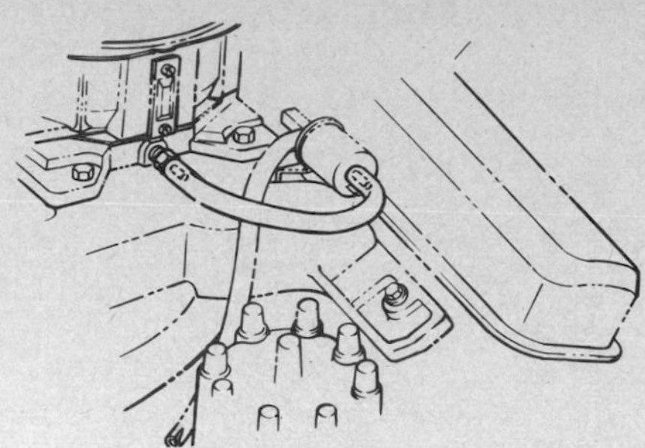

Pontiac vacuum solenoid location
(© G.M. Corp)

4. If the switch proves not to be defective when tested in step 3, reconnect it after removing the jumper lead.
5. Cool the switch, using either ice, cold water, or an aerosol spray circuit tester, to below 63°F. Repeat the system test. If there is no vacuum below the specified speed, the switch is stuck closed and must be replaced.

Engine Temperature Switch—Pontiac

If vacuum advance is present when it should not be, i.e., below the speed specified in the chart, the temperature switch is defective if the other SCS System components are functioning properly and the engine temperature is 95–230°F. Replace it and repeat the system test.

If, on the other hand, vacuum is not being supplied when it should be, with the engine temperature below 95°F or above 230°F, and the other components are functioning properly, the fault again lies in the temperature switch. Replace it and repeat the system test with the engine below 95°F (cold). Vacuum advance should be present at all speeds.

Cadillac

The Cadillac speed-controlled spark system used on *rear*-wheel-drive models (all models except Eldorado) may be tested in a similar manner to the American Motors and Pontiac systems above.

NOTE: Since Cadillac does not use this component, the temperature switch tests are unnecessary.

Cadillac recommends a road test procedure because the front wheels of the Eldorado should not be raised off the ground for test purposes. The procedure outlined below may be used for rear-wheel-drive Cadillac models, as well.

Caution Never test the SCS system used on the Eldorado with its front (drive) wheels off the ground. Working near the front wheels while they are rotating could result in personal injury or vehicle damage.

1. Unfasten the double connector at the vacuum advance solenoid. Install a low-amperage test lamp,

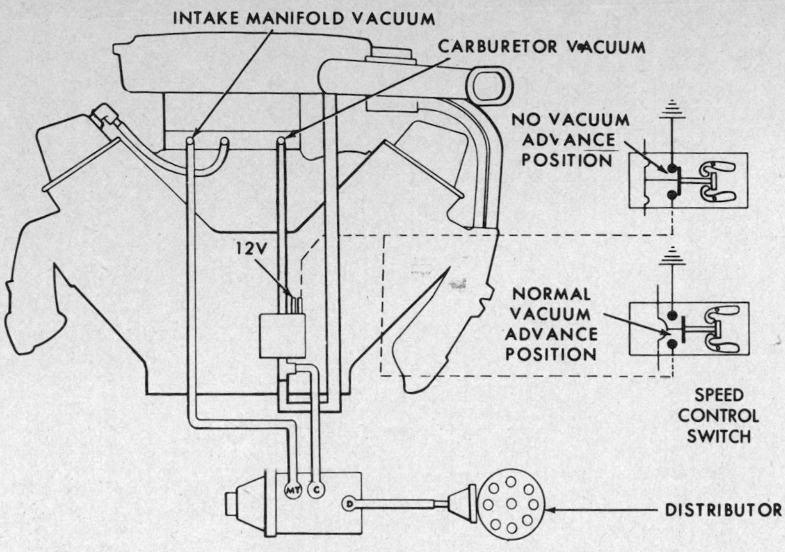

Cadillac SCS system (© G.M. Corp)

with long leads, between the wires on the connector.

2. Tape the test lamp to the car so that it is visible to the driver (hood, fender, cowl, etc.,) and close the hood.
3. Road-test the car while watching the test lamp (and traffic). Once 33 mph (± 2 mph) is reached, the test lamp should go out. Slow down; when 25 mph is reached, the lamp should come back on again.
4. If the test lamp fails to operate as indicated, jump the black wire to ground with the ignition turned on. If the lamp comes on now, replace the speed sensor switch and repeat step three. If the lamp does not come on, remove the jumper and proceed with the next step.
5. Install a jumper between one of the solenoid terminals and ground. Momentarily connect the other solenoid terminal to the positive (+) side of the battery.
6. The solenoid should energize when this is done, i.e., a "click" should be heard. If the solenoid fails to operate it is defective.

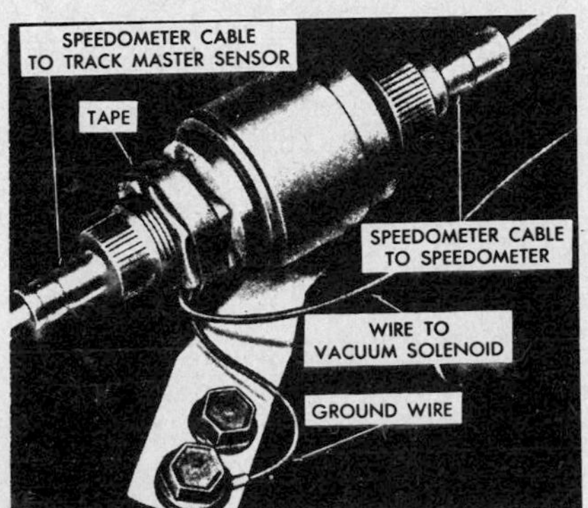

Speed control switch when used with Track-Master (except Eldorado) (© G.M. Corp)

SCS VACUUM ADVANCE

Make	*Year*	*No vacuum advance below*	*With engine temperature (deg F)*
American Motors	1971	30 mph	All temperatures①
	1972–73	34 mph	above 160①②
Cadillac	1972	33±2 mph	All temperatures
Pontiac	1972	38 mph	Between 95–230

①—Air temperature above 63°F
②—V8 only

7. If both the solenoid and transmission switch are functioning properly, reconnect the leads to the solenoid and check for faulty wiring.

1973 Ford Temperature Activated Vacuum System (TAV)

System Test

1. Disconnect the vacuum line from the primary port of the distributor. Connect a vacuum gauge to the line by means of a T-fitting. Connect the other end of the T-fitting to the distributor.
2. Be sure that the air temperature is above 65°F. Hot water may be used to warm the temperature switch, which is located in the front door pillar.
3. Place the transmission in Park or Neutral. Start the engine.
4. Run the engine at idle; the vacuum gauge should read zero.
5. Increase the engine speed to 1,500 rpm or slightly more. The gauge should read 5 in. Hg or better.
6. If there is no vacuum reading, check for leaking, plugged, or pinched lines and fittings.
7. Detach the EGR port hose and plug up the carburetor line. The vacuum gauge should read zero.
8. If it does not, check the lines and then proceed with the three-way vacuum valve test, below. If it does, go on to Step 9.
9. Next, detach one of the power leads from the three-way vacuum valve.
10. Speed the engine up to 1,500 rpm or more. The vacuum gauge should now read 6 in. Hg or better.
11. If the system fails to function as outlined, check the ambient temperature switch, the EGR valve, or the three-way vacuum valve.
12. If everything is functioning

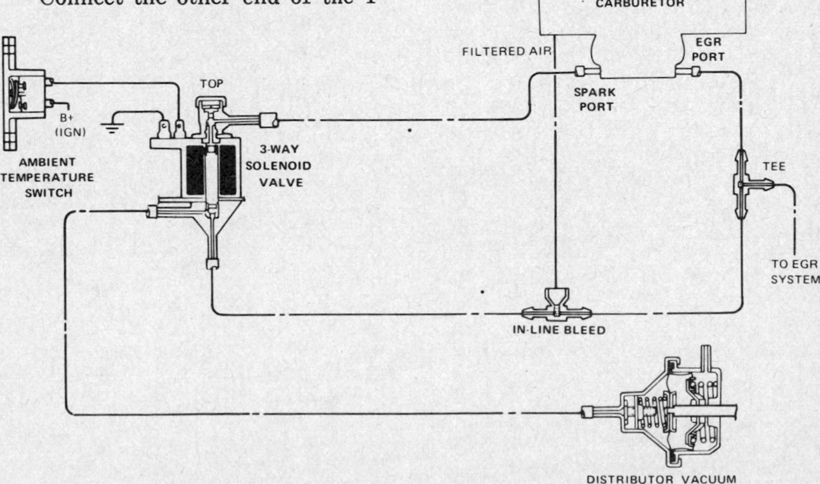

The temperature activated vacuum system used on some 1973 Fords (© Ford Motor Co)

properly, reconnect the leads and vacuum lines after disconnecting the vacuum gauge.

Temperature Switch Test

Test the door-mounted ambient temperature switch, as outlined under "Ford Electronic Spark Control—1972–73," above. The switch is in either the left or right front door pillar.

Three-way Vacuum Valve Test

1. Remove the three-way vacuum valve from the car.
2. Connect a vacuum gauge to the horizontal port at the *bottom* of the valve.
3. Apply a vacuum source to the horizontal port at the *top* of the valve.
4. Ground one of the valve terminals while connecting the other terminal to a 12V power supply. The vacuum gauge should read zero.
5. With the valve energized, connect the vacuum source to the bottom *vertical* port. The vacuum gauge should now indicate an amount of vacuum equal to the output of the vacuum source.
6. Disconnect the leads from the valve. The vacuum gauge reading should return to zero.
7. If the valve fails to function as outlined, replace it. If it is functioning correctly, check the EGR valve operation as detailed in the appropriate section below.

1973½-75 Ford Cold Temperature Activated Vacuum System (CTAV)

The cold temperature activated vacuum (CTAV) system is similar to the temperature activated system used on 1973 vehicles made before 15 March (see the previous section). On CTAV equipped vehicles, the temperature sensor has been moved from the door pillar to the air cleaner housing, and a latching relay has been added. The latching relay prevents variations in ambient temperature from affecting the system; once the CTAV system has been activated it cannot recycle until the ignition system has been shut off.

The CTAV system is tested in the same way as the TAV system. (except for the air cleaner mounted temperature switch). Follow the test procedure outlined in the TAV section. If all of the CTAV system components are working properly, then the latching relay must be defective; replace it and repeat the "System Test".

Air Cleaner-Mounted Temperature Switch—Normally Closed

The normally closed temperature switch may be identified by its rectangular connector.

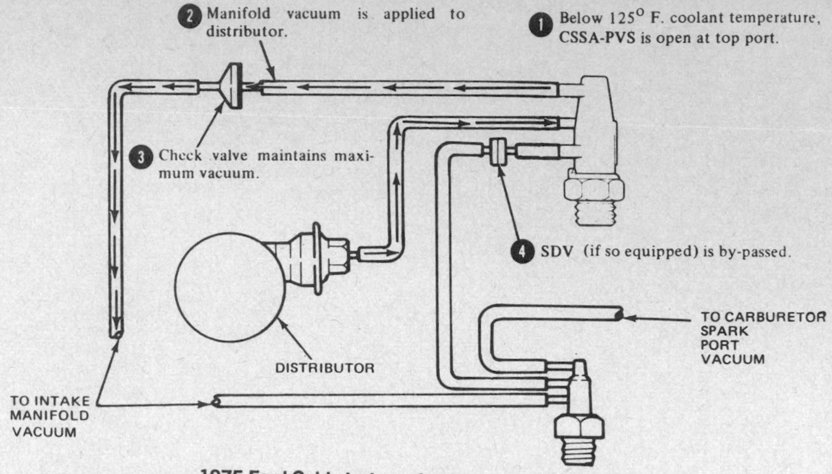

1975 Ford Cold start spark advance system (CSSA)
(© Ford Motor Co.)

1. Disconnect the temperature switch connector and remove the switch from the air cleaner.
2. Warm the switch in the palm of your hand.
3. Conect a self-powered test light between the terminals of the switch connector. The test light should glow.
4. Cool the switch with ice or aerosol circuit testing spray. The light should go off.
5. If the switch doesn't work as outlined, replace it.

Air Cleaner-Mounted Temperature Switch—Normally Opened

The normally opened temperature switch may be identified by its round connector.

1. Perform steps 1 and 2 of the test for the normally closed switch.
2. Connect a self-powered test light between the terminals on the switch connector. The test light should stay off.
3. Cool the switch with ice or aerosol circuit testing spray. The test light should come on.
4. If the switch doesn't work as outlined, replace it.

1975 Ford Cold Start Spark Advance (CSSA) System

System Test

1. Allow the engine to reach normal operating temperature. Stop the engine.
2. If the engine is equipped with a spark delay valve (SDV), remove it and test it separately. Use a fiitting to connect the two halves of the vacuum hose together where the SDV was mounted.
3. Using a T-fitting, connect a vacuum guage to the distributor vacuum unit.
4. Block the wheels, set the parking brake, place the transmission in Neutral (N), and start the engine. Open the throttle halfway and then allow it to close.
5. The vacuum guage should register a rise and then a fall in vacuum. If it doesn't, check for plugged vacuum fittings, and/or loose or misrouted hoses. If everything else checks out OK, then test the two coolant temperature operated vacuum valves (PVS) as outlined elsewhere in this section.

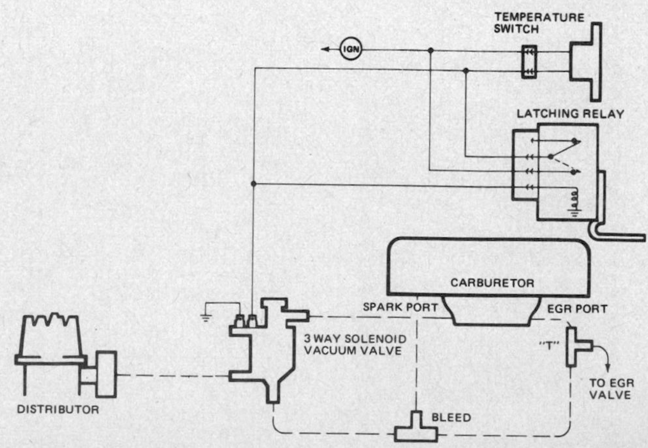

1973½-75 Ford cold temperature activated vacuum (CATV) system
(© Ford Motor Co)

6. Remove the T-fitting and vacuum gauge. Install the SDV, if so equipped.

Carburetor Controls

Antidieseling Solenoid Tests

NOTE: Antidieseling solenoids are also referred to as, "throttle stop" or "idle stop" solenoids.

Caution Chrysler Corp. cars that are equipped with catalytic converters have an additional solenoid; this is NOT an antidieseling solenoid, and no attempt to adjust the idle speed with it should be made. See "Catalytic Converters" for its operation.

1. Turn the ignition key on and open the throttle. The solenoid plunger should extend (solenoid energize).
2. Turn the ignition off. The plunger should retract, allowing the throttle to close.

NOTE: With the antidieseling solenoid de-energized, the carburetor idle speed adjusting screw must make contact with the throttle shaft to prevent the throttle plates from jamming in the throttle bore when the engine is turned off.

3. If the solenoid is functioning properly and the engine is still dieseling, check for one of the following:
   a. High idle or engine shut off speed;
   b. Engine timing not set to specification;
   c. Binding throttle linkage;
   d. Too low an octane fuel being used.

Correct any of these problems, as necessary.

4. If the solenoid fails to function as outlined in steps 1–2, disconnect the solenoid leads; the solenoid should de-enegerize. If it does not, it is jammed and must be replaced.
5. Connect the solenoid to a 12 V power source and to ground. Open the throttle so that the plunger can extend. If it does not, the solenoid is defective.
6. If the solenoid is functioning correctly and no other source of trouble can be found, the fault probably lies in the wiring between the solenoid and the ignition switch or in the ignition switch itself. Remember to reconnect the solenoid when finished testing.

NOTE: On some 1970–71 Ford models, dieseling may occur when the engine is turned off because of feedback through the alternator warning light circuit. A diode kit is available from Ford to cure this problem. A failure of this diode may also lead to a similar problem.

Combined antidieseling solenoid/dashpot used on some 1975 Ford products

Solenoid/Dashpot

Some 1975 Ford products use a combination antidieseling solenoid and dashpot. The antidieseling solenoid operation is tested in the same manner as any other antidieseling solenoid. See the previous section for the correct testing procedure.

A/C Operated Antidieseling Device Tests

1. Run the engine and turn off all of the air conditioning controls.
2. Turn the engine off. The air conditioner compressor clutch should engage for several sec-

A typical anti-dieseling solenoid installation (© G.M. Corp)

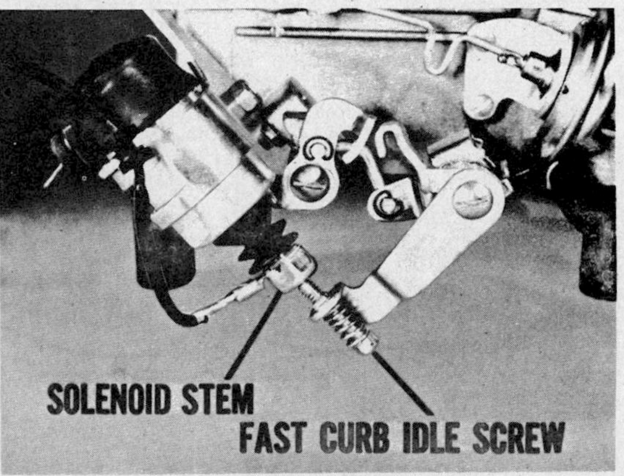

When the anti-dieseling solenoid is energized, its plunger should make contact with the (fast) curb idle screw (© Chrysler Corp)

onds to slow the engine down.

3. If the compressor clutch engagement does not occur, check the wiring for a loose connection, at either the compressor or the antidieseling relay.
4. Check to see that the relay is properly grounded to its mounting. Examine the air conditioner fuse(s) to see that they are not blown.
5. Start the engine and turn on the air conditioner. The clutch should engage. If it does not, the problem lies in the air conditioner circuit.
6. If the car is equipped with a blocking relay, remove it for bench-testing. Connect a 12 V test lamp between the two outboard connectors. Ground the mounting bracket. Connect a 12 V power source to the center terminal. The lamp should come on. If it does not, the blocking relay is defective and must be replaced.
7. If all of the other components are functioning properly, the antidieseling relay is defective and requires replacement.

CEC Solenoid Operation

The CEC solenoid is used on some GM models. It has two functions; one is to regulate distributor vacuum and the other is operate as a throttle positioner. When the solenoid is energized, the throttle blade is held off its seat by a plunger located at one end of the CEC solenoid. This provides higher engine rpm during deceleration, thus reducing exhaust emissions.

Because of its dual function, failure of this valve can lead to higher emission levels or an idle which is considerably faster than normal. If the CEC solenoid is suspected of not working properly, follow the complete set of test procedures for it in "Distributor Controls," above.

NOTE: On 1971 Buicks, the CEC solenoid is divided into two separate parts: a regular TCS solenoid and a solenoid to hold the throttle open during high gear deceleration. Testing and service should be carried out in the same manner as they would be for a regular CEC valve.

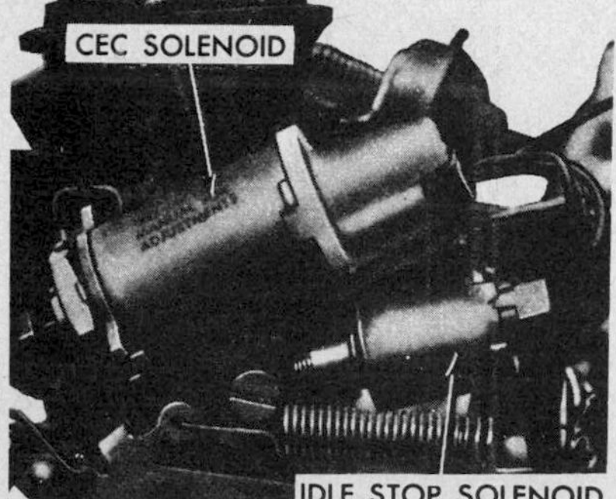

A typical CEC solenoid mounting (© G.M .Corp)

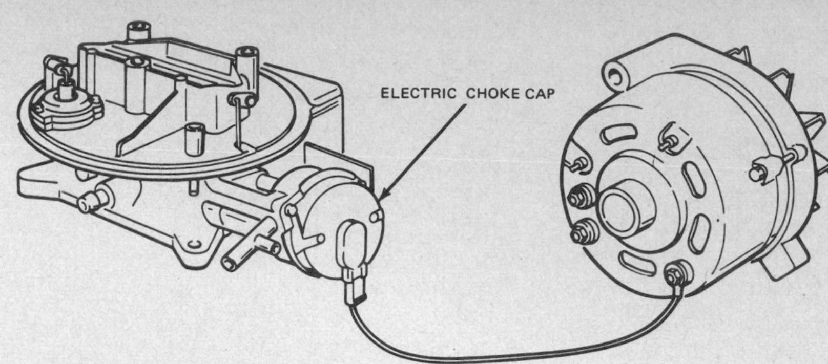

Ford and AMC electrically assisted choke hook-up (© Ford Motor Co)

Electrically Assisted Choke

Ford and AMC

1. Detach the electrical lead from the choke cap.
2. Use a jumper lead to connect the terminal on the choke cap and the wire terminal, so that the electrical circuit is still completed.
3. Start the engine.
4. Hook up a test light between the connector on the choke lead and ground.
5. The test light should glow. If it does not, current is not being supplied to the electrically assisted choke.
6. Connect the test light between the terminal on the alternator and the terminal on the choke cap. If the light now glows, replace the lead, since it is not passing current to the choke assist.

Caution Do not ground the terminal on the alternator while performing Step 6.

7. If the light still does not glow, the fault lies somewhere in the electrical system. Check the system out.

NOTE: Steps 8 through 12 do not apply to 1975 models equipped with 2300 four-cylinder engines.

If the electrically assisted choke receives power but still does not appear to be functioning properly, reconnect the choke lead and proceed with the rest of the test.

8. Tape the bulb end of the thermometer to the metallic portion of the choke housing.
9. If the electrically assisted choke operates below 55°F, it is defective and must be replaced.
10. Allow the engine to warm up to between 80 and 110°F; at these temperatures the choke should operate for about 1½ minutes.
11. If it does not operate for this length of time, check the bi-metallic spring to see if it is connected to the tang on the choke lever.
12. If the spring is connected and the choke is not operating properly, replace the cap assembly.

Chrysler Corp.

Caution Do not immerse the choke heating element in any type of liquid, especially solvent, for any reason.

NOTE: A short circuit in the choke wiring or in the heater will show up as a short in the ignition system.

1. Disconnect the electrical leads from the choke control switch

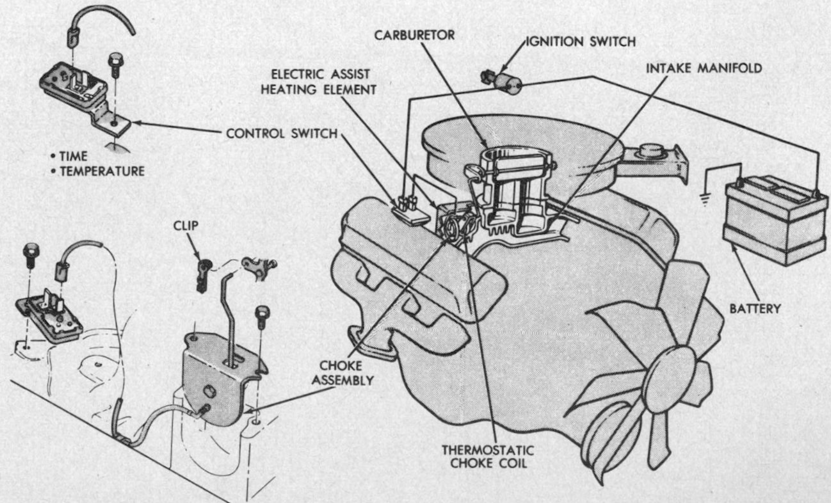

Chrysler electrically assisted choke system components (© Chrysler Corp)

before starting the engine.

2. Connect a test light between the smaller of the two terminals on the choke control switch and a ground.
3. Start the engine and run it until it reaches normal operating temperature.
4. Apply power from a 12V source to the terminal marked "BAT" on the choke control switch.
5. The test light should light for at least a few seconds or for as long as five minutes. If the light does not come on at all, glows dimly, or if it stays on longer than five minutes, replace the switch.
6. Disconnect the test light and reconnect the electrical leads to the choke switch, if it is functioning properly.
7. Detach the lead (B+) from the choke switch which runs to the choke heating element.
8. Connect the lead from an ohmmeter to the crimped section at the choke end of the wire, which was removed in Step 7.

Caution Do not connect the ohmmeter to the metallic heater housing.

9. Ground the other ohmmeter test lead to the engine manifold.
10. The meter should indicate a resistance of 4–6 ohms (1973) or 4–12 ohms (1974-76).
11. If the reading is not within specifications, or if it indicates an opened (zero resistance) or a shorted (infinite resistance) heater coil, replace the heater assembly.

NOTE: The electrically assisted choke does not change any carburetor service procedures. If any parts of the electrically assisted choke are defective, they must be replaced. Adjustment is not possible.

1975 Cadillac

1. At an engine compartment temperature of approximately 70° F (cold engine) the choke should open wide in approximately 1-½ minutes. The easiest way to make this test is to move the air cleaner to one side, open the throttle to allow the choke to close, and run a hot wire from the positive battery post to the choke terminal. Then time how long it takes the choke to open.
2. Off the car, the choke coil can be tested by connecting a hot wire to the coil terminal, and a ground wire to the choke cover grounding plate. Starting at a room temperature of 60–70°F the choke coil should rotate 45 degrees within 54–90 seconds after the connection is made. If not, the choke is defective, and the entire choke cover must be replaced.
3. If the choke coil is in good condition, but will not operate on the engine, it could be caused by:
   a. Broken or disconnected tan wire between oil pressure switch and choke coil.
   b. Poor ground between choke cover grounding plate and housing.
   c. Broken or disconnected wire in circuit from battery to oil pressure switch.
   d. Burned out "Backup-Trans" fuse in fuse block.
   e. Defective oil pressure switch.
   f. No oil pressure to switch. This could be caused by blocked oil passageways or sludged oil.
4. Repairs are limited to replacement.

1975 GM Secondary Choke Break Systems

System Test—2300-4

1. Start with a cold engine and allow it to idle.
2. The secondary vacuum break (1-bbl) or pull-off solenoid (2-bbl) should not operate.
3. Pull the connector off the temperature switch on the right side of the engine. The secondary vacuum break or solenoid should open the choke. If not, proceed with component checks.

NOTE: If the engine stalls in step 3 connect the temperature switch and depress the gas pedal before restarting the engine.

4. On a warm engine the secondary break or pull-off solenoid should be holding the choke in a nearly opened position when the engine is running.
5. Remove the connector on the temperature switch and ground the green wire with white stripe. The solenoid or vacuum break should de-engergize and you should be able to open the throttle and move the choke to the fully closed position.
6. Stop the engine and close the choke.
7. Start the engine. The choke should immediately be pulled open. If not, proceed with the component tests.

System Adjustments—2300-4

The amount of choke opening by the secondary vacuum break or pull-off solenoid is adjusted by bending its linkage. Choke plate-to-air horn wall clearances should be 0.450 in.

None of the other components are adjustable. If they are defective, they must be replaced.

Temperature Switch Test—2300-4

The switch is threaded into the water jacket on the right side of the engine. The green wire with the white stripe is the lead for the choke.

1. Connect a self-powered test light to the choke terminal and ground.
2. At normal operating temperature the light should stay off.
3. On a cold engine (below 93°F—automatic, or 120°F—manual) the light should come on.
4. If not, the switch is defective. Replace it.

Relay Test—2300-4 (2-bbl)

1. With the relay bracket pointing toward you and the terminals pointing up, connect the lower left terminal to a 12-volt power source.
2. Ground the relay bracket.
3. Connect a 12 volt non-powered test light between the upper left terminal and the relay bracket.
4. The test light should light. If not, the relay is defective.
5. Connect a jumper wire between the upper right terminal and the relay bracket. The light should go off. If not, the relay is defective.

Vacuum Solenoid Test—2300-4 (1-bbl)

1. Connect a vacuum gauge to the carburetor side of the solenoid.
2. Conect engine vacuum or an auxiliary source of vacuum to the other side.
3. Apply vacuum. The solenoid should hold the vacuum and not leak down. The gauge should register no vacuum.
4. Apply 12 volts to one solenoid terminal; ground the other. The solenoid should open and the gauge should indicate vacuum.
5. If the solenoid doesn't operate as outlined, replace it.

Testing Choke Pull-Off Solenoid—2300-4 (2-bbl)

1. Connect a 12-volt power source to the solenoid lead. Ground the body of the solenoid.
2. When the connection is completed, the solenoid stem should retract into the body. You should be unable to pull it out with your fingers.
3. If the stem is fully extended, it might be necessary to give it a push to make it retract.
4. Break the connections. You should be able to pull the solenoid out with your fingers.

NOTE: Don't expect the stem to jump out on its own. It is designed so that the choke linkage must pull it out.

5. If the solenoid dosen't operate as outlined, replace it.

System Test—GM 250-6 And Chevrolet V8 (4-bbl)

If the engine temperature is above 70°F, a timer starts as soon as the ignition switch is turned on. If you

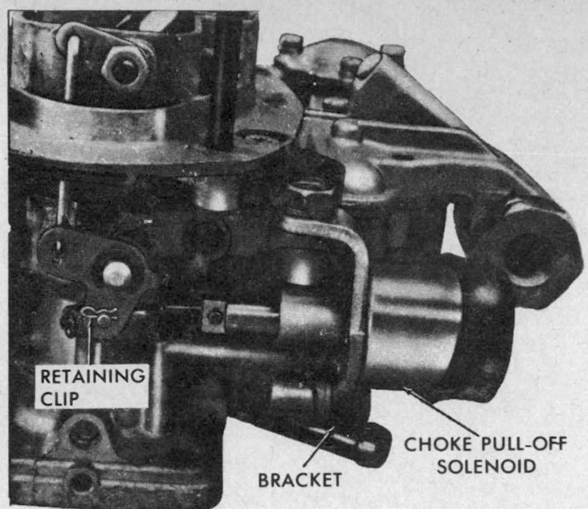

Choke pull-off solenoid—GM 2300 OHC 4-cylinder engine with 2-bbl carburetor
(© Pontiac Div., GM Corp.)

turn the ignition on but do not start the engine within 35 seconds, you will be attempting to start the engine with a wide-opened choke. To start the engine now, it will be necessary to turn the ignition off and start the engine immediately.

1. With the engine warmed-up and running, shut the ignition off.
2. Start the engine. It should take about 35 seconds for the secondary vacuum break to operate. If it doesn't the system is defective.
3. To simulate a cold engine, ground the temperature switch lead. Disconnect the lead from the temperature switch; there should be two terminals. Ground each terminal individually until you find the one that operates the red, "HOT" warning light on the dash. The *other* terminal is the timer terminal.
4. Ground the timer terminal with a jumper lead. Start the engine and watch the secondary vacuum break,, for at least one miunte. The break should not operate. If it does, proceed with the component tests.
5. Leave the engine running and disconect the ground wire. About 35 seconds later the vacuum break should operate. If, not, proceed with the component tests.
6. The simulated cold test will not check temperature switch operation. The temperature switch will either have to be checked on a cold engine or by removing it, as outlined below.

Temperature Switch Test—GM 250-6 and Chevrolet V8 (4-bbl)

1. Turn the ignition switch on.
2. Remove the connector from the temperature switch and ground each terminal. One terminal will cause the red "HOT" warning light to come on; the *other* terminal works the timer.
3. With the engine temperature below 70°F, connect a self-powered test light between the temperature switch timer terminal and ground. The light should come on.
7. With the engine temperature above 70°F, the light should go off.

NOTE: If necessary, remove the temperature switch to cool it. Relieve cooling system pressure first.

8. Replace the temperature switch if it doesn't work as outlined.

Vacuum Solenoid Test—GM 250-6 and Chevrolet V8 (4-bbl)

The solenoid for the secondary choke break system is the one next to the choke vacuum diaphragm. The one on the heat valve bracket is for the EFE system.

1. Remove the connector from the choke vacuum solenoid.
2. Connect one of the solenoid terminals to a 12 volt power source and ground the other terminal.
3. If the solenoid doesn't "click" on (energize) when the connection is made in step 2, the solenoid is defective. Replace it.
4. Leave the solenoid connected as in step 2. Disconnect the hose from the choke secondary vacuum break and connect a vacuum gauge to it.
5. With the engine running and the solenoid energized, the gauge should read zero.
6. Disconnect the jumper wires and the gauge should show full manifold vacuum.
7. Replace the solenoid if it is defective.

Timer Test—GM 250-6 and Chevrolet V8 (4-bbl)

If the secondary choke break vacuum solenoid and temperature switch are OK, and the system is not working, the problem is probably in the timer. Replace it and perform the system test again.

Adjusting the Secondary Choke Vacuum Diaphragm—GM 250-6 and Chevrolet V8 (4-bbl)

1. Disconnect the vacuum hose from the secondary choke break vacuum diaphragm.
2. Connect a hand-operated vacuum pump with a gauge to the diaphragm.
3. Cover the diaphragm bleed hole with your finger. Apply vacuum to the diaphragm. It should hold vacuum and not leak down. If it leaks it is defective.
4. Note the position of the choke cover and then remove it. Put the follower lever on the highest step of the fast idle cam.
5, Tape the bleed hole in the diaphragm. Use a hand pump to apply vacuum to the diaphragm. Apply enough vacuum to pull the diaphragm in all the way. It may take a few seconds for the diaphragm to make a full stroke.
6. Push the lever on the inside of the choke coil housing toward the closed position (up).
7. The choke rod should be in the bottom of the slot in the choke lever, and the choke plate wide-open.
8. If not, bend the rod at the first bend (next to the vacuum break diaphragm), until the choke plate is wide-open.
9. Remove the tape, install the hose and put the choke cover back in its original position.

The secondary choke vacuum break is the one on the left

System Test—400-V8 Olds and All Pontiac V8

1. Remove the air cleaner from the carburetor and move it to one side, so that you can watch the choke. Don't disconnect any of the air cleaner vacuum hoses.

NOTE: If necessary, remove the secondary choke break thermal vacuum valve from the air cleaner, but leave its hoses connected.

2. Start the engine and watch the choke. The main vacuum break (front) should partially open the choke.
3. If the air temperature is above 62°F the secondary (rear) vacuum break should (slowly) open the choke a bit further.
4. To check cold operation, remove the thermal vacuum from the air cleaner and drop it in an ice bath. Leave the vacuum hoses connected.
5. With the engine idling, you should see the vacuum break link move out, as the valve cools off.
6. If the system doesn't work as outlined, proceed with the component tests.

Testing the Vacuum Break—400-V8 400-V8 Olds and All Pontiac V8

1. Disconnect the vacuum hose from the secondary break vacuum unit. Connect the unit directly to manifold vacuum.
2. It should take less than 20 seconds for the vacuum break link to make a full stroke.
3. If is takes longer than 20 seconds, the vacuum break is defective and must be replaced.

Thermal Vacuum Valve Test—400-V8 Olds and All Pontiac V8

1. Connect a hand-operated vacuum pump with a gauge to the thermostatic vacuum valve (TVV) nipple marked "S". Connect another vacuum gauge to the nipple marked "E".
2. Warm the valve in your hand to above 62°F.
3. Apply vacuum to the TVV. Both gauges should read within 1 in. Hg of each other.
4. Cool the valve in an ice bath. Apply vacuum to it. Below 62° F, the vacuum gauge on the "E" nipple should read zero.
5. If the valve doesn't work as outlined, replace it.

1975 Chrysler Coolant Control Idle Enrichment (CCIE) System

California System Test

NOTE: The engine coolant temperature must be below 80°F for this test.

Hose with air bleed runs to carburetor idle enricher as part of 1975 Chrysler CCIE system

1. Disconnect the vacuum line, which runs from the two-nozzle coolant temperature operated vacuum valve to the CCIE valve on the carburetor, at the air bleed (on the vacuum valve side).
2. Connect a vacuum gauge to this line and start the engine.
3. The vacuum gauge should register manifold vacuum. If it does not, check the lines and fittings to see if they are pinched or plugged.
4. If everything is in good condition, replace the coolant temperature operated vacuum valve.
5. If the valve is OK, then run the engine until the coolant temperature goes above 90°F. Above this temperature, the vacuum gauge should read zero; if it does not, replace the vacuum valve.
6. Check the air bleed and the vacuum line which runs from it to the carburetor. Replace either if it is plugged.
7. Remove the vacuum gauge and connect the vacuum lines.

Federal (except California) System Test

NOTE: The engine coolant temperature must be below 150°F for this test.

1. Disconnect the vacuum line which runs from the two-nozzle coolant temperature operated vacuum valve to the CCIE valve on the carburetor, at the air bleed (on the vacuum valve side).
2. Connect a vacuum gauge to the disconnected line.
3. Start the engine, the gauge should register manifold vacuum for about 35 seconds, and then drop to zero.
4. If there is no vacuum, stop the engine. Check the vacuum lines and fittings. If these are in good shape, check the EGR delay timer and solenoid as detailed in the appropriate section.
5. If the delay timer, solenoid, fittings, and lines check out OK, then replace the two-nozzle coolant temperature operated vacuum valve.
6. If there was vacuum present long after 35 seconds in Step 3, then check the EGR delay timer and solenoid.
7. Start the engine and allow the coolant to warm-up to above 150°F, then stop the engine.
8. Start the engine again; there should be no vacuum reading on the gauge. If there is, replace the coolant temperature operated vacuum valve.
9. Check the air bleed and the vacuum line from it to the carburetor. Replace either if it is plugged.
10. Remove the vacuum gauge and connect the vacuum lines.

Ford Fuel Deceleration Valve—1971-76

Diaphragm Test

With the engine running, cover the small hole in the base of the valve. If the engine idle smoothes out or the speed decreases, the diaphragm is leaking and must be replaced.

Poppet Valve Test

If the engine idles excessively high, and it is not caused by improper carburetor adjustment, throttle linkage bind, or throttle plate bind, the poppet valve in the decel valve may be defective. With the engine running, disconnect the air-fuel line from the carburetor to the decel valve at the decel valve. Seal the opening where the line was disconnected. If the engine speed decreases noticeably, the poppet valve is hanging open and must be replaced.

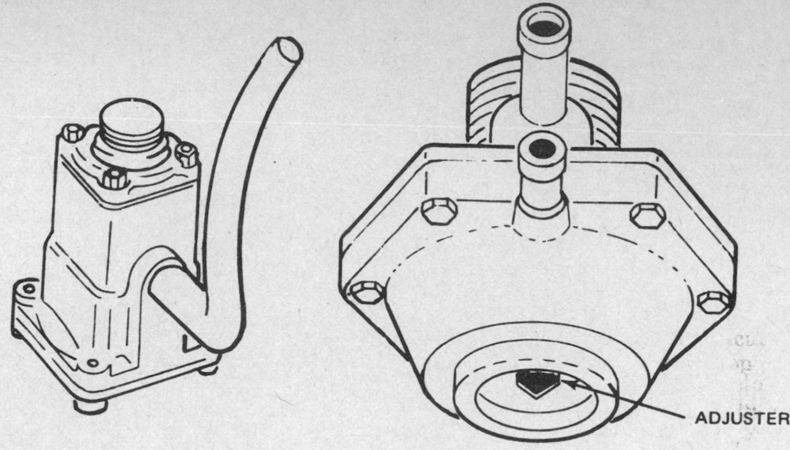

THIS VALVE DISCONTINUED FOR 1975

THIS TYPE USED IN 1975 IS NOW ADJUSTABLE.

The two sypes of Ford fuel decel valves
(© Ford Motor Co.)

Adjustment—1971-73

1. Install a vacuum gauge in the hose between the carburetor and the decel valve, using a T-fitting.
2. Attach a tachometer and run the engine at 3000 rpm.
3. Release the throttle and observe the time required for the vacuum gauge to drop to 0. Correct decel valve timing is 3-5 seconds on 1600 cc engines and 1½-5 seconds on 2000 cc engines.
4. The time delay can be adjusted by turning the nylon adjuster at the top of the decel valve body; clockwise to reduce the time, counterclockwise to increase.

   To gain access to the adjuster, unscrew the covering cap. Do not use a screwdriver to adjust the decel valve. It is recommended that a special tool be made from a ⅜ in. allen wrench. If the valve cannot be adjusted within specifications, it must be replaced as an assembly.

1974 Adjustment

1. Operate the engine to make sure that it is at normal operating temperature when performing the tests.
2. Attach a tachometer to the engine.
3. Disconnect the ruber hose between the decel valve and the carburetor at the decel valve and plug the nipple on the valve.
4. Make sure that the ignition timing, CO or idle mixture and idle speed are set to the correct specifications.
5. Increase the engine speed to 3000 rpm and hold for about 5 seconds, then release the throttle to make sure that the engine returns to normal idle speed.
6. Unplug the decel valve and install a vacuum gauge with a T-fitting into the hose between the decel valve and the carburetor.
7. On the 2300 cc engines, make sure that a 3/16 in. vacuum hose is conected between the small nipple on the valve to a manifold vacuum source.
8. Increase engine speed to 3000 rpm then release the throttle and measure the time required for the vacuum gauge reading to drop to 0. This should take 2-5 seconds.
9. The decel valve on the 2300 cc engine must be replaced if the time delay is not within specifications.
10. On the 2000 cc and 2800 cc engines the decel valve can be adjusted as required to meet the time specifications. Adjust the decel valve in the same manner as for models through 1973.

    If the valve closes too soon, emission levels will be high. If the valve closes too late (stays open too long), engine speed will be excessive.

    Advanced initial timing and/or too rich a mixture can cause the decel valve to remain open too long.

NOTE: The vacuum readings must not exceed 18.5 in. Hg for engines with dual-diaphragm distributors, or 19.5 in. Hg with single diaphragm distributor.

1975 Adjustment

NOTE: On 1975 models with a speed modulated fuel decel system, perform the system test (below) before adjusting the decel valve.

1. Allow the engine to reach normal operating temperature. Connect a tachometer and timing light. Set the timing and idle to specifications.
2. Remove the air cleaner assembly. Inspect the vacuum hoses.
3. Disconnect and plug the carburetor-to-decel valve hose at the carburetor end.
4. Place the transmission in Neutral (N) and apply the parking brake.
5. Increase the engine speed to 3000 rpm and hold for 5 seconds. Release the throttle. The engine should return to normal idle immediately. If not, check for a binding throttle or throttle linkage.
6. Unplug the decel valve-to-carburetor vacuum hose. Using a T-fitting, install a vacuum gauge in it.
7. Increase the engine speed to 300 rpm and hold it for 5 seconds. Release the throttle. It should take 2 to 3.5 seconds for the vacuum to return to zero.
8. If the time in step 7 was incorrect, adjust the decel valve. Rotate the adjuster with a ¼ in. allen key. Clockwise rotation of the adjuster reduces time and counterclockwise rotation increases time. Replace the valve if it can't be adjusted to specifications.
9. Disconnect the tachometer, vacuum gauge and timing light. Reconnect the vacuum hose.

Ford Speed Modulated Fuel Decel System

1975 Test

1. Raise the rear wheels of the vehicle off the ground and support it securely. Block the front wheels if they remain on the ground.
2. Using a T-fitting, install a vacuum gauge in the hose which runs between the fuel decel valve and the solenoid vacuum valve. Position the gauge so that it's visible from the driver's seat.
3. Start the engine and engage First gear or Drive (D). Bring the vehicle's indicated speed up to 11 mph. If the gauge shows vacuum below 11 mph and no vacuum above 11 mph, the system is working correctly. Disconnect the test equipment and lower the vehicle.
4. If there was no vacuum indicated at all in step 3, disconnect the solenoid vacuum valve leads. Connect the solenoid directly to battery voltage and a ground.
5. Run the engine at 1500 rpm with the transmisson in Neutral. If the gauge shows vacuum, replace the solenoid vacuum valve.
6. If there was no vacuum reading in step 5, connect a voltmeter or test light between the normal source of B+ (battery) voltage and the solenoid vacuum valve terminal. Ground the other terminal. Turn the ignition on. Voltage should be indicated. If not,

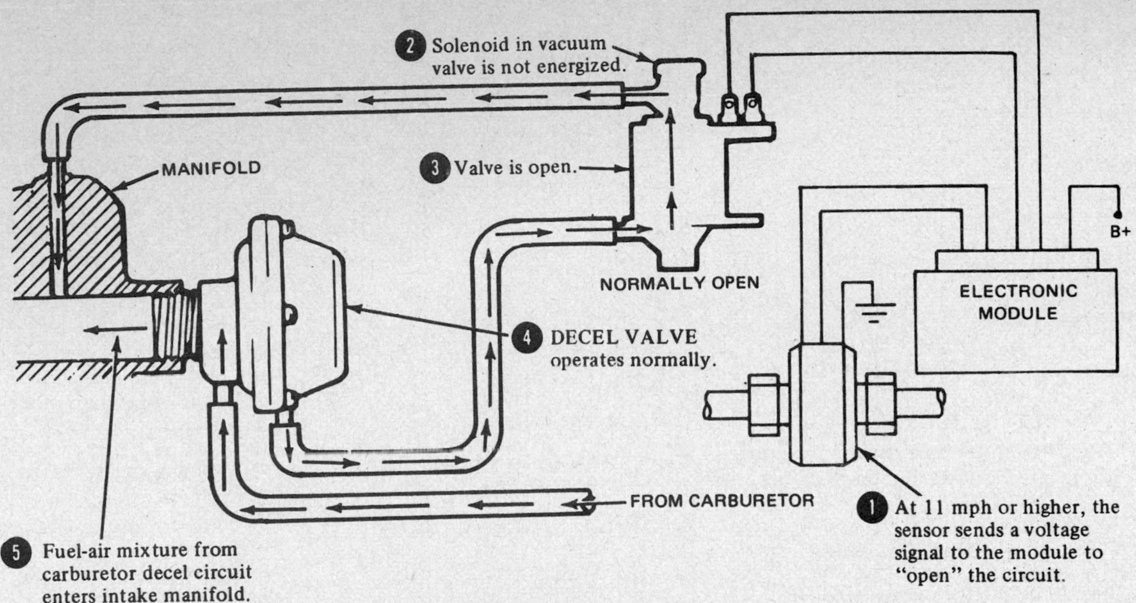

1975 Ford speed modulated fuel decel valve
(© Ford Motor Co.)

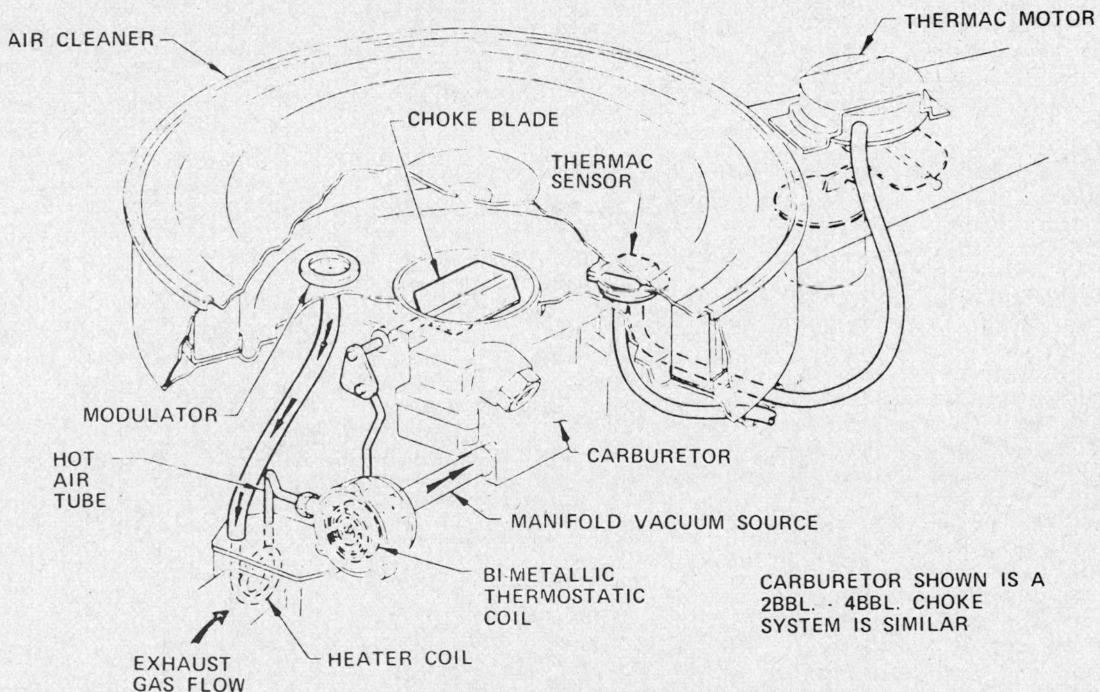

Choke hot air modulator system—1975 GM
(© Oldsmobile Div., GM Corp.)

check for an opened circuit.

7. If voltage was indicated in step 6, check the speed sensor (in the speedometer cable) with an ohmmeter. Replace the speed sensor if it shorted (infinite reading) or open (zero reading). If it is OK, check for a poor ground.
8. If everything else is working correctly, replace the electronic module and test the system again.
9. Remove the test equipment and lower the vehicle.

1975 GM Choke Hot Air Modulator System

Testing—All Buick V8 and V6, Omega, Ventura 350-V8 and Starfire 231-V6

1. Remove the air cleaner top.
2. Tape a thermometer of known accuracy to the inside of the air cleaner, near the modulator valve.
3. If the indicated temperature is less than 68°F, the valve should be closed.
4. If the temperature is greater than 68°F, the valve should be open.
5. Replace the modulator valve if does not work within ±7° of 68°F.
6. Remove the thermometer.

Evaporative Emission Control System

There are several things to check for if a malfunction of the evaporative emission control system is suspected.

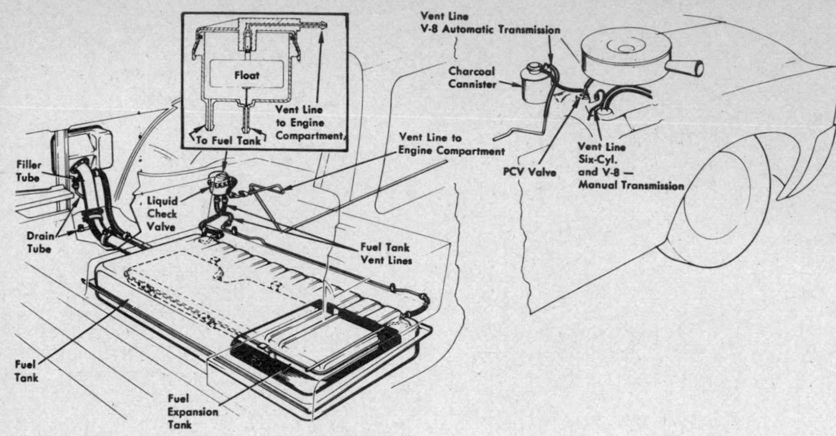

Vapor emission control system components (© American Motors Corp)

1. Leaks may be traced by using an infrared hydrocarbon tester. Run the test probe along the lines and connections. The meter will indicate the presence of a leak by a high hydrocarbon (HC) reading. This method is much more accurate than a visual inspection which would indicate only the presence of a leak large enough to pass liquid.
2. Leaks may be caused by any of the following, so always check these areas when looking for them:
   a. Defective or worn lines;
   b. Disconnected or pinched lines;
   c. Improperly routed lines;
   d. A defective filler cap.

NOTE: If it becomes necessary to replace any of the lines used in the evaporative emission control system, use only those hoses which are fuel resistant or are marked "EVAP."

3. If the fuel tank has collapsed, it may be the fault of clogged or pinched vent lines, a defective vapor separator, or a plugged or incorrect fuel filler cap.
4. To test the filler cap, clean it and place it against the mouth. Blow into the relief valve housing. If the cap passes pressure with light blowing or if it fails to release with hard blowing, it is defective and must be replaced.

NOTE: Replace the cap with one marked "pressure/vacuum" only. An incorrect cap will render the system inoperative or damage its components.

Exhaust Gas Recirculation (EGR) System

1972 Buick and 1973-75 GM EGR Valve Tests

NOTE: Skip steps 1-4 when checking early 1973 Pontiacs with combined EGR/TCS systems. Start with step 5. See TCS section above for further tests.

1. Start the engine. Allow it to warm up and reach normal idle speed.

NOTE: Some models are equipped with a temperature switch. This temperature switch may be coolant, block, or ambient temperature operated. Be sure that under-hood temperature is above 50-70°F, before testing the EGR valve.

2. Increase the engine speed to 1,200–1,500 rpm and watch the EGR valve shaft. The shaft should move upward at this speed.
3. Allow the engine to return to normal idle; the valve shaft should go down.
4. If the shaft fails to raise in step two, check the vacuum line which runs from the carburetor port to the valve. Make sure that it is not loose, clogged, or pinched. On models with temperature controls, disconnect the temperature switch and connect the two pieces of the vacuum hose. If the EGR valve now works, replace the temperature switch. If none of these conditions are present, proceed with the next step.

NOTE: On some models the temperature switch may operate other emission control systems as well. If more than one system is out, the fault probably lies in this switch.

5. Test the valve diaphragm by disconnecting the vacuum line and applying an outside vacuum source to the valve. The shaft should raise between 8–10 in. Hg. It should retain the pressure and not leak down.
6. If the valve shaft is frozen in the raised position, the valve is defective.
7. If the valve fails any of the above tests, it is defective. Replace it as an assembly; the valve cannot be disassembled and repaired.
8. In some cases the valve may be cleaned with a wire brush or in a spark plug cleaning machine, to loosen deposits which may cause the valve to stick.

NOTE: If the engine is to be tested by "shorting out" the cylinders when it is equipped with an EGR valve, first disconnect the vacuum hose at the valve and plug it. Failure to do this will cause uneven idling and indicate false test results.

1973½-74 Pontiac EGR System

NOTE: Pontiac models made on or after 15 March 1973 use separate systems for TCS and EGR. For TCS system checking procedures, see the appropriate section above.

PONTIAC'S EMISSIONS CONTROL SYSTEM
– PARTS LOCATION –

1973 LATE PRODUCTION (ON OR AFTER MARCH 15, 1973)

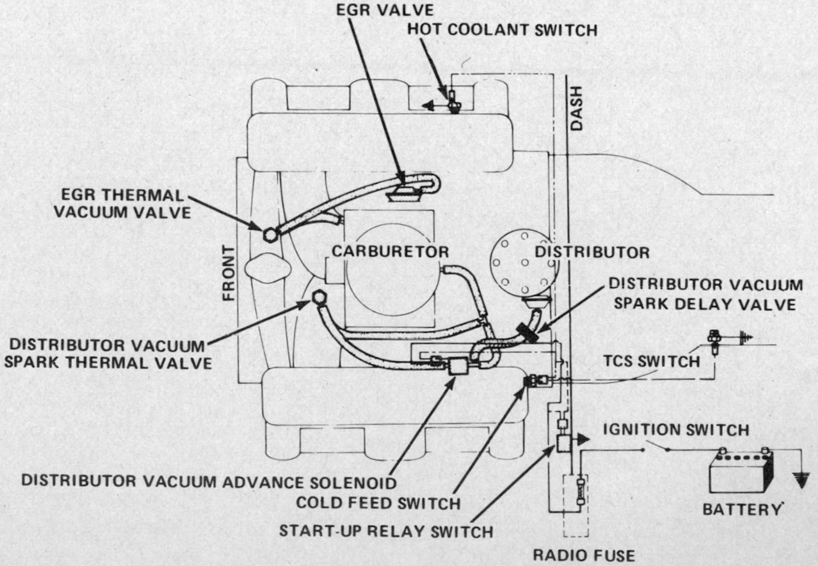

The testing procedure for the Pontiac EGR valve is basically the same as that outlined for the other GM cars, in the preceding section. However, there are several points which should be noted:

1. The engine must be warmed up until the coolant temperature is above 95°F.
2. The air cleaner must be removed in order to see the EGR valve shaft. Plug the manifold vacuum fitting.
3. If the EGR valve is not getting vacuum, check the vacuum hoses, then check the mixture thermal vacuum valve and/or the coolant temperature operated vacuum valve as outlined in the appropriate section above. The valve should work when the coolant temperature is above 95°F.

1974 GM Dual Diaphragm EGR Valve

A dual diaphragm EGR valve is used on some GM V8s which are sold in California. The dual diaphragm valve may be identified by the two vacuum hoses which run to it. To test, proceed as follows:

1. Shut the engine off.
2. Disconnect the *lower* vacuum line from the EGR valve.
3. Connect a hand-operated vacuum pump, which has a built in vacuum gauge, to the lower port on the EGR valve.
4. Draw about 14 in. Hg with the pump. There should be no drop in the gauge reading for at least 30 seconds.
   If the vacuum gauge shows a drop within 30 seconds, replace the EGR valve.
   If the valve is good, disconnect the pump and connect the vacuum line to the lower port.

1974-75 GM Backpressure Transducer Valve (BPV)

1. Take the air cleaner off of the carburetor and plug the manifold vacuum fitting.
2. Block the drive wheels, place the transmission in Park, and turn the air conditioner off.
3. Start the engine and allow it to reach normal operating temperature. Place the cam follower on the high step of the fast idle cam.
4. Connect a vacuum gauge to the carburetor side of the BPV. Note the reading. Reconnect the vacuum line.
5. Connect a vacuum gauge to the EGR valve side of the BPV with a T-fitting. The gauge should read 1.7-3.2 in. Hg; if it does not, replace the BPV.
6. With the vacuum gauge still connected, remove the vacuum line from the EGR valve and plug it; the gauge should read the same as in Step 4. If it does not read within 2-3 in. Hg of the figure obtained in Step 4, replace the BPV.
7. Remove the vacuum gauge, connect the vacuum lines, and replace the air cleaner.

1975-76 Cadillac with Electronic Fuel Injection

On models with electronic fuel injection (EFI) vacuum for the EGR valve is controlled by the fuel injection system.

A solenoid in the EGR valve vacuum line blocks its vacuum signal when coolant temperature is below 130°F. The solenoid is controlled by the fuel injection system computer.

The EGR valve is tested as outlined under "1972 Buick and 1973-75 GM EGR Valve Tests", except that the vacuum hose should be removed from the solenoid and its two halves joined. If the vacuum solenoid or its control circuit is suspected of faulty operation, they must be tested as part of the fuel injection system. Fuel injection system testing requires the use of a special factory checker.

The backpressure transducer valve (BPV) used with the fuel injection EGR system is tested by using the procedure outlined in the "1974-75 GM Backpressure Transducer Valve" test section.

Chrysler Corp. Floor Jet Service—1972-73

All six-cylinder engines have one floor jet, while all V8s have two.

1. Turn the engine off. Remove the air cleaner assembly from the carburetor.
2. Hold the choke and throttle valves open. Shine a flashlight through the carburetor to inspect the floor jet(s). The jet(s) is/are in satisfactory condition if the passage shows an open path to the orifice.
3. If the jet (s) is/are clogged, completely remove the carburetor. Withdraw the jet and clean it.

Caution Use care when handling the jets. They have very thin walls and are, therefore, easily damaged. Because they are made out of stainless steel, they are not magnetic and cannot be retrieved readily if dropped into the manifold.

4. Install the jet(s) and tighten to 25 ft lbs. Install the carburetor and attach the air cleaner.

NOTE: "Shorting out" cylinders on engines equipped with floor jets is not a reliable test proceedure. The unburned mixture is circulated to the other cylinders, causing the engine speed to fluctuate. Because of this, false test results may be obtained.

Chrysler Corp. 1973 (early) Proportional EGR System Tests

NOTE: Air temperature should be above 68°F for this test.

1. Check all of the vacuum hoses which run between the carburetor, intake manifold, EGR valve, and the vacuum amplifier (if so equipped). Replace the hoses and tighten the connections, as required.
2. Allow the engine to warm up. Connect a tachometer to it. Start with the engine idling in neutral and rapidly increase the engine speed to 2,000 rpm.
3. If the EGR valve stem moves (watch the groove on the stem), the valve and the rest of the system are functioning properly. If the stem does not move, proceed with the rest of the EGR system tests.

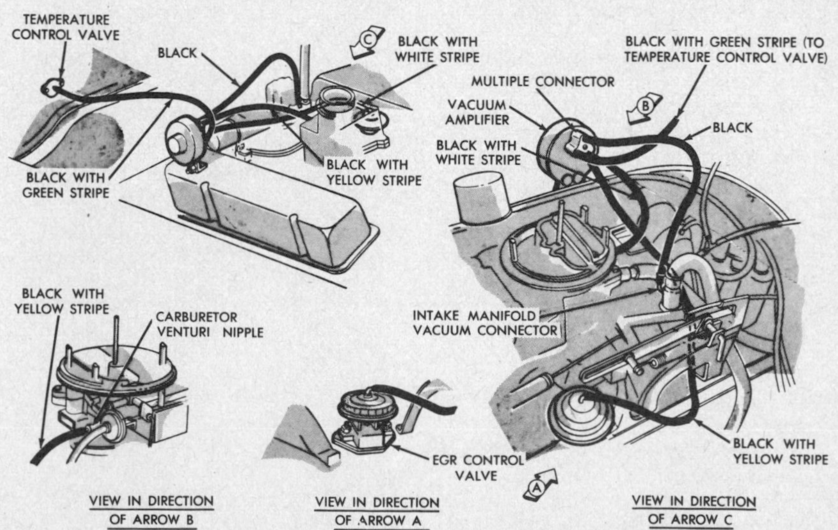

Typical hose routing and component layout of a Chrysler Proportional EGR system

Floor jet location in Chrysler Corp V8s—sixes use only one jet (© Chrysler Corp)

4. Disconnect the vacuum supply hose from the EGR valve. Apply a vacuum of at least 10 in. Hg to the valve with the engine warmed-up and idling and the transmission in neutral.

NOTE: A source of more than adequate vacuum is the intake manifold vacuum connection. Run a hose from the EGR valve directly to the connection.

5. When vacuum is applied to the EGR valve, the engine speed should drop at least 150 rpm. In some cases the engine may even stall. If the engine does not slow down and the EGR valve does not operate, the valve is defective or dirty. Replace it or remove the deposits from it.

NOTE: Always replace the EGR valve gasket with a new one when the valve is removed for service, even if the valve itself is not replaced.

6. If the EGR valve is functioning properly, reconnect its vacuum line and test the temperature control valve.
7. Disconnect the vacuum hose which runs to the temperature control valve and plug it. Repeat steps 2–3. If the EGR valve now functions, the temperature control valve is defective and must be replaced.
8. If everything else is functioning properly, the EGR system does not work and the engine is equipped with a vacuum amplifier (see the chart below), the amplifier is at fault. Replace it and repeat the system test.

NOTE: Before replacng the amplifier, check the vacuum port in the carburetor. If it is clogged, clean it with solvent; do not use a drill.

Engine	*Vacuum amplifier used on:*
225—6	All
318—V8	California only
360—V8	All
440—V8	All non-high-performance engines

Chrysler Corp. 1973 (late)-75 Proportional EGR System Tests

NOTE: This system is used starting with cars made on or after 15 March 1973. It replaces the system tested in the above section.

1. Perform Steps 1-6 of the 1973 proportional EGR system tests, detailed in the above section.
2. Depressurize the cooling system. Remove the coolant temperature operated EGR vacuum valve (CCEGR) from the top tank of the radiator. On 1975 360-V8 2-bbl engines, remove the CCEGR valve from the front of the block.
3. Place the CCEGR valve in an ice bath so that its threaded portion is covered. Cool it to less than 40°F.
4. Connect a hand-operated vacuum pump and gauge to the valve nipple which had the blue or yellow striped hose attached to it.
5. Apply at least 10 in. Hg vacuum to the valve. The gauge should show no more than a 1 in. Hg drop in vacuum in 1 minute.
6. If the reading drops off more than this, replace the CCEGR valve.
7. Proceed with step 8 in the preceding section.

Chrysler Corp. 1974-75 EGR Delay System

NOTE: Not all engines use an EGR delay timer; some 1975 engines also used the EGR delay timer to control the coolant control idle enrichment (CCIE) system as well.

1. Unfasten the distributor-to-coil lead.
2. Disconnect the vacuum line which runs from the delay solenoid to the vacuum amplifier at the amplifier end.
3. Turn the car's ignition switch to "START" and then release it, so that it returns to "RUN".
4. Suck on the end of the disconnected hose; the hose should be blocked.
5. After about 35 seconds from the time that the ignition switch was turned to "START", the solenoid should open, allowing air to flow through the line that you are sucking on.
6. If the system isn't working, disconnect the solenoid and connect it directly to a 12-volt power source, making and breaking the

The 1973½-75 EGR temperature control valve is located on the top tank of the radiator on most Chrysler products

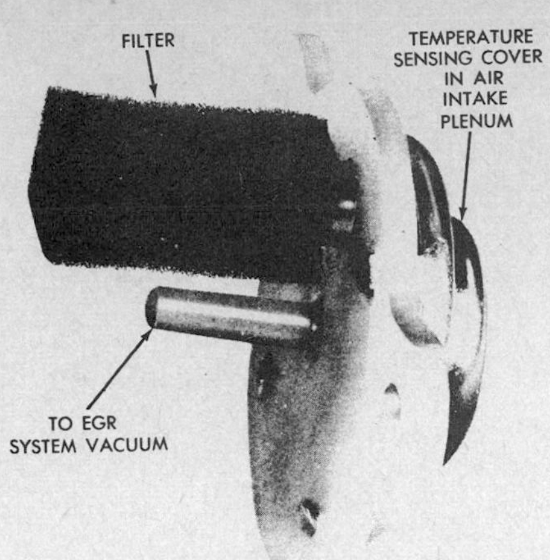

The temperature sensing valve used prior to 15 March 1973 on Chrysler EGR systems
(© Chrysler Corp)

circuit several times. If the solenoid works, replace the delay timer.

7. If the solenoid doesn't work, replace the solenoid.
8. Reconnect the vacuum lines and the coil after completing the test.

Chrysler Corp. 1975 EGR Reminder Light

NOTE: This light is designed to remind the driver that regularly scheduled service is due; it does not mean that the EGR system is not working properly.

1. After checking the EGR system for proper operation, slide the rubber boot on the EGR reminder odometer up, out of the way.
2. Reset the odometer with a small screwdriver.
3. Slide the boot back down over the odometer. The light will come on again when the next 15,000 mile check-up is due.

1973 Ford EGR System Tests

1. Allow the engine to warm up, so that the coolant temperature has reached at least 135°F.
2. Disconnect the vacuum hose which runs from the temperature cut-in valve to the EGR valve at the EGR valve end. Connect a vacuum gauge to this hose with a T-fitting.
3. Increase engine speed. The gauge should indicate a vacuum. If no vacuum is present, check the following:
   a. The carburetor—look for a clogged vacuum port.
   b. The vacuum hoses—including the vacuum hoses to the transmission modulator.
   c. The temperature cut-in valve —if no vacuum is present at its outlet with the engine temperature above 135°F and vacuum available from the carburetor, the valve is defective.
4. If all of the above tests are positive, check the EGR valve itself.
5. Connect an outside vacuum source and a vacuum gauge to the valve.
6. Apply vacuum to the EGR valve. The valve should open at 3–10 in. Hg, the engine idle speed should slow down, and the idle quality should become more rough.
7. If this does not happen, i.e., the EGR valve remains closed, the EGR valve is defective and must be replaced.

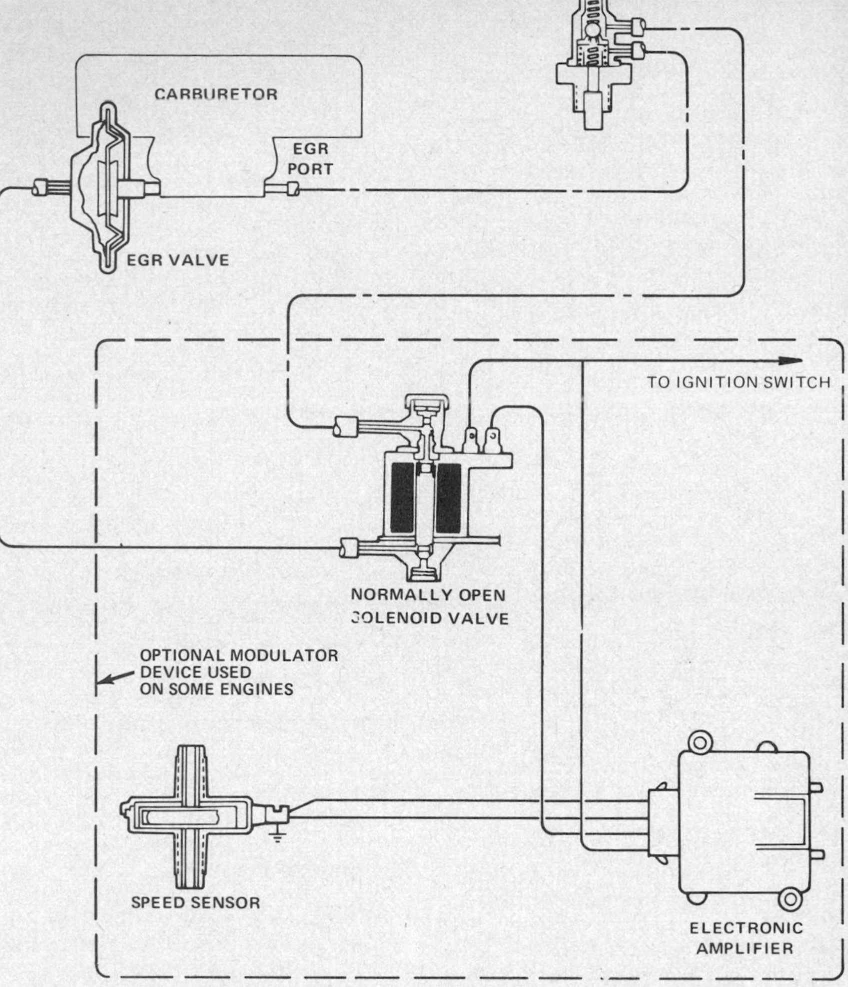

Ford exhaust gas recirculation (EGR) system (© Ford Motor Co)

Black cylinder (under steering shaft) is the EGR maintenance warning odometer used on 1975 Chrysler products

8. If the valve stem moves but the idle remains the same, the valve orifice is clogged and must be cleaned.

NOTE: If an outside vacuum source is not available, disconnect the hose which runs between the EGR valve and the temperature cut-in valve and plug the hose connections on the cut-in valve. Connect the EGR valve hose to a source of intake manifold vacuum and watch the idle. The results should be the same as in steps 6–7, above.

Vacuum Modulator—Bench Test

NOTE: The vacuum modulator is used only with an automatic transmission.

1. Remove the vacuum modulator from the car.
2. Connect the modulator to an outside vacuum source: a distributor tester, for example.

NOTE: The vacuum source should be adjusted to supply 18 in. Hg, with the end of the vacuum line blocked off.

3. Connect the vacuum line from the vacuum source to the EGR port on the vacuum modulator.
4. The vacuum modulator should hold the 18 in. Hg reading. If it does not, then the diaphragm is leaking and must be replaced.

Temperature Cut-In Valve—Bench Test

1. Remove the valve from the engine.
2. Connect an outside source of vacuum to the top port on the valve. Leave the bottom port vented to the atmosphere.
3. Use ice or an aerosol spray to cool the valve below 60°F.
4. Apply 20 in. Hg vacuum to the valve. The valve should hold a minimum of 19 in. Hg vacuum for five minutes without leaking down.
5. Leave the vacuum source connected to the valve and place it, along with a high temperature thermometer, into a non-metallic, heat-resistant container full of water.
6. Heat the water. The vacuum in the valve should drop to zero once the temperature of the water reaches about 125°F.
7. Replace the valve if it fails either of the tests.

1973 Ford High Speed EGR Modulator—System Tests

NOTE: Before beginning this test, check the EGR valve and the other related components as outlined in the section above.

1. Detach the line from the EGR valve. Connect a vacuum gauge to the line, using a T-fitting, and reconnect the EGR valve.

NOTE: Position the vacuum gauge so that it can be seen from the driver's seat.

2. Raise the rear wheels of the car off the ground, supporting it so that it cannot roll forward.
3. Start the engine and allow it to warm up at *fast* idle for 3–4 minutes.
4. Return the engine to normal idle; the vacuum gauge reading should return to zero.
5. Place the transmission in Third gear (manual) or Drive (automatic). Increase the engine speed; vacuum should also increase.
6. At an indicated speed of approximately 67 mph, the vacuum gauge reading should drop to zero.

If the system is functioning properly, lower the car, disconnect the vacuum gauge, and reconnect the vacuum lines. If the system is malfunctioning, proceed with the tests below.

Power Supply Tests

Caution Do not use a self-powered test light; damage to the amplifier could result.

1. Check the electrical leads which run to and from the vacuum solenoid valve with a low-amperage test light. The car should be running so that power is being supplied to the system.
2. If there is no current at the valve, trace the wiring back to its power source to determine the reason for the failure.
3. If there is current at the valve, remove the power connector from the amplifier and check for current at the connector. If there is none, replace the wiring between the amplifier and the vacuum valve.

Speed Sensor Tests

1. Check the resistance of the speed sensor by touching its leads with the test prods of an ohmmeter. The ohmmeter should read 40–60 ohms.
2. Replace the speed sensor if its resistance is not within specifications.
3. Check the connector on the speed sensor to be sure that it is tight. If the ground interlock loop between the connectors is loose, the circuit will not be grounded and the speed sensor will appear not to be functioning.

Vacuum Solenoid Valve Tests

1. Disconnect the leads from the vacuum solenoid valve which run to the amplifier.

Caution Never connect a jumper lead or a self-powered test light to the valve while it is still connected to the amplifier; damage to the amplifier could result.

2. Connect a vacuum gauge to the EGR valve port on the vacuum valve.
3. With the valve disconnected from the amplifier, connect the valve directly to a 12V power source (the battery) with jumper leads.
4. With the transmission in Neutral and current flowing to the valve, increase the engine speed to 1,500 rpm. The vacuum gauge should read zero. If it does not, replace the valve.
5. Disconnect the 12V power source from the valve. The gauge should show a vacuum reading with the engine speed at 1,500 rpm.

If the valve is not functioning properly, replace it. If it is functioning properly and the system still is not, the only other possible source of trouble is the amplifier; replace it.

NOTE: There is no way to test amplifier operation other than by process of elimination or by substitution. Attempts to check it will probably lead to its failure, if it is not already defective.

1974-75 Ford EGR System—Component Tests

1. Perform Steps 5-8 of the "1973 Ford EGR System Test". Replace the EGR valve and gasket, if necessary.
2. Connect a vacuum gauge to the EGR port on the carburetor, after disconnecting the EGR vacuum hose.
3. With the engine running (warmed-up), quickly open the throttle halfway. Allow the throttle to close.
4. If the vacuum gauge shows a quick rise and fall in vacuum, the EGR port is not clogged. No reading indicates a clogged port; if there is no reading, clean the port.
5. Check the coolant temperature operated vacuum valve (PVS) which controls the EGR system vacuum, when the engine is cold, as outlined in the appropriate section. Check the vacuum hoses for correct routing.

If everything else is in good working order, proceed with the vacuum amplifier tests (if so equipped):

6. Run the engine until normal operating temperature is reached.
7. Check the vacuum amplifier connections to be sure that they are tight and that the hoses are routed properly.
8. Remove the hose which runs from the EGR valve to the vacuum amplifier at the EGR valve end. Connect a vacuum gauge to this hose; the gauge *must* read in increments of 1 in. Hg or less.
9. Disconnect the venturi vacuum hose at the carburetor port.

10. With the engine at curb idle, the vacuum gauge should read either zero or show a small reading.
11. Increase the engine speed to 1500-2000 rpm, then allow it to return to idle.
12. If the vacuum reading increases more than 1 in. Hg or if it does not return to the same figure indicated in Step 10, replace the amplifier.
13. Reconnect the venturi hose to the carburetor port.
14. With the engine at curb idle, there should be no great increase in vacuum above the figure obtained in Step 10 (more than 0.5 in. Hg). If the vacuum increases greatly, check the idle speed, it is probably too high.
15. Unfasten the external reservoir hose from the amplifier and plug it.
16. Rapidly increase the engine speed to 1500-2000 rpm. The vacuum gauge reading should increase by at least 4 in. Hg; if it does not, replace the amplifier.
17. After completing the tests, remove the gauge and connect the vacuum hoses.
18. Check the external vacuum amplifier reservoir, if so equipped, by following the procedure outlined below.

External Amplifer Reservoir

Without Check Valve

1. Disconnect the reservoir-to-amplifier hose. Connect a vacuum gauge to it.
2. Using an external vacuum source, apply at least 14 in. Hg to the reservoir.
3. Trap the vacuum in the reservoir.
4. The vacuum should drop no more than 1 in. Hg in 1 minute. If it does, replace the reservoir.

With External Check Valve

1. Connect an external vacuum source and gauge to the amplifier side of the T-fitting in the reservoir-to-check valve hose.
2. Apply and trap 15 in. Hg to the line. Vacuum should leak down no more than 1 in. Hg in 1 minute. If it doesn't the system is OK. If it does, proceed with the rest of the test.
3. Remove the reservoir hose at the T-fitting and apply 15 in. Hg to the reservoir. Trap the vacuum in the reservoir.
4. The vacuum should drop no more than 1 in. Hg in 1 minute. If it does, replace the reservoir.
5. Remove the check valve hose. Apply 15 in. Hg vacuum to the check valve and trap it.
6. The vacuum should drop no more than 1 in. Hg in 1 minute. Replace the check valve if it does otherwise.
7. Remove the vacuum pump, and gauge. Reconnect the hoses.

Two-Nipple EGR/PVS

1. Disconnect the hoses from the EGR coolant temperature operated vacuum valve (PVS).
2. Connect a vacuum gauge to one of the nipples and an external vacuum source to the other (it dosn't matter which).
3. If the engine is cold, start it and allow the coolant temperature to reach at least 135°F.
4. If the vacuum dosen't indicate vacuum with the engine warm when vacuum is applied, the PVS is defective. Replace it.
5. If vacuum is indicated, the PVS is OK.

Three-Nipple EGR/PVS

1. Disconect the EGR vacuum hose, from the carburetor port. Connect the hose to either manifold vacuum or an auxiliary vacuum source.
2. Remove the vacuum hose from the EGR valve and connect a vacuum gauge to the hose.
3. If the engine is cold, start it and allow the coolant temperature to reach at least 135°F.
4. If the gauge doesn't indicate vacuum the PVS is defective and should be replaced.
5. If the gauge indicates vacuum the PVS is OK. Remove the gauge and reconnect the vacuum lines.

1973 American Motors EGR System Test

NOTE: Start the test with the engine cold.

1. Disconnect the vacuum line at the EGR valve. Connect a vacuum gauge to the vacuum line.
2. Heat the low ambient compensator (located in front of the radiator) in the palm of the hand, until it is above 60°F.
3. Start the engine; increase engine speed. There should be no vacuum reading on the gauge. Allow the engine to warm up to at least 125°F (160°F—304 V8/manual). With the ambient temperature compensator above 60°F and the engine coolant temperature above 125°F (160°F), vacuum should be present when the engine speed is increased.
4. Using a trouble light or some other suitable heat source, heat the *high* temperature compensator (mounted on the firewall) to above 115°F. Speed the engine up; the vacuum reading should be zero or quite low.
5. Cool the *high* temperature compensator to below 115°F, using ice; the gauge should now show a strong vacuum reading.
6. Using ice, cool the *low* ambient compensator to below 60°F; the vacuum reading should decrease.
7. If vacuum is present when it should not be, while one of the components is being tested, replace the component and repeat the system test.
8. If *no* vacuum is present when it should be, check the vacuum lines. If the lines are satisfactory, replace the suspect component and repeat the system test. Disconnect the vacuum gauge when the tests are completed.
9. Connect the EGR valve directly to the carburetor port or some other source of vacuum. Speed up the engine; the valve stem should move upward (8-10 in. Hg). Allow the engine to slow down; the valve stem should move down. If the valve is defective, replace it. Reconnect the vacuum lines.

The coolant temperature override switch is the only control for EGR vacuum used on AMC V8s after 15 March 1973

NOTE: The following components were dropped from the EGR system on, or after 15 March 1973:

1. *High temperature compensator—All engines.*
2. *Low temperature compensator—All engines.*
3. *Coolant temperature override switch — Six-cylinder engines only.*

Those steps of the test procedure which deal with these components are not required on models made after 15 March 1973.

1974-75 American Motors EGR System

EGR Valve Tests—All Engines

1. Start the engine and allow it to reach normal operating temperature.
2. Compress the EGR valve diaphragm by hand; the engine speed should drop by about 200 rpm.

Caution Be careful when depressing the valve diaphragm, the area around the valve gets very hot.

3. If the engine speed doesn't drop, but the engine is idling smoothly, the EGR passage to the intake manifold is plugged and must be cleaned.
4. If the engine idle is poor, and lifting the diaphragm has no effect on its speed, the EGR valve is probably plugged or defective. Clean or replace it, as necessary.
5. Insert a T-fitting in the EGR valve vacuum line and connect a vacuum gauge to the fitting.
6. Increase the engine speed slowly, while watching the vacuum gauge; at the same time either watch or feel the valve diaphragm.
7. The valve should start to open between 1.8-3.2 in. Hg and be fully opened at 3.8-7.3 in. Hg.
8. At wide-open throttle, the diaphragm should be fully depressed with no sign of leakage. Replace the valve if it is defective.

EGR Coolant Temperature Operated Vacuum Valve—All Engines

NOTE: Engine coolant temperature must be below 100°F before beginning this test.

1. Be sure that the lines are routed correctly and are not pinched, plugged, or leaking.
2. Unfasten the vacuum line from the EGR valve. Connect a vacuum gauge to this line.
3. Start the engine and increase its speed to 1500 rpm. The vacuum gauge should read zero; if it does not, replace the coolant temperature operated vacuum valve.
4. Allow the engine to run until the coolant temperature reaches 115°F or more.

NOTE: At 115°F, the needle on the car's temperature gauge should be halfway between "C" and the beginning of the band.

5. Increase the engine speed to 1500 rpm again. The vacuum gauge should show ported vacuum; if it doesn't, replace the vacuum valve.

Exhaust Backpressure Sensor Test—California Engines

1. Check all vacuum lines and fittings. Make sure that the vacuum line to the EGR valve is connected to the coolant temperature operated vacuum valve nipple with the 0.030 in. restriction.
2. Install a vacuum gauge, using a T-fitting, in the line which runs from the EGR valve to the backpressure sensor.
3. Start the engine and allow it to warm-up. With the engine at curb idle the vacuum gauge should read zero.
4. If vacuum is present, check the vacuum lines to be sure that manifold vacuum is *not* being used instead of carburetor ported vacuum. If the correct ported vacuum is being used, check to be sure that the throttle plate isn't sticking opened.
5. Increase the engine speed to 2000 rpm, while watching for one of the following:
   a. If the coolant temperature is less than 115°F, the gauge should read zero.
   b. If the coolant temperature is above 115°F, the gauge should show ported vacuum.
6. If vacuum is not shown when it should be, or vice versa, check the coolant temperature operated vacuum valve, as previously outlined.
7. If everything else is in good working order, remove the backpressure sensor. Check to see that the spacer port and tube are not blocked. Clean them with a spiral wire brush, as necessary. If this doesn't solve the problem, replace the backpressure sensor.

Catalytic Converters

Testing the Converter

At the present time there is no known way to reliably test catalytic converter operation in the field. The only reliable test is a 12 hour and 40 minute "soak test" (CVS) which must be done in a laboratory.

An infrared HC/CO tester is not sensitive enough to measure the higher tailpipe emissions from a partially-failed converter. Thus, a bad converter may allow enough HC and CO emissions to escape, so that the car is not in compliance with Federal (or state) standards, but still will not cause the needle on the HC/CO tester to move off zero.

You can check a converter for physical damage, such as a ripped skin or crushed shell. You can test for a plugged converter the same way you test for a plugged muffler. You can look for pellets coming out of the tailpipe, which means the pellets are breaking up. All such physical damage means the converter must be repaired, replaced, or recharged. But when it comes to testing the actual efficiency of the converter, or measuring the amount of HC and CO that it removes from the exhaust, forget it.

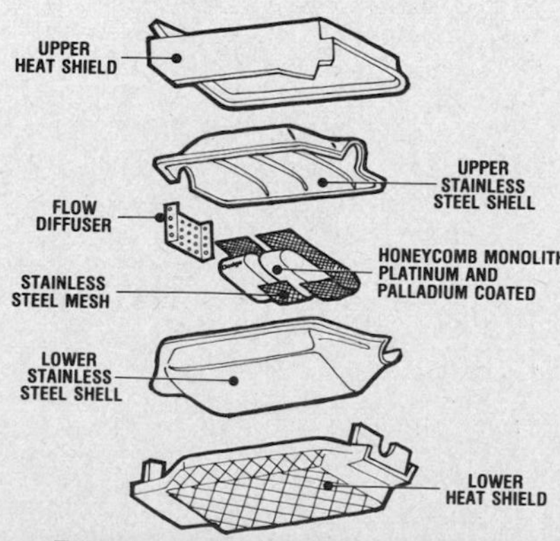

Typical monolithic catalytic converter construction
(© Chrysler Corp)

If you have a car with high HC or CO coming out the tailpipe, the problem has to be in the engine. If you took the converter off most 1975 cars, they would still be as clean as the 1974 cars. The converter removes so little HC and CO from the exhaust that even with the converter taken off, the car would still pass state or city emission control laws. The converter was put on the 1975 cars so they would pass the EPA and California laboratory test, which is much more severe than any state or city used car standards, including California.

If you discover the car has high tailpipe emissions, or if the car gets a citation for high emissions, it's easy to jump to the conclusion that the converter is to blame. *Do not replace or recharge a converter because of high tailpipe emissions.* The problem is in the engine, not the converter.

Following are the most common causes of high tailpipe emissions, as measured on an infra-red tester.

High HC	Missing cylinder Lean mixture screws Extreme flooding
High CO	Rich mixture screws Dirty air cleaner High float level

The only domestic car maker who gives idle CO settings is Chrysler. The mixture screws are set with the air pump disconnected, which reduces the efficiency of the converter and causes enough CO to go through that you get a reading. American Motors and General Motors use the lean drop method of setting idle mixture, and Ford uses the speed increase method of adding propane.

Recharging or Changing Converters

Because the converter cannot be tested in the field, many people wonder what should be done to it. We have established the following guidlines.

1. The car manufacturer requires it.
2. The converter is damaged beyond repair.
3. The law requires it.
4. The catalyst doesn't work.

So far, there is no requirement by either the car manufacturer or the law to change or recharge the converter according to mileage or time. General Motors and American Motors converters can be repaired if the bottom cover is damaged by installing a replacement cover.

We know of only two ways to tell if the catalyst isn't working. If *you* see pellets or pieces of the catalyst coming out the tailpipe, the catalyst is breaking up, and the converter must be recharged or changed. The other indication is the catalyst that melts and plugs the exhaust. In that case, you have to do something immediately, because the car probably won't run.

Leaded fuel will reduce the efficiency of the converter while the leaded fuel is being used. After the leaded fuel has been used up, and the car runs again on non-leaded fuel, the converter will recover its efficiency to a degree. How much the converter recovers depends on how long it was run on leaded fuel. How much efficiency is reduced you have no way of knowing.

Converter Removal

A new car dealer is prohibited by federal law from tampering with emission controls. If the catalyst melts or breaks up, he must replace or recharge the converter. An independent shop's work on emission controls is regulated by state and local laws. Before you remove a converter make sure that you are not breaking any state or local laws.

Catalyst Damage

Converters operate best at an internal temperature of 600-1500°F. At 1700°F or higher, the catalyst begins to melt or break up. The converter generates its own heat, according to how many hydrocarbons are fed through it. Hydracarbons are nothing more than raw, liquid fuel, so any excess of fuel will cause the converter to overheat. The following conditions will cause extra fuel to go through the converter, and may damage it.

1. Fast idle for a long time.
2. A missing plug or plugs, for a long time.
3. An extremely rich mixture for a long time.

How long is a long time? Only the converter knows. Garage testing may overheat the converter if carried on too long. Any testing that requires shorting out one or more cylinders will put raw fuel through the converter.

There is nothing wrong with these tests, as long as they are done quickly. The same applies to dynamometer tests. It isn't necessary to hold the engine at full throttle for more than a few seconds. There is no reason for changing normal dynamometer procedures. However, if you are doing experimental work that requires a lot of dyno running, the converter could overheat. For extensive experimental work, we suggest removing the converter temporarily and putting a length of empty tubing in its place.

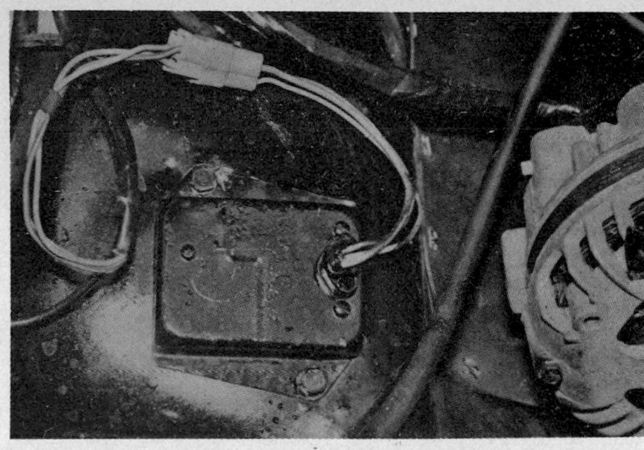

Speed switch for Chrysler catalyst protection system

On the dyno, you can remove the converter (if it isn't welded) and put your exhaust collector over the end of the exhaust pipe.

The following check list shows possible causes for catalyst damage:

- Excessive vibration
- Rich mixtures
- Leaded fuel
- Spark plug misfire
- Excessive fast idle
- Running out of gas (causes misfire)
- Fuel additives
- Carbon solvents
- Misuse of engine (turning key off at speed)
- Total ignition failure at speed

Catalyst Protection System Testing

Chrysler Corp.

1. Start the engine and allow it to warm up.
2. Connect a tachometer to the engine.
3. Increase the engine speed to 2,500 rpm; the solenoid plunger should extend.
4. Release the throttle, once the engine speed has dropped below 2,000 rpm; the plunger should retract.
5. If the solenoid doesn't work properly, disconnect it from the speed switch and connect it to a 12 volt power source. If the plunger extends, the solenoid is working and the speed switch is defective. Replace the speed switch.
6. If the plunger does not extend, the solenoid is defective and must be replaced.
7. With the solenoid connected to the 12 volt power source (energized) so that its plunger is out, adjust the engine speed to 1,500 rpm.

Caution *Do not* adjust the curb idle speed with the catalyst protection system solenoid. This is not an antidieseling solenoid. If the curb idle speed is adjusted with this solenoid, it wil be far above 2,000 rpm once the solenoid has been energized, creating a hazardous driving situation. The only way to stop an engine which has been adjusted in this manner, is to shut it off and not restart it until the solenoid has been correctly adjusted.

8. Reconnect the solenoid to the speed switch and disconnect the tachometer, once the proper setting has been obtained.

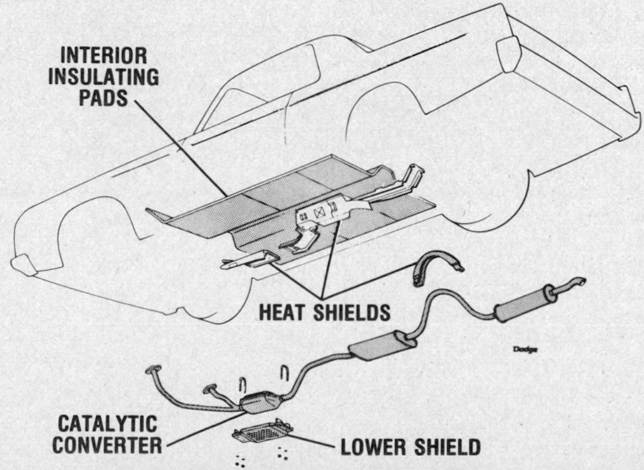

Typical Chrysler catalytic converter mounting
(© Chrysler Corp)

Replacing the Catalyst

Chrysler and Ford

The catalyst used in Ford and Chrysler products is the monolithic (one-piece) type which cannot be removed from the converter for replacement.

If the catalyst fails, it will be necessary to replace the entire converter assembly with a new one. To do so, proceed as follows:

Caution Allow the converter assembly to cool completely before attempting to service it; catalyst temperatures can reach 1500°-1600°F.

1. If a grass shield is used, remove the bolts which secure it and lower the shield from underneath the vehicle.
2. Unbolt the converter assembly at the mounting flanges, just as you would a normal exhaust pipe from the manifold.

NOTE: Support the exhaust pipe while the converter is removed.

3. Replace the old converter with a new unit which is the exact same size, part number, and type (or its *exact* equivalent) as was originally installed.
4. Remove the plastic plugs from the ends of the converter (if used) and install it in the reverse order of removal, being sure to use new gaskets to ensure a leak-free fit.
5. Install the grass shields.

Emptying the pellets from a GM catalytic converter
(© Cadillac Div, G.M. Corp)

Filling the GM converter
(© Cadillac Div, G.M. Corp)

This special vibrator is used in filling the GM catalytic converter
(© Cadillac Div, G.M. Corp)

GM and AMC

General Motors and American Motors cars use pellets in their converters, which may be replaced without replacing the whole catalytic converter assembly.

To replace the pellets, proceed as follows:

Caution Allow the converter assembly to cool completely before attempting to service it; catalyst temperatures can reach 1500°F.

1. Using a ¾ in. allen wrench, loosen, but do not remove the converter fill plug.
2. Remove the four nuts and bolts at each converter flange. Lower the converter being careful to note the position of, and saving any gaskets used.
3. Loosely install the upper rear flange nuts and bolts, to secure the exhaust system to the hanger while the converter is removed.
4. Place the converter on the workbench and remove the fill plug. Drain the old pellets into a container and discard them.
5. Inspect the converter housing for signs of damage. Replace the assembly, if necessary.
6. Clamp the special vibrator to the converter flange on the opposite end from the fill plug, with the mounting nuts and bolts.
7. Place the converter on a 30° angle with the fill plug end up. Fill the converter with new catalyst pellets through a funnel.
8. When it appears that the converter is full, connect the air supply to the vibrator and continue to add pellets in small amounts. Pack the pellets in tightly with your fingers.
9. Once the pellets are flush with the fill plug, remove the air supply from the vibrator. Coat the fill plug with an anti-seize compound and tighten it 50 ft lbs (GM) or 40 ft lbs (AMC).
10. Remove the vibrator.
11. Install the converter assembly on the car in the reverse order of removal, being sure to use all necessary gaskets. Tighten the flange nuts and bolts.

NOTE: GM makes a kit to replace the bottom converter cover should it become torn or damaged.

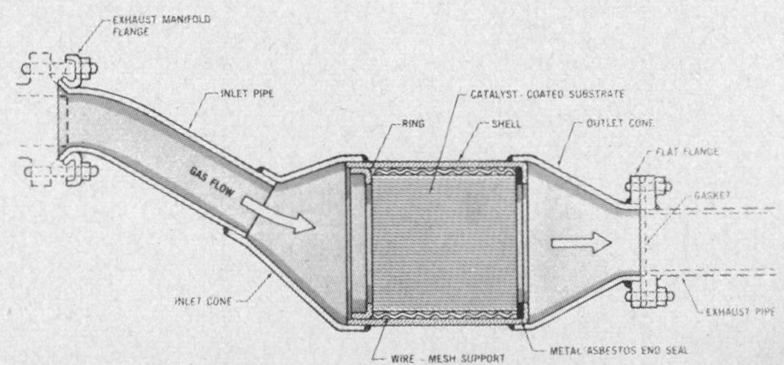

Ford monolithic converter—cutaway view
(© Ford Motor Co)

Vacuum-Operated Heat Risers

These valves are similar to the spring-operated heat risers used on American cars for many years. The old valve was operated by a bimetal spring. The type of valve is operated by a vacuum motor (diaphragm) which, in turn, is controlled by a vacuum valve that is temperature-sensitive. In some applications the vacuum is controlled by a solenoid that is hooked up to a temperature switch.

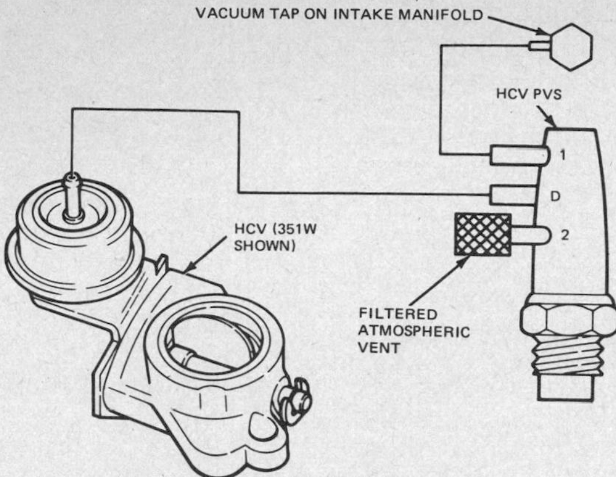

1975 Ford vacuum operated heat riser
(© Ford Motor Co.)

1975 Ford Vacuum Exhaust Heat Valve

Valve Test

1. With the engine off, look at the rod which connects the diaphragm with the valve lever. The rod should be fully extended (no vacuum applied).
2. Connect a hand-operated vacuum pump with a gauge to the diaphragm unit.

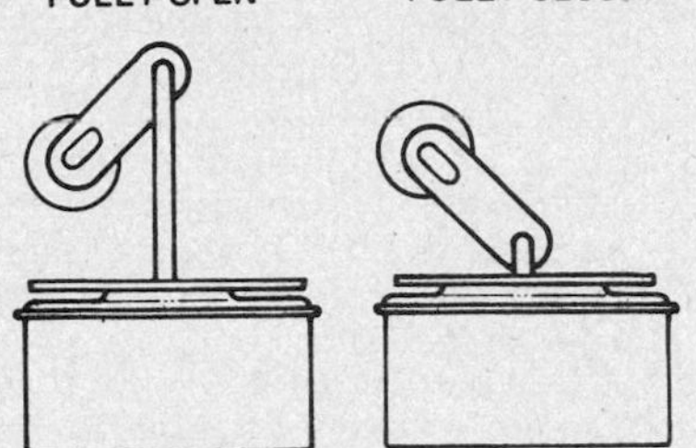

Ford vacuum operated heat riser rod operation
(© Ford Motor Co.)

3. Apply vacuum. Check the results against the chart below:

Engine	*Valve starts to close (in. Hg)*	*Valve Closed (in. Hg)*
302, 351W	1-3	6 or less
351M, 400	3-6	10 or less

4. If the valve rod doesn't extend fully when no vacuum is applied and doesn't close fully when vacuum is applied, tap the valve and apply heat riser lubricant to free it.
5. Apply 15-20 in. Hg vacuum to the diaphragm and trap it. If the vacuum leaks down more 2 in. Hg in one minute, replace the valve assembly.

Coolant Temperature Operated Vacuum Valve

1. Start with the engine cold.
2. Remove the vacuum line from the top nipple. Connect a hand-operated vacuum pump to the nipple.
3. Plug the middle nipple. Apply vacuum. The valve should hold the vacuum without leaking down.
4. With the engine at normal operating temperature, leave the middle nipple open and apply vacuum. The valve should hold vacuum and not leak down.
5. With the engine hot, remove the vacuum pump and connect the hose. Attach a hose to the middle nipple and blow through it. Air should come out through the valve vent.
6. If the valve doesn't work as outlined, replace it with a new one.

GM Early Fuel Evaporation (EFE) System

Starting in 1975, all 250-6, all 231-V6, and most GM V8 engines use a vacuum-operated heat riser valve. GM calls this system "Early Fuel Evaporation" or "EFE" for short.

With the exception of the 250-6 and the Chevrolet 454-V8, all engines use a coolant temperature operated vacuum valve (EFE/TVV) to control vacuum to the EFE valve vacuum motor. The 250-6 and 454-V8 use an oil temperature switch and vacuum solenoid, instead.

EFE Valve Test—All Engines

1. Inspect the manifold heat riser valve and linkage for damage and binding. Check for plugged, cracked, or misrouted vacuum hoses.
2. Connect external vacuum source and vacuum gauge to the EFE valve vacuum motor, after disconnecting the vacuum hose from from it.
3. Apply at least 10 in. Hg vacuum to the motor. The valve should move freely. The motor should hold the plunger in the retracted position for 1 minute without the aplication of additonal vacuum.
4. If the vacuum motor leaks down in less the 1 minute or fails to operate the EFE valve (linkage not binding), replace it.
5. If the valve or linkage binds, use heat riser lubricant on it. If the valve can't be freed by tapping it loose and lubricating it, replace the assembly.

GM vacuum operated heat riser (EFE) valve assembly
(© Oldsmobile Div., GM Corp.)

EFE Vacuum Solenoid Test—250-6 and Chevrolet 454-V8

1. Disconnect the engine harness wiring plug from the solenoid. Use a short jumper wire to connect one of the solenoid terminals to ground. Run a hot wire from the positive battery terminal to the other terminal.
2. The solenoid should click when the wire is connected. If not, the solenoid is defective.
3. To check for correct vacuum switching of the solenoid, connect an engine manifold vacuum hose to the nozzle that points straight down in the opposite direction from the wire terminals. Connect a vacuum gauge to the nozzle that points out to the side of he solenid.
4. With the engine running, energize the solenoid as described above. Full manifold vacuum should appear on the gauge.
5. De-energize the solenoid and the vacuum should drop to zero. If not, the solenoid is defective.
6. The manifold vacuum hose must connect to the bottom end nozzle, not to the side nozzle. If the hoses are hooked up backwards, the EFE valve may stay closed after the engine warms up.
7. Repairs are limited to replacement. Test the new solenoid to be sure it sends vacuum to the EFE actuator when energized. If it allows vacuum through when de-energized, it's the wrong solenoid.

Oil Temperature Switch Test—250-6 and Chevrolet 454-V8

1. Disconnect the oil temperature switch harness wiring.
2. Connect a self-powered test light between the switch terminal and ground.
3. If the engine is cold (below 150°—250-6 or 100°F—454-V8), the test light should come on.
4. Run the engine. When it reaches normal operating temperature, the light should go out.
5. Replace the switch if it doesn't work as outlined.

EFE Coolant Temperature Opearted Vacuum Valve Tests

5-Nozzle Valve

This valve may be identified by the nozzle on top and four nozzles down the side. A vent is also located on the other side.

1. Remove the vacuum hose from the top (vertical) nozzle and cap it.
2. Connect a hand-operated vacuum pump to the top nozzle on the side and a vacuum gauge to the next lower nozzle.
3. On a cold engine vacuum should register on the gauge.

EFE vacuum solenoid
(© Pontiac Div., GM Corp.)

4. Allow the engine to warm up to above 120°F.
5. The gauge should register zero. The valve should hold vacuum and not leak down.
6. Remove the vacuum gauge from the lower nozzle and blow through it. Air should come out of the vent.
7. Replace the valve if it doesn't work as outlined.

4-Nozzle Valve

This valve may be identified by the one vertical nozzle on top and the three nozzles down the side. There is also a vent on the side opposite the three nozzles.

1. Remove the hose from the top (vertical) nozzle. Connect a hand-operated vacuum pump to it.
2. Connect a vacuum gauge to the top nozzle on the side (marked "HV").
3. On a warm engine, about 120°F, the vertical nozzle should be closed and you should be able to get a reading on the hand pump gauge. The gauge connected to the "HV" nozzle should read zero.
4. Remove the vacuum gauge and blow through the "HV" nozzle; air should come out the vent.
5. Relieve the cooling system pressure and remove the coolant temperature operated vacuum valve.
6. Cool the valve in an ice bath. Below 120°F, you should get a reading on the gauge attached to the HV nozzle. The vacuum should not leak down.
7. Replace the valve if it doesn't work as oulined.

2-Nozzle Valve

This valve may be identified by the two nozzles on the one side with a vent on the opposite side.

1. Disconnect the vacuum hose from the top nozzle. Connect a hand-operated vacuum pump to the nozzle.
2. Connect a vacuum gauge to the lower nozzle.
3. On a cold engine the vacuum gauge on the lower nozzle should register when the vacuum is applied to the upper nozzle. The vent should be closed.
4. Warm the engine up, so that the coolant is above one of the following:
   Chevrolet V8—180°F
   Cadillac V8—150°F
   All other V8—120°
5. Apply vacuum to the uper nozzle. The gauge on the lower nozzle should register zero.
6. Remove the vacuum gauge from the lower nozzle. Blow through the nozzle, air should come out the vent.
7. Replace the valve if it doesn't work as outlined.

EFE Check Valve Test

Some engines have a check valve in the EFE vacuum line.

1. Remove the vacuum hose from the tappered end of the check valve.
2. Connect a hand-operated vacuum pump with gauge to the check valve. Apply vacuum and trap it.
3. The vacuum should not leak down. Replace the check valve if vacuum leaks down more than 0.5 in. Hg in one minute.

Engine Tune-Up

Engine tune-up is a procedure performed to restore engine performance, deteriorated due to normal wear and loss of adjustment. The three major areas considered in a routine tune-up are compression, ignition, and carburetion, although valve adjustment may be included.

A tune-up is performed in three steps: *analysis*, in which it is determined whether normal wear is responsible for performance loss, and which parts require replacement or service; *parts replacement or service*; and *adjustment*, in which engine adjustments are returned to original specifications. Since the advent of emission control equipment, precision adjustment has become increasingly critical, in order to maintain pollutant emission levels.

Analysis

The procedures below are used to indicate where adjustments, parts service or replacement are necessary within the realm of a normal tune-up. If, following these tests, all systems appear to be functioning properly, proceed to the Troubleshooting Section for further diagnosis.

—Remove all spark plugs, noting the cylinder in which they were installed. Remove the air cleaner, and position the throttle and choke in the full open position. Disconnect the coil high tension lead from the coil and the distributor cap. Insert a compression gauge into the spark plug port of each cylinder, in succession, and crank the engine with the starter to obtain the highest possible reading. Record the readings, and compare the highest to the lowest on the compression pressure limit chart. If the difference exceeds the limits on the chart, or if all readings are excessively low, proceed to a wet compression check (see Troubleshooting Section).

Maxi. Press. Lbs. Sq. In.	*Min. Press. Lbs. Sq. In.*	*Max. Press. Lbs. Sq. In.*	*Min. Press. Lbs. Sq. In.*
134	101	188	141
136	102	190	142
138	104	192	144
140	105	194	145
142	107	196	147
146	110	198	148
148	111	200	150
150	113	202	151
152	114	204	153
154	115	206	154
156	117	208	156
158	118	210	157
160	120	212	158
162	121	214	160
164	123	216	162
166	124	218	163
168	126	220	165
170	127	222	166
172	129	224	168
174	131	226	169
176	132	228	171
178	133	230	172
180	135	232	174
182	136	234	175
184	138	236	177
186	140	238	178

Compression pressure limits
© Buick Div. G.M. Corp.)

—Evaluate the spark plugs according to the spark plug chart in the Troubleshooting Section, and proceed as indicated in the chart.

—Remove the distributor cap, and inspect it inside and out for cracks and/or carbon tracks, and inside for excessive wear or burning of the rotor contacts. If any of these faults are evident, the cap must be replaced.

—Check the breaker points for burning, pitting or wear, and the contact heel resting on the distributor cam for excessive wear. If defects are noted, replace the entire breaker point set.

—Remove and inspect the rotor. If the contacts are burned or worn, or if the rotor is excessively loose on the distributor shaft (where applicable), the rotor must be replaced.

—Inspect the spark plug leads and the coil high tension lead for cracks or brittleness. If any of the wires appear defective, the entire set should be replaced.

—Check the air filter to ensure that it is functioning properly.

Parts Replacement and Service

The determination of whether to replace or service parts is at the mechanic's discretion; however, it is suggested that any parts in questionable condition be replaced rather than reused.

—Clean and regap, or replace, the spark plugs as needed. Lightly coat the threads with engine oil and install the plugs. CAUTION: *Do not over-torque taper-seat spark plugs, or plugs being installed in aluminum cylinder heads.*

SPARK PLUG TORQUE

Thread size	Cast-Iron Heads	Aluminum Heads
10 mm.	14	11
14 mm.	30	27
18 mm.	34*	32
7/8 in.—18	37	35

* 17 ft. lbs. for tapered plugs using no gaskets.

—If the distributor cap is to be reused, clean the inside with a dry rag, and remove corrosion from the rotor contact points with fine emery cloth. Remove the spark plug wires one by one, and clean the wire ends and the inside of the towers. If the boots are loose, they should be replaced.

If the cap is to be replaced, transfer the wires one by one, cleaning the wire ends and replacing the boots if necessary.

—If the original points are to remain in service, clean them lightly with emery cloth, lubricate the contact heel with grease specifically designed for this purpose. Rotate the crankshaft until the heel rests on a high point of the distributor cam, and adjust the point gap to specifications.

When replacing the points, remove the original points and condenser, and wipe out the inside of the distributor housing with a clean, dry rag. Lightly lubricate the contact heel and pivot point, and install the points and condenser. Rotate the crankshaft until the heel rests on a high point of the distributor cam, and adjust the point gap to specifications. NOTE: *Always replace the condenser when changing the points.*

—If the rotor is to be reused, clean the contacts with solvent. Do not alter the spring tension of the rotor center contact. Install the rotor and the distributor cap.

—Replace the coil high tension lead and/or the spark plug leads as necessary.

—Clean the carburetor using a spray solvent (e.g., Gumout Spray). Remove the varnish from the throttle bores, and clean the linkage. Disconnect and plug the fuel line, and run the engine until it runs out of fuel. Partially fill the float chamber with solvent, and reconnect the fuel line. In extreme cases, the jets can be pressure flushed by inserting a rubber plug into the float vent, running the spray nozzle through it, and spraying the solvent until it squirts out of the venturi fuel dump.

—Clean and tighten all wiring connections in the primary electrical circuit.

Additional Services

The following services *should* be performed in conjunction with a routine tune-up to ensure efficient performance.

—Inspect the battery and fill to the proper level with distilled water. Remove the cable clamps, clean clamps and posts thoroughly, coat the posts lightly with petroleum jelly, reinstall and tighten.

—Inspect all belts, replace and/or adjust as necessary.

—Test the PCV valve (if so equipped), and clean or replace as indicated. Clean all crankcase ventilation hoses, or replace if cracked or hardened.

—Adjust the valves (if necessary) to manufacturer's specifications.

Adjustment

—Connect a dwell-tachometer between the distributor primary lead and ground. Remove the distributor cap and rotor (unless equipped with Delco externally adjustable distributor). With the ignition off, crank the engine with a remote starter switch and measure the point dwell angle. Adjust the dwell angle to specifications. NOTE: *Increasing the gap decreases the dwell angle and vice-versa.* Install the rotor and distributor cap.

—Connect a timing light according to the manufacturer's specifications. Identify the proper timing marks with chalk or paint. NOTE: *Luminescent (day-glo) paint is excellent for this purpose.* Start the engine, and run it until it reaches operating temperature. Disconnect and plug any distributor vacuum lines, and adjust idle to the speed required to adjust timing, according to specifications. Loosen the distributor clamp and adjust timing to specifications by rotating the distributor in the engine. NOTE: *To advance timing, rotate distributor opposite normal direction of rotor rotation, and vice-versa.*

—Synchronize the throttles and mixture of multiple carburetors (if so equipped) according to procedures given in the individual car sections.

—Adjust the idle speed, mixture, and idle quality, as specified in the car sections. Final idle adjustments should be made with the air cleaner installed. CAUTION: *Due to strict emission control requirements on 1969 and later models, special test equipment (CO meter, SUN Tester) may be necessary to properly adjust idle mixture to specifications.*

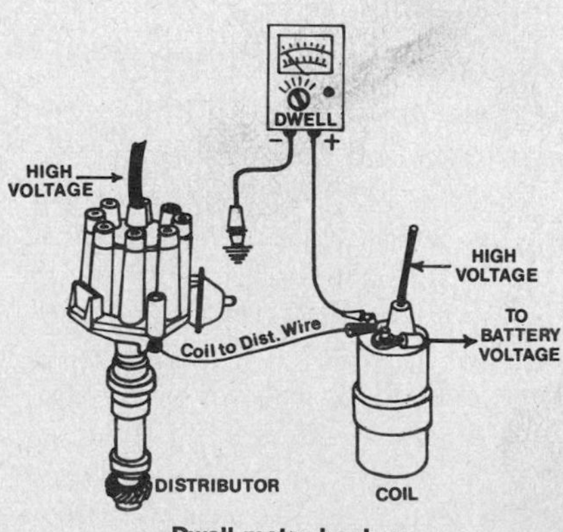

Dwell meter hook-up

Engine Troubleshooting

The following section is designed to aid in the rapid diagnosis of engine problems. The systematic format is used to diagnose problems ranging from engine starting difficulties to the need for engine overhaul. It is assumed that the user is equipped with basic hand tools and test equipment (tach-dwell meter, timing light, voltmeter, and ohmmeter).

Troubleshooting is divided into two sections. The first, *General Diagnosis*, is used to locate the problem area. In the second, *Specific Diagnosis*, the problem is systematically evaluated.

General Diagnosis

PROBLEM: Symptom	*Begin diagnosis at Section Two, Number ———*
Engine won't start:	
Starter doesn't turn	1.1, 2.1
Starter turns, engine doesn't	2.1
Starter turns engine very slowly	1.1, 2.4
Starter turns engine normally	3.1, 4.1
Starter turns engine very quickly	6.1
Engine fires intermittently	4.1
Engine fires consistently	5.1, 6.1
Engine runs poorly:	
Hard starting	3.1, 4.1, 5.1, 8.1
Rough idle	4.1, 5.1, 8.1
Stalling	3.1, 4.1, 5.1, 8.1
Engine dies at high speeds	4.1, 5.1
Hesitation (on acceleration from standing stop)	5.1, 8.1
Poor pickup	4.1, 5.1, 8.1
Lack of power	3.1, 4.1, 5.1, 8.1
Backfire through the carburetor	4.1, 8.1, 9.1
Backfire through the exhaust	4.1, 8.1, 9.1
Blue exhaust gases	6.1, 7.1
Black exhaust gases	5.1
Running on (after the ignition is shut off)	3.1, 8.1
Susceptible to moisture	4.1
Engine misfires under load	4.1, 7.1, 8.4, 9.1
Engine misfires at speed	4.1, 8.4
Engine misfires at idle	3.1, 4.1, 5.1, 7.1, 8.4

PROBLEM: Symptom	*Probable Cause*
Engine noises: ①	
Metallic grind while starting	Starter drive not engaging completely
Constant grind or rumble	*Starter drive not releasing, worn main bearings
Constant knock	Worn connecting rod bearings
Knock under load	Fuel octane too low, worn connecting rod bearings
Double knock	Loose piston pin
Metallic tap	*Collapsed or sticky valve lifter, excessive valve clearance, excessive end play in a rotating shaft
Scrape	*Fan belt contacting a stationary surface
Tick while starting	S.U. electric fuel pump (normal), starter brushes
Constant tick	*Generator brushes, shreaded fan belt
Squeal	*Improperly tensioned fan belt
Hiss or roar	*Steam escaping through a leak in the cooling system or the radiator overflow vent
Whistle	*Vacuum leak
Wheeze	Loose or cracked spark plug

①—It is extremely difficult to evaluate vehicle noises. While the above are general definitions of engine noises, those starred (*) should be considered as possibly originating elsewhere in the car. To aid diagnosis, the following list considers other potential sources of these sounds.

Metallic grind:
Throwout bearing; transmission gears, bearings, or synchronizers; differential bearings, gears; something metallic in contact with brake drum or disc.

Metallic tap:
U-joints; fan-to-radiator (or shroud) contact.

Scrape:
Brake shoe or pad dragging; tire to body contact; suspension contacting undercarriage or exhaust; something non-metallic contacting brake shoe or drum.

Tick:
Transmission gears; differential gears; lack of radio suppression; resonant vibration of body panels; windshield wiper motor or transmission; heater motor and blower.

Squeal:
Brake shoe or pad not fully releasing; tires (excessive wear, uneven wear, improper inflation); front or rear wheel alignment (most commonly due to improper toe-in).

Hiss or whistle:
Wind leaks (body or window); heater motor and blower fan.

Roar:
Wheel bearings; wind leaks (body and window).

Specific Diagnosis

This section is arranged so that following each test, instructions are given to proceed to another, until a problem is diagnosed.

INDEX

Group		Topic
1	*	Battery
2	*	Cranking system
3	*	Primary electrical system
4	*	Secondary electrical system
5	*	Fuel system
6	*	Engine compression
7	**	Engine vacuum
8	**	Secondary electrical system
9	**	Valve train
10	**	Exhaust system
11	**	Cooling system
12	**	Engine lubrication

*—The engine need not be running.
**—The engine must be running.

SAMPLE SECTION

Test and Procedure	*Results and Indications*	*Proceed to*
4.1—Check for spark: Hold each spark plug wire approximately ¼″ from ground with gloves or a heavy, dry rag. Crank the engine and observe the spark.	If no spark is evident:	4.2
	If spark is good in some cases:	4.3
	If spark is good in all cases:	4.6

DIAGNOSIS

Test and Procedure	Results and Indications	Proceed to
1.1—Inspect the battery visually for case condition (corrosion, cracks) and water level.	If case is cracked, replace battery:	1.4
	If the case is intact, remove corrosion with a solution of baking soda and water (CAUTION: *do not get the solution into the battery*), and fill with water:	1.2
1.2—Check the battery cable connections: Insert a screwdriver between the battery post and the cable clamp. Turn the headlights on high beam, and observe them as the screwdriver is gently twisted to ensure good metal to metal contact.	If the lights brighten, remove and clean the clamp and post; coat the post with petroleum jelly, install and tighten the clamp:	1.4
	If no improvement is noted:	1.3
1.3—Test the state of charge of the battery using an individual cell tester or hydrometer.	If indicated, charge the battery. NOTE: *If no obvious reason exists for the low state of charge (i.e., battery age, prolonged storage), the charging system should be tested:*	1.4

Testing battery cable connections using a screwdriver

Spec. Grav. Reading	*Charged Condition*
1.260-1.280	Fully Charged
1.230-1.250	Three Quarter Charged
1.200-1.220	One Half Charged
1.170-1.190	One Quarter Charged
1.140-1.160	Just About Flat
1.110-1.130	All The Way Down

State of battery charge

The effect of temperature on the specific gravity of battery electrolyte

Test and Procedure	*Results and Indications*	*Proceed to*
1.4—Visually inspect battery cables for cracking, bad connection to ground, or bad connection to starter.	If necessary, tighten connections or replace the cables:	2.1

Tests in Group 2 are performed with coil high tension lead disconnected to prevent accidental starting.

Test and Procedure	*Results and Indications*	*Proceed to*
2.1—Test the starter motor and solenoid: Connect a jumper from the battery post of the solenoid (or relay) to the ignition switch post of the solenoid (or relay).	If starter turns the engine normally:	2.2
	If the starter buzzes, or turns the engine very slowly:	2.4
	If no response, replace the solenoid (or relay).	3.1
	If the starter turns, but the engine doesn't, ensure that the flywheel ring gear is intact. If the gear is undamaged, replace the starter drive.	3.1
2.2—Determine whether ignition override switches are functioning properly (clutch start switch, neutral safety switch), by connecting a jumper across the switch(es), and turning the ignition switch to "start".	If starter operates, adjust or replace switch:	3.1
	If the starter doesn't operate:	2.3
2.3—Check the ignition switch "start" position: Connect a 12V test lamp between the starter post of the solenoid (or relay) and ground. Turn the ignition switch to the "start" position, and jiggle the key.	If the lamp doesn't light when the switch is turned, check the ignition switch for loose connections, cracked insulation, or broken wires. Repair or replace as necessary:	3.1
	If the lamp flickers when the key is jiggled, replace the ignition switch.	3.3

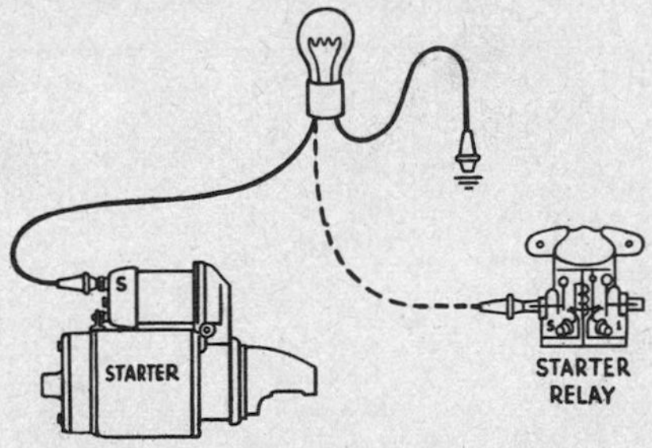

Checking the ignition switch "start" position

Test and Procedure	*Results and Indications*	*Proceed to*
2.4—Remove and bench test the starter, according to specifications in the car section.	If the starter does not meet specifications, repair or replace as needed:	3.1
	If the starter is operating properly:	2.5
2.5—Determine whether the engine can turn freely: Remove the spark plugs, and check for water in the cylinders. Check for water on the dipstick, or oil in the radiator. Attempt to turn the engine using an 18″ flex drive and socket on the crankshaft pulley nut or bolt.	If the engine will turn freely only with the spark plugs out, and hydrostatic lock (water in the cylinders) is ruled out, check valve timing:	9.2
	If engine will not turn freely, and it is known that the clutch and transmission are free, the engine must be disassembled for further evaluation:	Next Chapter

Tests and Procedures	*Results and Indications*	*Proceed to*
3.1—Check the ignition switch "on" position: Connect a jumper wire between the distributor side of the coil and ground, and a 12V test lamp between the switch side of the coil and ground. Remove the high tension lead from the coil. Turn the ignition switch on and jiggle the key.	If the lamp lights:	3.2
	If the lamp flickers when the key is jiggled, replace the ignition switch:	3.3
	If the lamp doesn't light, check for loose or open connections. If none are found, remove the ignition switch and check for continuity. If the switch is faulty, replace it:	3.3
Checking the ignition switch "on" position		
3.2—Check the ballast resistor or resistance wire for an open circuit, using an ohmmeter.	Replace the resistor or the resistance wire if the resistance is zero.	3.3
3.3—Visually inspect the breaker points for burning, pitting, or excessive wear. Gray coloring of the point contact surfaces is normal. Rotate the crankshaft until the contact heel rests on a high point of the distributor cam, and adjust the point gap to specifications.	If the breaker points are intact, clean the contact surfaces with fine emery cloth, and adjust the point gap to specifications. If pitted or worn, replace the points and condenser, and adjust the gap to specifications:	3.4
	NOTE: *Always lubricate the distributor cam according to manufacturer's recommendations when servicing the breaker points.*	
3.4—Connect a dwell meter between the distributor primary lead and ground. Crank the engine and observe the point dwell angle.	If necessary, adjust the point dwell angle: NOTE: *Increasing the point gap decreases the dwell angle, and vice-versa.*	3.6
	If dwell meter shows little or no reading:	3.5
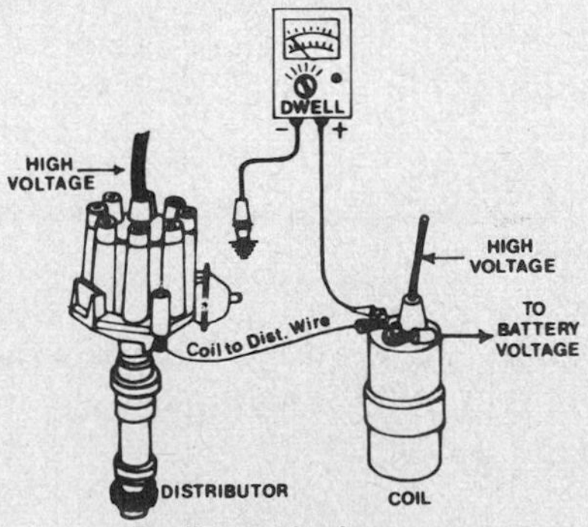 Dwell meter hook-up	Dwell angle	
3.5—Check the condenser for short: Connect an ohmmeter across the condenser body and the pigtail lead.	If any reading other than infinite resistance is noted, replace the condenser:	3.6
Checking the condenser for short		

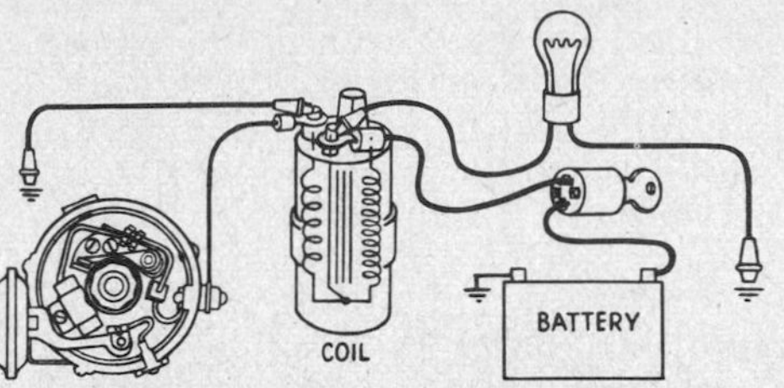

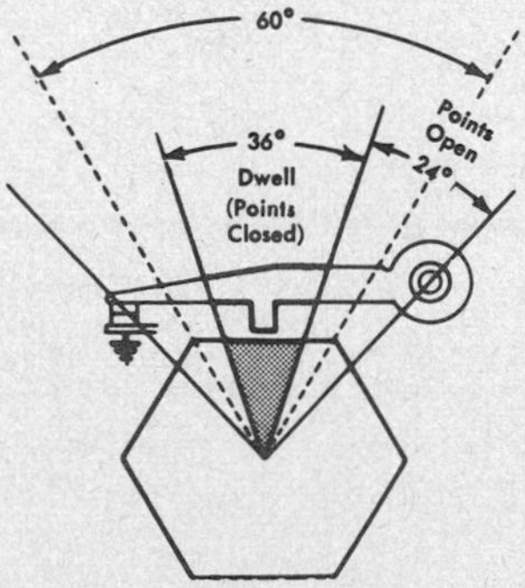

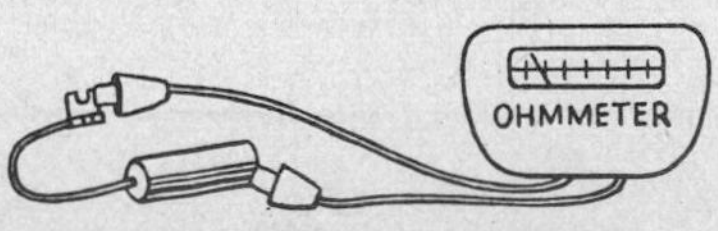

Test and Procedure	Results and Indications	Proceed to
3.6—Test the coil primary resistance: Connect an ohmmeter across the coil primary terminals, and read the resistance on the low scale. Note whether an external ballast resistor or resistance wire is utilized.	Coils utilizing ballast resistors or resistance wires should have approximately 1.0Ω resistance; coils with internal resistors should have approximately 4.0Ω resistance. If values far from the above are noted, replace the coil:	4.1
Testing the coil primary resistance		
4.1—Check for spark: Hold each spark plug wire approximately ¼″ from ground with gloves or a heavy, dry rag. Crank the engine, and observe the spark.	If no spark is evident:	4.2
	If spark is good in some cylinders:	4.3
	If spark is good in all cylinders:	4.6
4.2—Check for spark at the coil high tension lead: Remove the coil high tension lead from the distributor and position it approximately ¼″ from ground. Crank the engine and observe spark. CAUTION: *This test should not be performed on cars equipped with transistorized ignition.*	If the spark is good and consistent:	4.3
	If the spark is good but intermittent, test the primary electrical system starting at 3.3:	3.3
	If the spark is weak or non-existent, replace the coil high tension lead, clean and tighten all connections and retest. If no improvement is noted:	4.4
4.3—Visually inspect the distributor cap and rotor for burned or corroded contacts, cracks, carbon tracks, or moisture. Also check the fit of the rotor on the distributor shaft (where applicable).	If moisture is present, dry thoroughly, and retest per 4.1:	4.1
	If burned or excessively corroded contacts, cracks, or carbon tracks are noted, replace the defective part(s) and retest per 4.1:	4.1
	If the rotor and cap appear intact, or are only slightly corroded, clean the contacts thoroughly (including the cap towers and spark plug wire ends) and retest per 4.1:	
	If the spark is good in all cases:	4.6
	If the spark is poor in all cases:	4.5
4.4—Check the coil secondary resistance: Connect an ohmmeter across the distributor side of the coil and the coil tower. Read the resistance on the high scale of the ohmmeter.	The resistance of a satisfactory coil should be between 4KΩ and 10KΩ. If the resistance is considerably higher (i.e., 40KΩ) replace the coil, and retest per 4.1: NOTE: *This does not apply to high performance coils.*	4.1
Testing the coil secondary resistance		

Test and Procedure	Results and Indications	Proceed to
4.5—Visually inspect the spark plug wires for cracking or brittleness. Ensure that no two wires are positioned so as to cause induction firing (adjacent and parallel). Remove each wire, one by one, and check resistance with an ohmmeter.	Replace any cracked or brittle wires. If any of the wires are defective, replace the entire set. Replace any wires with excessive resistance (over 8000Ω per foot for suppression wire), and separate any wires that might cause induction firing.	4.6
4.6—Remove the spark plugs, noting the cylinders from which they were removed, and evaluate according to the chart below.	See below.	See below.

Condition	Cause	Remedy	Proceed to
Electrodes eroded, light brown deposits.	Normal wear. Normal wear is indicated by approximately .001″ wear per 1000 miles.	Clean and regap the spark plug if wear is not excessive: Replace the spark plug if excessively worn:	4.7
Carbon fouling (black, dry, fluffy deposits).	If present on one or two plugs:		
	Faulty high tension lead(s).	Test the high tension leads:	4.5
	Burnt or sticking valve(s).	Check the valve train: (Clean and regap the plugs in either case.)	9.1
	If present on most or all plugs: Overly rich fuel mixture, due to restricted air filter, improper carburetor adjustment, improper choke or heat riser adjustment or operation.	Check the fuel system:	5.1
Oil fouling (wet black deposits)	Worn engine components. NOTE: *Oil fouling may occur in new or recently rebuilt engines until broken in.*	Check engine vacuum and compression:	6.1
		Replace with new spark plug	
Lead fouling (gray, black, tan, or yellow deposits, which appear glazed or cinder-like).	Combustion by-products.	Clean and regap the plugs: (Use plugs of a different heat range if the problem recurs.)	4.7

Condition	Cause	Remedy	Proceed to
Gap bridging (deposits lodged between the electrodes).	Incomplete combustion, or transfer of deposits from the combustion chamber.	Replace the spark plugs:	4.7
Overheating (burnt electrodes, and extremely white insulator with small black spots).	Ignition timing advanced too far.	Adjust timing to specifications:	8.2
	Overly lean fuel mixture.	Check the fuel system:	5.1
	Spark plugs not seated properly.	Clean spark plug seat and install a new gasket washer: (Replace the spark plugs in all cases.)	4.7
Fused spot deposits on the insulator.	Combustion chamber blow-by.	Clean and regap the spark plugs:	4.7
Pre-ignition (melted or severely burned electrodes, blistered or cracked insulators, or metallic deposits on the insulator).	Incorrect spark plug heat range.	Replace with plugs of the proper heat range:	4.7
	Ignition timing advanced too far.	Adjust timing to specifications:	8.2
	Spark plugs not being cooled efficiently.	Clean the spark plug seat, and check the cooling system:	11.1
	Fuel mixture too lean.	Check the fuel system:	5.1
	Poor compression.	Check compression:	6.1
	Fuel grade too low.	Use higher octane fuel:	4.7

Test and Procedure	Results and Indications	Proceed to
4.7—Determine the static ignition timing: Using the flywheel or crankshaft pulley timing marks as a guide, locate top dead center on the *compression* stroke of the No. 1 cylinder. Remove the distributor cap.	Adjust the distributor so that the rotor points toward the No. 1 tower in the distributor cap, and the points are just opening:	4.8
4.8—Check coil polarity: Connect a voltmeter negative lead to the coil high tension lead, and the positive lead to ground (NOTE: *reverse the hook-up for positive ground cars*). Crank the engine momentarily. (Checking coil polarity)	If the voltmeter reads up-scale, the polarity is correct:	5.1
	If the voltmeter reads down-scale, reverse the coil polarity (switch the primary leads):	5.1

Test and Procedure	Results and Indications	Proceed to
5.1—Determine that the air filter is functioning efficiently: Hold paper elements up to a strong light, and attempt to see light through the filter.	Clean permanent air filters in gasoline (or manufacturer's recommendation), and allow to dry. Replace paper elements through which light cannot be seen:	5.2
5.2—Determine whether a flooding condition exists: Flooding is identified by a strong gasoline odor, and excessive gasoline present in the throttle bore(s) of the carburetor.	If flooding is not evident:	5.3
	If flooding is evident, permit the gasoline to dry for a few moments and restart.	
	If flooding doesn't recur:	5.6
	If flooding is persistant:	5.5
5.3—Check that fuel is reaching the carburetor: Detach the fuel line at the carburetor inlet. Hold the end of the line in a cup (not styrofoam), and crank the engine.	If fuel flows smoothly:	5.6
	If fuel doesn't flow (NOTE: *Make sure that there is fuel in the tank*), or flows erratically:	5.4
5.4—Test the fuel pump: Disconnect all fuel lines from the fuel pump. Hold a finger over the input fitting, crank the engine (with electric pump, turn the ignition or pump on), and feel for suction.	If suction is evident, blow out the fuel line to the tank with low pressure compressed air until bubbling is heard from the fuel filler neck. Also blow out the carburetor fuel line (both ends disconnected):	5.6
	If no suction is evident, replace or repair the fuel pump:	5.6
	NOTE: *Repeated oil fouling of the spark plugs, or a no-start condition, could be the result of a ruptured vacuum booster pump diaphragm, through which oil or gasoline is being drawn into the intake manifold (where applicable).*	
5.5—Check the needle and seat: Tap the carburetor in the area of the needle and seat.	If flooding stops, a gasoline additive (e.g., Gumout) will often cure the problem:	5.6
	If flooding continues, check the fuel pump for excessive pressure at the carburetor (according to specifications). If the pressure is normal, the needle and seat must be removed and checked, and/or the float level adjusted:	5.6
5.6—Test the accelerator pump by looking into the throttle bores while operating the throttle.	If the accelerator pump appears to be operating normally:	5.7
	If the accelerator pump is not operating, the pump must be reconditioned. Where possible, service the pump with the carburetor(s) installed on the engine. If necessary, remove the carburetor. Prior to removal:	5.7
5.7—Determine whether the carburetor main fuel system is functioning: Spray a commercial starting fluid into the carburetor while attempting to start the engine.	If the engine starts, runs for a few seconds, and dies:	5.8
	If the engine doesn't start:	6.1

Test and Procedures	Results and Indications	Proceed to
5.8—Uncommon fuel system malfunctions: See below:	If the problem is solved:	6.1
	If the problem remains, remove and recondition the carburetor.	

Condition	Indication	Test	Usual Weather Conditions	Remedy
Vapor lock	Car will not restart shortly after running.	Cool the components of the fuel system until the engine starts.	Hot to very hot	Ensure that the exhaust manifold heat control valve is operating. Check with the vehicle manufacturer for the recommended solution to vapor lock on the model in question.
Carburetor icing	Car will not idle, stalls at low speeds.	Visually inspect the throttle plate area of the throttle bores for frost.	High humidity, 32-40° F.	Ensure that the exhaust manifold heat control valve is operating, and that the intake manifold heat riser is not blocked.
Water in the fuel	Engine sputters and stalls; may not start.	Pump a small amount of fuel into a glass jar. Allow to stand, and inspect for droplets or a layer of water.	High humidity, extreme temperature changes.	For droplets, use one or two cans of commercial gas dryer (Dry Gas) For a layer of water, the tank must be drained, and the fuel lines blown out with compressed air.

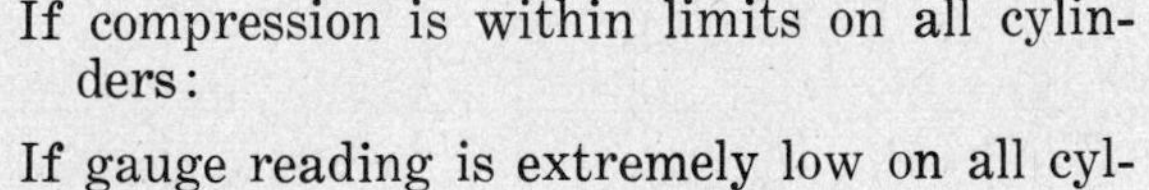

Test and Procedure	Results and Indications	Proceed to
6.1—Test engine compression: Remove all spark plugs. Insert a compression gauge into a spark plug port, crank the engine to obtain the maximum reading, and record.	If compression is within limits on all cylinders:	7.1
	If gauge reading is extremely low on all cylinders:	6.2
	If gauge reading is low on one or two cylinders:	6.2
	(If gauge readings are identical and low on two or more adjacent cylinders, the head gasket must be replaced.)	

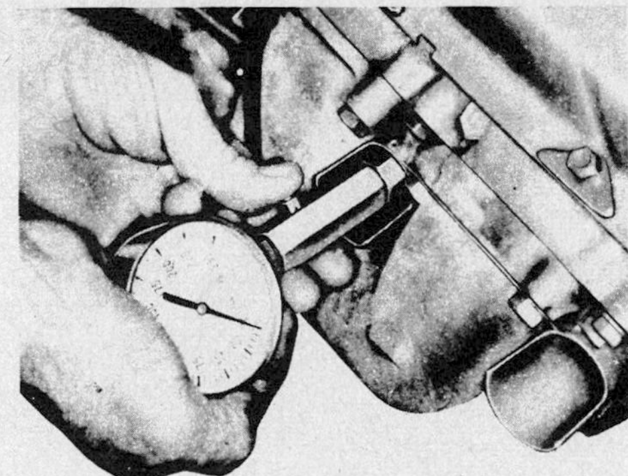

Testing compression
(© Chevrolet Div. G.M. Corp.)

Maxi. Press. Lbs. Sq. In.	Min. Press. Lbs. Sq. In.	Maxi. Press. Lbs. Sq. In.	Min. Press. Lbs. Sq. In.	Max. Press. Lbs. Sq. In.	Min. Press. Lbs. Sq. In.	Max. Press. Lbs. Sq. In.	Min. Press. Lbs. Sq. In.
134	101	162	121	188	141	214	160
136	102	164	123	190	142	216	162
138	104	166	124	192	144	218	163
140	105	168	126	194	145	220	165
142	107	170	127	196	147	222	166
146	110	172	129	198	148	224	168
148	111	174	131	200	150	226	169
150	113	176	132	202	151	228	171
152	114	178	133	204	153	230	172
154	115	180	135	206	154	232	174
156	117	182	136	208	156	234	175
158	118	184	138	210	157	236	177
160	120	186	140	212	158	238	178

Compression pressure limits
(© Buick Div. G.M. Corp.)

Test and Procedure	Results and Indications	Proceed to
6.2—Test engine compression (wet): Squirt approximately 30 cc. of engine oil into each cylinder, and retest per 6.1.	If the readings improve, worn or cracked rings or broken pistons are indicated: If the readings do not improve, burned or excessively carboned valves or a jumped timing chain are indicated: NOTE: *A jumped timing chain is often indicated by difficult cranking.*	Next Chapter 7.1
7.1—Perform a vacuum check of the engine: Attach a vacuum gauge to the intake manifold beyond the throttle plate. Start the engine, and observe the action of the needle over the range of engine speeds.	See below.	See below

Reading	Indications	Proceed to
 Steady, from 17-22 in. Hg.	Normal.	8.1
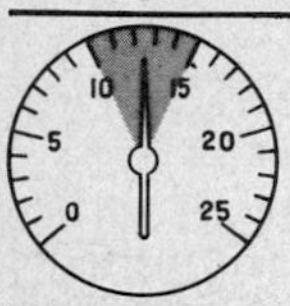 Low and steady.	Late ignition or valve timing, or low compression:	6.1
 Very low	Vacuum leak:	
 Needle fluctuates as engine speed increases.	Ignition miss, blown cylinder head gasket, leaking valve or weak valve spring:	6.1, 8.3
 Gradual drop in reading at idle.	Excessive back pressure in the exhaust system:	10.1
 Intermittent fluctuation at idle.	Ignition miss, sticking valve:	8.3, 9.1
 Drifting needle.	Improper idle mixture adjustment, carburetors not synchronized (where applicable), or minor intake leak. Synchronize the carburetors, adjust the idle, and retest. If the condition persists:	7.2
 High and steady.	Early ignition timing:	8.2

Test and Procedure	Results and Indications	Proceed to
7.2—Attach a vacuum gauge per 7.1, and test for an intake manifold leak. Squirt a small amount of oil around the intake manifold gaskets, carburetor gaskets, plugs and fittings. Observe the action of the vacuum gauge.	If the reading improves, replace the indicated gasket, or seal the indicated fitting or plug:	8.1
	If the reading remains low:	7.3
7.3—Test all vacuum hoses and accessories for leaks as described in 7.2. Also check the carburetor body (dashpots, automatic choke mechanism, throttle shafts) for leaks in the same manner.	If the reading improves, service or replace the offending part(s):	8.1
	If the reading remains low:	6.1
8.1—Check the point dwell angle: Connect a dwell meter between the distributor primary wire and ground. Start the engine, and observe the dwell angle from idle to 3000 rpm.	If necessary, adjust the dwell angle. NOTE: *Increasing the point gap reduces the dwell angle and vice-versa.* If the dwell angle moves outside specifications as engine speed increases, the distributor should be removed and checked for cam accuracy, shaft endplay and concentricity, bushing wear, and adequate point arm tension (NOTE: *Most of these items may be checked with the distributor installed in the engine, using an oscilloscope*):	8.2
8.2—Connect a timing light (per manufacturer's recommendation) and check the dynamic ignition timing. Disconnect and plug the vacuum hose(s) to the distributor if specified, start the engine, and observe the timing marks at the specified engine speed.	If the timing is not correct, adjust to specifications by rotating the distributor in the engine: (Advance timing by rotating distributor opposite normal direction of rotor rotation, retard timing by rotating distributor in same direction as rotor rotation.)	8.3
8.3—Check the operation of the distributor advance mechanism(s): To test the mechanical advance, disconnect all but the mechanical advance, and observe the timing marks with a timing light as the engine speed is increased from idle. If the mark moves smoothly, without hesitation, it may be assumed that the mechanical advance is functioning properly. To test vacuum advance and/or retard systems, alternately crimp and release the vacuum line, and observe the timing mark for movement. If movement is noted, the system is operating.	If the systems are functioning:	8.4
	If the systems are not functioning, remove the distributor, and test on a distributor tester:	8.4
8.4—Locate an ignition miss: With the engine running, remove each spark plug wire, one by one, until one is found that doesn't cause the engine to roughen and slow down.	When the missing cylinder is identified:	4.1

Test and Procedure	Results and Indications	Proceed to
9.1—Evaluate the valve train: Remove the valve cover, and ensure that the valves are adjusted to specifications. A mechanic's stethoscope may be used to aid in the diagnosis of the valve train. By pushing the probe on or near push rods or rockers, valve noise often can be isolated. A timing light also may be used to diagnose valve problems. Connect the light according to manufacturer's recommendations, and start the engine. Vary the firing moment of the light by increasing the engine speed (and therefore the ignition advance), and moving the trigger from cylinder to cylinder. Observe the movement of each valve.	See below	See below

Observation	Probable Cause	Remedy	Proceed to
Metallic tap heard through the stethoscope.	Sticking hydraulic lifter or excessive valve clearance.	Adjust valve. If tap persists, remove and replace the lifter:	10.1
Metallic tap through the stethoscope, able to push the rocker arm (lifter side) down by hand.	Collapsed valve lifter.	Remove and replace the lifter:	10.1
Erratic, irregular motion of the valve stem.*	Sticking valve, burned valve.	Recondition the valve and/or valve guide:	Next Chapter
Eccentric motion of the pushrod at the rocker arm.*	Bent pushrod.	Replace the pushrod:	10.1
Valve retainer bounces as the valve closes.*	Weak valve spring or damper.	Remove and test the spring and damper. Replace if necessary:	10.1

*—When observed with a timing light.

Test and Procedure	Results and Indications	Proceed to
9.2—Check the valve timing: Locate top dead center of the No. 1 piston, and install a degree wheel or tape on the crankshaft pulley or damper with zero corresponding to an index mark on the engine. Rotate the crankshaft in its direction of rotation, and observe the opening of the No. 1 cylinder intake valve. The opening should correspond with the correct mark on the degree wheel according to specifications.	If the timing is not correct, the timing cover must be removed for further investigation:	

Test and Procedure	*Results and Indications*	*Proceed to*
10.1—Determine whether the exhaust manifold heat control valve is operating: Operate the valve by hand to determine whether it is free to move. If the valve is free, run the engine to operating temperature and observe the action of the valve, to ensure that it is opening.	If the valve sticks, spray it with a suitable solvent, open and close the valve to free it, and retest.	
	If the valve functions properly:	10.2
	If the valve does not free, or does not operate, replace the valve:	10.2
10.2—Ensure that there are no exhaust restrictions: Visually inspect the exhaust system for kinks, dents, or crushing. Also note that gasses are flowing freely from the tailpipe at all engine speeds, indicating no restriction in the muffler or resonator.	Replace any damaged portion of the system:	11.1
11.1—Visually inspect the fan belt for glazing, cracks, and fraying, and replace if necessary. Tighten the belt so that the longest span has approximately ½″ play at its midpoint under thumb pressure.	Replace or tighten the fan belt as necessary:	11.2
11.2—Check the fluid level of the cooling system.	If full or slightly low, fill as necessary:	11.5
	If extremely low:	11.3
11.3—Visually inspect the external portions of the cooling system (radiator, radiator hoses, thermostat elbow, water pump seals, heater hoses, etc.) for leaks. If none are found, pressurize the cooling system to 14-15 psi.	If cooling system holds the pressure:	11.5
	If cooling system loses pressure rapidly, reinspect external parts of the system for leaks under pressure. If none are found, check dipstick for coolant in crankcase. If no coolant is present, but pressure loss continues:	11.4
	If coolant is evident in crankcase, remove cylinder head(s), and check gasket(s). If gaskets are intact, block and cylinder head(s) should be checked for cracks or holes.	
	If the gasket(s) is blown, replace, and purge the crankcase of coolant:	12.6
	NOTE: *Occasionally, due to atmospheric and driving conditions, condensation of water can occur in the crankcase. This causes the oil to appear milky white. To remedy, run the engine until hot, and change the oil and oil filter.*	

Checking the fan belt tension
(© Outboard Marine Corp.)

Test and Procedure	Results and Indication	Proceed to
11.4—Check for combustion leaks into the cooling system: Pressurize the cooling system as above. Start the engine, and observe the pressure gauge. If the needle fluctuates, remove each spark plug wire, one by one, noting which cylinder(s) reduce or eliminate the fluctuation. Radiator pressure tester (© American Motors Corp.)	Cylinders which reduce or eliminate the fluctuation, when the spark plug wire is removed, are leaking into the cooling system. Replace the head gasket on the affected cylinder bank(s).	
11.5—Check the radiator pressure cap: Attach a radiator pressure tester to the radiator cap (wet the seal prior to installation). Quickly pump up the pressure, noting the point at which the cap releases. Testing the radiator pressure cap (© American Motors Corp.)	If the cap releases within ± 1 psi of the specified rating, it is operating properly:	11.6
	If the cap releases at more than ± 1 psi of the specified rating, it should be replaced:	11.6
11.6—Test the thermostat: Start the engine cold, remove the radiator cap, and insert a thermometer into the radiator. Allow the engine to idle. After a short while, there will be a sudden, rapid increase in coolant temperature. The temperature at which this sharp rise stops is the thermostat opening temperature.	If the thermostat opens at or about the specified temperature:	11.7
	If the temperature doesn't increase: (If the temperature increases slowly and gradually, replace the thermostat.)	11.7
11.7—Check the water pump: Remove the thermostat elbow and the thermostat, disconnect the coil high tension lead (to prevent starting), and crank the engine momentarily.	If coolant flows, replace the thermostat and retest per 11.6:	11.6
	If coolant doesn't flow, reverse flush the cooling system to alleviate any blockage that might exist. If system is not blocked, and coolant will not flow, recondition the water pump.	—
12.1—Check the oil pressure gauge or warning light: If the gauge shows low pressure, or the light is on, for no obvious reason, remove the oil pressure sender. Install an accurate oil pressure gauge and run the engine momentarily.	If oil pressure builds normally, run engine for a few moments to determine that it is functioning normally, and replace the sender.	—
	If the pressure remains low:	12.2
	If the pressure surges:	12.3
	If the oil pressure is zero:	12.3

Test and Procedure	*Results and Indications*	*Proceed to*
12.2—Visually inspect the oil: If the oil is watery or very thin, milky, or foamy, replace the oil and oil filter.	If the oil is normal: If after replacing oil the pressure remains low: If after replacing oil the pressure becomes normal:	12.3 12.3 —
12.3—Inspect the oil pressure relief valve and spring, to ensure that it is not sticking or stuck. Remove and thoroughly clean the valve, spring, and the valve body. Oil pressure relief valve (© British Leyland Motors)	If the oil pressure improves: If no improvement is noted:	— 12.4
12.4—Check to ensure that the oil pump is not cavitating (sucking air instead of oil): See that the crankcase is neither over nor underfull, and that the pickup in the sump is in the proper position and free from sludge.	Fill or drain the crankcase to the proper capacity, and clean the pickup screen in solvent if necessary. If no improvement is noted:	12.5
12.5—Inspect the oil pump drive and the oil pump:	If the pump drive or the oil pump appear to be defective, service as necessary and retest per 12.1: If the pump drive and pump appear to be operating normally, the engine should be disassembled to determine where blockage exists:	12.1 Next Chapter
12.6—Purge the engine of ethylene glycol coolant: Completely drain the crankcase and the oil filter. Obtain a commercial butyl cellosolve base solvent, designated for this purpose, and follow the instructions precisely. Following this, install a new oil filter and refill the crankcase with the proper weight oil. The next oil and filter change should follow shortly thereafter (1000 miles).		

Engine Rebuilding

This section describes, in detail, the procedures involved in rebuilding a typical engine. The procedures specifically refer to an inline engine, however, they are basically identical to those used in rebuilding engines of nearly all design and configurations. Procedures for servicing atypical engines (i.e., horizontally opposed) are described in the appropriate section, although in most cases, cylinder head reconditioning procedures described in this chapter will apply.

The section is divided into two sections. The first, Cylinder Head Reconditioning, assumes that the cylinder head is removed from the engine, all manifolds are removed, and the cylinder head is on a workbench. The camshaft should be removed from overhead cam cylinder heads. The second section, Cylinder Block Reconditioning, covers the block, pistons, connecting rods and crankshaft. It is assumed that the engine is mounted on a work stand, and the cylinder head and all accessories are removed.

Procedures are identified as follows:

Unmarked—Basic procedures that must be performed in order to successfully complete the rebuilding process.

Starred (*)—Procedures that should be performed to ensure maximum performance and engine life.

Double starred (**)—Procedures that may be performed to increase engine performance and reliability. These procedures are usually reserved for extremely heavy-duty or competition usage.

In many cases, a choice of methods is also provided. Methods are identified in the same manner as procedures. The choice of method for a procedure is at the discretion of the user.

The tools required for the basic rebuilding procedure should, with minor exceptions, be those

TORQUE (ft. lbs.)*

U.S.

Bolt Diameter (inches)	Bolt Grade (SAE) 1 and 2	5	6	8	Wrench Size (inches) Bolt	Nut
1/4	5	7	10	10.5	3/8	7/16
5/16	9	14	19	22	1/2	9/16
3/8	15	25	34	37	9/16	5/8
7/16	24	40	55	60	5/8	3/4
1/2	37	60	85	92	3/4	13/16
9/16	53	88	120	132	7/8	7/8
5/8	74	120	167	180	15/16	1
3/4	120	200	280	296	1-1/8	1-1/8
7/8	190	302	440	473	1-5/16	1-5/16
1	282	466	660	714	1-1/2	1-1/2

Metric

Bolt Diameter (mm)	Bolt Grade 5D	8G	10K	12K	Wrench Size (mm) Bolt and Nut
6	5	6	8	10	10
8	10	16	22	27	14
10	19	31	40	49	17
12	34	54	70	86	19
14	55	89	117	137	22
16	83	132	175	208	24
18	111	182	236	283	27
22	182	284	394	464	32
24	261	419	570	689	36

*—Torque values are for lightly oiled bolts. CAUTION: Bolts threaded into aluminum require much less torque.

General Torque Specifications

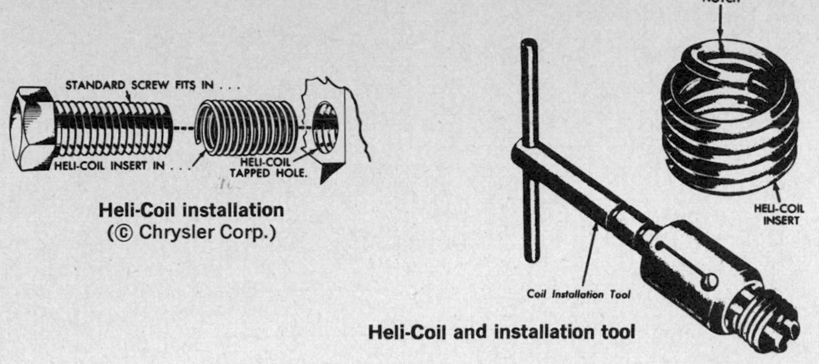

Heli-Coil installation
(© Chrysler Corp.)

Heli-Coil and installation tool

Heli-Coil Insert			*Drill*	*Tap*	*Insert. Tool*	*Extract-ing Tool*
Thread Size	*Part No.*	*Insert Length (In.)*	*Size*	*Part No.*	*Part No.*	*Part No.*
1/2 -20	1185-4	3/8	17/64(.266)	4 CPB	528-4N	1227-6
5/16-18	1185-5	15/32	Q(.332)	5 CPB	528-5N	1227-6
3/8 -16	1185-6	9/16	X(.397)	6 CPB	528-6N	1227-6
7/16-14	1185-7	21/32	29/64(.453)	7 CPB	528-7N	1227-16
1/2 -13	1185-8	3/4	33/64(.516)	8 CPB	528-8N	1227-16

Heli-Coil Specifications

included in a mechanic's tool kit. An accurate torque wrench, and a dial indicator (reading in thousandths) mounted on a universal base should be available. Bolts and nuts with no torque specification should be tightened according to size (see chart). Special tools, where required, all are readily available from the major tool suppliers (i.e., Craftsman, Snap-On, K-D). The services of a competent automotive machine shop must also be readily available.

When assembling the engine, any parts that will be in frictional contact must be pre-lubricated, to provide protection on initial start-up. Vortex Pre-Lube, STP, or any product specifically formulated for this purpose may be used. NOTE: *Do not use engine oil.* Where semi-permanent (locked but removable) installation of bolts or nuts is desired, threads should be cleaned and coated with Loctite. Studs may be permanently installed using Loctite Stud and Bearing Mount.

Aluminum has become increasingly popular for use in engines, due to its low weight and excellent heat transfer characteristics. The following precautions must be observed when handling aluminum engine parts:

—Never hot-tank aluminum parts.

—Remove all aluminum parts (identification tags, etc.) from engine parts before hot-tanking (otherwise they will be removed during the process).

—Always coat threads lightly with engine oil or anti-seize compounds before installation, to prevent seizure.

—Never over-torque bolts or spark plugs in aluminum threads. Should stripping occur, threads can be restored according to the following procedure, using Heli-Coil thread inserts:

Tap drill the hole with the stripped threads to the specified size (see chart). Using the specified tap (NOTE: *Heli-Coil tap sizes refer to the size thread being replaced, rather than the actual tap size*), tap the hole for the Heli-Coil. Place the insert on the proper installation tool (see chart). Apply pressure on the insert while winding it clockwise into the hole, until the top of the insert is one turn below the surface. Remove the installation tool, and break the installation tang from the bottom of the insert by moving it up and down. If the Heli-Coil must be removed, tap the removal tool firmly into the hole, so that it engages the top thread, and turn the tool counter-clockwise to extract the insert.

Snapped bolts or studs may be removed, using a stud extractor (unthreaded) or Vise-Grip pliers (threaded). Penetrating oil (e.g., Liquid Wrench) will often aid in breaking frozen threads. In cases where the stud or bolt is flush with, or below the surface, proceed as follows:

Drill a hole in the broken stud or bolt, approximately ½ its diameter. Select a screw extractor (e.g., Easy-Out) of the proper size, and tap it into the stud or bolt. Turn the extractor counter-clockwise to remove the stud or bolt.

Magnaflux and Zyglo are inspection techniques used to locate material flaws, such as stress cracks. Magnafluxing coats the part with fine magnetic particles, and subjects the part to a magnetic field. Cracks cause breaks in the magnetic field, which are outlined by the particles. Since Magnaflux is a magnetic process, it is applicable only to ferrous materials. The Zyglo process coats the material with a fluorescent dye penetrant, and then subjects it to blacklight inspection, under which cracks glow bright-

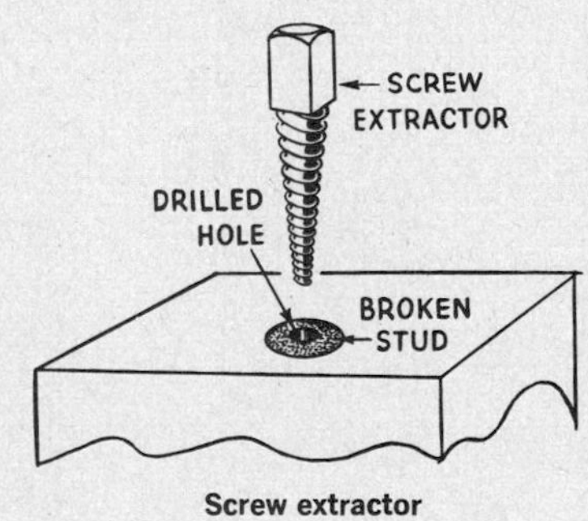

Screw extractor

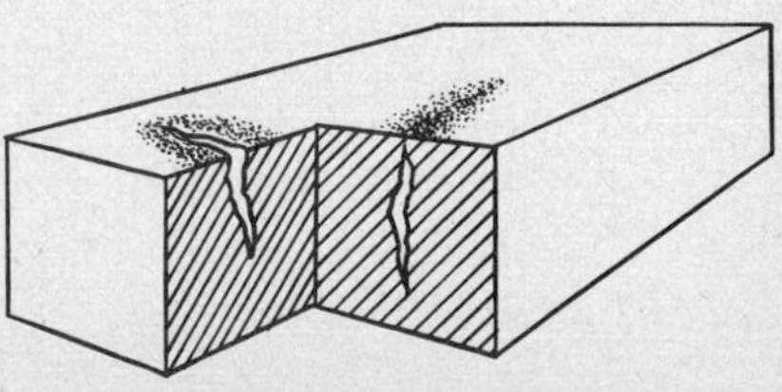
Magnaflux indication of cracks

ly. Parts made of any material may be tested using Zyglo. While Magnaflux and Zyglo are excellent for general inspection, and locating hidden defects, specific checks of suspected cracks may be made at lower cost and more readily using spot check dye. The dye is sprayed onto the suspected area, wiped off, and the area is then sprayed with a developer. Cracks then will show up brightly. Spot check dyes will only indicate surface cracks; therefore, structural cracks below the surface may escape detection. When questionable, the part should be tested using Magnaflux or Zyglo.

CYLINDER HEAD RECONDITIONING

Procedure	*Method*
Identify the valves:  Valve identification (© SAAB)	Invert the cylinder head, and number the valve faces front to rear, using a permanent felt-tip marker.
Remove the rocker arms:	Remove the rocker arms with shaft(s) or balls and nuts. Wire the sets of rockers, balls and nuts together, and identify according to the corresponding valve.
Remove the valves and springs:	Using an appropriate valve spring compressor (depending on the configuration of the cylinder head), compress the valve springs. Lift out the keepers with needlenose pliers, release the compressor, and remove the valve, spring, and spring retainer.
Check the valve stem-to-guide clearance:  Checking the valve stem-to-guide clearance (© American Motors Corp.)	Clean the valve stem with lacquer thinner or a similar solvent to remove all gum and varnish. Clean the valve guides using solvent and an expanding wire-type valve guide cleaner. Mount a dial indicator so that the stem is at 90° to the valve stem, as close to the valve guide as possible. Move the valve off its seat, and measure the valve guide-to-stem clearance by moving the stem back and forth to actuate the dial indicator. Measure the valve stems using a micrometer, and compare to specifications, to determine whether stem or guide wear is responsible for excessive clearance.
De-carbon the cylinder head and valves: 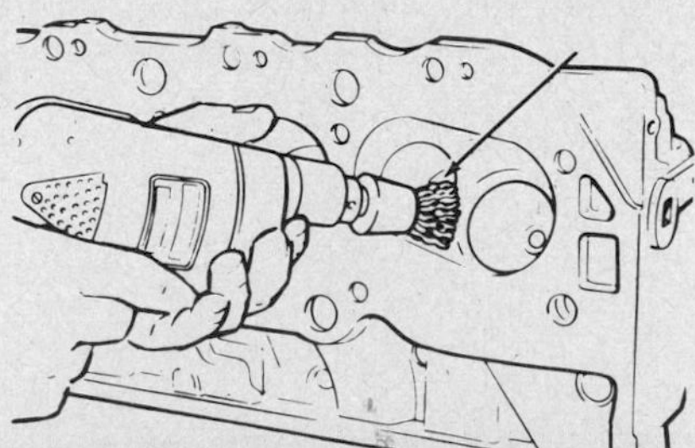 Removing carbon from the cylinder head (© Outboard Marine Corp.)	Chip carbon away from the valve heads, combustion chambers, and ports, using a chisel made of hardwood. Remove the remaining deposits with a stiff wire brush. NOTE: *Ensure that the deposits are actually removed, rather than burnished.*

Procedure	Method
Hot-tank the cylinder head:	Have the cylinder head hot-tanked to remove grease, corrosion, and scale from the water passages. NOTE: *In the case of overhead cam cylinder heads, consult the operator to determine whether the camshaft bearings will be damaged by the caustic solution.*
Degrease the remaining cylinder head parts:	Using solvent (i.e., Gunk), clean the rockers, rocker shaft(s) (where applicable), rocker balls and nuts, springs, spring retainers, and keepers. Do not remove the protective coating from the springs.
Check the cylinder head for warpage: 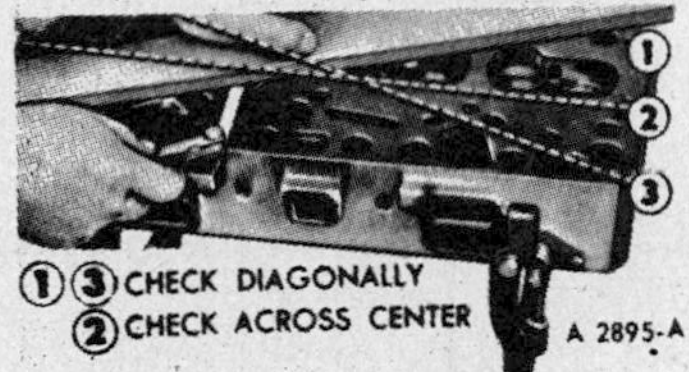 Checking the cylinder head for warpage (© Ford Motor Co.)	Place a straight-edge across the gasket surface of the cylinder head. Using feeler gauges, determine the clearance at the center of the straight-edge. Measure across both diagonals, along the longitudinal centerline, and across the cylinder head at several points. If warpage exceeds .003″ in a 6″ span, or .006″ over the total length, the cylinder head must be resurfaced. NOTE: *If warpage exceeds the manufacturers maximum tolerance for material removal, the cylinder head must be replaced.* When milling the cylinder heads of V-type engines, the intake manifold mounting position is altered, and must be corrected by milling the manifold flange a proportionate amount.
** Porting and gasket matching:  Marking the cylinder head for gasket matching (© Petersen Publishing Co.)  Port configuration before and after gasket matching (© Petersen Publishing Co.)	** Coat the manifold flanges of the cylinder head with Prussian blue dye. Glue intake and exhaust gaskets to the cylinder head in their installed position using rubber cement and scribe the outline of the ports on the manifold flanges. Remove the gaskets. Using a small cutter in a hand-held power tool (i.e., Dremel Moto-Tool), gradually taper the walls of the port out to the scribed outline of the gasket. Further enlargement of the ports should include the removal of sharp edges and radiusing of sharp corners. Do not alter the valve guides. NOTE: *The most efficient port configuration is determined only by extensive testing. Therefore, it is best to consult someone experienced with the head in question to determine the optimum alterations.*

Procedure | *Method*

** Polish the ports:

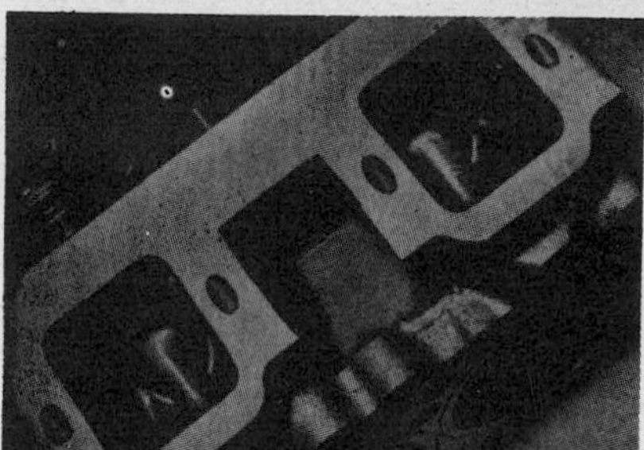
Relieved and polished ports
(© Petersen Publishing Co.)

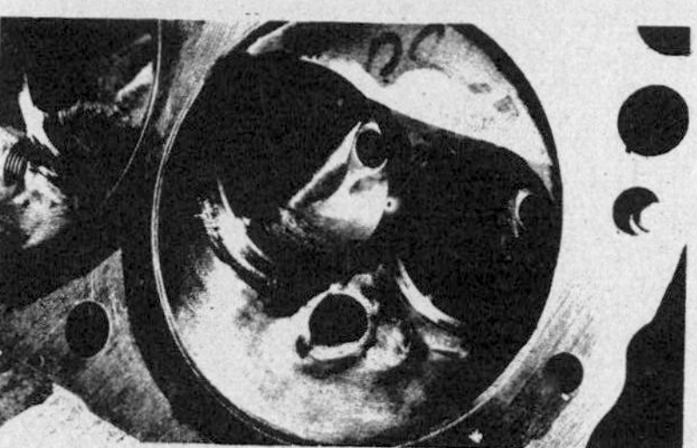
Polished combustion chamber
(© Petersen Publishing Co.)

** Using a grinding stone with the above mentioned tool, polish the walls of the intake and exhaust ports, and combustion chamber. Use progressively finer stones until all surface imperfections are removed. NOTE: *Through testing, it has been determined that a smooth surface is more effective than a mirror polished surface in intake ports, and vice-versa in exhaust ports.*

* Knurling the valve guides:

Cut-away view of a knurled valve guide
(© Petersen Publishing Co.)

* Valve guides which are not excessively worn or distorted may, in some cases, be knurled rather than replaced. Knurling is a process in which metal is displaced and raised, thereby reducing clearance. Knurling also provides excellent oil control. The possibility of knurling rather than replacing valve guides should be discussed with a machinist.

Replacing the valve guides: NOTE: *Valve guides should only be replaced if damaged or if an oversize valve stem is not available.*

B
A

A-VALVE GUIDE I.D.
B-SLIGHTLY SMALLER THAN VALVE GUIDE O.D.

Valve guide removal tool

WASHERS
B
A

A-VALVE GUIDE I.D.
B-LARGER THAN THE VALVE GUIDE O.D.

Valve guide installation tool (with washers used during installation)

Depending on the type of cylinder head, valve guides may be pressed, hammered, or shrunk in. In cases where the guides are shrunk into the head, replacement should be left to an equipped machine shop. In other cases, the guides are replaced as follows: Press or tap the valve guides out of the head using a stepped drift (see illustration). Determine the height above the boss that the guide must extend, and obtain a stack of washers, their I.D. similar to the guide's O.D., of that height. Place the stack of washers on the guide, and insert the guide into the boss. NOTE: *Valve guides are often tapered or beveled for installation.* Using the stepped installation tool (see illustration), press or tap the guides into position. Ream the guides according to the size of the valve stem.

Procedure	Method
Replacing valve seat inserts:	Replacement of valve seat inserts which are worn beyond resurfacing or broken, if feasible, must be done by a machine shop.
Resurfacing (grinding) the valve face:  Grinding a valve (© Subaru) 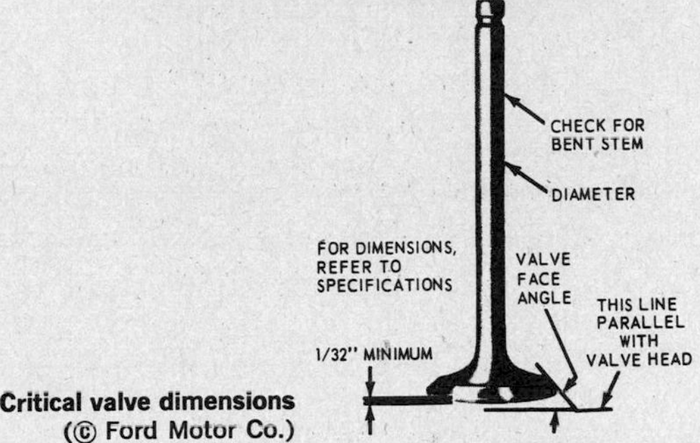 Critical valve dimensions (© Ford Motor Co.)	Using a valve grinder, resurface the valves according to specifications. CAUTION: *Valve face angle is not always identical to valve seat angle.* A minimum margin of 1/32" should remain after grinding the valve. The valve stem tip should also be squared and resurfaced, by placing the stem in the V-block of the grinder, and turning it while pressing lightly against the grinding wheel.
Resurfacing the valve seats using reamers: 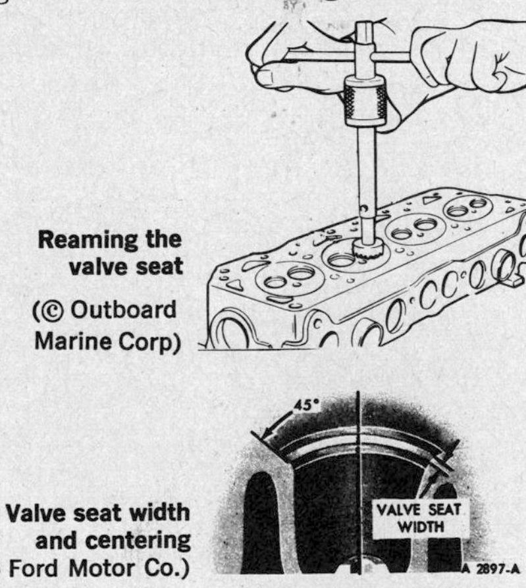 Reaming the valve seat (© Outboard Marine Corp) Valve seat width and centering (© Ford Motor Co.)	Select a reamer of the correct seat angle, slightly larger than the diameter of the valve seat, and assemble it with a pilot of the correct size. Install the pilot into the valve guide, and using steady pressure, turn the reamer clockwise. CAUTION: *Do not turn the reamer counter-clockwise.* Remove only as much material as necessary to clean the seat. Check the concentricity of the seat (see below). If the dye method is not used, coat the valve face with Prussian blue dye, install and rotate it on the valve seat. Using the dye marked area as a centering guide, center and narrow the valve seat to specifications with correction cutters. NOTE: *When no specifications are available, minimum seat width for exhaust valves should be 5/64", intake valves 1/16".* After making correction cuts, check the position of the valve seat on the valve face using Prussian blue dye.
* Resurfacing the valve seats using a grinder:  Grinding a valve seat (© Subaru)	Select a pilot of the correct size, and a coarse stone of the correct seat angle. Lubricate the pilot if necessary, and install the tool in the valve guide. Move the stone on and off the seat at approximately two cycles per second, until all flaws are removed from the seat. Install a fine stone, and finish the seat. Center and narrow the seat using correction stones, as described above.

Procedure	Method
Checking the valve seat concentricity:	Coat the valve face with Prussian blue dye, install the valve, and rotate it on the valve seat. If the entire seat becomes coated, and the valve is known to be concentric, the seat is concentric.
	* Install the dial gauge pilot into the guide, and rest the arm on the valve seat. Zero the gauge, and rotate the arm around the seat. Run-out should not exceed .002″.
* Lapping the valves: NOTE: *Valve lapping is done to ensure efficient sealing of resurfaced valves and seats. Valve lapping alone is not recommended for use as a resurfacing procedure.*	* Invert the cylinder head, lightly lubricate the valve stems, and install the valves in the head as numbered. Coat valve seats with fine grinding compound, and attach the lapping tool suction cup to a valve head (NOTE: *Moisten the suction cup*). Rotate the tool between the palms, changing position and lifting the tool often to prevent grooving. Lap the valve until a smooth, polished seat is evident. Remove the valve and tool, and rinse away all traces of grinding compound.
	** Fasten a suction cup to a piece of drill rod, and mount the rod in a hand drill. Proceed as above, using the hand drill as a lapping tool. CAUTION: *Due to the higher speeds involved when using the hand drill, care must be exercised to avoid grooving the seat.* Lift the tool and change direction of rotation often.
Check the valve springs:	Place the spring on a flat surface next to a square. Measure the height of the spring, and rotate it against the edge of the square to measure distortion. If spring height varies (by comparison) by more than 1/16″ or if distortion exceeds 1/16″, replace the spring.
	** In addition to evaluating the spring as above, test the spring pressure at the installed and compressed (installed height minus valve lift) height using a valve spring tester. Springs used on small displacement engines (up to 3 liters) should be ± 1 lb. of all other springs in either position. A tolerance of ± 5 lbs. is permissible on larger engines.

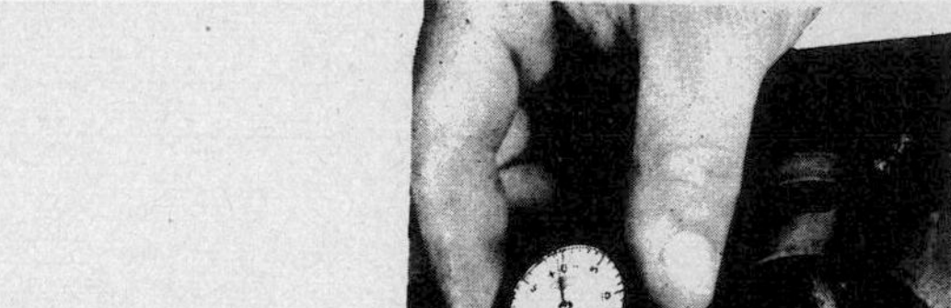

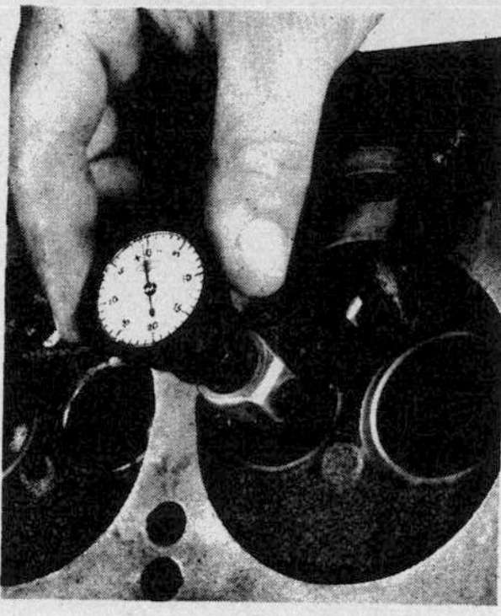

Checking the valve seat concentricity using a dial gauge (© American Motors Corp.)

Hand lapping the valves

HAND DRILL

ROD

SUCTION CUP

Home made mechanical valve lapping tool

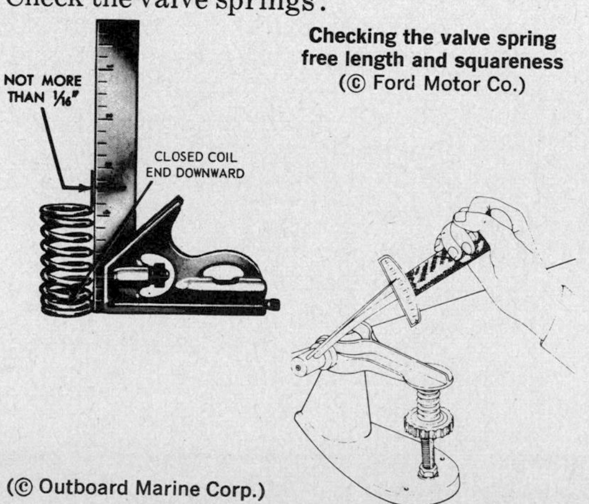

Checking the valve spring free length and squareness (© Ford Motor Co.)

(© Outboard Marine Corp.)

Procedure	Method
* Install valve stem seals:	* Due to the pressure differential that exists at the ends of the intake valve guides (atmospheric pressure above, manifold vacuum below), oil is drawn through the valve guides into the intake port. This has been alleviated somewhat since the addition of positive crankcase ventilation, which lowers the pressure above the guides. Several types of valve stem seals are available to reduce blow-by. Certain seals simply slip over the stem and guide boss, while others require that the boss be machined. Recently, Teflon guide seals have become popular. Consult a parts supplier or machinist concerning availability and suggested usages. NOTE: *When installing seals, ensure that a small amount of oil is able to pass the seal to lubricate the valve guides; otherwise, excessive wear may result.*
Install the valves:	Lubricate the valve stems, and install the valves in the cylinder head as numbered. Lubricate and position the seals (if used, see above) and the valve springs. Install the spring retainers, compress the springs, and insert the keys using needlenose pliers or a tool designed for this purpose. NOTE: *Retain the keys with wheel bearing grease during installation.*
Checking valve spring installed height:	Measure the distance between the spring pad and the lower edge of the spring retainer, and compare to specifications. If the installed height is incorrect, add shim washers between the spring pad and the spring. CAUTION: *Use only washers designed for this purpose.*
** CC'ing the combustion chambers:	** Invert the cylinder head and place a bead of sealer around a combustion chamber. Install an apparatus designed for this purpose (burette mounted on a clear plate; see illustration) over the combustion chamber, and fill with the specified fluid to an even mark on the burette. Record the burette reading, and fill the combustion chamber with fluid. (NOTE: *A hole drilled in the plate will permit air to escape*). Subtract the burette reading, with the combustion chamber filled, from the previous reading, to determine combustion chamber volume in cc's. Duplicate this procedure in all combustion

Valve stem seal installation
(© Ford Motor Co.)

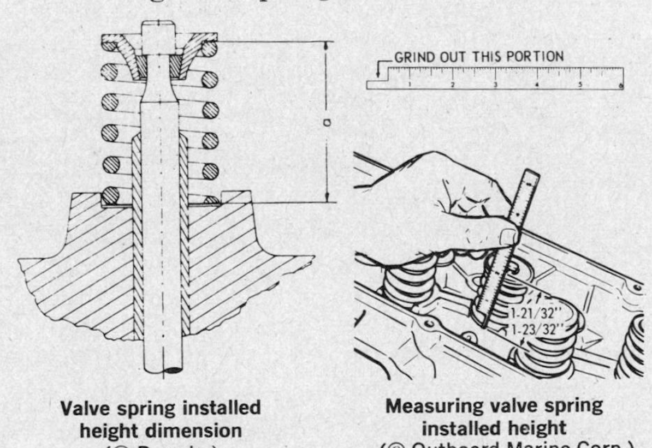

Valve spring installed height dimension
(© Porsche)

Measuring valve spring installed height
(© Outboard Marine Corp.)

Procedure	Method
 CC'ing the combustion chamber (© Petersen Publishing Co.)	chambers on the cylinder head, and compare the readings. The volume of all combustion chambers should be made equal to that of the largest. Combustion chamber volume may be increased in two ways. When only a small change is required (usually), a small cutter or coarse stone may be used to remove material from the combustion chamber. NOTE: *Check volume frequently.* Remove material over a wide area, so as not to change the configuration of the combustion chamber. When a larger change is required, the valve seat may be sunk (lowered into the head). NOTE: *When altering valve seat, remember to compensate for the change in spring installed height.*
Inspect the rocker arms, balls, studs, and nuts (where applicable):  Stress cracks in rocker nuts (© Ford Motor Co.)	Visually inspect the rocker arms, balls, studs, and nuts for cracks, galling, burning, scoring, or wear. If all parts are intact, liberally lubricate the rocker arms and balls, and install them on the cylinder head. If wear is noted on a rocker arm at the point of valve contact, grind it smooth and square, removing as little material as possible. Replace the rocker arm if excessively worn. If a rocker stud shows signs of wear, it must be replaced (see below). If a rocker nut shows stress cracks, replace it. If an exhaust ball is galled or burned, substitute the intake ball from the same cylinder (if it is intact), and install a new intake ball. NOTE: *Avoid using new rocker balls on exhaust valves.*
Replacing rocker studs: 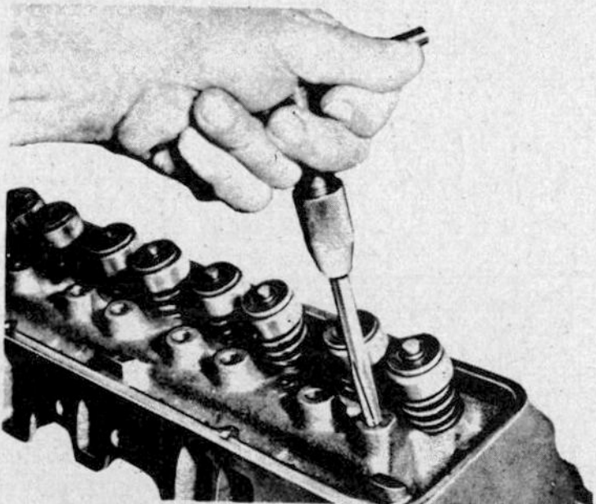 Reaming the stud bore for oversize rocker studs (© Buick Div. G.M. Corp.) 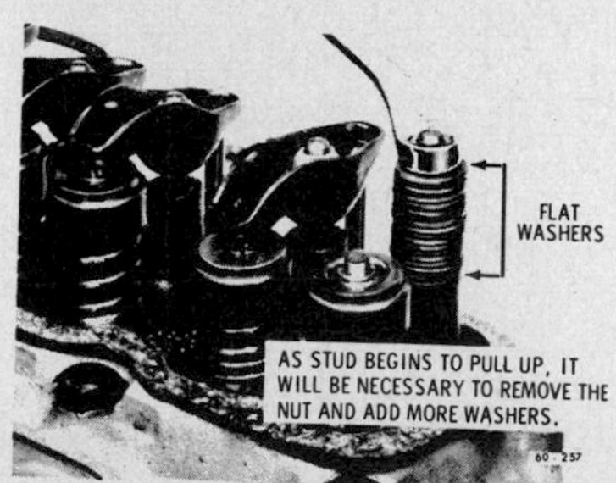 Extracting a pressed in rocker stud (© Buick Div. G.M. Corp.)	In order to remove a threaded stud, lock two nuts on the stud, and unscrew the stud using the lower nut. Coat the lower threads of the new stud with Loctite, and install. Two alternative methods are available for replacing pressed in studs. Remove the damaged stud using a stack of washers and a nut (see illustration). In the first, the boss is reamed .005-.006″ oversize, and an oversize stud pressed in. Control the stud extension over the boss using washers, in the same manner as valve guides. Before installing the stud, coat it with white lead and grease. To retain the stud more positively, drill a hole through the stud and boss, and install a roll pin. In the second method, the boss is tapped, and a threaded stud installed. Retain the stud using Loctite Stud and Bearing Mount.

Procedure	*Method*
Inspect the rocker shaft(s) and rocker arms (where applicable):	Remove rocker arms, springs and washers from rocker shaft. NOTE: *Lay out parts in the order they are removed.* Inspect rocker arms for pitting or wear on the valve contact point, or excessive bushing wear. Bushings need only be replaced if wear is excessive, because the rocker arm normally contacts the shaft at one point only. Grind the valve contact point of rocker arm smooth if necessary, removing as little material as possible. If excessive material must be removed to smooth and square the arm, it should be replaced. Clean out all oil holes and passages in rocker shaft. If shaft is grooved or worn, replace it. Lubricate and assemble the rocker shaft.
Inspect the camshaft bushings and the camshaft (overhead cam engines):	See next section.
Inspect the pushrods:	Remove the pushrods, and, if hollow, clean out the oil passages using fine wire. Roll each pushrod over a piece of clean glass. If a distinct clicking sound is heard as the pushrod rolls, the rod is bent, and must be replaced.
	* The length of all pushrods must be equal. Measure the length of the pushrods, compare to specifications, and replace as necessary.
Inspect the valve lifters:	Remove lifters from their bores, and remove gum and varnish, using solvent. Clean walls of lifter bores. Check lifters for concave wear as illustrated. If face is worn concave, replace lifter, and carefully inspect the camshaft. Lightly lubricate lifter and insert it into its bore. If play is excessive, an oversize lifter must be installed (where possible). Consult a machinist concerning feasibility. If play is satisfactory, remove, lubricate, and reinstall the lifter.
* Testing hydraulic lifter leak down:	Submerge lifter in a container of kerosene. Chuck a used pushrod or its equivalent into a drill press. Position container of kerosene so pushrod acts on the lifter plunger. Pump lifter with the drill press, until resistance increases. Pump several more times to bleed any air out of lifter. Apply very firm, constant pressure to the lifter, and observe rate at which fluid bleeds out of lifter. If the fluid bleeds very quickly (less than 15 seconds), lifter is defective. If the time exceeds 60 seconds, lifter is sticking. In either case, recondition or replace lifter. If lifter is operating properly (leak down time 15-60 seconds), lubricate and install it.

Disassembled rocker shaft parts arranged for inspection
(© American Motors Corp.)

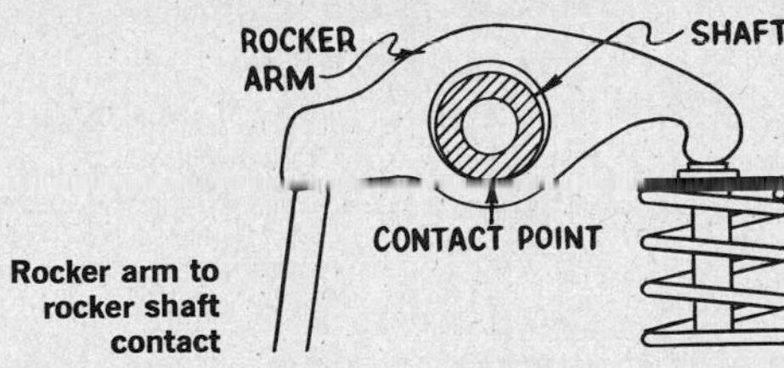

Rocker arm to rocker shaft contact

Checking the lifter face
(© American Motors Corp.)

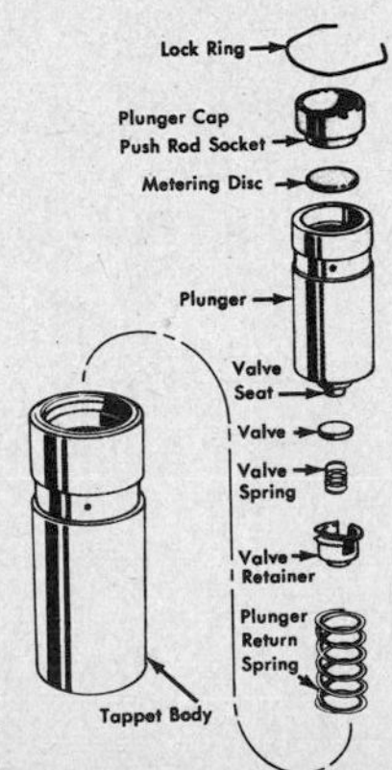

Exploded view of a typical hydraulic lifter
(© American Motors Corp.)

CYLINDER BLOCK RECONDITIONING

Procedure	*Method*
Checking the main bearing clearance:	Invert engine, and remove cap from the bearing to be checked. Using a clean, dry rag, thoroughly clean all oil from crankshaft journal and bearing insert. NOTE: *Plastigage is soluble in oil; therefore, oil on the journal or bearing could result in erroneous readings.* Place a piece of Plastigage along the full length of journal, reinstall cap, and torque to specifications. Remove bearing cap, and determine bearing clearance by comparing width of Plastigage to the scale on Plastigage envelope. Journal taper is determined by comparing width of the Plastigage strip near its ends. Rotate crankshaft 90° and retest, to determine journal eccentricity. NOTE: *Do not rotate crankshaft with Plastigage installed.* If bearing insert and journal appear intact, and are within tolerances, no further main bearing service is required. If bearing or journal appear defective, cause of failure should be determined before replacement.
	* Remove crankshaft from block (see below). Measure the main bearing journals at each end twice (90° apart) using a micrometer, to determine diameter, journal taper and eccentricity. If journals are within tolerances, reinstall bearing caps at their specified torque. Using a telescope gauge and micrometer, measure bearing I.D. parallel to piston axis and at 30° on each side of piston axis. Subtract journal O.D. from bearing I.D. to determine oil clearance. If crankshaft journals appear defective, or do not meet tolerances, there is no need to measure bearings; for the crankshaft will require grinding and/or undersize bearings will be required. If bearing appears defective, cause for failure should be determined prior to replacement.
Checking the connecting rod bearing clearance:	Connecting rod bearing clearance is checked in the same manner as main bearing clearance, using Plastigage. Before removing the crankshaft, connecting rod side clearance also should be measured and recorded.
	* Checking connecting rod bearing clearance, using a micrometer, is identical to checking main bearing clearance. If no other service

Plastigage installed on main bearing journal
(© Chevrolet Div. G.M. Corp.)

Measuring Plastigage to determine main bearing clearance
(© Chevrolet Div. G.M. Corp.)

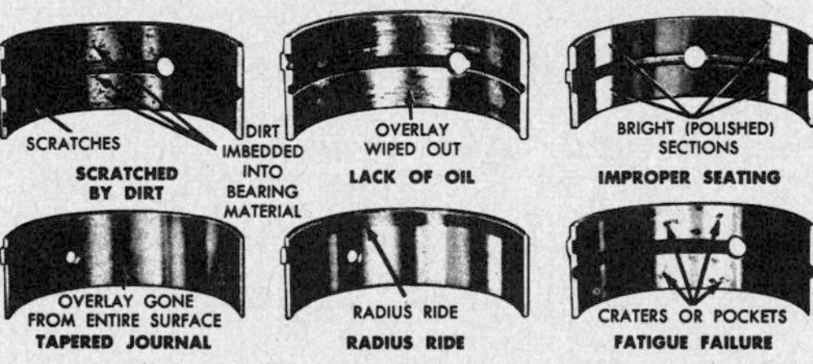

Causes of bearing failure
(© Ford Motor Co.)

Plastigage installed on connecting rod bearing journal
(© Chevrolet Div. G.M. Corp.)

Procedure	Method

is required, the piston and rod assemblies need not be removed.

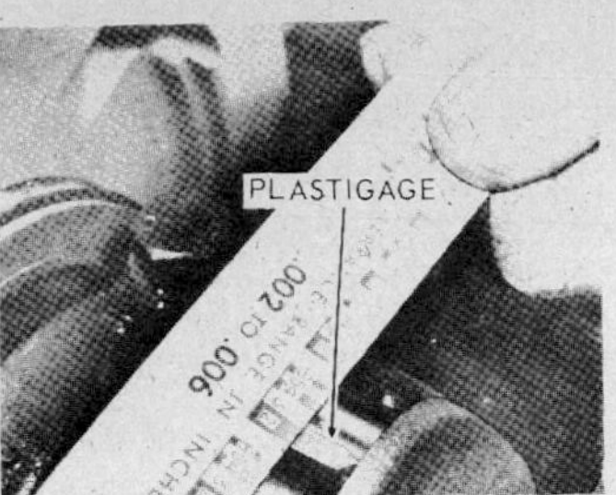

Measuring Plastigage to determine connecting rod bearing clearance
(© Outboard Marine Corp.)

Removing the crankshaft:

Connecting rod matching marks
(© Ford Motor Co.)

Using a punch, mark the corresponding main bearing caps and saddles according to position (i.e., one punch on the front main cap and saddle, two on the second, three on the third, etc.). Using number stamps, identify the corresponding connecting rods and caps, according to cylinder (if no numbers are present). Remove the main and connecting rod caps, and place sleeves of plastic tubing over the connecting rod bolts, to protect the journals as the crankshaft is removed. Lift the crankshaft out of the block.

Remove the ridge from the top of the cylinder:

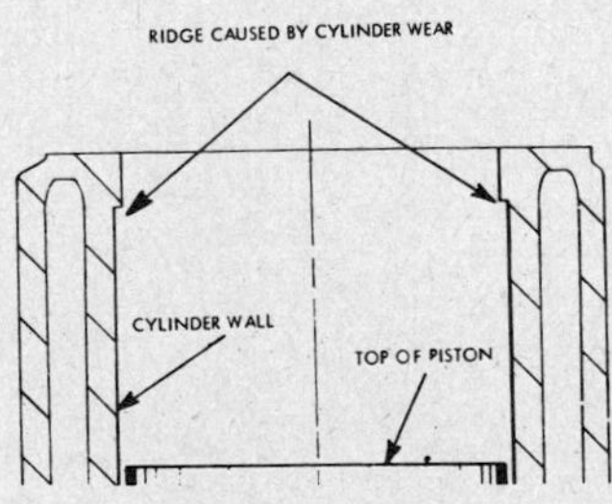

Cylinder bore ridge
(© Pontiac Div. G.M. Corp.)

In order to facilitate removal of the piston and connecting rod, the ridge at the top of the cylinder (unworn area; see illustration) must be removed. Place the piston at the bottom of the bore, and cover it with a rag. Cut the ridge away using a ridge reamer, exercising extreme care to avoid cutting too deeply. Remove the rag, and remove cuttings that remain on the piston. CAUTION: *If the ridge is not removed, and new rings are installed, damage to rings will result.*

Removing the piston and connecting rod:

Removing the piston
(© SAAB)

Invert the engine, and push the pistons and connecting rods out of the cylinders. If necessary, tap the connecting rod boss with a wooden hammer handle, to force the piston out. CAUTION: *Do not attempt to force the piston past the cylinder ridge* (see above).

Procedure	*Method*
Service the crankshaft:	Ensure that all oil holes and passages in the crankshaft are open and free of sludge. If necessary, have the crankshaft ground to the largest possible undersize.
	** Have the crankshaft Magnafluxed, to locate stress cracks. Consult a machinist concerning additional service procedures, such as surface hardening (e.g., nitriding, Tuftriding) to improve wear characteristics, cross drilling and chamfering the oil holes to improve lubrication, and balancing.
Removing freeze plugs:	Drill a hole in the center of the freeze plugs, and pry them out using a screwdriver or drift.
Remove the oil gallery plugs:	Threaded plugs should be removed using an appropriate (usually square) wrench. To remove soft, pressed in plugs, drill a hole in the plug, and thread in a sheet metal screw. Pull the plug out by the screw using pliers.
Hot-tank the block:	Have the block hot-tanked to remove grease, corrosion, and scale from the water jackets. NOTE: *Consult the operator to determine whether the camshaft bearings will be damaged during the hot-tank process.*
Check the block for cracks:	Visually inspect the block for cracks or chips. The most common locations are as follows: Adjacent to freeze plugs. Between the cylinders and water jackets. Adjacent to the main bearing saddles. At the extreme bottom of the cylinders. Check only suspected cracks using spot check dye (see introduction). If a crack is located, consult a machinist concerning possible repairs.
	** Magnaflux the block to locate hidden cracks. If cracks are located, consult a machinist about feasibility of repair.
Install the oil gallery plugs and freeze plugs:	Coat freeze plugs with sealer and tap into position using a piece of pipe, slightly smaller than the plug, as a driver. To ensure retention, stake the edges of the plugs. Coat threaded oil gallery plugs with sealer and install. Drive replacement soft plugs into block using a large drift as a driver.
	* Rather than reinstalling lead plugs, drill and tap the holes, and install threaded plugs.

Procedure	Method
Check the bore diameter and surface:	Visually inspect the cylinder bores for roughness, scoring, or scuffing. If evident, the cylinder bore must be bored or honed oversize to eliminate imperfections, and the smallest possible oversize piston used. The new pistons should be given to the machinist with the block, so that the cylinders can be bored or honed exactly to the piston size (plus clearance). If no flaws are evident, measure the bore diameter using a telescope gauge and micrometer, or dial gauge, parallel and perpendicular to the engine centerline, at the top (below the ridge) and bottom of the bore. Subtract the bottom measurements from the top to determine taper, and the parallel to the centerline measurements from the perpendicular measurements to determine eccentricity. If the measurements are not within specifications, the cylinder must be bored or honed, and an oversize piston installed. If the measurements are within specifications the cylinder may be used as is, with only finish honing (see below). NOTE: *Prior to submitting the block for boring, perform the following operation(s).*

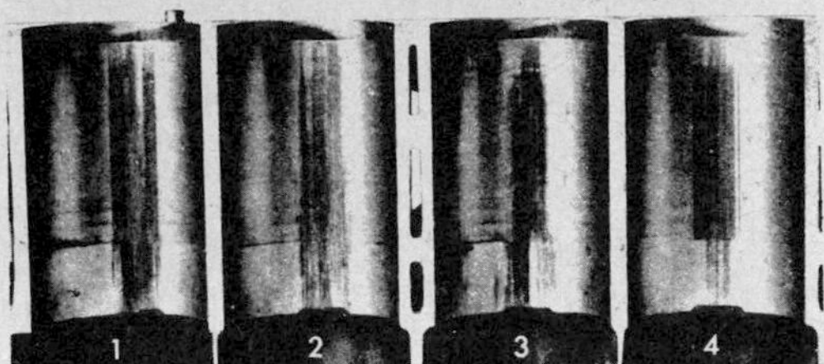

1, 2, 3 Piston skirt seizure resulted in this pattern. Engine must be rebored

4. Piston skirt and oil ring seizure caused this damage Engine must be rebored

5, 6 Score marks caused by a split piston skirt. Damage is not serious enough to warrant reboring

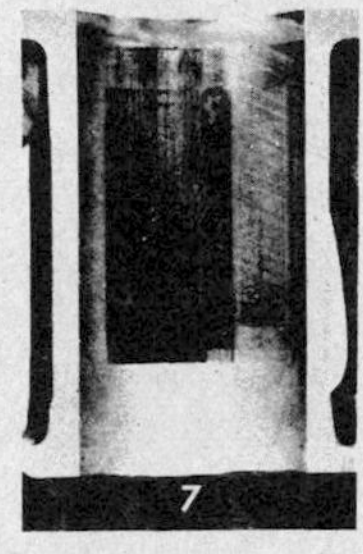

7. Ring seized longitudinally, causing a score mark 1 3/16" wide, on the land side of the piston groove. The honing pattern is destroyed and the cylinder must be rebored

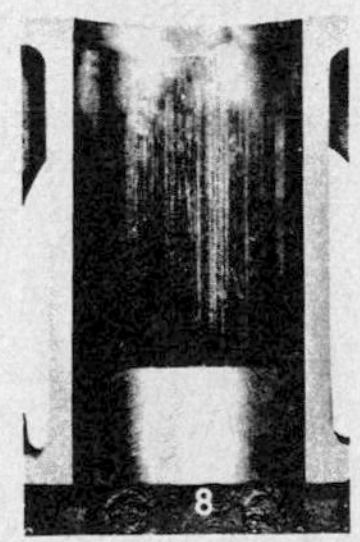

8. Result of oil ring seizure. Engine must be rebored

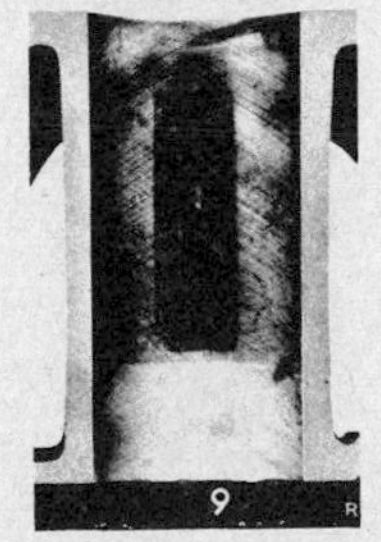

9. Oil ring seizure here was not serious enough to warrant reboring. The honing marks are still visible

Cylinder wall damage
(© Daimler-Benz A.G.)

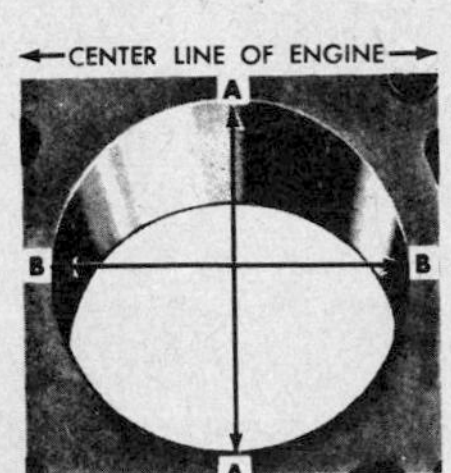

A AT RIGHT ANGLE TO CENTER LINE OF ENGINE
B PARALLEL TO CENTER LINE OF ENGINE

Cylinder bore measuring positions
(© Ford Motor Co.)

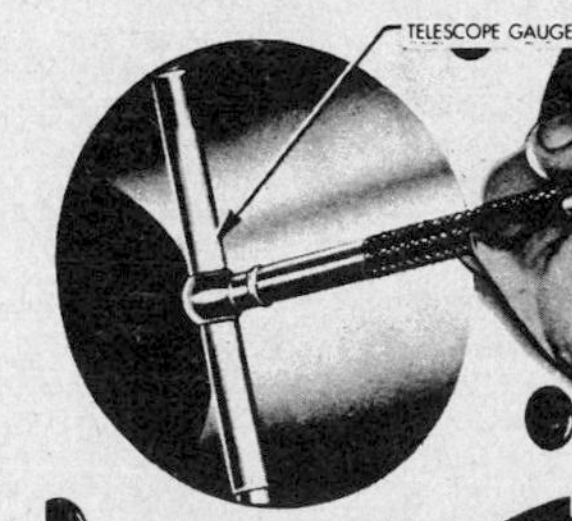

Measuring the cylinder bore with a telescope gauge
(© Buick Div. G.M. Corp.)

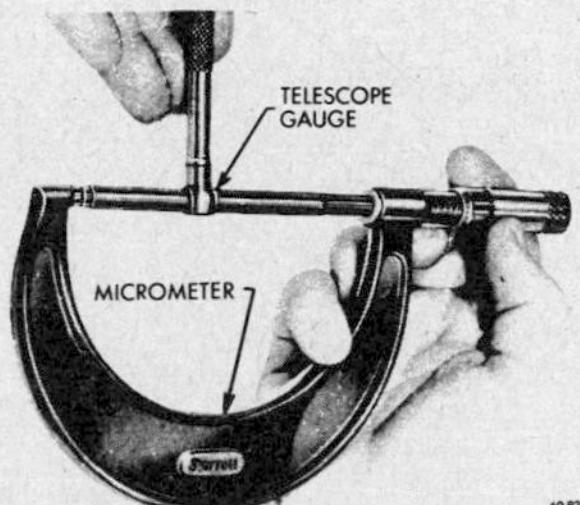

Determining the cylinder bore by measuring the telescope gauge with a micrometer
(© Buick Div. G.M. Corp.)

Measuring the cylinder bore with a dial gauge
(© Chevrolet Div. G.M. Corp.)

Procedure	Method
Check the block deck for warpage:	Using a straightedge and feeler gauges, check the block deck for warpage in the same manner that the cylinder head is checked (see Cylinder Head Reconditioning). If warpage exceeds specifications, have the deck resurfaced. NOTE: *In certain cases a specification for total material removal (Cylinder head and block deck) is provided. This specification must not be exceeded.*
* Check the deck height:	The deck height is the distance from the crankshaft centerline to the block deck. To measure, invert the engine, and install the crankshaft, retaining it with the center main cap. Measure the distance from the crankshaft journal to the block deck, parallel to the cylinder centerline. Measure the diameter of the end (front and rear) main journals, parallel to the centerline of the cylinders, divide the diameter in half, and subtract it from the previous measurement. The results of the front and rear measurements should be identical. If the difference exceeds .005″, the deck height should be corrected. NOTE: *Block deck height and warpage should be corrected concurrently.*
Check the cylinder block bearing alignment:  **Checking main bearing saddle alignment** (© Petersen Publishing Co.)	Remove the upper bearing inserts. Place a straightedge in the bearing saddles along the centerline of the crankshaft. If clearance exists between the straightedge and the center saddle, the block must be alignbored.
Clean and inspect the pistons and connecting rods: 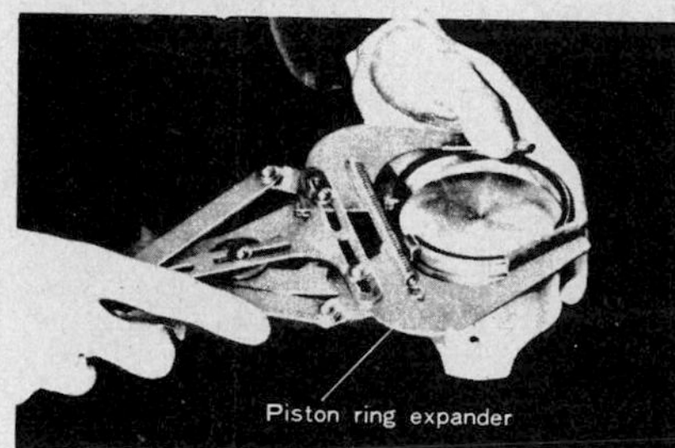 **Removing the piston rings** (© Subaru)	Using a ring expander, remove the rings from the piston. Remove the retaining rings (if so equipped) and remove piston pin. NOTE: *If the piston pin must be pressed out, determine the proper method and use the proper tools; otherwise the piston will distort.* Clean the ring grooves using an appropriate tool, exercising care to avoid cutting too deeply. Thoroughly clean all carbon and varnish from the piston with solvent. CAUTION: *Do not use a wire brush or caustic solvent on pistons.* Inspect the pistons for scuffing, scoring, cracks, pitting, or excessive ring groove wear. If wear is evident, the piston must be replaced. Check the connecting rod length by measuring the rod from the inside of the large end to the inside of the small end using calipers (see

Procedure	*Method*

Cleaning the piston ring grooves
(© Ford Motor Co.)

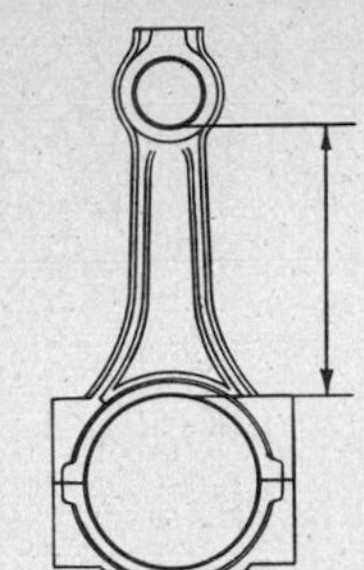

Connecting rod length checking dimension

illustration). All connecting rods should be equal length. Replace any rod that differs from the others in the engine.

* Have the connecting rod alignment checked in an alignment fixture by a machinist. Replace any twisted or bent rods.

* Magnaflux the connecting rods to locate stress cracks. If cracks are found, replace the connecting rod.

Fit the pistons to the cylinders:

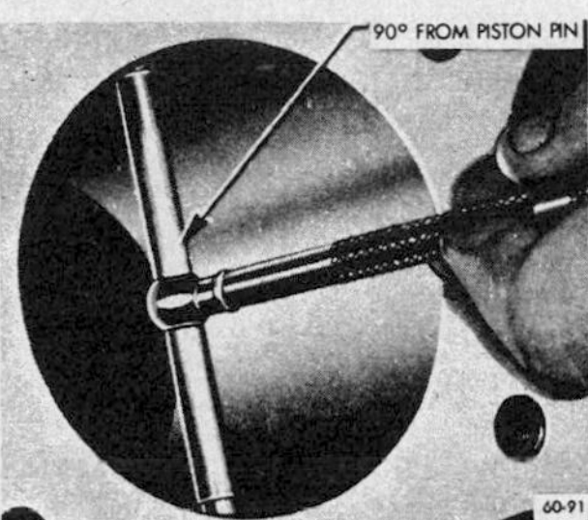

Measuring the cylinder with a telescope gauge for piston fitting
(© Buick Div. G.M. Corp.)

Measuring the piston for fitting
(© Buick Div. G.M. Corp.)

Using a telescope gauge and micrometer, or a dial gauge, measure the cylinder bore diameter perpendicular to the piston pin, 2½″ below the deck. Measure the piston perpendicular to its pin on the skirt. The difference between the two measurements is the piston clearance. If the clearance is within specifications or slightly below (after boring or honing), finish honing is all that is required. If the clearance is excessive, try to obtain a slightly larger piston to bring clearance within specifications. Where this is not possible, obtain the first oversize piston, and hone (or if necessary, bore) the cylinder to size.

Assemble the pistons and connecting rods:

Installing piston pin lock rings
(© Nissan Motor Co., Ltd.)

Inspect piston pin, connecting rod small end bushing, and piston bore for galling, scoring, or excessive wear. If evident, replace defective part(s). Measure the I.D. of the piston boss and connecting rod small end, and the O.D. of the piston pin. If within specifications, assemble piston pin and rod. CAUTION: *If piston pin must be pressed in, determine the proper method and use the proper tools; otherwise the piston will distort.* Install the lock rings; ensure that they seat properly. If the parts are not within specifications, determine the service method for the type of engine. In some cases, piston and pin are serviced as an assembly when either is defective. Others specify reaming the piston and connecting rods for an oversize pin. If the connecting rod bushing is worn, it may in many cases be replaced. Reaming the piston and replacing the rod bushing are machine shop operations.

Procedure	Method
Clean and inspect the camshaft:	Degrease the camshaft, using solvent, and clean out all oil holes. Visually inspect cam lobes and bearing journals for excessive wear. If a lobe is questionable, check all lobes as indicated below. If a journal or lobe is worn, the camshaft must be reground or replaced. NOTE: *If a journal is worn, there is a good chance that the bushings are worn.* If lobes and journals appear intact, place the front and rear journals in V-blocks, and rest a dial indicator on the center journal. Rotate the camshaft to check straightness. If deviation exceeds .001″, replace the camshaft.
	* Check the camshaft lobes with a micrometer, by measuring the lobes from the nose to base and again at 90° (see illustration). The lift is determined by subtracting the second measurement from the first. If all exhaust lobes and all intake lobes are not identical, the camshaft must be reground or replaced.
Replace the camshaft bearings:	If excessive wear is indicated, or if the engine is being completely rebuilt, camshaft bearings should be replaced as follows: Drive the camshaft rear plug from the block. Assemble the removal puller with its shoulder on the bearing to be removed. Gradually tighten the puller nut until bearing is removed. Remove remaining bearings, leaving the front and rear for last. To remove front and rear bearings, reverse position of the tool, so as to pull the bearings in toward the center of the block. Leave the tool in this position, pilot the new front and rear bearings on the installer, and pull them into position. Return the tool to its original position and pull remaining bearings into position. NOTE: *Ensure that oil holes align when installing bearings.* Replace camshaft rear plug, and stake it into position to aid retention.
Finish hone the cylinders:	Chuck a flexible drive hone into a power drill, and insert it into the cylinder. Start the hone, and move it up and down in the cylinder at a rate which will produce approximately a 60° cross-hatch pattern (see illustration). NOTE: *Do not extend the hone below the cylinder bore.* After developing the pattern, remove the hone and recheck piston fit. Wash the cylinders with a detergent and water solution to remove abrasive dust, dry, and wipe several times with a rag soaked in engine oil.

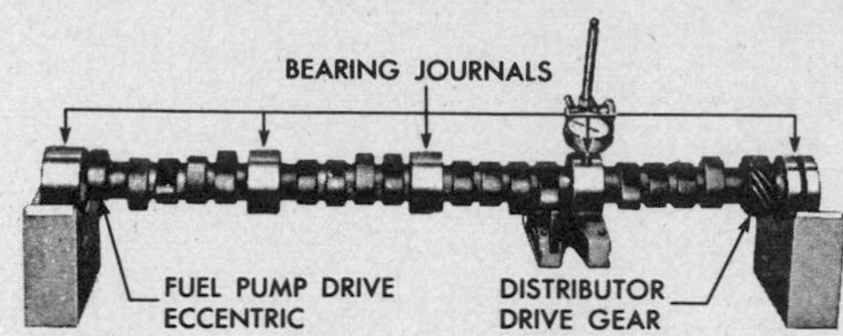

Checking the camshaft for straightness
(© Chevrolet Motor Div. G.M. Corp.)

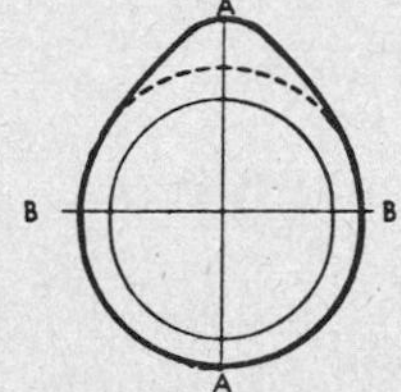

Camshaft lobe measurement
(© Ford Motor Co.)

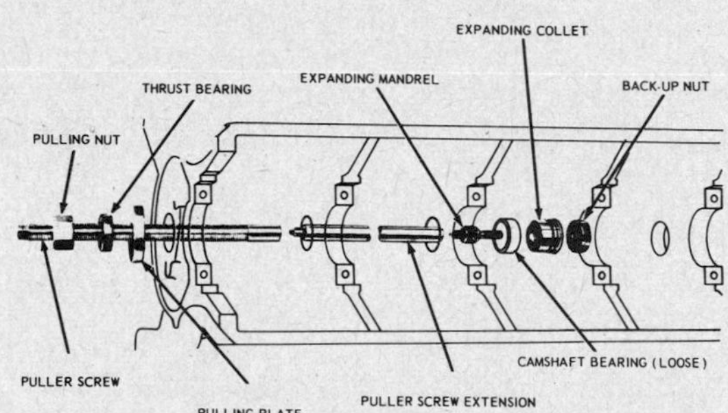

Camshaft removal and installation tool (typical)
(© Ford Motor Co.)

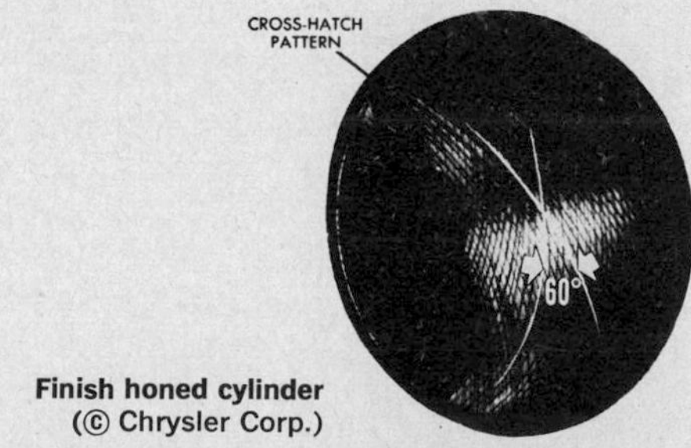

Finish honed cylinder
(© Chrysler Corp.)

Procedure	*Method*

Check piston ring end-gap:

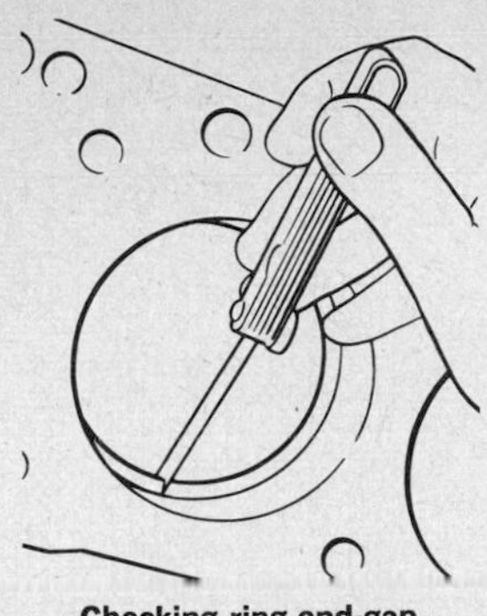

Checking ring end-gap
(© Outboard Marine Corp.)

Compress the piston rings to be used in a cylinder, one at a time, into that cylinder, and press them approximately 1″ below the deck with an inverted piston. Using feeler gauges, measure the ring end-gap, and compare to specifications. Pull the ring out of the cylinder and file the ends with a fine file to obtain proper clearance. CAUTION: *If inadequate ring end-gap is utilized, ring breakage will result.*

Install the piston rings:

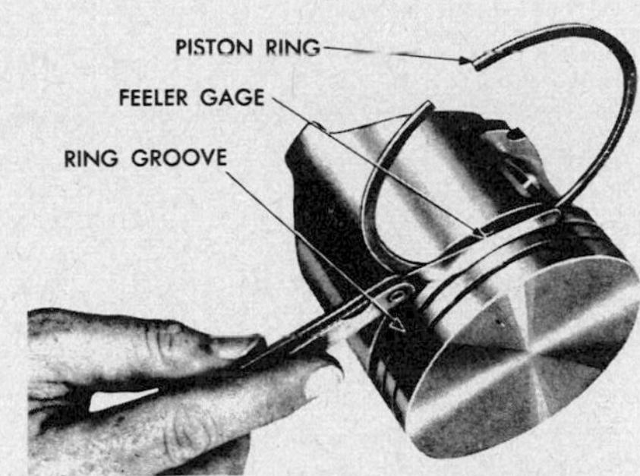

Checking ring side clearance
(© Chrysler Corp.)

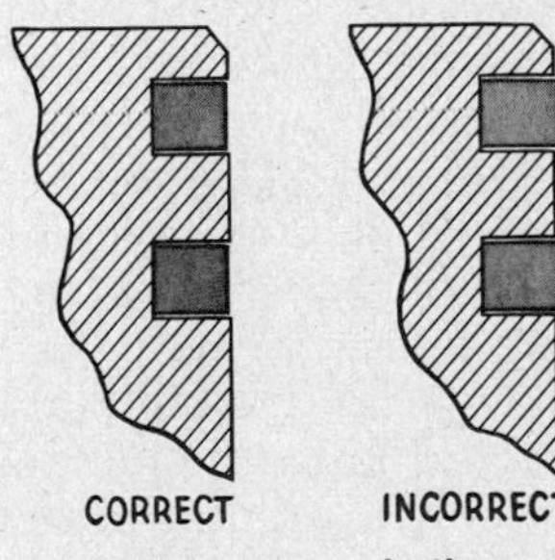

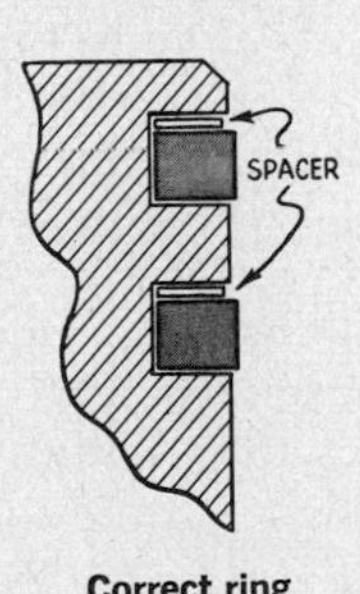

Piston groove depth

SPACER

Correct ring spacer installation

Inspect the ring grooves in the piston for excessive wear or taper. If necessary, recut the groove(s) for use with an overwidth ring or a standard ring and spacer. If the groove is worn uniformly, overwidth rings, or standard rings and spacers may be installed without recutting. Roll the outside of the ring around the groove to check for burrs or deposits. If any are found, remove with a fine file. Hold the ring in the groove, and measure side clearance. If necessary, correct as indicated above. NOTE: *Always install any additional spacers above the piston ring.* The ring groove must be deep enough to allow the ring to seat below the lands (see illustration). In many cases, a "go-no-go" depth gauge will be provided with the piston rings. Shallow grooves may be corrected by recutting, while deep grooves require some type of filler or expander behind the piston. Consult the piston ring supplier concerning the suggested method. Install the rings on the piston, lowest ring first, using a ring expander. NOTE: *Position the ring markings as specified by the manufacturer (see car section).*

Install the camshaft:

Liberally lubricate the camshaft lobes and journals, and slide the camshaft into the block. CAUTION: *Exercise extreme care to avoid damaging the bearings when inserting the camshaft.* Install and tighten the camshaft thrust plate retaining bolts.

Check camshaft end-play:

Checking camshaft end-play with a feeler gauge
(© Outboard Marine Corp.)

0.0025"-0.0075"

Using feeler gauges, determine whether the clearance between the camshaft boss (or gear) and backing plate is within specifications. Install shims behind the thrust plate, or reposition the camshaft gear and retest end-play.

Procedure	Method
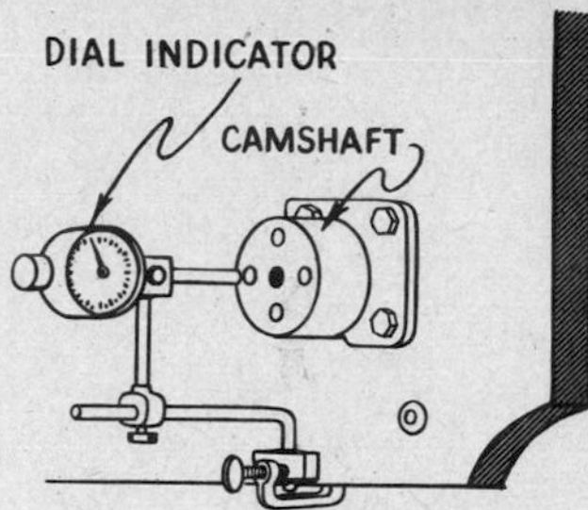 Checking camshaft end-play with a dial indicator	* Mount a dial indicator stand so that the stem of the dial indicator rests on the nose of the camshaft, parallel to the camshaft axis. Push the camshaft as far in as possible and zero the gauge. Move the camshaft outward to determine the amount of camshaft end-play. If the end-play is not within tolerance, install shims behind the thrust plate, or re-position the camshaft gear and retest.
Install the rear main seal (where applicable):  Seating the rear main seal (© Buick Div. G.M. Corp.)	Position the block with the bearing saddles facing upward. Lay the rear main seal in its groove and press it lightly into its seat. Place a piece of pipe the same diameter as the crankshaft journal into the saddle, and firmly seat the seal. Hold the pipe in position, and trim the ends of the seal flush if required.
Install the crankshaft: 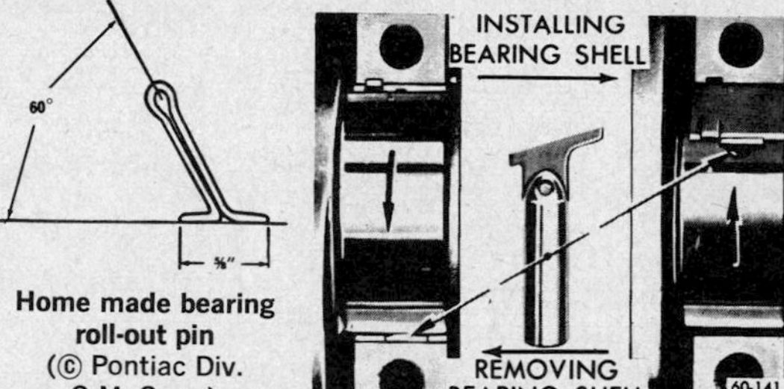 Home made bearing roll-out pin (© Pontiac Div. G.M. Corp.) Removal and installation of upper bearing insert using a roll-out pin (© Buick Div. G.M. Corp.)	Thoroughly clean the main bearing saddles and caps. Place the upper halves of the bearing inserts on the saddles and press into position. NOTE: *Ensure that the oil holes align.* Press the corresponding bearing inserts into the main bearing caps. Lubricate the upper main bearings, and lay the crankshaft in position. Place a strip of Plastigage on each of the crankshaft journals, install the main caps, and torque to specifications. Remove the main caps, and compare the Plastigage to the scale on the Plastigage envelope. If clearances are within tolerances, remove the Plastigage, turn the crankshaft 90°, wipe off all oil and retest. If all clearances are correct, remove all Plastigage, thoroughly

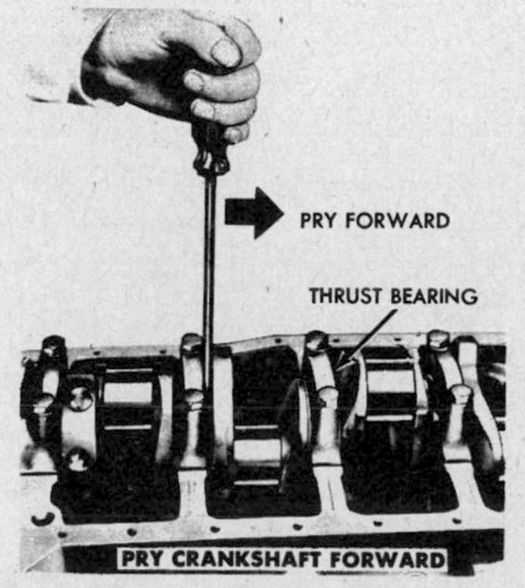

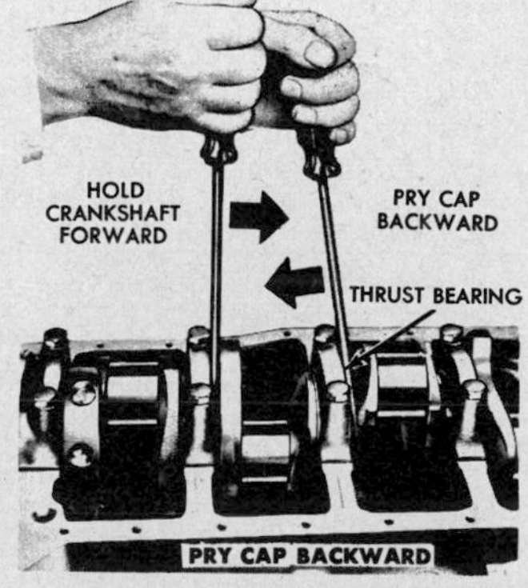

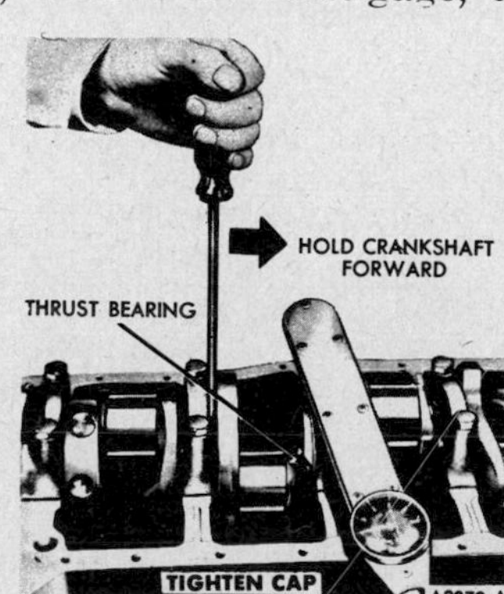

Aligning the thrust bearing
(© Ford Motor Co.)

Procedure	*Method*
	lubricate the main caps and bearing journals, and install the main caps. If clearances are not within tolerance, the upper bearing inserts may be removed, without removing the crankshaft, using a bearing roll out pin (see illustration). Roll in a bearing that will provide proper clearance, and retest. Torque all main caps, excluding the thrust bearing cap, to specifications. Tighten the thrust bearing cap finger tight. To properly align the thrust bearing, pry the crankshaft the extent of its axial travel several times, the last movement held toward the front of the engine, and torque the thrust bearing cap to specifications. Determine the crankshaft end-play (see below), and bring within tolerance with thrust washers.
Measure crankshaft end-play:  **Checking crankshaft end-play with a dial indicator** (© Ford Motor Co.) 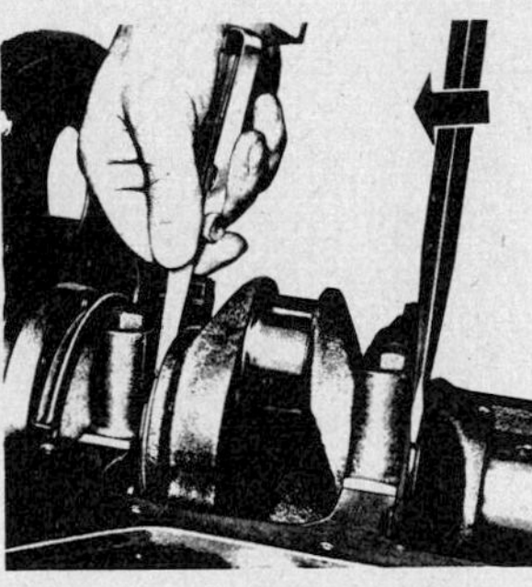 **Checking crankshaft end-play with a feeler gauge** (© Outboard Marine Corp.)	Mount a dial indicator stand on the front of the block, with the dial indicator stem resting on the nose of the crankshaft, parallel to the crankshaft axis. Pry the crankshaft the extent of its travel rearward, and zero the indicator. Pry the crankshaft forward and record crankshaft end-play. NOTE: *Crankshaft end-play also may be measured at the thrust bearing, using feeler gauges* (see illustration).
Install the pistons:	Press the upper connecting rod bearing halves into the connecting rods, and the lower halves into the connecting rod caps. Position the piston ring gaps according to specifications (see car section), and lubricate the pistons. Install a ring compresser on a piston, and press two long (8″) pieces of plastic tubing over the rod bolts. Using the plastic tubes as a guide, press the pistons into the bores and onto the crankshaft with a wooden hammer handle. After seating the rod on the crankshaft journal, remove the tubes and install the cap finger tight. Install the remaining pistons in the same man-

Procedure	Method

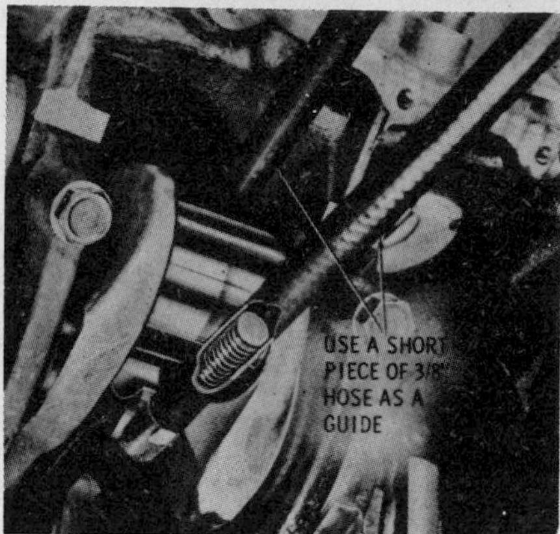

Tubing used as guide when installing a piston
(© Oldsmobile Div. G.M. Corp.)

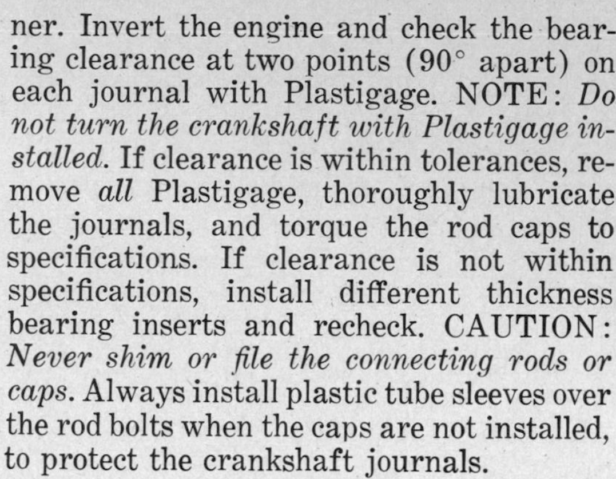
ner. Invert the engine and check the bearing clearance at two points (90° apart) on each journal with Plastigage. NOTE: *Do not turn the crankshaft with Plastigage installed.* If clearance is within tolerances, remove *all* Plastigage, thoroughly lubricate the journals, and torque the rod caps to specifications. If clearance is not within specifications, install different thickness bearing inserts and recheck. CAUTION: *Never shim or file the connecting rods or caps.* Always install plastic tube sleeves over the rod bolts when the caps are not installed, to protect the crankshaft journals.

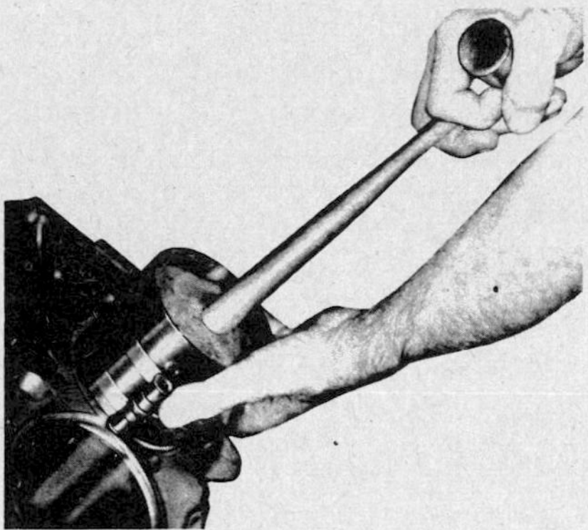
Installing a piston
(© Chevrolet Div. G.M. Corp.)

Check connecting rod side clearance:

Checking connecting rod side clearance
(© Chevrolet Div. G.M. Corp.)

Determine the clearance between the sides of the connecting rods and the crankshaft, using feeler gauges. If clearance is below the minimum tolerance, the rod may be machined to provide adequate clearance. If clearance is excessive, substitute an unworn rod, and recheck. If clearance is still outside specifications, the crankshaft must be welded and reground, or replaced.

Inspect the timing chain:

Visually inspect the timing chain for broken or loose links, and replace the chain if any are found. If the chain will flex sideways, it must be replaced. Install the timing chain as specified. NOTE: *If the original timing chain is to be reused, install it in its original position.*

Procedure	Method
Check timing gear backlash and runout:	Mount a dial indicator with its stem resting on a tooth of the camshaft gear (as illustrated). Rotate the gear until all slack is removed, and zero the indicator. Rotate the gear in the opposite direction until slack is removed, and record gear backlash. Mount the indicator with its stem resting on the edge of the camshaft gear, parallel to the axis of the camshaft. Zero the indicator, and turn the camshaft gear one full turn, recording the runout. If either backlash or runout exceed specifications, replace the worn gear(s).

Checking camshaft gear backlash
(© Chevrolet Div. G.M. Corp.)

Checking camshaft gear runout
(© Chevrolet Div. G.M. Corp.)

Completing the Rebuilding Process

Following the above procedures, complete the rebuilding process as follows:

Fill the oil pump with oil, to prevent cavitating (sucking air) on initial engine start up. Install the oil pump and the pickup tube on the engine. Coat the oil pan gasket as necessary, and install the gasket and the oil pan. Mount the flywheel and the crankshaft vibrational damper or pulley on the crankshaft. NOTE: *Always use new bolts when installing the flywheel.* Inspect the clutch shaft pilot bushing in the crankshaft. If the bushing is excessively worn, remove it with an expanding puller and a slide hammer, and tap a new bushing into place.

Position the engine, cylinder head side up. Lubricate the lifters, and install them into their bores. Install the cylinder head, and torque it as specified in the car section. Insert the pushrods (where applicable), and install the rocker shaft(s) (if so equipped) or position the rocker arms on the pushrods. If solid lifters are utilized, adjust the valves to the "cold" specifications.

Mount the intake and exhaust manifolds, the carburetor(s), the distributor and spark plugs. Adjust the point gap and the static ignition timing. Mount all accessories and install the engine in the car. Fill the radiator with coolant, and the crankcase with high quality engine oil.

Break-in Procedure

Start the engine, and allow it to run at low speed for a few minutes, while checking for leaks. Stop the engine, check the oil level, and fill as necessary. Restart the engine, and fill the cooling system to capacity. Check the point dwell angle and adjust the ignition timing and the valves. Run the engine at low to medium speed (800-2500 rpm) for approximately ½ hour, and retorque the cylinder head bolts. Road test the car, and check again for leaks.

Follow the manufacturer's recommended engine break-in procedure and maintenance schedule for new engines.

Clutch Problems

Problems and Solutions

When diagnosing problems in any area, there is no substitute for careful examination and experience. The following are some symptoms that may accompany clutch troubles.

1. Excessive noise.
2. Clutch chatter or grab.
3. Clutch slip.
4. Clutch drag or failure to release.
5. Pedal pulsation.
6. Low clutch facing life.
7. Gear lock up or hard shifting.
8. Hard pedal.

Excessive Noise

There are five common sources of clutch noise:

1. Release bearing.
2. Clutch shaft pilot bearing.
3. Transmission pinion shaft bearing.
4. Transmitted engine noises.
5. Clutch linkage noises.

Release Bearing

Release bearing noises vary with the degree of bearing failure. A dry or damaged bearing usually makes a shrill or scraping sound when depressing the clutch pedal to the point of release finger-to-bearing contact. This means that the noise should be audible at the lower end of clutch pedal free-play. Continued use of a car, with the release bearing in this condition, is damaging to the clutch release fingers.

Usual cause of release bearing failure is overwork—caused by riding the clutch. Other causes are not enough pedal free-play, lack of lubricant in the bearing, clutch release fingers worn or out of true.

Pilot Bearing

Clutch shaft pilot bearing noises can be heard only when the bearing is in operation. This is at any time crankshaft speed is different from that of the clutch shaft, (clutch disengaged with transmission in gear).

This is a high pitched squeal, caused by a dry bearing. Requires replacement.

Transmission Pinion Shaft Bearing

A rough, or otherwise damaged, transmission pinion (input) shaft bearing noise can be heard only when the clutch is engaged, with transmission in any shift position. The noise is usually quite noticeable with the gears in neutral. This noise should diminish and completely disappear as the transmission pinion gear slows down and stops after clutch release. This noise is easily distinguished from release bearing noise because of the opposite conditions of encounter.

Transmitted Engine Noises

Assuming that the clutch pedal has the required amount of free-play, there should be no objectionable amount of engine noise transmitted to the passenger area via the clutch. Some engine noises are transmitted through the positive pressure of the clutch release bearing and fingers to the clutch housing. Here they are amplified by the shape of the clutch housing and heard in the passenger compartment in the guise of clutch or transmission trouble. Engine noise transmission can usually be modified through clutch pedal manipulation.

Clutch Linkage Noise

Clutch linkage noise is usually a clicking or snapping sound that can be heard or felt in the pedal itself when moving it completely up or down. Locating the cause of trouble and correcting it is a matter of repositioning and lubrication. The trouble may be in the clutch assist spring, the retract spring, the release bearing lever, or even at the release bearing.

Clutch Chatter or Grab

Usually the cause of clutch chatter or grab can be located within the

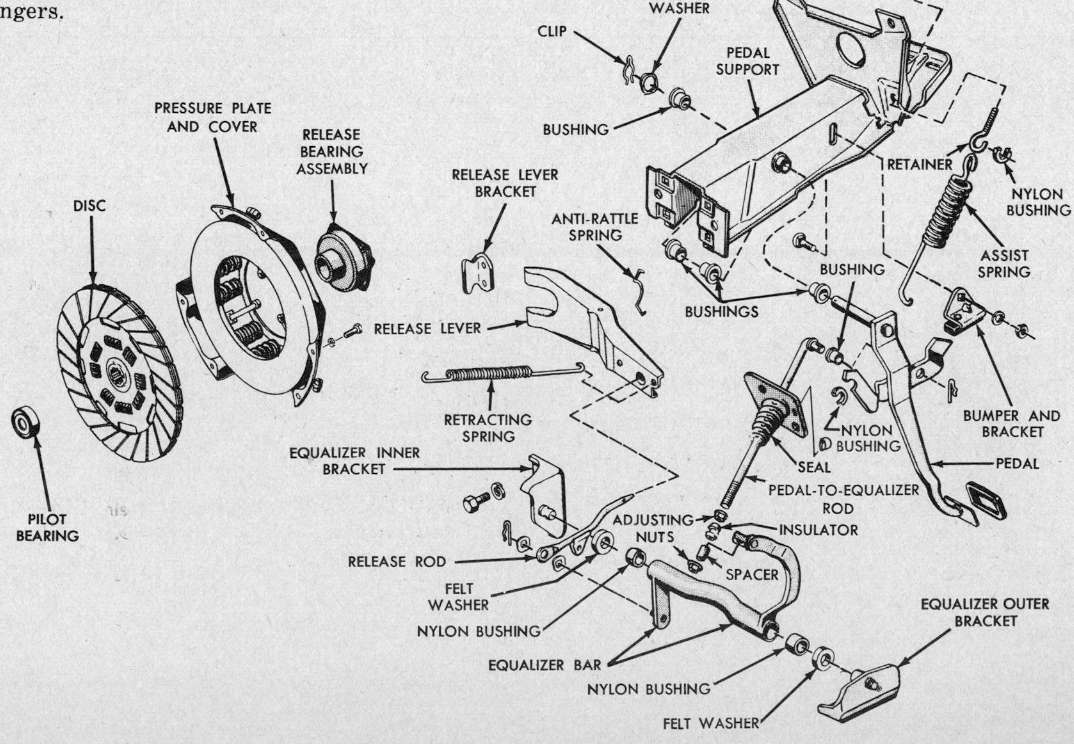

Typical clutch linkage (© Ford Motor Co)

clutch assembly. To correct the trouble will require the removal of the clutch. However, symptoms resembling clutch trouble may be misleading and originate in other areas.

In order to isolate the cause of the problem, we suggest that the following items be checked in this order.

1. Be sure that the clutch linkage is in adjustment and not binding. If necessary, lubricate, align and adjust linkage.
2. Check for worn or loose engine or transmission mounts. If necessary, tighten or replace mounts.
3. Check for wear, looseness or misalignment of universal joints. Check attaching bolts on clutch pressure plate, transmission and clutch housing. Tighten, align or replace as necessary.
4. Check freedom of movement of the clutch release bearing on its sleeve. Free up or replace as necessary.
5. Check for oil or grease on the flywheel, friction disc or pressure plate.
6. Check for trueness of the friction disc, and that the disc hub is not binding on the splines of the transmission input shaft (clutch shaft).
7. Be sure that the disc or the pressure plate is not broken.
8. Examine clutch pressure plate and cover plate assembly for cracks or heat discoloration.
9. Check pressure plate and flywheel for warpage.

Clutch Slip

Clutch slippage is usually most noticeable when pulling away, and during acceleration from a standing start. A severe, but positive, test for slippage is to start the engine, set the parking brake and apply the service brakes; shift the transmission into high gear and release the clutch pedal while accelerating the engine. A clutch in good condition should hold and stall the engine. If the clutch slips, the cause may be one or more of the following:

1. Improper linkage adjustment (not enough free-play).
2. Broken or disconnected parts.
3. Clutch linkage or lever mechanism binding or broken, not allowing full pressure plate application.
4. Friction disc oil-saturated or excessively worn.
5. Pressure plate worn, springs weak from temper loss or failure (damaging heat will usually cause parts to appear blue).
6. Clutch plate not seated (after installation of a new plate).

Clutch Drag or Failure to Release

There are many reasons for clutch drag (spin) or failure to release. The following conditions, therefore, apply to unmodified versions of standard vehicles. Changing the driven plate mass (replacing the standard driven plate with a heavy duty unit), changing transmission oil viscosity, etc. may influence clutch spin-time. Three seconds is a good, typical, spin-time for the standard transmission and clutch, driven under normal conditions, in average temperate zone climates.

The friction disc and some of the transmission gears spin briefly after clutch disengagement, so normal clutch action should not be confused with a dragging clutch.

Clutch drag, failure to release or abnormal spin-time may be caused by one or more of the following:

1. Improper clutch linkage adjustment or release fork off pivot.
2. Clutch plate hub binding on the transmission input (pinion) shaft.
3. A warped or bent friction disc or pressure plate; or loose friction material on the driven disc.
4. The transmission input shaft may be binding or sticking in the pilot bearing.
5. Misalignment of transmission to the engine.
6. Transmission lubricant low or not heavy enough.

Pedal Pulsation

This condition can be felt by applying light foot pressure to the clutch pedal with the engine idling. It may be caused by any of the following:

1. Bent or uneven clutch release finger adjustment.
2. Excessive flywheel runout due to bent wheel or crankshaft flange; or the flywheel may not be properly seated on the crankshaft flange.
3. Release bearing cocked on transmission bearing retainer.
4. Poor alignment of transmission with the engine.

Low Clutch Facing Life

This sort of complaint warrants a close study of the operator's driving habits. Poor clutch facing wear may be caused by any of the following:

1. Riding the clutch.
2. Drag strip type operation.
3. Continuous overloading, or the hauling of heavy trailers or other equipment.
4. Holding the car from drifting backward on a grade; by slipping the clutch instead of using the brakes.
5. Improper pedal linkage adjustment (free-play and pedal height).
6. Rough surface on flywheel or pressure plate.
7. Presence of oil or water on clutch facing.
8. Weak pressure plate springs, causing clutch creep or slip.

Gear Lock Up or Hard Shifting

This trouble is so closely related to Clutch Drag Or Failure To Release that diagnosis should be conducted in the same way as given under that heading. If, after checking the items listed and finding that the transmission still locks up or is hard to shift, the trouble probably lies in the transmission cover or shifter assembly, or in the transmission proper. In that case, transmission work is needed.

Hard Pedal

A stiff clutch pedal or a clutch release that requires abnormal pedal pressure may result from one or more of the following:

1. Dry and binding clutch linkage and levers.
2. Linkage out of alignment.
3. Improper (heavy) retracting spring.
4. Dry or binding release bearing sleeve or transmission bearing retainer.
5. Assist spring missing or improperly adjusted.
6. Wrong type clutch assembly (heavy duty) being used.

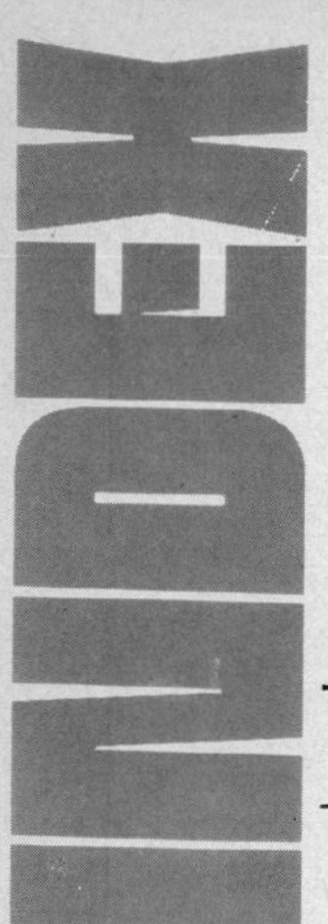

Manual Transmissions

Applicability Chart

Make	Model	TYPE 3-spd	TYPE 4-spd
American Motors	1969-72	16, 17	18
	1973	16	18
	1974	5, 16	18
	1975-76	5, 19	
Apollo	1973-76	11	
Astre	1975-76	11	13
Barracuda	1969	2	4
	1970-72	1, 3	4
	1973-74	1	4
Buick	1969-71	5	
Buick Special, Skylark, Century, GS	1969	5, 11	12
	1970-71	10, 11	12
	1972	11	12
	1973-76	11	
Camaro	1969-73	10, 11	12, 13
	1974-76	11	13, 18
Challenger	1970-72	1, 3	4
	1973-74	1	4
Chevelle	1969-74	10, 11	12, 13
	1975-76	11	
Chevrolet	1969	10, 11	12, 13
	1970-73	10, 11	
Chrysler	1969	2	
	1970-71	1	
Comet	1971-76	5	
Corvette	1969	11	12, 13
	1970-73		12, 13
	1974-76		13, 18
Cougar	1968-73	5	9
Dart, Demon	1969	2, 3	4
	1970-74	1, 3	4
	1975-76	1, 5	4
Dodge, Coronet, Charger	1969	2, 3	4
	1970-72	1, 3	4
	1973-74	1	4
	1975-76	1	
Fairlane, Falcon	1969-70	5	9
Firebird	1969	5, 11	12, 13
	1970-71	10, 11	12
	1972-73	10, 11	12, 13
	1974	10, 11	12, 13, 18

Make	Model	TYPE 3-spd	TYPE 4-spd
	1975-76	11	13, 18
Ford	1969-71	5	9
Granada	1975-76	5	
Maverick	1970-76	5	
Mercury	1969-71	5	9
Monarch	1975-76	5	
Monte Carlo	1970-71	10	12
	1972-74	10	
	1975-76	11	
Montego	1969-74	5	9
Monza	1975-76		13
Mustang	1969-73	5	9
Mustang II	1974-76		8
Nova	1969-74	10, 11	12, 13
	1975-76	11	13
Oldsmobile	1969-71	5	
Olds F-85, Cutlass, 4-4-2	1969	5, 11	12
	1970-71	10, 11	12
	1972-73	11	12
	1974-76	11	
Omega	1973-76	11	
Pinto	1971-73 1600		7
	1971-76 All		6
Plymouth, Belvedere, Satellite	1969	2, 3	4
	1970-72	1, 3	4
	1974	1	4
	1975-76	1	
Pontiac	1969-71	5, 10	12
Skyhawk, Starfire	1975-76		13
Tempest, GTO, LeMans	1969	5, 11	12, 13
	1970-74	10, 11	12, 13
	1975-76	11	
Torino	1971-74	5	9
Valiant, Duster	1969	2	4
	1970-74	1, 3	4
	1975-76	1, 5	4
Vega	1971-72	14	15
	1973-76	11	13
Ventura	1971-76	11	

Type Numbers Refer to Sections in Text

Section Page Numbers

Manual Transmissions

Diagnosis

Jumping out of High Gear

1. Misalignment of transmission case or clutch housing.
2. Worn pilot bearing in crankshaft.
3. Bent transmission shaft.
4. Worn high speed sliding gear.
5. Worn teeth in clutch shaft.
6. Insufficient spring tension on shifter rail plunger.
7. Bent or loose shifter fork.
8. End-play in clutch shaft.
9. Gears not engaging completely.
10. Loose or worn bearings on clutch shaft or mainshaft.

Sticking in High Gear

1. Clutch not releasing fully.
2. Burred or battered teeth on clutch shaft.
3. Burred or battered transmission main-shaft.
4. Frozen synchronizing clutch.
5. Stuck shifter rail plunger.
6. Gearshift lever twisting and binding shifter rail.
7. Battered teeth on high speed sliding gear or on sleeve.
8. Lack of lubrication.
9. Improper lubrication.
10. Corroded transmission parts.
11. Defective mainshaft pilot bearing.

Jumping out of Second Gear

1. Insufficient spring tension on shifter rail plunger.
2. Bent or loose shifter fork.
3. Gears not engaging completely.
4. End-play in transmission mainshaft.
5. Loose transmission gear bearing.
6. Defective mainshaft pilot bearing.
7. Bent transmission shaft.
8. Worn teeth on second speed sliding gear or sleeve.
9. Loose or worn bearings on transmission mainshaft.
10. End-play in countershaft.

Sticking in Second Gear

1. Clutch not releasing fully.
2. Burred or battered teeth on sliding sleeve.
3. Burred or battered transmission main-shaft.
4. Frozen synchronizing clutch.
5. Stuck shifter rail plunger.
6. Gearshift lever twisting and binding shifter rail.
7. Lack of lubrication.
8. Second speed transmission gear bearings locked will give same effect as gears stuck in second.
9. Improper lubrication.
10. Corroded transmission parts.

Jumping out of Low Gear

1. Gears not engaging completely.
2. Bent or loose shifter fork.
3. End-play in transmission mainshaft.
4. End-play in countershaft.
5. Loose or worn bearings on transmission mainshaft.
6. Loose or worn bearings in countershaft.
7. Defective mainshaft pilot bearing.

Sticking in Low Gear

1. Clutch not releasing fully.
2. Burred or battered transmission main-shaft.
3. Stuck shifter rail plunger.
4. Gearshift lever twisting and binding shifter rail.
5. Lack of lubrication.
6. Improper lubrication.
7. Corroded transmission parts.

Jumping out of Reverse Gear

1. Insufficient spring tension on shifter rail plunger.
2. Bent or loose shifter fork.
3. Badly worn gear teeth.
4. Gears not engaging completely.
5. End-play in transmission mainshaft.
6. Idler gear bushings loose or worn.
7. Loose or worn bearings on transmission mainshaft.
8. Defective mainshaft pilot bearing.

Sticking in Reverse Gear

1. Clutch not releasing fully.
2. Burred or battered transmission main-shaft.
3. Stuck shifter rail plunger.
4. Gearshift lever twisting and binding shifter rail.
5. Lack of lubrication.
6. Improper lubrication.
7. Corroded transmission parts.

Failure of Gears to Synchronize

1. Binding pilot bearing on mainshaft, will synchronize in high gear only.
2. Clutch not releasing fully.
3. Detent springs weak or broken.
4. Weak or broken springs under balls in sliding gear sleeve.
5. Binding bearing on clutch shaft.
6. Binding countershaft.
7. Binding pilot bearing in crankshaft.
8. Badly worn gear teeth.
9. Scored or worn cones.
10. Improper lubrication.
11. Constant mesh gear not turning freely on transmission mainshaft. Will synchronize in that gear only.

Gears Spinning When Shifting into Gear from Neutral

1. Clutch not releasing fully.
2. In some cases an extremely light lubricant in transmission will cause gears to continue to spin for a short time after clutch is released.
3. Binding pilot bearing in crankshaft.

Type-1 A-230 Fully Synchronized Chrysler 3-Speed

Application

Barracuda, 1970-74
Challenger, 1970-74
Charger, 1970-74
Chrysler, 1970-71
Dart, 1970-76
Dodge, 1970-76
Plymouth, 1970-76
Valiant, 1970-76

Disassembly

Shift Housing and Mechanism

1. Shift to second gear.
2. Unbolt and remove side cover with shift mechanism.

If shaft O-ring seals need replacement:

3. Pull shift forks out of shafts.
4. Remove nuts and operating levers from shafts.
5. Deburr shafts. Remove shafts.

Drive Pinion Retainer and Extension Housing

1. Unbolt pinion bearing retainer from front of transmission case. Remove retainer and gasket. Pry off retainer oil seal.

For clearance:

2. With a brass drift, tap drive pinion as far forward as possible. Rotate cut away part of second gear next to countershaft gear. Shift second-third synchronizer sleeve forward.
3. Remove speedometer pinion adapter retainer. Work adapter and pinion out of extension housing.
4. Unbolt extension housing. Break housing loose with plastic hammer and carefully remove.

Idler Gear and Mainshaft

1. Insert dummy shaft in case to push reverse idler shaft and key out of case.
2. Remove dummy shaft and idler gear together to prevent losing rollers.
3. Remove both tanged idler gear thrust washers.
4. Remove mainshaft assembly through rear of case.

Countershaft Gear and Drive Pinion

1. Using a mallet and dummy shaft, tap the countershaft rearward enough to remove key. Drive countershaft out of case, maintaining contact between countershaft and dummy shaft so that washers will not drop out.
2. Lower countershaft gear to bottom of case.
3. Remove snap-ring from pinion bearing outer race (outside front of case).
4. Drive pinion shaft into case with plastic hammer. Remove assembly through rear of case.
5. If bearing is to be replaced, remove snap-ring and press off bearing.
6. Lift countershaft gear and dummy shaft out through rear of case.

Mainshaft

1. Remove snap-ring from front end of mainshaft along with second gear stop ring. Remove sec-

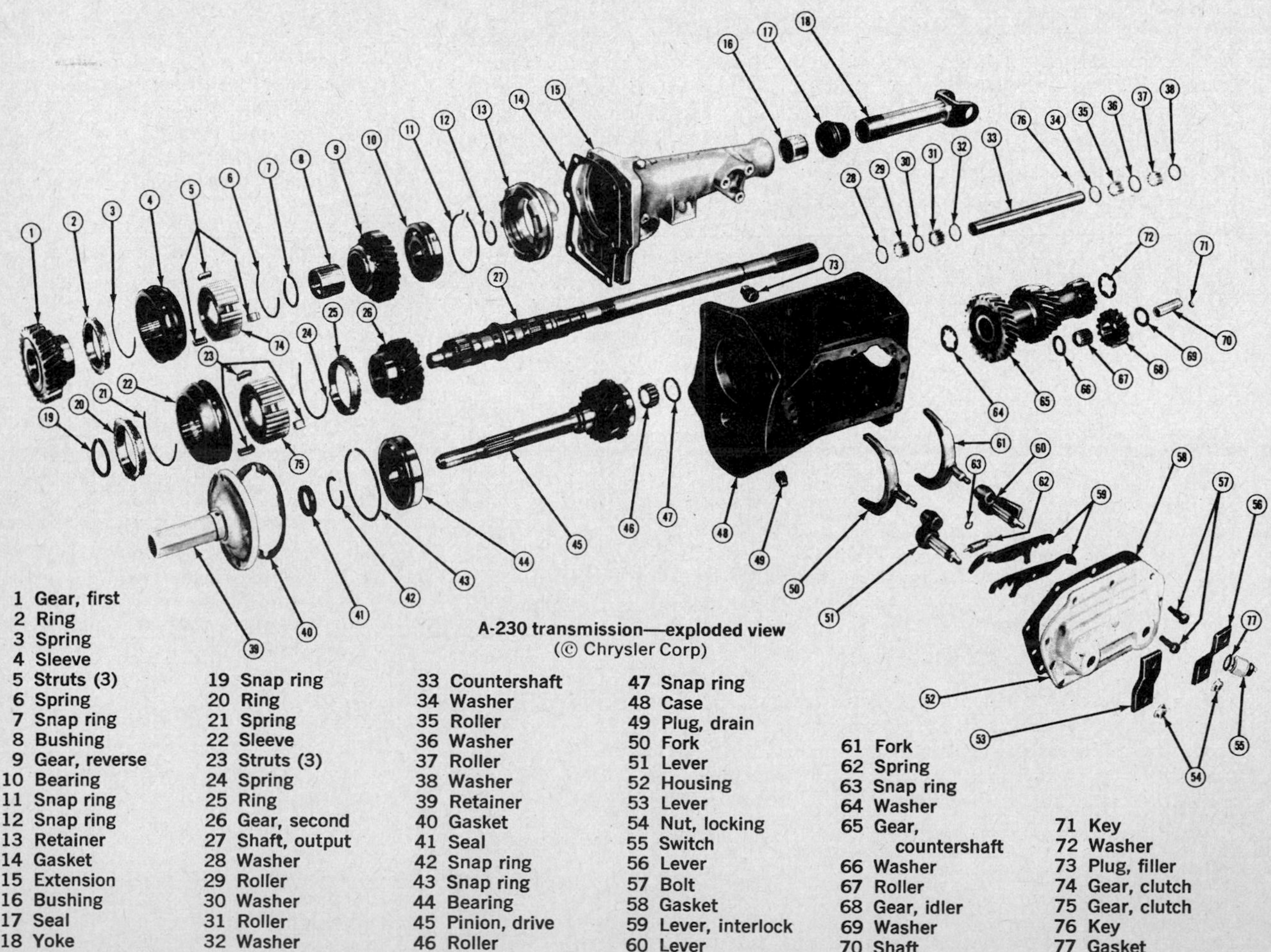

A-230 transmission—exploded view
(© Chrysler Corp)

1 Gear, first
2 Ring
3 Spring
4 Sleeve
5 Struts (3)
6 Spring
7 Snap ring
8 Bushing
9 Gear, reverse
10 Bearing
11 Snap ring
12 Snap ring
13 Retainer
14 Gasket
15 Extension
16 Bushing
17 Seal
18 Yoke
19 Snap ring
20 Ring
21 Spring
22 Sleeve
23 Struts (3)
24 Spring
25 Ring
26 Gear, second
27 Shaft, output
28 Washer
29 Roller
30 Washer
31 Roller
32 Washer
33 Countershaft
34 Washer
35 Roller
36 Washer
37 Roller
38 Washer
39 Retainer
40 Gasket
41 Seal
42 Snap ring
43 Snap ring
44 Bearing
45 Pinion, drive
46 Roller
47 Snap ring
48 Case
49 Plug, drain
50 Fork
51 Lever
52 Housing
53 Lever
54 Nut, locking
55 Switch
56 Lever
57 Bolt
58 Gasket
59 Lever, interlock
60 Lever
61 Fork
62 Spring
63 Snap ring
64 Washer
65 Gear, countershaft
66 Washer
67 Roller
68 Gear, idler
69 Washer
70 Shaft
71 Key
72 Washer
73 Plug, filler
74 Gear, clutch
75 Gear, clutch
76 Key
77 Gasket

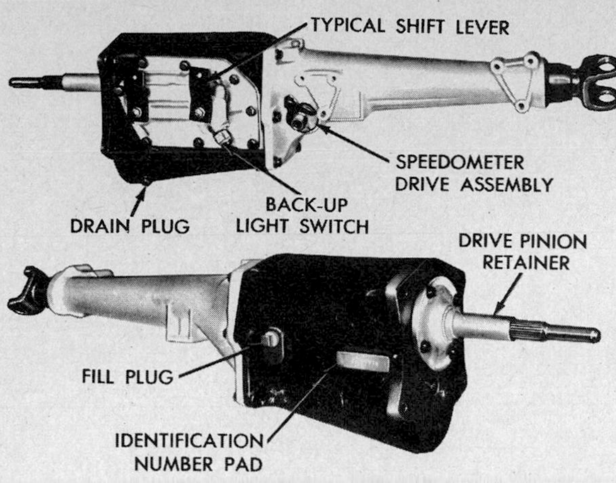

Side views of A-230 transmission
(© Chrysler Corp)

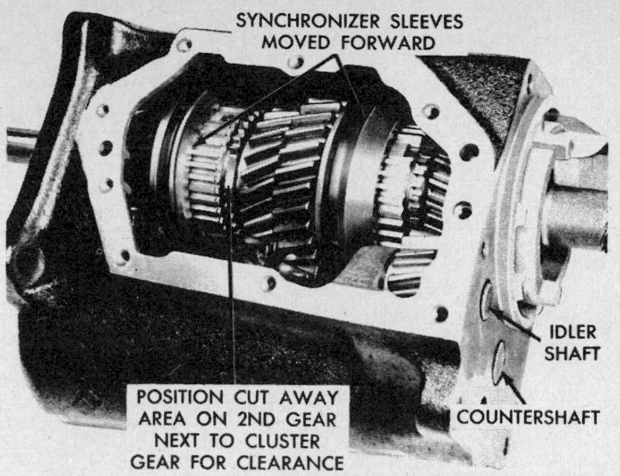

Positioning second gear and shift sleeves for clearance
(© Chrysler Corp)

ond gear from mainshaft.

2. Spread snap-ring in mainshaft bearing retainer. Slide retainer back off the bearing race.
3. Remove snap-ring at rear of mainshaft. Support front side of reverse gear. Press bearing off mainshaft. Be careful not to let parts drop when bearing clears shaft.
4. Remove from press. Remove mainshaft bearing and reverse gear from shaft.
5. Remove snap-ring from rear of shaft. Slide first-reverse synchronizer assembly off splines and remove rearward. Remove stop-ring and first gear through the rear.

Inspection

1. Clean all parts with solvent.
2. Dry with compressed air.

Case

1. Check for cracks, stripped threads, and burrs or nicks on machined surfaces. Dress off any burrs with a fine file. Stripped threads may be repaired by use of Helicoil inserts.

Ball Bearings

1. Do not spin bearings with air pressure; turn slowly by hand to avoid damage.
2. Lubricate with light engine oil.
3. Check for pitting.
4. Check fit on shafts.

Needle Bearings

1. Check rollers for flats or brinelling.
2. Check roller spacers for wear or galling.

Gears

1. Check gear splines on synchronizer clutch gears and stop-rings for chipping or worn teeth.
2. Be sure the clutch sleeve slides easily on clutch gear.
3. Check countershaft gear and all gear teeth for chipping, broken teeth, or excessive wear. Stone off small nicks or burrs.
4. If oil seal contact area on drive pinion shaft is pitted, rusted, or scratched, replace the pinion.

Synchronizer Stop Rings

1. Check for cracks or wear.
2. Check new rings for good fit on gear cones with minimum wobble.

Mainshaft

1. Check mainshaft gear and bearing mating surfaces for galling or excessive wear.
2. Check snap-rings for burred edges. Remove burrs with a fine file.
3. Check synchronizer clutch gear splines on shaft for burrs.

Assembly

Countershaft Gear

1. Slide dummy shaft into countershaft gear.
2. Slide one roller thrust washer over dummy shaft and into gear. followed by 22 greased rollers.
3. Repeat Step 2, adding one roller thrust washer on end.
4. Repeat steps 2 and 3 at other end of countershaft gear. There is a total of 88 rollers and 6 thrust washers.
5. Place greased front thrust washer on dummy shaft against gear with tangs forward.
6. Grease rear thrust washer and stick it in place in the case, with tangs rearward. Place countershaft gear assembly in bottom of transmission case until drive pinion is installed.

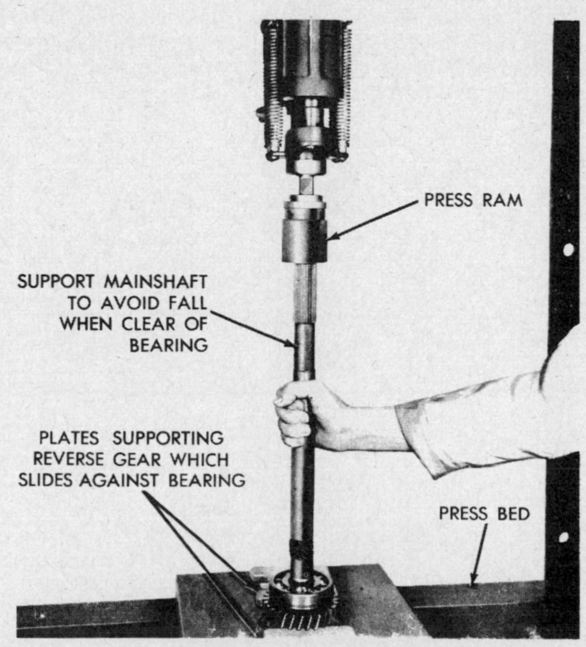

Pressing off mainshaft bearing
(© Chrysler Corp)

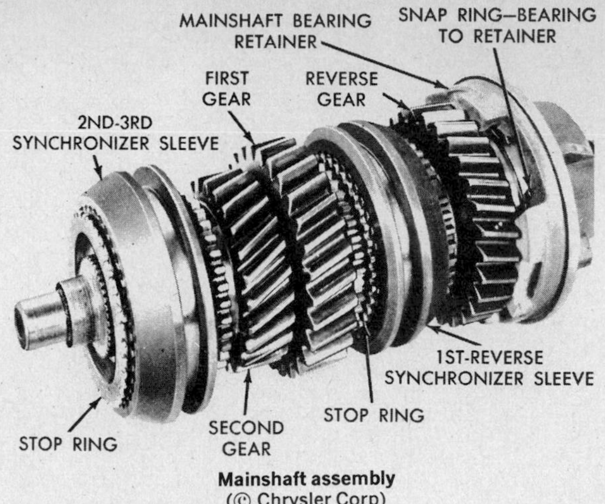

Mainshaft assembly
(© Chrysler Corp)

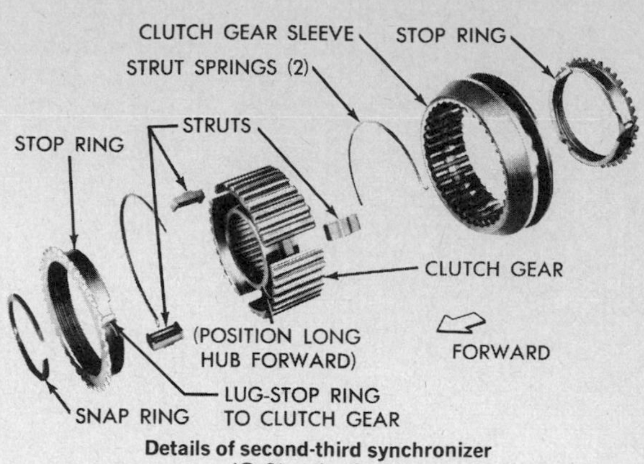

Details of second-third synchronizer
(© Chrysler Corp)

Pinion Gear

1. Press new bearing on pinion shaft with snap-ring groove forward. Install new snap-ring.
2. Install 15 rollers and retaining ring in drive pinion gear.
3. Install drive pinion and bearing assembly into case.
4. Install the countershaft gear assembly by positioning it and thrust washers so countershaft can be tapped into position. Be careful to keep the countershaft against the dummy shaft to keep parts from falling between them. Install key in countershaft.
5. Tap drive pinion forward for clearance.

Mainshaft

1. Place a stop-ring flat on the bench. Place a clutch gear and a sleeve on top. Drop the struts in their slots and snap in a strut spring placing the tang inside one strut. Turn the assembly over and install second strut spring, tang in a different strut.
2. Slide first gear and stop-ring over rear of mainshaft and against thrust flange between first and second gears on shaft.
3. Slide first-reverse synchronizer assembly over rear of mainshaft, indexing hub slots to first gear stop-ring lugs.
4. Install first-reverse synchronizer clutch gear snap-ring on mainshaft.
5. Slide reverse gear and mainshaft bearing into place. Press bearing on shaft, supporting inner race of bearing. Be sure snap-ring groove on outer race is forward.
6. Install bearing retaining snap-ring on mainshaft. Spread snap-ring in retainer groove and slide it over the bearing. Seat ring in groove.
7. Place second gear over front of mainshaft with thrust surface against flange.
8. Install stop-ring and second-third synchronizer assembly against second gear. Install second-third synchronizer clutch gear snap-ring on shaft.
9. Move second-third synchronizer sleeve forward as far as possible. Install front stop-ring, inside the sleeve with lugs indexed to struts. Coat the stop-ring with grease to hold it in position.
10. Rotate cut-out on second gear toward countershaft gear to provide clearance.
11. Insert mainshaft assembly into case. Tilt assembly to clear cluster gears and insert pilot rollers in drive pinion gear. If assembly is correct, the bearing retainer will bottom to the case without force. If not, check for a misplaced strut, pinion roller, or stop-ring.

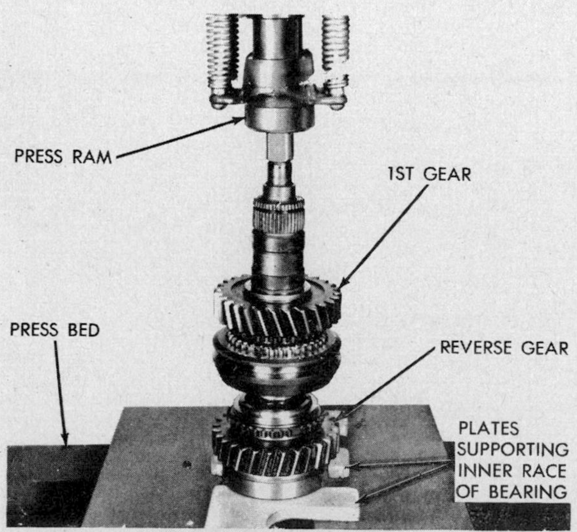

Pressing on mainshaft bearing
(© Chrysler Corp)

Reverse Idler Gear

1. Place dummy shaft into idler gear. Insert 22 greased rollers.
2. Position reverse idler thrust washers in case with grease.
3. Position idler gear and dummy shaft in case. Install idler shaft and key.

Extension Housing

1. Remove extension housing yoke seal. Drive bushing out from inside housing.
2. Align oil hole in bushing with oil slot in housing. Drive bushing into place. Drive new seal into housing.
3. Install extension housing and gasket to hold mainshaft and bearing retainer in place.

Drive Pinion Bearing Retainer

1. Install outer snap-ring on drive pinion bearing. Tap assembly back until snap-ring contacts case.
2. Install a new seal in retainer bore.
3. Position main drive pinion bearing retainer and gasket on front of case. Coat threads with sealing compound, install bolts, torque to 30 ft. lbs.

Gearshift Mechanism and Housing

1. If removed, place two interlock

levers on pivot pin with spring hangers offset toward each other, so that spring installs in a straight line. Place E-clip on pivot pin.
2. Grease and install new O-ring seals on both shift shafts. Grease housing bores. Push each shaft into its bore.
3. Install spring on interlock lever hangers.
4. Rotate each shift shaft fork bore to vertical position. Install shift forks through bores and under both interlock levers.
5. Position second-third synchronizer sleeve to rear, in second gear position. Position first-reverse synchronizer sleeve to middle of travel, in neutral position. Place shift forks in the same positions.
6. Install gasket and gearshift mechanism. The bolt with the extra long shoulder must be installed at the center rear of the case. Torque bolts to 15 ft. lbs.
7. Install speedometer drive pinion gear and adapter. Range number on adapter, which represents the number of teeth on the gear, should be in 6 o'clock position.

Exhaust Emission Control System Switch

Some models have a switch in the shift cover, adjacent to the 2-3 shift lever. It is actuated by a flat on the 2-3 shift lever, when in third gear. If vehicle is not equipped with Emission System, a plug is installed in the mounting hole. Torque the switch or plug to 15 ft. lbs.

Type-2
A-745 Chrysler 3-Speed

Application

Barracuda, 1969
Charger, 1969
Chrysler, 1969
Dart, 1969
Dodge, 1969
Plymouth, 1969
Valiant, 1969

Disassembly

1. Remove output flange nut, then the drum and flange assembly, if so equipped. Remove parking brake assembly, if so equipped.
2. Remove case cover. Measure synchronizer float with feeler gauges. This measurement is taken between the end of a synchronizer pin and the opposite synchronizer outer ring. The measurement should be .060-.117 in.
3. Remove five bolts and one nut attaching the extension housing to the transmission case.
4. Remove the extension housing.
5. Remove the mainshaft rear bearing, if it did not come off with the extension housing.
6. Remove transmission case cover and gasket.
7. Remove four bolts from the drive pinion bearing retainer, then remove the retainer.
8. When removing the drive pinion and bearing assembly from the transmission case, slide the front inner stop-ring from the short splines on the pinion as the assembly is being removed from the case.
9. Remove the snap-ring that holds the main drive pinion bearing onto the shaft.
10. Press bearing off pinion shaft and remove oil slinger.
11. Remove mainshaft pilot bearing snap-ring from the cavity of the pinion gear.
12. Remove the 15 pilot roller bearings.
13. Remove seal from pinion retainer.
14. Remove mainshaft rear bearing

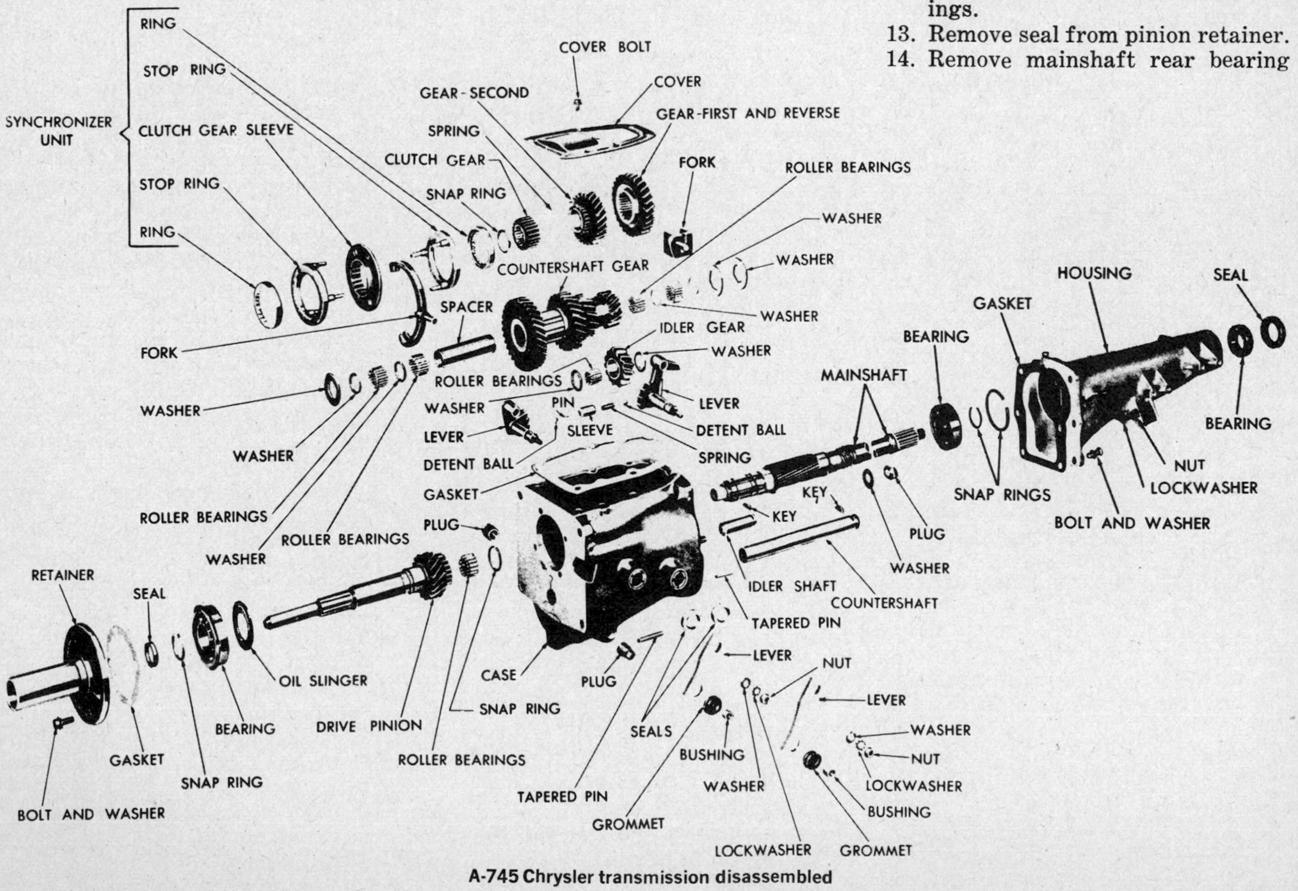

A-745 Chrysler transmission disassembled

snap-ring from groove in mainshaft rear bearing bore in the case.
15. Slide the mainshaft and rear bearing assembly to the rear, until the rear bearing is out of the case.
16. Remove synchronizer assembly from case.
17. Remove second and third-speed shift fork.
18. Remove synchronizer clutch gear snap-ring.
19. Remove synchronizer clutch gear, second-speed gear, and first and reverse sliding gear from the mainshaft.
20. Withdraw mainshaft and bearing out through the rear of the case.
21. Remove the synchronizer clutch gear, second-speed gear, low and reverse sliding gear, and low and reverse shift fork from the case.
22. With a dummy shaft, drive the countershaft toward the rear of the case until the small key can be removed from the countershaft.
23. Drive the countershaft the remaining way out of the case.
24. Lift the cluster gear, the thrust washers and the dummy shaft assembly out of the case.
25. Remove the cluster gear (88 rollers, four spacer rings) and the center spacer from the cluster.
26. With a blunt drift, drive the reverse idler shaft toward the rear of the case far enough to remove the key from the shaft.
27. Completely remove the shaft from the case, then remove the idler gear.
28. Remove the thrust washers and 22 rollers.
29. With a small punch, remove low and reverse gear lever shaft tapered lockpin by driving it toward the top of the transmission case.
30. Remove the second and third gear lever shaft in the same manner.
31. Remove the lever shafts from the transmission case. Don't lose the spring-loaded detent balls.
32. Remove the interlock sleeve, spring, pin and detent balls.
33. Remove both lever shaft seals and discard same.

Assembly

1. Place oil slinger on the main drive pinion with the offset outer portion next to the drive pinion teeth.
2. Place the main drive pinion bearing on the pinion shaft with the outer snap-ring away from the pinion gear.
3. Press the bearing into position so it is seated firmly against the oil slinger and pinion gear.
4. Install the bearing retaining snap-ring on the pinion shaft. Be sure the snap-ring is seated in its groove.
5. Coat the 15 pilot bearing rollers with heavy grease and install them in the cavity at the rear of the main drive pinion.
6. Install the snap-ring.
7. Place the bearing spacer in the center of the bore in the cluster gear and use the dummy shaft to assist in assembling the roller bearings.
8. Install a row of 22 rollers next to one end of the spacer, using heavy grease to hold them.
9. Place one of the four bearing spacer rings next to the row of rollers, and install another row of 22 rollers next to the spacer ring.
10. Install another spacer ring at the outside end of the second row of bearing rollers.
11. At the opposite end of the cluster gear bore, install the remaining spacer rings and bearing rollers in the same sequence as listed in Steps 8, 9, and 10.
12. With a small amount of grease, install the front thrust washer on the dummy shaft at the front end of the cluster gear, with the tabs outward.
13. Install the tabbed rear thrust washer onto the dummy shaft against the rear of the cluster gear with the tabs positioned in the grooves provided in the cluster gear.
14. Install the remaining rear thrust washer plate onto the rear of the gear and dummy shaft with the step in the washer facing upward, as viewed from the rear.
15. Align tabs of the front thrust washer vertically to index with notches in the transmission case and with the step in the rear thrust washer positioned upward. Insert the cluster gear and dummy shaft in the transmission case.
16. Using the countershaft, drive the dummy shaft forward, out of the case. Countershaft end-play should be .0045-.028 in.
17. Position a dummy shaft in the reverse idler gear and, using heavy grease, install the 22 roller bearings into the gear.
18. Place the thrust washers at each end of the reverse idler gear, then position the assembly in the transmission case with the chamfered end of the gear teeth toward the front.
19. Insert the reverse idler shaft into the bore at the rear of the case, with the keyway to the rear, pushing the dummy shaft forward and out of the front of the transmission.
20. With the keyway in proper align-

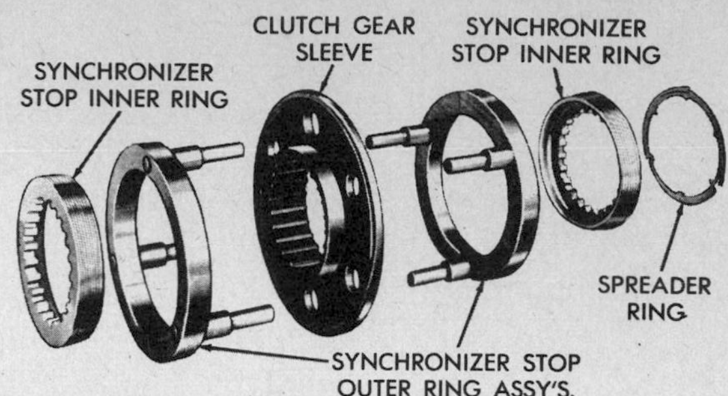

Synchromesh assembly

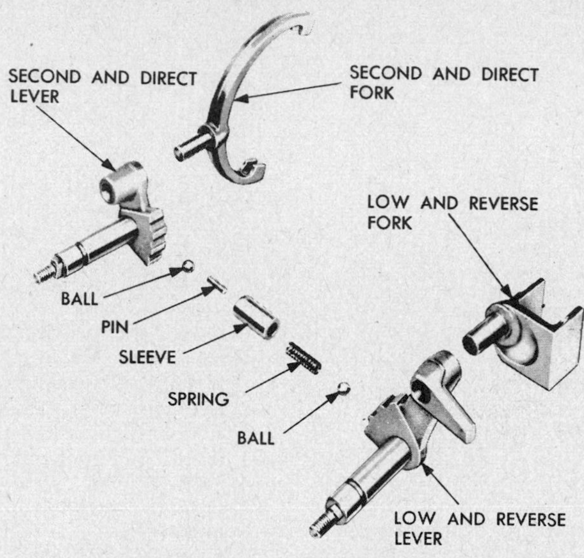

Shift forks and shafts

ment, insert the key and continue driving the shaft forward until the key seats in the recess.
21. Install two new lever shaft seals in the transmission case.
22. Lubricate and install second and third-speed lever shaft in the bores of the case.
23. Install the second and third speed lever shaft lockpin in the hole in the case. Drive it in firmly, in a downward direction.
24. Place interlock parts in the case in the following order: ball, sleeve, spring, pin and ball.
25. Enter low and reverse lever shaft in the case bore, depress the detent ball against spring tension and push the lever shaft firmly into position, in order to prevent the ball from escaping.
26. Install low and reverse lever shaft lockpin in the case by driving it downward.
27. Place low and reverse fork in the lever shaft, with the offset toward the rear.
28. While holding the low and reverse sliding gear in position in the fork, with the hub extension to the rear, insert the mainshaft with the rear bearing through the rear of the case and into the sliding gear.
29. Place synchronizer stop-ring spring, then the rear stop-ring, on the synchronizer splines of the second-speed gear. Install the second-speed gear onto the mainshaft. Synchronizer shims must be added if synchronizer float is more than the maximum in Step 2, disassembly. If float was less than minimum, the six pins must be shortened.
30. Install the synchronizer clutch gear on the mainshaft with the shoulder to the front.
31. Select the thickest synchronizer clutch gear snap-ring that can be used, and install it in the mainshaft groove.
32. Check clearance between clutch gear and second-speed gear. Clearance should be .004-.014 in.
33. Hold the synchronizer clutch gear sleeve and two outer rings together with pins properly entered into the holes in the clutch gear sleeve. The clutch gear sleeve should engage in the groove of the second- and third-speed shift fork. Position the fork in the second and third-speed lever shaft.
34. While holding the synchronizer parts and fork in position, slide the mainshaft forward, entering the synchronizer clutch gear into the clutch gear sleeve. At the same time, enter the mainshaft rear bearing in the case bore.
35. While still holding the synchronizer parts in position, tap the mainshaft forward until the rear bearing bottoms in the case bore.
36. Install the mainshaft rear bearing snap-ring into place in the case bore.
37. Install a new seal in the drive pinion retainer.
38. Place the synchronizer front inner ring in position in the front outer ring, and enter the main drive pinion through the case bore.
39. Engage the splines on the rear of the pinion with the inner stop ring, and tap the drive pinion into the case until the outer snap-ring on the pinion bearing is against the transmission case.
40. Place the drive pinion bearing retainer over the pinion shaft and against the transmission case. While holding the retainer against the transmission case, measure the clearance between the retainer and case.
41. Select a gasket .003-.005 in. thicker than the clearance found.
42. Install and tighten the front bearing retainer bolts to 30 ft. lbs. torque.
43. Install a new seal in the extension housing.
44. Install extension housing. Torque the attaching bolts and nuts to 50 ft. lbs.
45. Install the parking brake assembly, on vehicles so equipped.
46. Install the parking brake drum (if so equipped) and flange assembly. Install the washer and nut and torque to 175 ft. lbs.
47. Install the drain plug in the transmission case.
48. Install the gearshift operating levers, and torque to 12 ft. lbs.
49. Install the back-up light switch.
50. Install the speedometer cable and drive gear. Fill with transmission lubricant to the proper level.

Type-3

A-903 Chrysler 3-Speed

Application

Charger/Coronet (6 Cyl.), 1969-72
Challenger (6 Cyl.), 1970-72
Barracuda (6 Cyl.), 1969-72
Dart (6 Cyl.), 1969-72
Dodge (6 Cyl.), 1969-72
Belvedere/Satellite (6 Cyl.), 1969-72
Plymouth (6 Cyl.), 1969-72
Valiant (6 Cyl.), 1969-72

A-250 Chrysler 3-Speed

Application

Dart, (6 Cyl.), 1973-74
Valiant, (6 Cyl.), 1973-74

Disassembly

1. Remove output shaft yoke.
2. Remove the bolts that attach the extension housing to the transmission case. Remove the housing.
3. Remove extension housing oil seal.
4. Remove the transmission case cover. Measure synchronizer float with feeler gauges on A-903 models. This measurement is taken between the end of a synchronizer pin and the opposite synchronizer outer ring. This measurement should be .060-.117 in.
5. Remove the attaching bolts and remove the main drive pinion bearing retainer. Then grasp the pinion shaft and pull the assembly out of the case.

Caution Be careful not to bind the inner synchronizer ring on the drive pinion clutch teeth.

6. Remove the snap-ring that locks the main drive pinion bearing onto the pinion shaft. Remove the bearing washer, press the shaft out of the bearing and remove the oil slinger.
7. Remove the snap-ring from the pilot bearing in the end of the drive pinion and remove the 14 rollers.
8. With the transmission in reverse, remove the outer center bearing snap-ring, then partially remove the mainshaft.
9. Cock the mainshaft, then remove the clutch sleeve, the outer synchronizer rings, the front inner

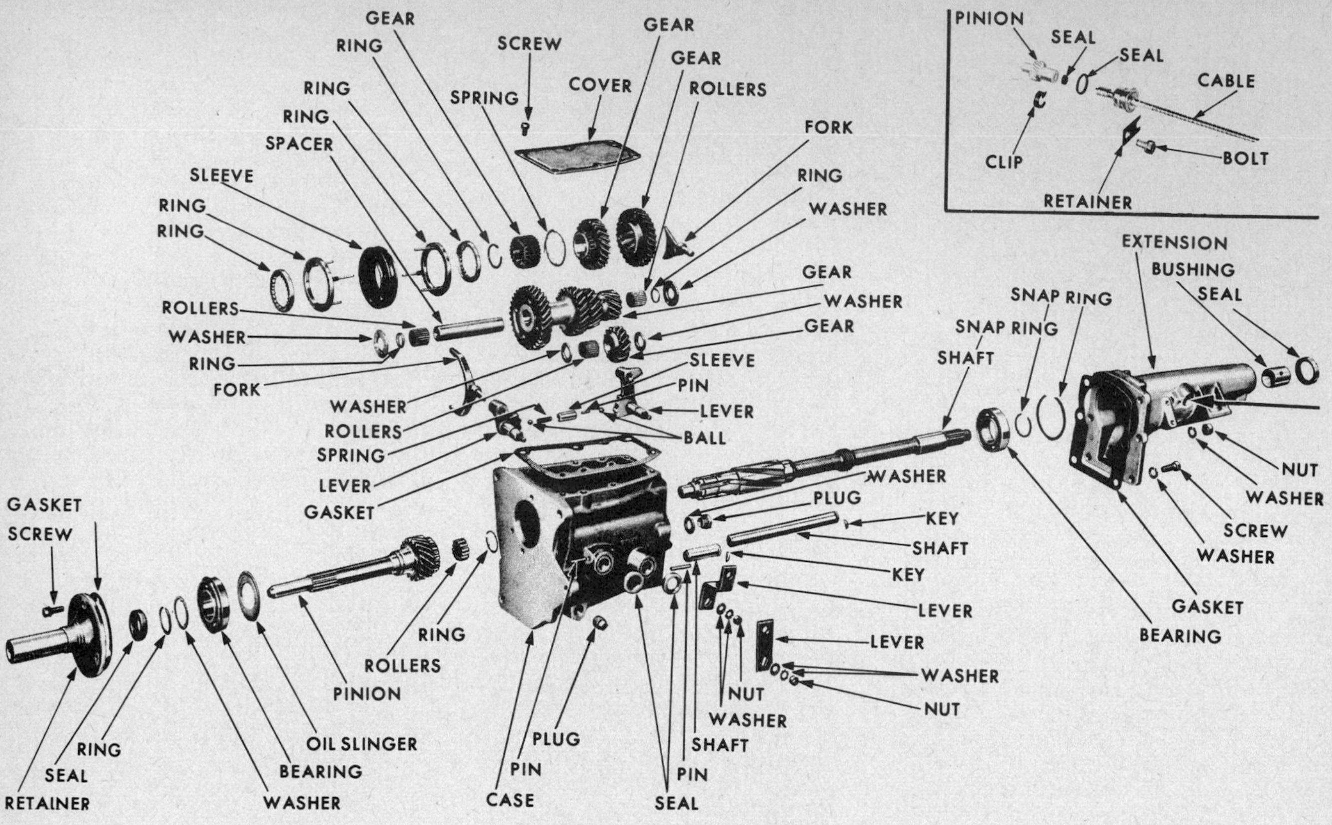

A-903, A-250 Chrysler transmission

ring and the second-third shift box.

10. Remove clutch gear retaining snap ring and slide the clutch gear off the end of the mainshaft.
11. Slide the second-speed gear, stop-ring and synchronizer spring off the mainshaft.
12. Remove the low and reverse sliding gear and shift fork, as the mainshaft is completely withdrawn from the case.
13. Check cluster gear end-play. End-play should be .005-.022 in. This measurement will determine thrust washer value at reassembly.
14. Drive the countershaft rearward, removing key, and out of the case.
15. Lift the gear cluster and thrust washers out of the case. Remove the needle bearings, (22 each end) and spacer from the cluster.
16. Drive the reverse idler shaft toward the rear and out of the case. Remove key.
17. Lift the reverse idler gear, thrust washers and 22 needle bearings out of the case.
18. Remove gearshift operating levers from their respective shafts. On an A-250 transmission, remove the tapered pins retaining the shift shafts to the case with a hammer and an 1/8 in. punch. Drive out the front pin to the front and the rear pin to the rear.
19. Drive out tapered retaining pin from either of the two lever shafts, then withdraw the shaft from inside the transmission case. (The detent balls are spring-loaded, as the shaft is being withdrawn, the balls will fall to the bottom of the case.)
20. Remove the interlock sleeve, spring, pin and both balls from the case. Drive out the remaining tapered pin, then slide the lever shaft out of the transmission.
21. Remove the lever shaft seals and discard them.

Assembly

1. Install two new shift lever shaft seals in the case.

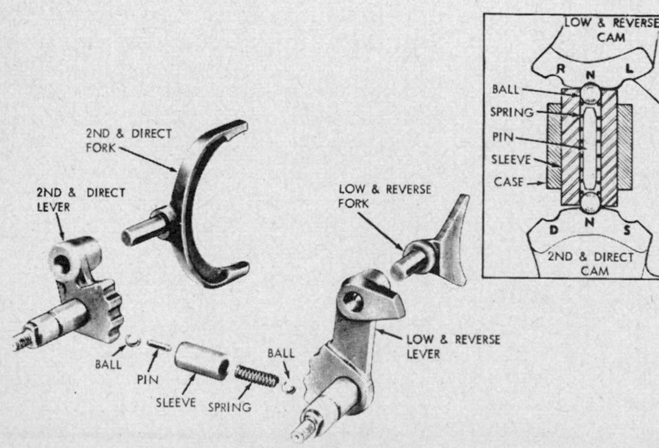

Shift forks and levers

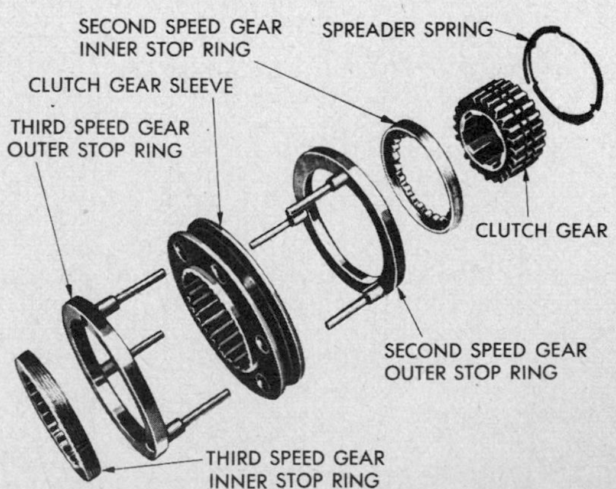

Synchronizer assembly

2. Carefully insert low and reverse lever shaft into the rear of the case, through the seal and into position. Lock with a tapered pin. Turn lever until the center detent is in line with the interlock bore.
3. Slide the interlock sleeve in its bore in the case, followed by one of the interlock balls. Then, install interlock spring and pin.
4. Place the remaining interlock ball on top of the interlock spring.
5. Depress the interlock ball and at the same time install the second and high lever shaft into the fully seated position, with the center detent aligned with the detent ball. Secure the shaft with the remaining tapered pin.
6. Install the operating levers and secure to the shafts with nuts. Torque the nuts to 18 ft. lbs.

Countershaft (Cluster) Gear

1. Slide the dummy shaft and tubular spacer into the bore of the countergear.
2. Grease and install 22 bearing rollers into each end of the countergear bore in the area around the arbor. Install the bearing retaining rings at each end of the gear, covering the bearings. If countershaft gear end-play measured over .022 in. at disassembly, install new thrust washers.
3. Install a thrust washer at each end of the countergear and over the arbor. Install the countergear assembly in the case, making sure the tabs on the thrust washers slide into the grooves in the case.

Reverse Idler Gear

1. Coat the bore of the reverse idler gear with grease, then slide dummy shaft into the bore, then install 22 bearing rollers in the bore and around the dummy shaft.
2. Install a new thrust washer at each end of the gear and over the arbor.
3. With the beveled end of the teeth forward, slide the gear into position in the case. Install the reverse idler shaft in its bore in the rear of the case. Install Woodruff key and align with the keyway in the case.
4. Align the idler gear with the shaft, then drive the shaft into the case and gear until the key seats in recess.

Mainshaft

1. Install rear bearing on mainshaft and install selective fit snap-ring.
2. Hold low and reverse sliding gear in position with shift fork. Insert mainshaft with rear bearing through rear of case and into the sliding gear. Both shift forks are offset toward rear of the case.
3. Place synchronizer spreader ring, and then rear stop ring, on synchronizer splines of second speed gear. Install second speed gear on mainshaft, with shims if required. Shims should be installed to correct excessive synchronizer float. If synchronizer float is below minimum, as measured on disassembly, shorten all six synchronizer pins.
4. Install synchronizer clutch gear on mainshaft. Install snap-ring.
5. Install second and direct fork in lever shaft with offset toward rear of transmission. Hold synchronizer clutch gear sleeve and two outer rings together, with pins in holes in clutch gear sleeve. Engage second and direct fork with clutch gear sleeve.
6. While holding synchronizer parts and fork in position, slide mainshaft forward, starting synchronizer clutch gear into clutch gear sleeve and mainshaft rear bearing into the case bore. Synchronizer parts must be correctly positioned before mainshaft is positioned.
7. While holding synchronizer parts in position, tap mainshaft forward until rear bearing bottoms in the case bore.
8. Install mainshaft rear bearing selective fit snap-ring into groove in case bore.

Drive Pinion (Clutch Shaft)

1. Slide the oil slinger over the pinion shaft and down against the gear.
2. Slide the bearing over the pinion shaft (ring groove away from the gear), then press to a firm seat against the oil slinger and gear.
3. Install the keyed washer, then the snap-ring. Four thicknesses of snap-ring are available to eliminate end-play. Install the large snap-ring onto the race of the ball bearing.
4. Install 14 greased bearing rollers in the bore of the pinion shaft gear. Install bearing roller retaining ring in the pinion gear bore.
5. Install third gear outer stop-ring and third gear inner stop-ring onto the mainshaft. Guide the drive pinion through the front of the case and engage the inner stop-ring with the clutch teeth, then seat the bearing so the large snap-ring is hard against the case.
6. Install a new seal in the pinion bearing retainer.
7. Install the gasket on the retainer and install with attaching bolts torqued to 30 ft. lbs.

Extension Housing

1. Install a new rear mainshaft bushing, and a new oil seal.
2. Protect the oil seal with thimble-type seal protector, and with gasket attached, slide the extension housing over the mainshaft and down against the case. Attach with bolts torqued to 50 ft. lbs.
3. Install flange assembly and secure with new washer and nut. Torque the nut to 140 ft. lbs.
4. Grease the cover gasket, and install gasket on cover. Torque attaching bolts to 12 ft. lbs.
5. Install drain plug and back-up light switch (if so equipped) and tighten securely. Refill transmission to proper level.

Exhaust Emission Control Switch

Some models have a switch mounted above the 2-3 shift lever, for emission control. In the absence of a switch a plug is substituted. Torque the plug or switch to 15 ft. lbs.

Type-4 A-833 Chrysler 4-Speed

Application

Barracuda, 1969-74
Challenger, 1970-74
Charger, 1969-74
Dart, 1969-76
Dodge, 1969-74
Plymouth, 1969-74
Valiant, 1969-76

This unit is used by Chrysler Corporation cars and varies somewhat with car application. However, illustrations and repair procedures may be considered as typical.

Disassembly

1. If available, mount transmission in a repair stand.
2. Disconnect gearshift control rods from the shift control levers and the transmission operating levers.
3. Remove the two gearshift control housing mounting bolts.
4. Remove gearshift control hous-

1 Bearing retainer
2 Bearing retainer gasket
3 Bearing retainer oil seal
4 Inner bearing snap-ring
5 Outer bearing snap-ring
6 Pinion bearing
7 Transmission case
8 Filler plug
9 2nd speed gear
10 Stop ring
11 Shift strut springs
12 Clutch gear
13 Shift struts (3)
14 Shift strut spring
15 Snap-ring
16 1st and 2nd clutch sleeve gear
17 Stop ring
18 1st speed gear
19 Bearing retainer ring
20 Rear bearing
21 Snap-ring
24 Baffle
25 Case to extension housing gasket
26 Lockwasher
27 Bolt
28 Extension housing
29 Mainshaft yoke bushing
30 Oil seal
31 Main drive pinion
33 Needle bearing rollers
34 Snap-ring
35 Stop ring
36 Snap-ring
37 Shift strut spring
38 Clutch gear
39 Shift strut spring
40 Clutch sleeve
41 Stop ring
42 3rd speed gear
43 Mainshaft (output)
44 Shift struts (3)
45 Woodruff key
46 Countershaft
47 Gear thrustwasher (1)
48 Needle roller bearing thrustwasher
49 Needle bearing rollers
50 Bearing spacer
51 Countershaft gear (cluster)

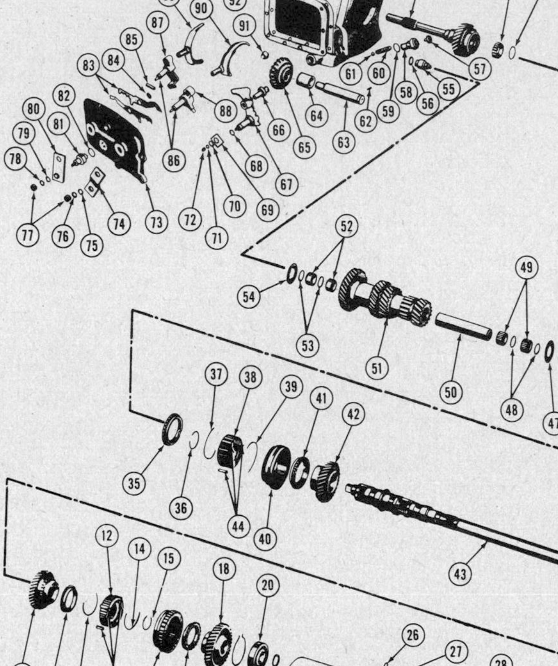

A-833 4-speed transmission disassembled

52 Needle bearing rollers
53 Needle roller bearing thrustwasher
54 Gear thrustwasher (1)
55 Backup light switch
56 Backup light switch gasket
57 Plug
58 Reverse detent ball spring retainer
59 Gasket
60 Reverse detent ball spring
61 Rerverse detent ball
62 Woodruff key
63 Reverse idler gear shaft
64 Reverse idler gear bushing
65 Reverse idler gear
66 Reverse shifter fork
67 Reverse lever
68 Reverse lever shaft oil seal
69 Reverse operating lever
70 Flatwasher
71 Lockwasher
72 Nut
73 Gearshift control housing
74 1st and 2nd operating lever
75 Flatwasher
76 Lockwasher lever
77 Lever nut
78 Lever lockwasher
79 Lever flatwasher
80 3rd and 4th operating lever
81 Switch
82 Gasket
83 Interlock lever (2)
84 E-ring
85 Spring
86 Oil seal (2)
87 3rd and 4th lever
88 Ist and 2nd lever
89 3rd and 4th speed fork
90 1st and 2nd speed fork
91 Drain plug
92 Shift control housing gasket

ing from the transmission extension housing or mounting bracket (if so equipped).

5. Remove the gearshift control housing mounting bracket bolts, then, remove the bracket (if so equipped).
6. Remove back-up light switch (if so equipped).
7. Remove output companion flange nut and washer, then pull the flange from the mainshaft (output shaft).
8. Remove gearshift housing-to-transmission case attaching bolts.
9. With all levers in the neutral detent position, pull housing out and away from the case.

NOTE: if first and second, or third and fourth shift forks remain in engagement with the synchronizer sleeves, work the sleeves and remove forks from the case.

10. Remove nuts, lock washers and flat washers that hold first-second, and third-fourth-speed shift operating levers to the shafts.
11. Disengage shift levers from the flats on the shafts and remove levers.
12. Remove gearshift lever shafts out of the housing, allowing detent balls to fall free. Remove seals and discard.
13. Slide interlock sleeve, interlock pin and spring from the housing.
14. Remove main drive pinion bearing retainer attaching bolts, then slide retainer and gasket from the main drive shaft. Remove the pinion oil seal.
15. Remove the attaching bolts that hold the tailshaft extension housing to the transmission case.
16. Slide the third-fourth synchronizer sleeve slightly forward, slide the reverse idler gear to the center of its shaft, then, using a soft hammer, tap rearward on the extension housing. Slide housing and mainshaft assembly out and away from the case.
17. Remove the snap-ring that holds the third-fourth synchronizer clutch gear and sleeve. Then,

slide third-fourth synchronizer assembly from the end of the mainshaft.

18. Slide third speed gear and stop-ring from the mainshaft.

NOTE: do not separate third-fourth-speed synchronizer clutch gear, sleeve, shift plates or spring unless replacement is required.

19. With long-nose pliers, compress the snap-ring that retains the mainshaft center bearing in the extension housing.
20. With snap-ring compressed, pull the mainshaft assembly and bearing out of the extension housing.
21. Remove and discard extension housing rear oil seal.
22. Remove rear bearing from the mainshaft by inserting steel plates on the front side of first-speed gear, then, with an arbor press, force the rear bearing from the mainshaft.
23. Remove the snap-ring that holds the mainshaft bearing onto the shaft.
24. Remove mainshaft bearing, retainer ring, first-speed gear, and first-speed stop-ring.
25. Remove the snap-ring that holds the first and second clutch sleeve gear and clutch to the mainshaft.
26. Slide the first and second clutch sleeve gear and clutch from the mainshaft.

NOTE: do not dismantle the clutch unless inspection reveals need for parts replacement.

27. With a feeler gauge, measure countershaft gear end-play. This measurement should be .015-.025 in. If measurement is greater than specified, a new thrust washer of desirable thickness must be installed at assembly.
28. Drive the reverse idler gear shaft, from front to rear, far enough out of the case to permit removal of the reverse idler gear.
29. Remove idler gear shaft from the case, then remove the Woodruff key from the shaft.
30. Remove reverse gearshift lever detent spring retainer, gasket, plug and detent ball spring from the rear of the case.
31. Push the reverse gearshift lever shaft into the case, and remove. Lift the detent ball from the bottom of the case.
32. Remove the shift fork from the shaft and detent plate.
33. Using a countershaft dummy, drive the countershaft from the gear and case, allowing the countergear and dummy assembly to rest on the bottom of the case.
34. Remove the main drive pinion bearing outer snap-ring, then with a soft hammer, drive the main drive pinion into the case and remove.
35. Remove the main drive pinion bearing outer snap-ring, then, with an arbor press, remove the bearing from the main drive pinion. Remove the oil slinger.
36. Lift the countergear cluster from the bottom of the case.
37. Remove the countergear dummy shaft, 76 bearing rollers, thrust washers and tubular spacer from the center of the countergear.

Assembly

1. Slide the second-speed gear over the mainshaft (synchronizer cone toward rear) and down into position against the shoulder on the shaft.
2. Slide first and second clutch sleeve gear assembly (including second gear stop-ring) over the mainshaft. Be sure shift fork groove is toward the front and down into position against second-speed gear, (stop-ring must be indexed with the shift plates). Install a new snap-ring to secure.
3. Slide low gear stop-ring over the shaft and down into position and index with the shift plates.
4. Slide first-speed gear, (synchronizer cone toward clutch sleeve gear) over the mainshaft and down into position against the clutch sleeve gear.
5. Install the mainshaft bearing retainer ring, followed by the mainshaft center bearing. Using an arbor or other suitable tool, press the bearing down into position. Install new snap-ring.
6. Slide the rear bearing over the mainshaft and drive, or press, into position.
7. Install partially assembled mainshaft into the extension housing far enough to engage the retaining ring in the slot in the extension housing. Compress the retaining ring and, at the same time, seat the mainshaft in the extension housing.
8. Slide third-speed gear over the mainshaft, synchronizer cone forward, followed by third gear stop-ring.
9. Install third and fourth-speed synchronizer clutch gear assembly onto the mainshaft (shift fork groove toward rear) down against third-speed gear. Be sure to index the rear stop-ring with the clutch shift plates.
10. Install retaining snap-ring, then, using heavy grease, position the front stop-ring over the clutch gear, indexing the ring slots with the shift plates.

NOTE: if above indexing of the stop-rings and the positioning of the gears and clutches is ignored at this point, damage will most likely result when mating the extension housing to the transmission case.

11. Grease the bore of the countergear at each end, then install the roller bearing tubular spacer (centered). Insert the countergear dummy shaft.
12. Grease each bearing roller, then install 19 bearing rollers at each end of the gear. Now, install a flat spacer onto each end of the dummy shaft and into the gear, followed by 19 more bearing rollers and a spacer ring into each end of the countergear.
13. Grease the tanged thrust washers and install them, one over each end of the dummy shaft, with the tangs toward the case (away from the gear).
14. Lay the countergear assembly into the bottom of the case.
15. To install the main drive pinion, slide the bearing oil slinger over the main drive pinion shaft, then, press the main drive pinion bearing on the pinion shaft. (Be sure the outer snap-ring groove is toward the front). Seat bearing all the way, against shoulder on gear.
16. Install a new inner snap-ring into the bearing retainer groove of the shaft.
17. Now, install the outer snap-ring into the main drive pinion bearing. Then, insert and tap the main drive pinion and bearing assembly into the front of the case.
18. Start the countershaft into its bore at the rear of the case. Raise the countergear cluster assembly until the gear bore is aligned with the countershaft bore in the case. (Be sure the thrust washer tangs are in place in the case recesses.)
19. Press the countershaft into the countergear, washer and bearings assembly while displacing the dummy shaft. Install Woodruff key into countershaft, then continue pressing the countershaft and key into its bore and recess.

NOTE: countergear end-play should not exceed .029 in.

20. Install a new oil seal onto the reverse gearshift lever shaft.
21. Lubricate and carefully install the lever shaft into the bore in the case. Insert reverse fork into the lever.
22. Install reverse shift detent ball and spring retainer gasket and retainer. Tighten securely.
23. Start reverse idler gear shaft into the end of the case, and press in far enough to position the reverse idler gear on the protruding end of the shaft. At the same time, engage the shifter groove with the reverse shift fork.
24. With reverse idler gear properly positioned, install Woodruff key into the sliding gear shaft, then finish seating the shaft and key

flush with the end of the case.

25. Grease, then position a new gasket on the end of the extension housing.
26. Center reverse sliding gear on its shaft, then carefully insert the mainshaft assembly into the case. (Be sure of the indexing of third and fourth-speed stop-rings and shifter plates.)
27. Move third and fourth - speed clutch sleeve slightly toward the front, and, at the same time, align the end of the mainshaft with the main drive pinion. Push in on the extension housing assembly until it is entirely seated against the rear of the case.
28. Install extension-to-case attaching bolts and torque to 50 ft. lbs.
29. Install back-up light switch (if so equipped).
30. Move reverse sliding gear ahead to neutral position.
31. Slide interlock sleeve into position in the gearshift housing. Lubricate and slide a new seal over a shifter shaft and down into its groove.
32. Install the gearshift lever shaft into position in the housing, then install the gearshift operating lever onto the flats of the shaft, (lever pointing up). Install flat washer, Lockwasher and nut. Tighten securely.
33. Place a detent ball in the sleeve, followed by the poppet spring and interlock pin.
34. Lubricate and slide a new seal over the other shifter shaft and down into its groove.
35. As with the first gearshift lever shaft, push the shaft into position in the housing, then install the operating lever onto the flats of the shaft (lever pointing up). Install flat washer, lockwasher and nut and tighten securely.
36. Place remaining detent ball on the poppet spring, compress the ball and spring with a small screwdriver, then, push the shafts in until seated. Turn the shafts until the balls drop into the neutral position detent.
37. Place transmission on its side, gearshift cover opening up.
38. Install a shift fork onto each synchronizer sleeve collar, and, with both sleeves in neutral position, install the shift housing and new gasket.
39. Install attaching bolts and tighten to 12 ft. lbs. (The center bolt on each side of the cover is a pilot bolt and should be installed first.)
40. Lubricate and install a new oil seal in the main drive pinion retainer bore, then install the retainer and gasket. Install attaching bolts, torqued to 15-20 ft. lbs.
41. Install gearshift control and rod assembly on the extension housing, then, secure rods with washers and clips.
42. Install output companion flange, washer and nut. Torque to 175 ft. lbs.

Type-5 3.03 Fully Synchronized Ford 3-Speed

Application

Buick LeSabre, Centurion, 1970-71
Buick Wildcat, 1969-70
Buick Special, 1969
Comet, 1971-76
Cougar, 1969-72
Fairlane, 1969-70
Firebird (V8), 1969
Ford, 1969-71
Granada, 1975-76
Maverick, 1970-76
Mercury, 1969-71
Monarch, 1975-76
Montego, 1969-74
Mustang, 1969-73
Oldsmobile, 1969-71
Olds F-85, 1969
Pontiac, 1969-71
Tempest, 1969
Torino, 1971-75

AMC 150T Fully Synchronized 3-Speed

Application
American Motors, 1975-76

A-390 Fully Synchronized Chrysler 3-Speed

Application
Dart (6 Cyl.), 1975-76
Valiant (6 Cyl.), 1975-76

Disassembly

1. Drain the lubricant, then remove the cover bolts and the case cover.
2. Remove the five attaching screws, then remove the extension housing from the transmission case. Remove a long spring which retains the detent plug in the case. Remove the detent plug with a small magnet.
3. Remove the four attaching screws, then remove the front bearing retainer from the case.
4. Remove the filler plug. Working through the filler plug hole, drive the roll pin out of the case and countershaft with a small punch.
5. With a dummy shaft, push the countershaft out of the rear of the case until the countershaft cluster gear can be lowered to the bottom of the case. Remove the countershaft from the rear of the case.
6. Remove the snap-ring. Lift the input gear and shaft from the front of the case. Press the shaft out of the bearing.
7. Remove the snap-ring that holds the speedometer gear onto the shaft. Slide the speedometer gear off the output shaft. Remove the speedometer gear lockball.
8. Remove the snap-ring that holds the output shaft bearing on the shaft. With a puller, remove the bearing from both the case and shaft.
9. Place both shaft levers in the neutral position.
10. Remove the set screw that holds the detent springs and plugs in the case. Remove a detent spring and plug from the case.
11. Remove the set screw that holds the first and reverse shift fork to the shift rail. Slide first and reverse shift rail out through the rear of the case.
12. Rotate the first and reverse shift fork upward, then lift it from the case.
13. Remove the set screw that holds the second and third shift fork to the shift rail. Rotate the shift rail 90°.
14. With a magnet, lift the interlock plug from the case.
15. Tap on the inner end of the second and third shift rail to remove the expansion plug from the front of the case. Remove the shift rail.
16. Remove second and third detent plug and spring from the detent bore.

NOTE: on 1971-72 RAT model transmissions, pull the input gear and shaft forward until the gear contacts the case. On all other models,

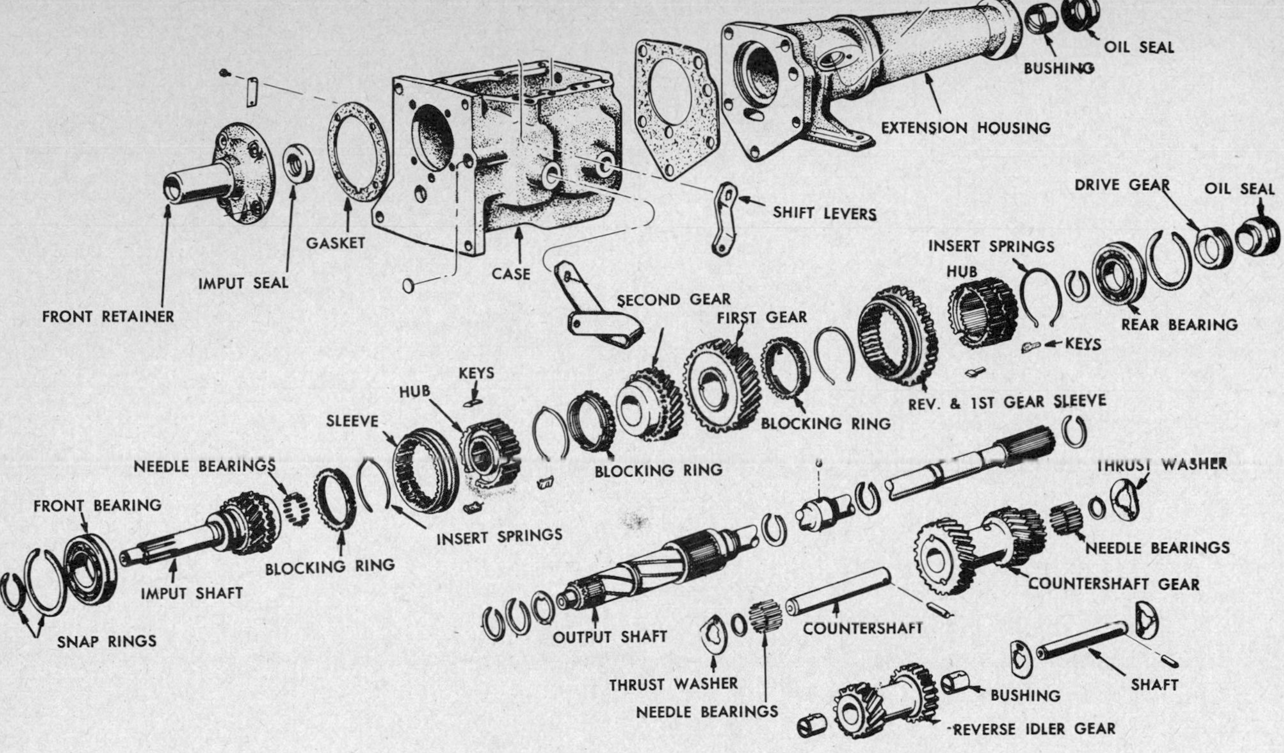

3.03 Ford 3-speed transmission disassembled (© Ford Motor Co)

remove the input gear and shaft through the front of the case.

17. Rotate the second and third shift fork upward, then lift it from the case.
18. Lift the output shaft out through the top of the case.
19. Working through the front bearing opening, drive the reverse idler shaft out through the rear of the case.
20. Lift the reverse idler gear and two thrust washers from the case.
21. Lift the countershaft gear and thrust washers from the case.
22. Remove the countershaft-to-case retaining pin and any needle bearings which may have fallen into the case.
23. Remove the shift levers and shafts from the case. Discard the O-rings.
24. Remove the snap-ring from the front of the output shaft, then slide the synchronizer and the second-speed gear from the shaft.
25. Remove the next snap-ring and thrust washer from the output shaft, then slide the first gear and blocking ring off the shaft.
26. Remove the next snap-ring from the output shaft, then press off the first-reverse synchronizer hub from the shaft.
27. Remove the dummy shaft, 50 bearing rollers and the two retainer washers from the countershaft gear.
28. Disassemble the synchronizers.

Assembly

1. Coat the bore in each end of the countershaft gear with grease. Hold the dummy shaft in the gear and install 25 bearing rollers and a retainer washer in each end of the gear. Install the countershaft gear, thrust washers and dummy shaft in the case. End-play is controlled with variable thickness thrust washers to .004-.018 in. Let the gear cluster assembly lie in the bottom of the case.
2. Install the idler gear, thrust washers and shaft in the case. Make sure that the thrust washer

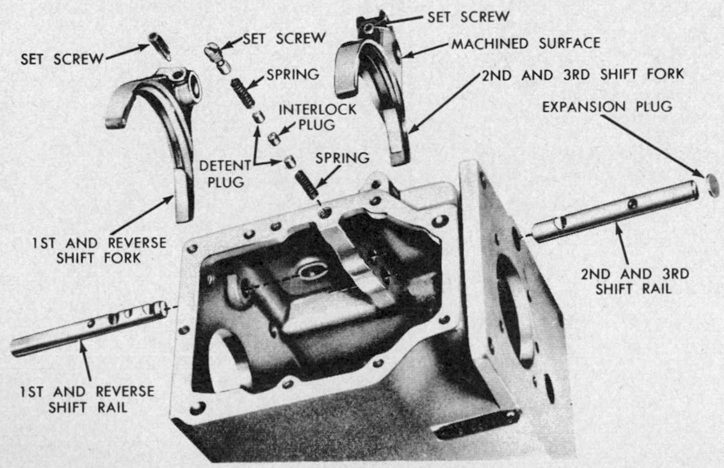

Shift rail and forks

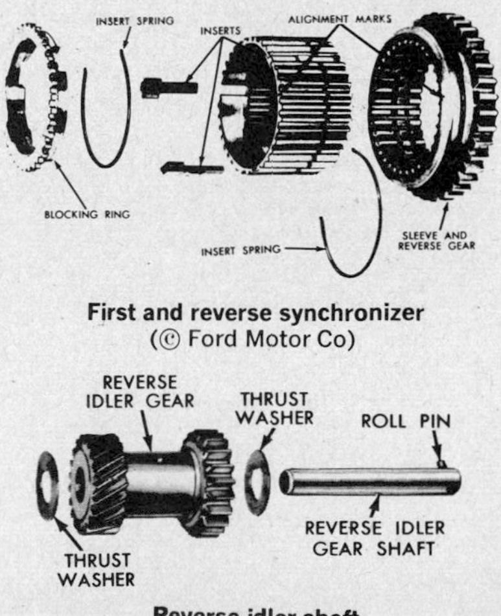

First and reverse synchronizer
(© Ford Motor Co)

Reverse idler shaft
(© Ford Motor Co)

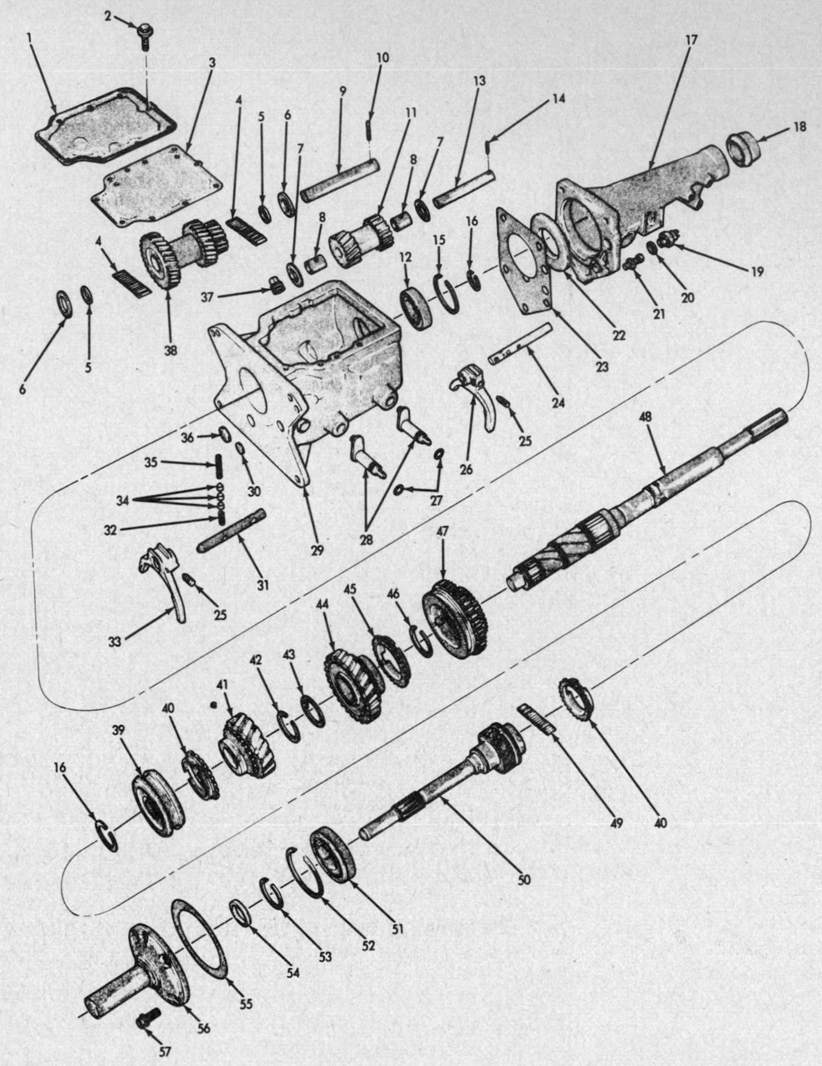

Exploded view of Chrysler A-390 fully synchronized three speed

1 Cover, Case
2 Screw, Case Cover
3 Gasket, Case Cover
4 Roller, Countershaft Brg.
5 Washer, Countershaft Brg.
6 Washer, Countershaft Thrust
7 Washer, Reverse Idler Thrust
8 Bushing, Reverse Idler
9 Countershaft
10 Pin, Countershaft Roll
11 Gear, Reverse Idler
12 Bearing, Output Shaft
13 Shaft, Reverse Idler
14 Pin, Reverse Idler Stop
15 Snap Ring, Output Shaft Brg., Outer
16 Snap Ring, Output Shaft, Inner
17 Extension
18 Seal, Extension
19 Switch, Back-Up Lamp
20 Gasket, Back-Up Lamp Switch
21 Screw, Extension
Lockwasher, Extension Screw
22 Retainer, Output Shaft Brg.
23 Gasket, Extension
24 Rail, Gearshift First and Reverse
25 Screw, Fork Set
26 Fork, Gearshift First and Reverse
27 Seal, Gearshift Lever Shaft Oil
28 Lever, Gearshift
29 Case
30 Plug
31 Rail, Gearshift Second and Third
32 Spring, Gearshift Detent Pin
33 Fork, Gearshift Second and Third
34 Pin, Gearshift Detent
35 Spring, Gearshift Detent Pin
36 Plug
37 Plug, Case Filler
38 Gear, Countershaft
39 Synchronizer Assy., Second and Third
40 Ring, Synchronizer Second and Third Stop
41 Gear, Second Speed
42 Snap Ring, Low Speed Gear Thrust Washer
43 Washer, Low Speed Gear Thrust
44 Gear, Low Speed
45 Ring, Synchronizer Low Stop
46 Snap Ring, Synchronizer Low and Reverse Clutch Gear
47 Synchronizer Assy., Low and Reverse
48 Shaft, Output
49 Roller, Output Shaft Pilot
50 Shaft, Input
51 Bearing, Input Shaft
52 Snap Ring, Bearing, Outer
53 Snap Ring, Bearing, Inner
54 Seal, Bearing Retainer Oil
55 Gasket, Bearing Retainer
56 Retainer, Bearing
57 Screw, Bearing Retainer

with the flat side, is at the web end and that the spur gear is toward the rear of the case. Idler gear end-play should be .004-.018 in.

3. Install an insert spring into the groove of the first and reverse synchronizer hub. Be sure that the spring covers all insert grooves. Start the hub in the sleeve, being sure the alignment marks are properly indexed. Position the three inserts in the hub and be sure the small end is over the spring and that the shoulder is on the inside of the hub. Slide the sleeve and reverse gear onto the hub until the detent is engaged. Install the other insert spring in the front of the hub to hold the inserts against it.
4. Install one insert spring into a groove of the second-third synchronizer hub. With the alignment marks on the hub and sleeve aligned, start the hub into the sleeve. Place the three inserts on top of the retaining spring and push the assembly together. Install the remaining insert spring, so that the spring ends cover the same slots as do the other spring. Do not stagger the springs. Place a synchronizer blocking ring in each end of the synchronizer sleeve.
5. Lubricate the output shaft splines and machined surfaces with transmission lubricant.
6. Press the first and reverse synchronizer hub onto the output shaft, with the teeth end of the gear facing toward the rear end of the shaft. Secure it with the snap-ring.
7. Place the blocking ring on the tapered machined surface of the first gear.
8. Slide the first gear onto the output shaft, with the blocking ring toward the rear of the shaft. Rotate the gear to engage the three notches in the blocking ring with the synchronizer inserts. Secure the first gear with the thrust washer and snap-ring.
9. Slide the blocking ring onto the tapered, machined surface of the second gear. Slide the second gear, with blocking ring and the second and third gear synchronizer, onto the mainshaft. The tapered machined surface of the second gear must be toward the front of the shaft. Secure the synchronizer with a snap-ring.

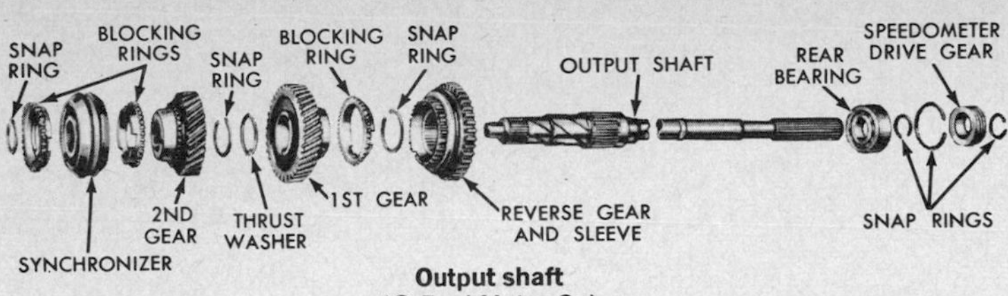

Output shaft
(© Ford Motor Co)

10. Install new O-rings onto the two shift lever shafts. Lubricate the shafts with transmission fluid and install them into the case. Secure each shift lever onto its shaft.
11. Coat the bore of the input shaft with a light coat of grease. Install the 15 bearing rollers into the bore.

NOTE: on RAT models (1971-72) install the input gear and bearing through the top of the case. On other models the input shaft is installed through the front of the transmission.

12. Position the output shaft assembly in the case.
13. Place a detent plug spring and a plug in the case. Place a second and third-speed shift fork in the synchronizer groove. Rotate the fork into position and install the second and third-speed shift rail. Move the rail inward until the detent plug engages the forward notch (second). Secure the fork to the shaft with a set screw. Move the synchronizer to the neutral position.
14. Install the interlock plug in the case.
15. Place first and reverse shift fork in the groove of the first and reverse synchronizer. Rotate the fork into position and install the first and reverse shift rail. Move the rail inward until the center notch is aligned with the detent bore. Secure the fork to the shaft with a set screw. Install the remaining detent plug and spring. Secure the detent spring with the slotted head set screw. Tighten set screw until the head is flush with the case.
16. Install a new expansion plug in the case front.
17. Install the input shaft and gear in the front of the case.
18. Place front bearing retainer (with new gasket in place) on the case with the oil return groove at the bottom. Torque attaching screws to 30 ft. lbs.
19. Install the large snap-ring on the rear bearing. Place the bearing on the output shaft, with the snap-ring end toward the rear of the shaft. Press bearing into place and secure with a snap-ring.
20. Hold the speedometer drive gear lock ball in the detent and slide the speedometer gear into place. Secure the gear with a snap-ring.
21. Lift the countershaft gear cluster up into place, and, by entering the countershaft at the rear of the case, push the dummy shaft out of the gear and transmission case. Before the countershaft is completely in place, align the roll pin hole in the shaft with the hole in the case.

NOTE: on all eight-cylinder vehicles and Ford six-cylinder models the countershaft is a press fit in the case. On Ford six-cylinder models with RAN transmissions, there is a radial clearance of .020 in. at front bore and .010 in. at rear.

22. Working through the filler hole, install a roll pin into the case and countershaft.
23. Install filler and drain plugs in the case.
24. Coat a new extension housing gasket with sealer and install it on the case.
25. Apply sealer to attaching screws and secure extension housing to the case by torqueing the screws to 42 to 50 ft. lbs.
26. With transmission in gear, pour lubricant over the entire gear train while rotating the input or output shaft.
27. Install the transmission cover, with a new sealer-coated gasket in place, and torque the nine attaching screws to 14-19 ft lbs.
28. Check operation of transmission in all of the gear positions.

Type-6
Ford 4-Speed
(German design)
Types 71 WG, 72 WG, 74 WT

***Application* Pinto, 1971-76**

NOTE: cars equipped with this transmission are identified by a transmission ID code suffix of AD or AE. The transmission ID code appears on a tag located under the left extension housing-to-case bolt.

Transmission Disassembly

1. Remove the clutch release bearing and detach the clutch housing.
2. Drain the lubricant and remove the cover and gasket from the case.
3. Remove the threaded plug, spring and shift rail detent plunger from the front of the case.
4. Drive the access plug from the rear of the case. Drive the interlock retaining pin from the case and remove the interlock plate.
5. Remove the roll pin from the selector lever arm.
6. Tap the front end of the shift rail, to displace the plug at the rear of the extension housing. Remove the shift rail from the rear of the extension housing.
7. Remove the selector arm and shift fork from the case.
8. Remove the extension housing attaching bolts. Loosen the extension housing and rotate the housing to align the countershaft with the cutaway in the extension housing flange.
9. Drive the countershaft rearward until the shaft clears the front of the case. Install a dummy shaft in the case and gear until the countershaft gear can be lowered to the bottom of the case. Remove the countershaft.
10. Lift the extension housing and mainshaft from the case as an assembly.
11. Remove the input shaft bearing retainer attaching bolts. Remove the input shaft and bearing retainer from the case as an assembly.
12. Remove the reverse idler gear and shaft from the rear of the case.
13. Remove the bearing retainers, bearings, dummy shaft and spacer from the countershaft gear.
14. Remove the pilot bearing and bearing retainer from the input shaft gear.
15. Do not remove the ball bearing from the input shaft unless replacement is necessary.

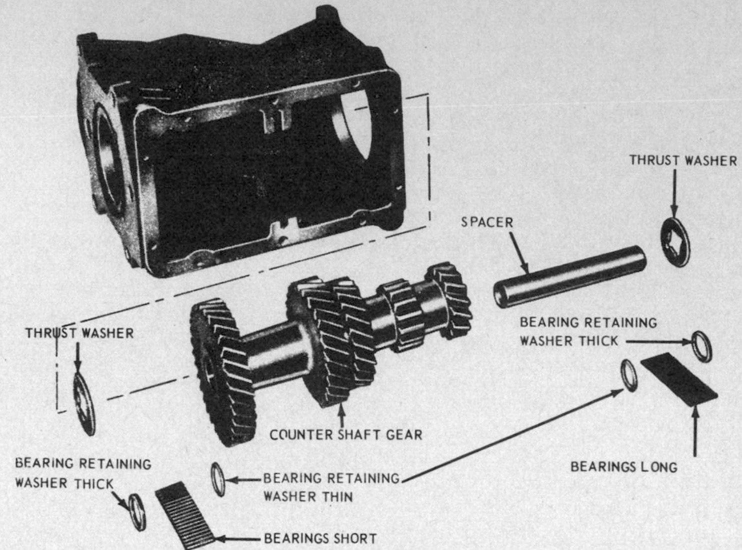

Countershaft gear disassembled (© Ford Motor Co)

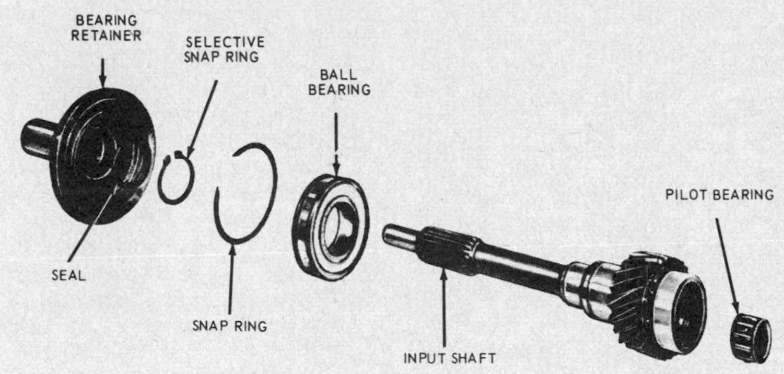

Input shaft disassembled —Types 71WG-AD and 72WG-AE
(© Ford Motor Co)

16. Pry the input shaft seal out of the bearing retainer.
17. Lift the fourth gear blocker ring from the front of the output shaft.
18. Remove the snap-ring from the forward end of the output shaft.
19. Support third gear on press plates and place the output shaft and extension housing in a press. Press the output shaft out of the third-fourth speed synchronizer and third gear, while supporting the extension housing and output shaft from beneath. Remove the snap-ring and washer and remove second gear and the blocker ring from the output shaft.
20. Disassemble the synchronizer assembly by pulling the sleeve from the hub and removing the inserts and spring.
21. Remove the snap-ring which retains the output shaft bearing to the extension housing.

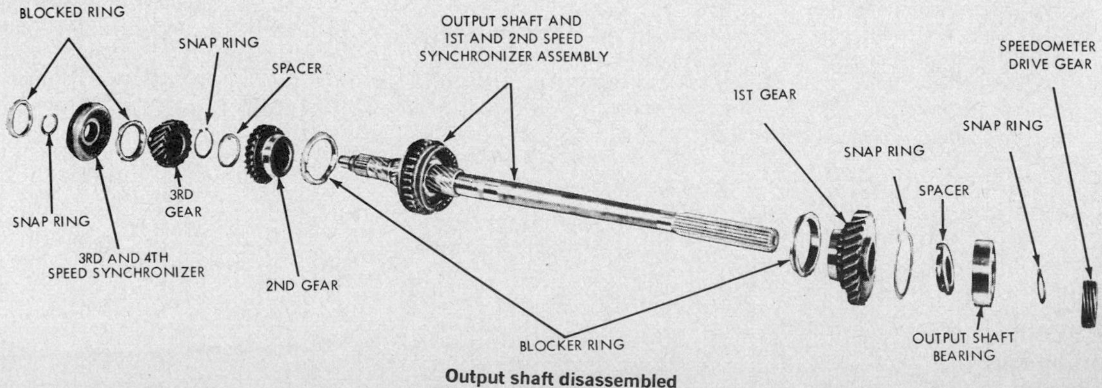

Output shaft disassembled —Types 71WG-AD and 72WG-AE
(© Ford Motor Co)

22. Use a plastic hammer and tap the output shaft assembly from the extension housing.
23. Position press plates behind first gear and place the assembly in a press. The first and second speed synchronizer are serviced as an assembly. No attempt should be made to separate the hub from the shaft. The only serviceable parts are the springs and inserts. If the hub or sleeve is worn, the shaft and synchronizer must be replaced as an assembly.
24. Drive the shift rail bushing from the rear of the extension housing, using a 9/16 in. socket. Do not remove serviceable bushings.
25. Pry the shift rail seal from the rear of the case.
26. Remove the remaining shaft linkage from the case. Do not remove the seat belt sensing switch unless it is damaged.

Transmission Assembly

1. Install a new shift rail seal in the rear of the case.
2. If the shift rail bushing was removed, drive a new one into position with a 9/16 in. socket.
3. Slide the synchronizer hub over the shaft, making sure that the shift fork groove is toward the front of the shaft. The sleeve and hub are select fit and must be assembled with the etch marks in the same relative locations. Locate an insert in each of three slots in the hub. Oil all parts, and install an insert spring inside the sleeve. The spring tab must locate in a section of an insert. Fit the other spring to the opposite face, making sure that the tab locates in the same insert. Both springs should be in the same rotational direction. The tab end of one spring should be aligned with the tab of the spring on the opposite side.
4. Assemble a blocker ring on the first gear side of the first-second synchronizer. Lubricate the cone surface of first gear and all output shaft gear journals, and slide the cone onto the output shaft, so that the cone surface engages the blocker ring.
5. Position the spacer on the output shaft, larger diameter rearward.
6. Install a snap-ring (selected from the chart) which will come closest to removing all end-play from the output shaft bearing. Position the output shaft bearing on the shaft and press the bearing into place. Secure the bearing with the thickest snap-ring that will fit the groove.

Installing speedometer driven gear (© Ford Motor Co)

Part No.	*Thickness*	*Identification*
D1FZ-7030-A	0.0679-	Color Coded—Copper
D1FZ-7030-B	0.0689-	Letter—W
D1FZ-7030-C	0.0699-	Letter-V
D1FZ-7030-D	0.0709-	Letter—U
D1FZ-7030-E	0.0719-	None
D1FZ-7030-F	0.0728-	Color Coded—Blue
D1FZ-7030-G	0.0738-	Color Coded—Black
D1FZ-7030-H	0.0748-	Color Coded—Brown

7. Slide the synchronizer over the hub and locate an insert in each of three slots in the sleeve. The sleeve and hub must be assembled with the etch marks in the same relative locations. Lightly oil all parts. Complete assembly of the synchronizer by following directions in previous Step 3.
8. Position second gear and the blocker ring on the output shaft, dog teeth facing rearward. Install the washer and snap-ring. Position third gear on the output shaft, dog teeth forward. Lubricate the gear cones and assemble a blocker ring on third gear cone.
9. Position the third-fourth synchronizer assembly on the output shaft, hub boss facing forward.
10. Install press plates against the boss on the synchronizer hub.
11. Place the entire unit in a press, extension end up, and press the synchronizer assembly onto the output shaft as far as possible.
12. Retain the third-fourth synchronizer assembly to the output shaft with a snap-ring. Pull up on the synchronizer so that the snap-ring is tight in the groove.
13. Lubricate the gear cone and place the blocker ring on the input shaft gear cone.
14. Press the speedometer drive gear onto the shaft.
15. Lubricate the bearing bore of the extension housing. Install the output shaft in the housing. It may be necessary to tap the shaft while holding the synchronizer sleeves firmly. Secure the shaft to the housing with the snap-ring previously installed.
16. Press the bearing on the input shaft. The snap-ring groove must be toward the front of the shaft. Use the thickest snap-ring that will fit.
17. Slide the spacer and dummy shaft into the countershaft gear. Position a thin bearing retaining washer on each end of the dummy shaft. Lubricate the roller bearings and load long bearings in the small end of the gear and short bearings in the long end of the gear. 19 needle bearings are used at either end of the gear on 71 WG and 72 WG series transmissions, and 21 needle bearings at either end of the gear on 74 WT series transmissions. Place a thick retaining washer over each end of the dummy shaft. Grease the thrust washers and place one on each end of the dummy shaft. The tabs must be in the same relative position to engage the slots in the case when the gear is lowered. Loop a piece of rope around each end of the gear and carefully install the gear and rope through the rear of the case. Lower the gear in place.
18. Lubricate the reverse idler gear shaft. Position the selector lever relay on the pivot pin. Secure with a spring clip. Hold the gear in the lever, long hub toward the rear of the case, and slide the re-

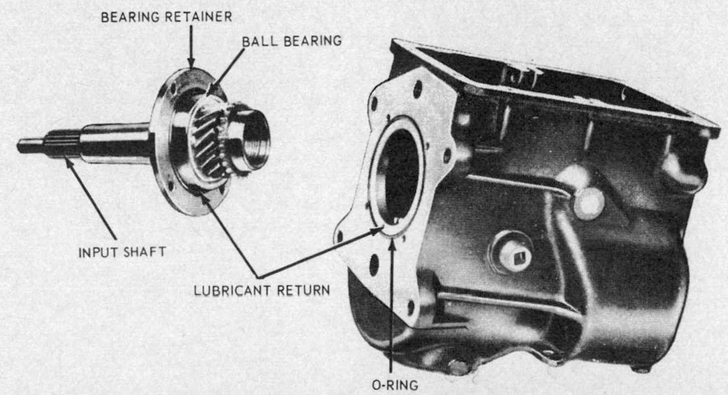

Installing input shaft gear (© Ford Motor Co)

verse idler shaft into place. Seat the shaft in the case with a brass hammer.

19. Install a new seal in the input shaft bearing retainer. Install the input shaft in the case with a new bearing retainer O-ring. Tap on the outer race of the bearing to seat the outer snap-ring.

Caution Use a soft hammer and do not tap on the input shaft itself.

20. Carefully slide third-fourth synchronizer sleeve into fourth speed position.
21. Place a new gasket on the extension housing.
22. Lubricate and install the input shaft pilot bearing on the shaft. Slide the extension housing and output shaft into place, being careful not to disturb the fourth speed synchronizer.
23. Align the cutaway in the extension housing flange with the countershaft bore in the rear of the case.
24. Lift the countershaft gear into place and install the countershaft, making sure that the thrust washers remain in place. The flat on the countershaft should be parallel to the top of the case. Tap the shaft with a brass hammer until the front of the shaft is flush with the case.
25. Rotate the extension housing to align the bolt holes and loosely install the attaching bolts. Make sure that the rail slides freely in its bore. Binding is remedied by slightly rotating the extension housing to free the rail, then pushing the housing into the case. Apply sealer to the attaching bolts and torque to 33-36 ft lbs. Place the shift forks in the synchronizer sleeves. Install the interlock lever and new retaining pin. Lubricate the shift rail oil seal and slide the shift rail through the extension housing, case and second and first speed shift forks. Position the selector arm on the rail and slide the rail through third and fourth speed shift fork. Slide the shift rail through the front of the case until the center detent bore is aligned with the detent plunger bore. Install a new retaining pin in the selector arm.
26. Install the detent plunger, spring and plug with sealer.
27. Install a new access plug in the rear of the case.
28. Position a new oil seal with tension spring and lip facing in the direction of the case.
29. Drive the seal in until it bottoms.
30. Position a new O-ring in the groove in the case. Position the input shaft bearing retainer with the groove in the retainer aligned with the oil passage in the case. Install the retaining bolts finger-tight.
31. Install the flywheel housing and tighten the retaining bolts and the front bearing retainer attaching bolts. Coat the retainer with grease.
32. Install the clutch release arm and bearing.
33. Install a new extension housing plug, using sealer.
34. Install a new cover gasket and cover, with the vent to the rear. Apply sealer to the left front cover attaching bolt. Torque to 8-10 ft lbs.
35. Install a new seat belt sensing switch if the old one was removed.

Type-7
Ford 4-Speed
(British Design)
Types 71 WG, 72 WG

Application

Pinto, 1971-73

NOTE: cars equipped with this transmission are identified by a transmission ID code suffix of BB or BC. The transmission ID code appears on a tag located under the left extension housing-to-case bolt.

Transmission Disassembly

1. Remove four bolts and top cover plate.

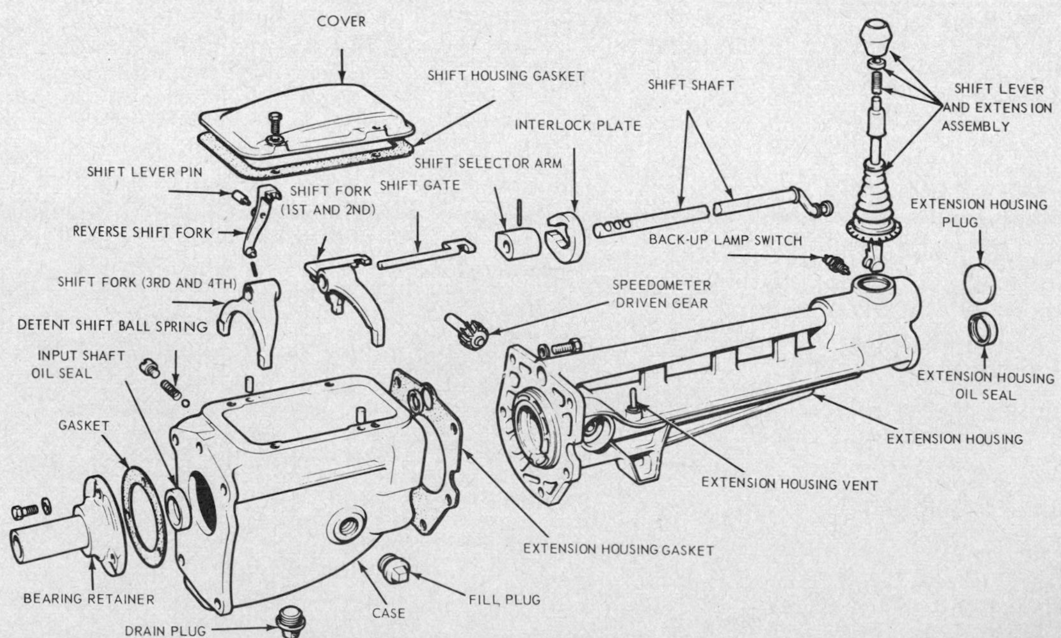

British 4-speed transmission disassembled—Types 71WG-BC and 72WG-BB
(© Ford Motor Co)

2. Pry plug from rear of extension housing.
3. Remove plunger screw from right side of case.
4. Working through the top cover opening, use a punch to remove the pin securing the shift selector arm to the shift shaft.
5. Pull the shift shaft rearward, being careful not to drop the shift selector arm and the interlock plate.
6. Move the first-second and third-fourth gear synchronizer hubs toward the input shaft bearing.
7. If necessary, remove the shift shaft plunger spring from the case. The plunger screw was removed in Step 3.
8. Remove the pin from the third-fourth shift fork. Remove the fork.
9. Unbolt extension housing from case. With a plastic hammer, tap the extension housing slightly rearward. Rotate the housing until the countershaft lines up with the notch in the housing flange.
10. Tap the countershaft rearward with a brass drift until it is just clear of the front of the case. Push the countershaft out with a dummy shaft. Lower the cluster gear to the bottom of the case.
11. Remove extension housing and output shaft assembly. The third-fourth synchronizer sleeve must be pushed forward for clearance.
12. Unbolt front bearing retainer from case. Remove retainer and gasket.
13. Remove input shaft oil seal.
14. Remove the snap ring around the input shaft bearing. Tap the input shaft gear and bearing assembly out of the transmission with a brass drift. Remove the needle roller bearing from the recess in the end of the input shaft gear.
15. Remove the cluster gear, two thrust washers, and the dummy shaft from the case. Remove 20 needle rollers and a retaining washer from each end of the cluster gear.
16. Assemble a nut, a flat washer, and a sleeve on a 5/16 in. x 24 UNF threaded bolt. Screw the bolt into the reverse idler shaft and tighten to pull out the shaft.
17. Remove the low-reverse shift fork from the lever pin inside the case. Do not remove the pin.

Component Disassembly

Third-Fourth Synchronizer

1. Remove fourth gear blocking ring from input shaft gear side of assembly.
2. Remove synchronizer hub snap-ring from forward end of output shaft and discard.
3. Support third gear. Press the output shaft out of the third-fourth gear synchronizer and third gear. Be careful not to drop the output shaft.
4. Pull the sleeve off the hub. Remove the inserts and springs.
5. Check all parts for wear. Synchronizer hub and sleeve should be replaced if worn or damaged.

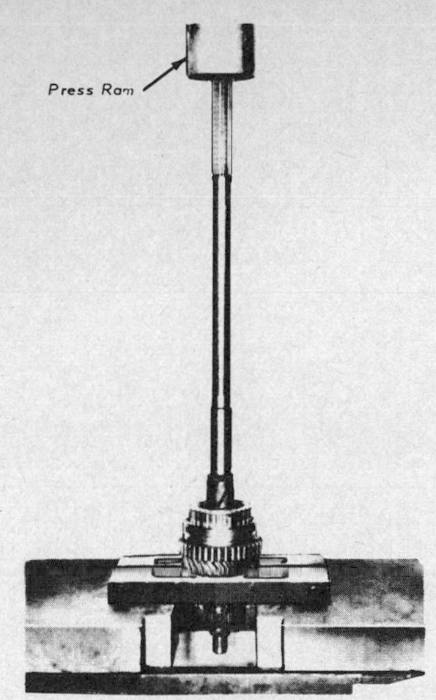

Removing low-reverse sliding gear, spacer and output shaft bearing
(© Ford Motor Co)

First-Second Synchronizer

1. Remove plug in extension housing. Remove speedometer driven gear.
2. Remove snap-ring holding output shaft bearing to extension housing. With a plastic hammer, tap output shaft assembly out of housing.
3. Remove snap-ring holding speedometer drive gear. Pull off gear. Remove snap-ring holding output shaft bearing.
4. Support low and reverse sliding gear. Press low and reverse sliding gear, spacer, and output shaft bearing from the output shaft.
5. Remove snap-ring holding first-second synchronizer assembly to output shaft.
6. Support second gear. Press second gear and first-second synchronizer assembly from output shaft.
7. Dismantle synchronizer assembly. Replace synchronizer hub or sleeve if worn or damaged. The output shaft bearing must be replaced.

Input Shaft and Gear

1. Remove and discard input shaft snap-ring.
2. Press off input shaft bearing.

Component Assembly

Third-Fourth Synchronizer

1. Slide gear over hub. Locate an insert in each slot.
2. Install a synchronizer spring inside the sleeve beneath the inserts; the spring tang should fit into an insert. Install the other spring on the opposite side, fitting the tang into the same insert. When viewed from the edge, the springs should run in opposite directions.
3. Place the third gear on the output shaft with the dog teeth forward. Assemble the blocking ring on the third gear cone.
4. Place the synchronizer assembly on the output shaft with the boss forward.
5. Support the hub. Press the hub on the output shaft and install a new snap-ring.

First-Second Synchronizer

1. Install the second gear on the output shaft with the cone and dog teeth to the rear.
2. Slide the synchronizer sleeve over the hub. Place an insert in each of the three slots.
3. Install synchronizer springs as for third-fourth synchronizer assembly.
4. Install a blocking ring to cone on second gear.
5. Install synchronizer assembly on output shaft with the gear teeth on the periphery of the synchronizer sleeve forward. Slide low and reverse sliding gear to the rear of the synchronizer hub.
6. Support the sliding gear. Press synchronizer assembly onto output shaft as far as possible.
7. Secure the synchronizer assembly with snap-ring.
8. Place a blocking ring on first gear side of first-second synchronizer assembly on output shaft. Install first gear, cone side forward.
9. Place the spacer with the larger diameter adjacent to first gear.
10. Select a snap-ring of the proper size to hold the output shaft bearing into the bearing recess with no end float.
11. Position the selected snap-ring loosely on the output shaft next to the spacer.
12. Support the bearing inner race. Press the bearing onto the shaft.
13. Select the thickest snap-ring that fits the groove to hold the bearing to the output shaft.
14. Locate output shaft ball bearing in shaft indent, push speedometer drive gear onto output shaft. Install new snap-ring.
15. Heat the end of the extension housing. Do not use a torch. A pan of hot water is recommended.

16. Install the output shaft into the extension housing. Install the snap-ring securing the output shaft bearing to the housing.
17. Replace the speedometer driven gear. Install a new plug, using sealer.

Input Shaft and Gear

1. Support the input shaft bearing inner race. Press the bearing onto the shaft.
2. Install the snap-ring securing the bearing to the input shaft.

Transmission Assembly

1. Slide the low-reverse lever onto the lever pin inside the case.
2. Push the idler shaft into the case. Place the reverse idler gear on the shaft. Locate the low-reverse lever in the gear groove. Tap the reverse idler shaft into position with a soft hammer.
3. Slide a dummy shaft into the cluster gear. Push a retainer washer into the gear bore. Grease and install 20 needle rollers and the second retaining washer. Install the washers and rollers at the other end of the gear. Grease and install the thrust washers with their convex side into the gear recess.
4. Place the cluster gear in the bottom of the case. Position the thrust washers with the flat upward.
5. Place the input shaft and gear in the case. Using a brass drift, tap bearing outer race into place. Be careful not to damage the dog teeth on the input shaft gear with the cluster gear. Install the bearing snap-ring.
6. Place the input shaft needle bearing in the input shaft gear recess.
7. Drive a new oil seal into the input shaft retainer. Cover the input shaft splines. Install a new gasket on the transmission front face. Check that the retainer oil groove is lined up with the oil passage in the case. Coat the bolts with sealer and install them with lock-washers.
8. Locate the fourth gear blocking ring on the input shaft gear cone.
9. Install a new oil seal in the shift shaft aperture. Drive the seal in with a socket.
10. Install a new sealer coated gasket to the extension housing.
11. Pull the third-fourth synchronizer sleeve forward. Slide the extension housing and output shaft into position. Align the cutaway on the extension housing with the countershaft aperture in the rear face of the case.

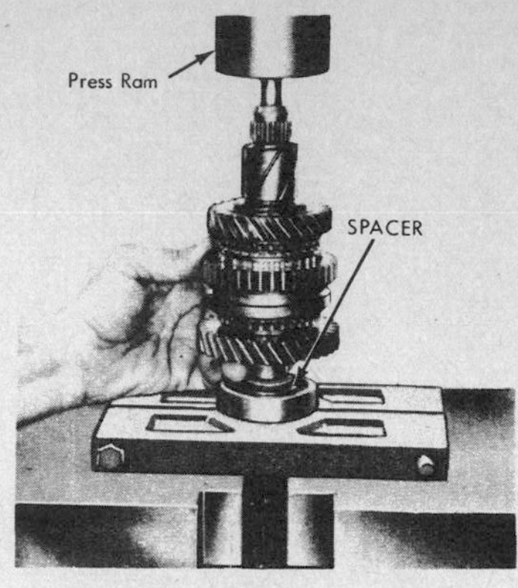

Replacing output shaft bearing
(© Ford Motor Co)

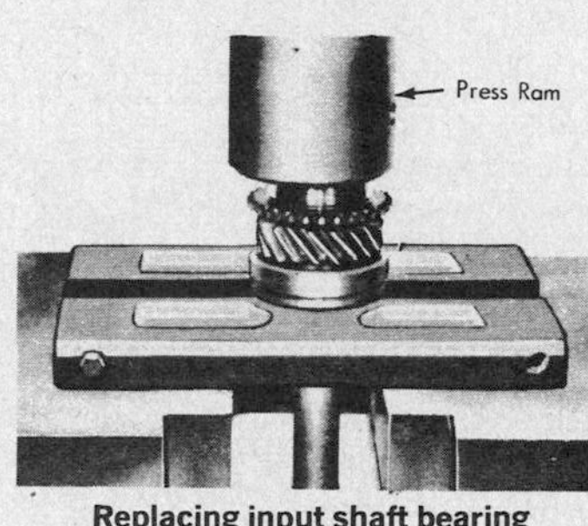

Replacing input shaft bearing
(© Ford Motor Co)

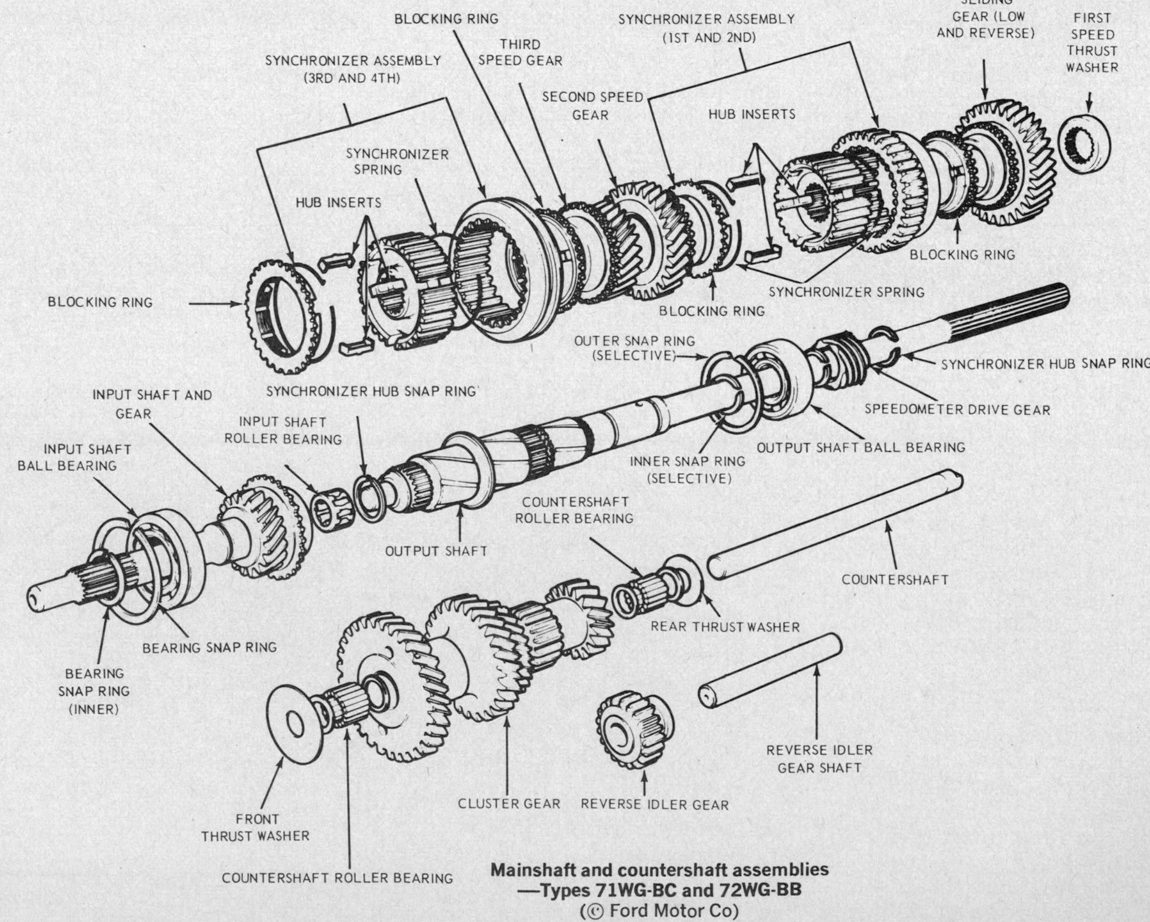

Mainshaft and countershaft assemblies —Types 71WG-BC and 72WG-BB
(© Ford Motor Co)

12. Using loops of cord, lift the cluster gear into mesh with the output and input shaft gears. Take care not to drop the countershaft thrust washers.
13. Tap the countershaft into place, driving out the dummy shaft, ensuring that the lug on the rear of the countershaft fits into the recess on the extension housing flange.
14. Push the extension housing onto the transmission case. Apply sealer to bolts. Torque to 30-35 ft. lbs.
15. Replace both shift forks. Secure third-fourth fork with a new pin.
16. Position shift forks to synchronizer sleeves. Move synchronizer hubs into neutral positions.
17. Grease shift shaft oil seal in rear of case. Slide shift shaft through extension housing. Position shift selector arm and interlock plate so that interlock plate locates in cutouts in shift forks. Pass the shift shaft through the shift selector arm and forks until the pin holes are aligned.
18. Replace the plunger ball and spring. Replace the retaining screw, using sealer.
19. Install the pin through the shift selector arm and shift shaft.
20. Apply sealer to plug. Tap plug into rear of extension housing.
21. Install top cover and gasket.
22. Refill transmission with 2.8 pints SAE 80 oil.

Type-8
Ford 4-Speed
Types RAD-B (2300) and RAD-C (2800)

***Application* Mustang II, 1974-76**

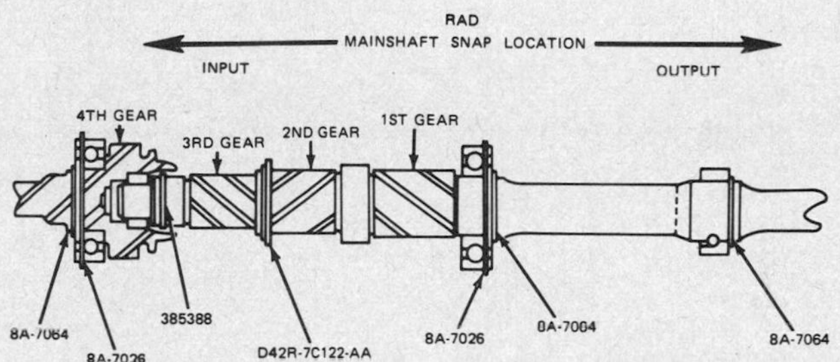

RAD mainshaft snap-ring locations (© Ford Motor Co)

Transmission Disassembly

1. Drain the lubricant by removing the lower extension housing bolt.
2. Drive the access plug from the rear of the extension housing. Remove the nut and washer securing the offset lever assembly. Remove the offset lever assembly.
3. Remove the remaining extension housing bolts and washers. Remove the extension from the case and discard the old gasket.
4. Remove the cap screws retaining the cover to the case. Remove the cover, shifter fork, shift rod assembly, and discard the old cover gasket.
5. Remove the bolts and washers attaching the front bearing retainer to the case. Remove the front bearing retainer and gasket.
6. Remove the spring clip retaining the reverse lever assembly to the pivot bolt. Remove the pivot and the reverse lever assembly.
7. Support the countershaft gear with a wire hook. To remove the countershaft, insert a dummy shaft in from the front of the case until the cluster gear falls to the bottom of the case. Then, remove the countershaft from the rear of the case. Lower the cluster gear to the bottom of the case.
8. Remove the input shaft from the front of the case.
9. Remove the snap-ring securing the speedometer drive gear on the output shaft. Slide the gear off and remove the lock ball from the shaft.
10. Remove the snap-ring retaining the output shaft bearing on the shaft. Use the outer snap-ring to pull the output shaft bearing from the shaft and case, then remove the snap-ring from the bearing. Carefully lift the output shaft and gear train assembly from the top of the case.
11. Slide out the reverse idler gear shaft through the rear of the case and remove reverse gear.
12. Remove the cluster gear and dummy shaft assembly from the bottom of the case. Remove the cluster gear thrust washers.
13. Clean and inspect all parts. If the back-up light switch was damaged, remove it at this time.

Component Disassembly

Cover Assembly

1. Remove the detent screw, spring and plunger.
2. Pull the shifter shaft rod rearward, rotating it counterclockwise.
3. Remove the spring pin retaining the manual selector and interlock to the shifter shaft.
4. Remove the shifter shaft from the cover taking care not to damage the seal.
5. Remove the manual selector and interlock plate.
6. Remove the first and second speed shifter fork. Remove the third and fourth speed shifter fork.
7. Clean and inspect all parts. Replace the shifter shaft seal and welch plug, if damaged.

Output Shaft

1. Scribe alignment marks on the synchronizer and blocker rings. Remove the snap-rings from the front of the output shaft. Slide the third and fourth speed synchronizer assembly, blocker rings and third gear off the shaft.
2. Remove the next snap-ring and the second gear thrust washer from the shaft. Slide second gear and the blocker ring off the shaft, taking care not to lose the sliding gear from the first and second speed synchronizer assembly. The first and second speed synchronizer hub cannot be removed from the output shaft.
3. Remove the first gear thrust washer (oil slinger) from the rear of the output shaft. Remove the spring pin retaining first gear onto the shaft.
4. Slide first gear off the output shaft, and remove the first speed blocker ring. Take care not to lose the sliding gear from the first and second speed synchronizer assembly.
5. Clean and inspect all parts.

Countershaft Gear Bearing Replacement

1. Remove the dummy shaft, bearing retainer washers and needle bearings from the countershaft gear. Clean and inspect the parts.
2. Coat the bore at each end of the countershaft gear with grease to retain the needle bearings.
3. While holding the dummy shaft

in the gear, install the needle bearings and retainer washers in each end of the gear.

Input Shaft Bearing Replacement

1. Remove the roller bearings from the input shaft.
2. Remove the snap-ring retaining the input shaft bearing. Press the input shaft out of the bearing. Clean and inspect all parts.
3. Press the input shaft bearing onto the input shaft, making sure that the snap-ring groove faces the front of the shaft. Install a new snap-ring to retain the bearing on the shaft.
4. Lightly coat the bore of the input shaft with grease.

NOTE: *If a thick film of grease, such as wheel bearing grease, is applied to the shaft, the lubrication holes may become clogged, thereby preventing transmission oil from reaching the bearings, possibly resulting in premature bearing failure.*

5. Install the roller bearings in the bore.

Synchronizer Replacement

1. Scribe alignment marks on the hub and sleeve of the synchronizer.
2. Push the synchronizer sleeve from each synchronizer hub.

NOTE: *The first and second speed*

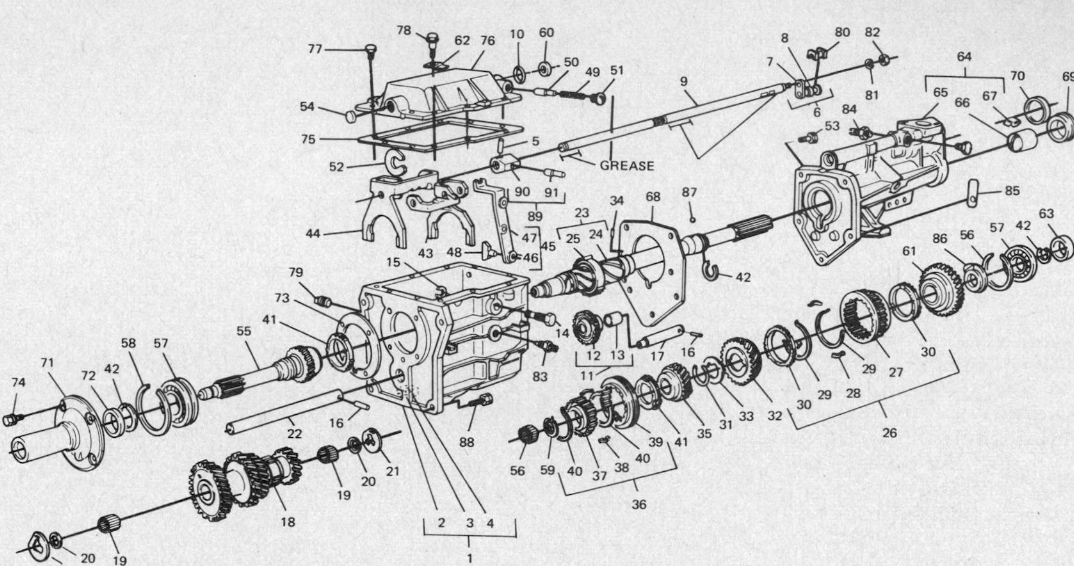

RAD transmission disassembled (© Ford Motor Co)

1 Case assembly—transmission
2 Case—transmission
3 Magnet—transmission case chip
4 Nut spring 9/64
5 Pin—3/16 diameter x 13/16 rolled spring
6 Lever assembly—transmission gearshift shaft offset
7 Lever transmission gearshift shaft offset
8 Pin—transmission gearshift shaft offset lever
9 Shaft—transmission shifter
10 Seal—O-ring
11 Gear & bush assembly—transmission reverse idler sliding
12 Gear—transmission reverse idler sliding
13 Bushing—transmission reverse idler gear
14 Pin—transmission reverse gear selector fork pivot
15 Ring—7/16 retaining
16 Pin—¼ x 1 spring
17 Shaft—transmission reverse idler gear
18 Gear—transmission countershaft
19 Roller—transmission countershaft bearing
20 Washer—208/.918 flat
21 Washer—transmission countershaft gear thrust
22 Countershaft—transmission
23 Shaft assembly—transmission output.
24 Shaft—transmission output
25 Hub—transmission synchronizer 1st & 2nd gear cluster
26 Shaft and gear assembly—transmission output
27 Gear—transmission reverse sliding
28 Insert—transmission synchronizer hub
29 Spring—transmission synchronizer retaining
30 Ring—transmission synchronizer blocking
31 Ring—transmission 2nd speed gear retaining snap
32 Gear—transmission 2nd speed
33 Washer—transmission 2nd speed gear thrust
34 Pin—⅛ x ¼ rolled spring
35 Gear—transmission 3rd speed
36 Synchronizer assembly—3rd & 4th speed
37 Hub—transmission synchronizer ; 4th gear clutch
38 Insert—transmission synchronizer hub
39 Sleeve—transmission 3rd & 4th gear clutch hub
40 Spring—transmission synchronizer retaining
41 Ring—transmission synchronizer blocking
42 Ring—transmission m/d gear bearing shaft snap
43 Fork—transmission 1st & 2nd gear shift
44 Fork—transmission 3rd & 4th gear shift
45 Lever assembly—transmission reverse gear shaft relay
46 Retaining—transmission reverse gear shaft relay lever
47 Lever—transmission reverse gear shaft relay
48 Fork—transmission reverse gear shift
49 Spring—transmission shifter interlock
50 Plunger—transmission meshlock
51 Screw—m12 x 10 round head flat
52 Plate—transmission gear selector interlock
53 Screw & washer assembly—m10 x 30 hex head
54 Plug—¾ diameter welch type
55 Shaft—transmission input
56 Roller—transmission mainshaft bearing
57 Bearing assembly—transmission m/d gear ball
58 Ring—m/d gear bearing retaining snap
59 Ring—1.00 retaining
60 Seal—transmission shift shaft
61 Gear—transmission 1st speed
62 Clip—spark control switch wire retaining
63 Gear—speedometer drive
64 Extension assembly—transmission
65 Extension—transmission
66 Bushing—transmission extension
67 Stop—transmission gear shift lever reverse
68 Gasket—transmission extension
69 Seal assembly—transmission extension oil
70 Plug—transmission extension
71 Retainer—transmission input shaft gear bearing
72 Seal assembly—transmission input shaft oil
73 Gasket—transmission input shaft bearing retainer
74 Bolt—M8 x 20 hex head-lock
75 Gasket—transmission case cover
76 Cover—transmission case
77 Screw—m6 x 20 hex head
78 Bolt—m6 x 32 hex washer HD shoulder
79 Plug—½-14 pipe (filler)
80 Bushing—transmission gear shift damper
81 Washer—spring lock
82 Nut—hexagon
83 Switch assembly—back-up lamp
84 Switch assembly—transmission seat belt warning sensor
85 Tag—transmission service identification
86 Washer—transmission 1st gear thrust
87 Ball—.25 diameter
88 Screw & lockwasher assembly—m12 x 40
89 Arm assembly—transmission control selector
90 Arm—transmission control selector
91 Pin—transmission gear shift

synchronizer hub cannot be removed from the output shaft.

3. Separate the inserts and insert springs from the hubs, taking care not to mix the parts of the first and second speed synchronizer with that of the third and fourth speed synchronizer. Clean and inspect all parts.
4. Position the sleeve on the hub, making sure that the alignment marks scribed prior to disassembly are aligned.
5. Position the 3 inserts on the hub. Install the insert springs, taking care to seat the bent tab in one of the inserts. The springs must face in opposite directions.

Component Assembly

Output Shaft

1. Place a blocker ring on the cone of first gear, and slide the gear and ring assembly onto the output shaft. Make sure that the inserts in the synchronizer engage in the blocker ring notches.
2. Install the spring pin retaining first gear to the output shaft.
3. Install a blocker ring on the cone of second gear, and slide the gear and ring assembly onto the output shaft. Make sure that the inserts in the synchronizer engage in the blocker ring notches.
4. Install the second gear thrust washer and new snap-ring on the shaft.
5. Install a blocker ring on the cone of third gear, and slide the gear and ring assembly onto the output shaft. Install the third and fourth speed synchronizer. Make sure that the inserts in the synchronizer engage in the blocker ring notches.
6. Install a new third and fourth gear synchronizer snap-ring.
7. Place the first gear thrust washer (oil slinger) on the shaft and on the spring pin retaining first gear.

CAUTION: *The oil grooves must be positioned against the gear.*

Cover Assembly

1. Install the third and fourth speed shifter fork into the cover.
2. Install the first and second speed shifter fork into the cover. Lubricate the shifter shaft bore with grease.

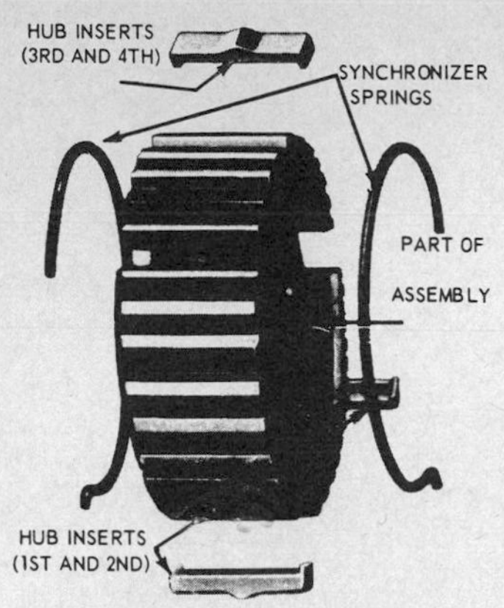

RAD synchronizer spring rotation
(© Ford Motor Co)

3. Install the manual selector arm through the interlock plate, and position the two pieces into the cover, with the wide leg of the interlock plate towards the inside of the transmission case.
4. Align the shifter shaft in the cover, and insert the shaft through the shifter forks and manual selector. Coat the shifter shaft with a light coating of grease.
5. Align the pin holes in the manual selector arm and shifter shaft. Install the spring pin flush with the surface of the selector arm.
6. Install the detent plunger, spring, and plug. Tighten the plug to 8-12 ft lbs.
7. Check the operation of the shift forks in each gear position.

Transmission Assembly

1. Position the reverse idler gear and shaft in place.
2. Coat the surfaces of the countershaft thrust washer with a thin film of grease and position in the case. Position the cluster gear assembly in the bottom of the case.
3. Position the output shaft assembly into the case through the cover opening. With the snap-ring groove facing rearward, place the rear bearing on the output shaft. Place the transmission in the vertical position and install the bearing. Position the first gear thrust washer on the roll pin carefully, holding it tightly during bearing installation. Install the rear bearing snap-rings.
4. Return the transmission to the horizontal position. Install the input shaft and blocker ring through the front of the case. Make sure that the blocker ring notches engage the synchronizer insert.
5. Install the front bearing retainer using a new gasket. Apply gasket sealer to the bolt threads and tighten to 11-15 ft lbs.
6. Place the transmission in the vertical position. Align the countershaft gear bore and thrust washers with the bore in the case. Install the countershaft from the rear of the case.
7. Install the reverse idler gear lever assembly, taking care to insert the fork in the reverse idler gear groove.
8. Apply gasket sealer to the reverse lever pivot bolt threads and install the bolt. Align the lever on the pivot bolt and torque the bolt to 15-25 ft lbs. Install the reverse lever retaining spring clip to the reverse gear pivot bolt. Tilt the transmission forward and pour a light coating of gear lube over the gear train.
9. Using a new cover gasket, install the cover assembly. Install the bolts and wiring clips and tighten to 7-10 ft lbs.

NOTE: *The two shouldered locating bolts must be installed first.*

Position the shift rail into first or third gear position.

10. Insert the speedometer drive gear lock ball into its hole. While holding the ball, slide the speedometer drive gear into place and secure it with a new snap-ring.
11. Using a new gasket, install the extension housing to the case. Using gasket sealer on the bolts, tighten them to 18-27 ft lbs. Take care not to damage the extension yoke seal.
12. Install the offset lever assembly onto the shift shaft, securing the assembly with a nut and flat washer. Tighten to 14-20 ft lbs.
13. Insert the gearshift lever into place. Check its operation in each gear position.
14. Install the access plug into the rear of the extension housing, using a soft mallet.

Type 9
Ford 4-Speed

Application

Cougar, 1969-73
Fairlane V8, 1969-70
Falcon V8, 1969-70
Ford, 1969-71
Mercury, 1969-70
Montego, 1969-73
Mustang V8, 1969-73
Torino V8, 1969-73

Disassembly

1. Remove retaining clips and flat washers from the shift rods at the levers.
2. Remove shift linkage control bracket attaching screws and remove shift linkage and control bracket.
3. Remove cover attaching screws. Then lift cover and gasket from the case.
4. Remove extension housing at-

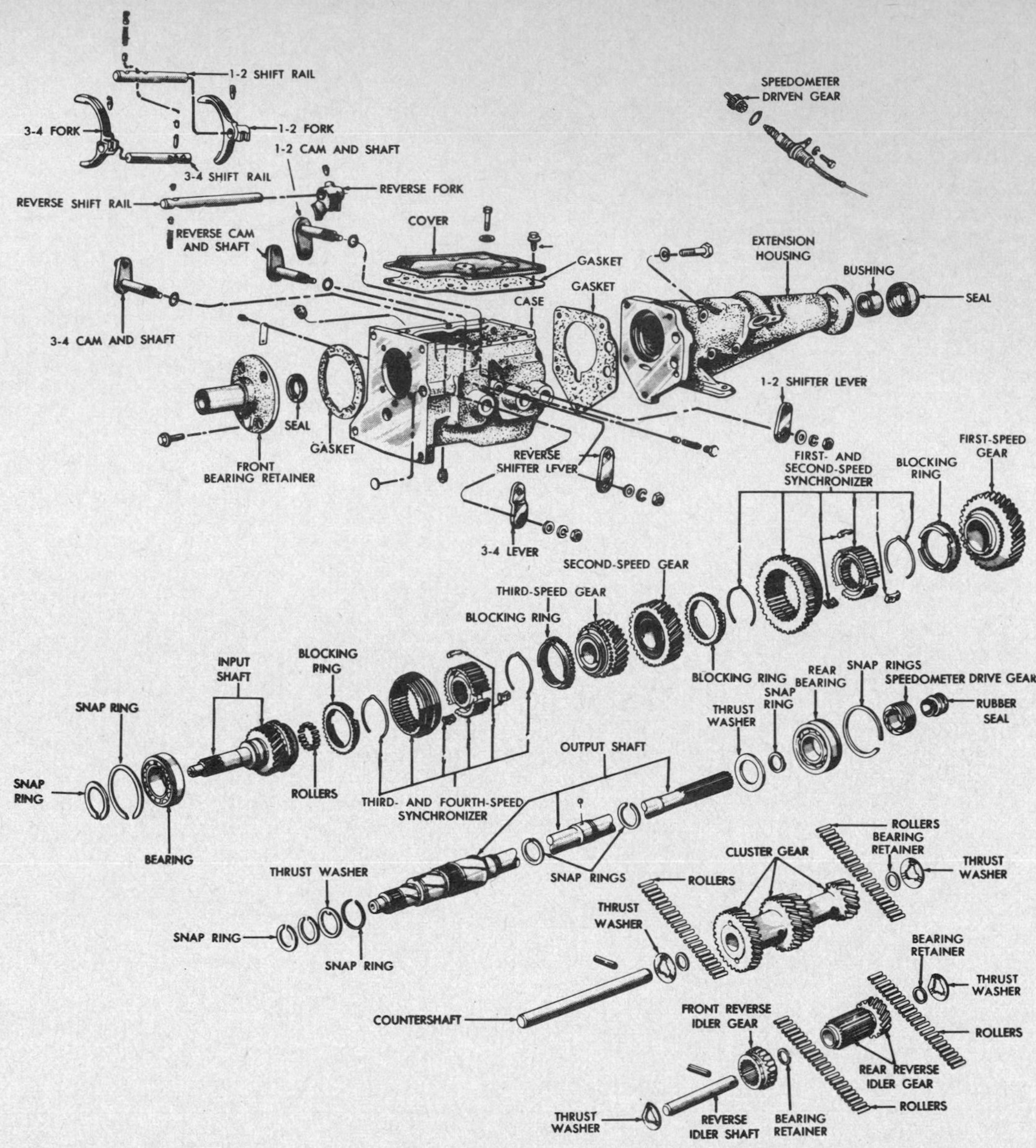

Ford 4-speed transmission disassembled (© Ford Motor Co)

taching screws. Then, remove extension housing and gasket.

5. Remove input shaft bearing retainer attaching screws. Then, slide retainer from the input shaft.
6. Working a dummy shaft in from the front of the case, drive the countershaft out the rear of the case. Let the countergear assembly lie in the bottom of the case.
7. Locate first-second-speed gear shift lever in neutral. Locate third fourth-speed gear shift lever in third-speed position.
8. Remove the lockbolt that holds the third-fourth-speed shift rail detent spring and plug the left side of the case. Remove spring and plug with a magnet.
9. Remove the detent mechanism set screw from top of case. Then, remove the detent spring and plug with a small magnet.
10. Remove attaching screw from the third-fourth-speed shift fork. Tap lightly on the inner end of the shift rail to remove the expansion plug from front of case. Then, withdraw the third-fourth-speed shift rail from the front. (Do not lose the interlock pin from rail.)
11. Remove attaching screw from the first and second-speed shift fork. Slide the first-second shift rail from the rear of case.
12. Remove the interlock and detent plugs from the top of the case with a magnet.
13. Remove the snap-ring or disengage retainer that holds the speedometer drive gear to the output shaft. Slide the gear from the shaft, then remove speedometer gear drive ball.
14. Remove the snap-ring used to hold the output shaft bearing to the shaft. Remove output shaft bearing.
15. Remove the input shaft bearing and blocking ring from the front of the case.
16. Move output shaft to the right side of case. Then, maneuver the forks to permit lifting them from the case.
17. Support first-speed gear to prevent it sliding from the shaft, then lift output shaft from the case.
18. Remove reverse gear shift fork attaching screw. Rotate the reverse shift rail 90°, then, slide the shift rail out the rear of the case. Lift out the reverse shift fork.
19. Remove the reverse detent plug and spring from the case with a magnet.
20. Using a dummy shaft, remove the reverse idler shaft from the case.
21. Lift reverse idler gear and thrust washers from the case. Be careful not to drop the bearing rollers or

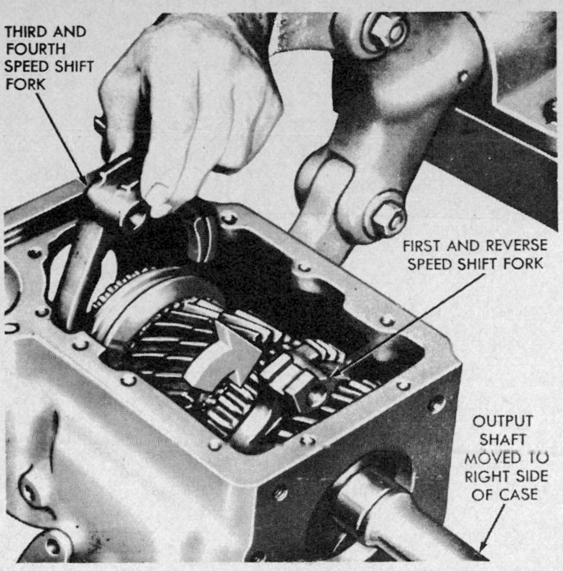

Removing shift forks
(© Ford Motor Co)

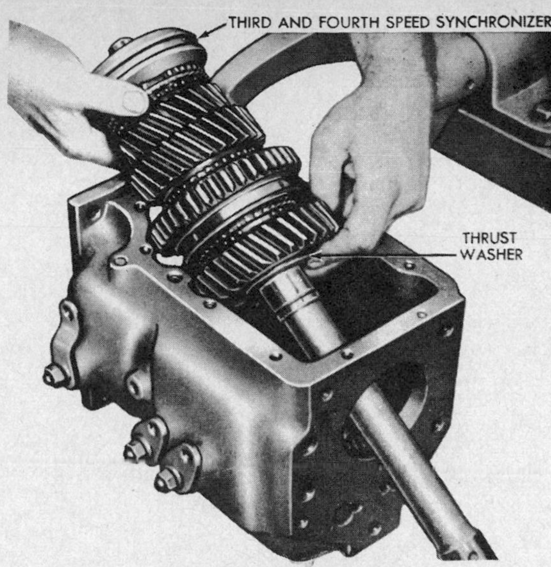

Removing output shaft
(© Ford Motor Co)

the dummy from the gear.

22. Lift the countergear, thrust washers, rollers and dummy shaft assembly from the case.
23. Remove the snap-ring from the front of the output shaft. Then, slide the third-fourth synchronizer blocking ring and the third-speed gear from the shaft.
24. Remove the next snap-ring and the second-speed gear thrust washer from the shaft. Slide the second-speed gear and the blocking ring from the shaft.
25. Remove the snap-ring, then slide the first-second synchronizer, blocking ring and the first-speed gear from the shaft.
26. Remove the thrust washer from rear of the shaft.

Unit Repairs

Cam and Shaft Seals

1. Remove attaching nut and washers from each shift lever, then remove the three levers.
2. Remove the three cams and shafts from inside the case.
3. Replace the old O-rings with new ones that have been well-lubricated.
4. Slide each cam and shaft into its respective bore in the transmission.
5. Install the levers and secure them with their respective washers and nuts.

Input Shaft Bearing

1. Remove the snap-ring that holds the bearing to the shaft.
2. Press the shaft gear from the bearing.
3. Press a new bearing onto the input shaft.
4. Secure the bearing with a snap-ring.

Synchronizers

1. Push the synchronizer hub from each synchronizer sleeve.
2. Separate the inserts and springs from the hubs. Do not mix parts of the first-second with parts of third-fourth synchronizers.
3. To assemble, position the hub in the sleeve. Be sure the alignment marks are properly indexed.
4. Place the three inserts into place on the hub. Install the insert springs so that the irregular surface (hump) is seated in one of the inserts. Do not stagger the springs.

Countershaft Gear

1. Dismantle the countershaft gear assembly.
2. Assemble the gear by coating each end of the countershaft gear bore with grease.
3. Install dummy shaft in the gear. Then install 21 bearing rollers and a retainer washer in each end of the gear.

Reverse Idler Gear

1. Dismantle reverse idler gear.
2. Assemble reverse idler gear by

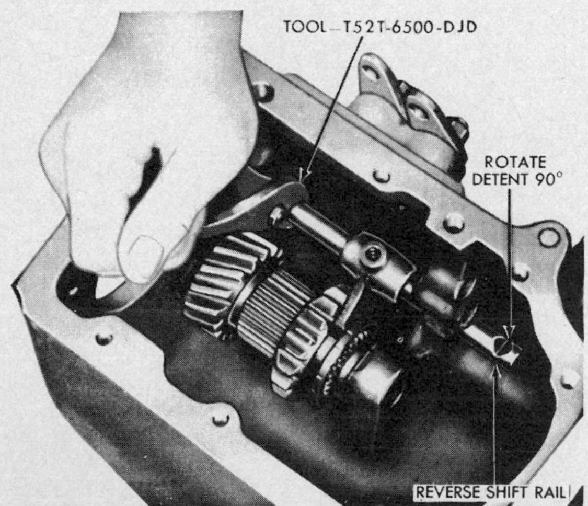

Rotating the reverse shift rail
(© Ford Motor Co)

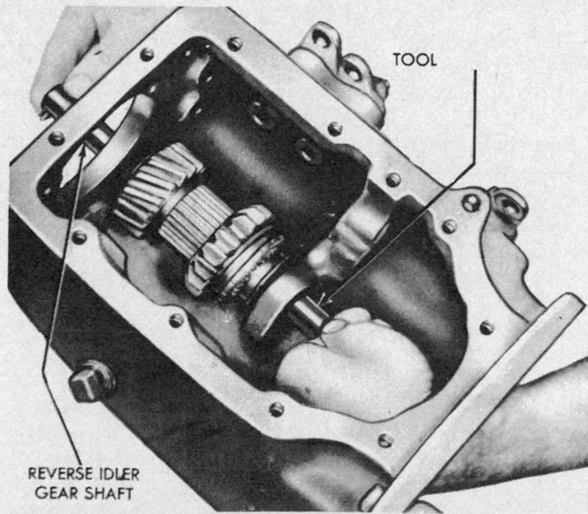

Removing reverse idler shaft
(© Ford Motor Co)

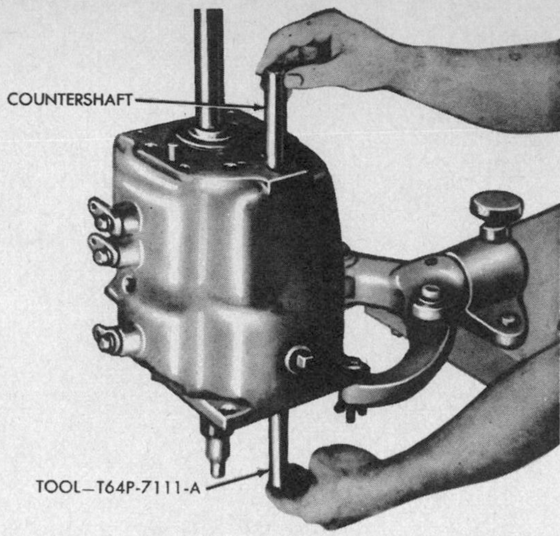

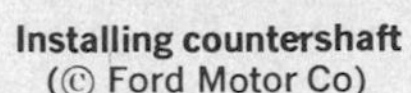

Installing countershaft
(© Ford Motor Co)

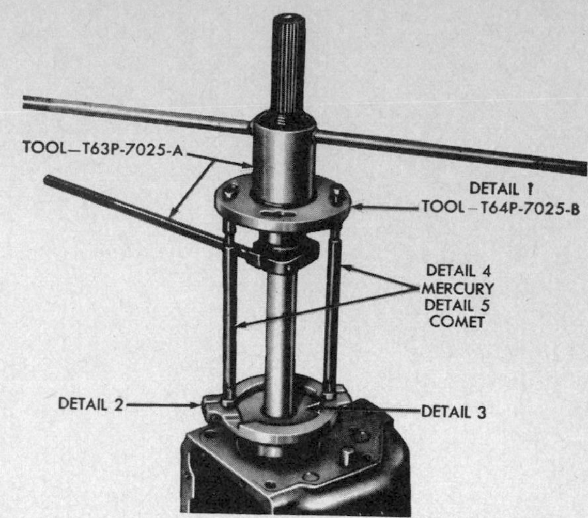

Installing output shaft bearing
(© Ford Motor Co)

coating the bore in each end of reverse idler gear with grease.

3. Hold the dummy shaft in the gear and install the 22 bearing rollers and the retainer washer into each end of the gear.
4. Install the reverse idler sliding gear on the splines of the reverse idler gear. Be sure the shift fork groove is toward the front.

Input Shaft Seal

1. Remove the seal from the input shaft bearing retainer.
2. Coat the sealing surface of a new seal with lubricant, then press the new seal into the input shaft bearing retainer.

Assembly

1. Grease the countershaft gear thrust surfaces in the case. Then, position a thrust washer at each end of the case.
2. Position the countershaft gear, dummy shaft, and roller bearings in the case.
3. Align the gear bore and thrust washers with the bores in the case. Install the countershaft.
4. With the case in a horizontal position, countershaft gear end-play should be from .004-.018 in. Use thrust washers to obtain play within these limits.
5. After establishing correct end-play, place the dummy shaft in the countershaft gear and allow the gear assembly to remain on the bottom of the case.
6. Grease the reverse idler gear thrust surfaces in the case, and position the two thrust washers.
7. Position the reverse idler gear, sliding gear, dummy, etc. in place. Make sure that the shift fork groove in the sliding gear is toward the front.
8. Align the gear bore and thrust washers with the case bores and install the reverse idler shaft.
9. Reverse idler gear end - play should be .004-.018 in. Use selective thrust washers to obtain play within these limits.
10. Position reverse gear shift rail detent spring and detent plug in the case. Hold the reverse shift fork in place on the reverse idler sliding gear and install the shift rail from the rear of the case. Lock the fork to the rail with the Allen head set screws.
11. Install the first-second synchronizer onto the output shaft. The first and reverse synchronizer hub are a press fit and should be installed with gear teeth facing the rear of the shaft.
12. Slide second-speed gear onto the front of the shaft with the synchronizer coned surface toward the rear.
13. Install the second-speed gear thrust washer and snap-ring.
14. Slide the third-speed gear onto the shaft with the synchronizer coned surface front.
15. Coat the cone of third-speed gear with grease. Place a blocking ring on the third-speed gear.
16. Slide the third-fourth speed gear synchronizer onto the shaft. Be sure that the inserts in the synchronizer engage the notches in the blocking ring. Install the snap-ring onto the front of the output shaft.
17. Coat the cone of second-speed gear with grease and position the blocking ring on the gear.
18. Slide the first-second speed synchronizer onto the rear of the output shaft. Be sure that the inserts engage the notches in the blocking ring and that the shift fork groove is toward the rear.
19. Coat the coned surface of first-speed gear with grease and position the blocking ring on it.
20. Slide the first-speed gear onto the rear of the output shaft. Be sure that the notches in the blocker ring engage the synchronizer inserts.
21. Install heavy thrust washer onto the rear of the output shaft.
22. Lower the output shaft assembly into the case.
23. Position the first-second speed shift fork and the third-fourth-speed shift fork in place on their respective gears. Rotate them into place.
24. Place a detent plug in the detent bore. Place the reverse shift rail into neutral position.
25. Coat the third-fourth-speed shift rail interlock pin with grease, then position it in the shift rail.
26. Align the third-fourth-speed shift fork with the shift rail bores and slide the shift rail into place. Be sure that the three detents are facing the outside of the case. Place the front synchronizer into third-fourth-speed position and install the set screw into the third - fourth - speed shift fork. Move the synchronizer to neutral position. Install the third-fourth-speed shift rail detent plug, spring and bolt into the left side of the transmission case. Place the interlock plug (tapered ends) in the detent bore.
27. Align first-second-speed shift fork with the case bores and slide the shift rail into place. Lock the fork with the set screw. Install the detent plug and spring into the detent bore. Thread the set screw into the case until the head is flush with the case.
28. Coat the input gear bore with a small amount of grease. Then install the 15 bearing rollers.
29. Place the input shaft gear in the case. Be sure that the output shaft pilot enters the roller bearing of the input shaft gear.
30. With a new gasket on the input bearing retainer, dip attaching

bolts in sealer, install bolts and torque to 30-36 ft. lbs.

31. Install the output shaft bearing, then install the snap-ring to hold the bearing.
32. Position the speedometer gear drive ball in the output shaft and slide the speedometer drive gear into place. Secure gear with snap-ring.
33. Align the countershaft gear bore and thrust washers with the bore in the case. Install the countershaft.
34. With a new gasket in place, install and secure the extension housing. Dip the extension housing screws in sealer, then torque screws to 42-50 ft. lbs.
35. Install the filler plug (torque 10-20 ft. lbs.) and the drain plug (torque 20-30 ft. lbs.), the drain plug is magnetic.
36. Pour in four pints of mild E.P. gear oil over the entire gear train while rotating the input shaft.
37. Place each shift fork in all positions to make sure they function properly.
38. With a new cover gasket in place, install the cover. Dip attaching screws in sealer, then torque screws to 14-19 ft. lbs.
39. Coat the third-fourth speed shift rail plug bore with sealer. Install a new plug.
40. Secure each shift rod to its respective lever with a spring washer, flat washer and retaining pin.
41. Position the shift linkage control bracket to the extension housing. Install and torque the attaching screws to 12-15 ft. lbs.

Type-10 Muncie Fully Synchronized 3-Speed

Application

Camaro, 1969-74
Chevelle, 1969-74
Chevrolet, 1969-73
Firebird, 1970-74
GTO, 1970-74
Monte Carlo, 1970-74
Nova, 1969-74
Olds F-85, 4-4-2, 1970-71
Pontiac Grand Prix, 1970-71
Tempest, 1970-71

Transmission Disassembly

1. Remove side cover and shift forks.
2. Unbolt extension. Rotate extension to line up groove in extension flange with reverse idler shaft. Drive reverse idler shaft and key out of case with a brass drift.
3. Move second-third synchronizer sleeve forward. Remove extension housing and mainshaft assembly.
4. Remove reverse idler gear from case.
5. Remove third speed blocker ring from clutch gear.
6. Expand snap-ring which retains mainshaft rear bearing. Tap gently on end of mainshaft to remove extension.
7. Remove clutch gear bearing retainer and gasket.
8. Remove snap-ring. Remove clutch gear from inside case by gently tapping on end of clutch gear.
9. Remove oil slinger. Remove 16 mainshaft pilot bearings from clutch gear cavity.
10. Slip clutch gear bearing out front of case. Aid removal with a screwdriver between case and bearing outer snap-ring.
11. Drive countershaft and key out to rear.
12. Remove countergear and two tanged thrust washers.

Mainshaft Disassembly

1. Depress speedometer drive gear retaining clip. Slide off gear. Some speedometer drive gears, made of metal, must be pulled off.
2. Remove rear bearing snap-ring.
3. Support reverse gear and press on rear of mainshaft to remove reverse gear, thrust washer, and rear bearing. Be careful not to cock the bearing on the shaft.
4. Remove first and reverse sliding clutch hub snap-ring.
5. Support first gear. Press on rear of mainshaft to remove clutch assembly, blocker ring, and first gear.
6. Remove second and third speed sliding clutch hub snap-ring.
7. Support second gear. Press on front of mainshaft to remove clutch assembly, second speed blocker ring, and second gear from shaft.

Inspection

1. Wash all parts in solvent.
2. Air dry.

Case

1. Check for cracks.
2. Check faces for burrs. Remove with a fine file.
3. Check bearing bores for damage. If they are damaged, replace case.

Front and Rear Bearings

1. Do not spin bearings with air pressure; turn them slowly by hand.
2. Lubricate bearings with light oil. Turn slowly to check for roughness.

Bearing Rollers

1. Check for wear; replace if worn.
2. Check countershaft and reverse idler shaft.
3. Replace all worn washers.

Gears

1. Check for wear, chips, or cracks.
2. If reverse gear bushing is worn or damaged, replace entire gear.
3. Check to see that both clutch sleeves slide freely on their hubs.

Reverse Idler Gear Bushing

This bushing may not be serviced separately. If the bushing requires replacement, replace the gear.

Countergear Anti-Lash Plate

1. Check the plate teeth for wear or damage.
2. Do not disassemble.

Repair

Clutch Keys and Springs

Keys and springs may be replaced if worn or broken, but the hubs and sleeves must be kept together as originally assembled.

1. Mark hub and sleeve for reassembly.
2. Push hub from sleeve. Remove keys and springs.
3. Place three keys and two springs, one on each side of hub, so all three keys are engaged by both springs. The tanged end of the springs should not be installed into the same key.
4. Slide the sleeve onto the hub, aligning the marks.

Extension Oil Seal and Bushing

1. Remove seal.
2. Using bushing remover and installer, or other suitable tool, drive bushing into extension housing.
3. Drive new bushing in from rear. Lubricate inside of bushing and seal. Install new oil seal with extension seal installer or suitable tool.

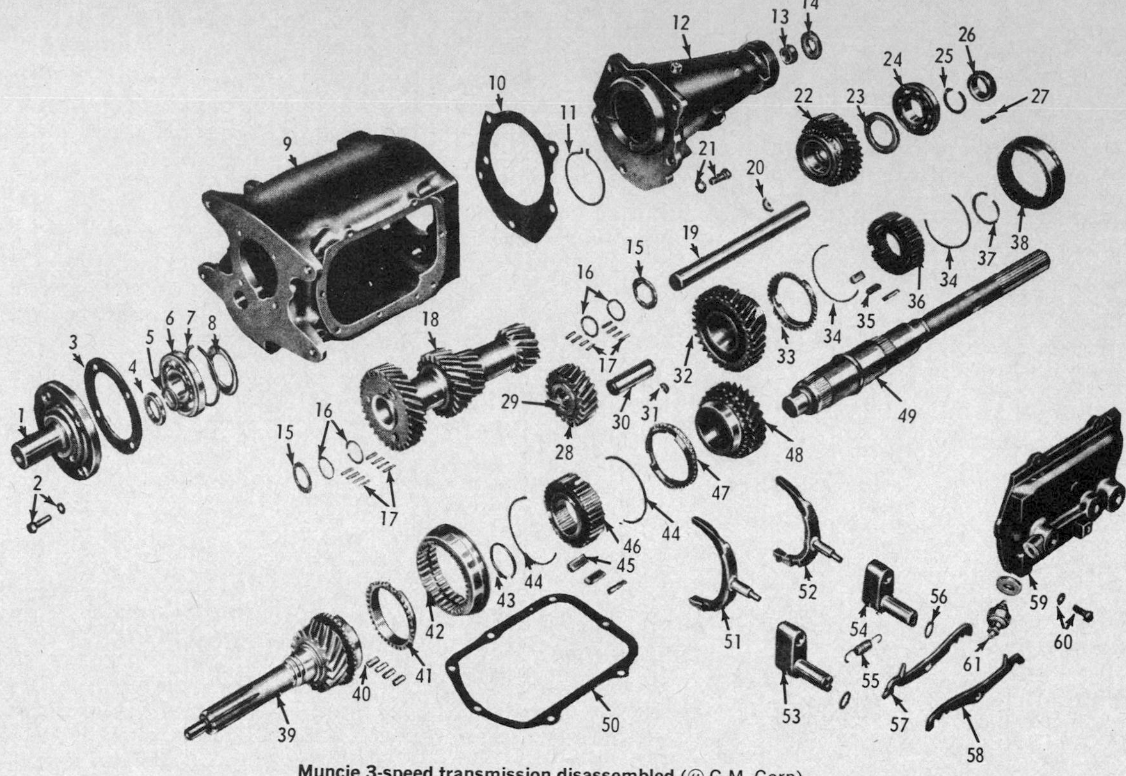

Muncie 3-speed transmission disassembled (© G.M. Corp)

1 Bearing retainer
2 Bolt and lock washer
3 Gasket
4 Oil seal
5 Snap ring (bearing-to-main drive gear)
6 Main drive gear bearing
7 Snap ring bearing
8 Oil slinger
9 Case
10 Gasket
11 Snap ring (rear bearing-to-extension)
12 Extension
13 Extension bushing
14 Oil seal
15 Thrust washer
16 Bearing washer
17 Needle bearings
18 Countergear
19 Countershaft
20 Woodruff key
21 Bolt (extension-to-case)
22 Reverse gear
23 Thrust washer
24 Rear bearing
25 Snap ring
26 Speedometer drive gear
27 Retainer clip
28 Reverse idler gear
29 Reverse idler bushing
30 Reverse idler shaft
31 Woodruff key
32 1st speed gear
33 1st speed blocker ring
34 Synchronizer key spring
35 Synchronizer keys
36 1st and reverse synchronizer hub assembly
37 Snap ring
38 1st and reverse synchronizer collar
39 Main drive gear
40 Pilot bearings
41 3rd speed blocker ring
42 2nd and 3rd synchronizer collar
43 Snap ring
44 Synchronizer key spring
45 Synchronizer keys
46 2nd and 3rd synchronizer hub
47 2nd speed blocker ring
48 2nd speed gear
49 Mainshaft
50 Gasket
51 2nd and 3rd shifter fork
52 1st and reverse shifter fork
53 2-3 shifter shaft assembly
54 1st and reverse shifter shaft assembly
55 Spring
56 O-ring seal
57 1st and reverse detent cam
58 2nd and 3rd detent cam
59 Side cover
60 Bolt and lock washer

Clutch Bearing Retainer Oil Seal

1. Pry old seal out.
2. Install new seal using seal installer or suitable tool. Seat seal in bore.

Mainshaft Assembly

1. Turn front of mainshaft up.
2. Install second gear with clutching teeth up; the rear face of the gear butts against the flange on the mainshaft.
3. Install a blocking ring with clutching teeth downward. All three blocking rings are the same.
4. Install second and third synchronizer assembly with fork slot down. Press it onto mainshaft splines. Both synchronizer assemblies are identical but are assembled differently. The second-third speed hub and sleeve is assembled with the sleeve fork slot toward the thrust face of the hub; the first-reverse hub and sleeve, with the fork slot opposite the thrust face. Be sure that the blocker ring notches align with the synchronizer assembly keys.
5. Install synchronizer snap-ring. Both synchronizer snap-rings are the same.
6. Turn rear of shaft up.
7. Install first gear with clutching teeth upward; the front face of the gear butts against the flange on the mainshaft.
8. Install a blocker ring with clutching teeth down.
9. Install first and reverse synchronizer assembly with fork slot up. Press it onto mainshaft splines. Be sure blocker ring notches align with synchronizer assembly keys and both synchronizer sleeves face front of mainshaft.
10. Install snap-ring.
11. Install reverse gear with clutching teeth down.
12. Install steel reverse gear thrust washer with flats aligned.
13. Press rear ball bearing onto shaft with snap-ring slot down.
14. Install snap-ring.
15. Install speedometer drive gear and retaining clip.

Transmission Assembly

1. Place a row of 29 roller bearings, a bearing washer, a second row of 29 bearings, and a second bearing washer at each end of the countergear. Hold in place with grease.
2. Place countergear assembly through rear case opening with a tanged thrust washer, tang away from gear, at each end. Install countershaft and key from rear of case. Be sure that thrust washer tangs are aligned with notches in case.
3. Place reverse idler gear in case. Do not install reverse idler shaft yet.

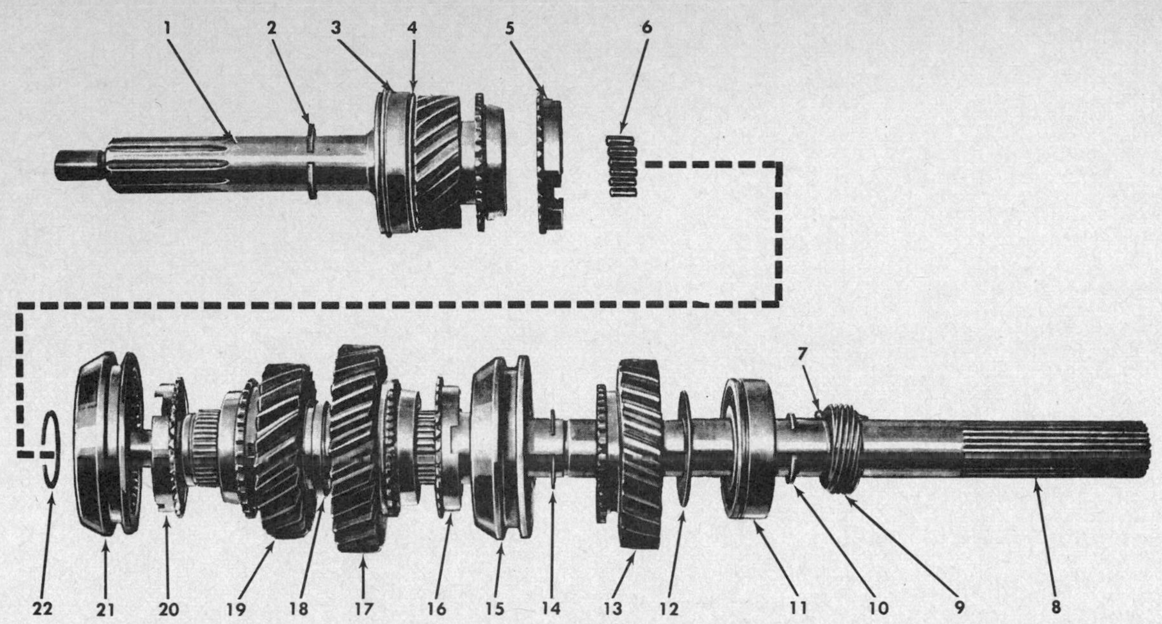

Clutch gear and mainshaft assembly (© G.M. Corp)

1 Clutch gear
2 Snap ring
3 Clutch gear bearing
4 Oil slinger
5 3rd speed blocker ring
6 Mainshaft pilot bearings (16)
7 Retaining clip
8 Mainshaft
9 Speedo drive gear
10 Snap ring
11 Rear bearing
12 Reverse gear thrust washer
13 Reverse gear
14 Snap ring
15 1st speed synchronizer assembly
16 1st speed blocker ring
17 1st speed gear
18 Shoulder (part of mainshaft)
19 2nd speed gear
20 2nd speed blocker ring
21 2-3 synchronizer assembly
22 Snap ring

4. Expand snap-ring in extension. Assemble extension over mainshaft and onto rear bearing. Seat snap-ring.
5. Load 16 mainshaft pilot bearings into clutch gear cavity. Assemble third speed blocker ring onto clutch gear clutching surface with teeth toward gear.
6. Place clutch gear assembly, without front bearing, over front of mainshaft. Make sure that blocker ring notches align with keys in second-third synchronizer assembly.
7. Stick gasket onto extension housing with grease. Assemble clutch gear, mainshaft, and extension to case together. Make sure that clutch gear teeth engage teeth of countergear anti-lash plate.
8. Rotate extension housing. Install reverse idler shaft and key.
9. Torque extension bolts to 45 ft. lbs.
10. Install oil slinger with inner lip facing forward. Install front bearing outer snap-ring to bearing. Slide bearing into case bore.
11. Install snap-ring to clutch gear stem. Install bearing retainer and gasket. Torque bolts to 20 ft. lbs. Retainer oil return hole must be at 6 o'clock.
12. Shift both synchronizer sleeves to neutral positions. Install side cover, aligning shifter forks with synchronizer sleeve grooves.
13. Torque side cover bolts to 20 ft. lbs.

Type-11
Saginaw Fully Synchronized 3-Speed

Application

Apollo, 1973-76
Astre, 1975-76
Buick Special, Skylark, Century, 1969-76
Camaro, 1969-76
Chevelle, 1969-76
Chevrolet, 1969-73
Corvette, 1969
Firebird, 1969-76
Monte Carlo, 1975-76
Nova, 1969-76
Olds F-85, Cutlass, 1969-76
Olds 4-4-2, 1972
Omega, 1973-76
Tempest, 1969-76
Ventura, 1971-76
Vega, 1973-76

Transmission Disassembly

1. Remove side cover assembly and shift forks.
2. Remove clutch gear bearing retainer.
3. Remove clutch gear bearing to gear stem snap-ring. Pull clutch gear outward until a screwdriver can be inserted between bearing and case. Remove clutch gear bearing.
4. Remove speedometer driven gear and extension bolts.
5. Remove reverse idler shaft snap-ring. Slide reverse idler gear forward on shaft.
6. Remove mainshaft and extension assembly.
7. Remove clutch gear and third speed blocker ring from inside case. Remove 14 roller bearings from clutch gear.
8. Expand the snap-ring which retains the mainshaft rear bearing. Remove the extension.
9. Using a dummy shaft, drive the countershaft and key out the rear of the case. Remove the gear, two tanged thrust washers, and dummy shaft. Remove bearing washer and 27 roller bearings from each end of countergear.
10. Use a long drift to drive the reverse idler shaft and key through the rear of the case.

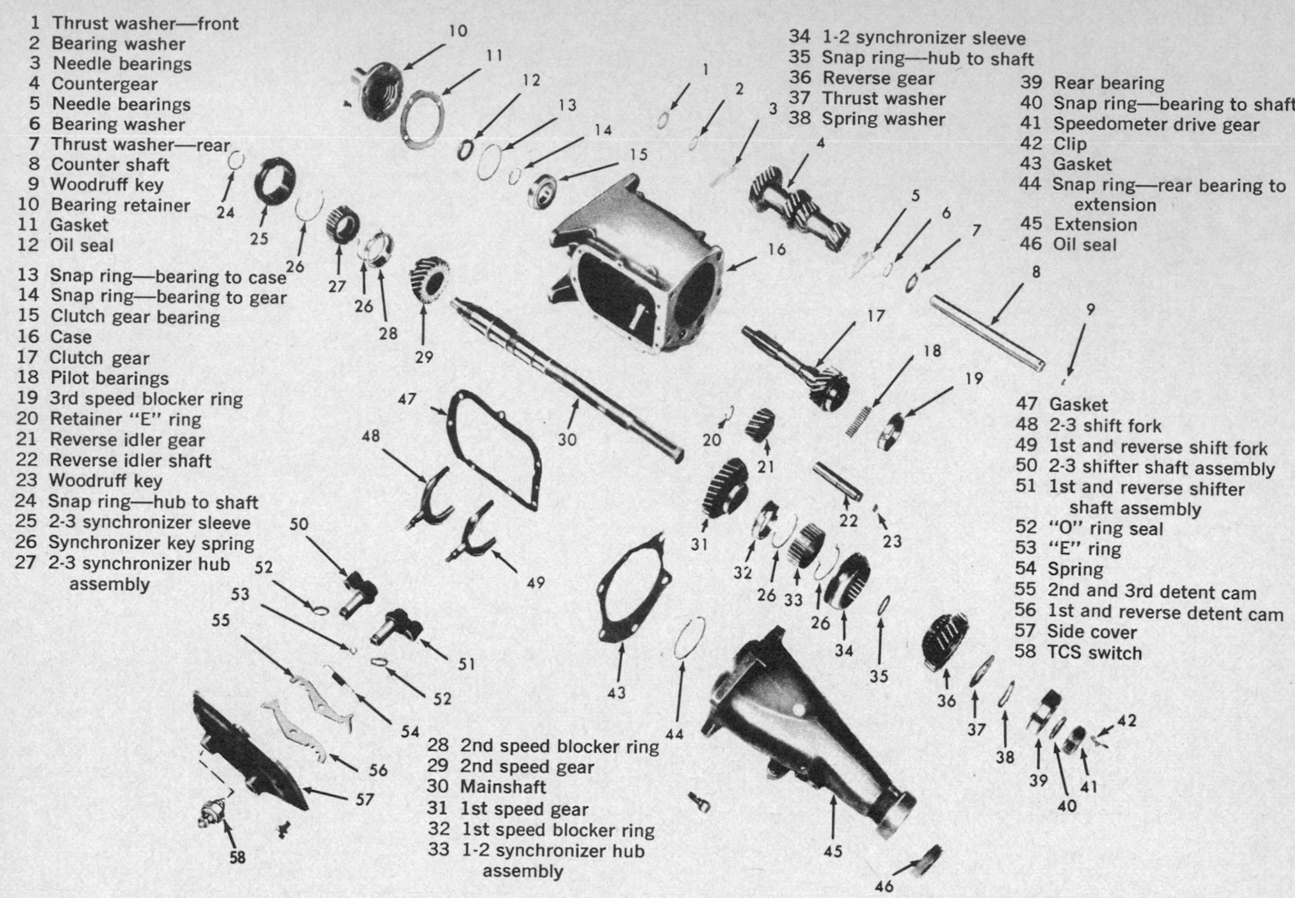

Saginaw transmission—exploded view (© G.M. Corp)

11. Remove reverse idler gear and tanged steel thrust washer.

Mainshaft Disassembly

1. Remove second and third speed sliding clutch hub snap-ring from mainshaft. Remove clutch assembly, second speed blocker ring, and second gear from front of mainshaft.
2. Depress speedometer drive gear retaining clip. Remove gear. Some units have a metal speedometer drive gear which must be pulled off.
3. Remove rear bearing snap-ring.
4. Support reverse gear. Press on rear of mainshaft. Remove reverse gear, thrust washer, spring washer, rear bearing, and snap-ring. When pressing off the rear bearing, be careful not to cock the bearing on the shaft.
5. Remove first and reverse sliding clutch hub snap-ring. Remove clutch assembly, first speed blocker ring, and first gear.

Inspection

1. Wash all parts in solvent.
2. Air dry.

Case

1. Check for cracks.
2. Check faces for burrs. Remove with a fine file.
3. Check bearing bores for damage. If they are damaged, replace case.

Front and Rear Bearings

1. Do not spin bearings with air pressure; turn them slowly by hand.
2. Lubricate bearings with light oil. Turn slowly to check for roughness.

Bearing Rollers

1. Check for wear; replace if worn.
2. Check countershaft and reverse idler shaft for wear or damage.
3. Replace all worn washers.

Gears

1. Check for wear, chips, or cracks.
2. If reverse gear bushing is worn or damaged, replace entire gear.
3. Check that both clutch sleeves slide freely on their hubs.

Reverse Idler Gear Bushing

This bushing may not be serviced separately. If the bushing requires replacement, replace the gear.

Countergear Anti-Lash Plate

1. Check the plate teeth for wear or damage.
2. Do not disassemble unit.

Repair

Clutch Keys and Springs

Keys and springs may be replaced if worn or broken, but the hubs and sleeves are matched pairs and must be kept together.

1. Mark hub and sleeve for reassembly.
2. Push hub from sleeve. Remove keys and springs.
3. Place three keys and two springs, one on each side of hub, in position, so all three keys are engaged by both springs. The tanged end of the springs should not be installed into the same key.
4. Slide the sleeve onto the hub, aligning the marks.

NOTE: a groove around the outside of the synchronizer hub marks the end that must be opposite the fork slot in the sleeve when assembled.

Extension Oil Seal and Bushing

1. Remove seal.
2. Using bushing remover and installer tool, or other suitable tool, drive bushing into extension housing.
3. Drive new bushing in from the rear. Lubricate inside of bushing and seal. Install new oil seal with extension seal installer tool or other suitable tool.

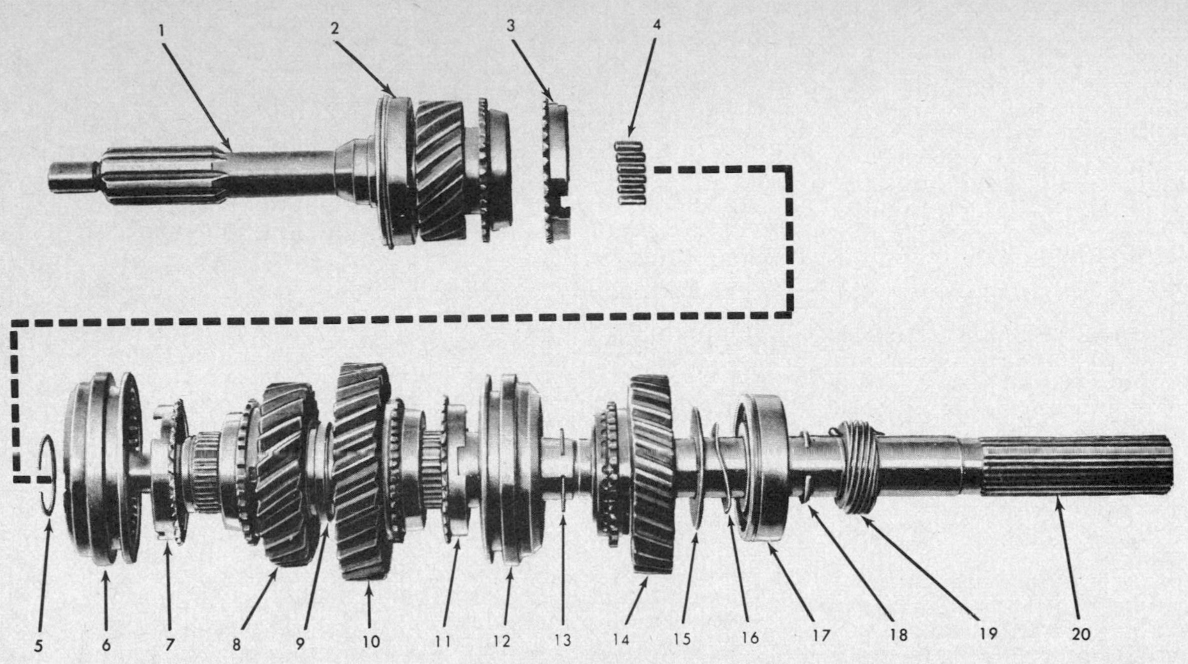

Clutch gear and mainshaft assembly (© G.M. Corp)

1 Clutch gear
2 Clutch gear bearing
3 3rd speed blocker ring
4 Mainshaft pilot bearings (14)
5 Snap ring
6 2-3 synchronizer assembly
7 2nd speed blocker ring
8 2nd speed gear
9 Shoulder (part of main shaft)
10 1st speed gear
11 1st speed blocker ring
12 1st speed synchronizer assembly
13 Snap ring
14 Reverse gear
15 Reverse gear thrust washer
16 Spring washer
17 Rear bearing
18 Snap ring
19 Speedo drive gear and clip
20 Mainshaft

Clutch Bearing Retainer Oil Seal

1. Pry old seal out.
2. Install new seal using seal installer or suitable tool. Seat seal in bore.

Mainshaft Assembly

1. Turn front of mainshaft up.
2. Install second gear with clutching teeth up; the rear face of the gear butts against the flange on the mainshaft.
3. Install a blocker ring with clutching teeth down. All three blocker rings are the same.
4. Install second and third speed synchronizer assembly with fork slot down. Press it onto mainshaft splines. Both synchronizer assemblies are the same. Be sure that blocker ring notches align with synchronizer assembly keys.
5. Install synchronizer snap-ring. Both synchronizer snap-rings are the same.
6. Turn rear of shaft up.
7. Install first gear with clutching teeth up; the front face of the gear butts against the flange on the mainshaft.
8. Install a blocker ring with clutching teeth down.
9. Install first and reverse synchronizer assembly with fork slot down. Press it onto mainshaft splines. Be sure blocker ring notches align with synchronizer assembly keys.
10. Install snap-ring.
11. Install reverse gear with clutching teeth down.
12. Install steel reverse gear thrust washer and spring washer.
13. Press rear ball bearing onto shaft with snap-ring slot down.
14. Install snap-ring.
15. Install speedometer drive gear and retaining clip. Press on metal speedometer drive gear.

Transmission Assembly

1. Using dummy shaft, load a row of 27 roller bearings and a thrust washer at each end of countergear. Hold in place with grease.
2. Place countergear assembly into case through rear. Place a tanged thrust washer, tang away from gear, at each end. Install countershaft and key, making sure that tangs align with notches in case.
3. Install reverse idler gear thrust washer, gear, and shaft with key from rear of case. Be sure thrust washer is between gear and rear of case with tang toward notch in case.
4. Expand snap-ring in extension. Assemble extension over rear of mainshaft and onto rear bearing. Seat snap-ring in rear bearing groove.
5. Install 14 mainshaft pilot bearings into clutch gear cavity. Assemble third speed blocker ring onto clutch gear clutching surface with teeth toward gear.
6. Place clutch gear, pilot bearings, and third speed blocker ring assembly over front of mainshaft assembly. Be sure blocker rings align with keys in second-third synchronizer assembly.
7. Stick extension gasket to case with grease. Install clutch gear, mainshaft, and extension together. Be sure clutch gear engages teeth of countergear anti-lash plate. Torque extension bolts to 45 ft. lbs.
8. Place bearing over stem of clutch gear and into front case bore. Install front bearing to clutch gear snap-ring.
9. Install clutch gear bearing retainer and gasket. The retainer oil return hole must be at the bottom. Torque retainer bolts to 10 ft. lbs.
10. Install reverse idler gear shaft E-ring.
11. Shift synchronizer sleeves to neutral positions. Install cover, gasket, and forks, aligning forks with synchronizer sleeve grooves. Torque side cover bolts to 10 ft. lbs.
12. Install speedometer driven gear.

Type-12
Muncie 4-Speed

Application

Buick Special, GS, 1969-72
Camaro, 1969-74
Chevelle, 1969-74
Chevrolet, 1969
Corvette, 1969-74
Firebird, 1969-74
GTO, 1971-74
Monte Carlo, 1970-71
Nova, 1969-74
Olds F-85, Cutlass, 4-4-2, 1969-73
Pontiac, 1969
Pontiac GP, 1969-71
Tempest, 1969-74

Disassembly

1. Remove side cover and shift controls after draining.
2. Remove bolts and bolt lock strips from front bearing retainer and remove retainer and gasket.
3. Lock up transmission by shifting into two gears and remove main drive gear retaining nut.

NOTE: this nut may have left-hand threads.

4. Return gears to neutral and remove lock pin from reverse shifter lever boss and pull shaft out about ⅛ in. This will disengage reverse shift fork from reverse gear.
5. Remove extension case attaching bolts. Tap extension with soft hammer toward rear. When idler shaft is out as far as it will go, move extension to left so reverse fork clears gear and remove extension and gasket.
6. Remove reverse idler gear, flat washer, shaft and roll spring pin.
7. Remove speedometer and reverse gears.

NOTE: slide third-fourth synchronizer clutch sleeve to fourth-speed gear position (forward) before trying to remove mainshaft assembly from case.

8. Remove rear bearing retainer and mainshaft assembly from case by tapping bearing retainer with soft hammer.
9. Unload bearing rollers from main drive gear and remove fourth-speed synchronizer blocking ring.
10. Lift front half of reverse idler gear with tanged thrust washer from case.
11. Press main drive gear down from bearing.
12. Tap front bearing and snap-ring from case.
13. From front of case, press out countershaft. Then, remove the countershaft gear and both tanged washers.
14. Remove the rollers (112), six spacers and roller spacer from countergear.
15. Remove mainshaft front snap-ring and slide third and fourth-speed clutch and third-speed gear and synchronizer ring from front of mainshaft.
16. Spread rear bearing retainer snap-ring and press mainshaft out of retainer.
17. Remove mainshaft snap-ring. Support second-speed gear and press on rear of mainshaft to remove rear bearing, first-speed gear and sleeve, first-speed syn-

Removing countershaft
(© G.M. Corp)

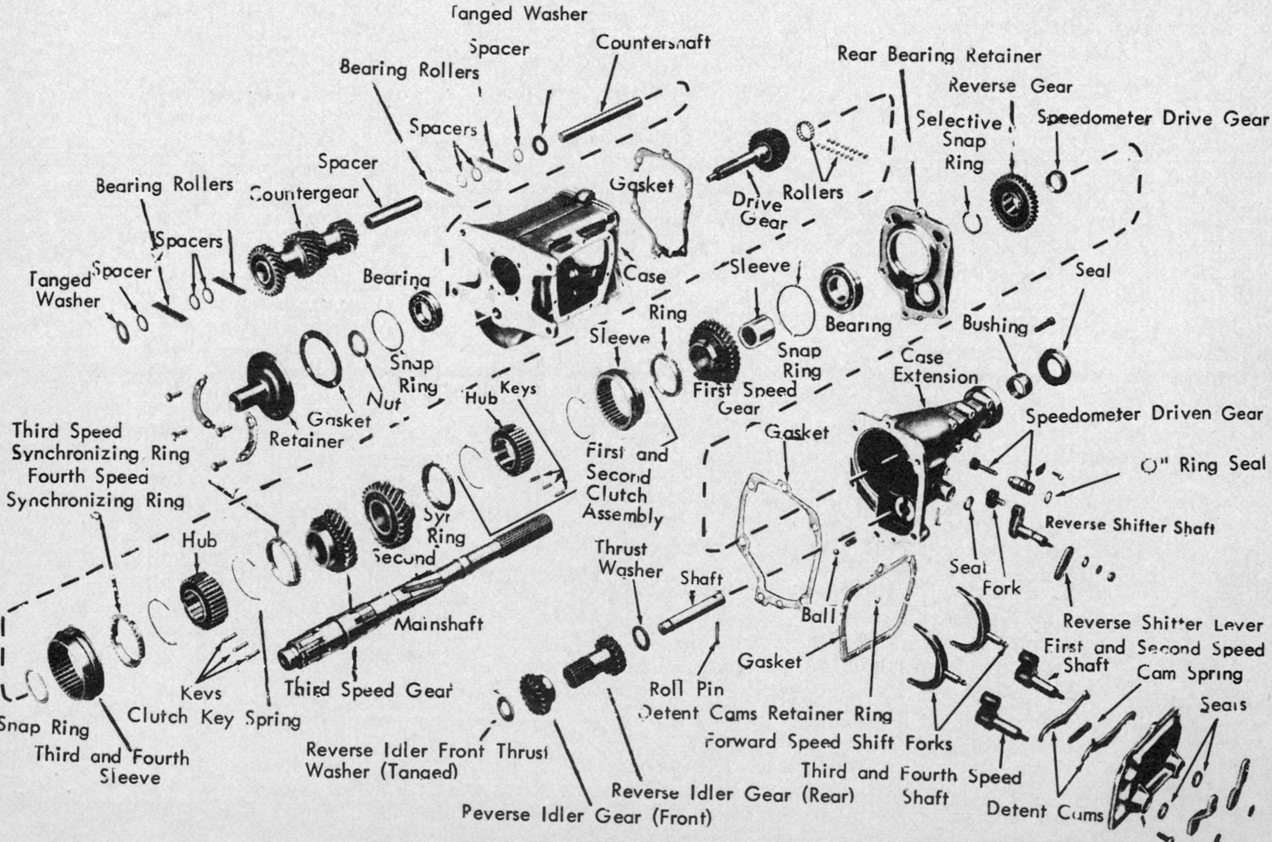

Muncie 4-speed transmission disassembled

chronizing ring, first-second-speed synchronizer clutch, second-speed synchronizer ring and second-speed gear.

After thoroughly cleaning case and all parts, make thorough inspection and replace required parts. In checking bearings do not spin at high speeds, but rather clean and rotate by hand to detect roughness and unevenness. Spinning can damage balls and races.

Assembly

Mainshaft

1. From rear of shaft, assemble second-speed gear (hub of gear toward rear of shaft).
2. Install first-second synchronizer clutch assembly onto mainshaft (sleeve taper toward rear, hub to front); together with a synchronizer ring on each side of clutch assembly so that keyways line up with clutch keys.
3. Press first-speed sleeve onto mainshaft. (A 1¾ in. or 1⅝ in. ID pipe cut to convenient length makes a suitable tool).
4. Install first-speed gear (hub toward front) and press onto the rear bearing with snap-ring grooves toward front of transmission. Be sure bearing is firmly seated.
5. Choose selective fit snap-ring (.087, .090, .093 or .096 in.) and install it into groove in mainshaft behind rear bearing. Maximum clearance of snap-ring and rear face should be between zero and .005 in.

NOTE: always use new snap-ring.

6. Install third-speed gear (hub to front of transmission) and third-speed gear synchronizing ring (notches to front).
7. Install third and fourth-speed gear clutch assembly with both sleeve taper and hub toward front.
8. Install snap-ring onto mainshaft in front of third and fourth-speed clutch, with ends of snap-ring seated behind spline teeth.
9. Install rear bearing retainer. Spread snap-ring in plate, to allow ring to drop around rear bearing, and press on the end of mainshaft until snap-ring engages the groove in rear bearing.
10. Install reverse gear (shift collar to rear).
11. Install speedometer drive gear.

Countergear

1. Install roller spacer into counter gear.
2. With heavy grease to assist, install a spacer in either end of countergear, 28 roller bearings, then a spacer and 28 more rollers. Then, install another spacer. In the other end of the counter-

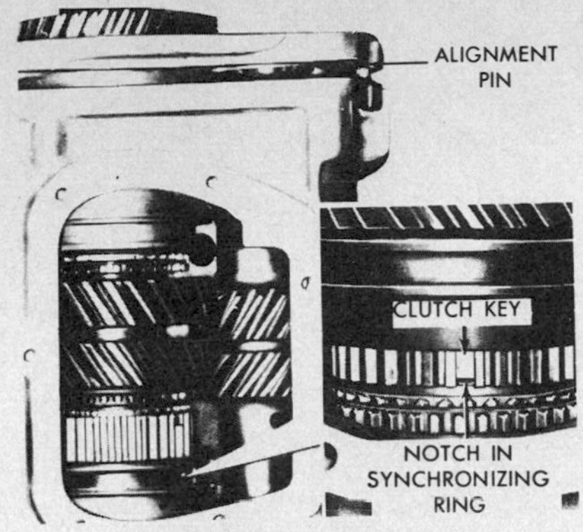

Installing mainshaft assembly
(© G.M. Corp)

gear, do the same.

3. Insert dummy shaft into counter gear.

Transmission

1. Rest case on side with cover opening toward mechanic. Install countergear tanged thrust washers in place, holding with heavy grease. Make sure tangs are in proper notches.
2. Set countergear in place. Use care not to disturb tanged washers.
3. Position transmission case so that it rests on front face.
4. Lubricate and insert countershaft in rear. Turn countershaft so flat on end of shaft is horizontal and facing bottom of case.

NOTE: the flat of shaft must be horizontal and toward bottom to mate with rear bearing retainer when installed.

5. Align countergear with shaft in rear and hole in front of case (pushing dummy shaft out front of case) until flat of shaft is flush with rear of case. Be sure thrust washers remain in place.
6. Check end-play in countergear (dial indicator should be used). If end-play is more than .025 in. install new thrust washer.
7. Install cage and 17 roller bearings into main drive gear. Use heavy grease to hold bearings.
8. Install main drive gear with bearings through side opening of case and into position in front bore.
9. Place gasket in position on rear bearing retainer.
10. Install fourth-speed synchronizing ring onto main drive gear (notches toward rear).
11. Position tanged thrust washer for reverse idler on machined face. Position front reverse idler gear next to thrust washer (hub facing toward rear of case).

Caution Before attempting to install mainshaft to case, slide the third-fourth synchronizer clutch sleeve forward into fourth-speed detent position.

12. Lower mainshaft assembly into case. Be sure notches on fourth-speed synchronizer ring correspond to keys in clutch assembly.
13. With guide pin in rear bearing retainer aligned with hole in rear of case, tap rear bearing retainer into position with soft hammer.
14. From rear of case, insert reverse idler gear, engaging splines with portion of front gear in case.
15. Place gasket in position on rear face of bearing retainer.
16. Install remaining flat washer on reverse idler shaft.
17. Install reverse idler shaft, roll pin, and thrust washer into gears and front boss of case. Make sure to pick up front tanged thrust washer.
18. Pull reverse shifter shaft to left side of extension and rotate shaft to bring reverse shift fork forward in extension (reverse detent position). Start extension onto transmission case, while slowly pushing in on shifter shaft to engage the shift fork with the reverse gear shift collar. Then, pilot the reverse idler shaft into the extension housing, permitting the extension to slide into the transmission case.
19. Install extension and retainer-to-case attaching bolts.
20. Push or pull reverse shifter shaft to line up grooves in the shaft with the holes in the boss and drive in the lockpin. Install shift lever.
21. Press bearing onto main drive gear (snap-ring groove in front), and into case until several main drive gear retaining nut threads are exposed.
22. Lock transmission by shifting into two gears. Install main drive gear retaining nut onto the gear shaft and draw it up tight. Be sure bearing is completely seated against shoulder. Torque retaining nut to 40 ft. lbs. and lock in place by staking into main drive gear shaft hole with punch. Do not damage shaft threads.
23. Install main drive gear bearing retainer, gasket attaching bolts and boltlock retainers. Use a suitable seal on bolts. Tighten to 20 ft. lbs.
24. Shift mainshaft third-fourth sliding clutch sleeve into neutral position and first-second sliding clutch into second gear (forward) detent position. Shift side cover third-fourth shift lever into neutral detent and first-second shift lever into second gear detent position.
25. Install side cover, with gasket, and carefully position in place. A dowel pin provides proper alignment position. Install bolts and tighten evenly to avoid distortion. Torque to 20 ft. lbs.

Type-13

Saginaw 4-Speed

Application

Astre, 1975-76
Camaro, 1969-76
Chevelle, 1969-74
Chevrolet, 1969
Corvette, 1969-76
Firebird, (6 Cyl.) 1969, V8 1972-76
Monza, 1975-76
Nova, 1969-76
Skyhawk, 1975-76
Starfire, 1975-76
Tempest, 1969-74
Vega, 1973-76

Disassembly

1. Remove the side cover and shift forks after draining the transmission.
2. Remove the clutch gear bearing retainer. Remove the bearing-to-gear stem snap-ring and pull out on the clutch gear until a screwdriver can be inserted between the bearing, large snap-ring, and case to pry the bearing off.

NOTE: the clutch gear bearing is a slip-fit on the gear and in the case. Removal of the bearing will provide clearance for clutch gear and mainshaft removal.

3. Remove the rear extension attaching bolts and remove the clutch gear, mainshaft, and extension as an assembly.
4. Spread the snap-ring which holds the mainshaft rear bearing and remove the extension case.
5. Remove the countershaft and its woodruff key by driving out of the rear of the case with a pipe or an old countershaft. Remove the countergear assembly and bearings.
6. Using a long drift, drive the reverse idler shaft and woodruff key through the rear of the case.
7. Expand and remove the third and fourth-speed sliding clutch hub snap-ring from the mainshaft. Remove the clutch assembly, third gear blocker ring, and third-speed gear from the front of the mainshaft.
8. Press in the speedometer gear retaining clip and slide the gear off the mainshaft. Remove the rear bearing snap-ring from its groove in the mainshaft.
9. With first gear supported on press plates, press first gear, thrust washer, spring washer, rear bearing, and snap-ring from the rear of the mainshaft.

Caution Be careful to center the gear, washers, bearings, and snap-ring when pressing the rear bearing.

10. Expand and remove the first and second sliding clutch hub snap-ring from the mainshaft and remove the clutch assembly, second-speed blocker ring, and second-speed gear from the rear of the mainshaft.

After thoroughly cleaning all parts and the transmission case, inspect and replace all damaged or worn parts. When checking the bearings, do not spin them at high speeds. Clean and rotate the bearings by hand to detect roughness and uneveness. Spinning can damage balls and races.

Assembly

Mainshaft

Install the following parts with the front of the mainshaft facing up:

1. Install the third-speed gear with the clutching teeth up; the rear face of the gear will abut with the mainshaft flange.
2. Install a blocking ring, clutching teeth down, over the third-speed gear synchronizing surface.

NOTE: all four blocker rings are the same.

3. Press the third and fourth synchronizer assembly, fork slot down, onto the mainshaft splines until it bottoms.

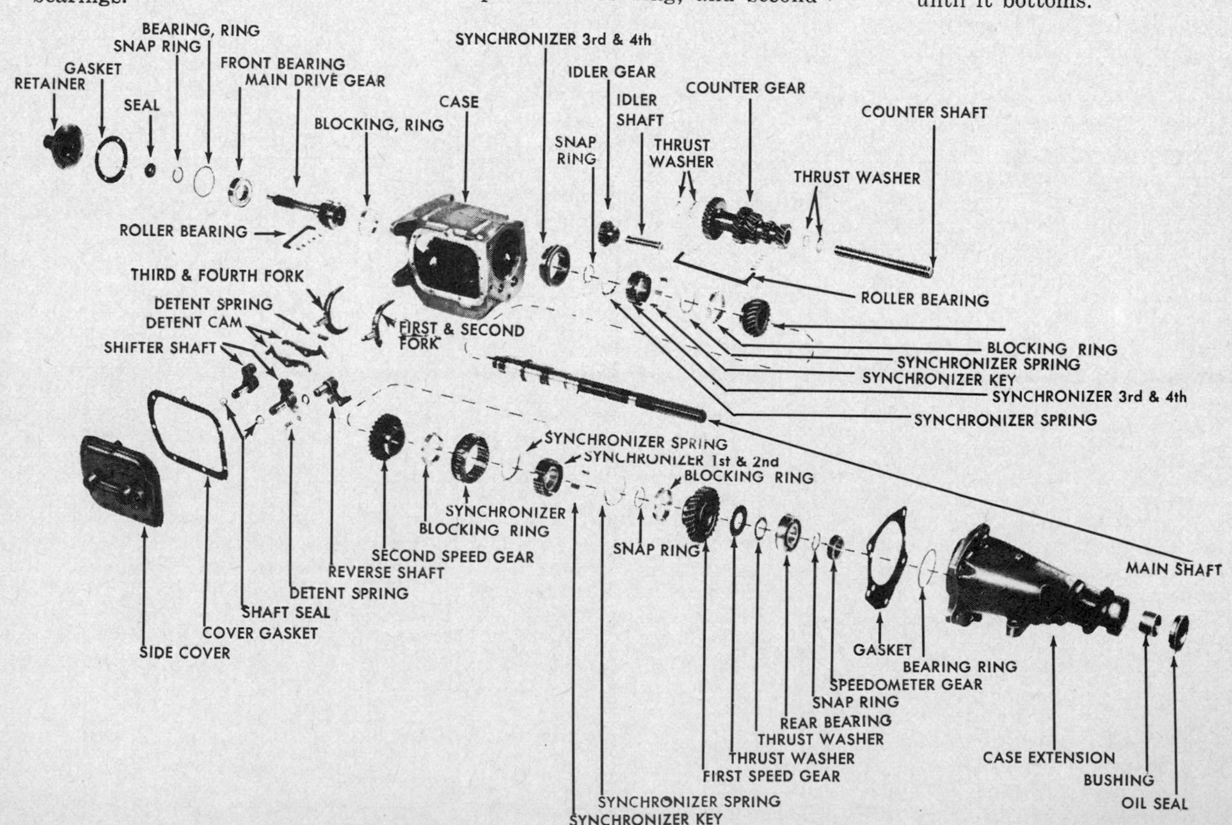

Saginaw 4-speed transmission disassembled

Removing clutch gear, mainshaft, and extension housing
(© G.M. Corp)

Clutch gear and mainshaft assembly
(© G.M. Corp)

1 Clutch gear bearing
2 Clutch gear
3 Mainshaft pilot bearings
4 3-4 synchronizer assembly
5 Third speed gear
6 Second speed gear
7 1-2 synchronizer and reverse gear assembly
8 First speed gear
9 Thrust washer
10 Spring washer
11 Rear bearing
12 Speedo drive gear
13 Mainshaft
14 Snap-ring
15 Synchronizing "blocker" ring

Caution The blocker ring notches must align with the synchronizer assembly keys.

4. Install the synchronizer hub-to mainshaft snap-ring. (Both synchronizer snap-rings are the same.)

Install the following parts with the rear of the mainshaft up.

5. Install the second-speed gear with the clutching teeth up; the front face of the gear will abut with the flange on the mainshaft.
6. Install a blocking ring, clutching teeth down, over the second-speed gear synchronizing surface.
7. Press the first and second synchronizer assembly, fork slot down, onto the mainshaft.

Caution The blocker ring notches must align with the synchronizer assembly keys.

8. Install the synchronizer hub-to-mainshaft snap-ring.
9. Install a blocker ring with the notches down so they align with the first/second synchronizer assembly keys.
10. Install first gear with the clutching teeth down. Install the first gear thrust washer and spring washer.
11. Press the rear ball bearing and snap-ring, slot down, onto the mainshaft. Install the snap-ring. Install the speedometer gear and clip.

Transmission

1. Using a dummy countergear shaft, load a row of roller bearings (27) and bearing thrust washers at each end of the countergear. Grease can be used to hold the bearings in place.
2. Position the countergear assembly into the case through the rear opening. Place a tanged thrust washer at each end of the countergear.
3. Install the countergear shaft and woodruff key from the rear of the case. Make sure that the shaft engages both thrust washers and that the tangs align with their notches in the case.
4. Install the reverse idler gear and shaft and the woodruff key. Install the extension-to-rear bearing snap-ring.
5. Install the fourteen mainshaft pilot bearings into the clutch opening and install the fourth-speed blocker ring onto the clutching surface of the clutch gear (clutching teeth toward the gear.)
6. Assemble the clutch gear, pilot bearings, and fourth-speed blocker ring unit over the front of the mainshaft. Do not assemble the bearing to the gear at this point.

Caution Be sure that the blocker ring notches line up with third/fourth synchronizer assembly keys.

7. Install the extension-to-case gasket and secure it with grease. Insert the clutch gear, mainshaft, and extension into the case as a unit. Install the extension-to-case bolts (apply sealer to the bottom bolt) and torque to 45 ft lbs.
8. Install the outer snap-ring on the front bearing and place the bearing over the stem of the clutch gear and into the case bore.
9. Install the snap-ring to the clutch gear stem. Install the clutch gear bearing retainer and gasket to the case, with the retainer oil return hole at the bottom.
10. Place the synchronizer sleeves into neutral positions and install the cover, gasket, and fork assemblies to the case. Be sure the forks align with their synchronizer sleeve grooves. Torque the cover bolts to 22 ft lbs.

Type-14

Vega 3-Speed

Application

Vega, 1971-72

Transmission Disassembly

1. Remove the shift lever boot. Remove the TCS switch and back-up light switch.
2. Remove the cotter pins from each end of the shift control rod. Remove washers and shift control rod.
3. Remove retaining rings, wave rings, and selector ring from selector shaft. Slide the selector lever and shift idler lever shaft from the intermediate shift lever assembly while simultaneously removing the selector ring.
4. Remove the transmission case cover and gasket.
5. Invert the transmission to drain the oil.
6. Remove the rear extension attaching bolts and rotate the extension until the countergear shaft is exposed.
7. From the front of the transmission, remove the countergear shaft. Lift the countergear from the case. Do not lose the lockball.
8. Engage second gear to prevent the second-third fork pin from binding against the case. Use a ⅛ in. pin punch to remove all lockpins.
9. Drive the lockpins from both shifter forks. Place the transmission in third gear and be sure that the second-third in-

1 Rear extension to case bolts
2 Back-up lamp switch and seal ring
3 Shift idler lever spring
4 Intermediate lever bushing snap-ring
5 Intermediate lever bushing
6 Shift idler lever
7 Rear extension
8 Rear extension gasket
9 Reverse idler gear shaft and lockball
10 Reverse idler gear and bushing assembly
11 2-3 speed shifter shaft
12 2-3 speed shift fork and spiral pin
13 Cotter pin
14 Waved washer

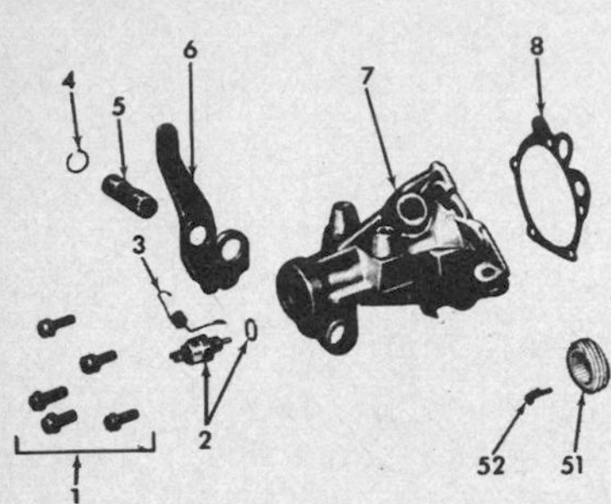

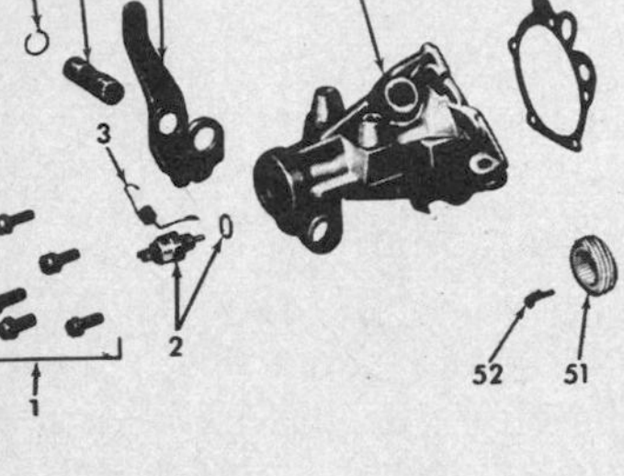

57 Countergear
58 Countergear bearing washer
59 Countergear roller bearings (24)
60 Countergear thrust washers
61 1st-reverse shift shaft
62 1st-reverse shift fork and spiral pin
63 Intermediate lever shaft and pin
64 TCS switch and gasket
65 2-3 shift detent ball, spring and hole plug
66 1st-reverse shift detent ball, spring and hole plug
67 Pivot pin lockring
68 Shift selector rod
69 Selector lever pivot pin
70 Oil filler plug
71 Selector shaft oil seal
72 Selector shaft lockring
73 Selector shaft ring
74 Belleville washer
75 Selector shaft lockring

15 Shift selector rod
16 Washer
17 Selector shaft
18 Selector shaft seal
19 2-3 intermediate shift lever and spiral pin
20 Ist-reverse intermediate shift lever and spiral pin
21 Cover gasket
22 Cover assembly
23 Cover-to-case screws
23a Clutch drive gear seal
24 Clutch drive gear assembly
25 Mainshaft pilot bearing assembly
26 Pilot bearing spacer ring
27 3rd gear synchronizer ring

28 Transmission case
29 2-3 speed synchronizer assembly retaining ring
30 2-3 speed synchronizer sleeve
31 Synchronizer spring
32 2-3 synchronizer hub
33 2-3 synchronizer keys
34 Synchronizer spring
35 2nd gear synchronizer ring
36 2nd speed gear
37 Mainshaft
38 1st speed gear
39 1st speed gear synchronizer ring
40. Synchronizer spring
41 1st-reverse synchronizer keys
42 Synchronizer spring

43 1st-reverse synchronizer hub
44 1st-reverse synchronizer sleeve
45 Rear bearing to extension locking ring
46 1st-reverse key stop-ring
47 Mainshaft rear bearing
48 Rear bearing spacer
49 Belleville washer
50 Rear bearing retaining ring
51 Speedo drive gear
52 Speedo drive clip
53 Countergear shaft and lockball
54 Countergear thrust washer
55 Countergear bearing washer
56 Countergear roller bearings (24)

Exploded view (inverted) of Vega 3-speed transmission
(© Chevrolet Div., G.M. Corp)

termediate lever engages the shifter shaft. This will allow the intermediate levers to pivot as the shifter shaft is removed.

10. Insert a long narrow drift through the bolt hole at the rear of the case and drive the second-third shifter shaft from the case. Remove the fork.
11. Drive the first-reverse shifter shaft from the front of the case and remove the fork from the case.
12. Remove the selector shaft intermediate lever lockpins. Remove the shaft and levers from the case.
13. Remove the snap-ring from the rear bearing retainer groove and slide the rear extension from the mainshaft assembly.
14. Remove the clutch drive gear from the case.
15. Position first-reverse sliding gear to the rear of the hub shaft and remove the mainshaft assembly from the case. Remove the lockpins and detent balls from the bottom of the case.
16. Drive the plugs and springs from the shift rail detent holes.
17. Remove the reverse idler gear and shaft from the case.

Mainshaft Disassembly

NOTE: the synchronizer hubs and sliding sleeves are a select assembly and kept together as originally assembled. Keys and springs may be replaced.

1. Remove the snap-ring from in front of the clutch hub.
2. Depress the retaining clip and slide the speedometer drive gear from the shaft.
3. Remove the snap-ring, spacer and Belleville washer from the shaft.
4. Support first gear and press the mainshaft until the bearing and synchronizers are free on the shaft. Remove all loose parts from the shaft.
5. Support second speed gear and press and shaft until second-third synchronizer assembly and second speed gear are free.

Inspection

1. Examine the shaft, bearing gear and hubs for excessive wear. Examine for chips, nicking or scoring. Wash ball bearings in solvent and blow dry. Replace worn synchronizer rings, clutch keys and hubs. Oil all parts with SAE 90 transmission fluid during assembly.

Mainshaft Assembly

1. From the front of the mainshaft, install the second speed gear. The gear must turn freely on the shaft.
2. Install the second-third synchronizer onto second speed gear cone.
3. Install front and rear synchronizer key springs into second-third speed synchronizer hubs, so that hooked spring ends are in the

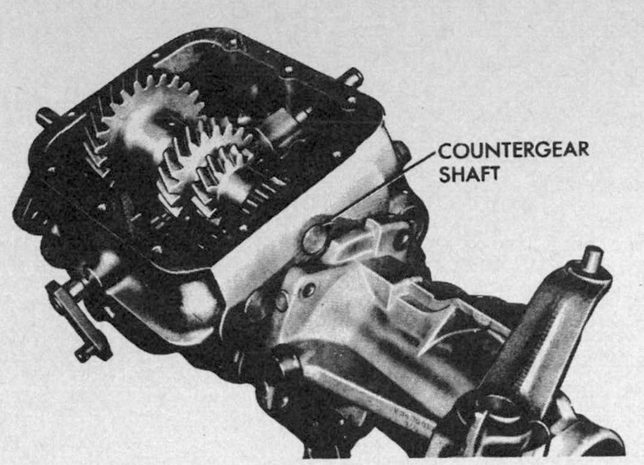

Counter gear shaft exposed for removal
(© Chevrolet Div., G.M. Corp)

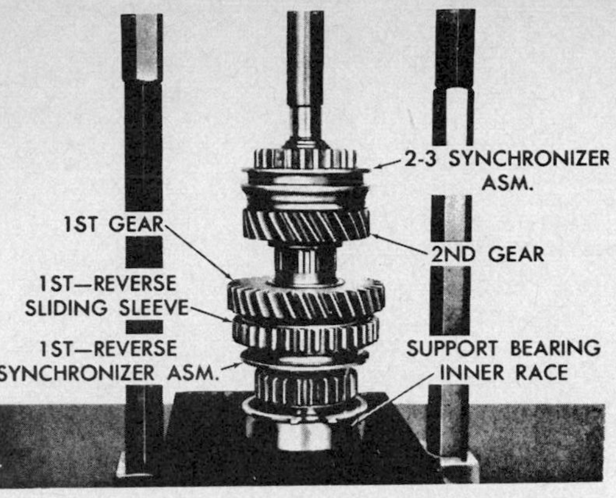

Assembling mainshaft components
(© Chevrolet Div., G.M. Corp)

same slot and raised ends are against the blocker rings.

4. Install sliding sleeve and keys on clutch hub. Arrows must point to front of shaft.
5. Press second-third speed synchronizer hub onto the mainshaft. Secure with a snap-ring.
6. Install both clutch key springs into first-reverse speed synchronizer hub. Hooks of both springs must rest in the same hub slot and raised spring ends should be positioned opposite each other against the blocker rings.
7. Assemble the sliding gear and keys on hub assembly with longer key flat and fork groove on gear toward the rear of the shaft.
8. From the rear of the mainshaft, slide on first gear. Gear must turn freely.
9. Place first-reverse speed synchronizer ring onto first speed gear cone.
10. Slide the first-reverse synchronizer assembly onto the mainshaft. Slide the stop-ring, rear extension retaining ring and rear bearing onto the shaft. Support the rear bearing inner race and press the components together.

Caution Align slots with synchronizer keys. The clutch drive bearing is used to service the mainshaft rear bearing. Install replacement bearing with shield side toward rear of shaft.

11. Place spacer and Belleville washer on the mainshaft. Secure with a snap-ring.
12. Position the speedometer drive gear retaining clip on shaft and install the speedometer drive gear.
13. Install the mainshaft into the extension housing up to the stop. Secure with a retaining ring.

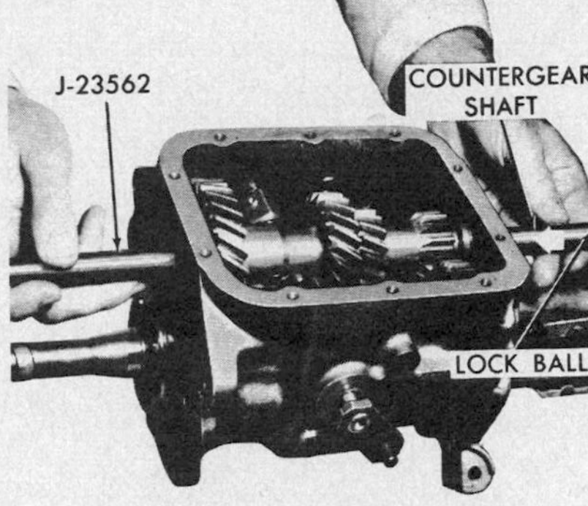

Installing countergear shaft
(© Chevrolet Div., G.M. Corp)

Transmission Assembly

1. Install a new gasket on the rear extension and slide mainshaft assembly into the case. Install one or two bolts to keep the extension from rotating.
2. Coat the pilot roller bearing with grease. From the front, slide the lockring and pilot roller bearing onto the mainshaft.
3. Install the blocker ring on clutch drive gear, and install the gear into the transmission case, up to the snap-ring stop.
4. Insert the first-reverse speed shifter shaft at the front of the case with the notches down, pushing it through the shifter fork. Position the fork shoulder toward the front of the case. Drive the lockpin in place.

NOTE: all lockpins should be installed protruding 1/16 in. to 5/16 in. above the fork or lever.

5. Insert the second-third speed shifter shaft, from the front of the case, with the notches down, pushing it through the shifter fork shoulder toward the front. Install the lockpin.
6. Install the selector shaft in the case. Push it through the second-third speed intermediate lever and the first-reverse lever. Install lockpins.
7. Install both lockballs and springs into the bores in the case and drive in the plugs.
8. Remove the rear extension bolt(s), pull back on the extension and rotate the extension until the bore for the reverse idler gear is exposed.
9. Install the lockball into the shaft from the rear of the case and install the shaft into the gear. Drive the shaft into place.
10. Using a dummy shaft, install a spacer at each end of the countergear. Hold them in place with heavy grease.
11. Coat the thrust washer with grease and stick it to the case. The lugs of the thrust washers must engage the slots in the case.
12. Turn the case extension until the countergear bore is exposed.
13. Place the lockball in the shaft. From the rear of the transmission, insert the shaft so that the thrust washer is held in position. Hold the opposite thrust washer in position with a short drift.
14. Insert the countergear into the case.
15. Insert the shaft into the countergear and push out the dummy shaft. Align the lockball with the groove in the case and tap the shaft into the case.
16. Align the rear bearing retainer and tighten the bolts.
17. Install the case cover gasket, cover and screws.
18. Install the gearshift linkages in reverse sequence to removal.

NOTE: start the idler lever shaft into the shift control simultaneously when installing selector ring.

Type-15

Vega 4-Speed

Application

Vega, 1971-72

Transmission Disassembly

1. Follow Steps 1-7 under early Vega 3-Speed transmission for removal of gearshift linkage, case cover and countergear shaft and countergear.
2. Drive out intermediate shift lever pin and remove intermediate lever. Use a 1/8 in. pin punch to drive out all pins.
3. Slide the reverse shaft to rear of the case so that the scallop in the selector shaft will clear the reverse shaft.
4. Shift transmission to neutral. Push in on the selector shaft and turn so that the lockpins are in the vertical position. Drive the lockpin out of the third-fourth speed intermediate lever cam and then from the first-second speed intermediate lever cam. Remove the selector shaft.
5. Pry the selector shaft seal rings out of the case.
6. Remove the lockball plugs with a slide hammer. Remove the thrust springs and balls.
7. Place the transmission in first gear and drive the lockpins out of the shifter forks and selector levers. Remove the first-second lever pin first.
8. From the rear of the transmission drive out the first-second shifter shaft with a brass drift. Remove the fork from the sliding sleeve.
9. Tap the third-fourth shifter shaft rearward until the fork can be removed from the shaft, then drive out the third-fourth shifter shaft through the front of the case.
10. Remove the clutch drive gear

1 Intermediate lever bushing snap-ring
2 Cotter pin
3 Shift idler lever and spring
4 Intermediate lever bushing
5 Rear extension and retaining bolts
6 Rear extension gasket
7 Reverse idler gear shaft and lockball
8 Reverse idler gear and bushing assembly

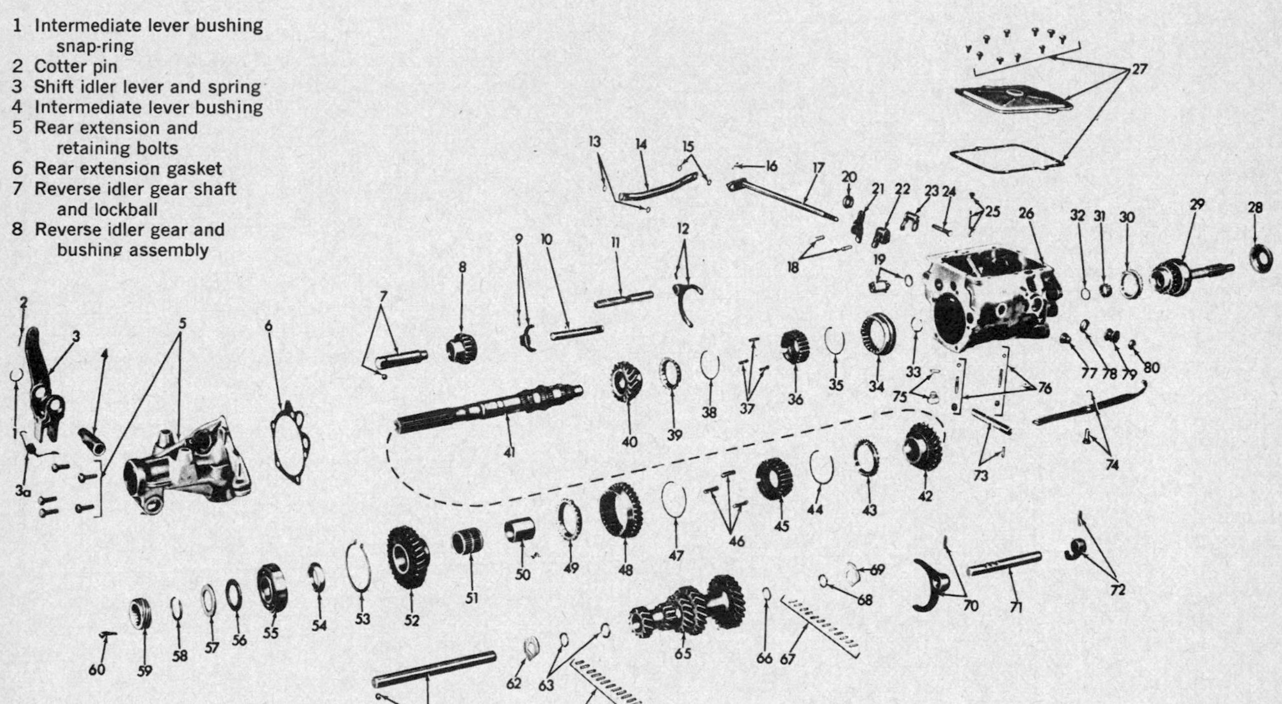

9 Reverse idler gear shift fork and spiral pin
10 Reverse idler gear shifter shaft
11 3-4 speed shifter shaft
12 3-4 speed shift fork and spiral pin
13 Washers
14 Shift control rod
15 Washers
16 Cotter pin
17 Selector shaft
18 Spiral pins
19 Back-up lamp switch and seal ring
20 Selector shaft oil seal
21 3rd-4th speed intermediate shifter lever
22 1st-2nd intermediate shift lever
23 Reverse intermediate lever
24 Reverse intermediate lever pin
25 Reverse shifter shaft detent ball, spring and cap
26 Transmission case
27 Cover gasket, cover, and screws
28 Clutch drive gear to housing seal
29 Clutch drive gear assembly
30 4th gear synchronizer ring
31 Mainshaft pilot bearing assembly
32 Pilot bearing spacer ring
33 3-4 speed synchronizer assembly retaining ring
34 3-4 speed synchronizer sleeve
35 Synchronizer spring
36 3-4 synchronizer hub
37 3-4 synchronizer keys
38 Synchronizer spring
39 3rd speed gear synchronizer ring
40 3rd speed gear
41 Mainshaft
42 2nd speed gear
43 2nd speed synchronizer ring
44 Synchronizer spring
45 1st-2nd synchronizer hub
46 1st-2nd synchronizer keys
47 Synchronizer spring
48 1st-2nd synchronizer sleeve
49 1st speed synchronizer ring
50 1st speed gear bushing
51 1st gear needle bearing assembly
52 1st speed gear
53 Rear bearing to extension locking ring
54 Rear bearing spacer ring (front)
55 Mainshaft rear bearing
56 Rear bearing spacer (rear)
57 Belleville washer
58 Rear bearing retaining ring (brg.-to-mainshaft)
59 Speedo drive gear
60 Speedo drive clip
61 Countergear shaft and lockball
62 Countergear thrust washer
63 Countergear bearing washers
64 Countergear roller bearings (24)
65 Countergear
66 Countergear bearing washer
67 Countergear roller bearings (24)
68 Countergear bearing washer
69 Countergear thrust washer
70 1st-2nd shift fork and spiral pin
71 1st-2nd shift shaft
72 1st-2nd selector lever cam and spiral pin
73 Intermediate lever shaft and pin
74 Shift selector rod, pivot pin and lock ring
75 TCS switch and gasket
76 Shifter shaft detent balls, springs and hole plugs
77 Oil filler plug
78 Selector shaft oil seal
79 Selector shaft adjusting ring
80 Selector shaft locknut

Exploded view (inverted) of Vega 4-speed transmission (© Chevrolet Div., G.M. Corp)

from the case.
11. Remove the rear extension and mainshaft from the case.
12. Push the reverse idler gear shaft toward the rear. Be sure that the lockball is not lost, and remove the reverse idler gear and shaft from the case.
13. From the front of the transmission, drive out the reverse shifter shaft with a brass drift. Remove the shifter fork from the case.

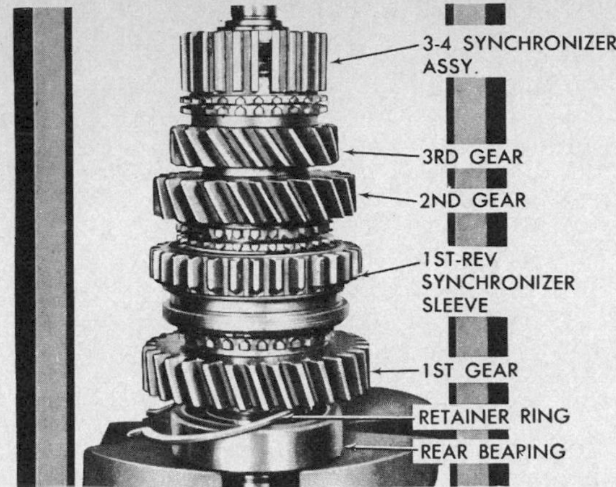

Assembling mainshaft components
(© Chevrolet Div., G.M. Corp)

Mainshaft Disassembly

1. Remove the snap-ring from the rear bearing retainer groove and remove the mainshaft assembly from the rear bearing retainer.
2. Depress the retaining clip and remove the speedometer driven gear.
3. Remove needle bearing, spacer ring and synchronizer ring. The sliding sleeve, keys and clutch keys can also be removed.

NOTE: the synchronizer hubs and sliding sleeves are a select assembly and should be kept together as originally assembled.

4. Remove the snap-ring from in front of the synchronizer hub.
5. Remove the snap-ring, spacer and Belleville washer from the shaft.
6. Support second gear and press the mainshaft until the bearing and synchronizers are free on the shaft. Remove all loose parts.
7. Remove third speed synchronizer hub snap-ring. Support third gear and press the mainshaft until the synchronizer and third gear are free.

Inspection

1. See inspection of components under early Vega 3-Speed transmission.

Mainshaft Assembly

1. From the front of the mainshaft, install the third speed gear. Gear must turn freely.
2. Install the third speed synchronizer ring onto the third speed gear cone.
3. Install the rear clutch key spring into the third-fourth speed synchronizer hub so that the hooked spring rests in one of the slots and the raised end is toward the blocker ring.
4. Press the third-fourth speed clutch hub onto the mainshaft.
5. Secure the third-fourth synchronizer hub with a snap-ring.
6. From the rear of the mainshaft slide on the second speed gear. Gear must turn freely.
7. Place the second speed synchronizer ring on the second speed gear cone.
8. Install both synchronizer key springs into the first-second speed synchronizer hub, so that the spring hooks rest in the same hub slot and the other spring ends are positioned opposite each other and toward the blocker rings. Install the sliding gear and keys on the hub.
9. Slide the first-second speed synchronizer hub, needle bearing and inner sleeve onto the mainshaft. Slide the spacer, rear extension retaining ring and rear bearing onto the shaft.
10. Support the rear bearing inner race and press the components together.

NOTE: align the slots in the synchronizer rings with the synchronizer keys.

11. Install the spacer and Belleville washer on the mainshaft and secure with snap-ring.

NOTE: the concave side of the Belleville washer should face the bearing.

12. Position the speedometer gear retaining clip on the shaft and install the gear.
13. Place the mainshaft assembly into the rear bearing retainer up to the stop. Secure with a snap-ring.
14. Assemble the third-fourth speed synchronizer assembly on hub with the raised end of the key springs toward the blocker ring.

NOTE: arrows on the keys point toward the shifter fork groove.

Transmission Assembly

1. Install a new gasket onto the rear extension.
2. Slide the mainshaft assembly into the transmission case.
3. From the front, slide the spacer ring and needle bearing onto the mainshaft. Coat the needle bearing and roller with grease.
4. Install the synchronizer blocker ring on the clutch drive gear and

Installing synchronizer key springs
(© Chevrolet Div., G.M. Corp)

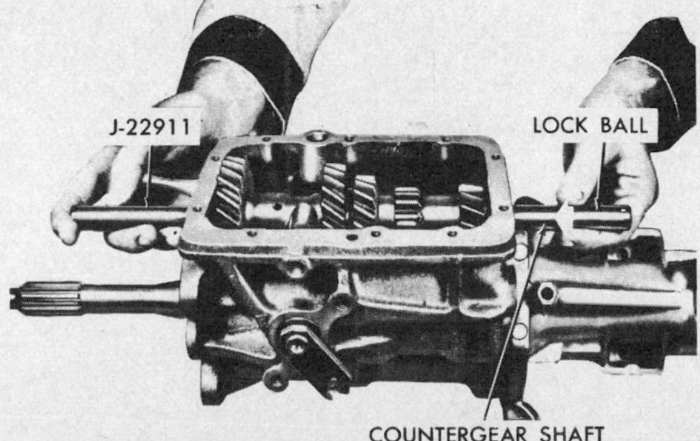

Installing counter gear shaft
(© Chevrolet Div., G.M. Corp)

install the gear into the case up to the stop.

5. Insert the first-second shifter shaft at the front of the case with the notches down, pushing it first through the L shaped selector dog. Push the first-second speed selector shaft through the shifter fork, positioning the shoulder toward the front of the case. Drive the lockpins in. Install selector dog pin first.

NOTE: all lockpins should protrude 1/16 in. to 5/64 in.

6. Insert the third-fourth speed shifter shaft from the front of the case. The notches should be down and it is pushed through the third-fourth speed shifter fork, positioning the shoulder toward the front. Install lockpin.
7. Install the reverse shifter shaft from the rear of the case with the notches up. Push it through the reverse shifter fork and install the lockpin. Position the shoulder of the shift fork toward the front of the case.
8. Insert the selector shaft into the case, through the third-fourth speed intermediate lever and through the first-second speed intermediate lever. Install lockpins.
9. Place the transmission in neutral and rotate the selector shaft to engage the levers with the shifter shafts.
10. Engage reverse speed intermediate levers with third-fourth speed intermediate lever and install pivot pin. Reverse speed intermediate lever end-play on the pin should be .004-.012 in.
11. Insert both lockballs and springs into their bores. Drive in plugs.
12. Turn the transmission case extension until the bore for the reverse idler gear shaft is exposed.
13. Place the lockball into the shaft and from the rear of the case, install the shaft into the gear.
14. Simultaneously, position the reverse idler gear and reverse shifter fork. The shifter fork groove of the reverse idler gear and the shoulder of the shifter fork should be toward the front of the mainshaft.
15. Follow Steps 10-18 under Transmission Assembly for early Vega 3-Speed transmission.

Type-16
Warner T-14, T-15 Fully Synchronized 3-Speed

T-14 Application
American Motors (6 Cyl.), 1969-74

T-15 Application
American Motors, 1969-74

Transmission Disassembly

1. Remove cover, front bearing cap, gasket, and two front bearing snap rings.
2. Align notch in clutch shaft third gear with countergear. Remove clutch shaft and front bearing. A puller may be needed.
3. Pull off front bearing.

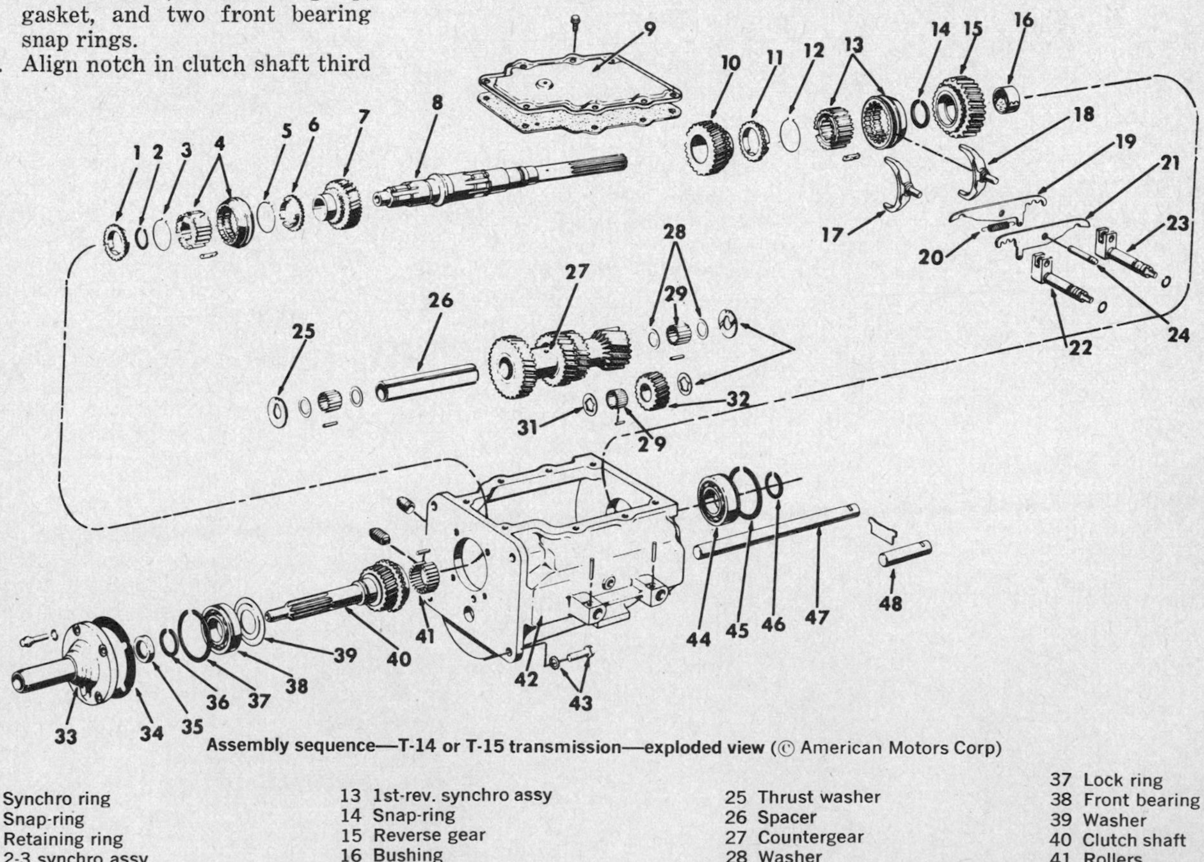

Assembly sequence—T-14 or T-15 transmission—exploded view (© American Motors Corp)

1 Synchro ring
2 Snap-ring
3 Retaining ring
4 2-3 synchro assy
5 Retaining ring
6 Synchro ring
7 2nd gear
8 Mainshaft
9 Cover
10 1st gear
11 Synchro ring
12 Retaining ring
13 1st-rev. synchro assy
14 Snap-ring
15 Reverse gear
16 Bushing
17 2nd-3rd fork
18 1st-rev. fork
19 1st-rev. lever
20 Interlock spring
21 2nd-3rd lever
22 2nd-3rd shaft
23 1st-rev. shaft
24 Interlock pin
25 Thrust washer
26 Spacer
27 Countergear
28 Washer
29 Rollers
30 Washer
31 Washer
32 Idler gear
33 Bearing cap
34 Gasket
35 Front seal
36 Snap ring
37 Lock ring
38 Front bearing
39 Washer
40 Clutch shaft
41 Rollers
42 Case
43 Case-to-bellhousing bolt (4)
44 Rear bearing
45 Snap-ring
46 Snap-ring
47 Countershaft
48 Idler shaft

4. Remove extension housing and gasket. Using oil seal remover and slide hammer, remove extension housing oil seal. Remove extension housing bushing. Install new bushing, aligning oil groove with housing slot.
5. Remove snap-ring, speedometer drive gear, and locating ball.
6. Remove two rear bearing snap-rings and pull off rear bearing.
7. Move mainshaft aside. Remove both shift forks.
8. Push front synchronizer toward rear. Tilt front of mainshaft up and out through top of case.
9. If necessary, remove the transmission controlled spark switch assembly.
10. Drive out roll pins. Push shift shafts into case. Remove shift shafts and detent assembly.
11. Tap reverse idler shaft and countershaft rearward. Remove shaft lockplate. Drive reverse idler shaft from case. Use dummy shaft to drive out countershaft.

Mainshaft Disassembly

1. From front of shaft, remove front snap-ring, second-third synchro-clutch assembly, and second gear.
2. From rear of shaft, remove reverse gear, rear snap-ring, rear synchro-clutch assembly, and low gear.

Inspection

1. Check gears for worn, chipped, or cracked teeth. Check fit to mainshaft.
2. Check bearings for smoothness and excessive play.
3. Check roller bearings for wear or damage.
4. Slide synchro-clutch and friction rings on gear cones and clutch shaft. Replace rings if taper is worn or pitted. There should be no play between hub and shaft splines.
5. Check case for cracks or damaged bearing bores.

Mainshaft Assembly

1. Install low gear and friction ring; friction ring hub to the rear.
2. Install low synchro-gear into synchro-collar so deep end of gear faces low gear. Install synchro-plates (dogs) and retainer ring with large end of plates toward low gear.
3. Place synchro-clutch assembly on mainshaft with synchro-collar groove toward low gear. Install the thickest snap-ring that will fit in groove.
4. Measure clearance between first gear and collar on mainshaft. The clearance should be .003-.012 in. for the T-14; .003-.014 in. for the T-15.
5. Place second gear and the friction ring on the front of the mainshaft with the gear hub and ring forward. Place second synchro-gear into synchro-collar with deep end of gear facing rear of shaft.
6. Hold synchro-clutch assembly with one synchro-plate, or dog, in 12 o'clock position. Install tang of retainer ring into the dog at 12 o'clock and install ring clockwise. On opposite side, start with the same dog and install ring clockwise.
7. Place second synchro assembly on shaft with deep end to rear. Install the thickest snap-ring that will fit into the groove.
8. Measure clearance between second gear and collar on mainshaft. It must be .003-.018 in.
9. Install reverse gear on rear of mainshaft.

Transmission Assembly

1. Install dummy shaft in countergear. Install spacer washers and roller bearings.
2. Place countergear in case. Align thrust washers at each end. Insert countershaft.
3. Install rollers in reverse idler gear. Hold rollers with petroleum jelly. Place gear in case. Position thrust washers. Insert shaft. Install shaft lockplate.
4. Insert shifter shafts in case. Position low-reverse lever to inside of case. Locate notches on top of levers to rear of case stud. Align shift detent assembly with shifter shafts and case stud. Push detent assembly and shifter shafts into place. Install shaft roll pins.
5. If removed, install the transmission controlled spark switch.
6. Place front synchronizer in second shift position. Place mainshaft assembly in case to one side.
7. Pull detent levers up. Place shift forks in shifting assembly.
8. Install mainshaft pilot end support in case. Install front bearing cap. Drive rear bearing on thickest rear bearing snap-ring with a 1¼ x 17 in. pipe. Install support and bearing cap.
9. Install locating ball, speedometer drive gear, and snap-ring.
10. Press front bearing onto clutch shaft.
11. Place rollers in clutch shaft. Hold with petroleum jelly.
12. Place friction ring on mainshaft. Slide clutch shaft into position from front.
13. Install thickest front bearing snap-ring that will fit in groove, gasket and cap. Align cap lubrication hole with hole in case.
14. Install extension housing. Install oil seal. Install shift lever, gaskets, and cover.

Type-17
Warner T-96 3-Speed

***Application* American Motors, 1969-72 (6 Cyl.)**

Disassembly

1. Remove top cover.
2. Remove front bearing cap, clutch shaft snap-ring, and bearing lockring.
3. Use a bearing puller and a thrust yoke to remove front bearing.
4. Remove oil slinger.
5. Remove extension housing. Replace rear bearing oil seal and extension housing bushing if necessary.
6. Remove speedometer drive gear snap-ring, drive gear, and retaining ball.
7. Move mainshaft assembly to rear ½ in. Lower front of clutch shaft and raise rear of countergear. Remove clutch shaft.
8. Check 21 roller bearings inside rear of clutch shaft for wear, pitting, or scoring.
9. Remove second-third shifter fork. Tilt mainshaft to remove synchro-clutch snap-ring.
10. Remove synchro-clutch, second gear, and low and reverse gear.
11. Remove low-reverse shifter fork.
12. Remove mainshaft and rear bearing from rear of case. Press rear bearing from shaft.
13. Remove reverse idler shaft and countershaft lockplate.
14. Drive countershaft out to rear with a dummy shaft. Lower dummy shaft and countergear to bottom of case.
15. Drive reverse idler shaft out to rear. Remove gear. Remove countergear.
16. Note position of reverse idler shaft thrust washers; check for wear or damage.
17. Remove outer shift levers and shifter shaft lockpin. Remove shifter shafts from inside case. Remove two interlock ball bearings. Remove interlock sleeve, pin, and spring. Remove shifter shaft O-rings.

Inspection

1. Wash all parts in solvent.
2. Air dry.

Gears and Mainshaft

1. Check for worn, cracked, or chipped teeth.
2. Check fit of gears to mainshaft. If gears are replaced, also replace the gear with which they mesh.

Bearings

1. Check for cracked races.
2. Check for worn or scored balls.

Synchro-Clutch and Friction Rings

1. Slide rings on cones of second gear and clutch shaft.
2. Replace rings if there is excessive wear or a pitted condition on the taper.

Case

1. Check for evidence of bearings turning in their bores.
2. Check for cracks.

Assembly

1. Install new shift shaft O-rings.
2. Install low-reverse shift shaft interlock sleeve, ball bearing, and spring.
3. Install second-third shift shaft. Place second ball bearing in position.
4. Place shifter mechanism in any gear. With one end of interlock sleeve against shifter shaft quadrant, measure clearance between opposite end of sleeve and the other quadrant. Clearance should be .001-.007 in. Selective lengths of interlock sleeves are available for adjustment. Install lockpins and shift levers.
5. Install dummy shaft in countergear. Install needle bearings, spacer, and washers. Install thrust washers. The bronze front washer must index with the case. Install countergear assembly in bottom of case.
6. Install reverse idler gear with chamfered side of teeth to front. Drive reverse idler shaft in from rear.
7. Drive countershaft into place. Install lockplate.
8. Press rear bearing on mainshaft. Install snap-rings. Place mainshaft in case.
9. Install shifter forks. Install first-reverse sliding gear, second gear, and synchro-clutch assembly, hub forward.
10. Install thickest mainshaft front snap-ring that will fit in groove.
11. There should be .003-.010 in. clearance between second gear and the mainshaft shoulder, with the synchro-clutch hub pressed against the snap-ring.
12. Hold the 21 clutch shaft bearings in place with petroleum jelly. Install front friction ring and clutch shaft on mainshaft.
13. Simultaneously install the mainshaft rear bearing, align the shifter forks and gears, and guide the mainshaft into the clutch shaft.
14. Install the thickest rear mainshaft snap-ring that will fit in the groove.
15. Install retaining ball, speedometer drive gear, and snap-ring.
16. Install extension housing with a new oil seal.
17. Place oil slinger on clutch shaft with concave side to rear. Install front bearing using thrust yoke. Install thickest snap-ring that will fit in the groove.
18. Install bearing cap and a new gasket.
19. Check clearance of synchro-clutch friction rings. Both clearances should be .036-.100 in.

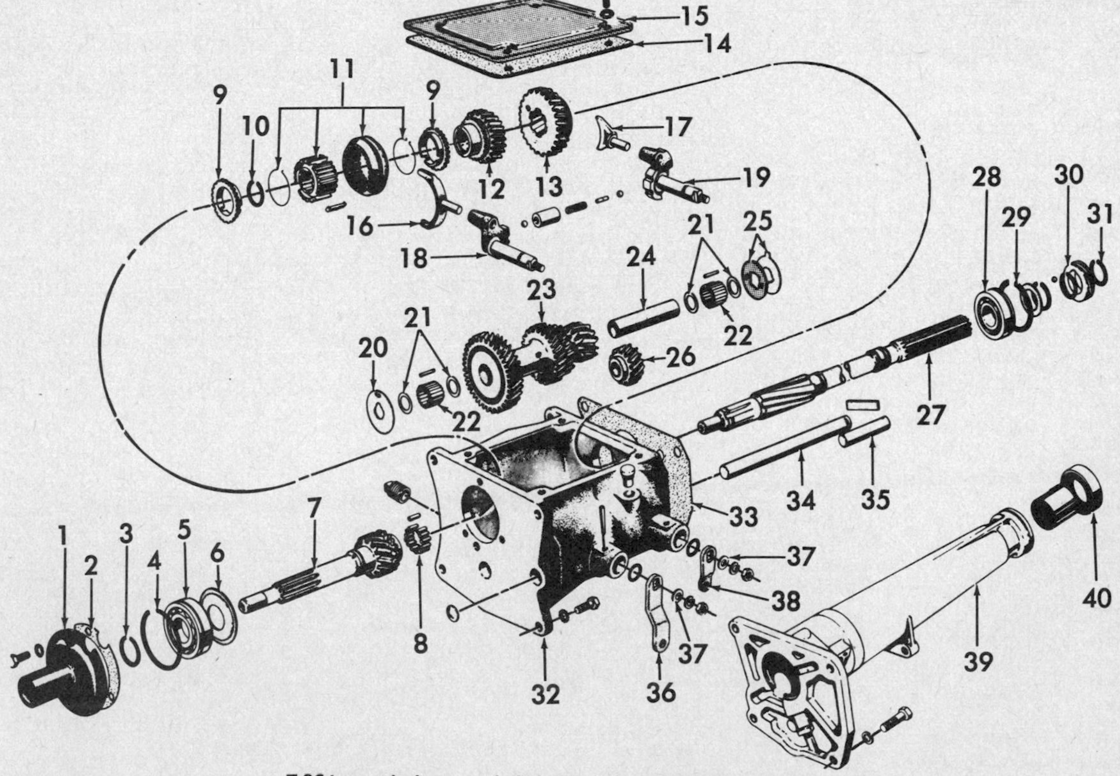

T-96 transmission—exploded view (© American Motors Corp)

1 Bearing cap
2 Gasket
3 Snap-ring
4 Lock ring
5 Bearing
6 Retaining washer
7 Clutch shaft
8 Bearing rollers
9 Friction ring set
10 Snap-ring
11 Synchronizer
12 Second gear
13 First and reverse gear
14 Cover gasket
15 Cover
16 Second and third fork
17 First and reverse fork
18 Second and third shaft
19 First and reverse shaft
20 Thrust washer
21 Bearing washers
22 Bearing rollers
23 Countershaft gear
24 Countershaft spacer
25 Thrust washer
26 Reverse idler gear
27 Mainshaft
28 Rear bearing
29 Lock ring
30 Speedometer drive gear
31 Snap-ring
32 Case
33 Extension gasket
34 Countershaft
35 Reverse idler shaft
36 Second and third lever
37 Shift lever seal
38 First and reverse lever
39 Extension
40 Extension seal

20. Check transmission operation in all gears; then install the case cover and gasket.

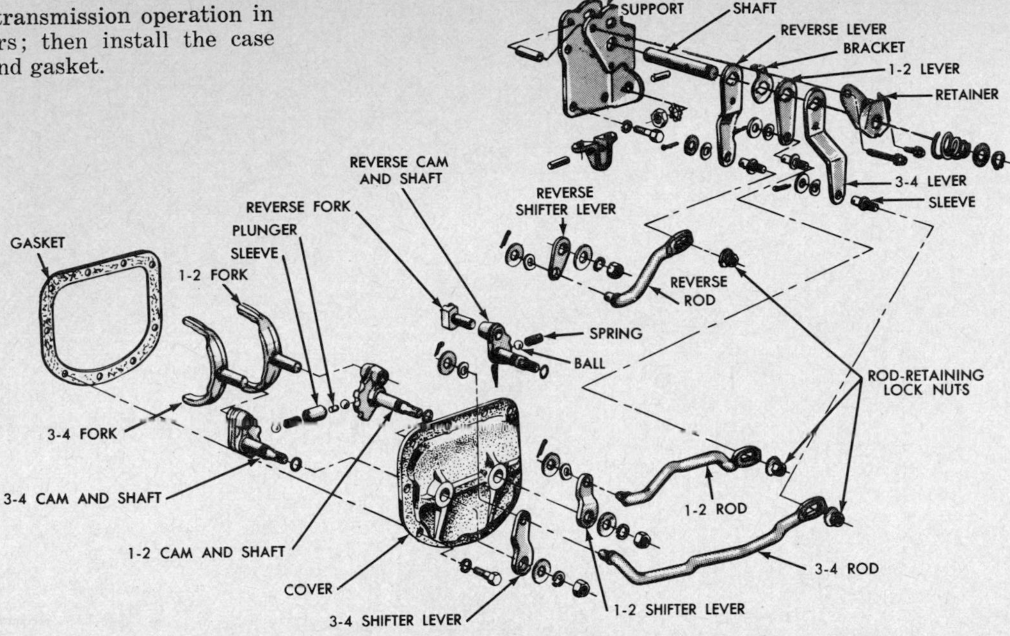

Linkage and cover

Type-18
Warner T-10 4-Speed

Application

American Motors, 1969-74
Camaro, 1974-76
Corvette, 1974-76
Firebird, 1974-76

Disassembly

1. Drain transmission, mount in adequate stand. Then remove the side cover and shift controls.
2. Remove four bolts from front bearing retainer, then remove retainer and gasket.
3. Remove output shaft companion flange.
4. Drive lockpin up from reverse shifter lever boss, then pull shift-shaft out about 1/8 in. to disengage shifter fork from reverse gear.
5. Remove five bolts from the case extension and tap the extension (with soft hammer) rearward. When idler gear shaft is out as far as it will go, move extension to the left so the reverse fork clears the reverse gear. Remove extension and gasket.
6. Remove rear bearing snap-ring from mainshaft.
7. Remove case extension oil seal.
8. Remove speedometer drive gear with puller.
9. Remove the reverse gear, reverse idler gear and tanged thrust washer.
10. Remove self-locking bolt holding the rear bearing retainer to transmission case.
11. Remove the entire mainshaft assembly.
12. Unload bearing rollers from main drive gear and remove fourth-speed synchronizer blocking ring.
13. Lift the front half of reverse idler gear and its thrust washer from the case.
14. Remove the main drive gear snap-ring and remove spacer washer.
15. With soft hammer, tap main drive gear toward rear and out of front bearing.
16. From inside the case, tap out front bearing and snap-ring.
17. From the front of the case, tap out the countershaft, using dummy shaft.
18. Then lift out the countergear assembly with both tanged washers.
19. Dismantle the countergear, consisting of 80 rollers, six .050 in. spacers and a roller tubular spacer.
20. Remove mainshaft front snap-ring and slide third and fourth-speed clutch assembly, third-speed gear and synchronizer ring, second and third-speed gear thrust bearing, second-speed gear and second-speed synchronizer ring from front of mainshaft.
21. Spread rear bearing retainer snap-ring and press mainshaft out of retainer.
22. Remove the mainshaft rear snap-ring.
23. Support first and second-speed clutch assembly and press on rear of mainshaft to remove shaft from rear bearing, first-speed gear, and synchromesh ring, first and second-speed clutch sliding sleeve and first-speed gear bushing.

Assembly

Mainshaft

1. From the rear of the mainshaft, assemble first and second-speed clutch assembly to mainshaft (sliding clutch sleeve taper toward the rear, hub to the front) and press the first-speed gear bushing onto the shaft.
2. Install first-speed gear synchronizing ring so notches in ring align with keys in hub.
3. Install first-speed gear (hub toward front) and the first-speed gear thrust washer. Be sure the grooves in the washer are facing first-speed gear.
4. Press on the rear bearing, with the snap-ring groove toward the front of the transmission. Be sure the bearing is firmly seated against the shoulder on the mainshaft.
5. Install the selective fit snap-ring onto the mainshaft behind the rear bearing. Use the thickest ring that will fit between the rear face of the bearing and the front face of the snap-ring.
6. From the front of the mainshaft, install the second-speed gear synchronizing ring so that notches in the ring correspond with the keys

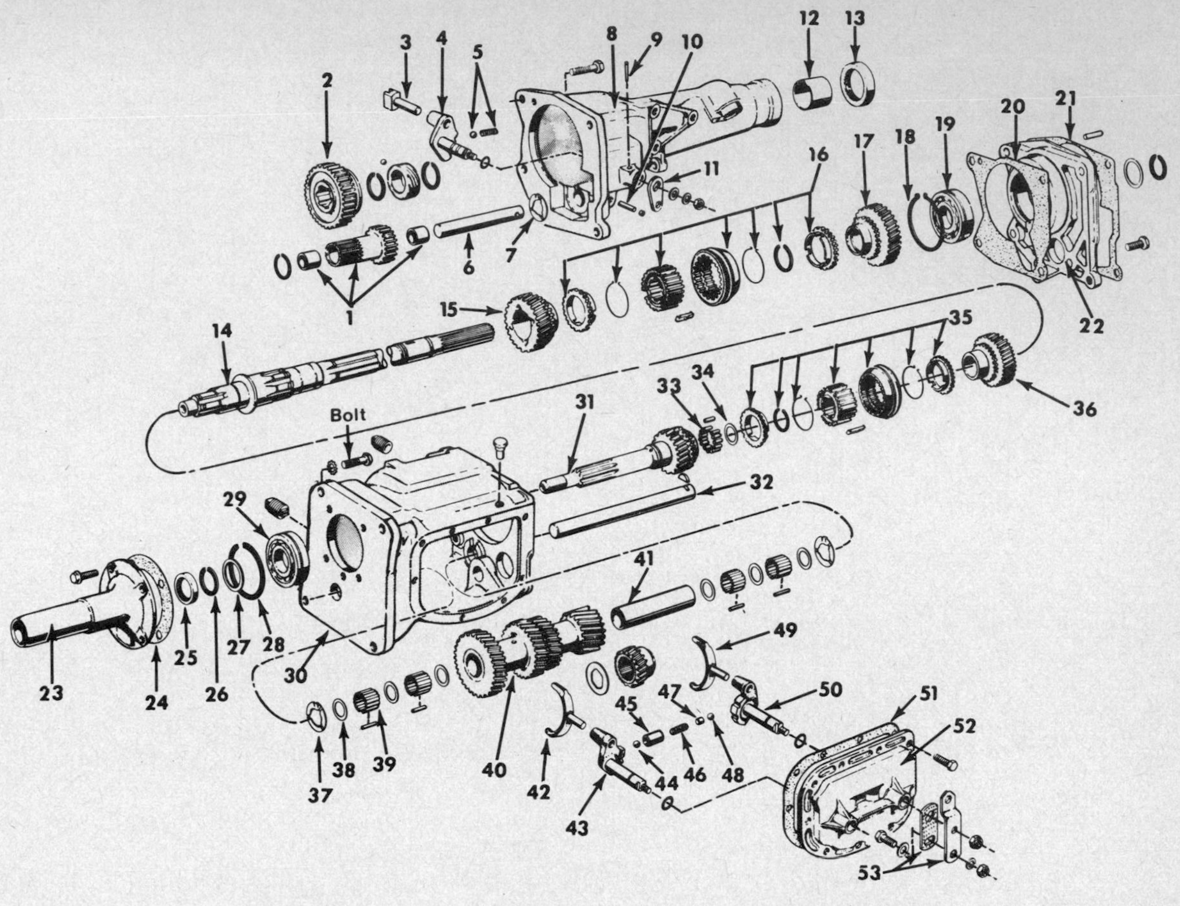

Warner T-10 transmission disassembled (American Motors application)

1 Reverse idler gear
2 Reverse gear
3 Reverse fork
4 Reverse shaft
5 Poppet ball and spring
6 Idler shaft
7 Thrust washer
8 Reverse housing
9 Reverse pin
10 Lock pin
11 Reverse lever
12 Bushing
13 Seal
14 Mainshaft
15 2nd gear
16 Synchro assy
17 1st gear
18 Snap-ring
19 Adapter bearing
20 Adapter
21 Gasket
22 Adapter
23 Front bearing cap
24 Gasket
25 Seal
26 Snap-ring
27 Washer
28 Lock ring
29 Front bearing
30 Case
31 Clutch shaft
32 Countershaft
33 Rollers
34 Roller spacer
35 Synchro assy
36 3rd gear
37 Countergear washer
38 Roller bearing washer
39 Rollers
40 Countergear
41 Spacer
42 3rd-4th fork
43 3rd-4th shaft
44 Poppet ball
45 Interlock sleeve
46 Poppet spring
47 Interlock
48 Poppet ball
49 1st-2nd fork
50 1st-2nd shaft
51 Cover gasket
52 Cover
53 Shift levers

in the hub.

7. Install the second-speed gear (hub toward the back) and install the second and third-speed gear thrust bearing.
8. Install third-speed gear (hub to front) and third-speed gear synchronizing ring (notches front).
9. Install third and fourth-speed gear clutch assembly (hub and sliding sleeve) with taper front, being sure keys in the hub correspond with notches in third-speed gear synchronizing ring.
10. Install snap-ring (.086-.088 in. thickness) into groove in mainshaft, in front of the third and fourth-speed clutch assembly.
11. Install rear bearing retainer plate. Spread the snap-ring on the plate to allow the snap-ring to drop around the rear bearing and press on the end of the mainshaft until the snap-ring engages the groove in the rear bearing.
12. Install reverse gear (shift collar to the rear).
13. Press speedometer drive gear onto the mainshaft. Position the speedometer gear to get a measurement of 4½ in. from the center of the gear to the flat surface of the rear bearing retainer.
14. Install special snap-ring into the groove at the rear of the mainshaft.

Countergear

1. Install countergear dummy and tubular roller bearing spacer into the countergear.
2. Using heavy grease to hold the rollers, install 20 bearing rollers in either end of the countergear, two spacers, 20 more rollers, then one spacer. Install the same combination of rollers and spacers in the other end of the countergear.
3. Set the countergear assembly in the bottom of the transmission case, be sure the tanged thrust washers are in their proper position.

Main Drive Gear

1. Press bearing (snap-ring groove front) onto main drive gear until the bearing fully seats against the shoulder on the gear.
2. Install spacer washer and selective fit snap-ring in the groove in the main drive gear shaft.

NOTE: variable thickness snap-rings are available to obtain a prescribed clearance of .000-.005 in. between the rear face of the snap ring and the front face of the spacer washer.

Transmission

1. Install main drive gear and bearing assembly through the side cover opening and into position in the transmission front bore. After assembly is in place, install snap-ring into groove in front bearing.
2. Lift countergear and thrust washers into place. Install Woodruff key into end of countershaft, then from the rear of the case, press the countershaft in until the end of the shaft is flush with

rear of transmission case and the dummy shaft is displaced. End-play in the countergear must not exceed .025 in.

3. Install the 14 bearing rollers into the grease-coated end of the main drive gear.
4. Using heavy grease, position gasket on front face of rear bearing retainer. Install the fourth-speed synchronizing ring onto main drive gear with clutch key notches toward rear of transmission.
5. Position the reverse idler gear thrust washer on the machined face of the gear cast in the case for the reverse idler shaft. Position the front reverse idler gear on top of the thrust washer, hub facing toward rear of case.
6. Lower the mainshaft assembly into the case, with the notches of the fourth-speed synchronizing ring corresponding to the keys in the clutch assembly.
7. Install self-locking bolt, holding the rear bearing retainer to the transmission case. Torque to 20-30 ft. lbs.
8. From the rear of the case, insert the rear reverse idler gear, engaging the splines with the portion of the gear within the case.
9. Grease gasket, and place in position on the rear face of the rear bearing retainer.
10. Install remaining tanged thrust washer into place on reverse idler shaft, being sure the tang on the thrust washer is in the notch in the idler thrust face of the extension.
11. Place the two clutches in neutral position.
12. Pull reverse shifter shaft to left side of extension and rotate shaft to bring reverse fork to extreme forward position in extension. Line up forward and reverse idler gears.
13. Start the extension onto the transmission case by inserting reverse idler shaft through reverse idler gears. Push in on shifter until shift fork engages reverse gear shift collar. When the fork engages, rotate the shifter shaft to move reverse gear rearward. This will allow the extension to slide onto the transmission case.
14. Install three extension and retainer to case attaching bolts and torque to 35-45 ft. lbs. Install two extension to retainer attaching bolts and torque to 20-30 ft. lbs. Use sealer on the lower, right attaching bolt.
15. Adjust reverse shift shaft so that groove in shaft lines up with hole in boss. Drive in lockpin from top of boss.
16. Install the main drive gear bearing retainer and gasket, being sure the oil well lines up with the oil outlet hole. Install four sealer-coated attaching bolts and torque to 15-20 ft. lbs.
17. Install a shift fork into each clutch sleeve.
18. With both clutches in neutral, install side cover gasket and lower side cover into place.
19. Install attaching bolts and torque to 10-20 ft. lbs. Use sealer on the lower right bolt.
20. Install first and second, and third and fourth shift levers, lockwashers and nuts.

Type-19
AMC Overdrive

Application American Motors (6 Cyl.), 1975-76

This unit uses an electrical solenoid valve to actuate a hydraulic circuit which engages and disengages a planetary gear system. Overdrive is available only in high gear.

NOTE: To make removal of the overdrive unit from the transmission easier, drive the car with overdrive engaged, then disengage it with the clutch pedal down. You can drain the transmission and overdrive by removing the transmission bottom extension housing bolt.

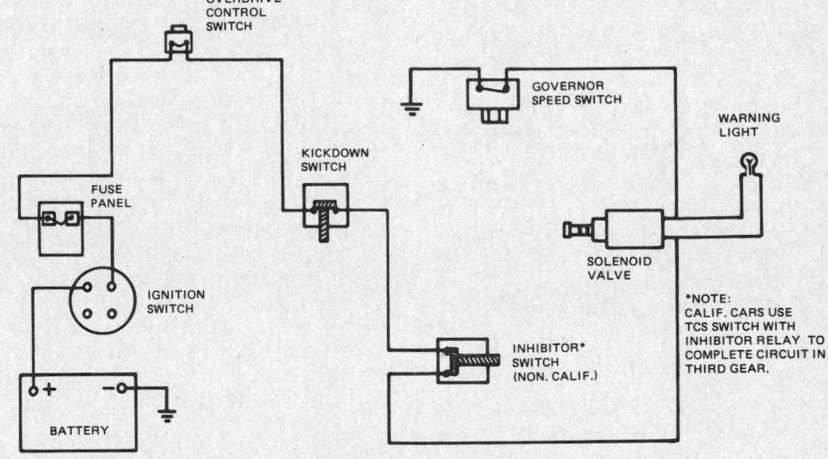

AMC overdrive electrical circuit

Disassembly

1. Use a 1/4 in. thick (or less) open end wrench to remove the solenoid valve.
2. At the front of the unit, remove the self-locking nuts holding the clutch piston apply bars to the thrust bearing cover pins. Discard the nuts; they can't be reused.
3. Remove the nuts and lockwashers from the case studs. Remove the copper gaskets used under the two top nuts. Separate the main and rear cases.
4. Remove the loose clutch return springs and the clutch brake ring and gaskets from the main case. If the brake ring is stuck, tap it with a plastic hammer; don't pry on it.
5. Remove the main case lower pan, gasket, filter, and pressure plug. A new gasket will be needed.
6. Use a spanner pin tool (one can be fabricated) to unscrew the pressure filter plug and remove the pressure filter and aluminum washer.
7. Use the spanner tool to unscrew the pump body plug and the non-return valve ball seat spring, check ball, and seat. Remove the O-ring from the plug.
8. Use pliers to carefully take the clutch apply pistons from their bores. Remove the piston O-rings.

Note: Don't remove the lubrication relief valve yet.

9. Pull the pump body up and slide the plunger out. Remove the body from the case, taking note of the flat side which must align with a lubrication feed hole. Remove the drive cam and key from the pump strap. Don't take apart the pump strap and plunger.
10. Now remove the relief valve piston plug with the spanner tool and take out the piston and spring. Remove the plug O-ring. Don't try to take the spring off the valve piston. Use a magnet or needlenose pliers to remove the relief valve and spring assembly. Don't try to remove the

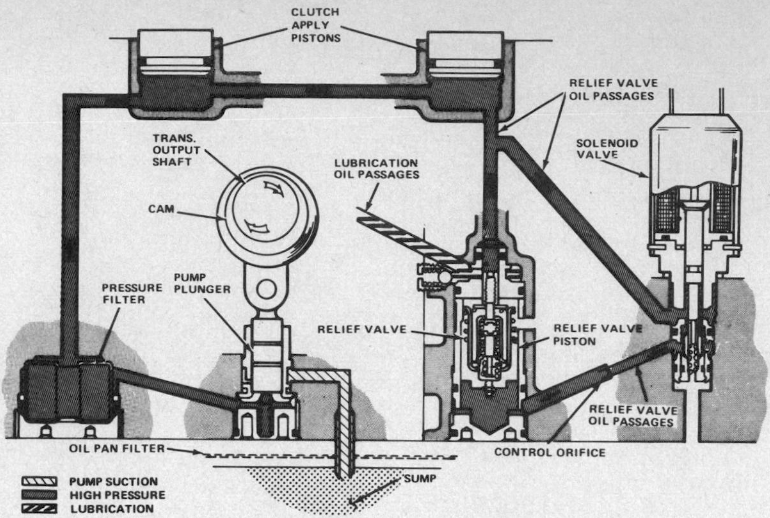

AMC overdrive hydraulic circuit, engaged

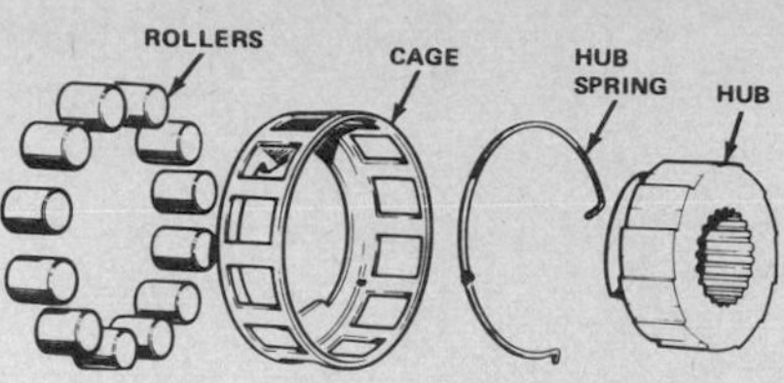

Overrunning clutch components

spring from the valve. A special tool is available to remove the relief valve sleeve and body; it is a hook device that pulls the valve body and sleeve out together. Don't jerk the body and sleeve out; they can easily be damaged.

Remove all the valve body, sleeve, and plug O-rings.

11. In the rear case, remove the sliding clutch, sun gear, and thrust bearing cover assembly from the mainshaft annulus gear. Remove the pinion carrier assembly from the gear.
12. Remove the sun gear snap-ring and the sliding clutch ring lock. Push the sun gear out of the hub.
13. Support the thrust bearing cover and gently drive the clutch hub from the bearing.
14. Remove the thrust bearing snap-ring and press the bearing from the cover, using an arbor press. Don't remove the thrust bearing cover bolts.
15. Remove the overrunning clutch snap-ring and the brass oil slinger.
16. Remove the overrunning clutch. Remove the mainshaft thrust washer from the recess in the annulus gear.
17. Pry the expansion plug out of the rear case. Place the rear case face down on two wood blocks, and using snap-ring pliers through the expansion plug hole, expand the mainshaft bearing snap-ring while tapping the mainshaft out of the case with a mallet.
18. Hold the splined end of the mainshaft and remove the drive gear locknut. Remove the speedometer drive gear tab washer and the gear. Press off the mainshaft bearing.
19. Pry the rear case oil seal out and remove the mainshaft bearing snap-ring. Don't remove the disc washer or rear bushing; the rear case must be replaced if these are damaged.

Assembly

1. Lubricate the mainshaft bearing with the lubricant to be used in the transmission and overdrive (SAE 80 gear lubricant is recommended). Put the bearing on the mainshaft with the snap-ring groove on the rear. Seat the bearing with a length of pipe.
2. Install the speedometer drive gear with the shoulder side toward the mainshaft bearing. Install a new drive gear washer on top of the gear with the tab in the mainshaft slot and finger tighten the drive gear locknut. Hold the mainshaft splines and torque the locknut to 55 ft lbs. Bend the washer against the nut in two places.
3. Put a new mainshaft bearing snap-ring in the groove in the rear case.
4. Place the mainshaft upright and lower the rear case over it. Tap the case with a soft hammer to start the bearing. Expand the snap-ring and tap the case down until the bearing and snap-ring are seated.
5. Lubricate the lip of the new rear case oil seal and install the seal. Install a new expansion plug in the case.
6. Lubricate the mainshaft thrust washer and place it in the recess in the annulus gear.
7. Assemble and lubricate the overrunning clutch. Install it in the bore of the annulus gear. Install the brass oil slinger, shoulder out, and the snap-ring.
8. Lubricate the pinion carrier assembly and install it in the annulus gear.
9. Press the thrust bearing into the thrust bearing cover and install the snap-ring. Lubricate the bearing. Position the bearing and clutch hub. Tap the cover to start the bearing onto the hub. Turn the assembly over, support the thrust bearing cover, and drive the hub into the bearing.
10. Install the sun gear into the sliding clutch hub. Install the ring lock, sharp edge up, and the snap-ring.
11. Engage the sun gear into the pinion gear and install the sliding clutch assembly onto the mainshaft annulus gear. Make sure the sliding clutch is seated and the gears fully engaged. Turning the shaft will make it easier.
12. Lubricate the clutch apply pistons, install new O-rings, and install the pistons with the counterbored end out.

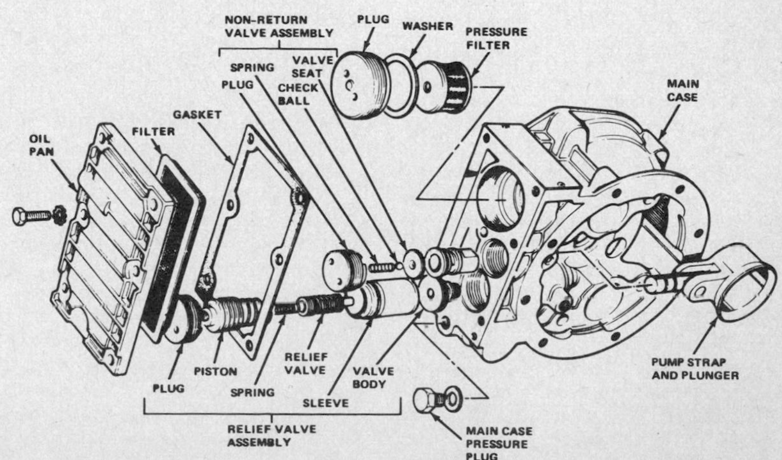

Lower main case details

1 Gasket Transmission to Adapter
2 Adapter, Transmission
3 Nut, Self Locking, Main Case Stud
4 Washer, Lock
5 Gasket, Main Case to Transmission Adaptor
6 Key, Pump Strap Cam Drive
7 Cam, Pump Strap
8 Strap, Pump
9 Bar, Clutch Piston Apply
10 Piston, Clutch Apply
11 Seal, Clutch Apply Piston O-Ring
12 Stud, Main Case to Transmission Adapter
13 Main Case
14 Gasket, Clutch Brake Ring (front)
15 Brake Ring, Clutch
16 Gasket, Clutch Brake Ring (rear)
17 Ring, Sun Gear Snap
18 Ring Lock, Sliding Clutch
19 Ring, Thrust Bearing Snap
20 Bearing, Thrust
21 Cover, Thrust Bearing
22 Clutch, Sliding
23 Sun Gear
24 Assembly,•Pinion Carrier
25 Bolt, Thrust Bearing Cover (4 reqd.)
26 Spring, Clutch Return (4 reqd.)
27 Solenoid Valve
28 Washer, Solenoid Valve
29 Seal, Solenoid Valve O-Ring
30 Seal, Solenoid Valve O-Ring
31 Gasket, Main Case Pressure Plug
32 Plug, Main Case Pressure
33 Ring, Overrunning Clutch Snap
34 Slinger, Overrunning Clutch Oil
35 Assembly, Overrunning Clutch
36 Washer, Mainshaft Thrust
37 Bushing, Mainshaft Support (Included in Mainshaft)
38 Main Shaft and Annulus Gear
39 Ring, Mainshaft Bearing Snap
40 Washer, Speedometer Drive Gear Tab
41 Nut, Speedometer Drive Gear Lock
42 Gear, Speedometer Drive
43 Bearing, Mainshaft
44 Bolt, Speedometer Adapter Clamp
45 Clamp, Speedometer Adapter
46 Adapter, Speedometer to Governor Speed Switch
47 Adapter, Speedometer Driven Gear
48 Gear, Speedometer Driven
49 Plug, Expansion
50 Bushing, Rear Case (included in Case)
51 Seal, Rear Case Oil
52 Nut, Self Locking, Main Case to Rear Case Stud
53 Washer, Lock
54 Rear Case
55 Stud, Main Case to Rear Case
56 Washer, Disc (not removed: included in rear case)
57 Seal, Speedometer Adapter O-Ring
58 Seal, Speedometer Adapter Oil
59 Seal, Relief Valve Body O-Ring (Inner)
60 Body, Relief Valve
61 Seal, Relief Valve Body O-Ring (Outer)
62 Assembly, Relief Valve and Spring
63 Spring, Relief Valve Residual Pressure

Exploded view, AMC overdrive

64 Sleeve, Relief Valve
65 Seal, Relief Valve Sleeve O-Ring
66 Piston, Relief Valve
67 Plug, Relief Valve Piston
68 Seal, Relief Valve Piston Plug O-Ring
69 Gasket, Oil Pan
70 Oil Pan
71 Bolt, Oil Pan
72 Washer, Lock
73 Filter, Oil Pan
74 Plug, Pressure Filter
75 Washer, Pressure Filter (Aluminum)
76 Filter, Pressure
77 Seal, Pump Body O-Ring
78 Plug, Pump Body
79 Spring, Non-return Valve Ball-seat
80 Ball, Non-return Valve Check
81 Seat, Non-return Valve
82 Body, Pump Plunger
83 Seal, Pump Plunger Body O-Ring
84 Ball, Lubrication Relief Valve Check
85 Spring, Lubrication Relief Valve
86 Plug, Lubrication Relief Valve
87 Nut, Self Locking, Clutch Piston Apply Bar
88 Plunger, Pump
89 Pin, Pump Plunger
90 Bolt, Gearshift Lever Retainer to Adapter
91 Washer, Lock
92 Washer, Lock
93 Bolt, Rear Support Cushion to Adapter
94 Switch, Back-up Light

13. Lubricate the relief valve components and install new O-rings. Insert the relief valve body into the case, align the sleeve hole with the bore oil hole and insert it with the O-ring end up. Push the sleeve firmly into the bore, install the valve and spring assembly in the body, install the residual pressure spring in the valve and spring assembly. Install the piston in the valve sleeve and install the plug, tightening it to 16 ft lbs.
14. Install the pressure filter, aluminum washer, and plug, torquing to 16 ft lbs.
15. Lubricate the pump plunger assembly, pump body, and non-return valve seat. Install new O-rings. Align the pump body flat with the main case bore oil hole and insert the body halfway. Insert the pump plunger into the body, then push the body completely into the case bore. Place the non-return valve seat on top of the body with the check ball seat up. Place the ball in the seat. Install the non-return valve ball seat spring. Install the plug and spring, tightening to 16 ft lbs.
16. Install the main case pressure plug, gasket, pan filter, new gasket, and cover. Tighten the pan bolts to 6 ft lbs and the plug to 16 ft lbs.
17. Place the rear case front up and install new clutch return springs on the thrust bearing cover bolts.
18. Install the first clutch brake ring gasket on the rear case. Install the clutch brake ring into the rear case with the tapered surface to the rear. Install the second new clutch brake ring gasket on the brake ring. Make sure the gaskets and the brake ring are aligned with the stud holes in the rear case.
19. Use sealer on the case studs. Lower the main case onto the rear case, aligning the thrust bearing cover bolts with the bolt holes in the main case.
20. Install the six nuts, four lockwashers, and two copper gaskets (on the upper studs). Tighten the nuts in a criss-cross pattern to 11 ft lbs.
21. Install the clutch apply bars on the thrust bearing cover bolts and fasten with new locknuts, tightened to 8 ft lbs.
22. Install the solenoid valve.
23. Lubricate the new drive cam and install it and the key on the output shaft. Install the snap-ring.
24. Pour about a pint of lubricant in through the access hole in the front of the main case. On installation, tighten the overdrive case to adapter nuts to 18 ft lbs. Check the lubricant level at the transmission filler plug; the two units have a common lubricant supply.

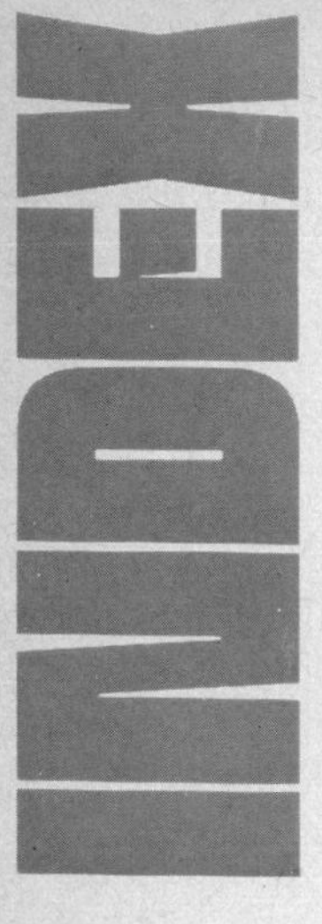

Front End Alignment

SERVICE PROCEDURE INDEX

Section Numbers Refer to Sections in Text

Car	Year	Caster, Chamber, and Toe-in
American Motors (all except Pacer)	1969-76	3
Plymouth Valiant, Duster, Barracuda; Dodge Dart, Demon, Challenger	1969-76	4
Plymouth Belvedere, Satellite, Road Runner, GTX; Dodge Coronet, Charger	1969-72	4
Plymouth Satellite, Fury (1975-76 only); Dodge Coronet, Charger; Chrysler Cordoba	1973-76	5
Plymouth Fury; Dodge Polara, Monaco	1969-73	4
Plymouth Fury (1974 only), Gran Fury; Dodge Monaco, Gran Monaco	1974-76	5
Chrysler, Chrysler Imperial	1969-73	4
Chrysler (full-size) Imperial	1974-76	5
Ford Pinto, Mustang II; Mercury Bobcat	1971-76	8
Ford Falcon, Fairlane, Torino; Mercury Montego	1969-71	3
Ford Torino; Mercury Montego	1972-76	7
Ford Mustang; Mercury Cougar	1969-73	3
Ford Elite; Mercury Cougar	1974-76	7
Ford Maverick; Mercury Comet	1971-76	3
Ford Granada; Mercury Monarch	1975-76	3
Ford (full-size); Mercury (full size)	1969-76	7
Ford Thunderbird; Lincoln Continental Mk III, Mk IV	1969-76	7
Lincoln Continental	1969	6
Lincoln Continental	1970-76	7
Chevrolet Vega, Monza; Pontiac Astre; Oldsmobile Starfire; Buick Skyhawk	1971-76	9
Chevrolet Nova; Pontiac Ventura; Oldsmobile Omega; Buick Apollo	1969-76	1
Chevrolet Chevelle, Monte Carlo; Pontiac Tempest, Le Mans, GTO, Grand Prix; Oldsmobile F-85, Cutlass 4-4-2; Buick Special, Skylark, GS, Century, Riviera	1969-76	1
Chevrolet Camaro; Pontiac Firebird	1969-76	1
Chevrolet Corvette	1969-76	1
Chevrolet (full-size)	1969-70	3
Chevrolet (full-size)	1971-76	1
Pontiac (full-size); Oldsmobile (full-size); Buick (full-size)	1969-76	1
Oldsmobile Toronado; Cadillac Eldorado	1969-76	See Car Section
Cadillac (except Eldorado)	1969-76	2

Section Page Numbers

Wheel Alignment

Front wheel alignment is the position of the front wheels relative to each other and to the vehicle. It is determined, and must be maintained to provide safe, accurate steering, directional stability, and minimum tire wear. Many factors are involved in wheel alignment, and adjustments are provided to return those that might change due to normal wear to their original value. The factors which determine wheel alignment are dependent on one another; therefore, when one of the factors is adjusted, the others must be adjusted to compensate.

Descriptions of these factors and their effects on the car are provided below. Adjustment specifications for each model year are given at the beginning of each Car Section.

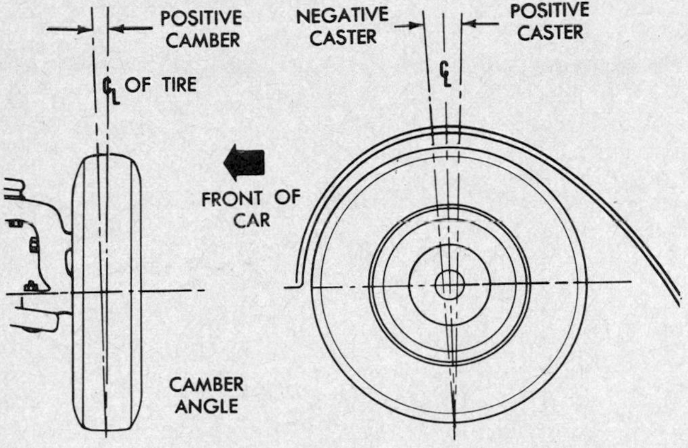

Caster and camber angles

Camber

Camber angle is the number of degrees that the centerline of the wheel is inclined from the vertical when viewed from the front. A small degree of positive camber reduces loading of the outer wheel bearing, and allows for easier steering.

Caster

Caster angle is the number of degrees that a line drawn through the steering knuckle pivots is inclined from the vertical, toward the front or rear of the car. A small degree of positive caster improves directional stability and decreases susceptibility to crosswinds or road surface deviations.

Steering Axis Inclination

Steering axis inclination is the number of degrees that a line drawn through the steering knuckle pivots is inclined to the vertical, when viewed from the front of the car. This, in combination with caster, is responsible for directional stability and self-centering of the steering. As the steering knuckle swings from lock to lock, the spindle generates an arc (see illustration), the high point being the straight ahead position of the wheel. Due to this arc, as the wheel turns, the front of the car is raised. The weight of the car acts against this lift, and attempts to return the spindle to the high point of the arc, resulting in self-centering when the steering wheel is released, and straight line stability.

Included Angle

Included angle is the sum of the camber angle and the steering axis inclination. This angle is determined by the design of the steering knuckle forging and must remain constant. Therefore, if a different camber angle is necessary to make the included angle on both sides identical, a bent spindle or steering knuckle is indicated. When indicated, the damaged suspension member must be replaced, to permit accurate front wheel alignment. Since steering knuckle damage is most commonly due to impact on the lower portion of the wheel (i.e., hitting curb), the side with the greater included angle (camber angle same on each side) will often be found to have a bent spindle.

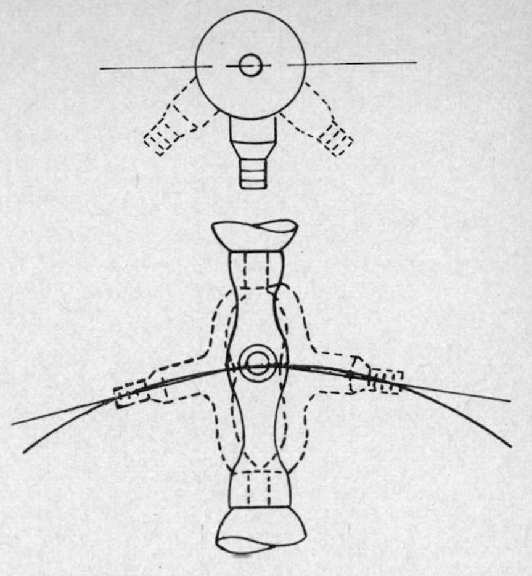

Arc generated by the spindle as the steering knuckle turns

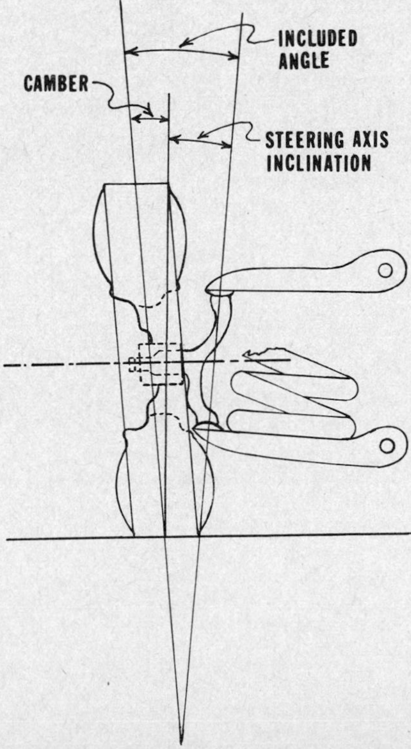

Camber, steering axis, and included angle

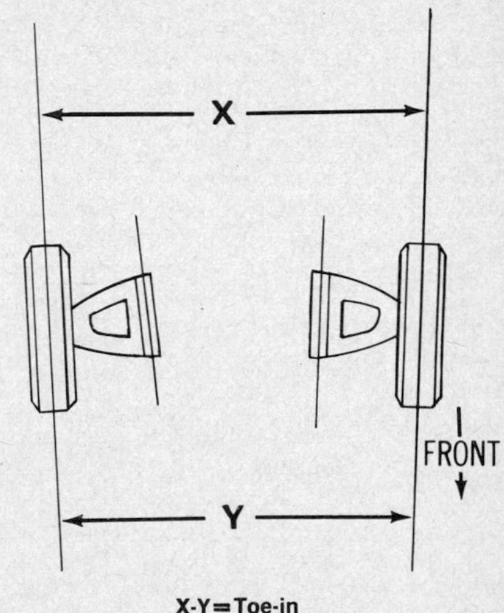

X-Y=Toe-in

Toe-In

Toe-in is the difference of the distance between the centers of the front and rear of the front wheels measured at spindle height. It is most commonly measured in inches, but is occasionally referred to as an angle between the wheels. Toe-in is necessary to compensate for the tendency of the wheels to deflect rearward while in motion. Due to this tendency, the wheels of a vehicle with properly adjusted toe-in are traveling straight forward when the vehicle itself is traveling straight forward, resulting in directional stability and minimum tire wear.

Steering wheel spoke misalignment is often an indication of incorrect front end alignment. Care should be exercised when aligning the front end to maintain steering wheel spoke position. When adjusting the tie rod ends, adjust each an equal amount (in the opposite direction) to increase or decrease toe-in. If, follow-

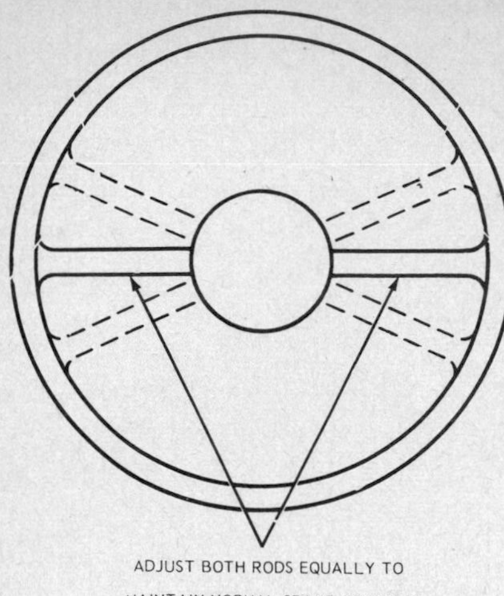

Steering wheel spoke alignment

ing toe-in adjustment, further adjustments are necessary to center the steering wheel spokes, adjust the tie rod ends an equal amount in the same direction.

Steering Radius

When a car is negotiating a turn, the outer wheel follows the path of a circle of a larger radius than the inner wheel (see illustration). For this reason, the inner wheel must be steered to a somewhat larger angle than the outer wheel. This value (known as the Ackerman effect) is designed into the steering linkage; therefore, if alignment is adjusted properly, and the steering radius (or toe-out on turns) appears to be incorrect, it is indicated that the steering arms or the linkage is bent.

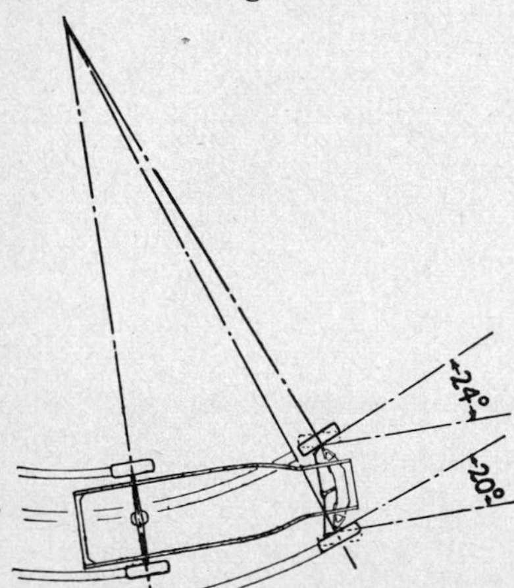

Toe-out. Inside wheel turns a greater number of degrees

Tracking

Tracking is the relationship between the paths traveled by the front and rear wheels when the vehicle is traveling in a straight line. When a car is tracking correctly, the path of the rear wheels will duplicate, or evenly straddle the path of the front wheels. Observing the car from the rear as it is driven away in a straight line will often make incorrect tracking evident.

If incorrect tracking is indicated, check as follows: Drop a plumb line from each lower ball joint, and from a point at each end of the rear axle, and mark the points on the ground with chalk. Measure these points from front to rear and diagonally. If the diagonal measurements are different (a tolerance of $+\frac{1}{4}''$ is acceptable), but the longitudinal measurements are the same, the frame is swayed (diamond shaped). If the diagonal and longitudinal measurements are both different, the rear axle is misaligned. If both diagonal and longitudinal measurements are different, but the car does not appear to be tracking incorrectly, a kneeback condition is indicated. Kneeback implies that one side of the front suspension is bent or pushed back. It is possible to align the front end to specifications, and, if kneeback exists, have very poor handling characteristics.

Diagnosis

Hard Ride

1. Excessive tire pressure
2. Shock absorbers malfunctioning
3. Broken spring
4. Worn suspension bushings

Soft Ride

1. Insufficient tire pressure
2. Worn shock absorbers
3. Collapsed or weak spring

Car Veers to One Side

1. Unequal tire pressures
2. Incorrect caster, camber or toe-in
3. Unequal spring rates
4. Unequal shock absorber control
5. Incorrect steering axis inclination (bent spindle)
6. Damaged suspension components or bushings
7. Incorrect tracking
8. Dragging brake
9. Grease on brake lining

Wander

1. Incorrect or unequal tire pressures
2. Incorrect caster or toe-in
3. Excessively worn or damaged suspension components

Hard or Erratic Steering

1. Insufficient tire pressure
2. Lack of lubrication
3. Binding or damaged steering column, steering gear, or linkage
4. Loose power steering pump belt, or poor pump operation
5. Worn or damaged suspension components

Tires Wear in Center

1. Excessive tire pressure

Tires Wear on Both Edges

1. Insufficient tire pressure

Tires Wear Evenly on One Edge

1. Incorrect camber or toe-in
2. Bent or damaged suspension components

Tires Wear Unevenly on One Edge

1. Insufficient tire pressure
2. Incorrect camber or toe-in
3. Out of round wheel and/or tire
4. Loose steering linkage
5. Severe cornering

Tires Wear Unequally

1. Unequal tire pressure
2. Unequal tire size
3. Incorrect toe-in or camber
4. Loose or bent steering linkage

Squeal on Cornering

1. Insufficient tire pressure
2. Incorrect toe-in or camber
3. Severe cornering

Caster, Camber and Toe-in Adjustment

Section 1

Caster and Camber are controlled by shims between the frame bracket

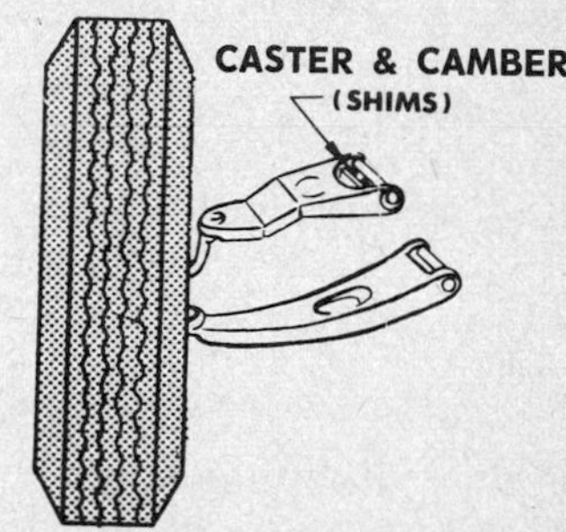

Location of caster and camber adjustments for type 1
(© Snap-On Tools Corp)

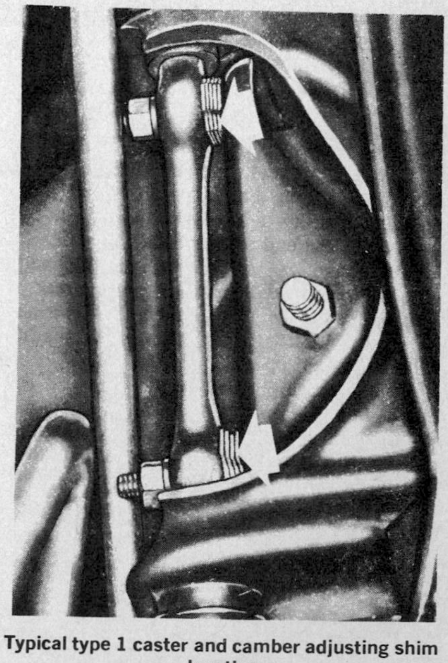

Typical type 1 caster and camber adjusting shim location
(© Chevrolet Div, G.M. Corp)

and the upper suspension arm pivot shaft.

To adjust caster, remove shims from the front bolt and replace them at the rear bolt, or vice versa. To adjust camber, add or remove the same number of shims from each bolt.

Keep in mind when loosening the bolts that the upper suspension arm is supporting the weight of the vehicle. Loosen the bolts only a sufficient amount to remove the shims.

Adjust toe-in by loosening the clamps on the sleeves at the outer ends of the tie-rod, and turning the sleeves an equal amount in the opposite direction, to maintain steering wheel spoke alignment while adjusting toe-in.

being careful not to strike the brake line or ball joint seal. Turn the eccentric until camber is within specifications. The stud must be positioned to the rear of the eccentric in order to maintain correct steering geometry. Tighten the ball joint stud nut to 60 ft. lbs.

Adjust toe-in by loosening the clamp bolts, and turning the adjuster sleeves at the outer ends of the tie rod. Turn each sleeve an equal amount in the opposite direction, in order to maintain steering wheel spoke alignment.

Section 3

Caster is adjusted by lengthening

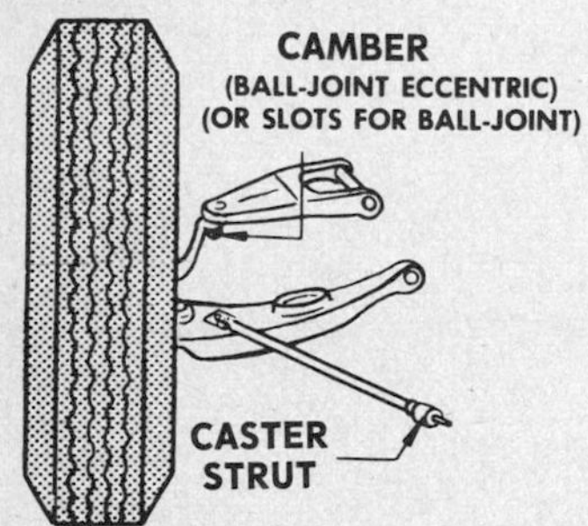

Location of caster and camber adjustments for type 2
(© Snap-On Tools Corp)

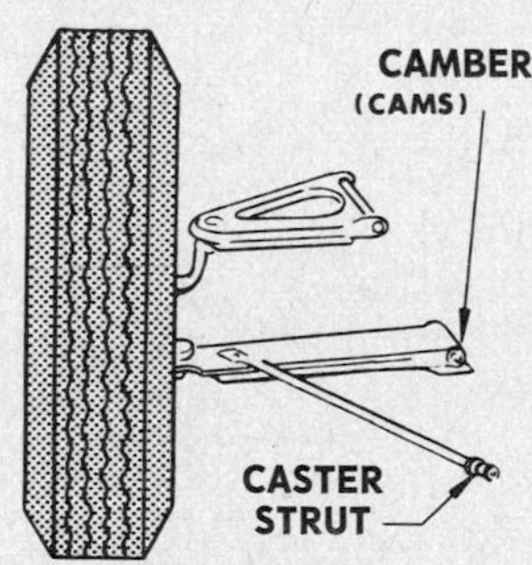

Location of caster and camber adjustments for type 3
(© Snap-On Tools Corp)

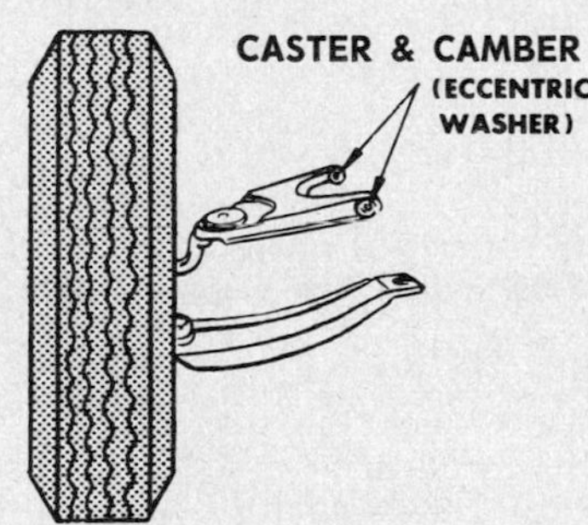

Location of caster and camber adjustment for type 4 (except Imperial)
(© Snap-On Tools Corp)

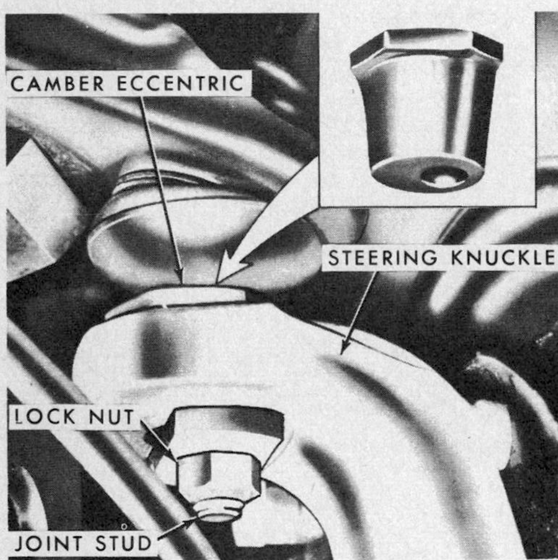

Details of type 2 camber adjustment
(© Cadillac Div, G.M. Corp)

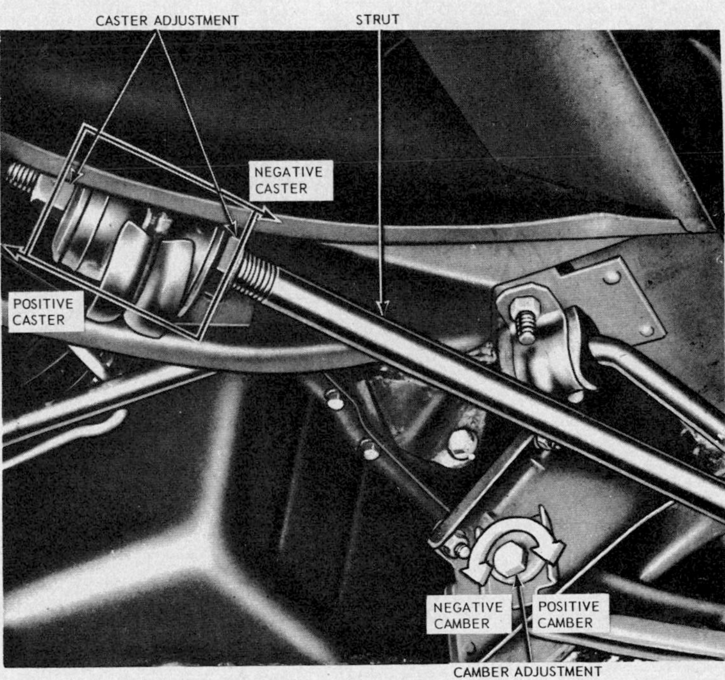

Type 3 caster and camber adjustment points (© Ford Motor Co)

Section 2

Caster is adjusted by lengthening or shortening the struts at the frame crossmember. To adjust, turn both nuts an equal number of turns in the same direction. Lengthening the strut increases negative caster. One turn of the nuts changes caster approximately ½°.

Camber is adjusted by turning the camber eccentric located in the steering knuckle upper support. Turning the eccentric changes the camber by moving the steering knuckle in or out. Loosen the ball joint stud locknut and tap the knuckle to free the eccentric,

or shortening the struts at the frame crossmember. To adjust, turn both nuts an equal number of turns in the same direction. Caster adjustments should be within ¼° of the opposing side of the car.

To adjust camber, loosen the lower control arm pivot bolt and rotate the eccentrics.

Adjust toe-in by loosening the clamp bolts, and turning the adjuster sleeves at the outer ends of the tie rod. Turn each sleeve an equal amount in the opposite direction, in order to maintain steering wheel spoke alignment.

Section 4

Caster and camber are controlled by eccentric (cam) bolts. The cam bolts are located at the ends of the upper control arm shafts on all models except the Imperial. They are on the underside of the upper control arm pivot bar attaching bracket on the Imperial. To adjust the caster, loosen the eccentric (cam) bolt nuts and turn either of the eccentric bolts. Camber is adjusted by turning both eccentrics an equal amount. Recheck caster after setting camber. Torque the eccentric (cam) bolts to 65–70 ft lbs (all Chrysler Corp. except Imperial), and 160 ft lbs (Imperial).

To adjust toe-in, loosen the tie rod clamp bolts and turn the adjuster sleeves at the outer ends of the tie-rod an equal amount in opposite directions so that steering wheel spoke alignment is maintained.

Section 5

Caster and camber are controlled by the positioning of the upper control arm pivot bar adjusting bolts. To adjust caster, loosen one of the pivot bar adjusting bolts or nuts and slide one end of the bar either inboard or outboard in its elongated mounting hole in the cross-member. Camber is adjusted by loosening both the pivot bar adjusting bolts or nuts and sliding both ends of the bar an equal amount.

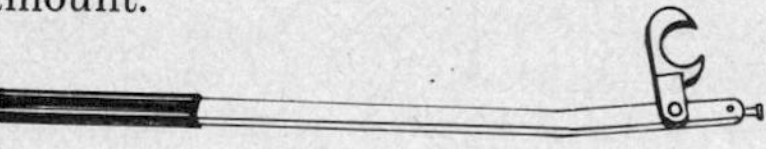

Type 5 caster and camber adjusting pry bar (© Chrysler Corp)

NOTE: Chrysler recommends the use of a special pry bar no. C-4196 for the adjusting operation on the upper control arm pivot bar.

Recheck caster after setting camber. Torque the pivot bar adjusting bolts or nuts to 160 ft lbs.

To adjust toe-in, loosen the tie rod clamp bolts and turn the adjuster sleeves at the outer ends of the tie rod an equal amount in opposite directions, so that steering wheel spoke alignment is maintained.

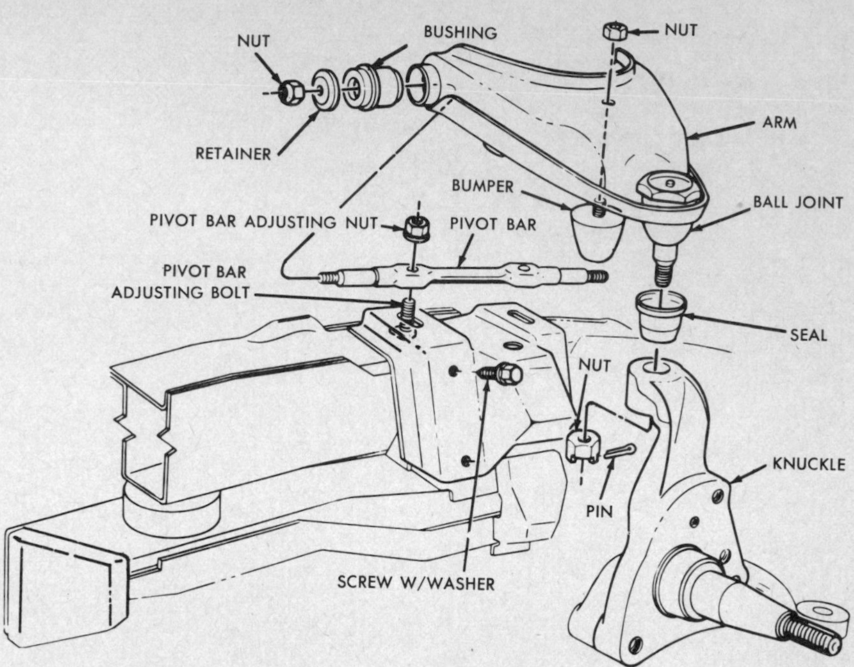

Type 5 upper control arm showing location of pivot bar and pivot bar adjusting nut and bolt (© Chrysler Corp)

Section 6

With the car positioned to adjust alignment, mark the position of the upper control arm pivot shaft, and loosen the pivot shaft retaining bolts. Lift the front end of the car and allow it to drop, to break the shaft loose from the frame. Using a pry bar, return the shaft to the index marks, and tighten the retaining bolts only enough to hold the shaft in position (loose enough to permit movement with the pry bar).

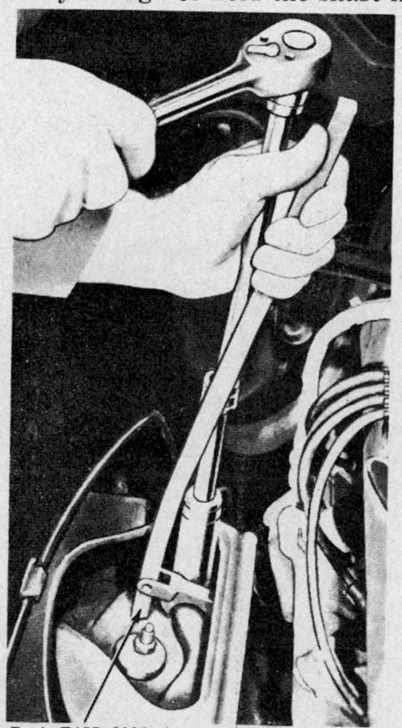

Type 6 caster and camber adjustment using pry bar (© Ford Motor Co)

To adjust caster, move either end of the pivot shaft in or out, using the pry bar. A movement of 3/32 in. at either bolt location will change caster approximately ½°. Camber is adjusted in a similar manner, by moving both ends of the shaft an equal distance. Moving the entire shaft 3/32 in. will change camber approximately ½°. After adjusting camber, tighten the retaining bolts to specifications and recheck caster.

To adjust toe-in, loosen the sleeve clamp bolts, and turn the adjuster sleeves at the outer ends of the tie-rod an equal amount in the opposite direction, to maintain steering wheel spoke alignment.

Section 7

Install Ford tool T65P-3000D or its equivalent on the frame rail, position the hooks around the upper control arm pivot shaft, and tighten the adjusting nuts of the tool slightly. Loosen the pivot shaft retaining bolts to permit adjustment.

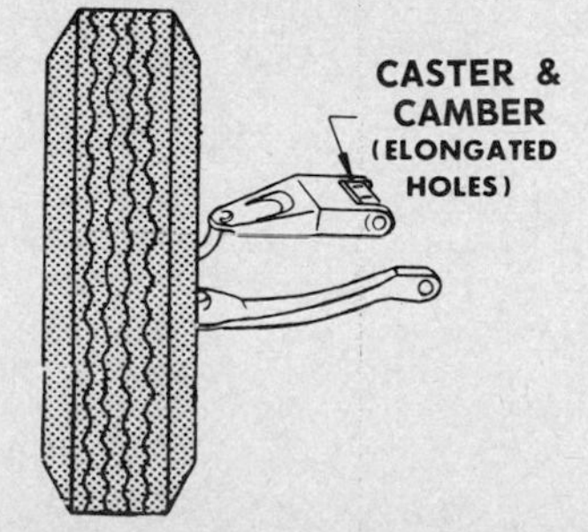

Location of caster and camber adjustments for type 7 (© Snap-On Tools Corp)

To adjust caster, loosen or tighten either the front or rear adjusting nut. After adjusting caster, adjust camber by loosening or tightening both nuts an equal amount. Tighten the shaft retaining bolts to specifications, remove the tool, and recheck the adjustments.

Adjust toe-in by loosening the clamp bolts, and turning the adjuster sleeves at the outer ends of the tie-rod. Turn the sleeves an equal amount in the opposite direction, to maintain steering wheel spoke alignment.

Section 8

Position one Ford tool T71P-3000-A at each end of the upper control arm, pivot shaft with the leg of the tools through the holes in the sheet metal (see illustration). Turn the adjusting bolts until they are solidly contacting sheet metal, and loosen the pivot shaft retaining bolts.

Caster is adjusted by turning the front and rear adjusting bolts in the opposite direction. Camber is adjusted by turning both bolts an equal amount in the same direction. Following the adjustments, tighten the pivot shaft retaining bolts, remove the adjusting tools, and recheck caster and camber.

Prior to adjusting toe-in, align the straight ahead marks at the base of the steering wheel and the head of the steering column. Loosen both the

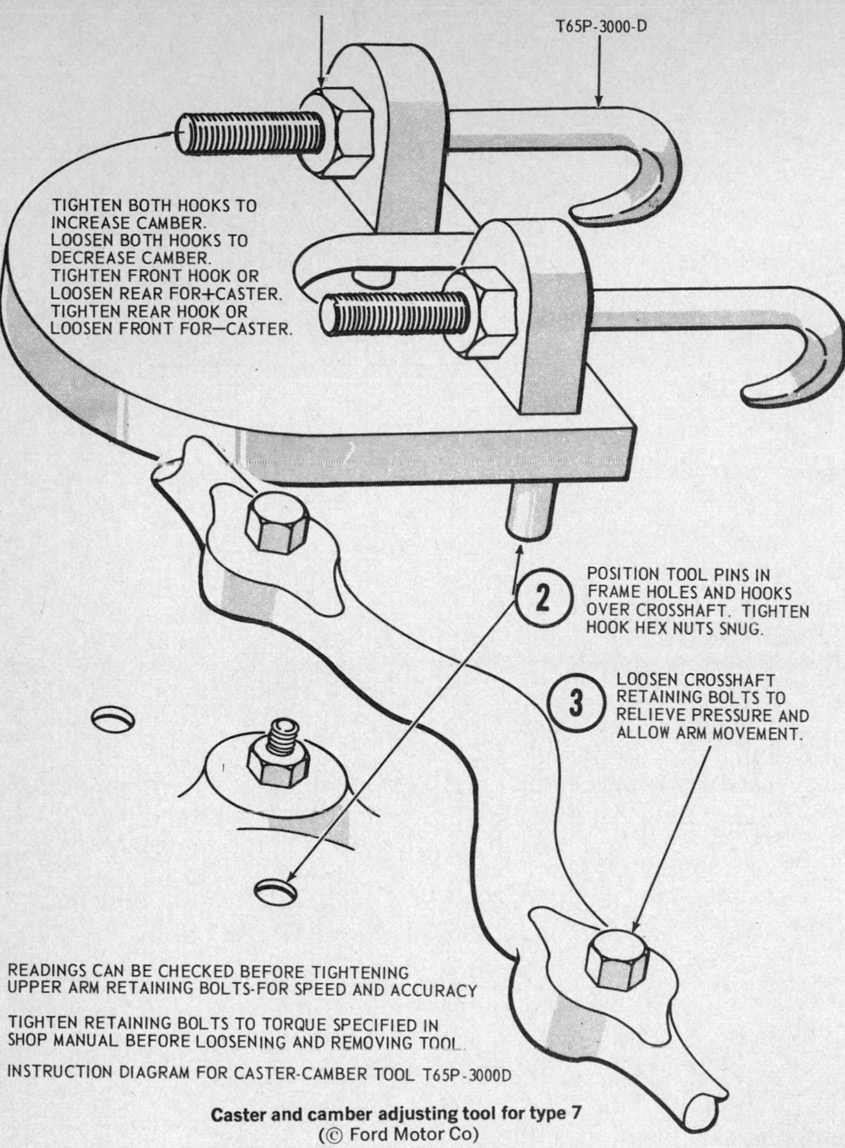

Caster and camber adjusting tool for type 7
(© Ford Motor Co)

clamp at the outer end of the rack bellows and the tie rod jam nuts. Using suitable pliers (i.e. Vise-Grips), turn the inner tie rod shafts to adjust toe-in. Turn the shafts an equal amount in the opposite direction, to maintain steering wheel spoke alignment. Following the adjustment, hold the inner shafts with pliers, and tighten the jam nuts.

Section 9

Camber and caster are adjusted using eccentrics on the lower control arm pivot bolts. Camber is adjusted first, by loosening the front pivot nut and rotating the eccentric. Tighten the front, and loosen the rear pivot nuts. Adjust caster by rotating the rear eccentric, and tighten the rear pivot nut while holding the bolt in position. Recheck camber and caster.

To adjust toe-in, loosen the clamps on the adjusting sleeves at the outer ends of the tie rod, and turn each sleeve an equal amount in the opposite direction, to maintain steering wheel spoke alignment while adjusting toe-in.

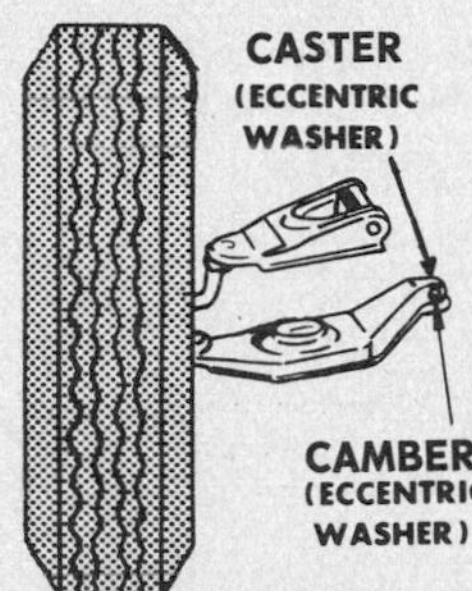

Location of caster and camber adjustments for type 9
(© Snap-On Tools Corp)

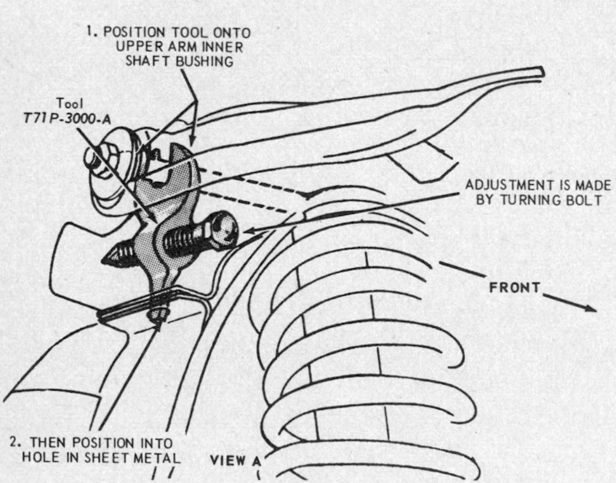

Type 8 caster and camber adjusting tool installation
(© Ford Motor Co)

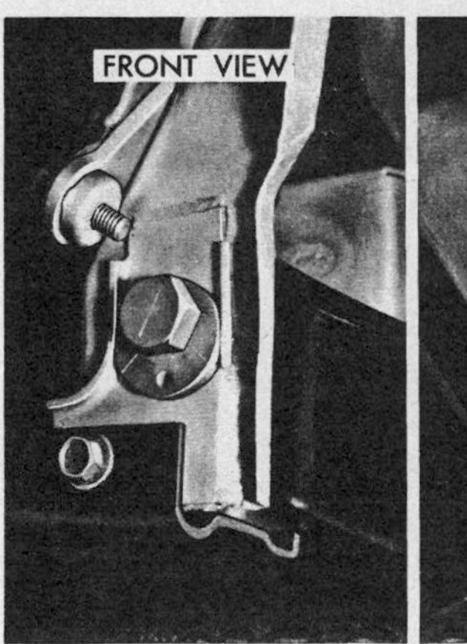

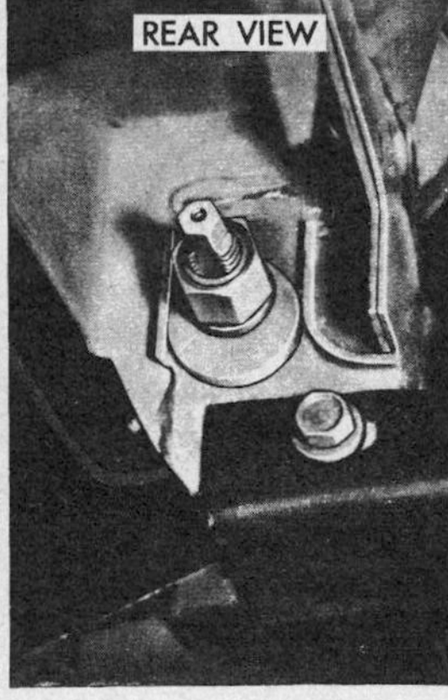

Type 9 camber (left) and caster (right) adjustments
(© Chevrolet Div, G.M. Corp)

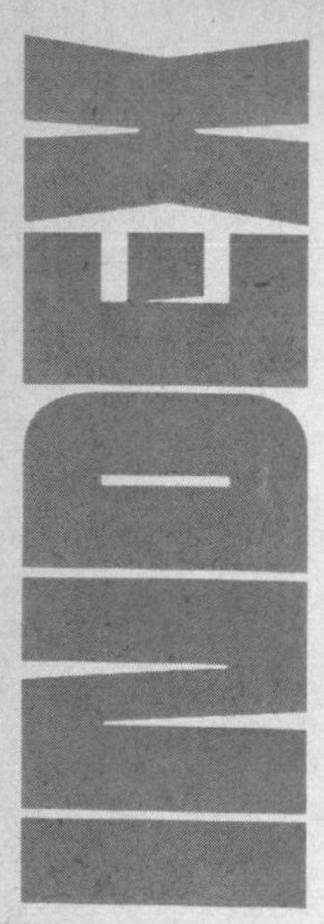

Brakes

DRUM BRAKE APPLICATION CHART

Car and Years	Brake Type	Self-Adjuster Type
AMERICAN MOTORS		
1969 6 cyl Rebel Sedan	Wagner Compound	Star & Screw
1969 all models except 6 cyl Rebel Sedan	Bendix Duo-Servo	Star & Screw
1970-76 all models	Bendix Duo-Servo	Star & Screw
CHRYSLER CORP.		
1969-76 all models	Bendix Duo-Servo	Star & Screw
FORD MOTOR CO.		
1969-76 all models	Bendix Duo-Servo	Star & Screw
GENERAL MOTORS CORP.		
1969-76 all models except below	Bendix Duo-Servo	Star & Screw
1971-76 Astre, Monza, Skyhawk, Starfire, Vega	Bendix Duo-Servo	Expanding Strut

Brakes

Brake Diagnosis Chart

Condition	*Mechanical*	*Hydraulic*	*Vacuum (Power Unit)*
Low pedal (Excessive pedal travel to apply brakes)	FGIMfg	T	k
Spongy Pedal (A springy sensation of pedal upon application)	I	PQU	
Hard Pedal (Excessive pedal pressure needed to stop vehicle)	AFGKVaf	RTUW	cehk
Fading Pedal (A falling away of pedal under steady foot pressure)	I	PQSTW	
Grabbing or Pulling	ADEGHIKL NVXYZa	RW	k
Noise (Squealing, clicking or scraping noise)	FGHILMN		
Chatter or Shudder (May be accompanied by brake roughness or pedal pumping)	DGILNO		
Dragging Brakes (Slow or incomplete release of brakes)	ABCFGHK LVafg	RUTW	k

A. Pedal linkage binding. (Check by bleeding one wheel cylinder using light pedal effort. Observe for smooth full travel of pedal)
B. Parking brake cables and linkage sticking, dirty or corroded.
C. Parking brake improperly adjusted (too loose or too tight).
D. Wheel bearings loose.
E. Front wheel alignment or uneven tire tread.
F. Brake shoes improperly adjusted. Automatic adjuster parts corroded, distorted or broken.
G. Brake linings or disc pads worn, contaminated or distorted.
H. Shoe return spring weak, broken, improperly installed.
I. Drums cracked, thin (beyond 0.060" of original specifications), scored, hard spotted, or out of round.
K. Brake support plate ledges rusted or grooved.
L. Support plate loose, worn, or distorted.
M. Disc brake pad "knock back" (loose or worn wheel bearings or steering parts).
N. Caliper not aligned with disc or loose.
O. Disc has excessive lateral runout. Excessively out of parallel.
P. Hydraulic system fluid has air in it, improper quality (low boiling point).
Q. Hoses and lines soft or weak (expanding under pressure).
R. Hose sand lines kinked, collapsed, dented, or clogged.
S. Hoses and lines loosely connected, ruptured, or damaged (causing leakage).
T. Master cylinder primary cup worn or damaged, bore worn, rough, corroded.
U. Master cylinder check valve faulty, or compensator port blocked.
V. Wheel or caliper cylinder pistons frozen or seized.
W. Wheel or caliper cylinder cups swollen, worn or damaged seals; bores rough or corroded.
X. Wheel or caliper cylinders mismatched (size).
Y. Check tire pressure.
Z. Rear wheels (both) grabbing. Rear brake line proportioning valve defective—replace.
a. Power unit valve rod linkage binding.
c. Vacuum lines loose, broken, collapsed. Engine vacuum low.
e. Vacuum check valve defective or sticking.
f. Power unit hydraulic pushrod improperly adjusted.
g. Air trapped in hub cavity of master cylinder. Inspect and remove master cylinder boot if installed.
h. Air filter dirty, clogged.
k. Corrosion or lack of lubrication in power cylinder. Control valve, power cylinder, piston or diaphragm defective.

Servicing Self-Adjusting Brakes

Bendix Duo-Servo Brake

Star and Screw Type

The Bendix duo-servo brake, with star and screw type self-adjusters, is by far the most common brake used on late-model American cars. The same basic brake unit has been used on all cars (except Vega) since 1970, and on most cars from 1966. General Motors cars use a rod-operated lever to turn the starwheel, while all others use a cable-operated lever. This is the only difference, other than size, between units used on different models.

Adjustment

1. Remove the access slot plug from the backing plate or front of drum on GM cars. On some late-model GM cars, there is no access slot in the backing plate or in the front of the drums. It has been filled in and must be punched out to gain access to the adjuster. Complete the adjustment and cover the hole with the plug to prevent entrance of dirt and water.
2. Using a brake adjusting spoon or screwdriver, pry downward on the end of the tool (starwheel teeth moving up) to tighten the brakes, or upward on the end of the tool (starwheel teeth moving down) to loosen the brakes.

NOTE: it will be necessary to use a small screwdriver to hold the adjusting lever away from the starwheel. Be careful not to bend the adjusting lever.

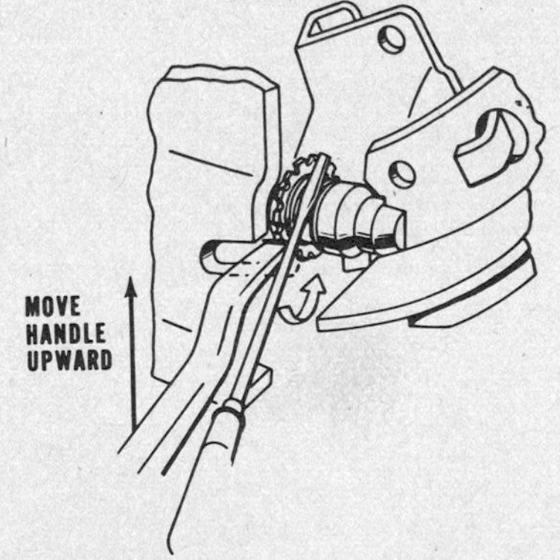

Self-adjuster method. Push the self-adjusting lever out of the way with a small screwdriver or ice pick to back off star wheel.

3. When the brakes are tight almost to the point of being locked, back off on the starwheel until the wheel is able to rotate freely. The starwheel on each set of brakes (front or rear) must be backed off the same number of turns to prevent brake pull from side to side.
4. When all four brakes are adjusted, check brake pedal travel and then make several stops, while backing the car up, to equalize all the wheels.

Testing Adjuster

1. Raise the vehicle on a hoist, with a helper in the car, to apply the brakes.
2. Loosen the brakes by holding the adjuster lever away from the starwheel and backing off the starwheel approximately 30 notches.
3. Spin the wheel and brake drum in reverse and apply the brakes. The movement of the secondary shoe should pull the adjuster lever up, and when the brakes are released the lever should snap down and turn the starwheel.

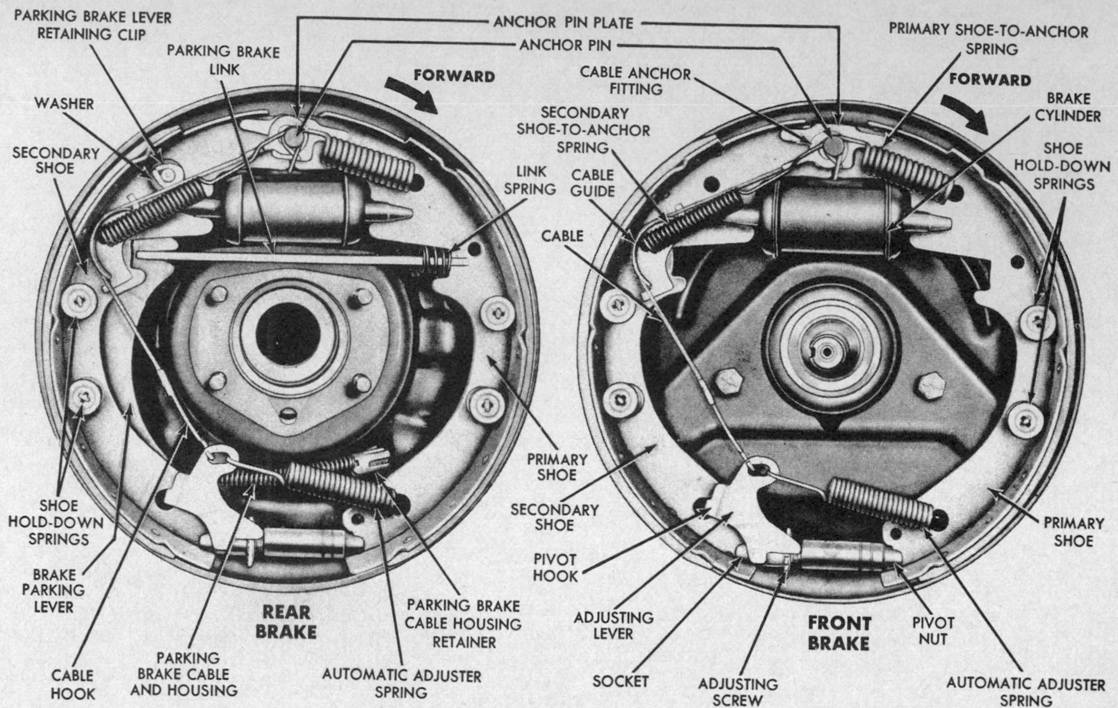

Bendix duo-servo self-adjusting brakes

4. If the automatic adjuster doesn't work, the drum must be removed and the adjuster components inspected carefully for breakage, wear, or improper installation.

Brake Shoe Removal

NOTE: if you are not thoroughly familiar with the procedures involved in brake replacement, disassemble and assemble one side at a time, leaving the other wheel intact, as a reference.

1. Remove the brake drum.
2. Place the hollow end of a brake spring service tool on the brake shoe anchor pin and twist it to disengage one of the brake retaining springs. Repeat this operation to remove the other spring. On GM cars, grasp the secondary shoe return spring with a pair of pliers and lift upward on the spring to disengage it from the automatic adjuster link.

Caution Be careful that the springs do not slip off the tool during removal, as the springs could break loose and cause personal injury.

3. Reach behind the brake backing plate and place a finger on the end of one of the brake hold-down mounting pins. Using a pair of pliers, grasp the washer on the top of the hold-down spring that corresponds to the pin that you are holding. Push

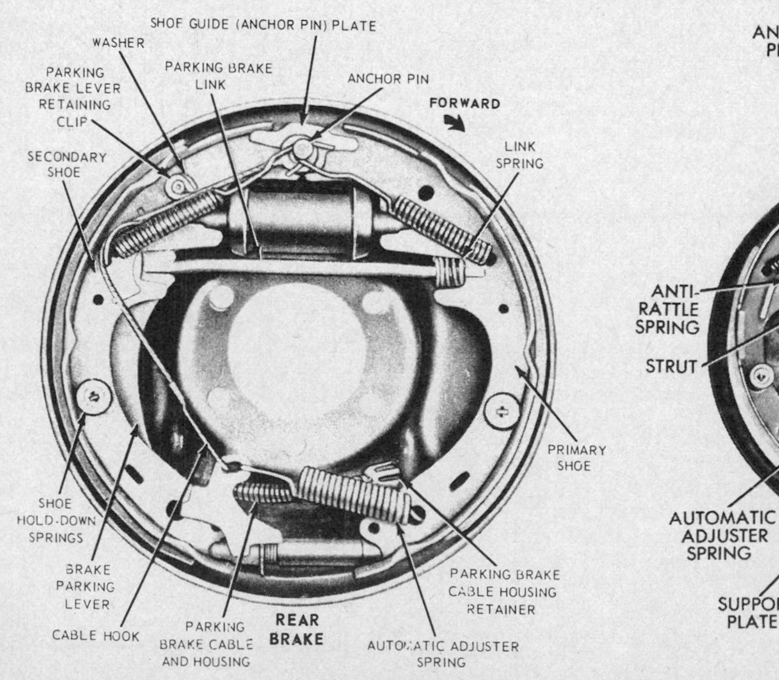

Bendix duo-servo self-adjusting brake—Ford type

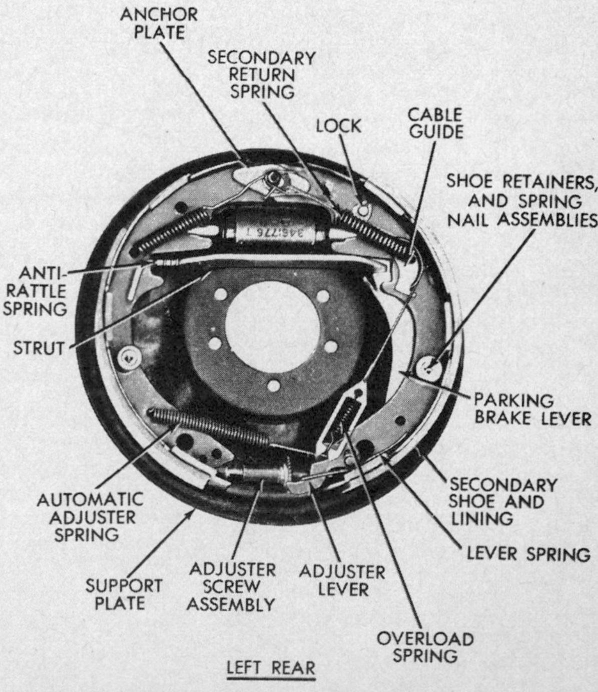

Bendix duo-servo self-adjusting brake—Chrysler Corp. 11 in. type

down on the pliers and turn them 90° to align the slot in the washer with the head on the spring mounting pin. Remove the spring and washer and repeat this operation on the hold-down spring of the other brake shoe.

4. Step 4 varies according to manufacturer:

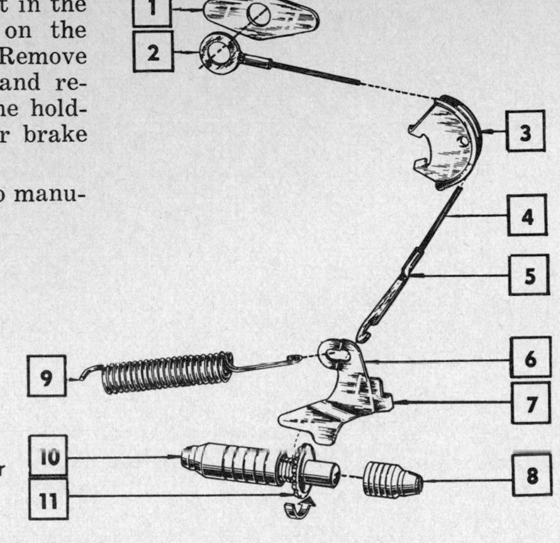

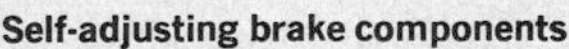

Self-adjusting brake components

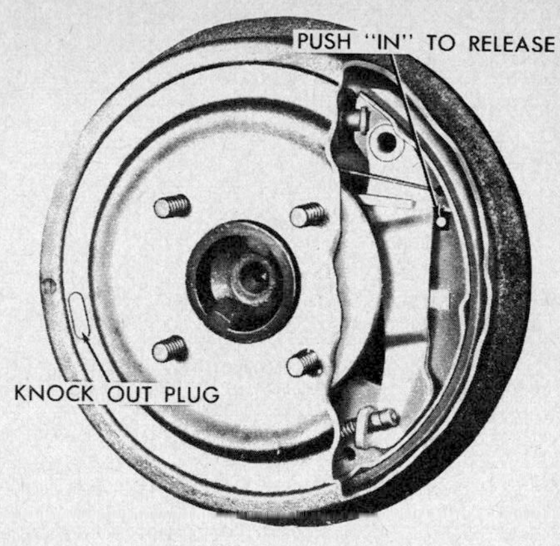

Release adjuster to remove drum on expanding strut rear brakes (© Chevrolet Div., G.M. Corp)

On Ford and American Motors cars, place the tip of a screwdriver on the top of the brake adjusting screw and move the screwdriver upward to lift up on the brake adjusting lever. When there is enough slack in the automatic adjuster cable, disconnect the loop on the top of the cable from the anchor. Grasp the top of each brake shoe and move them outward to disengage from the wheel cylinder and parking brake link (if working on rear wheels). When the brake shoes are clear, lift them from the backing plate. Twist the shoes slightly and the automatic adjuster assembly will disassemble itself.

On GM cars, remove the automatic adjuster link. Remove the automatic adjuster lever, pivot, and override spring from the secondary spring as an assembly. Move the top of each brake shoe outward to clear the wheel cylinder pins and parking brake link (rear brakes). Lift the brakes from the backing plate and remove the adjusting screw.

On Chrysler cars, slide the automatic adjuster cable from the anchor pin and disengage it from the adjusting lever. Remove the cable, overload spring, and cable guide. Disconnect the automatic adjuster lever return spring and remove the spring and lever. Move the top of the brake shoes outward to clear the wheel cylinder pins and parking brake link (rear brakes). Lift the brakes from the backing plate and remove the adjusting screw.

5. If you are working on rear brakes, grasp the end of the brake cable spring with a pair of pliers and, using the brake lever as a fulcrum, pull the end of the spring away from the lever. Disengage the cable from the brake lever.

Brake Shoe Installation

1. If you are working on rear brakes, the brake cable must be connected to the secondary brake shoe before the shoe is installed on the backing plate. To do this,

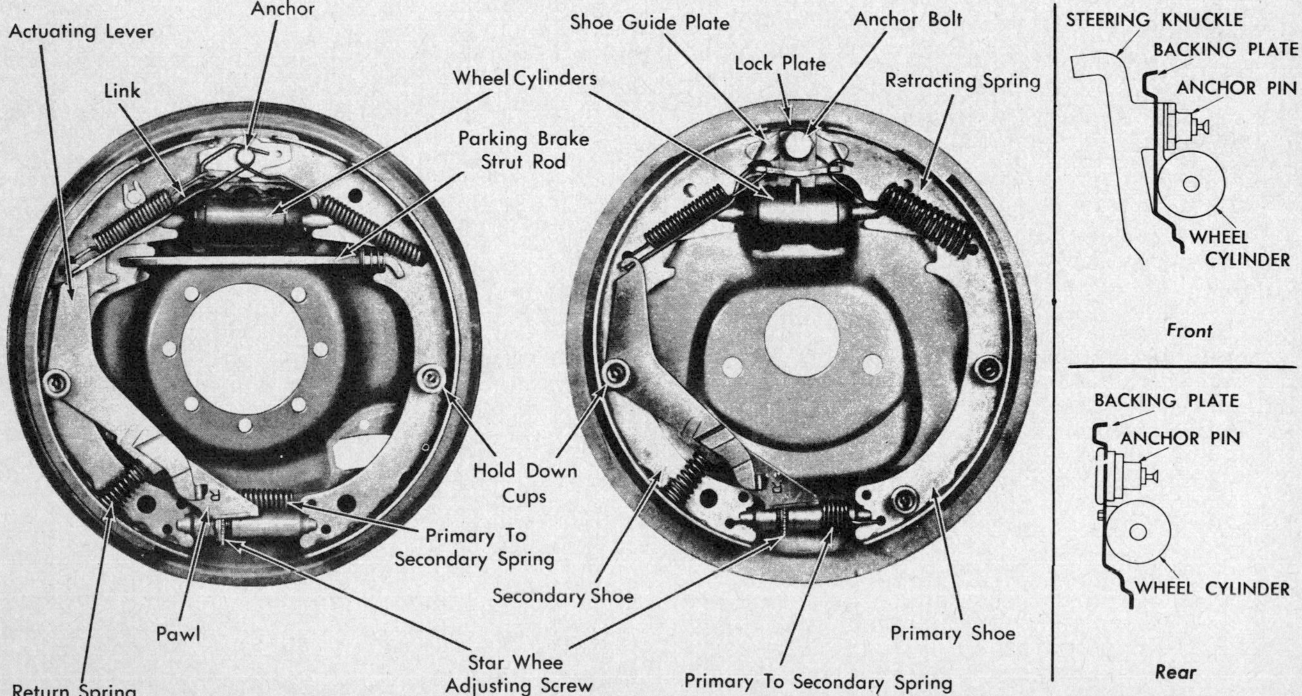

Bendix duo-servo self-adjusting brake—G.M. type

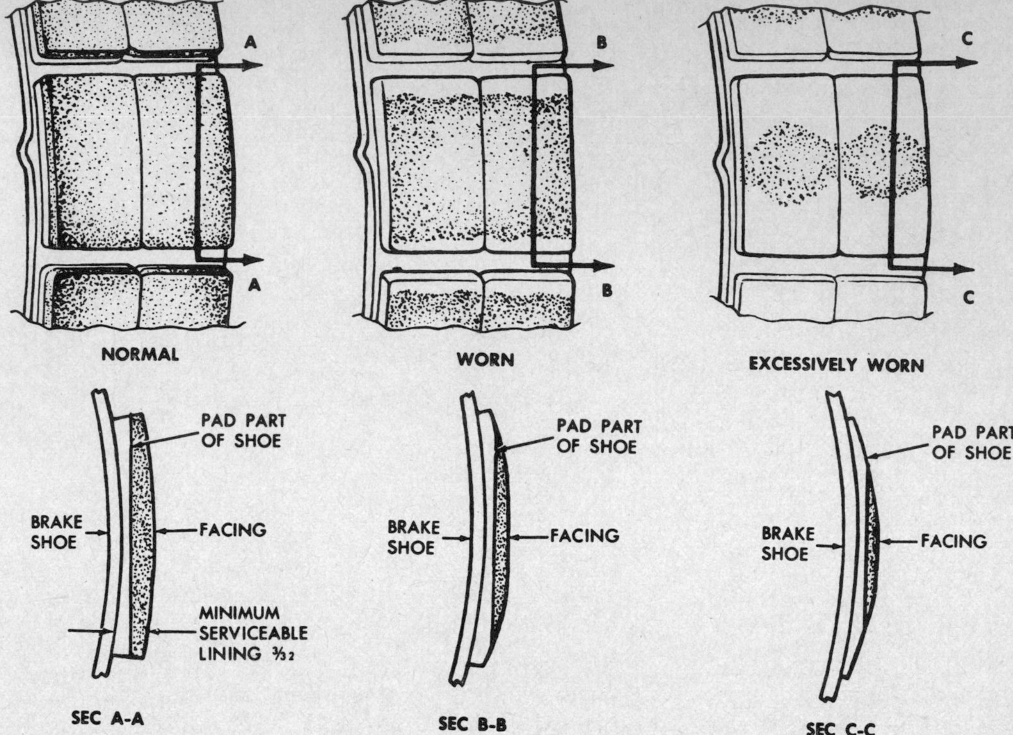

Metallic brake linings—Pontiac and Chevrolet

transfer the parking brake lever from the old secondary shoe to the new one. This is accomplished by spreading the bottom of the horseshoe clip and disengaging the lever. Position the lever on the new secondary shoe and install the spring washer and the horseshoe clip. Close the bottom of the clip after installing it. Grasp the metal tip of the parking brake cable with a pair of pliers. Position a pair of side cutters on the end of the cable coil spring and, using the pliers as a fulcrum, pull the coil spring back with the side cutters. Position the cable in the parking brake lever.

2. Apply a light coating of high-temperature grease to the brake shoe contact points on the backing plate. Position the primary brake shoe on the front of the backing plate and install the hold-down spring and washer over the mounting pin. Install the secondary shoe on the rear of the backing plate.
3. If working on rear brakes, install the parking brake link between the primary brake shoe and the secondary brake shoe.
4. Step 4 varies according to manufacturer:

   On Ford and American Motors cars, install the automatic adjuster cable loop end on the anchor pin. Make sure that the crimped side of the loop faces the backing plate.

   On GM cars, assemble the automatic adjuster lever, pivot, and override spring and install to the secondary spring as an assembly.

   On Chrysler, install the automatic adjuster lever and return spring. Install the adjuster overload spring and cable. One end of the cable engages with the adjusting lever while the other slips over the anchor pin underneath the primary and secondary return springs.
5. Install the return spring in the primary brake shoe and, using the tapered end of a brake spring service tool, slide the top of the spring onto the anchor pin.

Caution Be careful to make sure that the spring does not slip off the tool during installation, as the spring could break loose and cause personal injury.

6. Install the automatic adjuster cable guide in the secondary brake shoe, making sure that the flared hole in the cable guide is inside the hole in the brake shoe. Fit the cable into the groove in the top of the cable guide.
7. Install the secondary shoe return spring through the hole in the cable guide and the brake shoe. Using the brake spring tool, slide the top of the spring onto the anchor pin.
8. Clean the threads on the adjusting screw and apply a *light* coating of high-temperature grease to the threads. Screw the adjuster closed, then open it one-half turn.
9. Install the adjusting screw between the brake shoes with the star wheel nearest to the secondary shoe. Make sure that the star wheel is in a position that is accessible from the adjusting slot in the backing plate.
10. Install the short, hooked end of the automatic adjuster spring in the proper hole in the primary brake shoe.
11. Connect the hooked end of the automatic adjuster cable and the free end of the automatic adjuster spring in the slot in the top of the automatic adjuster lever.
12. Pull the automatic adjuster lever (the lever will pull the cable and spring with it) downward and to the left, and engage the pivot hook of the lever in the hole in the secondary brake shoe.

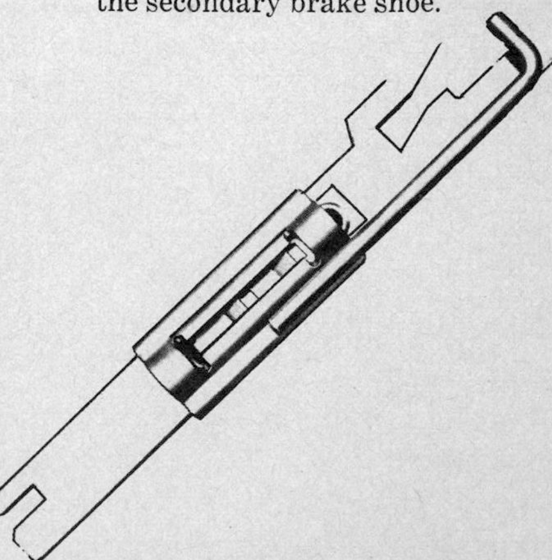

Adjuster properly positioned for installation—expanding strut rear brakes (© Chevrolet Div., G.M. Corp)

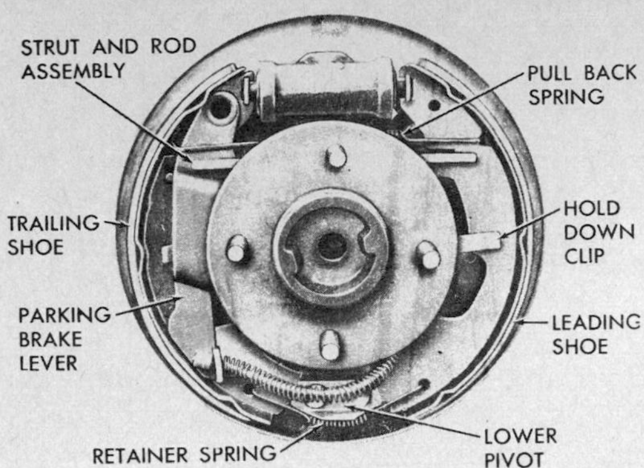

Bendix duo-servo self-adjusting brake—expanding strut type (© Chevrolet Div., G.M. Corp)

13. Check the entire brake assembly to make sure everything is installed properly. Make sure that the shoes engage the wheel cylinder properly and are flush on the anchor pin. Make sure that the automatic adjuster cable is flush on the anchor pin and in the slot on the back of cable guide. Make sure that the adjusting lever rests on the adjusting screw star wheel. Pull upward on the adjusting cable until the adjusting lever is free of the star wheel, then release the cable. The adjusting lever should snap back into place on the adjusting screw star wheel and turn the wheel one tooth.
14. Expand the brake adjusting screw until the brake drum will just fit over the brake shoes.
15. Install the wheel and drum and adjust the brakes. (See "Brake Adjustment.")

Expanding Strut Type

Bendix duo-servo brakes with expanding strut adjusters are used exclusively on GM subcompact cars.

Adjuster Disassembly

1. Remove the adjuster assembly from the wheel.
2. Separate the rod assembly from the adjuster locks.
3. Slide the rod off from the strut.

Assembly

1. Assemble the adjuster lock to the strut, making sure that the index hole in the lock is lined up and seated with the hole in the strut.
2. Slide the rod assembly onto the strut and over the adjuster locks. When properly installed, $\frac{1}{2}$ of the index hole in the adjuster lock should be covered by the rod assembly.

Shoe Replacement

1. If the drum does not slip off easily, it will be necessary to knock out the metal plug in the drum and push in on the adjuster rod so that the spring will pull the shoes away from the drum. Remove the drum. The adjuster rod is at the 2 o'clock position on the left wheel and at the 10 o'clock position on the right wheel.
2. Release all tension from the parking brake equalizer.
3. Remove the parking brake cable from the lever next to the shoe. Allowing the lever to swing forward will engage the adjuster rod and change the adjustment position.
4. Remove the pull-back spring.
5. Remove the shoes from under the clips and lift out with the strut and adjuster assembly attached.
6. Separate the shoes, and remove the strut and adjuster assembly.
7. Remove the parking brake lever.
8. Remove the shoe hold-down clips only if they are broken or worn.
9. Using white grease, lubricate the six contact surfaces on the backing plate. Do not allow any grease to contact the brake linings.
10. Install the parking brake lever to the rear brake shoe and install the parking brake strut and adjuster. The rear shoe can be identified as having a hole for the parking brake lever and one for the adjusting rod.
11. Connect both shoes with the lower spring.
12. Install both shoes with the spring onto the backing plate, placing the spring under the shoe anchor. Position the lever and adjuster assembly.
13. Engage the wheel cylinder links with the shoes.
14. Engage the parking brake strut to the leading shoe and install the pull-back spring.
15. Connect the parking brake cable to its lever, being careful not to activate the adjuster.
16. Install the drums and wheels, and adjust the parking brake equalizer. Lower the vehicle to the floor.
17. Adjust the parking brake and service brake by pulling and releasing the handle several times.
18. Seal the adjuster hole in the drum with a rubber or plastic replacement plug.

Wagner Compound Shoe Brake

Servicing and Adjustment

This brake unit is very similar to the Bendix duo-servo type with star and screw self-adjusters. Servicing and adjusting procedures are virtually the same, with these exceptions:

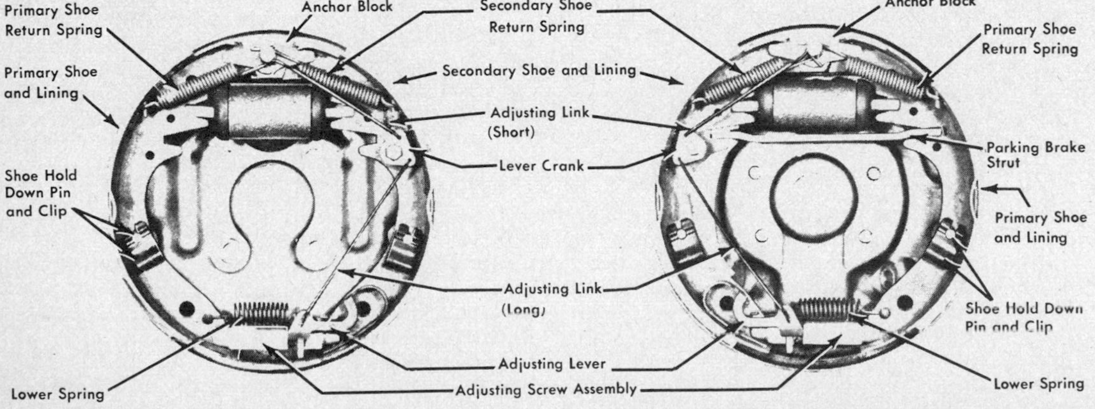

Wagner compound shoe self-adjusting brake (© Chevrolet Div., G.M. Corp)

1. Do not lift the adjusting lever off the starwheel when adjusting the brakes manually. The adjuster levers are painted red for right-side brakes and blue for left-side brakes. The lever crank (fits into the secondary shoe) is marked with a "R" (right) or "L" (left), depending upon the wheel in which it is used.
2. The lower brake spring should be installed with the long hook end in the secondary shoe and the hook facing out to prevent interference with the starwheel or the lever.
3. If the shoes have been removed for any reason, an initial adjustment must be made before drum installation. Adjust the screw assemblies so that approximately ¼ in. of threads are exposed between the starwheel and starwheel nut.
4. The anchor block must be installed with the arrow pointing in the direction of forward rotation.

NOTE: do not interchange the right-side adjuster assembly with the left-side assembly. Interchanging them will cause the shoe to retract rather than expand.

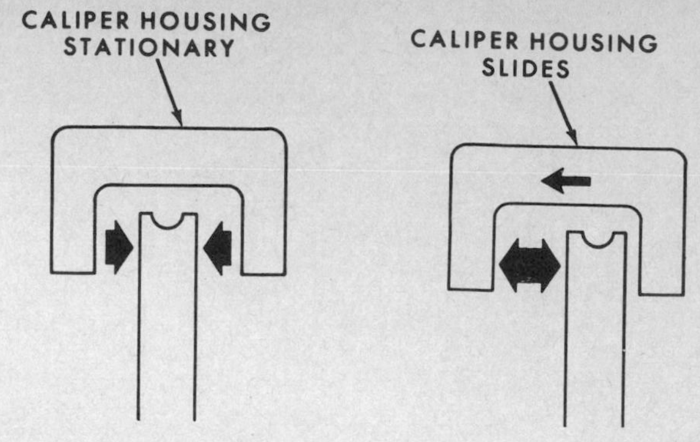

Fixed caliper disc brake operation

Floating caliper disc brake operation

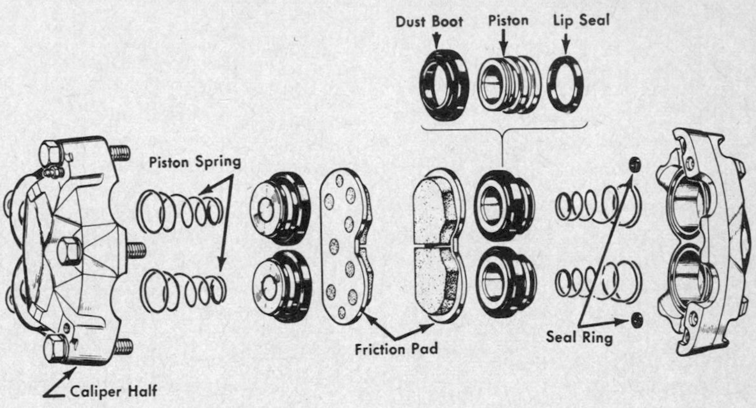

Bendix four piston disc brake (© American Motors Corp)

Servicing Disc Brakes

General Description and Inspection

Caliper disc brakes can be divided into three types: the four-piston, fixed-caliper type; the single-piston, floating-caliper type, and the single-piston sliding-caliper type.

In the four piston type (two in each side of the caliper) braking effect is achieved by hydraulically pushing both shoes against the disc sides. With the single piston type the inboard shoe is pushed hydraulically into contact with the disc, while the reaction force thus generated is used to pull the outboard shoe into frictional contact (made possible by letting the caliper move slightly along the axle centerline).

The sliding caliper (single piston) was used by Ford on the 1971 Pinto and many of its 1972 models. All 1973 Ford and Chrysler models, except Mustang and Cougar, equipped with disc brakes, use the sliding caliper design. The caliper assembly slides along the machined surfaces of the anchor plate. A steel key located between the machined surfaces of the caliper and the machined surfaces of the anchor plate is held in place with either a retaining screw or two cotter pins. The caliper is held in place against the anchor plate with one or two support springs.

To properly inspect disc pad wear it may be necessary to remove the pads. On some systems, it is necessary to remove the caliper to accomplish this. Disc pads (lining and shoe assemblies) should be replaced in axle sets (both wheels) when the lining on any pad is worn to ⅛ in. at any point. *If lining is allowed to wear past 1/16 in. minimum thickness severe damage to disc may result.* Note that disc pads in floating caliper type brakes may wear at an angle, and measurement should be made at the narrow end of the taper. Tapered linings should be replaced if the taper exceeds ⅛ in. from end to end (the difference betweeen the thickest and thinnest points).

Caution To prevent costly paint damage, remove some brake fluid (don't re-use) from the reservoir and install the reservoir cover before replacing the disc pads. When replacing the pads, the piston is depressed and fluid is forced back through the lines to squirt out of the fluid reservoir.

When the caliper is unbolted from the hub do not let it dangle by the brake hose; it can be rested on a suspension member or wired onto the frame. All disc brake systems are inherently self-adjusting and have no provision for manual adjustment.

Bendix 4 Piston Brake

Disc Pad Replacement

1. Raise the vehicle on a hoist and remove the front wheels.

See CAUTION under Delco-Moraine 4 Piston Brake.

2. Working on one side at a time only, remove the caliper mounting bolts and slide the caliper off of the disc.

NOTE: on American Motors cars the shims under the mounting bolts must be replaced exactly as removed. Remove the lower bolt, shake out the shims, and tag them as "lower." Remove the upper shims and tag them as "upper."

3. Remove the disc pads and inspect the caliper for damaged or leaking seals and casting cracks.
4. To install new pads insert the curved edge first (tabs, if any, should be up) and position the steel plate against the pistons.
5. Spread the pads apart until the pistons are bottomed in their bores and slide the caliper assembly over the disc.
6. Align the mounting holes and install shims (if used) and mounting bolts. Torque to specifications.
7. Check brake fluid level and pump the brake pedal to seat the linings against the disc. Replace the wheels and road test the vehicle.

DISC BRAKE SPECIFICATIONS

Manufacturer/Model/Year		Caliper Specifications: Fixed Caliper Four Piston	Caliper Specifications: Floating or Sliding Caliper Single Piston	Caliper Specifications: Mounting Bolts Torque ft lbs	Caliper Specifications: Bridge Bolts Torque ft lbs	Hydraulic Controls: Proportioning Valve	Hydraulic Controls: Metering Valve	Disc Specifications: Original Thickness (in.)	Disc Specifications: Resurfacing Min. Thickness (in.)	Disc Specifications: Parallel Variation (in.)	Disc Specifications: Runout Maximum (in.)
AMERICAN MOTORS											
All	1971-74		Kelsey-Hayes	upper: 105/lower: 85	30-35(2)	yes	yes	1.000	.940	.0005	.005
All	1968-70	Bendix		85	100-110	yes	no	.500	.450	.0005	.005
All	1975-76		Kelsey-Hayes sliding	80		yes	yes	1.190	1.130	.002	.003
CHRYSLER CORPORATION											
Imperial Full Size Models	1973-74 1973-76		Kelsey-Hayes sliding			yes(7)	yes	1.250	(8)	.0005	.0025(9)
Intermediates Barracuda, Challenger	1973-76 1973-76		Kelsey-Hayes			yes(7)	yes	1.000	(8)	.0005	.0025(9)
Valiant Dart	1973-76 1973-76		Kelsey-Hayes sliding	upper: 55/lower: 120		yes	no	1.000	(8)	.0005	.0025(9)
Imperial Full Size Models	1970-72 1969-72		Kelsey-Hayes	75-100	30-35(2)	no(4)	yes	1.250	1.200(5)	.0005	.0025
Intermediates Barracuda, Challenger	1970-72 1970-72		Kelsey-Hayes	75-100	35	yes	yes	1.000-1.010	.980(5)	.0005	.0025
Valiant, Dart Barracuda	1969-72 1969	Kelsey-Hayes		50-80	70-80	yes	yes	.810	.780	.0005	.0025
Imperial	1969	Budd		70-80(3)	7/16 in. 50-60 5/8 in. 140-160	no	yes	.8725-.8775	.829	.0005	.005
Intermediates	1968-69	Bendix		85-90(6)	120-140	yes	no	.886-.878	.816	.0005	.005
FORD MOTOR COMPANY											
Lincoln Full Size Models	1970-72 1968-72(1)		Kelsey-Hayes	upper: 125/lower: 105	25-35(2)	yes	yes	1.180	1.120	.0007	.003
All But Full Size	1969-72(1)		Kelsey-Hayes	upper: 120/lower: 70	25-35	yes	no	.935-.810 (68)	.875	.0007	.002
Lincoln	1969	Kelsey-Hayes		125	90	yes	yes	1.250	1.215	.0007	.002
Pinto	1971-72		Ford sliding			yes	no	.750	.685	.0007	.003
Mark IV	1972		Ford sliding			yes	yes	1.180	1.120	.0005	.003
Thunderbird	1972		Ford sliding			yes	yes	1.180	1.120	.0005	.003
Montego, Torino	1972		Ford sliding			yes	yes	1.180	1.120	.0005	.003
All Models	1973-76		Ford sliding			yes	yes	1.180	1.120	.0005	.003(10)
GENERAL MOTORS											
Buick (Full Size)	1970-76		Delco-Moraine		35	yes (no 1970)	yes	1.290	1.230 1.215 (73-74)	.0005	.005
Buick Special, Century	1969-76		Delco-Moraine	125	35	no	yes	1.040	.965	.0005	.004
Buick (Full Size)	1969	Bendix		70	125	no	yes	1.000	.965	.0005	.005
Skyhawk	1975-76		Delco-Moraine			yes	no	.500	.455	.0005	.005
Apollo, Skylark	1975-76		Delco-Moraine	35		yes	yes	1.040	.980	.0005	.005
Cadillac Eldorado	1969-76		Delco-Moraine	95	30	yes	yes	1.210	1.195	.0005	.008 (on hub)
Cadillac	1969-76		Delco-Moraine		35	yes (68-70 no)	yes	1.250	1.230	.0005	.0025 .005 (73)
Chevrolet (Full Size)	1969-76		Delco-Moraine	60-90	35	yes (69-70 no)	yes	1.250 (69-70) 1.285 (71-72)	1.215 (69-72) 1.230 (71-74)	.0005 .003 (73)	.002 .005 (73)
Corvette	1969-76	Delco-Moraine		60-90	F/130 R/60	yes (HD)	no	1.250	1.215	.0005 .003 (73)	.002 .005 (73)

Disc Brake Specifications

Chevelle, Nova Camaro	1969-76	Delco-Moraine	125	1969-70: 35 1971-76: 85	yes	yes	1969-70: 1.00 1971-76: 1.035	1969-70: .965 1971-76: .980	.0005 .003 (73)	.002 .005 (73)
Olds Toronado	1969-76	Delco-Moraine	55	40	yes	yes	1.205 ⑪	1.185 ⑫	.0005	.002
Olds 88 & 98	1969-76	Delco-Moraine		40	yes	yes	1.250 (69-70) 1.280 (71-74) 1.290 (75-76)	1.215 (69-73) 1.230 (74-76)	.0005 .0005	.004 .005
Olds F85, Cutlass	1969-76	Delco-Moraine	70	35	no	yes	1.035	.980	.0005	.004
Olds Starfire	1975-76	Delco-Moraine	40		yes	no	.500	.400	.0005	.005
Olds Omega	1973-76	Delco-Moraine	40		yes	yes	1.040	.965	.0005	.005
Pontiac (Full Size)	1969-76	Delco-Moraine		35	yes (no 69-70)	yes	1.250 (71-72) 1.285 (73-76) 1.230 (69-70)	1.230 (71-72) 1.215 (73-76) 1.195 (69-70)	.0005	.002 .004 (73-76)
Tempest, LeMans, Firebird	1969-76	Delco-Moraine		35	yes	yes	1.005 1.035 (73-76)	.960	.0007	.004
Pontiac Astre	1975-76	Delco-Moraine			yes	no	.500	.470	.0005	.005
Vega, Monza	1971-76	Delco-Moraine			yes	no	.500	.470	.0005	.005
Ventura	1971-76	Delco-Moraine	35		yes	yes	1.035	.965	.0007	.004

① Except 1972 Montego, Thunderbird, Torino, and Mark IV.
② Caliper guide pin torque.
③ 80-90 for 1969 models.
④ Yes for 1972 Fury, Chrysler (except wagon), Imperial, Polara, and Monaco (except wagon).
⑤ 1971-72 Chrysler, Imperial, and full-size Dodge and Plymouth minimum thickness is 1.180 in.
1971-72 Intermediates and Barracuda-Challenger minimum thickness is 0.940 in.
⑥ 1969 models 75-105.
⑦ No proportioning valve on station wagons (exc. Chrysler).
⑧ Resurfacing minimum thickness is cast on the disc.
⑨ .004 runout—1975-76.
⑨ Rear disc runout. 004—1975-76.
⑪ 1.245—1975-76.
⑫ 1.170—1975-76.

Servicing the Caliper Assembly

1. Raise the vehicle on a hoist and remove the front wheels.
2. Working on one side at a time only, disconnect the hydraulic inlet line from the caliper and plug the end. Remove the caliper mounting bolts and shims (if used) and slide the caliper off of the disc.
3. Remove the disc pads from the caliper. If the old ones are to be reused, mark them so that they can be reinstalled in their original positions.
4. Open the caliper bleed screw and drain the fluid. Clean the outside of the caliper and mount it in a vise with padded jaws.

Caution When cleaning any brake components, use only brake fluid or denatured alcohol. Never use a mineral-based solvent, such as gasoline or paint thinner, since it will swell and quickly deteriorate rubber parts.

5. Remove the bridge bolts, separate the caliper halves, and remove the two O-ring seals from the transfer holes.
6. Pry the lip on each piston dust boot from its groove and remove the piston assemblies and springs from the bores. If necessary, air pressure may be used to force the pistons out of the bores, using care to prevent them from popping out of control.
7. Remove the boots and seals from the pistons and clean the pistons in brake fluid. Blow out the caliper passages with an air hose.
8. Inspect the cylinder bores for scoring, pitting, or corrosion. Corrosion is a pitted or rough condition not to be confused with staining. Light rough spots may be removed by rotating crocus cloth, using finger pressure, in the bores. Do not polish with an in and out motion or use any other abrasive.
9. If the pistons are pitted, scored, or worn, they must be replaced. A corroded or deeply scored caliper should also be replaced.
10. Check the clearance of the pistons in the bores using a feeler gauge. Clearance should be 0.002-0.006 in. If there is excessive clearance the caliper must be replaced.
11. Replace all rubber parts and lubricate with brake fluid. Install the seals and boots in the grooves in each piston. The seal should be installed in the groove closest to the closed end of the piston with the seal lips facing the closed end. The lip on the boot should be facing the seal.
12. Lubricate the piston and bore with brake fluid. Position the

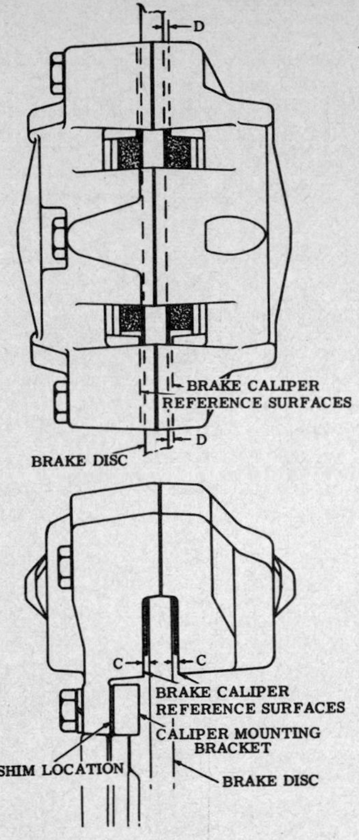

Alignment of caliper to disc—American Motors Cars

piston return spring, large coil first, in the piston bore.

13. Install the piston in the bore, taking great care to avoid damaging the seal lip as it passes the edge of the cylinder bore.
14. Compress the lip on the dust boot into the groove in the caliper. Be sure the boot is fully seated in the groove, as poor sealing will allow contaminants to ruin the bore.
15. Position the O-rings in the cavities around the caliper transfer holes, and fit the caliper halves together. Install the bridge bolts (lubricated with brake fluid) and be sure to torque to specification.
16. Install the disc pads in the caliper and remount the caliper on the hub (see Disc Pad Replacement). Connect the brake line to the caliper and bleed the brakes (see Brake Bleeding). Replace the wheels. Recheck the brake fluid level, check the brake pedal travel, and road test the vehicle.

Caliper Alignment Procedure for American Motors Cars

1. Check dimension "C" on either side of the disc (rotor). Both measurements should be within 0.010 in. of each other.
2. Check dimension "D" at both ends of the caliper. The measurements between the caliper reference surface and disc at both ends of the caliper should be within 0.005 in. of each other.
3. Add or remove shims as required to bring the dimensions to within the tolerance limits.

Budd 4 Piston Brake

Disc Pad Replacement

See Bendix 4 Piston Brake—Disc Pad Replacement. Procedure is identical except that the Budd brake has a retainer spring that must be unhooked to release the disc pads.

Servicing the Caliper Assembly

See Bendix 4 Piston Brake—Servicing the Caliper Assembly. Prodecure is identical except that:

1. The piston boot has a retaining spring. It can be removed and installed with a small screwdriver, and should be fully seated in its groove upon assembly of the caliper.

2. The piston dust boot should be installed so that the lip of the boot is toward the piston insulator pad.

3. The piston seal does not need to be installed in its groove in any special manner.

Delco-Moraine 4 Piston Brake

Disc Pad Replacement

1. Raise the car and remove the front wheels.

Caution To prevent paint damage from brake fluid, be sure to remove part of brake fluid (don't re-use) from master cylinder and to keep the master cylinder covered. Do not allow cylinder to drain too low or air will be pumped into system.

2. Remove and discard the cotter pin from the end of the pad retaining pin. Remove the retaining pin or pins. If old pads are to be re-used, mark them so that they can be returned to their original positions.

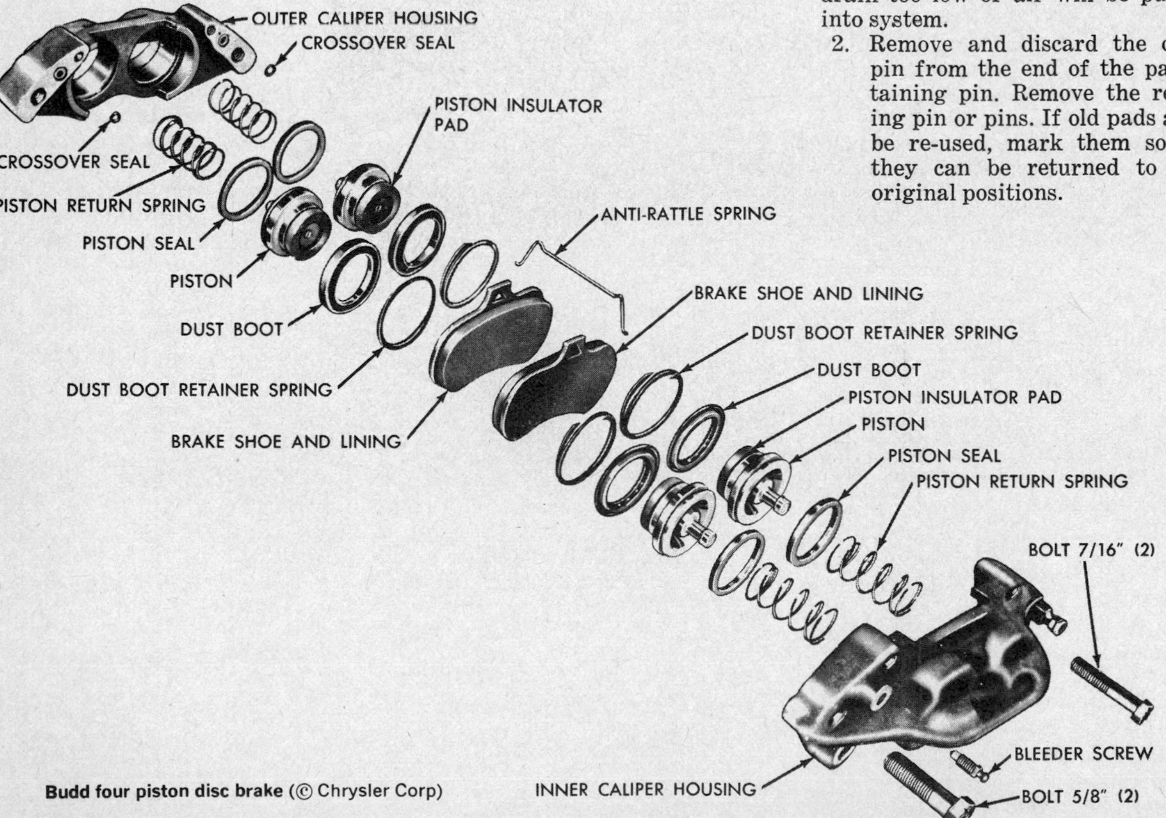

Budd four piston disc brake (© Chrysler Corp)

3. Push one pad back so that it is as far away from the disc as possible. Remove that pad and replace it with a new one. Replace the second pad in the same manner. Pistons are spring loaded so it will be difficult to insert the new pad. To facilitate this job, use a stiff, long-bladed putty knife to hold back the pistons while inserting the new pad. If this fails to work, it may be necessary to release some of the fluid pressure by loosening the bleeder screw. This will require bleeding air from the system later.

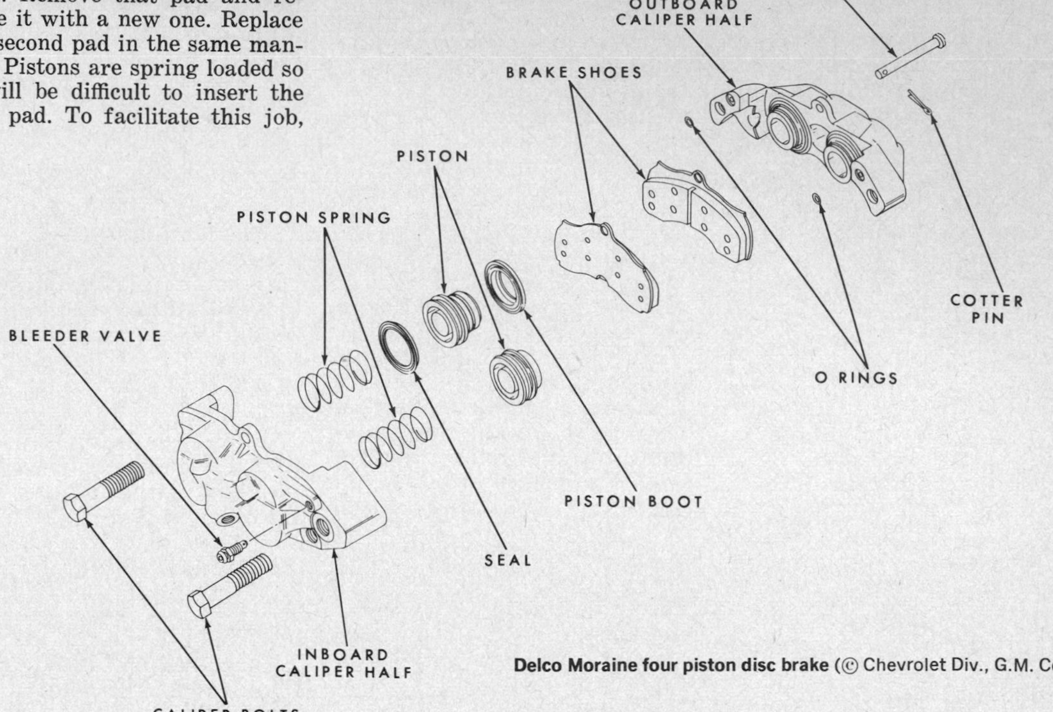

Delco Moraine four piston disc brake (© Chevrolet Div., G.M. Corp)

NOTE: pads are interchangeable from inboard to outboard and right to left on all cars except the Corvette. Disc pads for the Corvette have more metal showing (in relation to the lining centerline) at one end of the pad, and this end must be towards the front of the car. To remove Corvette pads lift straight out, to remove all others swivel one end up and lift out. Shims (if any) between the pads and pistons should be replaced in the exact position as removed.

4 With new pads in place install the retaining pin and lock it in place with a new cotter pin.
5. Replace the wheels, check the brake fluid level, check brake pedal travel, and road test the car.

Servicing the Caliper Assembly

See Bendix 4 Piston Brake—Servicing the Caliper Assembly. Procedure is identical except that:

1. When the pistons are installed in the caliper, a small screwdriver must be used to "tuck" the lip of the piston seal into the caliper bore (Step 13).
2. Corvette rear disc brakes have only one transfer hole and O-ring (Step 5).
3. Each piston boot has a retaining ring. It can be pried out using the piston as a fulcrum. When installing the ring in the piston bore make sure it is seated evenly flush or below the machined face of the caliper (Steps 6 & 13).
4. Piston to bore clearance should be from 0.0045-0.010 in. (except Corvette rear which is 0.0035-0.009 in. (Step 10).
5. The piston seal lip faces toward the spring end of the piston, and the fold in the piston boot faces toward the seal (Step 14).
6. Slide the caliper over the disc. A putty knife can be used to hold back the pistons so that the caliper can be completely lowered into position. The caliper should be positioned carefully to avoid tearing the rubber boot on the edge of the disc. Secure the caliper to the mounting bracket and torque to specifications. Install the pads as instructed earlier (Step 16).
7. When the brake hose is connected it should not be twisted or touch other parts at any time during suspension or steering travel (Step 16).

Kelsey-Hayes 4 Piston Brake

Disc Pad Replacement

See CAUTION under Delco-Moraine 4 Piston Brake.

1. Raise the car and remove the front wheels.
2. Remove the retainer bolts and the retainer(s).
3. Using two pairs of pliers, grasp the outer ends of one of the pads and pull straight out. Push the two pistons into their bores using a flat metal bar and install a new disc pad. Repeat for the second pad.
4. Install the retainer(s) and bolts.
5. Replace the wheels, check the brake fluid level, check brake pedal travel, and road test the car.

Servicing the Caliper Assembly

See Bendix 4 Piston Brake—Servicing the Caliper Assembly. Procedure is identical except that:

1. This unit does not use internal transfer passages with O-rings, an external crossover line is used instead. It must be removed before the caliper is disassembled.
2. The piston seal is not installed on the piston, but is installed in the groove in the piston bore.
3. This unit does not use piston return springs.
4. Caliper is mounted on disc and then pads are installed.

Delco-Moraine Single Piston Brake

Disc Pad Replacement

See CAUTION under Delco-Mo-

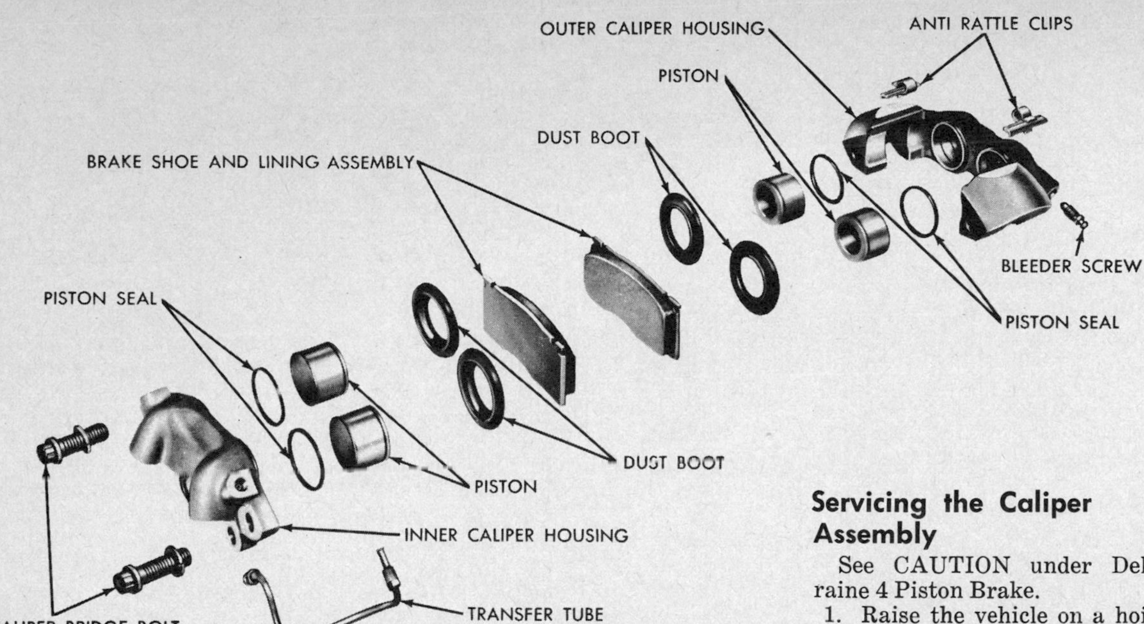

Kelsey-Hayes four piston disc brake (© Chrysler Corp)

raine 4 Piston Brake.

1. Drain about ⅔ of the fluid from the master cylinder. Discard the fluid. Raise the vehicle on a hoist and remove the front wheels.
2. Place a "C" clamp on the caliper so that the solid side of the clamp rests against the back of the caliper and the screw end rests against the metal part of the outboard shoe. Tighten the clamp until the caliper moves enough to bottom the piston in the bore. Remove the clamp.
3. Remove the caliper mounting bolts or guide pin retainers and guide pins (throw the old retainers away) and lift the caliper away from the disc.
4. Remove the disc pads (mark them as to location) and inspect the caliper for fluid leaks and damage. Lubricate with silicon and install new sleeves and bushings in caliper ears.
5. Place the inboard pad in the caliper so that the bottom edge contacts the piston and the two spring ends, and press the pad flat against the piston. When properly seated, the ends of the spring should not extend more than 0.10 in. beyond the metal part of the pad.

NOTE: most 1970 and later cars use a different type of spring to locate the pad. The clip-type spring must be assembled onto the pad before the pad is placed over the piston.

6. Place the outboard pad in the caliper so that the two ears on the pad fit over the ears on the caliper. Squeeze the ears on the pad tight around the caliper ears with a pair of pliers, except on subcompact cars.
7. Position the caliper assembly onto the disc, align the mounting holes, and make sure that the brake line isn't twisted.
8. Install the mounting bolts (making sure that they pass under the retaining ears on the inboard shoe) and torque to specification. On sub compacts, install the mounting pins with new retainers.
9. Check the brake fluid level and pump the brake pedal to seat the linings against the disc. Replace the wheels and road test the car.

Servicing the Caliper Assembly

See CAUTION under Delco-Moraine 4 Piston Brake.

1. Raise the vehicle on a hoist and remove the front wheels.
2. Working on one side at a time only, disconnect the brake hose from the steel brake line and cap the fittings. Remove the U-shaped retainer from the hose fitting (if applicable).
3. Remove the caliper mounting bolts or guide pin retainers and guide pins (throw the old retainers away) and lift the caliper away from the disc.
4. Clean the holes and the bushing grooves in the caliper ears, and wipe all dirt from the mounting bolts. If the bolts are corroded or damaged they should be replaced.

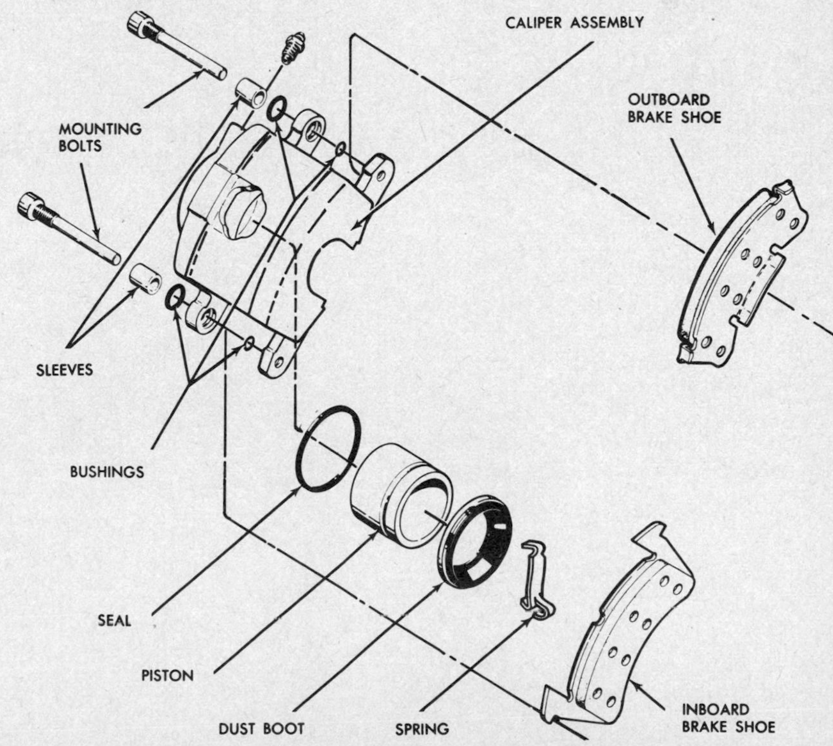

Delco-Moraine single piston disc brake (© Chevrolet Div., G.M. Corp)

5. Remove the shoe support springs (if applicable) from the piston.
6. Remove the sleeves from the ears of the caliper with a suitable drift pin. Remove the rubber bushings from the grooves in the caliper ears.
7. Remove the brake hose, drain the brake fluid, and clean the outside of the caliper.
8. Pad the inside of the caliper with towels and direct compressed air into the brake fluid inlet hole to remove the piston.

Caution To prevent damage to the piston use just enough air pressure to ease it out of the bore. Do not attempt to catch or protect the piston with the hand since this may cause serious injury.

9. Use a screwdriver to pry the boot out of the caliper. Avoid scratching the bore.
10. Remove the piston seal from its groove in the caliper bore. *Do not use a metal tool of any type for this operation.*
11. Blow out all passages in the caliper and bleeder valve. Clean the piston and piston bore with fresh brake fluid.
12. Examine the piston for scoring, scratches, or corrosion. If any of these conditions exist the piston must be replaced, as it is plated and cannot be refinished.
13. Examine the bore for the same defects. Light rough spots may be removed by rotating crocus cloth, using finger pressure, in the bore. Do not polish with an in and out motion or use any other abrasive.
14. Lubricate the piston bore and the new rubber parts with fresh brake fluid. Position the seal in the piston bore groove.
15. Lubricate the piston with brake fluid and assemble the boot into the piston groove so that the fold faces the open end of the piston.
16. Insert the piston into the bore, taking care not to unseat the seal.
17. Force the piston to the bottom of the bore. (This will require a force of 50-100 lbs.). Seat the boot lip around the caliper counterbore. Proper seating of the boot is very important for sealing out contaminants.
18. Install the brake hose into the caliper using a new copper gasket.
19. Lubricate the new sleeves and rubber bushings. Install the bushings in the caliper ears. Install the sleeves so that the end toward the disc pad is flush with the machined surface.

NOTE: lubrication of the sleeves and bushings is essential to ensure the proper operation of the sliding caliper design.

20. Install the shoe support spring (if applicable) in the piston.
21. Install the disc pads in the caliper and remount the caliper on the hub (see Disc Pad Replacement).
22. Reconnect the brake hose to the steel brake line. Install the retainer clip. Bleed the brakes (see Brake Bleeding).
23. Replace the wheels, check the brake fluid level, check the brake pedal travel, and road test the vehicle.

Kelsey-Hayes Single Piston Brake (Chrysler)

See CAUTION under Delco-Moraine 4 Piston Brake.

Disc Pad Replacement

Floating Caliper

1. Raise the vehicle on a hoist and remove front wheels.
2. Working on only one brake at a time, remove the caliper guide pins and positioners which attach caliper to adapter. Lift the caliper away from the disc.
3. Remove (and discard) the positioners and inner bushings from the guide pins, and the outboard bushings from the caliper.
4. Slide the disc pads out of the caliper, and carefully push the piston back into the bore.
5. Lubricate new outboard bushings and work them into position from the ouboard side of the caliper.
6. Slide the new disc pads into position (outboard pad in the retaining spring) and carefully slide the caliper assembly over the rotor.
7. Lubricate and install new inner bushings in the caliper. Install new positioners on the guide pins with the open ends toward the outside.
8. Install the assembled guide pins from the inboard side and press in while threading pin into adap-

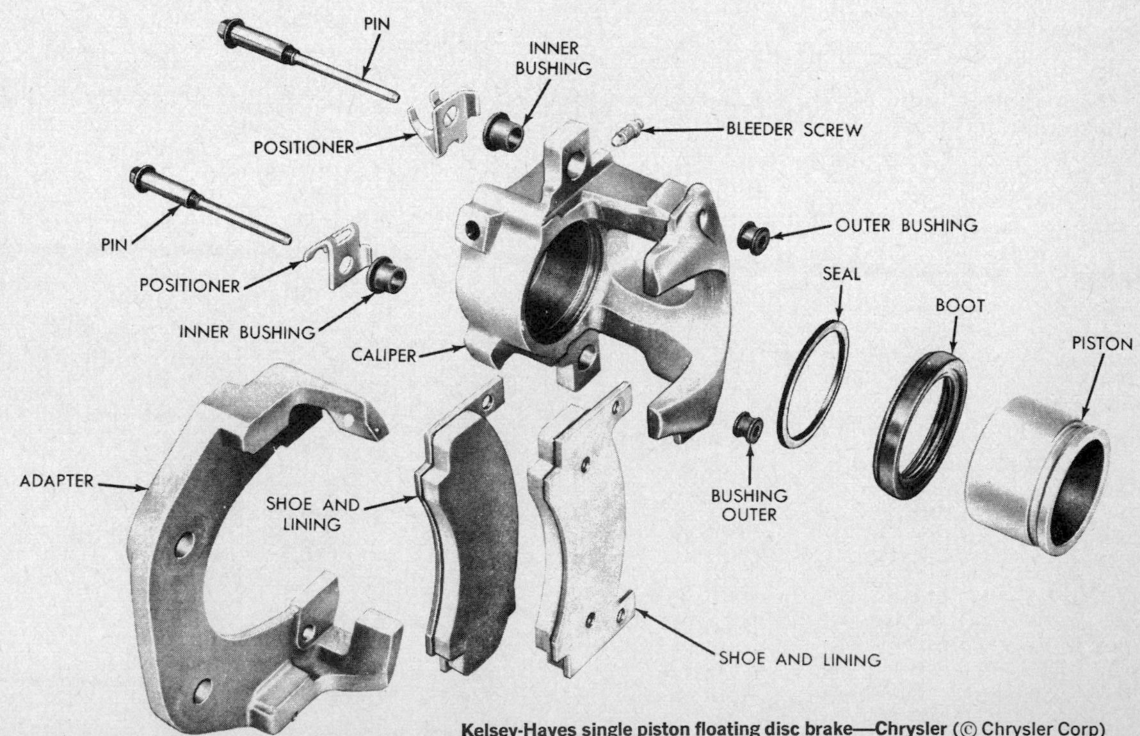

Kelsey-Hayes single piston floating disc brake—Chrysler (© Chrysler Corp)

ter. *Use extreme care to avoid crossing threads.* Tighten to specifications. Be sure the tabs of the positioners are over the machined surfaces of the caliper.

9. Check the brake fluid level and pump the brake pedal to seat the linings against the disc. Replace the wheels and road test the car.

Sliding Caliper

1. Jack up the car and remove the wheel and tire.
2. Remove the caliper retaining clips and anti-rattle springs.
3. Remove the caliper from the disc by slowly sliding the caliper and brake pad assembly out and away from the disc.
4. Remove the outboard pad from the caliper by prying between the pad and the caliper fingers. Remove the inboard pad from the caliper support by the same method.

NOTE: Safety-wire the caliper to the suspension while removing the inboard pad.

5. Push the pistons to the bottom of their bores. This may be done with a pair of large pliers or by placing a flat metal bar against the pistons and depressing the pistons with a steady force. This operation is much easier with the cover removed from the master cylinder.
6. Slide the new pads into the caliper and caliper support. The ears of the pad should rest on the bridges of the caliper.
7. Install the caliper on the disc and install the caliper retaining clips and anti-rattle springs. Pump the brake pedal until it is firm.
8. Check the fluid level in the master cylinder and add fluid as needed.
9. Install the wheel and tire.
10. Road-test the car. The car may pull to one side, but the pull should disappear shortly as the pads wear in.

Caliper Removal and Installation

1. Raise the car and support it securely with jackstands.
2. Remove the wheel and tire assembly from the car.
3. Detach the brake hose from the frame mounting bracket. Plug the brake tube to prevent fluid loss.
4. a. On 1969-72 models and all intermediates, remove the guide pins and positioners attaching the caliper to the adapter.
   b. On 1973 and later models (except intermediates), remove the screw, clip, and anti-rattle spring attaching the caliper to the adapter.
5. Slide the caliper assembly away from the disc. Hold the outboard pad while doing this so that it can't fall out.
6. Remove the pads if the caliper is being overhauled.
7. Install the calipers. Connect the brake hose and bleed the brake system.

Servicing the Caliper Assembly

Floating Caliper—1969-72 and All Intermediates

1. Remove the caliper assembly from the car *without* disconnecting the hydraulic line.
2. Support the caliper assembly on the upper control arm and surround it with shop towels to absorb any brake fluid. Slowly depress the brake pedal until the piston is pushed out of its bore.

Caution Do not use compressed air to force the piston from its bore; injury could result.

3. Disconnect the brake line from the caliper and plug it to prevent fluid loss.
4. Mount the caliper in a soft-jawed vise and clamp lightly. Do not tighten the vise too much or the caliper will become distorted.
5. Work the dust boot out with your fingers.
6. Use a small pointed *wooden* or *plastic* stick to work the piston seal out of the groove in the bore. Discard the seal.

Caution Using a screwdriver or other metal tool could scratch the piston bore.

7. Using the same wooden or plastic stick, press the outer bushings out of the housing. Discard the old bushings. Remove the inner bushings in the same manner. Discard them as well.
8. Clean all parts in denatured alcohol or brake fluid. Blow out all bores and passages with compressed air.
9. Inspect the piston and bore for scoring or pitting. Replace the piston if necessary. Bores with light scratches or corrosion may be cleaned with crocus cloth. Bores with deep scratches may be honed if you do not increase the bore diameter more than 0.002 in. Replace the housing if the bore must be enlarged beyond this.

NOTE: Black stains are caused by piston seals and are harmless.

10. If the bore had to be honed, clean its grooves with a stiff, non-metallic rotary brush. Clean the bore twice by flushing it out with brake fluid and drying it with a soft, lint-free cloth.

Caliper assembly is as follows:

1. Clamp the caliper in a soft-jawed vise; do not overtighten.
2. Dip a new piston seal in brake fluid or the lubricant supplied with the rebuilding kit. Position the new seal in one area of its groove and gently work it into place with clean fingers, so that it is correctly seated. Do not use an old seal.
3. Coat a new boot with brake fluid or lubricant (as above), leaving a generous amount inside.
4. Insert the boot in the caliper and work it into the groove, using your fingers only. The boot will snap into place once it is correctly positioned. Run your forefinger around the inside of the boot to make sure that it is correctly seated.
5. Install the bleed screw in its hole and plug the fluid inlet on the caliper.
6. Coat the piston with brake fluid or lubricant. Spread the boot with your fingers and work the piston into the boot.
7. Depress the piston; this will force the boot into its groove on the piston. Remove the plug and bottom the piston in the bore.
8. Compress the flanges of new guide pin bushings and work them into place by pressing *in* on the bushings with your fingertips, until they are seated. Make sure that the flanges cover the housing evenly on all sides.
9. Install the caliper on the car as previously outlined.

Sliding Caliper—1973-76 (Except Intermediates)

The overhaul procedure for these calipers is identical to that for the floating caliper, except that there are no guide pin bushings to be removed or installed.

Kelsey-Hayes Single Piston Brake (American Motors)

For disc brake service procedures for 1971-74 AMC models, see the floating caliper service sections for "Kelsey-Hayes Single Piston Brake (Chrysler)."

For 1975-76 AMC disc brake service procedures, see the sections for 1972-76 Continental, Thunderbird, etc. sliding caliper disc brakes, in the "Kelsey-Hayes Single Piston (Ford)" section.

Kelsey-Hayes Single Piston Brake (Ford)

Disc Pad Replacement—Floating Caliper

1969 (All Models)

1. Raise the vehicle on a hoist and remove the front wheels. Discon-

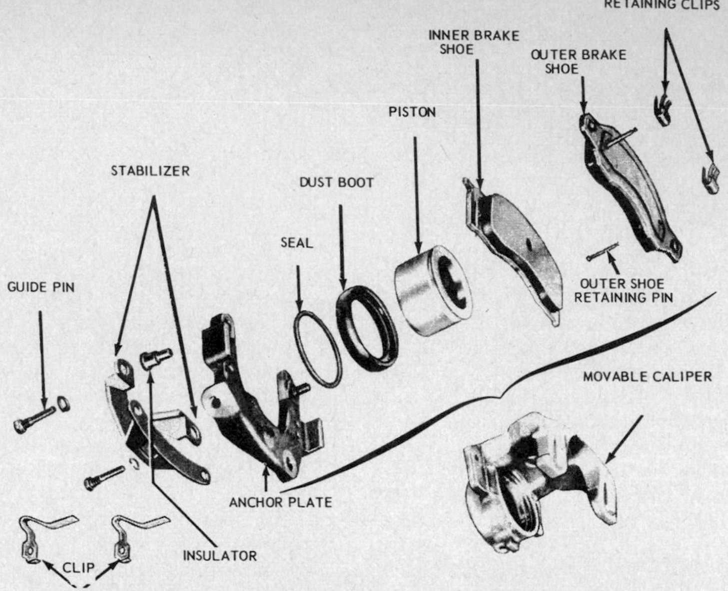

Kelsey-Hayes single piston disc brake—Ford (© Ford Motor Co)

nect the brake line from the caliper and cap the end to prevent leakage.

See CAUTION under Delco-Moraine 4 Piston Brake.

2. Remove the lockwires from the two mounting bolts and lift the caliper away from the rotor.
3. Remove the retaining clips with a screwdriver and slide the outboard pad and retaining pins out of the caliper. Remove the inboard pad. Loosen the bleed screw and drain fluid.
4. Slide the new inboard pad into the caliper so that the tabs are between the retaining clips and anchor plate and the backing plate lies flush against the piston.
5. Insert the outboard pad retaining pins into the outboard pad and position in caliper.

NOTE: stabilizer, insulators, pad clips and pins should always be replaced when disc pads are replaced.

6. Hold the retaining pins in place (one at a time) with a short drift pin or dowel and install the retaining clips.
7. Slide the caliper assembly over the disc and align the mounting bolt holes.
8. Install the lower bolt finger-tight. Install the upper bolt and torque to specification. Torque the lower bolt to specification. Safety wire both bolts.

Caution Do not deviate from this procedure. The alignment of the anchor plate depends on the proper sequence of bolt installation.

9. Check the brake fluid level and pump the brake pedal to seat the linings against the disc. Replace the wheels and road test the car.

1970-71 Thunderbird, Continental Mark III 1970-72 Ford, Mercury, Lincoln

1. Check brake fluid level in the large (primary) reservoir of the master cylinder. Remove enough fluid so that this reservoir is only half full. Do not re-use this fluid, throw it away.
2. Remove the wheel and tire assembly.
3. Remove the inboard pad hold down clips.
4. Using a small screwdriver, remove the retaining clips from the outboard pad and remove the pad.
5. Remove the caliper locating pins (2) from the back of the caliper.
6. Remove the upper stabilizer.
7. Remove the caliper assembly from the anchor plate and detach the outboard pad and retaining pins from the caliper.
8. Using a piece of wire, hang the caliper from the upper control arm.
9. Remove the caliper locating pin insulators from the anchor plate.
10. Remove the inboard pad and inspect the disc surfaces for wear.
11. Install the inboard pad to the anchor plate. Insert new locating pin insulators into the anchor plate.

NOTE: when replacing pads, install new stabilizer, insulators, shoe clips and pins. It may help to wet insulators with water before installing.

12. Install the inboard pad hold down clips and tighten bolts.
13. The piston must be fully retracted into the cylinder before the caliper and pad assembly will fit over the disc. Retracting the piston can be made easier by fabricating a retracting tool using a bolt, a nut, a used outer brake pad and a retaining spring.
14. Position the tool onto the caliper holding it in place with the retaining spring. Gradually turn in on the bolt pausing to allow the piston to pull in the seal. Make sure the piston is fully bottomed in the cylinder to create proper clearance between the pads. Inspect piston dust boot and replace if cracked. See Servicing the Caliper Assembly for replacement procedures.
15. Install the outer brake pad, retaining pins and new retainer clips.
16. Join the caliper assembly to the anchor plate.
17. Install the stabilizers to caliper.
18. Check the brake fluid level and pump the brake pedal to seat the pads against the disc. Install the wheels and road test the car.

1970 Fairlane 1970-71 Torino, 1970-71 Montego, 1970-73 Mustang and Cougar

1. Make sure large master cylinder

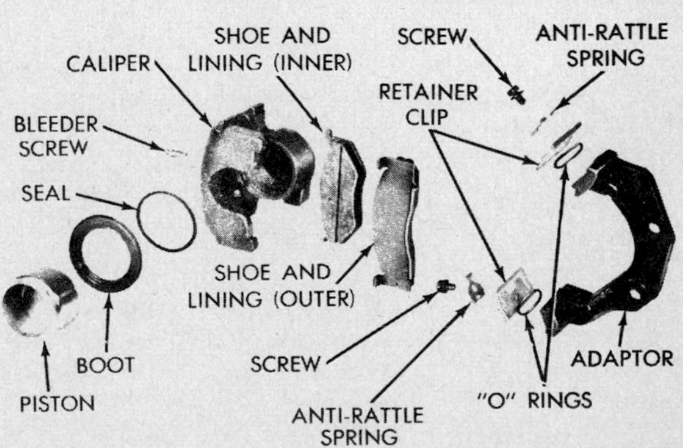

Kelsey-Hayes single piston sliding caliper disc brake—Chrysler (© Chrysler Corp)

reservoir is only half full.
2. Remove the front wheel and tire.
3. Disconnect and plug the brake line if necessary.
4. Remove the caliper locating pins and stabilizer bolts.
5. Lift caliper off disc. If working on both wheels, mark calipers right or left.
6. Remove the inboard pad hold down clips and the pin insulators from the anchor plate.
7. Remove the inboard pad.
8. Using a small screwdriver, lift the outer pad retaining clips off the retaining pins. Remove the outer pad.
9. Insert new caliper locating pin insulators in the anchor plate.
10. Install the inboard pad retaining clips.
11. Using a piston retracting tool (see steps 13 & 14 of Disc Pad Replacement for Ford, Mercury, etc.), push the piston completely into its cylinder.
12. Install outer pad and retaining clips.
13. Install the caliper onto the disc being careful not to pinch the piston boot between the inner pad and the piston.
14. Attach a new stabilizer to the caliper with clean locating pins.
15. Attach the stabilizer to the anchor plate.
16. Connect brake hose (if previously disconnected) using new copper washers, one on each side of the hose fitting. Bleed brakes.
17. Check the brake fluid level and pump the brake pedal to seat the pads against the disc. Install the wheels and road test the car.

Sliding caliper disc brake—1972-76 Mark IV, Thunderbird, Montego, Torino
(© Ford Motor Co)

Disc Pad Replacement—Sliding Caliper

1972-76 Continental Mark IV
1972-76 Thunderbird
1972-76 Montego
1972-76 Torino
1973-76 Continental
1973-76 Ford
1973-76 Mercury
1975-76 Cougar
1975-76 Maverick
1975-76 Comet

1. Raise the car, safely support it and remove the tire and wheel assembly.
2. Remove the retaining screw from the caliper retaining key.
3. Using a hammer and drift, remove the caliper retaining key and support spring from the anchor plate. Be careful not to damage key.
4. Push the caliper down against the anchor plate and rotate the upper end off the anchor plate.
5. Remove the inboard pad from the anchor plate. Do not lose the anti-rattle clip. Tap lightly on the outer pad to free it from the caliper. If the original pads are to be reused, mark them as to location for correct installation.
6. Clean all components and inspect for damage, leakage and excessive wear.

NOTE: if the pads on one wheel are replaced it is necessary to replace those on the other wheel to maintain equal braking action.

7. When installing new pads, use a 4 in. c-clamp and a block of wood measuring 1-¾ in. x 1 in. x ¾ in. thick. This will aid in seating the piston in its cylinder so that the caliper will fit over the new pads when installed.
8. Install the anti-rattle clip on the lower inboard pad support located on the anchor plate. The pigtail of the clip must be toward the inside of the plate. Place the inner pad on the anchor plate.
9. Install the outer pad with the upper flanges over the shoulders on the caliper legs. If the old pads are reused, be certain they are installed in their original positions.
10. If previously used, remove the C-clamp from the caliper since the piston will remain seated in its cylinder.
11. Position the caliper assembly lower V-groove on the anchor plate lower abutment surface.
12. Pivot the caliper housing upward toward the disc until the outer edge of the piston dust boot is about ¼ in. from the upper edge of inboard pad.
13. Place a piece of thin cardboard between the inboard pad and the lower half of the piston dust boot to prevent pinching of the boot when rotating the caliper onto the disc.
14. Continue to rotate the caliper onto the disc until a slight resistance is felt.
15. Gradually remove the cardboard as the caliper rotates onto the disc. Complete the rotation onto the disc and completely remove the cardboard.
16. Slide the caliper up against the upper anchor plate abutment and center it over the lower anchor plate abutment.
17. Install the caliper support spring and key into the opening between the lower end of the caliper and the lower anchor plate abutment. The hole in the slot must be centered over the threaded hole in the anchor plate.
18. Install the key retaining screw and torque to 12-16 ft. lbs.
19. Check the brake fluid level and pump the brake pedal to seat the pads against the disc. Install the wheels and road test the car.

1971-76 Pinto, 1974-76 Mustang II

1. Raise car and support safely. Remove wheel and tire assembly.
2. Remove the two cotter pins from the retaining key.
3. Using a hammer and drift, carefully remove the key.
4. Push in on the caliper assembly and lift it away from the anchor plate.

NOTE: do not stretch or twist the brake hose.

5. Using wire, temporarily suspend the caliper assembly from the upper suspension arms.
6. If brake pads are to be reused,

mark them as to correct location.

7. Remove the pads from the anchor plate.
8. Clean the caliper, anchor plate and disc and inspect them for leakage, damage or excessive wear.

NOTE: if the shoes are replaced on one wheel they must also be replaced on the other wheel to maintain balanced brake action.

9. When installing new pads, it is necessary to compress the piston in its cylinder to provide enough clearance for the caliper to fit over the pads. To perform this, place a block of wood (1-¾" x 1" x ¾" thick) on the piston and clamp down on it with a 4 in. C-clamp.
10. Place pads and anti-rattle clips in anchor plate.
11. Remove the C-clamp from the piston and remove the wire holding the caliper to the suspension arm.
12. Place the caliper on the anchor plate so that the lower edge of the caliper is on top of the rear caliper support spring.
13. Pivot the caliper over the pads until the upper edge of the caliper can be pushed over the forward caliper support spring.
14. Using a heavy screwdriver, hold the caliper over the upper support spring and against the anchor plate. Insert the retaining key.
15. Install two new stainless steel cotter pins in the key.
16. Check the brake fluid level and pump the brake pedal to seat the pads against the disc. Install the wheels and road test the car.

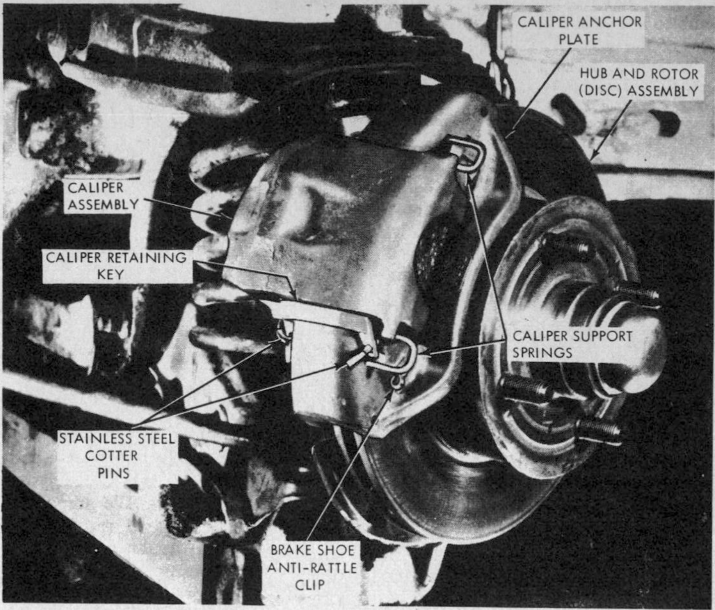

Pinto and Mustang II sliding caliper disc brake (© Ford Motor Co)

Servicing the Caliper Assembly—Floating Caliper

1969-71 All Models Except Pinto 1972 All Models Except Pinto, Continental Mark IV, Thunderbird, Montego, and Torino 1973 Mustang and Cougar

1. Raise the vehicle on a hoist and remove the front wheels.
2. Disconnect and plug the brake line.
3. Remove the lockwires from the two caliper mounting bolts and remove the bolt. Lift the caliper off the disc.
4. Remove and discard the locating pin insulators. Replace all rubber parts at reassembly.
5. Remove the retaining clips with a screwdriver and slide the outboard pad and retaining pins out of the caliper. Remove the inboard pad. Loosen the bleed screw and drain the brake fluid.
6. Remove the two small bolts and caliper stabilizers.
7. Remove the inboard pad retaining clips and bolts.
8. Clean and inspect all parts, and reinstall on anchor plate. Do not tighten stabilizer bolts at this time.
9. Remove the piston by applying compressed air to the fluid inlet hole. Use care to prevent the piston from popping out of control.

Caution Do not attempt to catch the piston with the hand. Use folded towels to cushion it.

10. Remove the piston boot. Inspect the piston for scoring, pitting, or corrosion. The piston must be replaced if there is any visible damage or wear.
11. Remove the piston seal from the cylinder bore. *Do not use any metal tools for this operation.*
12. Clean the caliper with fresh brake fluid. Inspect the cylinder bore for damage or wear. Light defects can be removed by rotating crocus cloth around the bore. Do not use any other type of abrasive.
13. Lubricate all new rubber parts in brake fluid. Install the piston seal in the cylinder groove. Install the boot into its piston groove.
14. Install the piston, open end out, into the bore while working the boot around the outside of the piston. Make sure boot lip is seated in the piston groove.
15. Slide the anchor plate assembly onto the caliper housing and reinstall the locating pins. Tighten pins to specification. Tighten stabilizer anchor plate bolts. Perform Steps 4-8 of Disc Pad Replacement.
16. Connect the brake line and bleed the brakes (see Brake Bleeding).
17. Install the front wheels, recheck the brake fluid level, and road test the car.

Servicing the Caliper Assembly—Sliding Caliper

1972-76 Lincoln-Continental, Continental Mark IV, Thunderbird, Montego, Pinto, Torino, Ford, 1974-76 Maverick, Comet, Cougar, Mercury

To service the caliper on these models, follow the instructions listed for the same models under Disc Pad Replacement—Sliding Caliper. The instructions are identical with one exception—caliper service requires you to disconnect and connect the brake hose from the caliper and bleed the brakes. If it is necessary to remove and install piston, follow steps 6-12 of 1971-75 Pinto.

1971-76 Pinto, 1974-76 Mustang II

1. Raise the car and support safely. Remove the wheel and tire assembly.
2. Disconnect the brake hose from the caliper.
3. Remove the two cotter pins from the retaining key.
4. Using a drift and hammer, remove the retaining key.
5. Press inward on the caliper assembly and lift it away from the anchor plate.
6. Remove the piston by applying air pressure to the caliper fluid port.

IMPORTANT: to prevent piston damage and possible personal injury, place a cloth over the piston before applying air pressure.

7. If the piston is seized in its cylinder, tap lightly around the piston while applying air pressure.

8. Remove and discard the piston dust boot and seal.
9. Clean (using alcohol) and inspect all parts for damage or excessive wear. Replace the piston if pitted or scored or if the chrome plating is worn off.
10. Lightly coat a new piston seal with clean brake fluid and seat it in the piston groove.
11. Install a new dust boot with its flange in the outer groove of the cylinder.
12. Coat the piston with fluid and install in the cylinder. Spread the dust boot over the piston while inserting it in cylinder and seat it in the piston groove.
13. Place the caliper on the anchor plate so that the lower edge of the caliper can be pushed over the forward caliper support spring.
14. Using a heavy screwdriver, hold the caliper over the upper support spring and against the anchor plate. Insert the retaining key.
15. Install two new stainless steel cotter pins in the key.
16. Connect the brake hose and bleed the brakes.
17. Check the brake fluid level and pump the brake pedal to seat the pads against the disc. Install the wheels and road test the car.

Servicing the Disc

Disc Replacement

1. Raise the vehicle on a hoist and remove the wheel.
2. Remove the caliper mounting bolts. Slide the caliper away from the disc and suspend it using a wire loop. On some cars, it is advisable to install a cardboard spacer between the pads to prevent the piston from coming out of its cylinder.
3. Remove the wheel bearing nut from the spindle and remove the outer wheel bearing roller assembly from the hub.

   On Ford sliding caliper brakes, remove the wheel bearing adjusting nut and pull the hub and disc assembly outward enough to loosen the washer and outer wheel bearing. Push the assembly back onto the spindle and remove the washer and outer wheel bearing from the spindle.
4. Remove the hub and disc assembly from the spindle.
5. Installation of hub and disc is in reverse order of removal.

Caution Alignment of the caliper assembly depends on proper sequence of bolt installations on some cars. Check caliper installation procedure under Disc Pad Replacement of proper brake type.

NOTE: the disc is removable from the hub on the Eldorado, Toronado, and Corvette (rear only).

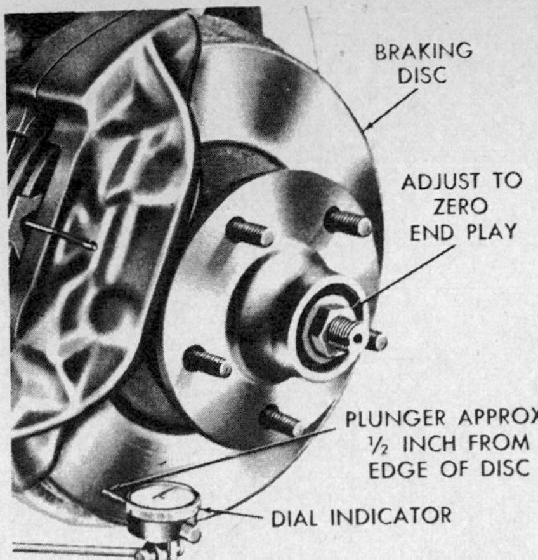

Checking disc runout
(© Chrysler Corp)

To separate the rear disc and hub on a Corvette the three hub-to-disc attaching rivets must be drilled out. This can be done with the hub and rotor mounted on the car. It is not necessary to install new rivets when the disc is installed.

Lateral Runout

Lateral runout is the movement of the disc from side to side (wobble) as it rotates. Excessive runout will result in brake chatter, pedal pumping, excessive pedal travel, or vibration during braking.

To check lateral runout:

1. Tighten the spindle nut until there is no end-play in the bearings, just loose enough to allow wheel to turn.
2. Fasten a dial indicator to the suspension so that the point contacts the disc face about ½ in. from the outer edge.
3. Set the dial to zero. Turn the disc through one complete revolution and check the indicator as the disc moves.

If the runout is more than the allowable maximum the disc and hub assembly should be replaced. Be sure to readjust the spindle nut if its setting was changed while checking the disc.

Parallelism

Parallelism refers to the variations in thickness of the disc. Excessive variation can cause pedal vibration and front end vibration during braking. Parallelism can be checked by measuring thickness at four or more equally spaced points around the braking surface of the disc. All measurements must be made at the same distance from the outer edge of the disc. The disc and hub should be replaced if variations in thickness exceed specification. Do not forget to adjust the spindle nut to specification if its setting was changed while checking the disc.

Rear Disc Brakes—Imperial

Brake Pads and Caliper Service

The sliding caliper which is used on the rear of 1974-76 Imperial models is serviced in the same manner as the Kelsey-Hayes sliding caliper which is used on the front. Disc brake pad changing and caliper removal procedures are identical, except that the rear caliper has a dust shield, which must be removed prior to caliper removal.

Parking Brakes

The disc used on the rear of 1974-76 Imperial has a 7 in. internal parking brake drum. The brake assembly itself is mounted on the rear axle flange and disc adapter.

See the car section for parking brake adjustment procedures.

Rear Disc/Drum Removal and Installation

1. Remove the caliper assembly. See the procedure for removing the sliding caliper from the front wheels of Chrysler products. Do not disconnect the caliper from the brake lines; safety wire it to the rear spring.
2. Remove the inboard pad.
3. Take the plug out of the parking brake adjuster access hole. Insert a brake adjusting tool into the hole and engage the notches on the starwheel. Pry down with the tool to release the adjustment.
4. Pull the disc/drum assembly off the studs.

Installation is the reverse of removal.

Drum Inspection

Measure drum runout and diameter. Variation in drum diameter should not exceed 0.006 in. Reface drums which exceed these specifications. Do not remove more than 0.060 in. from the standard drum diameter. The maximum allowable diameter of 7.090 in. is stamped on the drum.

Parking Brake Shoe Removal and Installation

1. Remove the caliper and disc/drum assembly.
2. Remove the lower brake shoe return spring.
3. Spread the shoes slightly and remove the starwheel adjuster assembly.
4. Remove the upper shoe return spring.
5. Move the shoes off the support and remove the retainers, springs and nails. Remove the shoes.

Installation is as follows:

1. Lubricate the shoe tab contact area on the support plate with

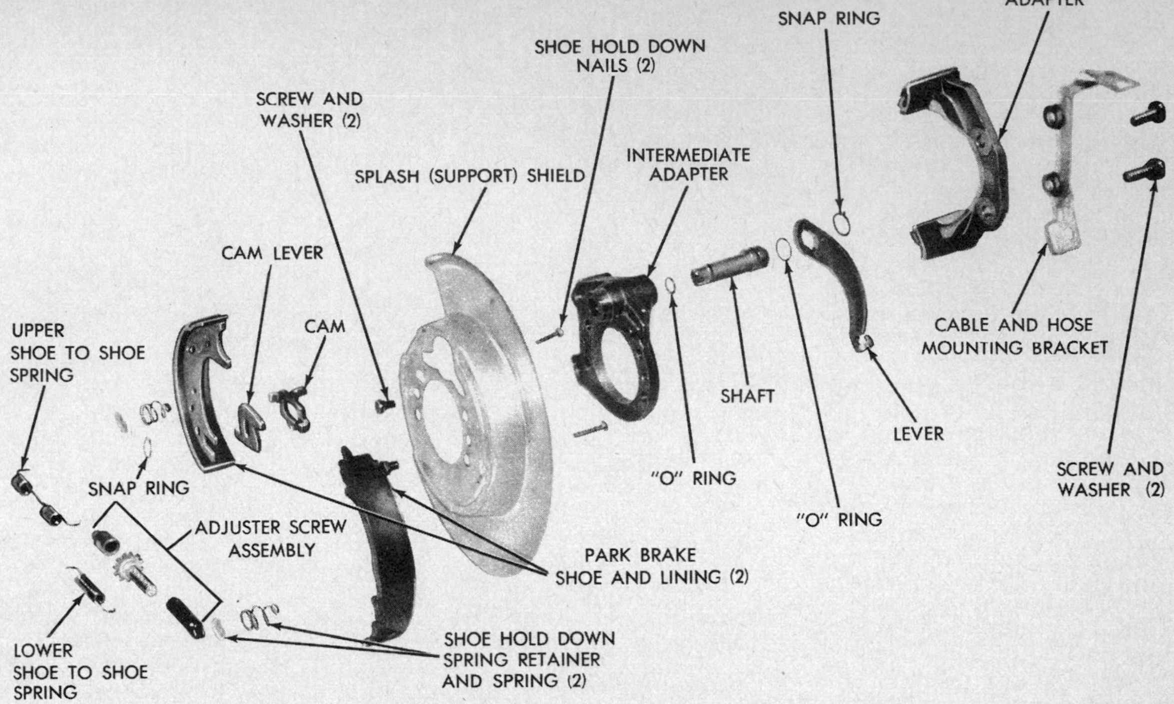

Rear wheel parking brake components—Imperial (© Chrysler Corp)

special brake grease.

2. Position the shoes on the support plate and install the nails, springs, and retainers.
3. Install the upper shoe return spring.
4. Install the starwheel adjuster. The starwheel goes forward on the left side and rearward in the right side.
5. Install the lower shoe return spring.
6. Install the disc/drum and caliper.

Lever, Cam and Shaft Removal and Installation

1. Detach the parking brake cable from the inner operating lever and separate the snap ring retainer from the shaft. Remove the operating lever.
2. Remove the inner shaft snapring and the cam lever. Remove the cam.
3. Pull out the shaft.

Installation is the reverse of removal. Lubricate the shaft with brake grease.

Rear Disc Brakes—Chevrolet Corvette

Pad Replacement and Caliper Service

The Corvette uses Delco-Moraine four-piston fixed caliper disc brakes on the rear wheels, as well as on the front. Rear disc brake pad replacement and caliper service procedures are the same as those for "Delco-Moraine 4 Piston Brake."

Parking Brakes

The discs used on the rear of the Corvette have integral drums which are used as parking brakes only. See the "Chevrolet-Corvette" section for parking brake adjustment procedures.

Corvette Parking Brake Shoe Removal and Installation

1. Jack the car up and remove the rear wheels and tires.
2. Remove the brake caliper from the disc. Do not disconnect the brake line, but remove the line clip from the control arm and hang the caliper above the disc with wire.
3. Drill the disc retaining rivets out and remove the disc from the axle hub. It is not necessary to replace the rivets when the disc is reinstalled.
4. Insert a screwdriver into the adjusting hole and turn the screw several times to expand the shoes.
5. Push the brake shoes forward until the front shoe hold-down spring can be seen through the adjusting hole.
6. Insert a pair of needle-nosed pliers through the hole and grasp the hold-down pin. Depress the spring with a screwdriver inserted from the side and turn the pin 90° to free the spring and retainer. Remove the spring and retainer.
7. Repeat this operation on the rear brake shoe.
8. Retract the shoes by turning the adjuster screw. Pull the shoes from the adjuster and remove the adjuster and spring.
9. Separate the shoes at the anchor pin and lift the shoes up and out of the housing, while allowing the straight part of the return spring to go between the outer

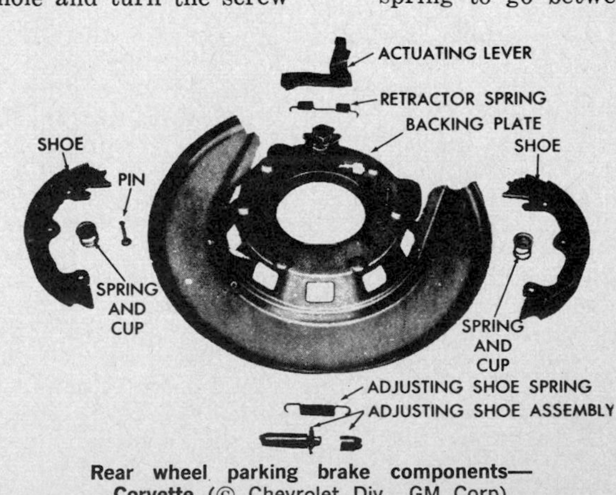

Rear wheel parking brake components—Corvette (© Chevrolet Div., GM Corp)

tip of the anchor pin and the axle flange plate.

10. Lightly lubricate the backing plate shoe contact surfaces, anchor pin, and adjusting screw threads.
11. Install the return spring on the replacement shoes and position the shoes on the anchor pin.
12. Install the adjuster spring and adjuster. Turn the adjuster screw to expand the shoes.
13. Turn the axle shaft flange so that the adjustment hole aligns with the front hold-down spring pin.
14. Push the shoe forward and over the hold-down pin.
15. Install the spring and retainer over the hold-down pin and using needle-nosed pliers and a screwdriver as in step 6, depress the spring and twist the pin 90°.
16. Repeat the above step on the rear shoe. Another pair of needle-nosed pliers will have to be utilized to hold the pin in position, as head of this pin is not accessible.
17. Turn the adjuster screw to retract the shoes.
18. Install the brake disc onto the studs, making sure that the adjustment holes in the disc and flange align.
19. Install the caliper.
20. Adjust the parking brake as described above.
21. Install the tire and wheel and lower the car.

Burnishing New Parking Brake Linings

Perform this procedure after new parking brake shoes have been installed:

1. Adjust the parking brakes.
2. Drive the car at a steady 50 mph and apply the parking brake lever 10 to 12 notches (until a light drag is felt).
3. Hold this speed with the brake applied for 50-60 seconds and then release the brake.

Rear Disc Brakes—Ford Motor Co.

Starting in 1975, rear disc brakes are standard equipment on Continental Mark IV models and are optional on Lincoln, Mercury, Thunderbird, Granada, and Monarch.

The rear sliding caliper assembly is similar to the one used on the front, except for the parking brake mechanism and a bigger anti-rattle spring. The parking brake lever on the caliper is cable-operated by depressing (or releasing) the parking brake pedal under the dash panel.

When the pedal is depressed, the cable rotates the parking brake lever (on the back of the caliper) and the operating shaft (inside the caliper). Three steel balls, which are located in pockets on the opposing heads of the shaft and thrust screw, roll between ramps formed in the pockets. The motion of the balls forces the thrust screw away from the shaft which, in turn, forces the piston and pad assembly against the disc to create braking action.

An automatic adjuster in the piston compensates for pad wear by moving the thrust screw.

Pad Replacement

NOTE: This procedure requires the use of a special service tool.

1. Raise the car and support it with jackstands. Block the front wheels if they remain on the ground.
2. Remove the wheel and tire.
3. Disconnect the cable from the caliper parking brake lever. Be careful not to kink or cut the cable and return spring.
4. Unfasten the setscrew which secures the caliper key. Use a hammer and soft brass drift (if necessary) to slide the support spring and retaining key out of the anchor plate.
5. Push the caliper against the anchor plate and rotate its upper end away from the plate. If a ridge of rust on the disc prevents caliper removal, scrape the rust away with a putty knife or similar blunt tool.
6. If the disc is scored to the point that the caliper still can't be removed, loosen the caliper end retainer ½-turn, after removing the retaining screw and caliper parking brake lever. Also, be sure to matchmark the caliper housing and end retainer to ensure that the retainer is only given ½-turn.

Caution Turning the end retainer more than ½-turn could cause internal fluid leaks in the caliper, which would make caliper rebuilding necessary.

7. Wire the caliper assembly out of the way to avoid stretching or kinking the brake hose.
8. Remove the inner pad assembly from the retaining clip. Tap lightly on the outer pad to free it from the caliper.
9. Mark the pads for proper installation if they are not going to be replaced. Used pads must be returned to the same side from which they were removed.
10. If the pad is worn to within 1/32 in. of any rivet head, replace all of the pads on both rear brakes. Do not replace just one pad or one set of pads; uneven braking will result.

NOTE: Pad replacement requires the use of a special tool to bottom the piston in its bore.

11. Inspect the caliper for leaks. Clean any rust off the caliper and anchor plate sliding surfaces or inner brake pad abutment surfaces on the anchor plate.

Installation is as follows:

1. If the end retainer was loosened in order to remove the caliper, perform the following:

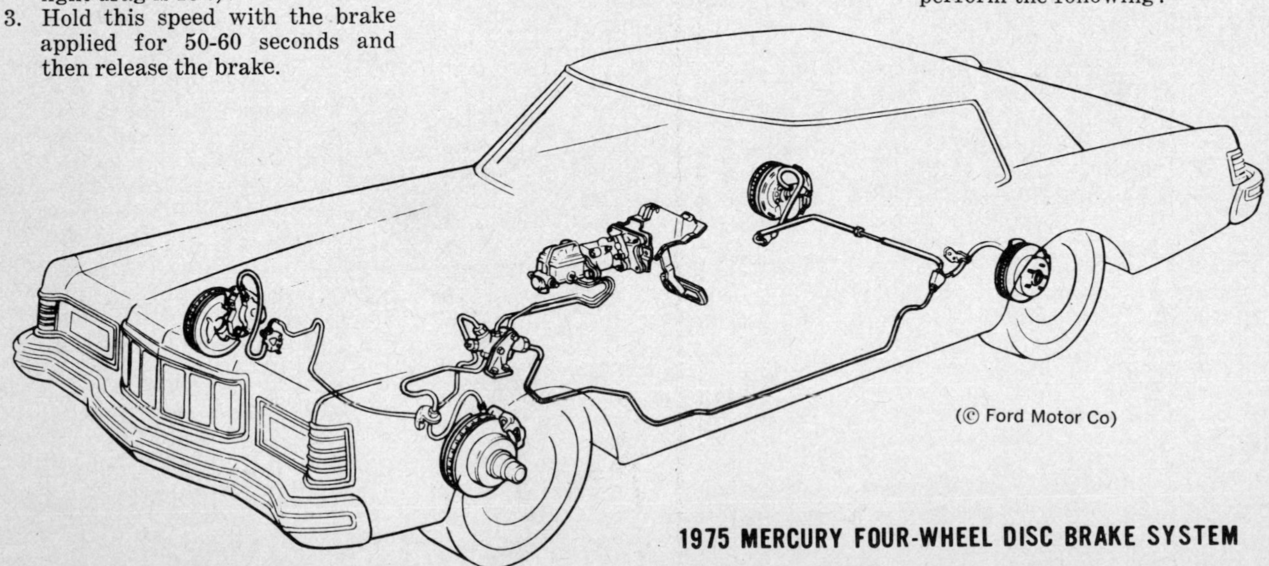

(© Ford Motor Co)

1975 MERCURY FOUR-WHEEL DISC BRAKE SYSTEM

pointing rearward and down. This allows the cable to pass under the axle.

d. Tighten the lever retaining screw to 16-22 ft lbs. Check for free rotation of the lever.

e. Remove the caliper.

2. The following special steps must be performed if new pads are being installed:

a. Remove the disc and install the caliper less the pads. Use only the key to retain the caliper.

b. Seat the special tool firmly against the piston by holding the shaft rotating the tool handle.

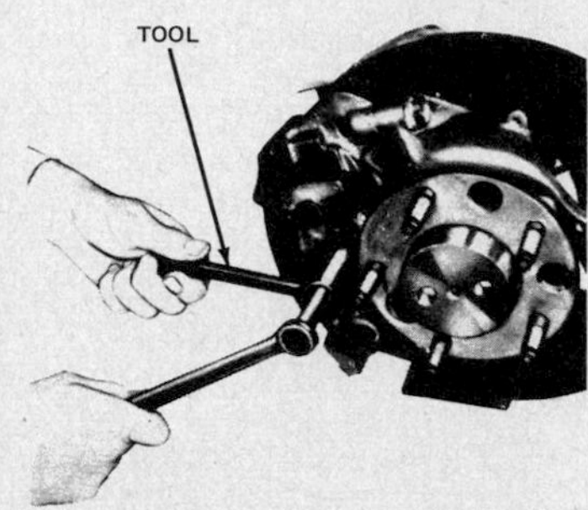

Adjusting the rear caliper piston depth with the special tool (© Ford Motor Co)

c. Loosen the handle ¼-turn. Hold the handle and rotate the tool shaft clockwise until the caliper piston bottoms (it will continue to turn after it bottoms).

d. Rotate the handle until the piston is firmly seated.

e. Remove the caliper and install the disc.

3. Confirm that the brake pad anti-rattle clip is correctly positioned in the lower inner brake pad support, the clip loop should face the inside of the anchor plate.

4. Fit the inner pad assembly on the anchor plate, with the lining facing the disc.

5. Install the outer brake pad with its lower flanges against the caliper leg abutments and its upper flanges against the machined shoulder surfaces.

6. Lubricate the caliper and anchor plate sliding surfaces with special brake lubricant. Keep the lubricant off the pad and disc.

7. Position the caliper housing lower groove against the anchor plate lower abutment surfaces. Rotate the housing until it is completely over the disc. Be careful not to damage the dust boot.

8. Slide the caliper outward until the inner pad is seated firmly against the disc. Measure the outer pad-to-disc clearance. It should be 1/16 in. or less. If it is more, adjust the piston *outward* with the special tool (See step 2). Each ¼-turn of the piston is about 1/16 in. of piston movement.

Caution If piston clearance is more than 1/16 in., the adjuster may pull out of the piston when the service brakes are applied, causing adjuster failure.

9. Center the caliper over the lower anchor plate abutment, while holding it over the upper abutment.

10. Install the retaining spring and key in the keyway and slide them into the opening at the lower end of the caliper and anchor plate abutment. Center the semi-circular slot in the key over the anchor plate setscrew hole. Tighten the setscrew to 12-16 ft lbs.

11. Attach the parking brake cable to the lower lever end.

12. If the caliper was completely removed (lines disconnected), bleed the hydraulic system. Run the engine and lightly pump the service brake pedal 40 times; allow one second between brake applications. Check the parking brake for too much travel or too light operating effort. Repeat the pumping and adjust the cable, if necessary.

13. Install the wheel and tire, remove the jacketstand and lower the car.

14. Make sure that the service brake pedal feels firm and then road-test the car. Check parking brake operation.

Caliper Removal and Installation

Perform all of the necessary procedures in the disc brake pad removal and installation section, and do the following:

1. Prior to removing the caliper, disconnect the rear brake pipe fitting from the hose end at the frame bracket.
2. Plug the brake pipe.
3. Unfasten the horseshoe clip from the hose fitting and separate the hose from the bracket. On Granadas and Monarchs, remove the hose bracket from the spring seat.
4. On Lincoln and Mercury models, unscrew the hose fitting from the caliper. On Mark IV, Granada, Monarch, and Thunderbird models, unfasten the hollow retaining nut which secures the fitting to the caliper.

When installing the caliper, perform the following additional steps.

a. Install the caliper on the anchor plate and secure it with the key, but do not install the pads.

b. Tighten the retainer end to 75-95 ft lbs.

c. Install the caliper parking brake lever with the arm

1. On Lincoln and Mercury models, put a new gasket on the fitting and screw the fitting into the caliper port; tighten to 20-30 ft lbs. On Mark IV, Granada, Monarch, and Thunderbird models; put new gaskets on either side of the fitting outlet and insert the hollow securing bolt through the washers and fitting; tighten to 17-20 ft lbs. On Granada and Monarch be sure to fit the hose pin in the hole on the caliper.
2. Fit the upper end of the flexible hose in the bracket and install the horseshoe clip. Do not twist or coil the brake hose; keep the stripe on the hose straight. On Granada and Monarch, install the hose bracket on the spring seat.
3. Unplug the pipe. Connect the hose to the pipe and tighten the fitting to 10-15 ft lbs.
4. Bleed the brake system.

Caliper Overhaul

1. Remove the caliper assembly from the car.
2. Remove the retaining screw, parking brake lever, and caliper end retainer.
3. Pull out the operating shaft, thrust bearing, and balls from the caliper.
4. Using either a magnet or tweezers, extract the thrust screw anti-rotation pin.
5. Using a ¼ in. Allen key, rotate the thrust screw counterclockwise to remove it.
6. Push the piston/adjuster assembly out of its bore from behind.

NOTE: A special tool is available to do this. Use care not to scratch the bore or press on the piston adjuster can while removing the piston.

7. Remove and discard the following:
   a. Piston seal
   b. Boot
   c. Thrust screw O-ring seal
   d. End retainer O-ring
   e. End retainer lip seal
8. Clean all metal parts in isopropyl alcohol. Dry them with compressed air. Be sure that no foreign material remains in the caliper.
9. Inspect the caliper bores. The thrust screw bore must be smooth and show no sign of pitting.
10. If the piston is pitted, scored, or the plating worn off, replace the piston/adjuster as an assembly. The adjuster can should not be loose, high, or damaged; if it is, replace the piston/adjuster assembly. If brake adjustment is incorrect, replace the piston-/adjuster assembly.

NOTE: The piston and the adjuster must be replaced as an assembly. No attempt to repair the adjuster

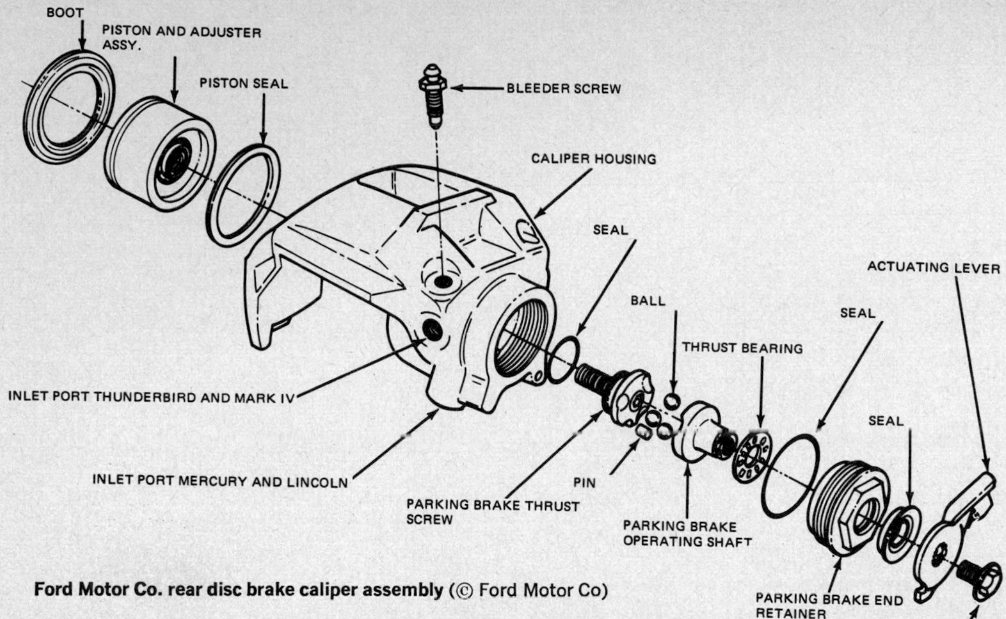

Ford Motor Co. rear disc brake caliper assembly (© Ford Motor Co)

should be made.

11. If in doubt about adjuster operation; check it as follows:
    a. Install the thrust screw in the piston/adjuster.
    b. Pull the two pieces apart about ¼ in. and release them.
    c. When the pieces are pulled apart, the brass drive ring should remain stationary, causing the nut to turn.
    d. When the pieces are released, the nut should remain stationary and the drive ring rotate.
    e. Replace the piston/adjuster if it fails to operate in this manner.
12. Inspect all bearing, sliding, rotating and rolling surfaces for wear, pitting or brinnelling. Replace any parts necessary. A polished appearance on ball paths or bearing surfaces is OK, as long as there is no sign of wear into the surface.

Assembly is as follows:

1. Coat a new piston seal with clean brake fluid. Seat the seal in the groove of the bore. Be sure it is not twisted.
2. Seat the flange of a new dust boot squarely in the caliper bore outer groove.
3. Coat the piston/adjuster assembly with clean brake fluid. Spread the dust boot over the piston and install the piston. Seat the dust boot in the piston-/adjuster groove.
4. Lay the caliper assembly (rear of bore up) in a soft-jawed vise. Do not tighten the vise; housing distortion will result.
5. Fill the piston/adjuster assembly up to the bottom edge of thrust screw bore with clean brake fluid.
6. Install a new O-ring in the thrust screw groove, after coating it with clean brake fluid. Use a ¼ in. Allen key to install the thrust screw in the piston adjuster assembly, until its top surface is flush with the bottom of the threaded bore. Align the notches on the thrust screw with those on the caliper housing. Install the anti-rotation pin.
7. Install one ball in each of the three thrust screw pockets. Coat all components of the parking brake mechanism with a liberal amount of silicone grease.
8. Install the parking brake operating shaft over the balls. Coat the thrust bearing with silicone grease and fit it on the shaft.
9. Install a new lip seal and O-ring on the caliper end retainer. Coat both seals with a light film of silicone grease and install the end retainer on the caliper; tighten it to 75-90 ft lbs. Hold the operating shaft so that it is securely seated against the parking brake mechanism during end retainer installation. If the lip seal is dislocated, reseat it.
10. Install the parking brake lever over its keyed spline, so that it points down and rearward. Torque the lever securing screw to 16-22 ft lbs. Check the lever for freedom of movement.
11. Support the caliper and bottom the piston with the special tool as in steps 2b through d of the disc brake pad replacement procedure.
12. Install the caliper.

Disc Removal and Installation

1. Remove the caliper assembly and wire it out of the way, unless it is to be serviced. Do not remove the anchor plate.
2. If corrosion makes identification difficult, mark the raised (not the braking) surface of the disc "RIGHT" or "LEFT" prior to removal.
3. Remove the securing nuts and take the disc off the axle shaft.

Installation is as follows:

1. If a new disc is being used, remove its protective coating with carburetor degreaser.
2. Identify the left and right discs before installation. The words "LEFT" and "RIGHT" are cast into the inner surface of the raised section of the disc. This is important, since the cooling vanes cast into the disc must face in the direction of forward rotation.
3. Install the two disc securing nuts.
4. Install the caliper.

Hydraulic Cylinders and Valves

Master Cylinders

Dual master cylinders, commonly in use since 1967, are actually two single master cylinders operating in the same bore. They are designed so that the front and rear brakes have separate hydraulic systems. Malfunction in either system has no effect on the other system but is immediately evident to the driver because of the additional pedal travel required to actuate the remaining half of the brake system. Service procedure for single master cylinders is identical, except

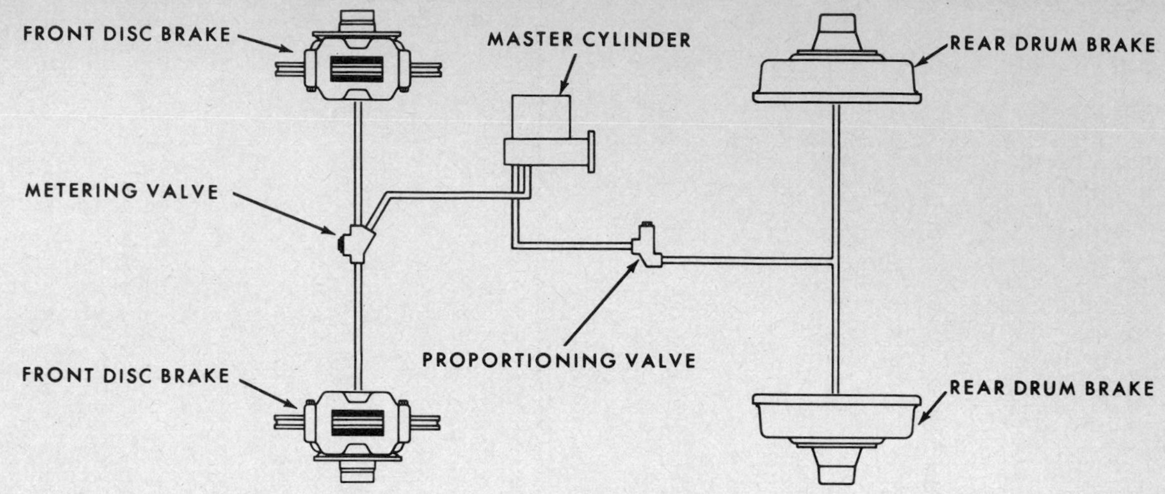

Disc brake hydraulic system

that there is only one piston assembly and no stop screw. Some master cylinders have bleed screws on the outlet flanges and may be bled without disturbing the wheel cylinders.

Servicing Master Cylinders

1. Remove the cylinder from the car and drain the brake fluid.
2. Mount the cylinder in a vise so that the outlets are up and remove the seal from the hub.
3. Remove the stop screw from the bottom of the front reservoir.
4. Remove the snap-ring from the front of the bore and remove the primary piston assembly.
5. Remove the secondary piston assembly using compressed air or a piece of wire. Cover the bore opening with a cloth to prevent damage to the piston.
6. Clean metal parts in brake fluid and discard rubber parts.
7. Inspect the bore for damage or wear, and check pistons for damage and proper clearance in the bore.
8. If the bore is only slightly scored or pitted it may be honed. Always use hones that are in good condition and completely clean the cylinder with brake fluid when honing is completed. If any evidence of contamination exists in the master cylinder the entire hydraulic system should be flushed and refilled with clean brake fluid. Blow out passages with compressed air.
9. Install new secondary seals in the two grooves in the flat end of the front piston. The lips of the seals will be facing away from each other.
10. Install a new primary seal and the seal protector on opposite end of the front piston with the lips of the seal facing outward.
11. Coat the seals with brake fluid. Install the spring on the front piston with the spring retainer in the primary seal.

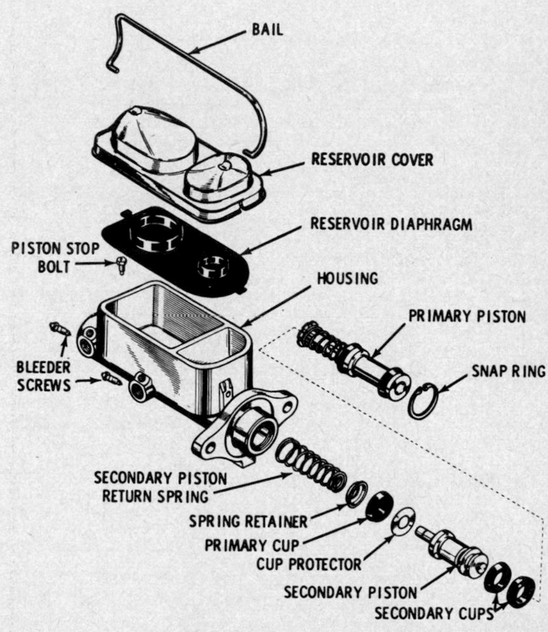

Bendix dual master cylinder
(© Oldsmobile Div., G.M. Corp)

12. Insert the piston assembly, spring end first, into the bore and use a wooden rod to seat it.
13. Coat the rear piston seals with brake fluid and install them into the piston grooves with the lips facing the spring end.
14. Assemble the spring onto the piston and install the assembly into the bore spring first. Install the snap-ring.
15. Hold the piston train at the bottom of the bore and install the stop screw. Install a new seal on the hub. Bench-bleed the cylinder or install and bleed the cylinder on the car.

Wheel Cylinders

Servicing Wheel Cylinders

1. Raise the vehicle on a hoist and remove the wheel and drum from the brake to be serviced.
2. Remove the brake shoes and clean the backing plate and wheel cylinder.
3. Disconnect the brake line from the brake hose. Remove the brake hose retainer clip at the frame bracket and remove the hose from the wheel cylinder. (On rear brakes it will only be necessary to remove the line from the cylinder.)
4. Remove the cylinder mounting bolts and remove the cylinder.
5. Remove the boots from the cylinder ends and discard. Remove the pistons, remove and discard the seal cups, and remove the expanders and spring.
6. Inspect the bore and pistons for damage or wear. Damaged pistons should be discarded, as they cannot be reconditioned. Slight bore roughness can be removed using a brake cylinder hone or

crocus cloth: (Cloth should be rotated in the bore under finger pressure. Do not slide lengthwise). Use only lint-free cloth for cleaning.

7. Clean the cylinder and internal parts *using only brake fluid or denatured alcohol.*
8. Insert the spring expander assembly. Lubricate all rubber parts using only fresh brake fluid.
9. Install new cups with the seal lips facing inwards.
10. Install the pistons and rubber boots. Install the cylinder on the car in reverse order of removal. Bleed the cylinder (see Brake Bleeding).

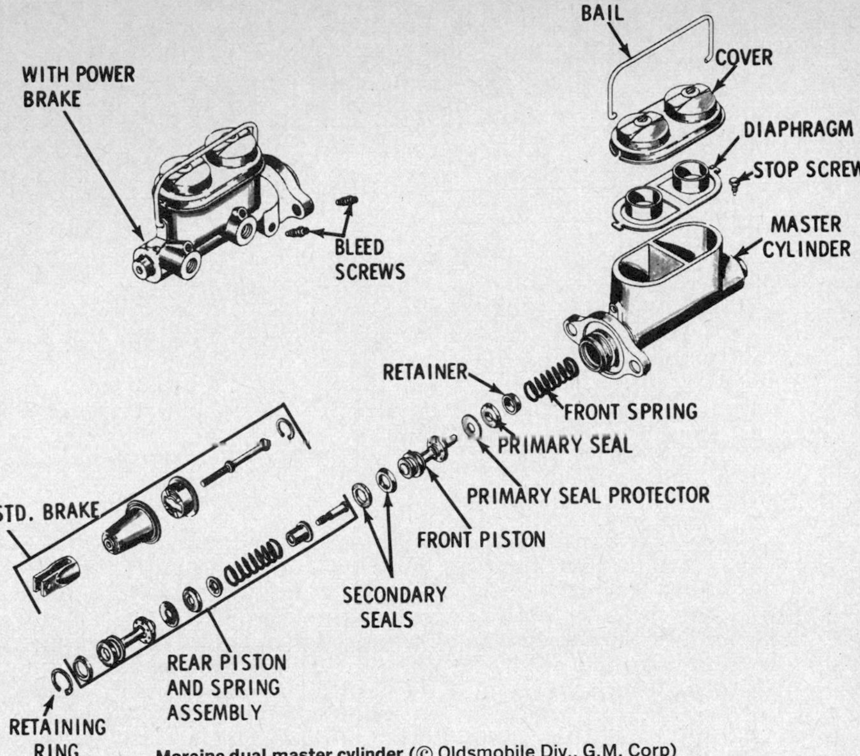

Moraine dual master cylinder (© Oldsmobile Div., G.M. Corp)

Proportioning Valves

On vehicles equipped with front disc and rear drum (or rear disc) brakes a proportioning valve is an important part of the system. It is installed in the hydraulic line to the rear brakes. Its function is to maintain the correct proportion between line pressures to the front and rear brakes. It prevents early lock-up of rear brakes and provides balanced braking during hard stops. *No attempt at adjustment of this valve should be made, as adjustment is pre-set and tampering will result in uneven braking action.*

To assure correct installation when replacing the valve, the outlet to the rear brakes is stamped with the letter "R". Replacement is a simple job requiring no special instructions.

Beginning with 1971 models, General Motors and American Motors installed a combination valve on their front disc (rear drum) brake cars.

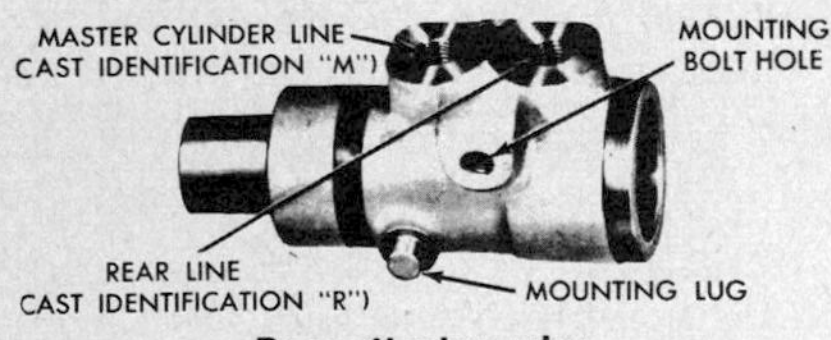

Proportioning valve

This valve combines in one unit, a metering valve, a proportioning valve and a pressure differential warning valve. Mounted on top of the unit is an electrical terminal which connects to the brake warning light on the dash. Ford introduced this unit to their cars in 1972. This unit is not serviceable and must be replaced if faulty.

Metering Valves

On some vehicles equipped with disc brakes a metering valve is used. This valve is installed in the hydraulic line to the front brakes, and functions to delay pressure buildup to the front brakes on application. It provides balanced braking during mild stops. Its purpose is to reduce front brake pressure until rear brake pressure builds up adequately to overcome the rear brake shoe return springs. In this way disc brake pad life is extended because it prevents the front disc brakes from carrying all or most of the braking load at low operating line pressures.

The metering valve can be checked very simply. With the car stopped, gently apply the brakes. At about one inch of travel a very small change in pedal effort (like a small bump) will be felt if the valve is operating properly. Metering valves are not serviceable, and must be replaced if defective.

Pressure Differential Warning Valves

Since the introduction of dual master cylinders to the hydraulic brake system, a pressure differential warning signal has been added. This signal consists of a warning light on the dashboard activated by a differential pressure switch located below the master cylinder. The signal indicates a loss of fluid pressure in either the front or rear brakes, and should warn the driver that a hydraulic failure has occurred.

The pressure differential warning valve is a housing with the brake warning light switch mounted centrally on top. Directly below the switch is a bore containing a piston assembly. The piston assembly is located in the center of the bore and kept in that position by equal fluid pressure on either side. Fluid pressure is provided by two brake lines, one coming from the rear brake system and one from the front brakes. If

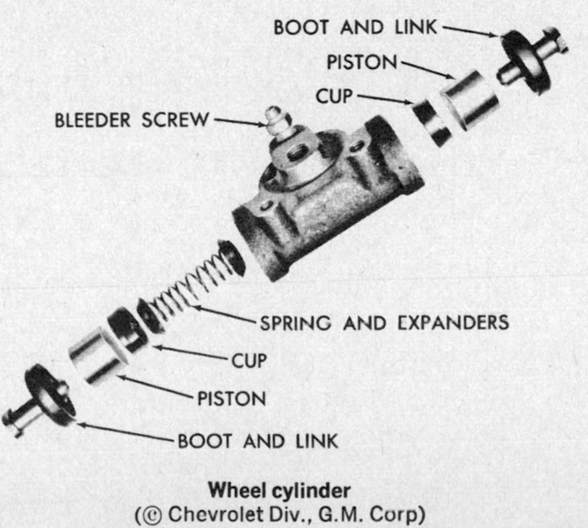

Wheel cylinder
(© Chevrolet Div., G.M. Corp)

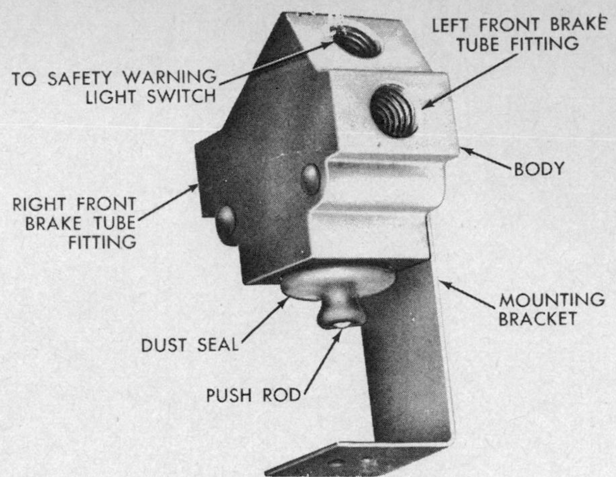

Kelsey-Hayes metering valve

a leak develops in either system (front or rear), fluid pressure to that side of the piston will decrease or stop causing the piston to move in that direction. The plunger on the end of the switch engages with the piston. When the piston moves off center, the plunger moves and triggers the switch to activate the warning light on the dash.

After repairing and bleeding any part of the hydraulic system the warning light may remain on due to the pressure differential valve remaining in the off-center position. To centralize the valve in 1969 Fords, a pressure difference (a leak) must be created in the opposite (rear or front) branch of the hydraulic system that was repaired or bled last. 1970-76 Ford products, General Motors cars, Chrysler products, 1971-76 American Motors cars (disc brakes), and all 1975-76 American Motors models have a self-centering valve. After repairs or bleeding have been performed, center the valve by applying moderate pressure on the brake pedal. This will turn out the light.

NOTE: front wheel balancing of cars equipped with disc brakes may also cause a pressure differential in the front branch of the system.

To centralize the valve on 1969 Fords:

1. Switch the ignition on and bleed brakes.
2. If the front brake system was repaired or bled, a leak must be created in the rear brake system and vice versa. Just open the bleed screw at one rear brake and have an assistant press the brake pedal slowly until the valve is centralized and the light goes out. Quickly close the bleed screw.
3. Check brake fluid level and brake pedal height and firmness. Road test the car.

To centralize the valve on 1969-1970 (drum and disc) and 1971-1974 (drum only) American Motors cars, perform the following procedure:

1. Before repairing or bleeding the brakes, disconnect the switch terminal wire and remove the nylon switch terminal, contact plunger spring, and nylon plunger with contact.
2. If the light had come on and actuated the valve, spring pressure may hold the plunger. To release the plunger, apply a small amount of brake pedal pressure.

NOTE: location of the leak can be determined by the position of the plunger in its bore. The top of the plunger will lean to the side (front or rear) which has the low pressure.

3. Make the repair and bleed the brakes. Install the spring and plunger in the valve with the contact down.
4. Install the nylon terminal and connect the warning light wire to the terminal.
5. Replace the valve assembly if any fluid leaks from the center terminal opening while removing the terminal.

IMPORTANT: the switch assembly is non-serviceable, replace if faulty.

Brake Bleeding

The purpose of bleeding brakes is to expel air trapped in the hydraulic system, and there are two methods of accomplishing this. The quickest and easiest of the two is pressure bleeding, but special pressure equipment is needed to externally pressurize the hydraulic system. The other, more commonly used method is gravity bleeding.

Gravity Bleeding Procedure

NOTE: when bleeding brakes on American Motors cars (1969-70 drum and disc, 1971-74 drum only), it is necessary to remove warning light switch terminal and plunger. For details, see Pressure Differential Warning Valves.

1. Clean the bleed screw at each wheel.
2. Attach a small rubber hose to one of the bleed screws and place the end in a container of brake fluid.
3. Top up the master cylinder with brake fluid. (Check often during bleeding). Pump up the brake pedal and hold.

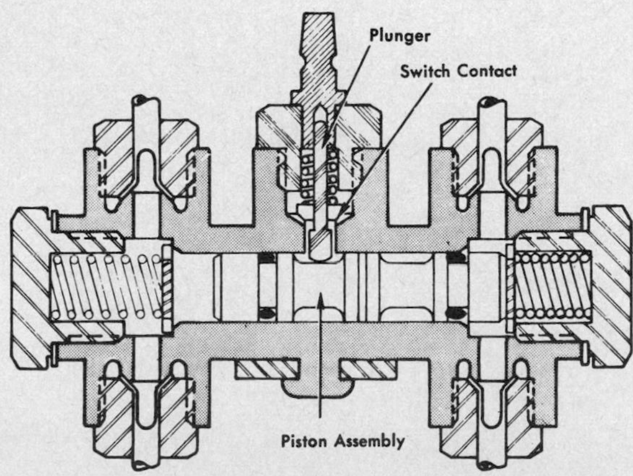

Pressure differential warning valve—ON position

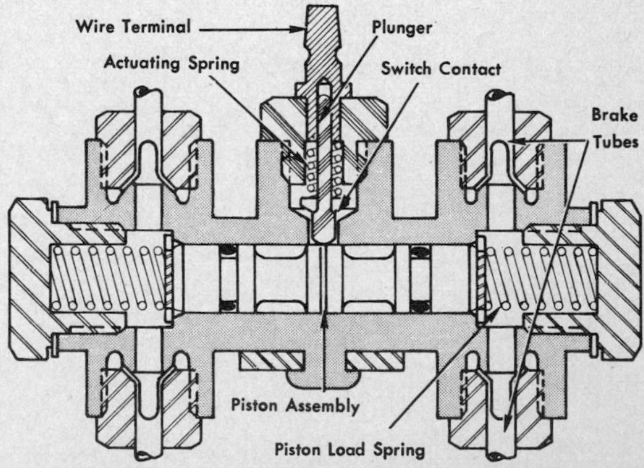

Pressure differential warning valve—OFF position

4. Open the bleed screw about one-quarter turn, press the brake pedal to the floor, close the bleed screw and slowly release the pedal. Continue until no more air bubbles are forced from the cylinder on application of the brake pedal.
5. Repeat procedure on remaining wheel cylinders.

Master cylinders equipped with bleed screws may be bled independently. When bleeding the Bendix-type dual master cylinder it is necessary to solidly cap one reservoir section while bleeding the other to prevent pressure loss through the cap vent hole.

Disc brakes may be bled in the same manner as drum brakes, except that:

1. It usually requires a longer time to bleed a disc brake thoroughly.
2. The disc should be rotated to make sure that the piston has returned to the unapplied position when bleeding is completed and the bleed screw closed.

Pressure Bleeding Disc Brakes

NOTE: see NOTE under Gravity Bleeding Procedure.

Pressure bleeding disc brakes will close the metering valve and the front brakes will not bleed. For this reason it is necessary to manually hold the metering valve open during pressure bleeding. Never use a block or clamp to hold the valve open, and never force the valve stem beyond its normal position. Two different types of valves are used. The most common type requires the valve stem to be held in while bleeding the brakes, while the second type requires the valve stem to be held out (.060 in. minimum travel). Determine the type by visual inspection.

Power Brakes

Vacuum Operated Booster

Power brakes operate just as standard brake systems except in the actuation of the master cylinder pistons. A vacuum diaphragm is located on the front of the master cylinder and assists the driver in applying the brakes, reducing both the effort and travel he must put into moving the brake pedal.

The vacuum diaphragm housing is connected to the intake manifold by a vacuum hose. A check valve is placed at the point where the hose enters the diaphragm housing, so that during periods of low manifold vacuum brake assist vacuum will not be lost.

Depressing the brake pedal closes off the vacuum source and allows atmospheric pressure to enter on one side of the diaphragm. This causes the master cylinder pistons to move and apply the brakes. When the brake pedal is released, vacuum is applied to both sides of the diaphragm, and return springs return the diaphragm and master cylinder pistons to the released position. If the vacuum fails, the brake pedal rod will butt against the end of the master cylinder actuating rod, and direct mechanical application will occur as the pedal is depressed.

The hydraulic and mechanical problems that apply to conventional brake systems also apply to power brakes, and should be checked for if the tests and chart below do not reveal the problem.

Test for a system vacuum leak as described below:

1. Operate the engine at idle with the transmission in Neutral without touching the brake pedal for at least one minute.
2. Turn off the engine, and wait one minute.
3. Test for the presence of assist vacuum by depressing the brake pedal and releasing it several times. Light application will produce less and less pedal travel, if vacuum was present. If there is no vacuum, air is leaking into the system somewhere.

Test for system operation as follows:

1. Pump the brake pedal (with engine off) until the supply vacuum is entirely gone.
2. Put a light, steady pressure on the pedal.
3. Start the engine, and operate it at idle with the transmission in Neutral. If the system is operating, the brake pedal should fall toward the floor if constant pressure is maintained on the pedal.

Power brake systems may be tested for hydraulic leaks just as ordinary systems are tested, except that the engine should be idling with the transmission in Neutral throughout the test.

Power Brake Booster Troubleshooting Chart

The following items are in addition to those listed in the "Brake Diagnosis Chart" at the front of the Hydraulic Brake Section. Check those items first.

Hard Pedal

1. Faulty vacuum check valve
2. Vacuum hose kinked, collapsed, plugged, leaky, or improperly connected.
3. Internal leak in unit
4. Damaged vacuum cylinder
5. Damaged valve plunger
6. Broken or faulty springs
7. Broken plunger stem

Grabbing Brakes

1. Damaged vacuum cylinder
2. Faulty vacuum check valve
3. Vacuum hose leaky or improperly connected
4. Broken plunger stem

Pedal Goes to Floor

Generally, when this problem occurs, it is not caused by the power brake booster. In rare cases, a broken plunger stem may be at fault.

Overhaul

Due to complex repair procedure and the need for special tools, it is suggested that the unit be replaced with a new or rebuilt unit or be taken to a shop with adequate facilities.

Hydro-Boost

Hydro-boost was first offered as a mid-year option on 1974 Continental Mark IV models. Starting 1975, it became standard on all Ford Motor Company cars equipped with four wheel disc brakes.

Hydro-boost differs from conventional power brake systems, in that it operates from power steering pump fluid pressure, rather than intake manifold vacuum.

The hydro-boost unit contains a spool valve with an open center which controls the strength of pump pressure whe nbraking occurs. A lever assembly controls the valve's position. A boost piston provides the force necessary to operate the conventional master cylinder on the front of the booster.

A reserve of at least two assisted brake applications is supplied by a spring-loaded accumulator, which retains power steering fluid under pressure.

The brakes can be operated without assist, once the reserve is depleted.

Hydro-Boost System Checks

1. A defective hydro-boost cannot cause any of the following conditions:
   a. Noisy brakes
   b. Fading pedal
   c. Pulling brakes

   If any of these occur, check elsewhere in the brake system.
2. Check the fluid level in the master cylinder. It should be within ¼ in. of the top. If it isn't, add only DOT-3 or DOT-4 brake fluid until the correct level is reached.
3. Check the fluid level in the power steering pump. The engine

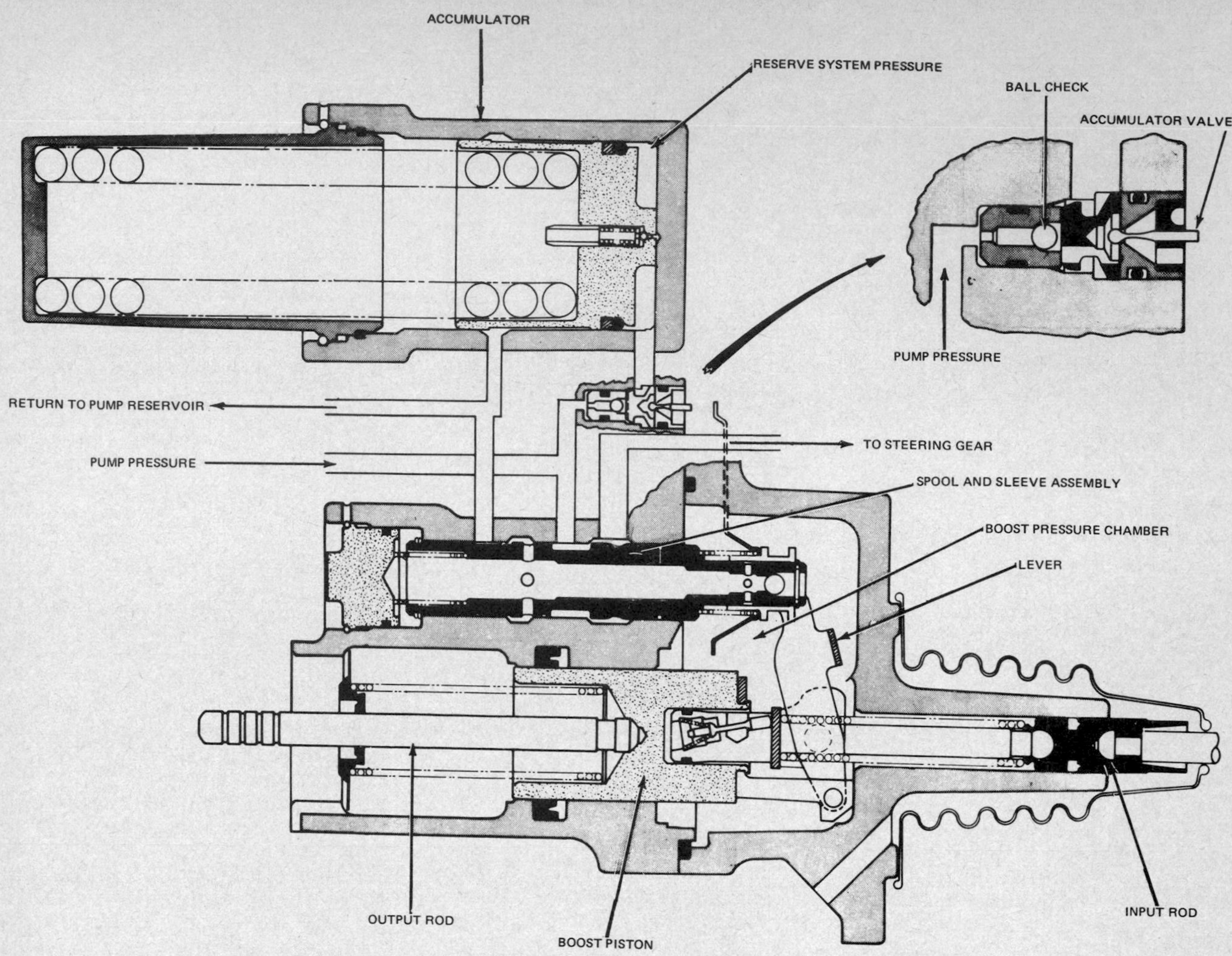

Cutaway view of the hydro-boost power brake unit and accumulator (© Ford Motor Co)

should be at normal running temperature and stopped. The level should register on the pump dipstick. Add power steering fluid to bring the reservoir level up to the correct level. Low fluid level will result in both poor steering and stopping ability.

Caution The brake hydraulic system uses brake fluid only, while the power steering and hydro-boost systems use power steering fluid only. Don't mix the two.

4. Check the power steering pump belt tension, and inspect all of the power steering/hydro-boost hoses for kinks or leaks.
5. Check and adjust the engine idle speed, as necessary.
6. Check the power steering pump fluid for bubbles. If air bubbles are present in the fluid, bleed the system:
   a. Fill the power steering pump reservoir to specifications with the engine at normal operating temperature.
   b. With the engine running, rotate the steering wheel through its normal travel 3 or 4 times, without holding the wheel against the stops.
   c. Check the fluid level again.
7. If the problem still exists, go on to the hydro-boost test sections and toubleshooting chart.

Hydro-Boost Tests

Functional Test

1. Check the brake system for leaks or low fluid level. Correct as necessary.
2. Place the transmission in Neutral and stop the engine. Apply the brakes 4 or 5 times to empty the accumulator.
3. Keep the pedal depressed with moderate (25-30 lbs) pressure and start the engine.
4. The brake pedal should fall slightly and then push back up against your foot. If no movement is felt, the hydro-boost system is not working.

Accumulator Leak Test

1. Run the engine at normal idle. Turn the steering wheel against one of the stops; hold it there for no longer than 5 seconds. Center the steering wheel and stop the engine.
2. Keep applying the brakes until a "hard" pedal is obtained. There should be a minimum of 2 power assisted brake applications when pedal pressure of 20-25 lbs is applied.
3. Start the engine and allow it to idle. Rotate the steering wheel against the stop. Listen for a light "hissing" sound; this is the accumulator being charged. Center the steering wheel and stop the engine.
4. Wait one hour and apply the brakes several times without starting the engine. As in step 2, there should be at least two stops with power assist. If not, the accumulator is defective and must be replaced.

Caution Do not attempt to disassemble the accumulator. It can be serviced as a unit only. Do not puncture the accumulator housing.

Hydro-Boost Troubleshooting Chart

High Pedal and Steering Effort (Idle)

1. Loose/broken power steering pump belt.
2. Low power steering fluid level
3. Leaking hoses or fittings
4. Low idle speed

5. Hose restriction
6. Defective power steering pump

High Pedal Effort (Idle)

1. Binding pedal/linkage
2. Fluid contamination
3. Defective hydro-boost unit

Poor Pedal Return

1. Binding pedal linkage
2. Restricted booster return line
3. Internal return system restriction

Pedal Chatter/Pulsation

1. Power steering pump drivebelt slipping
2. Low power steering fluid level
3. Defective power steering pump
4. Defective hydro-boost unit

Brakes Oversensitive

1. Binding pedal/linkage
2. Defective hydro-boost unit

Noise

1. Low power steering fluid level
2. Air in the power steering fluid
3. Loose power steering pump drivebelt
4. Hose restrictions

Overhaul

Neither the hydro-boost unit nor the accumulator can be dismantled and serviced. If either unit is defective, it must be replaced as a complete assembly. Attempts to disassemble the accumulator could result in personal injury.

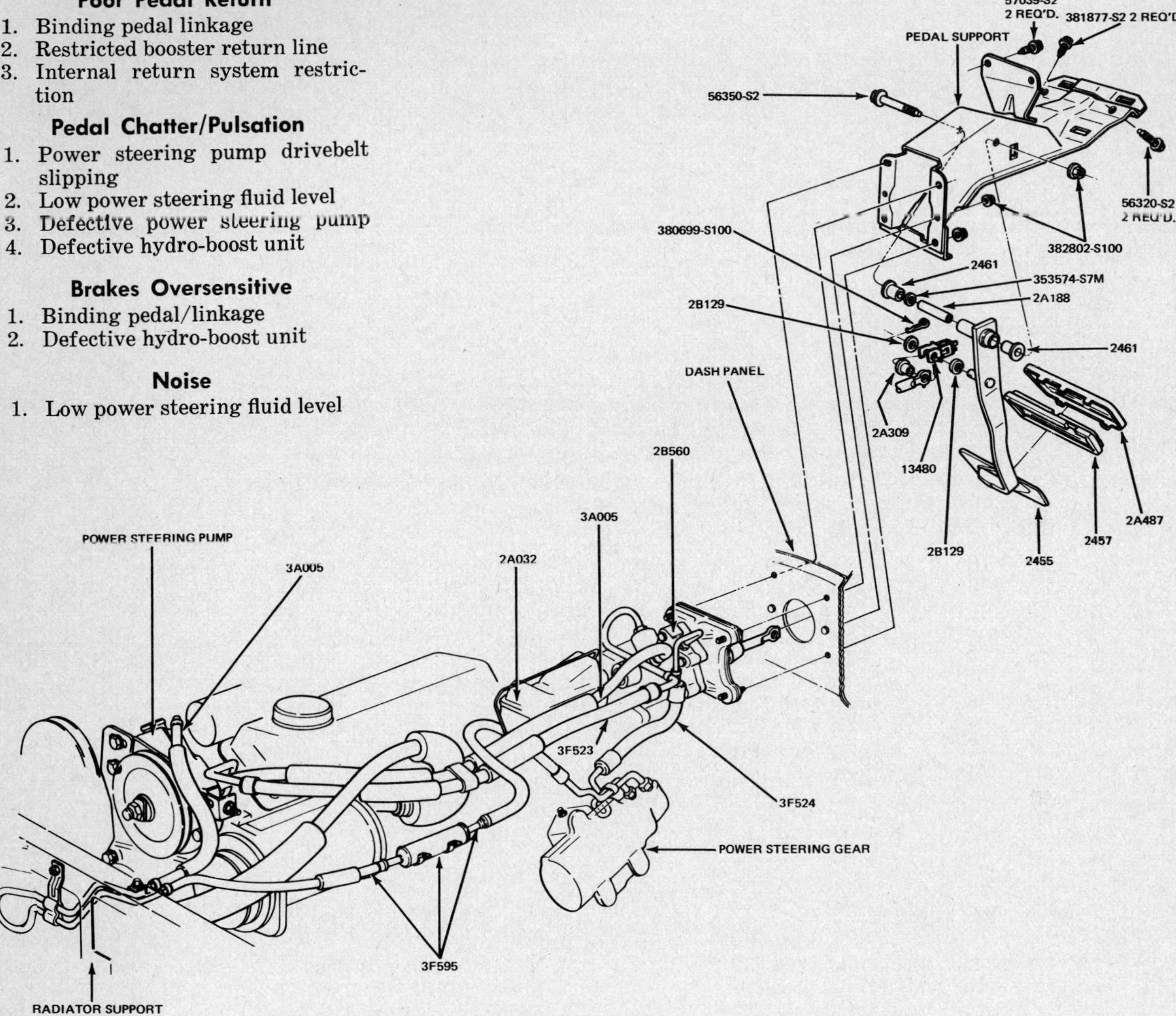

Hydro-boost component and related system locations (© Ford Motor Co)

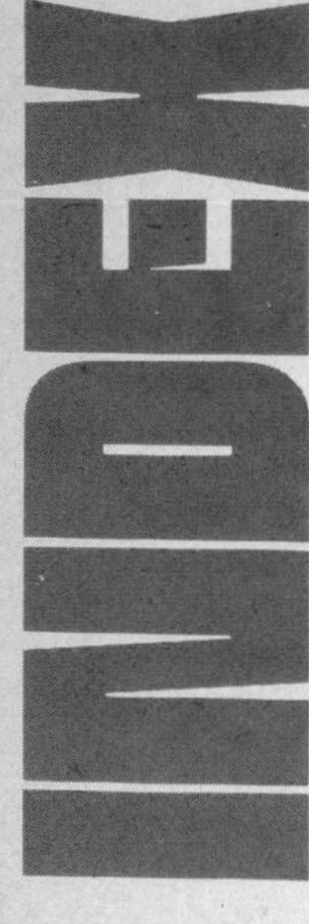

Manual Steering

GEAR APPLICATION INDEX

Listed below are the different types of steering gears and the make of car each is used in. Section numbers refer to the text sections that cover that particular type of steering gear.

Gear Type	Section	Make	Year
A	2	Ford Motor Co. and Lincoln-Mercury Division All models except Pinto, Mustang II, Lincoln Continental, Continental Mark III, IV, Thunderbird.	1969-76
B	3	General Motors Corp., All models	1969-76
		American Motors Corp., All models except Pacer	1969-76
C	4	Chrysler Corp., All models	1969-76
D	5	Ford Motor Co., Pinto and Mustang II	1971-76
E	6	American Motors Pacer	1975-76

Gear Types

A Ford steering gear, recirculating ball
B Saginaw steering gear, recirculating ball
C Chrysler steering gear, recirculating ball
D Ford rack and pinion steering gear
E AMC rack and pinion steering gear

Section Page Numbers

Manual Steering

Manual Steering Diagnosis

Condition	Possible Cause	Correction
Hard steering	(a) Low or uneven tire pressure.	(a) Inflate tires to recommended pressures.
	(b) Insufficient lubricant in the steering gear housing or in steering linkage.	(b) Lubricate as necessary.
	(c) Steering gear shaft adjusted too tight.	(c) Adjust according to instructions.
	(d) Front wheels out of line.	(d) Align the wheels. See the Front Suspension Section.
	(e) Steering column misaligned.	(e) See the Car Section for alignment procedures.
Excessive play or looseness in the steering wheel	(a) Steering gear shaft adjusted too loose or badly worn.	(a) Replace worn parts and adjust according to instructions.
	(b) Steering linkage loose or worn.	(b) Replace worn parts. See the Front Wheel Alignment Section.
	(c) Front wheel bearings improperly adjusted.	(c) Adjust according to instructions.
	(d) Steering arm loose on steering gear shaft.	(d) Inspect for damage to the gear shaft and steering arm, replace parts as necessary.
	(e) Steering gear housing attaching bolts loose.	(e) Tighten attaching bolts to specifications.
	(f) Steering arms loose at steering knuckles.	(f) Tighten according to specifications.
	(g) Worn ball joints.	(g) Replace the ball joints as necessary. See the Front Suspension Section.
	(h) Worm shaft bearing adjustment too loose.	(h) Adjust worm bearing preload according to instructions.

Section 1
Steering Gear Alignment

Before any steering gear adjustments are made, it is recommended that the front end of the car be raised and a thorough inspection be made for stiffness or lost motion in the steering gear, steering linkage and front suspension. Worn or damaged parts should be replaced, since a satisfactory adjustment of the steering gear cannot be obtained if bent or badly worn parts exist.

It is also very important that the steering gear be properly aligned in the car. Misalignment of the gear places a stress on the steering worm shaft, therefore a proper adjustment is impossible. To align the steering gear, loosen the mounting bolts to permit the gear to align itself. Check the steering gear mounting seat, and if there is a gap at any of the mounting bolts, proper alignment may be obtained by placing shims where excessive gap appears. Tighten the steering gear bolts. Alignment of the gear in the car is very important and should be done carefully so that a satisfactory, trouble-free gear adjustment may be obtained.

Section 2
Ford Recirculating Ball Type

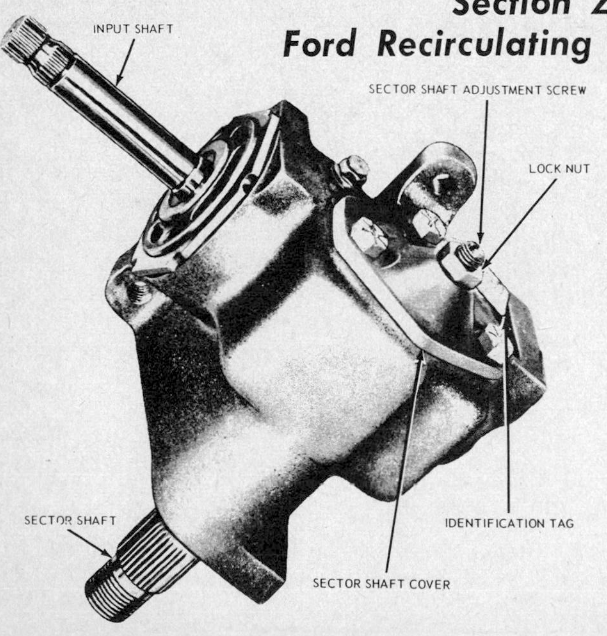

Ford manual steering gear, recirculating ball type

Steering Worm and Sector Gear Adjustments

The ball nut assembly and the sector gear must be adjusted properly to maintain a minimum amount of steering shaft end-play and a minimum amount of backlash between the sector gear and the ball nut. There are only two adjustments that may be done on this steering gear and they should be done as given below:

1. Disconnect the pitman arm from the steering pitman-to-idler arm rod.
2. Loosen the locknut on the sector shaft adjustment screw and turn the adjusting screw counterclockwise.
3. Measure the worm bearing preload by attaching an in. lbs. torque wrench to the steering wheel nut. With the steering wheel off

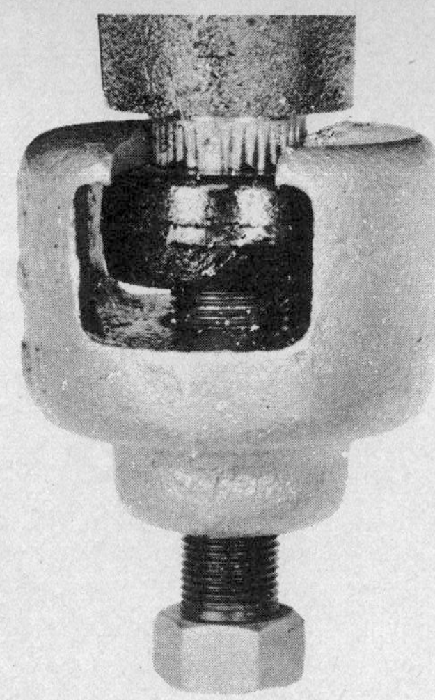

Removing pitman arm
(© Ford Motor Co)

Checking steering gear preload
(© Ford Motor Co)

center, note the reading required to rotate input shaft about 1½ turns either side of center. If the torque reading is not about 3-8 in. lbs., adjust the gear as given in the next step.

4. Loosen the steering shaft bearing adjuster locknut and tighten or back off the bearing adjusting screw until the preload is within the specified limits.
5. Tighten the steering shaft bearing adjuster locknut to 60-80 ft lbs, and recheck the preload torque.
6. Turn the steering wheel slowly to either stop. Turn *gently* against the stop to avoid possible damage to the ball return guides. Then rotate the wheel 2¾ turns to center the ball nut on Maverick and Comet, 3¼ turns on larger models.
7. Turn the sector adjusting screw clockwise until the proper torque (10-16 in. lbs.) is obtained that is necessary to rotate the worm gear past its center (high spot).
8. While holding the sector adjusting screw, tighten the sector screw adjusting locknut to 32-40 ft. lbs. and recheck the backlash adjustment.
9. Connect the pitman arm to the steering arm-to-idler arm rod.

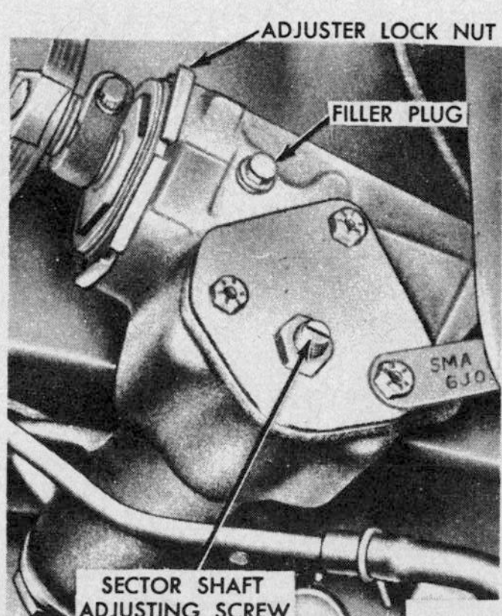

Steering gear adjustments
(© Ford Motor Co)

Steering Gear Disassembly and Assembly

1. Rotate the steering shaft to the center position.
2. Remove the sector shaft adjusting screw locknut and the housing cover bolts and remove the sector shaft with the cover. Remove the cover from the shaft by turning the screw clockwise. *Keep the shim with the screw.*
3. Loosen the worm bearing adjuster locknut and remove the adjuster assembly and wormshaft upper bearing.
4. Carefully pull the wormshaft and ball nut from the housing, and remove the wormshaft lower bearing. *Do not run the ball nut to either end of the worm gear to prevent damaging the ball return guides. Disassemble the ball nut only if there are signs of binding or tightness.*
5. To disassemble the ball nut, remove the ball return guide clamp and the ball return guides from the ball nut. *Keep ball nut clamp side up until ready to remove the balls.*
6. Turn the ball nut over and rotate the worm shaft from side to side until all the balls have dropped out into a clean pan. With all balls removed, the ball nut will slide off the wormshaft.
7. Remove the upper bearing cup from the bearing adjuster and the lower cup from the housing. It may be necessary to tap the housing or the adjuster on a wooden block to jar the bearing cups loose.
8. If the inspection shows bearing damage, the sector shaft bearing and the oil seal should be pressed out.
9. If the sector shaft bearing and oil seal have been removed, press a new bearing and oil seal into the housing. Do not clean, wash,

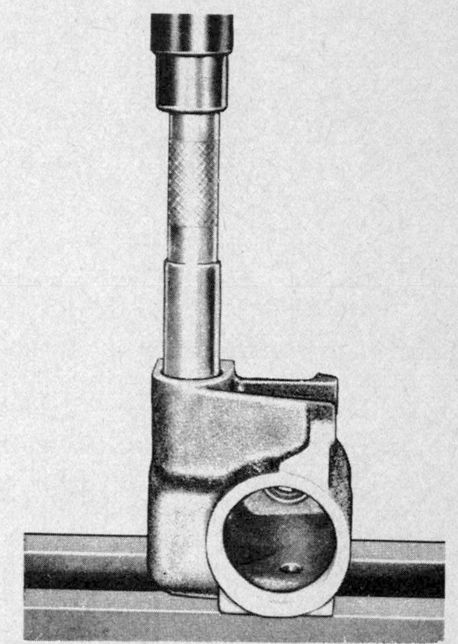

Removing oil seal and bearing
(© Ford Motor Co)

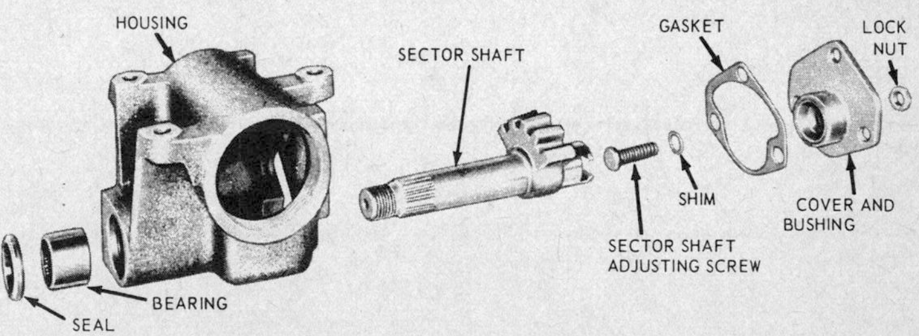

Sector shaft and housing disassembled (© Ford Motor Co)

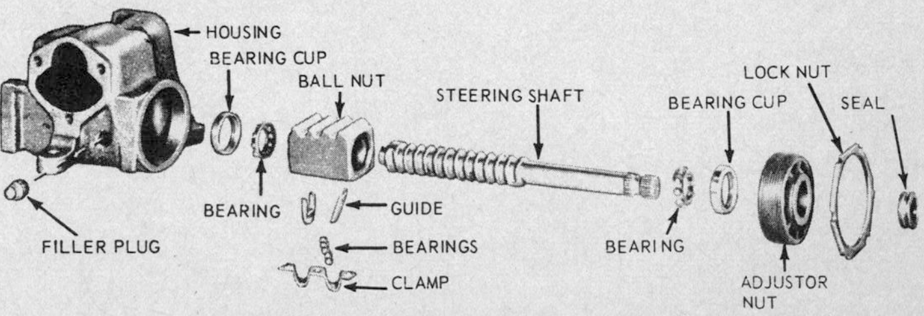

Steering shaft, ball nut, and bearings disassembled (© Ford Motor Co)

or soak seals in cleaning solvent. Apply steering gear lubricant to the housing and seals.

10. Install a bearing cup in the lower end of the housing and in the adjuster. This is a clearance fit not a press fit.
11. Install a new seal in the bearing adjuster if the old seal was removed.
12. Insert the ball guides into the holes in the ball nut, lightly tapping them if necessary to seat them.
13. Insert half of the balls into the hole in the top of each ball guide. If necessary, rotate the shaft slightly to distribute the balls evenly in the circuit.
14. Install the ball guide clamp, tightening the screws to 42-70 in. lbs for Maverick and Comet, and 18-42 in. lbs on larger models. Check that the wormshaft rotates freely.
15. Coat the threads of the steering shaft bearing adjuster, the housing cover bolts, and the sector adjusting screw with a suitable oil-resistant sealing compound. Do not apply sealer to female threads. *Do not get sealer on the steering shaft bearings.*
16. Coat the worm bearings, sector shaft bearings, and gear teeth with steering gear lubricant.
17. Clamp the housing in a vise, with the sector shaft axis horizontal, and place the wormshaft lower bearing in its cup. Place the wormshaft and ball nut assemblies in the housing.
18. Position the wormshaft upper bearing on top of the worm gear and install the wormshaft bearing adjuster, adjuster nut, and the bearing cup. Leave the nut loose.
19. Adjust the worm bearing preload according to the instructions given earlier.
20. Position the sector adjusting screw and adjuster shim, and check for a clearance of not more than 0.002 in. between the screw head and the end of the sector shaft. If the clearance exceeds 0.002 in., add enough shims to reduce the clearance to under 0.002 in. clearance.

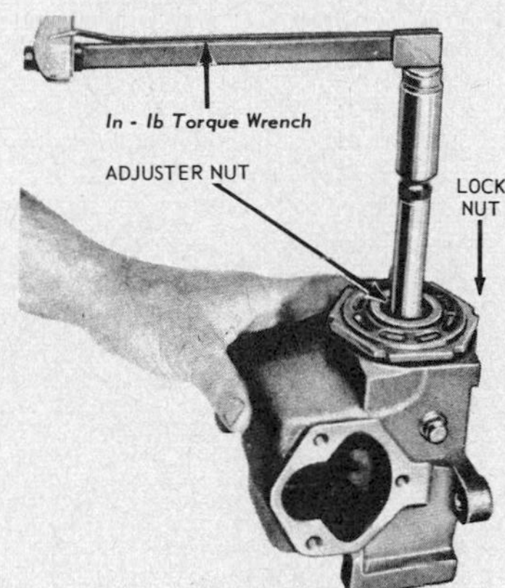

Checking steering shaft bearing preload (© Ford Motor Co)

21. Start the sector shaft adjusting screw into the housing cover. Install a new gasket on the cover.
22. Rotate the steering shaft until the ball nut teeth mesh with the sector gear teeth, tilting the housing so the ball will tip toward the housing cover opening.
23. Lubricate the sector shaft journal and install the sector shaft and cover. With the cover moved to one side, fill the gear with steering gear lubricant. Push the cover and the sector shaft into place, and install the two top housing bolts. Do not tighten the bolts until checking to see that there is some lash between the ball nut and the sector gear teeth. Hold or push the cover away from the ball nut and tighten the bolts to 17-25 ft lbs on Maverick and Comet, and 30-40 ft lbs on larger models.
24. Loosely install the sector shaft adjusting screw locknut and adjust the sector shaft mesh load as given earlier. Tighten the adjusting screw locknut.

Section 3
Saginaw Recirculating Ball Type

The steering gear is of the recirculating ball nut type. The ball nut, mounted on the worm gear, is driven by means of steel balls which circulate in helical grooves in both the worm and nut. Ball return guides attached to the nut serve to recirculate the two sets of balls in the grooves. As the steering wheel is turned to the right, the ball nut moves upward. When the wheel is turned to the left, the ball nut moves downward.

The sector teeth on the pinion shaft and the ball nut are designed so that they fit the tightest when the steering wheel is straight ahead. This mesh action is adjusted by an adjusting screw which moves the pinion shaft endwise until the teeth mesh properly. The worm bearing adjuster provides proper preloading of the upper and lower bearings.

Before doing the adjustment procedures given below, refer to Section 1 to ensure that the steering problem is not caused by faulty suspension components, bad front end alignment, etc. Then, proceed with the following adjustments.

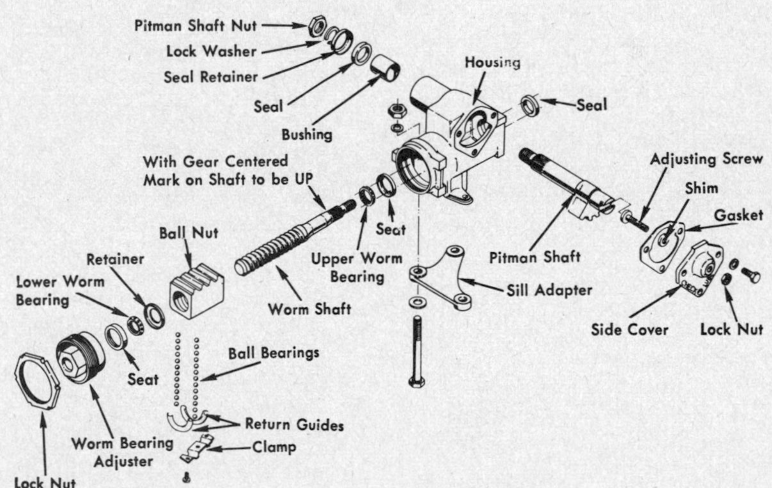

Saginaw steering gear, recirculating ball type (© American Motors Corp)

Worm Bearing Preload Adjustment

Caution Do not turn steering wheel hard against stops as damage to ball nut assembly may result. Use a torque wrench calibrated to 50 in. lbs or less.

1. Disconnect the steering linkage ball stud from the pitman arm.
2. Loosen the pitman shaft adjusting screw locknut and back off adjusting screw a few turns.
3. Install an in. lbs torque wrench to the steering wheel attaching nut and measure the pull needed to move the steering wheel when off the high point. The pull should be between 4 and 6 in. lbs on GM cars and 5 and 8 in. lbs on AMC

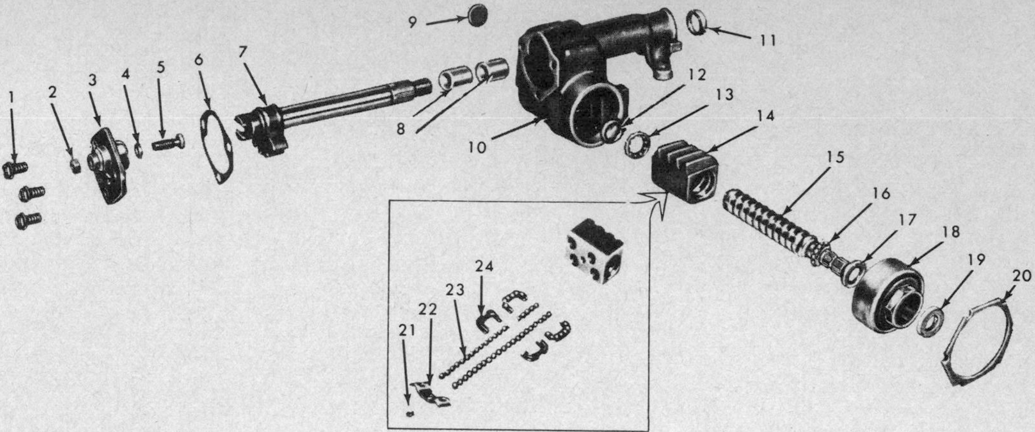

1. Side Cover Screws
2. Lash Adjuster Locknut
3. Side Cover and Bushing
4. Lash Adjuster Shim
5. Lash Adjuster Screw
6. Side Cover Gasket
7. Pitman Shaft
8. Pitman Shaft Bushings
9. Expansion Plug
10. Steering Gear Housing
11. Pitman Shaft Seal
12. Worm Bearing Race—Lower
13. Worm Bearing—Lower
14. Ball Nut
15. Wormshaft
16. Worm Bearing—Upper
17. Worm Bearing Race—Upper
18. Adjuster Plug
19. Wormshaft Seal
20. Adjuster Plug Locknut
21. Clamp Screw
22. Ball Guide Clamp
23. Balls
24 Ball Guides

Corvette steering gear, recirculating ball type (© G.M. Corp)

vehicles.

4. To adjust the worm bearing, loosen the worm bearing adjuster locknut with a brass drift and turn the adjuster screw until the proper pull is obtained. When adjustment is correct, tighten the adjuster locknut, and recheck with the torque wrench.

Sector and Ball Nut Backlash Adjustment

1. After the worm bearing preload has been adjusted correctly, loosen the pitman shaft adjusting screw locknut and turn the pitman shaft adjusting screw until a pull of 5 to 9 in. lbs on GM cars and 4 to 10 in. lbs on AMC

   cars is required to turn the steering wheel through the center of its travel. When the adjustment is correct, tighten the pitman shaft adjusting screw locknut and recheck the adjustment.

NOTE: This torque is in addition to Worm bearing preload torque Total torque required to turn the worm shaft should not exceed 16 in. lbs.

2. Turn the steering wheel to the center of its turning limits (pitman arm disconnected). If the steering wheel is removed, the mark on the steering shaft should be at top center.
3. Connect the ball stud to the pitman arm, tightening the attaching nut to 45-35 ft. lbs.

Steering Gear Disassembly and Assembly

1. After removing the steering gear from the car, place the steering gear assembly in a bench vise.

NOTE: worm seal may be replaced without disassembling gear. Be careful not to damage shaft or housing when removing seal.

2. Rotate the worm shaft until it is centered with the mark facing upward. Remove three cover attaching screws and the adjusting screw locknut. Remove the cover and gasket by turning adjusting screw clockwise through the cover.
3. Remove the adjusting screw with its shim from the slot in the end of the pitman shaft. Remove the pitman shaft from the housing being careful not to damage the seal in the housing.
4. Loosen the worm bearing adjuster locknut with a brass drift and remove the adjuster and bearing. Remove the bearing retainer with a screwdriver.
5. Remove the worm and shaft assembly with the ball nut assembly and bearing. Remove the ball nut return guide clamp by removing screws. Remove the guides, turn ball nut over, and remove the steel balls by rotating the shaft from side to side. After all steel balls have been removed, take the ball nut off the worm shaft.
6. Clean all parts in solvent. Inspect all bearings, bearing cups, bushings, seals, worm groove, and gear teeth for signs of wear, scoring, pitting, etc. If the pitman shaft bushings or seal, steering shaft seal, or upper and lower bearing cups need replacement, see the replacement procedures given below.
7. Remove the pitman shaft seal with a screwdriver or punch. If there is leakage around the threads of the bearing adjuster, apply a non-hardening sealer.
8. Remove faulty bushings from the pitman shaft with Puller and Slide Hammer. Install new bushings, seating the inner end of the bushing flush with the inside surface of the housing.
9. Remove the steering shaft seal with a punch or screwdriver. Tap new seal in place, using a section of tubing to seat the seal.
10. Remove the upper or lower bearing cup from the worm bearing adjuster or steering gear housing using Puller and Slide Hammer. Install the new bearing cups.
11. Lubricate all seals, bushings, and bearings before installing into the steering gear assembly.
12. Position the ball nut on the worm shaft. Install the steel balls in the return guides and the ball nut, placing an equal number in each circuit of the ball nut. Install the return guide clamp and screws.

Caution do not rotate the worm shaft while installing the steel balls since the balls may enter the crossover passage between the circuits, causing incorrect operation of the ball nut.

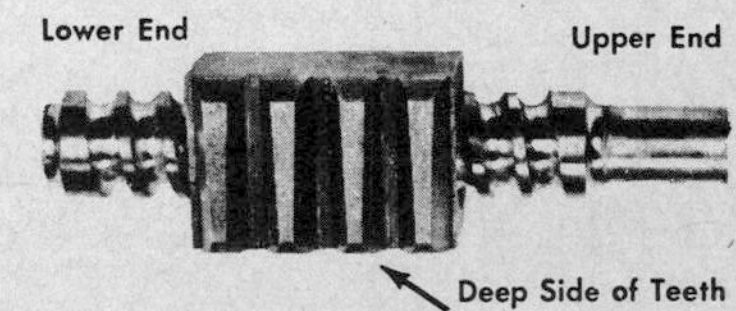

Ball nut properly installed on worm shaft (© American Motors Corp)

13. Place bearing on shaft above the worm gear, center ball nut on worm gear; then, slide the steering shaft, bearing, and ball nut into the housing. *Do not damage the steering shaft seal in the housing.*
14. Place the bearing in the worm adjuster, install the bearing retainer, and install the adjuster and locknut on the housing, tightening it just enough to hold the bearing in place.
15. Install the pitman shaft adjusting screw and selective shim in the pitman shaft. Be sure there is no more than 0.002 in. of end play of the screw in the slot. If the end-play is more than 0.002 in., install a new selective shim to get the proper clearance. Shims are available in four thicknesses: 0.063 in., 0.065 in., 0.067 in., and 0.069 in.
16. Install the pitman shaft and adjusting screw with the sector and ball nut positioned as shown.

Positioning the pitman shaft and ball nut in housing
(© American Motors Corp)

17. Install the cover and gasket on the adjusting screw, turning screw counterclockwise until it extends through the cover from 5/8 to 3/4 in. Install the cover attaching screws and torque to 35 ft. lbs. (Vega—18 ft. lbs.).
18. Tighten the pitman shaft adjusting screw so that the teeth on the shaft and the ball nut engage but do not bind. Final adjustment must be made later.
19. Wrap the pitman shaft splines with tape to protect the seal and install the seal.
20. Fill steering gear with a good quality steering gear lubricant. Turn the steering gear from one extreme to the other to make sure it does not bind. *Do not allow the ball nut to strike the ends of the ball races on the worm gear to avoid damaging the ball return guides.*
21. Install the steering gear as described previously. Perform the final adjustments on the worm bearing preload and the sector and ball nut backlash adjustments.

Section 4
Chrysler Recirculating Ball Type

This steering gear is quite similar to the Saginaw recirculating ball design. The main differences are adjustment and torque specifications. Refer to the introduction in Section 3 before proceeding with the adjustments below.

Worm Bearing Pre-load Adjustment

1. Remove the steering gear arm and lockwasher from the sector shaft, using a suitable gear puller.
2. Remove the horn button or horn ring.
3. Loosen the cross-shaft adjusting screw locknut, and back out the adjusting screw about two turns.

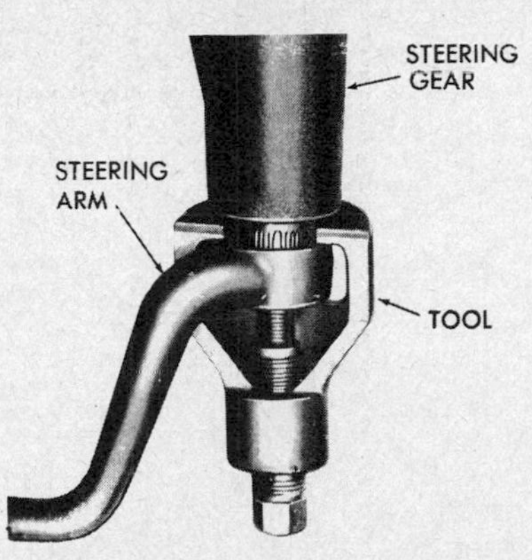

Removing steering gear arm
(© Chrysler Corp)

4. Turn the steering wheel two complete turns from the straight ahead position, and place an in. lb torque wrench on the steering shaft nut.
5. Rotate the steering shaft at least one turn toward the straight ahead position while measuring the torque on the torque wrench. The torque should be between 1 1/8 and 4 1/2 in. lbs. to move the steering wheel. If torque is not within these limits, loosen the worm shaft bearing adjuster locknut and turn the adjuster

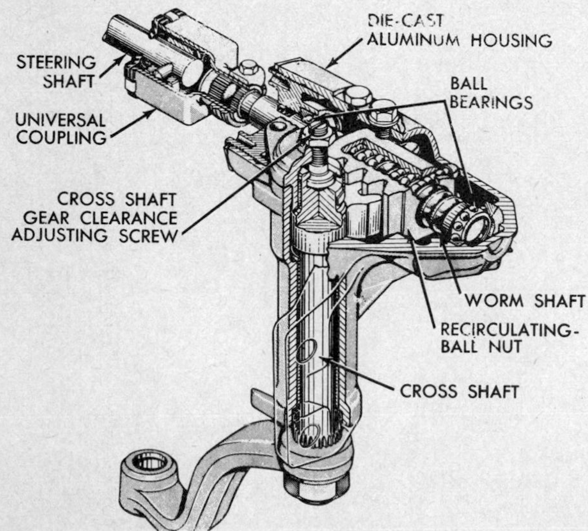

Chrysler steering gear, recirculating ball type
(© Chrysler Corp)

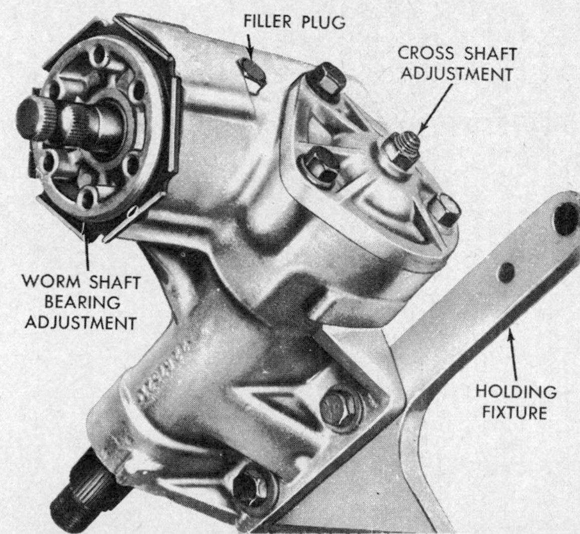

Steering gear adjustment locations
(© Chrysler Corp)

clockwise to increase the preload or counterclockwise to decrease the preload. When the preload is correct, hold the adjuster screw steady and tighten the locknut. Recheck preload.

Ball Nut Rack and Sector Mesh Adjustment

NOTE: this adjustment can be accurately made only after proper preloading of worm bearing.

1. Turn steering wheel gently from one stop to the other. counting the number of turns. Turn the steering wheel back exactly half way, to the center position.
2. Turn the cross-shaft adjusting screw clockwise to remove all lash between ball nut rack and the sector gear teeth, then tighten adjusting screw locknut to 35 ft. lbs.
3. Turn the steering wheel about ¼ turn away from the center or high spot position. With the torque wrench on the steering wheel nut measure the torque required to turn the steering wheel through the high spot at the center position. The reading should be between 8 and 11 in. lbs. This is the total of the worm shaft bearing preload and the ball nut rack and sector gear mesh load. Readjust the cross-shaft adjustment screw if necessary to obtain a correct torque reading.
4. After completing the adjustments, place the front wheels in a straight ahead position, and with the steering wheel and steering gear centered, install the steering arm on cross-shaft. Tighten the steering arm retaining nut to 180 ft. lbs.

Steering Gear Disassembly and Assembly

1. Attach the steering gear assembly to a holding fixture and put the holding fixture in a bench vise. Thoroughly clean the outside surface before disassembly.
2. Loosen the cross-shaft adjusting screw locknut, and back out the adjusting screw about two turns to relieve the mesh load between the ball nut rack and the sector gear teeth. Remove the cross-shaft seal as given in the procedure for cross-shaft seal replacement.
3. Position the steering gear worm shaft in a straight ahead position.
4. Remove the attaching bolts from the cross-shaft cover and slowly remove the cross-shaft while sliding arbor tool into the housing. Remove the locknut from the adjusting screw and remove the screw from the cover by turning it clockwise. Slide the adjustment screw and its shim out of the slot in the end of the cross-shaft.
5. Loosen the worm shaft bearing adjuster locknut with a brass drift (punch) and remove the locknut. Hold the worm shaft steady while unscrewing the adjuster. Slide the worm adjuster off the shaft.

Caution Handle the adjuster carefully to avoid damaging the aluminum threads.

Also, do not run the ball nut down to either end of the worm shaft to avoid damaging the ball guides.

6. Carefully remove the worm and ball nut assembly. This assembly is serviced as a complete assembly only and is not to be disassembled or the ball return guides removed or disturbed.

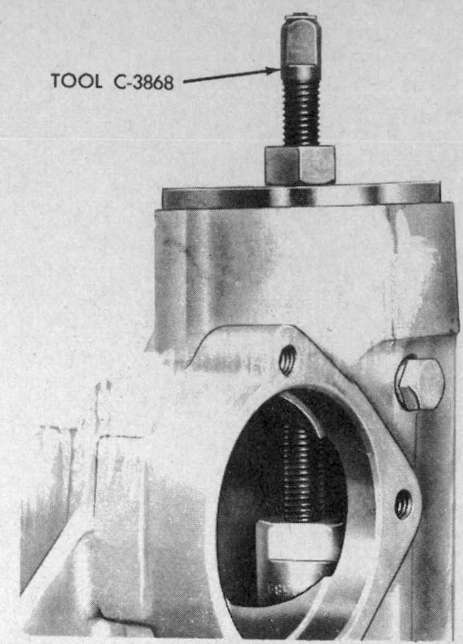

Removing the lower bearing cup
(© Chrysler Corp)

7. Remove the cross-shaft needle bearing by placing the gear housing in an arbor press; insert a tool in the lower end of the housing and press both bearings through the housing.
   The cross-shaft cover assembly, including a needle bearing or bushing, is serviced as an assembly.
8. Remove the worm shaft oil seal from the worm shaft bearing adjuster by inserting a blunt punch behind the seal and tapping alternately on each side of the seal until it is driven out of the adjuster.
9. Remove the worm shaft in the same manner as that given in step 8. *Be careful not to cock the*

Removing the cross shaft (© Chrysler Corp)

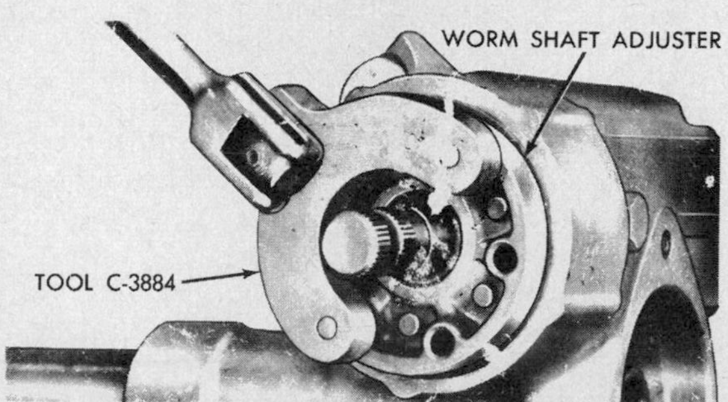

Removing the worm shaft adjuster (© Chrysler Corp)

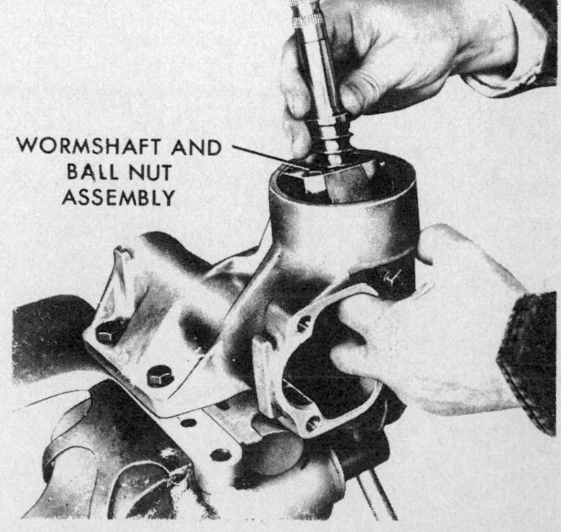

Removing the worm shaft and ball nut assembly
(© Chrysler Corp)

bearing cup and distort the adjuster counter bore.

10. Remove the lower cup if necessary by placing the locking head jaws of remover tool C-3868 behind the bearing cup and expanding the remover head by pressing down on the center plunger of the tool. Pull the bearing cup out by turning the remover screw clockwise while holding the center screw steady.
11. Wash all parts in clean solvent and dry thoroughly. Inspect all parts for wear, scoring, pitting, etc. Test operation of the worm shaft and ball nut assembly. If ball nut does not travel smoothly and freely on the worm shaft or if there is binding, replace the assembly.

NOTE: extreme care must be taken when handling the aluminum worm bearing adjuster to avoid thread damage. Also, be careful not to damage the threads in the gear housing. Always lubricate the worm bearing adjuster before screwing it into the housing.

12. Inspect the cross-shaft for wear and check the fit of the shaft in the housing bearings. Inspect the fit of the shaft pilot bearing in the housing. Be sure the worm shaft is not bent or damaged.
13. Install the cross-shaft lower needle bearing. Press the bearing into the housing about 7/16 in. below the end of the bore to leave space for the new oil seal.
14. Install the upper needle bearing in the same manner and press it into the inside end of the housing bore flush with the inside end of the bore surface.
15. Install the worm shaft bearing cups (upper and lower) by placing them and their spacers in the adjuster nut and press them into place.

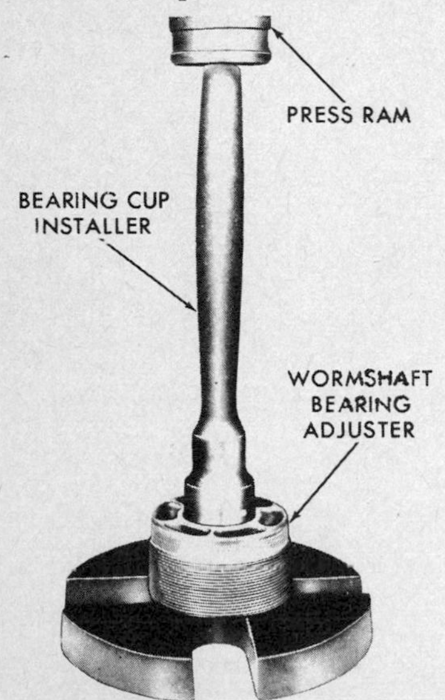

Installing the worm shaft upper bearing cup
(© Chrysler Corp)

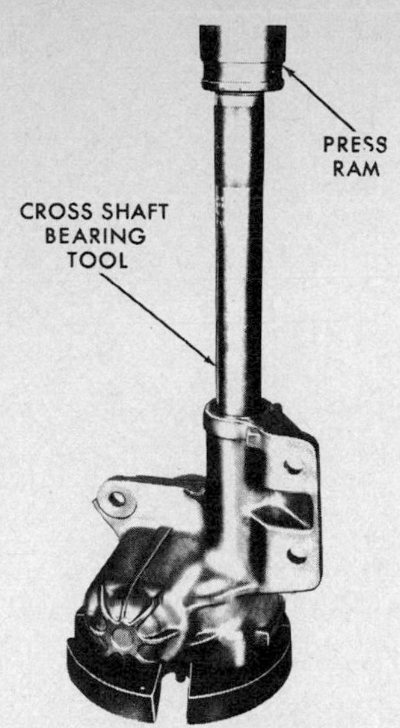

Removing the cross shaft inner and outer bearings
(© Chrysler Corp)

16. Install the worm shaft oil seal by placing the seal in the worm shaft adjuster with the metal seal retainer up. Drive the seal into place with a suitable sleeve until it is just below the end of the bore in the adjuster.

NOTE: apply a coating of steering gear lubricant to all moving parts during assembly. Also, put lubricant on and around oil seal lips.

17. Clamp the holding fixture and housing in a bench vise with the bearing adjuster opening upward. Place a thrust bearing in the lower cup in the housing.
18. Hold the ball nut from turning and insert the worm shaft and ball nut assembly into the housing with the end of the worm shaft resting in the thrust bearing. Place the upper thrust bearing on the worm shaft. Thoroughly lubricate the threads on the adjuster and the threads in the housing.
19. Place a protective sleeve of tape over the splines on the worm shaft to avoid damaging the seal. Slide the adjuster assembly over the shaft.
20. Thread the adjuster into the housing and, with Tool wrench C-3884 and the splined nut set, tighten the adjuster to 50 ft. lbs. while rotating the worm shaft to seat the bearings.
21. Loosen the adjuster so no bearing preload exists. Tighten the adjuster for a worm shaft bearing preload of 1⅛ to 4½ in. lbs. Tighten the bearing adjuster locknut and recheck the preload.
22. Before installing the cross-shaft, pack the worm shaft cavities in the housing above and below the ball nut with steering gear lubricant. A good grade of multi-purpose lubricant may be used if steering gear lubricant is not available. *Do not use gear oil.* Pack enough lubricant into the worm cavities to cover the worm.
23. Slide the cross-shaft adjusting screw and shim into the slot in the end of the shaft. Check the end clearance for no more than 0.004 in. clearance. If the clearance is not within the limit, remove old shim and install a new shim, available in three different thicknesses, to get the proper clearance.
24. Start the cross-shaft and adjuster screw into the bearing in the housing cover. Using a screwdriver through the hole in the cover, turn the screw counterclockwise to pull the shaft into the cover. Install the adjusting screw locknut, but do not tighten at this time.
25. Rotate the worm shaft to center the ball nut.
26. Place a new gasket on the housing cover and install the cross-shaft and cover assembly into the steering gear housing. *Be sure to coat the cross-shaft and sector teeth with steering gear lubricant before installing the cross-shaft in the housing.* Allow some lash between the cross-shaft sector teeth and the ball nut rack. Install and tighten the cover bolts to 25 ft. lbs.
27. Place the cross-shaft seal on the cross-shaft with the lip of the seal facing the housing. Press the seal in place.
28. Turn the worm shaft about ¼ turn away from the center of the high spot position. Using a

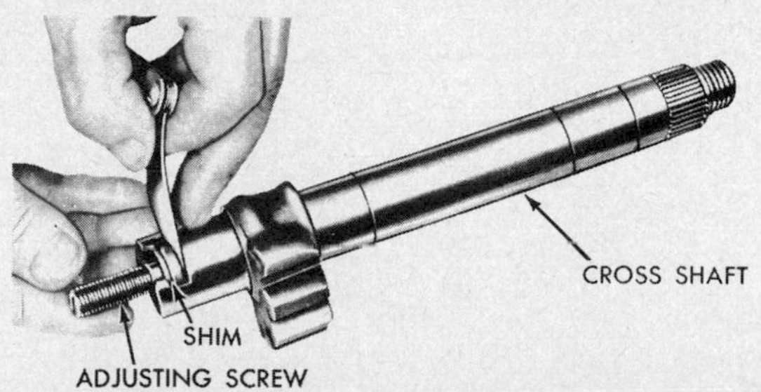

Measuring cross shaft adjusting screw end clearance
(© Chrysler Corp)

torque wrench and a ¾ in. socket on the worm shaft spline, check the torque needed to rotate the shaft through the high spot. The reading should be between 8 and 11 in. lbs. Readjust the cross-shaft adjusting screw until the proper reading is obtained. Tighten the locknut to 35 ft. lbs. and recheck cross-shaft torque.

Cross-Shaft Oil Seal Replacement

1. Remove the steering gear arm retaining nut and lockwasher.
2. Remove seal with a seal puller or other appropriate tool.
3. Place a new oil seal onto the splines of the cross-shaft with the lip of the seal facing the housing.
4. Remove the tool, and install the steering gear arm, lockwasher, and retaining nut. Tighten the nut to 180 ft. lbs. torque.

Section 5
Rack and Pinion Gear Type

The steering gear input shaft is connected to the steering shaft. A pinion gear is machined on the input shaft and engages the rack. Rotation of the input shaft pinion causes the rack to move from side to side.

A tie rod is attached at both ends of the rack by a moveable joint. The unit is sealed at each end with a rubber bellows. The steering gear is filled with SAE-90 oil at initial assembly and checking or refilling is not required unless leakage is evident.

Replacement of the inner tie rods, rack, housing, or upper pinion bearing, necessitates installation of new steering gear assembly.

It is important to remember that when the front wheels are off the ground, the steering wheel should not be moved quickly or forcefully from lock to lock. This could cause a build-up of hydraulic pressure within the assembly which could damage or blow off the bellows.

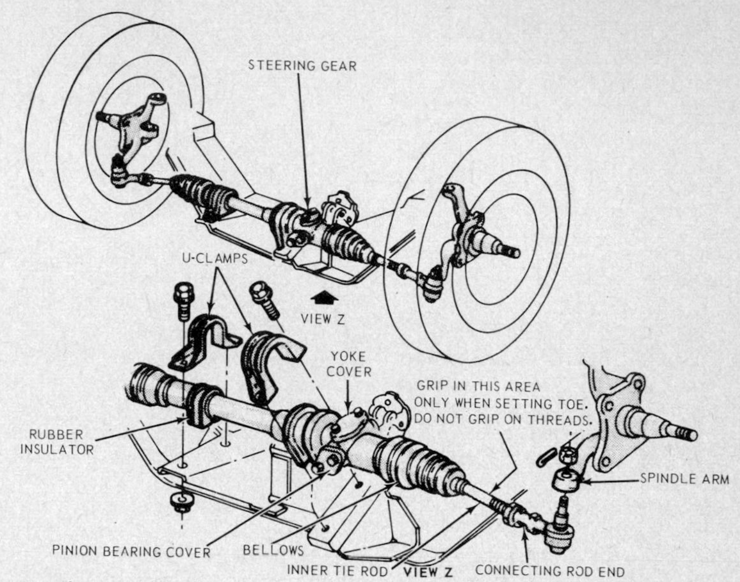

Pinto steering gear assembly, rack and pinion type (© Ford Motor Co)

With the front suspension and linkage in good condition and gear in proper adjustment, there should be no more than ⅜ in. free-play measured at the rim of the steering wheel.

When turning the steering wheel from one stop to the other in a stationary vehicle, there should be no knock produced by the steering gear.

All repair and adjustment procedures require the removal of the rack and pinion gear from the vehicle.

Support Yoke to Rack Adjustment

1. Clean the exterior of the gear thoroughly and place it, using the mounting pads, in a soft-jawed

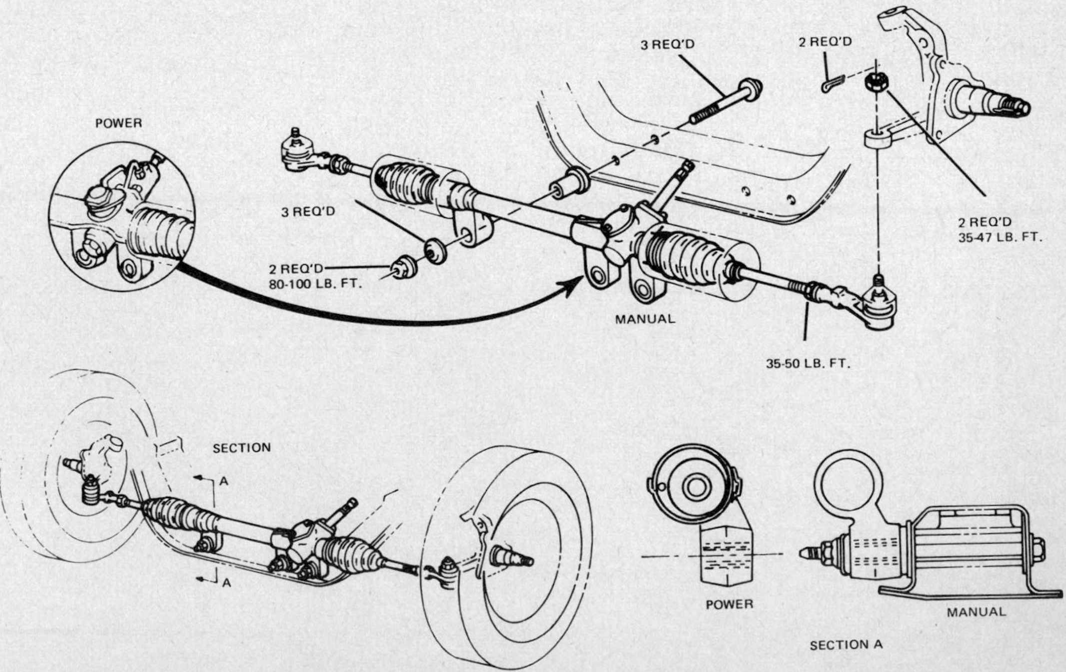

Mustang II rack and pinion steering gear (© Ford Motor Co)

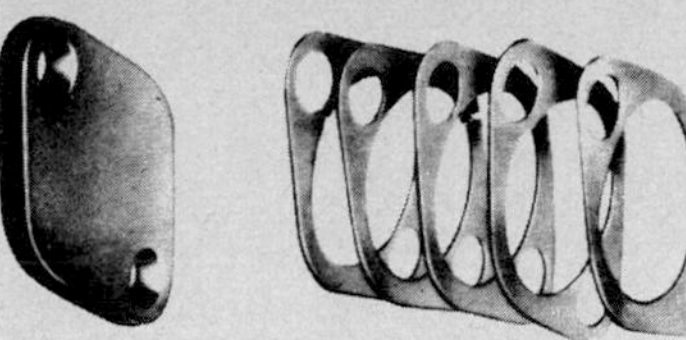

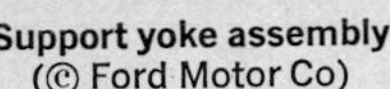

Support yoke assembly
(© Ford Motor Co)

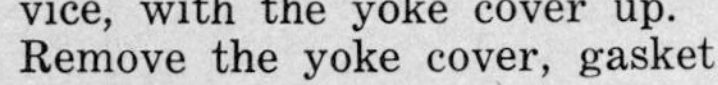

vice, with the yoke cover up.
2. Remove the yoke cover, gasket, shims, and yoke spring.
3. Clean the cover and housing flange areas thoroughly.
4. Reinstall the yoke and cover, omitting the gasket, shims, and spring. Tighten the cover bolts lightly, until the cover just touches the yoke.
5. Measure the gap between the cover and the housing flange with a feeler gauge. With the gasket, add selected shims to give a combined shim pack thickness of 0.005-0.006 in. more than the gap.
6. Remove the cover.
7. Assemble the gasket next to the housing flange and then assemble the selected shims, spring, and cover.
8. Add a sealant to cover the bolt threads and torque to 7-10 ft lbs through 1972, and 15-20 ft lbs on later models.
9. Check to see that gear operates smoothly without binding or slackness.

Pinion Bearing Preload Adjustment

1. Loosen the attaching bolts of the

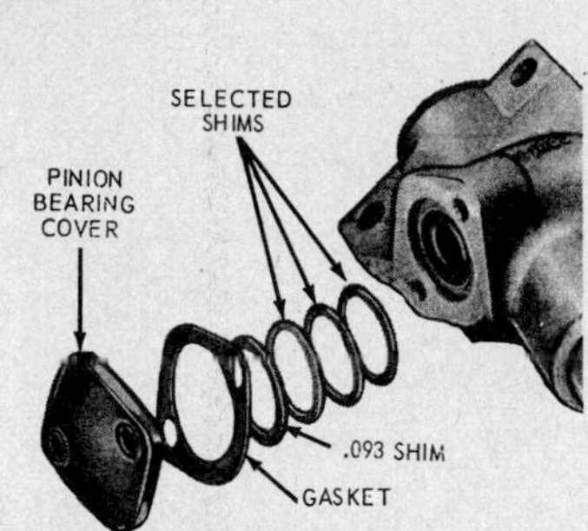

Pinion bearing preload cover and shims
(© Ford Motor Co)

yoke cover to relieve spring pressure on the rack.
2. Remove the pinion cover and clean area thoroughly. On some later models, beginning 1974, the input shaft passes through the pinion cover. The adjustment is made at this point rather than at a bottom cover.
3. Remove the gasket and shims. On later models, remove the spacer and shims.
4. Install a new gasket and fit shims until shim pack is flush with the gasket. On later models, the top of the spacer should be flush with the gasket. Check with a straightedge using light pressure. Install

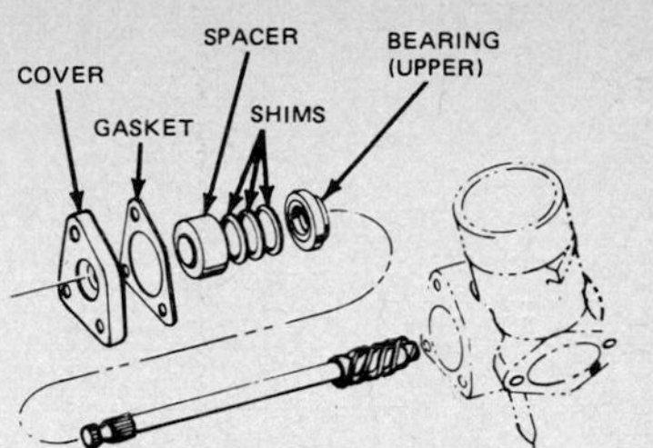

Pinion bearing preload is adjusted at the upper cover on later models
(© Ford Motor Co)

the thinnest of the selected shims first, then the 0.093 in. shim and cover.
5. Add one 0.005 in. shim to the pack, next to the pinion cover, in order to preload the bearing.
6. Add sealant to the bolt threads and install. Torque to 15-20 ft. lbs.
7. Torque yoke cover bolts to 7-10 ft lbs through 1972, and 15-20 ft lbs on later models.

Input Shaft Seal Replacement

1. Clean the area around the input shaft end-seal. Do not scratch or damage the pinion shaft.
2. Pry the pinion seal from its bore.
3. Lubricate the new pinion seal and install it over the shaft.
4. Use a piece of tubing to engage the outer flange of the seal and press or tap the seal into place so it is flush with shoulder of the bore.

Section 6
American Motors Pacer Rack and Pinion

Removal and Installation

1. Raise the front end of the car and support it. Unlock the steering column.
2. Remove the nuts that attach the flexible coupling to the intermediate shaft flange.
3. Disconnect the tie rod ends at the steering arms as follows:
   a. Turn the wheels to their stop in the direction of the tie rod end to be disconnected.
   b. Position a floor jack under the lower control arm and raise the arm at least 2 in.
   c. Remove the cotter pin and retaining nut from the tie rod end.
   d. Disconnect the tie rod end from the steering arm using a puller.
4. Remove the bolts that attach the steering gear to the front crossmember at the mounting bracket and housing and remove the steering gear. Loosen both mounting clamp bolts before removing to minimize stress on the clamp.
5. Install the steering gear in the reverse order of removal, tightening the mounting bracket bolts to 50 ft lbs, the housing bolts to 75 ft lbs, the tie rod end-to-steering arm nuts to 50 ft lbs, and the flexible coupling-to-intermediate shaft flange nuts to 25 ft lbs. Check and correct, the toe-in adjustment if necessary.

Overhaul

1. Remove the steering gear from the car and mount the assembly in a vise. Do not clamp any part of the tube in the vise; clamp only the housing.
2. Cut and remove the large diameter boot clamp from the boot on the housing end of the steering gear. Slide the boot away from the housing to expose the rack teeth.
3. Turn the flexible coupling to move the rack toward the housing end of the steering gear and expose as many teeth as possible.
4. Wipe the rack teeth clean with a clean cloth and inspect the rack for chipped, cracked, broken, flaking, or excessively worn teeth. If any of the above conditions exist, the steering gear assembly must be replaced. Machining marks or shiny and bright rack teeth are normal conditions.
5. Remove the flexible coupling pinch bolt and separate the coupling from the pinion shaft.
6. Remove the adjuster plug locknut at the pinion shaft.
7. Remove the pinion shaft from the housing by pulling upward and rotating the shaft counterclockwise slightly.
8. Clean and inspect the shaft for the same conditions as described

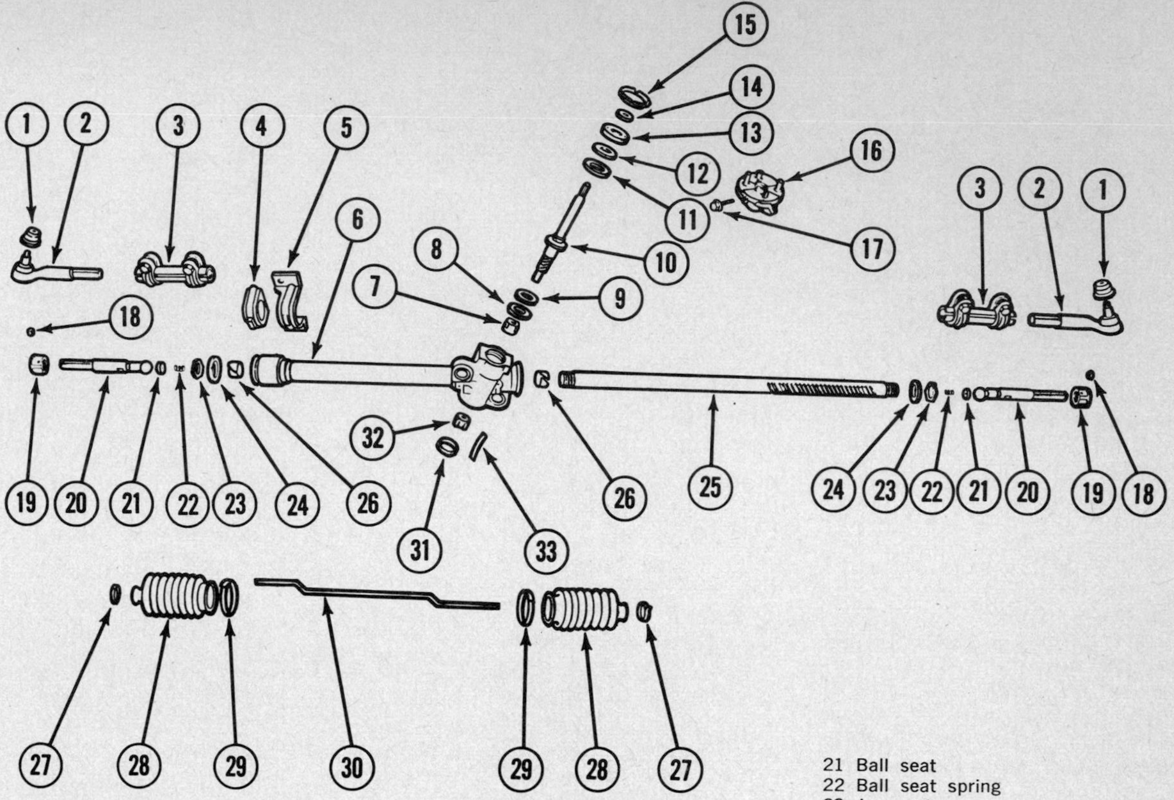

1 Tie rod seal
2 Tie rod end
3 Adjuster tube
4 Mounting grommet
5 Mounting clamp
6 Tube and housing assembly
7 Upper pinion bushing
8 Lower thrust bearing race
9 Lower thrust bearing
10 Pinion shaft
11 Upper thrust bearing
12 Upper thrust bearing race
13 Adjuster plug
14 Pinion shaft seal
15 Adjuster plug locknut
16 Flexible coupling
17 Pinch bolt
18 Set screw
19 Tie rod housing
20 Inner tie rod
21 Ball seat
22 Ball seat spring
23 Jam nut
24 Shock dampener ring
25 Steering rack
26 Rack bushing
27 Boot retainer
28 Boot
29 Boot clamp
30 Breather tube
31 Contraction plug
32 Lower pinion bushing
33 Preload spring

Exploded view of the American Motors Pacer manual rack and pinion steering gear
(© American Motors Corp)

in step 4.

9. Remove the contraction plug from the housing with a 1/4 in. brass rod inserted through the upper and lower pinion bushings. Tap the rod to remove the plug.
10. Remove the lower pinion bushing and preload spring from the housing with the brass rod.
11. Move the rack to the centered position in the tube and housing.
12. Install the pinion shaft and adjuster plug in the housing. Hand-tighten the adjuster plug.
13. Mark the position of the adjuster tubes on the inner tie rods for assembly and then loosen the adjuster tube clamp nuts on both sides. Remove the adjuster tubes and tie rod end assemblies from the inner tie rods. Use penetrating oil if the threads are corroded.
14. Mark the location of the breather tube on the housing and tube assembly. The end boots and breather tube must be installed

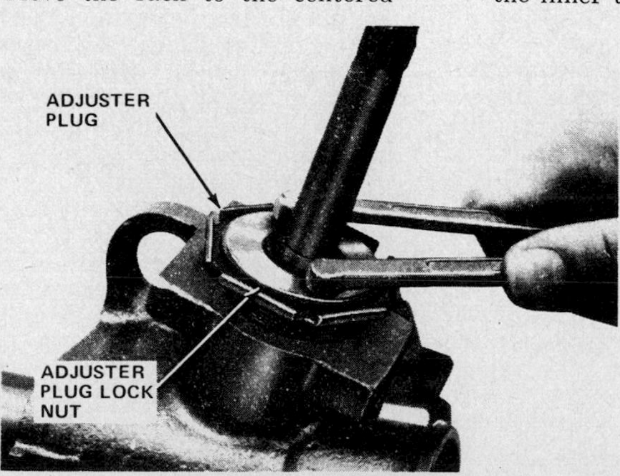

Removing the adjuster plug lock-nut and plug assembly
(© American Motors Corp)

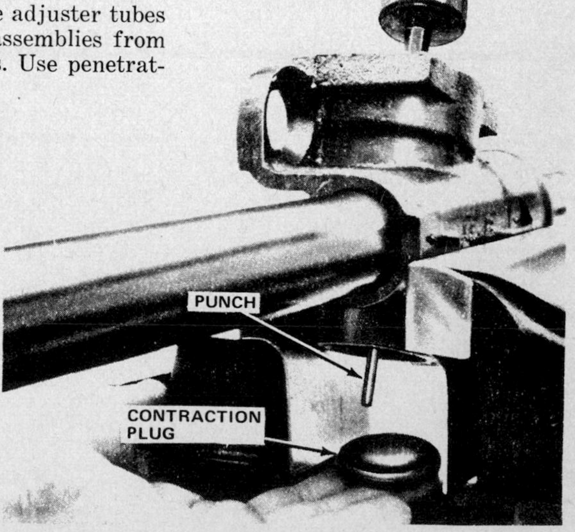

Removing the contraction plug (© American Motors Corp)

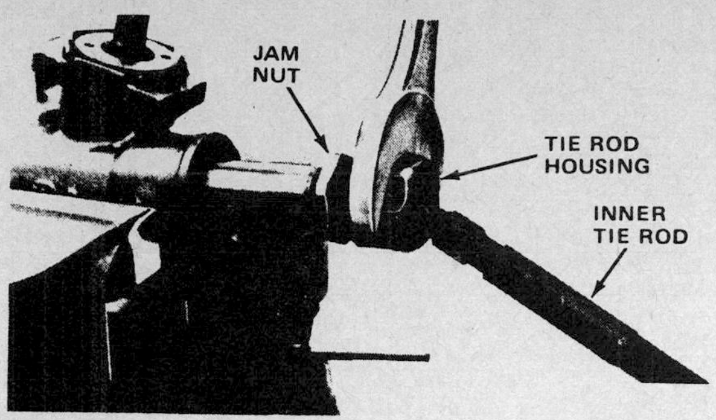

Removing the tie rod housing and inner tie rod
(© American Motors Corp)

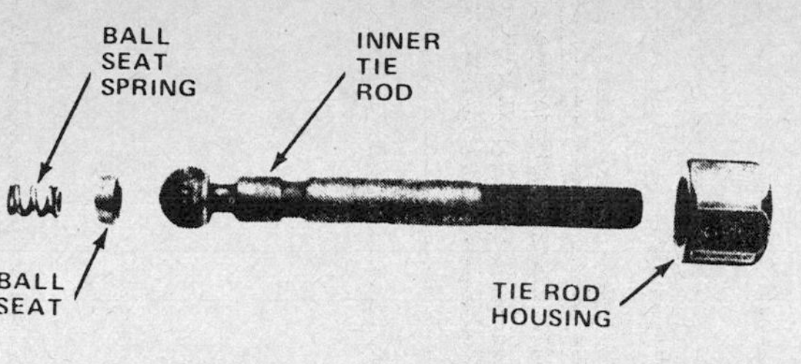

An exploded view of the inner tie rod assembly
(© American Motors Corp)

in the same position to insure proper sealing.

15. Cut and remove the remaining boot clamps and remove the boots. Take care not to cut the boot and do not turn the boot inside out.
16. Remove the breather tube from the hole in the mounting grommet and remove the breather tube. Do not disturb the position of the mounting clamp or the grommet unless they are to be replaced.
17. Move the shock dampener rings away from the jamnuts at both ends of the inner tie rod.
18. Clamp the inner tie rod housing in the vise and loosen the jamnut with a 1-½ in. open-end wrench. Do not use excessive pressure in clamping the inner tie rod housing in the vise. However, the housing must be held securely when the jamnut is loosened or tightened to prevent damage to the internal components of the steering gear.
19. Loosen, but do not remove, the tie rod housing set-screw.
20. Repeat steps 18 and 19 on the opposite end of the rack.
21. Remount the steering gear housing in the vise as originally placed.
22. Remove the inner tie rod housing and remove the ball seats, ball seat springs, jamnuts, and shock dampener rings from the rack. Remove the adjuster plug and remove the pinion shaft from the housing. Remove by pulling up and rotating counterclockwise.
23. Remove the pinion shaft lower thrust bearing and race.
24. Remove the upper pinion bushing from the housing.
25. Pull the steering rack from the tube and housing out either end.
26. Remove the rack bushings by inserting a knife blade under the bushings, grasping the bushings with a needlenose pliers and pulling them straight out.

Removing the upper pinion shaft bushing
(© American Motors Corp)

NOTE: If either of the bushings need replacing, replace both of them.

27. Remove the pinion shaft seal in the adjuster plug by threading the adjuster plug into the housing and prying the seal out with a screwdriver.
28. Wash all of the parts, except the rubber boots and nylon bushings in a suitable solvent and dry them with compressed air. Make sure you do not wash off the alignment marks for the breather tube and mounting clamp.
29. Inspect all of the parts for the conditions mentioned in step 4.

NOTE: If the tube and housing or steering rack and pinion shaft need replacing, replace the complete steering gear assembly, less the steering linkage components.

Bushings, thrust bearings, steering linkage components, the breather tube and boots, and the flexible coupling can all be replaced individually.

To assemble the steering gear:

30. Install a new pinion shaft seal in the adjuster plug using a suitable sized socket. Press the seal in until it is flush with the face of the adjuster plug. Do not press on the lip of the seal.
31. Replace the rack bushings, if removed. Compress the leading end and force them into the housing or tube opening. Once they are past the lip of the tube or housing, the bushing will snap back

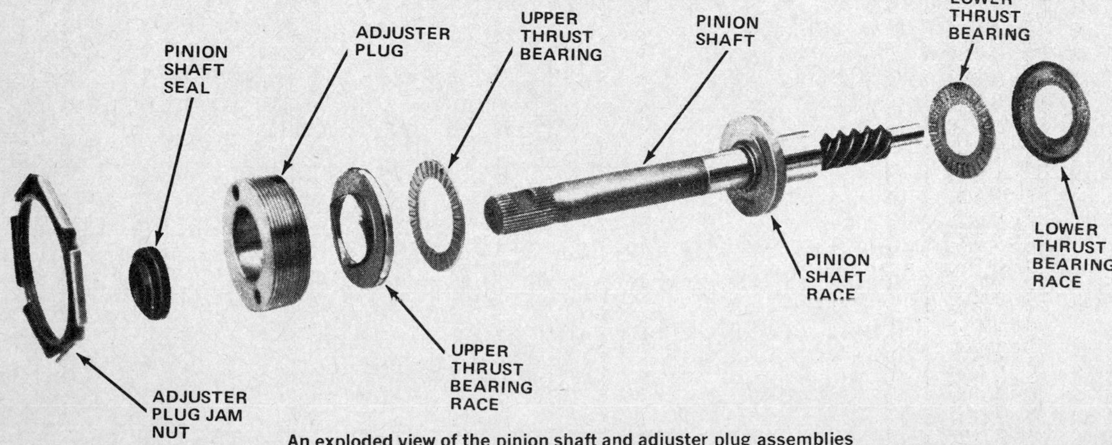

An exploded view of the pinion shaft and adjuster plug assemblies
(© American Motors Corp)

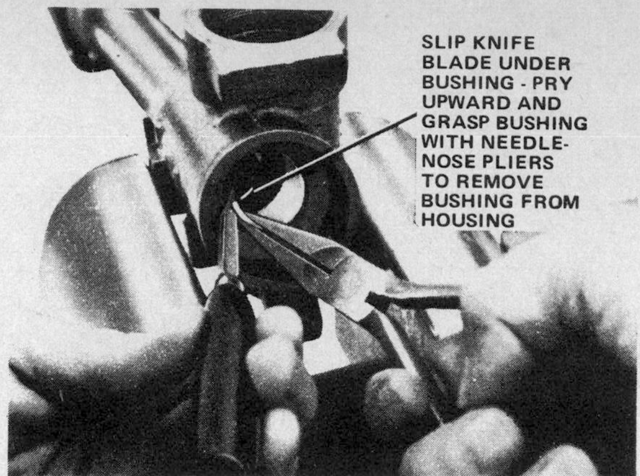

Removing the rack bushing(s) (© American Motors Corp)

Centering the steering rack in the tube and housing (© American Motors Corp)

to its original shape.

32. Coat the rack teeth with lithium based chassis grease and install the rack in the housing. Install the upper pinion bushing in the housing.
33. Lubricate the pinion shaft lower race and thrust bearing with the same type grease and install the race and thrust bearing in the housing with the flanged edge of the race facing up.
34. Center the steering rack in the housing. Set the distance between the end of the steering rack and the inner lip of the housing at 4 in.
35. Start the pinion shaft into the housing and rack with the flat on the splined end of the pinion shaft at about the 10 o'clock position. Turn the pinion shaft counterclockwise and push down until the pinion shaft race is bottomed on the thrust bearing.
36. Reset the distance between the end of the rack and the housing (step 34). The flat on the pinion shaft should be at the 3 o'clock position now. Be sure the pinion race is bottomed in the housing. If the flat on the pinion shaft is not at the 3 o'clock position with the rack set at 4 in., start over again at step 33.

NOTE: The rack must be centered, otherwise, the steering wheel travel from left to right will be unequal.

37. Install the adjuster plug using a spanner type tool that fits in the two holes in the top of the plug. Tighten the plug until it bottoms. Mark the adjuster plug and housing at a spanner hole. Back off the adjuster plug (counterclockwise) until the hole marked is 3/16 in. to ¼ in. past (counterclockwise) the reference mark made on the housing. Install and tighten the locknut to 50 ft lbs.
38. Turn the assembly over and mount it in a vise. Fill the space around the pinion shaft with the same type of grease (step 32).

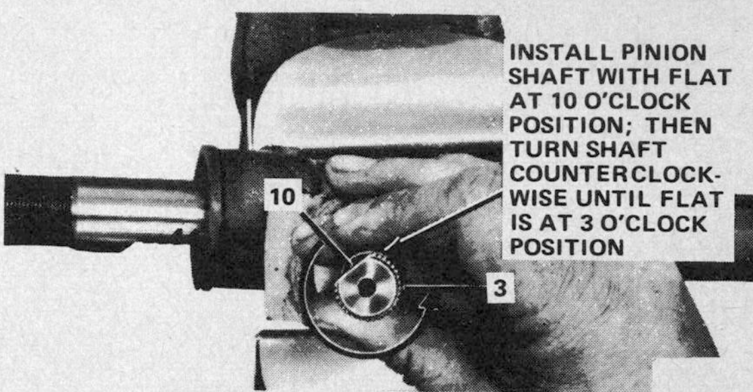

Installing the pinion shaft and engaging the rack (© American Motors Corp)

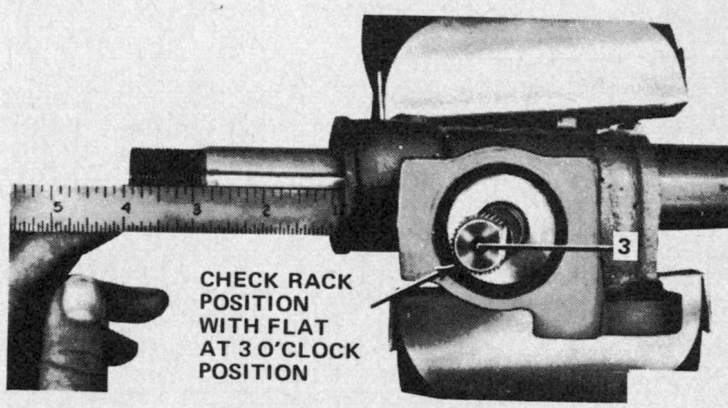

Checking the rack positioning after installation of the pinion shaft (© American Motors Corp)

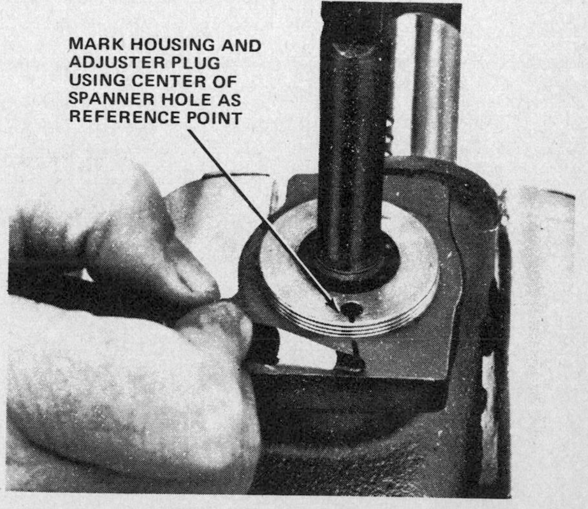

Marking the adjuster plug for adjustment (© American Motors Corp)

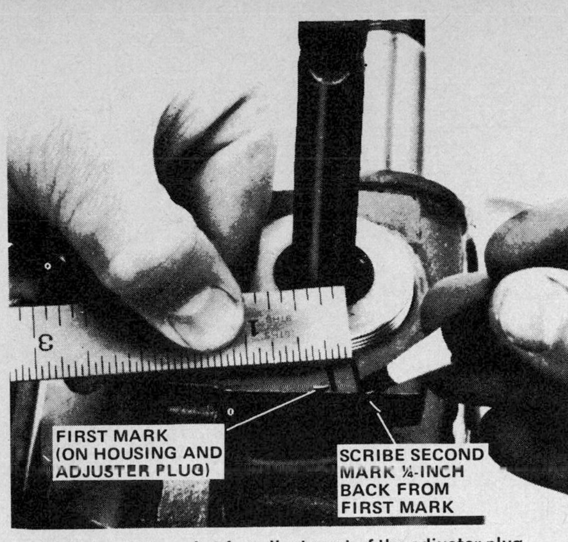

Marking the housing for adjustment of the adjuster plug
(© American Motors Corp)

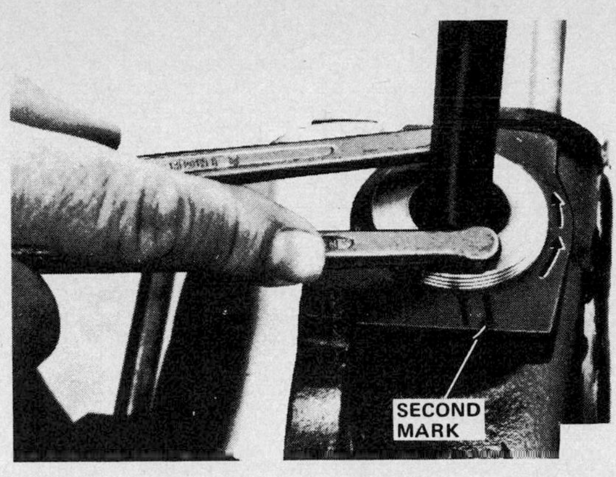

Backing off the adjuster plug to the proper adjustment
(© American Motors Corp)

Do not overfill because the pinion bushing and spring have to be installed yet.

39. Install the preload spring in the housing with the center hump of the spring bearing against the housing. Allow the spring to extend about 1/4 in. from the end of the housing.
40. Hold the top of the preload spring against the housing with needlenose pliers and install the busing in the housing with the chamfered end facing downward.
41. Seat the contraction plug in the housing using the brass rod from step 9 or a suitable size socket.
42. Install the shock dampener rings on each end of the steering rack with the open ends facing out and install both jamnuts.

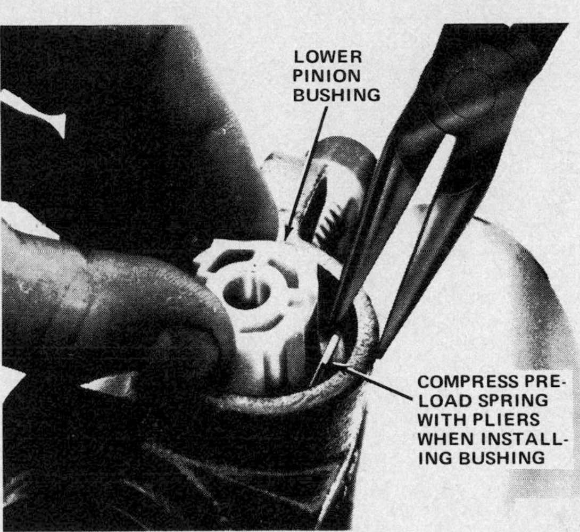

Installing the lower pinion bushing (© American Motors Corp)

42. Liberally apply some lithium based chassis lubricant to all of the inner tie rod assembly wear surfaces. Pack the tie rod housings with the same type grease.
44. Assemble and install the inner tie rod assemblies to the rack. tighten the tie rod housing to 75 in. lbs while rocking the inner tie rod to relieve grease lock, loosen 1/2 turn and retighten the housing to 50 in. lbs.
43. Tighten the housing setscrews to 60 in. lbs.
44. Clamp the tie rod housings in the vise (see step 18) and tighten the jamnuts to 100 ft lbs using a crow-foot adapter on the end of a torque wrench.
43. Slip the shock dampener rings over the jamnuts.
44. Install the mounting clamp and grommet on the tube using the alignment marks made during disassembly.
45. Install the boot on the mounting bracket side of the tube and housing in position so that the hole in the boot aligns with the hole in the mounting grommet. Slide the short end of the tube through the grommet and boot breather tube holes. The long end of the tube lies against the tube and housing.

NOTE: The breather tube transfers air from one boot to the other during the turning of the front wheels. If the tube is blocked in any way, dust and water could be drawn into the inner tie rod assemblies.

46. Install the opposite side boot with the hole in the boot aligned with the breather tube. The boot lip must fit into the housing flange to seat the tube.
47. Slide the small outer collars of the boots over the inner tie rod grooves. Install the small diameter boot clamps on the boots and tighten the clamps.
48. Install the adjuster tubes and tie rod ends on the inner tie rods. Align the tubes and tie rods using the marks made during disassembly. At least 3 threads should be visible at both ends of the adjuster tubes. The number of threads per side should not differ by more than 3.
49. Install the flexible coupling on the pinion shaft, flat to flat, and install the pinch bolt. Tighten the pinch bolt to 30 ft lbs.
50. Install the steering gear in the car and check the toe-in adjustment.

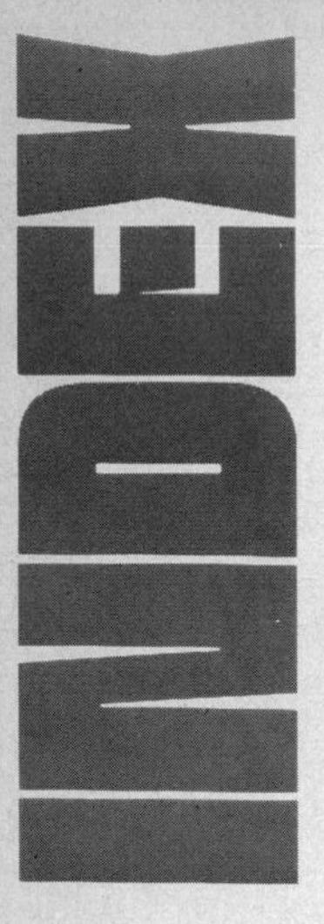

Power Steering

APPLICATION INDEX

Make	Year	Gear Type	Sections
American Motors			
All except Pacer	1969-76	D	2,6
Pacer	1975-76	G	2,10
Chrysler Corporation			
All	1969-76	C	2,7
Ford Motor Company			
Maverick-Comet	1970-76	A	2,4
Granada-Monarch	1976	A	2,4
Falcon	1969-70	A	2,4
Mustang-Cougar	1969-70	A	2,4
Cougar	1971-76	D	2,6
Torino-Montego	1972-76	E	2,8
Ford-Mercury	1969-76	E	2,8
Ford	1969	D	2,6
Thunderbird	1969-76	E	2,8
Lincoln, Mark III Mark IV	1969-76	E	2,8
Mustang II	1974-76	F	2,9
Bobcat	1975-76	F	2,9
Pinto	1975-76	F	2,9
General Motors			
Chevrolet	1969-76	D	2,6
Chevelle	1969-76	D	2,6
Nova	1969-76	D	2,6
Camaro	1969-76	D	2,6
Corvette	1969-76	B	2,5
Vega	1971-76	D	2,6
Monza	1975-76	D	2,6
Pontiac	1969-76	D	2,6
Ventura	1973-76	D	2,6
Astre	1975-76	D	2,6
Oldsmobile	1969-76	D	2,6
Omega	1973-76	D	2,6
Starfire	1975-76	D	2,6
Buick	1969-76	D	2,6
Apollo	1973-76	D	2,6
Skyhawk	1975-76	D	2,6
Cadillac	1969-76	D	2,6

A—Bendix linkage
B—Saginaw linkage
C—Chrysler constant control
D—Saginaw rotary
E—Ford torsion bar
F—Rack and Pinion—Ford
G—Rack and Pinion—AMC

Section Page Numbers

Power Steering

Preliminary

Before investigating any power steering system, first be sure of the general condition of the systems around it. Simple items such as tire pressure, loose belts, or faulty front end parts can have great effect on the function of the power steering system. After a common-sense general inspection has been made, consult Section 1 and proceed from there. Specific listings of make, model and year will be found in the Application Index.

Section 1 General Diagnosis

Hard Steering

1. Improper tire pressure.
2. Loose pump drive belt.
3. Low or incorrect hydraulic fluid.
4. Loose, bent or poorly lubricated front end parts.
5. Improper front end alignment, especially caster.
6. Bind in steering column or mechanism.
7. Air in hydraulic system.
8. Low pump output or leaks in system.
9. Obstruction in lines.
10. Pump valves sticking or out of adjustment.

Loose Steering

1. Loose wheel bearings.
2. Faulty shocks.
3. Worn Pitman arm or front end components.
4. Loose steering gear mountings or linkage points.
5. Steering mechanism worn or improperly adjusted.
6. Valve spool improperly adjusted.

Veer or Wander

1. Improper tire pressure.
2. Improper front end alignment.
3. Dragging brakes.
4. Bent frame.
5. Improper rear end alignment.
6. Faulty shocks or springs.
7. Loose or bent front end components.
8. Play in Pitman arm.
9. Loose wheel bearings.
10. Binding Pitman arm.
11. Spool valve sticking or improperly adjusted.

Wheel Oscillation

1. Improper tire pressure.
2. Loose wheel bearings.
3. Improper front end alignment.
4. Bent spindle.
5. Worn, bent or broken front end components.
6. Tires out of round or imbalanced.

Noises

1. Loose belts.
2. Low fluid, air in system.
3. Foreign matter in system.
4. Improper lubrication.
5. Interference or chafing in front end.
6. Steering gear mountings loose.
7. Incorrect adjustment or wear in mechanism.
8. Faulty valves or wear in pump.

Section 2 Preliminary Tests

NOTE: *The following tests are generally applicable to most power steering systems. If the specification required is not listed, then that test is only generally applicable to that system.*

Turning Effort

Check the effort required to turn the steering wheel after aligning the front wheels and inflating the tires to the proper pressure.

1. With the vehicle on dry pavement and the front wheels straight ahead, set the parking brake and turn the engine on.
2. After a short warm-up period turn the steering wheel back and forth several times to warm the steering fluid.
3. Attach a spring scale to the steering wheel rim and measure the pull required to turn the steering wheel one complete revolution in each direction. The effort needed to turn the steering wheel should not exceed the limits given in the specifications.

NOTE: this test may be done with torque wrench on the steering wheel nut. See the section on Manual Steering for a discussion of this test.

Checking the Oil Flow and Pressure Relief Valve in the Pump Assembly

When the wheels are turned hard right or hard left, against the stops, the oil flow and pressure relief valves come into action. If these valves are working, there should be a slight buzzing noise. Do not hold the wheels in the extreme position for over three or four seconds because, if the pressure relief valve is not working, the pressure could get high enough to damage the system.

Section 3 Power Steering Pumps

The power steering pump supplies all the power assist used in power steering systems of all designs. There are various designs of pumps used by the automobile manufacturers but all pumps supply power to operate the steering systems with the least effort. All power steering pumps have a reservoir tank built onto the pump. These pumps are driven by belts turned by pulleys on the front of the crankshaft.

With the engine at idle speed, the pump supplies high fluid pressure. When the car is moving straight ahead, less pressure is needed and the excess is relieved through a pressure relief and flow control valve. The pressure relief part of the valve is inside the flow control part and is basically the same for all pumps. The flow control valve regulates the constant flow of fluid from the pump to meet the demands of the steering gear. The pressure relief valve limits the hydraulic pressure built up when the steering gear is turned against its stops.

During all pump disassembly work, make sure all work is done on a clean work surface. Clean the outside of the pump thoroughly and do not allow dirt of any kind to get inside the pump. Do not immerse the

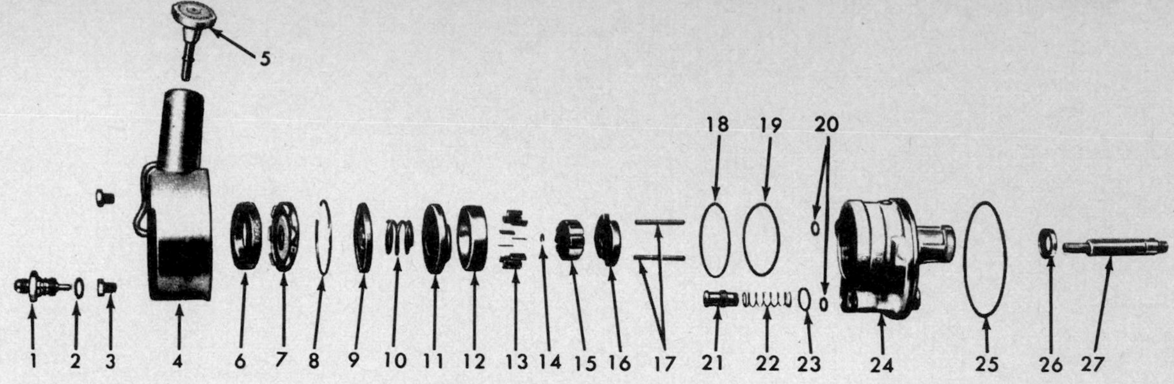

Vane type pump, exploded view (© Chevrolet Motor Div., G.M. Corp)

1 Union
2 Seal
3 Mounting studs
4 Reservoir
5 Dip stick and cover
6 Element (Chevy II and Corvette)
7 Filter assembly (Chevy II and Corvette)
8 End plate retaining ring
9 End plate
10 Spring
11 Pressure plate
12 Pump ring
13 Vanes
14 Drive shaft retaining ring
15 Rotor
16 Thrust plate
17 Dowel pins
18 End plate O-ring
19 Pressure plate O-ring
20 Mounting stud O-ring seals
21 Flow control valve
22 Flow control valve spring
23 Flow control valve O-ring seal
24 Pump housing
25 Reservoir O-ring seal
26 Shaft seal
27 Shaft

shaft oil seal in solvent.

When replacing the rotor shaft seal, be extremely careful not to scratch sealing surfaces.

Vane Type Power Steering Pump Overhaul

The vane type power steering pump is used in Saginaw steering systems. The operation is basically the same as that of the roller type pumps. Centrifugal force moves a number of vanes outward against the pump ring, pumping the fluid to the control valve.

Disassembly

1. Clean the outside of the pump in a non-toxic solvent before disassembling, and remove it from the engine.
2. Mount the pump in a vise, being careful not to distort the front hub of the pump. Remove pulley retaining nut and remove pulley.
3. Remove the union and seal.
4. Remove the reservoir retaining studs and separate the reservoir from the housing.
5. Remove the mounting bolt O-rings and the union O-rings.
6. Remove the filter and filter cage; discard the filter element.
7. Remove the end plate retaining ring by compressing the retaining ring and then prying it out with a screwdriver. The retaining ring may be compressed by inserting a small punch in the 1/8 in. diameter hole in the housing and pushing in until the ring clears the groove.
8. Remove the end plate. The end plate is spring-loaded and should rise above the housing level. If it is stuck inside the housing, gentle tapping should free the plate.
9. Remove the shaft Woodruff key and tap the end of the shaft gently to free the pressure plate, pump ring, rotor assembly, and thrust plate. Remove these parts as one unit.
10. Remove the end plate O-ring. Separate the pressure plate, pump ring, rotor assembly, and thrust plate.

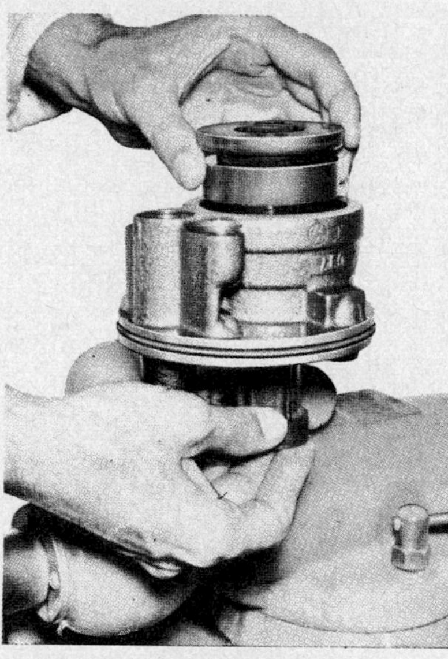

Removing impeller unit
(© Chevrolet Motor Div., G.M. Corp)

Removing end plate ring
(© Chevrolet Motor Div., G.M. Corp)

Inspection

Clean all metal parts in a non-toxic solvent and inspect them as noted below:

1. Check the flow control valve for free movement in the housing bore. If the valve is sticking, see if there is dirt or roughness in the bore.
2. Check the cap screw in the end of the flow control valve for looseness. Tighten if necessary, being careful not to damage the machined surfaces.
3. Inspect the pressure plate and pump plate surfaces for flatness, cracks, or scores. Do not mistake the normal wear marks for scoring.
4. Check the vanes in the rotor assembly for free movement. See that they were installed with the radiused edge toward the pump ring.
5. If the flow control valve plunger is defective, install a new part. It is factory calibrated and supplied as a unit.
6. Check the driveshaft for worn splines, cracks, bushing material pick-up, etc.
7. Check the reservoir, studs, casting, etc. for burrs and other defects that would impair operation.
8. Use new O-rings when assembling.

Assembly

1. Install a new shaft seal in the

housing and insert the shaft at the hub end of housing, splined end entering mounting face side.

2. Install the thrust plate on the dowel pins with the ported side facing the rear of the pump housing.
3. Install the rotor on the shaft, making sure it moves freely on the splines. Countersunk side must be toward the pulley.
4. Install the shaft retaining ring. Install the pump ring on the dowel pins with the direction of rotation arrow to the rear of the pump housing. Rotation is clockwise as seen from the pulley.
5. Install the vanes in the rotor slots with the radius edge towards the outside.
6. Lubricate the outside diameter and chamfer of the pressure plate with petroleum jelly so as not to damage the O-ring and install the plate on the dowel pins with the ported face toward the pump ring. Seat the pressure plate by placing a large socket on top of the plate and pushing down with hand.
7. Install the pressure plate spring in the center groove of the plate.
8. Install the end plate O-ring. Lubricate the outside diameter and chamfer of the end plate with petroleum jelly so as not to damage the O-ring and install the end plate in the housing using an arbor press. Install the end plate retaining ring while pump is in the arbor press. Be sure the ring is in the groove and the ring gap is positioned properly.

Installing thrust plate
(© Chevrolet Motor Div., G.M. Corp)

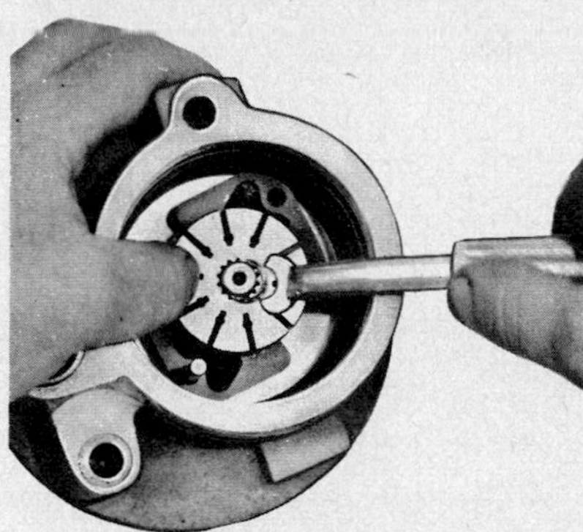
Installing shaft snap ring
(© Chevrolet Motor Div., G.M. Corp)

9. Install the flow control spring and plunger, hex head screw end in bore first. Install the filter cage, new filter stud seals and union seal.
10. Place the reservoir in the normal position and press down until the reservoir seats on the housing. Check the position of the stud seals and the union seal.
11. Install the studs, union, and driveshaft Woodruff key. Support the shaft on the opposite side of the key when tapping the key into place.

Roller Type Power Steering Pump Overhaul

The roller type power steering pump is similar to other constant flow centrifugal force pumps. A star-shaped rotor forces 12 steel rollers against the inside surface of a cam ring. As the rollers follow the ec-

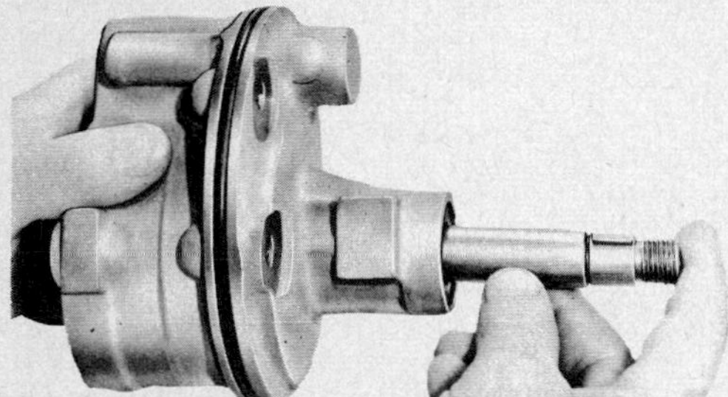
Shaft installation
(© Chevrolet Motor Div., G.M. Corp)

Installing vanes
(© Chevrolet Motor Div., G.M. Corp)

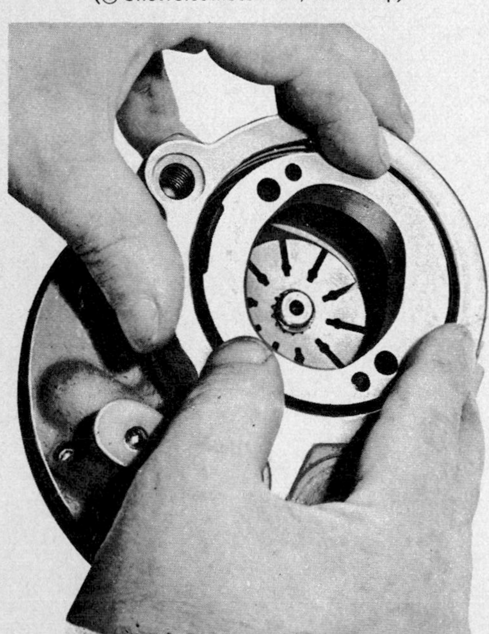
Installing pump ring
(© Chevrolet Motor Div., G.M. Corp)

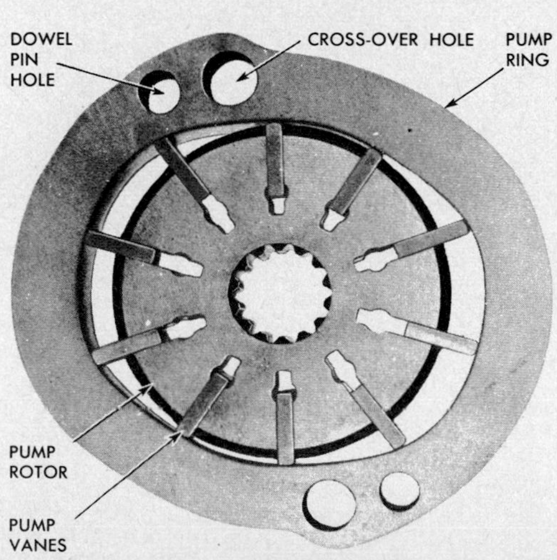

Correct vane assembly
(© Chevrolet Motor Div., G.M. Corp)

Installing pressure plate spring
(© Chevrolet Motor Div., G.M. Corp)

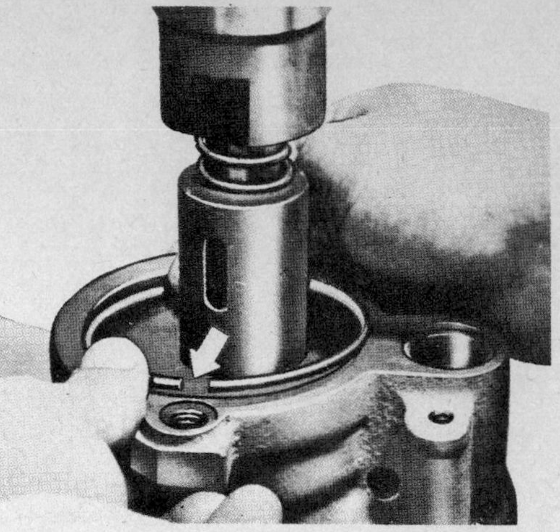

Installing end plate retaining ring
(© Chevrolet Motor Div., G.M. Corp)

centric pattern of the cam ring, fluid is drawn into the inlet ports and exhausted through the discharge ports while the rollers are forced into vee shaped cavities of the rotor, forcing fluid into the high pressure circuit. A flow control valve permits a regulated amount of fluid to return to the intake side of the pump when excess output is produced during high speed operation. This reduces the power needed to drive the pump and minimizes temperature build-up.

Under high pressure demand (such as turning the wheels against the stops), the pressure built up in the steering gear exerts force on the spring end of the flow control valve. This end of the valve contains the pressure relief valve. High pressure lifts the relief valve ball from its seat, allowing fluid to flow through a trigger orifice located in the front land of the flow control valve. This reduces pressure on the spring end of the valve which then opens and allows the fluid to return to the intake side of the pump. This action limits the maximum pressure output of the pump to a safe level.

Disassembly

1. Remove pump from engine, drain reservoir, and clean outside of pump. Clamp the pump in a vise at the mounting bracket.
2. Remove the drive pulley.
3. Remove the shaft seal.
4. Remove the pump from the vise and remove the bracket mounting bolts. Remove the bracket.
5. Remove the reservoir and place the pump in a soft-faced vise with the shaft down. Discard the mounting bolt and the reservoir O-rings.
6. Move the end cover retaining ring around until one end of the ring lines up with the hole in the pump body. Insert a small punch in the hole and push it in far enough to bend the ring so a screwdriver can be inserted to pry the ring loose.
7. Remove the end cover and

Installing flow control valve
(© Chevrolet Motor Div., G.M. Corp)

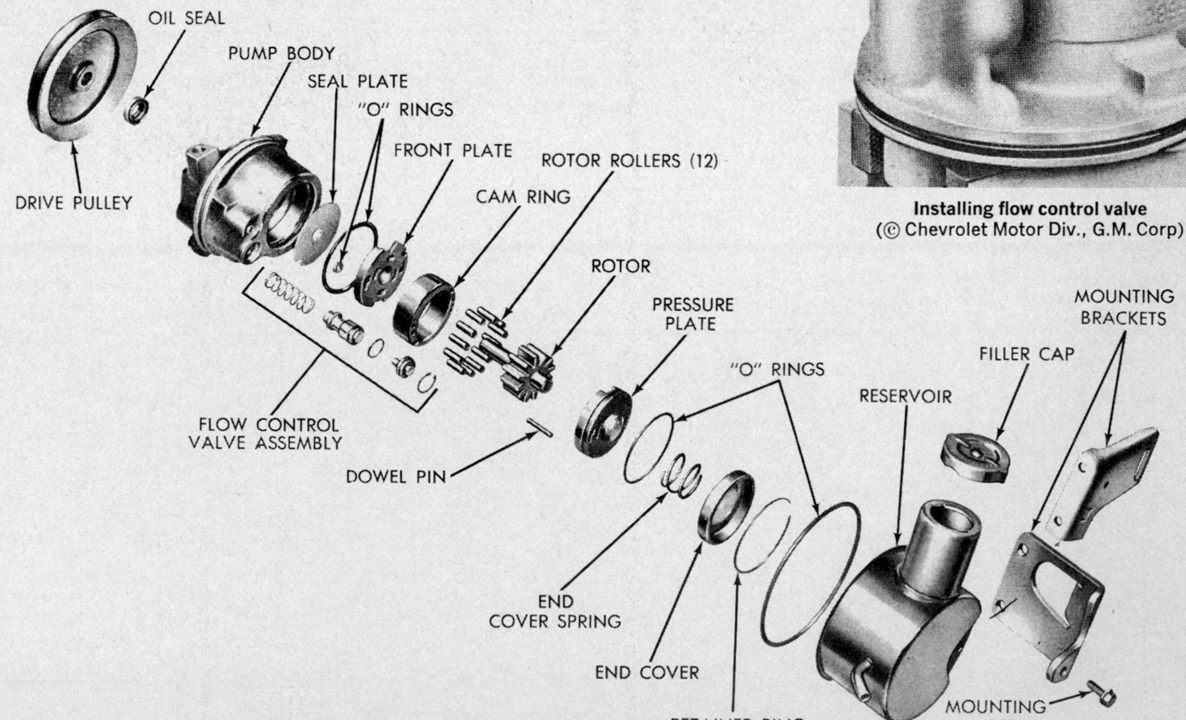

Chrysler 1.06 power steering pump, disassembled view (© Chrysler Corp)

spring from the housing. It may be necessary to tap the cover gently to loosen it.

8. Remove the pump from the vise and turn the pump over so the rotating group may come out of the housing. Tap the end of the driveshaft to loosen these parts. Lift the pump body off the rotating group. Check that the seal plate is removed from the bottom of the housing bore.
9. Discard the O-rings from the pressure plate and end cover.
10. Remove the snap ring, bore plug, flow control valve and spring from the housing. Discard the O-ring. If necessary to disassemble the flow control valve for cleaning, see the procedure for disassembly.

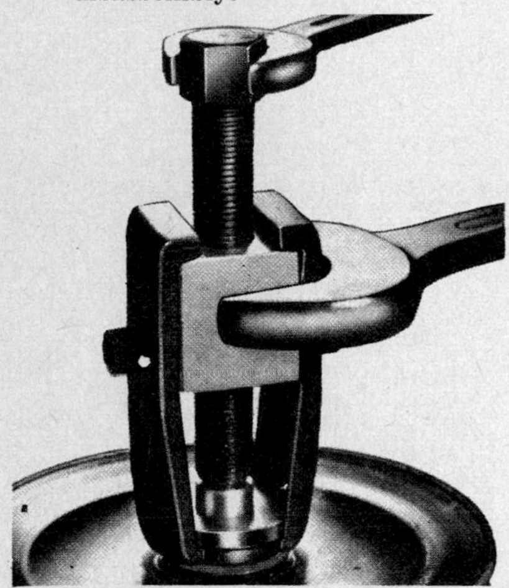

Removing drive pulley
(© Chrysler Corp)

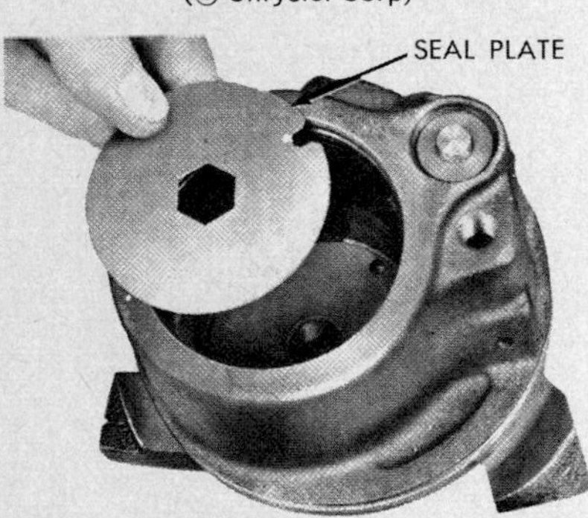

Installing seal plate
(© Chrysler Corp)

Inspection

1. Remove the clean out plug with an Allen wrench.
2. Wash all metal parts in clean, non-toxic solvent. Blow out all passages with compressed air and air dry all cleaned parts.
3. Inspect the driveshaft for excessive wear and the seal area for nicks or scoring. Replace if necessary.
4. Inspect the end plates, rollers, rotor and cam ring for nicks, burrs, or scratches. If any of the components are damaged enough to cause poor operation of the pump, all the internal parts may have to be replaced to prevent later failures.
5. Inspect the pump body drive shaft bushing for excessive wear. Replace the pump body and bushing as one assembly.

Assembly

1. Install the ⅛ in. pipe clean out plug, tightening it to 80 in. lbs.
2. Place the pump body on a clean flat surface and drive a new shaft seal into the bore.
3. Install a new lubricated end cover O-ring into the groove in the pump bore.
4. Lubricate and install a new O-ring on the pump body to reservoir joint.
5. Install a new fiber gasket and brass seal plate on bottom of housing floor, taking care to align correctly. Align the notch in the seal plate with the dowel pin hole in the housing.
6. Carefully install the front plate with the chamfered edge down in the pump bore. Align the index notch in the plate with the dowel pin hole in the housing.

Caution Be extremely careful to align the dowel pin properly. Pump can be completely assembled with the dowel pin improperly seated in the housing and positioned improperly in the end plates.

7. Place the dowel pin in the cam ring and position the cam ring inside the pump bore. Notch in the cam ring must be facing up (away from the pulley end of pump housing). If the cam ring has two notches, one machined and one cast, install with machined notch up. If dowel pin protrudes above cam ring surface by more than 3/16 in., the dowel pin is not seated in the index hole in the housing.
8. Install the rotor and shaft in the cam ring and carefully install the 12 steel rollers in the rotor. Lubricate the rotor, rollers, and the inside surface of the cam ring with power steering fluid. Rotate the shaft by hand to be sure all the rollers are seated and are not sticking or binding.
9. Position the pressure plate by carefully aligning the index notch on the plate with the dowel pin and inserting a clean drill (number 13 to 16) in the cam ring oil hole next to the dowel pin notch until it bottoms on the housing floor.
10. Lubricate and install a new O-ring on the pressure plate. Position the pressure plate in the pump bore so that the dowel pin is in the index notch on the plate and the drill extends through the oil passage in the pressure plate. Seat the pressure plate on the cam ring using a clean 1⅛ in. socket and a soft-faced hammer to tap it gently. Remove the drill and inspect the plate at both oil passage slots to be sure that the plate is squarely seated on the cam ring.
11. Place the large coil spring over the raised portion of the installed pressure plate.
12. Place the end cover, lip edge facing up, over the spring. Press the end cover down below the retaining ring groove. Install the retaining ring in the groove. Be sure the end cover chamfer is squarely seated against the snap-ring.
13. Replace the reservoir mounting bolt seal.
14. Lubricate the flow control valve assembly with power steering fluid and insert the valve spring and valve in the bore. Install a new O-ring on the bore plug, lubricate with fluid, and carefully install in the bore. Install the snap ring with the sharp edge up. *Do not depress the bore plug more than 1/16 in. below the snap-ring groove.*
15. Place the reservoir on the pump body and visually align the mounting bolt hole. Tap the reservoir down on the pump with a plastic-faced hammer.
16. Remove the pump from the vise and install the mounting brackets on the pump. Tighten to 18 ft. lbs.
17. Install the drive pulley by using the installer tool as follows.

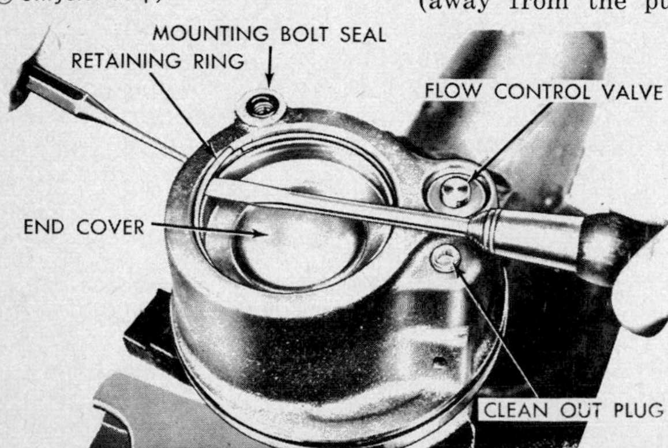

Removing end cover retaining ring
(© Chrysler Corp)

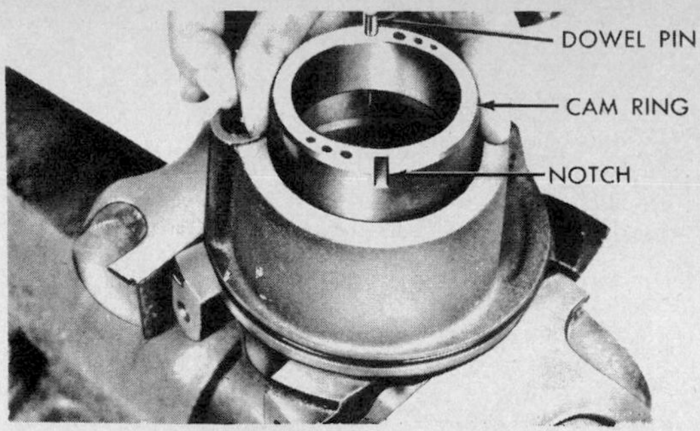

Installing cam ring
(© Chrysler Corp)

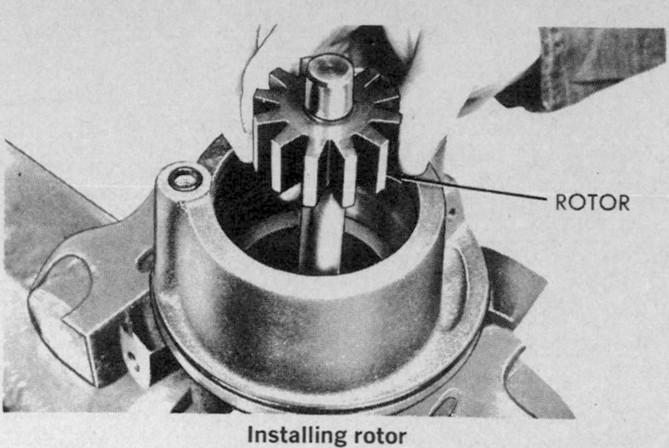

Installing rotor
(© Chrysler Corp)

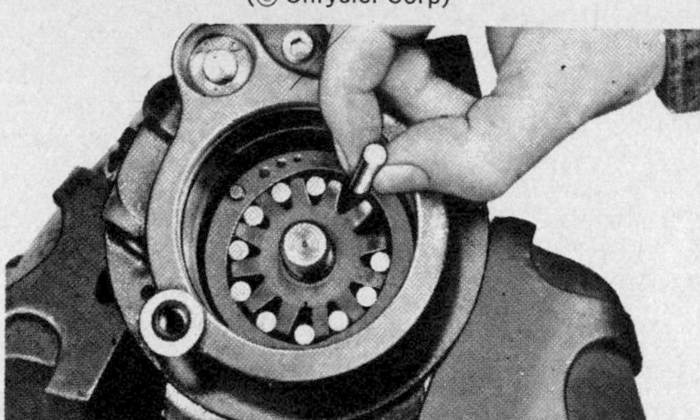
Installing rollers in rotor
(© Chrysler Corp)

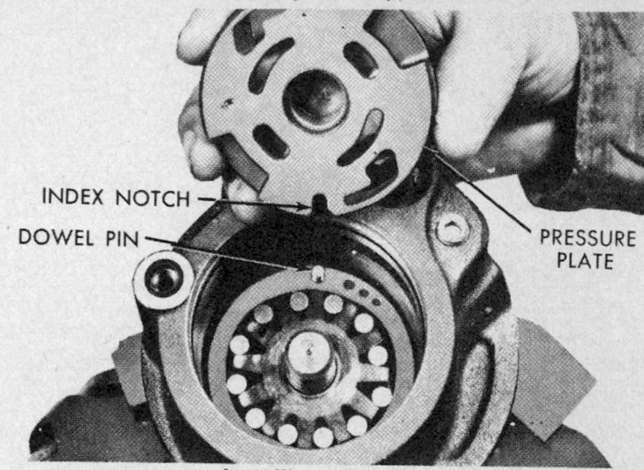

Installing pressure plate
(© Chrysler Corp)

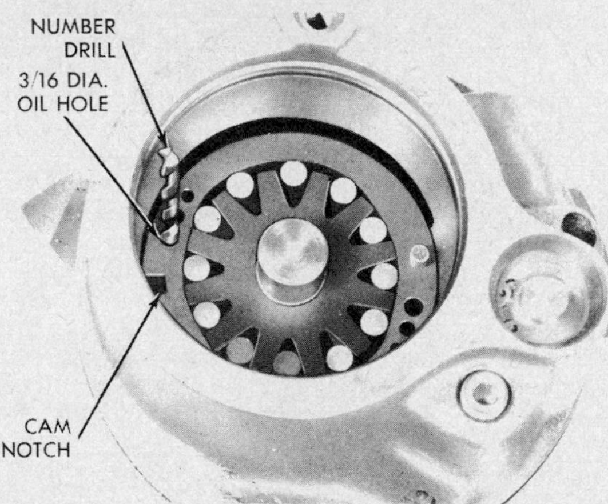

Aligning oil holes
(© Chrysler Corp)

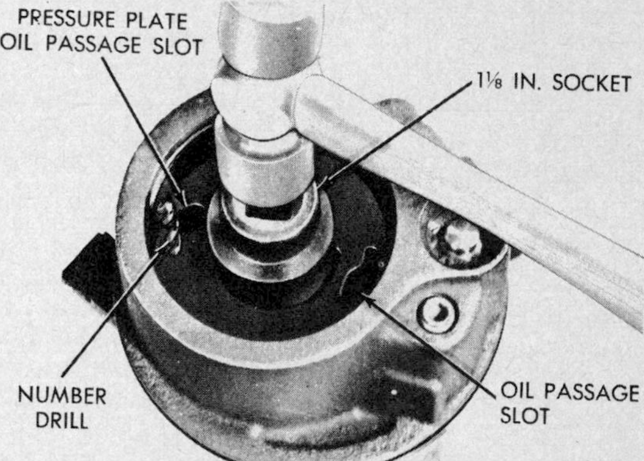

Seating pressure plate
(© Chrysler Corp)

Place the pulley on the end of the shaft and thread the installer tool into the ⅜ in. threaded hole in the end of the shaft. Put the installer shaft in a vise and tighten the drive nut against the thrust bearing, pressing the pulley on the shaft until it is flush with the end of the shaft. *Do not try to press the pulley on the shaft without the special installer tool since the pump will be damaged by any other installation procedure.* A small amount of driveshaft end-play will be seen when the pulley is installed. This end-play is necessary and will be minimized by a thin coat of oil between the rotor and the end plates when the pump is operating.

18. Install the pump assembly on the engine, install the drive belt and hoses (use new O-ring on pressure hose), and check for leaks.

Flow Control Valve Disassembly

1. After removing the pump from the engine and the reservoir from the pump, remove the snap-ring and plug from the flow bore. Discard the O-ring.
2. Depress the control valve against the spring pressure and allow the valve to spring out of the bore. If the valve is stuck in the bore or it did not come out far enough, it may be necessary to tap the housing lightly.
3. If the valve has dirt or foreign particles on it or in its bore, the rest of the pump needs cleaning. The hoses should be flushed and the steering gear valve body reconditioned. If the valve bore is badly scored, replace the pump body and the flow control valve.
4. Remove any nicks or burrs by gently rubbing the valve with crocus cloth. Clamp the valve land in a soft-jawed vise and remove the hex head ball seat and shims. Note the number and gauge (thickness) of the shims on the ball seat. They must be re-installed at the same shim thickness to keep the same value of relief pressure.
5. Remove the valve from the vise and remove the pressure relief ball, guide, and spring.

Flow Control Valve Assembly

1. Insert the spring, guide and pressure relief ball in the end of the flow control valve.
2. Install the hex head plug using the same number and thickness shim that were removed. Tighten the plug to 80 in. lbs.
3. Lubricate the valve with power steering fluid and insert the flow control valve spring and valve in the housing bore. Install a new O-ring on the bore plug, lubricate with fluid and carefully in-

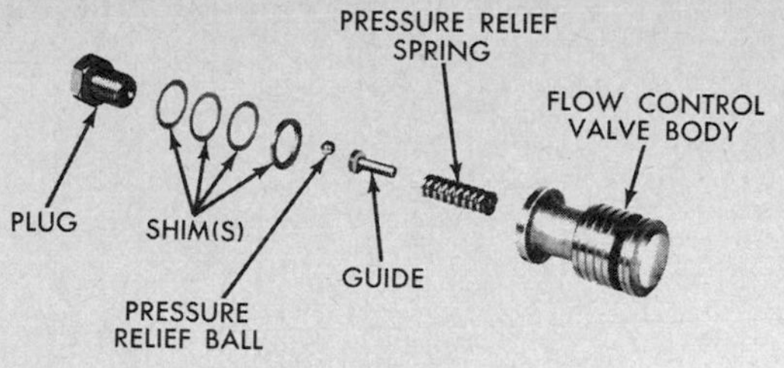

Flow control valve, disassembled view
(© Chrysler Corp)

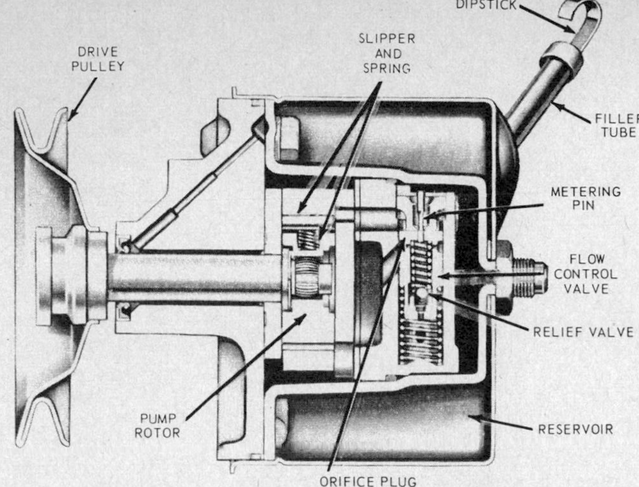

Ford-Thompson power steering pump, sectional view
(© Ford Motor Co)

stall into the bore. Install the snap ring. *Do not depress the bore plug more than 1/16 in. beyond the snap-ring groove.*

Slipper Type Power Steering Pump Overhaul

The slipper type power steering pump is a belt-driven constant displacement unit that uses a number of spring-loaded slippers in the pump rotor to force oil from the inlet side to the flow control valve. Openings in the metering pin allow a flow of about two gpm. of fluid to the steering gear before the flow control valve directs the excess fluid to the inlet side of the pump again. Maximum pressure in the pump is limited by the pressure relief valve which opens when the oil pressure exceeds the maximum pressure limits.

The slipper type power steering pump discussed in this section is used in some Ford cars and is called the Ford-Thompson or TRW power steering pump.

Disassembly

1. Drain as much fluid from the pump as possible after removing the pump from the car.
2. Install a 3/8-16 in. capscrew in the end of the pump shaft to avoid damaging the shaft. Install the pulley remover tool on the pulley hub and place the pump and remover tool in a vise as shown. Hold the pump steady and turn the tool nut counterclockwise to draw the pulley off the shaft. *The pulley must be removed without in and out pressure on the pump shaft to avoid damaging the internal thrust washers.*
3. Remove the pump reservoir by installing the pump in a holding fixture in a vise with the reservoir facing up.
4. Remove the outlet fitting hex nut and any other attaching parts from the reservoir case.
5. Invert the pump so the reservoir is now facing down. Using a wooden block, remove the reservoir by tapping around the flange until the reservoir is loose. Remove the reservoir O-ring seal and the outlet fitting gasket from the pump.
6. Again invert the pump assembly in the vise, remove the pump housing holding bolts, and the pump housing.
7. Remove the housing cover, the O-ring seal, and the pressure springs from inside the pump housing. Remove the pump cover gasket and discard it.
8. Remove the retainer end plate and upper pressure plate. In some pumps, the end plate and the upper pressure plate are one unit.
9. Remove the loose-fitting dowel pin. Be careful not to bend the fixed dowel pin which remains in the housing plate assembly.
10. Remove the rotor assembly, being careful not to let the slippers and springs fall out of the rotor. It may not be necessary to disassemble the rotor assembly unless the lower pressure plate, housing plate, rotor shaft and/or seal is to be replaced. However, the rotor assembly may be disassembled by removing the slippers and springs from the cam ring.
11. Clean any rust, dirt, burrs, or scoring from the pulley end of the rotor shaft before removing the shaft from the housing plate. The shaft must come out without restrictions to avoid scoring

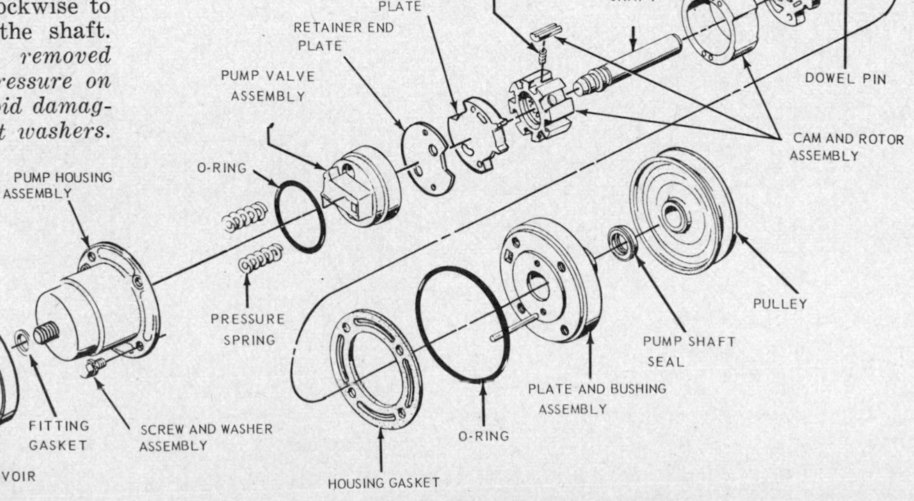

Ford-Thompson power steering pump, disassembled view (© Ford Motor Co)

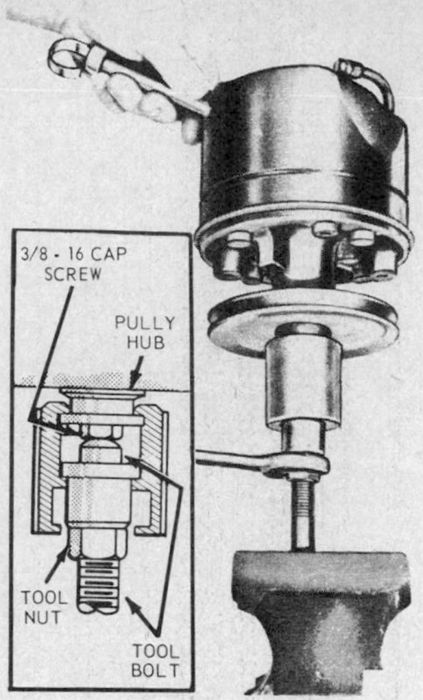

Removing drive pulley
(© Ford Motor Co)

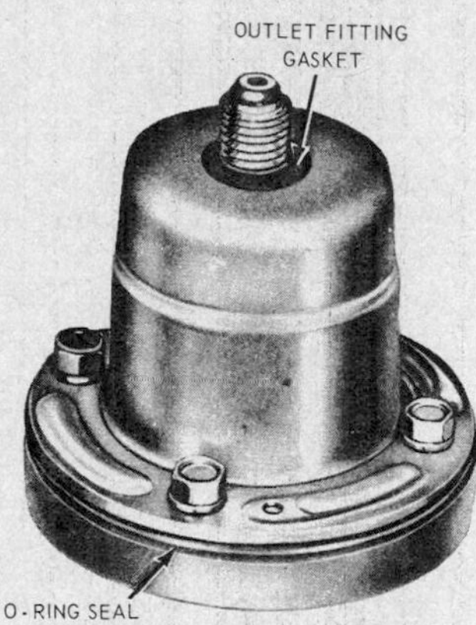

Pump gasket locations
(© Ford Motor Co)

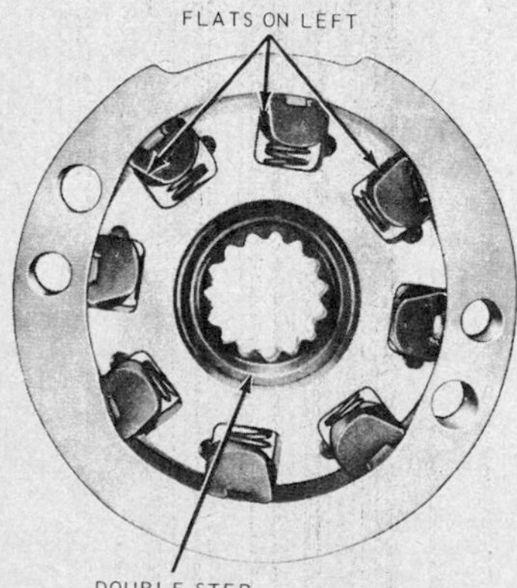

Correct slipper installation, Ford-Thompson power steering pump
(© Ford Motor Co)

or damaging the bushing. Remove the pump rotor shaft.

12. Remove the lower pressure plate.
13. Remove the rotor shaft seal after first wrapping a piece of 0.005 in. shim stock around the shaft and pushing it into the inside of the seal until it touches the bushing. With a sharp tool,

Removing pump reservoir
(© Ford Motor Co)

pierce the seal body and pry the seal out. *Do not damage the bushing, housing, or the shaft.* Install a new seal using the tool shown and a soft-faced hammer.

14. If the pump has a flow control valve, disassemble according to instructions given in the section on the roller type power steering pump.

Inspection

1. Wash all metal parts in clean, non-toxic solvent. Blow out all oil passages with compressed air and air dry all cleaned parts.
2. Inspect the driveshaft for excessive wear and the seal area for nicks or scoring. Replace if necessary.
3. Inspect the pressure plates, slippers, rotor, and cam ring for nicks, burrs, or scratches. If any

Cam and rotor installation
(© Ford Motor Co)

Upper pressure plate installation
(© Ford Motor Co)

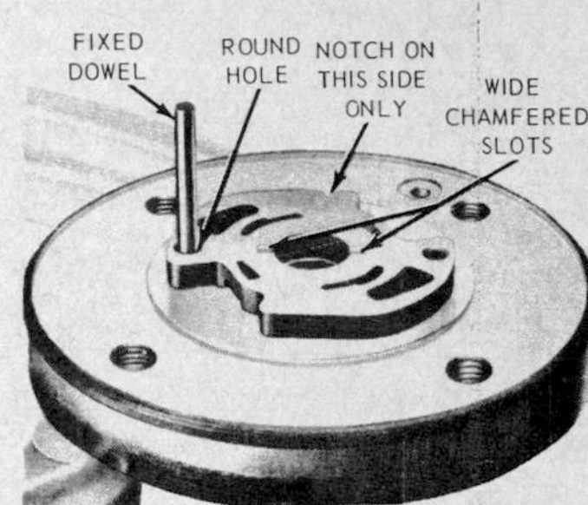

Low pressure plate installed
(© Ford Motor Co)

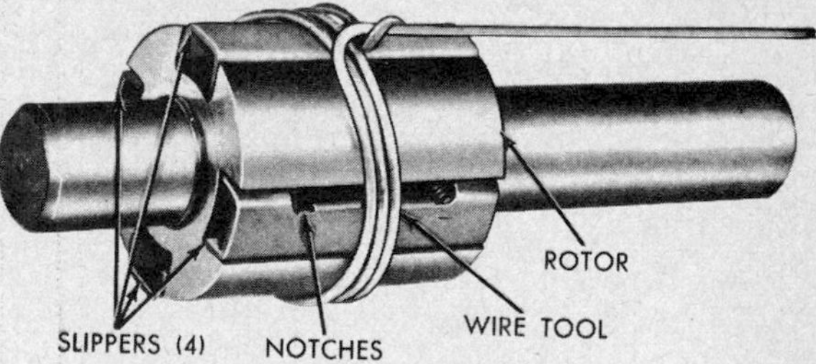

Slippers installed in rotor
(© Chrysler Corp)

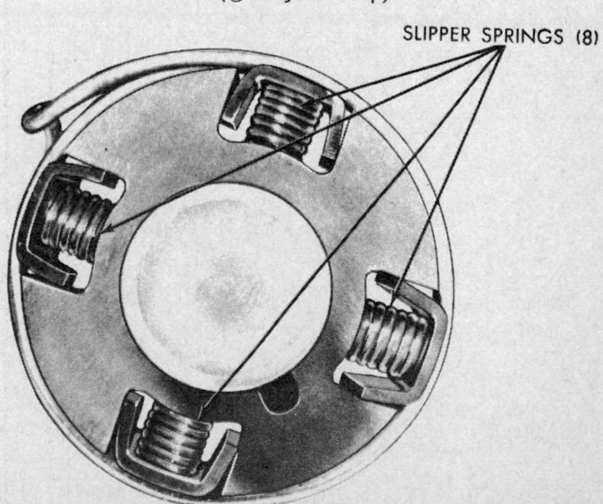

Correct slipper installation, Chrysler 1.2 power steering pump
(© Chrysler Corp)

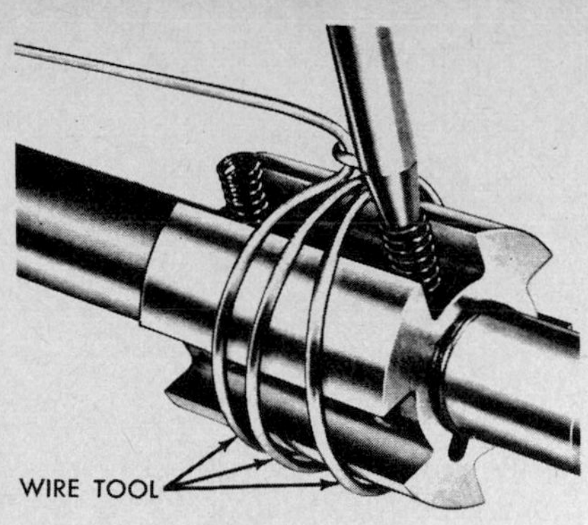

Installing slipper springs
(© Chrysler Corp)

of the parts are damaged enough to cause poor operation or binding of the pump, replace the defective part.

4. Inspect the driveshaft bushing in the pump body for excessive wear. Replace if necessary.

Assembly

1. With the pump assembly in the holding fixture, install the lower pressure plate on the anchor pin with the chamfered slots at the center hole facing up.
2. Lubricate the rotor shaft with power steering fluid and insert the shaft into the lower pressure plate and housing plate.
3. Assemble the rotor, slippers, and springs by wrapping a piece of wire around the rotor, installing the springs, and sliding a slipper into each groove of the rotor over the springs. Then, insert the assembly into the cam ring. Be sure the flat side of the slippers are toward the left side as shown. (Ford-Thompson power steering pump). The Chrysler power steering pump slippers are installed as shown. Be sure that the springs are installed straight and are not cocked to one side under the slippers.
4. Install the cam ring and rotor assembly on the driveshaft with the fixed dowel passing through the first hole to the left of the cam notch when the arrow on the cam outside diameter is pointing toward the lower pressure plate. If the cam and rotor assembly does not seat properly, turn the rotor shaft slightly until the spline teeth mesh, allowing the cam and rotor to drop into position.
5. Insert the loose-fitting dowel through the cam insert and lower pressure plate into the hole in the housing plate assembly. When both dowels are installed properly, they will be the same height.
6. Install the upper pressure plate so the tapered notch is facing down against the cam insert. The fixed dowel should pass through the round dowel hole and the loose dowel through the long hole. The slot between the ears on the outside of the pressure plate should match the notch on the cam insert.
7. Install the retainer end plate so the slot on the end plate matches the notches on the upper pressure plate and the cam insert..
8. Install the pump valve assembly O-ring seal on the pump valve assembly. *Do not twist the seal.*
9. Place the pump valve assembly on top of the retainer end plate with the large exhaust slot on the pump valve in line with the outside notches of the cam, upper pressure plate, and retainer end plate. All parts must be fully seated. If correctly installed, the relief valve stem will be in line with the lube return hole in the pump housing plate.
10. Put small amounts of vaseline on the pump housing plate to hold the cover gasket in place. Install the cover gasket.
11. Insert the pressure plate springs into the pockets in the pump valve assembly.
12. Block the intake hole in the housing.
13. Lubricate the inside of the housing and the housing cover seal with power steering fluid. Make and install two studs for use as positioning guides, one in the bolt hole nearest the drain hole and the other in the bolt hole on the opposite side of the housing plate.

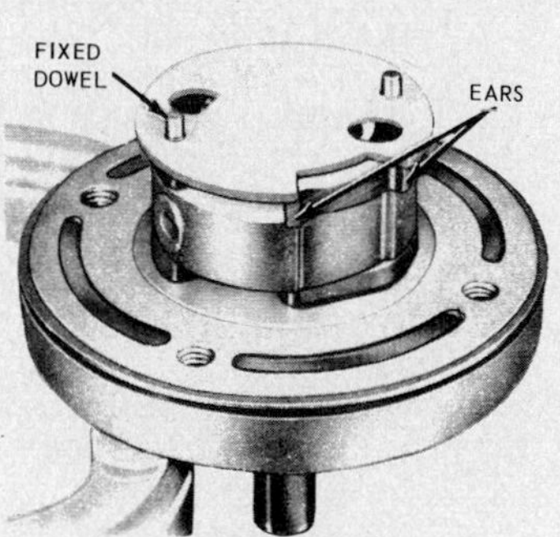

Retainer end plate installation
(© Ford Motor Co)

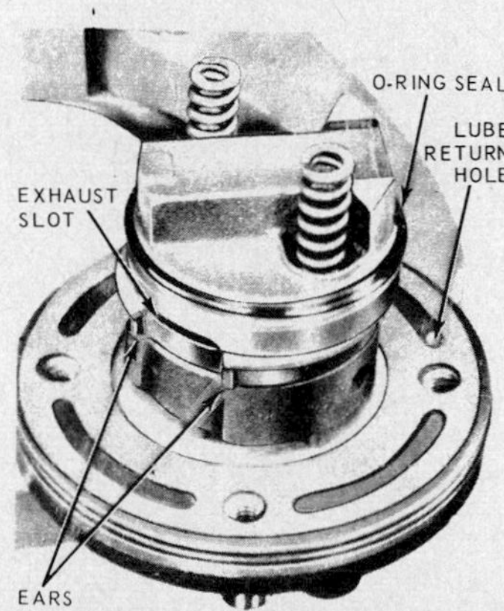

Valve and pressure spring installation
(© Ford Motor Co)

14. Align the small lube hole in the housing rim and the lube hole in the housing plate. Install the housing, using a steady, even, downward pressure. *Do not jar the pressure spring out of position.* Remove the guide studs and loosely install the housing retaining bolts finger tight. Remove the block from the intake hole.
15. Tighten the retaining bolts evenly to 28-32 ft. lbs. until the housing flange contacts the gasket.
16. Install a 3/8-16 hex head screw into the end of the rotor shaft. Check the amount of torque needed to rotate the shaft. If the torque is more than 15 in. lbs., loosen the retaining bolts slightly and rotate the rotor shaft. Then, retighten the retaining bolts evenly. *Do not use the pump if the shaft torque exceeds 15 in. lbs.*
17. Remove pump from the bench holding fixture and shake the assembly back and forth. If there is a rattle, the pressure springs have fallen out of their seats and must be reinstalled.
18. Install the reservoir O-ring seal on the housing plate without twisting it. Lubricate the seal and install the reservoir, aligning the notch in the reservoir flange with the notch in the outside edge of the pump housing plate and bushing assembly. Using a soft-faced hammer, tap at the rear outer corners of the reservoir. Inspect the assembly to be sure the reservoir is fully seated on the housing plate.
19. Install the identification tag (if any) on the outlet valve fitting. Install the outlet valve fitting nut and tighten to 43-45 ft. lbs.
20. Turn the pump assembly over and install the pulley with the tool used to remove it. Draw the pulley onto the shaft until it is flush with the shaft end. *Do not exert inward and outward pressures on the shaft to avoid damaging the internal thrust areas.*

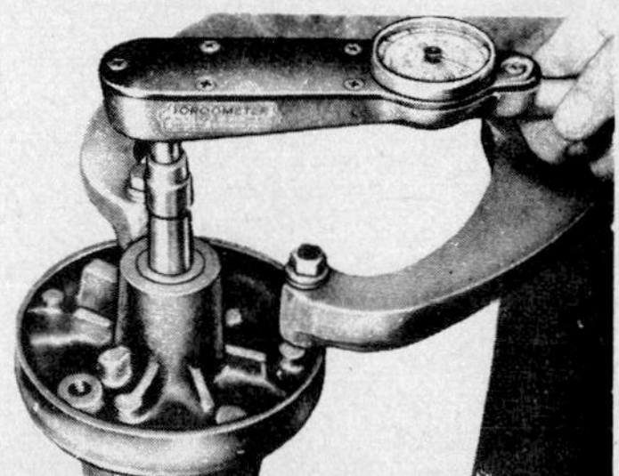
Checking pump rotational torque
(© Ford Motor Co)

Section 4
Bendix Linkage-Type Power Steering System

The Bendix linkage-type power steering system is a hydraulically controlled linkage-type system composed of an integral pump and fluid reservoir, a control valve, a power cylinder, connecting fluid lines, and the steering linkage. The hydraulic pump, which is driven by a belt turned by the engine, draws fluid from the reservoir and provides fluid pressure through hoses to the control valve and the power cylinder. There is a pressure relief valve to limit the pressures within the steering system to a safe level. After the fluid has passed from the pump to the control valve and the power cylinder, it returns to the reservoir.

The Bendix linkage-type steering system when used in Ford-built cars is called the Ford Non-Integral Power Steering System.

Control Valve Disassembly and Assembly

1. Clean the outside of the control valve of dirt and fluid.
2. Remove the control valve spring cap from the valve housing. The control valve should be put in a soft-faced bench vise during disassembly. Clamp the control valve around the sleeve flange only, to avoid damaging the housing, spool, or sleeve.
3. Remove the centering spring adjusting nut from the end of the valve spool bolt. Remove the washers, spacer, centering spring, adapter, and the bushing from the bolt and valve housing.
4. Remove the two bolts holding the valve housing and the sleeve together. Separate the valve housing and the sleeve.
5. Remove the plug from the sleeve. Push the valve spool out of the centering spring end of the valve housing, and remove the seal from the spool.
6. Remove the spacer, bushing, and seal from the sleeve end.
7. Drive the stop-pin out of the punch and hammer. *Pull the head of the valve spool bolt tightly against the travel regulator stop before driving out the pin.*
8. Turn the travel regulator stop counterclockwise in the valve sleeve to remove the stop from the sleeve.
9. Remove the valve spool bolt, spacer, and rubber washer from the stop.
10. Remove the rubber boot and clamp from the valve sleeve. Slide the bumper, spring, and ball stud seat out of the valve sleeve, and remove the ball stud socket from the sleeve.
11. Remove the return port hose seat and the return port relief valve.
12. Remove the spring plug and O-ring. Then, remove the reaction limiting valve.
13. Replace all worn or damaged hose seats by using an Easy-Out screw extractor or a bolt of proper size as a puller. Tap the existing hole in the hose seat, using a starting tap of the correct size. *Remove all metal chips from the hose seat after tapping.* Place a nut and washer on a bolt of the same size as the tapped hole. The washer must be large enough to cover the hose seat port. Insert the bolt in the tapped hole and remove the hose seat by turning the nut clockwise and drawing the bolt out. Install a new hose seal in the port, and thread a bolt of the correct size in the port. Tighten the bolt enough to bottom the seal in the port.
14. Coat all parts of the control valve assembly, except the seals, with power steering fluid. Use grease on the seals.
15. Install the reaction limiting valve, spring, and plug. Install the return port relief valve and the hose seat.
16. Insert one of the ball stud seats (flat end first) into the ball stud socket, and insert the threaded end of the ball stud into the socket.
17. Place the socket in the control valve sleeve so that the threaded end of the ball stud can be pulled out through the slot in the sleeve.
18. Place the other ball stud seat, spring, and bumper in the socket. Install and securely tighten the travel regulator stop.
19. Loosen the stop just enough to align the nearest hole in the stop with the slot in the ball stud socket, and install the stop pin in the ball stud socket, travel regulator stop, and valve spool bolt.
20. Install the rubber boot, clamp, and the plug on the control valve sleeve. Be sure the lubrication fitting is turned on tightly and does not bind on the ball stud socket.
21. Insert the valve spool in the valve housing, rotating it while installing.
22. Move the spool toward the centering spring end of the housing, and place the small seal, bushing, and spacer in the sleeve end of the housing.
23. Press the valve spool against the inner lip of the seal and, at the same time, guide the lip of the seal over the spool with a small screwdriver. *Do not nick or scratch the seal or spool during installation.*
24. Place the sleeve end of the housing on a flat surface so that the seal, bushing, and spacer are at the bottom end, and push down the valve spool until it stops.
25. Carefully install the spool seal and bushing in the centering spring end of the housing. Press the seal against the end of the spool, guiding the seal over the spool with a small screwdriver. *Do not nick or scratch the seal or the spool during installation.*
26. Pick up the housing, and slide the spool back and forth to check for free movement.
27. Place the body gasket and valve sleeve on the housing so that the ball stud is on the same side of the housing as the ports for the two power cylinder lines. Install the two bolts in the sleeve, and torque them to the proper specification.

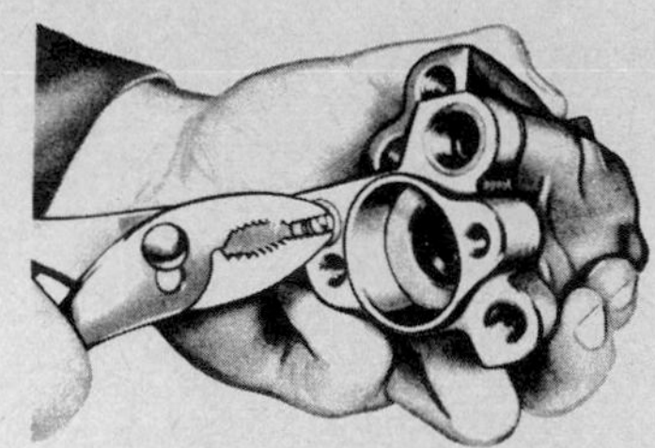

Removing the reaction valve plug
(© Ford Motor Co)

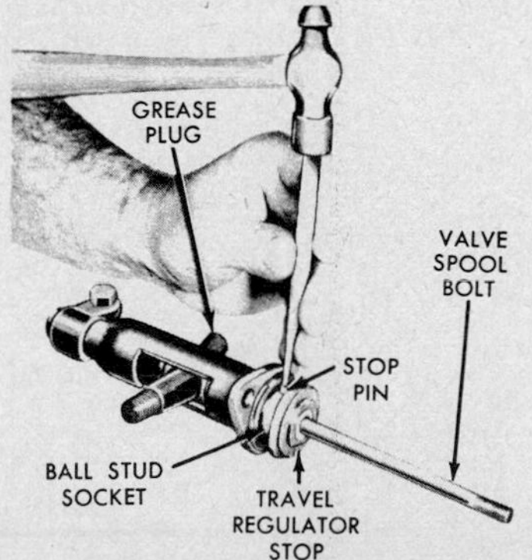

Removing the stop pin
(© Ford Motor Co)

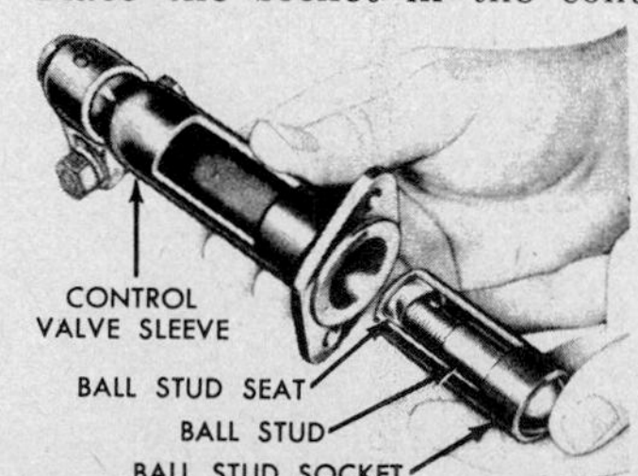

Installing ball socket, seal, and bracket
(© Ford Motor Co)

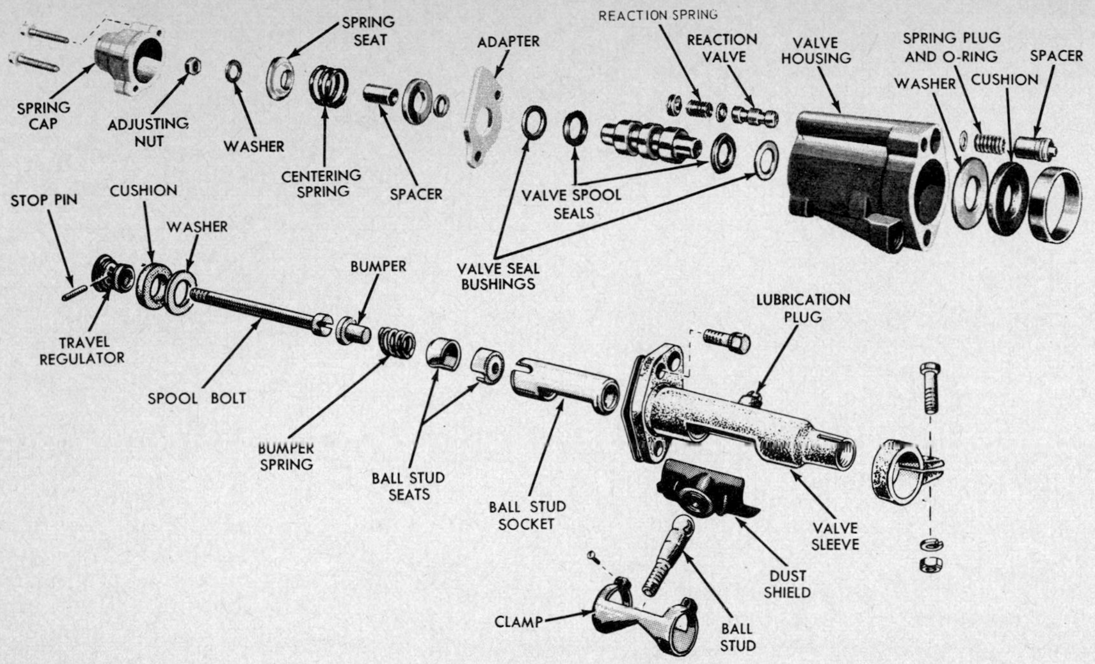

Control valve, disassembled view (© Ford Motor Co)

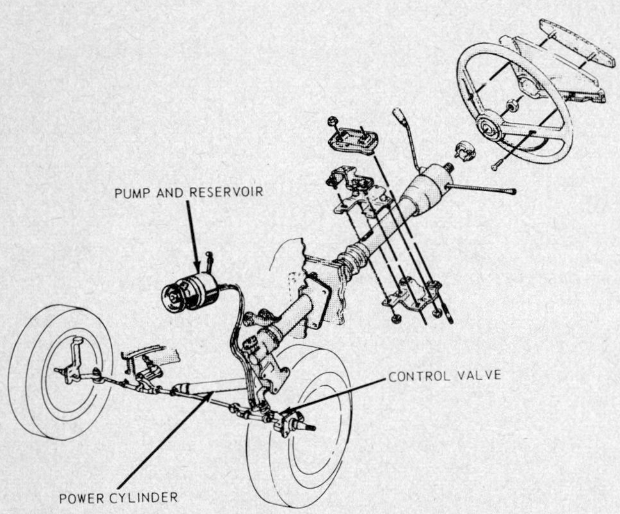

Bendix linkage-type power steering system (© Ford Motor Co)

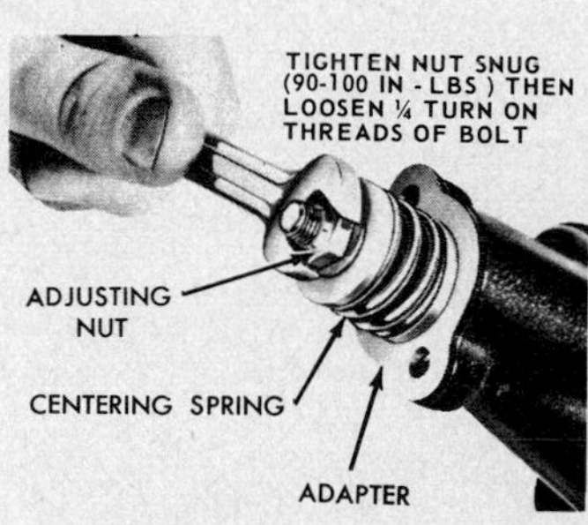

Adjusting centering spring (© Ford Motor Co)

28. Place the adapter on the centering spring end of the housing, and install the bushing, washers, spacers, and centering spring on the valve spool bolt.
29. Compress the centering spring, and install the nut on the bolt. Tighten the nut snug (90-100 in. lbs.) ; then, loosen it not more than 1/4 turn. *Do not overtighten, to avoid breaking the stop-pin at the travel regulator stop.*
30. Move the ball stud back and forth to check for free movement.
31. Lubricate the two cap attaching bolts. Install the centering spring cap on the valve housing, and tighten the two cap bolts to the proper torque.
32. Install the nut on the ball stud so that the valve can be put in a vise. Then, push forward on the cap end of the valve to check the valve spool for free movement.
33. Turn the valve around in the vise, and push forward on the sleeve end to check for free movement.

Power Cylinder Seal Removal and Installation

1. Clamp the power cylinder in a vise, and remove the snap-ring from the end of the cylinder. *Do not distort or crack the cylinder in the vise.*
2. Pull the piston rod out all the way to remove the scraper, bushing, and seals. If the seals cannot be removed in this manner, remove them by carefully prying them out of the cylinder with a sharp pick. *Do not damage the shaft or seal seat.*

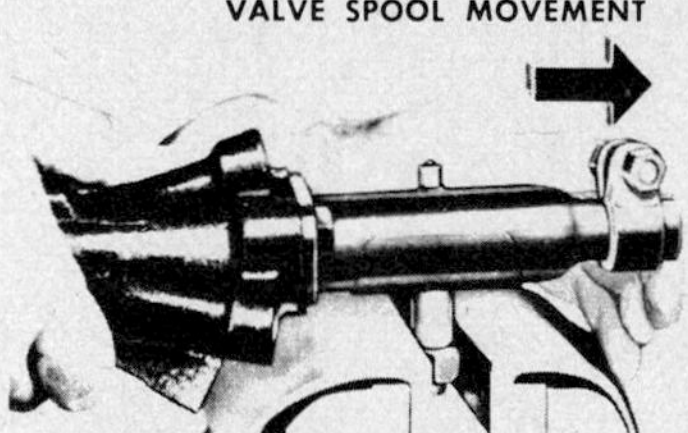

Inspecting valve spool movement (© Ford Motor Co)

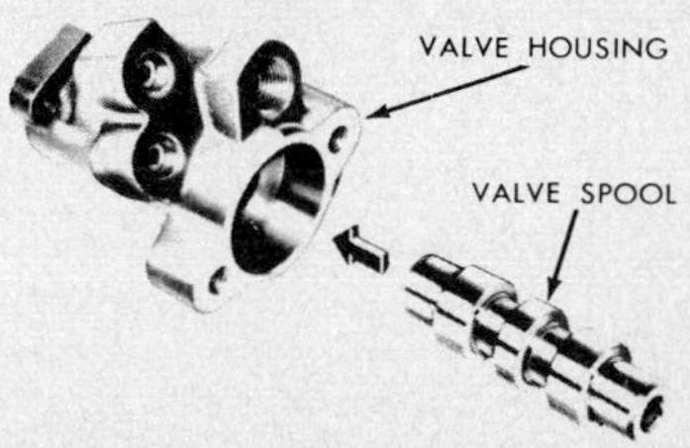

Inserting valve spool (© Ford Motor Co)

3. Coat the new seals with power steering fluid and place the parts on the piston rod, which should be lubricated.
4. Push the rod in all the way, and install the parts in the cylinder with a deep socket slightly smaller than the cylinder opening.

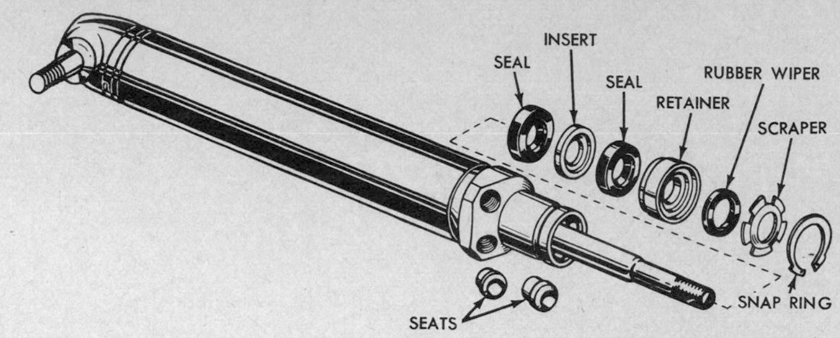

Power cylinder, disassembled view (© Ford Motor Co)

Section 5
Saginaw Linkage-Type Power Steering System

NOTE: Chevrolet Corvette is the only car that uses Saginaw Linkage-Type power steering.

Control Valve

Disassembly

1. Place valve assembly in vise with dust cap end up and remove dust cap.
2. Remove adjusting nut.
3 Remove valve-to-adapter bolts and remove valve housing and spool from adapter.
4. Remove spool from housing.
5. Remove spring, reaction spool, washer, reaction spring, and seal. O-ring may now be removed from reaction spool.
6. Remove annulus spacer, valve shaft washer, and plug-to-sleeve key. Remove the ball stud seal and ball stud seal clamp.
7. Carefully turn adjuster plug out of sleeve. Use care not to nick the top surface.
8. Remove adapter from vise and turn over to allow spring and one of the two ball seats to drop out.

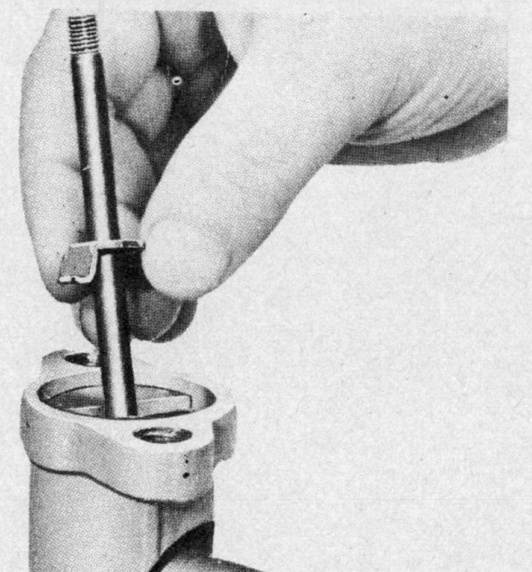

Removing plug-to-sleeve key
(© Chevrolet Motor Div., G.M. Corp)

9. Remove ball stud with other ball seat and allow sleeve to fall free.
10. If necessary to replace a connector seat, tap threads in center hole using a 5/16-18 tap. Thread a bolt with a nut and a flat washer into the tapped hole so the washer is against the face of the port boss and the nut is against the washer. Hold the bolt from turning while backing the nut off the bolt. This will force the washer against the port boss face and back out the bolt, drawing the connector seat from the top cover housing. Discard the old connector seat and clean the housing out thoroughly to remove any metal chips. Drive a new connector seat against the housing seat, being careful not to damage either the connector seat or the housing seat.

Inspection

1. Wash all parts in clean, non-toxic solvent and blow dry with air.
2. Inspect all parts for scratches, burrs, distortion, or excessive wear and replace worn or damaged parts.
3. Replace all seals and gaskets.

NOTE: Corvette valves incorporate a 55 or 40 pound centering spring which might be interchanged with earlier mode (pre-1969) Chevrolet, Chevelle and Chevy II springs. They should not be interchanged as the other springs are only 30 pounds. Corvette valves are stamped with an X (55 lbs) or a C (40 lbs) on the dust cover.

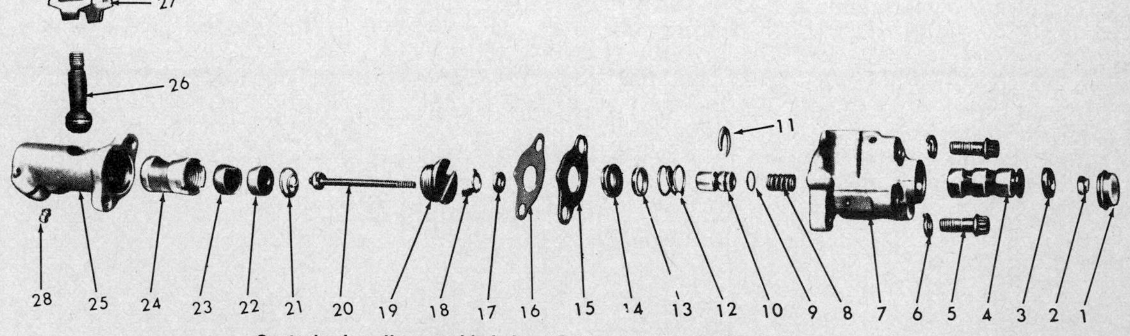

Control valve, disassembled view (© Chevrolet Motor Div., G.M. Corp)

1 Dust cover
2 Adjusting nut
3 Vee block seal
4 Valve spool
5 Valve mounting bolts
6 Lock washer
7 Valve housing
8 Valve adjustment spring
9 "O" ring seal
10 Valve reaction spool
11 Spring thrust washer
12 Valve spring
13 Spring retainer
14 Annulus seal
15 Annulus spacer
16 Gasket
17 Valve shaft washer
18 Plug to sleeve key
19 Ball adjuster nut
20 Valve shaft
21 Ball seat spring
22 Ball seat
23 Ball seat
24 Sleeve bearing
25 Adapter housing
26 Ball stud
27 Dust shield
28 Lubrication fitting

Assembly

1. Replace sleeve and ball seat in adapter, then the ball stud and then the other ball seat and spring. (small end down)
2. Place adapter in vise. Put the shaft through the seat in the adjuster plug and screw adjuster plug into sleeve.
3. Turn plug in until tight, then back off until slot lines up with notches in sleeve.
4. Insert key. Be sure small tangs on end of key fit into notches in sleeve.
5. Install valve shaft washer, annulus spacer, and reaction seal (lip up), spring retainer, reaction spring and spool, then washer and adjustment spring. Install

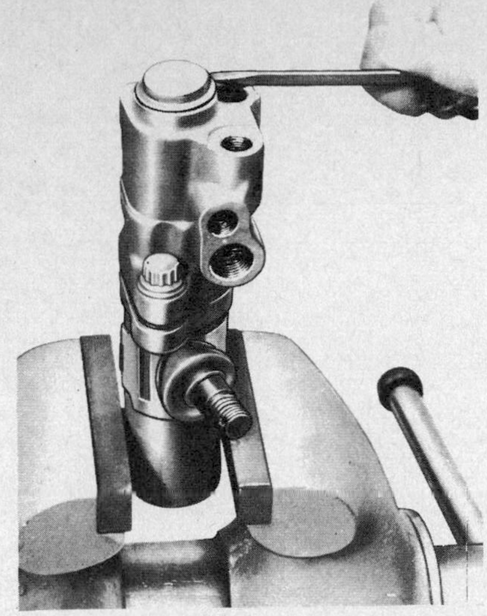
Dust cap removal
(© Chevrolet Motor Div., G.M. Corp)

Removing spool from housing
(© Chevrolet Motor Div., G.M. Corp)

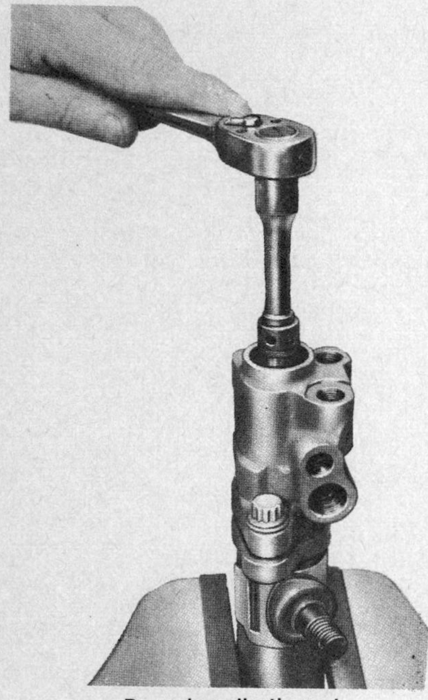
Removing adjusting nut
(© Chevrolet Motor Div., G.M. Corp)

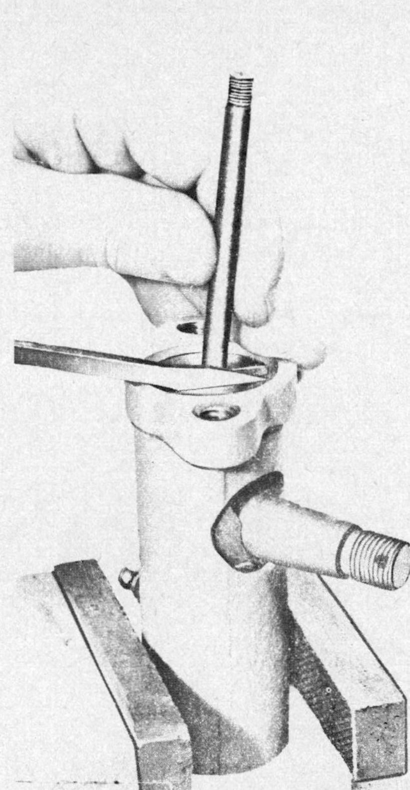
Turning adjuster plug out of sleeve
(© Chevrolet Motor Div., G.M. Corp)

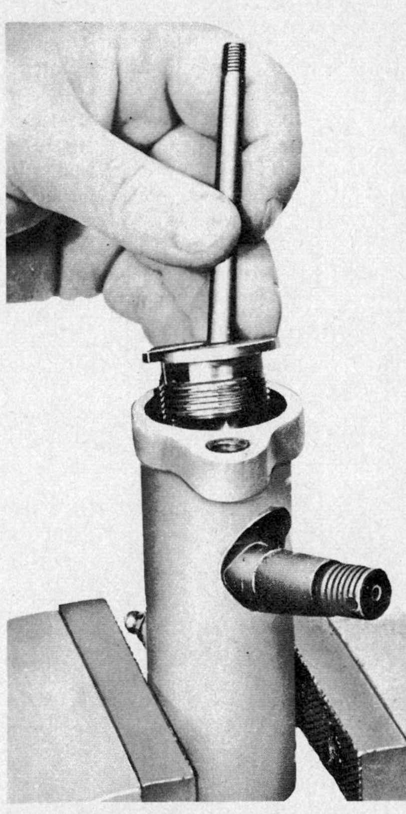
Replacing adjuster plug and shaft
(© Chevrolet Motor Div., G.M. Corp)

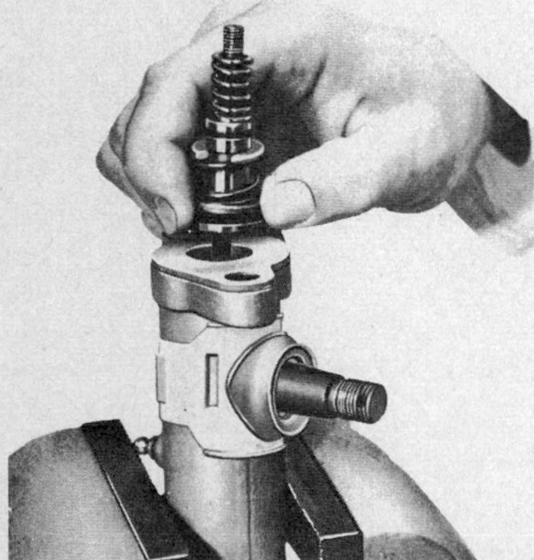
Removing valve parts from shaft
(© Chevrolet Motor Div., G.M. Corp)

Removing connector seat
(© Chevrolet Motor Div., G.M. Corp)

O-ring seal on reaction spool before installing spool on shaft. Install washer with chamfer up.

6. Install seal on valve spool with lip down. Then install spool, being careful not to jam spool in housing.
7. Install housing with spool onto adapter. The side ports should be on the same side as the ball stud. Bolt the housing to the adapter.
8. Depress the valve spool and turn the locknut into the shaft about four turns. Use a clean wrench or socket.

NOTE: always use a new nut.

Power Cylinder

Inspection

1. Check seals for leaks around cylinder rod. If leaks are found, replace seals.
2. Check hose connection seats for damage and replace if necessary.
3. For service other than seat or seal replacement, it is necessary to replace the power cylinder.
4. The ball stud may be replaced by removing snap-ring.

Disassembly and Reassembly

1. To remove piston rod seal, remove snap-ring and pull out on rod. Remove back-up washer, piston rod scraper, and piston rod seal from rod.
2. To remove the ball stud, depress the end plug and remove the snap ring. Push on the end of the ball stud and the end plug, spring, spring seat, and ball stud and seal may be removed. If the ball seat is to be replaced, it must be pressed out.
3. Reverse disassembly procedure. Be sure snap-ring is properly seated.

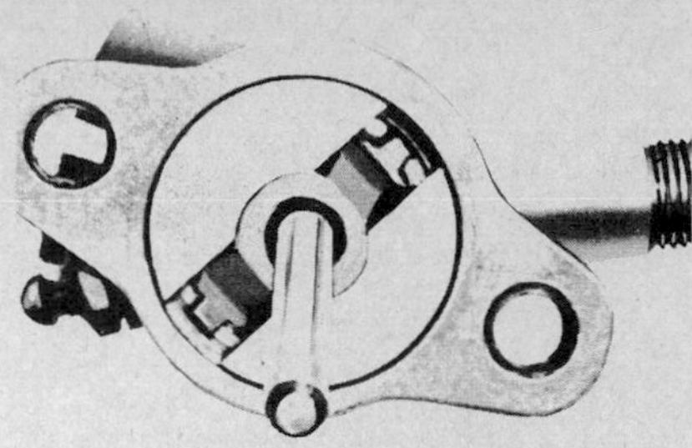

Proper key installation
(© Chevrolet Motor Div., G.M. Corp)

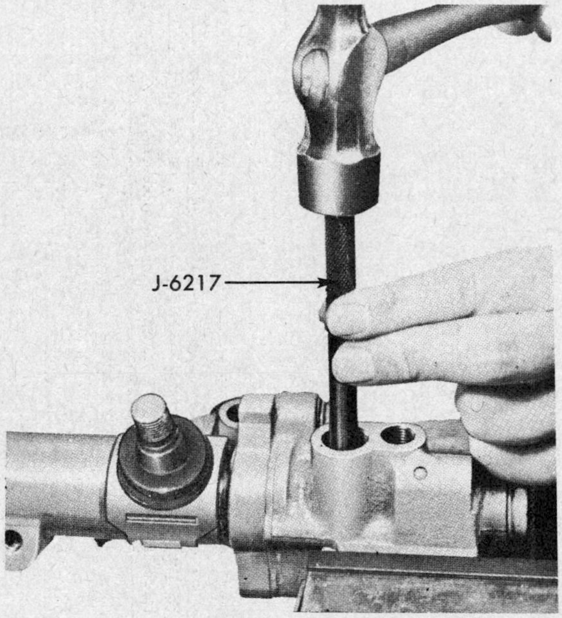

Installing connector seat
(© Chevrolet Motor Div., G.M. Corp)

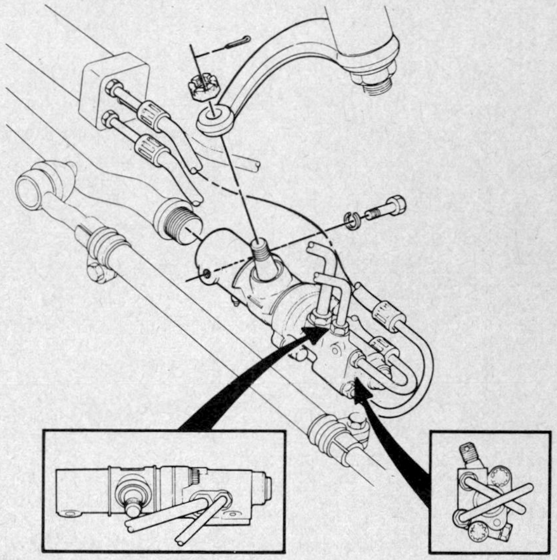

Power steering hose installation
(© Chevrolet Motor Div., G.M. Corp)

1 Lube fitting
2 Snap ring
3 End plug
4 O-ring
5 Spring
6 Spring seat
7 Ball stud
8 Ball seat
9 Ball stud shield
10 Piston body
11 Piston rod seal
12 Backup washer
13 Piston rod scraper
14 Snap ring
15 Piston rod

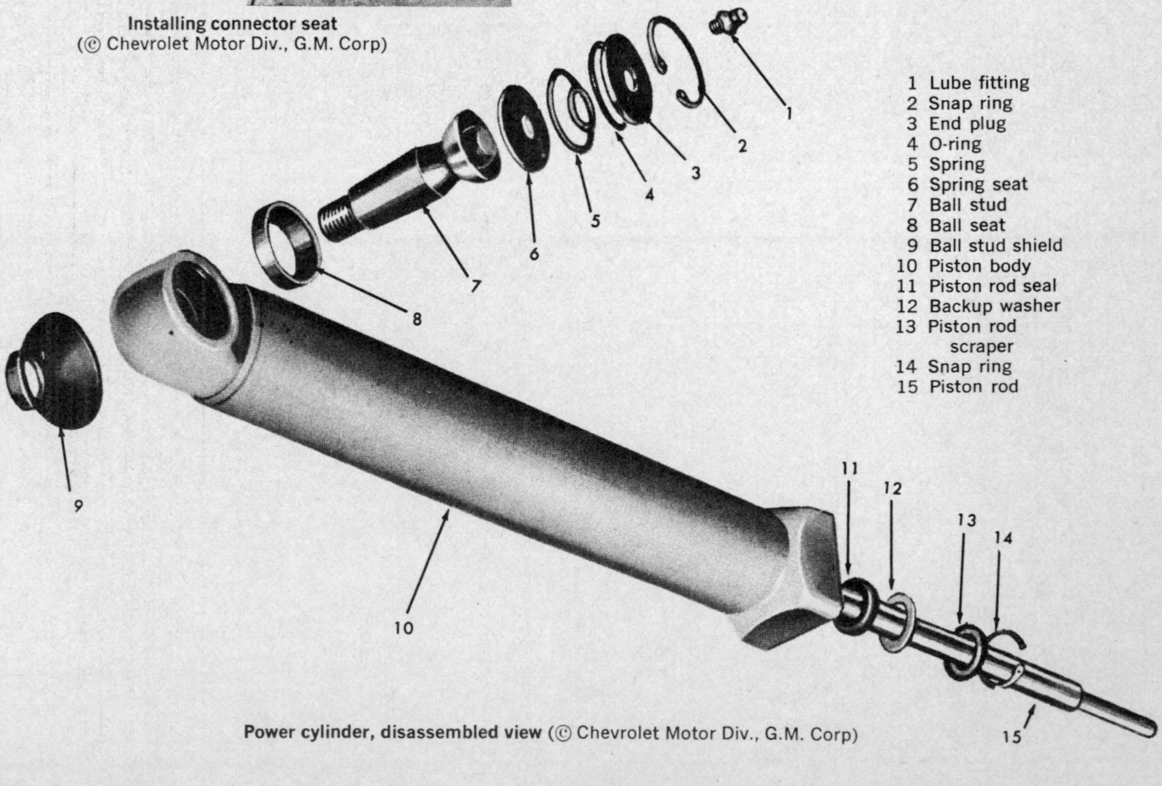

Power cylinder, disassembled view (© Chevrolet Motor Div., G.M. Corp)

Section 6
Saginaw Rotary-Type Power Steering

The rotary type power steering gear is designed with all components in one housing.

The power cylinder is an integral part of the gear housing. A double-acting piston allows oil pressure to be applied to either side of the piston. The one-piece piston and power rack is meshed to the sector shaft.

The hydraulic control valve is composed of a sleeve and valve spool. The spool is held in the neutral position by the torsion bar and spool actuator. Twisting of the torsion bar moves the valve spool, allowing oil pressure to be directed to either side of the power piston, depending on the directional rotation of the steering wheel, to give power assist.

On many General Motors cars a modified version of the system provides variable ratio steering for easier and safer control. The steering gear ratio will vary from a high ratio of about 16:1 while steering straight ahead to a lower gear ratio of about 12.4:1 while making a full turn to either side.

Power Steering Unit

Checking Steering Effort

Run the engine to attain normal operating temperatures. With the wheels on a dry floor, hook a pull scale to the spoke of the steering wheel at the outer edge. The effort required to turn the steering wheel should be 3½-5 lbs. If the pull is not within these limits, check the hydraulic pressure.

Pressure Test

To check the hydraulic pressure, disconnect the pressure hose from the gear. Now connect the pressure gauge between the pressure hose from the pump and the steering gear housing. Fill the fluid reservoir to the proper level. Run the engine and turn the wheel to a full right and a full left turn to the wheel stops to attain normal operating temperatures (150°F-170°F).

Hold the wheel in this position only momentarily.

The initial pressure gauge reading should be 80-125 psi. If the pressure reading is less than the minimum pressure needed for proper operation, check for hose restrictions. Close the valve at the gauge. Do not close the valve for more than 5 seconds. The

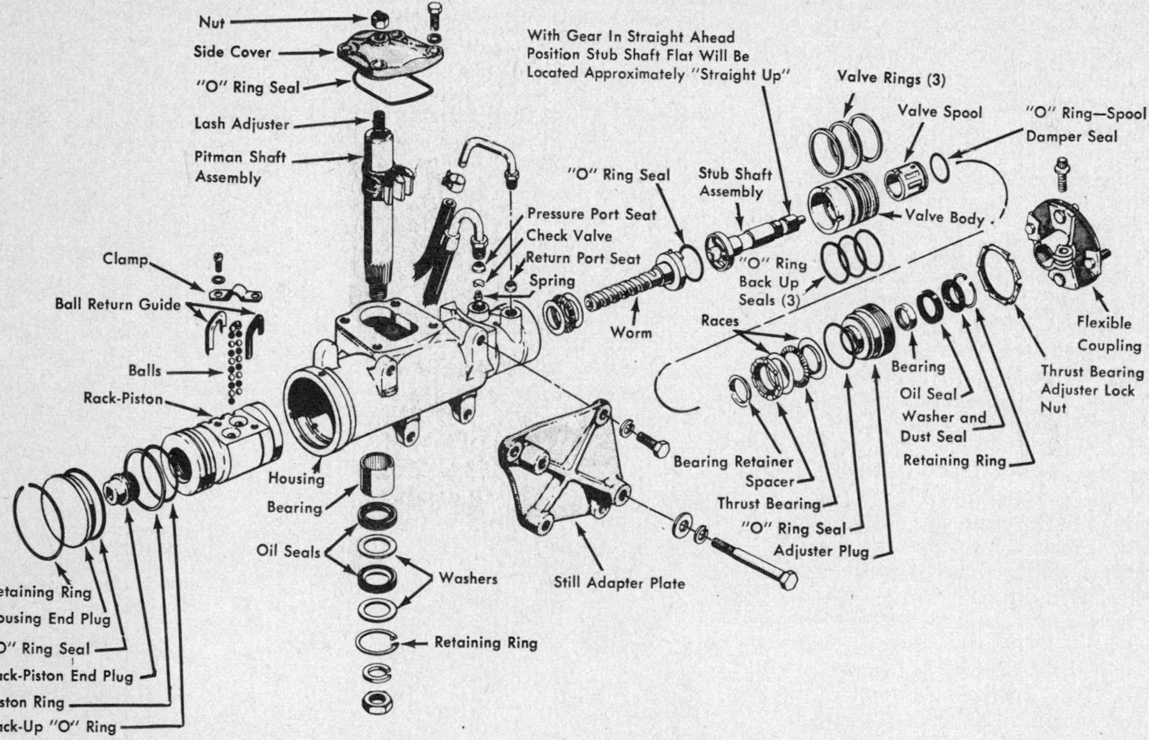

Saginaw rotary gear, exploded view (© American Motors Corp)

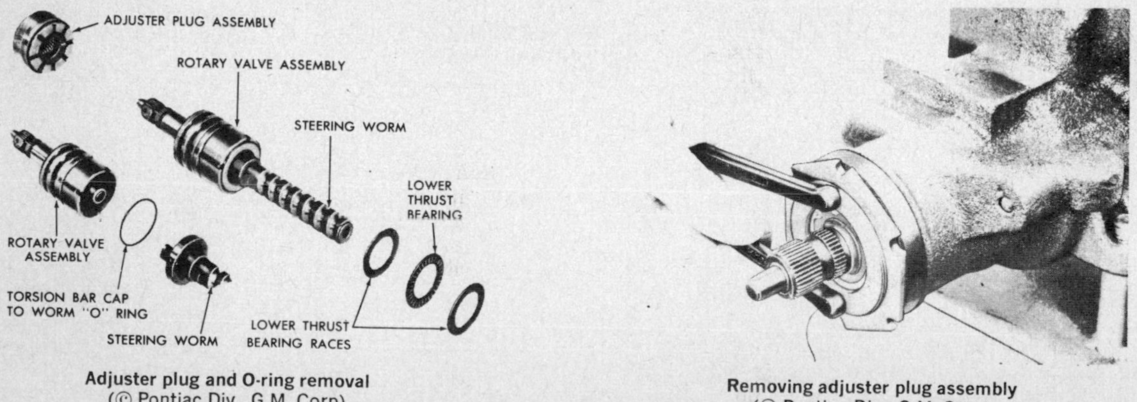

Adjuster plug and O-ring removal (© Pontiac Div., G.M. Corp)

Removing adjuster plug assembly (© Pontiac Div., G.M. Corp)

pressure reading should be within 50 psi of 1350 to 1450 psi (870-1000 psi on Corvette), 1200 to 1300 with 6-cylinder engines). If the pressure is 100 psi or more below specifications, the pump is defective and needs repair. If the pressure reading is within 50 psi of the minimum specifications, the pump is normal and needs only an adjustment of the power steering gear or flow control valve.

If the maximum pressure specification still cannot be obtained by turning the steering wheel against the stops momentarily, then the steering gear is leaking internally and must be disassembled and repaired.

Worm Bearing Preload and Sector Mesh Adjustments

NOTE: The steering gear must be out of the car to adjust it on 1974 and later models. On earlier models only the over-center preload (sector shaft) can be adjusted with the steering gear in the car.

Disconnect the Pitman arm from the sector shaft, then completely back off on the sector shaft adjusting screw on the sector shaft cover.

Center the steering on the high point, then attach an in. lb torque wrench to the steering wheel attaching nut. The torque required to keep the wheel moving for one complete turn should be ½-2 in. lbs.

If the torque is not within these limits, loosen the thrust bearing locknut and tighten or back off on the valve sleeve adjuster plug to bring the preload within limits. Tighten the thrust bearing locknut and recheck the preload.

Slowly rotate the steering wheel several times, then center the steering on the high point. Now, turn the sector shaft adjusting screw until a steering shaft torque of 3-6 in. lbs more is required to move the worm through the center point. Tighten the sector shaft adjusting screw locknut to 35 ft lbs and recheck the sector mesh adjustment. Total steering gear preload should be 14 in. lbs or less.

Install the pitman arm and draw the arm into position with the nut.

Repair Operations

Adjuster Plug and Rotary Valve Removal

1. Thoroughly clean exterior of gear assembly. Drain by holding valve ports down and rotating worm back and forth through entire travel.
2. Place gear in vise.
3. Loosen adjuster plug locknut with punch. Remove adjuster plug.
4. Remove rotary valve assembly by grasping stub shaft and pulling it out.

Adjuster Plug Disassembly

1. Remove upper thrust bearing retainer with screwdriver. Be careful not to damage bearing bore. Discard retainer. Remove spacer, upper bearing and races.
2. Remove and discard adjuster plug O-ring.
3. Remove stub shaft seal retaining ring (Truarc pliers will help) and remove and discard dust seal.
4. Remove stub shaft seal by pry-

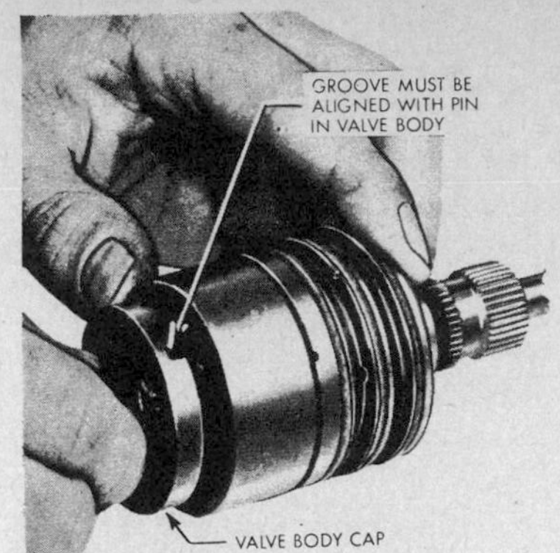

Assembling stub shaft, torsion bar, and cap assembly
(© Buick Motor Div., G.M. Corp)

Valve assembly installed in housing
(© Buick Motor Div., G.M. Corp)

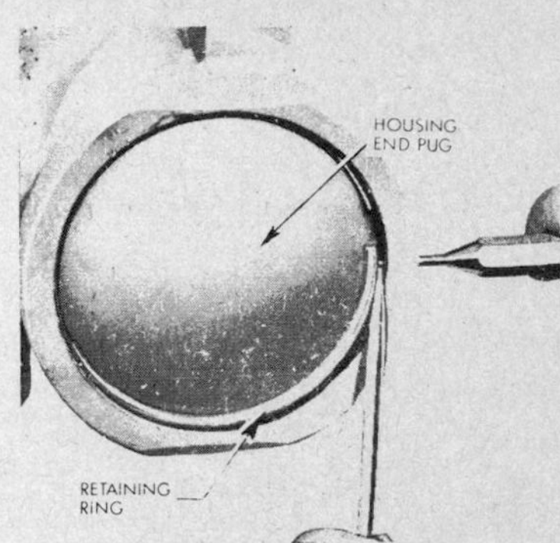

Removing housing end plug retaining ring
(© Buick Motor Div., G.M. Corp)

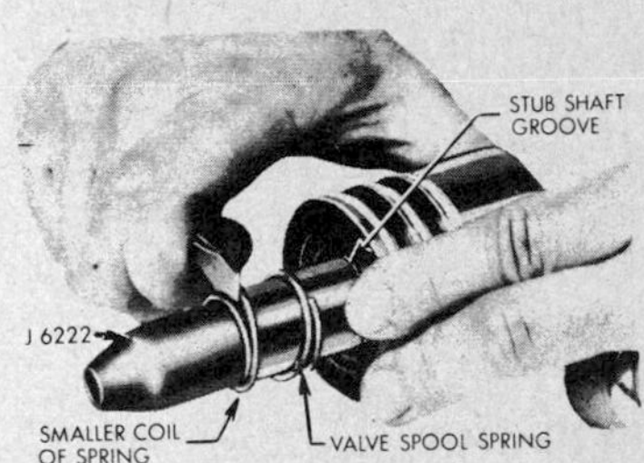

Installing valve spool spring
(© Buick Motor Div., G.M. Corp)

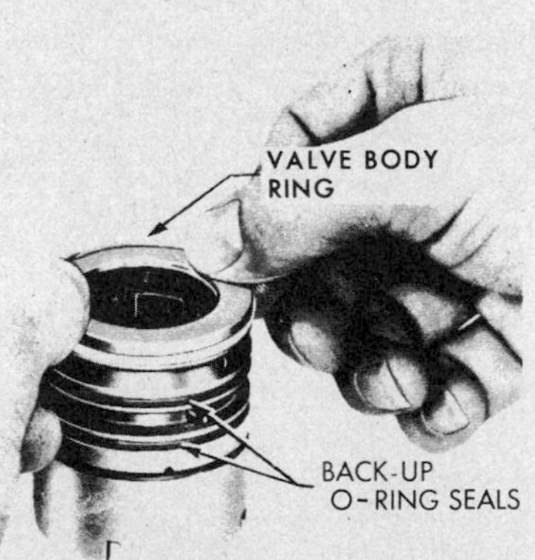

Installing valve body rings
(© Buick Motor Div., G.M. Corp)

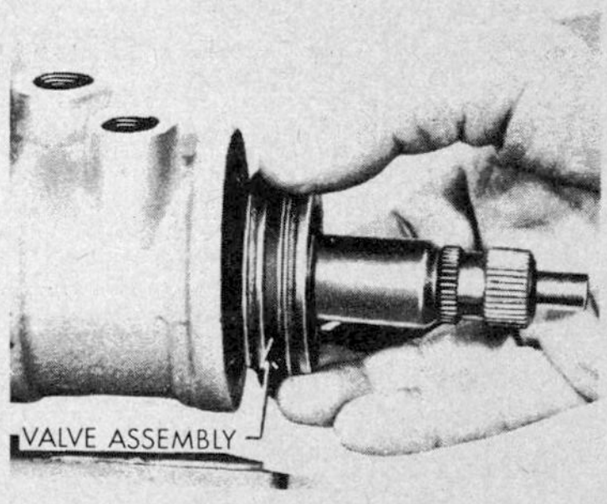

Inserting valve assembly in housing
(© Buick Motor Div., G.M. Corp)

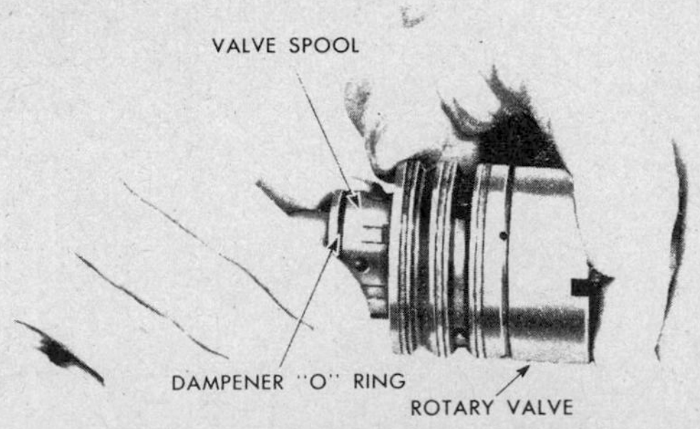

Removing valve spool from rotary valve
(© Pontiac Div., G.M. Corp)

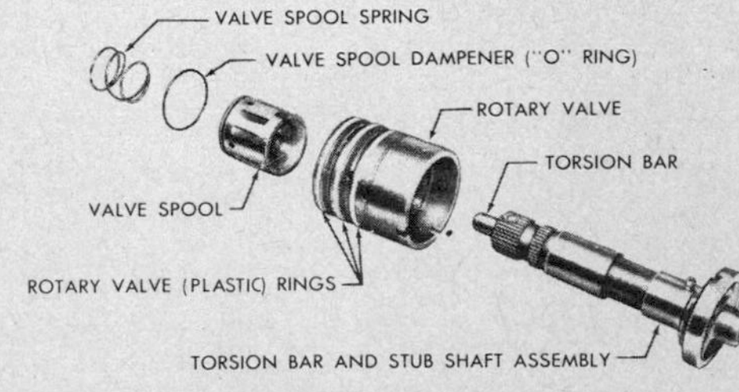

Rotary valve, disassembled view
(© Pontiac Div., G.M. Corp)

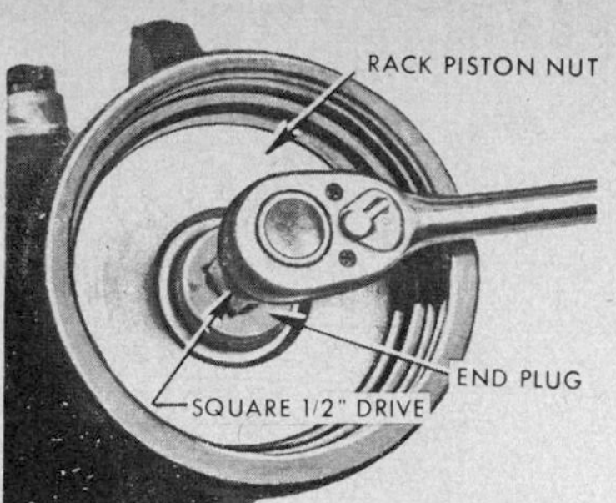

Removing rack-piston nut end plug
(© Buick Motor Div., G.M. Corp)

Installing pitman shaft seals
(© Buick Motor Div., G.M. Corp)

ing out with screwdriver and discard.

5. Examine needle bearing and, if required, remove same by pressing from thrust bearing end.
6. Inspect thrust bearing spacer, bearing rollers and races.
7. Reassemble in reverse of above.

Rotary Valve Disassembly

Repairs are seldom needed. Do not disassemble unless absolutely necessary. If the O-ring seal on valve spool dampener needs replacement, perform this portion of operation only.

1. Remove cap-to-worm O-ring seal and discard.
2. Remove valve spool spring by prying on small coil with small screwdriver to work spring onto bearing surface of stub shaft. Slide spring off shaft. Be careful not to damage shaft surface.
3. Remove valve spool by holding the valve assembly in one hand with the stub shaft pointing down. Insert the end of pencil or wood rod through opening in valve body cap and push spool until it is out far enough to be removed. In this procedure, rotate to prevent jamming. If spool becomes jammed it may be necessary to remove stub shaft, torsion bar and cap assembly.

Rotary Valve Reassembly

Caution All parts must be free of dirt, chips, etc., before assembly and must be protected after assembly.

1. Lubricate three new back-up O-ring seals with automatic transmission oil and reassemble in the ring grooves of valve body. Assemble three new valve body rings in the grooves over the O-ring seals by carefully slipping over the valve body.

NOTE: if the valve body rings seem loose or twisted in the grooves, the heat of the oil during operation will cause them to straighten.

2. Lubricate a new dampener O-ring with automatic transmission oil and install in valve spool groove.
3. Assemble stub shaft torsion bar and cap assembly in the valve body, aligning the groove in the valve cap with the pin in the valve body. Tap lightly with soft hammer until cap is against valve body shoulder. Valve body pin must be in the cap groove. Hold parts together during the remainder of assembly.
4. Lubricate spool. With notch in spool toward valve body, slide the spool over the stub shaft. Align the notch on the spool with the spool drive pin on stub shaft and carefully engage spool in valve body bore. Push spool evenly and with slight rotating motion until spool reaches drive pin. Rotate spool slowly, with some pressure, until notch engages pin. Be sure dampener O-ring seal is evenly distributed in the spool groove.

Caution Use extreme care because spool - to - valve body clearance is very small. Damage is easily caused.

5. With seal protector tool over stub shaft, slide valve spool spring over stub shaft, with small diameter of spring going over shaft last. Work spring onto shaft until small coil is located in stubshaft groove.
6. Lubricate a new cap-to-O-ring seal and install in valve body.

Adjuster Plug and Rotary Valve Installation

1. Align narrow pin slot on valve body with valve body drive pin on the worm. Insert the valve assembly into gear housing by pressing against valve body with finger tips. Do not press on stub shaft or torsion bar. The return hole in the gear housing should be fully visible when properly assembled.

Caution Do not press on stub shaft as this may cause shaft and cap to pull out of valve body, allowing the spool dampener O-ring seal to slip into valve body oil grooves.

2. With protector over end of stub shaft, install adjuster plug assembly snugly into gear housing then back plug off approximately one-eighth turn. Install plug locknut but do not tighten. Adjust preload as described in the adjustment section.
3. After adjustment, tighten locknut.

Pitman Shaft Removal and Installation

1. Completely drain the gear assembly and thoroughly clean the outside.
2. Place gear in vise.
3. Rotate stub shaft until pitman shaft gear is in center position. Remove side cover retaining bolts.
4. Tap end of pitman shaft with

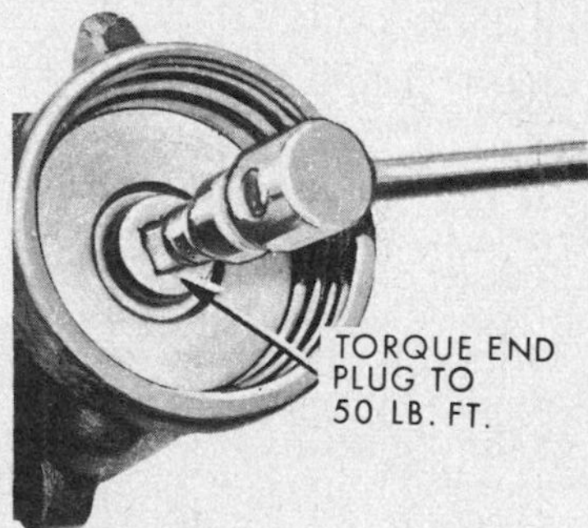

Torquing rack-piston nut end plug
(© Buick Motor Div., G.M. Corp)

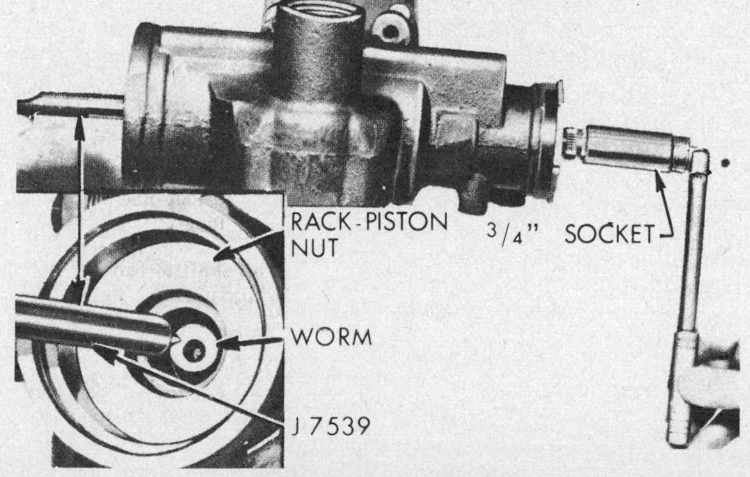

Removing rack-piston nut
(© Buick Motor Div., G.M. Corp)

soft hammer and slide shaft out of housing.
5. Remove and discard side cover O-ring seal.
6. The seals, washers, retainers and bearings may now be removed and examined.
7. Examine all parts for wear or damage and replace as required.
8. Install in reverse of above. Make proper adjustment as described in adjustment section.

Rack-Piston Nut and Worm Assembly Removal

1. Completely drain the gear assembly and thoroughly clean the outside.
2. Remove pitman shaft assembly, previously described.
3. Rotate housing end plug retaining ring so that one end of ring is over hole in gear housing. Spring one end of ring so screwdriver can be inserted to lift out ring.
4. Rotate stub shaft to full left turn position to force end plug out of housing.
5. Remove and discard housing end plug O-ring seal.
6. Remove rack-piston nut end plug with ½ in. square drive.
7. Insert tool in end of worm. Turn stub shaft so that rack-piston nut will go into tool and remove rack-piston nut from gear housing.
8. Remove adjuster plug and rotary valve assemblies as previously described.
9. Remove worm and lower thrust bearing and races.
10. Remove cap-to-O-ring seal and discard.

Rack-Piston Nut and Worm Disassembly and Reassembly

1. Remove and discard piston ring and back-up O-ring on rack-piston nut.
2. Remove ball guide clamp and return guide.
3. Place nut on clean cloth and remove ball retaining tool. Make sure all balls are removed.

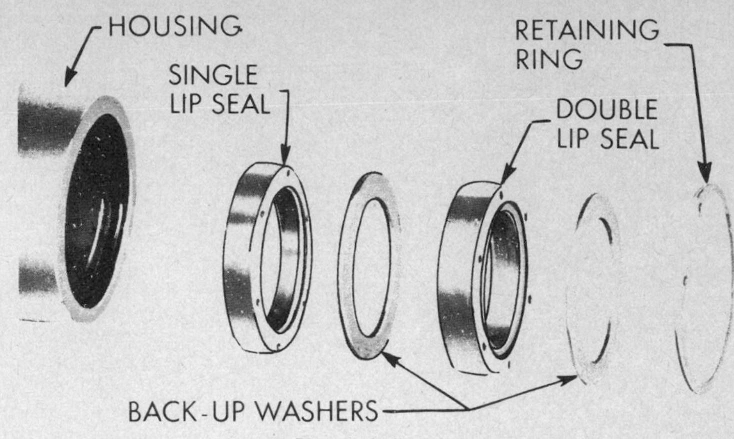

Pitman shaft seals
(© Buick Motor Div., G.M. Corp)

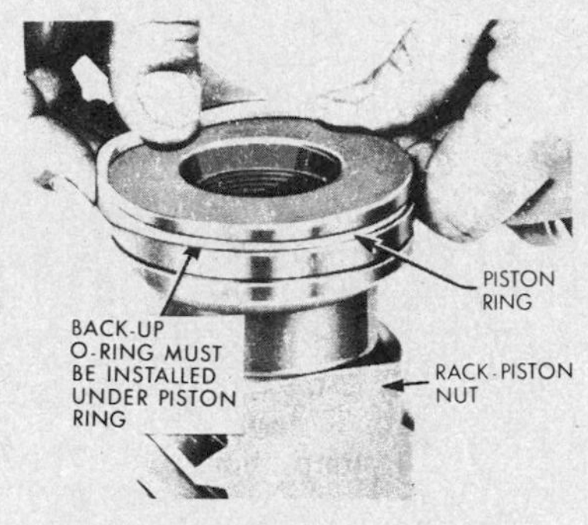

Installing rack-piston ring on rack-piston nut
(© Buick Motor Div., G.M. Corp)

Loading balls in rack-piston nut
(© Buick Motor Div., G.M. Corp)

Installing rack-piston nut
(© Buick Motor Div., G.M. Corp)

4. Inspect all parts for wear, nicks, scoring or burrs. If worm or rack-piston nut need replacing, both must be replaced as a matched pair.
5. In assembling, reverse the above.

NOTE: when assembling, alternate black and white balls, and install guide and clamp. Packing with grease helps in holding during assembly. When new balls are used, various sizes are available and a selection must be made to secure proper torque when making the high point adjustment.

Rack-Piston Nut and Worm Assembly Installation

1. Install in reverse of removal procedure.
2. In all cases use new O-ring seals.
3. Make adjustments as described in that section.

Section 7
Chrysler Full-Time Power Steering (Constant Control Type)

The power steering gear system for Chrysler Corporation cars is called the Constant Control type. This system consists of a hydraulic pressure pump, a power steering gear and connecting hoses.

The power steering gear housing contains a gear shaft and sector gear, a power piston with gear teeth milled into the side of the piston which is in constant mesh with the gear shaft sector teeth, a worm shaft which connects the steering wheel to the power piston through a coupling. The worm shaft is geared to the piston through recirculating ball contact.

A pivot lever is fitted into the spool valve at the upper end and into a drilled hole in the center thrust bearing race at the lower end. The center thrust bearing race is held firmly against the shoulder of the worm shaft by two thrust bearings, bearing races and an adjusting nut. The pivot lever pivots in the spacer which is held in place by the pressure plate.

When the steering wheel is turned to the left the worm shaft moves out of the power piston a few thousandths of an inch, the center thrust bearing race moves the same distance since it is clamped to the worm shaft. The race thus tips the pivot lever and moves the spool valve down, allowing oil under pressure to flow into the left-turn power chamber and force the power piston down. As the power piston moves, it rotates the cross-shaft sector gear and, through the steering

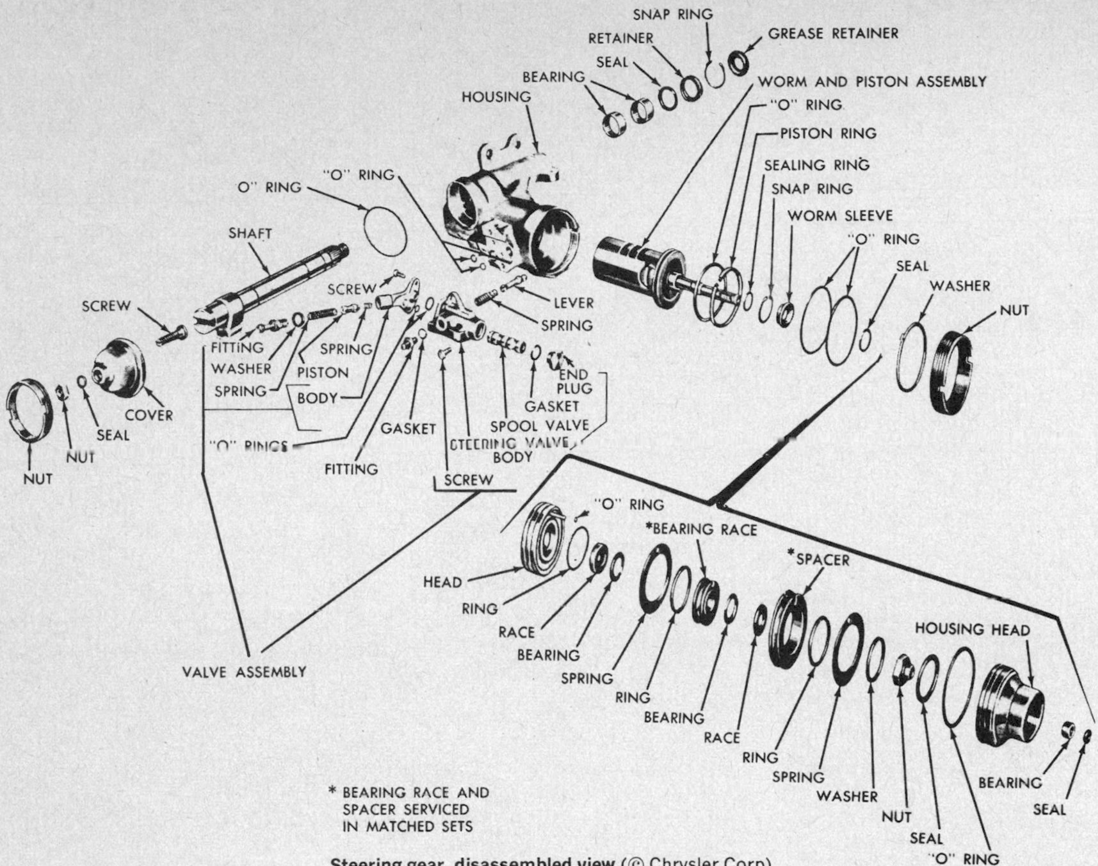

Steering gear, disassembled view (© Chrysler Corp)

linkage, turns the front wheels.

On a right turn the worm shaft moves into the power piston, the center thrust bearing race thus tips the pivot lever and moves the spool valve up, allowing oil under pressure to flow into the right power chamber and force the power piston up.

Pressure Test

Connect the pressure test hoses with the pressure gauge installed between the pump and steering gear.

Now, fill the reservoir to the level mark, then start the engine and bleed the system. Allow the engine to idle until the fluid in the reservoir is between 150° F. and 170° F. Now turn the steering wheel to the extreme right and check the pressure reading, then turn to the extreme left and check the reading again. The gauge reading should be equal in each direction. If not, it indicates excessive internal leakage in the unit.

The pressure should agree with the specifications in Pump Section for satisfactory power steering operation.

Repair Operations

Reconditioning

1. Drain gear by turning worm shaft from limit to limit with oil connections held downward. Thoroughly clean outside.
2. Remove valve body attaching screws, body and three O-rings.
3. Remove pivot lever and spring. Pry under spherical head with a screwdriver.

Caution Use care not to collapse slotted end of valve lever as this will destroy bearing tolerances of the spherical head.

4. Remove steering gear arm from sector shaft.
5. Remove snap-ring and seal back-up washer.
6. Remove seal, using proper tool to prevent damage to relative parts.
7. Loosen gear shaft adjusting screw locknut and remove gear shaft cover nut.
8. Rotate wormshaft to position sector teeth at center of piston travel. Loosen power train retaining nut.
9. Insert tools into housing until both tool and shaft are engaged with bearings.
10. Turn worm shaft either to full left or full right (depending on

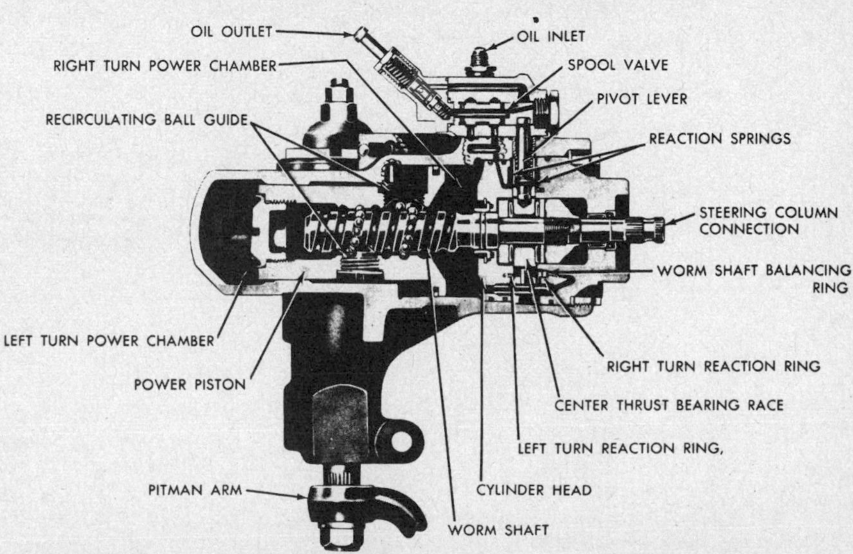

Chrysler power steering gear (© Chrysler Corp)

car application) to compress power train parts. Then remove power train retaining nut as mentioned above.

11. Remove housing head tang washer.
12. While holding power train completely compressed, pry on piston teeth with screwdriver, using shaft as a fulcrum, and remove complete power train.

Caution Maintain close contact between cylinder head, center race and spacer assembly and the housing head. This will eliminate the possibility of reactor rings becoming disengaged from their grooves in cylinder and housing head. It will prohibit center spacer from separating from center race and cocking in the housing. This could make it impossible to remove the power train without damaging involved parts.

13. Place power train in soft-jawed vise in vertical position. The worm bearing rollers will fall out. Use of arbor tool will hold roller when the housing is removed.
14. Raise housing head until wormshaft oil shaft just clears the top of wormshaft and position arbor tool on top of shaft and into seal. With arbor in position, pull up on housing head until arbor is positioned in bearing. Remove when the housing is removed.
15. Remove large O-ring from housing head groove.
16. Remove reaction seal from groove in face of head with air pressure directed into ferrule chamber.
17. Remove reactor spring, reactor ring, worm balancing ring and spacer.
18. While holding wormshaft from turning, turn nut with enough force to release staked portions from knurled section and remove nut.

NOTE: pay strict attention to cleanliness.

19. Remove upper thrust bearing race (thin) and upper thrust bearing.
20. Remove center bearing race.
21. Remove lower thrust bearing and lower thrust bearing race (thick).
22. Remove lower reaction ring and reaction spring.
23. Remove cylinder head assembly.
24. Remove O-rings from outer grooves in head.
25. Remove reaction O-ring from groove in face of cylinder head. Use air pressure in oil hole located between O-ring grooves.
26. Remove snap-ring, sleeve and rectangular oil seal from cylinder head counterbore.
27. Test wormshaft operation. Not

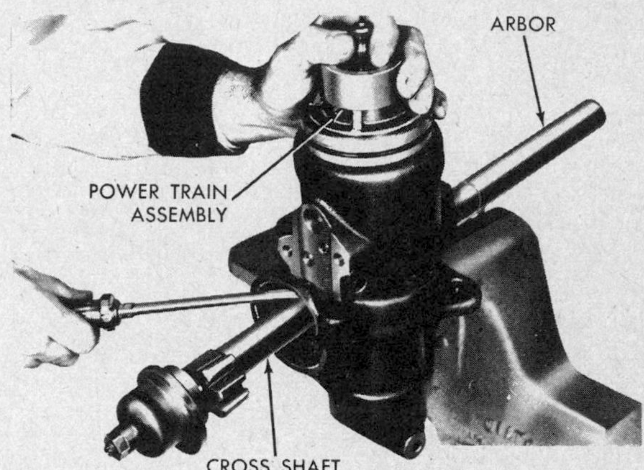

Removing power train
(© Chrysler Corp)

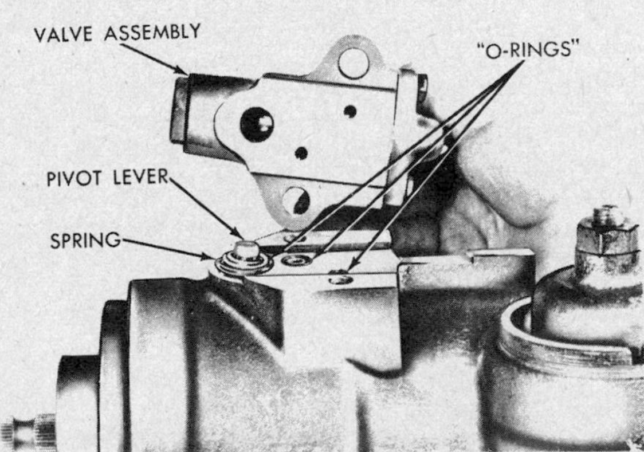

Removing valve body assembly
(© Chrysler Corp)

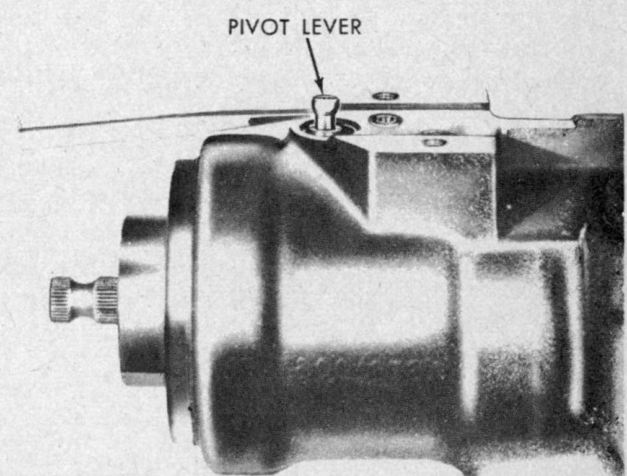

Removing pivot lever
(© Chrysler Corp)

Removing gear shaft retaining nut
(© Chrysler Corp)

Removing power train retaining nut
(© Chrysler Corp)

more than 2 in. lbs. should be required to turn it through its entire travel, and with a 15 ft. lb. side load.

NOTE: the worm and piston is serviced as a complete assembly and should not be disassembled.

28. Shaft side play should not exceed 0.008 in. under light pull applied 2 5/16 in. from piston flange.
29. Assemble in reverse of above, noting proper adjustments and preload requirements following.
30. When cover nut in installed, tighten to 20 ft-lbs. torque.
31. Valve mounting screws should be tightened to 200 in.-lbs. torque.
32. With hoses connected, system bled, and engine idling roughly, center valve unit until not self-steering. Tap on head of valve body attaching screws to move valve body up, and tap on end plug to move valve body down.
33. With steering gear on center, tighten gear shaft adjusting screw until lash just disappears.
34. Continue to tighten ⅜ to ½ turn and tighten locknut to 50 ft. lbs.

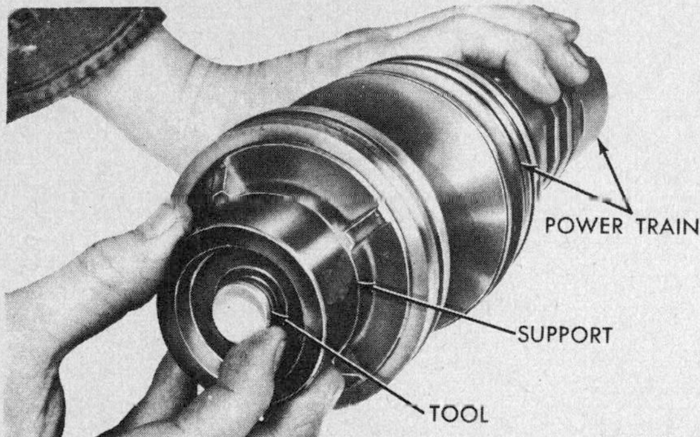

Retaining bearing rollers with arbor tool
(© Chrysler Corp)

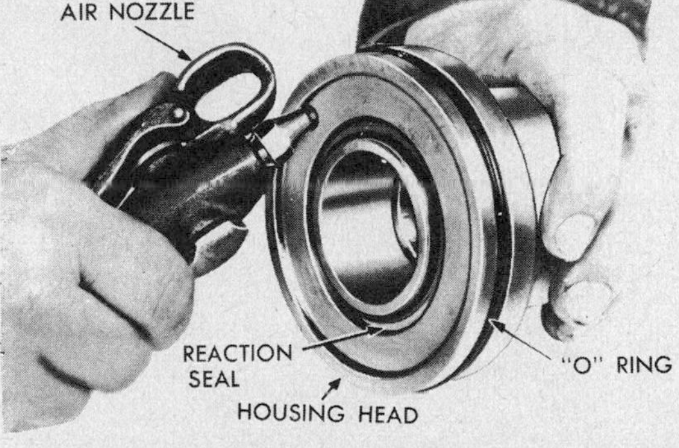

Removing reaction seal from wormshaft support
(© Chrysler Corp)

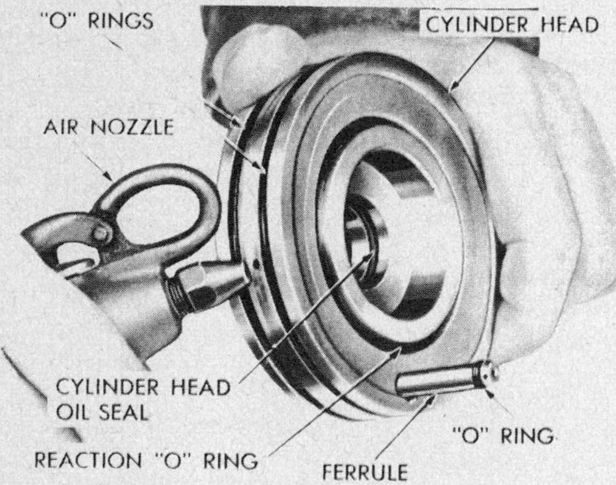

Removing reaction seal from cylinder head
(© Chrysler Corp)

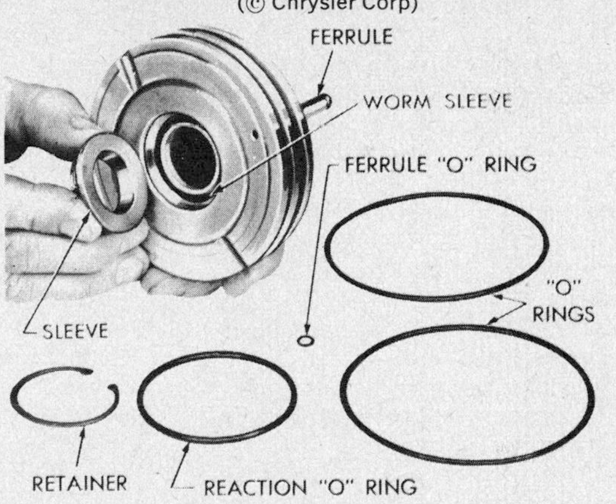

Removing cylinder head oil seal
(© Chrysler Corp)

Section 8
Ford Torsion Bar Power Steering

This is an integral type with steering gear, power unit and control valve combined as one unit.

Repair Operations

Disassembly

1. Remove housing mounting pads.
2. Invert steering gear and rotate shaft back and forth to completely drain. Thoroughly clean outside of housing to prevent dirt interference while working on assembly.
3. Mount in soft-jawed vise or special holding fixture.
4. Remove Teflon locknut and brass washer from adjusting screw.
5. Turn input shaft to either lock then back 1¾ turns to center the gear.
6. Remove sector shaft cover attaching screws and identifying tag.
7. Tap lower end of sector shaft with soft hammer to loosen it, then lift cover and shaft from housing as a unit. Discard O-ring.
8. Turn the sector shaft cover counterclockwise and remove from adjusting screw.
9. Remove valve housing attaching bolts. Lift valve housing from steering gear housing, while holding piston to prevent it from rotating off the worm shaft. Remove housing and passage O-rings and discard.
10. With valve body and piston on end (piston end down), rotate input shaft counterclockwise out of piston. Allow ball bearings to drop into piston.
11. With cloth over open end of piston, invert to remove balls.
12. Remove ball guide clamp and guides.
13. Install valve body in holding fixture. Do not use vise. Remove locknut and retaining nut.
14. Slide worm and valve assembly out of valve housing.
15. Remove shim from valve housing bore.

Valve Housing R & R

1. Remove dust seal from rear of housing.
2. Remove snap-ring from housing.
3. Turn fixture to invert valve housing.
4. From opposite the seal end, gently tap bearing and seal from housing. Discard seal. Use care

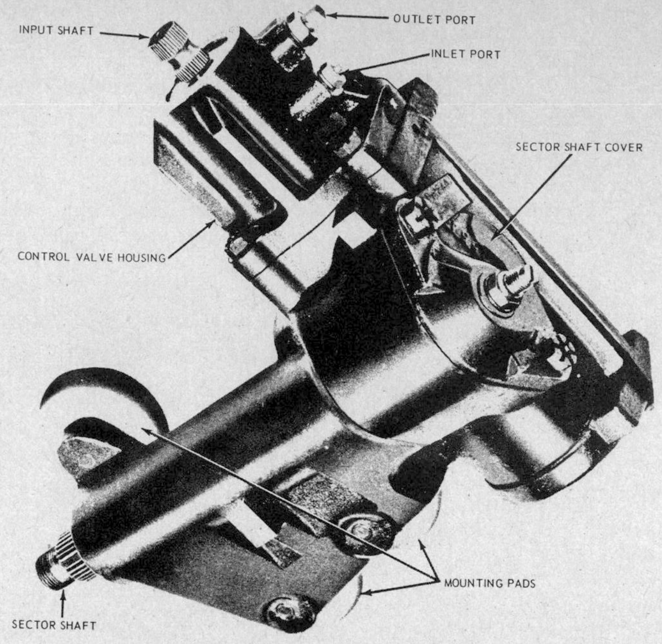

Power steering gear (© Lincoln-Mercury Div., Ford Motor Co)

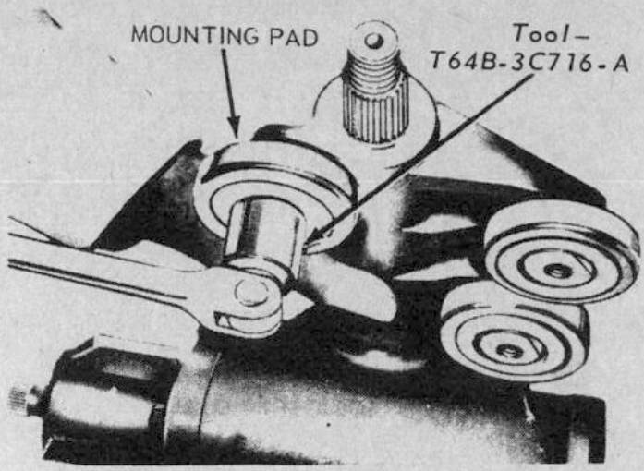

Removing or installing steering gear mounting pads
(© Lincoln-Mercury Div., Ford Motor Co)

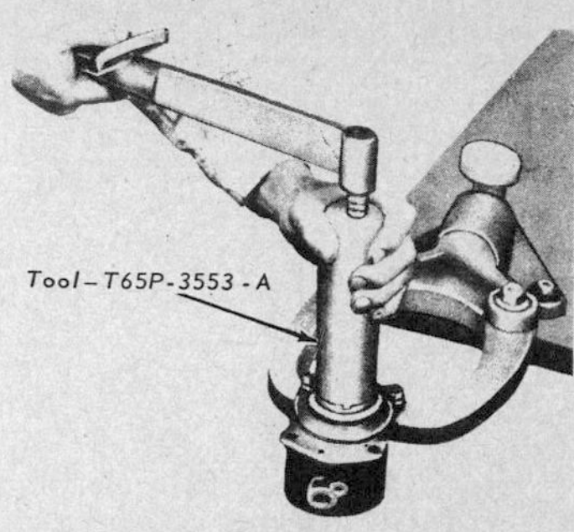

Removing or installing lock nut
(© Lincoln-Mercury Div., Ford Motor Co)

not to mar or damage the bore in housing.

5. Remove inlet and outlet seats if damaged. Use an Easy-out.
6. If installing new seats, coat with vaseline and position them in housing. Install and tighten tube nuts to press seats into proper position.
7. Coat bearing and seal surfaces with vaseline.
8. Position bearing in housing and, with proper tool, see that it is thoroughly seated.
9. Lubricate new seal with gear lubricant and place in housing with metal side of seal facing outward. Drive seal into housing until outer edge of seal does not quite clear the snap-ring groove.
10. Place snap-ring in housing and gently drive ring in until it seats in its groove. This will properly locate the seal.
11. Place dust seal in housing with rubber side out and drive into place. The seal must be located behind the undercut.

Worm and Valve R & R

1. Remove snap-ring from end of actuator.

NOTE: in 1971 Ford, Mercury, Thunderbird, Lincoln, Mark III and 1972 Torino and Montego, a Belleville spring is added to the actuator assembly. The addition of this spring eliminates the necessity for selective snap rings, so that only the (.048-.050) snap ring is needed. The Belleville spring is assembled beneath the tapered snap-ring with the convex side (color coded) away from the spool.

2. Slide control valve spool off of actuator.
3. Install valve spool evenly and slowly with slight oscillating motion into flanged end of housing with identification groove between the valve spool lands facing outward. Check for freedom of valve movement within working area. Spool should enter housing freely and fall by its own weight.
4. If spool is not free, check for burrs and remove with a hard stone.
5. Check valve for burrs and if burrs are found, stone valve in a radial direction only. Be sure valve is entirely free.
6. Remove spool from housing.
7. Slide spool into actuator, making sure groove in spool annulus is toward worm.
8. Install snap-ring to retain spool.
9. Check clearance between spool and snap-ring. It should be 0.0005-0.0035 in. If not within these limits, select snap-ring that will produce 0.002 in clearance.

Piston and Ball Nut R & R

1. Remove the Teflon ring and O-ring from piston and ball nut.
2. Dip new O-ring in gear lubricant and install on piston and ball nut.
3. Install new Teflon ring, using care not to stretch more than necessary.

Gear Housing R & R

1. Remove snap-ring and spacer washer from lower end of housing.
2. Remove outer seal from housing. Lift out spacer washer.
3. Remove upper seal in same manner as lower seal.
4. Press upper and lower bushings from housing if worn or defective.
5. Press new bushings into place.
6. Dip both sector shaft seals in gear lubricant.
7. Apply lubricant to sector shaft seal bore of housing and position sector shaft inner seal in housing with lip facing inward. Press

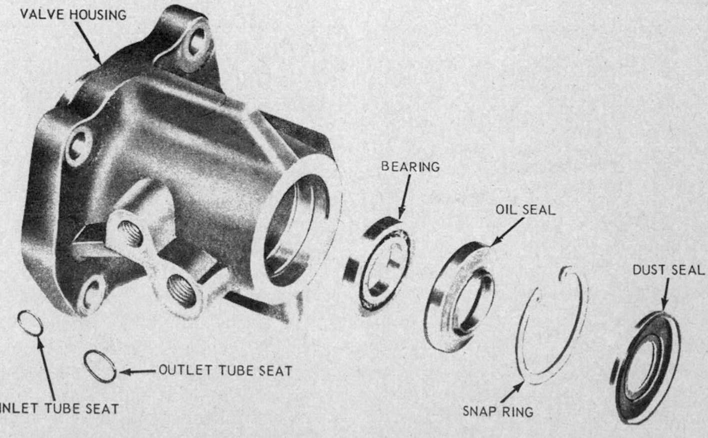

Valve housing, disassembled view (© Lincoln-Mercury Div., Ford Motor Co)

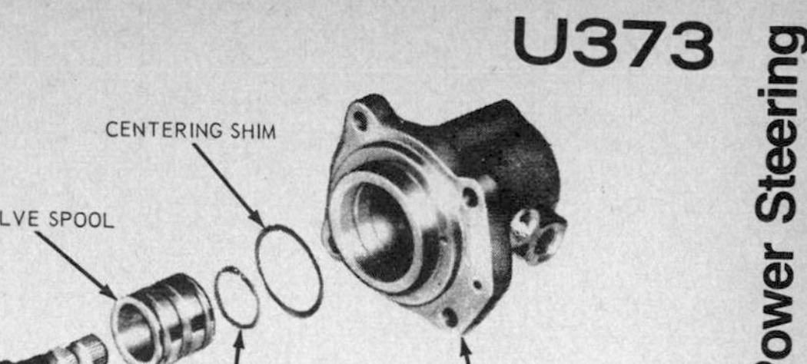

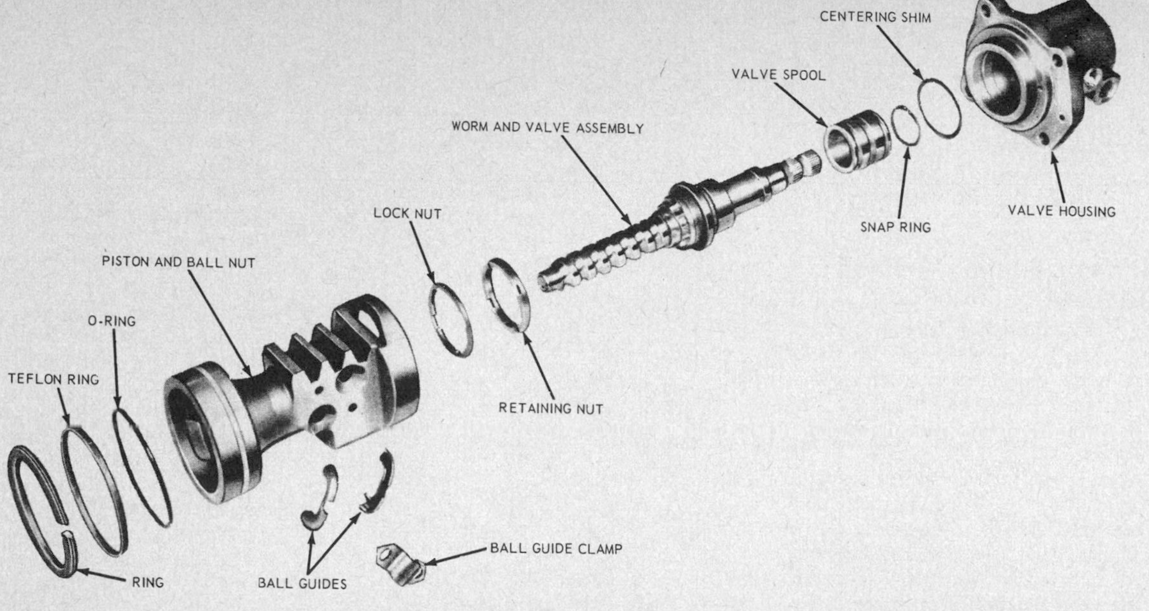

Ball nut and valve housing, disassembled view (© Lincoln-Mercury Div., Ford MotorCo)

into place.

8. Place a 0.090 in. thick spacer washer on top of seal and apply more lubricant to housing bore.
9. Place outer seal in housing with lip facing inward and press into place. Then place a 0.090 in. thick spacer washer on top of seal.
10. Place snap-ring in housing and press into position to locate seals and engage the snap-ring in groove.

Gear Assembly

1. Mount valve housing in fixture with flanged end up.
2. Place the same thickness valve spool centering shim in the housing as was removed. Use only one shim.
3. Install worm and valve in housing.
4. Install retaining nut in housing and torque to 55-65 ft. lbs.
5. Install locknut and tighten to 20-30 ft. lbs.
6. Place piston on bench with ball guide holes facing up. Insert worm shaft into piston so that first groove is in alignment with hole nearest to center of piston.
7. Place ball guide in position and feed balls into guide, turning worm clockwise. If all balls have not been fed into guide upon reaching stop, rotate shaft back and forth while installing balance of balls.
8. Secure guides in ball nut with the clamp.
9. Position new lube passage O-ring in counterbore of housing.
10. Apply vaseline to Teflon seal on piston.
11. Place new O-ring on valve housing.
12. Position housing spacer ring in housing and slide piston and valve into gear housing. Do not damage Teflon seal.
13. Align lube passage in valve housing with one in gear housing. Install, but do not tighten, attaching bolts.
14. Rotate ball nut so that teeth are in same plane as sector teeth. Tighten valve housing attaching bolts.
15. Position sector shaft cover O-ring in gear housing. Turn input shaft to center the piston.
16. Position sector shaft and cover in gear housing. Install identification tag and shaft cover attaching bolts and tighten. Make adjustments as described under "Adjustments."

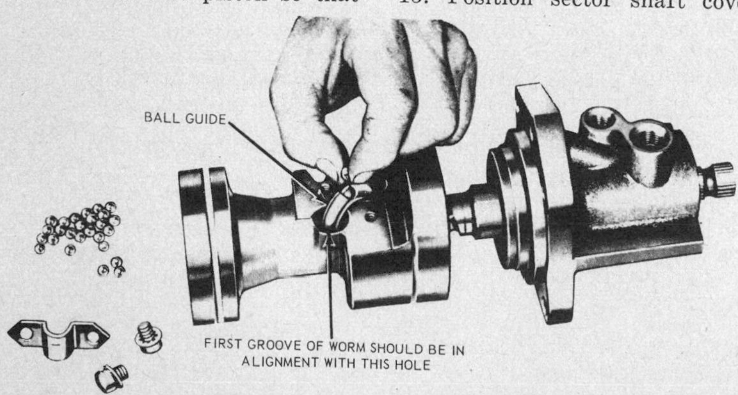

Assembling piston on wormshaft (© Lincoln-Mercury Div., Ford Motor Co)

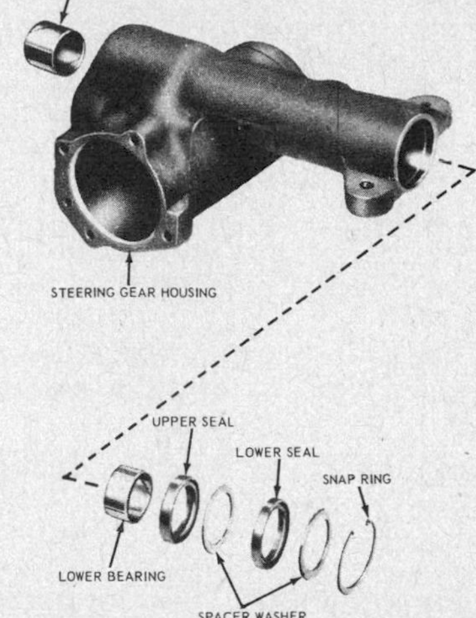

Steering gear housing, disassembled view (© Lincoln-Mercury Div., Ford Motor Co)

Over Center Position Load

1. With no fluid in gear and torque wrench on steering wheel nut, or on input shaft of gear if out of car, rotate the gear slowly through the high point of sector shaft mesh.
2. With no load required to turn through this position and with adjuster locknut loose, gradually turn the adjuster screw to produce 11-12 in. lbs. more than required to turn when mesh is at no contact. Tighten locknut and recheck the torque.

Section 9

Ford Integral Rack and Pinion Steering

This system was developed to provide a power steering system for those small Ford Motor Company cars equipped with rack and pinion steering.

Rack Yoke Bearing Preload Adjustment

The steering gear must be removed from the car to make this adjustment.

1. Remove the fluid lines from the gear and drain the fluid.
2. Fasten the unit down on the bench.
3. Attach an inch pound torque wrench to the input shaft.
4. Loosen the yoke plug locknut.
5. Attach an inch pound torque wrench to the yoke plug. Tighten the plug to 45-50 in. lbs with the rack at the center of travel.
6. Back off the yoke plug no more than 45 degrees until the torque required to turn the input shaft is 7-15 in. lbs.
7. Tighten the yoke plug locknut to 44-66 ft lbs, while holding the plug.
8. Recheck the adjustment after tightening the locknut.

Repair Operations

Tie-Rod Ends, Bellows, and Tie-Rod Ball Joint Socket Disassembly and Assembly

1. Loosen the jam nuts adjacent to the tie-rod sockets. Remove the sockets and jam nuts.
2. Remove the 4 clamps and remove the bellows and breather tube, after draining the fluid.
3. To remove the tie-rod and ball sockets, drill out the retaining pin in the ball socket.

Caution This hole must be drilled deeper than 3/8 in.

Remove the tie-rod and ball socket with a spanner wrench.

4. Remove the locknut, inner thrust bearing, and rack spring from the recess in the end of the rack.

To assemble:

5. Install a new rack spring in the recess in the end of the rack. Assemble the ball socket to the tie-rod.
6. Install a new inner thrust bearing in the ball socket.
7. Lubricate the spring, thrust bearing, tie-rod ball, and the ball socket.
8. Thread a new ball joint locknut onto the end of the rack .
9. Thread the ball socket onto the rack until the socket is tight.
10. Rotate the rod a few times. Adjust the ball socket until the effort

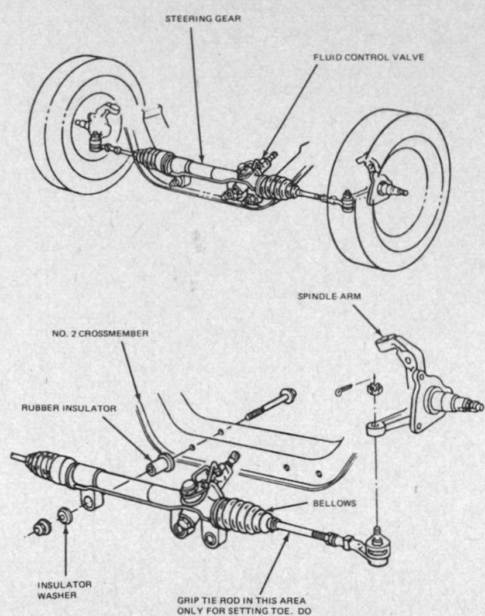

Ford integral rack and pinion steering gear (© Ford Motor Co)

required to move the tie-rod end with a spring scale is 4-6 lbs.

11. Hold the ball socket and tighten the locknut to 25-35 ft lbs. Repeat Step 10.
12. Drill a new hole, similar to that made in Step 3. It must not enter the notches of the locknut.
13. Install the retaining pin and stake it in place.
14. Install the bellows and the breather tube. Install new clamps. Put 2½ oz. of lubricant into each bellows.
15. Install the jam nuts and tie-rod sockets on the outer ends of the tie-rods.

Input Shaft and Valve Assembly, Disassembly and Assembly

1. Remove the fluid lines. Remove the flare gaskets from the ports.
2. Loosen the yoke plug locknut and yoke plug to relieve the rack preload.
3. Remove the pinion bearing plug.
4. Hold the input shaft and remove the pinion bearing locknut.
5. Remove the 3 bolts holding the valve housing to the gear unit. Move the rack to the left stop. Mark the relationship of the input shaft to the valve housing for reinstallation. Carefully work the input shaft and valve assembly out of the gear housing.
6. Remove the pinion bearing from the gear housing with a slide hammer. Remove the bearing-to-gear housing and valve housing-to-gear housing O-rings.
7. Remove the input shaft oil seal from the gear housing.
8. Slide the valve housing over the splined end of the input shaft to remove.
9. Remove the input shaft O-rings, being extremely careful not to damage the lands and grooves.
10. Remove the input shaft needle thrust bearing and the two thrust washers from the inside of the valve housing.
11. Use a slide hammer to remove the input shaft support bearing from the valve housing. Remove the input shaft oil seal also.
12. Pry the input shaft dust seal from the valve housing with a small sharp chisel.

To assemble:

13. Press the input shaft oil seal into the valve housing with a finger. Make sure that the lip faces in and that the seal bottoms in the bore.
14. Fill the input shaft dust seal bore with lubricant and install the dust seal.
15. Lubricate the input shaft support bearing with power steering fluid and install it in the valve housing. Avoid contact with the oil seal.
16. Install the 4 O-rings in the grooves on the valve.
17. Lubricate the two thrust washers and the needle thrust bearing with power steering fluid. Place a thrust washer on each side of the bearing and install over the input shaft.
18. Lubricate the O-rings and valve with power steering fluid. Insert the unit over the valve bore of the housing and push it through until it bottoms and the full spline passes through the dust seal.
19. Install the valve housing to gear housing O-ring on the flange protruding from the gear housing.
20. Use your fingers to install an input shaft oil seal in the gear housing. Make sure that the lip faces the input shaft and valve assembly.
21. Install the pinion bearing in the lower gear housing. Install an O-ring around the bearing adjacent to the gear housing.
22. Move the rack to the left stop. Install the input shaft and valve assembly in the gear housing bore. Align the marks made in Step 5.
23. Install the bolts holding the valve housing to the gear housing. Torque to 12-15 ft lbs.
24. Install the pinion bearing locknut on the pinion shaft. Drill a hole in a spare pinion bearing plug large enough to insert a 9/26 in. socket. Thread the plug into the housing bore and tighten to hold the bearing firmly. Hold the input

shaft and torque the pinion bearing locknut to 44-66 ft lbs. Make sure that the rack is away from the stop while doing this. Remove the drilled bearing plug.
25. Install the pinion bearing plug. Torque it to 60-100 ft lbs. Stake the plug in place.
26. Install the 4 small flare nuts in the pressure line fittings. Install the pressure lines.
27. Install the tube bracket with the tabs in the slots on the gear housing.
28. Install the yoke plug locknut. Make the rack yoke bearing preload adjustment described earlier, then torque the locknut to 44-66 ft lbs.

Section 10
American Motors Pacer Rack and Pinion

Removal and Installation

1. Raise the front of the car and support it. Unlock the steering column
2. Remove the nuts that attach the flexible coupling to the intermediate steering shaft flange.
3. Disconnect the tie rods at the steering arms by first turning the wheels to the stop in the direction of the tie rod end to be removed. Then, with a floor jack positioned under the lower control arm and raised at least 2 in., remove the cotter pin, nut, and remove the tie rod end with a puller.
4. Position a drain pan under the steering gear housing and disconnect the power steering hoses at the steering gear ,housing. Plug the hoses to prevent any dirt from entering.
5. Remove the bolts that attach the steering gear to the front crossmember at the mounting bracket and housing and remove the steering gear assembly.
6. Install the steering gear in the reverse order of removal, tightening the mounting bracket bolts to 50 ft lbs, the housing mounting bolts to 55 ft lbs, the tie rod ends-to-steering arm nuts to 50 ft lbs, and the flexible coupling-to-intermediate shaft flange nuts to 24 ft lbs.
7. Lower the car, fill the power steering fluid reservoir, and check the toe-in adjustment.

Overhaul

1. Remove the steering gear from the vehicle and mount the unit in a vise, clamping only the housing.
2. Cut and remove the two boot clamps from the housing end of the steering gear.
3. Slide the boot away from the housing to expose the rack teeth.
4. Turn the flexible coupling to move the rack toward the housing end of the steering gear and expose as many teeth as possible.

4a. Wipe the rack teeth clean with a clean cloth and inspect the rack for chipped, cracked, broken, flaking, or excessively worn teeth. If any of the above conditions exist, the steering gear assembly must be replaced. Machining marks or shiny and bright rack teeth are normal conditions.

5. Remove the flexible coupling pinch bolt and separate the coupling from the stub shaft.
6. Remove the adjuster plug lock nut and remove the adjuster plug with a spanner type tool that fits into the two holes in to top of the adjuster plug.
7. Remove the valve body assembly by pulling straight up on the stub shaft. Do not disassemble the valve body.
8. Remove the pinion shaft from the housing using pliers. Grip the pinion shaft at the drive tang and rotate the shaft clockwise while pulling up.
9. Clean and inspect the pinion shaft. If any of the conditions mentioned in step 4a exist, replace the steering gear.
10. Remove the contraction plug from the housing using a ¼ in. diameter brass rod. Insert the rod through the upper and lower pinion bushings and tap on the rod to remove the plug.
11. Remove the lower pinion bushing and preload spring from the housing with the brass rod.
12. Move the rack to the centered position in the tube and housing.
13. Install the pinion shaft in the housing. Be sure the pinion is fully seated.
14. Install the valve body and adjuster plug in the housing and hand tighten the plug only.

NOTE: Make sure that the valve body is seated in the housing. Do not press on the stub shaft to seat the valve body. Press directly on the valve body with only your thumbs.

13. Loosen, but do not remove, the adjuster tube clamp nuts and remove the tie rod ends and adjuster tubes as assemblies. Mark the position of the tubes and tie rods for reference during assembly. Use penetrating oil if the threads are corroded. Hold the inner tie rod with a 9/16 in. wrench while removing the tie rods and tubes.
16. Remove the remaining boot clamps and boot retainers.

Removing the adjuster plug (© American Motors Corp)

Removing the contraction plug (© American Motors Corp)

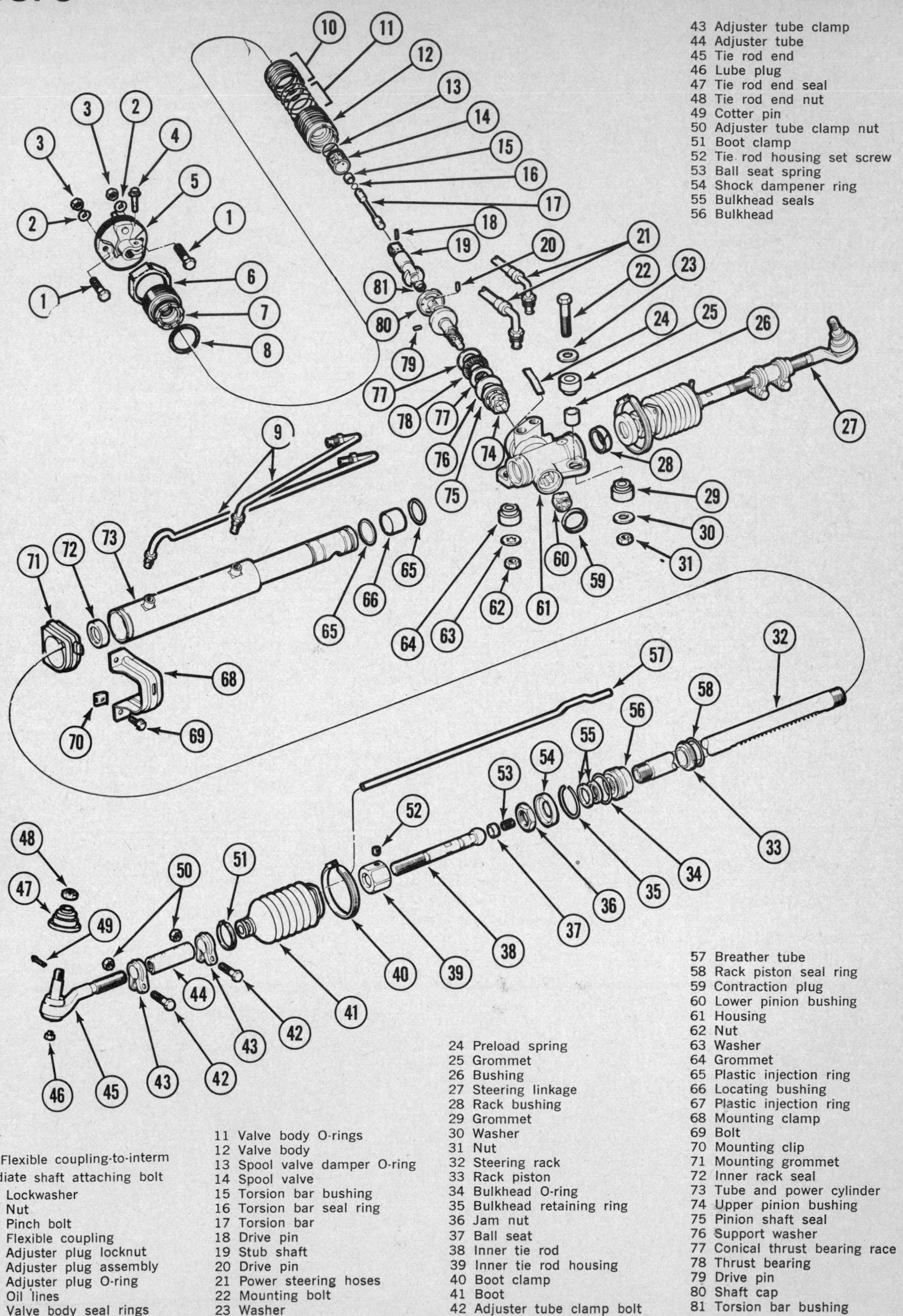

Exploded view of the American Motors Pacer power rack and pinion steering gear

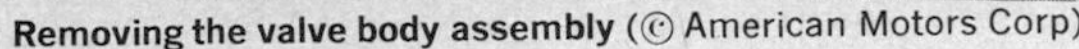
Removing the valve body assembly (© American Motors Corp)

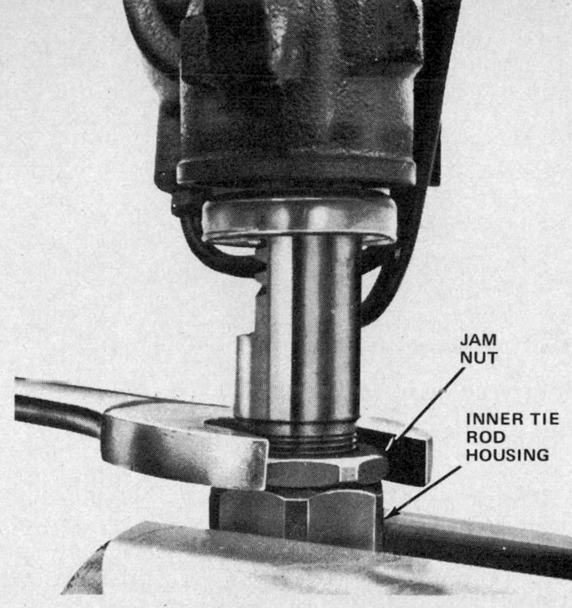

Loosening the inner tie rod housing jamnut(s)
(© American Motors Corp)

17. Remove both protective boots.
18. Slide the shock dampener rings back off the jamnuts by rotating and pushing them back.
19. Remove the steering gear from the vise, and clamp the inner tie rod housing. Loosen the jamnut using 1½ in. wrench. Loosen the jamnut at the opposite end of the rack also.

NOTE: The inner tie rod housings must be held in a vise while loosening the jamnuts to prevent damage to the rack, pinion, stub shaft and valve body.

20. Loosen but do not remove the set screw in each inner tie rod housing.
21. Reposition the steering gear in the vise as before, and remove the inner tie rod housings, inner tie rods, ball seats, ball seat springs, jamnuts, and shock dampener rings.
22. Remove the adjuster plug. Pull straight up and out on the stub shaft and remove the assembly.
23. Remove the pinion shaft from the housing with a pair of pliers. Grip the pinion shaft at the drive tang and rotate the shaft clockwise while pulling upward to remove the pinion shaft.
24. Remove the pinion thrust bearing conical thrust bearing races, and support washer from the housing with either your fingers, an external-type snap ring pliers, or a magnet.
25. Mark the position of the breather tube, mounting clamp and grommet on each end of the tube and housing for reference during assembly. The breather tube, grommet and mounting clamp must be reassembled in their original positions to ensure proper seating and sealing.
26. Remove the breather tube and the grommet and mounting clamp by pulling and twisting at the same time.
27. Remove the bulkhead retaining ring from the end of the tube by inserting a pin punch through the access hole in the end of the tube to force the retaining ring out of its groove. Then, place the blade of a screwdriver behind the ring and pry it out.

NOTE: Be careful not to scratch the bore of the tube when removing the retaining ring. Remove any scratches with crocus cloth.

28. Pull the steering rack and bulkhead out of the tube and housing assembly.

NOTE: Do not remove the steering rack unless a new inner rack seal is available as the seal is rendered useless when the rack is removed.

As the rack is removed, the rack piston will force the bulkhead out of the tube at the same time.

29. Remove the bulkhead from the steering rack.
30. Remove the plastic rack bushing from the housing. Insert a knife blade under the bushing and pry up. Grasp the bushing with a needlenose pliers and pull the bushing out of the housing.
31. Remove the inner rack seal by driving it out of the tube with a hammer and a brass rod 12 to 14 in. long.
32. Turn the steering gear over in the vise and remove the upper pinion bushing and pinion shaft seal with a ⅝ in. socket and extension. When the bushing separates from the housing, it will force the seal out also.
33. Remove the outer O-ring and two inner lip-type seals from the bulkhead. Note their positions for correct reassembly.
34. Using the blade of a small screwdriver or knife, carefully remove the seal from the rack piston. Be careful not to scratch the piston.

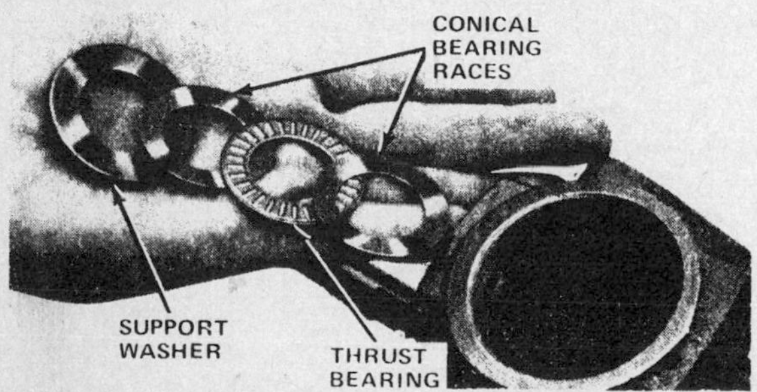

Removal of the thrust bearing and races (© American Motors Corp)

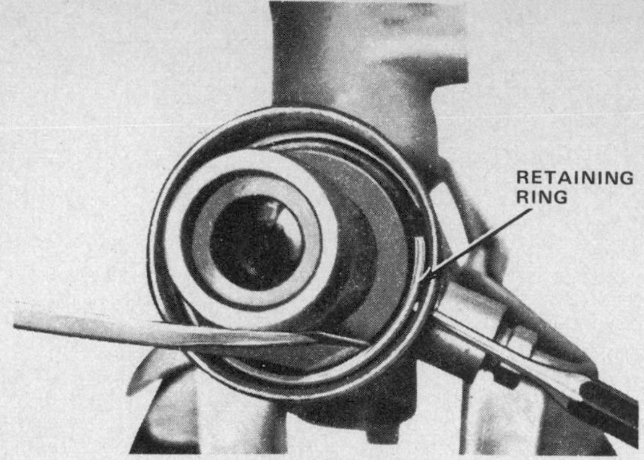

Removing the bulkhead retaining ring (© American Motors Corp)

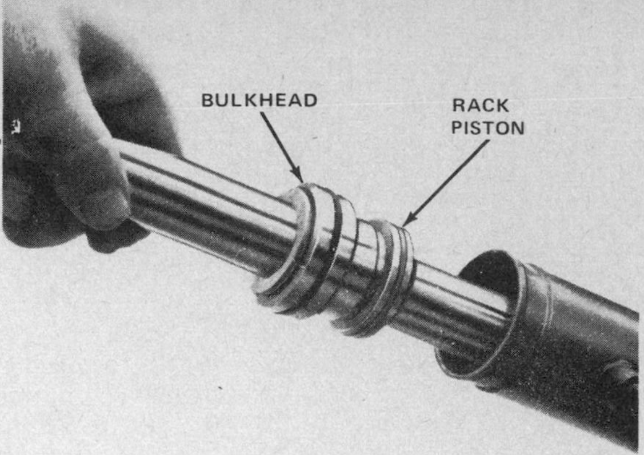

Removing the steering rack and bulkhead (© American Motors Corp)

35. To disassemble the adjuster plug:
    a. Remove the thrust bearing retainer with a screwdriver and discard the retainer. Be careful not to damage the needle bearing bore.
    b. Remove the thrust bearing spacer, bearing, and bearing races.
    c. Remove the adjuster plug O-ring seal and discard the seal.
    d. Remove the stub shaft seal retaining ring with snap ring pliers.
    e. Remove the stub shaft dust seal and oil seal by prying them out with a small screwdriver.
    f. Remove the needle bearing.
36. To disassemble the valve body and stub shaft assembly:

    NOTE: Do not disassemble the valve for any other reason than to replace the seals. If replacement of any valve part other than the seal rings or O-rings is necessary, replace the complete valve body assembly.

    a. Hold the valve body in your hand with the stub shaft pointing downward. Tap the stub shaft lightly against the workbench until the shaft cap is free of the valve body.
    b. Pull the stub shaft until the shaft cap clears the valve body by about 1/4 in. Do not pull the stub shaft out any further than 1/4 in. because the spool may become cocked in the body.
    c. Carefully remove the spool valve locating pin from the spool valve and remove the stub shaft.
    d. Remove the spool valve from the valve body by pushing and rotating the valve. If the valve becomes cocked, carefully align the valve, then remove it.
    e. Remove the damper O-ring from the spool valve and discard it.
    f. Carefully cut and remove the four seal rings and O-rings from the valve body.
37. To replace the housing hose connector seats:

    NOTE: The hose connector seats do not need to be replaced unless they are damaged and/or do not provide proper sealing.

    a. Insert a no. 4 screw extractor into the seat and turn counterclockwise to remove the seat.
    b. Install a new seat by driving it into place with a brass rod. Be sure the seat is bottomed in the housing and is not cocked.
38. Wash all of the parts, except the rubber boots and nylon bushings in a suitable solvent and dry them with compressed air. Make sure you do not wash off the alignment marks for the breather tube and mounting clamp.
39. Inspect all of the parts for the conditions mentioned in step 4a.

    NOTE: If the tube and housing or steering rack and pinion shaft need replacing, replace the complete steering gear assembly, less the steering linkage components.

    Bushings, thrust bearings, steering linkage components, the breather tube and boots, and the flexible coupling can all be replaced individually.

    The adjuster plug assembly components can be replaced separately.

    The valve body and stub shaft assembly must be replaced as a unit if found to be defective.

40. Install the split-type nylon rack bushing in the housing. Compress the leading edge of the bushing with your fingers and insert it into the housing. The bushing will snap into place once

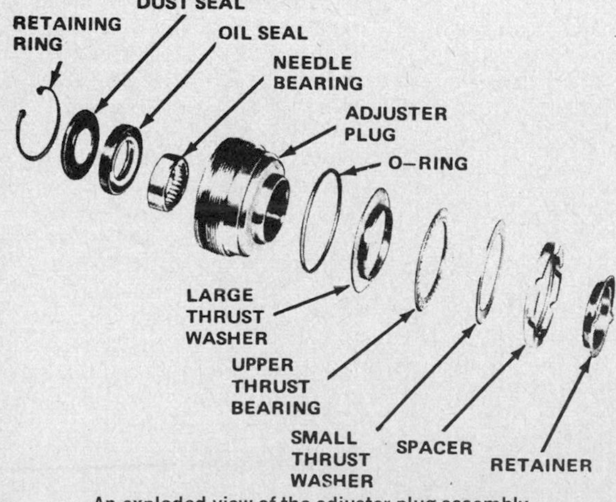

An exploded view of the adjuster plug assembly
(© American Motors Corp)

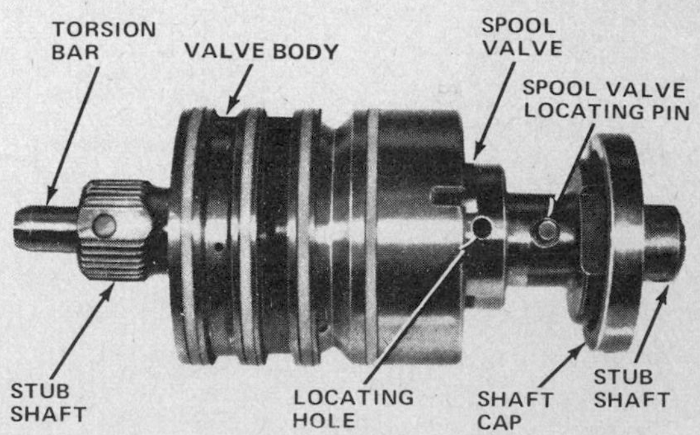

The valve body, stub shaft, and spool valve assembly
(© American Motors Corp)

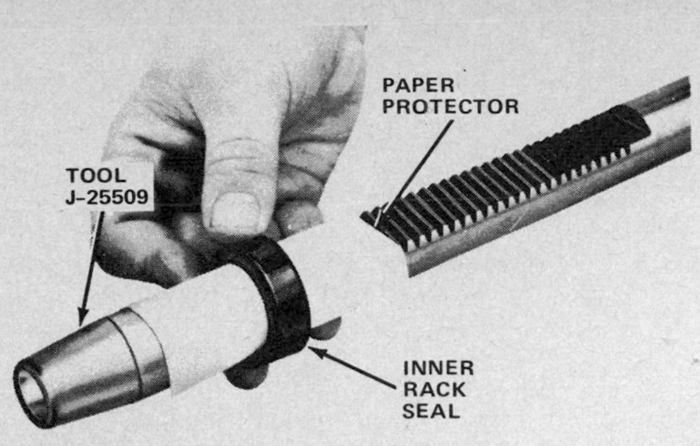

Installing the inner rack seal (© American Motors Corp)

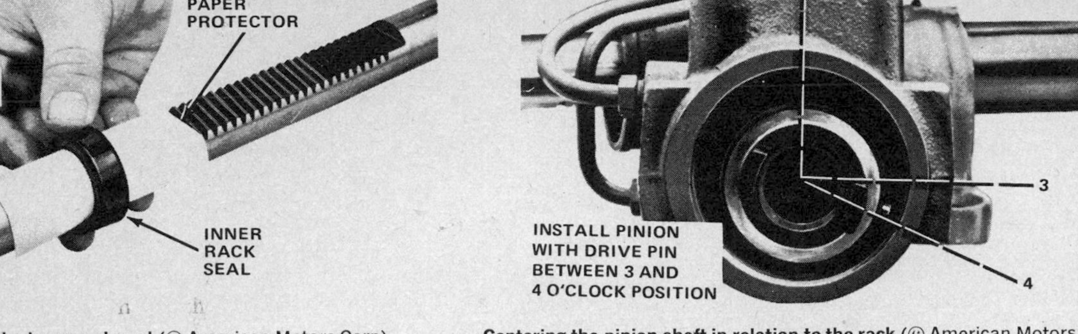

Centering the pinion shaft in relation to the rack (© American Motors Corp)

it is past the lip of the housing.

41. Install the inner rack seal on the steering rack by first cutting a $2\frac{1}{2}$ in. x 4 in. section of a manila envelope or similar cardboard-type paper. Form the paper over the rack teeth. The paper will protect the seal from the rack teeth during installation. Dip the seal in power steering fluid and slide it over the rack and onto the paper. Install the seal on the rack with the seal lip facing the rack piston and the metal surface of the seal facing away from the rack piston. remove the paper protector when the seal is over the rack teeth.
42. Lightly coat the outside diameter of the inner rack seal and bulkhead retaining ring groove in the tube with chassis grease.
43. Coat the rack teeth liberally with lithium base chassis lubricant.
44. Dip the rack piston seal ring in power steering fluid and install the seal ring on the rack piston. Be careful not to overstretch or twist the seal ring when installing it.
45. Carefully insert the steering rack into the tube. Push the steering rack into the tube as far as possible so that the rack piston will start the inner rack seal into its seat in the end of the tube. Bottom the seal in its seat. Install the upper pinion bushing with the chamfered side down, and start the pinion shaft seal, with the seal lip facing the bore, into the seat in the housing.
46. Place the support washer on top of the pinion shaft seal.
47. Using a $1\frac{1}{4}$ in. socket with an extension, lightly tap on the support washer until the pinion shaft seal and support washer are fully seated in the housing.
48. Lubricate the pinion shaft thrust bearing and races with petroleum jelly and install them on the pinion shaft. The bearing is installed between the two races.
49. Position the rack teeth parallel to the housing bore and set the end of the rack 4 in. from the machined inner face of the housing.
50. Install the pinion shaft into the housing bore with the drive pin located between the 3 and 4 o'clock position. Push the pinion down until it bottoms in the housing.
51. Center the steering rack to the 4 in. setting. With the rack centered, the pinion shaft drive pin should now be located at the 12 o'clock position. If the drive pin is positioned incorrectly either at the 11 o'clock or 1 o'clock position, remove the pinion shaft and start over again at step 49.
52. Assemble the valve body and stub shaft in the following manner:
    a. If the valve body O-rings and teflon rings were removed, install new O-rings in the oil ring grooves and lubricate them with power steering fluid.
    b. Lubricate the 4 teflon seal rings with power steering fluid and install them in the grooves over the O-rings. Do not be concerned if the teflon rings appear to be distorted; the heat of the fluid during operation will straighten them.
    c. Lubricate the spool valve dampener O-ring with power steering fluid and install it over the spool valve.
    d. Lubricate the spool valve and valve body with power steering fluid and slide the spool valve into the valve body. Rotate the spool valve while pushing it into the valve body. Push the spool valve on through the body until the shaft pin hole is visible from the opposite end. The spool valve should be flush with the shaft cap end of the valve body.
    e. Lubricate the stub shaft assembly with power steering fluid and carefully install it into the spool valve until the shaft pin can be placed into

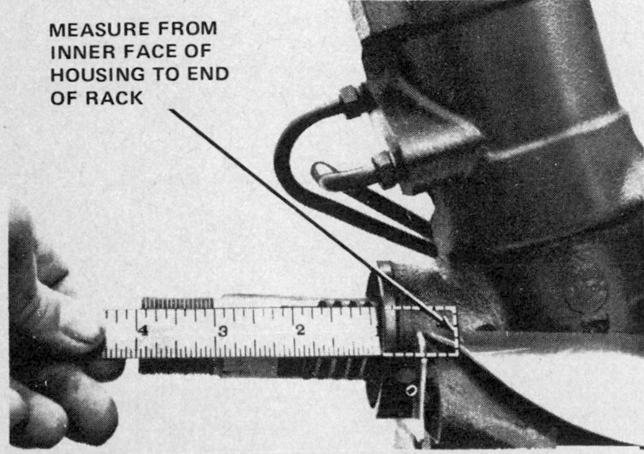

Centering the steering rack (© American Motors Corp)

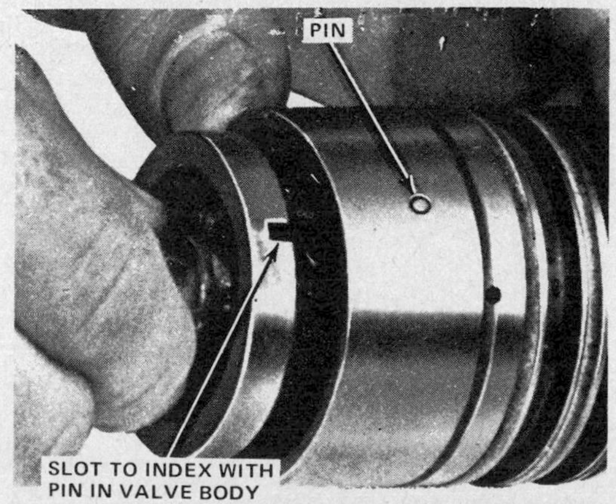

Installing the stub shaft in the valve body (© American Motors Corp)

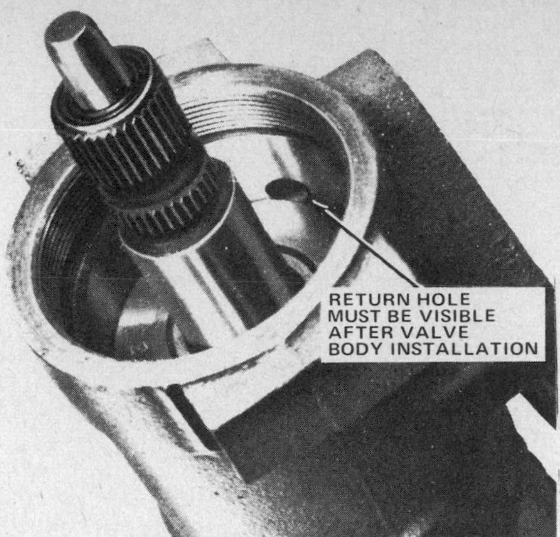

Installing the valve body assembly into the housing
(© American Motors Corp)

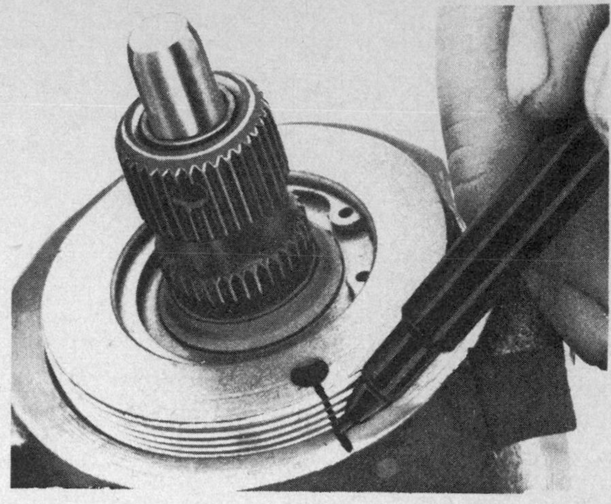

Marking the adjuster plug and housing for plug adjustment
(© American Motors Corp)

the spool valve.

f. Align the notch in the shaft cap with the pin in the valve body and press the spool valve and shaft assembly into the valve body. Make sure that the notch in the shaft cap mates with the valve body pin.

53. Align the notch in the valve body with the drive pin in the pinion shaft and install the valve body in the housing. Be sure the drive lugs on the pinion shaft fully engage the slots in the stub shaft. When the valve body is correctly installed, the fluid return hole in the housing will be exposed. If the hole is not visible, either the pinion shaft is not seated, the spool valve locating pins are misaligned, or the valve body stub shaft locating pins are misaligned.

NOTE: Do not press on the stub shaft to seat the valve body. Press only with your thumbs directly on the valve body.

54. Assemble the adjuster plug components as follows:
    a. If you are replacing the needle bearing, drive the new bearing into the plug bore with a soft drift until it bottoms. The bearing identification number faces up.
    b. Lubricate the new stub shaft oil seal and install the seal far enough to allow clearance for the dust seal and retaining ring.
    c. Lubricate the new dust seal and install it in the plug with the identification number facing outward.
    d. Install the retaining snap ring with snap ring pliers.
    e. Lubricate the new O-ring seal with petroleum jelly and install it into the groove on the adjuster plug.
    f. Assemble the large thrust bearing race, bearing, small bearing race and spacer on the plug. Press the bearing retainer into the needle bearing bore with a brass or wooden driver tool, being very careful not to damage the dimples. Radial location of the dimples is not important.

55. Install the adjuster plug in housing using a spanner type tool that fits into the two holes on the adjuster plug face. Tighten the plug until it is fully seated.

56. Adjust the thrust bearing preload by first measuring back (counterclockwise) 3/16 to ¼ in. from one of the adjuster plug holes and making a mark. Back the adjuster plug off (counterclockwise) so that the hole used for reference is opposite the mark. Install the adjuster plug locknut and tighten it to 80 ft lbs.

57. Install the O-ring and lip-type seals in the bulkhead. the lips of the seals must face the interior of the tube.

58. Slide the bulkhead into the tube and bottom it against the counterbore in the tube by tapping it with a brass rod.

59. Install the bulkhead retaining ring. The opening in the ring should be ¼ in. away from the access hole in the tube.

60. Turn the steering gear over in the vise and place some lithium base chassis grease in the housing bore. Do not overfill.

61. Install the preload spring in the housing with the center hump of the spring against the housing. The end of the spring must enter the upper pinion bushing. Allow about ¼ in. of spring to extend past the end of the housing.

62. Hold the preload spring against the housing with needlenose pliers, and install the lower pin-

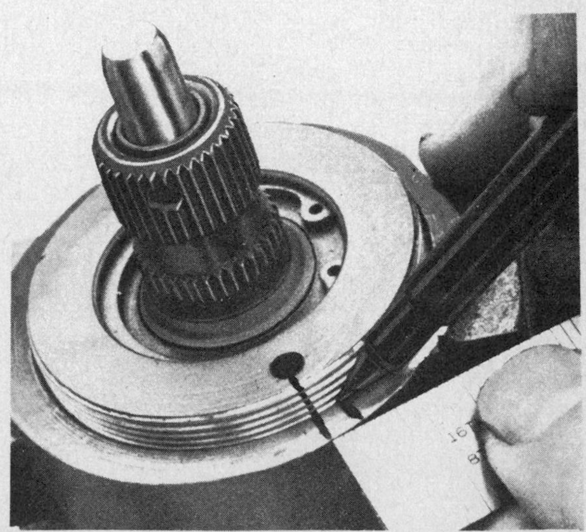

Marking the housing for adjuster plug adjustment (© American Motors Corp)

Backing off the adjuster plug to the proper adjustment (© American Motors Corp)

ion bushing. The chamfered end of the bushing faces inward toward the pinion shaft. Tap lightly on the spring and bushing until they are both seated.

63. Install the contraction plug in the housing and seat it using a brass rod or suitable size socket.
64. Install the mounting clamp and grommet on the tube. Position them according to the marks made during disassembly.
65. Install the shock dampener ring on each end of the steering rack with the open end facing out. Thread the jamnuts on the rack fully.
66. Liberally apply lithium base chassis grease to all wear surfaces of the inner tie rod assembly. Pack the tie rod housings with the same type grease.
67. Assemble the tie rod housing, inner tie rods, ball seats, ball seat springs, and install the assemblies on the steering rack. Tighten the inner tie rod housings to 75 in. lbs. while rocking the inner tie rods to prevent grease lock. Loosen the tie rod housings ½ of a turn and retighten the tie rod housings to 50 in. lbs.
68. Tighten the tie rod housing setscrews to 60 in lbs.
69. Clamp the tie rod housings in the vise and tighten the jamnuts to 100 ft lbs using a crow-foot adapter on the end of a torque wrench.
70. Slide the shock dampener rings over the jamnuts.
71. Install the mounting clamp and grommet on the tube end of the steering gear. Align the notch in the clamp with the oil line fitting boss in the tube.
72. Install the breather tube. Make sure the breather tube is not blocked in any way. The breather tube transfers air from one boot to the other during steering operation. Dust and air could be drawn into the inner tie rod assemblies if the tube is blocked.
73. Install the boot on the mounting bracket side of the tube and housing. Align the hole in the boot with the hole in the mounting grommet and breather tube. Install the boot clamp, but do not tighten it.
74. Install the opposite boot with the hole in the boot aligned with the breather tube. The boot lip must fit over the collar of the housing to seat the tube.
75. Slide the small ends of the boots over the inner tie rod undercuts and secure the boot with the small boot clamps. Tighten the clamps.
76. Secure the large end of the boot to the housing end of the steering gear. Fit the clamp over the groove in the boot with the clamp ear ¾ in. from the tube. Compress the clamp.
77. Install the adjuster tubes and tie rod ends on the inner tie rods using the alignment marks you made during disassembly. At least 3 threads should be visible at both ends of the adjuster tubes. The difference in the number of threads on each side should be no more than 3.
78. Install the flexible coupling on the stub shaft, flat to flat. Install the pinch bolt and tighten it to 30 ft lbs.
79. Install the steering gear and compress the boot clamps.

Ford Steering Wheel Turning Effort

Model	*Year*	*Lbs. Effort*
Lincoln Continental, Mark III, Thunderbird	through 1969	3.75
Lincoln Continental, Mark III, Mark IV	1970-up	4.0
Ford, Mercury	1972-up	4.0
Ford, Mercury	through 1971	5.0
Torino, Montego	1972-up	5.0
Mustang, Cougar —constant ratio	1972-up	5.0
Mustang, Cougar, Torino, Montego	1970-71	6.5
Maverick, Comet	1972-up	6.5
Mustang, Cougar —variable ratio	1972-up	6.5

Ford Power Steering Pump Service Specifications

Description	*Ford—Thompson*	*Eaton*
Pump Rotor Shaft End Play	.017 in. Max.—.003 in. Min.	
Max. Torque Allowed to Rotate Rotor Shaft	15 In-Lb.	
Stamped Housing-to-Plate Assy. Screw and Washer Assy.	28-32 Ft.-Lb.	
Stamped Housing-to-Plate Assy. Washer head hex bolt		38-47 Ft.-Lb.
Reservoir-to-Stamped Housing Nut	43-47 Ft.-Lb.	
Cam Ring-to-Pressure Plate Screw		20 In-Lb.

Ford Integral Power Steering Gear Specifications

Description	*Ford Design*	*Saginaw Design*
Type	Recirculating ball torsion bar	
Ratio	17:1	17.5:1
Turns of steering wheel (lock to lock-linkage disconnected)	4	4
Fluid capacity (included in pump reservoir fill)	1.6 Pints (Approx.)	
Sector shaft end play—linkage disconnected	None	.002 In. Max.
Sector shaft mesh load. Total over mechanical center position. Must be① greater than worm Bearing preload torque, shown below	17 In. Lb. (Max.)	14 In. Lb. (Max)
Worm bearing preload	2-8 In. Lb.	4-7 In. Lb. ②
Clearance between valve spool & retaining ring	.0035—.0005" Preferable .002"	—
Pressure variation between right & left turn (at 250 P.S.I.)— Check efforts each side of center	4 In. Lb. Max. Variation	—
Clearance between inner sector seal and housing	.025 In.	—

① 11-13 in. lb, 4-8 in. lb for Saginaw.
② 3 in lb in excess of valve assy. Drag total worm bearing preload and seal drag not to exceed 9 in. lb.

FORD INTEGRAL RACK AND PINION STEERING GEAR SPECIFICATIONS

Gear Ratio	19.03 on Center 16.24 at Stops
Number of Turns	3.3
Pinion, Rack, and Tie Rod Inner Ball Socket Lubricant Capacity	5.2 oz. or Approx. .33 pints (Divide Equally Between the Two Bellows
Power Steering Fluid Capacity (Including Steering Pump)	2.44 Pints
Pinion, Rack, Tie Rod Inner Ball Socket Lubricant	D2AZ-19580-B
Piston Seal Lubricant (Cavity under Dust Seal)	
Power Steering Fluid	D2AZ-19582-A
Effort Required to Initiate Proper Input Shaft Rotation (Rack Seals Filled with Lubricant, Power Cylinder Drained and Gear Removed from Vehicle)	10-15 In-Lb
Tie Rod Articulation Effort (on Pull Scale)	1½-6 Lbs.

Ford Steering Gear Torque Limits (Ft. Lbs.)

Description	*Non-integral*	*Ford Integral Power Steering*	*Saginaw Integral Power Steering*
Sector shaft cover bolts	17-25	55-70	30-45
Mesh load adjusting screw lock nut	32-40	35-45	27-37
Ball return guide clamp screw	18-42③	42-70③	3-6
Preload adjuster lock nut	60-80		50-110
Valve housing to gear housing screw		35-50	
Race retaining inner nut		①	
Race lock nut		15-25	③
Piston end cap		70-110	50-100
Lubricant fill plug and vent	3-9②		

① With tool T66P-3553-B - compute the torque as follows:

$$\text{Torque} = \frac{\text{Length of Torque Wrench} \times 72 \text{ Ft. Lb.}}{\text{Length of Torque Wrench} + 5.5 \text{ Inches}}$$

Example: With 13 inch torque wrench

$$\frac{13 \text{ In.} \times 72 \text{ Ft. Lb.}}{13 \text{ In.} + 5.5 \text{ In.}} = \frac{13 \times 72 \text{ Ft. Lb.}}{18.5} = 0.703 \times 72 = 50 \text{ (Ft. Lb.)}$$

② Minimum of one thread must remain exposed when installed.
③ In. Lbs.

Chevrolet Power Steering—Pump Pressure

Vehicle	*Constant Ratio Steering*	*Variable Ratio Steering*
Chevrolet		1350-1450
Chevelle		1200-1300 (L-6) 1350-1450 (V-8)
Station Wagon and Vega	900-1000	
Monte Carlo		1350-1450
Nova		1200-1300 (L-6) 1350-1450 (V-8)
Corvette	870-1000	

Chevrolet Adjustment Specifications—Power Steering

Ball drag	3 in. lb. max.
Thrust bearing preload	½ - 2 in. lb. in excess of valve assy. drag
Over center preload	3 - 6 in. lb. in excess of above
Total steering gear preload	14 in. lb. max.

Power Steering Gear—Chrysler

Type	Constant control full time power
Ratio	15.7 to 1
Wheel turns—stop to stop	3 ½
Worm shaft thrust bearing pre-load	16-24 ozs.
Cross shaft adjustment	Tighten adjusting screw ⅜ to ½ turn past zero back lash (center of high spot)
Type of fluid	Power steering fluid part No. 2084329 or equivalent; Do not use ATF

Pump

Type	Constant displacement—1.06 cu. in. per revolution	Constant displacement—.94 cu. in per revolution
Maximum pressure	1200 to 1300 PSI	950 to 1075 PSI
Pump output		2.1 to 2.6 gpm
High level	2.5 to 3.0 gpm	
Low level	1.4 to 1.8 gpm	
Type of fluid	Power steering—Part No. 2084329 or equivalent. Do not use Type "A" Transmission fluid	Power steering—Part No. 2084329 or equivalent Do not use Type "A" Transmission fluid

Power Steering Gear Torques

	Ft. Lbs.		*Pounds Foot*	*Pounds Inch*
Gear housing to frame bolt	100	Steering column support nut		140
Gear shaft adjusting screw lock nut	25-35	Steering shaft coupling bolts		200
Sector shaft cover nut	50	Valve body attaching bolts		200
Pump inlet fitting	30	Valve body end plug	30-40	
Steering arm nut	120	Steering wheel nut	60	

Pump Torques

Location	*Ft. Lbs.*
High pressure hose fittings	13
Pump bracket bolts	23
Flow control valve plug	7
Bracket mounting bolts	30
⅛ in. pipe clean out plug	7

Dash Gauges and Indicators

INDEX

There are various systems used to indicate values of heat, pressure, current flow and fuel supply. The following are the more popular systems used.

Bourdon Tube

This gauge consists of a flattened tube that is bent to form a curve. The curve tends to straighten under internal pressure caused by engine oil pressure. The curved tube is geared or linked to an indicator needle which may be read on a calibrated scale.

Bourdon tube oil pressure gauges are used on some Corvettes and the optional instrument panels on some Chevrolet sport models. This type of gauge may be easily distinguished from the electrical type by the small copper or nylon tube running from the gauge to the engine.

Bi-Metallic or Thermal

This gauge is activated by the difference in the expansion factors of a bi-metal bar. A sending unit, consisting of a variable resistance conductor, influences current flow to a voltage limiter, or directly to a heating element coiled around a bi-metal bar in the gauge. A bi-metallic gauge pointer will move slowly to its gauging position.

Magnetic

In this system, the indicator needle is moved by changing the balance between the magnetic pull of two coils built in the gauge. When the ignition switch is in the "off" position, the pointer may rest any place on the gauge dial. Balance is controlled by the action of a sending unit or a tank unit containing a rheostat, the value of which varies with temperature, pressure or movement of a float arm. A magnetic gauge will snap to its position when turned on.

Warning Lights

This system is quite popular and may be used to indicate heat, low pressure or as a battery discharge indicator. General Motors uses a two-light temperature indicator version of this unit in some models.

Section 1
Bourdon Tube

Oil Pressure

The gauge is the pressure expansion type and is activated by oil pressure developed by the oil pump, acting directly on the mechanism of the gauge. The gauge is connected by a small tube to the main oil passage in the engine oiling system. This design registers the full pressure of the oil pump.

Testing

A gauge pointer that flutters is usually an indication that oil has entered the gauge tube. The tube should contain trapped air to cushion the pulsations of the oil pump and relief valve. Oil can work up into the gauge line as a result of a gauge or tube leak or improper installation. To correct this condition, renew the unit or correct the leak; then, with the gauge line disconnected at both ends, blow the line clear. Connect line at gauge first and then at the engine.

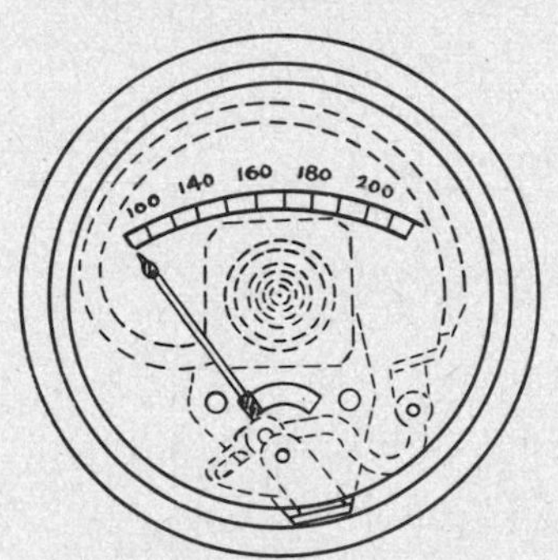

Bourdon tube gauge

If the gauge reads too low or reads no pressure, test for a possible obstruction by disconnecting the line at the gauge. Hold the end of the line over an empty container, then start the engine. After a few bubbles, oil should flow steadily.

If oil does not flow satisfactorily, first make sure that the oil level is correct and that the oil pump is functioning. Should the engine oil system be operating correctly, the problem is either with the gauge or the line.

Check the line for kinks, leaks, or blockage which would prevent oil from reaching the gauge. If the line is unobstructed, remove the gauge unit from the instrument panel. Check to make sure that the hole leading to the Bourdon tube is clear and be sure that the lever linkage and pointer gears operate freely. If none of these points is at fault, the Bourdon tube itself is defective and the gauge must be replaced.

Section 2
Bi-Metal

Fuel

Bi-metal or thermal type gauges operate on the principle of constant applied voltage and are sensitive only to changes originating at the sending unit.

The fuel gauge system consists of a sending unit, located in the fuel tank, and a registering unit mounted in the instrument cluster. The sending unit is a rheostat that varies its resistance depending on the amount of fuel in the tank.

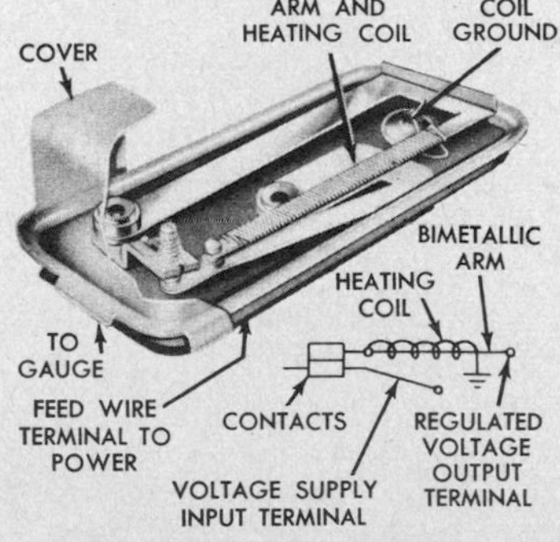

Constant voltage regulator

Testing the Dash Gauge

Caution Gauge systems using constant voltage regulators should not be grounded while testing. An excess of 5 volts is likely to burn out the unit.

To safely test this type of voltage regulated system:

1. Have the ignition switch in the "off" position.
2. Connect the terminals of four, series-connected, D-type flashlight batteries (total of six volts) to the terminals of the gauge to be tested. Three volts should cause the gauge to read

approximately half-scale.

If the gauge reads half-full and was not working properly before, the sending unit in the tank is probably defective.

If the gauge is inaccurate or does not register, replace it.

If both the fuel gauge and temperature gauge are in error, in the same manner, the constant voltage regulator is probably at fault.

While working under the dash, be careful not to ground any of the gauges. A full flow of current through the regulator to ground is likely to burn out the regulator.

Testing the Sending Unit

If the dash gauge test shows that unit to be satisfactory, the sending unit or gauge system wiring is faulty. Substitute a jumper wire between the gauge and the tank unit. If the gauge now functions, replace the wire. If the gauge still does not function correctly, replace the tank sending unit.

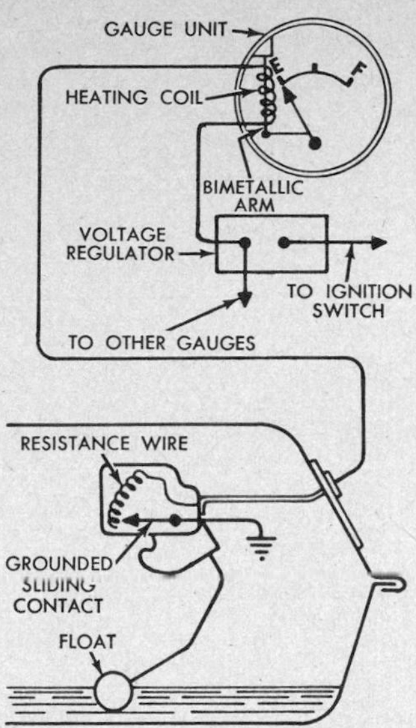

Bi-metallic fuel gauge system

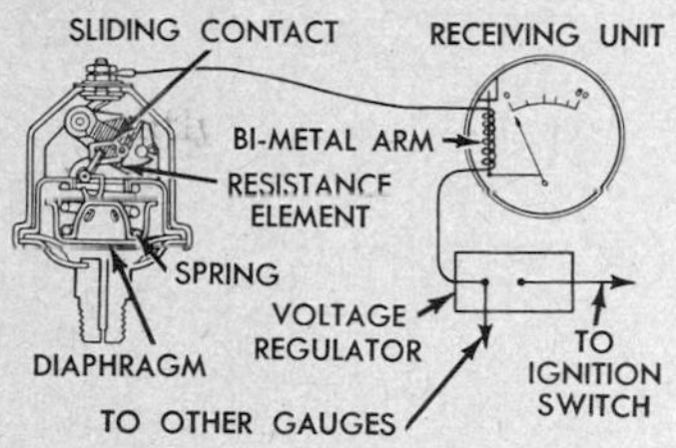

Bi-metallic oil gauge circuit

Oil Pressure

Oil pressure gauges of the bi-metal type operate on the same principle as gas gauges. They are activated by temperature and the difference in the expansion factors of a bi-metal bar.

The pressure sending unit consists of a pressure-activated variable resistor. This sealed unit is usually screwed into the engine oil pressure circuit. As pressure is applied to one side of a diaphragm, linkage advances a contact arm across the coils of a resistor. This action reduces resistance in the gauge circuit, thus increasing current flow and heat to the bi-metal arm in the gauge. The gauge is calibrated to read oil pressure in psi.

Run the engine and have an assistant watch the dash gauge. If the gauge reads zero, turn off the engine and remove the sending unit from the engine block. Restart the engine and allow it to idle for a minute. If there is oil pressure, oil should surge from the sending unit hole. If no oil flows from the hole, the problem is with the engine lubricating system. If oil flows, the fault lies with the sending unit, the wiring, or the dash gauge.

Check the gauge by grounding the connecting wire for an instant with the ignition switch turned on. A good gauge will go to the top of its scale.

Caution Grounding the connecting wire for any longer than a moment will damage the dash units.

If the gauge did not move when grounded, check the wiring to the dash unit for continuity. If the wiring is not faulty and the gauge doesn't register when grounded, replace the gauge. If the gauge functions when grounded, replace the sending unit.

Temperature

The temperature gauge consists of a sending unit, mounted in the cylinder head or block, and a remote resistor unit (temperature gauge) mounted on the instrument panel. The principle of operation is essentially the same as the bi-metallic fuel gauge, the exception being that the resistance of the sending unit is influenced by engine temperature instead of tank fuel level, as with the fuel gauge.

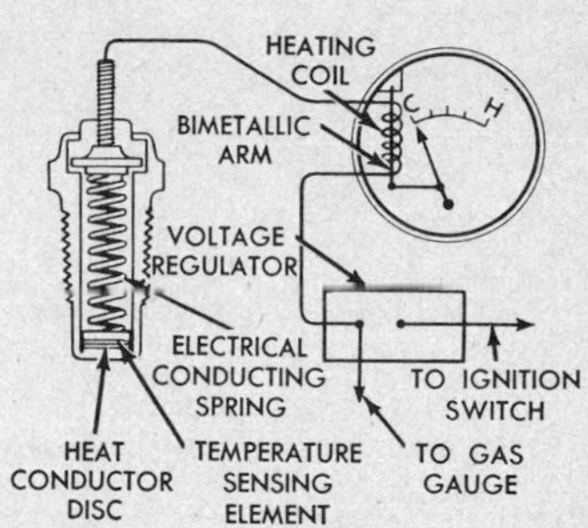

Bi-metallic temperature gauge

The temperature sending unit is constructed with a coil spring and sensing disc. Current passing through this coil encounters increased resistance, proportional to an increase in temperature. The gauge registers this resistance change and is calibrated to indicate the temperature.

Testing the Dash Gauge

Connect four D-cells (total of 6 volts) in series with the dash gauge, with the ignition switched off. A good gauge will register ½ on the scale. Replace the gauge if it does not move.

Testing the Sending Unit

Bring the engine to normal operating temperature (check with a thermometer). If the gauge doesn't register, disconnect the connecting wire from the engine sending unit and ground the connecting wire for an instant and have an assistant observe the gauge.

Caution Grounding the wire for any longer than a moment will damage the dash units.

If the gauge shows no reading, replace the connecting wire. If the gauge registers when grounded, replace the sending unit.

Section 3

Magnetic

Fuel

The magnetic fuel gauge consists of two units, the dash unit and the sending unit in the fuel tank. One terminal of the dash unit is connected to the ignition switch so that the system is active only when the ignition is on. With the ignition off, the pointer may come to rest at any position on the dial.

The gauge pointer is moved by varying the magnetic pull of two coils in the unit. The magnetic pull is controlled by the action of the tank unit which contains a variable rheostat, the value of which varies with movement of a float and arm.

When the ignition switch is on and the tank unit arm is in the full position, the current flow to ground is through the resistor, battery coil and the ground coil. Because the ground coil has more windings than the battery coil, it builds up a stronger magnetic field and the pointer is pulled to the full position.

When the tank unit arm is in the empty position, the current flow is through the resistor, the battery coil and the wire to ground at the tank unit. The pointer is thus pulled to the empty position. The resistor in series with the battery coil balances resistance between the two coils in the dash unit.

Testing the Dash Gauge

Disconnect the wire from the tank unit. Using a tank unit of known accuracy, clip a test wire from the body of the test unit to ground. Clip another test wire from the connector of the test unit to the tank unit wire. With the ignition on, moving the float arm through its entire range should cause the gauge to respond proportionally. If the dash gauge does not correspond to the movement of the test unit and the wiring to the gauge is OK, the dash unit is bad.

Testing the Tank Unit

If tests indicate that the trouble lies in the tank unit, remove the unit and check for mechanical failure. The unit may have either a ruptured or binding float.

An electrical check for circuit continuity may be made throughout the unit's range.

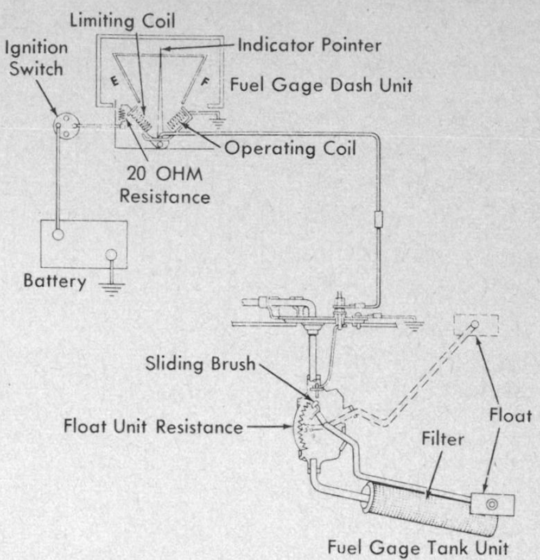

Magnetic fuel gauge circuit

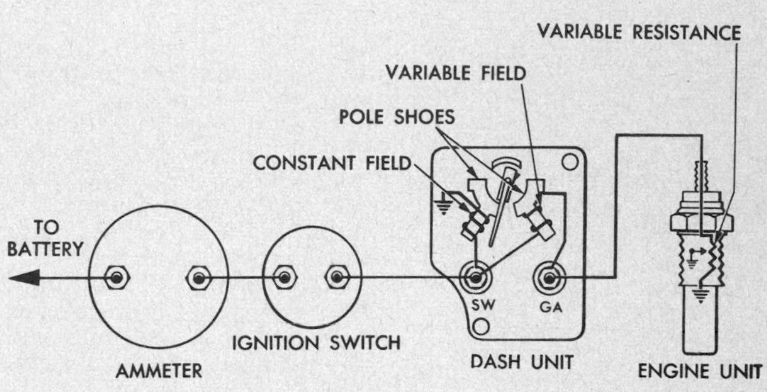

Magnetic temperature gauge

Temperature

The temperature gauge system consists of a magnetic dash unit and a resistance-type sending unit screwed into the water jacket of the cylinder head or the engine block.

The dash unit has two magnetic poles. One of the windings is connected to the ignition switch and ground. This electromagnet exerts a steady pull to hold the gauge pointer to the left or "cold" position when the ignition is on.

The other winding in the dash unit connects to a ground through the engine sending unit. This electromagnet exerts a steady pull on the gauge pointer toward the right, or "hot" side of the gauge. The strength of this pull is dependent upon the current allowed to pass through the engine unit (sending unit) resistor.

The sending unit, located in the engine cooling system, contains a flat disc (thermistor) that changes resistance as its temperature varies.

NOTE: this sending unit, while similar in appearance, is different and is not interchangeable with the unit used in systems using bi-metal or thermal dash gauges. The resistance of the thermistor disc is maximum when the temperature is cold and minimum when hot. The decrease in resistance allows more current to flow through the electromagnet connected to the engine unit. The resulting increase in magnetic pull causes the gauge pointer to move to the right, or "hot" side.

Tests

1. Disconnect the wire at the sending unit and turn on the ignition switch. The gauge hand should stay against the cold side stop pin.
2. Ground the wire disconnected from the sending unit. With the ignition switch still on, the gauge hand should swing across the dial to the hot stop pin.

Corrective Measures

If the gauge hand does not stay to the left, either the wire is grounded between the dash unit and the engine unit or the dash unit is defective.

Test further by disconnecting the sending unit wire at the gauge. Turn on the ignition. If the gauge hand stays on the left-hand stop pin, replace the disconnected wire. If the gauge still moves, replace the gauge.

If the gauge hand does not swing across the dial, there is an open circuit in the wire between the sending unit and gauge, the gauge is defective, or current is not reaching the dash gauge.

Test further by grounding the sending unit terminal of the dash gauge and turning on the ignition. If the gauge hand now moves, replace the disconnected wire. If the gauge hand does not move, connect a test lamp into the circuit. If the test lamp does not light, test the wire between the ignition switch and the dash unit by connecting the lamp to the accessory terminal at the ignition switch and ground. The test lamp should light.

If the gauge hand operates correctly, but the gauge does not indicate temperature correctly, either the sending unit is defective or the dash gauge is out of calibration. Replace sending unit with one of known accuracy. If gauge reading is still incorrect, replace the gauge.

If the gauge hand is at maximum at all times, and tests 1 and 2 indicate that the wiring and the dash unit are good, the sending unit must be replaced.

If the gauge hand will not move, the dash unit is bad, or incorrectly installed. Correct the installation or replace the gauge.

Oil Pressure

The warning or indicator light system supplies the driver with a visual signal of low engine oil pressure. The light usually lights at pressures below 5 psi.

The low pressure warning light is wired in series with an oil pressure sending unit. The sending unit is tapped into the main oil gallery and is sensitive to oil pressure. The unit contains a diaphragm, spring linkage and electrical contacts. When the ignition switch is on, the warning light circuit is energized and the circuit is completed through the closed contacts in the sending unit. When the engine starts, oil pressure will compress the diaphragm, opening the contact points and breaking the circuit.

Tests

The light should light when the engine is not running and the ignition switch is turned on. If the light does not go on, first substitute a new bulb. If there is still no light, check the wire from the light to the switch. If the wire is not at fault, disconnect the wire at the sending unit and ground it. Replace the sending unit if the light now lights.

Temperature

This system employs a heat sending unit with either one or two sets of contacts. Some systems use a green light to indicate subnormal, and a red light to warn of abnormal heat. The more common system, however, uses a simple make-and-break heat-sensitive sending unit screwed into the engine cooling system, and wired in series with the hot indicator light in the instrument panel.

The two-light system uses a bi-metal element mounted between two signal circuits. Normal operating temperature (somewhere between 120°F. and 250°F.) will cause the bi-metal bar to assume a position of no contact between the low and the high temperature circuit. When the ignition switch is turned on, with a cold engine, the cold (green) circuit is complete. If the engine becomes hot enough to move the bi-metal bar so that it touches the contacts of the hot circuit, the hot (red) light comes on. This hot signal indicates that temperatures are in the area of 250°F. in the sealed cooling system.

Tests

Use the same testing procedure given for oil pressure.

Charge Indicator

A light is used to indicate general charging system operation. When output is below battery potential, a red light is shown. When output is above battery potential, other factors (wiring, voltage regulator, etc.) be-

Section 4
Warning Lights

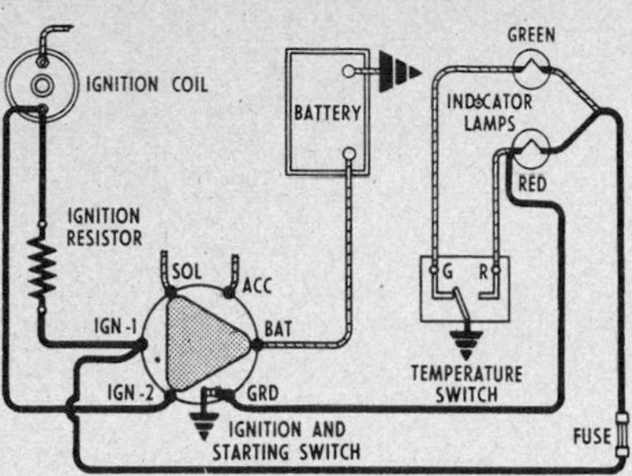

Cold and hot temperature indicator circuit

ing normal, the light is out.

The charge indicator bulb is connected to the charging circuit, obtaining its ground through the voltage regulator. When the output rises above battery potential, the current flow causes the light to go out.

When an alternator is used, it is necessary to supply a small amount of excitation current to the alternator field, due to the small amount of residual magnetism. Current can be supplied from the battery, through the indicator light, and to the regulator terminal on the alternator. This current has a value of about 12 volts at .25 amperes and will cause the indicator light to come on when the ignition switch is turned on.

When the alternator starts to generate, an output voltage is developed at the regulator terminal. When this voltage exceeds the battery voltage, current will pass from the alternator to the battery and to the system. This current is flowing in the reverse direction of the voltage supplied by the battery. The current flow coming from the alternator exceeds the battery current by a regulated 1 or 2 volts. This is not enough to light the indicator light, therefore, the light will go out when the alternator is supplying sufficient current.

If the alternator output current should drop below battery voltage, current will begin to flow in the opposite direction. If it exceeds 2 or 3 volts, the light will glow indicating that the alternator is not operating properly.

Caution In some instances, a glow of the indicator light will be noticed at night while cruising. This can exist in a system that is operating normally and with a fully charged battery. The condition, while of no great importance, is probably caused by an overload of equipment and accessories.

See "Charging and Starting Systems" for troubleshooting.

Coolant Level Indicator

Some GM models have a warning light which comes on if the coolant level in the radiator drops below a predetermined level. The coolant level indicator consists of three units; a sending unit which is threaded into the side tank of the radiator, a module which is mounted behind the instrument cluster, and a warning light. As a bulb test, the light is wired so that it comes on when the key is turned to the "START" position.

Light Doesn't Come On

Perform the following checks if the warning light won't come on when the key is turned to the "START" position:

1. With the ignition switch in the "ON" position, unfasten the lead from the coolant level sending unit. If the light comes on replace the sending unit.
2. If the light didn't come on in

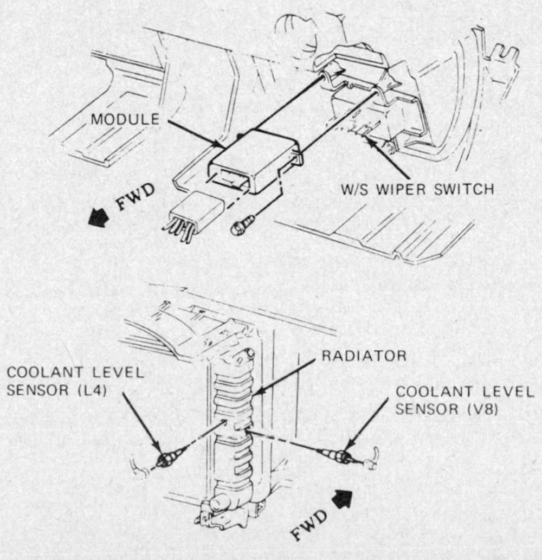

Coolant temperature sending unit and module (© Chevrolet Div., GM Corp)

step 1, check the light in the indicator and replace it, if necesary.

3. If the bulb is OK, check the wiring between the sending unit and module, and then between the module and light. If the wiring is not "open", replace the module.

Light Won't Go Out

Perform the following checks if the light won't go out when the coolant is at the specified level:

1. Detach the lead from the coolant level sending unit and ground the lead connector with a jumper wire. Turn the ignition switch to the "ON" position.
2. If the light doesn't come on, replace the sending unit. If the light remains on disconnect the jumper wire and proceed with the next step.
3. Check for a short in the sending unit-to-module wiring. If there is no short, replace the module.

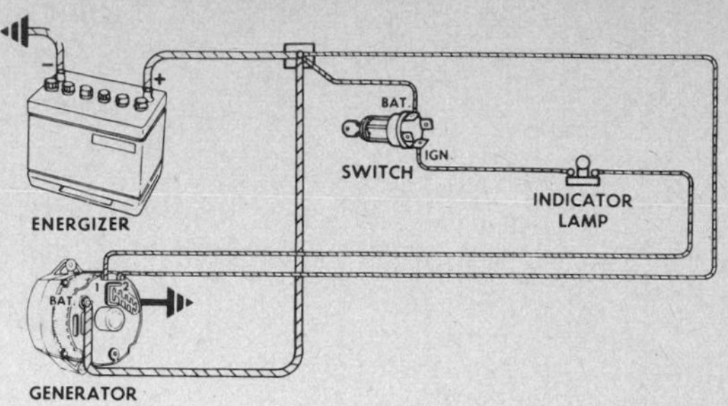

Charging indicator light circuit

Section 5

Ammeters

The automotive ammeter is a gauge or meter used to indicate direction and relative value of current flow. This type of charge indicator is usually equipped with a dampening device to reduce pointer fluctuation during current surge from the voltage regulator.

The meter will show charge when the battery is being charged and discharge when the battery is being discharged. It merely gives an indication of the state of charge of the battery, since it shows a relatively high charging rate when the battery is low, and a low charging rate when the battery is near full charge. An ammeter does not give a complete report of battery condition, whereas a voltmeter does. Just after cranking the engine, the meter will swing toward the charge side for a short time, if lights and accessories are turned off. As the energy spent in cranking is restored to the battery, the pointer will gradually move back toward center but should stay on the charge side. If the battery charge is low, however, the indicator will show a high charging rate for an indeterminate length of time.

The ammeter does not show the charging rate of the generator.

At speeds above 30-35 mph, with all lights and accessories on, the indicator should show a reading somewhere on the charge side, depending on the state of the battery. Above this speed, the indicator should never show a discharge reading; if it does, the generator and regulator should be tested. See "Charging and Starting Systems" for troubleshooting.

Section 6

Voltmeters

A voltmeter is used on some cars, instead of an ammeter. The voltmeter indicates regulated voltage, which shows the charging system's ability to keep the battery charged. Voltmeter readings that are continuously high or low, may indicate a defective regulator, broken or slipping alternator drivebelt, a faulty alternator, or a defective battery. For testing and service of these items, see "Charging and Starting Systems".

If a faulty voltmeter is suspected, check the voltage regulator output with a test voltmeter of known accuracy (See "Charging and Starting Systems"). If the voltage indicated on the test instrument is within specifications, and disagrees with the car's voltmeter reading, replace the car's voltmeter.

Diagnostic Charts

STARTING SYSTEM DIAGNOSIS

● Most probable causes
✓ Possible causes

Causes \ Problems	Repeated clicking from starter	Cranks very slowly	Starter Spins, but does not turn engine	Starter clunks, but does not turn engine	No sound from starter	Excessive Starter Current draw
Battery Not Fully Charged	●	●		●	●	
Loose Battery Cables	●	●		●	✓	✓
Defective Battery	✓	✓		✓	✓	✓
Shorted or Loose Starter Wire	✓	✓		✓	✓	✓
Defective Solenoid	✓				✓	✓
Engine Overheated		✓		✓		
Low Temperature		●		✓		
Thick Oil		✓		✓		
Internal Engine Malfunction		✓		✓		
Defective Starter		✓		✓		
Defective Starter Drive		✓	●			
Open Circuit in Solenoid Armature, or Field Coils				●		●
Short in Field or Armature Coils				●		●
Neutral Safety Switch Misadjusted					✓	
Fusible Link Melted					✓	
Defective Ignition Switch					✓	
Clutch Switch Misadjusted					✓	

CLUTCH AND MANUAL TRANSMISSION DIAGNOSIS

● Most probable causes
✓ Possible causes

Causes	Noisy in Forward Speeds	Noisy in Reverse	Noisy in Neutral	Hard Shifting	Jumping Out of Gear	Sticking in Gear	Gears Clash	Locks in Two Gears	Leaks
Low or Wrong Lubricant	✓	✓	✓	✓		✓	✓		✓
Transmission Misaligned or Loose	✓	✓	✓		✓				
Maindrive Gear or Bearing Damaged	●	✓	✓			✓	✓		
Speedometer Drive Noise	✓	✓							
Mainshaft Gears or Bearing Damaged	●	✓	✓		●				
Incorrect End Play on Shafts	✓	✓	✓		✓				
Reverse Idler Gear or Shaft Damaged		●	✓						
Incorrect Clutch Adjustment			●	✓		●	●		
Shift Linkage Misadjusted				●	✓	✓		●	
Bent Shifter Forks or Shafts				✓	✓	✓		✓	
Damaged Synchronizers				✓	✓	✓	●		
Speed Too High on Downshift				●			✓		
Front Main Bearing Damaged	✓	✓	✓		✓				
Bent Output Shaft					✓				
High Idle Speed							✓		
Wait 3-4 Sec. Before Shifting Into a Non-synchronized Gear							●		
Bent Shift Rods								✓	
Overfilled									●
Seals at Covers or Extension Housing Bad									✓
Loose Main Drive Gear Bearing Retainer									✓
Operating Shaft Seals Bad									✓
Worn Extension Housing Bushing									✓

CHRYSLER TORQUEFLITE AUTOMATIC TRANSMISSION DIAGNOSIS

Causes

✓ Possible causes

Problems	Oil level	Control linkage	Oil pressure check	Kickdown band	Low-reverse band	Improper engine idle	Servo linkage	Accumulator	Valve body assembly	Manual valve lever	Air pressure check	Servo link	Governor	Gear shift cable	Regulator valve	Strainer	Converter control valve	Breather clogged	Cooler or lines
Harsh N to D or N to R shift			✓	✓	✓	✓	✓		✓	✓									
Delayed Shift—N to D	✓		✓						✓										
Runaway on upshift—2-3 kickdown	✓	✓	✓	✓				✓	✓			✓							
Harsh upshift and 3-2 kickdown		✓	✓	✓				✓	✓			✓							
No upshift	✓	✓	✓	✓				✓	✓	✓	✓	✓	✓						
No kickdown on normal downshift	✓	✓	✓	✓				✓	✓		✓		✓	✓					
Erratic shifts	✓	✓	✓			✓								✓	✓	✓			
Slips in forward drive positions	✓		✓					✓	✓		✓								
Slips in Reverse only			✓		✓		✓		✓		✓								
Slips in all positions	✓		✓						✓		✓				✓				
No drive in any positions	✓		✓						✓	✓	✓					✓			
No drive in forward positions			✓	✓				✓	✓		✓	✓			✓				
No drive in Reverse			✓		✓		✓		✓		✓		✓						
Drives in Neutral									✓	✓				✓					
Drags or locks				✓	✓		✓					✓							
Noises	✓								✓	✓			✓		✓		✓		
Hard to fill or blows out	✓								✓							✓	✓	✓	✓
Transmission overheats	✓			✓	✓				✓				✓		✓		✓		✓

This transmission is used on all Chrysler Corporation cars since 1967 and on American Motors products since 1972.

FORD C-6 AUTOMATIC TRANSMISSION DIAGNOSIS

● Most probable causes
✓ Possible causes

Problems	Fluid level	Vacuum diaphragm	Manual linkage	Governor	Valve body	Pressure regulator	Intermediate band	Low-reverse clutch	Intermediate servo	Engine idle speed	Downshift linkage	Perform air pressure check	Extension rear oil seal	Perform pressure check	Engine performance
No drive in D, 2, and 1			✓		✓							✓		✓	
1-2 or 2-3 shift points erratic	✓	✓	✓	✓	✓						✓	✓		✓	
Rough 1-2 upshifts		✓			✓	✓	✓		✓			✓		✓	
Rough 2-3 upshifts		✓			✓	✓	✓		✓			✓		✓	
Dragged out 1-2 shift	✓	✓			✓	✓	✓		✓			✓		✓	
No 1-2 or 2-3 shift		✓	✓	✓	✓		✓		✓		✓	✓		✓	
No 3-1 shift in D				✓	✓										
No forced downshifts		✓			✓						✓				
Runaway engine on 3-2 downshift		✓			✓	✓	✓		✓			✓		✓	
Rough 3-2 or 3-1 shift at closed throttle		✓			✓	✓			✓	✓					
Shifts 1-3 in D		✓		✓	✓		✓		✓						
Creeps excessively										●					
Slips in first gear, D	✓	✓			✓	✓						✓		✓	
Slips in second gear	✓	✓			✓	✓	✓		✓			✓		✓	
Slips or chatters in R	✓	✓			✓	✓		✓				✓		✓	
No drive in D only			✓		✓							✓		✓	
No drive in 2 only	✓		✓		✓				✓			✓		✓	
No drive in 1 only	✓		✓		✓							✓		✓	
No drive in R only	✓		✓		✓			✓				✓		✓	
No drive in any lever position	✓		✓		✓	✓						✓		✓	
Lockup in 2 only								●							
Parking lock broken			✓												
Transmission overheats		✓				✓						✓		✓	
Maximum speed too low															✓
Transmission noisy in N and P	✓					✓									
Transmission noisy in all gears	✓					✓									
Fluid leak	✓	✓							✓				✓		
Car moves forward in N			✓												

This transmission is available on many Ford Motor Company cars from 1967.

GENERAL MOTORS TURBO HYDRA-MATIC 350 AUTOMATIC TRANSMISSION DIAGNOSIS

Causes

● Most probable causes
✓ Possible causes

Problems	Low oil level/water in oil	Vacuum leak	Modulator and/or valve	Strainer and/or gasket	Governor valve/screen	Valve body gasket/plate	Pressure regulator valve	1-2 shift valve	2-3 shift valve	Manual low-control valve	Detent valve and linkage	2-3 accumulator	Manual valve linkage	Pump gears	Gasket screen-pressure
Slips in all ranges	✓		✓	✓		✓	✓						✓		✓
Drive slips—no First gear	✓		✓	✓		✓	✓						✓		✓
No 1-2 upshift		✓			✓	✓	✓	✓							
Slips, 1-2 upshift	✓		✓			✓	✓	✓				✓			
Harsh 1-2 upshift		✓	✓				✓								
No 2-3 upshift						✓			✓						
2-3 upshift early or late		✓			✓	✓	✓		✓		✓				
Slips, 2-3 upshift	✓		✓			✓	✓		✓						
No full throttle downshift		✓	✓				✓		✓			✓			
2-3 upshift, full throttle only		✓									✓				
Car drives in Neutral											●				
Slips in Reverse	✓		✓	✓		✓	✓	✓					✓	✓	✓
1-2 or 2-3 shifts noisy	●														
Noisy in all ranges	✓			✓		✓									✓
Spews oil out of the breather	✓			✓											

This transmission is available on many General Motors cars since 1969.

BRAKE DIAGNOSIS

Problems

● Most probable causes
✓ Possible causes

Causes	Brake Tell-Tale Glows During Stop	Brakes Chatter (Roughness)	Brakes Squeak During Application	Scraping Noise from Brakes	Uneven Braking Action (Front to Rear)	Uneven Braking Action (Pulls to Side)	Brakes Drag	Brakes Slow to Release	Brakes Slow to Respond	Excessive Braking Action	Excessive Brake Pedal Effort	Pedal Travel Gradually Increases	Excessive Brake Pedal Travel
Leaking Brake Line or Connection	●				✓							●	✓
Leaking Wheel Cylinder or Piston Seal	✓					✓				✓		●	✓
Leaking Master Cylinder	✓											●	✓
Restricted Brake Fluid Passage					✓	✓	✓	✓	✓		✓	✓	
Air In Brake System	●				✓								●
Contaminated or Improper Brake Fluid	✓						✓	✓	✓				
Faulty Metering Valve (Disc Only)	✓				✓		✓	✓	✓	✓	✓		✓
Sticking Wheel Cylinder or Caliper Pistons					✓	✓	✓	✓			✓		
Improperly Adjusted Master Cylinder Push Rod	✓						●	✓					✓
Leaking Vacuum System									✓		●		
Restricted Air Passage In Power Unit								✓	●		✓		
Improperly Assembled Power Unit							●	✓	✓	✓	✓		
Damaged Power Unit							✓	✓	✓	✓	✓		
Brake Assembly Attachments—Missing or Loose		✓		✓	✓	✓	✓						✓
Brake Pedal Linkage Interference or Binding							●	●	✓		✓		
Worn Out Brake Lining—Replace			✓	✓	✓	✓					✓		
Uneven Brake Lining Wear—Replace	✓		✓	✓	✓	✓							✓
Glazed Brake Lining—Sand Lightly			✓		✓	✓			✓		●		
Incorrect Lining Material—Replace		✓	●		✓	✓			✓	✓	✓		
Contaminated Brake Lining—Replace		✓	✓	✓	●	●			✓	●			
Linings Damaged By Abusive Use—Replace			✓	✓	✓	✓				●	✓		
Excessive Brake Lining Dust—Remove with Air			✓		●	●				●	✓		
Brake Drums or Rotors Heat Spotted or Scored		●	✓		✓	✓				✓			
Out-of-Round or Vibrating Brake Drums		●											
Out-of-Parallel Brake Rotors		●											
Excessive Rotor Run-Out		✓											
Faulty Automatic Adjusters	✓				✓	✓	✓					●	✓
Weak or Incorrect Brake Shoe Return Springs			✓	●	✓	✓	●	✓		✓			
Drums Tapered or Threaded				●									
Incorrect Wheel Cylinder Sizes					✓	✓				✓	✓		
Improperly Adjusted Parking Brake							✓						
Incorrect Front End Alignment						●							
Incorrect Tire Pressure					✓	✓							
Incorrect Wheel Bearing Adjustment		✓		✓									✓
Loose Front Suspension Attachments		✓		●		✓							
Out-of-Balance Wheel Assemblies		●											
Driver Riding Brake Pedal					✓		✓				✓	✓	✓
Faulty Proportioning Valve							✓	✓	✓		✓		
Insufficient Brake Shoe Pad Lubricant			●	●	✓		✓	✓					

DISC BRAKE DIAGNOSIS

Problems

● Most probable causes
✓ Possible causes

Causes	Excessive Pedal Travel	Hard Pedal	Grabbing or Pulling	Fading Pedal	Noise and Chatter	Dragging Brakes
Master Cylinder Fluid Low	●		✓	✓		
Air in Hydraulic System	●		✓			
Hoses Soft or Weak	●			✓		
Caliper Seals Soft or Broken	●		●		✓	●
Power Brake Malfunctioning		●				
Lining Soiled With Brake Fluid		●	●			
Lines or Hoses Kinked or Collapsed		●	●			●
Caliper Pistons Frozen or Seized		●	●		✓	●
Master Cylinder Cups Swollen		●				●
Master Cylinder Bore Rough		●	●	●		
Caliper Cylinder Bore Rough or Worn		●	●	●	✓	●
Pedal Push Rod and Linkage Binding		●	✓			
Metering Valve Not Working		●	●			
Hydraulic Connections Loose or Ruptured	✓		✓	●		
Caliper Cylinder Seals Worn or Damaged	✓			●	✓	●
Bleed Screw Open	✓			●		
Lines or Hoses Ruptured	✓			●		
Disc Has Excessive Internal Runout					●	✓
Disc Out of Parallel			✓		●	✓
Disc Has Casting Imperfections					●	✓
Restricted Port in Master Cylinder		✓				●
Residual Pressure Check Valve		✓				●
Push Rod on Master Cylinder Out of Adjustment		✓				●
Caliper Loose			●		✓	
Poor Quality Brake Fluid				●		
Poor Quality Brake Lining				●	●	

AIR CONDITIONING DIAGNOSIS

● Most probable causes
✓ Possible causes

Causes \ Problems	Compressor Discharge Pressure Too High	Compressor Discharge Pressure Too Low	P.O.A. Valve Inlet Pressure Too High	P.O.A. Valve Inlet Pressure Too Low	Nozzle Outlet Temperature Too Warm	Nozzle Outlet Temperature Too Cold	Blown Thermal Limiter	Compressor Clutch Slips	Evaporator Pressure Too High	Water Blowing Out Discharge Nozzle	Compressor Not Operating	Water Drains Onto Floor
Engine Overheated	●				✓			✓	✓			
Overcharge of Refrigerant or Air in System	●				✓			✓	✓			
Restriction in Condenser	●				✓		✓	✓				
Restriction in Receiver-Dehydrator		●		✓	✓		✓					
Restriction in Any High Pressure Line	●	✓		✓	✓		✓	✓	✓			
Condenser Air Flow Blocked	●				✓		✓	✓	✓			
P.O.A. Valve Inlet Pressure Too High	●											
Insufficient Refrigerant		●		✓	●		●				✓	
Defective Compressor		●	✓		✓			✓	✓		●	
Plug in Refrigerant System	✓	●	✓	✓	✓		✓	✓	✓		✓	
P.O.A. Valve Inlet Pressure Too Low		●				✓	✓				✓	
P.O.A. Valve Stuck Open					✓	✓	✓				✓	
Capillary Tube to Evaporator Tube Contact	✓		●		✓	✓		●	✓			
Expansion Valve Inoperative	✓	✓	●	✓	●		●	✓	●		✓	
Inlet Screen Plugged or Valve Fails		✓		●	✓		✓				✓	
Restriction in System Hoses or Tubes	✓	✓		●	✓	✓	✓	✓	✓		✓	
Poor Seal Evaporator to Evaporator Inlet Case		✓		✓	●							
Poor Seal Evaporator to Heater Case		✓		✓	●							
Defective or Missing Evaporator Drain Hose										●		●
Air Ducts Not Properly Connected		✓		✓	●	✓						
Vacuum Hoses Not Connected Properly					●	✓						
P.O.A. Valve Faulty			●		●	●						
Low Charge or Discharged System		✓	✓	✓	✓		●		✓		✓	
Thermal Limiter Improperly Installed							●				✓	
Thermal Limiter Blown											●	
Faulty Superheat Shut Off Switch							●				✓	
Head Pressure Too High								●				
Pulley Wobbles								●				
Loose Compressor Drive Belt		✓	✓		✓				●		●	
Defective Clutch or Coil		✓	✓		✓				●		●	
Restriction in Suction Line		✓	✓		✓				●		✓	
Defective Suction Throttling Valve		✓	✓	●					✓			
Defective Expansion Valve	✓		●	✓	✓		✓		✓			
Plugged or Kinked Evaporator Drain Hose										●		
Broken Compressor Drive Belt											●	
No Power to Clutch							✓				●	
Faulty Switch or Wiring								✓			●	

COOLING SYSTEM DIAGNOSIS

● Most probable causes
✓ Possible causes

Causes \ Problems	External Leakage	Internal Leakage	Poor Circulation	Overheating	Overflow Loss	Corrosion	Temp Too Low (Slow Engine Warm Up)	Water Pump Noisy
Hose Leaking	●			●				
Water Pump Leaking	●			●				
Damaged Gasket	●	●		●				
Leaking Heater Core	●			✓				
Cracked Cylinder Block	●	●		✓				
Faulty Pressure Cap	●	●		●	●			
Oil Cooler Fittings Loose	●	●		✓				
Faulty Head Gasket	●	●		✓				
Loose Cylinder Head Bolts	●	●		✓				
Cracked Valve Port		●		✓				
Cracked Cylinder Wall		●		✓				
Leaking Oil Cooler		●						
Low Coolant Level			●	●				
Collapsed Radiator Hose			●	●				
Fan Belt Loose			●	✓				✓
Air Leak Through Bottom Hose	✓		●					
Faulty Thermostat			●	●			●	
Water Pump Impeller Broken			●					●
Restricted Radiator Core			●	●				
Restricted Engine Water Jacket			●					
Incorrect Ignition Timing				●				
Inaccurate Temperature Gauge				●			●	
Excessive Engine Idling				●				
Frozen Coolant				●				
Faulty Vacuum By Pass Valve			✓	●				
Overfilling					●			
Blown Head Gasket	✓				●			
Coolant Foaming					●			
Insufficient Corrosion Inhibitor			✓	✓		●		
Extended Use of Anti-Freeze			✓	✓		●		
High Mineral and Lime Content of Coolant			✓	✓		●		
Faulty Temperature Sending Unit							●	
Faulty Heater Controls			✓				●	
Defective Seal								●
Bearing Corroded								●

FRONT SUSPENSION DIAGNOSIS

Problems

● Most probable causes
✓ Possible causes

Causes	Front Wheel Shimmy	Pull to One Side	Excessive Play in Steering	Wheel Tramp	Excessive Tire Wear	Hard Steering	Wandering	Front End Noise
Out of Balance Tires	●			●	✓			
Worn or Out of Adjustment Wheel Bearings	✓					✓		
Worn Tie Rod Ends	✓							
Worn Ball Joints	✓							
Incorrect Wheel Alignment	●	✓			✓	✓	●	
Incorrect Ride Height	✓							
Low or Uneven Tire Pressures		●			●	●	✓	
Front or Rear Brake Dragging		✓						
Grease or Brake Fluid on Brake Linings		✓						
Broken or Sagging Front Spring		✓				✓	✓	
Incorrect Steering Gear Adjustment			✓					
Worn Front End Parts			●					●
Shock Absorber Inoperative or Loose				✓		✓	✓	✓
Ball Joint Needs Lubrication						✓		✓
Loose Stabilizer Bar								✓
Loose Lugnuts								✓
Loose Brake Parts								✓
Improper Tire Size					✓			
Bent or Worn Steering Linkage						✓	✓	

TIRE WEAR DIAGNOSIS

● Most probable causes
✓ Possible causes

Causes \ Problems	Rapid wear at shoulders	Rapid wear at center	Cracked Treads	Wear on one side	Feathered Edge	Bald spots
Underinflation	●		✓			
Overinflation		●				
Excessive speed			●			
Excessive camber				●		
Incorrect toe-in					●	
Wheel unbalanced						●
Corrections	Adjust pressure to specifications with tire cool	Adjust pressure to specifications with tire cool	Adjust pressure to specifications with tire cool or replace tire	Adjust camber to specifications	Adjust toe-in	Dynamic or static balance the wheels

ANTI-FREEZE INFORMATION

Freezing and Boiling Points of Solutions According to Percentage of Alcohol or Ethylene Glycol

Freezing Point of Solution	Alcohol Volume %	Alcohol Solution Boils at	Ethylene Glycol Volume %	Ethylene Glycol Solution Boils at
20°F.	12	196°F.	16	216°F.
10°F.	20	189°F.	25	218°F.
0°F.	27	184°F.	33	220°F.
−10°F.	32	181°F.	39	222°F.
−20°F.	38	178°F.	44	224°F.
−30°F.	42	176°F.	48	225°F.

Note: above boiling points are at sea level. For every 1,000 feet of altitude, boiling points are approximately 2°F. lower than those shown. For every pound of pressure exerted by the pressure cap, the boiling points are approximately 3°F. higher than those shown.

To Increase the Freezing Protection of Anti-Freeze Solutions Already Installed

Cooling System Capacity Quarts	Number of Quarts of **ETHYLENE GLYCOL** Anti-Freeze Required to Increase Protection													
	From +20°F. to					From +10°F. to					From 0°F. to			
	0°	−10°	−20°	−30°	−40°	0°	−10°	−20°	−30°	−40°	−10°	−20°	−30°	−40°
10	1¾	2¼	3	3½	3¾	¾	1½	2¼	2¾	3¼	¾	1½	2	2½
12	2	2¾	3½	4	4½	1	1¾	2½	3¼	3¾	1	1¾	2½	3¼
14	2¼	3¼	4	4¾	5½	1¼	2	3	3¾	4½	1	2	3	3½
16	2½	3½	4½	5¼	6	1¼	2½	3½	4¼	5¼	1¼	2¼	3¼	4
18	3	4	5	6	7	1½	2¾	4	5	5¾	1½	2½	3¾	4¾
20	3¼	4½	5¾	6¾	7½	1¾	3	4¼	5½	6½	1½	2¾	4¼	5¼
22	3½	5	6¼	7¼	8¼	1¾	3¼	4¾	6	7¼	1¾	3¼	4½	5½
24	4	5½	7	8	9	2	3½	5	6½	7½	1¾	3½	5	6
26	4¼	6	7½	8¾	10	2	4	5½	7	8¼	2	3¾	5½	6¾
28	4½	6¼	8	9½	10½	2¼	4¼	6	7½	9	2	4	5¾	7¼
30	5	6¾	8½	10	11½	2½	4½	6½	8	9½	2¼	4¼	6¼	7¾

Test radiator solution with proper hydrometer. Determine from the table the number of quarts of solution to be drawn off from a full cooling system and replace with undiluted anti-freeze, to give the desired increased protection. For example, to increase protection of a 22-quart cooling system containing Ethylene Glycol (permanent type) anti-freeze, from +20°F. to −20°F. will require the replacement of 6¼ quarts of solution with undiluted anti-freeze.

ANTI-FREEZE CHART

Temperatures Shown in Degrees Fahrenheit +32 is Freezing

Cooling System Capacity Quarts	Quarts of **ETHYLENE GLYCOL** Needed for Protection to Temperatures Shown Below													
	1	2	3	4	5	6	7	8	9	10	11	12	13	14
10	+24°	+16°	+ 4°	−12°	−34°	−62°								
11	+25	+18	+ 8	− 6	−23	−47								
12	+26	+19	+10	0	−15	−34	−57°							
13	+27	+21	+13	+ 3	− 9	−25	−45							
14			+15	+ 6	− 5	−18	−34							
15			+16	+ 8	0	−12	−26							
16			+17	+10	+ 2	− 8	−19	−34	−52°					
17			+18	+12	+ 5	− 4	−14	−27	−42					
18			+19	+14	+ 7	0	−10	−21	−34	−50°				
19			+20	+15	+ 9	+ 2	− 7	−16	−28	−42				
20				+16	+10	+ 4	− 3	−12	−22	−34	−48°			
21				+17	+12	+ 6	0	− 9	−17	−28	−41			
22				+18	+13	+ 8	+ 2	− 6	−14	−23	−34	−47°		
23				+19	+14	+ 9	+ 4	− 3	−10	−19	−29	−40		
24				+19	+15	+10	+ 5	0	− 8	−15	−23	−34	−46°	
25				+20	+16	+12	+ 7	+ 1	− 5	−12	−20	−29	−40	−50°
26					+17	+13	+ 8	+ 3	− 3	− 9	−16	−25	−34	−44
27					+18	+14	+ 9	+ 5	− 1	− 7	−13	−21	−29	−39
28					+18	+15	+10	+ 6	+ 1	− 5	−11	−18	−25	−34
29					+19	+16	+12	+ 7	+ 2	− 3	− 8	−15	−22	−29
30					+20	+17	+13	+ 8	+ 4	− 1	− 6	−12	−18	−25

For capacities over 30 quarts divide true capacity by 3. Find quarts Anti-Freeze for the ⅓ and multiply by 3 for quarts to add.

For capacities under 10 quarts multiply true capacity by 3. Find quarts Anti-Freeze for the tripled volume and divide by 3 for quarts to add.

MECHANICS' DATA

Tap Drill Sizes

National Coarse or U.S.S.

Screw & Tap Size	Threads Per Inch	Use Drill Number
No. 5	40	39
No. 6	32	36
No. 8	32	29
No. 10	24	25
No. 12	24	17
1/4	20	8
5/16	18	F
3/8	16	5/16
7/16	14	U
1/2	13	27/64
9/16	12	31/64
5/8	11	17/32
3/4	10	21/32
7/8	9	49/64
1	8	7/8
1 1/8	7	63/64
1 1/4	7	1 7/64
1 1/2	6	1 11/32

National Fine or S.A.E.

Screw & Tap Size	Threads Per Inch	Use Drill Number
No. 5	44	37
No. 6	40	33
No. 8	36	29
No. 10	32	21
No. 12	28	15
1/4	28	3
5/16	24	1
3/8	24	Q
7/16	20	W
1/2	20	29/64
9/16	18	33/64
5/8	18	37/64
3/4	16	11/16
7/8	14	13/16
1 1/8	12	1 3/64
1 1/4	12	1 11/64
1 1/2	12	1 27/64

Decimal Equivalent Size of the Number Drills

Drill No.	Decimal Equivalent	Drill No.	Decimal Equivalent	Drill No.	Decimal Equivalent
80	.0135	53	.0595	26	.1470
79	.0145	52	.0635	25	.1495
78	.0160	51	.0670	24	.1520
77	.0180	50	.0700	23	.1540
76	.0200	49	.0730	22	.1570
75	.0210	48	.0760	21	.1590
74	.0225	47	.0785	20	.1610
73	.0240	46	.0810	19	.1660
72	.0250	45	.0820	18	.1695
71	.0260	44	.0860	17	.1730
70	.0280	43	.0890	16	.1770
69	.0292	42	.0935	15	.1800
68	.0310	41	.0960	14	.1820
67	.0320	40	.0980	13	.1850
66	.0330	39	.0995	12	.1890
65	.0350	38	.1015	11	.1910
64	.0360	37	.1040	10	.1935
63	.0370	36	.1065	9	.1960
62	.0380	35	.1100	8	.1990
61	.0390	34	.1110	7	.2010
60	.0400	33	.1130	6	.2040
59	.0410	32	.1160	5	.2055
58	.0420	31	.1200	4	.2090
57	.0430	30	.1285	3	.2130
56	.0465	29	.1360	2	.2210
55	.0520	28	.1405	1	.2280
54	.0550	27	.1440		

Decimal Equivalent Size of the Letter Drills

Letter Drill	Decimal Equivalent	Letter Drill	Decimal Equivalent	Letter Drill	Decimal Equivalent
A	.234	J	.277	S	.348
B	.238	K	.281	T	.358
C	.242	L	.290	U	.368
D	.246	M	.295	V	.377
E	.250	N	.302	W	.386
F	.257	O	.316	X	.397
G	.261	P	.323	Y	.404
H	.266	Q	.332	Z	.413
I	.272	R	.339		

Decimal Equivalents of the Common Fractions

Fraction	Decimal	Fraction	Decimal	Fraction	Decimal
1/64	.0156	21/64	.3281	43/64	.6719
1/32	.0313	11/32	.3438	11/16	.6875
3/64	.0469	23/64	.3594	45/64	.7031
1/16	.0625	3/8	.3750	23/32	.7188
5/64	.0781	25/64	.3906	47/64	.7344
3/32	.0938	13/32	.4063	3/4	.7500
7/64	.1094	27/64	.4219	49/64	.7656
1/8	.1250	7/16	.4375	25/32	.7813
9/64	.1406	29/64	.4531	51/64	.7969
5/32	.1563	15/32	.4688	13/16	.8125
11/64	.1719	31/64	.4844	53/64	.8281
3/16	.1875	1/2	.5000	27/32	.8438
13/64	.2031	33/64	.5156	55/64	.8594
7/32	.2188	17/32	.5313	7/8	.8750
15/64	.2344	35/64	.5469	57/64	.8906
1/4	.2500	9/16	.5625	29/32	.9063
17/64	.2656	37/64	.5781	59/64	.9219
9/32	.2813	19/32	.5938	15/16	.9375
19/64	.2969	39/64	.6094	61/64	.9531
5/16	.3125	5/8	.6250	31/32	.9688
		41/64	.6406	63/64	.9844
		21/32	.6563		

SI Metric Tables

The following tables are given in SI (International System) metric units. SI units replace both customary (English) and the older gavimetric units. The use of SI units as a new worldwide standard was set by the International Committee of Weights and Measures in 1960. SI has since been adopted by most countries as their national standard.

These tables are general conversion tables which will allow you to convert customary units, which appear in the text, into SI units.

The following are a list of SI units and the customary units, used in this book, which they replace:

To measure:	Use SI units:	Which replace (customary units):
mass	kilograms (kg)	pounds (lbs)
temperature	Celsius (°C)	Fahrenheit (°F)
length	millimeters (mm)	inches (in.)
force	newtons (N)	pounds force (lbs)
capacities	liters (l)	pints/quarts/gallons (pts/qts/gals)
torque	newton-meters (N·m)	foot pounds (ft lbs)
pressure	kilopascals (kPa)	pounds per square inch (psi)
volume	cubic centimeters (cm^3)	cubic inches (cu in.)
power	kilowatts (kW)	horsepower (hp)

If you have had any prior experience with the metric system, you may have noticed units in this chart which are not familiar to you. This is because, in some cases, SI units differ from the older gravimetric units which they replace. For example, newtons (N) replace kilograms (kg) as a force unit, kilopascals (kPa) replace atmospheres or bars as a unit of pressure, and, although the units are the same, the name Celsius replaces centigrade for temperature measurement.

If you are not using the SI tables, have a look at them anyway; you will be seeing a lot more of them in the future.

ENGLISH TO METRIC CONVERSION: MASS (WEIGHT)

Current mass measurement is expressed in pounds and ounces (lbs. & ozs.). The metric unit of mass (or weight) is the kilogram (kg). Even although this table does not show conversion of masses (weights) larger than 15 lbs, it is easy to calculate larger units by following the data immediately below.

To convert ounces (oz.) to grams (g): multiply th number of ozs. by 28
To convert grams (g) to ounces (oz.): multiply the number of grams by .035

To convert pounds (lbs.) to kilograms (kg): multiply the number of lbs. by .45
To convert kilograms (kg) to pounds (lbs.): multiply the number of kilograms by 2.2

lbs	kg	lbs	kg	oz	kg	oz	kg
0.1	0.04	0.9	0.41	0.1	0.003	0.9	0.024
0.2	0.09	1	0.4	0.2	0.005	1	0.03
0.3	0.14	2	0.9	0.3	0.008	2	0.06
0.4	0.18	3	1.4	0.4	0.011	3	0.08
0.5	0.23	4	1.8	0.5	0.014	4	0.11
0.6	0.27	5	2.3	0.6	0.017	5	0.14
0.7	0.32	10	4.5	0.7	0.020	10	0.28
0.8	0.36	15	6.8	0.8	0.023	15	0.42

ENGLISH TO METRIC CONVERSION: TEMPERATURE

To convert Fahrenheit (°F) to Celsius (°C): take number of °F and subtract 32; multiply result by 5; divide result by 9

To convert Celsius (°C) to Fahrenheit (°F): take number of °C and multiply by 9; divide result by 5; add 32 to total

Fahrenheit (F)		Celsius (C)		Fahrenheit (F)		Celsius (C)		Fahrenheit (F)		Celsius (C)	
°F	°C	°C	°F	°F	°C	°C	°F	°F	°C	°C	°F
−40	−40	−38	−36.4	80	26.7	18	64.4	215	101.7	80	176
−35	−37.2	−36	−32.8	85	29.4	20	68	220	104.4	85	185
−30	−34.4	−34	−29.2	90	32.2	22	71.6	225	107.2	90	194
−25	−31.7	−32	−25.6	95	35.0	24	75.2	230	110.0	95	202
−20	−28.9	−30	−22	100	37.8	26	78.8	235	112.8	100	212
−15	−26.1	−28	−18.4	105	40.6	28	82.4	240	115.6	105	221
−10	−23.3	−26	−14.8	110	43.3	30	86	245	118.3	110	230
−5	−20.6	−24	−11.2	115	46.1	32	89.6	250	121.1	115	239
0	−17.8	−22	−7.6	120	48.9	34	93.2	255	123.9	120	248
1	−17.2	−20	−4	125	51.7	36	96.8	260	126.6	125	257
2	−16.7	−18	−0.4	130	54.4	38	100.4	265	129.4	130	266
3	−16.1	−16	3.2	135	57.2	40	104	270	132.2	135	275
4	−15.6	−14	6.8	140	60.0	42	107.6	275	135.0	140	284
5	−15.0	−12	10.4	145	62.8	44	112.2	280	137.8	145	293
10	−12.2	−10	14	150	65.6	46	114.8	285	140.6	150	302
15	−9.4	−8	17.6	155	68.3	48	118.4	290	143.3	155	311
20	−6.7	−6	21.2	160	71.1	50	122	295	146.1	160	320
25	−3.9	−4	24.8	165	73.9	52	125.6	300	148.9	165	329
30	−1.1	−2	28.4	170	76.7	54	129.2	305	151.7	170	338
35	1.7	0	32	175	79.4	56	132.8	310	154.4	175	347
40	4.4	2	35.6	180	82.2	58	136.4	315	157.2	180	356
45	7.2	4	39.2	185	85.0	60	140	320	160.0	185	365
50	10.0	6	42.8	190	87.8	62	143.6	325	162.8	190	374
55	12.8	8	46.4	195	90.6	64	147.2	330	165.6	195	383
60	15.6	10	50	200	93.3	66	150.8	335	168.3	200	392
65	18.3	12	53.6	205	96.1	68	154.4	340	171.1	205	401
70	21.1	14	57.2	210	98.9	70	158	345	173.9	210	410
75	23.9	16	60.8	212	100.0	75	167	350	176.7	215	414

ENGLISH TO METRIC CONVERSION: LENGTH

To convert inches (ins.) to millimeters (mm): multiply number of inches by 25.4

To convert millimeters (mm) to inches (ins.): multiply number of millimeters by .04

Inches	Decimals	Milli-meters	Inches to millimeters inches	mm
1/64	0.051625	0.3969	0.0001	0.00254
1/32	0.03125	0.7937	0.0002	0.00508
3/64	0.046875	1.1906	0.0003	0.00762
1/16	0.0625	1.5875	0.0004	0.01016
5/64	0.078125	1.9844	0.0005	0.01270
3/32	0.09375	2.3812	0.0006	0.01524
7/64	0.109375	2.7781	0.0007	0.01778
1/8	0.125	3.1750	0.0008	0.02032
9/64	0.140625	3.5719	0.0009	0.02286
5/32	0.15625	3.9687	0.001	0.0254
11/64	0.171875	4.3656	0.002	0.0508
3/16	0.1875	4.7625	0.003	0.0762
13/64	0.203125	5.1594	0.004	0.1016
7/32	0.21875	5.5562	0.005	0.1270
15/64	0.234375	5.9531	0.006	0.1524
1/4	0.25	6.3500	0.007	0.1778
17/64	0.265625	6.7469	0.008	0.2032
9/32	0.28125	7.1437	0.009	0.2286
19/64	0.296875	7.5406	0.01	0.254
5/16	0.3125	7.9375	0.02	0.508
21/64	0.328125	8.3344	0.03	0.762
11/32	0.34375	8.7312	0.04	1.016
23/64	0.359375	9.1281	0.05	1.270
3/8	0.375	9.5250	0.06	1.524
25/64	0.390625	9.9219	0.07	1.778
13/32	0.40625	10.3187	0.08	2.032
27/64	0.421875	10.7156	0.09	2.286
7/16	0.4375	11.1125	0.1	2.54
29/64	0.453125	11.5094	0.2	5.08
15/32	0.46875	11.9062	0.3	7.62
31/64	0.484375	12.3031	0.4	10.16
1/2	0.5	12.7000	0.5	12.70

Inches	Decimals	Milli-meters	Inches to millimeters inches	mm
33/64	0.515625	13.0969	0.6	15.24
17/32	0.53125	13.4937	0.7	17.78
35/64	0.546875	13.8906	0.8	20.32
9/16	0.5625	14.2875	0.9	22.86
37/64	0.578125	14.6844	1	25.4
19/32	0.59375	15.0812	2	50.8
39/64	0.609375	15.4781	3	76.2
5/8	0.625	15.8750	4	101.6
41/64	0.640625	16.2719	5	127.0
21/32	0.65625	16.6687	6	152.4
43/64	0.671875	17.0656	7	177.8
11/16	0.6875	17.4625	8	203.2
45/64	0.703125	17.8594	9	228.6
23/32	0.71875	18.2562	10	254.0
47/64	0.734375	18.6531	11	279.4
3/4	0.75	19.0500	12	304.8
49/64	0.765625	19.4469	13	330.2
25/32	0.78125	19.8437	14	355.6
51/64	0.796875	20.2406	15	381.0
13/16	0.8125	20.6375	16	406.4
53/64	0.828125	21.0344	17	431.8
27/32	0.84375	21.4312	18	457.2
55/64	0.859375	21.8281	19	482.6
7/8	0.875	22.2250	20	508.0
57/64	0.890625	22.6219	21	533.4
29/32	0.90625	23.0187	22	558.8
59/64	0.921875	23.4156	23	584.2
15/16	0.9375	23.8125	24	609.6
61/64	0.953125	24.2094	25	635.0
31/32	0.96875	24.6062	26	660.4
63/64	0.984375	25.0031	27	690.6

ENGLISH TO METRIC CONVERSION: TORQUE

To convert foot-pounds (ft./lbs.) to Newton-meters: multiply the number of ft./lbs. by 1.3

To convert inch-pounds (in./lbs.) to Newton-meters: multiply the number of in./lbs. by .11

in lbs	N-m	in lbs	N-m	in lbs	N-m	in lbs	N-m	in lbs	N-m
0.1	0.01	1	0.11	10	1.13	19	2.15	28	3.16
0.2	0.02	2	0.23	11	1.24	20	2.26	29	3.28
0.3	0.03	3	0.34	12	1.36	21	2.37	30	3.39
0.4	0.04	4	0.45	13	1.47	22	2.49	31	3.50
0.5	0.06	5	0.56	14	1.58	23	2.60	32	3.62
0.6	0.07	6	0.68	15	1.70	24	2.71	33	3.73
0.7	0.08	7	0.78	16	1.81	25	2.82	34	3.84
0.8	0.09	8	0.90	17	1.92	26	2.94	35	3.95
0.9	0.10	9	1.02	18	2.03	27	3.05	36	4.07

ENGLISH TO METRIC CONVERSION: TORQUE

Torque is now expressed as either foot-pounds (ft./lbs.) or inch-pounds (in./lbs.). The metric measurement unit for torque is the Newton-meter (Nm). This unit—the Nm—will be used for all SI metric torque references, both the present ft./lbs. and in./lbs.

ft lbs	N-m	ft lbs	N-m	ft lbs	N-m	ft lbs	N-m
0.1	0.1	33	44.7	74	100.3	115	155.9
0.2	0.3	34	46.1	75	101.7	116	157.3
0.3	0.4	35	47.4	76	103.0	117	158.6
0.4	0.5	36	48.8	77	104.4	118	160.0
0.5	0.7	37	50.7	78	105.8	119	161.3
0.6	0.8	38	51.5	79	107.1	120	162.7
0.7	1.0	39	52.9	80	108.5	121	164.0
0.8	1.1	40	54.2	81	109.8	122	165.4
0.9	1.2	41	55.6	82	111.2	123	166.8
1	1.3	42	56.9	83	112.5	124	168.1
2	2.7	43	58.3	84	113.9	125	169.5
3	4.1	44	59.7	85	115.2	126	170.8
4	5.4	45	61.0	86	116.6	127	172.2
5	6.8	46	62.4	87	118.0	128	173.5
6	8.1	47	63.7	88	119.3	129	174.9
7	9.5	48	65.1	89	120.7	130	176.2
8	10.8	49	66.4	90	122.0	131	177.6
9	12.2	50	67.8	91	123.4	132	179.0
10	13.6	51	69.2	92	124.7	133	180.3
11	14.9	52	70.5	93	126.1	134	181.7
12	16.3	53	71.9	94	127.4	135	183.0
13	17.6	54	73.2	95	128.8	136	184.4
14	18.9	55	74.6	96	130.2	137	185.7
15	20.3	56	75.9	97	131.5	138	187.1
16	21.7	57	77.3	98	132.9	139	188.5
17	23.0	58	78.6	99	134.2	140	189.8
18	24.4	59	80.0	100	135.6	141	191.2
19	25.8	60	81.4	101	136.9	142	192.5
20	27.1	61	82.7	102	138.3	143	193.9
21	28.5	62	84.1	103	139.6	144	195.2
22	29.8	63	85.4	104	141.0	145	196.6
23	31.2	64	86.8	105	142.4	146	198.0
24	32.5	65	88.1	106	143.7	147	199.3
25	33.9	66	89.5	107	145.1	148	200.7
26	35.2	67	90.8	108	146.4	149	202.0
27	36.6	68	92.2	109	147.8	150	203.4
28	38.0	69	93.6	110	149.1	151	204.7
29	39.3	70	94.9	111	150.5	152	206.1
30	40.7	71	96.3	112	151.8	153	207.4
31	42.0	72	97.6	113	153.2	154	208.8
32	43.4	73	99.0	114	154.6	155	210.2

ENGLISH TO METRIC CONVERSION: FORCE

Force is presently measured in pounds (lbs.). This type of measurement is used to measure spring pressure, specifically how many pounds it takes to compress a spring. Our present force unit (the pound) will be replaced in SI metric measurements by the Newton (N). This term will eventually see use in specifications for electric motor brush spring pressures, valve spring pressures, etc.

To convert pounds (lbs.) to Newton (N): multiply the number of lbs. by 4.45

lbs	N	lbs	N	lbs	N	oz	N
0.01	0.04	21	93.4	59	262.4	1	0.3
0.02	0.09	22	97.9	60	266.9	2	0.6
0.03	0.13	23	102.3	61	271.3	3	0.8
0.04	0.18	24	106.8	62	275.8	4	1.1
0.05	0.22	25	111.2	63	280.2	5	1.4
0.06	0.27	26	115.6	64	284.6	6	1.7
0.07	0.31	27	120.1	65	289.1	7	2.0
0.08	0.36	28	124.6	66	293.6	8	2.2
0.09	0.40	29	129.0	67	298.0	9	2.5
0.1	0.4	30	133.4	68	302.5	10	2.8
0.2	0.9	31	137.9	69	306.9	11	3.1
0.3	1.3	32	142.3	70	311.4	12	3.3
0.4	1.8	33	146.8	71	315.8	13	3.6
0.5	2.2	34	151.2	72	320.3	14	3.9
0.6	2.7	35	155.7	73	324.7	15	4.2
0.7	3.1	36	160.1	74	329.2	16	4.4
0.8	3.6	37	164.6	75	333.6	17	4.7
0.9	4.0	38	169.0	76	338.1	18	5.0
1	4.4	39	173.5	77	342.5	19	5.3
2	8.9	40	177.9	78	347.0	20	5.6
3	13.4	41	182.4	79	351.4	21	5.8
4	17.8	42	186.8	80	355.9	22	6.1
5	22.2	43	191.3	81	360.3	23	6.4
6	26.7	44	195.7	82	364.8	24	6.7
7	31.1	45	200.2	83	369.2	25	7.0
8	35.6	46	204.6	84	373.6	26	7.2
9	40.0	47	209.1	85	378.1	27	7.5
10	44.5	48	213.5	86	382.6	28	7.8
11	48.9	49	218.0	87	387.0	29	8.1
12	53.4	50	224.4	88	391.4	30	8.3
13	57.8	51	226.9	89	395.9	31	8.6
14	62.3	52	231.3	90	400.3	32	8.9
15	66.7	53	235.8	91	404.8	33	9.2
16	71.2	54	240.2	92	409.2	34	9.4
17	75.6	55	244.6	93	413.7	35	9.7
18	80.1	56	249.1	94	418.1	36	10.0
19	84.5	57	253.6	95	422.6	37	10.3
20	89.0	58	258.0	96	427.0	38	10.6

ENGLISH TO METRIC CONVERSION: LIQUID CAPACITY

Liquid or fluid capacity is presently expressed as pints, quarts or gallons, or a combination of all of these. In the metric system the liter (l) will become the basic unit. Fractions of a liter would be expressed as deciliters, centiliters, or most frequently (and commonly) as milliliters.

To convert pints (pts.) to liters (l): multiply the number of pints by .47
To convert liters (l) to pints (pts.): multiply the number of liters by 2.1
To convert quarts (qts.) to liters (l): multiply the number of quarts by .95

To convert liters (l) to quarts (qts.): multiply the number of liters by 1.06
To convert gallons (gals.) to liters (l): multiply the number of gallons by 3.8
To convert liters (l) to gallons (gals.): multiply the number of liters by .26

gals	liters	qts	liters	pts	liters
0.1	0.38	0.1	0.10	0.1	0.05
0.2	0.76	0.2	0.19	0.2	0.10
0.3	1.1	0.3	0.28	0.3	0.14
0.4	1.5	0.4	0.38	0.4	0.19
0.5	1.9	0.5	0.47	0.5	0.24
0.6	2.3	0.6	0.57	0.6	0.28
0.7	2.6	0.7	0.66	0.7	0.33
0.8	3.0	0.8	0.76	0.8	0.38
0.9	3.4	0.9	0.85	0.9	0.43
1	3.8	1	1.0	1	0.5
2	7.6	2	1.9	2	1.0
3	11.4	3	2.8	3	1.4
4	15.1	4	3.8	4	1.9
5	18.9	5	4.7	5	2.4
6	22.7	6	5.7	6	2.8
7	26.5	7	6.6	7	3.3
8	30.3	8	7.6	8	3.8
9	34.1	9	8.5	9	4.3
10	37.8	10	9.5	10	4.7
11	41.6	11	10.4	11	5.2
12	45.4	12	11.4	12	5.7
13	49.2	13	12.3	13	6.2
14	53.0	14	13.2	14	6.6
15	56.8	15	14.2	15	7.1
16	60.6	16	15.1	16	7.6
17	64.3	17	16.1	17	8.0
18	68.1	18	17.0	18	8.5
19	71.9	19	18.0	19	9.0
20	75.7	20	18.9	20	9.5
21	79.5	21	19.9	21	9.9
22	83.2	22	20.8	22	10.4
23	87.0	23	21.8	23	10.9
24	90.8	24	22.7	24	11.4
25	94.6	25	23.6	25	11.8
26	98.4	26	24.6	26	12.3
27	102.2	27	25.5	27	12.8
28	106.0	28	26.5	28	13.2
29	110.0	29	27.4	29	13.7
30	113.5	30	28.4	30	14.2

ENGLISH TO METRIC CONVERSION: PRESSURE

The basic unit of pressure measurement used today is expressed as pounds per square inch (psi). The metric unit for psi will be the kilopascal (kPa). This will apply to either fluid pressure or air pressure, and will be frequently seen in tire pressure readings, oil pressure specifications, fuel pump pressure, etc.

To convert pounds per square inch (psi) to kilopascals (kPa): multiply the number of psi by 6.89

Psi	kPa	Psi	kPa	Psi	kPa	Psi	kPa
0.1	0.7	37	255.1	82	565.4	127	875.6
0.2	1.4	38	262.0	83	572.3	128	882.5
0.3	2.1	39	268.9	84	579.2	129	889.4
0.4	2.8	40	275.8	85	586.0	130	896.3
0.5	3.4	41	282.7	86	592.9	131	903.2
0.6	4.1	42	289.6	87	599.8	132	910.1
0.7	4.8	43	296.5	88	606.7	133	917.0
0.8	5.5	44	303.4	89	613.6	134	923.9
0.9	6.2	45	310.3	90	620.5	135	930.8
1	6.9	46	317.2	91	627.4	136	937.7
2	13.8	47	324.0	92	634.3	137	944.6
3	20.7	48	331.0	93	641.2	138	951.5
4	27.6	49	337.8	94	648.1	139	958.4
5	34.5	50	344.7	95	655.0	140	965.2
6	41.4	51	351.6	96	661.9	141	972.2
7	48.3	52	358.5	97	668.8	142	979.0
8	55.2	53	365.4	98	675.7	143	985.9
9	62.1	54	372.3	99	682.6	144	992.8
10	69.0	55	379.2	100	689.5	145	999.7
11	75.8	56	386.1	101	696.4	146	1006.6
12	82.7	57	393.0	102	703.3	147	1013.5
13	89.6	58	399.9	103	710.2	148	1020.4
14	96.5	59	406.8	104	717.0	149	1027.3
15	103.4	60	413.7	105	723.9	150	1034.2
16	110.3	61	420.6	106	730.8	151	1041.1
17	117.2	62	427.5	107	737.7	152	1048.0
18	124.1	63	434.4	108	744.6	153	1054.9
19	131.0	64	441.3	109	751.5	154	1061.8
20	137.9	65	448.2	110	758.4	155	1068.7
21	144.8	66	455.0	111	765.3	156	1075.6
22	151.7	67	461.9	112	772.2	157	1082.5
23	158.6	68	468.8	113	779.1	158	1089.4
24	165.5	69	475.7	114	786.0	159	1096.3
25	172.4	70	482.6	115	792.9	160	1103.2
26	179.3	71	489.5	116	799.8	161	1110.0
27	186.2	72	496.4	117	806.7	162	1116.9
28	193.0	73	503.3	118	813.6	163	1123.8
29	200.0	74	510.2	119	820.5	164	1130.7
30	206.8	75	517.1	120	827.4	165	1137.6
31	213.7	76	524.0	121	834.3	166	1144.5
32	220.6	77	530.9	122	841.2	167	1151.4
33	227.5	78	537.8	123	848.0	168	1158.3
34	234.4	79	544.7	124	854.9	169	1165.2
35	241.3	80	551.6	125	861.8	170	1172.1
36	248.2	81	558.5	126	868.7	171	1179.0

ENGLISH TO METRIC CONVERSION: PRESSURE

The basic unit of pressure measurement used today is expressed as pounds per square inch (psi). The metric unit for psi will be the kilopascal (kPa). This will apply to either fluid pressure or air pressure, and will be frequently seen in tire pressure readings, oil pressure specifications, fuel pump pressure, etc.

To convert pounds per square inch (psi) to kilopascals (kPa): multiply the number of psi by 6.89

Psi	kPa	Psi	kPa	Psi	kPa	Psi	kPa
172	1185.9	216	1489.3	260	1792.6	304	2096.0
173	1192.8	217	1496.2	261	1799.5	305	2102.9
174	1199.7	218	1503.1	262	1806.4	306	2109.8
175	1206.6	219	1510.0	263	1813.3	307	2116.7
176	1213.5	220	1516.8	264	1820.2	308	2123.6
177	1220.4	221	1523.7	265	1827.1	309	2130.5
178	1227.3	222	1530.6	266	1834.0	310	2137.4
179	1234.2	223	1537.5	267	1840.9	311	2144.3
180	1241.0	224	1544.4	268	1847.8	312	2151.2
181	1247.9	225	1551.3	269	1854.7	313	2158.1
182	1254.8	226	1558.2	270	1861.6	314	2164.9
183	1261.7	227	1565.1	271	1868.5	315	2171.8
184	1268.6	228	1572.0	272	1875.4	316	2178.7
185	1275.5	229	1578.9	273	1882.3	317	2185.6
186	1282.4	230	1585.8	274	1889.2	318	2192.5
187	1289.3	231	1592.7	275	1896.1	319	2199.4
188	1296.2	232	1599.6	276	1903.0	320	2206.3
189	1303.1	233	1606.5	277	1909.8	321	2213.2
190	1310.0	234	1613.4	278	1916.7	322	2220.1
191	1316.9	235	1620.3	279	1923.6	323	2227.0
192	1323.8	236	1627.2	280	1930.5	324	2233.9
193	1330.7	237	1634.1	281	1937.4	325	2240.8
194	1337.6	238	1641.0	282	1944.3	326	2247.7
195	1344.5	239	1647.8	283	1951.2	327	2254.6
196	1351.4	240	1654.7	284	1958.1	328	2261.5
197	1358.3	241	1661.6	285	1965.0	329	2268.4
198	1365.2	242	1668.5	286	1971.9	330	2275.3
199	1372.0	243	1675.4	287	1978.8	331	2282.2
200	1378.9	244	1682.3	288	1985.7	332	2289.1
201	1385.8	245	1689.2	289	1992.6	333	2295.9
202	1392.7	246	1696.1	290	1999.5	334	2302.8
203	1399.6	247	1703.0	291	2006.4	335	2309.7
204	1406.5	248	1709.9	292	2013.3	336	2316.6
205	1413.4	249	1716.8	293	2020.2	337	2323.5
206	1420.3	250	1723.7	294	2027.1	338	2330.4
207	1427.2	251	1730.6	295	2034.0	339	2337.3
208	1434.1	252	1737.5	296	2040.8	240	2344.2
209	1441.0	253	1744.4	297	2047.7	341	2351.1
210	1447.9	254	1751.3	298	2054.6	342	2358.0
211	1454.8	255	1758.2	299	2061.5	343	2364.9
212	1461.7	256	1765.1	300	2068.4	344	2371.8
213	1468.7	257	1772.0	301	2075.3	345	2378.7
214	1475.5	258	1778.8	302	2082.2	346	2385.6
215	1482.4	259	1785.7	303	2089.1	347	2392.5

Turn Signal Flasher and Fuse Box Location Chart

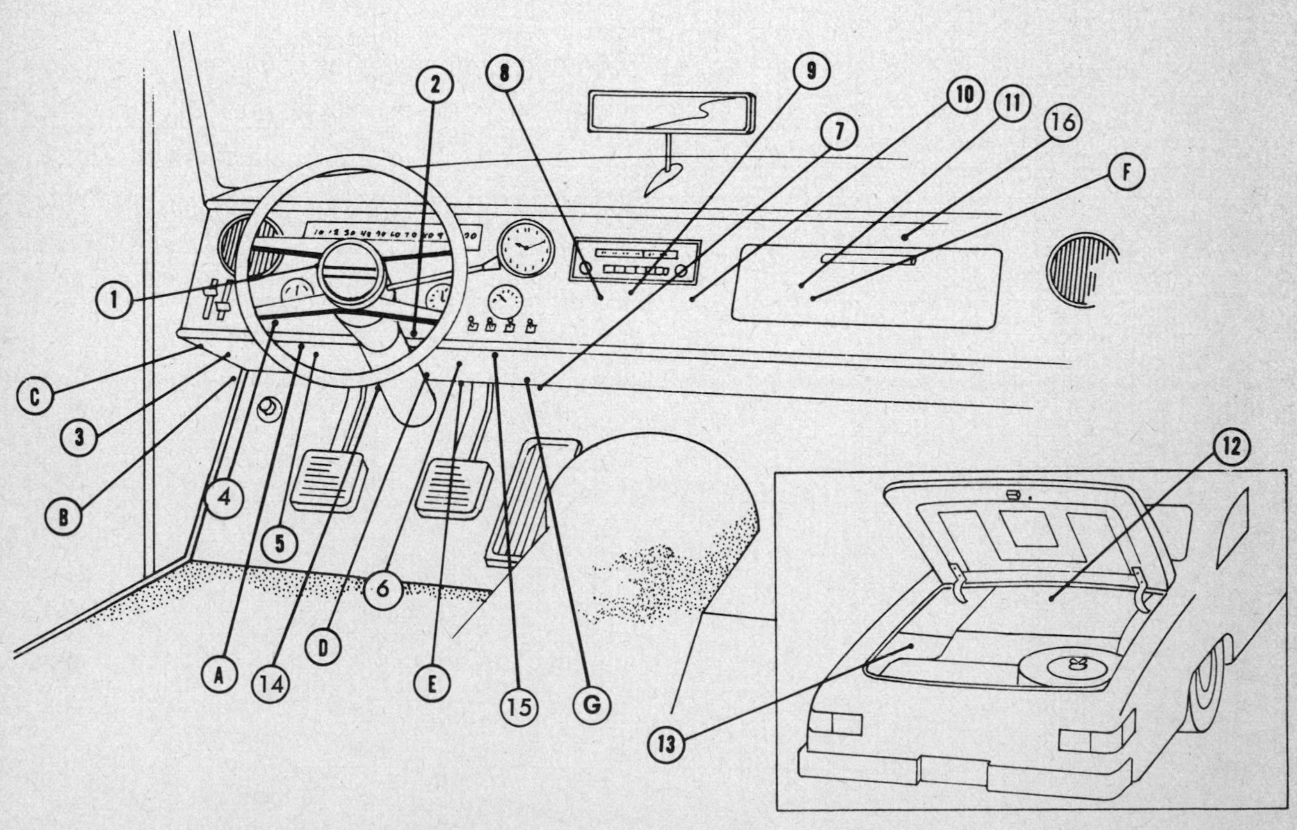

TURN SIGNAL FLASHER, HAZARD WARNING FLASHER, AND FUSE BLOCK LOCATION

	1969		1970		1971		1972		1973		1974		1975		Fuse Block Location	1974 Fuse Block Location	1975 Fuse Block Location
	TSF	HWF	TSF	HWF	TSF	HWF	TSF	HWF	TSF	HWF	TSF	HWF	TSF	HWF			
American Motors																	
Ambassador	2	3	2	3	2	3	2	3	2	3	2	3	3	1	C	F	F
AMX	2	3	2	3	—	—	—	—	—	—	—	—	—	—	C	—	—
Hornet, Gremlin	—	—	3	3	3	3	3	3	3	3	3	2	3	2	C	C	C
Javelin	3	3	3	3	3	3	3	3	3	3	3	3	—	—	C	C	C
Rebel, Matador	2	3	2	3	2	3	2	3	2	3	2	3	3	1	C	F	F
Pacer	—	—	—	—	—	—	—	—	—	—	—	—	2	14	—	—	F
Chrysler Corporation																	
Barracuda	8	5	8	6	8	6	10	6	8	6	6	6	—	—	D	G	—
Challenger	8	5	8	6	8	6	10	6	8	6	6	6	—	—	A	G	—
Chrysler	5	4	5	4	5	4	5	5	5	5	5	5	14	5	A	A	A
Cordoba	—	—	—	—	—	—	—	—	—	—	—	—	4	15	—	—	A
Dart	8	5	8	6	8	6	10	6	8	6	8	6	5	5	D	D	A
Dodge	4, 8	5, 10	5	6	5, 10	—	5, 10	5	8	6	8	6①	4③	15④	A	D②	A
Imperial	13	13	5	4	5	4	5	5	5	6	5	5	14	5	F	A	A
Plymouth	4, 8	4, 6	4, 8	6	5, 10	—	5, 10	5	8	6	8	6①	4③	15④	A	D②	A
Valiant	8	5	8	6	8	6	10	6	8	5	8	6	5	5	A	D	A
Ford Motor Company																	
Comet	—	—	—	—	5	5	5	5	5	5	5	5	5	3	E	E	E
Cougar	8	10	8	10	11	6	8	10	8	10	3	3	3	3	E	C	C
Fairlane, Torino	6	5	6	5	5	5	5	5	5	5	3	3	3	3	E	C	C
Falcon	6	5	—	—	—	—	—	—	—	—	—	—	—	—	F	—	—
Ford	6	5	11	3	8	3	8	3	8	3	8	3	3	3	E	C	A
Granada, Monarch	—	—	—	—	—	—	—	—	—	—	—	—	6	14	—	—	C
Lincoln Continental	11	11	3	3	6	6	3	3	3	3	3	5	10	5	F	A	E
Mark III, IV	11	11	11	3	11	3	3	3	3	3	3	3	3	5	F	C	A
Maverick	—	—	6	—	5	5	5	5	5	5	5	5	5	3	E	E	E
Mercury	4	6	11	3	8	3	8	3	8	3	8	3	3	3	E	C	A
Montego	6	5	6	5	5	5	5	5	5	5	3	3	3	3	E	C	C
Mustang	1	4	10	8	11	6	8	10	8	10	—	—	—	—	E	—	—
Mustang II	—	—	—	—	—	—	—	—	—	—	7	7	7	7	—	G	G
Pinto, Bobcat	—	—	—	—	10	10	10	10	10	10	10	10	16	16	E	E	E
Thunderbird	13	13	3	11	11	6	3	3	3	3	3	5	3	3	F	C	C
General Motors Corporation																	
Buick	3	3	3	3	3	3	3	3	3	3	3	3	3	3	—	—	B
Buick Apollo	—	—	—	—	—	—	—	—	5	3	5	3	3	3	B	B	B
Buick Skyhawk	—	—	—	—	—	—	—	—	—	—	—	—	3	3	C	C	B
Cadillac Eldorado	—	—	—	—	—	—	—	—	—	—	—	—	6	3	—	—	B
Cadillac Seville	—	—	—	—	—	—	—	—	—	—	—	—	5	6	—	—	E
Camaro	8	3	8	3	8	3	8	3	8	3	8	3	14	5	A	A	A
Chevelle	8	3	1	3	7	3	7	3	4	3	4	3	14	5	A	A	A
Chevrolet	8	3	10	3	7	3	7	3	6	3	6	3	14	5	A	A	A
Chevy II, Nova	8	3	10	3	7	3	7	3	10	3	10	3	14	5	A	A	A
Corvette	11	3	11	3	11	3	11	3	11	3	6	3	14	5	A	A	A
Monza	—	—	—	—	—	—	—	—	—	—	—	—	14	3	—	—	C
Vega	—	—	—	—	5	3	5	3	5	3	5	3	14	3	C	C	C
Oldsmobile	3	3	1	3	4	3	4	3	4	3	5	3	5	5	C	C	A
Oldsmobile F-85, Cutlass	3	3	3	3	4	3	4	3	4	3	14	3	14	3	C	C	C
Oldsmobile Omega	—	—	—	—	—	—	—	—	5	3	6	3	6	5	C	C	A
Oldsmobile Starfire	—	—	—	—	—	—	—	—	—	—	—	—	14	3	—	—	C
Oldsmobile Toronado	3	3	4	3	4	3	4	3	4	3	5	3	5	5	C	C	A
Pontiac Astre	—	—	—	—	—	—	—	—	—	—	—	—	14	3	—	—	C
Pontiac	3	3	3	3	3	3	3	3	3	3	3	3	5⑤	3	C	C	B
Firebird	3	3	3	3	3	3	3	3	3	3	3	3	5	3	C	C	B
Tempest, GTO, Grand Am	3	3	3	3	3	3	3	3	3	3	3	3	5	3	C	C	B
Ventura II	—	—	—	—	3	3	3	3	3	3	3	3	5	3	C	C	B

①—5 on Monaco, Fury
②—A on Monaco, Fury and Gran Fury
TSF—Turn Signal Flasher
HWF—Hazard Warning Flasher

③—14 on Gran Fury, Monaco
④—5 on Gran Fury, Monaco
⑤—B on Gran Prix

TOWING CARS WITH AUTOMATIC TRANSMISSIONS

When towing a disabled car, care must be used to avoid damage to the automatic transmission. None of the automatic transmission cars covered in this book can be push started. If it becomes necessary to tow one of these cars, the following chart should be used for reference.

Transmission	Towing	
	Maximum Speed	Maximum Distance (Miles)
AMC Shift Command	35	50
Torque-Command	30	①
Torqueflite	30	①
Ford FMX/CW	30	15
Ford C3, C4	30	15
Ford C6	30	15
Ford C4S	30	15
Powerglide	35	50
Torque Drive	35	50
G.M. Type 300	35	50
G.M. Type 250, 350, 375B	35	50
G.M. Type 375, 400, 425	35	50

①—Do not tow extended distances without disconnecting driveshaft or raising rear wheels.

Chilton's REPAIR MANUALS

IMPORT AUTOMOTIVE REPAIR MANUAL, 3rd Edition

Formerly titled CHILTON'S IMPORT CAR REPAIR MANUAL, this edition has been retitled and enlarged to include the popular import pick-up trucks. All of the information is contained in one volume and presented in the same three column format as the well-known CHILTON'S AUTO REPAIR MANUAL. In this edition the following popular import cars and trucks are covered from 1970 (or the date of importation) through the years in parentheses: Audi (1975), Capri (1976), Colt (1975), Courier (1975), Datsun (1975), Fiat (1974), Honda (1974), LUV (1975), Mazda (1975), Mercedes-Benz (1975), MG (1975), Opel (1975), Porsche (1975), Subaru (1975), Toyota (1975), Triumph (1975), Volvo (1975), VW—types 1, 2, 3, 4 (1975), VW Dasher/Scirocco/Rabbit (1975). A separate section for each car gives identification and tune-up procedures, specifications, and information for the repair and maintenance of the following: the engine electrical, mechanical, and cooling systems, emission controls, the fuel systems, transmissions, clutch, transaxle, drive axle, front and rear suspension, steering, brakes, and the chassis electrical system. The manual also includes three sections on engine tune-up, troubleshooting and rebuilding. Nearly 4000 photographs and drawings. $18.95

TRUCK REPAIR MANUAL: GASOLINE AND DIESEL POWERED LIGHT AND MEDIUM TRUCKS

This second edition has been updated to cover all maintenance and repair procedures on trucks with capacities from 1/2 to 2-1/2 tons for the years 1965 through 1974. It includes specifications and repair procedures for Chevrolet, Chevy Vans, Dodge, Dodge Vans, Ford, Ford Bronco, GMC, International, and Jeep. General sections cover overhaul procedures, testing, adjustments, and troubleshooting on all major systems. A complete section on diesel engines including specifications is also included. Many drawings, diagrams, illustrations, and troubleshooting charts are used throughout. $18.00

Chilton's EASY MECHANICAL AUTO CARE

Chilton's newest idea in do-it-yourself auto repair and maintenance is designed for use by the average car owner—you need no special technical or mechanical knowledge to perform simple automotive jobs and repairs. Each of Chilton's EASY MAC packages for a given car/model is presented on a 38" x 25" fold-out multi-colored chart. Each chart covers the eight basic areas of logical do-it-yourself car care, including Lubrication; Cooling System; Air Conditioning; Ignition and Tune-up; Fuel, Emission Controls and Carburetor; Tire and Suspension Systems; Electrical and Lighting Systems; and Safety Systems. Every chart provides comprehensive information on the tools, materials and precautions necessary to complete each job. Instructions are accompanied by clear and simple illustrations. CHILTON'S EASY MAC packages are available at $1.95 each for the following cars: Chevrolet 6; Chevrolet V-8; Comet 6; Comet V-8; Datsun 510 Series; Datsun 1200 Series; Ford 6; Ford V-8; Maverick 6; Maverick V-8; Pinto 1600, 2000, 2300; Toyota Corolla; Toyota Corona/Mark II; Vega; VW Type I; and VW Type II.

MOTORCYCLE REPAIR MANUAL

This new manual is a complete guide to the tune-up, maintenance, and general repair of all component systems of the most popular motorcycles now sold in the United States. The following makes are covered, from the date indicated in parentheses through 1973: BMW (1960); BSA singles, twins and triples (1963); Bultaco (1963); Harley Davidson singles and twins (1947); Honda singles, twins and fours, including the XL 250 and the MT 250 (1963); Kawasaki singles, twins, triples, and the 900 Z1 (1966); Montesa (1966); Moto Guzzi (1966); Norton 750 and 850 (1966); Ossa (1968); Suzuki singles, twins and triples (1963); Triumph singles, twins and triples (1963); and all Yamaha street and dirt bikes, including the TX 500, TX 650, and TX 750 (1964). All the necessary maintenance information, as well as removal, repair and installation procedures, and specifications are given. Also included are wiring diagrams and bulb charts for all models. $22.95